ABBREVIATIONS K...

ab.	about	fem.	feminine	obj.	objective
Abbr., abbr.	abbreviation	fig.	figurative	Obs., obs.	obsolete
abl.	ablative	fl.	flourished	orig.	originally
acc.	accusative	fol.	followed	pass.	passive
adj.	adjective	ft.	foot, feet	past part.	past participle
adv.	adverb	fut.	future	perh.	perhaps
Astron.	Astronomy	Gal.	Galatians	pers.	person
at. no.	atomic number	Gen.	Genesis	pl.	plural
at. wt.	atomic weight	gen.	genitive	Pop.	population
b.	blend	Geol.	Geology	poss.	possessive
b.	born	Geom.	Geometry	pp.	past participle
bef.	before	Gram.	Grammar	prec.	preceded
Biol.	Biology	Hos.	Hosea	prep.	preposition
Bot.	Botany	in.	inch(es)	pres.	present, present tense
c	circa	indic.	indicative	pres. part	present participle
Cap.	capital (city)	inf.	infinitive	prob.	probably
cap.	capital	interj.	interjection	Pron., pron	pronunciation, pronounced
caps.	capitals	irreg.	irregular	pron.	pronoun
cent.	century	Is.	Isaiah	prp.	present participle
Cf., cf	compare	Jer.	Jeremiah	Ps.	Psalms
Chem.	Chemistry	Judg.	Judges	pt.	preterit (past tense)
Chron.	Chronicles	km	kilometer(s)	ptp.	past participle
cm	centimeter(s)	Lam.	Lamentations	Rev.	Revelations
Col.	Colossians	Lev.	Leviticus	Rom.	Romans
compar.	comparative	l.c.	lowercase	Sam.	Samuel
conj.	conjunction	lit.	literally	S	south, southern
contr.	contraction	m	meter(s)	s.	stem
Cor.	Corinthians	masc.	masculine	sp.	spelling, spelled
Dan.	Daniel	Matt.	Matthew	sp. gr.	specific gravity
d.	died	Med.	Medicine	sq.	square
dat.	dative	mi.	mile(s)	subj.	subjunctive
def.	definition(s)	Mil.	Military	superl.	superlative
der.	derivative	mm	millimeter(s)	syll.	syllable
Deut.	Deuteronomy	mod.	modern	Thes.	Thessalonians
Dial., dial.	dialect, dialectal	Naut.	Nautical	Tim.	Timothy
dim.	diminutive	Neh.	Nehemiah	Usu., usu.	usually
E	east, eastern	N.	north, northern	v.	verb
Eccl.	Ecclesiastes	n.	noun	var.	variant
esp.	especially	neut.	neuter	v.i.	intransitive verb
etym.	etymology	nom.	nominative	v.t.	transitive verb
Ex.	Exodus	n.pl.	noun plural	W	west, western
Ezek.	Ezekiel	Num.	Numbers	yd.	yard(s)

WEBSTER'S AMERICAN FAMILY DICTIONARY

Webster's American Family Dictionary

Webster's American Family Dictionary

Copyright © 1998 by Random House, Inc.

All rights reserved under International and Pan-American Copyright Conventions. No part of this book may be reproduced in any form or by any means, electronic or mechanical, including photocopying, without the written permission of the publisher. All inquiries should be addressed to Random House Reference, Random House, Inc., New York, NY. Published in the United States by Random House, Inc., New York and simultaneously in Canada by Random House of Canada Limited.

Based on the *Random House Webster's College Dictionary* and the Random House Living Dictionary Database.

The *Random House Living Dictionary Database*™, the *Random House Living Database Dictionary*™, and the *Random House Living Dictionary Project*™ are trademarks of Random House, Inc. Random House and the house design are registered trademarks of Random House, Inc.

Library of Congress Cataloging-in-Publication Data is available.

Trademarks
A number of entered words which we have reason to believe constitute trademarks have been designated as such. However, no attempt has been made to designate as trademarks or service marks all terms or words in which proprietary rights might exist. The inclusion, exclusion, or definition of a word or term is not intended to affect, or to express a judgment on, the validity or legal status of the word or term as a trademark, service mark, or other proprietary term.

Please address inquiries about electronic licensing of this division's products, for use on a network or in software or on CD-ROM, to the Subsidiary Rights Department, Random House Reference, fax 212-940-7352.

This book is available for special purchases in bulk by organizations and institutions, not for resale, at special discounts. Please direct your sales inquiries to Random House Premium Sales, fax 212-572-4961.

Typeset and printed in the United States of America.

First Edition
0 9 8 7 6 5
ISBN 0-679-45801-8 (Hardcover)

New York   Toronto   London   Sydney   Auckland

CONTENTS

PREFACE

The aim of *Webster's American Family Dictionary* is unique and challenging: it is to record the standard vocabulary of American English in a way that reflects the common ethical, moral, religious, social, and civic values of mainstream Americans. In short, this dictionary aims to be both a lexical and cultural record of standard American speech and writing at the dawn of the 21st century.

That no similar dictionary exists is not entirely surprising—a result, perhaps, of both the secularization of our culture and the physical constraints of the printed page. Dictionaries, limited in size, traditionally avoid encyclopedic entries, terms that are not so much vocabulary items as references to objects in our culture. And so, in order to provide coverage of a wide range of terminology, some of which may offend some people, these dictionaries have largely been forced to exclude much of the basic vocabulary of American history, folklore, art, literature, and religion.

Yet the need for such a dictionary has long been felt by many educated Americans. The call for a value-centered, family-oriented dictionary, focusing on language that is suitable for the entire family, cannot be ignored. The fact is that most current dictionaries, based on a mandate to report on the English language in a scholarly and non-judgmental way, are directed at an adult market. To borrow a metaphor from the film and television industries, today's college-level dictionaries are R-rated rather than

G-rated. While such dictionaries provide an accurate reflection of the realities of the spoken and written language, they may not offer the most appropriate vocabulary source for families, especially those with young children who are not yet ready to encounter such realities.

In addition, these dictionaries do not contribute the rich lode of cultural referents that this one offers: from well-known proverbs, often linked to Biblical sources, and phrases of historical significance to the books and paintings that have become our cultural icons.

Parents should have a choice. They should be able to determine which reference books belong in their homes as their families evolve. And they themselves, as sentient adults, may well prefer a home library that reflects their own values and views of the world. Hence the need for an alternative dictionary.

To fill this need, the editors have created *Webster's American Family Dictionary*. As its name indicates, this dictionary has been designed as a new, comprehensive, and—yes—wholesome type of reference. The name *Webster's* in the title is itself significant. It serves as a reminder of Noah Webster, known as the "Father of American Lexicography," who viewed the dictionary as a moral guide as well as a practical reference book. He believed that, like the Bible, it should uplift the mind and inspire the soul. To Noah Webster, a dictionary was not simply a book of words, a lexicon; it was a teaching tool and textbook.

Webster was also an American patriot, who insisted on the equal status of American English and British English and sought to emphasize the differences between the two dialects. He was the creator of the first distinctly American English dictionary.

The purpose of *Webster's American Family Dictionary* is to integrate the traditional values espoused by Noah Webster into the framework of the modern standard dictionary. This is not a step backward but a new concept: the recognition that a dictionary can be modern, authoritative, and practical without compromising its moral character.

Thus, it is not the aim of this dictionary merely to exclude the most notoriously offensive words and meanings in the language. Its goal is also to include terms derived from our culture and history that elevate and inspire.

Users of this dictionary will find here thousands of entries and definitions from history, religion, folklore, and mythology that are not encountered in any other dictionary of this size. Some examples are inspiring hymns like the *Battle Hymn of the Republic* and *Amazing Grace*; inspiring figures from our folklore and literature like *Paul Bunyan* and *Horatio Alger*; allusions to the Bible such as *burning bush* and *crown of thorns*; important terms from American history like the *Alabama Claims* and the *Alien and Sedition Acts*; historical court cases like *Marbury v. Madison* and events like the *March on Washington*; popular proverbs and sayings like *All that glitters is not gold* and *Do not cast your pearls before swine*; titles of classic books, plays, paintings, films, etc., such as *Pilgrim's Progress, Hamlet, American Gothic,* and *The Birth of a Nation*; and many other categories.

The dictionary also includes practical charts and other supplements, among them the Declaration of Independence, a summary of the Amendments to the U.S. Constitution, (plus the full text of the first ten, the Bill of Rights), and the text of the Gettysburg Address.

In sum, this dictionary may be used with full confidence by all members of the family as a useful educational tool that upholds traditional standards and values.

vocabulary entry — **ab·a·cus** (ab′ə kəs, ə bak′əs), *n., pl.* **ab·a·cus·es, ab·a·ci** (ab′ə sī′, -kī′, ə bak′ī). **1.** a device for making arithmetical calculations, consisting of a frame set with rods on which balls or beads are moved. **2.** a **syllable dots** — slab forming the top of the capital of a column.

pronunciation — **ab·a·lo·ne** (ab′ə lō′nē), *n.* any gastropod mollusk of the family Haliotidae, having a flat, oval shell with a row of respiratory holes: the flesh is used for food and the shell as a source of mother-of-pearl.

homographs — **a·ban·don**[1] (ə ban′dən), *v.t.* **1.** to leave completely and finally; forsake utterly; desert: *to abandon a child; to abandon a sinking ship.* **2.** to give up; discontinue; withdraw from: *to abandon a project; to abandon hope.* **3.** to give up the control of: *to abandon a city to an enemy army.* **4.** to yield (oneself) without restraint or moderation, as to emotions or natural impulses: *to abandon oneself to grief.*

etymology — **a·ban·don**[2] (ə ban′dən), *n.* a complete surrender to natural impulses without restraint or moderation; freedom from constraint: *to dance with reckless abandon.*

ab·bot (ab′ət), *n.* a man who is the head or superior of a monastery.

cross reference to another entry for comparison — [< Latin < Greek < Aramaic *abbā* father]

A·bed·ne·go (ə bed′ni gō′), *n.* a companion of Daniel. Compare SHADRACH. Dan. 3:12–30.

italicized name of literary work — ***Abe′ Lin′coln in Illinois′,*** a play (1938) by Robert E. Sherwood.

numbered definitions — **ab·jure** (ab jŏŏr′, -jûr′), *v.t.,* **-jured, -jur·ing. 1.** to repudiate or retract, esp. with formal solemnity; recant. **2.** to renounce or give up under oath; forswear: *to abjure allegiance to a country.* **3.** to refrain from.

suffix — **-able,** a suffix meaning "capable of, susceptible of, fit for, tending to, given to," associated in meaning with the word ABLE, occurring in loanwords from Latin (*laudable*); used in English to form adjectives from stems of any origin (*teachable; photographable*). Compare -BLE, -IBLE.

Abom′inable Snow′man, *n.* a legendary large, hairy, humanoid creature said to inhabit the Himalayas. Also called **yeti.**

variant form — **ab·o·rig·i·ne** (ab′ə rij′ə nē), *n.* **1.** one of the original inhabitants of a country or region. **2.** (*usu. cap.*) a member of any of the peoples who **capitalization style** — are the aboriginal inhabitants of Australia. **3. aborigines,** the original, native fauna or flora of a region. [< Latin *ab origine* from the origin]

variant spelling — **a·bridg·ment** or **a·bridge·ment** (ə brij′mənt), *n.* **1.** a shortened or condensed form of a book, speech, etc., that still retains the basic contents. **2.** the act or process of abridging. **3.** the state of being abridged.

ab·sent (*adj., prep.* ab′sənt; *v.* ab sent′, ab′sənt), *adj.* **1.** not in a certain **example sentence or phrase** — place at a given time; away; missing; not present: *absent from class.* **2.** lacking; nonexistent: *Revenge was absent from his mind.* **3.** not attentive; preoccupied; absent-minded: *an absent expression.*

noun plurals, with variant plural pronounced — **a·can·thus** (ə kan′thəs), *n., pl.* **-thus·es, -thi** (-thī). **1.** any of several plants of the genus *Acanthus,* of the Mediterranean region, having toothed leaves and purplish flowers. **2.** an architectural ornament resembling the leaves of this plant. —**a·can′thine** (-thin, -thīn), *adj.*

taxonomic name —

illustration with caption —

leaf of plant,
Acanthus mollis

architectural ornament,
front and side views

acanthus

chemical formula — **a·ce·ta·min·o·phen** (ə sē′tə min′ə fən, as′i tə-), *n.* a crystalline substance, $C_8H_9NO_2$, used as a pain reliever and to reduce fever.

ac·co·lade (ak′ə lād′, -läd′; ak′ə lād′, -läd′), *n.* **1.** any award, honor, or laudatory notice. **2.** a light touch on the shoulder with the flat side of the sword, given in conferring knighthood.

variant pronunciation — **act** (akt), *n.* **1.** anything done, being done, or to be done; deed: *an act of mercy.* **2.** the process of doing: *caught in the act.* **3.** a formal deci**parts of speech** — sion, law, or the like, by a legislature, ruler, court, or other authority; decree or edict; statute. **4.** an instrument or document stating something done or transacted. **5.** one of the main divisions of a play or opera. **6. a.** a short performance by one or more entertainers, usu. part of a variety show, circus, etc. **b.** the routine or style by which an entertainer or group of entertainers is known: *a magic act.* **c.** the personnel of such a group. —*v.i.* **8.** to do someth ing; carry out an action; exert energy or force. **9.** to reach or issue a decision on some matter. **10.** to operate or function in a particular way: *to act as manager.* **11.** to produce an effect. **12.** to behave or conduct oneself in a particular fashion. **13.** to pretend; feign. **14.** to perform as an actor. **15.** to be capable of being performed: *His plays don't act well.* —*v.t.* **16.** to represent (a fictitious or historical character) with one's person: *to act Macbeth.* **17.** to feign; counterfeit. **18.** to behave as. **19.** to behave in a manner appropriate to: **phrasal verbs** — *to act one's age.* **20. act on** or **upon, a.** to act in accordance with; follow. **b.** to have an effect on; affect. **21. act out, a.** to illustrate by pantomime or other gestures. **b.** to express (repressed emotions) inappropriately and without conscious understanding. **22. act up, a.** to fail to **lettered subdefinitions** — function properly; malfunction. **b.** to behave willfully. **c.** (of a recurring ailment) to become painful or troublesome again. —*Idiom.* **23. clean up one's act,** *Informal.* to begin adhering to more acceptable rules of behavior. **24. get** or **have one's act together,** *Informal.* to behave or function responsibly and efficiently.

viii

SAMPLE PAGE

ac·tion (ak′shən), *n.* **1.** the process or state of acting or functioning; the state of being active: *We saw the team in action.* **2.** something done or performed; act; deed. **3.** a consciously willed act or activity. **4.** practical, often organized activity undertaken to deal with or accomplish something: *a crisis that requires immediate action.* **5. actions,** habitual or usual acts; conduct. **6.** energetic activity: *a man of action.* **7.** an exertion of power or force: *the destructive action of wind.* **8.** effect or influence: *the action of morphine.* **9.** a change in organs, tissues, or cells leading to performance of a function, as in muscular contraction. **10.** way or manner of moving: *the action of a horse.* **11.** the mechanism by which something is operated, as that of a gun or a piano. **12.** a military encounter, as a battle or skirmish. **13.** actual combat with enemy forces. **14.** the main subject or story line of a literary or dramatic work. **15. a.** an event or series of events that form part of a dramatic plot. **b.** (used as a command by a motion-picture director to begin the performance of a scene for filming). **16.** the gestures or deportment of an actor or speaker. **17.** a legal proceeding instituted by one party against another. **18.** *Slang.* **a.** interesting or exciting activity, sometimes of an illicit nature. **b.** gambling activity. —*Idiom.* **19.** piece of the action, *Informal.* a share of the proceeds or profits. **20. take action, a.** to start doing something. **b.** to start a legal procedure. —*Proverb.* **21. Actions speak louder than words,** deeds are more important than what is said. —**ac′tion·less,** *adj.*

ad (ad), *n.* **1.** an advertisement. **2.** advertising: *an ad agency.*

ad-, a prefix occurring in verbs or verbal derivatives borrowed from Latin, where it meant "toward" and indicated direction, tendency, or addition: *adjoin.*

ADD, attention deficit disorder.

ad·mire (ad mīᵊr′), *v.,* **-mired, -mir·ing.** —*v.t.* **1.** to regard with pleasure or approval, often mixed with wonder. **2.** to regard highly; respect; esteem. **3.** to regard with wonder or surprise. —*v.i.* **4.** to feel or express admiration. **5.** *Dial.* to take pleasure; like or desire: *I would admire to go.* —**ad·mir′er,** *n.* —**ad·mir′ing·ly,** *adv.*

adult′-on′set diabe′tes, *n.* See under DIABETES MELLITUS.

Ae·non (ē′non), *n.* a spring in Palestine where John the Baptist was baptizing during the ministry of Jesus in Judea. John 3:23.

a·gi·ta·to (aj′i tä′tō, ä′ji-), *adj. Music.* agitated; restless or hurried in movement or style.

ai·lan·thus (ā lan′thəs), *n., pl.* **-thus·es.** any of several wide-spreading trees of the genus *Ailanthus,* of the quassia family, with long leaves and dense flower clusters, esp. *A. altissima* **(tree of heaven),** an urban shade tree. —**ai·lan′thic,** *adj.*

air′ mile′, *n.* INTERNATIONAL NAUTICAL MILE.

air·y (âr′ē), *adj.,* **air·i·er, air·i·est. 1.** open to a free current of fresh air; breezy: *airy rooms.* **2.** consisting of or having the character of air; immaterial: *airy phantoms.* **3.** light in appearance; thin: *airy garments.* **4.** light in manner; sprightly; lively: *airy songs.* **5.** light in movement; graceful; delicate: *an airy step.* **6.** unsubstantial; unreal; imaginary: *airy dreams.* **7.** performed in the air; aerial. **8.** lofty; high in the air. **9.** snobbishly affected; haughty: *a model striking airy poses.*

al·a·me·da (al′ə mā′də), *n., pl.* **-das. 1.** *Chiefly Southwestern U.S.* a public walk shaded with trees. **2.** (in Latin America) a boulevard, park, or public garden having such a walk.

Al·drin (ôl′drin), *n.* **Edwin Eugene, Jr.** (*"Buzz"*), born 1930, U.S. astronaut: second person to walk on the moon, l969.

al·lit·er·a·tion (ə lit′ə rā′shən), *n.* **1.** repetition of the same sound, as a consonant or cluster, at the beginning of two or more stressed syllables, as in *from stem to stern.* Compare CONSONANCE (def. 4a). **2.** the commencement of two or more words of a word group with the same letter, as in *apt alliteration's artful aid.* —**al·lit′er·ate′,** *v.i., v.t.,* **-at·ed, -at·ing.** —**al·lit′er·a′tive** (-ə rā′tiv, -ər ə tiv), *adj.*

All′ Things′ Bright′ and Beau′tiful, a Christian hymn (1848) about creation with words by Cecil Alexander.

al·right (ôl rīt′), *adv., adj.* ALL RIGHT. —*Usage.* The form ALRIGHT as a one-word spelling of the phrase ALL RIGHT in all of its senses probably arose by analogy with such words as *already* and *altogether.* Although ALRIGHT is a common spelling in written dialogue and in other types of informal writing, it is often considered incorrect, and ALL RIGHT is used in more formal, edited writing.

an·cien ré·gime (än syaṅ rā zhēm′), *n. French.* **1.** the political and social system of France before the revolution of 1789. **2.** any former political and social system.

angio-, a combining form meaning "vessel, container" or "blood vessel": *angiology; angiosperm.*

An·go·la (ang gō′lə), *n.* a republic in SW Africa: formerly an overseas province of Portugal; gained independence Nov. 11, 1975. 10,623,994; 481,226 sq. mi. (1,246,375 sq. km). *Cap.:* Luanda. Formerly, **Portuguese West Africa.** —**An·go′lan,** *adj., n.*

a·poc·ry·pha (ə pok′rə fə), *n.* (*used with a sing. or pl. v.*) **1.** (*cap.*) a group of books not found in Jewish or Protestant versions of the Old Testament but included in the Septuagint and in Roman Catholic editions of the Bible. **2.** various religious writings of uncertain origin regarded by some as inspired, but rejected by most authorities. **3.** writings or statements of doubtful authorship or authenticity. Compare CANON¹ (defs. 5, 6, 8).

Ar·go·naut (är′gə nôt′, -not′), *n.* **1.** a member of the band of men who sailed to Colchis with Jason in the ship *Argo* in search of the Golden Fleece. **2.** (*sometimes l.c.*) a person in quest of something dangerous but rewarding; adventurer.

guide words

idioms

proverb

prefix

abbreviation

verb inflection

cross reference to hidden entry

Biblical citation

subject label

hidden entry

cross reference to another entry

adjective inflection

label of place

biographical entry

run-on derived entries

stressed multiple-word entry

usage note

foreign phrase

combining form

geographical term

grammatical information

lowercase style

HOW TO USE
THIS DICTIONARY

Entries: Where and How to Find Them

Guide words

Guide words, which are shown at the top left of even-numbered pages and the top right of odd-numbered pages, give the range of main entries covered on that page.

Main entries

To help you find the words you are looking for, all the main entries in the dictionary, including abbreviations, biographical and geographical terms, and the names of historical events, appear in a single alphabetical list.

Entries that would normally be italicized in print (or underlined in writing or typing)—such as foreign words and phrases not yet assimilated into English, book titles, and names of ships—are shown in boldface italics rather than the usual boldface roman type.

Variant forms

Variant forms are common alternatives to the entry term. If they have only minor spelling differences or a different suffix, they are shown at the top of the entry, following the

---

ad ma·jo·rem De·i glo·ri·am (äd mä yô′rem de′ē glô′rē äm′), *Latin.* for the greater glory of God: motto of the Jesuits.

Boldface italic entries

Mo·by-Dick (mō′bē dik′), a novel (1851) by Herman Melville.

Neg·ev (neg′ev) also **Neg·eb** (-eb), *n.* a partly desert region in S Israel, bordering on the Sinai Peninsula. 4700 sq. mi. (12,173 sq. km).

Equal variants

main entry, in the same large bold-face type, and are introduced by "or" or "also."

Variant forms that are consistently less common than the main-entry word are shown later in the entry, preceded by "Often" or "Sometimes."

Nouns that have the same meaning as the main-entry term, but that are substantially different in form, are preceded by "Also called."

In many cases, a variant form is listed as a main entry at its own alphabetical place and cross-referred to the more common form. Such cross references direct you to the entry with the definition and are normally shown in small capital letters.

Homographs

Homographs are words that are spelled identically but that differ in derivation. They have separate main entries and are marked with small superscript numbers.

Run-ons

Run-ons are words that are closely related to the main entry but often have a different grammatical function. Preceded by a lightface dash, these words appear at the end of an individual entry, following either the last definition or the bracketed etymology.

Run-ons are typically formed by adding a suffix. Although a run-on is not explicitly defined, its meaning can be understood by combining the senses of its root word and suffix, taking into account the part of speech. Thus the adverb *elaborately*, run-on to the adjective *elab-*

Less common variant

sym·bol·ic (sim bol′ik), *adj.* **1.** serving as a symbol of something (often fol. by *of*). **2.** of, pertaining to, or expressed by a symbol. **3.** characterized by or involving the use of symbols: *a highly symbolic poem.* Often, **sym·bol′i·cal.** —**sym·bol′i·cal·ly,** *adv.*

Different words for the same thing

ri·bo·fla·vin (rī′bō flā′vin, rī′bō flā′-, -bə-), *n.* a vitamin B complex factor essential for growth, occurring as a yellow crystalline compound, $C_{17}H_{20}N_4O_6$, abundant in milk, meat, eggs, and leafy vegetables and produced synthetically. Also called **vitamin B₂.**

A variant as a main entry

prus′sic ac′id (prus′ik), *n.* HYDROCYANIC ACID.

Homographs

loaf¹ (lōf), *n., pl.* **loaves** (lōvz). **1.** a portion of bread or cake usu. baked in an oblong mass with a rounded top. **2.** a shaped or molded mass of food, as of chopped meat: *a veal loaf.*
loaf² (lōf), *v.i.* **1.** to idle away time. **2.** to lounge or saunter lazily and idly. —*v.t.* **3.** to pass idly (usu. fol. by *away*): *to loaf one's life away.*

Run-ons

e·lab·o·rate (*adj.* i lab′ər it; *v.* -ə rāt′), *adj., v.,* **-rat·ed, -rat·ing.** —*adj.* **1.** worked out in great detail; painstaking: *elaborate preparations.* **2.** ornate, showy, or gaudy: *an elaborate costume.* —*v.t.* **3.** to work out in minute detail. **4.** to develop or expand. **5.** to produce or develop by labor. —*v.i.* **6.** to add details or information; expand (usu. fol. by *on*): *to elaborate on an idea.* —**e·lab′o·rate·ly,** *adv.* —**e·lab′o·rate·ness,** *n.* —**e·lab′o·ra′tion,** *n.* —**e·lab′o·ra′tive,** *adj.*

orate, is understood to mean "in an elaborate manner."

Some run-ons are formed in other ways, as by deleting or changing a suffix. Derivation of run-ons not involving suffixes follows standard conventions of English, as when a hyphenated adjective is formed from a two-word noun.

All suffixes used in forming run-ons are also listed as main entries, where their meanings are explained.

List words

Lists of undefined entries are shown using some common prefixes. In these lists, the words are formed by adding a prefix to the base word. The words can be understood by adding one of the meanings of the prefix to the meaning of the base word. Thus, *anti-* + *modern* as an adjective means "against (things that are) modern." These lists start at the bottom of the dictionary page where the prefix is entered and extend to following pages.

Hidden entries

Hidden entries are parenthesized boldface terms shown within the context of a definition, where the meaning of the hidden entry is made clear.

Phrasal verbs

Phrasal verbs, like *back off*, *clear up*, and *stand by* (sometimes known as two-word verbs), form a single vocabulary unit with a meaning that is often not predictable from the sum of its parts. Phrasal verbs are shown in bold-

---

anti-, a prefix meaning "against, opposed to, prejudicial to" (*antiabortion; anti-Semitic; antislavery*), "preventing, counteracting, or mitigating" (*anticoagulant; antifreeze*), "destroying or disabling" (*antiaircraft; antipersonnel*), "identical to in form or function, but lacking, opposite, or contrary in essential respects" (*anticlimax; antihero; antiparticle*), "an antagonist or rival of" (*Antichrist; antipope*), "situated opposite" (*Anti-Lebanon*). Also, *before a vowel*, **ant-**.

an′ti•spas•mod′ic, *adj., n.*
an′ti•spec′u•la′tion, *n., adj.*
an′ti•spend′ing, *adj.*
an′ti•stall′ing, *adj.*

— List words formed with prefix "anti"

Bun′ker Hill′, *n.* a hill in Charlestown, Mass., near Boston: the first major battle of the Revolutionary War **(Battle of Bunker Hill)** was fought on adjoining Breed's Hill on June 17, 1775.

— Hidden entry

wear (wâr), *v.,* **wore, worn, wear•ing,** *n.* —*v.t.* **1.** to carry or have on the body or about the person as a covering, support, ornament, or the like.... **12. wear down, a.** to make or become shabbier, smaller, or more aged by wearing. **b.** to make or become weary; tire. **c.** to prevail upon or over by persistence; overcome: *to wear down the opposition....* **14. wear out, a.** to make or become unfit or useless through hard or extended use: *to wear out clothes.* **b.** to expend, consume, or remove, esp. slowly or gradually. **c.** to exhaust, as by continued strain; weary....

— Phrasal verbs

face type and placed together as the final group of verb definitions in an entry.

Idioms

Idioms are fixed expressions whose meanings are not predictable from the usual senses of their component words. Idioms appear in a labeled group at or near the end of an entry.

Idiom ──

mile (mīl), *n.* **1.** Also called **statute mile.** a unit of distance on land in English-speaking countries equal to 5280 feet, or 1760 yards (1.609 kilometers).... *Abbr.:* mi, mi. **5.** a notable distance or margin: *missed it by a mile.* —*Idiom.* **6. go the extra mile,** to make an extra effort.

Proverbs and sayings

Proverbs and sayings are short, popularly known expressions that convey a truth based on common sense or practical experience. In this dictionary these expressions are labeled and grouped together at the end of an entry. If you can't find the saying you are looking for under one word, try looking under another word in the saying.

Proverb ──

leop•ard (lep′ərd), *n.* **1.** a large, powerful, spotted Asian or African cat, *Panthera pardus,* usu. tawny with black markings; the Old World panther. **2.** the fur or pelt of this animal. **3.** any similar cat, as the snow leopard. —*Proverb.* **4. A leopard can't change its spots,** someone's intrinsic nature can't be altered. Jer. 13:23.

Entries: How They Are Shown

Syllabification

All single-word entries of more than one syllable are syllabified, that is, divided into syllables by boldface centered dots. These dots indicate possible places where a word may break at the end of a line in printed or typed text.

Syllable dots ──

as•ter•oid (as′tə roid′), *n.* **1.** any of the thousands of small, solid bodies that revolve about the sun in orbits largely between Mars and Jupiter. —*adj.* **2.** starlike. —**as′ter•oi′dal,** *adj.*

Although the dictionary shows the total number of syllables into which a word may be broken, not all syllable breaks shown should be used as end-of-line divisions. It is not advisable to break the beginning or ending of a word before or after a single character: *nursery,* for example, should not be broken before the single character "y," or

Change in syllable division for different part of speech

prog·ress (*n.* prog′res, -rəs; *esp. Brit.* prō′gres; *v.* prə·gres′), *n.* **1.** advancement toward a goal or to a further or higher stage. **2.** the development of an individual or society in a direction considered superior to the previous level.... —*v.i.* **pro·gress 6.** to go forward or onward in space or time. **7.** to grow or develop; advance: *a disease progressing slowly....*

hap′py-go-luck′y, *adj.* trusting cheerfully to luck; happily unworried or unconcerned.

Stress marks

ba′sal metabol′ic rate′, *n.* the rate at which energy is expended while fasting and at rest, calculated as calories per hour per square meter of body surface.

a·cer·bic (ə sûr′bik), *adj.* **1.** sour or astringent in taste. **2.** sharply or bitterly severe, as temper or expression. —**a·cer′bi·cal·ly,** *adv.* —**a·cer′bi·ty,** *n.*

Pronunciation

alone after the single character "a." Hyphenated compounds, like *country-and-western* or *habit-forming* are best split after the hyphen.

Main entries are normally divided into syllables according to the first pronunciation shown. However, when both the pronunciation and syllable division shift for different parts of speech—as between *progress*, the noun and adjective, and *progress*, the verb— the entire entry is repeated to show the change in syllable division.

Stress

Primary and secondary stress marks replace centered dots at some syllable breaks. These marks serve as an aid to pronunciation for entries that are not pronounced fully by indicating the relative differences in emphasis between syllables. A primary stress mark (′) follows the syllable with greatest emphasis, and a secondary stress mark (‵) follows one with lesser emphasis.

Entries consisting of two or more words, where each is handled at its own entry, are not fully syllabified but are shown with a pattern of stress that reveals the relationship of each word to the others.

Pronunciation

Pronunciations are shown in parentheses immediately following the entry form, using a system of diacritical marks over vowels. A Pronunciation Key appears on page xxviii of this book.

Most entries show full pronunciations. Entries that are not pronounced fully have component parts pronounced elsewhere in the dictionary.

Parts of speech

Italicized part-of-speech labels, usually abbreviated, are given for main entries and run-ons to show their grammatical function in a sentence. Thus a main entry that is commonly used as a noun, whether spelled as a single solid word, a hyphenated form, or two or more words, would receive the label *n.*

Following are the most common of these labels, with the parts of speech they stand for:

adj. adjective
adv. adverb
conj. conjunction
interj. interjection
n. noun
n.pl. plural noun
prep. preposition
pron. pronoun
v. verb
v.i. intransitive verb
v.t. transitive verb

For verb definitions, the label *v.t.* is used at definitions for transitive verbs (verbs that take an object) and the label *v.i.* is used for intransitive verbs (verbs that do not take an object). Occasionally, a combined *v.t., v.i.* label will be used when the definition covers both transitive and intransitive uses.

Inflected forms

Inflected forms shown in this dictionary are, typically,

- plurals of nouns,

Transitive and intransitive definitions

tend[1] (tend), *v.i.* **1.** to be disposed or inclined in action, operation, or effect to do something: *The particles tend to unite.* **2.** to be disposed toward an idea, emotion, way of thinking, etc....
tend[2] (tend), *v.t.* **1.** to attend to by work or services, care, etc.: *to tend a fire.* **2.** to watch over and care for; minister to: *to tend the sick.* **3.** to handle or attend to (a rope). —*v.i.* **4.** to attend by action, care, etc.(usu. fol. by *to*).

pas•try (pā′strē), *n.*, *pl.* **-tries. 1.** a sweet baked food made of dough. **2.** a piece of such food.   **— Noun inflection**

go (gō), *v.*, **went, gone, go•ing,** *n.*, *pl.* **goes,** *adj.* **—***v.i.*   **— Verb inflection**
1. to move or proceed, esp. to or from something: *to go home....*

— Adjective inflection

ho•ly (hō′lē), *adj.*, **-li•er, -li•est. 1.** recognized as or declared sacred by religious use or authority; consecrated: *holy ground.* **2.** dedicated or devoted to the service of God, the church, or religion....

— Pronoun inflection

we (wē), *pron.pl.*, *poss.* **our** or **ours,** *obj.* **us. 1.** nominative plural of I. **2.** (used to denote oneself and another or others, specifically or generally): *We have two children. We often take good health for granted.* **3.** (used in the predicate following a linking verb): *It is we who should thank you....*

com•put•er (kəm pyōō′tər), *n.* **1.** a programmable   **— Regular noun:**
electronic device designed for performing prescribed   **no inflection**
operations on data at high speed, esp. one housed with
or linked to other devices for inputting, storing, retrieving, and displaying the data....

— Regular verb:
— no inflection

pack (pak), *n.* **1.** a group of things wrapped or tied together for easy handling or carrying; a bundle, esp. one carried on the back of an animal or person.... **—***v.t.* **13.** to make into a pack or bundle....

— Most common
senses given first

site (sīt), *n.*, *v.*, **sit•ed, sit•ing. —***n.* **1.** the position or location of a town, building, etc., esp. as to its environment. **2.** the area or exact plot of ground on which anything is, has been, or is to be located: *the site of ancient Troy.* **3.** Web site. **—***v.t.* **4.** to place in or provide with a site; locate. **5.** to put in position for operation, as artillery.

ra•tion•al (rash′ə nl, rash′nl), *adj.* **1.** based on or agreeable to reason: *a rational decision.* **2.** exercising reason: *a rational negotiator.* **3.** sane; lucid: *The patient   **— Specialized sense**
seems perfectly rational.* **4.** *Math.* **a.** capable of being   **given last**
expressed exactly by a ratio of two integers. **b.** (of a function) capable of being expressed exactly by a ratio of two polynomials. **—***n.* **5.** rational number. **—ra′tion•al•ly,** *adv.*

rev•o•lu•tion (rev′ə lōō′shən), *n.* **1.** a complete and   **— Subdefinitions**
forcible overthrow and replacement of an established
government or political system by the people governed.... **4. a.** a turning round or rotating, as on an axis. **b.** a moving in a circular or curving course, as about a central point. **c.** a single cycle in such a course. **5. a.** the orbiting of one heavenly body around another.   **— Italicized sense**
b. (not in technical use) the rotation of a heavenly body on its axis. **c.** a single course of such movement....

Twelfth′ Night′, *n.* **1.** the evening before Twelfth Day or the evening of Twelfth Day itself. **2.** (*italics*) a comedy (1602) by William Shakespeare.

ad•vent (ad′vent), *n.* **1.** an arrival; a start or com-   **— Capitalized sense**
mencement: *the advent of the holiday season.* **2. a.** (*usu. cap.*) the coming of Christ into the world. **b.** (*cap.*) the penitential period beginning four Sundays before Christmas, commemorating this.

- past-tense forms and past and present participles of verbs,
- comparative and superlative forms of adjectives that are formed by adding *-er* and *-est*, and
- the entire paradigm of pronoun forms.

Inflected forms are shown immediately after the part-of-speech label. The dictionary gives inflected forms for all words that form their inflections irregularly, as well as for many regular forms where confusion about spelling might occur.

Inflections are not given for regular verbs or for nouns that form their plurals by adding *-s* or *-es.*

Definitions

Definitions within an entry are individually numbered in a single sequence, regardless of their groupings according to part of speech. In general, the most common part of speech is listed first, as is the most frequent meaning within the part-of-speech group. Specialized senses follow those that are part of the general vocabulary.

Numbered definitions are sometimes divided into lettered subdefinitions so that related meanings can be grouped together.

When an italicized form applies only to a particular definition, the main entry remains in roman and the definition itself is labeled "*(italics).*"

If a word is spelled with a capital letter when used in a specific sense, this is noted at the beginning of the definition with the label (*cap.*). Similarly, when a word that is usually capitalized would not be capitalized for a specific sense, this is indicated by the label (*l.c.*) (lower case).

The word "Compare" at the end of a definition, preceding one or more terms in small capitals, indicates that related information may be found at other entries.

Labels

An italicized label preceding a definition or a group of definitions indicates that the word's use is limited in some way.

Subject labels

Entries or definitions restricted in use to a particular field are given an appropriate label.

Labels of place

Entries or definitions limited in use to a particular geographical location are given a regional label (for example, *Canadian, Chiefly Brit., South Midland U.S.*). Entries not so labeled are considered to be in general use in the U.S. A few terms too widespread to warrant specific geographical restriction or with a somewhat rural flavor are labeled "*Dial.*"

Labels of style or status

For entries not part of the standard vocabulary, these labels are given to aid in making useful judgments about the setting in which a term is appropriate, the kind of speaker who might use it, the kind of communication intended, and the likely effect on the listener or reader.

Lower case sense

Pu·ri·tan (py๐๐r′i tn), *n.* **1.** a member of a group of Protestants that arose in the 16th century within the Church of England,... **2.** (*l.c.*) a person who is strict in moral or religious matters, often to an excessive degree....

Reference to another entry

jet·sam or **jet·som** (jet′səm), *n.* goods that are cast overboard deliberately, as to lighten or stabilize a vessel in an emergency, and that sink where jettisoned or are washed ashore. Compare FLOTSAM.

Musical term

a·da·gio (ə dä′jō, -zhē ō′), *adv., adj., n., pl.* **-gios.** —*adv.* **1.** *Music.* in a leisurely manner; slowly. —*adj.* **2.** *Music.* slow. —*n.* **3.** an adagio movement or piece of music....

U.S. regional label

ap′ple pandow′dy, *n.* Chiefly New Eng. a deep-dish apple pie or cobbler, usually sweetened with molasses.

General dialect label

a·gin (ə gin′), *prep. Dial.* against; opposed to.

fla′vor of the month′, *n. Informal.* the subject of intense, usu. temporary interest; the current fashion. —— **Informal term**

no•how (nō′hou′), *adv. Nonstandard.* in no case; in no way. —— **Nonstandard term**

grunge (grunj), *n. Slang.* **1.** dirt; filth; rubbish. **2.** something unpleasant or of inferior quality. —**grun′gi•ness,** *n.* —**grun′gy,** *adj.,* **-i•er, -i•est.** —— **Slang term**

couth (kōōth), *Facetious.* —*adj.* **1.** showing or having good manners or sophistication; smooth. —*n.* **2.** good manners; refinement: *to be lacking in couth.* —— **Facetious usage**

Er•in (er′in), *n. Literary.* Ireland. —— **Literary usage**

luv (luv), *n. Eye Dialect.* love. —— **Eye dialect**

got•cha (goch′ə), *interj. Pron. Spelling.* got you (used to indicate comprehension, to exultingly point out a blunder, etc.). —— **Pronunciation spelling**

Informal. Not likely to occur in formal prepared speech or carefully edited writing except when used intentionally to convey a casual tone.

Nonstandard. Not conforming to the speech or grammar of educated people and often regarded as a marker of low social status.

Slang. Often metaphorical; vivid, playful, and elliptical. Much slang is ephemeral, becoming dated in a relatively short time, but some slang terms find their way into the standard language. Slang terms are used in formal speech and writing only for special effect.

Facetious. Used consciously for humorous or playful effect.

Literary. Used in contemporary speech or writing to create a poetic, evocative effect.

Eye Dialect. Used for deliberate misspellings in literature intended to convey a character's lack of education or habitual use of dialectal pronunciations, but in fact representing perfectly standard pronunciations.

Pron. Spelling. Terms with this label, which stands for Pronunciation Spelling, differ from those labeled "Eye Dialect" in that they are intended to convey not lack of education, but merely continuous rapid speech, and are often encountered in fiction. The relaxed pronunciations these forms reflect are used by speakers at all educational and social levels.

Etymologies

Etymologies, or word histories, appear in square brackets after the definitions. The etymology tells the language or languages from which the word came into English or the person or place that something is named after.

The word in the foreign language appears in italics. If there is a language label but no word in italics, it means that the word in the foreign language is the same as the main-entry word. Note that many words have come into English from Greek by way of Latin, or from Latin by way of French, etc.

Etymologies

Sab·bath (sab′əth), *n.* **1.** the seventh day of the week, Saturday, as the day of rest and religious observance among Jews and some Christians. Ex. 20:8–11. **2.** the first day of the week, Sunday, observed by most Christians in commemoration of the Resurrection of Christ. **3.** (*often l.c.*) a day of rest or prayer. [Old English < Latin *sabbatum* < Greek *sábbaton* < Hebrew *shabbāth* rest]

Mc·In·tosh (mak′in tosh′), *n.* a variety of red eating apple. [after John *McIntosh* of Ontario, who first cultivated it (1796)]

ad·vo·cate (*v.* ad′və kāt′; *n.* -kit, -kāt′), *v.*, **-cat·ed, -cat·ing,** *n.* —*v.t.* **1.** to support or urge by argument; recommend publicly: *to advocate higher salaries for teachers.* —*n.* **2.** a person who speaks or writes in support of a cause, person, etc.... **3.** a person who pleads for or in behalf of another ; intercessor.... **5.** (*cap.*) Jesus. I John 2:1. [< Latin *advocātus* legal counselor] —**ad′vo·ca′tion,** *n.* —**ad′vo·ca′tive,** *adj.* —**ad′vo·ca′tor,** *n.*

pa·dre (pä′drā, -drē), *n.*, *pl.* **-dres. 1.** a priest or clergyman. **2.** a military chaplain. [< Spanish, Portuguese, Italian: father < Latin *pater*]

SELECTED KEY TERMS—
TOPICAL INDEX

Bible Terms

Aaron
Abaddon
Abba
Abednego
Abigail
Abraham
Absalom
Aceldama
Acts of the Apostles
Admah
Adnah
Adoni-Bezek
Aenon
Ahab
Ahasuerus
Ahimelech
Ahithophel
Aijalon
Amalek
Amalekite
Amphipolis
Amos
Amram
Ananias
Ancient of Days
Andrew
Anna
Annas
apocalypse
apocrypha
Apollyon
Aquila
Aram
Archelaus
Ariel
Arimathaea
Armageddon
Asher
Athaliah
avenger of blood
Azazel
Babel
Barabbas
Barak
Bar-Jonah
Barnabas
Barsabbas
Bartholomew
Baruch
Bathsheba
Beelzebub

Beersheba
behemoth
Benjamin
Berea
Bernice
Bethany
Bethel
Bethesda
Beth Peor
Bethsaida
Beth Shemesh
Boaz
Bread of Life
burning bush
Caiaphas
Cain
Caleb
Calvary
Cana
Canaan
Capernaum
Cenchrea
Cephas
Chaldean
Chedorlaomer
Chronicles
Cities of Refuge
Cities of the Plain
Cleopas
coat of many colors
Colossians
Corinthians
Crispus
Curse of Cain
Dan
Daniel
Dathan
Daughter of Zion
David
Deborah
Delilah
Deuteronomy
Didymus
Dinah
Dives
Doeg
Dorcas
doubting Thomas
Drusilla
Ebal
Ebed-Melech
Ecclesiastes
Ecclesiasticus
Eden

Elihu
Elijah
Elimelech
Eliphaz
Elisabeth
Elisha
Elohim
Emmaus
Endor
Enoch
Enos
ephesians
Ephraim
epistle
Esau
Esdras
Eshcol
Esther
Eutychus
Evil-Merodach
Exodus
Ezekiel
Ezra
Felix
Four Horsemen of the
  Apocalypse
Gad
Gadara
Galatians
Gallio
Gamaliel
Gath
Gedaliah
Gehazi
Gehenna
Genesis
Gennesaret
Gershom
Gethsemane
Gibeon
Gideon
Gilboa
Gilgal
God and mammon
Gog and Magog
golden calf
golden rule
Golgotha
Goliath
Gomorrah
Goshen
Habakkuk
Haggai
Haman

Hannah
Hebrews
Hephzibah
Heptateuch
hermeneutics
hexaemeron
Hezekiah
Holofernes
Holy One
Horeb
Horite
Hosea
Huldah
Immanuel
Irijah
Isaac
Isaiah
Iscariot
Ishmael
Issachar
Jabal
Jabbok
Jacob
Jacob's well
Jael
James
Japheth
Jehoahaz
Jehoshaphat
Jehu
Jephthah
Jeremiah
Jeroboam
Jesse
Jesus
Jethro
Jezebel
Joab
Joanna
Joash
Job
Jochebed
Joel
John
John the Baptist
Jonah
Jonathan
Joram
Joseph
Joseph of Arimathaea
Joshua
Josiah
Jotham
Jubal

Judah
Judas
Jude
Judges
Judith
Kedar
Kenite
Keturah
Kidron
Kings
Kirjath Arba
Korah
Laban
Lachish
Lazarus
Leah
Lemuel
Levi
Leviticus
Light of the World
Lo-Ammi
Lois
lost tribes
Lot
Luke
Lystra
Machpelah
Magi
Major Prophet
Malachi
Malchus
Manasseh
manna
Manoah
Marah
mark of the beast
Martha
Mary
Matthew
Matthias
Megiddo
Melchizedek
Mephibosheth
Merab
Meshach
Methuselah
Micah
Michael
Michmash
Midian
Minor Prophet
Miriam
mixed multitude
Mizpah

United States History and Government

World History and Government

parliament
Pax Romana
peace dividend
peaceful coexistence
peace offensive
People's Liberation Army
Permanent Court of
   International Justice
Plantagenet
popular sovereignty
privy council
proportional representation
Prussia
realpolitik
Red Guard
regency

Reign of Terror
Renaissance
resistance
Riot Act
robber baron
Romanov
Russian Revolution
samurai
sans-culotte
Sandinista
Saracen
secretariat
Security Council
serf
Seven Years War
shogun

Sinn Fein
Slave Coast
Social Democratic Party
Solemn League and Covenant
Spanish-American War
Spanish Civil War
Stuart
suffragist
sultan
T'ang
Third Reich
Thirty Years War
Tory
Triple Alliance
Triple Entente
Tudor

ukase
UNICEF
V-E Day
Victorian
Vietcong
Viking
villein
V-J Day
War of the Spanish Succession
Wars of the Roses
Weimar Republic
World Bank
World War I
World War II
York

Proverbs and Sayings

Actions speak louder than words.

After a storm comes a calm.

After the feast comes the reckoning.

All that glitters is not gold.

The apple doesn't fall far from the tree.

Ask, and it shall be given you; seek, and you shall find; knock, and it shall be opened unto you.

As you sow, so shall you reap.

Beauty is in the eye of the beholder.

Beggars can't be choosers.

Better to light one little candle than to curse the darkness.

Beware of Greeks bearing gifts.

A bird in the hand is worth two in the bush.

Birds of a feather flock together.

A burnt child fears the fire.

Butter wouldn't melt in his (or her) mouth.

By their fruits shall ye know them.

Carry coals to Newcastle.

The cobbler should stick to his last.

Cream rises to the top.

Curiosity killed the cat.

The devil can cite scripture for his own purpose.

Discretion is the better part of valor.

Do not cast your pearls before swine.

Don't bite off more than you can chew.

Don't change horses in midstream.

Don't count your chickens before they hatch.

Don't kill the goose that laid the golden eggs.

Don't put all your eggs in one basket.

Don't take any wooden nickels.

The early bird catches the worm.

Early to bed and early to rise makes a man healthy, wealthy, and wise.

The emperor has no clothes on.

Every cloud has a silver lining.

Everyone to whom much is given, of him will much be required.

Experience is the best teacher.

An eye for an eye, a tooth for a tooth.

Facts are facts.

The family that prays together stays together.

First in war, first in peace, first in the hearts of his countrymen.

Fortune favors the brave.

For want of a nail the kingdom was lost.

A friend in need is a friend indeed.

From the sublime to the ridiculous is but a step.

The game is not worth the candle.

Get thee behind me, Satan.

Give me liberty, or give me death!

God helps those who help themselves.

God is in the details.

God's in his heaven, all's right with the world.

Good fences make good neighbors.

A good name is better than precious ointment.

Good things come to those who wait.

Government of the people, by the people, and for the people.

The grass is always greener on the other side of the fence.

Great oaks from little acorns grow.

Half a loaf is better than none.

Handsome is as handsome does.

Haste makes waste.

Here I stand, I can do no other, God help me.

He that is not with me is against me.

He who does not work, neither should he eat.

He who pays the piper calls the tune.

If a thing is worth doing, it's worth doing well.

If at first you don't succeed, try, try again.

If wishes were horses, beggars would ride.

If you can't stand the heat, get out of the kitchen.

If you want peace, prepare for war.

Imitation is the sincerest form of flattery.

In unity there is strength.

I only regret that I have but one life to lose for my country.

It is always darkest just before the dawn.

It is more blessed to give than to receive.

It never rains but it pours.

It's an ill wind that blows no good.

Jack of all trades and master of none.

Judge not according to appearances.

Judge not, that ye be not judged.

Justice is blind.

Least said, soonest mended.

A leopard can't change its spots.

Less is more.

Let him who is without sin cast the first stone.

Lightning never strikes twice in the same place.

The lion shall lie down with the lamb.

A little learning (or knowledge) is a dangerous thing.

Little pitchers have big ears.

Look before you leap.

The Lord gives and the Lord takes away.

Love thy neighbor as thyself.

Man does not live by bread alone.

Man proposes, God disposes.

A merry heart makes a cheerful countenance.

A miss is as good as a mile.

Murder will out.

Necessity is the mother of invention.

Never put off until tomorrow what you can do today.

Never say never.

Never sell America short.

A new broom sweeps clean.

No gain without pain.

No man is an island.

No news is good news.

Nothing ventured, nothing gained.

Oil and water don't mix.

Old habits die hard.

One's reach should exceed one's grasp.

One swallow does not make a summer.

Opportunity knocks but once.

An ounce of prevention is worth a pound of cure.

Out of sight, out of mind.

Out of the mouths of babes and sucklings come great truths.

The pen is mightier than the sword.

People who live in glass houses shouldn't throw stones.

Physician, heal thyself.

A place for everything and everything in its place.

A plague on both your houses.

Practice makes perfect.

Practice what you preach.

Praise the Lord and pass the ammunition.

Pride goes before a fall.

The proof of the pudding is in the eating.

A prophet is not without honor, save in his own country.

The race is not to the swift.

Rats desert a sinking ship.

Render unto Caesar the things that are Caesar's and unto God the things that are God's.

A rising tide lifts all boats.

A rolling stone gathers no moss.

A rotten apple spoils the barrel.

Seize the day.

The shoe is on the other foot.

Slow but steady wins the race.

A soft answer turneth away wrath.

Something is rotten in Denmark.

Spare the rod and spoil the child.

Speak softly and carry a big stick.

The spirit is willing, but the flesh is weak.

The squeaky wheel gets the grease.

Still waters run deep.

A stitch in time saves nine.

Strain at a gnat and swallow a camel.

That dog won't hunt.

There is nothing new under the sun.

There's always room at the top.

There's more than one way to skin a cat.

They that sow the wind shall reap the whirlwind.

Those who cannot remember the past are condemned to repeat it.

Time heals all wounds.

Time will tell.

To everything there is a season, and a time to every purpose under the heaven.

Tomorrow is another day.

Too many cooks spoil the broth.

To the victor belong the spoils.

The tree is known by its fruit.

The truth shall make you free.

Two wrongs don't make a right.

United we stand, divided we fall.

Vanity of vanities, all is vanity.

Variety is the spice of life.

Waste not, want not.

A watched pot never boils.

What's sauce for the goose is sauce for the gander.

When the cat's away, the mice will play.

When the going gets tough, the tough get going.

Where there is no vision, the people perish.

Where there's a will, there's a way.

Where there's smoke, there's fire.

Win this one for the Gipper.

A word to the wise (is sufficient).

Work never hurt anybody.

You can catch more flies with honey than with vinegar.

You can't fit a square peg into a round hole.

You can't make a silk purse out of a sow's ear.

You can't teach an old dog new tricks.

You have to crawl before you can walk.

ABBREVIATIONS KEY

ab.	about	fem.	feminine	obj.	objective
Abbr., abbr.	abbreviation	fig.	figurative	Obs., obs.	obsolete
abl.	ablative	fl.	flourished	orig.	originally
acc.	accusative	fol.	followed	pass.	passive
adj.	adjective	ft.	foot, feet	past part.	past participle
adv.	adverb	fut.	future	perh.	perhaps
Astron.	Astronomy	Gal.	Galatians	pers.	person
at. no.	atomic number	Gen.	Genesis	pl.	plural
at. wt.	atomic weight	gen.	genitive	Pop.	population
b.	blend	Geol.	Geology	poss.	possessive
b.	born	Geom.	Geometry	pp.	past participle
bef.	before	Gram.	Grammar	prec.	preceded
Biol.	Biology	Hos.	Hosea	prep.	preposition
Bot.	Botany	in.	inch(es)	pres.	present, present tense
c	circa	indic.	indicative	pres. part	present participle
Cap.	capital (city)	inf.	infinitive	prob.	probably
cap.	capital	interj.	interjection	Pron., pron	pronunciation, pronounced
caps.	capitals	irreg.	irregular	pron.	pronoun
cent.	century	Is.	Isaiah	prp.present	participle
Cf., cf	compare	Jer.	Jeremiah	Ps.	Psalms
Chem.	Chemistry	Judg.	Judges	pt.	preterit (past tense)
Chron.	Chronicles	km	kilometer(s)	ptp.	past participle
cm	centimeter(s)	Lam.	Lamentations	Rev.	Revelations
Col.	Colossians	Lev.	Leviticus	Rom.	Romans
compar.	comparative	l.c.	lowercase	Sam.	Samuel
conj.	conjunction	lit.	literally	S	south, southern
contr.	contraction	m	meter(s)	s.	stem
Cor.	Corinthians	masc.	masculine	sp.	spelling, spelled
Dan.	Daniel	Matt.	Matthew	sp. gr.	specific gravity
d.	died	Med.	Medicine	sq.	square
dat.	dative	mi.	mile(s)	subj.	subjunctive
def.	definition(s)	Mil.	Military	superl.	superlative
der.	derivative	mm	millimeter(s)	syll.	syllable
Deut.	Deuteronomy	mod.	modern	Thes.	Thessalonians
Dial., dial.	dialect, dialectal	Naut.	Nautical	Tim.	Timothy
dim.	diminutive	Neh.	Nehemiah	Usu., usu.	usually
E	east, eastern	N.	north, northern	v.	verb
Eccl.	Ecclesiastes	n.	noun	var.	variant
esp.	especially	neut.	neuter	v.i.	intransitive verb
etym.	etymology	nom.	nominative	v.t.	transitive verb
Ex.	Exodus	n.pl.	noun plural	W	west, western
Ezek.	Ezekiel	Num.	Numbers	yd.	yard(s)

PRONUNCIATION KEY

STRESS

Pronunciations are marked for stress to reveal the relative differences in emphasis between syllables. In words of two or more syllables, a primary stress mark (ˊ), as in *mother* (**muŧh′ər**), follows the syllable having greatest stress. A secondary stress mark (ˊ), as in *grandmother* (**grand′muŧh′ər**), follows a syllable having slightly less stress than primary but more stress than an unmarked syllable.

ENGLISH SOUNDS

a	act, bat, marry		**oi**	oil, joint, joy
ā	age, paid, say		**o͝o**	oomph, book, tour
â(r)	air, dare, Mary		**o͞o**	ooze, fool, too
ä	ah, part, balm		**ou**	out, loud, cow
b	back, cabin, cab		**p**	pot, supper, stop
ch	beach, child		**r**	read, hurry, near
d	do, madder, bed		**s**	see, passing, miss
e	edge, set, merry		**sh**	shoe, fashion, push
ē	equal, bee, pretty		**t**	ten, matter, bit
ēr	ear, mere		**th**	thin, ether, path
f	fit, differ, puff		**ŧh**	that, either, smooth
g	give, trigger, beg		**u**	up, sun
h	hit, behave		**ûr**	urge, burn, cur
hw	which, nowhere		**v**	voice, river, live
i	if, big, mirror		**w**	witch, away
ī	ice, bite, deny		**y**	yes, onion
j	just, tragic, fudge		**z**	zoo, lazy, those
k	keep, token, make		**zh**	treasure, mirage
l	low, mellow, bottle (bot′l)		**ə**	used in unaccented syllables to indicate
m	my, summer, him			the sound of the reduced vowel in
n	now, sinner, button (but′n)			alone, system, easily, gallop, circus
ng	sing, Washington		**ᵊ**	used between **i** and **r** and between **ou**
o	ox, bomb, wasp			and **r** to show triphthongal quality, as in
ō	over, boat, no			**fire** (fīᵊr), **hour** (ouᵊr)
ô	order, ball, raw			

NON-ENGLISH SOUNDS

A	as in French **ami** (A mēˊ)			Spanish and a sound in French and
KH	as in Scottish **loch** (lôKH)			German similar to KH but pronounced
N	as in French **bon** (bôN) [used to indicate that the preceding vowel is nasalized]			with voice]
			Y	as in French **tu** (tY)
Œ	as in French **feu** (fŒ)		**ᵊ**	as in French **bastogne**
R	[a symbol for any non-english **r** sound, including a trill or flap in Italian and			(ba stônˊyᵊ)

xxviii

A, a (ā), *n., pl.* **A's** or **As, a's** or **as.** **1.** the first letter of the English alphabet, a vowel. **2.** any spoken sound represented by this letter. **3.** something shaped like an A. **4.** a written or pr inted representation of the letter A or a. **—Idiom. 5. from A to Z,** completely; thoroughly.

a¹ (ə; *when stressed* ā), *indefinite article.* **1.** (used before a singular noun not referring to any specific member of a class or group or referring to a member not previously mentioned): *We need a new car. I spoke to a doctor.* **2.** any; every: *A dog has four legs.* **3.** one: *a hundred years; a yard of fabric.* **4.** (used indefinitely with certain quantifiers): *a great many years; a few stars.* **5.** the same: *two at a time.* **6.** a single portion, unit, type, or instance of: *two coffees and a tea.* **7.** a certain; a particular: *A Mr. Johnson called.* **8.** another; one resembling: *a Cicero in eloquence.* **9.** a work by: *a Van Gogh.* **10.** any; a single: *not a one.*

a² (ə; *when stressed* ā), *prep.* for or in each; for or in every; per: *ten cents a ride; three times a day.*

Å, *Physics Symbol.* angstrom.

A, *Symbol.* **1.** the first in order or in a series. **2.** (*sometimes l.c.*) (in some grading systems) a grade or mark indicating excellence or superiority. **3. a.** the sixth tone of the ascending C major scale. **b.** the tonality having A as the tonic. **4.** a major blood group. Compare ABO SYSTEM. **5.** adenine. **6.** alanine. **7.** (formerly) argon. **8.** mass number.

A-1 or **A 1** (ā′wun′), *adj.* A ONE.

AA, 1. administrative assistant. **2.** Alcoholics Anonymous. **3.** antiaircraft.

AAA, American Automobile Association.

aah (ä), *interj.* **1.** (used as an exclamation expressing surprise, delight, joy, etc.) **—n. 2.** the exclamation "aah." **—v.i. 3.** to exclaim or utter "aah": *We all oohed and aahed over the lovely birthday cake.*

A&M or **A and M,** Agricultural and Mechanical (college): *Texas A&M.*

aard·vark (ärd′värk′), *n.* a large burrowing African mammal, *Orycteropus afer,* the sole member of the order Tubulidentata, having a piglike snout and long sticky tongue for feeding on ants and termites. [< Afrikaans < Dutch, = *aarde* earth + *varken* pig]

aard·wolf (ärd′wŏolf′), *n., pl.* **-wolves.** a shaggy, striped African carnivore, *Proteles cristatus,* related to the hyena, that subsists largely on termites and insect larvae.

Aar·on (âr′ən, ar′-), *n.* **1.** the older brother of Moses, usu. regarded as the first high priest of the Hebrews. Ex. 28; 40:13–16. **2. Henry Louis** ("Hank"), born 1934, U.S. baseball player.

Aa·ron·ic (â ron′ik, a ron′-) also **Aa·ron′i·cal,** *adj.* **1.** of or pertaining to Aaron or the order of Jewish priests descended from him. **2.** of or pertaining to the lower order of Mormon priests.

AARP, American Association of Retired Persons.

A.A.S., Associate in Applied Science.

AAUP, American Association of University Professors.

AAUW, American Association of University Women.

AB, 1. airborne. **2.** Airman Basic. **3.** Alberta.

AB, *Symbol.* a major blood group. Compare ABO SYSTEM.

A.B., Bachelor of Arts. [< Latin *Artium Baccalaureus*]

a.b., *Baseball.* (times) at bat.

ab-, a prefix occurring in verbs or verbal derivatives borrowed from Latin, where it meant "off, away": *abhor; abjure; abrade.*

a·ba (ə bä′, ä′bə), *n., pl.* **a·bas. 1.** a coarse fabric woven of camel's or goat's hair. **2.** a loose, sleeveless outer garment made of this fabric or of silk, worn by Arabs.

ABA, 1. American Bankers Association. **2.** American Bar Association. **3.** American Basketball Association. **4.** American Booksellers Association.

a·ba·ca (ab′ə kä′, ä′bə-), *n., pl.* **-cas** or **-kas. 1.** a Philippine plant, *Musa textilis,* of the banana family. **2.** Also called **Manila hemp.** its fiber, used for rope, fabrics, etc.

a·back (ə bak′), *adv.* **1.** so that the wind presses against the forward side of the sail or sails. **2.** toward the back. **—Idiom. 3. take aback,** to surprise; disconcert.

a·bac·te·ri·al (ā′bak tēr′ē əl), *adj.* not caused by bacteria; free from the presence of bacteria.

ab·a·cus (ab′ə kəs, ə bak′əs), *n., pl.* **ab·a·cus·es, ab·a·ci** (ab′ə sī′, -kī′, ə bak′ī). **1.** a device for making arithmetical calculations, consisting of a frame set with rods on which balls or beads are moved. **2.** a slab forming the top of the capital of a column.

A·bad·don (ə bad′n), *n.* **1.** APOLLYON. **2.** a place of destruction; the depths of hell.

a·baft (ə baft′, ə bäft′), *Naut.* **—prep. 1.** to the rear of; aft of; behind. **—adv. 2.** toward the stern; astern.

ab·a·lo·ne (ab′ə lō′nē), *n.* any gastropod mollusk of the family Haliotidae, having a flat, oval shell with a row of respiratory holes: the flesh is used for food and the shell as a source of mother-of-pearl.

a·ban·don¹ (ə ban′dən), *v.t.* **1.** to leave completely and finally; forsake utterly; desert: *to abandon a child; to abandon a sinking ship.* **2.** to give up; discontinue; withdraw from: *to abandon a project; to abandon hope.* **3.** to give up the control of: *to abandon a city to an enemy army.* **4.** to

yield (oneself) without restraint or moderation, as to emotions or natural impulses: *to abandon oneself to grief.* **5.** to relinquish (insured property) in case of partial loss, so that the insured can claim a total loss. **—a·ban′doned,** *adj.* **—a·ban′don·ment,** *n.*

a·ban·don² (ə ban′dən), *n.* a complete surrender to natural impulses without restraint or moderation; freedom from constraint: *to dance with reckless abandon.*

a·ban·don·ee (ə ban′də nē′), *n.* **1.** the party to whom a right or property is abandoned, esp. an insurer to whom a property has been relinquished. **2.** a person who has been abandoned.

a·base (ə bās′), *v.t.,* **a·based, a·bas·ing.** to lower in rank, dignity, or estimation; humiliate; degrade. **—a·base′ment,** *n.* **—a·bas′er,** *n.*

a·bash (ə bash′), *v.t.* to destroy the self-confidence of; disconcert; make embarrassed. **—a·bash′ed·ly,** *adv.* **—a·bash′ment,** *n.*

a·bate (ə bāt′), *v.,* **a·bat·ed, a·bat·ing.** **—v.t. 1.** to reduce in amount, degree, intensity, etc.; lessen; diminish: *to abate a tax; to abate one's enthusiasm.* **2.** *Law.* **a.** to stop or suppress (an action, nuisance, etc.). **b.** to annul (a writ). **3.** to deduct or subtract: *to abate part of the price.* **—v.i. 4.** to diminish in intensity, violence, amount, etc.: *The storm has abated.* **5.** *Law.* to end; become null and void. **—a·bate′ment,** *n.* **—a·bat′er;** *Law.* **a·ba′tor,** *n.*

ab·a·tis (ab′ə tē′, -tis, ə bat′ē, ə bat′is), *n., pl.* **ab·a·tis** (ab′ə tēz′, ə bat′ēz)), **ab·a·tis·es** (ab′ə tis′iz, ə bat′ə siz). a defensive obstacle formed from rows of tree branches, with an end of each branch facing outward toward the enemy.

ab·at·toir (ab′ə twär′, ab′ə twär′), *n.* a slaughterhouse.

ab·ax·i·al (ab ak′sē əl), *adj.* being or situated away from the axis: *the abaxial surface of a leaf.*

Ab·ba (ab′ə), *n.* (*sometimes l.c.*) **1.** (in the New Testament) an intimate and respectful term for father, used by Jesus in addressing God and then taken up by the early Christians. Mark 14:36; Rom. 8:15; Gal. 4:6. **2.** a title of reverence for bishops and patriarchs in the Coptic, Ethiopian Christian, and Syriac churches. [< Aramaic *abbā* father]

ab·ba·cy (ab′ə sē), *n., pl.* **-cies. 1.** the rank, rights, or jurisdiction of an abbot. **2.** the term of office of an abbot.

Ab·bas·id (ə bas′id, ab′ə sid), *n.* a member of a dynasty of caliphs ruling at Baghdad, A.D. 750–1258, governing most of the Islamic world and claiming descent from Abbas, uncle of Muhammad.

ab·bess (ab′is), *n.* a woman who is the superior of a convent of nuns.

Abbe·vill·e·an or **Abbe·vill·e·an** (ab vil′ē ən, -vil′yən, ab′ə vil′-), *adj.* of or designating an early Lower Paleolithic industry of the middle Pleistocene Epoch in Europe, characterized by the manufacture of large flakes and hand axes.

ab·bey (ab′ē), *n., pl.* **-beys. 1.** a monastery under the supervision of an abbot or a convent under the supervision of an abbess. **2.** the church of an abbey.

ab·bot (ab′ət), *n.* a man who is the head or superior of a monastery. [< Latin < Greek < Aramaic *abbā* father]

Ab·bott (ab′ət), *n.* **Jacob,** 1803–79, and his son, **Lyman,** 1835–1922, U.S. clergymen and writers.

abbr. or **abbrev.,** abbreviation.

ab·bre·vi·ate (ə brē′vē āt′), *v.,* **-at·ed, -at·ing. —v.t. 1.** to shorten (a word or phrase) by omitting letters, substituting shorter forms, etc., so that the shortened form can represent the whole word or phrase. **2.** to reduce in length, duration, etc.; make briefer: *to abbreviate a speech.* **—v.i. 3.** to use abbreviations. **—ab·bre′vi·a·tor,** *n.* **—ab·bre′vi·a·to′ry** (-vē ə tôr′ē, -tōr′ē), *adj.*

ab·bre·vi·at·ed (ə brē′vē ā′tid), *adj.* **1.** shortened; made briefer. **2.** (of clothing) scanty; barely covering the body: *an abbreviated bathing suit.* **3.** constituting a shorter or smaller version.

ab·bre·vi·a·tion (ə brē′vē ā′shən), *n.* **1.** a shortened form of a word or phrase used to represent the whole, as *Dr.* for *Doctor, U.S.* for *United States, NW* for *Northwest, ft.* for *foot,* or *lb.* for *pound.* **2.** an act or result of abbreviating; reduction in length, duration, etc.; abridgment.

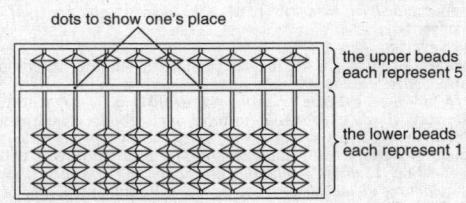

dots to show one's place

the upper beads each represent 5

the lower beads each represent 1

abacus

ABC, American Broadcasting Companies (a television network).

ABC's or **ABCs** (ā/bē/sēz/), *n.* (*used with a pl. v.*) **1.** the alphabet. **2.** the basic skills of spelling, reading, and writing. **3.** the basic facts, principles, or skills of any subject.

ABC soil, *n.* a soil with distinct A, B, and C horizons.

ABD, all but dissertation: applied to a person who has completed all requirements for a doctoral degree except for the writing of a dissertation.

ab·di·cate (ab/di kāt/), *v.,* **-cat·ed, -cat·ing.** —*v.t.* **1.** to give up or renounce (authority, duties, a high office, etc.), esp. in a voluntary, public, or formal manner. —*v.i.* **2.** to renounce or relinquish a throne, office, right, power, claim, or responsibility, esp. in a formal manner. —**ab/di·ca·ble** (-di kə bəl), *adj.* —**ab/di·ca/tion,** *n.* —**ab/di·ca/tive** (-kā/tiv, -kə-), *adj.* —**ab/di·ca/tor,** *n.*

ab·do·men (ab/də mən, ab dō/-), *n.* **1.** (in mammals) **a.** the part of the body between the thorax and the pelvis; belly. **b.** the cavity of this part of the body containing the stomach, intestines, etc. **2.** (in nonmammalian vertebrates) a region of the body corresponding to, but not coincident with, this part or cavity. **3.** (in arthropods) the posterior segment of the body, behind the thorax or cephalothorax.

ab·dom·i·nal (ab dom/ə nl), *adj.* **1.** of, in, on, or for the abdomen. —*n.* **2.** Usu., **abdominals.** the abdominal muscles. —**ab·dom/i·nal·ly,** *adv.*

Ab·don (ab/don), *n.* **1.** one of the minor judges of Israel. Judg. 12:13–15. **2.** a courtier of Josiah. II Chron. 34:20.

ab·duct (ab dukt/), *v.t.* **1.** to carry off or lead away (a person) illegally and in secret or by force, esp. to kidnap. **2.** to move or draw away from the axis of the body or a limb (opposed to *adduct*). —**ab·duct·ee/,** *n.* —**ab·duc/tion,** *n.*

a·beam (ə bēm/), *adv.* at right angles to the fore-and-aft line: *to sail with the wind abeam.*

a·be·ce·dar·i·an (ā/bē sē dâr/ē ən), *n.* **1.** a person learning the letters of the alphabet. **2.** a beginner in any field. —*adj.* **3.** of or pertaining to the alphabet. **4.** arranged in alphabetical order. **5.** elementary.

a/be·ce·dar/i·an hymn/ (ā/bē sē dâr/ē ən, ā/bē-), a hymn in which the lines begin in alphabetical order, as in the Hebrew version of Psalm 119.

A·bed·ne·go (ə bed/ni gō/), *n.* a companion of Daniel. Compare SHADRACH. Dan. 3:12–30.

A·bel (ā/bəl), *n.* the second son of Adam and Eve, slain by his brother, Cain. Gen. 4.

a·bele (ə bēl/, ā/bəl), *n.* the white poplar tree, *Populus alba.*

Abe/ Lin/coln in Illinois/, a play (1938) by Robert E. Sherwood.

A·bel-me·ho·lah (ā/bəl mi hō/lə), *n.* a city in ancient Palestine, east of the Jordan River: the home of Elisha. Judg. 7:22; I Kings 4:12; 19:16.

a·bel·mosk (ā/bəl mosk/), *n.* a tropical plant, *Abelmoschus moschatus,* of the mallow family, cultivated for its musky seeds, which yield an oil used in perfumery.

Ab/er·deen An/gus, *n.* one of a breed of hornless beef cattle having a smooth black coat, orig. raised in Scotland. Also called **Black Angus.**

ab·er·rant (ə ber/ənt, ab/ər-), *adj.* **1.** departing from the right, normal, or usual course. **2.** deviating from the ordinary, usual, or normal type; atypical; abnormal. —*n.* **3.** an aberrant person, thing, or group. —**ab·er/rance, ab·er/ran·cy,** *n.* —**ab·er/rant·ly,** *adv.*

ab·er·ra·tion (ab/ə rā/shən), *n.* **1.** deviation from the usual, normal, or right course. **2.** deviation from the ordinary, usual, or normal type. **3.** deviation from truth or moral rectitude. **4.** mental disorder, esp. of a minor or temporary nature; mental lapse. **5.** apparent displacement of a heavenly body, owing to the motion of the earth in its orbit. **6.** any disturbance of the rays of a pencil of light such that they can no longer be brought to a sharp focus or form a clear image. —**ab/er·ra/tion·al,** *adj.*

a·bet (ə bet/), *v.t.,* **a·bet·ted, a·bet·ting.** to encourage, support, or countenance by aid or approval, usu. in wrongdoing. —**a·bet/ment,** *n.* —**a·bet/tor, a·bet/ter,** *n.*

a·bey·ance (ə bā/əns), *n.* **1.** temporary inactivity, cessation, or suspension: *to hold a question in abeyance.* **2.** *Law.* the state of property whose title has not been vested in a known titleholder: *an estate in abeyance.* —**a·bey/ant,** *adj.*

ab·hor (ab hôr/), *v.t.,* **-horred, -hor·ring.** to regard with extreme repugnance or aversion; detest; loathe. —**ab·hor/rence,** *n.*

ab·hor·rent (ab hôr/ənt, -hor/-), *adj.* **1.** causing repugnance or aversion; detestable; loathsome: *an abhorrent deed.* **2.** utterly opposed or in conflict; contrary (usu. fol. by *to*): *abhorrent to reason.* **3.** feeling extreme repugnance or aversion (usu. fol. by *of*): *abhorrent of waste.* —**ab·hor/rent·ly,** *adv.*

A·bib (ä vēv/), *n.* AVIV.

a·bid·ance (ə bīd/ns), *n.* **1.** the act or state of abiding. **2.** conformity; compliance: *strict abidance by the rules.*

a·bide (ə bīd/), *v.,* **a·bode** or **a·bid·ed, a·bid·ing.** —*v.i.* **1.** to remain; continue; stay: *Abide with me.* **2.** to have one's abode; dwell; reside. **3.** to continue in a particular condition; last; endure. —*v.t.* **4.** to put up with; tolerate; stand: *I can't abide dishonesty!* **5.** to endure or withstand without yielding: *to abide a vigorous onslaught.* **6.** to wait for; await: *to abide the coming of the Lord.* **7.** to accept without opposition or question: *to abide the verdict of the judge.* **8. abide by, a.** to comply with; submit to: *to abide by the court's decision.* **b.** to remain steadfast or faithful to; keep: *to abide by a promise.* —**a·bid/ing,** *adj.*

Abide/ with Me/, a Christian hymn (1847) with words by Henry F. Lyte.

Ab·i·djan (ab/i jän/), *n.* a seaport in the Ivory Coast: the former capital. 1,850,000.

Ab·i·gail (ab/i gāl/), *n.* a wife of David. I Sam. 25.

A·bi·hu (ə bī/hyoo), *n.* a son of Aaron who, with Nadab, was destroyed by fire from heaven for disobeying the Lord. Lev. 10:1–5.

Ab·i·lene (ab/ə lēn/), *n.* a city in central Texas. 110,034.

a·bil·i·ty (ə bil/i tē), *n., pl.* **-ties. 1.** power or capacity to do or act physically, mentally, legally, morally, or financially. **2.** competence based on natural skill, training, or other qualification. **3. abilities,** talents; special skills or aptitudes.

-ability, a combination of -ABLE and -ITY, found on nouns corresponding to adjectives in -ABLE: *capability.*

A·bin·o·am (ə bin/ō am/), *n.* the father of Barak. Judg. 4:6; 12; 5:1.

a·bi·o·gen·e·sis (ā/bī ō jen/ə sis, ab/ē ō-), *n.* the production of living organisms by nonliving matter; spontaneous generation: a former belief. —**a/bi·o·ge·net/ic** (-jə net/ik), **a/bi·o·ge·net/i·cal,** *adj.* —**a/bi·o·ge·net/i·cal·ly,** *adv.* —**a/bi·o·ge·nist** (-oj/ə nist), *n.*

a·bi·o·gen·ic (ā/bī ō jen/ik, ab/ē ō-), *adj.* not resulting from the activity of living organisms. —**a/bi·o·gen/i·cal·ly,** *adv.*

a·bi·ot·ic (ā/bī ot/ik, ab/ē-), *adj.* of or characterized by the absence of life or living organisms. —**a/bi·ot/i·cal·ly,** *adv.*

Ab·i·shag (ab/ə shag/), *n.* a young maiden brought to David in his old age as a nurse and companion. I Kings 1:1–4.

ab·ject (ab/jekt, ab jekt/), *adj.* **1.** utterly hopeless, miserable, or wretched: *abject poverty.* **2.** contemptible; despicable; base-spirited: *an abject coward.* **3.** servile; submissive; slavish. —**ab·jec/tion,** *n.* —**ab·ject/ly,** *adv.* —**ab·ject/ness,** *n.*

ab·jure (ab joor/, -jûr/), *v.t.,* **-jured, -jur·ing. 1.** to repudiate or retract, esp. with formal solemnity; recant. **2.** to renounce or give up under oath; forswear: *to abjure allegiance to a country.* **3.** to refrain from; avoid. —**ab/ju·ra/tion,** *n.* —**ab·jur/a·to/ry,** *adj.*

ab·late (a blāt/), *v.,* **-lat·ed, -lat·ing.** —*v.t.* **1.** to remove or dissipate by melting, vaporization, erosion, etc. —*v.i.* **2.** to become ablated; undergo ablation.

ab·la·tion (a blā/shən), *n.* **1.** the act or process of ablating. **2.** the removal of organs, abnormal growths, or harmful substances from the body by mechanical means, as by surgery. **3.** the erosion of the protective outer surface (**ablator**) of a spacecraft or missile due to heat during reentry through the atmosphere.

ab·la·tive¹ (ab/lə tiv), *adj.* **1.** of or designating a grammatical case that is used to mark the starting point of an action and, in Latin, to indicate manner, instrument, or agent. —*n.* **2.** the ablative case. **3.** a word or other form in this case, as *Tusculō* "from Tusculum," *honōre* "with honor."

ab·la·tive² (a blā/tiv), *adj.* capable of or susceptible to ablation: *the ablative nose cone of a rocket.*

ab·la·tor (a blā/tər), *n.* See under ABLATION (def. 3).

ab·laut (äp/lout, ab/-, äb/-), *n.* (esp. in Indo-European languages) regular alternation of vowels in a word element, reflecting a change in grammatical function, as in English *sing, sang, sung, song.*

a·blaze (ə blāz/), *adj.* **1.** burning; on fire. **2.** gleaming with bright lights or bold colors. **3.** excited; eager; ardent.

a·ble (ā/bəl), *adj.,* **a·bler, a·blest. 1.** having the necessary power, skill, resources, or qualifications to do something: *able to read music; not able to vote.* **2.** having or showing unusual talent, intelligence, skill, or knowledge: *an able leader.*

-able, a suffix meaning "capable of, susceptible to, fit for, tending to, given to," associated in meaning with the word ABLE, occurring in loanwords from Latin (*laudable*); used in English to form adjectives from stems of any origin (*teachable; photographable*). Compare -BLE, -IBLE.

a/ble-bod/ied, *adj.* having a strong, healthy body; physically fit.

a·ble·ism (ā/bə liz/əm), *n.* discrimination against disabled people.

a/ble sea/man, *n.* an experienced seaman qualified to perform routine sea duties. Also called **a/ble-bod/ied sea/man.**

ab·lut·ed (ə bloo/tid), *adj.* thoroughly washed.

ab·lu·tion (ə bloo/shən), *n.* **1.** a cleansing with water or other liquid, esp. as a religious ritual. **2.** the liquid used. **3.** a washing of the hands, body, etc. —**ab·lu/tion·ar/y,** *adj.*

-ably, a suffix combining -ABLE and -LY that forms adverbs corresponding to adjectives ending in -ABLE: *dependably; tolerably.* Compare -IBLY.

ABM, antiballistic missile.

ab·ne·gate (ab/ni gāt/), *v.t.,* **-gat·ed, -gat·ing. 1.** to refuse or deny (rights, comforts, etc.) to oneself; renounce. **2.** to relinquish; give up. —**ab/ne·ga/tion,** *n.* —**ab/ne·ga/tor,** *n.*

Ab·ner (ab/nər), *n.* the commander of the Israelite army and a cousin of Saul. I Sam. 14:50; 26:5.

ab·nor·mal (ab nôr/məl), *adj.* **1.** not normal, average, typical, or usual; deviating from a standard or norm. **2.** unusually large: *abnormal profits.* —**ab·nor/mal·ly,** *adv.* —**ab·nor/mal·ness,** *n.*

ab·nor·mal·i·ty (ab/nôr mal/i tē), *n., pl.* **-ties. 1.** an abnormal condition, state, or quality. **2.** an abnormal thing or event.

ab·nor·mi·ty (ab nôr/mi tē), *n., pl.* **-ties.** an abnormal condition, quality, or thing; abnormality.

a·board (ə bôrd/, ə bōrd/), *adv.* **1.** on board; on, in, or into a ship, train, airplane, bus, etc.: *All aboard!* **2.** alongside; to the side. **3.** into a group as a new member: *The office manager welcomed him aboard.* —*prep.* **4.** on board of; on, in, or into: *aboard a ship.*

a•bode (ə bōd′), *n.* **1.** a place in which a person resides; residence; dwelling; home. **2.** an extended stay in a place; sojourn.

a•bol•ish (ə bol′ish), *v.t.* to do away with (a law, custom, etc.) completely; put an end to; annul: *to abolish slavery.* —**a•bol′ish•ment,** *n.*

ab•o•li•tion (ab′ə lish′ən), *n.* **1.** the act of abolishing or the state of being abolished; annulment; abrogation. **2.** (*sometimes cap.*) the legal termination of slavery in the U.S. —**ab′o•li′tion•ar′y,** *adj.*

ab•o•li•tion•ism (ab′ə lish′ə niz′əm), *n.* the principle or policy of abolition, esp. of slavery in the U.S. —**ab′o•li′tion•ist,** *n., adj.*

ab•o•ma•sum (ab′ə mā′səm), *n., pl.* **-sa** (-sə). the fourth or true stomach of the cow and other ruminants, from which partially fermented and digested food is passed to the small intestine.

A-bomb (ā′bom′), *n.* ATOMIC BOMB.

a•bom•i•na•ble (ə bom′ə nə bəl), *adj.* **1.** repugnantly hateful; detestable; loathsome. **2.** very unpleasant: *abominable weather.* **3.** very bad; inferior: *abominable taste in clothes.* —**a•bom′i•na•bly,** *adv.*

Abom′inable Snow′man, *n.* a legendary large, hairy, humanoid creature said to inhabit the Himalayas. Also called **yeti.**

a•bom•i•nate (ə bom′ə nāt′), *v.t.,* **-nat•ed, -nat•ing. 1.** to regard with intense aversion or loathing; abhor. **2.** to feel distaste for; dislike.

a•bom•i•na•tion (ə bom′ə nā′shən), *n.* **1.** something greatly disliked or abhorred. **2.** intense aversion or loathing; detestation. **3.** a vile or shameful action, condition, or habit.

abomina′tion of desola′tion, *n.* a heathen statue set up in a holy temple. Mark 13:14.

ab•o•ral (ab ôr′əl, -ōr′-), *adj.* opposite to or away from the mouth. —**ab•o′ral•ly,** *adv.*

ab•o•rig•i•nal (ab′ə rij′ə nl), *adj.* **1.** of or pertaining to aborigines. **2.** original or earliest known; native; indigenous. **3.** (*usu. cap.*) of or pertaining to the Aborigines of Australia. —*n.* **4.** ABORIGINE. —**ab′o•rig′i•nal′i•ty,** *n.* —**ab′o•rig′i•nal•ly,** *adv.*

ab•o•rig•i•ne (ab′ə rij′ə nē), *n.* **1.** one of the original or earliest known inhabitants of a country or region. **2.** (*usu. cap.*) a member of any of the peoples who are the aboriginal inhabitants of Australia. **3. aborigines,** the original, native fauna or flora of a region. [< Latin *ab origine* from the origin]

a•born•ing (ə bôr′ning), *adv.* **1.** in birth; before being carried out: *The scheme died aborning.* —*adj.* **2.** being born; coming into being, fruition, or realization: *A new era is aborning.*

a•bort (ə bôrt′), *v.i.* **1.** to bring forth a fetus before it is viable. **2.** to remain rudimentary, fail to develop, or develop incompletely. **3.** to fail or stop at an early or premature stage. **4.** to fail to accomplish a military objective for any reason other than enemy action. **5.** (of a missile) to stop before the scheduled flight is completed. —*v.t.* **6.** to cause to bring forth (a fetus) before it is viable. **7.** to cause (a pregnant female) to be delivered of a nonviable fetus. **8.** to cause to cease or end at an early or premature stage. **9.** to terminate (a missile flight, mission, etc.) before completion. —*n.* **10.** the termination of a missile flight, mission, etc., before completion. **11.** a missile, rocket, etc., that has aborted.

a•bor•tion (ə bôr′shən), *n.* **1.** the removal of an embryo or fetus from the uterus in order to end a pregnancy. **2.** any of various procedures for terminating a pregnancy. **3.** Also called **spontaneous abortion.** MISCARRIAGE (def. 1). **4.** an immature and nonviable fetus. **5.** a malformed or monstrous person or thing. **6.** the arrested development of an embryo or an organ at a more or less early stage. **7.** the stopping of an illness, infection, etc., at a very early stage. **8. a.** shambles; mess. **b.** anything that fails to develop, progress, or mature.

a•bor•tion•ist (ə bôr′shə nist), *n.* a person who performs or induces abortions.

abor′tion-on-demand′, *n.* the right of a woman to have an abortion during the first six months of a pregnancy.

a•bor•tive (ə bôr′tiv), *adj.* **1.** failing to succeed; unsuccessful; fruitless: *an abortive rebellion.* **2.** born prematurely. **3.** imperfectly developed; rudimentary. **4.** producing or intended to produce abortion. **5.** acting to halt progress of a disease. —**a•bor′tive•ly,** *adv.* —**a•bor′tive•ness,** *n.*

ABO system, *n.* a classification of human blood into four major groups, A, B, AB, and O, based on the presence on the surface of red blood cells of either of two antigens, A or B, or their absence, O: used in determining compatibility for transfusions.

a•bound (ə bound′), *v.i.* **1.** to occur or exist in great quantities or numbers: *a stream in which trout abound.* **2.** to be rich or well supplied (usu. fol. by *in*): *The region abounds in coal.* **3.** to be filled; teem (usu. fol. by *with*): *The ship abounds with rats.* —**a•bound′ing•ly,** *adv.*

a•bout (ə bout′), *prep.* **1.** concerning; on the subject of; in regard to: *a book about the Civil War.* **2.** connected or associated with: *an air of mystery about him.* **3.** near; close to: *about my height; about six o'clock.* **4.** in or somewhere near: *He is about the house.* **5.** on every side of; around. **6.** on or near (one's person): *They lost all they had about them.* **7.** so as to be of use to: *Keep your wits about you.* **8.** on the verge of (usu. fol. by an infinitive): *about to leave.* **9.** here or there in or on: *to wander about the castle.* **10.** engaged in or occupied with: *while you're about it.* **11.** having as a central concern or purpose: *That's not what life is all about.* —*adv.* **12.** near in time, number, degree, etc.; approximately: *about five miles from here.* **13.** nearly; almost: *Dinner is about ready.* **14.** nearby; not far off: *He is somewhere about.* **15.** on every side; in every direction; around: *to look about.* **16.** halfway around; in the opposite direction: *to turn a car about.* **17.** here and there: *to move furniture about; papers strewn about.* **18.** in rotation or succession; alternately: *Turn about is fair play.* **19.** in circumference. **20.** *Naut.* **a.** onto a new tack. **b.** onto a new course. —*adj.* **21.** moving around; astir: *She was up and about at dawn.* **22.** in existence; prevalent: *The flu is about.* —***Idiom.*** **23. not about to,** not intending or likely to.

a•bout-face (*n.* ə bout′fās′, ə bout′fās′; *v.* ə bout′fās′), *n., v.,* **-faced, -fac•ing.** —*n.* **1.** (in close-order drill) a 180° turn from the position of attention. **2.** a complete, sudden change in position, direction, principle, or attitude. —*v.i.* **3.** to perform an about-face.

a•bove (ə buv′), *adv.* **1.** in, at, or to a higher place. **2.** overhead or in the sky: *A flock of birds circled above.* **3.** upstairs: *the apartment above.* **4.** higher in rank, authority, or power: *the officer above.* **5.** higher in quantity or number: *books with 100 pages and above.* **6.** before or earlier, esp. in a book or other piece of writing: *the remark quoted above.* Compare BELOW (def. 6). **7.** in or to heaven: *gone to her eternal rest above.* **8.** higher than zero on the temperature scale. **9.** *Zool.* on the upper or dorsal side. **10.** upstage. Compare BELOW (def. 9). —*prep.* **11.** in or to a higher place than; over: *to fly above the clouds.* **12.** more in quantity or number than; in excess of: *all children above 6 years of age.* **13.** superior in rank, authority, or standing to. **14.** not subject or liable to: *to be above suspicion.* **15.** of too fine a character for: *above such trickery.* **16.** rather than; in preference to: *to favor one child above the other.* **17.** beyond, esp. north of: *six miles above Baltimore.* **18.** upstage of. —*adj.* **19.** said, mentioned, or written above; foregoing: *the above explanation.* —*n.* **20.** something that was said, mentioned, or written above. **21.** the person or persons previously indicated: *The above will stand trial.* **22.** heaven: *a gift from above.* **23.** a higher authority: *an order from above.* —***Idiom.*** **24. above all,** most importantly; principally.

a•bove•board (ə buv′bôrd′, -bōrd′), *adv., adj.* without tricks, concealment, or disguise; in the open: *Their actions are open and aboveboard.*

a•bove•ground (ə buv′ground′), *adj.* **1.** situated on or above the ground. **2.** not secret, hidden, or underground; open: *aboveground radical groups.*

a•bove•men•tioned (ə buv′men′shənd), *adj.* mentioned above.

abp., archbishop.

ab•ra•ca•dab•ra (ab′rə kə dab′rə), *n.* **1.** a mystical word used in incantations, on amulets, etc., as a magical means of warding off misfortune, harm, or illness. **2.** any charm or incantation using nonsensical or supposedly magical words. **3.** meaningless talk; gibberish; nonsense.

a•brade (ə brād′), *v.t., v.i.,* **a•brad•ed, a•brad•ing. 1.** to wear off or down by scraping or rubbing. **2.** to scrape or rub off.

A•bra•ham (ā′brə ham′, -həm), *n.* the first Biblical patriarch, the traditional founder of the Hebrew nation, and the father of Isaac: considered an ancestor of the Arab peoples through his son Ishmael. Gen. 11:26–25:10.

A′braham's bos′om, *n.* heaven, considered as the reward of the righteous. Luke 16:22.

A•bram (ā′brəm), *n.* an earlier name of Abraham. Gen. 17:5.

a•bra•sion (ə brā′zhən), *n.* **1.** a scraped spot or area; the result of rubbing or abrading: *abrasions on his leg.* **2.** the act or process of abrading.

a•bra•sive (ə brā′siv, -ziv), *adj.* **1.** tending to abrade; causing abrasion. **2.** tending to annoy or cause ill will; overly aggressive: *an abrasive personality.* —*n.* **3.** any material or substance used for grinding, polishing, smoothing, etc., as emery, pumice, or sandpaper. —**a•bra′sive•ly,** *adv.* —**a•bra′sive•ness,** *n.*

ab•re•ac•tion (ab′rē ak′shən), *n.* the release of emotional tension achieved through recalling a repressed traumatic experience, esp. during psychoanalysis. —**ab′re•act′,** *v.t.* —**ab′re•ac′tive,** *adj.*

a•breast (ə brest′), *adv., adj.* **1.** side by side: *They walked two abreast.* **2.** informed; aware; up-to-date: *to keep abreast of new developments.* **3.** equal to or alongside in progress or attainment.

a•bridge (ə brij′), *v.t.,* **a•bridged, a•bridg•ing. 1.** to shorten by omissions while retaining the basic contents: *to abridge a reference book.* **2.** to reduce or lessen in duration, scope, or extent; diminish; curtail: *to abridge a visit.* **3.** to deprive; cut off. [< Medieval Latin *abbreviāre* to shorten] —**a•bridg′a•ble, a•bridge′a•ble,** *adj.* —**a•bridg′er,** *n.*

a•bridg•ment or **a•bridge•ment** (ə brij′mənt), *n.* **1.** a shortened or condensed form of a book, speech, etc., that still retains the basic contents. **2.** the act or process of abridging. **3.** the state of being abridged. **4.** reduction or curtailment: *abridgment of civil rights.*

a•broad (ə brôd′), *adv.* **1.** in or to a foreign country or countries: *famous at home and abroad.* **2.** in or to another continent. **3.** out of doors; away from one's home: *There was no one abroad in the noonday heat.* **4.** spread around; in circulation: *Rumors of disaster were abroad.* **5.** broadly; widely; far and wide. **6.** wide of the mark; in error. —*n.* **7.** a foreign land or lands: *imports from abroad.*

ab•ro•gate (ab′rə gāt′), *v.t.,* **-gat•ed, -gat•ing. 1.** to abolish or annul by formal or official means; repeal: *abrogated a treaty.* **2.** to put aside; put an end to. —**ab′ro•ga′tion,** *n.* —**ab′ro•ga′tive,** *adj.*

ab•rupt (ə brupt′), *adj.* **1.** sudden or unexpected: *an abrupt departure.* **2.** curt or brusque in speech or manner: *an abrupt reply.* **3.** terminating or changing suddenly; sharp: *an abrupt turn in a road.* **4.** having many sudden changes from one subject to another; lacking in continuity or smoothness: *an abrupt writing style.* **5.** steep; precipitous: *an abrupt descent.* **6.** TRUNCATE (def. 3). —**ab•rupt′ly,** *adv.* —**ab•rupt′ness,** *n.*

ABS, antilock braking system.

abs., **1.** absent. **2.** absolute. **3.** abstract.

Ab•sa•lom (ab′sə ləm), *n.* the third son of David: he rebelled against his father and was slain by Joab. II Sam. 13–18.

ab•scess (ab′ses), *n.* a localized accumulation of pus in a body tissue. —**ab′scessed,** *adj.*

ab•scis•sa (ab sis′ə), *n., pl.* **-scis•sas, -scis•sae** (-sis′ē). (in plane Cartesian coordinates) the x-coordinate of a point: its distance from the y-axis measured parallel to the x-axis. Compare ORDINATE.

ab•scis•sion (ab sizh′ən, -sish′-), *n.* **1.** the act of cutting off; sudden termination. **2.** the normal separation of flowers, fruit, and leaves from plants.

ab•scond (ab skond′), *v.i.* to depart in a sudden and secret manner, esp. to avoid capture and legal prosecution. —**ab•scond′ence,** *n.* —**ab•scond′er,** *n.*

ab•sence (ab′səns), *n.* **1.** the state of being away or not being present. **2.** a period of being away: *an absence of several weeks.* **3.** failure to attend or appear when expected. **4.** lack; deficiency: *the absence of proof.* **5.** inattentiveness; preoccupation; absent-mindedness: *absence of mind.*

ab•sent (*adj., prep.* ab′sənt; *v.* ab sent′, ab′sənt), *adj.* **1.** not in a certain place at a given time; away; missing; not present: *absent from class.* **2.** lacking; nonexistent: *Revenge was absent from his mind.* **3.** not attentive; preoccupied; absent-minded: *an absent expression.* —*v.t.* **4.** to take or keep (oneself) away: *to absent oneself from a meeting.* —*prep.* **5.** in the absence of; without. —**ab′sen•ta′tion,** *n.* —**ab•sent′er,** *n.*

ab•sen•tee (ab′sən tē′), *n.* **1.** a person who is absent, esp. from work or school. **2.** a person who absents himself or herself, as a property owner who does not live on or near certain property owned.

ab′sentee bal′lot, *n.* the ballot used for an absentee vote.

ab•sen•tee•ism (ab′sən tē′iz əm), *n.* frequent or habitual absence from work, school, etc.

ab′sentee vote′, *n.* a vote cast by a person who, because of absence from the usual voting district, illness, etc., has been permitted to vote by mail. —**ab′sentee vot′er,** *n.*

ab′sent-mind′ed or **ab′sent•mind′ed,** *adj.* preoccupied with one's thoughts so as to be unaware or forgetful of other matters. —**ab′sent-mind′ed•ly,** *adv.* —**ab′sent-mind′ed•ness,** *n.*

ab′sent without′ leave′, *adj., adv.* See AWOL.

ab•sinthe or **ab•sinth** (ab′sinth), *n.* a strong green liqueur made with wormwood and other herbs, having a bitter licorice flavor: now banned in most Western countries.

ab•so•lute (ab′sə lo͞ot′, ab′sə lo͞ot′), *adj.* **1.** being fully or perfectly as indicated; complete; perfect. **2.** free from restriction, limitation, or exception: *absolute power; absolute freedom.* **3.** outright; unqualified: *an absolute lie; an absolute denial.* **4.** unrestrained in the exercise of governmental power; not limited by laws or a constitution: *an absolute monarchy.* **5.** viewed independently; not comparative or relative; ultimate: *absolute knowledge.* **6.** positive; certain; definite: *absolute in opinion; absolute proof.* **7.** not mixed or adulterated; pure. **8. a.** relatively independent syntactically in relation to other elements in a sentence, as the construction *It being Sunday* in *It being Sunday, I wasn't at work.* **b.** (of a usu. transitive verb) used without an object, as *give* in *Please give generously.* **c.** (of an adjective or possessive pronoun) used alone, with the noun that is modified understood but not expressed, as *hungry* in *to feed the hungry* or *mine* in *Take mine.* **9.** *Physics.* **a.** independent of arbitrary standards or of particular properties of substances or systems: *absolute humidity.* **b.** pertaining to a system of units, as the centimeter-gram-second system, based on some primary units, esp. units of length, mass, and time. **c.** pertaining to a measurement based on an absolute zero or unit. **10.** *Math.* (of an inequality) indicating that the expression is true for all values of the variable, as $x^2 + 1 > 0$ for all real numbers *x.* —*n.* **11.** something that is not dependent upon external conditions for existence or for its specific nature, size, etc. (opposed to *relative*). **12. the absolute, a.** something that is free from any restriction or condition. **b.** something that is independent of some or all relations. **c.** something that is perfect or complete. —**ab′so•lute′ly,** *adj., interj.* —**ab′so•lute′ness,** *n.*

ab′solute humid′ity, *n.* the mass of water vapor present in a unit volume of moist air. Compare RELATIVE HUMIDITY.

ab′solute mag′nitude, *n.* the magnitude of a star as it would appear to a hypothetical observer at a distance of 10 parsecs or 32.6 light-years.

ab′solute major′ity, *n.* **1.** a number of votes constituting more than half of the number cast. **2.** a number of voters constituting more than half of the number registered.

ab′solute mon′archy, *n.* a monarchy that is not limited or restrained by laws or a constitution.

ab′solute pitch′, *n.* **1.** the exact pitch of a tone in terms of vibrations per second. **2.** the ability to sing or recognize the pitch of a tone by ear.

ab′solute val′ue, *n.* **1.** the magnitude of a quantity, irrespective of sign; the distance of a quantity from zero. The absolute value of a number is symbolized by two vertical lines, as $|3|$ or $|-3|$ is three. **2.** the square root of the sum of the squares of the real and imaginary parts of a given complex number.

ab′solute ze′ro, *n.* the temperature of −273.16°C (−459.69°F), the hypothetical point at which all molecular activity ceases.

ab•so•lu•tion (ab′sə lo͞o′shən), *n.* **1.** the act of absolving; the state of being absolved. **2.** a remission of sin or of the punishment for sin, esp. as effected by a priest or bishop in the sacrament of penance. —**ab•sol′u•to′ry** (-sol′yə tôr′ē, -tōr′ē), *adj.*

ab•so•lut•ism (ab′sə lo͞o tiz′əm), *n.* **1.** the principle or the exercise of unrestricted power in government. **2.** any theory holding that values, principles, etc., are absolute and not relative, dependent, or changeable. —**ab′so•lut′ist,** *n., adj.* —**ab′so•lu•tis′tic,** *adj.*

ab•solve (ab zolv′, -solv′), *v.t.,* **-solved, solv•ing. 1.** to free from guilt or blame or their consequences. **2.** to set free or release from some duty, obligation, or responsibility (usu. fol. by *from*). **3.** to grant pardon for; excuse. **4. a.** to grant or pronounce remission of sins to. **b.** to remit (a sin) by absolution. —**ab•solv′a•ble,** *adj.* —**ab•solv′er,** *n.*

ab•sorb (ab sôrb′, -zôrb′), *v.t.* **1.** to suck up or drink in (a liquid); soak up: *A sponge absorbs water.* **2.** to take in and assimilate; incorporate: *The empire absorbed many nations.* **3.** to involve the full attention of; engross: *This book will absorb the serious reader.* **4.** to occupy or fill (time, attention, etc.). **5.** to assimilate by chemical or molecular action. **6.** to take in without echo, recoil, or reflection: *to absorb shock; to absorb sound.* **7.** to take in and utilize: *to absorb information.* **8.** to pay for (costs, taxes, etc.). —**ab•sorb′a•ble,** *adj.* —**ab•sorb′a•bil′i•ty,** *n.*

ab•sorbed (ab sôrbd′, -zôrbd′), *adj.* deeply interested or involved; engrossed. —**ab•sorb′ed•ly,** *adv.* —**ab•sorb′ed•ness,** *n.*

ab•sorb•ent (ab sôr′bənt, -zôr′-), *adj.* **1.** capable of absorbing heat, light, moisture, etc.; tending to absorb. —*n.* **2.** a substance that absorbs. —**ab•sorb′en•cy,** *n.*

ab•sorb•ing (ab sôr′bing, -zôr′-), *adj.* extremely interesting or involving; engrossing. —**ab•sorb′ing•ly,** *adv.*

ab•sorp•tion (ab sôrp′shən, -zôrp′-), *n.* **1.** the act of absorbing. **2.** the state or process of being absorbed. **3.** assimilation. **4.** complete involvement or preoccupation. **5.** assimilation by molecular or chemical action. **6.** the removal of energy or particles from a beam by the medium through which the beam propagates. —**ab•sorp′tive,** *adj., n.*

ab•stain (ab stān′), *v.i.* **1.** to refrain voluntarily, esp. from something regarded as improper or unhealthy (usu. fol. by *from*): *to abstain from eating meat.* **2.** to refrain from casting one's vote: *a referendum in which two delegates abstained.*

ab•ste•mi•ous (ab stē′mē əs), *adj.* **1.** sparing or moderate in eating and drinking; temperate. **2.** characterized by abstinence. **3.** sparing: *an abstemious diet.* —**ab•ste′mi•ous•ly,** *adv.* —**ab•ste′mi•ous•ness,** *n.*

ab•sten•tion (ab sten′shən), *n.* **1.** an act or instance of abstaining. **2.** the withholding of one's vote.

ab•ster•gent (ab stûr′jənt), *adj.* **1.** cleansing. **2.** purgative. —*n.* **3.** a cleansing agent, as a detergent.

ab•sti•nence (ab′stə nəns) also **ab′sti•nen•cy,** *n.* **1.** forbearance from indulgence of an appetite. **2.** abstention from a drug, as alcohol or heroin, esp. a drug on which one is dependent: *total abstinence.* **3.** any self-restraint, self-denial, or forbearance. **4.** the refraining from certain kinds of foods on certain days, as from meat during Lent. —**ab′sti•nent,** *adj.* —**ab′sti•nent•ly,** *adv.*

ab•stract (*adj.* ab strakt′, ab′strakt; *n.* ab′strakt; *v.* ab strakt′ *for 10–13,* ab′strakt *for 14*), *adj.* **1.** thought of apart from concrete realities, specific objects, or actual instances: *an abstract idea.* **2.** expressing a quality or characteristic apart from any specific object or instance: *an abstract word like* justice. **3.** theoretical; not applied or practical. **4.** difficult to understand; abstruse. **5.** emphasizing line, color, and nonrepresentational form: *abstract art.* —*n.* **6.** a summary of a text, technical article, speech, etc. **7.** an abstract idea or term. **8.** an abstract work of art. **9.** something that concentrates in itself the essential qualities of anything more extensive or more general. —*v.t.* **10.** to draw or take away; remove. **11.** to divert or draw away the attention of. **12.** to steal. **13.** to consider as a general quality or characteristic apart from specific objects or instances. **14.** to make an abstract of; summarize. —***Idiom.*** **15. in the abstract,** without reference to a specific object or instance; in theory. —**ab•stract′ly,** *adv.*

ab′stract expres′sionism, *n.* (*sometimes caps.*) experimental, nonrepresentational painting marked by technical freedom and spontaneous expression. —**ab′stract expres′sionist,** *n., adj.*

ab•strac•tion (ab strak′shən), *n.* **1.** an abstract or general idea or term. **2.** the act of considering something in terms of general qualities or characteristics, apart from concrete realities, specific objects, or actual instances. **3.** absent-mindedness; inattention. **4.** the act of taking away or separating; withdrawal. **5.** secret removal, esp. theft. **6.** the quality of being abstract. —**ab•strac′tion•al,** *adj.*

ab•strac•tion•ism (ab strak′shə niz′əm), *n.* the practice and theory of abstract art. —**ab•strac′tion•ist,** *n., adj.*

ab′stract noun′, *n.* a noun denoting something abstract, conceptual, or general, as *kindness, dread,* or *transportation.* Compare CONCRETE NOUN.

ab•struse (ab stro͞os′), *adj.* hard to understand; recondite; esoteric: *abstruse theories.* —**ab•struse′ly,** *adv.* —**ab•struse′ness,** *n.*

ab•surd (ab sûrd′, -zûrd′), *adj.* **1.** utterly or obviously senseless, illogical, or untrue; contrary to all reason; laughably foolish or false. —*n.* **2. the absurd,** the quality or condition of existing in a meaningless and irrational world. —**ab•surd′i•ty,** *n., pl.* **-ties.** —**ab•surd′ly,** *adv.*

ab•surd•ism (ab sûr′diz əm, -zûr′-), *n.* the philosophic and literary doctrine that humans live essentially isolated in a meaningless and irrational world. —**ab•surd′ist,** *n., adj.*

A•bu Dha•bi (ä′bo͞o dä′bē), *n.* **1.** a sheikdom in the N United Arab Emirates, on the S coast of the Persian Gulf. 670,125. **2.** the capital of this sheikdom and the capital of the United Arab Emirates. 242,975.

A·bu·ja (ə bŌŌ′jə), *n.* the capital of Nigeria, in the central part. 378,671.

a·bu·li·a (ə byŌŌ′lē ə, ə bŌŌ′-), *n.* a symptom of mental disorder involving impairment or loss of volition. —**a·bu′lic,** *adj.*

a·bun·dance (ə bun′dəns), *n.* **1.** an extremely plentiful or oversufficient quantity or supply. **2.** affluence; wealth. **3.** overflowing fullness: *abundance of the heart.*

a·bun·dant (ə bun′dənt), *adj.* **1.** present in great quantity; more than adequate: *an abundant supply of water.* **2.** well supplied; abounding: *a river abundant in salmon.* **3.** richly supplied: *an abundant land.* —**a·bun′dant·ly,** *adv.*

a·buse (*v.* ə byŌŌz′; *n.* ə byŌŌs′), *v.,* **a·bused, a·bus·ing,** *n.* —*v.t.* **1.** to use wrongly or improperly; misuse: *to abuse one's authority.* **2.** to treat in a harmful or injurious way: *to abuse a horse; to abuse one's eyesight.* **3.** to speak insultingly or harshly to or about; revile. **4.** to commit sexual assault upon. —*n.* **5.** wrong, improper, or excessive use; misuse: *the abuse of privileges; drug abuse.* **6.** harshly or coarsely insulting language. **7.** bad or improper treatment; maltreatment. **8.** a corrupt or improper practice or custom. **9.** rape or sexual assault. —**a·bus′a·ble** (-zə bəl), *adj.* —**a·bus′er,** *n.*

a·bu·sive (ə byŌŌ′siv), *adj.* **1.** using, containing, or characterized by harshly or coarsely insulting language. **2.** treating badly or injuriously; mistreating, esp. physically: *his abusive treatment of the horse.* **3.** wrongly used; corrupt: *an abusive exercise of power.* —**a·bu′sive·ly,** *adv.* —**a·bu′sive·ness,** *n.*

a·but (ə but′), *v.,* **a·but·ted, a·but·ting.** —*v.i.* **1.** to be adjacent; touch or join at the edge or border (often fol. by *on, upon,* or *against*). —*v.t.* **2.** to be adjacent to; border on; end at. **3.** to support by an abutment.

a·but·ment (ə but′mənt), *n.* **1. a.** a masonry mass supporting and receiving the thrust of part of an arch or vault. **b.** a mass, as of masonry, receiving the arch, beam, truss, etc., at each end of a bridge. **2.** the place where projecting parts abut.

a·but·tal (ə but′l), *n.* **1. abuttals,** those parts of a piece of land that abut on adjacent lands; boundaries. **2.** the act or state of abutting.

A·by·dos (ə bī′dəs), *n.* **1.** an ancient ruined city in central Egypt, near Thebes: temples and necropolis. **2.** an ancient town in NW Asia Minor, at the narrowest part of the Hellespont.

a·bys·mal (ə biz′məl), *adj.* **1.** of or like an abyss; immeasurably deep or great: *abysmal ignorance.* **2.** extremely or hopelessly bad or severe: *abysmal weather.* —**a·bys′mal·ly,** *adv.*

a·byss (ə bis′), *n.* **1.** a deep, immeasurable space, gulf, or cavity; vast chasm. **2.** anything profound, unfathomable, or infinite: *the abyss of time.* **3.** the lowest or most hopeless depths. **4.** (in ancient cosmogony) **a.** the primal chaos before Creation. **b.** the infernal regions; hell. **c.** a subterranean ocean.

a·byss·al (ə bis′əl), *adj.* **1.** of or like an abyss; immeasurable; unfathomable. **2.** of or pertaining to the biogeographic zone of the ocean bottom between the bathyal and hadal zones, from depths of approximately 13,000 to 21,000 ft. (4000 to 6500 m).

Ab·ys·sin·i·a (ab′ə sin′ē ə), *n.* **1.** ETHIOPIA (def. 1). **2.** ETHIOPIA (def. 2). —**Ab′ys·sin′i·an,** *adj., n.*

Abyssin′ian cat′, *n.* one of a breed of shorthaired domestic cats typically having reddish fur ticked with brown or black.

AC, 1. air conditioning. **2.** Also, **ac, a.c., A.C.** alternating current.

Ac, *Chem. Symbol.* actinium.

A/C or **a/c,** **1.** account. **2.** account current. **3.** air conditioning.

A.C., before Christ. [< Latin *ante Christum*]

a·ca·cia (ə kā′shə), *n., pl.* **-cias. 1.** a small tree or shrub of the genus *Acacia,* of the legume family, having clusters of small yellow flowers. **2.** any of several other plants, as the locust tree. **3.** GUM ARABIC.

ac·a·deme (ak′ə dēm′, ak′ə dēm′), *n.* **1.** the academic environment or community. **2.** (*sometimes cap.*) any place of instruction; school. **3.** (*cap.*) ACADEMY (def. 5b). **4.** a scholar or pedant.

ac·a·de·mi·a (ak′ə dē′mē ə, -dēm′yə, -dem′ē ə, -dem′yə), *n.* the academic world.

ac·a·dem·ic (ak′ə dem′ik), *adj.* Also, **ac′a·dem′i·cal. 1.** of or pertaining to a school, esp. one for higher education. **2.** of or pertaining to areas of study that are not primarily vocational or applied, as the humanities or pure mathematics. **3.** theoretical or hypothetical; not practical or directly useful: *an academic question.* **4.** learned or scholarly but lacking in worldliness, common sense, or practicality. **5.** conforming to set rules, standards, or traditions; conventional: *academic painting.* —*n.* **6.** a student or teacher at a college or university. **7.** a person who is academic in background, attitudes, methods, etc. **8. academics,** academic studies or subjects. —**ac′a·dem′i·cal·ly,** *adv.*

ac′adem′ic free′dom, *n.* freedom of a teacher or student to explore an idea or issue without interference from officials.

ac·a·de·mi·cian (ak′ə də mish′ən, ə kad′ə-), *n.* **1.** a member of an association or institution for the advancement of arts, sciences, or letters. **2.** a follower or promoter of traditional rules or trends in philosophy, art, or literature.

ac·a·dem·i·cism (ak′ə dem′ə siz′əm), *n.* **1.** traditionalism or conventionalism in art, literature, etc. **2.** thoughts, opinions, and attitudes that are purely speculative. **3.** a pedantic or formal quality.

a·cad·e·my (ə kad′ə mē), *n., pl.* **-mies. 1.** a secondary or high school, esp. a private one. **2.** a school or college for special instruction or training in a subject: *a military academy.* **3.** an association for the advance-

ment of art, literature, or science. **4.** a group of authorities and leaders in a field of scholarship, art, etc., who are often permitted to dictate standards, prescribe methods, and criticize new ideas. **5. the Academy, a.** the Platonic school of philosophy or its adherents. **b.** the public grove in Athens where Plato taught. [< Latin < Greek *akadēmeia* the garden where Plato taught]

Acad′emy Award′, *Trademark.* an annual award given to a performer, director, technician, etc., of the motion-picture industry for superior achievement in a specific category: judged by the voting members of the Academy of Motion Picture Arts and Sciences and symbolized by the presentation of an Oscar. Compare OSCAR.

A·ca·di·a (ə kā′dē ə), *n.* a region and former French colony on the N Atlantic coast of North America, including the present Canadian provinces of Nova Scotia, New Brunswick, and Prince Edward Island, and part of Maine: ceded to the British 1713.

a·can·thous (ə kan′thəs), *adj.* SPINOUS.

a·can·thus (ə kan′thəs), *n., pl.* **-thus·es, -thi** (-thī). **1.** any of several plants of the genus *Acanthus,* of the Mediterranean region, having spiny or toothed leaves and showy white or purplish flowers. **2.** an architectural ornament resembling the leaves of this plant. —**a·can′thine** (-thin, -thīn), *adj.*

leaf of plant,
Acanthus mollis

architectural ornament,
front and side views

acanthus

a cap·pel·la (ä′ kə pel′ə), *adv., adj.* without instrumental accompaniment.

ac·a·ri·a·sis (ak′ə rī′ə sis), *n., pl.* **-ses** (-sēz′). **1.** infestation with acarids, esp. mites. **2.** a skin disease caused by such infestation, as scabies.

ac·a·rid (ak′ə rid), *n.* any arachnid of the order Acarina, comprising the mites and ticks.

a·car·pous (ā kär′pəs), *adj.* not producing fruit; sterile; barren.

a·car·us (ak′ər əs), *n., pl.* **-a·ri** (-ə rī′). a mite, esp. of the genus *Acarus.* —**ac′a·roid′,** *adj.*

a·cat·a·lec·tic (ā kat′l ek′tik), *adj.* **1.** (of a line of verse) not catalectic; complete. —*n.* **2.** a verse having the complete number of syllables in the last foot.

ac·au·les·cent (ak′ô les′ənt, ā′kô-), *adj.* (of a plant) lacking a visible stem. —**ac′au·les′cence,** *n.*

ac·cede (ak sēd′), *v.i.,* **-ced·ed, -ced·ing. 1.** to give one's consent, approval, or adherence by yielding; give in; agree; assent: *to accede to a request; to accede to the terms of a contract.* **2.** to attain or assume an office, title, or dignity; succeed (usu. fol. by *to*): *to accede to the throne.* **3.** to become a party to an agreement or treaty. —**ac·ced′ence,** *n.*

ac·cel·er·an·do (ak sel′ə rän′dō, -rän′-, ä chel′-), *adv., adj.* gradually increasing in speed (used as a musical direction).

ac·cel·er·ant (ak sel′ər ənt), *n.* **1.** something that speeds up a process. **2.** ACCELERATOR (def. 3). **3.** a substance that intensifies a fire or accelerates its spread.

ac·cel·er·ate (ak sel′ə rāt′), *v.,* **-at·ed, -at·ing.** —*v.t.* **1.** to cause faster development, progress, or advancement in. **2.** to increase the speed or velocity of; cause to move faster. **3.** to hasten the occurrence of. **4.** to change the velocity of (a body) or the rate of (motion). **5.** to reduce the time required for (a course of study) by intensifying the work, eliminating detail, etc. —*v.i.* **6.** to move or go faster; increase in speed. **7.** to progress or develop faster. —**ac·cel′er·at′ed·ly,** *adv.*

ac·cel·er·a·tion (ak sel′ə rā′shən), *n.* **1.** the act of accelerating; increase of speed or velocity. **2.** a change in velocity. **3.** the time rate of change of velocity with respect to magnitude or direction; the derivative of velocity with respect to time.

accelera′tion of grav′ity, *n.* the acceleration of a falling body in the earth's gravitational field, approximately 32 ft. (9.8 m) per second per second. *Symbol:* g

ac·cel·er·a·tor (ak sel′ə rā′tər), *n.* **1.** a person or thing that accelerates. **2.** a device, usu. operated by the foot, for controlling the speed of a motor vehicle engine. **3.** a substance that increases the speed of a chemical change. **4.** a muscle, nerve, or activating substance that quickens a movement. **5.** PARTICLE ACCELERATOR.

ac·cent (*n.* ak′sent; *v.* also ak sent′), *n.* **1.** prominence of a syllable in terms of differential loudness, pitch, length, or a combination of these. **2.** degree of prominence of a syllable within a word or of a word within a phrase. **3.** a mark indicating stress (as ′, ′ or ·, ‚), vowel quality (as French grave `, acute ′, circumflex ^), pitch, distinction in meaning, or that an ordinarily silent vowel is to be pronounced. **4.** regularly recurring stress in verse. **5.** a mode of pronunciation characteristic of or distinctive to the speech of a particular person, group, or locality: *a Southern accent.* **6.** such a mode of pronunciation recognized as being of foreign origin: *She still speaks with an accent.* **7. a.** a stress or emphasis given to certain musical notes. **b.** a mark indicating this. **c.** stress or emphasis regularly recurring as a feature of rhythm. **8.** Often, **accents.** the tones, inflections, choice of words, etc., that identify a particular individual or express a particular emotion. **9.** special attention or emphasis: *an accent on accuracy.* **10.** a contrasting detail. **11.** a distinctive quality or feature. **12. a.** a symbol used to distinguish similar mathematical quantities that differ in value, as in b', b", b‴ (called *b prime, b second* or *b double prime, b third* or *b triple prime,* respectively). **b.** a symbol used to indicate a particular unit of measure, as feet (') or inches ("), minutes (') or seconds ("). **c.** a symbol used to indicate the order of a derivative of a function in calculus, as *f'* (called *f prime*) is the first derivative of a function *f.* **13. accents,** words; language; speech: *He spoke in accents bold.* —*v.t.* **14.** to pronounce with prominence (a syllable within a word or a word within a phrase): *Accent the first syllable.* **15.** to mark with a written accent or accents. **16.** to give emphasis or prominence to; accentuate. —**ac′cent•less,** *adj.*

ac•cen•tu•al (ak sen′cho͞o əl), *adj.* **1.** of or pertaining to accent or stress. **2.** pertaining to or based on stress rather than the number or duration of syllables: *accentual meter.* —**ac•cen′tu•al′i•ty,** *n.* —**ac•cen′tu•al•ly,** *adv.*

ac•cen•tu•ate (ak sen′cho͞o āt′), *v.t.,* **-at•ed, -at•ing. 1.** to give emphasis or prominence to. **2.** to mark or pronounce with an accent. —**ac•cen′tu•a′tion,** *n.* —**ac•cen′tu•a′tor,** *n.*

ac•cept (ak sept′), *v.t.* **1.** to take or receive (something offered). **2.** to receive with approval or favor: *to accept a proposal.* **3.** to receive or admit as adequate or satisfactory: *to accept an apology.* **4.** to respond or answer affirmatively to: *to accept an invitation.* **5.** to undertake the duties, responsibilities, or honors of: *to accept the office of president.* **6.** to admit formally, as to a college or club. **7.** to accommodate or reconcile oneself to: *to accept the situation.* **8.** to regard as true or sound; believe. **9.** to regard as normal, suitable, or usual. **10.** to receive as to meaning; understand. **11.** to agree to pay, as a draft. **12.** to receive or contain (something attached, inserted, etc.): *This socket won't accept a three-pronged plug.* **13.** to receive (a transplanted organ or tissue) without adverse reaction. Compare REJECT (def. 7). —*v.i.* **14.** to accept an invitation, gift, position, etc. (sometimes fol. by *of*). —**ac•cept′er,** *n.*

ac•cept•a•ble (ak sep′tə bəl), *adj.* **1.** capable or worthy of being accepted. **2.** pleasing to the receiver; agreeable; welcome. **3.** meeting only minimum requirements; barely adequate. **4.** capable of being endured; tolerable; bearable: *acceptable levels of radiation.* —**ac•cept′a•bil′i•ty,** *n.* —**ac•cept′a•bly,** *adv.*

ac•cept•ance (ak sep′təns), *n.* **1.** the act of taking or receiving something offered. **2.** favorable reception; approval; favor. **3.** the act of assenting or believing: *acceptance of a theory.* **4.** the fact or state of being accepted or acceptable. **5. a.** a pledge to pay an order, draft, or bill of exchange when it becomes due. **b.** an order, draft, or bill of exchange that has been accepted.

ac•cep•tor (ak sep′tər), *n.* **1.** one that accepts; accepter. **2.** a person who acccepts for payment a draft or bill of exchange. **3.** an atom that receives a pair of electrons to form a chemical bond. Compare DONOR (def. 3).

ac•cess (ak′ses), *n.* **1.** the ability or right to enter or use: *They have access to the files.* **2.** the right or opportunity to approach or speak with. **3.** the state or quality of being approachable: *The house was difficult of access.* **4.** a way or means of approach. **5.** an attack or onset, as of a disease. **6.** a sudden and strong emotional outburst. **7.** accession; increase. —*v.t.* **8.** to make contact with or gain access to. **9.** to locate (data) for transfer from one part of a computer system to another. —*adj.* **10.** (of television programming, time, etc.) available to the public.

ac•ces•si•ble (ak ses′ə bəl), *adj.* **1.** easy to approach, reach, enter, speak with, or use. **2.** able to be used, entered, or reached. **3.** obtainable; attainable: *accessible evidence.* **4.** readily understandable. **5.** open to the influence of (usu. fol. by *to*): *accessible to bribery.* —**ac•ces′si•bil′i•ty,** *n.* —**ac•ces′si•bly,** *adv.*

ac•ces•sion (ak sesh′ən), *n.* **1.** the act of coming into the possession of a right, title, office, etc.: *accession to the throne.* **2.** an increase by something added: *an accession of territory.* **3.** something added: *accessions to the library.* **4.** *Law.* addition to property by growth or improvement. **5.** consent; agreement; approval: *accession to a demand.* **6.** formal acceptance of a treaty or other agreement between states. **7.** approach or onset. —*v.t.* **8.** to make a record of (a book, painting, etc.) in the order of acquisition. **9.** to acquire (a book, painting, etc.), esp. for a permanent collection. —**ac•ces′sion•al,** *adj.*

ac•ces•so•rize (ak ses′ə rīz′), *v.,* **-rized, -riz•ing.** —*v.t.* **1.** to fit or equip with accessories. —*v.i.* **2.** to choose or wear accessories. —**ac•ces′so•ri•za′tion,** *n.*

ac•ces•so•ry (ak ses′ə rē), *n., pl.* **-ries,** *adj.* —*n.* **1.** a subordinate or supplementary part or object that adds to convenience, attractiveness, safety, etc. **2.** an article of dress, as gloves or earrings, that completes or enhances one's basic outfit. **3.** *Law.* **a.** Also called **acces′sory be•fore′ the fact′.** a person who, although not present during the commission of a felony, is guilty of having aided and abetted another, who committed the felony. **b.** Also called **acces′sory af′ter the fact′.** a person who knowingly conceals or assists another who has committed a felony. Compare PRINCIPAL (def. 7b). —*adj.* **4.** Also, **ac•ces•so•ri•al** (ak′sə sôr′ē əl, -sōr′-), contributing to a general effect; supplementary; subsidiary. **5.** *Law.* giving aid as an accessory. **6.** noting any mineral considered to be a nonessential constituent of a rock.

ac•ci•dence (ak′si dəns), *n.* **1.** the study of inflection as a grammatical device. **2.** the inflections so studied.

ac•ci•dent (ak′si dənt), *n.* **1.** an undesirable or unfortunate happening that occurs unintentionally and usu. results in injury, damage, or loss. **2.** an incident that results in injury, in no way the fault of the victim, for which compensation or indemnity is legally sought. **3.** any event that happens unexpectedly, without a deliberate plan or cause. **4.** chance; fortune; luck: *I was there by accident.* **5.** a nonessential or incidental feature or circumstance.

ac•ci•den•tal (ak′si den′tl), *adj.* **1.** happening by chance or accident. **2.** nonessential; incidental: *accidental benefits.* **3.** pertaining to or indicating sharps, flats, or naturals in music. —*n.* **4.** a nonessential or subsidiary circumstance or feature. **5.** a sign placed before a note indicating a chromatic alteration of its pitch. —**ac′ci•den′tal•ly,** *adv.*

ac′cident-prone′, *adj.* tending to have more accidents or mishaps than the average person.

ac•claim (ə klām′), *v.t.* **1.** to greet publicly with loud or enthusiastic approval or praise: *a widely acclaimed book.* **2.** to announce or proclaim with enthusiastic approval: *He was acclaimed the king.* —*v.i.* **3.** to make acclamation; applaud. —*n.* **4.** enthusiastic approval or praise. **5.** ACCLAMATION (defs. 1, 2).

ac•cla•ma•tion (ak′lə mā′shən), *n.* **1.** a loud or enthusiastic demonstration of welcome, goodwill, or approval. **2.** the act of acclaiming. —***Idiom.* 3. by acclamation,** by a majority voice vote, applause, or the like rather than a formal ballot. —**ac•clam•a•to•ry** (ə klam′ə tôr′ē, -tōr′ē), *adj.*

ac•cli•mate (ak′lə māt′, ə klī′mit), *v.t., v.i.,* **-mat•ed, -mat•ing.** to accustom or become accustomed to a new climate or environment. —**ac•cli′mat•a•ble,** *adj.* —**ac′cli•ma′tion,** *n.*

ac•cliv•i•ty (ə kliv′i tē), *n., pl.* **-ties.** an upward slope, as of ground; an ascent (opposed to *declivity*). —**ac•cliv′i•tous, ac•cli•vous** (ə klī′vəs), *adj.*

ac•co•lade (ak′ə lād′, -läd′; ak′ə lād′, -läd′), *n.* **1.** any award, honor, or laudatory notice. **2.** a light touch on the shoulder with the flat side of the sword, given in conferring knighthood. **3.** *Music.* a brace joining several staves. **4.** an ornamental molding over a door, window, or arch.

ac•com•mo•date (ə kom′ə dāt′), *v.,* **-dat•ed, -dat•ing.** —*v.t.* **1.** to do a kindness or a favor to; oblige. **2.** to provide suitably; supply. **3.** to lend money to. **4.** to provide with accommodations. **5.** to have or make room for: *This elevator accommodates 10 people.* **6.** to adjust or make suitable; adapt: *to accommodate oneself to circumstances.* **7.** to bring into harmony; reconcile: *to accommodate differences.* —*v.i.* **8.** to become adjusted, adapted, or reconciled. —**ac•com′mo•da′tive,** *adj.*

ac•com•mo•da•tion (ə kom′ə dā′shən), *n.* **1.** the act of accommodating; the state or process of being accommodated; adaptation. **2.** adjustment of differences; reconciliation. **3.** a process of mutual adaptation between persons or social groups, usu. achieved by eliminating or reducing hostility. **4.** anything that supplies a need, want, convenience, etc. **5.** Usu., **accommodations. a.** lodging. **b.** food and lodging. **c.** a seat, berth, etc., on a train, plane, or other public vehicle. **6.** readiness to aid others; obligingness. **7.** a loan. **8.** the automatic adjustment by which the eye adapts itself for distinct vision at different distances.

ac•com•pa•ni•ment (ə kum′pə ni mənt, ə kump′ni-), *n.* **1.** something incidental or added for ornament, symmetry, etc. **2.** a musical part supporting and enhancing the principal part.

ac•com•pa•nist (ə kum′pə nist, ə kump′nist) also **ac•com•pa•ny•ist** (-pə nē ist), *n.* a performer of musical accompaniments.

ac•com•pa•ny (ə kum′pə nē), *v.,* **-nied, -ny•ing.** —*v.t.* **1.** to go along or in company with. **2.** to exist or occur in association with: *Thunder accompanies lightning.* **3.** to cause to be associated with or attended by: *He accompanied his speech with gestures.* **4.** to perform musical accompaniment for. —*v.i.* **5.** to provide the musical accompaniment.

ac•com•plice (ə kom′plis), *n.* a person who knowingly helps another in a crime or wrongdoing.

ac•com•plish (ə kom′plish), *v.t.* **1.** to bring to a goal or successful conclusion; carry out; finish: *to accomplish one's mission.* **2.** to complete (a distance or period of time). —**ac•com′plish•a•ble,** *adj.*

ac•com•plished (ə kom′plisht), *adj.* **1.** completed; effected: *an accomplished fact.* **2.** highly skilled; expert: *an accomplished pianist.* **3.** having the social graces and other attainments of polite society.

ac•com•plish•ment (ə kom′plish mənt), *n.* **1.** an act or instance of carrying into effect; fulfillment. **2.** something done admirably or creditably. **3.** anything accomplished; achievement. **4.** a grace or skill expected in polite society. **5.** any acquired ability or skill.

ac•cord (ə kôrd′), —*v.i.* **1.** to be in agreement or harmony; agree. —*v.t.* **2.** to make agree or correspond; adapt. **3.** to grant; bestow: *to accord due praise.* —*n.* **4.** agreement; harmony. **5.** a harmonious union of sounds, colors, etc. **6.** concurrence of opinions or wills; agreement: *to reach an accord.* **7.** an international agreement. —***Idiom.* 8. of one's own accord,** without external compulsion or suggestion; voluntarily. **9. with one accord,** with unanimous agreement. —**ac•cord′a•ble,** *adj.*

ac•cord•ance (ə kôr′dns), *n.* **1.** agreement; conformity: *in accordance with the rules.* **2.** the act of granting.

ac•cord•ing•ly (ə kôr′ding lē), *adv.* **1.** in a way that is suitable or in accordance. **2.** therefore; so; in due course.

accord′ing to′, *prep.* **1.** in agreement or accord with: *according to his judgment.* **2.** consistent with; contingent on or in proportion to: *charge* *according to one's ability to pay.* **3.** on the authority of; as stated or reported by: *According to her, they have gone.*

ac•cor•di•on (ə kôr′dē ən), *n.* **1.** a portable wind instrument with a keyboard and a hand-operated bellows for forcing air through small metal reeds. —*adj.* **2.** having evenly spaced, parallel folds like the bellows of an accordion: *accordion pleats.* —**ac•cor′di•on•ist,** *n.*

ac•cost (ə kôst′, ə kost′), *v.t.* **1.** to confront boldly. **2.** to approach with a greeting, question, or remark. —*n.* **3.** a greeting.

ac•count (ə kount′), *n.* **1.** an oral or written description of particular events or situations; narrative. **2.** an explanatory statement of conduct, as to a superior. **3.** a statement of reasons, causes, etc., explaining some event. **4.** reason; basis: *On this account I'm refusing your offer.* **5.** importance; worth; value; consequence: *things of no account.* **6.** estimation; judgment: *In his account it was a miracle.* **7.** an amount of money deposited with a bank, as in a checking or savings account. **8.** an accommodation extended to a customer permitting the charging of goods or services. **9.** a statement of financial transactions. **10.** a formal record of the debits and credits relating to a particular person, business, etc. **11. a.** a business relation in which credit is used. **b.** a customer or client, esp. one carried on a regular credit basis. —*v.i.* **12.** to give an explanation (usu. fol. by *for*). **13.** to answer concerning one's conduct, duties, etc. (usu. fol. by *for*). **14.** to provide a report on money received, kept, and spent. **15.** to cause (usu. fol. by *for*): *The heat accounts for our discomfort.* —*v.t.* **16.** to regard; consider as: *I account myself well paid.* **17.** to assign or impute (usu. fol. by *to*). —***Idiom.*** **18. call to account, a.** to hold accountable; blame. **b.** to ask for an explanation of. **19. give a good account of oneself,** to behave or perform well. **20. hold to account,** to consider responsible and answerable. **21. on account,** as an installment or a partial payment. **22. on account of, a.** by reason of; because of. **b.** for the sake of. **23. on no account,** under no circumstances; absolutely not. **24. on someone's account,** for the sake of someone. **25. take account of, a.** to consider; make allowance for. **b.** Also, **take into account.** to notice. **26. turn to account,** to derive profit or use from.

ac•count•a•ble (ə koun′tə bəl), *adj.* **1.** subject to the obligation to report or justify something; responsible; answerable. **2.** capable of being explained. —**ac•count′a•bil′i•ty,** *n.* —**ac•count′a•bly,** *adv.*

ac•count•an•cy (ə koun′tn sē), *n.* the work or practice of an accountant.

ac•count•ant (ə koun′tnt), *n.* a person skilled or trained in accounting, esp. one in charge of the financial accounts of a company or organization. —**ac•count′ant•ship′,** *n.*

ac•count•ing (ə koun′ting), *n.* **1.** the system or occupation of setting up, maintaining, and auditing the books of a firm and of analyzing its financial status and operating results. **2.** a detailed report of the financial state or transactions of a person, company, etc.

account′ receiv′able, *n., pl.* **accounts receivable.** a claim against a debtor, usu. for the sale of goods or services.

ac•cou•ter•ment or **ac•cou•tre•ment** (ə ko͞o′trə mənt, -tər-), *n.* **1.** personal clothing, accessories, or equipment. **2.** the equipment, excluding weapons and clothing, of a soldier.

Ac•cra (ak′rə, ə krä′), *n.* a seaport in and the capital of Ghana, on the Gulf of Guinea. 867,459.

ac•cred•it (ə kred′it), *v.t.* **1.** to ascribe or attribute; credit. **2.** to provide or send with credentials; designate officially: *to accredit an envoy.* **3.** to certify (a school or college) as meeting official requirements for academic excellence, curriculum, facilities, etc. **4.** to make authoritative, creditable, or reputable; sanction. **5.** to regard as true; believe. —**ac•cred′it•a•ble,** *adj.* —**ac•cred′i•ta′tion,** *n.*

ac•cre•tion (ə krē′shən), *n.* **1.** an increase by natural growth or by gradual external addition. **2.** the result of this process. **3.** addition. **4.** the growing together of separate parts into a single whole. **5.** *Law.* increase of property by gradual natural additions, as of land by alluvion. —**ac•cre′tive, ac•cre′tion•ar′y,** *adj.*

ac•crue (ə kro͞o′), *v.,* **-crued, -cru•ing.** —*v.i.* **1.** to happen or result as a natural growth, addition, etc. **2.** to be added as a matter of periodic gain or advantage, as interest on money. **3.** *Law.* to become a present and enforceable right. —*v.t.* **4.** to accumulate or earn over time: *to accrue interest.* —**ac•cru′a•ble,** *adj.* —**ac•cru′al,** *n.*

acct., **1.** account. **2.** accountant.

ac•cul•tur•a•tion (ə kul′chə rā′shən), *n.* **1.** the process of adopting the cultural traits or social patterns of another group, esp. a dominant one. **2.** a restructuring or blending of cultures resulting from this. —**ac•cul′tur•ate′,** *v.t., v.i.,* **-at•ed, -at•ing.**

ac•cum•bent (ə kum′bənt), *adj.* **1.** reclining; recumbent: *accumbent posture.* **2.** *Bot.* lying against something. —**ac•cum′ben•cy,** *n.*

ac•cu•mu•late (ə kyo͞o′myə lāt′), *v.,* **-lat•ed, -lat•ing.** —*v.t.* **1.** to gather or collect, often in gradual degrees; heap up; amass: *to accumulate wealth.* —*v.i.* **2.** to gather into a heap or mass; form a steadily increasing quantity. —**accumulation,** *n.* —**ac•cu′mu•la′tive,** *adj.* —**ac•cu′mu•la′tive•ly,** *adv.*

ac•cu•ra•cy (ak′yər ə sē), *n., pl.* **-cies. 1.** the condition or quality of being true, correct, or exact; precision; exactness. **2.** the extent to which a given measurement agrees with the standard value for that measurement. **3.** *Math.* the degree of correctness of a quantity, expression, etc. Compare PRECISION (def. 4).

ac•cu•rate (ak′yər it), *adj.* **1.** free from error; conforming to truth: *an accurate description.* **2.** consistent with a standard, rule, or model: *an accurate scale.* **3.** not making mistakes; carefully precise; meticulous: *an accurate typist.* —**ac′cu•rate•ly,** *adv.* —**ac′cu•rate•ness,** *n.*

ac•curs•ed (ə kûr′sid, ə kûrst′) also **ac•curst** (ə kûrst′), *adj.* **1.** under a curse; ill-fated. **2.** damnable; detestable. —**ac•curs′ed•ly,** *adv.* —**ac•curs′ed•ness,** *n.*

ac•cu•sa•tion (ak′yo͝o zā′shən) also **ac•cu•sal** (ə kyo͞o′zəl), *n.* **1.** a charge of wrongdoing; imputation of guilt or blame. **2.** the specific offense charged. **3.** the act of accusing or the state of being accused.

ac•cu•sa•tive (ə kyo͞o′zə tiv), *adj.* **1.** of or designating a grammatical case that indicates the direct object of a verb or the object of certain prepositions. **2.** ACCUSATORY. —*n.* **3.** the accusative case. **4.** a word or other form in the accusative case. —**ac•cu•sa•ti•val** (ə kyo͞o′zə tī′vəl), *adj.* —**ac•cu′sa•tive•ly,** *adv.*

ac•cu•sa•to•ry (ə kyo͞o′zə tôr′ē, -tōr′ē) also **accusative,** *adj.* containing an accusation; accusing: *an accusatory look.*

ac•cuse (ə kyo͞oz′), *v.,* **-cused, -cus•ing.** —*v.t.* **1.** to charge with the fault, offense, or crime (usu. fol. by *of*): *He was accused of murder.* **2.** to blame. —*v.i.* **3.** to make an accusation. —**ac•cus′a•ble,** *adj.* —**ac•cus′er,** *n.* —**ac•cus′ing•ly,** *adv.*

ac•cused (ə kyo͞ozd′), *adj.* **1.** charged with a crime, wrongdoing, fault, etc. —*n.* **2. the accused,** a person charged in a court of law with a crime or offense.

ac•cus•tom (ə kus′təm), *v.t.* to familiarize by custom or use; habituate: *to accustom oneself to cold weather.* —**ac•cus′tomed,** *adj.*

AC/DC or **ac/dc,** alternating current or direct current.

ace (ās), *n., v.,* **aced, ac•ing,** *adj.* —*n.* **1.** a playing card or a die face bearing a single pip or spot. **2.** Also called **service ace.** (in tennis, badminton, handball, etc.) a point made on a serve that an opponent fails to touch. **3.** a fighter pilot who downs a specified number of enemy aircraft in combat. **4.** a very skilled person; expert; adept. **5. a.** Also called **hole in one.** a shot in which a golf ball is driven from the tee into the hole in one stroke. **b.** a score of one stroke made on such a shot. —*v.t.* **6.** (in tennis, badminton, handball, etc.) to win a point against (one's opponent) by an ace. **7.** to make an ace on (a hole) in golf. **8.** *Slang.* to defeat, supplant, or gain an advantage over by maneuvering (usu. fol. by *out*). **9.** *Slang.* **a.** to receive a grade of A in or on: *to ace a test.* **b.** to complete with great success. —*adj.* **10.** excellent; first-rate; outstanding. —***Idiom.*** **11. ace in the hole, a.** an ace in poker dealt and played facedown. **b.** Also, **ace up one's sleeve.** an advantage held in reserve. **12. be aces with,** *Slang.* to be highly regarded by. **13. within an ace of,** very close to: *within an ace of winning.*

ACE, American Council on Education.

a•ce•di•a (ə sē′dē ə), *n.* **1.** sloth (def. 1). Compare DEADLY SINS. **2.** sloth; spiritual torpor or indifference; apathy. [< Late Latin *acēdia* < Greek *akēdeia* negligence, indifference]

A•cel•da•ma (ə sel′də mə, ə kel′-), *n.* the place near Jerusalem purchased with the bribe Judas took for betraying Jesus. Acts 1:18, 19.

a•cel•lu•lar (ā sel′yə lər), *adj.* **1.** being without cells. **2.** composed of tissue not divided into cells, as striated muscle fibers.

a•cen•tric (ā sen′trik), *adj.* **1.** not centered; having no center. **2.** (of a chromosome) lacking a centromere.

-aceous, a suffix with the meanings "resembling, having the nature of," "made of," occurring in loanwords from Latin (*cretaceous; herbaceous*) and forming adjectives in English (*ceraceous*), esp. adjectival correspondents to taxonomic names ending in -ACEA and -ACEAE: *rosaceous.*

a•ceph•a•lous (ā sef′ə ləs), *adj.* **1.** Also, **a•ce•phal•ic** (ā′sə fal′ik). headless; lacking a distinct head. **2.** without a leader or ruler.

a•cer•bic (ə sûr′bik), *adj.* **1.** sour or astringent in taste. **2.** sharply or bitterly severe, as temper or expression. —**a•cer′bi•cal•ly,** *adv.* —**a•cer′bi•ty,** *n.*

ac•er•ose[1] (as′ə rōs′), *adj.* needle-shaped, as the leaves of the pine.

ac•er•ose[2] (as′ə rōs′), *adj.* **1.** resembling chaff. **2.** mixed with chaff.

a•cer•vate (ə sûr′vit, -vāt, as′ər vāt′), *adj.* growing in dense, heaped-up clusters. —**a•cer′vate•ly,** *adv.*

ac•e•tab•u•lum (as′i tab′yə ləm), *n., pl.* **-la** (-lə). **1.** the socket in the hipbone that connects with the head of the femur to form the hip joint. **2.** any of the suction appendages of a leech, octopus, etc. **3.** the depression on the body into which an insect's leg fits. —**ac′e•tab′u•lar,** *adj.*

ac•e•tal (as′i tal′), *n.* **1.** a colorless liquid, $C_6H_{14}O_2$, used chiefly as a solvent and in making perfume. **2.** any of a class of compounds of aldehydes with alcohols.

a•ce•ta•min•o•phen (ə sē′tə min′ə fən, as′i tə-), *n.* a crystalline substance, $C_8H_9NO_2$, used as a pain reliever and to reduce fever.

ac•e•tate (as′i tāt′), *n.* **1.** a salt or ester of acetic acid. **2.** a synthetic filament, yarn, or material derived from the acetic ester of cellulose. **3.** CELLULOSE ACETATE.

ace′tic ac′id, *n.* a colorless, pungent liquid, $C_2H_4O_2$, the essential constituent of vinegar: used chiefly in the manufacture of acetate fibers, solvents, and flavoring agents.

ac•e•tone (as′i tōn′), *n.* a volatile, flammable liquid, C_3H_6O, used in paints and varnishes, as a solvent, and in organic synthesis. —**ac′e•ton′ic** (-ton′ik), *adj.*

ac•e•tous (as′i təs, ə sē′-) also **ac•e•tose** (-tōs′, -tōs), *adj.* **1.** containing or producing acetic acid. **2.** sour; producing or resembling vinegar; vinegary.

a•ce•tyl (ə sēt′l, ə set′l, as′i tl), *n.* the univalent group CH_3CO-, derived from acetic acid.

a·ce·tyl·cho·line (ə sēt′l kō′lēn, ə set′-), *n.* a short-acting neurotransmitter, widely distributed in the body, that functions as a nervous system stimulant, a vasodilator, and a cardiac depressant. *Abbr.:* ACh —**a·ce′tyl·cho·lin′ic** (-lin′ik), *adj.*

a·cet·y·lene (ə set′l ēn′, -in), *n.* a colorless gas, C₂H₂, used esp. in metal cutting and welding, as an illuminant, and in organic synthesis. —**a·cet′y·len′ic** (-en′ik), *adj.*

A·chan (ā′kan), *n.* a member of the tribe of Judah who, with his family, was stoned to death for stealing forbidden spoils. Josh. 7:19–26.

ache (āk), *v.,* **ached, ach·ing.** —*v.i.* **1.** to have or suffer a continuous dull pain. **2.** to feel great sympathy, pity, or the like: *His heart ached for the starving animals.* **3.** to feel painful eagerness; yearn; long: *She ached to be the champion.* —*n.* **4.** a continuous dull pain. —**ach′ing·ly,** *adv.*

a·chene (ā kēn′, ə kēn′), *n.* any small, dry, hard, one-seeded, indehiscent fruit. —**a·che′ni·al,** *adj.*

A·cher·nar (ā′kər när′), *n. Astron.* a star of the first magnitude in the constellation Eridanus.

a·chieve (ə chēv′), *v.,* **a·chieved, a·chiev·ing.** —*v.t.* **1.** to bring to a successful end; succeed in doing or accomplishing: *The crackdown on speeders achieved its purpose.* **2.** to get or attain by effort: *to achieve victory.* —*v.i.* **3.** to accomplish some purpose or goal; perform successfully: *children who do not achieve in school.* —**a·chiev′a·ble,** *adj.* —**a·chiev′er,** *n.*

a·chieve·ment (ə chēv′mənt), *n.* **1.** something accomplished, as through great effort, skill, perseverance, or courage. **2.** the act of achieving; attainment or accomplishment.

A·chil·les (ə kil′ēz), *n.* the greatest Greek warrior in the Trojan War and hero of the *Iliad,* killed when Paris wounded him in the heel, his one vulnerable spot. —**Ach·il·le·an** (ak′ə lē′ən, ə kil′ē-), *adj.*

Achil′les (or **Achil′les′**) **heel′,** *n.* a vulnerable point.

Achil′les ten′don or **Achil′les′ ten′don,** *n.* the tendon joining the calf muscles to the heel bone.

ach·ing (ā′king), *adj.* **1.** causing physical pain or distress: *treatment for an aching back.* **2.** full of or precipitating nostalgia, grief, loneliness, etc.: *Her death left an aching void in his heart.* —**ach′ing·ly,** *adv.*

ach·ro·mat·ic (ak′rə mat′ik, ā′krə-), *adj.* **1.** free from color. **2.** able to emit, transmit, or receive light without separating it into colors. **3.** (of a cell structure) difficult to stain. **4.** without accidentals or changes in musical key. —**ach′ro·mat′i·cal·ly,** *adv.* —**a·chro·ma·tism** (ā krō′mə-tiz′əm), **a·chro′ma·tic′i·ty** (-tis′ə tē), *n.*

Ach·sah (ak′sə), *n.* the daughter of Caleb who was promised in marriage to the conqueror of the city of Debir. Josh. 15:16–19; Judg. 1:12–15.

ach·y (ā′kē), *adj.,* **ach·i·er, ach·i·est.** having or suffering from aches: *an achy back.* —**ach′i·ness,** *n.*

a·cic·u·lar (ə sik′yə lər), *adj.* needle-shaped. —**a·cic′u·lar′i·ty,** *n.* —**a·cic′u·lar·ly,** *adv.*

ac·id (as′id), *n.* **1.** a compound usu. having a sour taste and capable of neutralizing alkalis and turning blue litmus paper red, containing hydrogen that can be replaced by a metal or an electropositive group to form a salt, or containing an atom that can accept a pair of electrons from a base. **2.** a substance with a sour taste. **3.** biting criticism or sarcasm. **4.** *Slang.* the drug LSD. —*adj.* **5. a.** belonging or pertaining to acids or the anhydrides of acids. **b.** having only a part of the hydrogen of an acid replaced by a metal or its equivalent: *an acid phosphate.* **c.** having a pH value of less than 7. Compare ALKALINE. **6.** characterized by a high concentration of acid. **7.** sharp or biting to the taste; sour: *acid fruits.* **8.** sharp, biting, or ill-natured in mood or manner; caustic: *acid wit.* **9.** vividly intense in color: *acid green.* **10.** (of igneous rock) rich in silica. —**a·cid·ic** (ə sid′ik), *adj.* —**ac′id·ly,** *adv.* —**ac′id·ness,** *n.*

a·cid·i·fy (ə sid′ə fī′), *v.t., v.i.,* **-fied, -fy·ing. 1.** to make or become acid; convert into an acid. **2.** to make or become sour. —**a·cid′i·fi·a·ble,** *adj.* —**a·cid′i·fi·ca′tion,** *n.* —**a·cid′i·fi′er,** *n.*

a·cid·i·ty (ə sid′i tē), *n.* **1.** the quality or state of being acid. **2.** sourness; tartness. **3.** excessive acid quality.

ac·i·do·sis (as′i dō′sis), *n.* a blood condition in which the bicarbonate concentration is below normal. —**ac′i·dot′ic** (-dot′ik), *adj.*

ac′id rain′, *n.* precipitation containing acid-forming chemicals, chiefly industrial pollutants, that have been released into the atmosphere and combined with water vapor: ecologically harmful.

ac′id test′, *n.* a severe and conclusive test, as to establish quality, genuineness, or worth.

a·cid·u·late (ə sij′ə lāt′), *v.t.,* **-lat·ed, -lat·ing. 1.** to make somewhat acid. **2.** to sour; embitter. —**a·cid′u·la′tion,** *n.*

a·cid·u·lous (ə sij′ə ləs) also **a·cid·u·lent** (-lənt), *adj.* **1.** slightly sour. **2.** sharp; caustic: *acidulous criticism.* **3.** moderately acid or tart.

a·cin·i·form (ə sin′ə fôrm′), *adj.* clustered like grapes.

ac·i·nus (as′ə nəs), *n., pl.* **-ni** (-nī′). **1.** a small, rounded form, as a lobule, sac, seed, or berry. **2.** the smallest secreting portion of a gland. —**ac′i·nar** (-nər, -när′), **a·cin·ic** (ə sin′ik), *adj.*

-acity, a suffix forming nouns corresponding to adjectives ending in -ACIOUS: *tenacity.*

ack-ack (ak′ak′), *n.* (esp. during World War II) **1.** antiaircraft fire. **2.** antiaircraft arms.

Ack·ley (ak′lē), *n.* **1. Alfred,** 1887–1960, U.S. clergyman, musician, and hymn writer. **2.** his brother **Benton,** 1872–1958, U.S. musician and hymn writer.

ac·knowl·edge (ak nol′ij), *v.t.,* **-edged, -edg·ing. 1.** to admit to be real or true; recognize the existence, truth, or fact of. **2.** to show or express recognition or realization of: *to acknowledge applause by nodding.* **3.** to recognize the authority, validity, or claims of. **4.** to show or express appreciation or gratitude for: *to acknowledge a favor.* **5.** to indicate or make known the receipt of, as with a reply: *to acknowledge a letter.* **6.** *Law.* to confirm as binding or of legal force.

ac·knowl·edg·ment (ak nol′ij mənt), *n.* **1.** an act of acknowledging. **2.** recognition of the existence, truth, authority, or validity of something. **3.** an expression of appreciation. **4.** a thing done or given in appreciation or gratitude. **5.** a thing done or given to confirm receipt of something. **6. acknowledgments,** an author's statement expressing thanks to those who have assisted in the preparation of a book or article. **7. a.** a declaration before an official that one has executed a particular legal document. **b.** an official certificate of this. Also, *esp. Brit.,* **ac·knowl′edge·ment.**

a·clin′ic line′ (ā klin′ik), *n.* an imaginary line on the surface of the earth, close and approximately parallel to the equator, connecting all those points over which a magnetic needle shows no inclination from the horizontal. Also called **magnetic equator.**

ACLU or **A.C.L.U.,** American Civil Liberties Union.

ac·me (ak′mē), *n.* the highest point of attainment or development; peak: *The empire was at the acme of its power.*

ac·ne (ak′nē), *n.* any of various inflammatory skin eruptions involving breakdown of sebum from the sebaceous glands and characterized by pimples on the face, neck, and upper back. —**ac′ned,** *adj.*

a·coe·lo·mate (ā sē′lə māt′, ā′sē lō′mit), *adj.* **1.** lacking a body cavity or coelom. —*n.* **2.** any organism that lacks a cavity between the body wall and the digestive tract, as the flatworms, nemerteans, and jellyfishes.

ac·o·lyte (ak′ə līt′), *n.* **1.** an altar attendant in public worship; altar boy. **2.** any attendant, assistant, or follower.

ac·o·nite (ak′ə nīt′), *n.* any plant belonging to the genus *Aconitum,* of the buttercup family, having irregular flowers usu. in loose clusters, including species with poisonous and medicinal properties. Compare MONKSHOOD, WOLFSBANE.

a·corn (ā′kôrn, ā′kərn), *n.* the typically ovoid fruit or nut of an oak. —**a′corned,** *adj.*

a′corn squash′, *n.* a variety of winter squash resembling an acorn in shape, having dark green to orange-yellow ridged skin and deep yellow flesh.

a′corn worm′, *n.* any wormlike marine animal of the phylum Hemichordata, having gill slits and an acorn-shaped proboscis and collar.

a·cous·tic (ə koo′stik) also **a·cous′ti·cal,** *adj.* **1.** pertaining to the sense of hearing, to sound, or to the science of sound. **2.** (of a building material) designed for controlling sound. **3.** sounded without electric or electronic enhancement: *acoustic guitar.* —**a·cous′ti·cal·ly,** *adv.*

acous′tic cou′pler, *n.* a device designed to connect a telephone handset to a modem and a computer.

acous′tic phonet′ics, *n.* the branch of phonetics dealing with the transmission of speech sounds to the ear and with the physical properties of sounds, as their frequency, duration, and intensity.

a·cous·tics (ə koo′stiks), *n.* **1.** (*used with a sing. v.*) the branch of physics that deals with sound and sound waves. **2.** (*used with a pl. v.*) the qualities or characteristics of a room, auditorium, stadium, etc., that determine the audibility or fidelity of sounds in it.

ac·quaint (ə kwānt′), *v.t.* **1.** to make more or less familiar, aware, or conversant (usu. fol. by *with*): *to acquaint the mayor with our plan.* **2.** to furnish with knowledge; inform (usu. fol. by *with*): *to acquaint the manager with one's findings.* **3.** to bring into social contact; introduce (usu. fol. by *with*). —**ac·quaint′ed,** *adj.*

ac·quaint·ance (ə kwān′tns), *n.* **1.** a person known to one, but usu. not a close friend. **2.** the state of being acquainted. **3.** personal knowledge as a result of study, experience, etc. **4.** (*used with a pl. v.*) the persons with whom one is acquainted. Also, **ac·quaint′ance·ship′** (for defs. 2, 3).

ac·qui·esce (ak′wē es′), *v.i.,* **-esced, -esc·ing.** to assent tacitly; submit or comply silently or without protest (usu. fol. by *in* or *to*). —**ac′qui·esc′ing·ly,** *adv.*

ac·qui·es·cence (ak′wē es′əns), *n.* **1.** the act or condition of acquiescing. **2.** *Law.* failure to take legal proceedings, thereby implying the abandonment of a right.

ac·quire (ə kwīr′), *v.t.,* **-quired, -quir·ing. 1.** to come into possession or ownership of; get as one's own. **2.** to gain for oneself through one's actions or efforts: *to acquire learning.* **3.** to gain through experience of or exposure to something: *to acquire good taste.* **4.** *Ling.* to achieve native or nativelike command of (a language or a linguistic rule or element). **5.** to locate and track (a moving target) with a detector, as radar. —**ac·quir′a·ble,** *adj.* —**ac·quir′a·bil′i·ty,** *n.* —**ac·quir′er,** *n.*

acquired′ char′acter, *n.* a noninheritable trait that results from certain environmental influences.

acquired′ immune′ defi′ciency syn′drome, *n.* See AIDS. Also called **acquired′ immunodefi′ciency syn′drome.**

ac·quire·ment (ə kwīⁿr′mənt), *n.* **1.** the act of acquiring, esp. the gaining of knowledge or mental attributes. **2.** Often, **acquirements.** something that is acquired, esp. an acquired ability or attainment.

ac·qui·si·tion (ak′wə zish′ən), *n.* **1.** the act of acquiring or gaining possession. **2.** something acquired; addition. **—ac′qui•si′tion•al,** *adj.* **—ac•quis•i•tor** (ə kwiz′i tər), *n.*

ac•quis•i•tive (ə kwiz′i tiv), *adj.* tending or seeking to acquire and own, often greedily. **—ac•quis′i•tive•ly,** *adv.* **—ac•quis′i•tive•ness,** *n.*

ac•quit (ə kwit′), *v.t.,* **-quit•ted, -quit•ting. 1.** to declare not guilty of a crime; release or clear from a charge. **2.** to bear or conduct (oneself); behave. **3.** to release or discharge (a person) from an obligation. **4.** to settle or satisfy (a debt, obligation, claim, etc.). **—ac•quit′ter,** *n.*

ac•quit•tal (ə kwit′l), *n.* **1.** judicial deliverance from a criminal charge on a verdict or finding of not guilty. **2.** the act of acquitting; discharge. **3.** the state of being acquitted; release.

ac•quit•tance (ə kwit′ns), *n.* **1.** the discharge of a debt or obligation. **2.** a document giving evidence of this.

a•cre (ā′kər), *n.* **1.** a common variable unit of land measure, now equal in the U.S. and Great Britain to 43,560 square feet or 1/640 square mile (4047 square meters). **2. acres, a.** lands; landed property: *wooded acres.* **b.** *Informal.* large quantities: *acres of Oriental rugs.*

a•cre•age (ā′kər ij), *n.* extent or area in acres; acres collectively.

ac•rid (ak′rid), *adj.* **1.** harshly or bitterly pungent in taste or smell; irritating to the eyes, nose, etc. **2.** sharply stinging or bitter; caustic: *acrid remarks.* **—a•crid•i•ty** (ə krid′i tē), **ac′rid•ness,** *n.* **—ac′rid•ly,** *adv.*

ac•ri•mo•ni•ous (ak′rə mō′nē əs), *adj.* caustic, stinging, or bitter in nature, speech, behavior, etc.: *an acrimonious dispute.* **—ac′ri•mo′ni•ous•ly,** *adv.* **—ac′ri•mo′ni•ous•ness,** *n.*

ac•ri•mo•ny (ak′rə mō′nē), *n.* sharpness, harshness, or bitterness of nature, speech, disposition, etc.

acro-, a combining form with the meanings "height," "tip," "end," "extremities of the body": *acrophobia.*

ac•ro•bat (ak′rə bat′), *n.* a performer of gymnastic feats requiring agility, balance, and coordination.

ac•ro•bat•ics (ak′rə bat′iks), *n.* **1.** (*used with a pl. v.*) the feats of an acrobat; gymnastics. **2.** (*used with a sing. v.*) the art or practice of acrobatic feats. **3.** (*used with a pl. v.*) something performed with remarkable agility and ease: *verbal acrobatics.*

ac•ro•car•pous (ak′rə kär′pəs), *adj.* bearing the floral parts at the top of the main stem, as certain mosses.

ac•ro•lect (ak′rə lekt′), *n.* a variety of a language, esp. a creolized one, that is closest to the standard form of the language on which it is based. Compare BASILECT. **—ac′ro•lec′tal,** *adj.*

ac•ro•meg•a•ly (ak′rə meg′ə lē), *n.* a disorder of the pituitary gland involving excessive production of growth hormone and resulting in enlargement of the head, hands, and feet.

a•cro•mi•on (ə krō′mē ən), *n., pl.* **-mi•a** (-mē ə). a bony outer process of the shoulder blade that forms part of the shoulder joint.

ac•ro•nym (ak′rə nim), *n.* **1.** a word formed from the initial letters or groups of letters of the words in a name or phrase, as *Wac* from *Women's Army Corps,* or *loran* from *long-range navigation.* **2.** an acrostic.

a•crop•e•tal (ə krop′i tl), *adj.* (of a plant) exhibiting a pattern of growth or movement from the base of the stem to its apex (opposed to *basipetal*). **—a•crop′e•tal•ly,** *adv.*

ac•ro•pho•bi•a (ak′rə fō′bē ə), *n.* a pathological fear of heights.

a•crop•o•lis (ə krop′ə lis), *n.* **1.** the citadel or high fortified area of an ancient Greek city. **2. the Acropolis,** the citadel of Athens and the site of the Parthenon. **—ac•ro•pol•i•tan** (ak′rə pol′i tn), *adj.*

ac•ro•some (ak′rə sōm′), *n.* an organelle covering the head of animal sperm and containing enzymes that digest the egg cell coating, thus permitting the sperm to enter the egg.

ac•ro•spire (ak′rə spīər′), *n.* the first sprout appearing in the germination of seed.

a•cross (ə krôs′, ə kros′), *prep.* **1.** from one side to the other of: *a bridge across a river.* **2.** on or to the other side of; beyond: *across the sea.* **3.** into contact with; into the presence of, usu. by accident: *to come across an old friend.* **4.** crosswise of or transversely to the length of something; athwart. **—*adv.* 5.** from one side to another. **6.** on the other side: *We'll soon be across.* **7.** crosswise; transversely. **8.** so as to be understood or learned: *to get one's idea across.* **9.** into a desired or successful state.

across′-the-board′, *adj.* **1.** applying to all employees, members, groups, or categories; general: *an across-the-board pay increase.* **2.** (of a bet in a horse race) covering win, place, and show.

a•cros•tic (ə krô′stik, ə kros′tik), *n.* a series of lines or verses in which the first, last, or other particular letters form a word, phrase, etc.

ac•ry•late (ak′rə lāt′, -lit), *n.* a salt or ester of an acrylic acid.

a•cryl•ic (ə kril′ik), *adj.* **1.** of or derived from acrylic acid. **—*n.* 2.** any of a group of synthetic textile fibers, as Orlon. **3.** ACRYLIC RESIN. **4.** a paint with an acrylic resin as vehicle. **5.** a painting done in acrylic.

acryl′ic ac′id, *n.* a colorless, corrosive liquid, $C_3H_4O_2$, used esp. in the synthesis of acrylic resins.

acryl′ic res′in, *n.* any of a group of thermoplastic resins used to make paints, plastics, etc.

act (akt), *n.* **1.** anything done, being done, or to be done; deed: *an act of mercy.* **2.** the process of doing: *caught in the act.* **3.** a formal decision, law, or the like, by a legislature, ruler, court, or other authority; decree or edict; statute: *an act of Congress.* **4.** an instrument or document stating something done or transacted. **5.** one of the main divisions of a play or opera. **6. a.** a short performance by one or more entertainers, usu. part of a variety show, circus, etc. **b.** the routine or style by which an entertainer or group of entertainers is known: *a magic act.* **c.** the personnel of such a group. **7.** a display of insincere behavior assumed for effect; pretense. **—*v.i.* 8.** to do something; carry out an action; exert energy or force. **9.** to reach or issue a decision on some matter. **10.** to operate or function in a particular way: *to act as manager.* **11.** to produce an effect: *The medicine failed to act.* **12.** to behave or conduct oneself in a particular fashion. **13.** to pretend; feign. **14.** to perform as an actor. **15.** to be capable of being performed: *His plays don't act well.* **—*v.t.* 16.** to represent (a fictitious or historical character) with one's person: *to act Macbeth.* **17.** to feign; counterfeit: *to act outraged virtue.* **18.** to behave as: *to act the fool.* **19.** to behave in a manner appropriate to: *to act one's age.* **20. act on** or **upon, a.** to act in accordance with; follow. **b.** to have an effect on; affect. **21. act out, a.** to illustrate by pantomime or other gestures. **b.** to express (repressed emotions) inappropriately and without conscious understanding. **22. act up, a.** to fail to function properly; malfunction. **b.** to behave willfully. **c.** (of a recurring ailment) to become painful or troublesome again. **—*Idiom.* 23. clean up one's act,** *Informal.* to begin adhering to more acceptable rules of behavior. **24. get** or **have one's act together,** *Informal.* to behave or function responsibly and efficiently.

ACT, American College Test.

ACTH, a hormone of the anterior pituitary that stimulates the production of steroids in the cortex of the adrenal glands. Also called **adrenocorticotropic hormone, adrenocorticotropin.** [*a(dreno)c(ortico)t(ropic) h(ormone)*]

act•ing (ak′ting), *adj.* **1.** serving temporarily, esp. as a substitute during another's absence: *the acting mayor.* **2.** designed, adapted, prepared, or suitable for stage performance. **—*n.* 3.** the art, profession, or activity of those who perform in stage plays, motion pictures, etc.

ac′tinide se′ries, *n.* the series of mostly synthetic radioactive elements whose atomic numbers range from 89 (actinium) through 103 (lawrencium).

ac•tin•ism (ak′tə niz′əm), *n.* the property of radiation by which chemical effects are produced. **—ac•tin′ic,** *adj.*

ac•tin•i•um (ak tin′ē əm), *n.* a radioactive, silver-white, metallic element that glows blue in the dark, resembling the rare earths in chemical behavior and valence. *Symbol:* Ac; *at. no.:* 89; *at. wt.:* 227.

actino-, a combining form with the meaning "ray, beam."

ac•tin•o•lite (ak tin′l īt′), *n.* a variety of amphibole, occurring in greenish bladed crystals or in masses. **—ac•tin′o•lit′ic** (-it′ik), *adj.*

ac•tin•o•my•cete (ak tin′ō mī′sēt, -mī sēt′, ak′tə nō-), *n.* any of several rod-shaped or filamentous, aerobic or anaerobic bacteria of the phylum Chlamydobacteriae, or in some classification schemes, the order Actinomycetales, certain species of which are pathogenic for humans and animals. **—ac•tin′o•my•ce′tous,** *adj.*

ac•tin•o•my•cin (ak tin′ō mī′sin, ak′tə nō-), *n.* any of a group of related antibiotics derived from streptomyces bacteria, used against susceptible bacteria and fungi and in the treatment of various cancers.

ac•tion (ak′shən), *n.* **1.** the process or state of acting or functioning; the state of being active: *We saw the team in action.* **2.** something done or performed; act; deed. **3.** a consciously willed act or activity. **4.** practical, often organized activity undertaken to deal with or accomplish something: *a crisis that requires immediate action.* **5. actions,** habitual or usual acts; conduct. **6.** energetic activity: *a man of action.* **7.** an exertion of power or force: *the destructive action of wind.* **8.** effect or influence: *the action of morphine.* **9.** a change in organs, tissues, or cells leading to performance of a function, as in muscular contraction. **10.** way or manner of moving: *the action of a horse.* **11.** the mechanism by which something is operated, as that of a gun or a piano. **12.** a military encounter, as a battle or skirmish. **13.** actual combat with enemy forces. **14.** the main subject or story line of a literary or dramatic work. **15. a.** an event or series of events that form part of a dramatic plot. **b.** (used as a command by a motion-picture director to begin the performance of a scene for filming). **16.** a legal proceeding instituted by one party against another. **17.** *Slang.* **a.** interesting or exciting activity, sometimes of an illicit nature. **b.** gambling activity. **—*Idiom.* 18. piece of the action,** *Informal.* a share of the proceeds or profits. **19. take action, a.** to start doing something. **b.** to start a legal procedure. **—*Proverb.* 20. Actions speak louder than words,** deeds are more important than what is said. **—ac′tion•less,** *adj.*

ACTION (ak′shən), *n.* an independent agency created in 1971 to administer domestic volunteer programs. [named by analogy with the acronymic names of other agencies, but itself not an acronym]

ac•tion•a•ble (ak′shə nə bəl), *adj.* **1.** furnishing grounds for a lawsuit: *actionable negligence.* **2.** capable of being acted on or readily used: *actionable research.*

ac•ti•vate (ak′tə vāt′), *v.t.,* **-vat•ed, -vat•ing. 1.** to make active; cause to function or act. **2.** *Physics.* **a.** to render more reactive; excite: *to activate a molecule.* **b.** to induce radioactivity. **3.** *Chem.* **a.** to make (carbon, a catalyst, etc.) more active. **b.** to hasten (reactions), as by heating. **4.** to aerate (sewage) in order to accelerate decomposition by microorganisms. **5.** to place (a military unit) on an active status. **—ac′ti•va′tion,** *n.*

ac′tivated car′bon, *n.* a form of carbon having very fine pores, used chiefly for adsorbing gases or solutes, as in various filter systems for purification, deodorization, and decolorization. Also called **ac′tivated char′coal.**

ac•tive (ak′tiv), *adj.* **1.** engaged in action or activity; characterized by energetic work, motion, etc.: *an active life.* **2.** being in existence, progress, or motion: *active hostilities.* **3.** marked by or disposed to direct involvement or practical action: *active support.* **4.** involving physical action: *active sports.* **5.** agile; nimble. **6.** characterized by current activity, participation, or use: *an active member; an active account.* **7.** characterized by vigorous activity: *an active market in wheat.* **8.** capable of exerting influence (opposed to *passive*): *active treason.* **9.** effective (opposed to *inert*): *active ingredients.* **10. a.** of, pertaining to, or being a voice, verb form, or construction having a subject represented as performing or causing the action expressed by the verb, as the verb form *write* in *I write letters every day* (opposed to *passive*). **b.** (of a verb) expressing an action rather than a state. **11.** requiring or giving rise to action; practical. **12.** (of a volcano) in eruption or liable to erupt; not dormant or extinct. **13.** (of a fault) experiencing recurrent seismic movement. **14. a.** acting as a source of electrical energy, as a generator. **b.** capable of amplifying or converting voltages or currents, as a transistor or diode. **15.** (of military personnel) on active duty. **—***n.* **16.** the active voice. **17.** a form or construction in the active voice. **—ac′tive•ly,** *adv.*

ac′tive euthana′sia, *n.* See under EUTHANASIA.

ac•tiv•ism (ak′tə viz′əm), *n.* the doctrine or practice of vigorous action or involvement as a means of achieving political or other goals, as by demonstrations, protests, etc. **—ac′tiv•ist,** *n., adj.*

ac•tiv•i•ty (ak tiv′i tē), *n., pl.* **-ties. 1.** the state or quality of being active. **2.** energetic activity; animation; liveliness. **3.** a specific deed, action, function, or sphere of action: *social activities.* **4.** an educational task that involves direct experience and participation of the student. **5.** a use of energy or force; an active movement or operation. **6.** normal mental or bodily power, function, or process. **7.** the capacity of a chemical substance to react, corrected for the loss of reactivity due to the interaction of its constituents. **8. a.** the number of atoms of a radioactive substance that disintegrate per unit of time, usu. expressed in curies. **b.** RADIOACTIVITY. **9.** an organizational unit or the function it performs.

act′ of faith′, *n.* an act that demonstrates or tests the strength of one's convictions.

act′ of God′, *n.* a sudden action of natural forces that could not have been prevented, as an earthquake or hurricane.

act′ of war′, *n.* an act of aggression by a country against another with which it is nominally at peace.

ac•tor (ak′tər), *n.* **1.** a person who acts in stage plays, motion pictures, etc., esp. professionally. **2.** a person who does something; participant.

ac•tress (ak′tris), *n.* a woman who acts in stage plays, motion pictures, etc., esp. professionally.

Acts′ of the Apos′tles, *n.* a book of the New Testament. Also called **Acts.**

ac•tu•al (ak′cho͞o əl), *adj.* **1.** existing in act, fact, or reality; real: *an actual case; the actual cost.* **2.** existing now; present; current: *the ship's actual position.* **—actually,** *adv.*

ac•tu•al•i•ty (ak′cho͞o al′i tē), *n., pl.* **-ties. 1.** actual existence; reality. **2.** an actual condition or circumstance; fact.

ac•tu•al•ize (ak′cho͞o ə līz′), *v.t.,* **-ized, -iz•ing.** to make actual or real; turn into action or fact. **—ac′tu•al•i•za′tion,** *n.*

ac•tu•ary (ak′cho͞o er′ē), *n., pl.* **-ar•ies.** a person who computes insurance premium rates, dividends, risks, etc., based on statistical data. **—ac•tu•ar•i•al** (ak′cho͞o âr′ē əl), *adj.* **—ac′tu•ar′i•al•ly,** *adv.*

ac•tu•ate (ak′cho͞o āt′), *v.t.,* **-at•ed, -at•ing. 1.** to incite or move to action; impel; motivate: *actuated by selfish motives.* **2.** to put into action: *to actuate a machine.* **—ac′tu•a′tion,** *n.*

ac•u•ate (ak′yo͞o it, -āt′), *adj.* sharpened; pointed.

a•cu•i•ty (ə kyo͞o′i tē), *n.* sharpness; acuteness; keenness: *visual acuity; acuity of mind.*

a•cu•le•ate (ə kyo͞o′lē it, -āt′) also **a•cu′le•at′ed,** *adj.* **1.** *Biol.* having or being any sharp-pointed structure. **2.** having a slender ovipositor or sting, as the hymenopterous insects. **3.** pointed; stinging.

a•cu•men (ə kyo͞o′mən, ak′yə-), *n.* keen insight; shrewdness: *business acumen.* **—a•cu′mi•nous,** *adj.*

a•cu•mi•nate (*adj.* ə kyo͞o′mə nit, -nāt′; *v.* -nāt′), *adj., v.,* **-nat•ed, -nat•ing. —***adj.* **1.** tapering to a point, as a leaf. **—***v.t.* **2.** to make sharp or keen. **—a•cu′mi•na′tion,** *n.*

ac•u•pres•sure (ak′yo͝o presh′ər), *n.* **1.** a type of massage therapy using finger pressure on the bodily sites used in acupuncture. **2.** a procedure for stopping blood flow from an injured blood vessel by inserting needles into adjacent tissue.

ac•u•punc•ture (ak′yo͝o pungk′chər), *n.* a Chinese medical practice that treats illness or provides local anesthesia by the insertion of needles at specified sites of the body. **—ac′u•punc′tur•ist,** *n.*

a•cute (ə kyo͞ot′), *adj.* **1.** sharp or severe in effect; intense: *acute pain.* **2.** extremely great or serious; critical: *an acute shortage of oil.* **3.** (of disease) brief and severe (disting. from *chronic*). **4.** penetrating in intellect, insight, or perception. **5.** extremely sensitive even to slight details or impressions: *acute eyesight.* **6.** sharp at the end; pointed. **7. a.** (of an angle) less than 90°. **b.** (of a triangle) containing only acute angles. **8.** consisting of, indicated by, or bearing an acute accent. **—***n.* **9.** an acute accent. **—a•cute′ly,** *adv.* **—a•cute′ness,** *n.*

acute′ ac′cent, *n.* a mark (´) placed over a vowel, esp. to indicate that the vowel is close or tense, as in French *é,* or long, as in Hungarian, or that the vowel or the syllable it is in bears the word stress, as in Spanish, or is pronounced with raised pitch, as in Classical Greek.

a•cy•clic (ā sī′klik, ā sik′lik), *adj.* **1.** not cyclic: *an acyclic flower.* **2.** of or pertaining to a chemical compound not containing a closed chain or ring of atoms.

ac•yl (as′il, -ēl), *n.* the univalent group RCO–, where R is any organic group attached to one bond of the carbonyl group.

ad (ad), *n.* **1.** an advertisement. **2.** advertising: *an ad agency.*

ad-, a prefix occurring in verbs or verbal derivatives borrowed from Latin, where it meant "toward" and indicated direction, tendency, or addition: *adjoin.*

-ad, 1. a suffix occurring in loanwords from Greek denoting a group or unit comprising a certain number, sometimes of years: *myriad; Olympiad; triad.* **2.** a suffix meaning "derived from," "related to," "associated with," occurring in loanwords from Greek (*dryad; oread*) and in New Latin coinages on a Greek model (*bromeliad; cycad*). **3.** a suffix used, on the model of *Iliad,* in the names of epics, speeches, etc., derived from proper names: *Dunciad; jeremiad.*

A.D. or **AD, 1.** in the year of the Lord; since Christ was born: *Charlemagne was born in* A.D. *742.* [< Latin *annō Domini*] **2.** assembly district. **—Usage.** The abbreviation A.D. was orig. placed before a date and is still usu. so preferred in edited writing: *The Roman conquest of Britain began in* A.D. *43* (or, sometimes, *began* A.D. *43*). The abbreviation B.C. is always placed after a date: *Caesar was assassinated in 44* B.C. But by analogy with the position of B.C., A.D. is frequently found after the date in all types of writing, including historical writing: *Claudius I lived from 10* B.C. *to 54* A.D. This abbreviation may also designate centuries, being placed after the century specified: *the second century* A.D.

ad•age (ad′ij), *n.* a traditional saying expressing a common experience or observation; proverb. **—a•da•gi•al** (ə dā′jē əl), *adj.*

a•da•gio (ə dä′jō, -zhē ō′), *adv., adj., n., pl.* **-gios. —***adv.* **1.** *Music.* in a leisurely manner; slowly. **—***adj.* **2.** *Music.* slow. **—***n.* **3.** an adagio movement or piece of music. **4.** a technically demanding ballet movement danced by a man and woman or by a mixed trio. [Italian, for *ad agio* at ease]

Ad•am (ad′əm), *n.* **1.** the first man: husband of Eve and progenitor of the human race. Gen. 2:7; 5:1–5. **2. James,** 1730–94, and his brother **Robert,** 1728–92, English architects and furniture designers. **—***adj.* **3.** of or designating the style of architecture, decoration, and furniture originated by Robert and James Adam, characterized by freely adapted ancient Roman motifs and delicate ornamentation. **—*Idiom.* 4. not know someone from Adam,** to be completely unacquainted or unfamiliar with someone. **5. the old Adam,** the natural tendency toward sin. **—A•dam•ic** (ə dam′ik), **A•dam′i•cal,** *adj.*

ad•a•mant (ad′ə mənt, -mant′), *adj.* **1.** utterly unyielding in attitude or opinion; inflexible. **2.** hard; adamantine. **—***n.* **3.** any unyieldingly hard substance. **4.** a legendary stone of impenetrable hardness, formerly sometimes identified with the diamond. **—ad•a•man•cy** (ad′ə mən sē), **ad′a•mance,** *n.* **—ad′a•mant•ly,** *adv.*

ad•a•man•tine (ad′ə man′tēn, -tin, -tīn), *adj.* **1.** utterly unyielding. **2.** too hard to cut, break, or pierce. **3.** like a diamond in luster.

Ad•ams (ad′əmz), *n.* **1. Abigail (Smith),** 1744–1818, U.S. social and political figure (wife of John Adams). **2. Ansel,** 1902–84, U.S. photographer. **3. Brooks,** 1848–1927, U.S. historian (son of Charles Francis Adams). **4. Charles Francis,** 1807–86, U.S. statesman (son of John Quincy Adams). **5. Henry (Brooks),** 1838–1918, U.S. historian and writer (son of Charles Francis Adams). **6. John,** 1735–1826, 2nd president of the U.S. 1797–1801: a leader in the American Revolution. **7. John Quincy,** 1767–1848, 6th president of the U.S. 1825–29 (son of John Adams). **8. Samuel,** 1722–1803, a leader in the American Revolution. **9. Sarah F(lower),** 1805–48, U.S. hymn writer. **10. Mount,** a mountain in SW Washington, in the Cascade Range. 12,307 ft. (3751 m). **11. Mount,** a mountain in N New Hampshire, in the White Mountains. 5798 ft. (1767 m).

Ad′am's ap′ple, *n.* a projection of the thyroid cartilage at the front of the neck.

a•dapt (ə dapt′), *v.t.,* **1.** to make suitable to requirements or conditions; adjust or modify fittingly. **—***v.i.* **2.** to adjust oneself to different conditions, environment, etc.

a•dapt•a•ble (ə dap′tə bəl), *adj.* **1.** capable of being adapted. **2.** able to adjust oneself readily to different conditions: *an adaptable person.* **—a•dapt′a•bil′i•ty, a•dapt′a•ble•ness,** *n.*

ad•ap•ta•tion (ad′əp tā′shən), *n.* **1.** the act of adapting or the state of being adapted. **2.** something produced by adapting: *an adaptation of a play for television.* **3. a.** any beneficial alteration in an organism resulting from natural selection by which the organism survives and multiplies in its environment. **b.** a form or structure modified to fit a changed environment. **c.** the ability of a species to survive in a particular ecological niche, esp. because of alterations of form or behavior brought about through natural selection. **4.** the decrease in response of sensory receptor organs, as those of vision or touch, to changed, constantly applied environmental conditions. **5.** the regulating by the pupil of the quantity of light entering the eye. **6.** a slow, usu. unconscious modification of individual or collective behavior in adjusting to cultural surroundings. **—ad′ap•ta′tion•al,** *adj.*

a•dapt•er or **a•dap•tor** (ə dap′tər), *n.* **1.** one that adapts. **2.** a connector for joining parts of different sizes, designs, etc., enabling them to be fitted or to work together. **3.** an accessory to convert a machine, tool, or part to a new or modified use.

a·dap·tive (ə dap′tiv), *adj.* serving or able to adapt; showing or contributing to adaptation. —**a·dap′tive·ly,** *adv.* —**a·dap′tive·ness,** *n.* —**ad′ap·tiv′i·ty** (ad′ap-), *n.*

adap′tive radia′tion, *n.* the diversification of a group of organisms into separate species or subspecies adapted to different environments, each new group often further diversifying into more specialized types.

A·dar (ə där′), *n.* the sixth month of the Jewish calendar.

Adar′ She′ni (shā′nē, shä nē′), *n.* an intercalary month of the Jewish calendar, added between Adar and Nisan; Veadar.

ad·ax·i·al (ad ak′sē əl), *adj. Bot., Mycol.* situated on the side toward the axis or stem.

ADC, 1. advanced developing countries. **2.** Aid to Dependent Children. **3.** Air Defense Command. **4.** Also, **A.D.C.** aide-de-camp.

add (ad), —*v.t.* **1.** to unite or join so as to increase the number, quantity, size, or importance. **2.** to find the sum of (often fol. by *up*). **3.** to say or write further. **4.** to cause to have as an additional quality: *to add interest to a story.* **5.** to include (usu. fol. by *in*). —*v.i.* **6.** to perform the arithmetic operation of addition. **7.** to be or serve as an addition (usu. fol. by *to*): *His illness added to the family's troubles.* **8. add up, a.** to amount to the correct total. **b.** to seem reasonable or consistent; make sense. **9. add up to,** to signify; amount to.

ADD, attention deficit disorder.

Ad·dams (ad′əmz), *n.* **Jane,** 1860–1935, U.S. social worker.

ad·dax (ad′aks), *n.* a large, pale-colored antelope, *Addax nasomaculatus,* of North Africa, with loosely spiraled horns.

ad·dend (ad′end, ə dend′), *n.* any of a group of numbers or terms added together to form a sum.

ad·den·dum (ə den′dəm), *n., pl.* **-da** (-də). **1.** a thing to be added; an addition. **2.** an appendix to a book.

ad·der (ad′ər), *n.* **1.** the common European viper, *Vipera berus.* **2.** any of various snakes resembling the viper.

ad′der's-mouth′, *n., pl.* **-mouths.** any of several North American terrestrial orchids of the genus *Malaxis,* having tiny white or greenish flowers.

ad′der's-tongue′, *n.* **1.** any of various ferns of the genus *Ophioglossum* and family Ophioglossaceae, having a tall fruiting spike resembling a snake's tongue. **2.** any of several American dogtooth violets.

ad·dict (*n.* ad′ikt; *v.* ə dikt′), *n.* **1.** one who is addicted to a substance, activity, or habit. —*v.t.* **2.** to cause to become physiologically or psychologically dependent on an addictive substance, as alcohol or a narcotic. **3.** to habituate or abandon (oneself) to something compulsively or obsessively.

ad·dic·tion (ə dik′shən), *n.* dependence on or commitment to a habit, practice, or habit-forming substance to the extent that its cessation causes trauma.

ad·dic·tive (ə dik′tiv), *adj.* **1.** producing or tending to cause addiction: *an addictive drug.* **2.** more than normally susceptible to addiction: *an addictive personality.* —**ad·dic′tive·ness,** *n.*

Ad·dis A·ba·ba (ad′is ab′ə bə), *n.* the capital of Ethiopia, in the central part. 1,412,575.

Ad′dison's disease′, *n.* diminished function of the adrenal glands, resulting in low blood pressure, weight loss, anxiety, darkened skin, and other disturbances.

ad·di·tion (ə dish′ən), *n.* **1.** the act or process of adding or uniting. **2.** the process of uniting two or more numbers into one sum, represented by the symbol +. **3.** the result of adding. **4.** something added. **5.** a wing, room, etc., added to a building. **6.** a chemical reaction in which two or more substances combine to form another compound. —*Idiom.* **7. in addition,** besides; also. **8. in addition to,** as well as; besides. —**ad·di′tion·al,** *adj.*

ad·di·tive (ad′i tiv), *n.* **1.** something that is added, as one substance to another, to alter or improve the quality or to counteract undesirable properties. **2. a.** a substance added directly to food during processing, as for preservation, coloring, or stabilization. **b.** something that becomes part of food or affects it as a result of packaging or processing, as debris or radiation. —*adj.* **3.** characterized or produced by addition; cumulative: *an additive process.* **4.** (of a mathematical function) having the property that the function of the union or sum of two quantities is equal to the sum of the functional values of each quantity; linear. —**ad′di·tive·ly,** *adv.*

ad·dle (ad′l), *v.,* **-dled, -dling,** *adj.* —*v.t., v.i.* **1.** to make or become confused. **2.** to make or become rotten, as eggs. —*adj.* **3.** mentally confused; muddled (usu. used in combination): *addleheaded.* **4.** rotten: *addle eggs.*

add′-on′, *n.* **1.** a device or unit added to equipment or a construction. **2.** anything added on, as a charge, tax, rider, or provision. —*adj.* **3.** provided as an add-on.

ad·dress (*n.* ə dres′, ad′res; *v.* ə dres′), *n.* **1.** the place or the name of the place where a person, organization, or the like is located or may be reached. **2.** a direction as to the intended recipient, written on or attached to a piece of mail. **3.** a usu. formal speech or written statement directed to a particular group. **4.** skillful and expeditious management; ready skill. **5.** manner of speaking to others; personal bearing in conversation. **6.** the use of a name or title in speaking or writing to a person: *forms of address.* **7.** a label, as an integer or symbol, that designates the

location of information stored in computer memory. **8.** Usu., **addresses.** attentions paid by a suitor; courtship. **9.** to direct a speech or statement to. **10.** to use a specified form or title in speaking or writing to: *Address him as "Sir."* **11.** to direct to the attention: *She addressed her remarks to all.* **12.** to apply (oneself) in speech (usu. fol. by *to*). **13.** to deal with or discuss. **14.** to put the directions for delivery on: *to address a letter.* **15.** to direct the energy or efforts of (usu. fol. by *to*): *to address oneself to a task.* **16.** *Golf.* to take a stance and place the head of the club behind (the ball) preparatory to hitting it.

ad·dress·ee (ad′re sē′, ə dre sē′), *n.* the person, company, or the like to whom a piece of mail is addressed.

ad·duce (ə dōōs′, ə dyōōs′), *v.t.,* **-duced, -duc·ing.** to bring forward, as in evidence. —**ad·duc′i·ble,** *adj.* —**ad·duc′er,** *n.*

ad·duct (*v.* ə dukt′; *n.* ad′ukt), *v.t.* **1.** to move or draw toward the axis of the body or one of its parts (opposed to *abduct*). —*n.* **2.** a combination of two or more stable chemical compounds by means of van der Waals' forces, coordinate bonds, or covalent bonds. —**ad·duc′tive,** *adj.*

ad·duc·tor (ə duk′tər), *n.* any muscle that adducts (opposed to *abductor*).

-ade, 1. a suffix found in nouns denoting an action or process or the person or persons acting, appearing in loanwords from Romance languages (*cannonade; fusillade; renegade*), and occasionally productive in English (*blockade*). **2.** a noun suffix indicating a drink made of a particular fruit, normally a citrus: *lemonade.*

A·den (äd′n, ād′n), *n.* **1.** the economic capital of the Republic of Yemen, a seaport on the Gulf of Aden. 318,000. **2.** a former British colony and protectorate on the Gulf of Aden in SW Arabia: became People's Democratic Republic of Yemen in 1967; since 1990 part of the Republic of Yemen. **3. Gulf of,** an arm of the Arabian Sea between the E tip of Africa and the S coast of Arabia.

A·de·nau·er (ad′n ouᵊr, -ou′ər, äd′-), *n.* **Konrad,** 1876–1967, chancellor of the West German Federal Republic 1949–63.

ad·e·nine (ad′n in, -ēn′), *n.* a purine base, $C_5H_5N_5$, one of the fundamental components of nucleic acids, forming a base pair with thymine in DNA and pairing with uracil in RNA. *Symbol:* A

ad·e·noid (ad′n oid′), *n.* **1.** Usu., **adenoids.** growths of lymphoid tissue in the upper throat: when enlarged, they can block the back of the throat and cause the voice to have a nasal quality. —*adj.* **2.** LYMPHOID. **3.** of or pertaining to the adenoids. —**ad′e·noi′dal,** *adj.*

ad·e·no·ma (ad′n ō′mə), *n., pl.* **-mas, -ma·ta** (-mə tə). **1.** a benign tumor originating in a secretory gland. **2.** a benign tumor of glandlike structure. —**ad′e·nom′a·tous** (-om′ə təs, -ō′mə-), *adj.*

a·den·o·sine (ə den′ə sēn′, -sin), *n.* a white, crystalline, water-soluble nucleoside, $C_{10}H_{13}N_5O_4$, of adenine and ribose.

a·dept (*adj.* ə dept′; *n.* ad′ept, ə dept′), *adj.* **1.** very skilled; proficient; expert: *an adept juggler.* —*n.* **ad·ept 2.** a skilled or proficient person; expert. —**a·dept′ly,** *adv.* —**a·dept′ness,** *n.*

ad·e·quate (ad′i kwit), *adj.* **1.** as much or as good as necessary for some requirement or purpose; fully sufficient, suitable, or fit. **2.** barely sufficient or suitable. **3.** *Law.* reasonably sufficient for starting legal action. —**ad′e·quate·ly,** *adv.* —**ad′e·qua·cy, ad′e·quate·ness,** *n.*

à deux (ä dœ′; *Fr.* A dœ′), *adj., adv.* with just two persons present: *dinner à deux.*

ad·here (ad hēr′), *v.,* **-hered, -her·ing.** —*v.i.* **1.** to stay attached; stick fast; cling: *Mud adhered to my boots.* **2.** (of two or more dissimilar substances) to be united by adhesion. **3.** to hold closely or firmly: *to adhere to a plan.* **4.** to be devoted in support or allegiance: *to adhere to a party.* —*v.t.* **5.** to cause to adhere; make stick. —**ad·her′a·ble,** *adj.* —**ad·her′er,** *n.*

ad·her·ence (ad hēr′əns, -her′-), *n.* **1.** steady devotion, allegiance, or attachment. **2.** the act or state of adhering.

ad·her·ent (ad hēr′ənt, -her′-), *n.* **1.** a person who follows or supports a leader, cause, idea, etc.; follower. —*adj.* **2.** sticking; clinging; adhering. **3.** bound by contract or other formal agreement. —**ad·her′ent·ly,** *adv.*

ad·he·sion (ad hē′zhən), *n.* **1.** the act, state, or quality of adhering. **2.** steady or devoted attachment, support, etc.; adherence. **3.** assent; concurrence. **4.** the attractive molecular force that tends to hold together unlike bodies where they are in contact. **5. a.** the abnormal union of adjacent tissues. **b.** the tissue involved. —**ad·he′sion·al,** *adj.*

ad·he·sive (ad hē′siv, -ziv), *adj.* **1.** coated with glue, mastic, or other sticky substance: *adhesive bandages.* **2.** tending to adhere; sticking fast; clinging. —*n.* **3.** a substance that causes something to adhere, as glue. **4.** ADHESIVE TAPE. **5.** a postage or revenue stamp with a gummed back.

adhe′sive tape′, *n.* tape coated with an adhesive substance, as for holding a bandage in place.

ad hoc (ad hok′, hōk′), *adj.* **1.** for the special purpose or end presently under consideration. —*adj.* **2.** concerned or dealing with a specific subject, purpose, or end: *an ad hoc committee.*

ad ho·mi·nem (ad hom′ə nəm, -nem′), *adj.* **1.** appealing to one's prejudice, emotions, or special interests rather than to one's intellect or reason. **2.** attacking an opponent's character rather than answering an argument. —*adv.* **3.** in an ad hominem manner.

ad·i·a·bat·ic (ad′ē ə bat′ik, ā′dī ə-), *adj.* occurring without gain or loss of heat: *an adiabatic process.* —**ad′i·a·bat′i·cal·ly,** *adv.*

ad·i·aph·or·ism (ad′ē af′ə riz′əm), *n.* tolerance of actions or beliefs not specifically prohibited in the Scriptures; indifferentism. —**ad′i•aph′o•rist,** *n.* —**ad′i•aph′o•ris′tic,** *adj.*

a•dieu (ə do͞o′, ə dyo͞o′), *interj., n., pl.* **a•dieus, a•dieux.** good-bye; farewell. [< Middle French, = *a* (< Latin *ad* to) + *dieu* (< Latin *deus* god)]

ad in•fi•ni•tum (ad in′fə nī′təm, ad′ in-), *adv.* to infinity; endlessly; without limit.

ad in•te•rim (ad in′tə rim), *adv., adj.* in the meantime.

ad•i•os (ad′ē ōs′, ä′dē-), *interj.* good-bye; farewell. [< Spanish]

ad•i•pose (ad′ə pōs′), *adj.* **1.** consisting of, resembling, or pertaining to fat; fatty. —*n.* **2.** animal fat stored in the fatty tissue of the body. —**ad′i•pose′ness, ad′i•pos′i•ty** (-pos′i tē), *n.*

ad•it (ad′it), *n.* **1.** an entrance or a passage. **2.** a nearly horizontal passage leading into a mine. **3.** an approach or access.

ad•ja•cent (ə jā′sənt), *adj.* **1.** lying near, close, or contiguous; adjoining. **2.** just before, after, or facing: *an adjacent page.* —**ad•ja′cen•cy,** *n.* —**ad•ja′cent•ly,** *adv.*

ad•jec•tive (aj′ik tiv), *n.* **1.** a member of a class of words functioning as modifiers of nouns, typically by describing, delimiting, or specifying quantity, as *nice* in *a nice day, other* in *other people,* or *all* in *all dogs,* and in many languages having formal characteristics, as often in English the ability to be used in comparative and superlative forms. *Abbr.:* adj. —*adj.* **2.** of, pertaining to, or functioning as an adjective; adjectival: *an adjective phrase.* **3.** not able to stand alone; dependent. **4.** *Law.* pertaining to rules of procedure, rather than those of right (opposed to *substantive*). **5.** (of dye colors) requiring a mordant or the like to render them permanent (opposed to *substantive*). —**ad′jec•tive•ly,** *adv.*

ad•join (ə join′), *v.t.* **1.** to be close to or in contact with; abut. **2.** to attach or append; affix. —*v.i.* **3.** to be in connection or contact. —**ad•join′ing,** *adj.*

ad•journ (ə jûrn′), *v.t.* **1.** to suspend the meeting of (a legislature, court, committee, etc.) to a future time, another place, or indefinitely. **2.** to defer or postpone (a meeting) to a later time. **3.** to defer or postpone (a matter) to a future time. —*v.i.* **4.** to postpone, suspend, or transfer proceedings. **5.** to go to another place: *to adjourn to the living room.*

ad•judge (ə juj′), *v.t.,* **-judged, -judg•ing. 1.** to declare or pronounce formally; decree: *The will was adjudged void.* **2.** to award or assign judicially. **3.** to decide by a judicial opinion: *to adjudge a case.* **4.** to sentence or condemn. **5.** to deem; consider; think.

ad•ju•di•cate (ə jo͞o′di kāt′), *v.,* **-cat•ed, -cat•ing.** —*v.t.* **1.** to settle or determine (an issue or dispute) judicially. —*v.i.* **2.** to sit in judgment; act as judge (usu. fol. by *upon*). —**ad•ju′di•ca′tive** (-kā′tiv, -kə tiv), **ad•ju′di•ca•to′ry** (-kə tôr′ē, -tōr′ē), *adj.* —**ad•ju′di•ca′tor,** *n.*

ad•ju•di•ca•tion (ə jo͞o′di kā′shən), *n.* **1.** an act of adjudicating. **2. a.** the act of a court in making a judgment or decree. **b.** a judicial decision or sentence. **c.** a court decree in bankruptcy.

ad•junct (aj′ungkt), *n.* **1.** something added to another thing but not essential to it. **2.** a person associated with lesser rank, authority, etc., in some duty or service; assistant. **3.** a person working at an institution, as a college, without full or permanent status. **4. a.** a modifying word or phrase depending on some other word or phrase. **b.** an element of clause structure with adverbial function. —*adj.* **5.** joined or associated, esp. in an auxiliary or subordinate relationship. **6.** attached or belonging without full or permanent status: *adjunct professor.* —**ad•junc′tion,** *n.* —**ad•junc′tive,** *adj.* —**ad•junct′ly,** *adv.*

ad•jure (ə jo͝or′), *v.t.,* **-jured, -jur•ing. 1.** to charge, bind, or command earnestly and solemnly, often under oath or the threat of a penalty. **2.** to entreat or request solemnly. —**ad•ju•ra•tion** (aj′o͝o rā′shən), *n.* —**ad•jur′a•to′ry** (-tôr′ē, -tōr′ē), *adj.* —**ad•jur′er, ad•ju′ror,** *n.*

ad•just (ə just′), —*v.t.* **1.** to change (something) so that it fits, corresponds, or conforms; adapt; accommodate: *to adjust expenses to income.* **2.** to put in working order or in a proper state or position: *to adjust an instrument.* **3.** to settle or bring to a satisfactory state, so that parties are agreed in the result: *to adjust our differences.* **4.** to determine the amount to be paid in settlement of (an insurance claim). **5.** to systematize. —*v.i.* **6.** to adapt oneself; become adapted: *to adjust to new demands.* —**ad•just′a•ble,** *adj.* —**ad•just′a•bly,** *adv.* —**ad•just′er, ad•jus′tor,** *n.*

ad•just•ment (ə just′mənt), *n.* **1.** the act of adjusting; adaptation to a particular condition, position, or purpose. **2.** the state of being adjusted; orderly relation of parts or elements. **3.** a device, as a knob or lever on a machine, for adjusting. **4.** therapeutic manipulation of the vertebrae or joints to bring them into alignment. **5.** a modification of behavior and attitudes so as to achieve a balance between personal needs and interpersonal or societal demands. **6.** the settling of an insurance claim after determining the amount of indemnity an insured is entitled to receive. **7.** a change or concession, as in price or terms, in view of a minor defect or as a settlement. —**ad•just•ment′al** (-men′tl), *adj.*

ad•ju•tant (aj′ə tənt), *n.* **1.** a military staff officer who assists the commanding officer in issuing orders, handling correspondence, etc. **2.** an assistant.

ad′jutant gen′eral, *n., pl.* **adjutants general. 1. a. the Adjutant General,** the chief administrative officer of the U.S. Army. **b.** an adjutant of a unit having a general staff, usu. an officer of the Adjutant General's Corps. **2.** a high, often the highest, officer of the National Guard of a state or territory.

ad•ju•vant (aj′ə vənt), *adj.* **1.** serving to help or assist; auxiliary. **2.** utilizing drugs, radiation therapy, or other means of supplementary treatment following cancer surgery. —*n.* **3.** a person or thing that aids or assists. **4.** anything that aids in removing or preventing a disease, esp. a substance added to a prescription to aid the effect of the main ingredient. **5.** a substance admixed with an immunogen in order to elicit a more marked immune response.

Ad•ler (ad′lər; äd′lər), *n.* **1. Alfred,** 1870–1937, Austrian psychiatrist and psychologist. **2. Cyrus,** 1863–1940, U.S. religious leader and Jewish scholar. **3. Mortimer (Jerome),** 1902–91, U.S. philosopher, educator, and author.

ad lib (ad lib′, ad′), *n.* **1.** something improvised in speech, music, etc. —*adv.* **2.** at one's pleasure; without restriction. **3.** freely; as needed: *Water can be given to the patient ad lib.*

ad-lib (ad lib′, ad′-), *v.,* **-libbed, -lib•bing,** *adj.* —*v.t.* **1.** to improvise all or part of (a speech, a piece of music, etc.). —*v.i.* **2.** to act, speak, etc., without preparation. —*adj.* **3.** impromptu; extemporaneous: *ad-lib remarks.* —**ad-lib′ber,** *n.*

ad lib•i•tum (ad lib′i təm), *adj., adv.* (used as a musical direction) at one's pleasure; not obligatory or indispensable.

Adm. or **ADM, 1.** admiral. **2.** admiralty.

Ad•mah (ad′mə), *n.* one of the cities that was destroyed along with Sodom and Gomorrah. Deut. 29:23.

ad ma•jo•rem De•i glo•ri•am (äd mä yô′rem de′ē glô′rē äm′), *Latin.* for the greater glory of God: motto of the Jesuits.

ad•min•is•ter (ad min′ə stər), *v.t.* **1.** to direct or manage (affairs, a government, etc.); have executive charge of. **2.** to bring into use or operation: *to administer justice.* **3.** to dispense, esp. formally: *to administer the sacraments.* **4.** to give or apply: *to administer medicine.* **5.** to supervise the formal taking of (an oath or the like). **6.** *Law.* to manage or dispose of (an estate or a trust) as executor, administrator, or trustee. —*v.i.* **7.** to contribute assistance; bring aid or supplies; minister: *to administer to the poor.* **8.** to perform the duties of an administrator. —**ad•min′is•tra•ble,** *adj.* —**ad•min′is•trant,** *n.*

ad•min•is•trate (ad min′ə strāt′), *v.t.,* **-trat•ed, -trat•ing.** to administer.

ad•min•is•tra•tion (ad min′ə strā′shən), *n.* **1.** the management and direction of a government, business, institution, or the like. **2.** the function of a political state in exercising its governmental duties. **3.** the duty or duties of an administrator. **4.** a body of administrators or executive officials. **5.** (*often cap.*) the officials of the executive branch of a government. **6.** the period during which an administrator or body of administrators serves: *the Jefferson administration.* **7.** *Law.* the management of a decedent's estate by an executor or administrator, or of a trust estate by a trustee. **8.** the act or process of administering. —**ad•min′is•tra′tion•al,** *adj.*

ad•min•is•tra•tive (ad min′ə strā′tiv, -strə-), *adj.* of or pertaining to administration; executive. —**ad•min′is•tra′tive•ly,** *adv.*

ad•min•is•tra•tor (ad min′ə strā′tər), *n.* **1.** a person who administers, esp. one employed to manage the affairs of a government, business, institution, etc. **2.** *Law.* a person appointed by a court to take charge of the estate of a decedent, but not appointed in the decedent's will.

ad•mi•ra•ble (ad′mər ə bəl), *adj.* worthy of admiration; inspiring approval or respect; excellent. —**ad′mi•ra•bil′i•ty, ad′mi•ra•ble•ness,** *n.* —**ad′mi•ra•bly,** *adv.*

ad•mi•ral (ad′mər əl), *n.* **1.** the commander in chief of a fleet. **2.** (in the U.S. Navy) **a.** a high-ranking officer, next above vice-admiral. **b.** an officer of any of the four highest ranks: rear admiral, vice-admiral, admiral, and fleet admiral. **3.** any of several brightly colored butterflies of the genera *Vanessa* and *Basilarchia,* as the red admiral, *V. atalanta rubria.* —**ad′mi•ral•ship′,** *n.*

ad•mi•ral•ty (ad′mər əl tē), *n., pl.* **-ties. 1.** the office or jurisdiction of an admiral. **2.** the officials or the department of state having charge of naval affairs, as in Great Britain. **3.** a court dealing with maritime questions, offenses, etc. **4.** maritime law.

ad•mi•ra•tion (ad′mə rā′shən), *n.* **1.** a feeling of pleasure, approval, and often respect or wonder. **2.** an object of such feelings: *She was the admiration of all her friends.* **3.** the act of regarding with approval and pleasure.

ad•mire (ad mīər′), *v.,* **-mired, -mir•ing.** —*v.t.* **1.** to regard with pleasure or approval, often mixed with wonder. **2.** to regard highly; respect; esteem. **3.** to regard with wonder or surprise. —*v.i.* **4.** to feel or express admiration. **5.** *Dial.* to take pleasure; like or desire: *I would admire to go.* —**ad•mir′er,** *n.* —**ad•mir′ing•ly,** *adv.*

ad•mis•si•ble (ad mis′ə bəl), *adj.* **1.** able to be allowed or conceded; allowable. **2.** capable or worthy of being admitted: *admissible evidence.* —**ad•mis′si•bil′i•ty, ad•mis′si•ble•ness,** *n.* —**ad•mis′si•bly,** *adv.*

ad•mis•sion (ad mish′ən), *n.* **1.** the act of allowing to enter; entrance granted, as by permission or monetary means. **2.** right or permission to enter: *to grant admission.* **3.** the price paid for entrance, as to a theater. **4.** the act or condition of being received or accepted in a profession, office, etc. **5.** confession of a charge, error, or crime; acknowledgment. **6.** an acknowledgment of the truth of something. **7.** a point or statement admitted; concession. —**ad•mis′sive** (-mis′iv), *adj.*

Admis′sion Day′, *n.* any of several legal holidays set aside in various U.S. states to mark their admission into the Union.

ad•mit (ad mit′), *v.,* **-mit•ted, -mit•ting.** —*v.t.* **1.** to allow to enter; grant or afford entrance to: *to admit a student to college.* **2.** to give the right or means of entrance to: *This ticket admits two people.* **3.** to permit to exercise a certain function or privilege: *to admit someone to the* *bar.* **4.** to permit; allow. **5.** to allow or concede as valid: *to admit the force of an argument.* **6.** to acknowledge; confess: *He admitted his guilt.* **7.** to have capacity for: *The passage admits two abreast.* **—***v.i.* **8.** to permit entrance; give access: *This door admits to the garden.* **9.** to grant opportunity or permission; allow: *to admit of no other interpretation.* **10.** to confess or make acknowledgment: *to admit to a crime.* **—ad•mit•tee** (ad mit ē′, ad mit′ē), *n.* **—ad•mit′ter,** *n.*

ad•mit•tance (ad mit′ns), *n.* **1.** permission or right to enter, esp. a place: *admittance to the exhibit room.* **2.** an act of admitting. **3.** actual entrance. **4.** the measure of the ability of an electrical circuit to conduct an alternating current, consisting of two components, conductance and susceptance; the reciprocal of impedance. *Symbol:* Y

ad•mit•ted•ly (ad mit′id lē), *adv.* by acknowledgment; by one's own admission; confessedly.

ad•mix (ad miks′), *v.t., v.i.,* **-mixed** or **-mixt, -mix•ing.** to add to or mingle with something else.

ad•mix•ture (ad miks′chər), *n.* **1.** the act of mixing or the state of being mixed. **2.** anything added; an alien element or ingredient. **3.** a compound containing such an element or ingredient; mixture.

ad•mon•ish (ad mon′ish), *v.t.* **1.** to caution, advise, or counsel against something. **2.** to reprove or scold, esp. in a mild and good-willed manner. **3.** to urge to a duty or remind of an obligation. **—ad•mon′ish•er,** *n.* **—ad•mon′ish•ing•ly,** *adv.* **—ad•mon′ish•ment,** *n.*

ad•mo•ni•tion (ad′mə nish′ən), *n.* **1.** an act of admonishing. **2.** counsel, advice, or caution. **3.** a gentle reproof.

ad•mon•i•to•ry (ad mon′i tôr′ē, -tōr′ē), *adj.* tending or serving to admonish; warning. **—ad•mon′i•to′ri•ly,** *adv.*

Ad•nah (ad′nə), *n.* **1.** a Manassite deserter from Saul's to David's army. I Chron. 12:20. **2.** a commander in King Jehosaphat's army. II Chron. 17:14.

ad nau•se•am (ad nô′zē əm, -am′), *adv.* to a sickening degree.

a•do (ə do͞o′), *n.* busy or delaying activity; bustle; fuss.

a•do•be (ə dō′bē), *n., pl.* **-bes** for 3. **1.** sun-dried brick made of clay and straw. **2.** a yellow silt or clay, deposited by rivers, used to make bricks. **3.** a building constructed of adobe bricks. **4.** a dark, heavy soil, containing clay. [< Spanish < Arabic *al-ṭub* the brick]

ad•o•les•cence (ad′l es′əns), *n.* **1.** the transitional period between puberty and adulthood in human development, terminating legally when the age of majority is reached; youth. **2.** the process or state of growing to maturity. **3.** a period or stage of development, as of a society, preceding maturity. **—ad′o•les′cent,** *adj., n.*

A•do•nai (ä′dō nī′, -noi′), *n. Hebrew.* a title of reverence for God, serving also as a substitute pronunciation of the Tetragrammaton.

A•do•ni-Be•zek (ə dō′nī bē′zek), *n.* a king in Judah who was captured by the Hebrews. Judg. 1:5–6.

Ad•o•ni•jah (ad′n ī′jə), *n.* a son of David, put to death at the order of Solomon. II Sam. 3:4; I Kings 2:19–25.

A•don•is (ə don′is, ə dō′nis), *n.* **1.** a youth of Greek myth, slain by a wild boar, but brought back to life by Zeus and permitted to divide his time every year between Persephone and Aphrodite. **2.** a very handsome young man. **—A•don′ic,** *adj.*

a•dopt (ə dopt′), *v.t.* **1.** to choose or take and use as one's own: *to adopt a nickname.* **2.** to take and rear (the child of others) as one's own child, specifically by a formal legal act. **3.** to take or receive into any kind of new relationship. **4.** to take on or act in accordance with (an attitude, policy, course, etc.). **5.** to vote to accept: *The House adopted the report.* **6.** to select as a basic or required textbook in a course. **—a•dop′tion,** *n.*

a•dop•tive (ə dop′tiv), *adj.* **1.** of or involving adoption. **2.** acquired or related by adoption: *an adoptive father.* **3.** tending to adopt. **—a•dop′tive•ly,** *adv.*

a•dor•a•ble (ə dôr′ə bəl, ə dōr′-), *adj.* **1.** very attractive or charming: *an adorable child.* **2.** worthy of being adored. **—a•dor′a•bly,** *adv.*

ad•o•ra•tion (ad′ə rā′shən), *n.* **1.** the act of paying honor, as to a divine being; worship. **2.** reverent homage. **3.** fervent and devoted love.

a•dore (ə dôr′, ə dōr′), *v.,* **a•dored, a•dor•ing.** **—***v.t.* **1.** to regard with the utmost esteem, love, and respect. **2.** to pay divine honor to; worship. **3.** to like or admire very much: *I adore your new shoes.* **—***v.i.* **4.** to worship. **—a•dor′er,** *n.* **—a•dor′ing•ly,** *adv.*

a•dorn (ə dôrn′), *v.t.* **1.** to decorate or add beauty to, as by ornaments: *garlands of flowers adorning their hair.* **2.** to make more pleasing, attractive, impressive, etc.; enhance. **—a•dorn′er,** *n.*

ADP, **1.** adenosine diphosphate: a nucleotide that functions in the transfer of energy during the catabolism of glucose, formed by the removal of a phosphate from adenosine triphosphate and composed of adenine, ribose, and two phosphate groups. Compare ATP. **2.** automatic data processing.

ad rem (ad rem′, äd), *adj.* **1.** relevant; pertinent: *an ad rem argument.* **—***adv.* **2.** in a straightforward manner: *to reply ad rem.*

ad•re•nal (ə drēn′l), *adj.* **1.** of or produced by the adrenal glands. **2.** situated near or on the kidneys. **—***n.* **3.** ADRENAL GLAND.

adre′nal gland′, *n.* one of a pair of glands, located above the kidneys, consisting of a cortex, which produces steroidal hormones, and a medulla, which produces epinephrine and norepinephrine.

a•dren•a•line (ə dren′l in, -ēn′), *n.* **1.** EPINEPHRINE. **2.** something that excites or stimulates; energizer; stimulant.

a•dre•no•cor•ti•co•trop•ic (ə drē′nō kôr′ti kō trop′ik, -trō′pik) also **a•dre•no•cor•ti•co•troph•ic** (-trof′ik, -trō′fik) *adj.* stimulating the adrenal cortex.

adre′nocor′ticotrop′ic hor′mone, *n.* See ACTH. Also called **a•dre•no•cor•ti•co•tro•pin** (ə drē′nō kôr′ti kō trō′pin).

A′driat′ic Sea′, *n.* an arm of the Mediterranean between Italy and the Balkan Peninsula.

a•drift (ə drift′), *adj., adv.* **1.** floating without control; drifting; not anchored or moored. **2.** without aim, direction, or stability.

a•droit (ə droit′), *adj.* **1.** expert in using the hands or body; nimble **2.** cleverly skillful, resourceful, or ingenious. **—a•droit′ly,** *adv.* **—a•droit′ness,** *n.*

ad•sci•ti•tious (ad′si tish′əs), *adj.* added or derived from an external source; additional. **—ad′sci•ti′tious•ly,** *adv.*

ad•script (ad′skript), *adj.* **1.** written after. **—***n.* **2.** an adscript character or comment.

ad•sorb (ad sôrb′, -zôrb′), *v.t.* to hold (a gas, liquid, or dissolved substance) on a surface in a condensed layer: *Charcoal will adsorb gases.* **—ad•sorb′a•ble,** *adj.* **—ad•sorb′a•bil′i•ty,** *n.* **—ad•sorb′ent,** *adj., n.*

ad•sorp•tion (ad sôrp′shən, -zôrp′-), *n.* the process by which an ultrathin layer of one substance forms on the surface of another substance. **—ad•sorp′tive,** *adj.* **—ad•sorp′tive•ly,** *adv.*

ad•u•late (aj′ə lāt′), *v.t.,* **-lat•ed, -lat•ing.** to show excessive admiration of or devotion to; flatter or admire servilely. **—ad′u•la′tion,** *n.* **—ad′u•la′tor,** *n.* **—ad′u•la•to′ry** (-tôr′ē, -tōr′ē), *adj.*

A•dul•lam (ə dul′am), *n.* a cave where David hid after fleeing from King Saul. I Sam. 22:1; I Chron. 11:15.

a•dult (ə dult′, ad′ult), *adj.* **1.** having attained full size and strength; grown up; mature. **2.** of, pertaining to, or befitting adults. **3. a.** intended only for adults; not suitable for children. **b.** pornographic. **—***n.* **4.** a person who is fully grown or developed or of age. **5.** a person who has attained the legal age of majority. **6.** a full-grown animal or plant. **—a•dult′hood,** *n.* **—a•dult′like′,** *adj.*

a•dul•ter•ate (*v.* ə dul′tə rāt′; *adj.* -tər it, -tə rāt′), *v.,* **-at•ed, -at•ing,** *adj.* **—***v.t.* **1.** to debase or make impure by adding inferior, alien, or less desirable materials or elements. **—***adj.* **2.** adulterated. **3.** ADULTEROUS. **—a•dul′ter•a′tion,** *n.* **—a•dul′ter•a′tor,** *n.*

a•dul•ter•ous (ə dul′tər əs), *adj.* characterized by, involved in, or given to adultery; illicit. **—a•dul′ter•ous•ly,** *adv.*

a•dul•ter•y (ə dul′tə rē), *n., pl.* **-ter•ies.** voluntary sexual intercourse between a married person and someone other than his or her lawful spouse. **—a•dul′ter•er,** *n.*

adult′-on′set diabe′tes, *n.* See under DIABETES MELLITUS.

ad•um•bral (a dum′brəl), *adj.* shadowy; shady.

ad•um•brate (a dum′brāt, ad′əm brāt′), *v.t.,* **-brat•ed, -brat•ing.** **1.** to give a faint image or indication of; outline or sketch. **2.** to foreshadow; prefigure, esp. in an indistinct or formless way. **3.** to darken or conceal partially; overshadow. **—ad′um•bra′tion,** *n.*

ad va•lo•rem (ad və lôr′əm, -lōr′-), *adj., adv.* in proportion to the value: used esp. of a tax or duty fixed at a percentage of the value of the property or goods being taxed.

ad•vance (ad vans′, -väns′), *v.,* **-vanced, -vanc•ing,** *n., adj.* **—***v.t.* **1.** to move or bring forward in position. **2.** to bring into consideration; suggest; propose: *to advance reasons for a tax cut.* **3.** to further the development, progress, or prospects of; forward: *to advance one's interests.* **4.** to raise in rank; promote. **5.** to raise in rate or amount; increase. **6.** to bring forward in time; accelerate: *to advance a deadline.* **7.** to furnish or supply (money or goods) on credit. **8.** to schedule at a later time or date. **—***v.i.* **9.** to move or go forward; proceed. **10.** to increase in quantity, value, price, etc. **11.** to improve or make progress. **12.** to grow or rise in importance, status, etc. **—***n.* **13.** a forward movement: *the advance of the troops.* **14.** a development showing progress; step forward; improvement. **15.** Usu., **advances. a.** attempts at forming an acquaintanceship, reaching an agreement, etc., made by one party; overtures. **b.** actions or words intended to be sexually inviting. **16.** a rise in price, value, etc. **17. a.** a furnishing of something before an equivalent is received: *an advance on one's salary.* **b.** the money or goods thus furnished. **18.** news copy, a press release, etc., prepared before the event it describes has occurred. **19.** publicity done before the appearance of a noted person, the opening of a theatrical performance, etc. **20.** an adjustment made in the setting of the distributor of an internal-combustion engine to generate the spark for ignition in each cylinder earlier in the cycle. **—***adj.* **21.** going or placed before: *an advance guard.* **22.** made, given, or issued ahead of time: *an advance payment; an advance copy of a speech.* **—*Idiom.*** **23. in advance,** beforehand: *Get your tickets in advance.* **—ad•vanc′ing•ly,** *adv.*

ad•vanced (ad vanst′, -vänst′), *adj.* **1.** placed ahead or forward: *with one foot advanced.* **2.** beyond the beginning, elementary, or intermediate: *a course in advanced mathematics.* **3.** far or further along in progress, development, or growth. **4.** of or embodying modern, enlightened, or liberal ideas: *advanced theories of child care.* **5.** far along in time: *a person of advanced age.*

advance′ man′, *n.* a person who makes advance arrangements for an event, esp. the appearance of a politician.

ad•vance•ment (ad vans′mənt, -väns′-), *n.* **1.** an act of advancing or moving forward. **2.** promotion in rank or standing. **3.** furtherance; improvement: *the advancement of knowledge* **4.** *Law.* money or property given by a person during his or her lifetime to another as part of an inheritance.

ad·van·tage (ad van′tij, -vän′-), *n., v.,* **-taged, -tag·ing.** —*n.* **1.** any circumstance, opportunity, or means specially favorable to success or a desired end: *the advantages of a good education.* **2.** benefit; gain; profit: *It will be to your advantage to study Chinese.* **3.** a position of superiority or ascendancy (often fol. by *over* or *of*): *It gave him an advantage over his opponent.* **4.** the first point in tennis scored after deuce. —*v.t.* **5.** to be of service to; yield profit or gain to; benefit. —*Idiom.* **6.** take advantage of, a.** to make use of for gain: *to take advantage of an opportunity.* **b.** to impose upon, esp. unfairly, as by exploiting a weakness. **7. to advantage,** in such a way as to have beneficial effects.

ad·van·taged (ad van′tijd, -vän′-), *adj.* having greater advantages or resources; privileged; affluent.

ad·van·ta·geous (ad′vən tā′jəs), *adj.* providing an advantage; favorable; profitable; beneficial. —**ad′van·ta′geous·ly,** *adv.* —**ad′van·ta′geous·ness,** *n.*

ad·vec·tion (ad vek′shən), *n.* **1.** a shift in temperature, humidity, etc., resulting from horizontal movement of an air mass (disting. from *convection*). **2.** the horizontal flow of air, water, etc. —**ad·vec′tive,** *adj.*

ad·vent (ad′vent), *n.* **1.** an arrival; a start or commencement. **2.** the advent of the holiday season. **2. a.** (*usu. cap.*) the coming of Christ into the world. **b.** (*cap.*) the penitential period beginning four Sundays before Christmas, commemorating this.

Ad·vent·ist (ad′ven tist, ad ven′-), *n.* a member of any of certain Christian denominations that maintain that the Second Coming of Christ is imminent. —**Ad′vent·ism,** *n.*

ad·ven·ti·tious (ad′vən tish′əs), *adj.* **1.** associated by chance and not as an integral part; extrinsic. **2.** appearing in an unusual or abnormal place, as a root on a stem. —**ad′ven·ti′tious·ly,** *adv.*

ad·ven·tive (ad ven′tiv), *adj.* **1.** not native and usu. not yet well established, as exotic plants or animals. —*n.* **2.** an adventive plant or animal. —**ad·ven′tive·ly,** *adv.*

Ad′vent Sun′day, *n.* the first Sunday in Advent.

ad·ven·ture (ad ven′chər), *n., v.,* **-tured, -tur·ing.** —*n.* **1.** an exciting or very unusual experience. **2.** participation in exciting undertakings or enterprises: *the spirit of adventure.* **3.** an uncertain and usu. risky undertaking. **4.** a commercial or financial venture. —*v.t.* **5.** to risk or hazard. **6.** to take the chance of; dare. —*v.i.* **7.** to take the risk involved. **8.** to speculate; venture.

ad·ven·tur·er (ad ven′chər ər), *n.* **1.** a person who seeks out adventures. **2.** a soldier of fortune. **3.** a person who undertakes great commercial risk; speculator. **4.** a person who seeks power, wealth, or social rank by unscrupulous means.

ad·ven·ture·some (ad ven′chər səm), *adj.* bold; daring; adventurous. —**ad·ven′ture·some·ly,** *adv.* —**ad·ven′ture·some·ness,** *n.*

ad·ven·tur·ism (ad ven′chə riz′əm), *n.* rash or irresponsible actions, esp. in political or international affairs. —**ad·ven′tur·ist,** *n.*

ad·ven·tur·ous (ad ven′chər əs), *adj.* **1.** willing or eager to engage in adventures. **2.** requiring courage; hazardous: *an adventurous undertaking.* —**ad·ven′tur·ous·ly,** *adv.* —**ad·ven′tur·ous·ness,** *n.*

ad·verb (ad′vûrb), *n.* a member of a class of words functioning as modifiers of verbs, adjectives, other adverbs, or clauses, as *quickly, well, here, now,* and *very,* typically expressing some relation of place, time, manner, degree, means, cause, result, exception, etc., and in many languages distinguished by form, as often in English by the ending *-ly. Abbr.:* adv.

ad·ver·sar·y (ad′vər ser′ē), *n., pl.* **-sar·ies,** *adj.* —*n.* **1.** a person, group, etc., that opposes or attacks; opponent; enemy. **2.** an opponent in a contest; contestant. —*adj.* Also, **ad·ver·sar·i·al** (ad′vər sâr′ē əl). **3.** of or pertaining to an adversary. **4.** involving adversaries, as plaintiff and defendant in a legal proceeding. —**ad′ver·sar′i·ness,** *n.*

ad·ver·sa·tive (ad vûr′sə tiv), *adj.* **1.** expressing contrariety, opposition, or antithesis: *"But" is an adversative conjunction.* —*n.* **2.** an adversative word or proposition. —**ad·ver′sa·tive·ly,** *adv.*

ad·verse (ad vûrs′, ad′vûrs), *adj.* **1.** unfavorable or antagonistic: *adverse criticism.* **2.** opposing one's interests or wishes: *adverse circumstances.* **3.** being in an opposite or a contrary direction: *adverse winds.* —**ad·verse′ly,** *adv.* —**ad·verse′ness,** *n.*

ad·ver·si·ty (ad vûr′si tē), *n., pl.* **-ties** for 2. **1.** adverse fortune or fate; misfortune; calamity: *in times of adversity.* **2.** an adverse event or circumstance: *to cope with life's many adversities.*

ad·vert·ent (ad vûr′tnt), *adj.* attentive; heedful.

ad·ver·tise (ad′vər tīz′, ad′vər tīz′), *v.,* **-tised, -tis·ing.** —*v.t.* **1.** to announce or praise (a product, service, etc.) in some public medium in order to induce people to buy or use: *to advertise a new brand of toothpaste.* **2.** to give information to the public about, esp. in a newspaper or on radio or television. **3.** to call attention to, esp. in a boastful manner: *Stop advertising yourself!* —*v.i.* **4.** to request something, esp. by placing a notice in a newspaper: *to advertise for a house to rent.* **5.** to offer goods or services through advertisements. —**ad′ver·tis′er,** *n.*

ad·ver·tise·ment (ad′vər tīz′mənt, ad vûr′tis mənt, -tiz-), *n.* **1.** a paid announcement, as of goods for sale, in newspapers or magazines, on radio or television, etc. **2.** a public notice, esp. in print. **3.** the action of making generally known; a calling to the attention of the public: *The news of this event will receive wide advertisement.*

ad·ver·tis·ing (ad′vər tī′zing), *n.* **1.** the act or practice of offering goods or services to the public through announcements in the media. **2.** paid announcements; advertisements. **3.** the profession of planning, designing, and writing advertisements.

ad·vice (ad vīs′), *n.* **1.** an opinion or recommendation offered as a guide to action, conduct, etc.: *I acted on your advice.* **2.** a communication, esp. from a distance, containing information: *Advice from abroad states that the government has fallen.* **3.** an official notification.

advice′ and consent′, *n.* a phrase in the U.S. Constitution (Article II, Section 2) granting the U.S. Senate the power to approve or reject appointments and treaties made by a president. Also, rarely, **advise′ and consent′.**

ad·vis·a·ble (ad vī′zə bəl), *adj.* **1.** recommended or wise, as a course of action. **2.** open to or desirous of advice. —**ad·vis′a·bil′i·ty, ad·vis′a·ble·ness,** *n.* —**ad·vis′a·bly,** *adv.*

ad·vise (ad vīz′), *v.,* **-vised, -vis·ing.** —*v.t.* **1.** to give counsel to. **2.** to recommend as desirable, prudent, etc.: *to advise secrecy.* **3.** to give (a person, group, etc.) information or notice (often fol. by *of*): *Investors were advised of the risk.* —*v.i.* **4.** to take counsel; consult (usu. fol. by *with*): *to advise with one's friends.* **5.** to offer counsel; give advice: *I shall act as you advise.* —**ad·vis′er, ad·vi′sor,** *n.*

ad·vised (ad vīzd′), *adj.* **1.** considered (usu. used in combination): *ill-advised; well-advised.* **2.** informed; apprised: *The president must be kept advised.* —**ad·vis′ed·ness,** *n.*

ad·vise·ment (ad vīz′mənt), *n.* careful deliberation or consideration: *The petition was taken under advisement.*

ad·vi·so·ry (ad vī′zə rē), *adj., n., pl.* **-ries.** —*adj.* **1.** giving or containing advice: *an advisory letter to shareholders.* **2.** having the power or duty to advise: *an advisory council.* —*n.* **3.** a report on existing or predicted conditions, often with advice for dealing with them: *an investor's advisory.* **4.** an announcement or bulletin that serves to advise and usu. warn the public, as of some potential hazard. **5.** an announcement from the U.S. National Weather Service to keep the public informed about the progress of a potentially dangerous weather condition: *hurricane advisory; tornado advisory.* Compare WARNING (def. 3), WATCH (def. 21).

ad·vo·ca·cy (ad′və kə sē), *n., pl.* **-cies.** the act of pleading for, supporting, or recommending; active espousal: *their tireless advocacy of states' rights.*

ad·vo·cate (*v.* ad′və kāt′; *n.* -kit, -kāt′), *v.,* **-cat·ed, -cat·ing,** *n.* —*v.t.* **1.** to support or urge by argument; recommend publicly: *to advocate higher salaries for teachers.* —*n.* **2.** a person who speaks or writes in support of a cause, person, etc. (usu. fol. by *of*): *an advocate of military intervention.* **3.** a person who pleads for or in behalf of another; intercessor. **4.** a person who pleads the cause of another in a court of law. **5.** (*cap.*) Jesus. I John 2:1. [< Latin *advocātus* legal counselor] —**ad′vo·ca′tion,** *n.* —**ad′vo·ca′tive,** *adj.* —**ad′vo·ca′tor,** *n.*

ad·vow·son (ad vou′zən), *n.* the right to name a candidate for a vacant position in the Church of England.

advt., advertisement.

A′dy·gei Auton′omous Re′gion (ä′də gā′, ä′də gā′), *n.* an autonomous region in the Russian Federation, part of the Krasnodar territory, in the NW Caucasus Mountains. 432,000; 2,934 sq. mi. (7,600 sq. km). *Cap.:* Maikop.

ad·y·tum (ad′i təm), *n., pl.* **-ta** (-tə). **1.** (in an ancient temple) a sacred inner place that the public was forbidden to enter; inner shrine. **2.** the most sacred or reserved part of any place of worship.

adz or **adze** (adz), *n., v.,* **adzed, adz·ing.** —*n.* **1.** an axlike tool for dressing timbers roughly, with a curved chisellike steel head mounted at a right angle to the handle. —*v.t.* **2.** to shape (wood) with an adz.

a·e·des or **a·ë·des** (ā ē′dēz), *n.* any mosquito of the genus *Aedes,* esp. *A. aegypti,* a vector of yellow fever and dengue.

Aege′an Sea′, *n.* an arm of the Mediterranean Sea between Greece and Turkey.

ae·gis or **e·gis** (ē′jis), *n.* **1.** sponsorship; auspices: *a concert under the aegis of the Women's Club.* **2.** the shield or breastplate of Zeus or his daughter Athena, bearing at its center the head of the Gorgon. **3.** protection; support: *under the imperial aegis.*

Ae•ne•as (i nē′əs), *n.* a Trojan hero, the legendary ancestor of the Romans and protagonist of the *Aeneid.*

Ae•ne•id (i nē′id), *n.* a Latin epic poem by Virgil, recounting the adventures of Aeneas after the fall of Troy.

Ae•non (ē′non), *n.* a spring in Palestine where John the Baptist was baptizing during the ministry of Jesus in Judea. John 3:23.

aeo′lian harp′, *n.* a box with an opening across which are stretched a number of strings of equal length that are tuned in unison and sounded by the wind.

Ae•ol•ic or **E•ol•ic** (ē ol′ik), *n.* the group of ancient Greek dialects spoken in Aeolis, Lesbos, Thessaly, and Boeotia.

ae•o•ni•an or **e•o•ni•an** (ē ō′nē ən), *adj.* eternal; everlasting.

aer•ate (âr′āt, ā′ə rāt′), *v.t.,* **-at•ed, -at•ing. 1.** to expose to the action of air or to cause air to circulate through: *Breathe deep to aerate the lungs.* **2.** to change or treat with air or a gas, esp. with carbon dioxide. **—aer•a′tion,** *n.* **—aer′a•tor,** *n.*

aer•i•al (*adj.* âr′ē əl, ā ēr′ē əl; *n.* âr′ē əl), *adj.* **1.** of, in, or produced by the air: *aerial currents.* **2.** done in or from the air: *aerial photography; an aerial survey.* **3.** inhabiting or frequenting the air: *aerial creatures.* **4.** operating on a track or cable above the ground: *an aerial ski lift.* **5.** reaching far into the air; lofty: *aerial spires.* **6.** unsubstantial; visionary: *aerial fancies.* **7.** having a light and graceful beauty; ethereal: *aerial music.* **8.** growing in the air, as the adventitious roots of some trees. **9. a.** pertaining to aircraft; used by or in an aircraft. **b.** launched by or against an aircraft: *aerial bombs.* **c.** supplied or performed by aircraft: *aerial support; aerial combat.* **—n. 10.** a radio or television antenna. **—aer′i•al•ly,** *adv.*

aer•i•al•ist (âr′ē ə list, ā ēr′ē ə-), *n.* **1.** a trapeze artist. **2.** *Slang.* a burglar who gains entrance to a building by leaping from rooftop to rooftop, sliding down ropes, or the like.

aer•ie or **aer•y** or **ey•rie** (âr′ē, ēr′ē), *n., pl.* **aer•ies** or **ey•ries. 1.** the lofty nest of a bird of prey, as an eagle or a hawk. **2.** a lofty nest of any large bird. **3.** a house, fortress, or the like, located high on a hill.

aero-, a combining form meaning "air": *aerodynamics.* Also, *esp. before a vowel,* **aer-.**

aer•o•bal•lis•tics (âr′ō bə lis′tiks), *n.* (*used with a sing. v.*) the science of ballistics combined with that of aerodynamics and dealing primarily with the motion through the atmosphere of rockets, guided missiles, and other projectiles. **—aer′o•bal•lis′tic,** *adj.*

aer•o•bat•ics (âr′ə bat′iks), *n.* (*used with a pl. v.*) stunts performed in flight by an aircraft. **—aer′o•bat′ic,** *adj.*

aer•obe (âr′ōb), *n.* an organism, esp. a bacterium, that requires air or free oxygen to sustain life (opposed to *anaerobe*).

aer•o•bic (â rō′bik), *adj.* **1.** (of an organism or tissue) requiring the presence of air or free oxygen to sustain life. **2.** pertaining to or caused by the presence of oxygen. **3.** of or pertaining to aerobics: *aerobic dancing.* **—aer′o/bi•cal•ly,** *adv.*

aer•o•bics (â rō′biks), *n.* (*used with a pl. v.*) any of various sustained exercises, as jogging, calisthenics, and vigorous dancing, designed esp. to stimulate and strengthen the heart.

aer•o•cul•ture (âr′ə kul′chər), *n.* a method of growing plants without soil by suspending them above sprays that constantly moisten the roots with water and nutrients.

aer•o•dy•nam•ics (âr′ō dī nam′iks), *n.* (*used with a sing. v.*) the study of the motion of air and other gases and of the effects of such motion on bodies in the gas. **—aer′o•dy•nam′ic, aer′o•dy•nam′i•cal,** *adj.* **—aer′o•dy•nam′i•cal•ly,** *adv.*

aer•o•em•bo•lism (âr′ō em′bə liz′əm), *n.* **1.** an obstruction of the circulatory system caused by one or more air bubbles, as may arise during surgery. **2.** DECOMPRESSION SICKNESS.

aer•og•ra•phy (â rog′rə fē), *n.* the study of the air or atmosphere. **—aer•og′ra•pher,** *n.* **—aer•o•graph•ic** (âr′ə graf′ik), **aer′o•graph′i•cal,** *adj.*

aer•o•lite (âr′ə līt′) also **aer•o•lith** (-lith), *n.* a meteorite consisting mainly of stony matter. **—aer′o•lit′ic** (-lit′ik), *adj.*

aer•ol•o•gy (â rol′ə jē), *n.* the branch of meteorology involving the observation of the atmosphere by means of balloons, airplanes, etc. **—aer•o•log•ic** (âr′ə loj′ik), **aer′o•log′i•cal,** *adj.* **—aer•ol′o•gist,** *n.*

aer•o•nau•ti•cal (âr′ə nô′ti kəl, -not′i-) also **aer′o•nau′tic,** *adj.* of or pertaining to aeronautics or aeronauts. **—aer′o•nau′ti•cal•ly,** *adv.*

aer•o•nau•tics (âr′ə nô′tiks, -not′iks), *n.* (*used with a sing. v.*) the science or art of flight.

ae•ron•o•my (â ron′ə mē), *n.* the study of chemical and physical phenomena in the upper atmosphere.

aer•o•pause (âr′ə pôz′), *n.* the indefinite boundary in the upper atmosphere beyond which the air is too thin for conventional aircraft to operate.

aer•o•pho•bi•a (âr′ə fō′bē ə), *n.* an abnormal fear of drafts of air, gases, or airborne matter. **—aer′o•pho′bic** (-fō′bik), *adj.*

aer•o•plane (âr′ə plān′), *n. Brit.* AIRPLANE.

aer•o•pon•ics (âr′ə pon′iks), *n.* (*used with a sing. v.*) AEROCULTURE.

aer•o•sol (âr′ə sôl′, -sol′), *n.* **1.** a system of colloidal particles dispersed in a gas, as smoke or fog. **2.** a liquid substance sealed usu. in a metal container under pressure with an inert gas or other activating agent and released as a spray or foam through a push-button valve or nozzle. **—adj. 3.** of or containing a substance under pressure for dispensing as a spray or foam.

---

aer•o•space (âr′ō spās′), *n.* **1.** the atmosphere and the space beyond. **2.** the industry concerned with the design and manufacture of the aircraft, missiles, spacecraft, etc., that operate in aerospace. **—adj. 3.** of or pertaining to aerospace or the aerospace industry.

aer•o•stat (âr′ə stat′), *n.* any lighter-than-air aircraft, as a balloon or dirigible.

aer•o•stat•ics (âr′ə stat′iks), *n.* (*used with a sing. v.*) **1.** the science that deals with gases in equilibrium. **2.** the science of lighter-than-air aircraft.

aer•o•ther•mo•dy•nam•ics (âr′ō thûr′mō dī nam′iks), *n.* (*used with a sing. v.*) the science that deals with significant heat exchanges in gases or significant thermal effects between gases and solid surfaces, as in supersonic flight. **—aer′o•ther′mo•dy•nam′ic,** *adj.*

aer•y or **aër•y** (âr′ē, ā′ə rē), *adj.,* **aer•i•er, aer•i•est.** ethereal; aerial. **—aer′i•ly,** *adv.*

Aes•chy•lus (es′kə ləs), *n.* 525–456 B.C., Greek poet and dramatist. **—Aes′chy•le′an,** *adj.*

Ae•sop (ē′səp, ē′sop), *n.* c620–c560 B.C., Greek writer of fables. **—Ae•so•pi•an** (ē sō′pē ən, ē sop′ē-), **Ae•sop′ic** (ē sop′ik), *adj.*

aes•thete or **es•thete** (es′thēt; *esp. Brit.* ēs′-), *n.* **1.** a person who has or professes to have refined sensitivity toward the beauties of art or nature. **2.** a person who affects great love of art, music, poetry, etc., and indifference to practical matters.

aes•thet•ic or **es•thet•ic** (es thet′ik; *esp. Brit.* ēs-), *adj.* **1.** pertaining to a sense of beauty or to aesthetics. **2.** having a love of beauty. **3.** concerned with emotion and sensation as opposed to intellectuality. **—n. 4.** a theory or idea of what is aesthetically valid.

aes•thet•i•cism or **es•thet•i•cism** (es thet′ə siz′əm; *esp. Brit.* ēs-), *n.* **1.** the acceptance of aesthetic standards as of supreme importance. **2.** an exaggerated devotion to the artistic or beautiful. **3.** a late Victorian movement in British and American art characterized by a dedicatedly eclectic search for beauty and by an interest in old English, Japanese, and classical art.

aes•thet•ics or **es•thet•ics** (es thet′iks; *esp. Brit.* ēs-), *n.* (*used with a sing. v.*) **1.** the branch of philosophy dealing with taste and the study of beauty in nature and art. **2.** a particular theory of beauty or fine art.

AF, Air Force.

A.F. or **a.f.,** audio frequency.

a•far (ə fär′), *adv.* **1.** from, at, or to a distance; far away (often fol. by *off*): *He saw the castle afar off.* **—Idiom. 2. from afar,** from a long way off: *The princess saw him riding toward her from afar.*

AFB, Air Force Base.

AFBF, American Farm Bureau Federation.

af•fa•ble (af′ə bəl), *adj.* **1.** easy to approach and to talk to; friendly: *courteous and affable neighbors.* **2.** showing warmth and friendliness; pleasant: *an affable smile.* **—af′fa•bil′i•ty,** *n.* **—af′fa•bly,** *adv.*

af•fair (ə fâr′), *n.* **1.** anything requiring action or effort; business; concern: *Discuss the affair with your lawyer.* **2. affairs,** matters of commercial or public interest or concern: *affairs of state; to put one's affairs in order.* **3.** thing; matter (usu. used with a descriptive or qualifying term): *Our new computer is a complex affair.* **4.** a private or personal concern: *That's none of your affair.* **5.** a usu. brief amorous relationship. **6.** an incident that occasions notoriety, dispute, and often public scandal: *the Congressional bribery affair.* **7.** a social gathering or other organized festive occasion.

af•fect¹ (*v.* ə fekt′; *n.* af′ekt), *v.t.* **1.** to produce an effect or change in: *Cold weather affected the crops.* **2.** to impress the mind or move the feelings of: *The music affected him deeply.* **3.** (of pain, disease, etc.) to attack or lay hold of. **—n. 4.** feeling or emotion. **5.** *Psychiatry.* an expressed or observed emotional response: *the blunted affect of schizophrenia.* **—af•fect′a•ble,** *adj.* **—af•fect′a•bil′i•ty,** *n.* **—Usage.** Because of similarity in pronunciation, AFFECT and EFFECT are sometimes confused in writing. The spelling *affect* is used of two different words. The verb AFFECT¹ means "to act on" or "to move" (*His words affected the crowd so deeply that many wept*); the noun AFFECT¹, pronounced with the stress on the first syllable, refers to emotion or, in psychiatry, emotional response. AFFECT² is not used as a noun; as a verb it means "to pretend" or "to assume" (*new students affecting a nonchalance they didn't feel*). The verb EFFECT means "to bring about, accomplish": *Her administration effected radical changes.* The noun EFFECT means "result, consequence": *the serious effects of the oil spill.*

af•fect² (ə fekt′), *v.t.* **1.** to pretend or feign: *to affect knowledge of ancient history.* **2.** to assume artificially, pretentiously, or for effect: *to affect a British accent.* **3.** to use, wear, or adopt by preference: *to affect an outrageous costume.* **4.** to assume the character or attitude of: *to affect the freethinker.* **5.** (of substances) to tend toward habitually or naturally: *to affect colloidal form.* **—af•fect′•er,** *n.* **—Usage.** See AFFECT¹.

af•fec•ta•tion (af′ek tā′shən), *n.* **1.** the pretense of having a knowledge, standing, etc., not possessed: *the affectation of great wealth.* **2.** conspicuous artificiality of manner or appearance; pretension. **3.** an artificial trait, expression, or the like.

af•fect•ed¹ (ə fek′tid), *adj.* **1.** acted upon; influenced. **2.** harmed or impaired, as by climate or disease. **3.** (of the mind or feelings) impressed; moved.

af•fect•ed² (ə fek′tid), *adj.* **1.** characterized by affectation or pretension. **2.** assumed artificially; feigned: *an affected Southern accent.* **3.** inclined or disposed: *to be well affected toward the speaker's cause.* **4.**

A

held in affection; fancied: *a novel much affected by our grandparents.* —**af•fect′ed•ly,** *adv.* —**af•fect′ed•ness,** *n.*

af•fect•ing (ə fek′ting), *adj.* moving or stirring the feelings or emotions. —**af•fect′ing•ly,** *adv.*

af•fec•tion (ə fek′shən), *n.* **1.** fond attachment, devotion, or love. **2.** Often, **affections. a.** emotion; sentiment: *to let the affections sway our reason.* **b.** the emotional realm of love: *to hold a place in one's affections.* **3.** a disease or diseased condition: *a gouty affection.* **4.** the act of affecting, or the state of being affected. **5.** bent or disposition of mind. —**af•fec′tion•less,** *adj.*

af•fec•tion•ate (ə fek′shə nit), *adj.* **1.** showing affection or love; fondly tender: *an affectionate embrace.* **2.** having great affection or love; loving: *your affectionate brother.* —**af•fec′tion•ate•ly,** *adv.*

af•fec•tive (af′ek tiv), *adj.* **1.** caused by or expressing emotion or feeling; emotional. **2.** causing emotion or feeling. —**af′fec•tive•ly,** *adv.* —**af•fec•tiv•i•ty** (af′ek tiv′i tē), *n.*

af•fective disor′der, *n.* any of several mental disorders in which a major disturbance of emotions is predominant, as depression or bipolar disorder.

af•fer•ent (af′ər ənt), *adj.* **1.** bringing to or leading toward an organ or part, as a nerve or arteriole (opposed to *efferent*). —*n.* **2.** a nerve that conveys an impulse toward the central nervous system. —**af′fer•ent•ly,** *adv.*

af•fi•ance (ə fī′əns), *v.t.,* **-anced, -anc•ing.** to pledge by promise of marriage; betroth. —**af•fi′anced,** *adj.*

af•fi•da•vit (af′i dā′vit), *n.* a written declaration upon oath made before an authorized official. [< Medieval Latin: (he) has declared on oath]

af•fil•i•ate (*v.* ə fil′ē āt′; *n.* -it, -āt′), *v.,* **-at•ed, -at•ing,** *n.* —*v.t.* **1.** to bring into close association or connection: *The research center has been affiliated with the university.* **2.** to attach or unite on terms of fellowship; associate (usu. fol. by *with*): *The newcomers soon affiliated themselves with the church.* **3.** to trace the derivation or origin of: *to affiliate a language.* —*v.i.* **4.** to associate oneself; be united. —*n.* **5.** a branch organization. **6.** a business concern owned or controlled in whole or in part by another concern. **7.** an affiliated person; associate. —**af•fil′i•a•ble,** *adj.* —**af•fil′i•at•ed,** *adj.* —**af•fil′i•a′tive** (-ā′tiv,′-ə tiv), *adj.*

af•fine (ə fīn′, ə fīn′, af′īn), *n.* a relative by marriage. —*adj. Math.* **2.** assigning finite values to finite quantities. **3.** of or pertaining to a transformation that maps parallel lines to parallel lines and finite points to finite points. —**af•fine′ly,** *adv.*

af•fined (ə fīnd′), *adj.* **1.** closely related or connected. **2.** bound; obligated.

af•fin•i•ty (ə fin′i tē), *n., pl.* **-ties,** *adj.* —*n.* **1.** a natural liking for or attraction to a person, thing, idea, etc. **2.** the object of such liking or attraction. **3.** relationship by marriage or by ties other than those of blood (disting. from *consanguinity*). **4.** close resemblance, agreement, or connection. **5.** a resemblance of structure or behavior that results from or implies a phylogenetic relationship. **6.** the force by which atoms are held together in chemical compounds. —*adj.* **7.** designating persons who share the same interests. —**af•fin′i•tive,** *adj.*

af•firm (ə fûrm′), *v.t.* **1.** to assert positively; maintain as true: *to affirm one's loyalty.* **2.** to confirm or ratify: *The judgment of the lower court was affirmed.* **3.** to express agreement with; support; uphold. —*v.i.* **4. a.** to state something solemnly before a court or magistrate, but without oath. **b.** (of an appellate court) to determine that the action of the lower court shall stand. —**af•firm′a•ble,** *adj.* —**af•firm′a•bly,** *adv.* —**af•firm′er,** *n.* —**af•firm′ing•ly,** *adv.*

af•fir•ma•tion (af′ər mā′shən), *n.* **1.** the act of affirming; state of being affirmed. **2.** the assertion that something exists or is true. **3.** something that is affirmed or declared to be true. **4.** confirmation or ratification of a prior judgment, decision, etc. **5.** a solemn declaration accepted instead of a statement under oath.

af•firm•a•tive (ə fûr′mə tiv), *adj.* **1.** affirming or asserting the truth, validity, or fact of something. **2.** expressing agreement or consent; assenting: *an affirmative reply.* **3.** positive; not negative. **4.** *Logic.* noting a proposition in which a property of a subject is affirmed, as "All men are happy." —*n.* **5.** something that affirms or asserts; affirmation. **6.** a reply indicating assent, as *Yes* or *I do.* **7.** a manner or mode that indicates assent: *a reply in the affirmative.* **8.** the side, as in a debate, that defends a statement which the opposite side attacks. —*interj.* **9.** (used to indicate agreement, assent, etc.): *"Is this the road to Lake George?" "Affirmative."* —**af•firm′a•tive•ly,** *adv.*

affirm′ative ac′tion, *n.* a policy to increase opportunities for women and minorities, esp. in education and employment.

af•fix (*v.* ə fiks′; *n.* af′iks), —*v.t.* **1.** to fasten, join, or attach (usu. fol. by *to*): *to affix stamps to a letter.* **2.** to add on; append: *to affix a signature to a contract.* **3.** to attach (blame, reproach, etc.). —*n.* **4.** something that is joined or attached. **5.** a bound inflectional or derivational element, as a prefix, infix, or suffix, added to a base or stem to form a fresh stem or a word, as *-ed* added to *want* to form *wanted,* or *im-* added to *possible* to form *impossible.* —**af•fix′a•ble,** *adj.*

af•fix•a•tion (af′ik sā′shən), *n.* **1.** the process of inflection or derivation by adding affixes. **2.** the act of affixing.

af•fla•tus (ə flā′təs), *n.* inspiration, esp. as a result of divine communication.

af•flict (ə flikt′), *v.t.* to distress with bodily or mental pain; trouble

grievously: *to be afflicted with arthritis.* —**af•flict′ed•ness,** *n.* —**af•flict′er,** *n.*

af•flic•tion (ə flik′shən), *n.* **1.** a distressed or painful state; misery. **2.** a cause of mental or bodily pain, as sickness or calamity. —**af•flic′tive,** *adj.* —**af•flic′tive•ly,** *adv.*

af•flu•ence (af′lōō əns *or, sometimes,* ə flōō′-), *n.* **1.** abundance of money and other material goods; wealth. **2.** an abundant supply; profusion. **3.** a flowing to or toward some point; afflux.

af•flu•ent (af′lōō ənt *or, sometimes,* ə flōō′-), *adj.* **1.** having an abundance of material goods; wealthy. **2.** abounding in anything; abundant. **3.** flowing freely: *an affluent fountain.* —*n.* **4.** a tributary stream. **5.** an affluent person. —**af′flu•ent•ly,** *adv.*

af′fluent soci′ety, *n.* a prosperous society whose wealth is not shared by all. [from title of a book (1958) by J.K. Galbraith]

af•flux (af′luks), *n.* **1.** something that flows to or toward a point: *an afflux of blood to the head.* **2.** the act of flowing to or toward some point.

af•ford (ə fôrd′, ə fōrd′), *v.t.* **1.** to be able to undergo, manage, or the like, without serious consequence: *The country can't afford another drought.* **2.** to be able to meet the expense of or spare the price of: *Can I afford a new dress?* **3.** to furnish; supply: *The sale afforded us a good profit.* **4.** to give; confer upon: *to afford great pleasure to someone.*

af•ford•a•ble (ə fôr′də bəl), *adj.* **1.** considered to be within one's financial means: *new cars at affordable prices.* —*n.* **2.** Usu., **affordables.** items, expenses, etc., that one can afford. —**af•ford′a•bil′i•ty,** *n.* —**af•ford′a•bly,** *adv.*

af•fri•cate (*n.* af′ri kit; *v.* -kāt′), *n., v.,* **-cat•ed, -cat•ing.** —*n.* **1.** a composite speech sound in which a stop consonant is gradually released with audible friction, as the sound (ch) in *church* or (j) in *judge.* —*v.t.* **2.** to change the pronunciation of (a stop) to an affricate, esp. by releasing (the stop) slowly. —**af′fri•ca′tion,** *n.* —**af•fric•a•tive** (ə frik′ə tiv), *n., adj.*

af•front (ə frunt′), *n.* **1.** a deliberate act or display of disrespect; insult. —*v.t.* **2.** to offend by an open manifestation of disrespect or insolence.

af•fu•sion (ə fyōō′zhən), *n.* the pouring on of water or other liquid, as in baptism.

Af′ghan hound′, *n.* one of a breed of tall, slender hounds with a long, narrow head, a long, silky coat, and a topknot.

Af•ghan•i•stan (af gan′ə stan′), *n.* a republic in SW Asia, E of Iran, and NW of Pakistan. 23,738,085; 251,773 sq. mi. (652,090 sq. km). *Cap.:* Kabul.

a•fi•cio•na•do or **af•fi•cio•na•do** (ə fish′yə nä′dō, ə fish′ə-, ə fē′-sē ə-), *n., pl.* **-dos.** an ardent devotee; fan; enthusiast.

a•field (ə fēld′), *adv.* **1.** abroad; away from home. **2.** away from the subject; off the mark. **3.** in or to the field or countryside.

a•fire (ə fīr′), *adj.* on fire: *to set a house afire.*

AFL, 1. Also, **A.F.L. A.F. of L.** American Federation of Labor. **2.** American Football League.

AFL-CIO or **A.F.L.-C.I.O.,** American Federation of Labor and Congress of Industrial Organizations.

a•float (ə flōt′), *adv., adj.* **1.** floating or borne on the water. **2.** on board a ship; at sea: *cargo afloat and ashore.* **3.** covered with water; flooded: *The main deck was afloat.* **4.** drifting; adrift. **5.** circulating; in circulation. **6.** financially solvent.

a•flut•ter (ə flut′ər), *adj.* **1.** in a flutter; agitated or excited. **2.** fluttering or marked by fluttering: *Fingers aflutter, he typed the letter without a mistake.*

a•foot (ə fŏŏt′), *adv.* **1.** on foot; walking. **2.** astir; in progress.

a•fore•men•tioned (ə fôr′men′shənd, ə fōr′-; ə fôr′ men′shənd, ə fōr′-), *adj.* cited or mentioned earlier or previously.

a•fore•said (ə fôr′sed′, ə fōr′-), *adj.* said or mentioned earlier or previously.

a•fore•thought (ə fôr′thôt′, ə fōr′-), *adj.* thought of previously; premeditated: *with malice aforethought.*

a•foul (ə foul′), *adv., adj.* **1.** in a state of collision or entanglement: *a ship with its shrouds afoul.* —*Idiom.* **2. run** or **come** or **fall afoul of, a.** to become entangled with: *The boat ran afoul of the seaweed.* **b.** to come into conflict with.

AFP, alpha-fetoprotein.

Afr, African.

a•fraid (ə frād′), *adj.* **1.** feeling fear; filled with apprehension: *to be afraid to go.* **2.** feeling regret or unhappiness: *I'm afraid we can't go on Monday.* **3.** feeling reluctance or unwillingness: *He was afraid to show his emotions.*

A-frame (ā′frām′), *n.* **1.** any upright, rigid supporting frame in the form of a triangle or an inverted V, as Λ. **2.** a building constructed principally of such a frame, with a steep gabled roof resting directly on a foundation.

a•fresh (ə fresh′), *adv.* anew; once more: *to start afresh.*

Af•ri•ca (af′ri kə), *n.* a continent S of Europe and between the Atlantic and Indian oceans. 600,000,000; ab. 11,700,000 sq. mi. (30,303,000 sq. km).

Af•ri•can (af′ri kən), *adj.* **1.** of or pertaining to Africa, esp. sub-Saharan Africa, or the parts of Africa inhabited by blacks. —*n.* **2.** a native or inhabitant of Africa, esp. black Africa. **3.** a person of African ancestry, esp. a black.

Af·ri·can-Amer·i·can or **Af·ri·can Amer·i·can,** *n.* **1.** a black American of African descent. —*adj.* **2.** of or pertaining to African-Americans.

Af·ri·can buf·fa·lo, *n.* a large black buffalo, *Syncerus caffer,* of Africa, with thick horns that meet at the base. Also called **Cape buffalo.**

Af·ri·can gray′, *n.* an ash-gray African parrot, *Psittacus erithacus,* with a short red tail, noted for its ability to mimic speech. Also called **gray parrot.**

Af·ri·can hon′eybee, *n.* a small, highly mobile honeybee, *Apis mellifera adansonii,* of S Africa, that swarms readily when disturbed and is capable of stinging repeatedly. Compare AFRICANIZED HONEYBEE.

Af·ri·can·ize (af′ri kə nīz′), *v.t.,* **-ized, -iz·ing. 1.** to replace the European or white staff of (an organization in Africa) with black Africans. **2.** to bring under African, esp. black African, influence or to adapt to African needs. Also, *esp. Brit.,* **Af′ri·can·ise′.** —**Af′ri·can·i·za′tion,** *n.*

Af·ri·can·ized hon′eybee (af′ri kə nīzd′), *n.* an American hybrid of the African and European honeybees produced by the mingling of domesticated European colonies with an expanding and migrating African colony that escaped from an apiary in Brazil.

Af·ri·can Meth′odist Epis′copal Church′, *n.* one of the three largest Methodist groups in the U.S., begun in 1787 when members of a Methodist church in Philadelphia withdrew in protest against racial segregation: formally organized in 1816.

Af·ri·can Meth′odist Epis′copal Zi′on Church′, *n.* a Christian denomination, one of the three largest Methodist groups in the United States.

Af·ri·can vi′olet, *n.* a tropical African plant, *Saintpaulia ionantha,* of the gesneriad family, with hairy leaves and purple, pink, or white flowers.

Af·ri·kaans (af′ri käns′, -känz′), *n.* **1.** an official language of the Republic of South Africa, developed from the language of 17th-century Dutch settlers. —*adj.* **2.** of or pertaining to Afrikaans or Afrikaners.

Af·ri·kan·der or **Af·ri·can·der** (af′ri kan′dər), *n.* one of a breed of red beef cattle, raised orig. in S Africa, well adapted to heat.

Af·ri·ka·ner (af′ri kä′nər, -kan′ər), *n.* a white South African whose native language is Afrikaans.

Af·ro (af′rō), *adj., n., pl.* **-ros.** —*adj.* **1.** of or pertaining to African-Americans or to black traditions, culture, etc.: *Afro societies.* —*n.* **2.** a hairstyle of very curly or frizzy hair grown or cut into a full, bushy shape all over the head.

Af·ro·a·si·at·ic or **Af·ro-A·si·at·ic** (af′rō ā′zhē at′ik, -ā′shē-, -ā′zē-), *n.* **1.** a family of languages spoken or formerly spoken in SW Asia and Africa, having as branches Semitic, Egyptian, Berber, Cushitic, and Chadic. —*adj.* **2.** of or pertaining to Afroasiatic. [1955–1960]

Af·ro·cen·tric (af′rō sen′trik), *adj.* centered on Africa or on African-derived cultures, as those of Brazil, Cuba, and Haiti: *Afrocentric art.* —**Af′ro·cen′trism,** *n.* —**Af′ro·cen′trist,** *n.*

AFSC or **A.F.S.C.,** American Friends Service Committee.

aft (aft, äft), *adv.* **1.** at, close to, or toward the stern of a ship or tail of an aircraft. —*adj.* **2.** situated toward or at the stern or tail.

AFT or **A.F.T.,** American Federation of Teachers.

af·ter (af′tər, äf′-), *prep.* **1.** behind in place or position; following behind: *We marched one after the other.* **2.** following the completion of; in succession to: *Tell me after supper. Day after day he came to work late.* **3.** in consequence of: *After what has happened, I can never return.* **4.** below in rank or estimation: *placed after Shakespeare among English poets.* **5.** in imitation of: *fashioned after Raphael.* **6.** in pursuit or search of: *I'm after a better job.* **7.** concerning; about: *to inquire after a person.* **8.** in agreement or conformity with: *a man after my own heart.* **9.** in spite of: *After all her troubles, she's still optimistic.* —*adv.* **10.** behind; in the rear: *Jill came tumbling after.* **11.** later in time; afterward: *happily ever after.* —*adj.* **12.** later; subsequent: *In after years we never heard from him.* **13. a.** farther aft. **b.** located closest to the stern or tail; aftermost. **14.** subsequent to the time that: *after the boys left.* —*Idiom.* **15. after all,** despite what has occurred; nevertheless.

af·ter·birth (af′tər bûrth′, äf′-), *n.* the placenta and fetal membranes expelled from the uterus after childbirth.

af·ter·burn·er (af′tər bûr′nər, äf′-), *n.* a device for burning exhaust gases, as from a jet or internal-combustion engine.

af·ter·burn·ing (af′tər bûr′ning, äf′-), *n.* **1.** combustion in an afterburner that results from the injection of fuel into the exhaust gases of a jet engine to produce additional thrust. **2.** a similar process in an internal-combustion engine.

af·ter·damp (af′tər damp′, äf′-), *n.* an irrespirable mixture of gases, consisting chiefly of carbon dioxide and nitrogen, left in a mine after an explosion or fire.

af·ter·ef·fect (af′tər i fekt′, äf′-), *n.* a delayed effect, as one that follows at some interval after the stimulus that produced it.

af·ter·glow (af′tər glō′, äf′-), *n.* **1.** the glow frequently seen in the sky after sunset. **2.** the pleasant remembrance of a past experience, glory, etc. **3.** PHOSPHORESCENCE (def. 3).

af·ter·im·age (af′tər im′ij, äf′-), *n.* a visual image that persists after the stimulus that caused it is no longer operative.

af·ter·life (af′tər līf′, äf′-), *n.* **1.** Also called **future life.** life after death. **2.** the later part of a person's life, as following retirement.

af·ter·mar·ket (af′tər mär′kit, äf′-), *n.* the market for parts, accessories, etc., for maintaining the original product.

af·ter·math (af′tər math′, äf′-), *n.* **1.** something that follows and usu.

results from an event, esp. one of a calamitous nature; consequence: *the aftermath of war.* **2.** a new growth of grass or other crop following a mowing.

af·ter·most (af′tər mōst′, äf′-), *adj.* **1.** farthest aft; closest to the stern. **2.** hindmost; last.

af·ter·noon (af′tər nōōn′, äf′-), *n.* **1.** the time from noon until evening. **2.** the latter part: *the afternoon of life.* —*adj.* **3.** pertaining to or occurring during the latter part of the day: *afternoon tea.*

af·ter·shock (af′tər shok′, äf′-), *n.* **1.** a small earthquake or tremor that follows a major earthquake. **2.** the effect or repercussion of an event; aftermath.

af·ter·taste (af′tər tāst′, äf′-), *n.* **1.** a taste remaining after the substance causing it is no longer in the mouth. **2.** the remaining feeling or impression following an unpleasant experience.

af·ter·thought (af′tər thôt′, äf′-), *n.* **1.** a later or second thought; reconsideration. **2.** something added later, as a part or feature.

af·ter·ward (af′tər wərd, äf′-) also **af′ter·wards,** *adv.* at a later time; subsequently.

af·ter·word (af′tər wûrd′, äf′-), *n.* a concluding section, commentary, etc., as of a book or treatise; closing statement. Compare FOREWORD.

Ag, *Chem. Symbol.* silver. [< Latin *argentum*]

A.G. or **AG, 1.** Adjutant General. **2.** Attorney General.

a·ga or **a·gha** (ä′gə), *n.* (in Turkey and other Muslim countries) a title of honor for a high official, military commander, etc.

Ag·a·bus (ag′ə bəs), *n.* a Christian prophet who predicted a great famine. Acts 11:28.

A·gag (ā′gag), *n.* an Amalekite king who was captured and spared by Saul but later killed by Samuel. I Sam. 15.

a·gain (ə gen′, ə gān′), *adv.* **1.** once more; another time: *Spell your name again, please.* **2.** moreover; besides. **3.** on the other hand: *It might happen, and again it might not.* **4.** back; in reply: *to answer again.* **5.** to the same place or person: *to return again.* —*Idiom.* **6. again and again,** with many repetitions; often. **7. as much again,** twice as much.

a·gainst (ə genst′, ə gānst′), *prep.* **1.** in opposition to; contrary to: *twenty votes against ten.* **2.** in resistance to or defense from: *protection against mosquitos.* **3.** in an opposite direction to: *walking against the wind.* **4.** in or into contact with; upon: *The rain beat against the window. Don't lean against the door.* **5.** in preparation for: *money saved against a rainy day.* **6.** having as background: *a design of flowers against a dark wall.* **7.** as a charge or debit on: *an advance against one's salary.* **8.** in competition with: *a racehorse running against his own record time.* **9.** in contrast with: *reason as against emotion.* —*Idiom.* **10. over against,** in contrast with.

A·ga Khan (ä′gə kän′), *Islam.* the divinely ordained head of the Isma-′ili branch of Shi'ism.

ag·a·ma (ag′ə mə), *n., pl.* **-mas.** any Old World lizard of the family Agamidae, esp. of the genus *Agama:* many have the ability to change color. —**ag′a·mid,** *n., adj.*

Ag·a·mem·non (ag′ə mem′non, -nən), *n.* **1.** a legendary king of Mycenae who led the Greeks in the Trojan War and was murdered by his wife Clytemnestra. **2.** (*italics*) a tragedy (458 B.C.) by Aeschylus. Compare ORESTEIA.

a·gam·ete (ā gam′ēt, ā′gə mēt′), *n.* an asexual reproductive cell, as a spore, that forms a new organism without fusion with another cell.

A·ga·ña (ä gä′nyä), *n.* the capital of Guam. 2119.

a·gape¹ (ə gāp′, ə gap′), *adv., adj.* **1.** with the mouth wide open, as in wonder. **2.** wide open: *his mouth agape.*

a·ga·pe² (ä gä′pā, ä′gə pā′, ag′ə-), *n., pl.* **-pae** (-pī, -pī′, -pē′). **1.** nonerotic love, as of God for humankind or of humankind for God or for one another. **2.** LOVE FEAST (defs. 1, 2).

a·gar (ä′gär, ag′ər), *n.* **1.** Also, **a·gar-a′gar.** a gel prepared from the cell walls of various red algae, used in laboratories as a culture medium, in food processing as a thickener and stabilizer, and in industry as a filler, adhesive, etc. **2.** a culture medium having an agar base.

ag·a·ric (ag′ə rik, ə gar′ik), *n.* any of various gill fungi of the family Agaricaceae, including the meadow mushroom and other common edible mushrooms of the genus *Agaricus.*

a·gar·ose (ä′gə rōs′, -rōz′), *n.* a substance obtained from agar and used for chromatographic separations.

Ag·as·siz (ag′ə sē), *n.* **1. Alexander,** 1835–1910, U.S. oceanographer and marine zoologist, born in Switzerland. **2.** his father, **(Jean) Louis (Rodolphe)** (zhän), 1807–73, U.S. zoologist and geologist, born in Switzerland. **3. Lake,** a lake existing in the prehistoric Pleistocene Epoch in central North America. 700 mi. (1127 km) long.

ag·ate (ag′it), *n.* **1.** a variegated chalcedony showing curved, colored bands or other markings. **2.** a playing marble made of this substance, or of glass in imitation of it. **3.** *Print.* **a.** a 5½-point type. **b.** a type size smaller than that used for news text, esp. in classified advertisements. —**ag′ate·like′,** *adj.*

ag′ate line′, *n.* a measure of advertising space, one column wide and ¼ of an inch deep.

a·ga·ve (ə gä′vē, ə gā′-), *n.* any desert plant of the genus *Agave,* having a single tall flower stalk and thick leaves at the base.

agcy., agency.

age (āj), *n., v.,* **aged, ag·ing** or **age·ing.** —*n.* **1.** the length of time during which a being or thing has existed; length of life or existence to the time mentioned: *trees of unknown age.* **2.** a period of human life, measured by years from birth, when a person is regarded as capable of assuming certain privileges or responsibilities: *the age of consent.* **3.** the particular period of life at which a person becomes qualified or disqualified for something: *to be over the age for military service.* **4.** one of the periods or stages of human life: *a person of middle age.* **5.** advanced years; old age: *His eyes were dim with age.* **6.** a generation or a series of generations: *ages yet unborn.* **7.** the period of history in which an individual lives: *the most famous architect of the age.* **8.** (*often cap.*) a particular period of history; a historical epoch: *the Periclean Age.* **9.** Usu., **ages.** a long period of time: *You've been away for ages.* **10.** the average life expectancy of an individual or the individuals of a class or species: *The age of a horse is from 25 to 30 years.* **11.** (*often cap.*) **a.** a period of the history of the earth distinguished by some special feature: *the Ice Age.* **b.** a unit of geological time, shorter than an epoch, during which the rocks comprising a stage were formed. —*v.i.* **12.** to grow old: *She is aging gracefully.* **13.** to mature, as wine, cheese, or wood. —*v.t.* **14.** to cause to grow or seem old: *Fear aged him overnight.* **15.** to bring to maturity; make ready for use: *to age wine.* —***Idiom.*** **16. of age,** having reached adulthood, esp. as specified by law.

-age, a suffix typically forming mass or abstract nouns from various parts of speech, occurring orig. in loanwords from French (*courage; voyage*) and productive in English with the meanings "aggregate" (*coinage; peerage; trackage*), "process" (*coverage*), "the outcome of" as either "the fact of" or "the physical effect or remains of" (*spoilage; wreckage*), "place of living or business" (*brokerage; parsonage*), "social standing or relationship" (*bondage; marriage*), and "quantity, measure, or charge" (*footage; towage*).

a•ged (ā′jid *for 1, 2, 5, 6;* ājd *for 1, 3, 4*), *adj.* **1.** of advanced age; old. **2.** pertaining to or characteristic of old age: *aged wrinkles.* **3.** of the age of: *a man aged 40 years.* **4.** brought to maturity or mellowness, as wine, cheese, or wood. **5.** (of topography) old; approaching peneplanation. —*n.* **6. the aged,** (*used with a pl. v.*) old people collectively. —**a′ged•ly,** *adv.*

age•ism (ā′jiz əm), *n.* discrimination or prejudice against older persons.

age•less (āj′lis), *adj.* **1.** not aging or appearing to age. **2.** lasting forever; eternal. —**age′less•ly,** *adv.*

age•long (āj′lông′, -long′), *adj.* lasting for an age.

a•gen•cy (ā′jən sē), *n., pl.* **-cies. 1.** an organization, company, or bureau that provides a particular service: *a welfare agency.* **2.** a government bureau or administrative division. **3.** a company having a franchise to represent another. **4.** the place of business of an agent. **5.** a means of exerting power or influence; instrumentality: *to be rescued by the agency of Providence.*

a•gen•da (ə jen′də), *n., formally a pl. of* **agendum,** *but usu. used as a sing. with pl.* **-das** *or* **-da.** a list, plan, outline, or the like, of things to be done, matters to be acted or voted upon, etc.

a•gen•e•sis (ā jen′ə sis) also **a•ge•ne•sia** (ā′jə nē′zhə), *n.* absence or failed development of a body part.

a•gent (ā′jənt), *n.* **1.** a person or business authorized to act on another's behalf. **2.** a person or thing that acts or has the power to act. **3.** a natural force or object producing or used for obtaining specific results: *Many insects are agents of fertilization.* **4.** an active cause; an efficient cause. **5.** a person who works for or manages an agency. **6.** a person who acts in an official capacity for a government agency, as a law-enforcement officer or a spy: *an FBI agent.* **7.** a linguistic form or construction, usu. a noun or noun phrase, denoting an animate being that performs or causes the action expressed by the verb, as *the police* in *The car was found by the police.* **8.** a representative of a business firm, esp. a traveling salesperson. **9.** a substance that causes a chemical reaction. Compare REAGENT. **10.** a drug or chemical capable of eliciting a biological response. **11.** an organism that is a cause or vector of disease. —**a•gen•tial** (ā jen′shəl), *adj.*

a•gen•tive (ā′jən tiv), *adj.* **1.** of or designating a linguistic form, construction, or case that indicates the doer or causer of an action. —*n.* **2.** an agentive word or suffix, as the suffix *-er* in *painter.* **3.** the agentive case.

A′gent Or′ange, *n.* a powerful herbicide and defoliant containing trace amounts of dioxin, used heavily during the Vietnam War to deprive enemy troops of foliage cover.

a•gent pro•vo•ca•teur (ā′jənt prə vok′ə tûr′, -tŏŏr′, a zhäɴ′), *n., pl.* **a•gents pro•vo•ca•teurs** (ā′jənts prə vok′ə tûr′, -tŏŏr′, a zhäɴ′). a secret agent hired to incite suspected persons to some illegal action that will make them liable to punishment.

age′ of consent′, *n. Law.* the age at which a person is considered competent to consent to marriage or sexual intercourse.

Age′ of In′nocence, The, a novel (1920) by Edith Wharton.

Age′ of Rea′son, *n.* the 17th and 18th centuries in France, England, etc.

age′-old′, *adj.* ancient; from time immemorial.

ag•er•a•tum (aj′ə rā′təm, ə jer′ə-), *n.* **1.** any of several low-growing composite plants of the genus *Ageratum,* having heart-shaped leaves and dense, blue or white flower heads. **2.** any of various other composite plants, as the mistflower, having blue or white flowers.

Ag•ga•dah (ə gä′də) also **Haggadah,** *n.* (*often l.c.*) the nonlegal or narrative material, as parables, maxims, or anecdotes, in the Talmud and other rabbinical literature. [< Hebrew *haggādhāh,* der. of *higgīdh* to narrate] —**Ag•gad•ic, ag•gad•ic** (ə gad′ik, ə gä′dik), *adj.*

Ag•ga•dist (ə gä′dist), *n.* **1.** one of the writers of the Aggadah. **2.** a person who is versed in the Aggadah.

ag•gior•na•men•to (ə jôr′nə men′tō), *n., pl.* **-ti** (-tē). the act of bringing something up to date to meet current needs.

ag•glom•er•ate (*v.* ə glom′ə rāt′; *adj., n.* -ər it, -ə rāt′), *v.,* **-at•ed, -at•ing,** *adj., n.* —*v.t., v.i.* **1.** to collect or gather into a cluster or mass. —*adj.* **2.** gathered together into a cluster or mass. —*n.* **3.** a mass of things clustered together. **4.** rock composed of rounded or angular volcanic fragments. —**ag•glom′er•a′tive** (-ə rā′tiv, -ər ə tiv), *adj.* —**ag•glom′er•a′tion,** *n.* —**ag•glom′er•a′tor,** *n.*

ag•glu•ti•nate (*v.* ə glo͞ot′n āt′; *adj.* -it, -āt′), *v.,* **-nat•ed, -nat•ing,** *adj.* —*v.t.* **1.** to cause to adhere, as with glue. **2.** to cause (bacteria or cells) to undergo agglutination. **3.** *Ling.* to form by agglutination. —*v.i.* **4.** to become agglutinated; stick or clump. **5.** to form words by agglutination. —*adj.* **6.** united, as by glue. **7.** agglutinative. —**ag•glu′ti•nant,** *adj., n.*

ag•glu•ti•na•tion (ə glo͞ot′n ā′shən), *n.* **1.** the act or process of uniting by glue or other tenacious substance. **2.** the state of being thus united. **3.** a mass or group cemented together. **4.** the clumping of bacteria, red blood cells, or other cells, due to the introduction of an antibody. **5.** a process of word formation in which morphemes, each having a relatively constant shape and meaning, are combined without fusion or morphophonemic change.

ag•glu•ti•na•tive (ə glo͞ot′n ā′tiv, ə glo͞ot′n ə-), *adj.* **1.** tending or having power to agglutinate or unite. **2.** of or designating a language, as Turkish, characterized by agglutination.

ag•grade (ə grād′), *v.t.,* **-grad•ed, -grad•ing.** to raise the grade or level of (a river valley, a stream bed, etc.) by depositing detritus, sediment, or the like. Compare DEGRADE. —**ag•gra•da•tion** (ag′rə dā′shən), *n.* —**ag′gra•da′tion•al,** *adj.*

ag•gran•dize (ə gran′dīz, ag′rən dīz′), *v.t.,* **-dized, -diz•ing. 1.** to widen in scope; increase in size or intensity; enlarge; extend. **2.** to make great or greater in power, wealth, rank, or honor. **3.** to make (something) appear greater. —**ag•gran′dize•ment** (-diz mənt), *n.* —**ag•gran•diz•er** (ə gran′dī zər, ag′rən dī′-), *n.*

ag•gra•vate (ag′rə vāt′), *v.t.,* **-vat•ed, -vat•ing. 1.** to make worse or more severe; intensify, as anything evil, disorderly, or troublesome. **2.** to annoy; irritate; exasperate. **3.** to cause to become irritated or inflamed. —**ag′gra•va′tor,** *n.*

ag•gra•vat•ed (ag′rə vā′tid), *adj. Law.* characterized by some feature that makes the crime more serious: *aggravated assault.*

ag•gra•va•tion (ag′rə vā′shən), *n.* **1.** an increase in intensity, seriousness, or severity; act of making worse. **2.** the state of being aggravated. **3.** something that causes an increase in intensity, degree, or severity. **4.** annoyance; exasperation. **5.** a source or cause of annoyance or exasperation.

ag•gre•gate (*adj., n.* ag′ri git, -gāt′; *v.* -gāt′), *adj., n., v.,* **-gat•ed, -gat•ing.** —*adj.* **1.** formed by the conjunction or collection of particulars into a whole mass or sum; total; combined. **2. a.** (of a flower) formed of florets collected in a dense cluster but not cohering, as the daisy. **b.** (of a fruit) composed of a cluster of carpels belonging to the same flower, as the raspberry. **3.** (of a rock) consisting of a mixture of minerals separable by mechanical means. —*n.* **4.** a sum, mass, or assemblage of particulars; a total or gross amount. **5.** any of various loose, particulate materials, as sand, gravel, or pebbles, added to a cementing agent to make concrete, plaster, etc. —*v.t.* **6.** to bring together; collect into one sum, mass, or body. **7.** to amount to (the number of). —*v.i.* **8.** to combine and form a collection or mass. —***Idiom.*** **9. in the aggregate,** considered as a whole. —**ag′gre•gate•ly,** *adv.*

ag•gre•ga•tion (ag′ri gā′shən), *n.* **1.** a group or mass of distinct or varied things, persons, etc. **2.** collection into an unorganized whole. **3.** the state of being so collected. **4.** a group of organisms of the same or different species living closely together but less integrated than a society. —**ag′gre•ga′tion•al,** *adj.*

ag•gress (ə gres′), *v.i.* **1.** to commit the first act of hostility or offense; attack first. **2.** to begin to quarrel. —**ag•gres′sor,** *n.*

ag•gres•sion (ə gresh′ən), *n.* **1.** the action of a state in violating by force the rights of another state; an unprovoked attack, invasion, or the like. **2.** any offensive action, attack, or procedure; an inroad or encroachment. **3.** the practice of making assaults or attacks; offensive action in general. **4.** hostility toward or attack upon another, whether overt, verbal, or gestural.

ag•gres•sive (ə gres′iv), *adj.* **1.** characterized by or tending toward aggression. **2.** vigorously energetic, esp. in the use of initiative and forcefulness; boldly assertive: *an aggressive salesperson.* **3.** (of an investment) emphasizing maximum growth over assured income. —**ag•gres′sive•ly,** *adv.* —**ag•gres′sive•ness,** *n.*

ag•grieve (ə grēv′), *v.t.,* **-grieved, -griev•ing. 1.** to oppress or wrong grievously; injure by injustice. **2.** to afflict with pain, anxiety, etc. —**ag•grieve′ment,** *n.*

ag•grieved (ə grēvd′), *adj.* **1.** wronged, offended, or injured. **2.** *Law.* deprived of legal rights or claims. **3.** troubled; worried; disturbed.

a•ghast (ə gast′, ə gäst′), *adj.* struck with overwhelming shock or amazement; filled with sudden fright or horror.

ag•ile (aj′əl, -īl), *adj.* **1.** quick and well-coordinated in movement; nimble. **2.** active; lively. **3.** marked by an ability to think quickly; mentally acute or aware. —**ag′ile•ly,** *adv.* —**a•gil•i•ty** (ə jil′i tē), *n.*

a•gin (ə gin′), *prep. Dial.* against; opposed to.

Ag•in•court (aj′in kôrt′, -kōrt′, azh′in kŏŏr′), *n.* a village in N France, near Calais: victory of the English over the French 1415. 276.

ag•i•tate (aj′i tāt′), *v.,* **-tat•ed, -tat•ing.** —*v.t.* **1.** to move or force into violent, irregular action. **2.** to shake or move briskly: *The machine agitated the mixture.* **3.** to disturb or excite emotionally; perturb. **4.** to call attention to by speech or writing; discuss; debate. —*v.i.* **5.** to arouse or attempt to arouse public interest and support, as in a political or social cause: *to agitate for the repeal of a tax.*

ag•i•ta•tion (aj′i tā′shən), *n.* **1.** the act of agitating or the state of being agitated. **2.** persistent urging of a political or social cause or theory before the public. **3.** psychomotor restlessness, manifested by pacing, hand-wringing, or similar activity. —**ag′i•ta′tion•al,** *adj.*

a•gi•ta•to (aj′i tä′tō, ä′ji-), *adj. Music.* agitated; restless or hurried in movement or style.

ag•i•ta•tor (aj′i tā′tər), *n.* **1.** a person who stirs up others in favor of a political, social, or other cause or urges them to militant action. **2.** a machine or device for agitating and mixing.

ag•let (ag′lit) also **aiglet,** *n.* **1.** a tag or ornament at the ends of the lace, cord, or the like with which a shoe or garment is secured. **2.** AIGUILLETTE.

a•glos•si•a (ə glô′sē ə, ā glô′-, ə glos′ē ə, ā glos′-), *n.* **1.** absence of the tongue, esp. when congenital. **2.** inability to speak.

ag•nail (ag′nāl′), *n.* **1.** a hangnail. **2.** whitlow.

ag•nate (ag′nāt), *n.* **1.** a relative whose connection is traceable exclusively through males. **2.** any male relation on the father's side. —*adj.* **3.** related or akin through males or on the father's side. **4.** allied or akin. —**ag•nat′ic** (-nat′ik), **ag•nat′i•cal,** *adj.* —**ag•nat′i•cal•ly,** *adv.* —**ag•na′tion** (-nā′shən), *n.*

Ag•new (ag′nōō, -nyōō), *n.* **Spi•ro T(heodore)** (spēr′ō), 1918-96, U.S. vice president 1969-73; resigned 1973.

ag•no•men (ag nō′mən), *n., pl.* **-nom•i•na** (-nom′ə nə). **1.** an additional, fourth name given to a person by the ancient Romans in allusion to some achievement or other circumstance, as "Africanus" in "Publius Cornelius Scipio Africanus." Compare COGNOMEN (def. 2). **2.** a nickname. —**ag•nom′i•nal,** *adj.*

ag•nos•tic (ag nos′tik), *n.* **1.** a person who holds that the existence of the ultimate cause, as a god or God, and the essential nature of things are unknown and unknowable. —*adj.* **2.** of or pertaining to agnostics or agnosticism.

ag•nos•ti•cism (ag nos′tə siz′əm), *n.* the doctrine or belief of an agnostic.

Ag•nus De•i (ag′nəs dē′ī, de′ē; ä′nyŏŏs de′ē), *n.* **1.** a figure of a lamb as emblematic of Christ. **2.** a prayer addressed to Christ preceding the communion in the Mass. [< Latin: lamb of God]

a•go (ə gō′), *adj.* **1.** gone; gone by; past (usu. prec. by a noun): *five days ago.* —*adv.* **2.** in the past: *It happened long ago.*

a•gog (ə gog′), *adj.* highly excited by eagerness, curiosity, anticipation, etc.

ag•on (ag′ōn, -on, ä gōn′), *n., pl.* **a•go•nes** (ə gō′nēz). **1.** (in literature) conflict, esp. between the protagonist and the antagonist. **2.** (in ancient Greece) a contest in which prizes were awarded in any of a number of events, as athletics, drama, music, poetry, and painting.

ag•o•nal (ag′ə nl), *adj.* of, pertaining to, or symptomatic of agony, esp. paroxysmal distress, as the death throes.

a•gon•ic (ā gon′ik), *adj.* not forming an angle.

ag•o•nist (ag′ə nist), *n.* **1.** a person engaged in a contest, conflict, struggle, etc., esp. the protagonist in a literary work. **2.** a person who is torn by inner conflict. **3.** a contracting muscle whose action is opposed by another muscle. Compare ANTAGONIST (def. 3). **4.** a chemical substance capable of activating a receptor to induce a full or partial pharmacological response. Compare ANTAGONIST (def. 5).

ag•o•nis•tic (ag′ə nis′tik) also **ag•o•nis′ti•cal,** *adj.* **1.** combative; striving to overcome in argument. **2.** straining for effect: *agonistic humor.* **3.** of or pertaining to ancient Greek athletic contests. **4.** pertaining to a behavioral response to an aggressive encounter, as attack or appeasement. —**ag•o•nis′ti•cal•ly,** *adv.*

ag•o•nize (ag′ə nīz′), *v.,* **-nized, -niz•ing.** —*v.i.* **1.** to suffer extreme pain or anguish; be in agony. **2.** to put forth great effort of any kind. —*v.t.* **3.** to distress with extreme pain; torture. —**ag′o•niz′ing•ly,** *adv.*

ag′onizing reapprais′al, *n.* a painful process of reconsidering a policy. [used in 1953 by U.S. Secretary of State John Foster Dulles]

ag•o•ny (ag′ə nē), *n., pl.* **-nies. 1.** extreme and generally prolonged pain or suffering. **2.** the struggle preceding natural death: *mortal agony.* **3.** a violent struggle. **4.** a display or outburst of intense mental or emotional excitement.

ag′ony col′umn, *n.* a section or column in a newspaper containing advertisements by individuals seeking missing relatives or lost pets or possessions, announcing the end of a marriage, etc.

ag•o•ra (ag′ər ə), *n., pl.* **-o•rae** (-ə rē′). a marketplace or public square in ancient Greece serving as a center of civic life.

ag•o•ra•pho•bi•a (ag′ər ə fō′bē ə), *n.* an abnormal fear of being in crowds, public places, or open areas.

a•gou•ti (ə gōō′tē), *n., pl.* **-tis, -ties. 1.** any of several short-eared, rab-

bitlike New World rodents of the genus *Dasyprocta,* common from Mexico to Peru. **2.** an irregularly barred pattern of the fur of certain rodents.

a•graph•i•a (ā graf′ē ə, ə graf′-), *n.* a cerebral disorder characterized by total or partial inability to write. —**a•graph′ic,** *adj.*

a•grar•i•an (ə grâr′ē ən), *adj.* **1.** relating to land, land tenure, or the division of landed property. **2.** pertaining to the promotion of agricultural interests: *an agrarian movement.* **3.** composed of or pertaining to farmers: *an agrarian co-op.* **4.** rural; agricultural. —*n.* **5.** a person who favors the equal division of landed property and the promotion of agricultural interests. —**a•grar′i•an•ism,** *n.*

a•gree (ə grē′), *v.,* **a•greed, a•gree•ing.** —*v.i.* **1.** to be of one mind; harmonize in opinion or feeling (often fol. by *with*): *I agree with you.* **2.** to have the same opinion (often fol. by *on* or *upon*): *We don't agree on politics.* **3.** to give consent; assent (often fol. by *to*): *Do you agree to the conditions?* **4.** to arrive at a settlement or understanding: *They have agreed on the price.* **5.** to be consistent; correspond; harmonize (usu. fol. by *with*): *His story agrees with hers.* **6.** (of food or drink) to admit of digestion or absorption without difficulty (usu. fol. by *with*). **7.** to be suitable; comply with a preference (often fol. by *with*): *The climate did not agree with him.* **8.** to correspond in inflectional form, as in grammatical case, number, gender, or person: *In* he runs, *the third person singular verb* runs *agrees with the subject* he *in person and number.* —*v.t.* **9.** to concede; grant (usu. fol. by a noun clause): *I agree that he is the ablest of us.*

a•gree•a•ble (ə grē′ə bəl), *adj.* **1.** to one's liking; pleasing: *agreeable manners.* **2.** willing or ready to agree or consent: *Are you agreeable to my plans?* **3.** suitable; conformable (usu. fol. by *to*): *practice agreeable to theory.* —**a•gree′a•ble•ness,** *n.* —**a•gree′a•bly,** *adv.*

a•gree•ment (ə grē′mənt), *n.* **1.** the act of agreeing or of coming to a mutual arrangement. **2.** the state of being in accord. **3.** an arrangement that is accepted by all parties to a transaction. **4.** a contract or other document delineating such an arrangement. **5.** correspondence in grammatical case, number, gender, person, etc., between syntactically connected words.

ag•ri•cul•ture (ag′ri kul′chər), *n.* the science, art, or occupation concerned with cultivating land, raising crops, and feeding, breeding, and raising livestock; farming. —**ag′ri•cul′tur•al,** *adj.* —**ag′ri•cul′tur•al•ly,** *adv.*

ag•ri•cul•tur•ist (ag′ri kul′chər ist) also **ag•ri•cul•tur•al•ist** (-chər ə list), *n.* **1.** an expert in agriculture. **2.** a farmer.

ag•ri•mo•ny (ag′rə mō′nē), *n., pl.* **-nies.** any plant belonging to the genus *Agrimonia,* of the rose family, esp. the perennial *A. eupatoria,* having pinnate leaves and small, yellow flowers.

Ag•rip•pi•na II (ag′rə pī′nə, -pē′-), *n.* A.D. 16?-59?, mother of the Roman emperor Nero and sister of Caligula.

agro-, a combining form meaning "field," "soil," "crop production": *agronomy.*

ag•ro•bi•ol•o•gy (ag′rō bī ol′ə jē), *n.* the scientific study of plant life in relation to agriculture, esp. with regard to plant genetics, cultivation, and crop yield. —**ag′ro•bi′o•log′ic** (-bī′ə loj′ik), **ag′ro•bi′o•log′i•cal,** *adj.* —**ag′ro•bi•ol′o•gist,** *n.*

ag•ro•chem•i•cal (ag′rə kem′i kəl), *n.* **1.** any chemical used in agricultural production, as commercial fertilizer. —*adj.* **2.** of or pertaining to such a chemical.

ag•ro•in•dus•tri•al (ag′rō in dus′trē əl), *adj.* of or pertaining to the combined use of agricultural and industrial processes or methods, as in the production of food, chemicals, and fertilizers. —**ag′ro•in′dus•try** (-in′də strē), *n., pl.* **-tries.**

a•grol•o•gy (ə grol′ə jē), *n.* the branch of soil science dealing esp. with the production of crops. —**ag•ro•log′ic** (ag′rə loj′ik), **ag′ro•log′i•cal,** *adj.* —**a•grol′o•gist,** *n.*

a•gron•o•my (ə gron′ə mē), *n.* the science of farm management and the production of field crops. —**ag′ro•nom′ic, ag′ro•nom′i•cal,** *adj.* —**a•gron′o•mist,** *n.*

a•ground (ə ground′), *adv., adj.* **1.** with the bottom stuck on the ground beneath a body of water; stranded: *The ship ran aground.* **2.** on or onto the ground.

a•gue (ā′gyōō), *n.* **1.** chills, fever, and sweating associated with an active episode of malaria. **2.** any fever marked by fits of shivering. —**a′gu•ish,** *adj.* —**a′gue•like′,** *adj.*

a•gue•weed (ā′gyōō wēd′), *n.* **1.** a common boneset, *Eupatorium perfoliatum.* **2.** a gentian, *Gentianella quinquefolia,* having bristly blue flowers.

ah (ä), *interj.* (used as an exclamation of pain, surprise, pity, complaint, dislike, joy, etc., according to the manner of utterance.)

Ah or **a.h.,** ampere-hour.

A•hab (ā′hab), *n.* **1.** a king of Israel and husband of Jezebel, reigned 874?-853? B.C. I Kings 16-22. **2.** captain of the ship *Pequod* and tragic hero of Herman Melville's *Moby Dick,* obsessed with the pursuit of the white whale.

A•has•u•e•rus (ə haz′yŏŏ ēr′əs, ə has′-), *n.* a king of ancient Persia, usu. identified as Xerxes I: husband of Esther.

A•haz (ā′haz), *n.* a king of Judah, 735?-715? B.C. II Kings 16; II Chron. 28:9.

A•ha•zi•ah (ā′ə zī′ə, ā′hə-), *n.* **1.** a son of Ahab and his successor as king of Israel, reigned 853?-852? B.C. I Kings 22:40. **2.** a king of Judah, 846? B.C. II Kings 8:24.

a·head (ə hed′), *adv.* **1.** in or to the front; before. **2.** in a forward direction; onward. **3.** into or for the future: *Plan ahead.* **4.** so as to register a later time: *to set the clock ahead.* **5.** at or to a different time, either earlier or later. **6.** onward toward success: *to get ahead in the world.* —*adj.* **7.** having the highest score so far, as in a competition; presently winning. —*Idiom.* **8. ahead of,** before or further than.

A·hi·e·zer (ā′hī ē′zər), *n.* **1.** a Danite who assisted Moses with the census and was head of the tribe of Dan in the wilderness. Num. 1:12; 2:35; 10:25. **2.** a Benjaminite chief of a body of archers who came to David's aid while he was hiding from Saul. I Chron. 12:3.

A·him·a·az (ə him′ā az′), *n.* a priest who supported David during the revolt of Absalom. II Sam. 18:19–32.

A·him·e·lech (ə him′ə lek′), *n.* a priest who was killed by Saul for helping David. I Sam. 21:1–9; 22:9–23.

a·him·sa (ə him′sä, ə hing′-), *n.* the Hindu principle of noninjury to living beings.

A·hi·ra (ə hī′rə), *n.* a Naphtalite who assisted Moses with the census in the wilderness. Num. 1:15; 2:29.

A·hi·shar (ə hī′shär), *n.* a chamberlain in Solomon's household. I Kings 4:6.

a·his·tor·ic (ā′hi stôr′ik, -stor′-) also **a′his·tor′i·cal,** *adj.* without concern for history or historical development; indifferent to tradition.

A·hith·o·phel (ə hith′ə fel′), *n.* an adviser to David who later turned against him by joining the rebellion of Absalom. II Sam. 15–17.

Ahn′felt's sea′weed (än′felts), *n.* branching, bushy red algae, *Ahnfeltia plicata,* common along N Atlantic coasts.

-aholic, a combining form extracted from ALCOHOLIC, used in coinages having the general sense "a person who is addicted to or obsessed with an object or activity," as specified by the initial element: *chargeaholic; foodaholic.* Compare -HOLIC. [by extraction, orig. in WORKAHOLIC]

A horizon, *n.* the topsoil in a soil profile.

a·hoy (ə hoi′), *interj.* (used at sea to hail another ship, attract attention, etc.)

Ah·ri·man (ä′ri mən), *n. Zoroastrianism.* ANGRA MAINYU.

A·hu·na Var·ya (ä′hŏŏ nä vär′yä), *Zoroastrianism.* the best-known and most frequently recited prayer: equivalent to the Lord's Prayer for Christians. Also called **A·hun·var** (ä′hŏŏn vär′).

A′hu·ra Maz′da (ä′hŏŏ rə), *n.* the supreme creative deity in Zoroastrianism.

AI or **A.I.,** Amnesty International.

aid (ād), *v.t.* **1.** to provide support for or relief to; help. **2.** to promote the progress of; facilitate. —*v.i.* **3.** to give help or assistance. —*n.* **4.** help or support; assistance. **5.** a person or thing that aids or furnishes assistance; helper; auxiliary. **6.** AIDE-DE-CAMP. **7.** a payment made by feudal vassals to their lord on special occasions. **8.** (in medieval England after 1066) any of several revenues received by a king from his vassals and other subjects. —**aid′er,** *n.* —**aid′ful,** *adj.* —**aid′less,** *adj.*

aide (ād), *n.* **1.** an assistant or helper, esp. a confidential one. **2.** NURSE'S AIDE. **3.** AIDE-DE-CAMP.

aide-de-camp (ād′də kamp′), *n., pl.* **aides-de-camp** (ādz′-). a subordinate military officer acting as a confidential assistant, esp. to a general or admiral.

aide-mé·moire (ād′mem wär′), *n., pl.* **aides-mé·moire** (ādz′-). a memorandum summarizing a discussion, agreement, or action.

AIDS (ādz), *n.* a disease of the immune system characterized by increased susceptibility to opportunistic infections, to certain cancers, and to neurological disorders: caused by a retrovirus and transmitted chiefly through blood or blood products that enter the body's bloodstream, esp. by sexual contact or contaminated hypodermic needles. Compare **AIDS virus.** [*a(cquired) i(mmune) d(eficiency) s(yndrome)*]

AIDS′-relat′ed com′plex, a syndrome caused by the AIDS virus and characterized primarily by chronically swollen lymph nodes and persistent fever: sometimes a precursor of AIDS. *Abbr.:* ARC

AIDS′ vi′rus, *n.* a variable retrovirus that invades and inactivates helper T cells of the immune system and is a cause of AIDS and AIDS-related complex; HIV.

ai·glet (ā′glit), *n.* AGLET.

ai·grette (ā′gret, ā gret′), *n.* **1.** a plume of feathers, esp. from a heron, worn as a head ornament. **2.** an ornament depicting this, usu. for the hair or hat.

ai·guille (ā gwēl′, ā′gwēl), *n.* a needlelike rock mass or mountain peak.

ai·guil·lette (ā′gwi let′), *n.* an ornamental tagged cord or braid on the shoulder of a uniform; aglet. —**ai′guil·let′ted,** *adj.*

Ai·ja·lon (ā′jə lon′), *n.* an ancient city west of Jerusalem: one of the cities of refuge. Josh. 19:42; I Sam. 14:31.

ai·ki·do (ī kē′dō), *n.* a Japanese form of self-defense utilizing wrist, joint, and elbow grips to immobilize or throw one's opponent.

ail (āl), *v.t.* **1.** to cause pain, uneasiness, or trouble to. —*v.i.* **2.** to be unwell; feel pain; be ill.

ai·lan·thus (ā lan′thəs), *n., pl.* **-thus·es.** any of several wide-spreading trees of the genus *Ailanthus,* of the quassia family, with long leaves and dense flower clusters, esp. *A. altissima* **(tree of heaven),** an urban shade tree. —**ai·lan′thic,** *adj.*

ai·ler·on (ā′lə ron′), *n.* a movable surface near the trailing edge of an aircraft wing, used to control roll and to perform banks.

ail·ment (āl′mənt), *n.* a physical disorder or illness, esp. of a minor or chronic nature.

ai·lu·ro·phile (ī lŏŏr′ə fīl′, ā lŏŏr′-), *n.* a person who likes cats. —**ai·lu′ro·phil′ic** (-fil′ik), *adj.*

ai·lu·ro·phobe (ī lŏŏr′ə fōb′, ā lŏŏr′-), *n.* **1.** a person who has an abnormal fear of cats. **2.** a person who detests cats. —**ai·lu′ro·pho′bi·a,** *n.* —**ai·lu′ro·pho′bic,** *adj.*

aim (ām), *v.t.* **1.** to position or direct (a firearm, ball, rocket, etc.) so that the thing discharged or thrown will hit a target. **2.** to intend or direct for a particular effect or purpose: *to aim a satire at snobbery.* —*v.i.* **3.** to point or direct a gun, punch, etc. **4.** to strive; try (usu. fol. by *to* or *at*): *We aim at pleasing everyone.* **5.** to intend: *She aims to go tomorrow.* **6.** to direct efforts, as toward an object: *I aim at perfection.* —*n.* **7.** the act of directing anything at or toward a particular point or target. **8.** the direction in which a weapon or missile is pointed; line of sighting. **9.** the point intended to be hit: *to miss one's aim.* **10.** something intended to be attained by one's efforts; purpose. —*Idiom.* **11. take aim,** to sight a target.

aim·less (ām′lis), *adj.* purposeless. —**aim′less·ly,** *adv.* —**aim′less·ness,** *n.*

ain't (ānt), **1.** *Nonstandard except in some dialects.* am not; are not; is not. **2.** *Nonstandard.* have not; has not; do not; does not; did not. [1770–80; var. of *amn't* (contr. of AM NOT) by loss of *m* and raising with compensatory lengthening of *a;* cf. AREN'T] —*Usage.* As a substitute for *am not, is not,* and *are not* in declarative sentences, AIN'T is more common in uneducated speech than in educated, but it occurs with some frequency in the informal speech of the educated, esp. in the southern and south-central states. This is especially true of the interrogative *ain't I?* used as a substitute for the formal *am I not?* or for *aren't I?* (considered by some to be ungrammatical) or for the awkward *amn't I?* (which is rare in American speech). Some speakers avoid all of the preceding forms by substituting *Isn't that so (true, the case)?* AIN'T occurs in set phrases: *Ain't it the truth! That ain't chopped liver!* The word is also used for emphasis: *That just ain't so!* It does not appear in formal writing except for deliberate (often humorous) effect or to represent speech. As a substitute for *have not* or *has not* and—occasionally in Southern speech—*do not, does not,* and *did not,* it is nonstandard except in similar humorous uses: *You ain't seen nothin' yet!* See also **aren't.**

ai·o·li (ī ō′lē, ā ō′-), *n.* a garlic-flavored mayonnaise of Provence.

air (âr), *n.* **1.** a mixture of nitrogen, oxygen, and minute amounts of other gases that surrounds the earth and forms its atmosphere. **2.** a stir in the atmosphere; a light breeze. **3.** overhead space; sky. **4.** circulation; publication; publicity: *to give air to one's theories.* **5.** general character or appearance; aura: *an air of mystery about him.* **6. airs,** affected or unnatural manner; assumed haughtiness. **7. a.** a tune; melody. **b.** an Elizabethan accompanied song. **8.** aircraft as a means of transportation: *to ship by air.* **9.** the medium through which radio waves are transmitted. **10.** *Informal.* air conditioning or an air-conditioning system. —*v.t.* **11.** to expose to the air; ventilate (often fol. by *out*). **12.** to bring to public notice; display: *to air one's opinions.* **13.** to broadcast or televise. —*v.i.* **14.** to be exposed to the open air (often fol. by *out*): *Let the room air out.* **15.** to be broadcast or televised. —*adj.* **16.** operating by means of air pressure or by acting upon air: *an air drill; an air pump.* **17.** of or pertaining to aircraft or to aviation. **18.** taking place in the air; aerial. **19.** imaginary; imitated; mimicked (used before the name of a musical instrument): *to play the air guitar.* —*Idiom.* **20. clear the air,** to eliminate misunderstandings. **21. get the air,** to be rejected, esp. after a long association. **22. give someone the air,** to reject someone, as a lover. **23. in the air,** in circulation; current: *an interesting rumor in the air.* **24. into thin air,** so as to disappear completely: *to vanish into thin air.* **25. off the air,** not broadcasting or being broadcast. **26. on the air,** broadcasting or being broadcast. **27. up in the air,** not decided; unsettled. **28. walk** or **tread on air,** to feel elated. —*Proverb.* **29. Don't air your dirty linen in public,** don't tell the public about embarrassing private matters.

air′ bag′, *n.* an inflatable plastic bag mounted in the passenger compartment of a motor vehicle: it cushions the driver and passengers by inflating automatically in the event of a collision.

air′ base′, *n.* an operations center for units of an air force.

air′ blad′der, *n.* **1.** a vesicle or sac containing air. **2.** an air-filled sac at the top of the body cavity in bony fishes, serving in most to regulate hydrostatic pressure.

air·borne (âr′bôrn′, -bōrn′), *adj.* **1.** carried by the air, as pollen or dust. **2.** in flight; aloft. **3.** (of military ground forces) carried in airplanes or gliders.

air′-bound′, *adj.* stopped up by air.

air′ brake′, *n.* **1.** a brake or system of brakes operated by compressed air. **2.** a device for reducing the air speed of an aircraft by increasing its drag.

air·brush (âr′brush′), *n.* **1.** an atomizer for spraying paint. —*v.t.* **2.** to paint or decorate using an airbrush. **3.** to remove or alter by or as if by means of an airbrush.

air′bus′ or **air′ bus′,** *n.* a short-range or medium-range commercial passenger airplane, esp. one that is part of a frequent shuttlelike service between two popular destinations.

air′ cav′alry, *n.* an infantry or reconnaissance unit transported by air to combat areas.

air′ cham′ber, *n.* **1.** a chamber containing air, as in a pump, lifeboat, or organic body. **2.** a compartment of a hydraulic system containing air that by its elasticity equalizes the pressure and flow of liquid within the system.

air′ command′, *n.* a unit of U.S. Air Force command that is higher than an air force.

air′ condi′tioner, *n.* an air-conditioning device.

air′ condi′tioning, *n.* a system or process for reducing the temperature and humidity, and sometimes the impurities, of the air in an office, theater, house, etc. —**air′-condi′tioning,** *adj.*

air′-cool′, *v.t.* **1.** to remove the heat of combustion, friction, etc., from (a machine, engine, or device), as by air streams flowing over an engine jacket. **2.** to cool by means of air conditioning.

air′ cov′er, *n.* **1.** the protection by aircraft of ground or naval military operations. **2.** the aircraft providing this protection.

air·craft (âr′kraft′, -kräft′), *n.,* *pl.* **-craft.** any machine supported for flight in the air by buoyancy or by the dynamic action of air on its surfaces, esp. powered airplanes, gliders, and helicopters.

air′craft car′rier, *n.* a warship equipped with a large open deck for the taking off and landing of warplanes and with facilities to carry, service, and arm them.

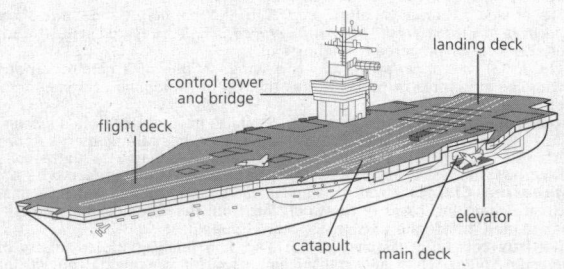

aircraft carrier

air′ cur′tain, *n.* compressed air directed, usu. downward, across a doorway so as to form a shield to exclude drafts, insects, etc.

air·date (âr′dāt′), *n.* the date of a broadcast.

air′ divi′sion, *n.* a unit of U.S. Air Force command within an air force, usu. composed of two or more wings.

air·drop (âr′drop′), *v.,* **-dropped, -drop·ping,** *n.* —*v.t.* **1.** to drop (persons, equipment, etc.) by parachute from an aircraft in flight. —*n.* **2.** the act or process of airdropping. —**air′-drop′pa·ble,** *adj.*

air′-dry′, *v.,* **-dried, -dry·ing,** *adj.* —*v.t., v.i.* **1.** to dry by exposure to the air. —*adj.* **2.** dry beyond further evaporation.

-aire, a suffix that forms nouns denoting a person characterized by or occupied with that named by the stem, occurring in loanwords from French: *concessionaire; doctrinaire; legionnaire; millionaire.*

Aire·dale (âr′dāl′), *n.* one of a breed of large terriers having a hard, wiry black-and-tan coat and a long, square muzzle with chin whiskers. Also called **Aire′dale ter′rier.**

air·fare (âr′fâr′), *n.* the price charged for transportation by airplane.

air·field (âr′fēld′), *n.* a level area, usu. equipped with paved runways, on which airplanes take off and land.

air·flow (âr′flō′), *n.* the air flowing past or through a moving body, as an airplane or automobile.

air·foil (âr′foil′), *n.* any surface, as a wing or stabilizer, designed to aid in lifting or controlling an aircraft by making use of the air currents through which it moves.

Air′ Force′, *n.* **1.** the U.S. department in charge of the nation's military air power. **2.** (*l.c.*) the military unit of a nation charged with carrying out air operations. **3.** (*l.c.*) a unit of U.S. Air Force command between an air division and an air command. **4.** (*l.c.*) (formerly) the largest unit in the U.S. Army Air Forces.

air·freight (âr′frāt′), *n.* **1.** a system of transporting freight by aircraft. **2.** freight transported by aircraft. **3.** the charge for such transportation. —*v.t.* **4.** to send or ship by air freight. —*v.i.* **5.** to ship cargo by air freight. Also, **air′-freight′** (for defs. 4, 5).

air·glow (âr′glō′), *n.* a dim light, usu. visible at night, that results from ionic radiation in the upper atmosphere.

air′ gun′, *n.* a gun operated by compressed air.

air·head¹ (âr′hed′), *n.* an area in enemy territory or in threatened friendly territory, seized by airborne troops for bringing in supplies and additional troops by airdrop or landing.

air·head² (âr′hed′), *n.* *Slang.* a scatterbrained, stupid, or simple-minded person; dolt. —**air′head′ed,** *adj.*

air′ hole′, *n.* **1.** an opening to admit or discharge air. **2.** an opening in the frozen surface of a river or pond. **3.** AIR POCKET.

air·i·ly (âr′ə lē), *adv.* **1.** in a gay or breezy manner; jauntily. **2.** lightly; delicately.

air·i·ness (âr′ē nis), *n.* **1.** openness to the air. **2.** sprightliness of manner. **3.** snobbishness; affectation.

air·ing (âr′ing), *n.* **1.** an exposure to the air, as for drying. **2.** a public discussion or disclosure, as of ideas, proposals, or facts. **3.** a period of leisure or physical activity in the open air, esp. to promote health. **4.** a broadcast on radio or television.

air·lift (âr′lift′), *n.* Also, **air′ lift′.** **1.** a system for transporting persons or cargo by aircraft, esp. in an emergency. **2.** the process of transporting such a load. —*v.t.* **3.** to transport (persons or cargo) by airlift.

air·line (âr′līn′), *n.* **1. a.** a system furnishing air transport, usu. scheduled, between specified points. **b.** the airplanes, airports, etc., of such a system. **c.** Often, **airlines.** a company that owns or operates such a system. **2.** Also, **air′ line′.** a direct line; beeline. —*adj.* **3.** of, for, or on an airline.

air·lin·er (âr′lī′nər), *n.* a passenger aircraft operated by an airline.

air′ lock′, *n.* **1.** an airtight chamber permitting passage to or from a space, as in a caisson, in which the air is kept under pressure. **2.** an impedance in the functioning of a pump or a system of piping caused by the presence of an air bubble.

air′-lock′, *v.t.* to place in or confine to an air lock: *to air-lock divers before they descend.*

air′mail′ or **air′-mail′,** *n.* Also, **air′ mail′.** **1.** the system, esp. a government postal system, of sending mail by airplane. **2.** the mail sent by this system. —*adj.* **3.** of or pertaining to airmail. —*adv.* **4.** by airmail: *to send letters airmail.* —*v.t.* **5.** to send via airmail.

air·man (âr′mən), *n., pl.* **-men. 1.** an aviator. **2.** *U.S. Air Force.* an enlisted person of one of the three lowest ranks (**air′man ba′sic, airman, air′man first′ class′**). **3.** a crewmember of a military aircraft.

air′ mass′, *n.* a body of air covering a wide area, exhibiting approximately uniform properties through any horizontal section.

air′ mat′tress, *n.* a mattress, usu. of plastic or rubber, that can be inflated for use and deflated for storage.

Air′ Med′al, *n.* an award given to a member of the U.S. armed forces for heroism or meritorious action in a military air operation.

air′ mile′, *n.* INTERNATIONAL NAUTICAL MILE.

Air′ Na′tional Guard′, *n.* a national guard organization similar to and coordinate with the U.S. Air Force.

air·pack (âr′pak′), *n.* an apparatus consisting of a face mask connected to a portable air supply, used esp. by firefighters in areas of smoke, poisonous fumes, etc.

air′ pi′racy, *n.* the hijacking of an airplane. —**air′ pi′rate,** *n.*

air·plane (âr′plān′), *n.* **1.** a heavier-than-air craft kept aloft by the upward thrust exerted by the passing air on its fixed wings and driven by propellers or jet propulsion. **2.** any similar heavier-than-air craft, as a glider or helicopter. Also, *esp. Brit.,* **aeroplane.**

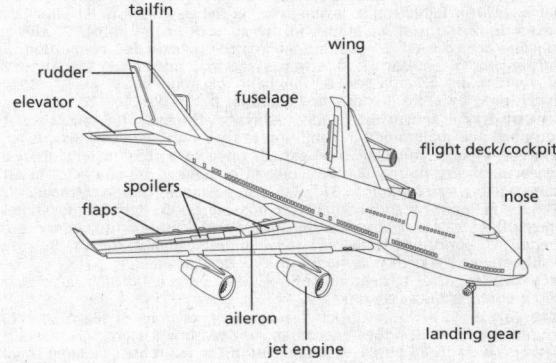

airplane

air′ plant′, *n.* **1.** an epiphyte. **2.** a tropical plant, *Kalanchoe pinnata,* of the stonecrop family, having pale-green flowers tinged with red and new plants sprouting at the leaf notches.

air·play (âr′plā′), *n.* the act or an instance of broadcasting recorded material over radio or television.

air′ pock′et, *n.* a nearly vertical air current that can cause an aircraft to lose altitude suddenly.

Air′ Police′, *n.* an organization of personnel in the U.S. Air Force or Air National Guard serving as police. *Abbr.:* AP

air·port (âr′pôrt′, -pōrt′), *n.* a facility for the landing, takeoff, shelter, supply, and repair of aircraft, esp. one used for transporting passengers and cargo at regularly scheduled times.

air′ pow′er, *n.* the total military capability of a nation for operations involving the use of aircraft and missiles.

air′ pres′sure, *n.* the force exerted by air, whether compressed or unconfined, on any surface in contact with it.

air′ pump′, *n.* an apparatus for drawing in, compressing, or exhausting air.

air′ raid′, *n.* a raid by aircraft, esp. for bombing a particular area.

air′ ri′fle, *n.* an air gun with rifled bore.

air′ right′, *n.* a right of way in the air space above a property, allowing the owner to build in such space, subject to legal restrictions.

air′ sac′, *n.* **1.** ALVEOLUS (def. 2). **2.** any of certain cavities in a bird's body connected with the lungs.

air·screw (âr′skrōō′), *n. Brit.* an airplane propeller.

air·ship (âr′ship′), *n.* a self-propelled, lighter-than-air craft with means of controlling the direction of flight; dirigible. Compare BLIMP.

air·sick·ness (âr′sik′nis), *n.* motion sickness induced by travel in an aircraft. **—air′sick′,** *adj.*

air·space (âr′spās′), *n.* **1.** a space made for or occupied by air. **2.** the region of the atmosphere above an area of land, esp. the region above a nation over which it has jurisdiction.

air′speed′ or **air′ speed′,** *n.* the forward speed of an aircraft relative to the air through which it moves. Compare GROUNDSPEED.

air′ sta′tion, *n.* an airfield having facilities for sheltering and servicing aircraft.

air·stream (âr′strēm′), *n.* any localized airflow.

air′ strike′ or **air′strike′,** *n.* the bombing or strafing of a city, enemy stronghold, etc., by military aircraft.

air·strip (âr′strip′), *n.* a small landing field having only one runway.

air′ tax′i, *n.* a small aircraft carrying passengers on short routes not serviced by airlines.

air·tight (âr′tīt′), *adj.* **1.** preventing the entrance or escape of air or gas. **2.** having no weak points or openings of which an opponent may take advantage: *an airtight contract.* **—air′tight′ness,** *n.*

air′time′ or **air′ time′,** *n.* **1.** the particular time scheduled for the broadcast of a radio or television program. **2.** the time during which broadcasting or a particular broadcast takes place on a given station. **3.** a block of such time sold or allotted by a station to an advertiser, political candidate, etc.

air′-to-air′, *adj.* **1.** operating between airborne objects, esp. aircraft: *air-to-air missiles; air-to-air communication.* **—adv. 2.** from one aircraft, missile, or the like to another while in flight: *They refueled air-to-air.*

air′-to-sur′face, *adj.* **1.** operating or directed from a flying aircraft to the surface: *air-to-surface missiles.* **—adv. 2.** from a flying aircraft to the surface of the earth: *They released the rockets air-to-surface.*

air′ traf′fic, *n.* aircraft moving in flight or on airport runways.

air′-traf′fic control′, *n.* a government service maintaining the safe and orderly movement of aircraft at and between airports. **—air′-traf′fic control′ler,** *n.*

air·waves (âr′wāvz′), *n.pl.* the medium of radio and television broadcasting: *airwaves filled with news of the crisis.*

air·way (âr′wā′), *n.* **1.** an air route equipped with emergency landing fields, beacon lights, radio beams, etc. **2.** the passageway by which air passes from the nose or mouth to the air sacs of the lungs. **3.** *Med.* a tubelike device used to maintain adequate, unobstructed respiration, as during general anesthesia. **4.** any passage in a mine used for purposes of ventilation. **5. airways, a.** the band of frequencies, taken collectively, used by radio broadcasting stations. **b.** AIRLINE (def. 1c).

air·wor·thy (âr′wûr′thē), *adj.,* **-thi·er, -thi·est.** (of an aircraft) equipped and maintained in condition to fly. **—air′wor′thi·ness,** *n.*

air·y (âr′ē), *adj.,* **air·i·er, air·i·est. 1.** open to a free current of fresh air; breezy: *airy rooms.* **2.** consisting of or having the character of air; immaterial: *airy phantoms.* **3.** light in appearance; thin: *airy garments.* **4.** light in manner; sprightly; lively: *airy songs.* **5.** light in movement; graceful; delicate: *an airy step.* **6.** unsubstantial; unreal; imaginary: *airy dreams.* **7.** performed in the air; aerial. **8.** lofty; high in the air. **9.** snobbishly affected; haughty: *a model striking airy poses.*

air′y-fair′y, *adj.* **1.** delicate or lovely. **2.** unrealistic: *airy-fairy ideas about winning the sweepstakes.*

aisle (īl), *n.* **1.** a walkway between or along sections of seats, shelves, counters, etc., as in a theater, church, or department store. **2.** a longitudinal division in a church, separated from the main area or nave by an arcade or the like. **—Idiom. 3. in the aisles,** (of an audience) convulsed with laughter. **—aisled,** *adj.*

ait (āt), *n. Brit.* a small island, esp. in a river.

a·jar[1] (ə jär′), *adj., adv.* neither entirely open nor entirely shut; partly open.

a·jar[2] (ə jär′), *adv., adj.* in contradiction to; at variance with: *a story ajar with the facts.*

AK, Alaska.

a.k.a. or **AKA** or **aka,** also known as.

a·ke·la (ə kē′lə), *n., pl.* **-las.** (in the cub scouts) a pack leader.

A·khe·na·ton or **A·khe·na·ten** (äk nät′n, ä′kə-), also **Akh·na·ton** (äk nät′n), *n.* (*Amenhotep IV*) died 1357? B.C., king of Egypt 1375?–1357?: reformer of ancient Egyptian religion (son of Amenhotep III).

Ak·hi·sar (äk′hi sär′), *n.* a town in W Turkey, NE of Izmir. 61,491. Ancient, **Thyatira.**

a·kim·bo (ə kim′bō), *adj., adv.* with hand on hip and elbow bent outward: *to stand with arms akimbo.*

a·kin (ə kin′), *adj.* **1.** of kin; related by blood. **2.** allied by nature or inclination; having the same or very similar properties, qualities, preferences, etc.

Ak·kad or **Ac·cad** (ak′ad, ä′käd), *n.* **1.** an ancient region in Mesopota-

mia, the N division of Babylonia. **2.** a city in this region: capital of the Akkadian empire c2350–2200 B.C.

Ak·ka·di·an or **Ac·ca·di·an** (ə kā′dē ən, ə kä′-), *n.* **1.** an extinct eastern Semitic language of Assyria and Babylonia, written in a cuneiform syllabary borrowed from Sumerian. **2.** a native or inhabitant of Akkad. **—adj. 3.** of or pertaining to the language Akkadian. **4.** of or pertaining to Akkad or its inhabitants.

Ak·mo·la (ak mō′lə), *n.* the capital of Kazakhstan, in the N central part. 276,000. Formerly, **Akmolinsk, Tselinograd.**

Ak·ron (ak′rən), *n.* a city in NE Ohio. 221,886.

-al[1], a suffix with the general sense "of the kind of, pertaining to, having the form or character of" that named by the stem, occurring in loanwords from Latin (*autumnal; natural; pastoral*), and productive in English on the Latin model, usu. with bases of Latin origin (*accidental; seasonal; tribal*).

-al[2], a suffix forming nouns from verbs, usu. verbs of French or Latin origin: *denial; refusal.*

AL, Alabama.

Al, *Chem. Symbol.* aluminum.

al., 1. other things. **2.** other persons.

A.L., 1. American League. **2.** American Legion.

à la or **a la** (ä′ lä, ä′ lə, al′ə), *prep.* **1.** in the manner or style of: *a short poem à la Ogden Nash; tuna à la provençale.* **2.** prepared with the ingredient of. **3.** prepared to the taste of.

a·la (ā′lə), *n., pl.* **a·lae** (ā′lē). **1.** a wing. **2.** one of a pair of various winglike structures or processes, as the top of a hipbone or a side petal of certain flowers.

Al·a·bam·a (al′ə bam′ə), *n.* **1.** a state in the SE United States. 4,273,084; 51,609 sq. mi. (133,670 sq. km). *Cap.:* Montgomery. *Abbr.:* AL, Ala. **2.** a river flowing SW from central Alabama to the Mobile River. 315 mi. (505 km) long. **—Al′a·bam′i·an, Al′a·bam′an,** *adj., n.*

Alaba′ma Claims′, *n.pl.* claims made by the United States against Great Britain for losses in the Civil War from the shipping raids of British-made Confederate vessels, esp. the *Alabama.*

al·a·bas·ter (al′ə bas′tər, -bä′stər), *n.* **1.** a finely granular variety of gypsum, often white and translucent, used for ornamental objects or work, as lamp bases and figurines. **2.** a variety of calcite, often banded, used or sold as alabaster. **—adj.** Also, **al·a·bas·trine** (al′ə bas′trin). **3.** made of alabaster. **4.** resembling alabaster; smooth and white.

à la carte or **a la carte** (ä′ lə kärt′, al′ə), *adv., adj.* with a separate price for each item on the menu.

a·lac·ri·ty (ə lak′ri tē), *n.* **1.** cheerful readiness, promptness, or willingness: *to do a favor with alacrity.* **2.** liveliness; briskness. **—a·lac′ri·tous,** *adj.*

A·lad·din (ə lad′n), *n.* (in *The Arabian Nights' Entertainments*) a youth who finds a magic lamp and ring with which he can command two jinns.

à la king (ä′ lə king′, al′ə), *adj.* diced and served in a cream sauce containing mushrooms, pimiento, and green pepper: *chicken à la king.*

al·a·me·da (al′ə mā′də), *n., pl.* **-das. 1.** *Chiefly Southwestern U.S.* a public walk shaded with trees. **2.** (in Latin America) a boulevard, park, or public garden having such a walk.

Al·a·mo (al′ə mō′), *n.* a Franciscan mission in San Antonio, Tex., taken by Mexicans in 1836 during the Texan war for independence.

à la mode or **a la mode** or **a·la·mode** (ä′ lə mōd′, al′ə-), *adj.* **1.** in or according to the fashion; fashionable. **2.** served with ice cream: *apple pie à la mode.* **3.** (of beef) braised in red wine with vegetables and served in a rich brown sauce. [< French]

al·a·nine (al′ə nēn′, -nin), *n.* any of several isomers of a colorless, crystalline, water-soluble amino acid, $CH_2CH(NH_2)COOH$, found in many proteins and produced synthetically: used chiefly in biochemical research. *Abbr.:* Ala; *Symbol:* A

a·lar (ā′lər), *adj.* **1.** of, pertaining to, or having wings. **2.** wing-shaped.

Al·a·ric (al′ər ik), *n.* A.D. c370–410, king of the Visigoths: captured Rome 410.

a·larm (ə lärm′), *n.* **1.** a sudden fear or distressing suspense due to awareness of danger; apprehension; fright. **2.** any sound, outcry, or information intended to warn of approaching danger. **3.** an automatic device that serves to warn of danger, as fire or an intruder, to arouse someone from sleep, or to call attention to a particular thing. **—v.t. 4.** to make fearful or apprehensive; distress. **5.** to warn of danger; rouse to vigilance or protective action. **6.** to equip with an alarm or alarms, as in case of fire or robbery. **—a·larm′ing,** *adj.*

alarm′ clock′, *n.* a clock with a bell or buzzer that can be set to sound at a particular time, as to awaken someone.

a·larm·ist (ə lär′mist), *n.* **1.** a person who tends to raise alarms, esp. without sufficient reason. **—adj. 2.** of or like an alarmist.

alar′ums and excur′sions, *n.pl.* noisy, frantic, or disorganized activities.

a·las (ə las′, ə läs′), *interj.* (used as an exclamation to express sorrow, pity, concern, apprehension, etc.)

A·las·ka (ə las′kə), *n.* **1.** a state of the United States in NW North America. 607,007; 586,400 sq. mi. (1,519,000 sq. km). *Cap.:* Juneau. *Abbr.:* AK, Alas. **2. Gulf of,** a gulf of the Pacific Ocean on the coast of S Alaska. **—A·las′kan,** *adj., n.*

Alas′ka-Hawai′i time′, *n.* the civil time officially adopted for the region of the 150th meridian, which includes the states of Alaska and Hawaii; two hours behind Pacific time.

Alas'ka High'way, *n.* a highway in NW Canada and Alaska, extending from E British Columbia to Fairbanks: built as a U.S. military supply route 1942. 1523 mi. (2452 km) long. Also called **Alcan Highway.**

Alas'kan king' crab', *n.* KING CRAB (def. 2).

Alas'kan mal'amute, *n.* one of an Alaskan breed of large dogs with a dense, coarse gray or black and white coat, erect ears, and a bushy tail carried over the back, raised orig. for pulling sleds.

Alas'ka Pur'chase, *n.* **1.** purchase of the territory of Alaska by the U.S. from Russia in 1867 for $7,200,000. Compare SEWARD'S FOLLY. **2.** the territory itself.

a·late (ā'lāt) also **a'lat·ed,** *adj.* **1.** having wings; winged. **2.** having membranous expansions like wings.

alb (alb), *n.* a long-sleeved linen vestment, worn chiefly by priests. [< Latin *alba* (*vestis*) white (garment)]

Alba., Alberta.

al·ba·core (al'bə kôr', -kōr'), *n.*, *pl.* **-cores,** (*esp. collectively*) **-core.** a long-finned tuna, *Thunnus alalunga.*

Al·ba·ni·a (al bā'nē ə, -bān'yə), *n.* a republic in S Europe, in the Balkan Peninsula between Yugoslavia and Greece. 3,293,252; 10,632 sq. mi. (27,535 sq. km). *Cap.:* Tiranë. —**Al·ba'ni·an,** *adj., n.*

Al·ba·ny (ôl'bə nē), *n.* **1.** the capital of New York, in the E part, on the Hudson. 104,828. **2.** a city in SW Georgia. 83,540. **3.** a river in central Canada, flowing E from W Ontario to James Bay. 610 mi. (980 km) long.

Al'bany Con'gress, *n.* a meeting of delegates from seven American colonies, held in 1754 at Albany, N.Y., at which Benjamin Franklin proposed a plan (**Al'bany Plan' of Un'ion**) for unifying the colonies.

al·ba·tross (al'bə trôs', -tros'), *n.*, *pl.* **-tross·es,** (*esp. collectively*) **-tross** for 1. **1.** any of several large, web-footed, mostly white birds of the family Diomedeidae, of S and tropical oceanic waters, having a large wingspread and able to remain aloft for long periods. **2.** a seemingly inescapable moral or emotional burden, as of guilt or responsibility. **3.** something burdensome that impedes action or progress.

al·be·do (al bē'dō), *n.*, *pl.* **-dos.** **1.** the ratio of the light reflected by a planet or satellite to that received by it. **2.** the white inner rind of a citrus fruit.

Al·bee (ôl'bē), *n.* **Edward,** born 1928, U.S. playwright.

al·be·it (ôl bē'it), *conj.* although; even if: *a peaceful, albeit brief retirement.*

Al·bert (al'bərt), *n.* **1. Prince** (*Albert Francis Charles Augustus Emanuel, Prince of Saxe-Coburg-Gotha*), 1819–61, consort of Queen Victoria. **2. Lake,** a lake in central Africa, between Uganda and Zaire: a source of the Nile. 100 mi. (160 km) long; 2061 sq. mi. (5338 sq. km); 2030 ft. (619 m) above sea level.

Al·ber·ta (al bûr'tə), *n.* a province in W Canada. 2,365,825; 255,285 sq. mi. (661,190 sq. km). *Cap.:* Edmonton. *Abbr.:* Alba., Alta. —**Al·ber'tan,** *adj., n.*

Al·ber·tus Mag·nus (al bûr'təs mag'nəs), *n.* **Saint** (*Count von Bollstädt*), 1193?–1280, German scholastic philosopher: teacher of Saint Thomas Aquinas. —**Al·ber'tist,** *n.*

al·bes·cent (al bes'ənt), *adj.* becoming white; whitish. —**al·bes'cence,** *n.*

Al·bi·gen·ses (al'bi jen'sēz), *n.pl.* members of an ascetic Christian sect that arose in Albi in the 11th century and was destroyed in the 13th century. —**Al'bi·gen'si·an** (-sē ən, -shən), *adj., n.* —**Al'bi·gen'si·an·ism,** *n.*

al·bi·no (al bī'nō; *esp. Brit.* -bē'-), *n.*, *pl.* **-nos.** **1.** a person with pale skin, white hair, pinkish eyes, and visual abnormalities resulting from a hereditary inability to produce the pigment melanin. **2.** an animal or plant with a marked deficiency in pigmentation. —**al·bin'ic** (-bin'ik), *adj.* —**bi'nal** (al'bə nl), *adj.*

al·bum (al'bəm), *n.* **1.** a bound or loose-leaf book consisting of blank pages, envelopes, etc., for storing or displaying photographs, stamps, or the like, or for collecting autographs. **2.** a recording or set of recordings containing musical selections, a complete play or opera, etc., released on compact disc, phonograph record, cassette tape, or other medium. **3.** the package or container for such an album. **4.** an anthology of artwork, songs, writings, etc. [< Latin *albus* white, i.e., a blank (tablet) painted white for writing on]

al·bu·men (al byōō'mən), *n.* **1.** the white of an egg. **2.** the nutritive matter around the embryo in a seed. **3.** ALBUMIN.

al·bu·min or **al·bu·men** (al byōō'mən), *n.* any of a class of simple, sulfur-containing, water-soluble proteins that coagulate when heated, occurring in egg white, milk, blood, and other animal and vegetable tissues and secretions. —**al·bu'mi·nous,** *adj.*

Al·bu·quer·que (al'bə kûr'kē), *n.* **1. Affonso de,** 1453–1515, founder of the Portuguese empire in the East. **2.** a city in central New Mexico. 411,994.

al·bur·num (al bûr'nəm), *n.* SAPWOOD. —**al·bur'nous,** *adj.*

al·cal·de (al kal'dē, -käl'-) also **al·cade** (-kād'), *n.*, *pl.* **-cal·des** also **-cades.** (in Spain and southwestern U.S.) a mayor having judicial powers.

Al'can High'way, *n.* ALASKA HIGHWAY.

Al·cá·zar (al'kə zär', al kaz'ər), *n.* **1.** a Moorish palace in Seville, later used by Spanish kings. **2.** (*l.c.*) a castle or fortress of the Spanish Moors.

al·che·mist (al'kə mist), *n.* a person who is versed in or practices alchemy.

al·che·my (al'kə mē), *n.*, *pl.* **-mies.** **1.** a form of chemistry and speculative philosophy of the Middle Ages that attempted to discover an elixir of life and a method for transmuting base metals into gold. **2.** any seemingly magical process of transmuting ordinary materials into something of true merit.

al·co·hol (al'kə hôl', -hol'), *n.* **1.** Also called **ethyl alcohol, grain alcohol, ethanol.** a colorless, volatile, flammable liquid, C_2H_5OH, produced by yeast fermentation of carbohydrates or, synthetically, by hydration of ethylene: used chiefly as a solvent and in beverages and medicines. **2.** an intoxicating liquor containing this liquid. **3.** any of a class of chemical compounds having the general formula ROH, where R represents an alkyl group and –OH a hydroxyl group. [< New Latin < Medieval Latin < Arabic *al-kuḥl* the powdered antimony]

al·co·hol·ic (al'kə hô'lik, -hol'ik), *adj.* **1.** of or pertaining to alcohol. **2.** containing or using alcohol. **3.** caused by alcohol. **4.** suffering from alcoholism. **5.** preserved in alcohol. —*n.* **6.** a person suffering from alcoholism. —**al'co·hol'i·cal·ly,** *adv.*

Alcohol'ics Anon'ymous, *n.* an international fellowship of alcoholics whose purpose is to stay sober and help others recover from alcoholism. *Abbr.:* AA

al·co·hol·ism (al'kə hô liz'əm, -ho-), *n.* a chronic disorder characterized by dependence on alcohol, repeated excessive use of alcoholic beverages, and decreased ability to function socially and vocationally.

Al·cott (ôl'kət, -kot), *n.* **1. (Amos) Bronson,** 1799–1888, U.S. educator and philosopher. **2. Louisa May,** 1832–88, U.S. author.

al·cove (al'kōv), *n.* **1.** a recess or small room adjacent to or opening out of a room: *a dining alcove.* **2.** a recess in a room for a bed, bookcases, or the like. **3.** an arbor or bower.

Al·cuin (al'kwin), *n.* (*Ealhwine Flaccus*) A.D. 735–804, English theologian and scholar: teacher and adviser of Charlemagne.

Al·deb·a·ran (al deb'ər ən), *n.* a first-magnitude star, orange in color, in the constellation Taurus.

al·de·hyde (al'də hīd'), *n.* any of a class of organic compounds containing the group – CHO, which yields acids when oxidized and alcohols when reduced. —**al'de·hy'dic,** *adj.*

al den·te (al den'tā, -tē), *adj., adv.* (esp. of pasta) cooked but still firm to the bite.

al·der (ôl'dər), *n.* any shrub or tree belonging to the genus *Alnus,* of the birch family, growing in moist places in N temperate or colder regions and having toothed, simple leaves and flowers in catkins.

al·der·fly (ôl'dər flī'), *n.*, *pl.* **-flies.** any of several dark-colored neuropterous insects of the family Sialidae, the larvae of which are aquatic and predatory on other aquatic insects.

al·der·man (ôl'dər mən), *n.*, *pl.* **-men.** a member of a municipal legislative body, esp. of a municipal council.

al·dol (al'dôl, -dol), *n.* a colorless, syrupy, water-soluble liquid, $C_4H_8O_2$, used chiefly in the manufacture of rubber vulcanizers and accelerators, and in perfumery.

al·do·ster·on·ism (al'dō ster'ə niz'əm, al dos'tə rō-), *n.* an abnormality of the body's electrolyte balance, caused by excessive secretion of aldosterone by the adrenal cortex and characterized by hypertension, low serum potassium, and excessive urination.

Al·drich (ôl'drich), *n.* **Thomas Bailey,** 1836–1907, U.S. short-story writer, poet, and novelist.

Al·drin (ôl'drin), *n.* **Edwin Eugene, Jr.** ("*Buzz*"), born 1930, U.S. astronaut: second person to walk on the moon, 1969.

ale (āl), *n.* **1.** a malt beverage, darker, heavier, and more bitter than beer.

a·le·a·to·ry (ā'lē ə tôr'ē, -tōr'ē, al'ē-) also **a·le·a·tor·ic** (ā'lē ə tôr'ik, -tor'-, al'ē-), *adj.* **1.** *Law.* depending on an uncertain event: *an aleatory contract.* **2.** of or pertaining to luck or chance; unpredictable. **3.** *Music.* employing the element of chance in the choice of tones, rests, durations, rhythms, dynamics, etc.

ale·house (āl'hous'), *n.*, *pl.* **-hous·es** (-hou'ziz). a tavern where ale or beer is sold; bar; pub.

a·lem·bic (ə lem'bik), *n.* **1.** a vessel with a beaked cap or head, formerly used in distilling. **2.** anything that transforms, purifies, or refines.

a·lert (ə lûrt'), *adj.* **1.** fully aware and attentive; wide-awake. **2.** quick to understand or respond; perceptive; acute. **3.** watchful and ready to act; vigilant. —*n.* **4.** a warning of an impending military attack, a storm, etc. **5.** the period such a warning or alarm is in effect. **6.** a state of vigilance or readiness, as before an expected attack. —*v.t.* **7.** to warn to prepare for an attack. **8.** to warn of an impending raid, storm, etc. **9.** to cause to be on guard; warn: *to alert gardeners to the dangers of some pesticides.* —*Idiom.* **10. on the alert,** ready, as for danger; vigilant. [< Italian *all'erta* = *all(a)* to, on the + *erta* lookout] —**a·lert'ly,** *adv.* —**a·lert'ness,** *n.*

al·eu·rone (al'yə rōn', ə loor'ōn) also **al·eu·ron** (-ron', -on), *n.* the granulated protein that forms the outermost layer of grain. —**al'eu·ron'ic** (-ron'ik), *adj.*

Al·eut (ə loot', al'ē oot'), *n.*, *pl.* **Al·euts,** (*esp. collectively*) **Al·eut. 1.** a member of a people inhabiting the Aleutian Islands and the W Alaska Peninsula. **2.** the language of the Aleuts, akin to the Eskimo languages.

Aleu·tian Is·lands, *n.pl.* an archipelago extending SW from the Alaska Peninsula: part of Alaska.

ale·wife (āl′wīf′), *n., pl.* **-wives.** a North American fish, *Alosa pseudoharengus*, similar to a shad.

Al·ex·an·der¹ (al′ig zan′dər, -zän′-), *n.* **1.** ALEXANDER THE GREAT. **2. Cecil,** 1818–95, English hymn writer. **3. William,** 1726–83, general in the American Revolution.

Al·ex·an·der² (al′ig zan′dər, -zän′-), *n.* **1. Alexander I,** (*Aleksandr Pavlovich*) 1777–1825, czar of Russia 1801–25. **2. Alexander II,** (*Aleksandr Nikolaevich*) 1818–81, czar of Russia 1855–81. **3. Alexander III,** **a.** died 1181, Italian ecclesiastic: pope 1159–81. **b.** (*Aleksandr Aleksandrovich*) 1845–94, czar of Russia 1881–94. **4. Alexander VI,** (*Rodrigo Borgia*) 1431?–1503, Italian ecclesiastic: pope 1492–1503 (father of Cesare and Lucrezia Borgia).

Alexan′der the Great′, *n.* 356–323 B.C., king of Macedonia 336–323: conqueror of Greek city-states and of the Persian Empire from Asia Minor and Egypt to India.

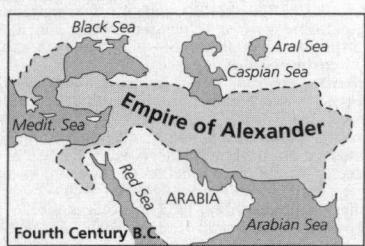

Al·ex·an·dri·a (al′ig zan′drē ə, -zän′-), *n.* **1.** a seaport in N Egypt, in the Nile delta: founded in 332 B.C. by Alexander the Great: ancient center of learning. 2,893,000. **2.** a city in NE Virginia, S of the District of Columbia. 112,879. **3.** a city in central Louisiana, on the Red River. 50,180.

Al·ex·an·dri·an (al′ig zan′drē ən, -zän′-), *adj.* **1.** of or pertaining to Alexandria, esp. Alexandria, Egypt. **2.** Hellenistic. **3.** of or pertaining to Alexander the Great or the period of his rule. —*n.* **4.** a native or resident of Alexandria, esp. Alexandria, Egypt.

al·ex·an·drine (al′ig zan′drin, -drēn, -zän′-), *n.* **1.** (*often cap.*) a line of poetry in iambic hexameter. —*adj.* **2.** (*often cap.*) of or pertaining to such a line.

al·ex·an·drite (al′ig zan′drīt, -zän′-), *n.* a variety of chrysoberyl, green by daylight and red-violet by artificial light, used as a gem.

a·lex·i·a (ə lek′sē ə), *n.* a neurologic disorder marked by loss of the ability to understand written or printed language, usu. resulting from a brain lesion or a congenital defect.

al·fal·fa (al fal′fə), *n., pl.* **-fas.** a plant, *Medicago sativa*, of the legume family, usu. having bluish purple flowers, originating in the Near East and widely cultivated as a forage crop.

alfal′fa wee′vil, *n.* a European weevil, *Hypera postica*, now an important pest of alfalfa in North America.

Al·fon·so (al fon′sō, -zō), *n.* **1. Alfonso I,** (*Alfonso Henriques*) 1109?–85, first king of Portugal 1139–85. **2. Alfonso XIII,** 1886–1941, king of Spain 1886–1930.

al·for·ja (al fôr′hä), *n., pl.* **-jas.** *Southwestern U.S.* a saddlebag, esp. a leather one.

al·fres·co or **al fres·co** (al fres′kō), *adv.* **1.** out-of-doors; in the open air: *to dine alfresco.* —*adj.* **2.** outdoor: *an alfresco café.*

al·gae (al′jē), *n.pl., sing.* **-ga** (-gə). any of numerous groups of eukaryotic one-celled or colonial organisms that contain chlorophyll, usu. flourishing in aquatic or damp environments and lacking true roots, stems, or leaves: includes seaweeds, pond scum, and many plankton.

al·gar·ro·ba or **al·ga·ro·ba** (al′gə rō′bə), *n., pl.* **-bas.** **1.** any of certain mesquites, esp. *Prosopis juliflora*, having pinnate leaves and yellowish flowers. **2.** the beanlike pod of this plant. **3.** the carob tree or fruit.

al·ge·bra (al′jə brə), *n.* **1.** the branch of mathematics that deals with general statements of relations, utilizing letters and other symbols to represent specific sets of numbers, values, vectors, etc., in the description of such relations. **2.** any special system of notation adapted to the study of a special system of relationship: *algebra of classes.* [< Medieval Latin < Arabic *al-jabr* lit., restoration] —**al′ge·bra′ist** (-brā′ist), *n.*

al·ge·bra·ic (al′jə brā′ik) also **al′ge·bra′i·cal,** *adj.* **1.** of, occurring in, or utilizing algebra. **2.** (of an equation) in the form of a polynomial with only a finite number of terms and equated to zero. **3.** using arbitrary letters or symbols in place of the letters, symbols, or numbers of an actual application. —**al′ge·bra′i·cal·ly,** *adv.*

al′gebra′ic num′ber, *n.* **1.** a root of an algebraic equation with integral coefficients. **2.** ROOT¹ (def. 9b).

Al·ger (al′jər), *n.* **Horatio, Jr.,** 1834–99, U.S. novelist: author of a series of books for boys emphasizing the achievement of success through industry and perseverance.

Al·ge·ri·a (al jēr′ē ə), *n.* a republic in NW Africa: gained independence from France 1962. 29,830,370; 919,352 sq. mi. (2,381,122 sq. km). *Cap.:* Algiers. —**Al·ge′ri·an,** *adj., n.*

-algia or **-algy,** a combining form meaning "pain" of the kind or in the body part or organ specified by the initial element: *causalgia; neuralgia.*

al·gi·cide (al′jə sīd′), *n.* a substance or preparation for killing algae. —**al′gi·cid′al,** *adj.*

al·gid (al′jid), *adj.* cold; chilly. —**al·gid′i·ty, al′gid·ness,** *n.*

Al·giers (al jērz′), *n.* **1.** the capital of Algeria, in the N part. 1,839,000. **2.** one of the former Barbary States: now Algeria.

al·gin (al′jin), *n.* any hydrophilic colloidal substance found in kelp, as alginic acid or one of its soluble salts.

al·gin′ic ac′id (al jin′ik), *n.* an insoluble colloidal acid, $(C_6H_8O_6)_n$, found in the cell walls of various kelps: used as a thickener or stabilizer, esp. in ice cream, and for sizing paper.

algo-, a combining form meaning "pain": *algometer.*

al·gol·o·gy (al gol′ə jē), *n.* the study of algae. Also called **phycology.** —**al′go·log′i·cal** (-gə loj′i kəl), *adj.* —**al·gol′o·gist,** *n.*

al·gom·e·ter (al gom′i tər), *n.* a device for determining sensitiveness to pain caused by pressure. —**al′go·met′ric** (al′gə me′trik), **al′go·met′ri·cal,** *adj.* —**al′go·met′ri·cal·ly,** *adv.* —**al·gom′e·try,** *n.*

Al·gon·qui·an (al gong′kē ən, -kwē ən) also **Al·gon·ki·an** (-kē ən), *n.* **1.** a family of American Indian languages spoken by nearly all the peoples of NE North America except the Iroquoians, in an area from Labrador S to North Carolina and W to Saskatchewan and the Mississippi River, and by several Plains Indian peoples, as the Arapaho, Cheyenne, and Blackfoot. **2.** a member of an Algonquian-speaking people.

al·go·rism (al′gə riz′əm), *n.* the Arabic system of arithmetical notation (with the figures 1, 2, 3, etc.). —**al′go·ris′mic,** *adj.*

al·go·rithm (al′gə rith′əm), *n.* **1.** a set of rules for solving a problem in a finite number of steps, as for finding the greatest common divisor. **2.** a sequence of steps designed for programming a computer to solve a specific problem. —**al′go·rith′mic,** *adj.*

al·gum (al′gəm, ôl′-), *n.* a Biblical tree, possibly the red sandalwood. II Chron. 2:8. Compare ALMUG.

-algy, var. of -ALGIA: *coxalgy.*

Al·ham·bra (al ham′brə), *n.* **1.** a palace and citadel of the Moorish kings in Granada, Spain: completed in the 14th century. **2.** a city in SW California, near Los Angeles. 64,615.

A·li (ä′lē, ä lē′ *for 1*; ä lē′ *for 2*), *n.* **1.** ('Alī ibn-abu-Talib), A.D. c600-61, fourth caliph of Islam 656-661 (cousin and son-in-law of Muhammad): considered the first caliph by Shi'ites. **2. Muhammad** (*Cassius Marcellus Clay, Jr.*), born 1942, U.S. boxer.

a·li·as (ā′lē əs), *n., pl.* **-as·es,** *adv.* —*n.* **1.** a false name used to conceal one's identity; an assumed name. —*adv.* **2.** at another time; in another place; in other circumstances; otherwise. "Simpson *alias* Smith" means that Simpson in other circumstances has called himself Smith.

al·i·bi (al′ə bī′), *n., pl.* **-bis,** *v.,* **-bied** (-bīd′), **-bi·ing.** —*n.* **1.** *Law.* the defense by an accused person of having been elsewhere when an offense was committed. **2.** an excuse, esp. to avoid blame. **3.** a person used as one's excuse. —*v.i.* **4.** to give an excuse; offer a defense. —*v.t.* **5. a.** to provide an alibi for (someone). **b.** to make or find (one's way) by using alibis.

Al′ice blue′, *n.* a pale grayish-blue color. [named after *Alice* Longworth (daughter of Theodore Roosevelt)]

Al′ice's Adven′tures in Won′derland, a story for children (1865) by Lewis Carroll. Also called **Al′ice in Won′derland.**

al·i·cy·clic (al′ə sī′klik, -sik′lik), *adj.* of or noting organic compounds having both aliphatic and cyclic properties.

al·i·dade (al′i dād′), *n.* **1.** a straightedge with a telescopic sight, used on a plane table for topographic surveying. **2.** the entire upper part of a theodolite or transit.

al·ien (āl′yən, ā′lē ən), *n.* **1.** a foreign-born resident who has not been naturalized and who owes allegiance to another country. **2.** a foreigner. **3.** a person who has been estranged or excluded. **4.** an extraterrestrial. —*adj.* **5.** owing allegiance to another country; not naturalized. **6.** belonging or relating to aliens. **7.** unlike one's own; strange. **8.** opposed; hostile (usu. fol. by *to* or *from*): *ideas alien to modern thinking.* **9.** extraterrestrial.

al·ien·a·ble (āl′yə nə bəl, ā′lē ə-), *adj. Law.* capable of being sold or transferred. —**al′ien·a·bil′i·ty,** *n.*

al·ien·age (āl′yə nij, ā′lē ə-), *n.* **1.** the state of being an alien. **2.** the legal status of an alien.

Al′ien and Sedi′tion Acts′, *n.pl.* four laws enacted by the U.S. Congress in 1798 that lengthened the residency requirement for citizenship and decreed penalties against critics of the government.

al·ien·ate (āl′yə nāt′, ā′lē ə-), *v.t.,* **-at·ed, -at·ing.** **1.** to turn away the affection of; make indifferent or hostile: *He has alienated most of his friends.* **2.** to transfer or divert: *to alienate funds from their intended purpose.* **3.** *Law.* to convey (title, property, etc.) to another: *to alienate lands.* —**al′ien·a′tor,** *n.*

al·ien·a·tion (āl′yə nā′shən, ā′lē ə-), *n.* **1.** the act of alienating; the state of being alienated. **2.** *Law.* a transfer of the title to property by one person to another; conveyance. **3.** the state of being withdrawn from the objective world, as through indifference.

al·ien·ee (āl′yə nē′, ā′lē ə-), *n. Law.* a person to whom property is alienated.

al′ien hand′ syn′drome, *n.* a neurological disorder in which the movements of the left and right hands are not coordinated.

al·ien·or (āl′yə nər, ā′lē ə-, āl′yə nôr′, ā′lē ə-) also **al·ien·er** (āl′yə-nər, ā′lē ə-), *n. Law.* a person who transfers property.

a·light¹ (ə līt′), *v.i.,* **a·light·ed** or **a·lit, a·light·ing. 1.** to dismount from a horse, descend from a vehicle, etc. **2.** to settle or stay after descending; come to rest: *The bird alighted on the sill.*

a·light² (ə līt′), *adv., adj.* **1.** provided with light. **2.** on fire; burning.

a·lign (ə līn′), *v.t.* **1.** to arrange in a straight line; adjust according to a line. **2.** to bring into a line or alignment. **3.** to bring into agreement with a particular group, cause, etc.: *He aligned himself with the liberals in the Senate.* **4.** to adjust (circuit components) to improve response over a frequency band. —*v.i.* **5.** to come into line; be in line. **6.** to join with others in a cause.

a·lign·ment (ə līn′mənt), *n.* **1.** an adjustment to a line; arrangement in a straight line. **2.** the line or lines so formed. **3.** the proper adjustment of the components of an electronic circuit, machine, etc., for coordinated functioning: *rear-wheel alignment.* **4.** a state of agreement or cooperation among persons, groups, nations, etc.: *an alignment of political parties.* **5.** a ground plan of a railroad or highway.

a·like (ə līk′), *adv.* **1.** in the same manner; similarly: *to treat all customers alike.* **2.** to the same degree; equally: *All three were guilty alike.* —*adj.* **3.** similar or comparable: *Not all twins are alike.*

al·i·ment (*n.* al′ə mənt; *v.* al′ə ment′), *n.* **1.** that which nourishes; nutriment; food. **2.** that which sustains; means of support. —*v.t.* **3.** to nourish or sustain; support.

al·i·men·ta·ry (al′ə men′tə rē), *adj.* **1.** concerned with the function of nutrition; nutritive. **2.** pertaining to food. **3.** providing sustenance or maintenance.

alimen′tary canal′, *n.* a tubular passage functioning in the digestion and absorption of food and the elimination of food residue, beginning at the mouth and terminating at the anus.

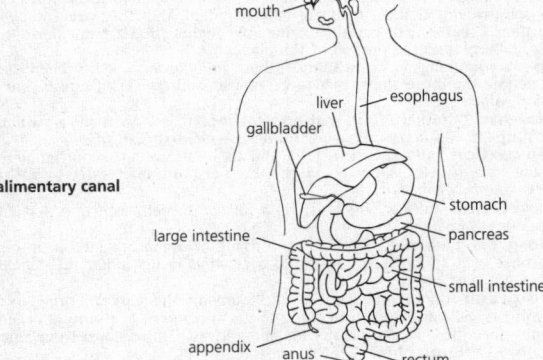

alimentary canal

(labels: mouth, liver, esophagus, gallbladder, stomach, pancreas, large intestine, small intestine, appendix, anus, rectum)

al·i·men·ta·tion (al′ə men tā′shən), *n.* **1.** nourishment; nutrition. **2.** sustenance; support.

al·i·mo·ny (al′ə mō′nē), *n.* **1.** *Law.* a periodic allowance ordered to be paid to a spouse or former spouse for maintenance following a divorce or legal separation or while such action is pending. **2.** supply of the means of living; maintenance.

al·i·phat·ic (al′ə fat′ik), *adj.* pertaining to nonaromatic hydrocarbon compounds in which the constituent carbon atoms form open chains.

al·i·quot (al′i kwət), *adj.* **1.** forming an exact proper divisor: *An aliquot part of 15 is 5.* **2.** comprising a known fraction of a whole and constituting a sample for chemical analysis.

a·live (ə līv′), *adj.* **1.** living; existing; not dead or lifeless. **2.** living (used for emphasis): *the proudest person alive.* **3.** in force or operation; active: *to keep hope alive.* **4.** full of energy and spirit; lively. **5.** having the quality of life; vivid; vibrant: *The room was alive with color.* —*Idiom.* **6.** alive to, alert or sensitive to; aware of. **7.** alive with, filled with; swarming with. —**a·live′ness,** *n.*

a·li·yah (ä′lē ä′; *for 2 usu.* ə lē′ə), *n., pl.* **a·li·yahs, a·li·yot** (ä′lē ōt′). **1.** the immigration of Jews to Israel. **2.** the honor of being called to the reading table in a synagogue to recite the blessings over the Torah.

al·ka·li (al′kə lī′), *n., pl.* **-lis, -lies,** *adj.* **—n. 1.** any of various bases, the hydroxides of the alkali metals and of ammonium, that neutralize acids to form salts and turn red litmus paper blue. **b.** any of various other active bases, as calcium hydroxide. **2.** a soluble mineral salt or a mixture of soluble salts, present in some soils, esp. in arid regions, and detrimental to the growing of most crops. —*adj.* **3.** ALKALINE.

al·kal·ic (al kal′ik), *adj.* (of igneous rock) containing a relatively high percentage of sodium and potassium alkali.

al′kali met′al, *n.* any of the group of univalent metals including potassium, sodium, lithium, rubidium, cesium, and francium, whose hydroxides are alkalis.

al·ka·line (al′kə līn′, -lin), *adj.* of, containing, or like an alkali, esp. in having a pH greater than 7. Compare ACID (def. 5c) —**al′ka·lin′i·ty** (-lin′i-), *n.*

al′kaline earth′, *n.* any of the oxides of barium, radium, strontium, calcium, and, sometimes, magnesium.

al·ka·lize (al′kə līz′) *v.t., v.i.,* **-lized** also **-lin·ized, -liz·ing** also **-lin·iz·ing.** to make or become alkaline. —**al′ka·liz′a·ble,** *adj.* —**al′ka·li·za′tion,** *n.* —**al′ka·liz′er,** *n.*

al·ka·loid (al′kə loid′), *n.* **1.** any of a large class of bitter-tasting, nitrogen-containing, alkaline ring compounds common in plants and including caffeine, morphine, nicotine, quinine, and strychnine. —*adj.* **2.** resembling an alkali; alkaline. —**al′ka·loi′dal,** *adj.*

al·kane (al′kān), *n.* any member of the homologous series of saturated, aliphatic hydrocarbons having a single covalent bond and the general formula C_nH_{2n+2}, as methane or ethane. Also called **paraffin.**

al·kene (al′kēn), *n.* any member of the homologous series of unsaturated, aliphatic hydrocarbons having at least one double bond and the general formula C_nH_{2n}, as ethylene.

al·kyd (al′kid), *n.* any of a group of sticky resins derived from dicarboxylic acids: used in adhesives and paints.

al·kyl (al′kəl), *n.* any of a series of univalent groups having the general formula C_nH_{2n+1}, as methyl or ethyl.

al·kyne (al′kīn), *n.* any member of the homologous series of unsaturated, aliphatic hydrocarbons having at least one triple bond and the general formula C_nH_{2n-2}, as acetylene.

all (ôl), *adj.* **1.** the whole or full amount of: *all the cake; all year.* **2.** the whole number of: *all students; all kinds.* **3.** the greatest possible: *with all speed.* **4.** any; any whatever: *beyond all doubt.* **5.** entirely; purely: *The coat is all wool.* **6.** dominated by a particular feature: *The colt was all legs.* **7.** *Pennsylvania German Area.* consumed; finished: *The pie is all.* —*pron.* **8.** the whole quantity or amount: *Did you eat all of the peanuts?* **9.** the whole number; every one: *all of us.* **10.** everything: *Is that all you've got to say?* **11.** one's whole interest, energy, or property: *Give it your all.* **12.** the entire area, place, environment, or the like: *all is calm, all is bright.* —*adv.* **13.** wholly; entirely; completely: *all alone.* **14.** each; apiece: *The score was one all.* —*Idiom.* **15.** all but, almost; very nearly: *These batteries are all but dead.* **16.** all in, very tired; exhausted. **17.** all in all, everything considered; in general: *All in all, her health is greatly improved.* **18.** all out, energetically and enthusiastically: *to go all out to win the game.* **19.** all the better, more advantageous; so much the better. **20.** all there, mentally competent. **21.** all things to all men, having appeal for all people. I Cor. 9:22. **22.** all up, *Informal.* with no vestige of hope remaining. **23.** and all, and so forth: *What with the late hour and all, we must leave.* **24.** at all, **a.** in the slightest degree. **b.** for any reason: *Why bother at all?* **c.** in any way: *no offense at all.* **25.** for all (that), in spite of (that); notwithstanding: *For all that, it was a good year.* **26.** in all, all included; all together. **27.** as all get-out, *Informal.* to an extreme degree, condition, etc.: *happy as all get-out; skinny as all get-out.* —*Proverb.* **28.** All that glitters is not gold, appearances can be deceiving. —*Usage.* Expressions like *all the farther* and *all the higher* occur chiefly in informal speech: *This is all the farther the bus goes. That's all the higher she can jump.* Elsewhere *as far as* and *as high as* are generally used: *as far as the bus goes; as high as she can jump.* The construction *all* (of *all of the students; all of the contracts*) is entirely standard. Some speakers object to it, however, and omit the *of.* See also already, ALRIGHT, ALTOGETHER.

Al·lah (al′ə, ä′lə), *n. Islam.* the Supreme Being; God.

all′-Amer′ican, *adj.* **1.** selected as the best in the United States, as in a sport: *the all-American college football team of 1990.* **2.** representing the entire United States. **3.** composed exclusively of American members or elements. —*n.* **4.** an all-American player or team.

al·lan·to·in (ə lan′tō in), *n.* a white powder, $C_4H_6N_4O_3$, produced by oxidation of uric acid: used as an emollient.

al·lan·to·is (ə lan′tō is, -tois), *n., pl.* **al·lan·to·i·des** (al′ən tō′i dēz′). a nourishing membrane surrounding the embryo, between the amnion and chorion, in birds and reptiles developing as a sac from the hindgut and in mammals developing as an inner layer of the placenta. —**al′lan·to′ic,** *adj.*

all′-around′ or **all-round,** *adj.* **1.** able to do many things; versatile: *an all-around athlete.* **2.** broadly applicable; not specialized: *an all-around education.* **3.** being so in all matters; complete: *an all-around failure.*

al·lay (ə lā′), *v.t.* **1.** to put (fear, doubt, etc.) to rest; calm. **2.** to lessen or relieve; mitigate; alleviate: *to allay pain.*

all′ clear′, *n.* the signal that an air raid or other danger is over.

al·le·ga·tion (al′i gā′shən), *n.* **1.** the act of alleging; an affirmation or assertion. **2.** an assertion made by a party in a legal proceeding, which the party then undertakes to prove. **3.** an assertion made with little or no proof.

al·lege (ə lej′), *v.t.,* **-leged, -leg·ing. 1.** to assert without proof. **2.** to declare with positiveness; affirm; assert. **3.** to declare before a court or elsewhere as if under oath. **4.** to offer as a reason or excuse. —**al·lege′a·ble,** *adj.* —**al·leg′er,** *n.*

al·leged (ə lejd′, ə lej′id), *adj.* **1.** declared or stated to be as described; asserted: *an alleged murderer.* **2.** doubtful; suspect; supposed: *an alleged cure.* —**al·leg′ed·ly,** *adv.*

Al′leghe′ny spurge′, *n.* a low, shrubby evergreen plant, *Pachysandra procumbens,* of the family Buxaceae, native to the southeastern U.S., and having spikes of white or purplish flowers.

al·le·giance (ə lē′jəns), *n.* **1.** the loyalty of citizens to their government or of subjects to their sovereign. **2.** loyalty or devotion to some person, group, cause, or the like.

al·le·gor·i·cal (al′i gôr′i kəl, -gor′-) also **al′le·gor′ic,** *adj.* of the nature of or containing allegory; figurative: *an allegorical poem.* —**al′le·gor′i·cal·ly,** *adv.* —**al′le·gor′i·cal·ness,** *n.*

al·le·go·ry (al′ə gôr′ē, -gōr′ē), *n., pl.* **-ries. 1.** the representation of spiritual, moral, or other abstract meanings through the actions of fictional characters that serve as symbols. **2.** an allegorical or figurative narrative, poem, or the like: *the allegory of* Piers Plowman. **3.** EMBLEM (def. 3). —**al′le·go·rize′,** *v.t., v.i.,* **-rized, -riz·ing.**

al·le·gret·to (al′i gret′ō), *adj., adv., n., pl.* **-tos.** *Music.* —*adj., adv.* **1.** light, graceful, and moderately fast in tempo. —*n.* **2.** an allegretto movement.

al·le·gro (ə lā′grō, ə leg′rō), *adj., adv., n., pl.* **-gros.** *Music.* —*adj., adv.* **1.** brisk or rapid in tempo. —*n.* **2.** an allegro movement.

al·lele (ə lēl′), *n.* one of two or more alternative forms of a gene occupying the same position on matching chromosomes: an individual normally has two alleles for each trait, one from either parent. —**al·lel·ic** (ə lē′lik, ə lel′ik), *adj.* —**al·lel′ism,** *n.*

al·le·lop·a·thy (ə lē lop′ə thē, al′ə lop′-), *n.* suppression of growth of a plant by a toxin released from a nearby plant. —**al·le·lo·path·ic** (ə lē′lə path′ik, ə lel′ə-), *adj.*

al·le·lu·ia (al′ə loo′yə), *interj., n., pl.* **-ias.** —*interj.* **1.** HALLELUJAH. —*n.* **2.** a song of praise to God.

al·le·mande (al′ə mand′, -mänd′), *n.* **1.** a 17th- and 18th-century dance in slow duple time. **2.** a piece of music based on its rhythm, often following the prelude in the classical suite. **3.** a figure performed in a quadrille. **4.** a German folk dance in triple meter.

all′-embrac′ing, *adj.* applying to all or everything; all-inclusive: *an all-embracing philosophy.*

Al·len (al′ən), *n.* **1. Ethan,** 1738–89, American soldier in the Revolutionary War: leader of the "Green Mountain Boys" of Vermont. **2. Fred** (*John Florence Sullivan*), 1894–1956, U.S. comedian. **3. Frederick Lewis,** 1890–1954, U.S. historian and editor. **4. Gracie** (*Grace Ethel Cecile Rosalie Allen*), 1905–64, U.S. comedian (partner and wife of George Burns). **5. Richard,** 1760–1831, U.S. clergyman: a founder of the African Methodist Episcopal Church. **6. Woody** (*Allen Stewart Konigsberg*), born 1935, U.S. comedian, author, actor, and filmmaker.

Al′len screw′, *n.* a screw turned by means of an axial hexagonal hole in its head.

Al·len·town (al′ən toun′), *n.* a city in E Pennsylvania. 105,339.

Al′len wrench′, *n.* a wrench for Allen screws, formed from a piece of hexagonal bar stock bent to a right angle.

al·ler·gen (al′ər jən, -jen′), *n.* any substance that induces an allergic reaction in a particular individual. —**al′ler·gen′ic,** *adj.*

al·ler·gic (ə lûr′jik), *adj.* **1.** of or pertaining to allergy: *an allergic reaction to wool.* **2.** having an allergy. **3.** *Informal.* having a strong dislike or aversion: *to be allergic to modern art.*

aller′gic rhini′tis, *n.* a condition characterized by head congestion, sneezing, tearing, and swelling of the nasal mucous membranes, caused by an allergic reaction. Compare HAY FEVER.

al·ler·gist (al′ər jist), *n.* a physician specializing in the diagnosis and treatment of allergies.

al·ler·gy (al′ər jē), *n., pl.* **-gies. 1.** an overreaction of the immune system to a previously encountered, ordinarily harmless substance, resulting in skin rash, swelling of mucous membranes, sneezing or wheezing, or other abnormal conditions. **2.** *Informal.* a strong dislike or aversion: *an allergy to hard work.*

al·le·vi·ate (ə lē′vē āt′), *v.t.,* **-at·ed, -at·ing.** to make easier to endure; lessen; mitigate: *to alleviate pain.* —**al·le′vi·ant,** *n., adj.* —**al·le′vi·a′tion,** *n.* —**al·le′vi·a′tive, al·le′vi·a·to·ry** (-tôr′ē, -tōr′ē), *adj.* —**al·le′vi·a′tor,** *n.*

al·ley[1] (al′ē), *n., pl.* **-leys. 1.** a passage, as behind a row of houses, permitting access from the street to backyards, garages, etc. **2.** a narrow back street. **3.** a walk, as in a garden, enclosed with hedges or shrubbery. **4.** *Bowling.* **a.** a long, narrow, wooden lane or floor along which the ball is rolled. **b.** (*often pl.*) a building for bowling. —*Idiom.* **5.** (**right**) **up** or **down one's alley,** highly compatible with one's interests or abilities.

al·ley[2] (al′ē), *n., pl.* **-leys.** *Northeastern U.S.* **1.** a large and choice playing marble. **2.** any playing marble.

al′ley cat′, *n.* a shorthaired domestic cat, esp. of unknown parentage.

all′-fired′, *adj., superl.* **-fired·est,** *adv. Informal.* —*adj.* **1.** extreme; excessive: *He had the all-fired gall to quit in the middle of the job.* —*adv.* **2.** extremely; excessively: *Don't be so all-fired sure of yourself.*

All′ Fools′ Day′, *n.* APRIL FOOLS′ DAY.

all′ fours′, *n.* **1.** all four limbs or extremities; the four feet of an animal or both hands and both feet of a person: *to walk or land on all fours.* **2.** (*used with a sing. v.*) Also called **pitch, seven-up.** a card game for two or three players or two partnerships in which special cards have scoring values, as the highest or lowest trump.

All·hal·lows (ôl′hal′ōz), *n.* ALL SAINTS′ DAY.

al·li·a·ceous (al′ē ā′shəs), *adj.* **1.** *Bot.* of or belonging to the genus *Allium.* Compare ALLIUM. **2.** having the odor or taste of garlic, onion, etc.

al·li·ance (ə lī′əns), *n.* **1.** the act of allying, or the state of being allied. **2.** a formal agreement or treaty between two or more nations to cooper-

ate for specific purposes. **3.** a merging of efforts or interests: *an alliance between church and state.* **4.** the persons or entities so allied. **5.** marriage or the family relationship created by marriage. **6.** close relationship or correspondence; affinity: *the alliance between logic and metaphysics.*

Alli′ance for Prog′ress, *n.* a program of foreign policy toward Latin America under the administration of John F. Kennedy, emphasizing democratic reform and economic development.

al·lied (ə līd′, al′īd), *adj.* **1.** joined by treaty, agreement, or common cause: *allied nations.* **2.** related; kindred: *allied species.* **3.** (*cap.*) of or pertaining to the Allies.

al·lies (al′īz, ə līz′), *n.* **1.** pl. of ALLY. **2.** (*cap.*) (in World War I) the nations that fought against the Central Powers: Great Britain, France, Russia, and the nations later allied with them, as Japan, Italy, and, loosely, the U.S. **3.** (*cap.*) (in World War II) the nations that fought against the Axis: Great Britain, the U.S., the Soviet Union, and others.

al·li·ga·tor (al′i gā′tər), *n.* either of two crocodilians of the genus *Alligator,* of the southeastern U.S. and E China, characterized by a broad snout. [< Spanish *el lagarto* the lizard < Latin *lacertus* lizard]

all′-impor′tant, *adj.* vitally important; essential.

all′-inclu′sive, *adj.* including everything; comprehensive.

al·lit·er·a·tion (ə lit′ə rā′shən), *n.* **1.** repetition of the same sound, as a consonant or cluster, at the beginning of two or more stressed syllables, as in *from stem to stern.* Compare CONSONANCE (def. 4a). **2.** the commencement of two or more words of a word group with the same letter, as in *apt alliteration's artful aid.* —**al·lit′er·ate′,** *v.i., v.t.,* **-at·ed, -at·ing.** —**al·lit′er·a′tive** (-ə rā′tiv, -ər ə tiv), *adj.*

al·li·um (al′ē əm), *n.* any bulbous plant of the genus *Allium,* of the amaryllis family, having an onion odor and flowers in a round cluster, including the onion, leek, shallot, garlic, and chive.

All′ men′ are creat′ed e′qual, a statement by Thomas Jefferson in the *Declaration of Independence* (1776) holding that human beings possess fundamental, equal rights from the start. "We hold these truths to be self-evident, that all men are created equal, that they are endowed by their Creator with certain unalienable Rights, that among these are Life, Liberty, and the pursuit of Happiness."

allo-, a combining form meaning "other" (*allopatric*); used in chemistry to denote the more stable of two geometric isomers. Also, *esp. before a vowel,* **all-.**

al·lo·cate (al′ə kāt′), *v.t.,* **-cat·ed, -cat·ing.** to set apart for a particular purpose: *to allocate space for storage.* —**al′lo·ca′tor,** *n.*

al·lo·ca·tion (al′ə kā′shən), *n.* **1.** the act of allocating; apportionment. **2.** the state of being allocated. **3.** the share or portion allocated. —**al′lo·ca′tive,** *adj.*

al·lo·cu·tion (al′ə kyoo′shən), *n.* a formal speech, esp. one that advises or exhorts.

al·lo·graft (al′ə graft′, -gräft′), *n.* a tissue or organ obtained from one member of a species and grafted to a genetically dissimilar member of the same species.

al·lo·graph (al′ə graf′, -gräf′), *n.* **1.** any of the variant forms of a grapheme, as *t* and *T* or *n* in *run* and *nn* in *runner.* **2.** a writing or signature inscribed by one person for another, as distinguished from autograph. —**al′lo·graph′ic** (-graf′ik), *adj.*

al·lom·e·try (ə lom′i trē) also **al·loi·om·e·try** (al′oi om′-), *n.* **1.** growth of a part of an organism in relation to the growth of the whole organism or some other part of it. **2.** the measurement or study of this growth. —**al·lo·met·ric** (al′ə me′trik), *adj.*

al·lo·morph (al′ə môrf′), *n.* **1.** any of two or more different forms of the same chemical compound. **2.** one of the alternate forms of a morpheme, as the plural form *-en* in *oxen,* the *-es* in *stitches,* and the vowel in *men.* —**al′lo·mor·phism,** *n.*

al·longe (ə lunj′; *Fr.* A lônzh′), *n., pl.* **al·long·es** (ə lun′jiz; *Fr.* A-lônzh′). *Law.* an addition to a negotiable instrument; rider.

al·lo·nym (al′ə nim), *n.* **1.** the name of another person taken by an author as a pen name. Compare PSEUDONYM. **2.** a work published under a name that is not that of the author. —**al·lon·y·mous** (ə lon′ə məs), *adj.*

al·lop·a·thy (ə lop′ə thē), *n.* the method of treating disease by the use of agents that produce effects different from those of the disease treated (opposed to *homeopathy*). —**al·lo·path·ic** (al′ə path′ik), *adj.* —**al′lo·path′i·cal·ly,** *adv.*

al·lo·phone (al′ə fōn′), *n.* **1.** a speech sound constituting one of the phonetic manifestations or variants of a phoneme, depending on its environment, as any of the *t*-sounds of *top, stop, tree, cat, button, metal,* or *city.* **2.** *Canadian.* a person whose native language is neither English nor French. —**al′lo·phon′ic** (-fon′ik), *adj.*

all′-or-none′, *adj.* **1.** of or pertaining to a process by which a muscle or nerve fiber either responds to a stimulus completely or not at all. **2.** ALL-OR-NOTHING.

all′-or-noth′ing, *adj.* not allowing qualification or compromise; either fully accepted or not at all: *an all-or-nothing approach.*

al·lo·saur (al′ə sôr′), *n.* any carnivorous theropod dinosaur of the genus *Antrodemus* (formerly *Allosaurus*), from the late Jurassic Period of North America.

al·lot (ə lot′), *v.t.,* **-lot·ted, -lot·ting. 1.** to assign as a portion; set apart: *to allot three weeks for vacation.* **2.** to appropriate for a special purpose: *to allot money for a park.* **3.** to divide or distribute by share or portion; apportion: *to allot the farmland among the heirs.* —**al•lot′ment,** *n.*

al•lot•tee (ə lot ē′), *n.* one to whom something is allotted.

all′-out′, *adj.* using all one's resources; complete.

all•ov•er (ôl′ō′vər), *adj.* **1.** repeated over the entire surface, as a decorative pattern. —*n.* **2.** a fabric with an allover pattern.

al•low (ə lou′), *v.t.* **1.** to give permission to or for; permit: *to allow a student to be absent; No smoking allowed.* **2.** to let have; give as one's share: *to allow a person $100 for expenses.* **3.** to permit by neglect or oversight: *to allow a door to remain open.* **4.** to admit; acknowledge; concede: *I had to allow that he was right.* **5.** to approve, as for payment: *to allow a claim.* **6.** to assign or allocate; set apart: *to allow an hour for changing trains.* **7.** *Older Use.* to say; think. —*v.i.* **8.** to permit or grant; admit (often fol. by *of*): *to spend more than one's budget allows; a premise that allows of only one conclusion.* **9. allow for,** to make provision for: *to allow for breakage.* —**al•low′a•ble,** *adj.*

al•low•ance (ə lou′əns), *n., v.,* **-anced, -anc•ing.** —*n.* **1.** the act of allowing. **2.** an amount or share allotted or granted: *a dietary allowance of 900 calories a day.* **3.** a sum of money allotted for a particular purpose: *an allowance of $200 for travel.* **4.** a sum of money allotted on a regular basis, as for personal or living expenses: *Each child got an allowance of $10 a week.* **5.** an additional sum allotted for specific circumstances: *an allowance for depreciation.* **6.** acknowledgment; concession. **7.** sanction or tolerance: *the allowance of slavery.* —*v.t.* **8.** to place on a fixed allowance, as of food or drink. **9.** to allocate (supplies, rations, etc.) in fixed or regular amounts. —***Idiom.*** **10. make allowance(s) for, a.** to excuse, taking mitigating factors into consideration. **b.** to allow for. **c.** to reserve time, money, etc., for.

al•loy (*n.* al′oi, ə loi′; *v.* ə loi′), *n.* **1.** a substance composed of two or more metals, or of a metal or metals with a nonmetal, intimately mixed, as by fusion. **2.** a less costly metal mixed with a more valuable one. **3.** standard; quality; fineness. **4.** admixture, as of good with evil. **5.** anything added that serves to reduce quality or purity. —*v.t.* **6.** to mix (metals or metal with nonmetal) so as to form an alloy. **7.** to reduce or debase by admixture; adulterate.

All′ Peo′ple That on Earth′ Do Dwell′, a Christian hymn (1561) with words by William Kethe: based on Psalm 100.

all′-points′ bul′letin, *n.* a broadcast alert from one police station to all others in an area, state, etc., as with instructions to arrest a particular suspect or suspects. *Abbr.:* APB

all′ right′, *adv.* **1.** yes; very well: *All right, I'll go with you.* **2.** (used as an interrogative) do you agree?: *We'll meet tomorrow, all right?* **3.** satisfactorily: *Her work is coming along all right.* **4.** without fail; certainly: *You'll hear about this, all right!* —*adj.* **5.** safe; sound: *Are you all right?* **6.** acceptable; passable: *His performance was all right.* **7.** reliable; good: *That fellow is all right.* —**Usage.** See ALRIGHT.

all′-right′, *adj.* very good; excellent: *an all-right guy.*

All′ Saints′′ Day′, *n.* a church festival celebrated Nov. 1 in honor of all the saints; Allhallows.

all′ sorts′ and condi′tions of men′, *n.pl.* everyone: a phrase in the *Book of Common Prayer.*

All′ Souls′′ Day′, *n.* a day of solemn prayer for all dead persons, usu. on Nov. 2.

all•spice (ôl′spīs′), *n.* **1.** the dried unripe berries of an aromatic tropical American tree, *Pimenta dioica,* of the myrtle family: used as a spice. **2.** the tree itself.

all′-star′, *adj.* **1.** consisting of athletes chosen as the best at their positions from all teams in a league or region: *an all-star team.* **2.** consisting entirely of star performers: *an all-star cast.* —*n.* **3.** a player selected for an all-star team.

all′-terrain′ ve′hicle, *n.* a vehicle with treads, wheels, or both, for traversing uneven terrain as well as roads. *Abbr.:* ATV

All′ the King's′ Men′, a novel (1946) by Robert Penn Warren.

All′ the News′ That's Fit′ to Print′, a slogan (1896) adopted by publisher Alfred Ochs for use on the front page of *The New York Times.*

All′ Things′ Bright′ and Beau′tiful, a Christian hymn (1848) about creation with words by Cecil Alexander.

all′-time′, *adj.* **1.** never equaled or surpassed: *Production will reach an all-time high.* **2.** regarded as such in its entire history: *an all-time favorite song.*

al•lude (ə lo͞od′), *v.i.,* **-lud•ed, -lud•ing.** to refer casually or indirectly: *to allude to one's childhood.*

al•lure (ə lo͝or′), *v.,* **-lured, -lur•ing,** *n.* —*v.t.* **1.** to attract or tempt by something flattering or desirable. **2.** to fascinate; charm. —*v.i.* **3.** to be attractive or tempting. —*n.* **4.** fascination; charm; appeal.

al•lur•ing (ə lo͝or′ing), *adj.* **1.** very attractive or tempting; enticing; seductive. **2.** fascinating; charming. —**al•lur′ing•ly,** *adv.*

al•lu•sion (ə lo͞o′zhən), *n.* **1.** a passing or casual reference to something, either directly or implied: *an allusion to Shakespeare.* **2.** the act of alluding.

al•lu•sive (ə lo͞o′siv), *adj.* containing or given to allusions. —**al•lu′sive•ly,** *adv.* —**al•lu′sive•ness,** *n.*

al•lu•vi•al (ə lo͞o′vē əl), *adj.* **1.** of or pertaining to alluvium. —*n.* **2.** alluvial soil.

al•lu•vi•on (ə lo͞o′vē ən), *n.* **1.** *Law.* a gradual increase of land on a shore or riverbank by the action of water. **2.** overflow; flood.

al•lu•vi•um (ə lo͞o′vē əm), *n., pl.* **-vi•ums, -vi•a** (-vē ə). **1.** a deposit of sand, mud, etc., formed by flowing water. **2.** the sedimentary matter deposited thus within recent times, esp. in the valleys of large rivers.

al•ly (*n.* al′ī, ə lī′; *v.* ə lī′), *n., pl.* **-lies,** *v.,* **-lied, -ly•ing.** —*n.* **1.** a nation, group, or person that is associated with another or others for some common cause or purpose: *Canada and the United States were allies in World War II.* **2.** a plant, animal, or other organism bearing a close taxonomic relationship to another. **3.** a person who associates or cooperates with another; supporter. —*v.t.* **4.** to unite formally, as by treaty, league, or marriage (usu. fol. by *with* or *to*): *Russia allied itself to France.* **5.** to associate or connect by some mutual relationship. —*v.i.* **6.** to enter into an alliance; unite. —**al•li′a•ble,** *adj.*

Al•ma-A•ta (al′mə ə tä′), *n.* former name of **Almaty.**

al•ma ma•ter (äl′mə mä′tər, al′-; al′mə mā′tər), *n.* a school, college, or university at which one has studied and, usu., from which one has graduated.

al•ma•nac (ôl′mə nak′), *n.* **1.** an annual publication containing a calendar for the coming year, important dates, and the times of such phenomena as sunrises and sunsets, phases of the moon, and tides. **2.** a publication containing astronomical or meteorological information, as future positions of celestial objects, star magnitudes, and culmination dates of constellations. **3.** an annual reference book of facts about countries, sports, entertainment, etc.

al•man•dine (al′mən dēn′, -dīn′, -din), *n.* a purple-red iron aluminum garnet.

Al•ma•ty (al′mə tē), *n.* a city in SE Kazakhstan: the former capital. 1,108,000. Formerly, **Alma-Ata.**

al•might•y (ôl mī′tē), *adj.* **1.** having unlimited power; omnipotent, as God. **2.** having very great power, influence, etc.: *the almighty press.* **3.** *Informal.* extreme; terrible: *He's in an almighty fix.* —*adv.* **4.** *Informal.* extremely: *It's almighty hot.* —*n.* **5. the Almighty,** God. —**al•might′i•ness,** *n.*

almight′y dol′lar, *n.* undue importance given to money.

al•mond (ä′mənd, am′ənd; *spelling pron.* al′mənd), *n.* **1.** the nutlike kernel of the fruit of either of two trees, *Prunus dulcis,* or *P. dulcis amara* **(bitter almond),** of the rose family. **2.** the tree itself. **3.** a pale tan. **4.** anything shaped like an almond. —*adj.* **5.** of the color, taste, or shape of an almond. **6.** made or flavored with almonds: *almond cookies.* —**al′mond•like′, al′mond•y,** *adj.*

al•mon•er (al′mə nər, ä′mə-), *n.* **1.** a person whose function or duty is the distribution of alms on behalf of an institution, a royal personage, etc. **2.** *Brit.* a social worker in a hospital.

al•most (ôl′mōst, ôl mōst′), *adv.* very nearly; all but: *almost every house; to pay almost nothing for a car.*

alms (ämz), *n.* (*used with a sing. or pl. v.*) money, food, or other donations given to the poor or needy.

al•mug (al′məg, ôl′-), *n.* a Biblical tree, possibly the red sandalwood. I Kings 10:12. Compare ALGUM.

al•oe (al′ō), *n., pl.* **-oes. 1.** any chiefly African shrub belonging to the genus *Aloe,* of the lily family, certain species of which yield a fiber. **2.** ALOE VERA. —**al′o•et′ic,** *adj.*

al′oe ver′a (ver′ə, vēr′ə), *n., pl.* **aloe ver•as.** any aloe of the species *Aloe vera,* the fleshy leaves of which yield a juice used as an emollient ingredient of skin lotions and for treating burns.

a•loft (ə lôft′, ə loft′), *adv.* **1.** high up; far above the ground. **2.** on the masts; in the rigging or upper rigging. **3.** in or into the air. —*prep.* **4.** on or at the top of: *flags flying aloft the castle.*

a•lo•ha (ə lō′ə, ä lō′hä), *n., pl.* **-has,** *interj.* **1.** hello; greetings. **2.** farewell. [< Hawaiian: lit., love]

a•lone (ə lōn′), *adj.* (used predicatively) **1.** separate, apart, or isolated from others. **2.** to the exclusion of all others or all else: *to live by bread alone.* **3.** unequaled; unexcelled: *alone among his peers in artistry.* —*adv.* **4.** solitarily; by oneself: *She prefers to live alone.* **5.** solely; exclusively: *It's sold by us alone.* **6.** without aid or help: *The baby can stand alone.* —***Idiom.*** **7. leave** or **let alone,** to refrain from bothering or interfering with. **8. let alone,** not to mention: *too tired to walk, let alone run.* **9. let well enough alone,** to leave things as they are. —**a•lone′ness,** *n.*

a•long (ə lông′, ə long′), *prep.* **1.** over the length or direction of: *walking along the highway.* **2.** in the course of: *I lost my hat along the way.* **3.** in conformity or accordance with: *along the lines suggested.* —*adv.* **4.** parallel in the same direction: *He ran along beside me.* **5.** so as to progress; onward: *Keep the line moving along.* **6.** in company; in agreement (usu. fol. by *with*): *He planned the project along with his associates.* **7.** as a companion; with one: *She took her brother along.* **8.** from one person or place to another: *The order was passed along from management to staff.* **9.** toward a goal or completion: *Work on the new ship is quite far along.* **10.** as an accompanying item: *Bring along your umbrella.* —***Idiom.*** **11. all along,** from the start. **12. be along,** *Informal.* to arrive at a place: *They should be along soon.*

a•long•side (ə lông′sīd′, ə long′-), *adv.* **1.** along or at the side of something: *We brought the boat alongside.* —*prep.* **2.** beside; by the side of: *The dog ran alongside me all the way.* **3. alongside of, a.** beside; alongside. **b.** *Informal.* compared with.

a•loof (ə lo͞of′), *adj.* **1.** reserved or reticent; indifferent: *to have the reputation of being aloof.* —*adv.* **2.** at a distance, esp. in feeling or interest; apart: *to stand aloof from one's classmates.* —**a•loof′ly,** *adv.* —**a•loof′ness,** *n.*

al·o·pe·ci·a (al′ə pē′shē ə, -sē ə), *n.* loss of hair; baldness. —**al′o·pe′cic** (-pē′sik), *adj.*

a·loud (ə loud′), *adv.* **1.** in the normal tone and volume of the speaking voice: *They could not speak aloud in the library.* **2.** vocally, as distinguished from mentally: *to read a book aloud.* **3.** in a loud voice; loudly: *to cry aloud in grief.*

alp (alp), *n.* a high mountain.

al·pac·a (al pak′ə), *n., pl.* **-pac·as. 1.** a domesticated South American hoofed mammal, *Lama pacos,* having long, soft, silky fleece, related to the llama and believed to be a variety of the guanaco. **2.** the fleece of this animal. **3.** a yarn or fabric made of it. **4.** any fabric simulating alpaca wool cloth.

al·pen·glow (al′pən glō′), *n.* a reddish glow often seen on the summits of mountains just before sunrise or just after sunset.

al·pen·horn (al′pən hôrn′), *n.* a very long, powerful horn used by Swiss herders and mountaineers.

al·pha (al′fə), *n., pl.* **-phas,** *adj.* —*n.* **1.** the first letter of the Greek alphabet (A, α). **2.** the first; beginning. **3.** (*cap.*) the brightest star in a constellation: *Alpha Centauri.* **4.** the first or foremost in a series of related items. —*adj.* **5.** (esp. of animals) having the highest rank of its sex in a dominance hierarchy: *the alpha female.* **6.** pertaining or linked to the carbon atom closest to a particular group in an organic molecule.

al′pha and ome′ga, *n.* **1.** the beginning and the end. Rev. 1:8. **2.** the basic or essential elements: *the alpha and omega of law.* **3.** (*cap.*) God. Rev. 1:8. **4.** (*cap.*) Jesus. Rev. 21:6; 22:13.

FOREIGN ALPHABETS

ARABIC			GERMAN[1]			GREEK			HEBREW			RUSSIAN		
Letter	Name	Transliteration	Letter		Transliteration	Letter	Name	Transliteration	Letter	Name	Transliteration	Letter		Transliteration
ا	alif	ʾ[1], a	𝔄 a	a	a	A α	alpha	a	א	aleph	- or ʾ	А а		a
ب	bā	b	𝔄̈ ä	ä	ae, ä	B β	beta	b	ב	beth	b, bh, v	Б б		b
ت	tā	t	𝔅 b	b	b	Γ γ	gamma	g				В в		v
ث	thā	th	ℭ c	c	c	Δ δ	delta	d	ג	gimel	g, gh	Г г		g
ج	jim	j	𝔇 d	d	d				ד	daleth	d, dh	Д д		d
ح	ḥā	ḥ[2]	ℭ̈ ë	e	e	E ε	epsilon	e				Е е		e, ye
خ	khā	kh	𝔉 f	f	f	Z ζ	zeta	z	ה	he	h	Ж ж		zh, ž
د	dāl	d	𝔊 g	g	g				ו	vav	v, w	З з		z
ذ	dhāl	dh	ℌ h	h	h	H η	eta	e (or ē)				И и		i
ر	rā	r	ℑ i	i	i	Θ θ	theta	th	ז	zayin	z	Й й		ĭ, y, j, i
ز	zā	z	ℑ̇ j	j	j	I ι	iota	i	ח	cheth	ḥ	К к		k
س	sin	s	𝔎 k	k	k				ט	teth	ṭ	Л л		l
ش	shin	sh	𝔏 l	l	l	K κ	kappa	k	י	yod	y, j, i	М м		m
ص	ṣād	ṣ	𝔐 m	m	m	Λ λ	lambda	l				Н н		n
ض	ḍād	ḍ	𝔑 n	n	n	M μ	mu	m	כ ך[1]	kaph	k, kh	О о		o
ط	ṭā	ṭ	𝔒 o	o	o	N ν	nu	n	ל	lamed	l	П п		p
ظ	ẓā	ẓ	𝔒̈ ö	ö	oe, ö				מ ם[1]	mem	m	Р р		r
ع	ʾain	ʿ[3]	𝔓 p	p	p	Ξ ξ	xi	x	נ ן[1]	nun	n	С с		s
غ	ghain	gh	𝔔 q	q	q	O o	omicron	o	ס	samekh	s	Т т		t
ف	fā	f	𝔑 r	r	r	Π π	pi	p	ע	ayin	ʿ	У у		u
ق	qāf	q[4]	𝔖 ſs[2]	ſs	s	P ρ	rho	r	פ ף[1]	pe	p, ph, f	Ф ф		f
ك	kāf	k	𝔗 t	t	t	Σ σ, ς[1]	sigma	s	צ ץ[1]	sadhe	ṣ	Х х		kh, x
ل	lām	l	𝔘 u	u	u	T τ	tau	t	ק	koph	q	Ц ц		ts, c
م	mim	m	𝔘̇ ü	ü	ue, ü	Y υ	upsilon	y	ר	resh	r	Ч ч		ch, č
ن	nūn	n	𝔙 v	v	v	Φ φ	phi	ph	שׁ	shin	sh, š	Ш ш		sh, š
ه	hā	h	𝔚 w	w	w	X χ	chi	ch, kh	שׂ	sin	ś	Щ щ		shch, šč
و	wāw	w, ū	𝔛 x	x	x	Ψ ψ	psi	ps	ת	tav	t	Ъ ъ[1]		″
ي	yā	y, i	𝔜 y	y	y	Ω ω	omega	o (or ō)				Ы ы		y, i
			𝔷 z	z	z							Ь ь[2]		′
												Э э		ė, eh, e
												Ю ю		yu, ju
												Я я		ya, ja

[1]Glottal stop.
[2]A voiceless pharyngeal fricative.
[3]A voiced pharyngeal fricative.
[4]A voiceless uvular stop.

[1]This type style, known as Fraktur or Gothic, was dropped in favor of conventional European type by government decree in 1941.
[2]At end of syllable.

[1]At end of word.

[1]At end of word.

[1]Represents the sound (y) between an unpalatalized consonant and a vowel.
[2]Indicates that the preceding consonant is palatalized, or represents (y) between a palatalized consonant and a vowel.

al•pha•bet (al′fə bet′, -bit), *n.* **1.** the letters of a language in their customary order. **2.** any system of letters or symbols with which a language is written: *the Greek alphabet.* See table on next page. **3.** any such system for representing the sounds of a language or languages: *a phonetic alphabet.* **4.** basic facts; rudiments; ABC's: *the alphabet of genetics.* [< Late Latin < Greek *alphábētos* = *alpha* + *bēta* first two letters of the Greek alphabet]

al•pha•bet•i•cal (al′fə bet′i kəl) also **al′pha•bet′ic,** *adj.* **1.** in the order of the letters of the alphabet. **2.** pertaining to, expressed by, or using an alphabet. **—al′pha•bet′i•cal•ly,** *adv.*

al•pha•bet•ize (al′fə bi tīz′), *v.t.*, **-ized, -iz•ing. 1.** to put or arrange in alphabetical order. **2.** to express by or furnish with an alphabet. **—al′pha•bet′i•za′tion** (-bet′ə zā′shən, -bi tə-), *n.*

al′phabet soup′, *n.* **1.** a soup containing small noodles in the shapes of letters of the alphabet. **2.** a jumble of abbreviations, as of names of government agencies.

Al′pha Centau′ri, *n.* a triple-star system that is the brightest celestial object in the constellation Centaurus.

al′pha-fe′to•pro′tein (fē′tō prō′tēn, -tē in), *n.* a serum protein produced during pregnancy, useful in the prenatal diagnosis of multiple births or birth defects. *Abbr.:* AFP

al•pha•nu•mer•ic (al′fə no͞o mer′ik, -nyo͞o-) also **al′pha•nu•mer′i•cal,** *adj.* utilizing letters, numbers, and often special characters or symbols: *an alphanumeric code.* **—al′pha•nu•mer′i•cal•ly,** *adv.*

al′pha par′ticle, *n.* a positively charged particle consisting of two protons and two neutrons, emitted in radioactive decay or nuclear fission; the nucleus of a helium atom.

al′pha ray′, *n.* a stream of alpha particles. Also called **al′pha radia′tion.**

al′pha rhythm′, *n.* a pattern of slow brain waves **(al′pha waves′)** in normal persons at rest with closed eyes, thought by some to be associated with an alert but daydreaming mind.

al′pha test′, *n.* **1.** *Psychol.* a set of mental tests designed to measure the general intelligence of individuals able to read and write, used by the U.S. Army in World War I. **2.** *Computers.* an early test of new or updated computer software conducted by the developers of the program prior to beta-testing by potential users. Compare BETA TEST.

al•pine (al′pīn, -pin), *adj.* **1.** of or pertaining to any lofty mountain. **2.** very high; elevated. **3.** (*cap.*) of or pertaining to the Alps. **4.** native to the heights above the timberline: *alpine plants.* **5.** (*often cap.*) of or pertaining to downhill or slalom skiing, esp. as a competitive event.

Alps (alps), *n.pl.* a mountain range in S Europe, extending from France through Switzerland and Italy into Austria and Yugoslavia. Highest peak, Mont Blanc, 15,781 ft. (4810 m).

al•read•y (ôl red′ē), *adv.* **1.** previously; prior to or at some specified or implied time. **2.** so soon; so early. **3.** *Informal.* (used as an intensifier to express exasperation or impatience): *Let's go already!* **—Usage.** The written forms ALREADY and ALL READY have distinct uses and meanings. ALREADY means "previously" (*The plane had already landed*) or "so soon" (*It's December already*). The phrase ALL READY means "entirely ready, prepared": *I was all ready to leave for church.*

al•right (ôl rīt′), *adv., adj.* ALL RIGHT. **—Usage.** The form ALRIGHT as a one-word spelling of the phrase ALL RIGHT in all of its senses probably arose by analogy with such words as *already* and *altogether.* Although ALRIGHT is a common spelling in written dialogue and in other types of informal writing, it is often considered incorrect, and ALL RIGHT is used in more formal, edited writing.

al′sike clo′ver (al′sīk, -sik, ôl′-), *n.* a European clover, *Trifolium hybridum,* having pink flowers: grown widely for forage. Also called **al′sike.**

Al Si•rat (al si rät′), *n.* *Islam.* **1.** the correct path of religion. **2.** the bridge over which all who enter paradise must pass. [< Arabic, = *al* the + *ṣirāṭ* road < Latin (*via*) *strāta* paved (way)]

al•so (ôl′sō), *adv.* **1.** in addition; too; besides: *He was thin, and he was also tall.* **2.** likewise; in the same manner: *Since you're having another cup of coffee, I'll have one also.*

al′so-ran′, *n.* **1.** (in a race) a contestant who fails to win or to place among the first three finishers. **2.** a person who loses a contest, election, or other competition. **3.** a person who attains little or no success.

Al•tair (al′târ, -tīᵊr, al târ′, -tīᵊr′), *n.* a first-magnitude star in the constellation Aquila.

al•tar (ôl′tər), *n.* **1.** an elevated place or structure, as a mound or platform, at which religious rites are performed or on which sacrifices are offered to gods, ancestors, etc. **—*Idiom.* 2. lead to the altar,** to marry.

al′tar boy′, *n.* ACOLYTE (def. 1).

al•tar•piece (ôl′tər pēs′), *n.* a painted or carved screen behind or above the altar or communion table in Christian churches.

al′tar rail′, *n.* the rail in front of an altar, separating the sanctuary from the rest of the church.

al•ter (ôl′tər), *v.t.* **1.** to make different in some particular, as size, style, course, or the like; modify: *to alter a coat; to alter a will.* **2.** to castrate or spay. **—*v.i.* 3.** to change; become different or modified. **—al′ter•a•ble,** *adj.* **—al′ter•a•bil′i•ty,** *n.*

al•ter•a•tion (ôl′tə rā′shən), *n.* **1.** the act of altering or the state of being altered. **2.** a change; modification or adjustment: *There has been an alteration in our plans.*

al•ter•cate (ôl′tər kāt′), *v.i.*, **-cat•ed, -cat•ing.** to argue or quarrel with intensity; wrangle.

al•ter•ca•tion (ôl′tər kā′shən), *n.* a heated or angry dispute; noisy argument or controversy.

al•ter e•go (ôl′tər ē′gō, eg′ō, al′-), *n.* **1.** an inseparable friend. **2.** a second self; a perfect substitute or deputy. **3.** another aspect of one's personality.

al•ter•nant (ôl′tûr nənt, al′-; *esp. Brit.* ôl tûr′-, al-), *adj.* **1.** alternating; alternate. **—*n.* 2.** a variant linguistic form that occurs in alternation with others.

al•ter•nate (*v.* ôl′tər nāt′, al′-; *adj., n.* -nit), *v.*, **-nat•ed, -nat•ing,** *adj., n.* **—*v.i.* 1.** to interchange repeatedly and regularly with one another in time or place (usu. fol. by *with*): *Day alternates with night.* **2.** to change back and forth between states, actions, etc.: *He alternates between hope and despair.* **3.** to take turns: *The children alternate in doing chores.* **4.** *Elect.* to reverse direction or sign periodically. **—*v.t.* 5.** to perform or do in succession or one after another. **6.** to interchange successively or regularly: *to alternate hot and cold compresses.* **—*adj.* 7.** interchanged repeatedly one for another: *Winter and summer are alternate seasons.* **8.** reciprocal; mutual: *alternate acts of kindness.* **9.** every second one of a series: *Read only the alternate lines.* **10.** ALTERNATIVE (def. 4). **11.** *Bot.* **a.** placed singly at different heights on the axis, on each side in succession, or at definite angular distances from one another, as leaves on a stem. **b.** opposite to the intervals between other parts: *petals alternate with sepals.* **—*n.* 12.** a person authorized to take the place of another who is temporarily absent. **—al′ter•nate•ly,** *adv.*

al′ternate an′gle, *n.* one of a pair of nonadjacent angles made by the crossing of two lines by a third line.

al′ternating cur′rent, *n.* an electric current that reverses direction at regular intervals, having a magnitude that varies continuously in a sinusoidal manner. *Abbr.:* AC Compare DIRECT CURRENT.

al•ter•na•tion (ôl′tər nā′shən, al′-), *n.* **1.** the act of alternating or the state of being alternated. **2.** alternate succession; repeated rotation: *the alternation of the seasons.* **3.** variation in the form of a linguistic unit as it occurs in different environments or under different conditions.

al•ter•na•tive (ôl tûr′nə tiv, al-), *n.* **1.** a choice limited to one of two or more possibilities: *the alternative of riding or walking.* **2.** one of these choices: *The alternative to riding is walking.* **3.** a possible or remaining choice: *no alternative but to walk.* **—*adj.* 4.** affording a choice between two or more things. **5.** (of two choices) mutually exclusive so that if one is chosen the other must be rejected. **6.** employing or following nontraditional or unconventional ideas, methods, etc.: *an alternative newspaper.* **—al•ter′na•tive•ly,** *adv.*

alter′native med′icine, *n.* health care and treatment practices, including traditional Chinese medicine, chiropractic, folk medicine, and naturopathy, that minimize or eschew the use of surgery and drugs.

al•ter•na•tor (ôl′tər nā′tər, al′-), *n.* a generator of alternating current.

al•the•a or **al•thae•a** (al thē′ə), *n., pl.* **-the•as** or **-thae•as. 1.** the rose of Sharon, *Hibiscus syriacus.* **2.** any plant belonging to the genus *Althaea,* of the mallow family, having lobed leaves and showy flowers in a spikelike cluster, including the hollyhocks and marsh mallows.

alt•horn (alt′hôrn′), *n.* a valved brass musical instrument that is the alto member of the cornet family.

al•though (ôl t͟hō′), *conj.* in spite of the fact that; even though; though.

alti- or **alto-,** a combining form meaning "height," "altitude": *altimeter.*

al•tim•e•ter (al tim′i tər, al′tə mē′tər), *n.* an aneroid or radio barometer used chiefly in aircraft to ascertain flight altitude.

al•tim•e•try (al tim′i trē), *n.* the science of measuring altitude, as by an altimeter. **—al′ti•met′ri•cal** (-tə me′tri kəl), *adj.*

al•ti•tude (al′ti to͞od′, -tyo͞od′), *n.* **1.** the height of a thing above a given planetary reference plane, esp. above sea level on earth. **2.** extent or distance upward; height. **3.** the angular distance of a heavenly body above the horizon. **4. a.** the perpendicular distance from the vertex of a geometric figure to the side opposite the vertex. **b.** the line through the vertex of a geometric figure perpendicular to the base. **5.** Usu., **altitudes.** a high place or region: *mountain altitudes.* **6.** high or exalted position, quality, etc.: *to rise in power to a certain altitude.*

al′titude sick′ness, *n.* a disorder associated with the low oxygen content of the atmosphere at high altitudes, in acute conditions resulting in prostration, shortness of breath, and cardiac disturbances, and in chronic conditions resulting in thickened and poorly circulating blood.

Alt•man (ôlt′mən), *n.* **Robert,** born 1922, U.S. film director.

al•to (al′tō), *n., pl.* **-tos,** *adj.* **—*n.* 1.** CONTRALTO. **2.** the second highest part of a four-part chorus. **3.** the second highest instrument in a family of musical instruments. **—*adj.* 4.** of, pertaining to, or having the range of an alto.

al′to clef′, *n.* a sign locating middle C on the third line of the staff.

al•to•cu•mu•lus (al′tō kyo͞o′myə ləs), *n., pl.* **-li** (-lī′). a cloud of a class characterized by globular masses or rolls in layers or patches: of medium altitude, about 8000–20,000 ft. (2450–6100 m).

al•to•geth•er (ôl′tə ge*th*′ər, ôl′tə ge*th*′ər), *adv.* **1.** wholly; entirely; completely: *an altogether fitting memorial.* **2.** with all or everything included: *The debt amounted altogether to twenty dollars.* **3.** with everything considered; on the whole: *Altogether, I'm glad it's over.* **—*Idiom.* 4. in the altogether,** *Informal.* nude. **—Usage.** The forms ALTOGETHER and ALL TOGETHER, though often indistinguishable in speech, are distinct in meaning. The adverb ALTOGETHER means "wholly, entirely, completely": *an altogether confused report.* The phrase ALL TOGETHER means "in a group": *The children were all together in the kitchen.*

al·to·stra·tus (al'tō strā'təs, -strat'əs), *n., pl.* **-stra·ti** (-strā'tī, -strat'ī). a cloud of a class characterized by a generally uniform gray sheet or layer: of medium altitude, 8000–20,000 ft. (2450–6100 m).

al·tru·ism (al'trōō iz'əm), *n.* **1.** the principle or practice of unselfish concern for the welfare of others (opposed to *egoism*). **2.** behavior by an animal that may be to its disadvantage but that benefits others of its kind. —**al'tru·ist,** *n.* —**al'tru·is'tic,** *adj.*

al·um[1] (al'əm), *n.* **1.** a crystalline solid, aluminum potassium sulfate, $K_2SO_4·Al_2(SO_4)_3·24H_2O$, used as an astringent and styptic and in dyeing and tanning.

a·lum[2] (ə lum'), *n.* an alumna or alumnus.

a·lu·mi·na (ə lōō'mə nə), *n.* the natural or synthetic oxide of aluminum, Al_2O_3, occurring in nature in a pure crystal form as corundum.

a·lu·mi·nate (ə lōō'mə nit', -nāt'), *n.* a salt of the acid form of aluminum hydroxide, containing the group AlO_2^- or AlO_3^{-3}.

al·u·min·i·um (al'yə min'ē əm), *n., adj. Chiefly Brit.* ALUMINUM.

a·lu·mi·no·sil·i·cate (ə lōō'mə nō sil'ə kit, -kāt'), *n.* any aluminum silicate containing alkali-metal or alkaline-earth-metal ions, as a feldspar, zeolite, or beryl.

a·lu·mi·num (ə lōō'mə nəm), *n.* **1.** a silver-white metallic element, light in weight, ductile, malleable, and not readily corroded or tarnished: used in alloys and for lightweight products. *Abbr.:* alum.; *Symbol:* Al; *at. wt.:* 26.98; *at. no.:* 13; *sp. gr.:* 2.70 at 20°C. —*adj.* **2.** of, pertaining to, or containing aluminum. Also, *esp. Brit.,* **aluminium.** —**al·u·min·ic** (al'yə min'ik), *adj.*

alu'minum hydrox'ide, *n.* a crystalline, water-insoluble powder, $Al(OH)_3$ or $Al_2O_3·3H_2O$, obtained chiefly from bauxite: used in the manufacture of glass, ceramics, and printing inks, in dyeing, and as an antacid.

alu'minum ox'ide, *n.* ALUMINA.

alu'minum sil'icate, *n.* any crystalline combination of silicate and aluminate.

a·lum·na (ə lum'nə), *n., pl.* **-nae** (-nē, -nī). a female graduate or former student of a specific school, college, or university.

a·lum·nus (ə lum'nəs), *n., pl.* **-ni** (-nī, -nē). **1.** a graduate or former student of a specific school, college, or university. **2.** a former associate, employee, member, or the like. ——**Usage.** ALUMNUS (in Latin a masculine noun) refers to a male graduate or former student; the plural is ALUMNI. An ALUMNA (in Latin a feminine noun) refers to a female graduate or former student; the plural is ALUMNAE. Traditionally, the masculine plural ALUMNI has been used for groups composed of both sexes and is still widely so used. Sometimes, to avoid any suggestion of sexism, both terms are used for mixed groups: the *alumni/alumnae* (or *the alumni and alumnae*) *of Indiana University.* While not quite equivalent in meaning, the terms *graduate* and *graduates* avoid both the complexities of the Latin forms and the use of a masculine plural form to refer to both sexes.

al·um·root (al'əm rōōt', -rŏŏt'), *n.* any of several North American plants belonging to the genus *Heuchera,* of the saxifrage family, esp. *H. americana,* having mottled foliage, greenish-white flowers, and an astringent root.

al·ve·o·lar (al vē'ə lər), *adj.* **1.** of or pertaining to an alveolus or to alveoli. **2.** (of a consonant sound) articulated with the tongue touching or close to the alveolar ridge behind the upper front teeth, as English (t), (d), or (n). —*n.* **3.** an alveolar sound.

alve'olar ridge', *n.* the ridgelike border of the upper and lower jaws containing the sockets of the teeth. Also called **alve'olar proc'ess.**

al·ve·o·late (al vē'ə lit, -lāt') also **al·ve·o·lat·ed,** *adj.* having alveoli; deeply pitted, as a honeycomb. —**al·ve·o·la'tion,** *n.*

al·ve·o·lus (al vē'ə ləs), *n., pl.* **-li** (-lī'). **1.** a little cavity, pit, or cell, as a cell of a honeycomb. **2.** any of the tiny bunched air sacs at the ends of the bronchioles of the lungs. **3.** the socket within the jawbone in which the root or roots of a tooth are set.

al·ways (ôl'wāz, -wēz), *adv.* **1.** every time; on every occasion: *We always sleep late on Saturday.* **2.** all the time; continuously; uninterruptedly: *The light is always burning.* **3.** forever: *Will you always love me?* **4.** in any event; if necessary: *I can always decide not to go.*

a·lys·sum (ə lis'əm), *n.* **1.** any of various plants of the mustard family, having gray leaves and clusters of small yellow or white flowers. **2.** SWEET ALYSSUM.

Alz'hei·mer's disease' (älts'hī mərz, alts'-, ôlts'-), *n.* a common form of dementia of unknown cause, usu. beginning in late middle age, characterized by progressive memory loss and mental deterioration associated with brain damage. [after A. *Alzheimer* (1864–1915), German neurologist]

am (am; *unstressed* əm, m), *v.* 1st pers. sing. pres. indic. of BE.

AM, 1. amplitude modulation: a method of impressing a signal on a radio carrier wave by varying its amplitude. **2.** a system of broadcasting using this method. Compare FM.

Am, *Chem. Symbol.* americium.

A.M., Master of Arts.

a.m. or **A.M., 1.** before noon. **2.** the period from midnight to noon, esp. the period of daylight prior to noon. [< L *ante meridiem*] Compare P.M. ——**Usage.** The abbreviation A.M. refers to the period from midnight until noon. One minute before noon is 11:59 a.m. One minute after

noon is 12:01 p.m. Many people distinguish between noon and midnight by saying *12 noon* and *12 midnight.* Expressions such as *6 a.m. in the morning* and *9 p.m. at night* are redundant.

-ama, var. of -ORAMA: *rollerama; Futurama.*

A.M.A., American Medical Association.

a·mah (ä'mə, am'ə), *n.* (in the Far East) a female servant, esp. a nursemaid.

Am·a·lek (am'ə lek'), *n.* **1.** the son of Eliphaz and grandson of Esau. Gen. 36:12; I Chron. 1:36. **2.** a nomadic tribe or nation descended from Amalek and hostile to Israel. Num. 24:20.

Am·a·lek·ite (am'ə lek'īt, ə mal'i kīt'), *n., pl.* **-ites,** (*esp. collectively*) **-ite.** a member of the tribe descended from Esau. Gen. 36:12.

a·mal·gam (ə mal'gəm), *n.* **1.** an alloy of mercury with another metal or metals. **2.** an alloy chiefly of silver mixed with mercury and variable amounts of other metals, used as a dental filling. **3.** a mixture or combination.

a·mal·ga·mate (ə mal'gə māt'), *v.,* **-mat·ed, -mat·ing.** —*v.t.* **1.** to mix or merge so as to make a combination; blend; unite: *to amalgamate two companies.* **2.** to mix or alloy (a metal) with mercury. —*v.i.* **3.** to combine, unite, merge, or coalesce: *The three schools decided to amalgamate.* —**a·mal'ga·ma·ble,** *adj.* —**a·mal'ga·ma'tor,** *n.*

a·mal·ga·ma·tion (ə mal'gə mā'shən), *n.* **1.** the act or process of amalgamating. **2.** the state or result of being amalgamated. **3.** the extraction of precious metals from their ores by treatment with mercury.

A·man'a Church' Soci'ety (ə man'ə), *n.* a religious group founded in Germany in 1714, moved to New York State in 1843, and then to Iowa in 1855, where its villages have flourished as cooperative corporations since 1932.

a·man·dine (ä'mən dēn', am'ən-), *adj.* served or prepared with almonds: *trout amandine.*

A·man·ite (ə man'īt), *n.* a member of the Amana Church Society.

a·man·ta·dine (ə man'tə dēn'), *n.* a water-soluble crystalline substance, $C_{10}H_{17}NHCl$, that inhibits penetration of viruses into cells and is used against influenza and in the treatment of parkinsonism.

a·man·u·en·sis (ə man'yōō en'sis), *n., pl.* **-ses** (-sēz). a person employed to write what another dictates or to copy what has been written by another; secretary.

am·a·ranth (am'ə ranth'), *n.* **1.** any plant of the genus *Amaranthus,* some species of which are cultivated as food and some for their showy flower clusters or foliage. **2.** an imaginary flower that never dies. **3.** a purplish red, water-soluble powder, $C_{20}H_{11}N_2O_{10}Na_3$, used as a dye.

am·a·ran·thine (am'ə ran'thin, -thīn), *adj.* **1.** of or like the amaranth. **2.** undying; everlasting. **3.** of purplish red color.

am·a·relle (am'ə rel'), *n.* any variety of the sour cherry, *Prunus cerasus,* having colorless juice.

am·a·ret·to (am'ə ret'ō, ä'mə-), *n.* an almond-flavored liqueur.

Am·a·ril·lo (am'ə ril'ō), *n.* a city in NW Texas. 165,036.

am·a·ryl·lis (am'ə ril'is), *n.* **1.** any of several bulbous plants of the genus *Hippeastrum,* esp. *H. puniceum,* which has large red or pink flowers: popular as a houseplant. **2.** Also called **belladonna lily.** a related plant, *Amaryllis belladonna,* having clusters of usu. rose-colored flowers. **3.** any of several other similar or related plants.

A·ma·sa (ə mā'sə, am'ə sə), *n.* the commander of Absalom's army and later of David's army. II Sam. 17:25; 19:13.

a·mass (ə mas'), *v.t.* **1.** to gather for oneself: *to amass a fortune.* **2.** to collect into a mass or pile; gather. —*v.i.* **3.** to come together; assemble: *A large crowd amassed for the parade.* —**a·mass'a·ble,** *adj.* —**a·mass'er,** *n.* —**a·mass'ment,** *n.*

am·a·teur (am'ə chŏŏr', -chər, -tər, am'ə tûr'), *n.* **1.** a person who engages in a study, sport, or other activity for pleasure rather than for financial benefit. Compare PROFESSIONAL (def. 11). **2.** an athlete who has never competed for payment or for a monetary prize. **3.** a person inexperienced or unskilled in a particular activity: *Detective work is not for amateurs.* **4.** a lover or devotee of an art, science, etc. —*adj.* **5.** pertaining to, characteristic of, or engaged in by an amateur: *amateur tennis.* **6.** composed of amateurs. **7.** being an amateur: *an amateur painter.* —**am'a·teur·ism,** *n.*

am·a·tive (am'ə tiv), *adj.* disposed to love; amorous.

am·a·to·ry (am'ə tôr'ē, -tōr'ē), *adj.* of or pertaining to lovers or love-making; expressive of love.

a·maze (ə māz'), *v.t.,* **a·mazed, a·maz·ing. 1.** to overwhelm with surprise or sudden wonder; astonish greatly. —*v.i.* **2.** to cause astonishment or amazement: *a show that delights and amazes.* —**a·maz'ed·ly,** *adv.* —**a·maz'ing,** *adj.*

a·maze·ment (ə māz'mənt), *n.* overwhelming surprise or astonishment.

Am·a·zi·ah (am'ə zī'ə), *n.* a son and successor of Joash as king of Judah. II Kings 14.

Amaz'ing Grace', a Christian hymn written by John Newton, an English seaman of the 1700s who became a minister of the Church of England.

Am·a·zon (am'ə zon', -zən), *n.* **1.** a river in N South America, flowing E from the Peruvian Andes through N Brazil to the Atlantic Ocean: the largest river in the world in volume of water carried. 3900 mi. (6280 km) long. **2.** (in legends of the ancient Greeks) a member of a nation of female warriors. **3.** (*often l.c.*) a tall, powerful, forceful woman. —**Am'a·zo'ni·an,** *adj.*

am·a·zon·ite (am′ə zə nīt′), *n.* a green feldspar, a variety of microcline, used as an ornamental material. Also called **Am′azon stone′.**

Am′azon par′rot, *n.* any of several tropical American green parrots of the genus *Amazona,* popular as pets.

am·bas·sa·dor (am bas′ə dər, -dôr′), *n.* **1.** a diplomatic official of the highest rank, sent by one sovereign or state to another as its resident representative **(ambas′sador extraor′dinary and plenipoten′tiary),** or sent on a special or temporary mission. **2.** a diplomatic official serving as permanent head of a country's mission to the United Nations or some other international organization. **3.** an authorized messenger or representative. —**am·bas′sa·do′ri·al** (-dôr′ē əl, -dōr′-), *adj.* —**am·bas′sa·dor·ship′,** *n.*

ambas′sador-at-large′, *n., pl.* **ambassadors-at-large.** an ambassador who is not assigned to a particular country.

am·ber (am′bər), *n.* **1.** a yellow, red, or brown translucent fossil resin of coniferous trees that readily becomes charged with static electricity when rubbed: used for jewelry. **2.** the yellowish brown color of resin. —*adj.* **3.** of the color of amber; yellowish brown. **4.** made of amber.

am·ber·gris (am′bər grēs′, -gris), *n.* an opaque, ash-colored secretion of the sperm whale intestine, usu. found floating on the ocean or cast ashore: used in perfumery.

am·ber·jack (am′bər jak′), *n., pl.* (*esp. collectively*) **-jack.** any of several yellow to coppery carangid fishes of the genus *Seriola,* as *S. dumerili* of warm Atlantic waters.

ambi-, a prefix occurring originally in loanwords from Latin, meaning "both" (*ambiguous; ambivalence*) and "around" (*ambient*).

am·bi·ance or **am·bi·ence** (am′bē əns; *Fr.* äN byäNs′), *n., pl.* **-bi·anc·es** or **-bi·enc·es** (-bē ən siz; *Fr.* -byäNs′). the mood, special quality, or atmosphere of a place, situation, etc.; environment; milieu: *The restaurant had a delightful ambiance.*

am·bi·dex·ter·i·ty (am′bi dek ster′i tē), *n.* **1.** ambidextrous ease, skill, or facility. **2.** unusual cleverness. **3.** duplicity; deceitfulness.

am·bi·dex·trous (am′bi dek′strəs), *adj.* **1.** able to use both hands equally well. **2.** unusually skillful; facile. **3.** double-dealing; deceitful. —**am′bi·dex′trous·ly,** *adv.* —**am′bi·dex′trous·ness,** *n.*

am·bi·ent (am′bē ənt), *adj.* **1.** of the surrounding area or environment: *the ambient temperature.* **2.** completely surrounding; encompassing: *the ambient air.*

am·bi·gu·i·ty (am′bi gyōō′i tē), *n., pl.* **-ties. 1.** doubtfulness or uncertainty of meaning or intention: *to speak with ambiguity.* **2.** the condition of admitting more than one meaning. **3.** an ambiguous word, expression, etc.: *a contract free of ambiguities.*

am·big·u·ous (am big′yōō əs), *adj.* **1.** open to or having several possible meanings or interpretations: *an ambiguous answer.* **2.** difficult to comprehend, distinguish, or classify: *a rock of ambiguous character.* **3.** lacking clearness or definiteness; obscure; indistinct: *an ambiguous shape.* —**am·big′u·ous·ly,** *adv.* —**am·big′u·ous·ness,** *n.*

am·bit (am′bit), *n.* **1.** a circumference; circuit. **2.** a boundary; limit. **3.** a sphere of operation or influence; scope.

am·bi·tion (am bish′ən), *n.* **1.** an earnest desire for some type of achievement or distinction, as wealth or fame, and the willingness to strive for it. **2.** the object or state desired or sought after: *A theatrical career is her ambition.* **3.** a desire for activity: *I awoke feeling tired and lacking in ambition.* —*v.t.* **4.** to seek earnestly; aspire to.

am·bi·tious (am bish′əs), *adj.* **1.** having ambition; eagerly desirous of achieving or obtaining success, power, wealth, etc.: *an ambitious student.* **2.** showing or caused by ambition; requiring exceptional effort, ability, etc.: *an ambitious program for fighting crime.* **3.** strongly desirous; eager: *ambitious of love.* —**am·bi′tious·ly,** *adv.*

am·biv·a·lence (am biv′ə ləns) also **am·biv′a·len·cy,** *n.* uncertainty or fluctuation, esp. when caused by inability to make a choice or by a simultaneous desire to say or do two opposite things. —**am·biv′a·lent,** *adj.* —**am·biv′a·lent·ly,** *adv.*

am·ble (am′bəl), *v.,* **-bled, -bling,** *n.* —*v.i.* **1.** to go at a slow, easy pace; stroll; saunter. **2.** (of a horse) to go at a slow pace with the legs moving in lateral pairs and usu. having a four-beat rhythm. —*n.* **3.** an ambling gait. **4.** a slow, easy walk or gentle pace.

am·bly·o·pi·a (am′blē ō′pē ə), *n.* dimness of sight without apparent organic defect. —**am′bly·op′ic** (-op′ik), *adj.*

Am·brose (am′brōz), *n.* **Saint,** A.D. 340?–397, bishop of Milan 374–397.

am·bro·sia (am brō′zhə), *n.* **1.** the food of the ancient Greek and Roman gods, ensuring their immortality. **2.** something esp. delicious to taste or smell. **3.** a dessert of oranges, shredded coconut, and often pineapple. —**am·bro′sial,** *adj.*

am·bry (am′brē), *n., pl.* **-bries.** a recess or cupboard in a church for sacred vessels, vestments, etc.

am·bu·lance (am′byə ləns), *n.* **1.** a specially equipped motor vehicle, airplane, ship, etc., for carrying sick or injured people, usu. to a hospital. **2.** (formerly) a field hospital.

am′bulance chas′er, *n.* a lawyer who seeks accident victims as clients and encourages them to sue for damages.

am·bu·lant (am′byə lənt), *adj.* **1.** moving from place to place; itinerant. **2.** AMBULATORY (def. 3).

am·bu·late (am′byə lāt′), *v.i.,* **-lat·ed, -lat·ing.** to walk about or move from place to place. —**am′bu·la′tion,** *n.* —**am′bu·la′tor,** *n.*

am·bu·la·to·ry (am′byə lə tôr′ē, -tōr′ē), *adj., n., pl.* **-ries.** —*adj.* **1.**

of, pertaining to, or capable of walking. **2.** moving about or from place to place; not stationary. **3.** Also, **ambulant.** **a.** not confined to bed; able or strong enough to walk: *an ambulatory patient.* **b.** serving patients who are able to walk: *an ambulatory care center.* **4.** *Law.* not fixed; alterable or revocable: *an ambulatory will.* —*n.* **5.** an aisle surrounding the end of the choir or chancel of a church. **6.** the covered walk of a cloister.

am·bu·lette (am′byə let′), *n.* a specially equipped motor vehicle for transporting handicapped people.

am·bush (am′bŏŏsh), *n.* **1.** an act or instance of lying concealed so as to attack by surprise: *The highwaymen waited in ambush near the road.* **2.** an act or instance of attacking unexpectedly from a concealed position. **3.** the concealed position itself: *They fired from ambush.* **4.** those who attack suddenly and unexpectedly from a concealed position. —*v.t.* **5.** to attack from ambush. —*v.i.* **6.** to lie in ambush. —**am′bush·er,** *n.*

A.M.E., African Methodist Episcopal.

a·me·ba or **a·moe·ba** (ə mē′bə), *n., pl.* **-bas, -bae** (-bē). **1.** any of numerous one-celled aquatic or parasitic protozoa of the order Amoebida, having a jellylike mass of cytoplasm that forms temporary pseudopodia, by which the organism moves and engulfs food particles. **2.** a protozoan of the genus *Amoeba,* inhabiting bottom vegetation of freshwater ponds and streams: used widely in laboratory studies. —**a·me′bic** or **a·moe′bic,** *adj.*

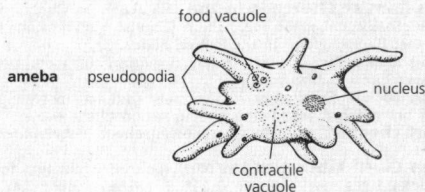

food vacuole

ameba   pseudopodia

nucleus

contractile vacuole

ame′bic dys′entery, *n.* a type of dysentery caused by the protozoan *Entamoeba histolytica,* characterized esp. by ulceration of the large intestine.

a·me·bo·cyte (ə mē′bə sīt′), *n.* a migratory white blood cell of invertebrates that has properties resembling those of an ameba.

a·me·boid (ə mē′boid), *adj.* resembling or related to amebas. —**a·me′boid·ism,** *n.*

a·mel·io·rate (ə mēl′yə rāt′, ə mē′lē ə-), *v.t., v.i.,* **-rat·ed, -rat·ing.** to make or become better or more satisfactory; improve; meliorate. —**a·mel′io·ra·ble,** *adj.* —**a·mel′io·ra′tion,** *n.* —**a·mel′io·ra′tive,** *adj.* —**a·mel′io·ra′tor,** *n.*

a·men (ā′men′, ä′men′), *interj.* **1.** it is so; so be it (used after a prayer, creed, or other formal statement to express solemn ratification or agreement). —*n.* **2.** an utterance of the interjection "amen." **3.** an expression of concurrence or assent: *The committee gave its amen to the proposal.* [< Late Latin < Greek < Hebrew *āmēn*]

A·men or **A·mon** (ä′mən), *n.* a primeval Egyptian deity, worshiped, esp. at Thebes, as the personification of air or breath and represented as either a ram or a goose: later identified with Amen-Ra.

A·men[1] (ā′men′, ä′men′), *n.* a traditional American spiritual.

a·me·na·ble (ə mē′nə bəl, ə men′ə-), *adj.* **1.** ready or willing to answer, act, agree, or yield; agreeable; tractable: *amenable to criticism.* **2.** liable to be called to account; answerable; responsible: *amenable to the law.* **3.** capable of being tested, tried, etc.: *a theory amenable to experimentation.* —**a·me′na·bil′i·ty,** *n.* —**a·me′na·bly,** *adv.*

amen′ cor′ner, *n. Chiefly Midland and Southern U.S.* **1.** a place in some Protestant churches, usually at one side of the pulpit, occupied by worshipers leading the responsive amens of the congregation. **2.** unconditional political support.

a·mend (ə mend′), *v.t.* **1.** to modify, rephrase, or add to or subtract from (a bill, constitution, etc.) by formal procedure: *Congress may amend the proposed tax bill.* **2.** to change for the better; improve. **3.** to remove or correct faults in; rectify. —*v.i.* **4.** to grow or become better by reforming oneself.

a·mend·a·to·ry (ə men′də tôr′ē, -tōr′ē), *adj.* serving to amend.

a·mend·ment (ə mend′mənt), *n.* **1.** the act of amending or the state of being amended. **2.** an alteration of or addition to a bill, constitution, etc. **3.** a change made by correction, addition, or deletion.

a·mends (ə mendz′), *n.* (*used with a sing. or pl. v.*) **1.** reparation or compensation for a loss, damage, or injury of any kind. —*Idiom.* **2.** **make amends,** to compensate, as for an injury, loss, or insult.

a·men·i·ty (ə men′i tē, ə mē′ni-), *n., pl.* **-ties. 1.** an agreeable way or manner; courtesy; civility: *social amenities.* **2.** any feature that provides comfort, convenience, or pleasure: *The hotel has a swimming pool and other amenities.* **3.** the quality of being pleasing or agreeable: *the amenity of a temperate climate.*

A·men-Ra or **A·mon-Ra** (ä′mən rä′), *n.* an Egyptian god in whom Amen and Ra were combined.

am·ent (am′ənt, ā′mənt), *n.* CATKIN.

a·men·tia (ā men′shə, ə men′-), *n.* lack of intellectual development; severe mental retardation.

a·merce (ə mûrs/), *v.t.* **1.** to punish by imposing a fine not fixed by statute. **2.** to punish by inflicting any discretionary or arbitrary penalty. —**a·merce/a·ble**, *adj.* —**a·merce/ment**, *n.*

A·mer·i·ca (ə mer/i kə), *n.* **1.** UNITED STATES. **2.** NORTH AMERICA. **3.** SOUTH AMERICA. **4.** Also called **the Americas.** North and South America, considered together. **5.** Also called "My Country, 'Tis of Thee." a U.S. patriotic hymn (1831) with words by Samuel Francis Smith. —*Saying.* **6.** Never sell America short, have faith in the American future.

Amer/ica First/ Commit/tee, *n.* a political pressure group that during 1940–41 urged the U.S. not to oppose fascism in Europe or enter World War II.

A·mer·i·can (ə mer/i kən), *adj.* **1.** of or pertaining to the United States of America or its inhabitants. **2.** of or pertaining to North or South America; of the Western Hemisphere. —*n.* **3.** a citizen of the United States of America. **4.** a native or inhabitant of the Western Hemisphere.

A·mer·i·ca·na (ə mer/i kan/ə, -kä/nə, -kā/nə), *n.pl.* books, papers, maps, etc., relating to America, esp. to its history, culture, and geography.

Amer/ican Antislav/ery Soci/ety, *n.* a society, founded in 1833 and led by William Lloyd Garrison, to abolish slavery.

Amer/ican Associa/tion of Retired/ Per/sons, *n.* an organization of retirement-age persons (aged 50 or over) devoted to informing its members of all rights and benefits to which they are entitled. *Abbr.:* AARP

American Baptist Churches in the U.S.A., *n.* a Christian denomination, originally called the Northern Baptist Convention, now the fourth-largest Baptist group in the United States.

Amer/ican Beau/ty, *n.* an American variety of rose, periodically bearing large crimson blossoms.

Amer/ican Bi/ble Soci/ety, *n.* a society founded in New York City in 1816 to bring about worldwide dissemination of the Bible.

Amer/ican cheese/, *n.* a mild processed cheddar-style cheese made in the U.S.

Amer/ican Civ/il Lib/erties Un/ion, *n.* an organization founded in 1920 to defend the civil rights of all U.S. citizens. *Abbr.:* ACLU, A.C.L.U.

Amer/ican depos/itory receipt/, *n.* a negotiable receipt similar to a stock certificate, registered in the owner's name and showing ownership of shares in a foreign company, held by a foreign branch of a U.S. bank or its overseas correspondent bank.

Amer/ican Dream/, *n.* **1.** the combination of freedom, equality, and opportunity traditionally held to be available to every American. **2.** a life of personal success and material comfort as sought by Americans, symbolized esp. by ownership of a home.

Amer/ican ea/gle, *n.* the bald eagle, esp. as depicted on the great seal of the U.S.

Amer/ican elm/, *n.* an elm, *Ulmus americana*, of North America, cultivated for shade and ornament.

Amer/ican Eng/lish, *n.* the English language as spoken and written in the U.S.

Amer/ican Expedi/tionary Forc/es, *n.pl.* troops sent to Europe by the U.S. Army during World War I. *Abbr.:* AEF

Amer/ican Farm/ Bu/reau Federa/tion, *n.* an organization founded in 1920 to promote the interests of farmers, esp. through state and national legislation. *Abbr.:* AFBF

Amer/ican Federa/tion of La/bor and Con/gress of Indus/trial Organiza/tions, *n.* a federation of trade unions formed in 1955 by merger. *Abbr.:* AFL-CIO

Amer/ican Friends/ Serv/ice Commit/tee, *n.* a social-service organization founded 1917 by the Religious Society of Friends: Nobel peace prize 1947. *Abbr.:* AFSC, A.F.S.C.

Amer/ican Goth/ic, *n.* a painting (1930) by Grant Wood, depicting a rural husband and wife standing in front of their home.

Amer/ican In/dian, *n.* a member of any of the indigenous peoples of North and South America, usu. excluding the Aleuts and Eskimos. —*Usage.* See INDIAN.

A·mer·i·can·ism (ə mer/i kə niz/əm), *n.* **1.** a custom, trait, or thing peculiar to the United States of America or its citizens. **2.** a word, phrase, or other language feature peculiar to American English. **3.** devotion to or preference for the U.S. and its institutions.

A·mer·i·can·ize (ə mer/i kə nīz/), *v.t., v.i.,* **-ized, -iz·ing.** to make or become American in character; assimilate to U.S. customs and institutions. —**A·mer/i·can·i·za/tion**, *n.*

Amer/ican League/, *n.* one of the two major professional U.S. baseball leagues, established in 1900. *Abbr.:* A.L.

Amer/ican Le/gion, *n.* a society, organized in 1919, composed of veterans of the U.S. armed forces.

Amer/ican Lu/theran Church/, *n.* a Christian denomination founded in 1960, the third-largest Lutheran group in the United States.

Amer/ican Na/tional Stand/ards In/stitute, *n.* a U.S. organization that recommends standards for many products in various industries. *Abbr.:* ANSI

Amer/ican plan/, *n.* (in hotels) a payment system that covers room and all meals. Compare EUROPEAN PLAN.

Amer/ican Revised/ Ver/sion, *n.* a revision of the Bible, based chiefly on the REVISED VERSION of the Bible, published in the U.S. in 1901.

Amer/ican Revolu/tion, *n.* the war between Great Britain and its American colonies, 1775–83, by which the colonies won independence.

Amer/ican sad/dle horse/, *n.* one of an American breed of horses, having a long neck, short back, and high-set tail. Also called **Amer/ican sad/dlebred horse/**.

Amer/ican Samo/a, *n.* the part of Samoa belonging to the U.S., comprising mainly Tutuila and the Manua Islands. 61,819; 76 sq. mi. (197 sq. km). *Cap.:* Pago Pago. *Abbr.:* AS

Amer/ican short/hair cat/, *n.* one of a breed of medium-sized, muscular shorthaired domestic cats with a broad head and a short, thick coat.

Amer/ican Sign/ Lan/guage, *n.* a visual-gesture language, having its own semantic and syntactic structure, used by deaf people in the U.S. and English-speaking parts of Canada. *Abbr.:* ASL

Amer/ican Staf/fordshire ter/rier, *n.* one of an American breed of strong, muscular terriers, orig. developed for dogfighting, having a short, stiff coat, broad head, neck, and chest, and wide-set forelegs. Also called **American pit bull terrier, pit bull terrier.**

Amer/ican Stock/ Exchange/, *n.* the second largest stock exchange in the U.S., located in New York City. *Abbr.:* ASE, A.S.E. Also called **AMEX, Amex.** Compare NEW YORK STOCK EXCHANGE.

Amer/ican wa/ter span/iel, *n.* one of an American breed of medium-sized water spaniels having a thick, curly chocolate- or liver-colored coat.

Amer/ica's Cup/, *n.* **1.** an international yachting trophy, originally offered as the Hundred Guinea Cup in 1851, but renamed for the yacht *America*, winner of it that year. **2.** the yacht race itself, the oldest and most prestigious event in international sailing, now restricted to 12-meter yachts.

Amer/ica the Beau/tiful, a patriotic song (1892) with words by Katharine Lee Bates.

am·er·i·ci·um (am/ə rish/ē əm), *n.* a transuranic element, one of the products of high-energy helium bombardment of uranium and plutonium. *Symbol:* Am; *at. no.:* 95.

Am·er·ind (am/ə rind), *n.* **1.** Also called **Am·er·in·di·an** (am/ə rin/dē ən). AMERICAN INDIAN. **2.** the indigenous languages of the Americas, taken collectively or as a hypothesized linguistic family. —*Usage.* See INDIAN.

AmerInd or **Amer. Ind.,** American Indian.

Am·e·slan (am/ə slan/, am/slan), *n.* AMERICAN SIGN LANGUAGE.

Ames/ test/ (āmz), *n.* a test that exposes a strain of bacteria to a chemical compound in order to determine the potential of the compound for causing cancer.

am·e·thyst (am/ə thist), *n.* **1.** a purple or violet quartz, used as a gem. **2.** a purplish tint. —*adj.* **3.** having the color of amethyst. **4.** containing or set with an amethyst or amethysts: *an amethyst brooch.* —**am/e·thys/tine** (-tin, -tīn), *adj.*

am·e·tro·pi·a (am/i trō/pē ə), *n.* faulty refraction of light rays by the eye, as in astigmatism. —**am/e·trop/ic** (-trop/ik, -trō/pik), *adj.*

AMEX or **A.M.E.X.** (am/eks), *n.* American Stock Exchange.

am/fm or **AM/FM** (ā/em/ef/em/), *adj.* (of a radio) able to receive both AM and FM stations.

a·mi·a·ble (ā/mē ə bəl), *adj.* **1.** having or showing agreeable personal qualities; pleasant; affable. **2.** friendly; sociable: *an amiable gathering.* **3.** agreeable; willing to accept the wishes, decisions, or suggestions of another or others. —**a/mi·a·bil/i·ty, a/mi·a·ble·ness,** *n.* —**a/mi·a·bly,** *adv.*

am·i·ca·ble (am/i kə bəl), *adj.* marked by goodwill; friendly; peaceable. —**am/i·ca·bil/i·ty,** *n.* —**am/i·ca·bly,** *adv.*

am·ice (am/is), *n.* an oblong ecclesiastical vestment of white cloth, worn at the neck and shoulders.

a·mi·cus cu·ri·ae (ə mī/kəs kyŏŏr/ē ē/, ə mē/kəs kyŏŏr/ē ī/), *n., pl.* **a·mi·ci cu·ri·ae** (ə mī/kī kyŏŏr/ē ē/, ə mē/kē kyŏŏr/ē ī/). *Law.* a person, not a party to the litigation, who volunteers or is invited by the court to give advice upon some matter pending before it. Also called **friend of the court.**

a·mid (ə mid/) also **amidst**, *prep.* **1.** in the middle of; surrounded by; among. **2.** in or throughout the course of; during.

am·ide (am/īd, -id), *n.* **1.** a metallic derivative of ammonia in which the −NH₂ group is retained, as potassium amide, KNH₂. **2.** an organic compound formed from ammonia by replacing a hydrogen atom by an acyl. —**a·mid·ic** (ə mid′ik), *adj.*

a·mid·ships (ə mid′ships′) also **a·mid′ship′**, *adv.* **1.** in or toward the middle part of a ship or aircraft. —*adj.* **2.** of, pertaining to, or located in the middle part of a ship or aircraft.

a·midst (ə midst′), *prep.* AMID.

a·mi·go (ə mē′gō, ä mē′-), *n., pl.* **-gos.** a male friend.

a·mil·len·ni·al·ism (ā′mi len′ē ə liz′əm), *n.* the belief that the spiritual rule of Christ in heaven is the millennium. Also called **nonmillennialism.**

Am′ I′ My′ Broth′er′s Keep′er? Must I care about my brother?: a question Cain asked God after he murdered his brother Abel. Gen. 4:9.

a·mine (ə mēn′, am′in), *n.* any of a class of compounds derived from ammonia by replacement of one or more hydrogen atoms with organic groups. —**a·min·ic** (ə mē′nik, ə min′ik), *adj.* —**a·min·i·ty** (ə min′i tē), *n.*

ami′no ac′id (ə mē′nō, am′ə nō′), *n.* any of a class of organic compounds that contains at least one amino group, –NH₂, and one carboxyl group, –COOH: the alpha-amino acids, RCH(NH₂)COOH, are the building blocks from which proteins are constructed.

A·mish (ä′mish, am′ish), *adj.* **1.** of or pertaining to any of the strict Mennonite groups in the U.S. and Canada that oppose ritualism and wear unadorned clothing. —*n.* **2.** (*used with a pl. v.*) the Amish Mennonites. [< German *amisch*, after Jakob *Ammann*, Swiss Mennonite bishop of the 17th cent.]

a·miss (ə mis′), *adv.* **1.** out of the right or proper course, order, or condition; wrongly: *to speak amiss.* —*adj.* **2.** improper; wrong; faulty. —*Idiom.* **3. take amiss,** to be mistakenly offended at or resentful of; misunderstand.

am·i·ty (am′i tē), *n.* a peaceful relationship, as between nations; friendship; harmony.

Am·man (ä män′, ä′män), *n.* the capital of Jordan, in the W part. 777,500. Also called **Rabbah, Rabbath.**

am·me·ter (am′mē′tər), *n.* an instrument for measuring current in amperes.

am·mine (am′ēn, ə mēn′), *n.* **1.** a complex containing one or more ammonia molecules in coordinate linkage. **2.** any complex containing one or more ammonia molecules bonded to a metal ion. —**am·mi′no**, *adj.*

Am·mon (am′ən), *n.* the ancient country of the Ammonites, east of the Jordan River.

am·mo·nia (ə mōn′yə, ə mō′nē ə), *n.* **1.** a colorless, pungent, suffocating, highly water-soluble, gaseous compound, NH₃, used chiefly for refrigeration and in the manufacture of commercial chemicals and laboratory reagents. **2.** Also called **ammonia water.** ammonia dissolved in water; ammonium hydroxide.

am·mo·ni·ac (ə mō′nē ak′), *n.* **1.** Also, **am·mo·ni·a·cum** (am′ə nī′ə-kəm). GUM AMMONIAC. —*adj.* **2.** consisting of, containing, using, or like ammonia.

am·mon·ic (ə mon′ik, ə mō′nik) also **am·mon′i·cal**, *adj.* of or pertaining to ammonia or ammonium.

am·mon·i·fy (ə mon′ə fī′, ə mō′nə-), *v.,* **-fied, -fy·ing.** —*v.t.* **1.** to combine or impregnate with ammonia. **2.** to form into ammonia or ammonium compounds. —*v.i.* **3.** to become ammonified. —**am·mon′i·fi′er**, *n.*

am·mo·nite¹ (am′ə nīt′), *n.* the coiled, chambered fossil shell of an extinct cephalopod mollusk. —**am′mo·nit′ic** (-nit′ik), *adj.* —**am·mon·i·toid** (ə mon′i toid′), *adj.*

am·mo·nite² (am′ə nīt′), *n.* a nitrogenous mixture consisting chiefly of dried animal fats, usu. obtained from livestock carcasses, and used as a fertilizer.

Am·mon·ite (am′ə nīt′), *n.* a member of a Semitic people inhabiting ancient Ammon.

am·mo·ni·um (ə mō′nē əm), *n.* the univalent ion, NH₄⁺, or group, NH₄, which plays the part of a metal in the salt formed when ammonia reacts with an acid.

ammo′nium hydrox′ide, *n.* a basic liquid compound, NH₄OH; ammonia water.

ammo′nium ni′trate, *n.* a white, crystalline, water-soluble powder, NH₄NO₃, used chiefly in explosives, fertilizers, freezing mixtures, and in the manufacture of nitrous oxide.

am·mu·ni·tion (am′yə nish′ən), *n.* **1.** fired or detonated material used in combat, as rockets or bombs, and esp. bullets or shells fired by guns. **2.** the means of detonating such material, as primers or fuzes. **3.** any weapon used in a conflict. **4.** any material used to defend or attack a viewpoint, claim, etc.: *These statistics are my ammunition.*

am·ne·sia (am nē′zhə), *n.* loss of a large block of interrelated memories; complete or partial loss of memory caused by brain injury, shock, etc. —**am·ne·si·ac** (am nē′zhē ak, -zē-), *adj., n.*

am·nes·ty (am′nə stē), *n., pl.* **-ties,** *v.,* **-tied, -ty·ing.** —*n.* **1.** a general pardon for offenses, esp. political offenses, against a government. **2.** a forgetting or overlooking of any past offense. —*v.t.* **3.** to grant amnesty to; pardon.

Am′nesty Interna′tional, *n.* an independent worldwide organization working against human-rights violations and for the release of persons imprisoned for political or religious dissent; Nobel peace prize 1977. *Abbr.:* AI, A.I.

am·ni·o·cen·te·sis (am′nē ō sen tē′sis), *n., pl.* **-ses** (-sēz). the surgical procedure of guiding a hollow needle through the abdomen of a pregnant woman into the uterus and withdrawing a sample of amniotic fluid for genetic diagnosis of the fetus.

am·ni·on (am′nē ən), *n., pl.* **-ni·ons, -ni·a** (-nē ə). the innermost membrane of the sac surrounding the embryo in reptiles, birds, and mammals, enclosing the amniotic fluid. —**am′ni·ot′ic** (-ot′ik), **am′ni·on′ic**, *adj.*

am′niot′ic flu′id, *n.* the watery fluid in the amnion, in which the embryo is suspended.

Am·non (am′non), *n.* the oldest son of David, who raped Tamar and was murdered by order of Absalom. II Sam. 3:2; I Chron. 3:1.

a·moe·ba (ə mē′bə), *n., pl.* **-bas, -bae** (-bē). AMEBA.

a·mok (ə muk′, ə mok′), *n.* Also, **amuck.** (in certain SE Asian cultures) a psychic disturbance characterized by depression followed by a manic urge to murder. —*adj., adv.* **2.** AMUCK.

a·mo·le (ə mō′lē), *n., pl.* **-les.** **1.** the root of any of several plants, as Mexican species of agaves, used as a substitute for soap. **2.** any such plant itself.

a·mong (ə mung′), *prep.* **1.** in, into, or through the midst of; surrounded by: *She was among friends.* **2.** in the midst of, so as to influence: *missionary work among the local people.* **3.** with a share for each of: *Divide the fruit among you.* **4.** in the class or group of: *That is among the things we must do.* **5.** with most or many of: *a candidate popular among the people.* **6.** by the joint or reciprocal action of: *Settle it among yourselves. They quarreled among themselves.* **7.** familiar to or characteristic of: *a proverb among the Spanish.*

a·mon·til·la·do (ə mon′tl ä′dō, -tē ä′-), *n.* a pale, dry Spanish sherry.

a·mor·al (ā môr′əl, a môr′-, ā mor′-, a mor′-), *adj.* **1.** without moral quality; neither moral nor immoral. **2.** lacking or indifferent to moral standards, criteria, or principles. —**a·mo·ral·i·ty** (ā′mə ral′i tē, am′ə-), *n.* —**a·mor′al·ly**, *adv.*

am·o·ret·to (am′ə ret′ō, ä′mə-), *n., pl.* **-ret·ti** (-ret′ē). a little cupid.

am·o·rist (am′ər ist), *n.* a person who is devoted to love or writes about love.

Am·o·rite (am′ə rīt′), *n.* **1.** a member of a culturally diverse population of western Semites prominent in the history of ancient Syria and adjacent areas, c2600–1200 B.C. **2.** the language of this population.

am·o·rous (am′ər əs), *adj.* **1.** inclined or disposed to love, esp. sexual love. **2.** showing, expressing, or pertaining to love. **3.** being in love; enamored (usu. fol. by *of*). —**am′o·rous·ly**, *adv.* —**am′o·rous·ness**, *n.*

a·mor pa·tri·ae (ä′môr pä′trē ī′; *Eng.* ā′môr pā′trē ē′), *n. Latin.* love of one's country; patriotism.

a·mor·phous (ə môr′fəs), *adj.* **1.** lacking definite form; having no specific shape: *amorphous clouds.* **2.** of no particular kind or character; indeterminate; unorganized: *an amorphous style.* **3.** *Chem.* not crystalline. —**a·mor′phous·ly**, *adv.* —**a·mor′phous·ness**, *n.* —**a·mor′phism**, *n.*

am·or·ti·za·tion (am′ər tə zā′shən, ə môr′-) also **am·or·tize·ment** (-tīz′mənt, ə môr′tiz-), *n.* **1.** an act or instance of amortizing a debt or other obligation. **2.** the sums devoted to this purpose.

am·or·tize (am′ər tīz′, ə môr′tīz), *v.t.,* **-tized, -tiz·ing.** **1.** to liquidate (a debt), esp. by periodic payments to the creditor. **2.** to write off a cost of (an asset) gradually. —**am′or·tiz′a·ble**, *adj.*

A·mos (ā′məs), *n.* **1.** a Minor Prophet of the 8th century B.C. **2.** a book of the Bible bearing his name.

a·mount (ə mount′), *n.* **1.** the sum total of two or more quantities or sums. **2.** quantity; measure: *a great amount of resistance.* **3.** the full effect, value, or significance. —*v.i.* **4.** to total; add (usu. fol. by *to*): *The bill amounts to $300.* **5.** to be equal in value, effect, or extent (usu. followed by *to*): *All those fine words amount to nothing.* **6.** to develop; attain (usu. fol. by *to*): *With his intelligence, he should amount to something one day.* —**Usage.** The traditional distinction between AMOUNT and NUMBER is that AMOUNT is used with mass or uncountable nouns (*the amount of paperwork; the amount of energy*) and NUMBER with countable nouns (*a number of songs; a number of days*). Although objected to, the use of AMOUNT instead of NUMBER with countable nouns occurs in both speech and writing, esp. when the noun can be considered as a unit or group (*the amount of people present; the amount of weapons*) or when it refers to money (*the amount of dollars paid; the amount of pennies in the till*).

a·mour (ə moŏr′), *n.* a love affair, esp. an illicit or secret one.

am·ox·i·cil·lin (am ok′sə sil′in, ə mok′-), *n.* a semisynthetic penicillin, C₁₆H₁₉N₃O₅S, taken orally as a broad-spectrum antibiotic.

amp¹ (amp), *n.* ampere.

amp² (amp), *n.* **1.** an amplifier. —*v.i., v.t.* **2.** to amplify.

AMP, adenosine monophosphate: a nucleotide composed of adenine, ribose, and one phosphate group, formed by the partial breakdown of adenosine triphosphate, usu. at an end point in the metabolic pathway. Compare ADP, ATP.

am·pere (am′pēr, am pēr′), *n.* the SI unit of electrical current, equal to a constant current that would produce a force of 2×10^{-7} newton per meter of length when maintained in two straight parallel conductors of infinite length and negligible circular cross section and placed one meter apart in a vacuum. *Abbr.:* A, amp.

am·per·sand (am′pər sand′), *n.* a character or symbol (& or ·) for *and,* as in *Smith & Jones, Inc.* [contr. of *and per se and* lit., (the symbol) & by itself (stands for) and]

am·phet·a·mine (am fet′ə mēn′, -min), *n.* a racemic drug, $C_9H_{13}N$, that stimulates the central nervous system: used in medicine chiefly to counteract depression and misused illegally as a stimulant.

amphi-, a prefix occurring originally in loanwords from Greek, meaning "two," "both," "on both sides": *amphibious; amphistylar.*

am·phib·i·an (am fib′ē ən), *n.* **1.** any cold-blooded vertebrate of the class Amphibia, including frogs, salamanders, and caecilians, usu. having an aquatic, gill-breathing tadpole stage and later developing lungs. **2.** an airplane designed for taking off from and landing on both land and water. **3.** a flat-bottomed military vehicle, equipped with both tracks and a rudder for traveling on land or in water. —*adj.* **4.** belonging or pertaining to the class Amphibia. **5.** AMPHIBIOUS.

am·phib·i·ous (am fib′ē əs), *adj.* **1.** living or able to live both on land and in water. **2.** capable of operating on both land and water: *amphibious vehicles.* **3.** pertaining to military operations by both land and naval forces, esp. to an assault by troops landed by naval ships. **4.** trained to fight on both land and sea. **5.** of or having a mixed or twofold nature. —**am·phib′i·ous·ly,** *adv.*

am·phi·bole (am′fə bōl′), *n.* any of a complex group of hydrous silicate minerals, containing chiefly calcium, magnesium, sodium, iron, and aluminum, and including hornblende, asbestos, etc., occurring as important constituents of many rocks.

am·phib·o·ly (am fib′ə lē) also **amphibology,** *n.,* *pl.* **-lies.** ambiguity of speech, esp. from uncertainty of the grammatical construction rather than of the meaning of the words, as in *The Duke yet lives that Henry shall depose.* —**am·phi·bol·ic** (am′fə bol′ik), *adj.*

am·phi·brach (am′fə brak′), *n.* a trisyllabic metrical foot whose syllables are short, long, short in quantitative meter, and unstressed, stressed, unstressed in accentual meter. —**am′phi·brach′ic,** *adj.*

am·phi·go·ry (am′fi gôr′ē, -gōr′ē), *n., pl.* **-ries.** a meaningless or nonsensical piece of writing, esp. one intended as a parody. —**am′phi·gor′ic** (-gôr′ik, -gor′-), *adj.*

am·phim·a·cer (am fim′ə sər), *n.* a trisyllabic metrical foot whose syllables are long, short, long in quantitative meter, and stressed, unstressed, stressed in accentual meter.

Am·phip·o·lis (am fip′ə lis) *n.* a city of Macedonia through which the Apostle Paul passed during his second missionary journey. Acts 17:1.

am·phi·the·a·ter (am′fə thē′ə tər, -thēᵊ′tər), *n.* **1.** an oval or round building with tiers of seats around a central open area, as those used in ancient Rome for contests and spectacles. **2.** any similar place for public contests, games, performances, etc. **3.** a room with tiers of seats around a central area for students and other observers. **4.** a level area surrounded by rising ground. Often, **am′phi·the′a·tre.** —**am′phi·the·at′ric** (-thē ā′trik), **am′phi·the·at′ri·cal,** *adj.*

am·pho·ra (am′fər ə), *n., pl.* **-pho·rae** (-fə rē′), **-pho·ras.** a large earthenware storage vessel of Greek and Roman antiquity, having an oval body with two handles extending from below the lip to the shoulder. —**am′pho·ral,** *adj.*

am·pho·ter·ic (am′fə ter′ik), *adj.* capable of functioning either as an acid or as a base.

am·pi·cil·lin (am′pə sil′in), *n.* a broad-spectrum semisynthetic penicillin, $C_{16}H_{19}N_3O_4S$, effective against certain susceptible bacteria.

am·ple (am′pəl), *adj.,* **-pler, -plest. 1.** fully sufficient for the purpose or need; plentiful. **2.** liberal; copious: *an ample reward.* **3.** large; roomy: *ample storage space.* —**am′ple·ness,** *n.* —**am′ply,** *adv.*

am·pli·fi·ca·tion (am′plə fi kā′shən), *n.* **1.** the act of amplifying or the state of being amplified. **2.** expansion of a statement, narrative, etc., as for rhetorical purposes. **3.** a statement, narrative, etc., so expanded. **4.** the matter or substance used to expand an idea, statement, or the like. **5. a.** increase in the strength of current, voltage, or power. **b.** (not in technical use) increase in the loudness of sound, esp. by mechanical or electronic means. —**am·plif′i·ca·to′ry** (-plif′i kə tôr′ē, -tōr′ē), *adj.*

am·pli·fi·er (am′plə fī′ər), *n.* **1.** a person or device that amplifies or enlarges. **2.** an electronic component or circuit for amplifying power, current, or voltage.

am·pli·fy (am′plə fī′), *v.,* **-fied, -fy·ing.** —*v.t.* **1.** to make larger, greater, or stronger; enlarge; extend. **2.** to expand in stating or describing, as by details or illustrations; clarify by expanding. **3. a.** to increase the amplitude of; cause amplification in. **b.** (not in technical use) to increase the loudness of (sound), esp. by mechanical or electronic means. —*v.i.* **4.** to discourse at length (usu. fol. by *on*). —**am′pli·fi′a·ble,** *adj.*

am·pli·tude (am′pli tood′, -tyood′), *n.* **1.** the state or quality of being ample, esp. as to breadth or width; largeness. **2.** large or full measure; abundance. **3.** mental range, scope, or capacity. **4.** the absolute value of the maximum displacement from a zero value during one period of an oscillation. **5.** the maximum deviation of an alternating current from its average value. **6.** the arc of the horizon measured from the east or west point to the point where a vertical circle through a heavenly body would intersect the horizon. **7.** ARGUMENT (def. 8b).

am·pule or **am·pul** or **am·poule** (am′pyool, -pool), *n.* a sealed glass or plastic bulb containing solutions for hypodermic injection.

am·pul·la (am pul′ə, -pool′ə), *n., pl.* **-pul·lae** (-pul′ē, -pool′ē). **1.** a dilated portion of a canal or duct, as of the semicircular canals of the ear. **2.** a bottle with a bulbous body and narrow neck, used by the ancient Romans for oil, wine, or other liquids.

am·pu·tate (am′pyoo tāt′), *v.t.,* **-tat·ed, -tat·ing.** to cut off (all or part of a limb or digit of the body), as by surgery. —**am′pu·ta′tion,** *n.* —**am′pu·ta′tive,** *adj.* —**am′pu·ta′tor,** *n.*

am·pu·tee (am′pyoo tē′), *n.* a person who has lost all or part of an arm, hand, leg, etc., by amputation.

Am·ram (am′ram), *n.* the father of Aaron and Moses. Ex. 6:20.

Am·rit·sar (əm rit′sər), *n.* a city in NW Punjab, in NW India: site of the holiest shrine of the Sikh religion. 432,663.

Am·ster·dam (am′stər dam′), *n.* the official capital of the Netherlands. 712,294. Compare HAGUE, The.

amt., amount.

Am·trak (am′trak′), *n.* a public corporation created by Congress in 1970 to operate a national passenger railroad system through contracts with existing railroads. [*Am(erican) tra(vel on trac)k*]

amu or **AMU,** atomic mass unit.

a·muck (ə muk′), *adj.* **1.** mad with murderous frenzy. —*n.* **2.** AMOK. —*adv.,* **Idiom. 3. run** or **go amuck** or **amok, a.** to rush about in a murderous frenzy. **b.** to go or rush about wildly. [< Malay]

am·u·let (am′yə lit), *n.* a charm worn to ward off evil or to bring good fortune; talisman.

a·muse (ə myooz′), *v.t.,* **a·mused, a·mus·ing. 1.** to hold the attention of (someone) pleasantly; entertain or divert: *to keep guests amused at dinner.* **2.** to cause mirth, laughter, or the like, in: *The comedian's jokes amused everyone.* —**a·mus′a·ble,** *adj.* —**a·mus′ed·ly,** *adv.* —**a·mus′er,** *n.*

a·muse·ment (ə myooz′mənt), *n.* **1.** anything that amuses; pastime; entertainment. **2.** the act of amusing. **3.** the state of being amused; enjoyment.

amuse′ment park′, *n.* a park equipped with such recreational devices as a Ferris wheel, roller coaster, etc., and usu. having booths for games and refreshments.

amuse′ment tax′, *n.* a tax levied on such forms of entertainment as motion pictures, theater, etc., and included in the total admission price.

a·mus·ing (ə myoo′zing), *adj.* **1.** pleasantly entertaining or diverting. **2.** causing laughter or mirth: *an amusing joke.* —**a·mus′ing·ly,** *adv.* —**a·mus′ing·ness,** *n.*

a·myg·da·la (ə mig′də lə), *n., pl.* **-lae** (-lē′). any of various almond-shaped anatomical parts, as a brain structure of the limbic system that is involved in emotions of fear and aggression.

am·yl (am′il, ā′mil), *n.* any of several univalent, isomeric groups with the formula C_5H_{11}. Also called **pentyl.**

am·y·la·ceous (am′ə lā′shəs), *adj.* like starch; starchy.

am′yl al′cohol, *n.* a colorless liquid, $C_5H_{12}O$, consisting of a mixture of two or more isomeric alcohols, derived from the pentanes, and used as a solvent and intermediate for organic synthesis.

am·yl·ase (am′ə lās′, -lāz′), *n.* any of several digestive enzymes that break down starches.

amylo-, a combining form representing AMYLUM: *amylolysis.*

am·y·lol·y·sis (am′ə lol′ə sis), *n.* the chemical conversion of starch into sugar. —**am′y·lo·lyt′ic** (-lō lit′ik), *adj.*

am·y·lo·pec·tin (am′ə lō pek′tin), *n.* the outer, insoluble component of starch granules. Compare AMYLOSE.

am·yl·ose (am′ə lōs′), *n.* the inner, soluble component of starch granules. Compare AMYLOPECTIN.

am·y·lum (am′ə ləm), *n.* STARCH (def. 1).

a·my·o·troph′ic lat′eral sclero′sis (ā′mī ə trof′ik, -trō′fik, ā mī′ə-), *n.* a nervous system disease in which degeneration of motor neurons in the brain stem and spinal cord leads to atrophy and paralysis of the voluntary muscles. *Abbr.:* ALS Also called **Lou Gehrig's disease.**

an (ən; *when stressed* an), *indefinite article.* the form of A[1] before an initial vowel sound (*an arch; an honor*) and sometimes, esp. in British English, before an initial unstressed syllable beginning with a silent or weakly pronounced *h*: *an historian.*

an-, a prefix occurring orig. in loanwords from Greek, with the meanings "not," "without," "lacking" (*anaerobic; anonymous*); regularly attached to words or stems beginning with a vowel or *h*. Compare A-[6].

-an[1], a suffix with the general sense "of, pertaining to, having qualities of," occurring orig. in adjectives borrowed from Latin and formed from nouns denoting places (*Roman; urban*) or persons (*Augustan*), now commonly forming adjectives and nouns denoting affiliation with a place or membership in a group (*crustacean; Episcopalian*); attached to personal names, it may additionally mean "contemporary with" (*Elizabethan*) or "proponent of" (*Freudian*). The suffix **-an**[1] also occurs in personal nouns denoting one who engages in, practices, or works with the referent of the base word (*comedian; historian*). See -IAN for relative distribution with that suffix. Compare -ENNE, -ARIAN, -ICIAN.

-an[2], a suffix used in the names of organic chemical compounds, esp. polysaccharides: *pentosan; xanthan.*

An, *Chem. Symbol.* actinon.

an·a (an′ə, ä′nə), *n.* **1.** a collection of miscellaneous information about a particular subject, person, place, or thing. **2.** an item in such a collection, as an anecdote, a memorable saying, etc.

ana-, a prefix occurring orig. in verbs and verbal derivatives borrowed from Greek, usu. denoting upward or backward motion (*anadromous*), completion (*analysis; anatomy*), or repetition (*anamorphosis*). Also, *before a vowel,* **an-.**

-ana or **-iana,** a suffix that forms collective nouns denoting an assembly of items representative of or associated with the place, person, or period named by the stem: *Americana; Shakespeareana; Victoriana.*

an·a·bae·na (an′ə bē′nə), *n., pl.* **-nas.** any blue-green algae of the genus *Anabaena,* sometimes contaminating drinking water and giving it a fishy taste.

An·a·bap·tist (an′ə bap′tist), *n.* **1.** a member of any of various 16th-century Protestant sects that baptized adult believers and advocated social reforms as well as separation of church and state. —*adj.* **2.** of or pertaining to Anabaptists or Anabaptism. —**An′a·bap′tism,** *n.*

an·a·bi·o·sis (an′ə bī ō′sis), *n.* **1.** reanimation after apparent death. **2.** *Zool.* a state of suspended animation under adverse environmental conditions. —**an′a·bi·ot′ic** (-ot′ik), *adj.*

an·a·bleps (an′ə bleps′), *n.* any small tropical American freshwater fish of the genus *Anableps,* having each eye divided horizontally for seeing above and below the water line simultaneously. Also called **four-eyes.**

an′abol′ic ster′oid, *n.* any of a class of steroid hormones, esp. testosterone, that promote growth of muscle tissue.

a·nab·o·lism (ə nab′ə liz′əm), *n.* constructive metabolism; the synthesis in living organisms of more complex substances from simpler ones (opposed to *catabolism*). —**an·a·bol′ic** (an′ə bol′ik), *adj.*

a·nach·ro·nism (ə nak′rə niz′əm), *n.* **1.** an error in chronology in which a person, object, event, etc., is assigned a date or period other than the correct one. **2.** a thing or person that belongs to another, esp. an earlier, time. —**a·nach′ro·nis′tic, a·nach′ro·nis′ti·cal, a·nach′ro·nous,** *adj.* —**a·nach′ro·nis′ti·cal·ly, a·nach′ro·nous·ly, an·a·chron·i·cal·ly** (an′ə kron′ik lē), *adv.*

an·a·con·da (an′ə kon′də), *n., pl.* **-das.** a South American boa, *Eunectes murinus,* that often grows to a length of more than 25 ft. (7.6 m).

an·a·cru·sis (an′ə krōō′sis), *n., pl.* **-cru·ses** (-krōō′sēz). **1.** an unstressed syllable or syllable group that begins a line of verse but is not counted as part of the first foot. **2.** UPBEAT (def. 1). —**an′a·crus′tic** (-krus′tik), *adj.* —**an′a·crus′ti·cal·ly,** *adv.*

an·a·di·plo·sis (an′ə di plō′sis), *n., pl.* **-plo·ses** (-plō′sēz). repetition of the last word or words of one clause at the beginning of the next clause, as in "To die, to sleep; to sleep!"

a·nad·ro·mous (ə nad′rə məs), *adj.* (of fish) migrating from salt water to spawn in fresh water, as salmon (disting. from *catadromous*).

an·aer·obe (an′ə rōb′, an âr′ōb), *n.* an organism, esp. a bacterium, that does not require air or free oxygen to live (opposed to *aerobe*).

an·aer·o·bic (an′ə rō′bik, an′â-), *adj.* **1.** (of an organism or tissue) living in the absence of air or free oxygen. **2.** pertaining to or caused by the absence of oxygen. —**an′aer·o′bi·cal·ly,** *adv.*

an·aes·the′sia (an′əs thē′zhə), *n.* ANESTHESIA. —**an′aes·thet′ic** (-thet′ik), *n., adj.* —**an·aes·the·tist** (ə nes′thi tist), *n.*

an·a·gram (an′ə gram′), *n.* **1.** a word, phrase, or sentence formed from another by rearranging its letters: "*Angel*" is an anagram of "*glean.*" **2. anagrams,** (used with a sing. v.) a game in which the players build words by transposing and, often, adding letters. —**an′a·gram·mat′ic** (-grə mat′ik), *adj.* —**an′a·gram·mat′i·cal·ly,** *adv.*

An·a·heim (an′ə hīm′), *n.* a city in SW California, SE of Los Angeles. 244,670.

An·a·heim (an′ə hīm′), *n.* a city in SW California, SE of Los Angeles. 282,133.

An·a·kim (an′ə kim), *n.pl.* tall people or giants who lived in S Palestine and were destroyed or scattered after the arrival of the Hebrews. Num. 13:28, 31; Deut. 2:21; 9:2.

a·nal (ān′l), *adj.* **1.** of, pertaining to, or near the anus. **2.** *Psychoanal.* **a.** of or pertaining to the second stage of psychosexual development, during which gratification is derived from the retention or expulsion of feces. **b.** of or pertaining to a group of adult behaviors and personality traits that include being rigid and ungenerous. —**a′nal·ly,** *adv.*

an·a·lects (an′l ekts′) also **an·a·lec·ta** (an′l ek′tə), *n.pl.* selected passages from the writings of an author or of different authors. —**an′a·lec′tic,** *adj.*

An′alects of Confu′cius, The, (Chinese, *Lun Yü*) a compilation of the discourses, maxims, and aphorisms of Confucius, dating from the 4th century B.C.

an·a·lep·tic (an′l ep′tik), *adj.* **1.** restoring; invigorating; giving strength after disease. **2.** awakening, esp. from drug stupor. —*n.* **3.** a nervous system stimulant.

an·al·ge·si·a (an′l jē′zē ə, -sē ə), *n.* absence of sense of pain.

an·al·ge·sic (an′l jē′zik, -sik), *n.* **1.** a remedy that relieves or allays pain. —*adj.* **2.** of, pertaining to, or causing analgesia.

an·a·log (an′l ôg′, -og′), *n.* **1.** ANALOGUE. —*adj.* **2.** of or pertaining to a mechanism that represents data by measurement to a continuous physical variable, as voltage or pressure. **3.** displaying a readout by a pointer or hands on a dial rather than by numerical digits: *an analog watch.*

an′alog comput′er, *n.* a computer that represents data by measurable quantities, as voltages, rather than by numbers. Compare DIGITAL COMPUTER.

a·nal·o·gism (ə nal′ə jiz′əm), *n.* reasoning or argument by analogy. —**a·nal′o·gist,** *n.* —**a·nal′o·gis′tic,** *adj.*

a·nal·o·gize (ə nal′ə jīz′), *v.,* **-gized, -giz·ing.** —*v.i.* **1.** to make use of analogy in reasoning, argument, etc. **2.** to be analogous; show analogy. —*v.t.* **3.** to make analogous; show an analogy between.

a·nal·o·gous (ə nal′ə gəs), *adj.* **1.** having analogy; corresponding in some particular: *A brain and a computer are analogous.* **2.** *Biol.* corresponding in function but of different origins and having evolved separately, as the wings of birds and insects (opposed to *homologous*). —**a·nal′o·gous·ly,** *adv.*

an·a·logue or **an·a·log** (an′l ôg′, -og′), *n.* **1.** something having analogy to something else. **2.** *Biol.* an organ or part analogous to another. **3.** one of a group of chemical compounds similar in structure but different in composition.

a·nal·o·gy (ə nal′ə jē), *n., pl.* **-gies. 1.** a similarity between like features of two things, on which a comparison may be based: *the analogy between the heart and a pump.* **2.** similarity or comparability: *I see no analogy between our situations.* **3.** a similarity of forms having a separate evolutionary origin (opposed to *homology*). **4.** a linguistic process by which words or phrases are created or re-formed according to existing patterns in the language, as when dialectal *shoon* was re-formed as *shoes.* **5.** a form of reasoning in which one thing is inferred to be similar to another thing in a certain respect, on the basis of known similarities in other respects.

an·al·pha·bet (an al′fə bet′, -bit), *n.* a person who cannot read or write; illiterate.

a·nal·y·sis (ə nal′ə sis), *n., pl.* **-ses** (-sēz′). **1.** the separating of any material or abstract entity into its constituent elements (opposed to *synthesis*). **2.** this process as a method of studying the nature of something or of determining its essential features and their relations. **3.** a presentation, usu. in writing, of the results of this process. **4. a.** an investigation based on the properties of numbers. **b.** the discussion of a problem by algebra, as opposed to geometry. **c.** the branch of mathematics consisting of calculus and its higher developments. **5. a.** intentionally produced decomposition or separation of materials into their ingredients or elements, as to find their kind or quantity. **b.** the ascertainment of the kind or amount of one or more of the constituents of materials. **6.** PSYCHOANALYSIS.

an·a·lyst (an′l ist), *n.* **1.** a person who analyzes or who is skilled in analysis. **2.** a psychoanalyst.

an·a·lyt·ic (an′l it′ik) also **an′a·lyt′i·cal,** *adj.* **1.** pertaining to or proceeding by analysis (opposed to *synthetic*). **2.** skilled in or habitually using analysis. **3.** (of a language) characterized by the use of function words and changes in word order, rather than inflected forms, to express syntactic relations. **4.** (of a proposition) necessarily true because its denial involves a contradiction, as "All husbands are married." —**an′a·lyt′i·cal·ly,** *adv.*

an·a·lyt·ics (an′l it′iks), *n.* (used with a sing. v.) the science of logical analysis.

an·a·lyze (an′l īz′), *v.t.,* **-lyzed, -lyz·ing. 1.** to separate (a material or abstract entity) into constituent parts or elements; determine the elements or essential features of (opposed to *synthesize*). **2.** to examine critically, so as to bring out the essential elements or give the essence of: *to analyze a poem.* **3.** to examine carefully and in detail so as to identify causes, key factors, possible results, etc.: *to analyze a situation.* **4.** to subject to mathematical, chemical, grammatical, etc., analysis. **5.** PSYCHOANALYZE. —**an′a·lyz′a·ble,** *adj.* —**an′a·lyz′a·bil′i·ty,** *n.* —**an·a·ly·za′tion,** *n.* —**an′a·lyz′er,** *n.*

an·am·ne·sis (an′am nē′sis), *n., pl.* **-ses** (-sēz). **1.** the recollection or remembrance of the past; reminiscence. **2.** the medical history of a patient. **3.** a prompt immune response to a previously encountered antigen, as after a booster shot in a previously immunized person. —**an′am·nes′tic** (-nes′tik), *adj.* —**an′am·nes′ti·cal·ly,** *adv.*

an·a·mor·phic (an′ə môr′fik), *adj.* **1.** *Optics.* having or producing unequal magnifications along two axes perpendicular to each other: *an anamorphic lens.* **2.** of or pertaining to anamorphosis.

an·a·mor·pho·sis (an′ə môr′fə sis, -môr fō′sis), *n., pl.* **-ses** (-sēz′, -sēz). **1.** a drawing presenting a distorted image that appears in natural form under certain conditions, as when reflected from a curved mirror. **2.** the gradual change in form from one type to another during the evolution of a group of organisms.

An·a·ni·as (an′ə nī′əs), *n.* **1.** a man who was struck dead for lying. Acts. 5:1–5. **2.** a liar.

an·a·pest or **an·a·paest** (an′ə pest′), *n.* a trisyllabic metrical foot whose syllables are short, short, long in quantitative meter and unstressed, unstressed, stressed in accentual meter. —**an′a·pes′tic,** *adj.* —**an′a·pes′ti·cal·ly,** *adv.*

an·a·phase (an′ə fāz′), *n.* the stage in mitosis or meiosis following metaphase in which the daughter chromosomes move away from each other to opposite ends of the cell. —**an′a·pha′sic,** *adj.*

a·naph·o·ra (ə naf′ər ə), *n.* **1.** the use of a word as a regular grammatical substitute for a preceding word or group of words, as the use of *it* and *do* in *I know it and they do, too.* **2.** repetition of a word or words at the beginning of two or more successive phrases, verses, clauses, or sentences, as in Shakespeare's "This blessed plot, this earth, this realm, this England." —**a·naph′o·ral,** *adj.*

an·a·phy·lax·is (an′ə fə lak′sis), *n.* a hypersensitive reaction to an allergen, as a severe bout of hay fever, the rapid appearance of wheals, or profound physiological changes and shock (**an′aphylac′tic shock′**). —**an′a·phy·lac′tic** (-lak′tik), *adj.* —**an′a·phy·lac′ti·cal·ly,** *adv.*

an·ar·chist (an′ər kist), *n.* **1.** a person who advocates or believes in anarchy or anarchism. **2.** a person who seeks to overturn by violence all constituted forms and institutions of society and government, with no purpose of establishing any other system of order. **3.** a person who promotes disorder or excites revolt against any established rule, law, or custom. —**an′ar·chis′tic,** *adj.*

an·ar·chy (an′ər kē), *n.* **1.** a state of society without government or law. **2.** political and social disorder due to the absence of governmental control. **3.** a theory that regards the absence of all direct or coercive government as a political ideal and that proposes the cooperative and voluntary association of individuals and groups as the principal mode of organized society. **4.** confusion; chaos; disorder. —**an·ar·chic** (an är′kik), **an·ar′chi·cal,** *adj.* —**an·ar′chi·cal·ly,** *adv.*

an·as·tig·mat·ic (an′ə stig mat′ik, a nas′tig-), *adj.* (of a lens) not having astigmatism; forming point images of a point object located off the axis of the lens.

a·nas·to·mo·sis (ə nas′tə mō′sis), *n., pl.* **-ses** (-sēz). **1.** interconnection between parts of any branching system, as between blood vessels or branches of a stream. **2.** a joining of or opening between two organs or spaces normally not connected. —**a·nas′to·mose′,** *v.t., v.i.,* **-mosed, -mos·ing.** —**a·nas′to·mot′ic** (-ə nat′ə mot′ik), *adj.*

a·nas·tro·phe (ə nas′trə fē), *n.* reversal of the usual order of words for rhetorical effect; inversion.

a·nath·e·ma (ə nath′ə mə), *n., pl.* **-mas. 1.** a person or thing detested or loathed: *That subject is anathema to them.* **2.** a person or thing condemned to damnation. **3.** a formal ecclesiastical curse of excommunication. **4.** any imprecation of divine punishment. **5.** a curse. —**a·nath′e·mat′ic** (-mat′ik), *adj.*

An·a·thoth (an′ə thoth′), *n.* the birthplace near Jerusalem of the prophet Jeremiah. Jer. 1:1, 29:27, 32:7–9.

An·a·to·li·a (an′ə tō′lē ə), *n.* a vast plateau between the Black and the Mediterranean seas: in ancient usage, synonymous with Asia Minor; in modern usage, applied to Turkey in Asia. Compare Asia Minor.

an·a·tom·i·cal (an′ə tom′i kəl) also **an′a·tom′ic,** *adj.* of or pertaining to anatomy. —**an′a·tom′i·cal·ly,** *adv.*

a·nat·o·mist (ə nat′ə mist), *n.* **1.** a specialist in anatomy. **2.** a person who analyzes something with particular care.

a·nat·o·mize (ə nat′ə mīz′), *v.t.,* **-mized, -miz·ing. 1.** to display the anatomy of; dissect. **2.** to examine in great detail; analyze minutely. —**a·nat′o·mi·za′tion,** *n.* —**a·nat′o·miz′er,** *n.*

a·nat·o·my (ə nat′ə mē), *n., pl.* **-mies. 1.** the science dealing with the structure of animals and plants. **2.** the structure of an animal or plant, or of any of its parts. **3.** dissection of all or part of an animal or plant in order to study its structure. **4.** *Informal.* the human body. **5.** an analysis or minute examination.

a·nat·to (ə nat′ō, ä nä′tō), *n., pl.* **-tos.** ANNATTO.

an·ces·tor (an′ses tər; *esp. Brit.* -sə stər), *n.* **1.** a person from whom one is descended; forebear; progenitor. **2. a.** the form or stock from which an organism has descended. **b.** the actual or assumed earlier type from which a species or other taxon evolved. **3.** an object, idea, style, or occurrence serving as a prototype, forerunner, or inspiration to a later one. **4.** a person from whom mental, artistic, spiritual, etc., descent is claimed.

an′cestor wor′ship, *n.* (in certain societies) the veneration of ancestors whose spirits are frequently held to possess the power to influence the affairs of the living.

an·ces·tral (an ses′trəl), *adj.* **1.** pertaining to ancestors; descending or claimed from ancestors. **2.** serving as a forerunner or inspiration. —**an·ces′tral·ly,** *adv.*

an·ces·try (an′ses trē; *esp. Brit.* -sə strē), *n., pl.* **-tries. 1.** ancestral descent; lineage. **2.** honorable or distinguished descent: *famous by title and ancestry.* **3.** a series of ancestors. **4.** the origin of a phenomenon, object, idea, or style. **5.** the history or developmental process of a phenomenon, object, idea, or style.

an·chor (ang′kər), *n.* **1.** a heavy device dropped by a chain, cable, or rope to the bottom of a body of water for restraining the motion of a vessel or other floating object. **2.** any similar device for holding fast or checking motion. **3.** a person or thing that can be relied on for support, stability, or security; mainstay. **4.** the main broadcaster on a program of

news, sports, etc., who often coordinates the reports of the program's other broadcasters. **5.** a television program that attracts many viewers who are likely to stay tuned to the network for the programs that follow. **6.** Also, **anchorman. a.** the person on a sports team, esp. a relay team, who competes last. **b.** the person farthest to the rear on a tug-of-war team. **7. anchors,** *Slang.* the brakes of an automobile. —*v.t.* **8.** to hold fast by an anchor. **9.** to fix or fasten; affix firmly: *to anchor a button to a sleeve.* **10.** to act or serve as a radio or television anchor for: *to anchor the evening news.* —*v.i.* **11.** to drop anchor; lie or ride at anchor. **12.** to keep hold or be firmly fixed. **13.** to act or serve as a radio or television anchor. —**Idiom. 14. at anchor,** kept in place by an anchor. —**an′chor·a·ble,** *adj.* —**an′chor·like′,** *adj.*

an·chor·age (ang′kər ij), *n.* **1.** a place for anchoring ships. **2.** a charge for occupying such an area. **3.** the act of anchoring or the state of being anchored. **4.** a means of securing. **5.** something providing security.

An·chor·age (ang′kər ij), *n.* a seaport in S Alaska. 253,649.

an·cho·ress (ang′kər is), *n.* a woman who is an anchorite.

an·cho·rite (ang′kə rīt′) also **an·cho·ret** (-kər it, -kə ret′), *n.* a person who has retired to a solitary place for a life of religious seclusion; hermit. —**an′cho·rit′ic** (-rit′ik), *adj.* —**an′cho·rit·ism** (-rī tiz′əm), *n.*

an·chor·man (ang′kər man′, -mən), *n., pl.* **-men** (-men′, -mən). **1.** ANCHOR (def. 6). **2.** a person who anchors a program of news, sports, etc.; anchor.

an·chor·wom·an (ang′kər wŏŏm′ən), *n., pl.* **-wom·en.** a woman who anchors a program of news, sports, etc.; anchor.

an·cho·vy (an′chō vē, -chə-, an chō′vē), *n., pl.* **-vies.** any small schooling fish of the family Engraulidae, as the European *Engraulis encrasicholus,* often salted and dried, canned, or made into a paste and used in cooking.

an·cien ré·gime (än syan′ Rā zhēm′), *n. French.* **1.** the political and social system of France before the revolution of 1789. **2.** any former political and social system.

an·cient (ān′shənt), *adj.* **1.** of or in time long past, esp. before the end of the Western Roman Empire A.D. 476. **2.** dating from a remote period: *ancient rocks.* **3.** very old; aged. **4.** old in wisdom and experience; venerable. **5.** old-fashioned or antique: *an ancient cooking stove.* —*n.* **6.** a person who lived in ancient times. **7. the ancients, a.** the civilized peoples or cultures of antiquity, as the Greeks, Romans, Hebrews, and Egyptians. **b.** the writers, artists, and philosophers of ancient times, esp. those of Greece and Rome. **8.** a very old or aged person.

an′cient his′tory, *n.* **1.** the study or a course of study of history before the end of the Western Roman Empire A.D. 476. **2.** information or an event that is common knowledge or no longer pertinent.

An′cient of Days′, *n.* God. Dan. 7:9, 13, 22.

an·cil·la (an sil′ə), *n., pl.* **-las.** an accessory; auxiliary or adjunct.

an·cil·lar·y (an′sə ler′ē; *esp. Brit.* an sil′ə rē), *adj., n., pl.* **-lar·ies.** —*adj.* **1.** subordinate; subsidiary. **2.** auxiliary; assisting. —*n.* **3.** something that serves in an ancillary capacity.

an·con (ang′kon), *n., pl.* **an·co·nes** (ang kō′nēz). **1.** the elbow. **2.** a bracket or console, as one supporting part of a cornice. —**an·co′nal,** **an·co′ne·al,** *adj.* —**an′con·oid′,** *adj.*

and (and; *unstressed* ənd, ən, *or, esp. after a homorganic consonant,* n), *conj.* **1.** (used to connect grammatically coordinate words, phrases, or clauses) with; as well as; in addition to: *pens and pencils.* **2.** added to; plus: *2 and 2 are 4.* **3.** then: *He finished and went to bed.* **4.** also, at the same time: *to sleep and dream.* **5.** (used to imply different qualities in things having the same name): *There are bargains and bargains, so watch out.* **6.** (used to introduce a sentence, implying continuation) also; then: *And he said unto Moses.* **7.** *Informal.* to (used between two finite verbs): *Try and do it.* **8.** (used to introduce a consequence or conditional result): *Say one more word and I'll scream.* **9.** but; on the contrary: *He tried to run five miles and couldn't.* —*n.* **10.** an added condition, stipulation, or particular: *no ands or buts about it.* **11.** *Logic.* the connective used in conjunction. —**Idiom. 12. and so forth** or **so on,** and the like; and more of the same; et cetera.

AND (and), *n.* a Boolean operator that returns a positive result when both operands are positive.

an·dan·te (än dän′tā, an dan′tē), *adj., adv., n., pl.* **-tes.** *Music.* —*adj., adv.* **1.** moderately slow and even. —*n.* **2.** an andante movement or piece.

An·der·sen (an′dər sən), *n.* **Hans Christian,** 1805–75, Danish author, esp. of fairy tales.

An·der·son (an′dər sən), *n.* **1. Carl David,** 1905–91, U.S. physicist. **2. Dame Judith,** 1898–1992, Australian actress. **3. Marian,** 1902–93, U.S. contralto. **4. Maxwell,** 1888–1959, U.S. dramatist. **5. Sherwood,** 1876–1941, U.S. author. **6.** a city in central Indiana. 60,720.

An·der·son·ville (an′dər sən vil′), *n.* a village in SW Georgia: site of a Confederate military prison. 267.

An·des (an′dēz), *n.pl.* a mountain range in W South America, extending ab. 4500 mi. (7250 km) from N Colombia and Venezuela south to Cape Horn. Highest peak, Aconcagua, 22,834 ft. (6960 m).

An·dhra Pra·desh (än′drə prə dāsh′), *n.* a state in SE India, formed from portions of Madras and Hyderabad states 1956. 53,593,000; 106,204 sq. mi. (275,068 sq. km). *Cap.*: Hyderabad.

and·i·ron (and′ī′ərn), *n.* one of a pair of metal stands, usu. of iron or brass, for holding logs in a fireplace.

and/or (and′ôr′), *conj.* (used to imply that either or both of the things

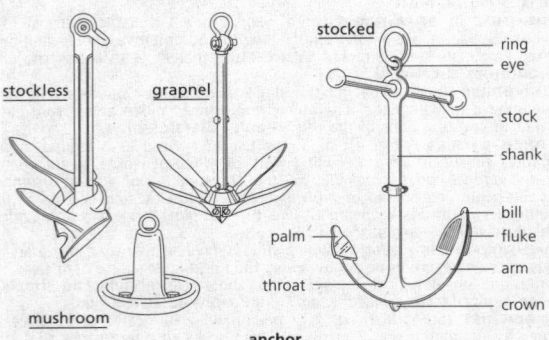

stockless   grapnel   stocked
ring
eye
stock
shank
bill
fluke
palm
arm
throat
crown
mushroom

anchor

mentioned may be affected or involved): *accident and/or health insurance.*

An·dor·ra (an dôr′ə, -dor′ə), *n.* **1.** a republic in the E Pyrenees between France and Spain. 74,839; 181 sq. mi. (468 sq. km). **2.** Also called **An·dor·ra la Ve·lla** (*Catalan.* än dôr′rä lä ve′lyä). the capital of this republic. 15,639. **—An·dor′ran**, *adj., n.*

An·drew (an′drōō), *n.* one of the 12 apostles of Jesus. Mark 3:18; John 1:40–42.

An·drewes (an′drōōz), *n.* **Lancelot,** 1555–1626, English theologian: one of the translators of the King James Version of the Bible.

An·drews (an′drōōz), *n.* **Julie,** born 1934, English singer and actress.

andro-, a combining form meaning "male," "male part or organ": *androgen.*

an·droe·ci·um (an drē′shē əm), *n., pl.* **-ci·a** (-shē ə). the stamens of a flower collectively. **—an·droe′cial** (-shəl), *adj.*

an·dro·gen (an′drə jən, -jen′), *n.* any substance, as testosterone or androsterone, that promotes male characteristics. **—an′dro·gen′ic** (-jen′ik), *adj.*

an·drog·e·nous (an droj′ə nəs), *adj.* pertaining to the production of or tending to produce male offspring.

an·drog·y·nous (an droj′ə nəs), *adj.* **1.** hermaphroditic. **2.** having both masculine and feminine characteristics. **—an′dro·gyne′** (-drə jīn′), *n.* **—an·drog′y·ny**, *n.*

an·droid (an′droid), *n.* an automaton in the form of a human being.

An·drom·e·da (an drom′i də), *n., gen.* **-dae** (-dē′) for 2. **1.** (in Greek myth) the daughter of Cassiopeia and wife of Perseus, by whom she had been rescued from a sea monster. **2.** a northern constellation between Pisces and Cassiopeia. **3.** (*l.c.*) any of several flowering evergreen shrubs of the genera *Andromeda* and *Pieris*, of the heath family.

Androm′eda strain′, *n.* an infectious pathogen that mutates unpredictably into new forms and shows extreme resistance to destruction by conventional means.

an·dros·ter·one (an dros′tə rōn′), *n.* an androgenic sex hormone that is a metabolite of testosterone and has much less effect.

-androus, a combining form meaning "having husbands" or "having stamens" of the kind or number specified by the initial element: *polyandrous.*

-andry, a combining form occurring in nouns corresponding to adjectives ending in -ANDROUS: *polyandry.*

ane (ān), *adj., n., pron. Chiefly Scot.* one.

an·ec·dot·age (an′ik dō′tij), *n.* anecdotes collectively.

an·ec·do·tal (an′ik dōt′l, an′ik dōt′l), *adj.* **1.** pertaining to, resembling, or containing anecdotes. **2.** based on incidental observations or reports rather than systematic evaluation. **—an′ec·do′tal·ism**, *n.* **—an′ec·do′tal·ly**, *adv.*

an·ec·dote (an′ik dōt′), *n.* a short account of an incident or event of an interesting or amusing nature, often biographical.

a·ne·mi·a (ə nē′mē ə), *n.* **1.** a reduction in the hemoglobin of red blood cells with consequent deficiency of oxygen in the blood, leading to weakness and pallor. **2.** a lack of power, vigor, vitality, or colorfulness.

a·ne·mic (ə nē′mik), *adj.* **1.** suffering from anemia. **2.** lacking power, vigor, vitality, or colorfulness; weak. **—a·ne′mi·cal·ly**, *adv.*

an·e·mom·e·ter (an′ə mom′i tər), *n.* any instrument for measuring the speed of wind. **—an′e·mo·met′ric** (-mō me′trik), **an′e·mo·met′ri·cal**, *adj.* **—an′e·mo·met′ri·cal·ly**, *adv.*

a·nem·o·ne (ə nem′ə nē′), *n.* **1.** any of various plants belonging to the genus *Anemone*, of the buttercup family, having petallike sepals in a variety of colors. **2.** SEA ANEMONE.

anem′one fish′, *n.* any small colorful tropical damselfish of the genus *Amphyprion*, that lives inside sea anemones.

an·en·ceph·a·ly (an′en sef′ə lē), *n.* the absence at birth of a portion of the skull and brain, caused by a failure of the embryonic upper neural tube to close and the consequent erosion of tissue. **—an′en·ce·phal′ic** (-sə fal′ik), *adj.*

an·er·oid (an′ə roid′), *adj.* using no fluid.

an′eroid barom′eter, *n.* a device for measuring atmospheric pressure, consisting of a chamber with a partial vacuum and an elastic cover and a pointer that registers compression of the cover by the air outside the chamber.

an·es·the·sia or **an·aes·the·sia** (an′əs thē′zhə), *n.* **1.** general or localized insensibility, induced by drugs or other intervention and used in surgery or other painful procedures. **2.** general loss of the senses of feeling, as pain, temperature, and touch.

an·es·the·si·ol·o·gy (an′əs thē′zē ol′ə jē), *n.* the science of administering anesthetics. **—an′es·the′si·ol′o·gist**, *n.*

an·es·thet·ic (an′əs thet′ik), *n.* **1.** a substance that produces anesthesia, as halothane, procaine, or ether. **—adj.** **2.** pertaining to or causing physical insensibility. **3.** physically insensitive: *an anesthetic state.* **—an′es·thet′i·cal·ly**, *adv.*

an·es·the·tist (ə nes′thi tist), *n.* a person who administers anesthetics, usu. a specially trained doctor or nurse.

an·es·the·tize (ə nes′thi tīz′), *v.t.*, **-tized, -tiz·ing.** to render physically insensible, as by an anesthetic. **—an·es′the·ti·za′tion**, *n.*

an·es·trus (an es′trəs), *n.* the interval of sexual inactivity in a female mammal between two periods of heat or rut.

an·eu·rysm or **an·eu·rism** (an′yə riz′əm), *n.* a permanent cardiac or arterial dilatation usu. caused by weakening of the vessel wall. **—an′eu·rys′mal**, **an′eu·ris′mal**, *adj.* **—an′eu·rys′mal·ly**, **an′eu·ris′mal·ly**, *adv.*

a·new (ə nōō′, ə nyōō′), *adv.* **1.** over again; once more: *to play the tune anew.* **2.** in a new form or manner: *to write the story anew.*

an·frac·tu·os·i·ty (an frak′chōō os′i tē), *n., pl.* **-ties.** **1.** the state or quality of being anfractuous. **2.** a channel, crevice, or passage full of windings and turnings.

an·frac·tu·ous (an frak′chōō əs), *adj.* characterized by windings and turnings: *an anfractuous path.*

an·gel (ān′jəl), *n.* **1.** a heavenly attendant or messenger of God; in the Old Testament, one of a class of spiritual beings who appear on earth to bring God's message to people; in medieval angelology, the lowest of the nine celestial orders (seraphim, cherubim, thrones, dominations, virtues, powers, principalities, archangels, and angels). **2.** a conventional representation of such a being, in human form, with wings. **3.** a person having qualities generally attributed to an angel, as beauty, purity, or kindliness. **4.** an attendant or guardian spirit. **5.** a deceased person whose soul is regarded as having been accepted into heaven. **6.** *Informal.* one who provides financial backing for some undertaking, as a play or political campaign. **7.** *Slang.* an image on a radar screen caused by a low-flying object, as a bird. **—v.t.** **8.** *Informal.* to provide financial backing for. **—Idiom.** **9.** **on the side of the angels,** holding a morally correct viewpoint. **—Proverb.** **10. to entertain an angel unaware,** to talk, meet, or offer hospitality to a stranger, who may be of great merit. Heb. 13:1. [Old English *engel* < Late Latin *angelus* < Greek *ángelos* messenger, trans. of Hebrew *malakh*] **—an·gel′ic** (an jel′ik), **an·gel′i·cal**, *adj.* **—an·gel′i·cal·ly**, *adv.*

NINE ORDERS OF ANGELS IN THREE HIERARCHIES
(in descending rank of importance)

First hierarchy:
Seraphim (highest angels of love, light, and fire)
Cherubim (angels who pray or intercede)
Thrones (angels who are in charge of justice)

Second hierarchy:
Dominations/Dominions (regulate angel duties)
Principalities (protect religion)
Powers (impose order on heavenly pathways)

Third hierarchy:
Virtues (work miracles on earth)
Archangels (minister and make propitiation for people's sins)
Angels (guard men and nations; act as messengers between God and man)

an·gel·fish (ān′jəl fish′), *n., pl.* (*esp. collectively*) **-fish,** (*esp. for kinds or species*) **-fish·es.** a South American freshwater fish, genus *Pterophyllum*, often kept in aquariums.

an′gel food′ cake′, *n.* a white sponge cake with a light, delicate texture obtained by using stiffly beaten egg whites and cream of tartar. Also called **an′gel cake′.**

an·gel·i·ca (an jel′i kə), *n., pl.* **-cas.** **1.** any plant belonging to the genus *Angelica*, of the parsley family, cultivated for its medicinal root and edible stalks. **2.** the candied stalks of this plant.

angel′ica tree′, *n.* HERCULES-CLUB (def. 2).

angel′ic hymn′, *n. Gloria in excelsis deo*, so called because it was sung by the angels who appeared to the shepherds at Bethlehem. Luke 2:14.

An·ge·li·co (an jel′i kō′), *n.* **Fra** (*Giovanni da Fiesole*), 1387–1455, Italian painter. **—An·gel′i·can**, *adj.*

An′gel of Death′, *n.* Azrael.

an·gel·ol·o·gy (ān′jə lol′ə jē), *n.* the study of angels.

An′gels, from the Realms′ of Glo′ry, a Christmas hymn (1816) with words by James Montgomery.

An·ge·lus (an′jə ləs), *n.* (*often l.c.*) **1.** a Roman Catholic devotion in honor of Annunciation and Incarnation. **2.** Also called **An′gelus bell′.** the bell announcing the Angelus. [< Late Latin, from the first word of the service: *Angelus* (*dominī nūntiāvit Mariae*). See ANGEL]

an·ger (ang′gər), *n.* **1.** a strong feeling of displeasure and belligerence aroused by a real or supposed wrong; wrath. **—v.t.** **2.** to arouse anger or wrath in. **—v.i.** **3.** to become angry.

An·ge·vin (an′jə vin) also **An·ge·vine** (-vin, -vīn′), *adj.* **1.** of or pertaining to Anjou or to the counts of Anjou or their descendants, esp. those who ruled in England, or to the period of their rule. **—n.** **2.** a member of an Angevin royal house, esp. a Plantagenet.

an·gi·na (an jī′nə; *in Med. often* an′jə nə), *n.* **1.** any attack of painful spasms or crushing pressure accompanied by a sensation of suffocating. **2.** ANGINA PECTORIS. **—an·gi′nal**, *adj.*

angi′na pec′to·ris (pek′tə ris), *n.* a sensation of crushing pressure in the chest, usu. at the sternum and sometimes radiating to the back or arm, caused by a sudden decrease of the blood supply to the heart muscle. [< New Latin: angina of the chest]

angio-, a combining form meaning "vessel, container" or "blood vessel": *angiology; angiosperm.*

an·gi·o·car·di·og·ra·phy (an′jē ō kär′dē og′rə fē), *n., pl.* **-phies.** x-ray examination of the heart and its blood vessels following intravenous injection of radiopaque fluid.

an·gi·o·gram (an′jē ə gram′), *n.* an x-ray produced by angiography.

an·gi·og·ra·phy (an′jē og′rə fē), *n., pl.* **-phies. 1.** x-ray examination of blood vessels or lymphatics following injection of a radiopaque substance. **2.** ANGIOCARDIOGRAPHY. —**an′gi·o·graph′ic** (-graf′ik), *adj.*

an·gi·ol·o·gy (an′jē ol′ə jē), *n.* the branch of anatomy dealing with blood vessels and lymph vessels.

an·gi·o·ma (an′jē ō′mə), *n., pl.* **-mas, -ma·ta** (-mə tə). a benign tumor consisting chiefly of dilated or newly formed blood vessels (**hemangioma**) or lymph vessels (**lymphangioma**). —**an′gi·om′a·tous** (-om′ə-təs, -ō′mə-), *adj.*

an·gi·o·plas·ty (an′jē ə plas′tē), *n., pl.* **-ties.** the surgical repair of a blood vessel, as by inserting a balloon-tipped catheter to unclog it or by replacing part of the vessel.

an·gi·o·sperm (an′jē ə spûrm′), *n.* any vascular plant of the phylum or division Anthophyta, having the seeds enclosed in a fruit, grain, pod, or capsule and comprising all flowering plants. —**an′gi·o·sper′mous,** *adj.*

an·gle¹ (ang′gəl), *n., v.,* **-gled, -gling.** —*n.* **1. a.** the space within two lines or three or more planes diverging from a common point, or within two planes diverging from a common line. **b.** the figure so formed. **c.** the amount of rotation needed to bring one line or plane into coincidence with another, generally measured in radians or degrees. **2.** an angular projection; a projecting corner. **3.** a viewpoint; standpoint: *She looked at the problem from a fresh angle.* **4.** the point of view from which journalistic copy is written; slant. **5.** one aspect of an event, problem, subject, etc. **6.** any of the four interceptions of the equatorial circle by the horizon and the meridian. **7.** ANGLE IRON (def. 2). —*v.t.* **8.** to move or bend in an angle. **9.** to set, direct, or adjust at an angle: *to angle a spotlight.* **10.** to slant (a piece of reporting) toward a particular point of view. —*v.i.* **11.** to turn sharply in a different direction: *The road angles to the right.* **12.** to move or go in angles or at an angle.

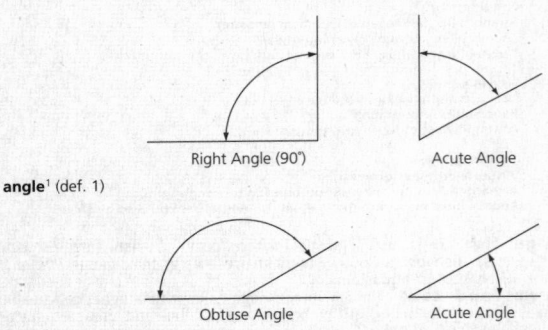

Right Angle (90°)   Acute Angle

Obtuse Angle   Acute Angle

angle¹ (def. 1)

an·gle² (ang′gəl), *v.i.,* **-gled, -gling. 1.** to fish with hook and line. **2.** to attempt to get something by sly or artful means; fish.

an′gle i′ron, *n.* **1.** an iron or steel bar, brace, or cleat in the form of an angle. **2.** a piece of structural iron or steel having a cross section in the form of an L.

an′gle of attack′, *n.* the acute angle between the chord of an aircraft wing or other airfoil and the direction of airflow.

an′gle of in′cidence, *n.* **1.** Also called **incidence.** the angle that a ray, as of light, makes with a normal to a surface at the point where the ray meets the surface. **2.** (on an airplane) the angle, usu. fixed, between a wing or tail root chord and the axis of the fuselage.

an′gle of reflec′tion, *n.* the angle that a reflected ray, as of light, makes with a normal to the surface at the point of reflection.

an′gle of refrac′tion, *n.* the angle between a refracted ray and a normal to the interface between two media at the point of refraction.

an·gler (ang′glər), *n.* **1.** a person who fishes with a hook and line. **2.** a person who tries to get something through scheming. **3.** any of various large-mouthed marine fishes of the family Lophiidae, having a wormlike lure dangling from the head for attracting prey.

an·gler·fish (ang′glər fish′), *n., pl.* (*esp. collectively*) **-fish,** (*esp. for kinds or species*) **-fish·es.** ANGLER (def. 3).

An·gli·can (ang′gli kən), *adj.* **1.** of or pertaining to the Church of England. **2.** related in origin to and in communion with the Church of England, as various Episcopal churches. **3.** ENGLISH (def. 8). —*n.* **4.** a member of the Church of England or of a church in communion with it. **5.** a person who upholds the teachings of the Church of England. [< Medieval Latin *Anglicānus* English] —**An′gli·can·ism,** *n.*

An′glican chant′, *n.* a harmonized, strictly metrical chant to which canticles, psalms, and other liturgical texts are sung in the Anglican Church.

An′glican Church′, *n.* the Church of England and those churches that are in communion with it.

An′glican Commun′ion, *n.* churches that are in communion with the Church of England, including the Church of Ireland, the Church in Wales, the Episcopal Church of Scotland, the Protesant Episcopal Church in the United States, the Churches of Pakistan, India, Burma,

and Ceylon, the Canadian Church, the Church of the West Indies, the Australian Church, the Church of New Zealand, the Church of the Province of South Africa, the Province of West Africa, and Nippon Sei Ko Kwai (Japan).

An·gli·cism (ang′glə siz′əm), *n.* (*sometimes l.c.*) **1.** a Briticism. **2.** an English word, idiom, etc., occurring in or borrowed by another language. **3.** the state of being English; characteristic English quality. **4.** any custom, manner, idea, etc., characteristic of the English people.

An·gli·cize (ang′glə sīz′), *v.t., v.i.,* **-cized, -ciz·ing.** (*sometimes l.c.*) to make or become English in form or character: *to Anglicize a foreign spelling.* —**An′gli·ci·za′tion,** *n.*

an·gling (ang′gling), *n.* the act or art of fishing with a hook and line, usu. attached to a rod.

An·glo (ang′glō), *n., pl.* **-glos,** *adj.* —*n.* **1.** a white American of non-Hispanic descent. **2.** a Canadian whose first language is English, as distinguished from French-speaking Canadians. **3.** ANGLO-AMERICAN. —*adj.* **4.** of or pertaining to Anglos.

Anglo-, a combining form of ENGLISH: *Anglo-Norman; Anglo-Catholic.*

An·glo-A·mer·i·can (ang′glō ə mer′i kən), *adj.* **1.** of, pertaining to, or involving England and America, esp. the United States, or their peoples: *the Anglo-American alliance.* —*n.* **2. a.** an American born in England or of English descent. **b.** any American whose first language is English. —**An′glo-A·mer′i·can·ism,** *n.*

An·glo-Cath·o·lic (ang′glō kath′ə lik, -kath′lik), *n.* **1.** a person who emphasizes the Catholic character of the Anglican Church. —*adj.* **2.** of or pertaining to Anglo-Catholicism or Anglo-Catholics. —**An′glo-Cathol′icism,** *n.*

An·glo·phile (ang′glə fīl′, -fil) also **An·glo·phil** (-fil), *n.* a person who is friendly to or admires England or English customs, institutions, etc. —**An′glo·phil′i·a** (-fil′ē ə), *n.* —**An′glo·phil′i·ac′, An′glo·phil′ic,** *adj.* —**An′glo·phil·ism,** *n.*

An·glo·phobe (ang′glə fōb′), *n.* a person who hates or fears England or anything English. —**An′glo·pho′bi·a,** *n.* —**An′glo·pho′bi·ac′, An′glo·pho′bic,** *adj.*

An·glo·phone (ang′glə fōn′), *n.* (*sometimes l.c.*) an English-speaking person, esp. a native speaker of English.

An·glo-Sax·on (ang′glō sak′sən), *n.* **1.** a native or inhabitant of any of the kingdoms formed by the West Germanic peoples who invaded and occupied Britain in the 5th and 6th centuries A.D. **2.** (formerly) OLD ENGLISH (def. 1). **3.** plain and simple English; blunt, monosyllabic, or vulgar language. **4.** a native of England, or a person of English ancestry, esp. in the U.S. —*adj.* **5.** of or pertaining to the Anglo-Saxons, or to the period of Anglo-Saxon dominance in Britain, ending with the Norman Conquest in 1066. **6.** of or pertaining to Great Britain together with countries colonized by Britons, where English is the dominant language and most of the population is of European descent, as the United States. **7.** of English ancestry.

An·go·la (ang gō′lə), *n.* a republic in SW Africa: formerly an overseas province of Portugal; gained independence Nov. 11, 1975. 10,623,994; 481,226 sq. mi. (1,246,375 sq. km). *Cap.:* Luanda. Formerly, **Portuguese West Africa.** —**An·go′lan,** *adj., n.*

An·go·ra (ang gôr′ə, -gōr′ə, an-), *n., pl.* **-ras,** *adj.* —*n.* **1.** Also called **Ango′ra cat′.** **a.** one of a breed of longhaired domestic cats with a long body and a wedge-shaped head, raised orig. in Turkey. **b.** any longhaired domestic cat. **2.** (*often l.c.*) Also called **Ango′ra wool′.** the hair of the Angora goat or of the Angora rabbit. **3.** (*often l.c.*) yarn, fabric, or a garment made from this. **4.** Also called **Ango′ra goat′.** a variety of domestic goat having long, silky hair called mohair. **5.** Also called **Ango′ra rab′bit.** one of a breed of European rabbits raised for its long, silky hair. —*adj.* **6.** (*usu. l.c.*) made from a yarn or fabric of Angora goat or Angora rabbit hair: *an angora hat.*

an′gos·tu′ra bark′ (ang′gə stŏŏr′ə, -styŏŏr′ə, ang′-), *n.* the bitter, aromatic bark of either of two South American citrus trees, *Galipea officinalis* or *G. cusparia,* used in medicine and in the preparation of liqueurs and bitters. Also called **angostura.**

An·gra Main·yu (ang′rə mīn′yŏŏ), *n.* Zoroastrianism. the evil spirit who contends against Spenta Mainyu. Also called **Ahriman.**

an·gry (ang′grē), *adj.,* **-gri·er, -gri·est. 1.** feeling anger or strong resentment: *to be angry at the dean; to be angry about the insult.* **2.** expressing, caused by, or characterized by anger; wrathful: *angry words.* **3.** *Chiefly New Eng. and Midland U.S.* inflamed, as a sore. **4.** exhibiting characteristics associated with anger or danger: *an angry sea.* —**an′gri·ly,** *adv.* —**an′gri·ness,** *n.*

angst (ängkst), *n.* a feeling of dread, anxiety, or anguish.

ang·strom (ang′strəm), *n.* (*often cap.*) a unit of length, equal to one ten millionth of a millimeter, primarily used to express electromagnetic wavelengths. *Symbol:* Å; *Abbr.:* A Also called **ang′strom u′nit.**

an·guish (ang′gwish), *n.* **1.** acute suffering or pain: *the anguish of grief.* —*v.t.* **2.** to inflict with suffering or pain. —*v.i.* **3.** to suffer or feel anguish.

an·gu·lar (ang′gyə lər), *adj.* **1.** having an angle or angles. **2.** consisting of, situated at, or forming an angle. **3.** pertaining to or measured by an angle. **4.** bony, lean, or gaunt: *a tall, angular man.* **5.** acting or moving awkwardly; stiff. —**an′gu·lar·ly,** *adv.* —**an′gu·lar·ness,** *n.*

an·gu·lar·i·ty (ang′gyə lar′i tē), *n., pl.* **-ties. 1.** the quality of being angular. **2.** angularities, sharp corners; angular outlines.

an′gular veloc′ity, *n.* the rate at which a body rotates about an axis, usu. expressed in radians per second.

an·gu·late (ang′gyə lit, -lāt′) also **an′gu·lat′ed,** *adj.* of angular form; angled: *angulate stems.* —**an′gu·late·ly,** *adv.*

an·gu·la·tion (ang′gyə lā′shən), *n.* **1.** an angular part, position, or formation. **2.** the exact measurement of angles.

an·hy·dride (an hī′drīd, -drid), *n.* **1.** a compound formed by removing water from a more complex compound. **2.** a compound from which water has been abstracted.

an·hy·drous (an hī′drəs), *adj.* (of a chemical compound) with all water removed, esp. water of crystallization.

a·ni (ä′nē, ä nē′), *n., pl.* **a·nis.** any of several black cuckoos of the genus *Crotophaga,* of the tropical and subtropical New World, having a prominent arched bill and usu. laying eggs in a large communal nest.

An′i·ak′chak Cra′ter (an′ē ak′chak, an′-), *n.* an active volcanic crater on the Alaskan Peninsula, with a diameter of 6 mi. (10 km).

an·il (an′l), *n.* **1.** a West Indian shrub, *Indigofera suffruticosa,* of the legume family, having clusters of small, reddish yellow flowers and yielding indigo. **2.** indigo; deep blue.

an·ile (an′īl, ā′nīl), *adj.* of or like a foolish, doddering old woman. —**a·nil·i·ty** (ə nil′i tē), *n.*

an·i·line (an′l in, -īn′) also **an·i·lin** (-in), *n.* a colorless, oily, slightly water-soluble liquid, $C_6H_5NH_2$, used chiefly in the synthesis of dyes and drugs.

an·i·ma (an′ə mə), *n., pl.* **-mas. 1.** soul; life. **2.** (in the psychology of C. G. Jung) **a.** the inner personality (contrasted with *persona*). **b.** the feminine principle, esp. as present in men (contrasted with *animus*).

an·i·mad·ver·sion (an′ə mad vûr′zhən, -shən), *n.* **1.** an unfavorable or censorious comment. **2.** the act of criticizing.

an·i·mad·vert (an′ə mad vûrt′), *v.i.* to comment unfavorably or critically (usu. fol. by *on* or *upon*).

an·i·mal (an′ə məl), *n.* **1.** any member of the kingdom Animalia, comprising multicellular organisms that have a well-defined shape and usu. limited growth, can move voluntarily, actively acquire food and digest it internally, and have sensory and nervous systems that allow them to respond rapidly to stimuli. **2.** any such living thing other than a human being. **3.** a mammal, as opposed to a fish, bird, etc. **4.** the physical or carnal nature of human beings; animality. **5.** an inhuman person; brutish or beastlike person. **6.** thing: *A perfect job? Is there any such animal?* —*adj.* **7.** of, pertaining to, or derived from animals: *animal fats.* **8.** pertaining to the physical or carnal nature of humans, rather than their spiritual or intellectual nature: *animal needs.* —**an′i·mal′ic** (-mal′ik), **an′i·ma′li·an** (-mā′lē ən, -māl′yən), *adj.*

an·i·mal·cule (an′ə mal′kyool), *n.* a minute or microscopic animal. —**an′i·mal′cu·lar, an′i·mal′cu·line** (-lin), *adj.*

An′imal Farm′, a political satire (1945) by George Orwell.

an′imal heat′, *n.* heat produced in a living animal by any of various metabolic activities.

an′imal hus′bandry, *n.* the scientific study or the practice of breeding and tending domestic animals, esp. farm animals.

An·i·ma·li·a (an′ə mā′lē ə, -māl′yə), *n.* (*used with a pl. v.*) the taxonomic kingdom comprising all animals.

an·i·mal·ism (an′ə mə liz′əm), *n.* preoccupation with or motivation by physical or carnal appetites rather than spiritual or intellectual forces. —**an′i·mal·ist,** *n.* —**an′i·mal·is′tic,** *adj.*

an·i·mal·ize (an′ə mə līz′), *v.t.,* **-ized, -iz·ing.** to excite the animal passions of; brutalize; sensualize. —**an′i·mal·i·za′tion,** *n.*

an′imal king′dom, *n.* **1.** ANIMALIA. **2.** the animals of the world collectively (contrasted with *mineral kingdom, vegetable kingdom*).

an′imal mag′netism, *n.* **1.** the power to attract others through physical presence, bearing, energy, etc. **2.** the power enabling one to induce hypnosis.

an′imal rights′, *n.pl.* the rights of animals, claimed on ethical grounds, to the same humane treatment and protection from exploitation and abuse that are accorded to humans.

an·i·mate (*v.* an′ə māt′; *adj.* -mit), *v.,* **-mat·ed, -mat·ing,** *adj.* —*v.t.* **1.** to give life to; make alive. **2.** to make lively or vigorous; enliven: *Her presence animated the party.* **3.** to encourage. **4.** to move or stir to action; motivate. **5.** to give motion to: *leaves animated by a breeze.* **6.** to prepare or produce as an animated cartoon. —*adj.* **7.** alive; possessing life. **8.** lively. **9.** of or relating to animal life. **10.** able to move voluntarily. **11.** (of a linguistic item) used with reference to living beings, esp. beings regarded as having perception and volition (opposed to *inanimate*): *an animate noun.* —**an′i·mate·ly,** *adv.*

an·i·mat·ed (an′ə mā′tid), *adj.* **1.** full of life, action, or spirit; lively: *an animated debate.* **2.** made to move in a lifelike fashion: *animated puppets.* **3.** containing objects that appear to move in a lifelike fashion: *an animated display.* —**an′i·mat′ed·ly,** *adv.*

an′imated cartoon′, *n.* a motion picture consisting of a sequence of drawings, each slightly different so that when filmed and run through a projector the figures appear to move.

an·i·ma·tion (an′ə mā′shən), *n.* **1.** animated quality; liveliness. **2.** an act or instance of animating. **3.** the state or condition of being animated. **4.** the process of preparing animated cartoons. **5. a.** ANIMATED CARTOON. **b.** a motion picture similar to an animated cartoon but using photographs of dolls, robots, etc., instead of drawings.

an·i·ma·tor (an′ə mā′tər), *n.* **1.** one that animates. **2.** an artist who draws animated cartoons. Sometimes, **an′i·mat′er.**

an·i·ma·tron·ics (an′ə mə tron′iks), *n.* (*used with a sing. v.*) the technology connected with the use of electronics to animate puppets or other figures, as for motion pictures.

an·i·mism (an′ə miz′əm), *n.* **1.** the belief that natural objects, natural phenomena, and the universe itself possess souls. **2.** the belief that souls may exist apart from bodies. **3.** belief in spiritual beings or agencies. —**an′i·mist,** *n., adj.* —**an′i·mis′tic,** *adj.*

an·i·mos·i·ty (an′ə mos′i tē), *n., pl.* **-ties.** a feeling of ill will that tends to display itself in action; strong hostility or antagonism.

an·i·mus (an′ə məs), *n.* **1.** strong dislike or enmity; animosity. **2.** purpose; intention; animating spirit. **3.** (in the psychology of C. G. Jung) the masculine principle, esp. as present in women (contrasted with *anima*).

an·i·on (an′ī′ən), *n.* **1.** a negatively charged ion that is attracted to the anode in electrolysis. **2.** any negatively charged ion (opposed to *cation*). —**an′i·on′ic** (-on′ik), *adj.* —**an·i·on′i·cal·ly,** *adv.*

an·ise (an′is), *n.* **1.** a Mediterranean plant, *Pimpinella anisum,* of the parsley family, having loose umbrels of small yellowish white flowers that yield aniseed. **2.** ANISEED. —**a·nis·ic** (ə nis′ik), *adj.*

an·i·seed (an′ə sēd′, an′is sēd′), *n.* the aromatic seed of anise, the oil of which is used in medicine as a carminative and expectorant, and in cooking and liqueurs for its licoricelike flavor.

an·i·sette (an′ə set′, -zet′; *Fr.* an′ə set′, -zet′), *n.* a liqueur flavored with aniseed.

An·ka·ra (ang′kər ə), *n.* the capital of Turkey, in the central part. 2,251,533. Formerly, **Angora.**

an·ker·ite (ang′kə rīt′), *n.* a carbonate mineral related to dolomite but with iron replacing part of the magnesium.

ankh (angk), *n.* a tau cross with a loop at the top, used esp. in ancient Egypt as a symbol of generation or enduring life.

ankh

an·kle (ang′kəl), *n.* **1.** the joint between the foot and leg. **2.** the slender part of the leg above the foot.

an′kle-bit′er, *n. Slang.* **1.** a toddler or small child. **2.** a minor official who obstructs superiors.

an·klet (ang′klit), *n.* **1.** a sock that reaches just above the ankle. **2.** an ornamental circlet worn around the ankle.

an·ky·lo·saur (ang′kə lō sôr′), *n.* any short-legged, plant-eating dinosaur of the suborder Ankylosauria, of the Cretaceous Period, being armored in thick bony plates.

an·ky·lose (ang′kə lōs′), *v.t., v.i.,* **-losed, -los·ing.** to unite, as the bones of a joint.

an·ky·lo·sis (ang′kə lō′sis), *n., pl.* **-lo·ses** (-lō′sēz). **1.** abnormal adhesion of the bones of a joint. **2.** the union or consolidation of two or more bones or other hard tissues into one. —**an′ky·lot′ic** (-lot′ik), *adj.*

An·na (an′ə), *n.* a woman with prophetic gifts who greeted Jesus as the Messiah. Luke 2:36–38.

An′na Ka·ren′i·na (kə ren′ə nə), a novel (1875–76) by Leo Tolstoy.

an·nal·ist (an′l ist), *n.* a writer of annals; historian.

an·nals (an′lz), *n.pl.* **1.** a record of events, esp. a yearly record, usu. in chronological order. **2.** historical records generally; chronicles: *the annals of war.* **3.** a journal containing the formal reports of an organization or learned field.

An·nap·o·lis (ə nap′ə lis), *n.* the capital of Maryland, in the central part, on Chesapeake Bay: U.S. Naval Academy. 33,360.

Ann Ar·bor (an är′bər), *n.* a city in SE Michigan. 108,817.

An·nas (an′əs), *n.* one of the high priests of Jerusalem when John the Baptist began his ministry. Luke 3:2.

an·nat·to or **a·nat·to** (ə nat′ō, ə nä′tō), *n., pl.* **-tos. 1.** a small tree, *Bixa orellana,* of the family Bixaceae, of tropical America. **2.** a yellowish red dye obtained from the pulp enclosing the seeds of this tree, used for coloring fabrics, butter, varnish, etc.

Anne (an), *n.* 1665–1714, queen of England 1702–14.

an·neal (ə nēl′), *v.t.* **1.** to heat (glass, earthenware, metals, etc.) to remove or prevent internal stress. **2.** to free from internal stress by heating and gradually cooling. **3.** to toughen or temper. **4.** to recombine (nucleic acid strands) at low temperature after separating by heat. **5.** to fuse colors onto (a vitreous or metallic surface) by heating. —**an·neal′er,** *n.*

an·ne·lid (an′l id) also **an·nel·i·dan** (ə nel′i dn), *n.* **1.** any segmented worm of the phylum Annelida, which includes the earthworms, leeches, and various marine forms. —*adj.* **2.** of or pertaining to the annelids.

an·nex (*v.* ə neks′, an′eks; *n.* an′eks), *v.t.* **1.** to attach, append, or add, esp. to something larger or more important. **2.** to incorporate (territory) into the domain of a city, country, or state: *Germany annexed part of Czechoslovakia.* **3.** to take or appropriate, esp. without permission: *planned to annex the private documents for their own use.* **4.** to attach as an attribute, condition, or consequence. —*n.* Also, *esp. Brit.,* **an′nexe. 5.** something annexed. **6.** a subsidiary building or an addition to a building. **7.** something added to a document; appendix; supplement: *an annex to a treaty.* —**an′nex•a′tion,** *n.*

An•nie (an′ē), a musical (1977) with lyrics by Martin Charnin and music by Charles Strouse.

an•ni•hi•late (ə nī′ə lāt′), *v.t.,* **-lat•ed, -lat•ing. 1.** to reduce to utter ruin or nonexistence; destroy utterly. **2.** to destroy the collective existence or main body of: *to annihilate an army.* **3.** to defeat completely; vanquish: *Our team was annihilated in the playoffs.* **4.** to annul; make void. **5.** to cancel the effect of; nullify. **6.** *Physics.* to convert rest mass into energy in the form of one or more photons: *a particle annihilates its antiparticle.* —**an•ni′hi•la′tion,** *n.* —**an•ni′hi•la′tor,** *n.*

an•ni•ver•sa•ry (an′ə vûr′sə rē), *n., pl.* **-ries,** *adj.* —*n.* **1.** the yearly recurrence of the date of a past event. **2.** the celebration or commemoration of such a date. **3.** a wedding anniversary. —*adj.* **4.** returning or recurring each year; annual. **5.** of or pertaining to an anniversary.

WEDDING ANNIVERSARIES AND GIFTS

Anniversary	Traditional Gift	Modern Gift
First	Paper	Clocks, plastics
Second	Cotton	China
Third	Leather	Crystal, glass
Fourth	Fruit, flowers*	Linen, appliances
Fifth	Wood	Silverware
Sixth	Candy**	Wood
Seventh	Wool	Copper, brass
Eighth	Bronze	Linen, lace
Ninth	Pottery	China, leather
Tenth	Tin, aluminum	Diamond jewelry
Eleventh	Steel	Fashion jewelry
Twelfth	Silk, linen	Pearls, colored gems
Thirteenth	Lace	Textiles
Fourteenth	Ivory	Gold jewelry
Fifteenth	Crystal	Glass, watches
Twentieth	China	Platinum
Twenty-fifth	Silver	Silver
Thirtieth	Pearl	Diamond
Thirty-fifth	Coral	Jade, coral
Fortieth	Ruby	Ruby
Forty-fifth	Sapphire	Sapphire
Fiftieth	Gold	Gold
Fifty-fifth	Emerald	Emerald
Sixtieth	Diamond	Diamond
Seventy-fifth	Diamond	Diamond

*Some references give this as Linen   **Some references give this as Iron

an•no Dom•i•ni (än′nō dō′mē nē′; *Eng.* an′ō dom′ə nī′, -nē′), *Latin.* See A.D. (def. 1).

an•no•na (ə nō′nə), *n., pl.* **-nas.** any of various trees and shrubs of the genus *Annona,* native to tropical America, grown for their edible fruits.

an•no•tate (an′ə tāt′), *v.,* **-tat•ed, -tat•ing.** —*v.t.* **1.** to supply (a text) with critical or explanatory notes; comment upon in notes. —*v.i.* **2.** to make annotations or notes. —**an′no•ta′tive,** *adj.*

an•no•ta•tion (an′ə tā′shən), *n.* **1.** a critical or explanatory note added to a text. **2.** NOTE (def. 1).

an•nounce (ə nouns′), *v.,* **-nounced, -nounc•ing.** —*v.t.* **1.** to make known publicly or officially; proclaim; give notice of: *to announce an engagement.* **2.** to state the approach or presence of: *to announce a guest.* **3.** to make known to the mind or senses. **4.** to serve as an announcer of: *to announce a program.* **5.** to state; declare. **6.** to state in advance; declare beforehand. —*v.i.* **7.** to be employed or serve as an announcer, esp. of a radio or television broadcast. **8.** to declare one's candidacy, as for a political office: *She is expected to announce for governor.* —**an•nounc′er,** *n.*

an•nounce•ment (ə nouns′mənt), *n.* **1.** a public or formal notice of something. **2.** a brief spoken message, esp. a radio commercial. **3.** a card or piece of stationery containing a formal declaration of an event, as a wedding. **4.** the act of announcing.

an•noy (ə noi′), *v.,* **-noyed, -noy•ing.** —*v.t.* **1.** to disturb or bother in a way that displeases, troubles, or irritates. **2.** to molest persistently; harass. —*v.i.* **3.** to be bothersome or troublesome.

an•noy•ance (ə noi′əns), *n.* **1.** a person or thing that annoys; nuisance. **2.** the feeling of being annoyed. **3.** an act or instance of annoying.

an•nu•al (an′yōō əl), *adj.* **1.** of, for, or pertaining to a year; yearly: *annual salary.* **2.** occurring or returning once a year: *an annual celebration.* **3.** (of a plant) living for only one growing season. **4.** performed or executed during a year: *the annual course of the sun.* —*n.* **5.** a plant that lives for one growing season. **6.** a publication issued annually. —**an′nu•al•ly,** *adv.*

an•nu•al•ize (an′yōō ə līz′), *v.,* **-ized, -iz•ing.** —*v.t.* **1.** to calculate for or as if for an entire year. —*v.i.* **2.** to become annualized.

an′nual ring′, *n.* a yearly formation of new wood in woody plants, observable as a ring on the cross section of a tree trunk. Also called **tree ring.**

an•nu•i•ty (ə nōō′i tē, ə nyōō′-), *n., pl.* **-ties. 1.** a specified income payable at stated intervals for a fixed or contingent period, often for the recipient's life, as in consideration of a premium paid. **2.** the right to receive such an income. **3.** the duty to make such a payment or payments.

an•nul (ə nul′), *v.t.,* **-nulled, -nul•ling. 1.** to make or declare void or null; invalidate: *to annul a marriage; to annul an agreement.* **2.** to abolish; cancel: *Joy annulled our cares.* **3.** to reduce to nothing; obliterate: *The news annulled all hope.* —**an•nul′la•ble,** *adj.*

an•nu•lar (an′yə lər), *adj.* having the form of a ring.

an′nular eclipse′, *n.* an eclipse of the sun in which a portion of its surface is visible as a ring surrounding the dark moon.

an•nu•late (an′yə lit, -lāt′), *adj.* **1.** formed of ringlike segments, as an annelid worm. **2.** having rings or ringlike bands. Also, **an′nu•lat′ed.** —**an′nu•la′tion,** *n.*

an•nul•ment (ə nul′mənt), *n.* **1.** an act of annulling. **2.** a formal declaration that annuls a marriage.

an•nu•lus (an′yə ləs), *n., pl.* **-li** (-lī′), **-lus•es. 1.** a ringlike part, band, or space; ring. **2.** the space between two concentric circles on a plane. **3.** the veil remnant on a mushroom stalk. **4.** a growth ring, as the annual ring of a tree trunk, that can be used to estimate age.

an•nun•ci•ate (ə nun′sē āt′), *v.t.,* **-at•ed, -at•ing.** to announce. —**an•nun′ci•a•tive, an•nun′ci•a•to′ry,** *adj.*

an•nun•ci•a•tion (ə nun′sē ā′shən), *n.* **1.** (*often cap.*) the announcement by the angel Gabriel to the Virgin Mary of her conception of Christ. **2.** (*cap.*) the church festival on March 25 in memory of this announcement. **3.** an act or instance of announcing; proclamation.

an•nun•ci•a•tor (ə nun′sē ā′tər), *n.* **1.** an announcer. **2.** a signaling apparatus, esp. in some doorbell systems, that uses lights or pointers to indicate the source of the signal.

an•ode (an′ōd), *n.* **1.** the electrode or terminal by which current enters an electrolytic cell, voltaic cell, battery, etc. **2.** the negative terminal of a voltaic cell or battery. **3.** the positive terminal, electrode, or element of an electron tube or electrolytic cell.

an•o•dize (an′ə dīz′), *v.t.,* **-dized, -diz•ing.** to coat a metal, esp. magnesium or aluminum, with a protective film by electrolytic means. —**an′o•di•za′tion,** *n.*

an•o•dyne (an′ə dīn′), *n.* **1.** anything that relieves pain or distress. —*adj.* **2.** relieving pain. **3.** soothing to the mind or feelings.

a•noint (ə noint′), *v.t.* **1.** to apply an ointment or oily liquid to by rubbing or sprinkling. **2.** to smear with any liquid. **3.** to consecrate or make sacred in a ceremony that includes the token applying of oil. **4.** to choose formally: *anointed a successor.*

anoint′ing of the sick′, *n.* a sacrament consisting of anointment with oil and the recitation of prayer by a priest to a person who is critically ill or dying. Also called **extreme unction.**

a•no•le (ə nō′lē), *n., pl.* **-les. 1.** a small green iguanid lizard, *Anolis carolinensis,* of the U.S. Gulf States, that changes skin color. **2.** any of numerous similar New World lizards of the genus *Anolis.*

a•nom•a•lis•tic (ə nom′ə lis′tik), *adj.* of or pertaining to an astronomical anomaly. —**a•nom′a•lis′ti•cal•ly,** *adv.*

a•nom•a•lous (ə nom′ə ləs), *adj.* **1.** deviating from the common order, form, or rule; irregular; abnormal. **2.** not fitting into a common, familiar, or expected type or pattern; unusual. **3.** incongruous or inconsistent.

a•nom•a•ly (ə nom′ə lē), *n., pl.* **-lies. 1.** a deviation from the common type, rule, arrangement, or form; irregularity; abnormality. **2.** someone or something anomalous. **3.** an unexpected, unusual, or strange condition, situation, or quality. **4.** *Astron.* a quantity measured in degrees, defining the position of an orbiting body with respect to the point at which it is nearest to or farthest from its primary.

a•no•mi•a (ə nō′mē ə), *n.* the inability to name objects or to recognize the written or spoken names of objects.

an•o•mie or **an•o•my** (an′ə mē′), *n.* a condition of an individual or of society characterized by a breakdown of norms and values or a sense of dislocation and alienation. —**a•nom•ic** (ə nom′ik), *adj.*

a•non (ə non′), *adv.* **1.** in a short time; soon. **2.** at another time. —*Idiom.* **3. ever and anon,** now and then; occasionally.

an•o•nym (an′ə nim), *n.* **1.** an assumed or false name. **2.** a pseudonym.

an•o•nym•i•ty (an′ə nim′i tē), *n., pl.* **-ties. 1.** the state or quality of being anonymous. **2.** an anonymous person.

a•non•y•mous (ə non′ə məs), *adj.* **1.** without any name acknowledged, as that of author, contributor, etc.: *an anonymous letter.* **2.** not named or identified: *an anonymous author.* **3.** lacking individuality, unique character, or distinction: *a row of drab, anonymous houses.* —**a•non′y•mous•ly,** *adv.*

a•noph•e•les (ə nof′ə lēz′), *n., pl.* **-les.** any of several mosquitoes of the genus *Anopheles,* certain species of which are vectors of the parasite causing malaria in humans.

an•o•rak (an′ə rak′), *n.* a hooded pullover jacket, usu. for wear in cold or stormy weather; parka.

an•o•rec•tic (an′ə rek′tik) also **an•o•ret•ic** (-ret′ik), *adj.* **1.** having no appetite. **2.** affected with anorexia nervosa. **3.** causing a loss of appetite. —*n.* **4.** a substance causing loss of appetite. **5.** an anorexic.

an•o•rex•i•a (an′ə rek′sē ə), *n.* **1.** loss of appetite and inability to eat. **2.** ANOREXIA NERVOSA.

anorex′ia ner•vo′sa (nûr vō′sə), *n.* an eating disorder characterized by a fear of becoming fat, a distorted body image, and excessive dieting leading to emaciation.

an·o·rex·ic (an′ə rek′sik), *n.* **1.** a person suffering from anorexia or esp. anorexia nervosa. —*adj.* **2.** ANORECTIC.

an·os·mi·a (an oz′mē ə, -os′-), *n.* absence or loss of the sense of smell. —**an·os·mat·ic** (an′əz mat′ik), **an·os′mic,** *adj.*

an·oth·er (ə nuth′ər), *adj.* **1.** being one more or more of the same; further; additional: *Please have another piece of cake.* **2.** different; distinct; of a different kind: *at another time; another man.* **3.** very similar to; of the same kind or category as: *another Martin Luther King, Jr.* —*pron.* **4.** one more; an additional one. **5.** a different one; something different: *going from one thing to another.* **6.** one like the first: *one copy for her and another for him.* **7.** a person other than oneself or the one specified: *He told her he loved another.* —**Idiom.** **8.** another day, another dollar, it's the end of an ordinary workday.

an·ov·u·la·tion (an′ov yə lā′shən, -ō vyə-, an ov′yə, -ō′vyə-), *n.* the absence of ovulation.

an·ox·e·mi·a (an′ok sē′mē ə), *n.* a deficiency of oxygen in the arterial blood. —**an′ox·e′mic,** *adj.*

an·sate (an′sāt), *adj.* having a handle or handlelike part.

An·schluss (än′shlŏŏs), *n.* union, esp. the political union of Austria with Germany in 1938. [< German: consolidation]

an·ser·ine (an′sə rīn′, -rin) also **an·ser·ous** (-sər əs), *adj.* **1.** of, pertaining to, or resembling a goose. **2.** stupid; foolish; silly.

ANSI, American National Standards Institute.

an·swer (an′sər, än′-), *n.* **1.** a spoken or written reply or response to a question, request, letter, etc. **2.** a correct response to a question. **3.** an equivalent or approximation; counterpart: *the French answer to the Beatles.* **4.** an action serving as a reply or response: *His answer was a stern look.* **5.** a solution to a problem, esp. in mathematics. **6.** a reply to a charge or accusation. **7.** the defendant's reply to the plaintiff's charge. —*v.i.* **8.** to speak or write in response; make answer; reply. **9.** to respond by an act or motion: *He answered with a quick shake of his head.* **10.** to act or suffer in consequence (usu. fol. by *for*). **11.** to be or declare oneself responsible or accountable (usu. fol. by *for*): *I will answer for his safety.* **12.** to be satisfactory or serve (usu. fol. by *for*). **13.** to conform; correspond (usu. fol. by *to*): *She answered to the description.* —*v.t.* **14.** to speak or write in response to; reply to. **15.** to act or move in response to: *Answer the doorbell.* **16.** to solve or present a solution of. **17.** to serve or fulfill: *This will answer the purpose.* **18.** to discharge (a responsibility, claim, debt, etc.). **19.** to conform or correspond to: *This dog answers your description.* **20.** to reply or respond favorably to: *to answer a request.* **21.** to atone for; make amends for. **22. answer back,** to reply impertinently. —*Proverb.* **23. A soft answer turneth away wrath,** gentle words deflect animosity. Prov. 15:1.

an·swer·a·ble (an′sər ə bəl, än′-), *adj.* **1.** liable to be asked to give account; responsible. **2.** capable of being answered. **3.** proportionate; correlative (usu. fol. by *to*). **4.** corresponding; suitable (usu. fol. by *to*): *an amount not answerable to my needs.*

an′swering machine′, *n.* a device that automatically answers telephone calls with a prerecorded message and records callers' messages for later playback.

an′swering serv′ice, *n.* a service that provides operators who take telephone messages for subscribers.

ant (ant), *n.* **1.** any of numerous hymenopterous insects of the widespread family Formicidae, that live in highly organized colonies containing wingless female workers of various castes, a winged queen, and during the breeding season winged males. —**Idiom.** **2. have ants in one's pants,** *Slang.* to be impatient or eager to act.

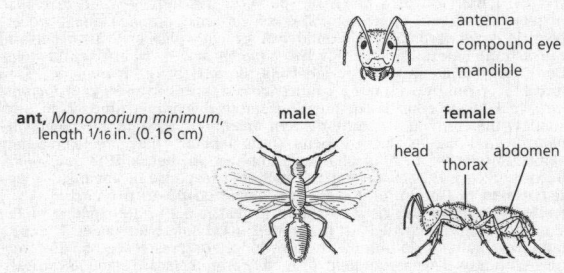

ant, *Monomorium minimum,*
length 1/16 in. (0.16 cm)

male   female

antenna
compound eye
mandible

head
thorax
abdomen

-ant, a suffix joined to verbs, with the general sense "performing" or "a person or thing that performs" the action denoted by the verb; often in nouns denoting participants in a formalized activity (*applicant; contestant; defendant*) or denoting substances that bring about a desired result (*coolant; deodorant; lubricant*). See also -ENT.

an·ta (an′tə), *n., pl.* **-tae** (-tē). a rectangular pier or pilaster, esp. one formed by thickening the end of a masonry wall.

ant·ac·id (ant as′id), *adj.* **1.** preventing, neutralizing, or counteracting acidity, as of the stomach. —*n.* **2.** an antacid agent.

an·tag·o·nism (an tag′ə niz′əm), *n.* **1.** an active hostility or opposition, as between unfriendly or conflicting groups. **2.** an opposing force, principle, or tendency. **3.** an opposing physiological action, as by one muscle in relation to another. **4.** the opposing action of substances, as drugs, that when taken together decrease the effectiveness of at least one of them (contrasted with *synergism*).

an·tag·o·nist (an tag′ə nist), *n.* **1.** a person who is opposed to or competes with another; opponent; adversary. **2.** (in drama or literature) the opponent of the hero or protagonist. **3.** a muscle that acts in opposition to another. Compare AGONIST (def. 2). **4.** a tooth in one jaw that articulates with a tooth in the other jaw. **5.** a drug that counteracts the effects of another drug. —**an·tag′o·nis′tic,** *adj.*

an·tag·o·nize (an tag′ə nīz′), *v.t.* **-nized, -niz·ing.** **1.** to cause to become hostile; make an enemy or opponent of: *His speech antagonized many voters.* **2.** to act in opposition to; oppose. —**an·tag′o·niz′a·ble,** *adj.* —**an·tag′o·ni·za′tion,** *n.*

ant·al·ka·li (ant al′kə lī′), *n., pl.* **-lis, -lies.** something that neutralizes alkalis or counteracts alkalinity. —**ant·al′ka·line′** (-līn′, -lin), *adj., n.*

An·ta·na·na·ri·vo (än′tə nä′nə rē′vō, an′tə nan′ə-), *n.* the capital of Madagascar, in the central part. 703,000. Formerly, **Tananarive.**

Ant·arc·ti·ca (ant ärk′ti kə, -är′ti-), *n.* the continent surrounding the South Pole: almost entirely covered by an ice sheet. ab. 5,000,000 sq. mi. (12,950,000 sq. km). Also called **Antarc′tic Con′tinent.**

Antarc′tic O′cean, *n.* the waters surrounding Antarctica, comprising the southernmost parts of the Pacific, Atlantic, and Indian oceans.

An·tar·es (an târ′ēz, -tar′-), *n.* a red supergiant star of the first magnitude in the constellation Scorpius.

ant·bird (ant′bûrd′), *n.* any of numerous suboscine birds of the family Formicariidae, of the New World tropics, some species of which follow army ant swarms to feed on insects disturbed by the ants.

ant′ cow′, *n.* an aphid that excretes honeydew and is tended by honeydew-gathering ants.

an·te (an′tē), *n., v.,* **-ted** or **-teed, -te·ing.** —*n.* **1.** a fixed but arbitrary stake in poker put into the pot by each player before the deal. **2.** an individual's share of the total expenses incurred by a group. **3.** the price or cost of something. —*v.t.* **4.** (in poker) to put (one's initial stake) into the pot. **5.** to produce or pay (one's share) (usu. fol. by *up*). —*v.i.* **6.** (in poker) to put one's initial stake into the pot. **7.** to pay (usu. fol. by *up*).

ante-, a prefix meaning "happening before" (*antediluvian*), "located in front of" (*anteroom*).

ant·eat·er (ant′ē′tər), *n.* **1.** any of several tropical New World edentate mammals of the family Myrmecophagidae, having a long snout, a sticky extensile tongue, and strong claws, and feeding on ants and termites. **2.** any of various other, unrelated mammals having similar adaptations for feeding on ants and termites, as the aardvark, echidna, and pangolin.

an·te·bel·lum (an′tē bel′əm), *adj.* before or existing before the war, esp. the American Civil War.

an·te·cede (an′tə sēd′), *v.t.,* **-ced·ed, -ced·ing.** to go before in time, order, rank, etc.; precede.

an·te·ced·ent (an′tə sēd′nt), *adj.* **1.** preceding; prior: *an antecedent event.* —*n.* **2.** a preceding circumstance, event, object, phenomenon, etc.; precursor. **3. antecedents, a.** ancestors. **b.** the history, events, conditions, etc., of one's earlier life. **4.** a word, phrase, or clause, usu. a substantive, that is replaced by a pronoun or other substitute, as *Jane* and *glove* in *Jane lost a glove and she can't find it.* **5.** *Math.* **a.** the first term of a ratio; the first or third term of a proportion. **b.** the first of two vectors in a dyad. **6.** the conditional element in a proposition introduced by "if." Compare CONSEQUENT (def. 5). —**an′te·ced′ence,** *n.* —**an′te·ce·den′tal** (an′tə sē den′tl), *adj.* —**an′te·ced′ent·ly,** *adv.*

an·te·ces·sor (an′tə ses′ər), *n.* a predecessor.

an·te·cham·ber (an′tē chām′bər), *n.* a room that serves as a waiting room and entrance to a larger room or an apartment; anteroom.

an·te·choir (an′tē kwīr′), *n.* an enclosed space in front of the choir of a church.

an·te·date (*v.* an′ti dāt′, an′ti dāt′; *n.* an′ti dāt′), *v.,* **-dat·ed, -dat·ing,** *n.* —*v.t.* **1.** to be of older date than; precede in time. **2.** PREDATE (def. 1). **3.** to assign to an earlier date: *to antedate a historical event.* **4.** to cause to happen sooner; accelerate. —*n.* **5.** a prior date.

an·te·di·lu·vi·an (an′tē di lōō′vē ən), *adj.* **1.** of or belonging to the period before the Flood. Gen. 7, 8. **2.** harking back to an earlier time; out of date; antiquated: *antediluvian ideas.* —*n.* **3.** a person who lived before the Flood. **4.** a very old or old-fashioned person or thing.

an·te·lope (an′tl ōp′), *n., pl.* **-lopes,** (*esp. collectively*) **-lope.** **1.** any of several ruminants of the family Bovidae, chiefly of Africa and Asia, having permanent, hollow, unbranched horns. **2.** PRONGHORN. **3.** leather made from the hide of an antelope. —**an′te·lo′pi·an, an′te·lo′pine** (-pin, -pīn), *adj.*

an·te·me·rid·i·an (an′tē mə rid′ē ən), *adj.* **1.** occurring before noon. **2.** of or pertaining to the forenoon.

an·te me·rid·i·em (an′tē mə rid′ē əm, -em′), *adj.* See A.M.

an·te·mor·tem or **an·te-mor·tem** (an′tē môr′təm), *adj.* before death: *an antemortem confession.*

an·te·na·tal (an′tē nāt′l), *adj.* prenatal: *an antenatal clinic.*

an·ten·na (an ten′ə), *n., pl.* **-ten·nas** for 1, **-ten·nae** (-ten′ē) for 2. **1.** a conductor by which electromagnetic waves are sent out or received, consisting commonly of a wire or set of wires often attached to metal rods; aerial. **2.** one of the jointed, movable sensory appendages occurring in pairs on the heads of insects and most other arthropods. **3.** a means or sense of perception. —**an·ten′nal,** *adj.*

an·te·pe·nult (an′tē pē′nult, -pi nult′), *n.* the third syllable from the end in a word, as *te* in *antepenult.*

an·te·ri·or (an tēr′ē ər), *adj.* **1.** situated before or at the front of; fore (opposed to *posterior*). **2. a.** (in animals and embryos) pertaining to or toward the head or forward end of the body. **b.** (in humans and other primates) pertaining to or toward the front plane of the body, equivalent to the ventral surface of quadrupeds. **3.** preceding in time or sequence; earlier.

an·te·room (an′tē rōōm′, -rŏōm′), *n.* **1.** a room that admits to a larger room. **2.** a waiting room.

an·te·type (an′tē tīp′), *n.* an earlier form; prototype.

ant·he·li·on (ant hē′lē an, an thē′-), *n., pl.* **-li·a** (-lē ə). a luminous white spot occasionally appearing in the sky opposite the sun.

an·them (an′thəm), *n.* **1.** a song, as of praise, devotion, or patriotism. **2.** a piece of sacred vocal music, usu. with words taken from the Scriptures. **3.** a hymn sung alternately by different sections of a choir or congregation. —*v.t.* **4.** to celebrate with or in an anthem.

an·ther (an′thər), *n.* the pollen-bearing part of a stamen. —**an′ther·al,** *adj.* —**an′ther·less,** *adj.*

an·ther·id·i·um (an′thə rid′ē əm), *n., pl.* **-ther·id·i·a** (-thə rid′ē ə). a male reproductive structure producing gametes, occurring in ferns, mosses, fungi, and algae. —**an′ther·id′i·al,** *adj.*

ant·hill (ant′hil′), *n.* a mound of earth formed by a colony of ants in digging or constructing their underground nest.

antho-, a combining form meaning "flower": *anthophore.*

an·tho·di·um (an thō′dē əm), *n., pl.* **-di·a** (-dē ə). the flower head of a composite plant, as the head of a dandelion.

an·thol·o·gy (an thol′ə jē), *n., pl.* **-gies. 1.** a book or other collection of selected writings, often in the same literary form, of the same period, or on the same subject. **2.** any collection of selected works, as songs, paintings, etc. —**an·thol′o·gize′,** *v.i., v.t.,* **-gized, -giz·ing.**

An·tho·ny (an′tə nē, -thə- for *1, 2;* an′thə nē for *3*), *n.* **1. Mark,** ANTONY, Mark. **2. Saint,** A.D. 251?–356?, Egyptian hermit: founder of Christian monasticism. **3. Susan Brownell,** 1820–1906, U.S. reformer and suffragist.

an·thoph·i·lous (an thof′ə ləs) also **an·thoph·a·gous** (-ə gəs), *adj.* feeding on flowers, as certain insects.

-anthous, a combining form meaning "having flowers" of the type or number specified by the initial element: *polyanthous.*

an·tho·zo·an (an′thə zō′ən), *n.* any sessile solitary or colonial marine polyp of the class Anthozoa, lacking a medusa stage, and including corals, sea anemones, and sea pens. —*adj.* **2.** Also, **an′tho·zo′ic.** belonging or pertaining to the anthozoans.

an·thra·cite (an′thrə sīt′), *n.* a hard coal low in volatile hydrocarbons and burning with little smoke or flame. —**an′thra·cit′ic** (-sit′ik), **an′thra·cit′ous** (-sī′təs), *adj.*

an·thrax (an′thraks), *n., pl.* **-thra·ces** (-thrə sēz′). **1.** an infectious disease of cattle, sheep, and other mammals caused by the bacterium *Bacillus anthracis,* transmitted to humans through wool and other animal products. **2.** any of the characteristic dark boils that erupt on the skin of humans infected with this.

an·throp·ic (an throp′ik) also **an·throp′i·cal,** *adj.* of or pertaining to human beings or their span of existence on earth.

anthropo-, a combining form meaning "human being": *anthropometry.*

an·thro·po·cen·tric (an′thrə pō sen′trik), *adj.* **1.** regarding the human being as the central fact of the universe. **2.** assuming human beings to be the final aim and end of the universe. **3.** viewing and interpreting everything in terms of human experience and values. —**an′thro·po·cen′tri·cal·ly,** *adv.* —**an′thro·po·cen′trism,** *n.*

an·thro·po·gen·ic (an′thrə pə jen′ik), *adj.* caused or produced by humans. —**an′thro·po·gen′i·cal·ly,** *adv.*

an·thro·pog·ra·phy (an′thrə pog′rə fē), *n.* the branch of anthropology that describes the varieties of humankind and their geographical distribution. —**an′thro·pog′ra·pher** (-pə graf′ik), *adj.*

an·thro·poid (an′thrə poid′), *adj.* **1.** resembling humans. **2.** resembling an ape; apelike. **3.** belonging or pertaining to the primate suborder Anthropoidea, characterized by a relatively flat face, dry nose, small immobile ears, and forward-facing eyes and comprising humans, apes, Old World monkeys, and New World monkeys. Compare PROSIMIAN. —*n.* **4.** ANTHROPOID APE. —**an′thro·poi′dal,** *adj.*

an′thropoid ape′, *n.* any ape of the families Pongidae and Hylobatidae, anatomically resembling humans and comprising the gorillas, chimpanzees, orangutans, gibbons, and siamangs.

anthropolog′ical linguis′tics, *n.* the study of language in relation to culture, including the recording and analysis of the languages of nonliterate societies.

an·thro·pol·o·gy (an′thrə pol′ə jē), *n.* the science that deals with the origins, physical and cultural development, biological characteristics, and social customs and beliefs of humankind. —**an′thro·po·log′i·cal** (-pə loj′i kəl), **an′thro·po·log′ic,** *adj.* —**an′thro·po·log′i·cal·ly,** *adv.* —**an′thro·pol′o·gist,** *n.*

an·thro·pom·e·try (an′thrə pom′i trē), *n.* the measurement of the size and proportions of the human body, esp. as an aid for comparative

study in physical anthropology. —**an′thro·po·met′ric** (-pə me′trik), **an′thro·po·met′ri·cal,** *adj.* —**an′thro·po·met′ri·cal·ly,** *adv.*

an·thro·po·mor·phic (an′thrə pə môr′fik) also **an′thro·po·mor′phous,** *adj.* **1.** ascribing human form or attributes to a thing or a being not human, as to a deity. **2.** resembling or made to resemble a human form: *an anthropomorphic carving.* —**an′thro·po·mor′phi·cal·ly,** *adv.* —**an′thro·po·mor′phism,** *n.*

an·thro·pop·a·thy (an′thrə pop′ə thē) also **an′thro·pop′a·thism,** *n.* ascription of human passions or feelings to a thing or a being not human, as to a deity.

an·thro·pos·o·phy (an′thrə pos′ə fē), *n.* a philosophy based on the teachings of Rudolf Steiner (1861–1925) which maintains that, by virtue of a prescribed method of self-discipline, cognitional experience of the spiritual world can be achieved. —**an′thro·po·soph·i·cal** (an′thrə pə sof′i kəl), **an′thro·po·soph′ic,** *adj.*

an·ti (an′tī, an′tē), *n., pl.* **-tis.** a person who is opposed to a particular practice, party, policy, action, etc.

anti-, a prefix meaning "against, opposed to, prejudicial to" (*antiabortion; anti-Semitic; antislavery*), "preventing, counteracting, or mitigating" (*anticoagulant; antifreeze*), "destroying or disabling" (*antiaircraft; antipersonnel*), "identical to in form or function, but lacking, opposite, or contrary in essential respects" (*anticlimax; antihero; antiparticle*), "an antagonist or rival of" (*Antichrist; antipope*), "situated opposite" (*Anti-Lebanon*). Also, *before a vowel,* **ant-.**

an·ti·air·craft (an′tē âr′kraft′, -kräft′, an′tī-), *adj.* **1.** designed for or used in defense against enemy aircraft. —*n.* **2.** artillery used against enemy aircraft.

an·ti·bac·te·ri·al (an′tē bak tēr′ē əl, an′tī-), *adj.* destructive to or inhibiting the growth of bacteria.

an·ti·bal·lis·tic (an′tē bə lis′tik, an′tī-), *adj.* designed to intercept and destroy ballistic missiles: *an antiballistic missile.*

an·ti·bi·o·sis (an′tē bī ō′sis, an′tī-), *n.* an association between organisms that is injurious to one of them.

an·ti·bi·ot·ic (an′tī bī ot′ik, -bē-, an′tē-, -tī-), *n.* **1.** any of a large group of chemical substances, as penicillin and streptomycin, that are produced by various microorganisms and fungi, have the capacity in dilute solutions to inhibit the growth of or to destroy bacteria and other microorganisms, and are used in the treatment of infectious diseases. —*adj.* **2.** of or involving antibiotics. —**an′ti·bi·ot′i·cal·ly,** *adv.*

an·ti·bod·y (an′ti bod′ē), *n., pl.* **-bod·ies. 1.** any of numerous protein molecules produced by B cells as a primary immune defense, each kind having a uniquely shaped site that combines with a foreign antigen, as of a virus, and disables it. **2.** antibodies of a particular type collectively.

an′tibody-me′diated immu′nity, *n.* immunity conferred to an individual through the activity of B cells and circulating antibodies. Compare CELL-MEDIATED IMMUNITY.

an·tic (an′tik), *n.* **1.** Usu., **antics. a.** a playful or silly trick or prank; caper. **b.** a grotesque, fantastic, or ludicrous gesture, act, or posture. —*adj.* **2.** ludicrous; funny; whimsical. **3.** fantastic; odd; grotesque. —**an′ti·cal·ly,** **an′tic·ly,** *adv.*

an·ti·chlor (an′ti klôr′, -klōr′), *n.* any of various substances, esp. sodium thiosulfate, used for removing excess chlorine from paper pulp, textiles, etc., after bleaching. —**an′ti·chlo·ris′tic** (-klô ris′tik, -klō-), *adj.*

an·ti·choice (an′tē chois′, an′tī-), *adj.* opposed to the idea that a pregnant woman has the right to choose abortion.

An·ti·christ (an′ti krīst′), *n.* **1.** a personage or power expected to corrupt the world but be conquered by Christ's Second Coming. **2.** (*often l.c.*) **a.** any opponent of or disbeliever in Christ. **b.** a false Christ.

an·tic·i·pant (an tis′ə pənt), *adj.* **1.** anticipative; expectant (usu. fol. by *of*). —*n.* **2.** a person who anticipates.

an·tic·i·pate (an tis′ə pāt′), *v.,* **-pat·ed, -pat·ing.** —*v.t.* **1.** to realize or feel beforehand; foretaste or foresee: *to anticipate pleasure.* **2.** to expect; look forward to, esp. confidently or with pleasure. **3.** to perform (an action) before another has had time to act. **4.** to answer (a question), obey (a command), or satisfy (a request) before it is made. **5.** to forestall or nullify by taking countermeasures in advance: *to anticipate an attack.* **6.** to consider or mention before the proper time. **7.** to foreshadow the creation of: *Many modern inventions were anticipated by Leonardo da Vinci.* **8. a.** to expend (funds) before they are legitimately available for use. **b.** to discharge (an obligation) before it is due. —*v.i.* **9.** to think, speak, act, or feel an emotional response in advance. —**an·tic′i·pa·to′ry** (-pə tôr′ē, -tōr′ē), *adj.* —**an·tic′i·pa·to′ri·ly,** *adv.*

an·tic·i·pa·tion (an tis′ə pā′shən), *n.* **1.** the act of anticipating or the state of being anticipated. **2.** realization in advance; foretaste. **3.** expectation or hope. **4.** intuition, foreknowledge, or prescience. **5.** a premature withdrawal or assignment of money from a trust estate. **6.** a musical tone introduced in advance of its harmony so that it sounds against the preceding chord.

an·ti·cli·max (an′tē klī′maks, an′tī-), *n.* **1.** an event, conclusion, statement, etc., that is far less important, powerful, or striking than expected. **2.** a descent in power, quality, or dignity; a disappointing, weak, or inglorious conclusion. **3.** a noticeable or ludicrous descent from lofty ideas or expressions to banalities or commonplace remarks. —**an′ti·cli·mac′tic** (-klī mak′tik, -klə-), *adj.*

an·ti·cli·nal (an′ti klīn′l), *adj.* **1.** inclining in opposite directions from a central axis. **2. a.** inclining downward on both sides from a median line or axis, as a fold of rock strata. **b.** pertaining to such a fold.

an·ti·co·ag·u·lant (an/tē kō ag/yə lənt, an/tī-), *adj.* **1.** Also, **an·ti·co·ag·u·la·tive** (-lā/tiv, -lə tiv). preventing coagulation, esp. of blood. —*n.* **2.** an anticoagulant agent, as heparin.

an·ti·co·don (an/tē kō/don, an/tī-), *n.* a set of three nucleotide bases at the loop end of tRNA that forms base pairs with the codon of messenger RNA.

an·ti·cy·clone (an/tē sī/klōn, an/tī-), *n.* a circulation of winds around a central region of high atmospheric pressure that is clockwise in the Northern Hemisphere and counterclockwise in the Southern Hemisphere. —**an/ti·cy·clon/ic** (-sī klon/ik), *adj.*

an·ti·de·pres·sant or **an·ti·de·pres·sant** (an/tē di pres/ənt, an/tī-), also **an·ti·de·pres·sive** (an/tē di pres/iv, an/tī-), *adj.* **1.** used to relieve or treat mental depression. —*n.* **2.** an antidepressant drug.

an·ti·di·u·ret·ic (an/tē dī/ə ret/ik), *adj.* **1.** of or pertaining to a substance that suppresses the formation of urine. —*n.* **2.** an antidiuretic substance.

an·ti·do·ron (än dē/thô rôn; *Eng.* an/tē dôr/on, -dōr/-), *n.* **1.** Also called **holy bread.** *Greek Orthodox Church.* bread blessed and distributed to the congregation at the end of the liturgy. **2.** *Eastern Church.* eulogia (def. 1).

an·ti·dote (an/ti dōt/), *n., v.,* **-dot·ed, -dot·ing.** —*n.* **1.** a medicine or other remedy for counteracting the effects of poison, disease, etc. **2.** something that prevents or counteracts injurious or unwanted effects: *an antidote to crime.* —*v.t.* **3.** to counteract with an antidote. —**an/ti·dot/al,** *adj.* —**an/ti·dot/al·ly,** *adv.*

an·ti·es·tab·lish·ment (an/tē i stab/lish mənt, an/tī-), *adj.* opposed to or working against the existing power structure or mores, as of society or government. —**an/ti·es·tab/lish·men·tar/i·an,** *n., adj.* —**an/ti·es·tab·lish·men·tar·i·an·ism,** *n.*

An·tie·tam (an tē/təm), *n.* a creek flowing from S Pennsylvania through NW Maryland into the Potomac: Civil War battle fought near here at Sharpsburg, Md., in 1862.

An·ti·fed·er·al·ist (an/tē fed/ər ə list, -fed/rə-, an/tī-), *n.* **1.** a member of a group that before 1789 opposed the adoption of the U.S. Constitution and after that favored its strict construction. **2.** (*l.c.*) an opponent of federalism. —**An/ti·fed/er·al·ism,** *n.*

an·ti·fer·til·i·ty (an/tē fər til/i tē, an/tī-), *adj.* of or being a substance that inhibits the ability to produce offspring; contraceptive.

an·ti·freeze (an/ti frēz/, an/tē-), *n.* a liquid, as ethylene glycol, used in the radiator of an internal-combustion engine to lower the freezing point of the cooling medium.

an·ti·gen (an/ti jən, -jen/), *n.* **1.** any substance that can stimulate the production of antibodies and combine specifically with them. **2.** any commercial substance that, when injected or absorbed into animal tissues, stimulates the production of antibodies. **3.** antigens of a particular type collectively. —**an/ti·gen/ic,** *adj.* —**an/ti·gen/i·cal·ly,** *adv.* —**an/ti·ge·nic/i·ty** (-jə nis/i tē), *n.*

An·tig·o·ne (an tig/ə nē/), *n.* (in Greek myth) a daughter of Oedipus and Jocasta who defied her uncle Creon by performing funeral rites over her brother Polynices.

an·ti·grav·i·ty (an/tē grav/i tē, an/tī-), *n.* **1.** the antithesis of gravity; a hypothetical force by which a body of positive mass would repel a body of negative mass. —*adj.* **2.** (not in technical use) counteracting the force of gravity.

Anti/gua and Barbu/da, *n.* an island state in the E West Indies, comprising Antigua, Barbuda, and a smaller island: formerly a British crown colony; gained independence 1981. 81,500; 171 sq. mi. (442 sq. km). *Cap.:* St. John's.

an·ti·he·ro (an/tē hēr/ō, an/tī-), *n., pl.* **-roes.** a protagonist who lacks the ennobling qualities of a hero.

an·ti·his·ta·mine (an/tē his/tə mēn/, -min, an/tī-), *n.* any of various synthetic compounds capable of blocking the action of histamines, used esp. for treating allergies and gastric ulcers. —**an/ti·his/ta·min/ic** (-min/ik), *adj.*

an·ti·hy·per·ten·sive (an/tē hī/pər ten/siv, an/tī-), *adj.* **1.** acting to reduce hypertension. —*n.* **2.** a drug used to treat hypertension.

an·ti·in·flam·ma·to·ry (an/tē in flam/ə tôr/ē, -tôr/ē, an/tī-), *adj., n., pl.* **-ries.** —*adj.* **1.** acting to reduce certain signs of inflammation, as swelling, tenderness, fever, and pain. —*n.* **2.** a medication, as aspirin, used to reduce inflammation.

an·ti·in·tel·lec·tu·al (an/tē in/tl ek/chōō əl, an/tī-), *adj.* opposed to, hostile to, or distrustful of intellectuals or intellectual pursuits, concerns, or points of view. —**an/ti·in/tel·lec/tu·al·ism,** *n.*

An·til·les (an til/ēz), *n.pl.* a chain of islands in the West Indies, divided into two parts, one including Cuba, Hispaniola, Jamaica, and Puerto Rico (**Greater Antilles**), the other including a large arch of smaller islands to the SE and S (**Lesser Antilles** or **Caribees**). —**An·til/le·an,** *adj., n.*

an/ti·lock brake/ (an/tē lok/, an/tī-), *n.* a brake equipped with a computer-controlled device that prevents the wheel from locking.

an·ti·log·a·rithm (an/ti lô/gə rith/əm, -rith/-, -log/ə-), *n.* the number of which a given number is the logarithm; antilog. —**an/ti·log/a·rith/mic,** *adj.*

an·ti·ma·cas·sar (an/ti mə kas/ər), *n.* a small, usu. ornamental covering placed on the backs and arms of upholstered furniture to prevent wear or soiling; a tidy.

an·ti·mag·net·ic (an/tē mag net/ik, an/tī-), *adj.* **1.** resistant to magnetization. **2.** (of a precision instrument, watch, etc.) having the critical parts composed of materials resistant to magnetization, and hence not seriously affected in accuracy by exposure to magnetic fields.

An/ti-Mason/ic par/ty, *n.* a former political party (1826–35) that opposed Freemasonry in civil affairs.

an·ti·mat·ter (an/tē mat/ər, an/tī-), *n.* matter composed only of antiparticles.

an·ti·mis·sile (an/tē mis/əl, an/tī-; *esp. Brit.* -mis/īl), *adj.* designed or used in defense against guided enemy missiles.

an·ti·mo·nous (an/tə mə nəs, -mō/nəs) also **an·ti·mo·ni·ous** (an/tə mō/nē əs), *adj.* of or containing antimony, esp. in the trivalent state.

an·ti·mo·ny (an/tə mō/nē), *n.* a brittle, lustrous, white metallic element occurring in nature free or combined, used chiefly in alloys and in compounds in medicine. *Symbol:* Sb; *at. no.:* 51; *at. wt.:* 121.75. —**an/ti·mo/ni·al,** *adj., n.*

an·ti·ne·o·plas·tic (an/tē nē/ō plas/tik, an/tī-), *adj.* **1.** destroying, inhibiting, or preventing the growth or spread of tumors. —*n.* **2.** an antineoplastic substance.

an·ti·neu·tron (an/tē nōō/tron, -nyōō/-, an/tī-), *n.* the antiparticle of the neutron, having zero charge and the same mass and spin of a neutron but with an opposite magnetic moment.

an·ti·node (an/ti nōd/), *n.* the region of maximum amplitude between two adjacent nodes in a standing wave. —**an/ti·nod/al,** *adj.*

an·tin·o·my (an tin/ə mē), *n., pl.* **-mies.** **1.** opposition between one law, principle, rule, etc., and another. **2.** a contradiction between two statements, both apparently obtained by correct reasoning. —**an/ti·nom/ic** (-ti nom/ik), —**an/ti·nom/i·cal,** *adj.*

an·ti·nu·cle·ar (an/tē nōō/klē ər, -nyōō/-, an/tī- *or, by metathesis,* -kyə lər), *adj.* opposed to the building or use of nuclear weapons or nuclear power plants.

An·ti·och (an/tē ok/), *n.* **1.** Arabic, **Antakiya.** Turkish, **Antakya.** a city in S Turkey: capital of the ancient kingdom of Syria 300–64 B.C. 94,942. **2.** a city in W California. 55,980. —**An/ti·o/chi·an** (-ō/kē ən), *n., adj.*

An·ti·o·chus (an tī/ə kəs), *n.* **1. Antiochus III,** (*"the Great"*) 241?–187

B.C., king of Syria 223–187. **2. Antiochus IV,** (*Antiochus Epiphanes*) died 164? B.C., king of Syria 175–164?.

an·ti·ox·i·dant (anʹtē okʹsi dənt, anʹtī-), *n.* **1.** a substance that inhibits oxidation. **2.** an enzyme or other organic substance, as vitamin E or beta carotene, capable of counteracting the damaging effects of oxidation in animal tissues.

an·ti·par·ti·cle (anʹtē pärʹti kəl, anʹtī-), *n.* a particle whose properties are identical in magnitude to those of a specific elementary particle but are of opposite sign.

an·ti·pas·to (anʹti päʹstō, -pasʹtō, änʹtē päʹ-), *n.*, *pl.* **-pas·tos, -pas·ti** (-päʹstē, -pasʹtē). an appetizer course in an Italian meal, often consisting of an assortment of foods, as olives, anchovies, salami, and peppers.

an·tip·a·thy (an tipʹə thē), *n.*, *pl.* **-thies. 1.** a natural, basic, or habitual repugnance; aversion. **2.** an object of natural aversion or habitual dislike.

an·ti·per·son·nel (anʹtē pûrʹsə nelʹ, anʹtī-), *adj.* designed to destroy or disable enemy troops rather than vehicles or matériel.

an·ti·per·spi·rant (anʹti pûrʹspər ənt), *n.* an astringent preparation for reducing perspiration, often containing aluminum.

an·ti·phon (anʹtə fonʹ), *n.* **1.** a verse, prayer, or song to be chanted or sung in response. **2.** a verse or text recited or sung before or after some part of the liturgical service.

an·tiph·o·ny (an tifʹə nē), *n.*, *pl.* **-nies.** alternate or responsive singing by a choir in two divisions. —**an·ti·phon·ic** (anʹtə fonʹik), *adj.* —**anʹti·phonʹi·cal·ly,** *adv.*

an·tiph·ra·sis (an tifʹrə sis), *n.* the use of a word in a sense opposite to its proper meaning, esp. for ironic effect. —**an·ti·phras·tic** (anʹti frasʹtik), *adj.* —**anʹti·phrasʹti·cal·ly,** *adv.*

an·tip·o·dal (an tipʹə dl), *adj.* **1.** on the opposite side of the globe; pertaining to the antipodes. **2.** diametrically opposite: *antipodal personalities.* **3.** opposed: *a view antipodal to the majority.*

an·ti·pode (anʹti pōdʹ), *n.* a direct or exact opposite.

an·ti·pope (anʹti pōpʹ), *n.* a person who is elected or claims to be pope in opposition to another held to be canonically chosen.

an·ti·pro·ton (anʹtē prōʹton, anʹtī-), *n.* the antiparticle of the proton, having negative charge but the mass and spin of the proton.

an·ti·py·ret·ic (anʹtē pī retʹik, anʹtī-), *adj.* **1.** checking or preventing fever. —*n.* **2.** an antipyretic agent. —**anʹti·py·reʹsis** (-rēʹsis), *n.*

an·ti·quar·i·an (anʹti kwârʹē ən), *adj.* **1.** pertaining to antiquaries or to the study of antiquities. **2. a.** of value because of age or rarity: *antiquarian books in fine leather bindings.* **b.** dealing or interested in such objects. —*n.* **3.** an antiquary.

an·ti·quark (anʹtē kwôrkʹ, -kwärkʹ, anʹtī-), *n.* the antiparticle of a quark.

an·ti·quar·y (anʹti kwerʹē), *n.*, *pl.* **-quar·ies. 1.** an expert on or student of antiquities. **2.** a collector of antiquities.

an·ti·quate (anʹti kwātʹ), *v.t.*, **-quat·ed, -quat·ing. 1.** to make obsolete or old-fashioned by replacing with something newer or better. **2.** to give an antique appearance to. —**anʹti·quaʹtion,** *n.*

an·ti·quat·ed (anʹti kwāʹtid), *adj.* **1.** surviving from, resembling, or adhering to the past; old-fashioned: *antiquated ideas.* **2.** no longer used; obsolete or obsolescent. **3.** aged; old.

an·tique (an tēkʹ), *adj.*, *n.*, *v.*, **-tiqued, -ti·quing.** —*adj.* **1.** of or belonging to the past; not modern. **2.** dating from a period long ago: *antique furniture.* **3.** in the tradition or style of an earlier period. **4.** old-fashioned; antiquated. **5.** of or belonging to the ancient Greeks and Romans. **6.** (of paper) neither calendered nor coated and having a rough surface. **7.** ancient. —*n.* **8.** a piece of furniture, decorative object, or work of art produced in a former period, or, according to U.S. customs laws, 100 years before date of purchase. **9.** the antique style, usu. Greek or Roman, esp. in art. —*v.t.* **10.** to finish or treat so as to give an antique appearance. —*v.i.* **11.** to shop for or collect antiques.

an·tiq·ui·ty (an tikʹwi tē), *n.*, *pl.* **-ties. 1.** the quality of being ancient; ancientness: *a bowl of great antiquity.* **2.** ancient times; former ages. **3.** the period of history before the Middle Ages. **4. antiquities,** things belonging to or remaining from ancient times, as monuments, relics, or customs. **5.** the peoples, nations, or cultures of ancient times.

An·ti-Sa·loonʹ Leagueʹ of Amerʹica (anʹtē sə lōōnʹ, anʹtī-), *n.* a national organization, founded in 1893 in Ohio, advocating the prohibition of the manufacture and sale of alcoholic beverages.

an·ti-Sem·i·tism (anʹtē semʹi tizʹəm, anʹtī-), *n.* discrimination against or prejudice or hostility toward Jews. —**anti-Semite,** *n.* —**anʹti-Semitʹic** (-sə mitʹik), *adj.* —**anʹti-Semʹit/i·cal·ly,** *adv.*

an·ti·sep·sis (anʹtə sepʹsis), *n.* destruction of the microorganisms that produce sepsis or septic disease.

an·ti·sep·tic (anʹtə sepʹtik), *adj.* **1.** pertaining to or effecting antisepsis. **2.** free from or cleaned of germs and other microorganisms. **3.** exceptionally clean or neat. **4.** free of contamination or pollution. **5.** lacking in warmth, vitality, emotion, or other humanizing qualities; cold. —*n.* **6.** an antiseptic agent. —**anʹti·sepʹti·cal·ly,** *adv.*

an·ti·se·rum (anʹtə sērʹəm), *n.*, *pl.* **-se·rums, -se·ra** (-sērʹə). animal or human serum that contains antibodies to a specific disease, used for injections to confer passive immunity to that disease.

an·ti·slav·er·y (anʹtē slāʹvə rē, -slāvʹrē, anʹtī-), *adj.* **1.** opposed to slavery. —*n.* **2.** opposition to slavery.

an·ti·so·cial (anʹtē sōʹshəl, anʹtī-), *adj.* **1.** unwilling or unable to associate in a normal or friendly way with other people. **2.** antagonistic, hostile, or unfriendly toward others. **3.** opposed or detrimental to social order or the principles on which society is constituted: *antisocial behavior.* —*n.* **4.** a person exhibiting antisocial traits. —**anʹti·soʹcial·ly,** *adv.*

an·ti·stat·ic (anʹtē statʹik, anʹtī-), *adj.* pertaining to a substance or procedure that inhibits the accumulation of static electricity, as on textiles, phonograph records, or paper products.

an·tith·e·sis (an tithʹə sis), *n.*, *pl.* **-ses** (-sēzʹ). **1.** opposition; contrast: *the antithesis of right and wrong.* **2.** the direct opposite: *Her behavior was the very antithesis of cowardly.* **3. a.** the placing of a sentence or one of its parts against another to which it is opposed to form a balanced contrast of ideas, as in "Give me liberty or give me death." **b.** the second sentence or part thus set in opposition, as "or give me death."

an·ti·thet·i·cal (anʹtə thetʹi kəl) also **anʹti·thetʹic,** *adj.* **1.** of the nature of or involving antithesis. **2.** directly opposed or contrasted.

an·ti·tox·in (anʹti tokʹsin, anʹtē-), *n.* **1.** a substance formed in the body that counteracts a specific toxin. **2.** the antibody formed in immunization with a given toxin, used in treating certain infectious diseases or in immunizing against them.

an·ti·trade (anʹti trādʹ), *n.* **1. antitrades,** westerly winds lying above the trade winds in the tropics. —*adj.* **2.** of, pertaining to, or characteristic of such a wind.

an·ti·trust (anʹtē trustʹ, anʹtī-), *adj.* opposing or intended to restrain trusts, monopolies, or other large combinations of business and capital, esp. to promote competition: *antitrust laws.*

an·ti·tus·sive (anʹtē tusʹiv, anʹtī-), *adj.* **1.** of or pertaining to a substance used to suppress coughing. —*n.* **2.** an antitussive substance.

an·ti·type (anʹti tīpʹ), *n.* **1.** something that is foreshadowed by a type or symbol, as a New Testament event prefigured in the Old Testament. **2.** an opposite type. —**anʹti·typʹic** (-tipʹik), **anʹti·typʹi·cal,** *adj.* —**anʹti·typʹi·cal·ly,** *adv.*

an·ti·ven·in (anʹtē venʹin, anʹtī-) also **an·ti·ven·om** (-venʹəm), *n.* an antitoxin that counteracts venom, as from snakebite, obtained from the serum of a large animal that has had a series of controlled venom injections: used for treating victims of severe venomous bites.

---

anʹti·medʹi·cal, *adj.;* -ly, *adv.*
anʹti·milʹi·ta·rism, *n.*
anʹti·milʹi·tar·y, *adj.*
anʹti·misʹce·ge·naʹtion, *n., adj.*
anʹti·modʹern, *n.*
anʹti·monʹar·chist, *n., adj.*
anʹti·mo·nopʹo·list, *n., adj.*
anʹti·nar·cotʹic, *adj., n.*
anʹti·naʹtion·al·ism, *n.*
anʹti-Naʹzi, *n., adj.*
anʹti·neuʹral·gic, *adj., n.*
anʹti·neuʹtral·i·ty, *n.*
anʹti·noiseʹ, *adj.*
anʹti·o·beʹsi·ty, *adj.*
anʹti·ob·scenʹi·ty, *adj.*
anʹti·orʹtho·doxʹ, *adj.*
anʹti·oxʹi·dizʹer, *n.*
anʹti·pacʹi·fism, *n.*
anʹti·parʹa·sitʹic, *n., adj.*
anʹti·parʹty, *n., adj.*
anʹti·pathʹo·gen, *n.*
anʹti·paʹtri·arʹchal, *adj.*
anʹti·paʹtri·ot, *n.*
anʹti·pleasʹure, *n., adj.*

anʹti·po·etʹic, *adj.*
anʹti·poʹlar, *adj.*
anʹti·po·litʹi·cal, *adj.;* -ly, *adv.*
anʹti·polʹi·tics, *adj.*
anʹti·pol·luʹtion, *adj.*
anʹti-Popʹu·list, *n., adj.*
anʹti·por·nogʹra·phy, *n., adj.*
anʹti·povʹer·ty, *adj.*
anʹti·pragʹma·tism, *n.*
anʹti·pro·gresʹsive, *adj.*
anʹti·proʹhi·biʹtion, *adj., n.*
anʹti·prosʹti·tuʹtion, *adj., n.*
anʹti·pro·tecʹtion·ist, *n., adj.*
anʹti·psy·chotʹic, *adj., n.*
anʹti·raʹbies, *adj., n.*
anʹti·raʹcism, *n.*
anʹti·raʹdar, *n.*
anʹti·ra·diʹa·tion, *adj.*
anʹti·rapeʹ, *adj., n.*
anʹti·ra·tionʹal, *adj.;* -ly, *adv.*
anʹti·reʹal·ism, *n.*
anʹti·re·cesʹsion, *n., adj.*
anʹti·re·flecʹtion, *adj.*
anʹti·re·formʹ, *adj.*
anʹti·regʹu·la·toʹry, *adj.*

anʹti·revʹo·luʹtion, *adj.*
anʹti·rheu·matʹic, *adj., n.*
anʹti·riʹot, *adj.*
anʹti·ro·manʹtic, *adj., n.*
anʹti·royʹal, *adj.*
anʹti·rustʹ, *adj.*
anʹti·sciʹence, *adj., n.*
anʹti·seg·re·gaʹtion, *n., adj.*
anʹti·sepʹa·raʹtist, *n.*
anʹti·sexʹism, *n.*
anʹti·skidʹ, *adj.*
anʹti·slipʹ, *adj.*
anʹti·smogʹ, *adj.*
anʹti·smokʹing, *adj.*
anʹti·smugʹgling, *adj.*
anʹti·soʹcial·ist, *n., adj.*
anʹti·spas·modʹic, *adj., n.*
anʹti·spendʹing, *adj.*
anʹti·spirʹit·u·al, *adj.*
anʹti·stimʹu·lant, *adj., n.*
anʹti·stressʹ, *adj.*
anʹti·stuʹdent, *n., adj.*
anʹti·sub·maʹrine, *adj.*
anʹti·sub·verʹsion, *n.*
anʹti·sufʹfrage, *adj.*

anʹti·suʹi·cide, *adj.*
anʹti·symʹme·try, *adj., n.*
anʹti·tankʹ, *adj.*
anʹti·tarʹnish, *adj.*
anʹti·taxʹ, *adj.*
anʹti·tech·nolʹo·gy, *n.*
anʹti·ter·rorʹist, *adj.*
anʹti·theftʹ, *adj.*
anʹti·to·bacʹco, *adj.*
anʹti·to·talʹi·tarʹi·an, *adj.*
anʹti·toxʹic, *adj.*
anʹti·tu·berʹcu·lar, *adj.*
anʹti·ulʹcer, *adj.*
anʹti·unʹion, *adj.*
anʹti·urʹban, *adj.*
anʹti·u·tilʹi·tarʹi·an, *adj., n.*
anʹti·viʹo·lence, *adj.*
anʹti·viʹral, *adj.*
anʹti·viʹrus, *adj.*
anʹti·viʹi·secʹtion, *n., adj.*
anʹti·warʹ, *adj.*
anʹti·welʹfare, *adj.*
anʹti·whalʹing, *adj.*
anʹti·womʹan, *adj.*
anʹti·wrinʹkle, *adj.*

A

ant•ler (ant′lər), *n.* one of the solid deciduous horns, usu. branched, of an animal of the deer family. **—ant′lered,** *adj.* **—ant′ler•less,** *adj.*

ant′ li′on or **ant′li′on,** *n.* any of several nocturnal insects of the family Myrmeleontidae, resembling a damselfly, which as a larva **(doodlebug)** preys upon ants and other insects by lying in wait at the bottom of a conical sand trap with only its mandibles exposed.

an•to•no•ma•sia (an′tə nə mā′zhə), *n.* **1.** the substitution of an epithet or appellative for an individual's name, as *his lordship.* **2.** the use of the name of a person or character noted for a particular characteristic, as Casanova or Walter Mitty, to designate a person or class having the same characteristic. **—an′to•no•mas′tic** (-mas′tik), *adj.* **—an′to•no•mas′ti•cal•ly,** *adv.*

An•to•ny (an′tə nē), *n.* **Mark** (*Marcus Antonius*), 83?–30 B.C., Roman general: friend of Caesar; rival of Augustus Caesar.

an•to•nym (an′tə nim), *n.* a word opposite in meaning to another: Fast *is an antonym of* slow. Compare SYNONYM (def. 1). **—an•ton•y•mous** (an ton′ə məs), **an′to•nym′ic,** *adj.* **—an•ton′y•my,** *n.*

an•tre (an′tər), *n.* a cavern; cave.

an•trum (an′trəm), *n., pl.* **-tra** (-trə). a cavity in a body organ, esp. a bony sinus. **—an′tral,** *adj.*

A•nu•bis (ə no͞o′bis, ə nyo͞o′-), *n.* the Egyptian god of tombs and weigher of the hearts of the dead: represented as having the head of a jackal.

an•u•ran (ə no͝or′ən, ə nyo͝or′-), *n.* **1.** any amphibian of the order Anura, comprising the frogs and toads. **—***adj.* **2.** belonging or pertaining to the Anura.

an•u•re•sis (an′yə rē′sis), *n.* retention of urine in the bladder. **—an′u•ret′ic** (-ret′ik), *adj.*

an•u•ri•a (ə no͝or′ē ə, ə nyo͝or′-, an yo͝or′-), *n.* the absence or suppression of urine. **—an•u′ric,** *adj.*

a•nus (ā′nəs), *n., pl.* **a•nus•es.** the excretory opening at the lower end of the alimentary canal.

an•vil (an′vil), *n.* **1.** a heavy iron block with a smooth face, frequently of steel, on which heated metals are hammered into desired shapes. **2.** the fixed jaw in certain measuring instruments. **3.** INCUS.

anx•i•e•ty (ang zī′i tē), *n., pl.* **-ties.** **1.** distress or uneasiness of mind caused by fear of danger or misfortune. **2.** earnest but tense desire; eagerness: *a keen anxiety to succeed.* **3.** a state of apprehension and psychic tension occurring in some forms of mental disorder.

anx•ious (angk′shəs, ang′-), *adj.* **1.** full of mental distress or uneasiness because of fear of danger or misfortune; worried. **2.** earnestly desirous; eager. **3.** attended with or showing solicitude or uneasiness: *anxious forebodings.* **—anx′ious•ly,** *adv.*

an•y (en′ē), *adj.* **1.** one, a, an, or some; one or more without specification or identification: *If you have any witnesses, produce them. Pick out any six you like.* **2.** whatever or whichever it may be: *at any price.* **3.** in whatever quantity or number, great or small; some: *Do you have any butter?* **4.** every; all: *Read any books you find on the subject.* **5.** (following a negative) at all: *She can't endure any criticism.* **—***pron.* **6.** an unspecified person or persons; anybody; anyone: *He did better than any before him.* **7.** a single one or ones; an unspecified thing or things; a quantity or number: *We don't have any left.* **—***adv.* **8.** in whatever degree; to some extent; at all: *Do you feel any better?* **—*Idiom.*** **9. any which way,** in any manner whatever; indifferently or carelessly. **—Usage.** See ANYBODY, ANYONE, ANYPLACE, ANYWAY, EITHER.

an•y•bod•y (en′ē bod′ē, -bud′ē), *pron., n., pl.* **-bod•ies.** **—***pron.* **1.** any person. **—***n.* **2.** a person of some importance: *If you're anybody, you'll get an invitation.* **—Usage.** The pronoun ANYBODY is always written as one word: *Is anybody home?* The two-word noun phrase ANY BODY means "any group" (*Any body of students will include a few dissidents*) or "any physical body": *The search continued for a week despite the failure to find any body.* If the word *a* can be substituted for *any* without seriously affecting the meaning, the two-word noun phrase is called for: *a body of students; failure to find a body.* If the substitution cannot be made, the spelling is ANYBODY. ANYBODY is less formal than ANYONE. See also ANYONE, EACH, THEY.

an•y•how (en′ē hou′), *adv.* **1.** in any way whatever. **2.** in any case; at all events. **3.** in a careless manner; haphazardly: *clothes strewn anyhow about the room.*

an•y•more (en′ē môr′, -mōr′), *adv.* **1.** any longer. **2.** nowadays; presently. **—Usage.** The adverb ANYMORE is used in negative constructions and in some types of questions: *She doesn't work here anymore. Do you play tennis anymore?* In some dialects, chiefly South Midland in origin, it is found in positive statements meaning "nowadays": *Baker's bread is all we eat anymore. Anymore we always take the bus.* The use of ANYMORE at the beginning of a sentence is almost exclusive to speech or to representations of speech.

an•y•one (en′ē wun′, -wən), *pron.* any person at all; anybody: *Did anyone see the accident?* **—Usage.** ANYONE as a pronoun meaning "anybody" or "any person at all" is written as one word. The two-word phrase ANY ONE means "any single member of a group of persons or things" and is often followed by *of: Any one of these books is exciting reading.* ANYONE is more formal than ANYBODY. See also EACH, THEY.

an•y•place (en′ē plās′), *adv.* ANYWHERE. **—Usage.** The adverb ANYPLACE is most often written as one word: *Anyplace you look there are ruins.* It occurs mainly in informal speech and only occasionally in writing. ANYWHERE is by far the more common form in formal speech and edited writing. The same holds true, respectively, of the adverbial pairs EVERYPLACE and EVERYWHERE; NOPLACE and NOWHERE; and SOMEPLACE and SOMEWHERE. The two-word noun phrases ANY PLACE, EVERY PLACE, NO PLACE, and SOME PLACE occur, however, in all contexts: *We can build the house in any place we choose. There's no place like home.*

an•y•thing (en′ē thing′), *pron.* **1.** any thing whatever; something, no matter what: *Do you have anything for a toothache?* **—***n.* **2.** a thing of any kind. **—***adv.* **3.** to any degree or extent; in any way; at all: *Does it taste anything like chocolate?* **—*Idiom.*** **4. anything but,** in no degree or respect; not in the least. **5. Anything goes,** anything is permissible.

an•y•time (en′ē tīm′), *adv.* **1.** at any time; whenever. **2.** invariably; without doubt or exception: *I can do better than that anytime.*

an•y•way (en′ē wā′), *adv.* **1.** in any case; anyhow; regardless. **2.** (used to continue or resume the thread of a story or account): *Anyway, we finally found it.* **—Usage.** The adverb ANYWAY is spelled as one word: *It was snowing hard, but we drove to the play anyway.* The two-word phrase ANY WAY means "in any manner": *Finish the job any way you choose.* If the words "in the" can be substituted for "any," the two-word phrase is called for: *Finish the job in the way you choose.* If the substitution cannot be made, the spelling is ANYWAY.

an•y•where (en′ē hwâr′, -wâr′), *adv.* **1.** in, at, or to any place. **2.** to any extent or degree: *I'm not anywhere near finished.* **—***n.* **3.** any place or direction: *The attack could come from anywhere.* **—*Idiom.*** **4. get anywhere,** to achieve success: *You'll never get anywhere with that attitude.* **—Usage.** See ANYPLACE.

an•y•wise (en′ē wīz′), *adv.* in any way or respect.

An•zi•o (an′zē ō′), *n.* a port in Italy, S of Rome on the Tyrrhenian coast: site of Allied beachhead in World War II. 27,094.

A/O or **a/o,** **1.** account of. **2.** and others.

A-OK or **A-O•kay** (ā′ō kā′), *adj., adv. Informal.* OK; perfect.

A one or **A 1** (ā′ wun′), *adj.* **1.** first-class; excellent. **2.** (of a ship) maintained in first-class condition.

a•or•ta (ā ôr′tə), *n., pl.* **-tas, -tae** (-tē). the main artery of the mammalian circulatory system, conveying blood from the left ventricle of the heart to all the other arteries except the pulmonary artery. **—a•or′tic, a•or′tal,** *adj.*

aor′tic valve′, *n.* the semilunar valve between the left ventricle and the aorta, controlling the flow of blood.

a•ou•dad (ä′o͞o dad′), *n.* a wild sheep, *Ammotragus lervia,* of N Africa, having a long fringe of hair on the throat, chest, and forelegs. Also called **Barbary sheep.**

AP, **1.** Advanced Placement. **2.** antipersonnel. **3.** Associated Press.

A/P or **a/p,** **1.** account paid. **2.** accounts payable.

a•pace (ə pās′), *adv.* with speed; quickly; swiftly.

a•pache (ə päsh′, ə pash′), *n.* a Parisian gangster, rowdy, or ruffian.

A•pach•e (ə pach′ē), *n., pl.* **A•pach•es,** (*esp. collectively*) **A•pach•e.** **1.** a member of any of a group of American Indian peoples of the U.S. Southwest and adjacent areas of the Great Plains. **2.** any of the Athabaskan languages spoken by the Apaches.

ap•a•nage (ap′ə nij), *n.* APPANAGE.

a•part (ə pärt′), *adv.* **1.** into pieces or parts; to pieces: *to take a watch apart; falling apart from decay.* **2.** separated or away from in place, time, or motion: *The cities are thousands of miles apart.* **3.** to or at one side, with respect to place, purpose, or function: *to keep apart from the group; space set apart for storage.* **4.** separately or individually in consideration: *each factor viewed apart from the others.* **5.** so as to distinguish one from another: *I can't tell the sisters apart.* **6.** aside (used with a gerund or noun): *Joking apart, what do you think?* **—***adj.* **7.** having independent or unique characteristics (usu. used following a noun): *a class apart.* **—*Idiom.*** **8. apart from,** aside from; besides.

a•part•heid (ə pärt′hāt, -hīt), *n.* **1.** (in the Republic of South Africa) a former rigid policy of segregation of the nonwhite population. **2.** any system or practice that separates people according to race, caste, etc.

a•part•ment (ə pärt′mənt), *n.* **1.** a room or a group of related rooms, usu. among similar sets in one building, having housekeeping facilities and used as a dwelling. **2.** a building made up of such rooms; apartment house.

apart′ment house′, *n.* a building containing a number of apartments. Also called **apart′ment build′ing.**

ap•a•thy (ap′ə thē), *n., pl.* **-thies.** **1.** absence or suppression of passion, emotion, or excitement. **2.** lack of interest in or concern for things that others find moving or exciting. **—apathetic,** *adj.*

ap•a•tite (ap′ə tīt′), *n.* a common mineral, calcium fluorophosphate, $Ca_5FP_3O_{12}$, occurring in individual crystals and in masses and varying in color, formerly used in the manufacture of phosphate fertilizers.

APB, *pl.* **APBs, APB's** all-points bulletin.

ape (āp), *n., v.,* **aped, ap•ing.** **—***n.* **1.** any of a group of anthropoid primates characterized by long arms, a broad chest, and the absence of a tail, comprising the great apes and lesser apes. **2.** (loosely) any monkey. **3.** an imitator; mimic. **4.** a large, clumsy, or coarse person. **—***v.t.* **5.** to imitate; mimic. **—ape′like′,** *adj.*

ape-man (āp′man′), *n., pl.* **-men.** **1.** a hypothetical primate representing a transitional form between true humans and the anthropoid apes, considered by some as constituting the genus *Australopithecus.* **2.** a human assumed to have been reared by apes.

a•pe•ri•od•ic (ā′pēr ē od′ik), *adj.* **1.** not periodic; irregular. **2.** *Physics.* of or pertaining to vibrations or oscillations with no apparent period. **—a•pe′ri•o•dic′i•ty** (-ə dis′i tē), *n.*

a·pé·ri·tif (ä per′i tēf′, ə per′-), *n.* an alcoholic drink taken to stimulate the appetite before a meal.

ap·er·ture (ap′ər chər), *n.* **1.** an opening, as a hole, slit, or gap. **2.** Also called **ap′erture stop′.** an opening, usu. circular, that limits the quantity of light that can enter an optical instrument, as the lens of a camera. —**ap′er·tured,** *adj.*

a·pex (ā′peks), *n., pl.* **a·pex·es, a·pi·ces** (ā′pə sēz′, ap′ə-). **1.** the highest point; vertex; summit. **2.** the tip or point: *the apex of the tongue.* **3.** climax; peak; acme: *the apex of a career.*

Ap′gar score′ (ap′gär), *n.* a quantitative evaluation of the health of a newborn, rating breathing, muscle tone, etc., on a scale of 1 to 10.

a·pha·sia (ə fā′zhə), *n.* the loss of a previously held ability to speak or understand spoken or written language, due to disease or injury of the brain. —**a·pha′sic,** *adj., n.*

a·phe·li·on (ə fē′lē ən, ə fēl′yən, ap hē′lē ən), *n., pl.* **a·phe·li·a** (ə fē′lē ə, ə fēl′yə, ap hē′lē ə). the point in the orbit of a planet or a comet at which it is farthest from the sun. Compare PERIHELION.

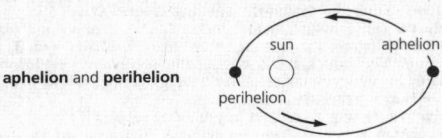

aphelion and **perihelion**

aph·e·sis (af′ə sis), *n.* the gradual disappearance or loss of an unstressed initial vowel or syllable. —**a·phet·ic** (ə fet′ik), *adj.* —**a·phet′i·cal·ly,** *adv.*

a·phid (ā′fid, af′id), *n.* any of numerous tiny soft-bodied insects of the family Aphididae that suck the sap from the stems and leaves of various plants. Also called **plant louse.** —**a·phid·i·an** (ə fid′ē ən), *adj., n.*

a·phis (ā′fis, af′is), *n., pl.* **a·phi·des** (ā′fi dēz′, af′i-). an aphid, esp. of the genus *Aphis.*

a·pho·ni·a (ā fō′nē ə), *n.* loss of voice, esp. due to an organic or functional disturbance of the vocal organs.

aph·o·rism (af′ə riz′əm), *n.* a terse saying embodying a general truth or astute observation, as "Art is long, life is short."

aph·o·ris·tic (af′ə ris′tik), *adj.* **1.** of, like, or containing aphorisms. **2.** given to using aphorisms. —**aph′o·ris′ti·cal·ly,** *adv.*

a·pho·tic (ā fō′tik), *adj.* lightless; dark.

aph·ro·dis·i·ac (af′rə dē′ze ak′, -diz′ē ak′), *adj.* **1.** Also, **aph·ro·di·si·a·cal** (af′rə də zī′ə kəl, -sī′-). arousing sexual desire. —*n.* **2.** a food, drug, or other agent that arouses or is reputed to arouse sexual desire.

Aph·ro·di·te (af′rə dī′tē), *n.* the ancient Greek goddess of love and beauty, identified by the Romans with Venus.

A·pi·a (ä pē′ä, ä′pē ä′), *n.* the capital of Western Samoa, 33,170.

a·pi·an (ā′pē ən), *adj.* of or pertaining to bees.

a·pi·ar·y (ā′pē er′ē), *n., pl.* **-ar·ies.** a place in which a colony or colonies of bees are kept, as a stand or shed for beehives.

a·pi·cal (ap′i kəl, ā′pi-), *adj.* **1.** of, at, or forming the apex. **2.** (of a speech sound) articulated principally with the tip of the tongue, as (t) or (d). —**a·pi′cal·ly,** *adv.*

a·pic·u·late (ə pik′yə lit, -lāt′), *adj.* tipped with a short, abrupt point, as a leaf.

a·pi·cul·ture (ā′pi kul′chər), *n.* beekeeping, esp. on a commercial scale for the sale of honey.

a·plas′tic ane′mia (ā plas′tik), *n.* severe anemia due to destruction or depressed functioning of the bone marrow.

a·plen·ty (ə plen′tē), *adj.* **1.** being in sufficient quantity; generous in amount (usu. following a noun): *He had troubles aplenty.* —*adv.* **2.** sufficiently; enough; more than sparingly.

a·plomb (ə plom′, ə plum′), *n.* imperturbable self-possession, poise, or assurance.

ap·ne·a (ap′nē ə, ap nē′ə), *n.* suspension of breathing. Compare SLEEP APNEA. —**ap·ne′ic,** *adj.*

a·poc·a·lypse (ə pok′ə lips), *n.* **1.** (*cap.*) REVELATION (def. 4). **2.** any of a class of Jewish or Christian writings of c200 B.C. to A.D. 350 that were assumed to make revelations of the ultimate divine purpose. **3.** a prophetic revelation, esp. concerning a cataclysm in which the forces of good triumph over the forces of evil. **4.** any universal or widespread destruction or disaster.

a·poc·a·lyp·tic (ə pok′ə lip′tik) also **a·poc′a·lyp′ti·cal,** *adj.* **1.** of or like an apocalypse. **2.** affording a revelation or prophecy, esp. of imminent destruction. —**a·poc′a·lyp′ti·cal·ly,** *adv.*

ap·o·car·pous (ap′ə kär′pəs), *adj.* (of a flower) having the carpels separate. —**ap′o·car′py,** *n.*

ap·o·chro·mat·ic (ap′ə krō mat′ik), *adj.* (of a lens) corrected for spherical aberration at two wavelengths or colors and for chromatic aberration at three wavelengths.

a·poc·o·pe (ə pok′ə pē′), *n.* the loss or omission of one or more letters or sounds at the end of a word.

ap·o·crine (ap′ə krin, -krīn′, -krēn′), *adj.* **1.** of or pertaining to certain glands whose secretions are acted upon by bacteria to produce the characteristic odor of perspiration (disting. from *eccrine*). **2.** of or pertaining to such secretions.

A·poc·ry·pha (ə pok′rə fə), *n.* (*used with a sing. or pl. v.*) **1.** (*cap.*) a group of books not found in Jewish or Protestant versions of the Old Testament but included in the Septuagint and in Roman Catholic editions of the Bible. **2.** various religious writings of uncertain origin regarded by some as inspired, but rejected by most authorities. **3.** writings or statements of doubtful authorship or authenticity. Compare CANON[1] (defs. 5, 6, 8).

a·poc·ry·phal (ə pok′rə fəl), *adj.* **1.** (*cap.*) of or pertaining to the Apocrypha. **2.** of doubtful authorship or authenticity. **3.** false; spurious.

ap·o·dal (ap′ə dl) also **ap·o·dous** (-dəs), *adj.* having no distinct feet or footlike members.

ap·o·dic·tic (ap′ə dik′tik) also **ap·o·deic·tic** (-dīk′-), *adj.* demonstrably or necessarily true.

ap·o·gee (ap′ə jē′), *n.* **1.** the point in the orbit of the moon or of a satellite at which it is farthest from the earth. Compare PERIGEE. **2.** the highest or most exalted point; climax: *an apogee of artistic development.*

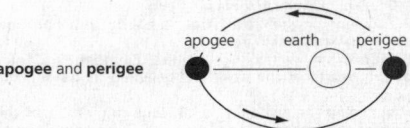

apogee and perigee

a·po·lit·i·cal (ā′pə lit′i kəl), *adj.* **1.** not involved or interested in politics. **2.** of no political significance. —**a′po·lit′i·cal·ly,** *adv.*

A·pol·lo (ə pol′ō), *n., pl.* **-los. 1.** the ancient Greek and Roman god of light, healing, music, and poetry. **2.** a handsome young man.

Apol′lo pro′gram, *n.* a U.S. program of space exploration, beginning in 1961, that made a landing on the moon, this being achieved by Neil Armstrong and Edwin E. ("Buzz") Aldrin on July 20, 1969.

A·pol·los (ə pol′əs), *n.* a Christian from Alexandria who was a leader in the early church. Acts 18:24.

A·pol·lyon (ə pol′yən), *n.* the angel of the bottomless pit. Rev. 9:11. [< Greek *apollýōn,* der. of *apollýnai* to utterly destroy]

ap·o·lo·get·ic (ə pol′ə jet′ik), *adj.* **1.** containing an apology or excuse for a fault or failure: *an apologetic letter for the delay.* **2.** presented in defense or vindication: *apologetic arguments.* **3.** seeming to offer apology: *an apologetic look.* **4.** regretful: *apologetic for the oversight.* —**a·pol′o·get′i·cal·ly,** *adv.*

ap·o·lo·get·ics (ə pol′ə jet′iks), *n.* (*used with a sing. v.*) the branch of theology concerned with the defense or proof of Christianity.

ap·o·lo·gi·a (ap′ə lō′jē ə), *n., pl.* **-gi·as.** a defense or justification of one's beliefs, attitudes, or actions.

a·pol·o·gist (ə pol′ə jist), *n.* a person who defends an idea, faith, cause, or institution.

a·pol·o·gize (ə pol′ə jīz′), *v.i.,* **-gized, -giz·ing.** to make an apology.

ap·o·logue (ap′ə lôg′, -log′), *n.* an allegorical fable typically containing a moral. —**ap′o·log′al,** *adj.*

a·pol·o·gy (ə pol′ə jē), *n., pl.* **-gies. 1.** an expression of regret for having committed an error or rudeness. **2.** a defense or justification of a cause or doctrine. **3.** an inferior substitute; makeshift.

ap·o·lune (ap′ə lōōn′), *n.* the point in a lunar orbit that is farthest from the moon.

ap·o·mix·is (ap′ə mik′sis), *n., pl.* **-mix·es** (-mik′sēz). any of several types of asexual reproduction.

a·poph·y·ge (ə pof′i jē′), *n.* a concave outward curve joining the shaft of a column to its base or capital.

a·poph·y·sis (ə pof′ə sis), *n., pl.* **-ses** (-sēz′). a small, usu. bony projection or protuberance, as on a vertebra.

ap·o·plec·tic (ap′ə plek′tik), *adj.* Also, **ap′o·plec′ti·cal. 1.** of or pertaining to apoplexy. **2.** having or inclined to apoplexy. **3.** intense enough to threaten or cause apoplexy: *an apoplectic rage.* —*n.* **4.** a person having or predisposed to apoplexy.

ap·o·plex·y (ap′ə plek′sē), *n.* **1.** STROKE[1] (def. 5). **2.** a sudden, usu. marked, loss of bodily function due to rupture or occlusion of a blood vessel. **3.** a hemorrhage into an organ cavity or tissue.

ap·o·si·o·pe·sis (ap′ə sī′ə pē′sis), *n., pl.* **-ses** (-sēz). a sudden breaking off in the midst of a thought, as if from inability or unwillingness to proceed, as in "You'll never believe—but of course you won't." —**ap′o·si·o·pet′ic** (-pet′ik), *adj.*

a·pos·ta·sy (ə pos′tə sē), *n., pl.* **-sies.** renunciation or abandonment of one's religious faith or of an object of one's previous loyalty.

a·pos·tate (ə pos′tāt, -tit), *n.* **1.** a person who commits apostasy. —*adj.* **2.** of or characterized by apostasy.

a pos·te·ri·o·ri (ā′ po stēr′ē ôr′ī, -ōr′ī, -ôr′ē, -ōr′ē), *adj.* **1.** from particular instances to a general principle or law; based on observation or experiment. Compare A PRIORI (def. 1). **2.** not existing in the mind prior to or apart from experience.

a·pos·tle (ə pos′əl), *n.* **1.** (*sometimes cap.*) any of the original 12 disciples called by Jesus to preach the gospel. The **Twelve Apostles** were Simon Peter, Andrew, James, John, Philip, Bartholomew, Matthew, Thomas, James the Less, Thaddeus, Simon the Zealot, and Judas Iscariot. **2.** any of the first or best-known Christian missionaries in a region, esp. an early follower of Christ, such as Saint Paul. **3.** one of the 12 ad-

ministrative officials of the Mormon Church. **4.** a pioneer of any reform movement. [Old English *apostol* < Late Latin *apostolus* < Greek *apóstolos,* lit., one who is sent out, der. of *apostéllein* to send off]

Apos′tles′ Creed′, *n.* a creed dating from about A.D. 500, traditionally ascribed to Christ's apostles and beginning with "I believe in God the Father Almighty."

a·pos·to·late (ə pos′tl it, -āt′), *n.* the mission or office of an apostle.

ap·os·tol·ic (ap′ə stol′ik) also **ap′os·tol′i·cal,** *adj.* **1.** of or characteristic of an apostle. **2.** derived from the apostles in regular succession. **3.** of or pertaining to the pope; papal. —**ap′os·tol′i·cal·ly,** *adv.*

Ap′ostol′ic Fa′thers, *n.pl.* the fathers of the early Christian church.

apostol′ic succes′sion, *n.* Rom. Cath. Ch., Orth. Ch., Anglican Ch. the unbroken line of succession beginning with the apostles and perpetuated through bishops, considered essential for orders and sacraments to be valid.

a·pos·tro·phe¹ (ə pos′trə fē), *n.* the sign (′), as used: to indicate the omission of one or more letters in a word, whether unpronounced, as in *o'er* for *over,* or pronounced, as in *gov't* for *government;* to indicate the possessive case, as in *woman's;* or to indicate plurals of abbreviations and symbols, as in *several M.D.'s, 3's.*

a·pos·tro·phe² (ə pos′trə fē), *n.* a digression in the form of an address to someone not present, or to a personified object or idea. —**ap·os·troph·ic** (ap′ə strof′ik), *adj.*

apoth′ecaries′ meas′ure, *n.* a system of units used chiefly in compounding and dispensing liquid drugs.

apoth′ecaries′ weight′, *n.* a system of weights used chiefly in compounding and dispensing drugs.

a·poth·e·car·y (ə poth′ə ker′ē), *n., pl.* **-car·ies. 1.** a druggist; pharmacist. **2.** a pharmacy; drugstore.

ap·o·thegm or **ap·o·phthegm** (ap′ə them′), *n.* a short, pithy saying; aphorism. —**ap′o·theg·mat′ic** (-theg mat′ik), *adj.*

a·poth·e·o·sis (ə poth′ē ō′sis, ap′ə thē′ə sis), *n., pl.* **-ses** (-sēz, -sēz′). **1.** the elevation or exaltation of a person to the rank of a god. **2.** the ideal example; epitome; quintessence: *This poem is the apotheosis of lyric expression.*

a·poth·e·o·size (ə poth′ē ə sīz′, ap′ə thē′ə sīz′), *v.t.,* **-sized, -siz·ing.** to deify; glorify.

Ap·pa·la·chi·a (ap′ə lā′chē ə, -chə, -lach′ē ə, -lach′ə), *n.* a region in the E United States, in the area of the S Appalachian Mountains, usu. including NE Alabama, NW Georgia, NW South Carolina, E Tennessee, W Virginia, E Kentucky, West Virginia, and SW Pennsylvania. —**Ap′pa·la′chi·an,** *adj., n.*

Ap′pala′chian Spring′, a dance (1944) choreographed by Martha Graham, with musical score by Aaron Copland.

ap·pall or **ap·pal** (ə pôl′), *v.t.,* **-palled, -pall·ing.** to fill or overcome with horror or fear; dismay: *I am appalled at your attitude.*

ap·pall·ing (ə pô′ling), *adj.* causing horror or dismay: *an appalling accident; an appalling lack of manners.* —**ap·pall′ing·ly,** *adv.*

Ap·pa·loo·sa (ap′ə lōō′sə), *n., pl.* **-sas.** one of a hardy breed of riding horses, developed in the North American West, having a mottled coat and vertically striped hoofs.

ap·pa·nage or **ap·a·nage** (ap′ə nij), *n.* **1.** land or some other source of revenue assigned for the maintenance of a member of a royal family. **2.** whatever belongs rightfully or appropriately to one's rank or station in life. **3.** a natural or necessary accompaniment; adjunct.

ap·pa·ra·tus (ap′ə rat′əs, -rā′təs), *n., pl.* **-tus, -tus·es. 1.** a group or combination of instruments, machinery, tools, or materials having a particular function: *firefighting apparatus.* **2.** any complex instrument or mechanism for a particular purpose: *the body's digestive apparatus.* **3.** the means by which a system functions: *the apparatus of government.*

ap·par·el (ə par′əl), *n., v.,* **-eled, -el·ing** or *(esp. Brit.)* **-elled, -el·ling.** —*n.* **1.** clothing, esp. outerwear; garments. **2.** something that decorates or covers: *woods in the white apparel of winter.* **3.** superficial appearance; guise. **4.** the sails, anchor, and other equipment of a ship. —*v.t.* **5.** to dress; clothe. **6.** to adorn; ornament.

ap·par·ent (ə par′ənt, ə pâr′-), *adj.* **1.** readily seen; open to view: *The crack in the wall was readily apparent.* **2.** capable of being easily understood; obvious: *The solution was apparent to all.* **3.** according to appearances: *He was the apparent winner of the election.* **4.** entitled by birth to inherit a throne, title, or other estate. —**ap·par′ent·ly,** *adv.*

ap·pa·ri·tion (ap′ə rish′ən), *n.* **1.** a ghostly appearance of a person or thing. **2.** something making a remarkable or incongruous appearance. **3.** an act of becoming visible; appearance.

ap·peal (ə pēl′), *n.* **1.** an earnest plea; entreaty; plea: *an appeal for help.* **2.** a request or reference to some authority for a decision, corroboration, or judgment. **3. a.** an application for review by a higher tribunal. **b.** (in a legislative body) a formal question as to the correctness of a ruling. **4.** the power or ability to attract or stimulate the mind or emotions: *The game has lost its appeal.* —*v.i.* **5.** to make an earnest plea: *appealed to the alumni for funds.* **6.** to apply for review of a case or particular issue to a higher tribunal. **7.** to have need of or ask for proof, a decision, corroboration, etc. **8.** to exert an attraction: *The red hat appeals to me.* —*v.t.* **9. a.** to apply for review of (a case) to a higher tribunal. **b.** to change with a crime. —**ap·peal′a·ble,** *adj.*

ap·peal·ing (ə pē′ling), *adj.* **1.** having great appeal; attractive. **2.** entreating; imploring: *the appealing look of a waif.* —**ap·peal′ing·ly,** *adv.*

ap·pear (ə pēr′), *v.i.* **1.** to come into sight; become visible: *A man sud-*

denly appeared in the doorway. **2.** to have the appearance of being: *to appear wise.* **3.** to be obvious or easily perceived: *It appears you are right.* **4.** to come before the public: *She appeared in several movies.* **5.** to put in an appearance; show up: *appeared briefly at the party.* **6.** to come into being: *Speech appears in the child's first or second year.* **7.** to come before a tribunal, esp. as a party or counsel to a proceeding.

ap·pear·ance (ə pēr′əns), *n.* **1.** the act or process of appearing. **2.** outward look or aspect: *a person of noble appearance.* **3.** outward show; semblance: *maintained an appearance of honesty.* **4.** the coming into court of either party to a suit or action. **5. appearances,** outward impressions, indications, or circumstances: *By all appearances, they enjoyed themselves.* **6.** the sensory aspect of existence. —*Idiom.* **7. put in an appearance,** to attend a gathering, esp. for a short time.

ap·pease (ə pēz′), *v.t.,* **-peased, -peas·ing. 1.** to bring to a state of peace, quiet, ease, calm, or contentment; pacify: *to appease an angry king.* **2.** to satisfy; relieve; assuage: *The fruit appeased his hunger.* **3.** to yield or concede to the belligerent demands of (a nation, group, person, etc.) in a conciliatory effort, sometimes at the expense of justice or other principles. —**ap·pease′ment,** *n.*

ap·pel·lant (ə pel′ənt), *n.* **1.** a person who appeals, as to a higher tribunal. —*adj.* **2.** pertaining to an appeal; appellate.

ap·pel·late (ə pel′it), *adj.* **1.** of or pertaining to appeals. **2.** (of a court) having the authority to review and decide appeals.

ap·pel·la·tion (ap′ə lā′shən), *n.* an identifying name, title, or designation.

ap·pel·la·tive (ə pel′ə tiv), *n.* **1.** APPELLATION. **2.** COMMON NOUN. —*adj.* **3.** tending toward or serving for the assigning of names: *the appellative function of some primitive rites.* **4.** of or pertaining to a common noun.

ap·pend (ə pend′), *v.t.* **1.** to add as a supplement or appendix: *to append a note to a letter.* **2.** to affix: *to append one's signature to a will.*

ap·pend·age (ə pen′dij), *n.* **1.** a limb or other subsidiary part that diverges from the central or principal structure. **2.** a person in a subordinate or dependent position. **3.** an adjunct to something greater: *wit as a natural appendage to wisdom.*

ap·pend·ant (ə pen′dənt), *adj.* **1.** attached; annexed. **2.** associated as an accompaniment or consequence: *the salary appendant to a position.* —*n.* **3.** a person or thing attached or added. **4.** a right historically annexed to a greater one and passing with it, as by sale or inheritance.

ap·pen·dec·to·my (ap′ən dek′tə mē), *n., pl.* **-mies.** surgical removal of the vermiform appendix.

ap·pen·di·ci·tis (ə pen′də sī′tis), *n.* inflammation of the vermiform appendix.

ap·pen·dic·u·lar (ap′ən dik′yə lər), *adj.* of or pertaining to an appendage or limb.

ap·pen·dix (ə pen′diks), *n., pl.* **-dix·es, -di·ces** (-də sēz′). **1.** supplementary material at the end of a text. **2.** any additional or supplemental part; appendage. **3.** Also called **vermiform appendix.** a wormlike tube, closed at the end, extending from the cecum of the large intestine. —*Usage.* APPENDICES, a plural borrowed directly from Latin, is sometimes used, to refer to supplementary material at the end of a book.

ap·per·ceive (ap′ər sēv′), *v.t.,* **-ceived, -ceiv·ing.** to comprehend (a new idea) by linkage with previous experience.

ap·per·cep·tion (ap′ər sep′shən), *n.* **1.** conscious perception. **2.** the act or process of apperceiving.

ap·per·tain (ap′ər tān′), *v.i.* to belong as a rightful attribute or part; pertain: *privileges that appertain to royalty.*

ap·pe·tence (ap′i təns) also **ap′pe·ten·cy,** *n., pl.* **-ten·ces** also **-ten·cies. 1.** strong natural craving; appetite. **2.** material or chemical attraction or affinity. —**ap′pe·tent,** *adj.*

ap·pe·tite (ap′i tīt′), *n.* **1.** a desire for food or drink. **2.** a desire to satisfy any bodily need or craving. **3.** a desire or inclination for something; taste: *an appetite for power.*

ap·pe·tiz·er (ap′i tī′zər), *n.* **1.** a small portion of a food or drink served before or at the beginning of a meal to stimulate the appetite. **2.** a sample of something that stimulates a desire for more.

ap·pe·tiz·ing (ap′i tī′zing), *adj.* **1.** appealing to or stimulating the appetite. **2.** appealing; tempting. —**ap′pe·tiz′ing·ly,** *adv.*

Ap′pi·an Way′ (ap′ē ən), *n.* an ancient Roman highway extending from Rome to Brundisium (now Brindisi): begun 312 B.C. by Appius Claudius Caecus. ab. 350 mi. (565 km) long.

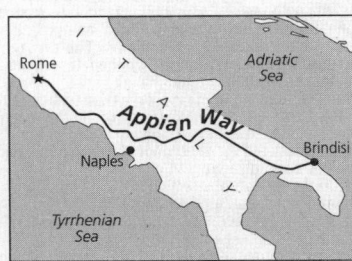

ap·plaud (ə plôd′), *v.i.* **1.** to clap the hands together in approval or appreciation. —*v.t.* **2.** to clap the hands together in approval or appreciation of: *to applaud a speech.* **3.** to express approval of; praise: *to applaud a person's ambition.*

ap·plause (ə plôz′), *n.* **1.** hand clapping as a demonstration of approval or appreciation. **2.** acclaim; acclamation. —**ap·plau·sive** (ə plô′siv, -ziv), *adj.*

ap·ple (ap′əl), *n.* **1.** the usu. round red or yellow edible fruit of a small tree, *Malus sylvestris,* of the rose family. **2.** the tree, cultivated in most temperate regions. **3.** the fruit of any of certain other species of tree of the same genus. **4.** any of various other similar fruits or plants, as the custard apple or May apple. **5.** something resembling an apple in size and shape, as a baseball. —*Proverb.* **6. The apple doesn't fall far from the tree,** children resemble their parents.

ap′ple but′ter, *n.* a creamy spread made from stewed and spiced apples.

ap′ple·jack (ap′əl jak′), *n.* a brandy distilled from fermented cider.

ap′ple of dis′cord, *n.* (in Greek myth) a golden apple inscribed "For the fairest," thrown by Eris, goddess of discord, among the gods. Its award by Paris to Aphrodite caused events that led to the Trojan War. Compare HELEN, PARIS.

ap′ple of one's eye′, *n.* something or someone very precious or dear: *His new baby girl was the apple of his eye.*

ap′ple pandow′dy, *n. Chiefly New Eng.* a deep-dish apple pie or cobbler, usually sweetened with molasses.

ap′ple-pie′, *adj.* pertaining to or embodying traditional American values: *the apple-pie fun of family get-togethers.*

ap′ple-pie′ or′der, *n.* a state of ideal orderliness.

ap′ple-pol′ish, *v.i.* **1.** to curry favor; toady. —*v.t.* **2.** to curry favor with.

ap·ple·sauce (ap′əl sôs′), *n.* **1.** apples stewed to a pulp and sometimes spiced with cinnamon. **2.** *Slang.* nonsense; bunk.

Ap·ple·seed (ap′əl sēd′), *n.* **Johnny** (*John Chapman*), 1774–1845, American pioneer and orchardist: prototype for character in American folklore.

app·let (ap′lit), *n. Computers.* a small application program that can be called up for use while working in another application.

ap·pli·ance (ə plī′əns), *n.* **1.** a device or machine used esp. in the home to carry out a specific function, as toasting bread or chilling food. **2.** any instrument, apparatus, or device for a particular purpose or use. **3.** the act of applying; application.

ap·pli·ca·ble (ap′li kə bəl, ə plik′ə-), *adj.* relevant; suitable; appropriate: *a solution applicable to the problem.*

ap·pli·cant (ap′li kənt), *n.* a person who applies for or requests something; a candidate: *an applicant for a position.*

ap·pli·ca·tion (ap′li kā′shən), *n.* **1.** the act of putting to a special use or purpose: *application of common sense to a problem.* **2.** the use to which something is put: *new applications of technology.* **3.** appropriateness; relevance: *This has no application to the case.* **4.** the act of requesting. **5.** petition; request: *application for college admission.* **6.** a form to be filled out by an applicant: *Sign the application.* **7.** persistent attention: *application to one's studies.* **8.** an act or instance of spreading or administering: *an application of varnish.* **9.** a salve, ointment, or the like, applied as a soothing or healing agent. **10.** a task that can be done by computer.

applica′tion pro′gram, *n.* a computer program used for a specific kind of task, as word processing.

ap·pli·ca·tive (ap′li kā′tiv, ə plik′ə-), *adj.* usable or capable of being used; practical. —**ap′pli·ca·tive·ly,** *adv.*

ap·pli·ca·tor (ap′li kā′tər), *n.* a simple device, as a rod or spatula, for applying medication, cosmetics, or other substance.

ap·plied (ə plīd′), *adj.* **1.** having a practical purpose or use; derived from or involved with actual phenomena: *applied mathematics.* **2.** having a primarily utilitarian function: *applied arts.*

ap·pli·qué (ap′li kā′), *n., v.,* **-quéd, -qué·ing.** —*n.* **1.** a cutout design that is sewn upon or otherwise applied to a piece of material. —*v.t.* **2.** to apply (a cutout) as an appliqué to.

ap·ply (ə plī′), *v.,* **-plied, -ply·ing.** —*v.t.* **1.** to make use of as relevant or suitable: *to apply a theory to a problem.* **2.** to put to use: *to apply pressure to open a door.* **3.** to use a label or other designation: *Don't apply any such term to me.* **4.** to assign to a specific purpose: *applied part of his salary to savings.* **5.** to put into effect: *applied the rules.* **6.** to employ diligently: *to apply oneself to a task.* **7.** to lay or spread on: *to apply paint to a wall.* **8.** to bring into contact: *to apply a match to gunpowder.* —*v.i.* **9.** to be pertinent or suitable: *The theory doesn't apply.* **10.** to make an application or request: *applied to college.* **11.** to lay or spread on: *The paint is easy to apply.*

ap·point (ə point′), *v.t.* **1.** to name or assign officially: *to appoint a new treasurer.* **2.** to fix; set: *to appoint a time for the meeting.* **3.** to designate (a person) to take the benefit of an estate created by a deed or will. **4.** to equip; furnish: *They appointed the house luxuriously.* —*v.i.* **5.** to use the power of appointment.

ap·point·ee (ə poin tē′, ap′oin tē′), *n.* **1.** a person who is appointed. **2.** a beneficiary under a legal appointment.

ap·poin·tive (ə poin′tiv), *adj.* pertaining to or filled by appointment: *an appointive office.*

ap·point·ment (ə point′mənt), *n.* **1.** a fixed mutual agreement for a

meeting; engagement: *an appointment to meet again.* **2.** a meeting set for a specific time or place: *I'm late for my appointment.* **3.** the act of appointing, as to an office or position. **4.** an office, position, or the like, to which a person is appointed: *an appointment as ambassador.* **5.** Usu., **appointments.** equipment, furnishings.

Ap·po·mat·tox (ap′ə mat′əks), *n.* a town in central Virginia where Lee surrendered to Grant on April 9, 1865, ending the Civil War. 1345.

ap·por·tion (ə pôr′shən, ə pōr′-), *v.t.* to distribute or allocate proportionally; divide and assign according to some rule of proportional distribution: *to apportion expenses among the three men.*

ap·por·tion·ment (ə pôr′shən mənt, ə pōr′-), *n.* **1.** the act of apportioning. **2.** the determination of the number of members of the U.S. House of Representatives according to the proportion of the population of each state to the total population of the U.S. **3.** the apportioning of members of any other legislative body.

ap·pose (ə pōz′), *v.t.,* **-posed, -pos·ing. 1.** to place side by side, as two things; place next to; juxtapose. **2.** to put or apply (one thing) to or near to another.

ap·po·site (ap′ə zit, ə poz′it), *adj.* suitable; apt; pertinent: *an apposite answer.* —**ap′po·site·ly,** *adv.* —**ap′po·site·ness,** *n.*

ap·po·si·tion (ap′ə zish′ən), *n.* **1.** the act of placing together or bringing into proximity; juxtaposition. **2.** the addition or application of one thing to another thing. **3.** a grammatical relation between expressions, usu. consecutive, that have the same referent and the same relation to other elements in the sentence, as between *our first president* and *Washington* in *Washington, our first president, was born in Virginia.* —**ap′po·si′tion·al,** *adj.*

ap·pos·i·tive (ə poz′i tiv), *n.* **1.** a word or phrase in apposition. —*adj.* **2.** of, pertaining to, or placed in apposition.

ap·prais·al (ə prā′zəl), *n.* **1.** the act of estimating or judging the nature or value of something or someone. **2.** a valuation, as for sale or taxation. **3.** an estimate or considered opinion of the nature, quality, importance, etc.: *the critics' appraisal of pop art; an incorrect appraisal of public opinion.*

ap·praise (ə prāz′), *v.t.,* **-praised, -prais·ing. 1.** to determine the worth, esp. monetary value, of. **2.** to estimate the nature, quality, importance, etc., of: *appraising the poetry of Milton.* —**ap·prais′a·ble,** *adj.* —**ap·prais′er,** *n.* —**ap·prais′ing·ly,** *adv.*

ap·pre·ci·a·ble (ə prē′shē ə bəl, -shə bəl), *adj.* sufficient to be readily perceived or estimated; considerable: *There is an appreciable difference between socialism and communism.* —**ap·pre′ci·a·bly,** *adv.*

ap·pre·ci·ate (ə prē′shē āt′), *v.,* **-at·ed, -at·ing.** —*v.t.* **1.** to be grateful or thankful for: *They appreciated his thoughtfulness.* **2.** to value or regard highly; place a high estimate on: *to appreciate good wine.* **3.** to be fully conscious of; be aware of; detect: *to appreciate the dangers of a situation.* **4.** to raise in value. —*v.i.* **5.** to increase in value: *Property values appreciated yearly.*

ap·pre·ci·a·tion (ə prē′shē ā′shən), *n.* **1.** gratitude; thankful recognition: *They showed their appreciation by giving him a gold watch.* **2.** the act of estimating the qualities of things and giving them their proper value. **3.** clear perception or recognition, esp. of historic importance and aesthetic quality: *a course in art appreciation.* **4.** an increase or rise in the value of property, goods, etc. **5.** critical notice; evaluation; opinion, as of a situation, person, etc. **6.** a critique or written evaluation, esp. when favorable.

ap·pre·cia·tive (ə prē′shə tiv, -shē ə-, -shē ā′-), *adj.* feeling or showing appreciation: *the applause of an appreciative audience.* —**ap·pre′cia·tive·ly,** *adv.*

ap·pre·hend (ap′ri hend′), *v.t.* **1.** to take into custody; arrest by legal warrant or authority: *The police apprehended the burglars.* **2.** to grasp the meaning of; understand, esp. intuitively; perceive. **3.** to expect with anxiety, suspicion, or fear; anticipate: *apprehending violence.* —*v.i.* **4.** to understand: *To apprehend was to forgive.* **5.** to be apprehensive, suspicious, or fearful; fear. —**ap′pre·hend′er,** *n.*

ap·pre·hen·sion (ap′ri hen′shən), *n.* **1.** fear of future trouble; foreboding. **2.** the faculty or act of understanding or perceiving. **3.** a view, opinion, or idea on any subject. **4.** the act of arresting; seizure.

ap·pre·hen·sive (ap′ri hen′siv), *adj.* **1.** uneasy or fearful about something that might happen. **2.** quick to learn or understand. **3.** perceptive; discerning. —**ap′pre·hen′sive·ly,** *adv.*

ap·pren·tice (ə pren′tis), *n., v.,* **-ticed, -tic·ing.** —*n.* **1.** a person who works for another in order to learn a trade: *an apprentice to a plumber.* **2.** a person legally bound through indenture to a master craftsman in order to learn a trade. **3.** learner; novice. —*v.t.* **4.** to bind to or place with an employer, master craftsman, or the like, for instruction in a trade. —*v.i.* **5.** to serve as an apprentice. —**ap·pren′tice·ship′,** *n.*

ap·prise (ə prīz′), *v.t.,* **-prised, -pris·ing.** to give notice to; inform.

ap·prize (ə prīz′), *v.t.,* **-prized, -priz·ing.** to appreciate; value. —**ap·priz′er,** *n.*

ap·proach (ə prōch′), *v.t.* **1.** to come nearer to: *The car approached the curb.* **2.** to come within range for comparison: *As a poet he can't approach Keats.* **3.** to make contact with: *to approach the company with an offer.* **4.** to begin work on; set about: *to approach a problem.* —*v.i.* **5.** to come nearer: *A storm approaches.* —*n.* **6.** an act or instance of approaching: *the approach of a train.* **7.** close approximation; nearness: *a fair approach to accuracy.* **8.** a means of access: *the approaches to a city.* **9.** the method used or steps taken in setting about a task. **10.** the course to be followed by an aircraft in making a landing. **—ap•proach′er,** n. **—ap•proach′less,** adj.

ap•proach•a•ble (ə prō′chə bəl), adj. **1.** capable of being approached; accessible. **2.** easy to meet and know. **—ap•proach′a•bil′i•ty, ap•proach′a•ble•ness,** n.

ap•pro•bate (ap′rə bāt′), v.t., **-bat•ed, -bat•ing.** to approve; sanction. **—ap′pro•ba′tor,** n. **—ap•pro•ba•to•ry** (ə prō′bə tôr′ē, -tōr′ē), adj.

ap•pro•ba•tion (ap′rə bā′shən), n. **1.** praise; commendation. **2.** approval; sanction.

ap•pro•pri•ate (adj. ə prō′prē it; v. -āt′), adj., v., **-at•ed, -at•ing.** —adj. **1.** particularly suitable; fitting; compatible: *remarks appropriate to the occasion.* —v.t. **2.** to set apart for a specific purpose or use: *to appropriate funds for an environmental study.* **3.** to take to or for oneself; take possession of. **4.** to take without permission; expropriate. **—ap•pro′pri•a•ble,** adj. **—ap•pro′pri•ate•ly,** adv. **—ap•pro′pri•ate•ness,** n. **—ap•pro′pri•a•tive** (-ā′tiv, -a tiv), adj. **—ap•pro′pri•a′tor,** n.

ap•pro•pri•a•tion (ə prō′prē ā′shən), n. **1.** the act of appropriating. **2.** anything appropriated for a special purpose, esp. money authorized to be paid from a public treasury.

ap•prov•al (ə prōō′vəl), n. **1.** the act of approving; approbation. **2.** permission; sanction. —**Idiom. 3. on approval,** subject to being tried or tested and rejected if not satisfactory.

ap•prove (ə prōōv′), v., **-proved, -prov•ing.** —v.t. **1.** to speak or think favorably of: *I approve your choice.* **2.** to find to be acceptable: *Do you approve the plan?* **3.** to confirm or sanction formally; ratify: *The Senate approved the bill.* —v.i. **4.** to have a favorable view: *They don't approve of my friends.* **—ap•prov′ed•ly,** adv. **—ap•prov′ing•ly,** adv.

ap•prox•i•mate (adj. ə prok′sə mit; v. -māt′), adj., v., **-mat•ed, -mat•ing.** —adj. **1.** nearly exact; not perfectly accurate: *The approximate time was 10 o'clock.* **2.** near; close together. **3.** very similar; nearly identical. —v.t. **4.** to approach closely to: *to approximate an ideal.* **5.** to estimate: *approximated the distance at a mile.* **6.** to simulate: *The motions of the stars can be approximated in a planetarium.* **7.** to bring near. —v.i. **8.** to come close. **—ap•prox′i•mate•ly,** adv.

ap•prox•i•ma•tion (ə prok′sə mā′shən), n. **1.** an inexact computation or result that still falls within the required limits of accuracy. **2.** the quality or state of being near or close: *an approximation to the facts.* **3.** the act of drawing together.

appt., 1. appoint. **2.** appointed. **3.** appointment.

ap•pur•te•nance (ə pûr′tn əns), n. **1.** something subordinate to another; adjunct. **2.** a legal right, privilege, or improvement belonging to and passing with a principal property. **3. appurtenances,** apparatus; accessories.

ap•pur•te•nant (ə pûr′tn ənt), adj. **1.** subsidiary; auxiliary. **2.** constituting a legal appurtenance. —n. **3.** APPURTENANCE.

a•près (ä′prā, ap′rā), prep. after; following (used in combination): *après-tennis clothes.*

ap•ri•cot (ap′ri kot′, ā′pri-), n. **1.** the downy, yellowish orange, peach-like fruit of a small tree, *Prunus armeniaca,* of the rose family. **2.** the tree itself. **3.** a pinkish yellow color.

A•pril (ā′prəl), n. the fourth month of the year, containing 30 days. *Abbr.:* Apr.

A′pril fool′, n. **1.** the victim of a joke or trick on April Fools' Day. **2.** a joke or trick played on that day.

A′pril Fools′ Day′, n. April 1, when jokes or tricks are traditionally played on the unsuspecting.

a pri•o•ri (ä′ prī ôr′ī, -ōr′ī, ā′ prē ôr′ē, -ōr′ē, ä′ prē ôr′ē, -ōr′ē), adj. **1.** from a general law to a particular instance; valid independently of observation. Compare A POSTERIORI (def. 1). **2.** existing in the mind independent of experience. **3.** conceived beforehand. **—a•pri•or•i•ty** (-ôr′i-tē, -or′-), n.

a•pron (ā′prən), n. **1.** a garment covering part of the front of the body and usu. tied at the back of the waist, worn to protect the clothing. **2.** a metal plate or cover, as on a machine, for protecting the operator. **3.** a paved area near an airfield's buildings and hangars where planes are parked. **4. a.** any device for protecting a surface of earth from the action of moving water. **b.** a platform to receive the water falling over a dam. **5.** the part of a stage floor in front of the curtain line. **6.** SKIRT (def. 5). **7.** the outer border of a green of a golf course. **8.** the part of the floor of a boxing ring that extends outside the ropes. **9.** the open part of a pier for loading and unloading vessels. **10.** the frill of long hairs on the throat and chest of certain long-haired dogs, as the collie.

ap•ro•pos (ap′rə pō′), adv. **1.** at the right time; opportunely. **2.** by the way. —adj. **3.** being appropriate and timely: *apropos remarks.* —**Idiom. 4. apropos of,** with reference to: *apropos of the preceding statement.*

apse (aps), n. **1.** a usu. vaulted semicircular or polygonal termination or recess in a building, esp. at the end of a church. **2.** APSIS (def. 1). **—ap′si•dal,** adj.

ap•sis (ap′sis), n., pl. **-si•des** (-si dēz′). **1.** either of the two points farthest or nearest the center of attraction in an eccentric astronomical orbit. **2.** APSE (def. 1).

apt (apt), adj. **1.** disposed; prone: *too apt to slander others.* **2.** likely: *Am I apt to find him at home?* **3.** being quick to learn; bright: *an apt pupil.* **4.** suited to the purpose: *an apt metaphor.* **—apt′ly,** adv. **—apt′ness,** n. —**Usage.** Some usage guides advise that APT followed by an infinitive should be used to mean only "inclined, disposed." In fact, APT is standard in all varieties of speech and writing as a synonym for *likely*

in suggesting probability without inclination: *She is apt to arrive any time now. Hostilities are apt to break out soon.* See also LIABLE.

apt., apartment.

ap•ter•ous (ap′tər əs), adj. wingless: *an apterous insect.*

ap•ti•tude (ap′ti tōōd′, -tyōōd′), n. **1.** innate ability; talent: *an aptitude for mathematics.* **2.** readiness or quickness in learning; intelligence. **3.** suitability; fitness. **—ap′ti•tu′di•nal,** adj. **—ap′ti•tu′di•nal•ly,** adv.

ap′titude test′, n. a test designed to measure skills and used to assist in the selection of a career.

A•qa•ba or **A•ka•ba** (ä′kə bə, ak′ə-), n. **1.** a seaport in SW Jordan at the N end of the Gulf of Aqaba. 10,000. **2. Gulf of,** an arm of the Red Sea between Saudi Arabia and Egypt. 100 mi. (160 km) long.

aq•ua (ak′wə, ä′kwə), n., pl. **aq•uae** (ak′wē, ä′kwē), **aq•uas. 1.** *Chiefly Pharm.* **a.** water. **b.** a liquid. **c.** a solution, esp. in water. **2.** a light greenish blue color.

aqua-, var. of AQUI-.

aq•ua•cul•ture (ak′wə kul′chər, ä′kwə-), n. the cultivation of aquatic animals or plants in a natural or controlled environment. **—aq′ua•cul′tur•al,** adj. **—aq′ua•cul′tur•ist,** n.

Aq′ua•lung′ (ak′wə, ä′kwə), *Trademark.* a brand of scuba apparatus.

aq•ua•ma•rine (ak′wə mə rēn′, ä′kwə-), n. **1.** a transparent light blue or greenish blue variety of beryl used as a gem. **2.** a light blue-green or greenish blue color.

aq•ua•naut (ak′wə nôt′, -not′, ä′kwə-), n. a scuba diver who works for an extended period of time in and around a submerged dwelling.

aq•ua•plane (ak′wə plān′, ä′kwə-), n., v., **-planed, -plan•ing.** —n. **1.** a board that skims over water when towed at high speed by a motor-boat, used to carry a rider in aquatic sports. —v.i. **2.** to ride an aquaplane.

aq′ua pu′ra (pyŏŏr′ə), n. pure water.

aq′ua re′gi•a (rē′jē ə), n. a mixture of nitric and hydrochloric acids used to dissolve precious metals.

aq•ua•relle (ak′wə rel′, ä′kwə-), n. a drawing using transparent watercolors. **—aq′ua•rel′list,** n.

a•quar•ist (ə kwâr′ist), n. a curator, collector, or ichthyologist working with an aquarium.

a•quar•i•um (ə kwâr′ē əm), n., pl. **a•quar•i•ums, a•quar•i•a** (ə kwâr′ē ə). **1.** a glass-sided tank, bowl, or the like, in which fish or other living aquatic animals or plants are kept. **2.** a building or institution in which fish or other aquatic animals or plants are kept for exhibit and study. **—a•quar′i•al,** adj.

A•quar•i•us (ə kwâr′ē əs), n. **1.** the Water Bearer, a zodiacal constellation between Capricorn and Pisces. **2.** the 11th sign of the zodiac. [< Latin: water carrier]

a•quat•ic (ə kwat′ik, ə kwot′-), adj. **1.** living or growing in water: *aquatic plant life.* **2.** taking place or practiced on or in water: *aquatic sports.* —n. **3.** an aquatic plant or animal. **4. aquatics,** sports practiced on or in water. **—a•quat′i•cal•ly,** adv.

aq•ua•vit (ä′kwə vēt′, ak′wə-), n. a dry Scandinavian liquor flavored with caraway seeds.

aq′ua vi′tae (vī′tē, vē′tī), n. a strong alcoholic liquor, as brandy or whiskey.

aq•ue•duct (ak′wi dukt′), n. **1. a.** a conduit or artificial channel for conducting water from a distance. **b.** a bridgelike structure that carries a water conduit or canal across a valley or over a river. **2.** *Anat.* a canal through which liquids pass.

a•que•ous (ā′kwē əs, ak′wē-), adj. **1.** of, like, or containing water; watery: *an aqueous solution.* **2.** (of rocks or sediments) formed of matter deposited in or by water. **—a′que•ous•ly,** adv. **—a′que•ous•ness,** n.

a′queous hu′mor, n. the watery fluid between the cornea and the lens of the eye.

aqui- or **aqua-,** a combining form meaning "water": *aquifer.*

aq•ui•cul•ture (ak′wi kul′chər), n. **1.** HYDROPONICS. **2.** AQUACULTURE. **—aq′ui•cul′tur•al,** adj. **—aq′ui•cul′tur•ist,** n.

aq•ui•fer (ak′wə fər), n. a geological formation of permeable rock, gravel, or sand containing or conducting groundwater, esp. one that supplies the water for wells, springs, etc.

Aq•ui•la (ak′wə lə), n. a Christian of Corinth, leader in the early church. Acts 18:2.

aq•ui•le•gi•a (ak′wə lē′jē ə, ä′kwə-), n., pl. **-gi•as.** any plant belonging to the genus *Aquilegia,* of the buttercup family, comprising the columbines.

aq•ui•line (ak′wə līn′, -lin), adj. **1.** pertaining to or resembling an eagle. **2.** curved like an eagle's beak: *an aquiline nose.* **—aq′ui•lin′i•ty** (-lin′i tē), n.

A•qui•nas (ə kwī′nəs), n. **Saint Thomas,** 1225?–74, Italian scholastic philosopher. **—A•qui′nist,** n.

Aq•ui•taine (ak′wi tān′), n. **1.** Latin, **Aq′ui•ta′ni•a.** a historic region in SW France, formerly an ancient Roman province and medieval duchy. **2.** a metropolitan region in SW France. 2,718,200; 15,949 sq. mi. (41,308 sq. km).

AR, 1. Arkansas. **2.** army regulation.

Ar, Arabic.

Ar, *Chem. Symbol.* argon.

ar., 1. arrival. **2.** arrive; arrives.

A/R, accounts receivable.

Ar•ab (ar′əb), n. **1.** a member of an Arabic-speaking people or citizen of an Arabic-speaking nation. **2.** a member of a Semitic people inhabiting since ancient times the Arabian Peninsula and the desert fringes of Mesopotamia and the Levant: after A.D. 632, spreading throughout SW Asia and N Africa. **3.** ARABIAN HORSE. —*adj.* **4.** of or pertaining to Arabs.

Arab., **1.** Arabia. **2.** Arabic.

ar•a•besque (ar′ə besk′), *n.* **1.** an ornamental style in which linear flowers, foliage, fruits, animals, and designs are represented in intricate patterns. **2.** a pose in ballet in which the dancer stands on one leg with one arm extended in front and the other leg and arm extended behind. **3.** a fanciful musical piece typically for piano.

A•ra•bi•a (ə rā′bē ə), *n.* a peninsula in SW Asia including Saudi Arabia, Yemen, Oman, the United Arab Emirates, Qatar, and Kuwait. ab. 1,000,000 sq. mi. (2,600,000 sq. km). Also called **Ara′bian Penin′sula.** —**A•ra′bi•an,** *adj.*

Ara′bian horse′, *n.* any of a breed of horses raised orig. in Arabia and noted for their intelligence, grace, and speed.

Ara′bian Nights′/ Entertain′ments, The, a collection of Eastern folk tales derived in part from Indian and Persian sources and dating from the 10th century A.D.

Ar•a•bic (ar′ə bik), *n.* **1.** a Semitic language that in its classical form reflects the speech of Arabia at the time of Muhammed: now spoken in a variety of dialects over much of North Africa, the Sahara, and SW Asia. —*adj.* **2.** of or pertaining to the Arabic language.

Ar′abic nu′merals, *n.pl.* the number symbols 0, 1, 2, 3, 4, 5, 6, 7, 8, 9, in general European use since the 12th century. Also called **Ar′abic fig′ures.**

ar•a•ble (ar′ə bəl), *adj.* **1.** capable of producing crops by plowing or tillage: *arable acreage.* **2.** land fit for cultivation. —**ar•a•bil′i•ty,** *n.*

Ar′ab Repub′lic of E′gypt, *n.* official name of EGYPT.

a•rach•nid (ə rak′nid), *n.* any of numerous wingless, carnivorous arthropods of the class Arachnida, comprising spiders, scorpions, mites, and ticks, characterized by a two-segmented body with eight appendages and no antennae. —**a•rach′ni•dan,** *adj., n.*

a•rach•noid (ə rak′noid), *adj.* **1.** of or belonging to the arachnids. **2.** of or pertaining to the arachnoid. **3.** *Bot.* formed of or covered with long, delicate hairs or fibers. —*n.* **4.** the serous membrane forming the middle of the three coverings of the brain and spinal cord. Compare DURA MATER, MENINGES, PIA MATER.

Ar•a•fat (ar′ə fat′, är′ə fät′), *n.* **Ya•sir** (yä′sər, -sir, yas′ər), born 1929, Palestinian leader: head of the Palestine Liberation Organization.

′A•ra•fat (är′ə fat′, ar′ə fat′), *n.* a hill 15 mi. (24 km) southeast of Mecca, in Saudi Arabia: site of Muslim pilgrimages.

a•rag•o•nite (ə rag′ə nīt′, ar′ə gə-), *n.* a carbonate mineral, CaCO₃, chemically identical with calcite but differing in key physical properties.

A•ram (ā′ram, âr′əm), *n.* Biblical name of ancient Syria.

Ar•a•mae•an or **Ar•a•me•an** (ar′ə mē′ən), *n.* **1.** a member of any of a group of western Semitic peoples prominent in the history of ancient Syria and Mesopotamia, c1100–700 B.C. —*adj.* **2.** of or pertaining to Aram or the Aramaeans.

Ar•a•ma•ic (ar′ə mā′ik), *n.* **1.** the western Semitic language of the Aramaeans, from Achaemenid times a lingua franca in SW Asia and the everyday speech of Palestine, Syria, and Mesopotamia: supplanted by Arabic. —*adj.* **2.** of or pertaining to Aramaic.

A•rap•a•ho or **A•rap•a•hoe** (ə rap′ə hō′), *n., pl.* **-hos** or **-hoes** (*esp. collectively*) **-ho** or **-hoe. 1.** a member of a Plains Indian people resident on the upper drainages of the Platte and Arkansas rivers in the mid-19th century: surviving groups live in Wyoming and Oklahoma. **2.** the Algonquian language or languages of the Arapaho.

Ar•a•rat (ar′ə rat′), *n.* a mountain in E Turkey, near the borders of Iran and Armenia: traditionally considered the landing place of Noah's Ark. 16,945 ft. (5165 m).

a•ra•ro•ba (ar′ə rō′bə), *n., pl.* **-bas.** a Brazilian tree, *Andira araroba,* of the legume family, from which Goa powder is derived.

arb (ärb), *n.* an arbitrager.

ar•bi•ter (är′bi tər), *n.* **1.** a person empowered to decide matters at issue; judge; umpire. **2.** a person or group having the sole or absolute power of judging or determining.

ar•bi•tra•ble (är′bi trə bəl), *adj.* capable of arbitration; subject to the decision of an arbiter or arbitrator: *an arbitrable dispute.*

ar•bi•trage (är′bi träzh′), *n., v.,* **-traged, -trag•ing.** —*n.* **1.** the simultaneous sale of a security or commodity in different markets to profit from unequal prices. —*v.i.* **2.** to engage in arbitrage.

ar•bit•ra•ment or **ar•bit•re•ment** (är bi′trə mənt), *n.* **1.** the act of arbitrating; arbitration. **2.** the decision or sentence pronounced by an arbiter. **3.** the power of absolute and final decision.

ar•bi•trar•y (är′bi trer′ē), *adj.* **1.** subject to individual will or judgment without restriction; contingent solely upon one's discretion: *an arbitrary decision.* **2.** decided by a judge or arbiter rather than by a law or statute. **3.** having unlimited power; uncontrolled or unrestricted by law; despotic: *an arbitrary government.* **4.** capricious; unreasonable; unsupported: *an arbitrary demand for payment.* **5.** *Math.* undetermined; not assigned a specific value: *an arbitrary constant.* —**ar′bi•trar′i•ly,** *adv.* —**ar′bi•trar′i•ness,** *n.*

ar•bi•trate (är′bi trāt′), *v.,* **-trat•ed, -trat•ing.** —*v.t.* **1.** to decide as arbitrator or arbiter; determine. **2.** to submit to arbitration; settle by arbitration: *to arbitrate a dispute.* —*v.i.* **3.** to act as arbitrator or arbiter; decide between opposing or contending parties or sides. **4.** to submit a matter to arbitration. —**ar′bi•tra′tive,** *adj.*

ar•bi•tra•tion (är′bi trā′shən), *n.* the hearing and determination of a dispute or the settling of differences between parties by a person or persons chosen or agreed to by them. —**ar′bi•tra′tion•al,** *adj.*

ar•bi•tra•tor (är′bi trā′tər), *n.* a person empowered to decide a dispute or settle differences, as contract terms involving labor and management.

ar•bor¹ (är′bər), *n.* **1.** a leafy, shady recess formed by tree branches, shrubs, etc. **2.** a latticework bower intertwined with vines. —**ar′bored,** *adj.*

ar•bor² (är′bər), *n.* **1.** a bar, shaft, or axis that holds, turns, or supports a rotating cutting tool or grinding wheel. **2.** a beam, shaft, axle, or spindle.

Ar′bor Day′, *n.* a day in spring observed by the planting of trees.

ar•bo•re•al (är bôr′ē əl, -bōr′-), *adj.* **1.** of or pertaining to trees; treelike. **2.** living in or among trees. **3.** adapted for living or moving about in trees, as the long arm of a monkey. —**ar•bo′re•al•ly,** *adv.*

ar•bo•re•ous (är bôr′ē əs, -bōr′-), *adj.* **1.** abounding in trees; wooded. **2.** ARBOREAL (def. 2). **3.** ARBORESCENT.

ar•bo•res•cent (är′bə res′ənt), *adj.* resembling a tree in size, appearance, or growth. —**ar′bo•res′cence,** *n.* —**ar′bo•res′cent•ly,** *adv.*

ar•bo•re•tum (är′bə rē′təm), *n., pl.* **-tums, -ta** (-tə). a parklike area in which many different trees or shrubs are grown for study or display.

ar•bor•i•cul•ture (är′bər i kul′chər, är bôr′-, -bōr′-), *n.* the cultivation of trees and shrubs. —**ar′bor•i•cul′tur•al,** *adj.*

ar•bor•ist (är′bər ist), *n.* a specialist in the cultivation and care of trees and shrubs.

ar•bor•vi•tae (är′bər vī′tē), *n.* **1.** any of several evergreen trees of the genus *Thuja,* of the cypress family, having a scaly bark and scalelike leaves on branchlets. **2.** Also, **ar′bor vi′tae.** a treelike longitudinal pattern formed by the white and gray matter of the brain.

ar•bo•vi•rus (är′bə vī′rəs), *n., pl.* **-rus•es.** any of several RNA-containing viruses that are transmitted by bloodsucking arthropods, as ticks, fleas, or mosquitoes, and may cause encephalitis, yellow fever, or dengue fever.

ar•bu•tus (är byōō′təs), *n., pl.* **-tus•es. 1.** any evergreen tree or shrub of the genus *Arbutus,* of the heath family, esp. *A. unedo,* of S Europe, with scarlet berries. **2.** TRAILING ARBUTUS.

arc (ärk), *n., v.,* **arced** (ärkt) or **arcked, arc•ing** (är′king) or **arck•ing.** —*n.* **1.** any unbroken part of the circumference of a circle or other curved line. **2.** a luminous bridge formed in a gap between two electrodes. **3.** the part of a circle representing the apparent course of a heavenly body. **4.** something curved or arched like a bow. **5.** a short set of episodes constituting a complete story line in a soap opera or other long serial. —*v.i.* **6.** to form an electric arc. **7.** to move in or describe an arched course.

ARC (ärk), *n.* AIDS-RELATED COMPLEX.

ARC or **A.R.C.,** American Red Cross.

ar•cade (är kād′), *n.* **1. a.** a series of arches supported on piers or columns. **b.** an arched, roofed-in gallery. **2.** an arched or covered passageway, usu. with shops on each side. **3.** an establishment or area with coin-operated games. —**ar•cad′ed,** *adj.*

ar•cane (är kān′), *adj.* known or understood by those with special knowledge; secret: *arcane rituals.*

ar•ca•num (är kā′nəm), *n., pl.* **-na** (-nə). **1.** a secret accessible only to the few; mystery. **2.** a powerful remedy; elixir.

Arc, d′ (DARK), **Jeanne** (zhän), JOAN OF ARC.

arch¹ (ärch), *n.* **1.** a curved construction spanning an opening and usu. supporting weight from above or the sides. **2.** a doorway or gateway having a curved head; archway. **3.** any overhead curvature resembling an arch. **4.** something bowed or curved: *the arch of the foot.* —*v.t.* **5.** to cover or span with an arch. **6.** to form into an arch: *a cat arching its back.* —*v.i.* **7.** to form an arch: *elms arching over the road.*

arch² (ärch), *adj.* **1.** coyly roguish or ironic. **2.** crafty; sly. —**arch′ly,** *adv.* —**arch′ness,** *n.*

arch-, a combining form used to create nouns that denote individuals or institutions directing or having authority over others of their class (*archbishop; archdiocese*); also meaning "principal" (*archenemy; archrival*) or "prototypical" and thus exemplary or extreme (*archconservative*).

-arch, a combining form meaning "leader, ruler": *matriarch; monarch.*

ar•chae•bac•te•ri•a (är′kē bak tēr′ē ə) also **ar•chae•o•bac•te•ri•a** (är′kē ō-), *n.pl., sing.* **-te•ri•um** (-tēr′ē əm). a group of microorganisms, including methanogens and halobacteria, that are genetically and functionally different from all other living forms, thrive in oxygen-poor environments, and are sometimes classified as a separate kingdom.

archaeo- or **archeo-,** a combining form meaning "ancient": *archaeopteryx; archaeology.*

ar•chae•o•as•tron•o•my (är′kē ō ə stron′ə mē), *n.* a branch of archaeology that deals with the use of astronomy by prehistoric civilizations. —**ar′chae•o•as•tron′o•mer,** *n.* —**ar′chae•o•as′tro•nom′i•cal** (-əs′trə nom′i kəl), *adj.*

ar•chae•ol•o•gy or **ar•che•ol•o•gy** (är′kē ol′ə jē), *n.* the scientific study of historic or prehistoric peoples and their cultures by analysis of their artifacts, inscriptions, monuments, and other remains. —**ar′chae•o•log′ic** (-ə loj′ik), **ar′chae•o•log′i•cal,** *adj.* —**ar′chae•o•log′i•cal•ly,** *adv.* —**ar′chae•ol′o•gist,** *n.*

ar·chae·om·e·try or **ar·che·om·e·try** (är′kē om′i trē), *n.* the branch of archaeology that deals with the dating of archaeological specimens, as by radiocarbon dating. —**ar′chae·om′e·trist,** *n.*

ar·chae·op·ter·yx (är′kē op′tə riks), *n.* a reptilelike feathered fossil bird of the genus *Archaeopteryx,* from the late Jurassic Period, having teeth and a long tail.

ar·cha·ic (är kā′ik), *adj.* **1.** marked by the characteristics of an earlier period; antiquated: *archaic ideas.* **2.** (of a linguistic form) commonly used in an earlier time but rare in present-day usage except to suggest an older time: used in this dictionary to indicate a word not current since c1900. **3.** forming the earliest stage: *an archaic period of technology.* **4.** primitive; ancient: *an archaic form of animal life.* —**ar·cha′i·cal·ly,** *adv.*

ar·cha·ism (är′kē iz′əm, -kā-), *n.* **1.** an archaic verbal usage. **2.** the use of archaic style or language. **3.** the survival or presence of something from the past.

arch·an·gel (ärk′ān′jəl), *n.* a chief or principal angel; one of the nine orders of celestial attendants on God. Compare ANGEL (def. 1). —**arch′an·gel′ic** (-an jel′ik), **arch′an·gel′i·cal,** *adj.*

arch·bish·op (ärch′bish′əp), *n.* a bishop of the highest rank who presides over an archbishopric or archdiocese.

arch′bish′op of Can′ter·bur·y, *n.* the head of the Anglican Communion.

arch·dea·con (ärch′dē′kən), *n.* an ecclesiastic who ranks next below a bishop and has administrative responsibility for a diocese.

arch·di·o·cese (ärch′dī′ə sēs′, -sis), *n.* the diocese of an archbishop. —**arch′di·oc′e·san** (-os′ə sən), *adj.*

arch·duch·ess (ärch′duch′is), *n.* **1.** the wife of an archduke. **2.** a princess of the Austrian imperial family.

arch·duch·y (ärch′duch′ē), *n., pl.* **-duch·ies.** the domain of an archduke or an archduchess.

arch·duke (ärch′dook′, -dyook′), *n.* a title of the sovereign princes of the former ruling house of Austria. —**arch′duke′dom,** *n.*

arche-, a combining form meaning "prior, original, first" (*archegonium; archetype*); in scientific coinages, a synonym of ARCHI- (*archesporium*).

Ar·che·la·us (är′ki lā′əs), *n.* the oldest son of Herod the Great. Matt. 2:22.

arch·en·e·my (ärch′en′ə mē), *n., pl.* **-mies.** a chief enemy.

Ar·che·o·zo·ic (är′kē ə zō′ik), *adj.* **1.** of or pertaining to the earlier half of the Precambrian Era, before 2.5 billion years ago, when the only life forms were blue-green algae and bacteria. —*n.* **2.** the Archeozoic division of geologic time or the rock systems formed then.

arch·er (är′chər), *n.* **1.** a person who shoots with a bow and arrow. **2.** (*cap.*) the constellation or sign of Sagittarius.

ar·cher·fish (är′chər fish′), *n., pl.* (*esp. collectively*) **-fish,** (*esp. for kinds or species*) **-fish·es.** a small fish, *Toxotes jaculator,* of SE Asia that catches spiders and insects by spitting drops of water at them and causing them to fall.

ar·cher·y (är′chə rē), *n.* **1.** the art, practice, or skill of shooting with a bow and arrow. **2.** an archer's equipment. **3.** a group of archers.

Arch′es Na′tional Park′, *n.* a national park in E Utah: natural arch formations. 114 sq. mi. (295 sq. km).

ar·che·type (är′ki tīp′), *n.* **1.** the original pattern or model from which all things of the same kind are copied or on which they are based; prototype. **2.** (in Jungian psychology) an inherited unconscious idea, pattern of thought, image, etc., universally present in individual psyches. —**ar′che·typ′al** (-tī′pəl), **ar′che·typ′i·cal** (-tip′i kəl), *adj.*

arch·fiend (ärch′fēnd′), *n.* **1.** a chief fiend. **2.** SATAN.

archi-, a combining form with the general sense "first, principal," prefixed to nouns denoting things that are earliest, most basic, or bottommost (*archiblast; archiphoneme; architrave*); or denoting individuals who direct or have authority over others of their class, usu. named by the base noun (*archimandrite; architect*).

ar·chi·man·drite (är′kə man′drīt), *n.* the head of a monastery or a group of monasteries in an Eastern church.

Ar·chi·me·des (är′kə mē′dēz), *n.* 287?–212 B.C., Greek mathematician, physicist, and inventor. —**Ar′chi·me·de′an,** *adj.*

Ar′chime′des′ screw′, *n.* a device consisting essentially of a spiral passage within an inclined cylinder for raising water to a height when rotated.

ar·chi·pel·a·go (är′kə pel′ə gō′), *n., pl.* **-gos, -goes. 1.** a large group or chain of islands. **2.** a large body of water with many islands. —**ar′chi·pe·lag′ic** (-pə laj′ik), **ar′chi·pe·la′gi·an** (-lā′jē ən, -jən), *adj.*

ar·chi·tect (är′ki tekt′), *n.* **1.** a person who engages in the profession of architecture. **2.** a person professionally engaged in the design of certain constructions other than buildings: *landscape architect.* **3.** planner; deviser; creator: *the architects of the report.*

ar·chi·tec·ton·ic (är′ki tek ton′ik), *adj.* **1.** of or pertaining to the principles of architecture. **2.** resembling architecture in disciplined organization and design. —**ar′chi·tec·ton′i·cal·ly,** *adv.*

ar·chi·tec·ton·ics (är′ki tek ton′iks), *n.* (*used with a sing. v.*) the science of planning and constructing buildings.

ar·chi·tec·ture (är′ki tek′chər), *n.* **1.** the profession of designing buildings, open areas, communities, and other artificial constructions and environments. **2.** the character or style of building: *Romanesque architecture.* **3.** the action or process of building; construction. **4.** the result or product of architectural work. **5.** buildings collectively. **6.** the

structure of something: *the architecture of a novel.* —**ar′chi·tec′tur·al,** *adj.*

ar·chi·trave (är′ki trāv′), *n.* **1.** the lowermost member of a classical entablature. **2.** a molded or decorated band framing a panel or an opening, as of a door or window. —**ar′chi·tra′val,** *adj.* —**ar′chi·traved′,** *adj.*

ar·chive (är′kīv), *n., v.,* **-chived, -chiv·ing.** —*n.* **1. archives,** a place where documents and other materials of public or historical importance are preserved. **2.** Usu., **archives.** the documents and other materials preserved in such a place. —*v.t.* **3.** to preserve in or as if in an archive. —**ar·chi′val,** *adj.*

arch·way (ärch′wā′), *n.* **1.** an entrance or passage under an arch. **2.** an arch over a passage.

-archy, a combining form meaning "rule," "government," forming abstract nouns usu. corresponding to personal nouns ending in -ARCH: *monarchy; oligarchy.*

arc′ light′, *n.* **1.** an electric lamp in which the light source is a high-intensity arc between carbon rods or metal electrodes. **2.** the light produced by such a lamp.

arc·tic (ärk′tik *or, esp. for 6,* är′tik), *adj.* **1.** (*often cap.*) of, pertaining to, or located at or near the North Pole: *the arctic region.* **2.** coming from the North Pole or the arctic region: *an arctic wind.* **3.** characteristic of the extremely cold, snowy, windy weather north of the Arctic Circle; frigid; bleak: *an arctic winter.* **4.** extremely cold in manner: *a look of arctic disdain.* —*n.* **5.** (*often cap.*) the region lying north of the Arctic Circle or of the northernmost limit of tree growth; the polar area north of the timberline. **6. arctics,** warm waterproof overshoes. [≪ Greek *arktikós* northern, lit., of the Bear (constellation)] —**arc′ti·cal·ly,** *adv.*

Arc′tic Cir′cle, *n.* an imaginary line drawn parallel to the equator, at 23°28′ S of the North Pole: between the North Frigid Zone and the North Temperate Zone.

arc′tic dai′sy, *n.* a daisy, *Chrysanthemum arcticum,* of arctic regions, having asterlike heads of white or lilac flowers.

arc′tic fox′, *n.* a thickly furred short-eared fox, *Alopex lagopus,* of the arctic regions that is brownish gray in summer and white in winter. Also called **white fox.**

Arc′tic O′cean, an ocean N of North America, Asia, and the Arctic Circle. ab. 5,540,000 sq. mi. (14,350,000 sq. km).

Arc·tu·rus (ärk tōōr′əs, -tyōōr′-), *n.* a first-magnitude star in the constellation Boötes. —**Arc·tu′ri·an,** *adj.*

ar·cu·ate (är′kyōō it, -āt′), *adj.* curved like a bow. —**ar′cu·ate·ly,** *adv.*

arc′ weld′ing, *n.* welding in which the heat for fusion is supplied by an electric arc.

-ard or **-art,** a suffix forming nouns that denote persons who regularly engage in an activity, or who are characterized in a certain way, as indicated by the stem; now usu. pejorative: *coward; dullard; wizard.*

Ar·dennes (är den′; *Fr.* AR den′), *n.* **Forest of,** a wooded plateau region in W Europe, in NE France, SE Belgium, and Luxembourg: World War I battle 1914; World War II battle 1944–45.

ar·dent (är′dnt), *adj.* **1.** characterized by intense feeling; fervent: *an ardent vow.* **2.** intensely devoted; zealous: *an ardent theatergoer.* **3.** fiercely bright: *ardent eyes.* **4.** fiery; hot: *the ardent core of a star.* —**ar′dent·ly,** *adv.* —**ar·den·cy** (är′dn sē), *n.*

ar·dor (är′dər), *n.* **1.** great warmth of feeling; fervor. **2.** intense devotion; zeal. **3.** burning heat. Also, *esp. Brit.,* **ar′dour.**

ar·du·ous (är′jōō əs; *esp. Brit.* är′dyōō-), *adj.* **1.** requiring great exertion; laborious: *arduous tasks.* **2.** using much energy; strenuous: *an arduous effort.* **3.** hard to climb; steep: *an arduous path.* **4.** severe: *an arduous winter.* —**ar′du·ous·ly,** *adv.* —**ar′du·ous·ness,** *n.*

are¹ (är; *unstressed* ər), *v.* pres. indic. pl. and 2nd pers. sing. of BE.

are² (âr, är), *n.* a surface measure equal to 100 square meters, equivalent to 119.6 sq. yds.; ¹⁄₁₀₀ of a hectare. *Abbr.:* a

ar·e·a (âr′ē ə), *n., pl.* **ar·e·as. 1.** an extent of space or surface: *the dark areas in the painting.* **2.** a geographical region: *the Chicago area.* **3.** a section reserved for a specific function: *the dining area.* **4.** extent; range; scope: *embraced the whole area of science.* **5.** field; sphere: *new areas of interest.* **6.** a piece of unoccupied ground. **7.** the yard attached to or surrounding a house. **8.** the quantitative measure of a plane or curved surface; two-dimensional extent.

ar′ea code′, *n.* a three-digit code that identifies one of the telephone areas into which the U.S. and certain other countries are divided, used when dialing a call between areas.

a·re·na (ə rē′nə), *n., pl.* **-nas. 1.** a central area used for sports or other forms of entertainment and surrounded by seats for spectators. **2.** the oval space in the center of a Roman amphitheater for gladiatorial combats or other spectacles. **3.** a field of competition or activity: *the arena of politics.*

ar·en·a·vi·rus (är′en ə′vī′rəs), *n., pl.* **-rus·es.** any of various RNA-containing viruses of the family Arenaviridae, usu. transmitted to humans by contact with excreta of infected rodents.

a·re·o·la (ə rē′ə lə), *n., pl.* **-lae** (-lē′), **-las. 1.** a ring of color, as around the human nipple. **2.** a small interstice, as between the fibers of connective tissue. —**a·re′o·lar,** *adj.*

Ar·es (âr′ēz), *n.* the ancient Greek god of war. Compare **Mars.**

a·re·te (är′i tā′), *n.* the aggregate of qualities making up good character.

a·rête (ə rāt′), *n.* a sharp rugged mountain ridge produced by glaciation.

ar·gent (är′jənt), *n.* **1.** the heraldic color silver or white. —*adj.* **2.** silvery; silvery white.

Ar·gen·ti·na (är′jən tē′nə), *n.* a republic in S South America. 35,797,536; 1,084,120 sq. mi. (2,807,870 sq. km). *Cap.:* Buenos Aires. Also called the **Argentine.**

ar·gen·tite (är′jən tīt′), *n.* a dark, lead-gray mineral, silver sulfide, Ag₂S, occurring in crystals and as formless aggregates: an important ore of silver.

ar·gil·la·ceous (är′jə lā′shəs), *adj.* of the nature of or resembling clay; clayey.

ar·gil·lite (är′jə līt′), *n.* any compact sedimentary rock composed mainly of clay materials; clay stone. —**ar′gil·lit′ic** (-lit′ik), *adj.*

ar·gol (är′gəl), *n.* a crude tartar produced as a by-product of grape fermentation.

ar·gon (är′gon), *n.* a colorless, odorless, chemically inactive, monatomic, gaseous element that is used for filling fluorescent and incandescent lamps and vacuum tubes. *Symbol:* Ar; *at. no.:* 18; *at. wt.:* 39.948.

Ar·go·naut (är′gə nôt′, -not′), *n.* **1.** a member of the band of men who sailed to Colchis with Jason in the ship *Argo* in search of the Golden Fleece. **2.** (*sometimes l.c.*) a person in quest of something dangerous but rewarding; adventurer.

Ar′gonne For′est (är′gon, är gon′), *n.* a wooded region in NE France: battles, World War I, 1918; World War II, 1944. Also called **Ar·gonne′.**

ar·go·sy (är′gə sē), *n., pl.* **-sies. 1.** a large merchant ship, esp. one with a rich cargo. **2.** a fleet of such ships. **3.** an opulent supply or collection.

ar·got (är′gō, -gət), *n.* **1.** a specialized vocabulary peculiar to a particular group of people, devised for private communication and identification: *thieves' argot.* **2.** the special vocabulary and idiom of a particular profession or social group. —**ar·got′ic** (-got′ik), *adj.*

ar·gu·a·ble (är′gyōō ə bəl), *adj.* **1.** doubtful; questionable: *It's arguable whether this is the best plan.* **2.** susceptible to persuasive argument; conceivable; possible: *It is arguable that Einstein was the greatest scientist of his time.* —**ar′gu·a·bly,** *adv.*

ar·gue (är′gyōō), *v.,* **-gued, -gu·ing.** —*v.i.* **1.** to present reasons for or against a thing: *to argue in favor of capital punishment.* **2.** to contend in oral disagreement; dispute: *to argue with a colleague; to argue about the new tax bill.* —*v.t.* **3.** to state the reasons for or against: *to argue a case.* **4.** to maintain in reasoning: *to argue that the news report was biased.* **5.** to persuade or compel by reasoning: *to argue someone out of a plan.* **6.** to show; indicate: *an intelligent answer that argues careful thought.*

ar·gu·ment (är′gyə mənt), *n.* **1.** an oral disagreement; contention; altercation. **2.** a discussion involving differing points of view; debate. **3.** a process of reasoning; series of reasons: *I couldn't follow his argument.* **4.** a statement, reason, or fact for or against a point: *a strong argument in favor of disarmament.* **5.** discourse intended to persuade: *became convinced through eloquent argument.* **6.** subject matter; theme. **7.** an abstract or summary of the major points of a literary work or sections of such a work. **8.** *Math.* **a.** an independent variable of a function. **b.** Also called **amplitude.** the angle made by a given vector with the reference axis. **c.** the angle corresponding to a point representing a given complex number in polar coordinates.

ar·gu·men·ta·tion (är′gyə men tā′shən), *n.* **1.** the process of developing or presenting an argument; reasoning. **2.** the premises and conclusion so set forth. **3.** discussion; debate. **4.** ARGUMENT (def. 5).

ar·gu·men·ta·tive (är′gyə men′tə tiv), *adj.* **1.** fond of or given to argument; disputatious. **2.** causing argument; controversial.

Ar′gus-eyed′, *adj.* vigilant; watchful.

ar·gyle or **ar·gyll** (är′gīl), *n.* (*often cap.*) **1.** (in knitting) a diamond-shaped pattern using two or more colors. **2.** an article knitted with this pattern.

a·ri·a (är′ē ə, âr′ē ə), *n., pl.* **a·ri·as. 1.** an air or melody. **2.** an elaborate melody sung solo with accompaniment, as in an opera or oratorio.

Ar·i·an·ism (âr′ē ə niz′əm, ar′-), *n.* the doctrine, taught by Arius, that Christ the Son was not consubstantial with God the Father. —**Ar′i·an·is′tic, Ar′i·an·is′ti·cal,** *adj.*

ar·id (ar′id), *adj.* **1.** extremely dry; parched: *arid land.* **2.** barren or unproductive due to lack of moisture: *arid farmland.* **3.** lacking vitality or imagination; sterile: *The book is spoiled by an arid treatment of an exciting topic.* —**a·rid·i·ty** (ə rid′i tē), *n.* —**ar′id·ly,** *adv.*

a·rid·i·sol (ə rid′ə sôl′, -sol′), *n.* a soil type common to the world's deserts, poor in organic matter and rich in salts.

A·ri·el (âr′ē əl′), *n.* Jerusalem. Is. 29:1–2, 7.

Ar·ies (âr′ēz, -ē ez′), *n.* **1.** the Ram, a zodiacal constellation between Pisces and Taurus. **2.** the first sign of the zodiac. [< Latin: ram]

ar·il (ar′il), *n.* a usu. fleshy appendage or covering of certain seeds, as of the bittersweet, *Celastrus scandens,* or of the nutmeg.

Ar·i·ma·thae·a or **Ar·i·ma·the·a** (ar′ə mə thē′ə), *n.* a town in ancient Palestine. Matt. 27:57. —**Ar′i·ma·thae′an,** *adj.*

a·ri·o·so (är′ē ō′sō, âr′-), *n., pl.* **-sos.** a musical passage having the character of a recitative or a simple aria.

a·rise (ə rīz′), *v.i.,* **a·rose, a·ris·en** (ə riz′ən), **a·ris·ing. 1.** to get up from sitting, lying, or kneeling; rise: *He arose from his chair.* **2.** to awaken; wake up. **3.** to move upward; ascend: *A thin curl of smoke arose from the chimney.* **4.** to appear; spring up: *New problems arise daily.* **5.** to result; spring or issue (sometimes fol. by *from*): *the consequences arising from this action.*

a·ris·ta (ə ris′tə), *n., pl.* **-tae** (-tē). **1.** a bristlelike appendage of the spikelets of grains or grasses. **2.** a prominent bristle on the antenna of some dipterous insects.

ar·is·toc·ra·cy (ar′ə stok′rə sē), *n., pl.* **-cies. 1.** a class of persons holding exceptional rank and privileges, esp. the hereditary nobility. **2.** a government or state ruled by an aristocracy, elite, or privileged upper class. **3.** government by the best or most able people in the state. **4.** a governing body composed of the best or most able people. **5.** any class or group regarded as superior because of education, ability, or wealth.

a·ris·to·crat (ə ris′tə krat′, ar′ə stə-), *n.* **1.** a member of a governing aristocracy. **2.** a hereditary noble. **3.** a person who has the taste, manners, etc., characteristic of members of an aristocracy. **4.** an advocate of an aristocratic form of government. **5.** a person of superior achievement. **6.** anything regarded as the best of its kind: *the aristocrat of California wines.* —**a·ris′to·crat′ic,** *adj.*

Ar·is·toph·a·nes (ar′ə stof′ə nēz′), *n.* 448?–385? B.C., Athenian comic dramatist. —**Ar·is·to·phan·ic** (ə ris′tə fan′ik), *adj.*

Ar·is·to·te·lian or **Ar·is·to·te·lean** (ar′ə stə tēl′yən, -tē′lē ən, ə ris′tə-), *adj.* **1.** of or based on Aristotle or his theories. —*n.* **2.** a follower of Aristotle. —**Ar′is·to·te′lian·ism,** *n.*

Ar·is·tot·le (ar′ə stot′l), *n.* 384–322 B.C., Greek philosopher: pupil of Plato; tutor of Alexander the Great.

a·rith·me·tic (*n.* ə rith′mə tik; *adj.* ar′ith met′ik), *n.* **1.** the method or process of computation with figures: the most elementary branch of mathematics. **2.** the theory of numbers; the study of the divisibility of whole numbers, the remainders after division, etc. **3.** a treatise on arithmetic. —*adj.* **ar·ith·met·ic** **4.** Also, **ar·ith·met′i·cal.** of, pertaining to, or in accordance with the rules of arithmetic.

ar′ithmet′ic mean′, *n.* the mean obtained by adding several quantities together and dividing the sum by the number of quantities: *The arithmetic mean of 1, 5, 2, and 8 is 4.* Also called **average.**

arithmet′ic progres′sion, *n.* a sequence in which each term is obtained by the addition of a constant number to the preceding term, as 1, 4, 7, 10, 13, and 6, 1, −4, −9, −14. Also called **ar′ithmet′ic se′ries.**

A·ri·us (ə rī′əs, âr′ē-), *n.* died A.D. 336, Christian priest at Alexandria: founder of Arianism.

Ar·i·zo·na (ar′ə zō′nə), *n.* a state in SW United States. 4,428,068; 113,909 sq. mi. (295,025 sq. km). *Cap.:* Phoenix. *Abbr.:* AZ, Ariz. —**Ar′i·zo′nan, Ar′i·zo′ni·an,** *adj., n.*

ark (ärk), *n.* **1.** (*sometimes cap.*) the vessel built by Noah for safety during the Flood. Gen. 6–9. **2.** Also called **ark of the covenant.** a sacred chest containing two stone tablets inscribed with the Ten Commandments, kept in the Biblical tabernacle and later in the Temple in Jerusalem. **3.** a refuge or asylum. **4.** (*cap.*) *Judaism.* HOLY ARK. **5.** a large, clumsy vehicle or vessel.

Ar·kan·sas (är′kən sô′; *also for 2* är kan′zəs), *n.* **1.** a state in S central United States; 2,509,793; 53,103 sq. mi. (137,537 sq. km). *Cap.:* Little Rock. *Abbr.:* AR, Ark. **2.** a river flowing E and SE from central Colorado into the Mississippi in SE Arkansas. 1450 mi. (2335 km) long. —**Ar·kan′san,** *n., adj.*

ark′ of the cov′enant, *n.* ARK (def. 2).

Ar·ling·ton (är′ling tən), *n.* **1.** a county in NE Virginia, opposite Washington, D.C.: site of national cemetery (**Ar′lington Na′tional Cem′etery**). 174,603. **2.** a city in N Texas. 286,922.

arm¹ (ärm), *n.* **1. a.** the upper limb of the human body. **b.** the upper limb from shoulder to elbow. **2. a.** the forelimb of any vertebrate. **b.** any similar structure in an invertebrate. **3.** any armlike part or attachment, as the tone arm of a phonograph. **4.** the sleeve of a garment. **5.** a projecting support for the forearm or elbow at the side of a chair, sofa, etc. **6.** an administrative or operational branch of an organization: *an investigative arm of the government.* **7.** a combat branch of the military service, as the infantry, cavalry, or field artillery. **8.** a curved piece on an anchor, terminating in a fluke. **9.** an inlet or cove: *an arm of the sea.* **10.** power; authority: *the long arm of the law.* —*Idiom.* **11.** an arm and a leg, a great deal of money: *to cost an arm and a leg.* **12. arm in arm,** with arms linked together or intertwined: *They walked along arm in arm.* **13. at arm's length,** on terms lacking in intimacy; at a distance: *to keep business associates at arm's length.* **14. in the arms of Morpheus,** asleep. **15. twist someone's arm,** to use force or coercion on someone. **16. with open arms,** cordially; with warm hospitality. —**armed,** *adj.*

arm² (ärm), *n.* **1.** Usu., **arms.** weapons, esp. firearms. **2. arms,** the heraldic devices of a person, family, or corporate body. —*v.i.* **3.** to make ready for war. —*v.t.* **4.** to equip with weapons: *to arm the troops.* **5.** to activate (a fuze) so that it will explode the charge at the time desired. **6.** to cover protectively. **7.** to equip or prepare for any specific purpose or effective use: *to arm a security system; to arm oneself with persuasive arguments.* —*Idiom.* **8. bear arms, a.** to carry weapons. **b.** to serve as a member of the armed forces. **9. take up arms,** to prepare for or go to war. **10. under arms,** (of troops) trained and equipped for battle. **11. up in arms,** provoked; indignant.

Ar·ma·da (är mä′də, -mā′-), *n., pl.* **-das. 1.** Also called **Spanish Armada.** the fleet sent against England by Philip II of Spain in 1588, defeated by the English navy. **2.** (*l.c.*) any fleet of warships. **3.** (*l.c.*)

large group or force of vehicles, airplanes, etc.: *an armada of transport trucks.*

ar·ma·dil·lo (är/mə dil/ō), *n.*, *pl.* **-los.** any of several New World burrowing mammals of the family Dasypodidae, related to the anteater, covered with jointed plates of bone and horn.

Ar·ma·ged·don (är/mə ged/n), *n.* **1.** the place where the final battle between good and evil will be fought (probably a reference to the battlefield of Megiddo. Rev. 16:16). **2.** a final, completely destructive battle. **3.** any large-scale and decisive conflict.

ar·ma·ment (är/mə mənt), *n.* **1.** the arms and equipment with which a military unit is supplied. **2.** a land, sea, or air force equipped for war. **3.** ARMOR (def. 5). **4.** Usu., **armaments.** military strength collectively. **5.** the process of arming for war.

ar·ma·men·tar·i·um (är/mə mən târ/ē əm, -men-), *n.*, *pl.* **-tar·i·a** (-târ/ē ə). **1.** the aggregate of equipment, methods, and techniques used to carry out one's duties: *The stethoscope is an essential part of the physician's armamentarium.* **2.** the array of devices or materials used or available for an undertaking.

ar·ma·ture (är/mə chər), *n.* **1.** the protective covering of an animal or plant, or any part serving for defense or offense. **2. a.** the part of a generator that includes the main current-carrying winding, in which the electromotive force is induced. **b.** the moving part in an electrical device, as a buzzer or relay, that is activated by a magnetic field. **c.** the iron or steel placed across the poles of a permanent magnet to close it. **3.** a framework on which a clay, wax, or plaster figure is supported while being sculpted.

arm·chair (ärm/châr/), *n.* **1.** a chair with sidepieces or arms to support a person's forearms or elbows. —*adj.* **2.** theorizing without the benefit of practical experience: *an armchair strategist.* **3.** participating vicariously: *an armchair traveler.*

armed (ärmd), *adj.* **1.** involving the use of weapons: *armed conflict.* **2.** maintained by arms: *armed peace.* **3.** equipped: *The students came armed with their pocket calculators.* **4.** fortified; made secure: *armed by an innate optimism.*

armed/ forc/es, *n.pl.* military, naval, and air forces, esp. of a nation or of a number of nations. Also called **armed/ serv/ices.**

Armed/ Forc/es Day/, *n.* the third Saturday in May, a U.S. holiday honoring the armed forces.

Ar·me·ni·a (är mē/nē ə, -mēn/yə), *n.* **1.** an ancient country in W Asia: now divided between Armenia, Turkey, and Iran. **2.** Also, **Arme/nian Repub/lic.** a republic in Transcaucasia, S of Georgia and W of Azerbaijan: a former constituent republic of the U.S.S.R. 3,465,611; ab. 11,490 sq. mi. (29,800 sq. km). *Cap.:* Yerevan. Former official name, **Arme/nian So/viet So/cialist Repub/lic.**

Arme/nian mas/sacres, *n.pl.* a series of massacres of Armenian Christians by Turkish government forces between 1895 and 1915, during which more than a million people were killed.

ar·mil·lar·y (är/mə ler/ē, är mil/ə rē), *adj.* consisting of hoops or rings.

ar/millary sphere/, *n.* an ancient astronomical instrument consisting of an arrangement of metal rings used to show the relative positions of the celestial equator, ecliptic, and other circles on the celestial sphere.

Ar·min·i·an·ism (är min/ē ə niz/əm), *n.* the doctrinal teachings of Jacobus Arminius or his followers, esp. that Christ died for all people, not only for the elect. Compare CALVINISM (def. 1). —**Ar·min/i·an,** *adj., n.*

Ar·min·i·us (är min/ē əs), *n.* **Jacobus,** (*Jacob Harmensen*), 1560–1609, Dutch Protestant theologian.

ar·mi·stice (är/mə stis), *n.* a temporary suspension of hostilities by agreement of the warring parties; truce: *the armistice of 1918 ending World War I.*

Ar/mistice Day/, *n.* former name of VETERANS DAY.

arm·let (ärm/lit), *n.* **1.** an ornamental band worn high on the arm. **2.** a small inlet or arm, as of the sea.

ar·moire (ärm wär/, ärm/wär), *n.* a large wardrobe or movable cupboard with doors and shelves.

ar·mor (är/mər), *n.* **1.** any covering worn as a defense against weapons. **2.** a suit of armor. **3.** a protective covering of metal, esp. metal plates, used on warships, armored vehicles, etc. **4.** mechanized units of military forces, as armored divisions. **5.** Also called **armament.** any protective covering, as on certain animals, insects, or plants. **6.** any quality, characteristic, situation, or thing that serves as protection. **7.** the outer, protective wrapping of metal, usu. fine, braided steel wires, on a cable. —*v.t.* **8.** to cover or equip with armor or armor plate. Also, *esp. Brit.,* **ar/mour.**

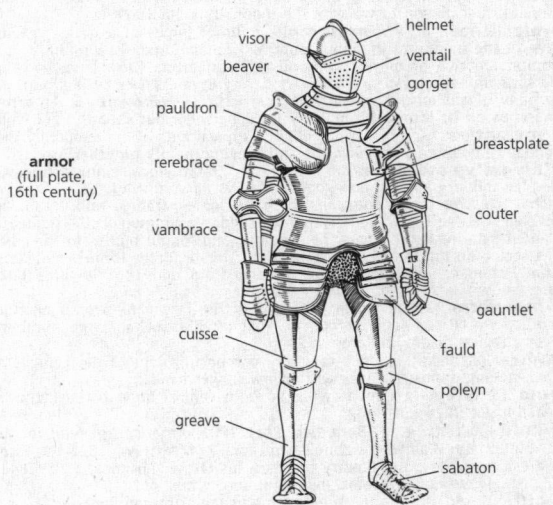

armor
(full plate,
16th century)

visor · helmet · beaver · ventail · gorget · pauldron · rerebrace · breastplate · vambrace · couter · cuisse · gauntlet · fauld · greave · poleyn · sabaton

ar/mored car/, *n.* **1.** an armor-plated truck for transporting money and valuables, as between banks. **2.** an enclosed, lightly armed and armored combat and reconnaissance vehicle.

ar·mor·er (är/mər ər), *n.* **1.** a maker or repairer of arms or armor. **2.** a person who manufactures, repairs, or services firearms.

COMPARATIVE RANKS IN THE UNITED STATES ARMED FORCES

Army	Navy	Air Force	Marine Corps
General of the Army	Fleet Admiral	General of the Air Force	NA
General	Admiral	General	General
Lieutenant General	Vice Admiral	Lieutenant General	Lieutenant General
Major General	Rear Admiral	Major General	Major General
Brigadier General	Commodore	Brigadier General	Brigadier General
Colonel	Captain	Colonel	Colonel
Lieutenant Colonel	Commander	Lieutenant Colonel	Lieutenant Colonel
Major	Lieutenant Commander	Major	Major
Captain	Lieutenant	Captain	Captain
First Lieutenant	Lieutenant Junior Grade	First Lieutenant	First Lieutenant
Second Lieutenant	Ensign	Second Lieutenant	Second Lieutenant
Chief Warrant Officer (in three grades)	Chief Warrant Officer (in three grades)	NA	Chief Warrant Officer (in three grades)
Warrant Officer	Warrant Officer	NA	Warrant Officer
Sergeant Major of the Army	Master Chief Petty Officer of the Navy	Chief Master Sergeant of the Air Force	Sergeant Major of the Marine Corps
Command Sergeant Major } Sergeant Major	Master Chief Petty Officer	Chief Master Sergeant	Sergeant Major } Master Gunnery Sergeant
First Sergeant } Master Sergeant	Senior Chief Petty Officer	Senior Master Sergeant	First Sergeant } Master Sergeant
Sergeant First Class	Chief Petty Officer	Master Sergeant	Gunnery Sergeant
Staff Sergeant	Petty Officer First Class	Technical Sergeant	Staff Sergeant
Sergeant	Petty Officer Second Class	Staff Sergeant	Sergeant
Corporal } Specialist 4	Petty Officer Third Class	Sergeant } Senior Airman	Corporal
Private First Class	Seaman	Airman First Class	Lance Corporal
Private	Seaman Apprentice	Airman	Private First Class
Private (no insignia)	Seaman Recruit	Airman Basic (no insignia)	Private (no insignia)

NA = not applicable

ar•mo•ri•al (är môr′ē əl, -mōr′-), *adj.* of, pertaining to, or bearing a coat of arms. —**ar•mo′ri•al•ly,** *adv.*

ar′mor plate′, *n.* a protective plating of hardened steel used esp. to cover warships, tanks, and aircraft. Also, **ar′mor plat′ing.** —**ar′mor-plat′ed,** *adj.*

ar•mor•y (är′mə rē), *n., pl.* **-mor•ies. 1.** a storage place for weapons and other war equipment. **2.** a building that is the headquarters and drill center of a National Guard unit. **3.** an armorer's shop or other place where arms and armor are made. **4.** the art of blazoning heraldic arms. **5.** heraldry. **6.** arms or armor collectively.

Ar′mory Show′, *n.* an international art show held in a New York City armory in 1913: considered a landmark in the public and critical acceptance of modern art.

Ar•mour (är′mər), *n.* **Philip Danforth,** 1832–1901, U.S. meat-packing industrialist.

arm•pit (ärm′pit′), *n.* the hollow under the arm at the shoulder; axilla.

arms′ race′, *n.* competition between countries for superiority in quantity and quality of military arms.

Arm•strong (ärm′strông′), *n.* **1. (Daniel) Louis** (*"Satchmo"*), 1900–71, U.S. jazz trumpeter. **2. Edwin Howard,** 1890–1954, U.S. electrical engineer: developed frequency modulation. **3. Neil A.,** born 1930, U.S. astronaut: first person to walk on the moon, July 20, 1969.

ar•my (är′mē), *n., pl.* **-mies. 1.** the military forces of a nation, exclusive of the navy and in some countries the air force. **2.** a military unit comprising two or more corps and a headquarters. **3.** a large body of persons trained and armed for war. **4.** any organized or large group: *an army of census takers; an army of cockroaches.* —***Proverb.*** **5. An army marches on its stomach,** an army must be well-nourished to fight well.

ar′my ant′, *n.* any of various chiefly tropical ants of the subfamily Dorylinae, traveling in vast swarms and preying mainly on other insects.

ar′my-na′vy store′ (är′mē nā′vē), *n.* a retail store selling a stock of surplus military apparel and goods, often at bargain rates.

Ar′my of the Poto′mac, *n.* **1.** Union forces, trained and organized by Gen. George B. McClellan, that guarded Washington, D.C., against a Confederate invasion across the Potomac and fought battles in the eastern sector during the Civil War. **2.** Confederate forces from the Alexandria, Potomac, and Shenandoah districts from mid-1861 to mid-1862: later known as Army of Northern Virginia.

ar•my•worm (är′mē wûrm′), *n.* any of the larvae of several noctuid moths, esp. *Pseudaletia unipuncta,* that often travel in large numbers over a region destroying crops.

ar•ni•ca (är′ni kə), *n., pl.* **-cas.** any composite plant of the genus *Arnica,* having opposite leaves and yellow flower heads.

Ar•no (är′nō), *n.* a river flowing W from central Italy to the Ligurian Sea. 140 mi. (225 km) long.

Ar•nold (är′nld), *n.* **1. Benedict,** 1741–1801, American general in the Revolutionary War who became a traitor. **2. Matthew,** 1822–88, English essayist, poet, and literary critic. **3.** his father, **Thomas,** 1795–1842, English clergyman, educator, historian, and writer.

ar•oid (ar′oid, âr′-), *adj.* **1.** belonging to the arum family. —*n.* **2.** any plant of the arum family.

a•ro•ma (ə rō′mə), *n., pl.* **-mas. 1.** a distinctive, usu. agreeable odor; fragrance: *the aroma of freshly brewed coffee.* **2.** the bouquet of a wine. **3.** a pervasive characteristic or quality: *an aroma of mystery.*

a•ro•ma•ther•a•py (ə rō′mə ther′ə pē), *n.* **1.** the use of fragrances to affect or alter a person's mood or behavior. **2.** treatment of facial skin by the application of fragrant floral and herbal substances.

ar•o•mat•ic (ar′ə mat′ik), *adj.* **1.** having an aroma; fragrant or sweet-scented; odoriferous. —*n.* **2.** a plant, drug, or medicine yielding a fragrant aroma.

ar′omat′ic com′pound, *n.* an organic compound that contains one or more benzene or equivalent heterocyclic rings: many such compounds have an agreeable odor.

a•rose (ə rōz′), *v.* pt. of ARISE.

a•round (ə round′), *adv.* **1.** in a circle, ring, or the like; so as to surround: *The crowd gathered around.* **2.** on all sides; about: *fenced in all around.* **3.** in all directions from a center or point of reference: *They own the land for miles around.* **4.** in a region about a place: *all the country around.* **5.** in circumference: *The tree was 40 inches around.* **6.** in a circular or rounded course: *to drive around the block.* **7.** through a sequence or series, as of places or persons: *to show someone around.* **8.** through a recurring period, as of time: *Lunchtime rolled around.* **9.** by a circuitous or roundabout course: *The lane goes around past the stables.* **10.** with a rotating course or movement: *The wheels turned around.* **11.** in or to another or opposite direction, course, opinion, etc.: *Sit still and don't turn around. After our arguments, she finally came around.* **12.** back into consciousness: *The smelling salts brought her around.* **13.** in circulation, action, etc.; nearby; about: *He hasn't been around lately.* **14.** somewhere near or about; nearby: *I'll be around till noon.* **15.** to a specific place: *Come around to see me.* —*prep.* **16.** about; on all sides; encircling: *a halo around his head.* **17.** so as to encircle, surround, or envelop: *to tie paper around a package.* **18.** on the edge, border, or outer part of: *a skirt with fringe around the bottom.* **19.** from place to place in; about: *to get around town.* **20.** in all or various directions from: *to look around one.* **21.** in the vicinity of: *the country around Boston.* **22.** approximately; about: *around five o'clock.* **23.** here and there in: *people around the city.* **24.** somewhere in or near: *to stay around the house.* **25.** to all or various parts of: *to wander around the park.* **26.** so as to make a circuit about or partial circuit to the other side of: *to sail around a cape.* **27.** reached by making a turn or partial circuit about: *the church around the corner.* **28.** so as to revolve or rotate about a center or axis: *the earth's motion around its axis.* **29.** personally close to: *all the advisers around the king.* **30.** so as to overcome a difficulty: *They got around the lack of chairs by sitting on the floor.* —***Idiom.*** **31. to have been around,** to have had much worldly experience.

around′-the-clock′, *adj.* all day and all night; constant.

a•rouse (ə rouz′), *v.,* **a•roused, a•rous•ing.** —*v.t.* **1.** to stir to action or strong response; excite: *to arouse a crowd; to arouse suspicion.* **2.** to stimulate sexually. **3.** to awaken; wake up. —*v.i.* **4.** to become awake or aroused. —**a•rous′a•ble,** *adj.* —**a•rous′al,** *n.*

ar•peg•gi•o (är pej′ē ō′, -pej′ō), *n., pl.* **-gi•os. 1.** the sounding of the notes of a chord in rapid succession instead of simultaneously. **2.** a chord thus sounded.

ar•que•bus (är′kwə bəs), *n., pl.* **-bus•es.** HARQUEBUS.

ar•raign (ə rān′), *v.t.* **1.** to bring before a court to answer an indictment. **2.** to accuse or charge in general; criticize adversely; censure. —**ar•raign′ment,** *n.*

ar•range (ə rānj′), *v.,* **-ranged, -rang•ing.** —*v.t.* **1.** to place in proper, desired, or convenient order. **2.** to come to an agreement or understanding regarding. **3.** to prepare or plan. **4. a.** to adapt (a musical work) for particular instrumentation. **b.** ORCHESTRATE. —*v.i.* **5.** to make plans or preparations: *They arranged for a conference on Wednesday.* **6.** to make a settlement; come to an agreement: *to arrange for regular service.* —**ar•range′a•ble,** *adj.* —**ar•rang′er,** *n.*

ar•range•ment (ə rānj′mənt), *n.* **1.** an act of arranging; state of being arranged. **2.** the manner or way in which things are arranged. **3.** an adjustment by agreement; settlement. **4.** Usu., **arrangements.** preparatory measures; plans; preparations: *Final arrangements have been made for the funeral.* **5.** something arranged in a particular way: *a floral arrangement.* **6.** a rescoring of a musical composition.

ar•rant (ar′ənt), *adj.* **1.** downright; thorough; unmitigated: *an arrant fool.* **2.** wandering; errant. —**ar′rant•ly,** *adv.*

ar•ras (ar′əs), *n.* **1.** a rich tapestry. **2.** a wall hanging, as a tapestry or similar object. **3.** a sturdy bobbin lace with a simple pattern. —**ar′rased,** *adj.*

ar•ray (ə rā′), *v.,* **-rayed, -ray•ing,** *n.* —*v.t.* **1.** to place in proper or desired order; marshal: *to array troops for battle.* **2.** to clothe with garments, esp. of an ornamental kind. —*n.* **3.** order or arrangement, as of troops drawn up for battle. **4.** military force, esp. a body of troops. **5.** a large and impressive grouping or organization: *an array of facts.* **6.** regular order or arrangement: *an array of figures.* **7.** a large group, number, or quantity of people or things. **8.** attire; dress: *in fine array.* **9.** a functional arrangement of interrelated objects or items of equipment: *an array of solar cells.* **10.** *Math., Statistics.* **a.** an arrangement of a series of terms according to value, as from largest to smallest. **b.** an arrangement of a series of terms in some geometric pattern, as in a matrix.

ar•rear (ə rēr′), *n.* **1.** Usu., **arrears.** the state of being late in repaying a debt: *to be in arrears with mortgage payments.* **2.** Often, **arrears.** a debt that remains unpaid.

ar•rear•age (ə rēr′ij), *n.* **1.** the condition of being in arrears. **2.** Usu., **arrearages.** the amount or amounts overdue.

ar•rest (ə rest′), *v.t.* **1.** to seize (a person) by legal authority; take into custody. **2.** to catch and hold; engage: *A noise arrested our attention.* **3.** to check the course of; stop: *to arrest a disease.* —*n.* **4.** the taking of a person into legal custody, as by the police. **5.** any seizure or taking by force. **6.** an act of stopping or the state of being stopped. —***Idiom.*** **7. under arrest,** in custody of the police or other legal authorities.

ar•rest•ant (ə res′tənt), *n.* a substance that interrupts the normal development of an insect.

ar•rest•ing (ə res′ting), *adj.* **1.** attracting or capable of attracting attention or interest; striking. **2.** making or having made an arrest: *the arresting officer.* —**ar•rest′ing•ly,** *adv.*

ar•rhyth•mi•a (ə rith′mē ə, ā rith′-), *n.* any disturbance in the rhythm of the heartbeat. —**ar•rhyth′mic, ar•rhyth′mi•cal,** *adj.*

ar•ri•val (ə rī′vəl), *n.* **1.** an act of arriving; a coming: *Their arrival was delayed by traffic.* **2.** the reaching or attainment of any object or condition: *arrival at a peace treaty.* **3.** the person or thing that arrives or has arrived.

ar•rive (ə rīv′), *v.i.,* **-rived, -riv•ing. 1.** to come to a certain point in the course of travel; reach one's destination: *We finally arrived in Rome.* **2.** to come to be present: *The moment to act has arrived.* **3.** to attain a position of success. **4. arrive at,** to reach or attain; come to.

ar•ri•viste (ar′ē vēst′), *n.* a person who has recently acquired unaccustomed status or wealth; upstart.

ar•ro•gance (ar′ə gəns), *n.* offensive display of superiority or self-importance; overbearing pride; haughtiness.

ar′rogance of pow′er, *n.* presumption on the part of a nation that its power gives it the right to intervene in the affairs of less powerful nations.

ar•ro•gant (ar′ə gənt), *adj.* **1.** making claims or pretensions to superior importance or rights. **2.** characterized by or proceeding from arrogance: *arrogant claims.* —**ar′ro•gant•ly,** *adv.*

ar•ro•gate (ar′ə gāt′), *v.t.,* **-gat•ed, -gat•ing. 1.** to claim unwarrantably or presumptuously; assume or appropriate to oneself without right. **2.** to attribute or assign to another; ascribe.

ar·ron·disse·ment (ə ron′dis mənt, ar′ən dēs′-; *Fr.* A RôN dēs mäN′), *n.*, *pl.* **-ments** (-mənts; *Fr.* -mäN′). **1.** the largest administrative division of a French department, comprising a number of cantons. **2.** an administrative district of certain large cities in France.

ar·row (ar′ō), *n.* **1.** a slender feathered and pointed shaft shot from a bow as a weapon or for sport. **2.** anything resembling an arrow in form, function, or character. **3.** a linear figure having a wedge-shaped end, as one used on maps or drawings to indicate direction or placement. —*v.t.* **4.** to indicate the proper position of (an insertion) by means of an arrow (often fol. by *in*).

ar·row·head (ar′ō hed′), *n.* **1.** a usu. wedge-shaped, pointed tip on an arrow. **2.** anything resembling or having the conventional shape of an arrowhead. **3.** any of various aquatic or bog plants of the genus *Sagittaria*, water plantain family, with arrowhead-shaped leaves and clusters of white flowers.

ar·row·root (ar′ō rōōt′, -rŏŏt′), *n.* **1.** a tropical American plant, *Maranta arundinacea*, cultivated for its fleshy tubers, which yield an edible starch. **2.** the fine-textured, readily digestible starch of this plant, used in cooking as a thickener and for bland diets. **3.** any of several similar starches obtained from other tuberous plants.

ar·row·wood (ar′ō wŏŏd′), *n.* any of several shrubs or small trees, esp. belonging to the genus *Viburnum*, of the honeysuckle family, having tough, straight shoots formerly used for making arrows.

ar·roy·o (ə roi′ō), *n.*, *pl.* **-os.** (chiefly in southwest U.S.) a small steep-sided watercourse or gulch with a nearly flat floor: usu. dry except after heavy rains.

ar·se·nal (är′sə nl, ärs′nəl), *n.* **1.** a military establishment for producing and storing weapons and munitions. **2.** a collection of weaponry. **3.** a supply of any useful item: *a critic's arsenal of vivid phrases.*

ar′senal of democ′racy, *n.* the role of the United States in supplying weapons and ammunition to nations fighting the Axis powers during World War II.

ar·se·nic (*n.* är′sə nik, ärs′nik; *adj.* är sen′ik), *n.* **1.** a grayish white element having a metallic luster, vaporizing when heated, and forming poisonous compounds. *Symbol:* As; *at. wt.:* 74.92; *at. no.:* 33. **2.** ARSENIC TRIOXIDE. —*adj.* **ar·sen·ic 3.** of or containing arsenic, esp. in the pentavalent state.

ar′senic triox′ide, *n.* a white, tasteless, poisonous powder, As₂O₃, used chiefly in the manufacture of pigments and glass and as an insecticide or weed-killer.

ar·sis (är′sis), *n.*, *pl.* **-ses** (-sēz). **1.** the upward stroke in conducting music; upbeat. Compare THESIS (def. 4). **2. a.** the part of a metrical foot that bears the ictus or stress. **b.** (less commonly) a part of a metrical foot that does not bear the ictus. Compare THESIS (def. 5).

ar·son (är′sən), *n.* the malicious burning of another's property or, sometimes, one's own property, as in an attempt to collect insurance. —**ar′son·ist,** *n.*

art (ärt), *n.* **1.** the quality, production, expression, or realm of what is beautiful or of more than ordinary significance. **2.** the class of objects subject to aesthetic criteria, as paintings, sculptures, or drawings. **3.** a field or category of art: *Dance is an art.* **4.** the fine arts collectively. **5.** any field using the skills or techniques of art: *industrial art.* **6.** (in printed matter) illustrative or decorative material. **7.** the principles or methods governing any craft or branch of learning: *the art of baking.* **8.** the craft or trade using these principles or methods. **9.** skill in conducting any human activity: *the art of conversation.* **10.** a branch of learning or university study, esp. one of the fine arts or the humanities, as music, philosophy, or literature. **11. arts, a.** (*used with a sing. v.*) the humanities. **b.** (*used with a pl. v.*) LIBERAL ARTS. **12.** skilled workmanship, execution, or agency, as distinguished from nature. **13.** trickery; cunning. **14.** studied action; artificiality in behavior. **15.** an artifice or artful device: *the arts and wiles of politics.*

Ar·ta·xerx·es (är′tə zûrk′sēz), *n.* **1.** Artaxerxes I, (*"Longimanus"*), died 424 B.C., king of Persia 464–24. **2.** Artaxerxes II, (*"Mnemon"*), died 359? B.C., king of Persia 404?–359?

art′ dec′o, *n.* (*often caps.*) a style of decorative art developed orig. in the 1920s and marked chiefly by geometric motifs, curvilinear forms, and sharply defined outlines.

Ar·te·mis (är′tə mis), *n.* an ancient Greek goddess, characterized as a virgin huntress and associated with the moon: identified by the Romans with Diana.

ar·te·mis·ia (är′tə mizh′ə, -mizh′ē ə-, -miz′ē ə), *n.*, *pl.* **-mis·ias.** any of several composite plants of the genus *Artemisia*, having aromatic foliage and small disk flowers, including the sagebrush and wormwood.

ar·te·ri·al (är tēr′ē əl), *adj.* **1.** of, pertaining to, or resembling the arteries. **2.** pertaining to the blood in the arteries and pulmonary veins, richer in oxygen and redder than venous blood. **3.** being or constituting a main route, channel, or other course of flow or access, often with many branches. —**ar·te′ri·al·ly,** *adv.*

ar·te·ri·og·ra·phy (är tēr′ē og′rə fē), *n.*, *pl.* **-phies.** x-ray examination of an artery following injection of a radiopaque substance. Compare ANGIOCARDIOGRAPHY. —**ar·te′ri·o·graph′ic** (-ə graf′ik), *adj.*

ar·te·ri·ole (är tēr′ē ōl′), *n.* any of the smallest branches of an artery. —**ar·te′ri·o′lar,** *adj.*

ar·te·ri·o·scle·ro·sis (är tēr′ē ō sklə rō′sis), *n.* abnormal thickening and loss of elasticity in the arterial walls. —**ar·te′ri·o·scle·rot′ic** (-rot′ik), *adj.*

ar·te·ri·o·ve·nous (är tēr′ē ō vē′nəs), *adj.* of, pertaining to, or affecting both arteries and veins.

ar·ter·y (är′tə rē), *n.*, *pl.* **-ter·ies. 1.** a blood vessel that conveys blood from the heart to any part of the body. **2.** a main channel or highway, esp. of a connected system with many branches.

ar·te′sian well′ (är tē′zhən), *n.* a well in which water rises under pressure from a permeable stratum overlaid by impermeable rock.

art′ form′, *n.* **1.** the structure of an artistic work. **2.** a medium for artistic expression. **3.** any medium regarded as having systematized rules, procedures, or formulations.

art·ful (ärt′fəl), *adj.* **1.** slyly crafty or cunning; deceitful; tricky. **2.** skillful or clever in adapting means to ends; ingenious. **3.** done with or characterized by art or skill.

ar·thrit·ic (är thrit′ik), *adj.* **1.** of, pertaining to, or afflicted with arthritis. —*n.* **2.** a person afflicted with arthritis.

ar·thri·tis (är thrī′tis), *n.* inflammation of one or more joints. Compare BURSITIS, OSTEOARTHRITIS, RHEUMATOID ARTHRITIS.

ar·thro·pod (är′thrə pod′), *n.* **1.** any invertebrate of the phylum Arthropoda, having a segmented body, jointed limbs, and a mineralized chitinous shell covering and including insects, spiders and other arachnids, crustaceans, and myriapods. —*adj.* **2.** Also, **ar·throp·o·dal** (är throp′ə dl), **ar·throp·o·dan** (är throp′ə dn). belonging or pertaining to the Arthropoda.

ar·thro·scope (är′thrə skōp′), *n.* an endoscope specialized for use in the diagnosis and surgical treatment of diseased or injured joints. —**ar·thros′co·py** (-thros′kə pē), *n.*

Ar·thur (är′thər), *n.* **1.** Chester Alan, 1830–86, 21st president of the U.S. 1881–85. **2.** a legendary king of Britain, whose life was based on the exploits of one or more historical figures of the 6th century A.D.

ar·ti·choke (är′ti chōk′), *n.* **1.** a tall thistlelike composite plant, *Cynara scolymus*, native to the Mediterranean region, of which the numerous scalelike bracts and receptacle of the immature flower head are eaten as a vegetable. **2.** JERUSALEM ARTICHOKE.

ar·ti·cle (är′ti kəl), *n.*, *v.*, **-cled, -cling.** —*n.* **1.** a factual piece of writing, usu. on a single topic, appearing in a newspaper, magazine, etc. **2.** an individual object, member, or portion of a class; item: *an article of clothing.* **3.** something of indefinite character or description. **4.** an item for sale; commodity. **5.** a member of a small class of words or affixes, as the words *a, an,* and *the* in English, that are linked to nouns and that typically function in identifying the noun as a noun and in indicating definiteness or indefiniteness of reference. Compare DEFINITE ARTICLE, INDEFINITE ARTICLE. **6.** a separate clause or section in a contract, treaty, statute, or other formal document. —*v.t.* **7.** to charge or accuse of specific offenses. **8.** to bind by the articles of a contract: *to article an apprentice.*

Ar′ticles of Confedera′tion, *n.pl.* the first constitution of the 13 American states, adopted in 1781 and replaced in 1789 by the Constitution of the United States.

Ar′ticles of War′, *n.pl.* the body of laws and legal procedures of the U.S. Army and Air Force, replaced in 1951 by the Uniform Code of Military Justice.

ar·tic·u·lar (är tik′yə lər), *adj.* of or pertaining to the joints.

ar·tic·u·late (*adj.* är tik′yə lit; *v.* -lāt′), *adj.*, *v.*, **-lat·ed, -lat·ing.** —*adj.* **1.** uttered clearly in distinct syllables. **2.** capable of speech. **3.** using language easily and fluently. **4.** expressed or presented with clarity and effectiveness. **5.** clear, distinct, and precise in relation to other parts: *an articulate shape.* **6.** organized into a coherent whole: *an articulate system of philosophy.* **7.** having joints, segments, or articulations. —*v.t.* **8.** to pronounce clearly and distinctly. **9.** to make the movements and adjustments of the speech organs necessary to utter (a speech sound). **10.** to give clarity or coherence to: *to articulate an idea.* **11.** to unite by a joint or joints. —*v.i.* **12.** to pronounce clearly each of a succession of speech sounds, syllables, or words. **13.** to articulate a speech sound. **14.** to form a joint.

ar·tic·u·lat·ed (är tik′yə lā′tid), *adj.* **1.** (of a vehicle) built in sections that are hinged or otherwise connected so as to allow flexibility of movement. **2.** jointed or segmented in a useful or logical way; articulate.

artic′ulated joint′, *n.* an artificial appendage, limb, or the like, esp. one activated and controlled by a computer, as the mechanical arm of a robot.

ar·tic·u·la·tion (är tik′yə lā′shən), *n.* **1.** the act or process of articulating. **2. a.** the act or process of articulating speech. **b.** the adjustments and movements of speech organs involved in pronouncing a sound. **c.** a speech sound, esp. a consonant. **3.** the act of jointing. **4.** a jointed state or formation; a joint. **5. a.** the point of attachment of a leaf. **b.** a node in a stem, or the stem between two nodes. **6.** a joint between bones or between movable segments of an exoskeleton. **7.** the relation of opposing tooth surfaces as they come into contact during jaw movement.

ar·ti·fact or **ar·te·fact** (är′tə fakt′), *n.* **1.** any object made by human beings, esp. with a view to subsequent use. **2.** a handmade object, as a tool, or the remains of one, as a shard of pottery, belonging to an earlier time or cultural stage, esp. such an object found at an archaeological excavation. **3.** a substance or structure not naturally present in the matter being observed but formed by artificial means, as during preparation of a microscope slide. **4.** a spurious observation or result arising from preparatory procedures. **5.** any feature that is not naturally present but is a product of an extrinsic agent. —**ar′ti·fac·ti′tious** (-fak tish′əs), adj. —**ar′ti·fac′tu·al** (-fak′chōō əl), adj.

ar·ti·fice (är′tə fis), n. **1.** a clever trick or stratagem. **2.** trickery; guile; craftiness. **3.** cleverness; ingenuity. **4.** a skillful or artful contrivance or expedient.

ar·ti·fi·cial (är′tə fish′əl), adj. **1.** made by human skill; produced by humans; not natural. **2.** imitation; simulated; sham: *artificial vanilla flavoring; artificial gemstones.* **3.** lacking naturalness or spontaneity; forced: *an artificial smile.* **4.** full of affectation; stilted. **5.** pertaining to a taxonomic classification that groups together unrelated organisms. —**ar′ti·fi′ci·al′i·ty,** n. —**ar′ti·fi′cial·ly,** adv.

artifi′cial insemina′tion, n. the injection of semen into the vagina or uterus by means of a syringe or the like.

artifi′cial intel′ligence, n. **1.** the collective attributes of a computer, robot, or other mechanical device programmed to perform functions analogous to learning and decision making. **2.** the field of study involved with the design of such programs and devices.

ar′tifi′cial lan′guage, n. an invented language intended for a special use, as in international communication or computer programming, and having no native speakers. Compare NATURAL LANGUAGE.

artifi′cial respira′tion, n. the stimulation of natural respiratory functions in a person whose breathing has failed by forcing air into and out of the lungs.

artifi′cial selec′tion, n. a process in the breeding of animals and in the cultivation of plants by which the breeder chooses to perpetuate only those forms having certain desirable inheritable characteristics.

ar·til·ler·y (är til′ə rē), n. **1.** mounted projectile-firing guns or missile launchers, light or heavy, as distinguished from small arms. **2.** the troops or the branch of an army concerned with the use and service of such weapons. **3.** the science that treats of the use of such weapons.

ar·ti·o·dac·tyl (är′tē ō dak′til), adj. **1.** having an even number of toes or digits on each foot. —n. **2.** a hoofed, even-toed mammal of the order Artiodactyla, as the cow and other ruminants, the pig, and the hippopotamus. Compare PERISSODACTYL.

ar·ti·san (är′tə zən), n. a person skilled in an applied art.

art·ist (är′tist), n. **1.** a person who practices or is proficient in one of the fine arts, esp. painting, sculpting, or drawing. **2.** a person proficient in a performing art, as an actor or musician. **3.** a person who exhibits exceptional skill.

ar·tiste (är tēst′), n. an artist, esp. an actor, singer, dancer, or other public performer.

ar·tis·tic (är tis′tik), adj. **1.** conforming to the standards of art. **2.** of or pertaining to the appreciation of art. **3.** of or characteristic of art or artists. **4.** showing skill in execution. —**ar·tis′ti·cal·ly,** adv.

art·ist·ry (är′ti strē), n. **1.** artistic workmanship, effect, or quality. **2.** artistic ability.

art·less (ärt′lis), adj. **1.** free from deceit, cunning, or craftiness; ingenuous. **2.** not artificial; natural; simple: *artless beauty.* **3.** lacking art, knowledge, or skill. **4.** poorly made; clumsy.

art nou·veau (ärt′ nōō vō′, är′), n. (*often caps.*) a style of fine and applied art current in the late 19th and early 20th centuries, characterized chiefly by curvilinear motifs derived from natural forms.

art·sy (ärt′sē), adj., **-si·er, -si·est.** *Informal.* ARTY. —**art′si·ness,** n.

art·sy-craft·sy (ärt′sē kraft′sē, -kräft′-), adj. *Informal.* pretending to artistry and craftsmanship or to an interest in arts and crafts.

art·work (ärt′wûrk′), n. **1.** the production of artistic or craft objects. **2.** an object or objects so produced. **3.** *Print.* **a.** the elements that constitute a mechanical, as type, proofs, and illustrations. **b.** a mechanical; paste-up.

art·y (är′tē) also **artsy,** adj., **art·i·er, art·i·est.** *Informal.* characterized by a pretentious display of artistic interest, manner, or mannerism.

a·ru·gu·la (ə rōō′gə lə), n. a Mediterranean plant, *Eruca vesicaria sativa,* of the mustard family, having pungent leaves used esp. in salads. Also called **rocket.**

-ary, a suffix with the general sense "pertaining to, connected with" the referent named by the base, occurring orig. in loanwords from Latin, as adjectives (*elementary; honorary*), personal nouns (*secretary*), or nouns denoting objects, esp. receptacles or places (*library; glossary*); in English it sometimes has the additional senses "contributing to," "for the purpose of," usu. forming adjectives: *complimentary; inflationary.*

Ar·y·an (âr′ē ən, ar′-, är′-, är′yən), n. **1.** a speaker of the languages ancestral to the Indo-Aryan or the Indo-Iranian languages. **2.** (in Nazi doctrine) a non-Jewish Caucasian, esp. of Nordic stock. —adj. **3.** of or pertaining to an Aryan or the Aryans. **4.** of or pertaining to Aryan as a language group.

ar·yl (ar′il), n. an organic group derived from an aromatic compound by removing a hydrogen atom, as phenyl from benzene.

as¹ (az; *unstressed* əz), adv. **1.** to the same degree or extent; equally: *It's not as hot today.* **2.** for example: *spring flowers, as the tulip.* **3.** thought or considered to be: *the square as distinct from the rectangle.* **4.** in the manner indicated: *She sang as promised.* —conj. **5.** to the same degree or extent that: *to run quick as a rabbit.* **6.** in the degree, manner, etc., of or that: *Do as we do.* **7.** at the same time that; while; when: *Pay as you enter.* **8.** since; because: *As you are leaving last, lock the door.* **9.** though: *Strange as it seems, it is so.* **10.** that the result or effect was: *His voice was so loud as to make everyone stare.* **11.** *Informal.* that: *I don't know as I do.* —pron. **12.** that; who; which (usu. prec. by *such* or

the same): *I have the same trouble as you had.* **13.** a fact that: *She spoke the truth, as can be proved.* —prep. **14.** in the role, function, or status of: *to act as leader.* —**Idiom. 15. as … as,** (used to express similarity or equality between one person or thing and another): *as rich as Croesus.* **16. as far as,** to the degree or extent that: *It is an excellent plan, as far as I can tell.* **17. as for** or **to,** with respect to; about; concerning: *As for staying away, I wouldn't think of it.* **18. as good as, a.** equivalent to: *as good as new.* **b.** true to; trustworthy as: *as good as his word.* **19. as if** or **though,** as it would be if: *It was as if the world had come to an end.* **20. as is,** in whatever condition something is in when offered, esp. if damaged. **21. as it were,** in a way; so to speak: *He became, as it were, a man without a country.* **22. as of,** beginning on; on and after; from: *This price is effective as of June 23.* **23. as such, a.** as being what is indicated; in that capacity: *An officer of the law, as such, is entitled to respect.* **b.** in itself or in themselves: *The job, as such, does not appeal to me.* **24. as yet,** up to the present time. —**Usage.** As a conjunction, one sense of AS is "because": *As she was bored, Sue left the room.* AS also has an equally common use in the sense "while, when": *As the parade passed by, the crowd cheered.* These two senses sometimes result in ambiguity: *As the gates were closed, he walked away.* (When? Because?) AS … AS is standard in both positive and negative constructions: *as happy as a lark; not as humid today as it was yesterday.* SO … AS is sometimes used in negative constructions (*not so humid as it was*) and in questions (*"What is so rare as a day in June?"*). The phrase AS FAR AS generally introduces a clause: *As far as money is concerned, the council has exhausted all its resources.* In some informal speech and writing, AS FAR AS is treated as a preposition and followed only by an object: *As far as money, the council has exhausted all its resources.* AS TO as a compound preposition has long been standard though occasionally criticized as a vague substitute for *about* or *concerning: As to your salary, that too will be reviewed.* See also AS, FARTHER, LIKE.

as² (as), n., pl. **as·ses** (as′iz, -ēz). **1.** a copper coin of ancient Rome. **2.** an ancient Roman unit of weight, equal to about 12 ounces.

As, *Chem. Symbol.* ARSENIC (def. 1).

A.S., Associate in Science.

A·sa (ā′sə), n. a king of Judah, 913?–873? B.C. I Kings 15:8–24.

As·a·hel (as′ə hel′), n. the half-brother of David and brother of Joab and Abishai, killed by Abner in battle. II Sam. 2:18–23.

ASAP (ā′sap), adv. without delay; promptly.

A.S.A.P. or **a.s.a.p.,** as soon as possible.

A·saph (ā′saf), n. a famous musician during the time of David. I Chron. 16:5.

A·sa·rah Be·te·vet (or **Be·te·bet**) (*Seph. Heb.* ä sä Rä′ bə te′vet; *Ashk. Heb.* ä sô′Rə bə tā′vās), n. a Jewish fast day observed on the 10th day of the month of Tevet in memory of the beginning of the siege of Jerusalem in 586 B.C. by the Babylonians under King Nebuchadnezzar.

as·bes·tos (as bes′təs, az-), n. **1.** a fibrous mineral, either amphibole or chrysotile, formerly used for making incombustible or fireproof articles and in building insulation. **2.** a fabric woven from asbestos fibers, formerly used for theater curtains, firefighters' gloves, etc.

as·bes·to·sis (as′be stō′sis, az′-), n. a lung disease caused by the inhalation of asbestos dust.

As·bur·y (az′bə rē), n. Francis, 1745–1816, English missionary: first bishop of the Methodist Church in America.

ASCAP (as′kap), n. American Society of Composers, Authors, and Publishers.

as·ca·rid (as′kə rid), n. any parasitic roundworm of the family Ascaridae.

as·ca·ris (as′kə ris), n., pl. **as·car·i·des** (a skar′i dēz′). any intestinal parasitic roundworm of the genus *Ascaris,* esp. the species causing colic and diarrhea in humans.

as·cend (ə send′), v.i. **1.** to move, climb, or go upward; mount; rise. **2.** to slant upward. **3.** to rise to a higher point, rank, degree, etc. **4.** to go toward the source or beginning; go back in time. —v.t. **5.** to go or move upward upon or along; climb; mount. **6.** to gain or succeed to: *to ascend the throne.*

as·cend·an·cy or **as·cend·en·cy** (ə sen′dən sē), also **as·cend′ance,** **as·cend′ence,** n. the state of being in the ascendant; governing or controlling influence; domination.

as·cend·ant or **as·cend·ent** (ə sen′dənt), n. **1.** a position of dominance or controlling influence; possession of power, superiority, or preeminence: *With his rivals in the ascendant, he soon lost his position.* **2.** an ancestor; forebear. **3.** the sign of the zodiac rising above the eastern horizon at the time of a birth or other event. —adj. **4.** ascending; rising. **5.** superior; predominant.

as·cend·er (ə sen′dər), n. **1.** a person or thing that ascends or causes ascension. **2. a.** the part of a lowercase letter, as *b, d, f,* or *h,* that rises above x-height. **b.** the letter itself.

as·cend·ing (ə sen′ding), adj. **1.** moving upward; rising. **2.** *Bot.* growing or directed upward.

as·cen·sion (ə sen′shən), n. **1.** the act of ascending; ascent. **2. the Ascension,** the bodily ascending of Christ from earth to heaven. **3.** (*cap.*) ASCENSION DAY. —**as·cen′sion·al,** adj.

As·cen·sion (ə sen′shən), n. a British island in the S Atlantic Ocean: constituent part of St. Helena. 1130; 34 sq. mi. (88 sq. km).

Ascen′sion Day′, n. the 40th day after Easter, commemorating the Ascension of Christ.

as•cent (ə sent′), *n.* **1.** the act of ascending; a rising or climbing movement. **2.** movement upward from a lower to a higher state, degree, grade, or status; advancement. **3.** a way or means of ascending; upward slope; acclivity. **4.** the degree of inclination; gradient: *a steep ascent.* **5.** a movement or return toward a source or beginning.

as•cer•tain (as′ər tān′), *v.t.,* to find out definitely; learn with certainty or assurance. —**as′cer•tain′a•ble,** *adj.*

as•cet•ic (ə set′ik), *n.* **1.** a person who practices self-denial and self-mortification for religious reasons. **2.** a person who leads an austerely simple, nonmaterialist life. **3.** (in the early Christian church) a monk; hermit. —*adj.* **4.** pertaining to asceticism. **5.** rigorously abstinent; austere. **6.** very strict or severe in religious exercises or self-mortification. —**as•cet′i•cism,** *n.*

asc•hel•minth (ask′hel minth′), *n.* any invertebrate of a former phylum, the Aschelminthes, including rotifers, nematodes, and gastrotrichs, all of which are now classified as separate phyla.

as•cid•i•um (ə sid′ē əm), *n., pl.* **-cid•i•a** (-sid′ē ə). a baglike or pitcherlike part of a plant or fungus.

ASCII (as′kē), *n.* a standardized code in which characters are represented for computer storage and transmission by the numbers 0 through 127.

a•scor•bate (ə skôr′bāt, -bit), *n.* a salt or other derivative of ascorbic acid.

a•scor′bic ac′id (ə skôr′bik), *n.* a white, crystalline, water-soluble vitamin, $C_6H_8O_6$, occurring naturally in citrus fruits, green vegetables, etc., and also produced synthetically, essential for normal metabolism: used in the prevention and treatment of scurvy, and in wound-healing and tissue repair. Also called **vitamin C.**

as•cot (as′kət, -kot), *n.* a tie or scarf with broad ends looped to lie flat one upon the other and sometimes held with a pin.

as•cribe (ə skrīb′), *v.t.,* **-cribed, -crib•ing. 1.** to credit or assign, as to a cause or source. **2.** to attribute or think of as belonging, as a quality or characteristic. —**a•scrip•tion** (ə skrip′shən), *n.*

asdic (az′dik), *n.* SONAR.

ASE or **A.S.E.,** American Stock Exchange.

a•sep•sis (ə sep′sis, ā sep′-), *n.* **1.** absence of the microorganisms that produce sepsis or septic disease. **2.** methods, as sterile surgical techniques, used to assure asepsis.

a•sep•tic (ə sep′tik, ā sep′-), *adj.* free from the living germs of disease, fermentation, or putrefaction. —**a•sep′ti•cal•ly,** *adv.*

a•sex•u•al (ā sek′sho͞o əl), *adj.* **1. a.** having no sex or sexual organs. **b.** independent of sexual processes, esp. not involving the union of male and female germ cells. **2.** free from or unaffected by sexuality: *an asexual friendship.* —**a•sex′u•al′i•ty,** *n.* —**a•sex′u•al•ly,** *adv.*

ash[1] (ash), *n.* **1.** the powdery residue of matter that remains after burning. **2.** finely pulverized lava thrown out by a volcano in eruption. **3.** a light, silvery gray color. **4. ashes, a.** deathlike grayness; extreme pallor. **b.** ruins, esp. the residue of something destroyed; remains; vestiges. **c.** mortal remains, esp. after decay or cremation. **d.** anything symbolic of penance, regret, remorse, or the like. —**ash′i•ness,** *n.* —**ash′less,** *adj.*

ash[2] (ash), *n.* **1.** any of various trees of the genus *Fraxinus,* of the olive family, esp. *F. excelsior,* of Europe and Asia, or *F. americana,* of North America, having opposite, pinnate leaves and purplish flowers in small clusters. **2.** the tough, straight-grained wood of any of these trees. **3.** the ligature or phonetic symbol "æ."

a•shamed (ə shāmd′), *adj.* **1.** feeling shame; distressed or embarrassed by feelings of guilt, foolishness, or disgrace. **2.** unwilling or restrained because of fear of shame, ridicule, or disapproval: *They were ashamed to show their work.* —**a•sham′ed•ly,** *adv.* —**a•sham′ed•ness,** *n.*

Ash•dod (ash′dod) also **Esdud,** *n.* a town in W Israel: an important ancient Philistine city; early center of Christianity. 64,400. Greek, **Azotos.**

ash•en[1] (ash′ən), *adj.* **1.** ash-colored; gray. **2.** extremely pale; pallid; pasty: *ashen cheeks.* **3.** consisting of ashes.

ash•en[2] (ash′ən), *adj.* **1.** pertaining to the ash tree or its timber. **2.** made of wood from the ash tree.

Ash•er (ash′ər), *n.* **1.** a son of Jacob and Zilpah. Gen. 30:12–13. **2.** one of the 12 tribes of Israel, traditionally descended from him.

Ash•ga•bat (ash′gə bät′, äsh′-), *n.* the capital of Turkmenistan, in the S part. 411,000. Formerly, **Ashkhabad, Poltoratsk.**

Ash•ke•lon (ash′ki lon′), *n.* a Philistine city near Gaza and the Mediterranean coast. I Sam. 6:17.

Ash•ke•naz•i (äsh′kə nä′zē), *n., pl.* **-naz•im** (-nä′zim). a Jew of central or E European origin or ancestry; a member of one of the two main branches of world Jewry distinguished from each other by liturgy, ritual, and pronunciation of Hebrew. Compare SEPHARDI. [< *ashkənaz* medieval Hebrew name for Germany] —**Ash′ke•naz′ic,** *adj.*

Ash•kha•bad (äsh′kə bäd′), *n.* a former name of **Ashgabat.**

ash•lar or **ash•ler** (ash′lər), *n.* **1.** a squared building stone cut more or less true on all faces adjacent to those of other stones so as to permit very thin mortar joints. **2.** masonry made of such stones.

a•shore (ə shôr′, ə shōr′), *adv.* **1.** to or onto the shore. **2.** on land rather than at sea or on the water.

ash•ram (äsh′rəm), *n.* **1.** a secluded place for retreat or instruction in Hinduism. **2.** the community living there.

Ash•to•reth (ash′tə reth′), *n.* an ancient Semitic goddess, identified with the Phoenician Astarte.

A•shur•ba•ni•pal (ä′sho͝or bä′nē päl′) also **Assurbanipal,** *n.* died 626? B.C., king of Assyria 668?–626? B.C.

Ash′ Wednes′day, *n.* the first day of Lent.

ash•y (ash′ē), *adj.,* **ash•i•er, ash•i•est. 1.** ash-colored; pale; wan. **2.** of or resembling ashes: *an ashy residue.* **3.** covered with ashes: *ashy ground.*

A•sia (ā′zhə, ā′shə), *n.* a continent bounded by Europe and the Arctic, Pacific, and Indian oceans. 3,069,000,000; ab. 16,000,000 sq. mi. (41,440,000 sq. km). —**A′sian,** *adj., n.*

A′sia Mi′nor, *n.* a peninsula in W Asia between the Black and Mediterranean seas, including most of Asian Turkey. Compare ANATOLIA.

a•side (ə sīd′), *adv.* **1.** on or to one side; to or at a short distance away. **2.** away from one's thoughts or consideration: *to put one's cares aside.* **3.** in reserve; in a separate place, as for safekeeping: *to put some money aside.* **4.** away from a present group or area, esp. for privacy: *He took her aside to discuss the plan.* **5.** put apart; notwithstanding: *all kidding aside.* —*n.* **6.** something spoken by an actor to or for the audience and supposedly not heard by others on stage. **7.** words spoken so as not to be heard by one or more persons present. **8.** a temporary departure from a main theme or topic; brief digression. —***Idiom.*** **9. aside from, a.** apart from; besides; excluding. **b.** except for.

as•i•nine (as′ə nīn′), *adj.* **1.** unintelligent; silly; stupid: *an asinine reason for quitting.* **2.** of or like an ass: *a beast that is more horselike than asinine.* —**as′i•nine′ly,** *adv.* —**as′i•nin′i•ty** (-nin′i tē), *n.*

ask (ask, äsk), *v.t.* **1.** to put a question to; inquire of: *I asked her but she didn't answer.* **2.** to request information about: *to ask the way.* **3.** to put into words so as to gain information, attention, etc.; utter; pose: *to ask the right questions.* **4.** to request: *to ask a favor.* **5.** to solicit from; request of: *Could I ask you a favor?* **6.** to demand; expect: *What price are they asking?* **7.** to set a price of: *to ask $40 for the hat.* **8.** to call for; need: *This experiment asks patience.* **9.** to invite: *to ask guests to dinner.* —*v.i.* **10.** to make inquiry; inquire. **11.** to request or petition (usu. fol. by *for*): *to ask for leniency.* —***Idiom.*** **12. ask for it,** to invite problems by persisting in risky or annoying behavior. Also, **ask for trouble.** —***Proverb.*** **13. Ask, and it shall be given you; seek, and you shall find; knock, and it shall be opened unto you,** know that what you ask for or seek will be given to you. Matt. 7:7. —**ask′er,** *n.*

a•skance (ə skans′) also **a•skant** (ə skant′), *adv.* **1.** with a side glance; obliquely. **2.** with suspicion or disapproval; skeptically: *The company may view askance your plan for early retirement.*

a•skew (ə skyo͞o′), *adv.* **1.** to one side; crookedly; awry: *a picture hanging askew.* **2.** askance. —*adj.* **3.** crooked; awry: *Your clothes are all askew.* —**a•skew′ness,** *n.*

ask′ing price′, *n.* the price at which something is offered by a seller, usu. subject to bargaining.

Ask not what your country can do for you; ask what you can do for your country, put your country's interests ahead of your own: from President John F. Kennedy's inaugural address (1961).

a•sleep (ə slēp′), *adv.* **1.** in or into a state of sleep: *to fall asleep quickly.* **2.** into a dormant or inactive state; to rest: *Put your doubts asleep.* **3.** into the state of death. —*adj.* **4.** sleeping: *He is asleep.* **5.** dormant; inactive. **6.** numb: *My foot is asleep.* **7.** dead.

As•ma•ra (äs mär′ə), *n.* the capital of Eritrea, in the N part. 276,355.

As•mo•de•us (az′mə dē′əs, as′-), *n. Jewish Demonology.* an evil spirit.

a•so•cial (ā sō′shəl), *adj.* **1.** not sociable or gregarious; withdrawn from society. **2.** indifferent to or unwilling to conform to conventional standards of behavior.

asp (asp), *n.* any of several venomous Eurasian snakes, esp. the horned viper. —**asp′ish,** *adj.*

as•par•a•gine (ə spar′ə jēn′, -jin), *n.* an essential amino acid, $NH_2COCH_2CH(NH_2)COOH$, abundant in legumes. *Abbr.:* Asn; *Symbol:* N

as•par•a•gus (ə spar′ə gəs), *n.* **1.** any plant of the genus *Asparagus,* of the lily family, esp. *A. officinalis,* cultivated for its edible shoots. **2.** the shoots, eaten as a vegetable.

aspar′agus fern′, *n.* a fernlike S African climbing vine, *Asparagus setaceus,* of the lily family, having very small, whitish flowers and pea-sized, purplish black berries: a popular houseplant.

as•par•tame (ə spär′tām, a spär′-, as′pər tām′), *n.* a white crystalline powder, $C_{14}H_{18}N_2O_5$, synthesized from amino acids, that is used as a low-calorie sugar substitute.

as•par′tic ac′id (ə spär′tik), *n.* a nonessential amino acid, $C_4H_7NO_4$, abundant in molasses. *Abbr.:* Asp; *Symbol:* D

ASPCA, American Society for the Prevention of Cruelty to Animals.

as•pect (as′pekt), *n.* **1.** appearance to the eye or mind; look: *the physical aspect of the country.* **2.** nature; quality; character: *the superficial aspect of the situation.* **3.** a way in which a thing may be regarded; interpretation; view: *both aspects of a decision.* **4.** part; feature; phase, as of a subject or problem. **5.** expression, air, or attitude; mien: *gloomy in aspect.* **6.** view commanded; exposure: *a house with a southern aspect.* **7.** the side or surface facing a given direction: *the dorsal aspect of a fish.* **8.** *Gram.* **a.** a category or set of categories for which a verb is inflected, serving typically to indicate the duration, repetition, beginning, or completion of the action or state denoted by the verb: *the Russian imperfective aspect.* **b.** a set of syntactic devices, as in the English progressive with *be* in *I am reading,* having similar functions. **9. a.** the angular distance between two points as seen from the earth. **b.** the astrological influence of any heavenly bodies located at such points.

As•per•ges (ə spûr′jēz), *n.* the rite of sprinkling holy water before high mass.

as•per•gil•lum (as′pər jil′əm), *n., pl.* **-gil•la** (-jil′ə), **-gil•lums.** a brush or instrument for sprinkling holy water.

as•per•gil•lus (as′pər jil′əs), *n., pl.* **-gil•li** (-jil′ī). any fungus of the genus *Aspergillus,* having sporophores with a bristly, knoblike top.

as•per•i•ty (ə sper′i tē), *n., pl.* **-ties. 1.** harshness or sharpness of tone, temper, or manner; severity; acrimony. **2.** hardship; difficulty; rigor. **3.** roughness of surface; unevenness. **4.** something rough or harsh.

as•perse (ə spûrs′), *v.t.,* **-persed, -pers•ing. 1.** to attack with false and damaging charges or insinuations; malign. **2.** to sprinkle; spatter.

as•per•sion (ə spûr′zhən, -shən), *n.* **1.** a damaging or derogatory remark or criticism; slander. **2.** the act of slandering; defamation; calumniation. **3.** the act of sprinkling with water, as in baptism.

as•phalt (as′fôlt; *esp. Brit.* -falt), *n.* **1.** any of various natural or synthetic, dark-colored, bituminous substances, composed mainly of hydrocarbon mixtures. **2.** a mixture of such substances with gravel, crushed rock, etc., used for paving. —*v.t.* **3.** to cover or pave with asphalt.

as′phalt jun′gle, *n.* a crowded urban area regarded as a dangerous place where people struggle constantly for survival.

a•spher•i•cal (ā sfer′i kəl, ā sfēr′-) also **a•spher′ic,** *adj.* (of a reflecting surface or lens) deviating slightly from a perfectly spherical shape and relatively free from aberrations.

as•phyx•i•a (as fik′sē ə), *n.* an extreme condition usu. involving loss of consciousness caused by lack of oxygen and excess of carbon dioxide in the blood, as from suffocation. —**as•phyx′i•al,** *adj.*

as•phyx•i•ate (as fik′sē āt′), *v.,* **-at•ed, -at•ing.** —*v.t.* **1.** to produce asphyxia in. **2.** to cause to die or lose consciousness by impairing normal breathing, as by gas or other noxious agents; choke; suffocate; smother. —*v.i.* **3.** to become asphyxiated. —**as•phyx′i•ant,** *adj., n.* —**as•phyx′i•a′tion,** *n.* —**as•phyx′i•a′tor,** *n.*

as•pic (as′pik), *n.* a savory jelly usu. made with meat or fish stock or tomato juice and gelatin.

as•pir•ant (as′pər ənt, ə spīər′ənt), *n.* **1.** a person who aspires, as one who seeks a career, advancement, status, etc. —*adj.* **2.** aspiring.

as•pi•rate (*v.* as′pə rāt′; *n., adj.,* -pər it), *v.,* **-rat•ed, -rat•ing,** *n., adj.* —*v.t.* **1. a.** to articulate (a speech sound, esp. a stop) so as to produce an audible puff of breath, as in the first *t* of *total.* **b.** to articulate (the beginning of a word or syllable) with an *h*-sound. **2. a.** to remove (a fluid) from a body cavity by aspiration. **b.** to inhale (fluid or a foreign body). **3.** to draw or remove by suction. —*n.* **4.** a speech sound produced with an audible puff of breath, as initial stop consonants in English or initial *h*-sounds. **5.** the substance or contents inhaled in aspiration. —*adj.* **6.** (of a speech sound) pronounced with or accompanied by aspiration; aspirated.

as•pi•ra•tion (as′pə rā′shən), *n.* **1.** a strong desire, longing, or hope; ambition. **2.** a goal or objective desired: *The presidency had been his aspiration since college.* **3.** an act of aspirating, esp. inhalation. **4. a.** the articulation of a speech sound accompanied by an audible puff of breath. **b.** the use of an aspirate in pronunciation. **5. a.** the act of removing a fluid, as pus or serum, from a cavity of the body by a hollow needle connected with a suction syringe. **b.** the act of inhaling fluid or a foreign body into the bronchi and lungs, often after vomiting.

as•pi•ra•tor (as′pə rā′tər), *n.* **1.** an apparatus or device employing suction. **2.** a suction pump that operates by the pressure differential created by the high-speed flow of a fluid past an intake orifice. **3.** a medical instrument used in aspirating fluids from the body.

as•pire (ə spīər′), *v.i.,* **-pired, -pir•ing.** to long, aim, or seek ambitiously: *to aspire after literary fame.*

as•pi•rin (as′pər in, -prin), *n., pl.* **-rin, -rins.** a white, crystalline substance, $C_9H_8O_4$, derivative of salicylic acid, used as an anti-inflammatory agent and to relieve pain and fever; acetylsalicylic acid.

ass (as), *n.* **1.** Also called **donkey.** a long-eared, slow, surefooted domesticated mammal, *Equus asinus,* related to the horse, used chiefly as a beast of burden. **2.** any wild species of the genus *Equus,* as the onager. **3.** a stupid, foolish, or stubborn person. —**ass′like′,** *adj.*

as•sail (ə sāl′), *v.t.* **1.** to attack vigorously or violently; assault. **2.** to attack verbally, as with arguments, criticism, or abuse. **3.** to make an impact on; beset: *The harsh light assailed their eyes.*

as•sail•ant (ə sā′lənt), *n.* a person who attacks.

as•sas•sin (ə sas′in), *n.* **1.** a murderer, esp. one who kills a politically prominent person for fanatical or monetary reasons. **2.** (*cap.*) one of an order of Muslim fanatics, active in Persia and Syria c1090–1272, whose chief object was to assassinate Crusaders. [< Medieval Latin *assassīnī* (pl.) < Arabic *ḥashshāshīn* lit., eaters of HASHISH]

as•sas•si•nate (ə sas′ə nāt′), *v.t.,* **-nat•ed, -nat•ing. 1.** to kill suddenly or secretively, esp. to murder a politically prominent person. **2.** to destroy or harm treacherously and viciously: *to assassinate a person's character.* —**as•sas′si•na′tion,** *n.* —**as•sas′si•na′tor,** *n.*

assas′sin bug′, *n.* any of various large bugs of the family Reduviidae, many of which kill and extract the blood of other insects and some of which are bloodsucking parasites of mammals.

as•sault (ə sôlt′), *n.* **1.** a sudden violent attack; onslaught. **2.** *Law.* an unlawful physical attack upon another, esp. an attempt or threat to do bodily harm. **3.** RAPE[1] (defs. 1, 2). —*v.t.* **4.** to make an assault upon; attack; assail. **5.** RAPE[1] (def. 6).

assault′ ri′fle, *n.* **1.** an automatic rifle firing high-powered ammunition that has features of a submachine gun. **2.** a nonmilitary weapon modeled on an assault rifle.

as•say (*v.* a sā′; *n.* as′ā, a sā′), *v.t.* **1.** to examine or analyze: *to assay a situation.* **2.** to analyze (an ore, alloy, etc.) to determine the content of gold, silver, or other metal. **3.** to analyze (a drug) to determine potency or composition. **4.** to test or evaluate: *to assay one's strength; to assay someone's efforts.* **5.** to attempt; try; essay: *to assay a dance step.* —*n.* **6.** an analysis of the composition or strength of a substance, esp. a determination of the amount of metal in an ore, alloy, etc. **7.** a substance undergoing analysis or trial. **8.** a detailed report of the findings in assaying a substance. —**as•say′a•ble,** *adj.* —**as•say′er,** *n.*

as•sem•blage (ə sem′blij; *for 3 also Fr.* A SÄN BLAZH′), *n.* **1.** a group of persons or things gathered or collected; an assembly; collection; aggregate. **2.** the act of assembling or the state of being assembled. **3. a.** a sculptural technique of organizing or composing into a unified whole a group of unrelated and often fragmentary or discarded objects. **b.** a work of art produced by this technique. —**as•sem•blag•ist** (ə sem′blə-jist, as′äm blä′zhist), *n.*

as•sem•ble (ə sem′bəl), *v.,* **-bled, -bling.** —*v.t.* **1.** to bring together or gather into one place, company, body, or whole. **2.** to put or fit together; put together the parts of: *to assemble a toy from a kit.* **3.** COMPILE (def. 4). —*v.i.* **4.** to come together; gather; meet.

Assem′blies of God′, *n.pl.* an evangelical Christian denomination founded in 1914: one of the largest Pentecostal groups in the United States.

as•sem•bly (ə sem′blē), *n., pl.* **-blies. 1.** an assembling or coming together of a number of persons, usu. for a particular purpose. **2.** a group of persons so gathered together, as for religious, political, or educational purposes. **3.** (*usu. cap.*) a legislative body, esp. the lower house of the legislature in certain states of the U.S. **4.** the putting together of complex machinery, as airplanes, from interchangeable parts of standard dimensions. **5.** the act of assembling.

assem′bly dis′trict, *n.* one of the districts into which a state is divided, each district electing one member to the lower house of the state legislature. Compare CONGRESSIONAL DISTRICT, SENATORIAL DISTRICT.

assem′bly line′, *n.* an arrangement of machines, tools, and workers in which a product is assembled in a particular sequence as it is moved along a direct line or route.

as•sent (ə sent′), *v.i.* **1.** to agree or concur; acquiesce; subscribe (often fol. by *to*): *to assent to a statement.* —*n.* **2.** agreement, as to a proposal; concurrence; acquiescence.

as•sert (ə sûrt′), *v.t.* **1.** to state strongly or positively; affirm; aver: *He asserted his innocence of the crime.* **2.** to maintain or defend (claims, rights, etc.). **3.** to state as having existence; affirm; postulate: *to assert a first cause as necessary.* —***Idiom.*** **4. assert oneself,** to claim one's rights or declare one's views firmly and forcefully.

as•ser•tion (ə sûr′shən), *n.* **1.** a positive statement or declaration, often without support or reason; allegation. **2.** an act of asserting.

as•ser•tive (ə sûr′tiv), *adj.* **1.** confidently aggressive or self-assured; forceful; dogmatic. **2.** having a distinctive or pronounced taste or aroma. —**as•ser′tive•ly,** *adv.* —**as•ser′tive•ness,** *n.*

asser′tiveness train′ing, *n.* behavior therapy in which one is taught how to assert oneself constructively through direct expression of both positive and negative feelings.

as•sess (ə ses′), *v.t.* **1.** to estimate officially the value of (property) for tax purposes. **2.** to determine the amount of (damages, a fine, etc.). **3.** to impose a tax or other charge on: *to assess members for painting the clubhouse.* **4.** to estimate or judge the value, character, etc., of; evaluate: *to assess one's efforts.*

as•sess•ment (ə ses′mənt), *n.* **1.** the act of assessing; appraisal; evaluation. **2.** an official valuation of property, used as a basis for levying a tax. **3.** an amount assessed as payable.

as•ses•sor (ə ses′ər), *n.* **1.** a person who makes assessments, esp. for tax purposes. **2.** an adviser or assistant to a judge.

as•set (as′et), *n.* **1.** a useful and desirable thing or quality: *Organizational ability is an asset.* **2.** a single item of ownership having exchange value. **3. assets, a.** the total resources of a person or business, as cash, notes and accounts receivable, securities, goodwill, or real estate (opposed to *liabilities*). **b.** the items detailed on a balance sheet, esp. in relation to liabilities and capital. **c.** all property available for the payment of debts, esp. of a bankrupt firm or person. **d.** property of a deceased that can be used to pay debts or legacies. **4.** *Slang.* an undercover or secret agent; spy: *an asset of the KGB.*

as•sev•er•ate (ə sev′ə rāt′), *v.t.,* **-at•ed, -at•ing.** to declare earnestly or solemnly; affirm; aver. —**as•sev′er•a′tion,** *n.*

As•si•de•an (as′i dē′ən), *n. Judaism.* a member of a sect, characterized by its religious zeal and piety, that flourished in the 2nd century B.C. during the time of the Maccabees and vigorously resisted the Hellenization of Jewish culture and religion.

as•si•du•i•ty (as′i do͞o′i tē, -dyo͞o′-), *n., pl.* **-ties. 1.** constant application or effort; diligence; industry. **2.** Often, **assiduities.** devoted or solicitous attention.

as•sid•u•ous (ə sij′o͞o əs), *adj.* **1.** constant; unremitting: *assiduous reading.* **2.** working diligently at a task; persevering; industrious: *an assiduous student.* —**as•sid′u•ous•ly,** *adv.*

as•sign (ə sīn′), *v.t.* **1.** to give or allocate; allot: *to assign rooms at a hotel.* **2.** to give out or announce as a task: *to assign homework.* **3.** to appoint, as to a post or duty. **4.** to designate; name; specify: *to assign a day for a meeting.* **5.** to bring forward; ascribe; attribute: *to assign a cause.* **6.** *Law.* to transfer (property, esp. in trust). —*v.i.* **7.** *Law.* to transfer property, esp. in trust or for the benefit of creditors. —*n.* **8.** Often, **assigns.** *Law.* a person to whom another's property is transferred; assignee. —**as•sign′a•ble,** *adj.* —**as•sign′a•bil′i•ty,** *n.* —**as•sign′a•bly,** *adv.* —**as•sign′er; Chiefly Law, as•sign•or** (ə sī nôr′, as′ə nôr′), *n.*

as•sig•na•tion (as′ig nā′shən), *n.* **1.** an appointment for a meeting, esp. a lover's secret rendezvous. **2.** the act of assigning.

as•sign•ee (ə sī′ nē′, as′ə nē′), *n.* a person to whom property is transferred, either in perpetuity or in trust.

as•sign•ment (ə sīn′mənt), *n.* **1.** something assigned, as a particular task or duty. **2.** a position of responsibility, post of duty, or the like, to which one is appointed. **3.** an act of assigning; appointment. **4. a.** the transfer of property, as to assignees for the benefit of creditors. **b.** the instrument of transfer.

as•sim•i•late (*v.* ə sim′ə lāt′; *n.* -lit, -lāt′), *v.,* **-lat•ed, -lat•ing,** *n.* —*v.t.* **1.** to take in and incorporate as one's own; absorb: *to assimilate new ideas.* **2.** to bring into conformity with the customs, attitudes, etc., of a dominant cultural group or national culture. **3.** to convert (ingested food) to substances suitable for incorporation into the body and its tissues. **4.** to cause to resemble; make similar. **5.** to compare; liken. **6.** to modify (a sound) by assimilation. —*v.i.* **7.** to be or become absorbed. **8.** to conform or adjust to the customs, attitudes, etc., of a dominant cultural group. **9.** (of ingested food) to be converted into the substance of the body. **10.** to bear a resemblance (usu. fol. by *to* or *with*). **11.** (of a sound) to become modified by assimilation. —*n.* **12.** something that is assimilated. —**as•sim′i•la•tive** (-lā′tiv, -lə tiv), *adj.*

as•sim•i•la•tion (ə sim′ə lā′shən), *n.* **1.** the act or process of assimilating or the state or condition of being assimilated. **2. a.** the conversion of absorbed food into the substance of the body. **b.** the process of plant nutrition, including photosynthesis and the absorption of nutrient matter. **3.** the merging of cultural traits from previously distinct cultural groups. **4.** the act or process by which a speech sound becomes identical with or similar to a neighboring sound, as in (gram′pā) for *grandpa.*

as•sist (ə sist′), *v.t.* **1.** to give support or aid to; help. **2.** to be associated with as an assistant or helper. —*v.i.* **3.** to give aid or help. **4.** to be present, as at a meeting or ceremony. —*n.* **5.** (in sports) **a.** a play helping a teammate to score. **b.** the official credit scored for such a play or pass. **6.** a helpful act. **7.** an electrical, hydraulic, or mechanical means of increasing power, efficiency, or ease of use.

as•sist•ant (ə sis′tənt), *n.* **1.** a person who gives aid and support; helper. **2.** a person who is subordinate to another in rank, function, etc.; aide; adjutant. **3.** something that aids and supplements another. **4.** a faculty member in a college or university ranking below an instructor. —*adj.* **5.** assisting; helpful. **6.** serving in an immediately subordinate position; of secondary rank.

assis′tant profes′sor, *n.* a college or university teacher ranking above an instructor and below an associate professor.

as•sist•ant•ship (ə sis′tənt ship′), *n.* a form of financial aid at graduate school in which a student assists a professor.

assist′ed su′icide, *n.* a form of euthanasia in which an incurably or terminally sick person commits suicide with the assistance of another person, such as a physician.

as•size (ə sīz′), *n.* **1.** Usu., **assizes.** (in England) trial sessions, civil or criminal, held periodically by a high court. **2.** an action, verdict, etc., of an assize. **3.** an inquest or other judicial inquiry. **4.** an enactment by a legislative assembly. **5.** a statute for the regulation and control of weights and measures or prices of general commodities in the market.

assn. or **Assn.,** association.

as•so•ci•ate (*v.* ə sō′shē āt′, -sē-; *n., adj.* -it, -āt′), *v.,* **-at•ed, -at•ing,** *n., adj.* —*v.t.* **1.** to connect or bring into relation in thought, feeling, memory, etc.: *to associate rainy days with depression.* **2.** to align or commit (oneself) as a companion, partner, or colleague. **3.** to unite; combine: *coal associated with shale.* —*v.i.* **4.** to keep company as a friend, companion, or ally. **5.** to join together as partners or colleagues. **6.** to enter into union; unite. —*n.* **7.** a person who shares actively in an enterprise; partner; colleague; coworker. **8.** a companion; comrade. **9.** anything usu. accompanying or associated with another; accompaniment; concomitant. **10.** a person admitted to a subordinate degree of membership in an association or institution. —*adj.* **11.** connected, joined, or related, esp. as a companion or colleague; having equal or nearly equal responsibility. **12.** having subordinate status; without full rights and privileges: *an associate member.* **13.** allied; concomitant.

asso′ciate profes′sor, *n.* a college or university teacher ranking above an assistant professor and below a professor.

asso′ciate's degree′, *n.* a degree granted by a junior college for the completion of two years of study.

as•so•ci•a•tion (ə sō′sē ā′shən, -shē-), *n.* **1.** an organization of people with a common purpose and having a formal structure. **2.** the act of associating or the state of being associated. **3.** connection, combination, or relationship. **4.** the connection or relation of ideas, feelings, sensations, etc.; correlation of elements of perception, reasoning, or the like. **5.** an idea, image, feeling, etc., suggested by or connected with something other than itself; an overtone or connotation. **6.** a group of plants of one or more species living together under uniform environmental conditions and having a distinctive aspect. **7.** a weak form of chemical bonding, as hydration. —**as•so′ci•a′tion•al,** *adj.*

as•so•ci•a•tive (ə sō′shē ā′tiv, -sē-, -shə tiv), *adj.* **1.** pertaining to or resulting from association. **2.** tending to associate or unite. **3.** *Math., Logic.* **a.** (of an operation on a set of elements) giving an equivalent expression when elements are grouped without change of order, as $(a + b) + c = a + (b + c)$. **b.** having reference to this property: *the associative law of multiplication.*

as•so•nance (as′ə nəns), *n.* **1.** similarity of sounds in words or syllables. **2.** rhyme in which the same vowel sounds are used with different consonants in the stressed syllables of the rhyming words, as in *penitent* and *reticence.*

as•sort (ə sôrt′), *v.t.* **1.** to distribute, place, or arrange according to kind or class; classify. **2.** to furnish with a suitable assortment or variety of goods.

as•sort•ed (ə sôr′tid), *adj.* **1.** consisting of different or various kinds; mixed or miscellaneous. **2.** matched; suited.

as•sort•ment (ə sôrt′mənt), *n.* **1.** the act of assorting; distribution; classification. **2.** a collection of various kinds of things.

asst., assistant.

as•suage (ə swāj′, ə swäzh′), *v.t.,* **-suaged, -suag•ing.** **1.** to make milder or less severe; relieve; ease; mitigate: *to assuage one's grief.* **2.** to appease; satisfy; allay: *to assuage one's hunger.* **3.** to soothe, calm, or mollify: *to assuage one's fears.* —**as•suage′ment,** *n.*

as•sume (ə soom′), *v.t.,* **-sumed, -sum•ing.** **1.** to take for granted or without proof; suppose; postulate; posit. **2.** to take upon oneself; undertake or accept: *to assume responsibility.* **3.** to take over the duties or responsibilities of. **4.** to adopt (a particular character, quality, mode of life, etc.): *to assume the role of patron of the arts.* **5.** to take on; become endowed with: *The situation assumed a threatening character.* **6.** to pretend to have or be; feign: *to assume a humble manner.* **7.** to seize; usurp: *to assume control.* **8.** to take upon oneself (the debts or obligations of another). —*v.i.* **9.** to take something for granted; presume. —**as•sum′a•ble,** *adj.*

as•sumed (ə soomd′), *adj.* **1.** adopted in order to deceive; fictitious; pretended; feigned. **2.** taken for granted; supposed. **3.** usurped. —**as•sum′ed•ly,** *adv.*

as•sum•ing (ə soo′ming), *adj.* taking too much for granted; presumptuous.

as•sump•tion (ə sump′shən), *n.* **1.** something taken for granted; a supposition. **2.** the act of taking for granted. **3.** the act of taking upon oneself. **4.** the act of taking possession of something. **5.** the taking over of another's debts or obligations. **6. a.** (*often cap.*) the bodily taking up into heaven of the Virgin Mary in Roman Catholic doctrine. **b.** (*cap.*) a feast commemorating this, celebrated on August 15.

as•sump•tive (ə sump′tiv), *adj.* **1.** taken for granted. **2.** characterized by assumption. **3.** presumptuous. —**as•sump′tive•ly,** *adv.*

as•sur•ance (ə shoor′əns, -shûr′-), *n.* **1.** a positive declaration intended to give confidence: *many assurances of support.* **2.** promise or pledge; guaranty: *to give one's assurance that a job will be done.* **3.** freedom from doubt; certainty: *to feel assurance of success.* **4.** freedom from timidity; self-confidence: *to enter a room with assurance.* **5.** the doctrine that believing Christians are assured of being saved. Col. 2:2.

As•sur•ba•ni•pal (ä′soor bä′nē päl′), *n.* ASHURBANIPAL.

as•sure (ə shoor′, ə shûr′), *v.t.,* **-sured, -sur•ing.** **1.** to declare earnestly or confidently to; tell positively: *She assured us of our welcome.* **2.** to cause to know surely; reassure: *He assured himself that the alarm was set.* **3.** to make (a future event) sure; ensure; guarantee. **4.** to secure; render safe or stable: *to assure a person's position.* **5.** to give confidence to; encourage.

as•sured (ə shoord′, ə shûrd′), *adj.* **1.** guaranteed; sure; secure. **2.** bold; confident; authoritative. **3.** boldly presumptuous. —*n.* **4. a.** the beneficiary of an insurance policy. **b.** the one whose life or property is insured. —**as•sur′ed•ly,** *adv.* —**as•sur′ed•ness,** *n.*

as•sur•gent (ə sûr′jənt), *adj. Bot.* curving or directed upward, as leaves; ascending. —**as•sur′gen•cy,** *n.*

As•syr•i•a (ə sēr′ē ə), *n.* an ancient kingdom and empire of SW Asia, centered in N Mesopotamia: greatest extent from c750 to 612 B.C. —**As•syr′i•an,** *adj., n.*

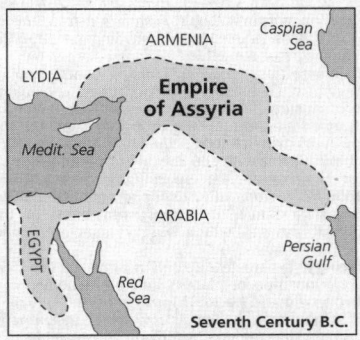

Seventh Century B.C.

As·tar·te (a stär′tē), *n.* a Semitic goddess of fertility and reproduction worshiped by the Phoenicians and Canaanites.

as·ta·tine (as′tə tēn′ -tin), *n.* a rare element of the halogen family. *Symbol:* At; *at. no.:* 85.

as·ter (as′tər), *n.* **1.** any composite plant of the genus *Aster*, having rays varying from white or pink to blue around a yellow disk. **2.** a plant of some allied genus, as the China aster. **3.** a structure formed in a cell during mitosis, composed of astral rays radiating about the centrosome. [< Latin < Greek *astḗr* star]

as·ter·isk (as′tə risk), *n.* **1.** a small starlike symbol (*), used in writing and printing as a reference mark or to indicate omission, doubtful matter, etc. **2. a.** this symbol used in linguistics to mark an ungrammatical or otherwise unacceptable utterance. **b.** this symbol used in historical linguistics to mark a hypothetical or reconstructed form that is not attested in written records. —*v.t.* **3.** to mark with an asterisk.

as·ter·ism (as′tə riz′əm), *n.* **1. a.** a group of stars. **b.** a constellation. **2.** a property of some crystallized minerals of showing a starlike luminous figure in transmitted light or, in a cabochon-cut stone, by reflected light. **3.** three asterisks (⁂ or ∴) printed before a passage to draw attention to it.

a·stern (ə stûrn′), *adv.* **1.** in a position behind a specified vessel or aircraft. **2.** in a backward direction.

as·ter·oid (as′tə roid′), *n.* **1.** any of the thousands of small, solid bodies that revolve about the sun in orbits largely between Mars and Jupiter. —*adj.* **2.** starlike. —**as′ter·oi′dal,** *adj.*

as·then·o·sphere (as then′ə sfēr′), *n.* the region below the lithosphere where rock is less rigid than that above and below it.

asth·ma (az′mə, as′-), *n.* a paroxysmal, often allergic disorder of respiration characterized by wheezing and difficulty in expiration.

asth·mat·ic (az math′ik, as-), *adj.* Also, **asth·mat′i·cal. 1.** suffering from asthma. **2.** pertaining to asthma. —*n.* **3.** a person suffering from asthma. —**asth·mat′i·cal·ly,** *adv.*

as·tig·mat·ic (as′tig mat′ik), *adj.* **1.** pertaining to, exhibiting, or correcting astigmatism. **2.** marked by rigidity or distortion, as in judgment or viewpoint; not objective or discriminating.

a·stig·ma·tism (ə stig′mə tiz′əm), *n.* **1.** Also called **a·stig·mi·a** (ə stig′mē ə). a refractive error of the eye in which parallel rays of light from an external source do not converge on a single focal point on the retina. **2.** an aberration of a lens or other optical system in which the image of a point is spread out along the axis of the system.

a·stir (ə stûr′), *adj.* **1.** moving or stirring, esp. with much activity or excitement. **2.** up and about; out of bed.

a·stom·a·tous (ā stom′ə təs, ā stō′mə-), *adj.* having no mouth, stoma, or stomata.

as·ton·ish (ə ston′ish), *v.t.* to fill with sudden and overpowering surprise or wonder; amaze.

as·ton·ish·ing (ə ston′i shing), *adj.* causing astonishment or surprise; amazing. —**as·ton′ish·ing·ly,** *adv.*

as·ton·ish·ment (ə ston′ish mənt), *n.* **1.** overpowering wonder or surprise; amazement. **2.** an object or cause of amazement.

As·tor (as′tər), *n.* **1.** John Jacob, 1763–1848, U.S. capitalist and fur merchant. **2.** Nancy (Langhorne), Viscountess, 1879–1964, first woman member of Parliament in England.

as·tound (ə stound′), *v.t.* to overwhelm with amazement; shock with wonder or surprise; astonish. —**as·tound′ment,** *n.*

as·tound·ing (ə stoun′ding), *adj.* capable of overwhelming with amazement; stunningly surprising. —**as·tound′ing·ly,** *adv.*

as·tral (as′trəl), *adj.* **1.** pertaining to, proceeding from, or like the stars; stellar. **2.** *Biol.* pertaining to, consisting of, or resembling an aster; having a discoid, radiate form. **3.** noting, in theosophy, a substance believed to pervade all space and to form a second body (**as′tral bod′y**) belonging to each individual through life and surviving death. —**as′tral·ly,** *adv.*

a·stray (ə strā′), *adv., adj.* **1.** out of the right way; off the correct or known path or route. **2.** away from that which is right; into error, confusion, or undesirable action or thought.

a·stride (ə strīd′), *prep.* **1.** with a leg on each side of; straddling: *to sit astride a fence.* **2.** on both sides of: *Budapest lies astride the river.* **3.** in a dominant position within: *Napoleon stands astride the early 19th century.* —*adv., adj.* **4.** in a posture of striding or straddling; with legs apart or on either side of something.

as·trin·gent (ə strin′jənt), *adj.* **1.** causing contraction or constriction of soft tissue; styptic. **2.** harshly biting; caustic: *astringent criticism.* **3.** stern or severe; austere. **4.** sharply incisive; pungent: *astringent wit.* —*n.* **5.** a substance that contracts the tissues or canals of the body. —**as·trin′gen·cy,** *n.* —**as·trin′gent·ly,** *adv.*

astro-, a combining form with the meaning "pertaining to stars or celestial bodies, or to activities, as spaceflight, taking place outside the earth's atmosphere": *astronautics; astrophotography.* Compare COSMO-.

as·tro·dome (as′trə dōm′), *n.* a transparent dome on top of the fuselage of an aircraft through which observations are made for celestial navigation.

as·tro·ge·ol·o·gy (as′trō jē ol′ə jē), *n.* the science dealing with the structure and composition of planets and other bodies in the solar system. —**as′tro·ge′o·log′ic** (-ə loj′ik), *adj.*

as·tro·labe (as′trə lāb′), *n.* an astronomical instrument used in ancient times to determine the position of the sun or stars.

as·trol·o·gy (ə strol′ə jē), *n.* the study that assumes and attempts to interpret the influence of the heavenly bodies on human affairs. —**as·trol′o·ger, as·trol′o·gist,** *n.* —**as·tro·log·i·cal** (as′trə loj′i kəl), **as′tro·log′ic,** *adj.* —**as′tro·log′i·cal·ly,** *adv.*

as·tro·naut (as′trə nôt′, -not′), *n.* a person engaged in or trained for spaceflight. —**as′tro·nau′ti·cal,** *adj.*

as·tro·nau·tics (as′trə nô′tiks, -not′iks), *n.* (*used with a sing. v.*) the science of or technology involved in travel beyond the earth's atmosphere, including interplanetary and interstellar flight.

as·tron·o·mer (ə stron′ə mər), *n.* an expert in astronomy; a scientific observer of the celestial bodies.

as·tro·nom·i·cal (as′trə nom′i kəl) also **as′tro·nom′ic,** *adj.* **1.** of, pertaining to, or connected with astronomy. **2.** extremely large; enormous: *astronomical costs.* —**as′tro·nom′i·cal·ly,** *adv.*

astronom′ical u′nit, *n.* a unit of length, equal to the mean distance of the earth from the sun: approximately 93 million miles (150 million km). *Abbr.:* AU

as·tron·o·my (ə stron′ə mē), *n.* the science that deals with the material universe beyond the earth's atmosphere.

as·tro·pho·tog·ra·phy (as′trō fə tog′rə fē), *n.* the photography of stars and other celestial objects. —**as′tro·pho·tog′ra·pher,** *n.* —**as′tro·pho′to·graph′ic** (-fō′tə graf′ik), *adj.*

as·tro·phys·ics (as′trō fiz′iks), *n.* (*used with a sing. v.*) the branch of astronomy that deals with the physical properties of celestial bodies and with the interaction between matter and radiation. —**as′tro·phys′i·cal,** *adj.* —**as′tro·phys′i·cist** (-ə sist), *n.*

as·tute (ə stōōt′, ə styōōt′), *adj.* **1.** keenly perceptive or discerning; sagacious: *an astute analysis.* **2.** clever; ingenious; shrewd; crafty. —**as·tute′ly,** *adv.* —**as·tute′ness,** *n.*

A·sun·ción (ä′sōōn syôn′), *n.* the capital of Paraguay, in the S part. 457,210.

a·sun·der (ə sun′dər), *adv., adj.* **1.** into separate parts; in or into pieces. **2.** apart or widely separated.

a·sy·lum (ə sī′ləm), *n.* **1.** (esp. formerly) an institution for the maintenance and care of the mentally ill, orphans, or other persons requiring specialized assistance. **2.** an inviolable refuge, as formerly for criminals and debtors; sanctuary. **3. a.** a refuge granted an alien by a sovereign state on its own territory. **b.** a temporary refuge granted political offenders, esp. in a foreign embassy. **4.** any secure retreat.

a·sym·met·ric (ā′sə me′trik, as′ə-) also **a′sym·met′ri·cal,** *adj.* **1.** not identical on both sides of a central line; lacking symmetry. **2. a.** having an unsymmetrical arrangement of atoms in a molecule. **b.** noting a carbon atom bonded to four different atoms or groups. **c.** (of a polymer) noting an atom or group that is within a polymer chain and is bonded to two different atoms or groups that are external to the chain. —**a·sym·me·try** (ā sim′i trē), *n.*

a·symp·to·mat·ic (ā simp′tə mat′ik, ā′simp-), *adj.* showing no evidence of disease. —**a·symp′to·mat′i·cal·ly,** *adv.*

as·ymp·tote (as′im tōt′), *n. Math.* a straight line approached by a given curve as one of the variables in the equation of the curve approaches infinity.

as·ymp·tot·ic (as′im tot′ik) also **as′ymp·tot′i·cal,** *adj.* **1.** of or pertaining to an asymptote. **2.** (of a function) approaching a given value as an expression containing a variable tends to infinity. **3.** coming into consideration as a variable approaches a limit, usu. infinity: *asymptotic property; asymptotic behavior.*

a·syn·chro·nous (ā sing′krə nəs), *adj.* **1.** not occurring at the same time. **2.** (of a computer or other electronic device) beginning each operation only after finishing the preceding one.

a·syn·de·ton (ə sin′di ton′, -tən), *n.* the omission of conjunctions, as in "He has provided the poor with jobs, with opportunity, with self-respect." —**as·yn·det·ic** (as′in det′ik), *adj.*

at (at; *unstressed* ət, it), *prep.* **1.** (used to indicate a point or place occupied in space); in, on, or near: *to stand at the door.* **2.** (used to indicate a location, as in time, on a scale, or in order): *at age 65; at zero; at the end.* **3.** (used to indicate incidence or occurrence): *at low tide.* **4.** (used to indicate presence or location): *at home; at hand.* **5.** (used to indicate amount, degree, or rate): *at great speed; at high altitudes.* **6.** (used to indicate a direction, goal, or objective); toward: *Look at that.* **7.** (used to indicate occupation or involvement): *at work; at play.* **8.** (used to indicate a state or condition): *at ease; at peace.* **9.** (used to indicate a cause or source): *She was annoyed at their carelessness.* **10.** (used to indicate relative quality or value): *at one's best; at cost.*

At, ampere-turn.

At, *Chem. Symbol.* astatine.

at′a·mas′co lil′y (at′ə mas′kō, at′-), *n.* a plant of the southeastern U.S., *Zephyranthes atamasco,* of the amaryllis family, bearing a single white lilylike flower sometimes tinged with purple.

at·a·rax·i·a (at′ə rak′sē ə) also **at′a·rax′y,** *n.* a state of freedom from emotional disturbance and anxiety; tranquillity. —**at′a·rac′tic** (-tik), **at′a·rax′ic,** *adj., n.*

A·ta·türk (at′ə tûrk′, ä′tə-), *n.* KEMAL ATATÜRK.

at·a·vism (at′ə viz′əm), *n.* **1. a.** the reappearance in an individual of characteristics of some remote ancestor that have been absent in intervening generations. **b.** an individual embodying such a reversion. **2.** reversion to an earlier type; throwback. —**at′a·vist,** *n.* —**at′a·vis′tic,** *adj.* —**at′a·vis′ti·cal·ly,** *adv.*

a·tax·i·a (ə tak′sē ə), *n.* loss of coordination of the muscles, esp. of the extremities. —**a·tax′ic,** *adj.*

ate (āt; *Brit.* et), *v.* pt. of EAT.

-ate[1], a suffix occurring orig. in loanwords from Latin, as adjectives (*literate; passionate*), nouns (*candidate; prelate*), and esp. past participles of verbs, which in English may function as verbs or adjectives (*consecrate; considerate; translate*); now used also as a verb-forming suffix in English (*calibrate; hyphenate*).

-ate[2], a suffix occurring orig. in nouns borrowed from Latin that denote offices or functions (*consulate; triumvirate*), as well as institutions or collective bodies (*electorate; senate*); sometimes extended to denote a person who exercises such a function (*magistrate; potentate*), an associated place (*consulate*), or a period of office or rule (*protectorate*); now joined to stems of any origin and denoting the office, term of office, or territory of a ruler or official (*caliphate*).

at·el·ier (at′l yā′, at′l yā′), *n.* a workshop or studio, esp. of an artist, artisan, or designer.

Ath·a·li·ah (ath′ə lī′ə), *n.* a daughter of Ahab and Jezebel and usurper of the throne of Judah, reigned 842–837 B.C. II Kings 11:1–3.

Ath·ana′sian Creed′, *n.* a creed or formulary of Christian faith, of unknown authorship, formerly ascribed to Athanasius.

Ath·a·na·sius (ath′ə nā′shəs), *n.* **Saint,** A.D. 296?–373, bishop of Alexandria: opponent of Arianism. —**Ath′a·na′sian** (-zhən), *adj.*

a·the·ism (ā′thē iz′əm), *n.* the belief that there is no God.

a·the·ist (ā′thē ist), *n.* a person who denies or disbelieves the existence of a supreme being or beings. —**a′the·is′tic,** *adj.*

A·the·na (ə thē′nə), *n.* a virgin deity of the ancient Greeks, worshiped as the goddess of wisdom, fertility, the useful arts, and prudent warfare; identified by the Romans with Minerva.

ath·e·nae·um or **ath·e·ne·um** (ath′ə nē′əm, -nā′-), *n.* an institution for the promotion of literary or scientific learning. **2.** a free library or reading room maintained by such an institution.

Ath·ens (ath′inz), *n.* **1.** Greek, **A·the·nai** (ä thē′ne). the capital of Greece, in the SE part. 885,136: ancient city-state. **2.** a city in N Georgia. 42,549. —**A·the·ni·an** (ə thē′nē ən), *adj., n.*

ath·lete (ath′lēt), *n.* a person trained or gifted in exercises or contests involving physical agility, coordination, stamina, or strength. ——**Pronunciation.** ATHLETE, ATHLETIC, and ATHLETICS are normally pronounced (ath′lēt), (ath let′ik), and (ath let′iks). The pronunciations (ath′ə lēt′), (ath′ə let′ik), and (ath′ə let′iks), with an unstressed vowel inserted between the first and second syllables, are usu. considered nonstandard.

ath′lete's foot′, *n.* a contagious disease of the feet, caused by a fungus that thrives on moist surfaces; ringworm of the feet.

ath·let·ic (ath let′ik), *adj.* **1.** physically active and strong; good at athletics or sports: *an athletic child.* **2.** of, like, or befitting an athlete. **3.** of, pertaining to, or involving athletes or their physical skills or capabilities. **4.** for athletics: *an athletic field; athletic shoes.* **5.** pertaining to or having a sturdy or well-proportioned physique; mesomorphic. —**ath·let′i·cal·ly,** *adv.* —**ath·let′i·cism** (-ə siz′əm), *n.* ——**Pronunciation.** See ATHLETE.

ath·let·ics (ath let′iks), *n.* **1.** (*usu. used with a pl. v.*) athletic sports, as running, rowing, or boxing. **2.** *Brit.* track-and-field events. **3.** (*usu. used with a sing. v.*) the practice of athletic exercises; the principles of athletic training. ——**Pronunciation.** See ATHLETE.

athlet′ic shoe′, *n.* a shoe for exercise or sport; sneaker.

athlet′ic support′er, *n.* JOCKSTRAP.

at-home′, *n.* **1.** Also, **at home′.** a reception of visitors at certain hours at one's home. —*adj.* **2.** done or used in the home; intended for one's home.

a·thwart (ə thwôrt′), *adv.* **1.** from side to side; crosswise. **2.** perversely; awry; wrongly. —*prep.* **3.** from side to side of; across. **4.** in opposition to; contrary to.

At·lan·ta (at lan′tə), *n.* the capital of Georgia, in the N part. 396,052.

Atlan′tic Char′ter, *n.* the joint declaration of President Roosevelt and Prime Minister Churchill (August 14, 1941) resulting from a conference at sea, setting forth the peace aims of their governments for the period following World War II. The declaration was later endorsed by a number of countries and incorporated in the purposes of the United Nations.

Atlan′tic Commu′nity, *n.* the member countries of NATO, esp. the United States, Great Britain, and Canada.

Atlan′tic croak′er, *n.* a food fish, *Micropogonias undulatus,* inhabiting Atlantic coastal waters of the southern U.S.

Atlan′tic O′cean, *n.* an ocean bounded by North America and South America on the Western Hemisphere and by Europe and Africa in the Eastern Hemisphere. ab. 31,530,000 sq. mi. (81,663,000 sq. km); greatest known depth, 30,246 ft. (9219 m).

Atlan′tic salm′on, *n.* a salmon, *Salmo salar,* of N coastal Atlantic seas and their freshwater tributaries.

At·lan·tis (at lan′tis), *n.* a legendary island, first mentioned by Plato, said to have existed in the Atlantic Ocean W of Gibraltar and to have sunk beneath the sea.

at·las (at′ləs), *n., pl.* **at·las·es** for 1–3, **at·lan·tes** (at lan′tēz) for 4. **1.** a bound collection of maps. **2.** a bound volume of charts, plates, or tables illustrating any subject. **3.** the first cervical vertebra, which supports the head. **4.** Also called **telamon.** a sculptural figure of a man used as a column. Compare CARYATID.

At·las (at′ləs), *n., pl.* **At·las·es. 1.** (in Greek myth) a Titan, condemned by Zeus to support the sky on his shoulders: identified by the ancients with the Atlas Mountains. **2.** a person who supports a heavy burden; mainstay. **3.** a liquid-propellant booster rocket, originally developed as the first U.S. ICBM, used to launch satellites into orbit around the earth and send probes to the moon and planets; also used to launch the Mercury spacecraft into orbit around the earth.

ATM, automated-teller machine. [*a(utomated)-t(eller) m(achine)*]

at. m., atomic mass.

at·man (ät′mən), *n. Hinduism.* the individual self, known after enlightenment to be identical with Brahman.

at·mos·phere (at′məs fēr′), *n.* **1.** the gaseous envelope surrounding the earth or a heavenly body; the air. **2.** any gaseous envelope or medium. **3.** a conventional unit of pressure, the normal pressure of the air at sea level, about 14.7 pounds per square inch, equal to the pressure exerted by a column of mercury 29.92 in. (760 mm) high. **4.** a surrounding or pervading mood, environment, or influence: *an atmosphere of tension.* **5.** the dominant mood or tone of a work of art, as of a play or novel. **6.** a distinctive quality, as of a place; character.

at·mos·pher·ic (at′məs fer′ik, -fēr′-) also **at′mos·pher′i·cal,** *adj.* **1.** pertaining to, existing in, produced by, or consisting of the atmosphere: *atmospheric storms.* **2.** resembling or suggestive of the atmosphere; softened and muted; hazy: *atmospheric effects.* **3.** having or producing a distinct emotional or esthetic tone, mood, or quality: *atmospheric lighting.*

at′mospher′ic pres′sure, *n.* **1.** the pressure exerted by the earth's atmosphere at any given point. **2.** a value of standard or normal atmospheric pressure, equivalent to the pressure exerted by a column of mercury 29.92 in. (760 mm) high, or 1013 millibars (101.3 kilopascals). Also called **barometric pressure.**

at·mos·pher·ics (at′məs fer′iks, -fēr′-), *n.* **1.** (*used with a pl. v.*) noise in a radio receiver or spots or bands on the screen of a television receiver, caused by interference from natural electromagnetic disturbances in the atmosphere. **2.** (*used with a sing. v.*) the study of such phenomena. **3.** (*used with a pl. v.*) mood or atmosphere.

at. no., atomic number.

at·oll (at′ôl, -ol, -ōl), *n.* a ring-shaped coral reef or a string of closely spaced small coral islands, enclosing a shallow lagoon.

at·om (at′əm), *n.* **1.** the smallest component of an element having the chemical properties of the element, consisting of a positively charged nucleus of neutrons and protons that exerts an electrical attraction on one or more electrons in motion around it. **2.** this component as the source of nuclear energy. **3.** a hypothetical particle of matter so minute as to admit of no division. **4.** anything extremely small; a minute quantity; speck; scintilla: *not an atom of truth in that statement.*

a·tom·ic (ə tom′ik), *adj.* **1.** of, pertaining to, resulting from, or using atoms, atomic energy, or atomic bombs: *an atomic explosion; atomic structure; atomic theory.* **2.** existing as free, uncombined atoms: *atomic hydrogen.* **3.** extremely minute. —**a·tom′i·cal·ly,** *adv.*

atom′ic bomb′, *n.* **1.** a bomb whose potency is derived from nuclear fission of atoms of fissionable material with the consequent conversion of part of their mass into energy. **2.** a bomb whose explosive force comes from a chain reaction based on nuclear fission in U-235 or plutonium. Also called **A-bomb.**

atom′ic clock′, *n.* an accurate electronic clock regulated by the resonance frequency of atoms or molecules of certain substances, as cesium.

atom′ic en′ergy, *n.* the energy released by reactions in atomic nuclei; nuclear energy.

at·o·mic·i·ty (at′ə mis′i tē), *n.* **1.** the number of atoms in a molecule of a gas. **2.** valence.

atom′ic mass′, *n.* the mass of an isotope of an element measured in units based on $1/12$ the mass of the carbon-12 atom. *Abbr.:* at. m.

atom′ic mass′ u′nit, *n.* a unit of mass, equal to $1/12$ the mass of the carbon-12 atom and used to express the mass of atomic and subatomic particles. Also called **dalton.**

atom′ic num′ber, *n.* the number of protons in the nucleus of an atom of a given element, used to locate the element in the periodic table. *Abbr.:* at. no.; *Symbol:* Z

atom′ic vol′ume, *n.* the atomic weight of a chemical element divided by its density. *Abbr.:* at. vol.

atom′ic weight′, *n.* the average weight of an atom of an element, based on $1/12$ the weight of the carbon-12 atom. *Abbr.:* at. wt.

at·om·ism (at′ə miz′əm), *n.* the theory that minute, discrete, finite, and indivisible elements are the ultimate constituents of all matter. —**at′om·ist,** *n.* —**at′om·is′tic,** *adj.*

at·om·ize (at′ə mīz′), *v.t.,* **-ized, -iz·ing. 1.** to reduce to fine particles or spray. **2.** to destroy (a target) by bombing, esp. with an atomic bomb. **3.** to split into many sections, groups, factions, etc.; fragmentize: *The group became atomized by disagreements among the members.* —**at′om·i·za′tion,** *n.*

at·om·iz·er (at′ə mī′zər), *n.* an apparatus for reducing liquids to a fine spray, as for medicinal or cosmetic application.

A·ton or **A·ten** (ät′n), *n.* an Egyptian solar deity declared by Amenhotep IV to be the only god, represented as a solar disk with rays ending in human hands.

a·to·nal·i·ty (ā′tō nal′i tē), *n.* music composed without reference to traditional tonality and employing the chromatic pitches on a free and equal basis.

a•tone (ə tōn′), *v.*, **a•toned, a•ton•ing.** —*v.i.* **1.** to make amends, as for an offense or error or for an offender (usu. fol. by *for*): *to atone for one's sins.* —*v.t.* **2.** to make amends for; expiate.

a•tone•ment (ə tōn′mənt), *n.* **1.** satisfaction or reparation for a wrong or injury; amends. **2.** (*sometimes cap.*) the Christian doctrine that the reconciliation of God and humankind will be accomplished through Christ. **3.** (in Christian Science) the state in which humankind exemplifies the attributes of Christ.

a•top (ə top′), *adj., adv.* **1.** on or at the top. —*prep.* **2.** on the top of: *atop the flagpole.*

-ator, a suffix that forms nouns corresponding to verbs ending in -ATE[1], denoting a human agent (*agitator; mediator*) or nonhuman entity, esp. a machine (*incubator*) performing the function named by the verb.

ATP, adenosine triphosphate: a nucleotide that is the primary source of energy in all living cells because of its function in donating a phosphate group during biochemical activities; composed of adenosine, ribose, and three phosphate groups and formed by enzymatic reaction from adenosine diphosphate and an orthophosphate. Compare ADP.

at•ra•bil•ious (a′trə bil′yəs) also **at′ra•bil′iar,** *adj.* **1.** gloomy; morose; melancholy; morbid. **2.** irritable; bad-tempered; splenetic.

a•tri•o•ven•tric•u•lar (ā′trē ō ven trik′yə lər), *adj.* of or pertaining to the atria and ventricles of the heart. *Abbr.:* AV, A-V

a•tri•um (ā′trē əm), *n., pl.* **a•tri•a** (ā′trē ə), **a•tri•ums. 1. a.** a usu. skylighted lobby or court, often several stories high, in an office building, hotel, etc. **b.** a central courtyard or patio open to the sky. **c.** the main or central room of an ancient Roman house, open to the sky at the center. **d.** a courtyard, flanked or surrounded by porticoes, in front of an early or medieval Christian church. **2. a.** a cavity of the body. **b.** Also called **auricle.** either of the two thin-walled upper chambers of the heart that receive blood from the veins and force it into the ventricles. —**a′tri•al,** *adj.*

a•tro•cious (ə trō′shəs), *adj.* **1.** extremely or shockingly wicked, cruel, or brutal: *an atrocious crime.* **2.** shockingly bad or tasteless; abominable: *atrocious manners.* —**a•tro′cious•ly,** *adv.*

a•troc•i•ty (ə tros′i tē), *n., pl.* **-ties. 1.** the quality or state of being atrocious. **2.** an atrocious act, thing, or circumstance.

at•ro•phy (a′trə fē), *n., v.,* **-phied, -phy•ing.** —*n.* Also, **a•tro•phi•a** (ə trō′fē ə). **1.** a wasting away of the body or of an organ or part, as from defective nutrition or nerve damage. **2.** degeneration or decline, as from disuse. —*v.t.* **3.** to affect with atrophy. —*v.i.* **4.** to undergo atrophy; wither; degenerate.

at•tach (ə tach′), *v.t.* **1.** to fasten or affix; join; connect: *to attach papers with a staple.* **2.** to join in action or function; make part of: *to attach oneself to a group.* **3.** to place on temporary duty with a military unit. **4.** to include as a quality or condition of something: *One proviso is attached to this legacy.* **5.** to assign or attribute: *to attach significance to a gesture.* **6.** to bind by ties of affection, regard, or the like. **7.** to take (persons or property) by legal authority. —*v.i.* **8.** to adhere; pertain; belong (usu. fol. by *to* or *upon*): *No blame attaches to him.*

at•ta•ché (a ta shā′, at′ə-; *esp. Brit.* ə tash′ā), *n., pl.* **-chés. 1.** a diplomatic official or a military officer assigned to an embassy or legation in a foreign country, esp. in a technical capacity: *a cultural attaché; a naval attaché.* **2.** Also, **at′ta•che′.** ATTACHÉ CASE.

attaché′ case′, *n.* a flat, usu. rigid briefcase for carrying business papers, documents, etc.

at•tached (ə tacht′), *adj.* **1.** joined; connected; bound. **2.** having a wall in common with another building. **3.** *Zool.* permanently fixed to the substratum; sessile.

at•tach•ment (ə tach′mənt), *n.* **1.** the act of attaching or the state of being attached. **2.** a feeling that binds one to a person, thing, cause, ideal, or the like; devotion; regard. **3.** something that attaches; a fastening or tie. **4.** an additional or supplementary device: *attachments for an electric drill.* **5.** seizure of property or persons by legal authority, esp. seizure of a defendant's property as security for debt. **6.** something attached, as a document added to a letter.

at•tack (ə tak′), *v.t.* **1.** to set upon in a forceful, violent, hostile, or aggressive way, with or without a weapon; begin fighting with: *The guard dog attacked the prowler.* **2.** to begin hostilities against; start an offensive against: *to attack the enemy.* **3.** to accuse, blame, or criticize severely; abuse verbally. **4.** to try to harm, undermine, or destroy, esp. with verbal abuse: *to attack someone's reputation.* **5.** to set about doing or working on vigorously. **6.** (of disease, destructive agencies, etc.) to begin to affect. —*v.i.* **7.** to make an attack; begin hostilities. —*n.* **8.** the act of attacking; onslaught; assault. **9.** a military offensive against an enemy or enemy position. **10.** seizure by disease, illness, or other condition: *an attack of indigestion; an attack of hiccups.* **11.** an experiencing of some sensation or response: *an attack of remorse; an attack of the giggles.* **12.** the beginning or initiating of some action; onset. **13.** an aggressive move in a performance or contest. **14.** the approach or manner of approach in beginning a musical phrase. —**at•tack′er,** *n.*

at•tain (ə tān′), *v.t.* **1.** to reach, achieve, or accomplish; gain; obtain: *to attain one's goals.* **2.** to come to or arrive at, esp. after some labor or tedium; reach: *to attain the mountain peak.* —*v.i.* **3.** to arrive at or succeed in reaching or obtaining something: *to attain to knowledge.* **4.** to reach in the course of development or growth: *These trees attain to remarkable height.* —**at•tain′a•ble,** *adj.* —**at•tain′a•bil′i•ty,** *n.*

at•tain•der (ə tān′dər), *n.* the extinction of a person's civil rights upon being sentenced to death or outlawry for treason or a felony.

at•tain•ment (ə tān′mənt), *n.* **1.** the act of attaining. **2.** something attained; a personal acquirement; achievement.

at•tar (at′ər), *n.* a perfume or essential oil obtained from flowers.

at•tempt (ə tempt′), *v.t.* **1.** to make an effort at; try; undertake: *to attempt a difficult task; to attempt to walk six miles a day.* —*n.* **2.** an effort made to accomplish something. **3.** an attack or assault: *an attempt on a person's life.*

at•tend (ə tend′), *v.t.* **1.** to be present at: *to attend school.* **2.** to go with as a concomitant or result; accompany: *Fever may attend a cold.* **3.** to take care of; minister to: *a nurse attending a patient.* **4.** to wait upon; accompany or serve: *The retainers attended their lord.* **5.** to look after; guard: *to attend one's health.* **6.** to listen to; give heed to: *to attend a warning.* —*v.i.* **7.** to take care or charge: *to attend to a sick person.* **8.** to apply oneself: *to attend to one's work.* **9.** to pay attention; listen or watch alertly: *to attend to a speaker.* **10.** to be present. **11.** to be present and ready to serve; wait: *to attend upon the queen.* **12.** to follow; be consequent (usu. fol. by *on* or *upon*).

at•tend•ance (ə ten′dəns), *n.* **1.** the act of attending. **2.** the persons or number of persons present.

at•tend•ant (ə ten′dənt), *n.* **1.** a person who attends another, as to perform a service; escort or servant: *a royal attendant; the ship's attendants.* **2.** a corollary or concomitant thing; consequence. **3.** a person who is present, as at a meeting. —*adj.* **4.** being present or in attendance; accompanying. **5.** consequent; associated; related: *poverty and its attendant hardships.* —**at•tend′ant•ly,** *adv.*

at•tend•ee (ə ten dē′, at′en-, ə ten′dē), *n.* a person who is present at a specific time or place.

at•tend•ing (ə ten′ding), *adj.* (of a physician) **1.** having primary responsibility for a patient. **2.** holding a staff position in an accredited hospital: *an attending physician.*

at•ten•tion (*n.* ə ten′shən; *interj.* ə ten′shun′), *n.* **1.** the act or faculty of mentally concentrating on a single object, thought, or event, esp. in preference to other stimuli. **2.** a state of consciousness characterized by such concentration. **3.** observant care or consideration: *to give a matter personal attention.* **4.** civility or courtesy; regard: *attention to a guest.* **5.** notice or awareness: *to catch someone's attention.* **6. attentions,** acts of courtesy or devotion indicating affection. **7.** a position assumed while standing in military formation, with eyes to the front, arms to the sides, and heels together (often used as a command). —**at•ten′tion•al,** *adj.*

atten′tion def′icit disor′der, *n.* a developmental disorder of children characterized by inattention, impulsiveness, distractibility, and often hyperactivity.

at•ten•tive (ə ten′tiv), *adj.* **1.** characterized by or giving attention; observant; mindful. **2.** thoughtful of others; considerate; polite; courteous. —**at•ten′tive•ly,** *adv.* —**at•ten′tive•ness,** *n.*

at•ten•u•ate (*v.* ə ten′yo͞o āt′; *adj.* -it, -āt′), *v.,* **-at•ed, -at•ing,** *adj.* —*v.t.* **1.** to weaken or reduce in force, intensity, effect, quantity, or value: *to attenuate desire.* **2.** to make thin. **3.** to render less virulent, as a strain of pathogenic virus or bacterium. **4.** to reduce the amplitude of (an electronic signal) without distortion. —*v.i.* **5.** to become thin or fine; lessen. —*adj.* **6.** weakened; diminishing. **7.** *Bot.* tapering gradually to a narrow extremity. —**at•ten′u•a′tion,** *n.*

at•test (ə test′), *v.t.* **1.** to bear witness to; declare to be correct, accurate, or genuine, in words or writing, esp. officially: *to attest the truth of a statement.* **2.** to give proof or evidence of; manifest: *This essay attests your talent.* **3.** to put on oath. —*v.i.* **4.** to testify or bear witness: *to attest to a person's reliability.*

at•tic (at′ik), *n.* **1.** the part of a building, esp. of a house, directly under a roof; garret. **2.** a room or rooms in an attic. **3.** a low story or decorative wall above an entablature or the main cornice of a building.

At•ti•la (at′l ə, ə til′ə), *n.* (*"Scourge of God"*) A.D. 406?–453, king of the Huns who invaded Europe: defeated by the Romans and Visigoths in 451.

at•tire (ə tīᵊr′), *v.,* **-tired, -tir•ing,** *n.* —*v.t.* **1.** to dress, array, or adorn, esp. for fancy or ceremonial occasions. —*n.* **2.** clothes or apparel, esp. rich or splendid garments. **3.** the horns of a deer.

at•ti•tude (at′i to͞od′, -tyo͞od′), *n.* **1.** manner, disposition, feeling, position, etc., with regard to a person or thing; tendency or orientation, esp. of the mind: *a cheerful attitude.* **2.** position or posture of the body appropriate to or expressive of an action, emotion, etc.: *to assume a threatening attitude.* **3.** the inclination of the three principal axes of an aircraft relative to the wind, to the ground, etc. **4.** *Ballet.* a pose in which the dancer stands on one leg, the other bent behind. **5.** *Slang.* a testy, uncooperative disposition. —**at′ti•tu′di•nal,** *adj.*

Att•lee (at′lē), *n.* **Clement (Richard),** 1883–1967, British prime minister 1945–51.

attn., attention.

at•tor•ney (ə tûr′nē), *n., pl.* **-neys.** a lawyer; attorney-at-law. [< Anglo-French *attourne* lit., (one who is) turned to] —**at•tor′ney•ship′,** *n.*

attor′ney-at-law′, *n., pl.* **attorneys-at-law.** an officer of the court authorized to appear before it as a representative of a party to a legal controversy.

attor′ney gen′eral, *n., pl.* **attorneys general, attorney generals.** (*often caps.*) the chief law officer of a country or state and head of its legal department: the U.S. Attorney General is the head of the Department of Justice and a member of the president's cabinet.

at·tract (ə trakt′), v.t. **1.** to draw by a physical force causing or tending to cause to approach, adhere, or unite; pull (opposed to *repel*): *The gravitational force of the earth attracts smaller bodies to it.* **2.** to draw by appealing to the emotions or senses, by stimulating interest, or by exciting admiration; allure; invite: *to attract attention; to attract admirers.* —v.i. **3.** to possess or exert the power of attraction.

at·trac·tion (ə trak′shən), n. **1.** the act, power, or property of attracting. **2.** attractive quality; magnetic charm; allurement. **3.** a person or thing that draws, attracts, or entices. **4.** a characteristic or quality that provides pleasure; attractive feature: *The chief attraction of the party was the good food.* **5.** the electric or magnetic force that acts between oppositely charged bodies, tending to draw them together. **6.** an entertainment offered to the public; spectacle. —**at·trac′tion·al·ly,** adv.

at·trac·tive (ə trak′tiv), adj. **1.** providing pleasure or delight, esp. in appearance or manner; charming; alluring: *an attractive personality.* **2.** arousing interest or engaging one's thought, consideration, etc.: *an attractive idea.* **3.** having the quality of attracting. —**at·trac′tive·ly,** adv. —**at·trac′tive·ness,** n.

at·trib·ute (v. ə trib′yo͞ot; n. a′trə byo͞ot′), v., **-ut·ed, -ut·ing,** n. —v.t. **1.** to regard as resulting from a specified cause; consider as caused by something indicated: *She attributes his bad temper to ill health.* **2.** to consider as a quality or characteristic of the person, thing, group, etc., indicated: *to attribute intelligence to one's colleagues.* **3.** to regard as made or produced by or originating in the person, time, place, etc., indicated: *to attribute a painting to an artist; to attribute a discovery to a certain century.* —n. **at·tri·bute 4.** a quality, character, characteristic, or property attributed as belonging to a person, thing, group, etc.: *Sensitivity is one of his attributes.* **5.** an object associated with a character, office, or quality, as the lion skin of Hercules. **6.** a subordinate word or phrase that serves to limit, particularize, or supplement the meaning of another: In *the red house, red* is an attribute of *house.* —**at·trib′ut·a·ble,** adj. —**at·trib′ut·er, at·trib′u·tor,** n.

at·tri·bu·tion (a′trə byo͞o′shən), n. **1.** the act of attributing; ascription. **2.** something ascribed; an attribute.

at·trib·u·tive (ə trib′yə tiv), adj. **1.** pertaining to or having the character of attribution or an attribute. **2.** of or pertaining to an adjective or noun that is directly adjacent to, in English usu. preceding, the noun it modifies, without any intervening linking verb, as the adjective *sunny* in *a sunny day* or the noun *television* in *a television screen.* —n. **3.** an attributive word, esp. an adjective. —**at·trib′u·tive·ly,** adv.

at·tri·tion (ə trish′ən), n. **1.** a reduction or decrease in numbers, size, or strength: *a high rate of attrition in union membership.* **2.** a wearing down or weakening of resistance, esp. as a result of continuous pressure or harassment: *The enemy conducted a war of attrition against the town.* **3.** a gradual reduction in work force without firing of personnel, as when workers retire and are not replaced. **4.** the act of rubbing against something; friction. **5.** a wearing down or away by friction; abrasion. —**at·tri′tion·al,** adj.

at·tune (ə toōn′, ə tyoōn′), v.t., **-tuned, -tun·ing.** to bring into accord, harmony, or sympathetic relationship; adjust: *to attune oneself to country living.*

atty., attorney.

ATV, all-terrain vehicle. [*a(ll)-t(errain) v(ehicle)*]

at. vol., atomic volume.

at. wt., atomic weight.

a·typ·i·cal (ā tip′i kəl), adj. not typical; irregular; abnormal. —**a·typ′i·cal′i·ty,** n. —**a·typ′i·cal·ly,** adv.

AU, astronomical unit.

Au, Chem. Symbol. gold. [< Latin *aurum*]

A.U. or **a.u.,** angstrom unit.

au·bade (ō bäd′), n. music suitable to greeting the dawn or the morning.

au·ber·gine (ō′bər zhēn′, -jēn′, ō′ber-), n. Chiefly Brit. EGGPLANT. **2.** a dark purplish color.

au·burn (ô′bərn), n. **1.** a reddish brown or golden brown color. —adj. **2.** of this color: *auburn hair.*

au cou·rant (ō′ koō rän′), adj. **1.** up-to-date. **2.** fully aware or familiar; cognizant.

auc·tion (ôk′shən), n. **1.** Also called **public sale.** a publicly held sale at which property or goods are sold to the highest bidder. —v.t. **2.** to sell by auction (often fol. by *off*): *to auction off one's furniture.*

auc·tion·eer (ôk′shə nēr′), n. **1.** a person who conducts sales by auction. —v.t. **2.** to sell by auction.

auc·to·ri·al (ôk tôr′ē əl, -tōr′-, ouk′-), adj. of, by, or pertaining to an author: *auctorial rights.*

au·da·cious (ô dā′shəs), adj. **1.** extremely bold or daring; recklessly brave; fearless. **2.** extremely original or inventive; unrestrained by existing ideas, conventions, etc.; uninhibited. **3.** recklessly bold in defiance of convention, propriety, law, or the like; insolent; brazen. —**au·da′cious·ly,** adv.

au·dac·i·ty (ô das′i tē), n., pl. **-ties. 1.** boldness or daring, esp. with confident or arrogant disregard for personal safety, conventional thought, or other restrictions; nerve. **2.** effrontery or insolence; shameless boldness. **3.** Usu., **audacities.** audacious acts or statements.

Au·den (ôd′n), n. **W(ystan) H(ugh),** 1907–73, English poet in the U.S.

au·di·ble (ô′də bəl), adj. **1.** capable of being heard; loud enough to be heard; actually heard. —n. **2.** (in football) a change in play called out

orally after both teams have assumed their positions at the line of scrimmage. —**au/di·bil/i·ty,** n. —**au/di·bly,** adv.

au·di·ence (ô′dē əns), n. **1.** the group of spectators at a public event; listeners or viewers collectively, as in attendance at a play or concert. **2.** the persons reached by a book, television broadcast, etc.; public. **3.** a regular public that manifests interest, support, enthusiasm, or the like; following. **4.** opportunity to be heard; chance to speak; a hearing. **5.** a formal interview with a sovereign, high officer of government, or other high-ranking person: *an audience with the pope.* **6.** the act of hearing, or attending to, words or sounds. —**Usage.** See COLLECTIVE NOUN.

au·dile (ô′dil, -dīl), adj. auditory.

au·di·o (ô′dē ō′), adj. **1.** of, pertaining to, or employed in the transmission, reception, or reproduction of sound. **2.** of or pertaining to frequencies or signals in the audible range. **3.** designating an electronic apparatus using audio frequencies: *audio amplifier.* —n. **4. a.** the audio elements of television (disting. from *video*). **b.** the circuits in a receiver for reproducing sound. **5.** the field of sound recording, transmission, reception, and reproduction.

audio-, a combining form with the meanings "sound within the range of human hearing" (*audiometer*), "hearing" (*audiology*), "sound reproduction" (*audiophile*).

au′dio fre′quency, n. a frequency between 15 Hz and 20,000 Hz, within the range of normally audible sound.

au·di·o·lin·gual (ô′dē ō ling′gwəl), adj. of or pertaining to a method of teaching foreign languages that emphasizes listening comprehension and speaking over reading and writing.

au·di·ol·o·gy (ô′dē ol′ə jē), n. the study of hearing disorders, including evaluation of hearing function and rehabilitation of patients with hearing impairments. —**au/di·o·log/i·cal** (-ə loj′i kəl), adj. —**au/di·ol/o·gist,** n.

au·di·o·tape (ô′dē ō tāp′), n. magnetic tape on which sound is recorded.

au·di·o·vis·u·al or **au·di·o-vis·u·al** (ô′dē ō vizh′oō əl), adj. **1.** of, pertaining to, involving, or directed at both hearing and sight: *audiovisual facilities.* —n. **2.** Usu., **audiovisuals.** AUDIOVISUAL AIDS.

au′diovis′ual aids′, n.pl. training or educational materials directed at the sense of hearing and the sense of sight, as films, recordings, and photographs, esp. as used in classroom instruction.

au·dit (ô′dit), n. **1.** an official examination and verification of financial accounts and records. **2.** a final report detailing an audit. **3.** the inspection or examination of something, as a building, to determine its safety, efficiency, or the like: *an energy audit.* —v.t. **4.** to make an audit of (accounts, records, etc.). **5.** to attend (classes, etc.) as an auditor. **6.** to make an audit of (a building) to evaluate safety, efficiency, etc. —v.i. **7.** to perform an audit. —**au/dit·a·ble,** adj.

au·di·tion (ô dish′ən), n. **1.** a trial hearing or viewing of a performer, group, act, etc., as for casting or employment. **2.** a reading or other simplified rendering of a theatrical work, performed before a potential backer, producer, etc. **3.** the act, sense, or power of hearing. **4.** something that is heard. —v.t. **5.** to hear or view in an audition. —v.i. **6.** to compete in an audition.

au·di·tor (ô′di tər), n. **1.** a person authorized to examine accounts and give a report. **2.** a student who attends a course to listen but not receive credit. **3.** a hearer; listener. —**au/di·tor·ship/,** n.

au·di·to·ri·um (ô′di tôr′ē əm, -tōr′-), n., pl. **-to·ri·ums** or, sometimes, **-to·ri·a** (-tôr′ē ə, -tōr′-). **1.** the space set apart for the audience in a theater, school, or other public building. **2.** a building for public gatherings; hall.

au·di·to·ry (ô′di tôr′ē, -tōr′ē-), adj. **1.** pertaining to hearing, to the sense of hearing, or to the organs of hearing. **2.** perceived through or resulting from the sense of hearing: *auditory hallucinations.*

Au·du·bon (ô′də bon′, -bən), n. **John James,** 1785–1851, U.S. naturalist who painted and wrote about the birds of North America.

au·ger (ô′gər), n. **1.** a tool for boring holes in wood, similar to but larger than a gimlet, consisting of a bit rotated by a transverse handle. **2.** a drill for boring holes in the ground, as to tap a spring.

aught¹ or **ought** (ôt), n. anything whatever; any part: *for aught I know.*

aught² or **ought.** (ôt), n. a cipher (0); zero.

aug·ment (v. ôg ment′; n. ôg′ment), v.t. **1.** to make larger; enlarge in size, number, strength, or extent; increase. **2.** Music. **a.** to raise (the upper note of an interval or chord) by a half step. **b.** to double the note values of (a theme). **3.** Gram. to add an augment to. —v.i. **4.** to become larger. —n. **5.** a prefixed vowel or a lengthening of the initial vowel that characterizes certain forms in the nonpresent inflection of verbs in Greek, Sanskrit, etc. —**aug·ment′a·ble,** adj. —**aug/men·ta/tion,** n. —**aug·ment′er, aug·men′tor,** n.

aug·men·ta·tive (ôg men′tə tiv), adj. **1.** serving to augment. **2.** Gram. pertaining to or productive of a form denoting increased size or intensity, as the Spanish suffix -*ón* in *sillón* "armchair," from *silla* "chair." —n. **3.** an augmentative element or formation.

au grat·in (ō grat′n, ō grät′n), adj. topped with buttered breadcrumbs or grated cheese or both and browned in an oven or broiler. [< French]

Augs′burg Confes′sion, n. the statement of beliefs and doctrines of the Lutherans, formulated by Melanchthon and presented at the Diet of Augsburg in 1530.

au·gur (ô′gər), *n.* **1.** one of a group of ancient Roman officials charged with observing and interpreting omens for guidance in public affairs. **2.** soothsayer; prophet. —*v.t.* **3.** to divine or predict, as from omens; prognosticate. **4.** to serve as an omen or promise of; foreshadow. —*v.i.* **5.** to conjecture from signs or omens; predict. **6.** to be a sign; bode: *The movement of troops augurs ill for peace.*

au·gu·ry (ô′gyə rē), *n., pl.* **-ries. 1.** the practice of divination from omens or signs. **2.** an omen, token, or indication. —**au′gu·ral,** *adj.*

au·gust (ô gust′), *adj.* **1.** inspiring reverence or admiration; of supreme dignity or grandeur; majestic. **2.** venerable; eminent: *an august personage.* —**au·gust′ly,** *adv.* —**au·gust′ness,** *n.*

Au·gust (ô′gəst), *n.* the eighth month of the year, containing 31 days. *Abbr.:* Aug.

Au·gus·ta (ô gus′tə, ə gus′-), *n.* **1.** a city in E Georgia, on the Savannah River. 47,532. **2.** a city in and the capital of Maine, in the SW part, on the Kennebec River. 21,819.

Au·gus·tine (ô′gə stēn′, ô gus′tin, ə gus′-), *n.* **1. Saint,** A.D. 354–430, one of the Latin fathers in the early Christian Church; bishop of Hippo in N Africa. **2. Saint,** (*Austin*) died A.D. 604, Roman monk: headed group of missionaries who landed in England A.D. 597; first archbishop of Canterbury 601–604.

Au·gus·tin·i·an (ô′gə stin′ē ən), *adj.* **1.** pertaining to St. Augustine of Hippo, to his doctrines, or to any religious order following his rule. —*n.* **2.** a member of any of the Roman Catholic Augustinian orders. **3.** a follower of St. Augustine. —**Au′gus·tin′i·an·ism, Au·gus·tin·ism** (ô gus′tə niz′əm, ə gus′-), *n.*

Au·gus·tus (ô gus′təs, ə gus′-), *n.* **1.** Also called **Octavian** (*Gaius Julius Caesar Octavianus, Augustus Caesar*), 63 B.C.–A.D. 14, first Roman emperor 27 B.C.–A.D. 14: heir and successor to Julius Caesar. **2.** a title of office given to rulers of the Roman Republic after Octavianus.

au jus (ō zhōōs′, ō jōōs′; Fr. ō zhy′), *adj.* served in the meat's natural juices.

auk (ôk), *n.* any of several usu. black and white diving birds of the family Alcidae, of northern seas, having webbed feet and small wings. Compare GREAT AUK.

auld lang syne (ōld′ lang zīn′, sīn′), *n.* fondly remembered times.

au na·tu·rel (ō′ nach′ə rel′, -nat′yə-), *adj.* **1.** in the natural state. **2.** naked; nude. **3.** cooked plainly. **4.** uncooked.

Aung San Suu Kyi (oung′ sän′ sōō′ kē′), *n.* born 1945, Burmese opposition leader.

aunt (ant, änt), *n.* **1.** the sister of one's father or mother. **2.** the wife of one's uncle. **3.** *Chiefly New Eng. and South Midland U.S.* (used as a term of respectful address to an older woman unrelated to the speaker.) ——**Pronunciation.** In New England and E Virginia, a "broad *a*" pronunciation of AUNT, resembling either the (ä) of *car* or a vowel midway in quality between (ä) and the (a) of *hat,* occurs in the speech of all social groups, even those who do not use the sound in words like *dance* and *laugh.* For those accustomed to this pronunciation, it is natural and not an affectation.

au pair (ō pâr′), *n.* **1.** a person, usu. a young foreign visitor, employed to take care of children, do housework, etc., in exchange for room and board. —*adj.* **2.** of, pertaining to, or employed under such an arrangement.

au·ra (ôr′ə), *n., pl.* **au·ras** or, for 3, **au·rae** (ôr′ē). **1.** a distinctive and pervasive quality or character; atmosphere: *an aura of respectability.* **2.** a light or radiance claimed to emanate from the body and to be visible to certain individuals with psychic powers. **3.** a sensation, as of a glowing light or an aroma, preceding an attack of migraine or epilepsy.

au·ral¹ (ôr′əl), *adj.* of or pertaining to an aura.

au·ral² (ôr′əl), *adj.* of or pertaining to the ear or to the sense of hearing. —**au′ral·ly,** *adv.*

au·re·ate (ôr′ē it, -āt′), *adj.* **1.** golden or gilded. **2.** brilliant; splendid. **3.** characterized by ornate, often pompous language.

au·re·ole (ôr′ē ōl′) also **au·re·o·la** (ô rē′ə lə, ə rē′-), *n., pl.* **-oles** also **-o·las. 1.** a radiance surrounding the head or the whole figure in the representation of a sacred personage. **2.** any encircling ring of light or color; halo. **3.** CORONA (def. 2). **4.** a zone of altered country rock around an igneous intrusion.

au·ric (ôr′ik), *adj.* of or containing trivalent gold.

au·ri·cle (ôr′i kəl), *n.* **1.** the outer ear; pinna. **2.** (loosely) the atrium of the heart. **3.** a part like or likened to an ear. —**au′ri·cled,** *adj.*

au·ric·u·lar (ô rik′yə lər), *adj.* **1.** pertaining to the ear or to hearing; aural. **2.** perceived by or addressed to the ear; made in private: *an auricular confession.* **3.** dependent on hearing; understood or known by hearing: *auricular evidence.* **4.** resembling an ear. —*n.* **5.** Usu., **auriculars.** the feathers that cover a bird's ear.

au·rif·er·ous (ô rif′ər əs), *adj.* yielding or containing gold.

Au·ri·ga (ô rī′gə), *n., gen.* **-gae** (-jē). the Charioteer, a northern constellation between Perseus and Gemini, containing the bright star Capella.

Au·ro·ra (ə rôr′ə, ə rōr′ə), *n., pl.* **au·ro·ras, au·ro·rae** (ə rôr′ē, ə rōr′ē). **1.** the Roman goddess of the dawn. **2.** (*l.c.*) dawn. **3.** (*l.c.*) a radiant emission from the upper atmosphere that occurs as luminous streamers, bands, etc., caused when air molecules are excited by charged particles from the solar wind. **4.** a city in central Colorado, near Denver. 250,717. **5.** a city in NE Illinois. 112,313. —**au·ro′ral,** *adj.*

auro′ra aus·tra′lis (ô strā′lis), *n.* the aurora of the Southern Hemisphere. Also called **southern lights.**

auro′ra bo·re·al′is (bôr′ē al′is, -ā′lis, bōr′-), *n.* the aurora of the Northern Hemisphere. Also called **northern lights, auro′ra polar′is.**

Ausch·witz (oush′vits), *n.* a town in SW Poland: site of Nazi death camp during World War II. 39,600. Polish, **Oswięcim.**

aus·cul·ta·tion (ô′skəl tā′shən), *n.* the act of listening, either directly or through a stethoscope or other instrument, to sounds within the body as a method of diagnosis.

aus·land·er (ous′lan′dər, ô′slan′-), *n.* foreigner; alien; outlander.

aus·pice (ô′spis), *n., pl.* **aus·pic·es** (ô′spə siz). **1.** Usu., **auspices.** patronage; support; sponsorship: *under the auspices of the government.* **2.** Often, **auspices.** a favorable sign or propitious circumstance. **3.** a divination or prognostication.

aus·pi·cious (ô spish′əs), *adj.* **1.** promising success; propitious; opportune; favorable: *an auspicious occasion.* **2.** favored by fortune; prosperous; fortunate. —**aus·pi′cious·ly,** *adv.*

Aus·ten (ô′stən), *n.* **Jane,** 1775–1817, English novelist.

aus·tere (ô stēr′), *adj.* **1.** severe in manner or appearance; strict; forbidding. **2.** rigorously self-disciplined and severely moral; ascetic; abstinent. **3.** without excess, luxury, or ease: *an austere life.* **4.** without ornament or adornment; severely simple: *austere writing.* **5.** grave; sober; solemn. **6.** lacking softness; hard; rough. —**aus·tere′ly,** *adv.*

aus·ter·i·ty (ô ster′i tē), *n., pl.* **-ties. 1.** austere quality; severity of manner, life, etc.; sternness. **2.** Usu., **austerities.** ascetic practices. **3.** strict economy.

Aus·tin (ô′stən), *n.* **1. Alfred,** 1835–1913, English poet. **2. Stephen Fuller,** 1793–1836, American colonizer in Texas. **3.** AUGUSTINE, Saint (def. 2). **4.** the capital of Texas, in the central part, on the Colorado River. 514,013.

aus·tral¹ (ô′strəl), *adj.* **1.** southern. **2.** (*cap.*) Australian.

aus·tral² (ous träl′), *n., pl.* **-tra·les** (-trä′les). the basic monetary unit of Argentina.

Aus·tral·ia (ô strāl′yə), *n.* **1.** a continent SE of Asia, between the Indian and Pacific oceans. 15,763,000; 2,948,366 sq. mi. (7,636,270 sq. km). **2. Commonwealth of,** a nation consisting of the continent of Australia and the island of Tasmania: a member of the Commonwealth of Nations. 18,438,824; 2,974,581 sq. mi. (7,704,165 sq. km). *Cap.:* Canberra. —**Aus·tral′ian,** *adj., n.*

Aus·tra·lo·pith·e·cus (ô strā′lō pith′i kəs, -pə thē′kəs, ô′strə-), *n.* a genus of small-brained, large-toothed bipedal hominids that lived in Africa between one and four million years ago.

Aus·tri·a (ô′strē ə), *n.* a republic in central Europe. 8,054,078; 32,381 sq. mi. (83,865 sq. km). *Cap.:* Vienna. German, **Österreich.** —**Aus′tri·an,** *adj., n.*

Aus′tria-Hun′gary, *n.* a former monarchy (1867–1918) in central Europe that included what is now Austria, Hungary, the Czech Republic, Slovakia, and parts of Romania, Poland, Yugoslavia, and Italy. —**Aus′tro-Hungar′ian,** *adj., n.*

aut-, var. of AUTO-¹ before a vowel: *autacoid.*

au·tar·chy (ô′tär kē), *n., pl.* **-chies. 1.** absolute sovereignty. **2.** an autocratic government. **3.** AUTARKY.

au·tar·ky or **au·tar·chy** (ô′tär kē), *n., pl.* **-kies. 1.** the condition of self-sufficiency, esp. economic, as applied to a nation. **2.** a national policy of economic independence.

au·then·tic (ô then′tik), *adj.* **1.** not false or copied; genuine; real. **2.** having an origin supported by unquestionable evidence. **3.** entitled to acceptance or belief because of agreement with known facts or experience; reliable; trustworthy: *an authentic report.* —**au·then′ti·cal·ly,** *adv.* —**au·then·tic·i·ty** (ô then tis′i tē, ô′then-), *n.*

au·then·ti·cate (ô then′ti kāt′), *v.t.,* **-cat·ed, -cat·ing. 1.** to establish as genuine. **2.** to establish conclusively the authorship or origin of: *to authenticate a painting.* **3.** to make authoritative or valid. —**au·then′ti·ca′tion,** *n.*

au·thor (ô′thər), *n.* **1.** the composer of a literary work; writer. **2.** the writer of a software program. **3.** the literature produced by a writer: *to edit an author.* **4.** the maker of anything; creator; originator: *the author of a new tax plan.* —*v.t.* **5.** to be the author of: *to author a novel.* —**au·tho·ri·al** (ô thôr′ē əl, ô thōr′-), *adj.*

au·thor·i·tar·i·an (ə thôr′i târ′ē ən, ə thor′-), *adj.* **1.** of, favoring, or requiring complete obedience to authority: *an authoritarian military code.* **2.** pertaining to or being a government in which authority is centered in one person or in a small group not constitutionally accountable to the people. **3.** exercising control over the will of others: *an authoritarian parent.* —*n.* **4.** a person who favors or acts according to authoritarian principles. —**au·thor′i·tar′i·an·ism,** *n.*

au·thor·i·ta·tive (ə thôr′i tā′tiv, ə thor′-), *adj.* **1.** having the sanction or weight of authority; official. **2.** substantiated or supported by evidence and accepted by most authorities in a field: *the authoritative edition.* **3.** having an air of or exercising authority; peremptory; dictatorial. —**au·thor′i·ta′tive·ly,** *adv.*

au·thor·i·ty (ə thôr′i tē, ə thor′-), *n., pl.* **-ties. 1.** the power to determine, adjudicate, or otherwise settle issues; the right to control, command, or determine. **2.** a power or right delegated or given; authorization. **3.** a person or body of persons in whom authority is vested, as a governmental agency. **4.** Usu., **authorities.** persons having the legal power to make and enforce the law; government. **5.** an accepted source of information, advice, or substantiation. **6.** a quotation or citation from such a source. **7.** an expert on a subject. **8.** persuasive force: *to speak with authority.* **9.** a statute, court rule, or judicial decision that establishes a rule or principle of law. **10.** the right to respect or acceptance of one's word, command, thought, etc.; commanding influence. **11.** a warrant for action; justification. **12.** testimony; witness.

au·thor·ize (ô′thər rīz′), *v.t.,* **-ized, -iz·ing. 1.** to give authority or official power to; empower: *an employee authorized to sign purchase orders.* **2.** to give authority or formal permission for; sanction: *to authorize spending on defense.* **3.** to establish by authority or usage. **4.** to afford a ground for; warrant; justify. —**au′thor·i·za′tion,** *n.*

Au′thorized Ver′sion, *n.* KING JAMES VERSION.

au·thor·ship (ô′thər ship′), *n.* **1.** origin, esp. with reference to an author, creator, or producer of a work: *to establish the authorship of a medieval poem.* **2.** the occupation or career of writing.

au·tism (ô′tiz əm), *n.* a pervasive developmental disorder characterized by impaired communication, extreme self-absorption, and detachment from reality. —**au′tist,** *n.* —**au·tis′tic,** *adj.*

au·to (ô′tō), *n., pl.* **-tos.** an automobile.

auto-, a combining form meaning "self," "same," "spontaneous": *autograph.* Also, *esp. before a vowel,* **aut-.**

au·to·bahn (ô′tō bän′, ou′tō-), *n.* (in Germany and Austria) a superhighway; expressway.

au·to·bi·og·ra·phy (ô′tə bī og′rə fē, -bē-, ô′tō-), *n., pl.* **-phies.** a history of a person's life written or told by that person. —**au′to·bi·og′ra·pher,** *n.* —**au·to·bi·o·graph·i·cal** (ô′tə bī′ə graf′i kəl), *adj.*

au·to·ca·tal·y·sis (ô′tō kə tal′ə sis), *n., pl.* **-ses** (-sēz′). catalysis caused by a catalytic agent formed during a chemical reaction. —**au′to·cat′a·lyt′ic** (-kat′l it′ik), *adj.*

au·to·ceph·a·lous (ô′tə sef′ə ləs), *adj.* **1.** (of an Eastern church) having its own head bishop, though in communion with other Orthodox churches. **2.** (of an Eastern bishop) subordinate to no superior authority.

au·toch·thon (ô tok′thən), *n., pl.* **-thons, -tho·nes** (-thə nēz′). **1.** an aboriginal inhabitant. **2.** one of the indigenous animals or plants of a region.

au·toch·tho·nous (ô tok′thə nəs) also **au·toch·tho·nal,** *adj.* **1.** aboriginal; indigenous. **2.** native to or formed in the place where found. **3.** *Pathol.* located in a part of the body in which it originated, as a cancer or infection. **4.** of or pertaining to ideas that originate independently of normal modes of thought or influences, as an obsession or schizophrenic construct.

au·to·clave (ô′tə klāv′), *n., v.,* **-claved, -clav·ing.** —*n.* **1.** a heavy vessel for sterilizing or cooking by means of steam under pressure. **2.** a heavy vessel for conducting chemical reactions under high pressure. —*v.t.* **3.** to place in an autoclave.

au·toc·ra·cy (ô tok′rə sē), *n., pl.* **-cies. 1.** government in which one person has unlimited authority; the government of an autocrat. **2.** a nation, state, or community ruled by an autocrat. **3.** the unlimited power or authority of an autocrat.

au·to·crat (ô′tə krat′), *n.* **1.** an absolute ruler who holds unlimited powers as by inherent right. **2.** a person invested with or claiming to exercise absolute authority. **3.** a person who behaves in an authoritarian or domineering manner. —**au′to·crat′ic, au′to·crat′i·cal,** *adj.* —**au′to·crat′i·cal·ly,** *adv.*

au·to-da-fé (ô′tō də fā′), *n., pl.* **au·tos-da-fé. 1.** the public declaration and execution of a sentence imposed by the Spanish Inquisition, esp. the burning of heretics at the stake. **2.** the burning of a heretic.

au·to·di·dact (ô′tō dī′dakt, -dī dakt′), *n.* a person who has learned a subject without a teacher or formal education; self-taught person. —**au′to·di·dac′tic,** *adj.*

au·to·fo·cus (ô′tō fō′kəs), *adj.* **1.** having the ability to focus automatically: *an autofocus camera.* —*n.* **2.** the ability of a camera or lens to focus automatically.

au·to·graph (ô′tə graf′, -gräf′), *n.* **1.** a person's signature, esp. a signature of a famous person for keeping as a memento. **2.** something written in a person's own hand, as a manuscript or letter. —*v.t.* **3.** to write one's name on or in; sign, esp. as a memento. **4.** to write with one's own hand.

au·to·im·mune (ô′tō i myōōn′), *adj.* of or pertaining to the immune response of an organism against any of its own components.

autoimmune′ disease′, *n.* a disease resulting from a disordered immune reaction in which antibodies are produced that damage components of one's own body.

au·to·mate (ô′tə māt′), *v.,* **-mat·ed, -mat·ing.** —*v.t.* **1.** to apply the principles of automation to (a mechanical process, industry, office, etc.). **2.** to operate or control by automation. **3.** to displace or make obsolete by automation. —*v.i.* **4.** to install automatic procedures, as for manufacturing or servicing; undergo automation.

au·to·mat·ic (ô′tə mat′ik), *adj.* **1.** having the capability of starting, moving, etc., independently. **2.** occurring independently of volition, as certain muscular actions; involuntary; reflex. **3.** done unconsciously or from force of habit. **4.** occurring spontaneously. **5.** (of a firearm) utilizing the recoil or part of the force of the explosive to eject the spent cartridge shell, introduce a new cartridge, cock the arm, and fire it repeatedly. —*n.* **6.** a machine or device that operates automatically. **7.** an automatic pistol or rifle. **8.** an automobile equipped with automatic

transmission. —*Idiom.* **9. on automatic,** being operated or controlled by or as if by an automatic device. —**au′to·mat′i·cal·ly,** *adv.*

au′tomat′ic pi′lot, *n.* an electronic control system, as on an aircraft, spacecraft, or ship, that automatically maintains a preset heading and attitude. Also called **au·to·pi·lot** (ô′tō pī′lət).

automat′ic transmis′sion, *n.* an automotive transmission requiring either very little or no manual shifting of gears.

au·to·ma·tion (ô′tə mā′shən), *n.* **1.** the technique, method, or system of operating or controlling a process by highly automatic means, as by electronic devices, reducing human intervention to a minimum. **2.** the act or process of automating or making automatic. **3.** the state of being automated.

au·tom·a·tism (ô tom′ə tiz′əm), *n.* **1.** the action or condition of being automatic; mechanical or involuntary action. **2.** the theory that the activities of humans and animals are controlled by physical or physiological causes rather than by consciousness. **3.** the involuntary functioning of an organic process, esp. muscular, without apparent neural stimulation. **4.** *Psychol.* the performance of an act or actions without the performer's awareness or conscious volition. **5.** an artistic technique in which the impulses of the unconscious mind are freed to guide the hand in producing images.

au·tom·a·ton (ô tom′ə ton′, -tn), *n., pl.* **-tons, -ta** (-tə). **1.** a mechanical figure or contrivance constructed to act as if by its own motive power; robot. **2.** a person or animal that acts in a monotonous, routine manner, without active intelligence. **3.** a mechanical device, operated electronically, that functions automatically, without continuous input from an operator. **4.** anything capable of acting automatically or without an external motive force.

au·to·mo·bile (ô′tə mə bēl′, ô′tə mə bēl′), *n.* a passenger vehicle designed for operation on ordinary roads and typically having four wheels and a gasoline or diesel internal-combustion engine.

au·to·mo·tive (ô′tə mō′tiv, ô′tə mō′tiv), *adj.* **1.** of or pertaining to automobiles or other motor vehicles: *automotive parts.* **2.** propelled by a self-contained motor, engine, or the like. —*n.* **3.** an industry, store department, etc., specializing in appliances and parts for automobiles and other motor vehicles.

au·to·nom·ic (ô′tə nom′ik), *adj.* **1.** autonomous. **2.** of, pertaining to, or controlled by the autonomic nervous system. **3.** *Biol.* internally caused; spontaneous. —**au′to·nom′i·cal·ly,** *adv.*

au′tonom′ic nerv′ous sys′tem, *n.* the system of nerves and ganglia that innervates the blood vessels, heart, smooth muscles, viscera, and glands and controls their involuntary functions and consists of sympathetic and parasympathetic portions.

au·ton·o·mous (ô ton′ə məs), *adj.* **1.** self-governing; independent. **2.** of or pertaining to a self-governing or independent state, community, organization, etc. **3.** *Biol.* **a.** existing and functioning as an independent organism. **b.** spontaneous.

au·ton·o·my (ô ton′ə mē), *n., pl.* **-mies. 1.** independence or freedom, as of the will or one's actions. **2.** the condition of being autonomous; self-government or the right of self-government; independence. **3.** a self-governing community.

au·top·sy (ô′top sē, ô′təp-), *n., pl.* **-sies,** *v.,* **-sied, -sy·ing.** —*n.* **1.** the inspection and dissection of a body after death, as for determination of the cause of death; postmortem examination. **2.** a critical analysis of something after it has taken place or been completed. —*v.t.* **3.** to perform an autopsy on.

au·to·sug·ges·tion (ô′tō səg jes′chən, -sə-), *n.* suggestion arising from oneself, as the repetition of verbal messages as a means of changing behavior.

au·tot·o·my (ô tot′ə mē), *n., pl.* **-mies.** the breaking off of a damaged or trapped body appendage, as the tail of a lizard or the claw of a crab. —**au·to·tom·ic** (ô′tə tom′ik), **au·tot′o·mous,** *adj.*

au·to·tox·in (ô′tō tok′sin), *n.* a poisonous chemical formed within the body and acting against it. —**au′to·tox′ic,** *adj.*

Au·try (ô′trē), *n.* **Gene,** born 1907, U.S. actor and singer.

au·tumn (ô′təm), *n.* **1.** the season between summer and winter; fall: in the Northern Hemisphere, from the September equinox to the December solstice; in the Southern Hemisphere, from the March equinox to the June solstice. **2.** a time of full maturity, esp. the late stages of maturity or the early stages of decline. —**au·tum·nal** (ô tum′nl), *adj.*

autum′nal e′quinox, *n.* **1.** See under EQUINOX (def. 1). **2.** Also called **autum′nal point′.** the position of the sun at the time of the autumnal equinox.

au′tumn cro′cus, *n.* any of several bulbous plants of the genus *Colchicum,* of the lily family, esp. *C. autumnale,* bearing showy crocuslike flowers in autumn. Also called **meadow saffron.**

aux·il·ia·ry (ôg zil′yə rē, -zil′ə-), *adj., n., pl.* **-ries.** —*adj.* **1.** additional; supplementary; reserve: *an auxiliary police force.* **2.** used as a substitute or reserve in case of need: *an auxiliary power system.* **3.** subsidiary; secondary. **4.** (of a boat) having an engine that can be used to supplement the sails: *an auxiliary yawl.* **5.** giving support; serving as an aid. —*n.* **6.** a person or thing that gives aid; helper. **7.** a subsidiary organization allied with a main body of restricted membership: *the women's auxiliary.* **8.** AUXILIARY VERB. **9. auxiliaries,** foreign troops in the service of a nation at war. **10.** a naval vessel, as a supply ship, designed for other than combat purposes.

auxil′iary lan′guage, *n.* any language used for intercommunication by speakers of various other languages.

auxil′iary verb′, *n.* a verb used in construction with certain forms of other verbs, as infinitives or participles, to express distinctions of tense, aspect, mood, etc., as *did* in *Did you go?,* have in *We have spoken,* or *can* in *They can see.* Also called **helping verb.**

aux•in (ôk′sin), *n.* any of a class of substances that in minute amounts regulate or modify the growth of plants, esp. root formation, bud growth, and fruit and leaf drop. —**aux•in′ic,** *adj.*

Av (äv, ôv) also **Ab,** *n.* the eleventh month of the Jewish calendar.

AV, 1. arteriovenous. **2.** atrioventricular. **3.** audiovisual. **4.** Authorized Version (of the Bible).

av., 1. avenue. **2.** average. **3.** avoirdupois (weight).

A/V, 1. Also, **a.v.** ad valorem. **2.** audiovisual.

a•vail (ə vāl′), *v.t.* **1.** to be of use, advantage, or value to; profit: *All our efforts availed us little.* —*v.i.* **2.** to be of use; have force or efficacy; serve; help: *Nothing you do will avail.* **3.** to be of value or profit. —*n.* **4.** effective use in the achievement of a goal or objective; advantage; use: *His help was of no avail.* —**Idiom. 5. avail oneself of,** to use to one's advantage; make use of.

a•vail•a•ble (ə vā′lə bəl), *adj.* **1.** suitable or ready for use; at hand: *I used whatever tools were available.* **2.** readily obtainable; accessible: *no information available.* **3.** free or ready to be seen, spoken to, employed, etc.: *not available for comment.* **4.** having sufficient power or efficacy; valid. —**a•vail′a•bil′i•ty,** *n.*

av•a•lanche (av′ə lanch′, -länch′), *n., v.,* **-lanched, -lanch•ing.** —*n.* **1.** a large mass of snow, ice, etc., detached from a mountain slope and sliding suddenly downward. **2.** anything like an avalanche in suddenness and overwhelming quantity: *an avalanche of fan mail.* **3.** a cumulative ionization process in which the ions and electrons of one generation undergo collisions that produce a greater number of ions and electrons in succeeding generations. —*v.i.* **4.** to come down in or like an avalanche. —*v.t.* **5.** to overwhelm with an extremely large amount of anything; swamp.

a•vant-garde (ə vänt′gärd′, ə vant′-, av′änt-, ä′vänt-; *Fr.* ä vän gard′), *n.* **1.** the advance group in a field, esp. in the arts, whose works are unorthodox and experimental. —*adj.* **2.** characteristic of or belonging to the avant-garde.

av•a•rice (av′ər is), *n.* insatiable greed for riches; inordinate, miserly desire to gain and hoard wealth: one of the seven deadly sins. [< Latin *avāritia* < *avārus* greedy]

av•a•ri•cious (av′ə rish′əs), *adj.* characterized by avarice; greedy; covetous. —**av′a•ri′cious•ly,** *adv.* —**av′a•ri′cious•ness,** *n.*

av•a•tar (av′ə tär′, av′ə tär′), *n.* **1.** an incarnation of a Hindu god. **2.** an embodiment or personification, as of a principle or view of life.

avdp., avoirdupois (weight).

a•ve (ä′vā, ä′vē), *interj.* **1.** hail; welcome. **2.** farewell; good-bye. —*n.* **3.** the salutation "ave." **4.** (*cap.*) AVE MARIA.

A•ve Ma•ri•a (ä′vā mə rē′ə), *n.* a Roman Catholic prayer based on the salutation of the angel Gabriel to the Virgin Mary and the words of Elizabeth to her, meaning "Hail Mary." Also called **Hail Mary.**

a•venge (ə venj′), *v.t.,* **a•venged, a•veng•ing. 1.** to take vengeance or exact satisfaction for: *to avenge a murder.* **2.** to take vengeance on behalf of: *He avenged his brother.*

aveng′er of blood′, *n.* one who was entitled to take vengeance on a person who had slain one of his family. Josh. 20:5.

av•ens (av′inz), *n., pl.* **-ens.** any of various plants of the genus *Geum,* of the rose family, having yellow, white, or red flowers.

a•ven•tu•rine (ə ven′chə rēn′, -chər in) also **a•ven•tu•rin** (-chər in), *n.* **1.** an opaque brown glass containing fine, gold-colored particles. **2.** any of several varieties of minerals, esp. quartz or feldspar, spangled with bright particles of mica, hematite, or other minerals.

av•e•nue (av′ə nyŏŏ′, -nŏŏ′), *n.* **1.** a wide street or main thoroughfare. **2.** a means of access or attainment: *avenues of escape.* **3.** a way or means of entering into or approaching a place: *the avenues to India.* **4.** a suburban residential street.

a•ver (ə vûr′), *v.t.,* **a•verred, a•ver•ring. 1.** to assert or affirm with confidence; declare in a positive manner. **2.** *Law.* to allege as a fact.

av•er•age (av′ər ij, av′rij), *n., adj., v.,* **-aged, -ag•ing.** —*n.* **1. a.** a quantity, rating, or the like that represents or approximates an arithmetic mean: *a golf average in the 90's.* Compare GRADE POINT AVERAGE. **b.** ARITHMETIC MEAN. **c.** a number or value intermediate to a set of numbers or values. **2.** a typical or usual amount, rate, degree, level, etc.; norm. —*adj.* **3.** of, pertaining to, or forming an average; estimated by average: *the average rainfall.* **4.** typical; common; ordinary: *the average person.* —*v.t.* **5.** to find an average value for (a variable quantity); reduce to a mean. **6.** (of a variable quantity) to have as an arithmetic mean: *Wheat averages 56 pounds to a bushel.* **7.** to do or have on the average: *to average seven hours of sleep a night.* —*v.i.* **8.** to have or show an average. **9. average down,** to purchase more of a security or commodity at a lower price to reduce the average cost of one's holdings. **10. average out, a.** to come out of a security or commodity transaction with a profit or without a loss. **b.** to reach or show an average: *My taxes average out to a third of my income.* **11. average up,** to purchase more of a security or commodity at a higher price in anticipation of a further rise in prices. —**Idiom. 12. on the** or **an average,** usually; typically.

a•verse (ə vûrs′), *adj.* having a strong feeling of opposition, antipathy, or repugnance; opposed. —**a•verse′ly,** *adv.*

a•ver•sion (ə vûr′zhən, -shən), *n.* **1.** a strong feeling of dislike, repug-

nance, or antipathy toward something and a desire to avoid it: *an aversion to snakes.* **2.** a cause or object of such a feeling.

a•ver•sive (ə vûr′siv, -ziv), *adj.* **1.** of or pertaining to aversion. **2.** of or pertaining to aversive conditioning. —*n.* **3.** a reprimand, punishment, or agent used in aversive conditioning. —**a•ver′sive•ly,** *adv.*

aver′sive condi′tioning, *n.* conditioning by linking an unpleasant or noxious stimulus with the performance of undesirable behavior.

a•vert (ə vûrt′), *v.t.* **1.** to turn away or aside: *to avert one's eyes.* **2.** to ward off; prevent: *to avert an accident.* —**a•vert′i•ble, a•vert′a•ble,** *adj.*

avg., average.

avi-, a combining form meaning "bird": *aviculture.*

a•vi•an (ā′vē ən), *adj.* of or pertaining to birds.

a•vi•ar•y (ā′vē er′ē), *n., pl.* **-ar•ies.** a large cage or a house or enclosure in which birds are kept. —**a′vi•a•rist** (-arist), *n.*

a•vi•a•tion (ā′vē ā′shən, av′ē-), *n.* **1.** the design, development, production, operation, or use of aircraft, esp. heavier-than-air aircraft. **2.** military aircraft. [< French, = Latin *avi(s)* bird + *-ation*] —**a′vi•at′ic** (-at′ik), *adj.*

a•vi•a•tor (ā′vē ā′tər, av′ē-), *n.* a pilot of an airplane or other heavier-than-air aircraft.

Av•i•cen•na (av′ə sen′ə), *n.* A.D. 980–1037, Islamic physician and philosopher, born in Persia.

a•vi•cul•ture (ā′vi kul′chər), *n.* the rearing or keeping of birds.

av•id (av′id), *adj.* **1.** enthusiastic; ardent; keen: *an avid moviegoer.* **2.** keenly desirous; eager; greedy (often fol. by *for* or *of*). —**av′id•ly,** *adv.* —**a•vid•i•ty** (ə vid′i tē), *n.*

a•vi•on•ics (ā′vē on′iks, av′ē-), *n.* (*used with a sing. v.*) the science and technology of the development and use of electrical and electronic devices in aviation. —**a′vi•on′ic,** *adj.*

A•viv or **A•bib** (ä vēv′), *n.* the seventh month of the Jewish year, equivalent to Nisan of the modern Jewish calendar. Ex. 34:18.

av•o•ca•do (av′ə kä′dō, ä′və-), *n., pl.* **-dos. 1.** a large, usu. pear-shaped fruit having green to blackish skin, a single large seed, and soft, light green pulp, borne by the tropical American tree, *Persea americana,* of the laurel family; often eaten raw. **2.** the tree itself.

av•o•ca•tion (av′ə kā′shən), *n.* **1.** something a person does in addition to a principal occupation; hobby. **2.** a person's regular occupation or calling; vocation. —**av′o•ca′tion•al,** *adj.*

av•o•cet (av′ə set′), *n.* any of several long-legged shorebirds of the genus *Recurvirostra,* of both the Old and New Worlds, having a long, slender, upward-curving bill.

A′voga′dro's law′, *n.* the principle that equal volumes of all gases at the same temperature and pressure contain the same number of molecules.

A′voga′dro's num′ber, *n.* the constant, 6.02×10^{23}, representing the number of atoms in a gram atom or the number of molecules in a gram molecule. *Symbol:* N Also called **A′voga′dro con′stant.**

a•void (ə void′), *v.t.* **1.** to keep away from; keep clear of; shun: *to avoid a person; to avoid danger.* **2.** to prevent from happening: *to avoid falling.* **3.** *Law.* to make void or of no effect; invalidate; annul.

av•oir•du•pois (av′ər də poiz′), *n.* **1.** AVOIRDUPOIS WEIGHT. **2.** *Informal.* bodily weight; heaviness: *excess avoirdupois.*

avoirdupois′ weight′, *n.* the system of weights, based on the pound of 16 ounces, used in Great Britain and the U.S. for goods other than gems, precious metals, and drugs.

A•von (ā′vən, av′ən), *n.* **1.** a river in central England, flowing SE past Stratford-on-Avon to the Severn. 96 mi. (155 km) long. **2.** a river in S England, flowing W to the mouth of the Severn. ab. 75 mi. (120 km) long. **3.** a river in S England, flowing S to the English Channel. ab. 60 mi. (100 km) long.

a•vow (ə vou′), *v.t.* to declare frankly or openly; acknowledge; admit: *He avowed himself an opponent of all alliances.* —**a•vow′a•ble,** *adj.*

a•vow•al (ə vou′əl), *n.* an open statement of affirmation; frank acknowledgment or admission.

a•vul•sion (ə vul′shən), *n.* **1.** a tearing away. **2.** *Law.* the sudden removal of soil by change in a river's course or by a flood, from the land of one owner to that of another. **3.** a part torn off.

a•vun•cu•lar (ə vung′kyə lər), *adj.* of, pertaining to, or characteristic of an uncle: *avuncular affection.* —**a•vun′cu•lar•ly,** *adv.*

a.w., 1. actual weight. **2.** (in shipping) all water. **3.** atomic weight.

AWACS (ā′waks), *n.* an aircraft equipped with radar to track low-flying enemy aircraft and missiles and coordinate defensive measures.

a•wait (ə wāt′), *v.t.* **1.** to wait for; expect; look for: *still awaiting an answer.* **2.** to be in store for: *A pleasant surprise awaited her.* —*v.i.* **3.** to wait, as in expectation.

a•wake (ə wāk′), *v.,* **a•woke** or **a•waked, a•woke** or **a•waked** or **a•wo•ken, a•wak•ing,** *adj.* —*v.t.* **1.** to rouse from sleep. **2.** to make active or alert; rouse: *It awoke his flagging interest.* —*v.i.* **3.** to emerge from sleep. **4.** to become active or alert. **5.** to become conscious of something: *finally awoke to the facts.* —*adj.* **6.** waking; not sleeping. **7.** vigilant; alert: *not awake to the danger.*

a•wak•en (ə wā′kən), *v.t., v.i.* to awake; waken.

a•wak•en•ing (ə wā′kə ning), *adj.* **1.** rousing; quickening: *an awakening interest.* —*n.* **2.** the act of awaking from sleep. **3.** a revival of interest or attention. **4.** a recognition, realization, or coming into awareness of something: *a rude awakening to the facts.* **5.** a renewal of interest in religion, esp. in a community; revival.

a•ward (ə wôrd′), *v.t.* **1.** to give as due or merited; assign or bestow: *to award prizes.* **2.** to bestow or assign by judicial decree: *The plaintiff was awarded damages of $100,000.* —*n.* **3.** something awarded, as a payment or medal. **4. a.** a judicial decision. **b.** the decision of arbitrators on a matter submitted to them. —**a•ward′a•ble,** *adj.*

a•ware (ə wâr′), *adj.* **1.** having knowledge or realization; cognizant. **2.** informed; alert; knowledgeable: *politically aware.* —**a•ware′ness,** *n.*

a•wash (ə wosh′, ə wôsh′), *adj., adv.* **1.** just level with the surface of the water, so that waves break over the top. **2.** covered with water. **3.** tossed about by the waves. **4.** covered, filled, or crowded: *a garden awash in colors.*

a•way (ə wā′), *adv.* **1.** from this or that place; off: *to go away.* **2.** aside; to another place; in another direction: *to turn away customers.* **3.** far; apart: *away back; away from the subject.* **4.** out of one's possession or use: *to give money away.* **5.** in or into a place for storage or safekeeping: *filed away.* **6.** out of existence or notice; into extinction: *to fade away; to idle away the morning.* **7.** so as to be removed or separated: *to break away.* **8.** incessantly or relentlessly; repeatedly: *He kept hammering away.* **9.** without hesitation: *Fire away.* —*adj.* **10.** absent; gone: *to be away from home.* **11.** distant in place or time: *six miles away; Christmas is two months away.* **12.** immediately off and on one's way. **13.** played in a ballpark, arena, etc., other than a team's own, usu. at the ballpark or arena of the opponent: *away games.*

awe (ô), *n., v.,* **awed, aw•ing.** —*n.* **1.** an overwhelming feeling of reverence, admiration, fear, or wonder produced by that which is grand, sublime, extremely powerful, etc. —*v.t.* **2.** to inspire or fill with awe. **3.** to influence by awe: *awed them into obedience.*

awe•some (ô′səm), *adj.* **1.** inspiring awe: *an awesome sight.* **2.** showing or characterized by awe. **3.** *Slang.* very impressive.

awe•struck (ô′struk′) also **awe•strick•en** (ô′strik′ən), *adj.* filled with awe.

aw•ful (ô′fəl), *adj.* **1.** extremely bad; unpleasant; disagreeable. **2.** inspiring fear; dreadful; terrible: *an awful noise.* **3.** solemnly impressive; inspiring awe: *the awful majesty of the peaks.* **4.** extremely dangerous; risky, injurious, etc.: *an awful fall; to take an awful chance.* **5.** *Informal.* very great: *an awful lot of money.* **6.** full of awe; reverential.

aw•ful•ly (ô′fə lē, ô′flē), *adv.* **1.** very; extremely: *awfully excited.* **2.** in a manner provoking censure, disapproval, or the like; objectionably: *to behave awfully.*

a•while (ə hwīl′, ə wīl′), *adv.* for a short time or period: *Stay awhile.*

awk•ward (ôk′wərd), *adj.* **1.** lacking skill or dexterity; clumsy; inept. **2.** lacking grace or ease, as in movement or posture: *an awkward gesture.* **3.** lacking social graces or manners. **4.** ill-adapted for ease of use or handling; unwieldy: *an awkward tool.* **5.** requiring caution; somewhat hazardous; dangerous: *an awkward turn in the road.* **6.** hard to deal with; difficult; requiring skill or tact: *an awkward situation.* **7.** embarrassing or inconvenient; caused by lack of social grace: *an awkward moment.* —**awk′ward•ly,** *adv.* —**awk′ward•ness,** *n.*

awl (ôl), *n.* a pointed instrument for piercing small holes in leather, wood, etc.

awn (ôn), *n.* **1.** a bristlelike appendage of a plant, esp. on the glumes of grasses. **2.** any similar bristle. —**awned,** *adj.* —**awn′less,** *adj.*

awn•ing (ô′ning), *n.* a rooflike shelter of canvas or other material extending over a doorway, window, deck, etc., to provide protection from the sun or rain. —**awn′inged,** *adj.*

a•woke (ə wōk′), *v.* a pt. and pp. of AWAKE.

a•wo•ken (ə wō′kən), *v.* a pp. of AWAKE.

AWOL (*pronounced as initials or* ā′wôl, ā′wol), *adj., adv.* **1.** away from military duties without permission. —*n.* **2.** a person in the military who is absent from duty without leave.

a•wry (ə rī′), *adv., adj.* **1.** with a turn or twist to one side. **2.** away from the expected or proper direction; amiss: *Our plans went awry.*

ax or **axe** (aks), *n., pl.* **ax•es** (ak′siz), *v.,* **axed, ax•ing.** —*n.* **1.** a tool with a blade on a handle or helve, used for hewing, cleaving, chopping, etc. **2.** *Slang.* a jazz instrument, esp. a guitar or saxophone. **3. the ax, a.** a sudden, peremptory dismissal, as from a job. **b.** a usu. summary removal or curtailment. —*v.t.* **4.** to shape or trim with an ax. **5.** to chop, split, or break open with an ax. **6.** to dismiss, restrict, or remove, esp. brutally or summarily: *Congress axed the budget.* —**Idiom.** **7. have an ax to grind,** to have a particular personal or selfish motive.

ax•el (ak′səl), *n.* a figure skating jump in which the skater leaps from the front outer edge of one skate to make 1½ rotations of the body and lands on the back outer edge of the other skate.

ax•i•al (ak′sē əl), *adj.* **1.** of, pertaining to, characterized by, or forming an axis. **2.** situated in or on an axis. —**ax′i•al′i•ty,** *n.*

ax′ial skel′eton, *n.* the skeleton of the head and trunk.

ax•il (ak′sil), *n.* the angle between the upper side of a leaf or stem and the supporting stem or branch.

ax•il•la (ak sil′ə), *n., pl.* **ax•il•lae** (ak sil′ē). **1.** the armpit. **2.** the corresponding region under the wing of a bird.

ax•il•lar (ak′sə lər), *adj.* **1.** of or pertaining to an axilla. —*n.* **2.** an axillary feather.

ax•il•lar•y (ak′sə ler′ē), *adj., n., pl.* **-lar•ies.** —*adj.* **1.** of or pertaining to the axilla. **2.** pertaining to or growing from an axil. —*n.* **3.** AXILLAR.

ax′illary bud′, *n.* a bud that is borne at the axil of a leaf and is capable of developing into a branch shoot or flower cluster.

ax•i•ol•o•gy (ak′sē ol′ə jē), *n.* the branch of philosophy dealing with values, as those of ethics, aesthetics, or religion. —**ax′i•o•log′i•cal** (-ə loj′i kəl), *adj.* —**ax′i•ol′o•gist,** *n.*

ax•i•om (ak′sē əm), *n.* **1.** a self-evident truth that requires no proof. **2.** a universally accepted principle or rule. **3.** a proposition in logic or mathematics that is assumed without proof for the sake of studying the consequences that follow from it.

ax•i•o•mat•ic (ak′sē ə mat′ik) also **ax′i•o•mat′i•cal,** *adj.* **1.** pertaining to or of the nature of an axiom; self-evident. **2.** aphoristic.

ax•is (ak′sis), *n., pl.* **ax•es** (ak′sēz). **1.** the line about which a rotating body, such as the earth, turns. **2. a.** a central line that bisects a two-dimensional body or figure. **b.** a line about which a three-dimensional body or figure is symmetrical. **c.** any line used as a fixed reference for determining the position of a point or series of points, as the x- or y-axis in a system of Cartesian coordinates. **3.** *Anat.* **a.** a central or principal structure about which something turns or is arranged: *the skeletal axis.* **b.** the second cervical vertebra. **4.** *Bot.* **a.** the main support of a plant; the stem and root. **b.** the main support of an inflorescence. **5.** an imaginary line, in a given formal structure, about which a form, area, or plane is organized. **6. the Axis,** (in World War II) the nations that fought against the Allies: Germany, Italy, Japan, and others. **7.** an alliance of two or more nations to coordinate their foreign and military policies. **8.** a principal line of development, movement, etc.

ax•le (ak′səl), *n.* **1.** the pin, bar, shaft, or the like, on which or by means of which a wheel or pair of wheels rotates. **2.** the spindle at either end of an axletree. **3.** an axletree. —**ax′led,** *adj.*

ax•le•tree (ak′səl trē′), *n.* a bar, fixed crosswise under an animal-drawn vehicle, with a rounded spindle at each end upon which a wheel rotates.

ax•o•lotl (ak′sə lot′l), *n.* any of several salamanders of the genus *Ambystoma,* of Mexico and the western U.S., that remain in the larval stage as sexually mature adults.

ax•on (ak′son), *n.* the appendage of a neuron that transmits impulses away from the cell body. —**ax′on•al** (-sə nl, -son′l), *adj.*

a•ya•tol•lah (ä′yə tō′lə), *n.* **1.** a title for a Shi'ite cleric with advanced knowledge of Islamic law. **2.** any person in a position of great power or authority. [< Persian < Arabic *āyat allāh* sign of God]

aye or **ay** (ī), *adv.* **1.** yes. —*n.* **2.** an affirmative vote or voter.

AZ, Arizona.

a•zal•ea (ə zāl′yə), *n., pl.* **-eas.** any of numerous shrubs that constitute a group (Azalea) within the genus *Rhododendron,* of the heath family, with funnel-shaped flower clusters in a variety of colors.

a•zan (ä zän′), *n.* (in Islamic countries) the call to prayer proclaimed five times a day by the muezzin.

Az•a•ri•ah (az′ə rī′ə), *n.* Uzziah. II Kings 15:1–7.

A•za•zel (ə zā′zəl, az′ə zel′), *n.* **1.** the demon or place in the wilderness to which the scapegoat is released in an atonement ritual. Lev. 16:8, 10, 26. **2.** the scapegoat itself.

Az•er•bai•jan (az′ər bī jän′, ä′zər-), *n.* **1.** Also, **Az′er•bai•dzhan′.** Former official name, **Azerbaijan′ So′viet So′cialist Repub′lic.** a republic in Transcaucasia, N of Iran and W of the Caspian Sea: a former constituent republic of the U.S.S.R. 7,735,918; 33,430 sq. mi. (86,600 sq. km). *Cap.:* Baku. **2.** a region of NW Iran.

az•i•muth (az′ə məth), *n.* **1.** the arc of the horizon measured clockwise from the south point, in astronomy, or from the north point, in navigation, to the point where a vertical circle through a given heavenly body intersects the horizon. **2.** (in surveying) the angle of horizontal deviation, measured clockwise, of a bearing from a standard direction, as from north or south. —**az′i•muth′al** (-muth′əl), *adj.*

a•zon•al (ā zōn′l), *adj.* not divided into zones.

A•zo•tos (ə zō′tos), *n.* Greek name of ASHDOD. Acts 8:40.

Az•ra•el (az′rē əl, -rā-), *n.* (in Jewish and Islamic angelology) the angel who separates the soul from the body at the moment of death. Also called **Angel of Death, death angel.**

Az•tec (az′tek), *n.* **1.** a member of a Nahuatl-speaking ethnic group that ruled much of central and S Mexico prior to the Spanish conquest in 1521. **2.** any Nahuatl-speaking Indian of the Valley of Mexico in the period prior to and immediately following the Spanish conquest. —*adj.* **3.** of or pertaining to the Aztecs or the culture of central Mexico during the period of Aztec dominance. —**Az′tec•an,** *adj.*

az•ure (azh′ər), *n.* **1.** the blue of a clear or unclouded sky; a light, purplish shade of blue. **2.** the heraldic color blue. **3.** the clear, cloudless sky. —*adj.* **4.** of or having the color azure.

az•ur•ite (azh′ə rīt′), *n.* **1.** a blue mineral, a hydrous copper carbonate, $Cu_3(CO_3)_2(OH)_2$, an ore of copper. **2.** a gem of moderate value cut from this mineral.

az•y•gous (az′ə gəs, ā zī′-), *adj. Biol.* not being one of a pair; single.

B

B, b (bē), *n., pl.* **Bs** or **B's, bs** or **b's.** **1.** the second letter of the English alphabet, a consonant. **2.** any spoken sound represented by this letter. **3.** something shaped like a B. **4.** a written or printed representation of the letter *B* or *b.*

B, *Symbol.* **1.** the second in order or in a series. **2.** (*sometimes l.c.*) a grade or mark indicating that academic work, a product, etc., is good but not of the highest quality. **3.** a major blood group. See ABO SYSTEM. **4. a.** the seventh tone of the ascending C major scale. **b.** a tonality having B as the tonic. **5.** boron. **6.** magnetic induction. **7.** a designation for a motion picture made on a low budget.

B-, (in designations of aircraft) bomber: *B-29.*

B-1 (bē'wun'), *n., pl.* **B-1's.** a U.S. long-range bomber having sweptback wings.

ba (bä), *n.* in ancient Egypt, an aspect of the soul, represented as a human-headed bird.

Ba, *Chem. Symbol.* barium.

B.A., **1.** Bachelor of Arts. **2.** batting average. **3.** British Academy.

baa (ba, bä), *n.* **1.** the bleat of a sheep. —*v.i.* **2.** to utter such a bleat.

Ba·al (bā'əl, bāl), *n., pl.* **Ba·al·im** (bā'ə lim, bā'lim). **1.** any of numerous local ancient Semitic deities typifying the generative forces of nature. **2.** (*sometimes l.c.*) a false god. —**Ba'al·ish,** *adj.* —**Ba'al·ism,** *n.* —**Ba'al·ist, Ba'al·ite,** *n.*

Baal·bek (bäl'bek, bā'əl-, bāl'-), *n.* a town in E Lebanon: ruins of ancient city. 16,000. Ancient Greek name, **Heliopolis.**

Baal Shem Tov (bäl' shem' tôv'), *n.* (*Israel ben Eliezer*), c1700–60, Jewish religious leader in Poland: founder of the Hasidic movement.

Ba·a·sha (bā'ə shə), *n.* a wicked king of the northern kingdom of Israel. I Kings 15:16, 27–30; 16:5–7.

ba·ba (bä'bä, -bə), *n., pl.* **-bas.** a small yeast cake often containing raisins, usu. served soaked in a rum syrup.

Ba·bar (bä'bər), *n.* BABER.

ba·bas·su (bä'bə sōō'), *n., pl.* **-sus.** a palm, *Orbignya barbosiana,* of NE Brazil, bearing nuts that yield an oil used in the manufacture of soaps and cosmetics and as a cooking oil.

Bab·bage (bab'ij), *n.* **Charles,** 1792–1871, English mathematician: invented the precursor of the modern computer.

bab·bitt (bab'it), *n.* **1.** a bearing or lining of Babbitt metal. —*v.t.* **2.** to line, face, or furnish with Babbitt metal.

Bab·bitt (bab'it), *n.* **1. Irving,** 1865–1933, U.S. educator and critic. **2. Milton Byron,** born 1916, U.S. composer. **3.** (*often l.c.*) a self-satisfied person who conforms to conventional middle-class ideals, esp. of material success: from the title character of a novel (1922) by Sinclair Lewis.

Bab'bitt met'al, *n.* any of various alloys of tin with smaller amounts of antimony and copper.

bab·ble (bab'əl), *v.,* **-bled, -bling,** *n.* —*v.i.* **1.** to utter sounds or words imperfectly, indistinctly, or without meaning. **2.** to talk idly, irrationally, excessively, or foolishly; chatter or prattle. **3.** to make a continuous murmuring sound: *a babbling brook.* —*v.t.* **4.** to utter in an incoherent, foolish, or meaningless fashion. **5.** to reveal foolishly or thoughtlessly: *to babble a secret.* —*n.* **6.** inarticulate or imperfect speech. **7.** foolish, meaningless, or incoherent speech; prattle. **8.** a murmuring sound or sounds.

bab·bler (bab'lər), *n.* **1.** a person or thing that babbles. **2.** any of numerous usu. very vocal songbirds of the subfamily Timaliinae, of Asia and Africa.

Bab·cock (bab'kok), *n.* **Maltbie,** 1858–1901, U.S. clergyman and hymn writer.

babe (bāb), *n.* **1.** a baby or small child. **2.** an inexperienced or naive person. **3.** (*usu. cap.*) *Southern U.S.* (used as a familiar name for a boy or man, esp. the youngest of a family.) **4.** *Slang.* (*sometimes cap.*) an affectionate or familiar term of address (sometimes offensive when used to strangers, subordinates, etc.). —*Proverb.* **5.** Out of the mouths of **babes and sucklings come great truths,** children sometimes speak more wisely and truly than their elders. Ps. 8:2.

Ba·bel (bā'bəl, bab'əl), *n.* **1.** an ancient city in Shinar where people began building a tower (**Tower of Babel**) intended to reach heaven but were forced to abandon their work upon the confusion of their languages by God. Gen. 11:4–9. **2.** (*usu. l.c.*) a confused mixture of sounds or voices. **3.** (*usu. l.c.*) a scene of noise and confusion. —**Ba·bel'ic** (-bel'ik), *adj.*

Ba·ber or **Ba·bar** or **Ba·bur** (bä'bər), *n.* (*Zahir ed-Din Mohammed*), 1483–1530, founder of the Mogul Empire.

Ba·bi (bä'bē), *n., pl.* **-bis.** **1.** Also called **Bab·ism** (bä'biz əm). a Persian religion, founded in the 19th century, now supplanted by Baha'i. **2.** an adherent of Babi. —**Bab'ist, Bab'ite,** *adj., n.*

bab·ka (bäb'kə), *n., pl.* **-kas.** a sweet, spongy yeast cake, traditionally cylindrical, often made with raisins and flavored with rum.

ba·boon (ba bōōn'; *esp. Brit.* bə-), *n.* **1.** any of various large terrestrial monkeys of the genus *Papio* and related genera, of Africa and Arabia, having a doglike muzzle. **2.** a coarse, ridiculous, or brutish person. —**ba·boon'er·y,** *n.* —**ba·boon'ish,** *adj.*

ba·bul (bə bōōl', bä'bōōl), *n.* an acacia tree, *Acacia nilotica,* of tropical Africa, that yields gum arabic, tannin, and a hard wood.

ba·bush·ka (bə bōōsh'kə, -bōōsh'-), *n., pl.* **-kas.** a head scarf, shaped or folded in a triangle, worn with two ends tied under the chin.

ba·by (bā'bē), *n., pl.* **-bies,** *adj., v.,* **-bied, -by·ing.** —*n.* **1.** an infant or very young child. **2.** a newborn or very young animal. **3.** the youngest member of a family, group, etc. **4.** an immature or childish person. **5.** *Informal.* **a.** a person of whom one is deeply fond; sweetheart. **b.** (*sometimes cap.*) an affectionate or familiar term of address (sometimes offensive when used to strangers, subordinates, etc.). **c.** a project, creation, etc., that requires one's special attention or of which one is esp. proud. **d.** any person or object: *Is that car your baby?* —*adj.* **6.** of or for a baby: *baby clothes.* **7.** of or like a baby; infantile: *baby skin.* **8.** smaller than the usual: *a baby car; baby eggplants.* —*v.t.* **9.** to treat like a young child; pamper. **10.** to handle or use with special care; treat gently. —**ba'by·hood,** *n.* —**ba'by·ish,** *adj.* —**ba'by·like',** *adj.*

ba'by-blue'-eyes', *n., pl.* **-eyes.** (*used with a sing. or pl. v.*) a low-growing plant, *Nemophila menziesii,* of the waterleaf family, native to California, having blue flowers with white centers.

ba'by boom', *n.* (*sometimes caps.*) a period of sharp increase in the birthrate, as that in the U.S. following World War II.

ba'by boom'er, *n.* (*sometimes caps.*) a person born during a baby boom, esp. one born in the U.S. between 1946 and 1965.

ba'by car'riage, *n.* a conveyance for a baby resembling a basket set on four wheels, often with a hood, designed to be pushed by a person walking. Also called **ba'by bug'gy.**

ba'by grand', *n.* the smallest form of the grand piano.

Bab·y·lon (bab'ə lən, -lon'), *n.* **1.** an ancient city in SW Asia, on the Euphrates River: capital of Babylonia and later of the Chaldean empire. **2.** any city regarded as a place of excessive luxury and wickedness.

Bab·y·lo·ni·a (bab'ə lō'nē ə, -lōn'yə), *n.* any of a succession of states, having Babylon as their principal city, that existed in S Mesopotamia between c1900 B.C. and 539 B.C. —**Bab'y·lo'ni·an,** *adj., n.*

Bab·y·lo·ni·an (bab'ə lō'nē ən, -lōn'yən), *adj.* **1.** of or pertaining to Babylon or Babylonia. **2.** extremely luxurious. **3.** wicked; sinful. —*n.* **4.** a native or inhabitant of ancient Babylon or Babylonia. **5.** the dialect of Akkadian spoken in Babylonia.

Babylo'nian captiv'ity, *n.* **1.** the period of the exile of the Jews in Babylonia, 597–538 B.C. **2.** the exile of the popes at Avignon, 1309–77.

ba'by's-breath' or **ba'bies'-breath',** *n.* a tall plant, *Gypsophila paniculata,* of the pink family, having numerous small white or pink flowers.

ba'by-sit' or **ba'by·sit',** *v.,* **-sat, -sit·ting.** —*v.i.* **1.** to take charge of a child while the parents are temporarily away. —*v.t.* **2.** to baby-sit for (a child). **3.** to take watchful responsibility for; tend: *to baby-sit a car.* —**ba'by-sit'ter, ba'by·sit'ter,** *n.*

ba'by's-tears' or **ba'by-tears',** *n., pl.* **-tears.** (*used with a sing. or pl. v.*) a mosslike plant, *Soleirolia soleirolii,* of the nettle family, having small, roundish leaves and tiny flowers.

ba'by talk', *n.* **1.** the speech of children learning to talk, marked esp. by syntactic simplification and phonetic modifications like omission and substitution of sounds. **2.** a style of speech used by adults in imitation of this, esp. in addressing young children.

ba'by tooth', *n.* DECIDUOUS TOOTH.

BAC, blood-alcohol concentration: the percentage of alcohol in the bloodstream: in most U.S. states, a BAC of 0.10 is the legal definition of intoxication.

bac·ca·lau·re·ate (bak'ə lôr'ē it, -lor'-), *n.* **1.** BACHELOR'S DEGREE. **2.** a religious service held for a graduating class.

bac·ca·rat or **bac·ca·ra** (bä'kə rä', bak'ə-), *n.* a card game in which the designated banker deals three hands and other players bet that either one or both of the other hands will win against the banker's hand.

bac·cate (bak'āt), *adj.* **1.** berrylike. **2.** bearing berries.

bac·cha·nal (bä'kə näl', bak'ə nal', bak'ə nl; *adj.* bak'ə nl), *n.* **1.** a worshiper of Bacchus. **2.** a drunken reveler. **3.** an occasion of drunken revelry; orgy; bacchanalia. —*adj.* **4.** pertaining to Bacchus or the Bacchanalia.

Bac·cha·na·li·a (bak'ə nā'lē ə, -nāl'yə), *n., pl.* **-li·a, -li·as.** **1.** (*sometimes used with a pl. v.*) a festival in honor of Bacchus. Compare DIONYSIA. **2.** (*l.c.*) a drunken feast. —**bac'cha·na'li·an,** *adj., n.*

Bac·chus (bak'əs), *n.* DIONYSUS. —**Bac'chic,** *adj.*

Bach (bäKH), *n.* **1. Johann Sebastian,** 1685–1750, German organist and composer. **2.** his sons, **Carl Philipp Emanuel,** 1714–88, and **Johann Christian,** 1735–82, German organists and composers.

bach·e·lor (bach'ə lər, bach'lər), *n.* **1.** an unmarried man. **2.** a person who has been awarded a bachelor's degree. **3.** a young male fur seal kept from the breeding grounds by the older males. **4.** Also called **bachelor-at-arms.** a young knight who followed the banner of another. [<

Old French < Vulgar Latin *baccalār(is)* farmhand] —**bach′e·lor·hood′**, **bach′e·lor·dom**, *n.*

bach′elor (or **bach′elor's**) **chest′**, *n.* a low chest of drawers, orig. one with a top inclining to form a writing surface.

Bach′elor of Arts′, *n.* **1.** a bachelor's degree in the liberal arts. **2.** a person having this degree. *Abbr.:* A.B., B.A.

Bach′elor of Sci′ence, *n.* **1.** a bachelor's degree, usu. awarded for studies in science or technology. **2.** a person having this degree. *Abbr.:* B.S., B.Sc., S.B.

bach′elor's-but′ton, *n.* any of various plants with round flower heads, esp. the cornflower.

bach′elor's degree′, *n.* a degree awarded by a college or university to a person who has completed undergraduate studies.

bac·il·lar·y (bas′ə ler′ē, bə sil′ə rē) also **ba·cil·lar** (bə sil′ər, bas′ə-lar), *adj.* **1.** Also, **ba·cil·li·form** (bə sil′ə fôrm′). of or like a bacillus; rod-shaped. **2.** characterized by bacilli.

ba·cil·lus (bə sil′əs), *n., pl.* **-cil·li** (-sil′ī). **1.** any rod-shaped or cylindrical bacterium of the genus *Bacillus*, comprising spore-producing bacteria. **2.** (formerly) any bacterium.

bac·i·tra·cin (bas′i trā′sin), *n.* an antibiotic polypeptide derived by the hydrolytic action of *Bacillus subtilis* on protein, primarily used topically in the treatment of superficial infections.

back¹ (bak), *n.* **1.** the rear part of the human body, from the neck to the end of the spine. **2.** the part of the body of animals corresponding to the human back. **3.** the rear portion of any part of the body: *the back of the head.* **4.** the part opposite to or farthest from the front; rear: *the back of a hall.* **5.** the part that forms the rear of any object or structure. **6.** the part covering the back: *the back of a jacket.* **7.** the spine or backbone: *The fall broke his back.* **8.** any rear part of an object serving to support, protect, etc.: *the back of a chair.* **9.** the side of an object that is less functional, less often seen, etc.: *the back of an envelope.* **10.** the whole body, with reference to clothing: *the clothes on one's back.* **11.** ability for labor; effort; endurance: *to put one's back to a task.* **12.** the edge of a book formed where its sections are bound together. **13.** (in various sports, as football) **a.** a player stationed to the rear of front-line play. **b.** the position so occupied. —*v.t.* **14.** to support, as with authority, influence, help, or money: *to back a candidate.* **15.** to bet on: *to back a horse in the race.* **16.** to cause to move backward (often fol. by *up*): *to back a car into a garage.* **17.** to furnish with a back: *to back a book.* **18.** to lie at the back of; form a back or background for. **19.** to provide with an accompaniment: *a singer backed by piano and bass.* **20.** to get upon the back of; mount. **21.** to write or print on the back of; endorse; countersign. —*v.i.* **22.** to go or move backward (often fol. by *up*). **23.** (of wind) to change direction counterclockwise (opposed to *veer*). **24. back away**, to retreat; withdraw. **25. back down**, to abandon an argument or position. **26. back off**, **a.** to move back from something; retreat. **b.** to back down. **27. back out**, to fail to keep an engagement or promise; withdraw. **28. back up**, **a.** to move or cause to move backward. **b.** to reinforce. **c.** to support or confirm. **d.** to bring (a stream of traffic) to a standstill. **e.** to accumulate or become clogged due to a stoppage. **f.** to copy (a computer file or program) as a precaution against failure. —*adj.* **29.** situated at or in the rear: *the back door.* **30.** far away or removed from the front or main area, position, or rank; remote: *back streets.* **31.** of or belonging to the past: *back issues of a magazine.* **32.** in arrears; overdue: *back pay.* **33.** coming or going back; moving backward: *back current.* **34.** (of a speech sound) articulated with the tongue in the back part of the mouth, as either of the sounds of *go.* —*Idiom.* **35. back and fill**, **a.** to trim the sails of a boat so that the wind strikes them first on the forward and then on the after side. **b.** to change one's opinion or position; vacillate. **36. be (flat) on one's back**, to be ill, helpless, or overcome by circumstances. **37. behind one's back**, without one's knowledge, esp. treacherously or secretly. **38. break the back of**, to conquer the most difficult or resistant part of: *to break the back of urban crime.* **39. get one's back up**, to become annoyed; take offense. **40. have one's back to the wall**, to be in a difficult or hopeless situation. **41. (in) back of**, at the rear of; behind. **42. on someone's back**, *Informal.* nagging or criticizing someone. —**back′less**, *adj.*

back² (bak), *adv.* **1.** at, to, or toward the rear; backward: *to step back.* **2.** in or toward the past: *to look back on one's youth.* **3.** at or toward the original starting point, place, or condition: *to go back to one's home town; to put a coat back on.* **4.** in direct payment or return: *to pay back a loan; to answer back.* **5.** in a state of restraint or retention: *to hold back tears; to hold back salary.* **6.** in a reclining position: *to lean back; to lie back.* **7. go back on**, **a.** to fail to keep; renege on: *to go back on a promise.* **b.** to be faithless to; betray. —*Idiom.* **8. back and forth**, **a.** backward and forward; to and fro. **b.** from side to side. **c.** from one to the other. **9. back to square one**, beginning anew. **10. back to the drawing board**, rethinking is needed.

back³ (bak), *n.* a large tub or vat used to hold liquids.

back·ache (bak′āk′), *n.* a pain or ache in the back, usu. in the lumbar region.

back′-and-forth′, *adj.* backward and forward; to and fro.

back·beat (bak′bēt′), *n.* an accented secondary or supplementary beat, as by a jazz drummer.

back·bench·er (bak′ben′chər, -ben′-), *n.* a member of the British Parliament or a similar legislative body who is not a party leader.

back·bend (bak′bend′), *n.* an acrobatic feat in which one bends backward from a standing position until the hands touch the floor.

back·bite (bak′bīt′), *v.*, **-bit**, **-bit·ten** or (*Informal*) **-bit**; **-bit·ing**. —*v.t.* **1.** to attack the character or reputation of (a person not present); slander. —*v.i.* **2.** to slander an absent person.

back·board (bak′bôrd′, -bōrd′), *n.* **1.** a board placed at or forming the back of anything. **2.** the vertical board at the end of a basketball court to which the basket is attached.

back·bone (bak′bōn′), *n.* **1.** the spinal column; spine. **2.** strength of character; resolution. **3.** something resembling a backbone in appearance, position, or function. **4.** a back or bound edge of a book; spine.

back·break·ing (bak′brā′king), *adj.* demanding great effort, endurance, etc.: *a backbreaking job.* —**back′break′er**, *n.*

back′ burn′er, *n.* a condition of low priority or temporary deferment: *an issue put on the back burner until after the election.* —**back′-burn′er**, *v.t.*

back′-check′, *v.i.* to skate back toward one's defensive zone in ice hockey, obstructing or impeding the progress of opponents on attack. Compare FORE-CHECK.

back′ coun′try, *n.* a sparsely populated rural region remote from a settled area. —**back′-coun′try**, *adj.*

back·court (bak′kôrt′, -kōrt′), *n.* **1.** the half of a basketball court in which the basket being defended is located. **2.** the part of a tennis court between the base line and the line that marks the in-bounds limit of a service. Compare FORECOURT (def. 1).

back·date (bak′dāt′), *v.t.*, **-dat·ed**, **-dat·ing.** to date earlier than the actual date; predate; antedate.

back′ door′, *n.* a secret, furtive, illicit, or indirect method or means. —**back′door′**, *adj.*

back·draft (bak′draft′, -dräft′), *n.* an explosive surge in a fire occurring when air is suddenly mixed with a combustible gas.

back·drop (bak′drop′), *n., v.*, **-dropped** or **-dropt**, **-drop·ping.** —*n.* **1.** the rear curtain of a stage setting. **2.** the background of an event; setting. —*v.t.* **3.** to provide a setting or background for.

back·er (bak′ər), *n.* **1.** a person who supports or aids a cause, enterprise, etc. **2.** a person who bets on a competitor in a race or contest. **3.** canvas or other material used for backing.

back·field (bak′fēld′), *n.* **1.** the members of a football team who, on offense, are stationed behind the linemen and, on defense, behind the linebackers. **2.** their positions considered as a unit.

back·fill (bak′fil′), *n.* **1.** material used for refilling an excavation. —*v.t., v.i.* **2.** to refill (an excavation).

back·fire (bak′fī°r′), *v.*, **-fired**, **-fir·ing**, *n.* —*v.i.* **1.** (of an internal-combustion engine) to have a loud, premature explosion in the intake manifold. **2.** to bring a result opposite to that planned or expected: *The plot backfired.* **3.** to start a fire deliberately in order to check a forest or prairie fire by creating a barren area in advance of it. —*n.* **4.** (in an internal-combustion engine) a premature, explosive ignition of fuel in the intake manifold. **5.** an explosion coming out of the breech of a firearm. **6.** a fire started intentionally to check the advance of a forest or prairie fire.

back·flip (bak′flip′), *n.* **1.** a backward somersault. **2.** a dive executed by somersaulting backward. **3.** a complete reversal in attitude or policy.

back·gam·mon (bak′gam′ən, bak′gam′-), *n.* a game for two persons in which pieces are moved around a board having two tables or parts, and then removed according to throws of the dice.

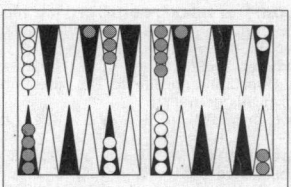

backgammon

back·ground (bak′ground′), *n.* **1.** the ground or parts, as of a scene, situated in the rear (opposed to *foreground*). **2.** the part of a painted or carved surface against which represented objects and forms are perceived or depicted. **3.** one's origin, education, experience, etc., in relation to one's present character or status: *a religious background.* **4.** the social, historical, and other antecedents or causes of an event or condition: *the background of the war.* **5.** the set of conditions against which an occurrence is perceived. **6. a.** Also called **back′ground radia′tion.** the natural low-intensity radiation from cosmic rays and naturally occurring radioisotopes in rocks, soil, etc. **b.** intrusive sound or radiation that tends to interfere with the transmission or reception of electronic signals. —*adj.* **7.** of, pertaining to, or serving as a background: *background noise.* —*v.t.* **8.** to supply a background for. —*Idiom.* **9. in** or **into the background**, in or into a state of less importance or visibility.

back·ground·er (bak′groun′dər), *n.* **1.** a briefing for the press in which an official, often from government or business, gives background information to clarify particular policies, actions, or newsworthy issues, with the understanding that the official will not be named or quoted directly in any resulting press reports. **2.** any briefing or report for the purpose of providing background information.

back•hand (bak/hand/), *n.* **1.** a stroke, slap, etc., made with the back of the hand turned forward. **2.** (in tennis, squash, etc.) a stroke made with the back of the hand facing the direction of movement. **3.** handwriting that slopes toward the left. —*adj.* **4.** backhanded. **5.** (in tennis, squash, etc.) of, pertaining to, or being a stroke made with the back of the hand facing the direction of movement. Compare FOREHAND (def. 1). —*adv.* **6.** with the back of the hand. **7.** backhanded: *She returned the ball backhand.* —*v.t.* **8.** to strike with the back of the hand. **9.** to hit, produce, or accomplish with a backhand. **10.** to catch (a ball or the like) backhanded.

back•hand•ed (bak/han/did), *adj.* **1.** performed with the back of the hand turned or facing forward: *a backhanded stroke.* **2.** sloping in a downward direction from left to right: *backhanded writing.* **3.** oblique or ambiguous in meaning: *a backhanded compliment.* —*adv.* **4.** with the hand across the body; backhand: *He caught the ball backhanded.* —**back/hand/ed•ly,** *adv.* —**back/hand/ed•ness,** *n.*

back•hoe (bak/hō/), *n.* an excavating machine with a bucket attached to a hinged boom that digs by being drawn toward the machine.

back•ing (bak/ing), *n.* **1.** aid or support of any kind. **2.** supporters or backers collectively. **3.** something that forms the back of anything, esp. for support or protection. **4.** a curtain or flat placed in a stage set, as behind a window, to conceal the offstage area.

back•lash (bak/lash/), *n.* **1.** a sudden, forceful backward movement; recoil. **2.** a strong negative reaction, as to some social or political change: *a backlash by voters to rising property taxes.* **3. a.** the difference between the thickness of a gear tooth and the width of the space between teeth in the mating gear, designed to allow room for lubricants, expansion, etc. **b.** play or lost motion between loosely fitting machine parts. **4.** a snarled line on the reel of a casting fisherman. —*v.i.* **5.** to make or undergo a backlash.

back•light (bak/līt/), *n., v.,* **-light•ed** or **-lit, -light•ing.** —*n.* **1.** a light source placed behind an object, person, or scene to create a highlight that separates the subject from the background. —*v.t.* **2.** to illuminate (something) from behind: *a backlit screen on a computer.*

back•list (bak/list/), *n.* **1.** the books that a publisher has kept in print over several years, as distinguished from newly issued titles. —*adj.* **2.** Also, **back/list/ed.** placed or maintained on a backlist. —*v.t.* **3.** to place on a backlist.

back•log (bak/lôg/, -log/), *n., v.,* **-logged, -log•ging.** —*n.* **1.** an accumulation, as of unfinished tasks. **2.** a large log at the back of a hearth to keep up a fire. —*v.i.* **3.** to accumulate in a backlog.

back/ mat/ter, *n.* the parts of a book that appear after the main text, as bibliography, index, and appendixes.

back/ or/der, *n.* an order placed for merchandise that is temporarily out of stock and will be delivered as soon as it is received. —**back/-or/der,** *v.t.*

back•pack (bak/pak/), *n.* **1.** a pack or knapsack, to be carried on one's back. **2.** a piece of equipment designed for use while being carried on the back. —*v.i.* **3.** to go on a hike using a backpack. —*v.t.* **4.** to place or carry in a backpack or on one's back. —**back/pack/er,** *n.*

back/-ped/al, *v.i.,* **-ped•aled, -ped•al•ing** or (*esp. Brit.*) **-ped•alled, -ped•al•ling.** **1.** to retard the forward motion of a bicycle by pressing backward on the pedal. **2.** to retreat from or reverse one's previous stand on a matter. **3.** to make quick steps backward, as in retreating against a boxing opponent.

back/ room/ or **back/room/,** *n.* **1.** a room in the rear of a building. **2.** a place from where powerful or influential persons exercise control in an indirect manner.

back•scat•ter (bak/skat/ər), *n.* **1.** the deflection of radiation by scattering in a direction opposite to the direction of incidence. **2.** radiation scattered in this manner.

back•seat (bak/sēt/), *n.* **1.** a seat at the rear. **2.** a secondary or inferior position.

back/seat driv/er, *n.* **1.** an automobile passenger who offers the driver unsolicited advice or criticism. **2.** any meddlesome person who offers unsolicited advice. —**back/seat driv/ing,** *n.*

back•side (bak/sīd/), *n.* **1.** the rear or back part or view of an object, person, scene, etc. **2.** rump; buttocks.

back•slap•ping (bak/slap/ing), *n.* the practice of making an effusive display of friendliness, as by slapping people on the back.

back•slash (bak/slash/), *n.* a short oblique stroke (\): used in some computer operating systems to mark the division between a directory and a subdirectory, as in typing a path.

back•slide (bak/slīd/), *v.,* **-slid, -slid** or **-slid•den, -slid•ing,** *n.* —*v.i.* **1.** to relapse into bad habits, sinful behavior, or undesirable activities. —*n.* **2.** an act or instance of backsliding.

back•space (bak/spās/), *v.,* **-spaced, -spac•ing,** *n.* —*v.i.* **1.** to move the typing element of a typewriter, the cursor on a computer display, etc., one space backward, as by depressing a special key. —*n.* **2.** the labeled key on a typewriter or computer keyboard used for backspacing.

back•spin (bak/spin/), *n.* reverse rotation of a ball causing it to bounce or roll backward or stop short.

back•stage (bak/stāj/), *adv.* **1.** behind the proscenium in a theater, esp. in the wings or dressing rooms. **2.** in private; behind the scenes. —*adj.* **3.** located or occurring backstage. **4.** of or pertaining to secret ac-

tivities. **5.** of or pertaining to the private lives of entertainers: *backstage gossip.* —*n.* **6.** a backstage area of a theater.

back•stairs (bak/stârz/) also **back/stair/,** *adj.* secret, underhanded, or scandalous: *backstairs gossip.*

back•stay (bak/stā/), *n.* **1.** a supporting or checking piece in a mechanism. **2.** a strip of leather at the back of a shoe, usu. serving as reinforcement.

back•stitch (bak/stich/), *n.* **1.** stitching or a stitch in which the thread is doubled back on the preceding stitch. —*v.t., v.i.* **2.** to sew by backstitch.

back•stop (bak/stop/), *n., v.,* **-stopped, -stop•ping.** —*n.* **1.** a wall, wire screen, or the like, serving to prevent a ball from going beyond the normal playing area. **2.** any support, safeguard, or reinforcement. —*v.t.* **3.** to act as a backstop to. —**back/stop/per,** *n.*

back•stretch (bak/strech/), *n.* the straight part of a race track opposite the part leading to the finish line. Compare HOMESTRETCH.

back•stroke (bak/strōk/), *n., v.,* **-stroked, -strok•ing.** —*n.* **1.** a backhanded stroke. **2.** a swimming stroke performed in a supine position. **3.** a blow or stroke in return; recoil. —*v.i.* **4.** to swim the backstroke.

back•swing (bak/swing/), *n.* the movement backward of a racket, bat, etc., preparatory to a forward stroke or swing.

back/ talk/, *n.* an impudent response; impudence. —**back/-talk/,** *v.i., v.t.*

back/ to back/ or **back/-to-back/,** *adj.* **1.** having the backs close together or adjoining. **2.** (of two similar events) following one immediately after the other; consecutive.

back-to-ba•sics (bak/tə bā/siks), *adj.* **1.** stressing simplicity and adherence to fundamental principles: *The movement suggests a back-to-basics approach to living for those whose lives have become complicated.* **2.** emphasizing or based upon the teaching of such basic subjects as reading, arithmetic, grammar, or history in a traditional way.

back/-to-the-land/, *adj.* of or pertaining to a move to a rural area to take up life there. —**back/-to-the-land/er,** *n.*

back•track (bak/trak/), *v.i.* **1.** to return over the same course or route. **2.** to withdraw from an undertaking, position, etc.; reverse a policy.

back•up (bak/up/), *n.* **1.** one that supports or reinforces, as a group of musicians supporting a soloist. **2.** an accumulation due to stoppage. **3.** an alternate or substitute kept in reserve.

back•ward (bak/wərd), *adv.* Also, **back/wards.** **1.** toward the back or rear. **2.** with the back foremost. **3.** in the reverse of the usual or right way: *counting backward from 100.* **4.** toward the past: *to look backward over one's earlier mistakes.* **5.** toward a less advanced state; retrogressively. —*adj.* **6.** directed toward the back or past. **7.** reversed; returning: *a backward movement.* **8.** behind in time, progress, or development: *a backward learner.* **9.** bashful or hesitant; shy: *a backward suitor.* —*Idiom.* **10.** backward(s) and forward(s), in every detail; thoroughly. **11.** bend, lean, or fall over backward, to exert oneself to the utmost; make a serious effort. —**back/ward•ly,** *adv.* —**back/ward•ness,** *n.*

back•wash (bak/wosh/, -wôsh/), *n.* **1.** water thrown backward by the motion of oars, propellers, etc. **2.** the portion of the wash of an aircraft that flows to the rear. **3.** a condition, usu. undesirable, that continues long after the event which caused it.

back•wa•ter (bak/wô/tər, -wot/ər), *n.* **1.** water held or forced back, as by a dam, flood, or tide. **2.** a place or state of stagnant backwardness.

back•woods (bak/woodz/), *n.* **1.** (*often used with a sing. v.*) wooded or partially uncleared and unsettled districts. **2.** any remote or isolated area. —*adj.* Also, **back/wood/, back/woods/y. 3.** of or pertaining to the backwoods. **4.** unsophisticated; uncouth.

back•yard (bak/yärd/), *n.* **1.** the yard behind a house. **2.** an area regarded as one's private property or domain.

ba•con (bā/kən), *n.* **1.** the back and sides of a hog, salted and dried or smoked, usu. sliced thin and fried. —*Idiom.* **2.** bring home the bacon, to support oneself or one's family; earn a living.

Ba•con (bā/kən), *n.* **1.** Francis (*Baron Verulam, Viscount St. Albans*), 1561–1626, English essayist, philosopher, and statesman. **2.** Francis, 1910–92, English painter, born in Ireland. **3.** Nathaniel, 1647–76, American colonist, born in England: leader of a rebellion in Virginia 1676. **4.** Roger, 1214?–94?, English philosopher and scientist.

Ba/con's Rebel/lion, *n.* an unsuccessful uprising by frontiersmen in Virginia in 1676, led by Nathaniel Bacon against the colonial government in Jamestown.

bac•te•ri•a (bak tēr/ē ə), *n.pl., sing.* **-te•ri•um** (-tēr/ē əm). any of numerous groups of microscopic one-celled organisms constituting the phylum Schizomycota, of the kingdom Monera, various species of

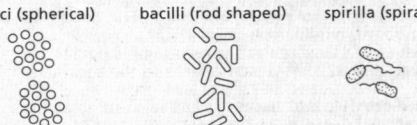

cocci (spherical)   bacilli (rod shaped)   spirilla (spiral)

bacteria (greatly magnified)

which are involved in infectious diseases, nitrogen fixation, fermentation, or putrefaction. —**bac•te′ri•al,** *adj.*

bac•te•ri•ol•o•gy (bak tēr′ē ol′ə jē), *n.* a branch of microbiology dealing with bacteria. —**bac•te′ri•o•log′i•cal** (-ə loj′i kəl), **bac•te′ri•o•log′ic,** *adj.* —**bac•te′ri•ol′o•gist,** *n.*

bac•te•ri•o•phage (bak tēr′ē ə fāj′), *n.* any of a group of viruses that infect specific bacteria, usu. causing their disintegration or dissolution. Also called **phage.**

Bac′trian cam′el, *n.* an Asian camel, *Camelus bactrianus,* having two humps on the back. Compare DROMEDARY.

bad (bad), *adj.,* **worse, worst,** *n., adv.* —*adj.* **1.** not good in any manner or degree. **2.** having a wicked or evil character; morally reprehensible. **3.** of inferior quality; inadequate; defective; deficient. **4.** disobedient or naughty. **5.** inaccurate or faulty: *a bad guess.* **6.** invalid or false: *bad judgment.* **7.** injurious or harmful: *Too much sugar is bad for your teeth.* **8.** suffering from sickness, pain, or injury. **9.** diseased, decayed, or physically weakened: *a bad heart.* **10.** tainted, spoiled, or rotten. **11.** having a detrimental effect, result, or tendency; unfavorable. **12.** disagreeable; unpleasant: *a bad night.* **13.** easily provoked to anger; irascible: *a bad temper.* **14.** severe: *a bad flood.* **15.** regretful or upset: *He felt bad about leaving.* **16.** disreputable or dishonorable: *a bad name.* **17.** displaying a lack of skill or competence. **18.** unfortunate or unfavorable: *bad news.* **19.** inclement, as weather. **20.** disagreeable or offensive to the senses: *a bad odor.* **21.** lacking aesthetic sensitivity: *bad taste.* **22.** not in keeping with a standard of behavior; coarse: *bad manners.* **23. a.** vulgar, obscene, or blasphemous: *a bad word.* **b.** not observing rules or customs of grammar, usage, spelling, etc.: *bad English.* **24.** marred by defects; blemished: *bad skin.* **25.** not profitable or worth the price paid: *The land was a bad buy.* **26.** (of a debt) deemed uncollectible and treated as a loss. **27.** counterfeit; not genuine. —*n.* **28.** that which is bad: *You have to take the bad with the good.* **29.** a bad condition, character, or quality. —*Idiom.* **30. bad** or **badly off,** poor; destitute. **31. not (half, so,** or **too) bad,** somewhat good; tolerable. **32. too bad,** unfortunate or disappointing. —**bad′ness,** *n.* —**Usage.** The adjective BAD meaning "unpleasant, unattractive, unfavorable, spoiled, etc.," is the usual form to follow such linking verbs as *sound, smell, look,* and *taste: After the rainstorm the water tasted bad. The locker room smells bad.* After the linking verb *feel,* the adjective BADLY in reference to physical or emotional states is also used and is standard, although BAD is more common in formal writing. BAD as an adverb appears mainly in informal contexts. See also BADLY, GOOD.

bad′ blood′, *n.* unfriendly or hostile relations; enmity.

bade (bad), *v.* a pt. of BID.

Ba•den-Pow•ell (bād′n pō′əl), *n.* Robert Stephenson Smyth (smĭth), **1st Baron,** 1857–1941, British general: founded the Boy Scouts and, with his sister Lady Agnes, the Girl Guides.

badge (baj), *n., v.,* **badged, badg•ing.** —*n.* **1.** a special mark, token, or device worn as a sign of membership, authority, achievement, etc. **2.** any emblem, token, or distinctive mark. —*v.t.* **3.** to furnish or mark with a badge.

badg•er (baj′ər), *n.* **1.** any of various burrowing, carnivorous mammals of the family Mustelidae, as *Taxidea taxus,* of North America, and *Meles meles,* of Europe and Asia. **2.** the fur of this mammal. —*v.t.* **3.** to harass or urge persistently; pester; nag.

bad•i•nage (bad′n äzh′, bad′n ij), *n., v.,* **-naged, -nag•ing.** —*n.* **1.** light, playful banter or raillery. —*v.t.* **2.** to banter with or tease (someone) playfully.

bad•lands (bad′landz′), *n.pl.* a barren area in which soft rock strata are eroded into varied, fantastic forms.

bad•ly (bad′lē), *adv.,* **worse, worst,** *adj.* —*adv.* **1.** in a defective or incorrect way. **2.** in an unsatisfactory, inadequate, or unskilled manner. **3.** unfavorably: *She spoke badly of him.* **4.** in a wicked, evil, or morally or legally wrong way. **5.** in a naughty or socially wrong way. **6.** very much; to a great extent or degree: *to want something badly.* **7.** severely; direly: *to be injured badly.* **8.** with great distress or emotional display: *She took the news badly.* —*adj.* **9.** in ill health; sick: *He felt badly.* **10.** sorry; regretful: *I feel badly about your loss.* **11.** dejected; downcast.

bad•min•ton (bad′min tn), *n.* a game played on a rectangular court by two players or two pairs of players equipped with light rackets used to volley a shuttlecock over a high net.

bad-mouth or **bad′mouth′** (bad′mouth′ or, *sometimes,* -mouth′), *v.t.* to criticize, often disloyally. —**bad′-mouth′er,** *n.*

baf•fle (baf′əl), *v.,* **-fled, -fling,** *n.* —*v.t.* **1.** to confuse, bewilder, or perplex. **2.** to frustrate or confound; thwart by creating confusion or bewilderment. **3.** to check or deflect the movement of (sound, light, gases, etc.). —*n.* **4.** something that balks, checks, or deflects. **5.** an artificial obstruction for checking or deflecting the flow of sounds, light, gases, etc. **6.** any boxlike enclosure or flat panel for mounting a loudspeaker. —**baf′fle•ment,** *n.*

bag (bag), *n., v.,* **bagged, bag•ging.** —*n.* **1.** a container or receptacle made of some pliant material and capable of being closed at the mouth; pouch. **2.** a piece of portable luggage. **3.** purse; handbag. **4.** the amount or quantity a bag can hold. **5.** an udder or pouch of an animal. **6.** something hanging in a loose, pouchlike manner, as skin or cloth. **7.** BASE¹ (def. 8b). **8.** a hunter's total amount of game taken. —*v.t.* **9.** to hang loosely. **10.** to pack items in a bag. **11.** to swell or bulge. —*v.t.* **12.** to put into a bag. **13.** to kill or catch, as in hunting. **14.** to cause to swell. —*Idiom.* **15. bag and baggage, a.** with all one's personal

property. **b.** completely, totally. **16. in the bag,** *Informal.* virtually certain to be attained. **17. leave holding the bag,** *Informal.* to force the consequences upon.

ba•gasse (bə gas′), *n.* **1.** crushed sugarcane or beet refuse from sugar making. **2.** paper made from fibers of bagasse.

bag•a•telle (bag′ə tel′), *n.* **1.** something of little value or importance; a trifle. **2.** a game similar to billiards played on a board with holes on one end. **3.** a short and light musical composition.

ba•gel (bā′gəl), *n.* a chewy, doughnut-shaped roll made of dough that is simmered in water and then baked.

bag•ful (bag′fŏŏl), *n., pl.* **-fuls. 1.** the contents of or amount held by a bag. **2.** a considerable amount.

bag•gage (bag′ij), *n.* **1.** trunks, suitcases, etc., used in traveling; luggage. **2.** the portable equipment of an army. **3.** things that encumber one's freedom; impediments.

bag•gy (bag′ē), *adj.,* **-gi•er, -gi•est.** baglike; hanging loosely.

Bagh•dad or **Bag•dad** (bag′dad, bəg dad′), *n.* the capital of Iraq, in the central part, on the Tigris. 4,648,609.

bag•pipe (bag′pīp′), *n.* Often, **bagpipes.** a reed instrument consisting of a melody pipe and one or more accompanying drone pipes protruding from a bag into which air is blown by the mouth or a bellows. —**bag′pip′er,** *n.*

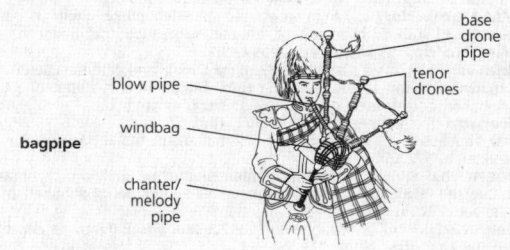

bagpipe

ba•guette or **ba•guet** (ba get′), *n.* **1.** a narrow rectangular shape given to a small gem, esp. a diamond, by cutting and polishing. **2.** a small convex molding, esp. one of semicircular section. **3.** a long, narrow loaf of French bread.

Ba•ha•′i (bə hä′ē, -hī′), *n., pl.* **-ha•′is,** *adj.* —*n.* **1.** a religion founded in Iran and teaching the essential worth of all races and religions and equality of the sexes. **2.** an adherent of Baha'i. —*adj.* **3.** pertaining to Baha'i or Baha'is. Also, **Ba•ha′i.** —**Ba•ha′ism,** *n.* —**Ba•ha′ist,** *adj.*

Ba•ha•mas (bə hä′məz, -hā′-), *n.pl.* an independent country comprising a group of islands (**Baha′ma Is′lands**) in the W Atlantic Ocean, SE of Florida: formerly a British colony; gained independence 1973. 262,034; 5353 sq. mi. (13,864 sq. km). *Cap.:* Nassau. Official name, **Com′monwealth of the Baha′mas.** —**Ba•ha′mi•an,** *n., adj.*

Ba•ha•ul•lah (bä hä′ŏŏl lä′), *n.* (Husayn 'Alī), 1817–92, Persian religious leader: founder of Baha'i.

Ba•hi′a grass′ (bə hē′ə), *n.* a lawn and pasturage grass, *Paspalum notatum,* native to tropical America.

Bah•rain or **Bah•rein** (bä rān′, -rīn′, bə-), *n.* **1.** a sheikdom in the Persian Gulf, consisting of a group of islands: formerly a British protectorate; declared independent 1971. 603,318; 266 sq. mi. (688 sq. km). *Cap.:* Manama. **2.** the largest island in this group: oil fields. 265,000; 213 sq. mi. (552 sq. km). —**Bah•rain′i,** *n., pl.* **-rain•is,** *adj.*

bail¹ (bāl), *n.* **1.** property or money given as surety that a person released from legal custody will return at an appointed time. **2.** a person who provides bail. **3.** the state of release upon being bailed. —*v.t.* **4.** to grant or obtain the liberty of (a person) on security for appearance in court as required. **5.** to deliver (goods) for storage, hire, or other special purpose. **6.** to assist in escaping a predicament (used with *out*). —*Idiom.* **7. jump bail,** to abscond while free on bail.

bail² (bāl), *n.* **1.** the semicircular handle of a kettle or pail. **2.** a hooplike support, as for the cover on a Conestoga wagon.

bail³ (bāl), *v.t.* **1.** to dip (water) out of a boat, as with a bucket. **2.** to clear of water by dipping: *to bail out a boat.* —*v.i.* **3.** to bail water. **4. bail out, a.** to make a parachute jump from an airplane. **b.** to give up on or abandon a difficult situation. —*n.* **5.** a bucket, dipper, or other container used for bailing.

bail•iff (bā′lif), *n.* an officer, similar to a sheriff, employed to keep order in the court, make arrests, etc.

bail•i•wick (bā′lə wik′), *n.* **1.** the district within which a bailiff has jurisdiction. **2.** a person's area of skill, knowledge, or authority.

bail•ment (bāl′mənt), *n.* the act of furnishing bail.

bail•out (bāl′out′), *n.* **1.** the act of parachuting from an aircraft. **2.** a rescue from financial distress. **3.** an alternative course out of a difficulty.

Baird (bârd), *n.* John Logie, 1888–1946, Scottish engineer, a pioneer in the development of television.

bairn (bârn), *n. Scot.* CHILD.

bait (bāt), *n.* **1.** food, or some substitute, used as a lure in fishing, trapping, etc. **2.** a poisoned lure used in exterminating pests. **3.** an allurement; enticement. —*v.t.* **4.** to prepare (a hook or trap) with bait. **5.** to lure, as with bait. **6.** to set dogs upon (an animal) for sport. **7.** to torment, esp. with malicious remarks; harass. **8.** to tease. **9.** to feed and water (an animal) during a journey. —**bait′er,** *n.*

bait′ and switch′, *n.* the practice of attracting customers to a store with bargain prices, then attempting to sell them higher-priced items.

baize (bāz), *n.* a soft feltlike fabric, usu. dyed green, commonly used for the tops of game tables.

bake (bāk), *v.,* **baked, bak·ing.** —*v.t.* **1.** to cook by dry heat in an oven or on heated metal or stones. **2.** to harden by heat, as pottery. **3.** to dry by or subject to heat: *The sun baked the land.* —*v.i.* **4.** to prepare food by baking it. **5.** to become baked. **6.** to feel hot; swelter.

Ba·ke·lite (bā′kə līt′, bāk′līt), *Trademark.* a brand name for any of a series of phenolic resins and plastics used as electrical insulators.

bak·er (bā′kər), *n.* **1.** a person who bakes, esp. one who makes and sells bread, cake, etc. **2.** a small portable oven.

Ba·ker (bā′kər), *n.* **1. Howard H(enry), Jr.,** born 1925, U.S. politician; senator 1967–85. **2. Josephine,** 1906–75, French entertainer, born in the U.S.

bak′er's doz′en, *n.* a group of 13; a dozen plus one.

Ba·kers·field (bā′kərz fēld′), *n.* a city in S California. 191,060.

bak·er·y (bā′kə rē, bāk′rē), *n., pl.* **-er·ies.** a place where baked goods are made or sold. Also called **bake·shop** (bāk′shop′).

bak′ing pow′der, *n.* a powder used as a leavening agent in baking, consisting of sodium bicarbonate, an acid substance, and a starch.

bak′ing so′da, *n.* SODIUM BICARBONATE.

ba·kla·va (bä′klə vä′, bä′klə vä′), *n.* a Greek and Middle Eastern pastry made of many layers of paper-thin dough with a filling of ground nuts, baked and drenched in honey or sugar syrup.

Ba·kon·go (bə kong′gō), *n.pl.* KONGO (def. 2).

Ba·ku (bu kōō′), *n.* the capital of Azerbaijan, in the E part, on the Caspian Sea. 1,757,000.

Ba·laam (bā′ləm), *n.* a Mesopotamian diviner who, when commanded to curse the Israelites, blessed them instead after being rebuked by the ass he rode. Num. 22–23.

Ba·lak (bā′lak), *n.* a Moabite king who sent for Balaam to come and curse the Israelites. Num. 22–23.

bal·a·lai·ka (bal′ə lī′kə), *n., pl.* **-kas.** a Russian stringed instrument with a triangular body and a guitarlike neck.

bal·ance (bal′əns), *n., v.,* **-anced, -anc·ing.** —*n.* **1.** a state of equilibrium or equipoise; equal distribution of weight, amount, etc. **2.** something used to produce equilibrium; counterpoise. **3.** the ability to maintain bodily equilibrium. **4.** mental or emotional steadiness. **5.** an instrument for determining weight, typically by the equilibrium of a bar, from each end of which is suspended a scale or pan. **6.** the remainder or rest. **7.** the power or ability to decide an outcome. **8. a.** equality between the totals of the two sides of an account. **b.** the difference between the debit total and the credit total of an account. **c.** unpaid difference represented by the excess of debits over credits. **9.** preponderating weight: *The balance of the blame is on your side.* **10.** the harmonious integration of components in an artistic work. **11.** a wheel that oscillates against the tension of a hairspring to regulate the beats of a watch or clock. **12.** (in a stereophonic sound system) the comparative loudness of two speakers. —*v.t.* **13.** to bring to or hold in equilibrium; poise: *to balance a book on one's head.* **14.** to arrange or adjust the parts of symmetrically. **15.** to be equal or proportionate to. **16.** to add up the two sides of (an account) and determine the difference. **17.** to weigh in a balance. **18.** to estimate the relative weight or importance of. **19.** to serve as a counterpoise to. —*v.i.* **20.** to have an equality or equivalence; be in equilibrium. **21.** to be in a state wherein debits equal credits. **22.** to waver or hesitate. —*Idiom.* **23. in the balance,** with the outcome in doubt. **24. on balance,** considering all aspects.

bal′ance beam′, *n.* a narrow wooden rail set horizontally on upright posts about 4 ft. (1.2 m) from the floor, used for performing feats of balancing and demonstrating gymnastic ability.

bal′anced tick′et, *n.* a slate of candidates chosen to appeal to a wide range of voters, esp. by including members of large regional, ethnic, or religious groups.

bal′ance of na′ture, *n.* population equilibrium among organisms and their environments resulting from interaction and interdependency.

bal′ance of pay′ments, *n.* the difference between a nation's payments to foreign countries and its receipts from foreign countries.

bal′ance of pow′er, *n.* a distribution of forces among nations or groups such that no single one is strong enough to assert its will or dominate the others.

bal′ance of ter′ror, *n.* the distribution of nuclear arms among nations such that no nation will initiate an attack for fear of retaliation: *maintaining the balance of terror between the United States and the Soviet Union.*

bal′ance of trade′, *n.* the difference in value between imports and exports, said to be favorable to a country when exports are greater.

bal′ance sheet′, *n.* a statement of the financial position of a business on a specified date, esp. a tabular statement showing the debit and credit balances to be equal in a set of accounts.

Bal·an·chine (bal′ən chēn′, bal′ən chēn′), *n.* **George,** 1904–83, U.S. choreographer, born in Russia.

ba·la·ta (bə lä′tə, bal′ə tə), *n., pl.* **-tas. 1.** BULLY TREE. **2.** a gum ob-

tained from the latex of the bully tree, used in golf ball covers and machinery belts.

Bal·bo·a (bal bō′ə), *n., pl.* **-bo·as. 1. Vasco Núñez de,** 1475?–1517, Spanish explorer who discovered the Pacific Ocean in 1513. **2.** (*l.c.*) the basic monetary unit of Panama.

bal·co·ny (bal′kə nē), *n., pl.* **-nies. 1.** a balustraded or railed elevated platform projecting from the wall of a building. **2.** a gallery in a theater. —**bal′co·nied,** *adj.*

bald (bôld), *adj.* **1.** having little or no hair on the scalp. **2.** destitute of some natural growth or covering: *a bald mountain.* **3.** plain: *a bald prose style.* **4.** undisguised: *a bald lie.* **5.** having white on the head: *the bald eagle.* **6.** (of a tire) having the tread worn away. —*v.i.* **7.** to become bald.

bal·da·chin or **bal·da·quin** (bal′də kin, bôl′-), *n.* **1.** a silk brocade woven or embroidered with gold threads. **2.** a permanent ornamental canopy, as of marble or stone, above an altar, throne, etc. **3.** a portable canopy carried in religious processions. —**bal′da·chined,** *adj.*

bald′ cy′press, *n.* a deciduous cone-bearing hardwood tree, *Taxodium distichum,* growing in southern U.S. swamplands.

bald′ ea′gle, *n.* a large fish-eating eagle, *Haliaeetus leucocephalus,* of the U.S. and Canada, having dark golden brown back and wings and white plumage on the head and tail in the adult: the national symbol of the United States.

bald eagle,
Haliaeetus leucocephalus,
length 2½ ft. (0.8 m);
wingspread to 7½ ft.
(2.3 m)

bal·der·dash (bôl′dər dash′), *n.* senseless, stupid, or exaggerated talk or writing; nonsense.

bald·pate (bôld′pāt′), *n.* **1.** a person with a bald head. **2.** the American wigeon, *Anas americana,* having a gray head and a white crown.

bale (bāl), *n., v.,* **baled, bal·ing.** —*n.* **1.** a large bundle, esp. one tightly compressed and secured by wires, cords, or the like: *a bale of cotton.* —*v.t.* **2.** to make into bales. —**bal′er,** *n.*

ba·leen (bə lēn′), *n.* WHALEBONE (def. 1).

bale·ful (bāl′fəl), *adj.* menacing or malign; threatening evil: *baleful glances.* —**bale′ful·ly,** *adv.* —**bale′ful·ness,** *n.*

Ba·li (bä′lē, bal′ē), *n.* an island in Indonesia, E of Java. 2,469,930; 2147 sq. mi. (5561 sq. km).

balk (bôk), *v.i.* **1.** to refuse curtly and firmly (usu. fol. by *at*): *He balked at making the speech.* **2.** to stop short and stubbornly refuse to go on. **3.** to commit a balk in baseball. —*v.t.* **4.** to place an obstacle in the way of; hinder; thwart. —*n.* **5.** a baseball pitcher's illegal motion or feint, penalized by awarding a runner or runners an advance to the next base. **6.** a check or hindrance; defeat; disappointment. **7.** a strip of land left unplowed. **8.** any heavy timber used for building purposes. —**balk′er,** *n.* —**balk′ing·ly,** *adv.*

Bal·kan (bôl′kən), *adj.* **1.** of or pertaining to the Balkan Peninsula or its inhabitants. —*n.* **2. the Balkans.** Also called **the Bal′kan States′.** the countries in the Balkan Peninsula: Yugoslavia, Romania, Bulgaria, Albania, Greece, and the European part of Turkey.

Bal·kan·ize (bôl′kə nīz′), *v.t.,* **-ized, -iz·ing.** to divide (a country, area, etc.) into small, often quarrelsome states. —**Bal′kan·i·za′tion,** *n.*

balk·y (bô′kē), *adj.,* **balk·i·er, balk·i·est.** given to balking; stubborn; obstinate. —**balk′i·ly,** *adv.* —**balk′i·ness,** *n.*

ball¹ (bôl), *n.* **1.** a spherical or approximately spherical body; sphere. **2.** a round or roundish body, of various sizes and materials, either hollow or solid, for use in games, as baseball, football, or golf. **3.** a pitched ball in baseball that is not swung at by the batter and does not pass through the strike zone. **4. a.** a solid, spherical projectile for a weapon. **b.** projectiles collectively. **5.** a part, esp. of the human body, that is rounded or protuberant: *the ball of the thumb.* **6.** a planetary or celestial body, esp. the earth. —*v.t.* **7.** to make into a ball or balls. —*v.i.* **8.** to form or gather into a ball. **9. ball up,** *Informal.* to make into a mess; confuse. —*Idiom.* **10. carry the ball,** to assume the responsibility; bear the burden. **11. get** or **start** (or **keep**) **the ball rolling,** to initiate (or continue) an activity. **12. on the ball, a.** alert or vital. **b.** into a state of alertness and efficiency: *to get on the ball.* **c.** indicating intelligence and ability: *to have a lot on the ball.* **13. play ball,** to work together; cooperate. **14. The ball is in one's court,** it is one's turn to take action.

ball² (bôl), *n.* **1.** a large, usu. lavish, formal party featuring social dancing, sometimes given to introduce debutantes or benefit a charitable organization. **2.** *Informal.* a thoroughly good time.

bal·lad (bal′əd), *n.* **1.** a simple song; air. **2.** a simple narrative poem, esp. of folk origin, composed in short stanzas and adapted for singing. **3.** a slow romantic or sentimental popular song.

bal·lade (bə läd′, ba-), *n.* **1.** a poem consisting commonly of three stanzas having an identical rhyme scheme, followed by an envoy, and having the same last line for each of the stanzas and the envoy. **2.** a romantic musical composition, esp. one for piano.

ball′ and chain′, *n.* a heavy iron ball fastened by a chain to a prisoner's leg.

ball′-and-sock′et joint′, *n.* **1.** an anatomical joint in which the rounded end of one bone fits into a cuplike end of the other bone. **2.** Also called **ball joint.** a similar mechanical joint used to connect rods, pipes, etc.

bal·last (bal′əst), *n.* **1.** a heavy material carried on a vessel to control draft and stability or a balloon to control altitude. **2.** gravel or broken stone placed under the ties of a railroad. **3.** a device that maintains the current in an electric circuit at a constant value and may also provide the starting voltage. —*v.t.* **4.** to furnish with ballast.

ball′ bear′ing, *n.* **1.** a bearing consisting of a number of hard balls running in grooves in the surfaces of two concentric rings, one of which is mounted on a rotating or oscillating shaft. **2.** any of the balls so used.

ball′car′ri·er or **ball′-car′rier,** *n. Football.* the offensive player having the ball and attempting to gain ground.

bal·le·ri·na (bal′ə rē′nə), *n., pl.* **-nas.** a female ballet dancer.

bal·let (ba lā′, bal′ā), *n.* **1.** a form of theatrical dance characterized by graceful, balanced movements with fully extended limbs, initiated from a restricted set of body positions. **2.** a theatrical work incorporating ballet dancing, music, and scenery to tell a story or convey a thematic atmosphere. —**bal·let·ic** (ba let′ik, bə-), *adj.*

bal·let·o·mane (ba let′ə mān′, bə-), *n.* a ballet enthusiast. —**bal·let′o·ma′ni·a,** *n.*

bal·lis·tic (bə lis′tik), *adj.* **1.** of or pertaining to ballistics. **2.** having its motion determined or describable by the laws of exterior ballistics. —*Idiom.* **3. go ballistic,** to become overwrought or irrational.

bal·lis·tics (bə lis′tiks), *n.* (*usu. used with a sing. v.*) **1.** the science or study of the motion of projectiles, as bullets, shells, or bombs. **2.** the art or science of designing projectiles for maximum flight performance. —**bal·lis·ti·cian** (bal′ə stish′ən), *n.*

ball′ of wax′, *n. Informal.* everything, including all details, parts, etc., relating to a particular matter: *contract for the whole ball of wax.*

bal·loon (bə lōōn′), *n.* **1.** an inflatable rubber bag used as a toy or for decoration. **2.** a fabric bag filled with heated air or a gas lighter than air, designed to rise and float, often with a gondola suspended under it for passengers or instruments. **3.** (in cartoons) an outline enclosing words represented as issuing from the mouth of a speaker. —*v.i.* **4.** to ride in a balloon. **5.** to puff out like a balloon. **6.** to increase at a rapid rate. —*v.t.* **7.** to inflate or distend (something) like a balloon. —*adj.* **8.** puffed out like a balloon: *balloon sleeves.* **9.** (esp. of a loan or mortgage) having a payment at the end of the term that is much bigger than the previous ones. —**bal·loon′like′,** *adj.*

balloon′ tire′, *n.* a broad tire filled with air at low pressure, used esp. in bicycles and early automobiles to cushion the shock of uneven surfaces.

balloon′ vine′, *n.* a tropical climbing plant, *Cardiospermum halicacabum,* of the soapberry family, bearing large bladderlike pods.

bal·lot (bal′ət), *n.* **1.** a sheet of paper or the like on which a voter marks his or her vote. **2.** the method of secret voting by printed or written ballot or by voting machine. **3.** a round of voting: *defeated on the third ballot.* **4.** the list of candidates to be voted on. **5.** the right to vote. **6.** the whole number of votes cast or recorded. **7.** a system or the practice of drawing lots: *chosen by ballot.* **8.** a little ball used in voting. —*v.i.* **9.** to vote by ballot. **10.** to draw lots: *to ballot for places.* —*v.t.* **11.** to canvass or solicit for votes. **12.** to vote on or select by ballot.

bal′lot box′, *n.* **1.** a receptacle for voters' ballots. **2.** a system or instance of voting by ballot. —*Idiom.* **3. stuff the ballot box, a.** originally, to insert prepared ballots illegally into a ballot box in order to distort the count of votes in favor of one candidate. **b.** in current usage, to commit any kind of electoral fraud.

ball·park (bôl′pärk′), *n.* **1.** a tract of land or a stadium where ball games, esp. baseball, are played. —*adj.* **2.** being an approximation; based on an educated guess: *a ballpark figure on expenses.* —*Idiom.* **3. in the ballpark, a.** within reasonable limits. **b.** close to the correct or expected amount.

ball′-peen ham′mer (bôl′pēn′), *n.* a hammer with a hemispherical peen (**ball′ peen′**) for beating metal.

ball·point (bôl′point′), *n.* a pen in which the point is a fine ball bearing that rotates against a supply of semisolid ink in a cartridge. Also called **ball′point pen′.**

ball′room dance′, *n.* any of a variety of dances performed by couples, as the waltz and tango. —**ball′room danc′ing,** *n.*

bal·ly·hoo (*n., v.* bal′ē hōō′; *v. also* bal′ē hōō′), *n., pl.* **-hoos,** *v.,* **-hooed, -hoo·ing.** —*n.* **1.** a clamorous and vigorous attempt to win customers or advance a cause; blatant advertising or publicity. **2.** clamor or outcry. —*v.t., v.i.* **3.** to promote with ballyhoo.

balm (bäm), *n.* **1.** any of various fragrant gum resins used in perfumery or medicine, esp. from tropical trees of the genus *Commiphora,* of the bursera family. **2.** a plant or tree yielding such a substance. **3.** any aromatic or fragrant ointment used for healing, soothing, or mitigating pain. **4.** aromatic fragrance. **5.** any of various aromatic plants of the mint family, esp. those of the genus *Melissa,* having ovate, scented leaves. **6.** anything that heals, soothes, or mitigates pain: *the balm of friendship.* [< Latin *balsamum* BALSAM]

balm′ in Gil′ead, *n.* a remedy or consolation. Jer. 8:22; 46:11.

balm′-of-Gil′ead, *n.* **1.** any of several plants of the genus *Commiphora,* of the bursera family, esp. *C. opobalsamum* and *C. meccanensis,* which yield a fragrant oleoresin. **2.** the resin itself, a turbid, viscid liquid used chiefly in perfumery. **3.** a hybrid North American poplar, *Populus gileadensis,* cultivated as a shade tree. [named after the balm referred to in Jer. 8:22; cf. BALM IN GILEAD]

balm·y (bä′mē), *adj.,* **balm·i·er, balm·i·est.** **1.** mild and refreshing; soft; soothing: *balmy weather.* **2.** *Informal.* crazy; foolish; eccentric.

bal·ne·ol·o·gy (bal′nē ol′ə jē), *n.* the study of the therapeutic effects of baths and bathing.

ba·lo·ney or **bo·lo·ney** (bə lō′nē), *n.* **1.** *Slang.* foolishness; nonsense. **2.** BOLOGNA. —*interj.* **3.** *Slang.* nonsense.

bal·sa (bôl′sə, bäl′-), *n., pl.* **-sas.** **1.** a tropical American tree, *Ochroma pyramidale* (*lagopus*), of the bombax family, yielding a light wood used for rafts, toy airplanes, etc. **2.** a life raft.

bal·sam (bôl′səm), *n.* **1.** any of various fragrant resins exuded from certain trees, esp. trees of the genus *Commiphora,* as balm-of-Gilead. Compare BALM (def. 1). **2.** any of various trees yielding a balsam, esp. the balsam fir. **3.** any of several plants belonging to the genus *Impatiens,* as *I. balsamina,* a common garden annual. **4.** any aromatic ointment for ceremonial or medicinal use. **5.** BALM (def. 6). —**bal·sa·ma·ceous** (bôl′sə mā′shəs), *adj.* —**bal·sam·ic** (bôl sam′ik), *adj.*

bal′sam fir′, *n.* **1.** a North American fir, *Abies balsamea,* having dark purplish cones and yielding Canada balsam. **2.** the wood of this tree.

balsam′ic vin′egar, *n.* a sweetish, aromatic vinegar made from the must of white grapes and aged in wood barrels.

bal′sam pop′lar, *n.* a North American poplar, *Populus balsamifera,* having sticky resinous buds and shiny ovate leaves; tacamahac.

Bal·tha·zar (bôl thaz′ər, bal-, bôl′thə zär′, bal′-), *n.* **1.** one of the three Magi. **2.** a wine bottle holding 13 quarts (12.3 liters).

Bal·tic (bôl′tik), *adj.* **1.** of or pertaining to the Baltic Sea and the land around it. **2.** of or pertaining to the language family Baltic and its speakers. —*n.* **3.** a branch of the Indo-European family of languages that includes Lithuanian, Latvian, and Old Prussian.

Bal′tic Sea′, *n.* a sea in N Europe, bounded by Denmark, Sweden, Finland, Estonia, Latvia, Lithuania, Poland, and Germany. ab. 160,000 sq. mi. (414,000 sq. km).

Bal·ti·more (bôl′tə môr′, -mōr′), *n.* **1.** Lord, CALVERT, Sir George. **2.** a seaport in N Maryland, near the Chesapeake Bay. 702,979.

Bal′timore o′riole, *n.* a North American oriole, *Icterus galbula galbula,* the eastern subspecies of the northern oriole, the male of which has a black head and upper body, bright orange underparts and tail, and a white wing bar.

bal·us·ter (bal′ə stər), *n.* **1.** any of a number of closely spaced supports for a railing. **2. balusters,** a balustrade. **3.** any of various symmetrical supports, as furniture legs or spindles, tending to swell toward the bottom or top. —**bal′us·tered,** *adj.*

bal·us·trade (bal′ə strād′, bal′ə strād′), *n.* a railing with its supporting balusters. —**bal′us·trad′ed,** *adj.*

Bal·zac (bôl′zak, bal′-; *Fr.* bAl zAk′), *n.* **Honoré de,** 1799–1850, French novelist.

Ba·ma·ko (bam′ə kō′, bä′mə kō′), *n.* the capital of Mali: inland port on the Niger River. 404,022.

bam·bi·no (bam bē′nō, bäm-), *n., pl.* **-nos, -ni.** (-nē). **1.** a small child or baby. **2.** an image of the infant Jesus.

bam·boo (bam bōō′), *n., pl.* **-boos. 1.** any of various tall, sometimes treelike tropical and semitropical grasses, as of the genera *Bambusa, Phyllostachys,* and *Dendrocalamus,* having woody, usu. hollow stems bearing stalks of narrow leaves. **2.** the stem of such a plant, used as a building material and for making furniture.

bam′boo cur′tain, *n.* a political and ideological barrier impeding relations between Communist China and the West.

bamboo′ shoot′, *n.* the young shoot produced by the rhizome of a bamboo, used as a vegetable.

bam·boo·zle (bam bōō′zəl), *v.,* **-zled, -zling.** —*v.t.* **1.** to deceive or get the better of by underhandedness; hoodwink. **2.** to perplex; mystify. —*v.i.* **3.** to practice trickery, deception, or the like. —**bam·boo′zle·ment,** *n.* —**bam·boo′zler,** *n.*

ban[1] (ban), *v.,* **banned, ban·ning,** *n.* —*v.t.* **1.** to prohibit, forbid, or bar; interdict: *to ban nuclear weapons.* —*n.* **2.** the act of prohibiting by law; interdiction. **3.** informal denunciation or prohibition, as by public opinion. **4.** a formal ecclesiastical condemnation or excommunication. **5.** a malediction; curse. —**ban′na·ble,** *adj.*

ban[2] (ban), *n.* **1.** the summoning of the sovereign's vassals for military service. **2.** the body of vassals summoned.

ba·nal (bə nal′, -näl′, bān′l), *adj.* devoid of freshness or originality; hackneyed; trite. —**ba·nal′i·ty,** *n.* —**ba·nal′ly,** *adv.*

ba·nal·ize (bə nal′īz, -nā′līz, bān′l īz′), *v.t.,* **-ized, -iz·ing.** to render or make banal; trivialize.

ba·nan·a (bə nan′ə), *n., pl.* **-nan·as. 1.** a tropical plant of the genus *Musa,* certain species of which are cultivated for their nutritious fruit. **2.** the fruit, esp. that of *M. paradisiaca,* with yellow or reddish rind. [< Spanish < Portuguese < a West African language]

banan′a oil′, *n.* a sweet-smelling liquid ester, $C_7H_{14}O_2$, having a bananalike odor: used as a paint solvent and in artificial fruit flavors.

B

banan′a split′, *n.* a dessert consisting of ice cream scoops placed on a banana sliced lengthwise and topped with syrup, whipped cream, etc.

ba•nau•sic (bə nô′sik, -zik), *adj.* serving utilitarian purposes only.

band¹ (band), *n.* **1.** a company of persons, animals, or things acting or functioning together; aggregation: *a band of protesters.* **2. a.** an orchestra composed chiefly of brass, woodwind, and percussion instruments. **b.** a musical group of a specialized type: *rock band.* **3.** a relatively small group of nomadic people who camp together and subsist by foraging. —*v.t.* **4.** to unite in a troop, company, or confederacy. —*v.i.* **5.** to unite; confederate (often fol. by *together*).

band² (band), *n.* **1.** a thin, flat strip of some material, as for binding or trimming. **2.** a fillet, belt, or strap: *a band for the hair.* **3.** a stripe, as of color. **4.** a plain or simply styled ring. **5.** a segment of a phonograph record on which sound has been recorded. **6.** Also called **wave band.** a specific range of frequencies, esp. a set of radio frequencies, as HF, VHF, and UHF. **7.** one or more tracks or channels on a computer's magnetic drum. —*v.t.* **8.** to mark or furnish with a band. —**band′er,** *n.*

band•age (ban′dij), *n., v.,* **-aged, -ag•ing.** —*n.* **1.** a strip of cloth or other material used to bind up a wound, sore, sprain, etc. **2.** anything used as a band or ligature. —*v.t.* **3.** to bind or cover with a bandage.

Band-Aid (band′ād′), **1.** *Trademark.* an adhesive bandage with a gauze pad in the center, used to cover minor abrasions and cuts. —*n.* **2.** (*often l.c.*) a makeshift, limited, or temporary aid or solution.

ban•dan•na or **ban•dan•a** (ban dan′ə), *n., pl.* **-dan•nas** or **-dan•as.** a large, usu. figured handkerchief often worn as a scarf.

Ban•dar Se•ri Be•ga•wan (bun′dər ser′ē bə gä′wən), *n.* the capital of the sultanate of Brunei, on the NW coast of Borneo, in the Malay Archipelago. 63,868.

B and B or **B&B,** bed-and-breakfast.

band•box (band′boks′), *n.* a box of pasteboard or thin wood for holding light articles of apparel.

ban•deau (ban dō′, ban′dō), *n., pl.* **-deaux** (-dōz′, -dōz). **1.** a headband. **2.** a narrow brassiere.

ban•de•role or **ban•de•rol** (ban′də rōl′), *n.* **1.** a small flag or streamer. **2.** a narrow scroll usu. bearing an inscription.

ban•der•snatch (ban′dər snach′), *n.* an imaginary wild animal of fierce disposition.

ban•di•coot (ban′di ko͞ot′), *n.* **1.** any of several large East Indian rats of the genera *Nesokia* and *Bandicota.* **2.** any of several insectivorous and herbivorous marsupials of the family Peramelidae, of Australia and New Guinea.

ban•dit (ban′dit), *n.* **1.** a robber, esp. a member of a gang or marauding band. **2.** an outlaw. **3.** *Informal.* a person who takes unfair advantage of others, as a merchant who overcharges; swindler; cheat.

band•lead•er (band′lē′dər), *n.* the leader of a musical band, esp. a dance band.

ban•do•leer or **ban•do•lier** (ban′dl ēr′), *n.* a broad belt with small loops or pockets for cartridges, worn over the shoulder by soldiers.

band′ saw′ or **band′saw′,** *n.* a saw consisting of an endless toothed steel band passing over two wheels.

band′ shell′, *n.* a concave, acoustically resonant structure at the back of an outdoor bandstand.

band•stand (band′stand′), *n.* a raised platform for the players in a band or orchestra.

band•wag•on (band′wag′ən), *n.* **1.** a large ornate wagon for carrying band musicians, as in a circus. —***Idiom.*** **2. climb** or **jump on the bandwagon,** to join a party, cause, movement, etc., that appears to be gaining popular support.

band•width (band′width′, -with′), *n.* **1.** the smallest range of electronic frequencies constituting a band, within which a particular signal can be transmitted without distortion. **2.** the capacity of a computer network to carry software programs and information.

ban•dy (ban′dē), *v.,* **-died, -dy•ing,** *adj., n., pl.* **-dies.** —*v.t.* **1.** to pass from one to another or back and forth; trade; exchange: *to bandy blows.* **2.** to throw or strike to and fro or from side to side, as a ball in tennis. **3.** to circulate freely: *to bandy gossip.* —*adj.* **4.** (of legs) having a bend or crook outward; bowed. —*n.* **5.** a game resembling ice hockey.

bane (bān), *n.* **1.** a person or thing that ruins or spoils: *Gambling was the bane of his existence.* **2.** a deadly poison (often used in the names of poisonous plants): *wolfsbane; henbane.* **3.** death; destruction; ruin.

bane•ber•ry (bān′ber′ē, -bə rē), *n., pl.* **-ries.** **1.** any plant belonging to the genus *Actaea,* of the buttercup family, having large compound leaves, spikes of small white flowers, and poisonous red or white berries. **2.** the berry of such a plant.

bane•ful (bān′fəl), *adj.* destructive, pernicious, or poisonous.

bang¹ (bang), *n.* **1.** a loud, sudden, explosive noise, as the discharge of a gun. **2.** a resounding stroke or blow: *a nasty bang on the head.* **3.** a sudden movement or show of energy. **4.** *Informal.* thrill; excitement: *to get a big bang out of movies.* **5.** *Computer and Printing Slang.* the exclamation point. —*v.t.* **6.** to strike or beat resoundingly; pound: *to bang a door.* **7.** to hit or bump painfully. **8.** to throw or set down roughly; slam. —*v.i.* **9.** to strike violently or noisily: *to bang on the door.* **10.** to make a loud, explosive noise. **11. bang up,** to damage, as through a hard blow. —*adv.* **12.** abruptly or violently: *She fell bang against the wall.* **13.** directly; precisely; right: *He stood bang in the middle of the flower bed.* —***Idiom.*** **14. bang for the buck,** *Slang.* value for money.

bang² (bang), *n.* Often, **bangs.** a fringe of hair cut or combed to fall over the forehead.

Bang•kok (bang′kok, bang kok′), *n.* the capital of Thailand, in the S central part, on the Chao Phraya. 5,609,352.

Ban•gla•desh (bäng′glə desh′, bang′-), *n.* a republic in S Asia, N of the Bay of Bengal: mem. of the Commonwealth of Nations; a former province of Pakistan. 125,340,261; 54,501 sq. mi. (141,158 sq. km). *Cap.:* Dhaka. —**Ban′gla•desh′i,** *n., pl.* **-desh•is,** *adj.*

ban•gle (bang′gəl), *n.* a rigid bracelet, usu. without a clasp.

Ban•gui (*Fr.* bäɴ gē′), *n.* the capital of the Central African Republic, in the SW part. 596,776.

bang′-up′, *adj. Informal.* excellent; extraordinary.

ban•ish (ban′ish), *v.t.* **1.** to expel from or relegate to a country or place by authoritative decree; condemn to exile. **2.** to send, drive, or put away: *to banish sorrow.* —**ban′ish•ment,** *n.*

ban•is•ter or **ban•nis•ter** (ban′ə stər), *n.* **1.** Sometimes, **banisters.** a handrail and its supporting posts, esp. on a staircase; balustrade. **2.** a handrail, esp. on a staircase. **3.** a baluster.

ban•jo (ban′jō), *n., pl.* **-jos, -joes.** a musical instrument of the guitar family, having a circular body covered in front with tightly stretched parchment and played with the fingers or a plectrum. —**ban′jo•ist,** *n.*

Ban•jul (bän′jo͞ol), *n.* the capital of The Gambia. 44,188.

bank¹ (bangk), *n.* **1.** a long pile or heap; mass: *a bank of earth; a bank of clouds.* **2.** a slope or acclivity. **3.** the slope immediately bordering a stream course along which the water normally runs. **4.** a broad elevation of the sea floor around which the water is relatively shallow. **5.** Also called **cant.** the inclination of the bed of a banked road or track. **6.** the lateral inclination of an aircraft, esp. during a turn. **7.** the cushion of a billiard table. —*v.t.* **8.** to border with or like a bank: *banking the flooded river with sandbags.* **9.** to form into a bank or heap: *to bank snow along a path.* **10.** to build (a road or track) with an upward slope from the inner edge to the outer edge at a curve. **11.** to tip or incline (an airplane) laterally. **12.** (in billiards or pool) **a.** to drive (a ball) to the cushion. **b.** to pocket (the object ball) by driving it against the bank. **13.** to cover (a fire) with ashes or fuel to make it burn long and slowly. —*v.i.* **14.** to build up in or form banks, as clouds or snow. **15.** (of an airplane) to tip or incline laterally. **16.** (of a road or track) to slope upward from the inner edge to the outer edge at a curve.

bank² (bangk), *n.* **1.** an institution for receiving, lending, and safeguarding money and transacting other financial business. **2.** the stock of pieces drawn upon by players in the course of a game, as dominoes. **3.** the person or office in a gambling establishment that holds and distributes cash. **4.** a special storage place: *a blood bank.* **5.** a reserve. —*v.i.* **6.** to keep money in or have an account with a bank. —*v.t.* **7.** to deposit in a bank. **8. bank on** or **upon,** to count on; depend on.

bank³ (bangk), *n.* **1.** an arrangement of objects in a line or in tiers: *a bank of lights.* **2.** a bench for rowers in a galley. **3.** the group of rowers on one bench or rowing one oar. **4.** a number of similar devices connected to act together: *a bank of transformers.* —*v.t.* **5.** to arrange in a bank.

bank•a•ble (bang′kə bəl), *adj.* **1.** acceptable for processing by a bank. **2.** considered powerful or prestigious enough to ensure profitability: *to hire bankable stars for a film.* —**bank′a•bil′i•ty,** *n.*

bank′ account′, *n.* ACCOUNT (def. 7).

bank•book (bangk′bo͝ok′), *n.* a book held by a depositor in which a bank enters a record of deposits and withdrawals.

bank′ draft′, *n.* a draft drawn by one bank on another.

bank•er (bang′kər), *n.* **1.** a person employed by a bank, esp. as an executive or other official. **2.** the keeper or holder of the bank in a game.

bank•ing (bang′king), *n.* the business carried on by or with a bank.

bank′note′, *n.* a promissory note, payable on demand, issued by an authorized bank and intended to circulate as money.

bank•roll (bangk′rōl′), *n.* **1.** money in one's possession; monetary resources. —*v.t.* **2.** to finance; provide funds for.

bank•rupt (bangk′rupt, -rəpt), *n.* **1.** a person who is adjudged insolvent by a court and whose property is divided among creditors under the bankruptcy laws. **2.** any insolvent debtor. **3.** a person lacking in a particular thing or quality: *a moral bankrupt.* —*adj.* **4.** subject to legal process because of insolvency; insolvent. **5.** lacking something; bereft (usu. fol. by *of* or *in*): *bankrupt of compassion.* **6.** pertaining to bankruptcy. —*v.t.* **7.** to make bankrupt. —**bank′rupt•cy,** *n., pl.* **-cies.**

bank′ shot′, *n.* a shot in billiards and pool in which the cue ball or object ball is banked.

bank•si•a (bangk′sē ə), *n., pl.* **-si•as.** any Australian shrub or tree of the genus *Banksia,* of the protea family, having alternate leaves and dense cylindrical flower heads.

Ban-Lon (ban′lon′), *Trademark.* a brand of multistranded, continuous-filament synthetic yarn modified by crimping to increase bulk.

Ban•ne•ker (ban′i kər), *n.* **Benjamin,** 1731–1806, U.S. mathematician, natural historian, and astronomer.

ban•ner (ban′ər), *n.* **1.** the flag of a country, army, troop, etc. **2.** an ensign or the like bearing some device, motto, or slogan, as one carried in religious processions or political demonstrations. **3.** a flag formerly used as the standard of a sovereign, lord, or knight. **4.** a sign painted on cloth and hung over a street, entrance, etc. **5.** anything regarded or displayed as a symbol of principles. **6.** a headline in large, bold type across the top of a newspaper page. **7.** a streamer with lettering, towed behind an airplane for advertising purposes. —*adj.* **8.** leading or foremost; outstanding: *a banner year for crops.*

Ban•nis•ter (ban′ə stər), *n.* **Sir Roger (Gilbert),** born 1929, English track and field athlete: first to run a mile in less than four minutes.

ban•nock (ban′ək), *n. Chiefly Scot.* a flat cake made of oatmeal, barley meal, etc., usu. baked on a griddle.

banns (banz), *n.* (*used with a pl. v.*) **1.** notice of an intended marriage posted by a church. **2.** any public announcement of a proposed marriage, made in a church or by church officials.

ban•quet (bang′kwit), *n.* **1.** a lavish meal; feast. **2.** a ceremonious public dinner, as to honor a person or benefit a charity.

ban•quette (bang ket′; *locally* bang′kit *for 2*), *n.* **1.** a long bench with an upholstered seat, esp. one along a wall, as in a restaurant. **2.** *Coastal Louisiana and East Texas.* a sidewalk, esp. a raised one of bricks or planks. **3.** a platform or step along the inside of a parapet, for soldiers to stand on when firing. **4.** a ledge running across the back of a buffet.

ban•shee or **ban•shie** (ban′shē, ban shē′), *n.* (in Irish folklore) a spirit in the form of a wailing woman who appears to or is heard by members of a family as a sign that one of them is about to die. [< Irish *bean sídhe* lit., woman of a fairy mound]

ban•tam (ban′təm), *n.* **1.** (*often cap.*) a chicken of any of several varieties or breeds characterized by very small size. **2.** a small and feisty or quarrelsome person. —*adj.* **3.** diminutive; tiny. **4.** feisty; combative.

ban•tam•weight (ban′təm wāt′), *n.* a boxer or weightlifter intermediate in weight between a flyweight and a featherweight, esp. a professional boxer weighing up to 118 pounds (53 kg).

ban•ter (ban′tər), *n.* **1.** an exchange of light, playful remarks. —*v.t.* **2.** to address with banter; chaff. —*v.i.* **3.** to use banter.

ban-the-bomb•er (ban′t͟hə bom′ər), *n. Informal.* a person who vigorously advocates banning the development or use of nuclear weapons.

Ban•ting (ban′ting), *n.* **Sir Frederick Grant,** 1891–1941, Canadian physician: one of the discoverers of insulin.

Ban•tu (ban′to͞o), *n., pl.* **-tus,** (*esp. collectively*) **-tu. 1.** a family of more than 200 languages, a branch of the Benue-Congo family, whose speakers make up most of the population of central and S Africa. **2.** (*used with a pl. v.*) the group of culturally diverse African peoples who speak Bantu languages. **3.** a member of a Bantu-speaking people.

ban•yan (ban′yən), *n.* an East Indian fig tree, *Ficus benghalensis,* of the mulberry family, having branches that send out adventitious roots to the ground and sometimes cause the tree to spread over a wide area.

ban•zai (bän zī′, bän′-), *interj.* **1.** (used as a Japanese patriotic cry or joyous shout.) **2.** (used as a Japanese battle cry.) [< Japanese, = *ban* ten thousand + *-zai,* year]

ba•o•bab (bā′ō bab′, bä′ō-, bou′bab), *n.* a large tropical African tree, *Adansonia digitata,* of the bombax family, that has an extremely thick trunk and bears a gourdlike fruit.

bap•tism (bap′tiz əm), *n.* **1.** a ceremonial immersion in water, or application of water, as an initiatory rite or sacrament of the Christian church. Some Christian churches restrict baptism to individuals, usually adults, who declare faith in Christ **(believer's baptism).** Other churches baptize children shortly after birth **(infant baptism)** though adults may also be baptized. **2.** any similar ceremony or action of initiation, dedication, etc. —**bap•tis′mal,** *adj.*

bap′tism of fire′, *n.* **1.** spiritual sanctification as a gift of the Holy Ghost. **2.** the first experience of a soldier in combat. **3.** any severe ordeal that tests one's endurance.

Bap•tist (bap′tist), *n.* **1.** a member of a Christian denomination that baptizes believers by immersion and that is usu. Calvinistic in doctrine. **2.** (*l.c.*) a person who baptizes. **3. the Baptist,** JOHN THE BAPTIST. —*adj.* **4.** of or pertaining to Baptists.

bap•tis•ter•y (bap′tə strē, -tis tə rē), *n., pl.* **-ter•ies. 1.** a building or a part of a church in which baptism is administered. **2.** (esp. in Baptist churches) a tank for administering baptism by immersion.

bap•tize (bap tīz′, bap′tīz), *v.,* **-tized, -tiz•ing.** —*v.t.* **1.** to immerse in water or sprinkle or pour water on in the Christian rite of baptism. **2.** to give a name to at baptism; christen. **3.** to initiate or dedicate by purifying. —*v.i.* **4.** to administer baptism. [< Greek *baptizein* to immerse]

bar[1] (bär), *n., v.,* **barred, bar•ring,** *prep.* —*n.* **1.** a relatively long, evenly shaped piece of some solid substance, as metal or wood, used as a guard or obstruction or for some mechanical purpose: *the bars of a prison.* **2.** an oblong piece of any solid material: *a bar of soap; a candy bar.* **3.** an ingot, lump, or wedge of gold or silver. **4.** a long ridge of sand, gravel, or other material near or slightly above the surface of a body of water, often an obstruction to navigation. **5.** any obstacle or barrier. **6.** a counter or place where beverages, esp. liquors, or light foods are served to customers: *a coffee bar, a wine bar.* **7.** a barroom or tavern. **8.** a counter, small wagon, or similar piece of furniture for serving food or beverages: *a breakfast bar.* **9. a.** the legal profession: *admitted to the bar.* **b.** a bar examination: *to pass the bar.* **c.** an objection that nullifies an action or claim. **d.** a railing in a courtroom separating the general public from the judges, jury, attorneys, etc. **e.** *Brit.* a wooden railing in front of the judge's bench. **f.** *Brit.* (formerly) a partition in the Inns of Court separating the readers from the general students. **10.** any tribunal: *the bar of justice.* **11.** a band or strip: *a bar of light.* **12.** a crowbar. **13. a.** the line marking the division between two measures of music. **b.** DOUBLE BAR. **c.** the unit of music contained between two bar lines; measure. **14.** BARRE. **15. a.** an iron or steel shape, as a T-bar. **b.** MUNTIN. **16.** one of a pair of metal or cloth insignia of rank worn by military officers. **17.** a space between the molar and canine teeth of a horse into which the bit is fitted. **18.** (in a bridle) the mouthpiece connecting the cheeks. **19.** a horizontal band on a heraldic shield. —*v.t.* **20.** to equip or fasten with a bar or bars: *to bar the door.* **21.** to block by or as if by bars: *to bar the exits.* **22.** to prevent or hinder: *to bar one's entrance.* **23.** to exclude or except: *barred from membership.* **24.** to mark with bars, stripes, or bands. —*prep.* **25.** except; omitting; but: *bar none.* —***Idiom.*** **26. behind bars,** in jail.

bar[2] (bär), *n.* a cgs unit of pressure, equal to one million dynes per square centimeter.

Bar., Baruch.

bar., **1.** barometer. **2.** barrel. **3.** barrister.

Bar•ab•bas (bə rab′əs), *n.* the criminal pardoned instead of Jesus to appease the mob. Mark 15:6–11, John 18:40.

Bar•ak (bâr′ək, bā′rak), *n.* a military commander who, with Deborah, destroyed the Canaanite army under Sisera. Judg. 4.

barb (bärb), *n.* **1.** a point or pointed part projecting backward from a main point, as of a fishhook or arrowhead. **2.** an obviously or openly unpleasant or carping remark. **3.** a hooked or sharp bristle. **4.** one of the series of paired parallel rods that attach to the central shaft of a feather and form its web. **5.** one of a breed of domestic pigeons, similar to the carriers or homers, having a short, broad bill. **6. a.** any of numerous small, Old World cyprinid fishes of the genera *Barbus* and *Puntius,* often kept in aquariums. **b.** BARBEL (def. 2). **7.** Also, **barbe.** a linen covering for the neck and breast, worn by women in mourning in the 14th to 16th centuries. —*v.t.* **8.** to furnish with a barb or barbs. —**barbed,** *adj.*

Bar•ba•dos (bär bā′dōz, -dōs, -dəs), *n.* an island in the E West Indies constituting an independent state in the Commonwealth of Nations: formerly a British colony. 257,731; 166 sq. mi. (430 sq. km). *Cap.:* Bridgetown. —**Bar•ba′di•an,** *adj., n.*

Bar•ba•ra Frietch•ie (bär′brə frich′ē, bär′bər ə), *n.* patriotic heroine of a poem (1863) by John Greenleaf Whittier, set during the Civil War.

bar•bar•i•an (bär bâr′ē ən), *n.* **1.** a person regarded as savage, primitive, or uncivilized, esp. a person belonging to a culture different from one's own. **2.** a person without culture, refinement, or education; philistine. **3.** (esp. in ancient and medieval times) a foreigner: applied orig. to non-Greeks and to those outside the Roman Empire. —*adj.* **4.** uncivilized; crude; savage. **5.** foreign; alien.

bar•bar•ic (bär bar′ik), *adj.* **1.** lacking civilizing influences; primitive: *barbaric raiders.* **2.** of or characteristic of barbarians. **3.** crudely rich or ornate: *barbaric splendor.* —**bar•bar′i•cal•ly,** *adv.*

bar•ba•rism (bär′bə riz′əm), *n.* **1.** a barbarous or uncivilized state or condition. **2.** a barbarous act. **3.** the use of words or constructions felt to be undesirably alien to the established standards of a language. **4.** such a word or construction.

bar•bar•i•ty (bär bar′i tē), *n., pl.* **-ties. 1.** brutal or cruel conduct. **2.** an act or instance of cruelty. **3.** crudity of style, expression, etc.

bar•ba•rize (bär′bə rīz′), *v.,* **-rized, -riz•ing.** —*v.t.* **1.** to make barbarous; brutalize; corrupt. —*v.i.* **2.** to become barbarous; lapse into barbarism. —**bar′ba•ri•za′tion,** *n.*

bar•ba•rous (bär′bər əs), *adj.* **1.** uncivilized; wild; savage. **2.** savagely cruel or harsh: *barbarous treatment of war prisoners.* **3.** full of harsh sounds; noisy; discordant: *wild and barbarous music.* **4.** not conforming to classical standards or accepted usage, as language. **5.** foreign; alien. —**bar′ba•rous•ly,** *adv.* —**bar′ba•rous•ness,** *n.*

Bar′bary ape′, *n.* a tailless macaque, *Macaca sylvanus,* of mountain ranges in NW Africa and Gibraltar.

Bar′bary States′, *n.pl.* Morocco, Algiers, Tunis, and Tripoli, c1520–1830, when they were the refuge of pirates.

bar•be•cue or **bar•be•que** (bär′bi kyo͞o′), *n., v.,* **-cued** or **-qued, -cu•ing** or **-qu•ing.** —*n.* **1.** pieces of meat, poultry, or fish roasted over an open hearth, esp. when basted with a sauce. **2.** a grill, spit, or fireplace for cooking food over an open fire. **3.** a meal, usu. outdoors, at which foods are so cooked. **4.** a dressed steer, lamb, or other animal, roasted whole. —*v.t.* **5.** to broil or roast over an open fire. —*v.i.* **6.** to have a barbecue. [< Spanish *barbacoa* < Taino (West Indian language): a raised frame of sticks] —**bar′be•cu′er,** *n.*

barbed′ wire′, *n.* strands of wire twisted together with small pieces of sharply pointed wire at short intervals, used for fencing. Also called **barb•wire** (bärb′ wīər).

bar•bel (bär′bəl), *n.* **1.** a slender, external process on the head of certain fishes. **2.** Also called **barb.** any European cyprinid fish of the genus *Barbus,* esp. *B. barbus,* having such processes.

bar•bell (bär′bel′), *n.* an apparatus used in weightlifting, consisting of a bar with disk-shaped weights attached to the ends.

bar•ber (bär′bər), *n.* **1.** a person whose occupation is to cut and dress the hair, esp. of male customers, and to shave or trim the beard. —*v.t.* **2.** to trim or dress the hair or beard of. —*v.i.* **3.** to work as a barber.

Bar•ber (bär′bər), *n.* **Samuel,** 1910–81, U.S. composer.

bar•ber•ry (bär′ber′ē, -bə rē), *n., pl.* **-ries. 1.** a shrub of the genus *Berberis,* esp. *B. vulgaris,* having yellow flowers in elongated clusters. **2.** the red fruit of this shrub.

bar•ber•shop (bär′bər shop′), *n.* **1.** Also called, *esp. Brit.,* **bar′ber's shop′.** the place of business of a barber. —*adj.* **2.** specializing in the singing of popular songs in a sentimental style of unaccompanied, four-part, close chromatic harmony: *a barbershop quartet.*

bar·bet (bär′bit), *n.* any of numerous typically stout, brightly colored arboreal birds of the family Capitonidae, of the Old and New World tropics, having bristles at the base of the large bill.

bar·bi·tal (bär′bi tôl′, -tal′), *n.* a barbiturate compound, $C_7O_3N_2H_{12}$, formerly used as a hypnotic.

bar·bi·tu·rate (bär bich′ər it, bär′bi tŏŏr′it, -tyŏŏr′-), *n.* any of a group of derivatives of a crystalline powder **(bar′bitur′ic ac′id)**, used as sedatives and hypnotics.

bar·bule (bär′byŏŏl), *n.* **1.** a small barb. **2.** any of the tiny branches that edge the barbs of a feather and attach the barbs to each other.

bar·ca·role or **bar·ca·rolle** (bär′kə rōl′), *n.* **1.** a boating song of the Venetian gondoliers. **2.** a piece of music in the style of such songs.

Bar·ce·lo·na (bar′sə lō′nə), *n.* a seaport in NE Spain, on the Mediterranean. 2,000,000.

Bar′ches·ter Tow′ers (bär′ches tər, -chi stər), a novel (1857) by Anthony Trollope.

bar′ code′, *n.* a series of contiguous lines of like height coded by width and applied to an item for identification by an optical scanner, as for registering the price of a product.

bar code

bard¹ (bärd), *n.* **1.** (formerly) a person who composed and recited epic or heroic poems, often while playing the harp, lyre, or the like. **2.** one of an ancient Celtic order of composers and reciters of poetry. **3.** any poet. **4. the Bard,** William Shakespeare.

bard² or **barde** (bärd), *n.* **1.** any of various pieces of defensive armor for a horse. **2.** a thin slice of fat or bacon secured to a roast to prevent its drying out while cooking. —*v.t.* **3.** to caparison (a horse) with bards. **4.** to cover with bards before cooking.

Bard′ of A′von, *n.* William Shakespeare: so called from his birthplace, Stratford-on-Avon.

bare (bâr), *adj.*, **bar·er, bar·est,** *v.*, **bared, bar·ing.** —*adj.* **1.** without covering or clothing; naked; nude: *bare legs.* **2.** without the usual furnishings, contents, etc.: *bare walls.* **3.** mere: *a bare three miles.* **4.** unadorned; bald; plain: *the bare facts.* **5.** constituting a minimum; scarcely sufficient: *the bare necessities of life.* —*v.t.* **6.** to reveal or divulge: *to bare damaging new facts.* —**bare′ness,** *n.*

bare·back (bâr′bak′) also **bare′backed′,** *adv., adj.* with the back of a horse, burro, etc., bare; without a saddle.

bare′ bones′, *n.pl.* the most essential facts or components: *Reduce this report to its bare bones.* —**bare′-bones′,** *adj.*

bare·faced (bâr′fāst′), *adj.* **1.** with the face uncovered. **2.** shameless; brazen: *a barefaced lie.* **3.** without concealment; boldly open: *barefaced bargaining.*

bare·foot (bâr′fŏŏt′) also **bare′foot′ed,** *adj., adv.* with the feet bare: *a barefoot boy; to walk barefoot.*

bare·hand·ed (bâr′han′did), *adj., adv.* **1.** with hands uncovered: *to catch a baseball barehanded.* **2.** without the necessary tools, weapons, or other means.

bare·knuck·le (bâr′nuk′əl) also **bare′knuck′led,** *adj.* **1.** (of a prizefight, prizefighter, etc.) without boxing gloves; using the bare fists. **2.** without conventional niceties: *bareknuckle bargaining.* —*adv.* **3.** in a rough-and-tumble manner.

bare·ly (bâr′lē), *adv.* **1.** scarcely; no more than: *I had barely enough money to pay the rent.* **2.** without disguise or concealment; openly. **3.** scantily; meagerly.

bar′ examina′tion (or **exam′**), *n.* a written examination to determine if one is qualified to practice law in a particular jurisdiction.

barf (bärf), *v.i., v.t., n. Slang.* VOMIT.

bar·fly (bär′flī′), *n., pl.* **-flies.** *Slang.* a person who frequents barrooms.

bar·gain (bär′gən), *n.* **1.** an advantageous purchase, esp. one acquired at less than the usual cost. **2.** an agreement between parties settling what each shall do, give, receive, etc., in a transaction. **3.** such an agreement as affecting one of the parties: *a losing bargain.* **4.** something acquired by bargaining. —*v.i.* **5.** to discuss the terms of a bargain; negotiate; haggle. **6.** to conclude a bargain. —*v.t.* **7.** to arrange by bargain; negotiate: *to bargain a new wage increase.* **8.** to anticipate as likely to occur; expect (usu. fol. by a clause): *I'll bargain that he's our next supervisor.* **9. bargain for** or **on,** to expect; anticipate: *I never bargained on a 12-hour day.* —**Idiom. 10. in** or **into the bargain,** over and above what has been stipulated; besides. —**bar′gain·er,** *n.*

bar′gaining chip′, *n.* something, as a concession or inducement, that can be used in negotiating.

barge (bärj), *n., v.,* **barged, barg·ing.** —*n.* **1.** a flat-bottomed vessel, usu. pushed or towed, for transporting freight or passengers. **2.** a vessel of state used in pageants. **3.** a naval vessel reserved for an admiral. —*v.i.* **4.** to move aggressively and clumsily: *to barge through.* **5.** to move in the slow, heavy manner of a barge. —*v.t.* **6.** to transport by barge. **7. barge in,** to intrude, esp. rudely. **8. barge into, a.** Also, **barge in on.** to interfere in, esp. rudely. **b.** to bump into; collide with.

bar′ graph′, *n.* a graph using parallel bars of varying lengths, as to illustrate comparative costs, exports, birthrates, etc.

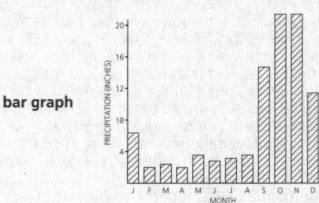

bar graph

bar·hop (bär′hop′), *v.i.,* **-hopped, -hop·ping.** to go to a succession of bars or nightclubs, with a brief stay at each.

bar·i·at·rics (bar′ē a′triks), *n.* (*used with a sing. v.*) a branch of medicine that deals with the treatment of obesity and allied diseases.

bar·ic¹ (bar′ik), *adj.* of or containing barium.

bar·ic² (bar′ik), *adj.* pertaining to weight, esp. of the atmosphere.

Bar·ing-Gould (bâr′ing gŏŏld′), *n.* **Sabine,** 1834–1924, English clergyman, writer, and hymn writer.

bar·ite (bâr′īt, bar′-), *n.* a mineral, barium sulfate, $BaSO_4$, occurring in white, yellow, or colorless tabular crystals: the principal ore of barium.

bar·i·tone (bar′i tōn′), *n.* **1.** a male voice or voice part intermediate between tenor and bass. **2.** a singer with such a voice. **3.** a large, valved brass instrument shaped like a trumpet or coiled in oval form, used esp. in military bands. —*adj.* **4.** of or pertaining to a baritone; having the compass of a baritone. —**bar′i·ton′al,** *adj.*

bar·i·um (bâr′ē əm, bar′-), *n.* a whitish, malleable, active, divalent, metallic element, occurring in combination chiefly as barite or as witherite. *Symbol:* Ba; *at. wt.:* 137.34; *at. no.:* 56; *sp. gr.:* 3.5 at 20°C.

Bar-Je·sus (bär′jē′zəs), *n.* a false prophet who opposed the apostles Paul and Barnabas during their mission to Cyprus. Acts 13:6–12. Also called **Elymas.**

Bar-Jo·nah (bär′jō′nə), *n.* "son of Jonah," the family name of the apostle Simon Peter. Matt. 16:17; John 1:42; 21:15–17.

bark¹ (bärk), *n.* **1.** the abrupt, explosive cry of a dog. **2.** a similar sound made by another animal, as a fox. **3.** a short, explosive sound, as of firearms. **4.** a brusque order, reply, etc. **5.** a cough. —*v.i.* **6.** (of a dog or other animal) to utter an abrupt, explosive cry. **7.** to make a similar sound: *The big guns barked.* **8.** to speak sharply or gruffly. **9.** to advertise some attraction, as a carnival sideshow, by standing outside and calling to passersby. **10.** to cough. —*v.t.* **11.** to utter in a harsh, shouting tone: *to bark orders at subordinates.* —**Idiom. 12. bark up the wrong tree,** to misdirect one's thoughts or efforts.

bark² (bärk), *n.* **1.** the external covering of the woody stems, branches, and roots of plants, as distinct and separable from the wood itself. **2.** a mixture of oak and hemlock barks used in tanning. **3.** candy, usu. of chocolate with large pieces of nuts, made in flat sheets. —*v.t.* **4.** to scrape the skin of, as by bumping into something: *to bark one's shins.* **5.** to treat with a bark infusion; tan. **6.** to strip the bark from; peel.

bark³ or **barque** (bärk), *n.* **1.** a sailing vessel having three or more masts, square-rigged on all but the aftermost. **2.** (formerly) any boat or sailing vessel.

bark′ bee′tle, *n.* any of numerous small, cylindrical beetles of the family Scolytidae that burrow under the bark of hardwood trees, leaving intricate tracings on the wood.

bark·er¹ (bär′kər), *n.* **1.** a person who stands at the entrance to a show, as in a carnival or fair, calling out its attractions to passersby. **2.** an animal or person that barks.

bark·er² (bär′kər), *n.* **1.** a person or thing that removes bark from trees. **2.** a person or thing that prepares bark for tanning.

Bark·ley (bärk′lē), *n.* **Al·ben William** (al′bən), 1877–1956, vice president of the U.S. 1949–53.

bar·ley (bär′lē), *n.* a widely distributed cereal plant belonging to the genus *Hordeum,* of the grass family, having awned flowers that grow in tightly bunched spikes. **2.** the grain of this plant, used as food and in making beer, ale, and whiskey.

bar·ley·corn (bär′lē kôrn′), *n.* **1.** barley. **2.** a grain of barley. **3.** a measure equal to ⅓ of an inch (8.5 mm).

barm (bärm), *n.* yeast formed on malt liquors while fermenting.

bar·maid (bär′mād′), *n.* a woman who bartends; bartender.

bar·man (bär′mən), *n., pl.* **-men.** a bartender.

Bar·me·cid·al (bär′mə sīd′l) also **Bar′me·cide′,** *adj.* giving only the illusion of plenty; illusory: *a Barmecidal banquet.*

bar mitz·vah (bär mits′və), *n., v.,* **-vahed, -vah·ing.** —*n.* (*often caps.*) **1.** a ceremony for admitting a boy of 13 as an adult member of the Jewish community. **2.** the boy participating in this ceremony. —*v.t.*

3. to administer this ceremony to: *Our son was bar mitzvahed last Saturday.*

barn[1] (bärn), *n.* **1.** a building for storing hay, grain, etc., and often for housing livestock. **2.** a very large garage for buses, trucks, etc. —*v.t.* **3.** to store (hay, grain, etc.) in a barn. —*Proverb.* **4. lock the barn door after the horse has fled,** to take action after a loss or damage has occurred rather than before.

barn[2] (bärn), *n.* a unit of area equal to 10^{-24} square centimeter, used in measuring cross sections of atomic nuclei.

Bar•na•bas (bär'nə bəs), *n.* surname of the Cyprian Levite Joseph, a companion of Paul on his first missionary journey. Acts 4:36, 37.

bar•na•cle (bär'nə kəl), *n.* **1.** any marine crustacean of the subclass Cirripedia, having a shell made up of separate plates, being either stalked and attaching itself to ship bottoms and floating timber, or stalkless. **2.** one that clings tenaciously. —**bar'na•cled,** *adj.*

bar'nacle goose', *n.* a wild goose of Arctic regions, *Branta leucopsis,* that winters in N Europe.

Bar•nard (bär'nərd), *n.* **Christiaan N(eethling),** born 1922, South African surgeon.

barn•burn•er (bärn'bûr'nər), *n.* **1.** *Informal.* something that is highly exciting, impressive, etc.: *The All Stars game was a real barnburner.* **2.** *Chiefly Pennsylvania.* a wooden friction match. **3.** (*cap.*) a member of the progressive faction in the Democratic party in New York State 1845–52. Compare HUNKER.

Barn•by (bärn'bē), *n.* **Joseph,** English musician and hymn writer.

barn' dance', *n.* a social gathering, orig. held in a barn, featuring square dances, round dances, and hoedown music.

Barnes (bärnz), *n.* **Albert,** 1798–1870, U.S. preacher and Bible expositor.

barn' owl', *n.* any of several owls of the family Tytonidae, having a heart-shaped facial disk, esp. *Tyto alba,* of the New World, Eurasia, and Africa.

barn' rais'ing, *n.* (in rural areas) a party, usu. providing food and drink, for the purpose of assisting a neighbor to put up a new barn.

barn•storm (bärn'stôrm'), *v.i.* **1.** to conduct a campaign or speaking tour in rural areas by making brief stops in many small towns. **2.** to tour small towns giving theatrical performances. **3.** (of a pilot) to do stunt flying or participate in races in the course of touring rural areas. **4.** (of a professional athletic team) to tour an area playing exhibition games. —*v.t.* **5.** to tour (a region, country, etc.) while barnstorming.

barn' swal'low, *n.* a common swallow, *Hirundo rustica,* of North America and Eurasia, that builds mud nests on the ledges and walls of buildings.

Bar•num (bär'nəm), *n.* **P(hineas) T(aylor),** 1810–91, U.S. showman and circus impresario.

barn•yard (bärn'yärd'), *n.* **1.** a yard next to or surrounding a barn. —*adj.* **2.** of, pertaining to, or typical of a barnyard.

barn'yard grass', *n.* a weedy, coarse grass, *Echinochloa crus-galli,* having a spikelike cluster of flowers.

bar•o•graph (bar'ə graf', -gräf'), *n.* a self-recording barometer. —**bar'o•graph'ic** (-graf'ik), *adj.*

ba•rom•e•ter (bə rom'i tər), *n.* **1.** an instrument that measures atmospheric pressure. **2.** anything that indicates changes. —**bar•o•met•ric** (bar'ə me'trik), *adj.*

bar'omet'ric pres'sure, *n.* ATMOSPHERIC PRESSURE.

bar•on (bar'ən), *n.* **1.** a member of the lowest grade of nobility. **2.** (in Britain) **a.** a feudal vassal holding his lands under a direct grant from the king. **b.** a direct descendant of such a vassal or his equal in the nobility. **c.** a member of the House of Lords. **3.** a powerful, wealthy man in some industry or activity: *the railroad barons of yesteryear.*

bar•on•age (bar'ə nij), *n.* **1.** the entire British peerage, including all dukes, marquesses, earls, viscounts, and barons. **2.** Also, **barony.** the dignity or rank of a baron.

bar•on•ess (bar'ə nis), *n.* **1.** the wife of a baron. **2.** a woman holding a baronial title.

bar•on•et (bar'ə nit, bar'ə net'), *n.* a member of a British hereditary order of honor, ranking below the barons and made up of commoners, designated by *Sir* before the name, and *Baronet,* usu. abbreviated *Bart.,* after: *Sir John Smith, Bart.*

ba•ro•ni•al (bə rō'nē əl), *adj.* **1.** pertaining to a baron or barony or to the order of barons. **2.** befitting a baron: *baronial splendor.*

bar•o•ny (bar'ə nē), *n., pl.* **-nies. 1.** the domain of a baron. **2.** BARONAGE (def. 2).

ba•roque (bə rōk'), *adj.* **1.** (*often cap.*) of or designating a style of architecture and art of the early 17th to mid-18th century, characterized by curvilinear shapes, exuberant decoration, and dramatic effect. **2.** (*sometimes cap.*) of or pertaining to the musical period following the Renaissance, extending roughly from 1600 to 1750. **3.** extravagantly ornate, florid, and convoluted in character or style: *the baroque writing of her earliest novels.* **4.** irregular in shape: *baroque pearls.* —*n.* **5.** (*often cap.*) the baroque style or period. **6.** an irregularly shaped pearl.

ba•rouche (bə rōosh'), *n.* a four-wheeled carriage with a high front seat for the driver, facing seats inside for two couples, and a calash top over the back seat.

bar•rack (bar'ək), *n.* Usu., **barracks. 1.** a building or group of buildings for lodging soldiers, esp. in garrison. **2.** any large, plain building in which many people are lodged. —*v.t., v.i.* **3.** to lodge in barracks.

bar•ra•cu•da (bar'ə kōo'də), *n., pl.* (*esp. collectively*) **-da,** (*esp. for kinds or species*) **-das** for 1; **-das** for 2. **1.** any of several long and slender, pikelike food and game fishes of the genus *Sphyraena,* of warm seas, noted for striking with sharp teeth at any moving object. **2.** *Slang.* a treacherous, greedy person.

bar•rage (bə räzh'; *esp. Brit.* bar'äzh *for 1, 2;* bär'ij *for 3), *n., v.,* **-raged, -rag•ing.** —*n.* **1.** a heavy barrier of artillery fire to protect troop movements or to stop an enemy advance. **2.** an overwhelming quantity or explosion, as of words, blows, or criticisms: *a barrage of questions.* **3.** an artificial obstruction in a watercourse to increase the depth of the water, facilitate irrigation, etc. —*v.t.* **4.** to subject to a barrage.

bar•ra•mun•da (bar'ə mun'də), *n., pl.* **-das,** (*esp. collectively*) **-da.** an Australian lungfish, *Neoceratodus forsteri.*

bar•ra•try (bar'ə trē), *n.* **1.** fraud by a master or crew at the expense of the owners of the ship or its cargo. **2.** the offense of frequently stirring up litigation. **3.** the purchase or sale of ecclesiastic preferments. —**bar'ra•trous,** *adj.*

barred (bärd), *adj.* **1.** provided with one or more bars: *a barred prison window.* **2.** striped; streaked: *barred fabrics.* **3.** (of feathers) marked with transverse bands of distinctive color.

barred' owl', *n.* a large owl, *Strix varia,* of E North America, having its breast barred and abdomen streaked with dark brown.

bar•rel (bar'əl), *n., v.,* **-reled, -rel•ing** or (*esp. Brit.*) **-relled, -rel•ling.** —*n.* **1.** a cylindrical wooden container with slightly bulging sides made of staves hooped together, and with flat, parallel ends. **2.** a standard quantity that such a vessel can hold, as, in the U.S., 31.5 gallons of liquid or 105 dry quarts of fruits or vegetables. **3.** any large quantity: *a barrel of fun.* **4.** any container, case, or part similar to a wooden barrel. **5.** the tubelike part of a gun from which the projectile emerges. **6.** the cylindrical case in a watch or clock within which the mainspring is coiled. **7.** the trunk of a quadruped, esp. of a horse or cow. **8.** Also called **throat.** a passageway in a carburetor that has the shape of a Venturi tube. —*v.t.* **9.** to put or pack in a barrel or barrels. **10.** to pursue (one's way) or to force (something) to go at high speed: *to barrel a car through traffic.* —*v.i.* **11.** to travel or drive very fast: *to barrel along the highway.* —*Idiom.* **12. over a barrel,** at the mercy of circumstances or one's adversaries; without choices.

bar'rel cac'tus, *n.* any of several large, cylindrical, ribbed, spiny cacti of the genera *Echinocactus* and *Ferocactus.*

bar•rel•house (bar'əl hous'), *n., pl.* **-hous•es** (-hou'ziz) for 1. **1.** a cheap saloon. **2.** a vigorous style of jazz originating in the barrelhouses of New Orleans in the early part of the 20th century.

bar'rel roll', *n.* a maneuver in which an airplane executes a complete roll by rotating once around its longitudinal axis while moving forward. —**bar'rel-roll',** *v.i.,* **-rolled, -roll•ing.**

bar•ren (bar'ən), *adj.* **1.** not producing or incapable of producing offspring; sterile. **2.** unproductive; unfruitful: *barren land.* **3.** without capacity to interest or attract: *a barren period in architecture.* **4.** bereft; lacking (usu. fol. by *of*): *barren of compassion.* —*n.* **5.** Usu., **barrens.** level or slightly rolling land, usu. with a sandy soil and few trees, and relatively infertile.

Bar'ren Fig' Tree', The, a parable of Jesus. Luke 13:6–9.

bar•rette (bə ret'), *n.* a clasp for holding hair in place.

bar•ri•cade (bar'i kād', bar'i kād'), *n., v.,* **-cad•ed, -cad•ing.** —*n.* **1.** a defensive barrier hastily constructed, as in a street, to stop an enemy. **2.** any barrier that obstructs passage. —*v.t.* **3.** to obstruct or block with a barricade: *Students had barricaded the streets.* **4.** to shut in and defend with or as if with a barricade: *Rebels barricaded themselves in the old city.*

Bar•rie (bar'ē), *n.* **Sir James M(atthew),** 1860–1937, Scottish writer.

bar•ri•er (bar'ē ər), *n.* **1.** anything built or serving to bar passage, as a railing, fence, or the like. **2.** any natural bar or obstacle: *a mountain barrier.* **3.** anything that obstructs progress, access, etc.: *trade barriers.* **4.** a limit or boundary of any kind: *the barriers of caste.* **5.** an antarctic ice shelf or its front.

bar•ring (bär'ing), *prep.* excepting; except for: *Barring accidents, I'll be there.*

bar•ri•o (bär'ē ō', bar'-), *n., pl.* **-ri•os. 1.** (in Spain and countries colonized by Spain) a division of a town or city, together with the contiguous rural territory. **2.** a section of a U.S. city inhabited chiefly by a Spanish-speaking population.

bar•ris•ter (bar'ə stər), *n.* (in England) a lawyer who is a member of one of the Inns of Court and who has the privilege of pleading in the higher courts. Compare SOLICITOR (def. 3).

bar•room (bär'rōom', -rŏom'), *n.* an establishment or room with a bar for the serving of alcoholic beverages.

bar•row[1] (bar'ō), *n.* WHEELBARROW.

bar•row[2] (bar'ō), *n.* a castrated male swine.

Bar•rows (bar'ōz), *n.* **Cliff,** born 1923, U.S. musical director in Billy Graham's evangelistic missions.

Bar•ry•more (bar'ə môr', -mōr'), *n.* **1. Maurice** (*Herbert Blythe*), 1847–1905, U.S. actor. **2.** his children: **Ethel,** 1879–1959, **John,** 1882–1942, and **Lionel,** 1878–1954, U.S. actors.

Bar•sab•bas (bär sab'əs, -sä'bəs), *n.* **1. Joseph the Just,** a candidate to replace Judas Iscariot as an apostle. Acts 1:23–26. **2. Judas,** a prophet who accompanied Paul, Barnabas, and Silas to Antioch in Syria. Acts 15:22, 27.

B

bar′ sin′ister, *n.* **1.** a putative heraldic charge presumed to indicate illegitimate birth. **2.** the proof, condition, or stigma of illegitimate birth.

Bart., Baronet.

bar′ tack′, *n.* a close series of short stitches in cloth, as in a garment, for reinforcement at a point of strain.

bar·tend·er (bär′ten/dər), *n.* a person who mixes and serves alcoholic drinks at a bar. —**bar′tend′,** *v.i.*

bar·ter (bär′tər), *v.i.* **1.** to trade by exchange of commodities rather than by the use of money. —*v.t.* **2.** to exchange in trade, as one commodity for another; trade. **3.** to bargain away unwisely or dishonorably (usu. fol. by *away*): *bartering away one's pride for material gain.* —*n.* **4.** the act or practice of bartering. **5.** items or an item for bartering. —**bar′ter·er,** *n.*

Barth (bärt, bärth), *n.* **Karl,** 1886–1968, Swiss theologian. —**Barth′i·an,** *adj., n.*

Bar·thol·di (bär thol′dē, -tol′-), *n.* **Frédéric Auguste,** 1834–1904, French sculptor: designed Statue of Liberty.

Bar·thol·o·mew (bär thol′ə myoo′), *n.* one of the 12 apostles: sometimes called Nathanael. Mark 3:18.

Bart·lett (bärt′lit), *n.* a large, yellow, juicy variety of pear.

Bar·ton (bär′tn), *n.* **1. Clara,** 1821–1912, U.S. philanthropist who organized the American Red Cross in 1881. **2. Derek H(arold) R(ichard),** born 1918, English chemist.

Bar·uch (bâr′ək *for 1;* bə rook′ *for 2*), *n.* **1.** the amanuensis and friend of Jeremiah and nominal author of the book of Baruch in the Apocrypha. Jer. 32:12. **2. Bernard M(annes),** 1870–1965, U.S. financier.

bar·ware (bär′wâr′), *n.* glassware and other items for preparing and serving alcoholic drinks.

bar·y·on (bar′ē on′), *n.* any strongly interacting fermion, as a proton or neutron, that decays into a set of particles that includes a proton. —**bar′y·on′ic,** *adj.*

Ba·rysh·ni·kov (bə rish′ni kôf′, -kof′), *n.* **Mikhail,** born 1948, Russian ballet dancer, born in Latvia; in the U.S. since 1974.

Bar·zil·la·i (bär zil′ā ī′), *n.* a man who helped David after he fled from Absalom. II Sam. 17:27–29.

B.A.S., 1. Bachelor of Agricultural Science. **2.** Bachelor of Applied Science.

ba·sal (bā′səl, -zəl), *adj.* **1.** of, at, or forming the base. **2.** forming a basis; fundamental; basic: *a basal reader.* **3. a.** indicating a standard low level of activity of an organism, as during total rest. **b.** of an amount required to maintain this level. —**ba′sal·ly,** *adv.*

ba′sal bod′y, *n.* an organelle of ciliated or flagellated cells that forms the base of the cilia or flagella.

ba′sal cell′, *n.* any cell situated at the base of a multilayered tissue, as at the lowest layer of the epidermis.

ba′sal gang′lion, *n.* any of several masses of gray matter in the cerebral cortex, involved in the control of movement.

ba′sal metabol′ic rate′, *n.* the rate at which energy is expended while fasting and at rest, calculated as calories per hour per square meter of body surface.

ba′sal metab′olism, *n.* the minimal amount of energy necessary to maintain respiration, circulation, and other vital body functions while fasting and at total rest.

ba·salt (bə sôlt′, bas′ôlt, bā′sôlt), *n.* the dark, dense, igneous rock of a lava flow or minor intrusion, composed essentially of labradorite and pyroxene and often displaying a columnar structure. —**ba·sal′tic, ba·sal′tine** (-tin, -tīn), *adj.*

bas·cule (bas′kyool), *n.* a device operating like a balance or seesaw, esp. an arrangement of a movable bridge (**bas′cule bridge′**) by which the rising floor or section is counterbalanced by a weight.

base¹ (bās), *n., adj., v.,* **based, bas·ing.** —*n.* **1.** a bottom support; that on which a thing stands or rests. **2.** a fundamental principle; foundation; basis. **3.** the bottom layer or coating, as of makeup or paint. **4. a.** the distinctively treated portion of a column or pier below the shaft. **b.** the distinctively treated lowermost portion of any structure, as a monument or exterior wall. **5. a.** the part of an organ nearest its point of attachment. **b.** the point of attachment. **6.** the principal element or ingredient of anything, considered as its fundamental part: *house paint with a lead base.* **7.** a starting point or point of departure. **8. a.** any of the four corners of a baseball diamond, esp. first, second, or third base. Compare HOME PLATE. **b.** a square canvas sack marking first, second, or third base. **9. a.** a usu. fortified place from which military operations proceed. **b.** a supply installation for a large military force. **10. a.** the lower side or surface of a geometric figure; the side or surface to which an altitude can be drawn. **b.** the number that serves as a starting point for a logarithmic or other numerical system. **c.** the number of symbols used in a numerical system: *The base in the decimal system is 10, in the binary system 2.* **11.** Also called **baseline. 12.** a thin, flexible layer of cellulose triacetate or similar material on photographic film that holds the light-sensitive emulsion and other coatings. **13. a.** a chemical compound that reacts with an acid to form a salt. **b.** the hydroxide of a metal or of an electropositive element or group. **c.** a group or molecule that accepts protons. **d.** a molecule or ion containing an atom with a free pair of electrons that can be donated to an acid. **14.** *Genetics.* any of the purine or pyrimidine compounds that constitute a portion of the nucleotide molecule of DNA or RNA: adenine, guanine, cytosine, thymine, or uracil. Compare BASE PAIR. **15.** the part of a complex word, consisting of one or more morphemes, to which derivational or inflectional affixes may be added, as *want* in *unwanted* or *biolog-* in *biological.* Compare ROOT¹ (def. 10), STEM¹ (def. 10). **16.** the component of a generative grammar containing the lexicon and phrase-structure rules that generate the deep structure of sentences. **17.** *Heraldry.* the lower part of an escutcheon. **18.** PAVILION (def. 5). —*adj.* **19.** serving as or forming a base: *the explorer's base camp; a base coat of paint.* —*v.t.* **20.** to make or form a base or foundation for. **21.** to establish, as a fact or conclusion (usu. fol. by *on* or *upon*): *to base an assumption of guilt on overwhelming evidence.* **22.** to place or establish on a base or basis; ground; found (usu. fol. by *on* or *upon*): *Our plan is based on an upturn in the economy.* **23.** to station, place, or situate (usu. fol. by *at* or *on*): *The general is based at Fort Benning.* —*v.i.* **24.** to have a basis; be based. **25.** to have or maintain a base. —*Idiom.* **26. off base, a.** (in baseball) not touching a base. **b.** *Informal.* badly mistaken. **27. on base,** (in baseball) having reached a base or bases. **28. touch base,** to communicate; get into contact.

base² (bās), *adj.,* **bas·er, bas·est. 1.** morally low; contemptible: *a base nature; base motives.* **2.** of little or no value; worthless: *base materials.* **3.** debased or counterfeit: *base coinage.* **4.** of illegitimate birth. **5.** not classical or refined: *base language.* **6.** held by or characteristic of villeinage: *base tenure.* —**base′ly,** *adv.* —**base′ness,** *n.*

base·ball (bās′bôl′), *n.* **1.** a game involving the batting of a hard ball, played by two teams usu. of nine players each on a large field with a diamond-shaped circuit defined by four bases, to which batters run and advance to score runs. **2.** the horsehide-covered ball used in this game.

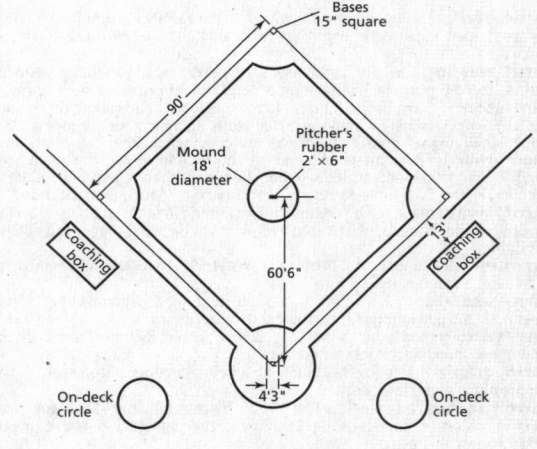

baseball diamond

base·board (bās′bôrd′, -bōrd′), *n.* a board or molding forming the foot of an interior wall.

base′burn′er or **base′ burn′er** or **base′-burn′er,** *n.* a stove with a self-acting fuel hopper over the fire chamber.

base′ hit′, *n.* a fair ball enabling the batter to reach base safely without the commission of an error in the field or a force-out or fielder's choice on a base runner.

Ba·sel (bä′zəl) also **Basle,** *n.* **1.** a city in NW Switzerland, on the Rhine River. 192,800. **2.** a canton in N Switzerland, divided into two independent areas. French, **Bâle.**

base·less (bās′lis), *adj.* having no base; without foundation; groundless: *a baseless claim.* —**base′less·ness,** *n.*

base·line (bās′līn′), *n.* Also, **base′ line′. 1.** the area on a baseball diamond within which a runner must keep when running from one base to another. **2.** the line at each end of a tennis court, parallel to the net, that marks the in-bounds limit of play. **3.** a basic standard or level; guideline: *a baseline for future studies.* **4.** a specific value or values serving as a comparison or control. **5.** See under TRIANGULATION (def. 1).

base·ment (bās′mənt), *n.* **1.** a story of a building, partly or wholly underground. **2.** (in classical and Renaissance architecture) the portion of a building beneath the principal story, treated as a single compositional unit. **3.** the lowermost portion of a structure. **4.** the undifferentiated assemblage of crystalline rock that underlies the sedimentary strata in any region.

base′ met′al, *n.* any metal other than a precious or noble metal, as copper, lead, zinc, or tin.

ba·sen·ji (bə sen′jē), *n., pl.* **-jis.** one of an African breed of dogs with a smooth chestnut coat and a curled tail, noted for their inability to bark.

base′ pair′, *n.* any two of the nucleotide bases that readily form weak bonds with each other, bringing together strands of DNA or RNA and linking codons with anticodons during translation of the genetic code: adenine pairs with thymine or uracil, and guanine pairs with cytosine.

BASE PAIRS

	Abbrev.	Base*		Abbrev.	Base*
DNA:	A	adenine ⌉	RNA:	A	adenine ⌉
	T	thymine ⌉		U	uracil ⌉
	C	cytosine ⌉		C	cytosine ⌉
	G	guanine ⌋		G	guanine ⌋

*A nucleotide base on a strand of DNA or RNA always pairs with its complementary base when the strand links with or forms another strand. Adenine (A) always pairs with thymine (T) in DNA and with uracil (U) in RNA. Cytosine (C) always pairs with guanine (G).

base′ pay′, *n.* pay received for a given work period, as an hour or week, but not including overtime, bonuses, and the like.

base′ run′ner, *n.* a baseball player of the team at bat who is on base or is trying to run from one base to another.

ba·ses[1] (bā′sēz), *n.* pl. of BASIS.

bas·es[2] (bā′siz), *n.* pl. of BASE[1].

base′ sta′tion, *n.* a unit functioning as a transmitter and receiver of broadcasting or other signals, as for a CB radio or mobile phone.

bash (bash), *v.t.* **1.** to strike with a crushing blow. **2. a.** to physically assault; beat up. **b.** to abuse verbally. —*n.* **3.** a crushing blow. **4.** a lively social event.

Ba·shan (bā′shən), *n.* a region in ancient Palestine, E of the Jordan River. Ps. 22:12; Is. 2:15; Jer. 50:19.

bash·ful (bash′fəl), *adj.* **1.** easily embarrassed; shy; timid: *a bashful child.* **2.** indicative of or proceeding from bashfulness: *a bashful manner.* —**bash′ful·ly,** *adv.* —**bash′ful·ness,** *n.*

bash·ing (bash′ing), *n.* **1.** the act of beating, whipping, or thrashing. **2.** a decisive defeat. **3.** (used in combination) **a.** unprovoked physical assaults against members of a specified group: *gay-bashing.* **b.** verbal abuse, as of a group or a nation: *feminist-bashing; China-bashing.*

ba·sic (bā′sik), *adj.* **1.** of or forming a base or basis; essential; fundamental: *a basic principle.* **2. a.** pertaining to a chemical base. **b.** not having all of the hydroxyls of the base replaced by the acid group. **c.** alkaline. **3.** (of a rock) having relatively little silica. **4.** of the lowest military rank: *airman basic.* —*n.* **5.** BASIC TRAINING. **6.** Often, **basics.** an essential ingredient, principle, procedure, etc.: *the basics of music.*

BASIC (bā′sik), *n.* a high-level programming language that uses English words, punctuation marks, and algebraic notation.

ba·si·cal·ly (bā′sik lē), *adv.* fundamentally; primarily.

ba′sic train′ing, *n.* a period following induction into the armed forces during which a recruit learns basic comportment, duties, and combat skills.

Ba·sie (bā′sē), *n.* **William** (*"Count"*), 1904–84, U.S. jazz pianist, bandleader, and composer.

bas·il (baz′əl, bas′-, bā′zəl, -səl), *n.* any of several aromatic herbs belonging to the genus *Ocimum,* of the mint family, as *O. basilicum* **(sweet basil),** having bright green to purplish green ovate leaves used in cooking.

Bas·il (baz′əl, bas′-, bā′zəl, -səl), *n.* **Saint** (*"the Great"*), A.D. 329?–379, bishop of Caesarea in Asia Minor (brother of Saint Gregory of Nyssa). Also called **Basilius.**

ba·si·lect (bā′zə lekt′, baz′ə-), *n.* a variety of a language, esp. a creolized one, that is most distinct from the acrolect.

ba·sil·i·ca (bə sil′i kə, -zil′-), *n., pl.* **-cas. 1.** an early Christian or medieval church characterized by an oblong plan including a nave with a clerestory, two or four side aisles, one or more vaulted semicircular apses, and often a narthex and atrium. **2.** one of the seven main churches of Rome or another Roman Catholic church accorded the same religious privileges. **3.** (in ancient Rome) an oblong building with a double colonnade used as a court of law and public meeting place. [< Latin < Greek *basilikḗ (oikía)* royal (house)] —**ba·sil′i·can,** *adj.*

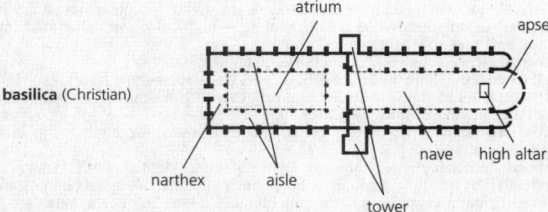

basilica (Christian)

atrium · apse · nave · high altar · narthex · aisle · tower

bas·i·lisk (bas′ə lisk, baz′-), *n.* **1.** a legendary creature, variously described as a serpent, lizard, or dragon, said to kill by its breath or look. **2.** any of several tropical American iguanid lizards of the genus *Ba-*

siliscus, noted for their ability to run across the surface of water on their hind legs. —**bas′i·lis′can,** *adj.*

ba·sin (bā′sən), *n.* **1.** a circular container with a greater width than depth, used chiefly to hold water for washing. **2.** the quantity held by such a container. **3.** a natural or artificial hollow place containing water. **4.** a partially enclosed, sheltered area along a shore where boats may be moored: *a yacht basin.* **5. a.** a hollow or depression in the earth's surface. **b.** an area in which rock strata dip inward toward a common center; a circular or elliptical syncline.

ba·sip·e·tal (bā sip′i tl, -zip′-), *adj.* (of a plant) exhibiting a pattern of growth or movement in a downward direction from the apex of the stem to its base (opposed to *acropetal*). —**ba·sip′e·tal·ly,** *adv.*

ba·sis (bā′sis), *n., pl.* **-ses** (-sēz). **1.** a bottom or base; the part on which something stands or rests. **2.** anything upon which something is based; a fundamental principle. **3.** the principal constituent; fundamental ingredient. **4.** a basic fact, amount, standard, etc., used in making computations, reaching conclusions, or the like: *to be paid on an hourly basis; to be chosen on the basis of merit.*

bask (bask, bäsk), *v.i.* **1.** to lie in or be exposed to a pleasant warmth: *to bask in the sun.* **2.** to take great pleasure; revel: *to bask in royal favor.*

bas·ket (bas′kit, bä′skit), *n.* **1.** a container made of twigs, rushes, or other flexible material woven together. **2.** a container made of pieces of thin veneer, used for packing berries, vegetables, etc. **3.** the amount contained in a basket; a basketful. **4.** anything like a basket in shape or use: *a wastepaper basket.* **5.** a group of similar or related things; unit; package: *a basket of industrial stocks.* **6.** the car or gondola suspended beneath a balloon. **7. a.** the goal on a basketball court, consisting of an open net suspended from a metal hoop attached to a backboard. **b.** FIELD GOAL (def. 2).

bas·ket·ball (bas′kit bôl′, bä′skit-), *n.* **1.** a game played on a rectangular court by two teams usu. of five players each, who attempt to score points by tossing a ball through a goal on the opponent's side of the court. **2.** the round, inflated ball used in this game.

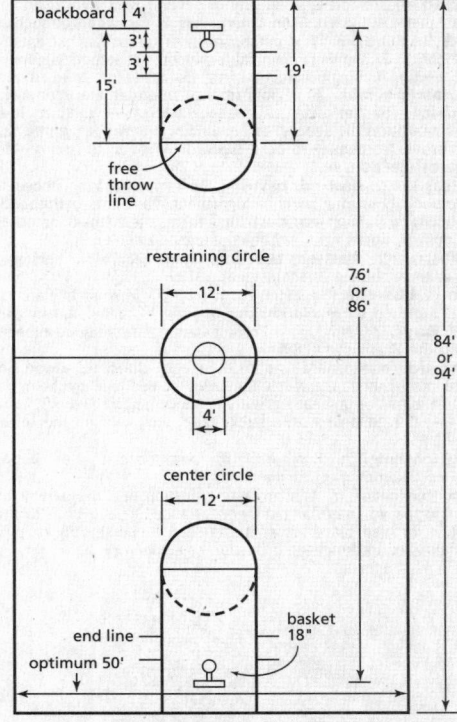

basketball court

bas′ket case′, *n. Slang.* **1.** a person who is incapable of functioning normally, as due to overwhelming stress or anxiety. **2.** anything that is impaired or incapable of functioning.

bas′ket-of-gold′, *n.* a widely cultivated alyssum, *Aurinia saxatilis* (or *Alyssum saxatile*), of the mustard family, growing in dense clumps and having clusters of small yellow flowers.

bas·ket·ry (bas′ki trē, bä′ski-), *n.* **1.** baskets collectively; basketwork. **2.** the art or process of making baskets.

B

bas′ket weave′, *n.* a plain weave with two or more yarns woven in a checkered, basketlike pattern.

bask′ing shark′ (bas′king, bä′sking), *n.* a large shark, *Cetorhinus maximus,* of cold and temperate seas, that often swims slowly or floats at the surface.

bas mitz•vah (bäs mits′və), *n.* (*often caps.*) BAT MITZVAH.

bas-re•lief (bä′ri lēf′, bas′-; bä′ri lēf′, bas′-), *n.* relief sculpture in which the figures project slightly from the background.

bass¹ (bās), *adj.* **1.** low in pitch; of the lowest pitch or range: *a bass clarinet.* **2.** of or pertaining to the lowest part in harmonic music. —*n.* **3.** the bass part. **4.** a bass voice, singer, or instrument. **5.** DOUBLE BASS. —**bass′ness,** *n.*

bass² (bas), *n., pl.* (*esp. collectively*) **bass,** (*esp. for kinds or species*) **bass•es.** any of numerous edible, spiny-finned, freshwater or marine fishes of the families Serranidae and Centrarchidae.

bass′ clef′ (bās), *n.* a symbol placed on the fourth line of a musical staff indicating that the fourth line corresponds to F below middle C.

bass′ drum′ (bās), *n.* the largest and lowest toned of drums, having a cylindrical body and two membrane heads.

Basse•terre (bäs târ′), *n.* the capital of St. Kitts-Nevis. 15,897.

Basse-Terre (bäs târ′), *n.* **1.** the capital of Guadeloupe, in the French West Indies. 15,690. **2.** See under GUADELOUPE.

bas′set hound′ (bas′it), *n.* one of a breed of short-legged, heavy-boned hounds with a long body, long, drooping ears, and usu. a black, tan, and white coat. Also called **bas′set.**

bass′ fid′dle (bās), *n.* DOUBLE BASS.

bass′ horn′ (bās), *n.* an obsolete wind instrument related to the tuba but resembling a bassoon in shape.

bas•si•net (bas′ə net′, bas′ə net′), *n.* **1.** a basket with a hood over one end, used as a baby's cradle. **2.** a style of perambulator resembling this.

bas•so (bas′ō, bä′sō), *n., pl.* **-sos, -si** (-sē). a bass singer, esp. of operatic caliber.

bas•soon (ba sōōn′, bə-), *n.* a large woodwind instrument of low range, with a doubled tube and a curved metal crook to which a double reed is attached. —**bas•soon′ist,** *n.*

bass•wood (bas′wŏŏd′), *n.* **1.** any of several New World linden trees, esp. the American linden, *Tilia americana.* **2.** the wood of such a tree.

bas•tard (bas′tərd), *n.* **1.** a person born of unmarried parents; an illegitimate child. **2.** a mean, despicable person. **3.** something spurious or inferior. —*adj.* **4.** illegitimate in birth. **5.** made or done in imitation; false: *bastard emeralds.* **6.** of abnormal or irregular shape or size.

bas•tard•ize (bas′tər dīz′), *v.,* **-ized, iz•ing.** —*v.t.* **1.** to lower the worth or condition of; debase: *to bastardize existing art forms.* **2.** to declare or prove (someone) to be a bastard. —*v.i.* **3.** to become debased. —**bas′tard•i•za′tion,** *n.*

baste¹ (bāst), *v.t.,* **bast•ed, bast•ing.** to sew with long, loose stitches, as in temporarily joining parts of a garment while it is being made.

baste² (bāst), *v.t.,* **bast•ed, bast•ing.** to moisten (meat or other food) with drippings, butter, etc., while cooking. —**bast′er,** *n.*

baste³ (bāst), *v.t.,* **bast•ed, bast•ing.** **1.** to beat with a stick; thrash; cudgel. **2.** to denounce or scold vigorously.

bas•tille or **bas•tile** (ba stēl′), *n.* **1.** (*cap.*) a fortress in Paris, used as a prison, captured by revolutionaries on July 14, 1789. **2.** any prison.

Bastille′ Day′, *n.* July 14, a French national holiday commemorating the fall of the Bastille in 1789.

bas•ti•na•do (bas′tə nā′dō, -nä′dō), *n., pl.* **-does,** *v.,* **-doed, -do•ing.** —*n.* **1.** a punishment in which the soles of the feet are beaten with a stick. **2.** a blow or a beating with a stick, cudgel, etc. **3.** a stick or cudgel. —*v.t.* **4.** to beat with a stick, cane, etc., esp. on the soles of the feet.

bast•ing (bā′sting), *n.* **1.** sewing with long, loose stitches. **2. bastings,** the stitches taken or the threads used.

bas•tion (bas′chən), *n.* **1.** a projecting portion of a rampart or fortification that forms an irregular pentagon attached at the base to the main work. **2.** a fortified place. **3.** anything seen as preserving or protecting some quality, condition, etc.: *a bastion of democracy.*

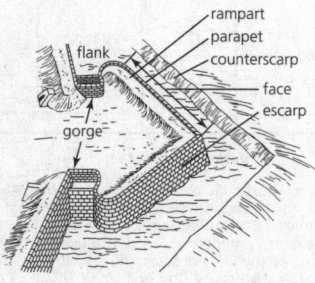

bastion (def. 1)

bat¹ (bat), *n., v.,* **bat•ted, bat•ting.** —*n.* **1.** the wooden club used in certain games, as baseball and cricket, to strike the ball. **2.** a racket, esp. one used in badminton or table tennis. **3.** a whip used by a jockey. **4.** a heavy stick, club, or cudgel. **5.** *Informal.* a blow, as with a bat. **6.** any fragment of brick or hardened clay. **7.** any of various slabs used in holding ceramic objects while they are being made. **8.** BATT. —*v.t.* **9.** to strike or hit with or as if with a bat or club. **10.** (of a baseball player) to have a batting average of; hit. —*v.i.* **11. a.** to strike at the ball with the bat. **b.** to take one's turn as a batter. **12.** *Slang.* to rush. **13. bat around, a.** *Slang.* to roam; drift. **b.** *Informal.* to discuss: *to bat around an idea.* **14. bat in,** to cause (a run in baseball) to be scored. **15. bat out,** to produce quickly. —*Idiom.* **16. at bat, a.** taking one's turn to bat in a game. **b.** an instance at bat officially charged to a batter. **17. go to bat for,** *Informal.* to intercede on behalf of. **18. (right) off the bat,** without delay; instantly.

bat² (bat), *n.* **1.** any of numerous flying mammals of the order Chiroptera, having large wings made of membranes extending from the forelimbs to the hind limbs and navigating, usu. at night, by echolocation. —*Idiom.* **2.** have bats in one's belfry, to have crazy ideas; behave insanely. —**bat′like′,** *adj.*

bat³ (bat), *v.t.,* **bat•ted, bat•ting.** **1.** to blink; wink; flutter. —*Idiom.* **2. not bat an eye,** to show no surprise or other emotion; maintain a calm exterior.

Ba•taan or **Ba•taán** (bə tan′, -tän′; *locally* bä′tä än′), *n.* a peninsula on W Luzon, in the Philippines: U.S. troops surrendered to Japanese April 9, 1942.

bat′ boy′, *n.* a boy who takes care of the bats and other equipment of a baseball team.

batch (bach), *n.* **1.** a quantity or number coming at one time or taken together; group; lot: *a batch of prisoners.* **2.** the quantity of bread, dough, etc., made at one baking: *a batch of cookies.* **3.** the quantity of material prepared or required for one operation: *a batch of concrete.* **4. a.** a group of jobs, data, programs, or commands treated as a unit for computer processing. **b.** BATCH PROCESSING. **5. a.** a quantity of raw materials mixed and prepared for fusion into glass. **b.** the material so mixed. —*v.t.* **6.** to combine, mix, or process in a batch.

batch′ proc′essing, *n.* a form of data processing in which a number of input jobs are run as a group.

bate¹ (bāt), *v.,* **bat•ed, bat•ing.** —*v.t.* **1.** to moderate or restrain: *to bate one's enthusiasm.* **2.** to lessen or diminish; abate. —*v.i.* **3.** to diminish or subside; abate. —*Idiom.* **4. with bated breath,** in a state of suspenseful anticipation.

bate² (bāt), *v.i.,* **bat•ed, bat•ing.** (of a hawk) to flutter the wings, as in anger or fear.

ba•teau (ba tō′), *n., pl.* **-teaux** (-tōz′). a small flat-bottomed rowboat used on rivers.

Bates (bāts), *n.* **Katharine Lee,** 1859–1929, U.S. teacher and hymn writer, author of *America the Beautiful.*

bat•fish (bat′fish′), *n., pl.* (*esp. collectively*) **-fish,** (*esp. for kinds or species*) **-fish•es.** **1.** any flat-bodied marine fish of the family Ogcocephalidae, as *Ogcocephalus vespertilio,* common in warm SW Atlantic coastal waters. **2.** a stingray, *Aetobatis californicus,* of California.

bat•fowl (bat′foul′), *v.i.* to catch birds at night by dazzling them with a light and then capturing them in a net. —**bat′fowl′er,** *n.*

bath (bath, bäth), *n., pl.* **baths** (baₜhz, bäₜhz, baths, bäths), *v.,* **bathed, bath•ing.** —*n.* **1.** a washing or immersion of something, esp. the body, in water, steam, etc., as for cleansing or medical treatment. **2.** a quantity of water or other liquid used for this purpose: *running a bath.* **3.** a container for water or other cleansing liquid, as a bathtub. **4.** Often, **baths.** one of the elaborate bathing establishments of the ancients. **5.** Usu., **baths.** a town or resort visited for medical treatment by bathing or the like; spa. **6.** a preparation, as an acid solution, in which something is immersed. **7.** the container for such a preparation. **8.** a device for controlling temperature by the use of a surrounding medium, as sand, water, or oil. **9.** the state of being covered by a liquid, as perspiration. —*v.t., v.i.* **10.** *Brit.* to wash or soak in a bath. —*Idiom.* **11. take a bath,** *Informal.* to suffer a large financial loss.

bathe (bāₜh), *v.,* **bathed, bath•ing,** *n.* —*v.t.* **1.** to immerse in water or some other liquid, as for cleansing or refreshment. **2.** to give a bath to; wash. **3.** to moisten or suffuse with any liquid. **4.** to apply water or other liquid to: *to bathe a wound.* **5.** to wash over or against, as by the action of the sea. **6.** to cover or surround: *sunlight bathing the room.* —*v.i.* **7.** to take a bath or sunbath. **8.** to swim for pleasure. **9.** to be covered or surrounded as if with water. —*n.* **10.** *Brit.* an act of bathing; bath; swim. —**bath′er,** *n.*

ba•thet•ic (bə thet′ik), *adj.* characterized by bathos.

bath•house (bath′hous′, bäth′-), *n., pl.* **-hous•es** (-hou′ziz). **1.** a structure, as at the seaside, containing dressing rooms for bathers. **2.** a building having bathing facilities.

bath′ing suit′ (bā′ₜhing), *n.* a garment worn for swimming. Also called **swimsuit.**

batho- or **bathy-,** a combining form meaning "depth": *bathometer.*

bath•o•lith (bath′ə lith), *n.* a large body of intrusive igneous rock believed to have crystallized at a considerable depth below the earth's surface. —**bath′o•lith′ic,** *adj.*

ba•thom•e•ter (bə thom′i tər), *n.* a device for ascertaining the depth of water, as in a lake or ocean.

ba•thos (bā′thos, -thôs, -thōs), *n.* **1.** a ludicrous descent from the exalted or lofty to the commonplace; anticlimax. **2.** insincere pathos; sentimentality. **3.** triteness or triviality in style.

bath·robe (bath′rōb′, bäth′-), *n.* a loose, coatlike garment worn before and after a bath, over sleepwear, or as casual attire at home.

bath·room (bath′rōōm′, -rŏŏm′, bäth′-), *n.* **1.** a room equipped with a bathtub or shower and usu. a sink and toilet. **2.** TOILET (def. 2). —*Idiom.* **3. go to** or **use the bathroom,** to urinate or defecate.

Bath·she·ba (bath shē′bə, bath′shə-), *n.* the wife of Uriah the Hittite and afterward of David: mother of Solomon. II Sam. 11, 12.

bath·tub (bath′tub′, bäth′-), *n.* a tub to bathe in, esp. one that is a permanent fixture in a bathroom.

bath′tub gin′, *n.* homemade gin, esp. gin made illegally during Prohibition.

bath·y·al (bath′ē əl), *adj.* of or pertaining to the biogeographic region of the ocean bottom between the sublittoral and abyssal zones, from depths of approximately 660 to 13,000 ft. (200 to 4000 m).

bath·y·scaphe (bath′ə skāf′, -skaf′) also **bath·y·scaph** (-skaf′) **bath·y·scape** (-skāp′), *n.* a navigable, submersible vessel for exploring the depths of the ocean, usu. having a spherical observation chamber under the hull.

bath·y·sphere (bath′ə sfēr′), *n.* a spherical diving apparatus from which to study deep-sea life.

ba·tik (bə tēk′, bat′ik), *n.* **1.** a technique of hand-dyeing fabric using wax as a dye repellent to cover those parts of the fabric not to be dyed. **2.** the design itself or a fabric so decorated. —*v.t.* **3.** to hand-dye (material) using batik.

ba·tiste (bə tēst′, ba-), *n.* a fine, often sheer fabric, constructed in either a plain or figured weave and made of any of various natural or synthetic fibers.

bat mitz·vah (bät mits′və, bäs) also **bas mitzvah,** *n.* (*often caps.*) **1.** a ceremony for a girl of 12 or 13, paralleling the bar mitzvah. **2.** the girl participating in this ceremony.

ba·ton (bə ton′, ba-, bat′n), *n.* **1.** a wand with which a conductor directs an orchestra or band. **2.** a metal rod fitted with a weighted bulb at each end and carried and twirled by a drum major or majorette. **3.** a thin cylinder that is passed from one member of a relay team to the member next to compete. **4.** a staff, club, or truncheon, esp. one serving as a mark of office or authority. **5.** a slender heraldic bend.

Bat·on Rouge (bat′n rōōzh′), *n.* the capital of Louisiana, in the SE part: a river port on the Mississippi. 227,482.

bats (bats), *adj. Slang.* insane; crazy.

bats·man (bats′mən), *n., pl.* **-men.** a batter, esp. in cricket.

batt or **bat** (bat), *n.* a sheet of matted cotton, wool, or synthetic fibers.

bat·tal·ion (bə tal′yən), *n.* **1.** a military unit of ground forces comprising a headquarters and two or more companies. **2.** an army in battle array. **3.** Often, **battalions,** a large number of persons or things; force: *battalions of sightseers.* [< Middle French *bataillon* < Italian *battaglione* large body of troops]

bat·ten¹ (bat′n), *n.* **1.** a small board or strip of wood used for various building purposes, as to cover joints between boards, reinforce doors, or supply a foundation for lathing. **2. a.** a strip of wood used to keep a sail flat. **b.** a length of wood or metal used on a ship, esp. to secure a tarpaulin over a hatch. —*v.t.* **3.** to furnish or bolster with battens. —*Idiom.* **4. batten down the hatches, a.** to cover a ship's hatches with tarpaulins held in place with battens. **b.** to prepare to meet an emergency.

bat·ten² (bat′n), *v.i.* **1.** to thrive by feeding; grow fat. **2.** to feed gluttonously or greedily. **3.** to thrive, prosper, or live in luxury, esp. at the expense of others. —*v.t.* **4.** to cause to thrive by or as if by feeding.

bat·ter¹ (bat′ər), *v.t.* **1.** to beat persistently or hard; pound repeatedly. **2.** to subject (a person, esp. a wife or child) to repeated beating or other abuse. **3.** to damage by beating or subjecting to rough usage. —*v.i.* **4.** to deal heavy, repeated blows; pound steadily. —**bat′ter·er,** *n.*

bat·ter² (bat′ər), *n.* **1.** a thin mixture typically of flour, milk or water, and eggs, beaten together and used to make cakes, pancakes, etc., or to coat foods before frying. —*v.t.* **2.** to coat with batter.

bat·ter³ (bat′ər), *n.* a player who swings a bat or whose turn it is to bat, as in baseball or cricket.

bat·ter⁴ (bat′ər), *v.i.* **1.** (of the face of a wall or the like) to slope backward and upward. —*n.* **2.** a backward and upward slope of the face of a wall or the like.

bat′tering ram′, *n.* **1.** an ancient military device with a heavy horizontal ram for battering down walls, gates, etc. **2.** any of various similar devices used in demolition, to force entrance to a building, etc.

bat·ter·y (bat′ə rē), *n., pl.* **-ter·ies. 1. a.** a combination of two or more cells connected to produce electric energy. **b.** CELL (def. 5). **2. a.** two or more pieces of artillery used for combined action. **b.** a tactical unit of artillery, usu. comprising six guns and the personnel and equipment to operate them. **3. a.** (on a warship) a group of guns having the same caliber or used for the same purpose. **b.** the whole armament of a warship. **4.** any group or series of similar or related things, esp. things used for a common purpose: *a battery of aptitude tests.* **5.** *Law.* an unlawful attack upon another person, esp. by beating or wounding. **6.** a baseball pitcher and catcher considered as a unit. **7.** the act of beating or battering. **8.** an instrument used in battering.

bat·ting (bat′ing), *n.* **1.** the use of a bat in a ball game. **2.** cotton, wool, or other fibers in batts, used for filling, padding, etc.

bat′ting av′erage, *n.* **1.** a measure of a baseball player's hitting ability, obtained by dividing base hits by number of times at bat. **2.** a degree of achievement or accomplishment in any activity.

bat·tle (bat′l), *n., v.,* **-tled, -tling.** —*n.* **1.** a hostile encounter between opposing military forces. **2.** participation in such an encounter or encounters: *wounds received in battle.* **3.** any fight, conflict, or struggle, as between two persons or teams. —*v.i.* **4.** to engage in battle. **5.** to struggle; strive. —*v.t.* **6.** to fight (a person, army, cause, etc.). **7.** to force or accomplish by fighting, struggling, etc. —*Idiom.* **8. give** or **do battle,** to engage in conflict; fight.

bat′tle cry′, *n.* **1.** a cry or shout of troops going into battle. **2.** a slogan used to arouse people in a contest or campaign.

bat·tle·dore (bat′l dôr′, -dōr′), *n.* **1.** Also called **bat′tledore and shut′tlecock.** a racket game from which badminton was developed. **2.** a light racket for striking the shuttlecock in this game.

bat′tle fatigue′, *n.* a posttraumatic stress disorder occurring among soldiers engaged in active and usu. prolonged combat. Also called **combat fatigue.**

bat·tle·field (bat′l fēld′), *n.* **1.** the field or ground on which a battle is fought. **2.** an area of contention, conflict, or hostile opposition. Also called **bat·tle·ground** (bat′l ground′).

Bat′tle Hymn′ of the Repub′lic, a hymn written during the American Civil War by the writer and reformer Julia Ward Howe. It is sung to the tune of "John Brown's Body," a popular song of the Civil War. Part of its refrain is "Glory, glory, hallelujah."

bat·tle·ment (bat′l mant), *n.* Often, **battlements.** a parapet of a fortification, with open spaces for shooting. —**bat′tle·ment′ed** (-men′tid), *adj.*

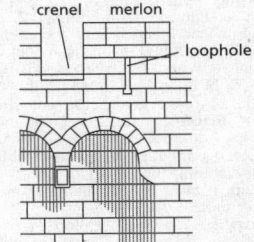

Battle of Bull Run, *n.* See under BULL RUN.

Battle of Bunker Hill, *n.* See under BUNKER HILL.

bat′tle roy′al, *n., pl.* **battles royal. 1.** a fight in which more than two combatants are engaged. **2.** a violent or noisy fight or dispute.

bat·tle·ship (bat′l ship′), *n.* any of a class of warships that are the most heavily armored and are equipped with the most powerful armament.

bau·ble (bô′bəl), *n.* **1.** a cheap, showy ornament; trinket. **2.** a scepter carried by a court jester.

Bau·cis (bô′sis), *n.* (in Greek myth) an aged Phrygian peasant woman who offered hospitality to the disguised Zeus and Hermes.

baud (bôd), *n.* a unit used to measure the speed of signaling or data transfer, equal to the number of pulses or bits per second: *baud rate.*

Bau·de·laire (bōd′l âr′), *n.* **Charles Pierre,** 1821–67, French poet.

Bau·haus (bou′hous′), *n.* **1.** a German school of design in existence from 1919 to 1933, established by Walter Gropius. —*adj.* **2.** of or pertaining to the styles developed at the Bauhaus, marked by an emphasis on functional design. [< German, = *Bau*- build, building + *Haus* house]

Baum (bôm, bäm), *n.* **L(yman) Frank,** 1856–1919, U.S. journalist, playwright, and author of children's books.

baux·ite (bôk′sīt, bō′zīt), *n.* a claylike rock consisting of aluminum oxides and hydroxides with various impurities: the principal ore of aluminum. —**baux·it·ic** (bôk sit′ik, bō zit′-), *adj.*

Ba·var·i·a (bə vâr′ē ə), *n.* a state in SE Germany. 11,082,600; 27,240 sq. mi. (70,550 sq. km). *Cap.:* Munich. German, **Bayern.** —**Ba·var′i·an,** *adj., n.*

bawd·y (bô′dē), *adj.,* **bawd·i·er, bawd·i·est,** *n.* —*adj.* **1.** indecent; lewd; obscene. —*n.* **2.** coarse or obscene talk or writing.

bawl (bôl), *v.i.* **1.** to cry or wail lustily. **2.** to cry out; shout. —*v.t.* **3.** to utter or proclaim by outcry; shout. **4.** to offer for sale by shouting, as a hawker. **5. bawl out,** *Informal.* to scold vigorously. —*n.* **6.** a loud shout; outcry. **7.** a period or spell of loud crying or weeping.

Bax·ter (bak′stər), *n.* **Richard,** 1615–91, English Puritan preacher, scholar, and writer.

bay¹ (bā), *n.* **1.** a body of water forming an indentation of the shoreline, larger than a cove but smaller than a gulf. **2.** a recess of land, partly surrounded by hills. **3.** an arm of a prairie or swamp, extending into woods and partly surrounded by them.

bay² (bā), *n.* **1. a.** any of a number of similar major vertical divisions of a large interior, wall, etc., defined by columns, vaulting, or the like. **b.** a recess in a wall, usu. containing a window. **2. a.** any portion of an airplane set off by two successive bulkheads or other bracing members. **b.** a compartment in an aircraft: *a cargo bay.* **3.** a compartment in a barn for storing hay. **4.**

bay³ (bā), *n.* **1.** a deep, prolonged howl, as of a hound on the scent. **2.** the position of an animal that is forced to face and resist pursuers, or of a person forced to face a foe or difficulty: *Hounds held the stag at bay. The escaped convicts were brought to bay.* **3.** the position of the pursuers or foe thus kept off: *The bear kept the hunters at bay.* —*v.i.* **4.** to howl, esp. with a deep, prolonged sound: *a hound baying at the moon.* —*v.t.* **5.** to assail with deep, prolonged howling. **6.** to express by howling. **7.** to bring to or to hold at bay.

bay⁴ (bā), *n.* **1.** LAUREL (def. 1). **2.** Also called **bayberry.** a tropical American shrub, *Pimenta racemosa,* of the myrtle family, having aromatic leaves that are used in making bay oil and bay rum. **3.** any of various laurellike trees or shrubs. **4.** an honorary garland or crown bestowed for military victory, literary excellence, etc. **5. bays,** fame; renown.

bay⁵ (bā), *n.* **1.** a horse having a reddish-brown body and black mane, tail, and lower legs. **2.** reddish brown. —*adj.* **3.** (esp. of a horse) reddish-brown.

bay•ber•ry (bā′ber′ē, -bə rē), *n., pl.* **-ries. 1.** any of several often aromatic trees or shrubs of the genus *Myrica,* as *M. pensylvanica,* of NE North America, bearing a grayish-white berry covered with a wax used in candle making. **2.** the berry of such a plant. **3.** BAY⁴ (def. 2).

bay′ leaf′, *n.* the dried leaf of the laurel, used as a flavoring.

Bay′ of Pigs′, *n.* a bay of the Caribbean Sea in SW Cuba: site of attempted invasion of Cuba by anti-Castro forces April 1961. Spanish, **Bahía de Cochinos.**

bay•o•net (bā′ə nit, -net′, bā′ə net′), *n., v.,* **-net•ed** or **-net•ted, -net•ing** or **-net•ting.** —*n.* **1.** a daggerlike steel weapon attached to the muzzle of a gun for hand-to-hand combat. **2.** a pin or flange that serves to lock in place a lens inserted into a camera or a flashbulb in a socket. —*v.t.* **3.** to kill or wound with a bayonet. [< French *baïonnette,* after Bayonne, France, where the weapon was first made or used]

bay•ou (bī′ōō, bī′ō), *n., pl.* **-ous.** (in the southern U.S.) a marshy arm, inlet, or outlet of a lake, river, etc., usu. sluggish or stagnant.

Bay′ Psalm′ Book′, a translation of the Psalms by John Eliot and others: the first book published (1640) in America.

bay′ rum′, *n.* a fragrant liquid used chiefly as an aftershave lotion, prepared by distilling the leaves of the tropical American bay, *Pimenta racemosa,* with rum or by mixing oil from the leaves with alcohol, water, and other oils.

bay′ scal′lop, *n.* **1.** a small scallop, *Pecten irradians,* of shallow North American Atlantic waters. **2.** the edible adductor muscle of this scallop, having a sweet and delicate flavor.

bay′ win′dow, *n.* **1.** a large window projecting from an outside wall and forming an alcove of a room. **2.** *Informal.* a protruding belly.

ba•zaar (bə zär′), *n.* **1.** a marketplace or shopping quarter, esp. one in the Middle East. **2.** a sale of miscellaneous articles to benefit some charity, cause, etc. **3.** a store in which many kinds of goods are sold. Sometimes, **ba•zar′.**

ba•zoo•ka (bə zōō′kə), *n., pl.* **-kas.** a tube-shaped, portable rocket launcher that fires a missile capable of penetrating the armor plate of a tank.

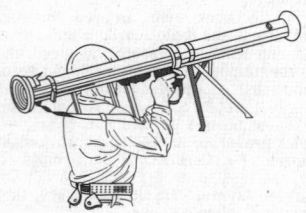

bazooka

BB (bē′bē′), *n.* **1.** a size of shot, 0.18 in. (0.46 cm) in diameter, fired from an air rifle (**BB gun**). **2.** Also called **BB shot.** shot of this size.

BBB, Better Business Bureau.

BBC, British Broadcasting Corporation.

BBS, bulletin board system: a computerized facility, accessible by modem, for collecting and relaying electronic messages and software programs. Also called **electronic bulletin board.**

B.C. or **BC, 1.** before Christ (used in indicating dates). **2.** British Columbia. —**Usage.** See A.D.

B.C.E., before the Christian (or Common) Era.

B cell, *n.* Also called **B lymphocyte.** a type of white blood cell that circulates in the blood and lymph and produces an antibody upon encountering any antigen that has a molecular arrangement complementary to the antibody.

bdel•li•um (del′ē əm, -yəm), *n.* **1.** a fragrant gum resin obtained from certain burseraceous plants, as of the genus *Commiphora.* **2.** a plant yielding this resin. **3.** a substance mentioned in the Bible. Gen. 2:12; Num. 11:7.

be (bē; *unstressed* bē, bi), *v.* and *auxiliary v., pres. sing. 1st pers.* **am,** *2nd* **are,** *3rd* **is,** *pres. pl.* **are;** *past sing. 1st pers.* **was,** *2nd* **were,** *3rd* **was,** *past pl.* **were;** *pres. subj.* **be;** *past subj. sing. 1st, 2nd, and 3rd pers.* **were;** *past subj. pl.* **were;** *past part.* **been;** *pres. part.* **be•ing.** —*v.i.* **1.** to exist or live: *Shakespeare's "To be or not to be" is the ultimate question.* **2.** to take place; occur: *The wedding was last week.* **3.** to occupy a place or position: *The book is on the table.* **4.** to continue or remain as before: *Let things be.* **5.** to belong; attend; befall: *May good fortune be with you.* **6.** (used as a copula to connect the subject with its predicate adjective, or predicate nominative, in order to describe, identify, or amplify the subject): *He is tall. She is president.* **7.** (used as a copula to introduce or form interrogative or imperative sentences): *Is that right? Be quiet!* —*auxiliary verb.* **8.** (used with the present participle of another verb to form progressive tenses): *I am waiting. We were talking.* **9.** (used with the infinitive of the principal verb to indicate a command, arrangements, or future action): *He is to see me today. You are not to leave before six.* **10.** (used with the past participle of another verb to form the passive voice): *The date was fixed.* **11.** (used in archaic or literary constructions with some intransitive verbs to form perfect tenses): *He is come.* —**Usage.** See ME.

Be, *Chem. Symbol.* beryllium.

be-, a prefix with the original sense "about," "around," "all over," hence having an intensive and often disparaging force; used as a verb formative (*besiege*), and often serving to form transitive verbs from intransitives or from nouns: *belabor; befriend; belittle.*

B/E or **b.e.,** bill of exchange.

B.E., 1. Bachelor of Education. **2.** Bachelor of Engineering.

beach (bēch), *n.* **1.** an expanse of sand or pebbles along a shore. **2.** the part of the shore of an ocean, sea, lake, etc., washed by the tide or waves. **3.** the area adjacent to a seashore. —*v.t.* **4.** to haul or run onto a beach: *to beach a boat.* **5.** to cause to be unemployed or idle.

beach•comb•er (bēch′kō′mər), *n.* **1.** a person who lives by gathering salable articles of jetsam, refuse, etc., from beaches. **2.** a vagrant who lives on the seashore, esp. a nonnative person on a South Pacific island. **3.** a long wave rolling in from the ocean onto the beach.

beach′ flea′, *n.* any of various tiny crustaceans that inhabit beaches and that jump like fleas.

beach•front (bēch′frunt′), *n.* **1.** land fronting on a beach. —*adj.* **2.** located on or adjacent to a beach: *beachfront property.*

beach′ grass′, *n.* any of several erect, strongly rooted grasses, esp. of the genus *Ammophila,* common on exposed sandy shores.

beach•head (bēch′hed′), *n.* **1.** the area that is the first objective of a military force landing on an enemy shore. **2.** a secure initial position that can be used for further advancement; foothold.

beach′ pea′, *n.* either of two seashore plants of the legume family, *Lathyrus japonicus* of N temperate regions or *L. littoralis* of the W coast of North America, both having oblong leaves and clusters of pealike flowers.

beach′ plum′, *n.* a small plum tree, *Prunus maritima,* that grows on seashores of NE North America.

beach′ worm′wood, *n.* a composite plant, *Artemisia stelleriana,* having yellow flowers and deeply lobed leaves covered with white fuzz.

bea•con (bē′kən), *n.* **1.** a guiding or warning signal, as a light or fire, esp. one in an elevated position. **2.** a tower or hill used for such purposes. **3.** a lighthouse, signal buoy, etc., on a shore or at sea to warn and guide vessels. **4.** a radar device transmitting a pulse from a fixed location as an aid to navigation. **5.** a person or thing that warns, guides, etc. —*v.t.* **6.** to serve as a beacon to. **7.** to furnish or mark with beacons. —*v.i.* **8.** to serve or shine as a beacon.

bead (bēd), *n.* **1.** a small, usu. round object of glass, wood, stone, or the like with a hole through it, often strung with others of its kind in necklaces, rosaries, etc. **2. beads, a.** a necklace of beads. **b.** a rosary. **3.** any small globular or cylindrical body, as a drop of liquid or a bubble in an effervescent liquid: *beads of sweat.* **4.** the front sight of a rifle or gun. **5.** a reinforced area of a rubber tire. **6.** a small molding having a convex circular section and, usu., a continuous cylindrical surface. **7.** a continuous deposit of fused metal formed by arc welding. —*v.t.* **8.** to ornament with beads. **9.** to form beads or a bead on. —*v.i.* **10.** to form beads; form in beads or drops. —*Idiom.* **11.** count, say, or tell one's beads, to say one's prayers, using rosary beads. **12.** draw or get a bead on, to take careful aim at (a target). —**bead′ed,** *adj.*

bead•ing (bē′ding), *n.* **1.** material made of or adorned with beads. **2.** openwork trimming run through with ribbon. **3. a.** BEAD (def. 6). **b.** all of the bead moldings in a single design.

bea•dle (bēd′l), *n.* **1.** a parish officer who performs various duties, as keeping order during the service. **2.** SEXTON (def. 1).

bead•y (bē′dē), *adj.,* **bead•i•er, bead•i•est. 1.** beadlike; small, round, and glittering: *beady eyes.* **2.** covered with or full of beads.

bea•gle (bē′gəl), *n.* one of a breed of small, compact hounds with drooping ears and usu. a black, tan, and white coat.

beak (bēk), *n.* **1.** the bill of a bird. **2.** any horny or stiff projecting mouthpart of an animal, fish, or insect. **3.** anything beaklike or ending in a point, as the spout of a pitcher. **4.** *Slang.* a person's nose. **5.** a projection from the bow of an ancient warship, used to ram enemy vessels. **6.** a narrow projecting molding resembling a bird's beak, forming a drip for shedding rainwater, as on a cornice.

beak•er (bē′kər), *n.* **1.** a large drinking cup or glass with a wide mouth. **2.** the contents of a beaker. **3.** a cuplike container, usu. with a pouring lip, esp. one used in a laboratory.

be′-all′ and end′-all′, *n.* the central and all-important part; the ultimate object.

beam (bēm), *n.* **1.** any of various relatively long pieces of metal, wood, etc., used esp. as rigid members or parts of structures or machines. **2.** a horizontal bearing member, as a joist or lintel, or a transverse supporting structural member on a ship. **3.** the extreme width of a ship. **4.** *Slang.* the measure across both hips or buttocks. **5. a.** (in a loom) a roller or cylinder on which the warp is wound before weaving. **b.** a similar cylinder on which cloth is wound as it is woven. **6.** the crossbar of a balance from which the scales or pans are suspended. **7.** a ray or stream of light or other radiation, as gamma rays, electrons, or subatomic particles. **8.** a group of nearly parallel rays. **9.** a radio signal transmitted along a narrow course, used to guide pilots. **10.** a radiant smile. **11.** the principal stem of the antler of a deer. —*v.t.* **12.** to emit in or as if in beams or rays. **13.** to transmit (a radio or television signal) in a particular direction. **14.** to direct (a radio or television program, commercial message, etc.) to a predetermined audience. —*v.i.* **15.** to emit beams, as of light. **16.** to smile radiantly or happily. —***Idiom.*** **17. off the beam, a.** not on the course indicated by a radio beam. **b.** *Informal.* wrong; incorrect. **18. on the beam, a.** on the course indicated by a radio beam. **b.** *Informal.* correct; exact.

beam•ing (bē′ming), *adj.* **1.** radiant; bright. **2.** smiling brightly; cheerful. —**beam′ing•ly,** *adv.*

bean (bēn), *n.* **1.** the edible nutritious seed of various plants of the legume family, esp. of the genus *Phaseolus.* **2.** a plant producing such seeds. **3.** the pod of such a plant, esp. when immature and eaten as a vegetable. **4.** any of various other beanlike seeds or plants, as the coffee bean. **5.** *Informal.* a person's head. **6. beans,** *Informal.* the slightest amount: *He doesn't know beans about navigation.* —*v.t.* **7.** *Informal.* to hit on the head, esp. with a baseball. —***Idiom.*** **8. full of beans,** *Informal.* **a.** overflowing with vitality. **b.** erroneous; misinformed. **9. spill the beans,** *Informal.* to disclose a secret.

Bean (bēn), *n.* **1. Alan L(aVern),** born 1932, U.S. astronaut. **2. Roy** (*"Judge"*), 1825?–1903, U.S. frontiersman and justice of the peace: called himself "the law west of the Pecos."

bean•bag (bēn′bag′), *n.* **1.** a small cloth bag filled with beans, used as a toy or in games. **2.** Also called **bean′bag chair′.** a chair in the form of a large bag filled with plastic or foam pellets that molds itself to the contours of the sitter.

bean′ ball′, *n.* a baseball pitch thrown at the batter's head.

bean′ ca′per, *n.* a small Mediterranean tree, *Zygophyllum fabago,* of the caltrop family, having flower buds that are sometimes used as a substitute for capers.

bean′ count′er, *n. Informal.* a person who makes judgments chiefly on the basis of numerical calculations, as an accountant, financial analyst, or statistician. —**bean′-count′ing,** *adj.*

bean′ curd′, *n.* TOFU.

bean•er•y (bē′nə rē), *n., pl.* **-er•ies.** *Informal.* a cheap, usu. inferior, restaurant.

bean•pole (bēn′pōl′), *n.* **1.** a tall pole for a bean plant to climb on. **2.** *Informal.* a tall, lanky person.

bean′ sprout′, *n.* the sprout of a newly germinated bean, esp. a mung bean, used as a vegetable.

bean•stalk (bēn′stôk′), *n.* the stem of a bean plant.

bean′ tree′, *n.* any of several trees bearing pods resembling those of a bean, as the catalpa and the carob tree.

bear[1] (bâr), *v.,* **bore, borne** or **born, bear•ing.** —*v.t.* **1.** to hold up or support: *The columns bear the weight of the roof.* **2.** to give birth to: *to bear a child.* **3.** to produce by natural growth: *a tree that bears fruit.* **4.** to sustain or be capable of: *This claim doesn't bear close examination.* **5.** to drive or push: *The crowd was borne back by the police.* **6.** to carry or conduct (oneself, one's body, etc.): *to bear oneself bravely.* **7.** to suffer; endure or tolerate: *He bore the blame. I can't bear your nagging.* **8.** to warrant or be worthy of: *It doesn't bear repeating.* **9.** to carry; bring: *to bear gifts.* **10.** to carry in the mind or heart: *to bear malice.* **11.** to transmit or spread (gossip, tales, etc.). **12.** to render; afford; give: *to bear testimony.* **13.** to have and be entitled to: *to bear title.* **14.** to exhibit; show: *to bear a resemblance.* **15.** to accept or have as an obligation: *to bear the cost.* **16.** to possess as a quality or characteristic; have in or on: *to bear traces; to bear an inscription.* —*v.i.* **17.** to tend in a course or direction; move; go: *to bear left.* **18.** to be situated: *The lighthouse bears due north.* **19.** to bring forth young, fruit, etc. **20. bear down, a.** to press or weigh down. **b.** to strive harder. **21. bear down on, a.** to press or weigh down on. **b.** to strive toward. **c.** to move toward rapidly and threateningly. **22. bear on** or **upon,** to be relevant to; affect. **23. bear out,** to substantiate; confirm. **24. bear up,** to face hardship bravely; endure. **25. bear with,** to be patient with. —***Idiom.*** **26. bear the burden and the heat of the day,** to endure hardship and adversity: said by Jesus in his parable of the workers in the vineyard. Matt. 20:12. **27. bring to bear,** to force to have an impact: *to bring pressure to bear on union members to end a strike.*

bear[2] (bâr), *n., pl.* **bears,** (*esp. collectively*) **bear,** *adj.* —*n.* **1.** any large, stocky, omnivorous mammal of the carnivore family Ursidae, with thick, coarse fur, a very short tail, and a plantigrade gait, inhabiting the Northern Hemisphere and N South America. **2.** a gruff, clumsy, or rude person. **3.** a person who believes that stock prices will decline (opposed to *bull*). **4.** (*cap.*) either of two constellations, Ursa Major or Ursa Minor. —*adj.* **5.** marked by declining prices, esp. of stocks: *a bear market.* —**bear′ish,** *adj.*

bear•a•ble (bâr′ə bəl), *adj.* capable of being endured or tolerated. —**bear′a•bly,** *adv.*

bear•ber•ry (bâr′ber′ē, -bə rē), *n., pl.* **-ries.** any of several prostrate shrubs of the genus *Arctostaphylos,* of the heath family, esp. *A. uva-ursi,* having tonic, astringent leaves and bright-red berries.

bear•cat (bâr′kat′), *n.* **1.** *Informal.* a person or thing that fights or acts with force or fierceness. **2.** PANDA (def. 2).

beard (bērd), *n.* **1.** hair growing on the lower part of the face, esp. on the face of a man, sometimes including a mustache. **2.** a similar growth on the chin of some animals or near the bill in some birds. **3.** a tuft or growth of awns or the like, as on wheat or barley. **4.** a barb or catch on an arrow, fishhook, etc. **5.** the sloping part of a printing type that connects the face with the shoulder of the body. —*v.t.* **6.** to seize, pluck, or pull the beard of. **7.** to oppose boldly; defy. **8.** to supply with a beard. —***Idiom.*** **9. beard the lion in its den,** to confront a fearsome, authoritative person in his or her own environment.

beard•tongue (bērd′tung′), *n.* PENSTEMON.

bear•er (bâr′ər), *n.* **1.** a person or thing that carries, upholds, or brings. **2.** the person who presents an order for money or goods. **3.** a tree or plant that yields fruit or flowers.

bear′ grass′ or **bear′grass′,** *n.* **1.** a tall W North American plant, *Xerophyllum tenax,* of the lily family, having grasslike foliage. **2.** any of several plants of the agave family, having linear, grasslike leaves, as those of the genera *Nolina* and *Dasylirion.*

bear′ hug′, *n.* a forcefully or heartily tight embrace.

bear•ing (bâr′ing), *n.* **1.** the manner in which one conducts or carries oneself, including posture and gestures: *a person of dignified bearing.* **2.** the act, capability, or period of producing or bringing forth. **3.** something that is produced; a crop. **4.** the act of enduring or the capacity to endure. **5.** reference or relation (usu. fol. by *on*): *It has no bearing on the problem.* **6. a.** a supporting part of a structure. **b.** the area of contact between a bearing member, as a beam, and a pier, wall, or other underlying support. **7.** the support and guide for a rotating, oscillating, or sliding shaft, pivot, or wheel. **8.** Often, **bearings.** direction or relative position: *The pilot radioed the plane's bearings.* **9.** a horizontal direction expressed in degrees east or west of a true or magnetic north or south direction. **10.** a device on a heraldic field.

bé•ar•naise′ sauce′ (ber nāz′, -nez′, bā′ər-), *n.* a thick sauce of egg yolks, butter, vinegar, wine, shallots, and tarragon.

bear•skin (bâr′skin′), *n.* **1.** the skin or pelt of a bear. **2.** a tall, black fur cap forming part of a dress uniform in some armies.

beast (bēst), *n.* **1.** any nonhuman animal, esp. a large, four-footed mammal. **2.** the crude animal nature common to humans and other animals. **3.** a cruel, coarse, or filthy person. **4.** any animal, as distinguished from a plant.

beast•ie (bē′stē), *n.* a small animal.

beast•ly (bēst′lē), *adj.,* **-li•er, -li•est,** *adv.* —*adj.* **1.** of or like a beast; bestial. **2.** nasty; unpleasant; disagreeable. —*adv.* **3.** *Chiefly Brit. Informal.* very; exceedingly: *It's beastly cold outside.*

beast′ of bur′den, *n.* an animal used for carrying heavy loads or pulling heavy equipment, as a donkey, mule, or ox.

beast′ of prey′, *n.* a predatory mammal.

beat (bēt), *v.,* **beat, beat•en** or **beat, beat•ing,** *n., adj.* —*v.t.* **1.** to strike forcefully and repeatedly: *to beat a toy drum.* **2.** to hit (a person or animal) repeatedly so as to cause painful injury; thrash (often fol. by *up*). **3.** to dash against: *rain beating the trees.* **4.** to flutter or flap: *a bird beating its wings.* **5.** to sound, as on a drum: *to beat a tattoo.* **6.** to stir vigorously: *Beat the egg whites well.* **7.** to break, forge, or make by blows: *to beat swords into plowshares.* **8.** to make (a path) by repeated treading. **9.** to mark (time) by strokes, as with the hand or a metronome. **10.** to scour (the forest, grass, or brush) in order to rouse game. **11.** to overcome, as in a contest; defeat. **12.** *Informal.* to be superior to: *Making reservations beats waiting in line.* **13.** *Informal.* to baffle: *It beats me how he got the job.* **14.** *Informal.* to mitigate or offset the effects of: *beating the hot weather.* **15.** *Slang.* to swindle; cheat (often fol. by *out*). **16.** *Slang.* to escape or avoid (blame or punishment). **17.** (in weaving) to strike (the loose pick) into its proper place in the woven cloth with the reed or other comblike device. —*v.i.* **18.** to strike with or as if with repeated blows. **19.** to throb or pulsate. **20.** to resound under blows, as a drum. **21.** to achieve victory in a contest; win. **22.** to play, as on a drum. **23.** to scour cover for game. **24.** (of a cooking ingredient) to permit beating. **25.** to tack to windward by sailing close-hauled. **26. beat about,** to search through; scour. **27. beat back,** to force back; compel to withdraw. **28. beat down, a.** to bring into subjection; subdue. **b.** *Informal.* to persuade (a seller) to lower the price. **29. beat off,** to ward off; repulse. **30. beat out, a.** to defeat; win or be chosen over. **b.** to create hurriedly; bat out. —*n.* **31.** a stroke or blow. **32.** the sound made by one or more such blows. **33.** a throb or pulsation: *a pulse of 60 beats per minute.* **34.** one's assigned or regular path or habitual round: *a police officer's beat.* **35. a.** the audible, visual, or mental marking of the metrical divisions of music. **b.** a stroke of the hand, baton, etc., marking the time division or an accent for music during performance. **36.** the accent stress, or ictus, in a foot or rhythmical unit of poetry. **37.** a variation in amplitude or volume caused by the interference of two waves that have slightly different frequencies. **38. a.** the reporting of a piece of news ahead of one's rivals; scoop. Compare EXCLU-SIVE (def. 10). **b.** Also called **newsbeat.** the news source, activity, etc., that a reporter is assigned to cover. **39.** (*often cap.*) BEATNIK. —*adj.* **40.** *Informal.* exhausted; worn out. **41.** (*often cap.*) of or characteristic of members of the Beat Generation or beatniks. —**Idiom. 42. beat all,** to be surprising or impressive: *Did he really? Well, if that doesn't beat all!* **43. beat it,** *Informal.* to go away. **44. beat swords into plowshares,** to turn from warfare to peaceful activities. Is. 2:4. **45. on the beat,** in the correct rhythm or tempo. —**beat′a•ble,** *adj.*

beat•en (bēt′n), *adj.* **1.** formed or shaped by blows; hammered: *a dish of beaten brass.* **2.** much trodden; commonly used: *a beaten path.* **3.** defeated; vanquished; thwarted. **4.** overcome by exhaustion; worn-out. **5.** mixed or made light by beating: *beaten eggs.* —**Idiom. 6. off the beaten track** or **path,** out of the ordinary; not well-known; unusual.

beat•er (bē′tər), *n.* **1.** one that beats. **2.** an implement or device for beating something. **3.** (in a hunt) a person who drives game from cover.

Beat′ Genera′tion, *n.* (*often l.c.*) members of the generation that came of age in the 1950s and espoused forms of mysticism and the relaxation of social inhibitions.

be•a•tif•ic (bē′ə tif′ik), *adj.* **1.** bestowing bliss, blessings, happiness, or the like: *beatific peace.* **2.** blissful; saintly: *a beatific smile.*

be•at•i•fy (bē at′ə fī′), *v.t.,* **-fied, -fy•ing. 1.** to make blissfully happy. **2.** (in the Roman Catholic Church) to declare (a deceased person) to be among the blessed and thus entitled to specific religious honor. —**be•at′i•fi•ca′tion,** *n.*

be•at•i•tude (bē at′i tōōd′, -tyōōd′), *n.* **1.** supreme blessedness; exalted happiness. **2.** (*often cap.*) any of the declarations of blessedness pronounced by Jesus in the Sermon on the Mount.

Bea•tles (bēt′lz), *n.pl.* **the,** British rock group (1962–70) including **George Harrison** (born 1943), **John (Winston) Len•non** (len′ən) (1940–80), **Paul (James) Mc•Cart•ney** (mə kärt′nē) (born 1942), and **Ringo Starr** (*Richard Starkey*) (born 1940).

beat•nik (bēt′nik), *n.* **1.** (*sometimes cap.*) a member of the Beat Generation. **2.** a person who rejects conventional behavior, dress, etc.

Be•a•trice (bē′ə tris, bē′tris), *n.* a Florentine woman represented in Dante's *Vita Nuova* and *Divine Comedy* as an ideal of womanhood.

beat-up (bēt′up′), *adj. Informal.* dilapidated; broken-down.

beau (bō), *n., pl.* **beaus, beaux** (bōz). **1.** a girl's or woman's sweetheart. **2.** a dandy; fop.

Beau′fort scale′ (bō′fərt), *n.* a scale for indicating the force or speed of wind, using numbers from 0 to 12 or, sometimes, 17.

beau′ ide′al, *n., pl.* **beaus ideal, beaux ideal** for 1; **beau ideals** for 2. **1.** a conception of perfect beauty. **2.** a model of excellence.

Beau•jo•lais (bō′zhə lā′), *n., pl.* **-laises** (-lāz′). **1.** a winegrowing region in E France. **2.** a red wine of this region.

beau′ monde′ (mond′, mônd′), *n.* the fashionable world; high society.

Beau•mont (bō′mont), *n.* **1. Francis,** 1584–1616, English dramatist who collaborated with John Fletcher. **2.** a city in SE Texas. 115,022.

Beau•re•gard (bō′ri gärd′), *n.* **Pierre Gustave Toutant,** 1818–93, Confederate general in the Civil War.

beaut (byōōt), *n. Informal.* (often used ironically) a beautiful or remarkable person or thing.

beau•te•ous (byōō′tē əs, -tyəs), *adj.* beautiful.

beau•ti•cian (byōō tish′ən), *n.* a person trained to style and dress the hair; hairdresser.

beau•ti•ful (byōō′tə fəl), *adj.* **1.** having beauty; delighting the senses or mind. **2.** excellent of its kind; wonderful; remarkable: *a beautiful putt on the seventh hole.* —*n.* **3. the beautiful,** beautiful things or people collectively. —*interj.* **4.** (often used ironically) wonderful; excellent; remarkable. —**beau′ti•ful•ly,** *adv.*

Beau′tiful Dream′er, a song (1864) by Stephen Foster.

beau′tiful peo′ple, *n.* (*often caps.*) wealthy or famous people, often members of the jet set, who mingle in glamorous social circles and who, because of their celebrity, often establish trends or fashions.

beau•ti•fy (byōō′tə fī′), *v.t., v.i.,* **-fied, -fy•ing.** to make or become beautiful. —**beau′ti•fi•ca′tion,** *n.* —**beau′ti•fi′er,** *n.*

beau•ty (byōō′tē), *n., pl.* **-ties. 1.** the quality present in a person or thing that gives intense aesthetic pleasure or deep satisfaction to the mind or the senses. **2.** a beautiful person, esp. a woman. **3.** a beautiful thing, as a work of art. **4.** Often, **beauties.** something that is beautiful in nature or in some natural or artificial environment. **5.** a particular advantage: *One of the beauties of this plan is its low cost.* **6.** (often used ironically) something remarkable or excellent: *a beauty of a bruise.* —**Proverb. 7. Beauty is in the eye of the beholder,** beauty depends on who perceives it. **8. Beauty is only skin-deep,** inner beauty is more important than physical appearance.

beau′ty-bush′, *n.* a Chinese ornamental shrub, *Kolkwitzia amabilis,* of the honeysuckle family, having tubular pink flowers.

beau′ty con′test, *n.* **1.** a competition in which the entrants, usu. women, are judged as to physical beauty and sometimes personality and talent. **2.** a contest, as a presidential primary, that is decided by popular vote.

beaux arts (bō zär′), *n.pl.* the fine arts.

bea•ver¹ (bē′vər), *n., pl.* **-vers,** (*esp. collectively*) **-ver** for 1. **1.** a large amphibious rodent of the genus *Castor,* having sharp incisors, webbed

hind feet, and a flattened tail, noted for its ability to dam streams with trees, branches, etc. **2.** the fur of this animal. **3.** a hat made of beaver fur or an imitation of it. **4.** TOP HAT. **5.** *Informal.* an exceptionally active or hardworking person. **6. a.** a thickly napped cotton cloth used chiefly for work clothes. **b.** (formerly) a thickly napped woolen cloth made to resemble beaver fur.

bea•ver² (bē′vər), *n.* **1.** plate armor covering the lower part of the face and the throat. **2.** a visor for a helmet.

be•bop (bē′bop′), *n.* BOP¹. —**be′bop′per,** *n.*

be•came (bi kām′), *v.* pt. of BECOME.

be•cause (bi kôz′, -koz′, -kuz′), *conj.* **1.** for the reason that; due to the fact that. —**Idiom. 2. because of,** by reason of; due to.

bé•cha•mel (bā′shə mel′, bā′shə mel′), *n.* a white sauce, sometimes seasoned with onion and nutmeg.

Bech•u•a•na•land (bech′ōō ä′nə land′, bek′yōō-), *n.* former name of BOTSWANA.

beck¹ (bek), *n.* **1.** a gesture used to signal, summon, or direct someone. —**Idiom. 2. at someone's beck and call,** subject to someone's every wish.

beck² (bek), *n. Brit.* CREEK.

Beck•et (bek′it), *n.* **Saint Thomas à,** 1118?–70, archbishop of Canterbury: murdered because of his opposition to Henry II's policies toward the church.

beck•on (bek′ən), *v.t., v.i.* **1.** to signal, summon, or direct by a gesture of the head or hand. **2.** to lure; entice. —*n.* **3.** a nod, gesture, etc., that signals, directs, or summons. —**beck′on•er,** *n.*

be•come (bi kum′), *v.,* **-came, -come, -com•ing.** —*v.i.* **1.** to come, change, or grow to be (as specified): *to become tired.* **2.** to come into being; develop or progress into: *She became a ballerina.* —*v.t.* **3.** to be attractive on; befit in appearance; suit: *That dress becomes you.* **4.** to be suitable to the dignity, situation, or responsibility of: *conduct that becomes an officer.* —**Idiom. 5. become of,** to happen to; be the fate of.

be•com•ing (bi kum′ing), *adj.* **1.** tending to suit or to give a pleasing effect or attractive appearance: *a becoming hairdo.* **2.** suitable; proper. —*n.* **3.** any process of change. —**be•com′ing•ly,** *adv.*

bed (bed), *n., v.,* **bed•ded, bed•ding.** —*n.* **1.** a piece of furniture upon which or within which a person sleeps, rests, or stays when not well. **2.** the mattress and bedclothes together with the bedstead of a bed. **3.** the bedstead alone. **4.** the act of or time for sleeping. **5.** the use of a bed for the night; lodging. **6.** the marital relationship. **7.** any place used for sleeping or resting. **8. a.** an area of ground in which plants, esp. flowering garden plants, are grown. **b.** the plants growing in such an area. **9.** the bottom of a lake, river, sea, or other body of water. **10.** an area on the bottom of a body of water abounding in a particular kind of plant or animal life: *an oyster bed.* **11.** a piece or part forming a foundation or base: *tuna on a bed of lettuce.* **12.** a layer of rock; stratum. **13.** a foundation surface of earth or rock supporting a track, pavement, or the like. **14. a.** the underside of a stone, brick, slate, tile, etc., laid in position. **b.** the layer of mortar in which a brick, stone, etc., is laid. **15.** the flat surface in a printing press on which the form of type is laid. **16.** the body or, sometimes, the floor or bottom of a truck or trailer. **17.** flesh enveloping the base of a claw, esp. the germinative layer beneath the claw. —*v.t.* **18.** to provide with a bed. **19.** to put to bed. **20.** to plant in or as if in a bed. **21.** to lay flat. **22.** to place in a bed or layer. **23.** to embed. —*v.i.* **24.** to have sleeping accommodations. **25.** to form a compact layer or stratum. **26. bed down,** to retire to bed. —**Idiom. 27. get up on the wrong side of the bed,** to be cranky and contrary from the moment one awakes. **28. make a bed,** to fit a bed with sheets and blankets. **29. put to bed, a.** to help (a child, invalid, etc.) go to bed. **b.** to lock up (forms) in a printing press in preparation for printing. **c.** to work on (an edition of a newspaper, periodical, etc.) up to the time of going to press.

B.Ed., Bachelor of Education.

bed′ and board′, *n.* **1.** living quarters and meals. **2.** one's home regarded as exemplifying the obligations of marriage.

bed′-and-break′fast, *n.* an inn providing guests with a room for the night and breakfast the next morning for one inclusive price. *Abbr.:* B and B, B&B

be•daz•zle (bi daz′əl), *v.t.,* **-zled, -zling. 1.** to impress forcefully, esp. so as to make oblivious to faults or shortcomings. **2.** to dazzle so as to blind or confuse. —**be•daz′zle•ment,** *n.*

bed′ board′ or **bed′board′,** *n.* a thin, rigid board placed between a mattress and bedspring to give firm support.

bed′bug′ or **bed′ bug′,** *n.* a flat, wingless, bloodsucking bug, *Cimex lectularius,* that infests houses and esp. beds.

bed•clothes (bed′klōz′, -klōᵺz′), *n.pl.* coverings for a bed, as sheets and blankets; bedding.

bed•ded (bed′id), *adj.* (of rocks) arranged in strata.

bed•ding (bed′ing), *n.* **1.** BEDCLOTHES. **2.** litter, straw, etc., used as a bed, as in a barn stall. **3.** arrangement of sedimentary rocks in strata. —*adj.* **4.** suitable for planting in a garden bed.

Bede (bēd) also **Baeda,** *n.* **Saint** (*"the Venerable Bede"*), A.D. 673?–735, English monk, historian, and theologian.

be•deck (bi dek′), *v.t.* to adorn, esp. in a showy or gaudy manner.

be•dev•il (bi dev′əl), *v.t.,* **-iled, -il•ing** or (*esp. Brit.*) **-illed, -il•ling. 1.** to torment or harass maliciously or diabolically. **2.** to possess as if with a devil; bewitch. **3.** to cause confusion or doubt in; muddle; confound.

4. to beset or hamper continuously: *a new building bedeviled by elevator failures.* —**be·dev′il·ment**, *n.*

bed·fel·low (bed′fel′ō), *n.* **1.** a person who shares one's bed. **2.** an associate or collaborator, esp. one who forms a temporary alliance for reasons of expediency.

be·di·zen (bi dī′zən, -diz′ən), *v.t.* to dress or adorn gaudily or tastelessly.

bed·lam (bed′ləm), *n.* a scene or state of wild uproar and confusion.

bed′ lin′en, *n.* sheets and pillowcases.

bed′ of ros′es, *n.* a situation of luxurious ease; a highly agreeable position.

Bed·ou·in or **Bed·u·in** (bed′ŏŏ in, bed′win), *n.*, *pl.* **-ins**, (*esp. collectively*) **-in. 1.** an Arab of the deserts of SW Asia and N Africa, traditionally tent-dwelling and dependent on animal herds for subsistence. **2.** a nomad; wanderer.

bed·pan (bed′pan′), *n.* a shallow toilet pan for use by persons confined to bed.

bed·post (bed′pōst′), *n.* one of the upright supports at the corners of a bedstead.

be·drag·gle (bi drag′əl), *v.t.,* **-gled, -gling.** to make limp and soiled, as with rain or dirt.

bed′ rest′, *n.* **1.** a prolonged rest in bed, as in the treatment of an illness. **2.** a device used to support a person sitting up in bed.

bed·rid·den (bed′rid′n), *adj.* confined to bed because of illness, injury, etc.

bed·rock (bed′rok′), *n.* **1.** unbroken solid rock, overlaid in most places by soil or rock fragments. **2.** the bottom layer; lowest stratum. **3.** any firm foundation or basis. **4.** the fundamental principles, as of a science.

bed·roll (bed′rōl′), *n.* bedding rolled for portability and used esp. for sleeping out-of-doors.

bed·room (bed′rŏŏm′, -rŏŏm′), *n.* **1.** a room furnished and used for sleeping. —*adj.* **2.** concerned mainly with love affairs or sex: *The movie is a typical bedroom comedy.* **3.** sexually inviting: *bedroom eyes.* **4.** inhabited largely by commuters: *bedroom suburbs.*

bed′side man′ner, *n.* the attitude, approach, and deportment of a doctor toward patients.

bed·sore (bed′sôr′, -sōr′), *n.* a skin ulcer over a bony part of the body, caused by immobility and prolonged pressure, as in bedridden persons.

bed·spread (bed′spred′), *n.* an outer covering for a bed.

bed·spring (bed′spring′), *n.* a set of springs for the support of a mattress.

bed·stead (bed′sted′, -stid), *n.* the framework of a bed supporting the springs and a mattress.

bed′ stone′, *n.* the fixed lower member of a pair of millstones. Compare RUNNER (def. 16).

bed·straw (bed′strô′), *n.* any of various plants belonging to the genus *Galium,* of the madder family, used as straw for stuffing mattresses.

bed·time (bed′tīm′), *n.* the time a person goes to bed.

bed·warm·er (bed′wôr′mər), *n.* WARMING PAN.

bed′wet′ting or **bed′-wet′ting**, *n.* urinating in bed during sleep, esp. habitually; enuresis. —**bed′wet′ter**, *n.*

bee (bē), *n.* **1.** any hymenopterous insect of the superfamily Apoidea, including social and solitary species of several families, as the bumblebees and honeybees. **2.** the common honeybee, *Apis mellifera.* **3.** a social gathering in order to perform some task, engage in a contest, etc.: *a quilting bee.* —*Idiom.* **4. have a bee in one's bonnet, a.** to be obsessed with a single idea. **b.** to be somewhat eccentric.

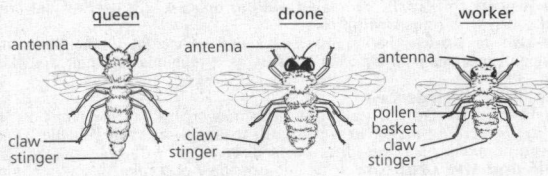

bee (def. 2)

bee′ balm′, *n.* **1.** OSWEGO TEA. **2.** a plant, *Melissa officinalis,* having broad, opposite, serrated leaves and tight clusters of white, lemon-scented flowers that attract bees.

beech (bēch), *n.* **1.** any tree of the genus *Fagus,* of temperate regions, having a smooth gray bark and bearing small, edible, triangular nuts. **2.** the wood of such a tree. —**beech′en**, *adj.*

Bee·cher (bē′chər), *n.* **1. Henry Ward,** 1813–87, U.S. preacher and writer. **2. Lyman,** 1775–1863, U.S. preacher and theologian (father of Harriet Beecher Stowe and Henry Ward Beecher).

beech·nut (bēch′nut′), *n.* the nut of the beech.

bee′-eat′er, *n.* any of numerous colorful birds of the family Meropidae, inhabiting warm regions of the Old World, that feed on flying insects.

beef (bēf), *n.,* *pl.* **beeves** (bēvz) for 2; **beefs** for 4, *v.,* **beefed, beef·ing.** —*n.* **1.** the flesh of a cow, steer, or bull raised and killed for its meat. **2.** an adult cow, steer, or bull raised for its meat. **3.** *Informal.* **a.** brawn; muscular strength. **b.** human flesh. **4.** *Slang.* a complaint.

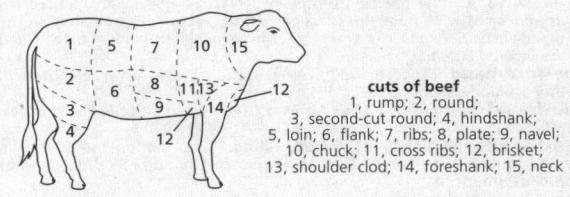

cuts of beef
1, rump; 2, round;
3, second-cut round; 4, hindshank;
5, loin; 6, flank; 7, ribs; 8, plate; 9, navel;
10, chuck; 11, cross ribs; 12, brisket;
13, shoulder clod; 14, foreshank; 15, neck

—*v.i.* **5.** *Slang.* to complain; grumble. **6. beef up,** to add strength, numbers, force, etc., to.

beef·eat·er (bēf′ē′tər), *n.* **1.** a yeoman of the English royal guard or a warder of the Tower of London. **2.** *Informal.* an Englishman. **3.** a person who eats beef.

bee′ fly′, *n.* any of numerous dipterous insects of the family Bombyliidae, some of which resemble bees.

beef′steak mush′room, *n.* an edible bracket fungus, *Fistulina hepatica,* that grows on trees and can rot the heartwood of living oaks and chestnuts. Also called **beef′steak fun′gus.**

beef′steak toma′to, *n.* **1.** any of several tomato plant varieties bearing fruit of large size with meaty flesh. **2.** the fruit of such a plant.

beef·y (bē′fē), *adj.,* **beef·i·er, beef·i·est. 1.** of or like beef. **2.** brawny; thickset; heavy. —**beef′i·ness**, *n.*

bee·hive (bē′hīv′), *n.* **1.** a natural or constructed dwelling place for bees. **2.** a crowded, busy place. **3.** something resembling the shape of an artificial beehive, as a high, domelike hairdo for women.

bee·keep·er (bē′kē′pər), *n.* a person who raises honeybees.

bee·line (bē′līn′), *n.* a direct course or route: *made a beeline for the refrigerator.*

Be·el·ze·bub (bē el′zə bub′, bēl′zə-), *n.* **1.** the chief devil; Satan. Mark 3:22–26; Matt. 12:26–27; Luke 11:15–19. **2.** a devil. **3.** (in Milton's *Paradise Lost*) one of the fallen angels, second only to Satan.

bee′ moth′, *n.* a moth, *Galleria mellonella,* the larvae of which feed on honeycombs in beehives. Also called **wax moth.**

been (bin), *v.* pp. of BE.

beep (bēp), *n.* **1.** a short, usu. high-pitched tone produced by an automobile horn, electronic device, etc., as a signal, summons, or warning. —*v.i.* **2.** to make or emit such a sound. —*v.t.* **3.** to sound (a horn, warning signal, etc.). **4.** to warn, summon, etc., by beeping.

beep·er (bē′pər), *n.* **1.** a pocket-size electronic device whose signal notifies the person carrying it of an important telephone message. **2.** any device that produces a beeping sound.

bee′ plant′, *n.* any of various plants frequented by bees as a source of nectar, esp. *Cleome serrulata,* of the caper family.

beer (bēr), *n.* **1.** an alcoholic beverage made by brewing and fermentation from cereals, usu. malted barley, and flavored with hops and the like for a slightly bitter taste. **2.** any of various beverages made from roots, molasses or sugar, yeast, etc., as root beer.

Beer·she·ba (bēr shē′bə, bēr′shə-), *n.* a city in Israel, near the N limit of the Negev desert: the southernmost city of ancient Palestine. 114,600.

bees·wax (bēz′waks′), *n.* WAX[1] (def. 1).

beet (bēt), *n.* **1.** any of various biennial plants of the genus *Beta,* of the goosefoot family, esp. *B. vulgaris,* having a fleshy red or white root and dark-green red-veined leaves. **2.** the edible root of such a plant.

Bee·tho·ven (bā′tō vən), *n.* **Ludwig van,** 1770–1827, German composer.

bee·tle[1] (bēt′l), *n.,* *v.,* **-tled, -tling.** —*n.* **1.** any of numerous insects of the order Coleoptera, characterized by hard, horny forewings that cover and protect the membranous flight wings. **2.** (loosely) any of various insects resembling a beetle, as a cockroach. —*v.i.* **3.** *Chiefly Brit.* to move quickly; scurry.

bee·tle[2] (bēt′l), *n.,* *v.,* **-tled, -tling.** —*n.* **1.** a heavy hammering or ramming instrument, usu. of wood. **2.** a machine for beetling. —*v.t.* **3.** to drive, ram, beat, or crush with a beetle. **4.** to finish (cloth) by beetling. —**bee′tler**, *n.*

bee·tle[3] (bēt′l), *adj.,* *v.,* **-tled, -tling.** —*adj.* **1.** projecting; overhanging: *beetle brows.* —*v.i.* **2.** to project or overhang.

bee′ tree′, *n.* a hollow tree used by wild bees as a hive.

beet′ sug′ar, *n.* sugar from the roots of the sugar beet.

be·fall (bi fôl′), *v.,* **-fell, -fall·en, -fall·ing.** —*v.t.* **1.** to happen to, esp. by chance or fate. —*v.i.* **2.** to happen or occur.

be·fit (bi fit′), *v.t.,* **-fit·ted, -fit·ting.** to be proper or appropriate for; suit; fit.

be·fog (bi fog′, -fôg′), *v.t.,* **-fogged, -fog·ging. 1.** to envelop in fog. **2.** to render unclear or confused.

be·fore (bi fôr′, -fōr′), *prep.* **1.** previous to; earlier than: *Call me before noon.* **2.** in front or ahead of: *She stood before the window.* **3.** awaiting: *The golden age is before us.* **4.** in preference to; rather than: *They would die before surrendering.* **5.** in precedence of, as in order or rank: *We put freedom before wealth.* **6.** in the presence or sight of: *to appear before an audience.* **7.** under the consideration or jurisdiction of: *summoned* *before a magistrate.* **8.** in the face of: *Before such wild accusations, he was speechless.* **9.** in the regard of: *a crime before God and humanity.* —*adv.* **10.** in time preceding; previously: *We've met before.* **11.** earlier or sooner. **12.** in front; in advance; ahead. —*conj.* **13.** previous to the time when: *See me before you go.* **14.** sooner than; rather than: *I will die before I submit.*

be·fore·hand (bi fôr′hand′, -fōr′-), *adv., adj.* in advance; ahead of time; in anticipation.

be·friend (bi frend′), *v.t.* to act as a friend to; help: *to befriend a new classmate.*

be·fud·dle (bi fud′l), *v.t.,* **-dled, -dling. 1.** to confuse, as with glib statements or arguments. **2.** to make muddled or stupidly drunk. —**be·fud′dle·ment,** *n.*

beg (beg), *v.,* **begged, beg·ging.** —*v.t.* **1.** to ask for as a gift, as charity, or as a favor: *to beg alms; to beg forgiveness.* **2.** to ask (someone) to give or do something; implore: *He begged me for help.* **3.** to avoid; evade: *a report that begs the whole problem.* —*v.i.* **4.** to ask alms or charity; live by asking alms. **5.** to ask humbly or earnestly. **6.** (of a dog) to sit up, as trained, in a posture of entreaty. **7. beg off,** to request release from an obligation. —**Idiom. 8. beg the question,** to assume the truth of the very point raised in a question. **9. go begging,** to remain unclaimed, unused, or unpurchased.

be·gan (bi gan′), *v.* pt. of BEGIN.

be·get (bi get′), *v.t.,* **be·got, be·got·ten** or **be·got, be·get·ting. 1.** (esp. of a male parent) to procreate or generate (offspring). **2.** to cause; produce as an effect: *a belief that power begets power.*

beg·gar (beg′ər), *n.* **1.** a person who begs alms or lives by begging. **2.** a penniless person. **3.** a rascal; rogue. **4.** a person; fellow. —*v.t.* **5.** to reduce to utter poverty; impoverish. **6.** to cause to seem inadequate; exhaust the resources of: *The place beggars description.* —*Proverb.* **7. Beggars can't be choosers,** one should not be fussy when in need.

beg·gar·ly (beg′ər lē), *adj.* **1.** like or befitting a beggar. **2.** meanly inadequate: *a beggarly salary.* —**beg′gar·li·ness,** *n.*

beg′gar's-lice′ or **beg′gar-lice′,** *n., pl.* **-lice.** (used with a sing. or pl.v.) **1.** any of several plants, esp. of the genera *Cynoglossum* and *Hackelia,* of the borage family, having small, prickly fruits that stick to clothing. **2.** the fruit or seed of such a plant.

beg′gar's-ticks′ or **beg′gar-ticks′,** *n., pl.* **-ticks.** (used with a sing. or pl. v.) **1.** any of several composite plants of the genus *Bidens,* having rayless yellow flowers and barbed achenes that cling to clothing. **2.** the fruit or seed of such a plant. **3.** any of several other plants having seeds or fruits that cling to clothing, as the tick trefoil.

beg·gar·weed (beg′ər wēd′), *n.* any of various tick trefoils, esp. *Desmodium tortuosum,* grown for forage in subtropical regions.

beg·gar·y (beg′ə rē), *n.* **1.** a state or condition of utter poverty or of being a beggar. **2.** beggars collectively.

be·gin (bi gin′), *v.,* **be·gan, be·gun, be·gin·ning.** —*v.i.* **1.** to proceed to perform the first or earliest part of an action; start. **2.** to come into existence; arise; originate: *The custom began during the war.* **3.** to have a first part: *The name begins with a C.* —*v.t.* **4.** to proceed to perform the first or earliest part of: *Begin the job tomorrow.* **5.** to originate; be the originator of: *those who began the reform movement.* **6.** to succeed to the slightest extent in (fol. by an infinitive): *The money won't begin to cover expenses.*

be·gin·ner (bi gin′ər), *n.* **1.** a person or thing that begins. **2.** a person who has just begun to learn something; novice.

be·gin·ning (bi gin′ing), *n.* **1.** an act of starting. **2.** the point of time or space at which anything starts. **3.** the first part. **4.** Often, **beginnings.** an initial or rudimentary stage: *the beginnings of science.* **5.** origin; source: *A misunderstanding was the beginning of their quarrel.*

be·gone (bi gôn′, -gon′), *v.i.* to go away; depart (usu. used in the imperative).

be·go·nia (bi gōn′yə, -gō′nē ə), *n., pl.* **-nias.** any of numerous tropical plants of the genus *Begonia,* including species cultivated for their ornamental leaves and flowers.

be·got (bi got′), *v.* pt. and a pp. of BEGET.

be·got·ten (bi got′n), *v.* a pp. of BEGET.

be·grudge (bi gruj′), *v.t.,* **-grudged, -grudg·ing. 1.** to envy or resent the pleasure or good fortune of: *She begrudged her friend the award.* **2.** to be reluctant to give, grant, or allow: *She did not begrudge the money spent on her children's education.* —**be·grudg′ing·ly,** *adv.*

be·guile (bi gīl′), *v.t.,* **-guiled, -guil·ing. 1.** to influence by guile; mislead; delude. **2.** to take away from by cheating or deceiving (usu. fol. by of): *to be beguiled of money.* **3.** to charm or divert: *attractions to beguile the tourist.* **4.** to pass (time) pleasantly. —**be·guile′ment,** *n.* —**be·guil′er,** *n.* —**be·guil′ing·ly,** *adv.*

be·gun (bi gun′), *v.* pp. of BEGIN.

be·half (bi haf′, -häf′), *n.* **1.** interest; support. —**Idiom. 2. in** or **on behalf of,** as a representative of or a proxy for. **3. in** or **on someone's behalf,** in someone's interests.

be·have (bi hāv′), *v.,* **-haved, -hav·ing.** —*v.i.* **1.** to act or react in a particular way: *The car behaves well in traffic.* **2.** to act properly: *Did the child behave?* —*v.t.* **3.** to conduct or comport (oneself) in a proper manner: *Sit quietly and behave yourself.*

be·hav·ior (bi hāv′yər), *n.* **1.** the manner of conducting oneself. **2.** *Psychol., Animal Behav.* **a.** observable activity in a human or animal. **b.** the aggregate of responses to internal and external stimuli. **c.** a stereo-

typed species-specific activity, as a courtship dance or startle reflex. **3.** the action or reaction of any material under given circumstances: *the behavior of tin under heat.* —**be·hav′ior·al,** *adj.*

behav′ioral sci′ence, *n.* a science or branch of learning, as psychology or sociology, that derives its concepts from observation of the behavior of living organisms. —**behav′ioral sci′entist,** *n.*

be·hav·ior·ism (bi hāv′yə riz′əm), *n.* the theory or doctrine that psychology can be accurately studied only through the examination and analysis of objectively observable and quantifiable behavioral events, in contrast with subjective mental states. —**be·hav′ior·ist,** *n., adj.*

behav′ior modifica′tion, *n.* the direct changing of unwanted behavior by means of biofeedback or conditioning.

be·head (bi hed′), *v.t.* to cut off the head of; decapitate.

be·held (bi held′), *v.* pt. and pp. of BEHOLD.

be·he·moth (bi hē′məth, bē′ə-), *n.* **1.** an animal, perhaps the hippopotamus, mentioned in Job 40:15–24. **2.** any creature or thing of monstrous size or power.

be·hest (bi hest′), *n.* **1.** a command; directive. **2.** an earnest request.

be·hind (bi hīnd′), *prep.* **1.** at or toward the rear of: *Look behind the house.* **2.** later than; after: *behind schedule.* **3.** in the state of making less progress than: *fell behind the competition.* **4.** on the farther side of; beyond: *behind the mountain.* **5.** in a role of originating or supporting: *Who's behind this program?* **6.** hidden or unrevealed by: *Malice lay behind her smile.* **7.** as a cause or latent feature of: *Fear lay behind their anger.* **8.** at the controls of: *behind the wheel of a car.* —*adv.* **9.** at or toward the rear; rearward: *to lag behind.* **10.** in a place or stage already passed. **11.** in arrears: *to be behind in one's rent.* **12.** slow; late: *We're running an hour behind.* **13.** in a situation existing afterward: *left behind a large family.* —*adj.* **14.** following: *the one behind.* —*n.* **15.** *Informal.* the buttocks. —*Proverb.* **16. Behind every great man is a great woman,** the success of a great man is often dependent on a woman's influence and help.

behind′-the-scenes′, *adj.* **1.** happening out of view of the public; done, held, or kept in secret. **2.** occurring backstage.

be·hold (bi hōld′), *v.,* **be·held, be·hold·ing, interj.** —*v.t.* **1.** to observe; look at; see. —*interj.* **2.** look; see: *And, behold, three sentries of the King did appear.*

be·hold·en (bi hōl′dən), *adj.* obligated; indebted: *beholden to no one.*

be·hoof (bi hŏof′), *n., pl.* **-hooves** (hŏovz′). advantage; benefit.

be·hoove (bi hŏov′), *v.,* **-hooved, -hoov·ing.** (chiefly in impersonal use) —*v.t.* **1.** to be necessary or proper for: *It behooves us to reconsider.* —*v.i.* **2.** to be necessary, proper, or due.

beige (bāzh), *n.* **1.** a very light grayish brown, as the color of undyed wool. —*adj.* **2.** of the color beige.

bei·gnet (ben yā′), *n.* a square doughnut or fritter dusted with powdered sugar.

Bei·jing (bā′jing′) also **Peking,** *n.* a city in and the capital of the People's Republic of China, in the NE part, in central Hebei province. 5,860,000. Formerly (1928–49), **Peiping.**

be·ing (bē′ing), *n.* **1.** the fact of existing; existence. **2.** conscious, mortal existence; life. **3.** essential substance or nature: *the very core of my being.* **4.** something that exists: *inanimate beings.* **5.** a living thing. **6.** a human being; person. **7.** (*cap.*) God. **8.** *Philos.* absolute existence in a complete or perfect state; essence. —*conj.* **9.** *Chiefly Dial.* since; because; considering that (often fol. by *as, as how, or that*).

Bei·rut (bā rŏot′, bā′rŏot), *n.* the capital of Lebanon, a seaport. 702,000.

be·jew·el (bi jōō′əl), *v.t.,* **-eled, -el·ing** or (*esp. Brit.*) **-elled, -el·ling.** to adorn with or as if with jewels.

be·kah or **be·ka** (bā′kə, -kä), *n.* a unit of weight in the Bible, the weight in silver paid by each Israelite as a religious tax; half a shekel. Ex. 38:26.

bel (bel), *n.* ten decibels.

be·la·bor (bi lā′bər), *v.t.* **1.** to explain, worry about, or work at unduly: *belaboring an obvious point.* **2.** to assail, as with ridicule. **3.** to beat; pummel. Also, *esp. Brit.,* **be·la′bour.**

Bel′ and the Drag′on, *n.* a book of the Apocrypha that is included as chapter 14 of Daniel in the Douay Bible.

Be·la·rus (byel′ə rōōs′, bel′-), *n.* a republic in N central Europe: formerly a constituent republic of the U.S.S.R. 10,439,916; 80,134 sq. mi. (207,600 sq. km). *Cap.:* Minsk. Formerly, **Belorussia, Byelorussia.**

be·lat·ed (bi lā′tid), *adj.* **1.** coming or being after the customary, useful, or expected time: *a belated birthday card.* **2.** delayed; detained. —**be·lat′ed·ly,** *adv.* —**be·lat′ed·ness,** *n.*

be·lay (bi lā′), *v.,* **-layed, -lay·ing, n.** —*v.t.* **1.** to fasten (a rope) by winding around a pin or short rod. **2. a.** to secure (a person) by one end of a rope. **b.** to secure (a rope) by attaching to a person or to an object. —*v.i.* **3.** to belay a rope. **4.** (used chiefly in the imperative) to stop; cease; quit. —*n.* **5.** something, as a rock or bush, sturdy enough to anchor a rope in mountain climbing.

belch (belch), *v.i.* **1.** to expel gas noisily from the stomach through the mouth. **2.** to explode or erupt violently. **3.** to gush forth: *Smoke belched from the chimney.* —*v.t.* **4.** to eject spasmodically or violently. —*n.* **5.** an act or instance of belching.

be·lea·guer (bi lē′gər), *v.t.* **1.** to surround with military forces. **2.** to beset, as with difficulties; harass: *beleaguered taxpayers.*

Bel·fast (bel′fast, -fäst, bel fast′, -fäst′), *n.* the capital of Northern Ireland, on the E coast. 374,300.

bel·fry (bel′frē), *n., pl.* **-fries. 1.** a bell tower either attached to a church or other building or standing apart. **2.** the part of a steeple or other structure in which a bell is hung. **3.** a frame of timberwork that holds or encloses a bell.

Bel·gian (bel′jən), *n.* **1.** a native or inhabitant of Belgium. **2.** one of a breed of large, strong draft horses raised orig. in Belgium. —*adj.* **3.** of or pertaining to Belgium or its inhabitants.

Bel′gian en′dive, *n.* ENDIVE (def. 2).

Bel′gian hare′, *n.* one of a breed of red-brown domestic rabbits raised for meat.

Bel′gian sheep′dog, *n.* one of a Belgian breed of dogs with a long black coat and erect ears, raised orig. for herding sheep.

Bel·gium (bel′jəm), *n.* a kingdom in W Europe, bordering the North Sea, N of France. 10,203,683; 11,779 sq. mi. (30,508 sq. km). *Cap.:* Brussels. French, **Bel·gique** (bel zhēk′); Flemish, **Bel·gi·ë** (bel′кнē ə).

Bel·grade (bel′grād, -gräd, -grad, bel grād′, -gräd′, -grad′), *n.* the capital of Yugoslavia and the republic of Serbia, at the confluence of the Danube and Sava rivers. 1,470,073.

Be·li·al (bē′lē əl, bēl′yəl), *n.* **1.** the spirit of evil personified; the devil; Satan. **2.** (in John Milton's *Paradise Lost*) one of the fallen angels. [Late Latin < Hebrew *baliyya'al* = *balī* without + *ya'al* worth, use]

be·lie (bi lī′), *v.t.* **-lied, -ly·ing. 1.** to show to be false; contradict: *His trembling hands belied his calm voice.* **2.** to give a false impression of; misrepresent. **3.** to be false to or disappoint: *to belie one's faith.*

be·lief (bi lēf′), *n.* **1.** something believed; opinion; conviction. **2.** confidence in the truth or existence of something not immediately susceptible to rigorous proof. **3.** confidence; faith; trust: *children's belief in parents.* **4.** a religious creed or tenet.

be·lieve (bi lēv′), *v.,* **-lieved, -liev·ing.** —*v.i.* **1.** to have confidence in the truth, existence, reliability, or value of something. **2.** to have religious faith. —*v.t.* **3.** to have confidence or faith in the truth of: *I can't believe that story.* **4.** to have confidence in the assertions of (a person). **5.** to hold as an opinion; suppose; think. —*Idiom.* **6. believe it or not,** odd though it may sound, it's true. —**be·liev′a·bil′i·ty,** *n.* —**be·liev′a·ble,** *adj.* —**be·liev′a·bly,** *adv.* —**be·liev′er,** *n.*

believer's baptism, *n.* See under BAPTISM.

be·lit·tle (bi lit′l), *v.t.,* **-tled, -tling.** to regard or portray as less impressive or important than appearances indicate; disparage.

Be·lize (bə lēz′), *n.* **1.** Formerly, **British Honduras.** a parliamentary democracy in N Central America: a former British crown colony; gained independence 1981. 224,663; 8867 sq. mi. (22,966 sq. km). *Cap.:* Belmopan. **2.** Also called **Belize′ Cit′y.** a seaport in and the main city of Belize. 48,400. —**Be·li·ze·an** (bə lē′zē ən), *adj., n.*

bell¹ (bel), *n., v.,* **belled, bell·ing.** —*n.* **1.** a hollow metal instrument, typically cup-shaped with a flaring mouth, that produces a ringing sound when struck. **2.** any device, as an electronic circuit, that produces a similar sound. **3.** the stroke or sound of a bell. **4.** something having the form of a bell, as the flared end of a musical instrument. **5.** any of the half-hour units of nautical time rung on the bell of a ship. —*v.t.* **6.** to cause to flare like a bell. **7.** to put a bell on. —*v.i.* **8.** to have the form of a bell. —*Idiom.* **9. bell the cat,** to attempt something dangerous. **10. with bells on,** eagerly; ready to enjoy oneself.

bell² (bel), *v.,* **belled, bell·ing,** *n.* —*v.i.* **1.** to bellow; bay. —*n.* **2.** a bellowing or baying sound, esp. of a stag in rut or a hunting dog.

Bell (bel), *n.* **Alexander Graham,** 1847–1922, U.S. scientist, born in Scotland: inventor of the telephone.

bel·la·don·na (bel′ə don′ə), *n.* Also called **deadly nightshade.** a poisonous plant, *Atropa belladonna,* of the nightshade family, having purplish red flowers and black berries.

bel′ladon′na lil′y, *n.* AMARYLLIS (def. 2).

bell′-bot′tom, *adj.* **1.** Also, **bell′-bot′tomed.** (of trousers) wide and flaring at the bottoms of the legs. —*n.* **2. bell-bottoms,** (*used with a pl. v.*) bell-bottom trousers.

bell′ bu′oy, *n.* a buoy having a bell that is rung by the motion of the buoy.

bell′ curve′, *n.* a frequency distribution in statistics that resembles the outline of a bell when plotted on a graph. Also called **bell-shaped curve.**

bell curve

belle (bel), *n.* a woman or girl much admired for her beauty and charm: *the belle of the ball.*

belle é·poque (bel′ ā pôk′), *n.* the period of peace and cultural productivity in W Europe before the outbreak of World War I.

belles-let·tres (Fr. bel le′tR°), *n.* (*used with a sing. v.*) literature that

is polished and elegant and often inconsequential in subject or scope. —**bel·let′rist** (-trist), *n.* —**bel′let·ris′tic** (-li tris′tik), *adj.*

bell·flow·er (bel′flou′ər), *n.* any of numerous plants of the genus *Campanula,* usu. having bell-shaped blue flowers.

bell·hop (bel′hop′), *n.* a person who is employed, esp. by a hotel, to carry guests' luggage and run errands.

bel·li·cose (bel′i kōs′), *adj.* inclined or eager to fight; aggressively hostile. —**bel′li·cose′ly** (-kos′i tē), *n.*

bel·lig·er·ent (bə lij′ər ənt), *adj.* **1.** waging war; engaged in warfare. **2.** showing readiness to fight; aggressively hostile; truculent: *a belligerent tone.* —*n.* **3.** a state or nation at war. **4.** a person engaged in fighting. —**bel·lig′er·ence,** *n.*

bell′ jar′, *n.* a bell-shaped glass cover designed esp. for protecting objects or for containing gases or a vacuum in chemical experiments.

bel·low (bel′ō), *v.i.* **1.** to emit the loud hollow cry typical of a bull. **2.** to roar; bawl. —*v.t.* **3.** to utter in a loud deep voice. —*n.* **4.** an act or sound of bellowing.

Bel·low (bel′ō), *n.* **Saul,** born 1915, U.S. novelist, born in Canada.

bel·lows (bel′ōz, -əz), *n.* (*used with a sing. or pl. v.*) **1.** a device for producing a strong current of air, consisting of a chamber that can be expanded to draw in air through a valve and contracted to expel it through a tube. **2.** something resembling a bellows in form, as the collapsible part of some cameras. **3.** the lungs.

bell′ pep′per, *n.* SWEET PEPPER.

bells′ and whis′tles, *n.pl. Informal.* features added to a product; special parts or functions; extras.

Bell's′ pal′sy, *n.* suddenly occurring paralysis that distorts one side of the face, caused by a lesion of the facial nerve.

bell·weth·er (bel′weth′ər), *n.* **1.** a person or thing that assumes leadership. **2.** a person or thing that indicates a trend. **3.** a sheep wearing a bell and leading a flock.

bell·wort (bel′wûrt′, -wôrt′), *n.* a plant of the genus *Uvularia,* of the lily family, having delicate bell-shaped yellow flowers.

bel·ly (bel′ē), *n., pl.* **-lies,** *v.,* **-lied, -ly·ing.** —*n.* **1.** the abdomen or underpart of an animal. **2.** the stomach with its adjuncts. **3.** appetite or capacity for food; gluttony. **4.** the womb; uterus. **5.** the interior of something: *a ship's belly.* **6.** a protuberant surface of something: *the belly of a flask.* **7.** the fleshy part of a muscle. **8.** the front, inner, or under surface or part, as distinguished from the back. **9.** the underpart of the fuselage of an airplane. —*v.t.* **10.** to fill out; swell: *Wind bellied the sails.* —*v.i.* **11.** to swell out: *sails bellying in the wind.* **12. belly up,** *Informal.* to approach very closely: *bellied up to a bar.* —*Idiom.* **13. go** or **turn belly up,** *Informal.* to come to an end; die; fail.

bel·ly·ache (bel′ē āk′), *n., v.,* **-ached, -ach·ing.** —*n.* **1.** a pain in the abdomen or bowels. —*v.i.* **2.** *Informal.* to complain; grumble.

bel′ly dance′, *n.* a solo dance performed by a woman, emphasizing sinuous movements of the hips and abdomen. —**bel′ly danc′er,** *n.* —**bel′ly danc′ing,** *n.*

bel′ly flop′, *n.* an awkward dive in which the front of the body strikes flat against the water or other surface. —**bel′ly-flop′,** *v.i.,* **-flopped, -flop·ping.**

bel·ly·ful (bel′ē fool′), *n., pl.* **-fuls.** an intolerable amount.

bel′ly laugh′, *n.* a loud hearty laugh.

Bel·mo·pan (bel′mō pan′), *n.* the capital of Belize, in the central part. 3500.

be·long (bi lông′, -long′), *v.i.* **1.** to be properly or suitably placed or situated: *The book belongs on the shelf. You belong in a better job.* **2.** to be appropriate or suitable: *That shirt doesn't belong with that jacket.* **3. belong to, a.** to be the property of: *The scarf belongs to me.* **b.** to be a part or adjunct of: *That cover belongs to this jar.* **c.** to be a member: *They belong to three clubs.*

be·long·ing (bi lông′ing, -long′-), *n.* **1. belongings,** possessions; personal effects. **2.** close relationship: *a sense of belonging.*

Be·lo·rus·sia (byel′ə rush′ə, bel′ə-), *n.* a former name of BELARUS. Also, **Byelorussia.** Former official name, **Belorus′sian So′viet So′cialist Repub′lic.**

be·lov·ed (bi luv′id, -luvd′), *adj.* **1.** greatly loved; dear to the heart. —*n.* **2.** a person who is beloved.

Belov′ed Disci′ple, *n.* the apostle John. John 13:23; 19:26; 20:2; 21:7, 20–21.

Belov′ed Physi′cian, *n.* the apostle Luke. Col. 4:14.

be·low (bi lō′), *adv.* **1.** in or toward a lower place: *Look out below!* **2.** on, in, or toward a lower deck or floor. **3.** beneath the surface of the water: *Divers were sent below to view the wreck.* **4.** on earth: *the fate of creatures here below.* **5.** in hell or the infernal regions. **6.** at a later point on a page or in a text: *See the illustration below.* Compare ABOVE (def. 6). **7.** in a lower rank or grade: *a class below.* **8.** under zero on the temperature scale. **9.** downstage. Compare ABOVE (def. 10). **10.** *Zool.* on the lower or ventral side. **11.** beneath the surface of the water. —*prep.* **12.** lower down than: *below the knee.* **13.** lower in rank, degree, amount, rate, etc.: *below cost.* **14.** too undignified to be worthy of; beneath. **15.** downstage of. **16.** downstream or south of.

Bel·sen (bel′zən), *n.* locality in NW Germany: site of Nazi concentration camp (**Bergen-Belsen**) during World War II.

Bel·shaz·zar (bel shaz′ər), *n.* the last king of Babylon and a son of Nebuchadnezzar. Dan. 5.

belt (belt), *n.* **1.** a band of flexible material, as leather or cord, for en-

B

circling the waist. **2.** any encircling or transverse band, strip, or stripe. **3.** an often extended region having distinctive properties or characteristics: *a belt of cotton plantations.* **4.** an endless flexible band passing about two or more pulleys, used to transmit motion or to convey materials and objects. **5.** a road, railroad, or the like encircling an urban center to handle peripheral traffic. **6.** *Slang.* **a.** a hard blow; punch. **b.** a swallow of liquor. **—***v.t.* **7.** to gird or furnish with a belt. **8.** to mark as if with a belt or band. **9.** to fasten on by means of a belt. **10.** to thrash with or as if with a belt. **11.** to sing (a song) loudly and energetically. **12.** *Slang.* **a.** to swallow (a drink of liquor). **b.** to hit; strike. **—*Idiom.*** **13. below the belt,** unfair or unfairly. **14. under one's belt, a.** in one's stomach, as food or drink. **b.** as part of one's background: *Get some experience under your belt.* **—belt′less,** *adj.*

Bel•te•shaz•zar (bel′tə shaz′ər), *n.* the Babylonian name given to Daniel. Dan. 1:7.

belt′-tight′ening, *n.* a curtailment in spending.

belt•way (belt′wā′), *n.* **1.** a highway around the perimeter of an urban area. **2. the Beltway,** a circumferential highway around Washington, D.C., that passes through Maryland and Virginia.

be•lu•ga (bə lo͞o′gə), *n., pl.* **-gas,** (*esp. collectively*) **-ga. 1.** a large white sturgeon, *Huso huso,* of the Black and Caspian seas, valued esp. as a source of caviar. **2.** Also called **white whale.** a small white toothed whale, *Delphinapterus leucas,* of northern seas, having a rounded head and upward-curving mouth.

bel•ve•dere (bel′vi dēr′, bel′vi dēr′), *n.* a structure, as a turret, cupola, or gazebo, designed and situated to look out upon a pleasing view.

be•ma (bē′mə), *n., pl.* **-ma•ta** (-mə tə), **-mas. 1.** the enclosed space around the altar in an Eastern church. **2.** Also, **bimah.** a platform in a synagogue for the table used when reading from the Torah.

be•moan (bi mōn′), *v.t.* **1.** to express distress or grief over; lament: *to bemoan one's fate.* **2.** to regard with regret or disapproval.

be•muse (bi myo͞oz′), *v.t.,* **-mused, -mus•ing. 1.** to bewilder; confuse. **2.** to cause to become lost in thought. **—be•mus′ed•ly** (-myo͞o′zid lē), *adv.* **—be•muse′ment,** *n.*

Be•na•res (bə när′is, -ēz), *n.* former name of Varanasi.

bench (bench), *n.* **1.** a long usu. hard seat for several people: *a park bench.* **2.** a seat occupied by an official, esp. a judge. **3.** such a seat regarded as a symbol of the office and dignity of the judiciary. **4.** the office or dignity of various other officials, or the officials themselves. **5. a.** the seat on which the players of a team sit during a game while not playing. **b.** the players of a team who are usu. used only as substitutes. **6.** a worktable, as of a carpenter; workbench. **7.** a platform on which animals are placed for exhibition, esp. at a dog show. **8.** a dog show. **9.** a step or working elevation in a mine. **—***v.t.* **10.** to furnish with benches. **11.** to seat on a bench. **12.** to exhibit (a dog or other animal) at a show. **13.** to remove from or keep from participating in a game.

bench′ mark′, *n.* **1.** a mark of known or assumed elevation from which other elevations may be established. **2.** benchmark.

bench′mark′ or **bench′ mark′,** *n.* a standard or reference by which others can be measured or judged.

bench′ press′, *n.* a weightlifting exercise in which a barbell is raised and lowered above the chest while the lifter lies supine on a bench. **—bench′-press′,** *v.t., v.i.*

bench′ show′, *n.* a dog show in which the animals of each breed are judged and awarded prizes on the basis of standards established for that breed.

bench′ war′rant, *n.* a warrant issued or ordered by a judge or court for the apprehension of an offender.

bend[1] (bend), *v.,* **bent, bend•ing,** *n.* **—***v.t.* **1.** to force from a straight form into a curved or angular one or from a curved or angular form into a different form: *to bend an iron rod into a hoop.* **2.** to guide in a particular direction: *to bend one's energies to the task.* **3.** to cause to submit: *to bend someone to one's will.* **4.** to modify or relax (restrictions): *to bend the rules.* **5.** to pull back the string of (a bow) in preparation for shooting. **6.** to fasten: *to bend ropes together.* **—***v.i.* **7.** to become curved or bent: *a bow that bends easily.* **8.** to assume a bent posture; stoop. **9.** to bow in submission or reverence. **10.** to turn or incline in a particular direction: *The road bent south.* **11.** to yield; submit. **12.** to direct one's energies. **—***n.* **13.** the act of bending. **14.** something that bends: *a bend in the road.* **15.** a knot for joining two rope ends or a rope to an object. **16. the bends,** decompression sickness. **—*Idiom.*** **17. around** or **round the bend,** *Informal.* insane; crazy. **18. bend** or **lean** or **fall over backward,** to exert oneself to the utmost. **19. bend someone's ear,** to talk to someone at often tiresome length. **—bend′a•ble,** *adj.*

bend[2] (bend), *n.* half of a trimmed butt or hide.

bend•ed (ben′did), *v.* **—*Idiom.*** **on bended knee(s), 1.** kneeling on the knee or knees. **2.** with great urgency or intense emotion: *to beg for help on bended knee.*

bend•er (ben′dər), *n.* a person or thing that bends.

bene-, a combining form occurring in loanwords from Latin, where it meant "well": *benediction.*

be•neath (bi nēth′, -nēth′), *adv.* **1.** in or to a lower position; below. **2.** underneath. **—***prep.* **3.** below; under: *beneath the same roof.* **4.** farther down than: *The drawer beneath the top one.* **5.** lower down on a slope than: *beneath the crest of a hill.* **6.** less important than; inferior to, as in rank or power: *A captain is beneath a major.* **7.** below the level or dignity of: *behavior beneath contempt.*

Beneath′ the Cross′ of Je′sus, a Christian hymn (1868) with words by Elizabeth C. Clephane.

Ben•e•dict[1] (ben′i dikt), *n.* **1. Ruth (Fulton),** 1887–1948, U.S. anthropologist. **2. Saint,** A.D. 480?–543?, Italian monk: founded Benedictine order.

Ben•e•dict[2] (ben′i dikt), *n.* **1. Benedict XIV,** (*Prospero Lambertini*) 1675–1758, Italian ecclesiastic: pope 1740–58. **2. Benedict XV,** (*Giacomo della Chiesa*) 1854–1922, Italian ecclesiastic: pope 1914–22.

Ben•e•dic•tine (ben′i dik′tin, -tēn, -tīn *for 1, 2;* ben′i dik′tēn *for*), *n.* **1. a.** a member of an order of monks founded at Monte Cassino by St. Benedict about A.D. 530. **b.** a member of any congregation of nuns following the rule of St. Benedict. **—***adj.* **2.** of or pertaining to St. Benedict or the Benedictines.

ben•e•dic•tion (ben′i dik′shən), *n.* **1.** an utterance of good wishes. **2.** the invocation of a blessing, esp. the short blessing at the close of a religious service. **3.** (*usu. cap.*) a Roman or Anglo-Catholic service that includes a blessing of the congregation with the Host in the monstrance. **4.** something that imparts a benefit or improvement. **—ben•e•dic•to•ry** (ben′i dik′tə rē), *adj.*

Ben•e•dic•tus (ben′i dik′təs), *n.* **1.** the short hymn beginning "Blessed is he that cometh in the name of the Lord." **2.** the hymn beginning "Blessed be the Lord God of Israel." [< Latin: blessed, der. of *benedīcere* to commend, bless = *bene-* + *dīcere* to say, speak]

ben•e•fac•tion (ben′ə fak′shən, ben′ə fak′-), *n.* **1.** an act of conferring a benefit. **2.** a benefit conferred; charitable donation.

ben•e•fac•tive (ben′ə fak′tiv), *adj.* **1.** of or designating a linguistic form or construction that denotes the person for whom an action is performed, as *for his son* in *He opened the door for his son.* **—***n.* **2.** a benefactive form or construction.

ben•e•fac•tor (ben′ə fak′tər, ben′ə fak′-), *n.* **1.** a person who confers a benefit. **2.** a person who makes a bequest or endowment, as to an institution.

ben•e•fice (ben′ə fis), *n., v.,* **-ficed, -fic•ing. —***n.* **1.** a position or post granted to an ecclesiastic that guarantees a fixed amount of property or income. **2.** the revenue itself. **3.** the equivalent of a fief in the early Middle Ages. **—***v.t.* **4.** to invest with a benefice.

be•nef•i•cent (bə nef′ə sənt), *adj.* **1.** doing good or causing good to be done; charitable. **2.** beneficial. **—be•nef′i•cent•ly,** *adv.*

ben•e•fi•cial (ben′ə fish′əl), *adj.* **1.** conferring benefit; advantageous; helpful: *the beneficial effect of sunshine.* **2.** *Law.* **a.** helpful in the meeting of needs. **b.** involving the personal enjoyment of proceeds.

ben•e•fi•ci•ar•y (ben′ə fish′ē er′ē, -fish′ə rē), *n., pl.* **-ar•ies. 1.** a person or group that receives benefits, profits, or advantages. **2.** a person designated as the recipient of funds or other property under a will, trust, or the like.

ben•e•fit (ben′ə fit), *n.* **1.** something that is advantageous or good; an advantage. **2.** a payment made to help someone or given by a benefit society, insurance company, or public agency. **3.** a social event or a performance for raising money for an organization, cause, or person. **—***v.t.* **4.** to do good to; be of service to: *a health program to benefit everyone.* **—***v.i.* **5.** to derive benefit; profit: *to benefit from experience.*

ben′efit of cler′gy, *n.* **1.** the rites or sanctions of a church: *living together without benefit of clergy.* **2.** the medieval privilege of clerics to be tried by ecclesiastic rather than secular courts.

Be•nét (bi nā′), *n.* **1. Stephen Vincent,** 1898–1943, U.S. poet. **2.** his brother **William Rose,** 1886–1950, U.S. poet and critic.

be•nev•o•lence (bə nev′ə ləns), *n.* **1.** desire to do good to others; goodwill; charity. **2.** an act of kindness; charitable gift. **3.** (formerly) a forced contribution to an English sovereign.

be•nev•o•lent (bə nev′ə lənt), *adj.* **1.** characterized by or expressing goodwill or kindly feelings: *a benevolent smile.* **2.** desiring to help others; charitable. **3.** established for good works: *a benevolent society.* **—be•nev′o•lent•ly,** *adv.*

Ben•gal (ben gôl′, -gäl′, beng-; ben′gəl, beng′-), *n.* **1.** a former province in NE India, now divided between India and Bangladesh. Compare East Bengal, West Bengal. **2. Bay of,** a part of the Indian Ocean between India and Burma. **—Ben•ga′li,** *adj., n.*

Ben-Gu•rion (ben go͝or′ē ən; *Seph. Heb.* ben′go͞o ʀyôn′), *n.* **David,** 1886–1973, Israeli statesman, born in Poland: prime minister of Israel 1948–53, 1955–63.

Ben Hur (ben′ hûr′), a historical novel (1880) by Lew Wallace.

be•night•ed (bi nī′tid), *adj.* **1.** intellectually or morally ignorant; unenlightened. **2.** overtaken by darkness or night.

be•nign (bi nīn′), *adj.* **1.** of kindly disposition; gracious: *a benign king.* **2.** showing gentleness or kindness: *a benign smile.* **3.** favorable; propitious: *benign omens.* **4.** clement: *benign weather.* **5.** not malignant: *benign tumors.* **—be•nig′ni•ty** (-nig′ni tē), *n.* **—be•nign′ly,** *adv.*

be•nig•nant (bi nig′nənt), *adj.* **1.** benign; gracious: *a benignant sovereign.* **2.** exerting a good influence; beneficial. **—be•nig′nan•cy,** *n.* **—be•nig′nant•ly,** *adv.*

benign′ neglect′, *n.* the practice of ignoring a problem in the hope that it will right itself.

Be•nin (be nēn′), *n.* **1.** Formerly, **Dahomey.** a republic in W Africa: formerly part of French West Africa; gained independence in 1960. 4,440,000; 44,290 sq. mi. (114,711 sq. km). *Cap.:* Porto Novo. **2. Bight of,** a bay in N Gulf of Guinea in W Africa. **3.** a historic kingdom of W Africa centered in Edo-speaking regions W of the Niger River. **4.** a river in S Nigeria flowing into the Bight of Benin. —**Be·ni·nese** (bə nēn'ēz, -ēs, ben'ə nēz', -nēs'), *adj., n., pl.* **-nese.**

Ben·ja·min (ben'jə mən), *n.* BENZOIN[1] (def. 2).

Ben·ja·min (ben'jə mən), *n.* **1.** the youngest son of Jacob and Rachel, and the brother of Joseph. Gen. 35:18. **2.** one of the 12 tribes of Israel, traditionally descended from him. **3. Judah Philip,** 1811–84, Confederate statesman.

Ben·nard (bə närd'), *n.* **George,** 1873–1958, U.S. clergyman and hymn writer.

ben·ne (ben'ē), *n.* the sesame plant or its seeds.

Ben·nett (ben'it), *n.* **1. (Enoch) Arnold,** 1867–1931, English novelist. **2. Floyd,** 1890–1928, U.S. aviator. **3. James Gordon,** 1795–1872, U.S. journalist. **4. Sanford F(illmore),** 1836–98, U.S. hymn writer.

Ben·ning·ton (ben'ing tən), *n.* a town in SW Vermont: defeat of British by the Green Mountain Boys 1777. 15,815.

Ben·ny (ben'ē), *n.* **Jack** (*Benjamin Kubelsky*), 1894–1974, U.S. comedian.

bent[1] (bent), *adj.* **1.** curved; crooked: *a bent back.* **2.** determined; set; resolved: *bent on succeeding.* **3.** *Chiefly Brit.* corrupt. —*n.* **4.** predilection; talent: *a bent for painting.* **5.** capacity of endurance. **6.** a transverse frame, as of a bridge or an aqueduct, designed to support either vertical or horizontal loads.

bent[2] (bent), *n.* **1.** BENT GRASS. **2.** a stalk of bent grass.

bent' grass', *n.* any grass of the genus *Agrostis,* esp. the redtop.

ben·thos (ben'thos), *n.* the biogeographic region that includes the bottom of a lake, sea, or ocean and the littoral and supralittoral zones of the shore. Also called **ben'thic divi'sion, benthon'ic zone'.**

bent·wood (bent'wŏŏd'), *n.* **1.** wood steamed and bent for use in furniture. —*adj.* **2.** designating furniture made principally of pieces of wood steamed and bent into curving shapes: *a bentwood chair.*

ben·zene (ben'zēn, ben zēn'), *n.* a colorless, slightly water-soluble, liquid aromatic compound, C_6H_6, obtained chiefly from coal tar: used in making chemicals and dyes and as a solvent.

ben'zene ring', *n.* the graphic representation of the structure of benzene as a hexagon with a carbon atom at each of its points, each carbon atom united with an atom of hydrogen, one or more of which may be replaced to form benzene derivatives.

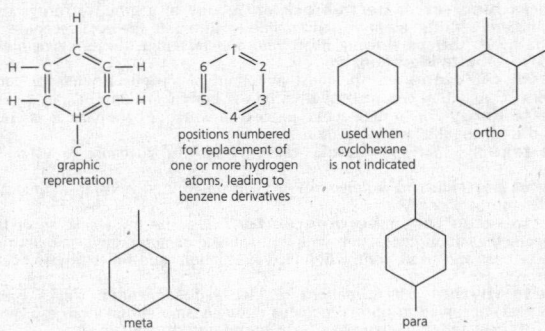

graphic reprentation

positions numbered for replacement of one or more hydrogen atoms, leading to benzene derivatives

used when cyclohexane is not indicated

ortho

meta

para

benzene ring (Kekulé's formula) double bonds are assumed

ben·zine (ben'zēn, ben zēn'), also **ben·zin** (ben'zin), *n.* a colorless liquid mixture of various hydrocarbons obtained in the distillation of petroleum: used in cleaning and dyeing.

ben·zo·ate (ben'zō āt', -it), *n.* a salt or ester of benzoic acid.

benzo'ic ac'id, *n.* a white, crystalline, slightly water-soluble powder, $C_7H_6O_2$, used chiefly as a preservative, in the synthesis of dyes, and in medicine as a germicide.

ben·zo·in[1] (ben'zō in, -zoin, ben zō'in), *n.* **1.** a reddish brown balsamic resin obtained from certain storax trees, used in medicine and perfumery. **2.** any plant belonging to the genus *Lindera (Benzoin),* of the laurel family, as the spicebush.

ben·zo·in[2] (ben'zō in, -zoin, ben zō'in), *n.* a white, water-soluble powder, $C_{14}H_{12}O_2$, used in organic synthesis.

ben·zo·yl (ben'zō il), *n.* the univalent group C_7H_5O-, derived from benzoic acid.

ben'zoyl perox'ide, *n.* a white, crystalline, water-insoluble, explosive solid, $C_7H_5O_4$, used esp. as a bleach and as a catalyst in polymerization reactions.

ben·zyl (ben'zil, -zēl), *n.* the univalent group C_7H_7-, derived from toluene. —**ben·zyl'ic,** *adj.*

Be·o·wulf (bā'ə wŏŏlf'), *n.* **1.** (*italics*) an English epic poem, probably written in the early 8th century A.D. **2.** the hero of *Beowulf.*

be·queath (bi kwēth', -kwēth'), *v.t.* **1.** to dispose of (property or money) by last will. **2.** to hand down; pass on. —**be·queath'a·ble,** *adj.* —**be·queath'al, be·queath'ment,** *n.* —**be·queath'er,** *n.*

be·quest (bi kwest'), *n.* **1.** the act of bequeathing. **2.** LEGACY.

be·rate (bi rāt'), *v.t.,* **-rat·ed, -rat·ing.** to scold; rebuke.

ber·ceuse (*Fr.* bɛʀ sœz'), *n., pl.* **-ceuses** (*Fr.* -sœz'). **1.** LULLABY. **2.** a soothing musical composition typically in ⁶⁄₈ time.

Berch·tes·ga·den (bɛʀкн'təs gäd'n), *n.* a town in SE Bavaria, in SE Germany: site of the fortified mountain chalet of Adolf Hitler. 39,800.

Be·re·a (bēr'ē ə), *n.* a city in Macedonia west of Salonika where the Apostle Paul preached on his first missionary journey. Acts 17:10.

be·reave (bi rēv'), *v.t.,* **-reaved** or **-reft, -reav·ing. 1.** to deprive and make desolate, esp. by death: *Illness bereaved them of their mother.* **2.** to deprive ruthlessly or by force: *War bereft us of our home.* —**be·reave'ment,** *n.* —**be·reav'er,** *n.*

be·reaved (bi rēvd'), *adj.* **1.** (of a person) greatly saddened at being deprived by death of a loved one. —*n.* **2. the bereaved,** a bereaved person or persons.

be·reft (bi reft'), *v.* **1.** a pt. and pp. of BEREAVE. —*adj.* **2.** deprived: *bereft of their senses.*

be·ret (bə rā'), *n.* a soft, visorless cap with a close-fitting headband and a flat or rounded top.

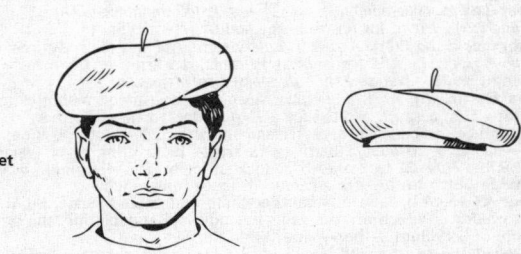

beret

berg (bûrg), *n.* an iceberg.

Ber·ga·ma (bɛʀ gä'mə, bûr'gə mə), *n.* a town in W Turkey in Asia. 24,121. Ancient, **Pergamum.**

ber·ga·mot (bûr'gə mot', -mət), *n.* **1.** a small citrus tree, *Citrus aurantium bergamia,* having fruit with a rind that yields a fragrant essential oil. **2.** any of various plants of the mint family, as *Monarda fistulosa,* yielding an oil resembling bergamot.

Ber·gen-Bel·sen (bûr'gən bel'sən, -zən, bâr'-), *n.* See under BELSEN.

Berg·man (bûrg'mən), *n.* **1. Ingmar,** born 1918, Swedish filmmaker. **2. Ingrid,** 1915–82, Swedish-born film actress.

Berg·son (bûrg'sən, berg'-), *n.* **Henri,** 1859–1941, French philosopher and writer. —**Berg·so'ni·an** (-sō'nē ən), *adj., n.*

ber·i·ber·i (ber'ē ber'ē), *n.* a disease of the peripheral nerves caused by a deficiency of vitamin B_1, leading to paralysis and congestive heart failure. —**ber'i·ber'ic,** *adj.*

Ber'ing Sea', *n.* a part of the N Pacific N of the Aleutian Islands. 878,000 sq. mi. (2,274,000 sq. km).

Ber'ing Strait', *n.* a strait between Alaska and the Russian Federation connecting the Bering Sea and the Arctic Ocean. 36 mi. (58 km) wide.

Berke·ley (bûrk'lē; *for 1, 2 also Brit.* bärk'-), *n.* **1. George,** 1685?–1753, Irish bishop and philosopher. **2. Sir William,** 1610–77, British colonial governor of Virginia 1642–76. **3.** a city in W California on San Francisco Bay. 103,660.

ber·ke·li·um (bər kē'lē əm), *n.* a transuranic element. *Symbol:* Bk; *at. no.:* 97.

Ber·lin (bər lin'), *n.* **1. Irving,** 1888–1989, U.S. songwriter. **2.** the capital of Germany, in the NE part: constitutes a state. 3,121,000; 341 sq. mi. (883 sq. km). Formerly (1948–90) divided into a western zone, West Berlin, the capital of West Germany; and an eastern zone, East Berlin, the capital of East Germany.

Ber'lin Air'lift, *n.* the air shipment of necessities to West Berlin from 1948 through 1949, chiefly by the United States: mounted as a response to the blockade of the city by the Soviet Union.

Ber'lin Wall', *n.* a guarded concrete wall 28 mi. (45 km) long, with minefields and controlled checkpoints, erected across Berlin by East Germany in 1961, dismantled in 1989.

berm (bûrm), *n.* **1.** a level strip of ground at the summit or sides, or along the base, of a slope. **2.** a nearly flat back portion of a beach formed of material deposited by the action of the waves. **3.** the shoulder of a road. **4.** a mound of snow or dirt.

Ber·mu·da (bər myŏŏ'də), *n.* a group of islands in the Atlantic, 580 mi. (935 km) E of North Carolina: a British colony; resort. 62,569; 19 sq. mi. (49 sq. km). *Cap.:* Hamilton. —**Ber·mu'dan, Ber·mu'di·an,** *adj., n.*

Bermu'da grass', *n.* a creeping grass, *Cynodon dactylon,* of S Europe, grown in the southern U.S. and Bermuda for lawns and pastures.

Bermu'da lil'y, *n.* a lily, *Lilium longiflorum eximium,* having white, funnel-shaped flowers.

Bermu'da on'ion, *n.* a large, mild, yellow-skinned onion.

Bern or **Berne** (bûrn, bârn), *n.* **1.** the capital of Switzerland, in the W part: capital of Bern canton. 136,300. **2.** a canton in W Switzerland.

928,800; 2658 sq. mi. (6885 sq. km). *Cap.:* Bern. —**Ber•nese** (bûr′nēz, -nēs, bûr nēz′, -nēs′), *adj., n., pl.* **-nese.**

San Ber•nar•di•no (san′ bûr′nər dē′nō, -bûr′nə-), *n.* a city in S California. 181,718.

Ber′nese moun′tain dog′, *n.* one of a Swiss breed of large, strong, longhaired dogs having a black coat with white and russet or tan markings, formerly used as draft animals.

Ber•ni•ce (bûr nī′sē), *n.* the oldest daughter of Herod Agrippa. Acts 25:13.

Bernoul′li effect′, *n.* the decrease in pressure as the velocity of a fluid increases.

Bern•stein (bûrn′stīn, -stēn), *n.* **Leonard,** 1918–90, U.S. conductor and composer.

ber•ry (ber′ē), *n., pl.* **-ries,** *v.,* **-ried, -ry•ing.** —*n.* **1.** any small usu. stoneless juicy fruit irrespective of botanical structure, as the huckleberry, strawberry, or hackberry. **2.** a simple fruit having a pulpy pericarp in which the seeds are embedded, as the grape, gooseberry, currant, or tomato. **3.** a dry seed or kernel, as of wheat. **4.** one of the eggs of a lobster, crayfish, etc. —*v.i.* **5.** to gather or pick berries. **6.** to bear or produce berries. —**ber′ry•less,** *adj.* —**ber′ry•like′,** *adj.*

ber•seem (bər sēm′), *n.* a clover, *Trifolium alexandrinum,* of Egypt and Syria grown for forage in the southwestern U.S.

ber•serk (bər sûrk′, -zûrk′), *adj.* violently or destructively frenzied: *to go berserk.* [< Old Norse *berserkr* frenzied warrior = *ber-* bear + *serkr* shirt, skin] —**ber•serk′ly,** *adv.* —**ber•serk′ness,** *n.*

berth (bûrth), *n.* **1.** a shelflike sleeping space, as on a ship or railroad car. **2. a.** a space allotted for a ship to dock or lie at anchor. **b.** a safe distance, as between a vessel and the shore. **3.** a job; position; place. —*v.t.* **4. a.** to allot a berth to (a ship). **b.** to bring to or install in a berth. —*v.i.* **5.** to come to a dock or moorage. —***Idiom.*** **6. give a wide berth to,** to keep a careful distance from; shun.

ber•yl (ber′əl), *n.* a mineral, beryllium aluminum silicate, $Be_3Al_2Si_6O_{18}$, varieties of which are the gems emerald and aquamarine: the principal ore of beryllium. —**ber•yl•ine** (ber′ə lin, -līn′), *adj.*

be•ryl•li•um (bə ril′ē əm), *n.* a hard, light metallic element, used chiefly in copper alloys to reduce fatigue. *Symbol:* Be; *at. wt.:* 9.0122; *at. no.:* 4; *sp. gr.:* 1.8 at 20° C.

be•seech (bi sēch′), *v.,* **-sought** or **-seeched, -seech•ing.** —*v.t.* **1.** to implore urgently: *They besought us to go at once.* **2.** to beg eagerly for; solicit. —*v.i.* **3.** to make urgent appeal. —**be•seech′er,** *n.* —**be•seech′ing•ly,** *adv.*

be•set (bi set′), *v.t.,* **-set, -set•ting. 1.** to attack on all sides: *The foe beset them.* **2.** to surround; hem in: *a village beset by dense forest.* **3.** to stud: *a gold bracelet beset with jewels.*

be•side (bi sīd′), *prep.* **1.** by or at the side of; near: *Sit down beside me.* **2.** compared with: *Beside her other writers seem amateurish.* **3.** apart from: *beside the point.* **4.** BESIDES (defs. 4, 5). —***Idiom.*** **5. beside oneself,** frantic; distraught. —**Usage.** For the prepositional meanings "over and above, in addition to" and "except" BESIDES is preferred, esp. in edited writing. However, BESIDE sometimes occurs with these meanings as well, even in formal writing.

be•sides (bi sīdz′), *adv.* **1.** moreover; furthermore; also: *Besides, I promised them we would come.* **2.** in addition: *There are three elm trees and two maples besides.* **3.** otherwise; else: *They had a roof over their heads but not much besides.* —*prep.* **4.** over and above; in addition to: *Besides his mother he has a sister to support.* **5.** other than; except: *no one here besides us.* —**Usage.** See BESIDE.

be•siege (bi sēj′), *v.t.,* **-sieged, -sieg•ing. 1.** to lay siege to. **2.** to crowd around; crowd in upon; surround: *Vacationers besieged the travel office.* **3.** to importune, as with requests. —**be•siege′ment,** *n.* —**be•sieg′er,** *n.* —**be•sieg′ing•ly,** *adv.*

be•som (bē′zəm), *n.* a broom, esp. one of brush or twigs.

be•sot (bi sot′), *v.t.,* **-sot•ted, -sot•ting. 1.** to stupefy with drink. **2.** to make stupid or foolish, esp. with infatuation. —**be•sot′ted•ly,** *adv.*

be•sought (bi sôt′), *v.* a pt. and pp. of BESEECH.

be•speak (bi spēk′), *v.t.,* **-spoke, -spo•ken** or **-spoke, -speak•ing. 1.** to ask for in advance; request. **2.** to reserve beforehand: *to bespeak a seat in a theater.* **3.** to speak to formally; address. **4.** to show; indicate: *This bespeaks a kindly heart.* **5.** to foretell.

be•spec•ta•cled (bi spek′tə kəld), *adj.* wearing eyeglasses.

Bes′semer proc′ess, *n.* a process of producing steel in which impurities are removed by forcing air through molten iron in a refractory-lined metal container (**Bes′semer convert′er**).

best (best), *adj., superl. of* **good** *with* **better** *as compar.* **1.** of the highest quality or standing: *the best students.* **2.** most advantageous or suitable: *the best way.* **3.** largest: *the best part of a day.* —*adv., superl. of* **well** *with* **better** as compar. **4.** most excellently or suitably: *an opera role that best suits her voice.* **5.** in or to the highest degree: *best-known; best-loved.* —*n.* **6.** someone or something that is best: *The best of us make mistakes.* **7.** a person's finest clothing. **8.** a person's highest degree of competence, inspiration, or health. **9.** the highest quality to be found in a given activity: *cabinetmaking at its best.* **10.** the best effort that a person, group, or thing can make: *Their best fell far short of excellence.* **11.** salutations: *Give them my best.* —*v.t.* **12.** to get the better of; beat. —***Idiom.*** **13. as best one can,** in the best way possible under the circumstances. **14. at best,** even under the most favorable circumstances possible: *The job won't be finished for a month at best.* **15. get** or **have the best of, a.** to gain the advantage over. **b.** to defeat; subdue: *The pain can get the best of him.* **16. make the best of,** to cope with; accept.

best′ boy′, *n.* the first assistant to the head electrician on a television or motion-picture production.

best′-case′, *adj.* being the best result that could be expected under the circumstances: *The best-case scenario shows her winning the nomination easily.* Compare WORST-CASE.

bes•tial (bes′chəl, bēs′-), *adj.* **1.** of, pertaining to, or having the form of a beast. **2.** lacking reason or intelligence. **3.** marked by base behavior or desires; debased; inhuman. —**bes′tial•ly,** *adv.*

bes•ti•al•i•ty (bes′chē al′i tē, bēs′-), *n., pl.* **-ties. 1.** brutish or beastly character or behavior. **2.** indulgence in beastlike appetites. **3.** an instance of bestial character or behavior.

bes•ti•ar•y (bes′chē er′ē, bēs′-), *n., pl.* **-ar•ies.** a collection of moralizing tales about real and mythical animals. —**bes•ti•a•rist** (bes′chē ər-ist, -chər-, bēs′-), *n.*

Be′ Still′, My′ Soul′, a Christian hymn with words (1752) by Katharine von Schlegel and music by Jean Sibelius.

best′ man′, *n.* the chief attendant of the bridegroom at a wedding.

be•stow (bi stō′), *v.t.* **1.** to present as a gift; confer. **2.** to put to use; apply: *Bestow your time well.* **3. a.** to provide quarters for; lodge. **b.** to stow; store. —**be•stow′al, be•stow′ment,** *n.*

best•sell•er (best′sel′ər), *n.* a product, as a book, that among those of its class sells very well at a given time.

bet (bet), *v.,* **bet** or **bet•ted, bet•ting,** *n.* —*v.t.* **1.** to wager with (someone). **2.** to maintain in or as if in a bet: *I bet you forgot it.* **3.** *Informal.* to be able to feel certain that (used in the phrase *you bet*): *You bet we care about it.* —*v.i.* **4.** to make a wager: *Do you want to bet?* —*n.* **5.** a pledge of a forfeit risked on some uncertain outcome; wager. **6.** a thing pledged: *a two-dollar bet.* **7.** something that is bet on: *That looks like a good bet.* **8.** an act of betting. **9.** a person or thing considered a good choice. —***Idiom.*** **10. bet one's boots,** to be sure of something.

BET, *Trademark.* Black Entertainment Television.

be•ta (bā′tə; *esp. Brit.* bē′-), *n., pl.* **-tas,** *adj.* —*n.* **1.** the second letter of the Greek alphabet (β, Β). **2.** (*cap.*) the second brightest star in a constellation: *Beta Tauri.* **3.** the second of any series. —*adj.* **4. a.** pertaining to one of the possible positions of an atom or group in a compound. **b.** pertaining to one of two or more isomeric compounds.

be′ta block′er or **be′ta-block′er,** *n.* any of a group of drugs that interfere with the ability of adrenaline to stimulate the beta receptors of the heart, thereby slowing heart rate and lessening the force of blood flow. —**be′ta-block′ing,** *adj.*

be′ta car′otene, *n.* the most abundant of various isomers of carotene, $C_{40}H_{56}$, that can be converted by the body to vitamin A.

be′ta decay′, *n.* a radioactive process in which a beta particle is emitted from the nucleus of an atom.

be•take (bi tāk′), *v.t.,* **-took, -tak•en, -tak•ing.** to cause (oneself) to go.

be′ta par′ticle, *n.* an electron or positron emitted from an atomic nucleus in beta decay.

be′ta recep′tor or **be′ta-recep′tor,** *n.* a site on a cell, as of the heart, that upon interaction with epinephrine or norepinephrine controls heartbeat and heart contractibility, vasodilation, and other physiological processes.

be′ta rhythm′, *n.* a pattern of high-frequency brain waves (**beta waves**) observed in normal persons upon sensory stimulation, esp. with light, or when they are engaging in purposeful mental activity.

be′ta test′, *n.* a test of new or updated computer software or hardware conducted at select user sites just prior to release of the product.

be•tel (bēt′l), *n.* an East Indian pepper plant, *Piper betle,* the leaves of which are chewed with other ingredients. Also called **be′tel pep′per.**

Be•tel•geuse or **Be•tel•geux** (bēt′l jo͞oz′, bet′l jœz′), *n.* a first-magnitude red supergiant in the constellation Orion.

be′tel palm′, *n.* a tropical Asian palm, *Areca catechu,* cultivated in the Old World tropics for its seeds, the kernels of which are chewed in combination with slaked lime and the leaves of the betel plant.

bête noire (bāt′ nwär′, bet′), *n., pl.* **bêtes noires** (bāt′ nwärz′, bet′). a person or thing esp. disliked or dreaded; bane; bugbear. [< French]

Beth•a•ny (beth′ə nē), *n.* a village in W Jordan, near Jerusalem, at the foot of the Mount of Olives; home of Lazarus; site ofJesus' ascension into heaven. Mark 11:1; Matt. 21:17; 16:6; John 12:1; Luke 24:50–51.

beth•el (beth′əl), *n.* **1.** a sacred area or sanctuary. Gen. 28:19. **2.** a church or hostel for sailors. [< Hebrew *bēth 'ēl* house of God]

Beth•el (beth′əl, -el, beth′el′), *n.* a village in W Jordan, near Jerusalem; dream of Jacob. Gen. 28:19.

Be•thes•da (bə thez′də), *n.* **1.** a pool in Biblical Jerusalem believed to have healing powers. John 5:2–4. **2.** a city in central Maryland: residential suburb of Washington, D.C. 62,736.

Beth Hil•lel (*Seph.* bet′ hē lel′), *n. Hebrew.* the school of Jewish legal thought and hermeneutics founded in Jerusalem in the 1st century B.C. by the Jewish spiritual leader Hillel and characterized by its systematic use of interpretive principles and a certain flexibility in interpreting the oral and written law. Compare BETH SHAMMAI.

Beth•le•hem (beth′li hem′, -lē əm), *n.* **1.** a town in NW Jordan, near Jerusalem, occupied by Israel 1967: birthplace of Jesus and David. 16,313. **2.** a city in E Pennsylvania. 72,490.

Beth Mid•rash (*Seph.* bet′ mē dʀäsh′), *n. Hebrew.* a place where Jews gather to study the Talmud and other religious writings; a small synagogue.

Beth′ Pe′or (pē′ôr), *n.* the place where Moses delivered his final exhortation to the Israelites and where he was later buried. Deut. 4:44–46; 34:1–6.

Beth·sa·i·da (beth sā′i də), *n.* an ancient town in N Israel, near the N shore of the Sea of Galilee.

Beth Sham·mai (Seph. bet′ shä mī′), *n. Hebrew.* the school of Jewish legal thought and hermeneutics founded in Jerusalem in the 1st century B.C. by the Jewish teacher Shammai and characterized by an austere or rigid interpretation of Jewish law and tradition. Compare BETH HILLEL.

Beth′ She′mesh (shē′mesh), *n.* **1.** sometimes assumed to be the birthplace of Samson. Judg. 13–16. **2.** the place where men died after looking into the ark of the covenant. I Sam. 6:19–21.

bet·o·ny (bet′n ē), *n., pl.* **-nies. 1.** a plant, *Stachys* (formerly *Betonica*) *officinalis,* of the mint family, having dense spikes of purple flowers, formerly used in medicine and dyeing. **2.** any of various similar plants, esp. of the genus *Pedicularis.*

be·tray (bi trā′), *v.t.* **1.** to deliver or expose to an enemy by treachery. **2.** to be unfaithful in guarding or fulfilling: *to betray a trust.* **3.** to be disloyal to: *to betray one's friends.* **4.** to reveal in violation of confidence: *to betray a secret.* **5.** to exhibit; disclose: *a remark that betrays indifference.* **6.** to lead astray; deceive. **7.** to seduce and desert. —**be·tray′al,** *n.*

be·troth·al (bi trō′thəl, -trô′thəl), *n.* the act or state of being betrothed; engagement. Sometimes, **be·troth′ment.**

be·trothed (bi trōthd′, -trôtht′), *adj.* **1.** engaged to be married. —*n.* **2.** the person to whom one is betrothed.

bet·ta (bet′ə), *n.* FIGHTING FISH.

bet·ter¹ (bet′ər), *adj., compar. of* **good** *with* **best** *as superl.* **1.** of superior quality or excellence: *a better coat.* **2.** morally superior: *no better than thieves.* **3.** of superior suitability; preferable: *a better time for action.* **4.** larger; greater: *the better part of a lifetime.* **5.** improved in health; healthier than before. —*adv., compar. of* **well** *with* **best** *as superl.* **6.** in a more appropriate manner: *to behave better.* **7.** to a greater degree; more completely: *knows the way better than I.* **8.** more: *lives better than a mile away.* —*v.t.* **9.** to make better; improve: *to better the lot of the needy.* **10.** to improve upon: *bettered last year's production record.* —*n.* **11.** something that is preferable: *the better of two choices.* **12.** Usu., **betters.** those superior to oneself. —*Idiom.* **13. better off, a.** in better circumstances. **b.** more fortunate; happier. **14. get** or **have the better of, a.** to get an advantage over. **b.** to prevail against. **15. go (someone) one better,** to exceed another's efforts; surpass. **16.** had **better** or **best,** ought to. —*Saying.* **17. better safe than sorry,** precautions should be taken to avoid misfortune.

bet·ter² (bet′ər), *n.* BETTOR.

bet·ter·ment (bet′ər mənt), *n.* **1.** the act of bettering; improvement. **2.** an improvement that increases the value of a property.

bet′ter-off′, *adj.* being in better circumstances, esp. economically.

bet·tor or **bet·ter** (bet′ər), *n.* a person who bets.

be·tween (bi twēn′), *prep.* **1.** in the space separating: *between New York and Chicago.* **2.** intermediate in time, quantity, or degree: *between twelve and one o'clock.* **3.** linking; connecting: *air service between cities.* **4.** in equal portions for each of: *The couple split the profits between them.* **5.** among: *sharing responsibilities between the five of us.* **6.** by the common participation of: *Between us, we can finish the job.* **7.** in the choice or contrast of: *the difference between good and bad.* **8.** by the combined effect of. **9.** existing confidentially for: *We'll keep this between ourselves.* **10.** involving; concerning: *war between nations.* —*adv.* **11.** in the intervening space or time: *visits that were far between.* —**Usage.** By traditional usage rules, AMONG expresses relationship when more than two are involved and BETWEEN is used for only two: *to decide between tea and coffee.* BETWEEN, however, continues to be used, as it has been throughout its history, to express relationship of persons or things considered individually, no matter how many: *Between holding public office, teaching, and raising a family, she has little free time.* By the rules of grammar, any and all pronouns that are the object of a preposition must be in the objective case: *between you and me; between her and them.* The construction BETWEEN EACH (or EVERY) is fully standard when the sense indicates that more than one thing is meant: *Marigolds peeked between each row of vegetables.*

be·twixt (bi twikst′), *prep., adv.* **1.** between. —*Idiom.* **2. betwixt and between,** neither the one nor the other; in a middle position.

Beu·lah (byōō′lə), *n.* **1.** the land of Israel. Isa. 62:4. **2.** the peaceful land at the end of the pilgrim's journey in John Bunyan's *Pilgrim's Progress* (1678). [< Hebrew *bə′ūlāh* lit., married woman]

BeV or **Bev** or **bev,** billion electron-volts.

bev·el (bev′əl), *n., v.,* **-eled, -el·ing** or (*esp. Brit.*) **-elled, -el·ling,** *adj.* —*n.* **1.** the inclination that one line or surface makes with another when not at right angles. **2.** a surface that does not form a right angle with adjacent surfaces. —*v.t.* **3.** to cut at a bevel. —*v.i.* **4.** to slant; display incline. —*adj.* **5.** Also, **beveled;** *esp. Brit.,* **bevelled.** oblique; slanted; sloping. —**bev′el·er;** *esp. Brit.,* **bev′el·ler,** *n.*

bev′el gear′, a gear having teeth cut into a conical surface, usu. meshing with a similar gear set at right angles.

bev′el joint′, a miter joint, esp. one in which two pieces meet at other than a right angle.

bev′el square′, *n.* an adjustable tool used by woodworkers for laying out angles and for testing the accuracy of surfaces worked to a slope.

bev·er·age (bev′ər ij, bev′rij), *n.* any drinkable liquid, esp. other than water. [< Anglo-French, = *be(i)vre* to drink (< Latin *bibere*) + *-age*]

bev·y (bev′ē), *n., pl.* **bev·ies. 1.** a group of birds, as larks or quail, or animals, as roebuck, in close association. **2.** a large group or collection: *a bevy of sailors.*

be·wail (bi wāl′), *v.t.* to express deep sorrow for; lament: *a child bewailing the loss of her dog.*

be·ware (bi wâr′), *v.* (usu. used in the imperative or infinitive) —*v.t.* **1.** to be wary of: *Beware his waspish wit.* —*v.i.* **2.** to be cautious or careful: *Beware of the dog.* —*Saying.* **3. Beware of Greeks bearing gifts,** be extremely cautious in accepting gifts from enemies. Virgil, *The Aeneid,* Book II.

be·wil·der (bi wil′dər), *v.t.* to confuse or puzzle completely; perplex. —**be·wil′der·ing·ly,** *adv.*

be·wil·der·ment (bi wil′dər mənt), *n.* **1.** the state of being bewildered. **2.** a confusing maze or tangle.

be·witch (bi wich′), *v.t.* **1.** to affect by witchcraft or magic; cast a spell over. **2.** to enchant; charm; fascinate. —**be·witch′ing·ly,** *adv.*

Beyle (bāl), *n.* **Marie Henri,** real name of STENDHAL.

be·yond (bē ond′, bi yond′), *prep.* **1.** on, at, or to the farther side of: *beyond the fence.* **2.** more distant than: *beyond the horizon.* **3.** outside the limits or reach of: *beyond endurance.* **4.** superior to; surpassing: *wise beyond her peers.* —*adv.* **5.** farther on or away: *as far as the house and beyond.* —*Idiom.* **6. beyond the pale,** outside the bounds of decency or good taste. **7. the beyond, a.** that which is at a great distance. **b.** Also, **the great beyond.** the afterlife; life after death.

Beyond′ the Sun′set, a Christian hymn (1936) with words by Virgil Brock and music by Blanche Brock.

Be·zal·e·el (bi zal′ē əl), *n.* the chief architect of the tabernacle. Ex. 31:1–11. —**Be·zal·e·el·i·an** (bi zal′ē el′ē ən, bez′ə lē′ēl-), *adj.*

bez·el (bez′əl), *n.* **1.** the diagonal face at the end of the blade of a chisel or the like. **2.** CROWN (def. 17). **3.** a grooved ring or rim holding a gem, watch crystal, etc., in its setting.

be·zique (bə zēk′), *n.* a card game resembling pinochle but played with more cards.

be·zoar (bē′zôr, -zōr), *n.* a calculus or concretion found in the stomach or intestines of certain animals, esp. ruminants, formerly reputed to be an effective remedy for poison.

BF, black female.

b.f. or **bf,** *Printing.* boldface.

B.F.A., Bachelor of Fine Arts.

BHA, butylated hydroxyanisole: the antioxidant $C_{11}H_{16}O_2$, used to retard rancidity in products containing fat or oil.

Bha·ga·vad-Gi·ta (bug′ə vəd gē′tä), *n. Hinduism.* a portion of the Mahabharata, having the form of a dialogue between the hero Arjuna and his charioteer, the avatar Krishna, in which a doctrine combining Brahmanical and other elements is evolved. Also called **Gita.** [< Sanskrit: Song of the Blessed One]

bhak·ti (buk′tē), *n.* (in Hinduism) selfless devotion as a means of reaching Brahman.

B horizon, *n.* the subsoil in a soil profile.

BHT, butylated hydroxytoluene: the antioxidant $C_{15}H_{24}O$, used to retard rancidity in products containing fat or oil.

Bhu·tan (bōō tän′), *n.* a kingdom in the Himalayas, NE of India: foreign affairs under Indian jurisdiction. 1,865,191; ab. 19,300 sq. mi. (50,000 sq. km). *Cap.:* Thimphu. —**Bhu·tan·ese** (bōōt′n ēz′, -ēs′), *n., pl.* **-ese,** *adj.*

Bi, *Chem. Symbol.* bismuth.

bi-, a combining form meaning "twice," "two": *bifacial; bicarbonate.* —**Usage.** Most words referring to periods of time and prefixed by BI- are potentially ambiguous. Since BI- can be taken to mean either "twice each" or "every two," a word like *biweekly* can be understood as "twice each week" or "every two weeks." Confusion is often avoided by using the prefix SEMI- meaning "twice each" (*semiweekly; semimonthly; semiannual*) or by using the appropriate phrases: *twice a week; twice each month; every two months; every two years.*

BIA, Bureau of Indian Affairs.

bi·an·gu·lar (bī ang′gyə lər), *adj.* having two angles or corners.

bi·an·nu·al (bī an′yōō əl), *adj.* **1.** occurring twice a year; semiannual. **2.** occurring every two years; biennial. —**bi·an′nu·al·ly,** *adv.* —**Usage.** See BI-¹.

bi·as (bī′əs), *n., adj., adv., v.,* **bi·ased, bi·as·ing** or (*esp. Brit.*) **bi·assed, bi·as·sing.** —*n.* **1.** an oblique or diagonal line of direction, esp. across a woven fabric. **2.** a particular tendency or inclination; prejudice. **3.** a systematic as opposed to a random distortion of a statistic as a result of sampling procedure. **4.** the application of a steady voltage or current to an active device, as a diode or transistor, to produce a desired mode of operation. —*adj.* **5.** (of the cut of a fabric or garment) diagonal; oblique. —*adv.* **6.** in a diagonal manner; obliquely; slantingly: *to cut material bias.* —*v.t.* **7.** to cause partiality in; influence, often unfairly: *a tearful plea designed to bias the jury.* —*Idiom.* **8. on the bias, a.** in the diagonal direction of the cloth. **b.** out of line; slanting.

bi·ased (bī′əst), *adj.* having or showing bias: *a biased report.* Also, *esp. Brit.,* **bi′assed.** —**bi′ased·ly;** *esp. Brit.,* **bi′assed·ly,** *adv.*

bi·ath·lon (bī ath′lon), *n.* a contest in which cross-country skiers car-

B

rying rifles shoot at targets at four stops along a 12.5-mi. (20 km) course.

bi•ax•i•al (bī ak/sē əl), *adj.* **1.** having two axes. **2.** (of a crystal) having two optical axes along which double refraction does not occur. —**bi•ax/i•al/i•ty,** *n.* —**bi•ax/i•al•ly,** *adv.*

bib (bib), *n., v.,* **bibbed, bib•bing.** —*n.* **1.** a shield of cloth, paper, or other material tied under the chin to protect the clothing during a meal. **2.** the front part of an apron, overalls, or the like above the waist. —*v.t., v.i.* **3.** to drink; imbibe.

bib/ and tuck/er, *n. Informal.* clothes: *one's best bib and tucker.*

Bibb/ let/tuce (bib), *n.* a variety of lettuce having a small tapering head and light-green leaves.

bib•cock (bib/kok/), *n.* a faucet having a nozzle bent downward.

bi•be•lot (bib/lō, bē/bə lō/), *n.* a small object of curiosity, beauty, or rarity.

Bi•ble (bī/bəl), *n.* **1.** the collection of sacred writings of the Christian religion, comprising the Old and New Testaments. **2.** Also called **Hebrew Scriptures.** the collection of sacred writings of Judaism, known as the Old Testament. **3.** (*often l.c.*) the sacred writings of any religion. **4.** (*l.c.*) a reference publication esteemed for its usefulness and authority: *a bird-watchers' bible.* [< Old French < Middle Latin *biblía* (fem sing.) < Greek, in *tà biblía tà hagía* the holy books; *biblía,* pl. of *biblíon* papyrus roll, der. of *býblos* papyrus, after *Býblos,* Phoenician port where papyrus was exported]

Bi/ble Belt/, *n.* an area chiefly in the S and midwestern U.S. noted for religious fundamentalism.

Bib•li•cal (bib/li kəl), *adj.* (*often l.c.*) **1.** of or in the Bible: *a Biblical name.* **2.** in accord with the Bible. —**Bib/li•cal•ly,** *adv.*

biblio-, a combining form meaning "book" (*bibliophile*) or "Bible" (*bibliolatry*).

bib•li•og•ra•phy (bib/lē og/rə fē), *n., pl.* **-phies. 1.** a complete or selective list of works compiled upon some common principle, as authorship, subject, or printer. **2.** a list of source materials that are used or consulted in the preparation of a work or that are referred to in the text. **3.** the discipline that deals with the physical description, comparison, and classification of books and other printed matter. —**bib/li•og/ra•pher,** *n.*

bib•li•o•man•cy (bib/lē ō man/sē), *n.* divination by means of a book, esp. the Bible, opened at random to some verse or passage.

bib•li•o•ma•ni•a (bib/lē ō mā/nē ə, -mān/yə), *n.* powerful enthusiasm for collecting books. —**bib/li•o•ma/ni•ac,** *n.*

bib•li•op•e•gy (bib/lē op/ə jē), *n.* the art of binding books.

bib•li•o•phile (bib/lē ə fīl/, -fil), *n.* one who loves or collects books.

bib•li•ot•ics (bib/lē ot/iks), *n.* (*used with a sing. or pl. v.*) the analysis of handwriting and documents, esp. for authentication of authorship. —**bib/li•ot/ic,** *adj.* —**bib/li•o•tist** (-ə tist), *n.*

bib•u•lous (bib/yə ləs), *adj.* **1.** fond of or addicted to drink. **2.** absorbent; spongy.

bi•cam•er•al (bī kam/ər əl), *adj.* having two branches, chambers, or houses, as a legislative body. —**bi•cam/er•al•ism,** *n.*

bi•car•bo•nate (bī kär/bə nit, -nāt/), *n.* a salt of carbonic acid, containing the HCO₃⁻ group.

bicar/bonate of so/da, *n.* SODIUM BICARBONATE.

bi•cen•ten•ar•y (bī/ sen ten/ə rē, bī sen/tn er/ē; *esp. Brit.* bī/sen tē/nə rē), *adj., n., pl.* **-ar•ies.** BICENTENNIAL.

bi•cen•ten•ni•al (bī/sen ten/ē əl), *adj.* **1.** pertaining to or in honor of a 200th anniversary. **2.** lasting 200 years. **3.** occurring every 200 years. —*n.* **4.** a 200th anniversary. —**bi/cen•ten/ni•al•ly,** *adv.*

bi•cen•tric (bī sen/trik), *adj.* (of a taxon) having two centers of evolution. —**bi•cen/tri•cal•ly,** *adv.*

bi•ceph•a•lous (bī sef/ə ləs), *adj.* having two heads.

bi•ceps (bī/seps), *n., pl.* **-ceps, -ceps•es** (-sep siz). a muscle with two points of origin, as the flexor at the front of the upper arm and the similar flexor at the back of the thigh.

bi•chon fri•se (bē shôn/ frē zā/), *n., pl.* **bi•chons fri•ses** (bē shôn/ frē zāz/). one of a breed of small dogs of Mediterranean origin having a loosely curled, thick white coat, a topknot, and hanging ears.

bick•er (bik/ər), *v.i.* **1.** to engage in peevish argument; wrangle. **2.** to run or flow rapidly: *a bickering stream.* **3.** to flicker; glitter. —*n.* **4.** a peevish quarrel.

bi•coast•al (bī kōs/tl), *adj.* occurring or existing on two coasts, esp. on both the E and W coasts of the U.S. —**bi•coast/al•ism,** *n.*

bi•col•or (bī/kul/ər), *adj.* **1.** Also, **bi/col/ored.** having two colors: *a bicolor flower.* —*n.* **2.** a flag divided into two major areas of color. Also, *esp. Brit.,* **bi/col/our.**

bi•con•cave (bī kon/kāv, bī/kon kāv/), *adj.* concave on both sides. —**bi/con•cav/i•ty** (-kən kav/i tē), *n.*

bi•con•di•tion•al (bī/kən dish/ə nl), *n.* a proposition expressing equivalence, as "A if and only if B."

bi•con•vex (bī kon/veks, bī/kon veks/), *adj.* convex on both sides. —**bi/con•vex/i•ty,** *n.*

bi•cus•pid (bī kus/pid), *adj.* **1.** Also, **bi•cus/pi•date/.** having or terminating in two cusps or points, as certain teeth. —*n.* **2.** PREMOLAR (def. 3).

bi•cy•cle (bī/si kəl, -sik/əl, -sī/kəl), *n., v.,* **-cled, -cling.** —*n.* **1.** a vehicle with two wheels in tandem, pedals connected to the rear wheel by a chain, handlebars for steering, and a saddlelike seat. —*v.i.* **2.** to ride a bicycle. —**bi/cy•clist, bi/cy•cler,** *n.*

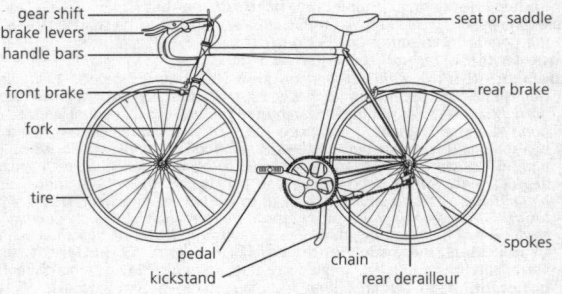

bicycle

bi/cycle kick/, *n.* an exercise performed by lying on one's back with the hips and legs in the air, supported by the hands, and moving the legs as if pedaling a bicycle.

bi•cy•clic (bī sī/klik, -sik/lik), *adj.* **1.** Also, **bi•cy/cli•cal.** consisting of or having two cycles or circles. **2.** containing two rings of atoms in a molecule.

bid (bid), *v.,* **bade** or **bid, bid•den** or **bid, bid•ding,** *n.* —*v.t.* **1.** to command; order; direct: *to bid them depart.* **2.** to say as a greeting, wish, etc.: *to bid good night.* **3.** to offer (a certain sum) as the price one will charge or pay: *They bid $25,000 and got the contract.* **4.** to enter a bid of (a given quantity or suit at cards). **5.** to offer or declare: *to bid defiance.* **6.** to invite. —*v.i.* **7.** to command; order; direct: *Do as I bid.* **8.** to make a bid. **9. bid up,** to increase the market price of by increasing bids. —*n.* **10.** an act or instance of bidding. **11. a.** an offer to make a specified number of points or to take a specified number of card tricks. **b.** the amount of such an offer. **c.** the turn of a person to bid. **12.** an invitation: *a bid to join a club.* **13.** an attempt to attain some goal or purpose: *a bid for election.* **14.** the highest price a prospective buyer is willing to pay for a security during a trading period. —*Idiom.* **15. bid fair,** to seem likely: *bids fair to win first prize.* —**bid/der,** *n.*

b.i.d., (in prescriptions) twice a day.

BOOKS OF THE BIBLE

Old Testament

Genesis	Joshua	I Kings	Nehemiah	Ecclesiastes	Ezekiel	Obadiah	Zephaniah
Exodus	Judges	II Kings	Esther	Song of Solomon	Daniel	Jonah	Haggai
Leviticus	Ruth	I Chronicles	Job	Isaiah	Hosea	Micah	Zechariah
Numbers	I Samuel	II Chronicles	Psalms	Jeremiah	Joel	Nahum	Malachi
Deuteronomy	II Samuel	Ezra	Proverbs	Lamentations	Amos	Habakkuk	

Apocrypha

I Esdras	Tobit	(additional parts	Wisdom of	Ecclesiasticus	(additional parts	Prayer of	I Maccabees
II Esdras	Judith	of Esther)	Solomon	Baruch	of Daniel)	Manasseh	II Maccabees

New Testament

Matthew	The Acts	Galatians	I Thessalonians	II Timothy	Hebrews	II Peter	III John
Mark	Romans	Ephesians	II Thessalonians	Titus	James	I John	Jude
Luke	I Corinthians	Philippians	I Timothy	Philemon	I Peter	II John	Revelation
John	II Corinthians	Colossians					

bid·da·ble (bid′ə bəl), *adj.* **1.** willing to do what is asked; obedient: *a biddable child.* **2.** capable of being bid or bid on.

bid·den (bid′n), *v.* a pp. of BID.

bid·ding (bid′ing), *n.* **1.** command; summons: *I went there at his bidding.* **2.** bids collectively, or a period during which bids are made or received. —*Idiom.* **3. do someone's bidding,** to submit to someone's orders or wishes.

bid·dy (bid′ē), *n., pl.* **-dies. 1.** HEN. **2.** a newly hatched or day-old chick.

bide (bīd), *v.,* **bid·ed** or **bode, bid·ed, bid·ing.** —*v.i.* **1.** to wait; remain. —*Idiom.* **2. bide one's time,** to wait for a favorable opportunity. —**bid′er,** *n.*

bi·det (bē dā′, bi det′), *n.* a low basinlike bathroom fixture with spigots, used for bathing the genital and perineal areas.

bi·di·rec·tion·al (bī′di rek′shə nl, -dī-), *adj.* capable of reacting or functioning in two, usu. opposite, directions. —**bi′di·rec′tion·al′i·ty,** *n.* —**bi′di·rec′tion·al·ly,** *adv.*

bi·en·ni·al (bī en′ē əl), *adj.* **1.** happening every two years: *biennial games.* **2.** lasting or enduring for two years: *a biennial life cycle.* **3.** (of a plant) requiring two years to complete a life cycle; blooming and forming seeds in the second year. —*n.* **4.** an event occurring once in two years. **5.** a biennial plant. Also, **biyearly** (for defs. 1, 2). —**bi·en′ni·al·ly,** *adv.*

bi·en·ni·um (bī en′ē əm), *n., pl.* **-en·ni·ums, -en·ni·a** (-en′ē ə). a period of two years.

bier (bēr), *n.* **1.** a frame or stand on which a corpse or the coffin containing it is laid before burial. **2.** such a stand together with the corpse or coffin.

bi·face (bī′fās′), *n.* a bifacial tool.

bi·fa·cial (bī fā′shəl), *adj.* **1.** (of a stone tool) having two opposing surfaces formed by flaking so as to meet in a sharp edge. **2.** having two faces or fronts. —**bi·fa′cial·ly,** *adv.*

biff (bif), *Slang.* —*n.* **1.** a blow; punch. —*v.t.* **2.** to hit; punch.

bi·fid (bī′fid), *adj.* separated or cleft into two equal parts or lobes. —**bi·fid′i·ty,** *n.* —**bi′fid·ly,** *adv.*

bi·fo·cal (bī fō′kəl, bī′fō′-), *adj.* **1.** having two foci. **2.** (of an eyeglass or contact lens) having two portions, one for near and one for far vision. —*n.* **3. bifocals,** bifocal eyeglasses or contact lenses.

bi·func·tion·al (bī fungk′shə nl), *adj. Chem.* having or involving two functional groups. —**bi·func′tion·al·ly,** *adv.*

bi·fur·cate (*v., adj.* bī′fər kāt′, bī fûr′kāt; *adj. also* -kit), *v.,* **-cat·ed, -cat·ing,** *adj.* —*v.t., v.i.* **1.** to divide or fork into two branches. —*adj.* **2.** divided into two branches.

big (big), *adj.,* **big·ger, big·gest,** *adv., n.* —*adj.* **1.** large in size, height, width, or amount: *a big house; a big batch.* **2.** of major concern or importance: *a big problem.* **3.** outstanding: *a big success.* **4.** important; influential: *a big activist in politics.* **5.** grown-up; mature: *big enough to know better.* **6.** elder: *my big sister.* **7.** large-scale and powerful; exercising substantial control and influence: *big government.* **8.** known or used widely; popular: *Jazz became big in the 1920s.* **9.** magnanimous: *big enough to forgive.* **10.** boastful; pompous: *a big talker.* **11.** loud; orotund: *a big voice.* **12.** filled; brimming: *eyes big with tears.* **13.** *Chiefly South Midland and Southern U.S.* pregnant. —*adv.* **14.** boastfully; pretentiously: *to talk big.* **15.** successfully: *to go over big.* —*n. Informal.* **16.** a person of importance or power: *She lunched with a Hollywood big.* **17. the bigs,** the highest level of competition, esp. baseball's major leagues. —*Idiom.* **18. be big on,** *Informal.* to have a special liking or enthusiasm for. —*Proverb.* **19. The bigger they are, the harder they fall,** failure is more conspicuous in the wealthy and powerful.

big·a·my (big′ə mē), *n., pl.* **-mies.** the act of marrying one person while still being legally married to another. Compare MONOGAMY, POLYGAMY (def. 1). —**big′a·mist,** *n.* —**big′a·mous,** *adj.*

Big′ Ap′ple, the, *n. Informal.* New York City.

big′ band′, *n.* an orchestra specializing in arrangements of swing or jazz, typically for dancing.

big′ bang′ the′ory, *n.* a theory that the universe began with an explosion of a dense mass of matter and is still expanding from the force of that explosion.

Big′ Bend′ Na′tional Park′, *n.* a national park in W Texas, on the Rio Grande. 1080 sq. mi. (2800 sq. km).

big′ broth′er, *n.* **1.** an elder brother. **2.** (*sometimes caps.*) a man who undertakes to sponsor or assist a boy in need of help or guidance. **3.** (*caps.*) **a.** the head of a totalitarian regime that keeps its citizens under close surveillance. **b.** the aggregate of powerful officials and policymakers of a totalitarian state.

Big′ Broth′er is watch′ing you′, —*Saying.* the government observes everything you do. [from George Orwell's novel *1984,* written in 1949]

big′ busi′ness, *n.* large commercial and financial firms considered as a group, esp. in regard to their influence over economic, social, or political policy.

big′ deal′, *n. Informal.* something or someone important or impressive.

Big′ Dip′per, *n.* the group of seven bright stars in Ursa Major resembling a dipper in outline.

big·eye (big′ī′), *n., pl.* (*esp. collectively*) **-eye,** (*esp. for kinds or spe-*

cies) **-eyes.** any of several red fishes of the family Priacanthidae, of warm Pacific seas, having a compressed oval body and large eyes.

Big′ Five′, *n.* **1.** the United States, Great Britain, France, Italy, and Japan during World War I and at the Paris Peace Conference in 1919. **2.** (after World War II) the United States, Great Britain, the Soviet Union, China, and France.

Big′ Foot′ or **Big′foot′,** *n.* a very large, hairy, humanoid creature reputed to inhabit wilderness areas of the U.S. and Canada, esp. the Pacific Northwest. Also called **Sasquatch.** Compare ABOMINABLE SNOWMAN.

big·foot (big′fŏŏt′), *n. Slang.* a prominent political journalist or news analyst.

big′ game′, *n.* **1.** large wild animals, esp. when hunted for sport. **2.** a major objective, esp. one that involves risk.

big′ gov′ernment, *n.* large, centralized government, esp. one that is wasteful and inefficient.

big·head (big′hed′, -hed′), *n.* **1.** *Informal.* self-importance; conceit. **2. a.** inflammation of the head in sheep, caused by a bacterial infection. **b.** enlargement of the head in horses, caused by nutritional hypothyroidism. —**big′head′ed,** *adj.*

big·heart·ed (big′här′tid), *adj.* generous; kind.

big·horn (big′hôrn′), *n., pl.* **-horns,** (*esp. collectively*) **-horn.** a wild sheep, *Ovis canadensis,* of the Rocky Mountains, with large, curving horns. Also called **Rocky Mountain sheep.**

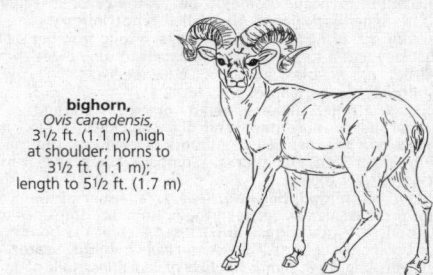

bighorn,
Ovis canadensis,
3½ ft. (1.1 m) high
at shoulder; horns to
3½ ft. (1.1 m);
length to 5½ ft. (1.7 m)

bight (bīt), *n.* **1.** a loop or slack part in a rope. **2.** a bend or curve in the shore of a sea or river. **3.** a body of water bounded by such a bend. **4.** a bay or gulf. —*v.t.* **5.** to fasten with a bight of rope.

big′ league′, *n.* **1.** MAJOR LEAGUE (defs. 1, 2). **2.** Often, **big leagues.** the area of greatest competition, highest achievement or rewards, etc. —**big′-league′,** *adj.* —**big′-lea′guer,** *n.*

big′ lie′, *n.* a false statement of outrageous magnitude employed as a propaganda measure in the belief that a lesser falsehood would not be credible.

big·mouthed (big′moutht′, -mouthd′), *adj.* **1.** very talkative; indiscreet; loudmouthed. **2.** having a very large mouth.

Big′ Mud′dy, *n.* a nickname of the Missouri River.

big′ name′, *n.* a recognized leader in a particular field: *one of the big names in education.* —**big′-name′,** *adj.*

big·no·ni·a (big nō′nē ə), *n., pl.* **-ni·as.** any chiefly tropical American climbing shrub of the genus *Bignonia,* cultivated for its showy, trumpet-shaped flowers.

big′ one′, *n. Informal.* **1.** a one-thousand-dollar bill or the sum of $1000. **2.** a major, often catastrophic event that is the culmination of a series of less significant like events.

big·ot (big′ət), *n.* a person who is extremely intolerant of another's creed, belief, or opinion. —**big′ot·ed,** *adj.*

big·ot·ry (big′ə trē), *n.* **1.** extreme intolerance of any creed, belief, or opinion that differs from one's own. **2.** the actions, prejudices, etc., of a bigot.

big′ shot′, *n. Informal.* an important or influential person.

big′ stick′, *n.* political or military force used as a threat.

big′ talk′, *n. Informal.* exaggeration; bragging.

big′ tent′, *n. Informal.* a political party that welcomes members with a wide range of opinions and viewpoints.

big′-tick′et, *adj.* costly; expensive.

big′ time′, *n.* **1.** *Informal.* the highest or most important level in any profession or occupation. **2.** a circuit of vaudeville theaters presenting just two performances daily and featuring only the most successful entertainers. —**big′-time′,** *adj.* —**big′-tim′er,** *n.*

big′ top′, *n.* **1.** the main tent of a circus. **2.** a circus.

big′ tree′, *n.* a large sequoia, *Sequoiadendron giganteum,* growing to 300 ft. (91 m) high, having reddish brown bark and scalelike blue-green leaves. Also called **giant sequoia.**

big′ wheel′, *n. Informal.* an important or influential person.

big·wig (big′wig′), *n. Informal.* an important person, esp. an official: *senators and other political bigwigs.* [from phrase *big wig,* i.e., person important enough to wear such a wig] —**big′wigged′,** *adj.* —**big·wig′ged·ness** (big′wig′id nis), *n.*

bi·jou (bē′zhŏŏ, bē zhŏŏ′), *n., pl.* **-joux** (-zhŏŏz, -zhŏŏz′). **1.** a jewel. **2.** something small, delicate, and exquisitely wrought.

B

bike (bīk), *n., v.,* **biked, bik·ing.** —*n.* **1.** a bicycle, motorbike, or motorcycle. —*v.i.* **2.** to ride a bike.

bik·er (bī′kər), *n.* **1.** a person who rides a bicycle, motorcycle, or motorbike. **2.** *Informal.* a member of a motorcycle gang.

bi·ki·ni (bi kē′nē), *n., pl.* **-nis. 1.** a very brief, close-fitting, two-piece bathing suit for women or girls. **2.** a very brief, close-fitting pair of bathing trunks for men or boys. **3.** Often, **bikinis.** underwear briefs that are fitted low on the hip or below it.

Bi·ki·ni (bi kē′nē), *n.* an atoll in the N Pacific, in the Marshall Islands: atomic bomb tests 1946. 3 sq. mi. (8 sq. km).

bi·la·bi·al (bī lā′bē əl), *adj.* **1.** (of a speech sound) produced with the lips close together or touching, as the sounds (p), (b), (m), and (w). —*n.* **2.** a bilabial speech sound.

bi·lat·er·al (bī lat′ər əl), *adj.* **1.** pertaining to or involving two or both sides, factions, or the like: *a bilateral agreement.* **2.** located on opposite sides of an axis. **3.** *Biol.* pertaining to the right and left sides of a structure, plane, etc. **4.** *Law.* (of a contract) binding the parties to reciprocal obligations. **5.** through both parents equally: *bilateral affiliation.* Compare UNILATERAL (def. 6). —**bi·lat′er·al·ism,** *n.* —**bi·lat′er·al·ly,** *adv.*

bilat′eral sym′metry, *n.* a basic body plan in which the left and right sides of the organism can be divided into approximate mirror images of each other along the midline. Compare RADIAL SYMMETRY.

bil·ber·ry (bil′ber′ē, -bə rē), *n., pl.* **-ries. 1.** a low-growing blueberry shrub, *Vaccinium myrtillus,* common on heaths of Great Britain and N Europe. **2.** its blue-black berry. Also called **whortleberry.**

bil·bo (bil′bō), *n., pl.* **-boes** Usu., **bilboes.** a long iron bar or bolt with sliding shackles and a lock, formerly attached to the ankles of prisoners.

bil·by (bil′bē), *n., pl.* **-bies.** RABBIT-EARED BANDICOOT.

Bil·dad (bil′dad), *n.* a friend of Job. Job 2:11.

bile (bīl), *n.* **1.** a bitter, alkaline, yellow or greenish liquid, secreted by the liver, that aids in absorption and digestion, esp. of fats. **2.** ill temper; peevishness. **3.** either of two humors of medieval physiology associated with anger and gloominess. Compare BLACK BILE, YELLOW BILE. —**bil·i·ar·y** (bil′ē er′ē), *adj.*

bilge (bilj), *n., v.,* **bilged, bilg·ing.** —*n.* **1. a.** either of the rounded areas that form the transition between the bottom and the sides on the exterior of a hull. **b.** Also, **bilges.** an enclosed area at the bottom of a vessel where seepage collects. **2.** Also called **bilge water.** seepage accumulated in bilges. **3.** *Slang.* foolish or worthless talk or ideas; nonsense. **4.** the widest circumference or belly of a cask. —*v.i.* **5.** to leak in the bilge. —*v.t.* **6.** to damage (a hull bottom) so that water comes in.

Bil·hah (bil′hä), *n.* the mother of Dan and Naphtali. Gen. 30:1–8.

Bil·horn (bil′hôrn), *n.* **Peter,** 1865–1936, U.S. musician and hymn writer.

bi·lin·e·ar (bī lin′ē ər), *adj.* **1.** of or pertaining to two lines: *bilinear coordinates.* **2.** of the first degree in each of two variables.

bi·lin·gual (bī ling′gwəl), *adj.* **1.** able to speak two languages, esp. with the facility of a native speaker. **2.** expressed in, involving, or using two languages: *a bilingual dictionary; bilingual schools.* —*n.* **3.** a bilingual person. —**bi·lin′gual·ly,** *adv.*

bil·ious (bil′yəs), *adj.* **1.** pertaining to bile or to excess secretion of bile. **2.** suffering from or caused or attended by trouble with the bile or liver. **3.** peevish; irritable; cranky. **4.** unattractive or distasteful: *a bilious green scarf.* —**bil′ious·ly,** *adv.*

bil·i·ru·bin (bil′ə rōō′bin, bil′ə rōō′bin), *n.* a reddish bile pigment, $C_{33}H_{36}O_6N_4$, at a high level in the blood producing the yellow skin symptomatic of jaundice.

bilk (bilk), *v.t.* **1.** to defraud; cheat. **2.** to evade payment of or to: *to bilk a creditor.* **3.** to frustrate: *a career bilked by poor health.* **4.** to escape from; elude. —*n.* **5.** a cheat; swindler. **6.** a trick; fraud; deceit. —**bilk′er,** *n.*

bill¹ (bil), *n.* **1.** a statement of money owed for goods or services supplied. **2.** a piece of paper money worth a specified amount: *a ten-dollar bill.* **3.** a form or draft of a proposed statute presented to a legislature, but not yet enacted or passed and made law. **4.** a written or printed public notice or advertisement. **5.** any written statement of particulars. **6.** a written statement, usu. of complaint, presented to a court. **7.** PLAYBILL. **8.** entertainment scheduled for presentation; program: *a good bill at the movies.* —*v.t.* **9.** to send a list of charges to. **10.** to enter (charges) in a bill. **11.** to advertise (something) by bill or public notice. **12.** to schedule on a program: *to bill the play for two weeks.* —*Idiom.* **13. fill the bill,** to fulfill a particular purpose or need. —**bill′er,** *n.*

bill² (bil), *n.* **1.** the parts of a bird's jaws that are covered with a horny or leathery sheath; beak. **2.** the visor of a cap. **3.** a beaklike headland. —*v.i.* **4.** to join bills, as doves. —*Idiom.* **5. bill and coo,** to kiss or fondle and whisper endearments.

bill³ (bil), *n.* **1.** a medieval shafted weapon having at its head a hooklike cutting blade with a beak at the back. **2.** Also called **billhook.** a sharp, hooked instrument used for pruning, cutting, etc.

bil·la·bong (bil′ə bông′, -bong′), *n. Australian.* a stagnant backwater formed by receding floodwater.

bill·board (bil′bôrd′, -bōrd′), *n.* **1.** a flat surface or board, usu. outdoors, on which large advertisements or notices are posted. —*v.t.* **2.** to advertise on or as if on a billboard.

bill·bug (bil′bug′), *n.* any of several weevils, esp. of the genus *Calendra,* that feed on various grasses.

bil·let¹ (bil′it), *n.* **1.** lodging for a soldier, student, etc., as in a private home or nonmilitary public building. **2.** an official order directing the addressee to provide such lodging. **3.** a bunk, berth, or the like, assigned to a member of a ship's crew. **4.** job; position; appointment. —*v.t.* **5.** to direct (a soldier) by ticket, note, or verbal order, where to lodge. **6.** to provide lodging for; quarter. —*v.i.* **7.** to be quartered; stay. —**bil′let·er,** *n.*

bil·let² (bil′it), *n.* **1.** a small chunk of wood, esp. a short section of a log cut for fuel. **2.** a narrow steel bar, esp. one rolled or forged from an ingot. **3.** one of a series of closely spaced cylinders, often in several rows, forming a molding or cornice.

bil·let-doux (bil′ā dōō′, bil′ē-), *n., pl.* **bil·lets-doux** (bil′ā dōōz′, -dōō′, bil′ē-). a love letter. [< French]

bill·fish (bil′fish′), *n., pl.* (*esp. collectively*) **-fish,** (*esp. for kinds or species*) **-fish·es.** any of various fishes having long pointed jaws, as a gar.

bill·fold (bil′fōld′), *n.* **1.** a thin, flat, folding case for carrying paper money and other items. **2.** WALLET (def. 1).

bil·liards (bil′yərdz), *n.* (*used with a sing. v.*) any of several games played with hard balls that are driven with a cue on a cloth-covered table, esp. a game played with a cue ball and two object balls on a table without pockets. Compare POOL² (def. 1). —**bil′liard·ist,** *n.*

bill·ing (bil′ing), *n.* **1.** the listing of the name of a performer, act, or the like, on a marquee, poster, handbill, etc., esp. in regard to prominence: *got top billing.* **2.** advertising; publicity: *Advance billing made the show a sellout.* **3.** the preparing or sending out of bills or invoices. **4.** the amount of business done by a firm within a specified period of time: *billings of $10 million a year.* **5.** the cost of goods or services billed to a customer within a specified period.

Bil·lings (bil′ingz), *n.* a city in S Montana. 78,020.

bil·lings·gate (bil′ingz gāt′; *esp. Brit.* -git), *n.* coarse or vulgar abusive language. [after the kind of speech customary at *Billingsgate,* a London fish market]

bil·lion (bil′yən), *n., pl.* **-lions,** (*as after a numeral*) **-lion,** *adj.* —*n.* **1.** a cardinal number represented in the U.S. by 1 followed by 9 zeros, and in Great Britain by 1 followed by 12 zeros. **2.** any vaguely large number: *I've told you a billion times.* —*adj.* **3.** equal in number to a billion. —**bil′lionth,** *adj., n.*

bil·lion·aire (bil′yə nâr′, bil′yə nâr′), *n.* a person with assets worth a billion or more, as of dollars, francs, or pounds.

bill′ of attain′der, *n.* a legislative act finding a person guilty of treason or felony without trial.

bill′ of exchange′, *n.* a written order to pay a specified sum of money to the person indicated.

bill′ of fare′, *n.* **1.** a menu. **2.** a program of entertainment.

bill′ of goods′, *n.* **1.** a quantity of salable items, as an order or shipment. **2.** a misrepresented, fraudulent, or defective article. —*Idiom.* **3. sell someone a bill of goods,** to defraud or deceive someone: *He sold me a bill of goods about that used car.*

bill′ of health′, *n.* **1.** a certificate attesting to the health of a ship's crew and the health conditions at the previous port. —*Idiom.* **2. clean bill of health,** an attestation of fitness or qualification; a commendation.

bill′ of indict′ment, *n.* a written accusation submitted to a grand jury for its decision.

bill′ of lad′ing, *n.* a receipt given by a carrier for goods accepted for transportation.

Bill′ of Rights′, *n.* **1.** a formal statement of the rights of the people of the United States, incorporated in the Constitution as Amendments 1–10, and in all state constitutions. **2.** (*l.c.*) a statement of the fundamental rights of any group of people: *a student bill of rights.* **3.** an English statute of 1689 confirming the rights and liberties of the people.

bill′ of sale′, *n.* a document transferring title in personal property from seller to buyer.

bil·lon (bil′ən), *n.* an alloy of gold or silver with a larger amount of base metal, esp. copper.

bil·low (bil′ō), *n.* **1.** a great wave or surge of the sea. **2.** any surging mass: *billows of smoke.* —*v.i.* **3.** to rise or roll in billows; surge. **4.** to swell out, puff up, etc.: *flags billowing in the breeze.* —*v.t.* **5.** to cause to billow. —**bil′low·y,** *adj.*

bil·ly (bil′ē), *n., pl.* **-lies.** Also called **bil′ly club′.** a heavy wooden stick used as a weapon, esp. by the police.

bil′ly goat′, *n.* a male goat.

Bil′ly the Kid′, *n.* **1.** (*William H. Bonney*) 1859–81, U.S. outlaw. **2.** (*italics*) a ballet (1938) choreographed by Eugene Loring, with musical score by Aaron Copland.

bi·lo·bate (bī lō′bāt) also **bi·lo′bat·ed, bi·lobed′,** *adj.* consisting of or divided into two lobes.

bi·lo·ca·tion (bī′lō kā′shən), *n.* the state of being or the ability to be in two places at the same time.

bi·mah (bē′mə), *n.* BEMA (def. 2).

bi·man·u·al (bī man′yōō əl), *adj.* involving or requiring the use of both hands. —**bi·man′u·al·ly,** *adv.*

bim·bo (bim′bō), *n., pl.* **-bos, -boes.** *Slang.* a foolish, stupid, or inept person.

bi·mes·ter (bī mes′tər, bī′mes-), *n.* a two-month period.

bi·mes·tri·al (bī mes′trē əl), *adj.* **1.** occurring every two months; bimonthly. **2.** lasting two months.

bi·met·al (bī met′l), *n.* a material made by the bonding of two sheets or strips of different metals, each metal having a different coefficient of thermal expansion. —**bi·me·tal·lic** (bī′mə tal′ik), *adj.*

bi·met·al·lism (bī met′l iz′əm), *n.* **1.** the use of two metals, ordinarily gold and silver, at a fixed relative value, as the monetary standard. **2.** the doctrine or policies supporting such a standard. —**bi·met′al·list,** *n.* —**bi·met′al·lis′tic,** *adj.*

bi·mil·le·nar·y (bī mil′ə ner′ē) also **bi·mil·len·ni·al** (bī′mi len′ē-əl), *adj., n., pl.* **-le·nar·ies** also **-len·ni·als.** —*adj.* **1.** of or pertaining to a bimillennium. —*n.* **2.** BIMILLENNIUM.

bi·mil·len·ni·um (bī′mi len′ē əm) also **bimillenary, bimillennial,** *n., pl.* **-len·ni·ums, -len·ni·a** (-len′ē ə). **1.** a period of two thousand years. **2.** a two-thousandth anniversary.

bi·mod·al (bī mōd′l), *adj.* **1.** having or providing two modes, methods, systems, etc. **2.** (of a distribution in statistics) having or occurring with two modes. —**bi·mo·dal′i·ty,** *n.*

bi·month·ly (bī munth′lē), *adj., n., pl.* **-lies,** *adv.* —*adj.* **1.** occurring every two months. **2.** occurring twice a month; semimonthly. —*n.* **3.** a bimonthly publication. —*adv.* **4.** every two months. **5.** twice a month; semimonthly. —**Usage.** See BI-¹.

bin (bin), *n., v.,* **binned, bin·ning.** —*n.* **1.** a box or enclosed place for storing grain, coal, or the like. —*v.t.* **2.** to store in a bin.

bi·na·ry (bī′nə rē, -ner ē), *adj., n., pl.* **-ries.** —*adj.* **1.** consisting of, indicating, or involving two. **2. a.** of or pertaining to a system of numerical notation to the base 2, in which each place of a number, expressed as 0 or 1, corresponds to a power of 2. **b.** of or pertaining to the digits or numbers used in binary notation. **c.** of or pertaining to a binary system. **3.** noting a chemical compound containing only two elements or groups, as sodium chloride or methyl bromide. **4.** of, pertaining to, or involving a relationship between two alternatives existing in opposition to each other. —*n.* **5.** a whole composed of two. **6.** BINARY STAR. **7.** Also called **bi′nary num′ber.** a number expressed in the binary system of notation.

bi′nary dig′it, *n.* either of the digits 0 or 1 when used in the binary number system.

bi′nary fis′sion, *n.* fission into two organisms roughly equal in size.

bi′nary star′, *n.* a system of two stars that revolve about their common center of mass.

bi·nate (bī′nāt), *adj. Bot.* produced or borne in pairs. —**bi′nate·ly,** *adv.*

bin·au·ral (bī nôr′əl, bin ôr′əl), *adj.* **1.** having two ears. **2.** of, with, or for both ears. **3.** (of sound) recorded through two separate microphones and transmitted through two separate channels to produce a stereophonic effect.

bind (bīnd), *v.,* **bound, bind·ing,** *n.* —*v.t.* **1.** to fasten or secure with or as if with a band. **2.** to encircle with a band or ligature: *to bind one's hair with a ribbon.* **3.** to bandage (often fol. by *up*): *to bind up one's wounds.* **4.** to fix in place by girding: *They bound his hands behind him.* **5.** to cause to cohere: *Ice bound the soil.* **6.** to unite by any legal or moral tie: *to be bound by a contract.* **7.** to place under obligation (usu. used passively): *We are bound to obey the laws.* **8.** to put under legal obligation, as to appear as witness: *to be bound over to the grand jury.* **9.** to make binding on both buyer and seller: *to bind an order with a deposit.* **10.** to secure within a cover: *to bind a book in leather.* **11.** to cover the edge of: *to bind a carpet.* **12.** (of clothing) to chafe or restrict (the wearer). **13.** to constipate. **14.** to indenture as an apprentice: *bound as a child to a blacksmith.* —*v.i.* **15.** to become compact or solid; cohere. **16.** to be obligatory. **17.** to chafe or restrict, as poorly fitting garments. **18.** to stick fast, as a drill in a hole. **19.** **bind off,** *Knitting* (def. 35d). —*n.* **20.** the act of binding, or the state of being bound. **21.** something that binds. **22.** a difficult situation or predicament: *This schedule has us in a bind.* —**bind′a·ble,** *adj.*

bind·er (bīn′dər), *n.* **1.** a person or thing that binds. **2.** a detachable cover, resembling the cover of a notebook or book, with clasps or rings for holding loose papers together: *a three-ring binder.* **3.** a bookbinder. **4.** an agreement granting coverage pending the issuance of an insurance policy. **5. a.** a sum of money given as a pledge of intent to purchase a piece of property. **b.** a written receipt acknowledging this payment and granting the right to purchase the property. **6.** any substance that causes the components of a mixture to cohere. **7.** a vehicle in which the pigment of a paint is suspended.

bind·er·y (bīn′də rē, -drē), *n., pl.* **-er·ies.** a place where books are bound.

bind·ing (bīn′ding), *n.* **1.** the act of fastening, uniting, etc. **2.** anything that binds. **3.** the covering within which the leaves of a book are bound. **4.** a strip of material that protects the edge of a tablecloth, rug, etc. **5.** a fastening to lock a boot onto a ski. —*adj.* **6.** able to bind; restrictive. **7.** having power to bind; obligatory. —**bind′ing·ly,** *adv.*

bind·weed (bīnd′wēd′), *n.* any of various twining or vinelike plants, esp. certain species of the genera *Convolvulus* and *Calystegia,* of the morning glory family.

bine (bīn), *n.* **1.** a twining plant stem, as of the hop or bindweed. **2.** WOODBINE.

Bi·net (bi nā′), *n.* **Alfred,** 1857–1911, French psychologist.

Bi·net′-Si′mon scale′ (or **test′**), *n.* a test for determining the relative development of intelligence, esp. of children, consisting of a series of questions and tasks graded with reference to the ability of the normal child at successive age levels. Compare STANFORD-BINET TEST. [after A. BINET and Théodore *Simon* (1873–1961)]

Bing (bing), *n.* a variety of dark red or blackish sweet cherry. Also called **Bing′ cher′ry.**

binge (binj), *n., v.,* **binged, bing·ing.** —*n.* **1.** a bout of excessive indulgence in eating or drinking; spree. —*v.i.* **2.** to go on a binge.

bin·go (bing′gō), *n.* (*sometimes cap.*) **1.** a game of chance in which each player has a card bearing rows of numbers in unique sequence and a set of numbered markers, a caller announces numbers drawn at random, and a game is won when a player can match and cover five numbers in a row. —*interj.* **2.** (used to call a win in bingo).

bin′go card′, *n.* a prepaid postcard inserted in a magazine by its publisher to enable a reader to order free information about advertised products.

bin·na·cle (bin′ə kəl), *n.* a stand or housing for a nautical compass.

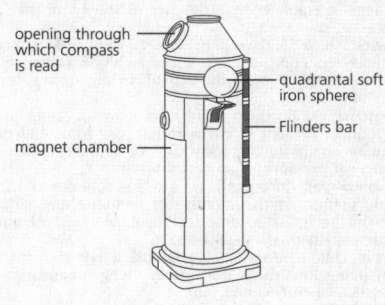

opening through which compass is read

quadrantal soft iron sphere

Flinders bar

magnet chamber

binnacle¹

bin·oc·u·lar (bə nok′yə lər, bī-), *n.* **1.** Usu., **binoculars.** an optical instrument for use with both eyes, consisting of two small telescopes fitted together side by side, each having two prisms between the eyepiece and objective for righting the image. —*adj.* **2.** involving both eyes: *binocular vision.* [< Latin *bin-* double + *oculus* eye]

bi·no·mi·al (bī nō′mē əl), *n.* **1.** an algebraic expression that is a sum or difference of two terms, as $3x + 2y$ and $x^2 - 4x.$ **2.** a taxonomic name consisting of a generic and a specific term, used to designate species. —*adj.* **3.** of or pertaining to a term, expression, or quantity that has two parts. —**bi·no′mi·al·ism,** *n.* —**bi·no′mi·al·ly,** *adv.*

bino′mial distribu′tion, *n.* a statistical distribution giving the probability of obtaining a specified number of successes in a finite set of independent trials in which the probability of a success remains the same from trial to trial.

bino′mial no′menclature, *n.* a naming system in biology in which each species is assigned a unique name consisting of two parts, the name of the genus and another, often descriptive, term.

bi·o (bī′ō), *n., pl.* **bi·os.** **1.** biography. **2.** biology.

bio-, a combining form meaning "life," "living organism," "biology": *biodegradable; biosphere.* Also, *esp. before a vowel,* **bi-.**

bi·o·a·cous·tics (bī′ō ə kōō′stiks; *esp. Brit.* -ə kou′-), *n.* (*used with a sing. v.*) a science dealing with the sounds produced by or affecting living organisms. —**bi′o·a·cous′ti·cal,** *adj.*

bi·o·ac·tiv·i·ty (bī′ō ak tiv′i tē), *n.* any effect on, interaction with, or response from living tissue. —**bi′o·ac′tive,** *adj.*

bi·o·as·say (*n.* bī′ō ə sā′, -as′ā; *v.* bī′ō ə sā′), *n., v.,* **-sayed, -say·ing.** —*n.* **1.** determination of the biological activity or potency of a substance, as a vitamin or hormone, by testing its effect on the growth of an organism. —*v.t.* **2.** to subject to a bioassay.

bi·o·as·tro·nau·tics (bī′ō as′trə nô′tiks), *n.* (*used with a sing. v.*) the science dealing with the effects of space travel on life. —**bi′o·as′tro·nau′tic, bi′o·as′tro·nau′ti·cal,** *adj.*

bi·o·au·tog·ra·phy (bī′ō ô tog′rə fē), *n.* an analytical technique in which organic compounds are separated by chromatography and identified by studying their effects on microorganisms. —**bi′o·au′to·graph** (-ô′tə graf′, -gräf′), *n.* —**bi′o·au′to·graph′ic,** *adj.*

bi·o·a·vail·a·bil·i·ty (bī′ō ə vā′lə bil′i tē), *n.* the extent to which a nutrient or medication can be used by the body. —**bi′o·a·vail′a·ble,** *adj.*

bi·o·cen·tric (bī′ō sen′trik), *adj.* centered in life; having life as its principal fact.

bi·o·chem·is·try (bī′ō kem′ə strē), *n.* the scientific study of the chemical substances and processes of living matter. —**bi′o·chem′i·cal** (-i kəl), *adj., n.* —**bi′o·chem′ist,** *n.*

bi·o·de·grad·a·ble (bī′ō di grā′də bəl), *adj.* capable of decaying through the action of living organisms: *biodegradable paper; biodegradable detergent.* —**bi′o·de·grad′a·bil′i·ty,** *n.*

bi·o·di·ver·si·ty (bī′ō di vûr′si tē, -dī-), *n.* diversity of plant and animal species in an environment.

bi·o·dy·nam·ics (bī′ō dī nam′iks, -dī-), *n.* (*used with a sing. v.*) the branch of biology dealing with energy or the activity of living organisms. —**bi′o·dy·nam′ic,** *adj.*

bi·o·e·lec·tric (bī′ō i lek′trik) also **bi·o·e·lec′tri·cal,** *adj.* of or per-

B

taining to electric phenomena occurring in living organisms. —**bi′o·e·lec·tric′i·ty** (-i lek tris′i tē, -ē′lek-), *n.*

bi·o·e·lec·tron·ics (bī′ō i lek tron′iks, -ē′lek-), *n.* (*used with a sing. v.*) **1.** the study of electron transfer reactions as they occur in biological systems. **2.** the application of electronic devices to living organisms for clinical testing, diagnosis, and therapy.

bi·o·en·er·get·ics (bī′ō en′ər jet′iks), *n.* (*used with a sing. v.*) the study of energy transformation in living systems.

bi·o·en·gi·neer·ing (bī′ō en′jə nēr′ing), *n.* the application of engineering principles and techniques to problems in medicine and biology, as the design and production of artificial limbs and organs. —**bi′o·en′gi·neer′,** *n.*

bi·o·eth·ics (bī′ō eth′iks), *n.* (*used with a sing. v.*) a field of study concerned with the implications of certain medical procedures, as organ transplants, genetic engineering, and care of the terminally ill. —**bi′o·eth′i·cist** (-ə sist), *n.*

bi·o·feed·back (bī′ō fēd′bak′), *n.* **1.** a method of learning to modify a particular body function, as temperature, blood pressure, or muscle tension, by monitoring it with the aid of an electronic device. **2.** the feedback thus obtained.

bi·o·fla·vo·noid (bī′ō flā′və noid′), *n.* any of a group of water-soluble compounds, present in citrus fruits, rose hips, and other plants, that in mammals maintain the resistance of capillary walls to permeation and change of pressure. Also called **vitamin P.**

bi·o·gas or **bi·o-gas** (bī′ō gas′), *n.* any gas fuel derived from the decay of organic matter, as the mixture of methane and carbon dioxide produced by the bacterial decomposition of sewage, manure, garbage, or plant crops. —**bi′o·gas′i·fi·ca′tion,** *n.*

bi·o·gen·e·sis (bī′ō jen′ə sis) also **bi·og·e·ny** (bī oj′ə nē), *n.* the production of living organisms from other living organisms. —**bi′o·ge·net′ic** (-jə net′ik), **bi·og′e·nous,** *adj.*

bi·o·ge·net·ics (bī′ō jə net′iks), *n.* (*used with a sing. v.*) GENETIC ENGINEERING. —**bi′o·ge·net′ic,** *adj.* —**bi′o·ge·net′i·cist,** *n.*

bi·o·gen·ic (bī′ō jen′ik), *adj.* **1.** resulting from the activity of living organisms, as fermentation. **2.** necessary for the life process, as food.

bi·o·ge·o·chem·is·try (bī′ō jē′ō kem′ə strē), *n.* the science dealing with the relationship between the geochemistry of a given region and its flora and fauna. —**bi′o·ge·o·chem′i·cal** (-i kəl), *adj.*

bi·o·ge·og·ra·phy (bī′ō jē og′rə fē), *n.* the study of the geographical distribution of living things. —**bi′o·ge·og′ra·pher,** *n.* —**bi′o·ge·o·graph′ic** (-ə graf′ik), **bi′o·ge′o·graph′i·cal,** *adj.*

bi·o·graph·i·cal (bī′ə graf′i kəl) also **bi′o·graph′ic,** *adj.* **1.** of or pertaining to a person's life. **2.** pertaining to or containing biography: *a biographical dictionary.* —**bi′o·graph′i·cal·ly,** *adv.*

bi·og·ra·phy (bī og′rə fē, bē-), *n.,* *pl.* **-phies. 1.** a written account of another person's life. **2.** an account of the history of an organization, society, etc. **3.** such writings collectively. **4.** the writing of biography as an occupation. —**bi·og′ra·pher,** *n.*

bi·o·haz·ard (bī′ō haz′ərd), *n.* **1.** a pathogen, esp. one used in or produced by biological research. **2.** the health risk posed by the release of such a pathogen into the environment. —**bi′o·haz′ard·ous,** *adj.*

bi·o·log·i·cal (bī′ə loj′i kəl) also **bi′o·log′ic,** *adj.* **1.** pertaining to biology. **2.** of or pertaining to the products and operations of applied biology: *a biological test.* **3.** related by blood rather than by adoption: *biological father.* —*n.* **4.** a medical product that is derived from biological sources. —**bi′o·log′i·cal·ly,** *adv.*

biolog′ical clock′, *n.* **1.** an innate mechanism of the body that regulates its rhythmic and periodic cycles, as that of sleeping and waking. **2.** such a mechanism perceived as inexorably marking the passage of one's youth and esp. one's ability to bear children.

biolog′ical control′, *n.* the control of pests by interference with their ecological status, as by introducing a natural enemy or a pathogen into the environment.

biolog′ical par′ent, *n.* BIRTH PARENT.

biolog′ical war′fare, *n.* the use in war of pathogenic organisms or toxins to disable an enemy or destroy resources.

bi·ol·o·gy (bī ol′ə jē), *n.* **1.** the scientific study of life or living matter in all its forms and processes. **2.** the living organisms of a region. **3.** the biological phenomena characteristic of an organism or a group of organisms. —**bi·ol′o·gist,** *n.*

bi·o·lu·mi·nes·cence (bī′ō lōō′mə nes′əns), *n.* a phosphorescent glow or similar emission of light from a living organism. —**bi′o·lu′mi·nes′cent,** *adj.*

bi·o·mass (bī′ō mas′), *n.* **1.** the amount of living matter in a given habitat, expressed either as the weight of organisms per unit area or as the volume of organisms per unit volume of habitat. **2.** organic matter that can be converted to fuel and is therefore regarded as a potential energy source.

bi·o·math·e·mat·ics (bī′ō math′ə mat′iks), *n.* (*used with a sing. v.*) mathematical methods applied to the study of living organisms.

bi·ome (bī′ōm), *n.* a major geographic region, as a grassland or rain forest, that contains a distinctive community of plants, animals, etc.

bi·o·me·chan·ics (bī′ō mi kan′iks), *n.* (*used with a sing. v.*) **1. a.** the study of the action of external and internal forces on the living body, esp. on the skeletal system. **b.** the development of prostheses. **2.** the study of the mechanical nature of biological processes, as heart action and muscle movement. —**bi′o·me·chan′i·cal,** *adj.*

bi·o·med·i·cine (bī′ō med′ə sin), *n.* the application of the natural sciences, esp. the biological and physiological sciences, to clinical medicine. —**bi′o·med′i·cal,** *adj.*

bi·o·me·te·or·ol·o·gy (bī′ō mē′tē ə rol′ə jē), *n.* the scientific study of the effects of natural or artificial atmospheric conditions, as temperature and humidity, on living organisms. —**bi′o·me′te·or·o·log′i·cal** (-ər ə loj′i kəl), *adj.* —**bi′o·me′te·or·ol′o·gist,** *n.*

bi·om·e·ter (bī om′i tər), *n.* an instrument for measuring the amount of carbon dioxide given off by an organism, tissue, etc.

bi·om·e·try (bī om′i trē), *n.* the calculation of the probable duration of human life.

bi·o·morph (bī′ō môrf′), *n.* a painted, drawn, or sculptured free form suggestive in shape of a living organism, esp. an ameba. —**bi′o·mor′phic,** *adj.*

bi·on·ic (bī on′ik), *adj.* having normal functions enhanced by electronic devices and mechanical parts for dangerous or intricate tasks: *a bionic hand.* —**bi·on′i·cal·ly,** *adv.*

bi·on·ics (bī on′iks), *n.* (*used with a sing. v.*) the study of the means by which humans and animals perform tasks and solve problems, and of the application of the findings to the design of electronic devices and mechanical parts.

bi·o·nom·ics (bī′ō nom′iks), *n.* (*used with a sing. v.*) ECOLOGY (def. 1). —**bi′o·nom′ic, bi′o·nom′i·cal,** *adj.* —**bi′o·nom′i·cal·ly,** *adv.* —**bi·on′o·mist** (-on′ə mist), *n.*

bi·o·phys·ics (bī′ō fiz′iks), *n.* (*used with a sing. v.*) the branch of biology that applies the methods of physics to the study of biological structures and processes. —**bi′o·phys′i·cal,** *adj.* —**bi′o·phys′i·cal·ly,** *adv.* —**bi′o·phys′i·cist** (-fiz′ə sist), *n.*

bi·o·proc·ess (bī′ō pros′es; *esp. Brit.* -prō′ses), *n.* **1.** a method or procedure for preparing biological material, esp. a product of genetic engineering, for commercial use. —*v.t.* **2.** to treat or prepare through bioprocess.

bi·op·sy (bī′op sē), *n.,* *pl.* **-sies,** *v.,* **-sied, -sy·ing.** —*n.* **1.** the removal for diagnostic study of a piece of tissue from a living body. **2.** a specimen obtained from a biopsy. —*v.t.* **3.** to remove (living tissue) for diagnostic evaluation.

bi·o·rhythm (bī′ō riŧH′əm), *n.* an innate periodicity in an organism's physiological processes, as sleep and wake cycles. —**bi′o·rhyth′mic,** *adj.* —**bi′o·rhyth·mic′i·ty** (-mis′i tē), *n.*

BIOS (bī′ōs), *n.* computer firmware that directs many basic functions of the operating system. [*B(asic) I(nput)/O(utput) S(ystem)*]

bi·o·safe·ty (bī′ō sāf′tē), *n.* the maintenance of safe conditions in biological research to prevent harm to workers, nonlaboratory organisms, or the environment.

bi·o·sci·ence (bī′ō sī′əns), *n.* any science that deals with the biological aspects of living organisms. —**bi′o·sci′en·tif′ic** (-ən tif′ik), *adj.* —**bi′o·sci′en·tist,** *n.*

bi·o·sphere (bī′ə sfēr′), *n.* **1.** the part of the earth's crust, waters, and atmosphere that supports life. **2.** the ecosystem comprising the entire earth and the living organisms that inhabit it. —**bi′o·spher′ic** (-sfer′ik), *adj.*

bi·o·sta·tis·tics (bī′ō stə tis′tiks), *n.* (*used with a sing. v.*) the application of statistics to biological and medical data. —**bi′o·stat′is·ti′cian** (-stat′ə stish′ən), *n.*

bi·o·stra·tig·ra·phy (bī′ō strə tig′rə fē), *n.* a branch of geology dealing with the differentiation of sedimentary rock on the basis of the fossils they contain. —**bi′o·strat′i·graph′ic** (-strat′i graf′ik), *adj.*

bi·o·syn·the·sis (bī′ō sin′thə sis), *n.* **1.** the formation of chemical compounds by the action of living organisms. **2.** the laboratory preparation of biological molecules.

bi·o·ta (bī ō′tə), *n.* the animals, plants, fungi, etc., of a region or period.

bi·o·tech·nol·o·gy (bī′ō tek nol′ə jē), *n.* the use of living organisms or other biological systems in the manufacture of drugs or other products or for environmental management. —**bi′o·tech′ni·cal** (-ni kəl), **bi′o·tech′no·log′i·cal** (-nl oj′i kəl), *adj.* —**bi′o·tech·nol′o·gist,** *n.*

bi·ot·ic (bī ot′ik) also **bi·ot′i·cal,** *adj.* pertaining to life or living beings.

bi·o·tin (bī′ə tin), *n.* a crystalline, water-soluble vitamin, $C_{10}H_{16}O_3N_2S$, of the vitamin B complex, present in all living cells. Also called **vitamin H.**

bip·a·rous (bip′ər əs), *adj.* **1.** bringing forth offspring in pairs. **2.** *Bot.* bearing two branches or axes.

bi·par·ti·san (bī pär′tə zən), *adj.* representing or including members from two parties or factions. —**bi·par′ti·san·ship′,** *n.*

bi·par·tite (bī pär′tīt), *adj.* **1.** divided into or consisting of two parts. **2.** shared by two; joint. **3.** divided into two parts nearly to the base, as certain leaves. —**bi·par′ti·tion** (-tish′ən), *n.*

bi·ped (bī′ped), *n.* **1.** a two-footed animal. —*adj.* **2.** Also, **bi·ped′al.** having two feet. —**bi·ped·al·ism** (bī ped′l iz′əm), *n.*

bi·phen·yl (bī fen′l, -fēn′l), *n.* a water-insoluble powder, $C_{12}H_{10}$: used chiefly as a heat-transfer agent and in organic synthesis.

bi·plane (bī′plān′), *n.* an airplane with two sets of wings, one above and usu. slightly forward of the other.

bi·po·lar (bī pō′lər), *adj.* **1.** having two poles, as the earth. **2.** pertaining to both polar regions. **3.** characterized by opposite extremes. —**bi′po·lar′i·ty,** *n.*

bipo/lar disor/der, *n.* an affective disorder characterized by periods of mania alternating with depression, usu. interspersed with relatively long intervals of normal mood; manic-depressive illness.

bi·ra·cial (bī rā/shəl), *adj.* consisting of, representing, or combining members of two separate races. —**bi·ra/cial·ism,** *n.*

bi·ra·mous (bī rā/məs) also **bi·ra·mose** (-mōs), *adj.* consisting of or divided into two branches: *a biramous appendage.*

biretta

birch (bûrch), *n.* **1.** any tree or shrub of the genus *Betula,* comprising species with a smooth, laminated outer bark and close-grained wood. **2.** the wood itself. **3.** a birch rod, or a bundle of birch twigs. —*adj.* **4.** Also, **birch/en.** of, pertaining to, or made of birch. —*v.t.* **5.** to beat or punish with or as if with a birch.

birch/ beer/, *n.* a usu. carbonated drink containing an extract from the bark of the birch tree.

bird (bûrd), *n.* **1.** any warm-blooded, egg-laying vertebrate of the class Aves, having feathers, forelimbs modified into wings, scaly legs, and a beak. **2.** a fowl or game bird. **3.** CLAY PIGEON. **4.** a shuttlecock. **5.** *Slang.* a person, esp. one having some peculiarity: *He's a queer bird.* **6.** *Informal.* an aircraft, spacecraft, or guided missile. —*v.i.* **7.** to catch or shoot birds. **8.** to bird-watch. —*Idiom.* **9. for the birds,** *Informal.* worthless; not to be taken seriously. —*Proverb.* **10. A bird in the hand is worth two in the bush,** it's better to possess something in fact now than to count on possessing something better in the future. **11. Birds of a feather flock together,** those with similar concerns tend to congregate.

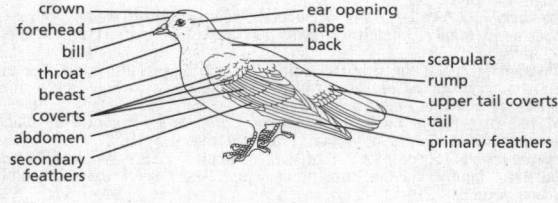

bird

bird/ call/ or **bird/call/,** *n.* **1.** a sound made by a bird. **2.** a sound imitating that of a bird. **3.** a device used to imitate the sound of a bird.

bird·er (bûr/dər), *n.* **1.** a bird-watcher. **2.** a person who raises birds.

bird·ie (bûr/dē), *n., v.,* **bird·ied, bird·ie·ing.** —*n.* **1.** a small bird. **2.** a score of one stroke under par on a golf hole. **3.** a shuttlecock. —*v.t.* **4.** to make a birdie on (a golf hole).

bird·ing (bûr/ding), *n.* the identification and observation of birds as a recreation; bird-watching.

bird·lime (bûrd/līm/), *n.* a sticky material prepared from holly, mistletoe, or other plants, and smeared on twigs to catch small birds.

bird/ of par/adise, *n.* any of various songbirds of the family Paradisaeidae, of New Guinea and adjacent regions, the males of which typically have elegant plumes used in mating displays.

bird-of-par·a·dise (bûrd/əv pär dīs/, -dīz/), *n., pl.* **birds-of-paradise.** a S African plant, *Strelitzia reginae,* of the family Strelitziaceae, having a stiff flower with five stamens and two erect, pointed orange-and-blue petals. Also called **bird/-of-par/adise flow/er.**

bird/ of pas/sage, *n.* **1.** a bird that migrates seasonally. **2.** a transient or migratory person.

bird/ of prey/, *n.* any of the carnivorous birds that seize and fly off with their prey, as an owl or hawk; raptor.

bird/ pep/per, *n.* a variety of pepper, *Capsicum anuum glabriusculum,* having small, elongated berries.

bird·seed (bûrd/sēd/), *n.* any seeds used for feeding birds.

Birds·eye (bûrdz/ī/), *n.* **Clarence,** 1886–1956, U.S. inventor and businessman: developer of food-freezing process.

bird's/-eye/, *adj., n., pl.* **-eyes.** —*adj.* **1.** seen from above; panoramic: *a bird's-eye view of the city.* **2.** superficial; general: *a bird's-eye view of ancient history.* **3.** having markings resembling birds' eyes: *bird's-eye tweed.* —*n.* **4.** any of various plants having small, round, bright-colored flowers, as a primrose, *Primula farinosa,* or a speedwell, *Veronica cha-*

maedrys. **5.** a woven, allover pattern in fabric, typically a small diamond with a center dot.

bird's/-eye/ ma/ple, *n.* a cut of sugar maple wood used esp. for veneers, having a wavy grain with many dark, circular markings.

bird's/-foot/ vi/olet, *n.* a violet, *Viola pedata,* of the E and midwestern U.S., having single flowers with a yellow center, two purple upper petals, and three lavender lower petals.

bird/-watch/ or **bird/watch/,** *v.i.* to identify and observe birds in their natural habitat. —**bird/-watch/er, bird/watch/er,** *n.*

bi·reme (bī/rēm), *n.* a galley having two tiers of oars.

bi·ret·ta (bə ret/ə), *n., pl.* **-tas.** a stiff square cap with three or four upright projecting pieces, worn by ecclesiastics.

birl (bûrl), *v.t.* to cause (a floating log) to rotate rapidly by treading upon it. —**birl/er,** *n.*

birl·ing (bûr/ling), *n.* a competition for lumberjacks, in which each tries to balance longest on a floating log while rotating the log with the feet.

Bir·ming·ham (bûr/ming əm *for 1;* bûr/ming ham/ *for 2*), *n.* **1.** a city in West Midlands, in central England. 1,084,600. **2.** a city in central Alabama. 264,527.

birr (bûr), *n.* **1.** force; energy; vigor. **2.** a whirring sound. —*v.i.* **3.** to move with or make a whirring sound.

birth (bûrth), *n.* **1.** an act or instance of being born: *day of birth.* **2.** the act or process of bearing or bringing forth offspring; childbirth; parturition. **3.** lineage; extraction; descent. **4.** high or noble lineage. **5.** heritage: *a musician by birth.* **6.** any coming into existence: *the birth of an idea.* —*v.t. Chiefly Dial.* **7.** to give birth to. —*Idiom.* **8. give birth to, a.** to bear (a child). **b.** to initiate; originate. —**birth/ing,** *n.*

birth/ canal/, *n.* the passage through which the young of mammals pass during birth, formed by the cervix, vagina, and vulva.

birth/ certif/icate, *n.* an official form recording the birth of a baby and containing pertinent data.

birth/ control/, *n.* regulation of the number of children born through control or prevention of conception.

birth/-control/ pill/, *n.* an oral contraceptive for women, usu. containing estrogen and progesterone or progesterone alone, that inhibits ovulation, fertilization, or implantation of a fertilized ovum, causing temporary infertility.

birth·day (bûrth/dā/), *n.* **1.** the anniversary of a birth. **2.** the day of a person's birth. **3.** a day commemorating the founding or beginning of something.

birth/day suit/, *n. Informal.* bare skin; nakedness.

birth/ defect/, *n.* any physical, mental, or biochemical abnormality present at birth.

birth·mark (bûrth/märk/), *n.* a minor disfigurement or blemish on a person's skin at birth; nevus.

Birth/ of a Na/tion, The, an American film (1915), directed by D. W. Griffith.

birth/ par/ent, *n.* a parent who has conceived or sired rather than adopted a child and whose genes are therefore transmitted to the child. Also called **biological parent.**

birth·place (bûrth/plās/), *n.* place of birth or origin.

birth·rate (bûrth/rāt/), *n.* the proportion of births to the total population in a place in a given time, usu. expressed as a quantity per 1000 of population.

birth·right (bûrth/rīt/), *n.* any right or privilege to which a person is entitled by birth.

birth·root (bûrth/rōōt/, -rŏŏt/), *n.* **1.** Also called **purple trillium.** a trillium, *Trillium erectum,* the roots of which were formerly used in medicine as an astringent. **2.** any of certain other trilliums.

birth·stone (bûrth/stōn/), *n.* a precious or semiprecious stone traditionally associated with the month of one's birth.

BIRTHSTONES

Month	Birthstone
January	Garnet
February	Amethyst
March	Aquamarine or Bloodstone
April	Diamond
May	Emerald
June	Pearl, Alexandrite, or Moonstone
July	Ruby
August	Peridot or Sardonyx
September	Sapphire
October	Opal or Tourmaline
November	Topaz
December	Turquoise or Zircon

birth·weight (bûrth/wāt/), *n.* the weight of an infant at birth.

birth·wort (bûrth/wûrt/, -wôrt/), *n.* any of various plants of the genus *Aristolochia,* esp. *A. clematitis,* an Old World species reputed to facilitate childbirth.

bis (bis), *adv.* **1.** twice. **2.** again (used as a direction in music to repeat a passage or interjectionally as a call for the repetition of a performance).

bis·cuit (bis/kit), *n.* **1.** a small, soft, raised bread, usu. leavened with baking powder or soda. **2.** a pale brown color. **3.** Also called **bisque.** unglazed earthenware or porcelain after firing. [< Middle French *biscuit* seamen's bread, lit., twice cooked]

bi•sect (bī sekt′, bī′sekt), *v.t.* **1.** to cut or divide into two equal or approximately equal parts: *to bisect an angle.* **2.** to intersect or cross. —*v.i.* **3.** to split into two, as a road; fork. —**bi•sec′tion,** *n.* —**bi•sec′tion•al,** *adj.* —**bi•sec′tion•al•ly,** *adv.*

bi•ser•rate (bī ser′āt, -it), *adj.* notched like a saw, with the teeth also notched, as some leaves.

bi•sex•u•al (bī sek′sho͞o əl), *adj.* **1.** of both sexes. **2.** combining male and female organs in one individual; hermaphroditic. **3.** sexually responsive to both sexes. —*n.* **4.** an animal or plant that has the reproductive organs of both sexes. **5.** a person sexually responsive to both sexes. —**bi′sex•u•al′i•ty,** *n.*

Bish•kek (bish kek′), *n.* the capital of Kyrgyzstan, in the N part. 616,000. Formerly, **Pishpek** (until 1926), **Frunze** (1926–91).

bish•op (bish′əp), *n.* **1.** a person who supervises a number of local churches or a diocese, being in the Greek, Roman Catholic, Anglican, and other churches a member of the highest order of the ministry. **2.** a spiritual supervisor, overseer, or the like. **3.** one of two chess pieces of the same color that may be moved any unobstructed distance diagonally, one on white squares and the other on black. **4.** a hot drink of port wine, oranges, and cloves. [< Late Latin *episcopus* < Greek *epískopos* overseer]

Bish•op (bish′əp), *n.* **Elizabeth,** 1911–79, U.S. poet.

bish•op•ric (bish′əp rik), *n.* the see, diocese, or office of a bishop.

Bish′ops′ Bi′ble, *n.* an English translation of the Bible made under the direction of Matthew Parker and published in 1568: the recognized translation of the Bible in England until the Authorized (King James) Version of 1611. [so called because a number of the scholars who worked on the translation were Anglican bishops]

Bis•marck (biz′märk), *n.* **1. Otto von,** 1815–98, German statesman: first chancellor of modern German Empire 1871–90. **2.** the capital of North Dakota, in the central part. 44,485.

bis•muth (biz′məth), *n.* a brittle, grayish white, red-tinged, metallic element used in the manufacture of fusible alloys and in medicine. *Symbol:* Bi; *at. wt.:* 208.980; *at. no.:* 83. —**bis′muth•al,** *adj.*

bi•son (bī′sən, -zən), *n., pl.* **-son. 1.** a North American buffalo, *Bison bison,* having a large head and high, humped shoulders. **2.** Also called **wisent.** a related buffalo, *Bison bonasus,* of Europe, less shaggy and slightly larger than the American bison: nearly extinct in the wild. —**bi′son•tine′** (-tīn′), *adj.*

bisque¹ (bisk), *n.* **1.** a thick cream soup. **2.** ice cream made with powdered macaroons or nuts.

bisque² (bisk), *n.* **1.** BISCUIT (def. 4). **2.** vitreous china that is left unglazed. **3.** pinkish-tan.

Bis•sau (bi sou′) also **Bis•são** (bē souɴ′), *n.* a seaport in and the capital of Guinea-Bissau, in the W part. 109,214.

bis•sex•tile (bī seks′til, -tīl, bi-), *adj.* **1.** containing or noting the extra day of leap year. —*n.* **2.** LEAP YEAR.

bis•sex•tus (bī seks′təs, bi-), *n.* February 29th: the extra day added to the Julian calendar every fourth year (except centenary years not divisible by 400) to compensate for the approximately six hours a year by which the common year of 365 days falls short of the solar year.

bis•tro (bis′trō, bē′strō), *n., pl.* **-tros. 1.** a small, modest, European-style restaurant or café. **2.** a small nightclub or bar.

bi•sul•fate (bī sul′fāt), *n.* a salt of sulfuric acid; an acid sulfate.

bi•sul•fide (bī sul′fīd, -fid), *n.* a disulfide.

bi•sul•fite (bī sul′fīt), *n.* a salt of sulfurous acid; an acid sulfite.

bit¹ (bit), *n., v.,* **bit•ted, bit•ting.** —*n.* **1.** the mouthpiece of a bridle, having fittings at each end to which the reins are fastened. **2.** anything that curbs or restrains. **3.** a removable drilling or boring tool for use in a brace, drill press, or the like. **4.** the cutting part of an ax or hatchet. **5.** the wide portion at the end of an ordinary key that moves the bolt. —*v.t.* **6.** to put a bit in the mouth of (a horse). **7.** to curb with or as if with a bit. **8.** to grind a bit on (a key). —***Idiom.*** **9. chafe** or **champ at the bit,** to become restless because of delay. **10. take the bit in** or **between one's teeth,** to reject control; go one's own way.

bit² (bit), *n.* **1.** a small piece or quantity of something. **2.** a short time: *Wait a bit.* **3.** a stereotypic set of behaviors, attitudes, or actions associated with a particular role, situation, etc.: *the whole Wall Street bit.* **4.** Also called **bit part.** a very small role containing few or no lines. Compare WALK-ON (def. 1). **5.** *Informal.* an amount equivalent to 12½ cents (used only in even multiples): *two bits.* **6.** *Brit.* any small coin: *a threepenny bit.* **7.** a former Spanish or Mexican silver real worth 12½ cents. —***Idiom.*** **8. a bit,** somewhat; a little: *a bit sleepy.* **9. a bit much,** somewhat overdone or beyond tolerability. **10. bit by bit,** by degrees; gradually. **11. do one's bit,** to contribute one's share to an effort. **12. every bit,** quite; just: *every bit as good.*

bit³ (bit), *n.* a single, basic unit of computer information, valued at either 0 or 1 to signal binary alternatives. [*b*(*inary*) + *d*(*igi*)*t*]

bit⁴ (bit), *v.* pt. and a pp. of BITE.

bitch (bich), *n.* **1.** a female dog. **2.** a female of canines generally.

bite (bīt), *v.,* **bit, bit•ten** or **bit, bit•ing,** *n.* —*v.t.* **1.** to cut, wound, or tear with the teeth. **2.** to sever with the teeth (often fol. by *off*). **3.** to grip with the teeth. **4.** to sting, as an insect. **5.** to cause to sting: *faces bitten by the icy wind.* **6.** *Informal.* **a.** to cheat; deceive: *bitten in a mail-order swindle.* **b.** to annoy or upset: *What's biting you?* **7.** to eat into; corrode. **8.** to cut or pierce with or as if with a weapon. **9.** to take firm hold of: *a clamp to bite the wood.* **10.** to make an impression on; affect. —*v.i.* **11.** to press the teeth into something; attack with the jaws, bill, sting, etc. **12.** (of fish) to take the bait. **13.** to accept a deceptive offer or suggestion. **14.** to take a firm hold. —*n.* **15.** the act of biting. **16.** a wound made by biting. **17.** a cutting, stinging, or nipping effect. **18.** a piece bitten off. **19.** a small meal. **20.** a morsel of food. **21.** an exacted portion: *the tax bite.* **22.** the occlusion of the teeth. **23.** a short excerpt, fragment, or bit: *a visual bite from a film.* **24. a.** the catch or hold that one object or one part of a mechanical apparatus has on another. **b.** a surface brought into contact to obtain a hold or grip, as in a lathe chuck. **25.** sharpness; incisiveness. **26.** the roughness of the surface of a file. —***Idiom.*** **27. bite one's lip** or **tongue,** to repress one's anger or other emotions. **28. bite someone's head off,** to respond with anger or impatience to someone's question or comment. **29. bite the hand that feeds one,** to repay kindness with malice or injury. **30. put the bite on,** *Slang.* to try to borrow or extort money from. **31. Don't bite off more than you can chew,** don't attempt something that exceeds your capacity. —**bit′a•ble, bite′a•ble,** *adj.*

bite′wing′ or **bite′-wing′,** *n.* dental x-ray film with a projecting tab that is held between the teeth during radiography to capture structures of the upper and lower jaws in one image.

bit•ing (bī′ting), *adj.* **1.** nipping; smarting; keen: *biting cold.* **2.** cutting; sarcastic: *a biting remark.* —**bit′ing•ly,** *adv.*

bit′ map′, *n.* a piece of text, a drawing, etc., represented, as on a computer display, by the activation of certain dots in a rectangular matrix of dots. —**bit′-mapped′,** *adj.*

bit•ter (bit′ər), *adj.* **1.** having a harsh, disagreeably acrid taste. **2.** producing one of the four basic taste sensations; not sour, sweet, or salt. **3.** hard to bear; grievous: *a bitter sorrow.* **4.** causing pain: *a bitter chill.* **5.** characterized by or showing intense hostility: *bitter enemies.* **6.** experienced at great cost: *a bitter lesson.* **7.** resentful or cynical: *bitter words.* —*n.* **8.** that which is bitter; bitterness. **9.** *Brit.* an ale bitter with hops. —*v.t.* **10.** to make bitter. —*adv.* **11.** extremely; very: *a bitter cold night.* **12. take the bitter with the sweet,** to accept unpleasant as well as pleasant things. —**bit′ter•ly,** *adv.* —**bit′ter•ness,** *n.*

bit′ter al′mond, *n.* See under ALMOND (def. 1).

bit′ter cress′, *n.* any plant of the genus *Cardamine,* of the mustard family, having clusters of white, pink, or purple flowers.

bit•ter end (bit′ər end′ *for 1;* bit′ər end′ *for 2*), *n.* **1.** the conclusion of a difficult or unpleasant situation. **2.** the inboard end of an anchor chain or other line.

bit•tern¹ (bit′ərn), *n.* any of several brown-and-buff wading birds of the heron family, inhabiting reedy marshes in both the Old and New Worlds.

bit•tern² (bit′ərn), *n.* a bitter solution remaining in saltmaking after the salt has crystallized out of seawater or brine, used as a source of bromides, iodides, and certain other salts.

bit•ter•nut (bit′ər nut′), *n.* a hickory, *Carya cordiformis,* of the E and southern U.S., bearing a smooth, gray, bitter seed.

bit•ter•root (bit′ər ro͞ot′, -ro͝ot′), *n.* a plant, *Lewisia rediviva,* of the purslane family, having pink flowers and fleshy roots that are edible when young.

bit•ters (bit′ərz), *n.* (*used with a pl. v.*) **1.** a usu. alcoholic liquor flavored with bitter herbs and used in mixed drinks or as a tonic. **2. a.** a usu. alcoholic liquid impregnated with a bitter medicine, as gentian or quassia, used to increase the appetite or as a tonic. **b.** bitter medicinal substances in general, as quinine.

bit•ter•sweet (*adj.* bit′ər swēt′, bit′ər swēt′; *n.* bit′ər swēt′), *adj.* **1.** both bitter and sweet to the taste: *bittersweet chocolate.* **2.** both pleasant and painful or regretful: *a bittersweet memory.* —*n.* **3.** a climbing or trailing plant, *Solanum dulcamara,* of the nightshade family, having small, violet, star-shaped flowers with a protruding yellow center and scarlet berries. **4.** any climbing plant of the genus *Celastrus,* of the staff-tree family, esp. *C. scandens,* bearing orange capsules opening to expose red-coated seeds. **5.** pleasure mingled with pain or regret. —**bit′ter•sweet′ly,** *adv.*

bit•ty (bit′ē), *adj.,* **-ti•er, -ti•est. 1.** tiny; itty-bitty. **2.** *Chiefly Brit.* containing or consisting of small bits.

bi•tu•men (bī to͞o′mən, -tyo͞o′-, bi-, bich′o͞o-), *n.* **1.** any of various natural substances, as asphalt, consisting mainly of hydrocarbons. **2.** (formerly) an asphalt of Asia Minor used as cement and mortar. —**bi•tu′mi•noid′,** *adj.*

bi•tu•mi•nous (bī to͞o′mə nəs, -tyo͞o′-, bi-), *adj.* **1.** resembling or containing bitumen: *bituminous shale.* **2.** of or pertaining to bituminous coal.

bitu′minous coal′, *n.* a soft coal rich in volatile hydrocarbons and tarry matter and burning with a yellow, smoky flame.

bi•va•lent (bī vā′lənt, biv′ə-), *adj.* **1. a.** having a valence of two. **b.** having two valences. —*n.* **2.** DYAD (def. 2). —**bi•va′lence, bi•va′len•cy,** *n.*

bi•valve (bī′valv′), *n.* **1.** any mollusk, as the oyster, clam, scallop, or mussel, of the class Bivalvia (also called Lamellibranchia or Pelecypoda), having hinged lateral shells, a soft body enclosed by a mantle, sheetlike gills, and often a retractile foot. —*adj.* **2.** having two shells, usu. united by a hinge. **3.** having two similar parts hinged together.

biv•ou•ac (biv′o͞o ak′, biv′wak), *n., v.,* **-acked, -ack•ing.** —*n.* **1.** a military encampment made with improvised shelters. **2.** the place used for such an encampment. —*v.i.* **3.** to assemble in a bivouac.

bi·week·ly (bī wēk′lē), *adj., n., pl.* **-lies,** *adv.* —*adj.* **1.** occurring every two weeks. **2.** occurring twice a week; semiweekly. —*n.* **3.** a periodical issued every other week. —*adv.* **4.** every two weeks. **5.** twice a week. —**Usage.** See BI-¹.

bi·year·ly (bī yēr′lē), *adj.* **1.** happening every two years; biennial. **2.** happening twice a year; biannual. —*adv.* **3.** every two years. **4.** twice yearly. —**Usage.** See BI-¹.

biz (biz), *n. Informal.* business.

bi·zarre (bi zär′), *adj.* markedly unusual in appearance, style, or general character; strange; odd. —**bi·zarre′ly,** *adv.*

Bk, *Chem. Symbol.* berkelium.

bk., **1.** bank. **2.** book.

bkpg., bookkeeping.

bkt., **1.** basket. **2.** bracket.

b/l or **B/L,** bill of lading.

blab (blab) also **blab·ber** (blab′ər), *v.,* **blabbed** also **blab·bered, blab·bing** also **blab·ber·ing.** —*v.t.* **1.** to reveal indiscreetly and thoughtlessly: *to blab secrets.* —*v.i.* **2.** to talk or chatter indiscreetly or thoughtlessly. —*n.* **3.** idle, indiscreet chattering. **4.** a blabbermouth.

blab·ber·mouth (blab′ər mouth′), *n., pl.* **-mouths** (-mouŧhz′, -mouths′). one who talks too much, esp. indiscreetly.

black (blak), *adj.* **1.** lacking hue and brightness; absorbing light without reflecting any of the rays composing it. **2.** characterized by absence of light; enveloped in darkness: *a black night.* **3.** (*sometimes cap.*) **a.** pertaining or belonging to any of the various populations having dark skin pigmentation, specifically the dark-skinned peoples of Africa, Oceania, and Australia. **b.** AFRICAN-AMERICAN (def. 2). **4.** soiled or stained with dirt. **5.** gloomy; pessimistic; dismal: *a black future.* **6.** sullen or hostile: *black words.* **7.** (of coffee or tea) served without milk or cream. **8.** harmful, evil, or wicked: *a black heart.* **9.** indicating censure, disgrace, etc.: *a black mark on one's record.* **10.** marked by disaster or misfortune: *black areas of drought.* **11.** wearing black or dark clothing or armor: *the black prince.* **12.** morbidly or grimly satirical: *black comedy.* **13.** secret; covert: *a black program to rebuild air defenses.* —*n.* **14.** the color opposite to white, absorbing all wavelengths of light. **15.** (*sometimes cap.*) **a.** a member of any of various dark-skinned peoples, esp. those of Africa, Oceania, and Australia. **b.** AFRICAN-AMERICAN (def. 1). **16.** black clothing, esp. as a sign of mourning. **17.** the dark-colored pieces or squares in checkers or chess. **18.** black pigment: *lamp black.* **19.** a horse or other animal that is entirely black. —*v.t.* **20.** to make black; put black on; blacken. **21.** to polish (shoes, boots, etc.) with a black polish. —*v.i.* **22.** to become black; take on a black color; blacken. **23. black out, a.** to lose consciousness or memory temporarily. **b.** to obliterate or suppress. **c.** to extinguish (all the stage lights). **d.** to make or become inoperable. **e.** to obscure by concealing all light in defense against air raids. **f.** to impose a broadcast blackout on (an area). —*Idiom.* **24. in black and white,** in print or writing: *I want that agreement in black and white.* **25. in the black,** operating at a profit. —**black′ish,** *adj.* —**Usage.** BLACK, COLORED, and NEGRO have all been used to describe or name the dark-skinned African peoples or their descendants. COLORED, now somewhat old-fashioned, is often offensive. In the late 1950s BLACK began to replace NEGRO and is still the most widely used and accepted term. Common as both adjective and noun, BLACK is usu. not capitalized except in proper names or titles (*Black Muslim; Black English*). By the close of the 1980s AFRICAN-AMERICAN, urged by leaders in the American black community, had begun to supplant BLACK in both print and speech, esp. as a term of self-reference.

Black (blak), *n.* **1. Hugo Lafayette,** 1886–1971, associate justice of the U.S. Supreme Court 1937–71. **2. James M(ilton),** 1856–1938, U.S. hymn writer.

black′ al′der, *n.* **1.** a holly, *Ilex verticillata,* of E and midwestern North America, bearing red fruit that remains through early winter. **2.** a European alder, *Alnus glutinosa,* having a gray bark and sticky foliage.

black′-and-blue′, *adj.* discolored, as by bruising.

Black′ and Tan′, *n., pl.* **Black and Tans.** a member of an armed force sent by the British government to Ireland in 1920 to suppress revolutionary activity: so called from the color of their uniforms.

black′ and tan′ coon′hound, one of an American breed of large, powerful hound dogs having a short, dense, black coat with tan markings above the eyes and on the muzzle, chest, legs, feet, and breech, and low-set, drooping ears, used for hunting raccoons, opossums, and other larger game.

black′-and-white′, *adj.* **1.** displaying only black and white tones; lacking color. **2.** partly black and partly white: *black-and-white shoes.* **3.** pertaining to or constituting a two-valued system, as of logic or morality; absolute: *To those who think in black-and-white terms, a person must be either entirely good or entirely bad.*

Black′ An′gus, *n.* ABERDEEN ANGUS.

black·ball (blak′bôl′), *v.t.* **1.** to vote against (an applicant, candidate, etc.). **2.** to exclude socially. —*n.* **3.** a negative vote. —**black′ball′er,** *n.*

black′ bear′, *n.* a medium-sized North American bear, *Ursus (Euarctos) americanus,* of wooded areas, ranging from gray to black and having a straight brown muzzle.

black belt (blak′ belt′, belt′ *for 1;* blak′ belt′ *for 2*), *n.* **1. a.** a black cloth waistband conferred upon a participant in a martial art to indicate the highest level of expertise. **b.** a person at this level. Compare BROWN

BELT, WHITE BELT. **2.** (*caps.*) a narrow belt of dark-colored, calcareous soils in central Alabama and Mississippi highly adapted to agriculture, esp. the growing of cotton.

black·ber·ry (blak′ber′ē, -bə rē), *n., pl.* **-ries. 1.** the black or dark purple fruit of certain brambles belonging to the genus *Rubus,* of the rose family. **2.** a plant bearing blackberries.

black′ bile′, *n.* one of the four elemental bodily humors of medieval physiology, regarded as causing gloominess.

black·bird (blak′bûrd′), *n.* **1.** any of several birds of the New World subfamily Icterinae (family Emberizidae) having shiny black or mostly black plumage, as the red-winged blackbird. **2.** a common European thrush, *Turdus merula,* the male of which is black with a yellow bill.

black·board (blak′bôrd′, -bōrd′), *n.* a sheet of smooth, hard material, esp. dark slate, used for writing or drawing on with chalk.

black′board jun′gle, *n. Informal.* a school or school system characterized by lack of discipline and by juvenile delinquency. [on the model of ASPHALT JUNGLE; popularized by the novel of the same name (1954) by American author Evan Hunter (b. 1926)]

black′ book′, *n.* a book of names of people liable to censure or punishment.

black′ box′, *n.* **1.** any unit that forms part of an electronic circuit and has its function but not its components specified. **2.** any small, usu: black, box containing a secret, mysterious, or complex mechanical or electronic device. **3.** FLIGHT RECORDER.

Black′ Boy′, an autobiography (1945) by Richard Wright.

black′ bread′, *n.* a coarse-grained dark bread, often sour and made from whole-grain rye flour.

black′buck′ or **black′ buck′,** *n.* a blackish brown antelope, *Antilope cervicapra,* of India.

Black′ Can′yon, *n.* a canyon of the Colorado River between Arizona and Nevada: site of Boulder Dam.

black·cap (blak′kap′), *n.* **1.** any of various small songbirds having a black crown, esp. the Old World warbler *Sylvia atricapilla.* **2.** BLACK RASPBERRY.

black′ cap′italism, *n.* the ownership of businesses and industries by African-Americans.

black′ cher′ry, *n.* **1.** a North American cherry, *Prunus serotina,* having drooping clusters of fragrant white flowers and bearing a sour, edible black fruit. **2.** the fruit itself.

black′ cur′rant, *n.* **1.** the small, round, blackish, edible fruit of a widely cultivated shrub, *Ribes nigrum,* of the saxifrage family. **2.** the shrub itself.

Black′ Death′, *n.* an outbreak of bubonic plague that spread over Europe and Asia in the 14th century and killed an estimated quarter of the population.

black′ dia′mond, *n.* **1.** CARBONADO¹. **2. black diamonds,** coal, esp. anthracite.

black·en (blak′ən), *v.t.* **1.** to make black; darken. **2.** to speak evil of; defame; slander. —*v.i.* **3.** to become black. —**black′en·er,** *n.*

black·ened (blak′ənd), *adj.* (esp. of fish) coated with spices and sautéed quickly over high heat so that the outside chars.

black′ eye′, *n.* **1.** discoloration of the skin around the eye, resulting from a blow, bruise, etc. **2.** a damaged reputation.

black′-eyed′ pea′, *n.* COWPEA.

black′-eyed′ Su′san, *n.* any of a number of composite plants having daisylike flowers with a dark center disk and usu. yellow ray flowers, esp. *Rudbeckia hirta:* the state flower of Maryland.

black·face (blak′fās′), *n.* **1. a.** black facial makeup, orig. burnt cork, worn by theatrical performers. **b.** a performer wearing such makeup. **2.** a heavy-faced type.

black·fish (blak′fish′), *n., pl.* (*esp. collectively*) **-fish,** (*esp. for kinds or species*) **-fish·es. 1.** any of various dark-colored fishes, as the tautog, *Tautoga onitis,* or the sea bass, *Centropristis striata.* **2.** a small, freshwater food fish, *Dallia pectoralis,* found in Alaska and Siberia, noted for its ability to survive frozen in ice.

black′ fly′ or **black′fly′,** *n.* any of various black biting gnats, of the family Simuliidae, that deposit their eggs in forest streams and are aquatic as larvae.

Black·foot (blak′fõõt′), *n., pl.* (*esp. collectively*) **-foot. 1.** a member of a Plains Indian people resident on the upper drainages of the Saskatchewan and Missouri rivers in the mid-19th century: later on reserves in N Montana and Alberta. **2.** the Algonquian language of the Blackfeet.

black′ gold′, *n.* petroleum.

black′ grouse′, *n.* a large grouse, *Lyrurus tetrix,* of Europe and W Asia.

black·guard (blag′ärd, -ərd, blak′gärd′), *n.* **1.** a contemptible person; scoundrel. **2.** a person who uses scurrilous language. —*v.t.* **3.** to speak to or of in scurrilous language; revile. —**black′guard·ly,** *adj., adv.*

Black′ Hand′, *n.* **1.** Italian, *La Mano Nera.* any of various secret criminal groups organized in Italy and operating in the U.S. in the late 19th and early 20th centuries, practicing blackmail and violence. **2.** an anarchistic society in Spain, suppressed in 1883. **3.** a nationalist society in Serbia, suppressed in 1914. —**Black′hand′er,** *n.*

Black′ Hawk′ War′, *n.* a war fought in northern Illinois and present-day southern Wisconsin, 1831–32, in which U.S. regulars and militia with Indian allies defeated the Sauk and Fox Indians, led by Chief Black Hawk, attempting to recover lost hunting grounds.

black•head (blak′hed′), *n.* **1.** a small, black-tipped fatty mass in a skin follicle, esp. of the face. **2.** any of several birds having a black head. **3.** an intestinal and liver disease of turkeys, chickens, and related birds, caused by the protozoan *Histomonas meleagridas*, often darkening the skin of the head.

black•heart (blak′härt′), *n.* a nonparasitic disease of plants, as of potatoes and various trees, in which internal plant tissues blacken, usu. as a result of extremes in temperature.

black′-heart′ed, *adj.* disposed to doing or wishing evil; malevolent. —**black′-heart′ed•ly,** *adv.*

black′ hole′, *n.* **1.** a theoretical massive object, formed at the beginning of the universe or by the gravitational collapse of a star exploding as a supernova, whose gravitational field is so intense that no electromagnetic radiation can escape. **2.** a void into which things vanish permanently.

Black′ Hole′ of Calcut′ta, *n.* a small cell in Calcutta in which in 1756 the nawab of Bengal reputedly imprisoned 146 British soldiers, most of whom died of suffocation.

black•jack (blak′jak′), *n.* **1.** a short, leather-covered club, consisting of a heavy head on a flexible handle, used as a weapon. **2. a.** Also called **twenty-one.** a gambling game at cards, in which a player needs to get more points than the dealer to win, but not more than 21. **b.** an ace together with a ten or a face card as the first two cards dealt in a hand of this game. **3.** a small oak, *Quercus marilandica*, of the eastern U.S., having a nearly black bark. —*v.t.* **4.** to strike or beat with a blackjack. **5.** to compel by threat.

black•leg (blak′leg′), *n.* **1.** an infectious, often fatal disease of cattle and sheep caused by the soil bacterium *Clostridium chauvoei* and characterized by darkened and swollen upper legs. **2. a.** a disease of cabbage and other cruciferous plants, characterized by dry, black lesions on the base of the stem, caused by a fungus, *Phoma lingam*. **b.** a disease of potatoes, characterized by wet, black lesions on the base of the stem, caused by a bacterium, *Erwinia atroseptica*. **3.** a swindler.

black′ let′ter, *n.* a heavy-faced type in a style like that of early European hand lettering and the earliest printed books. Also called **text.**

black′ light′, *n.* invisible infrared or ultraviolet light.

black•list (blak′list′), *n.* **1.** a list of persons who are under suspicion, disfavor, or censure, or who are not to be hired, served, or otherwise accepted. —*v.t.* **2.** to put on a blacklist.

black′ lo′cust, *n.* a North American tree, *Robinia pseudoacacia*, of the legume family, having pinnate leaves and clusters of white flowers.

black′ lung′, *n.* pneumoconiosis caused by coal dust.

black′ mag′ic, *n.* magic used for evil purposes; sorcery.

black•mail (blak′māl′), *n.* **1.** a payment extorted by intimidation, as by threats of prosecution or injurious revelations. **2.** the extortion of such payment. **3.** a tribute formerly exacted in the north of England and in Scotland by freebooting chiefs for protection from pillage. —*v.t.* **4.** to subject to blackmail. [*black* + *mail* rent, tribute (now dial.) < Old Norse] —**black′mail′er,** *n.*

black′ mark′, *n.* an indication of failure or censure.

black′ mar′ket, *n.* **1.** the illicit buying and selling of goods in violation of legal price controls, rationing, etc. **2.** a place where such activity is carried on.

Black′ Mass′, *n.* a travesty of the Christian Mass, esp. one by alleged worshipers of Satan.

Black′ Mus′lim, *n.* a member of the Nation of Islam.

Black′ Na′tional An′them, The, LIFT EVERY VOICE AND SING.

black′ na′tionalism, *n.* (*often caps.*) a social and political movement advocating the separation of blacks and whites and self-government for black people. —**black′ na′tionalist,** *n.*

black′ night′shade, *n.* a common weed, *Solanum nigrum*, of the nightshade family, having poisonous leaves, white flowers, and edible black berries.

black′ oak′, *n.* any of several oak trees, as *Quercus velutina*, characterized by a blackish bark.

black•out (blak′out′), *n.* **1.** the extinguishing or concealment of all visible lights, usu. as a precaution against air raids. **2.** a period of failure of all electrical power. **3.** the extinguishing of all stage lights, as in closing a vaudeville skit or separating the scenes of a play. **4. a.** temporary loss of consciousness or vision. **b.** a period of total memory loss, as one induced by an accident or prolonged alcoholic drinking. **5.** a brief, passing lapse of memory. **6.** complete stoppage of a communications medium: *a radio blackout.* **7.** a stoppage, suppression, or obliteration: *a news blackout.* **8.** a prohibition imposed on the televising of an event, as a prizefight, so as to encourage or ensure ticket sales.

Black′ Pan′ther, *n.* a member of a militant black American organization active in the 1960s and 1970s.

black′ pep′per, *n.* a hot, sharp condiment prepared from the dried berries of a tropical vine, *Piper nigrum*.

black′poll war′bler (blak′pōl′), *n.* a North American warbler, *Dendroica striata*, the male of which has a black crown.

black′ pop′lar, *n.* a poplar, *Populus nigra*, characterized by spreading branches, triangular leaves, and a gray bark.

black′ pow′er, *n.* (*often caps.*) the political and economic power of

black Americans as a group, esp. such power used for achieving racial equality.

black′ rasp′berry, *n.* the edible fruit of a prickly North American clambering shrub, *Rubus occidentalis*, of the rose family, resembling a raspberry in form and a blackberry in color.

black′ rot′, *n.* any of various fungal or bacterial diseases of plants characterized by black discoloration and decay.

Black′ Sea′, *n.* a sea between Europe and Asia, bordered by Turkey, Romania, Bulgaria, Ukraine, Georgia, and the Russian Federation. 164,000 sq. mi. (424,760 sq. km). Ancient, **Pontus Euxinus.**

black′ sheep′, *n.* a person who causes shame or embarrassment because of deviation from the accepted standards.

black′ skim′mer, *n.* a black-and-white New World skimmer, *Rynchops nigra*, having a bill with a reddish orange base.

black•smith (blak′smith′), *n.* **1.** a person who makes horseshoes and shoes horses. **2.** a person who forges objects of iron. —**black′smith′ing,** *n.*

black′snake′ or **black′ snake′,** *n.* **1.** a slender, harmless blackskinned racer, *Coluber constrictor*, of E North America. **2.** any of various other black snakes. **3.** a heavy, tapering whip of braided cowhide or the like.

black′ spruce′, *n.* a spruce, *Picea mariana*, of North America, having bluish green leaves and grayish brown bark.

black′strap molas′ses (blak′strap′), *n.* molasses remaining after maximum extraction of sugar from the raw product.

black′ stud′ies, *n.* a program of studies in black history and culture offered by a school or college.

black′-tailed′ (or **black′tail′**) **deer′,** *n.* a variety of mule deer, *Odocoileus hemionus columbianus*, of the W slope of the Rocky Mountains, having a tail that is black above.

black′ tea′, *n.* tea allowed to wither and ferment before being heated and dried.

black•thorn (blak′thôrn′), *n.* a thorny Old World shrub, *Prunus spinosa*, of the rose family, having white flowers and small plumlike fruits. Also called **sloe.**

black′ tie′, *n.* **1.** a black bow tie, worn with semiformal evening dress. **2.** semiformal evening dress for men (disting. from *white tie.*) Compare TUXEDO (def. 2).

black•top (blak′top′), *n., v.,* **-topped, -top•ping.** —*n.* **1.** a bituminous paving substance, as asphalt. **2.** a road covered with blacktop. —*v.t.* **3.** to pave with blacktop.

black′ vul′ture, *n.* a common New World vulture, *Coragyps atratus*, having a bald black head and black plumage.

black′ wal′nut, *n.* **1.** a large North American walnut tree, *Juglans nigra*. **2.** the nut or wood of this tree.

black•wa•ter (blak′wô′tər, -wot′ər), *n.* any of several diseases characterized by the production of dark urine as a result of the rapid breakdown of red blood cells.

black′ wid′ow, *n.* **1.** a venomous black spider, *Latrodectus mactans*, of warm regions, including the U.S. **2.** any venomous spider of the cosmopolitan genus *Latrodectus*.

blad•der (blad′ər), *n.* **1. a.** a distensible saclike organ serving as a receptacle for liquids or gases. **b.** URINARY BLADDER. **c.** an air-filled float, as in certain seaweeds. **2.** something resembling a bladder, as the inflatable lining of a football or basketball. —**blad′der•like′,** *adj.*

blad•der•nut (blad′ər nut′), *n.* **1.** the fruit capsule of a shrub or small tree of the genus *Staphylea*. **2.** the shrub or tree itself.

blad•der•wort (blad′ər wûrt′, -wôrt′), *n.* any aquatic, terrestrial, or epiphytic plant of the genus *Utricularia*, having threadlike leaves bearing many small bladders.

blade (blād), *n.* **1.** the flat cutting part of an implement, as a knife. **2.** SWORD. **3.** a similar part, as of a mechanism, used for clearing, wiping, scraping, etc. **4.** the arm of a propeller or other similar rotary mechanism, as an electric fan. **5. a.** the leaf of a plant, esp. of a grass or cereal. **b.** the broad part of a leaf. **6.** the metal part of an ice skate that comes into contact with the ice; runner. **7.** a thin, flat part of something, as of an oar or a bone: *shoulder blade*. **8.** a dashing, swaggering, or jaunty young man. **9.** SWORDSMAN. **10. a.** the upper surface of the tongue directly behind the tip. **b.** the foremost portion of the tongue, including the upper and lower surfaces and the tip. **11.** the elongated hind part of a fowl's single comb. —**blade′less,** *adj.*

blade•let or **blade•lette** (blād′lit), *n.* a small, blade-shaped piece of stone used as the cutting edge of a weapon or tool by Stone Age peoples. Also called **microblade.**

blad•ing (blā′ding), *n.* the act of skating on in-line skates. —**blad′er,** *n.*

blah (blä), *Informal.* —*n.* **1.** meaningless chatter; nonsense. **2. the blahs,** a feeling of physical uneasiness, general discomfort, or mild depression; malaise. —*adj.* **3.** insipid; dull; uninteresting.

blah-blah-blah (blä′blä′blä′), *n. Slang.* meaningless chatter; idle gossip: *the blah-blah-blah of gossip columnists.* Also, **blah′-blah′.**

Blair (blâr), *n.* **Anthony Charles Lynton** (*Tony*), born 1953: British political leader: prime minister since 1997.

blame (blām), *v.,* **blamed, blam•ing,** *n.* —*v.t.* **1.** to hold responsible: *Don't blame me for the delay.* **2.** to find fault with; censure: *I don't blame you for leaving.* **3.** to place the responsibility for (a fault, error, etc.) (usu. fol. by *on*): *to blame a mistake on someone.* **4.** blast; damn (used as a mild curse): *Blame the rotten luck.* —*n.* **5.** an act of attributing fault; censure; reproof. **6.** responsibility for anything deserving of censure: *to take the blame for an error.* —***Idiom.*** **7. to blame,** responsible; at fault; culpable. —**blam′a•ble,** *adj.* —**blame′less,** *adj.* —**blame′less•ly,** *adv.*

blame•wor•thy (blām′wûr′thē), *adj.* deserving blame; blamable. —**blame′wor′thi•ness,** *n.*

blanch (blanch, blänch), *v.t.* **1.** to whiten by removing color; bleach. **2.** to boil (food) briefly, as to whiten, facilitate removal of skins, remove strong flavors, or prepare for freezing. **3.** to whiten or prevent the greening of (the stems or leaves of plants, as lettuce) by excluding light. **4. a.** to give a white luster to (metals), as by means of acids. **b.** to coat (sheet metal) with tin. **5.** to make pale, as with sickness or fear. —*v.i.* **6.** to become white; turn pale. —**blanch′er,** *n.*

bland (bland), *adj.*, **-er, -est. 1.** pleasantly gentle or agreeable: *a bland, affable manner.* **2.** soothing or balmy, as air. **3.** nonirritating, as food or medicines. **4.** not highly flavored; mild; tasteless: *a bland sauce.* **5.** lacking in special interest, liveliness, individuality, etc.; insipid; dull. **6.** unemotional, casual: *a bland acknowledgment of guilt.* —**bland′ly,** *adv.* —**bland′ness,** *n.*

Bland′-Al′li•son Act′ (bland′al′ə sən), *n.* an act of Congress (1878) requiring the federal government to purchase at the market price from two to four million dollars' worth of silver monthly for conversion into silver dollars containing 16 times more silver per coin than gold in dollar coins of gold.

blan•dish (blan′dish), *v.t.* **1.** to coax or influence by gentle flattery; cajole. —*v.i.* **2.** to use flattery or cajolery. —**blan′dish•er,** *n.* —**blan′dish•ing•ly,** *adv.*

blan•dish•ment (blan′dish mənt), *n.* Often, **blandishments.** something, as an action or speech, that tends to flatter, coax, or entice.

blank (blangk), *adj.* **1.** having no marks; not written or printed on: *blank pages.* **2.** not filled in: *a blank check.* **3.** unrelieved or unbroken by ornament or opening: *a blank wall.* **4.** containing no recorded sound or images: *blank tape; blank film.* **5.** void of interest or variety: *to pass blank days reading trashy novels.* **6.** expressionless: *a blank look on her face.* **7.** nonplussed: *He looked blank when I asked for his ticket.* **8.** complete; utter: *blank stupidity.* —*n.* **9.** a place where something is lacking; an empty space. **10.** a space in a printed form, test, etc., to be filled in. **11.** a printed form containing such spaces. **12.** a dash put in place of an omitted letter or letters, esp. to avoid writing a word considered profane or obscene. **13.** a piece of metal ready to be drawn, pressed, or machined into a finished object. **14.** BLANK CARTRIDGE. —*v.t.* **15.** to keep (an opponent) from scoring in a game. **16.** to stamp or punch out of flat stock, as with a die. **17. blank out, a.** to cross out or delete: *to blank out an entry.* **b.** to suffer a loss of memory or concentration. —***Idiom.*** **18. draw a blank, a.** to be unsuccessful: *to draw a blank in an investigation.* **b.** to fail to comprehend or remember: *I drew a blank on his phone number.* —**blank′ly,** *adv.* —**blank′ness,** *n.*

blank′ car′tridge, *n.* a cartridge containing powder only, without a bullet.

blank′ check′, *n.* **1.** a bank check bearing a signature but no stated amount. **2.** unrestricted authority; free hand.

blan•ket (blang′kit), *n.* **1.** a large, rectangular piece of soft fabric, often with bound edges, used esp. for warmth as a bed covering. **2.** a similar piece of fabric used as a cover, garment, or the like. **3.** any extended covering or layer; mantle: *a blanket of snow.* —*v.t.* **4.** to cover with or as if with a blanket. **5.** to interrupt; obstruct (usu. fol. by *out*): *a storm that blanketed out TV reception.* —*adj.* **6.** covering or intended to cover a large group or class of things, conditions, situations, etc.: *a blanket proposal.*

blan′ket-flow′er or **blan′ket•flow′er,** *n.* any of several gaillardias with showy heads of yellow or red flowers.

blan′ket stitch′, *n.* a basic sewing stitch in which widely spaced, interlocking loops are formed, used for cutwork, as a decorative finish for edges, etc. —**blan′ket-stitch′,** *v.i.*, *v.t.*

blank′ verse′, *n.* unrhymed verse, esp. the iambic pentameter used in English dramatic and epic verse.

blare (blâr), *v.*, **blared, blar•ing,** *n.* —*v.i.* **1.** to emit a loud, raucous sound; blast. —*v.t.* **2.** to sound loudly; proclaim noisily: *a radio blaring rock music.* —*n.* **3.** a loud, raucous noise; clamor. **4.** glaring intensity of light or color. **5.** fanfare; ostentation; flamboyance.

blar•ney (blär′nē), *n.*, *v.*, **-neyed, -ney•ing.** —*n.* **1.** flattery; cajolery. **2.** misleading nonsense; humbug. —*v.t.*, *v.i.* **3.** to flatter or deceive with blarney.

bla•sé (blä zā′, blä′zā), *adj.* **1.** indifferent to or bored with life, as or as if from an excess of worldly pleasures; jaded. **2.** not concerned, perturbed, or excited about something; unmoved.

blas•pheme (blas fēm′, blas′fēm), *v.*, **-phemed, -phem•ing.** —*v.t.* **1.** to speak impiously or irreverently of (God or sacred things). **2.** to speak evil of; slander; abuse. —*v.i.* **3.** to speak irreverently of God or sacred things; utter impieties. —**blas•phem′er,** *n.* —**blas′phe•mous** (-fə məs), *adj.* —**blas′phe•my** (-fə mē), *n.*

blast (blast, bläst), *n.* **1.** a sudden and violent gust of wind. **2.** the blowing of a trumpet, whistle, etc. **3.** a loud, sudden sound or noise: *a harsh blast from the radio.* **4.** a forcible stream of air from the mouth, bellows, or the like. **5. a.** air forced into a furnace by a blower to increase the rate of combustion. **b.** a jet of steam directed up a smokestack, as of a steam locomotive, to increase draft. **6.** a forceful throw, hit, etc.: *a blast down to third base.* **7.** *Slang.* something that gives great pleasure, esp. a party. **8.** a vigorous outburst of criticism; attack. **9.** the charge explosive used at one firing in blasting operations. **10.** the act of exploding; explosion. **11.** any pernicious or destructive influence, esp. on animals or plants; a blight. **12.** the sudden death of buds, flowers, or young fruit. —*v.t.* **13.** to make a loud noise on; blow: *to blast a horn.* **14.** to cause to shrivel or wither. **15.** to ruin; destroy. **16.** to shatter by or as if by an explosion. **17.** to make, form, or open up by blasting: *to blast a tunnel.* **18.** to curse; damn: *Blast it, there's the phone again!* **19.** to criticize vigorously; denounce. **20.** to hit or propel with great force. **21.** to shoot. —*v.i.* **22.** to produce a loud, blaring sound. **23.** to shoot. **24.** to use or detonate explosives, as a charge of dynamite. **25. blast off, a.** (of a self-propelled rocket) to leave a launch pad. **b.** (of an astronaut) to travel aloft in a rocket. —***Idiom.*** **26. (at) full blast,** at maximum capacity; at or with full volume or speed.

B

blast•ed (blas′tid, blä′stid), *adj.* **1.** blighted; ruined. **2.** damned; confounded. **3.** *Slang.* drunk.

blast′ fur′nace, *n.* a large vertical furnace for smelting iron from ore.

blasto-, a combining form meaning "bud, sprout," "embryo," "formative cells or cell layer": *blastosphere.* Compare -BLAST.

blast•off (blast′ôf′, -of′, bläst′-), *n.* the launching of a rocket, guided missile, or spacecraft.

blas•tu•la (blas′chə lə), *n.*, *pl.* **-las, -lae** (-lē′). the early developmental stage of an animal, consisting of a single spherical layer of cells enclosing a hollow, central cavity. —**blas′tu•lar,** *adj.* —**blas′tu•la′tion** (-lā′shən), *n.*

bla•tant (blāt′nt), *adj.* **1.** brazenly obvious: *a blatant error.* **2.** offensively noisy or loud. **3.** tastelessly conspicuous: *blatant colors.* —**bla′tan•cy,** *n.* —**bla′tant•ly,** *adv.*

blath•er (blath′ər), *n.* **1.** foolish, voluble talk. —*v.i.* **2.** to talk foolishly; babble. —**blath′er•er,** *n.*

blath•er•skite (blath′ər skīt′), *n.* **1.** a person given to voluble, empty talk. **2.** nonsense; blather.

blaze[1] (blāz), *n.*, *v.*, **blazed, blaz•ing.** —*n.* **1.** a bright flame or fire. **2.** a bright, hot gleam or glow: *the blaze of day.* **3.** a vivid coruscation: *a blaze of jewels.* **4.** a sudden, intense outburst, as of passion or fury. **5. blazes,** hell: *Go to blazes!* —*v.i.* **6.** to burn brightly (sometimes fol. by *away, up,* or *forth*): *The bonfire blazed away for hours.* **7.** to shine like flame (sometimes fol. by *forth*). **8.** to burst out suddenly or intensely, as a fire or flame does; flare (sometimes fol. by *up*). **9.** to shoot steadily or continuously (usu. fol. by *away*). **10.** to be brilliantly conspicuous.

blaze[2] (blāz), *n.*, *v.*, **blazed, blaz•ing.** —*n.* **1.** a distinctive mark made on a tree, as with paint or by chipping off some bark, to indicate a trail or boundary. **2.** a white area down the center of the face of a horse, cow, etc. —*v.t.* **3.** to indicate or mark with blazes: *to blaze a trail; to blaze trees.* **4.** to lead in forming or finding: *research that blazed the way for space travel.*

blaze[3] (blāz), *v.t.*, **blazed, blaz•ing.** to make known; proclaim; publish.

blaz•er (blā′zər), *n.* **1.** something that blazes or shines brightly. **2.** a solid color or striped sports jacket with metal buttons, patch pockets, and sometimes an insignia on the breast pocket.

blaz′ing star′, *n.* a plant with showy flower clusters, as *Chamaelirium luteum,* of the lily family, or the composite plant *Liatris spicata.*

bla•zon (blā′zən), *v.t.* **1.** to set forth publicly; proclaim. **2.** to adorn or embellish, esp. brilliantly or showily. **3.** to describe in heraldic terminology. **4.** to depict (heraldic arms) in proper form and color. —*n.* **5.** COAT OF ARMS (def. 2). **6.** the heraldic description of armorial bearings. **7.** conspicuous display. —**bla′zon•er,** *n.*

bldg., building.

-ble, var. of -ABLE (*soluble*).

bleach (blēch), *v.t.* **1.** to make whiter or lighter in color; remove the color from, as by exposure to sunlight or a chemical agent. —*v.i.* **2.** to become whiter or lighter in color. —*n.* **3.** a bleaching agent. **4.** degree of paleness achieved in bleaching. **5.** an act of bleaching. —**bleach′a•ble,** *adj.*

bleach•er (blē′chər), *n.* **1.** Usu., **bleachers.** a typically roofless section of low-priced, tiered seating, usu. made of boards, esp. at an athletic field or stadium. **2.** a person or thing that bleaches.

bleak[1] (blēk), *adj.*, **-er, -est. 1.** bare, desolate, and often windswept: *a bleak plain.* **2.** cold and piercing; raw: *a bleak wind.* **3.** without hope or encouragement; depressing; dreary: *a bleak future.* —**bleak′ish,** *adj.* —**bleak′ly,** *adv.* —**bleak′ness,** *n.*

bleak[2] (blēk), *n.* a European freshwater fish, *Alburnus alburnus,* having scales with a silvery pigment used in the production of artificial pearls.

blear (blēr), *v.t.* **1.** to make dim, as with tears or inflammation. —*adj.* **2.** (of the eyes) dim from tears. **3.** dim; indistinct. —*n.* **4.** a blur; cloudiness; dimness.

blear•y (blēr′ē), *adj.*, **blear•i•er, blear•i•est. 1.** (of the eyes or sight) blurred or dimmed, as from sleep or weariness. **2.** indistinct; unclear: *a bleary view of the horizon.* **3.** fatigued; worn-out. —**blear′i•ly,** *adv.* —**blear′i•ness,** *n.*

bleat (blēt), *v.i.* **1.** to utter the cry of a sheep or goat, or a sound resembling such a cry. **2.** to talk in a whining, complaining tone. **3.** to babble; prate. —*v.t.* **4.** to utter with or as if with a bleat. —*n.* **5.** the cry of a sheep or goat. **6.** any similar sound: *the bleat of distant horns.* **7.** foolish or complaining talk; babble. —**bleat′er,** *n.* —**bleat′ing•ly,** *adv.*

bleed (blēd), *v.*, **bled** (bled), **bleed•ing,** *n.* —*v.i.* **1.** to lose, discharge, or exude blood. **2.** (of a plant) to exude sap, resin, etc., from a wound. **3. a.** to run or become diffused: *The colors bled when the dress was washed.* **b.** to lose or yield a substance, esp. dye: *dark blue towels bleeding in hot water.* **4.** (of a liquid) to ooze or flow out. **5.** to feel pity, sorrow, or anguish: *My heart bleeds for you.* **6.** to suffer wounds or death, as in battle. **7.** (of printed matter) to run off the edges of a page. **8.** to pay out money, as when overcharged. —*v.t.* **9.** to cause to lose blood; to draw blood from (a vein). **10.** to lose or emit (blood or sap). **11.** to drain or draw sap, water, etc., from. **12.** to remove trapped air from, as by opening a valve: *to bleed the brakes.* **13.** to extort money from, as by blackmail or usury. **14.** to permit (printed matter) to run off the page or sheet. **15. bleed off,** to draw or extract: *to bleed off sap from a maple tree.* —*n.* **16.** an instance of bleeding; hemorrhage: *an intracranial bleed.* —***Idiom.*** **17. bleed white** or **dry,** to deplete of all resources, money, etc., as through excessive demands.

bleed•ing (blē′ding), *adv. Brit. Slang.* (used as an intensifier): *a bleeding silly idea.*

bleed′ing heart′, *n.* **1.** any of various plants belonging to the genus *Dicentra,* of the fumitory family, esp. *D. spectabilis,* having long clusters of rose or red heart-shaped flowers. **2.** a person who makes an ostentatious display of pity or concern for others.

bleep (blēp), *n.* **1.** a brief beeping sound, usu. of a high pitch and generated by an electronic device. **2.** such a sound used to replace objectionable material, as in a broadcast. —*v.i.* **3.** (of an electronic device) to emit a series of bleeps as an audible signal. —*v.t.* **4.** to delete or block (sound, esp. speech) from a recording, broadcast, or the like.

blem•ish (blem′ish), *v.t.* **1.** to destroy or diminish the perfection of; mar; sully. —*n.* **2.** a mark that detracts from appearance, as a pimple or a scar. **3.** a defect or flaw; stain; blight: *a blemish on one's record.* —**blem′ish•er,** *n.*

blench[1] (blench), *v.i.* to shrink; flinch; quail.

blench[2] (blench), *v.t., v.i.* to whiten; blanch.

blend (blend), *v.t.* **1.** to mix smoothly and inseparably. **2.** to prepare by mixing various sorts or grades: *I blend this tea by mixing chamomile with pekoe.* —*v.i.* **3.** to intermingle smoothly and inseparably. **4.** to fit or relate harmoniously: *The voices blend beautifully.* **5.** to have no perceptible separation: *Sea and sky seemed to blend.* —*n.* **6.** a mixture or kind produced by blending. **7.** a word made by putting together parts of other words, as *motel,* made from *motor* and *hotel,* or *guesstimate,* from *guess* and *estimate.* **8.** a sequence of two or more consonant sounds within a syllable, as the *bl* in *blend;* cluster.

blend•er (blen′dər), *n.* **1.** a person or thing that blends. **2.** an electric appliance consisting of a tall container with motor-driven blades that chop, purée, liquefy, or mix foods.

blend′ing inher′itance, *n.* inheritance in which contrasting parental characters appear as a blend in the offspring.

blen•ny (blen′ē), *n., pl.* **-nies.** any of several small, spiny-finned fishes of the family Blenniidae, having a long, tapering body.

bless (bles), *v.t.,* **blessed** or **blest, bless•ing. 1.** to consecrate or sanctify by a religious rite; make or pronounce holy. **2.** to request God's divine favor upon or for: *Bless this house.* **3.** to bestow some benefit upon; endow: *Nature blessed me with strong teeth.* **4.** to extol as holy; glorify: *Bless the name of the Lord.* **5.** to protect or guard from evil (usu. used interjectionally): *Bless you!* **6.** to make the sign of the cross over or upon.

bless•ed (bles′id; *esp. for 3* blest), *adj.* **1.** consecrated; sacred; holy; sanctified. **2.** worthy of adoration, reverence, or worship: *the Blessed Trinity.* **3.** divinely or supremely favored; fortunate: *Blessed with common sense, she handled the problem neatly.* **4.** blissfully happy. **5.** beatified. **6.** bringing happiness and thankfulness: *the blessed assurance of a steady income.* **7.** (used as an intensifier): *every blessed cent.* —**bless′ed•ly,** *adv.*

Bless′ed Assur′ance, a Christian hymn with words by Fanny Crosby and music by Phoebe P. Knapp.

bless′ed event′, *n.* the birth of a child.

Bless′ed Redeem′er, a Christian hymn (1920) with words by Avis Christiansen.

Bless′ed Sac′rament, *n.* the consecrated Host.

Bless′ed Vir′gin, *n.* the Virgin Mary.

bless•ing (bles′ing), *n.* **1.** the act or words of a person who blesses. **2.** a special favor, mercy, or benefit: *the blessings of liberty.* **3.** a favor or gift bestowed by God, thereby bringing happiness. **4.** the invoking of God's favor upon a person. **5.** praise; devotion; worship, esp. grace said before a meal. **6.** approval or good wishes: *The law has the governor's blessing.* —***Idiom.*** **7. blessing in disguise,** a misfortune that has brought some unanticipated benefit.

blest (blest), *v.* **1.** a pt. and pp. of BLESS. —*adj.* **2.** BLESSED.

Blest′ Be′ the Tie′ That′ Binds′, a Christian hymn (1782) with words by John Fawcett.

blew (blo͞o), *v.* **1.** pt. of BLOW[2]. **2.** pt. of BLOW[3].

blight (blīt), *n.* **1. a.** the rapid and extensive discoloration, wilting, and death of plant tissues. **b.** any of various plant diseases so characterized. **2.** any cause of impairment or frustration. **3.** the state or result of being deteriorated or ruined: *urban blight.* —*v.t.* **4.** to cause to wither or decay. **5.** to destroy; ruin; frustrate: *Illness blighted her hopes.* —*v.i.* **6.** to suffer blight.

blimp (blimp), *n.* a small, nonrigid airship or dirigible.

blind (blīnd), *adj.* **1.** unable to see; lacking the sense of sight. **2.** unwilling or unable to perceive or understand: *parents blind to their children's faults.* **3.** not characterized or determined by reason or control: *blind chance.* **4.** not requiring a basis in reason or intelligence; absolute and unquestioning: *blind faith.* **5.** lacking all consciousness or awareness: *a blind stupor.* **6.** drunk. **7.** hard to see or understand: *blind reasoning.* **8.** hidden from immediate view, esp. from oncoming motorists: *a blind corner.* **9.** of concealed or undisclosed identity; sponsored anonymously: *a blind ad signed only with a box number.* **10.** having no outlets; closed at one end: *a blind passage.* **11.** (of an archway, arcade, etc.) having no windows, passageways, or the like. **12.** done by instruments alone: *blind flying.* **13.** made without some prior knowledge: *a blind purchase.* **14.** of or pertaining to an experimental design that prevents investigators or subjects from knowing the hypotheses or conditions being tested. **15.** of, pertaining to, or for blind persons. —*v.t.* **16.** to make sightless permanently or temporarily, as by injuring, dazzling, or bandaging the eyes. **17.** to make obscure or dark: *The room was blinded by heavy curtains.* **18.** to deprive of discernment, reason, or judgment. **19.** to outshine; eclipse: *a radiance that doth blind the sun.* —*n.* **20.** something that obstructs vision, as a blinker for a horse. **21.** a window covering with horizontal or vertical slats. **22.** VENETIAN BLIND. **23.** WINDOW SHADE. **24.** a lightly built structure of brush or other growths, esp. one in which hunters conceal themselves. **25.** an activity, organization, or the like for concealing a true action or purpose; subterfuge. **26. the blind,** persons who lack the sense of sight. —*adv.* **27.** to the point of losing consciousness: *to drink oneself blind.* **28.** without the ability to see clearly; blindly: *to drive blind through a storm.* **29.** without guidance, proper information, etc.: *to work blind.* **30.** to an extreme degree; completely: *to cheat someone blind.* —***Idiom.*** **31. fly blind,** to pilot an airplane during conditions of poor visibility with only instruments for guidance. —***Proverb.*** **32. If the blind lead the blind, both shall fall into the ditch,** leadership is disastrous if it is ignorant. Matt. 15:14. **33. There are none so blind as those who will not see,** those who remain wilfully ignorant are the blindest of all. —**blind′ing•ly,** *adv.* —**blind′ly,** *adv.* —**blind′ness,** *n.*

blind′ al′ley, *n.* **1.** a roadway that is open at only one end. **2.** a situation or path offering no help, opportunity, or reward.

blind′ date′, *n.* **1.** a social appointment or date arranged, usu. by a third person, between two people who have not met. **2.** either of the participants in such an arrangement.

blind•er (blīn′dər), *n.* **1. blinders,** something that impedes vision or discernment. **2.** a blinker for a horse.

blind•fish (blīnd′fish′), *n., pl.* **-fish•es,** (*esp. collectively*) **-fish.** any of several fishes that live in cave waters, as species of the genus *Amblyopsis,* having rudimentary, functionless eyes.

blind•fold (blīnd′fōld′), *v.t.* **1.** to prevent or obstruct sight by covering (the eyes) with a cloth, bandage, or the like. **2.** to impair the awareness or clear thinking of. —*n.* **3.** a cloth for covering the eyes. —*adj.* **4.** done with the eyes covered: *a blindfold test.* **5.** rash; unthinking.

blind•man's buff (blīnd′manz′ buf′), *n.* a game in which a blindfolded player must catch and identify one of the other players.

blind′ side′, *n.* **1.** the part of one's field of vision, as to the side or rear, where one cannot see approaching objects. **2.** the side opposite that toward which a person is looking.

blind•side (blīnd′sīd′), *v.t.,* **-sid•ed, -sid•ing. 1.** to hit or attack from the blind side. **2.** to attack where a person is vulnerable.

blind′ spot′, *n.* **1.** a small area of the retina, where it continues to the optic nerve, that is insensitive to light. **2.** an area or subject about which one is uninformed, prejudiced, or unappreciative.

blind′ trust′, *n.* a trust in which the financial investments of a public official are administered solely by a trustee, without the official's knowledge or participation, so as to avoid conflict of interest.

blind•worm (blīnd′wûrm′), *n.* a limbless European lizard, *Anguis fragilis.*

blin•i (blin′ē, blē′nē), *n., pl.* **blin•i, blin•is.** a small yeast-raised pancake.

blink (blingk), *v.i.* **1.** to open and close the eye, esp. involuntarily. **2.** to be startled or dismayed (usu. fol. by *at*): *She blinked at his outburst.* **3.** to look evasively or with indifference; ignore (often fol. by *at*): *to blink at another's eccentricities.* **4.** to shine unsteadily, dimly, or intermittently; twinkle. —*v.t.* **5.** to open and close (the eye or eyes), usu. rapidly and repeatedly; wink. **6.** to cause (something) to blink: *to blink a flashlight as a signal.* **7.** to ignore deliberately; disregard; evade. —*n.* **8.** an act of blinking; flicker; flutter. **9.** a gleam; glimmer. —***Idiom.*** **10. on the blink,** not working properly; in need of repair.

blink•er (bling′kər), *n.* **1.** a device for flashing light signals. **2.** a flashing light, as for regulating traffic. **3.** either of two leather flaps on a bridle, to prevent a horse from seeing sideways; blinder. —*v.t.* **4.** to put blinkers on.

blintze (blints, blint′sə) also **blintz** (blints), *n.* a thin pancake folded around a filling, as of cheese or fruit, and sautéed or baked.

blip (blip), *n., v.,* **blipped, blip•ping.** —*n.* **1.** a spot of light on a radar screen. **2.** a brief interruption, as in the continuity of a recorded sound or a motion-picture film. **3.** a brief upturn, as in revenue or income. **4.** BLEEP (def. 1). —*v.i.* **5.** to move or proceed in short, erratic movements. —*v.t.* **6.** BLEEP (def. 4).

bliss (blis), *n.* **1.** supreme happiness; utter joy or contentment. **2.** heaven; paradise. —**bliss′ful,** *adj.*

Bliss (blis), *n.* **Philip P(aul),** 1838–76, U.S. musician and hymn writer.

bliss•ful (blis′fəl), *adj.* full of, abounding in, enjoying, or conferring bliss. —**bliss′ful•ly,** *adv.* —**bliss′ful•ness,** *n.*

blis•ter (blis′tər), *n.* **1.** a thin vesicle on the skin containing watery matter or serum, as from a burn or other injury. **2.** any similar swelling, as an air bubble in a coat of paint. **3.** a transparent dome on the fuselage of an airplane, usu. for mounting a gun. **4.** the plastic overlay of a blister pack. —*v.t.* **5.** to raise a blister on. **6.** to subject to intense heat: *Heat blistered the coast.* **7.** to criticize or rebuke severely. —*v.i.* **8.** to become blistered. —**blis′ter•y,** *adj.*

blis′ter pack′, *n.* a package with a clear plastic overlay affixed to a cardboard backing for protecting and displaying a product.

blis′ter rust′, *n.* a disease, esp. of white pines, characterized by cankers and in the spring by blisters on the stems, caused by a rust fungus of the genus *Cronartium.*

blithe (blīth, blīth), *adj.* **1.** lighthearted in disposition; cheerful. **2.** carefree; heedless: *a blithe disregard for someone's feelings.* —**blithe′ful,** *adj.* —**blithe′ly,** *adv.* —**blithe′ness,** *n.*

blitz (blits), *n.* **1.** a sudden, swift, and overwhelming military attack, usu. using tanks and aerial bombardment. **2. the Blitz,** the intensive aerial bombing of British cities by the Germans in 1940–41. **3.** any swift, vigorous attack, barrage, or defeat. **4.** *Football.* a direct charge upon the passer as soon as the ball is snapped. **5.** a shutout in gin rummy. —*v.t.* **6.** to attack, defeat, or destroy with or as if with a blitz. **7.** *Football.* to charge (the passer) as soon as the ball is snapped. [shortening of *blitzkrieg,* < German, = *Blitz* lightning + *Krieg* war] —**blitz′er,** *n.*

blitz•krieg (blits′krēg′), *n.* BLITZ (defs. 1, 3).

bliz•zard (bliz′ərd), *n.* **1. a.** a storm with dry, driving snow, strong winds, and intense cold. **b.** a heavy and prolonged snowstorm covering a wide area. **2.** an inordinately large amount of something all at one time; avalanche.

bloat (blōt), *v.t.* **1.** to expand or distend, as with air or water; puff up. —*v.i.* **2.** to become swollen. —*n.* **3.** a gassy distension of the abdomen or other part of the digestive system. **4.** a sheep, cow, or the like affected by bloat.

blob (blob), *n., v.,* **blobbed, blob•bing.** —*n.* **1.** a small lump or drop of a thick or glutinous substance. **2.** a small splotch or daub, as of color. **3.** an object, esp. a large one, having no distinct shape or definition. —*v.t.* **4.** to mark or splotch with blobs.

bloc (blok), *n.* **1.** a group of persons, businesses, etc., united for a particular purpose, esp. a group of legislators of different parties who vote together for some interest. **2.** a group of nations that share common interests and usu. act in concert in international affairs: *the former Soviet bloc.*

block (blok), *n.* **1.** a solid mass of wood, stone, etc., usu. with one or more flat or approximately flat faces. **2.** a hollow masonry building unit of cement, terra cotta, etc. **3.** one of a set of cube-shaped pieces used as a child's toy in building. **4.** a mold or piece on which something is shaped or kept in shape. **5.** a piece of wood used in the art of making woodcuts. **6.** a structure on which a condemned person is beheaded. **7.** a platform for an auctioneer. **8.** CYLINDER BLOCK. **9.** a part enclosing one or more freely rotating, grooved pulleys, about which ropes or chains pass to form a hoisting or hauling tackle. **10.** an obstacle, obstruction, or hindrance. **11.** a stoppage in or difficulty in proceeding with mental processes, speech, or writing: *writer's block.* **12.** *Sports.* a hindering of an opponent or an opponent's play. **13.** a quantity, portion, or section taken as a unit or dealt with at one time: *a block of theater tickets.* **14.** a small section of a city, town, etc., enclosed by neighboring and intersecting streets. **15.** the length of one side of such a section: *to walk two blocks.* **16.** a large building divided into separate apartments, offices, shops, etc. **17.** a group of computer data stored and processed as a unit. **18.** the base on which a printing plate is mounted to make it type-high. **19.** any of the short lengths into which a railroad track is divided for signaling purposes. **20.** a group of four or more unseparated stamps not in a strip. **21.** *Slang.* a person's head. —*v.t.* **22.** to obstruct by placing obstacles in the way: *to block one's exit.* **23.** to fit with blocks; mount on a block. **24.** to shape or prepare on or as if on a block: *to block a sweater.* **25.** to plot stage movements of or for (often fol. by *out*). **26.** to mark off (a portion of text or data) for moving, deleting, printing, etc., as in word processing. **27.** to stop the passage of impulses in (a nerve). **28. a.** to obstruct or impede (an opposing player) by physical contact. **b.** to deflect (an opponent's pass, kick, or shot) during play. **29.** *Metall.* to give (a forging) a rough form before finishing. —*v.i.* **30.** *Sports.* to obstruct an opposing player physically or deflect an opponent's pass, kick, or shot. **31.** to block a play, performer, scene, stage, etc. **32.** to suffer a block. **33. block in** or **out,** to sketch or outline roughly or generally, without details. —*Idiom.* **34. on the block,** for sale at auction. —**block′a•ble,** *adj.*

block•ade (blo kād′), *n., v.,* **-ad•ed, -ad•ing.** —*n.* **1.** the closing off of a port, city, etc., by hostile ships or troops to prevent entrance or exit. **2.** any obstruction of passage or progress. **3.** interruption or inhibition of a normal physiological signal, as a nerve impulse. —*v.t.* **4.** to subject to a blockade. —**block•ad′er,** *n.*

block•age (blok′ij), *n.* **1.** an act of blocking. **2.** the state of being blocked. **3.** something that blocks; obstruction.

block′ and tack′le, *n.* the ropes or chains and blocks used in a hoisting tackle.

block•bust•er (blok′bus′tər), *n.* **1.** a huge aerial demolition bomb. **2.** a motion picture, novel, etc., esp. one lavishly produced, that has wide popular appeal or financial success. **3.** a person or thing that is overwhelmingly impressive, effective, or influential. **4.** one who practices blockbusting.

block•bust•ing (blok′bus′ting), *n.* the practice of inducing homeowners to sell their properties at prices below value by exploiting fears that members of minority groups will be moving into the neighborhood, and then reselling these homes at inflated prices. —**block′bust′,** *v.t., v.i.*

block′ di′agram, *n.* a chart or diagram using labeled blocks connected by straight lines to represent the relationship of parts or phases.

block′ grant′, *n.* a federal grant that a state or local government may use at its discretion for a wide range of programs.

block•head (blok′hed′), *n.* a stupid person. —**block′head′ed,** *adj.*

block•house (blok′hous′), *n., pl.* **-hous•es** (hou′ziz). **1.** a building of hewn timbers, usu. with a projecting upper story, having loopholes for musketry: formerly used as a fort. **2.** a defensive military structure, as of concrete, used for observation and directing gunfire. **3.** a concrete structure for housing and protecting personnel and controls during rocket launchings.

block•ish (blok′ish), *adj.* like a block; dull; stupid.

block′ let′ter, *n.* **1.** a usu. compressed sans-serif typeface or letter. **2.** a simple, hand-printed capital letter.

block′ print′, *n.* a design printed by means of one or more blocks of wood or metal.

bloke (blōk), *n. Chiefly Brit.* man; fellow; guy.

blond (blond), *adj.* **1.** (of hair, skin, etc.) light-colored: *the child's soft blond curls.* **2.** (of a person) having light-colored hair and skin. **3.** (of furniture wood) light in tone. —*n.* **4.** a blond person. —**blond′ness,** *n.*

blonde (blond), *adj.* **1.** (of a woman or girl) having fair hair and usu. fair skin and light eyes. —*n.* **2.** a woman or girl having this coloration. —**blonde′ness,** *n.*

blood (blud), *n.* **1.** the red fluid that circulates through the heart, arteries, and veins of vertebrates, consisting of plasma in which red blood cells, white blood cells, and platelets are suspended. **2.** a comparable circulating fluid in many invertebrates. **3.** the vital principle; life. **4.** a person or group regarded as a source of vitality: *The company needs new blood.* **5.** one of the four elemental bodily humors of medieval physiology, regarded as causing cheerfulness. **6.** bloodshed; slaughter. **7.** the juice or sap of plants. **8.** temperament: *a person of hot blood.* **9.** human nature; humanity: *the frailty of our blood.* **10.** descent from a common ancestor; ancestry: *related by blood.* **11.** the people of one's lineage; kindred. **12.** royal extraction: *a prince of the blood.* **13.** purebred breeding. **14.** a profligate or rake. **15.** *Chiefly Brit.* a high-spirited, adventuresome youth. —*v.t.* **16.** to give (hounds) a first sight or taste of blood. **17.** to stain with blood. —*Idiom.* **18. bad blood,** longstanding mutual animosity. **19. blood, sweat, and tears,** extreme effort. **20. in cold blood,** with malign and merciless lack of feeling. **21. make one's blood boil,** to inspire resentment, anger, or indignation: *Such carelessness makes my blood boil.* **22. make one's blood run cold,** to fill with terror; frighten: *The threat in his voice made her blood run cold.* **23. taste blood,** to experience a new, usu. violent or destructive sensation and acquire an appetite for it. —*Proverb.* **24. Blood is thicker than water,** family ties are stronger than any others. —*Saying.* **25. I have nothing to offer but blood, toil, tears, and sweat,** patriots should be willing to sacrifice their time, efforts, and even their lives for their country, especially in a time of crisis: from a speech in the House of Commons by Winston Churchill, on becoming Prime Minister, May 13, 1940.

blood-and-guts (blud′n guts′), *adj.* **1.** dealing with or depicting war or violence, esp. in a lurid manner: *a blood-and-guts movie.* **2.** concerned with fundamental needs, problems, values, etc.: *The blood-and-guts issues will determine the election.*

blood′ bank′, *n.* **1.** a place where blood or blood plasma is collected, processed, stored, and distributed. **2.** the supply of blood or blood plasma at such a place.

blood•bath (blud′bath′, -bäth′), *n., pl.* **-baths** (-bathz′, -bäthz′, -baths′, -bäths′). a ruthless slaughter; massacre.

blood′ broth′er, *n.* **1.** a person's brother by birth. **2.** a male in a close relationship with another male through the performance of a specific ritual, as the commingling of blood.

blood′ cell′, *n.* any of the cellular elements of the blood, as white blood cells or red blood cells. Also called **blood′ cor′puscle.**

blood′ count′, *n.* the count of the number of red and white blood cells and platelets in a specific volume of blood.

blood•cur•dling (blud′kûrd′ling, -kûr′dl ing), *adj.* arousing terror; horrifying.

blood′ feud′, *n.* FEUD[1] (def. 1).

blood′ group′, *n.* any of various classes into which human blood can be divided according to immunological compatibility based on the presence or absence of specific antigens on red blood cells. Also called **blood type.** Compare ABO SYSTEM, RH FACTOR.

blood•hound (blud′hound′), *n.* **1.** one of a breed of large dogs with very long ears, loose skin, a usu. black-and-tan coat, and an acute sense of smell, often used in tracking humans. **2.** a person who is a steadfast pursuer.

blood•less (blud′lis), *adj.* **1.** without blood. **2.** very pale: *a bloodless face.* **3.** accomplished without violence or killing: *a bloodless coup.* **4.**

spiritless; without vigor or zest. **5.** without emotion or feeling. —**blood′less•ly,** *adv.* —**blood′less•ness,** *n.*

Blood′less Revolu′tion, *n.* ENGLISH REVOLUTION.

blood•let•ting (blud′let′ing), *n.* **1.** the act of letting blood by opening a vein; phlebotomy. **2.** BLOODSHED. **3.** severe reduction, as in personnel or appropriations. —**blood′let′ter,** *n.*

blood•line (blud′līn′), *n.* **1.** (usu. of animals) the line of descent; pedigree; strain. **2.** ancestry; family.

blood•mo•bile (blud′mə bēl′), *n.* a small truck with medical equipment for receiving blood donations.

blood′ mon′ey, *n.* **1.** a fee paid to a hired murderer. **2.** compensation paid to the next of kin of a slain person by the slayer or the slayer's relatives. **3.** money obtained ruthlessly and at a cost of suffering to others.

blood′ plas′ma, *n.* the liquid portion of vertebrate blood.

blood′ plate′let, *n.* any of the minute, nonnucleated cellular elements in mammalian blood essential for coagulation.

blood′ poi′soning, *n.* invasion of the blood by toxic matter or microorganisms, characterized by chills, sweating, fever, and prostration; toxemia; septicemia; pyemia.

blood′ pres′sure, *n.* the pressure of the blood against the inner walls of the blood vessels, esp. of the arteries during different phases of contraction of the heart. Compare DIASTOLE, SYSTOLE.

blood′ pud′ding, *n.* BLOOD SAUSAGE.

blood′ rela′tion, *n.* a person related by birth rather than by marriage. Also called **blood′ rel′ative.**

blood•root (blud′ro͞ot′, -ro͝ot′), *n.* a North American plant, *Sanguinaria canadensis,* of the poppy family, having a red root and root sap and a solitary white flower.

blood′ sau′sage, *n.* a very dark sausage made with pig's blood, diced pork fat, and chopped onions, usu. stuffed in a casing.

blood•shed (blud′shed′), *n.* **1.** destruction of life; slaughter. **2.** the shedding of blood, as by injury or wound.

blood•shot (blud′shot′), *adj.* (of the eyes) red because of dilated blood vessels.

blood′ sport′, *n.* any sport involving killing or the shedding of blood, as bullfighting, cockfighting, or hunting.

blood•stone (blud′stōn′), *n.* a greenish variety of chalcedony spotted with red jasper; heliotrope.

blood•stream (blud′strēm′), *n.* the blood flowing through the circulatory system.

blood•suck•er (blud′suk′ər), *n.* **1.** any animal that sucks blood, esp. a leech. **2.** an extortioner or usurer. —**blood′suck′ing,** *adj.*

blood′ sug′ar, *n.* **1.** glucose in the blood. **2.** the quantity or percentage of glucose in the blood.

blood′ test′, *n.* a test of blood sample, as to determine blood group, presence of infection or other pathology, or parentage.

blood•thirst•y (blud′thûr′stē), *adj.* **1.** eager to shed blood; murderous: *a bloodthirsty criminal.* **2.** indicating or marked by a desire for bloodshed or violence: *the bloodthirsty cries of the enraged mob.* —**blood′thirst′i•ly,** *adv.* —**blood′thirst′i•ness,** *n.*

blood′ typ′ing, *n.* the process of classifying blood into blood groups through laboratory tests for particular antigens on the surface of red blood cells.

blood′ ves′sel, *n.* any channel through which the blood normally circulates; an artery, vein, or capillary.

blood•worm (blud′wûrm′), *n.* **1.** any of several small red annelid worms, esp. various earthworms. **2.** the freshwater larva of midges.

blood•wort (blud′wûrt′, -wôrt′), *n.* any of various plants having red roots, markings, or juices, as the redroot or bloodroot.

blood•y (blud′ē), *adj.*, **blood•i•er, blood•i•est,** *v.*, **blood•ied, blood•y•ing.** —*adj.* **1.** stained or covered with blood. **2.** bleeding: *a bloody nose.* **3.** characterized by bloodshed: *bloody battles.* **4.** inclined to bloodshed; bloodthirsty. **5.** containing or composed of blood. —*v.t.* **6.** to stain or smear with blood. **7.** to cause to bleed, as by a blow or accident.

bloom[1] (blo͞om), *n.* **1.** the flower of a plant. **2.** flowers collectively, as of a plant or tree. **3.** the state of flowering: *lilacs in bloom.* **4.** a flourishing, healthy condition; the time of greatest beauty, vigor, or freshness: *the bloom of youth.* **5.** a glowing or glossiness indicative of health, vigor, or youth, esp. a flush on the cheek. **6.** a whitish, powdery coating on the surface of certain fruits, as the grape, or some leaves. **7.** any similar surface coating or appearance, as on newly minted coins or on rocks or minerals. **8.** a clouded or dull area on a varnished or lacquered surface. **9.** the sudden development of conspicuous masses of organisms, as algae on the surface of a lake. —*v.i.* **10.** to produce or yield blossoms. **11.** to flourish or thrive. **12.** to be in or achieve a state of healthful beauty and vigor. **13.** to glow with warmth or with a warm color. —*v.t.* **14.** to cause to yield blossoms. **15.** to make bloom or give bloom to; cause to flourish or glow.

bloom[2] (blo͞om), *n.* **1.** a piece of steel, square or slightly oblong in section, reduced from an ingot to dimensions suitable for further rolling. **2.** a large lump of iron and slag, of pasty consistency when hot, hammered into wrought iron.

bloo•mer[1] (blo͞o′mər), *n.* **1.** a costume for women, introduced about 1850, consisting of a short skirt and loose trousers gathered and buttoned at the ankle. **2.** **bloomers,** (*used with a pl. v.*) **a.** loose trousers gathered at the knee, formerly worn by women for gymnastics or sports. **b.** women's underpants of similar, but less bulky, design. **c.** the trousers of a bloomer costume. —*adj.* **3.** (of a woman's garment) having full-cut legs gathered at the bottom edge: *bloomer shorts.* [after A. *Bloomer,* U.S. social reformer and advocate of the costume]

bloom•er[2] (blo͞o′mər), *n.* **1.** a plant that blooms: *a night bloomer.* **2.** a person who develops skills to the fullest capacity.

bloom•er[3] (blo͞o′mər), *n.* a foolish mistake; blunder.

Bloo•mer (blo͞o′mər), *n.* **Amelia Jenks,** 1818–94, U.S. social reformer and women's-rights leader.

bloop (blo͞op), *v.t.* **1.** *Baseball.* to hit (a pitched ball) as a blooper. **2.** to ruin; botch. —*n.* **3.** BLOOPER (def. 2).

bloop•er (blo͞o′pər), *n.* **1.** an embarrassing mistake, as something said on a radio or television broadcast. **2.** *Baseball.* **a.** a fly ball that carries just beyond the infield. **b.** a pitched ball with backspin, describing a high arc in flight.

blos•som (blos′əm), *n.* **1.** the flower of a plant, esp. of one producing an edible fruit. **2.** the state of flowering: *cherry trees in blossom.* —*v.i.* **3.** to produce or yield blossoms. **4.** to open up; bloom. **5.** to develop successfully; flourish (often fol. by *into* or *out*). **6.** to appear; become manifest.

blot[1] (blot), *n.*, *v.*, **blot•ted, blot•ting.** —*n.* **1.** a spot or stain, esp. of ink or chemicals on paper. **2.** a blemish on a person's character or reputation. —*v.t.* **3.** to spot, stain, or soil; sully. **4.** to dry with absorbent paper or the like: *to blot the wet pane.* **5.** to remove with absorbent paper or the like. —*v.i.* **6.** to make a blot; spread ink, dye, etc., in a stain. **7.** to become blotted or stained. **8.** to transfer components of a mixture to a chemically treated paper for analysis. **9.** **blot out, a.** to make indistinguishable; obscure. **b.** to destroy completely; obliterate; wipe out.

blot[2] (blot), *n.* an exposed backgammon piece liable to be taken or forfeited.

blotch (bloch), *n.* **1.** a large, irregular spot or blot; stain. **2.** a discolored spot on the skin; blemish. **3.** any of several plant diseases caused by fungi and characterized by cankers and lesions. —*v.t.* **4.** to mark with blotches. —**blotch•y,** *adj.*, **blotch•i•er, blotch•i•est.** —**blotch′i•ly,** *adv.*

blot•ter (blot′ər), *n.* **1.** a piece of blotting paper used to absorb ink, to protect a desk top, etc. **2.** a book in which transactions or events are recorded as they occur: *a police blotter.*

blot′ting pa′per, *n.* a soft, absorbent paper, used esp. to dry ink.

blouse (blous, blouz), *n.*, *v.*, **bloused, blous•ing.** —*n.* **1.** a garment, usu. for women and children, covering the body from the neck or shoulders to the waistline, with or without a collar and sleeves; waist. **2.** a single-breasted, semifitted military jacket. **3.** a loose outer garment, reaching to the hip or thigh or below the knee, and sometimes belted. —*v.i.* **4.** to puff out in a drooping fullness, as a blouse above a fitted waistband. —*v.t.* **5.** to dispose (a garment or its material) in loose folds.

blous•on (blou′son, -zon, blo͞o zōn′, blo͞o′zon), *n.* **1.** a woman's garment with a drawstring, belt, or similar closing at or below the waist that makes the fabric above it blouse. —*adj.* **2.** having or suggesting the style of this garment.

blow[1] (blō), *n.* **1.** a sudden, hard stroke with a hand, fist, or weapon. **2.** a sudden shock, calamity, reversal, etc. **3.** a sudden attack or drastic action: *The army struck a blow to the south.* —***Idiom.*** **4.** **come to blows,** to begin to fight, esp. physically.

blow[2] (blō), *v.*, **blew, blown** or, for 21, **blowed, blow•ing,** *n.* —*v.i.* **1.** (of the wind or air) to be in motion. **2.** to move along, carried by or as if by the wind. **3.** to produce or emit a current of air. **4.** (of a horn, trumpet, etc.) to give out sound. **5.** to make a blowing sound; whistle: *The sirens blew at noon.* **6.** (of horses) to breathe hard or quickly; pant. **7.** to boast; brag. **8.** (of a whale) to spout. **9.** (of a fuse, light bulb, tire, etc.) to stop functioning or be destroyed, as by bursting, exploding, or melting (often fol. by *out*). **10.** *Slang.* to leave; depart. —*v.t.* **11.** to drive by means of a current of air: *A breeze blew dust into my eyes.* **12.** to clear or empty by forcing air through: *Try blowing your nose.* **13.** to shape (glass, smoke, etc.) with a current of air. **14.** to cause to sound, as by a current of air: *to blow a horn.* **15.** to cause to explode: *A mine blew the ship to bits.* **16.** to cause or undergo the bursting, melting, burning, or disfunctioning of, as by strain or overload (often fol. by *out*): *to blow a tire.* **17.** to cause to fall by a current of air; topple or demolish (usu. fol. by *down, over,* etc.): *A windstorm blew down the tent.* **18.** to spread: *Growing panic blew the rumor about.* **19.** *Informal.* **a.** to squander; spend quickly or extravagantly: *I blew $100 on dinner.* **b.** to treat; bear the expense for: *I'll blow you to a movie.* **20.** *Informal.* **a.** to mishandle, ruin, or botch: *You blew your last chance.* **b.** to waste or lose: *The team blew the lead in the third quarter.* **21.** to damn: *Blow the cost! Well, I'll be blowed!* **22.** to put (a horse) out of breath by fatigue. **23.** *Slang.* to depart from: *to blow town.* **24.** **blow away, a.** to kill, esp. by gunfire. **b.** to defeat decisively; trounce. **c.** to overwhelm with emotion, astonishment, etc. **25.** **blow in,** to arrive at a place, esp. unexpectedly. **26.** **blow out, a.** to extinguish or become extinguished. **b.** to lose or cause to lose force or to cease: *The storm has blown itself out.* **c.** (of an oil or gas well) to lose oil or gas uncontrollably. **27.** **blow over, a.** to pass away; subside: *The storm blew over in minutes.* **b.** to be forgotten: *The scandal will blow over eventually.* **28.** **blow up, a.** to explode or cause to explode. **b.** to exaggerate; enlarge. **c.** to lose one's temper. **d.** to fill with air or gas; inflate: *to blow up a balloon.* **e.** to distend or become distended; swell. **f.** to make an enlarged reproduction of (a photograph). **g.** to come into being: *A storm suddenly blew up.* —*n.* **29.** a blast of air or wind. **30.** a violent windstorm, gale, hurricane, or the like. **31.** an act of producing a blast of air, as in playing a wind instrument. **—Idiom. 32. blow hot and cold,** to favor and then reject something by turns; vacillate. **33. blow off steam,** to reduce or release tension, as by loud talking. **34. blow one's cool,** to lose one's composure. **35. blow one's cover,** to divulge one's secret identity, esp. inadvertently. **36. blow one's mind, a.** to overwhelm one, as with excitement, pleasure, or dismay. **b.** to cause one to suffer extreme hallucinatory shifts in perception, as through the use of drugs. **37. blow one's stack** or **top,** to become enraged; lose one's temper. **38. blow the lid off,** to expose (scandal or illegal actions) to public view.

blow³ (blō), *n.* **1.** a display of blossoms. **2.** the state of blossoming: *tulips in full blow.*

blow'-by-blow', *adj.* precisely detailed; describing every minute detail and step: *a blow-by-blow account of a tennis match.*

blow'-dry'er, *n.* a small, usu. hand-held electrical appliance that emits a flow of heated air, used to dry and often style the hair.

blow•fish (blō'fish'), *n., pl.* (*esp. collectively*) **-fish,** (*esp. for kinds or species*) **-fish•es.** PUFFER (def. 2).

blow'-hard', *n.* a very boastful and talkative person.

blow•hole (blō'hōl'), *n.* **1.** either of two nostrils or spiracles, or a single one, at the top of the head in whales and dolphins, through which they breathe. **2.** a hole in the ice to which whales or seals come to breathe. **3.** a defect in a metal casting caused by the escape of gas.

blown¹ (blōn), *adj.* **1.** inflated; swollen. **2.** out of breath. **3.** formed by blowing: *blown glass.*

blown² (blōn), *adj.* fully expanded or opened, as a flower.

blow•off (blō'ôf', -of'), *n.* **1.** a current of escaping surplus steam, water, etc. **2.** a device that permits and channels such a current. **3.** a temporary, sudden surge, as in prices.

blow•out (blō'out'), *n.* **1.** a sudden bursting or rupture of an automobile tire. **2.** a sudden or violent escape of air, steam, or liquid, esp. an uncontrollable escape of oil, gas, or water from a well. **3.** FLAME-OUT. **4.** a lavish party or entertainment.

blow•pipe (blō'pīp'), *n.* **1.** a tube through which a stream of air or gas is forced into a flame to concentrate and increase its heating action. **2.** a long metal pipe used to gather and blow molten glass.

blow•torch (blō'tôrch'), *n.* **1.** a small portable apparatus that gives an extremely hot gasoline flame intensified by a blast, used esp. in metalworking. **—v.t. 2.** to weld, burn, or ignite with or as if with a blowtorch.

blow•up (blō'up'), *n.* **1.** an explosion. **2.** a violent argument, outburst of temper, or the like, esp. one resulting in estrangement. **3.** Also, **blow'-up'.** an enlargement of a photograph.

blowz•y or **blows•y** (blou'zē), *adj.,* **blowz•i•er** or **blows•i•er, blowz•i•est** or **blows•i•est. 1.** having a coarse, ruddy complexion. **2.** disheveled in appearance; unkempt. **—blowz'i•ly,** *adv.*

BLT, *n., pl.* **BLTs, BLT's.** a bacon, lettuce, and tomato sandwich.

blub•ber (blub'ər), *n.* **1.** the layer of fat below the skin of the whale or other large marine mammal. **2.** excess body fat. **3.** an act of noisy, unrestrained weeping. **—v.i. 4.** to weep noisily and without restraint. **—v.t. 5.** to utter, esp. incoherently, while weeping. **6.** to contort or disfigure (the features) with weeping. **—adj. 7.** fatty or swollen; puffed out: *blubber-faced.* **—blub'ber•er,** *n.*

blu•cher (blōō'kər, -chər), *n.* a shoe having the vamp and tongue made of one piece and overlapped by the quarters, which lace across the instep.

bludg•eon (bluj'ən), *n.* **1.** a short, heavy club with one end weighted or thicker and heavier than the other. **—v.t. 2.** to strike or knock down with a bludgeon. **3.** to force into something; coerce.

blue (blōō), *n., adj.,* **blu•er, blu•est,** *v.,* **blued, blu•ing** or **blue•ing. —n. 1.** the pure color of a clear sky; the primary color between green and violet in the visible spectrum, an effect of light with a wavelength between 450 and 500 nm. **2.** BLUING. **3.** something having a blue color. **4.** a person wearing blue or belonging to a group identified by some blue symbol. **5.** (*often cap.*) a member of the Union army in the American Civil War, or the army itself. Compare GRAY¹ (def. 11). **6.** any of several blue-winged butterflies of the family Lycaenidae. **7. the blue, a.** the sky. **b.** the sea. **c.** the remote distance. **—adj. 8.** of the color blue. **9.** (of the skin) discolored by cold, contusion, fear, or vascular collapse. **10.** depressed in spirits; dejected; melancholy. **11.** holding or offering little hope; dismal; bleak: *a blue outlook.* **12.** adhering to or stemming from rigid moral or religious observance; puritanical. **13.** indecent; suggestive or obscene; risqué: *a blue joke.* **14.** marked by blasphemy: *The air was blue with oaths.* **—v.t. 15.** to make blue; dye a blue color. **16.** to tinge with bluing. **—v.i. 17.** to become or turn blue. **—Idiom. 18. blue in the face,** at an extreme point of frustration, irritation, discouragement, etc.: *to argue till one is blue in the face.* **19. out of the blue,** suddenly and unexpectedly. **—blue'ly,** *adv.* **—blue'ness,** *n.*

blue' ba'by, *n.* an infant born with cyanosis resulting from a congenital heart or lung defect.

blue•bell (blōō'bel'), *n.* **1.** any of numerous plants of the bellflower family, having blue, bell-shaped flowers, as the harebell. **2.** an Old World plant, *Endymion nonscriptus,* of the lily family, having blue, bell-shaped flowers. **3.** any of various other plants having blue flowers, as those belonging to the genus *Mertensia,* of the borage family.

blue•ber•ry (blōō'ber'ē, -bə rē), *n., pl.* **-ries. 1.** the edible, usu. bluish berry of various shrubs belonging to the genus *Vaccinium,* of the heath family. **2.** any of these shrubs.

blue•bill (blōō'bil'), *n.* any of various North American ducks having blue bills, as the scaup.

blue•bird (blōō'bûrd'), *n.* any of several North American songbirds of the genus *Sialia,* of the thrush family, the male of which is predominantly or entirely blue.

blue blood (blōō' blud' *for 1;* blōō' blud' *for 2*), *n.* **1.** an aristocrat, noble, or member of a socially prominent family. **2.** aristocratic or noble lineage. **—blue'-blood'ed,** *adj.*

blue•bon•net (blōō'bon'it), *n.* **1.** CORNFLOWER (def. 1). **2.** a blue-flowered lupine, esp. *Lupinus subcarnosus,* having spikes of light blue flowers with a white or yellow spot: the state flower of Texas. **3.** a broad, flat cap of blue wool, formerly worn in Scotland. **4.** a Scottish soldier who wore such a cap. **5.** any Scot. Also called **blue•cap** (blōō'-kap').

blue' book' or **blue'book',** *n.* **1.** a register or directory, esp. of socially prominent persons. **2.** a blank book for taking college examinations, usu. with a blue cover. **3.** a manual listing the current market value of any of various consumer items, as appliances.

blue' cat'fish, *n.* a large freshwater catfish, *Ictalurus furcatus,* popular as a food fish in the Mississippi River valley. Also called **blue' cat'.**

blue' cheese', *n.* any of various usu. rich, strong-flavored cheeses streaked with blue or greenish veins of mold.

blue' chip', *n.* **1.** a blue-colored chip of high value, used esp. in poker. **2.** a common stock issued by a major company with a reputation for stability and financial strength and a good record of dividend payments: regarded as a low-risk investment. **3.** a secure and valuable item or property held in reserve. **—blue'-chip',** *adj.*

blue•coat (blōō'kōt'), *n.* **1.** a person who wears a blue coat or uniform. **2.** a police officer.

blue'-col'lar, *adj.* pertaining to or designating factory workers, manual laborers, or the like, who usu. wear work clothes and earn weekly wages. Compare WHITE-COLLAR.

blue' crab', *n.* an edible crab, *Callinectes sapidus,* of the North American Atlantic coast, having a greenish shell and blue legs.

Blue' Cross' and Blue' Shield', *Trademark.* a nonprofit organization that offers its members health insurance covering hospitalization, surgical, and medical expenses.

blue'-eyed' grass', *n.* any of numerous plants belonging to the genus *Sisyrinchium,* of the iris family, having grasslike leaves and small, usu. blue flowers.

blue•fin tu'na (blōō'fin'), *n.* a large tuna, *Thunnus thynnus,* common in temperate seas.

blue•fish (blōō'fish'), *n., pl.* (*esp. collectively*) **-fish,** (*esp. for kinds or species*) **-fish•es. 1.** a blue or greenish food and game fish, *Pomatomus saltatrix,* of the Atlantic and Indian oceans, that travels in schools and is a voracious predator. **2.** any of various other bluish fishes.

blue' flag', *n.* any of several North American irises having blue flowers, esp. *Iris versicolor,* the state flower of Tennessee.

blue' flu', *n.* organized absenteeism among police officers or firefighters, esp. to circumvent laws prohibiting a formal strike.

blue' fox', *n.* **1.** a permanent bluish gray color phase of the arctic fox, *Alopex lagopus.* **2.** the arctic fox in summer pelage. **3.** the blue fur of this animal or a fur dyed to imitate it.

blue•gill (blōō'gil'), *n.* a bluish freshwater sunfish, *Lepomis macrochirus,* of the Mississippi River valley.

blue•grass (blōō'gras', -gräs'), *n.* **1.** any grass of the genus *Poa,* as the Kentucky bluegrass, *P. pratensis,* having dense tufts of bluish green blades and creeping rhizomes. **2.** country music, polyphonic in character, played on unamplified stringed instruments, esp. the solo banjo.

blue'-green' al'gae, *n.pl.* any of various groups of prokaryotic microorganisms of the phylum Cyanophyta, containing chlorophyll and a blue pigment, occurring singly or in colonies in diverse habitats.

blue' gum', *n.* a large, extensively planted eucalyptus, *Eucalyptus globulus.*

blue•head (blōō'hed'), *n.* a wrasse, *Thalassoma bifasciatum,* of Atlantic seas, the adult male of which has a brilliant blue head.

blue•jack (blōō'jak'), *n.* a small oak, *Quercus incana,* of the southern U.S., having crooked branches and blue-green leaves. Also called **blue'jack oak'.**

blue' jay', *n.* a common crested jay, *Cyanocitta cristata,* of E North America, having a bright blue back and a gray breast.

blue' jeans', *n.* (*used with a pl. v.*) close-fitting trousers of blue denim, often reinforced with rivets, orig. worn as work pants.

blue' law', *n.* **1.** any law that forbids certain practices, as doing business, drinking, or dancing, on Sunday. **2.** any of the puritanical laws of colonial New England regulating personal conduct.

blue' line', *n.* either of two parallel lines that extend the width of an ice-hockey rink and divide it into three zones.

blue' mold', *n.* any fungus of the genus *Penicillium* forming a bluish green, furry coating on foodstuffs inoculated by its spores.

blue•nose (blōō'nōz'), *n.* a puritanical person; prude.

blue' note', *n.* a lowered third, seventh, or fifth degree of a musical major scale.

blue'-pen'cil, *v.t.,* **-ciled, -cil•ing** or (*esp. Brit.*) **-cilled, -cil•ling.** to alter, delete, or edit with or as if with a blue pencil.

blue' pe'ter, *n.* a blue flag with a white square in the center, designating the letter *P* in the International Code of Signals, flown by a vessel in port to indicate its imminent departure.

blue′ plate′ spe′cial, *n.* a specially priced main course on a restaurant menu, typically of meat, potatoes, and a vegetable.

blue′ point′, *n.* a Siamese cat having a light-colored body and darker, bluish gray points.

blue•point (blōō′point′), *n.* an edible Atlantic oyster, *Crassotrea virginica,* esp. one from off Blue Point, Long Island.

blue•print (blōō′print′), *n.* **1.** a photographic print made by a process that produces white lines on a blue background, used chiefly in copying architectural and mechanical drawings. **2.** a detailed outline or plan of action: *a blueprint for success.* **3.** a model; prototype. —*v.t.* **4.** to make a blueprint of. —**blue′print′er,** *n.*

blue′ rib′bon, *n.* **1.** a blue ribbon given as the first prize in a contest. **2.** the highest award or distinction. **3.** a blue ribbon worn as a badge of honor by members of the British Order of the Garter.

blue′-rib′bon, *adj.* of superior or unmatched quality or eminence; specially selected: *a collection of blue-ribbon recipes.*

blue′-rib′bon pane′l, *n.* a specially qualified jury or committee chosen to examine a complex case or issue.

blues (blōōz), *n.* **1. the blues,** (*used with a pl. v.*) depressed spirits; melancholy. **2.** (*used with a sing. v.*) a song of woe and yearning marked by persistent blue notes and structured in a 12-bar chorus with three-line stanzas of which the third line typically repeats the first. **3.** any of various blue military uniforms worn by members of the U.S. armed services. **4.** a blue work uniform.

blue′ shark′, *n.* a slender shark, *Prionace glauca,* that is deep blue above and pure white below.

blue′-sky′, *adj.* fanciful; impractical: *blue-sky ideas.*

blue′ spruce′, *n.* a spruce, *Picea pungens,* of W North America, having bluish green leaves, grown as an ornamental.

blue•stem (blōō′stem′), *n.* any of several prairie grasses of the genus *Andropogon,* having bluish leaf sheaths, grown for forage.

blue•stone (blōō′stōn′), *n.* a bluish, argillaceous sandstone used for building purposes, flagging, etc.

blue′ streak′, *n.* **1.** something that moves along very quickly. —*Idiom.* **2. talk a blue streak,** to talk rapidly and continuously.

blu•et (blōō′it), *n.* **1.** Usu., **bluets.** a low-growing North American plant, *Houstonia caerula,* of the madder family, with small four-petaled blue flowers. **2.** any of various other plants having blue flowers.

blue•weed (blōō′wēd′), *n.* a bristly European weed, *Echium vulgare,* of the borage family, having large blue flowers: naturalized in E North America.

blue′ whale′, *n.* a whale, *Balaenoptera musculus,* having furrowed, slate-blue skin with the underparts mottled yellow from a coating of microorganisms: at up to 100 ft. (30.5 m) long, the largest mammal ever known.

bluff¹ (bluf), *adj.* **1.** good-naturedly direct, blunt, or frank; heartily outspoken. **2.** presenting a bold and nearly perpendicular front: *a bluff, precipitous headland.* —*n.* **3.** a cliff, headland, or hill with a broad, steep face. —**bluff′ness,** *n.*

bluff² (bluf), *v.t.* **1.** to mislead or intimidate by a display of strength, self-confidence, or the like. **2.** to achieve by bluffing: *to bluff one's way into a job.* **3.** to deceive (an opponent in poker) by betting heavily on a weak hand. —*v.i.* **4.** to put on a bold or self-confident front in order to mislead. —*n.* **5.** an act or instance of bluffing. **6.** a person who bluffs; bluffer. —*Idiom.* **7. call someone's bluff,** to challenge someone to carry out a threat. —**bluff′er,** *n.*

blu•ing or **blue•ing** (blōō′ing), *n.* a substance, as indigo, used to whiten clothes or give them a bluish tinge.

blu•ish or **blue•ish** (blōō′ish), *adj.* rather or slightly blue.

blun•der (blun′dər), *n.* **1.** a gross, stupid, or careless mistake. —*v.i.* **2.** to move or act clumsily or stupidly: *We blundered into the wrong room.* **3.** to make a mistake, esp. through carelessness, stupidity, or confusion. —*v.t.* **4.** to bungle; botch. **5.** to utter thoughtlessly; blurt out. —**blun′der•er,** *n.* —**blun′der•ing•ly,** *adv.*

blun•der•buss (blun′dər bus′), *n.* **1.** a short musket used to scatter shot at close range. **2.** an insensitive, blundering person.

blunt (blunt), *adj.* **1.** having an obtuse, thick, or dull edge or point: *a blunt pencil.* **2.** abrupt and direct in address or manner; frank. **3.** slow in perception or understanding; obtuse. —*v.t.* **4.** to make blunt; dull. **5.** to weaken or impair the force, keenness, or susceptibility of: *Wine in excess can blunt the senses.* —*v.i.* **6.** to become blunt. —*n.* **7.** something blunt, as a small-game arrow, a short sewing needle, or a short, thick cigar. —**blunt′ly,** *adv.* —**blunt′ness,** *n.*

blur (blûr), *v.,* **blurred, blur•ring.** —*v.t.* **1.** to obscure or make indistinct, as by smearing or staining: *The fog blurred the outline of the car.* **2.** to obscure or sully by smearing or applying a smeary substance. **3.** to dull the perception or susceptibility of: *vision blurred by tears.* —*v.i.* **4.** to become indistinct. **5.** to make blurs. —*n.* **6.** a smudge or smear that obscures: *a blur of smoke.* **7.** a blurred condition; indistinctness. **8.** something seen or remembered indistinctly: *The ship was a blur on the horizon.* —**blur′ry,** *adj.,* **-ri•er, -ri•est.**

blurb (blûrb), *n.* **1.** a brief advertisement or notice, as on a book jacket, esp. one full of praise. —*v.t.* **2.** to advertise or praise in the manner of a blurb. —**blurb′ist,** *n.*

blurt (blûrt), *v.t.* to utter suddenly and impulsively or inadvertently (usu. fol. by *out*).

blush (blush), *v.i.* **1.** to redden, as from embarrassment. **2.** to feel shame or embarrassment (often fol. by *at* or *for*). **3.** (of the sky, flowers, etc.) to become rosy. **4.** (of new house paint or lacquer) to become cloudy or dull, esp. through moisture. —*v.t.* **5.** to make red; flush. **6.** to make known by a blush. —*n.* **7.** a reddening, as of the face. **8.** a rosy or pinkish tinge. **9.** BLUSHER (def. 2). —*Idiom.* **10. at first blush,** at first glance or consideration.

blush•er (blush′ər), *n.* **1.** a person who blushes, esp. readily. **2.** a cosmetic similar to rouge. **3.** an edible mushroom, *Amanita rubescens,* that turns from yellow to red when touched.

blush′ wine′, *n.* a pale pink wine resembling white wine in taste, made from red grapes by removing the skins from the must before fermentation is completed.

blus•ter (blus′tar), *v.i.* **1.** to roar and be tumultuous, as wind. **2.** to be loud, noisy, or swaggering; utter loud, empty threats or protests. —*v.t.* **3.** to force or accomplish by blustering: *He blustered his way through the crowd.* —*n.* **4.** boisterous noise and violence: *the bluster of a storm at sea.* **5.** noisy, empty threats or protests. —**blus′ter•er,** *n.* —**blus′ter•y,** *adj.*

blvd., boulevard.

B lymphocyte or **B-lymphocyte,** *n.* B CELL.

BM, 1. bench mark. **2.** black male. **3.** *Informal.* bowel movement.

B.M., 1. Bachelor of Medicine. **2.** Bachelor of Music.

B.M.E., 1. Bachelor of Mechanical Engineering. **2.** Bachelor of Mining Engineering. **3.** Bachelor of Music Education.

B movie, *n.* B PICTURE.

B.Mus., Bachelor of Music.

B.N., Bachelor of Nursing.

bo•a (bō′ə), *n., pl.* **bo•as. 1.** any nonvenomous, chiefly tropical constrictor of the family Boidae, esp. of the New World subfamily Boinae. **2.** a scarf or stole, usu. of feathers or fur.

bo′a constric′tor, *n.* a snake, *Constrictor constrictor,* of tropical America, noted for its large size and its ability to suffocate a prey by coiling around it.

Bo•a•ner•ges (bō′ə nûr′jēz), *n.* a surname given by Jesus to James and John. Mark 3:17.

boar (bōr, bôr), *n.* **1.** the uncastrated male swine. **2.** WILD BOAR.

board (bôrd, bōrd), *n.* **1.** a long rectangular piece of wood sawed thin. **2.** a flat slab of wood or other hard material for some specific purpose: *a cutting board; a diving board.* **3.** a sheet of wood, cardboard, etc., often with markings, on which a game is played: *a Scrabble board.* **4. boards, a.** the stage of a theater. **b.** the wooden fence surrounding the playing area of an ice-hockey rink. **c.** a racing course made of wood, used esp. in track meets held indoors. **5.** stiff cardboard or other material covered with paper, cloth, or the like to form the covers for a book. **6.** composition material made in large sheets, as plasterboard or corkboard. **7.** a table, esp. to serve food on. **8.** an official group of persons who direct or supervise some activity: *a board of directors.* **9.** daily meals, esp. as provided for pay: *room and board.* **10. a.** the side of a ship. **b.** one tack of the course of a ship beating to windward. **11.** a flat surface, as an object of rectangular shape, on which something is posted: *a bulletin board.* **12.** SURFBOARD. **13. a.** a piece of fiberglass or other material upon which an array of computer chips is mounted. **b.** CIRCUIT BOARD (def. 1). **14.** a switchboard. —*v.t.* **15.** to cover or close with boards (often fol. by *up* or *over*): *to board up a house.* **16.** to furnish with meals, or with meals and lodging, esp. for pay. **17.** to go on board of (a ship, plane, train, etc.). **18.** to allow on board: *to board passengers.* **19.** to come up alongside (a ship), as to attack or to go on board. —*v.i.* **20.** to take one's meals or receive food and lodging at a fixed price. —*Idiom.* **21. across the board, a.** (of a bet) so as to cover the first, second, or third place finish in a race. **b.** so as to apply to all equally or proportionately: *to raise salaries across the board.* **22. go by the board,** to be destroyed, wasted, or forgotten. **23. on board, a.** on or in a ship, plane, or other vehicle. **b.** *Baseball.* on base. **24. tread the boards,** to appear on the stage, esp. as a professional performer. —**board′a•ble,** *adj.* —**board′like′,** *adj.*

board•er (bôr′dər, bōr′-), *n.* a person, esp. a lodger, who is supplied with regular meals.

board′ foot′, *n.* the basic unit of board measure, equal to the cubic contents of a piece of lumber one foot square and one inch thick. *Abbr.:* bd. ft.

board′ game′, *n.* any game played on a board, esp. one in which pieces are moved, as chess or checkers.

board•ing (bôr′ding, bōr′-), *n.* **1.** wooden boards collectively. **2.** a structure of boards, as in a fence. **3.** the act of a person who boards a ship, train, airplane, or the like.

board′ing•house′ or **board′ing house′,** *n., pl.* **-hous•es** (-hou′ziz). a house at which meals, or meals and lodging, may be obtained for payment.

board′ing pass′, *n.* a pass that authorizes a passenger to board an aircraft.

board′ing ramp′, *n.* a movable staircase providing passengers and crew with access to the cabin of an aircraft.

board′ing school′, *n.* a school at which the pupils receive meals and lodging (disting. from *day school*).

board′ of educa′tion, *n.* an appointive or elective body that directs and administers chiefly the primary and secondary public schools in a town, city, county, or state.

board′ of trade′, *n.* an association of businesspeople.

board′ of trustees′, *n.* an appointed or elective board that supervises the affairs of a public or private organization.

board′room′ or **board′ room′,** *n.* a room set aside for meetings of a board, esp. of a corporation.

board·sail·ing (bôrd′sā′ling, bōrd′-), *n.* the sport of sailing a boat that has no cockpit, as in windsurfing.

board·walk (bôrd′wôk′, bōrd′-), *n.* a promenade made of wooden boards, usu. along a beach or shore.

Bo·as (bō′az), *n.* **Franz** (fränts), 1858–1942, U.S. anthropologist, born in Germany.

boast[1] (bōst), *v.i.* **1.** to speak with exaggeration and excessive pride, esp. about oneself; brag. —*v.t.* **2.** to speak of with excessive pride or vanity. **3.** to be proud in the possession of: *The town boasts two new schools.* —*n.* **4.** a thing boasted of; a cause for pride. **5.** exaggerated speech; bragging: *empty boasts and threats.* —**boast′er,** *n.* —**boast′ing·ly,** *adv.*

boast[2] (bōst), *v.t.* to dress or shape (stone) roughly.

boast·ful (bōst′fəl), *adj.* given to or characterized by boasting. —**boast′ful·ly,** *adv.* —**boast′ful·ness,** *n.*

boat (bōt), *n.* **1.** a vessel for transport by water, propelled by rowing, sails, or a motor. **2.** a small ship, generally for specialized use: *a fishing boat.* **3.** a boat-shaped serving dish: *a gravy boat.* —*v.i.* **4.** to go in a boat. —*v.t.* **5.** to transport or place in a boat. **—*Idiom.* 6. in the same boat,** in similar difficult circumstances.

boat·el (bō tel′), *n.* a waterside hotel with dock space for persons who travel by boat.

boat·er (bō′tər), *n.* **1.** a person who boats. **2.** a stiff straw hat with a shallow, flat-topped crown, ribbon band, and straight brim.

boat′ hook′, *n.* a hook mounted on a pole, used to maneuver boats, pick up a mooring, etc.

boat·house (bōt′hous′), *n., pl.* **-hous·es** (-hou′ziz). a building or shed, usu. built partly over water, for sheltering boats.

boat·ing (bō′ting), *n.* **1.** the use of boats, esp. for pleasure. —*adj.* **2.** of or pertaining to boats: *boating clothes.*

boat·lift (bōt′lift′), *n.* **1.** the act or process of transporting persons or cargo by ships or boats, esp. in an emergency. —*v.t.* **2.** to transport by boatlift.

boat′ nail′, *n.* a nail with a convex head and a chisel point.

boat′ peo′ple, *n.pl.* refugees who have fled a country by boat, usu. without sufficient resources.

boat·swain or **bo′s'n** or **bo·sun** (bō′sən), *n.* a warrant officer on a warship, or a petty officer on a merchant vessel, in charge of rigging, anchors, cables, etc.

Bo·az (bō′az), *n.* husband of Ruth. Ruth 2–4.

bob[1] (bob), *n., v.,* **bobbed, bob·bing.** —*n.* **1.** a short, jerky motion: *a bob of the head.* —*v.t.* **2.** to move quickly down and up: *to bob the head.* **3.** to indicate with such a motion: *to bob a greeting.* —*v.i.* **4.** to make a jerky motion with the head or body. **5.** to move about with jerky, usu. rising and falling motions: *The ball bobbed upon the waves.* **6. bob up,** to appear unexpectedly.

bob[2] (bob), *n., v.,* **bobbed, bob·bing.** —*n.* **1.** a short, caplike haircut. **2.** a docked horse's tail. **3.** a dangling or terminal object, as the weight on a pendulum or a plumb line. **4.** a float for a fishing line. **5.** a bobsled. —*v.t.* **6.** to cut short; dock: *to bob one's hair.* —*v.i.* **7.** to try to snatch floating or dangling objects with the teeth: *to bob for apples.*

bob[3] (bob), *n., v.,* **bobbed, bob·bing.** —*n.* **1.** a polishing wheel of leather, felt, or the like. —*v.t.* **2.** to tap; strike lightly.

bob·bin (bob′in), *n.* a reel, cylinder, or spool upon which yarn or thread is wound.

bob′bin lace′, *n.* lace made by hand with bobbins of thread, the thread being twisted around pins stuck into a pattern placed on a pillow or pad. Also called **pillow lace.**

bob·ble (bob′əl), *n., v.,* **-bled, -bling.** —*n.* **1.** a repeated, jerky movement; bob. **2.** a momentary fumbling or juggling of a batted or thrown baseball. **3.** an error; mistake. **4.** a small ball of fabric, esp. when set in rows and used as a trimming. —*v.t.* **5.** to juggle or fumble (a batted or thrown baseball) momentarily.

Bobb′sey twins′ (bob′zē), *n.pl.* two people who are often together or seem to resemble each other, as in appearance or actions: *We called them the Bobbsey twins, because they always had the same opinions.* [from the central characters in a series of children's books by Laura Lee Hope, pen name of a literary syndicate; some of the books are attributed to U.S. author Lillian C. Garis (1873–1954)]

bob·by (bob′ē), *n., pl.* **-bies.** *Brit.* POLICEMAN. [generic use of *Bobby,* for Sir *Robert* Peel, who set up the Metropolitan Police system of London in 1828]

bob′by pin′, *n.* a flat, springlike metal hairpin having the prongs held close together by tension.

bob·by·socks or **bob·by·sox** (bob′ē soks′), *n.pl.* socks that reach above the ankle and are sometimes folded down to the ankle, esp. as worn by bobbysoxers.

bob′by·sox′er or **bob′by sox′er** (-sok′sər), *n.* an adolescent girl, esp. during the 1940s, following youthful fads.

bob·cat (bob′kat′), *n., pl.* **-cats,** (*esp. collectively*) **-cat.** a North American lynx, *Lynx rufus,* having a brownish coat with black spots. Also called **bay lynx.**

bo·bèche (bō besh′), *n.* a slightly cupped ring placed over the socket of a candleholder to catch the drippings of a candle.

bob·o·link (bob′ə lingk′), *n.* a meadow-dwelling North American songbird, *Dolichonyx oryzivorus,* of the subfamily Icterinae, the male of which is black, white, and buff.

bob·sled (bob′sled′), *n., v.,* **-sled·ded, -sled·ding.** —*n.* **1.** a long sled for two or four riders, equipped with two pairs of runners one behind the other, a brake, and a steering wheel or other steering mechanism that enables the front rider to direct the sled down a steeply banked run or chute. **2.** a sled formed of two short sleds in tandem. —*v.i.* **3.** to ride on a bobsled. —**bob′sled′der,** *n.*

bob·tail (bob′tāl′), *n.* **1.** a short or docked tail. **2.** an animal with such a tail. —*adj.* Also, **bob′tailed′. 3.** having a bobtail. **4.** cut short; abbreviated; curtailed. —*v.t.* **5.** to cut short the tail of; dock.

bob·white (bob′hwīt′, -wīt′), *n.* any of several small New World quails of the genus *Colinus,* esp. *C. virginianus,* having mottled plumage.

bo·cac·cio (bə kä′chō, -chē ō′, bō-), *n., pl.* **-cios.** a large, brown, bigmouthed rockfish, *Sebastes paucispinis,* of California coastal waters.

boc·cie or **boc·ci** or **boc·ce** (boch′ē), *n.* a variety of lawn bowling played usu. on a long, narrow dirt court.

bock′ beer′ (bok), *n.* a strong, dark beer traditionally brewed in the fall for spring consumption. Also called **bock.**

bode[1] (bōd), *v.,* **bod·ed, bod·ing.** —*v.t.* **1.** to be an omen of; portend: *news that bodes evil for humanity.* —*v.i.* **2.** to portend: *The promotion bodes well for his future.*

bode[2] (bōd), *v.* a pt. of BIDE.

bo·de·ga (bō dā′gə), *n., pl.* **-gas. 1.** (esp. among Spanish-speaking Americans) a grocery store. **2.** a wineshop. **3.** a warehouse for storing or aging wine.

bode·ment (bōd′mənt), *n.* **1.** a foreboding; presentiment. **2.** a prophecy or prediction.

bod·ice (bod′is), *n.* **1.** the part of a woman's dress covering the body above the waistline. **2.** a woman's cross-laced, sleeveless outer garment covering the waist and bust.

bod·ied (bod′ēd), *adj.* having a body of a specific kind (used in combination): *a flat-bodied fish; a wide-bodied car.*

bod·i·ly (bod′l ē), *adj.* **1.** of the body. **2.** corporeal or material, as contrasted with spiritual or mental. —*adv.* **3.** as a physical entity: *The tornado picked the car up bodily.* **4.** in person.

bod·kin (bod′kin), *n.* **1.** a small, pointed instrument for making holes in cloth, leather, etc. **2.** a blunt, needlelike instrument for drawing tape, cord, etc., through a loop, hem, or the like. **3.** a long pin used by women to fasten up the hair.

bod·y (bod′ē), *n., pl.* **bod·ies,** *v.,* **bod·ied, bod·y·ing,** *adj.* —*n.* **1. a.** the physical structure and material substance of an animal, plant, or other organism. **b.** the trunk, torso, or main mass of an animal, as opposed to the head, limbs, or appendages. **c.** a corpse; carcass. **2.** the main or central mass of a thing. **3.** the section of a vehicle, usu. in the shape of a box, cylindrical container, or platform, in or on which passengers or the load is carried. **4.** *Print.* the shank of a type, supporting the face. **5.** a geometric figure having the three dimensions of length, breadth, and thickness; a solid. **6.** *Physics.* a mass, esp. one considered as a whole. **7.** the major portion of an army, population, etc. **8.** the principal part of a speech or document. **9.** *Informal.* a person: *What's a body to do?* **10.** *Law.* the physical person of an individual. **11.** a collective group: *the student body.* **12.** substance; consistency or richness: *a wine with good body.* **13.** the basic material of which a ceramic article is made. —*v.t.* **14.** to provide with or as if with a body. **15.** to represent in bodily form (usu. fol. by *forth*). —*adj.* **16.** of or pertaining to the body; bodily. **17.** of or pertaining to the main reading matter of a book, article, etc., as distinguished from headings, prefaces, or the like. **—*Idiom.* 18. in a body,** as a group; together; collectively. **19. keep body and soul together,** to support oneself; maintain life.

bod′y bag′, *n.* a zippered bag made of rubberized material, used to transport a dead body, as from the scene of an accident.

bod′y·build′ing or **bod′y-build′ing,** *n.* the developing of muscles and physique through exercise, weight training, etc. —**bod′y·build′er, bod′y-build′er,** *n.*

bod′y check′, *n. Ice Hockey.* an impeding with the body of the movement of an opponent. —**bod′y-check′,** *v.t., v.i.*

bod′y count′, *n.* the number of military personnel killed in a particular action or during a specified period.

bod′y Eng′lish, *n.* a twisting of the body by a player as if to help a ball hit, thrown, etc., to travel in the desired direction.

bod·y·guard (bod′ē gärd′), *n.* **1.** a person or group of persons employed to guard an individual from bodily harm. —*v.t., v.i.* **2.** to provide with or act as a bodyguard.

bod′y lan′guage, *n.* nonverbal, usu. unconscious, communication through the use of gestures, facial expressions, etc.

bod′y mike′, *n.* a small, wireless microphone worn inconspicuously, as by a performer. —**bod′y-mike′,** *v.t.,* **-miked, -mik·ing.**

bod′y pol′itic, *n.* a people regarded as a political body under an organized government.
bod′y-search′, *v.t.* to search all parts of the body of: *Police body-searched the suspects for concealed narcotics.*
bod′y shop′, *n.* a shop where bodies of automotive vehicles are repaired, manufactured, etc.
bod′y snatch′er, *n.* a person who steals corpses from graves, esp. to use them for dissection. **—bod′y snatch′ing,** *n.*
bod′y stock′ing, *n.* a close-fitting, one-piece garment of knitted or stretch material, usu. covering the feet, legs, and trunk.
bod′y•suit′ or **bod′y suit′,** *n.* a close-fitting, one-piece garment for the torso, usu. sleeved and having a snap crotch.
bod′y-surf′, *v.i.* to ride the crest of a wave without a surfboard. **—bod′y-surf′er,** *n.*
bod′y wave′, *n.* a permanent with little or no curl, designed to give fullness and body to the hair.
bod•y•work (bod′ē wûrk′), *n.* the work of making or repairing automobile or other vehicle bodies.
Boer′ War′, *n.* a war in which Great Britain fought against the Transvaal and Orange Free State, 1899–1902.
boeuf bour•gui•gnon (bœf′ bo͝or′gēn yun′, -yôɴ′), *n.* beef cubes cooked in red wine with with small onions and mushrooms.
boff (bof), *Slang.* **—***n.* **1.** *Theat.* **a.** a box-office hit. **b.** a joke or humorous line producing hearty laughter. **2.** a loud hearty laugh; belly laugh. **3.** something very successful; a hit. **—***v.t.* **4.** to cause to be overcome with laughter. **5.** to hit; strike.
bog (bog, bôg), *n., v.,* **bogged, bog•ging.** **—***n.* **1.** wet, spongy ground with soil composed mainly of decayed vegetable matter. **2.** an area or stretch of such ground. **—***v.t., v.i.* **3.** to sink in or as if in a bog (often fol. by *down*): *We were bogged down with a lot of work.* **—bog′gish,** *adj.* **—bog′gy,** *adj.,* **-gi•er, -gi•est. —bog′gi•ness,** *n.*
bo•gey•man (bo͝og′ē man′, bō′gē-, bo͞o′-) also **boogeyman,** *n., pl.* **-men.** an imaginary evil character of supernatural powers, esp. a mythical hobgoblin supposed to carry off naughty children.
bog•gle (bog′əl), *v.,* **-gled, -gling,** *n.* **—***v.t.* **1.** to overwhelm or bewilder, as with magnitude or complexity: *The distance of the stars boggles the imagination.* **2.** to bungle; botch. **—***v.i.* **3.** to be overwhelmed or bewildered: *The mind boggles at the thought of such vast distances.* **4.** to hesitate or waver because of scruples, fear, etc. **5.** to start or jump, as with fear or surprise. **6.** to bungle. **—***n.* **7.** an act of boggling. **8.** a bungle; botch. **—bog′gler,** *n.*
bo•gie or **bo•gy** (bō′gē), *n., pl.* **-gies. 1.** (on a truck) a rear-wheel assembly composed of four wheels on two axles. **2.** any low, strong cart or truck.
Bog•o•mil (bog′ə mil) also **Bog•o•mile** (bog′ə mīl′), *n.* a member of a dualistic sect, flourishing chiefly in Bulgaria in the Middle Ages, that rejected most of the Old Testament and was strongly anticlerical in polity. [from the name of a 10th cent. Bulgarian priest alleged to have founded the sect] **—Bog′o•mil′i•an,** *adj.* **—Bog′o•mil•ism,** *n.*
Bo•go•tá (bō′gə tä′, bō′gə tä′), *n.* the capital of Colombia, in the central part. 3,982,941.
bo•gus (bō′gəs), *adj.* not genuine; counterfeit; phony.
bo•gy or **bo•gey** or **bo•gie** (bō′gē; *for 1, 2 also* bo͝og′ē, bo͞o′gē), *n., pl.* **-gies** or **-geys. 1.** a hobgoblin. **2.** anything that haunts, frightens, or harasses. **3.** a real or imagined barrier that must be overcome.
bo•he•mi•an (bō hē′mē ən), *n.* **1.** a person, as an artist or writer, who lives and acts without regard for conventional rules and practices. **—***adj.* **2.** pertaining to or characteristic of a bohemian.
Bohe′mian Breth′ren, *n.* a Christian denomination formed in Bohemia in 1467 and reorganized in 1722 as the Moravian Church.
Bohr (bôr, bōr), *n.* **1. Aage Niels,** born 1922, Danish physicist. **2.** his father, **Niels Henrik David,** 1885–1962, Danish physicist.
boil[1] (boil), *v.i.* **1.** to change from a liquid to a gaseous state, typically as a result of heat, producing bubbles of gas that rise to the surface of the liquid. **2.** to reach the boiling point. **3.** to be in an agitated or violent state: *The sea boiled in the storm.* **4.** to be deeply angry or upset. **5.** to contain, or be contained in, a liquid that boils: *The kettle is boiling. Don't let the vegetables boil.* **—***v.t.* **6.** to bring to the boiling point. **7.** to cook (something) in boiling water: *to boil eggs.* **8.** to separate (salt, sugar, etc.) from a solution containing it by boiling off the liquid. **9. boil down, a.** to reduce or lessen by boiling. **b.** to shorten; abridge. **10. boil down to,** to be reduced to; amount to: *It boils down to a question of ethics.* **11. boil over, a.** to overflow while or as if while boiling; erupt. **b.** to be unable to repress anger, excitement, etc. **—***n.* **12.** the act or state of boiling: *Bring the water to a boil.* **13.** an area of agitated, swirling water.
boil[2] (boil), *n.* a painful circumscribed inflammation of the skin with a pus-filled inner core, usu. caused by a local infection.
boiled′ din′ner, *n.* a meal of meat and vegetables, as corned beef, cabbage, and potatoes, boiled together.
boil•er (boi′lər), *n.* **1.** a closed vessel in which water is heated to make steam for powering turbines, supplying heat, etc. **2.** a vessel, as a kettle, for boiling or heating. **3.** a tank in which water is heated and stored, as for supplying hot water. **—boil′er•less,** *adj.*
boil•er•mak•er (boi′lər mā′kər), *n.* **1.** a person who makes and repairs boilers. **2.** a drink of whiskey with beer as a chaser.
boil′er•plate′ or **boil′er plate′,** *n.* **1.** plating of iron or steel for making the shells of boilers, covering the hulls of ships, etc. **2. a.** syndicated or ready-to-print copy, used esp. by weekly newspapers. **b.** trite, hackneyed writing. **3.** phrases used repeatedly, as in correspondence. **4.** the detailed standard wording of a contract, warranty, etc.
boil•ing (boi′ling), *adj.* **1.** having reached the boiling point: *boiling water.* **2.** fiercely churning or swirling: *the boiling seas.* **3.** (of anger, rage, etc.) intense; fierce. **—***adv.* **4.** to an extreme extent: *I was boiling mad.*
boil′ing point′, *n.* **1.** the temperature at which the vapor pressure of a liquid is equal to the pressure of the atmosphere on the liquid, equal to 212°F (100°C) for water at sea level. *Abbr.:* b.p. **2.** the point beyond which one becomes visibly angry, outraged, or the like. **3.** the point at which matters reach a crisis.
Boi•se (boi′zē *or, esp. locally,* -sē), *n.* the capital of Idaho, in the SW part. 145,987.
bois•ter•ous (boi′stər əs, -strəs), *adj.* **1.** rough and noisy; clamorous: *boisterous laughter.* **2.** (of waves, wind, etc.) turbulent and stormy. **—bois′ter•ous•ly,** *adv.* **—bois′ter•ous•ness,** *n.*
bok choy or **bok-choy** (bok′ choi′), *n.* an Asian plant, *Brassica rapa chinensis,* of the mustard family, having a loose cluster of dark green leaves on white stalks, used as a vegetable.
bold (bōld), *adj.* **1.** not hesitating or fearful in the face of danger; courageous. **2.** scorning or ignoring the rules of propriety; forward; impudent. **3.** requiring courage and daring: *bold deeds.* **4.** beyond the usual limits of conventional thought or action; inventive or imaginative: *a bold solution to a perplexing problem.* **5.** striking or conspicuous to the eye; flashy; showy: *a bold pattern.* **6.** steep; abrupt: *a bold promontory.* **7.** typeset in boldface. **—bold′ly,** *adv.* **—bold′ness,** *n.*
bold•face (bōld′fās′), *n.* **1.** type or print that has thick, heavy lines, used for emphasis, headings, etc. **This is a sample of boldface.** **—***adj.* **2.** typeset or printed in boldface.
bold′-faced′, *adj.* **1.** impudent; brazen. **2.** (of type) having thick, heavy lines. **—bold′-fac′ed•ly,** *adv.*
bole (bōl), *n.* the stem or trunk of a tree.
bo•le•ro (bə lâr′ō, bō-), *n., pl.* **-ros. 1.** a lively Spanish dance in triple meter. **2.** the music for this dance. **3.** a waist-length jacket, with or without collar, lapels, and sleeves, worn open in front.
bo•le•tus (bō lē′təs), *n., pl.* **-tus•es, -ti** (-tī). any mushroom of the genus *Boletus,* having an easily separable layer of tubes on the underside of the cap or pileus.
bol•i•var or **bol•í•var** (bol′ə vər, bə lē′vär), *n., pl.* **bol•i•vars, bo•lí•va•res** (bol′ə vär′ās, bə lē′vä rās′). the basic monetary unit of Venezuela.
Bol•í•var (bol′ə vər, bə lē′vär), *n.* **Si•món** (sī′mən, sē mōn′), (*"El Libertador"*), 1783–1830, Venezuelan statesman: leader of revolt of South American colonies against Spanish rule.
Bo•liv•i•a (bə liv′ē ə, bō-), *n.* a republic in W South America. 7,669,868; 404,388 sq. mi. (1,047,370 sq. km). *Caps.:* La Paz and Sucre. **—Bo•liv′i•an,** *adj., n.*
boll (bōl), *n.* a rounded seed vessel or pod of a plant, as of flax.
bol•lard (bol′ərd), *n.* **1.** a thick low post, usu. of iron or steel, mounted on a wharf or the like, to which mooring lines from vessels are attached. **2.** *Brit.* one of a series of short posts, esp. for excluding motor vehicles from a road.
bol•lix (bol′iks), *Informal.* **—***v.t.* **1.** to botch or bungle (often fol. by *up*). **—***n.* **2.** a confused bungle.
boll′ wee′vil, *n.* a snout beetle, *Anthonomus grandis,* that attacks the bolls of cotton.
bo•lo•gna (bə lō′nē, -nə, -lōn′yə), *n.* a cooked and smoked sausage made usu. of finely ground beef and pork. [after *Bologna,* Italy, where first made]
Bol•she•vik (bōl′shə vik, -vēk′, bol′-), *n., pl.* **-viks, -vik•i** (-vik′ē, -vē′kē). **1. a.** a member of the radical majority wing of the Russian Social-Democratic Workers' Party, 1903–17, advocating abrupt, forceful seizure of power by the proletariat. **b.** (after 1918) a member of the Russian Communist Party. **2.** a member of any Communist Party. **—Bol′she•vism** (-viz′əm), *n.* **—Bol′she•vist,** *n., adj.* **—Bol′she•vis′tic,** *adj.*
bol•ster (bōl′stər), *n.* **1.** a long, often cylindrical cushion or pillow for a bed, sofa, etc. **2.** anything resembling this in form or in use as a support. **3.** any pillow, cushion, or pad. **4.** a horizontal timber on a post for lessening the free span of a beam. **—***v.t.* **5.** to support with or as if with a bolster. **6.** to add to, support, or uphold: *They bolstered their claim with new evidence.* **—bol′ster•er,** *n.*
bolt[1] (bōlt), *n.* **1.** any of several types of strong fastening rods, pins, or screws, usu. threaded to receive a nut. **2.** a movable bar or rod that is slid into a socket to fasten a door, gate, etc. **3.** the part of a lock that is shot from and drawn back into the case, as by the action of the key. **4.** a sudden dash, flight, or escape. **5.** a sudden desertion from a political party, social movement, etc. **6.** a length of woven goods, esp. as it comes on a roll from the loom. **7.** a roll of wallpaper. **8.** (on a breech-loading rifle) a sliding rod or bar that shoves a cartridge into the firing chamber and closes the breech. **9.** a short, heavy arrow for a crossbow. **10.** a thunderbolt. **—***v.t.* **11.** to fasten with or as if with a bolt. **12.** to discontinue support of or participation in; break with: *to bolt a political party.* **13.** to shoot or discharge (a missile), as from a crossbow or catapult. **14.** to say impulsively; blurt out. **15.** to swallow (one's food or drink) hurriedly: *He bolted his breakfast.* **16.** to make (cloth, wallpaper, etc.) into bolts. **—***v.i.* **17.** to make a sudden flight or escape. **18.** to break away, as from one's political party. **19.** to produce flowers or

seeds prematurely. **—Idiom. 20. bolt out of** or **from the blue,** a sudden and entirely unforeseen event. **21. bolt upright,** stiffly or rigidly straight: *to sit bolt upright.* **—bolt′er,** *n.*

bolt² (bōlt), *v.t.* **1.** to sift through a cloth or sieve. **2.** to examine or search into, as if by sifting. **—bolt′er,** *n.*

bol·to·ni·a (bōl tō′nē ə), *n., pl.* **-ni·as.** any of several North American composite plants of the genus *Boltonia,* with white, blue, or purple asterlike flower heads.

bo·lus (bō′ləs), *n., pl.* **-lus·es. 1.** a round mass of medicinal material, larger than an ordinary pill. **2.** a soft, roundish mass or lump, esp. of chewed food.

bomb (bom), *n.* **1.** a case filled with a bursting charge and exploded by means of a detonating device or by impact, esp. one designed to be dropped from an aircraft. **2.** any explosive device used as a weapon: *a time bomb; a smoke bomb; a car bomb.* **3.** a rough spherical or ellipsoidal mass of lava, ejected from a volcano and hardened while falling. **4.** an aerosol can and its contents. **5.** a long forward pass in football, esp. one to a teammate who scores a touchdown. **6.** *Slang.* an absolute failure. **7. the bomb, a.** ATOMIC BOMB. **b.** nuclear weapons collectively. **—v.t. 8.** to hurl bombs at or drop bombs upon, as from an airplane; bombard. **9.** *Slang.* to defeat decisively; trounce. **—v.i. 10.** to hurl or drop bombs. **11.** *Slang.* to fail decisively; flop (sometimes fol. by *out*): *The play bombed in Boston.* **12.** *Informal.* to move very quickly.

bom·bard (*v.* bom bärd′, bəm-; *n.* bom′bärd), *v.t.* **1.** to attack or batter with artillery fire. **2.** to attack with bombs. **3.** to assail vigorously: *bombarded me with questions.* **4.** to direct high-energy particles or radiation against: *to bombard a nucleus.* **—n. 5.** the earliest kind of cannon, orig. throwing stone balls. **—bom·bard′er,** *n.* **—bom·bard′ment,** *n.*

bom·bar·dier (bom′bər dēr′, -bə-), *n.* the crew member of a bombing plane who operates the bombsight and the bomb-release mechanism.

bom·bast (bom′bast), *n.* pompous oratory or pretentious writing. **—bom·bas′tic,** *adj.*

bom′bax fam′ily (bom′baks), *n.* a family, Bombacaceae, of tropical trees with palmate leaves, often showy flowers, and dry fruit with a woody pulp: includes the balsa, baobab, and the silk-cotton tree.

Bom·bay (bom bā′), *n.* a seaport in and the capital of Maharashtra, in W India, on the Arabian Sea. 8,227,000.

bom·ba·zine (bom′bə zēn′, bom′bə zēn′), *n.* a twill fabric constructed of a silk warp and worsted filling, often dyed black for mourning wear.

bombe (bom, bônb), *n.* a frozen round mold of ice cream usu. filled with custard.

bom·bé (bom bā′, bôn-), *adj.* (of furniture) curving or swelling outward.

bomb·er (bom′ər), *n.* **1.** an airplane equipped to carry and drop bombs. **2.** a person who drops or sets bombs.

bomb·shell (bom′shel′), *n.* **1.** a bomb. **2.** something or someone having a sudden and sensational effect.

bomb·sight (bom′sīt′), *n.* a device installed in an aircraft for guiding the release of bombs, esp. one utilizing radar to locate the target and to compensate for speed, winds, etc.

bom·by·cid (bom′bə sid), *n.* a moth of the family Bombycidae, comprising a single species, *Bombyx mori,* the Chinese silkworm moth.

Bon (bon; *Fr.* bôN), *n.* **Cape,** a cape on the NE coast of Tunisia: surrender of the German African forces, May 12, 1943. Also called **Ras Addar.**

bo·na fide or **bo·na-fide** (bō′nə fīd′, bon′ə; bō′nə fī′dē), *adj.* **1.** made, done, etc., in good faith; without deception or fraud: *a bona fide statement of intent to sell.* **2.** authentic; genuine; real: *a bona fide sample of Lincoln's handwriting.*

bo·na fi·des (bō′nə fī′dēz, fē′dās *or, esp. for 2,* bō′nə fīdz′, bon′ə), *n.* **1.** (*italics*) *Latin.* (*used with a sing. v.*) good faith; absence of fraud or deceit; genuineness: *The bona fides of this contract is not in question.* **2.** (*sometimes italics*) (*used with a pl. v.*) official documents or other items that prove authenticity, legitimacy, etc.; credentials. **—Usage.** At least partially because it looks and sounds like an English plural, the Latin phrase BONA FIDES has developed the plural sense "credentials," taking a plural verb. Although criticized by some usage guides, this use has been increasing in recent decades.

bo·nan·za (bə nan′zə, bō-), *n., pl.* **-zas. 1.** a rich mass of ore, as found in mining. **2.** a source of great and sudden wealth or luck; a spectacular windfall.

Bo·na·parte (bō′nə pärt′), *n.* **1. Charles Louis Napoléon,** NAPOLEON III. **2. François Charles Joseph,** NAPOLEON II. **3. Jérôme,** 1784–1860, king of Westphalia 1807 (brother of Napoleon I). **4. Joseph,** 1768–1844, king of Naples 1806–08; king of Spain 1808–13 (brother of Napoleon I). **5. Louis,** 1778–1846, king of Holland 1806–10 (brother of Napoleon I). **6. Lucien,** 1775–1840, prince of Canino, a principality in Italy (brother of Napoleon I). **7. Napoléon,** NAPOLEON I. Italian, **Buonaparte. —Bo′na·par′te·an,** *adj.*

Bon·ar (bon′ər), *n.* **Horatius,** 1808–89, Scottish hymn writer.

bon·bon (bon′bon′), *n.* **1.** a small fondant- or chocolate-coated candy with a fondant, fruit, or nut center. **2.** any candy.

bond (bond), *n.* **1.** something that binds, fastens, confines, or holds together. **2.** a cord, rope, band, or ligament. **3.** something that binds a person or persons to a certain circumstance or line of behavior: *the bond of matrimony.* **4.** something, as an agreement or friendship, that unites individuals or peoples into a group; covenant. **5.** binding security; firm assurance: *My word is my bond.* **6.** a sealed instrument under which a person, corporation, or government guarantees to pay a stated sum of money on or before a specified day. **7.** any written obligation under seal. **8.** the state of dutiable goods stored without payment of duties or taxes until withdrawn: *goods in bond.* **9.** Also called **bonded whiskey,** a 100-proof whiskey that has been aged at least four years in a bonded warehouse before bottling. **10.** a certificate of ownership of a specified portion of a debt due to be paid by a government or corporation to an individual holder and usu. bearing a fixed rate of interest. **11. a.** a surety agreement. **b.** the money deposited under such an agreement. **12.** a substance that causes particles to adhere; binder. **13.** adhesion between two substances or objects. **14.** the attraction between atoms in a molecule or crystalline structure: *covalent bond.* **15.** a patterned arrangement of overlapping bricks, stones, etc., in a construction, intended esp. to provide strength. **—v.t. 16.** to put (goods, an employee, official, etc.) on or under bond. **17.** to connect or bind. **18.** to join (two materials). **19.** to overlap (bricks, stones, etc.) so as to produce a strong construction. **20.** to restore the discolored or damaged surface of (a tooth) by coating it with a durable material that adheres to the existing enamel. **—v.i. 21.** to hold together or cohere, as bricks in a wall or particles in a mass. **22.** to establish a bond or attachment, as between a parent and offspring.

bond·age (bon′dij), *n.* **1.** slavery or involuntary servitude. **2.** the state of being bound by or subjected to some external power or control.

bond·ed (bon′did), *adj.* **1.** secured by bonds: *bonded debt.* **2.** placed in bond: *bonded goods.* **3.** made of two layers of the same fabric or of a fabric and a lining material attached to each other by a chemical process or adhesive: *bonded wool.*

bond·hold·er (bond′hōl′dər), *n.* a holder of a bond or bonds issued by a government or corporation. **—bond′hold′ing,** *adj., n.*

bond·ing (bon′ding), *n.* **1. a.** a relationship that usu. begins at the time of birth between a parent and offspring and that establishes the basis for an ongoing mutual attachment. **b.** the establishment of a pair bond. **2.** a close friendship that develops between adults, often as a result of shared experiences.

bond′ serv′ant or **bond′-serv′ant,** *n.* **1.** a slave. **2.** a person bound to service without wages.

bone (bōn), *n., v.,* **boned, bon·ing,** *adv.* **—n. 1. a.** one of the structures composing the skeleton of a vertebrate. **b.** the hard connective tissue forming these structures, composed of cells enclosed in a calcified matrix. **2.** such a structure from an edible animal, usu. with meat adhering to it, as an article of food: *a ham bone.* **3.** any of various similarly hard or structural animal substances, as ivory or whalebone. **4.** something resembling such a substance. **5. bones, a.** the skeleton. **b.** a body: *to rest one's weary bones.* **c.** dice. **d.** a simple rhythm instrument consisting of two bars of bone, ivory, or wood, held between the fingers and clacked together. **6.** the color of bone; ivory or off-white. **7.** a flat strip of whalebone or other material for stiffening corsets, petticoats, etc.; stay. **—v.t. 8.** to remove the bones from: *to bone a turkey.* **9.** to put whalebone or another stiffener into (clothing). **10. bone up,** *Informal.* to study intensely; cram: *to bone up for an exam.* **—adv. 11.** completely; absolutely: *bone tired.* **—Idiom. 12.** **feel in one's bones,** to be sure intuitively. **13. have a bone to pick with someone,** to have cause for reproaching someone. **14. make no bones about, a.** to act or speak openly and decisively about. **b.** to have no fear of or objection to. **15. throw a bone,** to give a small concession as a sop.

bone′ ash′, *n.* a white ash obtained by calcining bones, used as a fertilizer and in the making of bone china.

bone′ black′, *n.* a black carbonaceous substance obtained by calcining bones in closed vessels, used esp. as a pigment.

bone′ chi′na, *n.* a fine, naturally white china made with bone ash.

boned (bōnd), *adj.* **1.** having a particular kind of bone or bony structure (used in combination): *small-boned.* **2.** having the bones removed before cooking or serving: *boned chicken.* **3.** braced or supported with stays, as a corset.

bone′-dry′, *adj.* **1.** very dry. **2.** very thirsty.

bone·fish (bōn′fish′), *n., pl.* **-fish·es,** (*esp. collectively*) **-fish.** a silver game and food fish, *Albula vulpes,* of warm coastal seas. Also called **ladyfish.**

bone·head (bōn′hed′), *Slang.* **—n. 1.** a foolish or stupid person; blockhead. **—adj. 2.** Also, **bone′head′ed.** characteristic of or done by such a person. **—bone′head′ed·ness,** *n.*

bone′ meal′ or **bone′meal′,** *n.* bones ground to a coarse powder, used as fertilizer or feed.

bone′ of conten′tion, *n.* *Informal.* the subject or focal point of a dispute: *The will has been a bone of contention to the heirs.*

bon·er (bō′nər), *n.* a stupid mistake; blunder.

bone·set (bōn′set′), *n.* any composite plant of the genus *Eupatorium,* esp. *E. perfoliatum,* of North America, having white flowers in a flat-topped cluster. Also called **thoroughwort.**

bone·yard (bōn′yärd′), *n.* **1.** a cemetery. **2.** a place where the bones of wild animals accumulate. **3.** a place where old or discarded cars, etc., are collected before being disposed of.

bon·fire (bon′fī°r′), *n.* a large fire built in the open air, for warmth, entertainment, or as a signal.

bong¹ (bong, bông), *n.* **1.** a dull, resonant sound, as of a bell. **—v.i. 2.** to produce this sound.

bong² (bong, bông), *n.* a type of hookah or water pipe for smoking marijuana or other drugs.

bon·go¹ (bong′gō, bông′-), *n., pl.* **-gos,** (*esp. collectively*) **-go.** a reddish brown antelope, *Tragelaphus euryceros,* of tropical Africa, having white stripes and large, spirally twisted horns.

bon·go² (bong′gō, bông′-), *n., pl.* **-gos, -goes.** one of a pair of small tuned drums, played by beating with the fingers.

Bon·hoef·fer (bon′hoe′fər, -hō′-), *n.* **Dietrich,** 1906–45, German Lutheran theologian killed by the Nazis.

bon·ho·mie (bon′ə mē′, bō′na-), *n.* a good-natured manner; geniality. **—bon′ho·mous** (-məs), *adj.*

bo·ni·to (bə nē′tō), *n., pl.* (*esp. collectively*) **-to,** (*esp. for kinds or species*) **-tos. 1.** any mackerellike fish of the genus *Sarda,* as *S. sarda,* of the Atlantic Ocean. **2.** any of several related species, as the skipjack, *Euthynnus pelamis.*

bon·kers (bong′kərz), *adj. Slang.* mentally unbalanced; mad; crazy.

bon mot (bôn mō′), *n., pl.* **bons mots** (bôn mōz′). a witty remark or comment; witticism.

Bonn (bon, bôn), *n.* a city in W Germany, on the Rhine: seat of the government. 291,400.

bon·net (bon′it), *n.* **1.** a hat, usu. tying under the chin and often framing the face, formerly much worn by women but now worn mostly by children. **2.** any hat worn by women. **3.** any bonnetlike headdress. **4.** a cowl, hood, or cap for stabilizing the draft in a fireplace or chimney. **5.** a covering for a valve stem. **6.** a supplementary piece of canvas laced to the foot of a fore-and-aft sail, esp. a jib, in light winds. **—v.t. 7.** to put a bonnet on.

bon·ny (bon′ē), *adj.,* **-ni·er, -ni·est.** *Chiefly Brit.* **1.** attractive; handsome; pretty. **2.** pleasing; agreeable.

bon·sai (bon sī′, bōn-, bon′sī, bōn′-), *n., pl.* **-sai. 1.** a tree or shrub that has been dwarfed, as by pruning the roots and pinching the shoots and branches. **2.** the art of growing such a plant.

bon·te·bok (bon′tē bok′), *n., pl.* **-boks,** (*esp. collectively*) **-bok.** a purplish red antelope, *Damaliscus dorcas,* of S Africa, having a white face and rump.

bon ton (bon′ ton′, bôn tôn′), *n.* **1.** good or elegant form or style. **2.** something regarded as fashionably correct. **3.** fashionable society.

bo·nus (bō′nəs), *n., pl.* **-nus·es. 1.** something given or paid over and above what is due. **2.** a sum of money given in addition to regular pay, usu. for outstanding work. **3.** a sum of money paid by a state or federal government to a veteran for war service, usu. based on length of service. **4.** something extra or additional given freely: *The cookies are a bonus when you buy a jar of coffee.*

Bo′nus Ar′my, *n.* a group of 12,000 World War I veterans who massed in Washington, D.C., the summer of 1932 to induce Congress to appropriate moneys for the payment of bonus certificates granted in 1924.

bon vi·vant (*Fr.* bôn vē vän′), *n., pl.* **bons vi·vants** (*Fr.* bôn vē vän′). a person who lives luxuriously and enjoys good food and drink. [< French]

bon vo·yage (*Fr.* bôn vwa yazh′), *interj.* (used to wish someone a pleasant trip.)

bon·y (bō′nē), *adj.,* **bon·i·er, bon·i·est. 1.** of or like bone. **2.** full of bones. **3.** having prominent bones; big-boned. **4.** skinny; gaunt; emaciated. **—bon′i·ness,** *n.*

bon′y fish′, *n.* any fish of the class Osteichthyes, characterized by gill covers, an air bladder, and a skeleton composed chiefly of bone.

bonze (bonz), *n.* a Buddhist monk, esp. of Japan or China.

boo (boo), *interj., n., pl.* **boos,** *v.* **—interj. 1.** (used to express contempt or disapproval or to startle or frighten.) **—n. 2.** an exclamation of contempt or disapproval: *a loud boo from the bleachers.* **—v.i. 3.** to cry "boo" in derision. **—v.t. 4.** to show disapproval of by booing.

boo·by (boo′bē), *n., pl.* **-bies. 1.** a stupid person; dunce. **2.** any of several usu. black- or brown-and-white, goose-sized seabirds of the family Sulidae, of tropical oceans, that dive for fish from high over the water.

boo′by prize′, *n.* a prize given in good-natured ridicule to the worst player or team in a game or contest.

boo′by trap′, *n.* **1.** a hidden bomb or mine that can be set off by an unsuspecting person who steps on it, touches a tripwire, or the like. **2.** any hidden trap set for an unsuspecting person. **—boo′by-trap′,** *v.t.,* **-trapped, -trap·ping.**

boo·dle (bood′l), *n.* **1.** the lot, pack, or crowd: *Send the whole boodle back to the factory.* **2.** a large quantity of something, esp. money: *worth a boodle.* **3.** a bribe or other illicit payment; graft. **4.** stolen goods; loot.

boog·ie (boog′ē, boo′gē), *n., v.,* **-ied, -ie·ing. —n. 1.** BOOGIE-WOOGIE. **2.** a lively form of rock, based on the blues. **—v.i. 3.** to dance to rock music. **4.** *Slang.* to go: *Let's boogie down to the corner.*

Boog′ie Board′, *Trademark.* a small, flexible plastic surfboard.

boog·ie-woog·ie (boog′ē woog′ē, boo′gē woo′gē), *n.* a style of jazz piano blues featuring a constantly repeated bass figure and melodic improvisation in the treble.

book (book), *n.* **1.** a long written or printed work, usu. on sheets of paper fastened or bound together within covers: *a book of poems; a book of short stories.* **2.** a number of sheets of blank or ruled paper bound together for writing, recording business transactions, etc. **3.** a division of a literary work, esp. one of the larger divisions. **4. the Book,** the Bible. **5. the book, a.** a set of rules, conventions, or standards: *to go according to the book; to know every trick in the book.* **b.** the telephone book. **6.** the text or libretto of an opera, operetta, or musical. **7. books,** the financial records of a business, institution, etc. **8.** a script or story for a play. **9.** the number of tricks that must be taken before any trick counts in the score of a card game. **10.** a set or packet of tickets, checks, stamps, matches, etc., bound together like a book. **11.** anything that serves for the recording of facts or events: *The petrified tree was a book of nature.* **12.** gathered information and recommended strategy regarding a task, problem, opponent, etc., as in sports. **13.** a pile or package of leaves, as of tobacco. **—v.t. 14.** to enter in a book or list; record; register. **15.** to reserve or make a reservation for (a hotel room, passage on a ship, etc.). **16.** to register or list (a person) for a place, transportation, appointment, etc.: *The travel agent booked us on the next cruise.* **17.** to engage for one or more performances. **18.** to enter a charge against (an arrested person) on a police register. **—v.i. 19.** to register one's name. **20.** to engage a place, services, etc.: *Book early if you want a good table.* **21. book in** (or **out**), to sign in (or out), as at a job. **22. book up,** to sell or buy out, fill up, or the like: *Baseball fans have booked up the hotel for a week.* **—adj. 23.** pertaining to or dealing with books: *the book department; a book salesman.* **24.** derived or learned entirely from books: *book knowledge.* **25.** shown on a company's books: *The firm's book profit was $53,680.* **—Idiom. 26. bring to book,** to bring to justice. **27. by the book,** according to the correct or established form. **28. close the books,** to balance accounts at the end of an accounting period; settle accounts. **29. in one's book,** according to one's personal judgment. **30. in someone's good** (or **bad**) **books,** in (or out of) favor; liked (or disliked). **31. know** or **read like a book,** to know or understand completely: *She knew the city like a book.* **32. make book, a.** to take bets and give odds. **b.** to wager; bet. **33. off the books,** without being part of an official payroll, income report, etc.: *to pay someone off the books.* **34. one for the book(s),** a noteworthy incident; something extraordinary. **35. throw the book at,** *Informal.* to punish severely, esp. with the maximum sentence allowable. **—Proverb. 36. Don't judge a book by its cover,** don't be misled by appearances.

book·bind·ing (book′bīn′ding), *n.* **1.** the process or art of binding books. **2.** the binding of a book. **—book′bind′er,** *n.* **—book′bind′er·y,** *n., pl.* **-er·ies.**

book′ burn′ing, *n.* the destruction of writings of which the subject, the view of the author, or the like is considered politically or socially objectionable: used as a means of censorship or oppression.

book·case (book′kās′), *n.* a set of shelves for books.

book′ club′, *n.* a company or other organization that sells books to its subscribers, usu. through the mail and often at a discount.

book·end (book′end′), *n.* an often decorative support placed at each end of a row of books to hold them upright.

book·ie (book′ē), *n.* BOOKMAKER (def. 1).

book·ing (book′ing), *n.* **1.** a contract, engagement, or scheduled performance of a professional entertainer. **2.** RESERVATION (def. 5). **3.** the act of a person who books.

book·ish (book′ish), *adj.* **1.** given or devoted to reading or study. **2.** more acquainted with books than with real life. **3.** literary. **4.** stilted; pedantic. **—book′ish·ness,** *n.*

book·keep·ing (book′kē′ping), *n.* the system or occupation of keeping detailed records of a company's transactions, esp. its purchases and sales. **—book′keep′er,** *n.*

book·let (book′lit), *n.* a little book, esp. one with paper covers; pamphlet.

book′louse′ or **book′ louse′,** *n., pl.* **-lice** (-līs′). any of numerous minute wingless insects of the order Psocoptera, often living among books or papers.

book′ lung′, *n.* the respiratory organ of many arachnids, composed of thin, paperlike layers of tissue.

book·mak·er (book′mā′kər), *n.* **1.** a person who makes a business of accepting the bets of others on the outcome of sports contests, esp. of horse races. **2.** a person who designs, prints, or manufactures books. **—book′mak′ing,** *n., adj.*

book·mark (book′märk′), *n.* a ribbon or other marker placed between the pages of a book to mark a place.

book·mo·bile (book′mə bēl′, -mō-), *n.* a motor vehicle designed to carry books and serve as a traveling library.

Book′ of Books′, *n.* the Bible.

Book′ of Com′mon Prayer′, *n.* the service book of the Church of England, first composed in 1549: still in use, with revisions, by all branches of the Anglican Communion.

book′ of hours′ or **Book′ of Hours′,** *n.* a book containing the prescribed order of prayers, readings from Scripture, and rites for the canonical hours.

Book′ of Mor′mon, *n.* a sacred book of the Mormon Church, believed by Mormons to be an abridgment by a prophet (**Mormon**) of a record of certain ancient peoples in America, written on golden plates, and discovered and translated (1827–30) by Joseph Smith.

Book′ of the Dead′, a collection of ancient Egyptian papyrus books, many with elaborate illustrations, each containing prayers, hymns, incantations, and formulas for the behavior of the souls of the dead.

book·plate (book′plāt′), *n.* a label bearing the owner's name and often a design, for pasting on the front endpaper of a book.

book·rack (book′rak′), *n.* **1.** a support for an open book. **2.** a rack for holding books.

book·rest (book'rest'), *n.* a support for an open book, usu. holding it at a slight angle.

book' review', *n.* **1.** a critical analysis of a book. **2.** a section of a newspaper or magazine devoted to such analysis, esp. of new books. —**book' review·er,** *n.* —**book' review'ing,** *n.*

book·sell·er (book'sel'ər), *n.* a person who sells books, esp. the proprietor of a bookstore. —**book'sell'ing,** *n.*

book·stall (book'stôl'), *n.* **1.** a booth or stall at which books are sold, usu. secondhand. **2.** *Brit.* NEWSSTAND.

book·stand (book'stand'), *n.* **1.** a bookrack. **2.** a bookstall.

book·store (book'stôr', -stōr'), *n.* a store where books are sold. Also called **book·shop** (book'shop').

book' val'ue, *n.* **1.** the value of a business, property, etc., as shown on a financial statement, based on cost less depreciation (disting. from *market value*). **2.** total assets minus all liabilities.

book·worm (book'wûrm'), *n.* **1.** a person devoted to reading. **2.** any of various insects that feed on books, esp. a booklouse.

Bool'e·an al'gebra (boo'lē ən), *n.* a system of symbolic logic dealing with the relationship of sets: the basis of logic gates in computers.

Bool'ean opera'tion, *n.* any logical operation in which each of the operands and the result take one of two values, as "true" and "false" or "circuit on" and "circuit off." —**Bool'ean op'erator,** *n.*

boom¹ (boom), *v.i.* **1.** to make a deep, prolonged, resonant sound. **2.** to move with a great rush. **3.** to progress, grow, or flourish vigorously: *Business is booming since we enlarged the store.* —*v.t.* **4.** to announce with a booming sound (often fol. by *out*). **5.** to boost; campaign for vigorously. —*n.* **6.** a deep, prolonged, resonant sound. **7.** the resonant cry of a bird or animal. **8.** a rapid increase in sales, worth, development, etc.: *a housing boom.* **9.** a period of rapid economic growth, prosperity, high wages and prices, and relatively full employment. —**boom'ing·ly,** *adv.*

boom² (boom), *n.* **1.** any of various spars or poles projecting from a ship's mast and used to extend sails, handle cargo, etc. **2.** a chain, cable, etc., serving to obstruct navigation. **3.** a spar or beam projecting from the mast of a derrick for supporting or guiding the weights to be lifted. **4.** (on a motion-picture or television stage) a spar or beam on a mobile crane for holding or manipulating a microphone or camera. —*v.t.* **5.** to manipulate (an object) by or as if by means of a crane or derrick. —*Idiom.* **6. lower the boom,** to act decisively to punish wrongdoing.

boom-and-bust or **boom-or-bust** (boom'ən bust'), *adj.* characteristic of a period of economic prosperity followed by a depression.

boom' box' or **boom'box',** *n.* BOX¹ (def. 10).

boom·er (boo'mər), *n.* **1.** a person or thing that booms. **2.** a person who settles in areas or towns that are booming. **3.** *Informal.* BABY BOOMER. **4.** an itinerant or migratory worker.

boo·mer·ang (boo'mə rang'), *n.* **1.** a bent or curved piece of tough wood used by the Australian Aborigines as a throwing club, one form of which can be thrown so as to return to the thrower. **2.** something, as a scheme or argument, that does injury to the originator. —*v.i.* **3.** to come back or return, as a boomerang. **4.** to cause harm to the originator; backfire.

boomerang (def. 1)

boom·let (boom'lit), *n.* a brief increase, as in business activity or political popularity.

boom' town' or **boom'town',** *n.* a town that has grown very rapidly as a result of sudden prosperity.

boon¹ (boon), *n.* **1.** something to be thankful for; blessing; benefit. **2.** something that is asked; a favor sought. —**boon'less,** *adj.*

boon² (boon), *adj.* jolly; jovial; convivial: *boon companions.*

boon·docks (boon'doks'), *n.* **the,** *(used with a pl. v.)* **1.** an uninhabited area with thick natural vegetation, as a backwoods or marsh. **2.** a remote rural area.

boon·dog·gle (boon'dog'əl, -dô'gəl), *n.* **1.** work of little or no value done merely to keep or look busy. **2.** a project funded by the federal government out of political favoritism that is of no real value to the community or the nation. **3.** a plaited leather cord for the neck made typically by a camper or a scout. —*v.t.* **4.** to deceive or attempt to deceive. —*v.i.* **5.** to do work of little value merely to keep or look busy. —**boon'dog'gler,** *n.*

Boone (boon), *n.* **1. Daniel,** 1734–1820, American pioneer, esp. in Kentucky. **2. Pat,** born 1934, U.S. singer.

boon·ies (boo'nēz), *n.* **the,** *(used with a pl. v.)* *Informal.* a remote area; boondocks

boor (boor), *n.* **1.** a churlish, rude, or unmannerly person. **2.** a country bumpkin; rustic; yokel. **3.** peasant. —**boor'ish,** *adj.*

boost (boost), *v.t.* **1.** to lift or raise by pushing from behind or below. **2.** to advance or aid by speaking well of; promote. **3.** to increase; raise: *to boost prices.* —*n.* **4.** an upward shove or raise; lift. **5.** an increase;

rise: *a boost in food prices.* **6.** an act, remark, or the like, that helps one's progress, morale, efforts, etc.

boost·er (boo'stər), *n.* **1.** a person or thing that boosts, esp. an energetic and enthusiastic supporter. **2.** a device connected in series with a current for increasing or decreasing the nominal circuit voltage. **3.** an explosive more powerful than a primer, for ensuring the detonation of the main charge of a shell. **4. a.** the first stage of a multistage rocket, used as the principal source of thrust in takeoff and early flight. **b.** LAUNCH VEHICLE. **5.** Also called **boost'er dose', boost'er shot'.** a dose of an immunizing substance given to maintain or renew the effect of a previous one. **6.** a drug, medicine, etc., that serves as a synergist. **7.** a radio-frequency amplifier for a radio or television antenna and the receiving set.

boost'er ca'ble, *n.* either of a pair of electric cables used for starting the engine of a vehicle whose battery is dead. Also called **jumper.**

boot¹ (boot), *n.* **1.** a covering of leather, rubber, or the like, for the foot and all or part of the leg. **2.** an overshoe, esp. one of rubber or other waterproof material. **3.** any sheathlike protective covering: *a boot for a weak automobile tire.* **4. a.** the receptacle or place into which the top of a convertible car fits when lowered. **b.** a cloth covering for this receptacle or place. **5.** a metal device that, when attached to a wheel, immobilizes an illegally parked car. **6.** a U.S. Navy or Marine recruit. **7.** a kick. **8. the boot,** *Slang.* a dismissal; discharge: *to give someone the boot for being always late.* **9.** *Informal.* a sensation of pleasure or amusement: *I get a big boot from the kids.* **10.** a fumble of a baseball batted on the ground, usu. to the infield. —*v.t.* **11.** to kick; drive by kicking. **12.** to fumble (a ground ball). **13.** to put boots on; equip or provide with boots. **14.** Also, **bootstrap.** to start (a computer) by loading the operating system. **15.** *Slang.* to dismiss; discharge. —*Idiom.* **16. bet your boots,** to be sure; be certain. **17. die with one's boots on,** to die while still active in one's work. **18. lick someone's boots,** to be subservient to someone; toady.

boot² (boot), *v.* —*Idiom.* **to boot,** in addition; besides.

boot·black (boot'blak'), *n.* a person who shines shoes and boots for a living.

boot' camp', *n.* a camp for training U.S. Navy or Marine recruits.

boot·ee (boo tē' *or, esp. for 1, 3* boo'tē), *n.* **1.** Also, **bootie.** a baby's socklike shoe, usu. knitted or crocheted, and calf-length or shorter. **2.** any boot having a short leg. **3.** BOOTIE (def. 1).

booth (booth), *n., pl.* **booths** (boothz, booths). **1.** a stall or light structure for the sale of goods or for display purposes, as at a market or exhibition. **2.** a small compartment or boxlike room for a specific use by one occupant: *a telephone booth; a voting booth.* **3.** a partly enclosed compartment or partitioned area, as in a restaurant, music store, etc. **4.** any temporary structure, as of boughs or canvas, used esp. for shelter.

Booth (booth; *Brit.* booth), *n.* **1. Ballington,** 1859–1940, founder of the Volunteers of America, 1896 (son of William Booth). **2. Catherine Mumford,** 1829–90, English religious leader (wife of William Booth). **3. Evangeline Cory,** 1865?–1950, general of the Salvation Army 1934–39 (daughter of William Booth). **4. John Wilkes,** 1838–65, U.S. actor: assassin of Abraham Lincoln. **5. William** ("*General Booth*"), 1829–1912, English religious leader: founder of the Salvation Army 1865.

boot·ie (boo'tē), *n.* Also, **bootee.** **1.** a usu. soft, sometimes disposable sock or bootlike covering for the foot or shoe, as for informal wear, warmth, or protection. **2.** BOOTEE (def. 1).

boot·jack (boot'jak'), *n.* a yokelike device for catching the heel of a boot, as a riding boot, to aid in removing it.

boot·leg (boot'leg'), *n., v.,* **-legged, -leg·ging,** *adj.* —*n.* **1.** alcoholic liquor unlawfully made, sold, or transported. **2.** something, as a recording, made, reproduced, or sold unlawfully or without authorization. —*v.t.* **3.** to deal in (liquor or other goods) unlawfully. —*v.i.* **4.** to make, transport, or sell something, esp. liquor, unlawfully or without registration or payment of taxes. —*adj.* **5.** made, sold, or transported unlawfully. **6.** unlawful or clandestine. —**boot'leg'ger,** *n.*

boot·less (boot'lis), *adj.* without result, gain, or advantage; useless.

boot·lick (boot'lik'), *v.t.* **1.** to seek the favor or goodwill of in a servile, degraded way; toady to. —*v.i.* **2.** to be a toady. —**boot'lick'er,** *n.*

boot·strap (boot'strap'), *n., adj., v.,* **-strapped, -strap·ping.** —*n.* **1.** a loop of leather or cloth sewn at the top rear, or sometimes on each side, of a boot to facilitate pulling it on. —*adj.* **2.** relying entirely on one's efforts and resources: *a bootstrap operation.* **3.** self-generating or self-sustaining: *a bootstrap process.* —*v.t.* **4.** to help (oneself) without the aid of others. **5.** *Computers.* BOOT¹ (def. 14). —*Idiom.* **6. pull oneself up by one's (own) bootstraps,** to become a success through one's own efforts.

boo·ty (boo'tē), *n., pl.* **-ties.** **1.** spoil taken from an enemy in war; plunder; pillage. **2.** something that is seized by violence and robbery. **3.** any prize or gain.

booze (booz), *n., v.,* **boozed, booz·ing.** *Informal.* —*n.* **1.** any alcoholic drink, as whiskey. **2.** a drinking bout or spree. —*v.i.* **3.** to drink alcoholic liquor, esp. to excess. —*Idiom.* **4. booze it up,** to drink excessively. —**booz'er,** *n.* —**booz'y,** *adj.,* **-i·er, -i·est.**

bop¹ (bop), *n., v.,* **bopped, bop·ping.** —*n.* **1.** Also called **bebop.** jazz marked by often dissonant harmony, fast tempos, eccentric rhythms, and melodic intricacy. —*v.i.* **2.** to dance or move to bop music. **3.** *Slang.* to move, go, or proceed.

bop² (bop), *v.,* **bopped, bop·ping,** *n. Slang.* —*v.t.* **1.** to strike, as with the fist or a stick; hit. —*n.* **2.** a blow.

bor•age (bôr′ij, bor′-, bûr′-), *n.* a plant, *Borago officinalis,* native to S Europe, having hairy leaves and stems, and used medicinally and in salads.

bo•rate (*n.* bôr′āt, -it, bôr′-; *v.* bôr′āt, bōr′-), *n., v.,* **-rat•ed, -rat•ing.** —*n.* **1.** a salt or ester of boric acid. —*v.t.* **2.** to treat with borate, boric acid, or borax.

bo•rax[1] (bôr′aks, -əks, bōr′-), *n., pl.* **bo•rax•es, bo•ra•ces** (bôr′ə sēz′, bōr′-). a white, water-soluble powder or crystals, hydrated sodium borate, Na₂B₄O₇·10H₂O, used as a flux, as a cleansing agent, in glassmaking, and in tanning.

bo•rax[2] (bôr′aks, -əks, bōr′-), *n.* cheap, showy, poorly made merchandise, esp. cheaply built furniture of an undistinguished style.

bor•de•laise′ sauce′ (bôr′dl āz′, -ez′), *n.* a brown sauce flavored with red wine and shallots.

Bor•den (bôr′dn), *n.* **1. Gail,** 1801–74, U.S. inventor: developed technique for condensing milk. **2. Lizzie (Andrew),** 1860–1927, defendant in U.S. 1893 trial: acquitted of ax murder of father and stepmother. **3. Sir Robert Laird** (lârd), 1854–1937, Canadian statesman: prime minister 1911–20.

bor•der (bôr′dər), *n.* **1.** the part or edge of a surface or area that forms its outer boundary. **2.** the line that separates one country, state, province, etc., from another; frontier line. **3.** the district or region that lies along the boundary line of another. **4.** brink; verge. **5.** an ornamental design along the edge of a printed page, a drawing, a fabric, etc., or a piece of ornamental trimming around the edge of a rug, garment, article of furniture, etc. **6.** a long, narrow bed of plantings, as along a garden pathway. —*v.t.* **7.** to make a border around; adorn with a border. **8.** to form a border or boundary to. **9.** to lie on the border of; adjoin. —*v.i.* **10.** to form or constitute a border; abut. **11.** to approach closely in character; verge: *The situation borders on comedy.*

bor•der•line (bôr′dər līn′), *n.* **1.** Also, **bor′der line′.** a boundary line; frontier. —*adj.* **2.** on or near a border or boundary. **3.** not quite meeting accepted, expected, or average standards; indefinite or indeterminate: *borderline cases; borderline alcoholism.*

Bor′der State′, *n.* (*sometimes l.c.*) any of the Slave States bordering on the North before the Civil War, usu. including Delaware, Maryland, Kentucky, Missouri, and Virginia: only Virginia seceded.

bore[1] (bôr, bōr), *v.,* **bored, bor•ing.** —*v.t.* **1.** to pierce (a solid substance) with some rotary cutting instrument. **2.** to make (a hole) with such an instrument. **3.** to make (a tunnel, mine, passage, etc.) by hollowing out, cutting through, or removing a core of material. **4.** to enlarge (a hole) to a precise diameter with a cutting tool within the hole, by rotating either the tool or the work. **5.** to force (an opening), as through a crowd, by persistent forward thrusting (usu. fol. by *through* or *into*). —*v.i.* **6.** to make a hole in a solid substance with a rotary cutting instrument. **7.** a hole made or enlarged by boring. **8.** the inside diameter of a hole or hollow cylindrical object, such as an engine cylinder or a gun barrel.

bore[2] (bôr, bōr), *v.,* **bored, bor•ing,** *n.* —*v.t.* **1.** to weary by dullness, repetition, unwelcome attentions, etc.: *The long speech bored me.* —*n.* **2.** a dull, tiresome, or uncongenial person. **3.** a cause of ennui or petty annoyance: *The play was a bore.* —**bor′ing,** *adj.*

bore[3] (bôr, bōr), *n.* an abrupt rise of tidal water moving rapidly inland from the mouth of an estuary.

bore[4] (bôr, bōr), *v.* pt. of BEAR[1].

bo•re•al (bôr′ē əl, bōr′-), *adj.* **1.** of or pertaining to the north wind. **2.** of or pertaining to the north.

bore•dom (bôr′dəm, bōr′-), *n.* the state of being bored; tedium; ennui.

bore•hole (bôr′hōl′, bōr′-), *n.* a hole drilled in the earth, as for the purpose of extracting a core or releasing gas, oil, water, etc.

bor•er (bôr′ər, bōr′-), *n.* **1.** a person or thing that bores or pierces. **2.** a tool used for boring; auger. **3.** any of various insects or their larvae that bore into trees, fruit, etc.

Bor•ghe•se (bôr gā′zē, -zä), *n.* a member of a noble Italian family, important in Italian politics and society from the 15th to the 19th century.

Bor•gia (bôr′jə, -zhə), *n.* **1. Cesare,** 1476?–1507, Italian cardinal, military leader, and politician. **2. Lucrezia** (*Duchess of Ferrara*), 1480–1519, sister of Cesare Borgia: patron of the arts. **3.** their father, **Rodrigo,** ALEXANDER VI.

bo•ric (bôr′ik, bōr′-), *adj.* of or containing boron.

bo•ric ac′id, *n.* **1.** a white, crystalline acid, H₃BO₃, used chiefly in the manufacture of ceramics, cements, and glass and as an antiseptic. **2.** any of a group of acids containing boron.

bor•ing (bôr′ing, bōr′-), *n.* **1. a.** the act or process of making or enlarging a hole. **b.** the hole so made. **2. borings,** the chips, fragments, or dust produced in boring.

bork (bôrk), *v.t.* to attack (a candidate or public figure) systematically, esp. in the media. [after Judge Robert H. *Bork,* whose appointment to the Supreme Court was blocked in 1987 after an extensive media campaign by his opponents]

born (bôrn), *adj.* **1.** brought forth by birth. **2.** possessing from birth the quality, circumstances, or character stated: *a born musician.* **3.** native to the locale stated: *a German-born scientist.* —*Idiom.* **4. born yesterday,** naive; inexperienced.

born′-again′, *adj.* **1.** committed or recommitted to faith through an intensely religious experience: *a born-again Christian.* **2.** reactivated or revitalized: *a born-again conservative.*

bo•ron (bôr′on, bōr′-), *n.* a nonmetallic element occurring naturally only in combination, as in borax or boric acid: used in alloys and nuclear reactors. *Symbol:* B; *at. wt.:* 10.811; *at. no.:* 5.

bor•ough (bûr′ō, bur′ō), *n.* **1.** (in certain U.S. states) an incorporated municipality smaller than a city. **2.** one of the five administrative divisions of New York City. **3.** (in Great Britain) **a.** a self-governing incorporated urban community. **b.** a town or constituency represented by a Member of Parliament. **c.** a medieval fortified town. **4.** (in Alaska) an administrative division similar to a county in other states.

bor•row (bor′ō, bôr′ō), *v.t.* **1.** to take or obtain with the promise to return the same or an equivalent: *to borrow a pencil.* **2.** to appropriate or introduce from another source or from a foreign source: *to borrow a word from French.* **3.** to take or adopt as one's own: *to borrow an idea from a competitor.* **4.** (in subtraction) to take from one denomination and add to the next lower. —*v.i.* **5.** to borrow something. —*Idiom.* **6. borrow trouble,** to do something unnecessary that may cause future harm or inconvenience. —**bor′row•a•ble,** *adj.* —**bor′row•er,** *n.* —**bor′row•ing,** *n.*

bor′rowed time′, *n.* time during which death or another inevitable event is postponed: *to live on borrowed time.*

borscht (bôrsht) also **borsch** (bôrsh), *n.* any of various E European soups made with beets, served hot or chilled, usu. with sour cream.

bor•zoi (bôr′zoi), *n., pl.* **-zois.** any of a breed of tall, slender, swift dogs with long, silky hair and a long, narrow head, raised orig. in Russia for hunting wolves. Also called **Russian wolfhound.**

bos•cage or **bos•kage** (bos′kij), *n.* a mass of trees or shrubs; wood, grove, or thicket.

Bos•ni•a (boz′nē ə), *n.* a historic region in S Europe: a former Turkish province; a part of Austria 1879–1918; now part of Bosnia and Herzegovina. —**Bos′ni•an,** *adj., n.*

Bos′nia and Herzegovi′na, *n.* a republic in S Europe: formerly (1945–92) a constituent republic of Yugoslavia. 2,607,734; 19,741 sq. mi. (51,129 sq. km). *Cap.:* Sarajevo.

bos•om (bŏŏz′əm, bōō′zəm), *n.* **1.** the breast of a human being: *The father held the baby to his bosom.* **2.** the part of a garment that covers the breast. **3.** the breast, conceived of as the center of feelings or emotions: *Anger lay in her bosom.* **4.** something likened to the human breast: *the bosom of the earth.* **5.** a state of enclosing intimacy; warm closeness: *the bosom of the family.* —*adj.* **6.** intimate: *a bosom friend.* —*v.t.* **7.** to take to the bosom; embrace; cherish. **8.** to hide from view.

Bos•po•rus (bos′pər əs) also **Bos•pho•rus** (-fər-), *n.* a strait connecting the Black Sea and the Sea of Marmara. 18 mi. (29 km) long. —**Bos′po•ran, Bos•po•ran•ic** (bos′pə ran′ik), **Bos•po•ri•an** (bo spôr′ē ən, -spōr′-), *adj.*

boss[1] (bôs, bos), *n.* **1.** a person who employs or superintends workers; foreperson or manager. **2.** a politician who controls the party organization, as in a particular district. **3.** a person who makes decisions, exercises authority, etc.: *I'm the boss in my house.* —*v.t.* **4.** to be master of or over; direct. **5.** to order about, esp. in an arrogant manner. —*v.i.* **6.** to be boss. **7.** to be too domineering and authoritative. —*adj.* **8.** chief; master. **9.** *Slang.* first-rate. [< Dutch *baas* master]

boss[2] (bôs, bos), *n.* **1.** a knoblike mass on the body or on some organ of an animal or plant. **2.** an ornamental protuberance of metal, ivory, etc.; stud. **3.** an ornamental, knoblike architectural projection, as a carved stone at the intersection of ribs in a vault. —*v.t.* **4.** to ornament with bosses. [< Anglo-French *boce* lump]

boss[3] (bos, bôs), *n.* a familiar name for a calf or cow.

bos•sa no•va (bos′ə nō′və, bô′sə), *n., pl.* **bossa no•vas. 1.** jazz-influenced music of Brazilian origin, rhythmically related to the samba. **2.** a dance performed to this music.

boss•y[1] (bô′sē, bos′ē), *adj.,* **boss•i•er, boss•i•est.** given to ordering people about; overly authoritative; domineering. —**boss′i•ly,** *adv.* —**boss′i•ness,** *n.*

boss•y[2] (bô′sē, bos′ē), *adj.,* **boss•i•er, boss•i•est.** studded with bosses.

Bos•ton (bô′stən, bos′tən), *n.* the capital of Massachusetts, in the E part. 547,725. —**Bos•to•ni•an** (bô stō′nē ən, bo stō′-), *adj., n.*

Bos′ton brown′ bread′, *n.* a dark-brown steamed bread made of cornmeal and rye meal or graham or wheat flour sweetened with molasses.

Bos′ton cream′ pie′, *n.* a two-layer cake with a cream or custard filling and often chocolate icing.

Bos′ton fern′, *n.* a variety of sword fern, *Nephrolepis exaltata bostoniensis,* having long, narrow, drooping fronds.

Bos′ton i′vy, *n.* a climbing woody vine, *Parthenocissus tricuspidata,* of the grape family, native to E Asia: grown as a wall covering. Also called **Japanese ivy.**

Bos′ton Mas′sacre, *n.* a riot (March 5, 1770) of Boston colonists against British troops quartered in the city, in which the troops fired on the mob and killed several persons.

Bos′ton Tea′ Par′ty, *n.* a raid on British tea ships in Boston Harbor (Dec. 16, 1773) in which Boston colonists, disguised as Indians, threw the tea into the water as a protest against British taxes on tea.

Bos′ton ter′rier, *n.* any of an American breed of small, shorthaired dogs with a short, square muzzle, erect ears, and a brindled or black coat with white markings.

Bos•well (boz′wel′, -wəl), *n.* **1. James,** 1740–95, Scottish author: biographer of Samuel Johnson. **2.** any devoted biographer of a specific person. —**Bos•well/i•an,** *adj.*

Bos'worth Field' (boz'wərth), *n.* a battlefield in central England where Richard III was defeated by the future Henry VII in 1485.

bo•tan•i•cal (bə tan'i kəl), *adj.* Also, **bo•tan'ic. 1.** of, pertaining to, or derived from plants. **2.** of or pertaining to botany: *botanical research.* **3.** of or belonging to a plant species. —*n.* **4.** a drug made from part of a plant, as from roots or bark.

botan'ical gar'den, *n.* a garden for the exhibition and scientific study of collected growing plants.

bot•a•ny (bot'n ē), *n.*, *pl.* **-nies. 1.** the science of plants; the branch of biology that deals with plant life. **2.** the plant life of a region. **3.** the biological characteristics of a plant or plant group. —**bot'a•nist,** *n.*

botch (boch), *v.t.* **1.** to spoil by poor work; bungle. **2.** to do or say in a bungling manner. **3.** to mend or patch in a clumsy manner. —*n.* **4.** a poor piece of work; mess; bungle. **5.** a clumsily added part or patch.

bot•fly (bot'flī'), *n.*, *pl.* **-flies.** any of several flies of the families Oestridae, Gasterophilidae, and Cuterebrídae, the larvae of which are parasitic in the skin or other parts of various mammals.

both (bōth), *adj.* **1.** one and the other; two together: *I met both sisters.* —*pron.* **2.** the one as well as the other: *Both of us were ill.* —*conj.* **3.** alike; equally: *I am both ready and willing.*

both•er (both'ər), *v.t.* **1.** to give trouble to; annoy; pester: *Noise bothers me.* **2.** to bewilder; confuse: *His inability to get the joke bothered him.* **3.** to worry; distress: *It bothers us that she is so careless.* —*v.i.* **4.** to take the trouble; trouble or inconvenience oneself: *Don't bother to call.* —*n.* **5.** something or someone troublesome or burdensome. **6.** effort, work, or worry: *Gardening takes more bother than it's worth.* **7.** a worried or perplexed state: *Don't get into such a bother about small matters.*

both•er•some (both'ər səm), *adj.* causing annoyance or worry; troublesome.

bo' tree' (bō), *n.* the pipal, or sacred fig tree, of India, under which the founder of Buddhism is reputed to have attained the Enlightenment that constituted him the Buddha.

Bot•swa•na (bot swä'nə), *n.* a republic in S Africa; formerly a British protectorate; gained independence 1966; member of the Commonwealth of Nations. 1,500,765; 275,000 sq. mi. (712,250 sq. km). *Cap.:* Gaborone. Formerly, **Bechuanaland.**

Bot•ti•cel•li (bot'i chel'ē), *n.* **Sandro** (*Alessandro di Mariano dei Filipepi*), 1444?–1510, Italian painter.

bot•tle (bot'l), *n.*, *v.*, **-tled, -tling.** —*n.* **1.** a portable container for holding liquids, having a neck and mouth and made of glass or plastic. **2.** the contents or capacity of such a container: *a bottle of wine.* **3.** bottled cow's milk, milk formulas, or substitute mixtures given to infants instead of mother's milk: *raised on the bottle.* **4.** the bottle, intoxicating beverages; liquor. —*v.t.* **5.** to put into or seal in a bottle: *to bottle grape juice.* **6. bottle up, a.** to repress, control, or restrain: *to bottle up anger.* **b.** to enclose or entrap: *Traffic was bottled up in the tunnel.* —**Idiom.** **7. hit the bottle,** *Slang.* to drink alcohol to excess.

bot•tle•brush (bot'l brush'), *n.* any Australasian tree or shrub of the genera *Callistemon* and *Melaleuca*, of the myrtle family, having a flower spike with pink or yellow brushlike tufts.

bot'tled gas', *n.* **1.** gas stored in portable cylinders under pressure. **2.** LIQUEFIED PETROLEUM GAS.

bot'tle gourd', *n.* a hard-shelled gourd, *Lagenaria siceraria,* whose dried shell is used for bowls and other utensils.

bot'tle green', *n.* a deep green. —**bot'tle-green',** *adj.*

bot•tle•neck (bot'l nek'), *n.* **1.** a narrow entrance or passageway. **2.** a place or stage at which progress is impeded. **3.** a method of guitar playing that produces a gliding sound by pressing a metal bar or glass tube against the strings. —*v.t.* **4.** to hamper or confine by or as if by a bottleneck. —*v.i.* **5.** to become hindered by or as if by a bottleneck.

bot'tle-nosed' dol'phin, *n.* any of several dolphins of the genus *Tursiops,* common in North Atlantic and Mediterranean waters, having a rounded forehead and well-defined beak.

bot•tom (bot'əm), *n.* **1.** the lowest or deepest part of anything, as distinguished from the top: *the bottom of a page; ice on the bottom of the glass.* **2.** the under or lower side; underside: *the bottom of a typewriter.* **3.** the ground under any body of water: *the bottom of the sea.* **4.** Usu., **bottoms,** low alluvial land next to a river. **5. a.** the part of a hull of a vessel that is immersed at all times. **b.** a cargo vessel. **6.** the seat of a chair. **7.** *Informal.* the buttocks; rump. **8.** the fundamental part; basic aspect. **9. bottoms,** (used with a pl. v.) the trousers or pants of a pair of pajamas. **10.** the cause; origin; basis. **11.** the second half of an inning in baseball. **12.** the lowest limit, esp. of dignity or status; nadir. **13.** the working part of a plow, comprising the plowshare, landside, and moldboard. —*v.t.* **14.** to furnish with a bottom. **15.** to base or found (usu. fol. by *on* or *upon*). **16.** to discover the full meaning of (something); fathom. —*v.i.* **17.** to be based; rest. **18.** to strike against or reach the bottom. **19. bottom out,** to reach the lowest state or level. —*adj.* **20.** of or pertaining to the bottom or a bottom. **21.** located on or at the bottom: *the bottom floor.* **22.** lowest: *bottom prices.* **23.** living near or on the bottom: *A flounder is a bottom fish.* **24.** fundamental: *the bottom cause.* —**Idiom.** **25. at bottom,** in reality; fundamentally. **26. at the bottom of,** really causing; responsible for. **27. bet one's bottom dollar, a.** to wager the last of one's money or resources. **b.** to be

positive or assured. **28. bottoms up,** (used interjectionally in downing a drink.)

bot•tom•less (bot'əm lis), *adj.* **1.** lacking a bottom. **2.** immeasurably deep. **3.** without bounds; unlimited: *a bottomless supply of money.* **4.** without basis, cause, or reason: *a bottomless accusation.*

bot'tomless pit', *n.* **1.** hell (def. 1). **2.** something that drains all one's energy or resources.

bot'tom line', *n.* **1.** the last line of a financial statement, used for showing net profit or loss. **2.** net profit or loss. **3.** the deciding or crucial factor. **4.** the result or outcome. —**bot'tom-line',** *adj.*

bot•tom•most (bot'əm mōst' *or, esp. Brit,* -məst), *adj.* **1.** of, pertaining to, or situated at the bottom. **2.** (of one of a series) farthest down; lowest. **3.** bottom.

bot'tom round', *n.* a cut of beef taken from the outer part of the round.

bot•u•lin (boch'ə lin), *n.* the toxin formed by botulinus and causing botulism.

bot•u•li•nus (boch'ə lī'nəs) also **bot•u•li•num** (-lī'nəm), *n.*, *pl.* **-nus•es** also **-nums.** a soil bacterium, *Clostridium botulinum,* that thrives and forms botulin under anaerobic conditions.

bot•u•lism (boch'ə liz'əm), *n.* a sometimes fatal disease of the nervous system acquired from spoiled foods in which botulin is present, esp. improperly canned or marinated foods.

bou•clé or **bou•cle** (bōō klā'), *n.*, *pl.* **-clés** or **-cles. 1.** yarn with loops producing a rough, nubby appearance on woven or knitted fabrics. **2.** a fabric made of this yarn.

bou•doir (bōō'dwär, -dwôr), *n.* a woman's bedroom or private sitting room. [< French: lit., a sulking space]

bouf•fant (bōō fänt', bōō'fänt), *adj.* **1.** puffed out; full: *a bouffant skirt.* —*n.* **2.** a woman's hairstyle in which the hair is teased to give an overall puffed-out appearance.

bou•gain•vil•le•a (bōō'gən vil'ē ə, -vil'yə, bō'-), *n.*, *pl.* **-le•as.** any of several South American shrubs or vines belonging to the genus *Bougainvillea,* of the four-o'clock family, having small flowers with showy, variously colored bracts.

bough (bou), *n.* a branch of a tree, esp. one of the larger branches. —**bough'less,** *adj.*

bought (bôt), *v.* pt. and pp. of BUY.

bouil•la•baisse (bōō'yə bās', bōōl'-, bōō'yə bäs', bōōl'-), *n.* a soup or stew containing several kinds of fish and often shellfish, usu. combined with olive oil, tomatoes, and saffron.

bouil•lon (bōōl'yon, -yən, bōō'-, bōō yôn'), *n.* a clear, usu. seasoned broth made by straining the liquid in which beef, chicken, etc., has been cooked.

boul•der (bōl'dər), *n.* a detached and rounded or worn rock, esp. a large one.

Boul'der Dam', *n.* a dam on the Colorado River, on the boundary between SE Nevada and NW Arizona. 726 ft. (221 m) high; 1244 ft. (379 m) long. Official name, **Hoover Dam.**

boule (bōōl), *n.* a single crystal of material produced by a fusion process and used for making synthetic gemstones.

boul•e•vard (bōōl'ə värd', bōō'lə-), *n.* a broad avenue in a city, usu. having areas at the sides or center for trees, grass, or flowers.

bounce (bouns), *v.*, **bounced, bounc•ing.** —*v.i.* **1.** to strike a surface and rebound; spring back: *The ball bounced once before she caught it.* **2.** to move or walk in a lively, exuberant, or energetic manner. **3.** to move along repeatedly striking a surface and rebounding: *The box bounced down the stairs.* **4.** (of a check) to be refused payment by a bank, due to insufficient funds in the account. —*v.t.* **5.** to cause to bound and rebound. **6.** to refuse payment on (a check) because of insufficient funds. **7.** *Slang.* to eject, expel, or dismiss summarily or forcibly. **8. bounce back,** to recover quickly. —*n.* **9.** a bound or rebound. **10.** a sudden spring or leap. **11.** ability to rebound; resilience. **12.** vitality; energy; liveliness. **13. the bounce,** *Slang.* a dismissal, rejection, or expulsion. —*adv.* **14.** with a bounce; suddenly. —**bounc'y,** *adj.*, **-i•er, -i•est.**

bounc•er (boun'sər), *n.* **1.** a person who is employed at a bar, nightclub, etc., to eject disorderly persons. **2.** a person or thing that bounces. **3.** something large of its kind.

bounc•ing (boun'sing), *adj.* **1.** stout, strong, or vigorous: *a bouncing baby.* **2.** exaggerated; hearty; noisy. —**bounc'ing•ly,** *adv.*

bound¹ (bound), *v.* **1.** pt. and pp. of BIND. —*adj.* **2.** tied; in bonds: *a bound prisoner.* **3.** made fast as if by a band or bond. **4.** secured within a cover, as a book. **5.** under a legal or moral obligation. **6.** destined or certain: *It is bound to happen.* **7.** determined or resolved: *He is bound to go.* **8.** constipated. **9.** held with another element, substance, or material in chemical or physical union. **10.** (of a linguistic form) occurring only in combination with other forms, never by itself, as most affixes: *The* -ed *in* seated *is a bound form.* Compare FREE (def. 31). **11.** (of a variable in logic) occurring within the scope of a quantifier. Compare FREE (def. 28). —**Idiom.** **12. bound up in** or **with, a.** inseparably connected with. **b.** devoted or attached to. —**bound'ness,** *n.*

bound² (bound), *v.i.* **1.** to move by leaps; spring. **2.** to rebound; bounce. —*n.* **3.** a leap onward or upward; jump. **4.** a rebound; bounce. —**bound'ing•ly,** *adv.*

bound³ (bound), *n.* **1.** Usu., **bounds.** limit or boundary: *within the bounds of reason.* **2.** something that limits, confines, or restrains. **3.**

bounds, a. territories on or near a boundary. **b.** land within boundary lines. **4.** a number greater than or equal to, or less than or equal to, all the numbers in a given set: *greatest lower bound.* —*v.t.* **5.** to limit by or as if by bounds. **6.** to form the boundary or limit of. **7.** to name or list the boundaries of. —*v.i.* **8.** to abut. —*Idiom.* **9.** **out of bounds, a.** beyond the official boundaries, prescribed limits, or restricted area. **b.** forbidden; prohibited. —**bound′a•ble,** *adj.*

bound⁴ (bound), *adj.* going or intending to go; destined (usu. fol. by *for*): *The train is bound for Denver.*

bound•a•ry (boun′də rē, -drē), *n., pl.* **-ries. 1.** something that indicates bounds or limits, as a line. **2.** *Math.* the collection of all points of a given set having the property that every neighborhood of each point contains points in the set and in the complement of the set.

bound•less (bound′lis), *adj.* having no bounds; infinite or vast; unlimited. —**bound′less•ly,** *adv.* —**bound′less•ness,** *n.*

boun•te•ous (boun′tē əs), *adj.* **1.** giving or disposed to give freely; generous; liberal. **2.** freely bestowed; plentiful; abundant. —**boun′te•ous•ly,** *adv.* —**boun′te•ous•ness,** *n.*

boun•ti•ful (boun′tə fəl), *adj.* **1.** liberal in bestowing gifts or favors; munificent; generous. **2.** abundant; ample: *a bountiful supply.* —**boun′ti•ful•ly,** *adv.*

boun•ty (boun′tē), *n., pl.* **-ties. 1.** a premium or reward, esp. one offered by a government. **2.** a generous gift. **3.** generosity.

boun′ty hunt′er, *n.* a person who hunts outlaws or wild animals for the bounty offered for capturing or killing them.

bou•quet (bō kā′, bōō- for 1, 3; bōō kā′ or, occas., bō- for 2), *n.* **1.** a bunch of flowers; nosegay. **2.** the characteristic aroma of wines, liqueurs, etc. **3.** a compliment.

bouquet′ gar•ni′ (gär nē′), *n., pl.* **bouquets gar•nis** (gär nē′). a small bunch of herbs tied together or wrapped in cheesecloth and used to flavor soups and stews.

Bour•bon (bōōr′bən, bōōr bôn′ for 1–3; bûr′bən for 4 or, occas., for 3), *n.* **1.** a member of a French royal family that ruled in France 1589–1792, 1814–1848. Branches of the family have ruled in Spain, Sicily, and Naples. **2. Charles,** (*"Constable de Bourbon"*), 1490–1527, French general. **3.** a person who is extremely conservative or reactionary. **4.** (*l.c.*) Also called **bour′bon whis′key.** a straight whiskey distilled from a mash having 51 percent or more corn: orig. the corn whiskey produced in Bourbon County, Ky.

bourg (bōōrg, bōōr), *n.* **1.** a town. **2.** a French market town.

bour•geois¹ (bōōr zhwä′, bōōr′zhwä), *n., pl.* **-geois,** *adj.* —*n.* **1.** a member of the bourgeoisie or middle class. **2.** a person who is generally materialistic and concerned with respectability and convention. **3.** a shopkeeper or merchant. —*adj.* **4.** belonging to, characteristic of, or consisting of the middle class. **5.** characterized by or concerned with materialism and convention.

bour•geois² (bər jois′), *n.* a size of type approximately 9-point, between brevier and long primer.

bour•geoi•sie (bōōr′zhwä zē′), *n.* **1.** the middle class. **2.** (in Marxist theory) the property-owning capitalist class in conflict with the proletariat.

bout (bout), *n.* **1.** a contest, as of boxing; match. **2.** period; spell: *a bout of illness.* **3.** a turn at work or any action. **4.** a going and returning across a field, as in mowing or reaping.

bou•tique (bōō tēk′), *n.* **1.** a small shop or specialty department within a larger store, esp. one that sells fashionable items. **2.** any small, exclusive business. **3.** a small business specializing in one aspect of a larger field: *a pension boutique.* —*adj.* **4. a.** exclusive, exotic, or small-scale: *boutique beer.* **b.** producing boutique products: *a boutique farm.*

bou•ton•niere (bōōt′n ēr′, bōō′tən yâr′), *n.* a flower or small bouquet worn, usu. by a man, in the buttonhole of a lapel.

bo•vine (bō′vīn, -vēn), *adj.* **1.** of or pertaining to the subfamily Bovinae, which includes cattle, buffalo, and kudus. **2.** oxlike; cowlike. **3.** stolid; dull. —*n.* **4.** a bovine animal.

bo′vine growth′ hor′mone, *n.* **1.** a growth hormone of cattle that regulates growth and milk production in cows. **2.** the same hormone, harvested in large quantities from genetically engineered bacteria for daily injection into dairy cows to increase milk production. *Abbr.:* bGH Also called **bo′vine somatotro′pin.**

bow¹ (bou), *v.i.* **1.** to bend the knee or body or incline the head, as in reverence, submission, or salutation. **2.** to yield; submit: *to bow to the inevitable.* **3.** to bend or curve downward; stoop: *The pines bowed low.* —*v.t.* **4.** to bend or incline (the knee, body, or head) in worship, submission, respect, civility, etc. **5.** to cause to submit; subdue; crush. **6.** to cause to stoop or incline. **7.** to express by a bow: *to bow one's thanks.* **8.** to usher (someone) with a bow: *They were bowed in by the footman.* **9.** to cause to bend; make curved or crooked. **10. bow out,** to withdraw by choice, as from a task; retire. —*n.* **11.** an inclination of the head or body in salutation, assent, thanks, reverence, submission, etc. —*Idiom.* **12. bow and scrape,** to be excessively polite or deferential. **13. take a bow,** to step forward or stand up to receive recognition, applause, etc.

bow² (bō), *n.* **1.** a flexible strip of wood or other material, bent by a string stretched between its ends, for shooting arrows. **2.** a bend or curve. **3.** a readily loosened knot for joining the ends of a ribbon or string, having two projecting loops. **4.** a loop or gathering of ribbon, paper, etc., used as a decoration. **5.** a flexible rod having horsehairs stretched from end to end, used for playing a musical instrument of the

viol or violin families. **6.** something curved or arc-shaped. **7.** an archer; bowman. **8.** TEMPLE² (def. 2). **9.** RAINBOW. **10.** a U-shaped piece for placing under an animal's neck to hold a yoke. —*adj.* **11.** curved outward at the center; bent: *bow legs.* —*v.t., v.i.* **12.** to bend into the form of a bow; curve. **13.** to perform with a bow on a stringed musical instrument.

bow³ (bou), *n.* **1.** the forward end of a vessel or airship. **2.** the foremost oar in rowing a boat. —*adj.* **3.** of or pertaining to the bow of a ship.

Bow•ditch (bou′dich), *n.* **Nathaniel,** 1773–1838, U.S. mathematician, astronomer, and navigator.

bowd•ler•ize (bōd′lə rīz′, boud′-), *v.t.,* **-ized, -iz•ing.** to expurgate (a written work) by removing or changing passages one considers vulgar or objectionable. [after T. *Bowdler* (1754–1825), English editor of an expurgated edition of Shakespeare] —**bowd′ler•i•za′tion,** *n.*

bow•el (bou′əl, boul), *n., v.,* **-eled, -el•ing** or (*esp. Brit.*) **-elled, -el•ling.** —*n.* **1.** Usu., **bowels.** the intestine. **2. bowels,** the inward or interior parts: *the bowels of the earth.* —*v.t.* **3.** to disembowel.

bow′el move′ment, *n.* the evacuation of the bowels; defecation.

bow•er¹ (bou′ər), *n.* **1.** a leafy shelter or recess; arbor. **2.** a rustic dwelling; cottage. **3.** a lady's boudoir in a medieval castle. —*v.t.* **4.** to enclose in or as if in a bower.

bow•er² (bou′ər), *n.* an anchor carried at a ship's bow.

bow•er³ (bou′ər), *n.* one that bows or bends.

bow•er•bird (bou′ər bûrd′), *n.* any of various songbirds of the Australian and Papuan family Ptilonorhynchidae, the males of which build bowerlike structures, often brightly decorated, to attract the female.

bow•fin (bō′fin′), *n.* a freshwater fish, *Amia calva,* of central and E North America, having a long, narrow dorsal fin. Also called **dogfish.**

bow•front (bō′frunt′), *adj.* having a horizontally convex front, as a piece of furniture.

bow•head (bō′hed′), *n.* a whalebone whale, *Balaena mysticetus,* of northern seas, having an enormous head and mouth.

bow′ie knife′ (bō′ē, bōō′ē), *n.* a heavy sheath knife having a long, single-edged blade. [after J. *Bowie* (1799–1836), U.S. pioneer, for whom the knife was designed]

bow•ing (bō′ing), *n.* the technique of using a bow in playing a stringed musical instrument.

bowl¹ (bōl), *n.* **1.** a rather deep, round dish or basin, used chiefly for holding liquids, food, etc. **2.** the contents of a bowl. **3.** a rounded, cuplike, hollow part: *the bowl of a pipe.* **4.** a large drinking cup. **5.** any bowl-shaped depression or formation. **6.** amphitheater; stadium.

bowl² (bōl), *n.* **1.** one of the biased or weighted balls used in lawn bowling. **2. bowls,** (*used with a sing. v.*) LAWN BOWLING. **3.** a delivery of the ball in bowling or lawn bowling. —*v.i.* **4.** to play at bowling or lawn bowling. **5.** to move along smoothly and rapidly. —*v.t.* **6.** to roll or trundle, as a ball or hoop. **7.** to attain by bowling: *She bowls a good game.* **8.** to knock or strike, as by the ball in bowling. **9. bowl over,** to surprise greatly.

bow•leg (bō′leg′), *n.* **1.** outward curvature of the legs causing a separation of the knees when the ankles are close or in contact. **2.** a leg so curved. —**bow′leg′ged,** *adj.* —**bow′leg′ged•ness,** *n.*

bow•line (bō′lin, -līn′), *n.* **1.** Also called **bow′line knot′.** a knot used to make a nonslipping loop on the end of a rope. **2.** a rope fastened to the leech of a square sail to keep the sail as flat as possible when sailing close-hauled.

bowl•ing (bō′ling), *n.* **1.** any of several games in which players roll balls at standing objects or toward a mark, esp. a game in which a heavy ball is rolled down a wooden alley at wooden pins. **2.** an act or instance of playing or participating in any such game.

bowl′ing al′ley, *n.* **1.** a long, narrow wooden lane or alley, for the game of tenpins. **2.** an establishment containing a number of such lanes.

bow•sprit (bou′sprit, bō′-), *n.* a spar projecting from the upper end of the bow of a sailing vessel, for holding the tacks of various jibs or stays.

bow•string (bō′string′), *n., v.,* **-stringed** or **-strung, -string•ing.** —*n.* **1.** the string of an archer's bow. **2.** a horsehair string on the bow of a musical instrument. —*v.t.* **3.** to strangle with a string.

bow′ tie′ (bō), *n.* **1.** a small necktie tied in a bow at the collar. **2.** something, as a sweet roll, shaped like this.

box¹ (boks), *n.* **1.** a container, case, or receptacle, usu. rectangular, and often with a lid or cover. **2.** the quantity contained in a box. **3.** a compartment for the accommodation of a small number of people, as in a theater. **4.** a small enclosure in a courtroom for witnesses or the jury. **5.** a small shelter: *a sentry's box.* **6. the box,** television. **7.** a part of a printed page containing material enclosed in a border, as an obituary or classified advertisement. **8.** any enclosing, protective case or housing. **9.** any of various spaces on a baseball diamond marking the playing positions of the pitcher, catcher, batter, or coaches. **10.** *Informal.* Also called **boom box.** a large, powerful portable radio or combination radio and cassette player. **11.** the driver's seat on a coach. **12.** the section of a wagon in which passengers or parcels are carried. —*v.t.* **13.** to put into a box. **14.** to enclose or confine as if in a box (often fol. by *in* or *up*). **15.** to furnish with a box. **16.** to form into a box or the shape of a box. **17.** to block so as to keep from passing or achieving a better position (often fol. by *in*). **18.** to group together for consideration as one unit: *to box bills in the legislature.* **19.** to enclose or conceal (a structure) as with boarding. —**box′like′,** *adj.*

box² (boks), *n.* **1.** a blow with the hand or fist: *a box on the ear.* —*v.t.* **2.** to strike with the hand or fist, esp. on the ear. **3.** to fight against (someone) in a boxing match. —*v.i.* **4.** to participate in a boxing match.

box³ (boks), *n.* **1.** any of various evergreen shrubs or small trees of the genus *Buxus,* esp. *B. sempervirens,* having shiny, elliptic, dark green leaves, used for ornamental borders and hedges and yielding a hard, durable wood. **2.** any of various other shrubs or trees, esp. species of eucalyptus.

box⁴ (boks), *v.t.* —**Idiom.** **box the compass, 1.** to recite the points of the compass in a clockwise order. **2.** to make a complete turn or reversal.

box′ cam′era, *n.* a simple, boxlike camera, sometimes allowing for adjustment of the lens opening but usu. not of shutter speed.

box•car (boks′kär′), *n.* **1.** a completely enclosed railroad freight car. **2. boxcars,** a pair of sixes on the first throw in craps.

box′ el′der, *n.* a North American maple, *Acer negundo,* having a light gray-brown bark and coarsely toothed leaves.

box•er (bok′sər), *n.* **1.** a person who fights as a sport, usu. with gloved fists, according to set rules; prizefighter; pugilist. **2.** any of a German breed of medium-sized, stocky, shorthaired dogs with a short, square muzzle, a brindled or tan coat, and a docked tail.

Box•er (bok′sər), *n.* a member of a Chinese secret society that carried on an unsuccessful uprising in 1900 **(Box′er Rebel′lion),** principally against foreigners.

box′er shorts′, *n.* (*used with a pl. v.*) men's loose-fitting undershorts with an elastic waistband.

box•ing¹ (bok′sing), *n.* **1.** the material used to make boxes or casings. **2.** a boxlike enclosure; casing. **3.** an act or instance of putting into or furnishing with a box.

box•ing² (bok′sing), *n.* the act, technique, or profession of fighting with the fists, with or without boxing gloves.

box′ lunch′, *n.* a lunch or light meal packed in a cardboard box or similar container.

box′ of′fice, *n.* **1.** the office of a theater, stadium, or the like, at which tickets are sold. **2. a.** receipts from a play or other entertainment. **b.** entertainment popular enough to attract paying audiences and make a profit: *This show will be good box office.* —**box′-of′fice,** *adj.*

box′ seat′, *n.* a seat in a box at the theater, opera, etc.

box′ spring′, *n.* an upholstered bedspring composed of a number of helical springs, each in a cylindrical cloth pocket.

box′ tur′tle, *n.* any chiefly terrestrial North American turtle of the genus *Terrapene,* having a hinged shell that can be tightly shut. Also called **box′ tor′toise.**

box•wood (boks′wŏŏd′), *n.* **1.** the hard, fine-grained, compact wood of the box shrub or tree, used esp. for wood-engravers' blocks and musical instruments. **2.** the tree or shrub itself. Compare BOX³.

box•y (bok′sē), *adj.,* **box•i•er, box•i•est.** like or resembling a box, esp. in shape. —**box′i•ness,** *n.*

boy (boi), *n.* **1.** a male child, from birth to full growth. **2.** a young man who lacks maturity, judgment, etc. **3.** *Informal.* a grown man, esp. when referred to familiarly. **4.** a son. **5.** a male who is from or native to a given place: *He's a country boy.* **6. boys,** (*used with a sing. or pl. v.*) **a.** a range of sizes from 8 to 20 in garments for boys. **b.** a garment in this range. —*interj.* **7.** an exclamation of wonder, approval, etc., or of displeasure or contempt.

boy•cott (boi′kot), *v.t.* **1.** to join together in abstaining from, or preventing dealings with, as a means of protest or coercion: *to boycott a store.* **2.** to abstain from buying or using: *to boycott imported goods.* —*n.* **3.** the practice of boycotting. **4.** an instance of boycotting. [after C.C. *Boycott* (1832–97), English estate manager, first victim]

boy•friend (boi′frend′), *n.* **1.** a frequent or favorite male companion; beau. **2.** a male friend. **3.** a male lover.

boy•hood (boi′hŏŏd), *n.* **1.** the state or period of being a boy. **2.** boys collectively.

boy•ish (boi′ish), *adj.* of or befitting a boy; engagingly youthful. —**boy′ish•ly,** *adv.* —**boy′ish•ness,** *n.*

Boyle′s′ law′, *n.* the principle that, for relatively low pressures, the pressure of an ideal gas kept at constant temperature varies inversely with the volume of the gas.

Boyne (boin), *n.* a river in E Ireland: William III defeated James II near here 1690. 70 mi. (110 km) long.

boy′ scout′, *n.* **1.** (*sometimes caps.*) a member of an organization of boys **(Boy′ Scouts′),** founded in England in 1908 by Lieut. Gen. Sir Robert S. S. Baden-Powell, that seeks to develop certain skills in its members, as well as character, self-reliance, and usefulness to others. **2.** a member of any similar society elsewhere.

boy•sen•ber•ry (boi′zən ber′ē, -sən-), *n., pl.* **-ries.** a blackberrylike fruit with a flavor similar to that of raspberries, developed by crossing various plants belonging to the genus *Rubus,* of the rose family.

boy′ won′der, *n.* a young man whose skills or accomplishments are precocious.

bo•zo (bō′zō), *n., pl.* **-zos.** *Slang.* **1.** a fellow, esp. a stupid one. **2.** a rude or annoying person.

B.P. or **BP,** before the present: (in radiocarbon dating) in a specified amount of time or at a specified point in time before A.D. 1950.

B picture, *n.* a low-budget, usu. mediocre motion picture made esp. to accompany a major feature film on a double bill. Also called **B movie.**

bps or **BPS,** *Computers.* bits per second.

Br, *Chem. Symbol.* bromine.

bra (brä), *n.* BRASSIERE. —**bra′less,** *adj.*

brace (brās), *n., v.,* **braced, brac•ing.** —*n.* **1.** something that holds parts together or in place. **2.** anything that imparts rigidity or steadiness. **3.** a device for holding and turning a bit for boring or drilling. **4.** a piece of timber, metal, etc., for supporting or positioning another part of a framework. **5.** (on a square-rigged ship) a rope by which a yard is swung about and secured horizontally. **6.** Usu. **braces.** an oral appliance consisting generally of wires or bands, used to correct misalignment of the teeth and jaws by exerting pressure on the teeth and their supporting structures. **7.** an orthopedic appliance for supporting a weak joint or joints. **8.** a pair; couple: *a brace of grouse.* **9. a.** one of two characters { or } used to enclose words or lines to be considered together. **b.** BRACKET (def. 4). **10.** a printed brace connecting musical staves. **11.** a protective band for the wrist or lower arm, esp. a bracer. **12.** *Mil.* a position of attention with exaggeratedly stiff posture. —*v.t.* **13.** to furnish, fasten, or strengthen with or as if with a brace. **14.** to steady (oneself). **15.** to make tight; increase the tension of. **16.** to act as a stimulant to. **17.** to swing or turn around (the yards of a ship) by means of the braces. **18. brace up,** *Informal.* to summon up one's courage; become resolute.

brace•let (brās′lit), *n.* **1.** an ornamental band or circlet for the wrist or arm or, sometimes, for the ankle. **2. bracelets,** *Slang.* a pair of handcuffs. —**brace′let•ed,** *adj.*

brac•er¹ (brā′sər), *n.* **1.** a stimulating drink, esp. one of liquor. **2.** a person or thing that braces, binds, or makes firm.

brac•er² (brā′sər), *n.* an archer's protective band worn on the wrist of the bow hand.

bra•chi•al (brā′kē əl, brak′ē-), *adj.* **1.** belonging or pertaining to the arm, foreleg, wing, or pectoral fin of a vertebrate. **2.** armlike, as an appendage.

bra•chi•ate (*adj.* brā′kē it, -āt′, brak′ē-; *v.* -āt′), *adj., v.,* **-at•ed, -at•ing.** —*adj.* **1.** *Bot.* having widely spreading branches in alternate pairs. **2.** *Zool.* having arms. —*v.i.* **3.** to progress by means of brachiation.

bra•chi•a•tion (brā′kē ā′shən, brak′ē-), *n.* locomotion accomplished by swinging by the arms from one hold to another. —**bra′chi•a′tor,** *n.*

bra•chi•o•pod (brā′kē ə pod′, brak′ē-), *n.* any superficially clamlike marine animal of the phylum Brachiopoda, having unequal dorsal and ventral shells enclosing a pair of ciliated food-gathering appendages.

bra•chi•o•saur (brā′kē ə sôr′, brak′ē-), *n.* a sauropod dinosaur of the genus *Brachiosaurus,* having nostrils on a knob above the eyes and a sloping, massive body, and reaching a length of about 80 ft. (24 m).

bra•chi•um (brā′kē əm, brak′ē-), *n., pl.* **bra•chi•a** (brā′kē ə, brak′ē ə). **1.** the part of the arm from the shoulder to the elbow. **2.** the corresponding part of any limb, as in the wing of a bird. **3.** an armlike part or process.

brach•y•ur•an (brak′ē yŏŏr′ən), *adj.* **1.** belonging or pertaining to the suborder Brachyura, comprising the true crabs. —*n.* **2.** a brachyuran crustacean.

brac•ing (brā′sing), *adj.* **1.** stimulating; invigorating. **2.** of, pertaining to, or serving as a brace. —*n.* **3.** a brace. **4.** braces collectively. **5.** material, as timber, used for braces. —**brac′ing•ly,** *adv.*

brack•en (brak′ən), *n.* **1.** a large, coarse, worldwide fern, *Pteridium aquilinum,* of the polypody family, having large, creeping rootstocks and triangular fronds. **2.** a cluster or thicket of such ferns.

brack•et (brak′it), *n.* **1.** a supporting piece projecting from a wall or the like to bear the weight of a shelf, cornice, etc., or to reinforce the angle between two members. **2.** a shelf or shelves so supported. **3.** a wall fixture for holding a lamp, clock, telephone, etc. **4.** Also called **square bracket.** one of two marks, [or], used in writing or printing to enclose parenthetical matter, interpolations, etc. **5.** *Math.* **brackets,** parentheses of various forms indicating that the enclosed quantity is to be treated as a unit. **6.** a class, division, or grouping, as of persons in relation to their income or age. **7.** a projecting fixture for gas or electricity. **8.** gun range or elevation producing both shorts and overs on a target. —*v.t.* **9.** to furnish with or support by a bracket or brackets. **10.** to place within brackets. **11.** to associate, mention, or class together: *The problems were bracketed together.* **12.** to place (gunshots) both beyond and short of a target. **13.** to photograph (additional shots) at exposure levels above and below the estimated correct exposure.

brack′et fun′gus, *n.* any of the leathery, corky, or woody mushrooms that grow shelflike on the trunks of trees.

brack•ish (brak′ish), *adj.* **1.** slightly salt; salty or briny. **2.** distasteful; unpleasant. —**brack′ish•ness,** *n.*

bract (brakt), *n.* a specialized leaflike plant part, sometimes large and showy, usu. situated at the base of a flower or inflorescence. —**brac′te•al,** *adj.* —**brac′te•ate** (-tē it, -āt′), **bract′ed,** *adj.*

brac•te•ole (brak′tē ōl′) also **bract•let** (brakt′lit), *n.* a small or secondary bract, as on a pedicel.

brad (brad), *n., v.,* **brad•ded, brad•ding.** —*n.* **1.** a slender wire nail having either a small, deep head or a projection to one side of the head end. —*v.t.* **2.** to fasten with brads.

Brad•bur•y (brad′ber′ē, -bə rē), *n.* **William B(atchelder),** 1816–68, U.S. musician and hymn writer.

B

Brad·ley (brad′lē), *n.* **Omar Nelson,** 1893–1981, U.S. general.

Brad·street (brad′strēt′), *n.* **Anne (Dudley),** 1612?–72, American poet.

Bra·dy (brā′dē), *n.* **1. James Buchanan** (*"Diamond Jim"*), 1856–1917, U.S. financier, noted for conspicuously extravagant living. **2. Mathew B.,** 1823?–96, U.S. photographer, of the Civil War.

brad·y·car·di·a (brad′i kär′dē ə), *n.* a slow heartbeat rate, usu. less than 60 beats per minute. —**brad′y·car′dic,** *adj.*

brag (brag), *v.,* **bragged, brag·ging,** *n., adj.* —*v.i.* **1.** to use boastful language; boast. —*v.t.* **2.** to declare boastfully. —*n.* **3.** a boast or vaunt. **4.** a thing to boast of. **5.** a boaster.

brag·ga·do·ci·o (brag′ə dō′shē ō′), *n., pl.* **-ci·os. 1.** empty boasting; bragging. **2.** a boasting person; braggart. —**brag′ga·do′ci·an,** *adj.*

brag·gart (brag′ərt), *n.* **1.** a person who does a lot of bragging. —*adj.* **2.** bragging; boastful. —**brag′gart·ly,** *adv.*

Brah·ma¹ (brä′mə), *n.* **1.** BRAHMAN (def. 2). **2.** "the Creator," the first member of the Hindu Trimurti, with Vishnu the Preserver and Shiva the Destroyer.

Brah·ma² (brä′mə, brä′-), *n., pl.* **-mas.** one of a breed of large Asian chickens, having feathered legs and small wings and tail.

Brah·ma³ (brä′mə, brä′-), *n., pl.* **-mas.** a Brahman bull, steer, or cow.

Brah·man (brä′mən), *n., pl.* **-mans. 1.** Also, **Brahmin.** a member of the highest, or priestly, class among the Hindus. **2.** Also, **Brahma.** (in Hinduism) the supreme being, the primal source and ultimate goal of all beings; atman. **3.** any of several breeds of cattle developed from Indian stock. —**Brah·man′ic** (-man′ik), **Brah·man′i·cal,** *adj.*

Brah·man·ism or **Brah·min·ism** (brä′mə niz′əm), *n.* **1.** the religious and social system of the Brahmans and orthodox Hindus, characterized by the caste system and diversified pantheism. **2.** the Hinduism of the Vedas, Brahmanas, and Upanishads. —**Brah′man·ist,** *n.*

Brah·min (brä′min), *n.* **1.** BRAHMAN (def. 1). **2.** (esp. in New England) a person from an upper-class family, esp. a family with considerable social and political power. **3.** an intellectually or socially aloof person. —**Brah·min′ic, Brah·min′i·cal,** *adj.*

Brah′mo Samaj′ (brä′mō), a modern Hindu movement advocating a monotheistic religion based on the Upanishads, and social and educational reforms according to Western principles. Also, **Brahma Samaj.** [< Bengali *brāhma samāj* assembly of Brahma]

Brahms (brämz), *n.* **Jo·han·nes** (yō hä′nəs), 1833–97, German composer. —**Brahms′i·an,** *adj.*

braid (brād), *v.t.* **1.** to weave together three or more strips or strands of; plait. **2.** to form by such weaving: *to braid a rope.* **3.** to trim with braid, as a garment. —*n.* **4.** a braided length or plait, esp. of hair. **5.** a ropelike band formed by plaiting strands of silk, cotton, or other material, used as trimming. —**braid′er,** *n.*

brail (brāl), *n.* **1.** any of several horizontal lines fastened to the edge of a fore-and-aft sail or lateen sail, for gathering in the sail. —*v.t.* **2.** to gather or haul in (a sail) by means of brails (usu. fol. by *up*).

Braille (brāl), *n., v.,* **Brailled, Brail·ing.** —*n.* **1. Louis,** 1809–52, French teacher of the blind. **2.** a system of writing, devised by L. Braille for use by the blind, in which combinations of raised dots represent letters, numbers, punctuation marks, etc., that are read by touch. —*v.t.* **3.** to write or transliterate in Braille. Also, **braille** (for defs. 2, 3).

brain (brān), *n.* **1.** the anterior part of the central nervous system enclosed in the cranium of vertebrates, consisting of a mass of nerve tissue organized for the perception of sensory impulses, the regulation of motor impulses, and the production of memory, learning, and consciousness. **2.** (in many invertebrates) a part of the nervous system comparable to the brain of vertebrates. **3.** Sometimes, **brains.** understanding; intellectual power; intelligence. **4.** the brain as the center of thought, understanding, etc.; mind; intellect. **5. brains,** *Slang.* a member of a group who is regarded as its intellectual leader or planner. **6.** *Informal.* an extremely intelligent person. **7. a.** the controlling or guiding mechanism in a computer, robot, pacemaker, etc. **b.** the part of a computer system for coordination or guidance, as of a missile. —*v.t.* **8.** to smash the skull of. **9.** *Slang.* to hit or bang on the head. —*Idiom.* **10. have on the brain,** to think about constantly; have an obsession about.

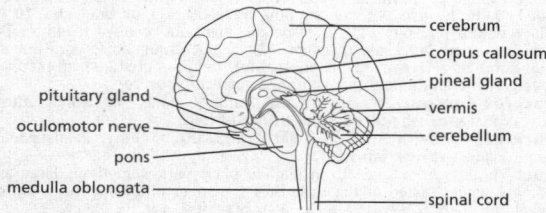

human brain (cross section)

Labels:
cerebrum
corpus callosum
pineal gland
vermis
cerebellum
spinal cord
pituitary gland
oculomotor nerve
pons
medulla oblongata

brain·child (brān′chīld′), *n., pl.* **-chil·dren.** a product of one's creative work or thought.

brain′ cor′al, *n.* any reef-building coral of the genera *Meandrina* and *Diploria,* having a highly convoluted surface.

brain′-dead′ or **brain′ dead′,** *adj.* **1.** having undergone brain death. **2.** (of a computer chip) relatively limited in capability; obsolescent.

brain′ death′, *n.* complete cessation of brain function as evidenced by absence of brain-wave activity on an electroencephalogram: sometimes used as a legal definition of death.

brain′ drain′, *n.* a loss of trained professional personnel to another company, nation, etc., that offers greater opportunity.

brain·pan (brān′pan′), *n.* the skull or cranium.

brain′-pick′ing, *n. Informal.* the act of obtaining information or ideas by questioning another person. —**brain′-pick′er,** *n.*

brain·pow·er (brān′pou′ər), *n.* **1.** intellectual capacity; mental ability. **2.** people with superior mental abilities.

brain′stem′ or **brain′ stem′,** *n.* the portion of the brain that is continuous with the spinal cord and in mammals comprises the medulla oblongata and parts of the midbrain.

brain·storm (brān′stôrm′), *n.* **1.** a sudden inspiration or idea. **2.** a fit of mental confusion or excitement. —*v.i.* **3.** to engage in brainstorming. —*v.t.* **4.** to subject (a problem) to brainstorming. —**brain′storm′er,** *n.*

brain·storm·ing (brān′stôr′ming), *n.* a group technique for solving problems, generating ideas, stimulating creative thinking, etc., by unrestrained spontaneous participation in discussion.

brain·teas·er (brān′tē′zər), *n.* a puzzle or problem whose solution requires great ingenuity.

brain′ trust′, *n.* a group of experts from various fields who act as unofficial consultants on matters of policy and strategy.

brain·wash·ing (brān′wosh′ing, -wô′shing), *n.* **1.** a method for systematically changing attitudes or altering beliefs, esp. through the use of torture, drugs, or psychological-stress techniques. **2.** any method of controlled indoctrination, esp. one based on repetition or confusion. **3.** an instance of subjecting to such techniques. —**brain′wash′,** *v.t.*

brain′ wave′, *n.* Usu. **brain waves.** electrical potentials or impulses given off by brain tissue.

braise (brāz), *v.t.,* **braised, brais·ing.** to cook (meat, fish, or vegetables) by sautéeing in fat and then simmering slowly in a small amount of liquid in a covered pot.

brake¹ (brāk), *n., v.,* **braked, brak·ing.** —*n.* **1.** a device for slowing or stopping a vehicle or other moving mechanism by the absorption or transfer of the energy of momentum, usu. by means of friction. **2. brakes,** the drums, shoes, tubes, levers, etc., making up such a device on a vehicle. **3.** anything that has a slowing or stopping effect. **4.** a tool or machine for breaking up flax or hemp, to separate the fiber. **5.** a machine for bending sheet metal to a desired shape. —*v.t.* **6.** to slow or stop by or as if by means of a brake. **7.** to furnish with brakes. **8.** to break up (flax or hemp) in a brake. —*v.i.* **9.** to use or run a brake. **10.** to stop or slow upon being braked. —**brake′less,** *adj.*

brake² (brāk), *n.* a place overgrown with bushes, brambles, or cane.

brake³ (brāk), *n.* **1.** BRACKEN (def. 1). **2.** any of numerous coarse tropical ferns of the genus *Pteris,* of the polypody family, cultivated as houseplants.

brake·age (brā′kij), *n.* the action of a brake or set of brakes as in stopping a vehicle.

brake′ drum′, *n.* a narrow metal cylinder, fixed to a rotating shaft or wheel, against which brake shoes act.

brake′ flu′id, *n.* the fluid used in a brake system to transmit pressure from the brake pedal to the pistons at each wheel.

brake′ lin′ing, *n.* a heat resistant padding, often of asbestos, attached to a brake shoe to produce friction.

brake·man (brāk′mən), *n., pl.* **-men.** a railroad worker who assists the conductor in the operation of a train.

brake′ shoe′, *n.* **1.** a rigid curved plate, usu. of steel coated with a friction-producing material, tightened against the inside of a brake drum to produce a braking action. **2.** (on a bicycle) a metal block holding a rubber pad, pressed against a rotating wheel to produce a braking action. Also called **shoe.**

bram·ble (bram′bəl), *n.* **1.** any prickly shrub belonging to the genus *Rubus,* of the rose family, as the blackberry. **2.** any rough, prickly shrub. —**bram′bly,** *adj.,* **-bli·er, -bli·est.**

bran (bran), *n.* the partly ground husk of wheat or other grain, separated from flour meal by sifting.

branch (branch, bränch), *n.* **1.** a division or subdivision of the stem or axis of a tree, shrub, or other plant. **2.** a limb, offshoot, or ramification of any main stem: *the branches of a deer's antlers.* **3.** any member or part of a body or system; a section or subdivision: *the various branches of medicine.* **4.** a local operating division of a business, library, etc. **5.** a line of family descent stemming from a particular ancestor. **6.** a tributary stream or any stream that is not a large river or a bayou. **7.** a group of related languages constituting a subdivision of a language family: *the Germanic branch of Indo-European.* **8.** a point in a computer program where the computer selects one of two or more instructions to execute, according to some criterion. —*v.i.* **9.** to put forth branches; spread in branches. **10.** to divide into separate parts or subdivisions; diverge: *The road branches off to the left.* **11.** to expand or extend, as business activities (usu. fol. by *out*). —*v.t.* **12.** to divide into branches or sections.

bran·chi·o·pod (brang′kē ə pod′), *n.* **1.** any crustacean of the class Branchiopoda, having gill-bearing appendages, as the fairy shrimp. —*adj.* **2.** of or belonging to the class Branchiopoda.

branch′ of gov′ernment, *n.* one of three branches of the U.S. government: the executive, legislative, or judicial.

branch′ wa′ter, *n.* **1.** water in or from a branch, creek, stream, etc.; pure, natural water. **2.** Also called **branch.** *Chiefly South Midland and Southern U.S.* (in a drink, highball, etc.) plain water as distinguished from soda water, ginger ale, or the like; ordinary water.

brand (brand), *n.* **1.** kind, grade, or make, as indicated by a stamp, trademark, or the like: *the best brand of coffee.* **2.** a mark made by burning or otherwise, to indicate kind, grade, make, ownership, etc. **3.** a mark formerly put upon criminals with a hot iron. **4.** any mark of disgrace; stigma. **5.** BRANDING IRON. **6.** a distinctive kind or variety: *an unfunny brand of humor.* **7.** a burning or partly burned piece of wood. —*v.t.* **8.** to label or mark with or as if with a brand. **9.** to mark with disgrace or infamy; stigmatize. **10.** to impress indelibly: *The plane crash was branded on her mind.*

Bran·den·burg (bran′dən bûrg′), *n.* **1.** a state in NE central Germany. 2,700,000; 10,039 sq. mi. (26,000 sq. km). *Cap.:* Potsdam. **2.** a city in NE Germany. 95,203. —**Bran′den·burg′er,** *n.*

brand′ing i′ron, *n.* a long-handled metal rod with a stamp at one end, used for branding livestock with a registered or recognized symbol.

bran·dish (bran′dish), *v.t.* **1.** to shake, wave, or display, esp. threateningly or ostentatiously, as a weapon; flourish. —*n.* **2.** a flourish or waving, as of a weapon. —**bran′dish·er,** *n.*

brand·ling (brand′ling), *n.* a small reddish brown earthworm, *Eisenia foetida,* having yellow markings, used as bait.

brand′ name′, *n.* **1.** a word, name, etc., used by a company to identify its products or services distinctively, usu. registered as a trademark. **2.** a product or service bearing a widely known brand name.

brand′-name′, *adj.* **1.** having or being a brand name: *brand-name products.* **2.** widely familiar; well-known: *brand-name actors.*

brand-new (bran′nōō′, -nyōō′, brand′-), *adj.* entirely new.

Brand X (eks), *n.* an unidentified or little-known brand name, product, etc., esp. one used as a basis of comparison or implied to be of inferior quality.

bran·dy (bran′dē), *n., pl.* **-dies,** *v.,* **-died, -dy·ing.** —*n.* **1.** a spirit distilled from wine or from fermented fruit juice. —*v.t.* **2.** to mix, flavor, or preserve with brandy. [short for *brandywine* < Dutch *brandewijn* burnt (i.e., distilled) wine]

Bran·dy·wine (bran′dē wīn′), *n.* a creek in SE Pennsylvania and N Delaware: British defeat of the Americans 1777.

bran·ni·gan (bran′i gən), *n.* **1.** a carousal. **2.** a squabble; brawl.

brant (brant), *n., pl.* **brants,** (*esp. collectively*) **brant.** a small, dark-colored goose of arctic regions, *Branta bernicla,* that winters along the Atlantic and Pacific coasts.

brash (brash), *adj.* **1.** impertinent; impudent; tactless: *a brash young man.* **2.** hasty; rash; impetuous. **3.** energetic or spirited, esp. in an irreverent way; zesty: *a brash new musical.* **4.** (esp. of wood) brittle. —*n.* **5.** a pile or mass of loose fragments or debris, as of rocks, hedge clippings, or ice. —**brash′ly,** *adv.* —**brash′ness,** *n.*

Bra·síl·i·a (brə zil′yə), *n.* the capital of Brazil, on the central plateau. 411,505.

brass (bras, bräs), *n.* **1.** any of various metal alloys consisting mainly of copper and zinc. **2. a.** an ornament, utensil, piece of hardware, or other article made of brass. **b.** such articles collectively. **3. a.** BRASS INSTRUMENT. **b.** Often, **brasses.** the brass instruments of a band or orchestra. **4.** metallic yellow; lemon, amber, or reddish yellow. **5. a.** high-ranking military officers. **b.** any very important officials. **6.** excessive self-assurance; impudence; effrontery. **7.** a semicylindrical shell, usu. of bronze, used to line a bearing. **8.** a brass memorial tablet. —*adj.* **9.** of, made of, or pertaining to brass. **10.** having the color brass. —*Idiom.* **11. get down to brass tacks,** to concentrate on essential matters.

bras·sard (bras′ärd, brə särd′), *n.* **1.** a decorative band worn around the upper arm, as to signify an affiliation. **2.** plate armor for the arm.

brass′ band′, *n.* a band made up principally of brass instruments.

bras·se·rie (bras′ə rē′), *n.* an unpretentious restaurant or tavern.

bras·si·ca (bras′i kə), *n., pl.* **-cas.** any plant belonging to the genus *Brassica,* of the mustard family, including cabbage, kale, broccoli, cauliflower, turnip, and mustard.

bras·siere or **bras·sière** (brə zēr′), *n.* a woman's undergarment for supporting the breasts.

brass′ in′strument, *n.* a musical wind instrument of brass or other metal with a cup-shaped mouthpiece, as the trombone, tuba, French horn, trumpet, or cornet.

brass′ knuck′les, *n.* (*used with a pl. v.*) a band of metal with four holes that fits over the upper fingers and is gripped when a fist is made, used as a weapon.

brass′ tacks′, *n.pl.* the most fundamental considerations; essentials; realities (usu. used in the phrase *get down to brass tacks*).

brass·y (bras′ē, brä′sē), *adj.,* **brass·i·er, brass·i·est. 1.** made of or covered with brass. **2.** resembling brass, as in color. **3.** harsh and metallic: *brassy tones.* **4.** brazen; bold. **5.** noisy; clamorous; loud. —**brass′i·ly,** *adv.* —**brass′i·ness,** *n.*

brat (brat), *n.* a child, esp. an annoying, spoiled, or impolite child. —**brat′tish,** *adj.,* **-ti·er, -ti·est.**

Bra·ti·sla·va (brat′ə slä′və, brä′tə-), *n.* the capital of Slovakia, in the SW part, on the Danube River: a former capital of Hungary. 440,421.

brat·tice (brat′is), *n.* **1.** a partition or lining, as of planks or cloth,

forming an air passage in a mine. **2.** (in medieval architecture) any temporary wooden fortification, esp. at the top of a wall.

brat·tle (brat′l), *n., v.,* **-tled, -tling.** —*n.* **1.** a clattering noise. —*v.i.* **2.** to scamper noisily.

brat·wurst (brat′wûrst, -wŏŏrst, -vŏŏrsht′, brät′-), *n.* a sausage made of pork, spices, and herbs.

bra·va (brä′vä, brä vä′), *interj., n., pl.* **-vas.** —*interj.* **1.** (used in praising a female performer.) —*n.* **2.** a shout of "brava!"

bra·va·do (brə vä′dō), *n., pl.* **-does, -dos.** an ostentatious display of courage.

brave (brāv), *adj.,* **brav·er, brav·est,** *n., v.,* **braved, brav·ing.** —*adj.* **1.** possessing or exhibiting courage or courageous endurance. **2.** making a fine appearance. —*n.* **3.** a brave person. **4.** a warrior, esp. among North American Indians. —*v.t.* **5.** to meet or face courageously: *to brave dangers.* **6.** to defy; challenge; dare. —**brave′ly,** *adv.* —**bravery,** *n.*

Brave′ New′ World′, a novel (1932) by Aldous Huxley.

bra·vis·si·mo (brä vis′ə mō′, -vē′sē-), *interj.* (used to express the highest praise to a performer.)

bra·vo (brä′vō; *for* 1, 2, 4 *also* brä vō′), *interj., n., pl.* **-vos** *for* 2, **-vos** or **-voes** *for* 3, *v.,* **-voed, -vo·ing.** —*interj.* **1.** (used in praising a performer.) —*n.* **2.** a shout of "bravo!" **3.** a bandit, assassin, or murderer, esp. a hired one. —*v.i.* **4.** to shout "bravo!"

bra·vu·ra (brə vyŏŏr′ə, -vŏŏr′ə, brä-), *n., pl.* **-ras. 1.** a florid musical passage or piece requiring great skill and spirit in the performer. **2.** a display of daring; brilliant performance.

brawl (brôl), *n.* **1.** a noisy fight or quarrel, esp. in a public place. **2.** a bubbling or roaring noise; clamor. **3.** *Slang.* a large, noisy party. —*v.i.* **4.** to fight or quarrel angrily and noisily; wrangle. **5.** to make a bubbling or roaring noise, as water flowing over a rocky bed. —**brawl′er,** *n.* —**brawl′y,** *adj.,* **-i·er, -i·est.**

brawn (brôn), *n.* **1.** strong, well-developed muscles. **2.** muscular strength. —**brawn′y,** *adj.,* **-i·er, -i·est.**

bray[1] (brā), *n., v.,* **brayed, bray·ing.** —*n.* **1.** the loud, harsh cry of a donkey. **2.** any similar sound. —*v.i.* **3.** to utter a bray. **4.** to make any similar sound. —*v.t.* **5.** to utter with a bray.

bray[2] (brā), *v.t.,* **brayed, bray·ing. 1.** to crush fine, as in a mortar. **2.** to thin (ink) on a slate before placing on the ink plate of a printing press.

braze[1] (brāz), *v.t.,* **brazed, braz·ing. 1.** to make of brass. **2.** to cover or ornament with or as if with brass. **3.** to make brasslike.

braze[2] (brāz), *v.t.,* **brazed, braz·ing.** to unite (metal objects) at high temperatures by applying any of various nonferrous solders. —**braz′er,** *n.*

bra·zen (brā′zən), *adj.* **1.** boldly shameless or impudent. **2.** made of brass. **3.** like brass, as in sound, color, or strength. —*v.t.* **4.** to make brazen or bold. —*Idiom.* **5. brazen it out** or **through,** to face something boldly or shamelessly. —**bra′zen·ly,** *adv.* —**bra′zen·ness,** *n.*

bra·zier[1] or **bra·sier** (brā′zhər), *n.* **1.** a metal receptacle for holding live coals or other fuel, as for heating a room. **2.** a container holding live coals covered by a grill on which food is cooked.

bra·zier[2] or **bra·sier** (brā′zhər), *n.* one who makes articles of brass.

Bra·zil (brə zil′), *n.* a federal republic in South America. 164,511,366; 3,286,170 sq. mi. (8,511,180 sq. km). *Cap.:* Brasília. Official name, **Fed′erative Repub′lic of Brazil′.** Portuguese, **Brasil.** —**Bra·zil′ian,** *adj., n.*

Brazil′ nut′, *n.* **1.** the three-sided, hard-shelled edible seed of a large South American tree, *Bertholletia excelsa,* of the lecythis family. **2.** the tree itself.

bra·zil·wood (brə zil′wŏŏd′), *n.* **1.** any of several tropical trees of the genus *Caesalpinia,* of the legume family, as *C. echinata,* having a wood used to make violins and from which a red dye is obtained. **2.** the wood of such a tree.

Braz·za·ville (braz′ə vil′, brä′zə-), *n.* the capital of the People's Republic of the Congo, in the S part, on the Congo (Zaire) River. 585,812.

breach (brēch), *n.* **1.** an infraction or violation, as of a law or promise. **2.** a gap made in a wall, fortification, etc.; rift; fissure. **3.** the act or a result of breaking; break or rupture. **4.** a severance of friendly relations. **5.** the leap of a whale above the surface of the water. —*v.t.* **6.** to make a breach or opening in. **7.** to break or act contrary to (a law, promise, etc.). —*v.i.* **8.** (of a whale) to leap out of the water and land with a loud splash. —**breach′er,** *n.*

breach′ of the peace′, *n.* a violation of the public peace, as by a riot, disturbance, or fighting.

bread (bred), *n.* **1.** a baked food made of a dough or batter containing flour or meal, milk or water, and often yeast or another leavening agent. **2.** food or sustenance; livelihood: *to earn one's bread.* **3.** *Slang.* money. **4.** *Eccles.* the wafer or bread used in a Eucharistic service. —*v.t.* **5.** to coat with breadcrumbs. —*Idiom.* **6. break bread,** to eat a meal, esp. with others. **7. know which side one's bread is buttered on,** to be aware of those things that are to one's own advantage. **8. take the bread out of someone's mouth,** to deprive someone of livelihood. —*Proverb.* **9. Cast thy bread upon the waters,** worthy actions will ultimately benefit you. Eccl. 11:1. **10. Man does not live by bread alone,** human beings have spiritual as well as physical needs. Deut. 8:3.

bread′ and but′ter, *n.* a basic means of support or income; source of livelihood; sustenance.

bread-and-but·ter (bred′n but′ər), *adj.* **1.** providing a livelihood or reliable income: *the agency's bread-and-butter accounts.* **2.** of or pertaining to the basic needs of life: *housing and other bread-and-butter issues.* **3.** basic or everyday; staple; routine. **4.** expressing thanks for hospitality: *a bread-and-butter letter.*

bread′-and-but′ter is′sue, *n.* a political issue directly concerning voters' income. Also called **pocketbook issue.**

bread′-and-but′ter pick′le, *n.* an unpeeled slice of cucumber marinated in salt water and boiled with vinegar, celery seed, spices, and brown sugar.

bread•bas•ket (bred′bas′kit, -bä′skit), *n.* **1.** a basket for bread or rolls. **2.** an area that produces large amounts of grain. **3.** *Slang.* the stomach or abdomen.

bread•board (bred′bôrd′, -bōrd′), *n.* **1.** a board on which dough is kneaded or bread is sliced. **2.** a circuit board on which electronic components can be easily rearranged or replaced for preliminary design or testing.

bread•fruit (bred′frōōt′), *n.* **1.** a large round starchy fruit borne by a tree, *Artocarpus altilis,* of the mulberry family, native to the Pacific islands: eaten baked or roasted. **2.** this tree itself.

bread′ line′, *n.* a line of people waiting for free food to be distributed by a government agency or charitable organization.

bread′ mold′, *n.* any fungus of the family Mucoraceae, esp. *Rhizopus nigricans,* that forms a black furry coating on foodstuffs.

Bread′ of Life′, *n.* **1.** Jesus Christ. John 6:35, 48. **2.** a parable of Jesus. John 6:32–58.

bread•root (bred′rōōt′, -rŏŏt′), *n.* the edible starchy root of *Psoralea esculenta,* of the legume family, native to central America.

bread•stick (bred′stik′), *n.* a slender sticklike piece of crisp bread.

bread•stuff (bred′stuf′), *n.* **1.** grain, flour, or meal for making bread. **2.** bread.

breadth (bredth, bretth, breth), *n.* **1.** the measure of the second largest dimension of a plane or solid figure; width. **2.** an extent or piece of something of definite or full width or as measured by its width: *a breadth of cloth.* **3.** freedom from narrowness, as of viewpoint or interests. **4.** size in general; extent; scope.

bread•win•ner (bred′win′ər), *n.* a person who earns a livelihood, esp. one who supports dependents. —**bread′win′ning,** *n.*

break (brāk), *v.,* **broke, bro•ken, break•ing,** *n.* —*v.t.* **1.** to smash, split, or divide into parts violently: *to break a vase.* **2.** to disable or destroy by or as if by shattering or crushing: *I broke my watch.* **3.** to violate or disregard (a law, promise, etc.). **4.** to fracture a bone of. **5.** to rupture the surface of: *to break the skin.* **6.** to destroy or disrupt the regularity, uniformity, or continuity of; interrupt: *A scream broke the silence.* **7.** to put an end to: *to break a tie.* **8.** to discover the system, key, etc., for decoding or deciphering (a code, cryptogram, etc.). **9.** to remove a part from (a set or collection). **10.** to exchange for or divide into smaller units: *to break a ten dollar bill.* **11.** to make a way through; penetrate: *The stone broke the surface of the water.* **12.** to escape from, esp. by force: *to break jail.* **13.** to better (a score or record). **14.** to disclose or reveal: *They broke the bad news to us.* **15.** to solve: *to break a murder case.* **16.** to ruin financially; bankrupt. **17.** to overcome or wear down the spirit, strength, or resistance of. **18.** to reduce in rank. **19.** to lessen or weaken the power, impact, or intensity of: *His arm broke the blow.* **20.** to train to obedience; tame: *to break a horse.* **21.** to train away from a habit or practice (usu. fol. by *of*). **22.** to contest (a will) successfully by judicial action. **23.** to render (an electronic circuit) incomplete; stop the flow of (a current). **24.** (in tennis and other racket games) to score frequently or win against (an opponent's serve). **25.** to prove the falsity of: *The FBI broke his alibi.* **26.** to begin or initiate (a plan or campaign). **27.** to open the breech or action of (a shotgun, rifle, or revolver). —*v.i.* **28.** to separate into parts or fragments, esp. suddenly and violently; shatter; burst. **29.** to become inoperative or malfunction, as through wear or damage. **30.** to become suddenly discontinuous or interrupted; stop abruptly. **31.** to become detached or disassociated: *to break with the past.* **32.** to begin uttering a sound or series of sounds suddenly: *to break into song.* **33.** to express or start to express an emotion or mood, esp. suddenly: *Her face broke into a smile.* **34.** (of a news item) to be released, published, or aired. **35.** to free oneself or escape suddenly, as from restraint. **36.** to run or dash toward something suddenly (usu. fol. by *for*): *He broke for the goal line.* **37.** to force a way: *The hunters broke through the underbrush.* **38.** to burst or rupture: *A blood vessel broke.* **39.** to interrupt an activity: *Let's break for lunch.* **40.** to appear suddenly: *A deer broke into the clearing.* **41.** to dawn: *The day broke hot.* **42.** to begin violently and suddenly: *The storm broke.* **43.** (of a storm, foul weather, etc.) to cease. **44.** to part the surface of water, as a jumping fish or surfacing submarine. **45.** to give way or fail, as health, strength, or spirit. **46.** to yield or submit to pressure, torture, etc.: *to break under questioning.* **47.** (of the heart) to be overwhelmed with sorrow. **48.** (of the voice or a musical instrument) to change harshly from one register or pitch to another. **49.** (of the voice) to cease, waver, or change tone abruptly. **50.** (of value or prices) to drop sharply and considerably. **51.** to disperse or collapse by colliding with something: *The waves broke on the shore.* **52.** (of a horse in a harness race) to fail to keep to a trot or pace, as by starting to gallop. **53.** (of a vowel) to undergo breaking. **54.** to make the opening play in pool by striking the racked balls with the cue ball and causing them to scatter. **55.** (of a pitched or bowled ball) to change direction: *The ball broke over the plate.* **56.** to leave the starting point in a race: *The horses broke from the gate.* **57.** (of boxers) to step back or separate from a clinch. **58.** to take place; occur. **59. break away, a.** to leave or escape, esp. suddenly or hurriedly. **b.** to sever connections or allegiance, as to tradition or a group. **c.** to start prematurely, as a horse from the starting gate. **60. break down, a.** to cease to function. **b.** to become ineffective; fail. **c.** to cause to collapse or become inoperative: *to break down resistance.* **d.** to separate into constituent parts. **e.** to lose control over one's emotions, esp. to cry. **f.** to have a complete physical or mental collapse. **g.** (of an insulator) to fail, as when subjected to excessively high voltage, permitting a current to pass. **61. break in, a.** to enter property by force or craft. **b.** to train or make accustomed to a new situation: *to break in a new assistant.* **c.** to wear or use (something new) and thereby ease stiffness, tightness, etc. **d.** to interrupt: *He broke in with an objection.* **62. break in on** or **upon,** to interrupt or intrude upon. **63. break into, a.** to interrupt. **b.** to begin abruptly. **c.** to enter (a business or profession). **d.** to enter (property) by force. **64. break off, a.** to sever by breaking. **b.** to stop suddenly; discontinue: *to break off relations.* **65. break out, a.** to begin abruptly; arise: *An epidemic broke out.* **b.** (of a person) to manifest a skin eruption. **c.** (of certain diseases) to appear in eruptions. **d.** to prepare for use: *to break out the parachutes.* **e.** to take out for consumption: *Let's break out the champagne.* **f.** to escape; flee. **g.** to separate by or into categories. **66. break up, a.** to separate; scatter. **b.** to put an end to; discontinue. **c.** to divide or become divided into pieces. **d.** to dissolve. **e.** to disrupt; upset: *breaking up the continuity.* **f.** (of a personal relationship) to end. **g.** to end a personal relationship. **h.** to be or cause to be overcome with laughter. **67. break with,** to sever relations with; separate from: *to break with one's family.* —*n.* **68.** an opening made by or as if by breaking; gap: *a break in the window.* **69.** an act or instance of breaking; separation of parts; fracture; rupture. **70.** an interruption of continuity: *a break with tradition.* **71.** a brief rest, as from work. **72.** a suspension of or sudden rupture in friendly relations. **73.** an abrupt or marked change: *a break in the weather.* **74.** an attempt to escape: *a prison break.* **75.** a sudden dash or rush: *Let's make a break for it!* **76.** a stroke of fortune, esp. a lucky one. **77.** a chance to improve one's lot, esp. one unlooked for or undeserved. **78. the breaks,** *Informal.* the way things happen; fate: *Those are the breaks.* **79.** a brief, scheduled interruption of a radio or television program, as for a commercial. **80.** a prosodic pause or caesura. **81.** a marked change in voice quality or pitch: *a break in her voice.* **82.** a usu. short solo instrumental passage in jazz or popular music. **83.** a sharp and considerable drop in prices. **84.** an opening or discontinuity in an electronic circuit. **85.** one or more blank lines between two printed paragraphs. **86.** the place, after a letter, where a word is or may be divided at the end of a line. **87.** the point at the bottom of a column where a printed story is broken off and continued on a subsequent page. **88.** a collapse of health, strength, or spirit; breakdown. **89.** the opening play in a game of pool, in which the cue ball is shot to scatter the balls. **90.** a change in direction of a pitched or bowled ball. **91.** (in harness racing) an instance of a horse's changing from a trot or pace into a gallop or other step. **92.** a failure to knock down all ten pins in a single frame in bowling. **93.** an act or instance of stepping back or separating from a clinch in boxing. **94.** *Mining.* a fault or offset, as in a vein or bed of ore. —***Idiom.*** **95. break camp,** to pack up tents and equipment and resume a journey or march. **96. break cover,** to emerge from a place of concealment. **97. break even,** to finish a business transaction, series of games, etc., with no loss or gain. **98. break service,** (in tennis) to win a game served by one's opponent. —**break′a•ble,** *adj.*

break•age (brā′kij), *n.* **1.** the act of breaking or the state of being broken. **2.** the amount or quantity of things broken. **3.** an allowance or compensation for articles broken, as in transit.

break•a•way (brāk′ə wā′), *n.* **1.** an act or instance of breaking away; secession; separation. **2.** a person or thing that breaks away. **3.** an object, as a theatrical prop, constructed so that it breaks or falls apart easily, esp. upon impact. —*adj.* **4.** of or designating something that separates or secedes: *the breakaway faction of the party.* **5.** built so as to come apart easily: *breakaway highway signposts.*

break′ danc′ing, *n.* vigorous acrobatic dancing often performed to rap music. —**break′ danc′er,** *n.* —**break′ dance′,** *v.i.*

break•down (brāk′doun′), *n.* **1.** an act or instance of breaking down, as a loss of ability to function effectively. **2.** a loss of mental or physical health; collapse. Compare NERVOUS BREAKDOWN. **3.** a division into parts, categories, processes, etc.; classification; analysis. **4.** *Chem.* **a.** decomposition. **b.** ANALYSIS (def. 5).

break•er (brā′kər), *n.* **1.** a person or thing that breaks. **2.** a wave that breaks or dashes into foam. **3.** a person indicating a wish to transmit a message on a CB radio, esp. on a channel already in use. **4.** a machine, implement, or structure used for breaking up rocks, soil, etc.

break′-e′ven or **break′e′ven,** *adj.* of or designating the point at which income, as from sales of a product or service, is exactly equal to expenditure, resulting in neither profit nor loss.

break•fast (brek′fəst), *n.* **1.** the first meal of the day; morning meal. —*v.i.* **2.** to eat breakfast. —*v.t.* **3.** to supply with breakfast.

break′fast food′, *n.* a cold or hot cereal eaten chiefly for breakfast.

break•front (brāk′frunt′), *n.* a cabinet, bookcase, etc., having a central section extending forward from those at either side.

break′-in′, *n.* **1.** an illegal forcible entry into a home, office, etc. **2.** a period of using or running something new, as an automobile, until normal operating conditions have been reached.

break•ing (brā′king), *n.* the change of a pure vowel to a diphthong, esp. under the influence of a neighboring sound.

break′ing and en′tering, *n.* forcible entry into the home or office of another.

break′ing point′, *n.* **1.** the point at which a person, object, or structure collapses under stress. **2.** the point at which a situation or condition becomes critical.

break•neck (brāk′nek′), *adj.* reckless or dangerous, esp. because of excessive speed: *running at breakneck speed.*

break′ of day′, *n.* dawn; daybreak.

break•out (brāk′out′), *n.* **1.** an escape, often by force, as from a prison. **2.** a sudden, often widespread appearance or occurrence, as of a disease; outbreak. **3.** an itemization; breakdown.

break•point (brāk′point′), *n.* a point at which a change, interruption, etc., can be made.

break•through (brāk′throo′), *n.* **1.** a significant or sudden advance, development, etc., as in scientific knowledge or diplomacy, that removes a barrier to progress. **2.** an act or instance of removing or surpassing an obstruction or restriction. **3.** a military advance through and beyond an enemy's defense.

break•up (brāk′up′), *n.* **1.** disintegration; disruption; dispersal. **2.** the ending of a personal, esp. a romantic, relationship. **3.** (in Alaska and Canada) the melting and loosening of ice in rivers and harbors during the early spring. **4.** an instance of being convulsed with laughter.

break•wa•ter (brāk′wô′tər, -wot′ər), *n.* a barrier that breaks the force of waves, as before a harbor.

bream (brim, brēm), *n., pl.* (*esp. collectively*) **bream,** (*esp. for kinds or species*) **breams. 1.** any carplike fish of the European genus *Abramis,* as *A. brama.* **2.** any of several porgies, as the sea bream, *Archosargus rhomboidalis.* **3.** any sunfish of the genus *Lepomis,* as the bluegill.

breast (brest), *n.* **1.** either of the pair of mammae occurring on the chest of human beings and other primates, esp. of the female after pubertal development. **2.** the outer, front part of the body from neck to midsection; chest. **3.** the bosom conceived of as the center of emotion. **4.** a projection from a wall, as part of a chimney. **5.** any surface or part resembling or likened to the human breast. **6.** FACE (def. 18). —*v.t.* **7.** to meet or oppose boldly; confront: *to breast hostile criticism.* **8.** to contend with or advance against: *The ship breasted the turbulent seas.* **9.** to climb or climb over (a mountain, obstacle, etc.). —*Idiom.* **10.** beat one's breast, to display grief, remorse, etc., loudly and demonstratively. **11.** make a clean breast of, to confess all of (one's wrongdoing).

breast•bone (brest′bōn′), *n.* the sternum.

breast′-feed′, *v.t.,* -fed, -feed•ing. to nurse (a baby) at the breast; suckle.

breast•plate (brest′plāt′), *n.* a piece of plate armor for protecting the front of the torso.

breast•stroke (brest′strōk′, bres′-), *n.* a swimming stroke, executed in a prone position, in which the two hands are extended forward, outward, and rearward from in front of the chest while the legs move in a frog kick. —**breast′strok′er,** *n.*

breath (breth), *n.* **1.** the air inhaled and exhaled in respiration. **2.** respiration, esp. as necessary to life. **3.** life; vitality. **4.** the ability to breathe easily and normally: *I stopped to regain my breath.* **5.** time to breathe; pause or respite. **6.** a single inhalation or respiration: *Take a deep breath.* **7.** the time required for a single respiration; moment. **8.** a slight suggestion or hint: *not touched by the breath of slander.* **9.** a light current of air. **10.** the audible expiration of air from the lungs generating voiceless speech sounds, as (p), (k), or (sh). **11.** moisture emitted in respiration, esp. when condensed and visible. **12.** an odorous exhalation, or the air impregnated by it. —*Idiom.* **13.** below or under one's breath, in a low voice or whisper. **14.** catch one's breath, to pause so as to rest. **15.** in the same breath, almost simultaneously. **16.** out of breath, breathless from exertion.

breath•a•ble (brē′thə bəl), *adj.* **1.** fit to be breathed. **2.** allowing the passage of air and moisture; porous: *breathable fabrics.*

breath′ an′alyzer, *n.* an instrument consisting of a small bag or tube filled with chemically treated crystals, into which a sample of a motorist's breath is taken as a test for intoxication.

breathe (brēth), *v.,* breathed (brēthd), breath•ing. —*v.i.* **1.** to take air, oxygen, etc., into the lungs and expel it; inhale and exhale; respire. **2.** to pause, as for breath; rest. **3.** to move or blow gently, as air. **4.** to live; exist. **5.** to be redolent of. **6.** (of a material) to allow air and moisture to pass through easily. **7.** (of the skin) to absorb oxygen and give off perspiration. **8.** (of a wine) to be exposed to air after being uncorked, in order to develop flavor and bouquet. —*v.t.* **9.** to inhale and exhale in respiration. **10.** to exhale: *breathing fire.* **11.** to inject as if by breathing; infuse: *to breathe life into a party.* **12.** to give utterance to; whisper: *Don't breathe a word of it.* **13.** to express; manifest. **14.** to allow to rest or recover breath: *to breathe a horse.* **15.** to deprive of breath, as by exercise; tire. —*Idiom.* **16.** breathe down someone's neck, a. to follow someone closely in pursuit. b. to watch someone closely so as to supervise or control. **17.** breathe freely, to have relief from anxiety, tension, or pressure. Also, breathe easily, breathe easy.

breath•er (brē′thər), *n.* **1.** a pause, as for breath; break. **2.** a person who breathes, esp. audibly or in a specified way. **3.** a vent in an otherwise airtight tank to relieve pressure.

breath•ing (brē′thing), *n.* **1.** the act of respiration. **2.** a single breath, or the short time required for this. **3.** a pause, as for breath. **4.** utterance or words. **5.** a gentle stirring, as of wind.

breath′ing space′, *n.* **1.** Also called **breath′ing spell′.** an opportunity to rest or think. **2.** sufficient space in which to move, work, etc. Also called **breath′ing room′.**

breath•less (breth′lis), *adj.* **1.** without breath or breathing with difficulty; gasping. **2.** with the breath held, as in suspense, astonishment, or fear. **3.** causing loss of breath, as from excitement, anticipation, or tension: *a breathless ride.* **4.** dead; lifeless. **5.** motionless or still, as air without a breeze. —**breath′less•ly,** *adv.* —**breath′less•ness,** *n.*

breath•tak•ing (breth′tā′king), *adj.* thrillingly or astonishingly beautiful, remarkable, exciting, etc. —**breath′tak′ing•ly,** *adv.*

breath′ test′, *n.* a test by breath analyzer.

breath•y (breth′ē), *adj.,* breath•i•er, breath•i•est. (of the voice) characterized by audible or excessive emission of breath. —**breath′i•ly,** *adv.* —**breath′i•ness,** *n.*

brec•ci•a (brech′ē ə, bresh′-), *n.* rock composed of angular fragments of older rocks melded together. —**brec′ci•ate′,** *v.t.,* -at•ed, -at•ing. —**brec′ci•a′tion,** *n.*

Brecht (brekt, brekHt), *n.* **Ber•tolt** (beR′tôlt), 1898–1956, German dramatist and poet. —**Brecht′i•an,** *adj.*

Breck•in•ridge (brek′ən rij′), *n.* **John Cabell,** 1821–75, vice president of the U.S. 1857–61; Confederate general.

bred (bred), *v.* pt. and pp. of BREED.

bred-in-the-bone (bred′n thə bōn′), *adj.* **1.** firmly instilled: *bred-in-the-bone integrity.* **2.** inveterate: *a bred-in-the-bone socialist.*

breech (*n.* brēch; *v.* brēch, brich), *n.* **1.** the rear part of the bore of a gun, esp. the opening that permits insertion of a projectile. **2.** the end of a block or pulley farthest from the supporting hook or eye. **3.** the buttocks. —*v.t.* **4.** to fit or furnish (a gun) with a breech. **5.** to clothe with breeches.

breech′ deliv′ery, *n.* the delivery of an infant with the feet or buttocks appearing first.

breech•es (brich′iz), *n.* (*used with a pl. v.*) **1.** knee-length trousers, often with buckles or decoration at the bottoms, worn by men in the 17th to early 19th centuries. **2.** *Informal.* TROUSERS. —*Idiom.* **3.** too big for one's breeches, more insolent and conceited than is warranted by one's position or abilities.

Breech′es Bi′ble, *n.* GENEVA BIBLE. [so called because of the translation of Gen. 3:7: "They sewed fig leaves together and made themselves breeches."]

breech′es bu′oy, *n.* a life preserver with a pantslike canvas seat for hauling a shipwrecked or disabled person on or off a vessel.

breed (brēd), *v.,* bred, breed•ing, *n.* —*v.t.* **1.** to produce (offspring); procreate. **2.** to produce by mating; propagate sexually; reproduce. **3.** to cause (plants or animals) to reproduce and usu. to be improved by selection. **4.** to give rise to; engender; produce: *Dirt breeds disease.* **5.** to develop by training or education; bring up; rear: *born and bred a gentleman.* **6.** to impregnate; mate: *to breed a mare.* **7.** to produce more fissile nuclear fuel than is consumed in a reactor. —*v.i.* **8.** to produce offspring. **9.** to be engendered or produced; grow; develop. —*n.* **10.** a relatively homogenous group of animals within a species, developed and maintained by humans. **11.** lineage; stock; strain. **12.** sort; kind; group: *Scholars are a quiet breed.* —**breed′a•ble,** *adj.*

breed•er (brē′dər), *n.* **1.** an animal, plant, or person that reproduces. **2.** a person who raises animals or plants primarily for breeding purposes. **3.** Also called **breed′er reac′tor.** a nuclear reactor in which more fissile material is produced than is consumed.

breed•ing (brē′ding), *n.* **1.** the producing of offspring. **2.** the improvement of breeds of livestock, as by selective mating and hybridization. **3.** the production of new forms of plants by selection, crossing, and hybridizing. **4.** training; nurture. **5.** the result of upbringing or training as shown in behavior, esp. in good manners.

breed′ing ground′, *n.* **1.** a place where animals breed or to which they return to breed. **2.** an environment suitable for or fostering the development of something.

Breed′s′ Hill′, *n.* a hill adjoining Bunker Hill, where the Battle of Bunker Hill was actually fought.

breeze[1] (brēz), *n., v.,* breezed, breez•ing. —*n.* **1.** a wind or current of air, esp. a light or moderate one. **2.** a wind of 4–31 mph (2–14 m/sec). **3.** an easy task. —*v.i.* **4.** to move in a carefree, self-confident, or jaunty manner. **5.** to proceed quickly and easily or effortlessly: *We breezed through the work.* —*Idiom.* **6.** shoot or bat the breeze, *Slang.* to talk aimlessly; chat. —**breeze′less,** *adj.*

breeze[2] (brēz), *n.* **1.** cinders, ash, or dust from coal, coke, or charcoal. **2.** concrete, brick, or cinder block in which such materials form a component.

breeze•way (brēz′wā′), *n.* an open-sided roofed passageway for connecting two buildings, as a house and garage.

breez•y (brē′zē), *adj.,* breez•i•er, breez•i•est. **1.** abounding in breezes; windy. **2.** sprightly; carefree; jauntily casual: *a breezy style of writing.* —**breez′i•ly,** *adv.* —**breez′i•ness,** *n.*

breth•ren (breth′rin), *n.pl.* male members, as of a congregation or fraternal organization; fellow members.

Bret′ton Woods′ Con′ference (bret′n), *n.* an international conference called at Bretton Woods, N.H., in July 1944 to deal with international monetary and financial problems: resulted in the creation of the International Monetary Fund and the World Bank.

Breu•ghel or **Breu•gel** or **Brue•ghel** (broiʹgəl, bro͞oʹ-, brœʹ-), *n.* **1. Pieter the Elder,** c1525–69, Flemish painter. **2.** his sons, **Jan,** 1568–1625, and **Pieter the Younger,** 1564–1637?, Flemish painters.

breve (brēv, brev), *n.* **1.** a mark (˘) over a vowel to show that it is short, or to indicate a specific pronunciation, as *ŭ* in (kŭt) *cut.* **2.** this same mark used to indicate a short or unstressed syllable in prosody. **3.** a musical note equivalent to two semibreves or whole notes.

bre•vet (brə vetʹ, brevʹit), *n., v.,* **-vet•ted, -vet•ting** or **-vet•ed, -vet•ing.** **—***n.* **1.** a commission promoting a military officer to a higher rank without increase of pay. **—***v.t.* **2.** to appoint, promote, or honor by brevet.

bre•vi•ar•y (brēʹvē erʹē, brevʹē-), *n., pl.* **-ar•ies.** a book containing the divine office of the Roman Catholic Church.

brev•i•ty (brevʹi tē), *n.* **1.** shortness of duration; briefness. **2.** the quality of expressing much in few words; terseness; succinctness.

brew (bro͞o), *v.t.* **1.** to make (beer, ale, etc.) by steeping, boiling, and fermenting malt and hops. **2.** to prepare (tea, coffee, etc.) by boiling, steeping, or the like. **3.** to contrive, plan, or bring about: *to brew mischief.* **—***v.i.* **4.** to make beer or ale. **5.** to boil, steep, soak, or cook. **—***n.* **6.** a quantity brewed in a single process. **7.** a brewed beverage. **8.** any concoction, esp. a liquid produced by a mixture of unusual ingredients: *a witches' brew.* **9.** *Informal.* beer or ale. **—*Idiom.* 10. be brewing,** to be forming or gathering: *Trouble was brewing.* **—brewʹer,** *n.*

brewʹer's yeastʹ, *n.* a yeast, as of the genus *Saccharomyces,* suitable for use as a ferment in the manufacture of wine and beer.

brew•er•y (bro͞oʹə rē, bro͝orʹē), *n., pl.* **-er•ies.** a building or establishment for brewing beer or other malt liquors.

Bri•and (brē ändʹ, -äNʹ), *n.* **Aristide,** 1862–1932, French statesman: minister of France 11 times; Nobel peace prize 1926.

bribe (brīb), *n., v.,* **bribed, brib•ing.** **—***n.* **1.** money or other valuable consideration given or promised with a view to corrupting the behavior of a person, as a public official. **2.** anything given or serving to persuade or induce. **—***v.t.* **3.** to give or promise a bribe to. **4.** to influence or corrupt by a bribe. **—***v.i.* **5.** to give a bribe; practice bribery. **—bribʹa•ble, bribeʹa•ble,** *adj.*

brib•er•y (brīʹbə rē), *n., pl.* **-er•ies.** the act or practice of giving or accepting a bribe.

bric-a-brac or **bric-à-brac** (brikʹə brakʹ), *n.* (*used with a sing. or pl. v.*) miscellaneous small articles collected for their decorative or other interest; knickknacks.

brick (brik), *n.* **1.** a block of clay hardened by drying in the sun or burning in a kiln and used for building, paving, etc. **2.** the material of which such blocks are made. **3.** any block or bar having a similar size and shape: *a gold brick.* **4.** *Informal.* an admirable person. **5.** *Brit.* BLOCK (def. 3). **—***v.t.* **6.** to pave, line, wall, fill, or build with brick. **—***adj.* **7.** made of, constructed with, or resembling bricks. **—*Idiom.* 8. drop a brick,** to make a social blunder, esp. an indiscreet remark. **9. hit the bricks, a.** to walk the streets. **b.** to go on strike.

brick•bat (brikʹbatʹ), *n.* **1.** a piece of broken brick, esp. one used as a missile. **2.** any rocklike missile. **3.** an unkind or unfavorable remark; caustic criticism.

brickʹ cheeseʹ, *n.* a semisoft American cheese with many small holes, produced in the shape of bricks.

brick•lay•ing (brikʹlāʹing), *n.* the act or occupation of laying bricks in construction. **—brickʹlayʹer,** *n.*

brickʹ redʹ, *n.* a yellowish or brownish red. **—brickʹ-redʹ,** *adj.*

brid•al (brīdʹl), *adj.* **1.** of or for a bride or a wedding: *a bridal gown.* **—***n.* **2.** a wedding.

bridʹal wreathʹ, *n.* a cultivated shrub, *Spiraea prunifolia,* of the rose family, having sprays of small white flowers.

bride (brīd), *n.* a newly married woman or a woman about to be married.

bride•groom (brīdʹgro͞omʹ, -gro͝omʹ), *n.* a newly married man or a man about to be married. [< Old English *brȳdguma* = *brȳd* bride + *guma* man]

brides•maid (brīdzʹmādʹ), *n.* **1.** a woman who attends the bride at a wedding ceremony. **2.** a person or group that never quite attains a goal.

bridge[1] (brij), *n., v.,* **bridged, bridg•ing.** **—***n.* **1.** a structure spanning and providing passage over a river, chasm, road, or the like. **2.** a connecting, transitional, or intermediate route, phase, etc. **3.** a raised transverse platform from which a power vessel is navigated and that often includes a pilot house. **4.** the ridge or upper line of the nose. **5.** the part of a pair of eyeglasses that joins the two lenses and spans the nose. **6.** an artificial replacement, fixed or removable, of a missing tooth or teeth, supported by adjacent natural teeth or roots. **7.** a thin fixed wedge or support raising the strings of a musical instrument above the sounding board. **8.** a transitional modulatory passage connecting sections of a musical composition. **9.** a transitional passage in a literary work connecting major sections. **10.** transitional material between two parts of a radio or television program. **11.** an electrical circuit or device for measuring resistance, capacitance, inductance, or impedance. **12.** a gantry over a railroad track for supporting waterspouts, signals, etc. **13. a.** the arch formed by the hand and fingers to support the striking end of a billiards or pool cue. **b.** a notched piece of wood with a long handle used to support the striking end of a cue. **14.** a gallery or platform that can be raised or lowered over a stage for use by technical crew members. **15.** a valence bond connecting two parts of a molecule. **16.** an archlike figure formed by acrobats, dancers, etc. **—***v.t.* **17.** to make a bridge or passage over; span. **18.** to join by or as if by a bridge. **19.** to make (a way) by a bridge. **—bridgeʹa•ble,** *adj.*

bridge[2] (brij), *n.* a card game derived from whist in which one partnership plays to fulfill a certain declaration against an opposing partnership.

bridge•head (brijʹhedʹ), *n.* **1.** a position secured on the enemy side of a river or other obstacle to cover the crossing of friendly troops. **2.** any position gained that can be used as a foothold for further advancement. **3.** a defensive work protecting the end of a bridge toward the enemy.

bridgeʹ loanʹ, *n.* a temporary, short-term loan, as for making the down payment on a new house while one's present house is being sold. Also called **swing loan.**

bridgeʹ taʹble, *n.* a square card table with folding legs.

Bridge•town (brijʹtounʹ), *n.* the capital of Barbados, on the SW coast. 7466.

bridge•work (brijʹwûrkʹ), *n.* **1. a.** a dental bridge. **b.** dental bridges collectively. **2.** the art or process of building bridges.

bridg•ing (brijʹing), *n.* a brace or an arrangement of braces fixed between floor or roof joists to keep them in place.

bri•dle (brīdʹl), *n., v.,* **-dled, -dling.** **—***n.* **1.** part of the tack or harness of a horse, consisting usu. of a headstall, bit, and reins. **2.** restraint; curb. **3.** a link, flange, or other attachment for limiting the movement of any part of a machine. **4.** a rope or chain secured at both ends to an object, and itself held or lifted by a rope or chain secured at its center. **—***v.t.* **5.** to put a bridle on. **6.** to control or hold back; restrain; curb. **—***v.i.* **7.** to draw up the head and draw in the chin, as in disdain or resentment. **8.** to show resentment. **—briʹdle•less,** *adj.* **—briʹdler,** *n.*

briʹdle pathʹ, *n.* a wide path for riding horses.

brief (brēf), *adj.* **1.** lasting or taking a short time. **2.** using few words; concise: *a brief report.* **3.** abrupt; curt. **4.** scanty: *a brief bathing suit.* **—***n.* **5.** a short and concise statement or written item. **6. a.** a memorandum of points of fact or of law for use in conducting a case. **b.** a written statement submitted to a court by counsel presenting the principal facts, points of law, and arguments related to a client's case. **7.** an outline, summary, or synopsis, as of a book. **8. briefs,** (*used with a pl.v.*) close-fitting legless underpants with an elastic waistband. **9.** a briefing. **10.** a papal letter less formal than a bull. **—***v.t.* **11.** to make an abstract or summary of. **12.** to instruct by a brief or briefing. **—*Idiom.* 13. hold a brief for,** to support or defend by argument; endorse. **14. in brief,** in a few words; in short. **—briefʹly,** *adv.* **—briefʹness,** *n.*

brief•case (brēfʹkāsʹ), *n.* a flat rectangular case with a handle, often of leather, for carrying books, papers, etc.

brief•ing (brēʹfing), *n.* **1.** a summary of events, details, or instructions. **2.** a meeting at which such information is given.

bri•er[1] or **bri•ar** (brīʹər), *n.* **1.** a prickly plant or shrub, esp. the sweetbrier or a catbrier. **2.** a tangled mass of prickly plants. **3.** a thorny stem or twig. **—briʹer•y,** *adj.*

bri•er[2] or **bri•ar** (brīʹər), *n.* **1.** the white heath, *Erica arborea,* of France and Corsica, the woody root of which is used for making tobacco pipes. **2.** a pipe made of brierroot.

bri•er•root or **bri•ar•root** (brīʹər ro͞otʹ, -ro͝otʹ), *n.* **1.** the root wood of the brier. **2.** certain other woods from which tobacco pipes are made. **3.** a pipe made of brierroot.

brig (brig), *n.* **1. a.** a two-masted vessel square-rigged on both masts. **b.** the compartment of a ship where prisoners are confined. **2.** a military prison; guardhouse.

bri•gade (bri gādʹ), *n., v.,* **-gad•ed, -gad•ing.** **—***n.* **1.** a military unit consisting of a headquarters and two or more regiments, squadrons, groups, or battalions. **2.** a large body of troops. **3.** a group of individuals organized for a particular purpose: *a rescue brigade.* **—***v.t.* **4.** to form into a brigade.

brig•a•dier (brigʹə dērʹ), *n.* **1.** a British military officer of the rank between colonel and major general. **2.** BRIGADIER GENERAL. **—brigʹa•dierʹship,** *n.*

brigʹadier genʹeral, *n., pl.* **brigadier generals.** an officer in the U.S. Army of the rank between colonel and major general.

brig•and (brigʹənd), *n.* a bandit, esp. one of a band of robbers in mountain or forest regions. **—brigʹand•age,** *n.*

bright (brīt), *adj.* **1.** radiating or reflecting light; luminous; shining. **2.** filled with light: *a bright, sunny room.* **3.** vivid or brilliant: *bright red.* **4.** quick-witted or intelligent. **5.** clever or witty, as a remark or idea. **6.** cheerful or lively: *a bright smile.* **7.** characterized by happiness or gladness. **8.** favorable or auspicious; promising: *a bright future.* **9.** radiant or splendid: *bright pageantry.* **10.** illustrious or glorious, as an era. **11.** clear or translucent, as liquid. **12.** clear and sharp in sound. **—***n.* **13. brights, a.** bright motor vehicle headlights used for driving esp. under conditions of low visibility. **b.** the level of intensity of these lights; high beams. **14.** flue-cured, light-hued tobacco. **—***adv.* **15.** in a bright manner; brightly. **—brightʹly,** *adv.* **—brightʹness,** *n.*

Bright (brīt), *n.* **William Rohl,** born 1921, U.S. evangelist.

bright•en (brītʹn), *v.i., v.t.* **1.** to become or make bright or brighter. **2.** to become or make more cheerful. **—brightʹen•er,** *n.*

brill (bril), *n., pl.* **brills,** (*esp. collectively*) **brill.** an edible European flatfish, *Scophthalmus rhombus.*

bril•liance (brilʹyəns), *n.* the state or quality of being brilliant.

bril·liant (bril′yənt), *adj.* **1.** shining brightly; sparkling; glittering: *brilliant jewels.* **2.** distinguished; outstanding: *a brilliant performance.* **3.** having or showing great intelligence, talent, etc. **4.** strong and clear in tone; vivid: *a brilliant blue.* **5.** splendid: *a brilliant social event.* —*n.* **6.** a gem, esp. a diamond, having any of several varieties of the brilliant cut. **7.** a size of type about 3½-point. —**bril′liant·ly,** *adv.*
bril′liant cut′, *n.* a cut intended to enhance the brilliance of a gem without sacrificing weight, characterized by a form resembling two pyramids set base to base and typically having 58 facets. Compare EMERALD CUT, MARQUISE (def. 3a). —**bril′liant-cut′,** *adj.*

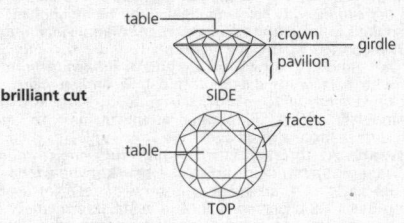

brilliant cut

brim (brim), *n., v.,* **brimmed, brim·ming.** —*n.* **1.** the upper edge of anything hollow; rim; brink: *the brim of a cup.* **2.** a projecting edge: *the brim of a hat.* **3.** a margin. —*v.i.* **4.** to be full to the brim. —*v.t.* **5.** to fill to the brim. —**brim′less,** *adj.* —**brim′ming·ly,** *adv.*
brim·stone (brim′stōn′), *n.* (not in technical use) SULFUR.
brin·dled (brin′dld), *adj.* gray or tawny with darker streaks.
brine (brīn), *n., v.,* **brined, brin·ing.** —*n.* **1.** water saturated or strongly impregnated with salt. **2.** a salt and water solution for pickling. **3.** the sea or ocean. **4.** the water of the sea. **5.** any saline solution. —*v.t.* **6.** to treat with or steep in brine.
brine′ shrimp′, *n.* any fairy shrimp of the genus *Artemia,* common to saline lakes.
bring (bring), *v.t.,* **brought, bring·ing. 1.** to carry, convey, conduct, or cause (someone or something) to come with, to, or toward the speaker. **2.** to cause to come to or toward oneself; attract: *The screams brought the police.* **3.** to cause to occur or exist: *The medicine brought rapid relief.* **4.** to cause to come into a particular position, state, or effect: *to bring a car to a stop.* **5.** to persuade, compel, or induce: *I couldn't bring myself to sell it.* **6.** to cause to come to mind; evoke; recall: *to bring back happy memories.* **7.** to sell for; fetch: *These lamps will bring a good price.* **8.** *Law.* to commence: *to bring an action for damages.* **9. bring about,** to accomplish; cause. **10. bring around** or **round, a.** to convince of a belief or opinion; persuade. **b.** to restore to consciousness, as after a faint. **11. bring down, a.** to injure, capture, or kill. **b.** to cause to fall. **c.** to cause to be in low spirits; depress. **12. bring forth, a.** to give birth to or produce; bear: *to bring forth young.* **b.** to give rise to; introduce. **13. bring forward, a.** to bring to view; show. **b.** to present for consideration; adduce. **14. bring in, a.** to yield, as profits or income. **b.** to present officially; submit: *to bring in a verdict.* **c.** to cause to operate or yield: *to bring in an oil well.* **d.** to introduce. **15. bring off,** to accomplish, carry out, or achieve. **16. bring on,** to cause to happen, appear, or exist: *to bring on a headache.* **17. bring out, a.** to reveal or expose. **b.** to make noticeable or conspicuous; emphasize. **c.** to cause to appear: *The clams I ate brought out a rash.* **d.** to publish or produce. **e.** to introduce formally into society. **18. bring to, a.** to bring back to consciousness; revive. **b.** to head (a vessel) close to or into the wind so as to halt. **19. bring up, a.** to care for during childhood; rear. **b.** to introduce or mention for attention or consideration. **c.** to vomit. **d.** to stop quickly or abruptly. —**bring′er,** *n.*
brink (bringk), *n.* **1.** the edge or margin of a steep place or of land bordering water. **2.** any extreme edge; verge. **3.** a critical point beyond which something will occur: *on the brink of disaster.* —**brink′less,** *adj.*
brink·man·ship (bringk′mən ship′) also **brinks·man·ship** (bringks′-), *n.* the technique of maneuvering a dangerous situation to the limits of tolerance in order to secure the greatest advantage.
brin·y¹ (brī′nē), *adj.,* **brin·i·er, brin·i·est.** of or like brine; salty. —**brin′i·ness,** *n.*
brin·y² (brī′nē), *n.* the ocean.
bri·o (brē′ō), *n.* vigor; vivacity.
bri·oche (brē ōsh′, -osh′, -ôsh′), *n.* a light, rich, sweet roll of yeast-leavened dough.
bri·o·lette (brē′ə let′), *n.* any pear-shaped gem having its entire surface cut with triangular facets.
bri·quette or **bri·quet** (bri ket′), *n.* **1.** a small block of compressed coal dust or charcoal used for fuel, esp. in barbecuing. **2.** a molded block of any material. —*v.t.* **3.** to mold into briquettes.
bris (bris), *n.* BRITH.
Bris·bane (briz′bān, -bən), *n.* the capital of Queensland, in E Australia. 1,171,300.
brisk (brisk), *adj.* **1.** quick and active; lively: *brisk trading; a brisk walk.* **2.** sharp and stimulating; invigorating: *brisk weather.* **3.** abrupt; curt: *a brisk tone of voice.* —*v.t., v.i.* **4.** to make or become brisk; liven (often fol. by *up*). —**brisk′ly,** *adv.* —**brisk′ness,** *n.*

bris·ket (bris′kit), *n.* **1.** the breast of an animal, or the part of the breast lying next to the ribs. **2.** a cut of meat, esp. beef, from this part.
bris·tle (bris′əl), *n., v.,* **-tled, -tling.** —*n.* **1.** one of the short, stiff, coarse hairs of certain animals, esp. hogs, used in making brushes. **2.** anything resembling these hairs. —*v.i.* **3.** to stand or rise stiffly, like bristles. **4.** to erect the bristles, as an irritated animal. **5.** to become rigid with anger or irritation: *He bristled when I asked him to move.* **6.** to be thickly set with something suggestive of bristles: *The plain bristled with bayonets.* —*v.t.* **7.** to erect like bristles. **8.** to furnish with bristles. **9.** to make bristly. —**bris′tle·less,** *adj.* —**bris′tle·like′,** *adj.*
bris′tlecone pine′, *n.* a small pine, *Pinus aristata,* of the high S Rocky Mountains, bearing cones with spine-tipped scales: believed to be the oldest living trees, with some 4,000-year-old specimens.
bris·tle·tail (bris′əl tāl′), *n.* any of various wingless insects of the order Thysanura, having long bristlelike caudal appendages, comprising the firebrats and silverfish.
bris·tly (bris′lē), *adj.,* **-tli·er, -tli·est. 1.** covered or rough with bristles. **2.** like or resembling bristles. **3.** easily antagonized. —**bris′tli·ness,** *n.*
Brit., 1. Britain. **2.** British.
Britan′nia met′al or **britan′nia met′al,** *n.* a white alloy of tin, antimony, and copper, sometimes with small amounts of zinc, lead, and bismuth.
britch·es (brich′iz), *n.* (*used with a pl. v.*) BREECHES.
brith (bris, brit) also **bris,** *n.* the Jewish rite of circumcising a male child as a sign of his becoming a Jew.
Brit·ish (brit′ish), *adj.* **1.** of or pertaining to Great Britain or its inhabitants. **2.** of or pertaining to the island of Britain and its inhabitants, esp. before the division of the island into the principalities of England, Wales, and Scotland in the Middle Ages. —*n.* **3.** (*used with a pl. v.*) **a.** the inhabitants of Great Britain, or natives of Great Britain living elsewhere; Britons. **b.** the Celtic-speaking inhabitants of Britain before the Germanic invasions of the 5th century A.D. —**Brit′ish·ness,** *n.*
Brit′ish Colum′bia, *n.* a province in W Canada on the Pacific coast. 2,883,367; 366,255 sq. mi. (948,600 sq. km). *Cap.:* Victoria. —**Brit′ish Colum′bian,** *n., adj.*
Brit′ish Guia′na, *n.* former name of GUYANA.
Brit′ish Hondu′ras, *n.* former name of BELIZE (def. 1). —**Brit′ish Hondu′ran,** *adj., n.*
Brit′ish Isles′, *n.pl.* a group of islands in W Europe: Great Britain, Ireland, the Isle of Man, and adjacent small islands. 53,978,538; 120,592 sq. mi. (312,300 sq. km).
Brit′ish North′ Amer′ica, *n.* **1.** Canada. **2.** all parts of the Commonwealth of Nations in or near North America.
Brit′ish North′ Amer′ica Act′, *n.* an act of the British Parliament that created the Dominion of Canada in 1867.
Brit′ish Vir′gin Is′lands, *n.pl.* a British colony comprising several small islands in the West Indies, E of Puerto Rico. 13,246; 67 sq. mi. (174 sq. km). *Cap.:* Road Town.
Brit′tany span′iel, *n.* a British breed of long-legged pointing spaniels with an orange- or liver-and-white coat.
brit·tle (brit′l), *adj.,* **-tler, -tlest,** *n.* —*adj.* **1.** having hardness and rigidity but little tensile strength; breaking readily with a comparatively smooth fracture, as glass. **2.** easily damaged or destroyed; fragile. **3.** lacking warmth, sensitivity, or compassion. **4.** having a sharp, tense quality: *a brittle tone of voice.* **5.** unstable or impermanent; evanescent. —*n.* **6.** a confection of melted sugar, usu. with nuts, brittle when cooled: *peanut brittle.*
brit·tle·bush (brit′l boosh′), *n.* any composite North American desert plant of the genus *Encelia,* having brittle leaves and flowers with yellow rays and a yellow or purple disk.
brit′tle star′ or **brit′tle·star′,** *n.* any echinoderm of the class Ophiuroidea, having the body composed of a central rounded disk from which radiate long, slender, flexible arms.
broach (brōch), *n.* **1.** an elongated, tapered, serrated cutting tool for shaping and enlarging holes. **2.** a spit for roasting meat. **3.** a gimlet for tapping casks. **4.** (in a lock) a pin receiving the barrel of a key. **5.** a pointed tool for the rough dressing of stone. **6.** BROOCH. —*v.t.* **7.** to mention or suggest for the first time: *to broach a subject.* **8.** to enlarge or finish with a broach. **9.** to draw (beer, liquor, etc.), as by tapping: *to broach beer from a keg.* **10.** to tap or pierce. —*v.i.* **11.** (of a sailing vessel) to veer to windward. **12.** to break the surface of water from below. —**broach′er,** *n.*
broad (brôd), *adj.* **1.** of great breadth. **2.** measured from side to side: *three feet broad.* **3.** of great extent; large: *a broad expanse of water.* **4.** widely diffused; open; full: *in broad daylight.* **5.** not limited or narrow; of extensive range or scope: *a broad range of interests.* **6.** liberal; tolerant. **7.** main or general: *the broad outlines of a subject.* **8.** plain or clear: *a broad hint.* **9.** indecent: *a broad joke.* **10.** unconfined; free; unrestrained. **11.** (of an actor or acting style) using or marked by exaggeration; lacking subtlety; not naturalistic. **12.** (of pronunciation) strongly dialectal: *a broad Scots accent.* **13.** (of a phonetic transcription) using one basic symbol to represent each phoneme. **14. broad a,** the *a*-sound (ä), esp. when used in place of the more common *a*-sound (a) in such words as *half* and *can't.* —*adv.* **15.** fully: *broad awake.* —*n.* **16.** the broad part of anything. —**broad′en,** *v.t.* —**broad′ly,** *adv.*
broad·ax or **broad·axe** (brôd′aks′), *n., pl.* **-ax·es** (-ak′siz). an ax with a broad head, used for hewing timber or as a battle-ax.

broad′ bean′, *n.* FAVA BEAN.

broad·bill (brôd′bil′), *n.* **1.** any of various typically brightly colored suboscine birds of the family Eurylaimidae, of the Old World tropics, having a flat, wide bill. **2.** any of various birds with a broad bill, as the scaup or shoveler.

broad·cast (brôd′kast′, -käst′), *v.,* **-cast** or **-cast·ed, -cast·ing,** *n., adj., adv.* —*v.t.* **1.** to transmit (programs) from a radio or television station. **2.** to speak, perform, or present on a radio or television program. **3.** to cast or scatter abroad over an area. **4.** to spread widely; disseminate: *to broadcast lies all over town.* —*v.i.* **5.** to transmit programs or signals from a radio or television station. **6.** to make something known widely; disseminate something. **7.** to speak, perform, or present all or part of a radio or television program. —*n.* **8.** something that is broadcast. **9.** a single radio or television program. **10.** a method of sowing by scattering seed. —*adj.* **11.** (of programs) transmitted from a radio or television station. **12.** of or pertaining to broadcasting. **13.** cast abroad or all over an area, as seed scattered widely. —*adv.* **14.** so as to reach or be cast abroad over a wide area. —**broad′cast′er,** *n.* —**broad′cast′ing,** *n.*

Broad′ Church′, *adj.* pertaining or belonging to a party in the Anglican Church emphasizing a liberal interpretation of ritual.

broad·cloth (brôd′klôth′, -kloth′), *n., pl.* **-cloths** (-klôthz′, -klothz′, -klôths′, -kloths′). **1.** a closely woven fabric of cotton, rayon, silk, or a mixture of these, having a soft mercerized finish, used for shirts, dresses, etc. **2.** a woolen or worsted fabric constructed in a plain or twill weave, having a smooth texture and lustrous finish.

broad′ jump′, *n.* LONG JUMP. —**broad′-jump′,** *v.i.* —**broad′ jump′er,** *n.*

broad·leaf (brôd′lēf′), *n., pl.* **-leaves** (-lēvz′), any of several cigar tobaccos having broad leaves.

broad·loom (brôd′lŏŏm′), *n.* **1.** any carpet woven on a wide loom and having no seams, generally no narrower than 54 in. (137 cm) and often as wide as 18 ft. (6 m). —*adj.* **2.** of or pertaining to rugs or carpets woven on a wide loom.

broad′-mind·ed, *adj.* free from prejudice or narrowness; liberal; tolerant. —**broad′-mind′ed·ly,** *adv.* —**broad′-mind′ed·ness,** *n.*

broad·side (brôd′sīd′), *n., adv., v.,* **-sid·ed, -sid·ing.** —*n.* **1.** the whole side of a ship above the water line. **2. a.** all the guns that can be fired from one side of a warship. **b.** a simultaneous discharge of all such guns. **3.** any strong or comprehensive attack, as by criticism. **4.** Also called **broad·sheet** (brôd′shēt′). **a.** a sheet of paper printed, orig. on one side only, as for distribution or posting. **b.** any printed advertising circular. **5.** a broad surface or side, as of a house. **6.** Also called **broad′side bal′lad.** a song, esp. in 16th- and 17th-century England, written on a topical subject and printed on broadsides. —*adv.* **7.** with the broader side facing toward a given point or object: *The truck hit the fence broadside.* **8.** in a wide-ranging manner: *to attack the policies broadside.* —*v.i.* **9.** to proceed broadside. **10.** to fire a broadside. —*v.t.* **11.** to collide with the side of. **12.** to make concerted verbal attacks on.

Broad·way (brôd′wā′), *n.* **1.** a major avenue in New York City. **2.** the professional or commercial theater in the U.S. as represented by the professional theater district in the vicinity of this avenue on the west side of the midtown area. —**Broad′way·ite′,** *n.*

bro·cade (brō kād′), *n., v.,* **-cad·ed, -cad·ing.** —*n.* **1.** fabric woven with an elaborate raised design, often using gold or silver thread. —*v.t.* **2.** to weave with a raised design or figure.

Bro′ca's ar′ea, *n.* a region of the left brain associated with the motor impulses necessary for speech.

broc·co·li (brok′ə lē, brok′lē), *n.* a form of cultivated cruciferous plant, *Brassica oleracea botrytis:* the leafy stalks and clusters of usu. green flower buds are eaten as a vegetable.

broc′coli rabe′ (or **raab′**) (räb′), *n.* a plant, *Brassica rapa ruvo:* the slightly bitter leaves and clustered flower buds are eaten as a vegetable.

bro·chette (brō shet′), *n.* **1.** a skewer. **2.** food, usu. in small pieces, broiled on a skewer.

bro·chure (brō shŏŏr′, -shûr′), *n.* a pamphlet or leaflet.

Brock (brok), *n.* **1. Blanche,** 1888–1958, U.S. musician and hymn writer. **2.** her husband **Virgil,** 1887–1978, U.S. clergyman and hymn writer.

Brock·en (brok′ən), *n.* a mountain in N central Germany: the highest peak in the Harz Mountains. 3745 ft. (1140 m).

brock·et (brok′it), *n.* **1.** any of several small, red South American deer of the genus *Mazama,* having short, unbranched antlers. **2.** the male red deer in the second year, with the first growth of straight horns.

Brod·sky (brod′skē), *n.* **Joseph,** 1940–96, Russian poet, U.S. citizen since 1977; Nobel prize 1987; U.S. poet laureate 1991.

brogue[1] (brōg), *n.* **1.** an Irish accent in the pronunciation of English. **2.** any strong regional accent.

brogue[2] (brōg), *n.* a durable, comfortable low-heeled shoe, often having decorative perforations and a wing tip.

broil[1] (broil), *v.t.* **1.** to cook by direct heat, as on a gridiron or in a broiler; grill. **2.** to make very hot; scorch. —*v.i.* **3.** to be subjected to great heat; become broiled. **4.** to burn with impatience, annoyance, etc. —*n.* **5.** the act of broiling or the state of being broiled. **6.** something broiled, esp. meat. —**broil′ing·ly,** *adv.*

broil[2] (broil), *n.* **1.** an angry quarrel or disturbance; tumult. —*v.i.* **2.** to quarrel; brawl.

broil·er (broi′lər), *n.* **1.** a small oven or a compartment in a stove in

which food is broiled by heat from above. **2.** a grate or pan used to broil food. **3.** a young chicken suitable for broiling.

broke (brōk), *v.* **1.** pt. of BREAK. —*adj.* **2.** without money; penniless. **3.** bankrupt. —*Idiom.* **4. go for broke,** *Slang.* to exert oneself or employ one's resources to the utmost.

bro·ken (brō′kən), *v.* **1.** pp. of BREAK. —*adj.* **2.** reduced to fragments; fragmented. **3.** ruptured; torn; fractured. **4.** not functioning properly; out of working order. **5.** infringed or violated: *a broken promise.* **6.** interrupted, disrupted, or disconnected: *a broken line.* **7.** changing direction abruptly. **8.** fragmentary or incomplete. **9.** weakened in strength, spirit, etc.: *broken health.* **10.** tamed, trained, or reduced to submission: *broken to the saddle.* **11.** (of language) imperfectly spoken: *broken English.* **12.** spoken in a halting or fragmentary manner, as under emotional strain. **13.** disunited or divided; disrupted, as by divorce: *broken families.* **14.** not smooth; rough or irregular: *broken ground.* **15.** overwhelmed with sorrow or disappointment: *a broken heart.* **16.** ruined; bankrupt: *broken fortunes.* —**bro′ken·ly,** *adv.* —**bro′ken·ness,** *n.*

bro′ken-down′, *adj.* **1.** dilapidated or infirm, as from age. **2.** out of working order, as from use or age.

bro·ken·heart·ed (brō′kən här′tid), *adj.* suffering from great sorrow, grief, or disappointment; heartbroken. —**bro′ken·heart′ed·ly,** *adv.*

bro·ker (brō′kər), *n.* **1.** an agent who buys or sells for a principal on a commission basis. **2.** a person who acts as an intermediary in arranging marriages, negotiating agreements, etc. **3.** STOCKBROKER. —*v.t.* **4.** to act as a broker for: *to broker the sale of a house.* **5.** to negotiate, arrange, or manipulate as a broker: *a presidential nomination brokered by party pros.* —*v.i.* **6.** to act as a broker. —**bro′ker·age** (-kər ij), *n.*

bro′kered conven′tion, *n.* a party convention in which many delegates are pledged to favorite sons who use their blocs of votes to bargain with leading candidates who lack a majority of delegate support. Compare OPEN CONVENTION.

brome·grass (brōm′gras′, -gräs′), *n.* any of various weeds and forage grasses of the genus *Bromus,* having flat blades and open clusters of flower spikelets.

bro·me·li·ad (brō mē′lē ad′), *n.* any plant of the pineapple family.

bro·mide (brō′mīd *or, for* 1, brō′mid), *n.* **1.** a compound containing bromine, as methyl bromide. **2.** potassium bromide, formerly used as a sedative. **3.** a trite saying; platitude. **4.** a boring, platitudinous person. —**bro·mid′ic** (-mid′ik), *adj.*

bro·mine (brō′mēn, -min), *n.* a dark reddish, toxic liquid element obtained from natural brines and ocean water and used chiefly in gasoline antiknock compounds, pharmaceuticals, and dyes. *Symbol:* Br; *at. wt.:* 79.909; *at. no.:* 35; *sp. gr.:* 3.119 at 20°C.

bron·chi (brong′kē, -kī), *n.* pl. of BRONCHUS.

bron·chi·al (brong′kē əl), *adj.* of or pertaining to the bronchi. —**bron′chi·al·ly,** *adv.*

bron·chi·ole (brong′kē ōl′), *n.* a small branch of a bronchus. —**bron′chi·o′lar,** *adj.*

bron·chi·tis (brong kī′tis), *n.* acute or chronic inflammation of the membrane lining of the bronchial tubes, caused by infection or inhalation of irritants. —**bron·chit′ic** (-kit′ik), *adj.*

bron·cho·pneu·mo·nia (brong′kō nŏŏ mōn′yə, -mō′nē ə, -nyŏŏ-), *n.* a form of pneumonia centering on bronchial passages.

bron·chus (brong′kəs), *n., pl.* **-chi** (-kē, -kī). either of the two branches of the trachea that extend into the lungs.

bron·co (brong′kō) also **bronc,** *n., pl.* **bron·cos** also **broncs.** a range pony or mustang of the western U.S., esp. one that is not broken or is imperfectly broken.

bron·co·bust·er (brong′kō bus′tər), *n.* a person who breaks broncos to the saddle. —**bron′co·bust′ing,** *n.*

Bron·të (bron′tē), *n.* **1. Anne** (*"Acton Bell"*), 1820–49, English novelist. **2.** her sister **Charlotte** (*"Currer Bell"*), 1816–55, English novelist. **3.** her sister **Emily Jane** (*"Ellis Bell"*), 1818–48, English novelist.

bron·to·saur (bron′tə sôr′), *n.* **1.** a huge sauropod dinosaur of the Jurassic genus *Apatosaurus* (formerly *Brontosaurus*), having a long, flexible neck and thick limbs. **2.** any sauropod. [< New Latin, = Greek *brontē* thunder + *saûros* lizard]

brontosaur, *Apatosaurus excelsus,* height 14 ft. (4.3 m); length 70 ft. (21.3 m)

Bronx′ cheer′, *n.* a loud, abrasive, spluttering noise made with the lips and tongue to express contempt. Also called **raspberry.**

bronze (bronz), *n., v.,* **bronzed, bronz·ing,** *adj.* —*n.* **1. a.** any of various alloys consisting essentially of copper and tin, the tin content not exceeding 11 percent. **b.** any of various other alloys having a large copper content. **2.** a metallic brownish color. **3.** a sculpture of bronze. —*v.t.* **4.** to give the appearance or color of bronze to. **5.** to coat with bronze. **6.** to make brown, as by exposure to the sun. —*adj.* **7.** of the color bronze. **8.** made of or coated with bronze. —**bronz′y, bronze′like′,** *adj.*

Bronze′ Age′, *n.* a period in the history of humankind, following the Stone Age and preceding the Iron Age, during which bronze weapons and implements were used: representative Old World cultures are the Minoan and Mycenaean.

bronze′ med′al, *n.* a medal, traditionally of bronze, awarded to the third-place winner in a competition. —**bronze′ med′alist,** *n.*

brooch (brōch, brōōch) also **broach,** *n.* a clasp or ornament having a pin at the back for passing through the clothing and a catch for securing the point of the pin.

brood (brōōd), *n.* **1.** a number of young produced or hatched at one time; family of offspring or young. **2.** a breed, species, group, or kind. —*v.t.* **3.** to sit upon (eggs) to hatch, as a bird; incubate. **4.** (of a bird) to warm, protect, or cover (young) with the wings or body. **5.** to think or worry persistently or moodily about; ponder: *to brood a problem.* —*v.i.* **6.** to sit upon eggs to be hatched, as a bird. **7.** to dwell on a subject or to meditate with morbid persistence (usu. fol. by *over* or *on*). —*adj.* **8.** kept for breeding: *a brood hen.* —**brood′less,** *adj.*

brood′ par′asitism, *n.* a form of social parasitism practiced by certain birds, as cuckoos and cowbirds, in which eggs are laid in the nests of other birds, causing them to be hatched and the young reared by the hosts.

brook[1] (brōōk), *n.* a small natural stream of fresh water.

brook[2] (brōōk), *v.t.* to bear; suffer; tolerate: *I will brook no interference.*

Brook′ Farm′, *n.* a farm in West Roxbury, Mass., where an experimental cooperative community was established from 1841 to 1847.

Brook′lyn Bridge′, *n.* a suspension bridge over the East River, in New York City, connecting Manhattan and Brooklyn: built 1867–84. 5989 ft. (1825 m) long.

Brooks (brōōks), *n.* **1. Gwendolyn,** born 1917, U.S. poet and novelist. **2. Phillips,** 1835–93, U.S. Protestant Episcopal bishop and orator. **3. Van Wyck** (wīk), 1886–1963, U.S. author and critic.

brook′ trout′, *n.* **1.** Also called **speckled trout.** a common trout, *Salvelinus fontinalis,* of E North America. **2.** BROWN TROUT.

broom (brōōm, brŏŏm), *n.* **1.** an implement for sweeping, consisting of a brush of straw or some other stiff material on a long handle. **2.** any of several flowering shrubs or small trees of the genera *Cytisus* and *Genista,* of the legume family, esp. *C. scoparius,* with yellow flowers borne on long branches. —*v.t.* **3.** to sweep. **4.** to splinter or fray mechanically. —*Saying.* **5. A new broom sweeps clean,** a new manager makes significant changes.

broom•corn (brōōm′kôrn′, brŏŏm′-), *n.* any of several varieties of sorghum having a long, stiff-branched panicle used in the manufacture of brooms.

broom•rape (brōōm′rāp′, brŏŏm′-), *n.* any of various parasitic plants, esp. of the genus *Orobanche,* living on the roots of broom and other plants.

broom•stick (brōōm′stik′, brŏŏm′-), *n.* the long slender handle of a broom.

broth (brôth, broth), *n.* **1.** a thin soup of concentrated meat or fish stock. **2.** water that has been boiled with meat, fish, vegetables, or grains; stock. **3.** a liquid medium containing nutrients suitable for culturing microorganisms. —**broth′y,** *adj.*

broth•el (broth′əl, brôth′-, brŏth′thəl, -thəl), *n.* a house of prostitution.

broth•er (bruth′ər *or, for 7,* bruth′ûr′), *n., pl.* **broth•ers,** *interj.* —*n.* **1.** a male offspring having both parents in common with another offspring; male sibling. **2.** HALF BROTHER. **3.** STEPBROTHER. **4.** a man or boy numbered in the same kinship group, nationality, race, church membership, society, etc., as another. **5.** (*often cap.*) **a.** a male numbered among the lay members of a religious organization that has a priesthood. **b.** a man who devotes himself to the duties of a religious order without taking holy orders, or while preparing for holy orders. **c.** (used as a title for a brother, monk, or friar.) **6.** *Slang.* fellow; buddy. —*interj.* **7.** (used to express disappointment, disgust, or surprise.)

broth•er•hood (bruth′ər hŏŏd′), *n.* **1.** the condition or quality of being a brother or brothers. **2.** the quality of being brotherly; fellowship. **3.** a fraternal or trade organization. **4.** all those engaged in a particular trade, profession, pursuit, etc. **5.** the belief that all people should act with warmth and equality toward one another.

broth•er-in-law′, *n., pl.* **broth•ers-in-law. 1.** the brother of one's husband or wife. **2.** the husband of one's sister. **3.** the husband of one's wife's or husband's sister.

Broth′er Jon′athan, *n. Brit.* a male native or resident of the United States.

broth•er•ly (bruth′ər lē), *adj.* **1.** of, like, or befitting a brother; affectionate and loyal; fraternal. —*adv.* **2.** as a brother; fraternally.

Broth′er of the Chris′tian Schools′, *n. Roman Catholic Church.* **1.** a member of a congregation of brothers, founded in France in 1684 for the education of the poor. **2.** Also, **Irish Christian Brother.** a member of a congregation of teaching brothers, founded in Ireland in 1802. Also called **Christian Brother.**

Broth′ers Kar•a•maz′ov, The (kar′ə mä′zôf, -zof, -maz′ôf, -of), a novel (1880) by Fyodor Dostoevsky.

brough•am (brōō′əm, brōōm, brŏŏ′əm), *n.* **1.** a four-wheeled, boxlike closed carriage with the driver's perch outside. **2. a.** (formerly) a limou-

sine with an open driver's compartment. **b.** an early type of automobile resembling a coupé.

brought (brôt), *v.* pt. and pp. of BRING.

brou•ha•ha (brōō′hä hä′, brōō′hä hä′, brōō hä′hä), *n., pl.* **-has. 1.** turmoil or clamor; uproar; hullabaloo. **2.** a minor episode involving excitement, confusion, etc.

brow (brou), *n.* **1.** the ridge over the eye. **2.** the hair growing on that ridge; eyebrow. **3.** the forehead. **4.** a person's countenance or mien. **5.** the edge of a steep place: *the brow of a hill.*

brow•beat (brou′bēt′), *v.t.,* **-beat, -beat•en, -beat•ing.** to intimidate by overbearing looks or words; bully. —**brow′beat′er,** *n.*

browed (broud), *adj.* having a brow of a specified kind (usu. used in combination): *shaggy-browed.*

brown (broun), *n.* **1.** a dark tertiary color with a yellowish or reddish hue. **2.** a person whose skin has a dusky or light brown pigmentation. —*adj.* **3.** of the color brown. **4.** having skin of this color. **5.** sunburned or tanned. —*v.t., v.i.* **6.** to make or become brown. **7.** to fry, sauté, roast, etc., to a brown color. —**brown′ish, brown′y,** *adj.*

brown′ al′gae, *n.pl.* any marine algae of the class Phaeophyceae, having brown pigments in addition to chlorophyll.

brown′-bag′, *v.t.,* **-bagged, -bag•ging. 1.** to bring (one's own liquor) to a restaurant or club, esp. one that has no liquor license. **2.** to bring (one's lunch) to work or elsewhere, usu. in a small brown paper bag.

brown′ bear′, *n.* any of various tan to near-black bears of the species *Ursus arctos,* having an upturned muzzle and a hump high on the back: subspecies include the brown bears of Eurasia and the grizzly bear and Kodiak bear of North America.

brown′ belt′, *n.* **1.** a brown cloth waistband conferred upon a participant in a martial art to indicate an intermediate level of expertise. **2.** a person at this level. Compare BLACK BELT (def. 1), WHITE BELT.

brown′ bet′ty (bet′ē), *n., pl.* **brown bet•ties.** a baked dessert made of apples or other fruit, breadcrumbs, sugar, butter, and spices.

Brown′ Bomb′er, *n.* nickname of Joe Louis.

brown′-eyed′ Su′san, *n.* a composite plant, *Rudbeckia triloba,* of the SE U.S., having a single flower with yellow rays darkening to an orange or brown at the base and a brownish black disk.

Brown′i•an mo′tion (brou′nē ən), *n.* the random motion of small colloidal particles suspended in a liquid or gas medium, caused by the collision of the medium's molecules with the particles. Also called **Brown′ian move′ment.**

brown•ie (brou′nē), *n.* **1.** a good-natured elf who secretly helps at night with household chores. **2.** a square piece of dense, chewy cake, usu. chocolate. **3.** (*sometimes cap.*) a member of the division of the Girl Scouts for girls 6–8 years old.

Brown′ie point′, *n. Informal.* a credit toward advancement or good standing gained esp. by currying favor.

Brown•ing (brou′ning), *n.* **1. Elizabeth Barrett,** 1806–61, English poet. **2. John Moses,** 1855–1926, U.S. designer of firearms. **3. Robert,** 1812–89, English poet.

Brown′ing au′tomatic ri′fle, *n.* an automatic rifle capable of firing 200 to 350 rounds per minute.

brown′ lung′, *n.* a chronic lung disease of textile workers caused by inhalation of cotton dust and other fine fibers.

brown′-nose′, *v.,* **-nosed, -nos•ing,** *n. Slang.* —*v.i.* **1.** to curry favor; behave obsequiously. —*v.t.* **2.** to seek favors from (a person) in an obsequious manner; fawn over. —*n.* **3.** Also, **brown′-nos′er.** a toady; sycophant.

brown•out (broun′out′), *n.* any curtailment of electric power, esp. a voltage reduction to prevent a blackout.

brown′ rice′, *n.* rice from which the bran layers and germs have not been removed by polishing.

brown′ sauce′, *n.* a sauce of browned roux and meat stock.

brown•stone (broun′stōn′), *n.* **1.** a reddish brown sandstone, used extensively as a building material. **2.** a building, esp. a row house, fronted with this stone.

brown′ stud′y, *n.* deep, serious absorption in thought.

brown′ sug′ar, *n.* sugar that retains some molasses or to which molasses has been added.

Browns•ville (brounz′vil), *n.* a seaport in S Texas, near the mouth of the Rio Grande. 112,362.

brown′-tail′ moth′, *n.* a white moth, *Euproctis chrysorrhoea,* having a brown tuft at the end of the abdomen, the larvae of which feed on the foliage of various shade and fruit trees.

brown′ trout′, *n.* a common trout, *Salmo trutta,* of N European streams: introduced in North America.

Brown v. Board of Education, *n.* a 1954 decision of the U.S. Supreme Court ruling that segregated schools are unequal and therefore violate the Fourteenth Amendment.

browse (brouz), *v.,* **browsed, brows•ing,** *n.* —*v.t.* **1.** to eat, nibble at, or feed on (foliage, berries, etc.). **2.** to graze; pasture on. **3.** to look through or glance at casually. —*v.i.* **4.** to feed on or nibble at foliage, lichen, berries, etc. **5.** to graze. **6.** to glance at random through a book, magazine, etc. **7.** to look leisurely at goods displayed for sale, as in a store. —*n.* **8.** tender shoots or twigs of shrubs and trees as food for cattle, deer, etc. **9.** an act or instance of browsing.

brows•er (brou′zər), *n.* **1.** a person or thing that browses. **2.** *Computers.* an application program that allows the user to examine encoded documents in a form suitable for display, esp. such a program for use on the World Wide Web.

Brue·ghel or **Brue·gel** (broi′gəl, brōō′-, brœ-), *n.* BREUGHEL.

bru·in (brōō′in), *n.* a bear, esp. a European brown bear.

bruise (brōōz), *v.*, **bruised, bruis·ing,** *n.* —*v.t.* **1.** to injure by striking or pressing, without breaking the skin. **2.** to injure or hurt slightly, as with an insult or unkind remark. **3.** to crush (drugs or food) by beating or pounding. —*v.i.* **4.** to develop or bear a discolored spot on the skin as the result of a blow, fall, etc. **5.** to become slightly injured: *feelings that bruise easily.* —*n.* **6.** an injury due to bruising; contusion.

bruis·er (brōō′zər), *n. Informal.* a strong, tough man.

bruit (brōōt), *v.t.* **1.** to voice abroad; rumor (used chiefly in the passive): *The report was bruited through the village.* —*n.* **2.** any generally abnormal sound or murmur heard on auscultation.

brume (brōōm), *n.* mist; fog. —**bru′mous,** *adj.*

brum·ma·gem (brum′ə jəm), *adj.* **1.** showy but inferior and worthless. —*n.* **2.** a showy but inferior and worthless thing.

brunch (brunch), *n.* **1.** a meal that serves as both breakfast and lunch. —*v.i.* **2.** to eat brunch.

Bru·nei (brōō nī′, -nā′), *n.* an independent sultanate on the NW coast of Borneo: a former British protectorate (1889–1983). 307,616; 2226 sq. mi. (5765 sq. km). *Cap.:* Bandar Seri Begawan. Official name, **Brunei Da·rus·sa·lam′** (dä′rōō sä läm′). —**Bru·nei′an,** *adj., n.*

bru·net (brōō net′), *adj.* **1.** (esp. of a male) brunette. —*n.* **2.** a person, usu. a male, with dark hair and, often, dark eyes and darkish skin.

bru·nette (brōō net′), *adj.* **1.** (of hair, eyes, skin, etc.) of a dark color or tone. **2.** (of a person) having dark hair and, often, dark eyes and darkish or olive skin. —*n.* **3.** a person, esp. a female, with such coloration.

Bruns′wick stew′, *n.* a stew orig. of squirrel and onions and now usu. of rabbit or chicken with lima beans, corn, tomatoes, onions, etc.

brunt (brunt), *n.* the main force or impact, as of an attack or blow.

brush[1] (brush), *n.* **1.** an implement consisting of bristles, hair, or the like and a handle, used for painting, cleaning, grooming, etc. **2.** either of a pair of wire-bristled, brushlike devices used to mark a soft rhythmic beat on drums or cymbals. **3.** the bushy tail of an animal, esp. a fox. **4.** an electrical conductor, often of carbon or copper, serving to maintain electric contact between stationary and moving parts of a motor, generator, etc. **5.** any feathery or hairy tuft or tassel. **6.** an act of brushing; application of a brush. **7.** a light, stroking touch. **8.** a close approach, esp. to something undesirable or harmful; skirmish: *a brush with disaster.* **9. the brush,** a rejection or rebuff: *to get the brush from one's lover.* —*v.t.* **10.** to sweep, paint, clean, polish, etc., with a brush. **11.** to touch lightly in passing; pass lightly over. **12.** to remove by brushing or by lightly passing over. —*v.i.* **13.** to move or skim with a slight contact. **14. brush aside,** to disregard; ignore. **15. brush back,** *Baseball.* to force (a batter) away from the plate with a fastball pitched high and inside. **16. brush off,** to rebuff; send away. **17. brush up (on),** to revive or review (studies, a skill, etc.).

brush[2] (brush), *n.* **1. a.** a dense growth of bushes, shrubs, etc.; scrub; thicket. **b.** dense, low-growing bushes and shrubs. **c.** land or area covered with dense, low growth. **2.** BRUSHWOOD (defs. 1, 2). —**brush′i·ness,** *n.*

brush·back (brush′bak′), *n. Baseball.* a fastball pitched high and inside, forcing the batter to lean away from the plate.

brushed (brusht), *adj.* having a nap produced by a brushing process: *brushed cotton.*

brush′ fire′, *n.* a fire in an area of bushes, shrubs, or brush, as distinct from a forest fire.

brush′-off′, *n.* an abrupt or final dismissal or rebuff.

brush·wood (brush′wŏŏd′), *n.* **1.** the wood of branches that have been cut or broken off. **2.** a pile of such branches. **3.** a thicket of bushes or shrubs; brush.

brush·work (brush′wûrk′), *n.* the use of a brush as a tool, as in painting.

brush·y[1] (brush′ē), *adj.*, **brush·i·er, brush·i·est.** resembling a brush, esp. in roughness or shagginess.

brush·y[2] (brush′ē), *adj.*, **brush·i·er, brush·i·est.** covered or overgrown with brush or brushwood. —**brush′i·ness,** *n.*

brusque or **brusk** (brusk; *esp. Brit.* brŏŏsk), *adj.* abrupt in manner; blunt; rough. —**brusque′ly,** *adv.* —**brusque′ness,** *n.*

Brus·sels (brus′əlz), *n.* the capital of Belgium, in the central part. 1,050,787 (with suburbs). Flemish, **Brus·sel** (brʏs′əl); French, **Brux·elles.**

Brus′sels lace′, *n.* **1.** a fine handmade lace in a floral pattern, orig. made in the area of Brussels. **2.** a modern machine-made net lace with appliquéd floral designs.

Brus′sels sprout′, *n.* **1.** Usu. **Brussels sprouts.** a plant, *Brassica oleracea gemmifera,* having small, cabbagelike heads or buds along the stalk. **2. Brussels sprouts,** the heads or buds, eaten as a vegetable.

brut (brōōt; *Fr.* brʏt), *adj.* (of wine, esp. champagne) very dry.

bru·tal (brōōt′l), *adj.* **1.** savage; cruel; inhuman. **2.** crude; coarse: *brutal language.* **3.** harsh; severe: *a brutal storm.* **4.** accurate or direct, but displeasing: *a brutal fact.* **5.** of or pertaining to animals; beastly. —**bru′tal·ly,** *adv.*

bru·tal·i·ty (brōō tal′i tē), *n., pl.* **-ties. 1.** the quality of being brutal; cruelty; savagery. **2.** a brutal act or practice.

bru·tal·ize (brōōt′l īz′), *v.t.,* **-ized, -iz·ing. 1.** to make brutal. **2.** to treat (someone) with brutality. —**bru′tal·i·za′tion,** *n.*

brute (brōōt), *n.* **1.** a nonhuman creature; beast. **2.** a savage, insensitive, or crude person. **3.** the animal qualities, desires, etc., of humankind: *to bring out the brute in someone.* —*adj.* **4.** animal; not human. **5.** not intelligent; irrational. **6.** savage; cruel: *brute force.* **7.** carnal; sensual. —**brute′ly,** *adv.* —**brut′ish,** *adj.*

Bry·an (brī′ən), *n.* **1. William Jennings,** 1860–1925, U.S. political leader. **2.** a city in E Texas. 60,410.

bryo-, a combining form meaning "moss, liverwort": *bryology.*

bry·ol·o·gy (brī ol′ə jē), *n.* the branch of botany dealing with bryophytes. —**bry′o·log′i·cal** (-ə loj′i kəl), *adj.* —**bry·ol′o·gist,** *n.*

bry·o·ny (brī′ə nē), *n., pl.* **-nies.** any Old World vine or climbing plant belonging to the genus *Bryonia,* of the gourd family, with acrid juice having emetic and purgative properties.

bry·o·phyte (brī′ə fīt′), *n.* any of the Bryophyta, a phylum of nonvascular plants comprising the true mosses and liverworts. —**bry′o·phyt′ic** (-fit′ik), *adj.*

bry·o·zo·an (brī′ə zō′ən), *n.* **1.** Also called **moss animal.** any marine or freshwater colonial animal of the phylum Bryozoa, forming branching, encrusting, or gelatinous mosslike masses. —*adj.* **2.** belonging to the Bryozoa.

B.S., Bachelor of Science.

B.S.A., Boy Scouts of America.

B.Sc., Bachelor of Science.

BST, bovine somatotropin. BOVINE GROWTH HORMONE.

Btu or **BTU,** British thermal unit.

bub·ble (bub′əl), *n., v.,* **-bled, -bling.** —*n.* **1.** a nearly spherical body of gas contained in a liquid. **2.** a small globule of gas in a thin liquid envelope. **3.** a globule of air or gas, or a globular vacuum, contained in a solid. **4.** anything that lacks firmness, substance, or permanence; delusion. **5.** an inflated speculation, esp. if fraudulent: *a real-estate bubble.* **6.** the act or sound of bubbling. **7.** a spherical or nearly spherical canopy or shelter; dome. —*v.i.* **8.** to form, produce, or release bubbles; effervesce. **9.** to flow or spout with a gurgling noise; gurgle. **10.** to boil. **11.** to issue forth in a lively, sparkling manner: *The play bubbled with fun.* **12.** to seethe or stir, as with excitement: *My mind bubbles with plans.* —*v.t.* **13.** to cause to bubble; make bubbles in. **14. bubble over,** to overflow with liveliness or zest.

bub′ble bath′, *n.* **1.** a crystal, powder, or liquid preparation that foams in scents, and softens bathwater. **2.** a bath with such a preparation added to the water.

bub·ble·gum (bub′əl gum′), *n.* a type of chewing gum that can be blown into large bubbles through the lips.

bub·bly (bub′lē), *adj.,* **-bli·er, -bli·est,** *n., pl.* **-blies.** —*adj.* **1.** full of or producing bubbles. **2.** lively; effervescent; enthusiastic. —*n.* **3.** *Informal.* CHAMPAGNE (defs. 1, 2). —**bub′bli·ness,** *n.*

Bu·ber (bōō′bər), *n.* **Martin,** 1878–1965, Jewish philosopher, theologian, and scholar: born in Austria.

bu·bo (byōō′bō, bōō′-), *n., pl.* **-boes.** an inflammatory swelling of a lymphatic gland, esp. in the groin or armpit. —**bu′boed,** *adj.*

bu·bon·ic (byōō bon′ik, bōō-), *adj.* **1.** of or pertaining to a bubo. **2.** accompanied by or affected with buboes.

bubon′ic plague′, *n.* a severe infection caused by the bacterium *Yersinia pestis,* transmitted by the bites of fleas from infected rats, characterized by the formation of buboes at the armpits and groin. Compare BLACK DEATH.

buc·cal (buk′əl), *adj.* **1.** of or pertaining to the cheek. **2.** pertaining to the mouth or the sides of the mouth. **3.** of or designating the surface of a tooth facing the cheek. Compare LABIAL (def. 4), LINGUAL (def. 4). —**buc′cal·ly,** *adv.*

buc·ca·neer (buk′ə nēr′), *n.* a pirate, esp. one who raided Spanish colonies and ships along the American coast in the second half of the 17th century. [< French *boucanier,* lit., barbecuer] —**buc′ca·neer′ish,** *adj.*

buc·ci·na·tor (buk′sə nā′tər), *n.* a thin, flat muscle of the cheek region, the action of which contracts and compresses the cheek. —**buc′ci·na·to′ry** (-nə tôr′ē, -tōr′ē), *adj.*

Bu·chan·an (byōō kan′ən, bə-), *n.* **James,** 1791–1868, 15th president of the U.S. 1857–61.

Bu·cha·rest (bōō′kə rest′, byōō′-), *n.* the capital of Romania, in the S part. 1,975,808. Romanian, **Bucureşti.**

Bu·chen·wald (bōō′kən wôld′, -vält′, -кнən-), *n.* the site of a former Nazi concentration camp in central Germany, near Weimar.

buck[1] (buk), *n.* **1.** the male of the deer, antelope, rabbit, hare, sheep, goat, and certain other animals. **2.** BUCKSKIN (defs. 1, 2). **3.** a casual oxford shoe made of buckskin, often in white or a neutral color. **4.** an impetuous, dashing, or spirited man or youth. —*adj.* **5.** of the lowest rank within a military designation: *buck private.*

buck[2] (buk), *v.i.* **1.** (of a saddle or pack animal) to leap with arched back and land with head low and forelegs stiff. **2.** to resist or oppose obstinately; object strongly: *to buck at a suggestion.* **3.** (of a vehicle, motor, or the like) to operate unevenly; move by jerks and bounces. —*v.t.* **4.** to throw or attempt to throw (a rider) by bucking. **5.** to force a way through or proceed against (an obstacle): *The plane bucked a strong headwind.* **6.** to strike with the head; butt. **7.** to resist or oppose obstinately; object strongly to. **8.** to gamble, play, or take a risk against:

to buck the odds. **9. buck for,** to strive or compete for (a promotion, raise, etc.). **10. buck up,** to make or become cheerful. —*n.* **11.** an act of bucking. —**buck′er,** *n.*

buck³ (buk), *n.* **1.** a sawhorse. **2.** a leather-covered block, used in gymnastics for vaulting. **3.** a doorframe of wood or metal. —*v.t.* **4.** to split or saw (logs, felled trees, etc.).

buck⁴ (buk), *n.* **1.** an object used by a poker player as a marker for who has the deal, for an ante, etc. **2.** ultimate responsibility: *The buck stops here.* —*v.t.* **3.** to pass (something) along to another, esp. as a means of avoiding responsibility or blame. —*Idiom.* **4. pass the buck,** to shift responsibility or blame to another person.

buck⁵ (buk), *n. Slang.* **1.** a dollar. —*Idiom.* **2. bang for the buck,** return for one's investment.

Buck (buk), *n.* **Pearl (Sydenstricker),** 1892–1973, U.S. novelist.

buck•a•roo (buk′ə rōō′, buk′ə rōō′), *n., pl.* **-roos.** *Western U.S.* a cowboy.

buck′ bean′, *n.* a bog plant, *Menyanthes trifoliata,* of the gentian family, having narrow clusters of white or pink flowers.

buck•board (buk′bôrd′, -bōrd′), *n.* a light, four-wheeled carriage in which a long elastic board or lattice frame is used in place of body and springs.

buck•et (buk′it), *n.* **1.** a deep, cylindrical container, usu. of metal, plastic, or wood, with a flat bottom and a semicircular bail. **2. a.** any of the scoops in certain types of conveyors or elevators. **b.** the scoop of a steam or power shovel. **c.** a vane or blade of a waterwheel, paddle wheel, or the like. **3.** a bucketful: *a bucket of sand.* —*v.t.* **4.** to lift, carry, or handle in a bucket (often fol. by *up* or *out*). —*Idiom.* **5. drop in the bucket,** a small, inadequate amount. **6. kick the bucket,** *Slang.* to die. —**buck′et•ful,** *n., pl.* **-fuls.**

buck′et seat′, *n.* an individual seat with a contoured back, as in some automobiles, often made to fold forward.

buck′et shop′, *n. Informal.* an overly aggressive brokerage house, esp. one that sells low-priced, highly speculative stocks by telephone.

buck•eye (buk′ī′), *n., pl.* **-eyes. 1.** any of various trees or shrubs of the genus *Aesculus,* of the horse chestnut family. **2.** the brown nut of any of these trees.

buck′ fe′ver, *n.* nervous excitement, esp. that felt by an inexperienced hunter at the approach of game.

buck•le (buk′əl), *n., v.,* **-led, -ling.** —*n.* **1.** a clasp consisting of a rectangular or curved rim with one or more movable tongues, fixed to one end of a belt or strap, used for fastening to the other end of the same strap or to another strap. **2.** an ornament of metal, beads, etc., of similar appearance. **3.** a bend, bulge, or kink, as in a board or saw blade. —*v.t.* **4.** to fasten with a buckle or buckles: *Buckle your seat belt.* **5.** to shrivel, by applying heat or pressure; bend; curl. **6.** to bend, warp, or cause to give way suddenly, as with heat or pressure. —*v.i.* **7.** to close or fasten with a buckle **8.** to bend, warp, bulge, or collapse. **9.** to yield, surrender, or give way to another (often fol. by *under*). **10. buckle down,** to set to work with vigor and determination. **11. buckle up,** to fasten one's belt, seat belt, or buckles.

Buck•ley (buk′lē), *n.* **William F., Jr.,** born 1925, U.S. writer and editor.

buck′ moth′, *n.* a saturniid moth, *Hemileuca maia,* having delicate, grayish wings with a white band.

buck•ram (buk′rəm), *n.* **1.** a stiffly sized fabric of cotton, linen, hemp, hair, or the like, used for interlinings, book bindings, etc. **2.** stiffness of manner; extreme preciseness or formality. —*v.t.* **3.** to strengthen with buckram.

buck•saw buk′sô′), *n.* a saw having a blade set across an upright frame or bow, used with both hands in cutting wood on a sawhorse.

bucksaw

buck•shot (buk′shot′), *n.* a large size of lead shot used in shotgun shells for hunting pheasants, ducks, etc.

buck•skin (buk′skin′), *n.* **1.** the skin of a buck or deer. **2.** a strong, soft, yellowish or grayish leather, orig. prepared from deerskins, now usu. from sheepskins. **3. buckskins,** breeches or shoes made of buckskin. **4.** a horse the color of buckskin. —*adj.* **5.** made of buckskin. **6.** having the color of buckskin.

buck•thorn (buk′thôrn′), *n.* **1.** any of several often thorny trees or shrubs of the genus *Rhamnus,* of the buckthorn family, esp. *R. frangula,* the bark of which is used in medicine. **2.** a thorny tree, *Bumelia lycioides,* of the sapodilla family, common in the southern U.S., having elliptical leaves and large clusters of white flowers.

buck•tooth (buk′tōōth′), *n., pl.* **-teeth** (-tēth′). a projecting tooth, esp. an upper front tooth. —**buck′toothed′,** *adj.*

buck•wheat (buk′hwēt′, -wēt′), *n.* **1.** any of several plants of the genus *Fagopyrum,* of the buckwheat family, cultivated for their edible triangular seeds. **2.** the seeds of this plant, made into flour or a cereal or used as animal feed. **3.** Also called **buck′wheat flour′.** flour made by grinding buckwheat seeds.

buck′wheat fam′ily, *n.* a family, Polygonaceae, of shrubs and non-woody plants having stems with enlarged joints, small petalless flowers, and dry, one-seeded fruit: includes buckwheat, dock, knotweed, rhubarb, and sorrel.

bu•col•ic (byōō kol′ik), *adj.* **1.** pertaining to shepherds; pastoral. **2.** pertaining to or suggesting an idyllic rural life. —*n.* **3.** a pastoral poem.

bud (bud), *n., v.,* **bud•ded, bud•ding.** —*n.* **1.** any of the small terminal bulges on a plant stem, from which leaves or flowers develop. **2.** a state of putting forth buds: *roses in bud.* **3.** a partially opened flower or leaf. **4.** a prominence that emerges or branches from the main body of certain relatively simple organisms, as sponges and yeasts, and develops asexually into a new individual. **5.** an immature or undeveloped person or thing. —*v.i.* **6.** to put forth or produce buds. **7.** to begin to develop. —*v.t.* **8.** to cause to bud. **9.** *Hort.* to graft by inserting a single bud into the stock. —*Idiom.* **10. nip in the bud,** to stop (something) in the earliest stages.

Bu•da•pest (bōō′də pest′, -pesht′, bōōd′ə-), *n.* the capital of Hungary, in the central part, on the Danube. 2,104,000.

Bud•dha (bōō′də, bōōd′ə), *n., pl.* **-dhas.** Also called **Gautama.** (*Prince Siddhätta* or *Siddhartha*) 566?–c480 B.C., Indian religious leader: founder of Buddhism.

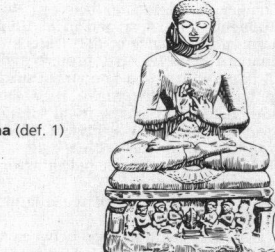

buddha (def. 1)

Bud•dhism (bōō′diz əm, bōōd′iz-), *n.* a religion, originated in India by Buddha (Gautama) and later spreading to China, Burma, Japan, Tibet, and parts of SE Asia, holding that life is full of suffering caused by desire and that the way to end this suffering is through Enlightenment that enables one to halt the endless sequence of births and deaths to which one is otherwise subject. —**Bud′dhist,** *n., adj.* —**Bud•dhis′tic,** *adj.*

bud•ding (bud′ing), *adj.* in an early, usu. promising stage of development: *a budding artist.*

bud•dle•ia (bud lē′ə, bud′lē ə), *n., pl.* **-ias.** any tropical shrub of the genus *Buddleia,* of the logania family, having lance-shaped leaves and clusters of showy flowers. Also called **butterfly bush.**

bud•dy (bud′ē), *n., pl.* **-dies,** *v.,* **-died, -dy•ing.** *Informal.* —*n.* **1.** a friend, comrade, or partner; chum. —*v.i.* **2.** to become friendly or work closely together (usu. fol. by *up* or *with*).

budge¹ (buj), *v.,* **budged, budg•ing.** (*often used negatively*) —*v.i.* **1.** to move slightly; begin to move: *The car wouldn't budge.* **2.** to change one's opinion or stated position; yield: *My mother said "no" and refused to budge.* —*v.t.* **3.** to cause to move. **4.** to cause (someone) to reconsider or change a decision, stated opinion, etc.

budge² (buj), *n.* a fur made from lambskin with the wool dressed outward.

budg•er•i•gar (buj′ə rē gär′, -ər i-), *n.* an Australian parakeet, *Melopsittacus undulatus,* having greenish plumage with black and yellow markings, bred as a pet in a variety of colors.

budg•et (buj′it), *n.* **1.** an estimate, often itemized, of expected income and expenses for a given period in the future. **2.** a plan of operations based on such an estimate. **3.** an itemized allotment of funds, time, etc., for a given period. **4.** a sum of money set aside or allowed for a particular purpose: *the construction budget.* **5.** a limited stock or supply of something. **6.** *Dial.* a small bag; pouch. —*adj.* **7.** reasonably or cheaply priced: *budget dresses.* —*v.t.* **8.** to plan an allotment of (funds, time, etc.). **9.** to deal with (specific funds) in a budget. —*v.i.* **10.** to subsist on or live within a budget. —**budg′et•ar′y** (-ter′ē), *adj.*

Bue′na Vis′ta (bwä′nə vis′tə, vēs′-), *n.* a village in NE Mexico, near Saltillo: site of U.S. victory in battle (1847) during the Mexican War.

Bue•nos Ai•res (bwä′nəs ēr′ēz, bō′nəs), *n.* the capital of Argentina, in the E part, on the Río de la Plata. 9,927,404.

buff¹ (buf), *n.* **1.** a soft, thick, light yellow leather with a napped surface, orig. made from buffalo skin. **2.** a brownish yellow color; tan. **3.** a stick, block, or wheel covered with leather or other soft material, used for polishing. **4.** a devotee or well-informed student of some activity or subject: *Civil War buffs.* **5.** *Informal.* the bare skin: *in the buff.* —*adj.* **6.** of the color buff. **7.** made of buff leather. —*v.t.* **8.** to clean, polish, or shine with or as if with a buff. **9.** to create a velvety surface on (leather), as by abrasion. —**buff'a·bil'i·ty,** n. —**buff'a·ble,** adj.

buff² (buf), v.t. to reduce or deaden the force of; act as a buffer.

buf·fa·lo (buf'ə lō'), n., pl. **-loes, -los,** (esp. collectively) **-lo,** v., **-loed, -lo·ing.** —n. **1.** any of several large wild oxen of the family Bovidae, as the bison or water buffalo. **2.** a buffalofish. —v.t. Informal. **3.** to puzzle or baffle; confuse. **4.** to intimidate by a display of power, importance, etc. —adj. **5.** patterned in buffalo plaid. [< Portuguese < Late Latin būfalus < Greek boúbalos]

Buf·fa·lo (buf'ə lō'), n. a port in W New York, on Lake Erie. 312,965.

buf'falo ber'ry, n. **1.** either of two North American shrubs, Shepherdia argentea or S. canadensis, of the oleaster family, having silvery, oblong leaves and edible yellow or red berries. **2.** the fruit itself.

Buf'falo Bill', n. Cody, William Frederick.

buf·fa·lo·fish (buf'ə lō'fish'), n., pl. (esp. collectively) **-fish,** (esp. for kinds or species) **-fish·es.** any of several large, carplike North American freshwater fishes of the genus Ictiobus, of the sucker family.

buf'falo grass', n. a short grass, Buchloë dactyloides, having gray-green blades, prevalent on the dry plains east of the Rocky Mountains.

buf'falo plaid', n. a plaid with large blocks formed by the intersection of two different-color yarns, typically red and black.

buf'falo wing', n. a deep-fried chicken wing served in a spicy sauce and usually with celery and blue cheese. [after a restaurant in Buffalo, which popularized the dish]

buff·er¹ (buf'ər), n. **1.** an apparatus at the end of a railroad car, railroad track, etc., for absorbing shock during coupling, collisions, etc. **2.** any device, material, or apparatus used as a shield, cushion, or bumper, esp. on machinery. **3.** any intermediate or intervening shield or device reducing the danger of interaction between two machines, chemicals, electronic components, etc. **4.** a person or thing that shields and protects against harm or annoyance or that lessens the impact of a shock or reversal. **5.** financial reserves that protect a person, organization, or country against bankruptcy. **6.** a temporary storage area that holds data until the computer is ready to process it. **7.** any substance capable of neutralizing both acids and bases in a solution without appreciably changing the solution's original acidity or alkalinity. —v.t. **8.** to cushion, shield, or protect. **9.** to treat with a buffer.

buff·er² (buf'ər), n. **1.** a device for polishing or buffing, as a buff. **2.** a person who uses such a device.

buff'er state', n. a nation lying between larger and potentially hostile nations.

buff'er zone', n. **1.** a neutral zone between two hostile nations, designed to prevent acts of aggression. **2.** any area serving to mitigate or neutralize potential conflict.

buf·fet¹ (buf'it), n. **1.** a blow, as with the hand or fist. **2.** a violent shock or concussion. —v.t. **3.** to strike, as with the hand or fist. **4.** to strike against or push repeatedly: The wind buffeted the house. **5.** to contend against; battle. —v.i. **6.** to force one's way, esp. by a struggle.

buf·fet² (bə fā', bŏŏ-; adj. also bŏŏ'fā), n. **1.** a sideboard or cabinet for holding china, table linen, etc. **2.** a meal laid out on a table or sideboard so that guests may serve themselves. **3.** a counter, bar, or table for food or refreshments. **4.** a restaurant with such a counter or table. —adj. **5.** served from or as a buffet: a buffet supper.

buf·fle·head (buf'əl hed'), n. a small North American duck, Bucephala albeola, the male of which has a large head with bushy plumage. —**buf'fle·head'ed,** adj.

buf·fo (bŏŏ'fō), n., pl. **-fi** (-fē). **-fos.** a male opera singer specializing in comic roles.

buf·foon (bə fŏŏn'), n. **1.** a person who amuses others by jokes, pranks, etc. **2.** a person given to coarse or offensive joking. —**buf·foon'er·y,** n. —**buf·foon'ish,** adj.

bug (bug), n., v., **bugged, bug·ging.** —n. **1.** Also called **true bug.** any insect of the order Hemiptera, characterized by sucking mouthparts and thickened, leathery forewings. **2.** (loosely) any insect or insectlike invertebrate. **3.** Informal. any microorganism, esp. a virus: an intestinal bug. **4.** a defect, error, or imperfection, as in computer software. **5.** Informal. **a.** an often short-lived enthusiasm; a craze or obsession: He's got the sports-car bug. **b.** an enthusiast; fan; hobbyist: a camera bug. **6.** a hidden microphone or other electronic eavesdropping device. **7.** Horse Racing. the five-pound weight allowance that can be claimed by an apprentice jockey. —v.t. **8.** to install a secret listening device in or on: The phone was bugged. **9.** Informal. to annoy or pester. —v.i. **10.** (of eyes) to bulge. **11. bug off,** Slang. to leave or depart (often used as a command). **12. bug out,** Slang. to flee in panic. —**Idiom. 13. put a bug in someone's ear,** to give someone a subtle suggestion.

bug·a·boo (bug'ə bŏŏ'), n., pl. **-boos.** something that causes fear or worry; bugbear; bogy.

bug·bane (bug'bān'), n. any of several tall E North American plants of the genus Cimicifuga, of the buttercup family, bearing erect spikes of white flowers that exude an unpleasant odor said to repel insects.

bug·bear (bug'bâr'), n. **1.** a persistent source or source of annoyance. **2.** any source, real or imaginary, of fright or fear. **3.** (in folklore) a goblin said to eat up naughty children.

bug'-eyed', adj. with bulging eyes, as from surprise or wonderment.

bug·ger (bug'ər, bŏŏg'-), n. **1.** Informal. a fellow or lad (used affectionately or abusively): a cute little bugger. **2.** Informal. any object or thing.

bug·gy (bug'ē), n., pl. **-gies.** a light, four-wheeled, horse-drawn carriage with a single seat and a transverse spring.

bu·gle¹ (byŏŏ'gəl), n., v., **-gled, -gling.** —n. **1.** a brass wind instrument resembling a cornet but usu. without keys or valves, used typically for sounding military signals. —v.i. **2.** to sound a bugle. **3.** (of bull elks) to utter a rutting call. —**bu'gler,** n.

bu·gle² (byŏŏ'gəl), n. any of various low-growing plants belonging to the genus Ajuga, of the mint family, usu. having blue flowers.

bu·gle³ (byŏŏ'gəl), n. **1.** Also called **bu'gle bead'.** a tubular glass bead used for ornamenting dresses. —adj. **2.** Also, **bu'gled.** ornamented with bugles.

bu·gle·weed (byŏŏ'gəl wēd'), n. a plant belonging to the genus Lycopus, of the mint family, esp. L. virginicus.

bu·gloss (byŏŏ'glos, -glôs), n. any of various erect, bristly plants of the borage family, with small blue flowers, common in sandy soil and open fields.

build (bild), v., **built, build·ing,** n. —v.t. **1.** to construct (esp. something complex) by assembling and joining parts or materials: to build a house. **2.** to establish, increase, or strengthen (often fol. by up): to build a business. **3.** to mold, form, or create: to build boys into men. **4.** to base; found: a relationship built on trust. —v.i. **5.** to engage in the art, practice, or business of building. **6.** to form or construct a plan, system of thought, etc. (usu. fol. by on or upon): to build on the philosophies of the past. **7.** to increase or develop in intensity, strength, etc. (often fol. by up): The drama builds steadily toward a climax. **8. build in** or **into,** to build or incorporate as part of something else: an allowance for travel built into the budget. **9. build up, a.** to develop or increase. **b.** to improve the strength or health of. **c.** to prepare in stages. **d.** to fill up with houses. **e.** to praise or promote. —n. **10.** the physical structure, esp. of a person; physique: a strong build. **11.** the manner or form of construction. —**build'a·ble,** adj.

build·ing (bil'ding), n. **1.** any relatively permanent enclosed structure on a plot of land, having a roof and usu. windows. **2.** anything built or constructed. **3.** the act, business, or practice of constructing houses, office buildings, etc.

build'ing block', n. **1.** BLOCK (defs. 2, 3). **2.** a basic element or component: the building blocks of proteins.

build'up' or **build'-up',** n. **1.** an increase, as in amount, number, strength, or intensity: a buildup of military forces; a buildup of suspense. **2.** an accumulation, as of a material: a buildup of salt deposits. **3.** a progressive or sequential development. **4.** praise or publicity designed to enhance a reputation or popularize someone or something. **5.** preparation designed to make possible the achievement of an objective: the buildup to a sales pitch.

built (bilt), v. **1.** pt. and pp. of BUILD. —adj. **2.** of sound or sturdy construction. **3.** having a good physique or figure.

built'-in', adj. **1.** built so as to be an integral and permanent part of a larger construction: built-in bookcases. **2.** existing as a natural or characteristic part; inherent: a built-in contempt for daydreamers. —n. **3.** a built-in appliance, piece of furniture, or feature.

built'-up', adj. **1.** built by the fastening together of several parts or enlarged by the addition of layers: a shoe with a built-up heel. **2.** (of an area) filled in with houses.

Bu·jum·bu·ra (bŏŏ'jŏŏm bŏŏr'ə), n. the capital of Burundi, in the W part, on Lake Tanganyika. 272,600. Formerly, **Usumbura.**

Bul (bŏŏl), n. Chiefly Biblical. a month equivalent to Heshvan of the modern Jewish calendar. I Kings 6:38.

bulb (bulb), n. **1. a.** a swollen, usu. underground stem having fleshy scalelike leaves that contain stored food, as in the onion or daffodil. **b.** a plant growing from such a bulb. **2.** any round, enlarged part, esp. at the end of a cylindrical object: the bulb of a thermometer. **3. a.** the glass housing, in which a partial vacuum has been established, that contains the filament of an incandescent lamp. **b.** an incandescent lamp. **4.** any of various small, bulb-shaped anatomical structures or protuberances: olfactory bulb. **5.** MEDULLA OBLONGATA. **6.** a camera shutter setting in which the shutter remains open as long as the shutter release is depressed.

bul·bar (bul'bər, -bär), adj. of or pertaining to a bulb, esp. to the medulla oblongata.

bulb·let (bulb'lit), n. a small bulb or bulblike structure, esp. one growing in the axils of leaves, as in the tiger lily, or replacing flowers, as in the onion.

bul·bous (bul'bəs), adj. **1.** bulb-shaped. **2.** having or growing from bulbs. —**bul'bous·ly,** adv.

bul·bul (bŏŏl'bŏŏl), n. **1.** any of various medium-sized songbirds of the family Pycnonotidae, inhabiting warmer regions of the Old World east to the Moluccas. **2.** a songbird often mentioned in Persian poetry, probably the nightingale.

Bul·gar·i·a (bul gâr'ē ə, bŏŏl-), n. a republic in SE Europe. 8,652,745; 42,800 sq. mi. (110,850 sq. km). Cap.: Sofia. —**Bul·gar'i·an,** adj., n.

bulge (bulj), n., v., **bulged, bulg·ing.** —n. **1.** a rounded projection or protruding part, often the result of internal pressure; protuberance. **2.** a sudden increase, as in numbers or volume. —v.i. **3.** to swell or bend outward; protrude. **4.** to be filled to capacity. —v.t. **5.** to make protuberant; cause to swell. —**bulg'ing·ly,** adv.

Bulge (bulj), n. **Battle of the,** the final major German counteroffensive in World War II, in the Ardennes Forest in Belgium and Luxembourg: begun in 1944 and repulsed by the Allies in January, 1945; so called from the "bulge" in the German lines caused by the territories they seized.

bul·gur (bul′gər, bŏŏl′-), *n.* a form of wheat that has been parboiled, cracked, and dried.

bu·lim·i·a (byŏŏ lim′ē ə, -lē′mē ə, bŏŏ-), *n.* **1.** Also called **bulim′ia ner′vo′sa** (nûr vō′sə). a habitual disturbance in eating behavior characterized by bouts of excessive eating followed by self-induced vomiting, purging with laxatives, strenuous exercise, or fasting. **2.** abnormally voracious appetite or unnaturally constant hunger. —**bu·lim′ic,** *adj., n.*

bulk¹ (bulk), *n.* **1.** magnitude in three dimensions; esp. when great. **2.** the greater part; main mass or body: *The bulk of the debt was paid.* **3.** goods or cargo not in packages or boxes, usu. transported in large volume, as grain, coal, or petroleum. **4.** FIBER (def. 4). **5.** the body of a living creature, esp. when large or heavy. **6.** BULK MAIL. —*adj.* **7.** being or involving material in bulk. —*v.i.* **8.** to increase in size; expand; swell. **9.** to be of great weight, size, or importance: *The problem bulks large in his mind.* —*v.t.* **10.** to cause to swell, grow, or increase in weight or thickness (often fol. by *up*). **11.** to gather, bring together, or mix. —*Idiom.* **12. in bulk, a.** unpackaged: *rice sold in bulk.* **b.** in large quantities. —**bulk′y,** *adj.,* **-i·er, -i·est.**

bulk² (bulk), *n.* a structure, as a stall, projecting from the front of a building.

bulk·head (bulk′hed′), *n.* **1.** a wall-like construction inside a ship or airplane, as for forming watertight compartments or strengthening the structure. **2.** a partition built in a subterranean passage to prevent the passage of air, water, or earth. **3.** a retaining structure of timber, steel, or reinforced concrete used for shore protection. **4.** a horizontal or inclined outside door over a stairway leading to a cellar. **5.** a boxlike structure, as on a roof, covering a stairwell or other opening.

bulk′ mail′, *n.* a category of mail for mailing large numbers of identical printed items, as circulars, to individual addressees at less than first-class rates. —**bulk′-mail′,** *v.*

bull¹ (bŏŏl), *n.* **1.** the male of a bovine mammal, esp. of the genus *Bos,* with sexual organs intact and capable of reproduction. **2.** the male of certain other animals, as the elephant and moose. **3.** a large, solidly built person. **4.** a person who believes that stock prices will increase (opposed to *bear*). **5.** a bulldog. —*adj.* **6.** male. **7.** pertaining to or resembling a bull, as in size or strength. **8.** marked by rising prices, esp. of stocks: *a bull market.* —*v.t.* **9.** to accomplish by forcing or shoving: *to bull one's way through a crowd.* —*Idiom.* **10. bull in a china shop,** an extremely awkward or clumsy person. **11. take the bull by the horns,** to attack a difficult or risky problem fearlessly. —**bull′ish,** *adj.*

bull² (bŏŏl), *n.* a formal papal document having a bulla attached.

bull³ (bŏŏl), *Slang.* —*n.* **1.** exaggerations; lies; nonsense. —*v.i.* **2.** to engage in foolish or exaggerated talk. —*v.t.* **3.** to try to fool or impress by lies or exaggeration.

bul·la (bŏŏl′ə, bul′ə), *n., pl.* **bul·lae** (bŏŏl′ē, bul′ē). **1.** a seal attached to an official document, as a papal bull. **2.** a large blister or vesicle.

bull·bait·ing (bŏŏl′bā′ting), *n.* the action or sport of setting dogs upon a bull in a pen or arena.

bull·dog (bŏŏl′dôg′, -dog′), *n., adj., v.,* **-dogged, -dog·ging.** —*n.* **1.** one of an English breed of stocky, muscular shorthaired dogs having wide-set legs and a large head with prominent undershot jaws and a short, wrinkled muzzle, raised orig. for bullbaiting. **2.** a stubbornly persistent person. —*adj.* **3.** like or characteristic of a bulldog or of a bulldog's jaws: *bulldog obstinacy.* —*v.t.* **4.** to attack in the manner of a bulldog. **5.** *Western U.S.* to throw (a calf, steer, etc.) to the ground by seizing the horns and twisting the head.

bull·doze (bŏŏl′dōz′), *v.t.,* **-dozed, -doz·ing. 1.** to clear, move, level, or reshape the contours of with or as if with a bulldozer. **2.** to coerce or intimidate; bully. **3.** to force in the manner of a bulldozer.

bull·doz·er (bŏŏl′dō′zər), *n.* **1.** a large, powerful tractor having a vertical blade at the front end for moving earth, rocks, tree stumps, etc. **2.** a person who intimidates or coerces.

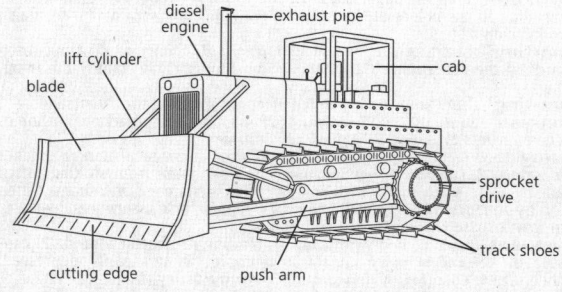

bulldozer (def. 1)

bul·let (bŏŏl′it), *n.* **1.** a small metal projectile, part of a cartridge, for firing from small arms. **2.** a cartridge. **3.** something resembling a bullet, as in shape or speed. **4.** a heavy dot for calling attention to particular

sections of text. —*Idiom.* **5. bite the bullet,** to force oneself to perform a painful, difficult task or to endure an unpleasant situation.

bul·le·tin (bŏŏl′i tn, -tin), *n.* **1.** a brief usu. official statement issued for the information of the public. **2. a.** a brief, prominently featured newspaper account, based upon information received just before the edition went to press. **b.** a similar brief account broadcast over radio or television pending further information. **3.** a journal or brochure regularly issued by an organization, government agency, etc. **4.** a catalog describing the courses taught at a college or university. —*v.t.* **5.** to publish by means of a bulletin.

bul′letin board′, *n.* **1.** a board for the posting of bulletins, notices, announcements, etc. **2.** See BBS.

bul·let·proof (bŏŏl′it prŏŏf′), *adj.* **1.** (of vehicles, glass, clothing, etc.) capable of resisting or absorbing the impact of a bullet. **2.** safe from criticism as well as failure: *a bulletproof budget.* —*v.t.* **3.** to make (something) bulletproof.

bul′let train′, *n.* a high-speed passenger train, esp. on certain routes in Japan.

bull·fight (bŏŏl′fīt′), *n.* a traditional Spanish, Portuguese, or Latin American spectacle in which a bull is fought in a prescribed way by a matador, and is usu. killed with a sword. —**bull′fight′er,** *n.* —**bull′-fight′ing,** *n.*

bull·finch (bŏŏl′finch′), *n.* a Eurasian finch, *Pyrrhula pyrrhula,* the male of which has a black, white, and gray back with a rosy breast.

bull·frog (bŏŏl′frog′, -frôg′), *n.* a large North American frog, *Rana catesbeiana,* having a deep voice.

bull·head·ed (bŏŏl′hed′id), *adj.* unreasonably or stupidly obstinate.

bull′horn′ or **bull′ horn′,** *n.* a directional, high-powered, electrical loudspeaker or megaphone.

bul·lion (bŏŏl′yən), *n.* **1.** gold or silver considered in mass rather than in value. **2.** gold or silver in the form of bars or ingots. **3.** lace, embroidery, or trimming worked with gold or silver threads, wire, or cord.

bull′ mas′tiff or **bull′mas′tiff,** *n.* one of an English breed of large, powerful dogs with a short fawn or brindled coat, produced by crossing bulldogs and mastiffs.

Bull′ Moose′, *n.* a member of the Progressive Party under the leadership of Theodore Roosevelt. Also called **Bull′ Moos′er** (mŏŏ′sər).

Bul′lock's o′riole (bŏŏl′əks), *n.* a North American oriole, *Icterus galbula bullockii,* the western subspecies of the northern oriole, distinguished from the similar Baltimore oriole by a black-crowned head, orange cheeks, and a large white patch on each wing.

bull′ pen′ or **bull′pen′,** *n.* **1. a.** a place where relief pitchers warm up during a baseball game. **b.** the relief pitchers on a team. **2.** *Informal.* **a.** a large cell for the temporary detention of prisoners. **b.** any temporary or crowded quarters, as sleeping quarters in a lumber camp. **3.** a pen for bulls.

Bull′ Run′, *n.* a creek in NE Virginia, near Washington, D.C.: the first battle of the American Civil War **(Battle of Bull Run)** was fought near there in 1861, and resulted in the defeat of the Union forces; a second battle, fought in the same place in 1862, ended in another Confederate victory. Also called **Manassas.**

bull′ ses′sion, *n.* an informal, spontaneous group discussion.

bull's′-eye′, *n., pl.* **-eyes. 1.** the circular spot, usu. black or outlined in black, at the center of a target. **2.** a shot that hits this. **3. a.** the center of a military target in a bombing raid. **b.** a missile that strikes the center of a target. **c.** an instance of aiming and firing a missile that results in its hitting the center of a target. **4.** any statement or act that is precisely to the point or achieves a desired result directly. **5.** a small circular opening, window, or disk of glass inserted in a roof, ship's deck, etc., to admit light.

bull′snake′ or **bull′ snake′,** *n.* any large, harmless North American constrictor of the genus *Pituophis,* as the gopher snake or pine snake, that feeds chiefly upon small rodents.

bull′ ter′rier, *n.* one of an English breed of strong medium-sized dogs with an oval head, small high-set eyes, and a short, often white coat, produced by crossing bulldogs and terriers.

bull′ this′tle, *n.* a tall, spiny thistle, *Cirsium vulgare,* having heads of pink to purple flowers: a common weed in North America.

bull′whip′ or **bull′-whip′,** *n.* a rawhide whip having a short handle and a long, plaited lash. Also called **bull-whack** (bŏŏl′hwak′, -wak′).

bul·ly (bŏŏl′ē), *n., pl.* **-lies,** *v.,* **-lied, -ly·ing,** *adj., interj.* —*n.* **1.** a quarrelsome, overbearing person who badgers and intimidates smaller or weaker people. —*v.t.* **2.** to intimidate or terrorize. —*v.i.* **3.** to be loudly arrogant and overbearing. —*adj.* **4.** *Informal.* fine; excellent. —*interj.* **5.** (used to express approval).

bul′ly pul′pit, *n.* a position of authority or public visibility, esp. a political office, from which one may express one's views.

bul′ly tree′, *n.* any of several tropical American trees of the sapodilla family, esp. of the genus *Manilkara,* that yield the gum balata.

bul·rush (bŏŏl′rush′), *n.* any of various rushes of the genera *Scirpus,* of the sedge family, and *Typha,* of the cattail family.

Bult·mann (bŏŏlt′män′), *n.* **Rudolf,** 1884–1976, German theologian.

bul·wark (bŏŏl′wərk, -wôrk, bul′-), *n.* **1.** a wall of earth or other material built for defense; rampart. **2.** any protection against external danger, injury, or annoyance. **3.** any person or thing giving strong support or encouragement in time of need, danger, or doubt. **4.** Usu., **bulwarks.**

(on a ship) a wall enclosing the perimeter of a weather or main deck. —*v.t.* **5.** to fortify or protect with a bulwark.

bum (bum), *n.*, *v.*, **bummed, bum·ming,** *adj.*, **bum·mer, bum·mest.** —*n.* **1.** a person who avoids work and sponges on others; loafer; idler. **2.** a tramp, hobo, or derelict. **3.** *Informal.* a single-minded enthusiast of a specific sport: *a ski bum.* **4.** *Informal.* an incompetent person. —*v.t.* **5.** *Informal.* to borrow without expectation of returning. —*v.i.* **6.** to sponge on others for a living. **7.** to live as a hobo. **8. bum around,** *Informal.* to spend time or wander aimlessly. —*adj. Slang.* **9.** of poor or miserable quality; worthless. **10.** disappointing; unpleasant. **11.** false or misleading: *a bum rap.* **12.** lame: *a bum leg.*

bum·ble[1] (bum′bəl), *v.*, **-bled, -bling,** *n.* —*v.i.* **1.** to bungle or blunder awkwardly; muddle. **2.** to stumble or stagger. **3.** to mumble. —*v.t.* **4.** to bungle or botch. —*n.* **5.** an awkward blunder. —**bum′bler,** *n.*

bum·ble[2] (bum′bəl), *v.i.*, **-bled, -bling.** to make a buzzing, humming sound, as a bee.

bum·ble·bee or **bum′ble bee′,** *n.* any of several large, hairy social bees of the family Apidae.

bum·bling (bum′bling), *adj.* **1.** tending to make awkward blunders. **2.** clumsily incompetent or ineffectual.

bum·mer[1] (bum′ər), *n.* a person who bums.

bum·mer[2] (bum′ər), *n. Slang.* **1.** the unpleasant aftermath of taking narcotic drugs, esp. frightening hallucinations. **2.** any unpleasant or disappointing experience.

bump (bump), *v.t.* **1.** to collide with; strike: *The car bumped a truck.* **2.** to cause to strike or collide: *He bumped the car against a tree.* **3.** to dislodge or displace by the force of collision. **4.** *Informal.* to remove, dismiss, or eject: *The airline bumped me from the flight.* **5.** *Informal.* to force upward; raise: *Demand from abroad bumped up the price of corn.* **6.** *Poker.* RAISE (def. 22). —*v.i.* **7.** to come in contact or collide with: *She bumped into me.* **8.** to bounce along; proceed in a series of jolts: *The old car bumped down the road.* **9. bump into,** to meet by chance. **10. bump off,** *Slang.* to murder. —*n.* **11.** a collision; blow. **12.** a swelling or contusion from a blow. **13.** a small area raised above the level of the surrounding surface; protuberance. **14.** a rapidly rising current of air that gives an airplane a severe upward thrust.

bump·er (bum′pər), *n.* **1.** a person or thing that bumps. **2.** a metal guard, usu. horizontal, for protecting the front or rear of an automobile, truck, etc. **3.** any protective guard, pad, or disk for absorbing shock and preventing damage from bumping. **4.** a cup or glass filled to the brim. **5.** *Informal.* something unusually large. —*adj.* **6.** unusually abundant: *a bumper crop.*

bump′er stick′er, *n.* an adhesive-backed strip of paper for sticking onto the rear bumper of an automobile, bearing a printed advertisement, political slogan, etc.

bump′er-to-bump′er, *adj.* marked by a long line of cars moving slowly or with many stops and starts: *bumper-to-bumper traffic.*

bump·kin (bump′kin), *n.* an awkward, simple rustic; yokel.

bump·tious (bump′shəs), *adj.* offensively self-assertive.

bump·y (bum′pē), *adj.*, **bump·i·er, bump·i·est. 1.** of uneven surface; full of bumps: *a bumpy road.* **2.** full of jolts: *a bumpy ride.* **3.** marked by failures as well as successes: *a bumpy career.* —**bump′i·ly,** *adv.* —**bump′i·ness,** *n.*

bum′s′ rush′, *n. Slang.* **1.** forcible and swift ejection from a place. **2.** any rude or abrupt dismissal.

bun (bun), *n.* **1.** any of various usu. round bread rolls, plain or sweetened and sometimes containing spices, raisins, etc. **2.** hair gathered into a round coil or knot, as at the nape of the neck.

bunch (bunch), *n.* **1.** a connected group; cluster: *a bunch of grapes.* **2.** a group of people or things: *a bunch of papers.* **3.** a large quantity; lots: *Thanks a bunch.* **4.** a knob, lump, or protuberance. —*v.t.* **5.** to group together; make a bunch of. —*v.i.* **6.** to gather together. **7.** (of fabric or clothing) to gather into folds (often fol. by *up*).

bunch·ber·ry (bunch′ber′ē, -bə rē), *n., pl.* **-ries.** a dwarf dogwood, *Cornus canadensis,* bearing clusters of bright red berries.

bunch·flow·er (bunch′flou′ər), *n.* a stout North American plant, *Melanthium virginicum,* of the lily family, having grasslike leaves and an open cluster of small greenish flowers.

bunch′ grass′, *n.* any of various grasses in different regions of North America, growing in distinct clumps.

bun·dle (bun′dl), *n., v.,* **-dled, -dling.** —*n.* **1.** several objects or a quantity of material gathered or bound together: *a bundle of hay.* **2.** an item or quantity wrapped for carrying; package. **3.** a number of things considered together: *a bundle of ideas.* **4.** *Slang.* a great deal of money. **5.** *Bot.* an aggregation of strands of specialized conductive and mechanical tissues. **6.** *Anat.* an aggregation of fibers, as of nerves or muscles. —*v.t.* **7.** to tie together or wrap in a bundle. **8.** to send away hurriedly or unceremoniously (usu. fol. by *off, out,* etc.): *They bundled her off to the country.* **9.** to supply (related products or services) in a single transaction at one all-inclusive price. —*v.i.* **10.** to leave hurriedly or unceremoniously (usu. fol. by *off, out,* etc.). **11. bundle up,** to dress warmly or snugly. —**bun′dler,** *n.*

Bundt′ cake′ (bunt, boont), *n.* a ring-shaped cake baked in a tube pan with fluted sides.

bung[1] (bung), *n.* **1.** a stopper for the opening of a cask. —*v.t.* **2.** to close with or as if with a bung; plug (often fol. by *up*).

bung[2] (bung), *v.t.* to beat; maul (often fol. by *up*).

bun·ga·low (bung′gə lō′), *n.* **1.** a small house or summer cottage, usu. of one or one and a half stories, sometimes with a veranda. **2.** (in India) a one-storied thatched or tiled house, usu. surrounded by a veranda.

bun′gee cord′ (bun′jē), *n.* an elasticized cord, typically with a hook at each end, used chiefly as a fastener. Also called **bun′gee.**

bun′gee jump′ing, *n.* the sport of jumping off a high structure to which one is attached by bungee cords, so that the body springs back just short of hitting the ground or water.

bun·gle (bung′gal), *v.,* **-gled, -gling,** *n.* —*v.t.* **1.** to do clumsily or awkwardly; botch. —*v.i.* **2.** to perform or work clumsily or inadequately. —*n.* **3.** something done clumsily or inadequately.

bun·ion (bun′yən), *n.* an inflammation of the synovial bursa of the great toe, usu. resulting in enlargement of the joint and lateral displacement of the toe.

bunk[1] (bungk), *n.* **1.** a built-in platform bed, as on a ship. **2.** *Informal.* any bed. **3.** a bunkhouse. —*v.i.* **4.** to occupy a bunk or bed. —*v.t.* **5.** to provide with a place to sleep.

bunk[2] (bungk), *n. Informal.* humbug; nonsense.

bunk′ bed′, *n.* either of two platformlike single beds connected one above the other.

bun·ker (bung′kər), *n.* **1.** a large bin or receptacle; a fixed chest or box: *a coal bunker.* **2.** a partially underground chamber, often of reinforced concrete, built as a bomb shelter or as part of a fortification. **3.** *Golf.* any obstacle, as a sand trap or mound of dirt, constituting a hazard. —*v.t.* **4.** to provide fuel for (a vessel). —*adj.* **5.** characterized by or given to desperate or extreme measures to avoid defeat: *a bunker mentality.*

Bun′ker Hill′, *n.* a hill in Charlestown, Mass., near Boston: the first major battle of the Revolutionary War **(Battle of Bunker Hill)** was fought on adjoining Breed's Hill on June 17, 1775.

bunk·house (bungk′hous′), *n., pl.* **-hous·es** (-hou′ziz). a rough building, often with bunk beds, used for sleeping quarters, as for ranch hands, migratory workers, or campers.

bunk·mate (bungk′māt′), *n.* a person who shares sleeping quarters with another or others, as in a bunkhouse.

bun·ko or **bun·co** (bung′kō), *n., pl.* **-kos** or **-cos,** *v.,* **-koed** or **-coed, -ko·ing** or **-co·ing.** *Informal.* —*n.* **1.** a swindle in which a person is cheated at gambling, persuaded to buy a nonexistent or worthless object, or otherwise victimized. —*v.t.* **2.** to victimize by a bunko.

bun·kum or **bun·combe** (bung′kəm), *n.* **1.** insincere speechmaking by a politician intended merely to please local constituents. **2.** insincere talk; claptrap; humbug. [after a pointless speech in Congress by F. Walker, who explained that he was expected to make a speech for his constituents in *Buncombe,* a county in North Carolina]

bun·ny (bun′ē), *n., pl.* **-nies,** *adj.* —*n.* **1.** a rabbit, esp. a small or young one. —*adj.* **2.** designed for or used by beginners in skiing: *a bunny slope.*

Bun′sen burn′er, *n.* a gas burner with a hot, almost nonluminous flame, commonly used in laboratories. [after R. W. *Bunsen* (1811–99), German chemist]

bunt[1] (bunt), *v.t.* **1.** (of a goat or calf) to push with the horns or head; butt. **2.** to tap (a pitched baseball) close to home plate, usu. by facing the pitcher and allowing the ball to bounce off the bat. —*v.i.* **3.** to push something with the horns or head; butt. **4.** to bunt a baseball. —*n.* **5.** a push with the head or horns; butt. **6. a.** the act of bunting a baseball. **b.** a bunted baseball. —**bunt′er,** *n.*

bunt[2] (bunt), *n.* **1.** the middle part of a square sail. **2.** the part of a fishing net in which the catch is made.

bunt[3] (bunt), *n.* a smut disease of wheat in which the kernels are replaced by the black foul-smelling spores of fungi of the genus *Tilletia.* Also called **stinking smut.**

bun·ting[1] (bun′ting), *n.* **1.** a coarse, open fabric of worsted or cotton for flags, signals, etc. **2.** patriotic and festive decorations made from such cloth, or from paper, usu. in the form of draperies, wide streamers, etc., in the colors of the national flag. **3.** flags, esp. a vessel's flags, collectively.

bun·ting[2] (bun′ting), *n.* any of various small, chiefly seed-eating songbirds of the subfamilies Cardinalinae and Emberizinae (family Emberizidae).

bun·ting[3] (bun′ting), *n.* a hooded sleeping garment for infants.

Bun·yan (bun′yən), *n.* **1. John,** 1628–88, English preacher: author of *The Pilgrim's Progress.* **2. Paul.** PAUL BUNYAN.

bu·oy (boo′ē, boi), *n.* **1.** an anchored float used as a marker or as a mooring. **2.** LIFE BUOY. —*v.t.* **3.** to keep afloat; keep from sinking (often fol. by *up*). **4.** to mark with buoys. **5.** to sustain or encourage (often fol. by *up*): *Her courage was buoyed by the doctor's assurances.* —*v.i.* **6.** to float or rise by reason of lightness.

buoy·ant (boi′ənt, boo′yənt), *adj.* **1.** tending to float in a fluid. **2.** capable of keeping a body afloat, as a liquid. **3.** not easily depressed; cheerful. **4.** cheering or invigorating. —**buoy′an·cy,** *n.*

bur (bûr), *n., v.,* **burred, bur·ring.** —*n.* **1.** a rough prickly case around the seeds of certain plants, as the chestnut. **2.** any bur-bearing plant. **3.** something that adheres like a bur. **4.** BURR[1] (defs. 1, 3). **5.** a rotary cutting tool for removing carious material from teeth and preparing cavities for filling. **6.** a surgical cutting tool resembling this, used for the excavation of bone. —*v.t.* **7.** to extract or remove burs from.

Bur·bage (bûr′bij), *n.* **Richard,** 1567?–1619, English actor.

Bur·bank (bûr′bangk′), *n.* **1. Luther,** 1849–1926, U.S. horticulturist and plant breeder. **2.** a city in SW California. 91,960.

bur·ble (bûr′bəl), *v.*, **-bled, -bling,** *n.* —*v.i.* **1.** to make a bubbling sound; bubble; gurgle. **2.** to speak in an excited manner; babble. —*n.* **3.** a bubbling or gentle flow. **4.** an excited flow of speech.

bur·bot (bûr′bət), *n.*, *pl.* **-bots,** (*esp. collectively*) **-bot.** a freshwater cod, *Lota lota*, of Europe, Asia, and North America, having an elongated body and a barbel on the chin.

bur·den[1] (bûr′dn), *n.* **1.** that which is carried; load. **2.** that which is borne with difficulty; onus: *the burden of leadership.* **3.** the weight of a ship's cargo. **4.** OVERBURDEN (def. 3). —*v.t.* **5.** to load heavily. **6.** to load oppressively; trouble.

bur·den[2] (bûr′dn), *n.* **1.** an often repeated main point, message, or idea. **2.** a musical refrain; chorus.

bur·den of proof′, *n.* the obligation to offer credible evidence in a court of law in support of a contention or accusation.

bur·den·some (bûr′dn səm), *adj.* oppressive; onerous.

bur·dock (bûr′dok), *n.* a composite plant of the genus *Arctium*, esp. *A. lappa*, a coarse broad-leaved weed bearing prickly heads of burs that stick to clothing.

bu·reau (byŏŏr′ō), *n.*, *pl.* **bu·reaus, bu·reaux** (byŏŏr′ōz). **1.** a chest of drawers, often with a mirror at the top. **2.** a division of a government department or an independent administrative unit. **3.** an office that collects and distributes information or performs specified services; agency.

bu·reauc·ra·cy (byŏŏ rok′rə sē), *n.*, *pl.* **-cies. 1.** government by a rigid hierarchy of bureaus, administrators, and petty officials. **2.** a body of officials and administrators, esp. in a government. **3.** excessive multiplication of, and concentration of power in, bureaus or administrators. **4.** administration characterized by excessive red tape and routine.

bu·reau·crat (byŏŏr′ə krat′), *n.* **1.** an official of a bureaucracy. **2.** an official who works by fixed routine without exercising intelligent judgment. —**bu′reau·crat′ic,** *adj.* —**bu′reau·crat′i·cal·ly,** *adv.*

bu·rette or **bu·ret** (byŏŏ ret′), *n.* a graduated glass tube with a stopcock at the bottom, used in a laboratory to measure or dispense liquids.

burg (bûrg), *n.* **1.** *Informal.* a small, quiet city or town. **2.** a fortified town.

burg·eon or **bour·geon** (bûr′jən), *v.i.* **1.** to grow or develop quickly; flourish: *The town burgeoned into a city.* **2.** to begin to grow, as a bud; put forth buds, shoots, etc., as a plant (often fol. by *out, forth*). —*v.t.* **3.** to put forth, as buds. —*n.* **4.** a bud; sprout.

burg·er (bûr′gər), *n.* a hamburger.

Burg·er (bûr′gər), *n.* **Warren Earl,** born 1907, U.S. jurist: Chief Justice of the U.S. 1969–86.

bur·gess (bûr′jis), *n.* **1.** a representative in the House of Burgesses. **2.** (formerly) a representative of a borough, corporate town, or university in the British Parliament.

Bur·gess (bûr′jis), *n.* **1. (Frank) Gelett,** 1866–1951, U.S. illustrator and humorist. **2. Thornton Waldo,** 1874–1965, U.S. author.

burgh·er (bûr′gər), *n.* an inhabitant of a town or borough, esp. a well-to-do member of the middle class. —**burgh′er·ship′,** *n.*

bur·glar (bûr′glər), *n.* a person who commits burglary.

bur·glar·ize (bûr′glə rīz′), *v.*, **-ized, -iz·ing.** —*v.t.* **1.** to break into and steal from. —*v.i.* **2.** to commit burglary.

bur·glar·proof (bûr′glər prŏŏf′), *adj.* safeguarded or secure against burglary.

bur·gla·ry (bûr′glə rē), *n.*, *pl.* **-ries.** the felony of breaking into and entering the house, office, etc., of another with intent to steal.

bur·gle (bûr′gəl), *v.t.*, *v.i.*, **-gled, -gling.** *Informal.* to burglarize.

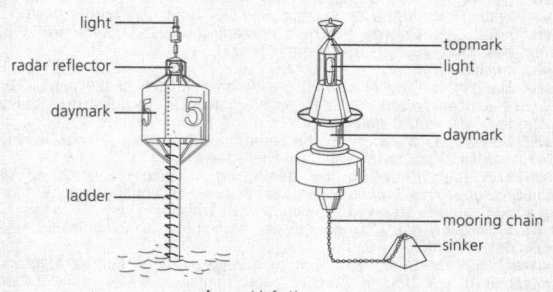

buoy (def. 1)

(labels: light, radar reflector, daymark, ladder, topmark, light, daymark, mooring chain, sinker)

bur·go·mas·ter (bûr′gə mas′tər, -mä′stər), *n.* the chief magistrate of a municipal town of Holland, Flanders, Germany, or Austria.

bur·goo (bûr′gŏŏ, bûr gŏŏ′), *n.*, *pl.* **-goos** for 2b. **1.** a thick oatmeal gruel, esp. as eaten by sailors. *Chiefly Kentucky and Tennessee.* **a.** a thick, highly seasoned soup or stew, usually made of chicken or small game and corn, tomatoes, and onions. **b.** a picnic or other gathering at which burgoo is served.

Bur·goyne (bər goin′), *n.* **John,** 1722–92, British general: surrendered at Saratoga in the American Revolution.

Bur·gun·dy (bûr′gən dē), *n.*, *pl.* **-dies** for 3. **1.** a historic region in central France: a former kingdom, duchy, and province. **2.** a metropolitan region in central France. 1,607,200; 12,194 sq. mi. (31,582 sq. km). **3.** any of the red or white wines produced in this region.

bur·i·al (ber′ē əl), *n.* **1.** the act or ceremony of burying. **2.** the place of burying; grave.

bu·rin (byŏŏr′in, bûr′-), *n.* **1.** a tempered steel tool with a lozenge-shaped point and a rounded handle, used for engraving metal and marble. **2.** a prehistoric pointed or chisellike flint tool.

Bur·ki·na Fa·so (bər kē′nə fä′sō), *n.* a republic in W Africa: formerly part of French West Africa. 10,891,159; 106,111 sq. mi. (274,827 sq. km). *Cap.:* Ouagadougou. Formerly, **Upper Volta.**

burl (bûrl), *n.* **1.** a small knot or lump in wool, thread, or cloth. **2.** a dome-shaped growth on the trunk of a tree, sliced to make veneer. —*v.t.* **3.** to remove burls from (cloth) in finishing.

bur·lap (bûr′lap), *n.* **1.** a plain-woven coarse fabric of jute, hemp, or the like; gunny. **2.** a lightweight fabric made in imitation of this.

bur·lesque (bər lesk′), *n.*, *adj.*, *v.*, **-lesqued, -lesquing.** —*n.* **1.** a comic literary or dramatic piece that vulgarizes lofty material or elevates the ordinary. **2.** any ludicrous parody or grotesque caricature. **3.** a stage show featuring comic, usu. bawdy skits and striptease acts. —*adj.* **4.** involving ludicrous or mocking treatment of a solemn subject. **5.** of, pertaining to, or like stage-show burlesque. —*v.t.* **6.** to make ridiculous by mocking representation. —*v.i.* **7.** to use burlesque or caricature.

bur·ley (bûr′lē), *n.*, *pl.* **-leys.** (*often cap.*) an American tobacco with thin leaves and light color, grown esp. in Kentucky and nearby regions, used mostly in cigarettes.

bur·ly (bûr′lē), *adj.*, **-li·er, -li·est. 1.** large in bodily size; stout; sturdy. **2.** bluff; brusque. —**bur′li·ness,** *n.*

Bur·ma (bûr′mə), *n.* a republic in SE Asia, on the Bay of Bengal. 46,821,943; 261,228 sq. mi. (676,577 sq. km). *Cap.:* Yangon. Official name, **Union of Myanmar.**

bur′ mar′igold, *n.* any of various composite plants of the genus *Bidens*, esp. those having conspicuous yellow flowers.

Bur′mese cat′, *n.* one of a breed of shorthaired domestic cats having a compact body, sable-brown coat, and yellow eyes.

burn[1] (bûrn), *v.*, **burned** or **burnt, burn·ing,** *n.* —*v.i.* **1.** to consume fuel and give off heat, gases, and usu. light; be on fire. **2. a.** to undergo combustion; oxidize. **b.** to undergo fission or fusion. **3.** (of a fireplace, furnace, etc.) to contain a fire. **4.** to give off light; glow brightly: *The lights burned all night.* **5.** to be hot: *The pavement burned in the noon sun.* **6.** to produce or feel sharp pain or a stinging sensation: *The whiskey burned in his throat.* **7.** to be injured, damaged, scorched, or destroyed by fire, heat, or acid. **8.** to feel extreme anger. **9.** to feel strong emotion: *to burn with desire.* **10.** to sunburn. **11.** *Slang.* to die in an electric chair. **12.** to be engraved by or as if by burning: *His words burned into her heart.* —*v.t.* **13.** to cause to undergo combustion or be consumed partly or wholly by fire. **14.** to use as fuel or as a source of light: *to burn coal.* **15.** to sunburn. **16.** to injure, damage, scorch, or destroy with or as if with fire. **17.** to execute by burning at the stake. **18.** to produce with or as if with fire: *to burn a hole.* **19.** to cause sharp pain or a stinging sensation in: *The iodine burned his cut.* **20.** *Slang.* to cheat, deceive, or swindle: *burned by a phony stock deal.* **21. burn down,** to burn to the ground. **22. burn in, a.** (in printing from a photographic negative) to expose (parts of an image) to more light for increased density. **b.** to run (a new computer or other electronic system) continuously for several hours or days, as a test of quality before delivery to the purchaser. **23. burn out, a.** to cease operating or functioning because of heat, friction, or lack of fuel. **b.** to deprive of a place to live, work, etc., by reason of fire. **c.** to exhaust (oneself) or become exhausted or apathetic through overwork, stress, or intense activity. **24. burn up, a.** to burn completely. **b.** *Informal.* to make or become angry. —*n.* **25.** a burned place or area. **26.** an injury caused by heat, abnormal cold, chemicals, poison gas, or electricity, and characterized by a painful reddening and swelling of the epidermis **(first-degree burn),** damage extending into the dermis, usu. with blistering **(second-degree burn),** or destruction of the epidermis and dermis extending into the deeper tissue **(third-degree burn). 27.** the process or an instance of burning or baking, as in brickmaking. **28.** the firing of a rocket engine. **29.** *Slang.* a swindle. —*Idiom.* **30. burn a hole in someone's pocket,** (of accessible money) to provoke someone to spend quickly. **31. burn one's fingers,** to suffer injury or loss by meddling or by acting rashly. **32. burn the candle at both ends,** to use up one's strength or energy by immoderation. **33. burn the midnight oil,** to work, study, etc., until late at night. —**burn′a·ble,** *adj.*

burn[2] (bûrn), *n.* *Scot.* a brook or rivulet.

Burne-Jones (bûrn′jōnz′), *n.* **Sir Edward Coley,** 1833–98, English painter and designer.

burn·er (bûr′nər), *n.* **1.** a person or thing that burns. **2.** the part of a gas or electric fixture or appliance from which flame or heat issues. **3.** any apparatus in which fuel or refuse is burned.

bur·net (bûr net′, bûr′nit), *n.* any of several plants belonging to the genera *Sanguisorba* and *Poterium*, of the rose family, having pinnate leaves and dense heads of small flowers.

Bur·nett (bər net′), *n.* **Frances Hodgson,** 1849–1924, U.S. novelist, born in England.

Bur·ney (bûr′nē), *n.* **Fanny** or **Frances** (*Madame D'Arblay*), 1752–1840, English novelist and diarist.

burn·ing (bûr′ning), *adj.* **1.** intense; passionate: *a burning desire.* **2.** urgent or crucial: *a burning question.*

burn′ing bush′, *n.* **1.** a desert bush that burned but was not consumed, and from which an angel of God appeared to Moses. Ex. 3:2-4. **2.** a shrubby plant, *Kochia scoparia,* of the goosefoot family, having dense, feathery foliage that turns red in autumn. **3.** any of various plants of the genus *Euonymus,* of the staff-tree family, that have bright red foliage in autumn.

bur·nish (bûr′nish), *v.t.* **1.** to polish (a surface) by friction. **2.** to make smooth and bright, esp. by rubbing with a tool. —*n.* **3.** brightness; luster.

bur·noose or **bur·nous** (bər nōōs′, bûr′nōōs), *n.* a hooded mantle or cloak, as that worn by Arabs. —**bur·noosed′,** *adj.*

burn·out (bûrn′out′), *n.* **1.** the termination of effective combustion in a rocket engine, due to exhaustion of propellant. **2.** the breakdown of a lamp, motor, or other electrical device due to heat caused by current flow. **3.** fatigue, frustration, or apathy resulting from prolonged stress, overwork, or intense activity.

Burns (bûrnz), *n.* **1. Arthur F(rank),** born 1904, U.S. economist, born in Austria: chairman of the Federal Reserve Board 1970-78. **2. George** (*Nathan Birnbaum*), born 1896, U.S. comedian (partner and husband of Gracie Allen). **3. Robert,** 1759-96, Scottish poet.

Burn·side (bûrn′sīd′), *n.* Ambrose E., 1824-81, Union general in the Civil War.

burn·sides (bûrn′sīdz′), *n.pl.* full whiskers and a mustache worn with the chin clean-shaven.

burnsides

burnt (bûrnt), *v.* a pt. and pp. of BURN[1].

burnt′ of′fering, *n.* an offering burnt upon an altar in sacrifice to a deity.

burnt′ sien′na, *n.* an intense dark reddish brown color.

bur′ oak′, *n.* an oak tree, *Quercus macrocarpa,* of E North America, having shiny dark green leaves, light gray deeply ridged bark, and large acorns with a fringed cup.

burp (bûrp), *Informal.* —*n.* **1.** a belch; eructation. —*v.i.* **2.** to belch; eruct. —*v.t.* **3.** to cause (a baby) to belch by patting the back, esp. to relieve gas after feeding.

burr[1] (bûr), *n.* **1.** a protruding ragged edge raised on metal during drilling, shearing, punching, or engraving. **2.** a rough protuberance on any object. **3.** a hand-held rotary power tool used to cut small recesses. —*v.t.* **4.** to form a rough point or edge on. **5.** to remove burrs from. Also, **bur** (for defs. 1, 3).

burr[2] (bûr), *n.* **1.** a washer placed at the head of a rivet. **2.** a blank punched out of sheet metal.

burr[3] (bûr), *n.* **1.** a pronunciation of (r) as a uvular trill, as in some Northern English dialects. **2.** a pronunciation of (r) as an alveolar flap or trill, as in Scottish English. **3.** a whirring noise. —*v.i.* **4.** to speak with a burr. **5.** to make a whirring sound. —*v.t.* **6.** to pronounce with a burr.

Burr (bûr), *n.* Aaron, 1756-1836, vice president of the U.S. 1801-05.

bur′ reed′, *n.* any of various plants of the genus *Sparganium,* bur reed family, having ribbony leaves and bearing burlike fruit.

bur·ri·to (bə rē′tō), *n., pl.* **-tos.** a flour tortilla folded over a filling, as of beef, cheese, or refried beans.

bur·ro (bûr′ō, bōōr′ō, bur′ō), *n., pl.* **-ros. 1.** a small donkey, esp. one used as a pack animal. **2.** any donkey.

Bur·roughs (bûr′ōz, bur′-), *n.* **1. Edgar Rice,** 1875-1950, U.S. novelist. **2. John,** 1837-1921, U.S. naturalist and essayist. **3. William Seward,** 1855-98, U.S. inventor of the adding machine. **4.** his grandson **William S(eward),** 1914-97, U.S. novelist.

bur·row (bûr′ō, bur′ō), *n.* **1.** a hole or tunnel in the ground made by an animal, as a rabbit, for habitation and refuge. **2.** a place of retreat. —*v.i.* **3.** to dig a burrow. **4.** to lodge or hide in a burrow. **5.** to proceed by or as if by digging. —*v.t.* **6.** to dig a burrow into. **7.** to hide in a burrow. **8.** to make by or as if by digging. —**bur′row·er,** *n.*

bur·sa (bûr′sə), *n., pl.* **-sae** (-sē), **-sas.** a pouch, sac, or vesicle, esp. a sac containing synovia, to facilitate motion, as between a tendon and a bone. —**bur′sal,** *adj.* —**bur′sate** (-sāt), *adj.*

bur·sar (bûr′sər, -sär), *n.* a treasurer or business officer, esp. of a college or university. —**bur·sar′i·al** (bər sâr′ē əl), *adj.*

bur·seed (bûr′sēd′), *n.* a stickseed, *Lappula echinata,* introduced into North America from Europe.

bur·si·tis (bər sī′tis), *n.* inflammation of a bursa.

burst (bûrst), *v.,* **burst** or, often, **burst·ed, burst·ing,** *n.* —*v.i.* **1.** to break, break open, or fly apart with sudden violence. **2.** to issue forth suddenly and forcibly. **3.** to give sudden expression to or as if to emotion: *to burst into tears.* **4.** to be extremely full, as if ready to break open: *a room bursting with people.* **5.** to appear suddenly: *The sun burst through the clouds.* —*v.t.* **6.** to cause to break suddenly and violently. **7.** to cause or suffer the rupture of: *to burst a blood vessel.* **8.** to separate (the sheets of a multipart copy). —*n.* **9.** an act or instance of bursting. **10.** a sudden, intense display, as of energy or effort: *a burst of speed.* **11.** a sudden expression or manifestation, as of emotion: *a burst of affection.* **12. a.** the explosion of a projectile, esp. in a specified place: *an air burst.* **b.** a rapid sequence of shots: *a machine gun burst.* **13.** breach; gap: *to plug a burst in the dike.* —**Idiom. 14. burst at the seams,** to be filled beyond normal capacity; be stuffed. —**burst′er,** *n.*

Bur·ton (bûr′tn), *n.* **1. Richard** (*Richard Jenkins*), 1925-84, English actor, born in Wales. **2. Sir Richard Francis,** 1821-90, English explorer, Orientalist, and writer. **3. Robert** (*"Democritus Junior"*), 1577-1640, English clergyman and author.

Bu·run·di (bōō rōōn′dē), *n.* a republic in central Africa, E of Zaire: formerly the S part of the Belgian trust territory of Ruanda-Urundi; gained independence 1962. 6,052,614; 10,747 sq. mi. (27,834 sq. km). *Cap.:* Bujumbura. —**Bu·run′di·an,** *adj., n.*

bur·weed (bûr′wēd′), *n.* any of various plants bearing a burlike fruit, as the cocklebur.

bur·y (ber′ē), *v.t.,* **bur·ied, bur·y·ing. 1.** to put in the ground and cover with earth. **2.** to put (a corpse) in the ground or a vault, or into the sea, often with ceremony. **3.** to plunge in deeply; cause to sink in. **4.** to conceal from sight: *to bury a card in the deck.* **5.** to immerse (oneself): *He buried himself in his work.* **6.** to cause to appear insignificant: *buried in small print.* —**Idiom. 7. bury one's head in the sand,** to avoid reality; ignore the facts of a situation. **8. bury the hatchet,** to become reconciled or reunited.

bus[1] (bus), *n., pl.* **bus·es, bus··ses,** *v.,* **bused** or **bussed, bus·ing** or **bus·sing.** —*n.* **1.** a large, long-bodied motor vehicle equipped with seating for passengers, usu. operating as part of a scheduled service. **2.** a similar horse-drawn vehicle. **3.** a passenger automobile or airplane used in a manner resembling that of a bus. **4.** a heavy bar of copper or other conducting material, used to collect, carry, and distribute powerful electric currents. **5.** a circuit that connects the CPU with other devices in a computer. —*v.t.* **6.** to convey or transport by bus. **7.** to transport (pupils) to school by bus, esp. as a means of achieving racial integration. —*v.i.* **8.** to travel on or by means of a bus. [short for *omnibus*]

bus[2] (bus), *v.i., v.t.,* **bused** or **bussed, bus·ing** or **bus·sing.** to work as a busboy or busgirl.

bus·boy′ or **bus′ boy′,** *n.* a waiter's helper in a restaurant or other public dining room.

bus·by (buz′bē), *n., pl.* **-bies.** a tall military hat of fur or feathers with a baglike ornament hanging from the top over the right side.

bus·girl′ or **bus′ girl′,** *n.* a girl or woman who works as a waiter's helper.

bush[1] (bōōsh), *n.* **1.** a low plant with many branches that arise from or near the ground. **2.** a small cluster of shrubs appearing as a single plant. **3.** something resembling or suggesting this, as a shaggy head of hair. **4.** a fox's tail. **5. a.** a large uncleared area covered with mixed plant growth, as a jungle. **b.** a large, sparsely populated, mostly uncleared area, as areas of Australia. —*v.i.* **6.** to branch or spread as or like a bush. —*v.t.* **7.** to cover, support, or mark with bushes. —*adj.* **8.** BUSH-LEAGUE. —**Idiom. 9. beat around** or **about the bush,** to avoid talking about a subject directly. **10. beat the bushes,** to search far and wide. —**bush′less,** *adj.* —**bush′like′,** *adj.*

bush[2] (bōōsh), *n.* **1.** a lining of metal or the like set into an orifice to guard against wearing. **2.** a bushing. —*v.t.* **3.** to furnish with a bush.

Bush (bōōsh), *n.* George (Herbert Walker), born 1924, vice president of the U.S. 1981-89; 41st president 1989-93.

bush., bushel.

bush′ ba′by, *n.* any of several prosimian primates of the genus *Galago,* of African forests, with large eyes and ears, woolly fur, and a bushy tail. Also called **galago.**

bush′ bean′, *n.* a variety of the common edible bean, *Phaseolus vulgaris humilis,* characterized by its bushy growth.

bush·buck (bōōsh′buk′), *n., pl.* **-bucks,** (*esp. collectively*) **-buck.** an African antelope, *Tragelaphus scriptus,* of wooded and bushy regions, having a reddish body streaked or spotted with white.

bushed (bōōsht), *adj.* **1.** overgrown with bushes. **2.** *Informal.* exhausted; tired out.

bush·el[1] (bōōsh′əl), *n.* **1.** a unit of dry measure containing 4 pecks, equivalent in the U.S. to 2150.42 cubic inches or 35.24 liters and in Great Britain to 2219.36 cubic inches or 36.38 liters (**imperial bushel**). *Abbr.:* bu., bush. **2.** a container of this capacity. **3.** a unit of weight equal to the weight of a bushel of a given commodity. **4.** a large, unspecified amount or number: *a bushel of kisses.*

bush·el[2] (bōōsh′əl), *v.t.,* **-eled, -el·ing** or (*esp. Brit.*) **-elled, el·ling.** to alter or repair (a garment).

bush·fire (bōōsh′fīr′), *n.* an uncontrolled fire in the trees and bushes of scrubland.

bush·ing (bōōsh′ing), *n.* **1.** a lining for a hole, intended to insulate and protect from abrasion one or more conductors that pass through it. **2. a.** a replaceable thin tube or sleeve, usu. of bronze, mounted in a case or housing as a bearing. **b.** a replaceable hardened steel tube used as a guide for various tools or parts, as a drill or valve rod.

bush′ jack′et, *n.* a belted shirtlike jacket, usu. with four patch pockets and a notched collar, adapted from a coat worn in the African bush. Also called **safari jacket.**

bush′ league′, *n.* MINOR LEAGUE.

bush′-league′, *adj.* inferior or amateurish; mediocre.

bush·man (boŏsh′mən), *n., pl.* **-men. 1.** a woodsman. **2.** *Australian.* a dweller in the bush.

bush·mas·ter (boŏsh′mas′tər, -mä′stər), *n.* a large tropical American pit viper, *Lachesis muta.*

Bush·nell (boŏsh′nəl), *n.* **Horace,** 1806–76, U.S. clergyman.

bush′ pi/lot, *n.* a pilot who flies small aircraft into remote areas.

bush·rang·er (boŏsh′rān′jər), *n.* **1.** a person who lives in the bush or woods. **2.** *Australian.* a person who lives by robbing residents of the bush. **—bush′rang′ing,** *n.*

bush·tit (boŏsh′tit′), *n.* a small songbird, *Psaltriparus minimus,* of the western U.S. and Mexico, that constructs long, pendent nests.

bush·whack (boŏsh′hwak′, -wak′), *v.i.* **1.** to make one's way through woods by cutting at undergrowth, branches, etc. **2.** to pull a boat upstream from on board by grasping bushes, rocks, etc., on the shore. **3.** to fight as a bushwhacker or guerrilla in the bush. **—v.t. 4.** to fight as a bushwhacker; ambush.

bush·whack·er (boŏsh′hwak′ər, -wak′-), *n.* **1.** a person or thing that bushwhacks. **2.** a Confederate guerrilla during the Civil War. **3.** any guerrilla or outlaw.

bush·y (boŏsh′ē), *adj.,* **bush·i·er, bush·i·est. 1.** resembling a bush; thick and shaggy: *bushy whiskers.* **2.** full of or overgrown with bushes. **—bush′i·ly,** *adv.*

busi·ness (biz′nis), *n.* **1.** an occupation, profession, or trade. **2.** the purchase and sale of goods in an attempt to make a profit. **3.** a person, partnership, or corporation engaged in commerce, manufacturing, or a service. **4.** volume of trade; patronage or custom. **5.** a store, office, factory, etc., where commerce is carried on. **6.** that with which a person is principally and seriously concerned: *Words are a writer's business.* **7.** something with which a person is rightfully concerned: *Their decision is none of my business.* **8.** affair; project: *fed up with the whole business.* **9. the business, a.** harsh or duplicitous treatment. **b.** a severe scolding: *to give someone the business.* **10.** a movement or gesture used by an actor to create an effect in a scene, help portray a character, etc. **11.** excrement: used as a euphemism. **—adj. 12.** of or pertaining to business or its procedures. **13.** suitable for or conducive to doing business. **—Idiom. 14. business as usual, a.** complacency **b.** determination to continue despite dangers. **15. get down to business,** to apply oneself to serious matters; concentrate on work. **16. have no business,** to have no right. **17. mean business,** to be in earnest; be entirely serious. **18. mind one's own business,** to refrain from meddling in the affairs of others.

busi′ness administra′tion, *n.* a program of studies at the university level covering business theory, management, etc.

busi′ness cy′cle, *n.* a recurrent fluctuation in the total business activity of a country.

busi′ness en′velope, *n.* a postal envelope for standard-size business letters 8½ × 11 in. (20 × 28 cm), measuring about 4⅛ × 9½ in. (11 × 23 cm).

busi·ness·like (biz′nis līk′), *adj.* **1.** showing attributes prized in business, as practicality, thoroughness, and purposefulness. **2.** efficient but impersonal.

busi·ness·man (biz′nis man′), *n., pl.* **-men.** a man regularly employed in business, esp. an executive or owner.

busi′ness park′, *n.* **1.** OFFICE PARK. **2.** INDUSTRIAL PARK.

busi·ness·per·son (biz′nis pûr′sən), *n.* a person regularly employed in business.

busi·ness·wom·an (biz′nis woŏm′ən), *n., pl.* **-wom·en.** a woman regularly employed in business, esp. an executive or owner.

bus·ing or **bus·sing** (bus′ing), *n.* the transporting of students by bus to public schools outside their neighborhoods, esp. in an effort to achieve racial balance.

bus·kin (bus′kin), *n.* **1.** a thick-soled, laced boot or half boot. **2.** Also called **cothurnus.** the high, thick-soled shoe worn by ancient Greek and Roman tragedians. **3.** tragic drama; tragedy. Compare SOCK[1] (def. 3). **—bus′kined,** *adj.*

bus′man's hol′iday, *n.* a vacation or day off from work spent in an activity closely resembling one's work.

buss (bus), *n., v.t., v.i.* KISS.

bust[1] (bust), *n.* **1.** a sculptured, painted, drawn, or engraved representation of the upper part of the human figure, esp. the head and shoulders. **2.** the chest or breast, esp. a woman's bosom.

bust[2] (bust), *v.i. Informal.* **1.** to burst. **2.** to break or separate; split (usu. fol. by *up*). **3.** to go bankrupt. **4.** to collapse from the strain of making a supreme effort. **—v.t. 5.** *Informal.* **a.** to burst. **b.** to bankrupt; ruin financially. **6.** to demote, esp. in military rank. **7.** to tame; break: *to bust a bronco.* **8.** *Slang.* **a.** to place under arrest. **b.** to subject to a police raid. **9.** *Informal.* **a.** to hit. **b.** to break: *I fell and busted my arm.* **10.** to damage or destroy (usu. fol. by *up*). **—n. 11.** a failure. **12.** *Informal.* a hit; sock; punch. **13.** a sudden economic decline; depression. **14.**

Slang. **a.** an arrest. **b.** a police raid. **15.** *Informal.* a drinking spree; binge. **—adj. 16.** *Informal.* bankrupt; broke.

bus·tard (bus′tərd), *n.* any of various chiefly terrestrial birds of the family Otididae, of the Old World and Australia.

bus·tier (boŏs tyā′), *n.* a woman's close-fitting, sleeveless, strapless top, usu. with boning to give it shape, worn as a blouse.

bus·tle[1] (bus′əl), *v.,* **-tled, -tling,** *n.* **—v.i. 1.** to move or act with a great show of energy (often fol. by *about*): *bustling about in the kitchen.* **2.** to abound in something: *an office bustling with activity.* **—v.t. 3.** to cause to bustle; hustle. **—n. 4.** energetic and often noisy activity. **—bus′tler,** *n.* **—bus′tling·ly,** *adv.*

bus·tle[2] (bus′əl), *n.* a projecting pad or framework formerly worn under the back of a woman's skirt to support and display the drape of the fabric. **—bus′tled,** *adj.*

bust·line (bust′līn′), *n.* **1.** the outline or shape of a woman's bust. **2.** the part of a garment covering the breasts.

bust·y (bus′tē), *adj.,* **bust·i·er, bust·i·est.** (of a woman) having a large bust; bosomy. **—bust′i·ness,** *n.*

bus·y (biz′ē), *adj.,* **bus·i·er, bus·i·est,** *v.,* **bus·ied, bus·y·ing. —adj. 1.** actively and attentively engaged, esp. in work. **2.** not at leisure; otherwise engaged: *He's busy and can't see you.* **3.** full of activity: *a busy life.* **4.** (of a telephone line) in use. **5.** meddlesome; prying. **6.** cluttered with small, fussy details: *The rug is too busy for this room.* **—v.t. 7.** to keep occupied; make or keep busy.

bus·y·bod·y (biz′ē bod′ē), *n., pl.* **-bod·ies.** a person who pries into or meddles in the affairs of others.

bus′y sig′nal, *n.* (on a telephone line) a rapid succession of buzzing tones, indicating that the number called is in use.

bus·y·work (biz′ē wûrk′), *n.* work often of little productive value assigned so that a person will be occupied or look busy.

but (but; *unstressed* bət), *conj.* **1.** on the contrary: *My brother went, but I did not.* **2.** and yet; nevertheless: *strange but true.* **3.** except; save: *did nothing but complain.* **4.** without the circumstance that: *It never rains but it pours.* **5.** otherwise than: *There is no hope but by prayer.* **6.** that (used esp. after *doubt, deny,* etc., with a negative): *I don't doubt but you'll do it.* **7.** that ... not: *No leaders ever existed but they were optimists.* **8.** (used to introduce an exclamatory expression): *But that's wonderful!* **9.** *Informal.* than: *It no sooner started raining but it stopped.* **—prep. 10.** with the exception of: *No one replied but me.* **11.** other than: *nothing but trouble.* **—adv. 12.** only; just: *There is but one answer.* **—n. 13.** buts, reservations or objections: *You'll do as you're told, no buts about it.* **—Idiom. 14. but for,** except for; were it not for. **—Usage.** When BUT is understood as a conjunction and the pronoun following it is understood as the subject of an incompletely expressed clause, the pronoun is in the subjective case: *Everyone lost faith in the plan but she (did not lose faith).* In virtually identical contexts, when BUT is understood as a preposition, the pronoun following it is in the objective case: *Everyone lost faith but her.* The prepositional use is more common. However, when prepositional BUT and its following pronoun occur near the beginning of a sentence, the subjective case often appears: *Everyone but she lost faith in the plan.* See also AND, DOUBT, THAN.

bu·tane (byoŏ′tān, byoŏ tān′), *n.* a colorless, flammable gas, C₄H₁₀, used chiefly in the manufacture of rubber and as fuel.

bu·ta·nol (byoŏt′n ôl′, -ol′), *n.* BUTYL ALCOHOL.

butch (boŏch), *adj.* **1.** *Slang.* **a.** (of a woman) having traits of behavior, dress, etc., usu. associated with males. **b.** (of a male) exaggeratedly masculine in appearance or manner. **2.** of or designating a haircut in which the hair is closely cropped. **—n. 3.** *Slang.* a butch person.

butch·er (boŏch′ər), *n.* **1.** a retail or wholesale dealer in meat. **2.** a person who slaughters certain animals or dresses their flesh for food or market. **3.** a person guilty of brutal or indiscriminate murder. **4.** a vendor who hawks refreshments, newspapers, etc., as on a train. **—v.t. 5.** to slaughter or dress (animals) for market. **6.** to kill indiscriminately or brutally. **7.** to bungle; botch: *to butcher a job.*

butch·er·bird (boŏch′ər bûrd′), *n.* **1.** any of several Eurasian or North American shrikes of the genus *Lanius.* **2.** any of various large, heavy-billed, highly vocal songbirds of the genus *Cracticus,* of Australia and New Guinea.

butch′er block′, *n.* **1.** a slab of wood formed by bonding or gluing together thick laminated strips of unpainted wood in alternating light and dark shades. **2.** a material, as vinyl, made to resemble this in color and pattern. **—butch′er-block′,** *adj.*

butch·er·y (boŏch′ə rē), *n., pl.* **-er·ies. 1.** brutal or wanton slaughter of animals or humans; carnage. **2.** the trade or business of a butcher. **3.** the act of bungling or botching.

bu·tene (byoŏ′tēn), *n.* BUTYLENE.

bu·te·o (byoŏ′tē ō′), *n., pl.* **-te·os.** any of various soaring hawks of the genus *Buteo,* of both the Old and New Worlds, having broad wings and a wide, rounded tail.

but·ler (but′lər), *n.* **1.** the chief male servant of a household, usually in charge of serving food, the care of silverware, etc. **2.** a male servant having charge of the wines and liquors. **—but′ler·like′,** *adj.*

But·ler (but′lər), *n.* **1. Benjamin Franklin,** 1818–93, U.S. politician and a Union general in the Civil War. **2. Joseph,** 1692–1752, English bishop, theologian, and author. **3. Nicholas Murray,** 1862–1947, U.S. educator: president of Columbia University 1902–45; Nobel peace prize 1931. **4. Samuel,** 1835–1902, English novelist, essayist, and satirist.

but'ler's pan'try, *n.* a service room between a kitchen and dining room.

butt¹ (but), *n.* **1.** the end or extremity of anything, esp. the thicker, larger, or blunt end considered as a base, support, or handle: *the butt of a rifle.* **2.** an end that is not used or consumed: *a cigar butt.* **3.** a lean cut of pork shoulder. **4.** *Slang.* the buttocks. **5.** *Slang.* a cigarette.

butt² (but), *n.* **1.** an object of witticisms, ridicule, etc. **2.** a target. **3.** (on a target range) a wall of earth or other backstop located behind the targets to stop bullets, arrows, etc. **4. butts,** a target range. —*v.i.* **5.** to abut. —*v.t.* **6.** to position or fasten an end (of something). **7.** to join the ends of (two things); set end to end.

butt³ (but), *v.t.* **1.** to strike or push with the head or horns. —*v.i.* **2.** to strike or push at something with the head or horns. **3.** to project. **4. butt in** (or **out**), to interfere (or stop interfering) in the affairs or conversation of others. —*n.* **5.** a push or blow with the head or horns.

butt⁴ (but), *n.* **1.** any of various units of capacity, usu. considered equal to two hogsheads. **2.** a large cask for wine, beer, or ale.

butte (byōōt), *n.* an isolated hill or mountain rising abruptly above the surrounding land, esp. in the western U.S. and Canada.

but·ter (but'ər), *n.* **1.** a soft whitish or yellowish fatty solid that separates from milk or cream when it is churned, processed for cooking and table use. **2.** any of various other soft spreads for bread: *apple butter; peanut butter.* **3.** any of various substances of butterlike consistency, as certain vegetable oils solid at ordinary temperatures: *cocoa butter.* —*v.t.* **4.** to put butter on or in. **5.** to apply a liquefied bonding material to (a piece or area), as mortar to a course of bricks. **6. butter up,** to flatter, esp. so as to gain a favor from. —**Saying. 7. Butter wouldn't melt in his** (or **her**) **mouth,** he (or she) is so eager to please as to inspire lack of trust.

but'ter-and-eggs', *n., pl.* **but·ter-and-eggs.** (*used with a sing. or pl. v.*) any of several plants whose flowers are of two shades of yellow, as the toadflax.

but'ter bean' or **but'ter-bean',** *n.* **1.** a variety of small-seeded lima bean, *Phaseolus lunatus,* grown in the southern U.S. **2.** *Midland and Southern U.S.* any type of lima bean.

but·ter·bur (but'ər bûr'), *n.* any of several composite plants of the genus *Petasites,* having large, woolly leaves said to have been used to wrap butter.

but·ter·cup (but'ər kup'), *n.* any of numerous plants of the genus *Ranunculus,* having glossy yellow flowers and deeply cut leaves.

but'ter·fat', *n.* the fatty portion of milk, from which butter is made.

but·ter·fin·gers (but'ər fing'gerz), *n., pl.* **-gers.** (*used with a sing. v.*) a person who frequently drops things; clumsy person. —**but'ter·fin·gered,** *adj.*

but·ter·fish (but'ər fish'), *n., pl.* (*esp. collectively*) **-fish·es,** (*esp. for kinds or species*) **-fish.** a small, flattened marine food fish, *Peprilus triacanthus,* of U.S. Atlantic coastal waters, having small scales and smooth skin.

but·ter·fly (but'ər flī'), *n., pl.* **-flies,** *v.,* **-flied, -fly·ing.** —*n.* **1.** any of numerous flying insects of the order Lepidoptera that are active by day, characterized by clubbed antennae, a slender body, and broad, often conspicuously marked wings. **2.** a person who flits aimlessly from one interest or group to another: *a social butterfly.* **3. butterflies,** (*used with a pl. v.*) *Informal.* a queasy feeling, as from nervousness or excitement. **4.** a racing breaststroke in which the swimmer brings both arms out of the water in forward, circular motions and kicks the legs up and down together. —*v.t.* **5.** to slit open and flatten (food) to resemble the spread wings of a butterfly: *butterflied shrimp.*

but'terfly fish' or **but'ter·fly·fish',** *n.* any of various small, brightly colored tropical fishes of the family Chaetodontidae, having deep, narrow bodies and darting movements suggestive of a butterfly.

but'terfly valve', *n.* a clack valve having two flaps with a common hinge. **2.** a valve, as the throttle valve in a carburetor, that swings about a central axis across its face.

but'terfly weed', *n.* a North American milkweed, *Asclepias tuberosa,* having clusters of bright orange flowers. Also called **orange milkweed.**

but·ter·head let'tuce (but'ər hed'), *n.* any of several varieties of lettuce, as Bibb or Boston lettuce, having a relatively small head of loosely-packed soft leaves.

but·ter·milk (but'ər milk'), *n.* **1.** the acidulous liquid remaining after butter has been separated from milk or cream. **2.** a similar liquid made by adding a bacterial culture to whole or skim milk.

but·ter·nut (but'ər nut'), *n.* **1.** the edible oily nut of an American tree, *Juglans cinerea,* of the walnut family. **2.** the tree itself, whose bark and husks yield a light brown dye. **3.** a Confederate soldier or partisan in the Civil War, esp. one whose uniform was dyed with this extract. **4.** a light brown color.

but'ternut squash', *n.* a long, pear-shaped winter squash with yellowish tan skin and sweet, orange-colored flesh.

but·ter·scotch (but'ər skoch'), *n.* **1.** a flavor produced in puddings, ice cream, etc., by combining brown sugar, butter, and vanilla. **2.** a hard, brittle taffy made with butter, brown sugar, etc. **3.** a golden brown color.

but'ter·weed', *n.* any of various wild plants having conspicuous yellow flowers, as the groundsel or ragwort.

but·ter·wort (but'ər wûrt', -wôrt'), *n.* any of various small carnivorous bog plants of the genus *Pinguicula,* of the bladderwort family, having leaves that secrete a sticky substance in which small insects are caught.

but·ter·y¹ (but'ə rē), *adj.* **1.** like, containing, or spread with butter. **2.** resembling butter, as in smoothness or softness of texture: *buttery leather.* **3.** grossly flattering; smarmy. —**but'ter·i·ness,** *n.*

but·ter·y² (but'ə rē, bu'trē), *n., pl.* **-ter·ies.** *Chiefly New Eng.* a storeroom for provisions, wines, and liquors; pantry or larder.

butt' hinge', *n.* a hinge for a door or the like, secured to the butting surfaces rather than to the adjacent sides of the door and its frame.

butt' joint', *n.* a joint formed by two pieces of wood or metal united end to end without overlapping.

but·tock (but'ək), *n.* Usu., **buttocks. 1.** (in humans) either of the two fleshy protuberances forming the lower and back part of the trunk. **2.** (in animals) the rump. —**but'tocked,** *adj.*

but·ton (but'n), *n.* **1.** a small disk, knob, or the like attached to an article, as of clothing, and serving as a fastener when passed through a buttonhole or loop. **2.** anything resembling a button, esp. in being small and round, as a candy, ornament, or marker. **3.** a badge or emblem bearing a name, slogan, or the like, for wear on the lapel, dress, etc.: *campaign buttons.* **4.** a small knob or disk pressed to activate an electric circuit, operate a machine, open a door, etc. **5.** a young or undeveloped mushroom. **6.** any of various small parts or structures resembling a button, as the rattle at the tip of the tail in a very young rattlesnake. **7.** *Informal.* the point of the chin. **8.** (in assaying) a small globule or lump of metal at the bottom of a crucible after fusion. **9.** the protective, blunting knob fixed to the point of a fencing foil. —*v.t.* **10.** to fasten with or as if with a button or buttons: *Button your coat.* **11.** to insert (a button) in a buttonhole or loop. —*v.i.* **12.** to be capable of being buttoned: *This coat buttons up the front.* —**Idiom. 13. button up, a.** Also, **button one's lip.** to become or keep silent. **b.** to complete successfully; finish. **14. have all one's buttons,** *Informal.* to be mentally competent; have all one's wits. **15. (right) on the button,** exact; correct. —**but'ton·er,** *n.* —**but'ton·less,** *adj.*

but·ton·bush (but'n bŏŏsh'), *n.* a North American shrub, *Cephalanthus occidentalis,* of the madder family, with globular flower heads.

but'ton-down', *adj.* **1.** (of a collar) having buttonholes at the ends with which it can be buttoned to the front of the garment. **2.** (of a garment) having a button-down collar. **3.** Also, **but'toned down'.** conventional, unimaginative, or conservative.

but·ton·hole (but'n hōl'), *n., v.,* **-holed, -hol·ing.** —*n.* **1.** the hole, slit, or loop through which a button is passed and by which it is secured. —*v.t.* **2.** to sew with a buttonhole stitch. **3.** to make buttonholes in. **4.** to accost and detain (someone) in conversation. —**but'ton·hol'er,** *n.*

but'tonhole stitch', *n.* a looped stitch used to strengthen and secure the edge of a material, as around a buttonhole.

but'ton quail', *n.* any of various terrestrial birds of the family Turnicidae, inhabiting warmer parts of the Old World, that resemble but are not related to true quails.

but'ton snake'root, *n.* **1.** any composite plant of the genus *Liatris,* having narrow, alternate leaves and spikelike heads of rose-purple flowers. **2.** a plant, *Eryngium yuccifolium,* of the parsley family, native to the southeastern U.S., having bristly leaves.

but·tress (bu'tris), *n.* **1.** a projecting support built into or against the outside of a masonry wall to steady a structure by opposing its outward thrusts. **2.** any prop or support. **3.** something resembling a buttress in shape or position. **4.** a bony or horny protuberance, esp. on a horse's hoof. —*v.t.* **5.** to support by a buttress; prop up. **6.** to give encouragement or support to.

buttress

bu·tyl (byōō'til, byōōt'l), *n.* any of four univalent isomeric groups with the formula C_4H_9.

bu'tyl al'cohol, *n.* any of four flammable isomeric liquid alcohols having the formula C_4H_9OH, used as solvents and in organic synthesis. Also called **butanol.**

bu·tyl·ene (byōōt'l ēn') also **butene,** *n.* any of three isomeric gaseous alkenes having the formula C_4H_8.

bux·om (buk'səm), *adj.* **1.** (of a woman) full-bosomed. **2.** (of a woman) plump and cheerful.

Bux·te·hu·de (bŏŏk′stə hōō′də), *n.* **Dietrich,** 1637–1707, Danish organist and composer, in Germany after 1668.

buy (bī), *v.,* **bought, buy·ing,** *n.* —*v.t.* **1.** to acquire the possession of, esp. by paying an equivalent in money; purchase. **2.** to acquire by exchange or concession: *to buy favor with flattery.* **3.** to hire or obtain the services of. **4.** to bribe. **5.** to be the purchasing equivalent of: *A dollar doesn't buy much these days.* **6.** *Theol.* to redeem; ransom. **7.** *Informal.* to accept or believe: *I don't buy that explanation.* —*v.i.* **8.** to be or become a purchaser. **9. buy into,** to purchase a share, interest, or membership in. **10. buy off,** to get rid of (a claim, opposition, etc.) by payment; bribe. **11. buy out,** to purchase all the business shares belonging to (another). **12. buy up,** to buy as much of (something) as is available. —*n.* **13.** an act or instance of buying. **14.** something bought; a purchase. **15.** a bargain: *The couch was a real buy.* —*Idiom.* **16. buy it,** *Slang.* to get killed. —**buy′a·ble,** *adj.*

buy·back (bī′bak′), *n.* **1.** the buying of something that one previously sold. **2.** any arrangement to take back something as a condition of a sale. **3.** a repurchase by a company of its own stock.

buy·er (bī′ər), *n.* **1.** a person who buys; purchaser. **2.** a purchasing agent, as for a department or chain store.

buy′ers′ mar′ket, *n.* a market in which goods and services are plentiful and prices relatively low. Compare SELLERS′ MARKET.

buy·off (bī′ôf′, -of′), *n.* an act or instance of buying off; a payment or bribe.

buy·out (bī′out′), *n.* an act or instance of buying out, esp. of buying all or a controlling percentage of the shares in a company.

buzz (buz), *n.* **1.** a low, vibrating, humming sound, as of bees or machinery. **2.** a rumor or report. **3.** *Informal.* a phone call: *I'll give you a buzz tonight.* **4.** *Slang.* a feeling of exhilaration or pleasant intoxication. —*v.i.* **5.** to make a low, vibrating, humming sound. **6.** to be filled with such a sound, as a room. **7.** to whisper; gossip: *The town is buzzing about the scandal.* **8.** to move busily from place to place. **9.** *Slang.* to go; leave (usu. fol. by *along* or *off*). —*v.t.* **10.** to cause to buzz: *The fly buzzed its wings.* **11.** to tell or spread secretively. **12.** to signal or summon with a buzzer: *She buzzed her secretary.* **13.** *Informal.* to make a phone call to. **14.** to fly a plane very low over: *to buzz a stadium.*

buz·zard (buz′ərd), *n.* **1.** any of several broad-winged Old World hawks of the genus *Buteo* and allied genera, esp. *B. buteo,* of Eurasia. **2.** any of several New World vultures, esp. the turkey vulture. **3.** a cantankerous or grasping person.

buzz·er (buz′ər), *n.* **1.** a person or thing that buzzes. **2.** a signaling apparatus similar to an electric bell but without hammer or gong, producing a buzzing sound by the vibration of an armature.

buzz′ saw′, *n.* a power-operated circular saw.

buzz·word (buz′wûrd′), *n.* a word or phrase, often sounding authoritative or technical, that has come into vogue in popular culture or a particular profession.

B.V., Blessed Virgin. [< Latin *Beāta Virgō*]

B.V.M., Blessed Virgin Mary. [< Latin *Beāta Virgō Marīa*]

by¹ (bī), *prep., adv., adj., n., pl.* **byes.** —*prep.* **1.** near to or next to: *a home by a lake.* **2.** over the surface of, through the medium of, along, or using as a route: *She came by air.* **3.** on, as a means of conveyance: *to arrive by ship.* **4.** to and beyond a place; past: *We drove by the church.* **5.** during: *by day; by night.* **6.** not later than: *I'll be done by five o'clock.* **7.** to the extent or amount of: *taller by three inches.* **8.** from the evidence or authority of: *By his own account he was there.* **9.** according to: *a bad movie by any standards.* **10.** through the agency of: *The booklet was issued by the government.* **11.** from the hand or invention of: *a poem by Emily Dickinson.* **12.** as a result or on the basis of: *We met by chance.* **13.** in support of; for: *to do well by one's children.* **14.** (of things in succession) after; next after: *piece by piece.* **15.** (in multiplication) taken the number of times as that specified by the second number, or multiplier: *Multiply 18 by 57.* **16.** (in measuring shapes, spaces, etc.) with another dimension of: *a room 10 feet by 12 feet.* **17.** (in division) separated into the number of equal parts as that specified by the second number, or divisor: *Divide 99 by 33.* **18.** in terms or amounts of: *Apples are sold by the bushel.* **19.** begot or born of: *She had a son by her first husband.* **20.** (of quadrupeds) having as a sire: *Equipoise II by Equipoise.* **21.** one point toward on the compass: *N by NE.* **22.** to, into, or at: *Come by my office this afternoon.* —*adv.* **23.** at hand; near: *The school is close by.* **24.** to and beyond a point; past: *The car drove by.* **25.** aside; away: *to lay by money for retirement.* **26.** to or at someone's home, office, etc.: *Stop by later.* **27.** past; over: *in times gone by.* Also, **bye. 28.** situated to one side: *a by passage.* **29.** incidental: *a by comment.* —*Idiom.* **31. by and by,** before long; presently. **32. by and large,** in general; on the whole.

by² (bī), *interj.* BYE².

by-and-by, *n.* the future: *to meet in the sweet by-and-by.*

bye¹ (bī), *n.* Also, **by. 1.** (in a tournament) the preferential status of a player or team not paired with a competitor in an early round and thus automatically advanced in play in the next round. **2.** something subsidi-

ary or secondary. —*adj.* **3.** BY¹. —*Idiom.* **4. by the bye,** by the way; incidentally.

bye² or **by** (bī), *interj.* GOOD-BYE.

bye-, var. of BY-: *bye-election.*

bye-bye (*interj.* bī′bī′; *n., adv.* bī′bī′), *interj.* **1.** GOOD-BYE. —*n.* **2.** *Baby Talk.* sleep. —*Idiom.* **3. go bye-bye,** *Baby Talk.* to leave; depart; go out.

by′-elec′tion or **bye′-elec′tion,** *n.* a special election held between general elections to fill a vacancy, esp. in the British Parliament.

by·gone (bī′gôn′, -gon′), *adj.* **1.** earlier; former; past: *bygone days.* —*n.* **2.** Usu., **bygones.** previous times or experiences. —*Idiom.* **3. let bygones be bygones,** to disregard past disagreements; reconcile.

by·law or **bye·law** (bī′lô′), *n.* **1.** a standing rule governing the regulation of internal affairs of a corporation or society. **2.** a subsidiary law.

by′line′ or **by′-line′,** *n., v.,* **-lined, -lin·ing.** —*n.* **1.** a printed line in a newspaper or magazine, usu. below the title or subhead of a story, giving the author's name. —*v.t.* **2.** to accompany with a byline.

BYOB, bring your own bottle (as of wine or liquor).

by′pass′ or **by′-pass′,** *n., v.,* **-passed, -passed** or **-past, -pass·ing.** —*n.* **1.** a road enabling motorists to avoid a city or other heavy traffic points. **2.** a surgical procedure in which a diseased or obstructed hollow organ is temporarily or permanently circumvented. Compare CORONARY BYPASS. **3.** a secondary pipe or other channel connected with a main passage. **4.** SHUNT (def. 7). —*v.t.* **5.** to avoid by following a bypass. **6.** to cause (fluid or gas) to follow a secondary pipe or bypass. **7.** to neglect to consult or to ignore the opinion or decision of: *I bypassed the manager and took my complaint straight to the owner.* —**by′pass′er,** *n.*

by·past (bī′past′, -päst′), *adj.* bygone.

by′play′ or **by′-play′,** *n.* an action or speech carried on to the side while the main action proceeds, esp. on the stage.

by′-prod′uct, *n.* **1.** a secondary or incidental product, as in a process of manufacture. **2.** the result of another action, often unforeseen or unintended.

Byrd (bûrd), *n.* **1. Richard Evelyn,** 1888–1957, rear admiral in the U.S. Navy: polar explorer. **2. William,** c1540–1623, English composer.

by′-road′ or **by′road′,** *n.* a side road.

By·ron (bī′rən), *n.* **George Gordon, Lord** (*6th Baron Byron*), 1788–1824, English poet.

by·stand·er (bī′stan′dər), *n.* a person present but not involved; onlooker.

byte (bīt), *n.* a group of adjacent bits, usu. eight, processed by a computer as a unit. [perh. alteration (influenced by BIT³) of BITE]

by·way (bī′wā′), *n.* **1.** a secluded, obscure, or little-used road. **2.** a subsidiary or obscure field of research, endeavor, etc.

by·word (bī′wûrd′), *n.* **1.** a word or phrase associated with some person or thing. **2.** a common saying; proverb. **3.** a person regarded as the embodiment of a particular quality. **4.** an object of reproach or scorn. **5.** an epithet.

Byz·an·tine (biz′ən tēn′, -tīn′, bī′zan-, bi zan′tin), *adj.* **1.** of or pertaining to Byzantium or the Byzantine Empire. **2.** of or in the style of architecture developed in the Byzantine Empire, characterized by masonry construction, round arches, low domes on pendentives, and the extensive use of mosaics. **3.** (*sometimes l.c.*) **a.** extremely complex or intricate. **b.** characterized by elaborate scheming and intrigue, esp. to obtain political advantage. —*n.* **4.** a native or inhabitant of Byzantium.

Byz′antine Church′, *n.* ORTHODOX CHURCH (def. 1).

Byz′antine Em′pire, *n.* the Eastern Roman Empire after the fall of the Western Empire in A.D. 476: became extinct after the fall of Constantinople, its capital, in 1453.

By·zan·ti·um (bi zan′shē əm, -tē əm), *n.* an ancient Greek city on the Bosporus and the Sea of Marmara: rebuilt by Constantine I and renamed Constantinople A.D. 330. Compare ISTANBUL.

C

C, c (sē), *n., pl.* **Cs** or **C's, cs** or **c's** for 1–4. **1.** the third letter of the English alphabet, a consonant. **2.** any spoken sound represented by this letter. **3.** something shaped like a C. **4.** a written or printed representation of the letter *C* or *c.* **5.** (*cap.*) a powerful high-level computer programming language suited for creating operating systems and complex applications.

C, *Symbol.* **1.** the third in order or in a series. **2.** (*sometimes l.c.*) (in some grading systems) a grade or mark indicating fair or average quality. **3. a.** the tonic note of the C major scale. **b.** a tonality having C as the tonic. **c.** a written or printed note representing this tone. **d.** (in the fixed system of solmization) the first tone of the scale of C major, called *do.* **e.** the tonality having C as the tonic note. **f.** a symbol indicating quadruple time and appearing after the clef sign on a musical staff. **4.** (*sometimes l.c.*) the Roman numeral for 100. **5.** Celsius. **6.** centigrade. **7.** capacitance. **8.** carbon. **9. a.** cysteine. **b.** cytosine. **10.** Also, **C-note.** *Slang.* a hundred-dollar bill.

c, 1. the velocity of light in a vacuum: approximately 186,000 miles per second or 299,793 kilometers per second. **2.** the velocity of sound.

c., 1. calorie. **2.** *Optics.* candle. **3.** carat. **4.** cent. **5.** centigrade. **6.** centimeter. **7.** century. **8.** chapter. **9.** (with a year) about: *c. 1775.* **10.** cognate. **11.** gallon. **12.** copyright. **13.** cubic. **14.** cycle.

CA, California.

Ca, *Chem. Symbol.* calcium.

ca-, var. of KER-.

ca or **ca.,** (with a year) about: *ca 476 B.C.*

cab¹ (kab), *n., v.,* **cabbed, cab·bing.** —*n.* **1.** a taxicab. **2.** a horse-drawn vehicle, as a hansom, for public hire. **3.** the covered or enclosed part of a locomotive, truck, crane, etc., where the operator sits. —*v.i.* **4.** to ride in a taxicab or horse-drawn cab.

cab² (kab), *n.* an ancient Hebrew measure equal to about 2 quarts (1.9 liters).

CAB or **C.A.B.,** Civil Aeronautics Board.

ca·bal (kə bal′), *n., v.,* **-balled, -bal·ling.** —*n.* **1.** a small group of secret plotters, as against a government or authority. **2.** the plots and schemes of such a group. **3.** a clique, as in literary or artistic circles. —*v.i.* **4.** to form a cabal.

cab·a·la or **cab·ba·la** or **kab·a·la** or **kab·ba·la** (kab′ə lə, kə bä′-), *n., pl.* **-las. 1.** (*often cap.*) a system of esoteric philosophy developed by rabbis, reaching its peak in the Middle Ages and based on a mystical method of interpreting the Scriptures. **2.** any occult doctrine or science.

cab·a·lism (kab′ə liz′əm), *n.* **1.** the principles or doctrines of the cabala. **2.** an interpretation according to the cabala. **3.** any mystic or occult doctrine. —**cab′a·list,** *n.* —**cab′a·lis′tic,** *adj.*

ca·bal·le·ro (kab′əl yâr′ō, -ə lâr′ō), *n., pl.* **-ros. 1.** a Spanish gentleman. **2.** *Southwestern U.S.* **a.** a horseman. **b.** a woman's escort; cavalier.

ca·ban·a (kə ban′ə, -ban′yə), *n., pl.* **-ban·as. 1.** a small cabin or tent-like structure for use as a bathhouse, esp. on a beach or by a swimming pool. **2.** a cabin or cottage.

cab·a·ret (kab′ə rā′), *n.* **1.** a restaurant providing food, drink, and often a floor show or other entertainment; nightclub or café. **2.** the entertainment at a cabaret.

cab·bage (kab′ij), *n.* **1.** any of several cultivated varieties of a plant, *Brassica oleracea capitata,* of the mustard family, having a short stem and leaves formed into a compact, edible head. **2.** the head or leaves of this plant, eaten cooked or raw. [< Old French < Latin *caput* head]

cab′bage but′terfly, *n.* any white or chiefly white butterfly of the family Pieridae, as *Pieris rapae,* the larvae of which feed on the leaves of cabbages and related plants.

cab′bage palm′, *n.* any of several palms, esp. those of the genus *Euterpe,* having terminal leaf buds.

cab′bage palmet′to, *n.* a fan palm, *Sabal palmetto,* of the southeastern U.S.

cab′bage rose′, *n.* a rose, *Rosa centifolia,* having large and fragrant pink flowers, cultivated in many varieties.

cab·bage·worm (kab′ij wûrm′), *n.* a caterpillar, esp. of the genus *Pieris,* that feeds on cabbages.

cab·by or **cab·bie** (kab′ē), *n., pl.* **-bies.** *Informal.* a cabdriver.

cab·driv·er (kab′drī′vər), *n.* a driver of a taxicab or horse-drawn carriage.

cab·in (kab′in), *n.* **1.** a small house or cottage, usu. of simple design and construction: *a log cabin.* **2.** an enclosed space for more or less temporary occupancy, as the living quarters in a trailer or the passenger space in a cable car. **3.** the enclosed space for the pilot, cargo, or esp. passengers in an air or space vehicle. **4.** an apartment or room in a ship, as for passengers. —*adv.* **5.** in cabin-class accommodations: *to travel cabin.*

cab′in class′, *n.* the class of accommodations on a passenger ship less luxurious than first class but more so than tourist class. Compare SECOND CLASS (def. 1). —**cab′in-class′,** *adj., adv.*

cab′in cruis′er, *n.* a power-driven pleasure boat having a cabin equipped for living aboard.

cab·i·net (kab′ə nit, kab′nit), *n.* **1.** a piece of furniture with shelves, drawers, etc., for holding or displaying items: *a file cabinet; a curio cabinet.* **2.** a wall cupboard used for storage, as of kitchen utensils or toilet articles. **3.** the case enclosing a radio, television, loudspeaker, etc. **4.** (*often cap.*) a council advising a sovereign or a chief executive; the group of persons who help to manage a government. **5.** (*often cap.*) (in the U.S.) an advisory body to the president, consisting of the heads of the executive departments of the federal government. **6.** a small case with compartments for valuables or other small objects. **7.** a small chamber or booth for special use, esp. a shower stall. **8.** a premium dry white wine produced in Germany. —*adj.* **9.** of or pertaining to a political cabinet: *a cabinet meeting.* **10.** of, pertaining to, or used by a cabinetmaker or in cabinetmaking.

CABINET OF THE UNITED STATES

Department of	Abbrev.	Created in
Agriculture	USDA	1889
Commerce	DOC	1913
Defense	DOD	1949
Education	ED	1979
Energy	DOE	1977
Health and Human Services*	HHS	1980
Housing and Urban Development	HUD	1965
The Interior	DOI	1849
Justice	DOJ	1870
Labor	DOL	1913
State	DOS	1789
Transportation	DOT	1966
The Treasury	TD	1789
Dept. of Veterans Affairs	DVA	1989

*Originally created in 1953 as the Department of Health, Education, and Welfare (HEW).

cab·i·net·mak·er (kab′ə nit mā′kər), *n.* a person who makes fine furniture and other woodwork. —**cab′i·net·mak′ing,** *n.*

cab·i·net·ry (kab′ə ni trē), *n.* fine furniture or other woodwork.

cab′in fe′ver, *n.* mounting boredom, restlessness, and anxiety resulting from a prolonged stay in a remote or confined place.

ca·ble (kā′bəl), *n., v.,* **-bled, -bling.** —*n.* **1.** a heavy, strong rope. **2.** a very strong rope made of strands of metal wire, used to support cable cars, suspension bridges, etc. **3.** a cord of metal wire used to operate or pull a mechanism. **4.** *Naut.* **a.** a thick hawser made of rope, strands of metal wire, or chain. **b.** a nautical unit of length equal to 720 feet (219 m). **5.** an insulated electrical conductor, often in strands, or a combination of electrical conductors insulated from one another. **6.** an ornament or molding resembling the twisted strands of a rope. —*v.t.* **7.** to send (a message) by cable. **8.** to send a cablegram to. **9.** to fasten or furnish with a cable. **10.** to work or fashion with cable stitch. —*v.i.* **11.** to send a message by cable. **12.** to cable-stitch.

ca′ble car′ or **ca′ble-car′,** *n.* a vehicle, usu. enclosed, used on a cable railway or tramway.

ca·ble·gram (kā′bəl gram′), *n.* a telegram sent by underwater cable.

ca′ble-read′y, *adj.* (of a television or VCR) able to receive cable television directly, without the need for special reception or decoding equipment.

ca′ble stitch′, *n.* a series of stitches used in knitting to produce a cable effect. —**ca′ble-stitch′,** *v.i., v.t.*

ca′ble tel′evision, *n.* a system of televising programs to private subscribers by means of coaxial cable. Also called **cable TV.**

ca·ble·way (kā′bəl wā′), *n.* a system for hoisting and hauling bulk materials by a bucket on a cable suspended between two towers.

cab·o·chon (kab′ə shon′, -shôn′), *n.* **1.** a gemstone, usu. round or oval, cut so as to have a domed surface that is polished but not faceted. —*adv.* **2.** in the form of a cabochon: *a turquoise cut cabochon.* —*adj.* **3.** cut in the form of a cabochon.

ca·boo·dle (kə bōōd′l), *n.* *Informal.* the lot, pack, or crowd: *Get rid of the whole caboodle.*

ca·boose (kə bōōs′), *n.* **1.** a car on a freight train, used chiefly as the crew's quarters and usu. attached to the rear of the train. **2.** a ship's galley.

Cab·ot (kab′ət), *n.* **1. John** (*Giovanni Caboto*), c1450–98?, Italian navigator for England: discoverer of North American mainland 1497. **2.** his son, **Sebastian,** 1474?–1557, English navigator and explorer.

cab·o·tage (kab′ə tij, kab′ə tăzh′), *n.* navigation or trade along the coast.

ca·bril·la (kə bril′ə), *n., pl.* **-las.** any of several sea basses, esp. *Epinephelus analogus,* of tropical E Pacific seas.

Ca·bri·ni (kə brē′nē), *n*. **Saint Frances Xavier** ("*Mother Cabrini*"),1850–1917, U.S. nun, born in Italy; founder of the Missionary Sisters of the Sacred Heart of Jesus.

cab·ri·ole (kab′rē ōl′), *n*. a leap by a ballet dancer in which one leg is raised in the air and the other is brought up to beat against it.

cab′riole leg′, *n*. a curved, tapering furniture leg curving outward at the top and inward farther down, usu. terminating in an ornamental foot: used esp. in the 18th century.

cab·ri·o·let (kab′rē ə lā′), *n*. **1.** a light, two-wheeled, one-horse carriage with a folding top, capable of seating two persons. **2.** an automobile resembling a coupe but with a folding top.

ca·ca·o (kə kä′ō, -kā′ō), *n., pl.* **-ca·os. 1.** a small tropical American evergreen tree, *Theobroma cacao*, of the sterculia family, cultivated for its seeds, the source of cocoa and chocolate. **2.** Also, **cocoa.** the fruit or seeds of this tree.

caca′o (or **co′coa**) **bean′,** *n*. a seed of the cacao tree.

cac·cia·to·re (kä′chə tôr′ē, -tōr′ē), *adj.* cooked with tomatoes, mushrooms, herbs, and usu. wine: *chicken cacciatore*.

cache (kash), *n., v.,* **cached, cach·ing.** —*n.* **1.** a hiding place for ammunition, food, treasures, etc. **2.** anything hidden in a caché. **3.** a piece of computer hardware or a section of RAM dedicated to selectively storing and speeding access to frequently used program commands or data. —*v.t.* **4.** to hide in a cache.

ca·chet (ka shā′, kash′ā), *n*. **1.** an official seal, as on a letter or document. **2.** an official sign of approval. **3.** superior status; prestige: *a job with a certain cachet.* **4.** a distinguishing mark or feature. **5.** a hollow wafer for enclosing an ill-tasting medicine. **6.** a design, slogan, or other device drawn or printed on an envelope for philatelic purposes, as for a first-day cover.

ca·chex·i·a (kə kek′sē ə) also **ca·chex·y** (-sē), *n*. general ill health with emaciation, usu. occurring in association with a disease. —**ca·chec′tic** (-tik), *adj.*

cach·in·nate (kak′ə nāt′), *v.i.,* **-nat·ed, -nat·ing.** to laugh loudly or immoderately.

ca·chou (kə shoo′, ka-, kash′oo), *n., pl.* **-chous.** a lozenge for sweetening the breath.

ca·cique (kə sēk′), *n*. **1.** a chief of an Indian clan or tribe in Mexico and the West Indies. **2.** (in Spain and Latin America) a political boss on a local level. **3.** any of various tropical and subtropical New World blackbirds of the genera *Cacicus* and *Amblycercus*, that typically construct long, pendent nests.

cack·le (kak′əl), *v.,* **-led, -ling,** *n*. —*v.i.* **1.** to utter a shrill, broken cry, as of a hen. **2.** to laugh in a shrill, broken manner. **3.** to chatter noisily. —*v.t.* **4.** to express with a cackling sound: *They cackled their disapproval.* —*n.* **5.** the act or sound of cackling. **6.** chatter; idle talk.

caco-, a combining form meaning "bad": *cacography.*

cac·o·de·mon or **cac·o·dae·mon** (kak′ə dē′mən), *n*. an evil spirit; demon. —**cac′o·de·mon′ic** (-di mon′ik), *adj.*

ca·cog·ra·phy (kə kog′rə fē), *n*. **1.** bad handwriting. **2.** poor spelling. —**ca·cog′ra·pher,** *n*. —**cac·o·graph·ic** (kak′ə graf′ik), **cac′o·graph′i·cal,** *adj.*

ca·col·o·gy (ka kol′ə jē, kə-), *n*. defective pronunciation or socially unacceptable speech.

cac·o·mis·tle or **cac·o·mix·le** (kak′ə mis′əl), *n*. a slender, raccoonlike carnivorous mammal, *Bassariscus astutus*, of Mexico and the southwestern U.S., with a long tail.

ca·coph·o·ny (kə kof′ə nē), *n., pl.* **-nies. 1.** harsh discordance of sound; dissonance. **2.** a discordant and meaningless mixture of sounds. —**ca·coph′o·nous,** *adj.*

cac·tus (kak′təs), *n., pl.* **-ti** (-tī), **-tus·es, -tus.** any of numerous New World flowering plants of the family Cactaceae, of warm and arid regions, with succulent, leafless stems usu. bearing spines. —**cac′toid,** *adj.*

cad (kad), *n*. a man who behaves dishonorably or irresponsibly toward women. —**cad′dish,** *adj.*

CAD (kad), *n*. computer-aided design.

ca·dav·er (kə dav′ər), *n*. a dead body, esp. a human body to be dissected; corpse. —**ca·dav′er·ous,** *adj.*

CAD/CAM (kad′kam′), *n*. computer-aided design and computer-aided manufacturing.

cad·die or **cad·dy** (kad′ē), *n., pl.* **-dies,** *v.,* **-died, -dy·ing.** —*n.* **1.** a person hired to carry a golf player's clubs, find the ball, etc. **2.** a wheeled device for moving heavy objects: *a luggage caddie.* —*v.i.* **3.** to work as a caddie.

cad·dis or **cad·dice** (kad′is), *n*. a kind of woolen braid, ribbon, or tape. —**cad′dised,** *adj.*

cad·dis·fly or **cad·dice·fly** (kad′is flī′), *n., pl.* **-flies.** any of numerous aquatic insects constituting the order Trichoptera, having two pairs of membranous, often hairy wings and superficially resembling moths. Compare CADDISWORM.

cad·dis·worm (kad′is wûrm′), *n*. the aquatic larva of a caddisfly, having an armored head and a pair of abdominal hooks, and typically living in a case built from sand or plant debris.

Cad·do (kad′ō), *n., pl.* **-dos,** (*esp. collectively*) **-do** for 1. **1.** a member of any of several North American Indian tribes formerly located in Arkansas, Louisiana, and eastern Texas, and now living in Oklahoma. **2.** the Caddoan language of the Caddo.

cad·dy (kad′ē), *n., pl.* **-dies. 1.** a container for holding or storing items. **2.** TEA CADDY.

cade (kād), *adj. New Eng., Brit.* (of the young of animals) abandoned by the mother and raised by humans.

ca·delle (kə del′), *n*. a small black beetle, *Tenebroides mauritanicus*, that feeds on grain both as a larva and an adult.

ca·dence (kād′ns), *n., v.,* **-denced, -denc·ing.** —*n.* **1.** rhythmic flow of sounds or words: *the cadence of language.* **2.** the beat, rate, or measure of any rhythmic movement. **3.** the flow or rhythm of events: *the frenetic cadence of modern life.* **4.** a slight falling in pitch of the voice in speaking. **5.** a sequence of musical chords moving toward a harmonic point of rest or closing. —*v.t.* **6.** to make rhythmical. —**ca·den·tial** (kə den′shəl), *adj.*

ca·det (kə det′), *n*. **1.** a student in a national service academy or private military school or on a training ship. **2.** a student in training for service as a commissioned officer in the military. **3.** a trainee in a profession. **4.** a younger son or brother. **5.** the youngest son.

cad·mi·um (kad′mē əm), *n*. a white, ductile, divalent metallic element resembling tin, used in plating and in making certain alloys. *Symbol:* Cd; *at. wt.:* 112.41; *at. no.:* 48; *sp. gr.:* 8.6 at 20°C. —**cad′mic,** *adj.*

ca·dre (kad′rē, kä′drā), *n*. **1.** the key group of officers and enlisted personnel necessary to establish and train a new military unit. **2.** any core group qualified to form, train, and lead an expanded organization or work force. **3.** a cell of trained workers in a Communist Party. **4.** a member of a cadre. **5.** a framework or scheme.

ca·du·ce·us (kə doo′sē əs, -syoos, -shəs, -dyoo′-), *n., pl.* **-ce·i** (-sē ī′). **1.** the winged staff carried by Mercury as messenger of the gods. **2.** a representation of this staff used as a symbol of the medical profession. —**ca·du′ce·an,** *adj.*

caduceus (def. 2)

ca·du·ci·ty (kə doo′si tē, -dyoo′-), *n*. **1.** senility. **2.** transitoriness; fleetingness: *the caducity of life.*

cae·cil·i·an (sē sil′ē ən), *n*. a wormlike, burrowing tropical amphibian of the order Gymnophiona.

cae·cum (sē′kəm), *n., pl.* **-ca** (-kə). CECUM.

Cae·sar (sē′zər), *n*. **1.** Gaius Julius, c100–44 B.C., Roman general, statesman, and historian. **2.** a title of the Roman emperors from Augustus to Hadrian, and later of the heirs presumptive. **3.** any emperor. **4.** any temporal ruler; civil authority. Matt. 22:21.

Caes·a·re·a (sē′zə rē′ə, ses′ə-, sez′ə-), *n*. an ancient seaport in NW Israel: Roman capital of Palestine.

Cae′sar sal′ad, *n*. a salad of romaine leaves tossed with olive oil, lemon juice, garlic, grated cheese, a raw or coddled egg, croutons, and often anchovies.

cae·si·um (sē′zē əm), *n*. CESIUM.

cae·su·ra (si zhoor′ə, -zoor′ə, siz yoor′ə), *n., pl.* **cae·su·ras** or **ce·su·ras, cae·su·rae** or **ce·su·rae** (si zhoor′ē, -zoor′ē, siz yoor′-ē). **1.** a break or pause in a line of verse, marked in scansion by a double vertical line. **2.** any pause or interruption. —**cae·su′ral, cae·su′ric,** *adj.*

ca·fé or **ca·fe** (ka fā′, kə-), *n., pl.* **-fés** or **-fes. 1.** a restaurant, often with an enclosed or outdoor section extending onto the sidewalk. **2.** a restaurant, usu. small and unpretentious. **3.** a barroom, cabaret, or nightclub. [< French: lit., coffee]

ca·fé au lait (kaf′ā ō lā′, ka fā′, kə-), *n*. **1.** hot coffee served with an equal amount of hot or scalded milk. **2.** a light brown color.

caf·e·te·ri·a (kaf′i tēr′ē ə), *n., pl.* **-ri·as. 1.** a restaurant in which patrons select food at a counter and carry it to tables. **2.** a lunchroom, as for employees or students.

caf·feine (ka fēn′, kaf′ēn), *n*. a white, crystalline, bitter alkaloid, $C_8H_{10}N_4O_2$, usu. derived from coffee or tea, used medicinally as a stimulant. —**caf·fein·at·ed** (-di nā′tid), *adj.*

caf·tan or **kaf·tan** (kaf′tan, kaf tan′), *n*. **1.** a long garment with long sleeves, sometimes sashed at the waist, worn in the Middle East. **2.** a long full robe worn for lounging, as beachwear, etc.

cage (kāj), *n., v.,* **caged, cag·ing.** —*n.* **1.** a boxlike enclosure with wires, bars, or the like, for confining birds or animals. **2.** a prison. **3.** a cagelike enclosure for a cashier or bank teller. **4.** an elevator car. **5.** a similar enclosure for raising and lowering workers in a mine shaft. **6.** any skeleton framework, esp. in construction. **7.** a movable mesh backstop used for baseball batting practice. **8.** a frame with a net attached to it, forming the goal in ice hockey and field hockey. —*v.t.* **9.** to put or confine in or as if in a cage.

cag·ey or **cag·y** (kā′jē), *adj.,* **cag·i·er, cag·i·est.** cautious, wary, or shrewd: *a cagey manner; a cagey reply.* —**cag′i·ly,** *adv.*

ca·hier (ka yā′, kä-; *Fr.* ka yā′), *n., pl.* **-hiers** (-yāz′; *Fr.* -yā′). **1.** a number of sheets of paper or leaves of a book placed together, as for binding. **2.** a report of the proceedings of any body.

Caho′kia Mounds′, *n.pl.* a group of very large prehistoric Indian earthworks in southwestern Illinois, consisting of mounds with flat tops that supported temples and other structures of mud and thatch.

ca·hoot (kə hōōt′), *n. Informal.* —**Idiom. in cahoots,** in partnership or conspiracy; in league: *in cahoots with the mob.*

ca·how (kə hou′), *n.* a rare petrel, *Pterodroma cahow,* of islets off Bermuda.

Cai·a·phas (kā′ə fəs, kī′-), *n.* a high priest of the Jews who presided over the assembly that condemned Jesus to death. Matt. 26.

cai·man or **cay·man** (kā′mən), *n., pl.* **-mans.** any of several tropical American crocodilians of the genus *Caiman* and allied genera.

cai′man liz′ard, a large South American lizard, *Dracaena guianensis,* resembling a crocodile.

Cain[1] (kān), *n.* **1.** the first son of Adam and Eve, who murdered his brother Abel. Gen. 4. —**Idiom. 2. raise Cain,** to behave boisterously or violently; make a disturbance. —**Cain·it′ic,** *adj.*

Cain,[2] James M., 1892–1977, U.S. novelist.

Cain·ite (kā′nīt), *n.* a member of a Gnostic sect that exalted Cain and regarded the God of the Old Testament as responsible for evil.

cairn (kârn) *n.* a heap of stones set up as a landmark, monument, etc. —**cairned,** *adj.*

cairn′ ter′rier, *n.* one of a Scottish breed of small, short-legged terriers with a broad head and a rough coat.

Cai·ro (kī′rō), *n.* the capital of Egypt, in the N part on the E bank of the Nile. 6,325,000.

cais·son (kā′son, -sən), *n.* **1.** any of various structures used as a protective environment for workers, esp. one consisting of a pressurized, watertight chamber for use in underwater construction. **2. a.** a float for raising a sunken vessel. **b.** a watertight structure built against a damaged hull to render it watertight. **3.** a two-wheeled wagon, used for carrying artillery ammunition. **4.** an ammunition chest. **5.** COFFER (def. 4). —**cais′soned,** *adj.*

ca·jole (kə jōl′), *v.t., v.i.,* **-joled, -jol·ing.** to persuade by flattery or promises; wheedle; coax. —**ca·jole′ment,** *n.* —**ca·jol′er,** *n.* —**ca·jol′er·y,** *n.* —**ca·jol′ing·ly,** *adv.*

Ca·jun (kā′jən), *n.* **1.** a member of the traditionally Roman Catholic, French-speaking population of rural S Louisiana, descended largely from French colonists expelled from Acadia in 1755–63. **2.** the form of French spoken by the Cajuns.

cake (kāk), *n., v.,* **caked, cak·ing.** —*n.* **1.** a sweet, baked, breadlike food, usu. containing flour, sugar, eggs, and flavoring and often shortening and baking powder or soda. **2.** a flat, thin mass of bread, esp. unleavened bread. **3.** a pancake; griddlecake. **4.** a shaped or molded mass of other food: *a fish cake.* **5.** a shaped or compressed mass: *a cake of soap.* —*v.t., v.i.* **6.** to form into a crust or compact mass. —**Idiom. 7. piece of cake,** something that can be done easily, often with enjoyment. **8. take the cake,** to be extraordinary or unusual; win the hypothetical prize (often used sarcastically).

cake·walk (kāk′wôk′), *n.* **1.** a musical promenade of black American origin with the prize of a cake awarded to couples who demonstrated the most intricate or imaginative dance figures and steps. **2.** a dance with a strutting step based on this promenade. **3.** syncopated music suitable for a cakewalk. **4.** *Informal.* something easy or certain. —*v.i.* **5.** to perform a cakewalk.

Cal, kilocalorie.

Cal′abar bean′, *n.* the poisonous seed of an African climbing plant, *Physostigma venenosum,* of the legume family, the active principle of which is physostigmine.

cal·a·bash (kal′ə bash′), *n.* **1.** any of various gourds, esp. the bottle gourd, *Lagenaria siceraria.* **2.** a tropical American tree, *Crescentia cujete,* bearing large, gourdlike fruit. **3.** the fruit of any of these plants. **4.** the dried, hollowed-out shell of any of these fruits, used as a container or utensil.

ca·la·di·um (kə lā′dē əm), *n.* any of several tropical American plants of the genus *Caladium,* of the arum family, cultivated for their variegated, colorful leaves.

Cal·ais (kal′ā, ka lā′, kal′is), *n.* a seaport in N France, on the Strait of Dover: the French port nearest England. 76,935.

cal·a·man·der (kal′ə man′dər), *n.* the hard, mottled brown and black wood of any of several ebony trees of the genus *Diospyros,* used for cabinetry.

cal·a·mar·i (kal′ə mär′ē, kä′lə-), *n.* squid, esp. in Italian cooking.

cal·a·mar·y (kal′ə mer′ē, -mə rē) also **cal·a·mar** (-ə mär′), *n., pl.* **-mar·ies** also **-mars.** a squid, esp. of the genus *Loligo.*

cal·a·mine (kal′ə mīn′, -min), *n.* a pink, water-insoluble powder consisting of zinc oxide and about 0.5 percent ferric oxide, used in ointments, lotions, or the like, for the treatment of skin eruptions.

cal·a·mint (kal′ə mint′), *n.* any of several aromatic plants of the genera *Calamintha* and *Satureja,* of the mint family, having drooping flower clusters.

cal·a·mite (kal′ə mīt′), *n.* any fossil plant of the genus *Calamites* and related genera of the Carboniferous Period, resembling oversized horsetails and constituting much of the coal used as fuel. —**cal′a·mi′te·an,** *adj.* —**ca·lam·i·toid** (kə lam′i toid′), *adj.*

ca·lam·i·tous (kə lam′i təs), *adj.* causing or involving calamity; disastrous. —**ca·lam′i·tous·ly,** *adv.* —**ca·lam′i·tous·ness,** *n.*

ca·lam·i·ty (kə lam′i tē), *n., pl.* **-ties. 1.** a great misfortune or disaster; catastrophe. **2.** grievous affliction; misery.

Calam′ity Jane′, *n.* (Martha Jane Canary Burke) 1852?–1903, U.S. frontier markswoman.

cal·a·mon·din (kal′ə mun′dən), *n.* **1.** a small citrus tree, *Citrofortunella mitis,* of the Philippines. **2.** the small, tart fruit of this tree.

cal·a·mus (kal′ə məs), *n., pl.* **-mi** (-mī′). **1.** the sweet flag, *Acorus calamus.* **2.** its aromatic root. **3.** any of various tropical Asian palms of the genus *Calamus,* some of which are a source of rattan. **4.** the hollow base of a feather; a quill.

ca·lash (kə lash′), *n.* **1.** Also, **calèche.** a light two- or four-wheeled vehicle pulled by one or two horses, seating two to four passengers, and often having a folding top. **2.** a folding top of a carriage. **3.** a bonnet that folds back like the top of a calash, worn by women in the 18th century.

calc (kalk), *n. Informal.* **1.** a calculator, esp. a small portable one. **2.** calculus (def. 1).

cal·ca·ne·us (kal kā′nē əs), *n., pl.* **-ne·i** (-nē ī′). the largest tarsal bone, forming the prominence of the heel. —**cal·ca′ne·al, cal·ca′ne·an,** *adj.*

cal·car·e·ous (kal kâr′ē əs), *adj.* of, containing, or like calcium carbonate; chalky: *calcareous earth.* —**cal·car′e·ous·ly,** *adv.*

cal·ce·o·lar·i·a (kal′sē ə lâr′ē ə), *n., pl.* **-lar·i·as.** any of numerous plants of the genus *Calceolaria,* figwort family, many species of which are cultivated for their slipperlike flowers.

cal·ces (kal′sēz), *n.* a pl. of CALX.

calci-, a combining form meaning "calcium," "calcium salt," "calcite": *calciferous.* Also, *esp. before a vowel,* **calc-.**

cal·cic (kal′sik), *adj.* of or containing lime or calcium.

cal·cif·er·ol (kal sif′ə rôl′, -rol′), *n.* a fat-soluble, crystalline, unsaturated alcohol, $C_{28}H_{43}OH$, occurring in milk, fish-liver oils, etc., and used as a dietary supplement. Also called **vitamin D₂.**

cal·cif·er·ous (kal sif′ər əs), *adj.* **1.** forming salts of calcium, esp. calcium carbonate. **2.** containing calcium carbonate.

cal·ci·fi·ca·tion (kal′sə fi kā′shən), *n.* **1.** a changing into lime. **2.** the deposition of lime or insoluble salts of calcium and magnesium, as in a tissue. **3.** *Anat., Geol.* a calcified formation. **4.** a soil process in which the surface soil is supplied with calcium in such a way that the soil colloids are always close to saturation. **5.** a hardening or solidifying; rigidity.

cal·ci·fy (kal′sə fī′), *v.t., v.i.,* **-fied, -fy·ing. 1.** to make or become calcareous or bony; harden by the deposit of calcium salts. **2.** to make or become rigid or inflexible, as in an intellectual position.

cal·cite (kal′sīt), *n.* a common mineral, calcium carbonate, $CaCO_3$, found in a great variety of crystalline forms: a major constituent of limestone, marble, and chalk. —**cal·cit′ic** (-sit′ik), *adj.*

cal·cit·ri·ol (kal si′trē ôl′, -ol′), *n.* **1.** a vitamin D compound derived from cholesterol, involved in the regulating and absorption of calcium. **2.** a preparation of this compound, used in the treatment of osteoporosis and bone fracture.

cal·ci·um (kal′sē əm), *n.* a silver-white divalent metal, combined in limestone, chalk, etc., occurring also in animals in bone, shell, etc. *Symbol:* Ca; *at. wt.:* 40.08; *at. no.:* 20; *sp. gr.:* 1.55 at 20°C.

cal′cium car′bonate, *n.* a white powder, $CaCO_3$, occurring in nature as calcite, chalk, etc., used in dentifrices and polishes and in manufacturing lime and cement.

cal′cium chlo′ride, *n.* a deliquescent crystalline compound, $CaCl_2$, used as a drying agent and preservative.

cal′cium fluor′ide, *n.* a white, crystalline compound, CaF_2, used as a decay preventive in dentifrices.

cal′cium hydrox′ide, *n.* a white powder, $Ca(OH)_2$, used in mortar, plaster, and cement.

cal·cu·la·ble (kal′kyə bəl), *adj.* **1.** determinable by calculation; ascertainable. **2.** able to be counted on; reliable.

cal·cu·late (kal′kyə lāt′), *v.,* **-lat·ed, -lat·ing.** —*v.t.* **1.** to determine or ascertain by mathematical methods; compute: *to calculate the velocity of light.* **2.** to determine by reasoning or practical experience; estimate; gauge. **3.** to make suitable or fit for a purpose; adapt: *The remarks were calculated to inspire confidence.* **4.** *Chiefly Northern U.S.* to think; guess. **b.** to intend; plan. —*v.i.* **5.** to make a calculation. **6.** to count or rely (usu. fol. by *on* or *upon*).

cal·cu·lat·ed (kal′kyə lā′tid), *adj.* **1.** arrived at by mathematical calculation. **2.** carefully thought out or planned. **3.** deliberate; intentional. —**cal′cu·lat′ed·ly,** *adv.*

cal′culated risk′, *n.* a chance of failure, the probability of which is estimated before some action is undertaken.

cal·cu·lat·ing (kal′kyə lā′ting), *adj.* **1.** capable of performing arithmetic calculations. **2.** shrewd or cautious. **3.** selfishly scheming. —**cal′cu·lat′ing·ly,** *adv.*

cal·cu·la·tion (kal′kyə lā′shən), *n.* **1.** the act or process of calculating; computation. **2.** the result or product of calculating. **3.** an estimate based on the known facts; forecast. **4.** forethought; prior or careful planning. **5.** scheming selfishness. —**cal′cu·la·tive** (-lā′tiv, -lə tiv), **cal′cu·la·to′ry** (-lə tôr′ē, -tōr′ē), *adj.*

cal·cu·la·tor (kal′kyə lā′tər), *n.* **1.** a small, hand-operated electronic or mechanical device that performs calculations. **2.** a set of tables that facilitate calculation. **3.** a person who calculates or computes.

cal·cu·lous (kal′kyə ləs), *adj.* characterized by the presence of calculus, or stone.

cal·cu·lus (kal′kyə ləs), *n., pl.* **-li** (-lī′), **-lus·es. 1.** a method of calculation, esp. one of several highly systematic methods of treating problems by a special system of algebraic notations, as differential or integral calculus. **2.** a stone, or concretion, formed in the gallbladder, kidney, or other part of the body. **3.** a hard, yellowish to brownish black deposit on teeth formed largely through the calcification of dental plaque; tartar. [< Latin: pebble, small stone (used in calculating)]

Cal·cut·ta (kal kut′ə), *n.* the capital of West Bengal state, in E India, on the Hooghly River: former capital of British India. 9,166,000.

Cal·der (kôl′dər), *n.* **Alexander,** 1898–1976, U.S. sculptor; originator of mobiles.

cal·de·ra (kal der′ə, kôl-), *n., pl.* **-ras.** a large, basinlike depression resulting from the explosion or collapse of the center of a volcano.

Ca·leb (kā′ləb), *n.* a Hebrew leader, sent as a spy into the land of Canaan. Num. 13:6.

cal·e·fac·tion (kal′ə fak′shən), *n.* **1.** the act of heating. **2.** a heated state. —**cal′e·fac′tive,** *adj.*

cal·en·dar (kal′ən dər), *n.* **1.** a table or register with the days of each month and week in a year. **2.** any of various systems of reckoning time, esp. with reference to the beginning, length, and divisions of the year. **3.** a list or register, esp. one arranged chronologically. —*v.t.* **4.** to enter in a calendar; register.

cal′endar day′, *n.* the period from one midnight to the following midnight.

cal·en·der (kal′ən dər), *n.* **1.** a machine in which cloth, paper, or the like is smoothed, glazed, etc., by pressing between rotating cylinders. **2.** a machine for impregnating fabric with rubber. —*v.t.* **3.** to press in a calender.

cal·ends or **kal·ends** (kal′əndz), *n.* (*often cap.*) (*usu. with a pl. v.*) the first day of the month in the ancient Roman calendar.

ca·len·du·la (kə len′jə lə), *n., pl.* **-las. 1.** a composite plant, *Calendula officinalis,* with many-rayed orange or yellow flowers. **2.** the dried florets of this plant, sometimes used medicinally. **3.** any other plant of the genus *Calendula.*

calf¹ (kaf, käf), *n., pl.* **calves** (kavz, kävz). **1.** the young of the domestic cow or other bovine animal. **2.** the young of certain other mammals, as the elephant, seal, and whale. **3.** calfskin leather. **4.** a mass of ice detached from a glacier, iceberg, or floe. —*Idiom.* **5. kill the fatted calf,** to prepare an elaborate feast in welcome.

calf² (kaf, käf), *n., pl.* **calves** (kavz, kävz). the fleshy part of the back of the human leg below the knee.

calf·skin (kaf′skin′, käf′-), *n.* **1.** the skin or hide of a calf. **2.** leather made from this skin.

Cal·ga·ry (kal′gə rē), *n.* a city in S Alberta, in SW Canada. 636,104.

Cal·houn (kal hōōn′, kəl-), *n.* **John Caldwell,** 1782–1850, vice president of the U.S. 1825–32.

cal·i·ber (kal′ə bər), *n.* **1.** the diameter of a circular section, esp. the inside of a tube. **2.** the diameter of the bore of a gun taken as a unit of measurement. **3.** degree of capacity or competence; ability. Also, *esp. Brit.,* **cal′i·bre.**

cal·i·brate (kal′ə brāt′), *v.t.,* **-brat·ed, -brat·ing. 1. a.** to set or check the graduation of (a quantitative measuring instrument). **b.** to mark (a thermometer or other instrument) with indexes of degree or quantity. **2.** to determine the correct range for (a gun, mortar, etc.) by observing where the fired projectile hits. —**cal′i·bra′tion,** *n.* —**cal′i·bra′tor, cal′i·brat′er,** *n.*

cal·i·ces (kal′ə sēz′), *n.* pl. of CALIX.

ca·li·che (kə lē′chē), *n.* **1.** a surface deposit of sodium nitrate found in South American desert areas: formerly a major source of chemical fertilizer. **2.** a zone of calcium carbonate or other carbonates in soils of semiarid regions.

cal·i·co (kal′i kō′), *n., pl.* **-coes, -cos,** *adj.* —*n.* **1.** a plain-woven cotton cloth printed with a figured pattern, usu. on one side. **2.** an animal having a spotted or particolored coat. —*adj.* **3.** made of calico. **4.** mottled

or variegated in color. **5.** (of a domestic cat) having a variegated white, black, red, and cream coat.

Cal·i·for·nia (kal′ə fôrn′yə, -fôr′nē ə), *n.* **1.** a state in the W United States, on the Pacific coast. 31,878,234; 158,693 sq. mi. (411,015 sq. km). *Cap.:* Sacramento. *Abbr.:* CA, Cal., Calif. **2. Gulf of,** an arm of the Pacific Ocean, extending NW between the coast of W Mexico and the peninsula of Baja California. ab. 750 mi. (1207 km) long; 62,600 sq. mi. (162,100 sq. km). —**Cal′i·for′nian,** *adj., n.*

Cal′ifor′nia con′dor, *n.* See under CONDOR (def. 1).

Cal′ifor′nia lau′rel, *n.* a tree, *Umbellularia californica,* of the laurel family, native to the W coast of the U.S., having aromatic leaves, umbels of yellowish green flowers, and hard wood.

Califor′nia live′ oak′, *n.* an evergreen oak, *Quercus agrifolia,* of the W coast of the U.S., having leathery leaves and a short, stout trunk.

Cal′ifor′nia pop′py, *n.* a poppy, *Eschscholzia californica,* having feathery bluish foliage and orange-yellow flowers.

cal·i·for·ni·um (kal′ə fôr′nē əm), *n.* a transuranic element. *Symbol:* Cf; *at. no.:* 98.

Ca·lig·u·la (kə lig′yə lə), *n.* (*Gaius Caesar*), A.D. 12–41, emperor of Rome 37–41.

cal·i·per or **cal·li·per** (kal′ə pər), *n.* **1.** Usu., **calipers.** an instrument for measuring thicknesses and diameters, consisting usu. of a pair of adjustable pivoted legs. **2.** a calibrated instrument for measuring thickness or distances between surfaces, usu. having a screwed or sliding adjustable piece. **3.** thickness or depth, as of paper or a tree. **4.** the part of a disc-brake assembly that presses the brake pads against the disc. —*v.t.* **5.** to measure with calipers.

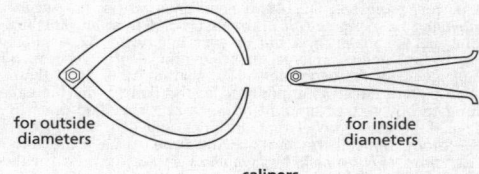

for outside
diameters

for inside
diameters

calipers

ca·liph (kā′lif, kal′if), *n.* **1.** a spiritual leader of Islam, claiming succession from Muhammad. **2.** any of the former Muslim rulers of Baghdad (until 1258) and of the Ottoman Empire (from 1571 until 1924). Also, **calif, kalif, kaliph, khalif.** [< Arabic *khalīf(a)* successor (of Muhammad)] —**cal·iph·al** (kal′ə fal, kā′lə-), *adj.*

cal·is·then·ics or **cal·lis·then·ics** (kal′əs then′iks), *n.* **1.** (*used with a pl. v.*) gymnastic exercises designed to develop physical health and vigor. **2.** (*used with a sing. v.*) the art, practice, or a session of such exercises. —**cal′is·then′ic, cal′is·then′i·cal,** *adj.*

ca·lix (kā′liks, kal′iks), *n., pl.* **cal·i·ces** (kal′i sēz′). a cup or chalice.

call (kôl), *v.t.* **1.** to cry out in a loud voice: *to call someone's name.* **2.** to summon or invite to come: *to call a witness; to call the family to dinner.* **3.** to communicate or try to communicate with by telephone. **4.** to rouse from sleep, as by a call; waken. **5.** to read over (a roll or a list) in a loud voice. **6.** to convoke; convene: *to call a meeting.* **7.** to announce authoritatively; proclaim: *to call a strike.* **8.** to schedule: *to call a rehearsal.* **9.** to summon by or as if by divine command: *felt called to the ministry.* **10.** to summon to an office, duty, etc.: *He was called to the army.* **11.** to cause to come; bring: *to call a forgotten episode to mind.* **12.** to bring under consideration or discussion: *The judge called the case.* **13.** to attract or lure (birds or animals) by imitating characteristic sounds. **14.** to direct or attract (attention). **15.** to name or address (someone) as. **16.** to designate as something specified: *She called me a liar.* **17.** to think of as something specified; consider: *I call that a mean remark.* **18.** to demand of (someone) fulfillment of a promise, evidence for a statement, etc.: *They called him on his story.* **19.** to criticize; censure: *She called them on their vulgar language.* **20.** to demand payment or fulfillment of (a loan). **21.** to forecast correctly. **22.** (of a sports official) **a.** to pronounce a judgment on (a shot, pitch, batter, etc.). **b.** to

---

MONTHS OF PRINCIPAL CALENDARS

GREGORIAN				JEWISH				ISLAMIC			
Month	Number of Days	Month	Number of Days	Month	Number of Days	Month	Number of Days	Month	Number of Days	Month	Number of Days
January	31	July	31	Tishri[1]	30	Adar[2]	29	Moharram	30	Shaban	29
February	28	August	31	Heshvan	29	(in leap years:	30)	Safar	29	Ramadan	30
(in leap years:	29)	September	30	(in some years:	30)	Nisan[3]	30	Rabi I	30	Shawwal	29
March	31	October	31	Kislev	29	Iyar	29	Rabi II	29	Dhu 'l-Qa'da	30
April	30	November	30	(in some years:	30)	Sivan	30	Jumada I	30	Dhu 'l-hijjah	29
May	31	December	31	Tevet	29	Tammuz	29	Jumada II	29	(in leap years:	30)
June	30			Shevat	30	Av	30	Rajab	30		
						Elul	29				

[1]The beginning of the civil year, corresponding to September—October.
[2]In leap years Adar is followed by the intercalary month of Veadar or Adar Sheni, having 29 days.
[3]The beginning of the ecclesiastical year, corresponding to March—April.

put an end to (a contest) because of inclement weather, poor field conditions, etc. **23. a.** to equal (a bet) or equal the bet made by (the preceding bettor) in a round of poker. **b.** to signal one's partner in bridge for a lead of (a certain card or suit). —*v.i.* **24.** to speak loudly, as to attract attention: *She called to the children.* **25.** to make a short visit. **26.** to telephone or try to telephone a person. **27. a.** to equal a bet in poker. **b.** to bid or pass in bridge. **28.** (of a bird or animal) to utter its characteristic cry. **29. call back, a.** to request or demand to return; recall. **b.** to return the telephone call of. **30. call down, a.** to request or pray for; invoke: *to call down the wrath of God.* **b.** to reprimand; scold. **31. call for, a.** to go or come to get; pick up; fetch. **b.** to request; summon. **c.** to require; demand; need. **32. call forth,** to summon into action; bring into existence. **33. call in, a.** to request payment for. **b.** to withdraw from circulation: *to call in gold certificates.* **c.** to appeal to for consultation; ask for help from. **34. call off, a.** to summon or take away: *Please call off your dog.* **b.** to cancel (something planned). **35. call on** or **upon, a.** to ask; appeal to. **b.** to visit for a short time. **36. call out, a.** to speak in a loud voice; shout. **b.** to summon into service or action: *Call out the militia!* **37. call up, a.** to bring forward or make available for consideration or action. **b.** to cause to remember; evoke. **c.** to make a telephone call to. **d.** to summon for action, esp. military service. —*n.* **38.** a cry or shout. **39.** the vocal sound of a bird or other animal. **40.** an instrument for imitating this sound and luring an animal. **41.** an act or instance of telephoning. **42.** a short visit. **43.** a summons or signal sounded by a bugle, bell, etc. **44.** a summons, invitation, or bidding. **45.** ROLL CALL. **46.** fascination or appeal: *the call of the sea.* **47.** a mystic experience of divine appointment to a vocation or service: *a call to the ministry.* **48.** an invitation to accept a job as pastor, professor, etc. **49.** a need or occasion: *no call for panic.* **50.** a demand or claim: *a call on one's time.* **51. a.** an equaling of the preceding bet in poker. **b.** a bid or pass in bridge. **52.** a judgment or decision by an umpire, referee, or other official of a contest. **53. a.** a notice of rehearsal for performance. **b.** CURTAIN CALL. **54.** a figure or direction in square dancing, announced to the dancers by the caller. **55.** an option to buy a fixed amount of stock at a specified price by a certain date: done in the belief that the price will rise. Compare PUT (def. 37). —*Idiom.* **56. call the shots** or **the tune,** to have the authority to make decisions. **57. on call, a.** payable or subject to return without notice. **b.** readily available for summoning upon short notice. **58. within call,** close enough to be spoken to or summoned.

cal•la (kal′ə), *n., pl.* **-las. 1.** Also called **cal′la lil′y.** any of several plants belonging to the genus *Zantedeschia,* of the arum family, esp. *Z. aethiopica,* having arrow-shaped leaves and a large white spathe enclosing a yellow spike. **2.** a related plant, *Calla palustris,* of cold marshes of Europe and North America, having heart-shaped leaves.

call•a•ble (kô′lə bəl), *adj.* **1.** capable of being called. **2.** subject to redemption prior to maturity, as a corporate bond. **3.** subject to payment on demand.

call′back′ or **call′-back′,** *n.* **1.** an act of calling back. **2.** a summoning of workers back to work after a layoff. **3.** a request to a performer to return for further auditioning. **4.** a return telephone call. —*adj.* **5.** of or pertaining to such a call.

call′ box′, *n.* **1.** an outdoor telephone or signal box for summoning aid. **2.** *Brit.* TELEPHONE BOOTH.

call•boy (kôl′boi′), *n.* **1.** a boy or man who summons performers to go on stage as needed. **2.** a bellhop.

call•er (kô′lər), *n.* **1.** a person who makes a short visit. **2.** a person who gives the calls at a square dance.

caller ID, *n.* a telephone service that allows a subscriber to identify a caller before answering by displaying the caller's telephone number on a small screen.

call′ for′warding, *n.* a telephone service that allows a customer to have calls automatically rerouted to another designated number.

calli-, a combining form meaning "beautiful": *calligraphy.*

cal•lig•ra•phy (kə lig′rə fē), *n.* **1.** fancy penmanship or the art of writing beautifully. **2.** handwriting; penmanship. **3.** a script produced chiefly by brush, esp. Chinese, Japanese, or Arabic writing of high aesthetic value. —**cal•lig′ra•pher, cal•lig′ra•phist,** *n.* —**cal•li•graph•ic** (kal′i graf′ik), *adj.*

call•ing (kô′ling), *n.* **1.** a vocation, profession, or trade. **2.** a divine call or summons: *a calling to the priesthood.* **3.** a strong impulse or inclination: *an inner calling.*

call′ing card′, *n.* **1.** a small card with a person's name and often address presented on a social visit. **2.** any trace or characteristic by which someone or something can be recognized.

cal•li•o•pe (kə lī′ə pē), *n.* a musical instrument consisting of a set of harsh-sounding steam whistles that are activated by a keyboard.

cal•li•op•sis (kal′ē op′sis), *n., pl.* **-op•sis.** any of several species of coreopsis, esp. *Coreopsis tinctoria.*

call′ let′ters, *n.pl.* letters of the alphabet or letters and numbers used esp. for identifying a radio or television station.

call′ num′ber, *n.* a number, letter, symbol, or combination of these, indicating the specific location of a work in a library.

Call′ of the Wild′, The, a novel (1903) by Jack London.

cal•los•i•ty (kə los′i tē), *n., pl.* **-ties. 1.** a callous condition. **2.** a hardened or thickened part of a plant. **3.** CALLUS (def. 1a).

cal•lous (kal′əs), *adj.* **1.** made hard; hardened. **2.** insensitive; indifferent; unsympathetic. **3.** having a callus; indurated, as parts of the skin

exposed to friction. —*v.t., v.i.* **4.** to make or become hard or callous. —**cal′lous•ly,** *adv.* —**cal′lous•ness,** *n.*

cal•low (kal′ō), *adj.* **1.** immature or inexperienced: *a callow youth.* **2.** (of a young bird) featherless; unfledged. —**cal′low•ness,** *n.*

cal•lus (kal′əs), *n., pl.* **-lus•es,** *v.,* **-lused, -lus•ing.** —*n.* **1. a.** a hardened or thickened part of the skin; callosity. **b.** a new growth of osseous matter at the ends of a fractured bone, serving to unite them. **2.** the tissue that forms over the wounds of plants, protecting the inner tissues and causing healing. —*v.i.* **3.** to form a callus. —*v.t.* **4.** to produce a callus or calluses on.

call′ wait′ing, *n.* a telephone service whereby a person engaged in a phone call is notified by a tone that a second call is being made to the same number.

calm (käm; *older* kam; *spelling pron.* kälm), *adj.* **1.** without rough motion; still or nearly still: *a calm sea.* **2.** not windy: *a calm day.* **3.** free from excitement or passion; tranquil: *a calm manner.* —*n.* **4.** freedom from motion or disturbance; stillness. **5.** wind speed of less than 1 mph (0.447 m/sec). **6.** freedom from agitation or excitement; tranquillity. —*v.t.* **7.** to make calm. —*v.i.* **8.** to become calm (usu. fol. by *down*). —*Idiom.* **9. calm before the storm,** a period of deceptive tranquillity before an anticipated crisis. —**calm′ing•ly,** *adv.* —**calm′ly,** *adv.* —**calm′ness,** *n.*

ca•lor•ic (kə lôr′ik, -lor′-), *adj.* **1.** of or pertaining to calories. **2.** of or pertaining to heat. **3.** high in calories: *a caloric meal.* —*n.* **4.** heat. **5.** a hypothetical fluid whose presence in matter was once thought to determine its thermal state. —**ca•lor′i•cal•ly,** *adv.* —**ca•lo•ric•i•ty** (kal′ə ris′i tē), *n.*

cal•o•rie or **cal•o•ry** (kal′ə rē), *n., pl.* **-ries. 1. a.** Also called **gram calorie, small calorie.** an amount of heat exactly equal to 4.1840 joules. *Abbr.:* cal **b.** (*usu. cap.*) KILOCALORIE. *Abbr.:* Cal **2. a.** a unit equal to the kilocalorie, used to express the heat output of an organism and the energy value of food. **b.** a quantity of food capable of producing such an amount of energy.

cal•o•rif•ic (kal′ə rif′ik), *adj.* pertaining to conversion into heat. —**cal′o•rif′i•cal•ly,** *adv.*

cal•o•rim•e•ter (kal′ə rim′i tər), *n.* an apparatus for measuring quantities of heat.

CALS (kalz), *n.* a set of standards mandated by the U.S. Department of Defense for technical documentation in electronic form, including SGML markup of the document structure.

cal•trop or **cal•trap** (kal′trəp), also **cal•throp** (-thrəp), *n.* **1.** any of several plants having spiny heads or fruit, as those of the genera *Tribulus* and *Kallstroemeria.* **2.** an iron ball with four projecting spikes, one of which always points upward when the ball is placed on the ground: used to obstruct cavalry, vehicles, etc.

cal•u•met (kal′yə met′, kal′yə met′), *n.* a long, ornamented tobacco pipe used ceremonially by North American Indians.

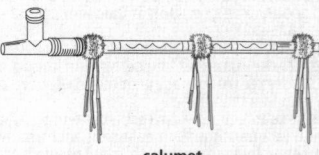

calumet

ca•lum•ni•ate (kə lum′nē āt′), *v.t.,* **-at•ed, -at•ing.** to make false and malicious statements about; slander. —**ca•lum′ni•a′tion,** *n.* —**ca•lum′ni•a′tor,** *n.*

cal•um•ny (kal′əm nē), *n., pl.* **-nies. 1.** a false and malicious statement designed to injure a reputation. **2.** slander; defamation.

Cal•va•ry (kal′və rē), *n., pl.* **-ries. 1.** the place where Jesus was crucified, near Jerusalem. Luke 23:33, Matt. 27:33. **2.** (*often l.c.*) a representation of the Crucifixion. **3.** (*l.c.*) an experience of extreme suffering. [< Late Latin *Calvāria;* Latin: skull, trans. of Greek *kraníon,* itself a trans. of the Aramaic name; see GOLGOTHA] —**Pronunciation.** See IRRELEVANT.

calve (kav, käv), *v.,* **calved, calv•ing.** —*v.i.* **1.** to give birth to a calf. **2.** (of a glacier, an iceberg, etc.) to break up so as to produce a detached piece. —*v.t.* **3.** to give birth to (a calf). **4.** (of a glacier, an iceberg, etc.) to produce (a detached piece) by calving.

Cal•vert (kal′vərt), *n.* **1. Sir George** (*1st Baron Baltimore*), c1580–1632, British founder of the colony of Maryland. **2.** his son, **Leonard,** 1606–47, first colonial governor of Maryland 1634–47.

calves (kavz, kävz), *n.* pl. of CALF.

Cal•vin (kal′vin), *n.* **1. John** (*Jean Chauvin* or *Caulvin*), 1509–64, French theologian and reformer in Switzerland: leader in the Protestant Reformation. **2. Melvin,** 1911–97, U.S. chemist.

Cal•vin•ism (kal′və niz′əm), *n.* **1.** the doctrines and teachings of John Calvin or his followers, emphasizing predestination, supreme authority of the Scriptures, and irresistibility of grace. **2.** adherence to these doctrines. —**Cal′vin•ist,** *n., adj.* —**Cal′vin•is′tic,** *adj.* —**Cal′vin•is′ti•cal•ly,** *adv.*

calx (kalks), *n., pl.* **calx•es, cal•ces** (kal′sēz). the oxide or ashy substance that remains after metals, minerals, etc., have been burned.

cal•y•ces (kal′ə sēz′, kā′lə-), *n.* a pl. of CALYX.

ca•lyx (kā′liks, kal′iks), *n., pl.* **ca•lyx•es, cal•y•ces** (kal′ə sēz′, kā′lə-). **1.** the outermost group of floral parts; the sepals collectively. **2.** *Anat., Zool.* a cuplike part. —**cal•y•cate** (kal′i kāt′), *adj.*

cal•zone (kal zō′nē, -nā, -zōn′), *n.* a turnover made of pizza dough filled with cheese, ham, etc., and baked or deep-fried.

cam (kam), *n.* a disk or cylinder having an irregular form such that its motion, usu. rotary, gives a rocking or reciprocating motion to any contiguous part.

ca•ma•ra•de•rie (kä′mə rä′də rē, -rad′ə-, kam′ə-), *n.* comradeship; good-fellowship.

cam•ass or **cam•as** (kam′əs), *n.* **1.** any of several plants of the genus *Camassia,* of the lily family, esp. *C. quamash,* of W North America, having long clusters of blue to white flowers and edible bulbs. **2.** DEATH CAMASS.

cam•ber (kam′bər), *v.t., v.i.* **1.** to arch slightly; curve upward in the middle. —*n.* **2.** a slight arching, upward curve, or convexity, as of the deck of a ship. **3.** a slightly arching piece of timber. **4.** the rise of the curve of an airfoil, usu. expressed as the ratio of the rise to the length of the chord of the airfoil. **5.** the tilt of an automotive wheel, measured as the angle between the vertical and a plane through the wheel's circumference.

cam•bi•um (kam′bē əm), *n., pl.* **-bi•ums, -bi•a** (-bē ə). a layer of meristematic plant tissue, between the inner bark and wood, that produces new bark and wood cells, causing the stem or trunk to grow in diameter and forming the annual ring in trees.

Cam•bo•di•a (kam bō′dē ə), *n.* **State of,** a republic in SE Asia: formerly part of French Indochina. 11,163,861; 69,866 sq. mi. (180,953 sq. km). *Cap.:* Phnom Penh. Formerly, **People's Republic of Kampuchea, Khmer Republic.** —**Cam•bo′di•an,** *adj., n.*

Cam•bri•a (kam′brē ə), *n.* medieval name of WALES.

Cam•bri•an (kam′brē ən), *adj.* **1.** noting or pertaining to a period of the Paleozoic Era, occurring from 570 million to 500 million years ago, when algae and marine invertebrates were the predominant form of life. **2.** of or pertaining to Cambria; Welsh. —*n.* **3.** the Cambrian Period or System. **4.** a native or inhabitant of Wales.

cam′bric tea′, *n.* a beverage of sweetened hot water and milk and often weak tea.

Cam•bridge (kām′brij), *n.* **1.** a city in Cambridgeshire, in E England: famous university founded in 12th century. 98,400. **2.** a city in E Massachusetts, near Boston. 90,290. **3.** CAMBRIDGESHIRE. **4.** a city in SE Ontario, in S Canada. 79,920.

Cam•bridge•shire (kām′brij shēr′, -shər), *n.* a county in E England. 642,400; 1316 sq. mi. (3410 sq. km). Also called **Cambridge.**

cam•cord•er (kam′kôr′dər), *n.* a lightweight hand-held television camera with an incorporated VCR.

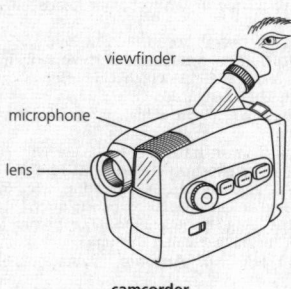

viewfinder

microphone

lens

camcorder

came (kām), *n.* a slender, grooved bar of lead for holding together the pieces of glass in windows of latticework or stained glass.

cam•el (kam′əl), *n.* **1.** either of two large, humped ruminants of the genus *Camelus,* of the Old World. Compare BACTRIAN CAMEL, DROMEDARY. **2.** a color ranging from yellowish tan to yellowish brown. **3.** a spin in skating done in an arabesque position. **4.** a float for increasing the buoyancy of a heavily laden vessel. —*Proverb.* **5. It is easier for a camel to go (or pass) through the eye of a needle than it is for a rich man to enter the kingdom of Heaven,** the rich will not have treasure in heaven unless they share their wealth with the poor. Matt. 19:24. —**cam′el•like′,** *adj.*

ca•mel•lia (kə mēl′yə, -mē′lē ə), *n., pl.* **-lias.** any of several shrubs of the genus *Camellia,* of the tea family, having glossy evergreen leaves and roselike flowers of white, pink, or red. [after G. J. *Camellus* (1661–1706), Jesuit missionary who brought it to Europe]

Cam•e•lot (kam′ə lot′), *n.* **1.** the legendary site of King Arthur's palace and court, possibly near Exeter, England. **2.** any idyllic place or period, esp. one of great happiness. **3.** the glamorous ambience of Washington, D.C., during the administration of President John F. Kennedy, 1961–63. **4.** (*italics*) a musical (1960) with lyrics by Alan Jay Lerner and music by Frederick Loewe. —**Cam′e•lot′i•an,** *adj.*

cam′el's hair′ or **camelhair,** *n.* **1.** the hair of the camel, used esp.

for cloth, painters' brushes, and Oriental rugs. **2.** a soft cloth made of this hair, or of a substitute. —**cam′el's-hair′,** *adj.*

Cam•em•bert (kam′əm bâr′), *n.* a soft cow's-milk cheese with a creamy golden center and a whitish rind. [after *Camembert,* France]

cam•e•o (kam′ē ō′), *n., pl.* **cam•e•os,** *adj.* —*n.* **1.** a gemstone or other hard substance, as coral, carved with a design in low relief, usu. so that an underlying darker layer of the material forms a background for the lighter tone of the design. **2.** a jewel with a central ornament having a head in profile set in relief. **3.** an effective literary sketch or small dramatic scene. **4.** Also called **cam′eo role′.** a small but notable part in a film, play, or television show, played esp. by a prominent performer, often in a single scene. —*adj.* **5.** of or pertaining to a cameo role: *a cameo appearance.*

cam•er•a (kam′ər ə, kam′rə), *n., pl.* **-er•as. 1.** a hand-held photographic device with an aperture controlled by a shutter that opens to admit light: focused by a lens, the light forms an image on a light-sensitive film or plate loaded through the back or top. **2.** (in a television transmitting apparatus) the device in which the picture to be televised is formed before it is changed into electric impulses. —*Idiom.* **3. in camera, a.** in the privacy of a judge's chambers. **b.** privately. **4. off camera,** out of the range of a television or motion-picture camera. **5. on camera,** being filmed or televised by a live camera.

cam•er•al (kam′ər əl, kam′rəl), *adj.* of or pertaining to a judicial or legislative chamber or to a chamber.

cam•er•a•man (kam′ər ə man′, -mən, kam′rə-), *n., pl.* **-men** (-men′, -mən). a person who operates a camera, esp. a motion-picture or television camera.

cam′era ob•scu′ra (ob skyŏor′ə), *n., pl.* **camera ob•scu•ras.** a darkened boxlike device in which images of external objects, received through an aperture, as with a convex lens, are exhibited in their natural colors on a surface.

cam′era-read′y, *adj.* (of text or illustrations) ready to be photographed.

Cam•e•roon (kam′ə rōōn′), *n.* **1.** a republic in W equatorial Africa: formed in 1960 by the French trusteeship of Cameroun; joined in 1961 by the S part of the British trusteeship of Cameroons. 14,677,510; 179,558 sq. mi. (465,054 sq. km). *Cap.:* Yaoundé. **2. Mount,** an active volcano in W Cameroon: highest peak on the coast of W Africa. 13,370 ft. (4075 m). —**Cam′e•roon′i•an,** *adj., n.*

cam•i•sole (kam′ə sōl′), *n.* **1.** a woman's waist-length garment with shoulder straps, worn underneath a sheer bodice to conceal the underwear. **2.** a woman's negligee jacket.

cam•o (kam′ō), *adj., n., pl.* **cam•os.** —*adj.* **1.** having a usu. green and brown mottled design, like that of military camouflage: *a camo fabric.* —*n.* **2.** a camo pattern, cloth, or garment.

Cam•o•ëns (kam′ō ens′) also **Ca•mões** (kə moinsh′), *n.* **Luis Vaz de** (väzh), 1524?–80, Portuguese poet.

cam•o•mile (kam′ə mīl′), *n.* CHAMOMILE.

cam•ou•flage (kam′ə fläzh′), *n., v.,* **-flaged, -flag•ing.** —*n.* **1. a.** the act or technique of disguising elements of a military installation so as not to be detectable. **b.** the constructing of decoy objects that from a distance give the appearance of a military installation. **2.** concealment by some means that alters or obscures the appearance. **3.** a device or stratagem used for concealment. **4.** clothing made of fabric with a mottled design, usu. green and brown, like that of military camouflage materials. —*v.t.* **5.** to disguise, hide, or deceive by means of camouflage. —*v.i.* **6.** to use camouflage.

camp¹ (kamp), *n.* **1. a.** a place where an army or other group of persons is lodged in tents or other temporary shelters. **b.** such tents or shelters collectively. **c.** the persons so sheltered. **2.** any temporary structure, as a tent or cabin, used on an outing or vacation. **3.** a group of troops, workers, etc., camping and moving together. **4.** army life. **5. a.** a group of people favoring the same ideals, doctrines, etc. **b.** the position held by such a group. **6. a.** a recreation area in the country, equipped with extensive facilities for sports. **b.** SUMMER CAMP. —*v.i.* **7.** to establish or pitch a camp. **8.** to live temporarily in or as if in a camp: *They camped out by the stream.* **9.** to reside or lodge somewhere indoors temporarily or irregularly. **10.** to become ensconced. —*v.t.* **11.** to put or station (troops) in a camp; shelter. [< Latin *campus* field]

camp² (kamp), *n.* **1.** something that provides amusement by virtue of its being contrived, overdone, or tasteless. **2.** a person who adopts a teasing, theatrical manner. **3.** Also, **camp it up.** to speak or behave in a coquettishly playful or extravagantly theatrical manner. —*adj.* **4.** campy: *camp musicals of the 1930s.*

cam•paign (kam pān′), *n.* **1.** a series of military operations for a specific objective. **2.** a systematic course of aggressive activities for some specific purpose: *a sales campaign; a campaign for mayor.* —*v.i.* **3.** to serve in or go on a campaign. —*adj.* **4.** of or designating furniture characterized as having metal strips on the corners and handles on the sides: *a campaign chest.* —**cam•paign′er,** *n.*

campaign′ but′ton, *n.* a disk-shaped pin worn by a supporter of a political candidate, usually bearing the name of the candidate and often a slogan or the candidate's picture.

campaign′ chest′, *n.* **1.** money collected and set aside for use in a campaign, esp. a political one; a campaign fund. **2.** a low chest of drawers having handles at each side for lifting.

campaign′ fund′, *n.* money for a campaign, as of a political candidate, usually acquired through contributions by supporters.

campaign′ hat′, *n.* **1.** a felt hat with a broad, stiff brim and four dents in the crown, formerly worn by personnel in the U.S. Army and Marine Corps. **2.** a hat resembling this, worn as part of a uniform by forest rangers, state troopers, boy scouts, and other groups.

campaign′ train′, *n.* a train that carries a candidate, advisers, supporters, and the press to meet voters during a political campaign.

cam•pa•ni•le (kam′pə nē′lē, -lā, -nēl′), *n., pl.* **-ni•les, -ni•li** (-nē′lē). a bell tower, esp. one freestanding from a church.

cam•pa•nol•o•gy (kam′pə nol′ə jē), *n.* the art of bell ringing. **—cam′-pa•nol′o•gist,** *n.*

cam•pan•u•la (kam pan′yə lə), *n., pl.* **-las.** any of numerous plants of the genus *Campanula,* of the bellflower family.

cam•pan•u•late (kam pan′yə lit, -lāt′), *adj.* bell-shaped, as a corolla.

camp′ bed′, *n.* a light folding cot or bed.

Camp•bell (kam′bəl, kam′əl), *n.* **1. Alexander,** 1788–1866, U.S. religious leader, born in Ireland: a founder of the Disciples of Christ Church. **2. Joseph,** 1904–87, U.S. mythologist.

Camp′ Da′vid (dā′vid), *n.* U.S. presidential retreat in the Catoctin Mountains, Md.

Cam•pe•che (käm pe′che), *n.* **1.** a state in SE Mexico, on the peninsula of Yucatán. 592,933; 19,672 sq. mi. (50,950 sq. km). **2.** the capital of this state. 151,805. **3. Gulf of,** the SW part of the Gulf of Mexico.

camp•er (kam′pər), *n.* **1.** a person who camps out for recreation, esp. in the wilderness. **2.** a person who attends a summer camp or day camp. **3.** a trucklike vehicle, van, or trailer fitted or suitable for recreational camping.

cam•pes•tral (kam pes′trəl), *adj.* of or pertaining to fields or open country.

camp•fire (kamp′fīər′), *n.* **1.** an outdoor fire for warmth or cooking, as at a camp. **2.** a reunion of soldiers, scouts, etc.

camp•ground (kamp′ground′), *n.* a place for a camp or for a camp meeting.

cam•phene (kam′fēn, kam fēn′), *n.* a colorless, crystalline, water-insoluble substance, $C_{10}H_{16}$, used in the manufacture of camphor.

cam•phor (kam′fər), *n.* a white, pleasant-smelling terpene ketone, $C_{10}H_{16}O$, used chiefly in making celluloid, as a counterirritant, and as a moth repellent. **—cam•phor′ic** (-fôr′ik, -for′-), *adj.*

cam′phor tree′, *n.* a tree, *Cinnamomum camphora,* of the laurel family, grown in E Asia and yielding camphor.

cam•pi•on (kam′pē ən), *n.* a plant of the genera *Lychnis* and *Silene,* of the pink family, having white, pink, or reddish flowers.

camp′ meet′ing, *n.* a religious gathering held in a tent or in the open air.

cam•po (kam′pō, käm′-), *n., pl.* **-pos.** (in South America) an extensive, nearly level grassland plain.

camp•o•ree (kam′pə rē′), *n.* a small camp gathering of boy scouts or girl scouts, usu. from a region or district (disting. from *jamboree*).

camp′site′ or **camp′-site′,** *n.* a place used for camping.

camp•stool (kamp′stōol′), *n.* a lightweight folding stool, usu. with a canvas seat.

cam•pus (kam′pəs), *n., pl.* **-pus•es. 1.** the grounds of a college or other school. **2.** a college or university.

camp•y (kam′pē), *adj.,* **camp•i•er, camp•i•est.** pertaining to or characterized by camp: *a campy spoof of romantic operetta.*

cam•shaft (kam′shaft′, -shäft′), *n.* an engine shaft fitted with cams.

can[1] (kan; *unstressed* kən), *auxiliary v.* and *v., pres.* **can,** *past* **could.** *For auxiliary v.:* imperative, infinitive, and participles lacking. **—***auxiliary verb.* **1.** to be able to; have the ability, power, or skill to: *She can solve the problem easily.* **2.** to know how to: *I can play chess, but not very well.* **3.** to have the power or means to: *a dictator who can impose his will on the people.* **4.** to have the right or qualifications to: *He can change whatever he wishes in the script.* **5.** may; have permission to: *Can I speak to you for a moment?* **6.** to have the possibility: *A coin can land on either side.* **—Idiom. 7. can but,** to be able to do nothing else except; can only: *We can but try.* **—Usage.** CAN and MAY are often interchangeable in the sense of possibility: *A power failure can (or may) occur at any time.* Despite the traditional insistence that only MAY conveys permission, both words are regularly used in this sense: *Can (or May) I borrow your tape recorder?* CAN occurs this way chiefly in spoken English; MAY occurs more frequently in formal speech and writing. In negative constructions, CAN'T or CANNOT is more common than MAY NOT; the contraction MAYN'T is rare: *You can't park in the driveway.* CAN BUT and CANNOT BUT are formal, now somewhat old-fashioned expressions suggesting that there is no alternative to doing something. See also CAN-NOT, HELP.

can[2] (kan), *n., v.,* **canned, can•ning. —***n.* **1.** a sealed container for food, beverages, etc., as of aluminum, sheet iron coated with tin, or other metal. **2.** a receptacle for garbage, ashes, etc. **3.** a bucket or other container for holding or carrying liquids. **4.** a metal or plastic container for holding film on cores or reels. **—***v.t.* **5.** to preserve by sealing in a can, jar, etc. **6.** *Slang.* to put a stop to: *Can that noise!* **7.** to record, as on film or tape. **—Idiom. 8. can of worms,** a source of complicated, entangled problems. **9. in the can,** (of a commercial film, scene, etc.) completed.

Ca•na (kā′nə), *n.* an ancient town in N Israel, in Galilee: scene of Jesus' first miracle. John 2:1, 11.

Ca•naan (kā′nən), *n.* **1.** the ancient region lying between the Jordan,

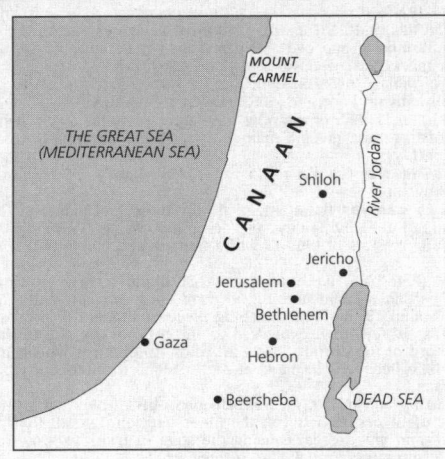

the Dead Sea, and the Mediterranean: the land promised by God to Abraham. Gen. 12:5–10. **2.** Biblical name of PALESTINE (def 1).

Ca•naan•ite (kā′nə nīt′), *n.* **1.** a member of any of the western Semitic peoples inhabiting Canaan at the time of its occupation by the Israelites. **2.** the language or languages of these peoples, ancestral to Hebrew, Phoenician, and Moabite. **—***adj.* **3.** of or pertaining to Canaan, the Canaanites, or their speech.

Can•a•da (kan′ə də), *n.* a nation in N North America: a member of the Commonwealth of Nations. 29,123,194; 3,690,410 sq. mi. (9,558,160 sq. km). *Cap.:* Ottawa. **—Ca•na•di•an** (kə nā′dē ən), *adj., n.*

Can′ada bal′sam, *n.* a water-soluble resin obtained from the balsam fir, *Abies balsamea,* used as a cement for lenses.

Can′ada Day′, *n.* a Canadian national holiday, July 1, celebrating the formation of the Dominion on July 1, 1867. Formerly (until 1982), **Dominion Day.**

Can′ada goose′, *n.* a common wild goose, *Branta canadensis,* of North America, with white cheek patches.

Can′ada lynx′, *n.* a North American lynx, *Lynx lynx,* having tufted ears and a grayish-tan coat.

Can′ada this′tle, *n.* an Old World prickly composite plant, *Cirsium arvense,* having small purple or white flower heads, now a troublesome weed in North America.

Cana′dian ba′con, *n.* bacon from the pork loin.

Cana′dian foot′ball, *n.* a game similar to American football, played by teams of 12 players each, in which the offense is allowed only 3 downs to advance the ball 10 yards.

Cana′dian whis′ky, *n.* a rye whiskey made entirely from cereal grain.

ca•naille (kə nī′, -nāl′), *n.* riffraff; rabble.

ca•nal (kə nal′), *n., v.,* **-nalled** or **-naled, -nal•ling** or **-nal•ing. —***n.* **1.** an artificial waterway for navigation, irrigation, etc. **2.** a tubular passage for food, air, etc., in an animal or plant; duct. **3.** channel; watercourse. **4.** one of the long, dark lines on the planet Mars, as viewed from Earth. **—***v.t.* **5.** to make a canal through.

Ca•na•let•to (kan′l et′ō), *n.* **Antonio,** (*Canale*), 1697–1768, Italian painter.

Canal′ Zone′, *n.* a zone in central Panama, including the Panama Canal: governed by the U.S. 1903–1979; partial control of the zone was returned to Panama, entire control to be returned by 2000; ab. 10 mi. (16 km) wide; excludes the cities of Panama and Colón. *Abbr.:* CZ, C.Z.

can•a•pé (kan′ə pē, -pā′), *n., pl.* **-pés. 1.** a cracker or piece of bread topped with cheese, caviar, or other savory food. **2.** a French sofa.

ca•nard (kə närd′, -när′), *n.* a false or baseless, usu. derogatory story, report, or rumor.

ca•nar•y (kə nâr′ē), *n., pl.* **-nar•ies. 1.** a small, sweetly singing greenish yellow finch, *Serinus canaria,* of the Canary Islands and vicinity, often a brilliant to pale yellow in varieties bred as cage birds. **2.** a light, clear yellow color. **3.** *Slang.* INFORMER (def. 1). **4.** a sweet white wine of the Canary Islands.

canar′y grass′, *n.* a grass, *Phalaris canariensis,* native to the Canary Islands, bearing seeds used as food for cage birds.

Canar′y Is′lands, *n.pl.* a group of mountainous islands in the Atlantic Ocean, near the NW coast of Africa, comprising two provinces of Spain. 1,614,882; 2894 sq. mi. (7495 sq. km). Spanish, **Islas Canarias. —Canar′i•an,** *adj., n.*

ca•nas•ta (kə nas′tə), *n.* a variety of rummy played with two decks of cards plus jokers.

Ca•nav•er•al (kə nav′ər əl), *n.* **Cape,** a cape on the E coast of Florida: site of John F. Kennedy Space Center. Formerly (1963–73), **Cape Kennedy.**

Can•ber•ra (kan′ber ə, -bər ə), *n.* the capital of Australia, in the SE part, in the Australian Capital Territory. 285,800 (with suburbs).

can•can (kan′kan′), *n.* a lively high-kicking dance that came into vogue about 1830 in Paris.

can•cel (kan′səl), *v.*, **-celed, -cel•ing** or (*esp. Brit.*) **-celled, -cel•ling,** *n.* —*v.t.* **1.** to make void; revoke; annul. **2.** to decide or announce that (a planned event) will not take place; call off. **3.** to mark or perforate (a postage stamp, admission ticket, etc.) so as to render invalid for reuse. **4.** to neutralize; counterbalance; compensate for: *His sincere apology canceled his sarcastic remark.* **5.** to eliminate by striking out a factor common to both the denominator and numerator of a fraction, equivalent terms on opposite sides of an equation, etc. **6.** to cross out (words, letters, etc.) by drawing a line over the item. —*v.i.* **7.** to counterbalance or compensate for one another; become neutralized. **8.** (of common factors in fractions, equations, etc.) to be equivalent; allow cancellation. —*n.* **9.** an act of canceling.

can•cel•la•tion or **can•cel•a•tion** (kan′sə lā′shən), *n.* **1.** an act of canceling. **2.** the marks or perforations made in canceling. **3.** something canceled, as a reservation for a hotel room or an airplane ticket, allowing someone else to obtain the accommodation.

can•cer (kan′sər), *n.* **1. a.** a malignant and invasive growth or tumor, esp. one originating in epithelium, tending to recur after excision and to metastasize to other sites. **b.** any disease characterized by such growths. **2.** any evil condition or thing that spreads destructively; blight. **3.** (*cap.*) the Crab, a zodiacal constellation between Gemini and Leo. **4.** (*cap.*) the fourth sign of the zodiac. [< Latin: crab] —**can′cer•ous,** *adj.*

can•de•la (kan dē′lə), *n.*, *pl.* **-las.** a unit adopted in 1979 as the international standard of luminous intensity, defined as the luminous intensity of a source that emits monochromatic radiation of frequency 540 × 10^{12} hertz and that has a radiant intensity of 1/683 watt/steradian. *Abbr.:* cd

can•de•la•bra (kan′dl ä′brə, ab′rə, -dl ā′brə), *n.*, *pl.* **-bras** for 2. **1.** a pl. of CANDELABRUM. **2.** a candelabrum.

can•de•la•brum (kan′dl ä′brəm, -dl ā′-), *n.*, *pl.* **-bra** (-brə), **-brums.** an ornamental branched holder for more than one candle.

can•des•cent (kan des′ənt), *adj.* glowing; incandescent. —**can•des′cence,** *n.* —**can•des′cent•ly,** *adv.*

can•did (kan′did), *adj.* **1.** frank; outspoken; open and sincere: *a candid critic.* **2.** free from reservation, disguise, or subterfuge; straightforward: *a candid opinion.* **3.** informal; unposed: *a candid photo.* **4.** honest; impartial: *a candid mind.* —*n.* **5.** an unposed photograph. —**can′did•ly,** *adv.* —**can′did•ness,** *n.*

can•di•date (kan′di dāt′, -dit), *n.* **1.** a person who seeks or is selected by others for an office, honor, etc. **2.** a person deserving of or destined for a certain fate: *a candidate for the poorhouse.* **3.** a student studying for a degree. [< Latin *candidātus* clothed in white (in reference to the white togas worn by those seeking office)] —**can′di•da•cy** (-də sē), *n.*

can•di•di•a•sis (kan′di dī′ə sis), *n.*, *pl.* **-ses** (-sēz′). any of a variety of infections caused by fungi of the genus *Candida,* occurring most often in the mouth, respiratory tract, or vagina.

can•died (kan′dēd), *adj.* **1.** impregnated or incrusted with sugar: *candied ginger.* **2.** cooked in sugar or syrup: *candied yams.* **3.** honeyed; flattering: *candied words.*

can•dle (kan′dl), *n.*, *v.*, **-dled, -dling.** —*n.* **1.** a long piece of tallow or wax with an embedded wick that is burned to give light. **2.** something resembling this in appearance or use. **3.** any of various former international standard units of luminous intensity. *Abbr.:* c., c Compare CANDELA. —*v.t.* **4.** to examine (eggs) for freshness, fertility, etc., by holding them up to a bright light. —***Idiom.*** **5. hold a candle to,** to compare favorably with (usu. in the negative). **6. worth the candle,** worth the trouble or effort involved (usu. in the negative).

can•dle•fish (kan′dl fish′), *n.*, *pl.* (*esp. collectively*) **-fish,** (*esp. for kinds or species*) **-fish•es.** a small, edible, smeltlike fish, *Thaleichthys pacificus,* of NW coastal waters of North America, being so oily that when dried it can be used as a candle.

Can•dle•mas (kan′dl məs, -mas′), *n.* a church festival, Feb. 2, in honor of the presentation of Jesus in the Temple and the purification of the Virgin Mary.

can•dle•nut (kan′dl nut′), *n.* the oily fruit or nut of a SE Asian tree, *Aleurites moluccana,* of the spurge family, the kernels of which when strung together are used locally as candles.

can•dle•pins (kan′dl pinz′), *n.* **1.** (*used with a sing. v.*) a game like tenpins played with a bowling pin that is almost cylindrical and can be set up on either end. **2. candlepin,** a pin used in this game.

can′dle•pow′er or **cand′le pow′er,** *n.* (formerly) a measure of luminous intensity expressed in candles.

can•dle•stick (kan′dl stik′), *n.* a device having a socket or a spike for holding a candle.

can•dle•wick (kan′dl wik′), *n.* **1.** the wick of a candle. **2.** Also, **can′dle•wick′ing. a.** Also called **can′dlewick yarn′.** loosely twisted yarn, usu. of cotton, used to form small decorative tufts on the surface of a fabric. **b.** a fabric with such tufts on its surface.

can•dle•wood (kan′dl wo͝od′), *n.* **1.** any resinous wood used for torches or as a substitute for candles. **2.** any of various trees or shrubs yielding such wood.

can′-do′, *Informal.* —*adj.* **1.** marked by purposefulness and efficiency. —*n.* **2.** the quality of being efficient and enthusiastic.

can•dor (kan′dər), *n.* **1.** the state or quality of being frank, open, and sincere in speech or expression; candidness. **2.** freedom from bias; fairness; impartiality. Also, *esp. Brit.,* **can′dour.**

can•dy (kan′dē), *n.*, *pl.* **-dies,** *v.*, **-died, -dy•ing.** —*n.* **1.** any of various confections made with sugar or syrup, often combined with chocolate, fruit, nuts, etc. **2.** a single piece of such a confection. —*v.t.* **3.** to cook in sugar or syrup until glazed, as sweet potatoes. **4.** to preserve by cooking in heavy syrup until translucent, as fruit or fruit peel. **5.** to reduce (sugar, syrup, etc.) to a crystalline form, usu. by boiling down. **6.** to roll in granulated sugar. **7.** to make sweet, palatable, or agreeable. —*v.i.* **8.** to become covered with sugar. **9.** to crystallize into sugar. [Middle English *sugre candi* candied sugar < Middle French < Arabic *qandī* < Sanskrit *khaṇḍakaḥ* sugar candy] —**can′dy•like′,** *adj.*

can′dy strip′er, *n.* a teenage volunteer worker at a hospital.

can•dy•tuft (kan′dē tuft′), *n.* any of various small plants of the genus *Iberis,* of the mustard family, with tufted white, pink, or lavender flowers.

cane (kān), *n.*, *v.*, **caned, can•ing.** —*n.* **1.** a stick or short staff used to assist one in walking; walking stick. **2.** a long, hollow or pithy, jointed woody stem, as that of bamboo, rattan, sugarcane, and certain palms. **3.** a plant having such a stem. **4.** split rattan woven or interlaced for chair seats, wickerwork, etc. **5.** any of several tall bamboolike grasses, esp. of the genus *Arundinaria.* **6.** the stem of a raspberry or blackberry. **7.** SUGARCANE. **8.** a rod used for flogging. —*v.t.* **9.** to flog with a cane. **10.** to furnish or make with cane: *to cane chairs.*

cane′ sug′ar, *n.* sugar obtained from sugarcane, identical with that obtained from the sugar beet. Compare SUGAR (def. 1).

can•id (kan′id, kā′nid), *n.* any member of the dog family Canidae, including the wolves, jackals, coyotes, foxes, and domestic dogs.

ca•nine (kā′nīn), *adj.* **1.** of or like a dog; pertaining to or characteristic of dogs: *canine loyalty.* **2.** of or pertaining to any of the four single-cusped, pointed teeth, esp. prominent in dogs, situated in the upper and lower jaws next to the incisors. —*n.* **3.** a canid. **4.** a dog. **5.** one of the four pointed teeth of the jaws. —**ca•nin′i•ty** (-nin′i tē), *n.*

Ca•nis Ma•jor (kā′nis mā′jər), *n.*, *gen.* **Ca•nis Ma•jo•ris** (kā′nis mə jôr′is, -jōr′-). a southern constellation containing Sirius, the brightest star. [< Latin: larger dog]

Ca•nis Mi•nor (kā′nis mī′nər), *n.*, *gen.* **Ca•nis Mi•no•ris** (kā′nis mī nôr′is, -nōr′-). the Little or Lesser Dog, a southern constellation containing the bright star Procyon. [< Latin: smaller dog]

can•is•ter (kan′ə stər), *n.* **1.** a small box or jar, often one of a kitchen set, for holding tea, coffee, flour, sugar, etc. **2.** (on a gas mask) the container of neutralizing substances through which poisoned air is filtered.

can•ker (kang′kər), *n.* **1.** a gangrenous or ulcerous sore. **2.** a defined area of diseased tissue, esp. in woody stems. **3.** something that corrupts or destroys; blight. —*v.t.* **4.** to infect with canker. **5.** to corrupt; destroy slowly. —*v.i.* **6.** to become infected with or as if with canker. Also called **can′ker sore′** (for defs. 1, 2). —**can′ker•ous,** *adj.*

can•ker•worm (kang′kər wûrm′), *n.* the striped green caterpillar of any of several geometrid moths: a foliage pest of trees.

can•na (kan′ə), *n.*, *pl.* **-nas.** any of various tropical plants of the genus *Canna,* of the canna family, cultivated for their large, brightly colored leaves and showy flowers.

can•nab•i•noid (kə nab′ə noid′, kan′ə bə-), *n.* any of the chemical compounds that are the active principles of marijuana.

can•na•bis (kan′ə bis), *n.* **1.** the hemp plant, *Cannabis sativa.* **2.** the flowering tops of the plant. **3.** any of the various parts of the plant from which hashish, marijuana, and similar drugs are prepared.

canned (kand), *adj.* **1.** preserved in a can or jar: *canned peaches.* **2.** recorded or prerecorded: *canned music; canned laughter.* **3.** prepared in advance for repeated use: *a canned speech.*

can•nel•lo•ni (kan′l ō′nē), *n.* (*used with a sing. or pl. v.*) large, tubular pieces of pasta filled usu. with chopped meat and baked in a sauce.

can•ner•y (kan′ə rē), *n.*, *pl.* **-ner•ies.** a factory where foodstuffs, as meat, fish, or fruit, are canned.

can•ni•bal (kan′ə bəl), *n.* **1.** a person who eats human flesh, esp. for magical or religious purposes. **2.** any animal that eats its own kind. —*adj.* **3.** pertaining to or like a cannibal.

can•ni•bal•ism (kan′ə bə liz′əm), *n.* **1.** the eating of human flesh by another human being, esp. for magical or religious purposes. **2.** the eating of the flesh of an animal by another animal of its own kind. **3.** the removal of elements from one thing for use in another. —**can′ni•bal•is′tic,** *adj.*

can•ni•bal•ize (kan′ə bə līz′), *v.*, **-ized, -iz•ing.** —*v.t.* **1.** to subject to cannibalism. **2.** to remove parts from (a machine, vehicle, etc.) in order to repair or make a similar unit. **3.** to remove employees from (a business) in order to build a similar one. **4.** to use material from (other writers or works) in developing a text. **5.** to cut into; cause to become diminished: *new products cannibalizing sales from existing lines.* —*v.i.* **6.** to practice cannibalism.

can•ning (kan′ing), *n.* the act, process, or business of preserving cooked food by sealing in cans or jars.

can•no•li (kə nō′lē), *n.*, *pl.* **-li, -lis.** a deep-fried tubular pastry shell filled with sweetened ricotta and bits of citron, chocolate, or nuts.

can•non (kan′ən), *n.*, *pl.* **-nons,** (*esp. collectively*) **-non,** *v.*, **-noned, -non•ing.** —*n.* **1.** a mounted gun for firing heavy projectiles; gun, howitzer, or mortar. **2.** the metal loop on a bell by which it is hung. **3. a.**

C

CANNON BONE. **b.** the part of the leg in which the cannon bone is situated. —*v.i.* **4.** to discharge cannon.

can·non·ade (kan′ə nād′), *n.*, *v.*, **-ad·ed, -ad·ing.** —*n.* **1.** a continued discharge of cannon, esp. during an attack. **2.** an attack, as of invective or censure; barrage. —*v.t.* **3.** to attack continuously with or as if with cannon. —*v.i.* **4.** to discharge like continuous cannon fire.

can·non·ball (kan′ən bôl′), *n.* **1.** a missile, usu. round and made of iron or steel, designed to be fired from a cannon. **2.** something that moves with great speed, as an express train. **3.** a dive made in a curled-up position with the arms pressing the knees against the chest.

can′non bone′, *n.* the greatly developed middle metacarpal or metatarsal bone of hoofed mammals, extending from the hock to the fetlock.

can′non fod′der, *n.* soldiers, esp. the infantry, who run the greatest risk of being wounded or killed in warfare.

can·non·ry (kan′ən rē), *n.*, *pl.* **-ries.** a discharge of artillery.

can·not (kan′ot, ka not′, kə-), *v.* **1.** a form of *can not.* —**Idiom. 2. cannot but,** to have no alternative but to; cannot help but: *We cannot but choose otherwise.* —**Usage.** CANNOT is sometimes spelled CAN NOT. The one-word spelling is more common by far. Its contraction, *can't,* is found chiefly in speech and informal writing. See also CAN[1], HELP.

can·ny (kan′ē), *adj.,* **-ni·er, -ni·est. 1.** careful; cautious; prudent. **2.** astute; shrewd; knowing. **3.** skilled; expert. **4.** frugal; thrifty. —**can′ni·ly,** *adv.* —**can′ni·ness,** *n.*

ca·noe *n.*, *v.,* **-noed, -noe·ing.** —*n.* **1.** any of various slender boats tapering at both ends, traditionally built with a light frame covered with bark, skins, etc., and now usu. made from molded aluminum, plastic, etc. —*v.i.* **2.** to paddle a canoe. **3.** to go in a canoe. —*v.t.* **4.** to transport or carry by canoe. —**Idiom. 5. paddle one's own canoe,** *Informal.* **a.** to handle one's own affairs; manage independently. **b.** to mind one's own business. —**ca·noe′ist,** *n.*

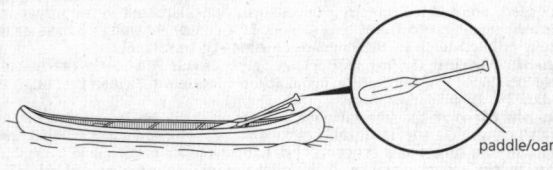

canoe

can·o·la (kan′l ə, kə nō′lə), *n.* a variety of rapeseed containing an oil low in erucic acid, used in cooking.

can·on[1] (kan′ən), *n.* **1.** an ecclesiastical rule or law enacted by a council or other competent authority. **2.** the body of ecclesiastical law. **3.** a body of rules, principles, or standards accepted as axiomatic and universally binding, esp. in a field of study or art. **4.** a principle, rule, or standard: *the canons of good behavior.* **5.** the books of the Bible recognized by any Christian church as genuine and inspired. **6.** any officially recognized set of sacred books. **7.** any comprehensive list of books within a field. **8.** the works of an author that have been accepted as authentic. **9.** the list of saints acknowledged by the Roman Catholic Church. **10.** the part of the mass between the Sanctus and the communion. **11.** *Eastern Ch.* a liturgical sequence sung at matins, usu. consisting of nine odes arranged in a fixed pattern. **12.** consistent, note-fornote imitation of one melodic line by another, in which the second line starts after the first.

can·on[2] (kan′ən), *n.* **1.** a member of the chapter of a cathedral or a collegiate church. **2.** one of the members of certain Roman Catholic religious orders.

ca·ñon (kan′yən), *n.* CANYON.

ca·non·i·cal (kə non′i kəl), *adj.* Also, **ca·non′ic. 1.** pertaining to, established by, or conforming to a canon or canons. **2.** included in the canon of the Bible. **3.** authorized; recognized; accepted. **4.** (of a mathematical equation, coordinate, etc.) in simplest or standard form. **5.** of or pertaining to a form cited as the characteristic, basic form of an item in a language: *the canonical syllable in Japanese.* —*n.* **6. canonicals,** garments prescribed by canon law for clergy when officiating. —**ca·non′i·cal·ly,** *adv.*

canon′ical hour′, *n.* any of certain periods of the day set apart for prayer and devotion: these are matins and lauds, prime, tierce, sext, nones, vespers, and compline.

can·on·ize (kan′ə nīz′), *v.t.,* **-ized, -iz·ing. 1.** to place (a dead person) in the canon of saints; declare officially as a saint. **2.** to place or include within a canon, esp. of scriptural works. **3.** to consider or treat as holy, authoritative, etc. **4.** to sanction authoritatively, esp. ecclesiastically. —**can′on·i·za′tion,** *n.* —**can′on·iz′er,** *n.*

can′on law′, *n.* the body of codified ecclesiastical law, esp. of the Roman Catholic Church as promulgated in ecclesiastical councils and by the pope.

ca·no′pic (or **Ca·no′pic) jar′,** (kə nō′pik, -nop′ik), *n.* a jar used in ancient Egypt to contain the entrails of an embalmed body.

Ca·no·pus (kə nō′pəs), *n.* **1.** a first-magnitude star in the constellation Carina: the second brightest star in the heavens. **2.** an ancient seacoast city in Lower Egypt, 15 mi. (24 km) E of Alexandria.

can·o·py (kan′ə pē), *n.,* *pl.* **-pies,** *v.,* **-pied, -py·ing.** —*n.* **1.** a covering, usu. of fabric, supported on poles or suspended above a bed, throne, exalted personage, or sacred object. **2.** a long awning stretching from the doorway of a building to a curb. **3.** an ornamental projection or covering. **4.** the cover formed by the leafy upper branches of the trees in a forest. **5.** the part of a parachute that opens up and fills with air. **6.** the transparent cover over the cockpit of an airplane. —*v.t.* **7.** to cover with or as if with a canopy.

cant[1] (kant), *n.* **1.** insincere or hypocritical statements, esp. pious platitudes. **2.** the private language of the underworld. **3.** the words and phrases peculiar to a particular class, profession, etc. **4.** whining or singsong speech. —*v.i.* **5.** to talk piously or hypocritically. **6.** to beg in a whining or singsong tone.

cant[2] (kant), *n.* **1.** a salient angle. **2.** a sudden movement that tilts or overturns a thing. **3.** a slanting or tilted position. **4.** an oblique line or surface, as one formed by cutting off the corner of a square or cube. **5.** BANK[1] (def. 5). **6.** a sudden pitch or toss. **7.** a partly trimmed log. —*adj.* **8.** oblique or slanting. —*v.t.* **9.** to bevel; form an oblique surface upon. **10.** to put in an oblique position; tilt; tip. **11.** to throw with a sudden jerk. —*v.i.* **12.** to take or have an inclined position; tilt; turn. —**cant′ic,** *adj.*

can't (kant, känt), contraction of *cannot.* —**Usage.** See CAN[1], CANNOT.

can·ta·bi·le (kän tä′bi lā′, -bē-), *Music.* —*adj.* **1.** songlike and flowing in style. —*adv.* **2.** in a cantabile manner.

Can·ta·brig·i·an (kan′tə brij′ē ən), *adj.* **1.** of or pertaining to Cambridge, England, or Cambridge University. **2.** of or pertaining to Cambridge, Mass., or Harvard University. —*n.* **3.** a native or resident of Cambridge. **4.** a student at or graduate of Cambridge University or Harvard University.

can·ta·la (kan tä′lə), *n.,* *pl* **-las. 1.** a cordage fiber obtained from the leaves of a tropical plant, *Agave cantala.* **2.** the plant itself. Also called **maguey.**

can·ta·loupe or **can·ta·loup** (kan′tl ōp′), *n.* **1.** a variety of melon, *Cucumis melo cantalupensis,* of the gourd family, having a hard scaly or warty rind, grown chiefly in Europe. **2.** a muskmelon having a reticulated rind and pale-orange flesh.

can·tan·ker·ous (kan tang′kər əs), *adj.* quarrelsome; irritable. —**can·tan′ker·ous·ly,** *adv.* —**can·tan′ker·ous·ness,** *n.*

can·ta·ta (kən tä′tə), *n.,* *pl.* **-tas.** a choral composition, either sacred and resembling a short oratorio, or secular, as a lyric drama set to music but not to be acted.

can·teen (kan tēn′), *n.* **1.** a small container used esp. by soldiers and hikers for carrying water or other liquids. **2.** a general store and cafeteria at a military base. **3.** a place where free entertainment is provided for military personnel. **4.** a snack bar, as in a factory or school. [< French *cantine* < Italian *cantina* cellar]

can·ter (kan′tər), *n.* **1.** an easy gallop. —*v.i.* **2.** to move or ride at a canter. —*v.t.* **3.** to cause to move at a canter.

Can·ter·bur·y (kan′tər ber′ē, -bə rē; *esp. Brit.* -brē), *n.* a city in E Kent, in SE England: early ecclesiastical center of England. 129,500. —**Can′ter·bu′ri·an** (-byŏŏr′ē ən), *adj.*

Can′terbury bells′, *n.* (*used with a sing. or pl. v.*) a plant, *Campanula medium,* of the bellflower family, cultivated for its bell-shaped violet-blue, pink, or white flowers.

Can′terbury Tales′, The, an uncompleted sequence of tales by Geoffrey Chaucer, written for the most part after 1387.

can·thus (kan′thəs), *n.,* *pl.* **-thi** (-thī). the angle or corner on each side of the eye, formed by the junction of the upper and lower lids. —**can′thal,** *adj.*

can·ti·cle (kan′ti kəl), *n.* one of the nonmetrical hymns or chants, chiefly from the Bible, used in church services.

Can′ticle of Can′ticles, *n.* SONG OF SOLOMON, The.

Can·ti·gny (kän tē nyē′), *n.* a village in N France, S of Amiens: first major battle of U.S. forces in World War I, May 1918.

can·ti·le·ver (kan′tl ē′vər, -ev′ər), *n.* **1.** any rigid structural member, esp. one projecting from a vertical support, in which the fixed end is in compression and the free end in tension. **2.** any rigid construction extending well beyond its support, used as a structural element of a bridge, building foundation, dam, etc. **3.** a form of aeronautical wing construction in which no external bracing is used. **4.** a projecting bracket supporting a balcony, cornice, etc. —*v.i.* **5.** to project in the manner of a cantilever. —*v.t.* **6.** to construct with or in the manner of a cantilever.

can·ti·na (kan tē′nə), *n.,* *pl.* **-nas.** *Southwestern U.S.* a saloon; bar.

can·tle (kan′tl), *n.* **1.** the hind part of a saddle, usu. curved upward. **2.** a corner; piece; portion: *a cantle of land.*

can·to (kan′tō), *n.,* *pl.* **-tos.** one of the main or larger divisions of a long poem.

can·ton (kan′tn, -ton, kan ton′), *n.* **1.** a small territorial district, esp. one of the states of the Swiss confederation. **2.** a division of a French arrondissement. **3.** the dexter chief area of a heraldic field. —**can′ton·al,** *adj.*

Can·ton (kan ton′, kan′ton *for 0;* kan′tn *for*), *n.* GUANGZHOU.

Can·ton·ese (kan′tn ēz′, -ēs′), *n.,* *pl.* **-ese,** *adj.* —*n.* **1. a.** a Yue dialect of Chinese spoken in Guangzhou, Hong Kong, and Macao. **b. 2.** a native or inhabitant of Guangzhou. —*adj.* **3.** of or pertaining to Guangzhou, its inhabitants, or their dialect.

can·ton·ment (kan ton′mənt, -tōn′-; *esp. Brit.* kən tōōn′-), *n.* **1.** a usu. large camp for training military personnel. **2.** military quarters. **3.** the winter quarters of an army.

can·tor (kan′tər, -tôr), *n.* **1.** the religious official of a synagogue who sings or chants the prayers to be performed as solos. **2.** PRECENTOR. —**can·to′ri·al** (-tôr′ē əl, -tōr′-), *adj.*

can·tus fir·mus (kan′təs fûr′məs), *n., pl.* **cantus firmus. 1.** PLAINSONG. **2.** a fixed melody to which other voices are added, typically in polyphonic treatment.

can·vas (kan′vəs), *n.* **1.** a closely woven, heavy cloth of cotton, hemp, or linen, used esp. for tents, sails, etc. **2.** a piece of this or similar material on which a painting is made. **3.** a painting on canvas. **4.** a tent, or tents collectively. **5.** sails collectively. **6.** any mesh-weave fabric of linen, hemp, etc., esp. one used as a ground in needlepoint.

can·vas·back (kan′vəs bak′), *n., pl.* **-backs,** (*esp. collectively*) **-back.** a North American duck, *Aythya valisineria,* the male of which has a whitish back and a reddish brown head and neck.

can·vass (kan′vəs), *v.t.* **1.** to solicit votes, opinions, sales orders, etc., from (a district or group of people). **2.** to investigate by inquiry; discuss; debate. —*v.i.* **3.** to solicit votes, opinions, etc. —*n.* **4.** a soliciting of votes, opinions, etc. **5.** close inspection; scrutiny. —**can′vass·er,** *n.*

can·yon (kan′yən), *n.* a deep valley with steep sides, often with a stream flowing through it; gorge. [< Mexican Spanish < Spanish *cañón* a long tube, a hollow]

Can′yon·lands Na′tional Park′ (kan′yən landz′), *n.* a national park in SE Utah, at the junction of the Colorado and Green rivers: site of geologic interest. 527 sq. mi. (1366 sq. km).

cap[1] (kap), *n., v.,* **capped, cap·ping.** —*n.* **1.** a close-fitting covering for the head, usu. of soft, supple material and having no brim but sometimes having a visor. **2.** a headdress denoting rank, occupation, religious order, or the like: *a nurse's cap.* **3.** MORTARBOARD (def. 2). **4.** anything resembling a covering for the head in shape, use, or position: *a bottle cap.* **5.** summit; top; acme. **6.** a maximum limit, as one set by law or agreement on prices, wages, spending, etc.; ceiling. **7.** the pileus of a mushroom. **8.** a noise-making device for toy pistols, made of a small quantity of explosive wrapped in paper. —*v.t.* **9.** to provide or cover with or as if with a cap. **10.** to complete. **11.** to follow with something better; outdo: *to cap one joke with another.* **12.** to serve as a cap, covering, or top to. **13.** to put a maximum limit on (wages, spending, etc.). —*Idiom.* **14. set one's cap for,** to pursue as a lover or husband.

cap[2] (kap), *n., v.,* **capped, cap·ping.** —*n.* **1.** a capital letter. **2.** Usu., **caps.** uppercase: *Set the underlined in caps.* —*v.t.* **3.** to write or print with a capital letter or letters; capitalize.

ca·pa·ble (kā′pə bəl), *adj.* **1.** having power and ability; efficient; competent: *a capable instructor.* **2. capable of, a.** having the ability for: *capable of writing music.* **b.** susceptible of: *a situation capable of improvement.* **c.** predisposed to: *capable of murder.* —**ca′pa·bil′i·ty,** *n.* —**ca′pa·bly,** *adv.*

ca·pa·cious (kə pā′shəs), *adj.* capable of holding much; roomy: *a capacious closet.* —**ca·pa′cious·ly,** *adv.* —**ca·pa′cious·ness,** *n.*

ca·pac·i·tor (kə pas′i tər), *n.* a device for accumulating and holding a charge of electricity, consisting of two equally charged conducting surfaces having opposite signs and separated by a dielectric. Also called **condenser.** —**ca·pac′i·tance,** *n.*

ca·pac·i·ty (kə pas′i tē), *n., pl.* **-ties,** *adj.* —*n.* **1.** the ability to receive or contain: *This hotel has a large capacity.* **2.** the maximum amount or number that can be received or contained; cubic contents; volume: *a jug with a capacity of two quarts.* **3.** power of receiving impressions, knowledge, etc.; mental ability. **4.** actual or potential ability to perform, yield, or withstand. **5.** quality or state of being susceptible to a given treatment or action: *Steel has a high capacity to withstand pressure.* **6.** position; function; role: *to serve in an advisory capacity.* **7.** legal qualification. **8.** maximum possible electrical output. —*adj.* **9.** reaching maximum capacity: *a capacity crowd.*

cap′ and gown′, *n.* a ceremonial mortarboard and gown worn by faculty, students, etc., as at commencement.

cap-a-pie or **cap-à-pie** (kap′ə pē′), *adv.* from head to foot.

ca·par·i·son (kə par′ə sən), *n.* **1.** a decorative covering for a horse or for the tack or harness of a horse; trappings. **2.** rich and sumptuous clothing or equipment. —*v.t.* **3.** to cover with a caparison. **b.** to dress richly; deck.

cape[1] (kāp), *n.* a sleeveless garment of variable length, fastened at the neck and falling loosely from the shoulders, worn separately or attached to another garment. —**caped,** *adj.*

cape[2] (kāp), *n.* a piece of land jutting into the sea or some other large body of water; point; headland.

Cape′ buf′falo, *n.* AFRICAN BUFFALO.

Cape′ Canav′eral, *n.* CANAVERAL, Cape.

Cape′ Cod′, *n.* **1.** a sandy peninsula in SE Massachusetts between Cape Cod Bay and the Atlantic Ocean: resort towns. **2.** a style of house developed mainly on Cape Cod, typically a rectangular one- or one-and-a-half-story cottage with a gable roof and a central chimney.

Cape′ Fear′, *n.* **1.** a river in SE North Carolina. 202 mi. (325 km) long. **2.** FEAR, Cape.

Cape′ Horn′, *n.* a headland on a small island at the S extremity of South America: belongs to Chile.

cape·let (kāp′lit), *n.* a short cape usu. covering just the shoulders.

cap·e·lin (kap′ə lin), *n.* a small food fish, *Mallotus villosus,* of North American coastal waters, related to the smelt.

Ca·pel·la (kə pel′ə), *n.* a first-magnitude star in the constellation Auriga.

Cape′ of Good′ Hope′, *n.* **1.** a cape in S Africa, in the SW Republic of South Africa. **2.** Also called **Cape′ Prov′ince.** Formerly, **Cape Colony.** a province in the Republic of South Africa. 7,443,500; 277,169 sq. mi. (717,868 sq. km). *Cap.:* Cape Town.

ca·per[1] (kā′pər), *v.i.* **1.** to leap or skip about in a sprightly manner; prance; frisk; gambol. —*n.* **2.** a playful leap or skip. **3.** a prank or trick; harebrained escapade.

ca·per[2] (kā′pər), *n.* **1.** a spiny shrub, *Capparis spinosa,* of Mediterranean regions, having roundish leaves and solitary white flowers. **2.** its flower bud, pickled and used for garnish or seasoning.

cap·er·cail·lie (kap′ər kāl′yē) also **cap·er·cail·zie** (-kāl′zē), *n.* a large grouse, *Tetrao urogallus,* of Eurasian forests.

Ca·per·na·um (kə pûr′nā əm, -nē-), *n.* an ancient site in N Israel, on the Sea of Galilee: center of Jesus' ministry in Galilee.

cape·skin (kāp′skin′), *n.* a light, pliable leather made from lambskin or sheepskin and used esp. for gloves.

Cape′ Town′, *n.* the legislative capital of the Republic of South Africa, in the SW part: also capital of Cape of Good Hope province. 789,580. —**Cape·to′ni·an** (kāp tō′nē ən), *n.*

Cape′ Verde′ (vûrd), *n.* an island republic (**Cape′ Verde′ Is′lands**) in the Atlantic, W of Senegal in W Africa: formerly an overseas territory of Portugal; gained independence in 1975. 393,843; 1557 sq. mi. (4033 sq. km). *Cap.:* Praia. —**Cape′ Ver′de·an** (vûr′dē ən), *n.*

cap·il·lar·i·ty (kap′ə lar′i tē), *n.* the elevation or depression of part of a liquid surface coming in contact with a solid.

cap·il·lar·y (kap′ə ler′ē), *n., pl.* **-lar·ies,** *adj.* —*n.* **1.** one of the minute blood vessels between the terminations of the arteries and the beginnings of the veins. **2.** Also called **cap′illary tube′.** a tube with a small bore. —*adj.* **3.** pertaining to a capillary or capillaries. **4.** pertaining to a tube of fine bore. **5.** resembling a strand of hair; hairlike. **6. a.** pertaining to capillarity. **b.** of or pertaining to the apparent attraction or repulsion between a liquid and a solid.

cap·i·tal[1] (kap′i tl), *n.* **1.** the city or town that is the official seat of government of a country, state, etc. **2.** a city regarded as being of special eminence in some field of activity: *the dance capital.* **3.** CAPITAL LETTER. **4.** the wealth, as in money or property, owned or employed in business by an individual, firm, etc. **5. a.** assets remaining after deduction of liabilities; the net worth of a business. **b.** the ownership interest in a business. **6.** any source of profit, advantage, power, etc.; asset. —*adj.* **7.** pertaining to financial capital. **8.** principal; primary: *a subject of capital concern.* **9.** chief, esp. as being the official seat of government of a country, state, etc.: *a capital city.* **10.** excellent or first-rate: *a capital hotel.* **11.** of or indicating a capital letter; uppercase. **12.** involving the loss of life: *capital punishment.* **13.** punishable by death: *a capital crime.* [< Anglo-French < Latin *capitālis* of the head]

cap·i·tal[2] (kap′i tl), *n.* the distinctively treated upper end of a column, pilaster, or the like. [≪ Late Latin *capitellum* little head]

cap′ital as′set, *n.* FIXED ASSET.

cap′ital expen′diture, *n.* an addition to the value of fixed assets, as by the purchase of a new building.

cap′ital gain′, *n.* profit from the sale of assets, as bonds or real estate.

cap′ital goods′, *n.pl.* machines and tools used in the production of other goods.

cap·i·tal·ism (kap′i tl iz′əm), *n.* an economic system in which investment in and ownership of the means of production, distribution, and exchange of wealth is made and maintained chiefly by private individuals or corporations.

cap·i·tal·ist (kap′i tl ist), *n.* **1.** a person who invests capital in business enterprises. **2.** an advocate of capitalism. **3.** a very wealthy person.

cap·i·tal·is·tic (kap′i tl is′tik), *adj.* **1.** pertaining to capital or capitalists. **2.** founded on or supporting capitalism: *a capitalistic system.* —**cap′i·tal·is′ti·cal·ly,** *adv.*

cap·i·tal·i·za·tion (kap′i tl ə zā′shən), *n.* **1.** the act or process of capitalizing. **2.** the authorized or outstanding stocks and bonds of a corporation. **3. a.** the total investment of the owner or owners in a business enterprise. **b.** the total corporate liability, including borrowed capital. **c.** the total of these amounts.

cap·i·tal·ize (kap′i tl īz′), *v.t.,* **-ized, -iz·ing. 1.** to write or print in capital letters or with an initial capital. **2.** to capitalize a certain amount of stocks and bonds in the corporate charter of: *to capitalize a corporation.* **3.** to supply with capital. **4. capitalize on,** to take advantage of: *to capitalize on one's opportunities.*

cap′ital let′ter, *n.* a letter of the alphabet that usu. differs from its corresponding lowercase letter in form and height, as *A, B, Q,* and *R* as distinguished from *a, b, q,* and *r.*

cap′ital loss′, *n.* loss from the sale of assets, as of bonds or real estate.

cap·i·tal·ly (kap′i tl ē), *adv.* **1.** excellently; very well. **2.** in a manner involving capital punishment.

cap′ital sins′, *n.pl.* DEADLY SINS.

cap′ital stock′, *n.* **1.** the total stock authorized or issued by a corporation. **2.** the book value of such stock.

cap•i•tate (kap′i tāt′), *adj.* **1.** globose, as certain leaf or flower clusters. **2.** enlarged or knob-shaped at the end, as a bone.

cap•i•ta•tion (kap′i tā′shən), *n.* **1.** a poll tax. **2.** a fee or payment of a uniform amount for each person. —**cap′i•ta′tive,** *adj.*

Cap•i•tol (kap′i tl), *n.* **1.** the building in Washington, D.C., in which the U.S. Congress holds its sessions. **2.** (*often l.c.*) a building occupied by a state legislature. **3.** the ancient temple of Jupiter at Rome, on the Capitoline. **4.** the Capitoline. [< Latin *capitōlium* temple of Jupiter on Capitoline hill, Rome < *caput* head]

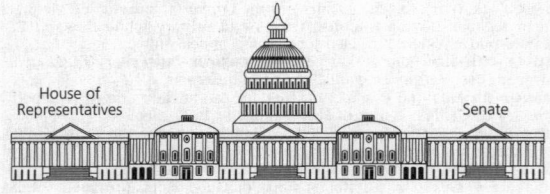

House of Representatives   Senate

Capitol

Cap′itol Hill′, *n.* **1.** the small hill in Washington, D.C., on which the Capitol stands. **2.** the U.S. Congress.

Cap•i•to•line (kap′i tl īn′), *n.* **1.** one of the seven hills on which ancient Rome was built. —*adj.* **2.** of or pertaining to the Capitoline or to the ancient temple of Jupiter that stood on this hill.

ca•pit•u•lar (kə pich′ə lər), *adj.* **1.** pertaining to an ecclesiastical or other chapter. **2.** CAPITATE (def. 1). —**ca•pit′u•lar•ly,** *adv.*

ca•pit•u•lar•y (kə pich′ə ler′ē), *n.,* *pl.* **-lar•ies. 1.** a member of a chapter, esp. of an ecclesiastical one. **2.** an ordinance or law of a Frankish sovereign.

ca•pit•u•late (kə pich′ə lāt′), *v.i.,* **-lat•ed, -lat•ing. 1.** to surrender unconditionally or on stipulated terms. **2.** to give up resistance; yield: *to capitulate to someone's pleas.*

ca•pit•u•la•tion (kə pich′ə lā′shən), *n.* **1.** the act of capitulating. **2.** the document containing the terms of a surrender. **3.** a list of the headings or main divisions of a subject; summary or enumeration. —**ca•pit′u•la•to′ry** (-lə tôr′ē, -tōr′ē), *adj.*

ca•piz (kə pēz′, ka-), *n.* a Pacific bivalve mollusk of the genus *Placuna,* common in Philippine waters, having a translucent inner shell used in making lamps and decorative objects.

cap•let (kap′lit), *n.* an oval-shaped tablet that is coated to facilitate swallowing.

cap′n (kap′m), *n.* captain.

ca•po (kā′pō), *n.,* *pl.* **-pos.** any of various devices for a guitar, lute, banjo, etc., that when clamped or screwed down across the strings will raise each string a corresponding number of half tones.

Ca•pone (kə pōn′), *n.* **Al**(phonse) (*"Scarface"*), 1899–1947, U.S. gangster and Prohibition-era bootlegger, probably born in Italy.

ca•pote (kə pōt′), *n.* a long cloak with a hood.

Capp (kap), *n.* **Al** (*Alfred Gerald Caplin*), 1909–79, U.S. comic-strip artist: creator of "Li'l Abner."

cap•puc•ci•no (kap′ə chē′nō, kä′pə-), *n.* hot espresso coffee with foaming steamed milk added, often sprinkled with cinnamon.

ca•pric•ci•o (kə prē′chē ō′, -prē′chō), *n.,* *pl.* **-ci•os, -ci** (-chē). **1.** an instrumental composition in a free and usu. lively style. **2.** a caper; prank. **3.** a whim; caprice.

ca•price (kə prēs′), *n.* **1.** a sudden, unpredictable change, as of one's mind or of the weather; vagary. **2.** a tendency to change one's mind without apparent or adequate motive; whimsicality; capriciousness. **3.** CAPRICCIO (def. 1).

ca•pri•cious (kə prish′əs, -prē′shəs), *adj.* subject to, led by, or indicative of caprice or whim; erratic; mercurial. —**ca•pri′cious•ly,** *adv.* —**ca•pri′cious•ness,** *n.*

Cap•ri•corn (kap′ri kôrn′), *n.* **1.** the Goat, a zodiacal constellation between Sagittarius and Aquarius. **2.** the tenth sign of the zodiac. [< Latin: goat]

cap•ri•fig (kap′rə fig′), *n.* the wild fig, *Ficus carica,* bearing an inedible fruit used in pollination of the edible fig.

cap•ri•ole (kap′rē ōl′), *n.,* *v.,* **-oled, -ol•ing.** —*n.* **1.** a caper or leap. **2.** a movement in manège in which the horse jumps completely off the ground, kicks its hind legs out horizontally in the air, and then lands again on the same spot. —*v.i.* **3.** to execute a capriole.

cap•si•cum (kap′si kəm), *n.* **1.** any plant of the genus *Capsicum,* of the nightshade family, as *C. annuum,* the common pepper of the garden, occurring in many varieties. **2.** the fruit of such a plant or some preparation of it, used as a condiment and intestinal stimulant.

cap•size (kap′sīz, kap sīz′), *v.i.,* *v.t.,* **-sized, -siz•ing.** to turn bottom up; overturn: *The boat capsized. They capsized their boat.*

cap•stan (kap′stən, -stan), *n.* **1.** any of various windlasses, rotated in a horizontal plane by hand or machinery, for winding in ropes, cables, etc. **2.** a rotating spindle or shaft, powered by an electric motor, that

capstan (def. 1)

transports magnetic tape past the heads of a tape recorder at a constant speed.

cap•stone (kap′stōn′), *n.* **1.** a finishing stone of a structure. **2.** the crowning achievement, point, element, or event.

cap•su•lar (kap′sə lər, -syŏŏ-), *adj.* of, in, or like a capsule.

cap•su•late (kap′sə lāt′, -lit, -syŏŏ-) also **cap•su•lat•ed** (-lā′tid), *adj.* enclosed in or formed into a capsule. —**cap′su•la′tion,** *n.*

cap•sule (kap′sal, -sŏŏl, -syŏŏl), *n.,* *v.,* **-suled, -sul•ing,** *adj.* —*n.* **1.** a gelatinous case enclosing a dose of medicine. **2. a.** a membranous sac or integument of the body. **b.** either of two strata of white matter in the cerebrum. **c.** the sporangium of various spore-producing organisms, as ferns, mosses, algae, and fungi. **3.** a dry dehiscent fruit, composed of two or more carpels. **4.** a small case, envelope, or covering. **5.** Also called **space capsule.** a sealed cabin, container, or vehicle in which a person or animal can ride in flight in space or at very high altitudes within the earth's atmosphere. **6.** a similar cabin in a military aircraft, which can be ejected in an emergency. **7.** a concise report; brief outline. —*v.t.* **8.** to furnish with or enclose in or as if in a capsule; encapsulate. **9.** to capsulize. —*adj.* **10.** small and compact. **11.** short and concise; briefly summarized: *a capsule report.*

cap•sul•ize (kap′sə līz′, -syŏŏ-), *v.t.,* **-ized, -iz•ing.** to summarize or make concise. —**cap′sul•i•za′tion,** *n.*

capt., captain.

cap•tain (kap′tən, -tin), *n.* **1.** a person in authority over others; chief; leader. **2.** an army officer ranking next above a first lieutenant. **3.** a commissioned naval officer ranking above a commander. **4.** an officer of any rank who commands a military vessel. **5.** an officer in a police or fire department ranking next above a lieutenant. **6.** the commander of a merchant vessel. **7.** the pilot of an airplane. **8.** the field leader of a sports team. **9.** a person of great power and influence, esp. based on wealth. **10.** HEADWAITER. —*v.t.* **11.** to lead or command as a captain. —**cap′tain•cy,** *n.*

cap′tain's bed′, *n.* a bed consisting of a shallow box with drawers in the side and a mattress on top.

cap′tain's chair′, *n.* a chair having a rounded back formed by a rail resting upon spindles and coming forward to form the arms.

cap•tan (kap′tan, -tən), *n.* a white powder, $C_9H_8Cl_3NO_2S$, used as a fungicide on vegetables, fruit, and flowers.

cap•tion (kap′shən), *n.* **1.** a title or explanation for a picture or illustration, esp. in a magazine. **2.** a heading or title, as of a chapter or page. **3.** a title, the text of dialogue, or other words projected onto a motion-picture or television screen. **4.** the heading of a legal document, stating when and where it was executed, etc. —*v.t.* **5.** to supply a caption or captions for; entitle.

cap•tious (kap′shəs), *adj.* **1.** apt to focus on trivial faults or defects; faultfinding. **2.** proceeding from a faultfinding disposition. **3.** apt or designed to ensnare or perplex: *captious questions.* —**cap′tious•ly,** *adv.* —**cap′tious•ness,** *n.*

cap•ti•vate (kap′tə vāt′), *v.t.,* **-vat•ed, -vat•ing.** to attract intensely and fixedly, as by beauty or some special quality; enchant; fascinate. —**cap′ti•vat′ing•ly,** *adv.* —**cap′ti•va′tor,** *n.*

cap•tive (kap′tiv), *n.* **1.** a prisoner. **2.** a person who is enslaved or dominated: *a captive of one's own fears.* —*adj.* **3.** made or held prisoner, esp. in war. **4.** kept in confinement or restraint: *captive animals.* **5.** enslaved by love, beauty, etc.; captivated. **6.** unable to avoid listening or attending to something: *a captive audience.*

cap′tive can′didate, *n.* a political candidate who is dominated by a group or interest.

cap•tiv•i•ty (kap tiv′i tē), *n.,* *pl.* **-ties.** the state or period of being held, imprisoned, enslaved, or confined; servitude or bondage; imprisonment.

cap•tor (kap′tər), *n.* a person who has captured a person or thing.

cap•ture (kap′chər), *v.,* **-tured, -tur•ing,** *n.* —*v.t.* **1.** to take by force or stratagem; take prisoner; seize; apprehend. **2.** to gain control of or exert influence over: *to capture someone's attention.* **3.** to take possession of, as in a game or contest: *to capture a pawn in chess.* **4.** to represent or record in lasting form: *a movie that captures Berlin in the 1930s.* **5. a.** to enter (data) into a computer for processing or storage. **b.** to record (data) in preparation for such entry. —*n.* **6.** the act of capturing; seizure. **7.** the person or thing captured. **8.** the process in which an atomic or nuclear system acquires an additional particle.

cap•u•chin (kap′yŏŏ chin, -shin), *n.* **1.** any New World monkey of the genus *Cebus,* having a prehensile tail and tufts of hair on the head. **2.** a hooded cloak for women. **3.** (*cap.*) a friar belonging to the branch of the Franciscan order that observes vows of poverty and austerity.

cap·y·ba·ra (kap/ə bär/ə), *n., pl.* **-ras.** a large South American aquatic rodent, *Hydrochoerus capybara.*

car (kär), *n.* **1.** an automobile. **2.** a vehicle running on rails, as a streetcar or railroad car. **3.** the part of a conveyance, as an elevator or balloon, that carries the passengers, freight, etc. **4.** any wheeled vehicle. [< Anglo-French < Latin *carra* < Celtic]

ca·ra·ba·o (kär/ə bä/ō), *n., pl.* **-ba·os.** (in the Philippines) the water buffalo.

car·a·bi·ner or **kar·a·bi·ner** (kar/ə bē/nər), *n.* a D-shaped ring with a spring catch on one side, used for fastening ropes in mountaineering.

car·a·cal (kar/ə kal/), *n.* a wildcat, *Felis (Lynx) caracal,* of S Asia and Africa, with a reddish brown coat and tufted ears.

ca·ra·ca·ra (kär/ə kär/ə, kar/ə kar/ə), *n., pl.* **-ras.** any of several typically large, long-legged, barefaced birds of prey of the falcon family, inhabiting tropical and subtropical regions of the New World.

Ca·ra·cas (kə rä/kəs), *n.* the capital of Venezuela, in the N part. 1,044,851.

car·a·cole (kar/ə kōl/), *n., v.,* **-coled, -col·ing.** —*n.* **1.** a half turn executed by a horse and rider. —*v.i.* **2.** to execute caracoles; wheel.

ca·rafe (kə raf/, -räf/), *n.* a wide-mouthed glass or bottle with a lip or spout, for holding and serving beverages.

ca·ram·bo·la (kar/əm bō/lə), *n., pl.* **-las. 1.** a SE Asian tree, *Averrhoa carambola,* of the family Oxalidaceae, bearing deeply ridged, yellow-brown fruit. **2.** Also called **star fruit.** the fruit itself.

car·a·mel (kar/ə məl, -mel/, kär/məl), *n.* **1.** a liquid made by cooking sugar until it darkens, used for coloring and flavoring food. **2.** a chewy candy made from sugar, butter, milk, etc.

car·a·mel·ize (kar/ə mə līz/, kär/mə-), *v.t., v.i.,* **-ized, -iz·ing.** to convert or be converted into caramel. —**car/a·mel·i·za/tion,** *n.*

ca·ran·gid (kə ran/jid), *n.* **1.** any of numerous fishes of the family Carangidae, comprising the jacks, scads, pompanos, and king mackerels. —*adj.* **2.** belonging or pertaining to the carangids.

car·a·pace (kar/ə pās/), *n.* a bony or chitinous shield, test, or shell covering some or all of the dorsal part of an animal, as of a turtle. —**car/a·paced/,** *adj.*

car·at (kar/ət), *n.* a unit of weight in gemstones, 200 milligrams (about 3 grains of troy or avoirdupois weight). *Abbr.:* c., ct.

car·a·van (kar/ə van/), *n., v.,* **-vaned** or **-vanned, -van·ing** or **-van·ning.** —*n.* **1.** a group of travelers journeying together for safety in passing through deserts, hostile territory, etc. **2.** any group traveling in or as if in a caravan, as pack animals or motor vehicles. **3.** a large covered vehicle for conveying passengers, goods, a sideshow, etc.; van. —*v.t.* **4.** to carry in or as if in a caravan. —*v.i.* **5.** to travel in or as if in a caravan. [< Italian *carovana* < Persian *kāwān*]

car·a·van·sa·ry (kar/ə van/sə rē) also **car·a·van·se·rai** (-sə rī/, -rā/), *n., pl.* **-sa·ries** also **-se·rais. 1.** (in the Near East) an inn, usu. with a large courtyard, for the overnight accommodation of caravans. **2.** any large inn or hotel.

car·a·vel (kar/ə vel/) also **carvel,** *n.* a small Spanish or Portuguese sailing vessel of the Middle Ages and later.

car·a·way (kar/ə wā/), *n.* **1.** a plant, *Carum carvi,* of the parsley family, native to Europe, having finely divided leaves and umbels of white or pinkish flowers. **2.** Also called **car/away seed/.** the aromatic seedlike fruit of this plant, used in cooking and medicine.

car·bam/ic ac/id (kär bam/ik), *n.* a compound, NH_3CO_2, known only in the form of its salts or its esters.

car·bide (kär/bīd, -bid), *n.* **1.** a compound of carbon with a more electropositive element or group. **2.** a very hard mixture of sintered carbides of various heavy metals, esp. tungsten carbide, used for cutting edges and dies.

car·bine (kär/bēn, -bīn), *n.* **1.** a light, gas-operated semiautomatic rifle. **2.** any of various short-barreled muskets or rifles used, orig. by cavalry troops, since c1600.

car·bi·nol (kär/bə nôl/, -nol/), *n.* **1.** METHYL ALCOHOL. **2.** an alcohol derived from methyl alcohol.

car·bo (kär/bō), *n., pl.* **-bos. 1.** carbohydrate. **2.** a food having a high carbohydrate content.

carbo-, a combining form used in the names of chemical compounds in which carbon is present: *carbohydrate.* Also, *esp. before a vowel,* **carb-.**

car·bo·hy·drate (kär/bō hī/drāt, -bə-), *n.* any of a class of organic compounds composed of carbon, hydrogen, and oxygen, including starches and sugars, produced in green plants by photosynthesis: important source of food for animals and people.

car·bol/ic ac/id (kär bol/ik), *n.* PHENOL (def. 1).

car/bo-load/ing, *n. Informal.* the practice of eating large amounts of carbohydrates for a few days before competing in a strenuous athletic event, as a marathon, to provide energy reserves in the form of glycogen. —**car/bo-load/,** *v.i.*

car·bon (kär/bən), *n.* **1.** a nonmetallic element found combined with other elements in all organic matter and in a pure state as diamond and graphite. *Symbol:* C; *at. wt.:* 12.011; *at. no.:* 6; *sp. gr.:* (of diamond) 3.51 at 20°C; (of graphite) 2.26 at 20°C. **2.** CARBON COPY. **3.** a sheet of carbon paper. **4. a.** the current-bearing carbon rod used in arc lights and in welding. **b.** the rod or plate, composed in part of carbon, used in batteries. —**car/bon·less,** *adj.*

carbon 12 or **carbon-12,** *n.* the isotopic carbon atom used as the standard for atomic weight.

carbon 14 or **carbon-14,** *n.* RADIOCARBON (def. 1).

carbon-14 dating, *n.* RADIOCARBON DATING.

car·bo·na·ceous (kär/bə nā/shəs), *adj.* of, like, or containing carbon.

car·bo·na·do[1] (kär/bə nā/dō), *n., pl.* **-dos, -does.** a massive, black variety of diamond, found chiefly near São Salvador, Brazil, used for drilling and other cutting purposes.

car·bo·na·do[2] (kär/bə nā/dō), *n., pl.* **-does, -dos,** *v.,* **-doed, -do·ing.** —*n.* **1.** a piece of meat, fish, etc., scored and broiled. —*v.t.* **2.** to score and broil.

car·bo·na·ra (kär/bə när/ə), *adj.* served with a sauce of beaten eggs, grated cheese, and chopped bacon: *spaghetti carbonara.*

car·bon·ate (*n.* kär/bə nāt/, -nit; *v.* -nāt/), *n., v.,* **-at·ed, -at·ing.** —*n.* **1.** a salt or ester of carbonic acid. —*v.t.* **2.** to charge or impregnate with carbon dioxide: *carbonated drinks.* —**car/bon·a/tion,** *n.*

car/bon cop/y, *n.* **1.** a duplicate, as of something typewritten, made with carbon paper. **2.** any near or exact duplicate; replica.

car/bon cy/cle, *n.* **1.** the biological cycle by which atmospheric carbon dioxide is converted to carbohydrates by plants and other photosynthesizers, consumed and metabolized by organisms, and returned to the atmosphere through respiration, decomposition, and the combustion of fossil fuels. **2.** a cycle of nuclear transformations in stellar interiors through which hydrogen is converted into helium.

car/bon-date/, *v.t.,* **-dat·ed, -dat·ing.** to estimate the age of (an object of plant or animal origin) by radiocarbon dating.

car/bon diox/ide, *n.* a colorless, odorless, incombustible gas, CO_2, present in the atmosphere and formed during respiration: used as dry ice and in carbonated beverages and fire extinguishers.

car/bon disul/fide, *n.* a clear flammable liquid, CS_2, used in making cellophane, rayon, and pesticides and as a solvent.

carbon/ic ac/id, *n.* the acid, H_2CO_3, formed when carbon dioxide dissolves in water, known in the form of its salts and esters, the carbonates.

Car·bon·if·er·ous (kär/bə nif/ər əs), *adj.* **1.** noting or pertaining to a period of the Paleozoic Era, including the Pennsylvanian and Mississippian periods as epochs, occurring from 345 million to 280 million years ago. **2.** (*l.c.*) producing carbon or coal. —*n.* **3.** the Carboniferous Period or System.

car·bon·ize (kär/bə nīz/), *v.,* **-ized, -iz·ing.** —*v.t.* **1.** to char (organic matter) until it forms carbon. **2.** to coat or enrich with carbon. —*v.i.* **3.** to become carbonized. —**car/bon·iz/a·ble,** *adj.*

car/bon monox/ide, *n.* a colorless, odorless, poisonous gas, CO, produced when carbon burns with insufficient air: used chiefly in organic synthesis and metallurgy.

car/bon pa/per, *n.* paper faced with a preparation of carbon or other material, used between two sheets of plain paper in order to reproduce on the lower sheet whatever is written on the upper.

car/bon tetrachlo/ride, *n.* a colorless, nonflammable, vaporous, toxic liquid, CCl_4, used mainly as a refrigerant, fire extinguisher, cleaning fluid, solvent, and insecticide.

car·bon·yl (kär/bə nil), *n.* a compound containing metal combined with carbon monoxide, as nickel carbonyl, $Ni(CO)_4$.

Car·bo·run·dum (kär/bə run/dəm), *Trademark.* any of various abrasives of silicon carbide, fused alumina, and other materials.

car·bun·cle (kär/bung kəl), *n.* **1.** a local skin inflammation of deep interconnected boils. **2.** a gemstone, esp. a garnet, cut with a convex back and a cabochon surface. —**car·bun/cu·lar,** *adj.*

car·bu·re·tor or **car·bu·ret·ter** (kär/bə rā/tər, -byə-), *n.* a device for mixing vaporized fuel with air to produce a combustible or explosive mixture, as for an internal-combustion engine. Also, *esp. Brit.,* **car·bu·ret/tor, car·bu·ret·ter** (kär/byə ret/ər).

car·bu·rize (kär/bə rīz/, -byə-), *v.t.,* **-rized, -riz·ing.** to cause to unite with carbon. —**car/bu·ri·za/tion,** *n.* —**car/bu·riz/er,** *n.*

car·cass (kär/kəs), *n.* **1.** the dead body of an animal, esp. of a slaughtered animal after removal of the offal. **2.** *Slang.* the body of a human being, whether living or dead. **3.** the physical or structural remnant of something stripped, plundered, or decayed; shell. **4.** an unfinished skeleton or framework, as of a house or ship. **5.** the inner body of a pneumatic tire.

car·cin·o·gen (kär sin/ə jən, -jen/, kär/sə nə jen/), *n.* any substance that tends to produce a cancer. —**car/cin·o·gen/ic,** *adj.*

car·ci·noid (kär/sə noid/), *n.* a small, yellowish amino-acid- and peptide-secreting tumor usu. found in the gastrointestinal tract and the lung.

car·ci·no·ma (kär/sə nō/mə), *n., pl.* **-mas, -ma·ta** (-mə tə). a malignant tumor composed of epithelial tissue.

card[1] (kärd), *n.* **1.** a usu. rectangular piece of stiff paper, thin pasteboard, or plastic for various uses, to record information or, when preprinted, to identify the holder. **2.** one of a set of cards with spots, figures, etc., used in playing various games. **3.** cards, (*usu. with a sing. v.*) **a.** a game or games played with such a set. **b.** the playing of such a game: *to win at cards.* **4.** something useful in attaining an objective, comparable to a high card held in a game. **5.** GREETING CARD. **6.** POST-CARD. **7.** CALLING CARD (def. 1). **8.** CREDIT CARD. **9.** a card with a picture of a sports or other figure on one side and information about the figure on the other, used as a collectible: *baseball cards.* **10.** a program of the events at races, boxing matches, etc. **11.** BOARD (def. 13a). **12.** an amusing, witty, or prankish person. —*v.t.* **13.** to provide with a card.

14. to fasten on a card. **15.** to write, list, etc., on cards. **16.** to ask (a youth) to produce identification, esp. to check whether the person is of legal drinking age. —*Idiom.* **17. in the cards,** destined to occur. **18. put** or **lay one's cards on the table,** to be completely straightforward; conceal nothing.

card² (kärd), *n.* Also called **carding machine. 1.** a machine for combing and paralleling fibers of cotton, flax, wool, etc., prior to spinning in order to remove short, undesirable fibers and produce a sliver. **2.** a similar implement for raising the nap on cloth. —*v.t.* **3.** to dress (wool or the like) with a card. —**card′er,** *n.*

car•da•mom (kär′də məm) also **car•da•mon** (-mən), **car′da•mum,** *n.* **1.** the aromatic seed capsules of a tropical Asian plant, *Elettaria cardamomum,* of the ginger family, used as a spice and in medicine. **2.** the plant itself. **3.** a related plant, *Amomum compactum,* or its seeds, used as a substitute for true cardamom.

card•board (kärd′bôrd′, -bōrd′), *n.* **1.** a thin, stiff pasteboard, used for signs, boxes, etc. —*adj.* **2.** resembling cardboard, esp. in flimsiness: *an apartment with cardboard walls.* **3.** not fully lifelike; two-dimensional: *a silly movie with a cardboard hero.*

card′-car′ry•ing, *adj.* **1.** admittedly belonging to a group or party: *a card-carrying Communist.* **2.** identified with or dedicated to an ideal, profession, or interest: *a card-carrying humanist.*

card′ cat′a•log, *n.* a file of cards arranged in some definite order and listing the items in the collection of a library.

card•hold•er (kärd′hōl′dər), *n.* a person to whom a card has been issued, esp. a credit card.

car•di•a (kär′dē ə), *n., pl.* **-di•ae** (-dē ē′), **-di•as.** an opening that connects the esophagus and the upper part of the stomach.

car•di•ac (kär′dē ak′), *adj.* **1.** of or pertaining to the heart: *cardiac disease.* **2.** of or pertaining to the esophageal portion of the stomach. —*n.* **3.** a person suffering from heart disease.

car′diac arrest′, *n.* abrupt cessation of heartbeat.

car′diac mus′cle, *n.* **1.** a specialized form of striated muscle in the hearts of vertebrates. **2.** the myocardium.

car•di•gan (kär′di gən), *n.* a usu. collarless knitted sweater or jacket that opens down the front. [after the Earl of *Cardigan* (1797–1868), British hero in Crimean War]

car•di•nal (kär′dn l), *adj.* **1.** of prime importance; chief; principal. **2.** of the color cardinal. —*n.* **3.** a high ecclesiastic appointed by the pope to the College of Cardinals. **4.** a common crested songbird, *Cardinalis cardinalis,* of North America, the male of which is bright red. **5.** a deep, rich red color. **6.** CARDINAL NUMBER. —**car′di•nal•ship′,** *n.*

car′dinal flow′er, *n.* a North American plant, *Lobelia cardinalis,* of the lobelia family, with showy red tubular flowers in an elongated cluster.

car′dinal num′ber, *n.* any of the numbers that express amount, as *one, two, three* (disting. from *ordinal number*).

car′dinal points′, *n.pl.* the north, south, east, and west points of the compass.

car′dinal vir′tue, *n.* **1.** anything considered to be an important or characteristic virtue: *Tenacity is his cardinal virtue.* **2. cardinal virtues,** *Ancient Philos.* justice, prudence, temperance, and fortitude.

cardio-, a combining form meaning "heart": *cardiogram.* Also, *esp. before a vowel,* **cardi-.**

car•di•o•gram (kär′dē ə gram′), *n.* ELECTROCARDIOGRAM.

car•di•o•graph (kär′dē ə graf′, -gräf′), *n.* ELECTROCARDIOGRAPH. —**car′di•og′ra•phy** (-og′rə fē), *n.*

car•di•ol•o•gy (kär′dē ol′ə jē), *n.* the study of the heart and its functions. —**car′di•o•log′ic** (-ə loj′ik), **car′di•o•log′i•cal,** *adj.* —**car′di•ol′o•gist,** *n.*

car•di•o•my•op•a•thy (kär′dē ō mī op′ə thē), *n.* any disease of the heart muscle.

car•di•op•a•thy (kär′dē op′ə thē), *n.* any disorder of the heart.

car•di•o•pul•mo•nar•y (kär′dē ō pul′mə ner′ē, -pōol′-), *adj.* of, pertaining to, or affecting the heart and lungs.

cardiopul′monary resuscita′tion, *n.* emergency procedure for reviving heart and lung function.

car•di•o•res•pi•ra•to•ry (kär′dē ō res′pər ə tôr′ē, -tōr′ē, -ri spīr′ə-), *adj.* of or affecting the heart and respiratory system.

car•di•o•vas•cu•lar (kär′dē ō vas′kyə lər), *adj.* of, pertaining to, or affecting the heart and blood vessels.

-cardium, a combining form occurring in compounds that denote tissue or organs associated with the heart, as specified by the initial element: *myocardium.*

car•doon (kär dōōn′) also **car•don** (-dōn′), *n.* a composite plant, *Cynara cardunculus,* of the Mediterranean area, having a root and leafstalks eaten as a vegetable.

card′sharp (kärd′shärp′) also **card′sharp′er,** *n.* a person, esp. a professional gambler, who cheats at card games. Also called **card′ shark′.** —**card′sharp′ing,** *n.*

card′ ta′ble, *n.* a small square table usu. with folding legs and a surface suitable for card games.

care (kâr), *n., v.,* **cared, car•ing.** —*n.* **1.** a troubled state of mind; worry or concern. **2.** a cause or object of worry or concern. **3.** serious attention; caution: *to devote great care to one's work.* **4.** protection; charge: *under the care of a doctor.* **5.** temporary keeping: *We left our cat in the care of friends.* —*v.i.* **6.** to be concerned; have thought or regard. **7.** to

object or mind: *I don't care if you come late.* **8.** to make provision: *Will you care for the children while I am away?* **9.** to have an inclination or liking: *Would you care for dessert?* —*v.t.* **10.** to feel concern about: *to care what others say.* **11.** to desire; like: *Would you care to dance?* —*Idiom.* **12. could(n't) care less,** to be completely unconcerned. **13. take care,** to guard oneself against harm (sometimes used as a conventional expression of parting). **14. take care of, a.** to watch over; be responsible for: *to take care of an invalid.* **b.** to deal with; attend to: *to take care of all the bills.*

CARE or **Care** (kâr), *n.* a private organization for the collection of funds, goods, etc., for distribution to the needy in foreign countries. [C(ooperative for) A(merican) R(elief) E(verywhere)]

ca•reen (kə rēn′), *v.i.* **1.** to lean or tip to one side while in motion; sway: *The car careened around the corner.* **2.** (of a ship) to heel over or list. **3.** CAREER (def. 5). —*v.t.* **4.** to cause (a ship) to lie over on a side, as for repairs or cleaning. **5.** to clean or repair (a careened ship). **6.** to cause (a ship) to heel over or list. —*n.* **7.** the act or position of careening. —**ca•reen′er,** *n.*

ca•reer (kə rēr′), *n.* **1.** an occupation or profession followed as one's lifework. **2.** a person's general course of action through some or all of life: *a short career as a soldier.* **3.** a course, esp. a swift one. **4.** speed, esp. full speed. —*v.i.* **5.** to go at full speed. —*adj.* **6.** having a career; professional: *a career diplomat.*

ca•reer•ism (kə rēr′iz əm), *n.* devotion to a successful career, often at the expense of one's personal life or ethics.

care•free (kâr′frē′), *adj.* being without anxiety or worry.

care•ful (kâr′fəl), *adj.* **1.** cautious in one's actions: *Be careful when you cross the street.* **2.** taking pains in one's work: *a careful typist.* **3.** done with accuracy or caution: *careful research.* **4.** solicitously mindful: *careful about one's behavior.* —**care′ful•ly,** *adv.*

care•giv•er (kâr′giv′ər), *n.* **1.** a person who cares for someone who is sick or disabled. **2.** an adult who cares for a child.

care•less (kâr′lis), *adj.* **1.** not paying enough attention to what one does. **2.** not exact or accurate: *careless work.* **3.** heedless; unconsidered: *a careless remark.* **4.** not caring or troubling; unconcerned. **5.** artless; unstudied: *careless beauty.* —**care′less•ly,** *adv.* —**care′less•ness,** *n.*

ca•ress (kə res′), *n.* **1.** a light stroking gesture expressing affection. —*v.t.* **2.** to touch or stroke lightly in or as if in affection. **3.** to treat with favor or kindness. —**ca•ress′ing•ly,** *adv.*

car•et (kar′it), *n.* a mark (^) made in written or printed matter to show the place where something is to be inserted. [< Latin: (there) is lacking]

care•tak•er (kâr′tā′kər), *n.* **1.** a person in charge of the maintenance of a building, estate, etc. **2.** a person or group that temporarily performs the duties of an office: *a caretaker government.* **3.** a person who takes care of another. —**care′tak′ing,** *n.*

Car•ey (kâr′ē, kar′ē), *n.* **George,** born 1935, English clergyman: archbishop of Canterbury since 1991.

car•fare (kär′fâr′), *n.* the amount charged for a ride on a subway or bus.

car•go (kär′gō), *n., pl.* **-goes, -gos.** the load of goods carried by a ship, airplane, etc.; freight.

Car′ibbe′an Sea′, *n.* a part of the Atlantic Ocean bounded by Central America, the West Indies, and South America. ab. 750,000 sq. mi. (1,943,000 sq. km); greatest known depth 22,788 ft. (6946 m).

car•i•bou (kar′ə bōō′), *n., pl.* **-bous,** (*esp. collectively*) **-bou.** the reindeer of North America.

caribou, *Rangifer tarandus,* about 4 ft. (1.2 m) high at shoulder; length to 6 ft. (1.8 m)

car•i•ca•ture (kar′i kə chər, -chōōr′), *n., v.,* **-tured, -tur•ing.** —*n.* **1.** a picture or description ludicrously exaggerating the peculiarities or defects of a person or thing. **2.** the art or process of producing such pictures or descriptions. **3.** any imitation so distorted or inferior as to be ludicrous. —*v.t.* **4.** to make a caricature of. —**car′i•ca•tur•ist,** *n.*

car•ies (kâr′ēz, -ē ēz′), *n., pl.* **-ies. 1.** decay, as of bone or of plant tissue. **2.** DENTAL CARIES. —**car′i•ous,** *adj.*

car•il•lon (kar′ə lon′, -lən; *esp. Brit.* kə ril′yən), *n.* **1.** a set of stationary bells hung in a tower and sounded by manual or pedal action or by machinery. **2.** an electronic instrument imitative of the sound of the carillon.

car·i·o·ca (kar′ē ō′kə), *n.*, *pl.* **-cas.** a dance based on the samba.

car′jack′ing (kär′jak′ing), *n.* the forcible stealing of a vehicle from a motorist. —**car′jack′er,** *n.*

car·load (kär′lōd′), *n.* **1.** the amount carried by a car, esp. a freight car. **2.** the minimum weight required to ship a load by rail at a discount rate (**car′load rate′**).

Car·mel (kär′məl, kär mel′), *n.* **Mount,** a mountain ridge in NW Israel, near the Mediterranean coast. Highest point, 1818 ft. (554 m).

Car·mel·ite (kär′mə līt′), *n.* **1.** a mendicant friar belonging to a religious order founded at Mt. Carmel, Palestine, in the 12th century. **2.** a nun belonging to this order. —*adj.* **3.** of or pertaining to Carmelites or their order.

Car·mi·chael (kär′mī kəl), *n.* **1. Hoagland Howard,** (*"Hoagy"*), 1899–1981, U.S. songwriter and musician. **2. Stokely,** born 1941, U.S. civil-rights leader, born in Trinidad: chairman of the Student Nonviolent Coordinating Committee 1966–67.

car·mine (kär′min, -mīn), *n.* **1.** a crimson or purplish red color. **2.** a crimson pigment obtained from cochineal.

car·nage (kär′nij), *n.* the slaughter of a great number of people, as in battle; massacre.

car·nal (kär′nl), *adj.* **1.** pertaining to or characterized by the passions and appetites of the flesh or body; sensual. **2.** not spiritual; temporal; worldly. —**car·nal′i·ty,** *n.* —**car′nal·ly,** *adv.*

car·na·tion (kär nā′shən), *n.* **1.** any of numerous cultivated varieties of the clove pink, *Dianthus caryophyllus,* having long-stalked fragrant flowers in a variety of colors. **2.** pink; light red.

car·nau·ba (kär nou′bə, -nô′-, -nōō′-), *n.*, *pl.* **-bas. 1.** a palm, *Copernicia prunifera,* of Brazil, having palmate leaves covered with wax. **2.** Also called **carnau′ba wax′.** a hard lustrous wax obtained from the leaves of this tree and used as a polish and floor wax.

car·nel·ian (kär nēl′yən), *n.* a reddish variety of chalcedony used in jewelry.

car·net (kär nā′), *n.* a customs document allowing an automobile to be driven at no cost across international borders.

car·ni·val (kär′nə vəl), *n.* **1.** a traveling amusement show having sideshows and rides. **2.** a festival: *a winter carnival of sports and games.* **3.** the season immediately preceding Lent, often observed with merrymaking. [< Italian *carnevale,* taking meat away]

car·ni·vore (kär′nə vôr′, -vōr′), *n.* **1.** an animal that eats flesh. **2.** a flesh-eating mammal of the order Carnivora, comprising the dogs, cats, bears, seals, and weasels. **3.** an insectivorous plant. —**car·niv·o·rous** (kär niv′ər əs), *adj.*

car·no·tite (kär′nə tīt′), *n.* a yellow earthy ore of uranium, hydrous potassium uranium vanadate.

car·ny or **car·ney** (kär′nē), *n.*, *pl.* **-nies** or **-neys. 1.** a person employed by a carnival. **2.** CARNIVAL (def. 1).

car·ob (kar′əb), *n.* **1.** a Mediterranean tree, *Ceratonia siliqua,* of the legume family, bearing long leathery pods containing hard seeds and sweet edible pulp. **2.** the pod of this tree. **3.** the pulp of the pods, often used as a substitute for chocolate.

car·ol (kar′əl), *n.*, *v.*, **-oled, -ol·ing** or (*esp. Brit.*) **-olled, -ol·ling.** —*n.* **1.** a song, esp. of joy. **2.** a Christmas song or hymn. —*v.i.* **3.** to sing Christmas songs, esp. in a group outdoors. **4.** to sing, esp. in a lively, joyous manner. —*v.t.* **5.** to sing joyously. **6.** to celebrate in song. —**car′ol·er;** *esp. Brit.,* **car′ol·ler,** *n.*

Car·o·li·na (kar′ə lī′nə; *for 2 also Sp.* kä′rō lē′nä), *n.* **1.** a former English colony on the Atlantic coast of North America, divided into North Carolina and South Carolina in 1729. **2.** a city in NE Puerto Rico, SE of San Juan. 162,888. **3. the Carolinas,** North Carolina and South Carolina.

Car′oli′na par′akeet, *n.* a small parrot, *Conuropsis carolinensis,* of the eastern U.S., having a green body, yellow head, and pink cheeks: extinct since 1918.

Car′oli′na wren′, *n.* a common wren, *Thryothorus ludovicianus,* of the eastern U.S. and parts of Mexico, having a cheerful two- or three-note song.

car·om (kar′əm), *n.* **1.** a shot in billiards or pool in which the cue ball hits two balls in succession. **2.** any hit and rebound. —*v.i.* **3.** to make a carom. **4.** to hit and rebound.

car·o·tene (kar′ə tēn′) also **car·o·tin** (-tin), *n.* any of three yellow or orange fat-soluble pigments having the formula $C_{40}H_{56}$, found in many plants, esp. carrots, and transformed into vitamin A in the liver; provitamin A.

ca·rot·e·noid or **ca·rot·i·noid** (kə rot′n oid′), *n.* **1.** any of a group of red and yellow pigments, chemically similar to carotene, contained in animal fat and some plants. —*adj.* **2.** similar to carotene. **3.** pertaining to carotenoids.

ca·rot·id (kə rot′id), *n.* **1.** Also called **carot′id ar′tery.** either of two large arteries, one on each side of the neck, that carry blood from the aorta to the head. —*adj.* **2.** pertaining to a carotid artery.

ca·rous·al (kə rou′zəl), *n.* a noisy or drunken gathering; revel.

ca·rouse (kə rouz′), *v.*, **-roused, -rous·ing,** *n.* —*v.i.* **1.** to engage in a drunken revel. **2.** to drink deeply and frequently. —*n.* **3.** CAROUSAL. —**ca·rous′er,** *n.* —**ca·rous′ing·ly,** *adv.*

car·ou·sel (kar′ə sel′, kar′ə sel′), *n.* **1.** MERRY-GO-ROUND (def. 1). **2.** a

continuously revolving conveyor on which items are placed: *a baggage carousel at an airport.*

carp¹ (kärp), *v.i.* **1.** to find fault; complain unreasonably; cavil. —*n.* **2.** a peevish complaint. —**carp′er,** *n.*

carp² (kärp), *n.*, *pl.* (*esp. collectively*) **carp,** (*esp. for kinds or species*) **carps. 1.** a large freshwater cyprinid fish, *Cyprinus carpio,* native to Asia but widely cultivated as a food fish. **2.** any of various other fishes of the family Cyprinidae.

-carp, a combining form occurring in words that denote a part of a fruit or fruiting body: *endocarp.*

car·pal (kär′pəl), *adj.* **1.** pertaining to the carpus: *the carpal joint.* —*n.* **2.** any of the bones of the carpus; a wrist bone.

car′pal tun′nel syn′drome, *n.* a disorder of the hand characterized by pain, weakness, and numbness in the thumb and other fingers, caused by an inflamed ligament that presses on a nerve in the wrist.

car·pel (kär′pəl), *n.* a simple pistil or a single member of a compound pistil. —**car′pel·lar·y** (-ler′ē), *adj.* —**car′pel·late′,** *adj.*

car·pen·ter (kär′pən tər), *n.* **1.** a person who builds or repairs wooden structures, as houses, scaffolds, or shelving. —*v.i.* **2.** to do carpenter's work. —*v.t.* **3.** to make by carpentry. **4.** to construct in a mechanical or unoriginal fashion: *to carpenter a soap opera script.* —**car′pen·try,** *n.*

car′penter ant′, *n.* a black or brown ant of the genus *Camponotus* that nests in decaying wood.

car′penter bee′, *n.* any of several solitary bees of the family Apidae that build nests by boring tunnels in wood.

car·pet (kär′pit), *n.* **1.** a heavy woven or felted fabric for covering floors. **2.** a covering of this. **3.** any surface or covering resembling a carpet. —*v.t.* **4.** to cover or furnish with or as if with a carpet. —*Idiom.* **5. on the carpet,** summoned for a reprimand.

car·pet·bag·ger (kär′pit bag′ər), *n.* **1.** a Northerner who went to the South after the Civil War to profit from the unsettled conditions. **2.** any person, esp. a politician, who takes up residence in a place opportunistically. —**car′pet·bag′ger·y,** *n.*

car′pet bee′tle, *n.* any of several small beetles of the family Dermestidae, the larvae of which feed on fur and wool fabrics, esp. rugs. Also called **car′pet bug′.**

car′pet sweep′er, *n.* a long-handled implement for removing dirt and lint from rugs and carpets, consisting of a metal case enclosing one or more rotating brushes.

car·pet·weed (kär′pit wēd′), *n.* a North American prostrate weed, *Mollugo verticillata,* having whorled leaves and small whitish flowers.

car·pi (kär′pī), *n.* pl. of CARPUS.

-carpic, a combination of -CARP and -IC used in the formation of adjectives from nouns ending in -CARP: *endocarpic.*

carp·ing (kär′ping), *adj.* characterized by or inclined to petty or fussy faultfinding. —**carp′ing·ly,** *adv.*

carpo-, a combining form meaning "fruit," "fruiting body": *carpogonium.*

car·pol·o·gy (kär pol′ə jē), *n.* the branch of botany dealing with fruits and seeds.

car·pool (kär′pōōl′), *n.* Also, **car′ pool′. 1.** an arrangement among automobile owners by which each in turn drives the others to and from a designated place. **2.** those included in such an arrangement. —*v.i.* **3.** Also, **car′-pool′.** to form or participate in a carpool. —**car′pool′er,** *n.*

car·port (kär′pôrt′, -pōrt′), *n.* a simple shed or a roof projecting from the side of a building for sheltering an automobile.

car·po·spore (kär′pə spôr′, -spōr′), *n.* a nonmotile spore of the red algae. —**car′po·spor′ic** (-spôr′ik, -spor′-), **car·pos′po·rous** (-pos′pər əs), *adj.*

-carpous, a combining form meaning "having fruit, fruiting bodies, or carpels" of the kind specified by the initial element: *apocarpous.*

car·pus (kär′pəs), *n.*, *pl.* **-pi** (-pī). **1.** the wrist. **2.** the wrist bones collectively.

car·rel or **car·rell** (kar′əl), *n.* a cubicle or desk partitioned off for private study in a library.

car·riage (kar′ij; *for 6 also* kar′ē ij), *n.* **1.** a wheeled vehicle for conveying persons, as one drawn by horses and designed for comfort and elegance. **2.** a wheeled support, as for a cannon. **3.** a movable part, as of a machine, designed for carrying something: *a wide carriage on a dot-matrix printer.* **4.** bearing of the head and body; posture. **5.** the act of transporting; conveyance. **6.** the price or cost of transportation.

car·ri·er (kar′ē ər), *n.* **1.** an employee of the post office who delivers or collects mail. **2.** a person who delivers newspapers or magazines. **3.** an individual or company engaged in transporting passengers or goods for profit. **4.** an underwriter or insurer. **5.** a frame attached to a vehicle for carrying luggage or skis. **6.** AIRCRAFT CARRIER. **7.** an individual harboring a disease who may be immune to the disease but transmits it to others. **8. a.** an individual with an unexpressed recessive genetic trait. **b.** the bearer of a defective gene. **9.** Also called **car′rier wave′.** the radio wave whose amplitude, frequency, or phase is to be varied or modulated to transmit a signal. **10.** a mechanism by which something is carried or moved. **11.** *Chem.* **a.** a catalytic agent responsible for the transfer of an element or molecule from one compound to another. **b.** a usu. inactive substance that serves as a vehicle for an active substance.

car′rier pig′eon, *n.* **1.** one of a breed of domestic pigeons having a large wattle. **2.** a homing pigeon.

car·ri·on (kar/ē ən), *n.* **1.** dead and putrefying flesh. —*adj.* **2.** feeding on carrion.

car/rion crow/, *n.* a crow of W and central Europe, *Corvus corone corone.*

car/rion flow/er, *n.* **1.** any of several North American climbing plants belonging to the genus *Smilax,* of the lily family, esp. *S. herbacea,* having small white flowers with an odor of carrion. **2.** any of various similar flowers that have a foul odor.

Car·roll (kar/əl), *n.* **1. Charles,** 1737–1832, American patriot and legislator. **2. Lewis,** pen name of Charles Lutwidge DODGSON.

car·rot (kar/ət), *n.* **1.** a plant, *Daucus carota,* of the parsley family, having fernlike leaves and umbels of small white flowers. **2.** the orange to yellow root of this plant, eaten raw or cooked. **3.** something offered as an incentive. —**car/rot·y,** *adj.*

car·ry (kar/ē), *v.,* **-ried, -ry·ing,** *n., pl.* **-ries.** —*v.t.* **1.** to move while supporting or holding; take from one place to another; transport: *to carry groceries home.* **2.** to wear, hold, or have around one: *to carry a cane.* **3.** to contain or be capable of containing; hold: *This suitcase can carry enough clothes for a week.* **4.** to serve as a medium for the transmission of: *The networks carried her speech.* **5.** to be the means of conveying: *The space shuttle carried a satellite.* **6.** to be pregnant with. **7.** to continue or transfer to a subsequent time, page, or column: *to carry a number in adding.* **8.** to transfer to a higher authority: *to carry a case to appellate court.* **9.** to bear the weight or burden of. **10.** to sing (a melody) on pitch. **11.** to hold (the body or head) in a certain manner. **12.** to bear or comport (oneself) in a specified manner: *carries herself with dignity.* **13.** to secure the passage of (a motion or bill). **14.** to gain a majority of votes in (a district). **15.** to extend in a given direction or to a certain point: *to carry the war into enemy territory.* **16.** to transmit or communicate. **17.** to influence by emotional or intellectual appeal. **18.** to dominate by superior talent or determination: *The star carried the play.* **19.** to drive or impel. **20.** to have as an attribute or consequence: *Violation carries a stiff penalty.* **21. a.** to keep on hand or in stock for sale. **b.** to keep on the account books. **22.** to bear as a crop. **23.** to sustain or support, esp. financially. **24.** to advance beyond (an object or expanse) with one golf stroke. —*v.i.* **25.** to act as a bearer or conductor. **26.** to have or exert propelling force. **27.** to be transmitted, propelled, or sustained: *Sounds carry well in the desert.* **28.** (of a horse) to bear the head in a particular manner. **29.** to rush with the football from scrimmage. **30. carry away,** to stir strong emotions in; provoke to excessive behavior: *Don't get carried away—it's only a movie.* **31. carry back,** to apply (an unused credit or operating loss) to the net income of a prior period in order to reduce the tax for that period. **32. carry forward, a.** to make progress with. **b.** to transfer (a total) to the next page, column, or book. **c.** to apply (an unused credit or operating loss) to the net income of a succeeding period in order to reduce the tax for that period. **33. carry off, a.** to win (a prize or honor). **b.** to cause the death of. **c.** to deal with successfully. **34. carry on, a.** to manage; conduct. **b.** to continue without stopping; persevere. **c.** to be disruptive; act up. **35. carry out, a.** to put into operation. **b.** to effect or accomplish. **36. carry over, a.** to hold until a later time; postpone. **b.** to remain. **c.** to carry forward. **d.** to extend from one activity or time to another. **37. carry through, a.** to accomplish; complete. **b.** to support or help through a difficult situation. **c.** to be prevalent in; persist throughout. —*n.* **38.** range, as of a gun. **39.** the distance a stroked golf ball travels. **40.** land that separates navigable waters and over which a canoe or boat must be carried; portage. **41.** an instance of rushing with the football from scrimmage. —*Idiom.* **42. carry the can,** to bear responsibility. **43. carry the day,** to win the contest or be triumphant; prevail. *The Republicans carried the day.*

car·ry·all¹ (kar/ē ôl/), *n.* a large bag or lightweight piece of luggage.

car·ry·all² (kar/ē ôl/), *n.* **1.** a four-wheeled covered carriage having seats for four persons. **2.** an automobile or bus having two facing benches running the length of the body.

car/rying capac/ity, *n.* the maximum population of a species that can be supported in a given environment. *Symbol:* K

car/rying-on/, *n., pl.* **carryings-on. 1.** irresponsible or overwrought behavior. **2.** improper or immoral behavior.

car/ry-on/, *adj.* **1.** of a size suitable for being carried onto an airplane: *carry-on luggage.* —*n.* **2.** a piece of carry-on luggage.

car/ry-out/ or **car/ry-out/,** *n., adj.* TAKEOUT (defs. 2, 3).

car·ry·o·ver (kar/ē ō/vər), *n.* something carried over or postponed to a later time.

car/ seat/, *n.* a removable seat designed to hold a small child safely while riding in an automobile.

car·sick (kär/sik/), *adj.* ill with motion sickness during automobile travel. —**car/sick/ness,** *n.*

Car·son (kär/sən), *n.* **1. Christopher** (*"Kit"*), 1809–68, U.S. frontiersman and scout. **2. Rachel Louise,** 1907–1964, U.S. marine biologist and author. **3.** a city in SW California. 89,380.

Car/son Cit/y, *n.* a town in and the capital of Nevada, in the W part. 36,650.

cart (kärt), *n.* **1.** a heavy two-wheeled vehicle, commonly without springs, drawn by draft animals and used to convey heavy goods. **2.** a light two-wheeled vehicle with springs, drawn by a horse or pony. **3.** any small vehicle pushed or pulled by hand. —*v.t.* **4.** to haul, as in a cart or truck. **5. cart off** or **away,** to take away, in an unceremonious manner: *The police carted them off to jail.* —*Idiom.* **6. put the cart**

before the horse, to reverse priorities; do or place things in improper or illogical order. —**cart/er,** *n.*

cart·age (kär/tij), *n.* the act or cost of carting.

carte blanche (kärt/ blänch/, bläNSH/), *n.* unconditional authority; full discretionary power.

carte du jour (kärt/ də zhŏŏr/, dōō), *n., pl.* **cartes du jour** (kärts, kärt). MENU (def. 1).

car·tel (kär tel/), *n.* **1.** an international syndicate, formed esp. to control prices and output in some field of business. **2.** an association of political groups acting as a unit toward a common goal. **3.** a written agreement between belligerents, esp. for the exchange of prisoners. —**car·tel/ism,** *n.* —**car·tel/ist,** *n.*

Car·ter (kär/tər), *n.* **1. Bennett Lester** (*Benny*), born 1907, U.S. jazz saxophonist and composer. **2. Hod·ding** (hod/ing), 1907–72, U.S. journalist and publisher. **3. James Earl, Jr.** (*Jimmy*), born 1924, 39th president of the U.S. 1977–81. **4. R(ussell) Kelso,** 1849–1928, U.S. clergyman and hymn writer.

Carte/sian coor/dinates, *n.pl.* a system of coordinates for locating a point on a plane by its distance from each of two intersecting lines, or in space by its distance from each of three planes intersecting at a point.

Car·thage (kär/thij), *n.* an ancient city-state in N Africa near modern Tunis: founded by the Phoenicians in the 9th cent. B.C.; destroyed 146 B.C. in the last Punic War. —**Car·tha·gin·i·an** (kär/thə jin/ē ən), *n., adj.*

Car·thu·sian (kär thōō/zhən), *n.* **1.** a member of a monastic order founded by St. Bruno in 1086 near Grenoble, France. —*adj.* **2.** pertaining to the Carthusians.

Car·tier (kär/tē ā/, kär tyā/), *n.* **Jacques,** 1491–1557, French navigator: discovered the St. Lawrence River.

car·ti·lage (kär/tl ij, kärt/lij), *n.* **1.** a firm, elastic, whitish type of connective tissue; gristle. **2.** a part or structure composed of cartilage. —**car·ti·lag·inous** (kär/tl aj/ə nəs), *adj.*

car·ti·lag·i·nous (kär/tl aj/ə nəs), *adj.* pertaining to, composed of, or resembling cartilage.

cartilag/inous fish/, *n.* any of various fishes of the class Chondrichthyes, including the sharks, skates, and rays, having a skeleton composed mainly of cartilage.

car·tog·ra·phy (kär tog/rə fē), *n.* the production of maps, including construction of projections, design, compilation, drafting, and reproduction. —**car·tog/ra·pher,** *n.*

car·ton (kär/tn), *n.* **1.** a cardboard or plastic box used typically for storage or shipping. **2.** the amount a carton can hold. **3.** the contents of a carton. —*v.t.* **4.** to pack in a carton. —*v.i.* **5.** to make or form cardboard sheets into cartons.

car·toon (kär tōōn/), *n.* **1.** a drawing symbolizing, satirizing, or caricaturing some action, subject, or person. **2.** COMIC STRIP. **3.** ANIMATED CARTOON. **4.** a preliminary pictorial design, as for a fresco. —*v.i.* **5.** to draw cartoons. —**car·toon/ist,** *n.*

car·touche or **car·touch** (kär tōōsh/), *n.* **1.** a rounded panel often containing an inscription, decoration, or coat of arms. **2.** an oblong figure, as on ancient Egyptian monuments, enclosing the name of a sovereign. **3.** CARTRIDGE (def. 1).

car·tridge (kär/trij), *n.* **1.** a cylindrical case for holding a charge of powder and usu. a bullet or shot for a rifle or other small arm. **2.** a case containing any explosive charge, as for blasting. **3.** any small container for powder, liquid, or gas, made for ready insertion into some device or mechanism: *an ink cartridge for a pen.* **4.** a lightproof twin-spool container in which a roll of film is wound, designed for loading directly into a camera without threading the film. **5.** PICKUP (def. 7). **6.** a flat, compact container enclosing an endless loop of audiotape or videotape, operated by inserting into a slot in a player.

cart·wheel (kärt/hwēl/, -wēl/), *n.* **1.** an acrobatic movement in which the upright body wheels sideways, landing first on the hands and then on the feet. **2.** *Slang.* any large coin. —*v.i.* **3.** to perform cartwheels. **4.** to roll forward end over end.

car·un·cle (kar/ung kəl, kə rung/-), *n.* a fleshy outgrowth, as on the head of a bird; a fowl's comb. —**ca·run·cu·lar** (kə rung/kyə lər), **ca·run/cu·lous,** *adj.*

carve (kärv), *v.,* **carved, carv·ing.** —*v.t.* **1.** to cut (a solid material) so as to form something: *to carve a piece of pine.* **2.** to form from a solid material by cutting: *to carve a statue out of stone.* **3.** to cut into pieces or slices, as meat. **4.** to decorate with designs or figures cut on the surface. **5.** to make or create for oneself (often fol. by *out*): *He carved out a career in business.* —*v.i.* **6.** to form figures, designs, etc., by carving. **7.** to carve meat. —**carv/er,** *n.*

car·vel (kär/vəl), *n.* CARAVEL.

car/vel-built/, *adj.* (of a ship's hull) formed of planks laid close on the frames so as to present a smooth exterior.

Car·ver (kär/vər), *n.* **1. George Washington,** 1864?–1943, U.S. botanist and chemist. **2. John,** 1575?–1621, Pilgrim leader: first governor of Plymouth Colony 1620–21. **3. Raymond,** 1938–88, U.S. short-story writer and poet.

carv·er·y (kär/və rē), *n., pl.* **-er·ies.** a restaurant or hotel dining room in which roasted meat is carved to the diner's request.

carv·ing (kär/ving), *n.* **1.** the act of fashioning or producing by cutting into or shaping solid material. **2.** a carved design or figure.

car′ wash′ or **car′wash′,** *n.* a place or structure having special equipment for washing automobiles.

car·y·at·id (kar′ē at′id), *n., pl.* **-ids, -i·des** (-i dēz′). a sculptured female figure used as a column. Compare ATLAS (def. 4).

caryatids

car·y·op·sis (kar′ē op′sis) *n., pl.* **-ses** (-sēz), **-si·des** (-si dēz′). a small, one-celled, one-seeded, dry indehiscent fruit with the pericarp fused to the seed coat: the typical fruit of grasses and grains.

ca·sa·ba or **cas·sa·ba** (kə sä′bə), *n., pl.* **-bas.** a variety of the winter melon, *Cucumis melo inodorus,* having a wrinkled, yellow rind and sweet, juicy, greenish flesh. [after *Kassaba* (now Turgutlu), Turkey, which exported it]

Cas·a·blan·ca (kas′ə blang′kə, kä′sə bläng′kə), *n.* a seaport in NW Morocco. 2,139,204.

Ca·sals (kə salz′, -sälz′), *n.* **Pablo,** 1876–1973, Spanish cellist, conductor, and composer; in France after 1936; in Puerto Rico after 1956.

cas·cade (kas kād′), *n., v.,* **-cad·ed, -cad·ing.** —*n.* **1.** a waterfall descending over a steep, rocky surface. **2.** a series of shallow or steplike waterfalls, either natural or artificial. **3.** anything that resembles a waterfall, esp. in seeming to flow or fall in abundance; torrent. **4.** an arrangement of a lightweight fabric in folds falling one over another. **5.** an arrangement of component devices, as electrolytic cells, each of which feeds into the next in succession. **6.** a series of reactions catalyzed by enzymes that are activated sequentially by successive products of the reactions, resulting in an amplification of the initial response. —*v.i., v.t.* **7.** to fall or cause to fall in or like a cascade.

cas·car·a (kas kâr′ə), *n., pl.* **-car·as.** a buckthorn, *Rhamnus purshiana,* of the northwestern U.S., yielding cascara sagrada.

cas·ca·ril·la (kas′kə ril′ə), *n., pl.* **-las. 1.** Also called **cascaril′la bark′.** the bitter, aromatic bark of a West Indian shrub, *Croton eluteria,* of the spurge family, used as a tonic. **2.** the shrub itself.

case¹ (kās), *n.* **1.** an instance of the occurrence, existence, etc., of something: *a case of poor judgment.* **2.** the actual state of things: *That is not the case.* **3.** situation; circumstance; plight: *a sad case.* **4.** a patient or client, as of a physician or social worker. **5.** a specific occurrence or matter requiring discussion, decision, or investigation. **6.** a statement of facts, reasons, etc., used to support an argument: *We presented a strong case against the proposed law.* **7.** an instance of disease, injury, etc., requiring medical or surgical attention. **8. a.** a suit or action at law; cause. **b.** a set of facts making up a claim or defense. **9. a.** a category or set of categories in the inflection of nouns, pronouns, and adjectives serving to indicate the syntactic relation of these words to other words in a sentence. **b.** the indication of such relations by other devices, as by the position of words in a sentence. **10.** *Informal.* a peculiar or unusual person. —*Idiom.* **11. in any case,** regardless of circumstances; anyhow. **12. in case,** if it should happen that; if. **13. in case of,** in the event of; if there should be. **14. in no case,** under no condition; never.

case² (kās), *n., v.,* **cased, cas·ing.** —*n.* **1.** a container for enclosing something, as for carrying or safekeeping; receptacle. **2.** a sheath or outer covering: *a knife case.* **3.** a box with its contents: *a case of soda.* **4.** the amount contained in a box or other container. **5.** a pair or couple; brace: *a case of pistols.* **6.** a surrounding frame or framework, as of a door. **7.** a completed book cover ready to be fitted to form the binding. **8.** a compartmentalized tray for holding printer's type, usu. arranged with one section **(upper case)** for capital letters and another **(lower case)** for small letters. **9.** a cavity in the skull of a sperm whale, containing an oil from which spermaceti is obtained. **10.** the hard outer part of a piece of casehardened steel. —*v.t.* **11.** to put or enclose in a case. **12.** *Slang.* to examine or survey (a house, bank, etc.) esp. in planning a crime (sometimes fol. by *out*).

ca·se·a·tion (kā′sē ā′shən), *n.* **1.** transformation of tissue into a soft cheeselike mass, as in tuberculosis. **2.** the formation of cheese from casein during the coagulation of milk.

case·book (kās′book′), *n.* a book containing detailed records of one or more cases, as in law or medicine.

case·hard·en (kās′här′dn), *v.t.* **1.** to harden the surface of (an iron-based alloy) by carburizing and heat treatment, leaving the interior tough and ductile. **2.** to make callous.

case′ his′tory, *n.* (in medicine, social work, etc.) a record of the relevant facts and information about an individual, family, or group, serving as a basis for analysis or treatment.

ca·sein (kā′sēn, -sē in, kā sēn′), *n.* **1.** a protein precipitated from milk, as by rennet, and forming the basis of cheese and certain plastics. **2. a.**

an emulsion made from a solution of this precipitated protein, water, and ammonia carbonate. **b.** a paint in which this emulsion is used as a binder.

ca·sein·ate (kā′sē nāt′, -sē ə-, kā sē′nāt), *n.* a metallic salt of casein.

case′ law′, *n.* law based on judicial decisions rather than legislative action.

case′load′ or **case′ load′,** *n.* the number of cases handled by a court, agency, social worker, etc., over a stated period.

case·ment (kās′mənt), *n.* **1.** a window sash opening on hinges that are generally attached to the upright side of its frame. **2.** Also called **case′ment win′dow.** a window with such a sash or sashes. **3.** a casing or covering. —**case′ment·ed,** *adj.*

ca·se·ous (kā′sē əs), *adj.* of or like cheese.

case′ stud′y, *n.* **1.** (in the social sciences) an analytical study of the development of an individual unit, as a person, family, or social institution. **2.** CASE HISTORY.

case′ sys′tem, *n.* a method of teaching law that focuses on analysis and discussion of selected cases rather than on textbook instruction.

case·work (kās′wûrk′), *n.* social work involving direct contact between the social worker and the individual or family being helped. —**case′work′er,** *n.*

Ca′sey at the Bat′, a humorous poem (1888) about the baseball player "Mighty Casey" and his turn at bat.

cash (kash), *n.* **1.** money in the form of coins or banknotes, esp. that issued by a government. **2.** money or an equivalent, as a check, paid at the time of making a purchase. —*v.t.* **3.** to give or obtain cash for (a check, money order, etc.). **4. a.** to win (a card trick) by leading an assured winner. **b.** to lead (an assured winner) in order to win a trick. **5. cash in, a.** to turn in and get cash for (one's chips), as in a gambling casino. **b.** to convert one's assets into cash. **6. cash in on,** to profit from; use to one's advantage. —**cash′less,** *adj.*

cash′-and-car′ry, *adj., n., pl.* **-car·ries.** —*adj.* **1.** sold for cash payment and including no delivery service. **2.** operated on such a basis: *a cash-and-carry business.* —*n.* **3.** a store that operates on a cash-and-carry basis.

cash·book (kash′book′), *n.* a book in which to record money received and paid out.

cash′ cow′, *n. Slang.* any business venture, operation, or product that is a dependable source of income or profit.

cash′ crop′, *n.* **1.** any crop that is considered easily marketable, as wheat or cotton. **2.** a crop for direct sale in a market, as distinguished from a crop for livestock feed or personal use.

cash′ dis′count, *n.* discount allowed a buyer from the amount due if paid within a specified period.

cash·ew (kash′ōō, kə shōō′), *n.* **1.** a tropical American tree, *Anacardium occidentale,* with milky juice, leathery leaves, and yellowish pink flowers in open clusters. **2.** Also called **cash′ew nut′.** the small, kidney-shaped, edible nut of this tree.

cash′ flow′, *n.* the funds available within a company for dividends, purchase of new equipment, etc., usu. the after-tax profit plus noncash charges, such as depreciation.

cash·ier¹ (ka shēr′), *n.* **1.** an employee, as in a market, who totals purchases and collects payment from customers. **2.** an executive who superintends the financial transactions of a company.

cash·ier² (ka shēr′), *v.t.* **1.** to dismiss from a position of command or trust, esp. with disgrace. **2.** to discard; reject.

cashier's′ check′, *n.* a check drawn by a bank on its own funds and signed by its cashier.

cash·mere or **kash·mir** (kazh′mēr, kash′-), *n.* **1.** the fine, downy wool at the roots of the hair of the Kashmir goat. **2.** a yarn made from this wool. **3.** a fabric made from this or a similar yarn.

Cash·mere (kash mēr′), *n.* KASHMIR.

cash′ on deliv′ery. See C.O.D.

cash′ reg′ister, *n.* a business machine that indicates the amounts of individual sales, that records and totals receipts, and that has a money drawer from which to make change.

cas·ing (kā′sing), *n.* **1.** a case or covering; housing. **2.** material for a case or covering. **3.** the framework around a door or window. **4.** the outermost covering of an automobile tire. **5.** any frame or framework. **6.** a steel pipe or tubing, esp. as used in oil and gas wells. **7.** the tubular intestinal membrane of sheep, cattle, or hogs, or a synthetic facsimile, for encasing sausage, salami, etc. **8.** a channel created in a garment or other article to carry a drawstring or elastic.

ca·si·no (kə sē′nō), *n., pl.* **-nos. 1.** a building or large room used for meetings, dancing, or esp. for professional gambling. **2.** (in Italy) a small country house or lodge.

cask (kask, käsk), *n.* **1.** a container made and shaped like a barrel but larger and stronger, esp. one for holding liquids. **2.** the quantity such a container holds. —*v.t.* **3.** to place or store in a cask.

cas·ket (kas′kit, kä′skit), *n.* **1.** a coffin. **2.** a small chest or box, as for jewels. —*v.t.* **3.** to put or enclose in a casket.

Cas′pi·an Sea′, (kas′pē ən), *n.* a salt lake between SE Europe and Asia: the largest inland body of water in the world. ab. 169,000 sq. mi. (438,000 sq. km); 85 ft. (26 m) below sea level.

casque (kask), *n.* **1.** an armored headpiece, esp. a medieval helmet. **2.** *Zool.* a process or formation resembling a helmet. —**casqued,** *adj.*

cas·sa·ba (kə sä′bə), *n., pl.* **-bas.** CASABA.

Cas•san•dra (kə san′drə), *n., pl.* **-dras. 1.** (in Greek myth) a daughter of King Priam of Troy, endowed with prophetic powers, but fated never to be believed. **2.** a person who prophesies doom or disaster.
Cas•satt (kə sat′), *n.* **Mary,** 1845–1926, U.S. painter.
cas•sa•va (kə sä′və), *n., pl.* **-vas. 1.** any of several tropical American plants belonging to the genus *Manihot,* of the spurge family, having tuberous roots. **2.** a nutritious starch from the roots, the source of tapioca.
cas•se•role (kas′ə rōl′), *n., v.,* **-roled, -rol•ing.** **—***n.* **1.** a usu. large covered baking dish of glass, pottery, etc. **2.** any food, esp. a mixture, baked in such a dish. **3.** a small dish with a handle, used for heating substances in a chemical laboratory. **—***v.t.* **4.** to bake (food) in a casserole.
cas•sette (kə set′, ka-), *n.* **1.** a plastic case in which audiotape or videotape runs between two reels for use in recording or playing back. **2.** a lightproof container for a roll of photographic film, having a single spool for supplying and rewinding the film.
cas•sia (kash′ə, kas′ē ə), *n., pl.* **-sias. 1.** any plant, tree, or shrub belonging to the genus *Cassia,* of the legume family, several species of which yield medicinal products. **2.** Also called **cas′sia pods′.** the pods of *Cassia fistula,* a tree widely cultivated as an ornamental. **3.** Also called **cas′sia pulp′.** the pulp of these pods, used medicinally and as a flavoring.
Cas•si•o•pe•ia (kas′ē ə pē′ə), *n., gen.* **-pe•iae** (-pē′ē) for 1. **1.** a northern constellation between Cepheus and Perseus. **2.** (in Greek myth) the wife of Cepheus and mother of Andromeda. **—Cas′si•o•pe′ian,** *adj.*
cas•sock (kas′ək), *n.* a long, close-fitting garment worn by clerics or other participants in church services.
cas•so•war•y (kas′ə wer′ē), *n., pl.* **-war•ies.** any of several large flightless birds of the family Casuariidae, of New Guinea, N Australia, and adjacent islands, having a bare neck and head topped by a bony casque.
cast (kast, käst), *v.t.* **1.** to throw or hurl; fling: *to cast dice; to cast aside the newspaper.* **2.** to direct (the eye, a glance, etc.). **3.** to cause to fall; put or send forth: *to cast a soft light; to cast a spell; to cast doubts.* **4.** to draw (lots), as in telling fortunes. **5.** to throw out (a fishing line, a net, bait, etc.). **6.** to shed or drop: *The snake cast its skin.* **7.** (of an animal) to bring forth (young), esp. abortively. **8.** to send off (a swarm), as bees do. **9.** to set aside; reject; dismiss: *She cast the problem from her mind.* **10.** to throw up (earth, sod, etc.), as with a shovel. **11.** to put or place, esp. forcibly: *to cast someone in prison.* **12.** to deposit or give (a ballot or vote). **13.** to bestow; confer: *to cast blessings.* **14.** to form or arrange; plan out: *He cast his remarks to fit the occasion.* **15. a.** to select actors for (a play, motion picture, etc.). **b.** to assign a role to (an actor). **16.** to form (an object) by pouring metal, plaster, etc., into a mold and letting it harden. **17.** to form (metal, plaster, etc.) by this process. **18.** to compute, as a column of figures. **19.** to calculate (a horoscope). **20.** to turn or twist; warp. **21.** to turn the head of (a ship), esp. away from the wind in getting under way. **—***v.i.* **22.** to throw. **23.** to receive form in a mold. **24.** to calculate or add. **25.** to conjecture; forecast. **26.** (of hounds) to search an area for scent. **27.** to warp, as timber. **28.** (of a ship) to turn, esp. to get the head away from the wind; tack. **29.** to select the actors for a play, motion picture, or the like. **30. cast about** or **around, a.** to search; seek. **b.** to devise a plan; scheme. **31. cast away, a.** Also, **cast aside.** to reject; discard. **b.** to shipwreck. **32. cast back,** to refer to something past; revert. **33. cast down,** to lower; humble. **34. cast off, a.** to discard; reject. **b.** to let go or let loose, as a ship from a mooring. **c.** to estimate the space a typeset manuscript will occupy. **d.** to complete a knitted fabric by looping over (the final stitches); bind off. **35. cast on,** (in knitting) to set (yarn) on a needle in order to form the initial stitches. **36. cast out,** to force to leave; expel; banish. **—***n.* **37.** the act of throwing. **38.** that which is thrown. **39.** the distance to which a thing may be thrown. **40. a.** a throw of dice. **b.** the number rolled. **41.** the act of throwing a fishing line or net onto the water. **42.** the group of performers in a play, motion picture, etc.; players. **43.** a searching of an area by hounds for a scent. **44.** a stroke of fortune; lot. **45.** the form in which something is made or written; arrangement. **46. a.** the act of founding. **b.** the quantity of metal cast at one time. **47.** something made in a mold; casting. **48.** an impression or mold: *the cast of a fossil.* **49.** a rigid surgical dressing, usu. made of bandage treated with plaster of Paris. **50.** outward form; appearance: *of a sinister cast.* **51.** sort; kind; style: *a hero of the cast of Don Quixote.* **52.** tendency; inclination: *minds of a philosophical cast.* **53.** a permanent twist or turn: *to have a cast in one's eye.* **54.** a warp. **55.** a slight tinge of some color; hue; shade: *a yellowish cast.* **56.** a dash or trace; a small amount. **57.** a computation; calculation. **58.** a conjecture or forecast. **59.** something that is shed, ejected, or cast off or out, as molted skin, feathers, food from a bird's crop, or the coil of sand and waste passed by certain earthworms. **60.** a pair of falcons put in flight together. **61.** effused plastic matter produced in the hollow parts of various diseased organs. **—***adj.* **62.** (of an animal, esp. a horse) lying in such a position that it is unable to return to its feet without assistance.
cas•ta•net (kas′tə net′), *n.* Usu., **castanets.** a small percussion instrument consisting of two concave shells of wood held in the palm of the hand and clicked rhythmically together.
cast•a•way (kast′ə wā′, käst′-), *n.* **1.** a shipwrecked person. **2.** anything cast adrift or thrown away. **3.** an outcast. **—***adj.* **4.** cast adrift. **5.** thrown away.
caste (kast, käst), *n.* **1.** any of the hereditary social divisions of traditional Hindu society. **2.** an endogamous social group limited to persons of the same hereditary rank, occupation, economic position, etc., and having distinctive mores. **3.** any rigid system of social distinctions. **4.** social position conferred upon one by a caste system: *to lose caste.* **5.** one of the distinct forms among polymorphous social insects, performing a specialized function in the colony, as a queen, worker, or soldier.
cas•tel•lan (kas′tl n, ka stel′ən), *n.* the governor of a castle.
cast•er (kas′tər, kä′stər), *n.* **1.** a person or thing that casts. **2.** a small wheel on a swivel, set under a piece of furniture, a machine, etc., to facilitate moving it. **3.** a bottle or cruet for holding a condiment. **4.** a stand containing such bottles. **5.** a container for sugar, pepper, etc., having a perforated top. **6.** the angle that an automobile's kingpin makes with the vertical. Also, **castor** (for defs. 2–5).
cas•ti•gate (kas′ti gāt′), *v.t.,* **-gat•ed, -gat•ing. 1.** to criticize or reprimand severely. **2.** to punish in order to correct. **—cas′ti•ga′tion,** *n.* **—cas′ti•ga′tor,** *n.*
cast•ing (kas′ting, kä′sting), *n.* **1.** the act of one that casts. **2.** something that has been cast in a mold. **3.** the act or process of choosing actors for a play, motion picture, etc. **4.** the act or skill of throwing a fishing line by means of a rod and reel.
cast′ i′ron, *n.* an alloy of iron, carbon, and other elements, cast as a soft and strong, or as a hard and brittle iron.
cast′-i′ron, *adj.* **1.** made of cast iron. **2.** not subject to change or exception: *a cast-iron rule.* **3.** hardy: *a cast-iron stomach.*
cas•tle (kas′əl, kä′səl), *n., v.,* **-tled, -tling.** **—***n.* **1.** a fortified, usu. walled residence, as of a prince or noble in feudal times. **2.** the chief and strongest part of the fortifications of a medieval city. **3.** a strongly fortified, permanently garrisoned stronghold. **4.** a large and stately residence, esp. one that imitates the forms of a medieval castle. **5.** any place providing security and privacy. **6.** *Chess.* the rook. **—***v.t.* **7.** to place or enclose in or as if in a castle. **8.** *Chess.* to move (the king) in castling. **—***v.i. Chess.* **9.** to move the king two squares horizontally and bring the appropriate rook to the square the king has passed over. **10.** (of the king) to be moved in this manner. **—*Idiom.* 11. to build castles in the air,** to be unrealistic. [< Latin *castellum* fortress]
Castle, The, (German, *Das Schloss*), a novel (1926) by Franz Kafka.
cast•off (kast′ôf′, -of′, käst′-), *adj.* **1.** thrown away; rejected; discarded. **—***n.* **2.** a person or thing that has been cast off. **3.** the estimate by a compositor of how many pages copy will occupy when set in type.
cas•tor[1] (kas′tər, kä′stər), *n.* **1.** a pungent, brownish, oily substance secreted by glands in the groin of the beaver, used in medicine and perfumery. **2.** a hat made of beaver or rabbit fur. **3.** a beaver.
cas•tor[2] (kas′tər, kä′stər), *n.* CASTER (defs. 2–5).
Cas′tor and Pol′lux, *n.pl.* (in Greek myth) twin sons of Leda and brothers of Helen, famous for their fraternal affection and regarded as the protectors of persons at sea; the Dioscuri.
cas′tor bean′, *n.* the seed of the castor-oil plant.
cas′tor oil′, *n.* a colorless or pale oil expressed from the castor bean, used as a lubricant and cathartic.
cas′tor-oil′ plant′, a tall plant, *Ricinus communis,* of the spurge family, cultivated for its ornamental foliage and having poisonous seeds that are the source of castor oil. Also called **castor bean.**
cas•trate (kas′trāt), *v.,* **-trat•ed, -trat•ing,** *n.* **—***v.t.* **1.** to remove the testes of; emasculate; geld. **2.** to remove the ovaries of. **3.** to render impotent by psychological means, as disparagement. **4.** to deprive of strength, power, or efficiency; weaken. **—***n.* **5.** a castrated person or animal. **—cas•tra′tion,** *n.* **—cas′tra•tor,** *n.*
Cas•tries (kas′trēz, -trēs, kä strē′), *n.* the capital of St. Lucia, on the NW coast. 52,868.
Cas•tro (kas′trō), *n.* **Fi•del** (fi del′), (*Fidel Castro Ruz*) born 1927, Cuban revolutionary leader: prime minister 1959–76; president since 1976.
cas•u•al (kazh′o͞o əl), *adj.* **1.** happening by chance: *a casual meeting.* **2.** without definite or serious intention; offhand: *a casual remark.* **3.** seeming or tending to be indifferent; apathetic: *a casual air.* **4.** appropriate for wear or use on informal occasions; not dressy. **5.** irregular; occasional: *a casual visitor.* **—***n.* **6.** a worker employed only irregularly. **—cas′u•al•ly,** *adv.* **—cas′u•al•ness,** *n.*
cas•u•al•ty (kazh′o͞o əl tē), *n., pl.* **-ties. 1.** *Mil.* **a.** a member of the armed forces removed from service by death, wounds, sickness, etc. **b. casualties,** loss in numerical strength through any cause. **2.** one who is injured or killed in an accident. **3.** any person or thing that is harmed or destroyed as a result of some act or event: *Their house was one of the casualties of the new highway cutting through the town.* **4.** a serious accident, esp. one involving bodily injury or death.
cas•u•is•tic (kazh′o͞o is′tik) also **cas′u•is′ti•cal,** *adj.* **1.** pertaining to casuists or casuistry. **2.** oversubtle; intellectually dishonest; sophistical. **—cas′u•is′ti•cal•ly,** *adv.*
cas•u•ist•ry (kazh′o͞o ə strē), *n., pl.* **-ries. 1.** oversubtle, fallacious, or dishonest reasoning; sophistry. **2.** the application of general ethical principles to particular cases of conscience or conduct.
cat (kat), *n., v.,* **cat•ted, cat•ting.** **—***n.* **1.** a small domesticated carnivore, *Felis domestica* or *F. catus,* bred in a number of varieties. **2.** any carnivore of the family Felidae, as the lion, tiger, leopard, or jaguar, and including numerous small wild cats. **3.** *Slang.* **a.** a person, esp. a man.

b. a devotee of jazz. **4.** a woman given to spiteful or malicious gossip. **5.** a cat-o'-nine-tails. **6.** a catfish. —*v.t.* **7.** to flog with a cat-o'-nine-tails. —*Idiom.* **8. let the cat out of the bag,** to divulge a secret. —*Proverb.* **9. When the cat's away, the mice will play,** people will take advantage of an overseer's absence.

CAT, computerized axial tomography. Compare CAT scan, CAT scanner.

cata- or **kata-,** a prefix meaning "down," "against," "back," occurring orig. in loanwords from Greek: *cataclysm; catalog; catalepsy.* Also, *esp. before a vowel or h,* CAT-.

ca•tab•o•lism (kə tab′ə liz′əm), *n.* destructive metabolism; the breaking down in living organisms of more complex substances into simpler ones, with the release of energy (opposed to *anabolism*). —**cat′a•bol•ic** (kat′ə bol′ik), *adj.* —**cat′a•bol/i•cal•ly,** *adv.* —**ca•tab/o•lize′,** *v.i., v.t.,* **-lized, -liz•ing.**

cat•a•chre•sis (kat′ə krē′sis), *n.* misuse or strained use of words, as in a mixed metaphor, occurring either in error or for rhetorical effect. —**cat′a•chres/tic** (-kres′tik), *adj.*

cat•a•clysm (kat′ə kliz′əm), *n.* **1.** any violent upheaval, esp. one of a social or political nature. **2.** a sudden and violent physical action producing changes in the earth's surface. **3.** an extensive flood; deluge. —**cat′a•clys/mic,** *adj.* —**cat′a•clys/mi•cal•ly,** *adv.*

cat•a•comb (kat′ə kōm′), *n.* **1.** Usu., **catacombs.** an underground cemetery, esp. one consisting of tunnels and rooms with recesses dug out for coffins and tombs. **2. the Catacombs,** the subterranean burial chambers of the early Christians in and near Rome, Italy. **3.** an underground passageway, esp. one full of twists and turns.

ca•tad•ro•mous (kə tad′rə məs), *adj.* (of fish) migrating from fresh water to spawn in the sea (disting. from *anadromous*).

cat•a•falque (kat′ə fôk′, -fôlk′, -falk′), *n.* a raised structure on which the body of a deceased person lies or is carried in state.

cat•a•lec•tic (kat′l ek′tik), *adj.* **1.** (of a line of verse) lacking part of the last foot. —*n.* **2.** a catalectic line of verse.

cat•a•lep•sy (kat′l ep′sē) also **cat/a•lep/sis,** *n.* a seizure or abnormal condition characterized by postural rigidity and mental stupor, associated with certain brain disorders. —**cat′a•lep/tic,** *adj., n.* —**cat/a•lep/ti•cal•ly,** *adv.*

cat•a•log (kat′l ôg′, -og′), *n.* **1.** a list or record, as of items for sale or courses at a university, systematically arranged and often including descriptive material. **2.** something, as a book or pamphlet, that contains such a list or record. **3.** a list of the contents of a library or a group of libraries, arranged according to any of various systems. Compare CARD CATALOG. **4.** any list or record: *a catalog of complaints.* —*v.t.* **5.** to enter (items) in a catalog; make a catalog of. —*v.i.* **6.** to produce a catalog. **7.** to have a specified price as listed in a catalog. —**cat′a•log/er,** *n.* —**cat/a•log/ic** (-oj′ik), *adj.*

cat•a•logue (kat′l ôg′, -og′), *n., v.t., v.i.,* **-logued, -logu•ing.** CATALOG.

Cat•a•lo•ni•a (kat′l ō′nē ə, -ōn′yə), *n.* a region in NE Spain, bordering on France and the Mediterranean: formerly a province. Spanish, **Ca•ta•lu•ña** (kä′tä lōō′nyä). —**Cat′a•lo/ni•an,** *adj., n.*

ca•tal•pa (kə tal′pə), *n., pl.* **-pas.** any of several trees of the genus *Catalpa,* native to North America and E Asia, having white flower clusters and long, beanlike seed pods.

ca•tal•y•sis (kə tal′ə sis), *n., pl.* **-ses** (-sēz′). **1.** the causing or accelerating of a chemical change by the addition of a catalyst. **2.** an action between two or more persons or forces, initiated by an agent remaining unaffected by the action. —**cat•a•lyt/ic** (kat′l it′ik), *adj., n.* —**cat/a•lyt/i•cal•ly,** *adv.*

cat•a•lyst (kat′l ist), *n.* **1.** a substance that causes or speeds a chemical reaction without itself being affected. **2.** a person or thing that precipitates an event or change. —**cat•a•lyze** (kat′l īz′), *v.t.,* **-lyzed, -lyz•ing**

catalyt/ic convert/er, *n.* an automotive antipollution device that renders some pollutants in the exhaust gases harmless.

cat•a•ma•ran (kat′ə mə ran′), *n.* **1.** a sailboat whose frame is set on two parallel hulls or floats. **2.** a float or raft formed of logs lashed together.

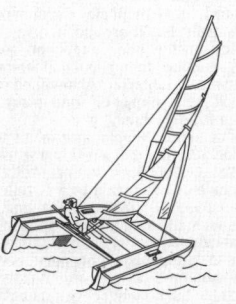

catamaran (def. 1)

cat•a•mount (kat′ə mount′), *n.* **1.** a wild cat, esp. the cougar or the lynx. **2.** CATAMOUNTAIN.

cat•a•moun•tain (kat′ə moun′tn), *n.* any wild cat, esp. the European wildcat.

cat•a•pult (kat′ə pult′, -pŏŏlt′), *n.* **1.** an ancient military engine for hurling stones, arrows, etc. **2.** a device for launching an airplane from the deck of a ship. —*v.t., v.i.* **3.** to hurl or be hurled from or as if from a catapult. **4.** to move quickly, suddenly, or forcibly.

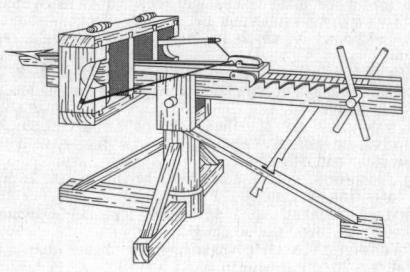

catapult (def. 1)

cat•a•ract (kat′ə rakt′), *n.* **1.** a descent of water over a steep surface; a waterfall, esp. one of considerable size. **2.** any furious rush or downpour of water; deluge. **3. a.** an abnormality of the eye characterized by opacity of the lens. **b.** the opaque area.

ca•tarrh (kə tär′), *n.* inflammation of a mucous membrane, esp. of the respiratory tract, causing excessive secretions. —**ca•tarrh/al, ca•tarrh/-ous,** *adj.* —**ca•tarrh/al•ly,** *adv.*

ca•tas•tro•phe (kə tas′trə fē), *n.* **1.** a sudden and widespread disaster. **2.** any misfortune or failure; fiasco. **3.** a disastrous end. **4.** the point in a drama following the climax and introducing the conclusion. **5.** a sudden, violent disturbance, esp. of a part of the surface of the earth; cataclysm. —**cat•a•stroph•ic** (kat′ə strof′ik), *adj.* —**cat/a•stroph/i•cal•ly,** *adv.*

cat•a•to•ni•a (kat′ə tō′nē ə, -tōn′yə), *n.* a psychotic syndrome, esp. in schizophrenia, characterized by muscular rigidity and mental stupor, sometimes alternating with excitability and confusion. —**cat/a•ton/ic** (-ton′ik), *adj., n.*

Ca•taw•ba (kə tô′bə), *n., pl.* **-bas,** (*esp. collectively*) **-ba** for 3. **1.** a reddish variety of grape, grown in the eastern U.S. **2.** a dry white wine made from this grape. **3.** a member of an American Indian people who lived in the Catawba River valley of the Carolinas in the early 18th century: later dispersed, with some communities remaining in N South Carolina.

cat•bird (kat′bûrd′), *n.* any of various songbirds with catlike vocalizations, esp. a common slate-colored member of the mockingbird family, *Dumetella carolinensis,* inhabiting the E and central U.S.

cat′bird seat′, *n. Informal.* an advantageous situation or condition: *His appointment as acting dean put him in the catbird seat.*

cat•bri•er (kat′brī′ər), *n.* any of numerous prickly vines of the genus *Smilax,* of the lily family, esp. *S. rotundifolia,* growing in tangled masses. Also called **greenbrier.**

cat′ bur′glar, *n.* a burglar who breaks into buildings by climbing through upstairs windows, across roofs, etc.

cat•call (kat′kôl′), *n.* **1.** a shrill sound or raucous shout expressing disapproval at a theater, meeting, etc. —*v.i.* **2.** to sound catcalls. —*v.t.* **3.** to express disapproval of by catcalls.

catch (kach), *v.,* **caught, catch•ing,** *n., adj.* —*v.t.* **1.** to seize or capture, esp. after pursuit: *to catch a thief.* **2.** to trap or ensnare: *to catch fish.* **3.** to take and hold (something thrown, falling, etc.): *to catch the ball.* **4.** to surprise or detect, as in some action: *I caught them cheating.* **5.** to receive or contract: *to catch a cold.* **6.** to be in time to get aboard (a train, boat, etc.). **7.** to lay hold of; clasp: *He caught her in an embrace.* **8.** to grip, hook, or entangle: *The closing door caught my arm.* **9.** to allow to become gripped, hooked, snagged, or entangled: *He caught his coat on a nail.* **10.** to attract: *to catch our attention.* **11.** to check or restrain suddenly (often used reflexively). **12.** to see or attend: *to catch a show.* **13.** to strike; hit: *The blow caught him on the head.* **14.** to become inspired by or aware of: *to catch the spirit.* **15.** to fasten with or as if with a catch. **16.** to deceive: *No one was caught by his sugary words.* **17.** to attract the attention of; charm: *caught by his winning smile.* **18.** to grasp with the intellect; comprehend: *I caught the meaning.* **19.** to hear clearly. **20.** to record; capture: *The painting caught her expression.* —*v.i.* **21.** to become gripped, hooked, or entangled. **22.** to take hold: *The lock won't catch.* **23.** to play the position of catcher in baseball. **24.** to become lighted; ignite. **25. catch at,** to grasp at eagerly; accept readily. **26. catch on, a.** to become popular. **b.** to fathom the meaning; understand. **27. catch out,** to catch or discover in deceit or an error. **28. catch up, a.** to overtake someone or something moving (often fol. by *with* or *to*). **b.** to lift up or snatch suddenly. **c.** to do enough so that one is no longer behind: *to catch up on one's work.* **d.** to involve or interest intensely (usu. in the passive): *caught up in the moment.* —*n.* **29.** the act of catching. **30.** anything that catches, esp. a device for checking motion, as a latch on a door. **31.** any tricky or concealed drawback: *There must be a catch somewhere.* **32.** a slight, momentary break or crack in the voice. **33.** something caught, as a quantity of fish. **34.** a person or thing worth getting, esp. a person regarded as a desirable matrimonial prospect. **35.** a game in which a ball is thrown from one person to another. **36.** a fragment: *catches of a song.* **37.** the catching and holding of a batted or thrown ball before it touches the ground. **38.** a musical round for male voices with the words in overlapping parts contrived to produce humorous or bawdy effects. —*adj.* **39.** CATCHY (def. 3). —*Idiom.* **40. catch it,** *Informal.* to receive a reprimand or punishment.

catch•er (kach′ər), *n.* **1.** a person or thing that catches. **2.** the baseball player stationed behind home plate, whose chief duty is to catch pitches not hit by the batter.

catch•fly (kach′flī′), *n., pl.* **-flies.** any of various plants of the pink family, esp. of the genera *Silene* and *Lychnis,* that have a viscid secretion on the stem and calyx.

catch•ing (kach′ing), *adj.* **1.** contagious or infectious. **2.** attractive; alluring. —**catch′ing•ly,** *adv.*

catch•ment (kach′mənt), *n.* **1.** something for catching water, as a reservoir or basin. **2.** the water so caught.

catch′ phrase′ or **catch′phrase′,** *n.* a phrase that attracts or is meant to attract attention; slogan.

Catch-22 (kach′twen′tē tōō′), *n., pl.* **Catch-22's, Catch-22s. 1.** a frustrating situation in which one is trapped by contradictory regulations or conditions. **2.** any illogical or paradoxical problem or situation; dilemma. **3.** a condition, regulation, etc., preventing the resolution of a problem or situation; catch. [from a military regulation in J. Heller's novel of the same name (1961)]

catch•word (kach′wûrd′), *n.* **1.** a memorable word or phrase that is repeated so often that it becomes a slogan. **2.** Also called **headword, guide word.** a word printed at the top of a page in a reference book to indicate the first or last entry or article on that page.

catch•y (kach′ē), *adj.,* **catch•i•er, catch•i•est. 1.** pleasing and easily remembered: *a catchy tune.* **2.** likely to attract interest or attention: *a catchy title.* **3.** tricky; deceptive: *a catchy question.* **4.** occurring in snatches; fitful: *a catchy wind.*

cat•e•che•sis (kat′i kē′sis), *n., pl.* **-ses** (-sēz). oral religious instruction, formerly esp. before baptism or confirmation.

cat•e•chism (kat′i kiz′əm), *n.* **1.** an elementary book containing a summary of the principles of a Christian religion, in the form of questions and answers. **2.** instruction by question and answer. **3.** a series of formal questions used to elicit views. —**cat′e•chis′mal,** *adj.*

cat•e•chist (kat′i kist), *n.* a person appointed to instruct catechumens. —**cat′e•chis′tic, cat′e•chis′ti•cal,** *adj.*

cat•e•chu•men (kat′i kyōō′mən), *n.* **1.** a person under instruction in the rudiments of Christianity; neophyte. **2.** a person being taught the rudiments of any subject.

cat•e•gor•i•cal (kat′i gôr′i kəl, -gor′-) also **cat′e•gor′ic,** *adj.* **1.** without exceptions or conditions; absolute: *a categorical denial.* **2.** *Logic.* **a.** (of a proposition) analyzable into a subject and an attribute related by a copula, as in the proposition "All humans are mortal." **b.** (of a syllogism) having categorical propositions as premises. **3.** belonging to a category. —**cat′e•gor′i•cal•ly,** *adv.*

cat•e•go•rize (kat′i gə rīz′), *v.t.,* **-rized, -riz•ing. 1.** to arrange in categories or classes; classify. **2.** to describe by labeling or giving a name to; characterize. —**cat′e•go′rist** (-gôr′ist, -gōr′-), *n.* —**cat′e•go•ri•za′tion,** *n.*

cat•e•go•ry (kat′i gôr′ē, -gōr′ē), *n., pl.* **-ries. 1.** any division in a system of classification; class; group. **2.** any of the classes, concepts, or terms that are basic in a field of knowledge.

cat•e•nar•y (kat′n er′ē; *esp. Brit.* kə tē′nə rē), *n., pl.* **-nar•ies,** *adj.* —*n.* **1.** the curve assumed approximately by a heavy uniform cord or chain hanging freely from two points not in the same vertical line. Equation: $y = k \cosh(x/k)$. **2.** (in electric railroads) the cable, running above the track, from which the trolley wire is suspended. —*adj.* **3.** of, pertaining to, or resembling a catenary.

cat•e•nate (kat′n āt′), *v.t.,* **-nat•ed, -nat•ing.** to link together; form into a connected series: *catenated cells.* —**cat′e•na′tion,** *n.*

ca•ter (kā′tər), *v.i.* **1.** to provide food, service, etc., as for a party. **2.** to provide or supply what is needed or gives pleasure, comfort, etc. (usu. fol. by *to* or *for*): *to cater to popular demand.* —*v.t.* **3.** to provide food and service for: *to cater a wedding.* —**ca′ter•er,** *n.*

cat•er-cor•nered (kat′i kôr′nərd, kat′ē-, kat′ər-) also **cat′er-cor′ner,** *adj.* **1.** diagonal. —*adv.* **2.** diagonally.

cat•er•pil•lar (kat′ə pil′ər, kat′ər-), *n.* the larva of a butterfly or a moth, having biting mouthparts, a long segmented body with several pairs of legs and prolegs, and a spinneret.

Cat′erpillar tread′, *n.* either of two endless tracks, passing over a number of wheels, on which vehicles intended for rough terrain run.

cat•er•waul (kat′ər wôl′), *v.i.* **1.** to utter long wailing cries, as cats in rutting time. **2.** to utter a similar sound; howl or screech. **3.** to quarrel like cats. —*n.* Also, **cat′er•waul′ing. 4.** the cry of a cat in rutting time. **5.** any similar sound.

cat•fish (kat′fish′), *n., pl.* (*esp. collectively*) **-fish,** (*esp. for kinds or species*) **-fish•es.** any of numerous scaleless fishes of the order Siluriformes, having barbels around the mouth that resemble a cat's whiskers.

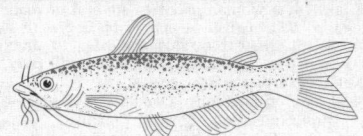
catfish, *Ictalurus punctatus,* length to 4 ft. (1.2 m)

cat•gut (kat′gut′), *n.* a strong cord made by twisting the dried intestines of animals, as sheep, used in stringing musical instruments and tennis rackets, for surgical sutures, etc.

ca•thar•sis (kə thär′sis), *n., pl.* **-ses** (-sēz). **1.** the purging of the emotions or relieving of emotional tensions, esp. through a work of art. **2.** *Med.* PURGATION. **3.** *Psychiatry.* a discharge of repressed or pent-up emotions resulting in the alleviation of symptoms or the elimination of the condition. —**ca•thar′tic,** *adj.*

ca•the•dra (kə thē′drə, kath′i-), *n., pl.* **-drae** (-drē, -drē′). the seat or throne of a bishop in the principal church of a diocese.

ca•the•dral (kə thē′drəl), *n.* **1.** the principal church of a diocese, containing the bishop's throne. **2.** (in nonepiscopal denominations) any of various important churches. —*adj.* **3.** pertaining to or containing a bishop's throne. **4.** authoritative.

cathe′dral ceil′ing, *n.* a high ceiling formed by or suggesting an open-timbered roof.

Cath•er (kath′ər; *often* kath′-), *n.* **Willa (Sibert),** 1876–1947, U.S. novelist.

Cath•er•ine (kath′ər in, kath′rin), *n.* **1. Catherine I,** (*Marfa Skavronskaya*) 1684?–1727, Lithuanian wife of Peter the Great: empress of Russia 1725–27. **2. Catherine II,** (*Sophia Augusta of Anhalt-Zerbst*) ("*Catherine the Great*") 1729–96, empress of Russia 1762–96.

Cath′erine de Mé•di•cis′ (də mā dē sēs′) also **Cath′erine de′** (or **de**) **Med′i•ci** (də med′i chē), *n.* (*Caterina de′ Medici*) 1518–89, queen of Henry II of France.

cath•e•ter (kath′i tər), *n.* a thin flexible tube inserted into a bodily passage, vessel, or cavity to allow fluids to pass into or out of it, to distend it, or to convey diagnostic or other instruments through it.

ca•thex•is (kə thek′sis), *n., pl.* **-thex•es** (-thek′sēz). *Psychoanal.* **1.** the investment of emotional significance in an activity, object, or idea. **2.** the charge of psychic energy so invested.

cath•ode (kath′ōd), *n.* **1.** the electrode or terminal by which current leaves an electrolytic cell, voltaic cell, battery, etc. **2.** the positive terminal of a voltaic cell or battery. **3.** the negative terminal, electrode, or element of an electron tube or electrolytic cell. —**ca•thod′ic** (ka thod′ik), *adj.*

cath′ode ray′, *n.* a flow of electrons emanating from a cathode in a vacuum tube and focused into a narrow beam.

cath′ode-ray′ tube′, *n.* a vacuum tube generating a focused beam of electrons, the terminus of which is visible as a luminescent spot or line on a screen at the broad end of the tube: used to display images on a television receiver or computer monitor. *Abbr.:* CRT

cath•o•lic (kath′ə lik, kath′lik), *adj.* **1.** universal in extent; encompassing all; wide-ranging: *catholic tastes and interests.* **2.** having broad sympathies; broad-minded; liberal. **3.** pertaining to the whole Christian body or church.

Cath•o•lic (kath′ə lik, kath′lik), *adj.* **1.** of or pertaining to the Roman Catholic Church. **2.** of or pertaining to the Christian Church that was formerly undivided or to all the modern orthodox churches that have kept the apostolic succession of bishops. —*n.* **3.** a member of a Catholic church.

Ca•thol•i•cism (kə thol′ə siz′əm), *n.* the faith, system, and practice of a Catholic church, esp. the Roman Catholic Church.

cath•o•lic•i•ty (kath′ə lis′i tē), *n.* **1.** broad-mindedness, as of tastes, interests, or views. **2.** universality. **3.** (*cap.*) the Roman Catholic Church, or its doctrines and usages.

cat•i•on (kat′ī′ən, -on), *n.* **1.** a positively charged ion that is attracted to the cathode in electrolysis. **2.** any positively charged ion (opposed to *anion*). —**cat′i•on′ic** (-on′ik), *adj.* —**cat′i•on′i•cal•ly,** *adv.*

cat•kin (kat′kin), *n.* a spike of unisexual flowers with scaly bracts and no petals, as on the willow or birch. Also called **ament.**

cat•nap (kat′nap′), *n., v.,* **-napped, -nap•ping.** —*n.* **1.** a short, light nap. —*v.i.* **2.** to sleep briefly; doze.

cat•nip (kat′nip), *n.* a plant, *Nepeta cataria,* of the mint family, having leaves containing aromatic oils that are a cat attractant.

cat-o'-nine-tails (kat′ə nīn′tālz′), *n., pl.* **-tails.** a whip, usu. having nine knotted thongs or cords fastened to a handle, used for flogging.

ca•top•trics (kə top′triks), *n.* (*used with a sing. v.*) the branch of optics dealing with the formation of images by mirrors. —**ca•top′tric, ca•top′tri•cal,** *adj.* —**ca•top′tri•cal•ly,** *adv.*

CAT′ scan′ (kat), *n.* **1.** an examination performed with a CAT scanner. **2.** an x-ray image obtained by examination with a CAT scanner. [C(OMPUTERIZED) A(XIAL) T(OMOGRAPHY)] Also called **CT scan.**

CAT′ scan′ner (kat), *n.* a tomographic device employing narrow beams of x-rays in two planes at various angles to produce computerized cross-sectional images of the body, including soft tissue. Also called **CT scanner.**

cat's′ cra′dle, *n.* a game in which two players alternately stretch a looped string over their fingers in such a way as to produce different designs.

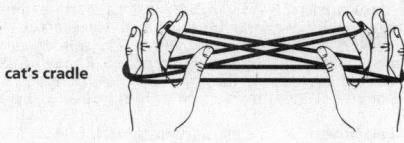

cat's cradle

cat's′-eye′, *n., pl.* **-eyes.** any of certain gems having a chatoyant luster, esp. chrysoberyl.

Cats′kill Moun′tains (kat′skil), *n.pl.* mountain range in E New York: resort area. Highest peak, 4204 ft. (1281 m). Also called **Cats′kills.**

cat's′ meow′, *n. Slang.* someone or something wonderful or remarkable. Also called **cat's pajamas.**

cat's′-paw′ or **cats′paw′,** *n.* **1.** a person who is exploited by another; tool. **2.** a light breeze that ruffles the surface of the water. **3.** a hitch made in the bight of a rope to hold the hook of a tackle.

cat•sup (kat′səp, kech′əp, kach′-), *n.* KETCHUP.

Catt (kat), *n.* **Carrie Chapman (Lane),** 1859–1947, U.S. leader in women's suffrage movements.

cat•tail (kat′tāl′), *n.* any tall, reedlike marsh plant of the genus *Typha,* of the cattail family, esp. *T. latifolia,* with long sword-shaped leaves that are used to make mats, and cylindrical clusters of minute brown flowers. Also called **bulrush.**

cat•tle (kat′l), *n. (used with a pl. v.)* bovine animals, esp. domesticated members of the genus *Bos,* as cows and steers.

cat′tle call′, *n. Slang.* a theatrical audition at which many performers are seen only briefly, often in groups.

cat′tle e′gret, *n.* a small egret of pastures and roadsides, *Bubulcus ibis,* orig. of Eurasia and Africa and now common in the New World.

cat′tle grub′, *n.* the larva or adult of a warble fly, esp. *Hypoderma lineatum,* a common pest of cattle in North America.

cat•tle•man (kat′l mən, -man′), *n., pl.* **-men** (-mən, -men′). **1.** the owner of a cattle ranch. **2.** a person who tends cattle.

cat′tle show′, *n.* **1.** an exhibition of prize cattle by cattle breeders, as at a livestock exposition. **2.** *Informal.* a public appearance by the contenders for a political office, a job, or the like, at which they may be judged by voters, prospective employers, etc.

cat′tle tick′, *n.* any tick of the genus *Boophilus* that is a vector for the protozoans that cause Texas fever.

catt•ley•a (kat′lē ə, kat lē′ə, -lā′ə), *n., pl.* **-ley•as.** any tropical American orchid of the genus *Cattleya,* having large, showy flowers.

Cat•ton (kat′n), *n.* **(Charles) Bruce,** 1899–1978, U.S. historian.

cat•ty (kat′ē), *adj.,* **-ti•er, -ti•est. 1.** slyly malicious; spiteful. **2.** catlike; feline. —**cat′ti•ly,** *adv.* —**cat′ti•ness,** *n.*

cat•ty-cor•nered (kat′ē kôr′nərd) also **cat′ty-cor′ner,** *adj., adv. Southern U.S.* CATER-CORNERED.

Ca•tul•lus (kə tul′əs), *n.* **Gaius Valerius,** 84?–54? B.C., Roman poet. —**Ca•tul′li•an,** *adj.*

CATV, community antenna television: a cable television service for areas where reception is ordinarily poor or impossible.

cat•walk (kat′wôk′), *n.* a narrow walkway, esp. one high above the surrounding area, used to provide access or allow movement.

Cau•ca•sia (kô kā′zhə, -shə), *n.* CAUCASUS (def. 2).

Cau•ca•sian (kô kā′zhən, -shən, -kazh′ən, -kash′-), *adj.* Also, **Cau•cas′ic** (kə kas′ik, -kā′-). **1.** of, designating, or characteristic of one of the traditional racial divisions of humankind, marked by fair to dark skin, straight to curly hair, and light to very dark eyes and orig. inhabiting Europe, parts of North Africa, W Asia, and India. **2.** of the Caucasus region, its peoples, or their culture. **3.** of or designating the non-Indo-European, non-Turkic languages spoken by the peoples of the Caucasus and adjacent areas. —*n.* **4.** a person having Caucasian physical characteristics. **5.** a native or inhabitant of the Caucasus.

Cau•ca•sus (kô′kə səs), *n.* **the, 1.** Also called **Cau′casus Moun′tains.** a mountain range in Caucasia, between the Black and Caspian seas, along the border between Russia, Georgia, and Azerbaijan. Highest peak, Mt. Elbrus, 18,481 ft. (5633 m). **2.** Also, **Caucasia.** a region between the Black and Caspian seas: divided by the Caucasus Mountains into Ciscaucasia in Europe and Transcaucasia in Asia.

cau•cus (kô′kəs), *n.* **1. a.** a meeting of the members of a political party to select candidates or convention delegates, determine policy, etc. **b.** a faction within a legislative body that pursues its interests through the legislative process: *the black caucus.* **2.** any group or meeting organized to further a special interest or cause. —*v.i.* **3.** to hold or meet in a caucus.

cau•dal (kôd′l), *adj.* **1.** of, at, or near the tail end of the body. **2.** taillike: *caudal appendages.* —**cau′dal•ly,** *adv.*

cau•date (kô′dāt) also **cau′dat•ed,** *adj.* having a tail or taillike appendage. —**cau•da′tion,** *n.*

cau•dil•lo (Sp. kou thē′lyô, -thē′yô), *n., pl.* **-dil•los** (Sp. -thē′lyôs, -thē′-

yôs). (in Spanish-speaking countries) a head of state, esp. a military dictator.

caught (kôt), *v.* pt. and pp. of CATCH.

caul (kôl), *n.* a part of the amnion sometimes covering the head of a child at birth.

caul•dron or **cal•dron** (kôl′drən), *n.* a large kettle or boiler.

cau•les•cent (kô les′ənt), *adj.. Bot.* having an obvious stem rising above the ground.

cau•li•flow•er (kô′lə flou′ər, -lē-, kol′ə-, kol′ē-), *n.* **1.** a form of a cultivated plant, *Brassica oleracea botrytis,* of the mustard family, whose inflorescence forms a compact, usu. whitish head. **2.** this head, used as a vegetable.

cau′liflower ear′, *n.* an ear that has been deformed by repeated injury, resulting in an irregular thickening of scar tissue.

caulk or **calk** (kôk), *v.t.* **1.** to fill or close seams or crevices of (a window, ship's hull, etc.) in order to make watertight, airtight, etc. **2.** to fill or close (a seam, joint, etc.), as in a boat. —*n.* **3.** Also, **caulking.** a material used to caulk. —**caulk′er,** *n.*

caus•al (kô′zəl), *adj.* **1.** of or pertaining to a cause. **2.** expressing a cause, as the conjunctions *because* and *since.* —**caus′al•ly,** *adv.*

cau•sal•gi•a (kô zal′jē ə, -jə), *n.* a neuralgia distinguished by a burning pain along certain nerves, usu. of the upper extremities. —**cau•sal′gic,** *adj.*

cau•sal•i•ty (kô zal′i tē), *n., pl.* **-ties. 1.** the relation of cause and effect. **2.** causal quality or agency.

cau•sa•tion (kô zā′shən), *n.* **1.** the act or fact of causing. **2.** the relation of cause to effect; causality. **3.** anything that produces an effect; cause.

caus•a•tive (kô′zə tiv), *adj.* **1.** acting as a cause; producing (often fol. by *of*): *a causative agent.* **2.** expressing causation, as the verb *fell* "to cause to fall" or the suffix *-en* in *sharpen* "to cause to become sharp." —*n.* **3.** a word or form expressing causation. —**caus′a•tive•ly,** *adv.*

cause (kôz), *n., v.,* **caused, caus•ing.** —*n.* **1.** a person that acts or a thing that occurs so as to produce a specific result: *the cause of the accident.* **2.** the reason or motive for some action: *a cause for rejoicing.* **3.** good or sufficient reason: *to complain without cause.* **4. a.** a ground of legal action. **b.** a case for judicial decision. **5.** a principle, ideal, goal, or movement to which a person or group is dedicated: *the human rights cause.* —*v.t.* **6.** to be the cause of; bring about. —**Idiom. 7. make common cause,** to unite in a joint effort.

cause cé•lè•bre (kôz′ sə leb′; *Fr.* kōz sā leb′ʳᵃ), *n., pl.* **causes cé•lè•bres** (kôz′ sə leb′; *Fr.* kōz sā leb′ʳᵃ). any controversy that attracts great public attention.

cause•way (kôz′wā′), *n.* a raised road, as over wet ground or a body of water.

caus•tic (kô′stik), *adj.* **1.** capable of burning or destroying living tissue. **2.** severely critical or sarcastic: *a caustic remark.* —*n.* **3.** a caustic substance, as potassium hydroxide. —**caus′ti•cal•ly,** *adv.*

caus′tic so′da, *n.* SODIUM HYDROXIDE.

cau•ter•ize (kô′tə rīz′), *v.t.,* **-ized, -iz•ing.** to burn with a hot iron, electric current, fire, or a caustic, esp. for curative purposes; treat with a cautery. —**cau′ter•i•za′tion,** *n.*

cau•ter•y (kô′tə rē), *n., pl.* **-ter•ies. 1.** any substance or instrument, as an electric current or hot iron, used to destroy tissue. **2.** the process of destroying tissue with a cautery.

cau•tion (kô′shən), *n.* **1.** alertness and prudence in a hazardous situation; care: *Proceed with caution.* **2.** a warning against danger or evil; anything serving as a warning. **3.** a person or thing that astonishes or causes mild apprehension: often used humorously. —*v.t.* **4.** to advise or urge to take heed. —*v.i.* **5.** to give a warning: *to caution against overoptimism.* —**Idiom. 6. throw caution to the wind,** to abandon all consideration of risks. —**cau′tious,** *adj.*

cau•tion•ar•y (kô′shə ner′ē), *adj.* serving as a warning: *a cautionary tale.*

cav•al•cade (kav′əl kād′, kav′əl kād′), *n.* **1.** a procession of persons riding on horses, in carriages or cars, etc. **2.** any procession. **3.** any noteworthy series, as of events or activities.

cav•a•lier (kav′ə lēr′, kav′ə lēr′), *n.* **1.** a horseman, esp. a mounted soldier; knight. **2.** one having the spirit or bearing of a knight; a courtly gentleman; gallant. **3.** the male escort or dancing partner of a woman. —*adj.* **4.** haughty, disdainful, or supercilious. **5.** casual; lighthearted. —*v.i.* **6.** to play the cavalier. [< Middle French: horseman < Late Latin *caballārius* groom] —**cav′a•lier•ly,** *adv.*

cav•al•ry (kav′əl rē), *n., pl.* **-ries. 1. a.** a unit of troops serving on horseback. **b.** motorized infantry units. **2.** horsemen, horses, etc., collectively.

cave (kāv), *n., v.,* **caved, cav•ing.** —*n.* **1.** a hollow in the earth, esp. one opening more or less horizontally into a hill, mountain, etc. **2.** a storage cellar, esp. for wine. —*v.t.* **3.** *Mining.* to cause (overlying rock) to collapse into a stope or sublevel; undermine. —*v.i.* **4.** to collapse (often fol. by *in*). **5. cave in, a.** to fall in; collapse. **b.** to cause to fall in or collapse. **c.** to yield; surrender. —**cave′like,** *adj.*

ca•ve•at (kav′ē ät′, -at′, kä′vē-, kä-), *n.* **1.** a warning or caution; admonition. **2.** a legal notice to a court or public officer to suspend a proceeding until the notifier is given a hearing.

ca′veat emp′tor (emp′tôr), let the buyer beware: the principle that the seller of a product cannot be held responsible for its quality unless it is guaranteed in a warranty. [< Latin]

cave′ dwell′er, *n.* **1.** a person, as a prehistoric human, living in a cave. **2.** a person living in an apartment building.

cave-in′, *n.* **1.** a collapse, as of anything hollow. **2.** a site of such a collapse. **3.** submission to the demands, policies, etc., of another.

Cav·ell (kav′əl), *n.* **Edith Louisa,** 1865–1915, English nurse: executed by the Germans in World War I.

cave′ man′, *n.* **1.** a cave dweller, esp. of the Stone Age. **2.** a man who behaves in a rough, primitive manner, esp. toward women.

cav·ern (kav′ərn), *n.* **1.** a cave, esp. one that is large and mostly underground. —*v.t.* **2.** to enclose in or as if in a cavern. **3.** to form a cavern of (often fol. by *out*). —**cav′ern·ous,** *adj.*

ca·vet·to (kə vet′ō, kä-), *n., pl.* **-ti** (-tē), **-tos.** a concave architectural molding the outline of which is a quarter circle.

cav·i·ar or **cav·i·are** (kav′ē är′, kav′ē är′), *n.* the roe of sturgeon, salmon, etc., eaten esp. as an appetizer.

cav·il (kav′əl), *v.,* **-iled, -il·ing** or (*esp. Brit.*) **illed, -il·ling,** *n.* —*v.i.* **1.** to raise trivial and unnecessary objections (usu. fol. by *at* or *about*). —*v.t.* **2.** to oppose by trivial or frivolous objections. —*n.* **3.** a trivial and annoying objection. **4.** the raising of such objections. —**cav′il·er;** *esp. Brit.,* **cav′il·ler,** *n.*

cav·i·ta·tion (kav′i tā′shən), *n.* **1.** the rapid formation and collapse of vapor pockets in a flowing liquid in regions of very low pressure, often causing structural damage to propellers, pumps, etc. **2.** the formation of cavities, esp in a part of the body. —**cav′i·tate′,** *v.t., v.i.,* **-tat·ed, -tat·ing.**

cav·i·ty (kav′i tē), *n., pl.* **-ties. 1.** any hollow place; hollow. **2.** a hollow space within the body, an organ, a bone, etc. **3.** a pit in a tooth, commonly produced by decay. —**cav′i·tied,** *adj.*

ca·vort (kə vôrt′), *v.i.* **1.** to prance or caper about. **2.** to make merry. —**ca·vort′er,** *n.*

ca·vy (kā′vē), *n., pl.* **-vies.** any of several short-tailed or tailless South American rodents of the family Caviidae, as the guinea pig.

caw (kô), *n.* **1.** the loud harsh call of the crow. —*v.i.* **2.** to utter this cry.

Cax·ton (kak′stən), *n.* **William,** 1422?–91, English printer: established first printing press in England 1476. —**Cax·to·ni·an** (kak stō′nē ən), *adj.*

cay (kā, kē), *n.* a small low island; key.

cay·enne (kī en′, kā-), *n.* **1.** a hot, biting condiment composed of the ground pods and seeds of the pepper *Capsicum annuum longum.* **2.** the long, wrinkled fruit of this plant. Also called **cayenne′ pep′per.**

Cay·enne (kī en′, kā-), *n.* the capital of French Guiana. 38,135.

cay·man (kā′mən), *n., pl.* **-mans.** CAIMAN.

Cay·man Is′lands (kā′mən′, -mən), *n.pl.* three islands in the West Indies, NW of Jamaica: a British crown colony. 23,700; 104 sq. mi. (269 sq. km).

Ca·yu·ga (kā yōō′gə, kī-), *n., pl.* **-gas,** (*esp. collectively*) **-ga. 1.** a member of an American Indian people, orig. residing near Cayuga Lake in New York: one of the Iroquois Five Nations. **2.** the Iroquoian language of the Cayugas.

cay·use (kī yōōs′, kī′ōōs), *n. Western U.S.* a horse, esp. an Indian pony.

CB, citizens band.

Cb, *Chem. Symbol.* columbium.

CBC or **C.B.C.,** Canadian Broadcasting Corporation.

CB radio, *n.* **1.** a device that transmits and receives citizens band radio signals. **2.** a system of private radio communication built around such a device.

CBT, Chicago Board of Trade.

cc, 1. carbon copy. **2.** copies. **3.** cubic centimeter.

cc. or **c.c., 1.** carbon copy. **2.** copies. **3.** cubic centimeter.

C-clamp (sē′klamp′), *n.* a C-shaped clamp having a screw threaded through one tip in the direction of the other tip.

C clef, *n.* a movable musical clef locating middle C on the first, third, or fourth line of the staff.

CCU, coronary-care unit.

CD, 1. certificate of deposit. **2.** Civil Defense. **3.** compact disc.

Cd, *Chem. Symbol.* cadmium.

cd, candela.

C.D., Civil Defense.

CDC, Centers for Disease Control.

cDNA, complementary DNA: a DNA molecule that is complementary to a specific messenger RNA.

CD player, *n.* COMPACT DISC PLAYER.

Cdr. or **CDR,** Commander.

CD-ROM (sē′dē′rom′), *n.* a compact disc on which a large amount of digitized read-only data can be stored. Compare ROM.

Ce, *Chem. Symbol.* cerium.

C.E., 1. Church of England. **2.** common era.

cease (sēs), *v.,* **ceased, ceas·ing,** *n.* —*v.i.* **1.** to stop; discontinue. **2.** to come to an end. —*v.t.* **3.** to put a stop or end to; halt: *to cease hostilities.* —*n.* **4.** cessation: *The noise went on for hours without cease.*

cease′-fire′, *n.* **1.** a cessation of hostilities; truce. **2.** an order issued for a cease-fire.

cease·less (sēs′lis), *adj.* without stop; unending; incessant. —**cease′less·ly,** *adv.* —**cease′less·ness,** *n.*

ce·cro′pi·a moth′ (si krō′pē ə), *n.* a large North American silkworm moth, *Hyalophora cecropia,* the larvae of which feed on tree leaves. Also called **ce·cro′pi·a.**

ce·cum or **cae·cum** (sē′kəm), *n., pl.* **-ca** (-kə). an anatomical cul-de-sac, esp. that in which the large intestine begins. —**ce′cal,** *adj.*

ce·dar (sē′dər), *n.* **1.** any of several Old World coniferous trees of the genus *Cedrus,* having wide, spreading branches. **2.** any of various other coniferous trees that resemble the true cedar, as the juniper. **3.** the fragrant wood of any of these trees, used in furniture and as a moth repellent.

ce′dar of Leb′anon, *n.* a cedar, *Cedrus libani,* of Asia Minor, having horizontally spreading branches.

Ce′dar Rap′ids, *n.* a city in E Iowa. 113,438.

ce′dar wax′wing, *n.* a North American waxwing, *Bombycilla cedrorum,* having yellowish brown plumage. Also called **ce′dar bird′.**

cede (sēd), *v.t.,* **ced·ed, ced·ing. 1.** to yield or formally surrender to another: *to cede territory.* **2.** to grant or transfer, as by a will. —**ced′er,** *n.*

ce·dil·la (si dil′ə), *n., pl.* **-las.** a mark (,) placed under a letter to indicate its pronunciation, as under *c* in French or Portuguese to indicate that it is pronounced (s) rather than (k), as in *façade.*

cei·ba (sā′bə *or, for 2,* sī′-), *n., pl.* **-bas. 1.** a silk-cotton tree, *Ceiba pentandra.* **2.** silk cotton; kapok.

ceil·ing (sē′ling), *n.* **1.** the overhead interior surface of a room. **2.** an upper limit on the amount of money that can be charged or spent, the quantity of goods produced or sold, etc.: *a ceiling on government spending.* **3. a.** the maximum altitude from which the earth can be seen from an aircraft. **b.** the maximum altitude at which an aircraft can operate under specified conditions. **4.** the height above ground level of the lowest layer of clouds that cover more than half of the sky. —**ceil′inged,** *adj.*

cel·a·don (sel′ə don′, -dn), *n.* **1.** any of several Chinese porcelains having a translucent, pale green glaze. **2.** a pale gray-green.

cel·an·dine (sel′ən dīn′, -dēn′), *n.* **1.** Also called **swallowwort.** an Old World plant, *Chelidonium majus,* of the poppy family, having yellow flowers. **2.** an Old World plant, *Ranunculus ficaria,* of the buttercup family, having fleshy, heart-shaped leaves and solitary yellow flowers.

cel·e·brant (sel′ə brənt), *n.* **1.** a participant in any celebration. **2.** the officiating priest in the celebration of the Eucharist.

cel·e·brate (sel′ə brāt′), *v.,* **-brat·ed, -brat·ing.** —*v.t.* **1.** to observe (a day) or commemorate (an event) with ceremonies or festivities: *to celebrate Christmas; to celebrate an anniversary.* **2.** to make known publicly; proclaim; praise widely: *a book celebrating the joys of country life.* **3.** to perform with appropriate rites and ceremonies; solemnize: *to celebrate Communion.* —*v.i.* **4.** to observe a day or commemorate an event with ceremonies or festivities. **5.** to perform a religious ceremony. **6.** to have or participate in a party or good time. —**cel′e·brat′ed,** *adj.* —**cel′e·bra′tion,** *n.* —**cel′e·bra′tive,** *adj.* —**cel′e·bra′tor, cel′e·brat′er,** *n.* —**cel′e·bra·to′ry** (-brə tôr′ē, -tōr′ē), *adj.*

ce·leb·ri·ty (sə leb′ri tē), *n., pl.* **-ties. 1.** a famous or well-known person. **2.** fame; renown.

ce·ler·i·ac (sə ler′ē ak′, -lēr′-), *n.* a variety of celery, *Apium graveolens rapaceum,* having a large, edible, turniplike root.

ce·ler·i·ty (sə ler′i tē), *n.* swiftness; speed.

cel·er·y (sel′ə rē, sel′rē), *n.* a plant, *Apium graveolens,* of the parsley family, with stiff clustered leafstalks eaten raw or cooked.

cel′ery cab′bage, *n.* CHINESE CABBAGE.

ce·les·tial (sə les′chəl), *adj.* **1.** of or pertaining to the sky or visible heaven: *a celestial body.* **2.** pertaining to the spiritual or invisible heaven; heavenly; divine. **3.** of or pertaining to celestial navigation. —*n.* **4.** an inhabitant of heaven. —**ce·les′tial·ly,** *adv.*

Celes′tial Cit′y, *n.* **1.** the goal of Christian's journey in Bunyan's *Pilgrim's Progress;* the heavenly Jerusalem. **2.** NEW JERUSALEM.

celes′tial equa′tor, *n.* the great circle of the celestial sphere, lying in the same plane as the earth's equator.

celes′tial hori′zon, *n.* See under HORIZON (def. 2b).

celes′tial mechan′ics, *n.* the branch of astronomy that applies the laws of dynamics and gravitation to the motions of heavenly bodies.

celes′tial naviga′tion, *n.* navigation by means of observations made of the apparent position of heavenly bodies.

celes′tial pole′, *n.* each of the two points in which the extended axis of the earth cuts the celestial sphere and about which the stars seem to revolve.

ce·li·ac or **coe·li·ac** (sē′lē ak′), *adj.* of, pertaining to, or located in the cavity of the abdomen.

ce′liac disease′, *n.* a hereditary digestive disorder involving intolerance to gluten, malnutrition and fatty stools.

cel·i·bate (sel′ə bit, -bāt′), *n.* **1.** a person who abstains from sexual relations. **2.** a person who remains unmarried, esp. for religious reasons. —*adj.* **3.** observing or pertaining to sexual abstention or a religious vow not to marry. **4.** not married. —**cel′i·ba·cy** (-bə sē), *n.*

cell (sel), *n.* **1.** a small room, as in a convent or prison. **2.** any of various small compartments or bounded areas forming part of a whole. **3.** a usu. microscopic structure containing nuclear and cytoplasmic material enclosed by a semipermeable membrane and, in plants, a cell wall; the basic structural unit of all organisms. **4.** a small group acting as a unit within a larger organization. **5.** a device that converts chemical energy into electricity, usu. consisting of two different kinds of conductors surrounded by an electrolyte; battery. **6.** Also called **electrolytic cell**. a device for producing electrolysis, consisting essentially of the electrolyte, its container, and the electrodes. **7.** a monastery or nunnery, dependent on a larger religious house. **8.** one of the areas into which the wing of an insect is divided by the veins. **9.** LOCULE. **10.** one of the separate areas covered by a radio transmitter in a cellular phone system. —**cel·lu·lar** (sel′yə lər), *adj.*

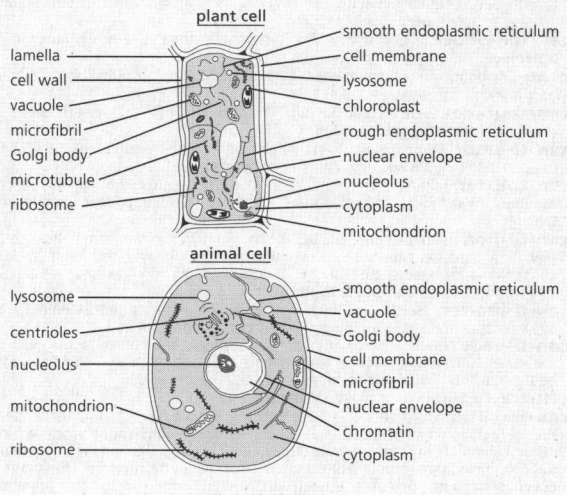

plant cell

lamella — smooth endoplasmic reticulum
cell wall — cell membrane
vacuole — lysosome
microfibril — chloroplast
Golgi body — rough endoplasmic reticulum
microtubule — nuclear envelope
ribosome — nucleolus
— cytoplasm
— mitochondrion

animal cell

lysosome — smooth endoplasmic reticulum
centrioles — vacuole
nucleolus — Golgi body
mitochondrion — cell membrane
— microfibril
ribosome — nuclear envelope
— chromatin
— cytoplasm

cells (def. 3)

cel·lar (sel′ər), *n.* **1.** a room, or set of rooms, wholly or partly underground and usu. beneath a building. **2.** an underground room or story. **3.** WINE CELLAR. **4.** the last place in a competitive ranking or standings. —*v.t.* **5.** to place or store in a cellar. —**cel′lar·less,** *adj.*

cell′ biol′ogy, *n.* the branch of biology dealing with the study of cells, esp. their formation, structure, and function.

cell·block (sel′blok′), *n.* a unit or section of a prison consisting of a number of cells.

cell′ bod′y, *n.* the compact area of a nerve cell that constitutes the nucleus and surrounding cytoplasm, excluding the axons and dendrites. Also called **perikaryon.**

cell′ cy′cle, *n.* the cycle of growth and asexual reproduction of a cell, consisting of interphase followed in actively dividing cells by prophase, metaphase, anaphase, and telophase.

cell′ divi′sion, *n.* the division of a cell or cells in reproduction or growth.

cell′ fu′sion, *n.* the fusion of the nuclei of two types of cells in the laboratory to form a new and genetically distinct cell.

Cel·li·ni (chə lē′nē), *n.* **Benvenuto,** 1500–71, Italian metalsmith, sculptor, and autobiographer.

cel·list (chel′ist), *n.* a person who plays the cello.

cell·mate (sel′māt′), *n.* a fellow inmate in a prison cell.

cell′-me′diated immu′nity, *n.* immunity conferred to an individual through the activity of T cells, involving the direct destruction of viruses, foreign particles, etc. Compare ANTIBODY-MEDIATED IMMUNITY.

cell′ mem′brane, *n.* the semipermeable membrane enclosing the cytoplasm of a cell.

cel·lo (chel′ō), *n., pl.* **-los.** the second largest member of the violin family, rested vertically on the floor between the performer's knees when played; violoncello.

cel·lo·phane (sel′ə fān′), *n.* a transparent, moistureproof paperlike product made from viscose, used to wrap and package food and other products.

cell′ the′ory, *n.* the tenet in biology that cells are the basic units of structure and function in living organisms.

cel′lular phone′, *n.* a mobile telephone using a system of radio transmitters, each covering separate areas, and computers for switching calls from one area to another. Also called **cell′ular tel′ephone.**

cel′lular respira′tion, *n.* the oxidation of organic compounds that occurs within cells, producing energy for cellular processes.

cel·lu·lite (sel′yə līt′, -lēt′), *n.* (not used scientifically) lumpy fat deposits, esp. in the thighs and buttocks.

cel·lu·loid (sel′yə loid′), *n.* **1.** a tough, flammable thermoplastic consisting of nitrocellulose and camphor, formerly used as a base for motion-picture film. **2.** motion-picture film: *captured the drama on celluloid.*

cel·lu·lose (sel′yə lōs′), *n.* an inert carbohydrate, $(C_6H_{10}O_5)_n$, the chief constituent of the cell walls of plants and of wood, cotton, hemp, paper, etc. —**cel′lu·los′i·ty** (-los′i tē), *n.*

cel′lulose ac′etate, *n.* any of a group of acetic esters of cellulose, used to make yarns, textiles, and photographic films.

cell′ wall′, *n.* the definite boundary or wall that is part of the outer structure of certain cells, as a plant cell.

Cel·si·us (sel′sē əs), *adj.* pertaining to or noting a temperature scale **(Cel′sius scale′)** in which 0° represents the ice point and 100° the steam point; Centigrade. *Symbol:* C [after Anders *Celsius* (1701–44), Swedish astronomer who devised the scale]

celt (selt), *n.* a prehistoric ax of stone or metal without perforations or grooves, for hafting.

Celt (kelt, selt) also **Kelt,** *n.* **1.** a member of any of a group of Indo-European peoples inhabiting the British Isles and large areas of W and central Europe in antiquity. **2.** a member of any of several modern peoples descended from the ancient Celts and speaking Celtic languages, including the Irish, Scots of the Scottish Highlands and Hebrides, Welsh, and Bretons.

Celt·ic (kel′tik, sel′-) also **Keltic,** *n.* **1.** a family of languages, a branch of the Indo-European family, spoken by the Celts and including the modern languages Irish, Scottish Gaelic, Welsh, and Breton. —*adj.* **2.** of or pertaining to the Celts or their languages.

Celt′ic cross′, *n.* a cross shaped like a Latin cross and having a ring that intersects each segment of the shaft and crossbar at a point equidistant from their junction.

ce·ment (si ment′), *n.* **1.** any of various calcined mixtures of clay and limestone, usu. mixed with water and sand, gravel, etc., to form concrete, that are used as a building material. **2.** any of various soft, sticky substances that dry hard or stonelike, used esp. for mending broken objects or for making things adhere. **3.** the compact groundmass surrounding and binding together the fragments of clastic rocks. **4.** anything that binds or unites. **5.** a hardening, adhesive, plastic substance, used in the repair of teeth. —*v.t.* **6.** to unite by or as if by cement: *an experience that cemented our friendship.* **7.** to coat or cover with cement. —*v.i.* **8.** to become cemented; cohere.

ce·men·ta·tion (sē′mən tā′shən, -men-, sem′ən-), *n.* **1.** the act, process, or result of cementing. **2.** the heating of two substances in contact in order to effect some change in one of them, esp. the formation of steel by heating iron in powdered charcoal.

ce·ment·ite (si men′tīt), *n.* an iron carbide, Fe_3C, a constituent of steel and cast iron, sometimes with part of its iron replaced by another metal, as manganese.

ce·men·tum (si men′təm), *n.* the bonelike tissue that forms the outer surface of the root of a tooth.

cem·e·ter·y (sem′i ter′ē), *n., pl.* **-ter·ies.** a burial ground for the dead.

cem′etery vote′, *n.* electoral fraud in which a vote is cast in the name of a dead person.

Cen·chre·a (sen′krē ə), *n.* a town in Greece near Corinth from which the Apostle Paul sailed on his second missionary journey. Acts 18:18.

ce·no·bite or **coe·no·bite** (sē′nə bīt′, sen′ə-), *n.* a member of a religious order living in a convent or community.

cen·o·taph (sen′ə taf′, -täf′), *n.* a sepulchral monument erected in memory of a deceased person whose body is buried elsewhere.

ce·no·te (sə nō′tē), *n.* a deep natural well or sinkhole of the Yucatán Peninsula, formed by the collapse of surface limestone.

Ce·no·zo·ic (sē′nə zō′ik, sen′ə-), *adj.* **1.** pertaining to the present era, beginning 65 million years ago and characterized by the ascendancy of mammals. —*n.* **2.** the Cenozoic Era or group of systems.

cen·ser (sen′sər), *n.* a container in which incense is burned.

censer

cen·sor (sen′sər), *n.* **1.** an official who examines literature, television programs, etc., for the purpose of suppressing or deleting parts deemed objectionable on moral, political, military, or other grounds. **2.** an adverse critic; faultfinder. —*v.t.* **3.** to examine and act upon as a censor. —**cen·sor′i·ous** (-sôr′ē əs, -sōr′-), *adj.* —**cen′sor·ship′,** *n.*

cen·sure (sen′shər), *n., v.,* **-sured, -sur·ing.** —*n.* **1.** strong or vehement expression of disapproval. **2.** an official reprimand, as by a legislative body or one of its members. —*v.t.* **3.** to criticize or reproach in a harsh manner. —*v.i.* **4.** to give censure. —**cen′sur·a·ble,** *adj.*

cen·sus (sen′səs), *n., pl.* **-sus·es. 1.** an official enumeration of the population, with details as to age, sex, occupation, etc. **2.** (in ancient Rome) the registration of citizens and their property, for purposes of taxation. —**cen′su·al** (-shōō əl), *adj.*

cent (sent), *n.* **1.** a bronze coin and monetary unit of the U.S., equal to ¹/₁₀₀ of a dollar. *Symbol:* **Ā 2.** a monetary unit of various other nations, including Ethiopia, the Netherlands, South Africa, and many Commonwealth nations, equal to ¹/₁₀₀ of the basic currency. [< Latin *centēsimus* hundredth]

cent., **1.** centigrade. **2.** central. **3.** centum. **4.** century.

cen•tal (sen′tl), *n.* HUNDREDWEIGHT.

cen•taur (sen′tôr), *n.* **1.** a race of creatures in Greek myth having the head and upper torso of a man and the body and legs of a horse. **2.** (*cap.*) CENTAURUS.

centaur (def. 1)

cen•tau•re•a (sen tôr′ē ə), *n., pl.* **-re•as.** any of numerous composite plants of the genus *Centaurea,* having tubular flowers in a variety of colors, as the cornflower and knapweed.

Cen•tau•rus (sen tôr′əs), *n., gen.* **-tau•ri** (-tôr′ī). the Centaur, a southern constellation containing Alpha Centauri and Beta Centauri.

cen•tau•ry (sen′tô rē), *n., pl.* **-ries.** **1.** any of various plants belonging to the genus *Centaurium,* of the gentian family, having clusters of small pink or red flowers. **2.** any of several allied or similar plants.

cen•ta•vo (sen tä′vō), *n., pl.* **-vos.** a monetary unit of the Philippines, Portugal, and various Latin American nations, equal to ¹/₁₀₀ of the basic currency.

cen•ten•ar•y (sen ten′ə rē, sen′tn er′ē; *esp. Brit.* sen tē′nə rē), *adj., n., pl.* **-ar•ies.** **1.** of or pertaining to a period of 100 years. **2.** recurring once in every 100 years. —*n.* **3.** a centennial. **4.** a period of 100 years; century. —**cen•te•nar•i•an** (sen′tn âr′ē ən), *adj.*

cen•ten•ni•al (sen ten′ē əl), *adj.* **1.** pertaining to or marking the completion of a period of 100 years. **2.** pertaining to a 100th anniversary. **3.** lasting 100 years. **4.** 100 years old. —*n.* **5.** a 100th anniversary or its celebration. —**cen•ten′ni•al•ly,** *adv.*

cen•ter (sen′tər), *n.* **1.** the point within a circle or sphere equally distant from all points of the circumference or surface, or the point within a regular polygon equally distant from the vertices. **2.** a pivot or axis around which something revolves. **3.** the middle of something. **4.** the source of an influence, action, or force: *the center of a problem.* **5.** a focus of interest or concern. **6.** a principal point, place, or object: *a shipping center.* **7.** a building or part of a building used as a meeting place or having facilities for certain activities. **8.** an office or other facility providing a service. **9.** a person, thing, or group occupying the middle position. **10.** an establishment devoted to a particular subject or hobby: *a garden center.* **11.** SHOPPING CENTER. **12.** (*usu. cap.*) **a.** (esp. in continental Europe) the members of a legislative assembly who hold views intermediate between those of the Right and Left, customarily seated in the center of the chamber. **b.** individuals or groups holding moderate views, esp. in politics. **c.** the moderate position held by these people. **13. a.** a football lineman who occupies a position in the middle of the line and who puts the ball into play by tossing it between his legs to a back. **b.** the position played by this lineman. **14. a.** a basketball player who plays close to and in front of the basket. **b.** this position or role. **15.** an ice hockey player who participates in a face-off at the beginning of play. **16.** *Math.* **a.** the mean position of a figure or system. **b.** the set of elements of a group that commute with every element of the group. —*v.t.* **17.** to place in or on a center. **18.** to collect around a center; focus: *He centered his novel on the Civil War.* **19.** to determine or mark the center of. **20.** to adjust or shape (an object, part, etc.) so that its axis or the like is in a central or normal position. —*v.i.* **21.** to be at or come to a center. **22.** to come to a focus; concentrate (fol. by *at, about, around, in,* or *on*). **23.** to gather in a cluster; collect (fol. by *at, about, around, in,* or *on*). Also, *esp. Brit.,* **centre.**

cen•tered (sen′tərd), *adj.* **1.** having a central axis: *a centered arc.* **2.** equidistant from all adjacent areas; situated in the center. **3.** inwardly calm and steady; having one's mental and emotional energies well-balanced.

cen′ter field′, *n.* **1.** the area of a baseball outfield beyond second base and between right field and left field. **2.** the position of the player covering this area. —**cen′ter field′er,** *n.*

cen•ter•fold (sen′tər fōld′), *n.* the pair of pages facing each other, or

a foldout, at the center of a magazine or newspaper, printed and made up as a single unit.

cen′ter for′ward, *n.* (in soccer) an offensive player who covers the center of the field and who usu. starts the kickoff.

cen′ter of grav′ity, *n.* **1.** the center of mass with reference to gravity as the external force. **2.** the focus of significance or stability: *The monarchy was that nation's center of gravity.*

cen•ter•piece (sen′tər pēs′), *n.* **1.** an ornamental object used on the center of a dining table. **2.** the central point or feature.

Cen′ters for Disease′ Control′, *n.* an agency of the U.S. Public Health Service charged with the investigation and control of contagious disease in the nation. *Abbr.:* CDC

cen′ter wheel′, *n.* the wheel driving the minute and hour hands of a timepiece.

centi-, a combining form meaning "hundredth" or "hundred": *centiliter; centimeter; centipede.*

cen•ti•grade (sen′ti grād′), *adj.* **1.** divided into 100 degrees, as a scale. **2.** (*cap.*) CELSIUS. *Symbol:* C

cen•ti•gram (sen′ti gram′), *n.* 1/100 of a gram, equivalent to 0.1543 grain. *Abbr.:* cg Also, *esp. Brit.,* **cen′ti•gramme′.**

cen•ti•li•ter (sen′tl ē′tər), *n.* 1/100 of a liter, equivalent to 0.6102 cubic inch, or 0.338 U.S. fluid ounce. *Abbr.:* cl Also, *esp. Brit.,* **cen′ti•li′tre.**

cen•til•lion (sen til′yən), *n., pl.* **-lions,** (as after a numeral) **-lion,** *adj.* —*n.* **1.** a cardinal number represented in the U.S. by 1 followed by 303 zeros, and in Great Britain by 1 followed by 600 zeros. —*adj.* **2.** amounting to one centillion in number.

cen•ti•me•ter (sen′tə mē′tər), *n.* 1/100 of a meter, equivalent to 0.3937 inch. *Abbr.:* cm Also, *esp. Brit.,* **cen′ti•me′tre.**

cen•ti•pede (sen′tə pēd′), *n.* any predaceous segmented arthropod of the class Chilopoda, with a pair of legs on each segment, the first pair being modified into poison fangs.

cen•tra (sen′trə), *n.* a pl. of CENTRUM.

cen•tral (sen′trəl), *adj.* **1.** of or forming the center. **2.** in, at, or near the center: *a central position.* **3.** constituting something from which other related things proceed or upon which they depend: *a central office.* **4.** principal; chief; dominant. **5.** of or pertaining to the central nervous system. **6.** (of a vowel) articulated with the tongue approximately midway between the front and back of the mouth, as the vowel (u) of *shut.* —*n.* **7.** (formerly) **a.** a main telephone exchange. **b.** a telephone operator at such an exchange. —**cen′tral•ly,** *adv.*

Cen′tral Af′rican Repub′lic, *n.* a republic in central Africa: a member of the French Community. 3,342,051; 238,000 sq. mi. (616,420 sq. km). *Cap.:* Bangui.

Cen′tral Amer′ica, *n.* continental North America S of Mexico, usu. considered as comprising Guatemala, Belize, El Salvador, Honduras, Nicaragua, Costa Rica, and Panama. 29,000,000; 227,933 sq. mi. (590,346 sq. km). —**Cen′tral Amer′ican,** *n., adj.*

cen′tral heat′ing, *n.* a system that supplies heat to an entire building from a single source through ducts or pipes.

Cen′tral Intel′ligence A′gency, *n.* See CIA.

cen•tral•ism (sen′trə liz′əm), *n.* a centralizing system; centralization. —**cen′tral•ist,** *n., adj.* —**cen′tral•is′tic,** *adj.*

cen•tral•i•ty (sen tral′i tē), *n., pl.* **-ties.** **1.** a central position or state. **2.** a vital, critical, or important position.

cen•tral•ize (sen′trə līz′), *v.,* **-ized, -iz•ing.** —*v.t.* **1.** to draw to or gather about a center. **2.** to bring under one control, esp. in government. —*v.i.* **3.** to come together at or to form a center. —**cen′tral•i•za′tion,** *n.* —**cen′tral•iz′er,** *n.*

cen′tral nerv′ous sys′tem, *n.* the part of the nervous system comprising the brain and spinal cord.

cen′tral proc′essing u′nit, *n.* See CPU. Also called **cen′tral proc′essor.**

cen′tral time′, *n.* See under STANDARD TIME. Also called **Cen′tral Stand′ard Time′.**

cen•tre (sen′tər), *n., v.,* **-tred, -tring.** Chiefly Brit. CENTER.

centri- or **centro-,** a combining form representing CENTER: *centrifuge.*

cen•tric (sen′trik) also **cen′tri•cal,** *adj.* pertaining to or situated at the center; central. —**cen•tric′i•ty** (-tris′i tē), *n.*

cen•trif•u•gal (sen trif′yə gəl, -ə gəl), *adj.* **1.** directed outward from the center (opposed to *centripetal*). **2.** pertaining to or operated by centrifugal force: *a centrifugal pump.* **3.** *Physiol.* efferent. —*n.* **4.** CENTRIFUGE.

centrif′ugal force′, *n.* the force, equal and opposite to the centripetal force, experienced by a body moving along a curved path and appearing to propel the body outward.

cen•tri•fuge (sen′trə fyōōj′), *n., v.,* **-fuged, -fug•ing.** —*n.* **1.** an apparatus that rotates at high speed and separates substances of different densities. —*v.t.* **2.** to subject to the action of a centrifuge.

cen•tri•ole (sen′trē ōl′), *n.* a small cylindrical cell organelle, seen near the nucleus in the cytoplasm of most eukaryotic cells, that divides perpendicularly during mitosis.

cen•trip•e•tal (sen trip′i tl), *adj.* **1.** directed toward the center (opposed to *centrifugal*). **2.** pertaining to or operated by centripetal force. **3.** *Physiol.* afferent. —**cen•trip′e•tal•ly,** *adv.*

centrip′etal force′, *n.* the force, acting upon a body moving along a curved path, that is directed toward the center of curvature of the path and constrains the body to the path.

cen•trist (sen′trist), *n.* (*sometimes cap.*) a person with moderate political views. —**cen′trism,** *n.*

cen•trum (sen′trəm), *n.*, *pl.* **-trums, -tra** (-trə). **1.** a center. **2.** the body of a vertebra, the part cushioned by the spinal disk.

cen•tu•ri•on (sen tŏŏr′ē ən, -tyŏŏr′-), *n.* (in the ancient Roman army) the commander of a century.

cen•tu•ry (sen′chə rē), *n.*, *pl.* **-ries. 1.** a period of 100 years. **2.** one of the successive periods of 100 years reckoned forward or backward from a recognized chronological epoch, esp. from the assumed date of the birth of Jesus. **3.** any group or collection of 100. **4.** a subdivision of the Roman legion, orig. consisting of 100 men. **5.** one of the voting divisions of the ancient Roman people.

cen′tury plant′, *n.* a desert agave, *Agave americana,* having a tall flower stalk emerging from a rosette of leaves, that requires a decade or more to mature and blooms only once.

CEO or **C.E.O.,** chief executive officer.

cep or **cèpe** (sep), *n.* a brown-capped boletus mushroom, *Boletus edulis,* prized for its flavor.

ce•phal•ic (sə fal′ik), *adj.* **1.** of or pertaining to the head. **2.** situated or directed toward the head. —**ce•phal′i•cal•ly,** *adv.*

cephal′ic in′dex, *n.* the ratio of the greatest breadth of the head to its greatest length from front to back, multiplied by 100.

cephalo-, a combining form meaning "head": *cephalothorax.*

ceph•a•lo•pod (sef′ə lə pod′), *n.* any mollusk of the class Cephalopoda, having tentacles attached to the head, including the squid, octopus, and nautilus.

Ce•phas (sē′fəs), *n.* the name Jesus gave to Simon Peter. John 1:42.

Ce•phe•us (sē′fē əs, -fyŏŏs), *n.*, *gen.* **-phe•i** (-fē ī′) for 1. **1.** a northern circumpolar constellation between Cassiopeia and Draco. **2.** a legendary king of Joppa, the husband of Cassiopeia and father of Andromeda. —**Ce′phe•id** (-id), *adj.*

ce•ra•ceous (sə rā′shəs), *adj.* waxlike; waxy.

ce•ram•ic (sə ram′ik), *adj.* **1.** of or pertaining to products made from clay and similar materials, as pottery and brick, or to their manufacture. —*n.* **2.** ceramic material.

ce•ram•ics (sə ram′iks), *n.* **1.** (*used with a sing. v.*) the art or technology of making objects of clay and similar materials treated by firing. **2.** (*used with a pl. v.*) articles of earthenware, porcelain, etc. —**ce•ram•ist** (sə ram′ist, ser′ə mist), **ce•ram•i•cist** (sə ram′ə sist), *n.*

ce•ras•tes (sə ras′tēz), *n.*, *pl.* **-tes.** **1.** HORNED VIPER. **2.** any of several small African vipers of the genus *Cerastes.*

ce•rate (sēr′āt), *n.* an unctuous, often medicated, preparation for external application, consisting of lard or oil mixed with wax, rosin, or the like.

cer•car•i•a (sər kâr′ē ə), *n.*, *pl.* **-car•i•ae** (-kâr′ē ē′). the free-swimming, tailed larva of parasitic trematodes. —**cer•car′i•al,** *adj.* —**cer•car′i•an,** *adj.*, *n.*

cer•cis (sûr′sis), *n.* any of several shrubs or small trees belonging to the genus *Cercis,* of the legume family, as the redbud or Judas tree.

cere (sēr), *n.* a fleshy covering at the top of the beak of certain birds, as raptors or parrots, through which the nostrils open. —**cered,** *adj.*

ce•re•al (sēr′ē əl), *n.* **1.** any plant of the grass family, as wheat, rye, oats, or corn, yielding an edible grain. **2.** the grain itself. **3.** some edible preparation of it, esp. a breakfast food. —*adj.* **4.** of or pertaining to grain or the plants producing it.

cer•e•bel•lum (ser′ə bel′əm), *n.*, *pl.* **-bel•lums, -bel•la** (-bel′ə). the rounded portion of the brain, directly behind the cerebrum in birds and mammals, that serves mainly to coordinate movement, posture, and balance. —**cer′e•bel′lar,** *adj.*

ce•re•bral (sə rē′brəl, ser′ə-), *adj.* **1.** of or pertaining to the cerebrum or the brain. **2.** characterized by the use of the intellect rather than intuition or instinct. **3.** RETROFLEX (def. 2). —*n.* **4.** a retroflex speech sound. —**ce•re′bral•ly,** *adv.*

cere′bral cor′tex, *n.* the outer layer of gray matter in the cerebrum associated with the higher brain functions, as voluntary movement, sensory perception, and learning.

cere′bral hem′isphere, *n.* either of the rounded halves of the cerebrum connected by the corpus callosum. Compare LEFT BRAIN, RIGHT BRAIN.

cere′bral pal′sy, *n.* a condition of muscular weakness and difficulty in coordinating voluntary movement owing to developmental or congenital damage to the brain. —**cere′bral pal′sied,** *adj.*

cer•e•brate (ser′ə brāt′), *v.i.,* **-brat•ed, -brat•ing.** to use the mind; think. —**cer′e•bra′tion,** *n.* —**cer′e•bra′tion•al,** *adj.*

ce•re•bro•spi•nal (sə rē′brō spīn′l, ser′ə-), *adj.* **1.** pertaining to or affecting the brain and the spinal cord. **2.** of or pertaining to the central nervous system.

ce•re•bro•vas•cu•lar (sə rē′brō vas′kyə lər, ser′ə-), *adj.* of or pertaining to the cerebrum and its associated blood vessels.

ce•re•brum (sə rē′brəm, ser′ə-), *n.*, *pl.* **-brums, -bra** (-brə). the forward and upper part of the brain, involved with voluntary movement and conscious processes, in mammals and birds being greatly enlarged. Compare CEREBRAL HEMISPHERE.

cer•e•mo•ni•al (ser′ə mō′nē əl), *adj.* **1.** of, pertaining to, or characterized by ceremony; formal; ritual: *a ceremonial occasion.* **2.** used in or in

connection with ceremonies: *ceremonial robes.* —*n.* **3.** a ceremonial act or system of rites or formalities. —**cer′e•mo′ni•al•ism,** *n.* —**cer′e•mo′ni•al•ly,** *adv.*

cer•e•mo•ni•ous (ser′ə mō′nē əs), *adj.* **1.** carefully observant of ceremony. **2.** marked by or consisting of ceremony; formal. —**cer′e•mo′ni•ous•ly,** *adv.*

cer•e•mo•ny (ser′ə mō′nē), *n.*, *pl.* **-nies. 1.** the formal activities conducted on some solemn or important public or state occasion. **2.** a formal religious or sacred observance; a solemn rite: *a marriage ceremony.* **3.** any formal act or observance, esp. a meaningless one: *His bow was mere ceremony.* **4.** a gesture or act of politeness or civility: *the ceremony of a handshake.* **5.** strict adherence to conventional forms; formality: *to leave without ceremony.* —*Idiom.* **6. stand on ceremony,** to behave in a formal or ceremonious manner.

ce•re•us (sēr′ē əs), *n.*, *pl.* **-us•es.** any of various plants of the genus *Cereus,* of the cactus family, having large, usu. white, funnel-shaped flowers.

ce•rise (sə rēs′, -rēz′), *adj.*, *n.* moderate to deep red.

ce•ri•um (sēr′ē əm), *n.* a steel-gray, ductile metallic element of the rare-earth group found only in combination. *Symbol:* Ce; *at. wt.:* 140.12; *at. no.:* 58.

cer•met (sûr′met), *n.* a durable, heat-resistant alloy formed by compacting and sintering a metal and a ceramic substance.

cer•tain (sûr′tn), *adj.* **1.** free from doubt or reservation; confident. **2.** destined; sure to happen: *She is certain to be there.* **3.** inevitable; bound to come: *Death and taxes are certain.* **4.** established as true or sure; indisputable: *It is certain that you tried.* **5.** fixed; agreed upon; settled: *for a certain amount.* **6.** definite or particular, but not named or specified: *A certain person phoned.* **7.** trustworthy; unfailing; reliable: *His aim was certain.* **8.** some though not much: *a certain reluctance.* —*pron.* **9.** certain ones: *Certain of the members abstained.* —*Idiom.* **10. for certain,** certainly; for sure. —**cer′tain•ly,** *adv.* —**cer′tain•ty,** *n.*, *pl.* **-ties.**

cer•tif•i•cate (*n.* sər tif′i kit; *v.* -kāt′), *n.*, *v.*, **-cat•ed, -cat•ing.** —*n.* **1.** a document providing evidence of status or qualifications, as one attesting to the completion of a course or the truth of facts stated. **2.** a gold or silver certificate. —*v.t.* **3.** to furnish with or authorize by a certificate. —**cer′ti•fi•ca′tion,** *n.*

certif′icate of depos′it, *n.* a written acknowledgment from a bank for money deposited, indicating the percentage of interest to be paid for a specified period.

cer′tified check′, *n.* a check drawn by a bank against funds made available by the depositor authorizing the check.

cer′tified mail′, *n.* uninsured first-class mail requiring proof of delivery.

cer′tified pub′lic account′ant, *n.* an accountant certified by a state examining board as having fulfilled the requirements of state law to be a public accountant. *Abbr.:* CPA, C.P.A.

cer•ti•fy (sûr′tə fī′), *v.t.,* **-fied, -fy•ing. 1.** to attest as certain; confirm: *He certified the truth of her claim.* **2.** to testify to or vouch for in writing. **3.** to guarantee; endorse: *to certify a document with an official seal.* **4.** to guarantee (a check) as to authenticity of signature and sufficiency of funds to cover payment. **5.** to declare (a person) legally insane and committable to a mental institution. **6.** to certificate; license. **7.** to assure or inform with certainty. —**cer′ti•fi′a•ble,** *adj.* —**cer′ti•fi′a•bly,** *adv.*

cer•ti•tude (sûr′ti tōōd′, -tyōōd′), *n.* freedom from doubt, esp. in matters of faith or opinion; certainty.

ce•ru•le•an (sə rōō′lē ən), *adj.*, *n.* deep blue; sky blue; azure.

ce•ru•men (si rōō′mən), *n.* EARWAX. —**ce•ru′mi•nous,** *adj.*

Cer•van•tes (sər van′tēz, -vän′tās), *n.* **Miguel de,** (*Miguel de Cervantes Saavedra*), 1547–1616, Spanish novelist.

cer•vi•cal (sûr′vi kəl), *adj.* of or pertaining to the cervix or neck.

cer′vical cap′, *n.* a contraceptive device made of rubberlike plastic and fitted over the cervix.

cer•vix (sûr′viks), *n.*, *pl.* **cer•vix•es, cer•vi•ces** (sûr′və sēz′, sər vī′sēz). **1.** the neck, esp. the back part. **2.** any necklike part, esp. the constricted lower end of the uterus.

Ce•sar•e•an (si zâr′ē ən), *n.* (*sometimes l.c.*) **1.** Also called **Cesar′ean sec′tion.** an operation by which a fetus is taken from the uterus by cutting through the walls of the abdomen and uterus. —*adj.* **2.** (*sometimes l.c.*) of or pertaining to a Cesarean. Also, **Caesarean, Ce•sar′i•an.**

ce•si•um (sē′zē əm), *n.* a rare highly reactive soft metallic element of the alkali metal group used chiefly in photoelectric cells. *Symbol:* Cs; *at. wt.:* 132.905; *at. no.:* 55; *sp. gr.:* 1.9 at 20°C; melts at 28.5°C.

ces•sa•tion (se sā′shən), *n.* a temporary or complete stopping; discontinuance: *a cessation of hostilities.*

ces•sion (sesh′ən), *n.* **1.** the act of ceding, as by treaty. **2.** something that is ceded, as territory.

cess•pool (ses′pōōl′), *n.* **1.** a reservoir for receiving the sewage from a house. **2.** a place of filth or immorality.

ces•tode (ses′tōd), *n.* **1.** a parasitic flatworm of the class Cestoda, which comprises the tapeworms. —*adj.* **2.** belonging or pertaining to cestodes.

ce•su•ra (sə zhōŏr′ə, -zōŏr′ə, siz yŏŏr′ə), *n.*, *pl.* **ce•su•ras, ce•su•rae** (sə zhōŏr′ē, -zōŏr′ē, siz yŏŏr′ē). CAESURA.

ce•ta•cean (si tā′shən), *adj.* **1.** belonging to the Cetacea, an order of aquatic, chiefly marine mammals, including the whales and dolphins. —*n.* **2.** a cetacean mammal. —**ce•ta′ceous,** *adj.*

ce•tol•o•gy (sē tol′ə jē), *n.* the branch of zoology dealing with whales and dolphins. —**ce•to•log•i•cal** (sēt′l oj′i kəl), *adj.* —**ce•tol′o•gist,** *n.*

Cey•lon (si lon′, sā-), *n.* former name of SRI LANKA. —**Cey•lon•ese** (sē′lə nēz′, -nēs′), *adj., n., pl.* **-ese.**

Cé•zanne (sā zan′, -zän′), *n.* **Paul,** 1839–1906, French painter.

CF, 1. Christian female. **2.** Also, **cf** cubic foot; cubic feet.

Cf, *Symbol, Chem.* californium.

cf., compare. [< Latin *confer*]

CFC, chlorofluorocarbon.

cfm, cubic feet per minute.

CFO or **C.F.O.,** chief financial officer.

cfs, cubic feet per second.

CFS, chronic fatigue syndrome.

Cha•blis (sha blē′, shə-, shä-, shab′lē), *n.* **1.** a dry white wine from the Burgundy region of France. **2.** a similar wine produced elsewhere.

cha-cha (chä′chä′), *n., pl.* **-chas,** *v.,* **-chaed, -cha•ing.** —*n.* **1.** a rhythmic ballroom dance of Latin American origin based upon a quick three-step movement. —*v.i.* **2.** to dance the cha-cha.

chac•ma (chak′mə), *n., pl.* **-mas.** a large, brownish gray baboon, *Papio (Chaeropithecus) ursinus,* of S Africa.

Chad (chad), *n.* **1. Lake,** a lake in Africa at the junction of Cameroon, Chad, Niger, and Nigeria. 5000 to 10,000 sq. mi. (13,000 to 26,000 sq. km) (seasonal variation). **2. Republic of,** a republic in N central Africa, E of Lake Chad: a member of the French Community. 7,166,023; 501,000 sq. mi. (1,297,590 sq. km). *Cap.:* N'Djamena. French, **Tchad.** —**Chad′i•an,** *n., adj.*

chad•or (chud′ər), *n.* the traditional garment of Muslim and Hindu women, consisting of a long, usually black or drab-colored cloth or veil that envelops the body from head to foot and covers all or part of the face. Also **chad′ar, chad′dar, chuddar.**

chae•ta (kē′tə), *n., pl.* **-tae** (-tē). a bristle or seta, esp. of an annelid worm.

chafe (chāf), *v.,* **chafed, chaf•ing,** *n.* —*v.t.* **1.** to wear away by rubbing; abrade. **2.** to make sore by rubbing. **3.** to irritate; annoy. **4.** to warm by rubbing: *to chafe cold hands.* —*v.i.* **5.** to rub with frictional force: *The horse chafed against his stall.* **6.** to become annoyed: *He chafed at their remarks.* —*n.* **7.** irritation; annoyance. **8.** heat, wear, or soreness caused by rubbing.

Cha•fer (chā′fər), *n.* **Lewis Sperry,** 1871–1952, U.S. clergyman and educator.

chaff[1] (chaf, chäf), *n.* **1.** the husks of grains and grasses that are separated during threshing. **2.** straw cut up for fodder. **3.** worthless matter; refuse. **4.** the membranous, usu. dry, brittle bracts of the flowers of certain plants. **5.** strips of metal foil dropped by an aircraft to confuse enemy radar. —**chaff′y,** *adj.* —**chaff•i•er, chaff•i•est.**

chaff[2] (chaf, chäf), *v.t., v.i.* **1.** to tease; banter. —*n.* **2.** good-natured teasing; raillery.

chaf•finch (chaf′inch), *n.* a common Eurasian finch, *Fringilla coelebs,* often kept as a pet.

chaf′ing dish′ (chā′fing), *n.* a metal pan mounted atop a heating device for preparing or warming food at the table.

cha•grin (shə grin′), *n., v.,* **-grined** or **-grinned, -grin•ing** or **-grin•ning.** —*n.* **1.** a feeling of vexation marked by disappointment or humiliation. —*v.t.* **2.** to vex by disappointment or humiliation.

chain (chān), *n.* **1.** a series of metal rings passing through one another, used either for hauling, supporting, or confining, or as decoration. **2. chains, a.** shackles or fetters. **b.** bondage; servitude: *to live one's life in chains.* **3.** a series of things connected or following in succession: *a chain of events.* **4.** a range of mountains. **5.** a number of establishments under one ownership or management. **6.** two or more atoms of the same element, usu. carbon, attached as in a chain. Compare RING[1] (def. 14). **7. a.** a distance-measuring device used by surveyors, consisting of a chain of 100 links of equal length. **b.** a unit of length equal to 100 feet (30 m) or 66 feet (20 m). —*v.t.* **8.** to fasten or secure with a chain. **9.** to confine or restrain: *His work chained him to his desk.* **10.** to chain-stitch. —*v.i.* **11.** to form or make a chain.

chain′ gang′, *n.* a group of convicts chained together, esp. when working outside.

chain′ let′ter, *n.* a letter sent to a number of people each of whom is asked to make and mail copies to others who are to do likewise.

chain′-link′ fence′, *n.* a mesh fence made of thick steel wire woven in a diamond-shaped pattern.

chain′ mail′, *n.* MAIL[2] (def. 1).

chain′ reac′tion, *n.* **1.** a nuclear or chemical reaction in which the reaction products in turn trigger additional reactions. **2.** a series of events in which each event is the result of the one preceding and the cause of the one following. —**chain′ re•ac′tor,** *n.*

chain′ saw′, *n.* a usu. portable power saw having teeth set on an endless chain. —**chain′-saw′,** *v.t., v.i.*

chain′ stitch′, *n.* **1.** a decorative hand stitch that forms a line of single stitches looped like a chain. **2.** a basic crochet stitch in which the yarn is formed into a strand of interlocking single loops. —**chain′-stitch′,** *v.t., v.i.*

chain′ store′, *n.* a retail store that is part of a chain.

chair (châr), *n.* **1.** a seat, esp. for one person, usu. having four legs for support and a rest for the back and often having rests for the arms. **2.** a seat of office or authority. **3.** a position of authority. **4.** the person occupying a seat of office or authority, esp. the chairperson of a meeting. **5.** (in an orchestra) the position of a player, assigned by rank; desk. —*v.t.* **6.** to place or seat in a chair. **7.** to install in office. **8.** to preside over; act as chairperson of. —*v.i.* **9.** to preside over a meeting, committee, etc. —*Idiom.* **10. take the chair,** to open or preside at a meeting; act as chairperson.

chair•lift (châr′lift′), *n.* a series of chairs suspended from an endless cable driven by motors, for conveying skiers up the side of a slope.

chair•man (châr′mən), *n., pl.* **-men,** *v.,* **-maned** or **-manned, -man•ing** or **-man•ning.** —*n.* **1.** the presiding officer of a meeting, committee, etc., or the head of a board or department. —*v.t.* **2.** CHAIR (def. 8). —**chair′man•ship′,** *n.*

chair•per•son (châr′pûr′sən), *n.* a person who presides over a meeting, committee, etc., or heads a board or department.

chair′ rail′, *n.* a molding, usu. of wood, placed along an interior wall to protect it from being damaged by the backs of chairs.

chair•wom•an (châr′wŏom′ən), *n., pl.* **-wom•en.** a woman who presides over a meeting, committee, etc., or heads a board or department.

chaise (shāz), *n.* **1.** a light, open carriage, usu. with a hood, esp. a one-horse, two-wheeled carriage for two persons. **2.** POST CHAISE. **3.** a chaise longue, esp. a light one used out of doors.

chaise longue (shāz′ lông′) *n., pl.* **chaise longues, chaises longues** (shāz′). a chair with or without arms for reclining, having a seat lengthened to form a complete leg rest and sometimes an adjustable back. Also called **chaise lounge** (shāz′ lounj′, chās′).

chak•ra (chuk′rə, chä′krə), *n., pl.* **-ras.** (in yoga) any of the points located along the body, usu. seven in number, considered as energy centers.

chal•ced•o•ny (kal sed′n ē, kal′si dō′nē), *n., pl.* **-nies.** a microcrystalline translucent variety of quartz, often milky or grayish. —**chal′ce•don′ic** (-si don′ik), **chal•ced′o•nous,** *adj.*

chal•cid (kal′sid), *n.* any of various tiny wasps of the family Chalcididae, many having larvae that are parasitic on pest insects. Also called **chal′cid fly′, chal′cid wasp′.**

chal•co•cite (kal′kə sīt′), *n.* a common mineral, cuprous sulfide, Cu_2S: an important ore of copper.

Chal•de•an (kal dē′ən), *n.* **1.** a Semitic people of Chaldea who seized Babylon from the Assyrians in the 7th century B.C., giving rise to the Neo-Babylonian or Chaldean dynasty (625–539 B.C.). **2.** an astrologer or soothsayer. Dan. 1:4; 2:2. —*adj.* **3.** of or pertaining to Chaldea, the Chaldeans, or the Babylonian state ruled by Chaldeans.

Chal•dee (kal′dē), *n.* (in the King James Version of the Bible) a Chaldean.

cha•let (sha lā′, shal′ā), *n.* **1.** a wooden house common in rural Alpine regions, having very wide eaves, exposed structural members, and often decoratively carved brackets, stair and balcony railings, etc. **2.** any cottage, house, ski lodge, etc., built in this style. **3.** a herder's hut in the Swiss Alps.

chalet (def. 1)

chal•ice (chal′is), *n.* **1.** a cup for the wine of the Eucharist. **2.** a drinking cup or goblet. **3.** a cuplike blossom. —**chal′iced,** *adj.*

chalk (chôk), *n.* **1.** a soft, white, powdery limestone consisting chiefly of fossil shells of foraminifers. **2.** a piece of chalk or chalklike substance for marking, as a blackboard crayon. **3.** a mark made with chalk. **4.** a score or tally. —*v.t.* **5.** to mark with chalk. **6.** to rub over or whiten with chalk. —*v.i.* **7.** (of paint) to powder from weathering. **8. chalk up, a.** to score or earn, as points in a game. **b.** to attribute. —**chalk′like′,** *adj.* —**chalk′y,** *adj.,* **-i•er, -i•est.**

chalk•board (chôk′bôrd′, -bōrd′), *n.* a blackboard, esp. a green or other light-colored one.

chalk•stone (chôk′stōn′), *n.* a chalklike concretion in the tissues or small joints of a person with gout.

chal•lah (кнä′lə, hä′), *n.* a rich, leavened, often braided white bread made with eggs, eaten esp. on the Jewish Sabbath.

chal•lenge (chal′inj), *n., v.,* **-lenged, -leng•ing.** —*n.* **1.** a summons to engage in a contest, as of skill or strength. **2.** something that by its nature or character serves as a serious test: *Space exploration offers a challenge to humankind.* **3.** a call to fight, as in a duel. **4.** a demand to explain, justify, etc. **5.** difficulty in a job or undertaking that is stimulating to one engaged in it. **6.** the demand of a military sentry for identifica-

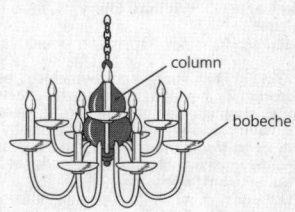

tion or a countersign. **7.** a formal objection to the qualifications of a juror or jury. **8.** the assertion that a vote is invalid or that a voter is not legally qualified. **9.** the assessment of a specific function in an organism by exposing it to a provocative substance or activity. —*v.t.* **10.** to summon to a contest. **11.** to take exception to; call in question. **12.** to demand as something due or rightful. **13.** to halt and demand identification or a countersign from. **14.** to take formal exception to (a juror or jury). **15.** to invite; arouse: *a matter which challenges attention.* **16.** to assert that (a vote) is invalid. **17.** to assert that (a voter) is not qualified to vote. **18.** to inject (an organism) with a specific substance in order to assess its physiological or immunological activity. —*v.i.* **19.** to make or issue a challenge. —**chal′leng·er,** *n.*

chal·lis (shal′ē), *n.* a soft plain-weave fabric in wool, cotton, or rayon, usu. in a small print.

cham·ber (chām′bər), *n.* **1.** a usu. private room in a house or apartment, esp. a bedroom. **2.** a room in a palace or official residence. **3. a.** a legislative, judicial, or other assembly, or a branch of such an assembly: *the upper and lower chambers of a legislature.* **b.** a room housing such an assembly. **4. chambers,** a place where a judge hears matters not requiring action in open court. **5.** an enclosed space; cavity: *a chamber of the heart.* **6.** a receptacle for one or more cartridges in a firearm, or for a shell in a gun. —*adj.* **7.** of, pertaining to, or performing chamber music: *chamber players.* —*v.t.* **8.** to put or enclose in or as if in a chamber. **9.** to provide with a chamber.

cham′bered nau′tilus, *n.* NAUTILUS (def. 1).

cham·ber·lain (chām′bər lin), *n.* **1.** an official who manages the living quarters of a sovereign or member of the nobility. **2.** the high steward of a member of the nobility. **3.** a high official of a royal court.

Cham·ber·lain (chām′bər lin), *n.* **(Arthur) Neville,** 1869–1940, British prime minister 1937–40.

cham·ber·maid (chām′bər mād′), *n.* a maid who cleans bedrooms and bathrooms, as in a hotel.

cham′ber mu′sic, *n.* music suited for performance in a room or a small concert hall and played by a small ensemble.

cham′ber of com′merce, *n.* an association, primarily of people in business, to promote the commercial interests of an area.

cham′ber or′chestra, *n.* a small orchestra commonly of about 25 players.

cham′ber pot′, *n.* a portable container, esp. for urine, used in bedrooms.

Cham·bers (chām′bərz), *n.* **Whittaker** (*Jay David Chambers*), 1901–61, U.S. journalist, Communist spy, and accuser of Alger Hiss.

cham′ber tomb′, *n.* a tomb of late Neolithic and Bronze Age Europe, usu. lined with megalithic slabs and covered by a mound, used for burials over successive generations.

cham·bray (sham′brā), *n.* a fine cloth of cotton, silk, or linen, commonly of plain weave with a colored warp and white weft.

cha·me·le·on (kə mēl′ē ən, -mēl′yən), *n.* **1.** any Old World lizard of the family Chamaeleontidae, characterized by very slow locomotion, a projectile tongue, and the ability to change color. **2.** ANOLE. **3.** a changeable or fickle person. [< Middle French < Latin < Greek *chamailéon* lit., dwarf lion] —**cha·me′le·on′ic** (-on′ik), *adj.*

cham·fer (cham′fər), *n.* a cut that is made in wood or some other material, usu. at a 45° angle to the adjacent principal faces.

cham·ois (sham′ē; *for 1 also* sham wä′), *n., pl.* **cham·ois, cham·oix** (sham′ēz; *for 1 also* sham wä′), *v.,* **cham·oised** (sham′ēd), **cham·ois·ing** (sham′ē ing). —*n.* **1.** an agile goat antelope, *Rupicapra rupicapra,* of high mountains of Europe. **2.** a soft, pliable leather from any of various skins dressed with oil. **3.** a cotton cloth simulating this leather. —*v.t.* **4.** to dress (a pelt) to produce chamois. **5.** to rub or buff with a chamois. Also, **shammy** (*for defs. 2–5*).

chamois, *Rupicapra rupicapra,* about 2 1/2 ft. (0.8 m) high at shoulder; horns to 8 in. (20 cm); length 4 ft. (1.2 m)

cham·o·mile or **cam·o·mile** (kam′ə mīl′, -mēl′), *n.* **1.** a composite plant, *Chamaemelium nobile* (or *Anthemis nobilis*), native to the Old World, having strongly scented foliage and white ray flowers with yellow centers used medicinally and as a tea. **2.** any of several allied plants of the genera *Matricaria* and *Tripleurospermum.*

champ (champ, chomp) also **chomp,** *v.t.* **1.** to bite upon or grind, esp. impatiently: *The horses champed the oats.* **2.** to crush with the teeth and chew vigorously or noisily. **3.** to mash; crush. —*v.i.* **4.** to make vigor-

ous chewing or biting movements with the jaws and teeth. —*n.* **5.** the act of champing.

cham·pac or **cham·pak** (cham′pak, chum′puk), *n.* a S Asian tree, *Michelia champaca,* of the magnolia family, having yellow or orange flowers and yielding a fragrant oil.

cham·pagne (sham pān′), *n.* **1.** (*cap.*) the sparkling dry white wine from the region of Champagne in France. **2.** a similar sparkling wine produced elsewhere. **3.** a very pale yellow or greenish yellow color.

cham·paign (sham pān′), *n.* **1.** level, open country; plain. —*adj.* **2.** level and open: *champaign fields.*

cham·pi·gnon (sham pin′yən, sham′pin yôn′), *n., pl.* **-pi·gnons** (-pin′yənz, -pin yôn′). an edible mushroom.

cham·pi·on (cham′pē ən), *n.* **1.** a person who has defeated all competing opponents so as to hold first place. **2.** anything that takes first place in competition. **3.** an animal that has won a certain number of points in officially recognized shows. **4.** a person who fights for or defends any person or cause: *a champion of the oppressed.* **5.** a fighter or warrior. —*v.t.* **6.** to act as champion of; defend; support. —*adj.* **7.** first among all contestants or competitors.

cham·pi·on·ship (cham′pē ən ship′), *n.* **1.** the distinction or condition of being a champion. **2.** advocacy or defense: *championship of the underdog.* **3.** a contest to determine a champion.

Cham·plain (sham plān′), *n.* **1. Samuel de,** 1567–1635, French explorer: founder of Quebec; first colonial governor 1633–35. **2. Lake,** a lake between New York and Vermont. 125 mi. (200 km) long; ab. 600 sq. mi. (1550 sq. km).

champ·le·vé (shăn lə vā′), *adj., n., pl.* **-vés** (-vā′, -vāz′). —*adj.* **1.** being or made by an enameling technique in which the enamel is fused onto incised or hollowed areas of a metal base. —*n.* **2.** the technique itself.

chance (chans, chäns), *n., v.,* **chanced, chanc·ing,** *adj.* —*n.* **1.** the unpredictable and uncontrollable element of an event or occurrence. **2.** luck or fortune: *a game of chance.* **3.** a possibility of anything happening: *a fifty-percent chance of success.* **4.** an opportunity: *Now is your chance.* **5.** a risk or hazard: *Take a chance.* **6.** a ticket in a lottery or prize drawing. **7. chances,** probability: *The chances are that the train hasn't left yet.* —*v.i.* **8.** to happen or occur by chance: *It chanced that our arrivals coincided.* —*v.t.* **9.** to take the chances or risks of; risk (often fol. by impersonal *it*): *I'll have to chance it, whatever the outcome.* **10. chance on** or **upon,** to meet unexpectedly and accidentally. —*adj.* **11.** not planned or expected; accidental: *a chance occurrence.* —*Idiom.* **12. by chance,** unintentionally; accidentally. **13. on the (off) chance,** counting on the (slight) possibility.

chan·cel (chan′səl, chän′-), *n.* the space around the altar of a church, usu. enclosed, for the use of the clergy and other officials.

chan·cel·ler·y (chan′sə lə rē, -slə rē, -səl rē, chän′-), *n., pl.* **-ler·ies. 1.** the position, office, or department of a chancellor. **2.** the staff or office of an embassy or consulate. **3.** a building or room occupied by a chancellor's department.

chan·cel·lor (chan′sə lər, -slər, chän′-), *n.* **1.** the chief minister of state in some parliamentary governments, as in Germany. **2.** the chief administrative officer in some American universities. **3.** the chief secretary of a king or noble, or of an embassy. **4.** the priest in charge of a Roman Catholic chancery. **5.** the title of various important officials in the British government. **6.** (in some states) the judge of a court of equity. —**chan′cel·lor·ship′,** *n.*

Chan′cellor of the Excheq′uer, *n.* the minister of finance in the British government.

Chan·cel·lors·ville (chan′sə lərz vil′, -slərz-, chän′-), *n.* a village in NE Virginia: site of a Confederate victory 1863.

chan·cer·y (chan′sə rē, chän′-), *n., pl.* **-cer·ies. 1.** the office or department of a chancellor; chancellery. **2.** an office of public records. **3. a.** a court of equity. **b.** EQUITY (defs. 3a, b). **4.** the administrative office of a diocese. —*Idiom.* **5. in chancery,** in litigation in a court of equity or chancery.

chan·cre (shang′kər), *n.* the initial lesion of certain infectious diseases, commonly a distinct sore with a hard base. —**chan′crous,** *adj.*

chanc·y (chan′sē, chän′-), *adj.,* **chanc·i·er, chanc·i·est. 1.** hazardous or risky; uncertain. **2.** subject to chance; random; haphazard.

chan·de·lier (shan′dl ēr′), *n.* a decorative, sometimes ornate light fixture suspended from a ceiling, usu. having branched supports for a number of lights. —**chan′de·liered′,** *adj.*

column

bobeche

chandelier

chan•dler (chand′lər, chänd′-), *n.* **1.** a person who makes or sells items of tallow or wax, as candles or soap. **2.** a dealer or trader in supplies, esp. of a specialized type: *a ship chandler.* —**chan′dler•y,** *n., pl.* **-dler•ies.**

Chan•dler (chand′lər, chänd′-), *n.* **1. Raymond (Thornton),** 1888–1959, U.S. writer of detective novels. **2.** a town in central Arizona. 119,227.

change (chānj), *v.,* **changed, chang•ing,** *n.* —*v.t.* **1.** to make different in form: *to change one's name.* **2.** to transform (usu. fol. by *into*): *The witch changed the prince into a toad.* **3.** to exchange for another or others: *to change shoes.* **4.** to give and take reciprocally: *to change places with someone.* **5.** to transfer from one (conveyance) to another. **6.** to give or get smaller money in exchange for. **7.** to give or get foreign money in exchange for. **8.** to remove and replace the coverings or garments of: *to change a bed; to change a baby.* —*v.i.* **9.** to become different: *The nation's mood has changed.* **10.** to become altered or modified: *Colors change when exposed to the sun.* **11.** to become transformed (usu. fol. by *into*): *The toad changed back into a prince.* **12.** to pass gradually into (usu. fol. by *to* or *into*): *Summer changed to autumn.* **13.** to make an exchange. **14.** to transfer between conveyances. **15.** to change one's clothes. **16.** (of the moon) to pass from one phase to another. **17.** (of the voice) to become deeper in tone. **18. change off, a.** to take turns with another, as at doing a task. **b.** to alternate between two tasks or between a task and a rest break. —*n.* **19.** the act of changing or the result of being changed. **20.** a transformation or modification: *a change of expression.* **21.** a variation or deviation: *a change in one's routine.* **22.** the substitution of one thing for another. **23.** a replacement or substitution. **24.** a fresh set of clothes. **25.** variety or novelty: *He's not one who likes change.* **26.** the passing from one state, phase, etc., to another: *social change.* **27.** a modulation in jazz. **28.** the money returned when the sum offered in payment is larger than the sum due. **29.** coins of low denomination. **30.** any of the various sequences in which a peal of bells may be rung. —***Idiom.* 31. change one's mind,** to modify or reverse one's opinions or intentions. **32. Don't change horses in midstream,** it is not wise to change leaders in the midst of a crisis. —**change′a•ble,** *adj.* —**change′less,** *adj.*

change•ling (chānj′ling), *n.* an infant exchanged by stealth for another child.

change′ of heart′, *n.* a reversal of feelings or opinions.

change′ of life′, *n.* MENOPAUSE.

change′ of pace′, *n.* **1.** a temporary variation in a normal routine. **2.** Also called **change′-up′.** a baseball pitch that is thrown like a fastball but, because of the pitcher's grip, is deceptively slower.

change•o•ver (chānj′ō′vər), *n.* a conversion from one condition, system, or apparatus to another.

chan•nel[1] (chan′l), *n., v.,* **-neled, -nel•ing** or (*esp. Brit.*) **-nelled, -nel•ling.** —*n.* **1.** the bed of a stream, river, or other waterway. **2.** a navigable route between two bodies of water. **3.** the deeper part of a waterway. **4.** a wide strait, as between a continent and an island. **5.** a course into which something may be directed: *to direct a conversation to a new channel.* **6.** a route through which anything passes or progresses: *channels of trade.* **7. channels,** the official course or means of communication: *going through channels to reach the governor.* **8.** a means of access: *The Senate is his channel to the White House.* **9.** a flute in a column. **10.** a frequency band of sufficient width for one- or two-way communication from or to a transmitter used for television, radio, CB radio, telephone, or telegraph communication. **11.** BUS[1] (def. 5). **12.** either of the two signals in stereophonic or any single signal in multichannel sound recording and reproduction. **13.** a transient opening made by a protein structure embedded in a cell membrane, permitting passage of specific ions or molecules into or out of the cell: *calcium channel.* **14.** a tubular passage for liquids or fluids. **15. a.** any structural member, as one of reinforced concrete, having the form of three sides of a rectangle. **b.** a number of such members. **c.** a flanged metal beam or bar with a U-shaped cross section. —*v.t.* **16.** to convey through or as if through a channel. **17.** to direct toward or into some particular course: *to channel one's interests.* **18.** to excavate as a channel. **19.** to form a channel in; groove. —*v.i.* **20.** to become marked by a channel: *Soft earth has a tendency to channel during a heavy rain.*

chan•nel[2] (chan′l), *n.* a horizontal timber or ledge built outboard from the side of a sailing vessel to spread shrouds and backstays outward.

chan′nel cat′fish, *n.* a freshwater food fish of the central U.S., *Ictalurus punctatus.* Also called **chan′nel cat′.**

Chan•ning (chan′ing), *n.* **William Ellery,** 1780–1842, U.S. Unitarian clergyman and writer.

chan•son (*Fr.* shäɴ sôɴ′), *n., pl.* **-sons** (*Fr.* -sôɴ′). a song, esp. an intimate ballad.

chant (chant, chänt), *n.* **1.** a short, simple melody, esp. the monodic intonation of plainsong. **2.** a psalm, canticle, or the like, chanted or for chanting. **3.** a song; singing: *the chant of a bird.* **4.** a phrase, slogan, or the like, repeated rhythmically and insistently, as by a crowd. —*v.t.* **5.** to sing to a chant, or in the manner of a chant, esp. in a church service. **6.** to repeat (a phrase, slogan, etc.) rhythmically and insistently. —*v.i.* **7.** to utter a chant. —**chant′a•ble,** *adj.*

chant•er (chan′tər, chän′-), *n.* **1. a.** a person who chants. **b.** CHORISTER (def. 1). **c.** CANTOR (def. 1). **2.** the pipe of a bagpipe provided with finger holes for playing the melody.

chan•te•relle (shan′tə rel′, chan′-), *n.* an edible mushroom, *Cantharellus cibarius,* having a bright yellow-to-orange funnel-shaped cap.

chan•teuse (shäɴ tœz′, -to͞oz′), *n., pl.* **-teuses** (-tœz′, -to͞o′ziz). a female singer in a nightclub or cabaret.

chant•ey or **chant•y** (shan′tē, chan′-), *n., pl.* **chant•eys** or **chant•ies.** a sailors' song, esp. one sung in rhythm to work.

chan•ti•cleer (chan′ti klēr′) also **chan•te•cler** (-klâr′), *n.* a rooster: used as a proper name in medieval fables.

chan•try (chan′trē, chän′-), *n., pl.* **-tries.** **1.** an endowment for the singing or saying of mass for the souls of the founders or of persons named by them. **2.** a chapel or the like so endowed. **3.** a chapel attached to a church, used for minor services.

Cha•nu•kah (KHä′nə kə, hä′-), *n.* HANUKKAH.

cha•os (kā′os), *n.* **1.** a state of utter confusion or disorder. **2.** any confused, disorderly mass. **3.** the infinity of space or formless matter supposed to have preceded the creation of the universe. **4.** *Physics, Math.* **a.** the nonlinear, deterministic behavior of certain systems, as the appearance of strange attractors or fractal structure in graphical representations of a system's evolution. **b.** the discipline that studies such behavior. —**cha•ot′ic** (-ot′ik), *adj.*

chap[1] (chap), *v.,* **chapped, chap•ping,** *n.* —*v.t.* **1.** to crack, roughen, and redden (the skin). **2.** to cause (the ground, etc.) to split or crack. —*v.i.* **3.** to become chapped. —*n.* **4.** a crack, esp. in the skin.

chap[2] (chap), *n. Informal.* fellow; guy.

chap[3] (chop, chap), *n.* CHOP[3] (def. 1).

chap•a•ra•jos or **chap•a•re•jos** (shap′ə rā′ōs, -hōs, chap′-), *n.* (*used with a pl. v.*) CHAPS.

chap•ar•ral (shap′ə ral′, chap′-), *n.* a dense growth of shrubs or small trees.

chaparral′ bird′, *n.* ROADRUNNER. Also called **chaparral′ cock′.**

chaparral′ pea′, *n.* a spiny bush, *Pickeringia montana,* of the legume family, having large purple flowers and sometimes forming dense thickets in the Pacific coast regions of the U.S.

cha•peau (sha pō′), *n., pl.* **-peaux** (-pōz′, -pō′), **-peaus.** a hat.

chap•el (chap′əl), *n.* **1.** a private or subordinate place of prayer or worship; oratory. **2.** a separately dedicated part of a church, or a small independent churchlike edifice, devoted to special services. **3.** a room or building for worship in an institution, palace, etc. **4.** a separate place of public worship dependent on the church of a parish.

chap•er•on or **chap•er•one** (shap′ə rōn′), *n., v.,* **-oned, -on•ing.** —*n.* **1.** a person who, for propriety, accompanies a young unmarried woman in public or who attends a party of young unmarried men and women. —*v.t.* **2.** to attend or accompany as chaperon. —*v.i.* **3.** to act as chaperon. —**chap′er•on′age** (-rō′nij), *n.*

chap•lain (chap′lin), *n.* **1.** an ecclesiastic associated with the chapel of a royal court, college, or military unit. **2.** a person who says the prayer, invocation, etc., for an organization or at an assembly. —**chap′lain•cy, chap′lain•ship′,** *n.*

chap•let (chap′lit), *n.* **1.** a wreath or garland for the head. **2.** a string of beads. **3. a.** a string of beads, one-third of the length of a rosary, for counting prayers. **b.** the prayers recited over such beads. **4.** a small molding carved to resemble a string of beads.

Chap•lin (chap′lin), *n.* **Sir Charles Spencer** (*Charlie*), 1889–1977, English film actor, producer, and director; in the U.S. 1910–52.

Chap•man (chap′mən), *n.* **1. George,** 1559–1634, English poet, dramatist, and translator. **2. John,** APPLESEED, Johnny.

chaps (chaps, shaps), *n.* (*used with a pl. v.*) sturdy trouserlike leather leggings, often widely flared, worn over work pants, typically by cowboys.

chap•ter (chap′tər), *n.* **1.** a main division of a book, treatise, or the like, usu. bearing a number or title. **2.** a branch of a society, fraternity, etc. **3.** an important portion or division of anything: *a new chapter in evolution.* **4. a.** an assembly of the monks in a monastery, in a province, or of the entire order. **b.** a general assembly of the canons of a church. **c.** the body of such monks or canons collectively. **5.** any general assembly. **6.** a short scriptural quotation read at various parts of the office. —*v.t.* **7.** to arrange in chapters. —**chap′ter•al,** *adj.*

Chapter 11 or **Chapter XI,** *n.* a section of the U.S. Bankruptcy Code that provides for the reorganization of an insolvent corporation under court supervision.

chap′ter and verse′, *n.* **1.** any specific chapter and verse of the Bible, as used when citing the text. **2.** full, cited authority, as for any quotation, opinion, action, etc.

chap′ter house′, *n.* **1.** a building attached to a cathedral or monastery, used as a meeting place for the chapter. **2.** a building used by a chapter of a fraternity, sorority, etc.

Cha•pul•te•pec (chə pul′tə pek′, -po͝ol′-), *n.* a castle-fortress and military school on the outskirts of Mexico City: captured by U.S. forces (1847) in the Mexican War; now a park.

char[1] (chär), *v.,* **charred, char•ring,** *n.* —*v.t.* **1.** to burn or reduce to charcoal. **2.** to burn slightly; scorch: *The flame charred the steak.* —*v.i.* **3.** to become charred. —*n.* **4.** a charred material or surface. **5.** charcoal.

char[2] (chär), *n., pl.* (*esp. collectively*) **char,** (*esp. for kinds or species*) **chars.** any trout of the genus *Salvelinus* (or *Cristovomer*).

char•ac•ter (kar′ik tər), *n.* **1.** the aggregate of features and traits that form the individual nature of a person or thing. **2.** one such feature or trait; characteristic. **3.** moral or ethical quality: *a woman of strong char-*

acter. **4.** qualities of honesty, fortitude, etc.; integrity. **5.** reputation: *a stain on one's character.* **6.** distinctive, often interesting qualities: *an old pub with a lot of character.* **7.** a person, esp. with reference to behavior or personality: *a suspicious character.* **8.** an odd, eccentric, or unusual person. **9.** a person represented in a drama, story, etc. **10.** a role, as in a play or film. **11.** status or capacity: *in his character of a justice of the peace.* **12.** a symbol used in a system of writing: *Chinese characters.* **13.** a significant visual mark or symbol. **14.** an account of a person's qualities, abilities, etc.; reference. **15.** (in 17th- and 18th-century literature) a sketch of a particular virtue or vice represented in a person or type. **16.** any trait, function, structure, or substance of an organism resulting from the effect of one or more genes. **17.** any encoded unit of computer-usable data representing a symbol, as a letter, number, or punctuation mark, or a space, carriage return, etc. **18.** a cipher or cipher message. —*adj.* **19.** (of a theatrical role) having or requiring eccentric, comedic, ethnic, or other distinctive traits. **20.** (of an actor) acting or specializing in such roles. —*Idiom.* **21. in** (or **out of**) **character, a.** in accord with (or in violation of) one's usual behavior and disposition. **b.** in accordance with (or deviating from) behavior appropriate to the role assumed by an actor. —**char′ac·ter·less,** *adj.*

char′acter assassina′tion, *n.* a slandering attack, esp. one intended to damage the reputation of a public or political figure.

char′acter educa′tion, *n.* the development of good character in children, esp. as part of a curriculum.

char′acter is′sue, *n.* the moral credentials of a political candidate in an election.

char·ac·ter·is·tic (kar′ik tə ris′tik), *adj.* **1.** indicating the character or distinctive quality of a person or thing; typical. —*n.* **2.** a distinguishing feature or quality. **3. a.** the integral part of a common logarithm. **b.** the exponent of 10 in a number expressed in scientific notation. —**char′ac·ter·is′ti·cal·ly,** *adv.*

char·ac·ter·ize (kar′ik tə rīz′), *v.t.,* **-ized, -iz·ing. 1.** to be a characteristic of; distinguish; mark. **2.** to describe the character of. **3.** to attribute a specific character to: *characterized him as a scoundrel.* —**char′ac·ter·i·za′tion,** *n.*

char′acter sketch′, *n.* a literary sketch describing a person.

char′acter wit′ness, *n.* a person summoned to give testimony regarding the moral character and reputation of a litigant during a legal proceeding.

cha·rade (shə rād′; *esp. Brit.* shə räd′), *n.* **1. charades,** (*used with a sing. v.*) a game in which players act out in pantomime a word, phrase, title, etc., often syllable by syllable, for members of their team to guess. **2.** a word or phrase acted out in pantomime. **3.** a blatant pretense or deception; travesty.

char·broil (chär′broil′), *v.t.* to broil on a grill over a charcoal fire.

char·coal (chär′kōl′), *n.* **1.** the carbonaceous material obtained by heating an organic substance, as wood, in the absence of air. **2.** a drawing pencil of charcoal. **3.** a drawing made with charcoal. —*v.t.* **4.** to draw or blacken with charcoal. **5.** to cook over a charcoal fire, esp. on a grill.

char·cu·te·rie (shär kōō′tə rē′, shär kōō′tə rē), *n.* **1.** a store where pork products, as hams, sausages, and pâtés, are sold. **2.** the items sold in such a store.

chard (chärd), *n.* a variety of beet, *Beta vulgaris cicla,* having leaves and leafstalks that are used as a vegetable. Also called **Swiss chard.**

Char·don·nay (shär′dn ā′), *n.* **1.** a white grape used in winemaking. **2.** a dry white wine made from this grape.

charge (chärj), *v.,* **charged, charg·ing,** *n.* —*v.t.* **1.** to impose or ask as a price or fee. **2.** to ask a price of (someone): *Did he charge you for it?* **3.** to defer payment for (a purchase) until a bill is rendered by the creditor: *to charge a coat.* **4.** to hold liable for payment; enter a debit against. **5.** to attack by rushing violently against: *The cavalry charged the enemy.* **6.** to accuse formally or explicitly (usu. fol. by *with*): *They charged her with theft.* **7.** to instruct authoritatively, as a judge does a jury. **8.** to lay a command or injunction upon. **9.** to fill or refill so as to make ready for use: *to charge a musket.* **10.** to supply with a quantity of electric charge or electrical energy: *to charge a battery.* **11.** to suffuse, as with emotion: *The air was charged with excitement.* **12.** to fill (air, water, etc.) with foreign matter in a state of diffusion or solution. **13.** to load (materials) into a furnace, converter, etc. **14.** to load or burden (the mind, heart, etc.). **15.** to put a load or burden on or in. **16.** to place charges on (an escutcheon). —*v.i.* **17.** to make an onset; rush, as to an attack. **18.** to require payment: *to charge for a service.* **19.** to place the price of a thing to one's debit. **20.** (in certain sports) to run or skate into an opposing defensive player, esp. in such a way as to incur a foul. **21. charge off, a.** to write off as an expense or loss. **b.** to attribute; chalk up. **22. charge up,** to agitate, stimulate, or excite. —*n.* **23.** a fee or price asked or imposed: *a charge of six dollars for admission.* **24.** expense or cost. **25.** an entry in an account of something due. **26.** an impetuous onset or attack, as of soldiers. **27.** a signal by bugle, drum, etc., for a military charge. **28.** a duty or responsibility entrusted to one. **29.** care, custody, or superintendence. **30.** someone or something committed to one's care. **31.** a parish or congregation committed to the spiritual care of a pastor. **32.** a command or injunction. **33.** an accusation: *a charge of theft.* **34.** the instructions given by a judge to a jury concerning points of law, the weight of evidence, etc., before deliberation begins. **35.** the quantity of anything that an apparatus is fitted to hold, or holds, at one time: *a charge of coal for a fur-*

nace. **36.** a quantity of explosive to be set off at one time. **37. a.** ELECTRIC CHARGE. **b.** the process of charging a storage battery. **38.** *Informal.* a pleasurable thrill; kick. **39.** a load or burden. **40.** any distinctive figure borne on an escutcheon. —*Idiom.* **41. in charge,** in command; having the care or supervision: *Who's in charge here?* **42. take charge,** to assume control, care, or responsibility.

char·gé (shär zhā′, shär′zhä), *n., pl.* **-gés** (-zhāz′; -zhäz). a chargé d'affaires.

charge′ account′, *n.* an account, esp. in retailing, that permits a customer to buy goods and be billed at a later date.

charge′ card′, *n.* an identification card used to make purchases on a charge account.

charged (chärjd), *adj.* **1.** fraught with emotion; intense. **2.** capable of arousing violent emotion or controversy. **3.** pertaining to a particle, body, or system possessing a net positive or negative electric charge.

chargé′ d'af·faires′ (də fâr′), *n., pl.* **chargés d'af·faires** (də fâr′). **1.** an official placed in charge of diplomatic business during the temporary absence of the ambassador or minister. **2.** an envoy to a state to which a diplomat of higher grade is not sent.

Charge′ of the Light′ Brigade′, The, a poem (1854) by Alfred, Lord Tennyson, celebrating the British cavalry attack on the Russian position at Balaklava during the Crimean War.

charg·er (chär′jər), *n.* **1.** a horse suitable to be ridden in battle. **2.** an apparatus for charging storage batteries.

char·i·ot (char′ē ət), *n.* **1.** a light horse-drawn vehicle of the ancient world, usu. two-wheeled and carrying no more than two standing riders, employed in warfare, hunting, races, and processions. **2.** a light four-wheeled carriage of the 18th century. —*v.t.* **3.** to convey in a chariot. —*v.i.* **4.** to ride in or drive a chariot.

chariot (def. 1)

char·i·ot·eer (char′ē ə tēr′), *n.* a chariot driver.

cha·ris·ma (kə riz′mə), *n., pl.* **-ma·ta** (-mə tə). **1.** a special quality conferring extraordinary powers of leadership and the ability to inspire veneration. **2.** a personal magnetism that enables an individual to attract or influence people. **3.** Also, **char·ism** (kar′iz əm). a divinely conferred gift or power.

char·is·mat·ic (kar′iz mat′ik), *adj.* **1.** of, having, or characteristic of charisma. **2.** characterizing Christians of various denominations who seek an ecstatic religious experience. —*n.* **3.** a Christian who emphasizes such a religious experience.

char·i·ta·ble (char′i tə bəl), *adj.* **1.** generous in gifts to aid the indigent, ill, homeless, etc. **2.** kindly or lenient in judging people. **3.** of or concerned with charity: *a charitable institution.* —**char′i·ta·bly,** *adv.*

char·i·ty (char′i tē), *n., pl.* **-ties. 1.** donations or generous actions to aid the poor, ill, or helpless. **2.** a charitable act or work. **3.** a charitable fund, foundation, or institution. **4.** benevolent feeling, esp. toward those in need: *to do something out of charity.* **5.** leniency in judging others; forbearance. **6.** alms. **7.** Christian love; agape: one of the three Christian virtues. —*Proverb.* **8. Charity begins at home,** love should first apply to the ones nearest us. [< Latin *cāritās,* der. of *cārus* dear]

cha·ri·va·ri (shiv′ə rē′, shiv′ə rē′; *esp. Brit.* shär′ə vär′ē) *n., pl.* **-ris,** *v.t.,* **-ried, -ri·ing.** SHIVAREE.

char·la·tan (shär′lə tn), *n.* a person who pretends to special knowledge or skill that he or she does not possess; quack; fraud.

Char·le·magne (shär′lə mān′), *n.* (*"Charles the Great"*) A.D. 742–814, king of the Franks 768–814; as Charles I, first emperor of the Holy Roman Empire 800–814.

Charles (chärlz), *n.* **1.** (*Prince of Edinburgh and of Wales*) born 1948, heir apparent to the throne of Great Britain (son of Elizabeth II). **2. Ray** (*Ray Charles Robinson*), born 1930, U.S. blues singer and pianist. **3.** a river in E Massachusetts, flowing between Boston and Cambridge into the Atlantic. 47 mi. (75 km) long.

Charles·ton[1] (chärlz′tən, chärl′stən), *n.* **1.** a seaport in SE South Carolina. 81,030. **2.** the capital of West Virginia, in the W part. 55,730.

Charles·ton[2] (chärlz′tən, chärl′stən), *n.* **1.** a vigorous, rhythmic ballroom dance popular in the 1920s. —*v.i.* **2.** to dance the Charleston. [after CHARLESTON[1], South Carolina]

char′ley horse′ (chär′lē), *n.* a cramp or a sore muscle, esp. in the leg, resulting from overuse or strain.

char·lock (chär′lək, -lok), *n.* a wild mustard, *Brassica kaber,* having lobed, ovate leaves and clusters of small yellow flowers: a weed in grain fields.

char·lotte (shär′lət), *n.* any of various desserts usu. made by lining a mold with cake or bread and filling it with fruit, whipped cream, custard, or gelatin.

Char·lotte (shär′lət), *n.* a city in S North Carolina. 437,797.

Char·lotte A·ma·li·e (shär′lət ə mä′lē ə), *n.* the capital of the Virgin Islands of the U.S., on St. Thomas. 12,372. Formerly, **St. Thomas.**

char′lotte russe′ (rōōs), *n.* a chilled dessert made by lining a mold with cake or ladyfingers and filling it with Bavarian cream.

charm (chärm), *n.* **1.** a power of pleasing or attracting, as through personality or beauty. **2.** a trait or feature imparting this power. **3. charms,** attractiveness. **4.** a trinket to be worn on a bracelet, necklace, etc. **5.** something worn or carried on one's person to bring good luck or ward off evil; amulet. **6.** a formula or action credited with magical power. **7.** the chanting or recitation of magic words; incantation. **8.** *Physics.* the quantum property assigned to the charmed quark. —*v.t.* **9.** to delight or please greatly by attractiveness; enchant. **10.** to act upon (someone or something) with or as if with a magical force. **11.** to gain or influence through personal charm. **12.** to endow with or protect by supernatural powers. —*v.i.* **13.** to be fascinating or pleasing. **14.** to use charms. —**charm′er,** *n.* —**charm′less,** *adj.*

char·nel (chär′nl), *n.* **1.** CHARNEL HOUSE. —*adj.* **2.** of, like, or fit for a charnel house.

char′nel house′, *n.* a house or place in which the bodies or bones of the dead are deposited.

char·o·phyte (kar′ə fīt′), *n.* any green algae of the class Charophyceae (or group Charophyta), comprising the stoneworts.

char·qui (chär′kē), *n.* JERKY[2].

chart (chärt), *n.* **1.** a sheet giving information in tabular or diagrammatic form. **2.** a graphic representation, as by curves, of a dependent variable, as temperature or price; graph. **3.** a map, esp. a hydrographic or marine map. **4.** an outline map showing special conditions or facts: *a weather chart.* **5. the charts,** a ranking of the most popular musical recordings, usu. based on sales for the week. —*v.t.* **6.** to make a chart of. **7.** to plan: *to chart a course of action.* **8.** to rank in the musical charts. —**chart′a·ble,** *adj.*

char·ter (chär′tər), *n.* **1.** a document issued by a sovereign or state outlining the conditions under which a business, city, or other corporate body is organized, and defining its rights and privileges. **2.** a document defining the formal organization of a corporate body; constitution: *the Charter of the United Nations.* **3.** an authorization from a central or parent organization to establish a new branch, chapter, etc. **4.** a document issued by a sovereign power granting certain rights or privileges to a group or individual. **5.** an arrangement by which all or part of a ship, airplane, etc., is leased for a particular group or journey. **6.** a tour, vacation, or trip using such an arrangement. **7.** a special privilege or immunity. —*v.t.* **8.** to issue by charter; establish by charter: *to charter a bank.* **9.** to lease or hire for exclusive use: *The company chartered a bus for the picnic.* —*adj.* **10.** pertaining to or involving transportation that is specially leased and not part of a regularly scheduled service: *a charter flight to Europe.* **11.** available for lease or hire by private individuals: *a charter boat for fishing.*

char′ter col′ony, *n.* (in colonial America) a colony, as Rhode Island or Connecticut, governed under a charter from the British crown and allowed much autonomy.

char′ter mem′ber, *n.* one of the original or founding members of a club, organization, etc. —**char′ter mem′bership,** *n.*

chart·ist (chär′tist), *n.* **1.** a specialist in the stock market who studies and draws charts of trading actions. **2.** a cartographer.

Char·treuse (shär trōōz′, -trōōs′), *Trademark.* **1.** an aromatic yellow or green liqueur made by Carthusian monks. —*n.* **2.** (*l.c.*) a clear light green with a yellowish tinge.

char·wom·an (chär′wŏŏm′ən), *n., pl.* **-wom·en.** a woman hired to do general cleaning, as in an office.

char·y (châr′ē), *adj.,* **char·i·er, char·i·est. 1.** cautious or careful; wary. **2.** shy; timid. **3.** particular; choosy. **4.** sparing; frugal (often fol. by *of*): *chary of his praise.* —**char′i·ly,** *adv.* —**char′i·ness,** *n.*

chase[1] (chās), *v.,* **chased, chas·ing,** *n.* —*v.t.* **1.** to follow rapidly or intently to seize, overtake, etc.; pursue: *to chase a thief.* **2.** to pursue with intent to capture or kill, as game; hunt. **3.** to follow or devote one's attention to with the hope of attracting, winning, etc. **4.** to drive or expel forcibly: *to chase the cat out.* —*v.i.* **5.** to follow in pursuit: *to chase after someone.* **6.** to rush; hasten: *chasing around all afternoon looking for a gift.* —*n.* **7.** the act of chasing; pursuit. **8.** an object of pursuit. **9.** *Brit.* a private game preserve. **10.** STEEPLECHASE. **11. the chase,** the sport or occupation of hunting. —*Idiom.* **12. give chase,** to go in pursuit. —**chase′a·ble,** *adj.*

chase[2] (chās), *n.* **1.** a rectangular iron frame in which composed type is secured or locked for printing or platemaking. **2.** a groove, furrow, or channel, as one made in a wall for pipes or ducts. **3.** the forepart of a gun, containing the bore.

chase[3] (chās), *v.t.,* **chased, chas·ing. 1.** to ornament (metal) by engraving or embossing. **2.** to cut (a screw thread), as with a chaser or machine tool.

Chase (chās), *n.* **1. Sal·mon Portland** (sal′mən), 1808–73, Chief Justice of the U.S. 1864–73. **2. Samuel,** 1741–1811, U.S. jurist and leader in the American Revolution.

chas·er[1] (chā′sər), *n.* **1.** a person or thing that chases or pursues. **2.** a milder beverage taken after a drink of liquor. **3.** a hunter.

chas·er[2] (chā′sər), *n.* **1.** a person who engraves metal. **2.** a tool with multiple teeth for cutting screw threads.

Cha·sid or **Chas·sid** (ᴋʜä′sid, hä′-), *n., pl.* **Cha·sid·im** or **Chas·sid·im** (ᴋʜä sid′im, hä-). HASID.

chasm (kaz′əm), *n.* **1.** a yawning fissure or deep cleft in the earth's surface; gorge. **2.** any marked gap or break. **3.** a wide divergence of opinions, interests, etc., esp. producing a breach in relations.

chas·sé (sha sā′ *or, esp. in square dancing,* sa shā′), *n., v.,* **chas·séd, chas·sé·ing.** —*n.* **1.** a gliding dance step with one foot kept in advance of the other. —*v.i.* **2.** to execute a chassé.

chas·sis (chas′ē, -is, shas′ē), *n., pl.* **chas·sis** (chas′ēz, shas′-). **1.** the frame, wheels, and machinery of a motor vehicle, on which the body is supported. **2.** the framework on which a gun carriage moves backward and forward. **3.** the main landing gear of an aircraft. **4.** a frame for mounting the circuit components of a radio or television set.

chaste (chāst), *adj.,* **chast·er, chast·est. 1.** refraining from sexual intercourse, regarded as contrary to morality or religion. **2.** virginal. **3.** not engaging in sexual relations; celibate. **4.** decent and modest: *chaste conversation.* **5.** unsullied; undefiled: *chaste white snow.* **6.** pure in style; simple; unadorned: *a chaste design.* —**chaste′ly,** *adv.* —**chas·ti·ty** (chas′ti tē), *n.*

chas·ten (chā′sən), *v.t.* **1.** to inflict suffering or punishment upon to humble or improve. **2.** to restrain; subdue. **3.** to rid of excess; refine. —**chas′ten·er,** *n.* —**chas′ten·ing·ly,** *adv.*

chas·tise (chas tīz′, chas′tīz), *v.t.,* **-tised, -tis·ing. 1.** to discipline, esp. by corporal punishment. **2.** to criticize severely. —**chas·tise·ment** (chas′tiz mənt, chas tīz′-), *n.* —**chas·tis′er,** *n.*

chas·u·ble (chaz′yə bəl, -ə bəl, chas′-), *n.* a sleeveless outer vestment worn by the celebrant at mass.

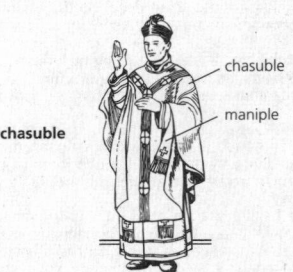

chasuble

chasuble

maniple

chat (chat), *v.,* **chat·ted, chat·ting,** *n.* —*v.i.* **1.** to converse informally. **2.** to engage in dialogue by exchanging electronic messages on a BBS. —*n.* **3.** informal conversation. **4. a.** any of several New World songbirds of the genera *Icteria* and *Granatellus.* **b.** any of various Eurasian songbirds, as the stonechat or whinchat.

châ·teau or **cha·teau** (sha tō′), *n., pl.* **-teaus** (-tōz′), **-teaux** (-tōz′, -tō′). **1.** a castle or fortress in France. **2.** a large country house or estate, esp. in France. **3.** a winegrower's estate, esp. in the Bordeaux region of France: often used as part of the name of a wine.

Châ·teau-Thier·ry (sha tō′tē′ə rē′, -tye rē′, shä-), *n.* a town in N France, on the Marne River: World War I battles. 13,856.

chat·e·lain (shat′l ān′), *n.* CASTELLAN.

chat·e·laine (shat′l ān′), *n.* **1.** the mistress of a castle or of a large and elegant household. **2.** a hooklike clasp with chains for suspending small objects, as keys and sewing implements, worn at the waist by women esp. in the 18th and 19th centuries.

cha·toy·ant (shə toi′ənt), *adj.* **1.** changing in luster or color: *chatoyant silk.* **2.** (of a gemstone) reflecting a single streak of light when cut in a cabochon. —*n.* **3.** a cabochon-cut gemstone having such a reflected streak, as a chrysoberyl cat's-eye. —**cha·toy′ance, cha·toy′an·cy,** *n.*

Chat·ta·noo·ga (chat′ə nōō′gə), *n.* a city in SE Tennessee, on the Tennessee River: Civil War battle 1863. 152,259. —**Chat′ta·noo′gan, Chat·ta·noo·gi·an** (chat′ə nōō′jē ən), *adj., n.*

chat·tel (chat′l), *n.* **1.** a movable article of personal property. **2.** any article of tangible property other than land and buildings.

chat·ter (chat′ər), *v.i.* **1.** to talk rapidly, continuously, and often purposelessly; jabber. **2.** to utter rapid, inarticulate speechlike sounds, as a monkey or bird. **3.** to make a rapid clicking noise by striking together: *teeth chattering from the cold.* **4.** (of a cutting tool or piece of metal) to vibrate during cutting. —*v.t.* **5.** to utter rapidly or inconsequentially. —*n.* **6.** rapid and often purposeless talk. **7.** the act or sound of chattering. —**chat′ter·er,** *n.*

chat·ter·box (chat′ər boks′), *n.* an excessively talkative person.

chat′tering class′, *n.* well-educated members of the upper-middle or upper class who readily opine on current issues.

chat·ty (chat′ē), *adj.,* **-ti·er, -ti·est. 1.** characterized by a friendly, informal conversational style: *a long, chatty letter.* **2.** given to chatting. —**chat′ti·ly,** *adv.* —**chat′ti·ness,** *n.*

Chau•cer (chô′sər), *n.* **Geoffrey,** 1340?–1400, English poet. —**Chau•ce′ri•an** (-sēr′ē ən), *adj., n.*

chauf•feur (shō′fər, shō fûr′), *n.* **1.** a person employed to drive an automobile for the owner. **2.** a person employed to drive a car or limousine for paying passengers. —*v.t.* **3.** to drive (a vehicle) as a chauffeur. **4.** to transport by car: *to chauffeur the kids to school.* —*v.i.* **5.** to work as a chauffeur.

Chau•tau•qua (shə tô′kwə, chə-), *n.* **1. Lake,** a lake in SW New York. 18 mi. (29 km) long. **2.** a village on this lake: summer educational center. **3.** an annual educational meeting, originating in this village in 1874, providing public lectures, concerts, and dramatic performances during the summer months, usually in an outdoor setting. **4.** (*usually l.c.*) any similar assembly, esp. one of a number meeting in a circuit of communities. —*adj.* **5.** of or pertaining to a system of education flourishing in the late 19th and early 20th centuries, originating at Lake Chautauqua, New York. **6.** (*usually l.c.*) pertaining to a chautauqua: *a chautauqua program.*

chau•vin•ism (shō′və niz′əm), *n.* **1.** zealous and aggressive patriotism or blind enthusiasm for military glory. **2.** biased devotion to any group, attitude, or cause. —**chau′vin•ist,** *n.* —**chau′vin•is′tic,** *adj.* —**chau′vin•is′ti•cal•ly,** *adv.*

cha•yo•te (chī ō′tē), *n.* **1.** a tropical American vine, *Sechium edule,* of the gourd family, having triangular leaves and small, white flowers. **2.** the green or white, furrowed, usu. pear-shaped edible fruit of this plant. Also called **mirliton.**

cha•zan (ᴋʜä′zən, ᴋʜä zän′), *n., pl.* ***cha•zan•im*** (ᴋʜä zô′nim, ᴋʜä′zä-nēm′), *Eng.* **cha•zans.** *Hebrew.* HAZAN.

cheap (chēp), *adj.* **1.** costing very little; relatively low in price; inexpensive. **2.** charging low prices: *a cheap store.* **3.** shoddy or inferior. **4.** costing little labor or trouble: *Talk is cheap.* **5.** mean or contemptible: *a cheap joke.* **6.** of little account or value: *Life was cheap.* **7.** embarrassed; sheepish. **8.** stingy; miserly. **9.** (of money) able to be borrowed at low interest. **10.** of decreased value or purchasing power. —*adv.* **11.** at a low price or small cost. —***Idiom.*** **12. on the cheap,** inexpensively; economically. —**cheap′ly,** *adv.* —**cheap′ness,** *n.*

cheap•en (chē′pən), *v.t.* **1.** to make cheap or cheaper. **2.** to lower in esteem. **3.** to decrease the quality of; make inferior or vulgar. —*v.i.* **4.** to become cheap. —**cheap′en•er,** *n.*

cheap′-jack′ or **cheap′jack′,** *n.* **1.** a peddler, esp. of inferior articles. —*adj.* **2.** cheap or inferior. **3.** unscrupulous or underhanded.

cheap′ shot′, *n.* **1.** (in sports) a blow, shove, or tackle maliciously directed against an opponent who is defenseless or off guard. **2.** any mean or unsportsmanlike remark or action, esp. one directed at a defenseless or vulnerable person.

cheap•skate (chēp′skāt′), *n. Informal.* a stingy or miserly person.

cheat (chēt), *v.t.* **1.** to defraud; swindle. **2.** to deceive; influence by fraud. **3.** to elude; escape: *to cheat death.* —*v.i.* **4.** to practice fraud or deceit. **5.** to violate rules or agreements: *to cheat at cards.* **6.** to take an examination in a dishonest way, as by having improper access to answers. **7.** to be sexually unfaithful (often fol. by *on*). —*n.* **8.** a person who cheats; swindler; deceiver; impostor. **9.** a fraud, swindle, or deception. —**cheat′er,** *n.*

check (chek), *v.t.* **1.** to stop or arrest the motion of suddenly or forcibly. **2.** to restrain; control: *to check an impulse.* **3.** to cause to diminish, as in rate or intensity. **4.** to verify the correctness of, as by comparison. **5.** to inquire into, search through, etc.: *to check the files for a missing letter.* **6.** to inspect or test the condition, performance, safety, etc., of. **7.** to mark so as to indicate choice, correctness, verification, etc. (often fol. by *off*). **8.** to leave in or accept for temporary custody: *Check your coats at the door.* **9.** to surrender (baggage) for conveyance. **10.** to mark with or in a pattern of squares: *to check fabric.* **11.** to plant in checkrows. **12.** (in chess) to place (an opponent's king) under direct attack. **13.** (in ice hockey) to obstruct or impede the movement or progress of (an opponent). —*v.i.* **14.** to prove to be right; correspond accurately. **15.** to make an inquiry or investigation, as for verification (often fol. by *up, into,* etc.): *Check into the matter.* **16.** to stop suddenly. **17.** (in chess) to make a move that puts the opponent's king under direct attack. **18.** to crack or split, as paint. **19.** (in poker) to decline to bet. **20. check in,** to register or report one's arrival, as at a hotel or airport. **21. check (up) on,** to investigate, scrutinize, or inspect. **22. check out, a.** to leave a hotel, hospital, etc., officially, esp. after settling one's account. **b.** to verify or become verified. **c.** to confirm or be confirmed as fulfilling necessary requirements, being in working condition, etc. **d.** to total the cost of purchases and collect payment from (a customer). **e.** to lend or borrow (an item) officially, as from a library. **f.** *Informal.* to depart quickly or abruptly. **23. check over,** to examine or investigate thoroughly. —*n.* **24.** Also, *Brit.,* **cheque.** a written order, usu. on a standard printed form, directing a bank to pay money. **25.** a slip showing an amount owed, esp. a bill as for food or beverages consumed. **26.** a ticket given for items left in a checkroom, to customers waiting to be served, etc. **27.** a criterion, standard, or means to insure against error, fraud, etc. **28.** an inquiry, search, or examination. **29.** a mark, often indicated by (✓), as on a list, to indicate that something has been noted, acted upon, approved, etc. **30.** a sudden arrest or stoppage. **31.** a means of stopping, limiting, or restraining. **32.** a test or inspection, as to ascertain quality or performance. **33.** a pattern formed of squares. **34.** one of the squares in such a pattern. **35.** a fabric having such a pattern. **36.** (in chess) the exposure of the king to direct attack. **37.** an ice hockey maneuver designed to obstruct or impede the movement of an opponent. **38.** a counter used in card games, as the chip in poker. **39.** a small crack, as in a painted surface. —*adj.* **40.** serving to check, control, verify, etc. **41.** ornamented with a checkered pattern; checkered. —*interj.* **42.** (used as a call in chess to warn that an opponent's king is in check.) **43.** *Informal.* all right! agreed! —***Idiom.*** **44. in check,** under restraint: *to hold one's anger in check.* —**check′a•ble,** *adj.* —**check′less,** *adj.*

check′ bit′, *n.* a binary digit used to check for errors in the electronic transmission or storage of a unit of information.

check•book (chek′bo͝ok′), *n.* a depositor's book containing blank checks to be drawn against an account.

checked (chekt), *adj.* **1.** having a pattern of squares; checkered: *a checked shirt.* **2. a.** (of a syllable) closed. **b.** (of a vowel) situated in a closed syllable (opposed to *free*).

check•er¹ (chek′ər), *n.* **1.** a small, usu. red or black disk of plastic or wood, used in playing checkers. **2. checkers,** Also called, *Brit.,* **draughts.** (*used with a sing. v.*) a game played by two persons, each with 12 playing pieces, on a checkerboard. **3.** a checkered pattern. **4.** one of the squares in such a pattern. —*v.t.* **5.** to mark like a checkerboard. **6.** to diversify in color; variegate. **7.** to diversify in character; subject to alternations. Also, *Brit.,* **chequer.**

check•er² (chek′ər), *n.* **1.** a person or thing that checks. **2.** a cashier, as in a supermarket. **3.** an employee of a checkroom.

check•er•ber•ry (chek′ər ber′ē), *n., pl.* **-ries. 1.** the red fruit of the American wintergreen, *Gaultheria procumbens.* **2.** the plant itself.

check•er•bloom (chek′ər blo͞om′), *n.* a W North American plant, *Sidalcea malviflora,* of the mallow family, having long, loose clusters of rose-colored flowers.

check•er•board (chek′ər bôrd′, -bōrd′), *n.* **1.** a board marked into 64 squares of two alternating colors, arranged in eight vertical and eight horizontal rows, on which checkers or chess is played. **2.** a design resembling this. —*v.t.* **3.** to arrange in or mark with a checkerboard pattern.

check•ered (chek′ərd), *adj.* **1.** marked by numerous shifts or changes: *a checkered career.* **2.** marked by dubious episodes: *a checkered past.* **3.** marked with squares. **4.** variegated in color or shading.

Check′ers Speech′, *n.* a television address given by Richard Nixon in the 1952 presidential campaign, in which he sentimentally and successfully defended himself against charges of bribery. [so called from Nixon's reference to his dog named Checkers]

check′-in′, *n.* the act or fact of checking in.

check′ing account′, *n.* a bank deposit against which checks can be drawn by the depositor.

check•list (chek′list′), *n.* **1.** Also, **check′ list′.** a list of items for comparison, verification, or other checking purposes. —*v.t.* **2.** to place on a checklist. —*v.i.* **3.** to make a checklist.

check•mate (chek′māt′), *n., v.,* **-mat•ed, -mat•ing,** *interj.* —*n.* **1. a.** an act or instance in chess of maneuvering the opponent's king into a check from which it cannot escape, thus bringing the game to a victorious conclusion. **b.** the position of the pieces when a king is checkmated. **2.** a thwarting or defeat. —*v.t.* **3.** to maneuver (an opponent's king in chess) into a check from which no escape is possible; mate. **4.** to check completely; defeat. —*interj.* **5.** (used by a chess player when placing the opponent's king in checkmate.)

check•off (chek′ôf′, -of′), *n.* **1.** the collection of union dues by employers through deductions from wages. **2.** a voluntary contribution from one's income tax, as for a political campaign fund.

check′out′ or **check′-out′,** *n.* **1.** the procedure of vacating and paying for one's quarters at a hotel. **2.** the time by which a hotel room must be vacated if another day's charge is not to be made. **3.** an examination, as of fitness for performance. **4.** a series of sequential actions to familiarize oneself with new equipment. **5.** the act of itemizing purchases and collecting the amount due. **6.** Also called **check′out count′er.** a counter where customers pay for purchases.

check•point (chek′point′), *n.* **1.** a place along a road, border, etc., where travelers are stopped for inspection. **2.** a point or item in a procedure for notation, inspection, or confirmation.

Check′point Char′lie, *n.* a checkpoint in Berlin at which passage was permitted between East and West Berlin.

check•room (chek′ro͞om′, -ro͝om′), *n.* a room where hats, coats, parcels, etc., may be checked.

checks′ and bal′ances, *n.pl.* limits imposed by the U.S. Constitution on all branches (executive, judicial, and legislative) of the government by vesting in each branch the right to amend or void those acts of another branch that fall within its purview.

check•up (chek′up′), *n.* **1.** a comprehensive physical examination. **2.** an examination, as to ascertain condition, accuracy, etc.

ched•dar (ched′ər), *n.* a hard smooth-textured cheese that varies in color from white to yellow or orange and in flavor from mild to sharp as it ages.

che•der (ᴋʜā′dər), *n.* HEDER.

Ched•or•la•o•mer, (ked′ər lā ō′mər), *n.* a king of Elam who did battle against Sodom and Gomorrah. Gen. 14:1–24.

cheek (chēk), *n.* **1.** either side of the face below the eye and above the jaw. **2.** the side wall of the mouth between the upper and lower jaws. **3.** something likened to the side of the face, as either of two parts forming corresponding sides of an object: *the cheeks of a vise.* **4.** impudence or effrontery. **5.** either of the buttocks. **6.** either of the sides of a pulley or block. —*Idiom.* **7. cheek by jowl,** in close intimacy; side by side.

cheek·bone (chēk′bōn′), *n.* the bony arch that forms the cheek prominence below the eye; zygomatic bone.

cheeked (chēkt), *adj.* having cheeks of the kind indicated (used in combination): *rosy-cheeked youngsters.*

cheek′ pouch′, *n.* a sac in the cheek of certain animals, as squirrels, in which food may be carried.

cheek·y (chē′kē), *adj.,* **cheek·i·er, cheek·i·est.** impudent; insolent. —**cheek′i·ly,** *adv.* —**cheek′i·ness,** *n.*

cheep (chēp), *v.i.* **1.** to chirp; peep. —*v.t.* **2.** to express by cheeps. —*n.* **3.** a chirp. —**cheep′er,** *n.*

cheer (chēr), *n.* **1.** a shout of encouragement, approval, etc. **2.** a set form of shout used by spectators to encourage an athletic team, contestant, etc. **3.** something that gives comfort or joy: *words of cheer.* **4.** a state of feeling or spirits: *Be of good cheer.* **5.** gladness, gaiety, or animation. **6.** food and drink: *to invite friends for Christmas cheer.* —*interj.* **7. cheers,** (used as a salutation or toast.) —*v.t.* **8.** to salute with shouts of approval, congratulation, triumph, etc. **9.** to gladden; raise the spirits of (often fol. by *up*): *The good news cheered her.* —*v.i.* **10.** to utter cheers of approval, encouragement, etc. **11. cheer on,** to encourage or urge on. **12. cheer up,** to become or make happier or more cheerful. —*Proverb.* **13. Be of good cheer,** be cheerful; don't worry. Matt. 14:27; John 16:33. —**cheer′ful,** *adj.* —**cheer′less,** *adj.*

cheer·lead·er (chēr′lē′dər), *n.* a person who leads spectators in organized cheering, esp. at an athletic event.

cheer·y (chēr′ē), *adj.,* **cheer·i·er, cheer·i·est. 1.** being in good spirits; cheerful. **2.** promoting cheer; enlivening: *a cheery letter.* —**cheer′i·ly,** *adv.* —**cheer′i·ness,** *n.*

cheese¹ (chēz), *n.* **1.** a food prepared from the curds of milk separated from the whey, often pressed and allowed to ripen. **2.** a definite mass of this substance, often shaped like a cylinder. **3.** something of similar shape or consistency. [< Latin *cāseus*]

cheese² (chēz), *n. Slang.* an important or powerful person (usu. prec. by *the big, the whole,* etc.).

cheese·burg·er (chēz′bûr′gər), *n.* a hamburger topped with a melted slice of cheese.

cheese·cake (chēz′kāk′), *n.* a cake with a firm custardlike texture made with sweetened cream cheese, cottage cheese, or the like.

cheese·cloth (chēz′klôth′, -kloth′), *n.* a lightweight cotton gauze of loose, open plain weave.

cheese·par·ing (chēz′pâr′ing), *adj.* **1.** parsimonious or stingy. —*n.* **2.** something of little or no value. **3.** pinchpenny economizing; stinginess; miserliness. —**cheese′par′er,** *n.*

cheese′ steak′ or **cheese′steak′,** *n.* a sandwich of sliced steak topped with melted cheese and fried onions, served on a long roll.

chee·tah (chē′tə), *n.* a swift, long-legged, black-spotted cat, *Acinonyx jubatus,* of SW Asia and Africa, with nonretractile claws.

Chee·ver (chē′vər), *n.* **John,** 1912–82, U.S. novelist and short-story writer.

chef (shef), *n.* **1.** the chief cook, esp. in a restaurant or hotel. **2.** any cook.

chef-d'oeu·vre (*Fr.* she dœ′vRə), *n., pl.* **chefs-d'oeu·vre** (she dœ′vRə). a masterpiece.

che·la (kē′lə), *n., pl.* **-lae** (-lē). a pincerlike organ or claw terminating certain limbs of crustaceans and arachnids.

che·late (kē′lāt), *adj., n., v.,* **-lat·ed, -lat·ing.** —*adj.* **1.** of or noting a heterocyclic compound having a central metallic ion attached by covalent bonds to two or more nonmetallic atoms in the same molecule. **2.** having a chela or chelae. —*n.* **3.** a chelate compound. —*v.i.* **4.** (of a heterocyclic compound) to form a chelate in a reaction. —*v.t.* **5.** to combine (an organic compound) with a metallic ion to form a chelate. —**che′lat·a·ble,** *adj.* —**che′la·tor,** *n.*

cheli-, a combining form meaning "claw," "chela": *cheliform.*

che·lic·er·a (kə lis′ər ə), *n., pl.* **-er·ae** (-ə rē′). one member of the first pair of usu. pincerlike appendages of spiders and other arachnids. —**che·lic′er·al,** *adj.* —**che·lic′er·ate′** (-ə rāt′, -ər it), *adj.*

chem·i·cal (kem′i·kal), *n.* **1.** a substance produced by or used in chemistry. **2. chemicals,** *Slang.* narcotic or mind-altering drugs or substances. —*adj.* **3.** of, used in, produced by, or concerned with chemistry or chemicals: *a chemical formula; chemical agents.* —**chem′i·cal·ly,** *adv.*

chem′ical engineer′ing, *n.* the science of applying chemistry to industrial processes. —**chem′ical engineer′,** *n.*

chem′ical war′fare, *n.* warfare with asphyxiating, poisonous, or corrosive gases, oil flames, etc.

che·min de fer (shə man′ də fâr′), *n.* a variation of baccarat.

che·mise (shə mēz′), *n.* **1.** a woman's loose-fitting, shirtlike or sliplike undergarment; shift. **2.** a dress designed to hang straight from the shoulders without fitting at the waist.

chem·ist (kem′ist), *n.* a specialist in chemistry.

chem·is·try (kem′ə strē), *n., pl.* **-tries. 1.** the science that systematically studies the composition, properties, and activity of organic and inorganic substances and various elementary forms of matter. **2.** chemical properties, reactions, phenomena, etc.: *the chemistry of carbon.* **3. a.**

sympathetic understanding; rapport. **b.** sexual attraction. **4.** the constituent elements of something: *the chemistry of love.*

chemo-, a combining form with the meanings "chemical," "chemically induced," "chemistry": *chemotherapy.* Also, *esp. before elements of Latin origin,* **chemi-.** Also, *esp. before a vowel,* **chem-.**

che·mo·sur·ger·y (kē′mō sûr′jə rē, kem′ō-), *n.* the use of chemical substances to destroy diseased tissue.

che·mo·ther·a·py (kē′mō ther′ə pē, kem′ō-), *n.* the treatment of disease by means of chemicals that have a specific toxic effect upon the disease-producing microorganisms or that selectively destroy cancerous tissue. —**che′mo·ther′a·peu′tic** (-pyōō′tik), *adj.* —**che′mo·ther′a·pist,** *n.*

chem·ur·gy (kem′ûr jē, kə mûr′-), *n.* a division of applied chemistry concerned with the industrial use of organic substances.

che·nille (shə nēl′), *n.* **1.** a yarn with a high velvety pile. **2.** a fabric made with such yarn, used in bedspreads, bathrobes, etc.

Che·nin Blanc (shen′in blängk′; *Fr.* shə naN blän′), *n.* a grape used in making white wine, esp. in the Loire Valley of France and in California.

che·no·pod (kē′nə pod′, ken′ə-), *n.* any plant of the goosefoot family Chenopodiaceae.

cher·i·moy·a (cher′ə moi′ə), *n., pl.* **-moy·as. 1.** a tropical American tree, *Annona cherimola,* of the annona family, having yellow-brown fragrant flowers and leaves with velvety undersides. **2.** the large edible fruit of this tree, having leathery skin and soft pulp.

cher·ish (cher′ish), *v.t.* **1.** to regard or treat as dear. **2.** to care for tenderly; nurture. **3.** to cling fondly to: *to cherish a memory.* —**cher′ish·a·ble,** *adj.* —**cher′ish·er,** *n.* —**cher′ish·ing·ly,** *adv.*

Cher·no·byl (chûr nō′bəl, cher-), *n.* a city in N Ukraine 80 mi. NW of Kiev: nuclear-plant accident 1986.

Cher·o·kee (cher′ə kē′), *n., pl.* **-kees,** (*esp. collectively*) **-kee. 1.** a member of an Native American people residing orig. in the W Carolinas and E Tennessee: surviving groups live in Oklahoma and North Carolina. **2.** the Iroquoian language of the Cherokee.

Cher′okee rose′, *n.* the fragrant white rose of a prickly, climbing shrub, *Rosa laevigata,* orig. from China and naturalized in the southern U.S.: the state flower of Georgia.

cher·ry (cher′ē), *n., pl.* **-ries,** *adj.* —*n.* **1.** the fruit of any of various trees belonging to the genus *Prunus,* of the rose family, consisting of a pulpy, globular drupe enclosing a one-seeded smooth stone. **2.** the tree bearing such a fruit. **3.** the reddish wood of the cherry tree, used in making furniture. **4.** a bright red; cerise. **5.** *Slang.* **a.** something new or unused. **b.** a novice. —*adj.* **6.** bright red; cerise. **7.** containing cherries or cherrylike flavoring. **8.** made of cherry wood. —*Saying.* **9. Life is just a bowl of cherries,** life is pleasant and enjoyable (song with words by Lew Brown and music by Ray Henderson, 1931).

cher′ry bomb′, *n.* a red, globular firecracker with a long fuse and high explosive capability.

cher′ry lau′rel, *n.* an evergreen shrub, *Prunus laurocerasus,* of the rose family, with clusters of white flowers and purple fruit.

cher′ry pep′per, *n.* a variety of pepper, *Capsicum annuum cerasiforme,* having rounded, usu. pungent fruit.

cher′ry pick′er, *n.* **1.** a movable boom topped with a bucketlike enclosure in which a worker stands while repairing telephone lines, pruning trees, etc. **2.** a vehicle equipped with such a boom.

cher′ry plum′, *n.* **1.** a small plum tree, *Prunus cerasifera,* bearing edible yellow or reddish fruit. **2.** the fruit of this tree. Also called **myrobalan.**

cher·ry·stone (cher′ē stōn′), *n.* the quahog clam, *Mercenaria mercenaria,* when larger than a littleneck.

cher′ry toma′to, *n.* a variety of tomato, *Lycopersicon lycopersicum cerasiforme,* as small and round as a large cherry.

chert (chûrt), *n.* a compact rock consisting essentially of microcrystalline quartz. —**chert′y,** *adj.*

cher·ub (cher′əb), *n., pl.* **cher·ubs** for 3; **cher·u·bim** (cher′ə bim, -yōō bim) for 1, 2. **1.** a celestial being. Gen. 3:24; Ezek. 1, 10. **2.** a member of the second order of angels, often represented as a winged child. **3.** a person, esp. a child, with a sweet, chubby, innocent face. —**che·ru·bic** (chə rōō′bik), *adj.* —**cher′ub·like′,** *adj.*

cherubim *n.* a plural of CHERUB.

cher·vil (chûr′vil), *n.* **1.** an herb, *Anthriscus cerefolium,* of the parsley family, having aromatic leaves used to flavor soups, salads, etc. **2.** any of several other plants of the same genus or allied genera.

Ches·a·peake (ches′ə pēk′), *n.* **1.** (*italics*) a U.S. frigate boarded in 1807 by the British, who removed part of its crew and impressed some members into British service: captured by the British in naval battle near Boston in 1813. **2.** a city in SE Virginia. 180,577.

Ches′apeake Bay′ retriev′er, *n.* one of an American breed of retrievers having a short, thick, oily coat ranging in color from brown to a light tan.

che sa·rà sa·rà (ke′ sä Rä′ sä Rä′), *Italian.* what will be, will be.

Chesh·van (KHesh′vən, -vän), *n.* HESHVAN.

chess (ches), *n.* a game played on a chessboard by two people who maneuver 16 pieces each according to rules governing movement of the six kinds of pieces (pawn, rook, knight, bishop, queen, king), the object being to bring the opponent's king into checkmate.

chess·board (ches′bôrd′, -bōrd′), *n.* a checkerboard used for playing chess.

chest (chest), *n.* **1.** the portion of the body enclosed by ribs; thorax. **2.** a box, usu. with a lid, for storage, safekeeping of valuables, etc. **3.** a box in which certain goods, as tea, are packed for shipping. **4.** CHEST OF DRAWERS. **5.** a small cabinet, esp. one hung on a wall, for storage, as of toiletries and medicines. —*Idiom.* **6. get something off one's chest,** to ease anxiety by finally discussing one's problems.

ches·ter·field (ches'tər fēld'), *n.* **1.** (*sometimes cap.*) a single- or double-breasted coat with a velvet collar. **2.** a large overstuffed sofa with high, often rounded arms.

Ches·ter·ton (ches'tər tən), *n.* G(ilbert) K(eith), 1874–1936, English essayist, critic, and novelist.

chest·nut (ches'nut', -nət), *n.* **1.** any of several tall trees of the genus *Castanea*, of the beech family, bearing edible nuts enclosed in a prickly bur, as *C. sativa*, of Europe, and *C. dentata*, an American tree virtually destroyed by chestnut blight. **2.** the edible nut of such a tree. **3.** the wood of any of these trees. **4.** any fruit or tree resembling the chestnut, as the horse chestnut. **5.** reddish brown. **6.** a stale joke, anecdote, etc. **7.** the callosity on the inner side of a horse's leg. **8.** a horse having a reddish brown or brown body with mane and tail of the same or a lighter color. —*adj.* **9.** reddish brown. —*Idiom.* **10. pull someone's chestnuts out of the fire,** to rescue someone from a difficulty. —chest'nut·ty, *adj.*

chest'nut oak', *n.* any of several North American oaks, as *Quercus prinus*, having serrate or dentate leaves resembling those of the chestnut.

chest' of drawers', *n.* a piece of furniture consisting of a set of drawers in a frame, often set on short legs, for holding clothing, household linens, etc.

che·val' glass' (shə val'), *n.* a full-length mirror mounted so that it can be tilted in a frame.

chev·a·lier (shev'ə lēr' *or, esp. for 1, 2,* shə val'yā, -väl'-), *n.* **1.** a member of certain orders of honor or merit, as of the Legion of Honor. **2.** the lowest title of rank in French nobility. **3.** a chivalrous man; cavalier.

chè·vre (shev'rə, shev) also **chev·ret** (shə vrā'), *n.* any cheese made from goat's milk.

chev·ron (shev'rən), *n.* **1.** a badge of one or more V-shaped stripes worn on the sleeve by noncommissioned officers to indicate rank, length of service, etc. **2.** an ornament in this form, as on a molding. **3.** Also called **chev'ron weave'.** HERRINGBONE (def. 2a). **4.** *Heraldry.* an ordinary in the form of an inverted V. —chev'roned, *adj.*

chevrons

chew (chōō), *v.t.* **1.** to crush or grind with the teeth; masticate. **2.** to tear or mangle, as if by chewing (often fol. by *up*): *The sorting machine chewed up the letters.* **3.** to make by or as if by chewing: *The puppy chewed a hole in the rug.* **4.** to meditate on; consider at length (often fol. by *over*): *to chew a problem over in one's mind.* —*v.i.* **5.** to perform the act of masticating. **6. chew out,** *Slang.* to scold harshly. —*n.* **7.** an act or instance of chewing. **8.** something chewed or intended for chewing. —chew'a·ble, *adj.*

chew·a·ble (chōō'ə bəl), *adj.* **1.** capable of being chewed. —*n.* **2.** something meant to be chewed.

chew'ing gum', *n.* a sweetened and flavored preparation for chewing, usu. made of chicle.

che·wink (chi wingk'), *n.* the rufous-sided towhee of E North America, *Pipilo erythrophthalmus.*

chew·y (chōō'ē), *adj.,* **chew·i·er, chew·i·est.** (of food) not easily chewed, esp. because of toughness or stickiness. —chew'i·ness, *n.*

Chey·enne (shī en', -an'), *n., pl.* **-ennes** (*esp. collectively*) **-enne. 1.** a member of a Plains Indian people resident on the upper drainages of the Platte and Arkansas rivers in the mid-19th century: surviving groups live in Montana and Oklahoma. **2.** the Algonquian language of the Cheyenne. **3.** the capital of Wyoming, in the S part. 54,010.

chi·a·ro·scu·ro (kē är'ə skyŏŏr'ō, -skôr'ō), *n., pl.* **-ros. 1.** the distribution of light and shade in a picture. **2.** the use of deep variations in and subtle gradations of light and shade, esp. to enhance the delineation of character and for general dramatic effect. **3.** a woodcut print in which the colors are produced by the use of different blocks with different colors.

chic (shēk), *adj.,* **-er, -est,** *n.* —*adj.* **1.** attractive and fashionable; stylish. —*n.* **2.** style and elegance, esp. in dress.

Chi·ca·go (shi kä'gō, -kô'-), *n.* a city in NE Illinois, on Lake Michigan: third largest city in the U.S. 2,731,743. —Chi·ca'go·an, *n.*

Chica'go Board' of Trade', *n.* a major exchange in the United States that deals in futures, notably of grains and metals. *Abbr.:* CBT

Chica'go Fire', *n.* a three-day fire in Chicago, Ill., in 1871 that largely destroyed the city and took several hundred lives.

Chica'go School', *n.* a group of Chicago architects active between c1880 and c1910 and known for major developments in skyscraper design and for experiments in a modern architectural style appropriate esp. to business and industrial buildings: two of the best-known members were Louis Sullivan and John Wellborn Root.

Chica'go style', *n.* a style of jazz flourishing in Chicago esp. in the early 1920s, constituting a direct offshoot of New Orleans style, and differing from its predecessor chiefly in the diminished influence of native folk sources, the greater tension of its group improvisation, the increased emphasis on solos, and the regular use of the tenor saxophone as part of the ensemble.

Chi·ca·na (chi kä'nə, -kan'ə), *n., pl.* **-nas.** a Mexican-American girl or woman.

chi·can·er·y (shi kā'nə rē, chi-), *n., pl.* **-er·ies. 1.** the use of sly or evasive language, reasoning, etc. to trick or deceive. **2.** a tricky or deceitful maneuver; subterfuge.

Chi·ca·no (chi kä'nō, -kan'ō), *n., pl.* **-nos.** a Mexican-American, esp. a male.

chi·chi (shē'shē'), *adj., n., pl.* **-chis.** —*adj.* **1.** pretentiously elegant or trendy; ostentatious. **2.** fashionable; smart. —*n.* **3.** a chichi person or thing. **4.** chichi quality.

chick (chik), *n.* **1.** a young chicken or other bird. **2.** a child.

chick·a·dee (chik'ə dē'), *n.* any of various North American birds of the genus *Parus*, of the titmouse family, with white cheeks and a dark-colored throat and cap.

Chick·a·mau·ga (chik'ə mô'gə), *n.* a creek in NW Georgia: scene of a Confederate victory 1863.

chick·a·ree (chik'ə rē'), *n.* RED SQUIRREL.

Chick·a·saw (chik'ə sô'), *n., pl.* **-saws,** (*esp. collectively*) **-saw. 1.** a member of an American Indian people orig. of N Mississippi, removed to the Indian Territory in 1837–47. **2.** a dialect of the Muskogean language shared by the Chickasaw and Choctaw.

chick·en (chik'ən), *n.* **1.** a domestic fowl, *Gallus domesticus*, descended from various jungle fowl of SE Asia and developed in a number of breeds for its flesh, eggs, and feathers. **2.** the young of this bird, esp. when less than a year old. **3.** the flesh of the chicken used as food. **4.** *Slang.* **a.** a cowardly or fearful person. **b.** a young or inexperienced person. **5.** a contest that threatens very serious, sometimes fatal consequences if one of the participants makes an error or does not yield. —*adj.* **6.** *Informal.* **a.** cowardly. **b.** frightened. **7.** *Slang.* **a.** petty or trivial: *a chicken regulation.* **b.** obsessed with petty details, regulations, etc. —*v.i.* **8. chicken out,** *Slang.* to withdraw from a commitment, esp. because of fear. —*Proverb.* **9.** Chickens come home to roost, one must eventually pay for one's past sins or errors. —*Saying.* **10. A chicken in every pot,** general prosperity: popularized in the 1928 U.S. presidential campaign.

chick'en feed', *n. Slang.* **1.** an insignificant sum of money. **2.** small change, as pennies and nickels.

chick'en-fried', *adj.* coated with batter or flour and fried: *chicken-fried steak.*

chick'en hawk', *n.* any of various hawks said to prey on poultry.

chick'en·pox' or **chick'en pox',** *n.* a disease, commonly of children, caused by the varicella zoster virus and characterized by fever and the eruption of blisters. Also called **varicella.**

chick'en wire', *n.* a light wire netting having a large hexagonal mesh, used esp. as fencing.

chick·pea (chik'pē'), *n.* **1.** a widely cultivated plant, *Cicer arietinum*, of the legume family, bearing pods containing pealike seeds. **2. chickpeas,** the seeds of this plant, used as a food. Also called **garbanzo.**

chick·weed (chik'wēd'), *n.* any of various plants of the genera *Stellaria* and *Cerastium*, of the pink family, as *S. media*, a common Old World weed whose leaves and seeds are relished by birds.

chic·le (chik'əl), *n.* a gumlike substance obtained from the latex of certain tropical American trees, as the sapodilla, used chiefly in the manufacture of chewing gum. Also called **chic'le gum'.**

chic·o·ry (chik'ə rē), *n., pl.* **-ries. 1.** a composite plant, *Cichorium intybus*, having blue flowers and toothed leaves, cultivated as a salad plant and for its root. Compare ENDIVE (def. 2). **2.** the root of this plant roasted and ground as a substitute for or additive to coffee.

chide (chīd), *v.,* **chid·ed** or **chid** (chid), **chid·ed** or **chid** or **chid·den** (chid'n), **chid·ing.** —*v.t.* **1.** to scold or reproach. **2.** to force by chiding: *to chide someone into apologizing.* —*v.i.* **3.** to find fault. —chid'ing·ly, *adv.*

chief (chēf), *n.* **1.** the head or leader of an organized body: *the chief of police.* **2.** the ruler of a tribe or clan: *an Indian chief.* **3.** *Informal.* BOSS[1]. **4.** the upper area of a heraldic field. —*adj.* **5.** highest in rank or authority. **6.** most important; principal: *the chief difficulty.* —*adv.* —*Idiom.* **7. in chief,** highest in rank (used in combination): *commander in chief.* —chief'dom, *n.*

Chief' Exec'utive, *n.* **1.** the president of the United States. **2.** (*l.c.*) the governor of a U.S. state. **3.** (*l.c.*) the head of a government.

chief' jus'tice, *n.* **1.** the presiding judge of a court having several members. **2.** (*caps.*) Official title, **Chief' Jus'tice of the Unit'ed States'.** the presiding judge of the U.S. Supreme Court.

chief·ly (chēf'lē), *adv.* **1.** primarily; essentially: *wanted chiefly for armed robbery.* **2.** mainly; mostly: *The dish consisted chiefly of noodles.* —*adj.* **3.** of, pertaining to, or like a chief: *chiefly duty.*

C

chief′ mas′ter ser′geant, *n.* the highest noncommissioned officer rank in the U.S. Air Force.

Chief′ of Na′val Opera′tions, *n.* the highest officer in the U.S. Navy and a member of the Joint Chiefs of Staff.

Chief′ of Staff′, *n.* **1.** the senior officer of the U.S. Army or Air Force and a member of the Joint Chiefs of Staff. **2.** (*l.c.*) the senior or principal staff officer in a division or unit of one of the service branches. **3.** (*l.c.*) the head of any staff.

chief′ of state′, *n.* the titular head of a nation, as a president or king.

chief′ pet′ty of′ficer, *n.* a noncommissioned rank in the U.S. Navy or Coast Guard next above petty officer first class. *Abbr.:* CPO

chief•tain (chēf′tən), *n.* **1.** the chief of a clan or a tribe. **2.** a leader of a group, band, etc.: *the robbers' chieftain.*

chief′ war′rant of′ficer, *n.* a warrant officer ranking immediately below a second lieutenant or ensign in the armed forces.

chiff•chaff (chif′chaf′, -chäf′), *n.* a greenish brown Old World warbler, *Phylloscopus collybita.*

chif•fon (shi fon′, shif′on), *n.* **1.** a sheer fabric of silk, nylon, or rayon. **2.** an ornamental ribbon, lace, etc., for a woman's dress. —*adj.* **3.** made of chiffon fabric. **4.** (of pies, cakes, etc.) having a light, fluffy texture, as from the addition of beaten egg whites.

chif•fo•nade (shif′ə nād′, -näd′), *n.* a mixture of vegetables or herbs cut into fine strips for use in soups, salads, etc.

chif•fo•nier or **chif•fon•nier** (shif′ə nēr′), *n.* **1.** a high chest of drawers, often with a mirror on top. **2.** a cabinet often combining open shelves with drawers or a closed cupboard below, for storage and display, as of books or china.

chif•fo•robe (shif′ə rōb′, shif′rōb′), *n.* a piece of furniture having both drawers and space for hanging clothes.

chig•ger (chig′ər), *n.* **1.** Also called **harvest mite.** the six-legged, bloodsucking larva of a mite of the family Trombiculidae, parasitic on humans and other mammals. **2.** CHIGOE.

chi•gnon (shēn′yon), *n.* a large smooth twist, roll, or knot of hair worn by women at the nape of the neck or the back of the head.

chig•oe (chig′ō), *n.* a flea, *Tunga penetrans,* of tropical America and Africa, the impregnated female of which embeds itself in the skin, esp. of the feet, of humans and animals and becomes greatly distended with eggs. Also called **chig′oe flea′, chigger, jigger, sand flea.**

child (chīld), *n., pl.* **chil•dren. 1.** a young boy or girl. **2.** a son or daughter. **3.** a baby or infant. **4.** a person who behaves in a childish manner. **5.** a descendant. **6.** any person or thing regarded as the product of particular circumstances or influences: *children of poverty; Abstract art is a child of the 20th century.* —*Idiom.* **7. great** or **big with child,** (of a human female) being in the late stages of pregnancy. **8. with child,** (of a human female) pregnant. —*Proverb.* **9. The child is father of the man,** adult characteristics are determined in childhood. —**child′less,** *adj.*

child′ abuse′, *n.* beating, neglect, or other mistreatment of a child by a parent or guardian.

child•bear•ing (chīld′bâr′ing), *n.* **1.** the act of producing or bringing forth children. —*adj.* **2.** capable of, suitable for, or relating to the bearing of a child or of children: *the childbearing years.*

child•bed (chīld′bed′), *n.* the condition of giving birth; parturition.

child•birth (chīld′bûrth′), *n.* an act or instance of bringing forth a child; parturition.

child•hood (chīld′hŏŏd′), *n.* **1.** the state or period of being a child. **2.** the early stage in the existence of something.

child•ish (chīl′dish), *adj.* **1.** of, like, or appropriate for a child: *childish games.* **2.** immature; foolish: *childish fears.* —**child′ish•ly,** *adv.*

child′ la′bor, *n.* the gainful employment of children below an age determined by law or custom.

child•like (chīld′līk′), *adj.* like or befitting a child: *childlike trust.*

child•ly (chīld′lē), *adj.* childlike.

child′proof′ or **child′-proof′,** *adj.* **1.** incapable of being opened, tampered with, or operated by a child. **2.** made free of hazard for a child. —*v.t.* **3.** to make childproof.

chil•dren (chil′drən), *n.* pl. of CHILD.

Chil′dren, Go′ Where′ I′ Send′ Thee′, a traditional American spiritual.

chil′dren of Is′rael, *n.pl.* the Hebrews; Jews.

child′s′ play′, *n.* something very easily done.

Chil•e (chil′ē), *n.* a republic in SW South America, on the Pacific Coast. 14,508,168; 286,396 sq. mi. (741,765 sq. km). *Cap.:* Santiago. —**Chil′e•an,** *adj., n.*

chil•e (or **chil′i**) **rel•le•no** (rə yā′nō, rəl yā′-), *n., pl.* **chil•es** (or **chil•is**) **rel•le•nos** (-nōz, -nōs). a green chili pepper stuffed with cheese or meat, dipped in batter, and fried.

chil•i (or **chil•e** (chil′ē), *n., pl.* **chil•ies** or **chil•es. 1.** Also called **chili pepper.** the pungent pod of any of several species of *Capsicum,* esp. *C. annuum longum:* used in cooking. **2.** CHILI CON CARNE. **3.** a dish similar to chili con carne but containing no beans.

chil•i (or **chil•e**) **con car′ne** (kon kär′nē), *n.* a highly seasoned dish made with ground or diced beef, chilies or chili powder, and often tomatoes and beans.

chil′i dog′ or **chil′i•dog′,** *n.* a hot dog topped with chili con carne.

chil′i pep′per, *n.* CHILI (def. 1).

chil′i pow′der, *n.* a powdered mixture of dried chilies, cumin, oregano, garlic, etc., used as a seasoning.

chil′i sauce′, *n.* a sauce of tomatoes cooked with chili peppers and spices.

chill (chil), *n.* **1.** an uncomfortably penetrating coldness. **2.** a sensation of cold, usu. with shivering. **3.** a sudden fear or alarm. **4.** a depressing influence or feeling: *His presence cast a chill over everyone.* **5.** unfriendliness; coolness. —*adj.* **6.** moderately cold; chilly. **7.** discouraging: *chill prospects.* **8.** distant or aloof; unfriendly. —*v.i.* **9.** to become cold. **10.** to be seized with a chill. —*v.t.* **11.** to affect with cold. **12.** to make cool: *Chill the wine before serving.* **13.** to depress; discourage; disturb. —**chill′ing•ly,** *adv.* —**chill′ness,** *n.*

chill•er (chil′ər), *n.* **1.** one that chills. **2.** a frightening or suspenseful story or film. **3.** a device for cooling or refrigerating.

chill′ fac′tor, *n.* WINDCHILL FACTOR.

chill′ing effect′, *n.* a discouraging or deterring effect, esp. one resulting from a restrictive law or regulation.

chill•y (chil′ē), *adj.,* **chill•i•er, chill•i•est,** *adv.* —*adj.* **1.** cool enough to cause shivering: *a chilly breeze.* **2.** feeling cold; sensitive to cold: *chilly hands.* **3.** without warmth of feeling: *a chilly reply.* **4.** frightening; disturbing. —**chill′i•ness,** *n.*

chi•lom•o•nad (kī lom′ə nad′), *n.* any colorless alga of the genus *Chilomonas,* common in stagnant waters and resembling a protozoan.

chi•lo•pod (kī′lə pod′), *n.* any arthropod of the class Chilopoda, comprising the centipedes. —**chi•lop′o•dous** (-lop′ə dəs), *adj.*

chi•mae•ra (ki mēr′ə, kī-), *n., pl.* **-ras. 1.** any fish of the family Chimaeridae, the male of which has a spiny clasping organ over the mouth. **2.** CHIMERA.

chime[1] (chīm), *n., v.,* **chimed, chim•ing.** —*n.* **1.** an apparatus for striking one or more bells, as a doorbell at the front door of a house. **2.** Often, **chimes. a.** a set of bells or of slabs of metal, stone, wood, etc., producing musical tones when struck. **b.** a musical instrument consisting of such a set, esp. a glockenspiel. **c.** the musical tone thus produced. **d.** CARILLON. **3.** harmonious sound in general; music; melody. **4.** harmonious relation; accord. —*v.i.* **5.** to sound harmoniously or in chimes, as a set of bells: *The church bells chimed at noon.* **6.** to produce a musical sound by striking a bell, gong, etc.; ring chimes: *The doorbell chimed.* **7.** to harmonize; agree. —*v.t.* **8.** to give forth (music, sound, etc.), as a bell or bells. **9.** to strike (a bell, set of bells, etc.) so as to produce musical sound. **10.** to indicate, announce, etc., by chiming: *Bells chimed the hour.* **11.** to speak in cadence or singsong. **12. chime in, a.** to enter a conversation, esp. to interrupt. **b.** to be compatible; agree (often fol. by *with*). **c.** to say or speak by chiming in (often fol. by *with*): *to chime in with a warning.* —**chim′er,** *n.*

chime[2] (chīm), *n.* the brim of a cask or barrel.

chi•me•ra or **chi•mae•ra** (ki mēr′ə, kī-), *n., pl.* **-ras. 1.** (*often cap.*) a monster of classical myth, with a lion's head, a goat's body, and a serpent's tail. **2.** any grotesque imaginary creature. **3.** a fancy or dream; an imagining. **4.** an organism composed of two or more genetically distinct tissues. —**chi•mer′i•cal** (-mer′i kəl, -mēr′-), *adj.*

chi•mi•chan•ga (chim′ē chäng′gə), *n., pl.* **-gas.** a deep-fried flour tortilla rolled around a filling.

chim•ney (chim′nē), *n., pl.* **-neys. 1.** a structure, usu. vertical, containing a passage by which the smoke, gases, etc., of a fire or furnace are carried off. **2.** the part of such a structure that rises above a roof. **3.** the smokestack or funnel of a locomotive, steamship, etc. **4.** a tube, usu. of glass, surrounding the flame of a lamp.

chim′ney pot′, *n.* an earthenware or metal pipe atop a chimney, esp. to increase the draft and disperse smoke.

chim′ney sweep′ (or **sweep′er**), *n.* a person whose work it is to clean the soot from the insides of chimneys.

chimp (chimp), *n.* a chimpanzee.

chim•pan•zee (chim′pan zē′, chim pan′zē), *n.* a large anthropoid ape, *Pan troglodytes,* of equatorial Africa, having a dark coat and a relatively bare face.

chin (chin), *n., v.,* **chinned, chin•ning.** —*n.* **1.** the lower extremity of the face, below the mouth. **2.** the prominence of the lower jaw. —*v.t.* **3.** to grasp an overhead bar and pull (oneself) upward until the chin is above or level with the bar: done as an exercise. **4.** to raise or hold to the chin, as a violin. —*v.i.* **5.** to perform chin-ups. **6.** *Slang.* to talk; chatter. —*Idiom.* **7. keep one's chin up,** to maintain one's courage and optimism during a period of adversity. **8. lead with one's chin,** to expose one's most vulnerable point to danger in order to show one's confidence. **9. take it on the chin,** *Informal.* **a.** to be defeated thoroughly. **b.** to endure punishment stoically.

chi•na (chī′nə), *n.* **1.** a translucent ceramic material, orig. imported from China; porcelain. **2.** any porcelain or ceramic tableware. **3.** figurines made of porcelain or ceramic material collectively.

Chi•na (chī′nə), *n.* **1. People's Republic of,** a country in E Asia. 1,221,591,778; 3,691,502 sq. mi. (9,560,990 sq. km). *Cap.:* Beijing. **2. Republic of,** a republic consisting mainly of the island of Taiwan off the SE coast of mainland China: under Nationalist control since 1948 but claimed by the People's Republic of China. 19,700,000; 13,885 sq. mi. (35,960 sq. km). *Cap.:* Taipei.

Chi•na as′ter, *n.* an asterlike composite plant, *Callistephus chinensis,* cultivated in numerous varieties having white, yellow, blue, red, or purple flowers.

chi′na bark′ (kī′nə, kē′nə), *n.* CINCHONA (def. 1).

chi·na·ber·ry (chī′nə ber′ē), *n., pl.* **-ries.** a tree, *Melia azedarach,* of the mahogany family, native to Asia but widely planted elsewhere for its ornamental yellow fruits and long clusters of fragrant purplish flowers. Also called **China tree.**

chi′na clos′et, *n.* a cabinet or cupboard for storing or exhibiting chinaware. Also called **chi′na cab′inet.**

Chi′na rose′, *n.* **1.** a rose, *Rosa chinensis,* of China, with crimson, pink, or white flowers. **2.** HIBISCUS (def. 1).

Chi′na tree′, *n.* CHINABERRY.

chin·bone (chin′bōn′), *n.* the anterior portion of the mandible, forming the prominence of the chin.

chinch′ bug′, *n.* a small lygaeid bug, *Blissus leucopterus,* that feeds on corn, wheat, and other grains.

chin·che·rin·chee (chin′chə rin chē′, -rin′chē, ching′kə-), *n.* a bulbous plant, *Ornithogalum thyrsoides,* of the lily family, native to S Africa, having dense clusters of cream-colored or white flowers.

chin·chil·la (chin chil′ə), *n., pl.* **-las. 1.** a small South American rodent, *Chinchilla laniger,* raised for its silvery gray fur. **2.** this fur. **3.** a woolen coat fabric with a curly nap.

Chin′coteague po′ny, *n.* a wild pony found on islands off the Virginia coast, apparently descended from shipwrecked Moorish ponies.

chine (chīn), *n., v.,* **chined, chin·ing.** —*n.* **1.** the backbone or spine, esp. of an animal. **2.** the angular intersection of the bottom and sides of a boat. —*v.t.* **3.** (in butchering) to sever the backbone of.

Chi·nese (chī nēz′, -nēs′), *n., pl.* **-nese,** *adj.* —*n.* **1.** a native or inhabitant of China. **2.** a Sino-Tibetan language or language family, comprising a wide variety of speech forms, many mutually unintelligible, that are traditionally labeled dialects, and are written with identical logographic characters. **3.** a member of the people who speak Chinese, collectively representing the great majority of the inhabitants of China and Taiwan, and forming a significant population element in Singapore, Thailand, Malaysia, Indonesia, and other countries of Southeast Asia. —*adj.* **4.** of or pertaining to China or its inhabitants. **5.** of or pertaining to the language Chinese or its speakers.

Chi′nese box′es, *n.pl.* a matched set of boxes, usu. decorated, that decrease in size so that each box fits inside the next larger one.

Chi′nese cab′bage, *n.* a plant, *Brassica rapa pekinensis,* of the mustard family, forming a long, dense head of broad, whitish leaves, used as a vegetable. Also called **celery cabbage.**

Chi′nese check′ers, *n.* (*used with a sing. v.*) a board game for two to six players in which marbles set in holes are moved to the opposite side of the board, a six-pointed star.

Chi′nese chest′nut, *n.* an Asian chestnut, *Castanea mollissima,* that is resistant to the chestnut blight.

Chi′nese Chip′pendale, *n.* a style of Chippendale furniture using Chinese or quasi-Chinese motifs.

Chi′nese date′, *n.* **1.** an Old World tree, *Ziziphus jujuba,* of the buckthorn family, that thrives in hot, dry regions. **2.** the edible plumlike fruit of this tree. Also called **jujube.**

Chi′nese Em′pire, *n.* China under the rule of various imperial dynasties: replaced by a republic in 1912.

Chi′nese ev′ergreen, *n.* a tropical Asian plant, *Aglaonema modestum,* of the arum family, often grown indoors for its glossy foliage.

Chi′nese gel′atin, *n.* AGAR (def. 1). Also called **Chi′nese i′singlass.**

Chi′nese goose′berry, *n.* a Chinese climbing shrub, *Actinidia chinensis,* of the family Actinidiaceae, cultivated in New Zealand for its edible fruit. Compare KIWI (def. 2).

Chi′nese lan′tern, *n.* a collapsible lantern of thin colored paper, often used for decorative lighting.

Chi′nese lan′tern plant′, *n.* a Eurasian ground cherry, *Physalis alkekengi,* of the nightshade family, bearing fruit enclosed in an orange-red inflated calyx.

Chi′nese pars′ley, *n.* CORIANDER (def. 1).

Chi′nese rad′ish, *n.* DAIKON.

Chinese′ Revolu′tion, *n.* **1.** the revolution in China in 1911, resulting in the overthrow of the Manchu dynasty and in the establishment of a republic in 1912. **2.** the events that culminated in the establishment of the People's Republic of China in 1949.

chink¹ (chingk), *n.* **1.** a crack or fissure: *a chink in a wall.* **2.** a narrow opening: *a chink between two buildings.* —*v.t.* **3.** to fill up chinks in.

chink² (chingk), *v.i., v.t.* **1.** to make or cause to make a short, sharp, ringing sound, as of glasses striking together. —*n.* **2.** a chinking sound.

chi·no (chē′nō), *n., pl.* **-nos. 1.** a twilled cotton cloth, often dyed khaki, used for uniforms, sportswear, etc. **2.** Usu., **chinos.** trousers of this cloth.

chi·noi·se·rie (shēn wä′zə rē, -wä′zə rē′), *n.* (*sometimes cap.*) **1.** a style of ornamentation using motifs identified as Chinese. **2.** an object decorated in this style.

Chi·nook (shi nŏŏk′, -nōŏk′, chi-), *n., pl.* **-nooks,** (*esp. collectively*) **-nook. 1. a.** a member of an American Indian people aboriginally inhabiting the N shore of the mouth of the Columbia River. **b.** a member of any of a group of peoples including the Chinook of the Columbia River mouth and related peoples to the S and W. **c.** either of two languages spoken by these peoples, one, now extinct, spoken on both sides of the Columbia estuary and the other spoken W of the estuary. **2.** (*l.c.*) a warm, dry wind that blows at intervals down the E slopes of the Rocky Mountains. —**Chi·nook′an,** *adj.*

chinook′ salm′on, *n.* a large salmon, *Oncorhynchus tshawytscha,* of the N Pacific Ocean. Also called **king salmon.**

chin·qua·pin (ching′kə pin), *n.* **1.** a shrubby chestnut, *Castanea pumila,* of the southeastern U.S., having toothed, oblong leaves and small edible nuts. **2.** a Pacific coast evergreen tree, *Castanopsis chrysophylla,* of the beech family, having deeply furrowed bark, dark green lance-shaped leaves, and inedible nuts. **3.** the nut of either of these trees.

chintz (chints), *n.* **1.** a cotton fabric, usu. glazed and often printed in bright patterns, used for apparel, draperies, slipcovers, etc. **2.** a painted or stained calico from India.

chintz·y (chint′sē), *adj.,* **chintz·i·er, chintz·i·est. 1.** of, like, or decorated with chintz. **2.** cheap, inferior, or gaudy. **3.** stingy; miserly.

chin′-up′, *n.* an act of chinning a horizontal bar or the like.

chip¹ (chip), *n., v.,* **chipped, chip·ping.** —*n.* **1.** a small, slender piece, as of wood, separated by chopping or breaking. **2.** a small piece of food, candy, etc.: *chocolate chips.* **3.** a flaw made by the breaking off or gouging out of a small piece: *This glass has a chip.* **4.** any of the small round disks, used as tokens for money in roulette, poker, and some other gambling games; counter. **5.** Also called **microchip.** a tiny slice of semiconducting material on which a transistor or an integrated circuit is formed. **6.** anything trivial or worthless. **7.** a piece of dried dung: *buffalo chips.* **8.** *Tennis.* a softly sliced return shot with heavy backspin. —*v.t.* **9.** to hew or cut with an ax, chisel, etc. **10.** to break off or gouge out (a bit or fragment): *to chip a piece of ice from a large block.* **11.** to cut or break a bit or fragment from: *to chip a tooth.* **12.** to shape or produce by cutting or flaking away pieces: *to chip a figure out of wood.* **13.** *Tennis.* to slice (a ball) on a return shot, producing backspin. —*v.i.* **14.** to break off in small pieces. **15.** to make a chip shot. **16. chip in, a.** to contribute: *We each chipped in five dollars.* **b.** to share a cost or burden by giving money, aid, or the like: *to chip in on a birthday cake.* —*Idiom.* **17. chip off the old block,** a person who strongly resembles one parent in appearance or behavior. **18. chip on one's shoulder,** a readiness to quarrel. **19. when the chips are down,** when the need for support is greatest, as during a disaster or crisis. **20. let the chips fall where they may,** to take action and disregard the consequences.

chip² (chip), *v.,* **chipped, chip·ping,** *n.* —*v.i.* **1.** to chirp or squeak; cheep. —*n.* **2.** a chirp or squeak; cheep.

chip·board (chip′bôrd′, -bōrd′), *n.* **1.** a thin, stiff sheet material made from wastepaper. **2.** a type of board made from compressed waste wood bound together with synthetic resin.

chip·munk (chip′mungk), *n.* any small, striped North American and Asian ground squirrel of the genera *Tamias* and *Eutamias.*

chipmunk, *Tamias striatus,*
head and body 6 in. (15 cm);
tail 4 in. (10 cm)

chip·per¹ (chip′ər), *adj.* marked by or being in sprightly good humor and health; jaunty.

chip·per² (chip′ər), *v.i.,* to chirp or twitter.

chip·per³ (chip′ər), *n.* a person or thing that chips or cuts.

Chip·pe·wa (chip′ə wä′, -wā′, -wə), *n., pl.* **-was,** (*esp. collectively*) **-wa.** the Ojibwa, esp. Ojibwas of the U.S.

chip′ping spar′row, *n.* a small, clear-breasted North American sparrow, *Spizella passerina.*

chi·ral (kī′rəl), *adj.* not able to be superimposed on its mirror image: *chiral molecules.* —**chi·ral·i·ty,** *n.*

chiro-, a combining form meaning "hand": *chiromancy.*

chi·rog·ra·phy (kī rog′rə fē), *n.* handwriting; penmanship. —**chi·rog′ra·pher,** *n.* —**chi′ro·graph′ic** (-rə graf′ik), *adj.*

chi·ro·man·cy (kī′rə man′sē), *n.* PALMISTRY. —**chi′ro·man′cer,** *n.*

chi·rop·o·dist (ki rop′ə dist, kī- *or, often,* shə-), *n.* PODIATRIST.

chi·rop·o·dy (ki rop′ə dē, kī- *or, often,* shə-), *n.* PODIATRY.

chi·ro·prac·tic (kī′rə prak′tik), *n.* a therapeutic system based upon adjusting the segments of the spinal column. —**chi′ro·prac′tor,** *n.*

chi·rop·ter (kī rop′tər), *n.* any mammal of the order Chiroptera, comprising the bats. —**chi·rop′ter·an,** *n., adj.*

chirp (chûrp), *n.* **1.** the short, sharp sound made by small birds and certain insects. **2.** any similar sound, esp. of a cheerful, excited tone. —*v.i.* **3.** to make the sound of a chirp. —*v.t.* **4.** to say or express with such a sound. —**chirp′er,** *n.*

chirp·y (chûr′pē), *adj.,* **chirp·i·er, chirp·i·est. 1.** chirping or tending to chirp: *chirpy birds.* **2.** cheerful; lively; gay. —**chirp′i·ly,** *adv.*

chirr (chûr), *v.,* **chirred, chirr·ing,** *n.* —*v.i.* **1.** to make a characteristic shrill, trilling sound, as a grasshopper does. —*n.* **2.** the sound of chirring.

chis·el (chiz′əl), *n., v.,* **-eled, -el·ing** or (*esp. Brit.*) **-elled, -el·ling.** —*n.* **1.** a wedgelike tool with a cutting edge at the end of the blade, often made of steel, used for cutting or shaping wood, stone, etc. **2.**

CHISEL PLOW. —*v.t.* **3.** to cut, shape, or fashion by or as if by carving with a chisel. **4.** *Slang.* **a.** to cheat or swindle (someone). **b.** to get by cheating or trickery. —*v.i.* **5.** to work with a (chisel). **6.** *Slang.* to trick; cheat. —**chis′el·er;** *esp. Brit.,* **chis′el·ler,** *n.*

chis·eled (chiz′əld) *adj.* **1.** cut, shaped, etc., with a chisel: *chiseled stone.* **2.** sharply or clearly shaped; clear-cut: *a finely chiseled profile.* Also, *esp. Brit.,* **chis′elled.**

chis′el plow′, *n.* a soil tillage device pulled by a tractor or animal, used to break up and stir soil a foot or more beneath the surface without turning it.

Chis·holm (chiz′əm), *n.* **1. Shirley (Anita St. Hill),** born 1924, U.S. politician: congresswoman 1969–83; first black woman elected to the House of Representatives. **2. Thomas (Obadiah),** 1866–1960, U.S. hymn writer.

Chis′holm Trail′, *n.* a cattle trail leading N from San Antonio, Tex., to Abilene, Kan.: used for about 20 years after the Civil War. [after Jesse *Chisholm* (1806–68), a scout]

Chi·şi·nă·u (*Romanian.* kē′shē nu′ōō), *n.* the capital of Moldova, in the central part. 700,000. Russian, **Kishinev.**

chi′-square′ (or **chi′-squared′**) **test′,** *n.* a test that uses the quantity chi-square for testing the mathematical fit of a frequency curve to an observed frequency distribution.

chit (chit), *n.* **1.** a signed note for money owed for food, drink, etc. **2.** any receipt, voucher, or similar document, esp. of an informal nature.

chit·chat (chit′chat′), *n., v.,* **-chat·ted, -chat·ting.** —*n.* **1.** light conversation; casual talk; gossip. —*v.i.* **2.** to converse lightly or casually.

chi·tin (kī′tin), *n.* a nitrogen-containing polysaccharide, related chemically to cellulose, that forms a semitransparent horny substance and is a principal constituent of the exoskeleton, or outer covering, of insects, crustaceans, and arachnids. —**chi′tin·ous,** *adj.* —**chi′tin·oid′,** *adj.*

chi·ton (kīt′n, kī′ton), *n.* **1.** any marine mollusk of the class Amphineura, having a dorsal shell of eight overlapping plates. **2.** a gown or tunic worn by both sexes in ancient Greece.

chit·ter (chit′ər), *v.i.* to twitter.

chit·ter·lings or **chit·lings** or **chit·lins** (chit′linz, -lingz), *n.* (*used with a sing. or pl. v.*) the small intestine of swine, esp. when prepared as food.

chiv·al·ry (shiv′al rē), *n.* **1.** the combination of qualities expected of a knight, including courage, generosity, and courtesy. **2.** the institution or customs of medieval knighthood. **3.** a group of knights or gallant gentlemen. —**chiv′al·rous,** *adj.*

chive (chīv), *n.* a small bulbous plant, *Allium schoenoprasum,* related to the leek and onion.

chiv·vy or **chiv·y** (chiv′ē), *v.,* **chiv·vied** or **chiv·ied, chiv·vy·ing** or **chiv·y·ing,** *n., pl.* **chiv·vies** or **chiv·ies.** *Brit.* —*v.t.* **1.** to chase; run after. **2.** to harass; torment. —*v.i.* **3.** to run; scamper. —*n.* **4.** a hunting cry. **5.** a hunt, chase, or pursuit.

chla·myd·i·a (klə mid′ē ə), *n., pl.* **-mid·i·ae** (-mid′ē ē′). **1.** any rickettsia of the genus *Chlamydia,* parasitic in birds and mammals, including humans, and causing various infections. **2.** a widespread, often asymptomatic sexually transmitted disease caused by *Chlamydia trachomatis.*

chlo·as·ma (klō az′mə), *n.* a condition in which light brown spots occur on the skin, caused by exposure to sun, dyspepsia, or certain specific diseases.

chlor·dane (klôr′dān, klōr′-) also **chlor·dan** (-dan), *n.* a colorless, toxic liquid, $C_{10}H_6Cl_8$, used as an insecticide.

chlo·rel·la (klə rel′ə), *n., pl.* **-las.** any of the freshwater unicellular green algae of the genus *Chlorella.*

chlo·ric (klôr′ik, klōr′-), *adj.* containing pentavalent chlorine.

chlo·ride (klôr′īd, -id, klōr′-), *n.* **1.** a salt of hydrochloric acid consisting of two elements, one of which is chlorine, as sodium chloride, NaCl. **2.** a compound containing chlorine, as methyl chloride, $CH_3Cl.$

chlo·ri·nate (klôr′ə nāt′, klōr′-), *v.t.,* **-nat·ed, -nat·ing.** **1.** to combine or treat with chlorine, esp. for disinfecting. **2.** to introduce chlorine atoms into (an organic compound) by addition or substitution. —**chlo′ri·na′tion,** *n.* —**chlo′ri·na′tor,** *n.*

chlo·rine (klôr′ēn, -in, klōr′-), *n.* a halogen element, a heavy, greenish yellow poisonous gas: used to purify water and to make bleach and various chemicals. *Symbol:* Cl; *at. wt.:* 35.453; *at. no.:* 17.

chlo·rite (klôr′īt, klōr′-), *n.* a salt containing the ClO_2 group.

chloro-, a combining form meaning "green": *chlorophyll.*

chlo·ro·fluor·o·car·bon (klôr′ō floor′ō kär′bən, -flôr′-; klōr′ō floor′-ō kär′bən, -flōr′-), *n.* any of several compounds of carbon, fluorine, chlorine, and hydrogen, used chiefly as refrigerants and formerly as aerosol propellants.

chlo·ro·form (klôr′ə fôrm′, klōr′-), *n.* **1.** a colorless volatile liquid, $CHCl_3,$ used chiefly in medicine as a solvent and formerly as an anesthetic. —*v.t.* **2.** to administer chloroform to, esp. in order to anesthetize, make unconscious, or kill. —**chlo′ro·for′mic,** *adj.*

chlo·ro·phyll or **chlo·ro·phyl** (klôr′ə fil, klōr′-), *n.* the green pigment of plant leaves and algae, essential to their production of carbohydrates by photosynthesis. —**chlo′ro·phyl′lous** (-fil′əs), **chlo′ro·phyl′lose** (-ōs), *adj.*

chlo·ro·plast (klôr′ə plast′, klōr′-), *n.* a plastid containing chlorophyll. —**chlo′ro·plas′tic,** *adj.*

chlo·ro·sis (klô rō′sis, klō-), *n.* **1.** an abnormally yellow color of plant tissues, resulting from partial failure to develop chlorophyll. **2.** Also called **greensickness.** a benign iron-deficiency anemia in adolescent girls, marked by a pale yellow-green complexion. —**chlo·rot′ic** (-rot′ik), *adj.* —**chlo·rot′i·cal·ly,** *adv.*

chock (chok), *n.* **1.** a wedge or block of wood, metal, or the like, for filling in a space, holding an object steady, etc. **2.** a heavy metal fitting on a deck or wharf that serves as a fairlead for a cable or chain. —*v.t.* **3.** to furnish with or secure by a chock or chocks. **4.** to place (a boat) upon chocks. —*adv.* **5.** as close or tight as possible: *chock against the edge.*

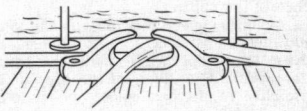

chock (def. 2)

chock·a·block or **chock-a-block** (chok′ə blok′), *adj.* **1.** extremely full; crowded; jammed. **2.** *Naut.* having the blocks drawn close together, as when the tackle is hauled to the utmost. —*adv.* **3.** in a crowded way; closely; tightly.

chock-full (chok′fŏŏl′, chuk′-), *adj.* full to the limit; crammed. Sometimes, **chock′-ful′, chock′full′.**

choc·o·hol·ic (chô′kə hô′lik, -hol′ik, chok′ə-), *n.* a person who is excessively fond of chocolate.

choc·o·late (chô′kə lit, chok′ə-, chôk′lit, chok′-), *n.* **1.** a preparation of the roasted, husked, and ground seeds of cacao, often sweetened and flavored, as with vanilla. **2.** a candy made from or coated with such a preparation. **3.** a syrup or flavoring made from such a preparation. **4.** a hot or cold beverage made by dissolving such a preparation in milk or water. **5.** a dark brown color. —*adj.* **6.** made or flavored with chocolate. **7.** having the color of chocolate; dark-brown. —**choc′o·lat·y, choc′o·lat·ey,** *adj.*

Choc·taw (chok′tô), *n., pl.* **-taws,** (*esp. collectively*) **-taw. 1.** a member of an American Indian people orig. of central and S Mississippi, removed in large part to the Indian Territory in 1831–33. **2.** a dialect of the Muskogean language shared by the Chickasaw and Choctaw.

choice (chois), *n., adj.,* **choic·er, choic·est.** —*n.* **1.** an act or instance of choosing; selection: *a wise choice of friends.* **2.** the right, power, or opportunity to choose; option. **3.** the person or thing chosen or eligible to be chosen: *Blue is my choice for the rug.* **4.** an alternative. **5.** an abundance or variety from which to choose: *a wide choice of styles.* **6.** something that is preferred or preferable to others; the best part. —*adj.* **7.** worthy of being chosen; excellent. **8.** carefully selected: *choice words.* **9.** (of meat) of or designating a grade between prime and good or prime and select. —*Idiom.* **10. of choice,** that is generally preferred: *the treatment of choice.* —**choice′ness,** *n.*

choir (kwīᵊr), *n.* **1.** a company of singers, esp. an organized group employed in church service. **2.** any group of musicians or musical instruments; a musical company or band, or a division of one: *string choir.* **3. a.** the part of a church occupied by the singers of the choir. **b.** the part of a cruciform church east of the crossing. **4.** (in medieval angelology) one of the orders of angels. —*v.t., v.i.* **5.** to sing or sound in chorus. [< Old French *cuer* < Latin *chorus* chorus]

choir′ loft′, *n.* a gallery in a church used by the choir.

choir·mas·ter (kwīᵊr′mas′tər, -mä′stər), *n.* the director of a choir.

choke (chōk), *v.,* **choked, chok·ing,** *n.* —*v.t.* **1.** to stop the breath of by squeezing or obstructing the windpipe; strangle; stifle. **2.** to stop by or as if by strangling or stifling: *The sudden wind choked his words.* **3.** to stop by filling; obstruct; clog: *Grease choked the drain.* **4.** to suppress (a feeling, emotion, etc.) (often fol. by *back* or *down*): *to choke back one's sobs.* **5.** to fill to the limit; pack: *The closet was choked with toys.* **6.** to enrich the fuel mixture of (an internal-combustion engine) by diminishing the air supply to the carburetor. **7.** to grip (a bat, racket, or the like) farther than usual from the end of the handle (often fol. by *up*). —*v.i.* **8.** to suffer from or as if from strangling or suffocating: *to choke on a peanut.* **9.** to become obstructed, clogged, or otherwise stopped: *The words choked in her throat.* **10.** to become too tense or nervous to perform well (sometimes fol. by *up*). **11. choke off,** to stop or obstruct by or as if by choking: *to choke off a nation's fuel supply.* **12. choke up,** to become or cause to become speechless, as from emotion or stress. —*n.* **13.** the act or sound of choking. **14.** any mechanism that regulates flow by blocking a passage, esp. the device in an automotive engine that controls how much air enters the carburetor. **15.** the bristly inner part of an artichoke head.

choke·ber·ry (chōk′ber′ē, -bə rē), *n., pl.* **-ries. 1.** any of several North American shrubs belonging to the genus *Aronia,* of the rose family. **2.** the red, purple, or black berrylike fruit of these shrubs.

choke·cher·ry (chōk′cher′ē), *n., pl.* **-ries.** *Chiefly Northern U.S.* **1.** any of several cherries, esp. *Prunus virginiana,* of North America, that bear an astringent fruit. **2.** the fruit itself.

choke′ col′lar, *n.* a nooselike collar for controlling untrained or powerful dogs. Also called **choke′ chain′.**

choke·point (chōk′point′), *n.* a place of greatest congestion and often hazard; bottleneck.

chok·er (chō′kər), *n.* **1.** one that chokes. **2.** something fitting snugly around the neck, as a necklace or high collar.

chol·er (kol′ər), *n.* **1.** irascibility; anger; wrath; irritability. **2.** YELLOW BILE.

chol·er·a (kol′ər ə), *n.* a severe contagious infection of the small intestine characterized by profuse watery diarrhea and dehydration, caused by *Vibrio cholerae* bacteria, and commonly transmitted through contaminated drinking water.

chol·er·ic (kol′ər ik, kə ler′ik), *adj.* extremely irritable or easily angered; irascible: *a choleric disposition.* —**chol′er·i·cal·ly, chol′er·ic·ly,** *adv.*

cho·les·ter·ol (kə les′tə rōl′, -rôl′), *n.* a sterol, $C_{27}H_{46}O$, abundant in animal fats, brain and nerve tissue, meat, and eggs, that functions in the body as a membrane constituent and as a precursor of steroid hormones: high levels in the blood are associated with arteriosclerosis and gallstones.

cho·line (kō′lēn, kol′ēn), *n.* a viscous fluid, $C_5H_{14}N^+O$, that is a constituent of lecithin and a primary component of the neurotransmitter acetylcholine: one of the B complex vitamins.

cho·lin·er·gic (kō′lə nûr′jik, kol′ə-), *adj.* **1.** resembling acetylcholine in physiological effect: *a cholinergic drug.* **2.** releasing acetylcholine: *a cholinergic neuron.* **3.** activated by acetylcholine or a substance with a similar effect: *a cholinergic receptor.*

cho·lin·es·ter·ase (kō′lə nes′tə rās′, -rāz′, kol′ə-), *n.* an enzyme, found esp. in the heart, brain, and blood, that hydrolyzes acetylcholine to acetic acid and choline.

chol·la (choi′ə), *n., pl.* **-las.** any of several cylindrical treelike cacti of the genus *Opuntia,* of Mexico and the southwestern U.S., having yellow spines.

Chom·sky (chom′skē), *n.* **(Avram) Noam** (nōm, nō′əm), born 1928, U.S. linguist and political writer. —**Chom′sky·an,** *adj., n.*

chon·drite (kon′drīt), *n.* a stony meteorite containing chondrules. —**chon·drit′ic** (-drit′ik), *adj.*

chon·dro·ma (kon drō′mə), *n., pl.* **-mas, -ma·ta** (-mə tə). a benign cartilaginous tumor or growth. —**chon·dro′ma·tous,** *adj.*

chon·drule (kon′drōōl), *n.* a small round mass of olivine or pyroxene found in stony meteorites.

choose (chōōz), *v.,* **chose, cho·sen, choos·ing.** —*v.t.* **1.** to select from a number of possibilities: *She chose July for her wedding.* **2.** to prefer or decide (to do something): *to choose to speak.* **3.** to want or desire, as one thing over another. —*v.i.* **4.** to make a choice: *to choose carefully.* **5.** to be inclined: *Stay or go, as you choose.* **6. choose up, a.** to select the team members of: *In the playground they chose up sides before the game.* **b.** to pick players for opposing teams. —**Idiom. 7. cannot choose but,** cannot do otherwise than: *We cannot choose but obey.*

choos·y (chōō′zē), *adj.,* **choos·i·er, choos·i·est.** hard to please; particular, esp. in making a selection. —**choos′i·ness,** *n.*

chop[1] (chop), *v.,* **chopped, chop·ping,** *n.* —*v.t.* **1.** to cut or sever with one or more quick, heavy blows, using a sharp tool (often fol. by *down, off,* etc.): *to chop down a tree.* **2.** to make or prepare for use by so cutting: *to chop logs.* **3.** to cut into smaller pieces; mince (often fol. by *up*): *to chop up celery.* **4.** to hit with a sharp, downward stroke. —*v.i.* **5.** to make one or more quick, heavy strokes, as with an ax. **6.** to deliver or administer a sharp, downward blow or stroke. **7.** to go, come, or move suddenly or violently. —*n.* **8.** an act or instance of chopping. **9.** a short downward cut, blow, or stroke. **10.** a piece chopped off. **11.** an individual cut or portion of lamb, mutton, pork, or veal, usu. containing a rib. **12.** crushed or ground grain used as animal feed. **13.** a short irregular motion, as of a wave. **14.** rough, turbulent water.

chop[2] (chop), *v.i.,* **chopped, chop·ping.** **1.** to turn, shift, or change suddenly, as the wind. **2.** to vacillate; change one's mind. —**Idiom. 3. chop logic,** to reason or dispute with needlessly fine or trivial distinctions.

chop[3] (chop), *n.* **1.** Usu., **chops. a.** the jaw. **b.** the lower part of the cheek; the flesh over the lower jaw. **2. chops,** the oral cavity; mouth.

chop[4] (chop), *n.* **1.** a stamp or seal used as an identification mark, esp. in the Far East. **2.** quality, class, or grade: *a musician of the first chop.*

chop-chop (chop′chop′), *adv.* with haste; quickly.

chop·house (chop′hous′), *n., pl.* **-hous·es** (-hou′ziz). a restaurant specializing in chops and steaks.

Cho·pin (shō′pan; *Fr.* shō paN′), *n.* **Frédéric François,** 1810–49, Polish composer and pianist, in France after 1831.

chop·per (chop′ər), *n.* **1.** a person or thing that chops. **2.** a short ax with a large blade, used for cutting up meat; butcher's cleaver. **3.** a helicopter. —*v.i.* **4.** to travel by helicopter or motorcycle.

chop′ping block′, *n.* a block of wood on which meat, vegetables, and the like are trimmed, chopped, etc.

chop·py (chop′ē), *adj.,* **-pi·er, -pi·est. 1.** (of the sea, a lake, etc.) forming short, irregular, broken waves. **2.** (of the wind) shifting or changing unpredictably; variable. **3.** uneven in style or quality: *a choppy first novel.* —**chop′pi·ly,** *adv.* —**chop′pi·ness,** *n.*

chop′ shop′, *n.* a garage where stolen cars are dismantled so that their parts can be sold separately.

chop·stick (chop′stik′), *n.* one of a pair of tapered sticks held in one hand between the thumb and fingers and used, esp. in some Asian countries, as an eating utensil.

chop′ su′ey (chop′sōō′ē), *n.* a Chinese-style dish of small pieces of meat, chicken, etc., cooked with onions, bean sprouts, and other vegetables, usu. served with rice.

cho·ral (*adj.* kôr′əl, kōr′-; *n.* kə ral′), *adj.* **1.** of a chorus or a choir: *a choral society.* **2.** sung by, adapted for, or containing a chorus or a choir. —*n.* **3.** CHORALE. —**cho′ral·ly,** *adv.*

cho·rale (kə ral′, -räl′), *n.* **1.** a hymn, esp. one with strong harmonization: *a Bach chorale.* **2.** a group of singers specializing in singing church music; choir.

chorale′ pre′lude, *n.* a contrapuntal musical composition for organ based on a chorale.

chord[1] (kôrd), *n.* **1.** a feeling or emotion: *Your story struck a sympathetic chord in me.* **2.** the line segment between two points on a given curve. **3.** a principal longitudinal member of a truss, usu. one of a pair connected by a web of compression and tension members. **4.** a straight line joining the trailing and leading edges of an airfoil section. **5.** CORD (def. 7). —**chord′ed,** *adj.*

chord[2] (kôrd), *n.* **1.** a combination of usu. three or more musical tones sounded simultaneously. —*v.t.* **2.** to harmonize or voice with chords.

chord·al (kôr′dl), *adj.* **1.** of, pertaining to, or resembling a chord. **2.** of or pertaining to music that is marked principally by vertical harmonic movement rather than by linear polyphony.

chor·date (kôr′dāt), *adj.* **1.** belonging or pertaining to the phylum Chordata, comprising the true vertebrates and those animals having a notochord, as the lancelets and tunicates. —*n.* **2.** a chordate animal.

chord′ or′gan, *n.* an electronic organ having a small keyboard for the right hand and for the left hand a set of buttons each of which produces a full chord when pushed.

chore (chôr, chōr), *n.* **1.** a small or routine task. **2. chores,** the everyday work around a house or farm. **3.** a hard or unpleasant task.

cho·re·a (kə rē′ə, kô-, kō-), *n.* **1.** any of several diseases of the nervous system characterized by jerky, involuntary movements, esp. of the face and extremities. **2.** Also called **St. Vitus's dance.** such a disease occurring chiefly in children and associated with rheumatic fever. —**cho·re′al, cho·re′ic, cho·re·at′ic** (kôr′ē at′ik, kōr′-), *adj.*

cho·re·og·ra·phy (kôr′ē og′rə fē, kōr′-), *n.* **1.** the art of composing dances and planning and arranging the movements, steps, and patterns of dancers. **2.** the movements, steps, and patterns composed for a dance, piece of music, show, etc. **3.** the technique of representing the various movements in dancing by a system of notation. **4.** the arrangement or manipulation of actions leading up to an event. —**chor′e·o·graph′** (-ə graf′, -gräf′), *v.t., v.i.* —**cho′re·og′ra·pher,** *n.*

cho·ri·on (kôr′ē on′, kōr′-), *n.* **1.** the outermost of the membranes enclosing the embryo in reptiles, birds, and mammals, developing into part of the eggshell or part of the placenta. **2.** a membrane enclosing the shell of an insect egg. —**cho′ri·on′ic, cho′ri·al,** *adj.*

chor·is·ter (kôr′ə stər, kor′-), *n.* a singer in a choir.

C horizon, *n.* the layer in a soil profile below the B horizon and immediately above the bedrock, consisting chiefly of weathered, partially decomposed rock.

cho·rog·ra·phy (kə rog′rə fē, kô-, kō-), *n., pl.* **-phies.** (formerly) a systematic description of regional geography, or the methods used to arrive at this.

chor·tle (chôr′tl), *v.,* **-tled, -tling,** *n.* —*v.i.* **1.** to chuckle gleefully. —*v.t.* **2.** to express with a gleeful chuckle: *to chortle one's joy.* —*n.* **3.** a gleeful chuckle. [b. of *chuckle* and *snort*; coined by Lewis Carroll in *Through the Looking-Glass* (1871)] —**chor′tler,** *n.*

cho·rus (kôr′əs, kōr′-), *n.* **1. a.** a group of persons singing in unison. **b.** (in an opera, oratorio, etc.) such a group singing choral parts in connection with soloists or individual singers. **c.** a piece of music for singing in unison. **2.** a part of a song that recurs at intervals, usu. following each verse; refrain. **2.** simultaneous utterance in singing, speaking, shouting, etc. **3.** the sounds so uttered: *a chorus of jeers.* **4.** (in a musical show) those performers in the company who sing or dance as a group and usu. do not play separate roles. **5.** (in ancient Greece) **a.** an ode or series of odes sung by a group of actors in a drama. **b.** the group itself. **6. a.** an actor or group of actors functioning like the ancient Greek chorus, as in Elizabethan drama. **b.** the role performed by this chorus. —*v.t., v.i.* **7.** to sing or speak simultaneously. —**Idiom. 8. in chorus,** with everyone speaking or singing simultaneously; in unison.

cho′rus boy′, *n.* a male singer or dancer of the chorus of a musical comedy, vaudeville show, etc.

cho′rus girl′, *n.* a female singer or dancer of the chorus of a musical comedy, vaudeville show, etc.

chose[1] (chōz), *v.* pt. of CHOOSE.

chose[2] (shōz), *n.* an article of personal property.

cho·sen (chō′zən), *v.* **1.** pp. of CHOOSE. —*adj.* **2.** selected from several; preferred: *my chosen profession.* **3.** ELECT (def. 8). —*n.* **4. the chosen,** ELECT (def. 9).

cho′sen peo′ple, *n.pl.* (*often caps.*) the Israelites. Ex. 19.

Chou or **Zhou** (jō), *n.* a dynasty in China, 1122?–256? B.C., marked by the emergence of Confucianism and Taoism.

chough (chuf), *n.* either of two crowlike birds of the jay family, *Pyrrhocorax pyrrhocorax* and *P. graculus,* inhabiting mountains and seaside cliffs from W Europe to E Asia.

chow[1] (chou), *n.* **1.** food, esp. hearty dishes or a meal. —*v.i.* **2.** to eat, esp. heartily (usu. fol. by *down*).

chow[2] (chou), *n.* (*often cap.*) CHOW CHOW.

chow chow (chou′ chou′), *n.* (*often caps.*) one of a Chinese breed of medium-sized dogs with a stocky body, a large head, a thick coat forming a ruff around the neck, and a blue-black tongue.

chow chow
20 in. (51 cm) high at the shoulder

chow′-chow′, *n.* a relish of chopped mixed pickles in mustard sauce.
chow·der (chou′dər), *n.* a thick soup of clams, fish, or vegetables, usu. with potatoes, milk, and various seasonings.
chow′ mein′ (mān), *n.* a Chinese-style dish of steamed or stir-fried vegetables, topped with shredded chicken, shrimp, etc., and served with fried noodles.
Chré·tien (krā tyen′, -tyan′), *n.* **(Joseph Jacques) Jean** (zhäN), born 1934, prime minister of Canada since 1993.
chrism (kriz′əm), *n.* **1.** a consecrated oil used by certain churches in various rites, as in baptism. **2.** a sacramental anointing.
chris·om (kriz′əm), *n.* **CHRISM. 2.** a white cloth or robe put on a person at baptism to signify innocence.
Christ (krīst), *n.* **1.** Jesus of Nazareth, held by Christians to be the fulfillment of prophecies in the Old Testament regarding the coming of a Messiah. **2.** (chiefly in versions of the New Testament) the Messiah prophesied in the Old Testament. **3.** someone regarded as similar to Jesus of Nazareth. [< Latin *Chrīstus* < Greek *Chrīstós* lit., anointed] —**Christ′hood,** *n.* —**Christ′less,** *adj.* —**Christ′ly, Christ′like,** *adj.*
chris·ten (kris′ən), *v.t.* **1.** to receive into the Christian church by baptism; baptize. **2.** to give a name to at baptism. **3.** to name and dedicate: *to christen a ship.* **4.** to make use of for the first time.
Chris·ten·dom (kris′ən dəm), *n.* **1.** Christians collectively. **2.** the Christian world.
chris·ten·ing (kris′ə ning, kris′ning), *n.* **1.** the ceremony of baptism, esp. as accompanied by the giving of a name to a child. **2.** a public ceremony in which a new ship is formally named and launched. **3.** an act or instance of naming or dedicating something new.
Chris·tian (kris′chən), *adj.* **1.** of, pertaining to, or derived from Jesus Christ or His teachings. **2.** of, pertaining to, or adhering to the religion based on the teachings of Jesus Christ. **3.** of or pertaining to Christians. **4.** exhibiting a spirit proper to a follower of Jesus Christ, as in having a loving regard for others. **5.** humane; decent; generous. —*n.* **6.** a person who believes in Jesus Christ; an adherent of Christianity. **7.** a person who exemplifies in his or her life the teachings of Christ. —**Chris′tian·ly,** *adj., adv.*
Chris′tian Broth′er, *n.* BROTHER OF THE CHRISTIAN SCHOOLS.
Chris′tian Church′, *n.* a Christian fellowship founded in 1811, the sixth-largest denomination in the United States. Also called **Disciples of Christ.**
Chris′tian Endeav′or, *n.* an organization of young people of various evangelical Protestant churches, formed in 1881 to promote Christian principles and service.
Chris′tian E′ra, *n.* the period since the assumed year of Jesus' birth.
Chris·ti·an·i·ty (kris′chē an′i tē), *n.* **1.** the Christian religion, including the Catholic, Protestant, and Eastern Orthodox churches. **2.** Christian beliefs or practices; Christian quality or character. **3.** the state of being a Christian.
Chris·tian·ize (kris′chə nīz′), *v.t.,* **-ized, -iz·ing. 1.** to make Christian. **2.** to imbue with Christian principles. —**Chris′tian·i·za′tion,** *n.* —**Chris′tian·iz′er,** *n.*
Chris′tian name′, *n.* **1.** the name given to one at baptism, as distinguished from the family name. **2.** GIVEN NAME.
Chris′tian Reformed′ Church′, *n.* a strict Protestant denomination founded in the Netherlands in 1816.
Chris′tian Sci′ence, *n.* a religion founded by Mary Baker Eddy in 1866 that is based on the Scriptures and emphasizes spiritual healing. —**Chris′tian Sci′entist,** *n.*
Chris·tian·sen (kris′chən sən), *n.* **Avis,** 1895–1985, U.S. hymn writer.
Chris′tian vir′tues, *n.pl.* the virtues of faith, hope, and charity. I Cor. 13:13.
Chris′tian year′, *n.* a year in the ecclesiastical calendar, used esp. in reference to the various feast days and special seasons. Also called **church year.**
Chris·tie (kris′tē), *n.* **Agatha,** 1891–1976, English mystery writer.
Christ·mas (kris′məs), *n.* the annual festival of the Christian church commemorating Jesus' birth: celebrated in the Western Church on December 25.
Christ′mas cac′tus, *n.* a cactus, *Schlumbergera bridgesii,* native to

Brazil, having stems with leaflike segments and bearing showy usu. purplish red flowers.
Christ′mas Car′ol, A, a story (1843) by Dickens.
Christ′mas club′, *n.* a savings account in which a person deposits a fixed amount of money regularly, usu. for a year, the sum accumulated being paid out to the depositor for use at Christmas.
Christ′mas Eve′, *n.* the evening or the day preceding Christmas.
Christ′mas rose′, *n.* a European hellebore, *Helleborus niger,* having evergreen leaves and white to purplish flowers that bloom in the winter.
Christ′mas tree′, *n.* an evergreen tree decorated at Christmastime with ornaments and lights.
Chris·tol·o·gy (kri stol′ə jē), *n., pl.* **-gies.** theological interpretation of the nature, person, and deeds of Christ. —**Chris·to·log·i·cal** (kris′tl oj′i kəl), *adj.* —**Chris·tol′o·gist,** *n.*
Chris·to·pher (kris′tə fər), *n.* **Saint,** died A.D. c250, Christian martyr.
Christ′s-thorn′, *n.* any of various Old World thorny shrubs or small trees supposed to have been used for Christ's crown of thorns, as the Jerusalem thorn, *Paliurus spina-christi,* or the jujube, *Ziziphus jujuba.*
Christ′ the Lord′ Is Ris′en Today′, a Christian hymn (1739) with words by Charles Wesley: usually sung at Easter.
Christ′ Within′, *n.* INNER LIGHT.
chro·ma (krō′mə), *n.* **1.** the purity of a color or its freedom from white or gray. **2.** intensity of hue.
chro·mate (krō′māt), *n.* a salt of chromic acid, as potassium chromate, K_2CrO_4.
chro·mat·ic (krō mat′ik, krə-), *adj.* **1.** pertaining to color. **2. a.** of, pertaining to, or involving the musical chromatic scale. **b.** marked by the use of musical accidentals. —**chro·mat′i·cal·ly,** *adv.*
chro·ma·tic·i·ty (krō′mə tis′i tē), *n.* the quality of a color as determined by its dominant wavelength and its purity.
chro·mat·ics (krō mat′iks, krə-), *n.* (*used with a sing. v.*) the science of colors. —**chro·ma·tist** (krō′mə tist), *n.*
chromat′ic scale′, *n.* a musical scale progressing by semitones.
chro·ma·tid (krō′mə tid), *n.* either of two identical chromosomal strands into which a chromosome splits before cell division.
chro·ma·tin (krō′mə tin), *n.* the readily stainable substance of a cell nucleus that consists of DNA, RNA, and various proteins, and forms chromosomes during cell division.. —**chro′ma·tin′ic,** *adj.* —**chro′ma·toid′,** *adj.*
chro·ma·tism (krō′mə tiz′əm), *n.* the abnormal coloration of leaves or other normally green parts of a plant.
chro·ma·tog·ra·phy (krō′mə tog′rə fē), *n.* a technique for identifying the components of chemical mixtures separated by preferential adsorption on an adsorbent medium, as a column of silica, a strip of filter paper, or a gel. —**chro′ma·tog′ra·pher,** *n.* —**chro·mat·o·graph·ic** (krə mat′ə graf′ik), *adj.*
chrome (krōm), *n., v.,* **chromed, chrom·ing.** —*n.* **1.** (not in technical use) CHROMIUM (def. 1). **2.** chromium-plated or other bright metallic trim, as on an automobile. **3.** (in dyeing) the dichromate of potassium or sodium. —*v.t.* **4.** to plate, dye, or treat with a compound of chromium.
chrome′ green′, *n.* a permanent green color made from chromic oxide or a chromic oxide pigment and used chiefly in printing textiles.
chrome′ red′, *n.* a bright red pigment consisting of the basic chromate of lead.
chrome′ yel′low, *n.* any of several pigments composed chiefly of chromates of lead, barium, or zinc.
chro·mi·nance (krō′mə nəns), *n.* the difference in color quality between a color and a reference color that has an equal brightness and a specified chromaticity.
chro·mi·um (krō′mē əm), *n.* **1.** a lustrous metallic element used in making alloy steels hard and corrosion-resistant and in plating other metals. Symbol: Cr; *at. wt.:* 51.996; *at. no.:* 24; *sp. gr.:* 7.1. **2.** (not in technical use) CHROME (def. 2).
chromo- or **chromato-,** a combining form meaning "color," "pigment" (*chromophil*) or, by extension, "chromosome" (*chromonema*).
chro·mo·plast (krō′mə plast′), *n.* a plastid containing coloring matter other than chlorophyll.
chro·mo·some (krō′mə sōm′), *n.* one of a set of threadlike structures, composed of DNA and a protein, that form in the nucleus when the cell begins to divide and that carry the genes which determine an individual's hereditary traits. —**chro′mo·so′mal,** *adj.*
chron·ic (kron′ik), *adj.* **1.** being such habitually or for a prolonged period: *a chronic liar.* **2.** continuing a long time or recurring frequently: *a chronic state of war.* **3.** having long had a disease, habit, weakness, or the like: *a chronic invalid.* **4.** (of a disease) having long duration (disting. from *acute*). —**chron′i·cal·ly,** *adv.* —**chro·nic·i·ty** (kro nis′i tē), *n.*
chron′ic fatigue′ syn′drome, *n.* a viral disease of the immune system, usu. characterized by debilitating fatigue and flu-like symptoms.
chron·i·cle (kron′i kəl), *n., v.,* **-cled, -cling.** —*n.* **1.** a chronological record of events; a history. —*v.t.* **2.** to record in or as if in a chronicle. —**chron′i·cler,** *n.*
Chron·i·cles (kron′i kəlz), *n.* (*used with a sing. v.*) either of two books of the Old Testament, I Chronicles or II Chronicles.
Chron′icles of Nar′ni·a, The, (när′nē ə), a series of allegorical novels (1950) for children by C.S. Lewis.

chrono-, a combining form meaning "time": *chronometer*. Also, *esp. before a vowel*, **chron-**.

chron•o•bi•ol•o•gy (kron′ō bī ol′ə jē), *n.* the science or study of the effect of time, esp. rhythms, on living systems. —**chron′o•bi′o•log′i•cal** (-ə loj′i kəl), *adj.*

chron•o•gram (kron′ə gram′), *n.* **1.** an inscription in which letters express a date or epoch on being added together by their values as Roman numerals. **2.** a record made by a chronograph. —**chron′o•gram•mat′ic** (-ō grə mat′ik), **chron′o•gram•mat′i•cal**, *adj.*

chron•o•graph (kron′ə graf′, -gräf′), *n.* **1.** a timepiece fitted with a recording device, as a stylus and rotating drum, used to mark the exact instant of an occurrence. **2.** a timepiece, as a stopwatch, capable of measuring extremely brief intervals of time. —**chro•nog•ra•pher** (krə nog′rə fər), *n.* —**chron′o•graph′ic** (-graf′ik), *adj.* —**chron′o•graph′i•cal•ly**, *adv.* —**chro•nog′ra•phy**, *n.*

chro•nol•o•gy (krə nol′ə jē), *n., pl.* **-gies.** **1.** the sequential order in which things occur. **2.** a table or list of this order. **3.** the science of arranging time in periods and ascertaining the dates and historical order of past events. **4.** a reference work organized according to the dates of events. —**chron•o•log•i•cal** (kron′l oj′i kəl), *adj.* —**chron′o•log′i•cal•ly**, *adv.* —**chro•nol′o•gist, chro•nol′o•ger**, *n.*

chro•nom•e•ter (krə nom′i tər), *n.* **1.** a timepiece or timing device for use in determining longitude at sea or for any purpose where very exact measurement of time is required. **2.** any timepiece, esp. a wristwatch, designed for the highest accuracy. —**chron•o•met•ric** (kron′ə me′trik), *adj.* —**chron′o•met′ri•cal•ly**, *adv.*

chrys-, var. of CHRYSO- before a vowel: *chryselephantine*.

chrys•a•lis (kris′ə lis), *n., pl.* **chrys•a•lis•es, chry•sal•i•des** (kri sal′i dēz′). **1.** the hard-shelled pupa of a moth or butterfly. **2.** a protected stage of development.

chry•san•the•mum (kri san′thə məm), *n.* **1.** any cultivated variety of a composite plant, *Chrysanthemum morifolium*, native to China, and of related species, bearing autumn flowers in a diversity of color and size. **2.** the flower of any such plant.

chrys•el•e•phan•tine (kris′el ə fan′tin, -tīn), *adj.* made of or overlaid with gold and ivory, as certain objects made in ancient Greece.

chryso-, a combining form meaning "gold": *chrysolite*. Also, *esp. before a vowel*, **chrys-**.

chrys•o•lite (kris′ə līt′), *n.* olivine. —**chrys•o•lit•ic** (kris′ə lit′ik), *adj.*

chry•som•o•nad (kri som′ə nad′), *n.* any golden-yellow to brown freshwater algae of the class Chrysomonadales living singly or in colonies and having blooms that may color water brown.

chrys•o•phyte (kris′ə fīt′), *n.* any algae of the phylum Chrysophyta, comprising the yellow-green and the golden-brown algae and diatoms, distinguished by having the three pigment groups chlorophyll, carotene, and xanthophyll.

chrys•o•prase (kris′ə prāz′), *n.* a green variety of chalcedony, sometimes used as a gem.

chthon•ic (thon′ik) also **chtho•ni•an** (thō′nē ən), *adj.* of or characteristic of deities and supernatural beings thought to dwell in or under the earth.

chub (chub), *n., pl.* (*esp. collectively*) **chub**, (*esp. for kinds or species*) **chubs.** **1.** a European freshwater cyprinid fish, *Leuciscus cephalus*, having a thick body. **2.** any of various related fishes. **3.** any of several unrelated American fishes, esp. the tautog and whitefishes of the genus *Coregonus*, of the Great Lakes.

chub•by (chub′ē), *adj.*, **-bi•er, -bi•est.** round and plump: *a chubby child; a chubby face*. —**chub′bi•ly**, *adv.* —**chub′bi•ness**, *n.*

chuck¹ (chuk), *v.t.* **1.** to toss; throw. **2.** to throw away. **3.** to eject from a public place (often fol. by *out*). **4.** to resign from: *He's chucked his job.* **5.** to pat or tap lightly, as under the chin. —*n.* **6.** a light pat or tap. **7.** a toss; pitch.

chuck² (chuk), *n.* **1.** the cut of beef between the neck and the shoulder blade. **2.** a block or log used as a chock. **3. a.** a device for centering and clamping work in a lathe or other machine tool. **b.** a device for holding a drill bit.

chuck³ (chuk), *v.t., v.i.* **1.** to cluck. —*n.* **2.** a clucking sound.

chuck⁴ (chuk), *n.* food; provisions.

chuck•hole (chuk′hōl′), *n.* a hole in a road; pothole.

chuck•le (chuk′əl), *v.*, **chuck•led, chuck•ling**, *n.* —*v.i.* **1.** to laugh in a softly moderated manner. —*n.* **2.** a softly moderated laugh.

chuck′ wag′on, *n. Western U.S.* a wagon carrying cooking facilities and food for people working outdoors, as at a ranch.

chuck•wal•la (chuk′wä′lə), *n., pl.* **-las.** an iguanid lizard, *Sauromalis obesus*, of arid parts of southwestern U.S. and Mexico.

chuck′-will's-wid′ow (chuk′wilz′), *n.* a large nightjar, *Caprimulgus carolinensis*, of the southern U.S.

chuff¹ (chuf), *n.* a boor; churl.

chuff² (chuf), *n.* **1.** a sound of or like the exhaust of a steam engine. —*v.i.* **2.** to emit or proceed with chuffs: *a train chuffing along*.

chug¹ (chug), *n., v.*, **chugged, chug•ging**. —*n.* **1.** a short, dull, explosive sound: *the steady chug of an engine*. —*v.i.* **2.** to make this sound: *The motor chugged.* **3.** to move while making this sound: *The train chugged along.* —**chug′ger**, *n.*

chug² (chug), *v.t., v.i.*, **chugged, chug•ging**, to chug-a-lug.

chug-a-lug (chug′ə lug′), *v.*, **-lugged, -lug•ging**, *Slang*. —*v.t.* **1.** to

drink (a container of beverage) in one continuous draught. —*v.i.* **2.** to drink a beverage in one continuous draught.

chu•kar (chu kär′), *n.* a gray Eurasian partridge, *Alectoris chukar*, established in W North America.

Chuk′chi Penin′sula, *n.* a peninsula in the NE Russian Federation across the Bering Strait from Alaska.

Chuk′chi Sea′, *n.* a part of the Arctic Ocean, N of the Bering Strait.

chuk′ka boot′ (chuk′ə), *n.* an ankle-high shoe laced through two pairs of eyelets and often made of suede.

Chu•la Vis•ta (chōō′lə vis′tə), *n.* a city in SW California near San Diego. 149,255.

chum¹ (chum), *n., v.*, **chummed, chum•ming**. —*n.* **1.** a close companion or friend; pal. —*v.i.* **2.** to associate closely. **3.** to room together.

chum² (chum), *n., v.*, **chummed, chum•ming**. —*n.* **1.** cut or ground bait dumped into the water to attract fish. **2.** fish refuse or scraps discarded by a cannery. —*v.i.* **3.** to attract fish with chum. —*v.t.* **4.** to attract with chum.

chum³ (chum), *n.* CHUM SALMON.

chum•my (chum′ē), *adj.*, **-mi•er, -mi•est.** friendly; intimate; sociable. —**chum′mi•ly**, *adv.* —**chum′mi•ness**, *n.*

chump (chump), *n.* **1.** *Informal.* a foolish or gullible person. **2.** a short, thick piece of wood. **3.** the thick, blunt end of anything.

chump′ change′, *n. Slang.* a small or insignificant amount of money.

chum′ salm′on, *n.* a Pacific salmon, *Oncorhynchus keta*, with fine speckles above.

chunk¹ (chungk), *n.* **1.** a thick mass or lump of anything; hunk. **2.** a strong and stoutly built horse or other animal. **3.** a substantial amount of something.

chunk² (chungk), *v.i.* to make a dull throbbing or explosive sound.

chunk•y (chung′kē), *adj.*, **chunk•i•er, chunk•i•est.** **1.** thick or stout; stocky. **2.** in chunks. **3.** full of chunks; coarse. —**chunk′i•ly**, *adv.* —**chunk′i•ness**, *n.*

Chun•nel or **chun•nel** (chun′l), *n.* a railroad tunnel under the English Channel between England and France. [b. CHANNEL¹ and TUNNEL]

church (chûrch), *n.* **1.** a building for public Christian worship. **2.** a religious service in such a building. **3.** (*sometimes cap.*) **a.** the whole body of Christian believers; Christendom. **b.** any major division of this body; a Christian denomination. **4.** a Christian congregation. **5.** organized religion as distinguished from the state. **6.** (*cap.*) **a.** the Christian Church before the Reformation. **b.** the Roman Catholic Church. **7.** the profession of an ecclesiastic. —*v.t.* **8.** to perform a church service of thanksgiving for (a woman after childbirth). [< Greek *kȳri(a)kón (dôma)* the Lord's (house)]

Church (chûrch), *n.* **Frank Pharcellus**, 1839–1906, U.S. newspaper editor, author of *Yes, Virginia, there is a Santa Claus*.

Church′es of Christ′, *n.* a Protestant denomination, orig. part of the Christian Church (Disciples of Christ), founded in 1906 in the United States.

church•go•er (chûrch′gō′ər), *n.* **1.** a person who goes to church, esp. regularly. **2.** *Chiefly Brit.* a member of the Established Church, in contrast to a Nonconformist. —**church′go′ing**, *n.*

Church•ill (chûr′chil, -chal), *n.* **1. John, 1st Duke of Marlborough,** ("*Corporal John*"), 1650–1722, British military commander. **2. Lord Randolph (Henry Spencer),** 1849–95, British statesman (father of Winston L. S. Churchill). **3. Sir Winston (Leonard Spencer),** 1874–1965, British prime minister 1940–45, 1951–55. **4.** a river in Canada flowing NE from E Saskatchewan through Manitoba to Hudson Bay. ab. 1000 mi. (1600 km) long.

church′ mode′, *n.* any of eight modal scales used in Gregorian chant and other liturgical music.

Church′ of Christ′, Sci′entist, *n.* the official name of the Christian Science Church.

Church′ of Eng′land, *n.* the established church in England, Catholic in faith and order, but incorporating many principles of the Protestant Reformation and independent of the papacy.

Church′ of God′, *n.* any of numerous Protestant churches that stress personal conversion, sanctification, the imminent return of Jesus, and baptism by immersion.

Church′ of God′ in Christ′, *n.* a Protestant denomination, a Pentecostal group, founded in 1906 in the United States.

Church′ of Ire′land, *n.* the Irish branch of the Anglican Communion.

Church′ of Je′sus Christ′ of Lat′ter-day Saints′, *n.* the name of the largest denomination of the Mormon Church.

Church′ of Rome′, *n.* ROMAN CATHOLIC CHURCH.

Church′ of Scot′land, *n.* a Presbyterian denomination, the established church in Scotland.

Church′ of the Breth′ren, *n.* the official name of the church of the Dunkers.

Church′ of the Naz′arene, *n.* a Protestant denomination, a holiness church, founded in 1908 in the United States.

Church′s One′ Founda′tion, The, a Christian hymn (1866) with words by Samuel Stone.

church•yard (chûrch′yärd′), *n.* the yard or ground adjoining a church, often used as a graveyard.

church′ year′, *n.* CHRISTIAN YEAR.

churl (chûrl), *n.* **1.** a rude, boorish, or surly person. **2.** a peasant; rustic. **3.** a niggard; miser. —**churl′ish**, *adj.*

churn (chûrn), *n.* **1.** a container or machine in which cream or milk is agitated to make butter. **2.** any of various similar machines, as for mixing beverages. —*v.t.* **3.** to agitate in order to make into butter: *to churn cream.* **4.** to make (butter) by the agitation of cream. **5.** to shake or agitate: *The storm churned the sea.* **6.** (of a stockbroker) to trade (a customer's securities) excessively in order to earn more in commissions. —*v.i.* **7.** to operate a churn. **8.** to move or shake in agitation. **9.** **churn out,** to produce mechanically and in abundance.

chute¹ (shōōt), *n., v.,* **chut·ed, chut·ing.** —*n.* **1.** an inclined channel, as a trough or shaft, for conveying water, grain, etc., to a lower level. **2.** a waterfall or steep descent, as in a river. **3.** a water slide, as at an amusement park. **4.** a steep slope, as for tobogganing. —*v.t.* **5.** to move or deposit, by or as if by means of a chute. —*v.i.* **6.** to descend by or as if by means of a chute.

chute² (shōōt), *n., v.,* **chut·ed, chut·ing.** —*n.* **1.** a parachute. —*v.i.* **2.** to descend from the air by or as if by parachute. —*v.t.* **3.** to drop from an aircraft by means of a parachute. —**chut′ist,** *n.*

chut·ney (chut′nē), *n.* a piquant relish or sauce of Indian origin, typically combining sweet and sour ingredients, as fruit and vinegar, with sugar and spices.

chutz·pa or **chutz·pah** (κHŏŏt′spə, hŏŏt′-), *n. Slang.* **1.** unmitigated effrontery or impudence; gall. **2.** audacity; nerve. [< Yiddish *chutspe* < Hebrew *ḥuṣpā*]

chy·trid (kī′trid, ki′-), *n.* any of the aquatic or soil fungi of the class Chytridiomycetes, having flagellated zoospores.

Ci, curie.

CIA or **C.I.A.,** Central Intelligence Agency: a federal agency that coordinates U.S. intelligence activities.

ciao (chou), *interj.* (used as a word of greeting or parting.)

ci·bo·ri·um (si bôr′ē əm, -bōr′-), *n., pl.* **-bo·ri·a** (-bôr′ē ə, -bōr′-). **1.** a permanent canopy over an altar; baldachin. **2.** a vessel for holding the consecrated bread or sacred wafers for the Eucharist.

ci·ca·da (si kā′də, -kä′-), *n., pl.* **-das, -dae** (-dē). a large homopterous insect of the family Cicadidae, maturing in cycles of 5 to 17 years, the adult male producing a prolonged shrill sound by vibrating a set of membranes on its underside.

cic·a·trix (sik′ə triks, si kā′triks) also **cic·a·trice** (sik′ə tris), *n., pl.* **cic·a·tri·ces** (sik′ə trī′sēz). **1.** new tissue that forms over a wound and later contracts into a scar. **2.** a scar left by a fallen leaf, seed, etc. —**cic′a·tri′cial** (-trish′əl), *adj.* —**ci·cat·ri·cose** (si ka′tri kōs′, sik′ə-), *adj.*

cic·e·ly (sis′ə lē), *n., pl.* **-lies.** a plant, *Myrrhis odorata,* of the parsley family, having a fragrant aroma and sometimes used as a potherb.

Cic·e·ro (sis′ə rō′), *n.* **Marcus Tullius,** ("Tully"), 106–43 B.C., Roman statesman, orator, and writer.

cich·lid (sik′lid), *n.* any freshwater fish of the family Cichlidae of South America, Africa, and S Asia, superficially resembling the American sunfishes and popular in home aquariums.

-cide, a combining form meaning "a person or thing that kills" or "the act of killing" that specified by the initial element: *homicide; pesticide.*

ci·der (sī′dər), *n.* the juice pressed from apples, used for drinking, either before fermentation **(sweet cider)** or after fermentation **(hard cider),** or for making applejack, vinegar, etc.

ci·gar (si gär′), *n.* **1.** a cylindrical roll of tobacco cured for smoking, usu. wrapped in a tobacco leaf. —*Idiom.* **2. no cigar,** (said to indicate that an effort was not good enough.)

cig·a·rette or **cig·a·ret** (sig′ə ret′, sig′ə ret′), *n.* a narrow, short roll of finely cut tobacco cured for smoking, usu. wrapped in thin paper.

cig·a·ril·lo (sig′ə ril′ō), *n., pl.* **-los.** a small thin cigar.

ci·lan·tro (si län′trō, -lan′-), *n.* CORIANDER (def. 1).

cil·i·a (sil′ē ə), *n.pl., sing.* **cil·i·um** (sil′ē əm). **1.** short, hairlike, rhythmically beating organelles on the surface of certain cells that provide mobility, as in protozoans, or move fluids and particles along ducts in multicellular forms. **2.** the eyelashes.

cil·i·ar·y (sil′ē er′ē), *adj.* **1.** pertaining to various anatomical structures in or about the eye, as the ciliary body. **2.** pertaining to cilia.

cil·i·ate (sil′ē it, -āt′), *n.* **1.** any protozoan of the phylum Ciliophora, characterized by cilia covering all or part of the body. —*adj.* **2.** Also, **cil·i·at·ed** (sil′ē ā′tid). having cilia. —**cil/i·a′tion,** *n.*

Ci·li·cia (si lish′ə), *n.* an ancient country in SE Asia Minor: at one time a Roman province. —**Ci·li′cian,** *adj., n.*

cil·i·um (sil′ē əm), *n.* sing. of CILIA.

Cim·me·ri·an (si mēr′ē ən), *adj.* very dark; gloomy: *deep, Cimmerian caverns.*

cinch (sinch), *n.* **1.** a strong girth for securing a pack or saddle. **2.** a firm hold or tight grip. **3.** *Informal.* **a.** something sure or easy: *Fixing this leak is a cinch.* **b.** a person or thing certain to fulfill an expectation: *She's a cinch to win the contest.* —*v.t.* **4.** to gird with a cinch; gird or bind firmly. **5.** *Informal.* to make sure of; guarantee: *Your support will cinch the deal.*

cin·cho·na (sing kō′nə, sin-), *n., pl.* **-nas. 1.** any of several trees or shrubs of the genus *Cinchona,* of the madder family, native to the Andes, esp. *C. calisaya,* whose bark yields quinine. **2.** the medicinal bark of such trees or shrubs. —**cin·chon′ic** (-kon′ik), *adj.*

Cin·cin·nat·i (sin′sə nat′ē), *n.* a city in SW Ohio, on the Ohio River. 358,170.

cinc·ture (singk′chər), *n., v.,* **-tured, -tur·ing.** —*n.* **1.** a belt or girdle. **2.** something that surrounds or encompasses, as a surrounding border.

3. the act of girding or encompassing. —*v.t.* **4.** to gird with or as if with a cincture; encircle; encompass.

cin·der (sin′dər), *n.* **1.** a partially or mostly burned piece of coal, wood, etc. **2.** cinders, **a.** any residue of combustion; ashes. **b.** coarse volcanic ejecta. **3.** a live, flameless coal; ember. **4.** a mixture of ashes and slag. —*v.t.* **5.** to spread cinders on.

cin′der block′, *n.* a concrete building block made with a cinder aggregate.

Cin·der·el·la (sin′də rel′ə), *n., pl.* **-las. 1.** a heroine of a fairy tale who is maltreated by a stepmother but achieves happiness and marries a prince through the intervention of a fairy godmother. **2.** a person who achieves sudden success, esp. after obscurity or neglect.

cine-, a combining form meaning "motion picture": *cinemicrography.*

cin·e·ma (sin′ə mə), *n., pl.* **-mas. 1. the cinema,** motion pictures, as an art or industry. **2.** a motion-picture theater. —**cin′e·mat′ic** (-mat′ik) *adj.* —**cin′e·mat′i·cal·ly,** *adv.*

cin·e·ma·tog·ra·phy (sin′ə mə tog′rə fē), *n.* the art or technique of motion-picture photography. —**cin′e·ma·tog′ra·pher,** *n.*

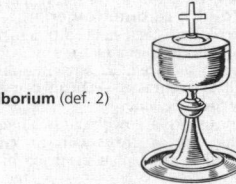

ciborium (def. 2)

cin·é·ma vé·ri·té′ (ver′i tā′; *Fr.* vā RĒ tā′), *n.* a technique of documentary filmmaking in which the camera records actual persons and events without directorial intervention.

cin·e·rar·i·a (sin′ə râr′ē ə), *n., pl.* **-rar·i·as.** any variety of a composite plant, *Senecio hybridus,* of the Canary Islands, having clusters of flowers with variegated rays.

cin·e·rar·i·um (sin′ə râr′ē əm), *n., pl.* **-rar·i·a** (-râr′ē ə). a place for depositing the ashes of the dead after cremation.

cin·e·rar·y (sin′ə rer′ē), *adj.* holding or intended for ashes, esp. the ashes of cremated bodies.

cin·na·bar (sin′ə bär′), *n.* **1.** a mineral, mercuric sulfide, HgS, occurring in red crystals or masses: the principal ore of mercury. **2.** red mercuric sulfide, used as a pigment. **3.** bright red; vermilion. —**cin′na·bar′ine** (-īn, -in), *adj.*

cin·na·mon (sin′ə mən), *n.* **1.** the aromatic inner bark of any of several East Indian trees belonging to the genus *Cinnamonum,* of the laurel family: used, in dried and often powdered form, as a spice. **2.** any tree yielding such bark. **3.** a yellowish or reddish brown. —*adj.* **4.** (of food) flavored with cinnamon. **5.** reddish brown or yellowish brown.

cin′namon bear′, *n.* a cinnamon-colored variety of the black bear of North America.

cin′namon fern′, *n.* a common coarse fern, *Osmunda cinnamomea,* having rusty-woolly stalks, growing in wet, low thickets.

cin·quain (sing kān′, sing′kān), *n.* **1.** a group of five. **2.** a stanza of five lines.

cinque·foil (singk′foil′), *n.* **1.** any of several plants belonging to the genus *Potentilla,* of the rose family, having yellow, red, or white five-petaled flowers. **2.** an architectural ornament consisting of five lobes, separated by cusps, radiating from a common center.

cinquefoil

cinquefoil

Cinque′ Ports′ (singk), *n.pl.* a former association of maritime towns in SE England, consisting of Hastings, Romney, Hythe, Dover, and Sandwich, formed in 1278 to assist in naval defense.

C.I.O. or **CIO,** CONGRESS OF INDUSTRIAL ORGANIZATIONS.

ci·pher (sī′fər), *n.* **1.** ZERO. **2.** any of the Arabic numerals or figures. **3.** a person or thing of no value or importance; nonentity. **4. a.** a secret method of writing, as by code. **b.** writing done by such a method; a coded message. **5.** the key to a secret method of writing. **6.** a combination of letters, as the initials of a name; monogram. —*v.i.* **7.** to use figures or numerals arithmetically. **8.** to write in or as in cipher. —*v.t.* **9.** to calculate numerically; figure. **10.** to convert into cipher; encipher. Also, *esp. Brit.,* **cypher.** —**ci′pher·a·ble,** *adj.* —**ci′pher·er,** *n.*

ci•pher•text (sī′fər tekst′), *n.* the encoded version of a message or other text, as opposed to the plaintext.

cir•ca (sûr′kə), *prep., adv.* about: used esp. in approximate dates. *Abbr.:* c, c., ca, ca., cir., circ.

cir•ca•di•an (sûr kā′dē ən, sûr′kə dē′ən), *adj.* of or pertaining to rhythmic cycles recurring at approximately 24-hour intervals: *the circadian biological clock.* —**cir•ca′di•an•ly,** *adv.*

cir•ci•nate (sûr′sə nāt′), *adj.* **1.** made round; ring-shaped. **2.** rolled up at the top of the axis, as the frond of a young fern.

cir•cle (sûr′kəl), *n., v.,* **-cled, -cling.** —*n.* **1.** a closed plane curve consisting of all points at a given distance from a point within it called the center. **2.** the portion of a plane bounded by such a curve. **3.** any circular or ringlike object, formation, or arrangement: *a circle of dancers.* **4.** a ring, circlet, or crown. **5.** the ring of a circus. **6.** a section of seats in a theater. Compare family circle (def. 2). **7.** the area within which something acts, exerts influence, etc.; realm; sphere: *a wide circle of influence.* **8.** a series ending where it began or forming a connected whole; cycle. **9.** an argument ostensibly proving a conclusion but actually assuming the conclusion as a premise; vicious circle. **10.** a number of persons bound by a common tie; coterie: *a circle of friends.* **11.** an administrative division, esp. of a province. **12.** a parallel of latitude. **13.** a sphere or orb: *the circle of the earth.* —*v.t.* **14.** to enclose in a circle; encircle: *Circle the correct answer.* **15.** to rotate or revolve around: *He circled the house cautiously.* **16.** to bypass; evade: *The ship carefully circled the iceberg.* —*v.i.* **17.** to move in a circle or circuit. —***Idiom.*** **18. come full circle, a.** to find oneself, after a series of events, back where one started. **b.** to reverse one's opinion. —**cir′cler,** *n.*

cir•clet (sûr′klit), *n.* **1.** a small circle. **2.** a ring or ring-shaped ornament.

cir•cuit (sûr′kit), *n.* **1.** an act or instance of going or moving around. **2.** a circular journey; round. **3.** a roundabout journey or course. **4. a.** a periodical journey from place to place, as by judges to hold court, ministers to preach, or salespeople covering a route. **b.** the persons making such a journey. **c.** the route followed or district covered. **5.** the line bounding any area or object. **6.** the complete path of an electric current, including the generating apparatus, intervening resistors, or capacitors. **7.** a means of transmitting communication signals or messages, usu. comprising two channels for interactive communication. **8.** a number of theaters, clubs, parks, or the like controlled by one management, devoted to one pursuit, or visited in turn by the same participants. **9.** a league or association: *a softball circuit.* —*v.t.* **10.** to go or move around; make the circuit of. —*v.i.* **11.** to go or move in a circuit. —**cir′cuit•al,** *adj.*

cir′cuit board′, *n.* **1.** a sheet of fiberglass or other material on which electronic components, as printed or integrated circuits, are installed. **2.** BOARD (def. 13a).

cir′cuit break′er, *n.* **1.** a device for interrupting an electric circuit to prevent excessive current, as that caused by a short circuit, from damaging the apparatus in the circuit or from causing a fire. **2.** any property-tax relief measure that reduces or limits property taxes for certain eligible taxpayers, as those with low income or the elderly.

cir′cuit court′, *n.* **1.** a court holding sessions at various intervals in different sections of a judicial district. **2.** (*caps.*) the court of general jurisdiction in a number of U.S. states.

cir′cuit judge′, *n.* a judge of a circuit court.

cir•cu•i•tous (sər kyōō′i təs), *adj.* roundabout; not direct. —**cir•cu′i•tous•ly,** *adv.* —**cir•cu′i•tous•ness,** *n.*

cir•cuit•ry (sûr′ki trē), *n.* **1.** the components of an electric circuit. **2.** the plan or system of such a circuit.

cir•cu•lar (sûr′kyə lər), *adj.* **1.** having the form of a circle; round. **2.** of or pertaining to a circle. **3.** moving in or forming a circle or a circuit. **4.** moving or occurring in a cycle or round: *the circular succession of the seasons.* **5.** circuitous; indirect. **6.** involving a vicious circle. **7.** (of a letter, notice, etc.) intended for general circulation. —*n.* **8.** a letter, advertisement, or notice intended for general circulation. —**cir′cu•lar′i•ty,** *n.* —**cir′cu•lar•ly,** *adv.*

cir•cu•lar•ize (sûr′kyə lə rīz′), *v.t.,* **-ized, -iz•ing. 1.** to circulate (a letter, memorandum, etc.). **2.** to send circulars to. **3.** to publicize, esp. by distributing circulars. **4.** to make circular. —**cir′cu•lar•i•za′tion,** *n.* —**cir′cu•lar•iz′er,** *n.*

cir′cular saw′, *n.* **1.** a power saw having a disk-shaped blade. **2.** the blade of such a saw.

cir•cu•late (sûr′kyə lāt′), *v.,* **-lat•ed, -lat•ing.** —*v.i.* **1.** to move in a circle or circuit; move or pass through a circuit back to the starting point, as blood in the body. **2.** to pass from place to place, from person to person, etc.: *I circulated among the guests.* **3.** to be distributed or sold, esp. over a wide area. **4.** (of library materials) to be available on loan for use outside library premises. —*v.t.* **5.** to cause to pass from place to place, person to person, etc.; disseminate; distribute: *to circulate a report.* **6.** LEND (def. 3). —**cir′cu•la′tive** (-lā′tiv, -lə tiv), *adj.* —**cir′cu•la•to′ry** (-tôr′ē, -tōr′ē), *adj.*

cir•cu•la•tion (sûr′kyə lā′shən), *n.* **1.** an act or instance of circulating. **2.** the continuous movement of blood through the heart and blood vessels, maintained chiefly by the action of the heart. **3.** any similar circuit, passage, or flow, as of the sap in plants or air currents in a room. **4.** the transmission or passage of anything from place to place or person to person; dissemination. **5.** the distribution of copies of a periodical among readers. **6.** the number of items distributed over a given period, as copies of a periodical sold by a publisher, or books lent by a library. **7.** the total of coins, notes, bills, etc., in use as money. —***Idiom.*** **8. in circulation,** participating actively in social or business life. —**cir•cu•la•ble** (sûr′kyə lə bəl), *adj.*

cir′culatory sys′tem, *n.* the system of organs and tissues, including the heart, blood, blood vessels, lymph, lymphatic vessels, and lymph glands, involved in circulating blood and lymph.

circum-, a prefix with the meaning "round about, around," found in Latin loanwords, esp. derivatives of verbs that had the general sense "to encompass or surround" (*circumference; circumstance*) or "to go around" in the manner specified by the verb (*circumnavigate; circumscribe*); on this basis forming adjectives in English with the meaning "surrounding" that named by the stem (*circumpolar*).

cir•cum•am•bu•late (sûr′kəm am′byə lāt′), *v.t., v.i.,* **-lat•ed, -lat•ing.** to walk or go around, esp. ceremoniously. —**cir′cum•am′bu•la′tion,** *n.* —**cir′cum•am′bu•la′tor,** *n.* —**cir′cum•am′bu•la•to′ry** (-lə tôr′ē, -tōr′ē), *adj.*

cir•cum•cise (sûr′kəm sīz′), *v.t.,* **-cised, -cis•ing.** to remove the prepuce of (a male), esp. as a religious rite. —**cir′cum•ci′sion** (-sizh′ən), *n.*

cir•cum•fer•ence (sər kum′fər əns), *n.* **1.** the outer boundary, esp. of a circular area; perimeter: *The circumference of a circle is equal to* π *times the diameter.* **2.** the length of such a boundary. —**cir•cum′fer•en′tial** (-fə ren′shəl), *adj.*

cir•cum•flex (sûr′kəm fleks′), *n.* **1.** a mark (ˆ, ˜, or ¯) placed over a vowel in some languages or phonetic systems to indicate that the vowel is long, as in French, pronounced with a rise and fall in pitch, as in Classical Greek, stressed, or pronounced with a particular quality, as the (â) in (âr) *air.* —*adj.* **2. a.** consisting of, indicated by, or bearing a circumflex. **b.** pronounced with or characterized by the quality, length, stress, or pitch indicated by a circumflex. **3.** bending or winding around. —*v.t.* **4.** to bend around.

cir•cum•fuse (sûr′kəm fyōōz′), *v.t.,* **-fused, -fus•ing. 1.** to pour around; spread. **2.** to surround as with a fluid; suffuse. —**cir′cum•fu′sion** (-fyōō′zhən), *n.*

cir•cum•ja•cent (sûr′kəm jā′sənt), *adj.* lying around; surrounding.

cir•cum•lo•cu•tion (sûr′kəm lō kyōō′shən), *n.* **1.** a roundabout or indirect way of speaking; the use of more words than necessary to express an idea. **2.** a roundabout expression. —**cir′cum•loc′u•to′ry** (-lok′yə tôr′ē, -tōr′ē), *adj.*

cir•cum•nav•i•gate (sûr′kəm nav′i gāt′), *v.t.,* **-gat•ed, -gat•ing. 1.** to sail or fly completely around. **2.** to go or maneuver around. —**cir′cum•nav′i•ga•ble** (-gə bəl), *adj.* —**cir′cum•nav′i•ga′tion,** *n.* —**cir′cum•nav′i•ga′tor,** *n.*

cir•cum•ro•tate (sûr′kəm rō′tāt), *v.i.,* **-tat•ed, -tat•ing.** to rotate like a wheel. —**cir′cum•ro•ta′tion,** *n.*

cir•cum•scribe (sûr′kəm skrīb′, sûr′kəm skrīb′), *v.t.,* **-scribed, -scrib•ing. 1.** to draw a line around; encircle. **2.** to enclose within bounds, esp. narrow ones; restrict. **3.** to mark off; define; delimit. **4. a.** to draw (a figure) around another figure so as to touch as many points as possible. **b.** (of a figure) to enclose (another figure) in this manner. —**cir′cum•scrib′a•ble,** *adj.*

cir•cum•scrip•tion (sûr′kəm skrip′shən), *n.* **1.** an act of circumscribing. **2.** circumscribed state; limitation. **3.** anything that surrounds or encloses; boundary. **4.** periphery; outline. **5.** a circumscribed area. **6.** a circular inscription on a coin, seal, etc. —**cir′cum•scrip′tive,** *adj.* —**cir′cum•scrip′tive•ly,** *adv.*

cir•cum•spect (sûr′kəm spekt′), *adj.* watchful and discreet; cautious; prudent: *circumspect behavior.* —**cir′cum•spec′tion,** *n.* —**cir′cum•spect′ly,** *adv.*

cir•cum•stance (sûr′kəm stans′; *esp. Brit.* -stəns), *n., v.,* **-stanced, -stanc•ing.** —*n.* **1.** a condition or attribute that accompanies, determines, or modifies a fact or event; an accessory or influencing factor. **2.** Usu., **circumstances.** the existing conditions or state of affairs surrounding and affecting an agent: *Circumstances permitting, we sail on Monday.* **3. circumstances,** the condition or state of a person with respect to income and material welfare: *a family in reduced circumstances.* **4.** an incident or occurrence: *His arrival was a fortunate circumstance.* **5.** detailed or circuitous narration. **6.** ceremonious accompaniment or display: *pomp and circumstance.* —*v.t.* **7.** to place in particular circumstances or relations. —***Idiom.*** **8. under** or **in the circumstances,** because of prevailing conditions. **9. under no circumstances,** never, regardless of events or conditions.

cir•cum•stan•tial (sûr′kəm stan′shəl), *adj.* **1.** of, pertaining to, or derived from circumstances: *a circumstantial result.* **2.** unessential; secondary; incidental. **3.** dealing with circumstances; detailed; particular. **4.** pertaining to conditions of material welfare. —**cir′cum•stan′tial•ly,** *adv.*

cir′cumstan′tial ev′idence, *n.* proof of facts offered as evidence from which other facts are to be inferred. Also called **indirect evidence.**

cir•cum•vent (sûr′kəm vent′, sûr′kəm vent′), *v.t.* **1.** to go around or bypass: *to circumvent the lake; to circumvent a problem.* **2.** to avoid by artfulness; elude: *to circumvent defeat.* **3.** to surround or encompass, as by stratagem; entrap. —**cir′cum•ven′tion,** *n.* —**cir′cum•ven′tive,** *adj.*

cir•cum•vo•lu•tion (sûr′kəm və lōō′shən), *n.* **1.** the act of rolling or turning around. **2.** a single complete turn or cycle. **3.** a winding or folding about something. **4.** a fold so wound: *the circumvolution of a snail shell.* **5.** a winding in a sinuous course. **6.** a roundabout course or procedure. —**cir′cum•vo•lu′to•ry** (-tə rē), *adj.*

cir·cus (sûr′kəs), *n.* **1. a.** a large public show or entertainment featuring performing animals, clowns, feats of skill and daring, pageantry, etc. **b.** the physical equipment, personnel, etc., of such a show. **c.** the place where such a show is held, usu. a circular arena surrounded by tiers of seats, often in a tent. 2. (in ancient Rome) **a.** a large, usu. U-shaped or oval roofless enclosure surrounded by tiers of seats on three or all sides, for chariot races, public games, etc. **b.** a game or spectacle presented in such an arena. **3.** *Brit.* an open circle or plaza where several streets converge. **4.** a display of rowdy sport or wild activity. —**cir′cus·y,** *adj.*

ci·ré (si rā′), *n.* **1.** a brilliant, highly glazed surface produced on fabrics by subjecting them to a wax, heat, and calendering treatment. **2.** a fabric with such a finish.

Cir·e·na·i·ca (sir′ə nā′i kə, sī′rə-), *n.* CYRENAICA.

cirque (sûrk), *n.* **1.** a bowl-shaped, steep-walled mountain basin carved by glaciation, often containing a small round lake. **2.** circle; ring.

cir·rho·sis (si rō′sis), *n.* a chronic disease of the liver in which fibrous tissue invades and replaces normal tissue, disrupting important functions, as digestion and detoxification. —**cir·rhot′ic** (-rot′ik), *adj.* —**cir·rhosed′,** *adj.*

cir·ri (sir′ī), *n.* a pl. of CIRRUS.

cir·ri·ped (sir′ə ped′), *n.* any crustacean of the class Cirripedia, comprising the barnacles and certain parasitic forms, typically free-swimming in the larval stage and attached as adults, with bristly food-gathering appendages.

cir·ro·cu·mu·lus (sir′ō kyōō′myə ləs), *n.,* *pl.* **-li** (-lī′). a high-altitude cloud composed of ice crystals and characterized by thin white patches. —**cir′ro·cu′mu·lar, cir′ro·cu′mu·la·tive** (-lā′tiv, -lə tiv), **cir′ro·cu′mu·lous,** *adj.*

cir·ro·stra·tus (sir′ō strā′təs, -strat′əs), *n.,* *pl.* **-stra·ti** (-strā′tī, -strat′ī). a high-altitude cloud composed of ice crystals and appearing as a thin white veil, often covering the entire sky.

cir·rus (sir′əs), *n.,* *pl.* **cir·ri** (sir′ī). **1.** a high-altitude cloud composed of ice crystals and characterized by thin white filaments or narrow bands. **2.** a tendril. **3. a.** a filament or slender appendage serving as a foot, tentacle, barbel, etc. **b.** the male copulatory organ of flatworms and various other invertebrates.

cis-, **1.** a prefix occurring in words meaning "on this side of" or "a place on this side of" the thing or place specified by the base word: *cisatlantic; cislunar.* **2.** a prefix used in the names of chemical compounds that are geometric isomers having two identical atoms or groups attached on the same side of a molecule divided by a given plane of symmetry. Compare TRANS- (def. 2).

CISC (sisk), *n.* complex instruction set computer: a computer whose central processing unit recognizes a relatively large number of instructions. Compare RISC

cis·co (sis′kō), *n.,* *pl.* (*esp. collectively*) **-co,** (*esp. for kinds or species*) **-coes, -cos.** any of several whitefishes of the genus *Coregonus,* of the Great Lakes and smaller lakes of E North America.

cist (sist, kist) also **kist,** *n.* a prehistoric sepulchral tomb or casket. —**cist′ed,** *adj.*

Cis·ter·cian (si stûr′shən), *n.* **1.** a member of a Benedictine order of monks and nuns founded in 1098 in France. —*adj.* **2.** of or pertaining to the Cistercians.

cis·tern (sis′tərn), *n.* **1.** a reservoir, tank, or container for storing or holding water or other liquid. **2.** a reservoir or receptacle of some natural fluid of the body.

cis·tron (sis′tron), *n.* a segment of DNA that codes for the formation of a specific protein. —**cis·tron′ic,** *adj.*

cit·a·del (sit′ə dl, -ə del′), *n.* **1.** a fortress for commanding or defending a city. **2.** any strongly fortified place; stronghold.

ci·ta·tion (sī tā′shən), *n.* **1.** the act of citing or quoting. **2.** a reference to an authority or a precedent, esp. in law. **3.** a passage cited; quotation. **4. a.** mention of a soldier or a unit in official dispatches, usu. for gallantry. **b.** an award, decoration, or the like, for exceptional military bravery. **5.** any award or commendation, esp. for outstanding service or devotion to duty. **6. a.** a summons, esp. to appear in court. **b.** a document containing such a summons. **7.** a quotation showing a particular word or phrase in context. **8.** mention or enumeration. —**ci·ta′tion·al,** *adj.*

cite (sīt), *v.t.,* **cit·ed, cit·ing.** **1.** to quote (a passage, book, author, etc.), esp. as an authority. **2.** to mention in support, proof, or confirmation; refer to as an example: *He cited instances of abuse.* **3.** to summon to appear in court. **4.** to call to mind; recall: *citing my gratitude to her.* **5.** to mention (a soldier, unit, etc.) in official dispatches, as for gallantry. **6.** to commend, as for outstanding service or devotion to duty. **7.** to summon or call; rouse to action. —**cit′a·ble, cite′a·ble,** *adj.* —**cit′er,** *n.*

cith·a·ra (sith′ər ə), *n.,* *pl.* **-ras.** KITHARA.

Cit′ies of Ref′uge, *n.pl.* six cities, three on each side of the Jordan River, reserved under Mosaic law to be a refuge for persons who committed accidental homicide. Josh. 20:2–9.

Cit′ies of the Plain′, *n.pl.* Sodom and Gomorrah. Gen. 14:2.

cit·i·fy (sit′i fī′), *v.t.,* **-fied, -fy·ing.** to cause to conform to city habits, fashions, etc. —**cit′i·fi·ca′tion,** *n.*

cit·i·zen (sit′ə zən, -sən), *n.* **1.** a native or naturalized member of a state or nation who owes allegiance to its government and is entitled to its protection. **2.** an inhabitant of a city or town, esp. one entitled to its

privileges or franchises. **3.** an inhabitant or denizen: *the wild citizens of our woods.* **4.** a civilian, as distinguished from a soldier, police officer, etc. —**cit′i·zen·ly,** *adj.*

Cit′izen Kane′, an American film (1941), directed by and starring Orson Welles.

cit′izen of the world′, *n.* an internationalist.

cit·i·zen·ry (sit′ə zən rē, -sən-), *n.,* *pl.* **-ries.** citizens collectively.

cit′izen's arrest′, *n.* an arrest made by a private citizen whose authority derives from the fact of citizenship.

cit′izens band′, *n.* (*often caps.*) a band of radio frequencies used for short-distance private communications between fixed or mobile stations. *Abbr.:* CB

cit′izens' commit′tee, *n.* **1.** a political group set up to support a political party or candidate, but functioning independently. **2.** an independent group of civic activists.

cit·i·zen·ship (sit′ə zən ship′, -sən-), *n.* **1.** the state of being vested with the rights and duties of a citizen. **2.** the character of an individual viewed as a member of society: *an award for good citizenship.*

cit·rate (si′trāt, sī′-), *n.* a salt or ester of citric acid.

cit·ric (si′trik), *adj.* of or derived from citric acid.

cit′ric ac′id, *n.* a white powder, $C_6H_8O_7 \cdot H_2O$, an intermediate in the metabolism of carbohydrates, occurring esp. in citrus fruits: used chiefly in flavorings and pharmaceuticals.

cit·rine (si′trēn, -trīn, si trēn′), *adj.* **1.** pale yellow; lemon-colored. —*n.* **2.** a translucent yellow variety of quartz, often sold as topaz.

cit·ron (si′trən), *n.* **1.** a pale yellow fruit resembling the lemon but larger and with thicker rind borne by a small tree, *Citrus medica,* allied to the lemon and lime. **2.** the tree itself. **3.** the rind of the fruit candied and preserved. **4.** CITRON MELON.

cit·ron·el·la (si′trə nel′ə), *n.* a fragrant, S Asian grass, *Cymbopogon nardus,* cultivated as the source of citronella oil.

cit′ron mel′on, *n.* a round hard-fleshed watermelon, *Citrullus lanatus citroides,* used candied or pickled.

cit·rus (si′trəs), *n.,* *pl.* **-rus·es,** *adj.* —*n.* **1.** any small tree or spiny shrub of the genus *Citrus,* of the rue family, including the lemon, lime, orange, tangerine, grapefruit, citron, kumquat, and shaddock. **2.** the fruit of any of these trees or shrubs, having a shiny, stippled skin, and tart-to-sweet juicy pulp. —*adj.* **3.** Also, **cit′rous.** of or pertaining to such trees or shrubs, or their fruit.

cit·tern (sit′ərn), *n.* an old musical instrument related to the guitar, having a flat, pear-shaped soundbox and wire strings.

cit·y (sit′ē), *n.,* *pl.* **cit·ies.** **1.** a large or important town. **2.** (in the U.S.) an incorporated municipality, usu. governed by a mayor and council. **3.** the inhabitants of a city collectively: *The entire city is celebrating.* **4.** (in Canada) a municipality of high rank, usu. based on population. **5.** (in Great Britain) a borough, usu. the seat of a bishop, having its title conferred by the Crown. **6.** a city-state.

cit′y clerk′, *n.* a city official who maintains public records and vital statistics, issues licenses, etc.

cit′y coun′cil, *n.* a municipal body with legislative and administrative powers, as passing ordinances and appropriating funds.

cit′y ed′itor, *n.* a newspaper editor in charge of local news and assignments to reporters.

cit′y fa′ther, *n.* any of the officials or prominent citizens of a city.

cit′y hall′, *n.* **1.** the administration building of a city government. **2.** a city government. **3.** *Informal.* bureaucratic rules and regulations, esp. of a city government: *You can't fight city hall.*

cit′y man′ager, *n.* a person appointed by a city council to manage a city.

Cit′y of Broth′erly Love′, *n.* Philadelphia, Pa. (used as a nickname).

Cit′y of Da′vid, *n.* **1.** Jerusalem. II Sam. 5:6–7. **2.** Bethlehem. Luke 2:4.

Cit′y of God′, *n.* the New Jerusalem; heaven.

Cit′y of the Lord′, *n.* Jerusalem. Also called **Cit′y of the Lord′ of Hosts′.**

cit′y on a hill′, *n.* an ideal or exemplar of civic achievement or virtue. Matt. 5:14.

cit′y plan′ning, *n.* the activity or profession of determining the future physical arrangement and condition of a community. —**cit′y plan′ner,** *n.*

cit′y room′, *n.* the department in which local news is handled for a newspaper, radio, television station, etc.

cit·y·scape (sit′ē skāp′), *n.* **1.** a view or picture of a city. **2.** the characteristic appearance of a city.

cit·y-state′, *n.* a sovereign state consisting of an autonomous city with its dependencies.

cit·y·wide (sit′ē wīd′), *adj.* **1.** occurring throughout a city. **2.** open to, including, or affecting all the inhabitants of a city.

civ·et (siv′it), *n.* **1.** Also called **civ′et cat′.** any of several catlike carnivores of the family Viverridae, esp. of the genera *Viverra* of the Orient and *Civettictis* of Africa. **2.** a musky secretion of civets, used in perfumery. —**civ′et·like′,** *adj.*

civ·ic (siv′ik), *adj.* **1.** of or pertaining to a city; municipal. **2.** of or pertaining to citizenship; civil. **3.** of citizens: *civic pride.*

civ′ic-mind′ed, *adj.* concerned with the well-being of the community. —**civ′ic-mind′ed·ly,** *adv.* —**civ′ic-mind′ed·ness,** *n.*

civ•ics (siv′iks), *n.* (*used with a sing. v.*) the study or science of the privileges and obligations of citizens.

civ•il (siv′əl), *adj.* **1.** of, pertaining to, or consisting of citizens: *civil life; civil society.* **2.** of the commonwealth or state: *civil affairs.* **3.** of the ordinary life and affairs of citizens, as distinguished from military and ecclesiastical life and affairs. **4.** befitting a citizen: *a civil duty.* **5.** of, or in a condition of, social order or organized government; civilized. **6.** adhering to the norms of polite social intercourse: *civil relations.* **7.** marked by benevolence: *He was a very civil sort.* **8.** (of divisions of time) legally recognized in the ordinary affairs of life: *the civil year.* **9.** of or pertaining to civil law.

civ′il defense′, *n.* plans and activities organized by civilians to protect people and property in case of natural disaster, war, or other emergency.

civ′il disobe′dience, *n.* the refusal to obey certain governmental laws or demands in order to influence legislation or policy, characterized by such nonviolent methods as nonpayment of taxes and boycotting.

civ′il engineer′ing, *n.* the applied science of the design of public works, as roads, bridges, dams, harbors, etc., and the supervision of their construction or maintenance. —**civ′il engineer′,** *n.*

ci•vil•ian (si vil′yən), *n.* **1.** a person who is not on active duty with a military, naval, police, or firefighting organization. **2.** a student of Roman or civil law. —*adj.* **3.** of, pertaining to, formed by, or administered by civilians.

civil′ian review′, *n.* a group of citizens who are appointed to hear complaints made against the police.

ci•vil•i•ty (si vil′i tē), *n., pl.* **-ties. 1.** courtesy; politeness. **2.** a polite action or expression.

civ•i•li•za•tion (siv′ə lə zā′shən), *n.* **1.** an advanced state of human society, in which a high level of culture, science, and government has been reached. **2.** those people or nations that have reached such a state. **3.** any type of culture, society, etc., of a specific place, time, or group: *Greek civilization.* **4.** the act or process of civilizing or being civilized. **5.** cultural and intellectual refinement. **6.** cities or populated areas in general, as opposed to unpopulated or wilderness areas. **7.** modern comforts and conveniences, as made possible by science and technology.

civ•i•lize (siv′ə līz′), *v.t.,* **-lized, -liz•ing.** to bring out of a savage, uneducated, or rude state; make civil; enlighten; refine: *Rome civilized the barbarians.*

civ•i•lized (siv′ə līzd′), *adj.* **1.** having an advanced or humane culture, society, etc. **2.** polite; well-bred; refined.

civ′il law′, *n.* **1.** the body of laws regulating private matters, as distinct from criminal, political, or military matters. **2.** the body of law proper to the city or state of ancient Rome, as distinct from that common to all nations. **3.** any of the systems of law derived from or influenced by Roman law and distinct from common law and canon law. —**civ′il-law′,** *adj.*

civ′il lib′erty, *n.* **1.** Often, **civil liberties.** a fundamental right, as freedom of speech, guaranteed to an individual by the laws of a country. **2.** the liberty of an individual to exercise such a right without unwarranted government interference. —**civ′il libertar′ian,** *n.*

civ•il•ly (siv′ə lē), *adv.* **1.** politely; courteously. **2.** in accordance with civil law.

civ′il mar′riage, *n.* a marriage performed by a government official, as distinguished from a member of the clergy.

civ′il rights′, *n.pl.* (*often caps.*) rights to personal liberty, esp. as established by the 13th and 14th Amendments to the U.S. Constitution and certain Congressional acts. —**civ′il-rights′,** *adj.*

civ′il serv′ant, *n.* a civil-service employee.

civ′il serv′ice, *n.* **1.** those branches of public service concerned with all governmental administrative functions outside the armed services. **2.** the body of persons employed in these branches.

civ′il war′, *n.* **1.** a war between political factions or regions within the same country. **2.** (*caps.*) the war in the U.S. between the North and the South, 1861–65.

civ•vies or **civ•ies** (siv′ēz), *n.pl. Informal.* civilian clothes, as distinguished from military uniforms.

Cl, *Chem. Symbol.* chlorine.

cl, centiliter.

clab•ber (klab′ər), *South Midland and Southern U.S.* —*n.* **1.** milk that has soured and thickened; curdled milk. —*v.i.* **2.** (of milk) to curdle; to become thick in souring.

clack (klak), *v.i.* **1.** to make a quick sharp sound, or a succession of such sounds, as by striking or cracking. **2.** to talk rapidly and continually or with sharpness and abruptness; chatter. —*v.t.* **3.** to utter by clacking. **4.** to cause to clack. —*n.* **5.** a clacking sound. **6.** something that clacks, as a rattle. **7.** rapid, continual talk; chatter.

clad (klad), *v.,* **clad, clad•ding,** *adj.* —*v.t.* **1.** a pt. and pp. of CLOTHE. **2.** to bond a metal to (another metal), esp. to provide with a protective coat. —*adj.* (usu. used in combination) **3.** dressed: *ill-clad vagrants.* **4.** covered: *vine-clad cottages.* **5.** bonded with a protective metallic coat: *copper-clad cookware.*

claim (klām), *v.t.* **1.** to demand by or as if by virtue of a right; demand as a right or as due: *to claim an estate by inheritance.* **2.** to assert or maintain as a fact: *She claimed that she was telling the truth.* **3.** to require as due or fitting: *to claim respect.* —*n.* **4.** a demand for something as due; an assertion of a right or an alleged right: *to make unreasonable claims on a doctor's time.* **5.** an assertion of something as a fact: *I make no claims to originality.* **6.** a right to claim or demand; a just title to something: *His claim to the heavyweight title is disputed.* **7.** something that is claimed, esp. a piece of public land for which formal request is made for mining or other purposes. **8.** a request or demand for payment in accordance with an insurance policy, a workers' compensation law, etc. —*Idiom.* **9. lay claim to,** to declare oneself entitled to. —**claim′a•ble,** *adj.* —**claim′er,** *n.*

claim•ant (klā′mənt), *n.* a person who makes a claim.

claim′ing race′, *n.* a race in which any horse entered can be purchased by anyone who has made a bid or claim before the start of the race.

clair•voy•ance (klâr voi′əns), *n.* **1.** the paranormal power of seeing objects or actions beyond the range of natural vision. **2.** quick, intuitive knowledge of things and people. —**clair•voy′ant,** *adj., n.*

clam (klam), *n., v.,* **clammed, clam•ming.** —*n.* **1.** any of various usu. edible bivalve mollusks with equal shells closed by two adductor muscles, inhabiting shallow seas or fresh waters. Compare QUAHOG. **2.** *Informal.* a secretive or silent person. **3.** *Slang.* a dollar or the sum of a dollar. —*v.i.* **4.** to gather or dig clams. **5. clam up,** *Informal.* to refuse to talk or reply: *so shy that he clams up in public.* —**clam′like′,** *adj.* —**clam′mer,** *n.*

cla•mant (klā′mənt, klam′ənt), *adj.* **1.** clamorous; noisy. **2.** compelling or pressing; urgent. —**cla′mant•ly,** *adv.*

clam•bake (klam′bāk′), *n.* **1.** a seaside picnic at which clams and other seafood are baked, traditionally on hot stones under a covering of seaweed. **2.** *Informal.* any social gathering.

clam•ber (klam′bər, klam′ər), *v.t., v.i.* **1.** to climb, using both feet and hands; climb with effort or difficulty. —*n.* **2.** an act or instance of clambering.

clam•my (klam′ē), *adj.,* **-mi•er, -mi•est. 1.** covered with a cold, sticky moisture; cold and damp: *clammy hands.* **2.** sickly; morbid: *a clammy feeling.* —**clam′mi•ly,** *adv.* —**clam′mi•ness,** *n.*

clam•or (klam′ər), *n.* **1.** a loud uproar, as from a crowd of people. **2.** a vehement expression of desire or dissatisfaction: *the clamor against higher taxation.* **3.** any loud and continued noise: *the clamor of traffic.* —*v.i.* **4.** to make a clamor; raise an outcry. —*v.t.* **5.** to drive, force, influence, etc., by clamoring: *The press clamored him out of office.* **6.** to utter noisily: *They clamored their demands at the meeting.* Also, *esp. Brit.,* **clam′our.** —**clam′or•er, clam′or•ist,** *n.*

clam•or•ous (klam′ər əs), *adj.* **1.** full of, marked by, or of the nature of clamor. **2.** vigorous in demands or complaints. —**clam′or•ous•ly,** *adv.* —**clam′or•ous•ness,** *n.*

clamp (klamp), *n.* **1.** a device, usu. of some rigid material, for strengthening or supporting objects or fastening them together. **2.** an appliance with opposite sides or parts that may be adjusted or brought closer together to hold or compress something. **3.** one of a pair of movable pieces, made of lead or other soft material, for covering the jaws of a vise and enabling it to grasp without bruising. —*v.t.* **4.** to fasten with or fix in a clamp. **5. clamp down,** to impose more strict control: *to clamp down on crime.*

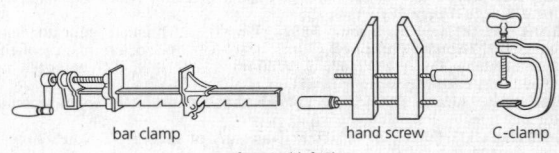

bar clamp   hand screw   C-clamp

clamps (def. 2)

clamp•er (klam′pər), *n.* a spiked metal plate worn on the sole of a shoe to prevent slipping on ice.

clam•shell (klam′shel′), *n.* **1.** the shell of a clam. **2. a.** Also called **clam′shell buck′et.** a dredging bucket opening at the bottom, consisting of two similar pieces hinged together at the top. **b.** a machine equipped with such a bucket.

clam•worm (klam′wûrm′), *n.* any of several polychaete worms of the genus *Nereis,* used as bait.

clan (klan), *n.* **1.** a group of families or households among the Scottish Highlanders, the heads of which claim descent from a common ancestor. **2.** a group of people of common descent; family: *Our whole clan gathers for Thanksgiving.* **3.** a clique, party, or other group united by some common interest. —**clan′less,** *adj.*

clan•des•tine (klan des′tin), *adj.* held or done in secrecy or concealment, esp. for purposes of subversion or deception; stealthy or surreptitious: *clandestine meetings.* —**clan•des′tine•ly,** *adv.*

clang (klang), *v.i.* **1.** to give out a loud, resonant sound, as that produced by a large bell or two heavy pieces of metal striking together. **2.** to move with such sounds: *The trolley clanged down the street.* —*v.t.* **3.** to cause to resound or ring loudly. —*n.* **4.** a clanging sound.

clang•or (klang′ər, klang′gər), *n.* **1.** a loud, resonant sound; clang. **2.** clamorous noise. —*v.i.* **3.** to make a clangor; clang. Also, *esp. Brit.,* **clang′our.** —**clang′or•ous,** *adj.* —**clang′or•ous•ly,** *adv.*

clank (klangk), *n.* **1.** a sharp, hard, nonresonant sound, like that produced by two pieces of metal striking, one against the other: *the clank of chains.* —*v.i.* **2.** to make such a sound. **3.** to move with such sounds: *The old truck clanked up the hill.* —*v.t.* **4.** to cause to make a sharp sound, as metal in collision. **5.** to place, set, etc., with a clank: *to clank the door shut.* —**clank′ing•ly,** *adv.*

clan•nish (klan′ish), *adj.* **1.** pertaining to or characteristic of a clan. **2.** inclined to associate exclusively with the members of one's own group. **3.** imbued with or influenced by the sentiments, prejudices, or the like, of a clan. —**clan′nish•ly,** *adv.* —**clan′nish•ness,** *n.*

clap (klap), *v.,* **clapped, clap•ping,** *n.* —*v.t.* **1.** to strike the palms of (one's hands) together, usu. repeatedly, esp. to express approval. **2.** to strike (someone) amicably with a light slap, as in greeting: *He clapped his friend on the back.* **3.** to strike (an object) against something quickly and forcefully, producing an abrupt, sharp sound. **4.** to bring together forcefully (facing surfaces of the same object): *She clapped the book shut.* **5.** to put or place quickly or forcefully. **6.** to make or arrange hastily (often fol. by *up* or *together*). **7.** to applaud (a performance, etc.) by clapping the hands. —*v.i.* **8.** to clap the hands, as to express approval; applaud. **9.** to make an abrupt, sharp sound, as of flat surfaces striking against one another: *The shutters clapped in the wind.* **10.** to move or strike with such a sound. —*n.* **11.** an act of clapping. **12.** the abrupt, sharp sound produced by clapping. **13.** a resounding blow; slap. **14.** a loud and abrupt or explosive noise, as of thunder. **15.** a sudden stroke, blow, or act.

clap•board (klab′ərd, klap′bôrd′, -bōrd′), *n.* **1.** a long, thin board, thicker along one edge than the other, used in covering the outer walls of buildings. —*adj.* **2.** of or made of clapboard.

clap•per (klap′ər), *n.* the tongue of a bell.

clap•trap (klap′trap′), *n.* **1.** pretentious and insincere or empty language. **2.** any artifice or expedient for winning applause.

Clare (klâr), *n.* a county in W Republic of Ireland. 87,489; 1231 sq. mi. (3190 sq. km).

Clar•en•don (klar′ən dən), *n.* **1. Edward Hyde, 1st Earl of,** 1609–74, British statesman and historian. **2. Council of,** the ecumenical council (1164) occasioned by the opposition of Thomas à Becket to Henry II.

Clare′ (or **Clar′a**) **of Assi′si** (klar′ə), *n.* **Saint,** 1194–1253, Italian nun: founder of the Franciscan order of nuns.

clar•et (klar′it), *n.* **1.** the dry red table wine produced in the Bordeaux region of France. **2.** a similar wine made elsewhere. **3.** Also called **clar′et red′.** a deep purplish red.

clar•i•fy (klar′ə fī′), *v.,* **-fied, -fy•ing.** —*v.t.* **1.** to make (an idea, statement, etc.) clear or intelligible; to free from ambiguity. **2.** to remove solid matter from (a liquid); to make into a clear or pellucid liquid. **3.** to free (the mind, intelligence, etc.) from confusion: *to clarify one's thoughts.* —*v.i.* **4.** to become clear, pure, or intelligible. —**clar′i•fi•ca′tion,** *n.* —**clar′i•fi′er,** *n.*

clar•i•net (klar′ə net′), *n.* a woodwind instrument in the form of a cylindrical tube with a single reed attached to its mouthpiece. —**clar′i•net′ist, clar′i•net′tist,** *n.*

clar•i•on (klar′ē ən), *adj.* **1.** clear and shrill: *the trumpet's clarion call.* —*n.* **2.** an ancient trumpet with a curved shape. **3.** the sound of this instrument. **4.** any similar sound.

clar•i•ty (klar′i tē), *n.* the state or quality of being clear; transparency; lucidity: *the clarity of pure water.*

Clark (klärk), *n.* **1. Glenn,** 1882–1956, U.S. Christian educator and writer. **2. Thomas Campbell** (*Tom*), 1899–1977, associate justice of the U.S. Supreme Court 1949–67. **3. William,** 1770–1838, U.S. explorer: on expedition with Meriwether Lewis.

Clarke, *n.* **Adam,** 1762–1832, English theologian and Bible commentator.

clark•i•a (klär′kē ə), *n., pl.* **clark•i•as.** any of several W North American wildflowers of the genus *Clarkia,* of the evening primrose family, having narrow leaves and red or purple flowers.

clar•y (klâr′ē), *n., pl.* **clar•ies.** a strongly fragrant sage, *Salvia scleria,* having hairy, heart-shaped leaves used chiefly to flavor certain wines.

clash (klash), *v.i.* **1.** to strike or collide with a loud, harsh, usu. metallic noise: *The cymbals clashed.* **2.** to conflict; disagree: *Your ideas often clash with mine.* **3.** (of juxtaposed colors) to be offensive to the eye. **4.** to engage in a physical conflict or contest (often fol. by *with*). —*v.t.* **5.** to strike with a loud, harsh, usu. metallic noise: *The tower bell clashed its mournful note.* —*n.* **6.** a loud, harsh, usu. metallic noise, as of a collision. **7.** a collision, esp. a noisy one. **8.** a conflict, esp. of views or interests. **9.** a battle, fight, or skirmish.

clasp (klasp, kläsp), *n.* **1.** a device, usu. of metal, for fastening together two or more things or parts of the same thing. **2.** a firm grasp or grip. **3.** a tight embrace. **4.** a small bar, star, etc., affixed to a military decoration to indicate that it has been awarded an additional time. —*v.t.* **5.** to fasten with or as if with a clasp. **6.** to furnish with a clasp. **7.** to grasp or grip with the hand. **8.** to hold in a tight embrace; hug: *He clasped the child to him.*

clasp′ knife′, *n.* a large pocket knife having a blade or blades that may be folded into the handle.

class (klas, kläs), *n.* **1.** a number of persons or things regarded as belonging together because of common attributes, qualities, or traits; kind; sort. **2. a.** a group of students meeting regularly to study a subject under the guidance of a teacher. **b.** the period in which they meet. **c.** a meeting of such a group. **d.** a classroom. **3.** a group of students ranked together or graduated in the same year: *the class of '92.* **4.** a social stratum sharing basic economic, political, or cultural characteristics, and having the same social position: *the blue-collar class.* **5.** the system of dividing society; caste. **6.** social rank, esp. high rank. **7.** the members of a given group in society, regarded as a single entity: *the academic class.* **8.** any division of persons or things according to rank or grade: *a hotel of the highest class.* **9.** *Informal.* elegance, grace, or dignity, as in dress and behavior. **10.** any of several grades of accommodations available on ships, airplanes, and the like. **11.** the usual major subdivision of a phylum or division in the classification of organisms, usu. consisting of several orders. **12.** *Math.* a set; a collection. —*adj.* **13.** *Informal.* of high quality, rank, or grade: *a class act; a class performer.* —*v.t.* **14.** to place or arrange in a class; classify: *to class doctors with lawyers.* —*v.i.* **15.** to take or have a place in a particular class: *those who class as believers.* —***Idiom.*** **16. in a class by itself** or **oneself,** having no peer; unequaled.

class′ ac′tion, *n.* a legal proceeding brought by one or more persons representing the interests of a large group of persons. —**class′-ac′tion,** *adj.*

clas•sic (klas′ik), *adj.* **1.** of the first or highest quality, class, or rank: *a classic piece of work.* **2.** serving as a standard, model, or guide: *a classic method of teaching.* **3.** CLASSICAL (defs. 1, 2). **4.** of or adhering to an established set of artistic or scientific standards or methods: *a classic example of cubism.* **5.** basic; fundamental: *the classic rules of conduct.* **6.** of enduring interest, quality, or style: *a classic design.* **7.** of literary or historical renown: *the classic haunts of famous writers.* **8.** traditional or typical: *a classic comedy routine.* **9.** definitive: *a classic text on biology.* **10.** of or pertaining to automobiles distinguished by excellent styling, engineering, and workmanship, esp. those built 1925–1948. —*n.* **11.** an author or a literary work of the first rank, esp. one of demonstrably enduring quality. **12.** an author or literary work of ancient Greece or Rome. **13. classics,** the literature and languages of ancient Greece and Rome (often prec. by *the*). **14.** an artist or artistic production considered a standard. **15.** a work honored as definitive in its field. **16.** something noteworthy of its kind and worth remembering: *Your reply was a classic.* **17.** an article, as of clothing, unchanging in style. **18.** a typical or traditional event, esp. one that is considered to be highly prestigious or the most important of its kind.

clas•si•cal (klas′i kəl), *adj.* **1.** of or characteristic of Greek and Roman antiquity: *classical literature; classical languages.* **2.** conforming to ancient Greek and Roman models in literature or art, or to later systems modeled upon them. **3.** marked by classicism: *classical simplicity.* **4. a.** of or being music of the European tradition marked by sophistication of structural elements and embracing opera, symphonic and chamber music, and works for solo instrument. **b.** of, characterized by, or adhering to a musical style of the latter half of the 18th and the early 19th centuries. **5. a.** of or pertaining to the architecture of ancient Greece and Rome. **b.** simple, well-proportioned, or symmetrical in a manner suggesting the architecture of ancient Greece and Rome. **6.** (*often cap.*) of or pertaining to a style of literature or art that adheres to established treatments and critical standards and that emphasizes formal simplicity, balance, and controlled emotion (contrasted with *romantic*). **7.** versed in the ancient classics: *a classical scholar.* **8.** relating to or teaching academic branches of knowledge. **9.** accepted as standard and authoritative: *classical physics.* —*n.* **10.** classical music. —**clas′si•cal•ly,** *adv.*

clas′sical mechan′ics, *n.* (*used with a sing. v.*) the mechanics of large systems for which Newton's laws of motion apply, as ballistics.

clas•si•cism (klas′ə siz′əm) also **clas•si•cal•ism** (-i kə liz′əm), *n.* **1.** the principles or styles characteristic of the literature and art of ancient Greece and Rome. **2.** adherence to such principles. **3.** the classical style in literature and art, or adherence to its principles (contrasted with *romanticism*). **4.** a Greek or Latin idiom or form, esp. one used in some other language. **5.** classical scholarship or learning.

clas•si•cist (klas′ə sist) also **clas•si•cal•ist** (-i kə list), *n.* **1.** an adherent of classicism in literature or art. **2.** an authority on the classics; a classical scholar.

clas•si•fi•ca•tion (klas′ə fi kā′shən), *n.* **1.** the act of classifying. **2.** the result of classifying or being classified. **3.** one of the groups or classes into which things may be or have been classified. **4.** the assignment of organisms to groups within a system of categories distinguished by structure, origin, etc.

clas•si•fied (klas′ə fīd′), *adj.* **1.** arranged in classes or according to class. **2.** containing advertisements or lists arranged by category: *a classified directory.* **3.** (of information, a document, etc.) assigned to a classification, as *restricted, confidential,* or *secret,* that limits its use to authorized persons. **4.** confidential. —*n.* **5.** CLASSIFIED AD.

clas′sified ad′, *n.* a brief advertisement in a newspaper, magazine, or the like, dealing with offers of or requests for jobs, houses, apartments, cars, etc. Also called **clas′sified advertise′ment, want ad.** —**clas′sified ad′vertising,** *n.*

clas•si•fi•er (klas′ə fī′ər), *n.* **1.** one that classifies. **2.** a device for separating solids of different characteristics by controlled rates of settling.

clas•si•fy (klas′ə fī′), *v.t.,* **-fied, -fy•ing. 1.** to arrange or organize by classes; order according to class. **2.** to limit the availability of (information, a document, etc.) to authorized persons. —**clas′si•fi′a•ble,** *adj.*

clas•sis (klas′is), *n., pl.* **clas•ses** (klas′ēz). (in certain Reformed churches) **1.** the organization of pastors and elders that governs a group of local churches; a presbytery. **2.** the group of churches governed by such an organization.

class•less (klas′lis, kläs′-), *adj.* **1.** having no economic or social distinctions: *a classless society.* **2.** (of an individual) not belonging to a social class or group. —**class′less•ness,** *n.*

class•mate (klas′māt′, kläs′-), *n.* a member of the same class at a school or college.

class•room (klas′ro͞om′, -ro͝om′, kläs′-), *n.* a room, as in a school or college, in which classes are held.

class′ strug′gle, *n.* (in Marxist theory) the struggle for political and economic power carried on between capitalists and workers.

class•work (klas′wûrk′, kläs′-), *n.* the work done in the classroom by students (disting. from *homework*).

class•y (klas′ē, klä′sē), *adj.*, **class•i•er, class•i•est.** *Informal.* having class; stylish; elegant: *a classy nightclub.*

clast (klast), *n.* a fragment of a clastic rock formation.

clas•tic (klas′tik), *adj.* **1.** composed of fragments or particles of older rocks or previously existing solid matter; fragmental. **2.** pertaining to an anatomical model made up of detachable pieces. **3.** *Biol.* breaking up into fragments or separate portions; dividing into parts.

clat•ter (klat′ər), *v.i.* **1.** to make a loud, rattling sound, as that produced by hard objects striking rapidly one against the other. **2.** to move rapidly with such a sound: *The train clattered down the track.* **3.** to talk fast and noisily; chatter. —*v.t.* **4.** to cause to clatter: *Stop clattering the pots and pans.* —*n.* **5.** a rattling noise or series of rattling noises. **6.** noisy disturbance; din; racket. **7.** idle talk; gossip.

Clau•di•us (klô′dē əs), *n.* **1. Claudius I,** 10 B.C.–A.D. 54, Roman emperor A.D. 41–54. **2. Claudius II,** (*"Gothicus"*) A.D. 214–270, Roman emperor 268–270.

clause (klôz), *n.* **1.** a syntactic construction containing a subject and predicate and forming part of a sentence or constituting a whole simple sentence. **2.** a distinct article or provision in a contract, treaty, will, or other formal or legal written document. —**claus′al,** *adj.*

claus•tro•pho•bi•a (klô′strə fō′bē ə), *n.* an abnormal fear of being in enclosed places. —**claus′tro•pho′bic,** *adj.*

clav•i•chord (klav′i kôrd′), *n.* an early keyboard instrument producing a soft sound by means of metal blades attached to the inner ends of the keys gently striking the strings. —**clav′i•chord′ist,** *n.*

clav•i•cle (klav′i kəl), *n.* either of two slender bones of the pectoral girdle that connect the sternum and the scapula; collarbone. —**cla•vic•u•lar** (klə vik′yə lər), *adj.* —**cla•vic′u•late′** (-yə lāt′), *adj.*

cla•vier[1] (klə vēr′, klav′ē ər, klā′vē-), *n.* the keyboard of a musical instrument.

cla•vier[2] (klə vēr′, klav′ē ər, klā′vē-), *n.* any keyboard instrument, esp. one with strings, as a harpsichord. —**cla•vier′ist,** *n.*

clav•i•form (klav′ə fôrm′), *adj.* club-shaped.

claw (klô), *n.* **1.** a sharp, usu. curved, nail on the foot of an animal, as on a cat, dog, or bird. **2.** a similar curved process at the end of the leg of an insect. **3.** the pincerlike extremity of specific limbs of certain arthropods: *lobster claws.* **4.** any part or thing resembling a claw, as the cleft end of the head of a hammer. —*v.t.* **5.** to tear, scratch, seize, pull, etc., with or as if with claws. **6.** to make by or as if by scratching, digging, etc., with hands or claws: *to claw a hole in the earth.* **7.** to proceed by or as if by using the hands or claws: *They clawed their way through the jungle.* —*v.i.* **8.** to scratch, tear, pull, or dig with or as if with claws. —**claw′less,** *adj.*

claw′ ham′mer, *n.* **1.** a hammer having a head with one end curved and cleft for pulling out nails. **2.** TAIL COAT.

clay (klā), *n.* **1.** a natural earthy material that is plastic when wet, consisting essentially of hydrated silicates of aluminum: used for making bricks, pottery, etc. **2.** earth; mud. **3.** earth regarded as the material from which the human body was formed. **4.** the human body, esp. as distinguished from the spirit or soul. —**clay′ish, clay′like′,** *adj.*

Clay (klā), *n.* **1. Cassius Marcellus,** 1810–1903, U.S. antislavery leader. **2. Cassius Marcellus, Jr.,** original name of Muhammad ALI. **3. Henry,** 1777–1852, U.S. statesman and orator. **4. Lucius (DuBignon),** 1897–1978, U.S. general.

clay′ pig′eon, *n.* a disk of baked clay or other material hurled into the air from a trap as a target in trapshooting or skeet.

Clay′ton Antitrust′ Act′, *n.* an act of Congress in 1914 supplementing the Sherman Antitrust Act and establishing the FTC.

Clay′ton-Bul′wer Trea′ty (klāt′n bo͝ol′wər), *n.* an agreement between the U.S. and Great Britain in 1850 guaranteeing that any canal built to connect the Atlantic and Pacific across Central America would be jointly controlled, open to all nations, and unfortified. Compare HAY-PAUNCEFOTE TREATY.

clay•to•ni•a (klā tō′nē ə), *n., pl.* **-ni•as.** any of several low, succulent plants belonging to the genus *Claytonia,* of the purslane family, having long clusters of white or rose-colored flowers.

clean (klēn), *adj.* **1.** free from dirt; unsoiled; unstained: *a clean dress.* **2.** free from foreign or extraneous matter; pure: *clean sound.* **3.** free from pollutants: *clean air; clean energy.* **4.** characterized by a fresh, wholesome quality. **5.** having few or no corrections: *The printer submitted clean proofs.* **6.** free from roughness: *He made a clean cut with a razor.* **7.** not ornate; trim: *the clean lines of a ship.* **8.** complete; unqualified: *a clean break with tradition.* **9.** morally pure; innocent; honorable: *to lead a clean life.* **10.** fair: *a clean fighter.* **11.** inoffensive in language or content; without obscenity. **12.** (of a document, record, etc.) bearing no marks of discreditable or unlawful conduct; listing no offenses. **13.** *Slang.* **a.** innocent of any crime. **b.** not having a criminal record. **c.** carrying or containing no evidence of unlawful activity or intent. **d.** not using narcotics. **14. a.** not radioactive. **b.** (of a nuclear weapon) producing little or no radioactive fallout. **15.** (of a document or financial instrument) free from qualifications or restrictions: *a clean bill of lading.* **16.** free from defects: *a clean diamond.* **17.** free from obstructions. **18.** made without any difficulty: *a clean getaway.* **19.** having no blemish so as to make impure according to dietary or ritual law. **20.** dexterously performed; adroit: *a clean serve in tennis.* **21.** *Slang.* without money or funds. —*adv.* **22.** in a clean manner. **23.** so as to be clean: *This shirt will never wash clean.* **24.** *Informal.* wholly; completely; quite: *The bullet passed clean through the wall.* —*v.t.* **25.** to make clean or clear. **26.** to dry-clean. **27.** to remove the entrails and other inedible parts from (poultry, fish, etc.); dress. **28.** *Slang.* to take away or win all or almost all the money or possessions of: *That last bet cleaned me out.* —*v.i.* **29.** to perform or undergo a process of cleaning. **30. clean out, a.** to empty in order to straighten or clean. **b.** to empty; deplete; evacuate. **31. clean up, a.** to wash or tidy up. **b.** to rid of undesirable features. **c.** to put an end to: *to clean up yesterday's chores.* **d.** to make a large profit. —***Idiom.*** **32. come clean,** *Slang.* to tell the truth, esp. to admit one's guilt. —**clean′a•ble,** *adj.* —**clean′ness,** *n.*

clean′ bill′ of health′, *n.* **1.** a certificate of health attesting the lack of a contagious disease. **2.** an assurance, as by a doctor, that one is in good health. **3.** Also, **clean′ bill′.** an assurance, esp. an official verdict by a committee, that a group or an individual has proved, under investigation, to be morally sound, fit for office, etc.

clean′-cut′, *adj.* **1.** having a distinct, regular shape. **2.** clearly outlined. **3.** neat and wholesome. **4.** unambiguously clear; clear-cut.

clean•er (klē′nər), *n.* **1.** a person who cleans, esp. as an occupation. **2.** an apparatus or machine for cleaning. **3.** a preparation for use in cleaning. **4.** the owner or operator of a dry-cleaning establishment. **5.** Usu., **cleaners.** a dry-cleaning establishment. —***Idiom.*** **6. take to the cleaners,** *Slang.* to take all the money or property of, esp. by cheating.

clean•li•ness (klen′lē nis), *n.* **1.** the quality or state of being cleanly. —***Proverb.*** **2. Cleanliness is next to godliness,** only religious devotion is more important than being personally and habitually neat.

clean•ly (*adj.* klen′lē; *adv.* klēn′-), *adj.*, **-li•er, -li•est,** *adv.* —*adj.* **1.** personally neat. **2.** habitually kept clean. —*adv.* **3.** in a clean manner.

clean′ room′, *n.* a room in which contaminants such as dust are reduced to create a sterile or nearly sterile environment for biological or manufacturing procedures.

cleanse (klenz), *v.*, **cleansed, cleans•ing.** —*v.t.* **1.** to make clean. **2.** to remove by or as if by cleaning: *to cleanse sin from the soul.* —*v.i.* **3.** to become clean. —**cleans′a•ble,** *adj.*

cleans•er (klen′zər), *n.* **1.** a preparation for cleansing, as a liquid or powder for scouring sinks, bathtubs, etc., or a cream for cleaning the face. **2.** a person or thing that cleanses.

clean′-shav′en, *adj.* having the beard and mustache shaved off.

clean′ sweep′, *n.* **1.** an overwhelming or decisive victory, as by a political candidate who wins in all or almost all election districts. **2.** the winning of all the prizes, rounds, contests, etc., in a competition or of all the games in a series. **3.** a thorough or sweeping change, esp. one effected by the large-scale removal or elimination of unwanted persons or things: *The new president made a clean sweep when he joined the company, replacing all the department heads.*

clean•up (klēn′up′), *n.* **1.** the act or process of cleaning up. —*adj.* **2.** (of a baseball batter) occupying the fourth position in the batting order.

clear (klēr), *adj.* **1.** free from darkness, obscurity, or cloudiness: *a clear day.* **2.** transparent; pellucid: *clear water.* **3.** without discoloration, defect, or blemish: *clear skin.* **4.** of a pure, even color: *a clear yellow.* **5.** easily seen; sharply defined: *a clear outline.* **6.** distinctly perceptible to the ear; easily heard: *a clear sound.* **7.** free from hoarse, harsh, or rasping qualities: *a clear voice.* **8.** easily understood: *clear answers.* **9.** entirely comprehensible: *The causes of inflation may never be clear.* **10.** distinct; evident; plain: *a clear case of misbehavior.* **11.** free from confusion, uncertainty, or doubt: *clear thinking.* **12.** perceiving or discerning distinctly: *a clear mind.* **13.** free from blame or guilt: *a clear conscience.* **14.** serene; untroubled: *a clear brow.* **15.** free from obstructions or obstacles; open: *a clear path.* **16.** free from entanglement or contact: *He kept clear of her after the argument.* **17.** without limitation or qualification; absolute: *a clear victory.* **18.** free from obligation, liability, or debt: *a return of 4 percent, clear of taxes.* **19.** without deduction or diminution: *a clear profit of $1000.* **20.** freed or emptied of contents, cargo, etc. **21.** (of tree trunks or timber) free from branches or protruding or rough parts. **22.** (of an *l*-sound) pronounced with the front of the tongue raised, giving front-vowel resonance, as the *l* in *leaf.* Compare DARK (def. 15). **23.** bright; shining: *a clear flame.* —*adv.* **24.** in a clear or distinct manner; clearly. **25.** so as not to be in contact with or near; away: *Stand clear of the closing doors.* **26.** entirely; completely; clean: *to cut a piece clear off.* —*v.t.* **27.** to remove people or objects from: *to clear the table of dishes.* **28.** to remove (people or objects): *to clear the press from the courtroom.* **29.** to make clear, transparent, or pellucid: *to clear a liquid.* **30.** to make free of confusion, doubt, or uncertainty: *to clear the mind.* **31.** to make understandable or lucid; free from ambiguity or obscurity: *Her reply cleared the confusion.* **32.** to make (a path, road, etc.) by removing any obstruction. **33.** to eat all the food on: *to clear one's* *plate.* **34.** to relieve (the throat) of some obstruction, as phlegm, by forcing air through the larynx, usu. producing a rasping sound. **35.** to make a similar rasping noise in (the throat), as to express disapproval or to attract attention. **36.** to free of anything defamatory or discrediting: *to clear one's name.* **37.** to free from suspicion, accusation, or imputation of guilt: *The jury cleared the defendant of the charge.* **38.** to remove instructions or data from (a computer, display screen, etc.). **39.** to pass by or over without contact or entanglement: *The ship cleared the reef.* **40.** to pass through or away from: *The bill cleared the Senate.* **41.** to pass (checks or other commercial paper) through a clearinghouse. **42.** (of mail, telephone calls, etc.) to process, handle, reroute, etc. **43.** to free from debt: *to clear an estate.* **44.** to gain as clear profit: *to clear $1000 in a transaction.* **45.** to pay (a debt) in full. **46.** to receive authorization before taking action on: *to clear a plan with headquarters.* **47.** to give clearance to; authorize. **48.** to authorize (a person, agency, etc.) to use classified information, documents, etc. **49.** to remove trees, buildings, or other obstructions from (land), as for farming or construction. **50.** to free (a ship, cargo, etc.) by satisfying customs and other requirements. **51.** to try or otherwise dispose of (the cases awaiting court action): *to clear the docket.* **52.** to jump (a specific height or distance): *He cleared 12 feet in the high jump.* —*v.i.* **53.** to become clear: *The sky cleared.* **54.** to disappear; vanish: *These problems will clear shortly.* **55.** to exchange checks and bills, and settle balances, as in a clearinghouse. **56.** to become free from doubt, anxiety, misunderstanding, etc. **57.** to pass an authority for review, approval, etc. **58.** to comply with customs and other legal requirements at port. **59.** (of a commodity for sale) to sell out; become bought out: *Wheat cleared rapidly.* **60. clear away** or **off, a.** to leave. **b.** to disappear. **61. clear out, a.** to remove the contents of: *Clear out the closet.* **b.** to remove; take away: *Clear out the mess in your room.* **c.** to go away, esp. quickly. **d.** to drive or force out. **62. clear up, a.** to make clear; explain. **b.** to put in order; tidy up. —*n.* **63.** a clear or unobstructed space. —*Idiom.* **64. clear the air** or **atmosphere,** to eliminate hidden feelings of anger, distrust, etc., by discussing them openly. **65. in the clear,** absolved of blame or guilt.

clear′-air′ tur′bulence, *n.* atmospheric turbulence in air devoid of clouds or other visible signs of disturbance. [1950–55]

clear•ance (klēr′əns), *n.* **1.** the act of clearing. **2.** the distance between two objects; an amount of clear space. **3.** a formal authorization permitting access to classified information, documents, etc. **4.** Also called **clear′ance sale′.** the disposal of merchandise at reduced prices to make room for new goods. **5.** a space between two moving machine parts, left to avoid clashing or to permit relatively free motion. **6. a.** the clearing of a ship at a port. **b.** Also called **clear′ance pa′pers.** the official papers certifying this.

clear-cut (klēr′kut′ for 1, 2; klēr′kut′ for 3–5), *adj., n., v.,* **-cut, -cutting.** —*adj.* **1.** formed with or having clearly defined outlines. **2.** completely evident; definite: *a clear-cut case of treason.* **3.** of or pertaining to a section of forest where all trees have been cut down for harvesting. —*n.* **4.** Also called **clear′ cut′ting.** a section of forest where all trees have been cut down for harvesting. —*v.t.* **5.** to fell all the trees in (a section of forest) for harvesting. Also, **clear/cut′** (for defs. 3–5).

clear•head•ed (klēr′hed′id), *adj.* having or showing an alert mind. —**clear′head′ed•ly,** *adv.* —**clear′head′ed•ness,** *n.*

clear•ing (klēr′ing), *n.* **1.** the act of a person or thing that clears; the process of becoming clear. **2.** a tract of land, as in a forest, that contains no trees or bushes. **3.** the reciprocal exchange between banks of checks and drafts, and the settlement of the differences. **4. clearings,** the total of claims settled at a clearinghouse.

clear′ing•house′ or **clear′ing house′,** *n., pl.* **-hous•es** (-hou′ziz). **1.** a place or institution where mutual claims and accounts are settled, as between banks. **2.** a central agency for the collection and distribution of materials, information, etc.

clear-sight•ed (klēr′sī′tid), *adj.* **1.** having clear or sharp eyesight. **2.** having or marked by keen perception or sound judgment. —**clear′-sight′ed•ly,** *adv.* —**clear′-sight′ed•ness,** *n.*

clear•wing (klēr′wing′), *n.* any moth of the family Aegeriidae, having transparent, scaleless wings.

cleat (klēt), *n.* **1.** a wedge-shaped block or strip of wood, metal, or the like, fastened to a surface to serve as a check or support. **2.** a strip of metal, wood, or the like, fastened across a surface to provide sure footing. **3.** a conical or rectangular projection, usu. of hard rubber, attached to the sole of a shoe to provide greater traction. **4.** a shoe fitted with such projections. **5.** an object of wood or metal having projecting horns to which ropes may be belayed. —*v.t.* **6.** to supply or strengthen with cleats; fasten to or with a cleat.

cleav•age (klē′vij), *n.* **1.** the act of cleaving or splitting. **2.** the state of being cleft. **3.** the area between a woman's breasts, esp. when revealed by a low-cut neckline. **4.** the tendency of crystals, certain minerals, rocks, etc., to break in preferred directions so as to yield more or less smooth surfaces **(cleav′age planes′). 5.** the breaking down of a molecule or compound into simpler structures. **6.** the series of cell divisions in mitosis that converts the fertilized egg into smaller cells.

cleave¹ (klēv), *v.i.,* **cleaved, cleav•ing. 1.** to adhere closely; cling (usu. fol. by *to*). **2.** to remain faithful: *to cleave to one's principles.* —**cleav′ing•ly,** *adv.*

cleave² (klēv), *v.,* **cleft** or **cleaved** or **clove, cleft** or **cleaved** or **cloven, cleav•ing.** —*v.t.* **1.** to split or divide by or as if by a cutting blow, esp. along a natural line of division, as the grain of wood. **2.** to make

by or as if by cutting: *to cleave a path through the wilderness.* **3.** to penetrate or pass through (air, water, etc.): *The bow of the boat cleaved the water cleanly.* **4.** to cut off; sever: *to cleave a branch from a tree.* —*v.i.* **5.** to part or split. **6.** to penetrate or advance by or as if by cutting (usu. fol. by *through*).

cleav•er (klē′vər), *n.* **1.** a heavy broad-bladed knife or long-bladed hatchet, esp. one used by butchers for cutting meat into joints or pieces. **2.** a person or thing that cleaves.

cleav•ers (klē′vərz), *n., pl.* **-ers.** a North American plant, *Galium aparine,* of the madder family, having short, hooked bristles on the stems and leaves and bearing very small white flowers. Also called **goose grass.**

clef (klef), *n.* a sign at the beginning of a musical staff to show the pitch of the notes.

cleft¹ (kleft), *n.* **1.** a space or opening made by cleavage; a split. **2.** a division formed by cleaving. **3.** a hollow area or indentation: *a chin with a cleft.*

cleft² (kleft), *v.* **1.** a pt. and pp. of CLEAVE². —*adj.* **2.** cloven; split; divided. **3.** (of plant parts, as a leaf) having divisions that extend more than halfway to the midrib or base.

cleft′ lip′, *n.* a congenital defect of the upper lip in which a longitudinal fissure extends into one or both nostrils.

cleft′ pal′ate, *n.* a congenital defect of the palate in which a longitudinal fissure exists in the roof of the mouth.

cleft′ sen′tence, *n.* a sentence in which a simpler sentence is paraphrased by being divided into two parts, each with its own verb, in order to emphasize certain information, as *It was a mushroom that Alice ate* instead of *Alice ate a mushroom.*

clem•a•tis (klem′ə tis, kli mat′is), *n.* any of numerous plants or woody vines belonging to the genus *Clematis,* of the buttercup family, including many species cultivated for their showy flowers.

clem•en•cy (klem′ən sē), *n., pl.* **-cies. 1.** the disposition to show forbearance, compassion, or forgiveness in judging or punishing; leniency; mercy. **2.** an act or deed of mercy or leniency. **3.** (of the weather) mildness or temperateness.

Clem•ens (klem′ənz), *n.* **Samuel Langhorne,** (*"Mark Twain"*), 1835–1910, U.S. author and humorist.

clem•ent (klem′ənt), *adj.* **1.** mild or merciful in disposition or character; lenient; compassionate: *A clement judge reduced his sentence.* **2.** (of the weather) mild or temperate; pleasant. [< Latin *clēmēns* gentle, merciful] —**clem′ent•ly,** *adv.*

Clem•ent (klem′ənt), *n.* **1. Clement I, Saint** (*Clement of Rome*), A.D. c30–c100, first of the Apostolic Fathers: pope 88?–97? **2. Clement VII,** (*Giulio de′ Medici*), 1478–1534, Italian ecclesiastic: pope 1523–34.

Clem′ent of Alexan′dria, *n.* (*Titus Flavius Clemens*) A.D. c150–c215, Greek Christian theologian and writer.

clench (klench), *v.t.* **1.** to close (the hands, teeth, etc.) tightly. **2.** to grasp firmly; grip. **3.** CLINCH (defs. 1, 2). —*v.i.* **4.** to close or knot up tightly. —*n.* **5.** the act of clenching. **6.** a tight hold; grip. **7.** something that clenches or holds fast. **8.** CLINCH (defs. 7, 9, 10).

cle•o•me (klē ō′mē), *n.* a strong-smelling plant or shrub of the genus *Cleome,* of the caper family, mostly natives of tropical regions, and often bearing showy flowers.

Cle•o•pas (klē′ə pas′), *n.* one of two disciples who met the resurrected Jesus on the road to Emmaus. Luke 24:13–35.

Cle•o•pa•tra (klē′ə pa′trə, -pä′-, -pā′-), *n.* 69–30 B.C., queen of Egypt 51–49, 48–30.

Clep•hane (klep′ən), *n.* **Elizabeth C(ecilia),** 1830–69, Scottish hymn writer.

clere•sto•ry (klēr′stôr′ē, -stōr′ē), *n., pl.* **-ries.** a portion of an interior rising above adjacent rooftops and having windows admitting daylight to the interior.

clerestory — triforium, gallery, ambulatory arcade

cler•gy (klûr′jē), *n., pl.* **-gies.** the group or body of ordained persons in a religion, as distinguished from the laity. —**Usage.** See COLLECTIVE NOUN.

cler•gy•man (klûr′jē mən), *n.*, *pl.* **-men.** a member of the clergy.

cler•gy•wom•an (klûr′jē wo͝om′ən), *n.*, *pl.* **-wom•en.** a woman who is a member of the clergy.

cler•ic (kler′ik), *n.* **1.** a member of the clergy. **2. clerics,** (*used with a pl. v.*) small-sized reading glasses, usu. rimless or with a thin metal frame. —*adj.* **3.** pertaining to the clergy; clerical.

cler•i•cal (kler′i kəl), *adj.* **1.** of, pertaining to, appropriate for, or assigned to an office clerk: *a clerical job.* **2.** doing the work of a clerk: *a clerical staff.* **3.** of, pertaining to, or characteristic of the clergy or a cleric. —*n.* **4.** a cleric. **5. clericals,** *Informal.* clerical garments.

cler′ical col′lar, *n.* a stiff, narrow, bandlike white collar fastened at the back of the neck, worn by certain clerics.

cler•i•cal•ism (kler′i kə liz′əm), *n.* **1.** power or influence of the clergy in government, politics, etc. **2.** a policy of supporting or advocating such power or influence. —**cler′i•cal•ist,** *n.*

clerk (klûrk; *Brit.* klärk), *n.* **1.** a person employed to keep records, file, type, or perform other general office tasks. **2.** a salesclerk. **3.** a person who keeps the records and performs the routine business of a court, legislature, etc. **4.** a member of the clergy; ecclesiastic. —*v.i.* **5.** to act or serve as a clerk. —**clerk′ish,** *adj.* —**clerk′ship,** *n.*

Cleve•land (klēv′lənd), *n.* **1. (Stephen) Grover,** 1837–1908, 22nd and 24th president of the U.S. 1885–89, 1893–97. **2.** a port in NE Ohio, on Lake Erie. 492,901.

clev•er (klev′ər), *adj.* **1.** mentally bright; having sharp or quick intelligence; able. **2.** superficially skillful or witty; facile: *a clever remark.* **3.** showing inventiveness or originality; ingenious: *a clever idea.* **4.** adroit with the hands or body; dexterous or nimble. —**clev′er•ish,** *adj.* —**clev′er•ly,** *adv.* —**clev′er•ness,** *n.*

clev•is (klev′is), *n.* a U-shaped yoke at the end of a chain or rod, between the ends of which a lever, hook, etc., can be pinned or bolted.

clew (klo͞o), *n.* **1.** CLUE (def. 1). **2.** either lower corner of a square sail or the after lower corner of a fore-and-aft sail. **3.** a ball or skein of thread, yarn, etc. **4.** Usu., **clews.** the rigging for a hammock. —*v.t.* **5.** to coil into a ball. **6.** CLUE (def. 3).

cli•ché or **cli•che** (klē shā′, kli-), *n.* **1.** a trite, stereotyped expression, as *sadder but wiser,* or *strong as an ox.* **2.** (in art, literature, drama, etc.) a trite or hackneyed plot, character development, use of form, musical style, etc. **3.** anything that has become trite or commonplace through overuse. **4.** *Print. Brit.* **a.** a stereotype. **b.** a reproduction made in a like manner. —*adj.* **5.** trite; hackneyed; stereotyped; clichéd.

cli•chéd (klē shād′, kli-), *adj.* **1.** full of or characterized by clichés. **2.** trite; hackneyed; commonplace: *a clichéd expression.*

click (klik), *n.* **1.** a slight, sharp sound: *the click of a latch.* **2.** a small device for preventing backward movement of a mechanism, as a detent or pawl. **3.** any of a variety of usu. implosive speech sounds, phonemic in some languages, produced by suction occlusion and plosive or affricative release. **4.** any of a variety of sounds used in calling or urging on horses or other animals, in expressing reprimand or sympathy, or produced in audible kissing. **5.** *Informal.* a sudden insight or realization. —*v.i.* **6.** to emit or make a slight, sharp sound, or series of such sounds, as by the cocking of a pistol. **7.** *Informal.* **a.** to succeed; make a hit. **b.** to fit together; function well together: *Their personalities don't really click.* **c.** to become suddenly clear or intelligible. **8.** *Computers.* to depress and release a mouse button rapidly, as to select an icon. —*v.t.* **9.** to cause to click. **10.** to strike together with a click: *He clicked his heels and saluted.* —**click′er,** *n.* —**click′less,** *adj.*

click′ bee′tle, *n.* any of numerous beetles of the family Elateridae, having the ability to spring up with a clicking sound when placed on their backs. Also called **snapping beetle.**

cli•ent (klī′ənt), *n.* **1.** a person or group that uses the professional advice or services of a lawyer, accountant, architect, etc. **2.** a person who is receiving the benefits, services, etc., of a social welfare agency, a government bureau, etc. **3.** a customer. **4.** anyone under the patronage of another; a dependent. **5.** CLIENT STATE. **6.** (in ancient Rome) a plebeian who lived under the patronage of a patrician. —**cli•en•tal** (klī en′tl, klī′ən tl), *adj.* —**cli′ent•less,** *adj.*

cli•en•tele (klī′ən tel′, klē′än-), *n.* the clients or customers, as of a professional person or shop, considered collectively; a group or body of clients: *a wealthy clientele.*

cli′ent state′, *n.* a country that is dependent on a richer or more powerful country for its political, economic, or military welfare.

cliff (klif), *n.* a high, steep rock face; precipice. —**cliff′like′,** *adj.*

cliff′ dwell′er, *n.* **1.** (*usu. caps.*) a member of a prehistoric people of the southwestern U.S. who were ancestors of the Pueblo Indians and built shelters in caves or on the ledges of cliffs. **2.** a person who lives in an apartment house. —**cliff′ dwell′ing,** *n.*

cliff′-hang′er or **cliff′hang′er,** *n.* **1.** a melodramatic adventure serial in which each installment ends in suspense. **2.** a situation or contest of which the outcome is uncertain up to the very last moment. —**cliff′-hang′ing,** *adj.*

cli•mac•ter•ic (klī mak′tər ik, klī′mak ter′ik), *n.* **1.** a period of decrease of reproductive capacity in men and women, culminating, in women, in the menopause. **2.** any critical period. **3.** a year in which important changes in health, fortune, etc., are held by some theories to occur, as one's sixty-third year **(grand climacteric).** —*adj.* **4.** Also, **cli′mac•ter′i•cal.** critical; crucial.

cli•mate (klī′mit), *n.* **1.** the composite or generally prevailing weather conditions of a region, as temperature, air pressure, humidity, precipitation, cloudiness, and winds, throughout the year, averaged over a series of years. **2.** a region or area characterized by a given climate: *to move to a warm climate.* **3.** the prevailing attitudes, standards, or conditions of a group, period, or place: *a climate of political unrest.* —**cli•mat′ic** (-mat′ik), *adj.*

cli•ma•tize (klī′mə tīz′), *v.t.*, **-tized, -tiz•ing. 1.** to acclimate to a new environment. **2.** to prepare or modify (a building, etc.) for use or comfort in a specific climate. —**cli′ma•ti•za′tion,** *n.*

cli•ma•tol•o•gy (klī′mə tol′ə jē), *n.* the science that deals with climates or climatic conditions. —**cli′ma•to•log′ic** (-tl oj′ik), *adj.* —**cli′ma•to•log′i•cal•ly,** *adv.* —**cli′ma•tol′o•gist,** *n.*

cli•max (klī′maks), *n.* **1.** the highest or most intense point in the development or resolution of something; culmination. **2.** (in a dramatic or literary work) a decisive moment that is of maximum intensity or is a major turning point in a plot. **3. a.** a rhetorical figure consisting of a series of related ideas so arranged that each surpasses the preceding in force or intensity. **b.** the last term or member of this figure. **4.** an orgasm. **5.** the stable and self-perpetuating end stage in the ecological succession of a plant and animal community. —*v.t., v.i.* **6.** to bring to or reach a climax. —**cli•mac′tic,** *adj.*

climb (klīm), *v.i.* **1.** to go up or ascend; move upward or toward the top of something: *The sun climbed over the hill.* **2.** to slope upward: *The road climbs steeply.* **3.** to ascend by twining or by means of tendrils, adhesive tissues, etc., as a plant. **4.** to proceed using the hands and feet (often fol. by *along, around, down, over,* etc.), esp. on or from an elevated area. **5.** to ascend in prominence, fortune, etc. —*v.t.* **6.** to ascend, go up, or get to the top of, esp. by the use of the hands and feet: *to climb a ladder; to climb the stairs.* **7.** to go to the top of and over: *The prisoners climbed the wall and escaped.* —*n.* **8.** an ascent by climbing: *a climb to the top of the hill.* **9.** a place to be climbed: *That peak is quite a climb.* —**climb′a•ble,** *adj.*

climb•er (klī′mər), *n.* **1.** a person or thing that climbs. **2.** a climbing plant. **3.** a device to assist in climbing, as a climbing iron.

climb′ing i′ron, *n.* one of a pair of spiked iron frames, strapped to the shoe, leg, or knee, to help in climbing trees, telephone poles, etc. Also called **climb′ing spur′, spur.**

climb′ing perch′, *n.* a brown labyrinth fish, *Anabas testudineus,* of SE Asia and the Malay Archipelago, having a specialized breathing apparatus that enables it to move about on land.

clinch (klinch), *v.t.* **1.** to settle (a matter) decisively. **2. a.** to secure (a nail, screw, etc.) in position by beating down the protruding point. **b.** to fasten (objects) together by nails, screws, etc., secured in this manner. —*v.i.* **3.** to engage in a clinch in boxing. **4.** *Slang.* to embrace, esp. passionately. **5.** (of a clinched nail, screw, etc.) to hold fast; be secure. —*n.* **6.** the act of clinching. **7.** an act or instance of one or both boxers holding the other about the arms or body to prevent or hinder the opponent's punches. **8.** *Slang.* a passionate embrace. **9.** a clinched nail or fastening. **10.** the bent part of a clinched nail, screw, etc. Also, **clench** (for defs. 1, 2, 7, 9, 10). —**clinch′ing•ly,** *adv.*

clinch•er (klin′chər), *n.* **1.** a person or thing that clinches. **2.** a statement, argument, fact, situation, or the like, that is decisive or conclusive. **3.** a nail, screw, etc., for clinching.

cling (kling), *v.*, **clung, cling•ing,** *n.* —*v.i.* **1.** to adhere closely; stick to: *Wet paper clings to glass.* **2.** to hold tight, as by grasping or embracing; cleave: *The child clung to her mother.* **3.** to remain attached, as to an idea, hope, memory, etc. **4.** to cohere. —*n.* **5.** the act of clinging; adherence. —**cling′er,** *n.* —**cling′ing•ly,** *adv.*

cling•fish (kling′fish′), *n.*, *pl.* (*esp. collectively*) **-fish,** (*esp. for kinds or species*) **-fish•es.** any fish of the family Gobiesocidae, having a sucking disk on the abdomen.

cling•stone (kling′stōn′), *n.* **1.** a peach or other fruit having a pit that clings to the pulp. **2.** the pit itself.

clin•ic (klin′ik), *n.* **1.** a place for the medical treatment of nonresident patients, sometimes at reduced cost. **2.** a group of physicians, dentists, or the like, working in cooperation and sharing facilities. **3.** a class or group convening for instruction or remedial work or for the diagnosis and treatment of specific problems: *a reading clinic.* **4.** the instruction of medical students by examining or treating patients in their presence or by their examining or treating patients under supervision. **5.** a class of students assembled for such instruction. —*adj.* **6.** of a clinic; clinical. [< Latin *clīnicus* < Greek *klīnikós* pertaining to a (sick) bed]

clin′ical psychol′ogy, *n.* the branch of psychology dealing with the diagnosis and treatment of behavioral and personality disorders. —**clin′ical psychol′ogist,** *n.*

clin′ical thermom′eter, *n.* a small thermometer used to measure body temperature.

cli•ni•cian (kli nish′ən), *n.* a physician or other qualified person who is involved in the treatment and observation of living patients, as distinguished from one engaged in research.

clink[1] (klingk), *v.i., v.t.* **1.** to make or cause to make a light, sharp, ringing sound: *The coins clinked together.* —*n.* **2.** a clinking sound.

clink[2] (klingk), *n. Slang.* a prison; jail; lockup.

clink•er[1] (kling′kər), *n.* **1.** a mass of incombustible matter fused together, as in the burning of coal. **2.** a hard Dutch brick, used esp. for paving.

clink•er[2] (kling′kər), *n.* a person or thing that clinks.

clink•er[3] (kling′kər), *n. Slang.* **1.** a wrong note in a musical perfor-

C

mance. **2.** any mistake or error. **3.** something that is a failure; a product of inferior quality.

cli·nom·e·ter (klī nom′i tər, kli-), *n.* an instrument for determining angles of inclination or slope. —**cli′no·met′ric** (-nə me′trik), *n., adj.* —**cli·nom′e·try,** *n.*

clin·quant (kling′kənt), *adj.* **1.** glittering, esp. with tinsel; decked with garish finery. —*n.* **2.** imitation gold leaf; tinsel; false glitter.

Clin·ton (klin′tn) *n.* **1. De Witt** 1769–1828, U.S. statesman. **2. George,** 1739–1812, vice president of the U.S. 1805–12. **3. Sir Henry,** 1738?–95, commander of the British forces in the American Revolutionary War. **4. Hillary Rodham,** born 1947, U.S. attorney and social reformer (wife of William J. Clinton). **5. William Jefferson** (*Bill*), born 1946, 42nd president of the U.S. since 1993.

clin·to·ni·a (klin tō′nē ə), *n., pl.* **-ni·as.** any plant of the genus *Clintonia,* of the lily family, having white or yellow flowers on a short stalk.

clip¹ (klip), *v.,* **clipped, clipped** or **clipt, clip·ping,** *n.* —*v.t.* **1.** to cut, or cut off or out, as with shears: *to clip a rose from a bush.* **2.** to trim by cutting: *to clip a hedge.* **3.** to cut or trim the hair or fleece of; shear. **4.** to cut short; curtail: *We clipped our visit by a week.* **5.** to shorten (a word or phrase) by dropping one or more syllables. **6.** *Informal.* to hit with a quick, sharp blow: *He clipped me on the jaw.* —*v.i.* **7.** to clip or cut something. **8.** to cut articles or pictures from a newspaper, magazine, etc. **9.** to move swiftly: *The motorcycle clipped along the highway.* —*n.* **10.** anything clipped off, esp. the wool shorn at a single shearing of sheep. **11.** the amount of wool shorn in one season. **12. clips,** (*used with a pl. v.*) an instrument for clipping; shears. **13.** FILM CLIP. **14.** *Informal.* CLIPPING (def. 2). **15.** *Informal.* a quick, sharp blow. **16.** rate; pace: *at a rapid clip.*

clip² (klip), *n., v.,* **clipped, clip·ping.** —*n.* **1.** a device that grips and holds tightly. **2.** a metal or plastic clasp for holding together papers, letters, etc. **3.** a frame holding cartridges for insertion into the magazine of a firearm. **4.** an article of jewelry or other decoration clipped onto clothing, shoes, hats, etc. —*v.t.* **5.** to fasten with or as if with a clip. **6.** to grip or hold tightly. **7.** to encircle; encompass. **8.** (in football) to block illegally by throwing one's body across a player's legs from behind. —*v.i.* **9.** to fasten or hold with or as if with a clip (often fol. by *on*). **10.** to clip a football player.

clip·board (klip′bôrd′, -bōrd′), *n.* a small board serving as a portable writing surface, with a clip at the top for holding papers.

clip′-on′, *adj.* **1.** designed to be clipped on easily, esp. by a self-attached clip: *a clip-on bow tie.* —*n.* **2.** a clip-on device, ornament, or the like.

clipped (klipt), *adj.* characterized by quick, terse, and clear enunciation.

clipped′ form′, *n.* a word formed by dropping one or more syllables from a longer word or phrase with no change in meaning, as *deli* from *delicatessen* and *flu* from *influenza.*

clip·per (klip′ər), *n.* **1.** a person or thing that clips or cuts. **2.** Often, **clippers.** (*often used with a pl. v.*) a cutting tool, esp. shears: *hedge clippers.* **3.** Usu., **clippers.** (*usu. used with a pl. v.*) a mechanical or electric tool for cutting hair, fingernails, or the like. **4.** a swift sailing vessel, a three-masted ship built in the U.S. c1845–70. **5.** a person or thing that moves along swiftly.

clip·ping (klip′ing), *n.* **1.** the act of a person or thing that clips. **2.** an article, advertisement, etc., clipped from a newspaper or magazine. —**clip′ping·ly,** *adv.*

clique (klēk, klik), *n., v.,* **cliqued, cli·quing.** —*n.* **1.** a small, exclusive group of people; coterie. —*v.i.* **2.** to form or associate in a clique. —**cli′quey, cli′quy,** *adj.* —**cli′quish,** *adj.* —**cli′quish·ness,** *n.*

clit·o·ris (klit′ər is, klī tôr′is, -tōr′-), *n., pl.* **clit·o·ris·es, cli·to·ri·des** (kli tôr′i dēz′, -tōr′-). the small erectile organ of the vulva. —**clit′o·ral,** (-tôr′ik), **clit′o·rid′e·an** (-ə rid′ē ən), *adj.*

Clive (klīv), *n.* **Robert** (*Baron Clive of Plassey*), 1725–74, British general and statesman in India.

cloak (klōk), *n.* **1.** a loose outer garment, as a cape or coat. **2.** something that covers or conceals; disguise; pretense. —*v.t.* **3.** to cover with or as if with a cloak. **4.** to hide; conceal. —**cloak′less,** *adj.*

cloak′-and-dag′ger, *adj.* pertaining to, characteristic of, or dealing in espionage or intrigue, esp. of a romantic or dramatic kind.

clob·ber (klob′ər), *v.t. Informal.* **1.** to batter severely; strike heavily. **2.** to defeat decisively; drub; trounce. **3.** to denounce or criticize vigorously.

cloche (klōsh, klôsh), *n.* a woman's close-fitting hat with a deep, bell-shaped crown and often a narrow, turned-down brim.

clock (klok), *n.* **1.** an instrument, normally larger than a watch, for measuring and recording time, usu. with hands or changing numbers to indicate the hour and minute. **2.** TIME CLOCK. **3.** a meter for measuring and recording speed, distance covered, or other quantitative functioning. **4.** BIOLOGICAL CLOCK. —*v.t.* **5.** to time, test, or determine by means of a clock or watch: *The racehorse was clocked at two minutes thirty seconds.* —*v.i.* **6. clock in** (or **out**), to begin (or end) the day's work, esp. by punching a time clock. —*Idiom.* **7. around the clock, a.** for the entire 24-hour day without pause. **b.** without stopping for rest; tirelessly. —**clock′er,** *n.*

clock·like (klok′līk′), *adj.* highly systematic, precise, and dependable.

clock′ ra′dio, *n.* a radio combined with an alarm clock serving as a timer to turn the radio on or off at a preset time.

clock·wise (klok′wīz′), *adv.* **1.** in the direction of the rotation of the

hands of a clock as viewed from the front or above. —*adj.* **2.** directed clockwise: *a clockwise movement.*

clock·work (klok′wûrk′), *n.* **1.** the mechanism of a clock. **2.** any mechanism similar to that of a clock. —*Idiom.* **3. like clockwork,** with perfect regularity or precision.

clod (klod), *n.* **1.** a lump or mass, esp. of earth or clay. **2.** a stupid person; dolt. **3.** earth; soil. —**clod′dish,** *adj.*

clod·hop·per (klod′hop′ər), *n.* **1.** a clumsy boor; rustic; bumpkin. **2. clodhoppers,** strong, heavy shoes.

clog (klog, klôg), *v.,* **clogged, clog·ging,** *n.* —*v.t.* **1.** to hinder or obstruct with thick or sticky matter; choke up: *to clog a drain.* **2.** to crowd excessively; overfill: *Cars clogged the highway.* **3.** to encumber; hamper; hinder. —*v.i.* **4.** to become clogged, encumbered, or choked up. **5.** to stick; stick together. —*n.* **6.** anything that impedes movement; encumbrance or hindrance. **7.** a shoe or sandal with a thick sole of wood, cork, rubber, or the like.

cloi·son·né (kloi′zə nā′; *Fr.* klwA zô nā′), *n.* enamelwork in which colored areas are separated by thin metal bands.

clois·ter (kloi′stər), *n.* **1.** a covered walk, esp. in a religious institution, having an open arcade or colonnade usu. opening onto a courtyard. **2.** a courtyard, esp. in a religious institution, bordered with such walks. **3.** a place of religious seclusion, as a monastery or convent. **4.** any quiet, secluded place. **5.** life in a monastery or convent. —*v.t.* **6.** to confine in a monastery or convent. **7.** to confine in retirement; seclude. **8.** to furnish with a cloister or covered walk. **9.** to convert into a monastery or convent. —**clois′tered,** *adj.*

cloister (def. 1)

clomp (klomp), *v.i.* CLUMP (def. 5).

clone (klōn), *n., v.,* **cloned, clon·ing.** —*n.* **1. a.** a cell, cell product, or organism that is genetically identical to the unit or individual from which it was asexually derived. **b.** a population of identical units, cells, or individuals that derive asexually from the same ancestral line. **2.** a person or thing that duplicates, imitates, or closely resembles another in appearance, function, etc.: *The new computers are clones of the original model.* —*v.t.* **3.** to produce a copy or imitation of. **4. a.** to cause to grow as a clone. **b.** to separate (a batch of cells or cell products) so that each portion produces only its own kind. —*v.i.* **5.** to grow as a clone. —**clon′al,** *adj.* —**clon′er,** *n.*

clop (klop), *n., v.,* **clopped, clop·ping.** —*n.* **1.** a sound made by or as if by a horse's hoof striking the ground. —*v.i.* **2.** to make or move with such a sound.

close (*v.* klōz; *adj., adv.* klōs; *n.* klōz for 52, 53, 56, klōs for 54, 55), *v.,* **closed, clos·ing,** *adj.,* **clos·er, clos·est,** *adv., n.* —*v.t.* **1.** to put (something) in a position to obstruct an entrance or opening; shut. **2.** to stop or obstruct (a gap, entrance, aperture, etc.): *to close a hole in the wall.* **3.** to block or hinder passage across or access to: *to close a border to tourists.* **4.** to stop or obstruct the entrances, apertures, or gaps in: *to close a box.* **5.** to make imperceptive or inaccessible: *to close one's mind to criticisms.* **6.** to bring together the parts of; join (often fol. by *up*): *Close up ranks!* **7.** to bring to an end: *to close a debate.* **8.** to conclude successfully; consummate: *to close a deal.* **9.** to stop rendering the customary services of: *to close a store for the night.* **10.** to terminate or suspend the operation of: *The police closed the bar for selling liquor to minors.* **11.** *Naut.* to come close to. —*v.i.* **12.** to become closed; shut: *The door closed with a bang.* **13.** to come together; unite: *Her lips closed firmly.* **14.** to come close: *His pursuers closed rapidly.* **15.** to grapple; engage in close encounter (often fol. by *with*): *to close with enemy troops.* **16.** to come to an end; terminate. **17.** to cease to offer the customary activities or services: *The school closed for the summer.* **18.** to cease to be performed: *The play closed yesterday.* **19.** to enter into or reach an agreement, usu. as a contract. **20.** (of a stock or group of stocks) to be priced or show a change in price as specified at the end of a trading period. **21. close down,** to terminate the operation of; discontinue. **22. close in on** or **upon, a.** to approach stealthily, as to capture. **b.** to envelop or seem to envelop, as if to suffocate. **23. close out, a.** to reduce the price of (merchandise) for quick sale. **b.** to dispose of completely; liquidate: *to close out a bank account.* —*adj.* **24.** having the parts or elements near to one another: *a close design.* **25.** compact; dense: *a close weave.* **26.** being in or having proximity in space or time. **27.** marked by similarity in degree, action, feeling, etc.: *Dark pink is close to red.* **28.** near, or near together, in kind or relationship: *a close relative.* **29.** intimate or confidential; dear. **30.** based on a strong uniting feeling of respect, honor, or love: *a close friend.* **31.** fitting tightly: *a close sweater.* **32.** cut so as to be left flush with the surface or very short. **33.** not deviating from the subject under consideration. **34.** strict; searching; minute: *close investigation.* **35.** not deviating from a model or original: *a close translation.* **36.** nearly even or equal: *a close contest.* **37.** strictly logical: *close reasoning.* **38.** shut; shut tight; not open: *a close hatch.* **39.** shut in; enclosed. **40.** completely enclosing or surrounding: *a close siege.* **41.** without opening; with all openings covered or closed. **42.** confined; narrow; stuffy: *close rooms.* **43.** heavy; oppressive: *close, sultry weather.* **44.** narrowly confined, as a prisoner. **45.** practicing or keeping secrecy; secretive; reticent. **46.** parsimonious; stingy. **47.** scarce, as money. **48.** not open to public or general admission, competition, etc. **49.** (of a vowel) articulated with a relatively small opening between the tongue and the roof of the mouth, as the vowel sound of *meet;* high. Compare OPEN (def. 25a). —*adv.* **50.** in a close manner; closely. **51.** near; close by. —*n.* **52.** the act of closing. **53.** the end or conclusion. **54.** an enclosed place or enclosure, esp. one beside a cathedral. **55.** any piece of land held as private property. **56. a.** the closing price on a stock. **b.** the closing prices on an exchange market. —*Idiom.* **57. close ranks,** to unite forces in a show of loyalty, esp. to deal with challenge or adversity. **58. close up,** from close range; in a detailed manner; intimately. —**close•ly** (klōs′lē) *adv.* —**close•ness** (klōs′nis), *n.*

close′-by′ (klōs), *adj.* nearby; adjacent; neighboring.

close′ call′ (klōs), *n.* a narrow escape from danger or trouble.

closed (klōzd), *adj.* **1.** having or forming a boundary or barrier: *a closed door.* **2.** brought to a close; concluded: *a closed incident.* **3.** not public; restricted; exclusive: *a closed meeting.* **4.** not open to new ideas or arguments. **5.** self-contained; independent or self-sufficient: *a closed system.* **6.** (of a syllable) ending with a consonant. Compare OPEN (def. 25b). **7. a.** (of a set in which a combining operation between members of the set is defined) such that performing the operation between members of the set produces a member of the set, as multiplication in the set of integers. **b.** (of a function or operator) having as its graph a closed set. **c.** (of a curve) not having endpoints; enclosing an area.

closed′-cap′tioned, *adj.* (of a television program) broadcast with captions that are visible only with the use of a decoder.

closed′-cir′cuit tel′evision, *n.* a system of televising by cable to designated viewing sets, as within a single building or school system.

closed′ (or **close′**) **corpora′tion,** *n.* an incorporated business the stock of which is owned by a small group.

closed′-door′, *adj.* held in strict privacy; not open to the press or the public: *a closed-door strategy meeting of banking executives.*

closed′ gen′tian, *n.* a gentian, *Gentiana andrewsii,* of the eastern and central U.S., having tight clusters of dark blue closed flowers.

closed′ shop′, *n.* a factory, office, or other business establishment in which union membership is a condition of being hired as well as of continued employment. Compare OPEN SHOP.

close-fist•ed (klōs′fis′tid), *adj.* stingy; miserly; tight. —**close′fist′ed•ness,** *n.*

close-fit•ting (klōs′fit′ing), *adj.* (of a garment) fitting tightly or snugly to the body: *a close-fitting jacket.*

close′-grained′ (klōs), *adj.* (of wood) fine in texture or having inconspicuous annual rings.

close′-knit′ (klōs), *adj.* tightly united or connected.

close•mouthed (klōs′mouthd′, -moutht′), *adj.* reticent; uncommunicative.

close•out (klōz′out′), *n.* **1.** a sale on all goods in liquidating a business. **2.** a sale on merchandise that will no longer be carried by the store.

close′ quar′ters (klōs), *n.pl.* **1.** a small, cramped place or position. **2.** direct and close contact in a fight.

close′ shave′ (klōs), *n. Informal.* a narrow escape from serious danger or trouble.

clos•et (kloz′it), *n.* **1.** a small room, enclosed recess, or cabinet for storing clothing, food, utensils, etc. **2.** a small private room, esp. one used for prayer, meditation, etc. **3.** a state or condition of secrecy or carefully guarded privacy. **4.** WATER CLOSET. —*adj.* **5.** private; secluded. **6.** suited for use or enjoyment in privacy: *closet prayer.* **7.** engaged in private study or speculation; speculative; impractical: *a closet thinker.* **8.** being or functioning as such in private; secret: *a closet homosexual.* —*v.t.* **9.** to shut up in a private room for a conference, interview, etc.: *The President was closeted with the senators for three hours.* —**clos′et•ful,** *n., pl.* **-fuls.**

close•up (klōs′up′), *n.* **1.** a photograph taken at close range or with a long focal-length lens. **2.** a movie or television shot in which some part of the subject, as the head of an actor, fills the entire frame. **3.** an intimate view or presentation of anything.

clos•ing (klō′zing), *n.* **1.** the end or conclusion, as of a speech. **2.** something that closes; a fastening, as of a purse. **3.** the final phase of a transaction, esp. the sale of real estate.

clos•trid•i•um (klo strid′ē əm), *n., pl.* **clos•trid•i•a** (klo strid′ē ə). any of several rod-shaped, spore-forming, anaerobic bacteria of the genus *Clostridium,* found in soil and in the intestinal tract. —**clos•trid′i•al, clos•trid′i•an,** *adj.*

clo•sure (klō′zhər), *n., v.,* **-sured, -sur•ing.** —*n.* **1.** the act of closing; the state of being closed. **2.** a bringing to an end; conclusion. **3.** something that closes or shuts. **4.** a blockage of the flow of air by contact between vocal organs in producing a sound. **5.** a cloture. **6.** the property of being closed with respect to a particular mathematical operation. **7. a.** the tendency to see an entire figure even though the picture of it is incomplete, based primarily on the viewer's past experience. **b.** a sense of certainty or completeness: *a need for closure.* —*v.t.* **8.** to cloture.

clot (klot), *n., v.,* **clot•ted, clot•ting.** —*n.* **1.** a mass or lump. **2.** a semisolid mass, as of coagulated blood. **3.** a small compact group of individuals; cluster. —*v.i.* **4.** to form into clots; coagulate. —*v.t.* **5.** to cause to clot. **6.** to cause to become blocked or obscured.

cloth (klôth, kloth), *n., pl.* **cloths** (klôŧħz, kloŧħz, klôths, kloths), *adj.* —*n.* **1.** a fabric made by weaving, felting, or knitting from wool, silk, cotton, flax, nylon, polyester, etc.: used for garments, upholstery, and many other items. **2.** a piece of such a fabric for a particular purpose: *an altar cloth.* **3.** the particular attire of any profession, esp. that of the clergy. **4. the cloth,** the clergy: *men of the cloth.* —*adj.* **5.** of or made of cloth. **6.** clothbound.

cloth•bound (klôth′bound′, kloth′-), *adj.* (of a book) bound with cloth rather than paper, leather, etc.

clothe (klōŧħ), *v.t.,* **clothed** or **clad, cloth•ing. 1.** to dress; attire. **2.** to provide with clothing. **3.** to cover with or as if with clothing.

clothes (klōz, klōŧħz), *n.pl.* **1.** garments for the body; articles of dress; wearing apparel. **2.** BEDCLOTHES.

clothes•horse (klōz′hôrs′, klōŧħz′-), *n.* **1.** a person whose chief interest and pleasure is dressing fashionably. **2.** a frame on which to hang wet laundry for drying.

clothes•line (klōz′līn′, klōŧħz′-), *n.* a strong narrow rope or cord on which clean laundry is hung to dry, usu. outdoors.

clothes′ moth′, *n.* any of several small moths of the family Tineidae, the larvae of which feed on wool, fur, etc.

clothes•pin (klōz′pin′, klōŧħz′-, klōs′-), *n.* a device, as a forked piece of wood or plastic, for fastening articles to a clothesline.

clothes′ tree′, *n.* an upright pole with hooks near the top for hanging coats, hats, etc.

cloth•ier (klōŧħ′yər, -ē ər), *n.* **1.** a retailer of clothing. **2.** a person who makes or sells cloth.

cloth•ing (klō′ŧħing), *n.* **1.** garments collectively; clothes; raiment; apparel. **2.** a covering.

clot′ted cream′, *n.* a thick, rich cream made by gently cooking unpasteurized milk and skimming off the layer of cream from the top. Also called Devonshire cream.

clo•ture (klō′chər), *n., v.,* **-tured, -tur•ing.** —*n.* **1.** a closing of debate in a legislative body in order to bring the question to a vote. —*v.t.* **2.** to close (a debate) by cloture.

cloud (kloud), *n.* **1.** a visible collection of particles of water or ice suspended in the air, usu. at an elevation above the earth's surface. **2.** any similar mass, esp. of smoke or dust. **3.** a dim or obscure area in something otherwise clear or transparent. **4.** anything that causes gloom, trouble, suspicion, etc. **5.** a great number of insects, birds, etc., flying together. —*v.t.* **6.** to cover with or as if with a cloud or clouds. **7.** to make gloomy. **8.** to make obscure or indistinct; confuse: *to cloud the issue with extraneous details.* **9.** to reveal distress, anxiety, etc., in (a part of one's face): *Worry clouded his brow.* **10.** to place under suspicion, disgrace, etc. —*v.i.* **11.** to grow cloudy. **12.** to reveal one's distress, anxiety, etc.: *Her brow clouded with anger.* —*Idiom.* **13. have one's head in the clouds, a.** to be lost in reverie; be daydreaming. **b.** to be impractical. **14. on a cloud,** *Informal.* exceedingly happy; in high spirits. **15. under a cloud,** in disgrace; under suspicion. —*Proverb.* **16. Every cloud has a silver lining,** even misfortune may contain something beneficial. —**cloud′less,** *adj.* —**cloud′less•ness,** *n.*

cloud•ber•ry (kloud′ber′ē, -bə rē), *n., pl.* **-ries.** an orange-yellow raspberry, *Rubus chamaemorus,* of northern regions.

cloud•burst (kloud′bûrst′), *n.* a sudden and very heavy rainfall.

cloud′ cham′ber, *n.* an apparatus containing a mixture of gas and vapor in which visible tracks of ions reveal the paths of charged particles through the mixture.

cloud-cuck•oo-land (kloud′koō′koō land′, -kŏŏk′oō-), *n.* an idealized, illusory domain of imagination; cloudland: *the cloud-cuckoo-land of technicolor cartoon whimsy.* [trans. of Greek *Nephelokokkȳgía,* the realm which separates the gods from mankind in Aristophanes' *The Birds*]

cloud′ nine′, *n. Informal.* a state of perfect happiness (usually in the phrase *on cloud nine*).

cloud•y (klou′dē), *adj.,* **cloud•i•er, cloud•i•est. 1.** covered with clouds: *a cloudy sky.* **2.** having little or no sunshine: *a cloudy day.* **3.** of or like

C

a cloud or clouds. **4.** not clear or transparent: *a cloudy liquid.* **5.** obscure; indistinct: *cloudy prospects.* **6.** darkened by gloom or trouble: *a cloudy look.* —**cloud′i•ness,** *n.*

clout (klout), *n.* **1.** a blow, esp. with the hand; cuff. **2.** *Informal.* influence upon, or the ability to influence, decisions made by public figures. **3.** a long hit in baseball. **4.** the mark or target shot at in archery, esp. in long-distance shooting. —*v.t.* **5.** to hit or cuff.

clove[1] (klōv), *n.* **1.** the dried flower bud of a tropical tree, *Syzygium aromaticum,* of the myrtle family, used whole or ground as a spice. **2.** the tree itself.

clove[2] (klōv), *n.* one of the small bulbs formed in the axils of the scales of a mother bulb, as in garlic.

clove[3] (klōv), *v.* a pt. of CLEAVE[2].

clove′ hitch′, *n.* a knot used to fasten a rope to a pole or larger rope.

clo•ven (klō′vən), *v.* **1.** a pp. of CLEAVE[2]. —*adj.* **2.** cleft; split; divided: *the cloven hoof of a goat.*

clo′ven-hoofed′, *adj.* **1.** having split hoofs, once assumed to represent the halves of a single undivided hoof, as in cattle. **2.** devilish; Satanic.

clove′ pink′, *n.* a pink, *Dianthus caryophyllus,* having a spicy scent resembling that of cloves.

clo•ver (klō′vər), *n., pl.* **-vers,** (*esp. collectively*) **-ver. 1.** any of various plants of the genus *Trifolium,* of the legume family, having trifoliolate leaves and dense flower heads, many species of which are cultivated as forage plants. **2.** any of various plants of allied genera, as melilot. —*Idiom.* **3. in clover,** luxuriating in a life of wealth and comfort.

clo•ver•leaf (klō′vər lēf′), *n., pl.* **-leafs, -leaves,** *adj.* —*n.* **1.** a road arrangement, resembling a four-leaf clover in form, for permitting traffic movement between two intersecting high-speed highways. —*adj.* **2.** shaped like a leaf of clover.

cloverleaf

clown (kloun), *n.* **1.** a comic performer, esp. in a circus, who wears an outlandish costume and makeup and pantomimes common situations in exaggerated fashion, often also juggling, tumbling, etc. **2.** a joker or buffoon; jester. **3.** a prankster or practical joker. **4.** *Slang.* a boor, oaf, or fool. **5.** a peasant; rustic. —*v.i.* **6.** to act like a clown. [perh. akin to Old Norse *klunni* boor] —**clown′ish,** *adj.* —**clown′ish•ly,** *adv.* —**clown′ish•ness,** *n.*

clown′ anem′one, *n.* a small anemone fish, *Amphiprion ocellaris,* having broad bands of orange and white.

cloy (kloi), *v.t.* **1.** to weary by excess; surfeit; satiate. —*v.i.* **2.** to become wearisome or distasteful through excess. —**cloy′ing,** *adj.*

cloze (klōz), *adj.* **1.** of or designating a procedure for measuring comprehension or text difficulty by requiring the reader to supply elements that have been systematically deleted from a text. —*n.* **2.** a cloze procedure or test.

club (klub), *n., v.,* **clubbed, club•bing.** —*n.* **1.** a heavy stick, usu. thicker at one end than the other, suitable for use as a weapon; cudgel. **2. a.** a stick or bat used to drive a ball in various games, as golf. **b.** INDIAN CLUB. **3.** a group of people organized for a social, literary, or other purpose: *an athletic club.* **4.** the building or rooms occupied by such a group. **5.** an organization that offers its subscribers certain benefits, as discounts on purchases: *a book club.* **6.** a group of nations associated in some way: *the European economic club.* **7.** a nightclub or cabaret. **8. a.** a black trefoil-shaped figure on a playing card. **b.** a card bearing such figures. **c. clubs,** (*used with a sing. or pl. v.*) the suit so marked. —*v.t.* **9.** to beat with or as if with a club. **10.** to gather or form into a clublike mass. **11.** to unite; join together. **12.** to contribute as one's share toward a joint expense. —*v.i.* **13.** to combine or join together. **14.** to gather into a mass. **15.** to attend a club or a club's activities. **16.** to contribute to a common fund.

club′ car′, *n.* a railroad passenger car equipped with easy chairs, card tables, a buffet, etc. Also called **lounge car.**

club′ chair′, *n.* a heavily upholstered chair with solid sides and a low back.

club•foot (klub′fŏot′), *n., pl.* **-feet. 1.** a congenitally deformed or distorted foot. **2.** the condition of having such a foot. —**club′foot′ed,** *adj.*

club′ fun′gus, *n.* any basidiomycete fungus belonging to the family Clavariaceae.

club•house (klub′hous′), *n., pl.* **-hous•es** (-hou′ziz). **1.** a building or room occupied by a club or used for recreational activities. **2.** the dressing room of an athletic team.

club′ moss′, *n.* **1.** any of various low, seedless, evergreen plants of the phylum Lycophyta, having a single vascular strand. **2.** Also called **lycopod.** any club moss of the genus *Lycopodium,* bearing cones at the tips of erect branches, as the ground pine.

club•root (klub′rŏot′, -rŏot′), *n.* a disease of plants of the cabbage family characterized by swollen roots, caused by a slime mold, *Plasmodiophora brassicae.*

club′ sand′wich, *n.* a sandwich typically consisting of three slices of toast or bread interlaid with chicken or turkey and bacon or ham, together with lettuce, tomato, and mayonnaise.

club′ so′da, *n.* SODA WATER (def. 1).

cluck (kluk), *v.i.* **1.** to utter the cry of a hen brooding or calling her chicks. **2.** to make a similar sound, esp. one expressing concern, approval, etc. —*v.t.* **3.** to call by clucking. **4.** to express by clucking. —*n.* **5.** the sound uttered by a hen when brooding, or in calling her chicks. **6.** any clucking sound.

clue (klŏo), *n., v.,* **clued, clu•ing.** —*n.* **1.** anything that serves to guide or direct in the solution of a problem, mystery, etc. **2.** CLEW (defs. 2–4). —*v.t.* **3.** to direct by a clue. **4.** CLEW (def. 5). **5. clue in,** to provide with necessary information: *Can you clue us in on the arrangements?*

clue•less (klŏo′lis), *adj. Informal.* ignorant; uninformed.

clump (klump), *n.* **1.** a small cluster, esp. of trees or other plants. **2.** a lump or mass. **3.** a heavy, thumping step, sound, etc. **4.** a cluster of agglutinated bacteria, red blood cells, etc. —*v.i.* **5.** Also, **clomp.** to walk heavily and clumsily. **6.** to gather or be gathered into clumps; agglutinate. —*v.t.* **7.** to form into a clump; mass. —**clump′y, clump′ish,** *adj.*

clum•sy (klum′zē), *adj.,* **-si•er, -si•est. 1.** awkward in movement or action; lacking skill or grace. **2.** awkwardly done; ill-contrived: *a clumsy apology.* —**clum′si•ly,** *adv.* —**clum′si•ness,** *n.*

clung (klung), *v.* pt. and pp. of CLING.

clunk (klungk), *v.i., v.t.* **1.** to hit hard, esp. on the head. —*n.* **2.** a hard hit, esp. on the head. **3.** *Informal.* a stupid person. **4.** *Informal.* CLUNKER (def. 2).

clunk•er (klung′kər), *n. Informal.* **1.** something worthless or inferior. **2.** an old, worn-out machine, esp. a car. **3.** CLUNK (def. 4).

clunk•y (klung′kē), *adj.,* **clunk•i•er, clunk•i•est.** *Informal.* awkwardly heavy; clumsy or unwieldy: *big clunky shoes.*

clu•pe•id (klŏo′pē id), *n.* any of the Clupeidae, a family of chiefly marine, teleostean fishes, including the herrings, sardines, menhaden, and shad.

clus•ter (klus′tər), *n.* **1.** a number of things of the same kind, growing or held together; a bunch. **2.** a group of persons or things close together. **3.** a small metal embellishment affixed to a military decoration to indicate its having been awarded again. **4.** a succession of two or more contiguous consonant sounds within a syllable, as the *str-* in *strap.* **5.** a group of stars, similar in age and composition, that are held together by gravitation. **6.** a group of classes or subjects that are administered or taught together. —*v.t.* **7.** to gather into a cluster. **8.** to furnish or decorate with clusters. —*v.i.* **9.** to form into a cluster.

clus′ter head′ache, *n.* a type of recurrent headache characterized by sudden attacks of intense pain on one side of the head.

clutch[1] (kluch), *v.t.* **1.** to seize with or as if with the hands or claws; snatch. **2.** to hold tightly. **3.** to spellbind; grip a person's interest or emotions. —*v.i.* **4.** to try to seize or grasp (usu. fol. by *at*): *to clutch at a fleeing child.* **5.** to operate the clutch in a vehicle. —*n.* **6.** the hand, claw, etc., when grasping. **7.** Often, **clutches.** power or control, esp. when inescapable: *to fall into the clutches of the enemy.* **8.** a tight grip or hold. **9.** a device for gripping something. **10. a.** a mechanism for readily engaging or disengaging a shaft that drives a mechanism or is driven by another part. **b.** a control for operating this. **11.** a critical point or moment. **12.** a woman's small handbag without a strap. —*adj.* **13.** done in a critical situation: *a clutch shot that won the game.* **14.** dependable in crucial situations: *a clutch player.* —**clutch′ing•ly,** *adv.*

clutch[2] (kluch), *n.* **1.** a hatch of eggs; the number of eggs produced or incubated at one time. **2.** a brood of chickens. **3.** a number of similar things or individuals. —*v.t.* **4.** to hatch (chickens).

clut•ter (klut′ər), *v.t.* **1.** to fill or litter with things in a disorderly manner: *Newspapers cluttered the living room.* —*n.* **2.** a disorderly heap or assemblage; litter. **3.** a confused state. **4.** echoes on a radar screen that do not come from the target.

Clydes•dale (klīdz′dāl′), *n.* any of a Scottish breed of strong, high-stepping draft horses with a feathering of long hairs along the backs of the legs. [after *Clydesdale,* the valley of the Clyde]

Cly•tem•nes•tra (klī′təm nes′trə), *n.* in ancient Greek legend, the wife of Agamemnon, who killed her husband and was herself killed by her son Orestes.

CM, 1. Christian male. **2.** Common Market.

Cm, *Symbol, Chem.* curium.

cm, centimeter; centimeters.

Cmdr., Commander.

cni•dar•i•an (nī dâr′ē ən), *n.* **1.** any radially symmetric invertebrate of the phylum Cnidaria, including the hydras, jellyfishes, sea anemones, and corals, characterized by stinging cells and a saclike digestive cavity with a single opening surrounded by tentacles. Compare COELENTERATE. —*adj.* **2.** of or pertaining to the cnidarians.

CO, Colorado.

Co, *Chem. Symbol.* cobalt.

co-, var. of COM- before a vowel, *h,* and *gn: coalesce; cohere; cognate.*

The prefix **co-**, with the sense "joint, jointly," now forms new words from bases beginning with any sound (*cochair; costar; coworker*), sometimes with the derived sense "auxiliary" (*copilot*), and, in mathematics and astronomy, with the sense "complement" (*codeclination*).

C/o or **c/o,** care of.

coach (kōch), *n.* **1.** a large, horse-drawn, four-wheeled carriage, usu. enclosed. **2.** a public motorbus. **3.** a class of airline travel less luxurious and less expensive than first class. **4.** a person who trains an athlete or team: *a football coach.* **5.** a private instructor for a student, singer, actor, etc. **6.** a type of inexpensive automobile with a boxlike, usu. two-door body manufactured esp. in the 1930s. —*v.t.* **7.** to instruct as a coach: *to coach golfers.* —*v.i.* **8.** to work as a coach. **9.** to go by or in a coach. —*adv.* **10.** in coach-class accommodations: *to fly coach.*

coach′-and-four′, *n.* a coach together with the four horses by which it is drawn.

coach•man (kōch′mən), *n., pl.* **-men.** a man employed to drive a coach or carriage.

co•ac•tion[1] (kō ak′shən), *n.* force or compulsion, either in restraining or in impelling.

co•ac•tion[2] (kō ak′shən), *n.* **1.** joint action or interaction. **2.** any interaction among organisms within an ecological community.

co•ad•ap•ta•tion (kō′ad əp tā′shən), *n.* **1.** the correlation of characteristics in two or more interacting organisms or organs resulting from progressive accommodation by natural selection. **2.** Also called **integration.** the accumulation in a population's gene pool of genes that interact by harmonious epistasis in the development of an organism. —**co′ad•ap•ta′tion•al,** *adj.* —**co′ad•ap•ta′tion•al•ly,** *adv.*

co•ad•ju•tant (kō aj′ə tənt), *n.* an assistant; aide.

co•ad•ju•tor (kō aj′ə tər, kō′ə jōō′tər), *n.* **1.** an assistant. **2.** a bishop who assists another bishop and has the right of succession.

co•ag•u•lant (kō ag′yə lənt), *n.* a substance that produces or aids coagulation.

co•ag•u•late (*v.* kō ag′yə lāt′; *adj.* -lit, -lāt′), *v.,* **-lat•ed, -lat•ing.** —*v.i., v.t.* **1.** to change from a fluid to a thickened mass; curdle; congeal. **2.** (of blood) to form or cause to form a clot. —**co•ag′u•la′tion,** *n.* —**co•ag′u•la′tor,** *n.* —**co•ag′u•la•to′ry** (-lə tôr′ē, -tōr′ē), **co•ag′u•la′tive** (-lā′tiv, -lə tiv), *adj.*

coal (kōl), *n.* **1.** a black or dark brown mineral substance consisting of carbonized vegetable matter, used as a fuel. **2.** a piece of glowing, charred, or burned wood or other combustible substance. **3.** CHARCOAL (def. 1). —*v.t.* **4.** to burn to coal or charcoal. **5.** to provide with coal. —*v.i.* **6.** to take in coal for fuel. —**Idiom. 7. rake** or **haul over the coals,** to reprimand severely.

co•a•lesce (kō′ə les′), *v.i.,* **-lesced, -lesc•ing. 1.** to grow together or into one body. **2.** to unite; join together: *The various groups coalesced into one party.* **3.** to blend or come together: *Their ideas coalesced into a new theory.* —**co′a•les′cence,** *n.* —**co′a•les′cent,** *adj.*

coal′ gas′, *n.* **1.** a gas used for illuminating and heating, produced by distilling bituminous coal. **2.** the gas formed by burning coal.

co•a•li•tion (kō′ə lish′ən), *n.* **1.** a combination or alliance, esp. a temporary one between factions, parties, states, etc. **2.** a union into one body or mass; fusion.

coal′ oil′, *n.* **1.** petroleum obtained by the destructive distillation of bituminous coal. **2.** KEROSENE.

coal′ tar′, *n.* a viscid black liquid obtained by distillation of coal, used in making dyes, drugs, and other synthetic compounds. —**coal′-tar′,** *adj.*

coam•ing (kō′ming), *n.* a raised border around an opening in a deck, roof, or floor, designed to keep water out.

co•an•chor (kō ang′kər), *v.t., v.i.,* **1.** (of a broadcast) to anchor jointly with another. —*n.* **2.** a person who coanchors.

coarse (kôrs, kōrs), *adj.,* **coars•er, coars•est. 1.** composed of relatively large parts or particles: *coarse sand.* **2.** lacking in fineness or delicacy of texture, structure, etc.: *coarse fabric.* **3.** harsh; grating. **4.** lacking refinement; unpolished: *coarse manners.* **5.** vulgar; obscene: *coarse language.* **6.** (of metals) unrefined. **7.** (of a metal file) having the maximum commercial grade of coarseness. —**coarse′ly,** *adv.* —**coarse′ness,** *n.*

coarse′-grained′, *adj.* **1.** of coarse texture or grain. **2.** crude; vulgar.

coast (kōst), *n.* **1.** the land next to the sea; seashore. **2.** the region adjoining it. **3.** a slide or ride down a hill or slope, as on a sled. —*v.i.* **4.** to slide on a sled down a snowy or icy incline. **5.** to descend a hill, as on a bicycle, without using pedals. **6.** to continue to move on acquired momentum: *We cut off the motor and coasted into town.* **7.** to progress with little or no effort: *to coast through school.* —*v.t.* **8.** to cause to move along under acquired momentum. **9.** to proceed along the coast of. —**Idiom. 10. the coast is clear,** nothing is present that would impede or endanger one's progress.

coast•al (kōs′tl), *adj.* pertaining to or bordering on a coast.

coast•er (kō′stər), *n.* **1.** a person or thing that coasts. **2.** a small dish or mat, esp. for placing under a glass. **3.** a ship engaged in coastwise trade. **4.** a sled for coasting. **5.** ROLLER COASTER.

coast′er brake′, *n.* a brake on the hub of the rear wheel of freewheel bicycles, operated by back pressure on the pedals.

Coast′ Guard′, *n.* **1.** a U.S. military service charged with enforcing maritime laws, saving lives and property at sea, etc., and which in wartime may augment the navy. **2.** (*l.c.*) any similar organization for aiding

navigation, preventing smuggling, etc. **3.** (*l.c.*) Also called **coastguards-man.** a member of any such organization.

coast•line (kōst′līn′), *n.* **1.** the outline or contour of a coast; shoreline. **2.** the land and water lying adjacent to a shoreline.

coast′-to-coast′, *adj.* covering the area between the E and W coasts of the U.S.: *a coast-to-coast broadcast.*

coast•ward (kōst′wərd), *adv.* **1.** Also, **coast′wards.** toward the coast. —*adj.* **2.** directed toward the coast.

coat (kōt), *n.* **1.** an outer garment with sleeves, covering at least the upper part of the body. **2.** a natural integument or covering, as the hair, fur, or wool of an animal, the bark of a tree, or the skin of a fruit. **3.** a layer of anything that covers a surface: *a coat of paint.* **4.** COAT OF ARMS. —*v.t.* **5.** to cover with a layer or coating: *The furniture was coated with dust.* **6.** to cover thickly, esp. with a viscous substance. **7.** to cover with a coat. —**Idiom. 8. cut one's coat according to one's cloth,** to adapt to existing circumstances and conditions. —**coat′less,** *adj.*

coat•ed (kō′tid), *adj.* **1.** having a coat. **2.** (of paper) having a polished coating applied to provide a smooth surface for printing.

co•a•ti (kō ä′tē), *n., pl.* **-tis.** a raccoonlike carnivore of the genus *Nasua,* of the New World tropics, with a ringed tail and a narrow, flexible snout. Also called **co•a•ti-mon•di, co•a•ti-mun•di** (kō ä′tē mun′dē).

coati, Nasua nasua,
1 ft. (0.3 m) high at shoulder;
head and body 1½ ft. (0.46 m);
tail to 2½ ft. (0.8 m)

coat•ing (kō′ting), *n.* **1.** a layer of any substance spread over a surface. **2.** fabric for making coats.

coat′ of arms′, *n.* **1.** a coat or tabard embroidered with heraldic devices, worn by medieval knights over their armor. **2.** a full display of the armorial bearings of a person, family, or corporation, usu. on an escutcheon.

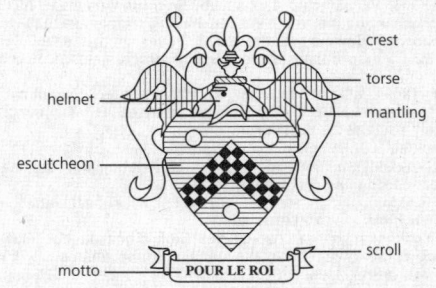

coat of arms (def. 2)

coat′ of mail′, *n.* an armored garment made of chain mail or metal scales.

coat′ of man′y col′ors, *n.* the coat that Jacob made for his son Joseph. Gen. 37:3–33.

coat•rack (kōt′rak′), *n.* a rack or stand for the temporary hanging or storing of coats, hats, etc.

coat•tail (kōt′tāl′), *n.* **1.** the back of the skirt on a man's coat or jacket. **2.** one of the two tails on a tail coat. —*adj.* **3.** gained by association with another: *coattail benefits.* —**Idiom. 4. on someone's coattails,** aided by association with another person: *The senator rode into office on the President's coattails.* **5. on the coattails of,** immediately after or as a direct result of.

co•au•thor (kō ô′thər, kō′ô′-), *n.* **1.** one of two or more joint authors. —*v.t.* **2.** to be a coauthor of.

coax[1] (kōks), *v.t.* **1.** to attempt to influence by gentle persuasion, flattery, etc.; cajole: *Maybe you can coax her to sing.* **2.** to obtain by coaxing: *to coax a secret from someone.* **3.** to maneuver into a desired position or end by adroit and persistent handling: *He coaxed the large chair through the door.* —*v.i.* **4.** to use gentle persuasion, flattery, etc. —**coax′ing•ly,** *adv.*

co•ax[2] (kō aks′, kō′aks), *n.* a coaxial cable.

co•ax•i•al (kō ak′sē əl) also **co•ax•al** (-səl), *adj.* having a common axis or coincident axes. —**co•ax′i•al•ly,** *adv.*

coax′ial ca′ble, *n.* a cable that consists of an insulated tube through which an insulated conductor runs, used for transmitting high-frequency telephone, telegraph, digital, or television signals.

cob (kob), *n.* **1.** CORNCOB (def. 1). **2.** a male swan. **3.** a short-legged, thick-set horse, often having a high gait. **4.** a mixture of clay and straw, used as a building material.

co·bal·a·min (kō bal′ə min) also **co·bal·a·mine** (-mēn′), *n.* VITAMIN B₁₂.

co·balt (kō′bôlt), *n.* a hard, ductile element occurring in compounds whose silicates afford important blue coloring substances for ceramics. *Symbol:* Co; *at. wt.:* 58.933; *at. no.:* 27; *sp. gr.:* 8.9 at 20°C.

co′balt blue′, *n.* **1.** a blue to greenish blue color. **2.** a pigment containing an oxide of cobalt.

Cobb (kob), *n.* **Ty(rus Raymond)** (*"the Georgia Peach"*), 1886–1961, U.S. baseball player.

cob·ble¹ (kob′əl), *v.t.,* **-bled, -bling. 1.** to mend (shoes, boots, etc.); patch. **2.** to put together roughly or clumsily.

cob·ble² (kob′əl), *n., v.,* **-bled, -bling.** —*n.* **1.** a cobblestone. —*v.t.* **2.** to pave with cobblestones.

cob·bler (kob′lər), *n.* **1.** a person who mends shoes. **2.** a deep-dish fruit pie with a thick biscuit crust, usu. only on top. —*Proverb.* **3. The cobbler should stick to his last,** one should concentrate on what one knows.

cob·ble·stone (kob′əl stōn′), *n.* a naturally rounded stone, larger than a pebble and smaller than a boulder, formerly used in paving. —**cob′ble·stoned′,** *adj.*

co·bi·a (kō′bē ə), *n., pl.* **-bi·as.** a large, perchlike game fish, *Rachycentron canadum,* of warm and temperate seas.

cob·nut (kob′nut′), *n.* **1.** the nut of certain cultivated varieties of hazel, *Corylus avellana grandis.* **2.** a tree bearing such nuts.

COBOL (kō′bôl), *n.* a high-level computer language suited for writing programs to process large files of data. [*co(mmon) b(usiness)-o(riented) l(anguage)*]

co·bra (kō′brə), *n., pl.* **-bras. 1.** any venomous Old World elapid snake of the genera *Naja* and *Ophiophagus,* characterized by the ability to flatten the neck into a hood. **2.** any of several related African snakes, as the ringhals.

cob·web (kob′web′), *n., v.,* **-webbed, -web·bing.** —*n.* **1.** a web, esp. when irregular, spun by a spider. **2.** a single thread spun by a spider. **3.** anything finespun, flimsy, or insubstantial. **4.** a network of plot or intrigue. **5. cobwebs,** confusion or indistinctness: *a head full of cobwebs.* —*v.t.* **6.** to cover with or as if with cobwebs. **7.** to confuse or muddle. —**cob′web·by,** *adj.*

co·ca (kō′kə), *n., pl.* **-cas. 1.** a shrub, *Erythroxylum coca,* of the family Erythroxylaceae, native to the Andes, having simple alternate leaves and small yellowish flowers. **2.** the dried leaves of this shrub, which are chewed for their stimulant properties and which yield cocaine and other alkaloids.

co·caine (kō kān′, kō′kān), *n.* a bitter, white, crystalline alkaloid, C₁₇H₂₁NO₄, obtained from coca leaves, used as a local anesthetic and also widely used as an illicit drug.

coc·ci (kok′sī, -sē), *n.* pl. of coccus.

coc·cid (kok′sid), *n.* any of various related bugs of the superfamily Coccoidea, comprising the scale insects.

coc·cus (kok′əs), *n., pl.* **-ci** (-sī, -sē). a spherical bacterium. —**coc′cal, coc′cic** (-sik), *adj.* —**coc′cous,** *adj.*

coc·cyx (kok′siks), *n., pl.* **coc·cy·ges** (kok sī′jēz, kok′si jēz′). a triangular bone at the lower end of the spinal column; tailbone. —**coc·cyg′e·al** (-sij′ē əl), *adj.*

co·chair (kō châr′), *v.t., v.i.* **1.** to chair along with another person or persons. —*n.* **2.** a person who cochairs.

co·chin (kō′chin, koch′in), *n.* one of an Asian breed of chickens, resembling the Brahma but slightly smaller.

coch·i·neal (koch′ə nēl′, kō′chə-, koch′ə nēl′, kō′chə-), *n.* a red dye prepared from the dried bodies of the females of the cochineal insect, *Dactylopius coccus,* which lives on cactuses of Mexico, Central America, and other warm regions.

coch′i·neal in′sect, *n.* any of various scale insects, of the family Dactylopiidae, that feed on cactus and have a bright red body fluid used as a dye.

coch·le·a (kok′lē ə, kō′klē ə), *n., pl.* **-le·ae** (-lē ē′, -lē ī′), **-le·as.** the fluid-filled, spiral-shaped part of the inner ear in mammals. —**coch′le·ar,** *adj.*

coch·le·ate (kok′lē it, -āt′) also **coch′le·at′ed,** *adj.* shaped like a snail shell; spiral.

cock¹ (kok), *n.* **1.** a male chicken; rooster. **2.** the male of any bird, esp. of the gallinaceous kind. **3.** Also called **stopcock.** a hand-operated valve or faucet that controls the flow of liquid or gas. **4.** (in a firearm) **a.** the part of the lock that, by its fall or action, causes the discharge; hammer. **b.** the position of the hammer preparatory to firing, usu. drawn completely back. **5.** WEATHERCOCK. **6.** chief; leader. —*v.t.* **7.** to draw back the hammer of (a firearm) preparatory to firing. **8.** to draw back in preparation for throwing or hitting. **9.** to set (a camera shutter) for tripping. —*v.i.* **10.** to cock the hammer of a firearm.

cock² (kok), *v.t.* **1.** to turn up or to one side, often in a jaunty manner: *The puppy cocked its ear at the sound.* —*v.i.* **2.** to stand up conspicuously. —*n.* **3.** the act of turning up or to one side, esp. in a jaunty manner.

cock³ (kok), *n. North Midland U.S.* a conical pile of hay, dung, etc.

cock·a·ma·mie or **cock·a·ma·my** (kok′ə mā′mē), *adj. Slang.* ridiculous; nonsensical: *another of his cockamamie ideas.*

cock′-and-bull′ sto′ry, *n.* an absurd, improbable story presented as the truth.

cock·a·poo (kok′ə pōō′), *n., pl.* **-poos.** a dog crossbred from a cocker spaniel and a miniature poodle.

cock·a·tiel or **cock·a·teel** (kok′ə tēl′), *n.* a crested Australian parrot, *Nymphicus hollandicus.*

cock·a·too (kok′ə tōō′, kok′ə tōō′), *n., pl.* **-toos.** any of several large, usu. white crested parrots of the genus *Cacatua* and allied genera, of Australia, New Guinea, and adjacent islands.

cockatoo, *Cacatua galerita,*
length 1 ½ ft. (0.5 m)

cock·a·trice (kok′ə tris), *n.* **1.** a legendary monster, part serpent and part fowl, that could kill with a glance. **2.** a venomous serpent. Is. 11:8.

cock·chaf·er (kok′chā′fər), *n.* any of certain scarab beetles, esp. the European species, *Melolontha melolontha,* which is destructive to forest trees.

cock·crow (kok′krō′) also **cock′ crow′ing,** *n.* daybreak; dawn.

cocked′ hat′, *n.* **1.** a man's hat, worn esp. in the 18th century, having a wide, stiff brim turned up on two or three sides toward a peaked crown. —*Idiom.* **2. knock into a cocked hat,** *Informal.* to destroy or defeat completely.

cocked hat

cock·er·el (kok′ər əl, kok′rəl), *n.* a young domestic cock.

cock′er span′iel, *n.* one of a breed of small spaniels having a long square muzzle, long drooping ears, and a soft flat or wavy coat.

cock·eye (kok′ī′), *n., pl.* **-eyes.** a squinting eye or one affected with strabismus.

cock·eyed (kok′īd′), *adj.* **1.** having a cockeye or cockeyes. **2.** *Slang.* **a.** off center; tilted or slanted to one side. **b.** foolish; absurd. **c.** intoxicated; drunk.

cock·fight (kok′fīt′), *n.* a fight between specially bred gamecocks usu. fitted with spurs. —**cock′fight′ing,** *n.*

cock·horse (kok′hôrs′), *n.* a rocking horse or hobbyhorse.

cock·le¹ (kok′əl), *n., v.,* **-led, -ling.** —*n.* **1.** any bivalve mollusk of the family Cardiidae having heart-shaped, usu. radially ribbed valves. **2.** COCKLESHELL (defs. 1, 2). **3.** a wrinkle or pucker, esp. in fabric. —*v.t., v.i.* **4.** to wrinkle or pucker. —*Idiom.* **5. cockles of one's heart,** the place of one's deepest feelings.

cock·le² (kok′əl), *n.* any of various weeds of grain fields, as the darnel.

cock·le·bur (kok′əl bûr′), *n.* any composite plant of the genus *Xanthium,* comprising coarse weeds with spiny burs.

cock·le·shell (kok′əl shel′), *n.* **1.** the shell of a cockle. **2.** the shell of any other bivalve mollusk. **3.** any light or frail boat.

cock·ney (kok′nē), *n., pl.* **-neys. 1.** (*sometimes cap.*) a member of the native-born working-class population of London, England, esp. an inhabitant of the East End district. **2.** (*sometimes cap.*) the speech of this population, typifying the broadest form of local London dialect.

cock′-of-the-rock′, *n., pl.* **cocks-of-the-rock.** either of two brilliant orange-red crested birds of South America, a Guianan species *Rupicola rupicola* and an Andean species *R. peruviana,* allied with or members of the cotinga family.

cock′ of the walk′, *n.* a domineering and overbearing person.

cock·pit (kok′pit′), *n.* **1.** a usu. enclosed space in the forward fuselage of an airplane containing the flying controls, instrument panel, and seats for the pilot and copilot or crew. **2.** a sunken open area in the aft of a small vessel, containing the steering wheel. **3.** the space, including the seat and instrumentation, surrounding the driver of a racing car or sports car. **4.** a pit or enclosed place for cockfights. **5.** a place noted as the site of many battles. **6.** (formerly) a space below the water line in a warship, occupied by the quarters of the junior officers and used as a dressing station for the wounded.

cock·roach (kok′rōch′), *n.* any of numerous orthopterous insects of the family Blattidae, characterized by a flattened body, rapid movements, and usu. nocturnal habits and including several common household pests. Also called **roach.**

cocks·comb (koks′kōm′), *n.* **1.** the comb or caruncle of a cock. **2.** the cap, resembling a cock's comb, formerly worn by professional fools. **3.** a garden plant, *Celosia cristata,* of the amaranth family with usu. crimson or purple flowers in a broad spike somewhat resembling the comb of a cock. **4.** COXCOMB (def. 1).

cock·spur (kok′spûr′), *n.* a North American hawthorne, *Crataegus crus-galli,* having leathery toothed leaves and red fruit.

cock·sure (kok′shoor′, -shûr′), *adj.* **1.** absolutely sure; certain. **2.** overconfident. —**cock′sure′ly,** *adv.* —**cock′sure′ness,** *n.*

cock·tail¹ (kok′tāl′), *n.* **1.** any of various chilled mixed drinks, consisting typically of an alcoholic liquor mixed with vermouth, fruit juice, or flavorings. **2.** any of various cold mixtures of small pieces of food, often served as an appetizer: *shrimp cocktail; fruit cocktail.* **3.** a beverage or solution concocted of various ingredients. —*adj.* **4.** styled for semiformal wear: *a cocktail dress.* **5.** used in or suitable for cocktails: *cocktail onions.*

cock·tail² (kok′tāl′), *n.* **1.** a horse with a docked tail. **2.** a horse of mixed breed.

cock·y (kok′ē), *adj.,* **cock·i·er, cock·i·est.** arrogant; conceited. —**cock′i·ly,** *adv.* —**cock′i·ness,** *n.*

co·co (kō′kō), *n., pl.* **-cos. 1.** COCONUT PALM. **2.** COCONUT (def. 1).

co·coa (kō′kō), *n.* **1.** a powder made from roasted, husked, and ground cacao seeds from which much of the fat has been removed. **2.** a beverage made by mixing cocoa powder with hot milk or water and sugar. **3.** yellowish or reddish brown.

co′coa bean′, *n.* CACAO BEAN.

co′coa but′ter, *n.* a fatty substance obtained from the seeds of the cacao, used esp. in making soaps and cosmetics.

co·co·nut or **co·coa·nut** (kō′kə nut′, -nət), *n.* **1.** the large hardshelled seed of the coconut palm, lined with a white edible meat, and containing a milky liquid. **2.** the meat of the coconut, often shredded and used in cooking. **3.** COCONUT PALM.

co′conut milk′, *n.* **1.** the potable liquid within the seed of the coconut palm. **2.** a potable liquid obtained by steeping grated coconut meat in boiling water.

co′conut oil′, *n.* a white semisolid fat or nearly colorless fatty oil extracted from coconut meat and used in foods and in making soaps, cosmetics, etc.

co′conut palm′, *n.* a tall tropical palm, *Cocos nucifera,* bearing large hard-shelled seeds enclosed in a thick fibrous husk.

co·coon (kə kōon′), *n.* **1.** the silky envelope spun by the larvae of many insects, as silkworms, serving as a covering while they are in the pupal stage. **2.** a similar protective covering in nature, as the silky case in which certain spiders enclose their eggs. **3.** a protective covering, usu. of polyvinyl chloride, sprayed over machinery, a ship's guns, etc., to provide an airtight seal and prevent rust. **4.** any wrapping or enclosure resembling a cocoon. —*v.i.* **5.** to produce a cocoon. —*v.t.* **6.** to wrap or enclose in or as if in a cocoon.

co·coon·ing (kə kōo′ning), *n.* the practice of spending leisure time at home, esp. watching television or using a VCR.

cod (kod), *n., pl.* (*esp. collectively*) **-cod,** (*esp. for kinds or species*) **-cods. 1.** any of several soft-rayed food fishes of the family Gadidae, esp. *Gadus morhua,* of cool, N Atlantic waters. **2.** a closely related fish, *Gadus macrocephalus,* of the N Pacific.

C.O.D. or **c.o.d.,** cash, or collect, on delivery (purchaser to pay for goods when delivered).

co·da (kō′də), *n., pl.* **-das. 1.** a concluding passage of a musical composition following the last formal section. **2.** a concluding section, esp. one serving as a summation of preceding themes, as in a drama. **3.** anything that serves as a conclusion or summation.

cod·dle (kod′l), *v.t.,* **-dled, -dling. 1.** to treat tenderly or indulgently; pamper. **2.** to cook (eggs, fruit, etc.) in water that is just below the boiling point. —**cod′dler,** *n.*

code (kōd), *n., v.,* **cod·ed, cod·ing.** —*n.* **1.** a system for communication by telegraph, heliograph, etc., in which the letters of a message are represented by long and short sounds, light flashes, etc.: *Morse code.* **2.** a system used for brevity or secrecy of communication, in which arbitrarily chosen words, letters, or symbols are assigned definite meanings. **3.** letters, numbers, or other symbols used in a code system to represent or identify something: *The code on the label shows the date of manufacture.* **4.** a systematically arranged collection of existing laws: *a local health code.* **5.** the symbolic arrangement of statements or instructions in a computer program or the set of instructions in such a program. **6.** any system of rules and regulations: *a code of behavior.* **7.** a directive or alert to a hospital team assigned to emergency resuscitation of patients. **8.** GENETIC CODE. **9.** *Ling.* the system of rules shared by the participants in an act of communication; a language, dialect, or language variety. —*v.t.* **10.** to translate (a message) into a code; encode. **11.** to put or arrange (rules, regulations, etc.) in a code. —*v.i.* **12.** to specify the amino acid sequence of a protein by the sequence of nucleotides comprising the gene for that protein: *a gene that codes for the production of insulin.* —**cod′er,** *n.*

code′ blue′, *n.* (*often caps.*) a medical emergency in which paramedics are dispatched to aid a person undergoing cardiac arrest.

co·de·fend·ant (kō′di fen′dənt), *n.* a joint defendant.

co·deine (kō′dēn), *n.* a white, crystalline alkaloid, $C_{18}H_{21}NO_3$, obtained from opium, used as an analgesic and cough suppressant.

Code Na·po·lé·on (kôd NA pô lā ôN′; *Eng.* kōd′ nə pō′lā ôN′), *n.* the civil code of France, enacted in 1804. Also called **Napoleonic Code.**

Code′ of Hammura′bi, *n.* a Babylonian legal code of the 18th century B.C. or earlier, instituted by Hammurabi and dealing with criminal and civil matters.

co·de·pend·ent (kō′di pen′dənt), *adj.* **1.** of or pertaining to a relationship in which one person is physically or psychologically addicted, as to alcohol or gambling, and the other person is psychologically dependent on the first in an unhealthy way. —*n.* **2.** one who is codependent. —**co′de·pend′en·cy, co′de·pend′ence,** *n.*

code′-switch′ing, *n.* the alternate use of two or more languages or varieties of language, esp. within the same discourse.

co·de·ter·mi·na·tion (kō′di tûr′mə nā′shən), *n.* the determination of policy through cooperation, as between management and labor.

code′ word′, *n.* a euphemistic or politically acceptable catchword or phrase used instead of a blunter or less acceptable term.

co·dex (kō′deks), *n., pl.* **co·di·ces** (kō′də sēz′, kod′ə-). a manuscript volume, usu. of an ancient classic or the Scriptures.

cod·fish (kod′fish′), *n., pl.* (*esp. collectively*) **-fish,** (*esp. for kinds or species*) **-fish·es.** COD.

codg·er (koj′ər), *n.* an eccentric man, esp. one who is old.

co·di·ces (kō′də sēz′, kod′ə-), *n.* pl. of CODEX.

cod·i·cil (kod′ə səl), *n.* **1.** a supplement to a will, containing an addition, modification, etc., of something in the will. **2.** any supplement; appendix.

cod·i·fy (kod′ə fī′, kō′də-), *v.t.,* **-fied, -fy·ing. 1.** to reduce (laws, rules, etc.) to a code. **2.** to make a digest or systematic arrangement of. —**cod′i·fi′a·bil′i·ty** (-ə bil′i tē), *n.* —**cod′i·fi′er,** *n.*

cod·ling (kod′ling), *n.* the young of the cod.

cod′ling moth′, *n.* a small olethreutid moth, *Carpocapsa pomonella,* the larvae of which feed on the pulp of apples and other fruits.

cod′-liv′er oil′, *n.* an oil extracted from the liver of cod and related fishes, used chiefly as a source of vitamins A and D.

co·don (kō′don), *n.* a triplet of adjacent nucleotides in the messenger RNA chain that codes for a specific amino acid in the synthesis of a protein molecule.

Co·dy (kō′dē), *n.* **William Frederick** (*"Buffalo Bill"*), 1846–1917, U.S. Army scout and showman.

co·ed or **co-ed** (kō′ed′, -ed′), *adj.* **1.** serving both men and women alike; coeducational. **2.** of or pertaining to a coed. —*n.* **3.** a female student in a coeducational institution.

co·ed·u·ca·tion (kō′ej ŏŏ kā′shən), *n.* the education of both sexes in the same institution and in the same classes. —**co′ed·u·ca′tion·al,** *adj.*

co·ef·fi·cient (kō′ə fish′ənt), *n.* **1.** a number or quantity placed generally before and multiplying another quantity, as *3* in the expression *3x.* **2.** *Physics.* a constant that is a measure of a property of a substance, body, or process: *coefficient of friction.* —*adj.* **3.** acting in consort; cooperating. —**co′ef·fi′cient·ly,** *adv.*

coe·la·canth (sē′lə kanth′), *n.* a heavy, hollow-spined fish, *Latimeria chalumnae,* of deep S African coastal seas, that crawls on the sea bottom with lobed, limblike fins: a living fossil of the order Crossopterygii, considered forerunners of the land vertebrates. —**coe′la·can′thine** (-kan′thīn, -thin), *adj.*

coelacanth, *Latimeria chalumnae,* length 5 to 6 ft. (1.5 to 1.8 m)

coe·len·ter·ate (si len′tə rāt′, -tər it), *n.* **1.** any of the invertebrate animals formerly included in the phylum Coelenterata, comprising the cnidarians and comb jellies. —*adj.* **2.** of or pertaining to the coelenterates.

co·en·zyme (kō en′zīm), *n.* a molecule that provides the transfer site for biochemical reactions catalyzed by an enzyme. —**co·en′zy·mat′ic** (-zī mat′ik, -zi-), *adj.* —**co·en′zy·mat′i·cal·ly,** *adv.*

co·e·qual (kō ē′kwəl), *adj.* **1.** equal with another or each other in rank, ability, etc. —*n.* **2.** a coequal person or thing. —**co′e·qual′i·ty** (-i kwol′i tē), *n.* —**co·e′qual·ly,** *adv.*

co·erce (kō ûrs′), *v.t.,* **-erced, -erc·ing. 1.** to compel by force or intimidation: *to coerce someone into signing a document.* **2.** to bring about through force; exact: *to coerce obedience.* **3.** to dominate or control, esp. by exploiting fear, anxiety, etc. —**co·er′cion,** *n.* —**co·er′cive,** *adj.*

co·es·sen·tial (kō′ə sen′shəl), *adj.* of the same essence or nature. —**co′es·sen′tial·ly,** *adv.*

co·e·ta·ne·ous (kō′i tā′nē əs), *adj.* of the same age or duration. —**co′e·ta′ne·ous·ly,** *adv.*

co·e·ter·nal (kō′i tûr′nl), *adj.* existing with another eternally. —**co′e·ter′nal·ly,** *adv.* —**co′e·ter′ni·ty,** *n.*

co·e·val (kō ē′vəl), *adj.* **1.** of the same age or duration; equally old:

This manuscript is coeval with that one. **2.** coincident or contemporaneous: *Leonardo da Vinci and Michelangelo were only approximately coeval.* —*n.* **3.** a contemporary. —**co•e′val•ly,** *adv.*

co•ev•o•lu•tion (kō′ev ə lōō′shən; *esp. Brit.* -ē və-), *n.* evolution involving a series of reciprocal changes in two or more noninterbreeding populations that have a close ecological relationship and act as agents of natural selection for each other, as the succession of adaptations of a predator for pursuing and of its prey for fleeing or evading.

co•ex•ec•u•tor (kō′ig zek′yə tər), *n.* a joint executor.

co•ex•ist (kō′ig zist′), *v.i.* **1.** to exist simultaneously. **2.** (esp. of nations) to exist together peacefully. —**co′ex•ist′ence,** *n*

co•ex•tend (kō′ik stend′), *v.t., v.i.* to extend equally through the same space or length of time. —**co′ex•ten′sion** (-sten′shən), *n.*

co•fac•tor (kō′fak′tər), *n.* **1.** a contributing factor. **2.** any of various organic or inorganic substances necessary to the function of an enzyme.

cof•fee (kô′fē, kof′ē), *n.* **1.** a beverage consisting of a decoction or infusion of the roasted ground or crushed seeds (**cof′fee beans′**) of the two-seeded fruit (**cof′fee ber′ry**) of certain coffee trees. **2.** the seeds or fruit themselves. **3.** any of various tropical trees of the madder family that yield coffee beans, as *Coffea arabica* and *C. canefora.* **4.** a cup of coffee. **5.** medium to dark brown. —*adj.* **6.** of a coffee color. **7.** flavored with coffee.

cof′fee break′, *n.* a break from work for coffee, a snack, etc.

cof•fee•cake (kô′fē kāk′, kof′ē-), *n.* a cake or sweetened bread often made or topped with nuts, raisins, and cinnamon and glazed with melted sugar.

cof•fee•house (kô′fē hous′, kof′ē-), *n., pl.* **-hous•es** (-hou′ziz). **1.** an establishment that serves coffee and other refreshments and sometimes provides informal entertainment. **2.** (in 17th- and 18th-century England) a similar establishment where groups met for informal discussions, card playing, etc.

cof′fee mill′, *n.* a small mill for grinding roasted coffee beans.

cof•fee•pot (kô′fē pot′, kof′ē-), *n.* a container, usu. with a handle and a spout or lip, in which coffee is made or served, or both.

cof′fee shop′, *n.* a restaurant, as in a hotel, where quick and inexpensive light refreshments or meals are served.

cof′fee spoon′, *n.* a small spoon used with demitasse cups.

cof′fee ta′ble, *n.* a low table, usu. placed in front of a sofa, for holding ashtrays, snack bowls, glasses, magazines, etc.

cof′fee-ta′ble book′, *n.* an oversize, expensive, and usu. illustrated book suitable for displaying, as on a coffee table.

cof′fee tree′, *n.* COFFEE (def. 3).

cof•fer (kô′fər, kof′ər), *n.* **1.** a box or chest, esp. one for valuables. **2.** **coffers,** a treasury, as of an organization; funds. **3.** COFFERDAM. **4.** one of a number of sunken panels, usu. square or octagonal, in a vault or ceiling. —*v.t.* **5.** to deposit in or as if in a coffer or chest. **6.** to ornament with coffers or sunken panels.

cof•fer•dam (kô′fər dam′, kof′ər-), *n.* **1.** a temporary watertight enclosure for construction or repairs in waterlogged soil or under water. **2.** a sealed void between two bulkheads that prevents the escape of liquids, heat, etc.

cof•fin (kô′fin, kof′in), *n.* **1.** the box in which the body of a dead person is buried; casket. **2.** the part of a horse's foot containing the coffin bone. —*v.t.* **3.** to put or enclose in or as if in a coffin.

co•func•tion (kō′fungk′shən), *n.* the trigonometric function of the complement of a given angle or arc: *cosθ is the cofunction of sinθ.*

cog¹ (kog, kôg), *n.* **1.** a gear tooth, esp. one of hardwood or metal, fitted into a slot in a gearwheel of less durable material. **2.** a cogwheel. **3.** a person who plays a minor part in an organization, activity, etc.

cog² (kog, kôg), *v.,* **cogged, cog•ging.** —*v.t.* **1.** to manipulate or load (dice) unfairly. —*v.i.* **2.** to cheat, esp. at dice.

cog³ (kog, kôg), *n., v.,* **cogged, cog•ging.** —*n.* **1.** the tongue in one timber, fitting into a corresponding slot in another to form a joint. —*v.t., v.i.* **2.** to join with a cog.

co•gen•cy (kō′jən sē), *n.* the quality or state of being cogent; power to convince.

co•gen•e•ra•tion (kō′jen ə rā′shən), *n.* utilization of the normally wasted heat energy produced by a power plant or industrial process, esp. to generate electricity.

co•gent (kō′jənt), *adj.* **1.** convincing; believable. **2.** relevant; pertinent. —**co′gent•ly,** *adv.*

Cog•gan (kog′ən), *n.* **(Frederick) Donald,** born 1909, English clergyman: archbishop of Canterbury 1974–80.

cog•i•tate (koj′i tāt′), *v.,* **-tat•ed, -tat•ing.** —*v.i.* **1.** to ponder; meditate. —*v.t.* **2.** to think about; devise. —**cog′i•ta•ble,** *adj.* —**cog′i•ta′tor,** *n.*

cog•i•ta•tion (koj′i tā′shən), *n.* **1.** an act of reflection or meditation; contemplation. **2.** the faculty of thinking. **3.** a thought, scheme, or plan. —**cog′i•ta′tive,** *adj.*

co•gnac (kōn′yak, kon′-, kôn′-), *n.* **1.** (*often cap.*) the brandy produced near the town of Cognac, in W central France. **2.** (loosely) any good brandy.

cog•nate (kog′nāt), *adj.* **1.** related by birth; of the same parentage or descent. **2.** descended from the same language or form: *such cognate languages as French and Spanish.* **3.** allied or similar in nature or quality. —*n.* **4.** a person or thing cognate with another. **5.** a cognate word:

The English word cold *is a cognate of German* kalt. —**cog′nate•ly,** *adv.* —**cog′nate•ness,** *n.*

cog•ni•tion (kog nish′ən), *n.* **1.** the act or process of knowing; perception. **2.** something known or perceived.

cog•ni•tive (kog′ni tiv), *adj.* **1.** of or pertaining to cognition. **2.** of or pertaining to the mental processes of perception, memory, judgment, and reasoning, as contrasted with emotional and volitional processes. —**cog′ni•tive•ly,** *adv.* —**cog′ni•tiv′i•ty,** *n.*

cog•ni•za•ble (kog′nə zə bəl, kon′ə-, kog nī′-), *adj.* **1.** capable of being perceived or known. **2.** being within the jurisdiction of a court. —**cog′ni•za•bly,** *adv.*

cog•ni•zance (kog′nə zəns, kon′ə-), *n.* **1.** awareness or realization; notice: *to take cognizance of a slighting remark.* **2. a.** judicial notice as taken by a court in dealing with a cause. **b.** the right of taking jurisdiction, as possessed by a court. **3.** the range or scope of a person's knowledge, observation, etc.: *Such perceptions are beyond my cognizance.* **4.** a heraldic emblem serving as an identifying mark.

cog•ni•zant (kog′nə zənt, kon′ə-), *adj.* **1.** having cognizance; aware (usu. fol. by *of*): *We were cognizant of the difficulty.* **2.** having legal cognizance.

cog•no•men (kog nō′mən), *n., pl.* **-no•mens, -nom•i•na** (-nom′ə nə). **1.** any name, esp. a nickname or epithet. **2.** the third and commonly the last name of a citizen of ancient Rome, indicating the person's house or family, as "Caesar" in "Gaius Julius Caesar." **3.** a surname. —**cog•nom′i•nal** (-nom′ə nəl, -nō′mə-), *adj.* —**cog•nom′i•nal•ly,** *adv.*

co•gno•scen•ti (kon′yə shen′tē, kog′nə-), *n.pl., sing.* **-te** (-tā, -tē). well-informed persons, esp. those who have superior knowledge of a particular field, as in the arts.

cog•wheel (kog′hwēl′, -wēl′), *n.* a gearwheel, esp. one having teeth of hardwood or metal inserted into slots.

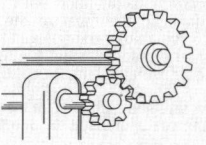

cogwheels

co•hab•it (kō hab′it), *v.i.* **1.** to live together as husband and wife, usu. without legal or religious sanction. **2.** to live together in an intimate relationship. **3.** to dwell with another or share the same place, as different species of animals. —**co•hab′it•ant, co•hab′it•er,** *n.* —**co•hab′i•ta′tion,** *n.*

co•hab•i•tate (kō hab′i tāt′), *v.i.,* **-tat•ed, -tat•ing.** COHABIT.

co•heir (kō âr′), *n.* a joint heir. —**co•heir′ship,** *n.*

co•heir•ess (kō âr′is), *n.* a joint heiress.

Co•hen (kō′ən, kō hen′), *n., pl.* **Co•ha•nim** (kō′hä nēm′), **Co•hens.** a member of the Jewish priestly class descended from Aaron, now having honorific duties and prerogatives. [< Hebrew *kōhēn* priest]

co•here (kō hēr′), *v.i.,* **-hered, -her•ing. 1.** to stick together; hold fast, as parts of the same mass. **2.** (of two or more similar substances) to be united within a body by the action of molecular forces. **3.** to be logically connected. **4.** to agree; be consistent.

co•her•ence (kō hēr′əns, -her′-) also **co•her′en•cy,** *n.* **1.** the act or state of cohering; cohesion. **2.** logical interconnection. **3.** congruity; consistency. **4.** *Physics, Optics.* (of waves) the state of being coherent.

co•her•ent (kō hēr′ənt, -her′-), *adj.* **1.** logically connected; consistent. **2.** cohering; sticking together. **3.** having a natural agreement of parts; harmonious. **4.** *Physics, Optics.* of or pertaining to waves that maintain a fixed phase relationship. —**co•her′ent•ly,** *adv.*

co•he•sion (kō hē′zhən), *n.* **1.** the act or state of cohering, uniting, or sticking together. **2.** the molecular force between particles within a body or substance that acts to unite them. **3.** *Bot.* the congenital union of one part with another. **4.** *Ling.* the property of unity in speech or writing that stems from links among surface elements, as in the reference of pronouns to elements in the surrounding discourse.

co•he•sive (kō hē′siv), *adj.* **1.** characterized by or causing cohesion. **2.** tending to unify, harmonize, or be consistent. **3.** of or pertaining to the molecular force within a body or substance acting to unite its parts. —**co•he′sive•ly,** *adv.* —**co•he′sive•ness,** *n.*

co•ho (kō′hō), *n., pl.* **-hos,** (*esp. collectively*) **-ho.** a small salmon, *Oncorhynchus kisutch,* of N Pacific coasts: introduced into the Great Lakes and other fresh waters. Also called **co′ho salm′on.**

co•hort (kō′hôrt), *n.* **1.** a companion, associate, or accomplice. **2.** a group or company. **3.** one of the ten divisions of a Roman legion. **4.** any group of soldiers or warriors. **5.** a group of persons sharing a particular statistical or demographic characteristic. **6.** an individual in a population of the same species.

co•hosh (kō′hosh, kō hosh′), *n.* either of two unrelated plants of the eastern U.S., *Cimicifuga racemosa,* of the buttercup family, or *Caulophyllum thalictroides,* of the barberry family: both used in folk medicine.

co-host (*v.* kō′hōst′, kō′hōst′; *n.* kō′hōst′), *v.t., v.i.* **1.** to host (a program) jointly with another. —*n.* **2.** a person who co-hosts.

coif (koif), *n.* **1.** any of various fitted or hoodlike caps worn alone or under another head covering by men or women. —*v.t.* **2.** to cover or dress with or as if with a coif.

coif•fure (kwä fyŏŏr′), *n., pl.* **-fures,** *v.,* **-fured, -fur•ing.** —*n.* **1.** a style of arranging or combing the hair. —*v.t.* **2.** to arrange (the hair) in a coiffure. —**coif•fur′ist,** *n.*

coil (koil), *v.t.* **1.** to wind into continuous rings one above the other or one around the other. **2.** to gather (rope, wire, etc.) into loops: *Coil the garden hose and hang it in the garage.* —*v.i.* **3.** to form rings, spirals, etc. **4.** to follow a winding course. —*n.* **5.** a series of spirals or rings into which something is wound: *a coil of rope.* **6.** a single such ring. **7.** an arrangement of pipes, coiled or in a series, as in a radiator. **8.** a continuous pipe having inlet and outlet, or flow and return ends. **9. a.** an electrical conductor, as a copper wire, wound up in a spiral or other form. **b.** a device composed essentially of such a conductor. **10.** a stamp issued in a rolled strip, usu. perforated vertically or horizontally only.

coin (koin), *n.* **1.** a piece of metal stamped and issued by the authority of a government for use as money. **2.** a number of such pieces. **3.** *Informal.* money; cash. **4.** QUOIN (defs. 1, 2). —*adj.* **5.** operated by or containing machines operated by the insertion of a coin or coins. —*v.t.* **6.** to make (coins) by stamping metal. **7.** to convert (metal) into money. **8.** to invent; fabricate: *to coin an expression.* —*Idiom.* **9. pay someone back in his or her own coin,** to retaliate against someone by using the person's own methods.

coin•age (koi′nij), *n.* **1.** the act or process of making coins. **2.** the types or amount of coins issued by a nation. **3.** coins collectively. **4.** the act or process of inventing words. **5.** an invented or newly created word or phrase: *"Ecdysiast" is a coinage of H. L. Mencken.* **6.** anything invented or fabricated.

co•in•cide (kō′in sīd′), *v.i.,* **-cid•ed, -cid•ing. 1.** to occupy the same location or period in time: *Our vacations coincided this year.* **2.** to correspond exactly, as in nature. **3.** to concur: *Our opinions coincide more often than not.* —**coincident, coincidental,** *adj.*

co•in•ci•dence (kō in′si dəns), *n.* **1.** a striking occurrence by mere chance of two or more events at one time: *Our meeting in Venice was pure coincidence.* **2.** the act, fact, or condition of coinciding.

co•in•ci•dent (kō in′si dənt), *adj.* **1.** happening at the same time. **2.** coinciding; occupying the same place or position. **3.** of like nature or agreeing (usu. fol. by *with*).

co•in•ci•den•tal (kō in′si den′tl), *adj.* **1.** being the result of coincidence: *a coincidental meeting.* **2.** occurring at the same time. —**co•in′ci•den′tal•ly, co•in′ci•dent•ly** (-dənt lē), *adv.*

coin′-op′erated, *adj.* activated by the insertion of a coin or coins into a slot: *a coin-operated washing machine.*

co•in•sur•ance (kō′in shŏŏr′əns, -shûr′-), *n.* **1.** insurance underwritten jointly with another insurer. **2.** property insurance in which liability is assumed only for a specified percentage of the property value.

co•in•sure (kō′in shŏŏr′, -shûr′), *v.t., v.i.,* **-sured, -sur•ing. 1.** to insure jointly. **2.** to insure on the basis of coinsurance. —**co′in•sur′er,** *n.*

coir (koir), *n.* the prepared fiber of the husk of the coconut, used in making rope, matting, etc.

co•i•tus (kō′i təs), *n.* sexual intercourse. —**co′i•tal,** *adj.*

co′itus in•ter•rup′tus (in′tə rup′təs), *n.* coitus that is intentionally interrupted by withdrawal before ejaculation of semen into the vagina.

coke¹ (kōk), *n., v.,* **coked, cok•ing.** —*n.* **1.** the solid carbonaceous product obtained by destructive distillation of coal: used chiefly as a fuel and reducing agent in metallurgy. —*v.t., v.i.* **2.** to convert into or become coke. —**coke′like′, cok′y,** *adj.*

coke² (kōk), *n., v.,* **coked, cok•ing.** *Slang.* —*n.* **1.** cocaine. —*v.t.* **2.** to affect with a narcotic drug, esp. with cocaine (usu. fol. by *up*).

Coke (kōk), *n.* **Thomas,** 1747–1814, first bishop of the Methodist Episcopal Church in the United States.

coke•head (kōk′hed′), *n. Slang.* a cocaine addict or habitual user.

col (kol), *n.* **1.** a pass or depression in a mountain range or ridge. **2.** the region of relatively low pressure between two anticyclones.

Col., 1. Colonel. **2.** Colorado. **3.** Colossians.

co•la (kō′lə), *n., pl.* **-las.** a carbonated soft drink containing an extract made from kola nuts, together with sweeteners and other flavorings.

col•an•der (kul′ən dər, kol′-), *n.* a usu. metal container with a perforated bottom and sides, for draining and straining foods.

col•by (kōl′bē), *n.* a mild cheese similar to cheddar but softer and more open in texture.

col•chi•cum (kol′chi kəm, kol′ki-), *n.* **1.** any Old World plant of the genus *Colchicum,* of the lily family, esp. the autumn crocus, *C. autumnale.* **2.** the dried seeds or corms of this plant. **3.** a medicine or drug prepared from these, used chiefly in the treatment of gout.

cold (kōld), *adj.* **1.** having a relatively low temperature. **2.** feeling an uncomfortable lack of warmth; chilled. **3.** having a temperature lower than the normal temperature of the human body: *cold hands.* **4.** lacking in passion, enthusiasm, etc.: *cold reason.* **5.** not affectionate or friendly: *a cold reply.* **6.** lacking sensual desire; frigid. **7.** depressing; dispiriting. **8.** unconscious because of a severe blow, shock, etc. **9.** lifeless or extinct; dead. **10.** (in games) distant from the object of search or the correct answer. **11. a.** COOL (def. 11). **b.** being a cool color. —*n.* **12.** the

absence of heat or warmth. **13.** the sensation produced by loss of heat from the body, as by contact with anything having a lower temperature than that of the body: *the cold of a steel door.* **14.** cold weather. **15.** Also called **common cold.** a respiratory disorder characterized by sneezing, sore throat, coughing, etc., caused by any of various viruses of the rhinovirus group. —*adv.* **16.** with complete competence; thoroughly: *He knew his speech cold.* **17.** without preparation or prior notice. **18.** abruptly; unceremoniously. **19.** *Metalworking.* at a temperature below that at which recrystallization can occur (sometimes used in combination): *to cold-hammer an iron bar; The wire was drawn cold.* —*Idiom.* **20. catch** or **take cold,** to become afflicted with a cold. **21. (out) in the cold,** neglected; ignored; forgotten. **22. throw cold water on,** to dampen someone's enthusiasm about. —**cold′ly,** *adv.* —**cold′ness,** *n.*

cold′-blood′ed or **cold′blood′ed,** *adj.* **1.** of or designating animals, as fishes and reptiles, whose blood temperature ranges from the freezing point upward, in accordance with the temperature of the surrounding medium. **2.** done or acting without emotion or feeling: *a cold-blooded killer.* **3.** sensitive to cold. —**cold′-blood′ed•ly,** *adv.* —**cold′-blood′ed•ness,** *n.*

cold′ call′, *n.* a visit or telephone call to a prospective customer without an appointment or a previous introduction.

cold′ com′fort, *n.* negligible comfort or consolation.

cold′ cream′, *n.* a creamy cosmetic for the face and neck, used to remove makeup or to cleanse or soothe the skin.

cold′ cuts′, *n.pl.* slices of various prepared meats, as salami, bologna, ham, etc., and sometimes cheeses, served cold.

cold′ duck′, *n.* **1.** a mixture of champagne and sparkling Burgundy, orig. from Germany. **2.** a drink typically of white wine, champagne, lemon juice, and sugar.

cold′ feet′, *n. Informal.* a lack of confidence or courage.

cold′ fish′, *n. Informal.* a person who is aloof and lacking in cordiality or sympathy.

cold′ frame′, *n.* a boxlike structure, usu. faced with glass, placed over a flower bed to protect plants, esp. seedlings.

cold′ front′, *n.* the zone separating two air masses, of which the cooler, denser mass is advancing and replacing the warmer.

cold′ fu′sion, *n.* a hypothetical form of nuclear fusion postulated to occur at relatively low temperatures and pressures, as at room temperature and at one atmosphere.

cold′-heart′ed, *adj.* lacking sympathy or feeling; indifferent; unkind. —**cold′-heart′ed•ly,** *adv.* —**cold′-heart′ed•ness,** *n.*

cold′ light′, *n.* emitted light that is not a result of incandescence or combustion, as phosphorescence.

cold′ pack′, *n.* **1.** a cold towel, ice bag, etc., applied to the body to reduce swelling, relieve pain, etc. **2.** a method of canning uncooked food by placing it in jars or cans and sterilizing in a bath of boiling water or steam. —**cold′-pack′,** *v.t.*

cold′ rub′ber, *n.* a low-temperature synthetic rubber used chiefly for retreading tires.

cold′ shoul′der, *n.* a show of deliberate indifference.

cold′ snap′, *n.* a sudden, relatively brief period of cold weather. Also called **cold′ spell′.**

cold′ sore′, *n.* See under ORAL HERPES. Also called **fever blister.**

cold′ stor′age, *n.* **1.** the storage of food, furs, etc., in an artificially cooled place. **2.** suspension of activity; abeyance.

cold′ tur′key, *Informal.* —*n.* **1.** abrupt and complete withdrawal from the use of an addictive substance, esp. a narcotic drug or nicotine. —*adv.* **2.** abruptly and completely: *to withdraw cold turkey from a drug.* **3.** without preparation; impromptu.

cold′ type′, *n.* type set by a method other than the casting of molten metal, as by photocomposition.

cold′ war′, *n.* **1.** intense political, military, and ideological rivalry between nations just short of armed conflict. **2.** (*caps.*) such rivalry after World War II between the Soviet Union and the U.S., and their respective allies. **3.** rivalry and tension between people or factions. —**cold′ war′rior,** *n.*

cold′-wa′ter flat′, *n.* an apartment, often in an unheated building, provided only with cold running water.

cold′ wave′, *n.* **1.** a rapid and considerable drop in temperature, usu. affecting a large area. **2.** a permanent wave set in the hair by chemical solutions without the aid of heat.

cole (kōl), *n.* any of various plants of the genus *Brassica,* of the mustard family, esp. kale or rape.

co•le•op•ter•an (kō′lē op′tər ən, kol′ē-), *n.* **1.** BEETLE¹ (def. 1). —*adj.* **2.** of or pertaining to a beetle.

Cole•ridge (kōl′rij, kō′lə-), *n.* **Samuel Taylor,** 1772–1834, English poet, critic, and philosopher. —**Cole•ridg′i•an,** *adj.*

cole•slaw (kōl′slô′), *n.* a salad of finely sliced or chopped raw cabbage, usu. dressed with a seasoned mayonnaise.

co•le•us (kō′lē əs), *n., pl.* **-us•es.** any of several Old World tropical plants of the genus *Coleus,* of the mint family, cultivated for their colorful leaves.

Col•fax (kōl′faks), *n.* **Schuyler,** 1823–85, U.S. political leader: vice president of the U.S. 1869–73.

col•ic (kol′ik), *n.* **1.** paroxysmal pain in the abdomen or bowels. **2.** a condition in young infants characterized by loud and prolonged crying, for which no physiological or other cause has been found. —*adj.* **3.** pertaining to or affecting the colon or the bowels. —**col′ick•y,** *adj.*

col•ic•root (kol′ik ro͞ot′, -ro͝ot′), *n.* **1.** a North American plant, *Aletris farinosa,* of the lily family, with yellow or white flower spikes and a root used in folk medicine to relieve colic. **2.** any of certain other plants having roots reputed to cure colic.

col•i•form (kol′ə fôrm′, kō′lə-), *adj.* of or pertaining to any of several bacilli, esp. *Escherichia coli* and members of the genus *Aerobacter,* that are normally present in the colon and that indicate fecal contamination when found in a water supply.

col•i•se•um (kol′i sē′əm), *n.* a stadium, large theater, or other special building for sporting events, exhibitions, etc.

co•li•tis (kə lī′tis, kō-), *n.* inflammation of the colon. —**co•lit′ic** (-lit′ik), *adj.*

col•lab•o•rate (kə lab′ə rāt′), *v.i.,* **-rat•ed, -rat•ing. 1.** to work, one with another; cooperate, as on a literary work. **2.** to cooperate with an enemy nation, esp. with an enemy occupying one's country. —**collaboration,** *n.* —**col•lab′o•ra′tor,** *n.*

col•lage (kə läzh′), *n.* **1.** a technique of composing a work of art by pasting on a surface various materials not normally associated with one another, as newspaper clippings or parts of photographs. **2.** a work produced by this technique. **3.** a film or other work that shifts suddenly or abruptly from one seemingly unrelated scene or image to another. —**col•lag′ist,** *n.*

col•la•gen (kol′ə jən), *n.* a strongly fibrous protein that is abundant in bone, tendons, cartilage, and connective tissue, yielding gelatin when denatured by boiling. —**col•lag•e•nous** (kə laj′ə nəs), *adj.*

col•lapse (kə laps′), *v.,* **-lapsed, -laps•ing,** *n.* —*v.i.* **1.** to fall or cave in; crumble suddenly. **2.** to be made so that sections or parts can be folded up, as for storage. **3.** to fall unconscious or fall down, as from a heart attack or exhaustion. **4.** (of lungs) to come into an airless state. **5.** to fall or decline suddenly, as in value. —*v.t.* **6.** to cause to collapse. —*n.* **7.** a falling in, down, or together: *trapped by the collapse of a tunnel.* **8.** a sudden, complete failure; breakdown. —**col•laps′i•ble,** *adj.*

col•lar (kol′ər), *n.* **1.** the part of a shirt, coat, dress, blouse, etc., that encompasses the neckline of the garment and is sewn permanently to it, often so as to fold or roll over. **2.** a similar but separate, detachable article of clothing worn around the neck or at the neckline of a garment. **3.** anything worn or placed around the neck. **4.** a leather or metal band or a chain, fastened around the neck of an animal, used esp. as a means of restraint or identification. **5.** the part of the harness that fits across the withers and over the shoulders of a draft animal. **6.** *Zool.* any of various collarlike markings or structures around the neck; torque. **7.** a raised area of metal for reinforcing a weld. **8.** a short ring formed on or fastened over a rod or shaft as a locating or holding part. **9.** the upper rim of a borehole or mine shaft. **10.** *Informal.* an arrest; capture. —*v.t.* **11.** to put a collar on; furnish with a collar. **12.** to seize by the collar or neck. **13.** to detain (someone) in conversation. **14.** *Informal.* to place under arrest.

col•lar•bone (kol′ər bōn′), *n.* the clavicle.

col•lard (kol′ərd), *n.* **1.** a variety of kale, *Brassica oleracea acephala,* grown in the southern U.S., having a rosette of green leaves. **2. collards.** Also called **col′lard greens′.** the leaves of this plant, eaten cooked as a vegetable.

col•late (kə lāt′, kō-, ko-, kō′lāt, kol′āt), *v.t.,* **-lat•ed, -lat•ing. 1.** to gather or arrange (pages) in their proper sequence. **2.** to verify the arrangement of (the gathered sheets of a book) before binding. **3.** to compare (texts, etc.) critically. **4.** to verify the number and order of the sheets of (a volume) as a means of determining its completeness. —**col•lat′a•ble,** *adj.* —**col•la′tor,** *n.*

col•lat•er•al (kə lat′ər əl), *n.* **1.** security pledged for the payment of a loan. **2.** *Anat.* **a.** a subordinate or accessory part. **b.** a side branch, as of a blood vessel or nerve. —*adj.* **3.** accompanying; auxiliary: *collateral aid.* **4.** additional; confirming: *collateral evidence.* **5.** secured by collateral. **6.** secondary or incidental. **7.** (of a relative) descended from the same stock, but in a different line. **8.** situated at the side. **9.** running side by side; parallel. —**col•lat′er•al′i•ty** (-ə ral′i tē), **col•lat′er•al•ness,** *n.* —**col•lat′er•al•ly,** *adv.*

collat′eral dam′age, *n.* **1.** the killing of civilians in a military attack. **2.** any damage incidental to an activity.

col•la•tion (kə lā′shən, kō-, ko-), *n.* **1.** the act of collating; fact or result of being collated. **2.** the verification of the number and order of the leaves and signatures of a volume. **3.** a light meal, esp. one that may be permitted on a fast day. **4.** (in a monastery) the practice of reading and conversing on the lives of the saints or the Scriptures at the close of the day.

col•league (kol′ēg), *n.* an associate; fellow worker or fellow member of a profession.

col•lect[1] (kə lekt′), *v.t.* **1.** to gather together; assemble. **2.** to make a collection of: *to collect stamps.* **3.** to demand and receive payment of. **4.** to regain control of (oneself or one's thoughts or emotions). **5.** to call for and take with one: *Did you collect your mail?* —*v.i.* **6.** to gather together; assemble. **7.** to accumulate. **8.** to receive payment (often fol. by *on*): *We collected on the damage to our house.* —*adj., adv.* **9.** requiring payment by the recipient: *a collect phone call; to call collect.*

col•lect[2] (kol′ekt), *n.* any of certain brief prayers used in Western churches esp. before the epistle in the communion service.

col•lec•ta•ne•a (kol′ek tā′nē ə), *n.pl.* collected passages, esp. as arranged in a miscellany or anthology.

col•lect•ed (kə lek′tid), *adj.* **1.** having control of one's faculties; self-possessed. **2.** brought together, as miscellaneous works: *collected essays.* —**col•lect′ed•ly,** *adv.* —**col•lect′ed•ness,** *n.*

col•lect•i•ble or **col•lect•a•ble** (kə lek′tə bəl), *adj.* **1.** able to be collected, as a debt. **2.** suitable for collecting. —*n.* **3.** an object suitable for a collection, as that of a hobbyist.

col•lec•tion (kə lek′shən), *n.* **1.** the act of collecting. **2.** something that is collected, as a group of objects or an amount of material accumulated in one place: *a stamp collection; a collection of rainwater.* **3.** the works of art constituting the holdings of an art museum. **4.** the clothes or other items produced by a designer, esp. for a specific season. **5.** a sum of money collected, esp. for church use.

col•lec•tive (kə lek′tiv), *adj.* **1.** formed by collection. **2.** forming a whole; combined: *our collective assets.* **3.** characteristic or expressive of a group: *their collective wishes.* **4.** organized according to the principles of collectivism. —*n.* **5.** an organization in a collectivist system, esp. a collective farm. **6.** COLLECTIVE NOUN. **7.** a collective body; aggregate. —**col•lec′tive•ly,** *adv.*

collec′tive bar′gaining, *n.* the process by which wages, working conditions, etc., are negotiated and agreed upon by union and employer for all employees under the union's jurisdiction.

collec′tive farm′, *n.* (esp. in Communist countries) a farm, or a number of farms organized as a unit, worked by a community under the supervision of the state.

collec′tive noun′, *n.* a noun, as *herd, jury,* or *clergy,* that appears singular in formal shape but denotes a group of individuals or objects. —**Usage.** Whether a COLLECTIVE NOUN will be used with a singular or plural verb depends on whether the word refers to the group as a unit or to its members as individuals. In American English a noun naming an organization regarded as a unit is usu. treated as singular: *The corporation is holding its annual meeting. The government has taken action.* In British English, such nouns are commonly treated as plurals: *The corporation are holding their annual meeting. The government are in agreement.* In formal speech and writing COLLECTIVE NOUNS are usu. not treated as both singular and plural in the same sentence: *The enemy is fortifying its position. The enemy are bringing up their heavy artillery.* When the nouns *couple* and *pair* refer to people, they are usu. treated as plurals: *The newly married couple have bought a house. The pair are busy furnishing their new home.* The COLLECTIVE NOUN *number,* when preceded by *a,* is treated as a plural: *A number of solutions were suggested.* When preceded by *the,* it is usu. treated as a singular: *The number of solutions offered was astounding.* Other common COLLECTIVE NOUNS are *audience, class, committee, crew, crowd, family, flock, group, panel,* and *staff.*

collec′tive uncon′scious, *n.* (in Jungian psychology) inborn unconscious psychic material common to humankind, accumulated by the experience of preceding generations. Compare ARCHETYPE (def. 2).

col•lec•tiv•ism (kə lek′tə viz′əm), *n.* the socialist principle of control by the people collectively, or the state, of all means of production or economic activity. —**col•lec′tiv•ist,** *n., adj.*

col•lec•tor (kə lek′tər), *n.* **1.** a person or thing that collects. **2.** a person employed to collect debts, duties, taxes, etc. **3.** a person who collects books, paintings, stamps, etc., as a hobby or investment. **4.** SOLAR COLLECTOR. —**col•lec′tor•ship′,** *n.*

col•leen (kol′ēn, ko lēn′), *n.* an Irish girl.

col•lege (kol′ij), *n.* **1.** an institution of higher learning that provides a general education in the liberal arts and sciences and grants a bachelor's degree. Compare UNIVERSITY. **2.** a constituent unit of a university offering instruction in a particular field of study. **3.** an institution for vocational, technical, or professional instruction: *a business college.* **4.** an endowed, self-governing association of scholars incorporated within a university, as at Oxford and Cambridge in England. **5.** the building or buildings occupied by an institution of higher education. **6.** the administrators, faculty, and students of a college. **7.** an organized association of persons having certain powers and rights, and performing certain duties or engaged in a particular pursuit: *the electoral college.* **8.** a company; assemblage. **9.** a body of clerics living in a funded institution. —**col•le•giate** (kə lē′jit, -jē it), *adj.*

Col′lege of Car′dinals, *n.* the chief ecclesiastical body of the Roman Catholic Church, electing and advising the pope and comprising all of the cardinals of the church.

col′lege try′, *n. Informal.* a maximum effort (usu. prec. by *the old*): *We may not finish on time, but let's give it the old college try.*

col•le•gial (kə lē′jəl, -jē əl; *for 2 also* kə lē′gē əl), *adj.* **1.** collegiate. **2.** (of colleagues) sharing responsibility in a group endeavor. —**col•le′gi•al•ly,** *adv.*

col•le•gian (kə lē′jən, -jē ən), *n.* a student in, or a recent graduate of, a college.

col•le•giate (kə lē′jit, -jē it), *adj.* **1.** of, pertaining to, or constituted as a college. **2.** of, characteristic of, or intended for college students. —**col•le′giate•ly,** *adv.*

colle′giate church′, *n.* **1.** a church that has a chapter of canons but no bishop's see. **2.** (in the U.S.) a church or group of churches governed by a consistory or session. **3.** (in Scotland) a church having two or more pastors.

col•le•gi•um (kə lē′jē əm), *n., pl.* **-gi•a** (-jē ə), **-gi•ums.** a group of officials with equal rank and power.

col•lem•bo•lan (kə lem′bə lən), *adj.* **1.** Also, **col•lem′bo•lous.** belonging or pertaining to the insect order Collembola, comprising the springtails. —*n.* **2.** a collembolan insect; springtail.

col•let (kol′it), *n.* **1.** a collar or enclosing band. **2.** the enclosing rim within which a gemstone is set. **3.** a slotted cylindrical clamp inserted into the tapered interior of a sleeve or chuck on a lathe to hold a cylindrical piece of work.

col•lide (kə līd′), *v.,* **-lid•ed, -lid•ing.** —*v.i.* **1.** to strike one another or one against the other with a forceful impact; crash. **2.** to clash; conflict. —*v.t.* **3.** to cause to collide.

col•lid•er (kə lī′dər), *n.* a particle accelerator in which oppositely charged particles circulate in opposite directions and collide head-on.

col•lie (kol′ē), *n.* one of a breed of large Scottish sheepherding dogs with a long, narrow, wedge-shaped head and either a long, thick, straight coat or a short, hard coat. —**col′lie•like′,** *adj.*

col•li•gate (kol′i gāt′), *v.,* **-gat•ed, -gat•ing.** —*v.t.* **1.** to bind or fasten together. **2.** to link (facts) together by a general description or by a hypothesis that applies to them all. —*v.i.* **3.** to become linked together. —**col′li•ga′tion,** *n.*

col•li•mate (kol′ə māt′), *v.t.,* **-mat•ed, -mat•ing.** **1.** to bring into line; make parallel. **2.** to adjust the line of sight of (a telescope or other optical instrument). —**col′li•ma′tion,** *n.*

col•lin•e•ar (kə lin′ē ər, kō-), *adj.* lying in the same straight line. —**col•lin′e•ar′i•ty,** *n.* —**col•lin′e•ar•ly,** *adv.*

col•lin•si•a (kə lin′sē ə, -zē ə), *n., pl.* **-si•as.** any plant belonging to the genus *Collinsia,* of the figwort family, having whorled leaves and usu. clusters of variously colored flowers.

col•li•sion (kə lizh′ən), *n.* **1.** the act of colliding; a crash. **2.** a conflict; clash. **3.** *Physics.* the meeting of particles or of bodies in which each exerts a force upon the other. —**col•li′sion•al,** *adj.*

col•lo•cate (kol′ə kāt′), *v.,* **-cat•ed, -cat•ing.** —*v.t.* **1.** to arrange in proper order, esp. to place side by side. —*v.i.* **2.** (of a word) to enter into a collocation.

col•lo•ca•tion (kol′ə kā′shən), *n.* **1.** the act of collocating. **2.** the state or manner of being collocated. **3.** the co-occurrence of words, esp. when habitual, as of *perform* with *operation* or *commit* with *crime.* —**col′lo•ca′tion•al, col′lo•ca′tive,** *adj.*

col•loid (kol′oid), *n.* **1.** a substance made up of a system of particles with linear dimensions in the range of about 10^{-7} to 5×10^{-5} cm dispersed in a continuous gaseous, liquid, or solid medium. **2.** a colloidal substance in the body, as a stored secretion. —*adj.* **3.** colloidal.

col•lo•qui•al (kə lō′kwē əl), *adj.* **1.** characteristic of or suitable to ordinary or familiar conversation or writing rather than formal speech or writing; informal. **2.** involving or using conversation. —**col•lo′qui•al•ly,** *adv.*

col•lo•qui•al•ism (kə lō′kwē ə liz′əm), *n.* **1.** a colloquial expression. **2.** colloquial style or usage. —**col•lo′qui•al•ist,** *n.*

col•lo•qui•um (kə lō′kwē əm), *n., pl.* **-qui•ums, -qui•a** (-kwē ə). a conference at which scholars or other experts present papers on and discuss a specific topic.

col•lo•quy (kol′ə kwē), *n., pl.* **-quies.** **1.** a conversational exchange; dialogue. **2.** a conference. —**col′lo•quist,** *n.*

col•lude (kə lo͞od′), *v.i.,* **-lud•ed, -lud•ing.** to conspire to commit a fraud. —**col•lud′er,** *n.*

col•lu•sion (kə lo͞o′zhən), *n.* a conspiracy for fraudulent purposes. —**col•lu′sive** (-siv), *adj.*

col•lu•vi•um (kə lo͞o′vē əm), *n., pl.* **-vi•a** (-vē ə), **-vi•ums.** loose earth material that has accumulated at the base of a slope; talus. —**col•lu′vi•al,** *adj.*

col•o•bus (kol′ə bəs, kə lō′-), *n., pl.* **-bus•es, -bi** (-bī′, -bī). any of several large, slender African monkeys of the genus *Colobus,* lacking thumbs and having long, silky fur.

col•o•cynth (kol′ə sinth), *n.* **1.** Also called **bitter apple.** a Mediterranean and S Asian plant, *Citrullus colocynthis,* of the gourd family, bearing a round, yellow or green fruit with a bitter pulp. **2.** a drug derived from the pulp of the fruit, used as a purgative.

co•log•a•rithm (kō lô′gə rith′əm, -rith′əm, -log′ə-), *n.* the logarithm of the reciprocal of a number, often used in expressing the logarithm of a fraction. *Abbr:* colog

co•logne (kə lōn′), *n.* a mildly perfumed toilet water; eau de Cologne. Also called **Cologne′ wa′ter.** —**co•logned′,** *adj.*

Co•logne (kə lōn′), *n.* a city in W Germany. 914,300. German, **Köln.**

Co•lom•bi•a (kə lum′bē ə), *n.* a republic in NW South America. 37,418,290; 439,828 sq. mi. (1,139,155 sq. km). *Cap.:* Bogotá. —**Co•lom′bi•an,** *adj., n.*

Co•lom•bo (kə lum′bō), *n.* the capital of Sri Lanka, on the W coast. 587,647.

co•lon[1] (kō′lən), *n.* **1.** the sign (:) used to mark a major division in a sentence to indicate that what follows is an elaboration, summation, interpretation, etc. of what precedes. **2.** the sign (:) used to separate groups of numbers, as hours from minutes in *5:30,* or the elements of a ratio or proportion in *1: 2:: 3: 6.*

co•lon[2] (kō′lən), *n., pl.* **-lons, -la** (-lə). the part of the large intestine extending from the cecum to the rectum.

colo•nel (kûr′nl), *n.* **1.** an officer in the U.S. Army, Air Force, or Marine Corps ranking above lieutenant colonel. **2.** a commissioned officer of similar rank in other nations. **3.** *Southern U.S.* **a.** an honorary title bestowed by some states, esp. on visiting dignitaries. **b.** (formerly) a title of respect for an elderly man. —**colo′nel•cy,** *n.* —**Pronunciation.** COLONEL (kûr′nl), with its medial *l* pronounced as (r), illustrates one source for the apparent vagaries of English spelling: divergence between a word's orthographic development and its established pronunciation. In this case, English borrowed from French two variant forms of the same word, one pronounced with medial and final (l), and a second reflecting dissimilation of the first (l) to (r). After a period of competition, the dissimilated form triumphed in pronunciation, while the spelling *colonel* became the orthographic standard.

co•lo•ni•al (kə lō′nē əl), *adj.* **1.** of or pertaining to a colony or colonies. **2.** (*often cap.*) of or pertaining to the 13 British colonies that became the United States of America, or to their period. **3.** (of an animal) **a.** having a way of life that requires being part of a community of its own kind: *Penguins are colonial birds.* **b.** being a partly attached life form. **4.** (*cap.*) of, pertaining to, or imitative of the styles of architecture, ornament, and furnishings of the British colonies in America in the 17th and 18th centuries. —*n.* **5.** an inhabitant of a colony. **6.** a house in or imitative of the Colonial style. —**co•lo′ni•al•ly,** *adv.*

co•lo•ni•al•ism (kə lō′nē ə liz′əm), *n.* the system or policy by which a nation seeks to extend or retain its authority over other peoples or territories. —**co•lo′ni•al•ist,** *n., adj.*

co•lo•ni•al•ize (kə lō′nē ə līz′), *v.t.,* **-ized, -iz•ing.** to make colonial. —**co•lo′ni•al•i•za′tion,** *n.*

col•o•nist (kol′ə nist), *n.* **1.** an inhabitant of a colony. **2.** a member of a colonizing expedition.

col•o•nize (kol′ə nīz′), *v.,* **-nized, -niz•ing.** —*v.t.* **1.** to establish a colony in; settle. **2.** to form a colony of. —*v.i.* **3.** to form a colony. **4.** to settle in a colony. —**col′o•ni•za′tion,** *n.* —**col′o•niz′er,** *n.*

col•on•nade (kol′ə nād′), *n.* **1.** a series of regularly spaced columns supporting an entablature and usu. one side of a roof. **2.** a row of trees, as on each side of a driveway or road. —**col′on•nad′ed,** *adj.*

col•o•ny (kol′ə nē), *n., pl.* **-nies.** **1.** a group of people who leave their native country to form in a new land a settlement subject to, or connected with, the parent nation. **2.** the country or district so settled. **3.** any people or territory separated from but subject to a ruling power. **4. the Colonies,** those British colonies that formed the original 13 states of the United States. **5.** a group of individuals having the same national origin or similar interests, occupations, etc., living in a particular locality: *the American colony in Paris; a colony of artists.* **6.** a group of people forced to live isolated from society, as because of disease or criminal behavior. **7.** the place or dwellings inhabited by such a group. **8.** an aggregation of bacteria growing together as the descendants of a single cell. **9.** a group of organisms of the same kind living or growing in close association.

col•o•phon (kol′ə fon′, -fən), *n.* **1.** a publisher's or printer's distinctive emblem, used as an identifying device on its books and other works. **2.** an inscription at the end of a book or manuscript, used esp. in the 15th and 16th centuries, giving its title, author, date, etc. —**col′o•phon′ic,** *adj.*

col•or (kul′ər), *n.* **1.** the quality of an object or substance with respect to light reflected by it, usu. determined visually by measurement of hue, saturation, and brightness of the reflected light; saturation or chroma; hue. **2.** the natural hue of the skin, esp. of the face; complexion. **3.** a ruddy complexion, usu. indicating good health. **4.** a blush. **5.** vivid or distinctive quality, as of a literary work. **6.** details in description, customs, speech, habits, etc., of a place or period: *a novel about the Pilgrims with much local color.* **7.** something that is used for coloring; pigment; dye. **8.** background information, as anecdotes or analyses of strategy, given by a sportscaster during a broadcast. **9. colors, a.** a colored badge, ribbon, or uniform worn or displayed to signify allegiance, membership, etc. **b.** viewpoint or attitude; character: *to show one's true colors under stress.* **c.** a flag, ensign, etc., particularly the national flag. **10.** skin tone other than caucasian as an indicator of racial or ethnic affiliation: *Persons of color had been denied their civil rights.* **11.** outward appearance or aspect; guise or show: *a lie that had the color of truth.* **12.** a pretext: *a mean trick under the color of a good deed.* **13.** *Law.* an apparent or evident right: *holding possession under color of title.* **14.** tonal shading and timbre in music. **15.** a trace or particle of valuable mineral, esp. gold, as shown by washing auriferous gravel. **16.** *Physics.* a theoretical property that distinguishes the various states in which quarks exist. —*adj.* **17.** involving, utilizing, yielding, or possessing color: *a color TV.* —*v.t.* **18.** to give or apply color to; tinge; paint; dye. **19.** to cause to appear different from the reality: *She colored her account of the incident in order to influence the jury.* **20.** to give a special character or quality to: *The author's personal feelings color his writing.* —*v.i.* **21.** to take on or change color. **22.** to flush; blush. —***Idiom.*** **23. change color, a.** to blush. **b.** to turn pale. Also, *esp. Brit.,* **colour.**

col•or•a•ble (kul′ər ə bəl), *adj.* **1.** capable of being colored. **2.** seemingly valid, true, or genuine; plausible. **3.** pretended; deceptive. —**col′or•a•bly,** *adv.*

Col•o•rad•o (kol′ə rad′ō, -rä′dō), *n.* **1.** a state in the W United States. 3,822,676; 104,247 sq. mi. (270,000 sq. km). *Cap.:* Denver. *Abbr.:* CO, Col., Colo. **2.** a river flowing SW from N Colorado through Utah and Arizona into the Gulf of California. 1450 mi. (2335 km) long. **3.** a river flowing SE from W Texas to the Gulf of Mexico. 840 mi. (1350 km) long. —Col′o·rad′an, Col′o·rad′o·an, *adj., n.*

Col·orad′o bee′tle, *n.* a black and yellow leaf beetle, *Leptinotarsa decemlineata,* orig. from the Colorado region, that is a common pest of potato plants. Also called **Colorad′o pota′to bee′tle, potatobug.**

Col·orad′o Springs′, *n.* a city in central Colorado: U.S. Air Force Academy. 316,480.

col·or·ant (kul′ər ənt), *n.* something used as a coloring matter; pigment; dye.

col·or·a·tion (kul′ə rā′shən), *n.* appearance with regard to color; coloring: *the bold coloration of some birds.*

col·or·a·tu·ra (kul′ər ə tŏŏr′ə, -tyŏŏr′ə, kol′-, kōl′-), *n., pl.* **-ras. 1.** runs, trills, and other florid decorations in vocal music. **2.** a lyric soprano of high range who specializes in such music.

col·or·bear·er (kul′ər bâr′ər), *n.* a person who carries the colors or standard, esp. of a military body.

col·or·blind′, *adj.* **1. a.** unable to distinguish one or more chromatic colors. **b.** unable to distinguish colors, seeing only shades of gray, black, and white. **2.** showing or characterized by freedom from racial bias. —col′or·blind′ness, *n.*

col′or·code′, *v.t.,* **-cod·ed, -cod·ing.** to distinguish or classify by a system of colored marks, labels, etc. —col′or code′, *n.*

col·ored (kul′ərd), *adj.* **1.** having color. **2.** influenced, biased, or distorted: *colored opinions.* —**Usage.** See BLACK.

col·or·fast (kul′ər fast′, -fäst′), *adj.* maintaining color without fading or running: *colorfast yarn.* —col′or·fast′ness, *n.*

col·or·ful (kul′ər fəl), *adj.* **1.** abounding in color: *colorful fabrics.* **2.** having vivid, striking, or spirited elements: *a colorful narrative; a colorful personality.* —col′or·ful·ly, *adv.* —col′or·ful·ness, *n.*

col′or guard′, *n.* military personnel or others who carry or escort the flag or colors in parades, reviews, etc.

col·or·if·ic (kul′ə rif′ik), *adj.* **1.** producing or imparting color. **2.** pertaining to color.

col·or·im·e·ter (kul′ə rim′i tər), *n.* a device that analyzes color by measuring a given color in terms of a standard color, a scale of colors, or certain primary colors. —col·or·i·met·ric (kul′ər ə me′trik), *adj.* —col′or·i·met′ri·cal·ly, *adv.* —col′or·im′e·try, *n.*

col·or·ing (kul′ər ing), *n.* **1.** the act or method of applying color. **2.** appearance as to color: *healthy coloring.* **3.** a substance used to color something: *food coloring.* **4.** aspect or tone. **5.** specious appearance; show.

col·or·ist (kul′ər ist), *n.* **1.** a person who uses or works with color or coloring materials, esp. with great skill. **2.** a hairdresser who is skilled in coloring or tinting women's hair. —col′or·is′tic, *adj.* —col′or·is′ti·cal·ly, *adv.*

col·or·ize (kul′ə rīz′), *v.t.,* **-ized, -iz·ing.** to cause to appear in color; enhance with color, esp. by computer: *to colorize black-and-white movies for television.* —col′or·i·za′tion, *n.*

col·or·less (kul′ər lis), *adj.* **1.** without color. **2.** pallid; dull in color: *a colorless complexion.* **3.** lacking vividness or excitement; drab; insipid; lackluster. —col′or·less·ness, *n.*

col·or·point (kul′ər point′), *adj.* (of a domestic cat) having a coat that is a light, solid color on the body with a contrasting darker color on the mask, ears, feet, and tail.

col′or transpar′ency, *n.* a positive color image photographically produced on transparent film or glass and viewed by transmitted light, usu. by projection.

Co·los·sae (kə los′ē), *n.* an ancient city in SW Phrygia. —Co·los′sian (-losh′ən), *adj., n.*

co·los·sal (kə los′əl), *adj.* **1.** extraordinarily great in size, extent, or degree; gigantic; huge. **2.** of or resembling a colossus. —co·los′sal·ly, *adv.*

Co·los·sians (kə losh′ənz), *n.* (*used with a sing. v.*) a book of the New Testament written by Paul to the church at Colossae.

co·los·sus (kə los′əs), *n., pl.* **-los·si** (-los′ī), **-los·sus·es. 1.** any statue of gigantic size. **2.** anything colossal, gigantic, or very powerful.

co·los·to·my (kə los′tə mē), *n., pl.* **-mies. 1.** the surgical construction of an artificial opening from the colon to the outside of the body, permitting passage of intestinal contents. **2.** the opening so constructed.

co·los·trum (kə los′trəm), *n.* a yellow fluid rich in protein and immune factors, secreted by the mammary glands during the first few days of lactation.

col·po·scope (kol′pə skōp′), *n.* a magnifying instrument used for examining the vagina and cervix, esp. to detect cancer cells. —col′po·scop′ic (-skop′ik), *adj.* —col·pos′co·py (-pos′kə pē), *n., pl.* **-pies.**

colt (kōlt), *n.* **1.** a young male animal of the horse family. **2.** a male horse of not more than four years of age. **3.** a young or inexperienced person.

Colt (kōlt), *n.* **Samuel,** 1814–62, U.S. inventor of the Colt revolver.

colt·ish (kōl′tish), *adj.* **1.** frolicsome. **2.** of, pertaining to, or resembling a colt. **3.** not trained or disciplined; unruly; wild. —colt′ish·ly, *adv.* —colt′ish·ness, *n.*

colts·foot (kōlts′fŏŏt′), *n., pl.* **-foots.** a composite plant, *Tussilago farfara,* with small daisylike yellow flowers and large leaves resembling the outline of a colt's foot.

col·u·brid (kol′yŏŏ brid, -yə-), *n.* **1.** any usu. nonvenomous snake of the family Colubridae. —*adj.* **2.** belonging or pertaining to the Colubridae.

col·u·brine (kol′ə brīn′, -brin, -yə-), *adj.* **1.** of or resembling a snake; snakelike. **2.** belonging or pertaining to the subfamily Colubrinae, comprising the typical colubrid snakes.

Co·lum·ba (kə lum′bə), *n.* **Saint,** A.D. 521–597, Irish missionary in Scotland.

Co·lum·bi·a (kə lum′bē ə), *n.* **1.** a river in SW Canada and the NW United States, flowing S and W from SE British Columbia through Washington along the boundary between Washington and Oregon and into the Pacific. 1214 mi. (1955 km) long. **2.** the capital of South Carolina, in the central part. 104,101. **3.** a city in central Missouri. 64,330. **4.** a city in central Maryland. 52,518. **5.** the United States of America. **6.** the first space shuttle to orbit and return to earth.

col·um·bine (kol′əm bīn′), *n.* **1.** a plant, *Aquilegia caerula,* of the buttercup family, having showy flowers with white to blue sepals that form long, backward spurs. **2.** any of various other plants of the genus *Aquilegia,* having showy flowers of various colors.

Co·lum·bus (kə lum′bəs), *n.* **1. Christopher** (Sp. *Cristóbal Colón;* It. *Cristoforo Colombo*), 1446?–1506, Italian navigator in Spanish service: traditionally considered the discoverer of America 1492. **2.** the capital of Ohio, in the central part. 635,913. **3.** a city in W Georgia. 186,470.

Colum′bus Day′, *n.* a holiday honoring Columbus's landing in the West Indies on Oct. 12, 1492: observed variously in the U.S. on Oct. 12 or on the second Monday in October.

col·umn (kol′əm), *n.* **1. a.** a rigid, slender upright support composed of relatively few pieces. **b.** a decorative pillar, often of stone, typically having a cylindrical or polygonal shaft with a capital and usu. a base. **2.** any columnlike object, mass, or formation: *a column of smoke.* **3.** a vertical row or list: *Add this column of figures.* **4.** a vertical arrangement on a page of horizontal lines of type, usu. typographically justified: *There are two columns on this page.* **5.** an article constituting a regular feature of a newspaper or magazine, and usu. reporting or commenting on political or social affairs, the arts, etc. **6.** a long, narrow file of troops (disting. from *line*). **7.** a formation of ships in single file. —columnar, *adj.* —col′umned, col·um·nat′ed (-nā′tid), *adj.*

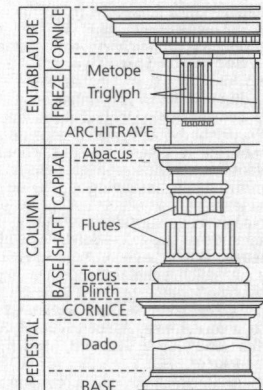

column (def. 1b)
(Roman Doric order)

ENTABLATURE / CORNICE / FRIEZE
Metope
Triglyph
ARCHITRAVE
Abacus
CAPITAL
COLUMN / SHAFT
Flutes
BASE
Torus
Plinth
CORNICE
PEDESTAL
Dado
BASE

col′umn inch′, *n.* type or space one column wide and 1 in. (2.54 cm) deep, used esp. in measuring advertisements.

col·um·nist (kol′əm nist, -ə mist), *n.* a person who writes a newspaper or magazine column.

co·ly (kō′lē), *n., pl.* **-lies.** any of several slender African birds comprising the order Coliiformes, having grayish brown plumage and a long tail.

com-, a prefix occurring in loanwords from Latin, where it and its variants meant "with," "together with," and denoted joint or simultaneous action (*colloquy; confer; convene*), partnership (*colleague*), union (*coitus; collect; combine*), or enclosure (*content*), or marked the telic or complete nature of the action of a verb (*conclude; confection*).

co·ma¹ (kō′mə), *n., pl.* **-mas.** a state of prolonged unconsciousness, including a lack of response to stimuli, from which it is impossible to rouse a person.

co·ma² (kō′mə), *n., pl.* **-mae** (-mē). **1.** the nebulous envelope around the nucleus of a comet. **2.** a monochromatic aberration of a lens or other optical system in which the image from a point source cannot be brought into focus. **3.** a tuft of hairs on a seed or a terminal cluster of leaves or bracts.

co·mak·er (kō mā′kər, kō′mā′kər), *n.* a person who formally agrees to fulfill the obligations of a financial instrument, esp. of a promissory note, in the event that the maker defaults.

Co·man·che (kə man′chē, kō-), *n., pl.* **-ches,** (*esp. collectively*) **-che. 1.** a member of a Plains Indian people ranging in the mid-19th century over a large area of the S Great Plains: later confined to a reservation in Oklahoma. **2.** the Uto-Aztecan language of the Comanche, closely related to Shoshone.

com•a•tose (kom′ə tōs′, kō′mə-), *adj.* **1.** affected with or characterized by coma. **2.** lacking vitality or alertness; torpid.

comb (kōm), *n.* **1.** a toothed strip of some hard material, as plastic, bone, or metal, used to untangle, arrange, or hold the hair. **2.** any comblike instrument, object, or formation. **3.** the fleshy outgrowth on the head of certain roosters. **4.** something resembling or suggesting this, as the crest of a wave. **5.** a honeycomb, or any similar group of cells. **6.** a machine for separating choice cotton or wool fibers from short ones. —*v.t.* **7.** to smooth, arrange, or adorn (the hair) with a comb. **8.** to use (something) in the manner of a comb. **9.** to remove (anything undesirable) with or as if with a comb: *to comb snarls from one's hair; to comb cowards from a group.* **10.** to search everywhere in: *to comb the files for a missing letter.* **11.** to separate (textile fibers) with a comb. **12.** to currycomb. **13.** to sweep across; rake: *High winds combed the seacoast.* —*v.i.* **14.** (of a wave) to roll over or break at the crest.

com•bat (*v.* kəm bat′, kom′bat; *n.* kom′bat), *v.*, **-bat•ed, -bat•ing** or (*esp. Brit.*) **-bat•ted, -bat•ting,** *n.* —*v.t.* **1.** to fight or contend against; oppose vigorously: *to combat crime.* —*v.i.* **2.** to battle; contend: *to combat with disease.* —*n.* **3.** active, armed fighting with enemy forces. **4.** a fight, struggle, or controversy, as between two persons, teams, or ideas. —**com•bat′a•ble,** *adj.*

com•bat•ant (kəm bat′nt, kom′bə tənt), *n.* **1.** a nation, group, or person prepared for or engaged in active fighting with an opposing force. —*adj.* **2.** engaged in combat; fighting. **3.** disposed to combat; combative.

com′bat boot′, *n.* a heavy, usu. laced and close-fitting boot of hard leather extending above the ankle and having a sole of hard rubber.

com′bat fatigue′, *n.* BATTLE FATIGUE.

com•bat•ive (kəm bat′iv), *adj.* ready or inclined to fight; pugnacious. —**com•bat′ive•ly,** *adv.* —**com•bat′ive•ness,** *n.*

com•bi•na•tion (kom′bə nā′shən), *n.* **1.** the act of combining or the state of being combined. **2.** a number of things combined; mixture: *a combination of ideas.* **3.** something formed by combining: *A chord is a combination of notes.* **4.** an alliance of persons, parties, countries, etc.: *a combination in restraint of trade.* **5.** the set or series of numbers or letters used in setting the mechanism of a combination lock. **6.** the parts of the mechanism operated by this. **7.** one-piece underwear uniting two garments, esp. a shirt and pants. **8.** *Math.* **a.** the act of arranging set elements together without regard to their order. **b.** an arrangement thus formed. Compare PERMUTATION (def. 2). —**com′bi•na′tion•al,** *adj.*

combina′tion lock′, *n.* a lock opened by rotating one or more dials through a set of positions in a prescribed order and direction.

combina′tion shot′, *n.* a shot in pool in which at least one object ball pockets another.

combina′tion square′, *n.* an adjustable device for carpenters, used as a try square, miter square, level, etc.

com•bi•na•tive (kom′bə nā′tiv, kəm bī′nə-), *adj.* **1.** tending or serving to combine. **2.** pertaining to or resulting from combination.

com•bi•na•to•ri•al (kəm bī′nə tôr′ē əl, -tōr′-, kom′bə-), *adj.* **1.** of, pertaining to, or involving the combination of elements, as in phonetics or music. **2.** of or pertaining to the enumeration of the number of ways of doing or arranging something in a specific way. **3.** of or pertaining to mathematical combinations.

combinato′rial anal′ysis, *n.* the branch of mathematics that deals with permutations and combinations, esp. used in statistics and probability.

com•bin•a•to•ry (kəm bī′nə tôr′ē, -tōr′ē), *adj.* **1.** combinative. **2.** combinatorial.

com•bine (*v.* kəm bīn′ *for 1, 2, 6,* kom′bīn *for 3, 7; n.* kom′bīn), *v.*, **-bined, -bin•ing,** *n.* —*v.t.* **1.** to bring into or join in a close union or whole; unite: *to combine the ingredients for a cake.* **2.** to possess or exhibit in union: *a plan that combines practicality and originality.* **3.** to harvest (grain) with a combine. —*v.i.* **4.** to unite; coalesce: *The clay and water combined into a thick paste.* **5.** to unite for a common purpose; join forces: *Two factions combined to defeat the proposal.* **6.** to enter into chemical union. **7.** to use a combine in harvesting. —*n.* **8.** a combination, esp. a combination of persons or groups for the furtherance of their own special interests, as a syndicate, cartel, or bloc. **9.** a harvesting machine for cutting and threshing grain in the field. —**com•bin′er,** *n.*

combin′ing form′, *n.* a linguistic form that occurs only in combination with other forms and may conjoin with an independent word (*mini-* + *skirt*) or another combining form (*photo-* + *-graphy*). Compare AFFIX (def. 5).

comb′ jel′ly (kōm), *n.* any marine invertebrate of the phylum Ctenophora, having an oval, transparent body with eight rows of comblike ciliated bands used for swimming. Also called **ctenophore**.

com•bo (kom′bō), *n.*, *pl.* **-bos.** *Informal.* **1.** a small jazz or dance band. **2.** a combination.

com•bus•ti•ble (kəm bus′tə bəl), *adj.* **1.** capable of catching fire and burning; inflammable; flammable. **2.** easily excited. —*n.* **3.** a combustible substance. —**com•bus′ti•bil′i•ty,** *n.*

com•bus•tion (kəm bus′chən), *n.* **1.** the act or process of burning. **2.** **a.** rapid oxidation accompanied by heat and, usu., light. **b.** chemical combination attended by production of heat and light. **c.** slow oxidation not accompanied by high temperature and light. **3.** violent excitement; tumult. —**com•bus′tive,** *adj.*

come (kum), *v.*, **came, come, com•ing,** *n.* —*v.i.* **1.** to approach or move toward someone or something: *Come a little closer.* **2.** to arrive by movement or progression: *The train is coming.* **3.** to approach or arrive in time, in succession, etc.: *Christmas comes once a year.* **4.** to move into view; appear: *The light comes and goes.* **5.** to extend; reach: *The dress comes to her knees.* **6.** to take place; occur; happen: *Her aria comes in the third act.* **7.** to be available, produced, offered, etc.: *Toothpaste comes in a tube.* **8.** to occur to the mind: *An idea came to me.* **9.** to befall: *They promised no harm would come to us.* **10.** to issue; emanate; be derived: *Pearls come from oysters.* **11.** to arrive or appear as a result: *This comes of carelessness.* **12.** to enter or be brought into a specified state or condition: *to come into popular use.* **13.** to do or manage; fare: *How are you coming with your term paper?* **14.** to enter into existence; be born: *The baby came at dawn.* **15.** to have been a resident or to be a native of (usu. fol. by *from*): *to come from Florida.* **16.** to become: *My shoe came untied.* **17.** to seem to become: *His fears made the menacing statues come alive.* **18.** (used imperatively to call attention or to express impatience, reproof, etc.): *Come, that will do!* —*v.t.* **19.** to assume the role or semblance of: *to come the grand inquisitor.* **20. come about, a.** to come to pass; happen. **b.** *Naut.* to tack. **21. come across, a.** Also, **come upon.** to find or encounter, esp. by chance. **b.** to do what one has promised or is expected to do. **c.** to be understandable or convincing: *The humor doesn't come across.* **d.** to make a particular impression: *He comes across as a cold person.* **22. come again,** (used as a request to repeat a statement.) **23. come along, a.** to accompany a person or group on a trip or the like. **b.** to proceed or advance: *The project is coming along on schedule.* **c.** to appear: *An opportunity came along to invest in real estate.* **24. come around** or **round, a.** to recover consciousness; revive. **b.** to change one's opinion, decision, etc., esp. to agree with another's. **c.** to visit. **d.** to cease being angry, hurt, etc. **25. come at, a.** to arrive at; attain. **b.** to rush at; attack. **26. come back, a.** to return, esp. to one's memory. **b.** to return to a former position or state. **27. come between,** to estrange; separate: *Jealousy came between the brothers.* **28. come by,** to obtain; acquire. **29. come down, a.** to lose wealth, rank, etc. **b.** to be handed down by tradition or inheritance. **c.** to be relayed or passed along from a higher authority: *Our orders will come down tomorrow.* **d.** to lead or point fundamentally: *It all comes down to a sense of pride.* **30. come down on** or **upon, a.** to voice one's opposition to. **b.** to reprimand; scold. **31. come down with,** to become afflicted with (an illness). **32. come in, a.** to enter. **b.** to arrive. **c.** to come into use or fashion. **d.** to begin to produce or yield: *The oil well finally came in.* **e.** to finish in a competition, as specified: *Our team came in fifth.* **33. come in for,** to receive; get; be subjected to: *to come in for much praise.* **34. come into, a.** to acquire; get. **b.** to inherit. **35. come off, a.** to happen; occur. **b.** to reach the end; acquit oneself: *to come off well.* **c.** to be effective or successful: *The last chapter just doesn't come off.* **36. come on, a.** Also, **come upon.** to meet or find unexpectedly. **b.** to make progress; develop; flourish. **c.** to appear on stage; make one's entrance. **d.** to begin to be shown, broadcast, etc.: *The game came on at one o'clock.* **e.** (used chiefly in the imperative) to hurry; begin: *Come on, before it rains!* **f.** please (used as an entreaty or in persuasion): *Come on, have dinner with us.* **37. come out, a.** to be published; appear. **b.** to become known; be revealed. **c.** to make a debut in society, the theater, etc. **d.** to end; terminate; emerge: *The lawsuit came out badly for both sides.* **38. come out with,** to reveal by stating; blurt out. **39. come over,** to happen to; affect: *What's come over him?* **40. come round, a.** (of a sailing vessel) to head toward the wind; come to. **b.** to come around. **41. come through, a.** to endure adversity, illness, etc., successfully. **b.** to fulfill needs or meet demands. **42. come to, a.** to recover consciousness. **b.** to amount to; total. **c.** to take the way off a vessel, as by bringing her head into the wind or anchoring. **43. come under,** to be the province or responsibility of: *This matter comes under the State Department.* **44. come up, a.** to be referred to; arise: *Your name came up in conversation.* **b.** to be presented for action or discussion: *The farm bill comes up on Monday.* **45. come up to, a.** to approach; near. **b.** to compare with as to quantity, excellence, etc.; equal. **46. come up with,** to produce; supply.

come•back (kum′bak′), *n.* **1.** a return to the higher status, prosperity, or success of a former time. **2.** a clever or effective retort; rejoinder; riposte. **3.** a basis or cause of complaint.

co•me•di•an (kə mē′dē ən), *n.* **1.** a professional entertainer who makes an audience laugh by telling jokes, doing impressions, etc. **2.** an actor in comedy. **3.** a person who amuses others.

come•down (kum′doun′), *n.* an unexpected or humiliating descent from dignity, importance, or wealth.

com•e•dy (kom′i dē), *n.*, *pl.* **-dies. 1.** a play, movie, etc., of light and humorous character with a cheerful ending. **2.** the branch of drama concerned with this form of composition. **3.** the comic element of literature generally or of life. **4.** any comic or humorous incident or series of incidents. —**co•me•dic** (kə mē′dik, -med′ik), *adj.*

come′-hith′er, *adj.* inviting or enticing, esp. in a sexually provocative manner: *a come-hither look.*

come•ly (kum′lē, kom′-, kōm′-), *adj.*, **-li•er, -li•est. 1.** pleasing in appearance; attractive; good-looking. **2.** proper; seemly; becoming. —**come′li•ness,** *n.*

come′-on′, *n.* an inducement or lure, esp. one intended to attract customers.

co•mes (kō′mēz), *n.*, *pl.* **com•i•tes** (kom′i tēz′). COMPANION[1] (def. 7).

co•mes•ti•ble (kə mes′tə bəl), *adj.* **1.** edible; eatable. —*n.* **2.** Usu., **comestibles.** articles of food; edibles.

com•et (kom′it), *n.* a celestial body that consists of a central solid mass and a tail of dust and gas and that orbits the sun along a highly eccentric course. —**com′et•ar′y** (-i ter′ē), *adj.*

come•up•pance (kum′up′əns), *n.* deserved reprimand or punishment.

com•fort (kum′fərt), *v.t.* **1.** to soothe, console, or reassure; bring solace or cheer to: *to comfort someone after a loss.* **2.** to make physically comfortable. —*n.* **3.** relief in affliction; consolation; solace. **4.** a feeling of relief or consolation. **5.** a person or thing that gives consolation or relief. **6.** a state of ease and satisfaction of bodily wants, with freedom from pain and anxiety. **7.** something that promotes such a state. **8.** *Chiefly Midland and Southern U.S.* a comforter or quilt. —**com′fort•ing•ly,** *adv.* —**com′fort•less,** *adj.*

com•fort•a•ble (kumf′tə bəl, kum′fər tə bəl), *adj.* **1.** (of clothing, furniture, etc.) producing or affording physical comfort, support, or ease. **2.** being in a state of physical or mental comfort; contented and undisturbed; at ease. **3.** (of a person, situation, etc.) producing mental comfort or ease; easy to associate or deal with. **4.** adequate or sufficient: *a comfortable salary.* —**com′fort•a•bly,** *adv.*

com•fort•er (kum′fər tər), *n.* **1.** one that comforts. **2.** a thick quilted bedcover. **3.** a long woolen scarf, usu. knitted. **4.** **the Comforter,** the Holy Spirit. John 14:16, 26; 16:7. [< Late Latin *confortare* to strengthen]

com′fort sta′tion, *n.* REST ROOM.

com•frey (kum′frē), *n., pl.* **-freys.** any of various coarse Eurasian plants of the genus *Symphytum,* borage family, having hairy leaves and drooping flower clusters.

com•fy (kum′fē), *adj.,* **-fi•er, -fi•est.** *Informal.* comfortable. —**com′fi•ness,** *n.*

com•ic (kom′ik), *adj.* **1.** pertaining to or characterized by comedy. **2.** performing in or writing comedy. **3.** provoking laughter; humorous; funny; laughable. —*n.* **4.** a comedian. **5. comics,** a section of a newspaper featuring comic strips. **6.** a comic book.

com•i•cal (kom′i kəl), *adj.* producing laughter; amusing; funny. —**com′i•cal•ly,** *adv.*

com′ic book′, *n.* a magazine of comic strips.

com′ic op′era, *n.* opera with spoken dialogue, comical scenes or characters, and a happy ending.

com′ic-op′era, *adj.* farcically inept or inane.

com′ic relief′, *n.* **1.** an amusing scene or incident in a serious or tragic setting, as in a play, providing temporary relief from tension or dramatic action. **2.** relief from tension caused by the introduction of a comic element.

com′ic strip′, *n.* a sequence of drawings relating a comic incident, an adventure, etc., often serialized in daily newspapers.

com•ing (kum′ing), *n.* **1.** approach; arrival; advent. —*adj.* **2.** following or impending; next; approaching: *the coming year.* **3.** promising future fame or success: *a coming actor.*

com′ing-out′, *n.* **1.** a debut into society, esp. a formal debut by a debutante. **2.** an acknowledgment of one's homosexuality, either to oneself or publicly.

com•i•ty (kom′i tē), *n., pl.* **-ties.** **1.** mutual courtesy; civility. **2.** Also called **com′ity of na′tions.** courtesy between nations, as in respect shown by one country for the laws and institutions of another.

com•ma (kom′ə), *n., pl.* **-mas.** **1.** the sign (,), a mark of punctuation used to indicate a division in a sentence, as in setting off a word, phrase, or clause, to separate items in a list, to mark off thousands in numerals, to separate types or levels of information in bibliographic and other data, and, in Europe, as a decimal point. **2.** a brown and black nymphalid butterfly, *Polygonia comma,* with a silver comma mark on the underwing.

com′ma fault′, *n.* the misuse of a comma, rather than a semicolon, colon, or period, to separate related main clauses not joined by a conjunction.

com•mand (kə mand′, -mänd′), *v.t.* **1.** to direct with specific authority or prerogative; order: *to command troops to march.* **2.** to require authoritatively; demand: *to command silence.* **3.** to deserve and receive (respect, sympathy, attention, etc.). **4.** to dominate by reason of location; overlook: *The hill commands the sea.* **5.** to have authority over and responsibility for (a military installation). **6.** to have control over; be master of: *The Pharaoh commanded 10,000 slaves.* —*v.i.* **7.** to issue an order or orders. **8.** to be in charge; have authority. **9.** to occupy a dominating position; look down upon or over a body of water, region, etc. —*n.* **10.** the act of commanding or ordering. **11.** an order given by one in authority. **12.** an order in prescribed words, as one given in a loud voice to troops at close-order drill: *The command was "Right shoulder arms!"* **13. a.** (*cap.*) a principal component of the U.S. Air Force: *Strategic Air Command.* **b.** a body of troops or a station, ship, etc., under a commander. **14.** the possession or exercise of controlling authority: *a lieutenant in command of a platoon.* **15.** expertise; mastery: *to have a command of four languages.* **16.** power of dominating a region by reason of location; extent of view or outlook: *the command of the valley from the hill.* **17.** a signal, as a keystroke, instructing a computer to perform a specific task. —*adj.* **18.** of, pertaining to, or resulting from a command. **19.** of or pertaining to a commander. **20.** ordered or requested: *a command performance.* —**com•mand′ing,** *adj.*

com•man•dant (kom′ən dant′, -dänt′, kom′ən dant′, -dänt′), *n.* the commanding officer of a place, group, etc., esp. the head of a military unit or school.

command′ econ′omy, *n.* an economic system that relies primarily on the planning and decisions of a central authority, as in China and Cuba.

com•man•deer (kom′ən dēr′), *v.t.* **1.** to order or force into active military service. **2.** to seize (private property) for military or other public use. **3.** to seize arbitrarily.

com•mand•er (kə man′dər, -män′-), *n.* **1.** a person who commands. **2.** a person who exercises authority; chief officer; leader. **3.** the commissioned officer in command of a military unit. **4.** an officer in the U.S. Navy or Coast Guard ranking below a captain and above a lieutenant commander. **5.** the chief officer of a medieval order of knights. **6.** a member of high rank in a modern fraternal order.

command′er in chief′, *n., pl.* **commanders in chief.** **1.** Also, **Command′er in Chief′.** the supreme commander of the armed forces of a nation or, sometimes, of several allied nations. **2.** an officer in command of a particular portion of an armed force.

command′ing of′ficer, *n.* an officer having command of a military unit, installation, etc.

com•mand•ment (kə mand′mənt, -mänd′-), *n.* **1.** a command or mandate. **2.** (*sometimes cap.*) any of the Ten Commandments. **3.** the act or power of commanding.

com•man•do (kə man′dō, -män′-), *n., pl.* **-dos, -does.** **1. a.** (in World War II) a combat unit specially trained for surprise raids against Axis forces. **b.** any military unit organized for similar operations. **c.** a member of such a unit. **2.** a member of an assault team trained to operate against terrorist attacks.

com•mem•o•rate (kə mem′ə rāt′), *v.t.,* **-rat•ed, -rat•ing.** **1.** to serve as a memorial or reminder of: *The monument commemorates a naval victory.* **2.** to honor the memory of by some observance: *to commemorate Bastille Day.* —**commemorative,** *adj.*

com•mem•o•ra•tive (kə mem′ə rā′tiv, -ər ə tiv), *adj.* **1.** Also, **com•mem•o•ra•to•ry** (-ər ə tôr′ē, -tōr′ē). serving to commemorate; specially arranged, produced, or devised for commemorating: *a commemorative dinner; a commemorative stamp.* —*n.* **2.** anything that commemorates. —**com•mem′o•ra′tive•ly,** *adv.*

com•mence (kə mens′), *v.i., v.t.,* **-menced, -menc•ing.** to begin; start. —**com•mence′a•ble,** *adj.* —**com•menc′er,** *n.*

com•mence•ment (kə mens′mənt), *n.* **1.** an act of commencing; beginning: *the commencement of hostilities.* **2.** the ceremony of conferring degrees or granting diplomas at the end of the academic year. **3.** the day on which this ceremony takes place.

com•mend (kə mend′), *v.t.* **1.** to present or mention as worthy of confidence, attention, kindness, etc.; recommend: *to commend one friend to another.* **2.** to entrust; deliver with confidence; consign. **3.** to cite with approval or special praise: *to commend a soldier for bravery.* —**com•mend′a•ble,** *adj.* —**com•mend′a•ble•ness,** *n.* —**com•mend′a•bly,** *adv.*

com•men•da•tion (kom′ən dā′shən), *n.* **1.** the act of commending; recommendation; praise. **2.** something that commends, as a formal recommendation or an official citation.

com•men•su•ra•ble (kə men′sər ə bəl, -shər ə-), *adj.* **1.** having the same measure or divisor: *The numbers 6 and 9 are commensurable since they are divisible by 3.* **2.** proportionate; commensurate. —**com•men′su•ra•bil′i•ty,** *n.* —**com•men′su•ra•bly,** *adv.*

com•men•su•rate (kə men′sər it, -shər-), *adj.* **1.** having the same measure; of equal extent or duration. **2.** corresponding in amount, magnitude, or degree; proportionate: *a sentence commensurate with the crime.* **3.** COMMENSURABLE (def. 2). —**com•men′su•rate•ly,** *adv.* —**com•men′su•rate•ness,** *n.* —**com•men′su•ra′tion** (-rā′shən), *n.*

com•ment (kom′ent), *n.* **1.** a remark, observation, or criticism: *a comment about the weather.* **2.** gossip; talk: *His absence gave rise to comment.* **3.** a criticism or interpretation, often by implication or suggestion: *The play is a comment on modern society.* **4.** a critical or explanatory annotation to a text or to a passage in a text. **5.** the part of a sentence that communicates new information about the topic. Compare TOPIC (def. 3). —*v.i.* **6.** to make remarks, observations, or criticisms. **7.** to write explanatory or critical notes upon a text; elucidate. —*v.t.* **8.** to make comments or remarks on. **9.** to furnish with comments; annotate (a text).

com•men•tar•y (kom′ən ter′ē), *n., pl.* **-tar•ies.** **1.** a series of comments, explanations, or annotations. **2.** an explanatory essay or treatise. **3.** anything serving to illustrate a point, prompt a realization, or exemplify: *The dropout rate is a sad commentary on our school system.* **4.** Usu., **commentaries.** a record of facts or events. —**com′men•tar′i•al** (-tär′ē əl), *adj.* —**commentate,** *v.t.,v.i.*

com•men•ta•tor (kom′ən tā′tər), *n.* **1.** a person who discusses news, sports events, or other topics on television or radio. **2.** a person who makes commentaries.

com•merce (kom′ərs), *n.* **1.** an interchange of goods or commodities between different countries or between areas of the same country; trade. **2.** social relations, esp. the exchange of views, attitudes, etc.

com•mer•cial (kə mûr′shəl), *adj.* **1.** of, pertaining to, or characteristic of commerce. **2.** produced, marketed, etc., with emphasis on salability, profit, or the like: *a commercial book.* **3.** able or likely to yield a profit. **4.** suitable for a wide popular market: *commercial uses for satellites.* **5.** engaged in, used for, or suitable to commerce or business, esp. of a public or nonprivate nature: *commercial vehicles.* **6.** not entirely or chemically pure: *commercial soda.* **7.** of or designating a grade of beef between standard and utility. **8.** paid for by advertisers: *commercial television.* —*n.* **9.** a paid advertisement or promotional announcement on radio or television. —**com•mer′ci•al/i•ty,** *n.* —**com•mer′cial•ly,** *adv.*

commer′cial art′, *n.* graphic art created for commercial uses, esp. for advertising, magazine illustrations, and the like. —**commer′cial art′ist,** *n.*

commer′cial bank′, *n.* a bank specializing in checking accounts and short-term loans.

com•mer•cial•ism (kə mûr′shə liz′əm), *n.* **1.** the principles, practices, and spirit of commerce. **2.** inappropriate or excessive emphasis on profit.

com•mer•cial•ize (kə mûr′shə līz′), *v.t.,* **-ized, -iz•ing. 1.** to make commercial in character, methods, etc.; make profitable or introduce profit into. **2.** to emphasize the profitable aspects of, esp. by sacrificing quality or debasing inherent nature: *to commercialize one's talent; to commercialize a religious holiday.* —**com•mer′cial•i•za′tion,** *n.* —**com•mer′cial•iz′er,** *n.*

commer′cial pa′per, *n.* **1.** negotiable paper, as drafts or bills of exchange. **2.** corporate promissory notes, usu. short-term and unsecured, sold at a discount in the open market.

com•mi•na•tion (kom′ə nā′shən), *n.* **1.** a threat of punishment or vengeance. **2.** a denunciation. —**com′mi•nate′,** *v.t., v.i.,* **-nat•ed, -nat•ing.** —**com′mi•na′tor,** *n.* —**com•min•a•to•ry** (kə min′ə tôr′ē, -tōr′ē, kom′ə nə-), *adj.*

com•min•gle or **co•min•gle** (kə ming′gəl), *v.t., v.i.,* **-gled, -gling.** to mix or mingle together; combine. —**com•min′gler,** *n.*

com•mi•nute (kom′ə nōōt′, -nyōōt′), *v.,* **-nut•ed, -nut•ing,** *adj.* —*v.t.* **1.** to pulverize, as in chemical processing; triturate. —*adj.* **2.** powdered or crushed; pulverized. —**com′mi•nu′tion,** *n.*

com•mis•er•ate (kə miz′ə rāt′), *v.,* **-at•ed, -at•ing.** —*v.t.* **1.** to feel or express sorrow or sympathy for; empathize with; pity. —*v.i.* **2.** to sympathize (usu. fol. by *with*): *to commiserate with someone over a loss.* —**com•mis′er•a′tion,** *n.*

com•mis•sar (kom′ə sär′, kom′ə sär′), *n.* **1.** the head of a major governmental division in the U.S.S.R. **2.** an official in any communist government whose duties include political indoctrination, detection of political deviation, etc.

com•mis•sar•i•at (kom′ə sâr′ē ət), *n.* **1.** a major governmental division in the U.S.S.R. **2.** the organized method by which food, equipment, etc., is delivered to armies. **3.** the department of an army charged with supplying provisions.

com•mis•sar•y (kom′ə ser′ē), *n., pl.* **-sar•ies. 1.** a store that sells food and supplies in a military post, mining camp, lumber camp, or the like. **2.** a dining room or cafeteria, esp. in a motion-picture studio. **3.** a person to whom some responsibility or role is delegated by a superior power; deputy. —**com′mis•sar′i•al** (-sâr′ē əl), *adj.*

com•mis•sion (kə mish′ən), *n.* **1.** the act of committing or giving in charge. **2.** an authoritative order, charge, or direction. **3.** authority granted for a particular action or function. **4.** a document granting such authority. **5.** a document conferring authority issued by the president of the U.S. to officers in the military services and by state governments to justices of the peace, etc. **6.** the position or rank of an officer in any of the armed forces. **7.** a group of persons authoritatively charged with particular functions: *a parks commission.* **8.** a task or matter committed to one's charge; official assignment: *The architect received a commission to design an office building.* **9.** the act of committing or perpetrating a crime, error, etc. **10.** authority to act as agent for another or others in commercial transactions. **11.** a sum allowed to agents, sales representatives, etc., for their services. —*v.t.* **12.** to give a commission to. **13.** to authorize; send on a mission. **14.** to order (a warship, military command, etc.) into readiness for active duty. **15.** to give a commission or order for: *to commission a painting for the lobby.* —*Idiom.* **16. in** (or **out of**) **commission, a.** in (or not in) service. **b.** in (or not in) operating order. **c.** Also, **into commission.** (of a ship) in condition for active naval service.

commis′sioned of′ficer, *n.* a military or naval officer holding rank by commission.

com•mis•sion•er (kə mish′ə nər), *n.* **1.** a person commissioned to act officially; member of a commission. **2.** a government official or representative in charge of a department or district: *the police commissioner.* **3.** an official chosen by an athletic association to exercise broad administrative or judicial authority: *the baseball commissioner.*

com•mit (kə mit′), *v.,* **-mit•ted, -mit•ting.** —*v.t.* **1.** to give in trust or charge; consign. **2.** to consign for preservation: *to commit ideas to writing.* **3.** to declare as having a certain opinion or position: *The senator would not commit herself on the upcoming vote.* **4.** to bind or obligate, as by pledge or assurance: *to commit oneself to a healthy lifestyle.* **5.** to entrust, esp. for safekeeping; commend: *to commit one's soul to God.* **6.** to assign or allot for a certain purpose: *to commit troops to battle.* **7.** to do; perform; perpetrate: *to commit murder.* **8.** to consign, as to a prison or mental institution, by or as if by legal authority. **9.** to deliver for treatment, disposal, etc.; relegate: *to commit a manuscript to the flames.* **10.** to refer (a legislative bill or proposal) to a committee for consideration. —*v.i.* **11.** to pledge or engage oneself. —**com•mit′ta•ble,** *adj.* —**com•mit′ter,** *n.*

com•mit•ment (kə mit′mənt), *n.* **1.** the act of committing. **2.** the state

of being committed. **3.** the act of committing, pledging, or engaging oneself. **4.** a pledge or promise; obligation: *to make a commitment to pay bills on time.* **5.** engagement; involvement: *a sincere commitment to religion.* **6.** perpetration or commission, as of a crime. **7.** consignment to or confinement in a prison, mental hospital, or other institution. **8.** a court order to confine someone in prison or a mental institution. **9.** the act of referring a bill or proposal to a committee.

com•mit•tee (kə mit′ē), *n.* a group of persons elected or appointed to perform some service or function, as to investigate or act upon a particular matter. —**Usage.** See COLLECTIVE NOUN.

Commit′tee of Correspond′ence, *n.* **1.** an intercolonial committee organized 1772 by Samuel Adams in Massachusetts to keep colonists informed of British anticolonial actions and to plan colonial resistance or countermeasures. **2.** (*sometimes l.c.*) any of various similar organizations formed for the same purpose during the late colonial period. Also called **Correspondence Committee.**

commit′tee of the whole′, *n.* a committee composed of all the members of a legislative body, meeting under relaxed rules in order to expedite business.

com•mix (kə miks′), *v.t., v.i.* to mix together; blend. —**com•mix′ture,** *n.*

com•mode (kə mōd′), *n.* **1.** a low cabinet or similar piece of furniture, often highly ornamented, containing drawers or shelves. **2.** a stand or cupboard containing a chamber pot or washbasin. **3.** TOILET (def. 1). **4.** a portable toilet, esp. one on a chairlike frame, as for an invalid.

com•mo•di•ous (kə mō′dē əs), *adj.* spacious and convenient; ample; roomy: *a commodious apartment.* —**com•mo′di•ous•ly,** *adv.* —**com•mo′di•ous•ness,** *n.*

com•mod•i•ty (kə mod′i tē), *n., pl.* **-ties. 1.** an article of trade or commerce, esp. a product as distinguished from a service. **2.** something of use, advantage, or value. **3.** any unprocessed or partially processed good, as a grain, fruit or vegetable, or a precious metal.

commod′ity exchange′, *n.* an exchange for the buying and selling of futures contracts on commodities.

com•mo•dore (kom′ə dôr′, -dōr′), *n.* **1.** an officer in the British navy in temporary command of a squadron. **2.** the senior captain when two or more ships of war are cruising in company. **3.** (in the U.S. Navy and Merchant Marine) the officer in command of a convoy. **4.** the senior captain of a line of merchant vessels. **5.** the head of a yacht or boat club.

com•mon (kom′ən), *adj.* **1.** belonging equally to, or shared alike by, two or more or all in question: *common objectives.* **2.** pertaining or belonging equally to an entire community, nation, or culture: *a common language.* **3.** joint; united: *a common defense.* **4.** widespread; general; universal: *common knowledge.* **5.** of frequent occurrence; usual; familiar: *a common mistake.* **6.** of mediocre or inferior quality; mean: *a rough, common fabric.* **7.** coarse; vulgar: *common manners.* **8.** lacking rank, station, distinction, etc.; ordinary: *a common soldier.* **9.** in keeping with accepted standards; fundamental: *common decency.* **10.** (of a syllable) able to be considered as either long or short. **11. a.** (of a grammatical case) fulfilling different functions that in some languages would require different inflected forms: *English nouns used as subject or object are in the common case.* **b.** of or pertaining to a word or gender that may refer to either a male or female: *French* élève *"pupil" has common gender.* **c.** constituting a gender comprising nouns that were formerly masculine or feminine: *Dutch nouns are either common or neuter in gender.* **12.** bearing a similar mathematical relation to two or more entities. **13.** of or pertaining to common stock. —*n.* **14.** Often, **commons.** a tract of land owned or used jointly by the residents of a community, as a central square or park in a city or town. **15.** the right, in common with other persons, to pasture animals on another's land or to fish in another's waters. **16. commons, a.** the common people; commonalty. **b.** the body of people not of noble birth, as represented by the House of Commons. **17. commons, a.** (*used with a sing. v.*) a large dining room, esp. at a university or college. **b.** (*usu. with a pl. v.*) food or provisions for any group. **18.** (*sometimes cap.*) **a.** an ecclesiastical office or form of service used on a festival of a particular kind. **b.** the ordinary of the Mass, esp. those parts sung by the choir. —*Idiom.* **19. in common,** in joint possession or use; shared equally. —**com′mon•ly,** *adv.* —**com′mon•ness,** *n.*

com•mon•al•i•ty (kom′ə nal′i tē), *n., pl.* **-ties. 1.** a sharing of features or characteristics in common; possession or manifestation of common attributes. **2.** a feature or characteristic held in common. **3.** COMMONALTY (def. 1).

com•mon•al•ty (kom′ə nl tē), *n., pl.* **-ties. 1.** the ordinary people, as distinguished from those with authority, rank, station, or the like; the common people. **2.** an incorporated body or its members.

com′mon car′rier, *n.* (in federal regulatory and other legal usage) a carrier offering its services at published rates for interstate transportation. **2.** a public service company, as a telephone company, engaged in transmitting messages for the public. —**com′mon car′riage,** *n.*

com′mon cold′, *n.* COLD (def. 15).

com′mon denom′inator, *n.* **1.** a number that is a multiple of all the denominators of a set of fractions. **2.** a trait, characteristic, belief, or the like common to or shared by all members of a group.

com•mon•er (kom′ə nər), *n.* a member of the commonalty; a person without a title of nobility.

com′mon frac′tion, *n.* a fraction represented as a numerator above and a denominator below a horizontal or diagonal line.

com′mon ground′, *n.* a foundation of common interest or comprehension, as in a social relationship or a discussion.

com′mon law′, *n.* the system of law originating in England, based on custom or court decision rather than civil or ecclesiastical law.

com′mon-law′ mar′riage, *n.* a marriage without a civil or ecclesiastical ceremony, usu. based on a couple's living together continuously as husband and wife.

Com′mon Mar′ket, *n.* **1.** EUROPEAN ECONOMIC COMMUNITY. **2.** (*often l.c.*) any economic association of nations.

com′mon noun′, *n.* a noun that may be preceded by an article or other limiting modifier and that denotes any or all of a class of entities and not an individual, as *man, city, horse, music.* Also called **com′mon name′.** Compare PROPER NOUN.

com·mon·place (kom′ən plās′), *adj.* **1.** ordinary; undistinguished or uninteresting. **2.** dull or platitudinous: *a commonplace remark.* —*n.* **3.** a well-known, customary, or obvious remark; a trite or uninteresting saying; platitude. **4.** anything common, ordinary, or uninteresting. —**com′mon·place′ness,** *n.*

com′mon room′, *n.* a room or lounge for informal use by all, esp. in a college.

com′mon sense′, *n.* sound practical judgment that is independent of specialized knowledge or training; normal native intelligence. —**com′mon-sense′,** *adj.* —**com′mon·sen′si·cal,** *adj.*

Com′mon Sense′, a pamphlet (1776) by Thomas Paine in which he asserts that the American colonies should be given independence.

com′mon stock′, *n.* the ordinary stock of a corporation, yielding to preferred stock in dividends.

com·mon·wealth (kom′ən welth′), *n.* **1.** the people of a nation or state; the body politic. **2.** a state in which the supreme power is held by the people; a republican or democratic state. **3.** (*cap.*) a group of sovereign states and their dependencies associated by their own choice and linked with common objectives and interests. **4.** (*cap.*) a federation of states: *the Commonwealth of Australia.* **5.** (*cap.*) a self-governing territory associated with the U.S.: official designation of Puerto Rico. **6.** (*cap.*) the official designation of Kentucky, Massachusetts, Pennsylvania, and Virginia.

Com′monwealth of Na′tions, *n.* a voluntary association of independent nations and their dependencies linked by historical ties as parts of the former British Empire and cooperating on matters of mutual concern. Formerly, **British Commonwealth of Nations.**

com′mon year′, *n.* an ordinary year of 365 days; a year having no intercalary period. Compare LEAP YEAR.

com·mo·tion (kə mō′shən), *n.* **1.** violent or tumultuous action or activity; agitation; noisy disturbance. **2.** political or social disturbance or upheaval. —**com·mo′tion·al,** *adj.* —**com·mo′tive,** *adj.*

com·move (kə mōōv′), *v.t.,* **-moved, -mov·ing.** to move violently or intensely; agitate; excite.

com·mu·nal (kə myōōn′l, kom′yə nl), *adj.* **1.** used or shared in common by everyone in a group: *a communal stove.* **2.** of, by, or belonging to the people of a community; public; common: *communal land.* **3.** pertaining to a commune or a community: *communal life.* **4.** engaged in by or involving two or more communities: *communal conflict.* —**com·mu′nal·ly,** *adv.*

com·mu·nal·ism (kə myōōn′l iz′əm, kom′yə nl-), *n.* **1.** a theory or system of government in which each commune is virtually an independent state, and the nation merely a federation of such states. **2.** the principles or practices of communal ownership. **3.** strong allegiance to one's own ethnic group rather than to society as a whole. —**com·mu′nal·ist,** *n.* —**com·mu′nal·is′tic,** *adj.*

com·mune¹ (*v.* kə myōōn′; *n.* kom′yōōn), *v.,* **-muned, -mun·ing,** *n.* —*v.i.* **1.** to converse or talk together, usu. intensely and intimately; interchange thoughts or feelings. **2.** to be in intimate communication or rapport: *to commune with nature.* —*n.* **3.** interchange of ideas or sentiments. —**com·mun′er,** *n.*

com·mune² (kə myōōn′), *v.i.,* **-muned, -mun·ing.** to partake of the Eucharist.

com·mune³ (kom′yōōn), *n.* **1.** a small group of persons living together, sharing possessions, work, income, etc. **2.** a close-knit community of people who share common interests. **3.** the smallest administrative division in France, Italy, Switzerland, etc., governed by a mayor and council. **4.** a community organized for the promotion of local interests. **5.** the government or citizens of a commune. **6. the Commune.** Also called **Com′mune of Par′is, Paris Commune. a.** a revolutionary committee that took control of the government of Paris from 1789 to 1794. **b.** a socialist government that controlled Paris from March 18 to May 27, 1871.

com·mu·ni·cant (kə myōō′ni kənt), *n.* **1.** a member of a church entitled to partake of the Eucharist. **2.** a person who communicates or informs. —*adj.* **3.** communicating; imparting.

com·mu·ni·cate (kə myōō′ni kāt′), *v.,* **-cat·ed, -cat·ing.** —*v.t.* **1.** to impart knowledge of; make known; divulge. **2.** to give to another; transmit: *to communicate a disease.* **3.** to administer the Eucharist to. —*v.i.* **4.** to give or interchange thoughts, feelings, information, or the like by writing, speaking, etc. **5.** to express thoughts, feelings, or information easily or effectively. **6.** to be joined or connected: *The rooms communicated by a hallway.* **7.** to partake of the Eucharist. —**communicable,** *adj.* —**com·mu′ni·ca′tor,** *n.*

com·mu·ni·ca·tion (kə myōō′ni kā′shən), *n.* **1.** the act or process of communicating; fact of being communicated. **2.** the imparting or interchange of thoughts, opinions, or information by speech, writing, or signs. **3.** something imparted, interchanged, or transmitted, esp. a document or message giving news, information, etc. **4.** passage, or an opportunity or means of passage, between places. **5. communications, a.** means of sending messages, orders, etc., including telephone, telegraph, radio, and television. **b.** routes and transportation for moving troops and supplies from a base to an area of operations. **c.** the professions of journalism, broadcasting, etc. **d.** the techniques used to communicate information. **e.** the study of these skills, as writing or broadcasting. **6. a.** activity by one organism that changes or has the potential to change the behavior of other organisms. **b.** transfer of information from one cell or molecule to another, as by chemical or electrical signals. —**com·mu′ni·ca′tion·al,** *adj.*

communica′tions sat′ellite, *n.* a satellite designed to facilitate radio, telephone, and television communication by retransmitting the signals it receives while orbiting the earth.

com·mu·ni·ca·tive (kə myōō′ni kā′tiv, -kə tiv) also **com·mu·ni·ca·to·ry** (-kə tôr′ē, -tōr′ē), *adj.* **1.** inclined to communicate or impart; talkative. **2.** of or pertaining to communication. —**com·mu′ni·ca′tive·ly,** *adv.* —**com·mu′ni·ca′tive·ness,** *n.*

com·mun·ion (kə myōōn′yən), *n.* **1.** (*often cap.*) Also called **Holy Communion. a.** the act of receiving the Eucharistic elements. **b.** the elements of the Eucharist. **c.** the celebration of the Eucharist. **d.** the antiphon sung at a Eucharistic service. **2.** a group of persons having a common religious faith; denomination: *Anglican communion.* **3.** intimate communication: *communion with nature.* **4.** the act of sharing, or holding in common; participation.

commun′ion of saints′, *n.* the spiritual fellowship existing among all faithful Christians, both living and dead: a phrase from the Nicene Creed.

commun′ion rail′, *n.* in a Christian church, the altar rail where communion is received by the congregation.

Commun′ion Sun′day, *n.* any Sunday on which communion is administered.

commun′ion ta′ble, *n.* the table used in the celebration of communion, or the Lord's Supper; the Lord's table.

com·mu·ni·qué (kə myōō′ni kā′, -myōō′ni kā′), *n.* an official bulletin or communication, usu. to the press or public.

com·mu·nism (kom′yə niz′əm), *n.* **1.** a theory or system of social organization based on the holding of all property in common, actual ownership being ascribed to the community as a whole or to the state. **2.** (*often cap.*) a political doctrine or movement based on Marxism and developed by Lenin and others, seeking a violent overthrow of capitalism and the creation of a classless society. **3.** (*often cap.*) a system of social organization in which all economic and social activity is controlled by a totalitarian state dominated by a single and self-perpetuating political party. **4.** (*often cap.*) the principles or practices of a Communist Party. **5.** COMMUNALISM. [< French < Latin *commūnis* common + -ISM]

com·mu·nist (kom′yə nist), *n.* **1.** (*cap.*) a member of a Communist Party. **2.** an advocate of communism. **3.** a person who is regarded as supporting politically leftist or subversive causes. —*adj.* **4.** (*cap.*) of or pertaining to a Communist Party or to Communism. **5.** pertaining to communists or communism. —**com′mu·nis′tic,** *adj.* —**com′mu·nis′ti·cal·ly,** *adv.*

Com′munist Manifes′to, a pamphlet (1848) by Karl Marx and Friedrich Engels: first statement of the principles of modern communism.

Com′munist Par′ty, *n.* a political party advocating the principles of communism, esp. as developed by Marx and Lenin.

com·mu·ni·ty (kə myōō′ni tē), *n., pl.* **-ties. 1.** a group of people who reside in a specific locality, share government, and often have a common cultural and historical heritage. **2.** a locality inhabited by such a group. **3.** a social, religious, occupational, or other group sharing common characteristics or interests: *the business community.* **4.** the public; society. **5.** a group of associated nations sharing common interests or a common heritage: *the Western European community.* **6.** an assemblage of interacting plant and animal populations occupying a given area. **7.** joint possession, enjoyment, liability, etc.: *community of property.* **8.** similar character; agreement: *community of interests.*

commu′nity cen′ter, *n.* a building in which members of a community may gather for social, educational, or cultural activities.

commu′nity col′lege, *n.* a nonresidential junior college supported in part by local government funds.

commu′nity prop′erty, *n.* property acquired by a husband and wife, considered in some states to be jointly owned.

commu′nity serv′ice, *n.* a punitive sentence requiring a convicted person to perform unpaid work for the community in lieu of imprisonment.

com·mu·ta·tion (kom′yə tā′shən), *n.* **1.** the act of substituting one thing for another; substitution; exchange. **2.** the changing of a prison sentence or other penalty to another less severe. **3.** the act of commuting, as to and from a place of work. **4.** the substitution of one kind of payment for another. **5.** the act or process of commutating.

commuta′tion tick′et, *n.* a ticket sold at a reduced rate, as by a railroad company, entitling the holder to travel a given route a fixed number of times or during a specified period.

com•mu•ta•tive (kə myōō′tə tiv, kom′yə tā′tiv), *adj.* **1.** of or pertaining to commutation, exchange, substitution, or interchange. **2. a.** (of a binary operation) having the property that one term operating on a second is equal to the second operating on the first, as $a \times b = b \times a$. **b.** having reference to this property: *the commutative law for multiplication.* —**com•mu′ta•tive•ly,** *adv.* —**com•mu′ta•tiv′i•ty,** *n.*

com•mu•ta•tor (kom′yə tā′tər), *n.* **1. a.** a device for reversing the direction of a current. **b.** (in a DC motor or generator) a ring or disk assembly that works to change the frequency or direction of current in the armature windings. **2.** *Math.* the element equal to the product of two given elements in a group multiplied on the right by the product of the inverses of the elements.

com•mute (kə myōōt′), *v.*, **-mut•ed, -mut•ing,** *n.* —*v.t.* **1.** to change (a prison sentence or other penalty) to a less severe form. **2.** to exchange for another or for something else; interchange. **3.** to change: *to commute base metal into gold.* **4.** to change (one kind of payment) into or for another, as by substitution. —*v.i.* **5.** to travel regularly over some distance, as from a suburb into a city and back. **6.** to make substitution; compensate. **7.** to serve as a substitute. **8.** to give the same mathematical result whether operating on the left or on the right. —*n.* **9.** a trip made by commuting. **10.** an act or instance of commuting. —**com•mut′a•ble,** *adj.* —**com•mut′er,** *n.*

commut′er tax′, *n.* an income tax imposed by a locality on those who work within its boundaries but reside elsewhere.

Com•o•ros (kom′ə rōz′), *n.* **Federal Islamic Republic of the,** a republic of three Comoro Islands: a former French territory; independence in 1975. 589,797; 719 sq. mi. (1862 sq. km). *Cap.:* Moroni.

comp¹ (komp), *Informal. n.* **1.** something, as a ticket or book, provided free of charge. —*adj.* **2.** complimentary; free of charge. —*v.t.* **3.** to provide with a comp. **4.** to provide free of charge.

comp² (komp), *n.* compensation: *unemployment comp.*

com•pact¹ (*adj.* kəm pakt′, kom-, kom′pakt; *v.* kəm pakt′; *n.* kom′pakt), *adj.* **1.** joined or packed together; dense; solid: *compact soil.* **2.** arranged within a relatively small space: *a compact kitchen.* **3.** designed to be small in size and economical in operation. **4.** solidly or firmly built: *a compact physique.* **5.** expressed concisely; pithy; terse: *a compact review of the news.* **6.** composed or made (usu. fol. by *of*): *a book compact of form and content.* —*v.t.* **7.** to join or pack closely together; consolidate; condense. **8.** to form or make by close union or conjunction; make up or compose. **9.** to crush or compress into a tight, solid form: *to compact rubbish.* —*n.* **10.** a small case containing a mirror, face powder, and sometimes rouge. **11.** an automobile that is larger than a subcompact but smaller than a midsize car. —**com•pact′ly,** *adv.* —**com•pact′ness,** *n.*

com•pact² (kom′pakt), *n.* a formal agreement between two or more parties, states, etc.; contract.

com′pact disc′, *n.* a small optical disc on which music, data, or images are digitally recorded for playback. *Abbr.:* CD

com′pact disc′ play′er, *n.* a device for playing compact discs. Also called **CD player.**

com•pac•tor (kəm pak′tər, kom′pak-), *n.* an appliance that crushes and compresses trash into small convenient bundles.

com•pa•dre (kəm pä′drā), *n. Chiefly Southwestern U.S.* a friend, companion, or close associate.

com•pan•ion¹ (kəm pan′yən), *n.* **1.** a person who frequently associates with or accompanies another; comrade; mate. **2.** a person in a usu. long-term, intimate relationship with another person; partner. **3.** a person employed to accompany, assist, or live with another as a helpful friend. **4.** a handbook or guide. **5.** a member of the lowest rank in an order of knighthood. **6.** Also called **comes.** the fainter of the two stars that constitute a double star. Compare PRIMARY (def. 11b). —*v.t.* **7.** to be a companion to; accompany.

com•pan•ion² (kəm pan′yən), *n.* **1.** COMPANIONWAY. **2.** a covering over the top of a companionway.

compan′ion piece′, *n.* a literary or musical work that has a close relationship to another work by the same author or composer.

com•pan•ion•way (kəm pan′yən wā′), *n.* a stair or ladder within the hull of a vessel.

com•pa•ny (kum′pə nē), *n., pl.* **-nies,** *v.,* **-nied, -ny•ing.** —*n.* **1.** a number of individuals assembled or associated together; group of people. **2.** a guest or guests: *We're having company tonight.* **3.** companionship; fellowship; association: *We always enjoy her company.* **4.** one's usual companions: *I dislike the company you keep.* **5.** a number of persons united or incorporated for joint action, esp. for business: *a publishing company; a dance company.* **6.** (*cap.*) the partners of a firm not specified in its title: *Jones & Company.* **7.** a basic unit of troops comprising a headquarters and two or three platoons. **8. the Company,** *Informal.* the CIA. **9.** a unit of firefighters. —*v.t.* —***Idiom.*** **10. keep company, a.** to associate in or as if in courtship: *She keeps company with a teacher.* **b.** (of a couple) to spend time together regularly; go out on dates, as in courtship. **11. keep someone company,** to associate with or be a companion to someone. **12. part company, a.** to separate: *We parted company at the airport.* **b.** to take an opposite view; differ.

com′pany grade′, *n.* military rank applying to army officers below major, as second and first lieutenants and captains. Compare FIELD GRADE.

com′pany un′ion, *n.* a labor union confined to employees of one company and often dominated by management.

com•pa•ra•ble (kom′pər ə bəl *or, sometimes,* kəm pâr′-), *adj.* **1.** capable of being compared; permitting comparison: *to consider the Roman and British empires comparable.* **2.** worthy of comparison: *shops comparable to those on Fifth Avenue.* **3.** usable for comparison; similar: *We have no comparable data on Russian farming.* —**com′pa•ra•bil′i•ty,** *n.* —**com′pa•ra•bly,** *adv.*

com•par•a•tive (kəm par′ə tiv), *adj.* **1.** of or pertaining to comparison. **2.** proceeding by, founded on, or using comparison as a method of study: *comparative anatomy.* **3.** estimated by comparison; not positive or absolute; relative: *to live in comparative luxury.* **4.** of or designating the intermediate degree of comparison of adjectives and adverbs, used to show an increase in quality, quantity, or intensity, as in *smaller, better,* and *more carefully,* the comparative forms of *small, good,* and *carefully.* Compare POSITIVE (def. 22), SUPERLATIVE (def. 2). —*n.* **5.** the comparative degree. **6.** the comparative form of an adjective or adverb. —**com•par′a•tive•ly,** *adv.* —**com•par′a•tive•ness,** *n.*

compar′ative reli′gion, *n.* a field of study seeking to derive general principles from a comparison and classification of the growth and influence of various religions.

com•pare (kəm pâr′), *v.,* **-pared, -par•ing,** *n.* —*v.t.* **1.** to examine (two or more objects, ideas, people, etc.) in order to note similarities and differences: *to compare two restaurants.* **2.** to consider or describe as similar; liken: *"Shall I compare thee to a summer's day?"* **3.** to form or display the degrees of comparison of (an adjective or adverb). —*v.i.* **4.** to be worthy of comparison: *Whose plays can compare with Shakespeare's?* **5.** to be in similar standing; be alike: *This recital compares with the one he gave last year.* **6.** to appear in quality, progress, etc., as specified: *Their development compares poorly with that of neighbor nations.* **7.** to make comparisons. —*n.* **8.** comparison: *a beauty beyond compare.* —**Usage.** The traditional rule states that COMPARE should be followed by *to* when it points out likenesses between unlike persons or things: *She compared his handwriting to knotted string.* It should be followed by *with,* the rule says, when it examines two entities of the same general class for similarities or differences: *She compared his handwriting with mine.* This rule is by no means always followed, even in formal speech and writing. Common practice is to use *to* for likeness between members of different classes: *to compare a language to a living organism.* Between members of the same category, both *to* and *with* are used: *Compare the Chicago of today with* (or *to*) *the Chicago of the 1890s.* After the past participle COMPARED, either *to* or *with* is used regardless of the type of comparison.

com•par•i•son (kəm par′ə sən), *n.* **1.** the act of comparing. **2.** the state of being compared. **3.** a likening; illustration by similitude; comparative estimate or statement. **4.** capability of being compared or likened; similarity. **5.** the inflection or other modification of an adjective or adverb to indicate degrees of superiority or inferiority in quality, quantity, or intensity, as in *mild, milder, mildest, less mild, least mild.* —***Saying.*** **6. Comparisons are odious,** one should judge people or things on their own merits, not by comparison with others.

com•part•ment (kəm pärt′mənt), *n.* **1.** a part or space that is marked or partitioned off. **2.** a separate room, section, etc.: *a baggage compartment.* —*v.t.* **3.** to divide into compartments. —**com•part•men•tal** (kəm pärt men′tl, kom′pärt-), *adj.* —**compartmentalize,** *v.t.*

com•pass (kum′pəs), *n.* **1.** an instrument for determining directions, as by means of a freely rotating magnetized needle that indicates magnetic north. **2.** Often, **compasses.** an instrument for drawing or describing circles, measuring distances, etc., consisting generally of two hinged, movable legs (often used with *pair of*). **3.** the enclosing line or limits of any area; perimeter. **4.** space within limits; area; extent; range; scope: *the broad compass of the novel.* **5.** due or proper limits; moderate bounds: *to act within the compass of propriety.* **6.** a passing round; circuit: *the compass of a year.* —*adj.* **7.** curved; forming a curve or arc: *a compass roof.* —*v.t.* **8.** to go or move around; make the circuit of: *to compass the city on foot.* **9.** to extend or stretch around; surround; encircle: *A stone wall compasses the property.* **10.** to attain or achieve; accomplish; obtain. **11.** to contrive; plot; scheme. **12.** to make curved or circular. **13.** to comprehend; grasp, as with the mind. —**com′pass•a•ble,** *adj.*

com•pas•sion (kəm pash′ən), *n.* a feeling of deep sympathy and sorrow for someone struck by misfortune, accompanied by a desire to alleviate the suffering; mercy. —**com•pas′sion•less,** *adj.*

com•pas•sion•ate (*adj.* kəm pash′ə nit; *v.* -nāt′), *adj., v.,* **-at•ed, -at•ing.** —*adj.* **1.** having or showing compassion; sympathetic: *a compassionate letter.* **2.** granted in an emergency: *compassionate military leave to attend a funeral.* —*v.t.* **3.** to have compassion for; pity. —**com•pas′sion•ate•ly,** *adv.*

com′pass plant′, *n.* an American prairie composite plant, *Silphium laciniatum,* with yellow flower heads and large, hairy leaves that tend to lie in a north-south plane.

com•pat•i•ble (kəm pat′ə bəl), *adj.* **1.** capable of living or existing together in harmony. **2.** able to exist together with something else: *Prejudice is not compatible with true religion.* **3.** consistent; congruous (often fol. by *with*): *Such claims are not compatible with the facts.* **4. a.** (of software) able to run on a specified computer. **b.** (of hardware) able to work with a specified device. **c.** (of a computer system) functionally equivalent to another, usu. widely used system. **5.** noting a television system in which color broadcasts can be received in black and white. —**com·pat′i·bil′i·ty**, *n.* —**com·pat′i·bly**, *adv.*

com·pa·tri·ot (kəm pā′trē ət; *esp. Brit.* -pa′-), *n.* **1.** a native or inhabitant of one's own country; fellow countryman or countrywoman. **2.** a colleague or companion; associate; peer. —*adj.* **3.** of the same country.

com·pel (kəm pel′), *v.t.*, **-pelled, -pel·ling. 1.** to force or drive, esp. to a course of action: *His unruliness compels us to dismiss him.* **2.** to secure or bring about by force or power: *to compel obedience.*

com·pel·ling (kəm pel′ing), *adj.* **1.** tending to compel; overpowering: *compelling reasons.* **2.** having a powerful and irresistible effect: *a compelling drama.* —**com·pel′ling·ly**, *adv.*

com·pen·di·ous (kəm pen′dē əs), *adj.* containing the substance of a subject, esp. an extensive one, in a concise form; succinct. —**com·pen′di·ous·ly**, *adv.*

com·pen·di·um (kəm pen′dē əm), *n.*, *pl.* **-di·ums, -di·a** (-dē ə). **1.** a brief treatment or account of a subject, esp. an extensive subject. **2.** a summary, epitome, or abridgment. **3.** a full list or inventory: *a compendium of their complaints.*

com·pen·sate (kom′pən sāt′), *v.*, **-sat·ed, -sat·ing.** —*v.t.* **1.** to recompense for something; pay: *Let me compensate you for your trouble.* **2.** to counterbalance; offset; make up for: *He compensated his homeliness with personal charm.* **3.** to counterbalance (a mechanical force), as by adjusting a mechanism to offset variations or produce equilibrium. —*v.i.* **4.** to provide or be an equivalent; make up; make amends (usu. fol. by *for*): *Apologies will not compensate for this damage.* **5.** to develop or employ mechanisms of psychological compensation. —**com′pen·sa′tor**, *n.* —**com·pen·sa·to·ry** (kəm pen′sə tôr′ē, -tōr′ē), **com·pen·sa·tive** (kom′pən sā′tiv, kəm pen′sə-), *adj.*

com·pen·sa·tion (kom′pən sā′shən), *n.* **1.** the act of compensating. **2.** the state of being compensated. **3.** something given or received as an equivalent for services, debt, loss, injury, etc.; indemnity; reparation; payment. **4.** *Biol.* the improvement of any defect by the excessive development or action of another part of the same structure. **5.** a psychological mechanism by which an individual attempts to make up for some personal deficiency by developing or stressing another aspect of personality or ability.

com·pete (kəm pēt′), *v.i.*, **-pet·ed, -pet·ing.** to strive to outdo another for acknowledgment, a prize, etc.; engage in a contest; vie: *to compete in business.* —**com·pet′er**, *n.* —**com·pet′ing·ly**, *adv.*

com·pe·tence (kom′pi təns), *n.* **1.** the quality of being competent; adequacy; possession of required skill, knowledge, or capacity. **2.** an income sufficient to furnish the necessities and modest comforts of life. **3.** the sum total of possible developmental responses of any group of blastemic cells under varied external conditions. **4.** the implicit internalized knowledge of a language that a speaker possesses and that enables the speaker to produce and understand the language. Compare PERFORMANCE (def. 8).

com·pe·tent (kom′pi tənt), *adj.* **1.** having suitable or sufficient skill, knowledge, experience, etc., for some purpose; properly qualified. **2.** adequate but not exceptional. **3.** (esp. of a witness) qualified as to age, soundness of mind, or the like. —**com′pe·tent·ly**, *adv.*

com·pe·ti·tion (kom′pi tish′ən), *n.* **1.** the act of competing; rivalry for supremacy, a prize, etc.: *competition between two teams.* **2.** a contest for some prize, honor, or advantage: *to enter a competition.* **3.** the rivalry offered by a competitor: *small businesses getting competition from the chain stores.* **4.** a competitor or competitors. **5.** the struggle among organisms, both of the same and of different species, for food, space, and other vital requirements.

com·pet·i·tive (kəm pet′i tiv), *adj.* **1.** of, pertaining to, involving, or decided by competition. **2.** well suited for competition; having a feature advantageous to competition: *a competitive price.* **3.** having a strong desire to compete or to succeed. —**com·pet′i·tive·ly**, *adv.* —**com·pet′i·tive·ness**, *n.*

com·pet·i·tor (kəm pet′i tər), *n.* a person, team, company, etc., that competes; rival. —**com·pet′i·tor·ship′**, *n.*

com·pi·la·tion (kom′pə lā′shən), *n.* **1.** the act of compiling. **2.** something compiled, as a reference book.

com·pile (kəm pīl′), *v.t.*, **-piled, -pil·ing. 1.** to put together (documents, selections, or other materials) in one book or work. **2.** to make (a book, writing, or the like) of materials from various sources: *to compile an anthology of plays.* **3.** to gather together: *to compile data.* **4.** to translate (a computer program) by means of a compiler.

com·pil·er (kəm pī′lər), *n.* **1.** a person who compiles. **2.** a computer program that translates a program written in a high-level language into another language. Compare INTERPRETER (def. 2).

com·pla·cen·cy (kəm plā′sən sē) also **com·pla·cence** (-səns), *n.*, *pl.* **-cies.** a feeling of quiet pleasure or security, often while unaware of, or unconcerned with, unpleasant realities or harmful possibilities; self-satisfaction; smugness.

com·pla·cent (kəm plā′sənt), *adj.* **1.** pleased, esp. with oneself or one's advantages or accomplishments; often without awareness of or concern for some defect, problem, or potential danger; self-satisfied; unconcerned. **2.** pleasant; complaisant. —**com·pla′cent·ly**, *adv.*

com·plain (kəm plān′), *v.i.* **1.** to express dissatisfaction, resentment, pain, grief, etc.; find fault. **2.** to make a formal accusation: *You must complain to the police about this vandalism.* —**com·plain′a·ble**, *adj.* —**com·plain′er**, *n.* —**com·plain′ing·ly**, *adv.*

com·plain·ant (kəm plā′nənt), *n.* a person, group, or company that makes a complaint, as in a legal action.

com·plaint (kəm plānt′), *n.* **1.** an expression of discontent, regret, pain, censure, resentment, or grief; lament; faultfinding. **2.** a cause of discontent, pain, grief, lamentation, etc. **3.** a cause of bodily pain or ailment; malady: *to suffer from a rare complaint.* **4.** (in a civil action) a statement by the plaintiff setting forth the cause of action.

com·plai·sant (kəm plā′sənt, -zənt, kom′plə zant′), *adj.* inclined or disposed to please; obliging; agreeable or gracious; compliant. —**com·plai′sance**, *n.* —**com·plai′sant·ly**, *adv.*

com·pleat (kəm plēt′), *adj.* highly skilled and accomplished in all aspects; expert: *the compleat actor, at home in comedy and tragedy.*

com·plect·ed (kəm plek′tid), *adj.* complexioned: *a light-complected child.* —**Usage.** Although criticized by some as a dialectal or nonstandard formation, COMPLECTED occurs in educated speech and occasionally in edited writing.

com·ple·ment (*n.* kom′plə mənt; *v.* -ment′), *n.* **1.** something that completes or makes perfect: *A good wine is a complement to a good meal.* **2.** the quantity or amount that completes anything: *We now have a full complement of packers.* **3.** either of two parts or things needed to complete the whole; counterpart. **4.** the full number of officers and crew required on a ship. **5. a.** a word or group of words that completes a grammatical construction in the predicate and that describes or is identified with the subject or object, as *small* in *The house is small* or *president* in *They elected him president.* Compare OBJECT COMPLEMENT, SUBJECT COMPLEMENT. **b.** any word or group of words used to complete a grammatical construction, esp. in the predicate, including adverbials, infinitives, and sometimes objects. **c.** COMPLEMENT CLAUSE. **6.** the quantity by which an angle or an arc falls short of 90° or a quarter of a circle. Compare SUPPLEMENT (def. 3). **7.** *Math.* the set of all the elements of a universal set not included in a given set. **8.** a musical interval that completes an octave when added to a given interval. **9. a.** a set of about 20 proteins that circulate in the blood and react in various combinations to promote the destruction of any cell displaying foreign surfaces or immune complexes. **b.** any of the proteins in the complement system, designated C1, C2, etc. **10.** COMPLEMENTARY COLOR. —*v.t.* **11.** to complete; form a complement to. —**com·ple·ment′er**, *n.*

com·ple·men·ta·ry (kom′plə men′tə rē, -trē), *adj.* **1.** forming a complement; completing. **2.** complementing each other. **3.** designating or consisting of a strand of DNA or RNA that can serve as a template for another strand.

com′plemen′tary an′gle, *n.* either of two angles that added together produce an angle of 90°. Compare SUPPLEMENTARY ANGLE.

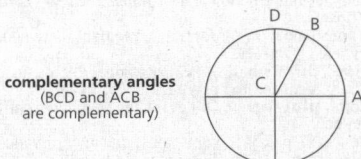

complementary angles
(BCD and ACB
are complementary)

com′plemen′tary col′or, *n.* **1.** one of a pair of colors opposed to the other member of the pair on a schematic chart or scale, as green opposed to red, that when mixed tend to neutralize each other. **2.** SECONDARY COLOR.

com·plement clause′, *n.* a subordinate clause that functions as the subject, direct object, or prepositional object of a verb, as *that you like it* in *I'm surprised that you like it.* Also called **com′plement sen′tence.**

com·plete (kəm plēt′), *adj.*, *v.*, **-plet·ed, -plet·ing.** —*adj.* **1.** having all parts or elements; lacking nothing; whole; entire; full: *a complete set of golf clubs.* **2.** finished; ended; concluded: *a complete orbit.* **3.** having all the required or customary characteristics, skills, or the like; consummate: *a complete scholar.* **4.** thorough; total; undivided; uncompromised, or unqualified: *a complete victory; a complete stranger.* **5.** (of a subject or predicate) having all modifying elements included: *The complete subject of* The dappled pony gazed over the fence *is* the dappled pony. Compare SIMPLE (def. 17a). **6.** (of a forward pass in football) caught by a receiver. **7.** accomplished; skilled; expert. —*v.t.* **8.** to make whole, entire, or perfect: *Hiking boots complete the outdoor look.* **9.** to bring to an end; finish: *to complete a task.* **10.** to consummate; fulfill. **11.** to execute (a forward pass) successfully. —**com·plete′ly**, *adv.* —**com·plete′ness**, *n.*

com·ple·tion (kəm plē′shən), *n.* **1.** the act of completing. **2.** the state of being completed. **3.** conclusion; fulfillment. **4.** (in football) a forward pass caught by the intended receiver.

com·plex (*adj.*, *v.* kəm pleks′, kom′pleks; *n.* kom′pleks), *adj.* **1.** composed of many interconnected parts; compound; composite: *a complex system.* **2.** characterized by a complicated or involved arrangement of parts, units, etc.: *complex machinery.* **3.** so complicated or intricate as to be hard to understand or deal with: *a complex problem.* **4.** (of a word) consisting of two or more parts, at least one of which is a bound form, as *childish*, which consists of the word *child* and the bound form *-ish.* **5.** pertaining to or using complex numbers: *complex methods; complex vector space.* —*n.* **6.** an often intricate or complicated association or assemblage of related things, parts, units, etc., forming a whole: *an apartment complex.* **7.** a cluster of interrelated, emotion-charged ideas, desires, and impulses that may be wholly or partly suppressed but influence attitudes, associations, and behavior. **8.** an obsessive notion or concern. **9.** Also called **coordination compound.** a chemical compound in which independently existing molecules or ions of a nonmetal form coordinate bonds with a metal atom or ion. Compare LIGAND (def. 2). **10.** an entity composed of molecules in which the constituents maintain much of their chemical identity: *receptor-hormone complex.* —*v.t.* **11.** *Chem.* to form a complex with. —*v.i.* **12.** *Chem.* to form a complex. —**com·plex′i·ty, com·plex′ness,** *n.* —**com·plex′ly,** *adv.*

com′plex frac′tion, *n.* a fraction in which the numerator or the denominator or both contain one or more fractions. Also called **compound fraction.**

com·plex·ion (kəm plek′shən), *n.* **1.** the natural color, texture, and appearance of the skin, esp. of the face. **2.** appearance; aspect; character: *This testimony put a different complexion on things.* **3.** viewpoint, attitude, or conviction: *one's political complexion.* **4.** (in medieval physiology) the constitution or nature of body and mind, regarded as the result of certain combined qualities.

com·plex·ioned (kəm plek′shənd), *adj.* having a specified complexion (usu. used in combination): *a light-complexioned person.*

com′plex sen′tence, *n.* a sentence containing one or more dependent clauses in addition to the main clause, as *When the bell rings* (dependent clause), *walk out* (main clause).

com·pli·ance (kəm plī′əns), *n.* **1.** the act of conforming, acquiescing, or yielding. **2.** a tendency to yield readily to others, esp. meekly. **3.** conformity; accordance: *in compliance with orders.* **4.** cooperation or obedience: *Compliance with the law is expected of all.*

com·pli·ant (kəm plī′ənt), *adj.* complying; obeying, obliging, or yielding, esp. in a submissive way: *a person with a compliant nature.* —**com·pli′ant·ly,** *adv.*

com·pli·cate (*v.* kom′pli kāt′; *adj.* -kit), *v.,* **-cat·ed, -cat·ing,** *adj.* —*v.t.* **1.** to make complex, intricate, involved, or difficult. —*adj.* **2.** complex; involved. **3.** folded longitudinally one or more times, as the wings of certain insects.

com·pli·ca·tion (kom′pli kā′shən), *n.* **1.** the act of complicating. **2.** a complicated or involved state or condition. **3.** a complex combination of elements or things. **4.** something that introduces a difficulty, problem, change, etc. **5.** a concurrent disease, accident, or adverse reaction that aggravates the original disease.

com·plic·i·ty (kəm plis′i tē), *n., pl.* **-ties.** the state of being an accomplice; partnership or involvement in wrongdoing.

com·pli·ment (*n.* kom′plə mənt; *v.* -ment′), *n.* **1.** an expression of praise, commendation, or admiration. **2.** a formal act or gesture of civility, respect, or regard: *The mayor paid her the compliment of a police escort.* **3. compliments,** a courteous greeting; good wishes; regards: *to send one's compliments.* —*v.t.* **4.** to pay a compliment to; commend; praise. **5.** to show kindness or regard for by a gift or other favor. **6.** to congratulate; felicitate. —*v.i.* **7.** to pay compliments.

com·pli·men·ta·ry (kom′plə men′tə rē, -trē), *adj., n., pl.* **-ries.** —*adj.* **1.** of the nature of, conveying, or expressing a compliment, often one that is politely flattering: *a complimentary remark.* **2.** given free as a gift or courtesy: *a complimentary ticket.* —*n.* **3.** something given or supplied without charge, esp. as an inducement to prospective customers. —**com′pli·men′ta·ri·ly,** *adv.*

com·pline (kom′plin, -plīn) also **com·plin** (-plin), *n.* the last of the seven canonical hours, or the service for it.

com·ply (kəm plī′), *v.i.,* **-plied, -ply·ing.** to act or be in accordance with wishes, requests, demands, requirements, or conditions (often fol. by *with*): *to comply with regulations.*

com·po·nent (kəm pō′nənt, kom-), *n.* **1.** a constituent part; element; ingredient. **2.** a part of a mechanical or electrical system: *hi-fi components.* **3.** the projection of a vector quantity, as force or velocity, along an axis; a coordinate of a vector. **4.** one of the set of the minimum number of chemical constituents by which every phase of a given system can be described. **5.** *Math.* a connected subset of a set, not contained in any other connected subset of the set. —*adj.* **6.** being or serving as an element in something larger; constituent: *component parts.* —**com·po·nen·tial** (kom′pə nen′shəl), *adj.* —**com·po′nent·ed,** *adj.*

com·port (kəm pôrt′, -pōrt′), *v.t.* **1.** to bear or conduct (oneself); behave: *to comport oneself with dignity.* —*v.i.* **2.** to be in agreement, harmony, or conformity (usu. followed by *with*): *Your statement does not comport with the facts.*

com·port·ment (kəm pôrt′mənt, -pōrt′-), *n.* bearing; demeanor; behavior.

com·pose (kəm pōz′), *v.,* **-posed, -pos·ing.** —*v.t.* **1.** to be or constitute the parts, elements, or materials of; make up; form the basis of: *a sauce composed of many ingredients.* **2.** to make or form by combining things, parts, or elements: *to compose a speech from research notes.* **3.** to create (a musical, literary, or choreographic work). **4.** to put or dispose in proper form or order. **5.** to arrange the elements of, esp. in an aesthetic manner. **6.** to end or settle (a quarrel, dispute, etc.): *The union and management composed their differences.* **7.** to bring (oneself, one's mind, etc.) to a condition of calmness, repose, etc.; calm; settle. **8. a.** to set (type). **b.** to set type for (an article, book, etc.). —*v.i.* **9.** to engage in composition, esp. musical composition. **10.** to enter into composition; fall into an arrangement.

com·posed (kəm pōzd′), *adj.* calm; tranquil; serene. —**com·pos′ed·ly,** *adv.*

com·pos·er (kəm pō′zər), *n.* **1.** a person or thing that composes. **2.** a person who writes music.

com·pos·ite (kəm poz′it), *adj., n., v.,* **-it·ed, -it·ing.** —*adj.* **1.** made up of disparate or separate parts or elements; compound: *a composite picture; a composite philosophy.* **2.** belonging to the composite family of plants. **3.** of or pertaining to a composite function or a composite number. —*n.* **4.** something composite; a compound. **5.** a composite plant. **6.** a picture, photograph, or the like, that combines several separate pictures or images. —*v.t.* **7.** to make a composite of.

compos′ite fam′ily, *n.* a large and varied plant family, Compositae, typified by nonwoody plants having flower heads composed of a disk containing tiny flowers, the flowers at the rim extending one petal outward to form a surrounding ray: includes the aster, daisy, dandelion, marigold, sunflower, thistle, and zinnia.

compos′ite num′ber, *n.* a number that is a multiple of at least two numbers other than itself and 1.

com·po·si·tion (kom′pə zish′ən), *n.* **1.** the manner of being composed; arrangement or combination of parts or elements. **2.** the parts or elements of which something is composed; makeup; constitution. **3.** the act of combining parts or elements to form a whole. **4.** the resulting state or product. **5.** an aggregate material formed from two or more substances. **6.** a short essay written as a school exercise. **7.** the act or process of producing a literary work. **8.** a piece of music. **9.** the act or art of composing music. **10.** the organization or grouping of the different parts of a work of art so as to achieve a unified whole. **11.** the process of forming compound words. **12.** a settlement by mutual agreement. **13. a.** the setting up of type for printing. **b.** the makeup of pages for printing.

com·pos·i·tor (kəm poz′i tər), *n.* a person who sets the type or text for printing. —**com·pos′i·to·ri·al** (-tôr′ē əl, -tōr′-), *adj.*

com·pos men·tis (kōm′pəs men′tis), *adj.* sane; mentally sound.

com·post (kom′pōst), *n.* **1.** a mixture of decaying organic matter, as decomposing leaves, manure, kitchen scraps, etc., used for fertilizing soil. **2.** a composition; compound. —*v.t.* **3.** to use in compost; make compost of. **4.** to apply compost to (soil). —**com′post·a·ble,** *adj.* —**com′post·er,** *n.*

com·po·sure (kəm pō′zhər), *n.* serene, self-controlled manner or state of mind; calmness; tranquillity.

com·pote (kom′pōt), *n.* **1.** fruit stewed or cooked in a syrup, usu. served as a dessert. **2.** a stemmed dish, often with a lid, for serving fruit, nuts, candy, etc.

com·pound[1] (*adj.* kom′pound, kom pound′; *n.* kom′pound; *v.* kəm pound′, kom′pound), *adj.* **1.** composed of two or more parts, elements, or ingredients: *Soap is a compound substance.* **2.** having or involving two or more actions or functions: *The mouth is a compound organ.* **3.** (of a word) **a.** consisting of two or more parts that are also words, as *housetop, many-sided, playact,* or *upon.* **b.** consisting of two or more parts that are also bases, as *biochemistry* or *ethnography.* **4.** (of a verb tense) consisting of an auxiliary verb and a main verb, as *are swimming, have spoken,* or *will write* (opposed to *simple*). **5.** composed of several similar parts that combine to form a whole: *a compound fruit.* **6.** composed of a number of distinct but connected individuals, as coral. —*n.* **7.** something formed by compounding or combining parts, elements, etc. **8.** a pure substance composed of two or more elements whose chemical composition is constant. **9.** a compound word, esp. one composed of two or more words that are otherwise unaltered, as *moonflower* or *rainstorm.* —*v.t.* **10.** to put together into a whole; combine: *to compound drugs to form a new medicine.* **11.** to make or form by combining parts, elements, etc.; construct: *a medicine compounded from various drugs.* **12.** to increase or add to, esp. so as to worsen: *a problem that was compounded by their isolation.* **13.** to settle or adjust by agreement, esp. for a reduced amount, as a debt. **14.** to agree, for a consideration, not to prosecute or punish a wrongdoer for: *to compound a crime or felony.* **15.** to pay (interest) on the accrued interest as well as the principal. —*v.i.* **16.** to make a bargain; come to terms; compromise. **17.** to form a compound. —**com·pound′a·ble,** *adj.*

com·pound[2] (kom′pound), *n.* a separate area, usu. fenced or walled, containing residences, business offices, barracks, or other structures.

com′pound eye′, *n.* an eye, typical of insects, composed of many individual light-sensitive units that form a mosaic of images on the retina.

com′pound flow′er, *n.* the flower head of a composite plant.

com′pound frac′tion, *n.* COMPLEX FRACTION.

com′pound frac′ture, *n.* a fracture in which the broken bone is exposed through a wound in the skin.

com′pound in′terest, *n.* interest paid on both the principal and on accrued interest.

com′pound leaf′, *n.* a leaf composed of a number of leaflets on a common stalk.

com′pound mi′croscope, *n.* an optical instrument for forming magnified images of small objects, consisting of an objective lens with a very short focal length and an eyepiece with a longer focal length, both lenses mounted in the same tube.

com′pound num′ber, *n.* a quantity expressed in more than one denomination or unit, as one foot six inches.

com′pound sen′tence, *n.* a sentence containing two or more coordinate independent clauses, usu. joined by one or more conjunctions, but no dependent clause, as *The lightning flashed* (independent clause) *and* (conjunction) *the rain fell* (independent clause).

com·pre·hend (kom′pri hend′), *v.t.* **1.** to understand the nature or meaning of; grasp with the mind; perceive. **2.** to take in or embrace; include; comprise. —**com′pre·hend′ing·ly,** *adv.*

com·pre·hen·si·ble (kom′pri hen′sə bəl), *adj.* capable of being comprehended; intelligible. —**com′pre·hen′si·bly,** *adv.*

com·pre·hen·sion (kom′pri hen′shən), *n.* **1.** the act or process of comprehending. **2.** the state of being comprehended. **3.** capacity of the mind to perceive and understand; power to grasp ideas. **4.** perception or understanding: *mature comprehension of a difficult subject.* **5.** inclusion. **6.** comprehensiveness.

com·pre·hen·sive (kom′pri hen′siv), *adj.* **1.** of large scope; covering much; inclusive: *a comprehensive study.* **2.** having or marked by an extensive mental range or grasp: *comprehensive understanding.* **3.** (of insurance) providing broad protection against loss. —*n.* **4.** Often, **comprehensives.** Also called **comprehen′sive examina′tion.** an extensive examination given to measure general progress or proficiency in a major field of study. —**com′pre·hen′sive·ly,** *adv.* —**com′pre·hen′sive·ness,** *n.*

com·press (*v.* kəm pres′; *n.* kom′pres), *v.t.* **1.** to press or squeeze together; force into less space. **2.** to cause to become a solid mass: *to compress cotton into bales.* **3.** to condense, shorten, or abbreviate: *The book was compressed by 50 pages.* —*n.* **4.** a soft pad or cloth held or secured on the body to provide pressure or to supply moisture, cold, heat, or medication. **5.** an apparatus for compressing cotton bales. —**com·press′i·ble,** *adj.* —**com·press′i·bil′i·ty,** *n.* —**com·press′ing·ly,** *adv.*

com·pressed (kəm prest′), *adj.* **1.** pressed into less space; condensed: *compressed gases.* **2.** pressed together: *compressed lips.* **3.** flattened by or as if by pressure: *compressed wallboard.* **4.** *Zool., Bot.* flattened laterally. —**com·press′ed·ly,** *adv.*

com·pres·sion (kəm presh′ən), *n.* **1.** the act of compressing. **2.** the state of being compressed. **3.** the effect or result of being compressed. **4.** (in internal-combustion engines) the reduction in volume and increase of pressure of the air or combustible mixture in the cylinder prior to ignition. Also, **com·pres′sure** (for defs. 1, 2). —**com·pres′sion·al,** *adj.*

com·pres·sor (kəm pres′ər), *n.* **1.** a person or thing that compresses. **2.** a muscle that compresses a part of the body. **3.** a pump or other machine for reducing volume and increasing pressure of gases in order to condense the gases, drive pneumatically powered machinery, etc.

com·prise (kəm prīz′), *v.t.,* **-prised, -pris·ing. 1.** to include or contain: *The Soviet Union comprised several republics.* **2.** to consist of; be composed of: *The advisory board comprises six members.* **3.** to form or constitute: *Seminars and lectures comprised the day's activities.* —**Idiom. 4. be comprised of,** to consist of; be composed of: *The sales network is comprised of independent outlets and chain stores.* —**com·pris′a·ble,** *adj.* —**com·pris′al,** *n.* —**Usage.** COMPRISE has had an interesting history of sense development. In addition to its original senses, dating from the 15th century, "to include" and "to consist of" (*The United States of America comprises 50 states*), COMPRISE has had since the late 18th century the meaning "to form or constitute" (*Fifty states comprise the United States of America*). Since the late 19th century it has also been used in passive constructions with a sense synonymous with one of its original meanings, "to consist of, be composed of": *The United States of America is comprised of 50 states.* These later uses are often criticized, but they occur with increasing frequency even in formal speech and writing.

com·pro·mise (kom′prə mīz′), *n., v.,* **-mised, -mis·ing. —*n.* 1.** a settlement of differences by mutual adjustment or modification of opposing claims, principles, demands, etc.; agreement by mutual concession. **2.** the result of such a settlement. **3.** something intermediate between different things. **4.** an endangering, esp. of reputation; exposure to danger, suspicion, etc. —*v.t.* **5.** to settle by a compromise. **6.** to expose or make vulnerable to danger, suspicion, scandal, etc.; jeopardize: *Such mistakes compromise our safety.* —*v.i.* **7.** to make a compromise or compromises. **8.** to make a dishonorable or shameful concession: *to compromise with one's principles.* —**com′pro·mis′er,** *n.* —**com′pro·mis′ing·ly,** *adv.*

com·pro·mised (kom′prə mīzd′), *adj.* unable to function optimally, esp. with regard to immune response, owing to underlying disease, harmful environmental exposure, or the side effects of a course of treatment.

comp·trol·ler (kən trō′lər; *spelling pron.* komp trō′lər), *n.* CONTROLLER (def. 1).

Comptrol′ler Gen′eral of the Unit′ed States′, *n.* the director of the General Accounting Office.

Comptrol′ler of the Cur′rency, *n.* an official of the U.S. Department of the Treasury who regulates the national banks and administers the issuance and redemption of Federal Reserve notes.

com·pul·sion (kəm pul′shən), *n.* **1.** the act of compelling; constraint; coercion. **2.** the state or condition of being compelled. **3.** a strong, usu. irresistible impulse to perform an act, esp. one that is irrational or contrary to one's will.

com·pul·sive (kəm pul′siv), *adj.* **1.** pertaining to, characterized by, or involving compulsion: *compulsive eating.* **2.** characterized by perfectionism, rigidity, conscientiousness, and an obsessive concern with order and detail. **3.** compelling; compulsory. —*n.* **4.** a compulsive person.

—**com·pul′sive·ly,** *adv.* —**com·pul′sive·ness, com·pul·siv′i·ty** (kəm pul siv′i tē, kom′pul-), *n.*

com·pul·so·ry (kəm pul′sə rē), *adj., n., pl.* **-ries. —*adj.* 1.** required; mandatory; obligatory: *compulsory education.* **2.** using compulsion; compelling; constraining: *compulsory measures to control rioting.* —*n.* **3.** something, as an athletic maneuver, that must be executed as part of a contest or competition. —**com·pul′so·ri·ly,** *adv.* —**com·pul′so·ri·ness,** *n.*

com·punc·tion (kəm pungk′shən), *n.* **1.** a feeling of uneasiness or anxiety of conscience for doing wrong or causing pain; contrition; remorse. **2.** any uneasiness or hesitation about the rightness of an action; qualm. —**com·punc′tious,** *adj.* —**com·punc′tious·ly,** *adv.*

com·pu·ta·tion (kom′pyŏŏ tā′shən), *n.* **1.** an act or method of computing; calculation. **2.** a result of computing. **3.** the amount computed. —**com′pu·ta′tion·al,** *adj.* —**com′pu·ta′tive,** *adj.*

computa′tional linguis′tics, *n.* the study of the applications of computers in processing and analyzing language, as in automatic machine translation and text analysis.

com·pute (kəm pyŏŏt′), *v.,* **-put·ed, -put·ing,** *n.* —*v.t.* **1.** to determine by calculation; reckon; calculate: *to compute the interest on a loan.* **2.** to determine by using a computer or calculator. —*v.i.* **3.** to reckon; calculate. **4.** to use a computer or calculator. —*n.* **5.** computation: *vast beyond compute.* —**com·put′a·ble,** *adj.* —**com·put′a·bil′i·ty,** *n.* —**com·put′a·bly,** *adv.*

com·put·er (kəm pyŏŏ′tər), *n.* **1.** a programmable electronic device designed for performing prescribed operations on data at high speed, esp. one housed with or linked to other devices for inputting, storing, retrieving, and displaying the data. **2.** one that computes. —**com·put′er·like′,** *adj.*

com·put·er·ese (kəm pyŏŏ′tə rēz′, -rēs′), *n.* the jargon and technical terms associated with computers and their operation.

comput′er graph′ics, *n.* (*used with a sing. v.*) **1.** pictorial computer output produced, through the use of software, on a display screen, plotter, or printer. **2.** the technique or process used to produce such output.

com·put·er·ize (kəm pyŏŏ′tə rīz′), *v.,* **-ized, -iz·ing.** —*v.t.* **1.** to control, process, or store by means of a computer. **2.** to equip with or automate by computers: *to computerize a business.* —*v.i.* **3.** to undergo automation by computers. —**com·put′er·i·za′tion,** *n.*

comput′erized ax′ial tomog′raphy, *n.* the process of producing a CAT scan. Compare CAT SCANNER.

comput′er lit′eracy, *n.* familiarity with computers and how they work. —**comput′er-lit′erate,** *adj.*

com·rade (kom′rad, -rid), *n.* **1.** a person who shares in one's activities, occupation, etc.; companion, associate, or friend. **2.** a fellow member of a fraternal group, political party, etc. **3.** (*often cap.*) a Communist or fellow Communist. —**com′rade·ship′,** *n.*

Com·stock (kum′stok, kom′-), *n.* Anthony, 1844–1915, U.S. author and reformer.

Com′stock Lode′, *n.* the most valuable deposit of silver ore ever recorded, discovered in 1859 by Henry T. P. Comstock near Virginia City, Nev. Also called **Com′stock Sil′ver Lode′.**

con[1] (kon), *adv.* **1.** against a proposition, opinion, etc.: *arguments pro and con.* —*n.* **2.** the argument, position, arguer, or voter against something. Compare PRO[1].

con[2] (kon), *v.t.,* **conned, con·ning. 1.** to peruse or examine carefully; study. **2.** to commit to memory; learn.

con[3] or **conn** (kon), *v.,* **conned, con·ning,** *n.* —*v.t.* **1.** to direct the steering of (a ship). —*n.* **2.** the station of the person who cons a ship.

con[4] (kon), *adj., v.,* **conned, con·ning,** *n.* —*adj.* **1.** involving abuse of confidence; deceitfully manipulative: *a con trick.* —*v.t.* **2.** to swindle; trick. **3.** to persuade by deception, cajolery, etc. —*n.* **4.** a confidence game or swindle. **5.** a lie, exaggeration, or glib self-serving talk.

con[5] (kon), *n. Informal.* a convict.

con-, var. of COM- before a consonant (except *b, h, l, p, r*): *convene; condone; connection.*

Co·na·kry (kon′ə krē), *n.* the capital of Guinea, in NW Africa. 705,280.

con a·mo·re (kon ə môr′e, -môr′ā, -mōr′e, -mōr′ā, kōn), *adv.* tenderly and lovingly (used esp. as a musical direction).

Co·nant (kō′nənt), *n.* James Bryant, 1893–1978, U.S. chemist and educator: president of Harvard University 1933–53.

con·cat·e·nate (kon kat′n āt′, kən-), *v.,* **-nat·ed, -nat·ing,** *adj.* —*v.t.* **1.** to link together, as in a series or chain. —*adj.* **2.** linked together. —**con·cat′e·na′tion,** *n.* —**con·cat′e·na′tor,** *n.*

con·cave (*adj., v.* kon kāv′, kon′kāv; *n.* kon′kāv), *adj., n., v.,* **-caved, -cav·ing.** —*adj.* **1.** curved or hollowed inward like the inside of a circle or sphere. Compare CONVEX (def. 1). **2.** (of a polygon) having at least one interior angle greater than 180°. —*n.* **3.** a concave surface, part, line, or thing. —*v.t.* **4.** to make concave.

con·cav·i·ty (kon kav′i tē), *n., pl.* **-ties. 1.** the state or quality of being concave. **2.** a concave surface or thing; cavity.

con·ceal (kən sēl′), *v.t.* **1.** to hide; cover or keep from sight: *A high wall concealed the house.* **2.** to keep secret; avoid disclosing or divulging: *to conceal one's true motives.* —**con·ceal′a·ble,** *adj.* —**con·ceal′er,** *n.* —**con·ceal′ment,** *n.*

con·cede (kən sēd′), *v.,* **-ced·ed, -ced·ing.** —*v.t.* **1.** to acknowledge as true, just, or proper; admit, often grudgingly: *He finally conceded that* *she was right.* **2.** to acknowledge (an opponent's victory, score, etc.) before it is officially established: *to concede an election.* **3.** to grant as a right or privilege; yield. —*v.i.* **4.** to make concession; yield; admit. —**con•ced′ed•ly,** *adv.*

con•ceit (kən sēt′), *n.* **1.** an excessively favorable opinion of one's own ability, importance, wit, etc.; vanity. **2.** a fancy; whim; fanciful notion. **3.** an elaborate, fanciful metaphor, esp. of a strained or far-fetched nature. **4.** something conceived in the mind; a thought; idea. **5.** a fancy, purely decorative article.

con•ceit•ed (kən sē′tid), *adj.* having an excessively favorable opinion of oneself; vain. —**con•ceit′ed•ly,** *adv.* —**con•ceit′ed•ness,** *n.*

con•ceiv•a•ble (kən sē′və bəl), *adj.* capable of being conceived; imaginable. —**con•ceiv′a•bly,** *adv.*

con•ceive (kən sēv′), *v.,* **-ceived, -ceiv•ing.** —*v.t.* **1.** to form (a notion, opinion, purpose, etc.): *He conceived the project while on vacation.* **2.** to form a notion or idea of; imagine: *Would you ever have conceived such behavior in public?* **3.** to hold as an opinion; think; believe: *I can't conceive that it would be of any use.* **4.** to experience or form (a feeling): *to conceive a great love for music.* **5.** to become pregnant with. **6.** to begin, originate, or found (something) in a particular way (usu. used in the passive): *a new nation conceived in liberty.* —*v.i.* **7.** to form an idea; think (usu. fol. by *of*). **8.** to become pregnant. —**conceivable,** *adj.* —**conceivably,** *adv.* —**con•ceiv′er,** *n.*

con•cen•trate (kon′sən trāt′), *v.,* **-trat•ed, -trat•ing,** *n.* —*v.t.* **1.** to bring or draw to a common center; direct toward one point; focus: *to concentrate one's attention on a problem.* **2.** to put or bring into a single place, group, etc.: *The population was concentrated in a few cities.* **3.** to intensify; make denser, stronger, or purer, esp. by the removal or reduction of liquid. **4.** to separate (metal or ore) from rock, sand, etc., so as to improve the quality of the valuable portion. —*v.i.* **5.** to bring all efforts, faculties, etc., to bear on one objective (often fol. by *on* or *upon*): *to concentrate on solving a problem.* **6.** to come to or toward a common center; converge; collect. **7.** to become more intense, stronger, or purer. —*n.* **8.** a concentrated form of something; product of concentration: *a juice concentrate.*

con•cen•trat•ed (kon′sən trā′tid), *adj.* **1.** applied with all one's attention, energy, etc.: *a concentrated effort to win.* **2.** clustered or gathered together closely. **3.** treated to remove or reduce an inessential ingredient, esp. liquid: *concentrated orange juice.*

con•cen•tra•tion (kon′sən trā′shən), *n.* **1.** the act of concentrating or the state of being concentrated. **2.** exclusive attention to one object; close mental application. **3.** something concentrated: *a concentration of stars.* **4.** (in a chemical solution) a measure of the amount of dissolved substance contained per unit of volume. **5.** a card game in which players try to find pairs of cards from a deck spread out face down by turning cards over, two at each turn.

concentra′tion camp′, *n.* a guarded compound for the confinement of political prisoners, minorities, etc.

con•cen•tric (kən sen′trik), *adj.* (esp. of circles or spheres) having a common center. —**con•cen′tri•cal•ly,** *adv.* —**con•cen•tric•i•ty** (kon′sən tris′i tē, -sen-), *n.*

con•cept (kon′sept), *n.* **1.** a general notion or idea; conception. **2.** an idea of something formed by mentally combining all its characteristics or particulars; a construct. **3.** a directly conceived or intuited object of thought. **4.** a theme or image, esp. as embodied in the design or execution of something. —**con•cep′tu•al,** *adj.*

con•cep•tion (kən sep′shən), *n.* **1.** the act of conceiving or the state of being conceived. **2.** fertilization; the formation of a zygote from the union of sperm and egg. **3.** a product of fertilization, as an embryo. **4.** a notion; idea; concept: *a strange conception of justice.* **5.** something that is conceived: *That theory is the conception of a genius.* **6.** origination; beginning. **7.** a design; plan. **8.** the act or power of forming notions, ideas, or concepts. —**con•cep′tion•al,** *adj.* —**con•cep′tive,** *adj.*

con•cep•tu•al•ism (kən sep′cho͞o ə liz′əm), *n.* any of several doctrines existing as a compromise between realism and nominalism and regarding universals as concepts. Compare NOMINALISM, realism (def. 5a). —**con•cep′tu•al•ist,** *n.* —**con•cep′tu•al•is′tic,** *adj.*

con•cep•tu•al•ize (kən sep′cho͞o ə līz′), *v.,* **-ized, -iz•ing.** —*v.t.* **1.** to form into a concept; make a concept of. —*v.i.* **2.** to form a concept; think in concepts. —**con•cep′tu•al•i•za′tion,** *n.*

con•cern (kən sûrn′), *v.t.* **1.** to be of interest or importance to; affect; involve: *Drug abuse concerns us all.* **2.** to relate to; be connected with. **3.** to interest or engage (used reflexively or in the passive): *to concern oneself with every aspect of a business.* **4.** to trouble, worry, or disquiet; disturb: *Your headaches concern me.* —*n.* **5.** something that relates or pertains to a person; business; affair. **6.** a matter that engages a person's attention, interest, or care, or that affects a person's welfare or happiness. **7.** worry, solicitude, or anxiety: *to show concern for the homeless.* **8.** important relation or bearing: *This news is of concern to both of us.* **9.** a commercial or manufacturing company or establishment; firm. **10.** any material object or contrivance.

con•cerned (kən sûrnd′), *adj.* **1.** interested or affected: *concerned citizens.* **2.** troubled or anxious: *a concerned look.* **3.** having a connection or involvement; participating: *all those concerned in the robbery.* —**con•cern′ed•ly,** *adv.* —**con•cern′ed•ness,** *n.*

con•cern•ing (kən sûr′ning), *prep.* relating to; regarding; about.

con•cert (*n., adj.* kon′sûrt, -sərt; *v.* kən sûrt′), *n.* **1.** a public performance of music or dancing. **2.** agreement of two or more individuals in a design or plan; combined action; accord or harmony. —*adj.* **3.** designed for or performing in music or dance concerts. —*v.t.* **4.** to contrive or arrange by agreement: *to concert a settlement of differences.* **5.** to plan; devise: *to concert a program of action.* —*v.i.* **6.** to plan or act together. —*Idiom.* **7. in concert,** together; jointly: *to act in concert.*

con•cert•ed (kən sûr′tid), *adj.* **1.** contrived or arranged by agreement; planned or devised together: *a concerted effort.* **2.** performed together or in cooperation: *a concerted attack.* **3.** arranged in parts for several voices or instruments. —**con•cert′ed•ly,** *adv.* —**con•cert′ed•ness,** *n.*

con′cert grand′, *n.* a grand piano of the largest size, being typically 9 ft. (2.7 m) in length.

con•cer•ti•na (kon′sər tē′nə), *n., pl.* **-nas,** *v.,* **-naed** (-nəd), **-na•ing** (-nə ing), *adj.* —*n.* **1.** a musical instrument resembling an accordion but having buttonlike keys, hexagonal bellows and ends, and a more limited range. —*v.i., v.t.* **2.** to fold or collapse in the manner of a concertina. —*adj.* **3.** of or resembling a concertina.

con•cer•to (kən cher′tō, -chûr′-), *n., pl.* **-tos, -ti** (-tē). a musical composition usu. in three movements for one or more principal instruments and orchestra.

con′cert pitch′, *n.* **1.** a standard of pitch used for tuning concert instruments, 440 vibrations per second for A above middle C. **2.** a state of heightened eagerness, readiness, or tension.

con•ces•sion (kən sesh′ən), *n.* **1.** the act of conceding or yielding, as a right, a privilege, or a point in an argument. **2.** the thing or point yielded. **3.** something conceded by a government or a controlling authority, as a grant of land, a privilege, or a franchise. **4.** a space or privilege within certain premises for a subsidiary business or service: *the refreshment concession at a theater.* —**con•ces′sion•al,** *adj.*

con•ces•sion•aire (kən sesh′ə nâr′) also **con•ces•sion•er** (-sesh′ə-nər), *n.* the owner, operator, or holder of a concession.

con•ces•sion•ar•y (kən sesh′ə ner′ē), *adj.* pertaining to concession; of the nature of a concession: *concessionary agreements.*

conces′sion speech′, *n.* a speech given by a political candidate when the votes are almost counted in which he or she concedes that defeat is inevitable.

conch (kongk, konch), *n., pl.* **conchs** (kongks), **con•ches** (kon′chiz). **1.** any marine gastropod mollusk of the family Strombidae, having a thick pointed spiral shell with a wide outer lip. **2.** any of various similar unrelated gastropods. **3.** the shell of a conch. [< Latin < Greek *kónchē* shell]

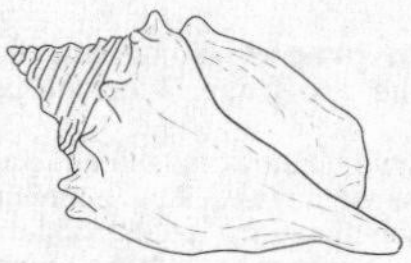

conch (def. 1),
Strombus alatus,
length 3 to 4 in. (8 to 10 cm)

con•chol•o•gy (kong kol′ə jē), *n.* the branch of zoology dealing with the shells of mollusks. —**con•chol′o•gist,** *n.*

con•cierge (kon′sē ârzh′; *Fr.* kôn syerzh′), *n., pl.* **-cierges** (-sē âr′zhiz; *Fr.* -syerzh′). **1.** (esp. in France) a person who has charge of the entrance of a building and is often the owner's representative or caretaker. **2.** a member of a hotel staff in charge of special services for guests, as arranging for theater tickets. **3.** an employee in an apartment house who directs or carries out various services relating to the building or its tenants.

con•cil•i•ate (kən sil′ē āt′), *v.,* **-at•ed, -at•ing.** —*v.t.* **1.** to overcome the distrust or hostility of; placate; win over: *to conciliate an angry competitor.* **2.** to win or gain (goodwill, regard, or favor). **3.** to make compatible; reconcile. —*v.i.* **4.** to become agreeable or reconciled. —**con•cil′i•a•ble** (-ə bəl), *adj.* —**con•cil′i•at′ing•ly,** *adv.* —**con•cil′i•a′tion,** *n.* —**con•cil′i•a′tor,** *n.*

con•cil•i•a•to•ry (kən sil′ē ə tôr′ē, -tōr′ē) also **con•cil•i•a•tive** (-ē ā′tiv, -ə tiv, -sil′yə-), *adj.* tending to conciliate: *a conciliatory manner.* —**con•cil′i•a•to′ri•ly,** *adv.* —**con•cil′i•a•to′ri•ness,** *n.*

con•cise (kən sīs′), *adj.* expressing much in few words; brief but comprehensive; succinct; terse. —**con•cise′ly,** *adv.* —**con•cise′ness,** *n.*

con•clave (kon′klāv, kong′-), *n.* **1.** a private or secret meeting. **2.** an assembly or gathering, esp. one that has special authority or influence: *a conclave of political leaders.* **3.** the assembly or meeting of the cardinals for the election of a pope.

con•clude (kən klo͞od′), *v.,* **-clud•ed, -clud•ing.** —*v.t.* **1.** to bring to an end; finish: *to conclude a speech with a quotation.* **2.** to say in conclusion. **3.** to bring to a decision or settlement: *to conclude a treaty.* **4.** to determine by reasoning; deduce; infer: *By your smile I conclude that the news is good.* **5.** to decide, determine, or resolve. —*v.i.* **6.** to come to an end; finish: *The meeting concluded at ten o'clock.* **7.** to arrive at an opinion, judgment, or decision; decide. —**con•clud′a•ble, con•clud′i•ble,** *adj.* —**con•clud′er,** *n.*

con•clu•sion (kən klo͞o′zhən), *n.* **1.** the end or close; final part. **2.** the last main division of a discourse, usu. containing a summary of points and a statement of opinion or decisions. **3.** a result, issue, or outcome. **4.** a reasoned deduction or inference. **5.** a final decision or judgment reached after consideration. **6.** a settlement or arrangement. **7.** a proposition concluded or inferred from the premises of an argument. **8. a.**

the formal closing of a plea, in which the jury is given an issue of fact to decide. **b.** the concluding matter in a complaint. —*Idiom.* **9. in conclusion,** lastly; to conclude.

con•clu•sive (kən klo͞o′siv), *adj.* **1.** serving to settle or decide a question; decisive: *conclusive evidence.* **2.** tending to terminate; closing. —**con•clu′sive•ly,** *adv.* —**con•clu′sive•ness,** *n.*

con•coct (kon kokt′, kən-), *v.t.* **1.** to prepare or make by combining ingredients: *to concoct a meal from leftovers.* **2.** to devise; contrive: *to concoct an excuse.* —**con•coc′tion,** *n.*

con•com•i•tance (kon kom′i təns, kən-), *n.* **1.** the quality or relation of being concomitant. **2.** CONCOMITANT (def. 2).

con•com•i•tant (kon kom′i tənt, kən-), *adj.* **1.** existing or occurring with something else, often in a lesser way; concurrent: *an event and its concomitant circumstances.* —*n.* **2.** a concomitant quality, circumstance, or thing. —**con•com′i•tant•ly,** *adv.*

con•cord (kon′kôrd, kong′-), *n.* **1.** agreement between persons, groups, etc. **2.** agreement between things. **3.** peace; amity. **4.** a treaty; compact. **5.** a stable, harmonious combination of musical tones; a chord requiring no resolution. [< Old French < Latin *concord* harmonious (*con-* + *cord-* HEART)] —**con•cord′al,** *adj.*

Con•cord (kong′kərd *for 1, 3–5;* kon′kôrd, kong′- *for 2; for 4, 5 also* kon′kôrd, kong′-), *n.* **1.** a city in W California, near San Francisco. 111,889. **2.** the capital of New Hampshire, in the S part. 30,400. **3.** a town in E Massachusetts, NW of Boston: second battle of the Revolution fought here April 19, 1775. 16,293. **4.** Also called **Con′cord grape′.** a cultivated variety of the fox grape used in making jelly, juice, and wine. **5.** a sweet red wine from the Concord grape.

con•cord•ance (kon kôr′dns, kən-), *n.* **1.** agreement; concord; harmony: *the concordance of the membership.* **2.** an alphabetical index of the principal words of a book, as of the Bible, with a reference to the passage in which each occurs. **3.** an alphabetical index of subjects or topics. **4.** (in genetic studies) the degree of similarity in a pair of twins with respect to the presence or absence of a particular disease or trait.

con•cord•ant (kon kôr′dnt, kən-), *adj.* agreeing; harmonious. —**con•cord′ant•ly,** *adv.*

con•cor•dat (kon kôr′dat), *n.* **1.** an agreement or compact, esp. an official one. **2.** an agreement between the pope and a secular government regarding the regulation of church matters. —**con•cor′da•to′ry** (-də tôr′ē, -tōr′ē), *adj.*

Con•corde (kon′kôrd, kong′-, kon kôrd′, kong-), *Trademark.* a supersonic passenger aircraft manufactured and operated jointly by England and France.

Con′cord grape′ (kong′kərd, kon′kôrd, kong′-), *n.* a cultivated variety of the fox grape, *Vitis labrusca,* used in making jelly, juice, and wine.

con•course (kon′kôrs, -kōrs, kong′-), *n.* **1.** an assemblage; gathering: *a concourse of people.* **2.** a boulevard or other broad thoroughfare. **3.** a large open space for accommodating crowds, as in a railroad station. **4.** an act or instance of coming together; confluence: *a concourse of events.*

con•cres•cence (kon kres′əns, kən-), *n.* a growing together, as of tissue or embryonic parts; coalescence. —**con•cres′cent,** *adj.*

con•crete (kon′krēt, kong′-, kon krēt′, kong-), *adj., n., v.,* **-cret•ed, -cret•ing.** —*adj.* **1.** constituting an actual thing or instance; real; perceptible; substantial: *concrete proof.* **2.** pertaining to or concerned with realities or actual instances rather than abstractions; particular as opposed to general: *concrete proposals.* **3.** referring to an actual substance or thing, as opposed to an abstract quality: *The words "cat," and "water," are concrete, whereas the words "truth,"and "excellence," are abstract.* **4.** made of concrete: *concrete blocks.* **5.** formed by coalescence of separate particles into a mass; united in a coagulated, condensed, or solid mass or state. —*n.* **6.** an artificial, stonelike building material made by mixing cement and various aggregates, as sand, gravel, or shale, with water and allowing the mixture to harden. Compare REINFORCED CONCRETE. **7.** any of various other artificial building or paving materials, as those containing tar. **8.** a concrete idea or term; a word or notion referring to an actual thing or instance. **9.** a mass formed by coalescence or concretion of particles of matter. —*v.t.* **10.** to treat or lay with concrete. **11.** to form into a mass by coalescence of particles; render solid. **12.** to make real, tangible, or particular. —*v.i.* **13.** to coalesce into a mass; become solid; harden. —**con•crete′ly,** *adv.* —**con•crete′ness,** *n.*

con′crete noun′, *n.* a noun denoting something material and nonabstract, as *chair* or *automobile.* Compare ABSTRACT NOUN.

con•cre•tion (kon krē′shən, kong-), *n.* **1.** the act or process of concreting or becoming substantial; coalescence; solidification. **2.** the state of being concreted. **3.** a solid mass formed by or as if by coalescence or cohesion: *a concretion of melted candies.* **4.** anything that is made real, tangible, or particular. **5.** a solid or calcified mass in the body formed by a disease process. **6.** a rounded mass of mineral matter occurring in sandstone, clay, etc., often in concentric layers about a nucleus. —**con•cre′tion•ar′y,** *adj.*

con•cu•bine (kong′kyə bīn′, kon′-), *n.* **1.** a woman who cohabits with a man to whom she is not legally married. **2.** (among polygamous peoples) a secondary wife, usu. of inferior rank.

con•cu•pis•cence (kon kyo͞o′pi səns, kong-), *n.* **1.** sexual desire; lust. **2.** ardent longing. —**con•cu′pis•cent,** *adj.*

con•cur (kən kûr′), *v.i.,* **-curred, -cur•ring.** **1.** to accord in opinion; agree: *Do you concur with that statement?* **2.** to cooperate; work or act together: *Both parties concurred in urging passage of the bill.* **3.** to coincide; occur at the same time. —**con•cur′ring•ly,** *adv.*

con•cur•rence (kən kûr′əns, -kur′-), *n.* **1.** the act of concurring. **2.** accordance in opinion; agreement. **3.** cooperation, as of agents or causes; combined action or effort. **4.** simultaneous occurrence; coincidence. **5.** *Law.* the equal sharing of a power or claim. Also, **con•cur′ren•cy.**

con•cur•rent (kən kûr′ənt, -kur′-), *adj.* **1.** occurring or existing simultaneously or side by side: *serving two concurrent prison sentences.* **2.** acting in conjunction; cooperating: *the concurrent efforts of medical researchers.* **3.** having equal authority or jurisdiction: *concurrent courts of law.* **4.** accordant or agreeing. **5.** intersecting or tending to intersect at the same point: *four concurrent lines.* —*n.* **6.** a concurrent action, process, effort, etc. —**con•cur′rent•ly,** *adv.*

concur′rent resolu′tion, *n.* a resolution adopted by both branches of a legislature but not having the effect of law.

con•cus•sion (kən kush′ən), *n.* **1.** injury to the brain or spinal cord due to jarring from a blow, fall, or the like. **2.** shock caused by the impact of a collision, blow, etc. **3.** the act or action of violently shaking or jarring. —**con•cus′sive,** *adj.*

con•demn (kən dem′), *v.t.* **1.** to express an unfavorable or adverse judgment on; indicate strong disapproval of; censure. **2.** to sentence to punishment, esp. a severe punishment: *to condemn a murderer to death.* **3.** to pronounce to be guilty. **4.** to force into a specified, usu. unhappy state: *condemned by lack of education to a life of poverty.* **5.** to give grounds for convicting or censuring: *His acts condemn him.* **6.** to judge or pronounce to be unfit for use or service: *to condemn an old building.* **7.** *Law.* to acquire ownership of for a public purpose under the right of eminent domain. —**con•dem′na•ble** (-nə bəl), *adj.* —**con•dem•na•to•ry** (-nə tôr′ē, -tōr′ē), *adj.* —**con•demn′er** (-dem′ər), **con•dem′nor** (-dem′ər, -dem nôr′), *n.*

con•dem•na•tion (kon′dem nā′shən, -dəm-), *n.* **1.** the act of condemning, esp. by law. **2.** the state of being condemned. **3.** strong censure; disapprobation. **4.** a reason for condemning.

con•den•sa•tion (kon′den sā′shən, -dən-), *n.* **1.** the act of condensing or the state of being condensed. **2.** the result or product of condensing. **3.** reduction of a book, speech, or the like to a shorter or terser form; abridgment. **4.** a condensed form, as of a book. **5.** a condensed mass. **6. a.** the act or process of reducing a gas or vapor to a liquid or solid form. **b.** a liquid or solid produced in this manner; condensate. **7.** a reaction between two or more organic molecules leading to the formation of a larger molecule and the elimination of a simple molecule such as water or alcohol. **8.** the process by which atmospheric water vapor liquefies to form fog, clouds, or the like, or solidifies to form snow or hail. —**con′den•sa′tion•al,** *adj.* —**con′den•sa′tive,** *adj.*

con•dense (kən dens′), *v.,* **-densed, -dens•ing.** —*v.t.* **1.** to make more dense or compact; reduce the volume or extent of; concentrate. **2.** to reduce (a text, speech, etc.) to a shorter form; abridge. **3.** to reduce to another and denser form, as a gas or vapor to a liquid or solid state. —*v.i.* **4.** to become denser or more compact. **5.** to reduce a book, speech, or the like to a shorter form. **6.** to become liquid or solid, as a gas or vapor: *The steam condensed into droplets.* —**con•den′sa•ble, con•den′si•ble,** *adj.* —**con•den′sa•bil′i•ty, con•den′si•bil′i•ty,** *n.*

con•densed (kən denst′), *adj.* **1.** reduced in volume, area, length, or scope. **2.** thickened by distillation or evaporation; concentrated. **3.** reduced from a gas to a liquid.

condensed′ milk′, *n.* whole milk reduced by evaporation to a thick consistency, with sugar added.

con•dens•er (kən den′sər), *n.* **1.** a person or thing that condenses. **2.** an apparatus for condensing, esp. for reducing gases or vapors to liquid or solid form. **3.** a lens or combination of lenses that gathers and concentrates light in a specified direction, often used to direct light onto the projection lens in a projection system. **4.** CAPACITOR.

con•de•scend (kon′də send′), *v.i.* **1.** to behave as if one is descending from a superior position, rank, or dignity. **2.** to stoop or deign to do something: *He would not condescend to misrepresent the facts.* **3.** to put aside one's dignity or superiority voluntarily and assume equality with one regarded as inferior.

con•de•scend•ing (kon′də sen′ding), *adj.* showing condescension; implying a descent from dignity or superiority; patronizing. —**con′de•scend′ing•ly,** *adv.*

Con′descend′ing Mas′ter, The, a parable of Jesus. Luke 17:7–10.

con•de•scen•sion (kon′də sen′shən), *n.* **1.** an act or instance of condescending. **2.** behavior that is patronizing or condescending. **3.** voluntary assumption of equality with a person regarded as inferior.

con•dign (kən dīn′), *adj.* well-deserved; fitting; adequate: *condign punishment.* —**con•dign′ly,** *adv.*

con•di•ment (kon′də mənt), *n.* something used to flavor food, as mustard, ketchup, salt, or spices.

con•di•tion (kən dish′ən), *n.* **1.** a particular mode of being of a person or thing; existing state; situation with respect to circumstances. **2.** state of health: *a patient in critical condition.* **3.** fit or requisite state: *to be in no condition to run.* **4.** social position. **5.** a restricting, limiting, or modifying circumstance: *It can happen only under certain conditions.* **6.** a circumstance indispensable to some result; prerequisite: *conditions of acceptance.* **7.** Usu., **conditions.** existing circumstances: *poor living conditions.* **8.** something demanded as an essential part of an agreement; provision; stipulation: *I accept on one condition.* **9.** *Law.* **a.** a stipulation that would alter an agreement should a specified event occur. **b.** the event itself. **10.** an abnormal or diseased state of part of the body: *heart condition; skin condition.* **11.** an academic grade that permits a student failing a course to earn credit for the course by later performance. **12.** ANTECEDENT (def. 6). —*v.t.* **13.** to put in a fit or proper state. **14.** to accustom or inure: *to condition oneself to the cold.* **15.** to form or be a condition of; determine, limit, or restrict as a condition. **16.** to impose a condition on (a student). **17.** to make (something) a condition; stipulate. **18.** to establish a conditioned response in (a subject). **19.** to apply a conditioner to: *to condition one's hair.* —*v.i.* **20.** to make conditions. —**con·di′tion·a·ble,** *adj.*

con·di·tion·al (kən dish′ə nl), *adj.* **1.** imposing, containing, subject to, or depending on a condition; not absolute: *conditional acceptance.* **2.** (of a sentence, clause, mood, or word) involving or expressing a condition, as the first clause in the sentence *If it rains, we won't go.* —*n.* **3.** a sentence, clause, or word expressing a condition. **4.** *Logic.* a proposition expressing implication, as "If A then B." —**con·di′tion·al′i·ty,** *n.* —**con·di′tion·al·ly,** *adv.*

con·di·tioned (kən dish′ənd), *adj.* **1.** existing under or subject to conditions. **2.** characterized by a predictable or consistent pattern of behavior or thought as a result of being subjected to certain circumstances or conditions. **3.** acquired through conditioning: *conditioned behavior patterns.* **4.** in a fit or suitable condition. **5.** accustomed.

condi′tioned response′, *n. Psychol.* a response that becomes associated with a previously unrelated stimulus as a result of pairing the stimulus with another stimulus normally yielding the response. Also called **condi′tioned re′flex.**

con·di·tion·er (kən dish′ə nər), *n.* **1.** a person or thing that conditions. **2.** something added to a substance to enhance its usability, as a water softener. **3.** a cream, lotion, or gel applied to the hair or skin to soften or smooth it.

con·di·tion·ing (kən dish′ə ning), *n.* **1.** a process of changing behavior by rewarding or punishing a subject each time an action is or is performed. **2.** Also called **classical conditioning.** a process in which a previously neutral stimulus comes to evoke a specific response by being repeatedly paired with another stimulus that evokes the response.

con·do (kon′dō), *n., pl.* **-dos.** CONDOMINIUM (defs. 1, 2).

con·do·lence (kən dō′ləns), *n.* Often, **condolences.** expression of sympathy with a person who is suffering sorrow, misfortune, or grief. Sometimes, **con·dole′ment.** —**con·dole′ment,** *adj.*

con·dom (kon′dəm, kun′-), *n.* a thin sheath, usu. of rubber, worn over the penis during sexual intercourse to prevent conception or sexually transmitted disease.

con·do·min·i·um (kon′də min′ē əm), *n.* **1.** an apartment house, office building, or other multiple-unit complex, the units of which are individually owned, with each owner receiving a deed to the unit purchased, including the right to sell or mortgage that unit, and sharing in joint ownership of any common grounds, passageways, etc. **2.** a unit in such a building. **3. a.** joint sovereignty over a territory by several states. **b.** the territory itself. **4.** joint or concurrent dominion.

con·done (kən dōn′), *v.t.,* **-doned, -don·ing.** **1.** to disregard or overlook (something illegal, objectionable, etc.). **2.** to give tacit approval to: *By his silence, he seemed to condone their behavior.* **3.** to pardon or forgive (an offense); excuse. —**con·don′a·ble,** *adj.*

con·dor (kon′dər, -dôr), *n.* either of two New World vultures of the family Cathartidae, *Gymnogyps californianus* (**California condor**) now extinct in the wild, or *Vultur gryphus* (**Andean condor**), the largest flying birds in the Western Hemisphere.

con·dot·tie·re (kon′də tyâr′ā, -tyâr′ē), *n., pl.* **-tie·ri** (-tyâr′ē). **1.** a leader of a private band of mercenary soldiers in Italy, esp. in the 14th and 15th centuries. **2.** any mercenary; soldier of fortune. [< Italian, < *condott(o)* < Latin *conductus* hired man]

con·du·cive (kən dōō′siv, -dyōō′-), *adj.* tending to produce; conducing; contributive (usu. fol. by *to*): *eating habits conducive to good health.* —**con·du′cive·ness,** *n.*

con·duct (*n.* kon′dukt; *v.* kən dukt′), *n.* **1.** personal behavior; way of acting; deportment. **2.** direction, management, or execution: *the conduct of a business.* **3.** the act of leading; guidance; escort. —*v.t.* **4.** to behave or manage (oneself). **5.** to direct in action or course; manage; carry on: *to conduct a test.* **6.** to direct (an orchestra, chorus, etc.) as leader. **7.** to lead or guide; escort: *to conduct a tour.* **8.** to serve as a channel or medium for (heat, electricity, sound, etc.): *Copper conducts electricity.* —*v.i.* **9.** to lead. **10.** to act as conductor, esp. of a musical group. —**con·duct′i·ble,** *adj.* —**con·duct′i·bil′i·ty,** *n.*

con·duct·ance (kən duk′təns), *n.* (esp. in alternating current) the conducting power of a conductor, equal to the real part of the admittance, and, in a circuit with no reactance, equal to the reciprocal of the resistance. *Symbol:* G

con·duc·tion (kən duk′shən), *n.* **1.** the act of conducting, as of water through a pipe. **2. a.** the transfer of heat between two parts of a stationary system at different temperatures. **b.** CONDUCTIVITY (def. 1). **3.** the carrying of sound waves, electrons, heat, or nerve impulses by a nerve or other tissue. —**con·duc′tion·al,** *adj.*

con·duc·tiv·i·ty (kon′duk tiv′i tē), *n., pl.* **-ties.** **1.** the property or power of conducting heat, electricity, or sound. **2.** a measure of the ability of a substance to conduct electric current, equal to the reciprocal of the substance's resistance. *Symbol:* σ

con·duc·tor (kən duk′tər), *n.* **1.** a person who conducts; a leader, guide, director, or manager. **2.** an employee on a bus, train, or other

public conveyance who is in charge of the conveyance and its passengers, collects fares or tickets, etc. **3.** a person who directs an orchestra, band, or chorus. **4.** a substance, body, or device that readily conducts heat, electricity, sound, etc. —**con·duc·to·ri·al** (kon′duk tôr′ē əl, -tōr′-), *adj.* —**con·duc′tor·ship′,** *n.*

con·duit (kon′dwit, -dōō it, -dyōō it, -dit), *n.* **1.** a pipe, tube, or natural channel for conveying water or other fluid. **2.** a channel through which anything is conveyed: *a conduit for information.* **3.** a structure containing ducts for electrical conductors or cables.

con·dyle (kon′dīl, -dl), *n.* **1.** the rounded process at the end of a bone, forming part of a joint. **2.** (in arthropods) a similar process formed from the hard integument. —**con′dy·lar,** *adj.* —**con′dy·loid′,** *adj.*

cone (kōn), *n., v.,* **coned, con·ing.** —*n.* **1. a.** a solid whose surface is generated by a line passing through a fixed point and a fixed plane curve not containing the point, consisting of two equal sections joined at a vertex. **b.** a plane surface resembling the cross section of a solid cone. **2.** anything shaped like a cone: *the cone of a volcano.* **3. a.** the reproductive structure of certain nonflowering trees and shrubs, as the pine, consisting of hard or papery scales bearing naked seeds and arranged in an overlapping whorl around an axis. Compare CONIFER. **b.** a similar structure, as in cycads or club mosses. **4.** one of the cone-shaped cells in the retina of the eye, sensitive to bright light and color. Compare ROD (def. 11). —*v.t.* **5.** to shape like a cone or a segment of a cone.

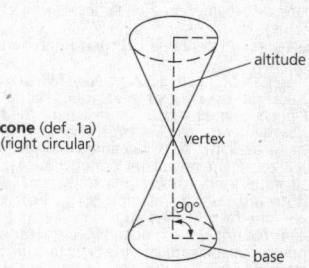

cone (def. 1a)
(right circular)

altitude
vertex
90°
base

cone·flow·er (kōn′flou′ər), *n.* any of several composite plants of the genus *Rudbeckia,* having flowers usu. with yellow rays and a brown or black disk.

cone′ shell′, *n.* any cone-shaped marine gastropod of the family Conidae, having a poison apparatus that fires a stinging dart. Also called **cone′ snail′.**

Con′es·to·ga wag′on (kon′ə stō′gə, kon′-), *n.* a large, broad-wheeled covered wagon, used to transport freight across North America during the early westward migration. Also called **Con′es·to·ga.**

co·ney (kō′nē, kun′ē), *n., pl.* **-neys.** a serranid fish, *Epinephelus fulvus,* of tropical American waters.

con·fab·u·late (kən fab′yə lāt′), *v.i.,* **-lat·ed, -lat·ing. 1.** to converse informally or privately. **2.** *Psychiatry.* to fill a gap in memory with a falsification that the falsifier believes to be true. —**con·fab′u·la′tion,** *n.* —**con·fab′u·la·to′ry** (-lə tôr′ē, -tōr′ē), *adj.*

con·fect (*v.* kən fekt′; *n.* kon′fekt), *v.t.* **1.** to make up, compose, or prepare from various ingredients or materials. **2.** to make into a preserve or confection. **3.** to construct; form; make. —*n.* **4.** a sweet, usu. preserved, confection.

con·fec·tion (kən fek′shən), *n.* **1.** a sweet preparation, as a candy or preserve. **2.** the process of confecting something. **3.** something, as a book or play, regarded as frivolous, amusing, or contrived. **4.** something made up or confected; concoction. **5.** something, as a garment, that is very delicate or elaborate. **6.** a medicinal preparation made with sugar, honey, or syrup.

con·fec·tion·ar·y (kən fek′shə ner′ē), *n., pl.* **-ar·ies,** *adj.* —*n.* **1.** a candy. **2.** a place where confections are kept or made. **3.** CONFECTIONERY (def. 3). —*adj.* **4.** of or like confections or their production.

con·fec·tion·er (kən fek′shə nər), *n.* a person who makes or sells candies and, sometimes, ice cream, cakes, etc.

confec′tioners′ sug′ar, *n.* extra-fine powdered sugar.

con·fec·tion·er·y (kən fek′shə ner′ē), *n., pl.* **-er·ies. 1.** confections or candies collectively. **2.** the work or business of a confectioner. **3.** a confectioner's shop.

con·fed·er·a·cy (kən fed′ər ə sē, -fed′rə sē), *n., pl.* **-cies. 1.** an alliance between persons, parties, states, etc., for some purpose. **2.** a group of persons, parties, states, etc., united by such a confederacy. **3.** a combination of persons for unlawful purposes; conspiracy. **4. the Confederacy,** CONFEDERATE STATES OF AMERICA.

con·fed·er·ate (*adj., n.* kən fed′ər it, -fed′rit; *v.* -fed′ə rāt′), *adj., n., v.,* **-at·ed, -at·ing.** —*adj.* **1.** united in a league, alliance, or conspiracy. **2.** (*cap.*) of or pertaining to the Confederate States of America. —*n.* **3.** a person, group, nation, etc., united with others in a confederacy; ally. **4.** an accomplice, esp. in a mischievous or criminal act. **5.** (*cap.*) a supporter of the Confederate States of America. —*v.t., v.i.* **6.** to unite in a league, alliance, or conspiracy.

Confed′erate Memo′rial Day′, *n.* MEMORIAL DAY (def. 2).

Confed′erate States′ of Amer′ica, *n.* the group of 11 Southern states that seceded from the U.S. in 1860–61.

con•fed•er•a•tion (kən fed′ə rā′shən), *n.* **1.** the act of confederating. **2.** the state of being confederated. **3.** an alliance. **4.** a group of confederates, esp. of states more or less permanently united for common purposes. **5. the Confederation,** the union of the 13 original U.S. states under the Articles of Confederation 1781–89. **6.** (*cap.*) the Canadian federation of Ontario, Quebec, New Brunswick, and Nova Scotia, formed in 1867 and since joined by six more provinces.

con•fer (kən fûr′), *v.*, **-ferred, -fer•ring.** **—***v.i.* **1.** to consult or discuss something together; compare ideas or opinions. **—***v.t.* **2.** to bestow upon as a gift, favor, honor, etc.: *to confer a degree on a graduate.* **—con•fer′•ra•ble,** *adj.* **—con•fer′ral, con•fer′ment,** *n.*

con•fer•ee or **con•fer•ree** (kon′fə rē′), *n.* **1.** a person on whom something is conferred. **2.** a person, group, etc., that confers or takes part in a conference.

con•fer•ence (kon′fər əns, -frəns), *n.*, *v.*, **-enced, -enc•ing.** **—***n.* **1.** a meeting for consultation or discussion: *a conference between a student and her adviser.* **2.** the act of conferring or consulting together; consultation, esp. on an important or serious matter. **3.** a meeting of members of both houses of a legislature to effect a compromise between different versions of a bill. **4.** an association of athletic teams; league. **5. a.** an official assembly of clergy or of clergy and laity. **b.** a group of churches whose representatives regularly meet in such an assembly. **—***v.i.* **6.** to hold or participate in a conference or series of conferences. **—con′fer•en′tial** (-fə ren′shəl), *adj.*

con′ference call′, *n.* a telephone call that interconnects three or more phones simultaneously.

con•fess (kən fes′), *v.t.* **1.** to acknowledge or avow (a fault, crime, misdeed, or weakness) by way of revelation. **2.** to own or admit as true; concede: *I must confess that I haven't read it.* **3.** to declare or acknowledge (one's sins), esp. to God or a priest. **4.** (of a priest) to hear the confession of (a person). **5.** to acknowledge one's belief or faith in; declare adherence to. **6.** to reveal by circumstances. **—***v.i.* **7.** to make confession; plead guilty; own: *to confess to a crime.* **8.** to make confession of sins, esp. to a priest. **9.** (of a priest) to hear confession. **—con•fess′a•ble,** *adj.* **—con•fess′ing•ly,** *adv.*

con•fes•sion (kən fesh′ən), *n.* **1.** acknowledgment; avowal; admission. **2.** acknowledgment or disclosure of sin, esp. to a priest to obtain absolution. **3.** something that is confessed. **4.** a formal, usu. written acknowledgment of guilt by a person accused of a crime. **5.** Also called **confes′sion of faith′.** a formal profession of religious belief. **6.** an organized religious group sharing the same beliefs and doctrines.

con•fes•sion•al (kən fesh′ə nl), *adj.* **1.** of, characteristic of, or based on confession. **—***n.* **2.** a place set apart for the hearing of confessions by a priest.

Con•fes•sions (kən fesh′ənz), an autobiography (A.D. 400) by St. Augustine.

con•fes•sor (kən fes′ər), *n.* **1.** a person who confesses. **2.** a priest authorized to hear confessions. **3.** a male saint who has suffered persecution but not martyrdom.

con•fet•ti (kən fet′ē), *n.* **1.** (*used with a sing. v.*) small bits of paper, usu. colored, thrown or dropped from a height at festive events, as parades or weddings. **2.** confections; bonbons.

con•fi•dant (kon′fi dant′, -dänt′, -dənt, kon′fi dant′, -dänt′), *n.* a person to whom secrets are confided or with whom private matters and problems are discussed.

con•fi•dante (kon′fi dant′, -dänt′, kon′fi dant′, -dänt′), *n.* a woman to whom secrets are confided or with whom private matters and problems are discussed.

con•fide (kən fīd′), *v.*, **-fid•ed, -fid•ing.** **—***v.i.* **1.** to impart secrets trustfully; discuss private matters or problems (usu. fol. by *in*). **2.** to have full trust; have faith. **—***v.t.* **3.** to tell in assurance of secrecy. **4.** to entrust; commit to the charge of another. **—con•fid′er,** *n.*

con•fi•dence (kon′fi dəns), *n.* **1.** belief in the powers, trustworthiness, or reliability of a person or thing; full trust; reliance. **2.** belief in oneself and one's powers or abilities; self-confidence; self-reliance; assurance. **3.** certitude; assurance: *to speak with confidence of a fact.* **4.** a confidential communication: *to exchange confidences.* **5.** (esp. in European politics) the wish to retain an incumbent government in office, as shown by a vote on a particular issue. **—*Idiom.*** **6. in confidence,** as a secret or private matter not to be divulged.

con′fidence game′, *n.* a swindle in which the swindler, after gaining the victim's confidence, robs the victim by cheating at a gambling game, appropriating funds entrusted for investment, or the like. Also called, *Brit.*, **con′fidence trick′.**

con•fi•dent (kon′fi dənt), *adj.* **1.** having strong belief or full assurance; sure: *confident of success.* **2.** sure of oneself and one's abilities, correctness, or likelihood of success; self-confident; assured. **3.** excessively bold; presumptuous. **—***n.* **4.** a confidant. **—con′fi•dent•ly,** *adv.*

con•fi•den•tial (kon′fi den′shəl), *adj.* **1.** spoken, written, or acted on in strict confidence; secret; private. **2.** indicating confidence or intimacy; imparting private matters: *a confidential tone of voice.* **3.** entrusted with secrets or private affairs: *a confidential secretary.* **4.** designating the category of security classification below secret, or a document assigned to this category. **—con′fi•den′ti•al′i•ty,** *n.* **—con′fi•den′tial•ly,** *adv.*

con•fig•u•ra•tion (kən fig′yə rā′shən), *n.* **1.** the relative disposition or arrangement of the parts or elements of a thing. **2.** external form, as resulting from this; conformation. **3.** an atomic spatial arrangement that is fixed by the chemical bonding in a molecule and that cannot be altered without breaking bonds (contrasted with *conformation*). **4.** a computer plus the equipment connected to it. **5.** GESTALT. **—con•fig′u•ra′•tion•al, con•fig′u•ra•tive** (-yər ə tiv, -yə rā′tiv), *adj.* **—con•fig′u•ra′•tion•al•ly,** *adv.*

con•fig•ure (kən fig′yər), *v.t.*, **-ured, -ur•ing.** to put together or arrange the parts of in a specific way or for a specific purpose; form into a configuration.

con•fine (kən fīn′ *for 1, 2;* kon′fīn *for 3, 4*), *v.*, **-fined, -fin•ing,** *n.* **—***v.t.* **1.** to enclose within bounds; limit or restrict: *Confine your remarks to the subject at hand.* **2.** to shut or keep in; prevent from leaving a place because of imprisonment, illness, discipline, etc. **—***n.* **3.** Usu., **confines.** a boundary or bound; limit; border. **4.** Often, **confines.** region; territory.

con•fined (kən fīnd′), *adj.* **1.** limited or restricted. **2.** kept from leaving a place by illness, imprisonment, etc. **3.** being in childbirth; being in parturition. **—con•fin′ed•ly,** *adv.* **—con•fin′ed•ness,** *n.*

con•fine•ment (kən fīn′mənt), *n.* **1.** the act of confining. **2.** the state of being confined. **3.** childbirth.

con•firm (kən fûrm′), *v.t.* **1.** to establish the truth, accuracy, validity, or genuineness of; corroborate; verify: *to confirm one's suspicions.* **2.** to acknowledge with definite assurance; make certain or definite: *to confirm a reservation.* **3.** to make valid or binding by some formal or legal act; sanction; ratify. **4.** to make firm or firmer; add strength to. **5.** to strengthen (a person) in habit, resolution, opinion, etc. **6.** to administer the rite of confirmation to. **—con•firm′a•ble,** *adj.* **—con•firm′a•bil′•i•ty,** *n.* **—con•firm′er;** *Law,* **con•fir•mor** (kon′fər môr′, kən fûr′mər), *n.*

con•fir•ma•tion (kon′fər mā′shən), *n.* **1.** the act of confirming. **2.** the state of being confirmed. **3.** something that confirms, as a corroborative statement or piece of evidence. **4.** a rite administered to baptized persons, as a Roman Catholic sacrament endowing gifts of the Holy Spirit or a ceremony of admission to full communion with a Protestant church. **5.** a ceremony among Reform and some Conservative Jews in which a young person is formally admitted as an adult member of the Jewish community. **—con′fir•ma′tion•al,** *adj.*

confirma′tion hear′ing, *n.* a proceeding to examine a nominee's fitness for public office.

con•firmed (kən fûrmd′), *adj.* **1.** made certain as to truth, accuracy, validity, etc. **2.** settled; ratified. **3.** firmly established in a habit or condition; inveterate: *a confirmed bachelor.* **4.** given additional determination; made resolute. **5.** having received the religious rite of confirmation. **—con•firm′ed•ly,** *adv.*

con•fis•cate (kon′fə skāt′, kən fis′kāt), *v.*, **-cat•ed, -cat•ing,** *adj.* **—***v.t.* **1.** to seize as forfeited to the public domain; appropriate, by way of penalty, for public use. **2.** to seize by or as if by authority; appropriate summarily. **—***adj.* **3.** seized. **—con′fis•cat′a•ble,** *adj.* **—con′fis•ca′•tion,** *n.* **—con′fis•ca′tor,** *n.*

con•fla•gra•tion (kon′flə grā′shən), *n.* a destructive fire, usu. an extensive one. **—con′fla•gra′tive,** *adj.*

con•flate (kən flāt′), *v.t.*, **-flat•ed, -flat•ing.** to fuse into one entity; merge; combine. **—con•fla′tion,** *n.*

con•flict (*v.* kən flikt′; *n.* kon′flikt), *v.i.* **1.** to be contradictory, at variance, or in opposition; clash; disagree. **2.** to fight or contend; do battle. **—***n.* **3.** a fight, battle, or struggle, esp. a prolonged one; strife. **4.** controversy; quarrel. **5.** antagonism or opposition, as between interests or principles: *a conflict of opinions.* **6.** discord of action, feeling, or effect. **7.** incompatibility or interference, as of one idea, event, or activity with another: *a conflict in the schedule.* **8.** a mental struggle arising from opposing demands or impulses. **9.** a striking together; collision. **—con•flict′ing,** *adj.*

con′flict of in′terest, *n.* the circumstance of a public officeholder, corporate officer, etc., whose personal interests might benefit from his or her official actions or influence.

con•flu•ence (kon′flo͞o əns), *n.* **1.** a flowing together of two or more streams, rivers, etc. **2.** their place of junction. **3.** a body of water formed by confluence. **4.** a coming together of people or things; concourse. **5.** a crowd or throng; assemblage. Sometimes, **con′flux** (-fluks).

con•flu•ent (kon′flo͞o ənt), *adj.* **1.** flowing or running together; blending into one: *confluent rivers; confluent ideas.* **2.** characterized by confluent efflorescences: *confluent smallpox.* **—***n.* **3.** a confluent stream. **4.** a tributary stream.

con•form (kən fôrm′), *v.i.* **1.** to act in accordance or harmony; comply (usu. fol. by *to*): *to conform to rules.* **2.** to act in accord with the prevailing standards, attitudes, practices, etc., of society or a group. **3.** to be or become similar in form, nature, or character. **4.** to be in harmony or accord. **5.** to comply with the usages of an established church, esp. the Church of England. **—***v.t.* **6.** to make similar in form, nature, or character. **7.** to bring into agreement, correspondence, or harmony. **—con•form′er,** *n.* **—con•form′ing•ly,** *adv.* **—con•form′ist,** *n.*, *adj.*

con•form•a•ble (kən fôr′mə bəl), *adj.* **1.** corresponding in form, nature, or character; similar. **2.** compliant; obedient; submissive. **3.** of or pertaining to an unbroken sequence of geologic strata or beds, characteristic of uninterrupted deposition.

con•for•mal (kən fôr′məl), *adj.* of or designating a map or transformation in which angles and scale are preserved.

con•for•ma•tion (kon′fôr mā′shən), *n.* **1.** manner of formation; structure; form, as of a physical entity. **2.** symmetrical disposition or arrangement of parts. **3.** the act or process of conforming; adaptation. **4.** the state of being conformed. **5.** an atomic spatial arrangement that results from rotation of carbon atoms about single bonds within an organic molecule (contrasted with *configuration*). **—con′for•ma′tion•al,** *adj.*

con•form•i•ty (kən fôr′mi tē), *n., pl.* **-ties. 1.** action in accord with prevailing social standards, attitudes, practices, etc. **2.** correspondence in form, nature, or character; agreement; congruity. **3.** compliance or acquiescence; obedience. **4.** the relationship between adjacent conformable geologic strata. Compare UNCONFORMITY (def. 2).

con•found (kon found′, kən-; *for 6 usu.* kon′found′), *v.t.* **1.** to perplex or amaze; bewilder; confuse. **2.** to throw into confusion or disorder. **3.** to throw into increased confusion or disorder. **4.** to treat or regard erroneously as identical; mix or associate by mistake: *truth confounded with error.* **5.** to mingle so that the elements cannot be distinguished or separated. **6.** to damn (used in mild imprecations): *Confound it!* **7.** to contradict or refute: *to confound their arguments.* **8.** to put to shame; abash. **—con•found′a•ble,** *adj.* **—con•found′er,** *n.* **—con•found′ing•ly,** *adv.*

con•found•ed (kon foun′did, kən-), *adj.* bewildered; confused; perplexed. **—con•found′ed•ly,** *adv.*

con•front (kən frunt′), *v.t.* **1.** to face in hostility or defiance; oppose. **2.** to present for acknowledgment, contradiction, etc.; set face to face: *They confronted him with the evidence.* **3.** to stand or come in front of; meet face to face. **4.** to encounter as something to be dealt with: *the obstacles that confronted us.* **5.** to bring together for examination or comparison. **—con•front′al,** *n.* **—con•front′er,** *n.*

con•fron•ta•tion (kon′frən tā′shən, -frun-), *n.* **1.** an act of confronting. **2.** the state of being confronted. **3.** a meeting of persons face to face. **4.** an open conflict of opposing ideas, forces, etc.

con•fron•ta•tion•al (kon′frən tā′shə nl, -frun-) also **con•fron•ta•tive** (kon′frən tā′tiv, kən frun′tə-), *adj.* tending toward or ready for confrontation or conflict.

Con•fu•cian•ism (kən fyōō′shə niz′əm), *n.* the teachings on ethics, education, and statesmanship of Confucius and his disciples, stressing love for humanity, ancestor worship, honoring parents, and harmony in thought and conduct. **—Con•fu′cian•ist,** *n., adj.*

Con•fu•cius (kən fyōō′shəs), *n.* 551?–478? B.C., Chinese philosopher and teacher. Chinese, **K'ung Fu-tzu. —Con•fu′cian,** *adj., n.*

con•fuse (kən fyōōz′), *v.t.,* **-fused, -fus•ing. 1.** to perplex or bewilder: *The flood of questions confused me.* **2.** to make unclear: *The new evidence tended to confuse the issue.* **3.** to fail to distinguish between; associate by mistake: *I always confuse the twins.* **4.** to disconcert or abash. **5.** to combine without order; jumble; disorder. **—con•fus′a•ble,** *adj.* **—con•fus′a•bil′i•ty,** *n.* **—con•fus′ed•ly,** *adv.*

con•fu•sion (kən fyōō′zhən), *n.* **1.** the act of confusing. **2.** the state of being confused. **3.** disorder; upheaval; tumult; chaos: *The army retreated in confusion.* **4.** lack of clearness or distinctness. **5.** perplexity; bewilderment. **6.** embarrassment or abashment. **7.** a disturbed mental state; disorientation. **—con•fu′sion•al,** *adj.*

con•fute (kən fyōōt′), *v.t.,* **-fut•ed, -fut•ing. 1.** to prove to be false, invalid, or defective; disprove: *to confute an argument.* **2.** to prove (a person) to be wrong by argument or proof. **—con•fut′a•ble,** *adj.* **—con•fut′er,** *n.*

con•ga (kong′gə), *n., pl.* **-gas,** *v.,* **-gaed, -ga•ing.** **—***n.* **1.** a Cuban ballroom dance that consists of three steps forward followed by a kick, characteristically performed by a group following a leader in a single line. **2.** a tall, conical Afro-Cuban drum played with the hands. **—***v.i.* **3.** to dance a conga.

con′ game′, *n.* CONFIDENCE GAME.

con•geal (kən jēl′), *v.t., v.i.* **1.** to change from a soft or fluid state to a rigid or solid state, as by cooling or freezing. **2.** to coagulate, as a fluid. **3.** to make or become fixed, as ideas, sentiments, or principles. **—con•geal′a•ble,** *adj.* **—con•geal′er,** *n.* **—con•geal′ment,** *n.*

con•gen•ial (kən jēn′yəl), *adj.* **1.** agreeable, suitable, or pleasing in nature or character; pleasant: *congenial surroundings.* **2.** suited or adapted in tastes, temperament, etc.; compatible: *a congenial couple.* **—con•ge′ni•al′i•ty** (-jē′nē al′i tē), **—con•gen′ial•ly,** *adv.*

con•gen•i•tal (kən jen′i tl), *adj.* **1.** present or existing at the time of birth: *a congenital abnormality.* **2.** having by nature a specified character: *a congenital fool.* **—con•gen′i•tal•ly,** *adv.*

con•ger (kong′gər), *n.* **1.** a large marine eel, *Conger conger,* reaching a length of up to 10 ft. (3 m), used for food. **2.** any other eel of the family Congridae. Also called **con′ger eel′.**

con•ge•ries (kon jēr′ēz, kon′jə rēz), *n.* (*used with a sing. or pl. v.*) a collection of items or parts in one mass; assemblage; aggregation; heap.

con•gest (kən jest′), *v.t.* **1.** to fill to excess; overcrowd or overburden; clog. **2.** to cause an unnatural accumulation of blood or other fluid in (a body part or blood vessel): *The cold congested her sinuses.* **—***v.i.* **3.** to become congested. **—con•gest′i•ble,** *adj.* **—con•ges′tion,** *n.* **—con•ges′tive,** *adj.*

con•ges•tion (kən jes′chən), *n.* **1.** overcrowding; clogging: *traffic congestion.* **2.** clogging in a blood vessel, duct, or other body part due to an accumulation of fluid, mucus, etc.: *nasal congestion.*

conges′tive heart′ fail′ure, *n.* HEART FAILURE (def. 2).

con•gi•us (kon′jē əs), *n., pl.* **-gi•i** (-jē ī′). **1.** (in prescriptions) a gallon (3.7853 liters). **2.** an ancient Roman unit of liquid measure equal to about 0.8 U.S. gallon (3.2 liters).

con•glom•er•ate (*n., adj.* kən glom′ər it, kəng-; *v.* -ə rāt′), *n., adj., v.,* **-at•ed, -at•ing. —***n.* **1.** anything composed of heterogeneous elements. **2.** a corporation consisting of a number of subsidiary companies or divisions in a variety of unrelated industries. **3.** a rock consisting of pebbles or the like embedded in a finer cementing material; consolidated gravel. **—***adj.* **4.** consisting of heterogeneous parts or elements. **5.** gathered into a rounded mass, or consisting of parts so gathered; clustered. **6.** of or pertaining to a corporate conglomerate. **—***v.t.* **7.** to bring together into a cohering mass. **8.** to gather into a ball or rounded mass. **—***v.i.* **9.** to collect or cluster together. **10.** (of a company) to become part of or merge with a conglomerate.

con•glom•er•a•tion (kən glom′ə rā′shən, kəng-), *n.* **1.** the act of conglomerating or the state of being conglomerated. **2.** a cohering mass; cluster. **3.** a heterogeneous combination: *a conglomeration of ideas.* **—con•glom′er•a•tive** (-ər ə tiv, -ə rā′tiv), *adj.*

Con•go (kong′gō), *n.* **1. Democratic Republic of the.** Formerly, **Zaire** (1971–97), **Democratic Republic of the Congo** (1960–71), **Belgian Congo** (1908–60), **Congo Free State** (1885–1908). a republic in central Africa: a former Belgian colony; gained independence 1960. 47,440,362; 905,568 sq. mi. (2,345,410 sq. km). *Cap.:* Kinshasa. **2. People's Republic of the,** a republic in central Africa, W of the Democratic Republic of the Congo: a former French territory; gained independence 1960. 2,583,198; 132,046 sq. mi. (341,999 sq. km). *Cap.:* Brazzaville. Formerly, **French Congo, Middle Congo. 3.** Also called **Zaire.** a river in central Africa, flowing in a great loop from SE Democratic Republic of the Congo to the Atlantic. ab. 3000 mi. (4800 km) long. **4.** KONGO (def. 1). **—Con′go•lese′** (-gə lēz′, -lēs′), *adj., n., pl.* **-lese.**

con•grat•u•late (kən grach′ə lāt′ *or, often,* -graj′-, kəng-), *v.t.,* **-lat•ed, -lat•ing. 1.** to express pleasure to (a person) on a happy occasion, praiseworthy accomplishment, or good fortune. **2.** to feel satisfaction or pride in (oneself) for an accomplishment or good fortune: *She congratulated herself on her narrow escape.* **—con•grat′u•la′tor,** *n.* **—con•grat′u•la•to′ry** (-tôr′ē, -tōr′ē), *adj.*

con•grat•u•la•tion (kən grach′ə lā′shən *or, often,* -graj′-, kəng-), *n.* **1.** the act of congratulating. **2. congratulations,** an expression of pleasure in the success or good fortune of another. **—***interj.* **3. congratulations,** (used to express pleasure in the success or good fortune of another.)

con•gre•gate (*v.* kong′gri gāt′; *adj.* kong′gri git, -gāt′), *v.,* **-gat•ed, -gat•ing,** *adj.* **—***v.i., v.t.* **1.** to come or bring together in a crowd, body, or mass; assemble, esp. in large numbers; collect. **—***adj.* **2.** congregated; assembled. **3.** formed by collecting; collective. **4.** of or pertaining to group housing that combines individual living quarters with communal facilities for food, care, and recreation. **—con′gre•ga′tive,** *adj.* **—con′gre•ga′tor,** *n.*

con•gre•ga•tion (kong′gri gā′shən), *n.* **1.** an assembly of people brought together or regularly meeting together for common religious worship. **2.** the act of congregating or the state of being congregated. **3.** a gathered or assembled body; assemblage. **4.** an organization formed for providing church services; a local church society. **5.** (in the Old Testament) the people of Israel. **6.** (in the New Testament) the Christian Church. **7.** (in Roman Catholicism) **a.** a committee of cardinals or other ecclesiastics. **b.** a community of men or women, either with or without vows, observing a common rule.

con•gre•ga•tion•al (kong′gri gā′shə nl), *adj.* **1.** of or pertaining to a congregation. **2.** (*cap.*) pertaining or adhering to a form of Protestant church government in which each local church acts as a self-governing body. **—con′gre•ga′tion•al•ly,** *adv.*

con•gre•ga•tion•al•ism (kong′gri gā′shə nl iz′əm), *n.* **1.** a form of church government in which each local religious society is self-governing. **2.** (*cap.*) the system of government and doctrine of Congregational churches. **—con′gre•ga′tion•al•ist,** *n., adj.*

con•gress (*n.* kong′gris; *v.* kən gres′, kəng-), *n.* **1.** (*cap.*) **a.** the national legislative body of the U.S., consisting of the Senate and the House of Representatives. **b.** this body as it exists for a period of two years during which it has the same membership: *the 100th Congress.* **c.** a session of this body. **2.** the national legislative body of a nation, esp. of a republic. **3.** a formal meeting of representatives for the discussion, arrangement, or promotion of some matter of common interest. **4.** the act of coming together; encounter; meeting. **5.** an association, esp. one composed of representatives of various organizations. **6.** familiar relations; dealings; intercourse. **7.** coitus; sexual intercourse. **—***v.i.* **8.** to assemble together; meet in congress.

con•gres•sion•al (kən gresh′ə nl, kəng-), *adj.* **1.** of or pertaining to a congress. **2.** (*cap.*) of or pertaining to the U.S. Congress. **—con•gres′sion•al•ist,** *n.* **—con•gres′sion•al•ly,** *adv.*

Congres′sional dis′trict, *n.* one of a fixed number of districts into which a state is divided, each district electing one member to the national House of Representatives. Compare ASSEMBLY DISTRICT, SENATORIAL DISTRICT.

Congres′sional Med′al of Hon′or, *n.* MEDAL OF HONOR.

Congres′sional Rec′ord, *n.* the record of the proceedings of the U.S. Congress, with a transcript of the discussion, published daily by the government while Congress is in session.

con•gress•man (kong′gris mən), *n., pl.* **-men.** (*often cap.*) a member of a congress, esp. of the U.S. House of Representatives.

Con′gress of Indus′trial Organiza′tions, *n.* a federation of affiliated industrial labor unions, founded 1935 within the American Federation of Labor but independent of it 1938–55. *Abbr.:* C.I.O., CIO

Con′gress of Vien′na, *n.* an international conference (1814–15) held at Vienna after Napoleon's banishment to Elba, aimed at territorial resettlement and restoration to power of the crowned heads of Europe.

con•gress•per•son (kong′gris pûr′sən), *n.* (*often cap.*) a member of a congress, esp. of the U.S. House of Representatives.

con•gress•wom•an (kong′gris wo͝om′ən), *n., pl.* **-wom•en.** (*often cap.*) a woman who is a member of a congress, esp. of the U.S. House of Representatives.

con•gru•ence (kong′gro͞o əns, kən gro͞o′-, kəng-), *n.* **1.** the quality or state of agreeing or corresponding. **2.** a relation between two numbers in which the numbers give the same remainder when divided by a given number. —**con′gru•ent,** *adj.* —**con•gru′i•ty,** *n.*

con•gru•ous (kong′gro͞o əs), *adj.* **1.** exhibiting harmony of parts. **2.** appropriate or fitting. —**con′gru•ous•ly,** *adv.*

con•ic (kon′ik), *adj.* **1.** Also, **con′i•cal.** having the form of, resembling, or pertaining to a cone. —*n.* **2.** CONIC SECTION. —**con′i•cal•ly,** *adv.* —**co•nic•i•ty** (ko nis′i tē), **con′i•cal•ness,** *n.*

con•ics (kon′iks), *n.* (*used with a sing. v.*) the branch of geometry that deals with conic sections.

con′ic sec′tion, *n.* a curve formed by the intersection of a plane with a right circular cone; an ellipse, a circle, a parabola, or a hyperbola. Also called **conic.**

co•ni•fer (kō′nə fər, kon′ə-), *n.* any of a class, Pinopsida, of chiefly evergreen trees and shrubs, as those of the pine and cypress families, that bear both seeds and pollen on dry scales arranged as a cone. —**co•nif•er•ous** (kō nif′ər əs, kə-), *adj.*

con•jec•tur•al (kən jek′chər əl), *adj.* **1.** of, of the nature of, or involving conjecture; problematical; speculative. **2.** given to making conjectures. —**con•jec′tur•al•ly,** *adv.*

con•jec•ture (kən jek′chər), *n., v.,* **-tured, -tur•ing.** —*n.* **1.** the formation or expression of an opinion or theory without sufficient evidence for proof. **2.** an opinion or theory so formed or expressed; speculation; surmise. —*v.t.* **3.** to conclude or suppose from evidence insufficient to ensure reliability. —*v.i.* **4.** to form conjectures. —**con•jec′tur•a•ble,** *adj.* —**con•jec′tur•a•bly,** *adv.* —**con•jec′tur•er,** *n.*

con•join (kən join′), *v.t., v.i.* **1.** to join together; unite; combine; associate. **2.** to link linguistic units of the same grammatical rank, as coordinate clauses. —**con•join′er,** *n.*

con•joint (kən joint′), *adj.* **1.** joined together; united; combined; associated. **2.** of, formed by, or involving two or more in combination; joint. —**con•joint′ly,** *adv.* —**con•joint′ness,** *n.*

con•ju•gal (kon′jə gəl), *adj.* **1.** of, pertaining to, or characteristic of marriage. **2.** of or pertaining to the relation of husband and wife. —**con′ju•gal′i•ty,** *n.* —**con′ju•gal•ly,** *adv.*

con′jugal rights′, *n.pl.* the sexual rights and privileges conferred on husband and wife by the marriage bond.

con•ju•gate (*v.* kon′jə gāt′; *adj., n.* kon′jə git, -gāt′), *v.,* **-gat•ed, -gat•ing,** *adj., n.* —*v.t.* **1. a.** to recite or display all or some subsets of the inflected forms of (a verb) in a fixed order: *to conjugate the present tense of the verb* be. **b.** to inflect (a verb). **2.** to join together, esp. in marriage. —*v.i.* **3.** *Biol.* to unite; to undergo conjugation. **4.** (of a verb) to be characterized by conjugation. —*adj.* **5.** joined together, esp. in a pair or pairs; coupled. **6.** (of words) having a common derivation. **7.** *Math.* **a.** (of two points, lines, etc.) so related as to be interchangeable in the enunciation of certain properties. **b.** (of two complex numbers) differing only in the sign of the imaginary part. **8.** (of an acid and a base) related by the loss or gain of a proton: *NH_3 is a base conjugate to NH_4^+.* —*n.* **9.** one of a group of conjugate words. **10.** *Math.* **a.** either of two conjugate points, lines, etc. **b.** either of a pair of complex numbers of the type $a + bi$ and $a - bi$, where a and b are real numbers and i is imaginary. —**con′ju•ga•ble** (-gə bəl), *adj.* —**con′ju•ga•bly,** *adv.* —**con′ju•ga′tive,** *adj.* —**con′ju•ga′tor,** *n.*

con•ju•ga•tion (kon′jə gā′shən), *n.* **1. a.** the inflection of verbs. **b.** the whole set of inflected forms of a verb or the recital or display thereof in a fixed order. **c.** a class of verbs having similar sets of inflected forms: *the Latin second conjugation.* **2.** an act of joining. **3.** the state of being joined together; union; conjunction. **4. a.** (in bacteria, protozoans, etc.) the temporary fusion of two organisms with an exchange of nuclear material. **b.** (in certain algae and fungi) the fusion of a male and female gamete as a form of sexual reproduction. —**con′ju•ga′tion•al,** *adj.*

con•junc•tion (kən jungk′shən), *n.* **1.** a member of a small class of words functioning as connectors between words, phrases, clauses, or sentences, as *and, because, but,* and *unless. Abbr.:* conj. **2.** the act of conjoining; combination. **3.** union; association: *The police worked in conjunction with the army.* **4.** a combination of events or circumstances. **5.** *Logic.* a compound proposition that is true only if all of its component propositions are true. **6. a.** the coincidence of two or more heavenly bodies at the same celestial longitude. **b.** such a coincidence regarded astrologically as a fusion of planetary influences. —**con•junc′tion•al,** *adj.* —**con•junc′tion•al•ly,** *adv.*

con•junc•ti•va (kon′jungk tī′və), *n., pl.* **-vas, -vae** (-vē). the mucous membrane that covers the exposed portion of the eyeball and lines the inner surface of the eyelids. —**con′junc•ti′val,** *adj.*

con•junc•tive (kən jungk′tiv), *adj.* **1.** serving to connect; connective: *conjunctive tissue.* **2.** conjoined; joint. **3. a.** pertaining to, being, or functioning like a conjunction. **b.** (of an adverb) serving to connect two clauses or sentences, as *however* or *furthermore.* —*n.* **4.** a conjunctive expression; conjunction. —**con•junc′tive•ly,** *adv.*

con•junc•ti•vi•tis (kən jungk′tə vī′tis), *n.* inflammation of the conjunctiva.

con•junc•ture (kən jungk′chər), *n.* **1.** a combination of circumstances; a particular state of affairs. **2.** a critical state of affairs; crisis. **3.** conjunction; joining. —**con•junc′tur•al,** *adj.*

con•jure (kon′jər, kun′- *for 1–5, 7–10;* kən jo͝or′ *for 6*), *v.,* **-jured, -jur•ing,** *n.* —*v.t.* **1.** to affect or influence by or as if by invocation or spell. **2.** to effect or produce by or as if by magic: *to conjure a miracle.* **3.** to call upon or command (a devil or spirit) by invocation or spell. **4.** to call or bring into existence by or as if by magic (usu. fol. by *up*). **5.** to bring to mind (usu. fol. by *up*). **6.** to appeal to or charge solemnly. —*v.i.* **7.** to call upon or command a devil or spirit by invocation or spell. **8.** to practice magic. **9.** to practice legerdemain. —*n.* **10.** *Chiefly Southern U.S.* an act or instance of witchcraft.

con•jur•er or **con•ju•ror** (kon′jər ər, kun′- *for 1, 2;* kən jo͝or′ər *for 3*), *n.* **1.** a person who conjures spirits or practices magic; magician. **2.** a person who practices legerdemain; juggler. **3.** a person who solemnly charges or entreats.

conk[1] (kongk, kôngk), *Slang.* —*v.t.* **1.** to strike on the head. —*n.* **2.** the head. **3.** a blow on the head.

conk[2] (kongk, kôngk), *v.i. Slang.* **1.** to break down or fail, as a machine or engine (often fol. by *out*). **2.** to slow down or stop; lose energy (often fol. by *out*). **3.** to go to sleep (usu. fol. by *off* or *out*). **4.** to lose consciousness; faint (usu. fol. by *out*). **5.** to die.

conk[3] (kongk, kôngk), *n.* the shelflike fruiting body of certain wood-decaying fungi; bracket. —**conk′y,** *adj.*

conk[4] (kongk, kôngk), *n.* Also called **process. 1.** a method of chemically straightening the hair. **2.** a hairstyle in which the hair is chemically straightened and sometimes set into waves. —*v.t.* **3.** to straighten (hair) by the use of chemicals; process.

Conn., Connecticut.

con•nate (kon′āt), *adj.* **1.** existing in a person or thing from birth or origin; inborn. **2.** associated in birth or origin. **3.** allied or agreeing in nature; cognate. **4.** (of anatomical parts) firmly united; fused. **5.** congenitally joined, as leaves. **6.** trapped in sediment at the time the sediment was deposited: *connate water.* —**con′nate•ly,** *adv.* —**con′nate•ness,** *n.* —**con•na•tion** (kə nā′shən), *n.*

con•nat•u•ral (kə nach′ər əl, -nach′rəl), *adj.* **1.** belonging to one by nature or from birth or origin; inborn. **2.** of the same or a similar nature. —**con•nat′u•ral•ly,** *adv.* —**con•nat′u•ral′i•ty,** *n.*

con•nect (kə nekt′), *v.t.* **1.** to join, link, or fasten together. **2.** to establish telephone communication between. **3.** to have as an accompanying or associated feature. **4.** to cause to be associated in a relationship. **5.** to associate mentally or emotionally. **6.** to link to an electrical or communications system; hook up. —*v.i.* **7.** to become connected; join or unite. **8.** (of trains, buses, etc.) to run so as to make connections (often fol. by *with*). **9.** to establish a sympathetic or harmonious relationship. **10.** *Informal.* to meet or establish communication; make contact. **11.** to make contact for the illegal sale or purchase of drugs. **12.** to hit successfully or solidly: *The batter connected for a home run.* —**con•nec′tor, con•nect′er,** *n.* —**con•nect′i•ble, con•nect′a•ble,** *adj.* —**con•nect′i•bil′i•ty, con•nect′a•bil′i•ty,** *n.*

Con•nect•i•cut (kə net′i kət), *n.* **1.** a state in the NE United States. 3,274,238; 5009 sq. mi. (12,975 sq. km). *Cap.:* Hartford. *Abbr.:* Conn., Ct., CT **2.** a river flowing S from N New Hampshire through Massachusetts and Connecticut into Long Island Sound. 407 mi. (655 km) long.

Connect′icut Com′promise, *n.* a compromise adopted at the Constitutional Convention, providing the states with equal representation in the Senate and proportional representation in the House of Representatives. Compare NEW JERSEY PLAN, VIRGINIA PLAN.

con•nec•tion (kə nek′shən), *n.* **1.** the act or state of connecting. **2.** the state of being connected. **3.** anything that connects; link: *an electrical connection.* **4.** association; relationship: *no connection with any other firm of the same name.* **5.** logical association or development; mental association: *to make a connection between two events; in connection with your last remark.* **6.** contextual relation; context, as of a word. **7.** Usu., **connections.** associates, relatives, or friends, esp. considered as having influence or power. **8.** the meeting of trains, planes, etc., for transfer of passengers. **9.** Often, **connections.** a transfer by a passenger from one conveyance to another: *to miss connections.* **10.** the conveyance boarded in making connections. **11.** a channel of communication: *a bad telephone connection.* **12.** a circle of friends or associates or a member of such a circle. **13.** a relative, esp. by marriage or distant blood relationship. **14.** a person who sells illegal drugs. **15.** a source of supply, esp. for scarce or illegal materials or goods. **16.** a group of persons connected as by political or religious ties. **17.** sexual intercourse. Also, *Brit.,* **connexion.** —**con•nec′tion•al,** *adj.*

con•nec•tive (kə nek′tiv), *adj.* **1.** serving or tending to connect. —*n.* **2.** something that connects. **3.** a word, as a conjunction, used to connect words, phrases, clauses, and sentences. **4.** *Bot.* the tissue joining the two cells of an anther. —**con•nec′tive•ly,** *adv.* —**con•nec•tiv•i•ty** (kon′ek tiv′i tē), *n.*

connec′tive tis′sue, *n.* a kind of tissue that connects, supports, or surrounds other tissues and organs, including tendons, bone, cartilage, and fatty tissue.

con•nip•tion (kə nip′shən), *n.* Often, **conniptions.** a fit of hysterical excitement or anger. Also called **connip′tion fit′.**

con•nive (kə nīv′), *v.i.*, **-nived, -niv•ing.** **1.** to cooperate secretly; conspire. **2.** to avoid noticing something one is expected to oppose or condemn; give aid to wrongdoing by forbearing to act or speak (usu. fol. by *at*). **3.** to be indulgent toward something others oppose or criticize (usu. fol. by *at*). [< Latin *co(n)nīvēre* to wink, turn a blind eye to] —**con•niv′er,** *n.* —**con•niv′ing•ly,** *adv.*

con•nois•seur (kon′ə sûr′, -so͝or′), *n.* **1.** a person esp. competent to pass critical judgments in an art or in matters of taste. **2.** a discerning judge of the best in any field. —**con′nois•seur′ship,** *n.*

con•no•ta•tion (kon′ə tā′shən), *n.* **1.** an act or instance of connoting. **2.** the associated or secondary meaning of a word in addition to its explicit or primary meaning: *The word* home *often has the connotation "a place of warmth and affection."* Compare DENOTATION (def. 1). **3.** INTENSION (def. 5). —**con•no•ta•tive** (kon′ə tā′tiv, kə nō′tə-), **con•no′tive,** *adj.* —**con′no•ta′tive•ly, con•no′tive•ly,** *adv.*

con•note (kə nōt′), *v.t.*, **-not•ed, -not•ing.** **1.** to signify or suggest (certain meanings, ideas, etc.) in addition to the explicit or primary meaning: *To me, a fireplace connotes comfort and hospitality.* **2.** to involve as a condition or accompaniment: *Injury connotes pain.*

con•nu•bi•al (kə no͞o′bē əl, -nyo͞o′-), *adj.* of marriage or wedlock; matrimonial; conjugal. —**con•nu′bi•al•ly,** *adv.*

con•quer (kong′kər), *v.t.* **1.** to acquire by force of arms; win in war: *to conquer a foreign land.* **2.** to overcome by force; vanquish: *to conquer an enemy.* **3.** to gain or win by effort, personal appeal, etc.: *conquered the hearts of the audience.* **4.** to gain a victory over; overcome: *to conquer one's fear.* —*v.i.* **5.** to be victorious; make conquests. —**con′quer•a•ble,** *adj.* —**con′quer•ing•ly,** *adv.* —**con′quer•or,** *n.*

con•quest (kon′kwest, kong′-), *n.* **1.** the act or process of conquering; vanquishment. **2.** the winning of favor, affection, love, etc. **3.** a person whose favor, affection, etc., has been won: *one of her many conquests.* **4.** anything acquired by conquering, as a nation, a territory, or spoils.

con•quis•ta•dor (kong kwis′tə dôr′, -kēs′-), *n.*, *pl.* **conquistadors, con•quis•ta•do•res** (kong kēs′tə dôr′ēz, -āz). one of the Spanish conquerors of the Americas, esp. of Mexico and Peru, in the 16th century.

Con•rad (kon′rad), *n.* **Joseph** (*Teodor Jozef Konrad Korzeniowski*), 1857–1924, English novelist, born in Poland.

con•san•guin•i•ty (kon′sang gwin′i tē), *n.* **1.** relationship by descent from a common ancestor; kinship (disting. from *affinity*). **2.** close relationship or connection.

con•science (kon′shəns), *n.* **1.** the inner sense of what is right or wrong in one's conduct or motives, impelling one toward right action: *to follow the dictates of conscience.* **2.** the complex of ethical and moral principles that controls or inhibits the actions or thoughts of an individual. **3.** an inhibiting sense of what is prudent. **4.** conscientiousness. —***Idiom.*** **5. in (all) conscience,** in all reason and fairness. **6. on one's conscience,** (of a wrongdoing) burdening one with guilt.

con•sci•en•tious (kon′shē en′shəs, kon′sē-), *adj.* **1.** meticulous; careful; painstaking. **2.** governed by or done according to conscience; scrupulous: *a conscientious judge.* —**con′sci•en′tious•ly,** *adv.* —**con′sci•en′tious•ness,** *n.*

conscien′tious objec′tion, *n.* refusal on moral or religious grounds to bear arms in a military conflict or to serve in the armed forces. —**conscien′tious objec′tor,** *n.*

con•scion•a•ble (kon′shə nə bəl), *adj.* being in conformity with one's conscience; just. —**con′scion•a•bly,** *adv.*

con•scious (kon′shəs), *adj.* **1.** aware of one's own existence, sensations, thoughts, surroundings, etc. **2.** fully aware of something: *not conscious of the passage of time.* **3.** having the mental faculties fully active: *to be conscious during an operation.* **4.** known to oneself; felt: *conscious guilt.* **5.** aware of what one is doing. **6.** aware of oneself; self-conscious. **7.** deliberate; intentional: *a conscious effort.* **8.** acutely aware of or concerned about: *money-conscious.* —*n.* **9. the conscious,** *Psychoanal.* the part of the mind comprising psychic material of which the individual is aware. —**con′scious•ly,** *adv.*

con•scious•ness (kon′shəs nis), *n.* **1.** the state of being conscious; awareness. **2.** the thoughts and feelings, collectively, of an individual or of an aggregate of people. **3.** full activity of the mind and senses, as in waking life: *to regain consciousness.* **4.** awareness of something for what it is: *consciousness of wrongdoing.* **5.** concern, interest, or acute awareness: *class consciousness.* **6.** the mental activity of which a person is aware, as contrasted with unconscious mental processes. **7.** *Philos.* the mind or the mental faculties as characterized by thought, feelings, and volition. —***Idiom.*** **8. raise one's consciousness,** to make or become aware of one's own or another's needs, attitudes, etc., esp. stemming from political or social repression.

con′sciousness-rais′ing, *n.* the process of learning to recognize, esp. through group discussion, one's own needs, goals, and problems or those of a group to which one or someone else belongs.

con•script (*v.* kən skript′; *n.*, *adj.* kon′skript), *v.t.* **1.** to draft for military service. **2.** to compel into service. —*n.* **3.** a recruit obtained by conscription. —*adj.* **4.** enrolled or formed by conscription; drafted: *a conscript soldier.* —**con•script′a•ble,** *adj.*

con•scrip•tion (kən skrip′shən), *n.* compulsory enrollment of persons for military or naval service; draft.

con•se•crate (kon′si krāt′), *v.*, **-crat•ed, -crat•ing,** *adj.* —*v.t.* **1.** to make or declare sacred; dedicate to the service of a deity. **2.** to make an object of honor or veneration; hallow: *a custom consecrated by time.* **3.** to devote or dedicate to some purpose. **4.** to admit or ordain to a sacred office, esp. to the episcopate. **5.** to change (bread and wine) into the Eucharist. —*adj.* **6.** consecrated; sacred. —**con′se•cra′tor,** *n.*

con•se•cra•tion (kon′si krā′shən), *n.* **1.** the act of consecrating; dedication to the service and worship of a deity. **2.** the act of consecrating the Eucharistic elements of bread and wine. **3.** ordination to a sacred office, esp. to the episcopate.

con•sec•u•tive (kən sek′yə tiv), *adj.* **1.** following one another in uninterrupted succession or order; successive: *consecutive numbers such as 5, 6, 7, 8.* **2.** marked by logical sequence. —**con•sec′u•tive•ly,** *adv.* —**con•sec′u•tive•ness,** *n.*

con•sen•su•al (kən sen′sho͞o əl), *adj.* **1.** formed or existing by mutual consent: *a consensual divorce.* **2.** involuntarily correlative with a voluntary action, as the contraction of the iris when the eye is opened. —**con•sen′su•al•ly,** *adv.*

con•sen•sus (kən sen′səs), *n.*, *pl.* **-sus•es.** **1.** collective judgment or belief; solidarity of opinion: *The consensus of the group was that they should meet twice a month.* **2.** general agreement or concord.

con•sent (kən sent′), *v.i.* **1.** to permit, approve, or comply; agree, as to an expressed wish or a proposed action (often fol. by *to* or an infinitive). —*n.* **2.** permission, approval, or agreement; compliance; acquiescence: *He gave his consent to the marriage.* **3.** agreement in sentiment, opinion, or a course of action: *by common consent.* —**con•sent′er,** *n.* —**con•sent′ing•ly,** *adv.*

con•se•quence (kon′si kwens′, -kwəns), *n.* **1.** the effect, result, or outcome of something occurring earlier. **2.** the conclusion reached by a line of reasoning; inference. **3.** importance or significance: *a matter of no consequence.* **4.** importance in rank or position: *a man of consequence.* —***Idiom.*** **5. in consequence,** consequently; as a result.

con•se•quent (kon′si kwent′, -kwənt), *adj.* **1.** following as an effect or result; resulting (often fol. by *on* or *to*). **2.** following as a logical conclusion. **3.** following or progressing logically. —*n.* **4.** anything that follows upon something else, with or without a causal relationship. **5.** the second member of a conditional proposition, as *he was a great general* in *If Caesar conquered Gaul, he was a great general.* Compare ANTECEDENT (def. 6). **6.** *Math.* **a.** the second term of a ratio. **b.** the second of two vectors in a dyad.

con•se•quen•tial (kon′si kwen′shəl), *adj.* **1.** following as an effect, result, or outcome; resultant; consequent. **2.** following as a logical conclusion or inference; logically consistent. **3.** of consequence or importance. **4.** self-important; pompous. —**con′se•quen′ti•al′i•ty, con′se•quen′tial•ness,** *n.* —**con′se•quen′tial•ly,** *adv.*

con•serv•an•cy (kən sûr′vən sē), *n.*, *pl.* **-cies.** **1.** conservation of natural resources. **2.** an association dedicated to the protection of the environment and its resources. —**con•serv′ant,** *adj.*

con•ser•va•tion (kon′sər vā′shən), *n.* **1.** the act of conserving; prevention of injury, decay, waste, or loss; preservation. **2.** the controlled utilization or official supervision of natural resources in order to preserve or protect them or to prevent depletion. **3.** the restoration and preservation of works of art. —**con′ser•va′tion•ist,** *n.*

conserva′tion law′, *n.* any physical law stating that a quantity or property remains constant during and after a process.

conserva′tion of en′ergy, *n.* the principle that in a system not subject to any external force, the amount of energy is constant despite its changes in form.

conserva′tion of mass′, *n.* the principle that in a system not subject to any external force, the mass is constant despite its changes in form. Also called **conserva′tion of mat′ter.**

con•serv•a•tive (kən sûr′və tiv), *adj.* **1.** disposed to preserve existing conditions, institutions, etc., or to restore traditional ones, and to limit change. **2.** cautiously moderate: *a conservative estimate.* **3.** traditional in style or manner; avoiding novelty or showiness: *a conservative suit.* **4.** (*cap.*) of or pertaining to a conservative political party, esp. the Conservative Party of Great Britain. **5.** of or pertaining to political conservatism. **6.** (*cap.*) conforming to or characteristic of Conservative Judaism. **7.** having the power or tendency to conserve; preservative. —*n.* **8.** a person who is conservative in principles, actions, habits, etc. **9.** a supporter of conservative political policies. **10.** (*cap.*) a member of a conservative political party, esp. the Conservative Party of Great Britain. **11.** a preservative. —**con•ser′va•tism,** *n.* —**con•serv′a•tive•ly,** *adv.*

Conserv′ative Bap′tist, *n.* a member of a Protestant denomination **(Conserv′ative Bap′tist Associa′tion of Amer′ica)** organized in Milwaukee, Wis., in 1948.

Conserv′ative Ju′daism, *n.* a branch of Judaism that adheres to most traditional beliefs and practices but permits some adaptation to the contemporary world. Compare ORTHODOX JUDAISM, REFORM JUDAISM.

Conserv′ative Par′ty, *n.* a political party in Great Britain founded about 1832 as successor to the Tories.

con•serv•a•tor (kən sûr′və tər, kon′sər vā′-), *n.* **1.** a person who conserves or preserves; preserver; protector. **2.** a person who repairs, restores, or maintains the condition of objects, as in a museum or library. **3.** *Law.* a guardian, esp. a person appointed to look after the affairs of one judged incompetent. —**con•serv′a•to′ri•al** (-tôr′ē əl, -tōr′-), *adj.* —**con•serv′a•tor•ship′,** *n.*

con•serv•a•to•ry (kən sûr′və tôr′ē, -tōr′ē), *n.*, *pl.* **-ries.** **1.** a school giving training in the fine or dramatic arts, esp. a school of music. **2.** a greenhouse, usu. attached to a dwelling, for growing plants.

con•serve (*v.* kən sûrv′; *n.* kon′sûrv, kən sûrv′), *v.*, **-served, -serv•ing,** *n.* —*v.t.* **1.** to prevent injury, decay, waste, or loss of: *Conserve your strength for the race.* **2.** to use or manage (natural resources) wisely; preserve; save. **3.** to hold (a physical or chemical property) constant during a process. **4.** to preserve (fruit) by cooking with sugar or syrup. —*n.* **5.** a mixture of fruits cooked with sugar to a jamlike consistency. —**con•serv′a•ble,** *adj.* —**con•serv′er,** *n.*

con•sid•er (kən sid′ər), *v.t.* **1.** to think carefully about, esp. in order to make a decision; contemplate; ponder. **2.** to regard as or deem to be: *I consider the matter settled.* **3.** to think, believe, or suppose. **4.** to bear in mind; make allowance for: *Her behavior was justified if you consider the provocation.* **5.** to regard with respect or thoughtfulness; show consideration for: *to consider other people's feelings.* **6.** to look at; regard: *He considered the man from a distance.* **7.** to regard with respect or honor; esteem. **8.** to think about (something that one might do, accept, buy, etc.): *I'm considering a job in Arizona.* —*v.i.* **9.** to think deliberately or carefully; reflect.

con•sid•er•a•ble (kən sid′ər ə bəl), *adj.* **1.** rather large or great, as in size, distance, or extent: *a considerable length of time.* **2.** worthy of respect or attention; important; distinguished. —*n.* **3.** *Informal.* much; not a little. —**con•sid′er•a•bly,** *adv.*

con•sid•er•ate (kən sid′ər it), *adj.* **1.** showing kindly regard for the feelings or circumstances of others; thoughtful. **2.** marked by or showing care. —**con•sid′er•ate•ly,** *adv.* —**con•sid′er•ate•ness,** *n.*

con•sid•er•a•tion (kən sid′ə rā′shən), *n.* **1.** the act of considering; careful thought or attention; deliberation. **2.** something kept in mind in making a decision: *Age was not a consideration.* **3.** thoughtful or sympathetic regard or respect; thoughtfulness. **4.** a thought or reflection; an opinion based upon reflection. **5.** a recompense or payment, as for work done; compensation. **6.** importance or consequence. **7.** estimation; esteem. **8.** something given in return, as a recompense, that suffices to make an informal promise legally binding. —*Idiom.* **9. in consideration of, a.** in view of. **b.** in return or recompense for. **10. take into consideration,** to consider; take into account.

con•sid•er•ing (kən sid′ər ing), *prep.* **1.** taking into account; in view of: *The campaign was a success, considering the initial opposition.* —*adv.* **2.** *Informal.* with all things considered (used after the statement it modifies): *He paints very well, considering.* —*conj.* **3.** taking into consideration that: *Considering they are newcomers, they've accomplished a lot.*

con•sign (kən sīn′), *v.t.* **1.** to hand over or deliver; assign. **2.** to transfer to another's custody or charge; entrust. **3.** to banish or set apart; relegate: *to consign unpleasant thoughts to oblivion.* **4.** to address or ship, esp. for the purpose of being sold. —**con•sign′a•ble,** *adj.* —**con•sig•na•tion** (kon′sig nā′shən), *n.*

con•sign•ment (kən sīn′mənt), *n.* **1.** the act of consigning. **2.** something that is consigned. **3.** property sent to an agent, esp. for sale. —*Idiom.* **4. on consignment,** (of goods) sent to an agent for sale, with title held by the consignor until a sale is made.

con•sist (kən sist′), *v.i.* **1.** to be made up or composed (usu. fol. by *of*): *This cake consists mainly of sugar, flour, and butter.* **2.** to be comprised or contained (usu. fol. by *in*): *The charm of Paris does not consist only in its beauty.* **3.** to be compatible, consistent, or harmonious (usu. fol. by *with*).

con•sist•en•cy (kən sis′tən sē) also **con•sist′ence,** *n., pl.* **-cies. 1.** degree of density, firmness, viscosity, etc.: *a liquid with the consistency of cream.* **2.** steadfast adherence to the same principles, course, form, etc.: *no consistency in his behavior.* **3.** agreement, harmony, or compatibility, esp. correspondence or uniformity among the parts of a complex thing. **4.** the condition of cohering or holding together and retaining form.

con•sist•ent (kən sis′tənt), *adj.* **1.** agreeing or accordant; compatible; not self-contradictory: *actions consistent with his views.* **2.** constantly adhering to the same principles, course, form, etc.: *a consistent opponent of capital punishment.* **3.** holding firmly together; cohering. —**con•sist′ent•ly,** *adv.*

con•sis•to•ry (kən sis′tə rē), *n., pl.* **-ries. 1.** any of various ecclesiastical councils or tribunals. **2.** the place where such a body meets. **3.** the meeting of any such body. **4.** a solemn assembly of Roman Catholic cardinals summoned and presided over by the pope. **5.** a bishop's court in the Anglican Church for dealing with ecclesiastical and spiritual questions. **6.** the local governing board of certain Reform churches. **7.** any assembly or council.

con•so•la•tion (kon′sə lā′shən), *n.* **1.** the act of consoling; solace. **2.** the state of being consoled. **3.** someone or something that consoles. **4.** a contest for tournament entrants eliminated before the final round.

consola′tion prize′, *n.* a prize, usu. of minor value, given to the loser or runner-up in a competition.

con•sole[1] (kən sōl′), *v.t.*, **-soled, -sol•ing.** to alleviate or lessen the grief, sorrow, or disappointment of; give solace or comfort. —**con•sol′a•ble,** *adj.* —**con•sol′er,** *n.* —**con•sol′ing•ly,** *adv.*

con•sole[2] (kon′sōl), *n.* **1.** a television, phonograph, or radio cabinet designed to stand on the floor. **2.** the control unit of a computer, including the keyboard and display screen. **3.** a desklike structure containing the keyboards, pedals, etc., by means of which an organ is played. **4.** a small cabinet standing on the floor and having doors. **5.** the control unit of a mechanical, electrical, or electronic system. **6.** a storage tray or container mounted between bucket seats in an automobile.

con•sol•i•date (kən sol′i dāt′), *v.*, **-dat•ed, -dat•ing.** —*v.t.* **1.** to bring together (separate parts) into a single or unified whole; unite; combine. **2.** to make solid, firm, or secure; solidify; strengthen: *to consolidate gains.* **3.** to organize into a more compact form. —*v.i.* **4.** to unite or combine. **5.** to become solid or firm. —**con•sol′i•da′tion,** *n.* —**con•sol′i•da′tor,** *n.*

con•som•mé (kon′sə mā′, kon′sə mā′), *n.* a clear soup made from rich stock.

con•so•nance (kon′sə nəns) also **con′so•nan•cy,** *n.* **1.** accord or agreement. **2.** correspondence of sounds; harmony of sounds. **3.** a simultaneous combination of musical tones conventionally accepted as being in a state of repose. Compare DISSONANCE (def. 2). **4. a.** a repetition of consonants, esp. those after a stressed vowel, as in *march, lurch,* but often of all the consonants, as in *stick, stuck.* Compare ALLITERATION (def. 1). **b.** the use of such repetition of consonants as a rhyming device.

con•so•nant (kon′sə nənt), *n.* **1.** a speech sound produced by occluding (p, b, t, d, k, g), diverting (m, n, ng), or obstructing (f, v, s, z, etc.) the flow of air from the lungs (opposed to *vowel*). **2.** a letter or other symbol representing or usu. representing a consonant sound. —*adj.* **3.** in accord: *behavior consonant with his character.* **4.** corresponding in sound, as words. **5.** pertaining to or being a musical consonance.

con•sort (*n.* kon′sôrt, *v.* kən sôrt′), *n.* **1.** a husband or wife; spouse, esp. of a reigning monarch. **2.** one ship accompanying another. **3. a.** a group of instrumentalists and singers who perform music, esp. old music. **b.** a group of instruments of the same family, as viols, played in concert. **4.** a companion, associate, or partner. **5.** accord or agreement. —*v.i.* **6.** to associate; keep company: *to consort with known criminals.* **7.** to agree or harmonize. —*v.t.* **8.** to associate, join, or unite.

con•sor•ti•um (kən sôr′shē əm, -tē-), *n., pl.* **-ti•a** (-shē ə, -tē ə). **1.** a combination, as of corporations, for carrying out a business venture requiring large amounts of capital. **2.** association; partnership. **3.** the right of husband and wife to companionship and conjugal intercourse with each other. —**con•sor′ti•al,** *adj.*

con•spec•tus (kən spek′təs), *n.* **1.** a general or comprehensive view; survey. **2.** a digest; summary; résumé.

con•spic•u•ous (kən spik′yo͞o əs), *adj.* **1.** easily seen or noticed; readily observable. **2.** attracting special attention, as by outstanding qualities or eccentricities; striking. —**con•spic′u•ous•ly,** *adv.* —**con•spic′u•ous•ness, con•spi•cu•i•ty** (kon′spi kyo͞o′i tē), *n.*

conspic′uous consump′tion, *n.* public enjoyment of possessions that are known to be costly so that one's ability to pay for such things is flaunted.

con•spir•a•cy (kən spir′ə sē), *n., pl.* **-cies. 1.** the act of conspiring. **2.** a plan or agreement formulated, esp. in secret, by two or more persons to commit an unlawful, harmful, or treacherous act. **3.** a combination of persons for a secret, unlawful, or evil purpose. **4.** any concurrence in action; combination in bringing about a given result. —**con•spir′a•tive,** *adj.* —**con•spir′a•to′ri•al** (-tôr′ē əl, -tōr′-), **con•spir′a•to′ry,** *adj.* —**con•spir′a•to′ri•al•ly,** *adv.*

conspir′acy of si′lence, *n.* a usually secret or unstated agreement to remain silent among those who know something whose disclosure might be damaging, harmful, or against their own best interest or that of their associates.

con•spire (kən spīər′), *v.*, **-spired, -spir•ing.** —*v.i.* **1.** to agree together, esp. secretly, to do something wrong, evil, or illegal. **2.** to act or work together toward the same goal. —*v.t.* **3.** to contrive; plot. —**con•spir•a•tor** (kən spir′ə tər), *n.* —**con•spir′er,** *n.* —**con•spir′ing•ly,** *adv.*

con•sta•ble (kon′stə bəl; *esp. Brit.* kun′-), *n.* **1.** an officer of the peace in a town or township, having minor police and judicial functions. **2.** an officer of high rank in medieval monarchies. **3.** the keeper or governor of a royal fortress or castle.

Con•sta•ble (kun′stə bəl, kon′-), *n.* **John,** 1776–1837, English painter.

con•stan•cy (kon′stən sē), *n.* **1.** the quality of being unchanging or unwavering, as in purpose, love, or loyalty. **2.** uniformity or regularity, as in qualities or conditions; stability.

con•stant (kon′stənt), *adj.* **1.** not changing; invariable: *Conditions remained constant.* **2.** continuing without pause; unceasing: *constant noise.* **3.** regularly recurrent; continual; persistent: *constant interruptions.* **4.** faithful; unswerving in love or devotion. **5.** steadfast; firm in mind or purpose; resolute. —*n.* **6.** something that does not or cannot change or vary. **7.** *Physics.* a number expressing a property, quantity, or relation that remains unchanged under specified conditions. **8.** *Math.* a quantity assumed to be unchanged throughout a given discussion. —**con′stant•ly,** *adv.*

Con•stan•tine[1] (kon′stən tēn′ *or, for 1,* -tīn′), *n.* **1.** died A.D. 715, pope 708–715. **2.** a city in NE Algeria. 448,578.

Con•stan•tine[2] (kon′stən tēn′, -tīn′), *n.* **1. Constantine I, a.** (*Flavius Valerius Aurelius Constantinus*) (*"the Great"*) A.D. 288?–337, Roman emperor 324–337: legally sanctioned Christian worship. **b.** 1868–1923, king of Greece 1913–17, 1920–22. **2. Constantine II,** born 1940, king of Greece 1964–74. —**Con′stan•tin′i•an** (-tin′ē ən), *adj.*

Con•stan•ti•no•ple (kon′stan tn ō′pəl), *n.* former name of ISTANBUL.

con•stel•la•tion (kon′stə lā′shən), *n.* **1. a.** any of various groups of stars that have been named, as Ursa Major, Boötes, or Orion. **b.** the section of the heavens occupied by such a group. **2.** the astrological grouping of the heavenly bodies, esp. at a person's birth. **3.** a group or configuration of ideas, qualities, objects, etc., that are related in some way. **4.** any brilliant, outstanding group or assemblage: *a constellation of great writers.*

con•ster•na•tion (kon′stər nā′shən), *n.* a sudden, alarming amazement or dread that results in utter confusion; dismay.

con•sti•pate (kon′stə pāt′), *v.t.,* **-pat•ed, -pat•ing. 1.** to cause constipation in. **2.** to cause to become slow-moving or immobilized; constrict.

con•sti•pa•tion (kon′stə pā′shən), *n.* **1.** a condition of the bowels in which the feces are dry and hardened and evacuation is difficult and infrequent. **2.** a state of sluggishness or inactivity.

con•stit•u•en•cy (kən stich′o͞o ən sē), *n., pl.* **-cies. 1.** a body of constituents; the voters or residents in a district represented by an elective officer. **2.** the district itself. **3.** any body of supporters, customers, etc.; clientele.

con•stit•u•ent (kən stich′o͞o ənt), *adj.* **1.** serving to make up a thing; component: *the constituent parts of a motor.* **2.** having power to frame or alter a political constitution or fundamental law, as distinguished from lawmaking power: *a constituent assembly.* —*n.* **3.** a constituent element, material, etc.; component. **4.** a person who authorizes another to act in his or her behalf, as a voter in a district represented by an elected official. **5.** a linguistic element considered as part of a construction.

con•sti•tute (kon′sti to͞ot′, -tyo͞ot′), *v.t.,* **-tut•ed, -tut•ing. 1.** to compose; form: *mortar constituted of lime and sand.* **2.** to appoint to an office or function: *He was constituted treasurer.* **3.** to establish, as a law. **4.** to give legal form to. **5.** to create or be tantamount to: *Imports constitute a challenge to local goods.*

con•sti•tu•tion (kon′sti to͞o′shən, -tyo͞o′-), *n.* **1.** the way in which a thing is composed or made up; makeup; composition. **2.** the physical character of the body as to strength, health, etc.: *a strong constitution.* **3.** the aggregate of a person's physical and psychological characteristics. **4.** the act of constituting; establishment. **5.** the state of being constituted; formation. **6.** any established arrangement or custom. **7.** (*cap.*) the fundamental law of the U.S., framed in 1787 and put into effect in 1789. **8.** the system of fundamental principles according to which a nation, state, corporation, or the like, is governed. **9.** the document embodying these principles.

con•sti•tu•tion•al (kon′sti to͞o′shə nl, -tyo͞o′-), *adj.* **1.** of or pertaining to the constitution of a state, organization, etc. **2.** subject to the provisions of such a constitution: *a constitutional monarchy.* **3.** provided by, in accordance with, or not prohibited by such a constitution: *the constitutional powers of the president; a constitutional law.* **4.** belonging to or inherent in the character or makeup of a person's body or mind: *a constitutional weakness for sweets.* **5.** pertaining to the constitution or composition of a thing; essential. **6.** beneficial to one's constitution; healthful: *constitutional exercise.* —*n.* **7.** a walk or other mild exercise taken for the benefit of one's health. —**con′sti•tu′tion•al•ly,** *adv.*

con•sti•tu•tion•al•i•ty (kon′sti to͞o′shə nal′i tē, -tyo͞o′-), *n.* **1.** the quality of being constitutional. **2.** accordance with the constitution of a country, state, etc.

Constitu′tional Un′ion par′ty, *n.* the political party formed in 1859 chiefly by former Whigs to rally moderates desirous of preserving the Union. In 1860 it nominated John Bell for president and Edward Everett for vice president.

Constitu′tion of the Unit′ed States′, *n.* the fundamental or organic law of the U.S., framed in 1787 by the Constitutional Convention. It went into effect March 4, 1789.

con•strain (kən strān′), *v.t.* **1.** to force, compel, or oblige: *He was constrained to admit the offense.* **2.** to confine forcibly, as by bonds. **3.** to repress or restrain. —**con•strain′a•ble,** *adj.* —**con•strain′ing•ly,** *adv.*

con•strained (kən strānd′), *adj.* **1.** compelled; obliged. **2.** stiff; uneasy: *a constrained manner.* —**con•strain′ed•ly,** *adv.*

con•straint (kən strānt′), *n.* **1.** limitation or restriction. **2.** repression of natural feelings and impulses. **3.** unnatural restraint in manner; embarrassment. **4.** something that constrains. **5.** the act of constraining. **6.** the condition of being constrained.

con•strict (kən strikt′), *v.t.* **1.** to draw or press in; compress. **2.** to cause to contract or shrink. **3.** to slow or stop the natural course or development of. —*v.i.* **4.** to become constricted. —**con•stric′tion,** *n.* —**con•stric′tive,** *adj.*

con•stric•tor (kən strik′tər), *n.* **1.** a snake, esp. of the family Boidae, that suffocates its prey in its coils. **2.** a muscle that constricts a hollow part of the body. **3.** a person or thing that constricts.

con•struct (*v.* kən strukt′; *n.* kon′strukt), *v.t.* **1.** to build or form by putting together parts. **2.** *Geom.* to draw (a figure) fulfilling certain given conditions. —*n.* **3.** something constructed. **4.** an image, idea, or theory, esp. a complex one formed from a number of simpler elements. —**con•struct′i•ble,** *adj.* —**con•struc′tor, con•struct′er,** *n.*

con•struc•tion (kən struk′shən), *n.* **1.** the process, or art of constructing. **2.** the way in which a thing is constructed: *a building of solid construction.* **3.** something that is constructed; structure. **4.** the occupation or industry of building. **5. a.** the arrangement of two or more words or morphemes in a grammatical unit. **b.** a group of words or morphemes consisting of two or more forms arranged in a particular way. **6.** an explanation or interpretation, as of a law, a text, or an action. —**con•struc′tion•al,** *adj.* —**con•struc′tion•al•ly,** *adv.*

construc′tion pa′per, *n.* a heavy groundwood paper used esp. in making posters and cutouts.

con•struc•tive (kən struk′tiv), *adj.* **1.** promoting further development or advancement; helping to improve (opposed to *destructive*): *constructive criticism.* **2.** of, pertaining to, or of the nature of construction; structural. **3.** deduced by inference or interpretation; inferential: *constructive permission.* —**con•struc′tive•ly,** *adv.* —**con•struc′tive•ness,** *n.*

con•strue (*v.* kən stro͞o′; *esp. Brit.* kon′stro͞o; *n.* kon′stro͞o), *v.,* **-strued, -stru•ing,** *n.* —*v.t.* **1.** to give or explain the meaning or intention of; interpret. **2.** to deduce by inference or interpretation; infer. **3.** to analyze the grammatical structure of: *to construe a Latin sentence.* **4.** to arrange or combine (words, phrases, etc.) syntactically. —*v.i.* **5.** to admit of grammatical analysis or interpretation. **6.** to analyze grammatical structure. —*n.* **7.** the act of construing. **8.** something that is construed. —**con•stru′a•ble,** *adj.* —**con•stru′al,** *n.*

con•sub•stan•tial (kon′səb stan′shəl), *adj.* of one and the same substance, essence, or nature. —**con′sub•stan′ti•al′i•ty,** *n.*

con•sub•stan•ti•a•tion (kon′səb stan′shē ā′shən), *n.* the doctrine that the substance of the body and blood of Christ coexist in and with the bread and wine of the Eucharist.

con•sue•tude (kon′swi to͞od′, -tyo͞od′), *n.* custom, esp. as having legal force. —**con′sue•tu′di•nar′y,** *adj.*

con•sul (kon′səl), *n.* an official appointed by the government of a country to look after its commercial interests and the welfare of its citizens in another country. —**con′su•lar,** *adj.* —**con′sul•ship′,** *n.*

con•su•late (kon′sə lit), *n.* **1.** the premises officially occupied by a consul. **2.** the position, authority, or term of service of a consul.

con′sulate gen′eral, *n., pl.* **consulates general.** the office or establishment of a consul general.

con′sul gen′eral, *n., pl.* **consuls general.** a consul of the highest rank, usu. stationed at a place of commercial importance.

con•sult (*v.* kən sult′; *n.* kon′sult, kən sult′), *v.t.* **1.** to seek guidance or information from: *to consult a lawyer.* **2.** to refer to for information: *to consult a dictionary.* **3.** to have regard for (a person's interest, convenience, etc.) in making plans. —*v.i.* **4.** to take counsel: *to consult with a doctor.* **5.** to give professional or expert advice; serve as consultant. —*n.* **6.** a consultation.

con•sult•ant (kən sul′tnt), *n.* **1.** a person who gives professional or expert advice. **2.** a person who consults someone or something. —**con•sult′ant•ship′,** *n.*

con•sul•ta•tion (kon′səl tā′shən), *n.* **1.** the act of consulting; conference. **2.** a meeting for deliberation or discussion. **3.** a meeting of physicians to evaluate a patient's case and treatment.

con•sult•ing (kən sul′ting), *adj.* **1.** giving professional advice to the public or to those practicing the profession: *a consulting physician.* **2.** of or used for consultation: *a physician's consulting room.*

con•sum•a•ble (kən so͞o′mə bəl), *adj.* **1.** able or liable to be consumed: *consumable goods.* —*n.* **2.** Usu., **consumables.** something produced to be consumed. —**con•sum′a•bil′i•ty,** *n.*

con•sume (kən so͞om′), *v.,* **-sumed, -sum•ing.** —*v.t.* **1.** to destroy or expend by use; use up. **2.** to eat or drink up; devour. **3.** to destroy, as by decomposition or burning: *Fire consumed the forest.* **4.** to spend (money, time, etc.) wastefully. **5.** to absorb; engross: *consumed with curiosity.* —*v.i.* **6.** to undergo destruction; waste away. **7.** to use or use up consumer goods.

con•sum•er (kən so͞o′mər), *n.* **1.** a person or thing that consumes. **2.** a person or organization that buys or uses a commodity or service. **3.** *Ecol.* an organism, usu. an animal, that feeds on plants or other animals.

consum′er cred′it, *n.* credit extended by a retail store, bank, etc., chiefly for the purchase of consumer goods.

consum′er goods′, *n.pl.* goods, as clothing and food, produced to satisfy human wants and not used in further production.

con•sum•er•ism (kən so͞o′mə riz′əm), *n.* **1.** a movement for the protection of the consumer against defective products, misleading advertising, etc. **2.** the concept that an ever-expanding consumption of goods is advantageous to the economy. **3.** a preoccupation with or emphasis on the consumption of goods. —**con•sum′er•ist,** *n., adj.*

consum′er price′ in′dex, *n.* an index in the changes of the cost of goods and services to a typical consumer based on the costs of the same items in a previous period. *Abbr.:* CPI

con•sum•ing (kən so͞o′ming), *adj.* strongly and urgently felt: *a consuming need.* —**con•sum′ing•ly,** *adv.*

con•sum•mate (*v.* kon′sə māt′; *adj.* kən sum′it, kon′sə mit), *v.,* **-mat•ed, -mat•ing,** *adj.* —*v.t.* **1.** to bring to a state of perfection; fulfill. **2.** to bring to a state of completion, as an arrangement or agreement. **3.** to complete (the union of a marriage) by the first marital sexual intercourse. —*adj.* **4.** complete or perfect; supremely skilled; superb: *a consummate master of the violin.* **5.** of the highest or most extreme degree: *a work of consummate skill; an act of consummate savagery.* —**con•sum′mate•ly,** *adv.* —**con′sum•ma′tion,** *n.*

con•sump•tion (kən sump′shən), *n.* **1.** the act of consuming, as by use, decay, or destruction. **2.** the amount consumed: *the high consumption of gasoline.* **3.** the using up of goods and services having an exchangeable value. **4. a.** *Older Use.* tuberculosis of the lungs. **b.** progressive wasting of the body.

con•sump•tive (kən sump′tiv), *adj.* **1.** tending to consume; destructive; wasteful. **2.** pertaining to or of the nature of consumption. **3.** disposed to or affected with consumption. **—*n.* 4.** *Older Use.* a person suffering from tuberculosis.

con•tact (kon′takt), *n.* **1.** the act or state of touching; a touching or meeting, as of two things or people. **2.** immediate proximity or association. **3.** the act or state of being in communication. **4.** a person one knows through whom one can gain access to information, favors, influential people, etc. **5.** a junction of electric conductors, usu. metal, that controls current flow, often completing or interrupting a circuit. **6.** the interface, generally a planar surface, between geologic strata that differ in lithology or age. **7.** a person who has lately been exposed to an infected person. **—*v.t.* 8.** to put or bring into contact. **9.** to communicate with: *We'll contact you by phone.* **—*v.i.* 10.** to enter into or be in contact. **—*adj.* 11.** involving or produced by touching or proximity: *a contact allergy.* **—con′tact•ee′,** *n.* **—con•tac•tu•al** (kon tak′cho͞o əl), *adj.*

con′tact lens′, *n.* either of a pair of small plastic disks that are held in place over the cornea by surface tension and correct vision defects inconspicuously.

con′tact sport′, *n.* any sport in which physical contact between players is an accepted part of play, as football, boxing, or hockey.

con•ta•gion (kən tā′jən), *n.* **1.** the communication of disease by direct or indirect contact. **2.** a disease so communicated. **3.** the medium by which a contagious disease is transmitted. **4.** harmful or undesirable contact or influence. **5.** the ready transmission or spread of an idea, emotion, etc.: *the contagion of fear.*

con•ta•gious (kən tā′jəs), *adj.* **1.** capable of being transmitted by bodily contact with an infected person or object: *contagious diseases.* **2.** carrying or spreading a contagious disease. **3.** tending to spread from person to person: *contagious fear.* **—con•ta′gious•ly,** *adv.*

con•ta•gium (kən tā′jəm, -jē əm), *n., pl.* **-gia** (-jə, -jē ə). the causative agent of a contagious or infectious disease, as a virus.

con•tain (kən tān′), *v.t.* **1.** to hold or include within its volume or area: *This glass contains water.* **2.** to have as contents or constituent parts; comprise; include. **3.** to be capable of holding; have capacity for. **4.** to keep under proper control; restrain: *He could not contain his amusement.* **5.** to prevent or limit the advance, spread, or influence of: *to contain an epidemic.* **6.** (of a number) to be a multiple of; be divisible by, without a remainder: *Ten contains five twice.* **7.** to be equal to: *A quart contains two pints.* **—con•tain′a•ble,** *adj.*

con•tained (kən tānd′), *adj.* showing restraint or calmness; controlled. **—con•tain′ed•ly,** *adv.*

con•tain•er (kən tā′nər), *n.* **1.** anything that contains something, as a carton, box, crate, or can. **2.** a large, vanlike, reusable box for consolidating smaller crates or cartons into a single shipment.

con•tain•er•i•za•tion (kən tā′nər ə zā′shən), *n.* a method of shipping freight in relatively uniform, sealed, movable containers whose contents do not have to be unloaded at each point of transfer.

con•tain•ment (kən tān′mənt), *n.* **1.** the act or condition of containing. **2.** an act or policy of restricting the territorial growth or ideological influence of a hostile power. **3.** an enclosure surrounding a nuclear reactor designed to prevent the accidental release of radioactive material.

con•tam•i•nate (*v.* kən tam′ə nāt′; *n., adj.* -nit, -nāt′), *v.,* **-nat•ed, -nat•ing,** *n., adj.* **—*v.t.* 1.** to make impure or unsuitable by contact or mixture with something unclean, bad, etc.; pollute; taint: *to contaminate a lake with sewage.* **2.** to render harmful or unusable by adding radioactive material to. **—*n.* 3.** something that contaminates or carries contamination; contaminant. **—con•tam′i•na•ble,** *adj.* **—con•tam′i•nant,** *n.* **—con•tam′i•na′tive,** *adj.* **—con•tam′i•na′tor,** *n.*

con•tam•i•na•tion (kən tam′ə nā′shən), *n.* **1.** the act of contaminating. **2.** the state of being contaminated. **3.** something that contaminates. **4.** an alteration in a linguistic form due to the influence of a related form, as the replacement in English of earlier *femelle* with *female* through the influence of *male.*

con•tem•plate (kon′təm plāt′, -tem-), *v.,* **-plat•ed, -plat•ing. —*v.t.* 1.** to look at or view with continued attention; observe thoughtfully. **2.** to consider thoroughly; think fully or deeply about. **3.** to have in view as a purpose; intend: *to contemplate bribery.* **4.** to have in view as a future event: *to contemplate buying a new car.* **—*v.i.* 5.** to think studiously; meditate; consider deliberately. **—con′tem•plat′ing•ly,** *adv.*

con•tem•pla•tion (kon′təm plā′shən, -tem-), *n.* **1.** the act of contemplating; thoughtful observation. **2.** full or deep consideration; meditation; reflection: *religious contemplation.* **3.** purpose or intention. **4.** prospect or expectation.

con•tem•pla•tive (kən tem′plə tiv, kon′təm plā′-, -tem-), *adj.* **1.** given to or characterized by contemplation. **—*n.* 2.** a person devoted to contemplation, as a monk. **—con•tem′pla•tive•ly,** *adv.*

con•tem•po•ra•ne•ous (kən tem′pə rā′nē əs), *adj.* living or occurring during the same period of time; contemporary. **—con•tem′po•ra′ne•ous•ness,** *n.* **—con•tem′po•ra′ne•ous•ly,** *adv.*

con•tem•po•rar•y (kən tem′pə rer′ē), *adj., n., pl.* **-rar•ies. —*adj.* 1.** existing, occurring, or living at the same time; belonging to the same period of time. **2.** of the present time; modern. **3.** of about the same age or date: *a Georgian table with a contemporary wig stand.* **—*n.* 4.** a person or thing belonging to the same time or period with another. **5.** a person of the same age as another. **—con•tem′po•rar′i•ly,** *adv.*

con•tempt (kən tempt′), *n.* **1.** a feeling of disdain for anything considered mean, vile, or worthless; scorn. **2.** disgrace. **3.** willful disobedience to or open disrespect for the rules or orders of a court or legislative body: *contempt of court.* **—con•tempt′i•ble,** *adj.*

con•temp•tu•ous (kən temp′cho͞o əs), *adj.* showing or expressing contempt; scornful. **—con•temp′tu•ous•ly,** *adv.*

con•tend (kən tend′), *v.i.* **1.** to struggle or vie in opposition or rivalry; compete: *to contend for first prize.* **2.** to strive in debate; dispute. **—*v.t.* 3.** to assert or maintain earnestly: *She contended that taxes were too high.* **—con•tend′er,** *n.*

con•tent[1] (kon′tent), *n.* **1.** Usu., **contents. a.** something that is contained: *the contents of a box.* **b.** the topics covered in a book or document. **c.** the chapters or other formal divisions of a book or document: *a table of contents.* **2.** something expressed through some medium, as speech, writing, or a work of art: *a poetic form adequate to the content.* **3.** significance or profundity: *a clever play that lacks content.* **4.** that which may be perceived in something: *the latent content of a dream.* **5.** power of containing; holding capacity. **6.** volume, area, or extent; size. **7.** the amount of a substance contained.

con•tent[2] (kən tent′), *adj.* **1.** satisfied with what one is or has; not wanting more or anything else. **2.** willing or resigned; assenting. **—*v.t.* 3.** to make content. **—*n.* 4.** the state or feeling of being contented; contentment. **—con•tent′ment,** *n.*

con•tent•ed (kən ten′tid), *adj.* satisfied; content. **—con•tent′ed•ly,** *adv.* **—con•tent′ed•ness,** *n.*

con•ten•tion (kən ten′shən), *n.* **1.** a struggling together in opposition; strife; conflict. **2.** a striving in rivalry; competition; contest. **3.** strife in debate; dispute; controversy. **4.** a point contended for or affirmed in controversy. **—con•ten′tion•al,** *adj.*

con•ten•tious (kən ten′shəs), *adj.* **1.** tending to argument or strife; quarrelsome: *a contentious crew.* **2.** causing, involving, or characterized by argument or controversy: *contentious issues.* **3.** pertaining to causes between contending parties involved in litigation. **—con•ten′tious•ly,** *adv.* **—con•ten′tious•ness,** *n.*

con′tent word′, *n.* a word, typically a noun, verb, adjective, or adverb, that carries semantic content, bearing reference to the world independently of its use within a particular sentence (disting. from *function word*).

con•ter•mi•nous (kən tûr′mə nəs) also **con•ter′mi•nal,** *adj.* **1.** having a common boundary; contiguous. **2.** meeting without an intervening gap: *The close of one year is conterminous with the beginning of the next.* **3.** coterminous. **—con•ter′mi•nous•ly,** *adv.*

con•test (*n.* kon′test; *v.* kən test′), *n.* **1.** a competition between rivals, as for a prize. **2.** struggle for victory or superiority. **3.** strife in argument; dispute. **—*v.t.* 4.** to struggle or fight for, as in battle. **5.** to argue against; dispute: *to contest a will.* **6.** to call in question; challenge: *They contested his right to speak.* **7.** to contend. **—*v.i.* 8.** to dispute; contend. **—con•test′a•ble,** *adj.* **—con•test′a•bly,** *adv.* **—con•test′er,** *n.*

con•test•ant (kən tes′tənt), *n.* **1.** a person who takes part in a contest or competition. **2.** a person who contests the results of an election. **3.** the party who contests the validity of a will in probate court.

con•text (kon′tekst), *n.* **1.** the parts of a written or spoken statement that precede or follow a specified word or passage and can influence its meaning or effect. **2.** the set of circumstances or facts that surround a particular event, situation, etc. **—con•tex′tu•al,** *adj.*

con•tig•u•ous (kən tig′yo͞o əs), *adj.* **1.** touching; in contact. **2.** adjacent in time: *contiguous events.* **—con•tig′u•ous•ly,** *adv.*

con•ti•nence (kon′tn əns) also **con′ti•nen•cy,** *n.* **1.** self-restraint or abstinence, esp. in regard to sexual activity; temperance; moderation. **2.** the ability to voluntarily control urinary and fecal discharge.

con•ti•nent (kon′tn ənt), *n.* **1.** one of the main landmasses of the globe, usu. reckoned as seven in number (Europe, Asia, Africa, North America, South America, Australia, and Antarctica). **2.** the mainland, as distinguished from islands or peninsulas. **3.** a continuous tract, as of land. **—*adj.* 4.** characterized by or exercising self-restraint. **5.** able to control urinary and fecal discharge. **—con′ti•nent•ly,** *adv.*

con•ti•nen•tal (kon′tn en′tl), *adj.* **1.** of or of the nature of a continent. **2.** (*usu. cap.*) of or pertaining to the mainland of Europe, to Europeans, or to European customs and attitudes. **3.** (*cap.*) of or pertaining to the 13 American colonies during and immediately after the American Revolution. **4.** of or pertaining to the continent of North America. **—*n.* 5.** (*cap.*) a soldier in the American army during the American Revolution. **6.** a piece of paper currency issued by the Continental Congress during the American Revolution. **7.** a small amount: *not worth a continental.* **8.** an inhabitant of a continent. **9.** (*usu. cap.*) an inhabitant of the mainland of Europe. **—con′ti•nen′tal•ly,** *adv.*

Con′tinen′tal Ar′my, *n.* the Revolutionary War Army, authorized by the Continental Congress in 1775 and led by George Washington.

con′tinen′tal break′fast, *n.* a light breakfast consisting typically of coffee and bread or rolls.

Con′tinen′tal Con′gress, *n.* either of two American legislative congresses during and after the American Revolution. The first met in 1774 to petition the British government for a redress of grievances. The second existed from 1775 to 1789 and adopted the Declaration of Independence and the Articles of Confederation.

continen′tal divide′, *n.* **1.** a divide separating river systems that flow to opposite sides of a continent. **2.** (*caps.*) Also called **Great Divide.** the watershed in North America formed by the Rocky Mountains, separating streams flowing west from those flowing east.

con'tinen'tal drift', *n.* the lateral movement of continents resulting from the motion of crustal plates.

con'tinen'tal shelf', *n.* the part of a continent that is submerged in relatively shallow sea.

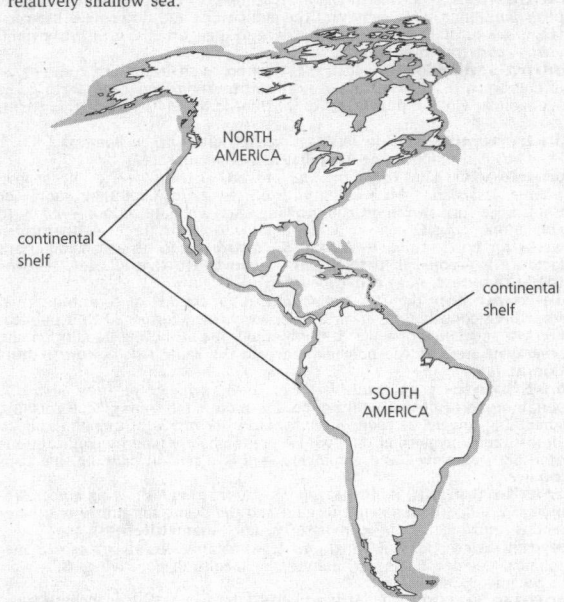

continental shelf

NORTH AMERICA

continental shelf

SOUTH AMERICA

continen'tal Unit'ed States', *n.* the states of the U.S. on the North American continent, usu. excluding Alaska; the 48 contiguous states (excluding Alaska and Hawaii).

con•tin•gence (kən tin′jəns), *n.* contact or tangency.

con•tin•gen•cy (kən tin′jən sē), *n., pl.* **-cies. 1.** dependence on chance or on the fulfillment of a condition; uncertainty. **2.** a contingent event; a chance, accident, or possibility conditional on something uncertain: *prepared with a plan for every contingency.* **3.** something incidental to something else.

contin'gency ta'ble, *n.* the frequency distribution for a two-way statistical classification.

con•tin•gent (kən tin′jənt), *adj.* **1.** dependent on something not yet certain; conditional: *plans contingent on the weather.* **2.** liable to happen or not; uncertain; possible: *contingent expenses.* **3.** happening by chance or without known cause; fortuitous; accidental. **4.** (of a proposition) neither logically necessary nor logically impossible, so that its truth or falsity can be established only by sensory observation. —*n.* **5.** a quota of troops furnished. **6.** any one of the representative groups composing an assemblage. **7.** a share to be contributed or furnished. —**con•tin′gent•ly**, *adv.*

con•tin•u•al (kən tin′yoo əl), *adj.* **1.** of regular or frequent recurrence; often repeated; very frequent: *continual bus departures.* **2.** happening without interruption or cessation; continuous in time. —**con•tin′u•al•ly**, *adv.* —**Usage.** Although the words are used interchangeably in all kinds of speech and writing, usage guides generally advise that CONTINUAL be used only to mean "intermittent" and CONTINUOUS only to mean "uninterrupted." To avoid confusion, some writers use instead the terms *intermittent* (*intermittent losses of power during the storm*) and *uninterrupted* (*uninterrupted reception during the storm*) or similar expressions. CONTINUOUS is never interchangeable with CONTINUAL in the sense of spatial relationship: *a continuous* (not *continual*) *series of passages.*

con•tin•u•ance (kən tin′yoo əns), *n.* **1.** a remaining in the same place, condition, etc. **2.** CONTINUATION (def. 3). **3.** adjournment of a legal proceeding to a future day.

con•tin•u•ant (kən tin′yoo ənt), *n.* **1.** a consonant sound, as (f), (l), or (s), that may be prolonged without change of quality. Compare STOP (def. 37). —*adj.* **2.** of or pertaining to a continuant.

con•tin•u•a•tion (kən tin′yoo ā′shən), *n.* **1.** the act of continuing; the state of being continued. **2.** extension or carrying on to a further point. **3.** something that continues a preceding thing by being of the same or a similar kind; supplement; sequel.

con•tin•ue (kən tin′yoo), *v.,* **-ued, -u•ing.** —*v.i.* **1.** to go on or keep on without interruption, as in some course or action: *The road continues for three miles.* **2.** to go on after suspension or interruption; resume. **3.** to last or endure: *The strike continued for two months.* **4.** to remain in a particular state or capacity: *He agreed to continue as commander.* **5.** to remain in a place; stay. —*v.t.* **6.** to go on with or persist in: *to continue reading.* **7.** to carry on from the point of suspension or interruption. **8.** to extend from one point to another in shape; prolong. **9.** to cause to continue; maintain or retain, as in a position. **10.** to carry over, postpone, or adjourn. —**con•tin′u•a•ble**, *adj.*

contin'uing (or **contin'ued**) **educa'tion**, *n.* a program of courses for adults offered by a university extension or other institution.

con•ti•nu•i•ty (kon′tn ōō′i tē, -tn yōō′), *n., pl.* **-ties. 1.** the state or quality of being continuous. **2.** a continuous or connected whole. **3.** a motion-picture scenario with all details of the action, dialogue, effects, etc., in order. **4.** (on a radio or television program) narration or music that serves as an introduction or transition. **5.** *Math.* the property of a continuous function.

con•tin•u•ous (kən tin′yōō əs), *adj.* **1.** uninterrupted in time; without cessation: *continuous noise during the movie.* **2.** being in immediate connection or spatial relationship: *a continuous row of warehouses.* **3.** PROGRESSIVE (def. 9). —**con•tin′u•ous•ly**, *adv.* —**con•tin′u•ous•ness**, *n.* —**Usage.** See CONTINUAL.

con•tin•u•um (kən tin′yōō əm), *n., pl.* **-tin•u•a** (-tin′yōō ə). **1.** a continuous extent, series, or whole, with no discernible division into parts. **2.** *Math.* **a.** a set of elements such that between any two of them there is a third element. **b.** the set of all real numbers.

con•tort (kən tôrt′), *v.t.* **1.** to twist, bend, or draw out of shape. —*v.i.* **2.** to become twisted. —**con•tor′tive**, *adj.*

con•tort•ed (kən tôr′tid), *adj.* **1.** twisted in a violent manner; distorted. **2.** twisted back on itself; convoluted. —**con•tort′ed•ly**, *adv.* —**con•tort′ed•ness**, *n.*

con•tor•tion•ist (kən tôr′shə nist), *n.* a person who performs gymnastic feats involving contorted postures. —**con•tor′tion•is′tic**, *adj.*

con•tour (kon′tŏŏr), *n.* **1.** the outline of a figure or body; the edge or line that defines or bounds a shape or object. **2.** CONTOUR LINE. **3.** a distinctive pattern of changes in pitch, stress, or tone extending across all or part of an utterance. —*v.t.* **4.** to mark with contour lines. **5.** to make or form the contour or outline of. **6.** to build (a road, railroad track, etc.) in conformity with the contour of the land. **7.** to mold or shape so as to fit a certain configuration or form: *seats contoured for comfort.* —*adj.* **8.** molded or shaped to fit a particular contour or form: *contour sheets.* **9.** of or pertaining to a system of plowing and cultivating hilly land along the natural contours of the slopes in order to prevent runoff and erosion.

con'tour line', *n.* a line representing the locus of points at the same elevation on a topographic surface.

con'tour map', *n.* a topographic map on which the shape of the land surface is shown by contour lines, the relative spacing of the lines indicating the relative slope of the surface.

con•tra¹ (kon′trə), *prep.* **1.** against; in opposition or contrast to. —*adv.* **2.** contrariwise; on or to the contrary.

con•tra² (kon′trə; *Sp.* kôn′trä), *n., pl.* **-tras** (-trəz; *Sp.* -träs). (*often cap.*) a member of a counterrevolutionary guerrilla group in Nicaragua. [< American Spanish, shortening of *contrarrevolucionario* COUNTERREVOLUTIONARY]

contra-¹, a prefix meaning "against," "opposite," "opposing": *contradistinction.*

contra-², a prefix meaning "pitched lower than" the voice or instrument specified by the following element: *contralto; contrabassoon.*

con•tra•band (kon′trə band′), *n.* **1.** anything prohibited by law from being imported or exported. **2.** goods imported or exported illegally. **3.** illegal or prohibited trade; smuggling. **4.** (during the Civil War) a black slave who escaped to or was brought within the Union lines. —*adj.* **5.** prohibited from export or import.

con•tra•bas•soon (kon′trə bə sōōn′, -bə-), *n.* a bassoon larger in size and an octave lower in pitch than the ordinary bassoon; a double bassoon. —**con′tra•bas•soon′ist**, *n.*

con•tra•cep•tion (kon′trə sep′shən), *n.* the deliberate prevention of conception or impregnation by any of various drugs, techniques, or devices; birth control.

con•tra•cep•tive (kon′trə sep′tiv), *adj.* **1.** tending or serving to prevent conception or impregnation. **2.** pertaining to contraception. —*n.* **3.** a contraceptive device, drug, foam, etc.

con•tract (*n., adj., and usu. for v.* 15–17, 21, 22 kon′trakt; *otherwise v.* kən trakt′), *n.* **1.** an agreement between two or more parties for the doing or not doing of something specified. **2.** an agreement enforceable by law. **3.** the written form of such an agreement. **4.** the division of law dealing with contracts. **5.** Also called **con'tract bridge'.** a variety of bridge in which the side that wins the bid can earn toward game only that number of tricks named in the contract, additional points being credited above the line. **6.** (in auction or contract bridge) **a.** a commitment by the declaring team to take six tricks plus the number specified by the final bid made. **b.** the final bid itself. **c.** the number of tricks so specified, plus six. **7.** the formal agreement of marriage; betrothal. —*adj.* **8.** under contract; governed or arranged by special contract: *a contract carrier.* —*v.t.* **9.** to draw together or into smaller compass; draw the parts of together: *to contract a muscle.* **10.** to wrinkle: *to contract the brows.* **11.** to shorten (a word, phrase, etc.) by combining or omitting some of its elements. **12.** to make narrow or illiberal; restrict. **13.** to get, as by exposure to something contagious: *to contract a disease.* **14.** to incur, as a liability or obligation: *to contract a debt.* **15.** to settle or establish by agreement: *to contract an alliance.* **16.** to assign (a job, work, project, etc.) by contract. **17.** to enter into an agreement with: *to* *contract a freelancer to do the work.* **18.** to enter into (friendship, acquaintance, etc.). **19.** to betroth. *—v.i.* **20.** to become drawn together or reduced in compass; become smaller; shrink: *His pupils contracted in the light.* **21.** to enter into an agreement. **22. contract out,** to hire an outside contractor to produce or do; subcontract. —**con′tract•ee′,** *n.* —**con•tract′i•ble,** *adj.* —**con•tract′i•bil′i•ty, con•tract′i•ble•ness,** *n.*

con•trac•tion (kən trak′shən), *n.* **1.** an act or instance of contracting. **2.** the quality or state of being contracted. **3.** a shortened form of a word or group of words, with the omitted letters often replaced in written English by an apostrophe, as *isn't* for *is not, they're* for *they are, e'er* for *ever.* **4.** the change in a muscle by which it becomes thickened and shortened. **5.** a decrease in economic and industrial activity (opposed to *expansion*). —**Usage.** Contractions *(isn't, couldn't, can't, he'll)* occur chiefly, although not exclusively, in informal speech and writing. They are common in personal letters, business letters, journalism, and fiction; rare in scientific and scholarly writing. Contractions in formal writing usu. represent speech.

con•trac•tor (kon′trak tər, kən trak′tər), *n.* **1.** a person who contracts to furnish supplies or perform work at a certain price, esp. in construction. **2.** something that contracts, esp. a muscle.

con•trac•tu•al (kən trak′cho͞o əl), *adj.* of, pertaining to, or secured by a contract. —**con•trac′tu•al•ly,** *adv.*

con•tra•dict (kon′trə dikt′), *v.t.* **1.** to assert the contrary or opposite of; deny categorically. **2.** to speak contrary to the assertions of: *to contradict oneself.* **3.** to imply a denial of: *His way of life contradicts his stated principles.* *—v.i.* **4.** to utter a contrary statement. —**con′tra•dict′a•ble,** *adj.* —**con′tra•dict′er, con′tra•dic′tor,** *n.*

con•tra•dic•tion (kon′trə dik′shən), *n.* **1.** the act of contradicting. **2.** assertion of the contrary or opposite; denial. **3.** a statement or proposition that contradicts or denies another or itself and is logically incongruous. **4.** direct opposition between things compared; inconsistency. **5.** a contradictory act, fact, etc.

con•tra•dic•to•ry (kon′trə dik′tə rē), *adj., n., pl.* **-ries.** *—adj.* **1.** involving contradiction; inconsistent: *contradictory statements.* **2.** tending or inclined to contradict. *—n.* **3.** *Logic.* a proposition so related to a second that it is impossible for both to be true or both to be false. —**con′tra•dic′to•ri•ly,** *adv.* —**con′tra•dic′to•ri•ness,** *n.*

con•tra•dis•tinc•tion (kon′trə di stingk′shən), *n.* distinction by opposition or contrast: *plants and animals in contradistinction to humans.* —**con′tra•dis•tinc′tive,** *adj.* —**con′tra•dis•tinc′tive•ly,** *adv.*

con•trail (kon′trāl), *n.* a visible condensation of water droplets or ice crystals from the atmosphere, occurring in the wake of an aircraft, rocket, or missile. [*con(densation) + trail*]

con•tra•in•di•cate (kon′trə in′di kāt′), *v.t.,* **-cat•ed, -cat•ing.** to make (a procedure or treatment) inadvisable: *That lung congestion contraindicates general anesthesia.*

con•tral•to (kən tral′tō), *n., pl.* **-tos. 1.** the lowest female voice or voice part, intermediate between soprano and tenor. **2.** a singer with a contralto voice.

con•tra•po•si•tion (kon′trə pə zish′ən), *n.* **1.** placement opposite or against. **2.** opposition, contrast, or antithesis. **3.** the inference drawn from a proposition by negating its terms and changing their order, as by inferring "not B implies not A" from "A implies B."

con•trap•tion (kən trap′shən), *n.* a mechanical contrivance; gadget; device.

con•tra•pun•tal (kon′trə pun′tl), *adj.* **1.** of, pertaining to, or involving musical counterpoint. **2.** composed of two or more relatively independent melodies sounded together. —**con′tra•pun′tal•ly,** *adv.*

con•trar•i•an (kən trâr′ē ən), *n.* a person who takes an opposing view, esp. one who rejects the majority opinion.

con•tra•ri•e•ty (kon′trə rī′i tē), *n., pl.* **-ties. 1.** the quality or state of being contrary. **2.** something contrary or of opposite character; a contrary fact or statement.

con•trar•i•ous (kən trâr′ē əs), *adj.* perverse; refractory.

con•trar•y (kon′trer ē; *for 5 also* kən trâr′ē), *adj., n., pl.* **-trar•ies,** *adv.* *—adj.* **1.** opposite in nature or character; diametrically or mutually opposed: *contrary to fact; contrary beliefs.* **2.** opposite in direction or position: *contrary motion.* **3.** being the opposite one of two. **4.** unfavorable or adverse: *contrary winds.* **5.** perverse; obstinate; stubbornly opposed or willful. *—n.* **6.** something that is contrary or opposite. **7.** either of two contrary things. **8.** *Logic.* a proposition so related to another proposition that both may not be true though both may be false, as with the propositions "All judges are male" and "No judges are male." *—adv.* **9.** in opposition; oppositely; counter: *to act contrary to one's principles.* —***Idiom.*** **10. on the contrary,** in opposition to what has been stated. **11. to the contrary,** to the opposite effect: *whatever you may say to the contrary.* —**con′trar•i•ly** (kon′trer ə lē, kən trâr′-), *adv.* —**con′trar•i•ness,** *n.*

con•trast (*v.* kən trast′, kon′trast; *n.* kon′trast), *v.t.* **1.** to compare in order to show unlikeness or differences; note the opposite qualities of. *—v.i.* **2.** to exhibit unlikeness on comparison with something else; form a contrast. **3.** (of linguistic elements, as speech sounds) to differ in a way that can serve to distinguish meanings. *—n.* **4.** the act of contrasting; the state of being contrasted. **5.** a striking exhibition of unlikeness. **6.** a person or thing that is strikingly unlike in comparison. **7.** opposition or juxtaposition of different forms, lines, or colors in a work of art. **8.** the relative difference between light and dark areas of a photographic print or negative. **9.** the brightness ratio of the lightest to the darkest part of a television screen image. **10.** a difference between linguistic elements, esp. sounds, that can serve to distinguish meanings. —**con•trast′a•ble,** *adj.* —**con•trast′ing•ly,** *adv.*

con•tras•tive (kən tras′tiv), *adj.* **1.** tending to contrast; contrasting. **2.** of or pertaining to the study of the similarities and differences between languages or dialects without reference to their origins: *contrastive analysis.* —**con•tras′tive•ly,** *adv.*

con•tra•vene (kon′trə vēn′), *v.t.,* **-vened, -ven•ing. 1.** to come or be in conflict with; deny or oppose: *to contravene a statement.* **2.** to go or act against; violate; transgress: *to contravene the law.* —**con′tra•ven′er,** *n.*

con•tre•temps (kon′trə täɴ′; *Fr.* kôɴtʀᵊ täɴ′), *n., pl.* **-temps** (-täɴz′; *Fr.* -täɴ′). an inopportune or embarrassing occurrence.

con•trib•ute (kən trib′yo͞ot), *v.,* **-ut•ed, -ut•ing.** *—v.t.* **1.** to give (money, assistance, etc.) along with others, as to a common supply or fund. **2.** to furnish (an article, drawing, etc.) for publication. *—v.i.* **3.** to give money, food, etc., to a common supply or fund. **4.** to furnish works for publication. —***Idiom.*** **5. contribute to,** to be an important factor in. —**con•trib′u•tive,** *adj.* —**con•trib′u•tive•ly,** *adv.* —**con•trib′u•tive•ness,** *n.* —**con•trib′u•tor,** *n.*

con•tri•bu•tion (kon′trə byo͞o′shən), *n.* **1.** the act of contributing. **2.** something contributed. **3.** an article, story, etc., furnished to a publication. **4.** an impost or levy. **5.** the method of distributing liability among several insurers whose policies attach to the same risk. —**con′tri•bu′tion•al,** *adj.*

con•trib•u•to•ry (kən trib′yə tôr′ē, -tōr′ē), *adj., n., pl.* **-ries.** *—adj.* **1.** pertaining to or of the nature of contribution; contributing. **2.** furnishing something toward a result: *a contributory factor.* **3.** of or pertaining to an insurance or pension plan whose premiums are paid by contributions from both employee and employer. *—n.* **4.** a person or thing that contributes.

con•trite (kən trīt′, kon′trīt), *adj.* **1.** caused by or showing sincere remorse. **2.** filled with a sense of guilt and the desire for atonement; penitent: *a contrite sinner.* —**con•trite′ly,** *adv.* —**con•trite′ness,** *n.*

con•triv•ance (kən trī′vəns), *n.* **1.** something contrived, esp. a mechanical device. **2.** the act, manner, or faculty of contriving. **3.** a plan or scheme; expedient.

con•trive (kən trīv′), *v.,* **-trived, -triv•ing.** *—v.t.* **1.** to plan with ingenuity; devise; invent: *to contrive a means of escape.* **2.** to bring about by a plan, scheme, etc.; manage: *He contrived to gain their votes.* **3.** to plot (evil, treachery, etc.). *—v.i.* **4.** to form designs; plan. **5.** to plot. —**con•triv′a•ble,** *adj.* —**con•triv′er,** *n.*

con•trol (kən trōl′), *v.,* **-trolled, -trol•ling,** *n.* *—v.t.* **1.** to exercise restraint or direction over; dominate, regulate, or command. **2.** to hold in check; curb: *to control one's emotions.* **3.** to test or verify (a scientific experiment) by a parallel experiment or other standard of comparison. **4.** to prevent the flourishing or spread of: *to control a forest fire.* *—v.i.* **5.** to exercise control. *—n.* **6.** the act or power of controlling; regulation; domination or command. **7.** check or restraint: *My anger was under control.* **8.** a legal or official means of regulation or restraint: *wage and price controls.* **9. a.** a standard of comparison in scientific experimentation. **b.** a person or subject that serves in such a comparison. **10.** a person who acts as a check; controller. **11.** a device for regulating, guiding, or directing the operation of a machine, apparatus, or vehicle. **12. controls,** a coordinated arrangement of such devices. **13.** prevention of the flourishing or spread of something undesirable: *rodent control.* **14.** a baseball pitcher's ability to place the ball or throw strikes. **15.** a spiritual agency believed to assist a medium at a séance. —**con•trol′la•ble,** *adj., n.* —**con•trol′la•bil′i•ty,** *n.* —**con•trol′la•bly,** *adv.* —**con•trol′ling•ly,** *adv.*

controlled′ sub′stance, *n.* any of a category of behavior-altering or addictive drugs whose possession and use are restricted by law.

con•trol•ler (kən trō′lər), *n.* **1.** a government official or an officer of a business firm who superintends financial accounts and transactions; comptroller. **2.** a person who regulates, directs, or restrains. **3.** a regulating mechanism; governor. —**con•trol′ler•ship′,** *n.*

con•tro•ver•sy (kon′trə vûr′sē; *Brit. also* kən trov′ər sē), *n., pl.* **-sies. 1.** a usu. prolonged public dispute concerning a matter of opinion. **2.** contention, strife, or argument. —**con′tro•ver′sial,** *adj.*

con•tro•vert (kon′trə vûrt′, kon′trə vûrt′), *v.t.* **1.** to argue against; dispute; deny; oppose. **2.** to argue about; debate; discuss. —**con′tro•vert′er,** *n.* —**con′tro•vert′i•ble,** *adj.* —**con′tro•vert′i•bly,** *adv.*

con•tu•ma•cious (kon′to͞o mā′shəs, -tyo͞o-), *adj.* stubbornly perverse or rebellious; willfully disobedient. —**con′tu•ma′cious•ly,** *adv.* —**con′tu•ma′cious•ness, con′tu•mac′i•ty** (-mas′i tē), *n.*

con•tu•me•ly (kon′to͞o mə lē, -tyo͞o-; kən to͞o′mə lē, -tyo͞o′-), *n., pl.* **-lies. 1.** insulting display of contempt in words or actions; contemptuous or humiliating treatment. **2.** a humiliating insult. —**con′tu•me′li•ous** (-mē′lē əs), *adj.* —**con′tu•me′li•ous•ly,** *adv.*

con•tuse (kən to͞oz′, -tyo͞oz′), *v.t.,* **-tused, -tus•ing.** to injure (tissue), esp. without breaking the skin; bruise. —**con•tu′sive** (-to͞o′siv, -tyo͞o′-), *adj.*

con•tu•sion (kən to͞o′zhən, -tyo͞o′-), *n.* an injury to the subsurface tissue without the skin being broken; bruise. —**con•tu′sioned,** *adj.*

co•nun•drum (kə nun′drəm), *n.* **1.** a riddle whose answer involves a pun. **2.** anything that puzzles.

con•ur•ba•tion (kon′ər bā′shən), *n.* an extensive urban area resulting from the expansion of several cities or towns so that they coalesce but usu. retain their separate identities.

con·va·les·cence (kon′və les′əns), *n.* **1.** the gradual recovery of health and strength after illness. **2.** the period during which one is recovering. —**con·va·lesce,** *v.i.* -lesced, -lesc·ing. —**con·va·les′cent,** *adj., n.*

con·vect (kən vekt′), *v.t.* **1.** to transfer (heat or a fluid) by convection. —*v.i.* **2.** (of a fluid) to transfer heat by convection. —**con·vec′tive,** *adj.* —**con·vec′tive·ly,** *adv.*

con·vec·tion (kən vek′shən), *n.* **1.** the transfer of heat by the circulation or movement of the heated parts of a liquid or gas. **2.** the vertical transport of atmospheric properties, esp. upward (disting. from *advection*). **3.** the act of conveying or transmitting. —**con·vec′tion·al,** *adj.*

convec′tion ov′en, *n.* an oven equipped with a fan that circulates the heated air, thereby decreasing normal cooking time.

con·ve·nance (kon′və näns′; *Fr.* kônvə näns′), *n., pl.* -nanc·es (-nän′siz; *Fr.* -näns′). **1.** suitability; propriety. **2. convenances,** social proprieties.

con·vene (kən vēn′), *v.,* -vened, -ven·ing. —*v.i.* **1.** to assemble, usu. for some public purpose. —*v.t.* **2.** to cause to assemble; convoke. **3.** to summon to appear, as before a judicial officer. —**con·ven′a·ble,** *adj.* —**con·ven′er, con·ve′nor,** *n.*

con·ven·ience (kən vēn′yəns), *n.* **1.** the quality of being convenient. **2.** anything, as an appliance, that saves or simplifies work or adds to one's ease or comfort. **3.** a convenient situation or time: *at your convenience.* **4.** advantage or accommodation; comfort. **5.** *Chiefly Brit.* LAVATORY.

conven′ience food′, *n.* any packaged food, as frozen food or instant cereal, that can be prepared quickly and easily.

conven′ience store′, *n.* a small market that carries a limited selection of goods and is open long hours.

con·ven·ient (kən vēn′yənt), *adj.* **1.** suitable or agreeable to the needs or purpose; well-suited with respect to facility or ease in use. **2.** at hand; easily accessible: *convenient to all transportation.* —**con·ven′ient·ly,** *adv.*

con·vent ·(kon′vent, -vənt), *n.* **1.** a community of people, esp. nuns, devoted to religious life under a superior. **2.** the building or complex occupied by such a society.

con·ven·tion (kən ven′shən), *n.* **1.** a meeting or formal assembly, as of members or delegates, to discuss or act on matters of common concern. **2.** an assembly of delegates of a political party to nominate candidates and adopt platforms and party rules. **3.** an agreement or contract; compact. **4.** an international agreement, esp. one dealing with a specific matter. **5.** a rule, method, or practice established by usage; custom: *the convention of showing north at the top of a map.* **6.** general agreement or consent; accepted usage, esp. as a standard of procedure. **7.** a bid or play in bridge that allows partners to convey information about their hands according to a prearranged system.

con·ven·tion·al (kən ven′shə nl), *adj.* **1.** conforming or adhering to accepted standards, as of conduct or taste. **2.** pertaining to or established by general consent or accepted usage: *conventional symbols.* **3.** ordinary rather than different or original. **4.** not using nuclear weapons or energy; nonnuclear: *conventional weapons; conventional warfare.* **5.** in accordance with an accepted manner, model, or tradition in art. **6.** of or pertaining to a compact or convention. **7.** of or pertaining to a convention or assembly. —**con·ven′tion·al·ism,** *n.* —**con·ven′tion·al·ly,** *adv.*

con·ven·tion·al·i·ty (kən ven′shə nal′i tē), *n., pl.* -ties. **1.** conventional quality or character. **2.** adherence to convention. **3.** a conventional practice, principle, or form.

conven′tional wis′dom, *n.* something that is generally believed; prudence.

conven′tion bounce′, *n.* a brief surge of popularity after a candidate has been nominated at a convention to run for the office of president.

con·verge (kən vûrj′), *v.,* -verged, -verg·ing. —*v.i.* **1.** to tend to meet in a point or line; incline toward each other, as lines that are not parallel. **2.** to tend toward a common result or conclusion. **3.** (of a mathematical sequence) to have values eventually arbitrarily close to some number; to have a finite limit. —*v.t.* **4.** to cause to converge.

con·ver·gence (kən vûr′jəns), *n.* **1.** an act or instance of converging. **2.** a convergent state or quality. **3.** the degree or point of converging. **4.** a coordinated turning of the eyes to bear upon a near point. **5.** a similarity of structure in unrelated organisms that is caused by similar environmental pressures. **6.** a net flow of air into a given region. Also, **con·ver′gen·cy** (for defs. 1–3).

con·ver·gent (kən vûr′jənt), *adj.* characterized by convergence; tending to come together; merging. —**con·ver′gent·ly,** *adv.*

con·ver·sant (kən vûr′sənt, kon′vər-), *adj.* familiar by use or study (usu. fol. by *with*): *conversant with Spanish history.* —**con·ver′sance, con·ver′san·cy,** *n.* —**con·ver′sant·ly,** *adv.*

con·ver·sa·tion (kon′vər sā′shən), *n.* **1.** informal spoken interchange of thoughts, information, etc.; oral communication between people. **2.** an instance of this. **3.** an interchange resembling spoken conversation. **4.** the ability to talk socially with others: *a person with no conversation.* **5.** association or social intercourse; intimate acquaintance. —**con′ver·sa′tion·al,** *adj.*

conversa′tion piece′, *n.* **1.** any object that arouses comment because

of some striking or unusual quality. **2.** a group portrait of people in their customary setting.

con·verse¹ (*v.* kən vûrs′; *n.* kon′vûrs), *v.,* -versed, -vers·ing, *n.* —*v.i.* **1.** to talk informally with another; exchange ideas by talking. —*n.* **2.** familiar discourse or talk; conversation. —**con·vers′er,** *n.*

con·verse² (*adj.* kən vûrs′, kon′vûrs; *n.* kon′vûrs), *adj.* **1.** opposite or contrary in direction, action, sequence, etc.; turned around. —*n.* **2.** something opposite or contrary. **3.** a logical proposition obtained from another proposition by conversion. **4.** a group of words correlative with a preceding group but having a significant pair of terms interchanged, as "hot in winter but cold in summer" and "cold in winter but hot in summer." —**con·verse′ly,** *adv.*

Con·verse (kon′vûrs), *n.* **Charles,** 1832–1918, U.S. musician and hymn writer.

con·ver·sion (kən vûr′zhən, -shən), *n.* **1.** the act or process of converting; the state of being converted. **2.** change in character, form, or function. **3.** change from one religion, political belief, viewpoint, course, etc., to another. **4.** a change from indifference, disbelief, or antagonism to acceptance, faith, or enthusiastic support, esp. such a change involving religious belief. **5.** a physical transformation from one material or state to another: *conversion of base metals into gold.* **6.** the act of obtaining equivalent value, as of money or units of measurement, in an exchange or calculation. **7.** a physical, structural, or design change, as in a building, to effect a change in function. **8.** a substitution of one component for another so as to effect a change: *conversion from oil heat to gas heat.* **9.** a change in the form or units of a mathematical expression. **10.** the transposition of the subject and predicate of a logical proposition, as in converting "No good man is unhappy" to "No unhappy man is good." **11. a.** unauthorized assumption and exercise of rights of ownership over personal property belonging to another. **b.** change from realty into personalty, or vice versa, as in the sale or purchase of land. **12.** the making of an additional score in certain sports, as on a try for a point after a touchdown in football or a free throw in basketball. **13.** *Psychoanal.* the process by which a repressed psychic event, idea, feeling, memory, or impulse is represented by a bodily change or symptom. **14.** the transformation of one radioactive material into another by neutron capture. **15. a.** the process of enabling software for one computer system to run on another. **b.** the transformation of data from a form compatible with one computer program to a form compatible with another. —**con·ver′sion·al, con·ver′sion·ar′y** (-zhə ner′ē, -shə-), *adj.*

con·vert (*v.* kən vûrt′; *n.* kon′vûrt), *v.t.* **1.** to change into something of different form or properties; transform. **2.** to cause to adopt a different religion, belief, political doctrine, course, etc. **3.** to cause a change from disbelief to faith. **4.** to turn to another use or purpose; modify so as to serve a different function: *to convert the study into a nursery.* **5.** to obtain an equivalent value for in an exchange or calculation, as money or units of measurement: *to convert yards into meters.* **6.** to exchange (a bond or preferred stock) for another security, esp. common stock. **7.** to cause (a substance) to undergo a chemical change: *to convert sugar into alcohol.* **8.** to invert or transpose. **9. a.** to assume unlawful rights of ownership of (personal property). **b.** to change the form of (property), as from realty to personalty or vice versa. **10.** to transpose the subject and predicate of (a logical proposition) by conversion. **11.** to transmute (fertile material) into fissile nuclear fuel by neutron bombardment. —*v.i.* **12.** to become converted. **13.** to make a conversion in football or basketball. —*n.* **14.** a person who has been converted, as to a religion or opinion.

con·vert·er (kən vûr′tər), *n.* **1.** a person or thing that converts. **2.** a device that converts alternating current to direct current or vice versa. **3.** DECODER (def. 3). **4.** an auxiliary device that permits a radio or television receiver to pick up frequencies or channels for which it was not orig. designed. **5.** a chamber or vessel through which an oxidizing blast of air is forced, as in making steel by the Bessemer process. **6.** a nuclear reactor for converting fertile material into fissile fuel.

con·vert·i·ble (kən vûr′tə bəl), *adj.* **1.** capable of being converted. **2.** having a folding top, as an automobile or boat. **3.** exchangeable for something of equal value: *a convertible currency.* **4.** having a seat, often with a mattress beneath it, that folds out for use as a bed: *a convertible sofa.* —*n.* **5.** an automobile or boat with a folding top. **6.** a convertible sofa. **7.** a convertible bond or security. —**con·vert′i·bil′i·ty,** *n.* —**con·vert′i·bly,** *adv.*

con·vex (*adj.* kon veks′, kən-; *n.* kon′veks), *adj.* **1.** curved or rounded outward like the outside of a circle or sphere. Compare CONCAVE (def. 1). **2.** (of a polygon) having all interior angles less than or equal to 180°. —*n.* **3.** a convex surface, part, line, or thing. —**con·vex′ly,** *adv.*

con·vex·i·ty (kən vek′si tē), *n., pl.* -ties. **1.** the state of being convex. **2.** a convex surface or thing.

con·vey (kən vā′), *v.t.* **1.** to carry or take from one place to another; transport; bear. **2.** to communicate; impart; make known: *to convey a wish.* **3.** to lead or conduct, as a channel or medium; transmit. **4.** *Law.* to transfer; pass the title to. —**con·vey′a·ble,** *adj.*

con·vey·ance (kən vā′əns), *n.* **1.** the act of conveying; transmission. **2.** a means of transporting, esp. a vehicle. **3. a.** the transfer of property from one person to another. **b.** the document accomplishing this.

convey′or belt′, *n.* an endless belt or chain, set of rollers, etc., for carrying materials or objects short distances.

con·vict (*v.* kən vikt′; *n.* kon′vikt), *v.t.* **1.** to prove or declare guilty of an offense, esp. after a legal trial. **2.** to impress with a sense of guilt.

—*n.* **3.** a person proved or declared guilty of an offense. **4.** a person serving a prison sentence.
con•vic•tion (kən vik′shən), *n.* **1.** a fixed or firm belief. **2.** the act of convicting. **3.** the state of being convicted. **4.** the state of being convinced. **5.** the act of convincing. —**con•vic′tion•al,** *adj.*
con•vince (kən vins′), *v.t.*, **-vinced, -vinc•ing. 1.** to move by argument or evidence to belief, agreement, consent, or a course of action: *to convince you of his guilt.* **2.** to persuade; cajole: *We finally convinced them to stay.* —**con•vinc′ed•ly,** *adv.* —**con•vinc′ed•ness,** *n.* —**con•vinc′er,** *n.* —**con•vin′ci•ble,** *adj.* —**con•vinc′i•bil′i•ty,** *n.*
con•vinc•ing (kən vin′sing), *adj.* **1.** persuading or assuring by argument or evidence: *a convincing demonstration of the car's safety.* **2.** appearing worthy of belief; plausible: *a convincing excuse for being late.* —**con•vinc′ing•ly,** *adv.*
con•viv•i•al (kən viv′ē əl), *adj.* **1.** friendly; agreeable: *a convivial atmosphere.* **2.** fond of feasting and merry company; jovial. **3.** of or befitting a feast; festive. —**con•viv′i•al′i•ty,** *n.* —**con•viv′i•al•ly,** *adv.*
con•vo•ca•tion (kon′və kā′shən), *n.* **1.** the act of convoking. **2.** a group of people gathered in answer to a summons; assembly. **3.** either of the two provincial synods of the Church of England. **4.** an assembly of the clergy of part of a diocese in the Episcopal Church. **5.** a formal assembly at a college or university, esp. for a graduation ceremony. —**con′vo•ca′tion•al,** *adj.*
con•voke (kən vōk′), *v.t.*, **-voked, -vok•ing.** to call together; summon to meet or assemble. —**con•vok′er,** *n.*
con•vo•lute (kon′və lo͞ot′), *v.*, **-lut•ed, -lut•ing,** *adj.* —*v.t., v.i.* **1.** to coil up; form into a twisted shape. —*adj.* **2.** coiled or rolled up together or with one part over another. —**con′vo•lute′ly,** *adv.*
con•vo•lut•ed (kon′və lo͞o′tid), *adj.* **1.** twisted; coiled. **2.** complicated; intricately involved: *convoluted reasoning.* —**con′vo•lut′ed•ly,** *adv.* —**con′vo•lut′ed•ness,** *n.*
con•vo•lu•tion (kon′və lo͞o′shən), *n.* **1.** a rolled up or coiled condition. **2.** a rolling or coiling together. **3.** a turn of anything coiled; whorl. **4.** one of the sinuous folds or ridges of the surface of the brain. —**con′vo•lu′tion•al, con′vo•lu′tion•ar•y** (-shə ner′ē), *adj.*
con•vol•vu•lus (kən vol′vyə ləs), *n., pl.* **-lus•es, -li** (-lī′). any of numerous twining or prostrate plants belonging to the genus *Convolvulus,* of the morning glory family, having trumpet-shaped flowers.
con•voy (kon′voi; *v. also* kən voi′), *n.* **1.** a ship or fleet accompanied by a protecting escort. **2.** a group of vehicles traveling together, sometimes for protection. **3.** the act of convoying or escorting. —*v.t.* **4.** to accompany or escort, usu. for protection.
con•vulse (kən vuls′), *v.t.*, **-vulsed, -vuls•ing. 1.** to shake violently; agitate. **2.** to cause to shake violently with laughter, anger, pain, etc. **3.** to cause to suffer violent, spasmodic contractions of the muscles. —**con•vuls′ed•ly,** *adv.*
con•vul•sion (kən vul′shən), *n.* **1.** contortion of the body caused by violent, involuntary muscular contractions. **2.** violent agitation or disturbance. **3.** an outburst of great, uncontrollable laughter.
con•vul•sive (kən vul′siv), *adj.* **1.** of the nature of or characterized by convulsions or spasms. **2.** accompanied by convulsions: *convulsive rage.* —**con•vul′sive•ly,** *adv.* —**con•vul′sive•ness,** *n.*
coo (ko͞o), *v.i.* **1.** to utter or imitate the soft, murmuring sound characteristic of doves. **2.** to murmur or talk fondly or amorously. —*v.t.* **3.** to utter by cooing. —*n.* **4.** a cooing sound. —**coo′er,** *n.* —**coo′ing•ly,** *adv.*
co-oc•cur or **co•oc•cur** (kō′ə kûr′), *v.i.*, **-curred, -cur•ring.** to appear together in sequence or simultaneously. —**co′-oc•cur′rence,** *n.*
cook (ko͝ok), *v.t.* **1.** to prepare (food) by the use of heat, as by boiling, baking, or roasting. **2.** to subject (anything) to the application of heat. **3.** *Slang.* to ruin; spoil. **4.** *Informal.* to falsify, as accounts: *to cook the books.* —*v.i.* **5.** to prepare food by the use of heat. **6.** (of food) to undergo cooking. **7.** *Informal.* to take place or develop: *What's cooking?* **8.** *Slang.* **a.** to perform or do extremely well or with energy and style: *The band is really cooking tonight.* **b.** to be full of activity and excitement. **9. cook up,** *Informal.* to concoct or contrive, esp. falsely: *to cook up an excuse.* —*n.* **10.** a person who cooks. —***Proverb.*** **11. Too many cooks spoil the broth,** having too many people work on a project results in confusion and inattention.
Cook (ko͝ok), *n.* **1. David Caleb,** 1850–1927, U.S. editor and publisher of Sunday School materials. **2. Captain James,** 1728–79, English explorer of the S Pacific, Antarctica, and the coasts of Australia and New Zealand. **3. Robert Andrew,** U.S. clergyman and Christian educator.
cook•book (ko͝ok′bo͝ok′), *n.* a book containing recipes and instructions for preparing and cooking food.
cook•er (ko͝ok′ər), *n.* **1.** an appliance or utensil for cooking: *pressure cooker.* **2.** a person employed in certain industrial processes, as in brewing or distilling, to operate cooking apparatus.
cook•er•y (ko͝ok′ə rē), *n., pl.* **-er•ies. 1.** the art or practice of cooking. **2.** a place equipped for cooking.
cook•ie or **cook•y** (ko͝ok′ē), *n., pl.* **cook•ies. 1.** a small, flat, sweetened cake, often round, made from stiff dough baked on a large, flat pan **(cook′ie sheet′). 2.** *Slang.* a person: *a smart cookie.* —***Idiom.*** **3. the way the cookie crumbles,** the way things happen.
cook•ing (ko͝ok′ing), *adj.* **1.** used in preparing foods: *a cooking utensil.* **2.** fit to eat when cooked (disting. from *eating*): *cooking apples.*
cook′off′ or **cook′-off′,** *n.* a cooking contest in which competitors gather to prepare their specialties.
cook•out (ko͝ok′out′), *n.* **1.** an outdoor gathering at which food is cooked and consumed. **2.** a meal cooked and eaten in the open.
cook•ware (ko͝ok′wâr′), *n.* pots, pans, and other cooking utensils.
cook•y (ko͝ok′ē), *n., pl.* **cook•ies.** COOKIE.
cool (ko͞ol), *adj.* **1.** moderately cold; neither warm nor cold. **2.** imparting a sensation of coolness: *a cool breeze.* **3.** permitting relief from heat: *a cool dress.* **4.** not excited; calm: *remained cool in the face of disaster.* **5.** not hasty; deliberate: *a cool and calculated action.* **6.** lacking in interest or enthusiasm: *a cool reply to an invitation.* **7.** lacking in cordiality: *a cool reception.* **8.** calmly audacious or impudent: *a cool lie.* **9.** unresponsive; indifferent: *cool to his passionate advances.* **10.** *Informal.* not exaggerated or qualified: *a cool million dollars.* **11.** (of colors) having green, blue, or violet predominating. **12.** *Slang.* **a.** great; excellent. **b.** highly skilled; adept: *cool maneuvers on the parallel bars.* **c.** socially adept: *It's not cool to arrive at a party too early.* —*adv.* **13.** *Informal.* coolly: *play it cool.* —*n.* **14.** a cool part, place, or time: *in the cool of the evening.* **15.** calmness; composure; poise: *an executive noted for maintaining her cool under pressure.* —*v.i.* **16.** to become cool: *cooled off in the mountain stream.* **17.** to become less ardent or cordial. —*v.t.* **18.** to make cool; impart a sensation of coolness to. **19.** to lessen the ardor or intensity of: *Disappointment cooled enthusiasm.* —***Idiom.*** **20. cool it,** *Slang.* calm down. —**cool′ly,** *adv.* —**cool′ness,** *n.*
cool•ant (ko͞o′lənt), *n.* **1.** a substance, as a liquid or gas, used to reduce the temperature of a system below a specified value. **2.** a lubricant that dissipates the heat caused by friction.
cool•er (ko͞o′lər), *n.* **1.** a container, as an insulated chest, for keeping something cool. **2.** a tall, iced, usu. alcoholic drink.
cool′-head′ed, *adj.* not easily excited. —**cool′-head′ed•ness,** *n.*
Cool•idge (ko͞o′lij), *n.* **Calvin,** 1872–1933, 30th president of the U.S. 1923–29.
coo•lie (ko͞o′lē), *n.* a laborer hired at subsistence wages for unskilled work, esp. formerly in the Far East.
cool′ing-off′ pe′riod, *n.* a period arranged by agreement to allow for negotiation and an abatement of tension between disputing parties: *The law calls for a cooling-off period before a strike can begin.*
coon (ko͞on), *n.* raccoon.
coon•hound (ko͞on′hound′), *n.* a hound of any of several breeds developed esp. for hunting raccoons.
coon's′ age′, *n. Informal.* a long period of time.
coon•skin (ko͞on′skin′), *n.* **1.** the pelt of a raccoon. **2.** an article of clothing made of coonskin, esp. a hat with a tail.
coon•tie (ko͞on′tē), *n.* **1.** either of two arrowroots, *Zamia integrifolia* or *Z. floridana,* of Florida, having a short trunk, pinnate leaves, and cones. **2.** flour produced from coontie starch.
co-op (kō′op), *n.* **1.** a cooperative enterprise, building, or apartment. —***Idiom.*** **2. go co-op,** (of an apartment building) to convert to a cooperative. —**co′-op•er,** *n.*
coop (ko͞op, ko͝op), *n.* **1.** an enclosure or cage in which poultry or small animals are penned. **2.** a confined space. —*v.t.* **3.** to place in or as if in a coop (often fol. by *up*).
coop•er (ko͞o′pər, ko͝op′ər), *n.* **1.** a person who makes or repairs casks, barrels, or tubs. —*v.t.* **2.** to work as a cooper on. —*v.i.* **3.** to work as a cooper.
Coo•per (ko͞o′pər, ko͝op′ər), *n.* **1. Gary,** 1901–60, U.S. actor and film maker. **2. James Fenimore,** 1789–1851, U.S. novelist. **3. Peter,** 1791–1883, U.S. inventor and philanthropist.
co•op•er•ate or **co-op•er•ate** (kō op′ə rāt′), *v.i.*, **-at•ed, -at•ing. 1.** to work or act together or jointly for a common purpose or benefit. **2.** to work or act with others willingly and agreeably.
co•op•er•a•tion or **co-op•er•a•tion** (kō op′ə rā′shən), *n.* **1.** the action of working or acting together for a common purpose or benefit. **2.** the combination of persons for purposes of production, purchase, or distribution for their joint benefit. **3.** *Ecol.* mutually beneficial interaction among organisms living in a limited area. —**co•op′er•a′tion•ist,** *n.*
co•op•er•a•tive or **co-op•er•a•tive** (kō op′ər ə tiv, -op′rə tiv, -op′ə-rā′tiv), *adj.* **1.** working or acting together for a common purpose or benefit. **2.** demonstrating a willingness to cooperate. **3.** pertaining to economic cooperation: *a cooperative business.* —*n.* **4.** a jointly owned enterprise engaging in the production or distribution of goods or the supplying of services, operated by its members for their mutual benefit. **5.** Also called **co-op, coop′erative apart′ment. a.** a building owned and managed by a corporation in which shares are sold, entitling the shareholders to occupy individual units in the building. **b.** an apartment in such a building. Compare CONDOMINIUM (defs. 1, 2). —**co•op′er•a•tive•ly,** *adv.*
Coo′per's hawk′, *n.* a North American hawk, *Accipiter cooperii,* having a gray back and a rusty breast.
co-opt (kō opt′), *v.t.* **1.** to elect or choose as a member. **2.** to assimilate or win over into a larger group. **3.** to appropriate as one's own; preempt. —**co-op′tion,** *n.* —**co-op′tive,** *adj.*
co•or•di•nate or **co-or•di•nate** (*adj., n.* kō ôr′dn it, -dn āt′; *v.* -āt′), *adj., n., v.*, **-nat•ed, -nat•ing.** —*adj.* **1.** of the same order or degree; equal in rank or importance. **2.** involving coordination. **3.** *Math.* using or pertaining to systems of coordinates. **4.** of the same grammatical rank in a construction, as *Jack* and *Jill* in the phrase *Jack and Jill,* or *got*

up and *shook hands* in the sentence *He got up and shook hands.* —*n.* **5.** *Math.* any of the magnitudes that serve to define the position of a point, line, or the like, by reference to a fixed figure, system of lines, etc. **6.** a person or thing of equal rank or importance; an equal. **7. coordinates,** articles, as of clothing, harmonizing in color, material, or style. —*v.t.* **8.** to place or class in the same order, rank, or division. **9.** to place or arrange in proper order or position. **10.** to combine in harmonious relation or action. —*v.i.* **11.** to become coordinate. **12.** to act in harmonious combination. —**co•or′di•nate•ly,** *adv.*

coor′dinating conjunc′tion, *n.* a conjunction that connects grammatical elements of equal rank, as *and* in *Sue and Andrea* or *or* in *I can't decide if I should stay or go.* Compare SUBORDINATING CONJUNCTION.

co•or•di•na•tion or **co-or•di•na•tion** (kō ôr′dn ā′shən), *n.* **1.** the act or state of coordinating or of being coordinated. **2.** proper order or relationship. **3.** harmonious combination or interaction, as of functions or parts.

co•or•di•na•tor or **co-or•di•na•tor** (kō ôr′dn ā′tər), *n.* **1.** a person or thing that coordinates. **2.** a coordinating conjunction.

coot (kōōt), *n.* **1.** any aquatic rail of the genus *Fulica,* as *F. americana,* of North America, and *F. atra,* of the Old World, characterized by lobate toes. **2.** any of various other swimming or diving birds, esp. the scoters. **3.** *Informal.* a foolish or crotchety person, esp. one who is old.

American coot, *Fulica americana,*
length 16 in. (41 cm)

coot•er (kōō′tər), *n.* any of several large freshwater turtles of the genus *Chrysemys,* of the S U.S., esp. *C. floridana.*

cop¹ (kop), *v.t.,* **copped, cop•ping.** *Informal.* **1.** to catch; nab. **2.** to steal; filch. **3. cop out,** to renege on a promise; avoid a responsibility. —*Idiom.* **4. cop a plea,** to plea-bargain.

cop² (kop), *n.* POLICE OFFICER.

co•pai•ba (kō pā′bə, -pī′bə), *n.* an oleoresin obtained from several tropical, chiefly South American trees belonging to the genus *Copaifera,* used chiefly in varnishes and in cleaning oil paintings.

co•pal (kō′pəl, -pal), *n.* a lustrous resin obtained from various tropical trees and used in making varnishes.

co•par•ent or **co•par•ent** (kō pâr′ənt, -par′-), *n.* **1.** a divorced or separated parent who shares equally with the other parent in the custody and care of a child. —*v.i.* **3.** to share equally with another parent in the care of (a child). —*v.i.* **3.** to act as a co-parent.

cope¹ (kōp), *v.i.,* **coped, cop•ing. 1.** to struggle esp. on fairly even terms or with some degree of success (usu. fol. by *with*): *I will try to cope with his rudeness.* **2.** to face and deal with responsibilities or problems esp. calmly or adequately: *After his breakdown he couldn't cope any longer.*

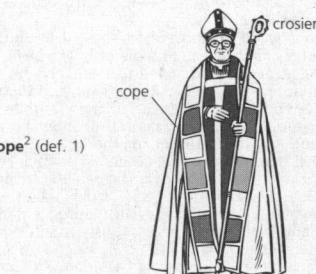

cope² (def. 1)

cope² (kōp), *n., v.,* **coped, cop•ing.** —*n.* **1.** a long mantle worn by an ecclesiastic, esp. in processions. **2.** any cloaklike or canopylike covering. **3.** COPING. —*v.t.* **4.** to furnish with a cope or coping.

Co•pen•ha•gen (kō′pən hā′gən, -hä′-, kō′pən hā′-, -hä′-), *n.* the capital of Denmark on the E coast of Zealand. 802,391; with suburbs, 1,380,204. Danish, **København.**

co•pe•pod (kō′pə pod′), *n.* any tiny marine or freshwater crustacean of the class Copepoda: some are abundant in plankton and others are parasitic.

Co•per•ni•cus (kō pûr′ni kəs, kə-), *n.* **Nicolaus** (*Mikołaj Kopernik*), 1473–1543, Polish astronomer who promulgated the theory that the earth and the other planets move around the sun (the **Coper′nican Sys′tem**). —**Co•per′ni•can,** *adj., n.*

cope•stone (kōp′stōn′), *n.* **1.** the top stone of a building or other

structure. **2.** a stone used for or in coping. **3.** the crown or completion; finishing touch.

cop•i•er (kop′ē ər), *n.* **1.** a person or thing that copies; copyist. **2.** PHOTOCOPIER. **3.** COPYING MACHINE.

co•pi•lot (kō′pī′lət), *n.* a pilot who is second in command of an aircraft.

cop•ing (kō′ping), *n.* **1.** a finishing or protective course or cap to an exterior masonry wall or the like. **2.** a piece of woodwork having its end shaped to fit together with a molding.

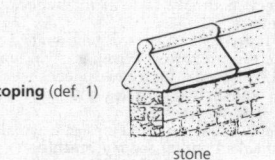 

coping (def. 1)   stone   tile

co•pi•ous (kō′pē əs), *adj.* **1.** large in quantity or number; abundant; plentiful: *copious amounts of food.* **2.** yielding an abundant supply: *a copious harvest.* **3.** exhibiting abundance or fullness, as of thoughts or words. —**co′pi•ous•ly,** *adv.* —**co′pi•ous•ness,** *n.*

co•pla•nar (kō plā′nər), *adj. Math.* being or operating in the same plane: *coplanar triangles.* —**co′pla•nar′i•ty,** *n.*

Cop•land (kōp′lənd), *n.* **Aaron,** 1900–90, U.S. composer.

co•pol•y•mer (kō pol′ə mər), *n.* a chemical compound of high molecular weight produced by polymerizing two or more different monomers.

cop′-out′, *n.* **1.** an act or instance of copping out. **2.** a person who cops out.

cop•per¹ (kop′ər), *n.* **1.** a malleable ductile metallic element having a characteristic reddish brown color: used in large quantities as an electrical conductor and in the manufacture of alloys, as brass and bronze. Symbol: Cu; *at. wt.:* 63.54; *at. no.:* 29; *sp. gr.:* 8.92 at 20°C. **2.** a metallic reddish brown. **3.** a coin composed of copper or bronze. **4.** any of several butterflies of the family Lycaenidae, as *Lycaena hypophleas* (**American copper**), having copper-colored wings spotted and edged with black. **5.** a tool partly or wholly made of copper: *a soldering copper.* **6.** *Brit.* a large kettle for cooking or for boiling laundry. —*v.t.* **7.** to cover, coat, or sheathe with copper. **8.** *Slang.* to bet against. [< Latin *cuprum*] —**cop′per•y,** *adj.*

cop•per² (kop′ər), *n. Slang.* POLICE OFFICER.

Cop′per Age′, *n.* a cultural period between the Neolithic and the Bronze ages, marked by the development and use of copper tools.

cop′per beech′, *n.* a variety of the European beech, *Fagus sylvatica atropunicea,* having purplish or copper-red leaves.

cop•per•head (kop′ər hed′), *n.* **1.** a venomous snake of the eastern and southern U.S., having a light-brown to copper-red body marked with darker bands. **2.** (*cap.*) a Northern Democrat who opposed the Civil War, advocating peace and restoration of the Union even if slavery continued.

cop•pice (kop′is), *n.* COPSE. —**cop′piced,** *adj.*

Cop•po•la (kop′ə lə), *n.* **Francis Ford,** born 1939, U.S. film director and screenwriter.

cop•ra (kop′rə, kō′prə), *n.* the dried meat of the coconut from which coconut oil is expressed.

cop•ro•lite (kop′rə līt′), *n.* a fossil consisting of animal fecal matter. —**cop′ro•lit′ic** (-lit′ik), *adj.*

copse (kops) also **coppice,** *n.* a thicket of small trees or bushes; a small wood.

Copt (kopt), *n.* an Egyptian who is a member of the Coptic Church. —**Cop′tic,** *adj., n.*

cop•ter (kop′tər), *n.* a helicopter.

Cop′tic Church′, *n.* the Christian church in Egypt, governed by a patriarch and characterized by an adherence to Monophysitism.

cop•u•la (kop′yə lə), *n., pl.* **-las, -lae** (-lē′). **1.** something that connects or links together. **2.** Also called **linking verb.** a verb, as *be, seem,* or *look,* that serves as a connecting link or establishes an identity between subject and complement. **3.** the connecting link between the subject and predicate of a proposition. —**cop′u•lar,** *adj.*

cop•u•late (*v.* kop′yə lāt′; *adj.* -lit), *v.,* **-lat•ed, -lat•ing,** —*v.i.* **1.** to engage in sexual intercourse. —*adj.* **2.** connected; joined. —**cop′u•la′tion,** *n.* —**cop′u•la•to′ry** (-lə tôr′ē, -tōr′ē), *adj.*

cop•u•la•tive (kop′yə lā′tiv, -lə tiv), *adj.* **1.** serving to unite or couple. **2. a.** (of a verb) pertaining to or serving as a copula. **b.** (of a conjunction) serving to connect words, phrases, or clauses of equal rank with a cumulative effect, as *and.* **3.** of or pertaining to sexual intercourse. —*n.* **4.** a copulative word.

cop•y (kop′ē), *n., pl.* **cop•ies,** for 1, 2, *v.,* **cop•ied, cop•y•ing.** —*n.* **1.** an imitation, reproduction, or transcript of an original: *a copy of a famous painting.* **2.** one of the various examples or specimens of the same book, engraving, or the like. **3.** matter intended to be reproduced in printed form. **4.** the text of a news story, advertisement, television commercial, or the like. **5.** something newsworthy: *Political gossip is always good copy.* **6.** REPLICATION (def. 6). —*v.t.* **7.** to make a copy of;

transcribe; reproduce. **8.** to follow as a pattern or model; imitate. —*v.i.* **9.** to make a copy or copies. **10.** to undergo copying: *It copied poorly.*

cop·y·boy (kop′ē boi′), *n.* an employee of a newspaper office who carries copy and runs errands, esp. a man.

cop·y·cat (kop′ē kat′), *n., adj., v.,* **-cat·ted, -cat·ting.** —*n.* Also, **cop′y cat′. 1.** a person or thing that imitates another persistently or exactly. —*adj.* **2.** imitating or repeating a well-known occurrence: *a copycat crime.* —*v.t.* **3.** to imitate; mimic; reproduce.

cop′y desk′, *n.* the desk in a newspaper office at which copy is edited and prepared for printing.

cop′y·ed′it or **cop′y-ed′it,** *v.t.* **1.** to edit (a text) for publication. **2.** to work on (copy) as a copyreader.

cop′y·ed′i·tor or **cop′y ed′itor,** *n.* **1.** a person who edits a manuscript, text, etc., for publication, esp. to correct errors in style, punctuation, and grammar. **2.** the head copyreader on a newspaper.

cop·y·girl (kop′ē gûrl′), *n.* a woman who carries copy and runs errands in a newspaper office. ——**Usage.** See GIRL.

cop′ying machine′, *n.* a machine that makes copies of original documents, esp. by xerography. Also called **copier, cop′y machine′.**

cop·y·ist (kop′ē ist), *n.* **1.** a person who transcribes copies, esp. of documents. **2.** an imitator.

cop′y protec′tion, *n.* a method of preventing users of a computer program from making unauthorized copies, usu. through hidden instructions contained in the program code. —**cop′y-protect′ed,** *adj.*

cop·y·read·er (kop′ē rē′dər), *n.* **1.** COPYEDITOR (def. 1). **2.** a newspaper employee who edits copy and writes headlines. —**cop′y·read′,** *v.t.,* **-read** (-red′), **-read·ing.**

cop·y·right (kop′ē rīt′), *n.* **1.** the exclusive ownership of and the right to make use of a literary, musical, or artistic work, protected by law for a specified period of time. —*adj.* **2.** Also, **cop′y·right′ed.** protected by copyright. —*v.t.* **3.** to secure a copyright on. —**cop′y·right′a·ble,** *adj.*

cop·y·writ·er (kop′ē rī′tər), *n.* a writer of copy, esp. for advertisements or publicity releases. —**cop′y·writ′ing,** *n.*

coq au vin (*Fr.* kôk ô vaN′), *n.* chicken cooked in red wine usu. with mushrooms, onions, and bacon.

co·quet (kō ket′), *v.,* **-quet·ted, -quet·ting,** *adj.* —*v.i.* **1.** to behave as a coquette; flirt. —*adj.* **2.** coquettish. —**co′quet·ry,** *n.*

co·quette (kō ket′), *n.* a woman who flirts insincerely with men to win their admiration and attention. —**co·quet′tish,** *adj.* —**co·quet′tish·ly,** *adv.* —**co·quet′tish·ness,** *n.*

co·qui·na (kō kē′nə), *n., pl.* **-nas. 1.** Also called **butterfly shell.** a small clam, *Donax variabilis,* having fanlike bands of various hues and common in intertidal zones of the E and S U.S. coasts. **2.** any similar clam. **3.** a soft whitish rock made up of fragments of marine shells and coral, used as a building material.

cor·al (kôr′al, kor′-), *n.* **1.** the hard, variously colored, calcareous skeleton secreted by certain marine polyps. **2.** such skeletons collectively, forming reefs, islands, etc. **3.** any of several solitary or colonial anthozoan marine polyps that secrete this calcareous skeleton. **4.** a color ranging from reddish to pinkish yellow. **5.** the roe of the lobster, resembling red coral when cooked. **6.** something made of coral. —*adj.* **7.** made of coral. **8.** making coral: *a coral polyp.* **9.** resembling coral, esp. in color.

cor′al bells′, *n.* an alumroot, *Heuchera sanguinea,* of SW North America, having drooping, bell-shaped flowers in coral hues.

cor·al·ber·ry (kôr′al ber′ē, kor′-), *n., pl.* **-ries.** a North American shrub, *Symphoricarpos orbiculatus,* of the honeysuckle family, having hairy leaves, inconspicuous white flowers, and reddish purple fruit.

cor′al fun′gus, *n.* any of a group of brightly colored, branching club fungi that resemble coral.

cor′al reef′, *n.* a reef composed mainly of coral skeletons and other calcareous materials.

cor·al·root (kôr′al rōōt′, -rŏot′, kor′-), *n.* a saprophytic orchid of the genus *Corallorhiza,* of the Northern Hemisphere, having elongated clusters of small flowers.

Cor′al Sea′, *n.* a part of the S Pacific, bounded by NE Australia, New Guinea, the Solomon Islands, and the New Hebrides: U.S. naval victory over the Japanese, May 1942.

cor′al snake′, *n.* any of several venomous elapid snakes often marked with bands of red, yellow, and black, as *Micrurus fulvius,* of the SE U.S.

cor·bel (kôr′bəl), *n., v.,* **-beled, -bel·ing** or (*esp. Brit.*) **-belled, -bel·ling.** —*n.* **1.** an architectural bracket or member, esp. of stone or brick, built into a wall and projecting from it to support a weight. **2.** a short horizontal timber supporting a girder. —*v.t.* **3.** to set (a stone, brick, etc.) so as to form a corbel. **4.** to support by means of a corbel.

cor·bie·step (kôr′bē step′), *n.* any of a series of steplike portions of a masonry gable that terminate the gable above the surface of the roof.

cor·bi·na (kôr bē′nə), *n., pl.* **-nas.** a dark gray, slender California croaker, *Menticirrhus undulatus,* with a chin barbel.

cord (kôrd), *n.* **1.** a string or thin rope made of several strands braided, twisted, or woven together. **2.** a small, flexible, insulated electrical cable. **3.** a ribbed fabric, esp. corduroy. **4.** a cordlike rib on the surface of cloth. **5. cords,** clothing, as trousers, of corded fabric, esp. corduroy. **6.** any influence that binds or restrains: *the spinal cord.* **8.** a unit of volume used chiefly for fuel wood, now generally equal to 128 cubic feet (3.6 cubic meters), usu. specified as 8 ft. long, 4 ft. wide, and 4 ft. high (2.4 m × 1.2 m × 1.2 m). *Abbr.:* cd, cd. —*v.t.*

9. to bind or fasten with a cord or cords. **10.** to pile or stack up (wood) in cords. **11.** to furnish with a cord. —**cord′er,** *n.* —**cord′like′,** *adj.*

cord·age (kôr′dij), *n.* **1.** lines, hawsers, etc., esp. on the rigging of a vessel. **2.** a quantity of wood measured in cords.

cor·date (kôr′dāt), *adj.* **1.** heart-shaped. **2.** (of leaves) heart-shaped, with the attachment at the notched end.

cord·ed (kôr′did), *adj.* **1.** furnished with, made of, or in the form of cords. **2.** ribbed, as a fabric. **3.** bound with cords. **4.** (of wood) stacked up in cords. **5.** stringy or ribbed in appearance.

cord·grass (kôrd′gras′, -gräs′), *n.* any of several grasses of the genus *Spartina,* of coastal wetlands.

cor·dial (kôr′jal; *esp. Brit.* -dē əl), *adj.* **1.** courteous and gracious; warm: *a cordial reception.* **2.** invigorating the heart. **3.** sincere; heartfelt: *a cordial dislike.* —*n.* **4.** a strong, sweetened, aromatic alcoholic liquor; liqueur. **5.** a stimulating medicine. —**cor′dial·ly,** *adv.*

cor·di·al·i·ty (kôr jal′i tē, kôr′jē al′-; *esp. Brit.* -dē al′-), *n., pl.* **-ties. 1.** cordial quality. **2.** an expression of cordial feeling.

cor·di·er·ite (kôr′dē ə rīt′), *n.* a strongly dichroic blue mineral consisting of a silicate of magnesium, aluminum, and iron: common in metamorphic rocks.

cor·dil·le·ra (kôr′dl yâr′ə, -âr′ə, kôr dil′ər ə), *n.* a chain of mountains, usu. the principal mountain system or mountain axis of a large landmass. —**cor′dil·le′ran,** *adj.*

Cor·dil·le·ras (kôr′dl yâr′əs, -âr′-, kôr dil′ər əz), *n.pl.* the entire chain of mountain ranges parallel to the Pacific coast, extending from Cape Horn to Alaska. —**Cor′dil·le′ran,** *adj.*

cord·ite (kôr′dīt), *n.* a smokeless, slow-burning, explosive powder composed of nitroglycerin, cellulose nitrate, and mineral jelly.

cord·less (kôrd′lis), *adj.* **1.** lacking a cord. **2.** (of an electrical appliance) requiring no wire leading to an external electricity source because of a self-contained power supply.

cor·don (kôr′dn), *n.* **1.** a line of police, sentinels, military posts, warships, etc., enclosing or guarding an area. **2.** a cord, braid, or ribbon worn as an ornament, fastening, or badge. **3.** a stringcourse, esp. one having little or no projection, on the face of a building. —*v.t.* **4.** to surround or blockade with or as if with a cordon (often fol. by *off*): *Police cordoned off the street.*

cor·don bleu (*Fr.* kôr dôn blœ′), *n., pl.* **cor·dons bleus** (*Fr.* kôr dôn blœ′), *adj.* —*n.* **1.** the sky-blue ribbon worn as a badge by knights of the highest order of French knighthood under the Bourbons. **2.** some similar high distinction. **3.** any person of great distinction in a field, esp. a chef. —*adj.* **4.** of or pertaining to gourmet cookery.

cor·don sa·ni·taire (*Fr.* kôr dôn sa nē ter′), *n., pl.* **cor·dons sa·ni·taires** (*Fr.* kôr dôn sa nē ter′). **1.** a line around a quarantined area guarded to prevent the spread of a disease by restricting passage into or out of the area. **2.** a group of neighboring, generally neutral states forming a geographical barrier between two states having aggressive military or ideological aims against each other.

cor·don vert (kôr dôn ver′), *adj.* of or pertaining to gourmet vegetarian cookery.

cor·du·roy (kôr′də roi′, kôr′də roi′), *n., adj., v.,* **-royed, -roy·ing.** —*n.* **1.** a cotton-filling pile fabric with lengthwise cords or ridges. **2. corduroys,** trousers made of this fabric. —*adj.* **3.** of, pertaining to, or resembling corduroy. **4.** constructed of logs laid together transversely, as a road across swampy ground. —*v.t.* **5.** to form (a road or the like) by laying logs transversely.

cord·wood (kôrd′wŏod′), *n.* **1.** wood stacked in cords for use as fuel. **2.** trees intended for timber but suitable only for fuel.

core (kôr, kōr), *n., v.,* **cored, cor·ing.** —*n.* **1.** the central part of a fleshy fruit, containing the seeds. **2.** the central, innermost, or most essential part of anything. **3.** the piece of iron, bundle of iron wires, or other ferrous material forming the central or inner portion in an electromagnet, induction coil, transformer, or the like. **4.** (in mining, geology, etc.) a cylindrical sample of earth, mineral, or rock extracted from the ground so that the strata are undisturbed in the sample. **5.** a lump of stone from which prehistoric humans struck flakes in order to make tools. **6.** the central portion of the earth, having a radius of about 2100 mi. (3379 km) and believed to be composed mainly of iron and nickel in a molten state. Compare CRUST (def. 7), MANTLE (def. 3). **7.** the region in a nuclear reactor that contains its fissionable material. **8.** an assemblage of small magnetized ferrite rings used as a data-storage medium in some computers. **9.** a thickness of base metal beneath a cladding. —*v.t.* **10.** to remove the core of (fruit). **11.** to cut from the central part. **12.** to remove (a cylindrical sample) from the interior, as of the earth or a tree trunk. —**core′less,** *adj.*

Co·re (kôr′ē, kōr′ē), *n.* Korah.

CORE or **C.O.R.E.** (kôr, kōr), *n.* Congress of Racial Equality.

core′ curric′ulum, *n.* a school curriculum in which the subjects are correlated to a central theme.

co·re·li·gion·ist (kō′ri lij′ə nist), *n.* an adherent of the same religion as another.

co·re·op·sis (kôr′ē op′sis, kōr′-), *n., pl.* **-op·sis.** any composite plant of the genus *Coreopsis,* including varieties with ray flowers of yellow, brown, or red and red.

cor·er (kôr′ər, kōr′-), *n.* **1.** a person or thing that cores. **2.** a knife or other instrument for coring apples, pears, etc.

co·re·spond·ent (kō′ri spon′dənt), *n.* a joint defendant, esp. a person charged with adultery in a divorce proceeding.

cor·gi (kôr′gē), *n.*, *pl.* **-gis.** WELSH CORGI.

co·ri·an·der (kôr′ē an′dər, kōr′-), *n.* **1.** Also called **cilantro.** an herb, *Coriandrum sativum,* of the parsley family, having strong-scented leaves used in cooking. **2.** the aromatic seeds of this herb, used whole or ground as a flavoring.

Cor·inth (kôr′inth, kor′-), *n.* **1.** an ancient city in Greece, on the Isthmus of Corinth. **2.** a port in the NE Peloponnesus, in S Greece: NE of the site of ancient Corinth. **3. Gulf of.** Also called **Gulf of Lepanto.** an arm of the Ionian Sea, N of the Peloponnesus. **4. Isthmus of,** an isthmus at the head of the Gulf of Corinth, connecting the Peloponnesus with central Greece.

Co·rin·thi·an (kə rin′thē ən), *adj.* **1.** of or pertaining to Corinth or its residents. **2.** of or designating one of the five classical orders of architecture, similar to the Ionic but usu. of slenderer proportions and characterized by a deep capital with a round bell decorated with acanthus leaves. —*n.* **3.** a native or resident of Corinth.

Co·rin·thi·ans (kə rin′thē ənz), *n.* (*used with a sing. v.*) either of two books of the New Testament, I Corinthians or II Corinthians, written by Paul.

cork (kôrk), *n.* **1. a.** Also called **phellem.** a layer of dead protective tissue between the bark and cadmium in woody plants. **b.** the thick lightweight layer of a Mediterranean oak, *Quercus suber* (**cork oak**), harvested commercially for making floats, stoppers for bottles, etc. **2.** something made of cork. **3.** a piece of cork, rubber, or the like used as a stopper, as for a bottle. **4.** a small float to buoy up a fishing line. —*v.t.* **5.** to provide or fit with cork or a cork. **6.** to stop with or as if with a cork (often fol. by *up*). **7.** to blacken with burnt cork.

cork·board (kôrk′bôrd′, -bōrd′), *n.* **1.** an insulating material made of compressed cork, used in building, for industrial purposes, etc. **2.** a bulletin board made of this material.

cork·screw (kôrk′skrōō′), *n.* **1.** an instrument typically consisting of a metal spiral with a sharp point at one end and a transverse handle at the other, used for drawing corks from bottles. —*adj.* **2.** resembling a corkscrew; helical; spiral. —*v.t., v.i.* **3.** to move in a spiral course.

cork·wood (kôrk′wŏŏd′), *n.* **1.** a small tree, *Leitneria floridana,* with light green leaves and woolly catkins. **2.** any of certain trees and shrubs yielding a light and porous wood, as the balsa.

corm (kôrm), *n.* an enlarged, fleshy, bulblike base of a plant stem that stores food, as in a crocus. —**corm′like′,** *adj.* —**cor′moid,** *adj.* —**cor′mous,** *adj.*

cor·mo·rant (kôr′mər ənt), *n.* **1.** any of various typically dark-plumaged diving seabirds of the family Phalacrocoracidae, of worldwide distribution, having a long neck and a throat pouch for holding fish. **2.** a greedy person.

corn[1] (kôrn), *n.* **1.** Also called **Indian corn**; *esp. technical and Brit.,* **maize. a.** a tall cereal plant, *Zea mays,* cultivated in many varieties, having a jointed, solid stem and bearing the kernels on large ears. **b.** the kernels of this plant, used for human food or for fodder. **c.** the ears of this plant. **2. a.** the edible seed of certain other cereal plants, esp. wheat in England and oats in Scotland. **b.** the plants themselves. **3.** *Informal.* old-fashioned, trite, or mawkishly sentimental material, as a joke, a story, or music. —*v.t.* **4.** to preserve and season with brine or with salt in grains.

corn[2] (kôrn), *n.* a horny growth of tissue with a tender core, formed over a bone, esp. on the toes, as a result of pressure or friction.

-corn, a combining form meaning "having a horn," of the kind or number specified by the initial element: *longicorn.*

Corn′ Belt′, *n.* a region in the midwestern U.S., esp. Iowa, Illinois, and Indiana, excellent for raising corn and cornfed livestock.

corn′ bread′ or **corn′bread′,** *n.* a bread made with cornmeal.

corn′ chip′, *n.* a thin, crisp piece of snack food made from cornmeal.

corn·cob (kôrn′kob′), *n.* **1.** the elongated woody core in which the grains of an ear of corn are embedded. **2.** Also called **corn′cob pipe′.** a tobacco pipe with a bowl made from a corncob.

corn′ cock′le, *n.* a plant, *Agrostemma githago,* of the pink family, having magenta-purple flowers: common in grainfields.

corn′ crake′, *n.* a short-billed Eurasian rail, *Crex crex,* frequenting meadows and grainfields.

corn′ dodg′er, *n.* **1.** *South Midland and Southern U.S.* a small, usually oval cake made of corn bread and baked or fried hard in a skillet. **2.** *Chiefly South Atlantic States and Eastern Virginia.* a boiled dumpling made of cornmeal.

cor·ne·a (kôr′nē ə), *n.*, *pl.* **-ne·as.** the transparent anterior part of the external coat of the eye covering the iris and the pupil and continuous with the sclera. —**cor′ne·al,** *adj.*

corned′ beef′, *n.* beef cured in a seasoned brine and cooked.

cor·nel (kôr′nl), *n.* any tree or shrub of the genus *Cornus;* dogwood.

Cor·nell (kôr nel′), *n.* **1. Ezra,** 1809–74, U.S. capitalist and philanthropist. **2. Katharine,** 1898–1974, U.S. stage actress.

cor·ner (kôr′nər), *n.* **1.** the place at which two converging lines or surfaces meet. **2.** the space between two converging lines or surfaces near their intersection; angle: *a chair in the corner of the room.* **3.** a projecting angle, esp. of a rectangular figure or object. **4.** the point where two streets meet. **5.** an end; margin; edge. **6.** any narrow, secluded, or secret place. **7.** an awkward or embarrassing position, esp. one from

which escape is impossible. **8.** a monopoly of the available supply of a stock or commodity. **9.** region; part; quarter: *from every corner of the empire.* **10.** a piece to protect the corner of anything. —*adj.* **11.** situated on or at a corner where two streets meet. **12.** made to fit in a corner. —*v.t.* **13.** to furnish with corners. **14.** to place in or drive into a corner. **15.** to force into an awkward, difficult, or inescapable position. **16.** to gain control of (a stock, commodity, etc.). —*Idiom.* **17. cut corners, a.** to use a shorter route. **b.** to reduce costs or care in execution.

cor·ner·back (kôr′nər bak′), *n.* a defensive back in football who covers the area behind the line of scrimmage near the sideline.

cor·nered (kôr′nərd), *adj.* **1.** having corners (usu. used in combination): *a six-cornered room.* **2.** having a given number of positions; sided (usu. used in combination): *a four-cornered debate.* **3.** forced into an awkward, embarrassing, or inescapable position.

cor′ner kick′, *n.* a free kick in soccer, taken from the corner by the offense after a defensive player has driven the ball out of bounds.

cor·ner·stone (kôr′nər stōn′), *n.* **1.** a stone uniting two masonry walls at an intersection. **2.** a stone representing the nominal starting place in the construction of a monumental building, usu. carved with the date. **3.** something that is essential or basic. **4.** the foundation on which something is constructed or developed. **5.** (*cap.*) Jesus Christ. Mark 12:10; I Peter 2:6.

cor·net (kôr net′; *esp. Brit.* kôr′nit), *n.* **1.** a valved wind instrument of the trumpet family. **2.** a small cone of paper twisted at the end and used for holding candy, nuts, etc. **3.** *Brit.* ICE-CREAM CONE.

corn·fed (kôrn′fed′), *adj.* **1.** fed on corn. **2.** having a well-fed, healthy, and guileless appearance.

corn′flakes′ or **corn′ flakes′,** *n.pl.* small toasted flakes made from corn and eaten usu. with milk as a breakfast cereal.

corn·flow·er (kôrn′flou′ər), *n.* **1.** a European composite plant, *Centaurea cyanus,* with blue flower heads, common in grainfields: often cultivated. **2.** Also called **corn′flower blue′.** a deep vivid blue.

corn·husk (kôrn′husk′), *n.* the husk of an ear of corn.

cor·nice (kôr′nis), *n., v.,* **-niced, -nic·ing.** —*n.* **1. a.** any prominent projecting molded feature surmounting a wall, doorway, or other construction. **b.** the uppermost member of a classical entablature, above the frieze. **2.** any of various other ornamental horizontal moldings or bands, as for concealing curtain hooks or rods. —*v.t.* **3.** to furnish or finish with a cornice.

cor·niche (kôr′nish, kôr nēsh′), *n.* a winding road cut into the side of a steep hill or along the face of a coastal cliff.

cor·nic·u·late (kôr nik′yə lit, -lāt′), *adj.* having horns or hornlike parts; horned.

Cor·nish (kôr′nish), *adj.* **1.** of or pertaining to Cornwall, England, its inhabitants, or the language Cornish. —*n.* **2.** the Celtic language of Cornwall, extinct since c1800. **3.** one of an English breed of small chickens raised chiefly for crossbreeding. Compare ROCK CORNISH.

Cor′nish game′ hen′, *n.* a market chicken that is four to five weeks old and weighs less than two pounds.

corn·meal (kôrn′mēl′), *n.* meal made of corn.

corn′ oil′, *n.* an oil obtained by expressing the germs of corn kernels.

corn′ pone′, *n.* *Southern U.S.* corn bread, esp. of a plain or simple kind.

corn′ pop′py, *n.* a red poppy, *Papaver rhoeas,* of Europe and Asia, common in grainfields. Also called **field poppy.**

corn·row (kôrn′rō′), *n.* **1.** a narrow braid of hair plaited tightly against the scalp. —*v.t.* **2.** to arrange (hair) in cornrows.

corn′ sal′ad, *n.* any of several plants of the genus *Valerianella,* of the valerian family, esp. *V. locusta,* having small light blue flowers and tender narrow leaves eaten in salads. Also called **mache.**

corn′ silk′, *n.* the long, threadlike, silky styles on an ear of corn.

corn′ snake′, *n.* a large harmless rat snake, *Elaphe guttata guttata,* of the SE U.S., yellow, tan, or gray in color.

corn·stalk (kôrn′stôk′), *n.* the stalk or stem of corn.

corn·starch (kôrn′stärch′), *n.* a starch or starchy flour made from corn and used for thickening gravies or sauces, making puddings, etc.

corn′ syr′up, *n.* syrup prepared from corn.

cor·nu·co·pi·a (kôr′nə kō′pē ə, -nyə-), *n., pl.* **-pi·as. 1.** a horn containing food and drink in endless supply, associated in classical mythology with the horn of the goat Amalthea. **2.** a representation of this horn, used as a symbol of abundance. **3.** an abundant, overflowing supply. **4.** a horn-shaped or conical receptacle or ornament. [< Latin *cornū* horn + *cōpiae* of plenty] —**cor′nu·co′pi·an,** *adj.* —**cor′nu·co′pi·ate** (-it), *adj.*

cornucopia (def. 2)

Corn·wall (kôrn′wôl; *esp. Brit.* -wəl), *n.* a county in SW England. 453,100; 1369 sq. mi. (3545 sq. km).

corn·y (kôr′nē), *adj.,* **corn·i·er, corn·i·est.** *Informal.* old-fashioned, trite, or mawkishly sentimental: *corny jokes.*

co·rol·la (kə rol′ə, -rō′lə), *n., pl.* **-las.** the inner whorl of floral leaves of a flower, usu. other than green; the petals collectively. **—cor·rol′late** (kə rol′it, kôr′ə lāt′, kor′-), *adj.*

cor·ol·lar·y (kôr′ə ler′ē, kor′-; *esp. Brit.* kə rol′ə rē), *n., pl.* **-lar·ies.** **1.** *Math.* a proposition that is incidentally proved in proving another proposition. **2.** an immediate consequence or easily drawn conclusion. **3.** a natural consequence or result.

cor·o·man·del (kôr′ə man′dl, kor′-), *n.* the hard brownish wood of a tropical Asian tree, *Diospyros melanoxylon.*

co·ro·na (kə rō′nə), *n., pl.* **-nas, -nae** (-nē). **1. a.** a white or colored circle or set of concentric circles of light seen around a luminous body, esp. around the sun or moon. **b.** a similar colored circle or set of circles visible in the atmosphere and attributable to the diffraction caused by thin clouds, mist, or sometimes dust (disting. from *halo*). **2.** a diffuse, hot envelope of ionized gas surrounding the sun that is visible during total solar eclipse. **3.** a long, straight, untapered cigar, rounded at the closed end. **4.** a crownlike appendage on a plant, esp. on the inner side of a corolla, as in the narcissus. **5.** the upper portion or crown of a part, as of the head. **6.** the projecting slablike member of a classical cornice, surmounted by the cymatium. **7.** a metal chandelier having the form of one or more concentric hoops, used esp. in churches.

Co·ro·na Bo·re·al·is (kə rō′nə bôr′ē al′is, -ā′lis, -bōr′-), *n., gen.* **Co·ro·nae Borealis** (kə rō′nē). the Northern Crown, a constellation between Hercules and Boötes. [< Latin: lit., northern crown]

Co·ro·na·do (kôr′ə nä′dō, kor′-), *n.* **Francisco Vásquez de,** 1510–54?, Spanish explorer in North America.

cor·o·nar·y (kôr′ə ner′ē, kor′-), *adj., n., pl.* **-nar·ies.** **—*adj.*** **1.** of or pertaining to the heart. **2. a.** pertaining to the coronary arteries. **b.** encircling like a crown, as certain blood vessels. **3.** of or like a crown. **—*n.*** **4.** a heart attack. **5.** a coronary artery.

cor′onary ar′tery, *n.* either of two arteries that originate in the aorta and supply the heart muscle with blood.

cor′onary by′pass, *n.* the surgical revascularization of the heart, using healthy blood vessels of the patient, performed to circumvent obstructed coronary vessels.

cor′onary-care′ u′nit, *n.* a specialized hospital unit for the early care and treatment of heart-attack patients.

cor′onary occlu′sion, *n.* partial or total obstruction of a coronary artery.

cor′onary thrombo′sis, *n.* a coronary occlusion in which there is blockage of a coronary arterial branch by a blood clot within the vessel.

cor·o·na·tion (kôr′ə nā′shən, kor′-), *n.* the act or ceremony of crowning a king, queen, or other sovereign.

cor·o·ner (kôr′ə nər, kor′-), *n.* an officer, as of a county or municipality, whose chief function is to investigate by inquest, as before a jury, any death not clearly resulting from natural causes.

cor·o·net (kôr′ə net′, kor′-), *n.* **1.** a small crown. **2.** a crown worn by nobles or peers. **3.** a crownlike ornament for the head, as of gold or jewels. **4.** the lowest part of the pastern of a horse or other hoofed animal, just above the hoof.

cor·po·ra (kôr′pər ə), *n.* a pl. of CORPUS.

cor·po·ral¹ (kôr′pər əl, -prəl), *adj.* **1.** of the human body; bodily; physical: *corporal punishment.* **2.** personal: *corporal possession.* **—cor′po·ral′i·ty,** *n.* **—cor′po·ral·ly,** *adv.*

cor·po·ral² (kôr′pər əl, -prəl), *n.* **1.** a noncommissioned U.S. Army officer ranking above a private first class. **2.** a noncommissioned officer in the U.S. Marine Corps ranking above a lance corporal. **3.** an officer of similar rank in the armed services of other countries. **—cor′po·ral·cy, cor′po·ral·ship′,** *n.*

cor·po·rate (kôr′pər it, -prit), *adj.* **1.** of, for, or belonging to a corporation or corporations: *a corporate executive.* **2.** pertaining to a united group, as of persons. **3.** united or combined into one. **—*n.*** **4.** Also called **cor′porate bond′.** a bond issued by a corporation. **—cor′po·rate·ly,** *adv.*

cor′porate raid′er, *n.* a person who seizes control of a company, as by secretly buying stock and gathering proxies.

cor′porate wel′fare, *n.* financial assistance, as tax breaks or subsidies, given by the government esp. to large companies.

cor·po·ra·tion (kôr′pə rā′shən), *n.* **1.** an association of individuals, created by law and having an existence apart from that of its members as well as distinct and inherent powers and liabilities. **2.** an incorporated business; company. **3.** (*often cap.*) the principal officials of a city or town. **4.** any group of persons united or regarded as united in one body. **5.** *Informal.* a paunch; potbelly. **—cor′po·ra′tion·al,** *adj.* **—Usage.** See COLLECTIVE NOUN.

cor·po·re·al (kôr pôr′ē əl, -pōr′-), *adj.* **1.** of the nature of the physical body; bodily. **2.** material; tangible: *corporeal property.* **—cor·po′re·al′i·ty, cor·po′re·al·ness,** *n.* **—cor·po′re·al·ly,** *adv.*

cor·po·re·i·ty (kôr′pə rē′i tē), *n.* material or physical nature or quality; materiality.

corps (kôr, kōr), *n., pl.* **corps** (kôrz, kōrz). **1. a.** an organization of officers and enlisted personnel or of officers alone: *the U.S. Marine Corps.* **b.** a combat unit comprising two or more divisions. **2.** a group of persons associated or acting together. **3.** a unit of type size in the Didot point system.

corps de bal·let (kôr′ də ba lā′, bal′ā, kôr′), *n.* the dancers in a ballet company who perform as a group and have no solo parts.

corpse (kôrps), *n.* a dead body, usu. of a human being.

corps·man (kôr′mən, kōr′-), *n., pl.* **-men.** **1.** an enlisted person in the U.S. Navy working as a pharmacist or hospital assistant. **2.** an enlisted person in the Medical Corps of the U.S. Army who gives first aid to the wounded on the battlefield. **3.** a member of any corps, as of the Peace Corps.

Corps′ of Engineers′, *n.* a branch of the U.S. Army responsible for military and many civil engineering projects.

cor·pu·lence (kôr′pyə ləns) also **cor′pu·len·cy,** *n.* bulkiness or largeness of body; fatness; portliness.

cor·pu·lent (kôr′pyə lənt), *adj.* large or bulky of body; portly; stout; fat. **—cor′pu·lent·ly,** *adv.*

cor·pus (kôr′pəs), *n., pl.* **-po·ra** (-pər ə) for 1–3, **-pus·es** for 4. **1.** a large or complete collection of writings: *the entire corpus of Old English poetry.* **2.** the body of a person or animal, esp. when dead. **3. a.** a mass of body tissue that has a specialized function. **b.** the main part of a bodily organ. **4.** a collection of utterances, as spoken or written sentences, taken as a representative sample of a given language or dialect and used for linguistic analysis.

cor·pus cal·lo·sum (kôr′pəs kə lō′səm), *n., pl.* **cor·po·ra cal·lo·sa** (kôr′pər ə kə lō′sə). the thick band of transverse nerve fibers between the two halves of the cerebrum in placental mammals.

Cor·pus Chris·ti¹ (kôr′pəs kris′tē, -tī), *n.* a Roman Catholic festival in honor of the Eucharist, celebrated on the Thursday after Trinity Sunday. [< Medieval Latin: lit., body of Christ]

Cor·pus Chris·ti² (kôr′pəs kris′tē), *n.* a seaport in S Texas. 275,419.

cor·pus·cle (kôr′pə səl, -pus əl), *n.* **1.** an unattached cell, esp. a blood or lymph cell. **2.** a small mass of cells forming a distinct anatomical part, as certain sensory receptors. **3.** any minute particle. **—cor·pus′cu·lar** (-kyə lər), *adj.*

cor·pus de·lic·ti (kôr′pəs di lik′tī), *n., pl.* **cor·po·ra delicti** (kôr′pər ə). **1.** the basic element of a crime, as, in murder, the fact that a death has occurred. **2.** the evidence, as a body, that proves a crime has been committed. [< New Latin: lit., body of the offense]

cor·pus lu·te·um (kôr′pəs loo′tē əm), *n., pl.* **cor·po·ra lu·te·a** (kôr′pər ə loo′tē ə). a yellowish structure that develops in the ovary on the site where an ovum is released and that secretes progesterone if fertilization occurs.

cor·pus stri·a·tum (kôr′pəs strī ā′təm), *n., pl.* **cor·po·ra stri·a·ta** (kôr′pər ə strī ā′tə). a mass of banded gray and white matter in front of the thalamus in each cerebral hemisphere.

cor·ral (kə ral′), *n., v.,* **-ralled, -ral·ling.** **—*n.*** **1.** an enclosure or pen for horses, cattle, etc. **2.** a circular enclosure of wagons, formed for defense against attack. **—*v.t.*** **3.** to confine in or as if in a corral. **4.** *Informal.* **a.** to seize; capture. **b.** to collect or garner: *to corral votes.* **5.** to form (wagons) into a corral.

cor·ra·sion (kə rā′zhən), *n.* the mechanical erosion of soil and rock by the abrasive action of particles set in motion by running water, wind, glacial ice, and gravity. **—cor·ra′sive** (-siv), *adj.*

cor·rect (kə rekt′), *v.t.* **1.** to set or make right; remove the errors or faults from. **2.** to point out or mark the errors in: *to correct examination papers.* **3.** to rebuke or punish in order to improve: *Don't correct your child in public.* **4.** to counteract the operation or effect of (something hurtful or undesirable). **5.** to alter or adjust so as to bring into accordance with a standard or with a required condition. **—*v.i.*** **6.** (of stock prices) to reverse a trend, esp. temporarily, as after a sharp advance or decline in previous trading sessions. **—*adj.*** **7.** conforming to fact or truth; accurate. **8.** in accordance with an acknowledged or accepted standard; proper: *correct behavior.* **—cor·rect′a·ble, cor·rect′i·ble,** *adj.* **—cor·rect′a·bil·i·ty, cor·rect′i·bil·i·ty,** *n.* **—cor·rect′ly,** *adv.* **—cor·rect′ness,** *n.* **—cor·rec′tor,** *n.*

cor·rec·tion (kə rek′shən), *n.* **1.** something given, done, or proposed as a substitute for what is wrong or inaccurate; emendation. **2.** the act of correcting. **3.** punishment or chastisement. **4.** Usu., **corrections.** the various methods by which society deals with convicted offenders. **5.** a quantity applied or other adjustment made in order to increase accuracy, as in the use of an instrument or the solution of a problem. **6.** a reversal of the trend of stock prices, esp. temporarily. **—cor·rec′tion·al,** *adj.*

cor·rec·tive (kə rek′tiv), *adj.* **1.** tending to correct or rectify; remedial. **—*n.*** **2.** a means of correcting; corrective agent. **—cor·rec′tive·ly,** *adv.*

cor·re·late (*v., adj.* kôr′ə lāt′, kor′-; *n.* -lit, -lāt′), *v.,* **-lat·ed, -lat·ing,** *adj., n.* **—*v.t.*** **1.** to place in or bring into mutual or reciprocal relation; establish in orderly connection: *to correlate expenses and income.* **—*v.i.*** **2.** to have a mutual or reciprocal relation; stand in correlation. **—*adj.*** **3.** mutually or reciprocally related. **—*n.*** **4.** either of two related things, esp. when one implies the other.

cor·re·la·tion (kôr′ə lā′shən), *n.* **1.** mutual relation of two or more things, parts, etc. **2.** the act of correlating or the state of being correlated. **3.** (in statistics) the degree to which two or more attributes or measurements on the same group of elements show a tendency to vary together. **—cor′re·la′tion·al,** *adj.*

cor·rel·a·tive (kə rel′ə tiv), *adj.* **1.** so related that each implies or complements the other. **2.** being in correlation; mutually related. **3.**

Gram. answering to or complementing one another and regularly used in association, as *either* and *or*, or *no sooner* and *than.* —*n.* **4.** either of two things, as two terms, that are correlative. **5.** a correlative expression.

correl′ative conjunc′tion, *n.* either member of a matched pair of words, of which the second is a coordinating conjunction, as *either … or, neither … nor, both … and,* and *not only … but.*

cor•re•spond (kôr′ə spond′, kor′-), *v.i.* **1.** to be in agreement or conformity; match (often fol. by *with* or *to*): *His actions don't correspond to his words.* **2.** to be similar or analogous (usu. fol. by *to*): *The U.S. Congress corresponds to the British Parliament.* **3.** to communicate by exchange of letters. —**cor′re•spond′ing•ly,** *adv.*

cor•re•spond•ence (kôr′ə spon′dəns, kor′-), *n.* **1.** communication by exchange of letters. **2.** a letter or letters that pass between correspondents. **3.** an instance of corresponding. **4.** similarity or analogy. **5.** agreement; conformity. **6.** FUNCTION (def. 4a).

Correspond′ence Commit′tee, *n.* COMMITTEE OF CORRESPONDENCE.

correspond′ence school′, *n.* a school from which students receive instructional materials through the mail as well as corrections on their work.

cor•re•spond•ent (kôr′ə spon′dənt, kor′-), *n.* **1.** a person who communicates by letters. **2.** a person employed by a newspaper, television network, etc., to gather and report news regularly from a distant place. **3.** a thing that corresponds to something else. —*adj.* **4.** consistent, similar, or analogous; corresponding.

cor•re•spond•ing (kôr′ə spon′ding, kor′-), *adj.* **1.** identical in all essentials or respects: *corresponding fingerprints.* **2.** similar in position, purpose, form, etc.: *corresponding officials in two states.* **3.** associated in a working or other relationship: *a bolt and its corresponding nut.* **4.** dealing with correspondence: *a corresponding secretary.* **5.** employing the mails as a means of association: *a corresponding member of a club.* —**cor′re•spond′ing•ly,** *adv.*

cor′respond′ing an′gles, *n.pl.* two nonadjacent angles made by the crossing of two lines by a third line, one angle being interior, the other exterior, and both being on the same side of the third line.

cor•ri•dor (kôr′i dər, -dôr′, kor′-), *n.* **1.** a passageway giving access to rooms, apartments, ship cabins, railway compartments, etc.; hallway. **2.** a narrow passageway of land, as between an inland country and an outlet to the sea. **3.** a densely populated region with major overland and air transportation routes: *the Northeast corridor.* **4.** a restricted path along which an aircraft must travel to avoid hostile action, other air traffic, etc.

cor′ridors of pow′er, *n.pl.* centers of political and governmental power.

cor•ri•gen•dum (kôr′i jen′dəm, kor′-), *n., pl.* **-da** (-də). **1.** an error to be corrected, esp. an error in print. **2.** corrigenda, a list of corrections of errors that is inserted in a book or other publication.

cor•ri•gi•ble (kôr′i jə bəl, kor′-), *adj.* **1.** capable of being corrected or reformed. **2.** submissive to correction. **3.** subject to being revised, improved, or made more accurate: *a corrigible theory.* —**cor′ri•gi•bil′i•ty,** *n.* —**cor′ri•gi•bly,** *adv.*

cor•rob•o•rant (kə rob′ər ənt), *adj.* corroborating; confirming.

cor•rob•o•rate (kə rob′ə rāt′), *v.t.,* **-rat•ed, -rat•ing.** to make more certain; confirm: *He corroborated my account of the accident.* —**cor•rob′o•ra′tion,** *n.* —**cor•rob′o•ra′tive** (-ə rā′tiv, -ər ə tiv), **cor•rob′o•ra•to′ry,** *adj.* —**cor•rob′o•ra′tor,** *n.*

cor•rode (kə rōd′), *v.,* **-rod•ed, -rod•ing.** —*v.t.* **1.** to eat or wear away gradually as if by gnawing, esp. by chemical action. **2.** to impair; deteriorate: *Jealousy corroded his character.* —*v.i.* **3.** to become corroded. —**cor•rod′i•ble,** *adj.*

cor•ro•sion (kə rō′zhən), *n.* **1.** the act or process of corroding; condition of being corroded. **2.** a product of corroding, as rust. —**cor•ro′sion•al,** *adj.*

cor•ro•sive (kə rō′siv), *adj.* **1.** having the quality of corroding or eating away. **2.** harmful or destructive; deleterious: *the corrosive effects of poverty.* **3.** sharply sarcastic; caustic: *corrosive comments.* —*n.* **4.** something corrosive, as an acid or drug. —**cor•ro′sive•ly,** *adv.* —**cor•ro′sive•ness, cor•ro•siv′i•ty** (kôr′ō siv′i tē, kor′-), *n.*

cor•ru•gate (*v.* kôr′ə gāt′, kor′-; *adj.* -git, -gāt′), *v.,* **-gat•ed, -gat•ing.** —*v.t.* **1.** to draw or bend into folds or alternate furrows and ridges; wrinkle. —*v.i.* **2.** to become corrugated; undergo corrugation. —*adj.* **3.** corrugated; wrinkled; furrowed. —**cor′ru•ga′tor,** *n.*

cor•ru•ga•tion (kôr′ə gā′shən, kor′-), *n.* **1.** the act or state of corrugating or of being corrugated. **2.** a wrinkle; fold; furrow; ridge.

cor•rupt (kə rupt′), *adj.* **1.** guilty of dishonest practices, as bribery; *a corrupt judge.* **2.** debased in character; depraved. **3.** infected; tainted. **4.** decayed; putrid. **5.** made inferior by errors or alterations, as a text. —*v.t.* **6.** to cause to be dishonest, disloyal, etc., esp. by bribery. **7.** to lower morally; pervert: *to corrupt youth.* **8.** to infect; taint. **9.** to alter (a language, text, etc.) for the worse; debase. —*v.i.* **10.** to become corrupt. —**cor•rupt′er, cor•rup′tor,** *n.* —**cor•rupt′i•ble,** *adj.* —**cor•rupt′i•bil′i•ty, cor•rupt′i•ble•ness,** *n.* —**cor•rupt′i•bly,** *adv.* —**cor•rup′tive,** *adj.* —**cor•rupt′ly,** *adv.* —**cor•rupt′ness,** *n.*

cor•rup•tion (kə rup′shən), *n.* **1.** the act of corrupting or the state of being corrupt. **2.** moral perversion; depravity. **3.** perversion of integrity. **4.** corrupt or dishonest proceedings. **5.** BRIBERY. **6.** debasement or alteration, as of language or a text. **7.** an altered or debased form of a word.

8. putrefactive decay; rottenness. **9.** any corrupting influence or agency. —**cor•rup′tion•ist,** *n.*

cor•sage (kôr säzh′), *n.* a small bouquet worn at the waist, on the shoulder, etc., by a woman.

cor•sair (kôr′sâr), *n.* **1.** a fast ship used for piracy. **2.** a pirate.

cor•set (kôr′sit), *n.* **1.** Sometimes, **corsets.** a close-fitting undergarment stiffened with whalebone or the like and often adjustable by lacing, worn esp. by women to shape and support the torso; stays. —*v.t.* **2.** to dress with or as if with a corset. **3.** to regulate strictly; constrict.

Cor•si•ca (kôr′si kə), *n.* a French island in the Mediterranean, N of Sardinia: constitutes a metropolitan region of France. 248,700; 3367 sq. mi. (8720 sq. km). *Cap.:* Ajaccio. French, **Corse.** —**Cor′si•can,** *adj., n.*

cor•tege or **cor•tège** (kôr tezh′, -tāzh′), *n.* **1.** a procession, esp. a ceremonial one: *a funeral cortege.* **2.** a line or train of attendants; retinue.

Cor•tes (kôr′tiz, -tez), *n.* the national legislature of Spain or Portugal.

Cor•tés or **Cor•tez** (kôr tez′), *n.* **Hernando** or **Hernán,** 1485–1547, Spanish conqueror of Mexico.

cor•tex (kôr′teks), *n., pl.* **-ti•ces** (-tə sēz′). **1.** the outer region of a body organ or structure, as the outer portion of the kidney. **2. a.** the portion of a plant stem or trunk between the epidermis and the vascular tissue; bark. **b.** any outer layer, as rind. **3.** the surface tissue layer of a fungus or lichen, composed of massed hyphal cells.

cor•ti•cal (kôr′ti kəl), *adj.* **1.** of, pertaining to, resembling, or consisting of cortex. **2.** resulting from the function or condition of the cerebral cortex. —**cor′ti•cal•ly,** *adv.*

cor•ti•co•ster•oid (kôr′ti kō ster′oid, -stēr′-), *n.* **1.** any of a class of steroid hormones formed in the cortex of the adrenal gland and having anti-inflammatory properties. **2.** any chemically similar synthesized hormone. Also called **cor•ti•coid** (kôr′ti koid′).

cor•ti•sone (kôr′tə zōn′, -sōn′), *n.* a corticosteroid, $C_{21}H_{28}O_5$, used chiefly in the treatment of autoimmune and inflammatory diseases and certain cancers.

co•run•dum (kə run′dəm), *n.* a mineral, aluminum oxide, Al_2O_3, noted for its hardness: transparent varieties, as sapphire and ruby, are used as gems, other varieties as abrasives.

cor•us•cate (kôr′ə skāt′, kor′-), *v.i.,* **-cat•ed, -cat•ing.** to emit vivid flashes of light; sparkle; scintillate; gleam.

cor•vette (kôr vet′) also **cor•vet** (kôr vet′, kôr′vet), *n.* **1.** a warship of the old sailing class, having a flush deck and usu. one tier of guns. **2.** a lightly armed ship, used esp. as a convoy escort and ranging in size between a destroyer and a gunboat.

cor•vi•na (kôr vē′nə), *n., pl.* **-nas.** any of various silvery gray croakers, esp. of the genera *Cynoscion* and *Micropogonias.*

cor•vine (kôr′vīn, -vin), *adj.* **1.** pertaining to or resembling a crow. **2.** belonging or pertaining to the Corvidae, a family of birds including crows, ravens, magpies, and jays.

co•ryd•a•lis (kə rid′l is), *n.* any of numerous erect or climbing plants of the genus *Corydalis,* fumitory family, with clusters of irregular spurred flowers.

Cos•by (kôz′bē, koz′-), *n.* **William Henry** (*Bill*), born 1937, U.S. comedian and actor.

co•sec (kō′sēk′), *n.* cosecant.

co•se•cant (kō sē′kant, -kənt), *n.* **1.** (in a right triangle) the ratio of the hypotenuse to the side opposite a given angle. **2.** the secant of the complement, or the reciprocal of the sine, of a given angle or arc. *Abbr.:* csc

co•sign•er (kō′sī′nər, kō sī′-), *n.* a joint signer of a negotiable instrument, esp. a promissory note. —**co′sign′,** *v.i., v.t.*

co•sine (kō′sīn), *n.* **1.** (in a right triangle) the ratio of the side adjacent to a given angle to the hypotenuse. **2.** the sine of the complement of a given angle or arc. *Abbr.:* cos

cos′ let′tuce, *n.* ROMAINE.

cos•met•ic (koz met′ik), *n.* **1.** a powder, lotion, cream, or other preparation for beautifying the face, skin, hair, nails, etc. **2. cosmetics,** superficial measures to make something seem better than it is. —*adj.* **3.** serving to impart or improve beauty, esp. of the face: *cosmetic surgery.* **4.** used or done superficially to make something seem better than it is. —**cos•met′i•cal•ly,** *adv.*

cos•me•tol•o•gy (koz′mi tol′ə jē), *n.* the art or profession of applying cosmetics. —**cos′me•to•log′i•cal** (-tl oj′i kəl), *adj.* —**cos′me•tol′o•gist,** *n.*

cos•mic (koz′mik) also **cos′mi•cal,** *adj.* **1.** of or pertaining to the cosmos: *cosmic laws.* **2.** characteristic of the cosmos or its phenomena: *cosmic events.* **3.** immeasurably extended in time and space; vast. **4.** forming a part of the material universe, esp. outside of the earth. —**cos′mi•cal•ly,** *adv.*

cos′mic ray′, *n.* a radiation of high penetrating power originating in outer space and consisting partly of high-energy atomic nuclei.

cosmo-, a combining form meaning "world," "universe" (*cosmography*); in contemporary usage, sometimes representing Russian *kosmo-,* it may mean "outer space," "space travel," or "cosmic ray" (*cosmonaut*). Compare ASTRO-.

cos•mo•chem•is•try (koz′mə kem′ə strē), *n.* the science dealing with the distribution of chemical elements in the universe. —**cos′mo•chem′i•cal** (-i kəl), *adj.* —**cos′mo•chem′ist,** *n.*

cos•mog•o•ny (koz mog′ə nē), *n., pl.* **-nies.** a theory or story of the origin and development of the universe, a solar system, etc. —**cos′mo•gon′ic** (-mə gon′ik), *adj.* —**cos•mog′o•nist,** *n.*

cos•mog•ra•phy (koz mog′rə fē), *n., pl.* **-phies. 1.** the study of the structure of the universe and its constituent parts, comprising astronomy, geography, and geology. **2.** a description or representation of the main features of the universe. —**cos•mog′ra•pher, cos•mog′ra•phist,** *n.* —**cos′mo•graph′ic** (-mə graf′ik), **cos′mo•graph′i•cal,** *adj.* —**cos′-mo•graph′i•cal•ly,** *adv.*

cos•mol•o•gy (koz mol′ə jē), *n.* **1.** the branch of philosophy dealing with the origin and general structure of the universe, esp. with such of its characteristics as space, time, causality, and freedom. **2.** the branch of astronomy that deals with the general structure and evolution of the universe. —**cos•mol′o•ger, cos•mol′o•gist,** *n.* —**cos′mo•log′i•cal** (-mə loj′i kəl), **cos′mo•log′ic,** *adj.* —**cos′mo•log′i•cal•ly,** *adv.*

cos•mo•naut (koz′mə nôt′, -not′), *n.* a Russian or Soviet astronaut.

cos•mop•o•lis (koz mop′ə lis), *n.* an internationally important city inhabited by many different peoples.

cos•mo•pol•i•tan (koz′mə pol′i tn), *adj.* **1.** belonging to all the world; not limited to the politics, interests, or prejudices of one part of the world. **2.** of or characteristic of a cosmopolite; worldly; sophisticated. **3.** (of an animal, plant, etc.) widely distributed over the globe. —*n.* **4.** a person who is free from local, provincial, or national bias or attachment; citizen of the world; cosmopolite.

cos•mop•o•lite (koz mop′ə līt′), *n.* **1.** a person who is sophisticated in outlook, lifestyle, etc.; citizen of the world. **2.** an animal or plant of worldwide distribution. —**cos•mop′o•lit•ism,** *n.*

cos•mos (koz′məs, -mōs), *n., pl.* **-mos, -mos•es** for 2, 4. **1.** the world or universe regarded as an orderly, harmonious system. **2.** a complete, orderly, harmonious system. **3.** order; harmony. **4.** any of a genus, *Cosmos,* of New World composite plants having open clusters of flowers with red or yellow disks and wide rays of white, pink, or purple. [< Greek *kósmos* order, form, arrangement]

Cos•sack (kos′ak, -ək), *n.* **1.** a member of any of a number of self-governing communities of varied ethnic affiliation that developed on the S and E frontiers of the Muscovite state and Poland-Lithuania after c1400: all were eventually incorporated into czarist Russia. **2.** a mounted soldier of a military unit drafted from these communities.

cos•set (kos′it), *v.t.* **1.** to treat as a pet; pamper; coddle. —*n.* **2.** a lamb brought up without its dam; pet lamb. **3.** any pet.

cost (kôst, kost), *n., v.,* **cost** or, for 9, 10, **cost•ed, cost•ing.** —*n.* **1.** the price paid to acquire, produce, accomplish, or maintain anything. **2.** an outlay or expenditure of money, time, labor, etc. **3.** a sacrifice, loss, or penalty: *to work at the cost of one's health.* **4. costs,** money awarded to a successful litigant for legal expenses, charged against the unsuccessful litigant. —*v.t.* **5.** to require the payment of (money or something else of value) in an exchange: *That camera cost $200.* **6.** to result in or entail the loss or injury of: *Carelessness costs lives.* **7.** to entail (effort or inconvenience): *Courtesy costs little.* **8.** to cause to pay or sacrifice: *That request will cost us two weeks' extra work.* **9.** to estimate or determine the cost of (manufactured articles, new processes, etc.). —*v.i.* **10.** to estimate or determine costs, as of manufacturing something. —*Idiom.* **11. at all costs,** regardless of the effort involved; by any means necessary.

cost′ account′ing, *n.* an accounting system that analyzes the cost of all items involved in production. —**cost′ account′ant,** *n.*

Cos•tain (kos′tān), *n.* **Thomas Bertram,** 1885–1965, U.S. novelist, historian, and editor, born in Canada.

co•star or **co-star** (*n.* kō′stär′; *v.* -stär′), *n., v.,* **-starred, -star•ring.** —*n.* **1.** a performer who shares star billing with another. —*v.i.* **2.** to be or have billing as a costar. —*v.t.* **3.** to present or bill as a costar or costars.

Cos•ta Ri•ca (kos′tə rē′kə, kô′stə, kō′-), *n.* a republic in Central America, between Panama and Nicaragua. 3,534,174; 19,238 sq. mi. (49,825 sq. km). *Cap.:* San José. —**Cos′ta Ri′can,** *adj., n.*

cost′-ben′efit, *adj.* of, pertaining to, or based on a cost-effective analysis.

cost′-effec′tive, *adj.* producing optimum results for the expenditure. —**cost′-effec′tively,** *adv.* —**cost′-effec′tiveness,** *n.*

cost•ly (kôst′lē, kost′-), *adj.,* **-li•er, -li•est. 1.** costing much; high in price. **2.** resulting in great detriment: *a costly mistake.* **3.** involving great expense; sumptuous. **4.** lavish; extravagant. —**cost′li•ness,** *n.*

cost•mar•y (kost′mâr′ē, kôst′-), *n., pl.* **-mar•ies.** a composite plant, *Chrysanthemum balsamita,* that has silvery, fragrant leaves and is used in salads and as a flavoring.

cost′ of liv′ing, *n.* the average that a person or family pays for such necessary goods and services as food, clothing, and rent.

cos•tume (kos′tōōm, -tyōōm; *v. also* ko stōōm′, -styōōm′), *n., v.,* **-tumed, -tum•ing,** *adj.* —*n.* **1.** style of dress, including accessories and hairdos, esp. that peculiar to a nation, group, or historical period. **2.** clothing of another period, place, etc., or for a particular occasion or season. **3.** a set of garments, esp. women's garments, selected for wear at a single time; outfit; ensemble. —*v.t.* **4.** to furnish with a costume; dress. —*adj.* **5.** of or characterized by the wearing of costumes: *a costume party.*

cos′tume jew′elry, *n.* inexpensive jewelry made of nonprecious metals and set with imitation or semiprecious stones, pearls, etc.

cos•tum•er (kos′tōō mər, -tyōō-; ko stōō′mər, -styōō′-), *n.* **1.** a person

who makes, sells, or rents costumes, as for theatrical productions. **2.** a clothes tree.

cot¹ (kot), *n.* **1.** a light portable bed, esp. one of canvas on a folding frame. **2.** *Brit.* a child's crib. **3.** a light bedstead.

cot² (kot), *n.* **1.** a small house; cottage; hut. **2.** a small place of shelter. **3.** a sheath or protective covering, as for an injured finger or toe.

co•tan•gent (kō tan′jənt, kō′tan′-), *n.* **1.** (in a right triangle) the ratio of the side adjacent to a given angle to the side opposite. **2.** the tangent of the complement, or the reciprocal of the tangent, of a given angle or arc. *Abbr.:* cot, ctn Also called **co•tan** (kō′tan′). —**co′tan•gen′tial** (-jen′shəl), *adj.*

cote (kōt), *n.* a coop or shed for sheep, pigs, pigeons, etc.

Côte d'I•voire (kōt dē vwAR′), *n.* French name of Ivory Coast.

co•te•rie (kō′tə rē), *n.* **1.** a group of people who associate closely. **2.** an exclusive group; clique. [< French: an association of tenant farmers]

co•ter•mi•nous (kō tûr′mə nəs) also **co•ter′mi•nal,** *adj.* **1.** having the same border or covering the same area. **2.** being the same in extent; coextensive. —**co•ter′mi•nous•ly,** *adv.*

co•til•lion (kə til′yən, kō-), *n.* **1.** a formal ball given esp. for debutantes. **2.** any of various dances resembling the quadrille. **3.** a formalized dance for a large number of people, in which a head couple leads the other dancers through elaborate and stately figures.

co•tin•ga (kō ting′gə, kə-), *n.* any of numerous suboscine birds comprising the family Cotingidae, of New World tropical forests: diverse in size and habits, with many species having spectacular plumage and far-carrying voices.

co•to•ne•as•ter (kə tō′nē as′tər, kot′n ē′stər), *n.* any of various shrubs of the genus *Cotoneaster,* rose family, having white or pink flowers and red or black berries.

Co•to•pax•i (kō′tə pak′sē, -pä′hē), *n.* a volcano in central Ecuador: highest active volcano in the world. 19,498 ft. (5943 m).

cot•tage (kot′ij), *n.* **1.** a small house, usu. of only one story. **2.** a small, modest vacation house, as at a lake or mountain resort. —**cot′-taged,** *adj.*

cot′tage cheese′, *n.* a soft, loose, white, mild-flavored unripened cheese made from skim-milk curds.

cot′tage fries′, *n.pl. Chiefly Northern and North Midland U.S.* HOME FRIES. Also called **cot′tage-fried′ pota′toes.**

cot′tage in′dustry, *n.* **1.** a business in which goods are produced in the home for commercial use or sale. **2.** any small-scale, loosely organized industry.

cot′tage tu′lip, *n.* a late-flowering type of tulip, usu. having pointed or elongated flowers.

cot•ter (kot′ər), *n.* **1.** a pin, wedge, or the like inserted into an opening to secure something or hold parts together. **2.** COTTER PIN.

cot′ter pin′, *n.* a cotter having a split end that is spread after being pushed through a hole to prevent it from working loose.

cot•ton (kot′n), *n.* **1.** a soft, white, downy substance consisting of the hairs or fibers attached to the seeds of plants belonging to the genus *Gossypium,* of the mallow family, used in making fabrics, thread, wadding, etc. **2.** the plant itself, having spreading branches and broad, lobed leaves. **3.** such plants collectively as a cultivated crop. **4.** cloth, thread, a garment, etc., of cotton. **5.** any soft, downy substance resembling cotton, but growing on other plants. —*v.i.* **6.** *Informal.* to get on well together; agree. **7. cotton to** or **on to,** *Informal.* **a.** to become fond of; begin to like. **b.** to approve of; agree with: *to cotton to a suggestion.*

Cot•ton (kot′n), *n.* **John,** 1584–1652, U.S. clergyman, colonist, and author (grandfather of Cotton Mather).

Cot′ton Belt′, *n.* (*sometimes l.c.*) the part of the southern U.S. where cotton is grown, orig. Alabama, Georgia, and Mississippi, but now often extended to include parts of Texas and California.

cot′ton can′dy, *n.* a fluffy, sweet confection whipped from spun sugar and wound around a stick or paper cone.

cot′ton gin′, *n.* a machine for separating the fibers of cotton from the seeds. Also called **gin.**

cot′ton grass′, *n.* any rushlike plant constituting the genus *Eriophorum,* of the sedge family, common in swampy places and bearing spikes resembling tufts of cotton.

cot′ton gum′, *n.* a tupelo tree, *Nyssa aquatica,* of swamps in the southeastern U.S.

cot•ton•mouth (kot′n mouth′), *n., pl.* **-mouths** (-mouths′, -mouthz′). a pit viper, *Agkistrodon piscivorus,* of southeastern U.S. swamps. Also called **water moccasin.**

cot′ton stain′er, *n.* any of several large red and black bugs of the genus *Dysdercus* that puncture oranges and cotton bolls and discolor cotton fiber.

cot•ton•tail (kot′n tāl′), *n.* any North American rabbit of the genus *Sylvilagus.*

cot•ton•weed (kot′n wēd′), *n.* any of various wild plants with a hoary down on the leaves and stems.

cot•ton•wood (kot′n wōōd′), *n.* any of several American poplars, as *Populus deltoides,* with cottony tufts on the seeds.

cot•y•le•don (kot′l ēd′n), *n.* the rudimentary leaf of the embryo of seed plants. —**cot′y•le′don•al, cot′y•le′don•ous,** *adj.*

cot•y•lo•saur (kot′l ə sôr′), *n.* any reptile of the extinct order Cotylosauria, comprising heavy-bodied splay-limbed forms that arose during the Pennsylvanian Period and that include the ancestors of all other reptiles. —**cot′y•lo•sau′ri•an,** *adj.*

couch (kouch), *n.* **1.** a piece of upholstered furniture for seating usu. two to four people, typically having a back and an armrest at one or both ends. **2.** a long upholstered seat with a headrest at one end, on which a person reclines; lounge. **3.** a bed or other place of rest; any place used for repose. **4.** the lair of a wild beast. —*v.t.* **5.** to arrange or frame (words, a sentence, etc.); express. **6.** to express indirectly or obscurely: *to couch a threat in pleasant words.* **7.** to lower or bend down, as the head. **8.** to lower (a spear, lance, etc.) to a horizontal position, as for attack. **9.** to put or lay down, as for rest or sleep; cause to lie down. —*v.i.* **10.** to lie at rest or asleep; repose; recline. **11.** to crouch; bend; stoop. **12.** to lie in ambush or in hiding; lurk. **13.** to lie in a heap for decomposition or fermentation, as leaves.

couch′ grass′ (kouch, ko͞och), *n.* any of various grasses that have rapidly spreading underground stems and are troublesome weeds. Compare QUACK GRASS.

couch′ pota′to, *n. Informal.* a person whose leisure time is spent watching television.

cou•gar (ko͞o′gər), *n., pl.* **-gars,** (*esp. collectively*) **-gar.** a large, tawny cat, *Felis concolor,* of North and South America. Also called **mountain lion, panther, puma.**

cough (kôf, kof), *v.i.* **1.** to expel air from the lungs suddenly with a harsh noise, often involuntarily. **2.** (of an internal-combustion engine) to make a similar noise as a result of the failure of one or more cylinders to fire in sequence. **3.** to make a similar sound, as a machine gun firing in spurts. —*v.t.* **4.** to expel by coughing (usu. fol. by *up* or *out*). **5. cough up,** *Informal.* to produce or relinquish, esp. reluctantly; hand over. —*n.* **6.** the act or sound of coughing. **7.** an illness characterized by frequent coughing. **8.** a sound similar to a cough, as of an engine firing improperly.

cough′ drop′, *n.* a small medicinal lozenge for relieving a cough, sore throat, hoarseness, etc.

cough′ syr′up, *n.* a medicated, syruplike fluid, usu. flavored and nonnarcotic or mildly narcotic, for relieving coughs or soothing irritated throats. Also called **cough′ med′icine.**

could (ko͝od; *unstressed* kəd), *v.* **1.** a pt. of CAN[1]. —*auxiliary verb.* **2.** (used to express possibility): *That could never be true.* **3.** (used to express conditional possibility or ability): *You could do it if you tried.* **4.** (used in making polite requests): *Could you open the door for me, please?* **5.** (used in asking for permission): *Could I borrow your pen?* **6.** (used in offering suggestions): *You could ask for information.*

cou•lee (ko͞o′lē), *n.* **1.** *Chiefly Western U.S. and Western Canada.* a deep ravine or gulch, usu. dry, that has been formed by running water. **2.** a small valley. **3.** a small intermittent stream.

coun•cil (koun′səl), *n.* **1.** an assembly of persons convened for consultation, deliberation, or advice. **2.** a body of persons appointed or elected to act in an advisory, administrative, or legislative capacity: *the governor's council on housing.* **3.** an ecclesiastical assembly for deciding matters of doctrine or discipline. —**Usage.** COUNCIL and COUNSEL are not interchangeable. COUNCIL is a noun. Its most common sense is "an assembly of persons convened for deliberation or the like." COUNSEL is both noun and verb. Its most common meaning as a noun is "advice given to another." In law, COUNSEL means "legal adviser or advisers" and can be either singular or plural. As a verb, COUNSEL means "to advise."

coun•ci•lor or **coun•cil•lor** (koun′sə lər, -slər), *n.* a member of a council. —**coun′ci•lor•ship′,** *n.*

coun•sel (koun′səl), *n., pl.* **-sel** for 3, *v.,* **-seled, -sel•ing** or (*esp. Brit.*) **-selled, -sel•ling.** —*n.* **1.** advice; opinion or instruction regarding the judgment or conduct of another. **2.** interchange of opinions as to future procedure; consultation. **3.** (*used with a sing. or pl. v.*) the lawyer or lawyers representing one party or the other in court. **4.** deliberate purpose; plan; design. —*v.t.* **5.** to advise. **6.** to urge the adoption of, as a course of action; recommend. —*v.i.* **7.** to give counsel or advice. **8.** to get or take counsel or advice. —***Idiom.*** **9. keep one's own counsel,** to remain silent. —**Usage.** See COUNCIL.

coun•se•lor (koun′sə lər), *n.* **1.** a person who counsels; adviser. **2.** a faculty member, as at a high school, who advises students on personal and academic problems. **3.** one of a number of supervisors at a children's camp. **4.** a lawyer, esp. a trial lawyer. **5.** an official of an embassy or legation who ranks below an ambassador or minister. Also, *esp. Brit.,* **coun′sel•lor.**

coun′selor-at-law′, *n., pl.* **counselors-at-law.** COUNSELOR (def. 4).

count[1] (kount), *v.t.* **1.** to check over one by one to determine the total number; add up; enumerate. **2.** to reckon up; calculate; compute. **3.** to list or name the numerals up to: *Close your eyes and count to ten.* **4.** to include in a reckoning; take into account: *Count her among the chosen.* **5.** to reckon to the credit of another; ascribe; impute. **6.** to consider or regard: *He counted himself lucky.* —*v.i.* **7.** to count the items of a collection to determine the total. **8.** to list or name numerals in order. **9.** to reckon numerically. **10.** to have a specified numerical value. **11.** to be accounted or worth something: *That try didn't count—I was practicing.* **12.** to have merit, importance, value, etc.; deserve consideration: *Every bit of help counts.* **13. count down,** to count backward, usu. by ones, from a given integer to zero. **14. count in,** to include. **15. count off,** to count aloud by turns, as to arrange positions within a group of persons; divide or become divided into groups: *Count off from the left by threes.* **16. count on** or **upon,** to depend or rely on. **17. count out, a.** to declare (a boxer) the loser in a bout because of inability to stand up before the referee has counted to 10. **b.** to exclude. **c.** to count and apportion or give out. **d.** to disqualify (ballots) illegally in counting, in order to control the election. —*n.* **18.** the act of counting; enumeration; reckoning; calculation. **19.** the number obtained by counting; the total. **20.** an accounting. **21.** *Baseball.* the number of balls and strikes that have been called on a batter during a turn at bat. **22.** a separate charge in a legal declaration or indictment: *two counts of embezzlement.* **23. a.** a single ionizing reaction registered by an ionization chamber, as in a Geiger counter. **b.** the total number of ionizing reactions so registered. **24. the count,** the calling out, by the referee, of the numbers from 1 to 10 when a boxer falls to the canvas. —*adj.* **25.** noting a number of items determined by an actual count: *The box is labeled 50 count.* —***Idiom.*** **26. count heads** or **noses,** to count the number of people present. —***Proverb.*** **27. Don't count your chickens before they hatch,** don't make rash predictions about results.

count[2] (kount), *n.* (in some European countries) a nobleman equivalent in rank to an English earl.

C

count•a•ble (koun′tə bəl), *adj.* **1.** able to be counted. **2.** *Math.* **a.** (of a set) having a finite number of elements. **b.** (of a set) having elements that form a one-to-one correspondence with the natural numbers; enumerable.

count•down (kount′doun′), *n.* **1.** the backward counting from the initiation of a project, as a rocket launching, with the moment of firing designated as zero. **2.** the final preparations made during this period. **3.** any period of increased activity before a deadline.

coun•te•nance (koun′tn əns), *n., v.,* **-nanced, -nanc•ing.** —*n.* **1.** appearance, esp. the expression of the face: *a sad countenance.* **2.** the face; visage. **3.** calm facial expression. **4.** approval or favor. —*v.t.* **5.** to permit or tolerate. **6.** to approve or encourage.

count•er[1] (koun′tər), *n.* **1.** a table or display case on which goods can be shown, business transacted, etc. **2.** (in restaurants, luncheonettes, etc.) a long, narrow table with stools or chairs along one side for the patrons, behind which refreshments or meals are prepared and served. **3.** a surface for the preparation of food in a kitchen, esp. on a low cabinet. **4.** anything used to keep account, esp. a disk or other small object used in games. —***Idiom.*** **5. over the counter, a.** (of the sale of stock) through a broker's office rather than through the stock exchange. **b.** (of the sale of merchandise) through a retail store rather than through a wholesaler. **c.** (of the sale of medicinal drugs) without requiring a prescription. **6. under the counter,** in a clandestine manner, esp. illegally.

count•er[2] (koun′tər), *n.* **1.** a person who counts. **2.** a device for counting revolutions of a wheel, items produced, etc. **3.** any of various instruments for detecting ionizing radiation and for registering counts, as a Geiger counter.

coun•ter[3] (koun′tər), *adv.* **1.** in the wrong way; in the reverse direction. **2.** contrary; in opposition. —*adj.* **3.** opposite; opposed. —*n.* **4.** something that is opposite or contrary to something else. **5.** a blow delivered in receiving or parrying another blow, as in boxing. **6.** a statement or action made to refute or oppose another statement or action. **7.** a circular parry in fencing. **8.** a piece of leather or the like inside the lining of the upper of a shoe or boot, around the heel, to keep it stiff. **9.** the part of a vessel's stern that overhangs and projects aft of the sternpost. —*v.t.* **10.** to go counter to; oppose; controvert. **11.** to meet or answer (a move, blow, etc.) by another in return. —*v.i.* **12.** to make a counter or opposing move. **13.** to give a blow while receiving or parrying one, as in boxing.

counter-, a prefix used in the formation of words that have the general senses "against" (*counterintuitive*), "in response or reply to" (*counterattack*), "thwarting, or designed to thwart, frustrate, or nullify" (*counterespionage*), "refuting" (*counterexample*), "opposite, in the reverse direction" (*counterclockwise*), "offsetting, complementary" (*counterbalance*), "occurring simultaneously" (*countermelody*).

coun•ter•act (koun′tər akt′), *v.t.* to act in opposition to; frustrate by contrary action. —**coun′ter•ac′tion,** *n.* —**coun′ter•ac′tive,** *adj.* —**coun′ter•ac′tive•ly,** *adv.*

coun•ter•ar•gu•ment (koun′tər är′gyə mənt), *n.* a contrasting, opposing, or refuting argument.

coun•ter•at•tack (koun′tər ə tak′), *n.* **1.** an attack made as an offset or reply to another attack. —*v.t.* **2.** to make a counterattack against. —*v.i.* **3.** to deliver a counterattack.

coun•ter•bal•ance (*n.* koun′tər bal′əns; *v.* koun′tər bal′əns), *n., v.,* **-anced, -anc•ing.** —*n.* **1.** a weight balancing another weight; an equal power or influence acting in opposition; counterpoise. —*v.t., v.i.* **2.** to oppose with an equal weight, force, or influence.

coun•ter•charge (*n.* koun′tər chärj′; *for v. also* koun′tər chärj′), *n., v.,* **-charged, -charg•ing.** —*n.* **1.** a charge by an accused person against the accuser. **2.** a retaliatory military attack or action. —*v.t.* **3.** to make an accusation against (one's accuser). **4.** to attack or take action against in retaliation.

coun•ter•claim (*n.* koun′tər klām′; *v.* koun′tər klām′), *n.* **1.** a claim made to offset another claim. **2.** a civil action brought by the defendant against the plaintiff. —*v.t., v.i.* **3.** to claim in answer to a previous claim. —**coun′ter•claim′ant,** *n.*

coun•ter•clock•wise (koun′tər klok′wīz′), *adj., adv.* in a direction opposite to that of the normal rotation of the hands of a clock.

coun•ter•cult′ move′ment (koun′tər kult′), *n.* a group of organizations and individuals who seek to reduce the influence of religious cults considered to be harmful.

coun·ter·cul·ture (koun′tər kul′chər), *n.* the culture and lifestyle of those people who reject the dominant values and behavior of society. —**coun′ter·cul′tur·al,** *adj.* —**coun′ter·cul′tur·ist,** *n.*

coun·ter·es·pi·o·nage (koun′tər es′pē ə näzh′, -nij), *n.* the detection and frustration of enemy espionage.

coun·ter·feit (koun′tər fit′), *adj.* **1.** made in imitation with intent to deceive; not genuine; forged. **2.** pretended; unreal: *counterfeit grief.* —*n.* **3.** an imitation intended to be passed off as genuine; forgery. —*v.t.* **4.** to make a counterfeit of; forge. **5.** to resemble. **6.** to simulate. —*v.i.* **7.** to make counterfeits, as of money. **8.** to feign; dissemble. —**coun′ter·feit′er,** *n.*

coun·ter·in·sur·gen·cy (koun′tər in sûr′jən sē), *n., pl.* **-cies.** a program or an act of combating guerrilla warfare and subversion. —**coun′ter·in·sur′gent,** *n., adj.*

coun·ter·in·tel·li·gence (koun′tər in tel′i jəns), *n.* **1.** the activity of an intelligence service engaged in thwarting the subversive or intelligence-gathering efforts of a foreign power. **2.** an organization engaged in counterintelligence.

coun·ter·mand (*v.* koun′tər mand′, -mänd′; *n.* koun′tər mand′, -mänd′), *v.t.* **1.** to revoke or cancel (a command, order, etc.). **2.** to recall or stop by a contrary order. —*n.* **3.** a command, order, etc., revoking a previous one.

coun·ter·meas·ure (koun′tər mezh′ər), *n.* an opposing, offsetting, or retaliatory measure.

coun·ter·mine (koun′tər mīn′), *n., v.,* **-mined, -min·ing.** —*n.* **1.** a mine intended to intercept an enemy mine. **2.** a counterplot. —*v.t.* **3.** to intercept by a countermine. —*v.i.* **4.** to counterplot.

coun·ter·of·fen·sive (koun′tər ə fen′siv, koun′tər ə fen′-), *n.* an attack by an army against an attacking enemy force.

coun·ter·of·fer (koun′tər ô′fər, -of′ər), *n.* an offer or proposal made to offset or substitute for an earlier offer made by another.

coun·ter·part (koun′tər pärt′), *n.* **1.** a person or thing closely resembling another, esp. in function. **2.** a copy or duplicate. **3.** one of two parts that fit, complete, or complement one another.

coun·ter·point (koun′tər point′), *n.* **1.** POLYPHONY (def. 1). **2.** the texture resulting from the combining of individual melodic lines. **3.** a melody composed to be combined with another melody. **4.** any element that is juxtaposed and contrasted with another. —*v.t.* **5.** to emphasize or set off by contrast or juxtaposition.

coun·ter·pro·duc·tive (koun′tər prə duk′tiv), *adj.* thwarting the achievement of an intended goal; tending to defeat one's purpose.

coun·ter·pro·pos·al (koun′tər prə pō′zəl), *n.* a proposal offered to offset or substitute for a preceding one.

Coun′ter Reforma′tion, *n.* the movement for reform within the Roman Catholic Church that followed the Protestant Reformation of the 16th century.

coun·ter·rev·o·lu·tion (koun′tər rev′ə lōō′shən), *n.* **1.** a revolution against a government recently established by a revolution. **2.** a political movement that resists revolutionary tendencies.

coun·ter·rev·o·lu·tion·ar·y (koun′tər rev′ə lōō′shə ner′ē), *adj., n., pl.* **-ar·ies.** —*adj.* **1.** characteristic of or resulting from a counterrevolution. **2.** opposing a revolution or revolutionary government. —*n.* **3.** Also, **coun·ter·rev·o·lu·tion·ist** (koun′tər rev′ə lōō′shə nist) a person who advocates or engages in a counterrevolution.

coun·ter·sign (koun′tər sīn′), *n.* **1.** a sign used in reply to another sign. **2.** a secret sign or signal that must be given by authorized persons seeking admission into a guarded area. **3.** a signature added to another signature, esp. for authentication. —*v.t.* **4.** to sign (a document that has been signed by someone else), esp. in confirmation or authentication. —**coun′ter·sig′na·ture** (-sig′nə chər), *n.*

coun·ter·sink (koun′tər singk′), *v.,* **-sank, -sunk, -sink·ing,** *n.* —*v.t.* **1.** to enlarge the upper part of (a hole) to receive the head of a screw or bolt. **2.** to set the head of (a screw or bolt) flush with or below the surface. —*n.* **3.** a tool for countersinking a hole.

coun·ter·suit (koun′tər sōōt′), *n.* COUNTERCLAIM (def. 2). —**coun′ter·sue′,** *v.t., v.i.,* **-sued, -su·ing.**

count·er·top (koun′tər top′), *n.* the flat, horizontal working surface of a counter, as in a kitchen.

coun·ter·type (koun′tər tīp′), *n.* **1.** a corresponding type. **2.** an opposite type.

coun·ter·vail (koun′tər vāl′), *v.t.* **1.** to act against with equal power or effect; counteract. **2.** to furnish an equivalent of or a compensation for; offset. —*v.i.* **3.** to be of equal force in opposition; avail.

coun·ter·weight (koun′tər wāt′), *n.* **1.** a weight used as a counterbalance. —*v.t.* **2.** to balance or equip with a counterweight.

count·er·word (koun′tər wûrd′), *n.* a word that has come to be used with meanings much less specific than that which it had originally, as *swell, awful,* or *terrific.*

count·ess (koun′tis), *n.* **1.** the wife or widow of a count in the nobility of continental Europe or of an earl in the British peerage. **2.** a woman having the rank of a count or earl in her own right.

count′ing house′, *n.* a building or office where the financial records of a business are maintained.

count·less (kount′lis), *adj.* too numerous to count; innumerable.

count′ noun′, *n.* a noun, as *apple, table,* or *birthday,* that typically re-

fers to a countable thing and that in English can be used in both the singular and the plural and can be preceded by the indefinite article *a* or *an* and by numerals. Compare MASS NOUN.

coun·tri·fied (kun′trə fīd′), *adj.* **1.** rustic or rural in appearance, conduct, etc. **2.** not sophisticated or cosmopolitan; provincial.

coun·try (kun′trē), *n., pl.* **-tries,** *adj.* —*n.* **1.** a state or nation: *European countries.* **2.** the territory of a nation. **3.** the people of a district, state, or nation. **4.** the land of one's birth or citizenship. **5.** rural districts, as opposed to cities or towns. **6.** any considerable territory demarcated by topographical conditions, by a distinctive population, etc. **7.** the public at large, as represented by a jury. **8.** COUNTRY MUSIC. —*adj.* **9.** of, from, or characteristic of the country; rural. **10.** rude; unpolished; rustic: *country manners.* **11.** of, from, or pertaining to a particular country. —*Saying.* **12. our country right or wrong,** patriotism is a paramount virtue.

coun′try club′, *n.* a suburban club with facilities for tennis, golf, swimming, etc.

coun′try cous′in, *n.* a person from a small town to whom city life is novel and bewildering.

coun′try mu′sic, *n.* music with roots in the folk music of the Southeast and the cowboy music of the West.

coun′try rock′, *n.* **1.** a style of popular music combining the features of country and rock music. **2.** the rock surrounding and penetrated by mineral veins or igneous intrusions.

coun·try·side (kun′trē sīd′), *n.* **1.** a particular section of a country, esp. a rural section. **2.** its inhabitants.

coun·ty (koun′tē), *n., pl.* **-ties. 1.** the largest local administrative division in most states of the U.S. **2.** a territorial division and unit of local government in Great Britain, Canada, etc. **3.** the territory of a county, esp. its rural areas. **4.** the inhabitants of a county. **5.** the domain of a count or earl.

coun′ty court′, *n.* **1.** a court of record having jurisdiction within a county over civil matters and some criminal matters. **2.** a judicial tribunal in some states with jurisdiction extending over one or more counties.

coun′ty fair′, *n.* a competitive exhibition of farm products, livestock, etc., often held annually in the same place in the county.

coun′ty seat′, *n.* **1.** the seat of government of a county. **2.** a building housing these offices; a county courthouse.

coup (kōō), *n., pl.* **coups** (kōōz; *Fr.* kōō). **1.** a highly successful, unexpected stroke, act, or move. **2.** (among the Plains Indians of North America) a daring deed performed in battle by a warrior, as touching an enemy without sustaining injury oneself. **3.** COUP D'ÉTAT.

coup de grâce (kōō′ də gräs′), *n., pl.* **coups de grâce** (kōō). **1.** a death blow, esp. one delivered mercifully to end suffering. **2.** any finishing or decisive stroke.

coup d'é·tat (kōō′ dā tä′), *n., pl.* **coups d'é·tat** (kōō′ dā täz′, -tä′). a sudden and decisive action in politics, esp. one resulting in a change of government illegally or by force.

coupe¹ (kōōp), *n.* Also, **coupé.** a closed two-door car shorter than a sedan of the same model.

coupe² (kōōp), *n.* **1.** ice cream or sherbet topped with fruit, syrup, whipped cream, etc. **2.** a glass container for serving such a dessert, usu. having a stem and a wide, deep bowl.

cou·pé (kōō pā′ *or, for 1, 3,* kōōp), *n.* **1.** a short, four-wheeled, closed carriage, usu. with a single seat for two passengers and an outside seat for the driver. **2.** the end compartment in a European railroad car. **3.** COUPE¹ (def. 1). Also, **coupe** (for defs. 1, 2).

cou·ple (kup′əl), *n., v.,* **-pled, -pling.** —*n.* **1.** a combination of two of a kind; pair. **2.** a grouping of two persons, as a married or engaged pair, lovers, or dance partners. **3.** any two persons considered together. **4.** a pair of equal, parallel forces acting in opposite directions and tending to produce rotation. **5.** something that joins two things together. —*v.t.* **6.** to fasten or associate together in a pair or pairs. **7.** to join; connect. **8.** to unite in marriage or in sexual union. **9. a.** to join or associate by means of a coupler. **b.** to bring (two electric circuits or circuit components) close enough to permit an exchange of electromagnetic energy. —*v.i.* **10.** to join in a pair; unite. **11.** to copulate. —*Idiom.* **12. a couple of,** more than two, but not many of; a small number of; a few.

cou·pler (kup′lər), *n.* **1.** a person or thing that couples or links together. **2.** a rod or link transmitting force and motion between a rotating part and a rotating or oscillating part. **3.** Also called **coupling.** **4.** a device for joining pieces of rolling stock. **4.** a device in an organ or harpsichord for connecting keys, manuals, or a manual and pedals, so that they are played together when one is played. **5.** a device for transferring electrical energy from one circuit to another, as a transformer that joins parts of a radio apparatus together by induction.

cou·plet (kup′lit), *n.* **1.** a pair of successive lines of verse, esp. a pair the same length that rhyme. **2.** a pair; couple. **3.** any of the contrasting sections of a musical rondo.

cou·pling (kup′ling), *n.* **1.** the act of a person or thing that couples. **2.** a device for joining two rotating shafts semipermanently at their ends so as to transmit torque from one to the other. **3.** COUPLER (def. 3). **4. a.** the association of two circuits or systems in such a way that power may be transferred from one to the other. **b.** a device or expedient to ensure this. **5.** the part of the body between the tops of the shoulder blades and the tops of the hip joints in a dog, horse, etc. **6.** LINKAGE (def. 5).

cou·pon (kōō′pon, kyōō′-), *n.* **1.** a detachable portion of a certificate, ticket, advertisement, or the like, entitling the holder to something, as a discount, or for use as an order blank, a contest entry form, etc. **2.** a separate certificate, ticket, etc., for the same purpose. **3.** a detachable certificate calling for a periodic payment of interest on a bearer bond. —**cou′pon·less,** *adj.* —**Pronunciation.** The American pronunciation variant (kyōō′pon), with a *y*-sound not justified by the spelling, is well-established and standard. It probably developed by analogy with words like *cupid* and *cute,* where the (y) is mandatory.

cour·age (kûr′ij, kur′-), *n.* **1.** the quality of mind or spirit that enables a person to face difficulty, danger, pain, etc., without fear; bravery. —*Idiom.* **2. have the courage of one's convictions,** to act in accordance with one's beliefs.

cou·ra·geous (kə rā′jəs), *adj.* possessing or characterized by courage; brave. —**cou·ra′geous·ly,** *adv.* —**cou·ra′geous·ness,** *n.*

cou·ri·er (kûr′ē ər, kŏŏr′-), *n.* **1.** a messenger, usu. bearing news, packages, diplomatic messages, etc. **2.** any means of carrying news, messages, etc., regularly. **3.** the conveyance used by a courier, as an airplane or ship. **4.** a tour guide for a travel agency.

course (kôrs, kōrs), *n., v.,* **coursed, cours·ing.** —*n.* **1.** a direction or route taken or to be taken. **2.** the path, route, or channel along which anything moves: *the course of a stream.* **3.** advance or progression in a particular direction. **4.** the continuous passage or progress through time or a succession of stages: *in the course of a year.* **5.** the track, water, etc., on which a race is run, sailed, etc. **6.** a particular manner of proceeding: *a course of action.* **7.** a customary manner of procedure; regular or natural order of events: *the course of a disease.* **8.** a mode of conduct; behavior. **9.** a systematized or prescribed series: *a course of treatment.* **10.** a program of instruction, as in a college. **11.** a prescribed number of classes in a particular field of study. **12.** a part of a meal served at one time. **13.** the lowermost sail on a fully square-rigged mast. **14.** a continuous and usu. horizontal range of bricks, shingles, etc., as in a wall or roof. —*v.t.* **15.** to run through or over. **16.** to chase; pursue. **17.** to hunt (game) with dogs by sight rather than by scent. **18.** to cause (dogs) to pursue game by sight rather than by scent. **19.** to lay (bricks, stones, etc.) in courses. —*v.i.* **20.** to follow a course; direct one's course. **21.** to run, race, or move swiftly. **22.** to take part in a hunt with hounds. —*Idiom.* **23. in due course,** in the proper or natural order of events; eventually. **24. of course, a.** certainly; definitely. **b.** in the usual or natural order of things.

cours·er¹ (kôr′sər, kōr′-), *n.* **1.** a person or thing that courses. **2.** a dog for coursing.

cours·er² (kôr′sər, kōr′-), *n.* a swift horse.

cours·er³ (kôr′sər, kōr′-), *n.* any of various swift-footed, ploverlike birds of the family Glareolidae, esp. of the genera *Cursorius* and *Rhinoptilus,* inhabiting arid regions of Africa and S Asia.

court (kôrt, kōrt), *n.* **1. a.** a place where legal justice is administered. **b.** a judicial tribunal duly constituted for the hearing and determination of cases. **c.** a session of a judicial assembly. **2.** an area open to the sky and mostly or entirely surrounded by buildings, walls, etc. **3.** a high interior usu. having a glass roof and surrounded by several stories of galleries or the like. **4.** a short street. **5. a.** a smooth, level quadrangle on which to play tennis, basketball, etc. **b.** one of the divisions of such an area. **6.** the residence of a sovereign or other high dignitary; palace. **7.** a sovereign's or dignitary's retinue. **8.** a sovereign and councilors as the political rulers of a state. **9.** a formal assembly held by a sovereign. **10.** devoted attention in order to win favor; homage: *to pay court to a beloved.* **11.** a branch or lodge of a fraternal society. **12.** the group of insects, as honeybees, surrounding the queen; retinue. —*v.t.* **13.** to try to win the favor or goodwill of: *to court the rich.* **14.** to seek the affections of; woo. **15.** (of animals) to attempt to attract (a mate) by engaging in certain species-specific behaviors. **16.** to attempt to gain (applause, favor, etc.). **17.** to hold out inducements to. **18.** to act so as to cause, lead to, or provoke: *to court disaster.* —*v.i.* **19.** to seek another's love; woo. **20.** (of animals) to attempt to attract individuals of the opposite sex for mating. —*Idiom.* **21. hold court,** to act as the center of attention for one's admirers. **22. out of court,** without a legal hearing; privately: *The case will be settled out of court.*

cour·te·ous (kûr′tē əs), *adj.* having or showing good manners; polite. —**cour′te·ous·ly,** *adv.* —**cour′te·ous·ness,** *n.*

cour·te·san (kôr′tə zən, kōr′-, kûr′-), *n.* a kept woman or prostitute associating with noblemen or men of wealth.

cour·te·sy (kûr′tə sē *or, for* **3,** kûrt′sē), *n., pl.* **-sies. 1.** excellence of manners or social conduct; polite behavior. **2.** a courteous, respectful, or considerate act or expression. **3.** indulgence, consent, or acquiescence: *a "colonel" by courtesy rather than by right.* **4.** favor, help, or generosity: *The actors appeared by courtesy of their union.*

cour′tesy card′, *n.* a card making the bearer eligible for special prices or privileges, as at a hotel, club, or bank.

cour′tesy ti′tle, *n.* a title allowed by custom, as to the children of dukes.

court·house (kôrt′hous′, kōrt′-), *n., pl.* **-hous·es** (-hou′ziz). **1.** a building in which courts of law are held. **2.** a county seat.

cour·ti·er (kôr′tē ər, kōrt′-), *n.* **1.** a person who is often in attendance at the court of a royal personage. **2.** a person who flatters.

court·ly (kôrt′lē, kōrt′-), *adj.,* **-li·er, -li·est,** *adv.* —*adj.* **1.** polite, refined, or elegant: *courtly manners.* **2.** flattering; obsequious. **3.** noting, pertaining to, or suitable for the court of a sovereign. —*adv.* **4.** in a courtly manner; politely or flatteringly. —**court′li·ness,** *n.*

court′ly love′, *n.* a highly stylized code of conduct between lovers, often the subject of medieval literature.

court′-mar′tial (kôrt′, kōrt′), *n., pl.* **courts-mar·tial, court-mar·tials,** *v.,* **-tialed, -tial·ing** or (*esp. Brit.*) **-tialled, -tial·ling.** —*n.* **1.** a military court appointed by a commander to try armed forces personnel charged with infractions of military law. **2.** a trial by such a court. —*v.t.* **3.** to arraign and try by court-martial.

court′ of appeals′, *n.* **1.** an appellate court intermediate between the trial courts and a court of last resort. **2.** the highest appellate court of New York State.

court′ of claims′, *n.* a court specializing in claims against the federal government, a state government, its agencies, etc.

court′ of domes′tic rela′tions, *n.* a court that handles family controversies.

court′ of hon′or, *n.* a body, esp. a military one, convened to hear complaints relating to personal honor.

Court′ of Hon′or, *n.* **1.** the planning body of a girl-scout troop, composed of patrol leaders, the troop scribe, the troop treasurer, and the adult troop leader. **2.** a body of officials of a boy-scout organization that awards honor medals and certificates of promotion.

court′ of in′quiry, *n.* a military board created to investigate and report on certain matters, as an accusation against an officer.

court′ of law′, *n.* an arm of the judicial branch of government that hears cases and administers justice, usu. on the basis of legislation or precedent.

court′ report′er, *n.* a stenographer employed to record the proceedings of a court.

court·room (kôrt′rōōm′, -rŏŏm′, kōrt′-), *n.* a room in which the sessions of a law court are held.

court·ship (kôrt′ship, kōrt′-), *n.* **1.** the wooing of one person by another. **2.** the period during which such wooing takes place. **3.** solicitation of favors, applause, etc. **4.** behavior in animals before and during mating, often including elaborate displays.

court·side (kôrt′sīd′, kōrt′-), *n.* the area adjoining the official playing area of a court, as in basketball or tennis.

court′ ten′nis, *n.* tennis played indoors on a court having a net and high cement walls off which the ball may also be played.

Court TV, *Trademark.* a cable television station featuring live coverage of courtroom trials.

court·yard (kôrt′yärd′, kōrt′-), *n.* a court open to the sky, esp. one enclosed on all four sides.

cous·cous (kŏŏs′kŏŏs), *n.* **1.** a North African dish of steamed semolina served usu. with a spicy stew. **2.** the granular semolina used in this dish.

cous·in (kuz′ən), *n.* **1.** the son or daughter of an uncle or aunt. **2.** one related by descent in a diverging line from a known common ancestor. **3.** a kinsman or kinswoman; relative. **4.** a person or thing related to another by similar natures, languages, geographical proximity, etc.

Cous·teau (kōō stō′), *n.* **Jacques Yves** (zhäk ēv), 1910–97, French naval officer, author, and undersea explorer: developed the Aqua-Lung.

couth (kōōth), *Facetious.* —*adj.* **1.** showing or having good manners or sophistication; smooth. —*n.* **2.** good manners; refinement: *to be lacking in couth.*

cou·ture (kōō tŏŏr′; *Fr.* kōō tYR′), *n.* **1.** the occupation or business of a couturier. **2.** fashion designers or couturiers collectively. **3.** the apparel created by such designers. —*adj.* **4.** created by a fashion designer or pertaining to or suggesting such creation: *couture clothes; the couture look.*

cou·tu·ri·er (kōō tŏŏr′ē ər, -ē ā′), *n.* a person who designs, makes, and sells fashionable, custom-made clothes for women.

cou·vade (kōō väd′), *n.* a practice among some peoples in which an expectant father takes to bed in an enactment of the birth and subjects himself to various pregnancy taboos.

co·va·lence (kō vā′ləns), *n.* the number of electron pairs that an atom can share with other atoms. —**co·va′lent,** *adj.*

cova′lent bond′, *n.* the bond formed by the sharing of a pair of electrons by two atoms.

cove (kōv), *n., v.,* **coved, cov·ing.** —*n.* **1.** a small indentation or recess in the shoreline of a sea, lake, or river. **2.** a sheltered nook. **3.** a hollow or recess in a mountain; cavern. **4.** a narrow pass or sheltered area between woods or hills. **5.** a concave architectural surface or molding, esp. one linking a ceiling and a wall. —*v.t., v.i.* **6.** to make or become a cove.

cov·en (kuv′ən, kō′vən), *n.* an assembly of witches.

cov·e·nant (kuv′ə nənt), *n.* **1.** an agreement, usu. formal, between two or more persons to do or not do something specified. **2.** (*cap.*) **a.** NATIONAL COVENANT. **b.** SOLEMN LEAGUE AND COVENANT. **3. a.** the conditional promises made to humanity by God, as revealed in Scripture. **b.** the agreement between God and the ancient Israelites, in which God promised to protect them if they kept His law and were faithful to Him. **4.** a formal agreement of legal validity, esp. one under seal. —*v.i.* **5.** to enter into a covenant. —*v.t.* **6.** to promise by covenant; pledge. **7.** to stipulate. [< Latin *convenīre* to come together, agree]

cov·e·nant·er (kuv′ə nən tər; *for 2 also Scot.* kuv′ə nan′tər), *n.* **1.** a person who makes a covenant. **2.** (*cap.*) *Scot. Hist.* a person who, by solemn agreement, pledged to uphold Presbyterianism, esp. an adherent of the National Covenant or the Solemn League and Covenant.

cov·er (kuv′ər), *v.t.* **1.** to be or serve as a covering for; extend over: *Snow covered the fields.* **2.** to place something over or upon, as for protection, concealment, or warmth. **3.** to provide with a covering: *Cover the pot with a lid.* **4.** to protect or conceal (the body, head, etc.) with clothes, a hat, etc; wrap. **5.** to bring upon (oneself): *He covered himself with honors at school.* **6.** to hide from view; screen. **7.** to spread on or over; put over the surface of: *to cover bread with honey.* **8.** to deal with or provide for; address: *The rules cover working conditions.* **9.** to suffice to defray or meet (a charge, expense, etc.): *Ten dollars should cover my expenses.* **10.** to offset (an outlay, loss, etc.). **11.** to achieve in distance traversed; pass or travel over. **12. a.** to act as a reporter or reviewer of (an event, performance, etc.). **b.** to publish or broadcast news of (an event, disaster, etc.). **13.** to pass or rise over and surmount or envelop: *The flooded river covered the town.* **14.** to insure against risk or loss. **15.** to shelter; protect; serve as a defense for. **16.** to protect (a soldier, position, etc.) during combat by taking a position from which hostile troops can be fired upon. **17.** to take temporary charge of or responsibility for in place of another. **18.** to extend over; comprise: *The book covers 18th-century England.* **19.** to be assigned to or responsible for, as a territory or field of endeavor. **20.** to aim at, as with a pistol. **21.** to play a card higher than (the one led or previously played in the round). **22.** to deposit the equivalent of (money deposited), as in wagering. **23.** to accept the conditions of (a bet, wager, etc.). **24.** (in short selling) to replace (borrowed securities). **25. a.** to defend (a base or an area of a field or court) in a sport. **b.** to guard (an opponent on offense). —*v.i.* **26.** to serve as a substitute for someone who is absent. **27.** to hide the wrongful or embarrassing action of another by providing an alibi or acting in the other's place. **28.** to play a card higher than the one led or previously played in the round. **29. cover up, a.** to cover completely; enfold. **b.** to keep secret; conceal. —*n.* **30.** something that covers, as the lid of a container or the binding of a book. **31.** a blanket, quilt, or the like. **32.** protection; shelter; concealment. **33.** anything that veils, screens, or shuts from sight: *under cover of darkness.* **34.** woods, underbrush, etc., serving to shelter and conceal wild animals or game; a covert. **35.** a set of eating utensils and the like, as plate, knife, fork, and napkin, for one person. **36.** an assumed identity, occupation, or business that masks the real one. **37.** a covering of snow, esp. when suitable for skiing. **38.** a pretense; feigning. **39. a.** an envelope or outer wrapping for mail. **b.** a letter folded so that the address may be placed on the outside and the missive mailed. —*Idiom.* **40. cover all bases,** to anticipate all possible eventualities. **41. take cover,** to seek shelter or safety. **42. under cover, a.** clandestinely; secretly. **b.** within an envelope: *mailed under separate cover.*

cov·er·age (kuv′ər ij, kuv′rij), *n.* **1.** protection against a risk or risks specified in an insurance policy. **2.** the reporting or broadcasting of news: *coverage of the Olympics.* **3.** the extent to which something is covered. **4.** the area or number of persons served or reached by a communications medium.

cov·er·all (kuv′ər ôl′), *n.* Often, **coveralls.** a one-piece work garment worn over other clothing as protection.

cov′er charge′, *n.* an additional charge made by a restaurant or nightclub for providing entertainment, as a floor show.

Cov·er·dale (kuv′ər dāl′), *n.* **Miles,** 1488–1569, English cleric: translator of the Bible into English 1535.

Cov′erdale Bi′ble, *n.* the first printed edition of an English Bible (1535): translated from German and Latin by Miles Coverdale.

cov′ered wag′on, a large wagon with a high, bonnetlike canvas top, esp. such a wagon used by pioneers to cross the North American plains in the 19th century.

cov·er·ing (kuv′ər ing), *n.* something laid over or wrapped around a thing, esp. for concealment, protection, or warmth.

cov′ering let′ter or **cov′er let′ter,** *n.* a letter that accompanies another letter, a package, or the like, to explain, commend, etc.

cov·er·let (kuv′ər lit), *n.* a bed quilt that does not cover the pillow; bedspread. Also, **cov·er·lid** (kuv′ər lid).

cov′er sto′ry, *n.* a magazine article highlighted by an illustration on the cover.

co·vert (adj. kō′vərt, kuv′ərt; n. kuv′ərt, kō′vərt), *adj.* **1.** concealed; secret; disguised. **2.** covered; sheltered. **3.** (of a wife) under the legal protection of a husband. —*n.* **4.** a covering; cover. **5.** a shelter or hiding place. **6.** concealment or disguise. **7.** a thicket giving shelter to wild animals or game. **8.** one of the small feathers that cover the bases of the large feathers of a bird's wings and tail. —**co′vert·ly,** *adv.*

cov·er-up, *n.* **1.** any action, stratagem, or other means of concealing or preventing investigation or exposure. **2.** any of various women's outer garments, as a loose blouse or caftan.

cov·et (kuv′it), *v.t.* **1.** to desire wrongfully, inordinately, or without due regard for the rights of others: *to covet another's property.* **2.** to wish for, esp. eagerly. —*v.i.* **3.** to have an inordinate or wrongful desire. —**cov′et·er,** *n.* —**cov′et·ous,** *adj.*

cov·ey (kuv′ē), *n., pl.* **-eys. 1.** a small group of game birds, esp. partridges or quail. **2.** a group, set, or company.

cow[1] (kou), *n.* **1.** the mature female of a bovine animal. **2.** the female of various other large animals, as the elephant or whale.

cow[2] (kou), *v.t.* to frighten with threats; intimidate; overawe.

cow·ard (kou′ərd), *n.* **1.** a person who shows shameful lack of courage or fortitude. —*adj.* **2.** of, pertaining to, or characteristic of a coward.

—*Proverb.* **3. Cowards die many times before their deaths,** the fear of death is almost as bad as death itself. Shakespeare, *Julius Caesar.*

cow·ard·ice (kou′ər dis), *n.* lack of courage or fortitude.

cow·ard·ly (kou′ərd lē), *adj.* **1.** characteristic of or befitting a coward. —*adv.* **2.** in a cowardly manner. —**cow′ard·li·ness,** *n.*

cow·bane (kou′bān′), *n.* any of several poisonous plants of the parsley family, as *Oxypolis rigidior*, of swampy areas of North America, or the water hemlock, *Cicuta maculata.*

cow·ber·ry (kou′ber′ē, -bə rē), *n., pl.* **-ries.** MOUNTAIN CRANBERRY.

cow·bird (kou′bûrd′), *n.* any of various New World blackbirds of the genera *Molothrus* and *Scaphidura,* noted for their brood parasitism, esp. the common North American species *M. ater.*

cow·boy (kou′boi′), *n.* **1.** a man who herds and tends cattle on a ranch, esp. in the western U.S., and who traditionally goes about most of his work on horseback. **2.** a man who exhibits the skills attributed to such cowboys, esp. in rodeos. **3.** *Chiefly Northeastern U.S.* a reckless or speedy automobile driver. **4.** *Informal.* a reckless or irresponsible person, esp. a show-off or one who undertakes a dangerous or sensitive task heedlessly: *They put foreign policy in the hands of cowboys.* **5.** (during the American Revolution) a member of a pro-British guerrilla band that operated between the American and British lines near New York City. —*v.i.* **6.** to work as a cowboy.

cow·catch·er (kou′kach′ər), *n.* a triangular frame at the front of a locomotive for clearing the track of obstructions.

cow·er (kou′ər), *v.i.* to crouch or shrink back, as in fear or shame. —**cow′er·ing·ly,** *adv.*

cow·fish (kou′fish′), *n., pl.* (*esp. collectively*) **-fish,** (*esp. for kinds or species*) **-fish·es.** any of several trunkfishes having hornlike projections over the eyes, esp. *Lactophrys quadricornus.*

cow·girl (kou′gûrl′), *n.* a woman who works as a cowhand.

cow·hand (kou′hand′), *n.* a person employed on a cattle ranch; cowboy or cowgirl.

cow·herb (kou′ûrb′, -hûrb′), *n.* a plant, *Vaccaria pyramidata,* of the pink family, having clusters of pink flowers.

cow·herd (kou′hûrd′), *n.* a person who tends cows.

cow·hide (kou′hīd′), *n., v.,* **-hid·ed, -hid·ing.** —*n.* **1.** the hide of a cow. **2.** the leather made from it. **3.** a strong, flexible whip made of rawhide or of braided leather. —*v.t.* **4.** to whip with a cowhide.

cowl (koul), *n.* **1.** a hooded garment worn by monks. **2.** the hood itself. **3.** a draped, hoodlike garment. **4.** the forward part of the body of a motor vehicle supporting the rear of the hood and the windshield and housing the pedals and instrument panel. **5.** a hoodlike covering for increasing the draft of a chimney or ventilator. —*v.t.* **6.** to cover with or as if with a cowl.

cowl (def. 1)

cow·lick (kou′lik′), *n.* a tuft of hair that grows in a direction different from that of the rest of the hair.

co·work·er (kō′wûr′kər, kō wûr′-), *n.* a fellow worker.

cow′ pars′nip, *n.* any of several tall, coarse plants of the genus *Heracleum,* of the parsley family, having large, flat heads of tiny white flowers. Also called **hogweed.**

cow·pea (kou′pē′), *n.* **1.** a forage plant, *Vigna unguiculata,* of the legume family, extensively cultivated in the southern U.S. **2.** the seed of this plant, used for food. Also called **black-eyed pea.**

Cow·per (kōō′pər, kou′-), *n.* **William,** 1731–1800, English poet.

Cow′per's gland′ (kou′pərz, kōō′-), *n.* either of two small glands that secrete a mucous substance into the male urethra during sexual excitement.

cow·pox (kou′poks′), *n.* a mild disease of cattle, now rare, characterized by a pustular rash on the teats and udder, caused by a virus that was formerly used for smallpox vaccinations.

cow·rie or **cow·ry** (kou′rē), *n., pl.* **-ries. 1.** any marine gastropod mollusk of the family *Cypraeidae,* having a glossy oval shell with a slit-like toothed opening. **2.** the shell of such a gastropod, sometimes used as currency in Asia and Africa.

cow·slip (kou′slip), *n.* **1.** an English primrose, *Primula veris,* having fragrant yellow flowers. **2.** the marsh marigold.

cox (koks), *n.* **1.** a coxswain. —*v.t.* **2.** to act as coxswain to (a boat).

cox·a (kok′sa), *n., pl.* **cox·ae** (kok′sē). **1.** the joint of the hip. **2.** the first or proximal segment of the leg of insects and other arthropods. —**cox′al,** *adj.*

cox•comb (koks′kōm′), *n.* a conceited, foolish dandy.
cox•sack•ie•vi•rus or **Cox•sack•ie vi•rus** (kok sak′ē vī′rəs, ko͝ok-sä′kē-), *n., pl.* **-rus•es.** any of a group of enteroviruses that may infect the intestinal tract, esp. in the summer months.
cox•swain (kok′sən, -swān′), *n.* **1.** the steersman of a racing shell. **2.** a person in charge of a ship's boat and who usu. steers it.
coy (koi), *adj.* **1.** affectedly shy or reserved; coquettish. **2.** shy; modest. **3.** reluctant to reveal one's plans, make a commitment, or take a stand. —**coy′ly,** *adv.* —**coy′ness,** *n.*
coy•o•te (kī ō′tē, kī′ōt), *n., pl.* **-tes,** (*esp. collectively*) **-te.** **1.** a wolf-like, medium-sized North American canid, *Canis latrans.* **2.** *Slang.* a person who smuggles Latin Americans into the U.S. for a fee. [< Mexican Spanish < Nahuatl *coyōtl*]
coz•en (kuz′ən), *v.t., v.i.* to cheat, deceive, or trick. —**coz′en•er,** *n.*
co•zy (kō′zē), *adj.,* **-zi•er, -zi•est,** *n., pl.* **-zies,** *v.,* **-zied, -zy•ing.** —*adj.* **1.** snugly warm and comfortable. **2.** convenient, beneficial, or opportunistic, esp. as a result of connivance: *a cozy agreement between competing firms.* —*n.* **3.** a padded covering for a teapot, chocolate pot, etc., to retain the heat. —*v.t.* **4.** to make more cozy (often fol. by *up*): *New curtains cozied the room up.* **5. cozy up, a.** to become more cozy: *to cozy up by the fire.* **b.** to try to ingratiate oneself: *to cozy up to the boss.* —**co′zi•ly,** *adv.* —**co′zi•ness,** *n.*
CPA or **C.P.A.,** certified public accountant.
CPR, cardiopulmonary resuscitation.
CPU, central processing unit: the key component of a computer system, containing the circuitry necessary to interpret and execute program instructions. Compare MICROPROCESSOR.
Cr, *Chem. Symbol.* chromium.
crab[1] (krab), *n., v.,* **crabbed, crab•bing.** —*n.* **1.** any decapod crustacean of the suborder Brachyura, having a wide and flattened body, with a small abdomen folded under the thorax. **2.** any of various crablike arthropods, as the horseshoe crab. **3.** a mechanical contrivance for hoisting or pulling heavy weights. **4.** a maneuver in which an aircraft is headed partly into the wind to compensate for drift. —*v.i.* **5.** to fish for crabs. **6.** to move sideways with short bursts of speed; scuttle. **7.** (of an aircraft) to head partly into the wind to compensate for drift. —*v.t.* **8.** to move (an object) sideways or obliquely, esp. with short, abrupt movements. **9.** to head (an aircraft) partly into the wind to compensate for drift. —**crab′ber,** *n.* —**crab′like′,** *adj.*
crab[2] (krab), *n., v.,* **crabbed, crab•bing.** —*n.* **1.** an ill-tempered person. —*v.i.* **2.** to find fault; complain. —*v.t.* **3.** to make ill-tempered. **4.** to find fault with. **5.** to spoil; ruin. —**crab′ber,** *n.*
crab′ ap′ple, *n.* **1.** any of various small, tart varieties of apple, used for making jelly and preserves. **2.** any tree bearing such fruit.
crab•bed (krab′id), *adj.* **1.** difficult to read, as handwriting. **2.** hard to understand; intricate and obscure. **3.** ill-tempered; surly.
crab•by (krab′ē), *adj.,* **-bi•er, -bi•est.** ill-tempered; peevish; grouchy. —**crab′bi•ly,** *adv.* —**crab′bi•ness,** *n.*
crab′ grass′, *n.* a weed grass, *Digitaria sanguinales,* that roots vigorously from the lower stem joints and grows in thick patches on lawns and uncultivated areas.
crab′ louse′, *n.* a crablike louse, *Phthirus pubis,* that infests pubic hair and other body hair in humans.
crab•meat (krab′mēt′), *n.* the edible parts of a crab.
crab•wise (krab′wīz′), *adv.* sideways.
crack (krak), *v.i.* **1.** to break without separation of parts; become fissured. **2.** to break with a sudden, sharp sound. **3.** to make a sudden, sharp sound; snap. **4.** (of the voice) to break abruptly and discordantly. **5.** to break down, esp. under severe psychological pressure. **6.** to decompose by being subjected to heat. —*v.t.* **7.** to cause to make a sudden sharp sound: *to crack a whip.* **8.** to break without separation of parts. **9.** to break into many parts; break open or splinter: *to crack walnuts.* **10.** to strike forcefully: *to crack someone on the jaw.* **11.** to recount or tell: *to crack jokes.* **12.** to cause to make a cracking sound: *to crack one's knuckles.* **13.** to damage or weaken. **14.** to make mentally unsound. **15.** to make (the voice) harsh or unmanageable. **16.** to solve: *to crack a murder case.* **17.** *Informal.* to break into (a safe, vault, etc.). **18.** to subject to the process of cracking, as in the distillation of petroleum. **19.** *Informal.* **a.** to open slightly, as a window or door. **b.** to open (a book) in order to study or read. **20. crack down,** to take severe measures, esp. in enforcing laws or regulations (often fol. by *on*): *to crack down on drug pushers.* **21. crack up,** *Informal.* **a.** to suffer a mental or emotional breakdown. **b.** to crash, as in an automobile or airplane. **c.** to wreck (an automobile, airplane, or other vehicle). **d.** to laugh or to cause to laugh unrestrainedly. —*n.* **22.** a break without separation of parts; fissure. **23.** a slight opening, as between boards in a floor or wall. **24.** a sudden, sharp noise. **25.** the snap of or as of a whip. **26.** a resounding blow. **27.** a witty or cutting remark. **28.** a break in the tone of the voice. **29.** a chance; try: *I'd like a crack at that job.* **30.** highly addictive cocaine in a form prepared for smoking. **31.** a shot, as with a rifle. —*adj.* **32.** first-rate; excellent: *a crack shot.* —*adv.* **33.** with a cracking sound. —***Idiom.*** **34. crack a smile,** *Informal.* to smile, esp. hesitantly. **35. crack the whip,** to goad one's subordinates to work harder. **36. get cracking,** to get moving; hurry up: *We're late—let's get cracking.* —**crack′a•ble,** *adj.* —**crack′less,** *adj.*
crack•down (krak′doun′), *n.* the severe or stern enforcement of laws or regulations.
cracked (krakt), *adj.* **1.** broken. **2.** broken without separation of parts; fissured. **3.** damaged; injured. **4.** *Informal.* eccentric; mad. **5.** broken in tone, as the voice. —***Idiom.*** **6. cracked up to be,** *Informal.* reputed to be (usu. used in the negative): *The play is not what it's cracked up to be.*
crack•er (krak′ər), *n.* **1.** a thin, crisp biscuit. **2.** a firecracker. **3.** Also called **crack′er bon′bon.** a small paper roll used as a party favor, that usu. contains candy, trinkets, etc., and that pops when pulled sharply at one or both ends. **4.** a person or thing that cracks. **5.** a chemical reactor used for cracking. **6.** HACKER (def. 3b). —*adj.* **7. crackers,** *Informal.* wild; crazy: *to go crackers over the new styles.*
crack′er-bar′rel, *adj.* suggesting the rustic informality of life around a country store: *stories full of homespun, cracker-barrel philosophy.*
crack•ing (krak′ing), *n.* **1.** (in the distillation of petroleum) the process of breaking down complex hydrocarbons into simpler compounds with lower boiling points, as gasoline. —*adv.* **2.** extremely; unusually: *a cracking good race.* —*adj.* **3.** done with precision: *a cracking salute.*
crack•le (krak′əl), *v.,* **-led, -ling,** *n.* —*v.i.* **1.** to make slight, sudden, sharp noises, rapidly repeated. **2.** (of ceramic glaze) to craze. **3.** to exhibit liveliness, vibrancy, or the like; sparkle: *The play crackled with wit.* —*v.t.* **4.** to break with a crackling noise. **5.** to craze (ceramic glaze). —*n.* **6.** the act or sound of crackling. **7.** a network of fine cracks, as in some glazes.
crack•ling (krak′ling *or, for 2, 3,* -lən), *n.* **1.** a series of slight cracking sounds. **2.** the crisp browned skin of roast pork. **3.** Usu., **cracklings.** the crisp residue left when fat, esp. pork or poultry fat, is rendered.
crack•pot (krak′pot′), *n.* **1.** a person who is eccentric, fanatical, or irrational. —*adj.* **2.** eccentric; fanatical; irrational.
crack•up (krak′up′), *n.* **1.** a crash; collision. **2.** a breakdown in health, esp. a mental breakdown. **3.** collapse or disintegration.
-cracy, a combining form meaning "rule," "government" by the agent specified by the initial element: *democracy; theocracy.* Compare -CRAT.
cra•dle (krād′l), *n., v.,* **-dled, -dling.** —*n.* **1.** a small bed for an infant, usu. on rockers. **2.** any of various supports for objects set horizontally, as the support for the handset or receiver of a telephone. **3.** the place where something is nurtured in its early years: *Boston is the cradle of the American Revolution.* **4. a.** a toothed frame attached to a scythe for laying grain in bunches as it is cut. **b.** a scythe together with this frame. **5.** a wire or wicker basket used at table to hold a wine bottle in a slightly upturned position. **6.** the part of a gun carriage on which a recoiling gun slides. **7.** a docklike structure in which a rigid or semirigid airship is built or is supported during inflation. **8.** a frame that prevents the bedclothes from touching an injured part of a bedridden patient. **9.** a box on rockers for washing sand or gravel to separate gold or other heavy metal. —*v.t.* **10.** to hold gently or protectively. **11.** to place or rock in or as if in an infant's cradle. **12.** to nurture during infancy. **13.** to cut (grain) with a cradle. —*v.i.* **14.** to lie in or as if in a cradle. **15.** to cut grain with a cradle scythe. —***Idiom.*** **16. from the cradle to the grave,** from birth to death. **17. rob the cradle,** to become romantically involved with a person much younger than oneself. —**cra′dler,** *n.*
cra′dle cap′, *n.* an inflammation of the scalp, occurring in infants and characterized by greasy, yellowish scales.
cra•dling (krād′l ing), *n.* a framework for supporting a dome or vaulted ceiling.
craft (kraft, kräft), *n., pl.* **crafts** or, for 5, 7, **craft,** *v.t.* —*n.* **1.** an art, trade, or occupation requiring special skill, esp. manual skill. **2.** skill; dexterity. **3.** cunning; deceit. **4.** the membership of a guild. **5.** a ship or other vessel. **6.** a number of ships or other vessels taken as a whole. **7.** an aircraft. **8.** aircraft collectively. —*v.t.* **9.** to make or manufacture (an object or objects) with great skill and care.
crafts•man (krafts′mən, kräfts′-), *n., pl.* **-men.** **1.** a person who is skilled in a craft; artisan. **2.** an artist. —**crafts′man•ship′,** *n.*
crafts•wom•an (krafts′wo͝om′ən, kräfts′-), *n., pl.* **-wom•en.** a woman who is skilled in a craft; artisan.
craft•y (kraf′tē, kräf′-), *adj.,* **-i•er, -i•est.** **1.** skillful in underhand or evil schemes; cunning; deceitful; sly. **2.** *Dial.* skillful; dexterous. —**craft′i•ly,** *adv.* —**craft′i•ness,** *n.*
crag (krag), *n.* **1.** a steep, rugged rock. **2.** a rough, broken, projecting part of a rock. —**crag′like′,** *adj.*
crag•gy (krag′ē) also **crag•ged** (krag′id), *adj.,* **-gi•er, -gi•est.** **1.** full of crags. **2.** rugged; rough-hewn. —**crag′gi•ness,** *n.*
crake (krāk), *n.* any of several short-billed rails, as the corn crake.
cram (kram), *v.,* **crammed, cram•ming,** *n.* —*v.t.* **1.** to fill (something) by force with more than it can easily hold. **2.** to force or stuff (usu. fol. by *into, down,* etc.). **3.** to fill with an excessive amount of food; overfeed. **4.** to prepare (a class, etc.) for an examination within a short period of time. —*v.i.* **5.** to eat greedily or to excess. **6.** to study for an examination by memorizing facts at the last minute. **7.** to crowd; jam: *A mob crammed into the hall.* —*n.* **8.** the act of cramming for an examination. **9.** a crammed state; crush.
cramp[1] (kramp), *n.* **1.** Often, **cramps. a.** an involuntary, usu. painful contraction or spasm of a muscle or muscles. **b.** a painful contraction of involuntary muscle in the wall of the abdomen, uterus, or other organ. —*v.t.* **2.** to affect with or as if with a cramp.
cramp[2] (kramp), *n.* **1.** a metal bar with bent ends for holding together building stones or for fastening them to a steel or concrete beam. **2.** a portable frame or tool with a movable part that can be screwed up to hold things together; clamp. **3.** anything that confines or restrains. **4.** a cramped state or part. —*v.t.* **5.** to fasten or hold with a cramp. **6.** to re-

strict or hamper. **7.** to steer (the wheels of a vehicle) in order to make a turn. —*Idiom.* **8. cramp one's style,** to prevent one from showing one's best abilities.

cramped (krampt), *adj.* **1.** confined or severely limited in space: *cramped closets.* **2. a.** (of handwriting) small and crowded. **b.** (of a style of writing) hard to understand; crabbed. —**cramped′ness,** *n.*

cram·pon (kram′pon) also **cram·poon** (kram pōōn′), *n.* **1.** a spiked iron plate worn on boots or shoes for aid in climbing or to prevent slipping on ice, snow, etc. **2.** a grapnel attached to a chain or cable, used esp. for lifting blocks of stone.

cran·ber·ry (kran′ber′ē, -bə rē), *n.,* *pl.* **-ries.** **1.** the sour red berry of certain plants belonging to the genus *Vaccinium,* of the heath family, as *V. macrocarpon* or *V. oxycoccos,* used esp. to make a sauce, relish, or juice. **2.** the plant itself, growing wild in bogs or cultivated in acid soils, esp. in the northeastern U.S.

cran′berry bush′, *n.* HIGHBUSH CRANBERRY.

crane (krān), *n., v.,* **craned, cran·ing.** —*n.* **1.** any of various large wading birds of the family Gruidae, with long legs, bill, and neck. **2.** (not used scientifically) any of various similar birds of other families, as the great blue heron. **3.** a device for lifting and moving heavy weights in suspension. **4.** a similar device used by a fireplace for suspending pots over the fire. **5.** a vehicle having a long boom on which a motion-picture camera can be mounted for taking shots from high angles. —*v.t.* **6.** to stretch (the neck) as a crane does. —*v.i.* **7.** to stretch out one's neck, esp. to see better. **8.** to hesitate at danger, difficulty, etc.

whooping crane, *Grus americana,*
height about 5 ft. (1.5 m);
wingspread 7 ½ ft. (2.3 m)

Crane (krān), *n.* **1.** (Harold) **Hart,** 1899–1932, U.S. poet. **2. Stephen,** 1871–1900, U.S. novelist and short-story writer.

crane′ fly′, *n.* any of numerous nonbiting insects constituting the family Tipulidae, resembling a large mosquito with long legs.

cra·ni·al (krā′nē əl), *adj.* of or pertaining to the cranium or skull.

cra·ni·ol·o·gy (krā′nē ol′ə jē), *n.* a science that deals with the size, shape, and other characteristics of human skulls. —**cra′ni·o·log′i·cal** (-ə loj′i kəl), *adj.* —**cra′ni·o·log′i·cal·ly,** *adv.* —**cra′ni·ol′o·gist,** *n.*

cra·ni·ot·o·my (krā′nē ot′ə mē), *n., pl.* **-mies.** the surgical opening of the skull, usu. for operations on the brain.

cra·ni·um (krā′nē əm), *n., pl.* **-ni·ums, -ni·a** (-nē ə). **1.** the skull of a vertebrate. **2.** Also called **braincase.** the part of the skull that encloses the brain.

crank[1] (krangk), *n.* **1.** any of several types of arms or levers for imparting rotary or oscillatory motion to a rotating shaft. **2.** *Informal.* an ill-tempered person. **3.** an unbalanced person who is overzealous in the advocacy of a private cause. **4.** a whimsical notion; conceit. **5.** a strikingly clever turn of speech or play on words. **6.** methamphetamine prepared for illicit use. **7.** a crankshaft. —*v.t.* **8.** to rotate (a shaft) by means of a crank. **9.** to start (an internal-combustion engine), esp. by turning the crankshaft manually. **10.** to shape like a crank. **11.** to furnish with a crank. —*v.i.* **12.** to turn a crank, as in starting an automobile engine. **13. crank out,** to produce in a mass-production or mechanical way: *to crank out a series of bestsellers.* **14. crank up, a.** to get started: *The new theater season is cranking up with a gala benefit.* **b.** to stimulate or produce: *to crank up enthusiasm for a new product.* —*adj.* **15.** of, pertaining to, or by an unbalanced or overzealous person: *a crank phone call.* **16.** unstable; loose; shaky. —**crank′less,** *adj.*

crank[2] (krangk) also **crank·y,** *adj.* tending to roll easily, as a boat; tender (opposed to *stiff*).

crank·case (krangk′kās′), *n.* (in an internal-combustion engine) the housing enclosing the crankshaft, connecting rods, and allied parts.

crank′pin′ or **crank′ pin′,** *n.* a short cylindrical pin at the outer end of a crank, held by and moving with a connecting rod or link. Compare WEB (def. 11).

crank·shaft (krangk′shaft′, -shäft′), *n.* a shaft having one or more cranks, usu. formed as integral parts.

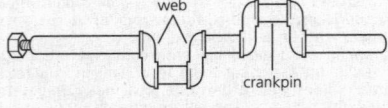

crankshaft

crank·y (krang′kē), *adj.,* **crank·i·er, crank·i·est.** **1.** ill-tempered; grouchy. **2.** eccentric; erratic. **3.** shaky; malfunctioning. **4.** full of bends or windings, as a road. —**crank′i·ly,** *adv.* —**crank′i·ness,** *n.*

Cran·mer (kran′mər), *n.* **Thomas,** 1489–1556, first Protestant archbishop of Canterbury and primary author of the *Book of Common Prayer* (1549).

Cran′mer's Bi′ble, *n.* the Great Bible in the edition of 1540.

cran·nog (kran′əg) also **cran·noge** (-əj), *n.* a small, artificial, fortified island constructed in bogs in ancient Scotland and Ireland.

cran·ny (kran′ē), *n., pl.* **-nies.** **1.** a small, narrow opening in a wall, rock, etc.; crevice. **2.** an out-of-the-way place or corner; nook.

crap[1] (krap), *n.* junk; litter.

crap[2] (krap), *n., v.,* **crapped, crap·ping.** —*n.* **1.** (in craps) a losing first throw of 2, 3, or 12. —*v.* **3. crap out, a.** to throw craps or a 7 rather than one's point. **b.** *Slang.* to abandon an undertaking; give up.

crape′ (or **crepe′**) **myr′tle,** *n.* a tall, ornamental Chinese shrub, *Lagerstroemia indica,* of the loosestrife family, having clusters of crinkled pink, purple, or white flowers.

crap·pie (krap′ē), *n., pl.* **-pies,** (*esp. collectively*) **-pie.** either of two large sunfishes of the central U.S., *Pomoxis nigromaculatus* (**black crappie**) or *P. annularis* (**white crappie**).

crap·py (krap′ē), *adj.,* **-pi·er, -pi·est.** *Slang.* extremely bad; inferior.

craps (kraps), *n.* (*usu. with a sing. v.*) **1.** a game in which two dice are thrown: a first throw of 7 or 11 wins, a first throw of 2, 3, or 12 loses, and a first throw of any other number can be won by throwing it again without throwing a 7. **2.** CRAP[2] (def. 1).

crap·shoot (krap′shōōt′), *Informal.* —*n.* anything unpredictable, risky, or problematical; gamble.

crap·u·lous (krap′yə ləs), *adj.* **1.** characterized by gross excess in drinking or eating. **2.** suffering from such excess. —**crap′u·lous·ly,** *adv.* —**crap′u·lous·ness,** *n.*

crash (krash), *v.i.* **1.** to make a loud, clattering noise, as of something dashed to pieces. **2.** to break or fall to pieces with noise. **3.** (of moving objects) to collide, esp. violently and noisily. **4.** to strike with a crash. **5.** to land an aircraft in such a way that damage is unavoidable. **6.** to collapse or fail suddenly, as a financial enterprise. **7.** *Slang.* **a.** to sleep. **b.** to stay or live temporarily without payment: *I crashed with my brother for a week.* **c.** to fall asleep. **8.** *Slang.* to experience unpleasant sensations, as sudden exhaustion or depression, when a drug, esp. an amphetamine, wears off. **9.** *Med. Slang.* to suffer cardiac arrest. **10.** (of a plant or animal population) to decline rapidly. **11.** (of a computer) to shut down because of a malfunction of hardware or software. —*v.t.* **12.** to break into pieces violently and noisily; shatter. **13.** to cause (a moving vehicle) to collide with or strike another object violently (usu. fol. by *into*): *He crashed his car into a tree.* **14.** to force or drive with violence and noise (usu. fol. by *in, through, out,* etc.): *to crash a truck through a gate.* **15.** to cause (an aircraft) to sustain severe damage in landing. **16.** to enter or force one's way into without invitation, payment, or pass. —*n.* **17.** an act or instance of crashing. **18.** a sudden loud noise, as of something being violently smashed. **19. a.** a collision, as of automobiles or trains. **b.** the emergency landing of an aircraft, space vehicle, etc., usu. causing severe damage. **20.** a sudden general collapse of a business, the stock market, etc. **21.** a sudden, rapid decline in the size of a plant or animal population. —*adj.* **22.** characterized by an intensive effort, esp. to deal with an emergency, meet a deadline, etc.: *a crash plan for flood relief; a crash diet.*

crash′-dive′, *v.i., v.t.,* **-dived** or **-dove, -dived, -div·ing.** to dive rapidly at a steep angle.

crash′ hel′met, *n.* a helmet to protect the head, worn by motorcyclists, automobile racers, etc.

crash′-land′, *v.t.* **1.** to land (an aircraft) in an emergency situation so that damage to the aircraft is unavoidable. —*v.i.* **2.** to crash-land an aircraft. —**crash′-land′ing,** *n.*

crash′ pad′, *n.* **1.** *Slang.* a place to sleep or live temporarily and at no cost. **2.** padding inside cars, airplanes, etc., for protecting passengers in the event of a crash.

crass (kras), *adj.,* **-er, -est.** without refinement or sensitivity; gross. —**crass′ly,** *adv.* —**crass′ness,** *n.*

-crat, a combining form meaning "ruler," "member of a ruling body," "advocate of a particular form of rule": *autocrat; Eurocrat; technocrat.* Compare -CRACY.

crate (krāt), *n., v.,* **crat·ed, crat·ing.** —*n.* **1.** a slatted wooden box for packing, shipping, or storing fruit, furniture, etc. **2.** an enclosed boxlike packing or shipping case. **3.** *Informal.* something rickety and dilapidated, esp. an automobile. **4.** the quantity, esp. of fruit, that is packed in a crate. —*v.t.* **5.** to pack in a crate.

cra·ter (krā′tər), *n.* **1.** the cup-shaped depression or cavity on the surface of the earth or other heavenly body marking the orifice of a volcano. **2.** (on the surface of the earth, moon, etc.) a bowl-shaped depression with a raised rim, formed by the impact of a meteoroid. **3.** the hole in the ground where a bomb, shell, or military mine has exploded. **4.** KRATER. —*v.t.* **5.** to make a crater or craters in. —*v.i.* **6.** to form a crater or craters. [< Latin *krātēr* < Greek *krātēr* mixing bowl] —**cra′ter·like′,** *adj.*

Cra′ter Lake′ Na′tional Park′, *n.* a national park in SW Oregon, in the Cascade Range: Crater Lake. 250 sq. mi. (648 sq. km).

C ration, *n.* canned ration used in the field by U.S. armed forces. Compare K RATION.

cra·ton (krā'ton), *n.* a relatively rigid and immobile region of continental portions of the earth's crust.

cra·vat (krə vat'), *n.* **1.** NECKTIE (def. 1). **2.** a scarf worn about the neck and folded at the front with the ends tucked into the neckline.

crave (krāv), *v.,* **craved, crav·ing.** —*v.t.* **1.** to long for; desire eagerly. **2.** to require; need: *a problem craving your prompt attention.* **3.** to ask earnestly for. —*v.i.* **4.** to beg or plead (usu. fol. by *for*). —**crav'er,** *n.*

cra·ven (krā'vən), *adj.* **1.** cowardly; contemptibly timid. —*n.* **2.** a coward. —**cra'ven·ly,** *adv.* —**cra'ven·ness,** *n.*

crav·ing (krā'ving), *n.* great or eager desire; yearning.

craw (krô), *n.* **1.** the crop of a bird or insect. **2.** the stomach of an animal.

craw·dad (krô'dad') also **craw'dad'dy,** *n., pl.* **-dads** also **-dad·dies.** CRAYFISH (def. 1).

craw·fish (krô'fish'), *n., pl.* (*esp. collectively*) **-fish,** (*esp. for kinds or species*) **-fish·es,** *v.* —*n.* **1.** CRAYFISH. —*v.i.* **2.** *Informal.* to back out of a commitment or retreat from a position.

crawl¹ (krôl), *v.i.* **1.** to move in a prone position with the body close to the ground, as a worm or caterpillar, or on the hands and knees. **2.** to move or progress slowly or laboriously: *a line of cars crawling toward the beach.* **3.** to behave in a remorseful or cringing manner. **4.** to be, or feel as if, overrun with crawling things: *The hut crawled with insects.* **5.** (of paint) to raise or contract because of an imperfect bond with the underlying surface. —*v.t.* **6.** to visit or frequent one after the other: *a night of crawling the pubs.* —*n.* **7.** a slow, crawling motion. **8.** a slow rate of progress. **9.** a swimming stroke in a prone position, characterized by alternate overarm movements combined with the flutter kick. **10.** text that moves slowly across a television or movie screen, giving information. —**crawl'ing·ly,** *adv.*

crawl² (krôl), *n. South Atlantic States.* an enclosure in shallow water on the seacoast, as for confining fish, turtles, etc.

crawl·er (krô'lər), *n.* **1.** a person or thing that crawls. **2.** Also called **crawl'er trac'tor.** a large, heavy vehicle or machine that travels on caterpillar treads, used esp. in construction.

crawl'space' or **crawl' space',** *n.* (in a building) an area accessible by crawling, having a clearance less than human height, for access to plumbing or wiring, storage, etc.

crawl·y (krô'lē), *adj.,* **crawl·i·er, crawl·i·est,** *n., pl.* **crawl·ies.** —*adj.* **1.** characterized by crawling, as worms or insects, and imparting a queasy feeling. —*n.* **2.** a crawling insect, small reptile, etc.

cray·fish (krā'fish') also **crawfish,** *n., pl.* (*esp. collectively*) **-fish,** (*esp. for kinds or species*) **-fish·es.** **1.** Also called **crawdad, crawdaddy.** any of various mainly freshwater decapod crustaceans, esp. of the genera *Astacus* and *Cambarus,* resembling small lobsters. **2.** (not in technical use) the spiny lobster.

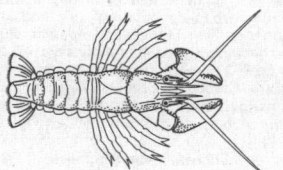

crayfish, (def. 1)
Cambarus diogenes,
length 3 ½ in. (8.9 cm)

Cray·o·la (krā ō'lə), *Trademark.* a brand of colored wax crayon.

cray·on (krā'on, -ən), *n.* **1.** a pointed stick or pencil, as of colored chalk or wax. **2.** a drawing in crayons. —*v.t.* **3.** to draw or color with a crayon or crayons.

craze (krāz), *v.,* **crazed, craz·ing,** *n.* —*v.t.* **1.** to make insane; derange. **2.** to make small cracks on the surface of (a ceramic glaze, paint, etc.); crackle. —*v.i.* **3.** to become insane. **4.** to become minutely cracked, as a ceramic glaze; crackle. **5.** *Metall.* (of a casehardened object) to develop reticulated surface markings. —*n.* **6.** a popular fad; mania. **7.** a minute crack or pattern of cracks in the glaze of a ceramic object.

cra·zy (krā'zē), *adj.,* **-zi·er, -zi·est,** *n., pl.* **-zies.** —*adj.* **1.** mentally deranged; insane. **2.** impractical; totally unsound: *a crazy scheme.* **3.** intensely enthusiastic. **4.** infatuated (usu. fol. by *about*). **5.** unusual; bizarre. —*n.* **6.** *Slang.* an unpredictable person; oddball: *one nice sister and two crazies.* —**Idiom.** **7.** crazy like a fox, ostensibly insane but in reality shrewd. **8.** like crazy, *Slang.* with great enthusiasm or energy: *We worked like crazy all morning.* —**cra'zi·ly,** *adv.* —**cra'zi·ness,** *n.*

Cra'zy Horse', *n.* (*Tashunca-Uitco*), c1849–77, Lakota Indian leader: defeated General George Custer.

cra'zy quilt', *n.* **1.** a patchwork quilt made of irregular patches combined with little or no regard to pattern. **2.** a conglomeration or hodgepodge; mishmash. —**cra'zy-quilt',** *adj.*

creak (krēk), *v.i.* **1.** to make a sharp, grating, or squeaking sound. **2.** to move slowly with or as if with such a sound. —*v.t.* **3.** to cause to creak. —*n.* **4.** a creaking sound. —**creak'ing·ly,** *adv.*

creak·y (krē'kē), *adj.,* **i·er, i·est.** **1.** creaking or apt to creak. **2.** rundown; dilapidated. —**creak'i·ly,** *adv.* —**creak'i·ness,** *n.*

cream (krēm), *n.* **1.** the fatty part of milk that rises to the surface when the liquid is allowed to stand and is not homogenized. **2.** a soft, solid or thick liquid containing medicaments or other specific ingredients, ap-

plied externally for a prophylactic, therapeutic, or cosmetic purpose. **3.** a purée containing cream or milk: *cream of tomato soup.* **4.** any of various foods made with cream or milk or having the consistency of cream: *pastry cream.* **5.** a soft-centered confection coated with chocolate. **6.** the best part of anything: *the cream of society.* **7.** a yellowish white. —*v.i.* **8.** to form cream. **9.** to froth; foam. —*v.t.* **10.** to work (butter and sugar, etc.) to a smooth mass. **11.** to prepare with cream, milk, or a cream sauce. **12.** to allow (milk) to form cream. **13.** to remove the cream from (milk); skim. **14.** to take the best part of. **15.** to use a cosmetic cream on. **16.** to add cream to (tea, coffee, etc.). **17.** *Slang.* **a.** to beat up; thrash. **b.** to win decisively over. —*adj.* **18.** of the color cream; cream-colored. —**Idiom.** **19.** cream of the crop, the best or choicest. —*Saying.* **20.** Cream rises to the top, the most accomplished will achieve success. —**cream·y,** *adj.,* **-i·er, -i·est.**

cream' cheese', *n.* a soft, white, spreadable unripened cheese made of sweet milk and sometimes cream.

cream·cups (krēm'kups'), *n., pl.* **-cups.** (*used with a sing. or pl. v.*) a Californian plant, *Platystemon californicus,* of the poppy family, having small, pale yellow or cream-colored flowers.

cream·er (krē'mər), *n.* **1.** a person or thing that creams. **2.** a small jug or pitcher for serving cream. **3.** an apparatus for separating cream from milk. **4.** a refrigerator in which milk is placed to facilitate the formation of cream. **5.** a nondairy product made chiefly from corn syrup solids, used esp. in coffee as a substitute for cream or milk.

cream·er·y (krē'mə rē), *n., pl.* **-er·ies.** **1.** a place where milk and cream are processed or where butter and cheese are produced. **2.** a place for the sale of milk and milk products.

cream' of tar'tar, *n.* a white, crystalline, water-soluble powder, $C_4H_5KO_6$, used chiefly as an ingredient in baking powders and in galvanic tinning of metals.

cream' puff', *n.* **1.** a light, hollow pastry filled with custard or whipped cream. **2.** a weak or timid person. **3.** a vehicle or machine that has been kept in unusually good condition.

cream' sauce', *n.* a white sauce made with butter, flour, and cream or milk.

cream' so'da, *n.* a carbonated soft drink flavored with vanilla.

crease (krēs), *n., v.,* **creased, creas·ing.** —*n.* **1.** a ridge or furrow produced in or on anything by folding, striking, etc. a wrinkle. **3.** a sharp, vertical edge pressed into the front and back of trousers, as with a steam iron. **4.** (in ice hockey) the marked rectangular or semicircular area in front of a goal cage. —*v.t.* **5.** to make a crease or creases in; wrinkle. **6.** to wound or stun by a superficial shot. —*v.i.* **7.** to become creased. —**crease'less,** *adj.*

cre·ate (krē āt'), *v.,* **-at·ed, -at·ing.** —*v.t.* **1.** to cause to come into being, as something unique. **2.** to evolve from one's imagination, as a work of art or an invention. **3.** to perform (a role) in the first production of a play or motion picture. **4.** to make by investing with new rank; designate: *to create a duke.* **5.** to arrange or bring about, as by intention or design: *to create confusion.* —*v.i.* **6.** to do something creative.

cre·a·tine (krē'ə tēn', -tin), *n.* an amino acid, $C_4H_9N_3O_2$, that is a constituent of the muscles of vertebrates.

cre·a·tion (krē ā'shən), *n.* **1.** the act of creating or engendering. **2.** the fact of being created. **3.** something that is created. **4. the Creation,** the original bringing into existence of the universe by God. **5.** the world; universe. **6.** creatures collectively.

cre·a·tion·ism (krē ā'shə niz'əm), *n.* **1.** the doctrine that matter and all things were created, substantially as they now exist, by an omnipotent Creator, and not gradually evolved or developed. **2.** (*sometimes cap.*) the doctrine that the true story of the creation of the universe is as it is recounted in the Bible, esp. in the first chapter of Genesis. **3.** the doctrine that God immediately creates out of nothing a new human soul for each individual born. Compare TRADUCIANISM. —**cre·a'tion·ist,** *n., adj.*

crea'tion sci'ence, *n.* the scientific study of the creation of the universe as recounted in the Bible.

cre·a·tive (krē ā'tiv), *adj.* **1.** having the quality or power of creating. **2.** resulting from originality of thought; imaginative. **3.** *Facetious.* producing deceptive or fraudulent information, etc.: *creative bookkeeping.* —**cre·a'tive·ly,** *adv.* —**cre·a·tiv'i·ty,** *n.*

cre·a·tor (krē ā'tər), *n.* **1.** a person or thing that creates. **2. the Creator,** God.

crea·ture (krē'chər), *n.* **1.** an animal, esp. a nonhuman. **2.** any unspecific being: *creatures of the imagination.* **3.** person; human being: *a lovely creature.* **4.** a person under the control or influence of another.

crea'ture com'forts, *n.pl.* things that contribute to bodily comfort and ease of mind, as food, warmth, or sleeping facilities.

crèche (kresh, krāsh), *n.* **1.** a representation or tableau of Mary, Joseph, and others around the crib of Jesus in the stable at Bethlehem. **2.** a home for foundlings. **3.** *Ethology.* an assemblage of dependent young animals that are cared for communally.

cre·dence (krēd'ns), *n.* **1.** belief as to the truth of something: *to give credence to a claim.* **2.** something that establishes a claim to belief or confidence: *letter of credence.* **3.** Also called **cre'dence ta'ble, cre·denza.** a small side table for holding articles used in the Eucharist service. **4.** CREDENZA (def. 1).

cre·den·tial (kri den'shəl), *n., v.,* **-tialed, -tial·ing,** *adj.* —*n.* Usu. **credentials.** **1.** evidence of entitlement to rights, privileges, or the like, usu. in written form: *No one admitted without credentials.* **2.** anything that provides the basis for confidence, belief, etc., or for extending credit. —*v.t.* **3.** to grant credentials to. —*adj.* **4.** entitled to or granting privileges, credit, etc.

cre•den•za (kri den′zə), *n., pl.* **-zas. 1.** Also, **credence.** a sideboard or buffet, esp. one without legs. **2.** a low, closed cabinet for papers, supplies, etc., in an office. **3.** CREDENCE (def. 3).

credibil′ity gap′, *n.* **1.** a lack of popular confidence in the truth of the claims or public statements made by the federal government, large corporations, politicians, etc.: *a credibility gap between the public and the power company.* **2.** a perceived discrepancy between statements and actual performance or behavior.

cred•i•ble (kred′ə bəl), *adj.* **1.** capable of being believed; trustworthy. **2.** effective or reliable: *credible new defense weapons.* —**cred′i•bil′i•ty,** *n.* —**cred′i•bly,** *adv.*

cred•it (kred′it), *n.* **1.** commendation given for some action, quality, etc. **2.** a source of pride or honor. **3. a.** the acknowledgment of something as due a person, institution, etc. **b. credits,** the names of all who contributed to a motion picture or a television program, usu. listed at the end. **4.** trustworthiness; credibility. **5. a.** permission for a customer to have goods or services that will be paid for at a later date. **b.** the reputation of a person or firm for paying bills or other financial obligations when due: *to ruin one's credit.* **6.** influence or authority resulting from a good reputation. **7.** a sum of money due to a person: *Your account shows a credit of $50.* **8. a.** official acceptance and recording of the work completed by a student in a particular course of study. **b.** CREDIT HOUR. **9. a.** an entry of payment or value received on an account. **b.** the right-hand side of an account on which such entries are made (opposed to *debit*). **c.** an entry, or the total shown, on the credit side. **10.** any deposit or sum of money against which a person may draw. —*v.t.* **11.** to believe or trust. **12.** to bring honor, esteem, etc., to; reflect well upon. **13.** to enter on the credit side of an account; give credit for or to. **14.** to award educational credits to. **15. credit to** or **with,** to ascribe: *a success credited to hard work; herbs credited with healing powers.* —*Idiom.* **16. do someone credit,** to be a source of honor or distinction for someone. Also, **do credit to someone. 17. on credit,** by deferred payment: *to buy a sofa on credit.* **18. to one's credit,** deserving of praise; admirable. —*Proverb.* **19. Give credit where credit is due,** acknowledge merit where it is found. Rom. 13:7.

cred•it•a•ble (kred′i tə bəl), *adj.* bringing or deserving credit, honor, or esteem. —**cred′it•a•bil′i•ty,** *n.* —**cred′it•a•bly,** *adv.*

cred′it card′, *n.* a card that entitles a person to make purchases on credit.

cred′it hour′, *n.* one unit of academic credit, usu. representing attendance at one scheduled period of instruction per week throughout a semester, quarter, or term.

cred′it line′, *n.* **1.** a line of text acknowledging the source or origin of published or exhibited material. **2.** the maximum amount of credit that a customer is authorized to use.

cred•i•tor (kred′i tər), *n.* a person or firm to whom money is due.

Cred′itor Who Had′ Two′ Debt′ors, The, a parable of Jesus. Luke 7:40–50.

cred′it rat′ing, *n.* an indication of the risk involved in granting credit to a person or firm: *an unblemished credit rating.*

cred′it un′ion, *n.* a cooperative group that makes loans to its members at low rates of interest.

cre•do (krē′dō, krā′-), *n., pl.* **-dos.** any creed or formula of belief.

cre•du•li•ty (krə dōo′li tē, -dyōo′-), *n.* willingness to believe or trust too readily; gullibility.

cred•u•lous (krej′ə ləs), *adj.* **1.** willing to believe or trust too readily; gullible. **2.** marked by or arising from credulity: *a credulous rumor.* —**cred′u•lous•ly,** *adv.* —**cred′u•lous•ness,** *n.*

creed (krēd), *n.* **1.** an authoritative formulated statement of the chief articles of Christian belief. **2.** an accepted system of religious or other belief. [< Latin *crēdō* I believe]

creek (krēk, krik), *n.* **1.** a stream smaller than a river. **2.** a stream or channel in a coastal marsh. **3.** a recess or inlet in the shore of the sea. **4.** an estuary. —*Idiom.* **5. up the creek,** *Slang.* in a difficult or seemingly hopeless situation.

Creek (krēk), *n., pl.* **Creeks,** (*esp. collectively*) **Creek. 1.** a member of a loose confederacy of American Indian peoples that in the 18th century occupied the greater part of Georgia and Alabama: forcibly removed to the Indian Territory in 1834–37. **2.** MUSKOGEE (def. 1a). **3.** the Muskogean language spoken by the Muskogee.

Creek′ War′, *n.* an uprising in 1813–14 of the Creek Indians against settlers in Alabama: frontier militia from Tennessee, Georgia, and Mississippi under Andrew Jackson helped defeat the Creek, who ceded two-thirds of their land to the U.S.

creel (krēl), *n.* **1.** a wickerwork basket, used esp. for carrying fish. **2.** a wicker trap for fish, lobsters, etc. **3.** a rack for holding bobbins in a machine. —*v.t.* **4.** to place or keep (caught fish) in a creel.

creep (krēp), *v.,* **crept** or, sometimes, **creeped; creep•ing,** *n.* —*v.i.* **1.** to move slowly with the body close to the ground, on hands and knees, or the like. **2.** to approach slowly and stealthily (often fol. by *up*). **3.** to advance slowly and often with difficulty: *The car crept up the hill.* **4.** to sneak up behind someone (usu. fol. by *up on*): *The prisoner crept up on the guard.* **5.** to become evident gradually (often fol. by *in* or *into*): *The writer's bias creeps into the story.* **6.** to grow along the ground, a wall, etc., as a plant. **7.** to slide or shift gradually. **8.** (of a metal object) to

become deformed, as under continuous loads or at high temperatures. —*n.* **9.** an act or instance of creeping. **10.** *Slang.* an obnoxious person. **11. a.** the gradual movement downhill of loose soil, rock, gravel, etc. **b.** the slow deformation of solid rock resulting from constant stress applied over long periods. **12.** *Mech.* the gradual, permanent deformation of a body produced by a continued application of heat or stress. **13. the creeps,** a sensation of fear, disgust, or the like, as of something crawling over the skin: *That movie gave me the creeps.* —*Idiom.* **14. make one's flesh creep,** to cause one to be frightened or repelled. —**creep′ing•ly,** *adv.*

creep•er (krē′pər), *n.* **1.** a person or thing that creeps. **2.** a plant that grows upon or just beneath the surface of the ground, sending out rootlets from the stem, as ivy. **3.** a spiked iron plate worn on the shoe to prevent slipping on ice, rock, etc. **4.** any of various songbirds that ascend the trunks and larger limbs of trees, esp. of the family Certhiidae. **5.** a grappling device for dragging a body of water.

creep′ing so′cialism, *n.* the gradually increasing growth of government power at the expense of private enterprise.

creep•y (krē′pē), *adj.,* **creep•i•er, creep•i•est. 1.** causing a creeping sensation of the skin, as from horror or fear: *a creepy story.* **2.** characterized by creeping: *a creepy insect.* **3.** *Slang.* (of a person) obnoxious; weird. —**creep′i•ly,** *adv.* —**creep′i•ness,** *n.*

creep′y-crawl′y, *n., pl.* **-crawl•ies,** *adj.,* **-crawl•i•er, -crawl•i•est.** *Informal.* —*n.* **1.** a creeping insect. —*adj.* **2.** CREEPY (def. 1).

cre•mate (krē′māt), *v.t.,* **-mat•ed, -mat•ing.** to reduce (a dead body) to ashes by fire, esp. as a funeral rite. —**cre•ma•tion** (kri mā′shən), *n.*

cre•ma•to•ry (krē′mə tôr′ē, -tōr′ē, krem′ə-), *n., pl.* **-ries,** *adj.* —*n.* **1.** a funeral establishment or the like where cremation is done. **2.** a furnace for cremating. —*adj.* **3.** of or pertaining to cremation.

crème or **creme** (krem, krēm), *n., pl.* **crèmes** (kremz, krēmz, krem). **1.** cream. **2.** a usu. thick, sweet liqueur.

crème ca•ra•mel (krem′ kar′ə mel′, krēm′; *Fr.* KREM KA RA mel′), *n.* a baked sweetened custard with a caramel sauce.

crème de ca•ca•o (krem′ də kō′kō, kä kä′ō, krēm′), *n.* a liqueur flavored with cacao and vanilla beans.

crème de la crème (krem′ də lä krem′), *n.* the choicest elements of something.

crème de menthe (krem′ də menth′, mint′, mänt′), *n.* a white or green liqueur flavored with mint.

crème fraîche (krem′ fresh′, krēm′), *n.* cream that has been thickened by a slight natural fermentation.

cre•nate (krē′nāt) also **cre′nat•ed,** *adj.* having the margin notched or scalloped so as to form rounded teeth, as a leaf.

Cren′shaw mel′on (kren′shô), *n.* a variety of melon resembling the casaba, having pinkish flesh.

Cre•ole (krē′ōl), *n.* **1.** (now usu. in historical contexts) a member of the French-speaking, generally urban population of Louisiana that claims descent from the region's earliest French and Spanish settlers. **2.** (*usu. l.c.*) a pidgin that has become the native language of a speech community. Compare PIDGIN (def. 1). —*adj.* **3.** (*sometimes l.c.*) of, pertaining to, or characteristic of a Creole or Creoles. **4.** (*usu. l.c.*) made with tomatoes, peppers, onions, and spices and, often, served with rice.

cre•o•sol (krē′ə sôl′, -sol′), *n.* a colorless oily liquid, $C_8H_{10}O_2$, used as a disinfectant and in making resins.

cre•o•sote (krē′ə sōt′), *n., v.,* **-sot•ed, -sot•ing.** —*n.* **1.** a strong-smelling, oily liquid obtained by the distillation of coal and wood tar, used as a wood preservative and as an antiseptic. —*v.t.* **2.** to treat with creosote. —**cre′o•sot′ic** (-sot′ik), *adj.*

cre′osote bush′, *n.* a shrub, *Larrea tridentata,* of the caltrop family, native to arid regions of the southwestern U.S. and Mexico, having yellow flowers and resinous foliage.

crepe (krāp; *for 3 also* krep), *n., pl.* **crepes** (krāps; *for 3 also* kreps *or* krep), *v.,* **creped, crep•ing.** —*n.* **1.** a lightweight fabric of silk, cotton, or other fiber, with a finely crinkled or pebbled surface. **2.** a usu. black band or piece of this material, worn as a token of mourning. **3.** a thin, light, delicate pancake. —*v.t.* **4.** to cover, drape, or clothe with crepe. Also, **crape** (for defs. 1, 2); **crêpe** (for defs. 1–3).

crepe de Chine (krāp′ də shēn′), *n.* a light, soft, silk or synthetic crepe used for dresses.

crepe′ pa′per (krāp), *n.* thin paper densely wrinkled to resemble crepe, used for decorating, wrapping, etc. Also called **crepe.** —**crepe′-pa′per,** *adj.*

crepe′ rub′ber (krāp), *n.* a crude rubber pressed into crinkled sheets and used esp. for shoe soles. Also called **crepe.**

crêpe (or **crepe**) **su•zette** (krāp′ sōo zet′, krep′), *n., pl.* **crêpe** (or **crepe**) **su•zettes, crêpes** (or **crepes**) **su•zette.** a thin dessert pancake heated in a sauce of butter and orange-flavored liqueur and served flambé.

crep•i•tate (krep′i tāt′), *v.i.,* **-tat•ed, -tat•ing.** to make a crackling sound; crackle. —**crep′i•tant,** *adj.* —**crep′i•ta′tion,** *n.*

crept (krept), *v.* pt. and pp. of CREEP.

cre•pus•cule (kri pus′kyōol, krep′ə skyōol′) also **cre•pus•cle** (kri-pus′əl), *n.* twilight; dusk.

cre•scen•do (kri shen′dō, -sen′dō), *n., pl.* **-dos, -di** (-dē), *adj., adv., v.,* **-doed, do•ing.** —*n.* **1.** a gradual increase in loudness. **2.** a musical passage characterized by such an increase. **3.** the climactic point in such an increase; peak. —*adj.*

adv. **4.** gradually increasing in force, volume, or loudness (opposed to *decrescendo* or *diminuendo*). **—v.i. 5.** to grow in force or loudness.

cres·cent (kres′ənt), *n.* **1.** a shape resembling a segment of a ring tapering to points at the ends. **2.** something, as a roll or cookie, having this shape. **3.** the figure of the moon in its first or last quarter, resembling such a shape. **4.** the emblem of Turkey or of Islam. **—adj. 5.** shaped like a crescent. **6.** increasing; growing. **—cres·cen·tic** (kri sen′-tik), *adj.*

cress (kres), *n.* a plant of the mustard family, esp. the watercress, having pungent-tasting leaves often used for salad and as a garnish. **—cress′y,** *adj.*

cres·set (kres′it), *n.* a metal cup or basket mounted on a pole or hung from above, containing oil or other illuminant, and burned as a light or beacon.

crest (krest), *n.* **1.** the highest part of a hill or mountain range; summit. **2.** the highest point or level: *riding the crest of popularity.* **3.** a ridge or ridgelike formation. **4.** the foamy top of a wave. **5.** the point of highest flood, as of a river. **6.** a tuft or other natural growth on the top of the head of an animal, as the comb of a rooster. **7.** the ridge of the neck of a horse, dog, etc. **8.** the mane growing from this ridge. **9.** an ornament or emblem on a knight's helmet. **10. a.** a heraldic device above the escutcheon on a coat of arms. **b.** COAT OF ARMS (def. 2). **11.** *Anat.* a ridge, esp. on a bone. **12.** a ridge or other prominence on any part of the body of an animal. **13.** CRESTING (def. 1). **—v.i. 14.** to form a crest, as a wave or river. **—v.t. 15.** to top with a crest. **16.** to reach the crest of (a hill, mountain, etc.). **—crest′ed,** *adj.* **—crest′less,** *adj.*

crest′ed wheat′grass, (hwēt′gras′, -gräs′, wēt′-), *n.* a forage grass, *Agropyron cristatum,* native to Eurasia.

crest·fall·en (krest′fô′lən), *adj.* **1.** dejected; discouraged. **2.** having a drooping crest or head. **—crest′fall′en·ly,** *adv.*

crest·ing (kres′ting), *n.* **1.** a decorative coping, balustrade, etc., usu. designed to give an interesting skyline to a building. **2.** ornamentation, usu. carved, on the top rail of a piece of furniture, as a chair.

cre·ta·ceous (kri tā′shəs), *adj.* **1.** resembling or containing chalk. **2.** (*cap.*) noting or pertaining to a period of the Mesozoic Era, from 140 million to 65 million years ago, characterized by the greatest development and subsequent extinction of dinosaurs and the advent of flowering plants and modern insects.

Crete (krēt), *n.* a Greek island in the Mediterranean, SE of mainland Greece. 502,165; 3235 sq. mi. (8380 sq. km). *Cap.:* Canea. Also called **Candia. —Cre′tan,** *adj., n.*

cre·tin (krēt′n; *esp. Brit.* kret′n), *n.* a stupid, obtuse, or boorish person. **—cre′tin·ous,** *adj.*

Creutz′feldt-Ja′kob disease′ (kroits′felt yä′kôp), *n.* a fatal degenerative disease of the human brain, thought to be caused by an abnormal, infectious form of cellular prion protein. [after German physicians Hans G. *Creutzfeldt* (1885–1964) and Alfons *Jakob* (1884–1931)]

cre·val·le (krə val′ē, -val′ə), *n., pl.* (*esp. collectively*) **-le,** (*esp. for kinds or species*) **-les.** a marine fish of the jack family, Carangidae.

cre·vasse (krə vas′), *n.* a fissure, or deep cleft, in glacial ice, the earth's surface, etc.

crev·ice (krev′is), *n.* a crack forming an opening; cleft; rift; fissure. **—crev′iced,** *adj.*

crew (krōō), *n.* **1.** a group of persons working together, esp. in a particular kind of work: *a demolition crew.* **2. a.** the people who operate a ship, aircraft, or spacecraft. **b.** the common sailors of a ship's company. **3.** the team that rows a racing shell. **4.** the sport of racing with racing shells. **5.** a company, crowd, or band. **—v.t. 6.** to serve as a member of a crew on. **—v.i. 7.** to serve as a member of a crew. **—crew′less,** *adj.* **—Usage.** See COLLECTIVE NOUN.

crew′ cut′, *n.* a haircut in which all the hair is very closely cropped. **—crew′-cut′, crew′-cut′,** *adj.*

crew·el (krōō′əl), *n.* Also called **crew′el yarn′.** a worsted yarn for embroidery and edging.

crew·man (krōō′mən), *n., pl.* **-men.** a member of a crew. **—crew′-man·ship′,** *n.*

crew′ neck′, *n.* **1.** a collarless, rib-knit neckline that fits snugly around the base of the neck. **2.** a garment with this neckline. **—crew′-neck′, crew′-necked′,** *adj.*

crew′ sock′, *n.* a short, thick, ribbed sock.

crib (krib), *n., v.,* **cribbed, crib·bing.** **—n. 1.** a child's bed with enclosed sides. **2.** a stall or pen for cattle. **3.** a rack or manger for fodder. **4.** a bin for storing grain, salt, etc. **5.** *Informal.* **a.** a translation, list of correct answers, or other illicit aid used by students while reciting, taking exams, or the like; pony. **b.** plagiarism. **c.** a petty theft. **6.** any of various cellular frameworks assembled in layers at right angles, used in construction of foundations, dams, etc. **7.** a barrier projecting part of the way into a river and then upward, acting to reduce the flow of water and as a storage place for logs being floated downstream. **8.** a lining for a well or other shaft. **9.** a set of cards in cribbage made up by equal contributions from each player's hand, and belonging to the dealer. **—v.t. 10.** to pilfer or steal, esp. to plagiarize. **11.** to confine in or as if in a crib. **12.** to provide with a crib or cribs. **13.** to line with timber or planking. **—v.i. 14.** *Informal.* **a.** to use a crib in, as in examinations. **b.** to steal; plagiarize. **15.** (of a horse) to practice cribbing. **—crib′ber,** *n.*

crib·bage (krib′ij), *n.* a card game, basically for two teams, in which

points for certain combinations of cards are scored on a small pegboard (**crib′bage board′**).

cri·ce·tid (krī sē′tid, -set′id, krī-), *n.* any rodent of the family Cricetidae, including gerbils, hamsters, New World rats and mice, lemmings, and voles.

crick (krik), *n.* **1.** a sharp, painful spasm of the muscles, as of the neck or back. **—v.t. 2.** to give a wrench to (the neck, back, etc.).

crick·et¹ (krik′it), *n.* **1.** any of several jumping orthopterous insects of the family Gryllidae, characterized by long antennae and stridulating organs on the forewings of the male. **2.** a small, hand-held metal toy that makes a clicking noise when pressed.

crick·et² (krik′it), *n.* **1.** a game, popular esp. in England, for two teams of 11 members each that is played on a field having two wickets 22 yards (20 m) apart, the object being to score runs by batting the ball far enough so that one is enabled to exchange wickets with the batsman defending the opposite wicket before the ball is recovered. **2.** fair play: *It's not cricket to ask such questions.* **—v.i. 3.** to play cricket.

cried (krīd), *v.* pt. and pp. of CRY.

cri·er (krī′ər), *n.* **1.** a person who cries. **2.** a court or town official who makes public announcements. **3.** a hawker.

crime (krīm), *n.* **1.** an action that is deemed injurious to the public welfare and is legally prohibited. **2.** criminal activity and those engaged in it: *to fight crime.* **3.** any serious wrongdoing. **4.** a foolish act or practice: *It's a crime to let that beautiful garden go to ruin.*

Cri·me·a (krī mē′ə, krī-), *n.* **the,** a peninsula in SE Ukraine, between the Black Sea and the Sea of Azov. Russian, **Krim, Krym. —Cri·me′an,** *adj.*

crime′ against′ human′ity, *n.* a crime, as genocide, directed against a people or group solely because of their race, religion, national origin, political beliefs, sexual orientation, etc.

Crime′ and Pun′ishment, a novel (1866) by Fyodor Dostoevsky.

Cri′me·an War′, *n.* a war involving Great Britain, France, Turkey, and Sardinia against Russia, fought chiefly in the Crimea 1853–56.

crim·i·nal (krim′ə nl), *adj.* **1.** of the nature of or involving crime. **2.** guilty of crime. **3.** dealing with crime or its punishment: *a criminal proceeding.* **4.** senseless; foolish: *a criminal waste of food.* **5.** exorbitant; outrageous: *criminal prices.* **—n. 6.** a person convicted of a crime. **—crim′i·nal·ly,** *adv.*

crim′inal code′, *n.* the body of laws, statutes, and the like, relating to criminal offenses.

crim′inal court′, *n.* a court of law in which criminal cases are tried and determined.

crim·i·nal·is·tics (krim′ə nl is′tiks), *n.* (*used with a sing. v.*) the scientific evaluation of physical evidence in criminal cases.

crim·i·nal·i·ty (krim′ə nal′i tē), *n., pl.* **-ties. 1.** the state of being criminal. **2.** a criminal act or practice.

crim′inal law′, *n.* the body of laws dealing with criminal offenses and their punishment. **—crim′inal law′yer,** *n.*

crim·i·nol·o·gy (krim′ə nol′ə jē), *n.* the sociological study of crime and criminals. **—crim′i·no·log′i·cal** (-nl oj′i kəl), *adj.* **—crim′i·nol′o·gist,** *n.*

crimp (krimp), *v.t.* **1.** to press into small regular folds; make wavy. **2.** to curl (hair), esp. with a curling iron. **3.** to seal by pressing together. **4.** to restrain or hinder. **5.** to corrugate (sheet metal, cardboard, etc.). **6.** to bend (leather) into shape. **7.** to fold the edges of (sheet metal) to make a lock seam. **—n. 8.** the act of crimping. **9.** a crimped condition or form. **10.** Usu. **crimps.** waves or curls, esp. in hair that has been crimped. **11.** the waviness of a fiber, either natural, as in the wool on a sheep, or produced by weaving, plaiting, or other processes. **12.** a crease formed in sheet metal or plate metal to make the material less flexible or for fastening purposes. **—Idiom. 13. put a crimp in,** to interfere with; impede.

crim·son (krim′zən, -sən), *adj.* **1.** deep purplish red. **—n. 2.** a crimson color, pigment, or dye. **—v.t., v.i. 3.** to make or become crimson.

cringe (krinj), *v.,* **cringed, cring·ing,** *n.* **—v.i. 1.** to shrink or crouch, esp. in fear or servility; cower. **2.** to fawn; toady. **—n. 3.** servile or fawning deference. **—cring′ing·ly,** *adv.*

crin·kle (kring′kəl), *v.,* **-kled, -kling,** *n.* **—v.t., v.i. 1.** to wrinkle; crimple; ripple. **2.** to make or cause to make slight, sharp sounds; rustle. **3.** to bend or twist. **—n. 4.** a wrinkle or ripple. **5.** a crinkling sound. **6.** a turn or twist. **—crin′kly,** *adj.,* **-kli·er, -kli·est.**

cri·noid (krī′noid, krin′oid), *n.* **1.** any echinoderm of the class Crinoidea, having a cup-shaped body with branched radiating arms, comprising the sea lilies and feather stars. **—adj. 2.** lilylike.

crin·o·line (krin′l in), *n.* **1.** a stiff, coarse fabric, often of cotton, used as interlining or for support in garments, hats, etc. **2.** a petticoat of stiff material worn to bell out an overskirt. **3.** a hoop skirt.

cri·num (krī′nəm), *n.* any of various bulbous plants of the genus *Crinum,* amaryllis family, having large, showy flowers.

crip·ple (krip′əl), *n., v.,* **-pled, -pling. —n. 1.** *Sometimes Offensive.* **a.** a lame or disabled person or animal. **b.** a person who is disabled in any way: *a mental cripple.* **2.** anything that is impaired or flawed. **—v.t. 3.** to make a cripple of; lame. **4.** to disable; impair. **—crip′pling·ly,** *adv.*

cri·sis (krī′sis), *n., pl.* **-ses** (-sēz). **1.** a turning point, as in a sequence of events, for better or for worse. **2.** a condition of instability, as in international relations, that leads to a decisive change. **3.** a personal tragedy, emotional upheaval, or the like. **4.** the point in the course of a serious disease at which a decisive change occurs, leading either to recovery or to death. **5.** the point, as in a play, at which the antagonistic elements confront each other.

cri′sis cen′ter, *n.* a facility that operates a telephone service from which people may obtain help and advice in a personal crisis.

cri′sis man′agement, *n.* the techniques used, as by an employer or government, to avert or deal with crisis situations, as strikes, riots, or violence. —**cri′sis man′ager,** *n.*

crisp (krisp), *adj.* **1.** hard but easily breakable; brittle: *crisp crackers.* **2.** firm and fresh; not soft or wilted: *crisp lettuce.* **3.** brisk; clear: *a crisp reply.* **4.** lively; pithy: *a crisp tempo.* **5.** clean-cut; well-groomed. **6.** bracing; invigorating: *crisp weather.* **7.** (of hair) lying in small, stiff curls. —*v.t., v.i.* **8.** to make or become crisp. **9.** to curl. —*n.* **10.** a dessert of apples or other fruit baked with a crunchy topping of crumbs, sugar, etc. —**crisp′er,** *n.* —**crisp′ly,** *adv.* —**crisp′ness,** *n.*

crisp•en (kris′pən), *v.t., v.i.* to make or become crisp.

Cris•pus (kris′pəs), *n.* a ruler of the Corinth synagogue who was converted to Christianity. Acts 18:8; I Cor. 1:14.

criss•cross (kris′krôs′, -kros′), *v.t.* **1.** to move back and forth over. **2.** to mark with crossing lines. —*v.i.* **3.** to pass back and forth; be arranged in a crisscross pattern. —*adj.* **4.** Also, **criss′crossed′.** having many crossing lines, paths, or the like. —*n.* **5.** a crisscross mark, pattern, etc. —*adv.* **6.** in a crisscross manner; crosswise.

cri•te•ri•on (krī tēr′ē ən), *n., pl.* **-te•ri•a** (-tēr′ē ə), **-te•ri•ons.** a standard of judgment or criticism; a rule or principle for evaluating or testing something. —**cri•te′ri•al,** *adj.* —**Usage.** Like some other nouns borrowed from the Greek, CRITERION has both a Greek plural, CRITERIA, and a plural formed on the English pattern, CRITERIONS. The plural in *-a* occurs with far greater frequency: *These are the criteria for the selection of candidates.* Although CRITERIA is sometimes used as a singular, most often in speech, it continues strongly in use as a plural in Standard English. See also MEDIA[1], PHENOMENON.

crit•ic (krit′ik), *n.* **1.** a person who judges, evaluates, or criticizes. **2.** a person who evaluates, analyzes, or judges literary or artistic works, dramatic or musical performances, etc., as for a newspaper. **3.** a person who tends to find fault or make harsh judgments; faultfinder.

crit•i•cal (krit′i kəl), *adj.* **1.** inclined to find fault or to judge severely. **2.** occupied with or skilled in criticism. **3.** involving or requiring skillful judgment as to truth, merit, etc. **4.** of or pertaining to critics or criticism: *critical essays.* **5.** providing textual variants, proposed emendations, etc.: *a critical edition of Chaucer.* **6.** caused by or constituting a crisis: *a critical shortage of food.* **7.** of decisive importance; crucial. **8.** of essential importance; indispensable: *a critical ingredient.* **9.** (of a patient's condition) having unstable and abnormal vital signs and one or more unfavorable indicators. **10.** *Physics.* **a.** pertaining to a state, value, or quantity at which one or more properties of a substance or system change. **b.** of a quantity of fissionable material large enough to sustain a chain reaction. —**crit′i•cal•ly,** *adv.*

crit′ical an′gle, *n.* **1.** the minimum angle of incidence beyond which total internal reflection occurs for light traveling from a medium of higher to one of lower index of refraction. **2.** the angle of attack at which a sudden change in airflow occurs around the wings of an aircraft, reducing lift and increasing drag.

crit′ical mass′, *n.* **1.** the amount of a given fissionable material necessary to sustain a chain reaction. **2.** an amount necessary or sufficient to have a significant effect or to achieve a result.

crit′ical point′, *n.* the point at which a substance in one phase, as the liquid, has the same density, pressure, and temperature as in another phase, as the gaseous.

crit•ic•as•ter (krit′i kas′tər), *n.* an incompetent critic.

crit•i•cism (krit′ə siz′əm), *n.* **1.** an act of passing judgment as to the merits of anything. **2.** an act of passing severe judgment; censure. **3.** an unfavorable comment or judgment. **4.** the act of analyzing and evaluating a literary or artistic work, musical or dramatic performance, etc. **5.** a critique. **6.** any of various methods of studying texts or documents for the purpose of dating them, evaluating their authenticity, etc.

crit•i•cize (krit′ə sīz′), *v.,* **-cized, -ciz•ing.** —*v.t.* **1.** to find fault with; censure. **2.** to judge or discuss the merits of; evaluate. —*v.i.* **3.** to judge unfavorably or harshly; find fault. **4.** to make judgments as to merits and faults.

cri•tique (kri tēk′), *n., v.,* **-tiqued, -ti•quing.** —*n.* **1.** an article or essay evaluating a literary or other work; review. **2.** a criticism or critical comment on some subject, problem, etc. —*v.t.* **3.** to review or analyze critically.

Crit′ten•den Com′promise (krit′n dən), a series of constitutional amendments proposed in Congress in 1860 to serve as a compromise between proslavery and antislavery factions, one of which would have permitted slavery in the territories south but not north of latitude 36°30′N. Also called **Crit′tenden Plan′.** [after its proponent, John J. Crittenden (1787–1863), U.S. Senator from Kentucky]

crit•ter (krit′ər), *n. Dial.* **1.** a domesticated animal. **2.** any creature.

croak (krōk), *v.i.* **1.** to utter a low-pitched, harsh cry, as the sound of a frog or a raven. **2.** to speak with a low, rasping voice. **3.** *Slang.* to die. —*v.t.* **4.** to utter by croaking. **5.** *Slang.* to kill. —*n.* **6.** the act or sound of croaking. —**croak′y,** *adj.,* **croak•i•er, croak•i•est.**

croak•er (krō′kər), *n.* **1.** a person or thing that croaks. **2.** any fish of the family Sciaenidae that produces sounds with its muscular swim bladder. **3.** *Slang.* a doctor.

Cro•at (krō′at, -ät), *n.* **1.** a member of a Slavic people of Croatia. **2.** a native or inhabitant of Croatia.

Cro•a•tia (krō ā′shə, -shē ə), *n.* a republic in S Europe: includes the historical regions of Dalmatia, Istria, and Slavonia; formerly (1945–91) part of Yugoslavia. 5,026,995; 21,835 sq. mi. (56,555 sq. km). *Cap.:* Zagreb. —**Cro•a′tian,** *adj., n.*

cro•chet (krō shā′), *n.* **1.** needlework done with a hooked needle **(cro-chet′ hook′** or **crochet′ nee′dle)** for drawing the thread or yarn through intertwined loops. —*v.i.* **2.** to do this needlework. —*v.t.* **3.** to form or work by crochet. —**cro•chet′er,** *n.*

crock[1] (krok), *n.* **1.** an earthenware pot, jar, or other container. **2.** a fragment of earthenware; potsherd.

crock[2] (krok), *n.* **1.** one that is old or decrepit. **2.** *Slang.* a person who complains about or insists on being treated for an imagined illness. **3.** an old worn-out horse.

crock[3] (krok), *n. Slang.* something false or exaggerated; humbug.

crock•er•y (krok′ə rē), *n.* earthenware.

crock•et (krok′it), *n.* a medieval architectural ornament, usu. in the form of a leaf that curves up and away from the supporting surface and returns partially upon itself.

Crock•ett (krok′it), *n.* **David** (*Davy*), 1786–1836, U.S. frontiersman, politician, and folklore hero.

Crock•pot (krok′pot′), *Trademark.* a brand of electric slow cooker.

croc•o•dile (krok′ə dīl′), *n.* **1.** any of various narrow-snouted crocodilians of the genus *Crocodylus* and related genera, found mainly in tropical waters of both hemispheres. **2.** any reptile of the order Crocodylia; crocodilian. **3.** the tanned skin or hide of these reptiles. **4.** *Brit.* a long line of people, esp. schoolchildren walking by twos. [< Latin < Greek *krokódelios* lizard]

croc′odile bird′, *n.* a short-legged African courser, *Pluvianus aegyptius,* inhabiting sandy riverbanks and lake shores.

croc′odile tears′, *n.pl.* tears that are not real; a hypocritical show of grief.

croc•o•dil•i•an (krok′ə dil′ē ən), *n.* **1.** any large reptile of the order Crocodylia, comprising the crocodiles, alligators, caimans, and gavials. —*adj.* **2.** of, like, or pertaining to a crocodile. **3.** hypocritical; insincere.

cro•cus (krō′kəs), *n., pl.* **-cus•es.** **1.** any of various small bulbous plants of the genus *Crocus,* of the iris family, cultivated for their showy, spring-blooming flowers. **2.** an orange yellow; saffron. **3.** a polishing powder consisting of iron oxide. —**cro′cused,** *adj.*

crois•sant (*Fr.* krwä säɴ′; *Eng.* krə sänt′, kwä-), *n., pl.* **-sants** (*Fr.* -säɴ′; *Eng.* -sänts′). a crescent-shaped roll of rich, flaky pastry.

Crom•well (krom′wəl, -wel, krum′-), *n.* **1. Oliver,** 1599–1658, English general and statesman: Lord Protector of England, Scotland, and Ireland 1653–58. **2.** his son, **Richard,** 1626–1712, Lord Protector of England 1658–59. **3. Thomas, Earl of Essex,** 1485?–1540, English statesman.

Crom′well's Bi′ble, *n.* GREAT BIBLE.

Cron•kite (kron′kīt, krong′-), *n.* **Walter,** born 1916, U.S. newscaster.

Cro•nus (krō′nəs), *n.* a Titan, son of Uranus and Gaea, who was dethroned by his son Zeus.

cro•ny (krō′nē), *n., pl.* **-nies.** a close friend or associate; companion; chum.

cro•ny•ism (krō′nē iz′əm), *n.* the practice of favoring one's close friends, esp. in political appointments.

crook (kro͝ok), *n.* **1.** a bent or curved implement, appendage, etc.; hook. **2.** the hooked part of anything. **3.** an instrument or implement having a curved part, as a shepherd's staff hooked at one end. **4.** a dishonest person, esp. a swindler or thief. **5.** a bend or curve. —*v.t.* **6.** to bend; curve: *to crook one's finger.* —*v.i.* **7.** to bend; curve.

crook•ed (kro͝ok′id *for 1–4;* kro͝okt *for 5*), *adj.* **1.** not straight; bending; curved. **2.** askew; awry. **3.** deformed. **4.** dishonest. **5.** bent, as a finger or neck. —**crook′ed•ly,** *adv.* —**crook′ed•ness,** *n.*

crook•neck (kro͝ok′nek′), *n.* **1.** any of several varieties of squash having a long, recurved neck. **2.** any plant bearing such fruit.

croon (kro͞on), *v.i.* **1.** to sing or hum in a soft, soothing voice. **2.** to sing in an evenly modulated, slightly exaggerated manner. —*v.t.* **3.** to sing (a song) in a crooning manner. **4.** to lull by singing to in a soft, soothing voice. —*n.* **5.** the act or sound of crooning. —**croon′er,** *n.*

crop (krop), *n., v.,* **cropped, crop•ping.** —*n.* **1.** the cultivated produce of the ground, while growing or when gathered: *the wheat crop.* **2.** the yield of such produce in one season. **3.** the yield of any product in a season. **4.** a group of persons or things appearing or occurring together: *the new crop of freshmen.* **5.** the stock or handle of a whip. **6.** Also called **riding crop.** a short riding whip consisting of a stock without a lash. **7.** Also called **craw.** **a.** a pouch in the esophagus of many birds, in which food is held for later digestion or for regurgitation to nestlings. **b.** a chamber in the foregut of some annelids and insects for holding and crushing food. **8.** a mark produced by clipping the ears, as of cattle. **9.** a close cutting of something, as the hair. —*v.t.* **10.** to cut or bite off the top of (a plant, grass, etc.): *sheep cropping the grass.* **11.** to cut off the ends or a part of: *to crop the ears of a dog.* **12.** to cut short. **13.** to trim (a photographic print or negative). **14.** to cause to bear a crop. —*v.i.* **15.** to yield a crop. **16.** to feed by cropping or grazing. **17. crop out, a.** to rise to the surface of the ground: *Veins of quartz crop out in the canyon walls.* **b.** to occur. **18. crop up,** to appear, esp. suddenly or unexpectedly. —**crop′less,** *adj.*

crop'-dust'ing, *n.* the spraying of powdered fungicides or insecticides on crops, usu. from an airplane. —**crop'-dust',** *v.t., v.i.*

crop' rota'tion, *n.* the system of varying successive crops in a definite order on the same ground, esp. to avoid depleting the soil and to control weeds, diseases, and pests.

cro·quet (krō kā′), *n.* a lawn game played by knocking wooden balls through metal wickets with mallets.

cro·quette (krō ket′), *n.* a small cake of minced meat, fish, vegetable, or other food coated with egg and breadcrumbs and deep-fried.

Cros·by (krôz′bē, kroz′-), *n.* **1. Bing** (*Harry Lillis Crosby*), 1904–77, U.S. singer and actor. **2. Fanny,** 1820–1915, U.S. hymn writer.

cro·sier or **cro·zier** (krō′zhər), *n.* **1.** a ceremonial staff carried by a bishop or an abbot, hooked at one end like a shepherd's crook. **2.** the coiled tip of a plant part, as a fern frond.

cross (krôs, kros), *n.* **1.** a figure or object consisting of two lines or pieces intersecting usu. at right angles. **2.** a wooden structure consisting of an upright and a transverse piece, upon which persons were formerly put to death. **3.** a mark, usu. an X, used as a signature or to indicate location, an error, etc. **4. the Cross,** the cross upon which Jesus died. **5.** a figure of the Cross as a Christian emblem, badge, etc. **6.** the Cross as the symbol of Christianity. **7.** CRUCIFIX (def. 1). **8.** a sign made with the hand outlining the figure of a cross as an act of devotion. **9.** a structure or monument in the form of a cross, set up for prayer, as a memorial, etc. **10.** a conventional representation or modification of the Christian emblem used as a symbol or ornament: *Maltese cross.* **11.** the crucifixion of Jesus as the culmination of His redemptive mission. **12.** any suffering endured for Jesus' sake. **13.** the teaching of redemption gained by Jesus' death. **14.** Christianity or Christendom. **15.** an opposition; thwarting. **16.** an affliction; misfortune; trouble. **17.** a crossing of animals or plants; a mixing of breeds. **18.** an animal, plant, breed, etc., produced by crossing; crossbreed. **19.** a person or thing that is intermediate in character between two others. **20.** a boxing punch thrown across and over the lead of an opponent. **21.** a cross-examination. **22.** a movement from one place or side to another; a crossing, as by an actor on stage. **23.** a place of crossing. **24.** a four-way plumbing joint or connection. **25.** (*cap.*) SOUTHERN CROSS. —*v.t.* **26.** to move or extend from one side to the other side of (a street, river, etc.). **27.** to put or draw a line across. **28.** to cancel by marking with a cross or drawing a line through (often fol. by *off* or *out*). **29.** to lie or pass across; intersect. **30.** to place across each other or crosswise: *to cross one's legs.* **31.** to meet and pass. **32.** to cause (members of different genera, species, breeds, varieties, or the like) to interbreed. **33.** to oppose openly; thwart. **34.** *Slang.* to betray; double-cross. **35.** to make the sign of the cross upon or over: *to cross oneself.* —*v.i.* **36.** to lie or be athwart; intersect. **37.** to move, pass, or extend from one side or place to another. **38.** to meet and pass. **39.** to interbreed. **40. cross over, a.** (of a chromosome segment) to undergo crossing over. **b.** to switch allegiance, as from one political party to another. **c.** to change successfully from one field of endeavor, genre, etc., to another. **41. cross up, a.** to deceive; double-cross. **b.** to confuse. —*adj.* **42.** angry and annoyed; ill-humored. **43.** lying crosswise; transverse. **44.** involving a reciprocal action or interchange (often used in combination): *cross-marketing of related services.* **45.** contrary; opposite. **46.** crossbred; hybrid. —**Idiom. 47. cross one's mind,** to occur to one: *The idea never crossed my mind.* **48. cross one's path,** to encounter or meet unexpectedly. **49. cross swords, a.** to engage in combat; fight. **b.** to disagree violently; argue. —**cross'ly,** *adv.* —**cross'ness,** *n.*

Latin cross · tau cross or St. Anthony's cross · cross of Calvary · cross of Lorraine · patriarchal cross · Greek cross · botonée

St. Andrew's cross · cross potent · papal cross · Maltese cross · Celtic cross · moline

crosses

cross·bar (krôs′bär′, kros′-), *n.* **1.** a horizontal bar, line, or stripe. **2. a.** the horizontal bar forming part of the goalposts. **b.** a horizontal bar used for gymnastics. **c.** a horizontal bar that must be cleared in performing the pole vault or high jump.

cross·beam (krôs′bēm′, kros′-), *n.* a transverse beam in a structure, as a joist.

cross·bill (krôs′bil′, kros′-), *n.* any bird of the genus *Loxia* (family Fringillidae), of coniferous forests of the Northern Hemisphere, having a bill with crossed tips used to extract seeds from cones.

cross·bones (krôs′bōnz′, kros′-), *n.pl.* a representation of two bones placed crosswise, usu. below a skull, to symbolize death.

cross·bow (krôs′bō′, kros′-), *n.* a medieval weapon consisting of a bow fixed transversely on a stock having a trigger mechanism to release the bowstring. —**cross'bow'man,** *n., pl.* **-men.**

cross·bred (krôs′bred′, kros′-), *adj.* **1.** produced by crossbreeding. —*n.* **2.** a crossbred plant or animal; hybrid.

cross·breed (krôs′brēd′, kros′-), *v.,* **-bred, -breed·ing,** *n.* —*v.t.* **1.** to produce (a hybrid); hybridize. —*v.i.* **2.** to undertake or engage in hybridizing; hybridize. —*n.* **3.** a crossbred.

cross·buck (krôs′buk′, kros′-), *n.* an X-shaped warning sign for vehicular traffic at a railroad grade crossing.

cross-check (*v.* krôs′chek′, kros′-; *n.* -chek′, -chek′), *v.t.* **1.** to determine the accuracy of (something) by checking it with various sources. **2.** (in ice hockey) to block (an opponent) by placing the stick across the opponent's body. —*n.* **3.** the act of cross-checking. —**cross'-check'er,** *n.*

cross-coun·try (*adj.* krôs′kun′trē, kros′-; *n.* -kun′trē, -kun′-), *adj., n., pl.* **-tries.** —*adj.* **1.** directed or proceeding over fields, through woods, etc., rather than on a road, track, or run: *a cross-country race.* **2.** from one end of the country to the other: *a cross-country flight.* —*n.* **3.** a cross-country sport or race.

cross'-coun'try ski'ing, *n.* the sport of skiing across the countryside using narrow skis with boots that can be raised off the ski at the heel when striding. —**cross'-coun'try ski'er,** *n.*

cross·court (krôs′kôrt′, -kōrt′, kros′-), *adj., adv.* to the opposite or diagonally opposite side of the court, as in tennis or basketball.

cross'-cul'tural, *adj.* pertaining to or contrasting cultures or cultural groups: *cross-cultural studies.* —**cross'-cul'turally,** *adv.*

cross·cur·rent (krôs′kûr′ənt, -kur′-, kros′-), *n.* **1.** a current, as in a stream, moving across the main current. **2.** Often, **crosscurrents.** a conflicting tendency or movement.

cross·cut (krôs′kut′, kros′-), *adj., n., v.,* **-cut, -cut·ting.** —*adj.* **1.** made or used for cutting crosswise. **2.** cut across the grain or on the bias. —*n.* **3.** a transverse cut or course. **4.** a shortcut diagonally across a network of roads or paths. **5.** a passageway in an underground mine, usu. from a shaft to a vein of ore or crosswise of a vein of ore. **6.** an act or instance of crosscutting. —*v.t.* **7.** to cut or go across. **8.** to insert into a particular film or television scene or sequence (portions of another scene). —*v.i.* **9.** to employ crosscutting. —**cross'cut'ter,** *n.*

cross'cut saw', *n.* a saw for cutting wood perpendicular to the grain.

cross'-dress', *v.i.* (esp. of a man) to dress in clothing typically worn by members of the opposite sex. —**cross'-dress'er,** *n.*

crosse (krôs, kros), *n.* a long-handled racket used in the game of lacrosse.

cross'-exam'ine, *v.t.,* **-ined, -in·ing. 1.** to examine (a witness called and examined by the opposing side), esp. for the purpose of checking, clarifying, or discrediting that witness's testimony. **2.** to question closely or minutely. —**cross'-examina'tion,** *n.* —**cross'-exam'iner,** *n.*

cross'-eye', *n.* strabismus, esp. the form in which one or both eyes turn inward. —**cross'-eyed',** *adj.*

cross'-fertiliza'tion, *n.* **1.** the fertilization of an organism by the fusion of an egg from one individual with a sperm or male gamete from a different individual. **2.** the fertilization of the flower of one plant by a gamete from the flower of a closely related plant. **3.** (not in technical use) CROSS-POLLINATION. **4.** interaction between two or more cultures, fields of study, or the like, that is mutually productive. —**cross'-fer'tilize,** *v.i., v.t.,* **-lized, -liz·ing.**

cross'-file', *v.i., v.t.,* **-filed, -fil·ing.** to register as a candidate in the primary elections of more than one party.

cross' fire' or **cross'fire',** *n.* **1.** gunfire issuing from two or more positions so that the lines of fire cross one another. **2.** a brisk or angry exchange of words or opinions. **3.** a situation involving conflicting claims, forces, etc.

cross'-grained', *adj.* **1.** (of timber) **a.** having the grain running transversely or diagonally. **b.** having an irregular or gnarled grain. **2.** stubborn; perverse.

cross' hairs', *n.pl.* fine wires or fibers crossing in a focal plane of an optical instrument to center a target or object or to define a line of sight.

cross·hatch (krôs′hach′, kros′-), *v.t.* **1.** to mark or shade with two or more intersecting series of parallel lines. —*n.* **2.** a pattern or mark made with such lines. —**cross'hatch'ing,** *n.*

cross·ing (krô′sing, kros′ing), *n.* **1.** the act of a person or thing that crosses. **2.** a place where lines, streets, tracks, etc., cross each other. **3.** a place at which a road, railroad track, river, etc., may be crossed. **4.** hybridization; crossbreeding. **5.** the act of opposing or thwarting. **6.** the intersection of nave and transept in a cruciform church.

cross'ing o'ver, *n.* the exchange of segments of chromatids between pairs of chromosomes during meiosis, resulting in a recombination of linked genes.

cross'-leg'ged (-leg′id, -legd′), *adj., adv.* **1.** having the knees wide apart and the ankles crossed. **2.** having one leg placed across the other.

cross' match'ing, *n.* the testing for compatibility of a donor's and a recipient's blood prior to transfusion.

cross' of Cal'vary, *n.* a Latin cross with a representation of steps beneath it.

cross' of gold', *n.* the gold standard, referred to in a speech (1896) by William Jennings Bryan: "You shall not crucify mankind upon a cross of gold."

cros·sop·te·ryg·i·an (kro sop′tə rij′ē ən), *n.* **1.** any fish of the group Crossopterygii, extinct except for the coelacanth, and including the ancestors of amphibians and other land vertebrates. —*adj.* **2.** pertaining to or resembling a crossopterygian.

cross·o·ver (krôs′ō′vər, kros′-), *n.* **1.** a bridge or other structure for crossing over a river, highway, etc. **2. a.** music that crosses over in style, sometimes sharing attributes with several musical styles and therefore often appealing to a broader audience. **b.** a performer of crossover. **3.** a member of one political party who votes in the primary of another party. **4.** *Genetics.* **a.** CROSSING OVER. **b.** a genotype resulting from crossing over. **5.** a track structure composed of two or more turnouts, permitting movement of cars from either of two parallel and adjacent tracks to the other. **6.** (in plumbing) a U-shaped pipe for bypassing another pipe.

cross′-pollina′tion, *n.* the transfer of pollen from the flower of one plant to the flower of a plant having a different genetic constitution. Compare SELF-POLLINATION.

cross′-pur′pose, *n.* **1.** an opposing or contrary purpose. —*Idiom.* **2. at cross-purposes,** in a way that involves mutual misunderstanding or produces mutual frustrations, usu. unintentionally.

cross·rail (krôs′rāl′, kros′-), *n.* a horizontal structural member or slat, as in a door or the back of a chair.

cross′ ref′erence, *n.* a reference from one part of a book, index, etc., to related material in another part.

cross′-ref′erence, *v.t.,* **-ref·er·enced, -ref·er·enc·ing.** to provide with cross references.

cross·road (krôs′rōd′, kros′-), *n.* **1.** a road that crosses another road, or one that runs transversely to main roads. **2.** Often, **crossroads.** (*used with a sing. or pl. v.*) **a.** a place where roads intersect. **b.** a point at which a vital decision must be made. **c.** a main center of activity or assembly.

cross′ sec′tion, *n.* **1.** a section made by a plane cutting something transversely, esp. at right angles to the longest axis. **2.** a diagram, photograph, or the like of such a section. **3.** a representative sample showing all characteristic parts, relationships, etc., of the whole. **4.** a vertical section of the ground surface taken at right angles to a survey line. **5.** *Physics.* a measure of the probability, expressed as the effective area of a given particle, that one particle will interact with another. —**cross′-sec′tion,** *v.t.* —**cross′-sec′tional,** *adj.*

cross′-stitch′, *n.* **1.** a stitch in which pairs of diagonal stitches of the same length cross each other in the middle to form an X. **2.** embroidery or needlepoint done with this stitch. —*v.t., v.i.* **3.** to work in cross-stitch.

cross′ street′, *n.* **1.** a street crossing another street. **2.** a short street connecting main streets.

cross′ talk′ or **cross′talk′,** *n.* **1.** interference heard on a telephone or radio because of unintentional coupling to another communication channel. **2.** *Brit.* witty, fast-paced dialogue; repartee.

cross·town (krôs′toun′, kros′-), *adj.* **1.** extending or traveling across to the opposite side of a town or city: *a crosstown bus.* —*adv.* **2.** across a town or city: *to hurry crosstown.*

cross-train (krôs′trān′, kros′-), *v.t.* to train (a worker, athlete, etc.) to be proficient at different, usu. related, skills, tasks, etc.

cross·walk (krôs′wôk′, kros′-), *n.* a lane marked off for pedestrians to use when crossing a street, as at an intersection.

cross′ wind′ or **cross′wind′** (wind), *n.* a wind blowing across the course or path of a ship, aircraft, etc.

cross·wise (krôs′wīz′, kros′-) also **cross·ways** (-wāz′), *adv.* **1.** across; transversely. **2.** contrarily. —*adj.* **3.** forming a cross; transverse.

cross′word puz′zle (krôs′wûrd′, kros′-), *n.* a puzzle in which words corresponding to numbered clues or definitions are fitted into a pattern of horizontal and vertical squares, one letter per square, so that most letters form parts of two words. Also called **cross′word′.**

crotch (kroch), *n.* **1.** a place where something divides, as the human body between the legs. **2.** the part of trousers, panties, etc., where the two legs or panels join. **3.** a piece of material serving as a juncture between the legs or panels of trousers, underpants, etc. **4.** the area of a tree at which a main branch joins the trunk. **5.** a forked object, as a staff with a forked top.

crotch·et (kroch′it), *n.* **1.** an odd fancy or whimsical notion. **2.** a small hook. **3.** a hooklike device or part.

crotch·et·y (kroch′i tē), *adj.* **1.** given to odd fancies or whims; eccentric. **2.** grouchy or cantankerous **3.** of the nature of a crotchet. —**crotch′et·i·ness,** *n.*

cro·ton (krōt′n), *n.* **1.** any of numerous chiefly tropical plants constituting the genus *Croton,* of the spurge family, several species of which, as *C. tiglium,* have medicinal properties. **2.** any of several related plants of the genus *Codiaeum,* cultivated for their ornamental foliage.

cro·ton·bug or **Cro′ton bug′** (krōt′n bug′), *n.* GERMAN COCKROACH. [allegedly after the *Croton* Reservoir in Westchester Co., N.Y.; its opening in 1842 was supposedly coincident with a rise in New York City's cockroach population]

crouch (krouch), *v.i.* **1.** to stoop low with the knees bent. **2.** to bend close to the ground preparing to spring, as a cat. **3.** to bow or stoop servilely; cringe. —*v.t.* **4.** to bend (the head or body) low. —*n.* **5.** the act of crouching. —**crouch′er,** *n.* —**crouch′ing·ly,** *adv.*

croup¹ (kroop), *n.* any condition of the larynx or trachea characterized by a hoarse cough and difficult breathing. —**croup′y,** *adj.,* **croup·i·er, croup·i·est.**

croup² (kroop), *n.* the highest part of the rump of a quadruped, esp. a horse.

crou·pi·er (kroo′pē ər, -pē ā′), *n.* an attendant who collects and pays the money at a gaming table.

crous·tade (kroo städ′), *n.* a shell, as of pastry or bread, baked or fried and filled with ragout or the like.

croûte (kroot), *n.* a pastry case or covering; crust.

crou·ton (kroo′ton, kroo ton′), *n.* a small cube of fried or toasted bread, used as a garnish for salads, soups, etc.

crow¹ (krō), *n.* **1.** any of various large, stout-billed, usu. gregarious songbirds of the genus *Corvus* (family Corvidae), typically black or drab-colored, and nearly worldwide in distribution. **2.** any of several other birds of the family Corvidae. **3.** CROWBAR. —*Idiom.* **4. as the crow flies,** in a straight line; by the most direct route. **5. eat crow,** to be forced to admit one's mistake; suffer humiliation.

crow² (krō), *v.,* **crowed** or, for 1, (*esp. Brit.*), **crew; crowed; crow·ing;** *n.* —*v.i.* **1.** to utter the characteristic cry of a rooster. **2.** to gloat or exult (often fol. by *over*). **3.** to boast or brag. **4.** to utter an inarticulate cry of pleasure. —*n.* **5.** the cry of a rooster. **6.** an inarticulate cry of pleasure. —**crow′er,** *n.*

Crow (krō), *n., pl.* **Crows,** (*esp. collectively*) **Crow. 1.** a member of a Plains Indian people of the Yellowstone River drainage basin in Montana and N Wyoming. **2.** the Siouan language of the Crow.

crow·bar (krō′bär′), *n.* a steel bar, usu. flattened and slightly bent at one or both ends, used as a lever.

crow·ber·ry (krō′ber′ē, -bə rē), *n., pl.* **-ries. 1.** a low evergreen shrub, *Empetrum nigrum,* of the crowberry family, bearing an edible black berry. **2.** the berry itself.

crowd (kroud), *n.* **1.** a large number of persons gathered together; throng. **2.** any group of persons having something in common: *the theater crowd.* **3.** a group of spectators; audience: *the opening night crowd.* **4.** the common people; the masses. **5.** a large number of things considered together. —*v.i.* **6.** to gather in large numbers; throng. **7.** to press forward; advance by pushing. —*v.t.* **8.** to press closely together; force into a small space; cram. **9.** to push, shove, or force. **10.** to fill, as by pressing or thronging into. **11.** to place under constant pressure. —**Usage.** See COLLECTIVE NOUN.

crow·foot (krō′foot′), *n., pl.* **-foots** for 1, **-feet** for 2. **1.** any of various plants of the genus *Ranunculus,* of the buttercup family, esp. one with divided leaves suggestive of a bird's foot. **2.** *Naut.* an arrangement of ropes for supporting an awning.

crown (kroun), *n.* **1.** any of various types of headgear, often made of precious metal and set with gems, worn by a monarch as a symbol of sovereignty. **2.** the power or dominion of a sovereign. **3.** (*often cap.*) the sovereign as head of the state, or the supreme governing power of a state under a monarchical government. **4.** an ornamental wreath or circlet for the head, conferred as a mark of victory or distinction. **5.** a distinction or award for a great achievement. **6.** a championship title. **7.** any crownlike emblem or design. **8.** the top or highest part of anything, as of a hat or the head. **9. a.** the part of a tooth that is covered by enamel. **b.** an artificial substitute, as of gold or porcelain, for the crown of a tooth. **10.** the highest or most nearly perfect state of anything; culmination. **11.** *Bot.* **a.** the leaves and living branches of a tree. **b.** the point at which the root of a seed plant joins the stem. **12.** the crest, as of a bird. **13.** a knurled knob for winding a watch. **14.** the part of a cut gem above the girdle; bezel. **15.** the part of an anchor at which the arms join the shank. —*v.t.* **16.** to invest with a regal crown, or with regal dignity and power. **17.** to place a crown or garland upon the head of. **18.** to honor or reward; invest with honor, dignity, etc. **19.** to be at the top or highest part of. **20.** to bring to a successful or triumphant conclusion. **21.** *Informal.* to hit on the top of the head. **22.** to give to (a construction) an upper surface of convex section or outline. **23.** to cap (a tooth) with a false crown. **24.** to change (a checker) into a king after having safely reached the last row. —**crown′less,** *adj.*

crown′ cap′, *n.* a cork-lined crimped metal bottle cap.

crown′ col′ony, *n.* a British colony in which the crown controls legislation and administration, as distinguished from one having a constitution and representative government.

crown′ jew′el, *n.* **1. crown jewels,** the ceremonial objects of a sovereign, as the crown and scepter, that are heavily jeweled. **2.** the most valued possession.

crown′ of glo′ry, *n.* **1.** heavenly rewards. I Peter 5:4. **2.** a triumph or great achievement.

crown′ of thorns′, *n.* **1.** a wreath made up of thorns with which Jesus was mockingly crowned by Roman soldiers before his crucifixion. Matt. 27:29. **2.** a climbing spurge, *Euphorbia milii splendens,* of Madagascar, having spiny stems and flowers with petallike red bracts. Also, **crown′-of-thorns′.** a starfish, *Acanthaster planci,* that feeds on living coral polyps, causing erosion and destruction of coral reefs.

crown′ prince′, *n.* a male heir apparent to a throne.

crown′ prin′cess, *n.* **1.** the wife of a crown prince. **2.** a female heir presumptive or heir apparent to a throne.

crown′ vetch′, *n.* an Old World low plant of the legume family, naturalized in the NE U.S. and planted as a ground cover.

crow's′-foot′, *n., pl.* **-feet. 1.** Usu., **crow's-feet.** any of the tiny wrinkles at the outer corners of the eyes resulting from age or constant squinting. **2.** an arrangement of ropes in which one main rope exerts pull at several points through a group of smaller ropes.

crow's′-nest′ or **crow's′ nest′,** *n.* **1.** a platform or shelter for a lookout high on a ship's mast. **2.** any similar platform raised high above the ground, as a lookout or a station for a traffic officer.

CRT, 1. cathode-ray tube. **2.** a computer terminal or monitor that includes a cathode-ray tube.

cru•ces (kro͞o′sēz), *n.* a pl. of CRUX.

cru•cial (kro͞o′shəl), *adj.* of vital or critical importance, esp. with regard to a decision or result: *a crucial experiment.* **—cru′ci•al′i•ty** (-shē al′i-tē, -shal′-), *n.* **—cru′cial•ly,** *adv.*

cru•ci•ate (kro͞o′shē it, -āt′), *adj.* **1.** cross-shaped. **2.** *Bot.* formed like a cross with equal arms, as mustard flowers. **3.** *Zool.* having wings that cross at the tips. **—cru′ci•ate•ly,** *adv.*

cru•ci•ble (kro͞o′sə bəl), *n.* **1.** a container of metal or refractory material employed for heating substances to high temperatures. **2.** a hollow area at the bottom of a furnace in which the metal collects. **3.** a severe test or trial, esp. one that causes a lasting change or influence.

cru•ci•fer (kro͞o′sə fər), *n.* **1.** a person who carries a cross, as in ecclesiastical processions. **2.** a cruciferous plant.

cru•cif•er•ous (kro͞o sif′ər əs), *adj.* **1.** bearing a cross. **2.** belonging to the Cruciferae, the mustard family of plants.

cru•ci•fix (kro͞o′sə fiks), *n.* **1.** a cross with the figure of Jesus crucified upon it. **2.** any cross.

cru•ci•fix•ion (kro͞o′sə fik′shən), *n.* **1.** the act of crucifying or the state of being crucified. **2.** (*cap.*) the death of Jesus upon the Cross. **3.** a picture or other representation of this. **4.** severe and unjust punishment or suffering.

cru•ci•form (kro͞o′sə fôrm′), *adj.* **1.** cross-shaped. **—*n.* 2.** a cross. **—cru′ci•for′mi•ty,** *n.* **—cru′ci•form′ly,** *adv.*

cru•ci•fy (kro͞o′sə fī′), *v.t.,* **-fied, -fy•ing. 1.** to put to death by nailing or binding the hands and feet to a cross. **2.** to persecute or torment. **3.** to subdue or repress (passion, sin, etc.). **4.** to punish or criticize severely. **—cru′ci•fi′er,** *n.*

crud (krud), *n., v.,* **crud•ded, crud•ding. —*n.*** *Slang.* **1.** a deposit of filth, incrusted matter, or other objectionable substance. **2.** a despicable or disagreeable person. **3.** something worthless or objectionable. **4.** lies, exaggeration, or flattery. **—crud′dy,** *adj.,* **-di•er, -di•est.**

crude (kro͞od), *adj.,* **crud•er, crud•est,** *n.* **—*adj.* 1.** in a raw or unrefined state: *crude sugar.* **2.** undeveloped. **3.** showing a lack of polish, completeness, or skill; rough: *a crude shelter.* **4.** lacking culture, refinement, etc.; vulgar: *crude behavior.* **5.** blunt; stark. **—*n.* 6.** CRUDE OIL. **—crude′ly,** *adv.* **—crude′ness,** *n.*

Cru•den (kro͞od′n), *n.* **Alexander,** 1701–70, Scottish compiler of a Bible concordance.

crude′ oil′, *n.* petroleum as it comes from the ground, before refining. Also called **crude′ petro′leum.**

cru•di•tés (kro͞o′di tā′; *Fr.* KRY dē tā′), *n.pl.* raw vegetables cut into pieces and served with a dip as an appetizer.

cru•el (kro͞o′əl), *adj.* **1.** willfully causing pain or distress to others. **2.** enjoying the pain or distress of others. **3.** causing or marked by great pain or distress. **4.** unrelentingly severe; merciless; brutal. **—cru′el•ly,** *adv.* **—cru′el•ty,** *n.*

cru•et (kro͞o′it), *n.* a glass bottle, esp. one for holding vinegar, oil, etc., for the table.

cruise (kro͞oz), *v.,* **cruised, cruis•ing,** *n.* **—*v.i.* 1.** to sail about on a pleasure trip. **2.** to patrol a body of water, as a warship. **3.** to fly, drive, or sail at a constant speed that permits maximum operating efficiency for sustained travel. **4.** to travel about slowly, looking for customers or to maintain order: *taxis and police cars cruising in the downtown area.* **5.** (of an infant) to take small steps while holding onto a wall or furniture for balance. **—*v.t.* 6.** to cruise in (a specified area). **7.** to inspect (a tract of forest) for the purpose of estimating lumber potential. **—*n.* 8.** a pleasure voyage on a ship.

cruise′ control′, *n.* a system on some motor vehicles that can be set to maintain a chosen speed automatically.

cruise′ miss′ile, *n.* a winged guided missile designed to fly at low altitudes to avoid radar detection.

cruis•er (kro͞o′zər), *n.* **1.** a person or thing that cruises. **2.** one of a class of warships of medium tonnage, designed for high speed and long cruising radius. **3.** CABIN CRUISER.

crul•ler (krul′ər), *n.* **1.** a twisted oblong pastry of doughnut dough, deep-fried and sugared. **2.** a light raised doughnut, usu. having a ridged surface and topped with white icing.

crumb (krum), *n.* **1.** a small particle of bread, cake, etc., that has broken off. **2.** a fragment of anything; bit. **3.** the soft inner portion of bread (disting. from *crust*). **4. crumbs,** a cake topping made of sugar, flour, butter, and spice. **—*v.t.* 5.** (in cooking) to top, coat, or prepare with crumbs. **6.** to break into crumbs or small fragments. **7.** to remove crumbs from. **—crumby,** *adj.,* **–i•er, –i•est.**

crum•ble (krum′bəl), *v.,* **-bled, -bling,** *n.* **—*v.i.* 1.** to break or collapse into small fragments. **2.** to decay or disintegrate gradually: *The ancient walls were crumbling.* **—*v.t.* 3.** to break into small particles or crumbs. **—*n.* 4.** a crumbly or crumbled substance.

crum•my (krum′ē), *adj.,* **-mi•er, -mi•est.** *Informal.* **1.** dirty and rundown; shabby. **2.** of little value; cheap; worthless. **3.** wretched; miserable. **—crum′mi•ness,** *n.*

crum•pet (krum′pit), *n.* a small, round, soft bread resembling an English muffin, cooked on a griddle and usu. served toasted.

crum•ple (krum′pəl), *v.,* **-pled, -pling,** *n.* **—*v.t.* 1.** to mash or crush into irregular folds or a compact mass. **2.** to cause to collapse. **—*v.i.* 3.** to contract into wrinkles; shrink or shrivel. **4.** to give way suddenly; collapse. **—*n.* 5.** an irregular fold or wrinkle. **—crum′ply,** *adj.*

crunch (krunch), *v.t.* **1.** to chew with a sharp crushing noise. **2.** to crush or grind noisily. **3.** to condense: *Crunch the first page into one paragraph.* **4.** to squeeze financially. **5.** to manipulate or process (numbers or data) extensively or in large amounts, esp. by computer. **—*v.i.* 6.** to chew with a crushing sound. **7.** to proceed with a crushing noise: *cars crunching along the gravel road.* **—*n.* 8.** an act or sound of crunching. **9.** a shortage or reduction: *the energy crunch.* **10.** distress due to such a shortage or reduction: *a budget crunch.* **11.** a critical or difficult situation: *when the crunch comes.*

crus (krus, kro͞os), *n., pl.* **cru•ra** (kro͝or′ə). **1.** the part of a leg or hind limb between the knee and the ankle; shank. **2.** any leglike part or process.

cru•sade (kro͞o sād′), *n., v.,* **-sad•ed, -sad•ing. —*n.* 1.** (*often cap.*) any of the military expeditions undertaken by the Christians of Europe in the 11th, 12th, and 13th centuries for the recovery of the Holy Land from the Muslims. **2.** any war carried on under papal sanction. **3.** any vigorous, aggressive movement for the defense or advancement of an idea, cause, etc.: *a crusade against child abuse.* **—*v.i.* 4.** to go on or engage in a crusade. **—cru•sad′er,** *n.*

cruse (kro͞oz, kro͞os), *n.* an earthen pot, bottle, etc., for liquids.

crush (krush), *v.t.* **1.** to press or squeeze with a force that destroys or deforms. **2.** to pound into small particles, as stone. **3.** to wrinkle or crease. **4.** to force out by pressing or squeezing. **5.** to hug or embrace tightly. **6.** to suppress utterly and often forcibly: *to crush a revolt.* **7.** to squelch or humiliate. **8.** to oppress grievously. **—*v.i.* 9.** to become crushed. **10.** to advance forcibly. **—*n.* 11.** the act of crushing or the state of being crushed. **12.** a great crowd; throng. **13.** *Informal.* **a.** an intense but usu. short-lived infatuation. **b.** the object of such an infatuation. **—crush′a•ble,** *adj.* **—crush′proof′,** *adj.*

crust (krust), *n.* **1.** the brown, hard outer surface of a loaf of bread. **2.** a slice of bread from the end of the loaf. **3.** a piece of stale bread. **4.** the pastry containing the filling of a pie or other dish. **5.** any hard external covering or coating, as of ice or snow. **6.** a scab. **7.** the outer layer of the earth, about 22 mi. (35 km) deep under the continents and 6 mi. (10 km) deep under the oceans. **8.** *Slang.* presumption; gall. **—*v.t., v.i.* 9.** to cover or become covered with a crust. **10.** to form into a crust. **—crust′al,** *adj.* **—crust′less,** *adj.*

crus•ta•cean (kru stā′shən), *n.* **1.** any chiefly aquatic arthropod of the class Crustacea, typically having the body covered with a hard shell, including lobsters, shrimps, crabs, barnacles, and wood lice. **—*adj.* 2.** belonging or pertaining to the Crustacea.

crus•ta•ceous (kru stā′shəs), *adj.* **1.** of the nature of or pertaining to a crust or shell. **2.** CRUSTACEAN. **3.** having a hard covering or crust.

crust•y (krus′tē), *adj.,* **crust•i•er, crust•i•est. 1.** having a crisp or thick crust: *crusty bread.* **2.** of the nature of or resembling a crust. **3.** testy; cantankerous. **—crust′i•ly,** *adv.* **—crust′i•ness,** *n.*

crutch (kruch), *n.* **1.** a staff or support to assist a lame or infirm person in walking, usu. having a crosspiece at one end to fit under the armpit. **2.** anything that serves as a temporary support; prop: *the use of liquor as a psychological crutch.* **3.** CROTCH (def. 1). **4.** a forked support for a boom, spar, oar, etc. **5.** a forked support for the legs on the left side of a sidesaddle. **—*v.t.* 6.** to support on or as if on crutches. **—crutch′like′,** *adj.*

crux (kruks), *n., pl.* **crux•es, cru•ces** (kro͞o′sēz). **1.** the central or pivotal point; essence: *the crux of the matter.* **2.** a perplexing and unresolved difficulty. **3.** a cross.

Crux (kruks), *n., gen.* **Cru•cis** (kro͞o′sis). *Astron.* SOUTHERN CROSS.

cru•zei•ro (kro͞o zâr′ō), *n., pl.* **-zei•ros.** the basic monetary unit of Brazil.

cry (krī), *v.,* **cried, cry•ing,** *n., pl.* **cries. —*v.i.* 1.** to utter inarticulate sounds, esp. of grief or suffering, usu. with tears. **2.** to shed tears, with or without sound; weep. **3.** to call loudly; shout (sometimes fol. by *out*). **4.** to manifest urgent need for attention (often fol. by *out*): *decaying streets that cry out for repair.* **5.** (of an animal) to give forth a vocal sound or characteristic call. **—*v.t.* 6.** to utter loudly; call out. **7.** to announce publicly: *to cry one's wares.* **8.** to beg or plead for: *to cry mercy.* **9.** to bring (oneself) to a specified state by weeping: *to cry oneself to sleep.* **10. cry down,** to disparage; belittle. **11. cry off,** to break a promise, agreement, etc. **12. cry up,** to praise; extol. **—*n.* 13.** the act or sound of crying; a shout, scream, or wail. **14.** a fit of weeping. **15.** the utterance or call of an animal. **16.** an entreaty; appeal. **17.** a political or party slogan. **18.** (in fox hunting) **a.** a continuous baying of a hound or a pack in following a scent. **b.** a pack of hounds. **—*Idiom.* 19. a far cry, a.** a long way. **b.** altogether different. **20. cry all the way to the bank,** (used ironically) to affect remorse while enjoying the fruit of one's wrongdoing. **21. cry havoc,** to warn of danger or disaster. **22. cry in the wilderness,** a prophet's outcry in the face of ignorance and sin. Is. 40:3; Matt. 3:3. **23. cry over spilled milk,** to regret what cannot be changed or undone. **24. in full cry,** in excited, intense pursuit.

cry•ba•by (krī′bā′bē), *n., pl.* **-bies.** a person who cries or complains readily or often, esp. with little cause.

cry•ing (krī′ing), *adj.* **1.** demanding attention or remedy: *a crying evil.* **2.** abominable; flagrant: *a crying shame.* **—cry′ing•ly,** *adv.*

cryo-, a combining form meaning "freezing cold," "frost": *cryogenics.*

cry·o·bi·ol·o·gy (krī′ō bī ol′ə jē), *n.* the study of the effects of very low temperatures on living organisms and biological systems. —**cry′o·bi′o·log′i·cal** (-ə loj′i kəl), *adj.* —**cry′o·bi·ol′o·gist**, *n.*

cry·o·gen·ic (krī′ə jen′ik), *adj.* of or pertaining to the production or use of extremely low temperatures. —**cry′o·gen′i·cal·ly**, *adv.*

cry·o·gen·ics (krī′ə jen′iks), *n.* (*used with a sing. v.*) the scientific study of extremely low temperatures.

cry·o·lite (krī′ə līt′), *n.* a mineral, sodium aluminum fluoride, Na$_3$AlF$_6$, occurring in white masses, used as a flux in the electrolytic production of aluminum.

cry·on·ics (krī on′iks), *n.* (*used with a sing. v.*) the deep-freezing of human bodies at death for preservation and possible revival in the future. —**cry·on′ic**, *adj.*

cry·o·phyte (krī′ə fīt′), *n.* **1.** any plant that grows on ice or snow, as certain algae, mosses, fungi, and bacteria. **2.** any low-growing plant of the genus *Cryophytum*, certain species of which form extensive mats along coastal lands.

cry·o·sur·ger·y (krī′ō sûr′jə rē), *n.* the use of extreme cold to destroy tissue for therapeutic purposes. —**cry′o·sur′gi·cal**, *adj.*

cry·o·ther·a·py (krī′ō ther′ə pē), *n.* medical treatment by means of applications of cold.

crypt (kript), *n.* **1.** a subterranean chamber or vault, esp. one beneath the main floor of a church, used as a burial place, a location for secret meetings, etc. **2.** *Anat.* **a.** any recess or depression. **b.** a small glandular cavity. [< Latin < Greek *kryptḗ* hidden place]

crypt·a·nal·y·sis (krip′tə nal′ə sis), *n.* **1.** the procedures, methods, etc., used to translate or interpret secret writings, as codes and ciphers, for which the key is unknown. **2.** the science or study of such procedures. Compare CRYPTOGRAPHY. —**crypt′an·a·lyt′ic** (-tan l it′ik), *adj.* —**crypt′an·a·lyt′i·cal·ly**, *adv.* —**crypt′an′a·lyst** (-ist), *n.*

cryp·tic (krip′tik) also **cryp′ti·cal**, *adj.* **1.** mysterious in meaning; puzzling. **2.** secret; occult: *cryptic writing.* **3.** involving or using cipher or code. **4.** *Zool.* fitted for concealing; serving to camouflage. —**cryp′ti·cal·ly**, *adv.*

crypto-, a combining form meaning "hidden," "not perceived immediately or with certainty" (*cryptocrystalline; cryptozoology*), "secret" (*cryptogram*), "not professing openly" (*crypto-fascist*), "pertaining to cryptograms" (*cryptology*).

cryp·to·gam (krip′tə gam′), *n.* a plant that bears no true flowers or seeds and that reproduces by spores, as the ferns, mosses, fungi, and algae. —**cryp′to·gam′ic**, **cryp·tog′a·mous** (-tog′ə məs), *adj.*

cryp·to·gram (krip′tə gram′), *n.* **1.** a message or writing in code or cipher. **2.** an occult symbol or representation. —**cryp′to·gram′mic**, **cryp′to·gram·mat′ic** (-grə mat′ik), *adj.*

cryp·to·graph (krip′tə graf′, -gräf′), *n.* **1.** CRYPTOGRAM (def. 1). **2.** a system of secret writing; cipher. **3.** a device for translating text into cipher.

cryp·tog·ra·phy (krip tog′rə fē), *n.* the study or the application of the techniques of secret writing, esp. code and cipher systems. Compare CRYPTANALYSIS. —**cryp·tog′ra·pher**, —**cryp′to·graph′ic** (-tə graf′ik), *adj.* —**cryp′to·graph′i·cal·ly**, *adv.*

cryp·tol·o·gy (krip tol′ə jē), *n.* the science and study of cryptanalysis and cryptography. —**cryp·tol′o·gist**, *n.* —**cryp′to·log′ic** (-tl oj′ik), **cryp′to·log′i·cal**, *adj.*

crys·tal (kris′tl), *n.* **1.** a clear, transparent mineral or glass resembling ice. **2.** the transparent form of crystallized quartz. **3.** a solid body having a characteristic internal structure and enclosed by symmetrically arranged plane surfaces, intersecting at definite and characteristic angles. **4.** a single grain or mass of a crystalline substance. **5.** glass of fine quality and a high degree of brilliance. **6.** glassware, esp. for the table and ornamental objects, made of such glass. **7.** the glass or plastic cover over the face of a watch. **8.** a quartz crystal shaped to vibrate at a particular frequency, used to control the frequency of an oscillator. **9.** *Slang.* any stimulant drug in solid form, as methamphetamine. —*adj.* **10.** composed or made of crystal. **11.** resembling crystal; clear; transparent. —**crys′tal·like′**, *adj.*

crys′tal ball′, **1.** a glass ball used in crystal gazing. **2.** a method or means of predicting the future.

crys′tal-clear′, *adj.* perfectly clear, transparent, or lucid.

crys′tal gaz′ing, *n.* **1.** the practice of staring into a crystal ball to divine distant events or the future. **2.** speculation about the future. —**crys′tal gaz′er**, *n.*

crys·tal·line (kris′tl in, -īn′, -ēn′), *adj.* **1.** of or like crystal; clear; transparent. **2.** formed by crystallization. **3.** composed of crystals. **4.** pertaining to crystals or their formation.

crys·tal·lize (kris′tl īz′), *v.*, **-lized, -liz·ing.** —*v.t.* **1.** to form into crystals; cause to assume crystalline form. **2.** to give definite or concrete form to: *to crystallize an idea.* **3.** to coat with sugar. —*v.i.* **4.** to form crystals; become crystalline in form. **5.** to assume definite or concrete form. —**crys′tal·li·za′tion**, *n.* —**crys′tal·liz′er**, *n.*

crys·tal·log·ra·phy (kris′tl og′rə fē), *n.* the study of crystallization and the forms and structure of crystals. —**crys′tal·log′ra·pher**, *n.* —**crys′tal·lo·graph′ic** (-ə graf′ik), **crys′tal·lo·graph′i·cal**, *adj.*

Cs, *Chem. Symbol.* cesium.

C/S, cycles per second.

C-sec·tion (sē′sek′shən), *n. Informal.* CESAREAN.

CST or **C.S.T.** or **c.s.t.**, Central Standard Time.

CT, **1.** Also **C.T.** Central time. **2.** Connecticut.

Ct., **1.** Connecticut. **2.** Count.

ct., **1.** carat. **2.** cent. **3.** centum. **4.** certificate. **5.** county. **6.** court.

cten·o·phore (ten′ə fôr′, -fōr′, tē′nə-), *n.* COMB JELLY.

CT scan, *n.* CAT SCAN.

CT scanner, *n.* CAT SCANNER.

Cu, *Chem. Symbol.* copper. [< Latin *cuprum*]

cub (kub), *n.* **1.** the young of certain animals, esp. the bear, wolf, lion, and whale. **2.** a young shark. **3.** a young and inexperienced person, esp. a callow youth or young man. **4.** a young person serving as an apprentice.

Cu·ba (kyōō′bə), *n.* **1.** an island of the Greater Antilles, in the West Indies, S of Florida. **2.** a republic in the Caribbean, including this island and several nearby islands. 10,999,041; 44,206 sq. mi. (114,524 sq. km). *Cap.:* Havana. —**Cu′ban**, *adj., n.*

Cu′ban mis′sile cri′sis, *n.* a confrontation in 1962 between the United States and the Soviet Union after the installation of Soviet ballistic missile sites began in Cuba.

Cu′ban sand′wich, *n. Chiefly Southern Florida and New York City.* a hero sandwich, esp. with ham, pork, cheese, and pickles, often grilled.

cub·by (kub′ē), *n., pl.* **-bies. 1.** a cubbyhole. **2.** a small, open, boxlike compartment or cupboard, as one used by children for storage.

cub·by·hole (kub′ē hōl′), *n.* **1.** a pigeonhole. **2.** a small, snug place.

cube[1] (kyōōb), *n., v.,* **cubed, cub·ing.** —*n.* **1.** a solid bounded by six equal squares, the angle between any two adjacent faces being a right angle. **2.** an object, either solid or hollow, having or approximating this form: *a sugar cube; plastic storage cubes.* **3.** the third power of a quantity, expressed as $a^3 = a \times a \times a$. **4.** *Slang.* one of a pair of dice; die. —*v.t.* **5.** to make into a cube or cubes. **6.** to cut into cubes. **7.** to raise (a quantity or number) to the third power. **8.** to measure the cubic contents of. **9.** to tenderize (meat) by scoring the fibers in a pattern of small squares. —**cub′er**, *n.*

cu·be[2] or **cu·bé** (kyōō′bā, kyōō bā′), *n., pl.* **-bes** or **-bés.** any of several tropical plants of the legume family, used in making poisons and insecticides.

cu·beb (kyōō′beb), *n.* the spicy fruit or drupe of an East Indian climbing shrub, *Piper cubeba*, of the pepper family.

cube′ root′, *n.* a quantity of which a given quantity is the cube: *The cube root of 64 is 4.*

cu·bic (kyōō′bik), *adj.* **1.** having three dimensions; solid. **2.** having the form of a cube; cubical. **3.** pertaining to the measurement of volume: *the cubic contents.* **4.** pertaining to a unit of linear measure that is multiplied by itself twice to form a unit of measure for volume: *a cubic foot; a cubic centimeter.* **5.** *Math.* of or pertaining to the third degree. **6.** belonging or pertaining to the isometric system of crystallization. —*n.* **7.** a cubic polynomial or equation.

cu·bi·cal (kyōō′bi kəl), *adj.* **1.** having the form of a cube. **2.** pertaining to volume. —**cu′bi·cal·ly**, *adv.* —**cu′bi·cal·ness**, *n.*

cu·bi·cle (kyōō′bi kəl), *n.* a small space or compartment partitioned off in a large room or area.

cu′bic zir·co′ni·a (zûr kō′nē ə), *n., pl.* **-ni·as.** an artificial crystal resembling a diamond in refraction, dispersion, hardness, and color, used in jewelry. *Abbr.:* CZ Sometimes, **cu′bic zirco′nium.**

cub·ism (kyōō′biz əm), *n.* (*sometimes cap.*) a style of painting and sculpture marked esp. by the reduction of natural forms to their geometrical equivalents and the reorganization of the planes of a represented object. —**cub′ist**, *n.* —**cub·is′tic**, *adj.*

cu·bit (kyōō′bit), *n.* an ancient linear unit based on the length of the forearm from the elbow to the tip of the middle finger, usu. from 17 to 21 inches (43 to 53 cm).

cu·boid (kyōō′boid), *adj.* Also, **cu·boi′dal. 1.** shaped like a cube. **2.** pertaining to the tarsal bone above the fourth metatarsal in mammals. —*n.* **3.** a rectangular parallelepiped. **4.** the cuboid bone.

cub′ report′er, *n.* a young, inexperienced newspaper reporter.

cub′ scout′, *n.* (*sometimes caps.*) a member of the junior division (ages 8–10) of the Boy Scouts.

cuck·old (kuk′əld), *n.* **1.** the husband of an unfaithful wife. —*v.t.* **2.** to make a cuckold of (a husband).

cuck·oo (kōō′kōō, kŏŏk′ōō), *n., pl.* **-oos,** *v.,* **-ooed, -oo·ing,** *adj.* —*n.* **1.** any of various usu. slim, stout-billed, long-tailed birds of the order Cuculiformes, of worldwide distribution: many species noted for their brood parasitism. **2.** a common Eurasian cuckoo, *Cuculus canorus,* with a monotonously repeated call. **3.** the call of this cuckoo, or an imitation of it. **4.** *Informal.* a crazy, silly, or foolish person. —*v.i.* **5.** to utter or imitate the call of the cuckoo. —*v.t.* **6.** to repeat monotonously. —*adj.* **7.** *Informal.* crazy; silly; foolish.

cuck′oo clock′, *n.* a clock that announces the hours by a sound like the call of the cuckoo, usu. accompanied by the appearance of an imitation bird through a little door.

cuck·oo·flow·er (kōō′kōō flou′ər, kŏŏk′ōō-), *n.* any of various plants, as the lady's-smock or ragged robin, whose time of blooming is associated with the cuckoo's spring call.

cu·cum·ber (kyōō′kum bər), *n.* **1.** a creeping plant, *Cucumis sativus,* of the gourd family, occurring in many cultivated forms. **2.** the edible fleshy green-skinned fruit of this plant, of a cylindrical shape with rounded ends.

cu′cumber tree′, *n.* any of several American magnolias, esp. *Magnolia acuminata,* having dark red conelike fruit.

cu·cur·bit (kyōō kûr′bit), *n.* **1.** a gourd. **2.** any plant of the gourd family. **3.** the gourd-shaped portion of an alembic.

cud (kud), *n.* **1.** the coarse food regurgitated by a ruminant from its first stomach for further chewing. **2.** *Dial.* QUID¹. —*Idiom.* **3.** chew one's or **the cud,** *Informal.* to meditate or ponder.

cud·bear (kud′bâr′), *n.* a violet coloring matter obtained from various lichens, esp. *Lecanora tartarea.*

cud·dle (kud′l), *v.,* **-dled, -dling,** *n.* —*v.t.* **1.** to hold close in an affectionate manner; hug tenderly; fondle. —*v.i.* **2.** to lie close and snug; nestle. —*n.* **3.** an act of cuddling; hug; embrace.

cudg·el (kuj′əl), *n., v.,* **-eled, -el·ing,** or (*esp. Brit.*) **-elled, -el·ling.** —*n.* **1.** a short, thick stick used as a weapon; club. —*v.t.* **2.** to strike with a cudgel; beat. —*Idiom.* **3. cudgel one's brains,** to try hard to comprehend or remember. **4. take up the cudgels,** to come to the defense or support of someone or something.

cud·weed (kud′wēd′), *n.* any of the woolly composite plants of the genus *Gnaphalium,* having simple leaves and tubular flowers.

cue¹ (kyōō), *n., v.,* **cued, cu·ing.** —*n.* **1.** anything said or done, on or off stage, that is followed by a specific line or action: *The gunshot is your cue to enter.* **2.** anything that excites to action; stimulus. **3.** a hint; intimation; guiding suggestion. **4.** a sensory signal that serves to elicit a behavioral response. **5.** the part a person is to play; a prescribed or necessary course of action. —*v.t.* **6.** to give a cue to; prompt. **7.** to insert, or direct to come in, in a specific place in a performance (often fol. by *in*): *to cue in a lighting effect.* **8.** to search for and reach (a track on a recording). **9. cue in,** *Informal.* to give information, news, etc., to; inform.

cue² (kyōō), *n., v.,* **cued, cu·ing.** —*n.* **1.** a tapering rod, tipped with leather, used to strike the ball in pool, billiards, etc. **2.** a stick used to propel the disks in shuffleboard. **3.** QUEUE (defs. 1, 2). —*v.t.* **4.** to strike with a cue. **5.** to tie (hair) into a queue.

cue³ (kyōō), *n.* the letter *Q, q.*

cue′ ball′, *n.* (in billiards or pool) the usu. white ball a player strikes with the cue, as distinguished from the object balls.

cues·ta (kwes′tə), *n., pl.* **-tas.** a long, low ridge with a relatively steep face or escarpment on one side and a long, gentle slope on the other.

cuff¹ (kuf), *n.* **1.** a fold or band serving as a trim or finish, esp. at the bottom of a sleeve. **2.** the turned-up fold at the bottom of a trouser leg. **3.** the part of a glove that extends over the wrist. **4.** a handcuff. **5.** a band of muscle encircling a joint. **6.** an inflatable wrap placed around the upper arm and used with a device for recording blood pressure. —*v.t.* **7.** to make a cuff on. **8.** to handcuff. —*Idiom.* **9. off the cuff,** *Informal.* extemporaneously; on the spur of the moment.

cuff² (kuf), *v.t.* **1.** to strike, esp. with the open hand. —*n.* **2.** a blow with the fist or the open hand.

cuff′ link′ or **cuff′link′,** *n.* one of a pair of linked ornamental buttons or buttonlike devices for fastening a shirt cuff.

cu. ft., cubic foot.

cui bo·no (kōōi bō′nō; *Eng.* kwē′ bō′nō, kī′-), *Latin.* for whose benefit?

cu. in., cubic inch.

cui·rass (kwi ras′), *n.* **1.** plate armor covering the torso from neck to waist. **2.** either of the two plates of a cuirass. **3.** any similar covering, as a ship's armor. **4.** a hard shell or other covering on an animal forming a defensive shield. —*v.t.* **5.** to equip or cover with a cuirass.

cui·sine (kwi zēn′), *n.* **1.** a style or manner of cooking: *Italian cuisine.* **2.** the food prepared, as by a restaurant.

cul-de-sac (kul′də sak′, -sak′, kōōl′-), *n., pl.* **culs-de-sac. 1.** a street, lane, etc., closed at one end; blind alley; dead-end street. **2.** any situation in which further progress is impossible. **3.** a saclike anatomical cavity or tube open at only one end, as the cecum.

cu·lex (kyōō′leks), *n., pl.* **-li·ces** (-lə sēz′). any of numerous mosquitoes constituting the genus *Culex,* standing with the body parallel to surfaces, including the common house mosquito, *C. pipiens.* —**cu′li·cine′** (-lə sīn′, -sin), *adj.*

cu·li·nar·y (kyōō′lə ner′ē, kul′ə-), *adj.* of, pertaining to, or used in cooking or the kitchen: *the culinary arts.* —**cu′li·nar′i·ly,** *adv.*

cull (kul), *v.t.* **1.** to choose; select; pick. **2.** to gather the choice things or parts from. **3.** to collect; gather; pluck. —*n.* **4.** the act of culling. **5.** something culled, esp. something picked out and put aside as inferior. —**cull′er,** *n.*

cul·let (kul′it), *n.* broken or waste glass suitable for remelting.

culm¹ (kulm), *n.* **1.** coal dust; slack. **2.** anthracite, esp. of inferior grade.

culm² (kulm), *n.* **1.** a stem or stalk, esp. the jointed and usu. hollow stem of grasses. **2.** a stem forming a culm.

cul·mi·nate (kul′mə nāt′), *v.,* **-nat·ed, -nat·ing.** —*v.i.* **1.** to reach the highest point or highest development (usu. fol. by *in*). **2.** to arrive at a final or climactic stage (usu. fol. by *in*). **3.** to rise to or form an apex; terminate (usu. fol. by *in*): *a tower culminating in a tall spire.* **4.** (of a celestial body) to be on the meridian, or reach the highest or the lowest altitude. —*v.t.* **5.** to bring to a close; complete.

cul·mi·na·tion (kul′mə nā′shən), *n.* **1.** the act or fact of culminating. **2.** that in which anything culminates; highest point; acme. **3.** the position of a celestial body when it is on the meridian.

cu·lottes (kōō lots′, kyōō-) also **cu·lotte′,** *n.* (*used with a pl. v.*) women's trousers, usu. knee-length or calf-length, cut full to resemble a skirt.

cul·pa (kul′pə, kōōl′-), *n., pl.* **-pae** (-pē, -pī). **1.** *Law.* negligence; neglect. **2.** fault; guilt.

cul·pa·ble (kul′pə bəl), *adj.* deserving blame or censure. —**cul′pa·bil′i·ty,** *n.* —**cul′pa·bly,** *adv.*

Cul·pep·er (kul′pep′ər), *n.* **Thomas** (*2nd Baron Culpeper of Thoresway*), 1635–89, English colonial governor of Virginia 1680–83.

cul·prit (kul′prit), *n.* **1.** a person guilty of an offense or fault. **2.** a person accused of or arraigned for an offense.

cult (kult), *n.* **1.** a particular system of religious worship, esp. with reference to its rites and ceremonies. **2.** a group that devotes itself to or venerates a person, ideal, fad, etc. **3. a.** a religion or sect considered to be false, unorthodox, or extremist. **b.** the members of such a religion or sect. —*adj.* **4.** of or pertaining to a cult. **5.** of, for, or attracting a small group of devotees: *a cult movie.* —**cul′tic,** *adj.* —**cult′ish,** *adj.* —**cult′ism,** *n.* —**cult′ist,** *n.*

cul·ti·vate (kul′tə vāt′), *v.t.,* **-vat·ed, -vat·ing. 1.** to prepare and work on (land) in order to raise crops; till. **2.** to use a cultivator on. **3.** to promote or improve the growth of (a plant or crop) by labor and attention. **4.** to produce by culture: *to cultivate a strain of bacteria.* **5.** to develop or improve by education or training: *to cultivate a talent.* **6.** to promote the growth or development of (an art, science, etc.); foster. **7.** to devote oneself to (an art, science, etc.). **8.** to seek to promote or foster (friendship, love, etc.). **9.** to seek the acquaintance or friendship of (a person). —**cul′ti·va·ble,** *adj.*

cul·ti·vat·ed (kul′tə vā′tid), *adj.* **1.** prepared and used for raising crops; tilled: *cultivated land.* **2.** produced or improved by cultivation, as a plant. **3.** educated; refined; cultured: *cultivated tastes.*

cul·ti·va·tion (kul′tə vā′shən), *n.* **1.** the act or art of cultivating. **2.** the state of being cultivated. **3.** culture; refinement.

cult′ of personal′ity, *n.* a cult promoting adulation of a living national leader or public figure, as one encouraged by Stalin to extend his power.

cul·trate (kul′trāt) also **cul′trat·ed,** *adj.* sharp-edged and pointed, as a leaf.

cul·tur·al (kul′chər əl), *adj.* **1.** of or pertaining to culture. **2.** of or pertaining to cultivation. —**cul′tur·al·ly,** *adv.*

cul′tural anthropol′ogy, *n.* the branch of anthropology dealing with the origins, history, and development of human culture, esp. its social forms and institutions. Compare PHYSICAL ANTHROPOLOGY. —**cul′tural anthropol′ogist,** *n.*

cul·tur·al·ize (kul′chər ə līz′), *v.t.,* **-ized, -iz·ing.** to expose or subject to the influence of culture. —**cul′tur·al·i·za′tion,** *n.*

cul′tural lag′ or **cul′ture lag′,** *n.* slowness in the rate of change of one part of a culture in relation to another part, resulting in a maladjustment within society.

Cul′tural Revolu′tion, *n.* a political movement in China (1966–69) launched by Mao Zedong to restore revolutionary zeal.

cul·ture (kul′chər), *n., v.,* **-tured, -tur·ing.** —*n.* **1.** artistic and intellectual pursuits and products. **2.** a quality of enlightenment or refinement arising from an acquaintance with and concern for what is regarded as excellent in the arts, letters, manners, etc. **3.** development or improvement of the mind by education or training. **4.** the sum total of ways of living built up by a group of human beings and transmitted from one generation to another. **5.** a particular form or stage of civilization, as that of a nation or period: *Greek culture.* **6.** the behaviors and beliefs characteristic of a particular social, ethnic, or age group: *youth culture; the drug culture.* **7. a.** the cultivation of microorganisms, as bacteria, or of tissues, for scientific study, medicinal use, etc. **b.** the product or growth resulting from such cultivation. **8.** the act or practice of cultivating the soil; tillage. **9.** the raising of plants or animals, esp. with a view to their improvement. —*v.t.* **10.** to subject to culture; cultivate. **11. a.** to grow (microorganisms, tissues, etc.) in or on a controlled or defined medium. **b.** to introduce (living material) into a culture medium.

cul·tured (kul′chərd), *adj.* **1.** enlightened; refined. **2.** artificially nurtured or grown: *cultured bacteria.* **3.** cultivated; tilled.

cul′tured pearl′, *n.* a pearl induced to form by placement of a grain of sand or another irritating object within the shell of a pearl oyster or mussel.

cul′ture shock′, *n.* a state of bewilderment and distress experienced by an individual who is exposed to a new, strange, or foreign culture.

cul·vert (kul′vərt), *n.* a drain or channel crossing under a road, sidewalk, etc.; sewer; conduit.

cum (kum, kōōm), *prep.* with; combined with; along with (usu. used in combination): *a garage-cum-workshop.*

Cu·mae (kyōō′mē), *n.* an ancient city in SW Italy, on the coast of Campania: believed to be the earliest Greek colony in Italy or Sicily. —**Cu·mae′an,** *adj.*

cum·ber (kum′bər), *v.t.* **1.** to hinder; hamper. **2.** to overload; burden. **3.** to inconvenience; trouble. —*n.* **4.** a hindrance. **5.** something that cumbers.

Cum′berland Gap′, *n.* a pass in the Cumberland Mountains at the junction of the Virginia, Kentucky, and Tennessee boundaries. 1315 ft. (401 m) high.

Cum′berland Moun′tains, *n.pl.* a plateau largely in Kentucky and

Tennessee, a part of the Appalachian Mountains: highest point, ab. 4000 ft. (1220 m). Also called **Cum′berland Plateau′.**

cum•ber•some (kum′bər səm), *adj.* **1.** burdensome; heavy or bulky. **2.** unwieldy; clumsy.

cum•brance (kum′brəns), *n.* **1.** trouble; bother. **2.** burden; encumbrance.

cum•in (kum′ən, kŏŏm′- *or, often,* kŏŏ′mən, kyŏŏ′-), *n.* **1.** a small plant, *Cuminum cyminum,* of the parsley family, bearing aromatic, seedlike fruit used as a spice in cooking. **2.** the fruit or seeds of this plant.

cum lau•de (kŏŏm lou′dä, -də, -dē; kum lô′dē), *adv.* with honor: used in diplomas to grant the lowest of three special honors for grades above the average. Compare MAGNA CUM LAUDE, SUMMA CUM LAUDE.

cum•mer•bund (kum′ər bund′), *n.* a wide sash worn at the waist, esp. a horizontally pleated one worn with a tuxedo.

cu•mu•late (*v.* kyŏŏ′myə lāt′; *adj.* -lit, -lāt′), *v.,* **-lat•ed, -lat•ing,** *adj.* —*v.t.* **1.** to heap up; amass; accumulate. —*adj.* **2.** heaped up. —**cu′mu•late•ly,** *adv.* —**cu′mu•la′tion,** *n.*

cu•mu•la•tive (kyŏŏ′myə lə tiv, -lā′tiv), *adj.* **1.** increasing or growing by accumulation or successive additions. **2.** formed by or resulting from accumulation or the addition of successive parts or elements. **3.** of or pertaining to interest or dividends that, if not paid when due, become a prior claim for payment in the future. —**cu′mu•la•tive•ly,** *adv.*

cu•mu•lo•nim•bus (kyŏŏ′myə lō nim′bəs), *n., pl.* **-bi** (-bī), **-bus•es.** a cloud indicative of thunderstorm conditions, characterized by large, dense towers that may penetrate the upper limits of the troposphere.

cu•mu•lus (kyŏŏ′myə ləs), *n., pl.* **-li** (-lī′). **1.** a cloud of a class characterized by dense individual elements in the form of puffs, mounds, or towers, with flat bases and tops that often resemble cauliflower. **2.** a heap; pile.

cu•ne•ate (kyŏŏ′nē it, -āt′) *also* **cu′ne•at′ed,** *adj.* **1.** wedge-shaped. **2.** (of leaves) triangular at the base and tapering to a point. —**cu′ne•ate•ly,** *adv.*

cu•ne•i•form (kyŏŏ nē′ə fôrm′, kyŏŏ′nē ə-), *adj.* **1.** having the form of a wedge; wedge-shaped. **2.** composed of slim triangular or wedge-shaped elements, as the characters used in writing by the ancient Akkadians, Assyrians, Babylonians, Persians, and others. **3.** of or pertaining to any wedge-shaped bone, as certain tarsal bones. —*n.* **4.** cuneiform characters or writing.

cuneiform inscription (Persian)

cun•ner (kun′ər), *n.* a small Atlantic wrasse.

cun•ning (kun′ing), *n.* **1.** skill employed in a shrewd or sly manner, as in deceiving; craftiness; guile. **2.** adeptness in performance; dexterity: *The weaver's hand lost its cunning.* —*adj.* **3.** showing or made with ingenuity. **4.** artfully subtle or shrewd; crafty; sly. **5.** charmingly cute or appealing: *a cunning little baby.* —**cun′ning•ly,** *adv.*

cup (kup), *n., v.,* **cupped, cup•ping.** —*n.* **1.** a small, open container made of china, glass, metal, etc., usu. with a handle, used chiefly as a drinking vessel for hot beverages. **2.** the bowllike part of a goblet or the like. **3.** a cup with its contents. **4.** the quantity contained in a cup. **5.** a unit of capacity equal to 8 fluid ounces (237 milliliters) or 16 tablespoons; half pint. **6.** an ornamental bowl, vase, etc., esp. of precious metal, offered as a prize for a contest. **7.** any of various mixed drinks, as wine with fruit and other ingredients. **8.** the chalice or wine used in the Eucharist. **9.** something to be partaken of or endured; one's portion, as of joy or suffering. **10. cups,** the drinking of intoxicating liquors. **11.** any cuplike utensil, organ, part, cavity, etc. **12.** either of the two forms that cover the breasts in a brassiere. **13.** an athletic supporter protectively reinforced with rigid plastic or metal. **14. a.** the metal receptacle within a golf hole. **b.** the hole itself. —*v.t.* **15.** to take, place, or hold in or as if in a cup. **16.** to form into a cuplike shape: *to cup one's hands.* **17.** to use a cupping glass on. —*Idiom.* **18. in one's cups,** intoxicated; drunk. **19. one's cup of tea,** something suited or attractive to one.

cup•board (kub′ərd), *n.* a closet with shelves for dishes, food, etc.

cup•cake (kup′kāk′), *n.* a small cake, the size of an individual portion, baked in a cup-shaped mold.

cup′ fun′gus, *n.* any small, cup-shaped, usu. brightly colored mushroom of the family Pezizaceae.

Cu•pid (kyŏŏ′pid), *n.* **1.** the Roman god of carnal love, the son of Venus, commonly represented as a winged, naked infant boy with a bow and arrows. **2.** (*l.c.*) a representation of Cupid, esp. as symbolic of love.

cu•pid•i•ty (kyŏŏ pid′i tē), *n.* eager or excessive desire, esp. to possess something; greed; avarice.

Cu′pid's bow′ (bō), *n.* **1.** a classical bow; the bow Cupid is traditionally pictured as bearing. **2.** a line or shape resembling this, esp. the line of the upper lip.

cu•po•la (kyŏŏ′pə lə), *n., pl.* **-las. 1. a.** a light structure on a dome or roof, serving as a belfry, lantern, or belvedere. **b.** a dome, esp. one covering a circular or polygonal area. **2.** any of various domelike structures. **3.** a vertical furnace for melting iron to be cast.

cupola (def. 1a)

cu•prite (kyŏŏ′prīt, kŏŏ′-), *n.* a mineral, cuprous oxide, Cu_2O, occurring in red crystals and brown to black granular masses: an ore of copper.

cu•pro•nick•el (kyŏŏ′prə nik′əl, kŏŏ′-), *n.* any of various alloys of copper containing up to 40 percent nickel.

cur (kûr), *n.* **1.** a mongrel dog, esp. a worthless or unfriendly one. **2.** a mean, cowardly person.

cu•ra•re *or* **cu•ra•ri** (kyŏŏ rär′ē, kŏŏ-), *n.* **1.** a blackish, resinlike substance derived chiefly from tropical plants belonging to the genus *Strychnos,* of the logania family, esp. *S. toxifera,* used as an arrow poison for its effect of arresting the action of motor nerves. **2.** a plant yielding this substance.

cu•ras•sow (kyŏŏr′ə sō′, kyŏŏ ras′ō), *n.* any of several large gallinaceous birds of the guan family, esp. of the genus *Crax,* typically crested, with bony knobs or casques above the bill.

cu•rate (kyŏŏr′it), *n.* **1.** a cleric assisting a rector or vicar. **2.** a cleric in charge of a parish. —**cu′rate•ship′,** *n.*

cu•ra•tive (kyŏŏr′ə tiv), *adj.* **1.** serving to cure or heal; pertaining to curing or remedial treatment; remedial. —*n.* **2.** a curative agent; remedy. —**cur′a•tive•ly,** *adv.*

cu•ra•tor (kyŏŏ rā′tər, kyŏŏr′ā-), *n.* **1.** the person in charge of a museum, art collection, zoo, etc. **2.** a manager or overseer; superintendent. —**cu′ra•to′ri•al** (-ə tôr′ē əl, -tōr′-), *adj.*

curb (kûrb), *n.* **1.** a rim, esp. of joined stones or concrete, along a street or roadway, forming an edge for a sidewalk. **2.** anything that restrains or controls; restraint; check. **3.** an enclosing framework or border. **4.** Also called **curb′ bit′.** a bit to which a chain (**curb′ chain′**) is hooked to control a horse. **5.** Also called **curb′ mar′ket.** a market, orig. on the sidewalk or street, for the sale of securities not listed on a stock exchange. **6.** a swelling on the lower part of the back of the hock of a horse, often causing lameness. —*v.t.* **7.** to control with or as if with a curb; restrain; check. **8.** to cause (a dog) to keep near the curb when defecating. **9.** to furnish with or protect by a curb. **10.** to put a curb on (a horse). Also, *Brit.,* **kerb** (for defs. 1, 5, 9). —**curb′a•ble,** *adj.*

curb•ing (kûr′bing), *n.* **1.** the material forming a curb, as along a street. **2.** a curb, or a section of a curb.

curb•side (kûrb′sīd′), *n.* **1.** a side of a pavement or street bordered by a curb. —*adj.* **2.** being adjacent to a curb: *the car's curbside door.*

cur•cu•li•o (kûr kyŏŏ′lē ō′), *n., pl.* **-li•os.** any of several weevils, esp. of the genus *Conotrachelus,* that feed on fruits.

cur•cu•ma (kûr′kyŏŏ mə), *n., pl.* **-mas.** any of various chiefly Old World plants belonging to the ginger family, yielding turmeric.

curd (kûrd), *n.* **1.** a substance consisting mainly of casein, obtained from milk by coagulation and used as food or made into cheese. **2.** any substance resembling this. —*v.t., v.i.* **3.** to turn into curd; curdle.

cur•dle (kûr′dl), *v.t., v.i.,* **-dled, -dling. 1.** to change into curd; coagulate. **2.** to spoil; turn sour or bad. —*Idiom.* **3. curdle one's blood,** to fill one with horror or fear. —**cur′dler,** *n.*

cure (kyŏŏr), *n., v.,* **cured, cur•ing.** —*n.* **1.** a means of healing or restoring to health; remedy. **2.** a method or course of remedial treatment, as for disease. **3.** successful remedial treatment; restoration to health. **4.** a means of correcting or relieving anything troublesome: *to seek a cure for inflation.* **5.** a process or method of preserving meat, fish, etc., by smoking, salting, or the like. **6.** spiritual or religious charge of the people in a certain district. **7.** the office or district of a curate or parish priest. —*v.t.* **8.** to restore to health. **9.** to relieve or rid of (an illness, bad habit, etc.). **10.** to prepare (meat, fish, etc.) for preservation by smoking, salting, etc. **11.** to process (rubber, tobacco, etc.) as by fermentation or aging. **12.** to promote hardening of (fresh concrete or mortar), as by keeping damp. —*v.i.* **13.** to effect a cure. **14.** to become cured. —**cur′a•ble,** *adj.* —**cure′less,** *adj.*

cure′-all′, *n.* a cure for all ills; panacea.

cu•ret•tage (kyŏŏr′i täzh′, kyŏŏ ret′ij), *n.* the process of curetting. Compare D AND C.

cu•rette *or* **cu•ret** (kyŏŏ ret′), *n., v.,* **-ret•ted, -ret•ting.** —*n.* **1.** a scoop-shaped surgical instrument for removing tissue from body cavities, as the uterus. —*v.t.* **2.** to scrape with a curette.

cur•few (kûr′fyŏŏ), *n.* **1.** an order establishing a time in the evening after which certain regulations apply, esp. that no unauthorized persons may be outdoors or that places of public assembly must be closed. **2.** a regulation requiring a person to be home at a stated time, as one imposed by a parent on a child. **3.** the time at which a daily curfew starts. **4.** the period during which a curfew is in effect. **5.** a signal, as the ringing of a bell, announcing the start of the time of a curfew. **6.** a bell for sounding a curfew. [< Anglo-French *coverfeu,* Old French *covrefeu* lit., (it) covers (the) fire; the curfew originally referred to the time in the evening when fires had to be extinguished]

cu•ri•a (kyŏŏr′ē ə), *n., pl.* **cu•ri•ae** (kyŏŏr′ē ē′). **1.** one of the ten political subdivisions of each of the three tribes of ancient Rome. **2.** the building in which such a division met, as for worship or public deliberation. **3.** the senate house in ancient Rome. **4.** (*sometimes cap.*) the body of congregations, offices, etc., that assist the pope in the administration of the Roman Catholic Church. —**cu′ri•al,** *adj.*

cu•rie (kyŏŏr′ē, kyŏŏ rē′), *n.* a unit of activity of radioactive substances equivalent to 3.70 × 10^{10} disintegrations per second. *Abbr.:* Ci [after Marie and Pierre CURIE]

Cu•rie (kyŏŏr′ē, kyŏŏ rē′), *n.* **1. Irène,** JOLIOT-CURIE. **2. Marie,** 1867–1934, Polish physicist and chemist in France: codiscoverer of radium 1898. **3.** her husband, **Pierre,** 1859–1906, French physicist and chemist: codiscoverer of radium.

cu•ri•o (kyŏŏr′ē ō′), *n., pl.* **-ri•os.** a usu. small article, object of art, etc., valued as a curiosity.

cu•ri•os•i•ty (kyŏŏr′ē os′i tē), *n., pl.* **-ties. 1.** the desire to learn or know about anything; inquisitiveness. **2.** a curious, rare, or novel thing. **3.** a strange, curious, or interesting quality. —***Saying.*** **4. Curiosity killed the cat,** being too inquisitive can have bad results.

cu•ri•ous (kyŏŏr′ē əs), *adj.* **1.** eager to learn or know; inquisitive. **2.** taking an undue interest in others' affairs; prying. **3.** arousing attention or interest through being unusual or hard to explain; odd; strange; novel. —**cu′ri•ous•ly,** *adv.*

cu•ri•um (kyŏŏr′ē əm), *n.* a synthetic radioactive element produced from plutonium. *Symbol:* Cm; *at. no.:* 96.

curl (kûrl), *v.t.* **1.** to form into coils or ringlets, as the hair. **2.** to form into a spiral or curved shape; coil. **3.** to adorn with or as if with curls or ringlets. —*v.i.* **4.** to grow in or form curls or ringlets, as the hair. **5.** to become curved or undulated. **6.** to coil. **7.** to play the game of curling. **8.** to move or progress in a curving direction or path. **9. curl up,** to sit or lie down cozily: *to curl up with a good book.* —*n.* **10.** a coil or ringlet of hair. **11.** anything of a spiral or curved shape. **12.** a coil. **13.** the act of curling or the state of being curled. **14.** any disease of plants characterized by curling of the leaves. **15.** a forearm lift in which a weight is raised from the level of the thighs to the chest or shoulders while keeping the legs, upper arms, and shoulders taut. —***Idiom.*** **16. curl one's** or **the hair,** to fill one with horror. **17. curl one's lip,** to raise a corner of one's lip, as in an expression of disdain.

curl•er (kûr′lər), *n.* **1.** a person or thing that curls. **2.** any of various pins, rollers, or appliances on which the hair is wound or clamped for curling. **3.** a player in the game of curling.

cur•lew (kûr′lōō), *n.* any of several large shorebirds of the genus *Numenius,* having a long, slender bill that curves down.

curl•i•cue or **cur•ly•cue** (kûr′li kyōō′), *n.* an ornamental, fancy curl or twist, as in a signature.

curl•ing (kûr′ling), *n.* a game played on ice in which two teams slide curling stones towards a mark in a circle.

curl′ing i′ron (or **i′rons**), *n.* a rod, usu. metal, used when heated to curl the hair, which is twined around it.

curl′ing stone′, *n.* an oblate stone or iron object having a handle on the top by which it is released in the game of curling.

curl•y (kûr′lē), *adj.,* **curl•i•er, curl•i•est. 1.** curling or tending to curl: *curly hair.* **2.** having curls. **3.** (of wood) having a grain with a rippled or undulating appearance: *curly maple.* —**curl′i•ness,** *n.*

curl′y-coat′ed retriev′er, *n.* one of a breed of large dogs with a dense, tightly curled coat, used esp. as a water retriever.

cur•mudg•eon (kər muj′ən), *n.* a bad-tempered, difficult, cantankerous person. —**cur•mudg′eon•ly,** *adj.*

cur•rant (kûr′ənt, kur′-), *n.* **1.** a small seedless raisin, produced chiefly in California and in the Levant, used in cooking. **2.** the small, round, sour berry of certain shrubs of the genus *Ribes,* of the saxifrage family. **3.** the shrub itself.

cur•ren•cy (kûr′ən sē, kur′-), *n., pl.* **-cies. 1.** any form of money that is in circulation as a medium of exchange in a country. **2.** general acceptance; prevalence; vogue. **3.** a time or period during which something is widely accepted. **4.** the fact or quality of being widely accepted and circulated from person to person. **5.** circulation, as of coin.

cur′rency bond′, *n.* a bond payable in legal tender.

cur•rent (kûr′ənt, kur′-), *adj.* **1.** belonging to the time actually passing; present: *the current month.* **2.** generally or commonly used or accepted; prevalent: *current usage in English.* **3.** popular; in vogue. **4.** most recent; new: *the current issue of a magazine.* **5.** publicly or commonly reported or known: *a rumor that is current.* **6.** in circulation, as a coin. —*n.* **7.** a flowing; flow, as of a river. **8.** something that flows, as a stream. **9.** the most rapidly moving part of a stream. **10.** a portion of a large body of water or mass of air moving in a certain direction. **11.** the speed at which such flow moves; velocity of flow. **12.** the movement or flow of electric charge. **13.** a general tendency or course. —**cur′rent•ly,** *adv.*

cur•ric•u•lum (kə rik′yə ləm), *n., pl.* **-la** (-lə), **-lums. 1.** the aggregate of courses given in a school, college, etc. **2.** the regular or a particular course of study in a school, college, etc. —**cur•ric′u•lar,** *adj.*

curric′ulum vi′tae (vī′tē, vē′tī, wē′tī), *n., pl.* **curricula vitae.** a brief biographical résumé of one's career and training, as prepared by a person applying for a job.

Cur•ri•er (kûr′ē ər, kur-), *n.* **Nathaniel,** 1813–88, U.S. lithographer: with James Merritt Ives produced prints showing American life.

Cur′rier and Ives′, *n.* the lithography firm of Nathaniel Currier and James Merritt Ives, founded originally by Currier (1835), which produced prints of American history, life, and manners.

cur•ry¹ (kûr′ē, kur′ē), *n., pl.* **-ries,** *v.,* **-ried, -ry•ing.** —*n.* **1.** a pungent dish of meat, fish, or vegetables cooked in a sauce with curry powder. **2.** a sauce containing curry powder. —*v.t.* **3.** to cook or flavor (food) with curry powder.

cur•ry² (kûr′ē, kur′ē), *v.t.,* **-ried, -ry•ing. 1.** to rub and clean (a horse) with a currycomb. **2.** to dress (tanned hides) by soaking, beating, coloring, etc. **3.** to beat; thrash. —***Idiom.*** **4. curry favor,** to seek to advance oneself through flattery or fawning.

cur•ry•comb (kûr′ē kōm′, kur′-), *n.* **1.** a comb, usu. with rows of metal teeth, for currying horses. —*v.t.* **2.** to clean with such a comb.

cur′ry pow′der, *n.* a pungent mixture of finely ground spices, as turmeric, coriander, cumin, pepper, etc.

curse (kûrs), *n., v.,* **cursed** or **curst, curs•ing.** —*n.* **1.** the expression of a wish that misfortune, evil, doom, etc., befall someone. **2.** a formula or charm intended to cause such misfortune to another. **3.** the act of reciting such a formula. **4.** a profane or obscene word, esp. as used in anger or for emphasis; swearword. **5.** an evil or misfortune that has been invoked upon one. **6.** the cause of evil, misfortune, or trouble. **7.** something accursed. **8.** an ecclesiastical censure or anathema. —*v.t.* **9.** to wish or invoke evil, calamity, injury, or destruction upon. **10.** to swear at. **11.** to blaspheme. **12.** to afflict with great evil. **13.** to excommunicate. —*v.i.* **14.** to utter curses; swear profanely. —**curs′er,** *n.*

curs•ed (kûr′sid, kûrst), *adj.* **1.** under a curse; damned. **2.** deserving a curse; hateful; abominable. —**curs′ed•ly,** *adv.*

Curse′ of Cain′, *n.* God's judgment that Cain should wander homeless. Gen. 4:11–12.

cur•sive (kûr′siv), *adj.* **1.** (of handwriting) in flowing strokes with the letters joined together. **2.** (of typed or typeset material) resembling handwriting. —*n.* **3.** a cursive letter or character. **4.** a style of typeface simulating handwriting.

cur•sor (kûr′sər), *n.* **1.** a movable, sometimes blinking, symbol used to indicate where data (as text, commands, etc.) may be input on a computer screen. **2.** a sliding object, as the lined glass on a slide rule, that can be set at any point on a scale.

cur•so•ri•al (kûr sôr′ē əl, -sōr′-), *adj.* **1.** (of a body part) adapted for running. **2.** having limbs adapted for running.

cur•so•ry (kûr′sə rē), *adj.* going rapidly over something, without noticing details; superficial: *a cursory glance.* —**cur′so•ri•ly,** *adv.*

curt (kûrt), *adj.* **1.** rudely brief in speech or abrupt in manner. **2.** brief; concise; terse. —**curt′ly,** *adv.* —**curt′ness,** *n.*

cur•tail¹ (kər tāl′), *v.t.* to cut short or cut off a part of; abridge; reduce. —**cur•tail′ment,** *n.*

cur•tail² (kûr′tāl′), *n.* a starting step of a flight of stairs having a scroll termination to one or both ends of the tread. Also called **cur′tail step′.**

cur•tain (kûr′tn), *n.* **1.** a hanging piece of fabric used to shut out the light from a window, adorn a room, increase privacy, etc. **2.** a movable or folding screen used for similar purposes. **3. a.** a movable drapery that hangs directly behind a proscenium arch and conceals the stage from the audience. **b.** the start or end of a performance, scene, act, or play, esp. the time at which a performance begins. **c.** an effect, line, or plot solution at the conclusion of a performance. **d.** (used as a direction in a script to indicate the end of a scene or act.) **4.** anything that shuts off, covers, or conceals: *a curtain of artillery fire.* **5.** the part of a wall or rampart connecting two bastions or towers. **6. curtains,** *Slang.* the end; death, esp. by violence. —*v.t.* **7.** to provide, shut off, conceal, or adorn with or as if with a curtain. —***Idiom.*** **8. draw the curtain on** or **over, a.** to bring to a close. **b.** to keep secret. **9. lift the curtain on, a.** to commence; start. **b.** to make known or public; disclose.

cur′tain call′, *n.* the appearance of a performer or group of performers at the conclusion of a play, program, etc., to receive the applause of the audience.

Cur•tis (kûr′tis), *n.* **Charles,** 1860–1936, vice president of the U.S. 1929–33.

Cur•tiss (kûr′tis), *n.* **Glenn Hammond,** 1878–1930, U.S. inventor: pioneer in the field of aviation.

curt•sy (kûrt′sē), *n., pl.* **-sies,** *v.,* **-sied, -sy•ing.** —*n.* **1.** a respectful bow made by women and girls, consisting of bending the knees and lowering the body. —*v.i.* **2.** to make a curtsy.

cur•va•ceous (kûr vā′shəs), *adj.* (of a woman) having a well-shaped figure with voluptuous curves. —**cur•va′ceous•ness,** *n.*

cur•va•ture (kûr′və chər, -chŏŏr′), *n.* **1.** the act of curving or the state of being curved. **2.** a curved condition, often abnormal: *curvature of the spine.* **3.** the degree of curving of a line or surface. **4.** *Geom.* **a.** (at a point on a curve) the derivative of the inclination of the tangent with respect to arc length. **b.** the absolute value of this derivative. **5.** something curved.

curve (kûrv), *n., v.,* **curved, curv•ing,** *adj.* **—***n.* **1.** a continuously bending line, without angles. **2.** the act or extent of curving. **3.** any curved outline, form, thing, or part. **4.** a curved section of a road, railroad track, path, etc. **5.** Also called **curve′ ball′.** a baseball pitch delivered with a spin that causes the ball to veer from a normal straight path, away from the side from which it was thrown. **6.** a graphic representation of the variations effected in something by the influence of changing conditions; graph. **7.** *Math.* a collection of points whose coordinates are continuous functions of a single independent variable. **8.** a misleading trick. **9.** an academic grading system based on the scale of performance of the group, so that those performing better, regardless of their actual knowledge, receive higher grades: *to mark on a curve.* **10.** a curved guide used in drafting. **—***v.i.* **11.** to bend in a curve; take the course of a curve. **—***v.t.* **12.** to cause to curve. **13.** to grade on a curve. **14.** to pitch a curve to in baseball. **—***adj.* **15.** curved. **—*Idiom.*** **16. throw someone a curve,** to take someone by surprise, esp. so as to cause chagrin. —**curv′y,** *adj.,* **•i•er, •i•est.**

cur•vet (kûr′vit; *for v. also* kər vet′), *n., v.,* **-vet•ted** or **-vet•ed, -vet•ting** or **-vet•ing.** **—***n.* **1.** a leap of a horse from a rearing position, in which it springs up with the hind legs outstretched as the forelegs descend. **—***v.i.* **2.** to leap in a curvet, as a horse. **3.** to leap and frisk. **—***v.t.* **4.** to cause to make a curvet.

cur•vi•lin•e•ar (kûr′və lin′ē ər) also **cur′vi•lin′e•al,** *adj.* **1.** consisting of or bounded by curved lines: *a curvilinear figure.* **2.** formed or characterized by curved lines.

cu•sec (kyo͞o′sek), *n.* a unit of flow of one cubic foot per second.

Cush or **Kush** (ko͝osh, kush), *n.* **1.** the eldest son of Ham. Gen. 10:6. **2.** an area mentioned in the Bible, sometimes identified with Upper Egypt. **3.** an ancient kingdom in North Africa, in the region of Nubia.

cu•shaw (kə shô′, ko͞o′shô), *n.* any of several squashes having long curved necks, esp. varieties of *Cucurbita mixta.*

Cush•ing (ko͝osh′ing), *n.* **William O(rcutt),** 1823–1902, U.S. clergyman and hymn writer.

cush•ion (ko͝osh′ən), *n.* **1.** a soft pad or bag filled with feathers, air, foam rubber, etc., used to sit, lie, or lean on. **2.** anything similar in form or function, as a pad used to prevent excessive pressure or chafing. **3.** something to absorb or counteract a shock, jar, or jolt, as a body of air or steam. **4.** something that lessens the effects of hardship or distress. **5.** any anatomical part resembling a pad. **6.** the resilient raised rim encircling the top of a billiard table. **7.** RAT (def. 5). **8.** a pillow used in lacemaking. **—***v.t.* **9.** to place on or support by a cushion. **10.** to furnish with a cushion or cushions. **11.** to lessen or soften the effects of: *to cushion a blow.* **12.** to cover or conceal with or as if with a cushion. **13.** to check the motion of (a piston or the like) by a cushion, as of steam. —**cush′ion•less,** *adj.* —**cush′ion•like′,** *adj.* —**cush′ion•y,** *adj.*

Cush•it•ic or **Kush•it•ic** (kə shit′ik), *n.* a language family of Africa, a branch of the Afroasiatic family, that includes Beja, Oromo, Somali, and a number of other languages, primarily of Ethiopia, Djibouti, Somalia, and NE Kenya.

cush•y (ko͝osh′ē), *adj.,* **i•er, i•est.** *Informal.* **1.** involving little effort for ample rewards; easy and profitable: *a cushy job.* **2.** soft and comfortable. —**cush′i•ness,** *n.*

cusk (kusk), *n., pl.* **cusks,** (*esp. collectively*) **cusk.** an edible North American codlike fish, *Brosme brosme.*

cusp (kusp), *n.* **1.** a point or pointed end. **2.** an anatomical point or prominence, as on the crown of a tooth or on a valve of the heart. **3.** a point where two branches of a curve meet, end, and are tangent. **4.** an architectural figure consisting of a pair of curves tangent to the line defining the area, decorated and meeting at a point within the area. **5.** a point of a crescent, esp. of the moon. **6. a.** the degree of the zodiac that marks the beginning of an astrological house or sign. **b.** the beginning, esp. the first day, of a new sign. **c.** a person born on the first day of a sign. **7.** a point that marks the beginning of a change: *on the cusp of a new era.*

cus•pid (kus′pid), *n.* any of the four canine teeth in humans. Also called **cuspid tooth.**

cus•pi•date (kus′pi dāt′) also **cus′pi•dat′ed,** *adj.* **1.** having a cusp or cusps. **2.** coming to a stiff point: *cuspidate leaves.*

cus•pi•dor (kus′pi dôr′), *n.* a large bowl, often of metal, serving as a receptacle for spit, esp. from chewing tobacco.

cuss (kus), *Informal.* **—***v.i.* **1.** to use profanity; curse; swear. **—***v.t.* **2.** to swear at; curse. **—***n.* **3.** a profane or obscene word; curse. **4.** a person or animal: *a strange old cuss.* —**cuss′er,** *n.*

cuss•ed (kus′id), *adj. Informal.* **1.** cursed. **2.** obstinate; stubborn; perverse. —**cuss′ed•ly,** *adv.* —**cuss′ed•ness,** *n.*

cus•tard (kus′tərd), *n.* a preparation, esp. a dessert, made with eggs, milk, and usu. sugar, baked or boiled until thickened.

cus′tard ap′ple, *n.* **1.** any of several trees of the genus *Annona,* as the cherimoya. **2.** any of several other trees, as the pawpaw, *Asimina triloba,* bearing fruit with soft, edible pulp. **3.** the fruit of these trees.

Cus•ter (kus′tər), *n.* **George Armstrong,** 1839–76, U.S. general: killed at the battle of Little Bighorn.

Cus′ter's Last′ Stand′, *n.* the annihilation of George Armstrong Custer and his military force by Sioux under Sitting Bull at the Battle of Little Big Horn (June 25, 1876).

cus•to•di•an (ku stō′dē ən), *n.* **1.** a person who has custody; keeper; guardian. **2.** a person entrusted with guarding or maintaining a property; caretaker. —**cus•to′di•an•ship′,** *n.*

cus•to•dy (kus′tə dē), *n., pl.* **-dies.** **1.** keeping; guardianship; care. **2.** the keeping or charge of officers of the law: *in the custody of the police.* **3.** imprisonment; legal restraint: *He was taken into custody.* **4.** (esp. in a divorce) the right of determining the residence, care, schooling, etc., of a child or children. —**cus•to′di•al,** *adj.*

cus•tom (kus′təm), *n.* **1.** a habitual practice; the usual way of acting in given circumstances. **2.** habits or usages collectively; convention. **3.** a practice so long established that it has the force of law. **4.** such practices collectively. **5. customs, a.** (*used with a sing. or pl. v.*) duties imposed by law on imported or, sometimes, exported goods. **b.** (*used with a sing. v.*) the government department that collects these duties. **c.** (*used with a sing. v.*) the section of an airport, station, etc., where baggage is checked for contraband and for goods subject to duty. **6.** regular patronage of a shop, restaurant, etc. **7.** customers or patrons collectively. **8.** a customary tax, tribute, or service due by feudal tenants to their lord. **—***adj.* **9.** made specially for individual customers: *custom shoes.* **10.** dealing in things so made, or doing work to order: *a custom tailor.*

cus•tom•ar•y (kus′tə mer′ē), *adj.* **1.** according to or depending on custom; usual; habitual. **2.** of or established by custom rather than law. **3.** *Law.* defined by long-continued practices: *the customary service due from tenants of a manor.* —**cus•tom•ar•i•ly** (kus′tə mer′ə lē; *for emphasis,* kus′tə mâr′ə lē), *adv.*

cus•tom•er (kus′tə mər), *n.* **1.** a person who purchases goods or services from another; buyer; patron. **2.** *Informal.* a person one has dealings with: *a tough customer.* **—*Saying.*** **3. The customer is always right,** even when customers are in the wrong, their good will is worth preserving.

cus•tom•ize (kus′tə mīz′), *v.t.,* **-ized, -iz•ing.** to modify, make, or build according to individual specifications or preference. —**cus′tom•iz′a•ble,** *adj.* —**cus′tom•i•za′tion,** *n.* —**cus′tom•iz′er,** *n.*

cus′tom-made′, *adj.* **1.** made to individual order: *custom-made shoes.* **—***n.* **2.** a custom-made item.

cus′tom-tai′lor, *v.t.* to modify for a specific use or need.

cut (kut), *v.,* **cut, cut•ting,** *adj., n.* **—***v.t.* **1.** to penetrate with or as if with a sharp-edged instrument or object. **2.** to divide with or as if with a sharp-edged instrument; sever; carve: *to cut a rope.* **3.** to detach or remove with or as if with a sharp-edged instrument; lop off; extract: *to cut a slice of bread; to cut an article from the newspaper.* **4.** to hew or saw down; fell: *to cut timber.* **5.** to trim by clipping, shearing, paring, or pruning: *to cut hair.* **6.** to mow; reap; harvest: *to cut grain.* **7.** to abridge or shorten; edit by omitting parts: *to cut a speech.* **8.** to lower, reduce, diminish, or curtail: *to cut prices.* **9.** to dilute or adulterate: *to cut whiskey.* **10.** to dissolve: *a detergent that cuts grease.* **11.** to intersect; cross. **12.** *Informal.* to cease; discontinue: *Cut the kidding.* **13.** to halt the running of, as a liquid or an engine; stop. **14.** to grow (a tooth) through the gum. **15.** to type or write on (a stencil) for mimeographing. **16.** to make or fashion by cutting, as a statue, jewel, or garment. **17.** to produce a pattern in (glass) by grinding and polishing. **18.** to refuse to recognize socially; shun: *Her friends began to cut her.* **19.** to strike sharply, as with a whip. **20.** to absent oneself from: *to cut classes.* **21. a.** to stop (a scene or shot being filmed). **b.** to edit (a film). **22.** to wound the feelings of severely. **23. a.** to divide (a pack of cards) at random into two or more parts, as by removing cards from the top. **b.** to take (a card) from a deck. **24. a.** to record a selection on (a phonograph record or magnetic tape). **b.** to make a recording of (a song, album of music, etc.). **25.** to castrate or geld. **26.** to hit (a ball) so as to change the course and often to cause spin. **27.** to hollow out; excavate; dig: *to cut a trench.* **28.** to perform or make: *to cut capers; to cut a deal.* **—***v.i.* **29.** to penetrate or divide something, as with a sharp-edged instrument. **30.** to admit of being cut. **31.** to move or cross, esp. in the most direct way: *to cut across an empty lot.* **32. a.** to shift suddenly from one film or television shot to another. **b.** to stop the action of a scene (used as a command by a director). **33.** to make a sudden or sharp change in direction; swerve: *We cut to the left.* **34.** to strike a person, animal, etc., sharply, as with a whip. **35.** to wound the feelings severely: *His criticism cut deep.* **36.** to cut a pack of cards. **37.** *Informal.* to leave hastily. **38. cut across,** to go beyond considerations of; transcend: *a tax program that cuts across party lines.* **39. cut back, a.** to shorten by cutting off the end. **b.** to curtail or discontinue: *to cut back steel production.* **c.** to return to an earlier event, as in the plot of a novel. **d.** *Football.* to reverse direction suddenly by moving in the diagonally opposite course. **40. cut down, a.** Also, **cut down on.** to lessen or curtail; decrease: *to cut down on snacks.* **b.** to strike and cause to fall. **c.** to destroy, kill, or disable: *The hurricane cut down everything in its path.* **d.** to remodel or reduce in size, as a garment. **41. cut in, a.** to move or thrust oneself, a vehicle, etc., abruptly between others. **b.** to interpose; interrupt: *to cut in with a remark.* **c.** to interrupt a dancing couple in order to dance with one of them. **d.** to include, as in a business deal or card game. **e.** to blend (shortening) into flour by means of a knife. **42. cut off, a.** to intercept. **b.** to interrupt. **c.** to stop suddenly; discontinue. **d.** to halt the operation of; turn off. **e.** to shut off or shut out. **f.** to disinherit. **g.** to sever; separate. **43. cut out, a.** to omit, delete, or remove; excise. **b.** to form by or as if by cutting. **c.** to refrain from; discontinue; stop: *to cut out smoking.* **d.** to oust and replace a rival; supplant. **e.** to part an animal from a herd. **f.** to plan; arrange: *You have your work cut out for you.* **g.** to move out of one's lane of traffic. **h.** *Slang.* to leave suddenly. **i.** (of an engine, machine, etc.) to stop running. **44. cut up, a.** to cut into pieces or sections. **b.** to lacerate; wound. **c.** to distress mentally; injure. **d.** *Informal.* to play pranks; misbehave. —*adj.* **45.** divided into pieces or detached by cutting: *cut flowers.* **46.** fashioned by cutting; having the surface shaped or ornamented by grinding, polishing, etc.: *cut diamonds.* **47.** reduced by or as if by cutting: *cut prices.* **48.** indented or cleft, as a leaf. —*n.* **49.** the result of cutting, as an incision, wound, passage, or channel. **50.** the act of cutting; a stroke or blow, as with a knife or whip. **51.** a piece cut off. **52.** a share, esp. of earnings or profits: *an agent's cut.* **53.** a haircut, often with a styling. **54.** a reduction in price, salary, etc. **55.** the manner or fashion in which anything is cut: *the cut of a dress.* **56.** style; manner; kind: *a man of his cut.* **57.** a passage or course straight across or through: *a cut through the woods.* **58.** an excision or omission of a part. **59.** a part or quantity of text deleted or omitted. **60.** a quantity cut, esp. of lumber. **61.** a refusal to recognize an acquaintance. **62.** an act, speech, etc., that wounds the feelings. **63.** an engraved plate or block of wood used for printing. **64.** a printed picture or illustration. **65.** an absence, as from a class, at which attendance is required. **66.** a part of an animal carcass usu. cut as one piece for meat. **67. a.** the act of cutting a ball. **b.** the spin imparted. **68.** a blow with the edge of the blade instead of the tip in fencing. **69.** one of several pieces of straw, paper, etc., used in drawing lots. **70. a.** the transition from one shot or scene to another in an edited film. **b.** an edited version of a film. **c.** an act or instance of editing a film. **71.** an individual song, musical piece, etc., on a record or tape. —*Idiom.* **72. a cut above,** somewhat superior to. **73. cut a figure,** to give a certain impression of oneself: *to cut a distinguished figure.* **74. cut and run,** to leave as hurriedly as possible; flee. **75. cut both ways,** to have or result in advantages as well as disadvantages. **76. cut fine,** to calculate precisely, without allowing for possible error or accident. **77. cut it,** *Informal.* to perform effectively or successfully. **78. cut off one's nose to spite one's face,** to damage oneself by acting spitefully against another. **79. cut one's eyeteeth,** to become sophisticated or experienced. **80. cut one's teeth on,** to do at an early stage or age. **81. cut out for,** fitted for; capable of: *not cut out for a military career.* **82. cut short,** to end abruptly before completion; interrupt.

cut′-and-dried′ or **cut′-and-dry′,** *adj.* **1.** prepared or settled in advance; not needing much thought or discussion. **2.** lacking in originality or spontaneity; routine.

cut′-and-paste′, *adj.* assembled from various existing elements.

cu•ta•ne•ous (kyōō tā′nē əs), *adj.* of, pertaining to, or affecting the skin. —**cu•ta′ne•ous•ly,** *adv.*

cut•a•way (kut′ə wā′), *n.* **1.** Also called **cut′away coat′.** a man's formal daytime coat with the front part of the skirt cut away from the waist so as to curve to the long tails at the back. **2.** a shot or scene in a film that shifts abruptly from the principal scene to a related action, esp. something occurring simultaneously. **3.** an illustration or scale model having the outer section removed to display the interior. —*adj.* **4.** having a part cut away.

cut•back (kut′bak′), *n.* **1.** a reduction in rate, quantity, etc.: *a cutback in production.* **2.** a return in the course of a story, film, etc., to earlier events.

cute (kyōot), *adj.,* **cut•er, cut•est,** *adv.* —*adj.* **1.** attractive, esp. in a dainty way; pleasingly pretty. **2.** charmingly attractive. **3.** affectedly pretty or clever; precious. **4.** mentally keen; clever; shrewd. —*adv.* **5.** *Informal.* in a cute manner; cutely. —**cute′ly,** *adv.* —**cute′ness,** *n.*

cut′ glass′, *n.* glass ornamented or shaped by cutting or grinding with abrasive wheels.

cut′-grass′, *n.* any of several grasses having blades with rough edges, esp. grasses of the genus *Leersia.*

cu•ti•cle (kyōo′ti kəl), *n.* **1.** the hardened skin that surrounds the edges of a fingernail or toenail. **2.** the epidermis. **3.** the outer, noncellular layer of the arthropod integument. **4.** a very thin waxy film covering the surface of plants, formed from the outer surfaces of the epidermal cells. —**cu•tic′u•lar** (-tik′yə lər), *adj.*

cut•ie (kyōo′tē), *n.* **1.** *Informal.* **a.** a charmingly attractive person. **b.** an affectionate or familiar term of address (sometimes offensive when used to strangers, subordinates, etc.). **2.** *Slang.* **a.** a person who tries to outsmart or outmaneuver others. **b.** a clever or cunning maneuver.

cut′-in′, *n.* **1.** the act of cutting in, as on a dancing couple. **2.** something inserted into another thing.

cu•tin (kyōo′tin), *n.* a transparent waxy substance constituting, together with cellulose, the cuticle of plants.

cu•tis (kyōo′tis), *n., pl.* **-tes** (-tēz), **-tis•es.** the dermis and epidermis of the skin together.

cut•lass or **cut•las** (kut′ləs), *n.* a short, heavy, slightly curved sword with a single cutting edge, formerly used by sailors.

cut•lass•fish (kut′ləs fish′), *n., pl.* (*esp. collectively*) **-fish,** (*esp. for kinds or species*) **-fish•es.** any compressed, ribbonlike fish of the genus *Trichiurus,* having daggerlike teeth.

cut•ler (kut′lər), *n.* a person who makes, sells, or repairs knives and other cutting instruments.

cut•ler•y (kut′lə rē), *n.* **1.** cutting instruments collectively, esp. knives for cutting food. **2.** utensils, as knives, forks, and spoons, used at the table for serving and eating food. **3.** the trade or business of a cutler.

cut•let (kut′lit), *n.* **1.** a slice of meat for broiling or frying. **2.** a flat croquette of minced food, as chicken, fish, or vegetables.

cut′ nail′, *n.* a nail having a tapering rectangular form with a blunt point, made by cutting from a thin rolled sheet of iron or steel.

cut•off (kut′ôf′, -of′), *n.* **1.** an act or instance of cutting off. **2.** something that cuts off. **3.** a point serving as the limit beyond which something is no longer effective, applicable, or possible. **4.** a road, passage, etc., that leaves another, usu. providing a shortcut. **5.** a new and shorter channel formed in a river by the water cutting across a bend in its course. **6. cutoffs,** shorts made by cutting the legs off a pair of trousers, esp. jeans. **7.** an infielder's interception of a baseball thrown from the outfield in order to relay it to home plate or keep a base runner from advancing. **8.** arrest of the steam moving the pistons of an engine, usu. occurring before the completion of a stroke. —*adj.* **9.** being or constituting a limit or ending: *the cutoff date for applications.*

cut•out (kut′out′), *n.* **1.** something cut out from something else, as a pattern or figure cut out or intended to be cut out of paper or other material. **2.** a valve in the exhaust pipe of an internal-combustion engine, which when open permits the engine to exhaust directly into the air. **3.** an act or instance of cutting out. **4.** *Slang.* an intermediary, as in espionage. **5.** a device for the manual or automatic interruption of electric current. **6.** a usu. discontinued record album that is for sale at a discount.

cut′-rate′, *adj.* **1.** offered at a reduced rate or price; inexpensive. **2.** offering goods or services at reduced prices.

cut•tage (kut′ij), *n.* the propagation of plants from cuttings.

cut•ter (kut′ər), *n.* **1.** a person who cuts, esp. as a job, as one who cuts fabric for garments or film for editing. **2.** a machine, tool, or other device for cutting. **3.** a single-masted sailing vessel, similar to a sloop but having its mast farther astern. **4.** a lightly armed government vessel. **5.** a small, light sleigh, usu. single-seated and pulled by one horse.

cut•throat (kut′thrōt′), *n.* **1.** a person who cuts throats; murderer. —*adj.* **2.** murderous. **3.** ruthless: *cutthroat competition.* **4.** of or designating a game, as of cards, played by three persons, each scoring individually.

cut•ting (kut′ing), *n.* **1.** the act of a person or thing that cuts. **2.** something cut, cut off, or cut out. **3.** a piece, as a root or leaf, cut from a plant and used for propagation. **4.** something made by cutting, as a recording. **5.** a clipping from a newspaper, etc. —*adj.* **6.** designed or used for cutting. **7.** penetrating or dividing by or as if by a cut. **8.** piercing, as a wind. **9.** sarcastic. —**cut′ting•ly,** *adv.*

cut′ting board′, *n.* a board on which something, as food, cloth, or leather, is cut.

cut′ting edge′, *n.* the most advanced position; lead: *on the cutting edge of computer technology.* —**cut′ting-edge′,** *adj.*

cut′ting horse′, *n.* a saddle horse trained to separate calves, steers, etc., from a herd.

cut•tle•fish (kut′l fish′), *n., pl.* (*esp. collectively*) **-fish,** (*esp. for kinds or species*) **-fish•es.** any flattened squidlike cephalopod of the family Sepiidae with a hard internal shell.

cut•work (kut′wûrk′), *n.* **1.** embroidery in which parts of the ground fabric are cut out within the design. **2.** fretwork formed by perforation or cut in low relief. **3.** POINT COUPÉ.

cut•worm (kut′wûrm′), *n.* the caterpillar of any of several noctuid moths that feeds at night on the stems of young plants, cutting them off at the ground.

cu•vée (kōō vā′, kyōō-), *n.* **1.** wine in vats or casks, blended, often from different vintages, for uniform quality. **2.** a blend resulting from the mixing of wines.

cu•vette (kōō vet′, kyōō-), *n.* a tube or vessel used in a laboratory.

CV, 1. cardiovascular. **2.** curriculum vitae.

cwt, hundredweight.

cy•an•a•mide or **cy•an•a•mid** (sī an′ə mid), *n.* a white crystalline solid, CH_2N_2, produced by the action of ammonia or sulfuric acid on cyanic compounds.

cy′an blue′, *n.* a moderate greenish blue to bluish green color.

cy•an•ic (sī an′ik), *adj.* **1.** blue: applied esp. to colors in flowers, including blues and colors tending toward blue. **2.** pertaining to or containing cyanogen.

cy•a•nide (sī′ə nīd′, -nid), *n., v.,* **-nid•ed, -nid•ing.** —*n.* **1.** Also, **cy•a•nid** (sī′ə nid). a highly poisonous compound containing sodium or potassium, as potassium cyanide, KCN. —*v.t.* **2.** to treat with a cyanide, as an ore in order to extract gold.

cy′anide proc′ess, *n.* a process for extracting gold or silver from ore by dissolving the ore in an alkaline solution of sodium or potassium cyanide and precipitating the gold or silver from the solution.

cyano-, a combining form meaning "blue, dark blue": *cyanobacteria.*

cy•a•no•co•bal•a•min (sī′ə nō kō bal′ə min, sī an/ō-), *n.* VITAMIN B₁₂.

cy•an•o•gen (sī an′ə jən, -jen′), *n.* **1.** a colorless, poisonous, flammable gas, C_2N_2, used chiefly in organic synthesis. **2.** the univalent group CN.

cy•a•no•phyte (sī′ə nō fīt′, sī an′ə-), *n.* any moneran of the phylum Cyanophyta, comprising the blue-green algae.

cy•a•no•sis (sī′ə nō′sis), *n.* blueness or lividness of the skin, caused by a deficiency of oxygen or defective hemoglobin in the blood. —**cy′a•not′ic** (-not′ik), *adj.*

cyber-, a combining form representing COMPUTER (*cybertalk; cyberart*) and by extension meaning "very modern" (*cyberfashion*).

cy•ber•na•tion (sī′bər nā′shən), *n.* the use of computers to control automatic processes, esp. in manufacturing. —**cy′ber•nate′**, *v.t.*, **-nat•ed, -nat•ing.**

cy•ber•net•ics (sī′bər net′iks), *n.* (*used with a sing. v.*) the comparative study of organic control and communication systems, as the brain and its neurons, and mechanical or electronic systems analogous to them, as robots or computers. —**cy′ber•net′ic, cy′ber•net′i•cal,** *adj.* —**cy′ber•net′i•cal•ly,** *adv.* —**cy′ber•net′i•cist, cy′ber•ne•ti′cian** (-ni-tish′ən), *n.*

cy•ber•punk (sī′bər pungk′), *n.* **1.** science fiction featuring extensive human interaction with supercomputers and a punk ambiance. **2.** *Slang.* a computer hacker.

cy•ber•space (sī′bər spās′), *n.* **1.** the realm of electronic communication. **2.** VIRTUAL REALITY.

cy•borg (sī′bôrg), *n.* a person whose physiological functioning is aided by or dependent upon a mechanical or electronic device.

cy•cad (sī′kad), *n.* any of several palmlike gymnospermous trees of the order Cycadales, having a thick, unbranched trunk, a crown of leathery pinnate leaves, and large cones. —**cy′cad•like′,** *adj.*

cy•cla•ble (sī′klə bəl), *adj.* fit or designed for bicycle riding.

cy•cla•mate (sī′klə māt′, sik′lə-), *n.* any of several compounds formerly used as a noncaloric sweetener in foods and beverages: now banned as a carcinogen.

cy•cla•men (sī′klə mən, -men′, sik′lə-), *n.* any plant of the genus *Cyclamen,* of the primrose family, having nodding white, purple, or red flowers with reflexed petals.

cy•cle (sī′kəl), *n., v.,* **-cled, -cling.** —*n.* **1.** any complete round or recurring series. **2.** a round of years or a recurring period of time, esp. one in which certain events or phenomena repeat themselves in the same order and at the same intervals. **3.** any long period of years; age. **4.** a bicycle, motorcycle, tricycle, or the like. **5.** a group of poems, stories, songs, etc., about a central theme or figure: *the Arthurian cycle.* **6.** *Physics.* **a.** a sequence of changing states that, upon completion, produces a final state identical to the original one. **b.** one of a succession of periodically recurring events. —*v.i.* **7.** to ride or travel by bicycle, motorcycle, or the like. **8.** to move or revolve in cycles; pass through cycles.

cy•clic (sī′klik, sik′lik), *adj.* **1.** revolving or recurring in cycles; characterized by recurrence in cycles. **2.** of, pertaining to, or being a cycle. **3.** of or pertaining to a chemical compound containing a closed chain or ring of atoms. **4. a.** pertaining to an algebraic system in which all the elements of a group are powers of one element. **b.** (of a set of elements) arranged as if on a circle, so that the first element follows the last. —**cy•clic′i•ty** (-klis′i tē), *n.*

cy•cli•cal (sī′kli kəl, sik′li-), *adj.* **1.** cyclic. **2.** (of earnings, value, etc.) fluctuating widely according to changes in the economy or the seasons. —*n.* **3.** Usu., **cyclicals.** stocks of companies with cyclical earnings. —**cy′cli•cal•ly,** *adv.*

cy•cling (sī′kling), *n.* **1.** the act or sport of riding or traveling by bicycle, motorcycle, or the like. **2.** the sport of touring or racing on usu. lightweight bicycles with low handlebars and multiple gears.

cy•clist (sī′klist) also **cy′cler,** *n.* a person who rides or travels by bicycle, motorcycle, or the like.

cyclo-, a combining form meaning "circle" (*cyclometer; cyclotron*); "cycle" (*cyclothymia*); "(of a chemical compound) structured in closed chains" (*cyclohexane*); "cyclone" (*cyclogenesis*).

cy•cloid (sī′kloid), *adj.* **1.** resembling a circle; circular. **2. a.** (of the scale of a fish) smooth-edged and more or less circular in form. **b.** (of a fish) having such scales. **3.** *Psychiatry.* of or denoting a personality type characterized by wide fluctuations in mood within the normal range. —*n.* **4.** a curve generated by a point on the circumference of a circle that rolls, without slipping, on a straight line. —**cy•cloi′dal,** *adj.* —**cy•cloi′dal•ly,** *adv.*

cy•clone (sī′klōn), *n.* **1.** a large-scale atmospheric wind-and-pressure system characterized by low pressure at its center and by circular wind motion, counterclockwise in the Northern Hemisphere, clockwise in the Southern Hemisphere. **2.** a device for removing small or powdered solids from air, water, or other gases or liquids by centrifugal force. [< Greek *kyklôn* revolving] —**cy•clon′ic** (-klon′ik), *adj.*

Cy•clops (sī′klops), *n., pl.* **Cy•clo•pes** (sī klō′pēz). a giant of Greek myth, having a single round eye in the middle of the forehead.

cy•clo•ram•a (sī′klə ram′ə, -rä′mə), *n., pl.* **-ram•as. 1.** a pictorial representation, in perspective, of a landscape, battle, etc., on the inner wall of a cylindrical room, viewed by spectators occupying a position in the center. **2.** a curved wall or drop at the back of a stage set, used to create the illusion of space or distance. —**cy′clo•ram′ic,** *adj.*

cy•clo•tron (sī′klə tron′, sik′lə-), *n.* an accelerator in which particles move in spiral paths in a constant magnetic field.

cyg•net (sig′nit), *n.* a young swan.

cyl•in•der (sil′in dər), *n.* **1.** a surface or solid bounded by two parallel planes and generated by a straight line moving parallel to the given planes and tracing a curve bounded by the planes and lying in a plane perpendicular or oblique to them. **2.** any cylinderlike object or part, whether solid or hollow. **3.** the rotating part of a revolver, containing the chambers for the cartridges. **4.** a cylindrical chamber in a pump in which a piston slides to move or compress a fluid. **5.** a cylindrical chamber in an engine in which the pressure of a gas or liquid moves a sliding piston. **6.** (in printing presses) **a.** a rotating cylinder that produces the impression and under which a flat form to be printed from passes. **b.** either of two cylinders, one carrying a curved form or plate

to be printed from, that rotate against each other. **7.** a cylindrical device in a lock that retains the bolt until tumblers have been pushed out of its way. —*v.t.* **8.** to furnish with a cylinder or cylinders. **9.** to subject to the action of a cylinder.

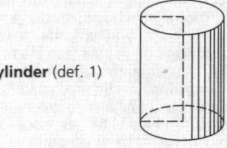

cylinder (def. 1)

cyl′inder block′, *n.* the metal casting in which the cylinders of an internal-combustion engine are bored.

cyl′inder head′, *n.* (in a reciprocating engine or pump) a detachable plate or cover on the end opposite to that from which the piston rod or connecting rod projects.

cyl′inder press′, *n.* a printing press in which a flat bed holding the printing form moves against a rotating cylinder that carries the paper. Also called **flat-bed press.** Compare ROTARY PRESS.

cy•lin•dri•cal (si lin′dri kəl) also **cy•lin′dric,** *adj.* of, pertaining to, or having the form of a cylinder. —**cy•lin′dri•cal•ly,** *adv.*

cy•ma•ti•um (si mā′shē əm, sī-), *n., pl.* **-ti•a** (-shē ə). the uppermost member of a classical cornice.

cym•bal (sim′bəl), *n.* a concave plate of brass or bronze that produces a sharp, ringing sound when struck: played either in pairs, by being struck together, or singly, by being struck with a drumstick or the like. —**cym′bal•ist,** *n.* —**cym′bal•like′,** *adj.*

cym•bid•i•um (sim bid′ē əm), *n.* any of various orchids of the genus *Cymbidium,* native to Asia and Australia, having long clusters of numerous flowers.

cyn•ic (sin′ik), *n.* **1.** a person who believes that only selfishness motivates human actions and who disbelieves in or minimizes selfless acts. **2.** a person who shows or expresses a bitterly or sneeringly cynical attitude. —*adj.* **3.** cynical. —**cyn′i•cism,** *n.*

cyn•i•cal (sin′i kəl), *adj.* **1.** distrusting or disparaging the motives or sincerity of others. **2.** showing contempt for accepted standards of honesty or morality, esp. by actions that exploit the scruples of others. **3.** bitterly or sneeringly distrustful, contemptuous, or pessimistic.

cy•no•sure (sī′nə shŏŏr′, sin′ə-), *n.* **1.** someone or something that strongly attracts attention or admiration: *the cynosure of all eyes.* **2.** something serving for guidance or direction. —**cy′no•sur′al,** *adj.*

cy pres or **cy•pres** (sē′ prā′), *Law.* —*adv.* **1.** as near as possible. —*n.* **2.** the doctrine, applied esp. to cases of charitable trusts or donations, that, in place of an impossible or illegal condition or object, allows the nearest practicable one to be substituted.

cy•press¹ (sī′prəs), *n.* **1.** any of several evergreen coniferous trees of the genus *Cupressus,* having dark-green, scalelike, overlapping leaves. **2.** any of various other coniferous trees of allied genera, as the bald cypress. **3.** the wood of these trees.

cy•press² or **cy•prus** (sī′prəs), *n.* a fine, thin fabric resembling lawn or crepe, formerly used in black for mourning garments.

cy′press vine′, *n.* a tropical American vine, *Ipomoea quamoclit,* of the morning glory family, having finely divided leaves and tubular scarlet flowers.

cyp•ri•nid (sip′rə nid), *n.* **1.** any of the freshwater fishes of the family Cyprinidae, including carps, minnows, bream, etc. —*adj.* **2.** Also, **cyp•ri•noid** (sip′rə noid′). carplike in form or structure.

cy•prin•o•dont (sip′rə dont′), *n.* any of the small, soft-rayed freshwater fishes of the family Cyprinodontidae, including the killifishes, topminnows, and guppies.

cyp•ri•pe•di•um (sip′rə pē′dē əm), *n.* any orchid of the genus *Cypripedium,* comprising the lady's-slippers.

cy•prus (sī′prəs), *n.* CYPRESS².

Cy•prus (sī′prəs), *n.* an island republic in the Mediterranean, S of Turkey: formerly a British colony; independent since 1960. 752,808; 3572 sq. mi. (9250 sq. km). *Cap.:* Nicosia.

Cyr•e•na•i•ca or **Cir•e•na•i•ca** (sir′ə nā′i kə, sī′rə-), *n.* **1.** an ancient district in N Africa. **2.** the E part of Libya. —**Cyr′e•na′ic,** *adj.*

Cy•re•ne (sī rē′nē), *n.* an ancient Greek city in N Africa, in Cyrenaica.

Cy•re•ni•us (sī rē′nē əs) also **Quirinius,** *n.* the Roman ruler of Syria at the time of Jesus' birth. Luke 2:1–5.

Cyr•il (sir′əl), *n.* Saint ("*Apostle of the Slavs*"), A.D. 827–869, Greek missionary to the Moravians.

Cy•ril•lic (si ril′ik), *adj.* **1.** of or designating an alphabet derived from Greek uncials, first used for the writing of Old Church Slavonic and adopted with minor modifications for the writing of Russian and many other languages of E Europe and Asia. **2.** of or pertaining to St. Cyril. —*n.* **3.** the Cyrillic alphabet.

Cy•rus (sī′rəs), *n.* **1.** ("*the Great*") c600-529 B.C., king of Persia c550-529: founder of the Persian Empire. **2.** ("*the Younger*") 424-401 B.C., Persian prince and satrap.

cyst (sist), *n.* **1.** any abnormal saclike growth of the body in which matter is retained. **2.** a bladder, sac, or vesicle. **3. a.** a protective capsule or spore surrounding an inactive or resting organism or enclosing a reproductive body. **b.** such a capsule and its contents. —**cyst′oid,** *adj.,* *n.*

cys•tec•to•my (si stek′tə mē), *n., pl.* **-mies. 1.** the surgical removal of a cyst. **2.** the surgical removal of the urinary bladder.

cys•te•ine (sis′tē ēn′, -in), *n.* a crystalline amino acid, $C_3H_7O_2NS$, a component of nearly all proteins, obtained by the reduction of cystine. *Symbol:* C —**cys′te•in′ic,** *adj.*

cys•tic (sis′tik), *adj.* **1.** pertaining to, of the nature of, or having a cyst or cysts. **2.** belonging or pertaining to the urinary bladder or gallbladder.

cys′tic fibro′sis, *n.* a hereditary disease of the exocrine glands characterized by the production of thickened mucus that chronically clogs the bronchi and pancreatic ducts, leading to breathing difficulties, infection, and fibrosis.

cys•tine (sis′tēn, -tin), *n.* a crystalline amino acid, $C_6H_{12}O_4N_2S_2$, occurring in most proteins, esp. the keratins.

cys•ti•tis (si stī′tis), *n.* inflammation of the urinary bladder.

cyto-, a combining form meaning "cell": *cytoplasm.* Compare -CYTE.

cy•to•chem•is•try (sī′tə kem′ə strē), *n.* the branch of cell biology dealing with the detection of cell constituents by means of biochemical analysis and visualization techniques.

cy•to•gen•e•sis (sī′tə jen′ə sis), *n.* the origin and development of cells.

cy•to•ge•net•ics (sī′tō jə net′iks), *n.* (*used with a sing. v.*) the branch of biology linking the study of genetic inheritance with the study of cell structure. —**cy′to•ge•net′ic,** *adj.* —**cy′to•ge•net′i•cal•ly,** *adv.* —**cy′to•ge•net′i•cist** (-ə sist), *n.*

cy•tol•o•gy (sī tol′ə jē), *n.* the study of the microscopic appearance of cells, esp. for the diagnosis of abnormalities and malignancies. —**cy•to•log•ic** (sīt′l oj′ik), **cy′to•log′i•cal,** *adj.* —**cy′to•log′i•cal•ly,** *adv.* —**cy•tol′o•gist,** *n.*

cy•to•meg•a•ly (sī′tō meg′ə lē) also **cy•to•me•ga•li•a** (-mi gā′lē ə), *n.* an abnormal enlargement of cells in the body. —**cy′to•me•gal′ic** (-mi gal′ik), *adj.*

cy•to•plasm (sī′tə plaz′əm), *n.* the cell substance between the cell membrane and the nucleus. —**cy′to•plas′mic,** *adj.*

cy•to•sine (sī′tə sēn′, -zēn′, -sin), *n.* a pyrimidine base, $C_4H_5N_3O$, that is one of the fundamental components of DNA and RNA, in which it forms a base pair with guanine. *Symbol:* C

cy•to•tax•on•o•my (sī′tō tak son′ə mē), *n.* classification of organisms on the basis of cellular structure, particularly chromosome structure. —**cy′to•tax′o•nom′ic** (-sə nom′ik), *adj.*

CZ or **C.Z., 1.** Canal Zone. **2.** cubic zirconia.

czar or **tsar** or **tzar** (zär, tsär), *n.* **1.** an emperor or king. **2.** (*often cap.*) the former emperor of Russia. **3.** an autocratic ruler or leader. **4.** any person exercising great authority or power: *a czar of industry.* [< Russian *tsar* < Latin *Caesar* Caesar] —**czar′dom,** *n.*

czar•e•vitch (zär′ə vich, tsär′-), *n.* a son of a Russian czar, esp. the eldest son.

cza•rev•na (zä rev′nə, tsä-), *n., pl.* **-nas. 1.** a daughter of a czar. **2.** the wife of the son of a czar.

cza•ri•na (zä rē′nə, tsä-), *n., pl.* **-nas.** the wife of a czar; Russian empress.

czar•ism (zär′iz əm, tsär′-), *n.* **1.** the system of government in Russia under the czars. **2.** dictatorship; despotic or autocratic government. —**czar′ist,** *adj., n.*

Czech•o•slo•va•ki•a (chek′ə slə vä′kē ə, -vak′ē ə), *n.* a former republic in central Europe: formed after World War I; comprised Bohemia, Moravia, Slovakia, and part of Silesia: a federal republic 1968–92. 49,383 sq. mi. (127,903 sq. km). *Cap.:* Prague. Formerly (1990–92), **Czech′ and Slo′vak Fed′erative Repub′lic;** (1948–89), **Czech′oslo′vak So′cialist Repub′lic.** —**Czech′o•slo•va′ki•an,** *adj.*

Czech′ Repub′lic, *n.* a republic in central Europe: includes the regions of Bohemia, Moravia, and part of Silesia; formerly part of Czechoslovakia; independent since 1993. 10,318,958; 30,449 sq. mi. (78,864 sq. km). *Cap.:* Prague.

C

D

D, d (dē), *n., pl.* **Ds** or **D's, ds** or **d's. 1.** the fourth letter of the English alphabet, a consonant. **2.** any spoken sound represented by this letter. **3.** something shaped like a D. **4.** a written or printed representation of the letter *D* or *d.*

d', *Pron. Spelling.* do (esp. before *you*): *How d'you like them?*

'd, 1. contraction of *had: They'd already left.* **2.** contraction of *would: I'd like to see it.* **3.** contraction of *did: Where'd you go?* **4.** contraction of *-ed: She OK'd the plan.*

D, 1. deep. **2.** depth. **3.** diopter. **4.** divorced. **5.** Dutch.

D, *Symbol.* **1.** the fourth in order or in a series. **2.** (*sometimes l.c.*) (in some grading systems) a grade or mark indicating poor or barely acceptable quality. **3. a.** the second note of the ascending C major scale. **b.** a tonality having D as the tonic. **4.** (*sometimes l.c.*) the Roman numeral for 500. Compare ROMAN NUMERALS. **5.** deuterium. **6.** aspartic acid.

D., 1. day. **2.** December. **3.** Democrat. **4.** Democratic. **5.** *Physics.* density. **6.** Doctor.

d., 1. date. **2.** daughter. **3.** day. **4.** deceased. **5.** deep. **6.** degree. **7.** delete. **8.** *Chiefly Brit.* penny. **9.** *Physics.* density. **10.** depth. **11.** deputy. **12.** dialect. **13.** diameter. **14.** died. **15.** dime. **16.** dividend. **17.** dollar. **18.** dose. **19.** drachma.

DA, District Attorney.

dab¹ (dab), *v.,* **dabbed, dab·bing,** *n.* —*v.t.* **1.** to pat or tap gently: *I dabbed my eyes with a handkerchief.* **2.** to apply (a substance) by light strokes. **3.** to strike, esp. lightly. —*v.i.* **4.** to strike lightly; make a dab; pat: *She dabbed at the stain on her dress.* —*n.* **5.** a quick or light pat, as with something soft. **6.** a small lump or quantity: *a dab of powder.* —**dab′ber,** *n.*

dab² (dab), *n.* any of several flatfishes of the genus *Limanda,* esp. the European flatfish, *L. limanda.*

dab·ble (dab′əl), *v.,* **-bled, -bling.** —*v.i.* **1.** to play and splash in or as if in water, esp. with the hands. **2.** to work at anything in an irregular or superficial manner: *to dabble in literature.* **3.** (of a duck) to feed on shallow-water vegetation with rapid, splashing movements of the bill. —*v.t.* **4.** to wet slightly in or with a liquid; splash; spatter. —**dab′bler,** *n.* —**dab′bling·ly,** *adv.*

dab′bling duck′, any shallow-water duck, esp. of the genus *Anas,* that feeds by upending and dabbling (contrasted with *diving duck*).

dab·chick (dab′chik′), *n.* any of various small grebes, esp. the little grebe, *Tachybaptus rufficollis,* of Europe.

Dac·ca (dak′ə, dä′kə), *n.* DHAKA.

dace (dās), *n., pl.* (*esp. collectively*) **dace,** (*esp. for kinds or species*) **dac·es. 1.** a small, stout European cyprinid fish, *Leuciscus leuciscus.* **2.** any of several North American minnows.

Da·chau (dä′кнou), *n.* a city in S Germany, near Munich: site of Nazi concentration camp. 33,950.

dachs·hund (däks′hŏŏnt′, -hŏŏnd′, -ənd, daks′-, dash′-), *n.* one of a German breed of dogs having very short legs, a long body and ears, and a usu. reddish brown or black-and-tan coat. [< Greek, = *Dachs* badger + *Hund* dog]

Da·cron (dā′kron, dak′ron), *Trademark.* a brand of polyester fiber.

dac·tyl (dak′til), *n.* **1.** a prosodic foot of three syllables, one long followed by two short in quantitative meter, or one stressed followed by two unstressed in accentual meter, as in *humanly.* **2.** a finger or toe.

dactylo-, a combining form meaning "finger," "toe": *dactylography.*

dac·ty·log·ra·phy (dak′tə log′rə fē), *n.* the study of fingerprints for purposes of identification. —**dac′ty·log′ra·pher,** *n.*

dac·ty·lol·o·gy (dak′tə lol′ə jē), *n., pl.* **-gies.** the technique of communicating by signs made with the fingers, esp. in the manual alphabets used by the deaf.

da·da (dä′dä), *n.* a movement in early 20th-century art and literature whose exponents challenged established canons of art, thought, and morality through nihilist works and outrageous behavior. —**da′da·ism,** *n.* —**da′da·ist,** *n., adj.* —**da′da·is′tic,** *adj.*

dad·dy (dad′ē), *n., pl.* **-dies.** *Informal.* father; dad.

dad′dy-long′legs′ or **dad′dy long′legs** (lông′legz′, long′-), *n., pl.* **-long·legs. 1.** any spiderlike arachnid of the order Opiliones, having a compact rounded body and usu. extremely long, slender legs. **2.** *Brit.* CRANE FLY.

da·do (dā′dō), *n., pl.* **-does, -dos,** *v.,* **-doed, -do·ing.** —*n.* **1.** Also called **die.** the part of a pedestal between the base and the cornice or cap. **2.** the lower broad part of an interior wall when distinctively finished with wallpaper, paneling, paint, etc. **3.** a groove or rectangular section in a board for receiving the end of another board. —*v.t.* **4.** to provide with a dado. **5. dado in,** to insert (a board or the like) into a dado.

dae·dal (dēd′l), *adj.* **1.** skillful; ingenious. **2.** cleverly intricate. **3.** diversified.

Daed·a·lus (ded′l əs; *esp. Brit.* dēd′l əs), *n.* a legendary Athenian who built the labyrinth for Minos and made wings for himself and his son Ic-

arus to escape from Crete. —**Dae·da·li·an, Dae·da·le·an** (di dā′lē ən), **Dae·dal·ic** (-dal′ik), *adj.*

daf·fo·dil (daf′ə dil), *n.* **1.** any plant of the genus *Narcissus,* of the amaryllis family, esp. species having solitary yellow flowers with a trumpetlike corona. **2.** the flower itself. **3.** clear yellow; canary.

daffodil

daf·fy (daf′ē), *adj.,* **-fi·er, -fi·est.** *Informal.* silly; weak-minded; crazy. —**daf′fi·ly,** *adv.* —**daf′fi·ness,** *n.*

daft (daft, däft), *adj.,* **-er, -est. 1.** senseless, stupid, or foolish. **2.** insane; crazy; mad. —**daft′ness,** *n.*

dag·ger (dag′ər), *n.* **1.** a short, swordlike weapon with a pointed blade and a handle, used for stabbing. **2.** a printer's mark (†) used esp. for references. —*v.t.* **3.** to stab with or as if with a dagger. **4.** to mark with a printer's dagger. —*Idiom.* **5. look daggers at,** to look with intense hostility or anger.

Da·gon (dā′gon), *n.* a Phoenician and Philistine god of the earth: the national god of the Philistines.

da·guerre·o·type (də gâr′ə tīp′, -ē ə tīp′), *n., v.,* **-typed, -typ·ing.** —*n.* **1.** an obsolete photographic process, invented in 1839, in which a picture made on a silver surface sensitized with iodine is developed by exposure to mercury vapor. **2.** a picture made by this process. —*v.t.* **3.** to photograph by this process. [after L. J. M. *Daguerre* (1789–1851), French inventor] —**da·guerre′o·typ′er, da·guerre′o·typ′ist,** *n.* —**da·guerre′o·typ′ic** (-tip′ik), *adj.* —**da·guerre′o·typ′y,** *n.*

Dag′wood sand′wich (dag′wŏŏd), *n.* a thick sandwich filled with a variety of meats, cheeses, dressings, and condiments. Also called **Dag′wood.** [named after *Dagwood* Bumstead, a character in the comic strip *Blondie,* who makes and eats such sandwiches]

dah (dä), *n.* an echoic word, the referent of which is a tone interval approximately three times the length of the dot, used to designate the dash of Morse code. Compare DIT.

dahl·ia (dal′yə, däl′-; *esp. Brit.* däl′-), *n., pl.* **-ias.** any composite plant of the genus *Dahlia,* native to Mexico and Central America, having tuberous roots and showy flowers. [after Anders *Dahl* (d. 1789), Swedish botanist]

Da·ho·mey (də hō′mē), *n.* former name of BENIN (def. 1). —**Da·ho′me·an, Da·ho′man,** *adj., n.*

da·hoon (də hōōn′), *n.* a southern U.S. evergreen shrub, *Ilex cassine,* of the holly family, having flat, leathery leaves and red or yellow berry clusters: cultivated for hedges.

dai·kon (dī′kən, -kon), *n.* a large, elongated, white winter radish, *Raphanus sativus longipinnatus,* used esp. in Japanese cooking.

dai·ly (dā′lē), *adj., n., pl.* **-lies, adv.** —*adj.* **1.** of, done, occurring, or issued each day or each weekday: *daily attendance; a daily newspaper.* **2.** computed or determined by the day: *a daily quota.* —*n.* **3.** a newspaper appearing each day or each weekday. **4. dailies,** the quickly printed film from one day's shooting of a motion picture, for review by the director; rushes. —*adv.* **5.** every day; day by day. —**dai′li·ness,** *n.*

dai′ly dou′ble, a betting system in horse or dog racing in which the bettor makes one bet on the winners of two races, usu. the first and second, and collects only if both choices win.

dai·myo (dī′myō), *n., pl.* **-myo, -myos.** one of the great feudal lords of Japan who were vassals of the shogun.

dain·ty (dān′tē), *adj.,* **-ti·er, -ti·est, n., pl.* **-ties.** —*adj.* **1.** of delicate beauty or form. **2.** pleasing to the taste and, often, temptingly served: *dainty pastries.* **3.** of delicate discrimination or taste; particular; fastidious: *a dainty eater.* **4.** overly particular; finicky. —*n.* **5.** something delicious to the taste; delicacy. —**dain′ti·ly,** *adv.* —**dain′ti·ness,** *n.*

dai·qui·ri (dī′kə rē, dak′ə-), *n., pl.* **-ris.** a cocktail of rum, lemon or lime juice, and sugar, sometimes with fruit added.

dair·y (dâr′ē), *n., pl.* **dair·ies, adj.** —*n.* **1.** a room, building, or group of buildings where milk and cream are kept and butter and cheese are made. **2.** a company that processes or distributes milk and milk products. **3.** a store that sells milk and milk products. **4.** the business of producing milk, butter, and cheese. **5.** (in the Jewish dietary laws) dairy products, in contrast to meat and meat products. —*adj.* **6.** of or pertaining to a dairy or to a farm devoted to the production of milk and milk products. **7.** of or pertaining to milk, cream, butter, cheese, etc.

dair•y cat•tle, *n.pl.* cows raised mainly for their milk.

dair•y farm, *n.* a farm devoted chiefly to the production of milk and milk products.

da•is (dā′is, dī′-, dās), *n.* a raised platform, as at the front of a room, for a lectern, throne, seats of honor, etc.

dai•sy (dā′zē), *n.*, *pl.* **-sies.** **1.** any of various composite plants that have flower heads of a yellow disk and white rays, as the English daisy and oxeye daisy. **2.** Also called **dai′sy ham′.** a small section of pork shoulder, usu. smoked and boned. **3.** *Slang.* someone or something of first-rate quality. —*Idiom.* **4. push up daisies,** *Informal.* to be dead and buried. —**dai′sied,** *adj.*

dai•sy wheel′, *n.* a small spoked wheel with raised numbers, letters, etc., on the tips of the spokes: used as the printing element in some typewriters and computer printers.

Da•kar (dä kär′), *n.* a seaport in and the capital of Senegal. 1,380,000; 68 sq. mi. (176 sq. km).

Da•ko•ta (də kō′tə), *n.*, *pl.* **-tas,** (*esp. collectively*) **-ta** for defs. 3, 4. **1.** a former territory in the U.S.: divided into the states of North Dakota and South Dakota 1889. **2. the Dakotas,** North Dakota and South Dakota. **3.** a member of an Native American people of Minnesota and the N Great Plains in the mid-19th century: later confined to reservations, mainly in the Dakotas, Montana, Nebraska, and Canada. **4.** the easternmost subgroup of the Dakota. **5.** the Siouan language of the Dakota. —**Da•ko′tan,** *adj.*, *n.*

dal, dekaliter.

Da•lai La•ma (dä′lī lä′mə), *n.* **1.** the title for the traditional ruler and chief monk of Tibet. **2.** (*Tenzin Gyatso*), born 1935, Tibetan religious and political leader, in exile since 1959: the Dalai Lama since 1940. [< Mongolian, = *dalai* ocean + *lama* a celibate priest]

dale (dāl), *n.* a valley, esp. a broad valley.

Dal•las (dal′əs), *n.* **1. George Mifflin,** 1792–1864, vice president of the U.S. 1845–49. **2.** a city in NE Texas. 1,022,830.

dal•li•ance (dal′ē əns, dal′yəns), *n.* **1.** a trifling away of time; dawdling. **2.** amorous toying; flirtation.

Dal′lis grass′ (dal′is), *n.* a pasture grass, *Paspalum dilatatum*, native to South America and naturalized in the southern U.S.

Dall′s′ sheep′ (dôlz) also **Dall′ sheep′,** *n.* a white-haired wild mountain sheep, *Ovis dalli*, of NW North America.

dal•ly (dal′ē), *v.*, **-lied, -ly•ing.** —*v.i.* **1.** to waste time; loiter; delay. **2.** to act playfully, esp. in an amorous or flirtatious way. **3.** to play mockingly; trifle: *to dally with danger.* —*v.t.* **4.** to waste (time) (usu. fol. by *away*). —**dal′li•er,** *n.* —**dal′ly•ing•ly,** *adv.*

Dal•ma•tian (dal mā′shən), *n.* **1.** a native or inhabitant of Dalmatia. **2.** one of a breed of medium-sized shorthaired dogs having a white coat marked with black or brown spots.

dal•mat•ic (dal mat′ik), *n.* **1.** an open-sided vestment worn over the alb by a deacon or bishop. **2.** a similar vestment worn by English sovereigns at their coronation.

dal•ton (dôl′tn), *n.* ATOMIC MASS UNIT.

dal•ton•ism (dôl′tn iz′əm), *n.* (*sometimes cap.*) color blindness, esp. the inability to distinguish red from green. —**dal•ton′ic** (-ton′ik), *adj.*

dam¹ (dam), *n.*, *v.*, **dammed, dam•ming.** —*n.* **1.** a barrier to obstruct the flow of water, esp. one of earth, masonry, etc., built across a stream or river. **2.** a body of water confined by a dam. **3.** any barrier resembling a dam. —*v.t.* **4.** to furnish with a dam; obstruct or confine with a dam. **5.** to stop up; block up.

dam² (dam), *n.* a female parent (used esp. of four-footed domestic animals).

dam•age (dam′ij), *n.*, *v.*, **-aged, -ag•ing.** —*n.* **1.** injury or harm that reduces value, usefulness, etc. **2. damages,** the estimated money equivalent for loss or injury sustained. **3.** Often, **damages.** *Informal.* cost; expense; charge: *What are the damages for the work on my car?* —*v.t.* **4.** to cause damage to. —*v.i.* **5.** to become damaged. —**dam′age•a•ble,** *adj.* —**dam′age•a•bil′i•ty,** *n.*

dam′age control′, *n.* any efforts, as by a politician or a company, to counteract unfavorable publicity, curtail losses, or the like.

dam•ag•ing (dam′i jing), *adj.* causing or capable of causing damage; harmful; injurious. —**dam′ag•ing•ly,** *adv.*

Da•mas•cus (də mas′kəs), *n.* the capital of Syria, in the SW part: reputed to be the oldest continuously existing city in the world. 1,251,000.

Damas′cus steel′, *n.* hand-wrought steel, repeatedly folded over and welded and finally etched to reveal the resulting grain: used esp. for sword blades. Also called **damask.**

dam•ask (dam′əsk), *n.* **1.** an elaborately patterned, usu. reversible fabric of linen, silk, cotton, wool, or synthetic fibers, woven on a Jacquard loom. **2. a.** Also called **dam′ask steel′.** DAMASCUS STEEL. **b.** the pattern or wavy appearance peculiar to the surface of such steel. **3.** the pink color of the damask rose. —*adj.* **4.** made of or resembling damask. **5.** of the pink color of the damask rose.

dam′ask rose′, *n.* a fragrant pink rose, *Rosa damascena*.

dame (dām), *n.* **1.** (*cap.*) (in Britain) **a.** the official title of a female member of the Order of the British Empire, equivalent to that of a knight. **b.** the official title of the wife of a knight or baronet. **2.** (for-

merly) a form of address to any woman of rank or authority. **3.** a matronly woman of advanced age; matron. **4.** *Slang* (*sometimes offensive*). a woman; female.

dames′ rock′et, *n.* a Eurasian plant, *Hesperis matronalis*, of the mustard family, having loose clusters of four-petalled purple or white fragrant flowers. Also called **dames′ vi′olet.**

Da•mien (dā′mē ən), *n.* **Father (Joseph de Veuster),** 1840–89, Belgian Roman Catholic missionary to the lepers of Molokai.

da•min•o•zide (də min′ə zīd′), *n.* a plant-growth retardant, $C_6H_{12}N_2O_3$, formerly used for controlling the ripening of apples.

dam•mar (dam′ər), *n.* a hard, lustrous resin derived from S Asian trees of the monkey puzzle family, used for making a colorless varnish.

damn (dam), *v.t.* **1.** to declare to be bad, unfit, invalid, or illegal. **2.** to condemn as a failure: *to damn a play.* **3.** to bring condemnation upon; ruin: *damned by his gambling habit.* **4.** to doom to eternal punishment or condemn to hell. —*Idiom.* **5. damn with faint praise,** to praise so moderately as, in effect, to condemn.

dam•na•ble (dam′nə bəl), *adj.* **1.** worthy of condemnation. **2.** detestable, abominable, or outrageous. —**dam′na•bly,** *adv.*

dam•na•tion (dam nā′shən), *n.* **1.** the act of damning or the state of being damned. **2.** a cause or occasion of being damned. **3.** condemnation to eternal punishment as a consequence of sin. —*interj.* **4.** (used as an oath expressing anger, upset, etc.)

damned (damd), *adj.*, *superl.* **damned•est, damnd•est,** *adv.* —*adj.* **1.** condemned or doomed, esp. to eternal punishment. **2.** detestable; loathsome: *Get that damned dog out of here!* **3.** complete; absolute; utter: *a damned nuisance.* —*adv.* **4.** extremely; very; absolutely: *a damned good singer; too damned lazy.*

damned•est (dam′dist), *adj.* **1.** most extraordinary or amazing: *It was the damnedest thing I'd ever seen.* —*n.* **2.** best; utmost: *We did our damnedest to finish on time.*

damn•ing (dam′ing, dam′ning), *adj.* causing incrimination: *damning evidence.* —**damn′ing•ly,** *adv.* —**damn′ing•ness,** *n.*

Dam•o•cles (dam′ə klēz′), *n.* a flatterer of classical legend who, having extolled the happiness of Dionysius, tyrant of Syracuse, was seated at a banquet with a sword suspended over his head by a single hair to show him the perilous nature of that happiness. Compare SWORD OF DAMOCLES.

Da′mon and Pyth′ias (dā′mən), *n.* two legendary Greeks of ancient Syracuse, whose mutual loyalty was shown by Damon's offer of his life as a pledge that Pythias, sentenced to death, would return from settling his affairs to face execution.

damp (damp), *adj.* **1.** slightly wet; moist: *a damp cellar; a damp towel.* **2.** unenthusiastic; dejected; depressed: *a rather damp reception.* —*n.* **3.** moisture; humidity; moist air. **4.** a noxious or stifling vapor or gas, esp. in a mine. **5.** depression of spirits; dejection. **6.** a restraining or discouraging force or factor. —*v.t.* **7.** to make damp; moisten. **8.** to check or retard the energy, action, etc., of; deaden; dampen. **9.** to stifle or suffocate; extinguish: *to damp a furnace.* **10.** to check or retard the action of (a vibrating string); dull; deaden. **11.** to cause a decrease in amplitude of (successive oscillations or waves). —**damp′ish,** *adj.* —**damp′ish•ly,** *adv.* —**damp′ish•ness,** *n.* —**damp′ly,** *adv.* —**damp′ness,** *n.*

damp•en (dam′pən), *v.t.* **1.** to make damp; moisten. **2.** to dull or deaden; depress: *to dampen one's spirits.* —*v.i.* **3.** to become damp. —**damp′en•er,** *n.*

damp•er (dam′pər), *n.* **1.** a person or thing that damps or depresses: *The bad news put a damper on the party.* **2.** a movable plate for regulating the draft in a stove, furnace, etc. **3. a.** a device in stringed keyboard instruments to deaden the vibration of the strings. **b.** the mute of a brass instrument, as a horn. **4.** an attachment to keep the indicator of a measuring instrument from oscillating excessively.

damp′er ped′al, *n.* a pedal on a piano that raises the dampers, allowing the strings to continue vibrating.

dam•sel (dam′zəl), *n.* a maiden, orig. one of gentle or noble birth.

dam•sel•fish (dam′zəl fish′), *n.*, *pl.* (*esp. collectively*) **-fish,** (*esp. for kinds or species*) **-fish•es.** any of several brilliantly colored coral reef fishes of the family Pomacentridae. Also called **demoiselle.**

dam•sel•fly (dam′zəl flī′), *n.*, *pl.* **-flies.** any of numerous slender, nonstinging insects of the order Odonata (suborder Zygoptera), distinguished from the dragonflies by having the wings folded back in line with the body when at rest.

dam•son (dam′zən, -sən), *n.* **1.** a small, dark blue or purple plum. **2.** the tree from which it comes, *Prunus insititia*, native to Asia Minor.

dan (dän, dan), *n.* a level of expertise in a martial art, as karate or judo, usu. signified by the wearing of a cloth belt of a particular color.

Dan (dan), *n.* **1.** a son of Jacob and Bilhah. Gen. 30:6. **2.** one of the 12 tribes of Israel, traditionally descended from him. **3.** the northernmost city of ancient Palestine. —*Idiom.* **4. from Dan to Beersheba,** from one outermost extreme or limit to the other. Judg. 20:1.

Dan., Daniel.

dance (dans, däns), *v.*, **danced, danc•ing,** *n.* —*v.i.* **1.** to move one's feet or body, or both, rhythmically in a pattern of steps, esp. to the accompaniment of music. **2.** to leap, skip, etc., as from excitement or emotion; move nimbly or quickly. **3.** to bob up and down: *The toy sailboats danced on the pond.* —*v.t.* **4.** to perform or take part in (a dance). **5.** to cause to dance: *He danced her around the room.* **6.** to cause to be in a specified condition by dancing: *She danced her way to stardom.*

—*n.* **7.** a successive group of rhythmical steps or bodily motions, or both, usu. executed to music. **8.** an act or round of dancing; set: *May I have this dance?* **9.** the art of dancing: *to study dance.* **10.** a social gathering or party for dancing; ball. **11.** a piece of music suited in rhythm or style to a particular form of dancing. **12.** a stylized pattern of movements performed by an animal, as a bird in a courtship display. —*Idiom.* **13.** dance attendance on, to lavish attention on obsequiously. **14.** dance to another tune, to change one's behavior, attitudes, etc. —dance′a•ble, *adj.* —dance′a•bil′i•ty, *n.* —danc′er, *n.*

dance′ hall′, *n.* a public establishment that, for a fee, provides music and space for dancing and, sometimes, dancing partners and refreshments.

dance′ of death′, *n.* a symbolic dance in which Death, represented as a skeleton, leads people to their grave. Also called **danse macabre.**

danc•er•cise (dan′sər sīz′, dän′-), *n.* vigorous dancing done as an exercise for physical fitness.

D and C, *n.* a surgical method for the removal of diseased tissue or an early embryo from the lining of the uterus by means of scraping.

D&D, Dungeons and Dragons.

dan•de•li•on (dan′dl ī′ən), *n.* any weedy composite plant of the genus *Taraxacum,* having edible, toothed leaves, golden-yellow flowers, and clusters of white, hairy seeds. [< Middle French *dent de lion* tooth of a lion, in allusion to the toothed leaves]

dan•der (dan′dər), *n.* **1.** loose scales formed on the skin and shed from the coat or feathers of various animals. **2.** *Informal.* anger; temper: *Don't get your dander up.*

dan•dle (dan′dl), *v.t.,* -dled, -dling. **1.** to move (as a child) lightly up and down, on one's knee or in one's arms. **2.** to pet; pamper. —dan′dler, *n.*

dan•druff (dan′drəf), *n.* a seborrheic scurf that forms on the scalp and comes off in small scales.

dan•dy (dan′dē), *n., pl.* -dies, *adj.,* -di•er, -di•est. —*n.* **1.** a man excessively concerned about his clothes and appearance; fop. **2.** something or someone of exceptional quality. —*adj.* **3.** characteristic of a dandy; foppish. **4.** fine; excellent; first-rate. —dan′di•ly, *adv.* —dan′dy•ish, *adj.* —dan′dy•ism, *n.*

Dane (dān), *n.* **1.** a native or inhabitant of Denmark. **2.** GREAT DANE.

dan•ger (dān′jər), *n.* **1.** liability or exposure to harm or injury; risk; peril. **2.** an instance or cause of peril; menace.

dan•ger•ous (dān′jər əs, dānj′rəs), *adj.* **1.** full of danger or risk; causing danger; perilous; risky; hazardous. **2.** able or likely to cause physical injury. —dan′ger•ous•ly, *adv.*

dan•gle (dang′gəl), *v.,* -gled, -gling, *n.* —*v.i.* **1.** to hang loosely, esp. with a jerking or swaying motion. **2.** to hang around or follow a person, as if seeking favor or attention. —*v.t.* **3.** to cause to dangle; hold or carry swaying loosely. **4.** to offer as an inducement. —*n.* **5.** the act of dangling. **6.** something that dangles. —*Idiom.* **7.** keep someone dangling, to keep someone in a state of uncertainty. —dan′gler, *n.*

dan′gling par′ticiple, *n.* a participle or participial phrase, often found at the beginning of a sentence, that appears from its position to modify an element of the sentence other than the one it was intended to modify, as *plunging* in *Plunging hundreds of feet into the gorge, we saw Yosemite Falls.*

Dan•iel (dan′yəl), *n.* **1.** a Hebrew prophet during the Babylonian captivity. **2.** the book of the Bible bearing his name.

Daniel in the lions' den, an episode in which the prophet Daniel was thrown into a den of lions but suffered no harm because he had prayed to God. Dan. 6.

Dan•ish (dā′nish), *adj.* **1.** of or pertaining to Denmark, the Danes, or the language Danish. —*n.* **2.** the Germanic language of the Danes. *Abbr.:* Dan **3.** DANISH PASTRY.

Dan′ish pas′try, *n.* a rich, flaky, yeast-leavened pastry, often filled with cheese, nuts, or fruit.

Dan•ite (dan′īt), *n.* **1.** a member of the tribe of Dan. **2.** a member of an alleged secret order of Mormons supposed to have been formed about 1837.

dank (dangk), *adj.* unpleasantly moist or humid; damp and, often, chilly: *a dank cellar.* —dank′ly, *adv.* —dank′ness, *n.*

danse ma•ca•bre (Fr. däns mA kA′brə), *n.* DANCE OF DEATH.

Dan•te (dän′tā, -tē, *Dante Alighieri*), 1265–1321, Italian poet: author of the *Divine Comedy.* —Dan•te•an (dan′tē ən, dan tē′-), *adj., n.* —Dan•tesque (dan tesk′), *adj.*

Dan•ube (dan′yōōb), *n.* a river in central and SE Europe, flowing E from S Germany to the Black Sea. 1725 mi. (2775 km) long. German, Donau. Hungarian, Duna. Czech and Slovak, Dunaj. Romanian, Dunărea. —Dan•u′bi•an, *adj.*

Dan•zig (dan′sig, dän′-), *n.* German name of GDANSK.

dap (dap), *v.i.,* dapped, dap•ping. **1.** to fish by letting the bait fall lightly on the water. **2.** to dip lightly or suddenly into water: *The bird dapped for the fish.* **3.** to bounce or skip, as on the surface of a body of water.

daph•ni•a (daf′nē ə), *n., pl.* -ni•as. any tiny freshwater branchiopod crustacean of the genus *Daphnia,* used as aquarium food.

dap•per (dap′ər), *adj.* **1.** neat, trim, or smart in dress or demeanor; spruce. **2.** lively and brisk: *to walk with a dapper step.* **3.** small and active. —dap′per•ly, *adv.* —dap′per•ness, *n.*

dap•ple (dap′əl), *n., adj., v.,* -pled, -pling. —*n.* **1.** a spot or mottled marking, usu. occurring in clusters. **2.** an animal with a mottled skin or coat. —*adj.* **3.** marked with spots; dappled: *a dapple horse.* —*v.t., v.i.* **4.** to mark or become marked with spots of a different shade or color from the background.

dap′ple-gray′, *adj.* gray with ill-defined mottling of a darker shade.

D.A.R., Daughters of the American Revolution.

Dar•by (där′bē), *n.* **John Nelson,** 1800–82, English religious leader, founder of the Plymouth Brethren.

dar•cy (där′sē), *n., pl.* -cies. a unit of permeability measuring the flow of fluid through a porous medium.

Dar•da•nelles (där′dn elz′), *n.* (*used with a pl. v.*) the strait between European and Asian Turkey, connecting the Aegean Sea with the Sea of Marmara. 40 mi. (64 km) long; 1–5 mi. (1.6–8 km) wide. Ancient, **Hellespont.**

dare (dâr), *v.,* dared, daring; *pres. sing. 3rd pers.* dares or dare, *n.* —*v.i.* **1.** to have the necessary courage or boldness for something; be bold enough: *You wouldn't dare!* —*v.t.* **2.** to have the boldness to try; venture; hazard. **3.** to meet defiantly; face courageously. **4.** to challenge or provoke (a person) into a demonstration of courage: *I dare you to climb that.* —*auxiliary v.* **5.** to have the necessary courage or boldness to (used chiefly in questions and negatives): *How dare you speak to me like that? He dare not mention the subject again.* —*n.* **6.** an act of daring or defiance; challenge. —*Idiom.* **7.** dare say, DARESAY. —dar′er, *n.*

Dare (dâr), *n.* **Virginia,** 1587–?, first child born of English parents in the Western Hemisphere.

DARE, Dictionary of American Regional English.

dare•dev•il (dâr′dev′əl), *n.* **1.** a recklessly daring person. —*adj.* **2.** recklessly daring. —dare′dev′il•try, dare′dev′il•ry, *n.*

dare•say (dâr′sā′), *v.i., v.t.* to venture to say (something); assume (something) as probable (used in pres. sing. 1st pers.): *I daresay it's too late now.* Also, dare′ say′.

Dar es Sa•laam or **Dar-es-Sa•laam** (där′ es sə läm′), *n.* a seaport in Tanzania, on the Indian Ocean. 757,346.

dar•ing (dâr′ing), *n.* **1.** adventurous courage; boldness; bravery. —*adj.* **2.** bold or courageous; fearless or intrepid; adventurous. —dar′ing•ly, *adv.* —dar′ing•ness, *n.*

Da•ri•us I (də rī′əs), *n.* (*Darius Hystaspes*) ("the Great"), 558?–486? B.C., king of Persia 521–486.

dark (därk), *adj.* **1.** having very little or no light: *a dark room.* **2.** radiating, admitting, or reflecting little light: *a dark color.* **3.** approaching black in hue: *a dark brown.* **4.** not pale or fair; swarthy: *a dark complexion.* **5.** brunette; dark-colored: *dark eyebrows.* **6.** having brunette hair: *She's dark but her children are blond.* **7.** (of coffee) containing only a small amount of milk or cream. **8.** gloomy; cheerless; dismal: *the dark days of the war.* **9.** sullen; frowning: *a dark expression.* **10.** evil; iniquitous; wicked: *a dark plot.* **11.** destitute of knowledge or culture; unenlightened. **12.** hard to understand; obscure. **13.** hidden; secret. **14.** (of a theater) offering no performances; closed. **15.** (of an *l*-sound) pronounced with the back of the tongue raised, giving back-vowel resonance, as the *l* in *full.* Compare CLEAR (def. 22). —*n.* **16.** the absence of light; darkness. **17.** night; nightfall: *to come home after dark.* **18.** a dark place. **19.** a dark color. —*Idiom.* **20.** in the dark, in ignorance; uninformed. —*Proverb.* **21.** It is always darkest just before the dawn, relief may come when things seem most hopeless.

dark′ adapta′tion, *n.* the reflex adjustment of the eye to dim light or darkness, consisting of a dilation of the pupil, an increase in the number of functioning rods, and a decrease in the number of functioning cones. —dark′-a•dapt′ed, *adj.*

Dark′ Ag′es, *n.* **1.** the period in European history from about A.D. 476 to about 1000. **2.** (*often l.c.*) a period or stage marked by repressiveness, a lack of advanced knowledge, etc.

dark•en (där′kən), *v.t., v.i.* **1.** to make or become dark or darker. **2.** to make or become obscure. **3.** to make or become less white or clear in color. **4.** to make or become gloomy; sadden or dampen. **5.** to make or become clouded, furrowed, etc., as with worry or anger. —dark′en•er, *n.*

dark′ horse′, *n.* **1.** a racehorse, competitor, etc., that is relatively unknown or that wins unexpectedly. **2.** a candidate who is unexpectedly nominated at a political convention.

dark′ lan′tern, *n.* a lantern having an opening with a shutter that can be slid across the opening to obscure the light.

dark′ling bee′tle, *n.* any brown or black beetle of the family Tenebrionidae, the larvae of which feed on decaying plant matter.

dark•ly (därk′lē), *adv.* **1.** so as to appear dark. **2.** vaguely; mysteriously. **3.** in a vaguely threatening or menacing manner: *to hint darkly of hidden dangers.* **4.** imperfectly; faintly.

dark′ mat′ter, *n.* a hypothetical form of matter invisible to electromagnetic radiation, postulated to account for gravitational forces observed in the universe.

dark•ness (därk′nis), *n.* **1.** absence or deficiency of light: *the darkness of night.* **2.** wickedness or evil: *the forces of darkness.* **3.** obscurity; concealment. **4.** lack of knowledge or enlightenment. **5.** lack of sight; blindness. —*Idiom.* **6.** cast into outer darkness, to reject and exclude. Matt. 8:12.

dark′ reac′tion, *n.* the phase of photosynthesis, not requiring light, in which carbohydrates are synthesized from carbon dioxide.

dark•room (därk′rōōm′, -rŏŏm′), *n.* a room in which film, photographic paper, etc., is made, handled, or developed and from which certain rays of light are excluded.

dar·ling (där′ling), *n.* **1.** a person very dear to another; one dearly loved. **2.** a person or thing in great favor; a favorite: *the darling of café society.* —*adj.* **3.** very dear; dearly loved; cherished: *my darling child.* **4.** charming; cute; lovable: *What a darling baby!* —**dar′ling·ly,** *adv.* —**dar′ling·ness,** *n.*

darn¹ (därn), *v.t.* **1.** to mend with rows of stitches, sometimes by crossing and interweaving rows. —*n.* **2.** a darned place, as in a garment. —**darn′er,** *n.*

darn² (därn), *adj., adv.* **1.** damned. —*v.t.* **2.** to curse; damn: *Darn that pesky fly!*

darned (därnd), *adj., adv.* damned.

dar·nel (där′nl), *n.* any weedy grass of the genus *Lolium,* having flat leaves and terminal spikes.

darn·ing (där′ning), *n.* articles to be darned.

darn′ing nee′dle, *n.* **1.** a long needle with a long eye used in darning. **2.** *Chiefly Northern and Western U.S.* a dragonfly.

Dar·row (dar′ō), *n.* **Clarence (Seward),** 1857–1938, U.S. lawyer.

dart (därt), *n.* **1.** a small, slender missile pointed at one end and usu. feathered at the other, propelled by hand, as in the game of darts. **2.** something similar in function to such a missile, as the stinging member of an insect. **3. darts,** (*used with a sing. v.*) a game in which darts are thrown at a target having a bull's-eye in the center. **4.** a sudden swift movement. **5.** a tapered seam of fabric for adjusting the fit of a garment. —*v.i.* **6.** to move swiftly; spring or start suddenly and run swiftly; dash. —*v.t.* **7.** to thrust or move suddenly or rapidly: *to dart one's eyes around the room.* —**dart′ing·ly,** *adv.*

dart·board (därt′bôrd′, -bōrd′), *n.* the target used in the game of darts.

dart·er (där′tər), *n.* **1.** a person or thing that darts. **2.** any of several small, darting, colorful North American perches.

Dar·win (där′win), *n.* **1. Charles (Robert),** 1809–82, English naturalist. **2.** his grandfather, **Erasmus,** 1731–1802, English naturalist and poet. —**Dar·win′i·an,** *adj., n.*

Dar·win·ism (där′wə niz′əm), *n.* the Darwinian theory that species originate by descent with slight variation from parent forms through the natural selection of individuals best adapted for survival and reproduction. —**Dar′win·ist,** *n., adj.* —**Dar′win·is′tic,** *adj.*

Dar′win's finch′es, *n.pl.* a group of Galapagos Island finches, esp. of the genus *Geospiza,* that were observed by Charles Darwin and provide a striking example of speciation.

dash (dash), *v.t.* **1.** to strike or smash violently, esp. so as to break to pieces: *to dash a plate against a wall.* **2.** to throw or thrust violently or suddenly: *to dash one stone against another.* **3.** to splash, often violently; spatter, as with water or mud. **4.** to apply roughly, as by splashing: *to dash paint on a wall.* **5.** to mix or adulterate by adding another substance: *wine dashed with water.* **6.** to ruin or frustrate: *The rain dashed our hopes for a picnic.* **7.** to depress; dispirit: *The failure dashed my spirits.* **8.** to confound or abash. —*v.i.* **9.** to strike with violence: *waves dashing against the cliff.* **10.** to move with violence; rush: *to dash around the corner.* **11. dash off, a.** to hurry away; leave. **b.** Also, **dash down,** to write, make, accomplish, etc., hastily: *to dash off a letter; to dash down a memo.* —*n.* **12.** a small quantity of anything thrown into or mixed with something else: *a dash of salt.* **13.** a hasty or sudden movement; a rush or sudden onset: *to make a dash for the door.* **14.** a mark or sign (—) used variously in printed or written matter, esp. to note a break, pause, or hesitation, to begin and end parenthetic text, to indicate omission of letters or words, to substitute for certain uses of the colon, and to separate elements of a sentence or series of sentences, as a question from its answer. **15.** the throwing or splashing of liquid against something. **16.** the sound of such splashing. **17.** spirited action; élan; vigor in action or style: *to perform with spirit and dash.* **18.** a short race: *the 100-yard dash.* **19.** DASHBOARD (def. 1). **20.** a signal of longer duration than a dot, used in groups of dots, dashes, and spaces to represent letters, as in Morse code. **21.** a hasty stroke, esp. of a pen.

dash·board (dash′bôrd′, -bōrd′), *n.* **1.** the instrument panel of an automotive vehicle. **2.** a board at the front of an open carriage to deflect mud or dirt.

da·sheen (da shēn′), *n.* TARO.

dash·er (dash′ər), *n.* **1.** a person or thing that dashes. **2.** a plunger with paddles at one end, as for churning butter or ice cream. **3.** a person of dashing appearance or manner.

da·shi·ki (də shē′kē, dä-) also **daishiki,** *n., pl.* **-kis.** a loose, often colorfully patterned pullover garment of African origin.

dashiki

dash·ing (dash′ing), *adj.* **1.** energetic and spirited; lively: *a dashing hero.* **2.** elegant and gallant in appearance and manner: *a dashing young cavalry officer.* —**dash′ing·ly,** *adv.*

das·tard·ly (das′tərd lē), *adj.* cowardly; meanly base; sneaking: *a dastardly act.* —**das′tard·li·ness,** *n.*

das·y·ure (das′ē yŏŏr′), *n.* any carnivorous marsupial of the family Dasyuridae, of Australia and nearby islands. —**das′y·u′rid,** *adj., n.* —**das′y·u′rine** (-īn, -in), *adj.* —**das′y·u′roid,** *adj., n.*

da·ta (dä′tə, dat′ə, dä′tə), *n.* **1.** a pl. of DATUM. **2.** (*used with a pl. v.*) individual facts, statistics, or items of information. **3.** (*used with a sing. v.*) a body or collection of facts or particulars; information. —**Usage.** DATA is a plural of DATUM, orig. a Latin noun meaning "a thing given." Today, DATA is used in English both as a plural noun meaning "facts or pieces of information" (*These data are described fully on page 8*) and as a singular mass noun meaning "information": *The data has been entered in the computer.* It is almost always treated as a plural in scientific and academic writing, as a singular or plural elsewhere depending on the context. The singular DATUM meaning "a piece of information" is now rare in all types of writing.

da′ta·base′ or **da′ta base′,** *n.* **1.** a collection of organized, related data, esp. one in electronic form that can be accessed and manipulated by specialized computer software. **2.** a fund of information on one or more subjects, as a collection of articles or précis, accessible by computer.

da′ta proc′essing, *n.* the automated processing of information, esp. by computers. —**da′ta proc′essor,** *n.*

date¹ (dāt), *n., v.,* **dat·ed, dat·ing.** —*n.* **1.** a particular month, day, and year at which some event happened or will happen: *July 4, 1776 is an important date in American history.* **2.** the day of the month: *Is today's date the 7th or the 8th?* **3.** an inscription on a writing, coin, etc., that shows the time, or time and place, of writing, casting, delivery, etc.: *a letter bearing the date January 16.* **4.** the time or period to which any event or thing belongs; period in general: *at a late date.* **5.** the time during which anything lasts; duration: *Childhood has so short a date.* **6.** an appointment for a particular time, esp. a social engagement or occasion arranged beforehand. **7.** a person with whom one has such an appointment: *Can I bring a date to the party?* **8.** an engagement to perform; booking. **9. dates,** the birth and death dates, usu. in years, of a person: *Dante's dates are 1265 to 1321.* —*v.i.* **10.** to have or bear a date: *The letter dates from 1873.* **11.** to belong to a particular period; have its origin: *The architecture dates as far back as 1830.* **12.** to reckon from some point in time: *The custom dates from the Victorian era.* **13.** to go out socially on dates. —*v.t.* **14.** to mark or furnish with a date. **15.** to ascertain or fix the period or point in time of: *to date the archaeological ruins.* **16.** to show the age of; show to be old-fashioned. **17.** to make a date with; go out on dates with: *He's dating his best friend's sister.* —**Idiom. 18. to date,** up to the present time; until now. **19. up to date,** in accord with the latest styles, information, or technology. —**dat′a·ble, date′a·ble,** *adj.* —**dat′er,** *n.*

date² (dāt), *n.* the oblong, fleshy fruit of the date palm.

date·book (dāt′bŏŏk′), *n.* a notebook for listing appointments, making entries of events, etc., usu. for the period of a year.

dat·ed (dā′tid), *adj.* **1.** having or showing a date. **2.** out-of-date; old-fashioned; outmoded. —**dat′ed·ness,** *n.*

date·less (dāt′lis), *adj.* **1.** lacking a date; undated. **2.** endless; limitless. **3.** so old as to be undatable. **4.** of permanent interest regardless of age: *a dateless work of art.* **5.** having no social engagement.

date·line (dāt′līn′), *n., v.,* **-lined, -lin·ing.** —*n.* **1.** a line at the beginning of a news dispatch, giving the place of origin and usu. the date. —*v.t.* **2.** to furnish (a news story) with a dateline.

date′ palm′, *n.* any date-bearing palm of the genus *Phoenix,* esp. *P. dactylifera,* having a tall trunk topped by a crown of pinnate leaves.

date′ rape′, *n.* sexual intercourse forced by a man upon the woman with whom he has a date.

Da·than (dā′thən), *n.* a leader of the tribe of Reuben who attempted to overthrow Moses and Aaron. Num. 16; 26:9; Deut. 11:6.

da·tive (dā′tiv), *adj.* **1.** of or designating a grammatical case that typically indicates the indirect object of a verb or the object of certain prepositions. —*n.* **2.** a word or other form in the dative case.

da·tum (dā′təm, dat′əm, dä′təm), *n., pl.* **da·ta** (dä′tə, dat′ə, dä′tə) for 1, 2, **da·tums** for . **1.** a single piece of information, as a fact, statistic, or code; an item of data. **2.** any proposition assumed or given, from which conclusions may be drawn.

da·tu·ra (də tŏŏr′ə, -tyŏŏr′ə), *n., pl.* **-ras.** any plant of the genus *Datura,* of the nightshade family, usu. having funnel-shaped flowers and prickly pods: a source of hallucinogenic alkaloids. Compare JIMSONWEED. —**da·tu′ric,** *adj.*

daub (dôb), *v.t.* **1.** to cover or coat with soft, adhesive matter, as plaster, paint, or mud. **2.** to smear, soil, or defile. **3.** to apply unskillfully, as paint or colors. —*v.i.* **4.** to daub something. **5.** to paint unskillfully. —*n.* **6.** material, esp. of an inferior kind, for daubing walls. **7.** something daubed on. **8.** an act of daubing. **9.** a crude, inartistic painting. —**daub′er,** *n.*

daube (dōb), *n.* a stew of meat, esp. beef, slowly braised in red wine with vegetables and seasonings.

daugh·ter (dô′tər), *n.* **1.** a girl or woman in relation to her parents. **2.** any female descendant. **3.** a person related as if by the ties binding daughter to parent: *a daughter of the church.* **4.** anything personified as female and considered with respect to its origin. **5.** an isotope formed by radioactive decay of another isotope. —*adj.* **6.** pertaining to a cell or other structure arising from division or replication: *daughter cell; daughter DNA.*

daugh′ter-in-law′, *n., pl.* **daugh·ters-in-law.** the wife of one's son.

Daugh′ter of Zi′on, *n.* Jerusalem and its inhabitants. Ps. 9:14; Is. 1:8.

Daugh′ters of the Amer′ican Revolu′tion, *n.* a patriotic society of women descended from Americans of the Revolutionary period, organized in 1890. *Abbr.:* D.A.R.

daunt (dônt, dänt), *v.t.* **1.** to overcome with fear; intimidate: *to daunt one's adversaries.* **2.** to lessen the courage of; dishearten: *Don't be daunted by the remaining work.* —**daunt′ing·ly,** *adv.*

daunt·less (dônt′lis, dänt′-), *adj.* not to be daunted or intimidated; fearless; intrepid; bold: *a dauntless hero.* —**daunt′less·ly,** *adv.* —**daunt′less·ness,** *n.*

dau·phin (dô′fin, dō faN′), *n.* the eldest son of a king of France, used as a title from 1349 to 1830.

da·ven or **do·ven** (dä′vən), *v.i.* to recite the Jewish prayers.

dav·en·port (dav′ən pôrt′, -pōrt′), *n.* **1.** a large sofa, often one convertible into a bed. **2.** *Chiefly Brit.* a small writing desk.

Da·vid (dä′vid *for 1, 2; Fr.* dá vēd′ *for 3*), *n.* **1.** died c970 B.C., the second king of Israel, reigned c1010–c970, successor to Saul. **2. Saint,** A.D. c510–601?, Welsh bishop: patron saint of Wales. **3. Jacques Louis,** 1748–1825, French painter.

Da·vid Cop·per·field (dä′vid kop′ər fēld′), a novel (1850) by Charles Dickens.

Da·vid·ic (də vid′ik), *adj.* of or pertaining to the Biblical David or his descendants.

Da·vis (dä′vis), *n.* **1. Bet·te** (bet′ē), (*Ruth Elizabeth Davis*), 1908–89, U.S. film actress. **2. Jefferson,** 1808–89, president of the Confederate States of America 1861–65. **3. Miles (Dewey, Jr.),** 1926–91, U.S. jazz trumpeter. **4. Owen,** 1874–1956, U.S. playwright. **5. Richard Harding,** 1864–1916, U.S. journalist, novelist, and playwright. **6. Sammy, Jr.,** 1925–90, U.S. singer and entertainer. **7. Stuart,** 1894–1964, U.S. painter and illustrator.

dav·it (dav′it, dä′vit), *n.* any of various cranelike devices used on a ship for supporting, raising, and lowering boats, anchors, etc.

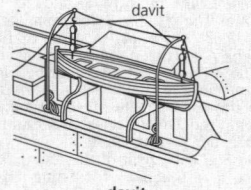

davit

Da·vy (dä′vē), *n.* **Sir Humphry,** 1778–1829, English chemist.

Da′vy Jones′ (jōnz), *n.* the personification of the sea.

Da′vy Jones′'s lock′er (jōn′ziz, jōnz), *n.* the bottom of the ocean, esp. when regarded as the grave of all who perish at sea.

daw·dle (dôd′l), *v.,* **-dled, -dling.** —*v.i.* **1.** to waste time; idle; loiter. **2.** to move slowly, languidly, or dilatorily; saunter. —*v.t.* **3.** to waste (time) by or as if by trifling (usu. fol. by *away*): *We dawdled away the whole morning.* —**daw′dler,** *n.* —**daw′dling·ly,** *adv.*

Dawes (dôz), *n.* **Charles Gates,** 1865–1951, vice president of the U.S. 1925–29.

dawn (dôn), *n.* **1.** the first appearance of daylight in the morning; daybreak; sunrise. **2.** the beginning or rise of anything; advent: *the dawn of civilization.* —*v.i.* **3.** to begin to grow light in the morning: *The day dawned cloudless.* **4.** to begin to open or develop. **5.** to begin to be perceived (usu. fol. by *on*): *The idea suddenly dawned on her.* —**dawn′like′,** *adj.*

day (dā), *n.* **1.** the interval of light between two successive nights; time between sunrise and sunset. **2.** the light of day; daylight. **3. a.** Also called **mean solar day.** a division of time equal to 24 hours and representing the average length of the period during which the earth makes one rotation on its axis. **b.** Also called **solar day.** a division of time equal to the time elapsed between two consecutive returns of the same terrestrial meridian to the sun. **c.** Also called **civil day.** a division of time equal to 24 hours but reckoned from one midnight to the next. **4.** an analogous division of time for a planet other than the earth: *the Martian day.* **5.** the portion of a day allotted to work: *an eight-hour day.* **6.** a time considered as propitious or opportune: *His day will come.* **7.** Often, **days.** a particular era: *in olden days.* **8.** Usu., **days.** period of life or activity: *His days are numbered.* **9.** period of existence or influence; heyday: *In my day we called them "hepcats."* **10.** the contest or battle at hand: *to win the day.* —*Idiom.* **11. call it a day,** to stop working for the rest of the day. **12. day in, day out,** every day without fail; regularly. Also, **day in and day out.**

day·bed (dā′bed′), *n.* **1.** a couch that can be used as a sofa by day and a bed by night. **2.** a couch, esp. of the 17th or 18th century, in the form

of a chair with a greatly elongated seat, used for reclining or sleeping during the day.

day·break (dā′brāk′), *n.* the first appearance of daylight in the morning; dawn.

day′ care′, *n.* supervised daytime care for preschool children, the elderly, or those with chronic disabilities, usu. provided at a center outside the home. —**day′-care′,** *adj.*

day·dream (dā′drēm′), *n.* **1.** a visionary fancy indulged in while awake; reverie. **2.** a fanciful notion, wish, or plan. —*v.i.* **3.** to indulge in daydreams. —**day′dream′er,** *n.* —**day′dream′y,** *adj.*

day·flow·er (dā′flou′ər), *n.* any of various plants of the genus *Commelina,* of the spiderwort family, usu. bearing clusters of small blue flowers that open only during the day.

day·fly (dā′flī′), *n., pl.* **-flies.** an adult mayfly.

Day-Glo (dā′glō′), *Trademark.* a brand of pigments and other products that exhibit fluorescence in daylight.

day′ in court′, *n.* a chance to present one's defense or argument.

Day-Lew·is (dā′lōō′is), *n.* **C(ecil),** 1904–72, British poet, born in Ireland: poet laureate 1968–72.

day·light (dā′līt′), *n., adj., v.,* **-light·ed** or **-lit, -light·ing.** —*n.* **1.** the period of light during a day. **2.** public knowledge or awareness; openness. **3.** DAYTIME. **4.** daybreak; dawn. **5.** a crack, break, or other space between any two parts that should be close together: *I can see daylight around the doorframe.* **6. daylights,** wits; sanity: *to scare the daylights out of someone.* —*adj.* **7.** done, used, or taking place in daylight: *the daylight shooting on a film.* —*v.t.* **8.** to expose to daylight by the removal of obstructions: *a railway tunnel daylighted by blasting the enclosing rock.*

day′light sav′ing (or **sav′ings**), *n.* the practice of advancing standard time by one hour in the spring of each year and of setting it back by one hour in the fall in order to gain an extra period of daylight during the early evening.

day′lil′y or **day′ lil′y,** *n.* any lily of the genus *Hemerocallis,* having short-lived yellow, orange, or red flowers.

day·lin′er or **day′ lin′er,** *n.* a train, boat, etc., having a regularly scheduled route during daylight hours.

day·mare (dā′mâr′), *n.* a distressing experience, similar to a bad dream, occurring while one is awake.

day′ name′, *n.* a name given at birth indicating the child's sex and the day of the week on which he or she was born.

day′ nurs′ery, *n.* a center for the care of small children during the day, esp. while their parents are at work.

Day′ of Atone′ment, *n.* YOM KIPPUR.

Day′ of In′famy, *n.* December 7, 1941, on which Japan attacked Pearl Harbor, bringing the United States into World War II: so referred to by President Franklin D. Roosevelt in his speech to Congress the next day, asking for a declaration of war on Japan.

Day′ of Judg′ment, *n.* JUDGMENT DAY.

Day′ of the Lord′, *n.* **1.** Also called **Day′ of Yah′weh.** (in Old Testament eschatology) a day of final judgment. Amos 5:18–21; Ezek. 30. **2.** Also called **Day′ of Christ′, Day of Je′sus Christ′.** the day of the Second Advent. II Peter 3:10; I Cor. 1:14; Phil. 1:10, 2:16.

day′ one′, *n.* (*often caps.*) the beginning; inception.

day′ room′ or **day′room′,** *n.* a room at an institution, as a hospital or military base, with facilities for leisure activities.

day′ school′, *n.* **1.** a school open for instruction on weekdays only. **2.** a private school for pupils living outside the school (disting. from *boarding school*).

day′ shift′, *n.* **1.** the work force scheduled to work during the daytime. **2.** the scheduled period of labor for this work force.

day·side (dā′sīd′), *n.* the side of a planet or moon illuminated by the sun.

days′ of grace′, *n.pl.* days, usu. three, allowed for payment after a bill or note falls due.

days′ of wine′ and ros′es, *n.pl.* a happy, prosperous period.

day·star (dā′stär′), *n.* **1.** a morning star. **2.** the sun.

day′ stu′dent, *n.* a regularly enrolled student at a preparatory school or college who does not live in a school residence but instead travels to class daily, as from the family home.

day·time (dā′tīm′), *n.* **1.** the time between sunrise and sunset. —*adj.* **2.** occurring, offered, or done during the day.

day′-to-day′, *adj.* **1.** occurring each day; daily. **2.** concerned only with immediate needs without regard for the future.

Day·ton (dāt′n), *n.* a city in SW Ohio. 178,540.

day′-trip′per, *n.* a person who goes on a trip, esp. an excursion, lasting all or part of a day.

daze (dāz), *v.,* **dazed, daz·ing,** *n.* —*v.t.* **1.** to stun or stupefy with a blow, shock, etc. **2.** to overwhelm; dazzle. —*n.* **3.** a dazed condition. —**daz′ed·ly,** *adv.* —**daz′ed·ness,** *n.*

daz·zle (daz′əl), *v.,* **-zled, -zling,** *n.* —*v.t.* **1.** to overpower the vision of by intense light. **2.** to impress deeply; astonish with delight. —*v.i.* **3.** to shine brilliantly. **4.** to excite admiration by brilliance. —*n.* **5.** an act or instance of dazzling. —**daz′zler,** *n.* —**daz′zling·ly,** *adv.*

dB or **db,** decibel.

dbl., double.

DBMS, database management system: a set of software programs for controlling the storage, retrieval, and modification of organized data in a computerized database.

DBS, direct broadcast satellite: a satellite that transmits television signals that can be picked up directly by a home viewer with a dish antenna.

DC, 1. Also, **dc, d.c., D.C.** direct current. 2. District of Columbia.

D.C., 1. da capo. 2. District of Columbia.

D.C.M., Distinguished Conduct Medal.

D.Cn.L., Doctor of Canon Law.

DD, dishonorable discharge.

dd or **dd.,** delivered.

D-day or **D-Day** (dē′dā′), *n.* 1. a day set for beginning something. 2. June 6, 1944, the day of the invasion of W Europe by Allied forces in World War II. [D (for *day*) + DAY]

D.D.S., 1. Doctor of Dental Science. 2. Doctor of Dental Surgery.

DDT, a toxic compound, $C_{14}H_9Cl_5$, formerly widely used as an insecticide.

de-, a prefix, occurring orig. in loanwords from Latin, used to form verbs that denote motion or conveyance down from, away, or off (*deflect; descend*); reversal or undoing of the effects of an action (*deflate*); extraction or removal of a thing (*decaffeinate*); thoroughness or completeness of an action (*despoil*).

DE, 1. Delaware. 2. destroyer escort.

de•a•cid•i•fy (dē′ə sid′ə fī′), *v.t.,* **-fied, -fy•ing.** to remove acid from or reduce the acidity of (a substance). —**de′a•cid′i•fi•ca′tion,** *n.*

dea•con (dē′kən), *n.* 1. (in hierarchical churches) a member of the clerical order next below that of a priest. 2. (in other churches) an appointed or elected officer having variously defined duties.

dea•con•ess (dē′kə nis), *n.* (in certain Protestant churches) a woman belonging to an order or sisterhood dedicated to social services.

de•ac•ti•vate (dē ak′tə vāt′), *v.,* **-vat•ed, -vat•ing.** —*v.t.* 1. to make inactive: *to deactivate a chemical.* 2. to demobilize or disband (a military unit). 3. to render (a bomb or shell) inoperative. —*v.i.* 4. to lose radioactivity. —**de•ac′ti•va′tion,** *n.* —**de•ac′ti•va′tor,** *n.*

dead (ded), *adj.* 1. no longer living; deprived of life. 2. brain-dead. 3. not endowed with life; inanimate. 4. resembling death; deathlike: *a dead faint.* 5. bereft of sensation or feeling; numb. 6. (of an emotion) no longer felt; extinguished: *a dead passion.* 7. obsolete; defunct. 8. inoperative: *a dead battery.* 9. stagnant or stale: *dead air.* 10. utterly tired; exhausted. 11. (of a language) no longer in use as a sole means of oral communication among a people. 12. dull or inactive: *a dead business day.* 13. complete; absolute: *dead silence.* 14. extinguished: *a dead cigarette.* 15. exact; precise: *the dead center of a target.* 16. flat rather than glossy: *dead white.* 17. lacking resonance: *dead sound.* 18. *Sports.* out of play: *a dead ball.* 19. (of type or copy) having been used or rejected. 20. **a.** free from any electric connection to a source of potential difference and from electric charge. **b.** not having a potential different from that of the earth. —*n.* 21. the period of greatest darkness, coldness, etc.: *the dead of night.* 22. **the dead,** dead persons collectively. —*adv.* 23. absolutely; completely: *dead tired.* 24. directly; straight: *dead ahead.* —*Idiom.* 25. **dead to rights,** in the very act of committing a crime. —*Proverb.* 26. **Let the dead bury the dead,** think of the future, not the past. Matt. 8:22.

dead′ air′, *n.* the loss or suspension of the video or audio signal during a television or radio transmission.

dead•beat (*n.* ded′bēt′; *adj.* -bēt′), *n.* 1. a person who avoids paying debts. 2. a sponger. —*adj.* 3. (of the indicator of an electric meter and the like) coming to a stop with little or no oscillation.

dead′beat dad′, *n.* a father who neglects his responsibilities as a parent, esp. one who does not pay child support to his estranged wife.

dead•bolt (ded′bōlt′), *n.* a lock bolt that is moved into position by the turning of a knob or key rather than by spring action.

dead′ cen′ter, *n.* 1. (in a reciprocating engine) either of two positions at which the crank cannot be turned by the connecting rod, occurring at each end of a stroke when the crank and connecting rod are in the same line. 2. a tapered rod mounted on the tailstock spindle of a lathe. —**dead′-cen′ter,** *adj.*

dead′ duck′, *n.* a person or thing that is beyond help or hope: *If the money doesn't arrive, you're a dead duck.*

dead•en (ded′n), *v.t.* 1. to make less sensitive, intense, or effective. 2. to make dull or lifeless. 3. to soundproof. —*v.i.* 4. to become deadened.

dead′ end′, *n.* 1. a street, corridor, etc., that has no exit. 2. a position with no hope of progress; blind alley.

dead′-end′, *adj.* 1. terminating in a dead end. 2. offering no possibility for advancement: *a dead-end job.* 3. living in the slums: *a dead-end kid.* —*v.i.* 4. to terminate in a dead end.

dead•en•ing (ded′n ing), *n.* material employed to deaden or prevent the transmission of sound; soundproofing.

dead′ heat′, *n.* a race in which two or more competitors finish in a tie.

dead′ let′ter, *n.* 1. a letter that is not deliverable or returnable because of incorrect address and that is sent to a special department (**dead′-let′ter of′fice**) of a post office. 2. a law no longer enforced but not formally repealed. —**dead′-let′ter,** *adj.*

dead•line (ded′līn′), *n.* 1. the time by which something must be finished, submitted, accomplished, etc. 2. a line or limit that must not be passed. 3. (formerly) a boundary around a military prison beyond which a prisoner could not venture without risk of being shot by the guards.

dead•lock (ded′lok′), *n.* 1. a state, as in negotiations, in which progress halts; stalemate. 2. (in sports) a tied score. 3. a maximum-security cell for the solitary confinement of a prisoner. —*v.t., v.i.* 4. to bring or come to a deadlock.

dead•ly (ded′lē), *adj.,* **-li•er, -li•est,** *adv.* —*adj.* 1. causing or tending to cause death; lethal. 2. aiming to kill or destroy; implacable: *a deadly enemy.* 3. like death; deathly. 4. excruciatingly boring. 5. excessive; inordinate: *deadly haste.* 6. extremely accurate: *a deadly shot.* —*adv.* 7. in a manner suggesting death: *deadly pale.* 8. excessively; completely: *deadly dull.* —**dead′li•ness,** *n.*

dead′ly night′shade, *n.* BELLADONNA (def. 1).

dead′ly sins′, *n.pl.* the seven sins of pride, covetousness, lust, anger, gluttony, envy, and sloth.

dead′-man′s′ float′, *n.* a prone floating position, with face downward, legs extended backward, and arms stretched forward.

dead′-on′, *adj. Informal.* exactly right; perfect.

dead•pan (ded′pan′), *adj., adv., v.,* **-panned, -pan•ning,** *n.* —*adj.* 1. marked by a fixed air of seriousness or calm detachment. —*adv.* 2. in a deadpan manner. —*v.i., v.t.* 3. to behave or perform in a deadpan manner. —*n.* 4. a deadpan face.

dead′ reck′oning, *n. Navig.* calculation of one's position on the basis of compass readings, speed, and distance run from a known point, with allowances for drift from wind, currents, etc. —**dead′-reck′on,** *v.t.*

dead′ ring′er, *n.* a person or thing that closely resembles another; twin; double.

Dead′ Sea′, *n.* a salt lake between Israel and Jordan: the lowest lake in the world. ab. 390 sq. mi. (1010 sq. km); 1293 ft. (394 m) below sea level.

Dead′ Sea′ Scrolls′, *n.pl.* a number of leather, papyrus, and copper scrolls dating from c100 B.C. to A.D. 135, containing partial texts of Old Testament books and some non-Biblical scrolls, in Hebrew and Aramaic, and including apocryphal writings, commentaries, hymns, and psalms: found in caves near the Dead Sea beginning in 1947.

dead′ weight′ or **dead′weight′,** *n.* 1. the heavy, unrelieved weight of anything inert. 2. a heavy burden or responsibility.

dead•wood (ded′wood′), *n.* 1. dead branches or trees. 2. useless or extraneous persons or things. 3. a reinforcing construction located between the keel of a ship and the stem or sternpost. 4. bowling pins knocked down but not cleared from the alley.

deaf (def), *adj.* 1. partially or wholly deprived of the sense of hearing. 2. refusing to heed or be persuaded; unyielding: *deaf to all advice.* —*n.* 3. **the deaf,** deaf persons collectively. —**deaf′ly,** *adv.* —**deaf′ness,** *n.*

deaf•en (def′ən), *v.t.* 1. to make deaf. 2. to stun with noise. 3. DEADEN (def. 3). —**deaf′en•ing•ly,** *adv.*

deaf•en•ing (def′ə ning), *n.* DEADENING.

deaf′-mute′, *adj.* 1. unable to hear and speak. —*n.* 2. a person who is unable to hear and speak, esp. one in whom inability to speak is due to congenital or early deafness.

deal¹ (dēl), *v.,* **dealt, deal•ing,** *n.* —*v.i.* 1. to occupy oneself or itself (usu. fol. by *with* or *in*): *Botany deals with the study of plants.* 2. to take action with respect to a thing or person (fol. by *with*): *Law courts must deal with such culprits.* 3. to conduct oneself toward persons. 4. to trade or do business (fol. by *with* or *in*): *to deal in used cars.* 5. to distribute, esp. the cards in a game. 6. *Slang.* to buy and sell drugs illegally. —*v.t.* 7. to give to one as a share; apportion. 8. **a.** to distribute among a number of recipients, as the cards required in a game. **b.** to give a player (a specific card) in dealing. 9. to deliver; administer: *to deal a blow.* 10. *Slang.* to buy and sell (drugs) illegally. 11. **deal off, a.** to deal the final hand of a poker game. **b.** *Slang.* to get rid of or trade (something or someone) in a transaction. —*n.* 12. a business transaction. 13. a bargain or arrangement for mutual advantage: *the best deal in town.* 14. a secret or underhand agreement or bargain: *They had to make some deals to get the bill passed.* 15. *Informal.* treatment received in dealing with another: *to get a raw deal.* 16. an indefinite but large quantity (usu. prec. by *good* or *great*): *a great deal of money.* 17. **a.** the distribution of cards to the players in a game. **b.** the set of cards in one's hand. **c.** the turn of a player to deal. 18. an act of dealing or distributing. —*Idiom.* 19. **deal someone in,** *Slang.* to include someone.

deal² (dēl), *n.* **1.** a board or plank, esp. of fir or pine, cut to any of various standard sizes. **2.** fir or pine wood.

deal·er (dē′lər), *n.* **1.** a trader or merchant, esp. a wholesaler. **2.** the player distributing the cards in a card game. **3.** a person who behaves or acts toward another or others in a specified manner: *a plain dealer.* **4.** *Slang.* a person who buys and sells drugs illegally.

deal·er·ship (dē′lər ship′), *n.* **1.** authorization to sell a commodity. **2.** a sales agency or distributor having such authorization.

deal·fish (dēl′fish′), *n., pl.* **-fish·es,** (*esp. collectively*) **-fish.** a ribbonfish, esp. *Trachipterus arcticus.*

deal·ing (dē′ling), *n.* **1.** Usu., **dealings.** interaction: *commercial dealings.* **2.** conduct in relations to others: *honest dealing.*

dealt (delt), *v.* pt. and pp. of DEAL¹.

dean (dēn), *n.* **1. a.** the head of faculty in a university or college. **b.** an official in a university or college in charge of discipline, counseling, or admissions. **2. a.** the head of the chapter of a cathedral or a collegiate church. **b.** a priest in the Roman Catholic Church appointed by a bishop to take care of the affairs of a division of a diocese. **3.** the senior member, in length of service, of any profession, field, etc.: *the dean of American composers.*

dean's′ list′, *n.* a list of students of high scholastic standing at a college or university.

dear (dēr), *adj.* **1.** beloved; loved. **2.** (used in the salutation of a letter as an expression of affection or respect or as a conventional greeting): *Dear Sir or Madam.* **3.** precious; cherished: *our dearest possessions.* **4.** heartfelt; earnest: *no dearer wish.* **5.** expensive. —*n.* **6.** a kind or generous person. **7.** a beloved one. **8.** (*sometimes cap.*) an affectionate or familiar term of address (sometimes offensive when used to a stranger, subordinate, etc.) —*adv.* **9.** dearly; fondly. **10.** at a high price: *I paid dear for that painting.* —*interj.* **11.** (used as an exclamation of surprise, distress, etc.): *Oh dear, I've lost the phone number.* —**dear′ly,** *adv.* —**dear′ness,** *n.*

Dear·born (dēr′bərn, -bôrn), *n.* **1.** Henry, 1751–1829, U.S. soldier and diplomat. **2.** a city in SE Michigan, near Detroit. 86,180.

dearth (dûrth), *n.* **1.** a scarcity or lack. **2.** FAMINE.

death (deth), *n.* **1.** the act of dying; the end of life. Compare BRAIN DEATH. **2.** the state of being dead. **3.** extinction; destruction. **4.** (*usu. cap.*) the agent of death personified, usu. represented as the Grim Reaper. **5.** loss or absence of spiritual life. **6.** massacre; mayhem. **7.** a cause of death: *You'll be the death of me yet!* —**Idiom. 8. at death's door,** in serious danger of dying; gravely ill. **9. be death on,** to handle with ruthless efficiency. **10. death by a thousand cuts,** an end of something by means of successive small reductions. **11. do to death, a.** to kill. **b.** to do so often that boredom or staleness sets in. **12. put to death,** to kill; execute. **13. to death,** to an intolerable degree: *sick to death of working.* —**death′less,** *adj.* —**death′like′,** *adj.* —**death′ly,** *adj.*

death′ an′gel, *n.* AZRAEL.

death·bed (deth′bed′), *n.* **1.** the bed on which a person dies. —*adj.* **2.** pertaining to or occurring in the last few hours of a person's life: *a deathbed confession.* —**Idiom. 3. on one's deathbed,** in the last few hours before death.

death′ ben′efit, *n.* the amount of money payable to a beneficiary upon the death of the insured.

death·blow (deth′blō′), *n.* **1.** a blow causing death. **2.** anything that ends hope, expectation, or the like; death warrant.

death′ cam′ass, *n.* **1.** a North American plant of the genus *Zigadenus,* of the lily family, having narrow leaves and clusters of flowers. **2.** the root of this plant, poisonous to animals.

death′ camp′, *n.* a concentration camp in which the inmates are likely to die or be executed.

death′ certif′icate, *n.* a certificate signed by a doctor, giving information about the time, place, and cause of a person's death.

death′ cham′ber, *n.* a place in which executions take place.

death′ rate′, *n.* the number of deaths per unit of population in a given place and time.

death′ row′, *n.* prison cells for inmates awaiting execution.

death′ tax′, *n.* **1.** ESTATE TAX. **2.** INHERITANCE TAX.

death·trap (deth′trap′), *n.* a structure, place, or situation where there is imminent risk of death.

Death′ Val′ley, *n.* an arid basin in E California and S Nevada: lowest land in North America. ab. 1500 sq. mi. (3900 sq. km); 280 ft. (85 m) below sea level.

Death′ Val′ley Na′tional Mon′ument, *n.* a national monument in E California, including most of Death Valley. 2980 sq. mi. (7718 sq. km).

death′ war′rant, *n.* **1.** a warrant authorizing the execution of a death sentence. **2.** a deathblow.

death·watch (deth′woch′, -wôch′), *n.* **1.** a vigil beside a dying or dead person. **2.** a guard set over a condemned person before execution. **3.** Also called **death′watch bee′tle.** any of several beetles of the family Anobiidae that make a ticking sound as they bore through wood: the sound was once believed to be an omen of death.

death′ wish′, *n.* **1.** a conscious desire for one's own death or for the death of another. **2.** *Psychiatry.* an unconscious desire for one's own death.

deb (deb), *n.* DEBUTANTE.

de·ba·cle (də bä′kəl, -bak′əl, dā-), *n.* **1.** a disaster or fiasco. **2.** a general rout or dispersal of troops. **3.** a breaking up of ice in a river.

de·bar (di bär′), *v.t.* **-barred, -bar·ring. 1.** to shut out or exclude. **2.** to hinder or prevent; prohibit. —**de·bar′ment,** *n.*

de·bark¹ (di bärk′), *v.i., v.t.* to disembark. —**de′bar·ka′tion,** *n.*

de·bark² (dē bärk′), *v.t.* to remove the bark from (a log).

de·base (di bās′), *v.t.* **-based, -bas·ing. 1.** to reduce in quality or value; adulterate. **2.** to lower in rank or dignity. —**de·bas′ed·ness,** *n.* —**de·base′ment,** *n.* —**de·bas′er,** *n.*

de·bate (di bāt′), *n., v.,* **-bat·ed, -bat·ing.** —*n.* **1.** a discussion, esp. of a public question in an assembly, involving opposing viewpoints. **2.** a formal contest in which the affirmative and negative sides of a proposition are advocated by opposing speakers. **3.** deliberation; consideration. —*v.i.* **4.** to engage in argument or discussion. **5.** to participate in a formal debate. **6.** to deliberate; consider. —*v.t.* **7.** to argue or discuss (a question, issue, or the like), as in an assembly. **8.** to dispute or disagree about. **9.** to engage in formal argumentation with. **10.** to deliberate upon; consider. —**de·bat′a·ble,** *adj.* —**de·bat′er,** *n.*

de·bauch (di bôch′), *v.t.* **1.** to corrupt (another's virtue or chastity) by sensuality, intemperance, etc.; seduce. **2.** to subvert (honesty, integrity, or the like). —*v.i.* **3.** to indulge excessively in sensual pleasures. —*n.* **4.** a period of intemperance or self-indulgence. **5.** an orgy. —**de·bauch′er,** *n.* —**de·bauch′er·y,** *n.*

de·ben·ture (di ben′chər), *n.* a short-term, negotiable, interest-bearing note representing indebtedness. —**de·ben′tured,** *adj.*

de·bil·i·tate (di bil′i tāt′), *v.t.* **-tat·ed, -tat·ing.** to make weak; enfeeble. —**de·bil′i·tant,** *n.* —**de·bil′i·ta′tion,** *n.* —**de·bil′i·ta′tive,** *adj.*

de·bil·i·ty (di bil′i tē), *n., pl.* **-ties. 1.** a weakened or enfeebled state; weakness. **2.** a handicap or disability.

De·bir (dē′bər), *n.* a royal city in the vicinity of Hebron, conquered by Othniel.

deb·it (deb′it), *n.* **1.** the record kept of another's indebtedness. **2. a.** a recorded item of debt. **b.** any entry or the total shown on the debit side. **c.** the left-hand, or debit, side of an account (opposed to *credit*). **3.** a failing or shortcoming. —*v.t.* **4.** to charge with or as a debt. **5.** to enter on the debit side of a bookkeeping account.

deb·o·nair (deb′ə nâr′), *adj.* **1.** suave; worldly. **2.** jaunty; carefree.

Deb·o·rah (deb′ər ə, deb′rə), *n.* a prophet of Israel. Judg. 4, 5.

de·bouch (di bouch′, *esp. for 1* -bōsh′), *v.i.* **1. a.** to emerge from a relatively narrow valley upon an open plain: *A river or glacier debouches on the plains.* **b.** to flow from a small valley into a larger one. **c.** (of a body of water) to empty into another body of water. **2.** to march out from a narrow or confined place into open country. **3.** to come forth; emerge. —**de·bouch′ment,** *n.*

de·brief (dē brēf′), *v.t.* **1.** to interrogate in order to obtain useful information or intelligence. **2.** to caution against revealing classified information after leaving a position of military or political sensitivity. —**de·brief′er,** *n.*

de·bris or **dé·bris** (də brē′, dā′brē; *esp. Brit.* deb′rē), *n.* **1.** the remains of anything destroyed; ruins; rubble. **2.** *Geol.* accumulated loose fragments of rock.

Debs (debz), *n.* **Eugene Victor,** 1855–1926, U.S. labor leader: Socialist candidate for president 1900–20.

debt (det), *n.* **1.** something that is owed or that one is bound to pay to or perform for another. **2.** a liability or obligation to pay or render something. **3.** a sin; trespass. —**debt′less,** *adj.*

debt·or (det′ər), *n.* a person, company, or nation in debt or under financial obligation.

de·bug (dē bug′), *v.t.,* **-bugged, -bug·ging. 1.** to detect and remove defects or errors from: *to debug a computer program.* **2.** to remove electronic bugs from (a room or building). **3.** to rid of insect pests. —**de·bug′ger,** *n.*

de·bunk (di bungk′), *v.t.* to expose as being false or exaggerated. —**de·bunk′er,** *n.*

De·bus·sy (deb′yōō sē′, dā′byōō-, də byōō′sē), *n.* **Claude Achille,** 1862–1918, French composer. —**De·bus′sy·an,** *adj.*

de·but or **dé·but** (dā byōō′, di-, dā′byōō), *n.* **1.** a first public appearance or presentation, as of a performer, artistic work, or new product. **2.** a formal introduction of a young woman into society. —*v.i.* **3.** to make a debut. —*v.t.* **4.** to perform (something) for the first time before an audience. **5.** to introduce, as a new product. —*adj.* **6.** of or constituting a first appearance.

deb·u·tante or **déb·u·tante** (deb′yōō tänt′), *n.* a young woman making a debut into society.

deca-, a combining form meaning "ten": *decapod.* Also, *esp. before a vowel,* **dec-.**

dec·ade (dek′ād), *n.* **1.** a period of ten years. **2.** a period of ten years beginning with a year whose last digit is zero: *the decade of the 1990s.* **3.** a set or series of ten.

dec·a·dence (dek′ə dəns, di kād′ns) also **dec·a·den·cy** (dek′ə dən-sē, di kād′n-), *n.* **1.** the act or process of falling into decay; deterioration. **2.** moral degeneration.

dec·a·dent (dek′ə dənt, di kād′nt), *adj.* **1.** characterized by or given to decadence. **2.** (*often cap.*) of or like the decadents. —*n.* **3.** a person who is decadent. **4.** (*often cap.*) any of a group of writers, esp. of late 19th-century France, whose work stressed refinement of style and a content of artificiality, perverseness, the bizarre, despair, etc. —**dec′a•dent•ly,** *adv.*

de•caf (dē′kaf′), *n.* **1.** decaffeinated coffee or tea. —*adj.* **2.** decaffeinated.

de•caf•fein•ate (dē kaf′ə nāt′, -kaf′ē ə-), *v.t.,* **-at•ed, -at•ing.** to remove caffeine from. —**de•caf′fein•a′tion,** *n.*

dec•a•gon (dek′ə gon′), *n.* a polygon having ten angles and ten sides. —**de•cag•o•nal** (də kag′ə nl), *adj.*

dec•a•gram (dek′ə gram′), *n.* DEKAGRAM.

dec•a•he•dron (dek′ə hē′drən), *n., pl.* **-drons, -dra** (-drə). a solid figure having ten faces. —**dec′a•he′dral** (-drəl), *adj.*

de•cal (dē′kal, di kal′), *n.* a picture or design on specially prepared paper for transfer to wood, metal, glass, etc.

de•cal•ci•fy (dē kal′sə fī′), *v.,* **-fied, -fy•ing.** —*v.t.* **1.** to deprive of lime or calcareous matter, as a bone. —*v.i.* **2.** to become decalcified. —**de•cal′ci•fi•ca′tion,** *n.* —**de•cal′ci•fi′er,** *n.*

de•ca•les•cence (dē′kə les′əns), *n.* absorption of heat without a corresponding increase in temperature when a metal has been heated to a critical point. —**de′ca•les′cent,** *adj.*

Dec•a•logue or **Dec•a•log** (dek′ə lôg′, -log′), *n.* (*often l.c.*) TEN COMMANDMENTS. Ex. 20:2–17. [< Late Latin *decalogus* < Greek *deká-* ten + *lógos* word, speech]

de•camp (di kamp′), *v.i.* **1.** to pack up equipment and leave a camping ground. **2.** to depart hastily and often secretly. —**de•camp′ment,** *n.*

de•cant (di kant′), *v.t.* **1.** to pour (a liquid) from one container to another. **2.** to pour gently so as not to disturb the sediment.

de•cant•er (di kan′tər), *n.* a vessel, usu. an ornamental glass bottle, for holding and serving wine, brandy, or the like.

de•cap•i•tate (di kap′i tāt′), *v.t.,* **-tat•ed, -tat•ing.** to cut off the head of. —**de•cap′i•ta′tion,** *n.* —**de•cap′i•ta′tor,** *n.*

dec•a•pod (dek′ə pod′), *n.* **1.** any crustacean of the order Decapoda, having five pairs of limbs, including the crabs, lobsters, crayfish, prawns, and shrimps. **2.** any cephalopod having ten arms, as a cuttlefish or squid. —*adj.* **3.** belonging or pertaining to the decapods. **4.** having ten feet or legs. —**de•cap•o•dan** (də kap′ə dn), *adj., n.* —**de•cap′o•dous,** *adj.*

De•cap•o•lis (di kap′ə lis), *n.* a region in the NE part of ancient Palestine: confederacy of ten cities in the 1st century B.C.

de•car•bon•ate (dē kär′bə nāt′), *v.t.,* **-at•ed, -at•ing.** to remove carbon dioxide from. —**de•car′bon•a′tion,** *n.*

de•car•bu•rize (dē kär′bə rīz′, -byə-), *v.t.,* **-rized, -riz•ing.** to remove carbon from (molten steel, automobile cylinders, etc.). —**de•car′bu•ri•za′tion,** *n.* —**de•car′bu•ra′tion,** *n.*

dec•ath•lon (di kath′lon), *n.* an athletic contest comprising ten different track-and-field events and won by the contestant amassing the highest total score.

De•ca•tur (di kā′tər), *n.* **1. Stephen,** 1779–1820, U.S. naval officer. **2.** a city in central Illinois. 88,220.

de•cay (di kā′), *v.i.* **1.** to become decomposed; rot. **2.** to decline in health, prosperity, etc.; deteriorate. **3.** (of an atomic nucleus) to undergo radioactive disintegration. —*v.t.* **4.** to cause to decompose; rot. —*n.* **5.** decomposition; rot. **6.** a gradual and progressive decline. **7.** the spontaneous radioactive transformation of a nucleus or particle into one or more different nuclei or particles. **8.** progressive change in the path of an earth-orbiting satellite due to atmospheric drag. —**de•cay′a•ble,** *adj.* —**de•cayed′ness** (di kād′nis, -kā′id-), *n.* —**de•cay′less,** *adj.*

decd., deceased.

de•cease (di sēs′), *n., v.,* **-ceased, -ceas•ing.** —*n.* **1.** the act of dying; death. —*v.i.* **2.** to depart from life; die.

de•ce•dent (di sēd′nt), *n. Law.* a deceased person.

de•ceit (di sēt′), *n.* **1.** the act or practice of deceiving. **2.** a stratagem intended to deceive. **3.** the quality of being deceitful; duplicity.

de•ceit•ful (di sēt′fəl), *adj.* **1.** given to deceiving. **2.** intended to deceive; misleading: *a deceitful action.* —**de•ceit′ful•ly,** *adv.* —**de•ceit′ful•ness,** *n.*

de•ceive (di sēv′), *v.,* **-ceived, -ceiv•ing.** —*v.t.* **1.** to mislead by a false appearance or statement; trick. **2.** to be unfaithful to (one's spouse or lover). —*v.i.* **3.** to practice deceit. —**de•ceiv′er,** *n.* —**de•ceiv′ing•ly,** *adv.*

de•cel•er•ate (dē sel′ə rāt′), *v.,* **-at•ed, -at•ing.** —*v.t.* **1.** to decrease the velocity of. **2.** to slow the rate of increase of: *efforts to decelerate inflation.* —*v.i.* **3.** to slow down. —**de•cel′er•a′tion,** *n.* —**de•cel′er•a′tor,** *n.*

De•cem•ber (di sem′bər), *n.* the 12th month of the year, containing 31 days. *Abbr.:* Dec.

de•cen•ni•um (di sen′ē əm), *n., pl.* **-cen•ni•ums, -cen•ni•a** (-sen′ē ə). a period of ten years.

de•cent (dē′sənt), *adj.* **1.** conforming to the recognized standard of propriety, as in behavior or speech. **2.** respectable; worthy. **3.** adequate; passable. **4.** kind; obliging. **5.** of reasonably attractive appearance. —**de′cen•cy,** *n.* —**de′cent•ly,** *adv.*

de•cen•tral•ize (dē sen′trə līz′), *v.,* **-ized, -iz•ing.** —*v.t.* **1.** to distribute the administrative powers or functions of (a central authority) throughout local or regional divisions, branches, etc. **2.** to disperse (something) from an area of concentration. —*v.i.* **3.** to undergo or achieve decentralization. —**de•cen′tral•ist,** *n.* —**de•cen′tral•i•za′tion,** *n.*

de•cep•tion (di sep′shən), *n.* **1.** the act of deceiving, or the state of being deceived. **2.** something that deceives or is intended to deceive; trick; ruse.

de•cep•tive (di sep′tiv), *adj.* **1.** likely to deceive; capable of deception. **2.** perceptually misleading. —**de•cep′tive•ly,** *adv.* —**de•cep′tive•ness,** *n.*

de•cer•ti•fy (dē sûr′tə fī′), *v.t.,* **-fied, -fy•ing.** to withdraw certification from. —**de•cer′ti•fi•ca′tion,** *n.*

deci-, a combining form used initially in the names of units of measurement that are one tenth the size of the unit denoted by the second element of the compound: *decibel; deciliter.*

dec•i•bel (des′ə bel′, -bəl), *n.* a unit used to express differences in power, esp. in acoustics or electronics: equal to ten times the common logarithm of the ratio of two signals. *Abbr.:* dB

de•cide (di sīd′), *v.,* **-cid•ed, -cid•ing.** —*v.t.* **1.** to solve or conclude (a dispute) by awarding victory to one side: *to decide a case in favor of the plaintiff.* **2.** to determine or settle (something in dispute): *to decide an argument.* **3.** to bring (a person) to a decision; persuade or convince: *What decided you to take the job?* —*v.i.* **4.** to settle something in dispute or doubt. **5.** to come to a conclusion. —**de•cid′a•ble,** *adj.* —**de•cid′er,** *n.*

de•cid•ed (di sī′did), *adj.* **1.** in no way uncertain or ambiguous: *a decided improvement.* **2.** free from hesitation or wavering; resolute; determined. —**de•cid′ed•ly,** *adv.* —**de•cid′ed•ness,** *n.*

de•cid•ing (di sī′ding), *adj.* settling a question or dispute; determining; decisive: *the deciding vote.* —**de•cid′ing•ly,** *adv.*

de•cid•u•ous (di sij′ōō əs), *adj.* **1.** shedding the leaves annually. **2.** falling off or shed at a particular season, stage of growth, etc., as leaves, horns, or teeth. **3.** impermanent; transitory. —**de•cid′u•ous•ly,** *adv.* —**de•cid′u•ous•ness,** *n.*

decid′uous tooth′, *n.* one of the temporary teeth of a mammal, in humans amounting to 20, that are replaced by the permanent teeth. Also called **baby tooth, milk tooth.**

dec•i•gram (des′i gram′), *n.* a unit of mass or weight equal to ¹⁄₁₀ gram (1.543 grains). *Abbr.:* dg

dec•i•li•ter (des′ə lē′tər), *n.* a unit of capacity equal to ¹⁄₁₀ liter (6.102 cu. in. or 3.381 U.S. fl. oz.). *Abbr.:* dl

dec•i•mal (des′ə məl, des′məl), *adj.* **1.** pertaining to tenths or to the number 10. **2.** proceeding by tens: *a decimal system.* —*n.* **3.** DECIMAL FRACTION. —**dec′i•mal•ly,** *adv.*

dec′imal frac′tion, *n.* a fraction whose denominator is some power of 10, usu. indicated by a dot (**dec′imal point′** or **point**) written before the numerator: as $0.4 = \frac{4}{10}$; $0.126 = \frac{126}{1000}$.

dec′imal sys′tem, *n.* **1.** a system of counting or measurement, the units of which are powers of ten. **2.** a system of classification, as in libraries, using numerals with decimals.

dec•i•mate (des′ə māt′), *v.t.,* **-mat•ed, -mat•ing.** **1.** to destroy a great number or proportion of: *Cholera decimated the population.* **2.** to take a tenth of or from. —**dec′i•ma′tion,** *n.* —**dec′i•ma′tor,** *n.*

dec•i•me•ter (des′ə mē′tər), *n.* a unit of length equal to ¹⁄₁₀ meter (3.937 in.). *Abbr.:* dm   Also, *esp. Brit.,* **dec′i•me′tre.**

de•ci•pher (di sī′fər), *v.t.* **1.** to make out the meaning of (something obscure or difficult to read or understand): *I couldn't decipher his handwriting.* **2.** to interpret by the use of a key, as something written in cipher: *to decipher a secret message.* —**de•ci′pher•a•ble,** *adj.* —**de•ci′pher•a•bil′i•ty,** *n.*

de•ci•sion (di sizh′ən), *n.* **1.** the act or process of deciding. **2.** the act of making up one's mind: *a difficult decision.* **3.** something that is decided; resolution. **4.** a judgment, as one pronounced by a court. **5.** the quality of being decided; firmness: *to speak with decision.* **6.** the final score in any sport or contest. **7.** the awarding of a victory in a boxing match when there is no knockout, based on scoring by the referee and judges. —**de•ci′sion•al,** *adj.*

de•ci•sive (di sī′siv), *adj.* **1.** having the power to decide, end a controversy, or determine a result; conclusive; crucial: *the decisive argument.* **2.** displaying decision and firmness; resolute: *a decisive manner.* **3.** unquestionable; definite: *a decisive lead.* —**de•ci′sive•ly,** *adv.* —**de•ci′sive•ness,** *n.*

deck (dek), *n.* **1. a.** a floorlike surface wholly or partially occupying one level of a hull, superstructure, or deckhouse of a vessel. **b.** the space between such a surface and the next such surface above. **2.** a platform, surface, or level suggesting the deck of a ship. **3.** an open, unroofed porch or platform extending from a house or other building. **4.** the roadway of a bridge. **5.** a pack of playing cards. **6.** a cassette deck or tape deck. —*v.t.* **7.** to clothe or array in something dressy or festive (often fol. by *out*): *all decked out for the party.* **8.** to furnish with a deck. **9.** *Informal.* to knock down; floor. —*Idiom.* **10. clear the decks, a.** to prepare for combat, as by removing all unnecessary gear. **b.** to prepare for some activity or work. **11. hit the deck, a.** to fall or drop to the floor or ground. **b.** to get out of bed. **12. on deck, a.** present and ready to act or work. **b.** *Baseball.* next at bat.

deck′ chair′, *n.* a folding chair, usu. with arms and a full-length leg rest, used for lounging.

deck•er (dek′ər), *n.* something having a specified number of decks, levels, etc. (used in combination): *a double-decker bus.*

deck′ hand′ or **deck′hand′,** *n.* a sailor given general duties that include maintenance, cargo storage, and line handling.

deck′ ten′nis, *n.* a game for two persons played on a small court, esp. on the deck of a ship, in which a rubber or rope ring is tossed back and forth over a net, using only one hand.

de•claim (di klām′), *v.i.* **1.** to speak aloud rhetorically. **2.** to inveigh (usu. fol. by *against*). **3.** to speak or write for oratorical effect. —*v.t.* **4.** to recite or utter aloud in an oratorical manner. —**de•claim′er,** *n.*

dec•la•ma•tion (dek′lə mā′shən), *n.* **1.** the act or art of declaiming. **2.** exercise in oratory or elocution, as in the recitation of a classic speech. **3.** speech or writing for oratorical effect.

dec•la•ra•tion (dek′lə rā′shən), *n.* **1.** the act of declaring; announcement. **2.** a formal statement; proclamation. **3.** something that is announced or proclaimed. **4.** a document containing an announcement or proclamation. **5.** *Law.* **a.** a formal statement of the plaintiff's claim in an action. **b.** an unsworn statement that may be admissible as evidence. **6.** a bid in bridge, esp. the successful bid. **7.** a statement of goods, income, etc., subject to a duty or tax.

Declara′tion of Indepen′dence, *n.* **1.** the public act by which the Second Continental Congress, on July 4, 1776, declared the Colonies to be free and independent of England. **2.** the document embodying it.

de•clar•a•tive (di klar′ə tiv), *adj.* **1.** Also, **de•clar•a•to•ry** (di klar′ə tôr′ē, -tōr′ē). serving to declare, state, or explain. **2.** pertaining to or having the form of a sentence used in making a statement. —**de•clar′a•tive•ly,** *adv.*

de•clare (di klâr′), *v.*, **-clared, -clar•ing.** —*v.t.* **1.** to make known; state clearly, esp. in formal terms. **2.** to announce officially; proclaim. **3.** to state emphatically. **4.** to reveal; indicate. **5.** to make due statement of (goods for duty, income for taxation, etc.). **6.** to make (a dividend) payable. **7.** to bid (a trump suit or no-trump) in bridge. —*v.i.* **8.** to make a declaration. **9.** to proclaim oneself: *to declare against a proposal.* —**de•clar′a•ble,** *adj.* —**de•clar′er,** *n.*

dé•clas•sé (dā′kla sā′, -klä-), *adj.* **1.** reduced to a lower status, rank, or social class. **2.** of a lower status, class, or rank.

de•clas•si•fy (dē klas′ə fī′), *v.t.*, **-fied, -fy•ing.** to remove the security classification that restricts access to (information, a document, etc.). —**de•clas′si•fi′a•ble,** *adj.* —**de•clas′si•fi•ca′tion,** *n.*

de•claw (dē klô′), *v.t.* to remove the claws from.

de•clen•sion (di klen′shən), *n.* **1. a.** the inflection of nouns, pronouns, and adjectives for categories such as case and number. **b.** the whole set of inflected forms of such a word, or the recital thereof in a fixed order. **c.** a class of such words having similar sets of inflected forms: *the Latin second declension.* **2.** a bending, sloping, or moving downward. **3.** deterioration; decline. —**de•clen′sion•al,** *adj.*

dec•li•na•tion (dek′lə nā′shən), *n.* **1.** a bending, sloping, or moving downward. **2.** DETERIORATION. **3.** deviation, as from a standard. **4.** a polite refusal. **5.** the angular distance of a heavenly body from the celestial equator, measured on the great circle passing through the celestial pole and the body. **6.** VARIATION (def. 8).

de•cline (di klīn′), *v.*, **-clined, -clin•ing,** *n.* —*v.t.* **1.** to withhold or deny consent to do; refuse. **2.** to refuse with courtesy. **3.** to cause to slope or incline downward. **4.** to recite or display the inflected forms of (a noun, pronoun, or adjective) in a fixed order. —*v.i.* **5.** to express usu. courteous refusal. **6.** to fail in strength, health, value, etc.; deteriorate. **7.** to diminish: *to decline in popularity.* **8.** to slope or sink downward. **9.** to draw toward the close, as the day. **10.** (of a noun, pronoun, or adjective) to be characterized by declension. —*n.* **11.** a downward slope; declivity. **12.** a downward movement, as of prices or population: *a decline in the stock market.* **13.** a deterioration, as in strength, power, or value. **14.** progress downward or toward the close. **15.** the later years or last part: *the decline of life.* —**de•clin′a•ble,** *adj.* —**de•clin′er,** *n.*

de•cliv•i•tous (di kliv′i təs), *adj.* having a somewhat steep downward slope. —**de•cliv′i•tous•ly,** *adv.*

de•cliv•i•ty (di kliv′i tē), *n.*, *pl.* **-ties.** a downward slope (opposed to *acclivity*).

de•coct (di kokt′), *v.t.* to extract the flavor or essence of by boiling.

de•code (dē kōd′), *v.*, **-cod•ed, -cod•ing.** —*v.t.* **1.** to translate (data or a message) from a code into the original language or form. **2.** to extract meaning from (spoken or written symbols). —*v.i.* **3.** to translate encoded messages, data, signals, etc.

de•cod•er (dē kō′dər), *n.* **1.** a person who decodes messages or the like. **2.** a device for decoding, as an electric or electronic apparatus that transforms arbitrary input signals into letters, words, etc. **3.** a boxlike device attached to a television set containing circuitry to unscramble encoded signals.

dé•col•le•tage or **de•col•le•tage** (dā′kol ə täzh′, dek′ə lə-), *n.* **1.** the neckline of a dress cut low in the front or back and often across the shoulders. **2.** a décolleté garment or costume.

dé•col•le•té or **de•col•le•te** (dā′kol ə tā′, dek′ə lə-), *adj.* **1.** (of a garment) low-necked. **2.** wearing a low-necked garment. [< French]

de•com•mis•sion (dē′kə mish′ən), *v.t.* **1.** to remove or retire (a ship, airplane, etc.) from active service. **2.** to deactivate; shut down.

de•com•pose (dē′kəm pōz′), *v.*, **-posed, -pos•ing.** —*v.t.* **1.** to separate or resolve into constituent parts or elements; disintegrate. —*v.i.* **2.** to rot; putrefy. —**de′com•pos′a•ble,** *adj.* —**de′com•pos′a•bil′i•ty,** *n.* —**de′com•po•si′tion** (-kom pə zish′ən), *n.*

de•com•pres•sion (dē′kəm presh′ən), *n.* **1.** the gradual reduction in atmospheric pressure experienced after working in deep water or breathing compressed air. **2.** the act or process of releasing from pressure or stress. **3.** a surgical procedure for relieving increased cranial, cardiac, or orbital pressure.

decompres′sion sick′ness, *n.* an acute disorder involving the formation of nitrogen bubbles in the body fluids, caused by a sudden drop in external pressure, as during a too-rapid ascent from diving, and resulting in pain in the lungs and joints and faintness.

de•con•di•tion (dē′kən dish′ən), *v.t.* **1.** to diminish the physical strength or stamina of; weaken. **2.** to diminish or eliminate the conditioned responses or behavior patterns of.

de•con•ges•tant (dē′kən jes′tənt), *adj.* **1.** relieving mucus congestion of the upper respiratory tract. —*n.* **2.** a decongestant agent.

de•con•struct (dē′kən strukt′), *v.t.* **1.** to break down into constituent parts; dissect; dismantle. **2.** to analyze (a text) by deconstruction.

de•con•struc•tion (dē′kən struk′shən), *n.* **1.** a theory of textual analysis positing that a text has no stable reference and questioning assumptions about the ability of language to represent reality. **2.** a philosophical and critical movement that started in France in the 1960s, holding such a theory. —**de′con•struc′tion•ist,** *n.*, *adj.*

de•con•struc•tiv•ism (dē′kən struk′ti viz′əm), *n.* a movement in modern architecture that challenges traditional architectural concepts of unity, harmony, balance, and the fundamentality of the right angle and is typically characterized by the use of fragmented forms, asymmetry, sloping surfaces, and oblique angles. —**de′con•struc′tiv•ist,** *n.*, *adj.*

de•con•tam•i•nate (dē′kən tam′ə nāt′), *v.t.*, **-nat•ed, -nat•ing.** **1.** to make (an object or area) safe by removing or neutralizing any harmful substance, as radioactive material or poisonous gas. **2.** to free from contamination; purify. —**de′con•tam′i•na′tion,** *n.* —**de′con•tam′i•na′tive,** *adj.* —**de′con•tam′i•na′tor,** *n.*

dé•cor or **de•cor** (dā kôr′, di-, dā′kôr), *n.* **1.** style or mode of decoration, as of a room, building, or the like. **2.** decoration in general; ornamentation. **3.** the scenic decoration of a stage; stage scenery.

dec•o•rate (dek′ə rāt′), *v.t.*, **-rat•ed, -rat•ing.** **1.** to furnish or adorn with something ornamental or becoming; embellish. **2.** to design the interior of (a room or building). **3.** to confer distinction upon by a badge, medal, or the like: *to decorate a soldier for bravery.*

dec•o•ra•tion (dek′ə rā′shən), *n.* **1.** something used for decorating; adornment; embellishment. **2.** the act of decorating. **3.** a badge, medal, etc., conferred and worn as a mark of honor.

Decora′tion Day′, *n.* former name of MEMORIAL DAY.

dec•o•ra•tive (dek′ər ə tiv, dek′rə-, dek′ə rā′-), *adj.* **1.** serving or tending to decorate. **2.** ornamental rather than functional in purpose. —**dec′o•ra•tive•ly,** *adv.* —**dec′o•ra•tive•ness,** *n.*

dec•o•ra•tor (dek′ə rā′tər), *n.* **1.** a person who decorates, esp. an interior decorator. —*adj.* **2.** harmonizing with a scheme of interior decoration: *appliances in decorator colors.*

dec•o•rous (dek′ər əs), *adj.* showing respect for social customs and manners. —**dec′o•rous•ly,** *adv.* —**dec′o•rous•ness,** *n.*

de•cor•ti•cate (dē kôr′ti kāt′), *v.t.*, **-cat•ed, -cat•ing.** **1.** to remove the bark, husk, or outer covering from. **2.** to remove the cortex from surgically, as an organ or structure. —**de•cor′ti•ca′tion,** *n.* —**de•cor′ti•ca′tor,** *n.*

de•co•rum (di kôr′əm, -kōr′-), *n.* **1.** dignified propriety of conduct, manners, or appearance. **2.** Usu., **decorums.** the customs and observances of polite society.

de•cou•page or **dé•cou•page** (dā′ko͞o päzh′), *n.*, *v.*, **-paged, -pag•ing.** —*n.* **1.** the art of decorating something with cutouts of paper, linoleum, plastic, or other flat material over which varnish or lacquer is applied. —*v.t.* **2.** to decorate by decoupage.

de•cou•ple (dē kup′əl), *v.*, **-pled, -pling.** —*v.t.* **1.** to cause to become separated, disconnected, or divergent; uncouple. **2.** to absorb the shock of (a nuclear explosion): *a surrounding mass of earth and rock can decouple a nuclear blast.* **3.** *Electronics.* to loosen or eliminate the coupling of (a signal between two circuits). —*v.i.* **4.** to separate or diverge from an existing connection; uncouple. —**de•cou′pler,** *n.*

de•coy (*n.* dē′koi, di koi′; *v.* di koi′, dē′koi), *n.*, *v.*, **-coyed, -coy•ing.** —*n.* **1.** a person who entices or lures another, as into danger or a trap. **2.** anything used as a lure. **3.** an artificial bird or a trained bird or other animal used to entice game into a trap or within gunshot. **4.** a pond into which wild fowl are lured for capture. **5.** an object capable of reflecting radar waves, as a spurious aircraft or missile, used for the deception of radar detectors. —*v.t.*, *v.i.* **6.** to lure or be lured by or as if by a decoy. [< Dutch *(de) kooi* (the) cage] —**de•coy′er,** *n.*

de•crease (*v.* di krēs′; *n.* dē′krēs, di krēs′), *v.*, **-creased, -creas•ing,** *n.* —*v.i.* **1.** to lessen, esp. by degrees, as in extent, quantity, strength, or power; diminish. —*v.t.* **2.** to make less; cause to diminish. —*n.* **3.** gradual reduction. **4.** the amount by which a thing is lessened. —**de•creas′ing•ly,** *adv.*

de•cree (di krē′), *n.*, *v.*, **-creed, -cree•ing.** —*n.* **1.** a formal order usu. having the force of law. **2.** a judicial decision or order. **3.** one of the eternal purposes of God, by which events are foreordained. —*v.t.*, *v.i.* **4.** to command, ordain, or decide by or as if by decree.

de•crep•it (di krep′it), *adj.* **1.** weakened by old age; feeble; infirm. **2.** worn out or broken down by long use; dilapidated. —**de•crep′it•ly,** *adv.* —**de•crep′it•ness,** *n.*

de•cre•scen•do (dē′kri shen′dō, dā′-), *adj.*, *adv.*, *n.*, *pl.* **-dos, -di** (dē). —*adj.*, *adv.* **1.** gradually decreasing in loudness. —*n.* **2.** a gradual decrease in loudness.

de·cres·cent (di kres′ənt), *adj.* waning; diminishing; decreasing. —**de·cres′cence,** *n.*

dec·re·to·ry (dek′ri tôr′ē, -tōr′ē), *adj.* **1.** pertaining to a decree. **2.** established by a decree; judicial.

de·crim·i·nal·ize (dē krim′ə nl īz′), *v.t.,* **-ized, -iz·ing.** to eliminate criminal penalties for: *to decriminalize marijuana.* —**de·crim′i·nal·i·za′tion,** *n.*

de·cry (di krī′), *v.t.,* **-cried, -cry·ing. 1.** to disparage openly; denounce. **2.** to depreciate by proclamation, as coins. —**de·cri′al,** *n.* —**de·cri′er,** *n.*

de·crypt (dē kript′, di-), *v.t.* to decode or decipher. —**de·cryp′tion,** *n.*

de·cus·sate (*v.* di kus′āt, dek′ə sāt′; *adj.* di kus′āt, -it), *v.,* **-sat·ed, -sat·ing,** *adj.* —*v.t., v.i.* **1.** to cross in the form of an X; intersect. —*adj.* **2.** arranged along the stem in pairs, each pair at right angles to the next pair, as leaves. —**de·cus′sate·ly,** *adv.*

decussate leaves

ded·i·cate (ded′i kāt′), *v.t.,* **-cat·ed, -cat·ing, 1.** to set apart and consecrate to a deity or sacred purpose. **2.** to devote wholly to some purpose or person: *to dedicate one's life to public service.* **3.** to offer formally (a book, piece of music, etc.) to a person, cause, etc., as on a prefatory page, in testimony of affection or respect. **4.** to mark the official opening of (a public building, highway, etc.), usu. by formal ceremonies. **5.** to set aside for a specific purpose. —**ded′i·ca′tor,** *n.*

ded·i·ca·tion (ded′i kā′shən), *n.* **1.** the act of dedicating or the state of being dedicated. **2.** an inscription, as in a book, dedicating it to a person, cause, etc. **3.** a ceremony marking the official completion or opening of a public building, monument, etc.

de·duce (di dōōs′, -dyōōs′), *v.t.,* **-duced, -duc·ing. 1.** to derive as a conclusion from something known or assumed; infer. **2.** to trace the derivation or course of. —**de·duc′i·ble,** *adj.*

de·duct (di dukt′), *v.t.* **1.** to take away from a total. **2.** to deduce; infer. —*v.i.* **3.** to detract.

de·duct·i·ble (di duk′tə bəl), *adj.* **1.** capable of being deducted. **2.** allowable as a tax deduction. —*n.* **3.** the amount for which the insured is liable on each claim made on an insurance policy. —**de·duct′i·bil′i·ty,** *n.*

de·duc·tion (di duk′shən), *n.* **1.** the act or process of deducting; subtraction. **2.** something that is or may be deducted. **3.** the act or process of deducing. **4.** something that is deduced. **5. a.** a process of reasoning in which a conclusion follows necessarily from the premises presented; inference from the general to the particular. **b.** a conclusion reached by this process. Compare INDUCTION (def. 3).

de·duc·tive (di duk′tiv), *adj.* based on deduction from accepted premises: *deductive reasoning.* —**de·duc′tive·ly,** *adv.*

deed (dēd), *n.* **1.** something that is done, performed, or accomplished; act: *a good deed.* **2.** an exploit or achievement; feat. **3.** action or performance, esp. as indicative of one's intentions. **4.** a document executed under seal and delivered to effect a conveyance, esp. of real estate. —*v.t.* **5.** to convey or transfer by deed. —*Saying.* **6. deeds, not words,** action is more important than talk. —**deed′less,** *adj.*

deem (dēm), *v.t.* to hold as an opinion; think: *I deemed it wise to refuse.*

de·em·pha·size (dē em′fə sīz′), *v.t.,* **-sized, -siz·ing.** to place less emphasis upon; reduce the importance of: *to de-emphasize sports.* —**de·em′pha·sis** (-sis), *n.*

deep (dēp), *adj.* **1.** extending far down from the top or surface: *a deep well; a deep cut.* **2.** extending far in or back from the front: *a deep shelf.* **3.** extending far in width; broad: *a deep border.* **4.** ranging far from the earth and sun: *a deep space probe.* **5.** having a specified dimension in depth: *a tank 10 feet deep.* **6.** immersed or submerged (usu. fol. by *in*): *a road deep in snow.* **7.** covered or immersed to a specified depth (often used in combination): *standing knee-deep in mud.* **8.** situated far back or within: *deep in the woods.* **9.** far back in geological history: *deep time.* **10.** coming from far down: *a deep breath.* **11.** made with the body bent or lowered to a considerable degree: *a deep curtsy.* **12.** difficult to understand; abstruse: *a deep allegory.* **13.** not superficial; profound: *deep thoughts.* **14.** heartfelt; sincere: *deep affections.* **15.** great in measure; intense: *deep sorrow.* **16.** sound and heavy; undisturbed: *deep sleep.* **17.** (of colors) dark and vivid: *a deep red.* **18.** low in pitch, as sound, a voice, or the like. **19.** mysterious; obscure: *deep, dark secrets.* **20.** involved or enveloped: *to be deep in debt.* **21.** absorbed; engrossed: *deep in thought.* **22.** *Baseball.* relatively far from home plate: *deep center field.* **23.** of or pertaining to the deep structure of a sentence. **24.** larger than usual: *deep discounts.* —*adv.* **25.** to or at a considerable or specified depth. **26.** to a depth or breadth of several such persons or

things (used in combination): *lined up three-deep around the block.* **27.** far on in time: *to look deep into the future.* **28.** *Baseball.* farther than usual from home plate: *The outfielders played deep.* —*n.* **29.** the deep part of a body of water. **30.** a vast extent, as of space or time. **31.** the part of greatest intensity, as of winter. **32.** any of the unmarked levels, one fathom apart, on a deep-sea lead line. Compare MARK[1] (def. 18). **33. the deep,** *Literary.* the sea or ocean: *The deep was his final resting place.* —*Idiom.* **34. go off the deep end, a.** to act without thought of the consequences. **b.** to become emotionally overwrought. **c.** to act without restraint, as by good sense or taste: *The committee went off the deep end with the Christmas decorations.* **35. in deep,** inextricably involved. **36. in deep water,** in serious trouble. —**deep′ly,** *adv.* —**deep′ness,** *n.*

deep′-dish′ pie′, *n.* a fruit pie baked in a deep dish, usu. with only a top crust.

deep·en (dē′pən), *v.t., v.i.* to make or become deep or deeper.

deep′ freeze′, *n.* COLD STORAGE (def. 2).

deep-freeze (dēp′frēz′), *v.t.,* **-freezed** or **-froze, -freezed** or **-fro·zen, -freez·ing. 1.** to quick-freeze (food). **2.** to store in a frozen state.

deep′-fry′, *v.t.,* **-fried, -fry·ing.** to fry in a quantity of hot oil or fat sufficient to cover the food being cooked.

deep′ pock′ets, *n.pl.* an abundance of money or wealth.

deep′-root′ed, *adj.* firmly implanted or established: *a deep-rooted suspicion.* —**deep′root′ed·ness,** *n.*

deep′-seat′ed, *adj.* firmly implanted or established: *a deep-seated loyalty.*

deep′-six′, *v.t. Slang.* **1.** to throw overboard; discard. **2.** to reject or abandon.

Deep′ South′, *n.* the southeastern section of the U.S., usu. including South Carolina, Georgia, Alabama, Mississippi, and Louisiana.

deep′ space′, *n.* space beyond the solar system. Also called **outer space.** —**deep′-space′,** *adj.*

deep′ struc′ture, *n.* (in transformational grammar) the underlying semantic or syntactic representation of a sentence from which the surface structure may be derived. Compare SURFACE STRUCTURE.

deer (dēr), *n., pl.* **deer,** (*occasionally*) **deers. 1.** any ruminant of the family Cervidae: in most species only the males grow and shed antlers. **2.** any of the smaller species of this family, as distinguished from the moose or elk.

deer·ber·ry (dēr′ber′ē, -bə rē), *n., pl.* **-ries.** either of two shrubs, *Vaccinium stamineum* or *V. caesium,* of the heath family, of the eastern U.S., having clusters of small white or greenish flowers and blue or greenish berries.

Deere (dēr), *n.* **John,** 1804–86, U.S. inventor and manufacturer of farm implements.

deer′ fly′, *n.* any of several tabanid flies of the genus *Chrysops,* the female of which is a vector of tularemia.

deer′ mouse′, *n.* WHITE-FOOTED MOUSE.

de·es·ca·late or **de·es·ca·late** (dē es′kə lāt′), *v.t., v.i.,* **-lat·ed, -lat·ing.** to decrease in intensity, magnitude, amount, or the like. —**de·es′ca·la′tion,** *n.* —**de·es′ca·la·to′ry** (-lə tôr′ē, -tōr′ē), *adj.*

de·face (di fās′), *v.t.,* **-faced, -fac·ing. 1.** to mar the surface or appearance of; disfigure. **2.** to make illegible: *to deface a bond.* —**de·face′a·ble,** *adj.* —**de·face′ment,** *n.* —**de·fac′er,** *n.*

de fac·to (dē fak′tō, dā), *adv.* **1.** in fact; in reality. —*adj.* **2.** actually existing, esp. without lawful authority (disting. from *de jure*): *de facto segregation.*

de·fal·ca·tion (dē′fal kā′shən, -fôl-), *n.* misappropriation of funds held by a trustee or other fiduciary.

def·a·ma·tion (def′ə mā′shən), *n.* the act of defaming, esp. unjustified injury to another's reputation, as by slander or libel. —**de·fam·a·to·ry** (di fam′ə tôr′ē, -tōr′ē), *adj.*

de·fame (di fām′), *v.t.,* **-famed, -fam·ing.** to attack the good name or reputation of; slander or libel. —**de·fam′er,** *n.* —**de·fam′ing·ly,** *adv.*

de·fault (di fôlt′), *n.* **1.** failure to act; inaction or neglect. **2.** failure to meet financial obligations. **3.** failure to comply with a legal obligation. **4.** *Sports.* failure to appear for or complete a match. **5.** a preset value that a computer system assumes or an action that it takes unless otherwise instructed. —*v.t.* **6.** to fail to perform or pay. **7.** to declare to be in default. **8.** *Sports.* to fail to compete in (a contest). —*v.i.* **9.** to fail to fulfill an obligation. —**de·fault′er,** *n.*

de·fea·sance (di fē′zəns), *n.* **1.** a condition rendering a deed or other instrument void. **2.** a document, as a deed, stipulating such a condition.

de·fea·si·ble (di fē′zə bəl), *adj.* capable of being annulled or terminated. —**de·fea′si·ble·ness, de·fea′si·bil′i·ty,** *n.*

de·feat (di fēt′), *v.t.* **1.** to overcome in a contest; vanquish. **2.** to frustrate; thwart. **3.** to deprive of something expected: *to defeat one's hopes.* **4.** *Law.* to annul. —*n.* **5.** the act of overcoming in a contest. **6.** an instance of defeat; setback. **7.** an overthrow or overturning; downfall; abolition. —**de·feat′er,** *n.*

de·feat·ism (di fē′tiz əm), *n.* the attitude or conduct of a person who is resigned to defeat and regards further struggle as futile. —**de·feat′ist,** *n., adj.*

def·e·cate (def′i kāt′), *v.,* **-cat·ed, -cat·ing.** —*v.i.* **1.** to void excrement from the bowels through the anus. —*v.t.* **2.** to clear of dregs, impurities, etc.; purify; refine. **3.** to void (excrement) through the anus. —**def′e·ca′tion,** *n.*

D

de•fect (*n.* dē′fekt, di fekt′; *v.* di fekt′), *n.* **1.** a fault or shortcoming; imperfection. **2.** lack of something essential; deficiency: *a defect in hearing.* **3.** a discontinuity in the lattice of a crystal caused by missing or extra atoms or ions, or by dislocations. —*v.i.* **4.** to desert a cause, country, etc.: *to defect to the West.*

de•fec•tion (di fek′shən), *n.* **1.** desertion from allegiance, loyalty, duty, or the like; apostasy. **2.** failure; lack; loss.

de•fec•tive (di fek′tiv), *adj.* **1.** faulty. **2.** subnormal in intelligence or behavior. **3.** lacking one or more of the inflected forms common to most words of the same class in a language, as *must,* which occurs only in the present tense. —*n.* **4.** a defective person or thing. —**de•fec′tive•ly,** *adv.* —**de•fec′tive•ness,** *n.*

de•fec•tor (di fek′tər), *n.* a person who defects from a cause or country.

de•fend (di fend′), *v.t.* **1.** to ward off attack from; guard against assault or injury. **2.** to maintain by argument, evidence, etc.; uphold. **3.** to contest (a legal charge, claim, etc.). **4.** to serve as attorney for (a defendant). **5.** to attempt to retain (a championship title) in competition against a challenger. —*v.i.* **6.** to make a defense. —**de•fend′a•ble,** *adj.* —**de•fend′er,** *n.*

de•fend•ant (di fen′dənt *or, esp. in court for 1,* -dant), *n.* **1.** one against whom a legal action or suit is brought in a court (opposed to *plaintiff*). —*adj.* **2.** making one's defense; defending.

Defend′er of the Faith′, *n.* a title conferred on Henry VIII by Pope Leo X in 1521, and retained by English sovereigns. [trans. of Latin *Fidēī dēfēnsor*]

de•fense (di fens′ *or, esp. for 8, 9,* dē′fens), *n., v.,* **-fensed, -fens•ing.** —*n.* **1.** resistance against attack; protection. **2.** something that defends, as a fortification or medication. **3.** the defending of a cause or the like by speech, argument, etc.: *to speak in defense of a cause.* **4.** the arms production of a nation: *spending billions on defense.* **5.** a speech, argument, etc., in vindication. **6. a.** the defendant's answer to the charge or claim made by the plaintiff. **b.** the strategy adopted by a defendant for defending against the plaintiff's charge. **c.** a defendant together with counsel. **7.** DEFENSE MECHANISM. **8. a.** the tactics of defending oneself or one's goal against attack. **b.** the team attempting to thwart the attack of the team having the ball or puck. **c.** the players of such a team or their positions. —*v.t.* **9.** to defend against (an opponent, play, etc.). —**de•fense′less,** *adj.* —**de•fense′less•ness,** *n.*

defense′ mech′anism, *n.* an unconscious process that protects an individual from unacceptable or painful ideas or impulses.

de•fen•si•ble (di fen′sə bəl), *adj.* **1.** capable of being defended against assault or injury. **2.** able to be defended in argument; justifiable. —**de•fen′si•bil′i•ty,** *n.* —**de•fen′si•bly,** *adv.*

de•fen•sive (di fen′siv), *adj.* **1.** serving or done for the purpose of resisting attack. **2.** of or pertaining to defense. **3.** sensitive to the threat of criticism or injury to one's ego. —*n.* **4.** a position or attitude of defense: *on the defensive about one's mistakes.* —**de′fen′sive•ly,** *adv.* —**de•fen′sive•ness,** *n.*

de•fer[1] (di fûr′), *v.,* **-ferred, -fer•ring.** —*v.t.* **1.** to postpone; delay. **2.** to exempt temporarily from induction into military service. —*v.i.* **3.** to put off action; delay. —**de•fer′ment,** *n.*

de•fer[2] (di fûr′), *v.,* **-ferred, -fer•ring.** —*v.i.* **1.** to yield respectfully in judgment or opinion. —*v.t.* **2.** to submit for decision; refer.

def•er•ence (def′ər əns), *n.* **1.** respectful yielding to the opinion, will, etc., of another. **2.** respectful or courteous regard.

def•er•ent[1] (def′ər ənt), *adj.* deferential.

def•er•ent[2] (def′ər ənt), *adj. Anat.* **1.** conveying away; efferent. **2.** of or pertaining to the vas deferens.

def•er•en•tial (def′ə ren′shəl), *adj.* showing deference; respectful. —**def′er•en′tial•ly,** *adv.*

de•fi•ance (di fī′əns), *n.* **1.** a bold resistance to authority or to any opposing force. **2.** open disregard; contempt (often fol. by *of*): *defiance of danger.* **3.** a challenge, as to meet in combat. —***Idiom.*** **4. in defiance of,** despite; notwithstanding.

de•fi•ant (di fī′ənt), *adj.* showing defiance; bold. —**de•fi′ant•ly,** *adv.* —**de•fi′ant•ness,** *n.*

de•fib•ril•late (dē fib′rə lāt′, -fī′brə-), *v.t.,* **-lat•ed, -lat•ing.** to arrest the fibrillation of (heart muscle) by applying electric shock across the chest. —**de•fib′ril•la′tion,** *n.*

de•fi•cien•cy (di fish′ən sē), *n., pl.* **-cies. 1.** the state of being deficient; lack; insufficiency. **2.** the amount or quality lacked.

de•fi•cient (di fish′ənt), *adj.* **1.** lacking some element or characteristic; defective. **2.** insufficient; inadequate. —*n.* **3.** a person who is deficient, esp. one who is mentally defective. —**de•fi′cient•ly,** *adv.*

def•i•cit (def′ə sit), *n.* **1.** the amount by which a sum of money falls short of the required amount. **2.** a loss, as in the operation of a business. **3.** the amount by which expenditures or liabilities exceed income or assets. **4.** a deficiency. **5.** a disadvantage.

def′icit spend′ing, *n.* the practice of spending funds in excess of income, esp. by a government, usu. requiring that such funds be raised by borrowing, as from the sale of long-term bonds.

de•file[1] (di fīl′), *v.t.,* **-filed, -fil•ing. 1.** to make foul, dirty, or unclean. **2.** to violate the chastity of. **3.** to desecrate. **4.** to sully, as a person's reputation. —**de•file′ment,** *n.* —**de•fil′er,** *n.*

de•file[2] (di fīl′, dē′fīl), *n., v.,* **-filed, -fil•ing.** —*n.* **1.** a narrow passage, esp. between mountains. —*v.i.* **2.** to march in a line or by files.

de•fine (di fīn′), *v.,* **-fined, -fin•ing.** —*v.t.* **1.** to state or set forth the meaning of (a word, phrase, etc.). **2.** to explain or identify the nature or essential qualities of; describe. **3.** to specify: *to define responsibilities.* **4.** to determine or fix the boundaries or extent of. **5.** to make clear the outline or form of. —*v.i.* **6.** to set forth the meaning of a word, phrase, etc. —**de•fin′a•ble,** *adj.* —**de•fin′a•bil′i•ty,** *n.* —**de•fin′a•bly,** *adv.* —**de•fin′er,** *n.*

defin′ing mo′ment, *n.* **1.** a point at which the essential nature or character of a person, group, etc., is revealed or identified. **2.** a significant incident, event, or episode, esp. in a political campaign.

def•i•nite (def′ə nit), *adj.* **1.** clearly defined or determined; precise. **2.** having fixed limits. **3.** positive; certain. **4.** defining; limiting. **5.** (of an inflorescence) determinate. —**def′i•nite•ness,** *n.*

def′inite ar′ticle, *n.* an article, as English *the,* that classes as identified or definite the noun it modifies.

def•i•nite•ly (def′ə nit lē), *adv.* **1.** in a definite manner; unambiguously. **2.** unequivocally; positively. —*interj.* **3.** (used to express complete agreement or strong affirmation.)

def•i•ni•tion (def′ə nish′ən), *n.* **1.** the act of making definite, distinct, or clear. **2.** the formal statement of the meaning or significance of a word, phrase, etc. **3.** the condition of being definite, distinct, or clear. **4.** sharpness of the image formed by an optical system. —**def′i•ni′tion•al,** *adj.* —**def′i•ni′tion•al•ly,** *adv.*

de•fin•i•tive (di fin′i tiv), *adj.* **1.** most reliable or complete, as of a text, author, study, or the like. **2.** serving to define, fix, or specify definitely: *a definitive statement.* **3.** satisfying all criteria: *the definitive treatment for an infection.* **4.** *Biol.* fully developed or formed; complete. —*n.* **5.** a postage stamp on sale for an extended period of time, usu. part of a set of similar design and differing denominations. —**de•fin′i•tive•ly,** *adv.* —**de•fin′i•tive•ness,** *n.*

def•la•grate (def′lə grāt′), *v.t., v.i.,* **-grat•ed, -grat•ing.** to burn, esp. suddenly and violently. —**def′la•gra′tion,** *n.*

de•flate (di flāt′), *v.,* **-flat•ed, -flat•ing.** —*v.t.* **1.** to release the air or gas from (something inflated, as a balloon). **2.** to depress or reduce (a person or a person's ego, hopes, etc.); puncture; dash. **3.** to reduce (currency, prices, etc.) from an inflated condition. —*v.i.* **4.** to become deflated. —**de•fla′tor,** *n.*

de•fla•tion (di flā′shən), *n.* **1.** the act of deflating or the state of being deflated. **2.** a fall in the general price level or a contraction of credit and available money (opposed to *inflation*). **3.** the erosion of soil by the wind. —**de•fla′tion•ar′y,** *adj.*

de•flect (di flekt′), *v.t., v.i.* to bend or turn aside; turn from a true course. —**de•flect′a•ble,** *adj.* —**de•flec′tive,** *adj.* —**de•flec′tor,** *n.*

de•flec•tion (di flek′shən), *n.* **1.** the act or state of deflecting or the state of being deflected. **2.** amount of deviation. **3.** the deviation of the indicator of an instrument from the position taken as zero. Also, *Brit.,* **de•flex′ion.**

de•flow•er (di flou′ər), *v.t.* **1.** to deprive (a woman) of virginity. **2.** to despoil of beauty, freshness, sanctity, etc. —**de•flow′er•er,** *n.*

De•foe or **De Foe** (di fō′), *n.* **Daniel,** 1659?–1731, English novelist and political journalist.

de•fog (dē fog′, -fôg′), *v.t.,* **-fogged, -fog•ging.** to remove the fog or moisture from (a window, mirror, etc.). —**de•fog′ger,** *n.*

de•fo•li•ant (dē fō′lē ənt), *n.* a preparation for defoliating plants.

de•fo•li•ate (dē fō′lē āt′), *v.,* **-at•ed, -at•ing.** —*v.t.* **1.** to strip of leaves. **2.** to destroy or cause widespread loss of leaves in (an area of jungle, forest, etc.), as to deprive an enemy of concealment. —*v.i.* **3.** to lose leaves. —**de•fo′li•a′tion,** *n.* —**de•fo′li•a′tor,** *n.*

de•for•est (dē fôr′ist, -for′-), *v.t.* to divest or clear of forests or trees. —**de•for′est•a′tion,** *n.* —**de•for′est•er,** *n.*

de•form (di fôrm′), *v.t.* **1.** to mar the natural form or shape of; disfigure. **2.** to mar the beauty of; spoil. **3.** to change the form of; transform. **4.** *Geol., Mech.* to subject to deformation. —*v.i.* **5.** to undergo deformation. —**de•form′er,** *n.*

de•for•ma•tion (dē′fôr mā′shən, def′ər-), *n.* **1.** the act of deforming; distortion; disfigurement. **2.** the result of deforming; change of form, esp. for the worse. **3.** an altered form. —**de′for•ma′tion•al,** *adj.*

de•formed (di fôrmd′), *adj.* having the form changed, esp. with loss of beauty; misshapen; disfigured. —**de•form′ed•ness,** *n.*

de•form•i•ty (di fôr′mi tē), *n., pl.* **-ties. 1.** the quality or state of being deformed, disfigured, or misshapen. **2.** an abnormally formed part of the body. **3.** a deformed person or thing.

de•fraud (di frôd′), *v.t.* to deprive of a right, money, or property by fraud. —**de•fraud′er,** *n.*

de•fray (di frā′), *v.t.,* **-frayed, -fray•ing.** to bear or pay all or part of: *to help defray some of the costs.* —**de•fray′a•ble,** *adj.*

de•frost (di frôst′, -frost′), *v.t.* **1.** to remove the frost or ice from. **2.** to thaw. —*v.i.* **3.** to become free of ice or frost. **4.** to thaw.

deft (deft), *adj.* skillful; nimble; facile. —**deft′ly,** *adv.* —**deft′ness,** *n.*

de•funct (di fungkt′), *adj.* **1.** no longer in effect or use; not operating or functioning: *a defunct law.* **2.** no longer in existence; dead; extinct. —**de•funct′ness,** *n.*

de•fuse (dē fyo͞oz′), *v.,* **-fused, -fus•ing** —*v.t.* **1.** to remove the fuze from (a bomb, mine, etc.). **2.** to make less dangerous, tense, or embarrassing: *to defuse a tense situation.* —*v.i.* **3.** to grow less dangerous; weaken. —**de•fus′er,** *n.*

de•fy (*v.* di fī′; *n. also* dē′fī), *v.,* **-fied, -fy•ing,** *n., pl.* **-fies.** —*v.t.* **1.** to challenge the power of; resist boldly or openly. **2.** to offer effective resistance to: *This fort defies attack.* **3.** to challenge (a person) to do something deemed impossible. —*n.* **4.** a challenge; a defiance. —**de·fi′a·ble,** *adj.* —**de·fy′ing·ly,** *adv.*

dé·ga·gé (dā′gä zhā′), *adj.* **1.** unconstrained; easy, as in manner or style. **2.** lacking emotional involvement; detached.

De·gas (dā gä′, də-), *n.* **Hilaire Germain Edgar,** 1834–1917, French impressionist painter.

de Gaulle (də gōl′, gôl′), *n.* **Charles André Joseph Marie,** 1890–1970, French general: president 1959–69.

de·gen·er·ate (*v.* di jen′ə rāt′; *adj., n.* -ər it), *v.,* **-at·ed, -at·ing,** *adj., n.* —*v.i.* **1.** to decline in physical, mental, or moral qualities; deteriorate. **2.** to diminish in quality; fall from a high or normal standard: *The debate degenerated into a brawl.* **3.** (of an organ or tissue) to lose structure or function. **4.** (of a species or any of its traits or structures) to lose function or structural organization in the course of evolution, as the vestigial wings of a flightless bird. —*adj.* **5.** having declined in physical or moral qualities; deteriorated; degraded. **6.** having lost the qualities proper to the race or kind: *a degenerate vine.* **7.** characterized by or associated with degeneracy. **8.** *Physics.* **a.** (of modes of vibration of a system) having the same frequency. **b.** (of quantum states of a system) having equal energy. —*n.* **9.** a person who has declined, esp. in morals, from a type considered standard. **10.** a person or thing that reverts to an earlier stage of culture, development, or evolution. —**de·gen′er·a·cy,** *n.*

de·glaze (dē glāz′), *v.t.,* **-glazed, -glaz·ing. 1.** to dissolve cooking juices and particles of food in (a pan in which food has been sautéed or roasted) by adding liquid and stirring. **2.** to remove the glaze from (porcelain or the like).

de·grade (di grād′ *or, for 3,* dē-), *v.,* **-grad·ed, -grad·ing.** —*v.t.* **1.** to lower in dignity or estimation; bring into contempt. **2.** to lower in character or quality; debase. **3.** to reduce (someone) to a lower rank, degree, etc., esp. as a punishment. **4.** to reduce in amount, strength, intensity, etc. **5.** to wear down by erosion, as hills. Compare AGGRADE. **6.** to break down (an organic compound). —*v.i.* **7.** to become degraded; weaken or worsen; deteriorate. **8.** (esp. of an organic compound) to break down or decompose. —**deg′ra·da′tion,** *n.* —**de·grad′ing·ly,** *adv.*

de·gree (di grē′), *n.* **1.** any of a series of steps or stages, as in a process or course of action; a point in any scale. **2.** a stage or point in or as if in progression or retrogression: *We followed the degrees of her recovery with joy.* **3.** a stage in a scale of intensity or amount: *a high degree of mastery.* **4.** extent, measure, scope, or the like. **5.** a stage in a scale of rank or station, as in society, business, etc.: *a lord of high degree.* **6.** an academic title conferred by universities and colleges upon the completion of studies, or as an honorary recognition of achievement. **7.** a unit of measure, esp. of temperature, marked on the scale of a measuring instrument. **8.** the 360th part of a complete angle or turn, often represented by the sign °, as in 45°. **9.** the distinctive classification of a crime according to its gravity. **10.** one of the parallel formations of adjectives and adverbs used to express differences in quality, quantity, or intensity, consisting in English of the comparative, positive, and superlative. **11. a.** the sum of the exponents of the variables in an algebraic term: x^3 and $2x^2y$ *are terms of degree three.* **b.** the term of highest degree of a given equation or polynomial: *The expression* $3x^2y + y^2 + 1$ *is of degree three.* **c.** the exponent of the derivative of highest order appearing in a given differential equation. **12.** a tone, step, or note of a musical scale. **13.** a certain distance or remove in the line of descent, determining the proximity of relationship: *a cousin of the second degree.* —*Idiom.* **14. by degrees,** by easy stages; gradually. **15. to a degree, a.** somewhat. **b.** exceedingly.

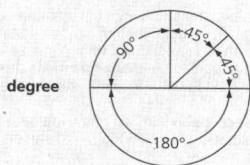

degree

de·gree-day (di grē′dā′), *n.* one degree of departure, on a single day, of the daily mean temperature from a given standard temperature.

de·gust (di gust′), *v.t.* to taste or savor carefully or appreciatively. —**de·gus·ta·tion** (dē′gu stā′shən), *n.*

de·hu·man·ize (dē hyōō′mə nīz′ *or, often,* -yōō′-), *v.t.,* **-ized, -iz·ing.** to deprive of human qualities or attributes; divest of individuality. —**de·hu′man·i·za′tion,** *n.*

de·hu·mid·i·fi·er (dē′hyōō mid′ə fī′ər, *or, often,* -yōō-), *n.* any device for removing moisture from indoor air. —**de′hu·mid′i·fy,** *v.t.,* **-fied, -fy·ing.** —**de′hu·mid′i·fi·ca′tion,** *n.*

de·hy·drate (dē hī′drāt), *v.,* **-drat·ed, -drat·ing.** —*v.t.* **1.** to free (fruit, vegetables, etc.) from moisture for preservation; dry. **2.** to cause abnormal loss of water from (the body or a tissue). **3.** to deprive (a chemical compound) of water or the elements of water. —*v.i.* **4.** to lose body fluids or water. —**de′hy·dra′tion,** *n.* —**de·hy′dra·tor,** *n.*

de·ice *or* **de-ice** (dē īs′), *v.t.,* **-iced, -ic·ing.** to free of ice; prevent or remove ice formation, as on the wing of an airplane. —**de·ic′er, de·ic′er,** *n.*

de·i·fy (dē′ə fī′), *v.t.,* **-fied, -fy·ing. 1.** to make a god of; exalt to the rank of a deity. **2.** to exalt as an object of worship: *to deify wealth.* —**de′i·fi·ca′tion,** *n.*

deign (dān), *v.i.* **1.** to think fit or in accordance with one's dignity; condescend: *She would not deign to visit us.* —*v.t.* **2.** to condescend to give or grant: *He deigned no reply.*

De·i gra·ti·a (dē′ē grä′tē ä′; *Eng.* dē′ī grā′shē ə, dē′ē), *Latin.* by the grace of God.

de·in·sti·tu·tion·al·ize (dē in′sti tōō′shə nl īz′, -tyōō′-, dē′in-), *v.,* **-ized, -iz·ing.** —*v.t.* **1.** to release (a mental patient, disabled person, etc.) from institutionalized care and treat or support with community resources. **2.** to free from the complexity of a bureaucracy. —**de·in′sti·tu′tion·al·i·za′tion,** *n.*

Deir·dre (dēr′drə, -drē), *n. Irish Legend.* the wife of Naoise, who killed herself after her husband was murdered by his uncle, King Conchobar.

de·ism (dē′iz əm), *n.* **1.** belief in the existence of a God on the evidence of reason and nature only, with rejection of supernatural revelation (distinguished from *theism*). **2.** belief in a God who created the world but has since remained indifferent to it. [< French *déisme* < Latin *deus* god]

de·i·ty (dē′i tē), *n., pl.* **-ties. 1.** a god or goddess. **2.** divine character or nature; divinity. **3.** the estate or rank of a god: *The king attained deity after his death.* **4.** a person or thing revered as supremely powerful or beneficent. **5. the Deity,** God.

dé·jà vu (dā′zhä vōō′, vyōō′; *Fr.* dā zhA vʏ′), *n.* **1.** the illusion of having previously experienced something actually being encountered for the first time. **2.** disagreeable familiarity or sameness. [< French: lit., already seen]

de·ject (di jekt′), *v.t.* to depress the spirits of; dispirit: *The bad news dejected me.*

de·ject·ed (di jek′tid), *adj.* depressed in spirits; disheartened; low-spirited. —**de·ject′ed·ly,** *adv.* —**de·ject′ed·ness,** *n.*

de ju·re (di jŏŏr′ē, dā jŏŏr′ā), *adv., adj.* according to law (disting. from *de facto*).

dek·a·gram *or* **dec·a·gram** (dek′ə gram′), *n.* a unit of mass or weight equal to 10 grams (0.3527 ounce avoirdupois). *Abbr.:* dag

dek·a·li·ter *or* **dec·a·li·ter** (dek′ə lē′tər), *n.* a unit of capacity equal to 10 liters (9.08 quarts U.S. dry measure or 2.64 gallons U.S. liquid measure). *Abbr.:* dal

dek·a·me·ter *or* **dec·a·me·ter** (dek′ə mē′tər), *n.* a unit of length equal to 10 meters (32.81 ft.). *Abbr.:* dam

del (del), *n. Math.* a differential operator. *Symbol:* ▽

De·la·croix (del′ə krwä′), *n.* **(Ferdinand Victor) Eugène,** 1798–1863, French painter.

de·lam·i·nate (dē lam′ə nāt′), *v.i.,* **-nat·ed, -nat·ing.** to split into laminae or thin layers.

De·la·ny (də lā′nē), *n.* **Martin Robinson,** 1812–85, U.S. physician and army officer: leader of black nationalist movement.

Del·a·ware (del′ə wâr′), *n., pl.* **-wares,** (*esp. collectively*) **-ware** for 3. **1.** a state in the E United States, on the Atlantic coast. 724,842; 2057 sq. mi. (5330 sq. km). *Cap.:* Dover. *Abbr.:* DE, Del. **2.** a river flowing S from SE New York, along the boundary between Pennsylvania and New Jersey into Delaware Bay. 296 mi. (475 km) long. **3.** a member of any of a group of American Indian peoples formerly of the drainage basin of the Delaware River, the lower Hudson River, and the intervening area. **4.** the Eastern Algonquian language of any of the Delaware peoples.

De La Warr *or* **Del·a·ware** (del′ə wâr′), *n.* **12th Baron** (*Thomas West*), 1577–1618, 1st English colonial governor of Virginia.

de·lay (di lā′), *v.,* **-layed, -lay·ing,** *n.* —*v.t.* **1.** to put off to a later time; postpone. **2.** to impede the process or progress of; retard: *The fog delayed the plane's landing.* —*v.i.* **3.** to put off action; linger; loiter. —*n.* **4.** the act of delaying; procrastination; loitering. **5.** an instance of being delayed. —**de·lay′a·ble,** *adj.* —**de·lay′er,** *n.* —**de·lay′ing·ly,** *adv.*

de·le (dē′lē), *v.,* **de·led, de·le·ing,** *n.* —*v.t.* **1.** to delete. —*n.* **2.** a mark, as ⟨⟩, used to indicate matter to be deleted.

de·lec·ta·ble (di lek′tə bəl), *adj.* **1.** delightful; highly pleasing. **2.** delicious. —*n.* **3.** an appetizing food or dish. —**de·lec′ta·ble·ness, de·lec′ta·bil′i·ty,** *n.* —**de·lec′ta·bly,** *adv.*

del·e·gate (*n.* del′i git, -gāt′; *v.* -gāt′), *n., v.,* **-gat·ed, -gat·ing.** —*n.* **1.** a person designated to act for or represent another or others, as at a conference or political convention. **2.** the representative of a Territory in the U.S. House of Representatives. **3.** a member of the lower house of the legislatures of Virginia, West Virginia, and Maryland. —*v.t.* **4.** to send or appoint as deputy or representative. **5.** to commit (powers, functions, etc.) to another as agent. —**del′e·ga·tee′** (-gə tē′), *n.* —**del′e·ga·tor,** *n.*

del·e·ga·tion (del′i gā′shən), *n.* **1.** a group or body of delegates. **2.** the body of delegates chosen to represent a political unit in an assembly. **3.** the act of delegating. **4.** the state of being delegated.

de Les·seps (də les′eps), *n.* **Vicomte Ferdinand Marie,** LESSEPS, Ferdinand Marie, Vicomte de.

de·lete (di lēt′), *v.t.,* **-let·ed, -let·ing.** to strike out or remove (something written or printed); cancel; erase; expunge. —**de•let′a•ble,** *adj.* —**de•le′tion,** *n.*

del•e•te•ri•ous (del′i tēr′ē əs), *adj.* **1.** injurious to health. **2.** harmful; injurious. —**del′e•te′ri•ous•ly,** *adv.* —**del′e•te′ri•ous•ness,** *n.*

Del•hi (del′ē), *n.* **1.** a union territory in N India. 6,220,400; 574 sq. mi. (1487 sq. km). **2.** the capital of this territory: former capital of the old Mogul Empire; administrative headquarters of British India 1912–29. 5,714,000. Compare NEW DELHI.

del•i (del′ē), *n., pl.* **del•is** (del′ēz). delicatessen.

de•lib•er•ate (*adj.* di lib′ər it; *v.* -ə rāt′), *adj., v.,* **-at•ed, -at•ing.** —*adj.* **1.** studied or intentional: *a deliberate lie.* **2.** characterized by deliberation; careful or slow in deciding: *a deliberate decision.* **3.** slow and even; unhurried: *a deliberate step.* —*v.t.* **4.** to weigh in the mind; consider: *to deliberate a question.* —*v.i.* **5.** to think carefully or attentively; reflect. **6.** to consult or confer formally: *The jury deliberated for three hours.* —**de•lib′er•ate•ly,** *adv.* —**de•lib′er•ate•ness,** *n.* —**de•lib′er•a′tor,** *n.*

de•lib•er•a•tion (di lib′ə rā′shən), *n.* **1.** careful consideration before decision. **2.** formal consultation or discussion. **3.** deliberate quality; leisureliness of movement or action; slowness.

de•lib•er•a•tive (di lib′ər ə tiv, -ə rā′tiv), *adj.* **1.** having the function of deliberating, as a legislative assembly. **2.** dealing with the wisdom and expediency of a proposal: *a deliberative speech.* —**de•lib′er•a•tive•ly,** *adv.* —**de•lib′er•a•tive•ness,** *n.*

del•i•ca•cy (del′i kə sē), *n., pl.* **-cies. 1.** fineness of texture, quality, etc.; softness; daintiness: *the delicacy of lace.* **2.** something delightful or pleasing, esp. a choice food considered with regard to its rarity, costliness, or the like. **3.** the quality of being easily broken or damaged; fragility. **4.** the quality of requiring or involving great care or tact: *negotiations of great delicacy.* **5.** precision of action or operation; minute accuracy. **6.** fineness of perception or feeling; sensitiveness. **7.** sensitivity with regard to what is fitting, proper, etc.: *Delicacy would not permit her to be rude.* **8.** bodily weakness; liability to sickness; frailty.

del•i•cate (del′i kit), *adj.* **1.** fine in texture, quality, construction, etc. **2.** fragile; easily damaged; frail. **3.** so fine as to be scarcely perceptible; subtle: *a delicate flavor.* **4.** soft or faint, as color. **5.** fine or precise in action or execution: *a delicate performance.* **6.** requiring great care, caution, or tact: *a delicate situation.* **7.** capable of distinguishing subtle differences: *a delicate sense of smell.* **8.** regardful of what is becoming or proper: *a delicate sense of propriety.* **9.** choice: *delicate tidbits.* **10.** squeamish: *not a movie for the delicate viewer.* —**del′i•cate•ly,** *adv.* —**del′i•cate•ness,** *n.*

del•i•ca•tes•sen (del′i kə tes′ən), *n.* **1.** a store selling prepared foods, as cooked meats, cheese, and salads. **2.** the products sold in a delicatessen.

de•li•cious (di lish′əs), *adj.* **1.** highly pleasing to the senses, esp. taste or smell. **2.** very pleasing; delightful: *delicious gossip.* —*n.* **3.** (*cap.*) a red or yellow variety of apple cultivated in the U.S. —**de•li′cious•ly,** *adv.* —**de•li′cious•ness,** *n.*

de•light (di līt′), *n.* **1.** a high degree of pleasure or enjoyment; joy; rapture. **2.** something that gives great pleasure. —*v.t.* **3.** to give delight to. —*v.i.* **4.** to have or take great pleasure: *She delights in walking.*

de•light•ed (di lī′tid), *adj.* highly pleased. —**de•light′ed•ly,** *adv.*

De•li•lah (di lī′lə), *n.* Samson's mistress, who betrayed him to the Philistines. Judg. 16.

de•lim•it (di lim′it), *v.t.* to fix or mark the limits or boundaries of. —**de•lim′i•ta′tion,** *n.* —**de•lim′i•ta′tive,** *n., adj.*

de•lim•it•er (di lim′i tər), *n.* a character or space indicating the beginning or end of a piece of computer data.

de•lin•e•ate (di lin′ē āt′), *v.t.,* **-at•ed, -at•ing. 1.** to trace the outline of; represent pictorially. **2.** to portray in words; describe with precision. —**de•lin′e•a•ble** (-ə bəl), *adj.* —**de•lin′e•a′tor,** *n.*

de•lin•e•a•tion (di lin′ē ā′shən), *n.* **1.** the act or process of delineating. **2.** a chart or diagram; sketch; rough draft. **3.** a description. —**de•lin′e•a′tive** (-ā′tiv, -ə tiv), *adj.*

de•lin•quen•cy (di ling′kwən sē), *n., pl.* **-cies. 1.** failure in or neglect of duty or obligation; dereliction; default: *delinquency in payment of dues.* **2.** wrongful, illegal, or antisocial behavior. **3.** any misdeed, offense, or misdemeanor. **4.** something, as a debt, that is past due or otherwise delinquent.

de•lin•quent (di ling′kwənt), *adj.* **1.** failing in or neglectful of a duty or obligation; guilty of a misdeed or offense. **2.** past due: *a delinquent account.* **3.** of or pertaining to delinquents or delinquency. —*n.* **4.** a person who is delinquent, esp. a juvenile delinquent. —**de•lin′quent•ly,** *adv.*

del•i•quesce (del′i kwes′), *v.i.,* **-quesced, -quesc•ing. 1.** to become liquid by absorbing moisture from the air, as certain salts. **2.** to melt away. **3.** *Bot.* **a.** to form many small divisions or branches. **b.** to become liquid in the course of maturity, as certain fungi. —**del′i•ques′cence,** *n.* —**del′i•ques′cent,** *adj.*

de•lir•i•ous (di lēr′ē əs), *adj.* **1.** affected with or characteristic of delirium. **2.** wild with excitement, enthusiasm, etc. —**de•lir′i•ous•ly,** *adv.* —**de•lir′i•ous•ness,** *n.*

de•lir•i•um (di lēr′ē əm), *n., pl.* **-lir•i•ums, -lir•i•a** (-lēr′ē ə). **1.** a temporary disturbance of consciousness characterized by restlessness, excitement, and delusions or hallucinations. **2.** a state of violent excitement or emotion.

delir′ium tre′mens (trē′mənz, -menz), *n.* a withdrawal syndrome occurring in persons who have developed physiological dependence on alcohol, characterized by tremor, visual hallucinations, and autonomic instability. Also called **the d.t.'s.**

de•liv•er (di liv′ər), *v.t.* **1.** to carry and turn over (letters, goods, etc.) to the intended recipient or recipients. **2.** to give into another's possession or keeping; hand over; surrender: *to deliver a prisoner to the police.* **3.** to bring (votes) to the support of a candidate or a cause. **4.** to give forth in words; utter or pronounce: *to deliver a speech.* **5.** to give forth or emit: *The oil well delivers 500 barrels a day.* **6.** to strike or throw: *to deliver a blow.* **7.** to set free or liberate; save: *delivered them from bondage.* **8.** to give birth to. **9. a.** to assist at the birth of: *The doctor delivered the baby.* **b.** to assist (a female) in bringing forth young. **10.** to disburden (oneself) of thoughts, opinions, etc. **11.** to make known; assert. —*v.i.* **12.** to give birth. **13.** to provide a delivery service for goods and products. **14.** to do or carry out something as promised. —**de•liv′er•a•ble,** *adj.* —**de•liv′er•er,** *n.*

de•liv•er•ance (di liv′ər əns), *n.* **1.** an act or instance of delivering. **2.** salvation. **3.** liberation. **4.** a thought or judgment expressed; a formal or authoritative pronouncement.

de•liv•er•y (di liv′ə rē), *n., pl.* **-er•ies. 1.** the carrying and turning over of letters, goods, etc., to a designated recipient or recipients. **2.** a giving up or handing over; surrender. **3.** the utterance or enunciation of words. **4.** vocal and bodily behavior during the presentation of a speech: *a speaker's fine delivery.* **5.** the act or manner of giving or sending forth: *the pitcher's fine delivery of the ball.* **6.** the state of being delivered of or giving birth to a child; parturition. **7.** something delivered: *The delivery is late today.* **8.** a shipment of goods from the seller to the buyer.

deliv′ery room′, *n.* an area in a hospital equipped for delivering babies.

dell (del), *n.* a small, usu. wooded valley; vale.

de•louse (dē lous′, -louz′), *v.t.,* **-loused, -lous•ing.** to free of lice; remove lice from.

Del•phi (del′fī), *n.* an ancient city in central Greece, on the slopes of Mount Parnassus: site of an oracle of Apollo.

Del•phic (del′fik), *adj.* **1.** of or pertaining to Delphi. **2.** (*often l.c.*) oracular: *Delphic pronouncements.* —**del′phi•cal•ly,** *adv.*

del•phin•i•um (del fin′ē əm), *n., pl.* **-i•ums, -i•a** (-ē ə). any of numerous plants of the genus *Delphinium,* of the buttercup family, esp. any of various tall, cultivated species having usu. blue, pink, or white flowers. Compare LARKSPUR.

del•ta (del′tə), *n., pl.* **-tas. 1.** the fourth letter of the Greek alphabet (Δ, δ). **2.** the fourth in a series of items. **3.** anything triangular, like the Greek capital delta (Δ). **4.** *Math.* an incremental change in a variable, as Δ or δ. **5.** a nearly flat plain of alluvial, often triangular deposit between diverging branches of the mouth of a river. —**del•ta′ic** (-tā′ik), *adj.*

del′ta rhythm′, *n.* a pattern of slow brain waves, less than 6 cycles per second, associated with the deepest phase of slow-wave sleep.

del′ta wing′, *n.* a triangularly shaped surface that serves as both wing and horizontal stabilizer of a space vehicle and some supersonic aircraft.

del•toid (del′toid), *n.* **1.** a large, triangular muscle covering the joint of the shoulder, the action of which raises the arm away from the side of the body. —*adj.* **2.** pertaining to or involving the deltoid. **3.** in the shape of a Greek capital delta (Δ); triangular.

de•lude (di lo͞od′), *v.t.,* **-lud•ed, -lud•ing.** to mislead the mind or judgment of; deceive. —**de•lud′er,** *n.* —**de•lud′ing•ly,** *adv.*

del•uge (del′yo͞oj, -yo͞ozh, -o͞oj, -o͞ozh, di lo͞oj′, -lo͞ozh′), *n., v.,* **-uged, -ug•ing.** —*n.* **1.** a great flood of water; inundation; flood. **2.** a drenching rain; downpour. **3.** anything that overwhelms like a flood: *a deluge of mail.* **4. the Deluge,** FLOOD (def. 3). —*v.t.* **5.** to flood; inundate. **6.** to overrun; overwhelm.

de•lu•sion (di lo͞o′zhən), *n.* **1.** an act or instance of deluding. **2.** the state of being deluded. **3.** a false belief or opinion: *delusions of grandeur.* **4.** a false belief that is resistant to reason or confrontation with actual fact: *a paranoid delusion.* —**de•lu′sion•al, de•lu′sion•ar′y,** *adj.*

de•luxe or **de luxe** (də luks′, -lo͝oks′), *adj.* of special elegance or sumptuousness.

delve (delv), *v.i.,* **delved, delv•ing.** to carry on intensive and thorough research for data, information, or the like. —**delv′er,** *n.*

dely., delivery.

de•mag•net•ize (dē mag′ni tīz′), *v.t.,* **-ized, -iz•ing.** to remove magnetization from. —**de•mag′net•iz′a•ble,** *adj.* —**de•mag′net•i•za′tion,** *n.* —**de•mag′net•iz′er,** *n.*

dem•a•gog•ic (dem′ə goj′ik, -gog′-, -gō′jik) also **dem′a•gog′i•cal,** *adj.* of, pertaining to, or characteristic of a demagogue. —**dem′a•gog′i•cal•ly,** *adv.*

dem•a•gogue or **dem•a•gog** (dem′ə gog′, -gôg′), *n., v.,* **-gogued, -gogu•ing.** —*n.* **1.** a person, esp. an orator or political leader, who gains power by arousing people's emotions and prejudices. **2.** (in ancient times) a leader of the people. —*v.i.* **3.** to speak or act like a demagogue.

de•mand (di mand′, -mänd′), *v.t.* **1.** to ask for with proper authority; claim as a right. **2.** to ask for peremptorily or urgently: *She demanded that we resign.* **3.** to call for or require as just, proper, or necessary: *This task demands patience.* —*v.i.* **4.** to make a demand; inquire; ask. —*n.* **5.** an urgent or pressing requirement. **6. a.** the desire and means to purchase goods. **b.** the amount of goods purchased at a specific price. **7.** the state of being wanted or sought for purchase or use: *an article in great demand.* **—Idiom. 8. on demand, a.** upon request for or presentation of payment. **b.** sanctioned by legal rights: *abortion on demand.* **—de•mand′a•ble,** *adj.*

demand′ depos′it, *n.* a bank deposit subject to withdrawal at the demand of the depositor without prior notice.

de•mand•ing (di man′ding, -män′-), *adj.* **1.** requiring or claiming more than is generally felt by others to be due: *a demanding teacher.* **2.** calling for intensive effort or attention; taxing: *a demanding job.* **—de•mand′ing•ly,** *adv.*

demand′-side′, *adj.* of or pertaining to an economic policy that stimulates consumer demand to increase production and employment. Compare SUPPLY-SIDE. **—demand′-sid′er,** *n.*

de•mar•cate (di mär′kāt, dē′mär kāt′), *v.t.,* **-cat•ed, -cat•ing. 1.** to determine or mark off the boundaries of. **2.** to separate distinctly: *to demarcate the lots with fences.* **—de•mar′ca•tor,** *n.*

de•mar•ca•tion or **de•mar•ka•tion** (dē′mär kā′shən), *n.* **1.** the determining and marking off of the boundaries of something. **2.** separation by distinct boundaries: *line of demarcation.*

De•mas (dē′mas, -məs), *n.* an unreliable fellow missionary with the Apostle Paul. II Tim. 4:10.

de•mean¹ (di mēn′), *v.t.* to lower in dignity or standing; debase.

de•mean² (di mēn′), *v.t.* to conduct or behave (oneself) in a specified manner.

de•mean•or (di mē′nər), *n.* **1.** conduct; behavior; deportment. **2.** facial appearance; mien. Also, *esp. Brit.,* **de•mean′our.**

de•ment•ed (di men′tid), *adj.* **1.** crazy; insane; mad. **2.** affected with dementia. **—de•ment′ed•ly,** *adv.* **—de•ment′ed•ness,** *n.*

de•men•tia (di men′shə, -shē ə), *n.* severely impaired memory and reasoning ability, usu. with disturbed behavior, associated with damaged brain tissue. **—de•men′tial,** *adj.*

de•mer•it (di mer′it), *n.* **1.** a mark against a person for misconduct or deficiency. **2.** the quality of being censurable or punishable; fault; culpability.

de•mesne (di mān′, -mēn′), *n.* **1.** possession of land as one's own. **2.** an estate occupied by and worked exclusively for the owner. **3.** the dominion or territory of a sovereign or state; domain. **4.** a district; region. **—de•mesn′i•al,** *adj.*

De•me•ter (di mē′tər), *n.* the ancient Greek goddess of agriculture, identified by the Romans with Ceres.

demi-, a combining form appearing in loanwords from French meaning "half" (*demilune*), "lesser" (*demitasse*), or sometimes used with a pejorative sense (*demimonde*); on this model, also prefixed to words of English origin (*demigod*).

dem•i•god (dem′ē god′), *n.* **1.** a mythological being who is partly divine and partly human. **2.** a deified mortal.

de•mil•i•ta•rize (dē mil′i tə rīz′), *v.t.,* **-rized, -riz•ing. 1.** to deprive of military character; place under civil control. **2.** to forbid military use of. **—de•mil′i•ta•ri•za′tion,** *n.*

De Mille (də mil′), *n.* **1. Agnes (George),** 1905–93, U.S. choreographer and dancer. **2.** her uncle, **Cecil B(lount),** 1881–1959, U.S. motion-picture producer and director.

dem•i•lune (dem′i lōōn′), *n.* a crescent or half-moon shape.

de•mise (di mīz′), *n., v.,* **-mised, -mis•ing. —***n.* **1.** death or decease. **2.** termination of existence or operation. **3. a.** a death or decease occasioning the transfer of an estate. **b.** a conveyance or transfer of an estate. **4.** the transfer of sovereignty, as by the death or abdication of the sovereign. **—***v.t.* **5.** to transfer (an estate or the like) by bequest or lease. **6.** to transfer (sovereignty), as by death or abdication. **—***v.i.* **7.** to pass by bequest or inheritance. **—de•mis′a•bil′i•ty,** *n.* **—de•mis′a•ble,** *adj.*

dem•i•tasse (dem′i tas′, -täs′, dem′ē-), *n.* **1.** a small cup for serving strong black coffee. **2.** the coffee served.

de•mo•bi•lize (dē mō′bə līz′), *v.t.,* **-lized, -liz•ing. 1.** to disband (troops). **2.** to discharge (a person) from military service. **—de•mo′bi•li•za′tion,** *n.*

de•moc•ra•cy (di mok′rə sē), *n., pl.* **-cies. 1.** government by the people; a form of government in which the supreme power is vested in the people and exercised directly by them or by their elected agents under a free electoral system. **2.** a state having such a form of government. **3.** a state of society characterized by formal equality of rights and privileges. **4.** political or social equality; democratic spirit. **5.** the common people, esp. with respect to their political power.

Democ′racy in Amer′ica, (French, *Démocracie en Amérique*), a study (1835) by Alexis de Tocqueville of American political institutions.

dem•o•crat (dem′ə krat′), *n.* **1.** an advocate of democracy. **2.** a person who believes in political or social equality. **3.** (*cap.*) a member of the Democratic Party.

dem•o•crat•ic (dem′ə krat′ik), *adj.* **1.** pertaining to or of the nature of democracy or a democracy. **2.** pertaining to or characterized by political or social equality. **3.** advocating or upholding democracy. **4.** (*cap.*) of, pertaining to, or characteristic of the Democratic Party. **—dem′o•crat′i•cal•ly,** *adv.*

Dem′ocrat′ic Par′ty, *n.* one of the two major political parties in the U.S., dating from a split in the Democratic-Republican Party in 1828.

Democrat′ic-Repub′lican par′ty, *n.* a U.S. political party opposed to the Federalist party.

de•moc•ra•tize (di mok′rə tīz′), *v.t.,* **-tized, -tiz•ing.** to make democratic. **—de•moc′ra•ti•za′tion,** *n.*

de•mod•u•late (dē moj′ə lāt′), *v.t.,* **-lat•ed, -lat•ing.** to extract the original information-bearing signal from (a modulated carrier wave or signal); detect. **—de•mod′u•la′tion,** *n.* **—de•mod′u•la′tor,** *n.*

de•mog•ra•phy (di mog′rə fē), *n.* the science of vital and social statistics, as of the births, deaths, diseases, marriages, etc., of populations. **—de•mog′ra•pher,** *n.* **—dem•o•graph•ic** (dem′ə graf′ik, dē′mə-), *adj.* **—dem′o•graph′i•cal•ly,** *adv.* **—dem•o•graph′ics,** *n.*

dem•oi•selle (dem′wə zel′, dem′ə-), *n.* **1.** an unmarried girl or young woman. **2.** a small gray crane, *Anthropoides virgo,* of N Africa and Eurasia, with white neck plumes. **3.** a damselfly, esp. of the genus *Agrion.* **4.** DAMSELFISH.

de•mol•ish (di mol′ish), *v.t.* **1.** to destroy or ruin (a building or other structure), esp. on purpose; tear down; raze. **2.** to put an end to; destroy; finish. **3.** to lay waste to; ruin utterly.

dem•o•li•tion (dem′ə lish′ən, dē′mə-), *n.* **1.** an act or instance of demolishing. **2.** the state of being demolished; destruction. **3.** destruction or demolishment by explosives. **4.** demolitions, explosives, esp. as used in war. **—dem′o•li′tion•ist,** *n.*

de•mon (dē′mən), *n.* **1.** an evil spirit; fiend. **2.** an evil passion or influence. **3.** a wicked or cruel person. **4.** one with great energy: *a demon for work.*

de•mo•ni•ac (di mō′nē ak′, dē′mə nī′ak), *adj.* Also, **de•mo•ni•a•cal** (dē′mə nī′ə kəl). **1.** of, pertaining to, or like a demon; demonic. **2.** possessed by or as if by an evil spirit; raging; frantic. **—de′mo•ni′a•cal•ly,** *adv.*

de•mon•ic or **dae•mon•ic** (di mon′ik), also **de•mon′i•cal,** *adj.* **1.** inspired as if by a demon, indwelling spirit, or genius. **2.** DEMONIAC (def. 2).

de•mon•stra•ble (di mon′strə bəl, dem′ən-), *adj.* **1.** capable of being demonstrated or proved. **2.** clearly evident; obvious. **—de•mon′stra•bil′i•ty, de•mon′stra•ble•ness,** *n.* **—de•mon′stra•bly,** *adv.*

dem•on•strate (dem′ən strāt′), *v.,* **-strat•ed, -strat•ing. —***v.t.* **1.** to describe, explain, or illustrate by examples, specimens, experiments, or the like. **2.** to make evident or establish by reasoning; prove. **3.** to display openly or publicly, as feelings. **4.** to exhibit the operation or use of (a product), esp. to a prospective customer. **—***v.i.* **5.** to make, give, or take part in a demonstration. **6.** to attack or make a show of military force to deceive an enemy. **—dem•on′strat′ed•ly,** *adv.*

dem•on•stra•tion (dem′ən strā′shən), *n.* **1.** the act of proving, as by reasoning or a show of evidence. **2.** something serving as proof or supporting evidence. **3.** a description or explanation, as of a process, illustrated by examples, specimens, or the like. **4.** the act of exhibiting the operation or use of a product, as to a prospective buyer. **5.** an exhibition, as of feeling; display: *a demonstration of affection.* **6.** a public exhibition of the attitude of a group toward a controversial issue or other matter, made by picketing, parading, etc. **7.** a show of military force made to deceive an enemy. **8.** Math. a logical presentation of the way in which given assumptions imply a certain result; proof.

de•mon•stra•tive (də mon′strə tiv), *adj.* **1.** characterized by or given to open exhibition or expression of one's emotions, attitudes, etc., esp. of love or affection. **2.** serving to demonstrate; explanatory or illustrative. **3.** serving to prove the truth of anything; conclusive. **4.** indicating or singling out the thing referred to. *This* is a demonstrative pronoun. **—***n.* **5.** a demonstrative word, as *this* or *there.* **—de•mon′stra•tive•ly,** *adv.* **—de•mon′stra•tive•ness,** *n.*

dem•on•stra•tor (dem′ən strā′tər), *n.* **1.** a person or thing that demonstrates. **2.** a person who takes part in a public demonstration, as by marching. **3.** a person who explains or teaches by practical demonstrations. **4.** a person who exhibits the use and application of (a product) to a prospective customer. **5.** the product actually used in demonstrations to prospective customers.

de•mor•al•ize (di môr′ə līz′, -mor′-), *v.t.,* **-ized, -iz•ing. 1.** to deprive (a person or persons) of spirit, courage, discipline, etc.; destroy the morale of. **2.** to throw (a person) into disorder or confusion; bewilder. **3.** to corrupt or undermine the morals of. **—de•mor′al•i•za′tion,** *n.* **—de•mor′al•iz′ing•ly,** *adv.*

De•mos•the•nes (di mos′thə nēz′), *n.* 384?–322 B.C., Athenian statesman and orator.

de•mote (di mōt′), *v.t.,* **-mot•ed, -mot•ing.** to reduce to a lower grade or rank. **—de•mo′tion,** *n.*

de•mot•ic (di mot′ik), *adj.* **1.** of or pertaining to the current, ordinary, everyday form of a language; vernacular. **2.** of or pertaining to the common people; popular.

Demp•sey (demp′sē), *n.* **Jack** (*William Harrison Dempsey*), 1895–1983, U.S. boxer: world heavyweight champion 1919–26.

de•mul•si•fy (dē mul′sə fī′), *v.t.,* **-fied, -fy•ing.** to break down (an emulsion) into substances incapable of re-forming the original emulsion. **—de•mul′si•fi•ca′tion,** *n.* **—de•mul′si•fi′er,** *n.*

de•mur (di mûr′), *v.,* **-murred, -mur•ring,** *n.* **—***v.i.* **1.** to make objection, esp. on the grounds of scruples; take exception; object. **2.** *Law.* to respond with a demurrer. **—***n.* **3.** the act of making objection. **4.** an objection raised. **5.** hesitation.

de•mure (di myŏŏr′), *adj.,* **-mur•er, -mur•est. 1.** characterized by shyness and modesty; reserved. **2.** affectedly or coyly decorous, sober, or sedate. **—de•mure′ly,** *adv.* **—de•mure′ness,** *n.*

de•mur•rer¹ (di mûr′ər), *n.* a person who demurs; objector.

de·mur·rer[2] (di mûr′ər), *n.* **1.** a pleading in response to another's complaint asserting that the complaint contains no cause for action. **2.** an objection raised; demur.

de·mys·ti·fy (dē mis′tə fī′), *v.t.,* **-fied, -fy·ing.** to rid of mystery; clarify. —**de·mys′ti·fi·ca′tion,** *n.* —**de·mys′ti·fi′er,** *n.*

den (den), *n., v.,* **denned, den·ning.** —*n.* **1.** the lair or shelter of a wild animal, esp. a predatory mammal. **2.** a room in a home designed to provide a comfortable and informal atmosphere for conversation, reading, etc. **3.** a cave used as a place of shelter or concealment. **4.** a squalid or vile abode or place: *dens of misery.* **5.** one of the units of a cub scout pack, analogous to a patrol in the Boy Scouts. —*v.i.* **6.** to live in or as if in a den.

De·na′li Na′tional Park′, *n.* a national park in S central Alaska, including Mount McKinley. 3030 sq. mi. (7850 sq. km). Formerly, **Mount McKinley National Park.**

de·nar·i·us (di nâr′ē əs), *n., pl.* **-nar·i·i** (-nâr′ē ī′). **1.** a silver coin of ancient Rome, orig. equal to 10 asses. **2.** a gold coin of ancient Rome equal to 25 silver denarii.

de·na·tion·al·ize (dē nash′ə nl īz′), *v.t.,* **-ized, -iz·ing. 1.** to remove (an industry or the like) from government ownership or control. **2.** to deprive of national status, attachments, or characteristics. —**de·na′tion·al·i·za′tion,** *n.*

de·na·ture (dē nā′chər), *v.t.,* **-tured, -tur·ing. 1.** to deprive (something) of its natural character, properties, etc. **2.** to render (any of various alcohols) undrinkable by adding an unwholesome substance. **3.** to treat (a protein or the like) by chemical or physical means so as to alter its original state. —**de·na′tur·ant,** *n.* —**de·na′tur·a′tion,** *n.*

dena′tured al′cohol, *n.* alcohol, esp. ethyl alcohol, that has been denatured: used chiefly as a solvent and in chemical synthesis.

den·drite (den′drīt), *n.* **1. a.** a branching figure or marking, resembling moss or a shrub or tree in form, found on or in certain stones or minerals due to the presence of a foreign material. **b.** any arborescent crystalline growth. **2.** any branching process of a neuron that conducts impulses toward the cell body.

dendro-, a combining form meaning "tree": *dendrology.*

den·dro·chro·nol·o·gy (den′drō krə nol′ə jē), *n.* the study of the annual rings of trees to determine the dates and chronology of past events. —**den′dro·chron′o·log′i·cal** (-kron′l oj′i kal), *adj.* —**den′dro·chron′o·log·i·cal·ly,** *adv.* —**den′dro·chro·nol′o·gist,** *n.*

den·drol·o·gy (den drol′ə jē), *n.* the branch of botany dealing with trees and shrubs. —**den′dro·log′i·cal** (-drə loj′i kal), **den′dro·log′ic,** *adj.* —**den·drol′o·gist,** *n.*

Den·eb (den′eb), *n.* a first-magnitude star in the constellation Cygnus.

den·e·ga·tion (den′i gā′shən), *n.* denial; contradiction.

den·gue (deng′gā, -gē), *n.* an infectious, eruptive fever of warm climates, usu. epidemic, characterized esp. by severe pains in the joints and muscles. Also called **dan′gue fe′ver.**

Deng Xiao·ping (dung′ shou′ping′), *n.* 1904–97, Chinese Communist leader.

de·ni·a·ble (di nī′ə bəl), *adj.* capable of being or liable to be denied or contradicted. —**de·ni′a·bil′i·ty,** *n.*

de·ni·al (di nī′əl), *n.* **1.** an assertion that an allegation is false. **2.** refusal to believe a doctrine, theory, or the like. **3.** disbelief in the existence or reality of a thing. **4.** the refusal to satisfy a claim, request, etc., or the refusal of a person making it. **5.** refusal to recognize or acknowledge; a disowning or disavowal: *Peter's denial of Christ.* **6.** *Law.* a plea that denies the alleged facts of an adversary's plea. **7.** *Psychol.* the reduction of anxiety by the unconscious exclusion from the mind of intolerable thoughts, feelings, or facts.

de·ni·er[1] (di nī′ər), *n.* a person who denies.

de·nier[2] (də nēr′, dən yā′ *or, esp. for 1,* den′yər), *n.* a unit of weight indicating the fineness of fiber filaments and yarns, both silk and synthetic, and equal to a yarn weighing one gram per each 9000 meters: used esp. for women's hosiery.

den·i·grate (den′i grāt′), *v.t.,* **-grat·ed, -grat·ing. 1.** to speak damagingly of; defame or disparage: *to denigrate someone's character.* **2.** to make black; blacken. —**den′i·gra′tion,** *n.* —**den′i·gra′tive,** *adj.* —**den′i·gra′tor,** *n.* —**den′i·gra·to′ry** (-grə tôr′ē, -tōr′ē), *adj.*

den·im (den′əm), *n.* **1.** a heavy twill fabric of cotton or other fibers woven with white and colored, often blue, threads, used esp. for jeans. **2.** a lighter, softer fabric resembling this, used for garments, upholstery, etc. **3. denims,** (*used with a pl. v.*) clothes of denim. [< French: short for *serge de Nîmes* serge of Nîmes (city in France)] —**den′imed,** *adj.*

Den·is (den′is; *Fr.* də nē′), *n.* **Saint,** died A.D. c280, 1st bishop of Paris; patron saint of France.

den·i·zen (den′ə zən), *n.* **1.** an inhabitant; resident. **2.** a person who regularly frequents a place; habitué. —*v.t.* **3.** to make a denizen of.

Den·mark (den′märk), *n.* a kingdom in N Europe, on the Jutland peninsula and adjacent islands. 5,268,775; 16,576 sq. mi. (42,930 sq. km). *Cap.:* Copenhagen.

den′ moth′er, *n.* a woman who serves as an adult leader of a cub scout den.

den′ of thieves′, *n.* a place where one must guard against theft or attack. Matt. 21:13.

de·nom·i·nate (di nom′ə nāt′), *v.t.,* **-nat·ed, -nat·ing.** to give a name to; denote; designate.

de·nom·i·na·tion (di nom′ə nā′shən), *n.* **1.** a religious group, usu.

including many local churches. **2.** one of the grades or degrees in a series of designations of quantity, value, measure, weight, etc.: *bills of small denomination.* **3.** a name or designation, esp. one for a class of things. **4.** a class or kind of persons or things distinguished by a specific name. **5.** the act of naming or designating a person or thing. —**de·nom′i·na′tion·al,** *adj.* —**de·nom′i·na′tion·al·ly,** *adv.*

de·nom·i·na·tive (di nom′ə nā′tiv, -nə tiv), *adj.* **1.** conferring or constituting a distinctive designation or name. **2.** (esp. of verbs) formed from a noun, as English *to man* from the noun *man.* —*n.* **3.** a denominative verb or other word. —**de·nom′i·na′tive·ly,** *adv.*

de·nom·i·na·tor (di nom′ə nā′tər), *n.* **1.** the term of a fraction, usu. written under or after the line, that indicates the number of equal parts into which the unit is divided; divisor. Compare NUMERATOR (def. 1). **2.** something shared or held in common; standard.

de·no·ta·tion (dē′nō tā′shən), *n.* **1.** the explicit or direct meaning or set of meanings of a word or expression, as distinguished from the ideas or meanings associated with or suggested by it. Compare CONNOTATION (def. 2). **2.** the act or fact of denoting; indication. **3.** a word that names or denotes something. **4.** a mark, sign, or symbol; indicator. **5.** *Logic.* EXTENSION (def. 11).

de·note (di nōt′), *v.t.,* **-not·ed, -not·ing. 1.** to be a mark or sign of; indicate: *A fever often denotes an infection.* **2.** to be a name or designation for; mean. **3.** to represent by a symbol; stand as a symbol for. —**de·not′a·ble,** *adj.* —**de·no′tive,** *adj.*

de·noue·ment or **dé·noue·ment** (dā′nōō män′), *n.* **1. a.** the final resolution of a plot, as of a drama or novel. **b.** the point at which this occurs. **2.** the outcome or resolution of a doubtful series of occurrences.

de·nounce (di nouns′), *v.t.,* **-nounced, -nounc·ing. 1.** to condemn or censure openly or publicly. **2.** to make a formal accusation against, as to the police or in a court. **3.** to give formal notice of the termination or denial of (a treaty, pact, or the like). —**de·nounce′ment,** *n.* —**de·nounc′er,** *n.*

de no·vo (dē nō′vō), *adv.* anew; from the beginning.

dense (dens), *adj.,* **dens·er, dens·est. 1.** having the component parts closely compacted together; crowded or compact: *a dense forest.* **2.** stupid; slow-witted; dull. **3.** intense; extreme. **4.** relatively opaque; transmitting little light. **5.** difficult to understand because of being closely packed with ideas or complexities of style. —**dense′ly,** *adv.* —**dense′ness,** *n.*

den·si·ty (den′si tē), *n., pl.* **-ties. 1.** the state or quality of being dense; compactness. **2.** stupidity; obtuseness. **3.** the average number of inhabitants, dwellings, or the like, per unit of area: *a population density of 100 persons per square mile.* **4.** *Physics.* mass per unit volume. **5.** the degree of opacity of a substance, medium, etc., that transmits light. **6.** the relative degree of opacity of an area of a photographic negative or transparency, often expressed logarithmically. **7.** a measure of how much data can be stored in a given amount of space on a disk, tape, or other computer storage medium.

dent (dent), *n.* **1.** a hollow or depression in a surface, as from a blow. **2.** a noticeable effect, esp. of reduction: *a dent in one's pride.* **3.** slight progress: *I haven't made a dent in this pile of work.* —*v.t.* **4.** to make a dent in or on; indent. **5.** to have the effect of reducing or slightly injuring: *The caustic remark dented my ego.* —*v.i.* **6.** to show dents; become dented.

den·tal (den′tl), *adj.* **1.** of or pertaining to the teeth. **2.** of or pertaining to dentistry or a dentist. **3.** (of a speech sound) articulated with the tongue tip touching or near the back of the upper front teeth, as *t* in French or the sound (th) in English. —*n.* **4.** a dental speech sound. —**den′tal·i·ty,** *n.* —**den′tal·ly,** *adv.*

den′tal car′ies, *n.* decay in teeth caused by bacteria that form acids in the presence of sucrose, other sugars, and refined starches.

den′tal floss′, *n.* a soft, strong thread used to dislodge food particles from between the teeth.

den′tal hygien′ist, *n.* a person who is trained and licensed to clean teeth, take dental x-rays, and otherwise assist a dentist.

den′tal techni′cian, *n.* a person who makes dentures, bridges, etc.

den·tate (den′tāt), *adj.* having a toothed margin or toothlike projections or processes: *a dentate leaf.* —**den′tate·ly,** *adv.*

dent′ corn′, *n.* a variety of field corn, *Zea mays indentata,* having yellow or white kernels that become indented as they ripen.

denti-, a combining form meaning "tooth": *dentiform.*

den·tic·u·late (den tik′yə lit, -lāt′) also **den·tic·u·lat·ed** (-lā′tid), *adj.* **1.** finely dentate, as a leaf. **2.** having dentils. —**den·tic′u·late·ly,** *adv.* —**den·tic′u·la′tion,** *n.*

den·ti·frice (den′tə fris), *n.* a paste, powder, liquid, or other preparation for cleaning the teeth.

den·til (den′tl, -til), *n.* one of a series of closely spaced small rectangular blocks, used esp. in classical architecture beneath the corona of a cornice.

den·tin (den′tn, -tin) also **den·tine** (-tēn), *n.* the hard, calcareous tissue that forms the major portion of a tooth, surrounds the pulp cavity, and is situated beneath the enamel. —**den′tin·al,** *adj.*

den·tist (den′tist), *n.* a person whose profession is dentistry.

den·tist·ry (den′tə strē), *n.* the science or profession dealing with the prevention or treatment of diseases of the teeth, gums, and oral cavity, the correction or removal of decayed, damaged, or malformed parts, and the replacement of lost structures.

den·ti·tion (den tish′ən), *n.* **1.** the makeup of a set of teeth including their kind, number, and arrangement. **2.** the cutting of the teeth.

den·ture (den′chər, -chŏŏr), *n.* **1.** an artificial replacement of one or more teeth. **2.** Often, **dentures.** a replacement of all the teeth of one or both jaws.

den·u·date (di nŏŏ′dāt, -nyŏŏ′-, den′yŏŏ dāt′), *v.,* **-dat·ed, -dat·ing,** *adj.* —*v.t.* **1.** to make bare; denude. —*adj.* **2.** denuded; bare.

de·nude (di nŏŏd′, -nyŏŏd′), *v.t.,* **-nud·ed, -nud·ing.** **1.** to make naked or bare; strip: *The storm denuded many trees.* **2.** to subject (rocks) to denudation. —**de·nud′er,** *n.*

de·nun·ci·ate (di nun′sē āt′, -shē-), *v.t., v.i.,* **-at·ed, -at·ing.** to denounce; condemn openly. —**de·nun′ci·a′tor,** *n.*

de·nun·ci·a·tion (di nun′sē ā′shən, -shē-), *n.* **1.** an act or instance of denouncing. **2.** an accusation of crime before a public prosecutor or tribunal. **3.** notice of the termination or the renouncement of an international agreement or part thereof.

Den·ver (den′vər), *n.* the capital of Colorado, in the central part. 493,559.

de·ny (di nī′), *v.t.,* **-nied, -ny·ing.** **1.** to state that (something declared or believed to be true) is not true: *to deny an accusation.* **2.** to refuse to agree or accede to: *to deny a petition.* **3.** to withhold the possession, use, or enjoyment of: *to deny access to information.* **4.** to withhold something from, or refuse to grant a request of: *to deny a beggar.* **5.** to refuse to recognize or acknowledge; disavow; repudiate: *to deny one's gods.* —*Idiom.* **6. deny oneself, a.** to refrain from satisfying one's desires. **b.** to refuse to indulge oneself in; abstain from.

de·o·dar (dē′ə där′), *n.* a large Himalayan cedar, *Cedrus deodara,* yielding a durable wood.

de·o·dor·ant (dē ō′dər ənt), *n.* **1.** an agent for destroying odors. **2.** a substance for inhibiting or masking perspiration or other bodily odors. —*adj.* **3.** capable of destroying odors.

de·o·dor·ize (dē ō′də rīz′), *v.t.,* **-ized, -iz·ing.** to rid of unpleasant odor. —**de·o′dor·i·za′tion,** *n.* —**de·o′dor·iz′er,** *n.*

de·on·tol·o·gy (dē′on tol′ə jē), *n.* ethics dealing esp. with duty, moral obligation, and right action. —**de′on·to·log′i·cal** (-tl oj′i kəl), *adj.* —**de′on·tol′o·gist,** *n.*

de·ox·i·dize (dē ok′si dīz′), *v.t.,* **-dized, -diz·ing.** to remove oxygen from. —**de·ox′i·di·za′tion,** *n.* —**de·ox′i·diz′er,** *n.*

de·ox·y·gen·ate (dē ok′si jə nāt′), *v.t.,* **-at·ed, -at·ing.** to remove oxygen from (blood, water, etc.). —**de·ox′y·gen·a′tion,** *n.*

de·ox′y·ri′bo·nu·cle′ic ac′id (dē ok′si rī′bō nŏŏ klē′ik, -nyŏŏ-, -ok′si rī′-), *n.* See DNA.

de·part (di pärt′), *v.i.* **1.** to go away; leave. **2.** to diverge or deviate (usu. fol. by *from*): *Our method departs from theirs in several respects.* **3.** to pass away, as from life or existence; die. —*v.t.* **4.** to go away from; leave.

de·part·ed (di pär′tid), *adj.* **1.** deceased; dead. **2.** gone; past. —*n.* **3. the departed,** a particular dead person or persons.

de·part·ment (di pärt′mənt), *n.* **1.** a distinct part of anything arranged in divisions; a division of a complex whole or organized system. **2.** one of the principal branches of a governmental organization. **3.** (*cap.*) one of the principal divisions of the U.S. government, headed by a secretary who is a member of the president's cabinet: *the Department of State.* **4.** a division of a company dealing with a particular activity. **5.** a section of a store selling a particular kind of goods. **6.** one of the sections of a school or college dealing with a particular field of knowledge. **7.** one of the large districts into which certain countries, as France, are divided for administrative purposes. **8.** a division of official business, duties, or functions. **9.** a sphere or province of activity, knowledge, or responsibility. —**de·part·men·tal** (di pärt men′tl, dē′pärt-), *adj.* —**de·part·men′tal·ly,** *adv.*

de·part·men·tal·ize (di pärt men′tl īz′, dē′pärt-), *v.t.,* **-ized, -iz·ing.** to divide into departments. —**de′part·men′tal·i·za′tion,** *n.*

Depart′ment of Ag′riculture, *n.* the department of the U.S. federal government that institutes and administers all federal programs dealing with agriculture. *Abbr.:* USDA

Depart′ment of Com′merce, *n.* the department of the U.S. federal government that promotes and administers domestic and foreign commerce. *Abbr.:* DOC

Depart′ment of Defense′, *n.* the department of the U.S. federal government charged with ensuring that the military capacity of the U.S. is adequate to safeguard the national security. *Abbr.:* DOD

Depart′ment of Educa′tion, *n.* the department of the U.S. federal government that administers federal programs dealing with education: created in 1979, largely by transfer from part of the former Department of Health, Education, and Welfare. *Abbr.:* ED

Depart′ment of En′ergy, *n.* the department of the U.S. federal government that sets forth and maintains the national energy policy, including energy conservation, environmental protection, etc. *Abbr.:* DOE

Depart′ment of Health′ and Hu′man Serv′ices, *n.* the department of the U.S. government that administers federal programs dealing with public health, welfare, and income security: created in 1979 from the reorganized Department of Health, Education, and Welfare. *Abbr.:* HHS

Depart′ment of Health′, Educa′tion, and Wel′fare, *n.* a former department of the U.S. government (1953–79) that administered federal programs dealing with health, education, welfare, and income security. *Abbr.:* HEW

Depart′ment of Hous′ing and Ur′ban Devel′opment, *n.* the department of the U.S. federal government that institutes and administers all federal programs dealing with better housing, urban renewal, and metropolitan planning. *Abbr.:* HUD

Depart′ment of Jus′tice, *n.* the department of the U.S. federal government charged with the responsibility for the enforcement of federal laws. *Abbr.:* DOJ

Depart′ment of La′bor, *n.* the department of the U.S. federal government that promotes and improves the welfare, opportunities, and working conditions of wage earners. *Abbr.:* DOL

Depart′ment of State′, *n.* the department of the U.S. federal government that sets forth and maintains the foreign policy of the U.S., esp. in negotiations with foreign governments and international organizations. *Abbr.:* DOS

Depart′ment of the Inte′rior, *n.* the department of the U.S. federal government charged with the conservation and development of the natural resources of the U.S. and its possessions. *Abbr.:* DOI

Depart′ment of the Treas′ury, *n.* the department of the U.S. federal government that collects revenue and administers the national finances. *Abbr.:* TD

Depart′ment of Transporta′tion, *n.* the department of the U.S. federal government that coordinates and institutes national transportation programs. *Abbr.:* DOT

depart′ment store′, *n.* a large retail store organized into various departments of merchandise.

de·par·ture (di pär′chər), *n.* **1.** an act or instance of departing. **2.** divergence or deviation, as from a standard or rule. **3.** the distance due east or west traveled by a vessel or aircraft. **4.** the length of the projection, on the east-west reference line, of a survey line.

de·pend (di pend′), *v.i.* **1.** to rely; place trust (usu. fol. by *on* or *upon*): *You may depend on our tact.* **2.** to rely for support or help (usu. fol. by *on* or *upon*). **3.** to be conditioned or contingent (usu. fol. by *on* or *upon*): *Our plans depend on the weather.* **4.** to be undetermined or pending. **5.** (of a word or other linguistic form) to be subordinate to another linguistic form in the same construction. **6.** to hang down; be suspended (usu. fol. by *from*).

de·pend·a·ble (di pen′də bəl), *adj.* capable of being depended on; worthy of trust; reliable: *a dependable employee.* —**de·pend′a·bil′i·ty,** *n.* —**de·pend′a·bly,** *adv.*

de·pend·ence (di pen′dəns), *n.* **1.** the state of relying on or needing someone or something for aid, support, or the like. **2.** reliance; confidence; trust. **3.** the state of being contingent on something: *the dependence of an effect upon a cause.* **4.** the state of being psychologically or physiologically dependent on a drug. **5.** subordination or subjection. Sometimes, **de·pend′ance.**

de·pend·en·cy (di pen′dən sē), *n., pl.* **-cies. 1.** the state of being dependent. **2.** something dependent or subordinate; appurtenance. **3.** a subject territory that is not an integral part of the ruling country. **4.** outbuilding; annex. Sometimes, **de·pend′an·cy.**

de·pend·ent (di pen′dənt), *adj.* **1.** relying on someone or something else for aid, support, etc. **2.** conditioned or determined by something else; contingent: *Our trip is dependent on the weather.* **3.** subordinate; subject: *a dependent territory.* **4.** used only in connection with other forms, not in isolation; subordinate. In *I walked out when the bell rang, when the bell rang* is a dependent clause. Compare INDEPENDENT (def. 10). **5.** hanging down; pendent. **6. a.** (of a variable) having values determined by one or more independent variables. **b.** (of an equation) having solutions that are identical to those of another equation or to those of a set of equations. —*n.* **7.** a person who depends on or needs someone or something for aid, support, favor, etc., esp. a child, spouse, or aged parent. Often, *esp. for def. 7,* **de·pend′ant.** —**de·pend′ent·ly,** *adv.*

de·per·son·al·ize (dē pûr′sə nl īz′), *v.t.,* **-ized, -iz·ing.** **1.** to make impersonal. **2.** to deprive of personality or individuality. —**de·per′son·a·li·za′tion,** *n.*

de·pict (di pikt′), *v.t.* **1.** to represent by or as if by painting; portray; delineate. **2.** to represent or characterize in words; describe. —**de·pic′tion,** *n.*

dep·i·late (dep′ə lāt′), *v.t.,* **-lat·ed, -lat·ing.** to remove the hair from (hides, skin, etc.). —**dep′i·la′tion,** *n.* —**dep′i·la′tor,** *n.*

de·pil·a·to·ry (di pil′ə tôr′ē, -tōr′ē), *adj., n., pl.* **-ries.** —*adj.* **1.** capable of removing hair. —*n.* **2.** a depilatory agent, esp. in a mild liquid or cream form for temporarily removing unwanted hair from the body.

de·plane (dē plān′), *v.i.,* **-planed, -plan·ing.** to disembark from an airplane.

de·plete (di plēt′), *v.t.,* **-plet·ed, -plet·ing.** to decrease seriously or exhaust the abundance or supply of. —**de·ple′tion,** *n.* —**de·ple′tive,** *adj.*

deple′tion allow′ance, *n.* a tax reduction allowed on income from exhaustible resources, as oil or timber.

de·plor·a·ble (di plôr′ə bəl, -plōr′-), *adj.* **1.** causing or being a subject for grief or regret; lamentable. **2.** worthy of censure or disapproval; wretched; very bad. —**de·plor′a·ble·ness,** *n.* —**de·plor′a·bly,** *adv.*

de·plore (di plôr′, -plōr′), *v.t.,* **-plored, -plor·ing.** **1.** to regret deeply or strongly; lament. **2.** to disapprove of; censure. —**de·plor′er,** *n.* —**de·plor′ing·ly,** *adv.*

D

de•ploy (di ploi′), *v.t.* **1.** to spread out (troops) so as to form an extended front or line. **2.** to arrange, place, or move strategically or appropriately: *to deploy missiles.* —*v.i.* **3.** to be or become deployed. —**de•ploy′a•ble,** *adj.* —**de•ploy′ment,** *n.*

de•plume (dē plo͞om′), *v.t.*, **-plumed, -plum•ing.** to deprive of feathers; pluck. —**de′plu•ma′tion,** *n.*

de•po•lar•ize (dē pō′lə rīz′), *v.t.*, **-ized, -iz•ing.** to deprive of polarity or polarization, esp. in eliminating a magnetic charge. —**de•po′lar•i•za′tion,** *n.* —**de•po′lar•iz′er,** *n.*

de•po•lit•i•cize (dē′pə lit′ə sīz′), *v.t.*, **-cized, -ciz•ing. 1.** to remove from the arena or influence of politics: *to depoliticize labor relations.* **2.** to deprive of involvement or interest in politics.

de•pone (di pōn′), *v.t., v.i.*, **-poned, -pon•ing.** to testify under oath; depose.

de•pop•u•late (dē pop′yə lāt′), *v.t.*, **-lat•ed, -lat•ing.** to remove or reduce the population of, as by destruction or expulsion. —**de•pop′u•la′tion,** *n.* —**de•pop′u•la′tor,** *n.*

de•port (di pôrt′, -pōrt′), *v.t.* **1.** to expel (an alien, criminal, etc.) from a country; banish. **2.** to bear, conduct, or behave (oneself) in a particular manner. —**de•port′a•ble,** *adj.* —**de•por•tee** (dē′pôr tē′, -pōr-), *n.* —**de•port′er,** *n.*

de•por•ta•tion (dē′pôr tā′shən, -pōr-), *n.* **1.** the lawful expulsion of an undesired alien or other person from a state. **2.** an act or instance of deporting.

de•port•ment (di pôrt′mənt, -pōrt′-), *n.* conduct; behavior.

de•pose (di pōz′), *v.*, **-posed, -pos•ing.** —*v.t.* **1.** to remove from office or position: *The people deposed the dictator.* **2.** to testify or affirm under oath, esp. in writing. —*v.i.* **3.** to give sworn testimony, esp. in writing. —**de•pos′a•ble,** *adj.* —**de•pos′er,** *n.*

de•pos•it (di poz′it), *v.t.* **1.** to place for safekeeping, esp. in a bank account. **2.** to deliver and leave (an item). **3.** to insert (a coin) in a coin-operated device. **4.** to put, place, or set down: *She deposited the baby in the crib.* **5.** to lay or throw down by a natural process; precipitate: *The river deposited soil at its mouth.* **6.** to give as security or in part payment. —*v.i.* **7.** to become deposited. —*n.* **8. a.** an instance of placing money in a bank account. **b.** the money placed there. **9.** anything given as security or in part payment: *a bottle deposit of five cents.* **10.** anything laid away or entrusted to another for safekeeping. **11.** a place for safekeeping; depository. **12.** something precipitated, delivered and left, or thrown down, as by a natural process: *a deposit of soil.* **13.** a coating of metal deposited on something, usu. by an electric current. **14.** a natural accumulation or occurrence, esp. of oil or ore: *gold deposits.*

de•pos•i•tar•y (di poz′i ter′ē), *n., pl.* **-tar•ies. 1.** one to whom anything is given in trust. **2.** DEPOSITORY (def. 1).

dep•o•si•tion (dep′ə zish′ən, dē′pə-), *n.* **1.** removal from an office or position. **2.** the act or process of depositing. **3.** the state of being deposited. **4.** something that is deposited. **5.** a statement under oath, taken down in writing, to be used in court. —**dep′o•si′tion•al,** *adj.*

de•pos•i•to•ry (di poz′i tôr′ē, -tōr′ē), *n., pl.* **-ries. 1.** a place where something is deposited or stored, as for safekeeping: *the night depository of a bank.* **2.** a depositary; trustee.

de•pot (dē′pō; *Mil. or Brit.* dep′ō), *n.* **1.** a railroad or bus station. **2. a.** a place in which supplies are stored for distribution. **b.** a place where military recruits are given basic training.

de•prave (di prāv′), *v.t.*, **-praved, -prav•ing.** to make morally bad or evil; vitiate; corrupt. —**dep•ra•va•tion** (dep′rə vā′shən), *n.* —**de•prav′er,** *n.*

de•prav•i•ty (di prav′i tē), *n., pl.* **-ties. 1.** the state of being depraved. **2.** a depraved act or practice.

dep•re•cate (dep′ri kāt′), *v.t.*, **-cat•ed, -cat•ing. 1.** to express earnest disapproval of. **2.** to urge reasons against; protest against (a scheme, purpose, etc.). **3.** to depreciate; belittle. —**dep′re•cat′ing•ly,** *adv.* —**dep′re•ca′tion,** *n.* —**dep′re•ca′tor,** *n.*

de•pre•ci•ate (di prē′shē āt′), *v.*, **-at•ed, -at•ing.** —*v.t.* **1.** to reduce the purchasing value of (money). **2.** to lessen the value or price of. **3.** to claim depreciation on (a property) for tax purposes. **4.** to represent as of little value or merit; belittle. —*v.i.* **5.** to decline in value. —**de•pre′ci•a•ble,** *adj.* —**de•pre′ci•at′ing•ly,** *adv.* —**de•pre′ci•a′tor,** *n.*

de•pre•ci•a•tion (di prē′shē ā′shən), *n.* **1.** a decrease in value due to wear and tear, decline in price, etc. **2.** such a decrease as allowed in computing the value of property for tax purposes. **3.** a decrease in the purchasing or exchange value of money. **4.** a lowering in estimation.

dep•re•date (dep′ri dāt′), *v.*, **-dat•ed, -dat•ing.** —*v.t.* **1.** to plunder or lay waste to; prey upon; pillage; ravage. —*v.i.* **2.** to plunder; pillage. —**dep′re•da′tion,** *n.* —**dep′re•da′tor,** *n.* —**dep•re•da•to•ry** (di pred′ə tôr′ē, -tōr′ē), *adj.*

de•press (di pres′), *v.t.* **1.** to make sad or gloomy; lower in spirits; dispirit. **2.** to lower in force, vigor, activity, etc.; weaken. **3.** to lower in amount or value. **4.** to put into a lower position; press down.

de•pres•sant (di pres′ənt), *adj.* **1.** tending to slow the activity of one or more bodily systems. **2.** causing a lowering in spirits; dejecting. **3.** causing a drop in value; economically depressing. —*n.* **4.** a drug or other agent that reduces irritability or excitement.

de•pressed (di prest′), *adj.* **1.** sad and gloomy; downcast. **2.** *Psychiatry.* suffering from depression. **3.** pressed down, or situated lower than the general surface. **4.** lowered in force, amount, etc. **5.** undergoing economic hardship. **6.** *Bot., Zool.* flattened down; greater in width than in height.

de•pres•sion (di presh′ən), *n.* **1.** the state of being depressed. **2.** a depressed or sunken place or part; an area lower than the surrounding surface. **3.** sadness; gloom; dejection. **4.** *Psychiatry.* a condition of general emotional dejection and withdrawal; sadness greater and more prolonged than that warranted by any objective reason. **5.** a low state of functional activity. **6.** dullness or inactivity, as of trade. **7.** a period during which business, employment, and stock-market values decline severely. **8.** the angular distance of a celestial body below the horizon. **9.** the angle between the line from an observer or surveying instrument to an object below either of them and a horizontal line. **10.** an area surrounded by higher land, ordinarily having interior drainage and not conforming to the valley of a single stream. **11.** an area of low atmospheric pressure.

de•pres•sur•ize (dē presh′ə rīz′), *v.*, **-ized, -iz•ing.** —*v.t.* **1.** to remove the air pressure from. —*v.i.* **2.** to lose air pressure. —**de•pres′sur•i•za′tion,** *n.* —**de•pres′sur•iz′er,** *n.*

dep•ri•va•tion (dep′rə vā′shən), *n.* **1.** the act of depriving. **2.** the fact of being deprived. **3.** dispossession; loss. **4.** privation.

de•prive (di prīv′), *v.t.*, **-prived, -priv•ing. 1.** to divest of something possessed or enjoyed; dispossess. **2.** to keep from possessing or enjoying something withheld: *to deprive a child of affection.* **3.** to remove from office. —**de•priv′a•tive** (-priv′ə tiv), *adj.*

de•prived (di prīvd′), *adj.* marked by deprivation; lacking the necessities of life.

de•pro•gram (dē prō′gram), *v.t.*, **-grammed** or **-gramed, -gram•ming** or **-gram•ing.** to free (a person) from the influence of a cult, sect, etc., by intensive and systematic reeducation. —**de•pro′gram•mer, de•pro′gram•er,** *n.*

dept., 1. department. 2. deputy.

depth (depth), *n.* **1.** a dimension taken through an object or body of material, usu. downward or inward. **2.** the quality of being deep; deepness. **3.** complexity or obscurity: *a question of great depth.* **4.** gravity; seriousness. **5.** emotional profundity: *the depth of one's feelings.* **6.** intensity, as of silence or color. **7.** lowness of tonal pitch: *the depth of a voice.* **8.** the amount of a person's intelligence, wisdom, insight, etc. **9.** Often, **depths.** a deep part or place. **10.** an unfathomable space; abyss: *the depth of time.* **11.** Sometimes, **depths.** the farthest, innermost, or extreme part or state: *the depths of the forest.* **12.** Usu., **depths.** a low intellectual or moral condition: *How could he sink to such depths?* **13.** the part of greatest intensity, as of night or winter. **14.** the strength of a team's lineup of substitute players. —***Idiom.*** **15. in depth,** extensively; thoroughly. **16. out of** or **beyond one's depth,** beyond one's knowledge or capability.

depth′ charge′, *n.* an explosive device used underwater, esp. against submarines, and set to detonate at a predetermined depth. Also called **depth′ bomb′.**

depth′ percep′tion, *n.* the ability to judge the dimensions and spatial relationships of objects.

depth′ poll′ing, *n.* detailed political polling that asks other questions besides those about voting intentions.

de•pute (də pyo͞ot′), *v.t.*, **-put•ed, -put•ing. 1.** to appoint as one's substitute, representative, or agent. **2.** to assign (authority, a function, etc.) to a deputy. —**dep•u•ta•ble** (dep′yə tə bəl, də pyo͞o′-), *adj.*

dep•u•tize (dep′yə tīz′), *v.*, **-tized, -tiz•ing.** —*v.t.* **1.** to appoint as deputy. —*v.i.* **2.** to act as a deputy; substitute. —**dep′u•ti•za′tion,** *n.*

dep•u•ty (dep′yə tē), *n., pl.* **-ties. 1.** a person appointed or authorized to act as a substitute for another or others. **2.** a person appointed or elected as assistant to a public official, serving as successor in the event of a vacancy. **3.** a person representing a constituency in certain legislative bodies. —*adj.* **4.** appointed, elected, or serving as an assistant or second-in-command. —**dep′u•ty•ship′,** *n.*

de•rac•i•nate (di ras′ə nāt′), *v.t.*, **-nat•ed, -nat•ing.** to pull up by or as if by the roots; uproot or displace. —**de•rac′i•na′tion,** *n.*

de•rail (dē rāl′), *v.t.* **1.** to cause (a train, streetcar, etc.) to run off the rails of a track. **2.** to cause to be deflected from a purpose or direction, permanently or temporarily: *A skiing accident derailed her dancing career.* —*v.i.* **3.** to run off the rails of a track. **4.** to become derailed; go astray. —**de•rail′ment,** *n.*

de•rail•leur (di rā′lər), *n.* a gear-shifting mechanism on a bicycle that shifts the drive chain from one sprocket wheel to another.

de•range (di rānj′), *v.t.*, **-ranged, -rang•ing. 1.** to throw into disorder; disarrange. **2.** to disturb the condition, action, or function of. **3.** to make insane. —**de•rang′er,** *n.*

Der•by¹ (dûr′bē; *Brit.* där′-), *n., pl.* **-bies. 1.** a race for three-year-old horses held annually at Epsom Downs, near London, England: first run in 1780. **2.** any of certain other annual horse races, esp. the Kentucky Derby. **3.** (*l.c.*) a race or contest, usu. one open to all entrants. **4.** (*l.c.*) a man's stiff felt hat with rounded crown and narrow brim; bowler. [after Edward Stanley, 12th Earl of *Derby* (d. 1834)]

Der•by² (dûr′bē; *Brit.* där′-), *n.* **1.** a city in Derbyshire, in central England. 215,200. **2.** DERBYSHIRE.

Der•by•shire (dûr′bē shēr′, -shər; *Brit.* där′-), *n.* a county in central England. 918,700; 1060 sq. mi. (2630 sq. km).

de•reg•u•late (dē reg′yə lāt′), *v.t.*, **-lat•ed, -lat•ing.** to halt or reduce government regulation of: *to deregulate the airline industry.* —**de•reg′u•la′tion,** *n.* —**de•reg′u•la′tor,** *n.*

der•e•lict (der′ə likt), *adj.* **1.** left or deserted, as by the owner or guardian; abandoned: *a derelict ship.* **2.** neglectful of duty; delinquent;

negligent. —*n.* **3.** a person who has no home or means of support; vagrant; bum. **4.** a vessel abandoned in open water. **5.** any abandoned or discarded possession. **6.** *Law.* land left dry by a change of the water line. —**der′e·lict·ly,** *adv.*

der·e·lic·tion (der′ə lik′shən), *n.* **1.** deliberate or conscious neglect; negligence; delinquency: *dereliction of duty.* **2.** the act of abandoning something. **3.** the state of being abandoned. **4.** *Law.* a leaving dry of land by recession of the water line.

de·ride (di rīd′), *v.t.,* **-rid·ed, -rid·ing.** to laugh at in scorn or contempt; mock. —**de·rid′er,** *n.* —**de·rid′ing·ly,** *adv.*

de ri·gueur (də ri gûr′, -rē) *adj.* strictly required, as by etiquette, usage, or fashion.

de·ri·sion (di rizh′ən), *n.* **1.** the act of deriding; ridicule; mockery. **2.** an object of ridicule. —**de·ris′i·ble** (-riz′ə bəl), *adj.*

de·ri·sive (di rī′siv) also **de·ri·so·ry** (-sə rē, -zə-), *adj.* characterized by or expressing derision; ridiculing; mocking: *derisive heckling.* —**de·ri′sive·ly,** *adv.* —**de·ri′sive·ness,** *n.*

der·i·va·tion (der′ə vā′shən), *n.* **1.** the act of deriving or the state of being derived. **2.** source; origin. **3.** something derived. **4.** development of a mathematical theorem. **5. a.** the process of adding affixes to or changing the shape of a base, thereby forming a word that may undergo further inflection or participate in different syntactic constructions, as in forming *service* from *serve, song* from *sing,* or *hardness* from *hard* (contrasted with *inflection*). **b.** the systematic description of such processes in a language. **6.** a set of forms showing the successive stages in the generation of a sentence as the rules of a generative grammar are applied to it. —**der′i·va′tion·al,** *adj.*

de·riv·a·tive (di riv′ə tiv), *adj.* **1.** not original; secondary. —*n.* **2.** a word that has undergone derivation from another, as *atomic* from *atom.* **3.** a chemical substance or compound obtained or regarded as derived from another substance or compound. **4.** *Math.* the instantaneous rate of change of one quantity in a function with respect to another. —**de·riv′a·tive·ly,** *adv.*

de·rive (di rīv′), *v.,* **-rived, -riv·ing.** —*v.t.* **1.** to receive or obtain from a source or origin (usu. fol. by *from*); gain; glean. **2.** to trace from a source or origin. **3.** to reach or obtain by reasoning; deduce; infer. **4.** to produce or obtain (a chemical substance) from another. —*v.i.* **5.** to come from a source or origin; originate (often fol. by *from*). —**de·riv′a·ble,** *adj.* —**de·riv′er,** *n.*

derm·a·bra·sion (dûr′mə brā′zhən), *n.* the removal of acne scars, dermal nevi, or the like, by abrading.

der·mal (dûr′məl), *adj.* of or pertaining to the skin.

der·ma·ti·tis (dûr′mə tī′tis), *n.* inflammation of the skin.

dermato-, a combining form meaning "skin": *dermatology.* Also, *esp. before a vowel,* **derm-.**

der·ma·tol·o·gy (dûr′mə tol′ə jē), *n.* the branch of medicine dealing with the skin and its diseases. —**der′ma·to·log′i·cal** (-tl oj′i kəl), **der′ma·to·log′ic,** *adj.* —**der′ma·tol′o·gist,** *n.*

der·mis (dûr′mis), *n.* the thick layer of skin beneath the epidermis.

der·nier cri (dern′yā krē′), *n.* the latest fashion; last word.

der·o·gate (der′ə gāt′), *v.,* **-gat·ed, -gat·ing.** —*v.i.* **1.** to detract, as from authority or estimation (usu. fol. by *from*). **2.** to stray in character or conduct; degenerate (usu. fol. by *from*). —*v.t.* **3.** to disparage or belittle. —**de·rog·a·tive** (di rog′ə tiv), *adj.* —**de·rog′a·tive·ly,** *adv.* —**de·rog′a·to·ry,** *adj.*

der·rick (der′ik), *n.* **1.** a boom for lifting cargo, as the arm of a jib crane or a boom pivoted to a ship's mast. **2.** the towerlike framework over an oil well or the like.

derrick

Der·ri·da (der′ē dä′), *n.* **Jacques,** born 1930, French philosopher and literary critic, born in Algiers.

der·ri·ère or **der·ri·ere** (der′ē âr′), *n.* the buttocks; rump.

der·ring-do (der′ing dōō′), *n.* daring deeds; heroic daring.

der·rin·ger (der′in jər), *n.* an early short-barreled pocket pistol. [after Henry *Deringer,* 19th-century U.S. gunsmith]

DES, diethylstilbestrol.

de·salt (dē sôlt′), *v.t.* to remove the salt from (esp. sea water), usu. to make it drinkable. —**de·salt′er,** *n.*

des·cant (*n.* des′kant; *v.* des kant′, dis-) also **discant,** *n.* **1. a.** a melody or counterpoint accompanying a simple musical theme and usu. written above it. **b.** (in part music) the soprano. **c.** a song or melody. **2.** a commentary upon a subject; discourse on a theme. —*v.i.* **3.** to comment or discourse at great length. —**des·cant′er,** *n.*

de·scend (di send′), *v.i.* **1.** to go or pass from a higher to a lower place; move or come down: *to descend from the mountaintop.* **2.** to pass from higher to lower in any scale or series. **3.** to go from generals to particulars, as in a discussion. **4.** to slope, tend, or lead downward: *The path descends to the pond.* **5.** to be inherited or transmitted, as through succeeding generations of a family: *The title descends through eldest sons.* **6.** to be derived from something remote in time, esp. through continuous transmission: *a festival descending from a druidic rite.* **7.** to attack or approach as if attacking (usu. fol. by *on* or *upon*): *Thrill-seekers descended upon the scene of the crime.* **8.** to settle, as a cloud or vapor. **9.** to sink or come down from a certain standard or level of behavior; stoop: *You must never descend to bickering.* **10.** to move downward upon or along; go or climb down (stairs, a hill, etc.). **11.** to extend or lead down along: *The path descends the hill.* **12. descend** or **be descended from,** to have a certain ancestor or ancestry: *We are descended from the kings of Ireland.* —**de·scend′i·ble, de·scend′a·ble,** *adj.* —**de·scend′ing·ly,** *adv.*

de·scend·ant (di sen′dənt), *n.* **1.** a person or animal that is descended from a specific ancestor; an offspring. **2.** something deriving in appearance, function, or character from an earlier form. **3.** the point of the ecliptic or the sign of the zodiac setting below the western horizon at the time of a birth or an event. —*adj.* **4.** DESCENDENT.

de·scend·ent (di sen′dənt), *adj.* **1.** descending; going or coming down. **2.** deriving or descending from an ancestor.

de·scend·er (di sen′dər), *n.* **1.** one that descends. **2.** the part of a lowercase letter, as *p, q, j,* or *y,* that goes below the body.

de·scen·sion (di sen′shən), *n.* **1.** (in astrology) the part of the zodiac in which the influence of a planet is weakest. Compare EXALTATION (def. 4). **2.** DESCENT.

de·scent (di sent′), *n.* **1.** the act, process, or fact of descending. **2.** a downward inclination or slope. **3.** a passage or stairway leading down. **4.** derivation from an ancestor; lineage; extraction. **5.** any passing from higher to lower in degree or state; decline. **6.** a sudden raid or hostile attack. **7.** transmission of real property by intestate succession.

de·scribe (di skrīb′), *v.t.,* **-scribed, -scrib·ing.** **1.** to tell or depict in words; give an account of: *to describe an accident in detail.* **2.** to pronounce, as by a designating term or phrase: *to describe someone as a tyrant.* **3.** to represent or delineate by a figure. **4.** to draw or trace the outline of: *to describe an arc.* —**de·scrib′a·ble,** *adj.* —**de·scrib′er,** *n.*

de·scrip·tion (di skrip′shən), *n.* **1.** a statement, picture in words, or account that describes; descriptive representation. **2.** sort; kind; variety: *dogs of every description.*

de·scrip·tive (di skrip′tiv), *adj.* **1.** serving to describe; characterized by description: *a descriptive passage in an essay.* **2. a.** (of an adjective or other modifier) expressing a quality of the word it modifies, as *fresh* in *fresh milk.* Compare LIMITING (def. 2). **b.** nonrestrictive: *a descriptive clause.* **3.** noting, concerned with, or based upon experience or observation. **4.** characterized by or based upon the classification and description of material in a given field: *descriptive botany.* **5.** based on or concerned with the actual usage of speakers of a language without reference to norms of correctness or advocacy of rules based on such norms: *descriptive grammar.* —**de·scrip′tive·ly,** *adv.* —**de·scrip′tive·ness,** *n.*

de·scrip·tor (di skrip′tər), *n.* a significant term used to categorize or locate material in an index or information retrieval system.

de·scry (di skrī′), *v.t.,* **-scried, -scry·ing.** **1.** to see (something unclear or distant) by looking carefully. **2.** to discover; detect. —**de·scri′er,** *n.*

des·e·crate (des′i krāt′), *v.t.,* **-crat·ed, -crat·ing.** **1.** to divest of sacred character or office. **2.** to divert from a sacred to a profane use or purpose. **3.** to treat with sacrilege; profane; defile. —**des′e·crat′er, des′e·cra′tor,** *n.* —**des′e·cra′tion,** *n.*

de·seg·re·gate (dē seg′ri gāt′), *v.,* **-gat·ed, -gat·ing.** —*v.t.* **1.** to eliminate racial or other segregation in: *to desegregate schools.* —*v.i.* **2.** to eliminate racial or other segregation.

de·seg·re·ga·tion (dē′seg ri gā′shən, dē seg′-), *n.* the elimination of laws, customs, or practices that restrict specific racial or other groups to separate public facilities, neighborhoods, organizations, etc. —**de′seg·re·ga′tion·ist,** *n.*

de·sen·si·tize (dē sen′si tīz′), *v.t.,* **-tized, -tiz·ing.** **1.** to lessen the sensitiveness of. **2.** to make indifferent, unaware, or the like, in feeling. **3.** to make less sensitive or wholly insensitive to light, as the emulsion on a film. —**de·sen′si·tiz′er,** *n.*

des·ert¹ (dez′ərt), *n.* **1.** an arid, sandy region capable of supporting only a few, usu. specialized, life forms. **2.** any area in which few forms of life can exist because of lack of water, permanent frost, or absence of soil. **3.** any place lacking in something desirable: *The town was a cultural desert.* —*adj.* **4.** of, pertaining to, or like a desert; desolate; barren.

5. occurring in the desert: *a desert palm.* **6.** suitable for use in the desert. —**de•ser•tic** (di zûr′tik), *adj.*

de•sert² (di zûrt′), *v.t.* **1.** to leave (a person, place, etc.) without intending to return, esp. in violation of a duty, promise, or the like: *He deserted his wife.* **2.** (of military personnel) to leave or run away from (service, duty, etc.) with the intention of never returning. **3.** to fail (someone) at a time of need: *None of his friends had deserted him.* —*v.i.* **4.** to forsake or leave one's duty, obligations, etc. **5.** (of military personnel) to leave service, duty, etc., with no intention of returning: *Troops were deserting to the enemy.* —**de•sert′er,** *n.*

de•sert³ (di zûrt′), *n.* **1.** Often, **deserts.** reward or punishment that is deserved: *to get one's just deserts.* **2.** the state or fact of deserving reward or punishment. **3.** the fact of deserving well; merit; virtue.

Des′ert Cul′ture, *n.* the nomadic hunting, fishing, and gathering preagricultural post-Pleistocene phase in the American West, characterized by an efficient exploitation of varied natural resources that was continued by Amerindian cultures into historic times.

des′ert fa′thers, *n.pl.* monks, as Saint Anthony or Saint Pachomius, who lived as hermits in the deserts of Egypt and founded the first Christian monasteries.

de•ser•tion (di zûr′shən), *n.* **1.** the act of deserting or the state of being deserted. **2.** willful abandonment of a spouse, dependent children, etc., in violation of legal or moral obligations.

des′ert lo′cust, *n.* a migratory locust, *Schistocerca gregaria,* of N Africa and Asia, associated with the plagues described in the Old Testament.

de•serve (di zûrv′), *v.,* **-served, -serv•ing.** —*v.t.* **1.** to merit, qualify for, or have a claim to (reward, punishment, aid, etc.) because of actions, qualities, or circumstances: *to deserve a pay raise; to deserve exile.* —*v.i.* **2.** to be worthy of, qualified for, or have a claim to reward, punishment, etc.: *an idea deserving of study.*

des•ha•bille (dez′ə bēl′, -bē′), *n.* DISHABILLE.

des•ic•cate (des′i kāt′), *v.,* **-cat•ed, -cat•ing.** —*v.t.* **1.** to dry thoroughly; dry up. **2.** to preserve (food) by removing moisture; dehydrate. —*v.i.* **3.** to become thoroughly dried or dried up. —**des′ic•ca′tion,** *n.* —**des′ic•ca′tive,** *adj.*

des•ic•ca•tor (des′i kā′tər), *n.* a chemical apparatus for absorbing moisture from a substance, esp. an airtight glass container containing calcium chloride.

de•sid•er•a•tum (di sid′ə rā′təm, -rä′-, -zid′-), *n., pl.* **-ta** (-tə). something wanted or needed.

de•sign (di zīn′), *v.t.* **1.** to prepare the preliminary sketch or the plans for (a work to be executed): *to design a new bridge.* **2.** to plan and fashion artistically or skillfully. **3.** to intend for a definite purpose: *a scholarship designed for foreign students.* **4.** to form or conceive in the mind; contrive; plan: *The prisoner designed an intricate escape.* **5.** to assign in thought or intention; purpose: *to design to be a veterinarian.* —*v.i.* **6.** to make drawings, preliminary sketches, or plans. **7.** to plan and fashion the form and structure of an object, work of art, decorative scheme, etc. —*n.* **8.** an outline, sketch, or scheme of something to be executed or constructed. **9.** organization or structure of formal elements in a work of art; composition. **10. a.** the combination of details or features of something executed or constructed: *the design of the master bedroom.* **b.** a pattern or motif: *the design on a bracelet.* **11. a.** the art of designing. **b.** the art or profession of decorative design, esp. in fashions or home furnishings. **12.** a plan or project: *a design for a new process.* **13.** a plot or intrigue. **14. designs,** a hostile or aggressive project or scheme with evil or selfish motives: *to have designs on someone's property.* **15.** intention; purpose; end. **16.** adaptation of means to a preconceived end.

des•ig•nate (*v.* dez′ig nāt′; *adj.* -nit, -nāt′), *v.,* **-nat•ed, -nat•ing,** *adj.* —*v.t.* **1.** to mark or point out; show; specify. **2.** to denote; signify; mean. **3.** to name; entitle; style. **4.** to nominate or select, as for a duty or office; appoint; assign. —*adj.* **5.** named or selected for an office, position, etc., but not yet installed (often used in combination following the noun it modifies): *ambassador-designate.* —**des′ig•na′tion,** *n.* —**des′ig•na′tive, des•ig•na•to•ry** (dez′ig nə tôr′ē, -tōr′ē), *adj.* —**des′ig•na′tor,** *n.*

des′ignated driv′er, *n.* a person who abstains from alcoholic beverages at a gathering in order to be fit to drive companions home safely.

des′ignated hit′ter, *n.* a player on a baseball team, selected prior to the game, who substitutes for the pitcher at bat but does not take the field defensively. *Abbr.:* DH, dh

de•sign•er (di zī′nər), *n.* **1.** a person who devises or executes designs, as for works of art or fashions. —*adj.* **2.** created by or as if by an eminent designer; fancy and expensive: *designer jeans.*

design′er drug′, *n.* a drug produced by a minor modification in the chemical structure of an existing drug, resulting in a new substance with similar pharmacological effects.

design′er gene′, *n.* a gene altered or created by genetic engineering, esp. for use in gene therapy.

de•sign•ing (di zī′ning), *adj.* **1.** scheming; crafty. **2.** showing or using forethought. —**de•sign′ing•ly,** *adv.*

de•sir•a•ble (di zīr′ə bəl), *adj.* **1.** pleasing; suitable; attractive: *a desirable apartment.* **2.** arousing desire or longing. **3.** advisable; recommendable: *a desirable law.* —**de•sir′a•bil′i•ty, de•sir′a•ble•ness,** *n.* —**de•sir′a•bly,** *adv.*

de•sire (di zīᵊr′), *v.,* **-sired, -sir•ing,** *n.* —*v.t.* **1.** to wish or long for; crave; want. **2.** to ask for; solicit; request: *The mayor desires your presence at the meeting.* —*n.* **3.** a longing or craving, as for something that brings satisfaction; hunger. **4.** an expressed wish; request. **5.** something desired. **6.** sexual appetite or a sexual urge. —**de•sir′er,** *n.* —**de•sir′ing•ly,** *adv.* —**de•sir′ous,** *adj.*

de•sist (di zist′, -sist′), *v.i.* to cease, as from some action or proceeding; stop. —**de•sist′ance,** *n.*

desk (desk), *n.* **1.** an article of furniture having a broad, usu. level, writing surface, as well as drawers or compartments for papers, writing materials, etc. **2.** a frame for supporting a book from which the service is read in a church. **3.** the section of a large organization, as a newspaper, having responsibility for particular operations: *the city desk.* **4.** a table or counter, as in a library or office, at which a specific job is performed or a service offered: *the information desk.* **5.** a stand used to support sheet music. **6.** (in an orchestra) a seat or position assigned by rank (usu. used in combination): *a first-desk flutist.* —*adj.* **7.** of a size or form suitable for use on a desk: *a desk dictionary.* **8.** done at or based on a desk, as in an office or schoolroom: *a desk job.*

desk•top (desk′top′), *adj.* made to fit or be used on a desk or table: *a desktop computer.*

desk′top pub′lishing, *n.* the design and production of publications by means of specialized software enabling a microcomputer to generate typeset-quality text and graphics.

des•man (des′mən), *n., pl.* **-mans.** either of two aquatic, insectivorous mammals, *Desmana moschata,* of SE Russia, or *Galemys pyrenaica,* of the Pyrenees, related to moles.

des•mid (dez′mid), *n.* any green algae of the family Desmidiaceae, each alga being composed of symmetrical half-cells bridged by a nucleus and usu. living colonially in a branching mat. —**des•mid′i•an,** *adj.*

Des Moines (də moin′), *n.* **1.** the capital of Iowa, in the central part,

NOTABLE DESERTS OF THE WORLD

Name	Location	Approximate Area sq. mi.	sq. km
Sahara	N Africa	3,500,000	9,065,000
Great Australian	Interior of Australia	1,480,000	3,830,000
Libyan	E part of Sahara Desert	650,000	1,683,500
Great Arabian	Arabian Peninsula, SW Asia	500,000	1,295,000
Gobi	Central Asia, Mongolia, and Inner Mongolia	500,000	1,295,000
Rub' al Khali	S Arabian Peninsula	250,000	647,500
Kalahari	S Botswana	200,000	518,000
Great Sandy	NW Australia	160,000	414,400
Nubian	NE Sudan	157,000	406,560
Great Victoria	SW central Australia	125,000	324,000
Syrian	N Saudi Arabia, SE Syria, W Iraq, and NE Jordan	125,000	324,000
Taklamakan	S central Xinjiang Uygur, China	125,000	324,000
Kara Kum	Turkmenistan	110,000	284,900
Thar	NW India and adjacent Pakistan	100,000	259,000
Kyzyl Kum	Uzbekistan and S Kazakhstan, SE of Aral Sea	90,000	233,100
Atacama	N Chile	70,000	181,300
Namib	W Namibia	50,000	129,500
Nefud	N Saudi Arabia	50,000	129,500
Dasht-i-Kavir	N central Iran	18,000	46,620
Sinai	Sinai Peninsula, E Egypt	17,000	44,000
Mojave	S California	15,000	38,850
Negev	S Israel	5000	12,950
Painted	NE Arizona	5000	12,950
Great Salt Lake	NW Utah	4000	10,360
Death Valley	E California and S Nevada	1500	3900

on the Des Moines River. 193,965. **2.** a river flowing SE from SW Minnesota through Iowa to the Mississippi River. ab. 530 mi. (850 km) long. —**Des Moines/i•an,** *n.*

des•o•late (*adj.* des/ə lit; *v.* -lāt/), *adj., v.,* **-lat•ed, -lat•ing.** —*adj.* **1.** barren or laid waste; devastated: *a treeless, desolate landscape.* **2.** deprived or destitute of inhabitants; deserted; lonely. **3.** feeling loveless, friendless, or hopeless; forlorn. **4.** dreary; dismal; gloomy: *desolate prospects.* —*v.t.* **5.** to lay waste; devastate. **6.** to deprive of inhabitants; depopulate. **7.** to make disconsolate; sadden. **8.** to forsake or abandon; desert. —**des/o•late•ly,** *adv.*

des•o•la•tion (des/ə lā/shən), *n.* **1.** an act of desolating. **2.** the state of being desolated. **3.** devastation; ruin. **4.** loneliness. **5.** sorrow; grief; woe. **6.** a desolate place.

De So•to (də sō/tō), *n.* **Hernando** or **Fernando,** c1500–42, Spanish explorer in America.

de•spair (di spâr/), *n.* **1.** loss of hope; hopelessness. **2.** a source of hopelessness: *to be the despair of one's teachers.* —*v.i.* **3.** to lose, give up, or be without hope: *to despair of humanity.* —**de•spair/er,** *n.*

de•spair•ing (di spâr/ing), *adj.* subject to or indicating despair or hopelessness: *a despairing look.* —**de•spair/ing•ly,** *adv.*

des•per•a•do (des/pə rä/dō, -rä/-), *n., pl.* **-does, -dos.** a bold, reckless outlaw, esp. in the early days of the American West.

des•per•ate (des/pər it, -prit), *adj.* **1.** reckless or dangerous because of despair or urgency: *a desperate killer.* **2.** having an urgent need, desire, etc.: *desperate for attention.* **3.** leaving little or no hope; very serious or dangerous: *a desperate illness.* **4.** making a final, ultimate effort; giving all: *a desperate attempt to save a life.* **5.** extreme or excessive: *desperate haste.* **6.** undertaken out of despair or as a last resort. **7.** having no hope; giving in to despair. **8.** extremely bad; intolerable or shocking. —**des/per•ate•ly,** *adv.*

des•per•a•tion (des/pə rā/shən), *n.* **1.** the state of being desperate or of having the recklessness of despair. **2.** the act or fact of despairing; despair.

des•pi•ca•ble (des/pi kə bəl, di spik/ə-), *adj.* deserving to be despised; contemptible. —**des/pi•ca•ble•ness,** *n.* —**des/pi•ca•bly,** *adv.*

de•spise (di spīz/), *v.t.,* **-spised, -spis•ing.** to regard with contempt or disdain; scorn. —**de•spis/a•ble,** *adj.* —**de•spis/er,** *n.*

de•spite (di spīt/), *prep., n., v.,* **-spit•ed, -spit•ing.** —*prep.* **1.** in spite of; notwithstanding. —*n.* **2.** contemptuous treatment; insult. **3.** malice, hatred, or spite. —*Idiom.* **4. in despite of,** in spite of; notwithstanding.

de•spoil (di spoil/), *v.t.* to strip of possessions, things of value, etc.; rob; plunder; pillage. —**de•spoil/er,** *n.* —**de•spoil/ment,** *n.*

de•spo•li•a•tion (di spō/lē ā/shən), *n.* **1.** the act of plundering. **2.** the fact or circumstance of being plundered.

de•spond•ent (di spon/dənt), *adj.* feeling or showing profound hopelessness, dejection, discouragement, etc. —**de•spond/ent•ly,** *adv.*

des•pot (des/pət, -pot), *n.* **1.** a king or other ruler with absolute, unlimited power; autocrat. **2.** any tyrant or oppressor. —**des•pot•ic** (di spot/ik), *adj.* —**des/pot•ism,** *n.*

des•qua•mate (des/kwə māt/), *v.i.,* **-mat•ed, -mat•ing.** to peel off in scales, as injured skin. —**des/qua•ma/tion,** *n.*

des•sert (di zûrt/), *n.* a usu. sweet food, as cake, pudding, ice cream, or fruit, served as the final course of a meal. [< French, der. of *desservir* to clear the table]

des•sert•spoon (di zûrt/spōon/), *n.* a spoon intermediate in size between a tablespoon and a teaspoon.

dessert/ wine/, *n.* a sweet wine served at the end of a meal, usu. with dessert.

de•sta•bi•lize (dē stā/bə līz/), *v.t.,* **-lized, -liz•ing.** to make (a government, economy, etc.) unstable; rid of stabilizing attributes. —**de•sta/bi•li•za/tion,** *n.*

des•ti•na•tion (des/tə nā/shən), *n.* **1.** the place to which a person or thing travels or is sent. **2.** the purpose for which something is destined.

des•tine (des/tin), *v.t.,* **-tined, -tin•ing. 1.** to set apart for a particular use, purpose, etc.; intend. **2.** to appoint or ordain beforehand; foreordain; predetermine.

des•ti•ny (des/tə nē), *n., pl.* **-nies. 1.** something that is to happen or has happened to a particular person or thing; lot or fortune. **2.** the predetermined, usu. inevitable or irresistible, course of events. **3.** the power or agency that determines the course of events.

des•ti•tute (des/ti tōot/, -tyōot/), *adj., v.,* **-tut•ed, -tut•ing.** —*adj.* **1.** without means of subsistence; lacking food, clothing, and shelter. **2.** deprived of, devoid of, or lacking (often fol. by *of*): *destitute of feeling.* —*v.t.* **3.** to leave destitute. —**des/ti•tute/ness,** *n.*

des•ti•tu•tion (des/ti tōo/shən, -tyōo/-), *n.* lack of the means of subsistence; utter poverty.

de•stroy (di stroi/), *v.t.* **1.** to reduce (a thing) to useless fragments or a useless form, as by smashing or burning; injure beyond repair; demolish. **2.** to put an end to; extinguish. **3.** to kill; slay. **4.** to render ineffective or useless; neutralize; invalidate. **5.** to defeat completely. —*v.i.* **6.** to engage in destruction. —**de•stroy/a•ble,** *adj.*

de•stroy•er (di stroi/ər), *n.* **1.** a person or thing that destroys. **2.** a fast, small warship armed mainly with 5-in. (13-cm) guns.

de•struct (di strukt/), *adj.* **1.** serving or designed to destroy: *a destruct mechanism.* —*n.* **2.** the act or process of intentional destruction, as of a

rocket or missile. —*v.t.* **3.** to destroy. —*v.i.* **4.** to be destroyed. —**de•struct/i•ble,** *adj.* —**de•struc/tion,** *n.* —**de•struc/tor,** *n.*

de•struc•tive (di struk/tiv), *adj.* **1.** tending to destroy; causing much damage: *bacteria destructive of tooth enamel.* **2.** tending to overthrow, disprove, or discredit; negative (opposed to *constructive*): *destructive criticism.* —**de•struc/tive•ly,** *adv.* —**de•struc/tive•ness, de•struc•tiv•i•ty** (dē/struk tiv/i tē), *n.*

destruc/tive distilla/tion, *n.* the decomposition of a substance, as wood or coal, by heating with a minimal exposure to air, and the collection of the volatile products formed.

des•ue•tude (des/wi tōod/, -tyōod/), *n.* the state of being no longer used or practiced.

des•ul•to•ry (des/əl tôr/ē, -tōr/ē), *adj.* **1.** lacking in consistency, method, purpose, or visible order; disconnected: *desultory conversation.* **2.** digressing from or unconnected with the main subject; random: *a desultory remark.* —**des/ul•to/ri•ly,** *adv.* —**des/ul•to/ri•ness,** *n.*

de•tach (di tach/), *v.t.* **1.** to unfasten and separate; disengage. **2.** to send (a regiment, ship, etc.) on a special mission. —**de•tach/a•ble,** *adj.* —**de•tach/a•bil/i•ty,** *n.* —**de•tach/a•bly,** *adv.*

de•tached (di tacht/), *adj.* **1.** not attached; separated: *a detached ticket stub.* **2.** having no wall in common with another building (opposed to *attached*): *a detached house.* **3.** impartial or objective; disinterested; unbiased: *a detached judgment.* **4.** not involved or concerned; aloof. —**de•tached/ly,** *adv.* —**de•tached/ness,** *n.*

de•tach•ment (di tach/mənt), *n.* **1.** the act of detaching or the condition of being detached. **2.** aloofness; disinterest. **3.** freedom from prejudice or partiality. **4.** a body of troops or ships detached for a special mission.

de•tail (di tāl/, dē/tāl), *n.* **1.** an individual part; particular. **2.** particulars collectively. **3.** attention to or treatment of a subject in individual parts. **4.** intricate, finely wrought decoration. **5.** any small section of a larger structure or whole, esp. an area of a drawing or photograph magnified to show what the eye would not otherwise distinguish. **6.** the property of an image or a method of image production making small, closely spaced elements individually distinguishable. **7. a.** an assignment, as of military personnel, for a special task. **b.** the party or person so selected: *the kitchen detail.* —*v.t.* **8.** to relate with all particulars; tell fully. **9.** to mention one by one; list. **10.** to appoint or assign for some particular duty. **11.** to provide with intricate, finely wrought decoration. —*Idiom.* **12. in detail,** item by item; with particulars.

de•tailed (di tāld/, dē/tāld), *adj.* **1.** thorough in the treatment of details: *a detailed report.* **2.** having many details.

de•tail•er (dē/tā lər), *n.* a manufacturer's representative who calls on customers to supply information on and promote products, monitor sales, etc. Also called **de/tail man/.**

de•tain (di tān/), *v.t.* **1.** to keep from proceeding; delay. **2.** to keep under restraint. —**de•tain/ment,** *n.*

de•tain•er (di tā/nər), *n.* **1.** a writ for the further detention of a person already in custody. **2.** the wrongful detaining or withholding of what belongs to another.

de•tect (di tekt/), *v.t.* **1.** to discover or notice the existence or presence of: *to detect the odor of gas.* **2.** to discover (a person) in some act or activity: *to detect someone cheating.* **3.** to discover the true, usu. concealed or underlying nature of. **4. a.** to rectify alternating signal currents in a radio receiver. **b.** to demodulate. —**de•tect/a•ble, de•tect/i•ble,** *adj.* —**de•tect/a•bil/i•ty, de•tect/i•bil/i•ty,** *n.*

de•tec•tion (di tek/shən), *n.* **1.** the act of detecting or the state of being detected. **2. a.** rectification of alternating signal currents in a radio receiver. **b.** the conversion of an alternating, modulated carrier wave or current into a direct, pulsating current equivalent to the transmitted information-bearing signal.

de•tec•tive (di tek/tiv), *n.* **1.** a police officer or a private investigator whose function is to obtain information and evidence, as of illegal activity. —*adj.* **2.** of or pertaining to detection or detectives.

de•tec•tor (di tek/tər), *n.* **1.** a person or thing that detects. **2.** any of various devices for detecting and registering the presence of or a change in something. **3. a.** a device for detecting electric oscillations or waves. **b.** a device, as a crystal detector or a vacuum tube, that rectifies the alternating current in a radio receiver.

de•tent (di tent/), *n.* a mechanism that temporarily keeps one part in a certain position relative to another, and can be released by applying force to one of the parts.

dé•tente or **de•tente** (dā tänt/, -tänt/), *n.* a relaxing of tension, esp. between nations.

de•ten•tion (di ten/shən), *n.* **1.** the act of detaining or the state of being detained. **2.** maintenance of a person in custody or confinement, as while awaiting a court decision. **3.** the keeping of a student after school hours as a punishment.

de•ter (di tûr/), *v.t.,* **-terred, -ter•ring. 1.** to discourage or restrain from acting or proceeding: *The large dog deterred trespassers.* **2.** to prevent; check; arrest: *face cream to deter wrinkles.* —**de•ter/ment,** *n.* —**de•ter/ra•ble,** *adj.* —**de•ter/rer,** *n.*

de•ter•gent (di tûr/jənt), *n.* **1.** any synthetic organic cleaning agent that is liquid or water-soluble and has wetting-agent and emulsifying properties. **2.** a similar substance that is oil-soluble, used in lubricating oils, dry-cleaning preparations, etc. **3.** any cleansing agent, including soap. —*adj.* **4.** cleansing; purging.

D

de·te·ri·o·rate (di tēr′ē ə rāt′), v.t., v.i., **-rat·ed, -rat·ing. 1.** to make or become worse or inferior in character, quality, value, etc. **2.** to disintegrate or wear away. **—de·te/ri·o·ra/tive,** adj.

de·te·ri·o·ra·tion (di tēr′ē ə rā′shən), n. **1.** the act or process of deteriorating. **2.** the state or condition of having deteriorated. **3.** a gradual decline, as in quality, serviceability, or vigor.

de·ter·mi·na·cy (di tûr′mə nə sē), n. **1.** the quality of being determinate. **2.** the condition of being determined or mandated.

de·ter·mi·nant (di tûr′mə nənt), n. **1.** a determining agent or factor. **2.** an algebraic expression of the sum of products of matrix elements used in the solution of systems of linear equations. **3.** GENE.

de·ter·mi·nate (di tûr′mə nit), adj. **1.** having defined limits. **2.** settled; positive. **3.** conclusive; final. **4.** (of an inflorescence) having the primary and each secondary stem ending in a flower or bud. **—de·ter/mi·nate·ly,** adv.

de·ter·mi·na·tion (di tûr′mə nā′shən), n. **1.** the act of coming to a decision or of resolving something. **2.** ascertainment, as by observation, investigation, or measurement. **3.** the information ascertained. **4.** the settlement of a dispute, question, etc., as by authoritative or judicial decision. **5.** the decision or settlement arrived at or pronounced. **6.** the quality of being resolute; firmness of purpose. **7.** a fixed purpose or intention: *a determination to fight.* **8.** the fixing or settling of amount, limit, character, etc. **9.** fixed direction or tendency toward something. **10.** *Law.* conclusion or termination. **11.** the fixation of the fate of a cell or group of cells, esp. before actual morphological or functional differentiation occurs. **12.** *Logic.* **a.** the act of rendering a notion more precise by adding differentiating characteristics. **b.** the definition of a concept in terms of its constituent elements.

de·ter·mi·na·tive (di tûr′mə nā′tiv, -nə tiv), adj. **1.** serving to determine; determining. **—n. 2.** something that determines. **—de·ter/mi·na/tive·ly,** adv. **—de·ter/mi·na/tive·ness,** n.

de·ter·mine (di tûr′min), v., **-mined, -min·ing. —v.t. 1.** to settle or resolve (a dispute, question, etc.) by an authoritative or conclusive decision. **2.** to conclude or ascertain, as after reasoning or observation. **3.** to fix the position of. **4.** to cause, affect, or control; fix or decide causally: *Demand usually determines supply.* **5.** to give direction or tendency to; impel. **6.** to lead or bring (a person) to a decision. **7.** to decide upon. **8.** *Logic.* to limit (a notion) by adding differentiating characteristics. **9.** *Law.* to put an end to; terminate. **—v.i. 10.** to come to a decision or resolution; decide. **11.** *Law.* to come to an end.

de·ter·mined (di tûr′mind), adj. **1.** resolute; staunch; unwavering. **2.** decided; settled; resolved. **—de·ter/mined·ly** (-mind lē, -mə nid lē), adv. **—de·ter/mined·ness,** n.

de·ter·min·er (di tûr′mə nər), n. **1.** one that determines. **2.** a member of a subclass of English limiting adjectival words that usu. precede descriptive adjectives, including the articles *the, a,* and *an,* and any words that may substitute for them, as *your, their, some,* and *each.*

de·ter·min·ism (di tûr′mə niz′əm), n. **1.** a doctrine that all facts and events exemplify natural laws. **2.** a doctrine that all events have sufficient causes. **—de·ter/min·ist,** n., adj. **—de·ter/min·is/tic,** adj. **—de·ter/min·is/ti·cal·ly,** adv.

de·ter·rence (di tûr′əns, -tur′-, -ter′-), n. the act of deterring, esp. of deterring a nuclear attack by the capability for retaliation.

de·ter·rent (di tûr′ənt, -tur′-, -ter′-), adj. **1.** serving or tending to deter. **—n. 2.** something that deters: *a deterrent to crime.* **3.** military strength or the capacity to retaliate strongly enough to deter an enemy from attacking. **—de·ter/rent·ly,** adv.

de·test (di test′), v.t. to feel abhorrence of; hate; dislike intensely. **—de·test/er,** n.

de·test·a·ble (di tes′tə bəl), adj. deserving to be detested; abominable; hateful. **—de·test/a·bil/i·ty, de·test/a·ble·ness,** n. **—de·test/a·bly,** adv.

de·throne (dē thrōn′), v.t., **-throned, -thron·ing.** to remove from a throne or position of power or authority; depose. **—de·throne/ment,** n.

det·i·nue (det′n ōō′, -yōō′), n. (in common law) an action to recover personal property wrongfully detained.

det·o·nate (det′n āt′), v., **-nat·ed, -nat·ing. —v.i. 1.** to explode with sudden violence. **—v.t. 2.** to cause to explode. **—det/o·na·ble** (-ə bəl), **det/o·nat/a·ble,** adj.

det·o·na·tor (det′n ā′tər), n. a device, as a percussion cap, used to make another substance explode.

de·tour (dē′tŏŏr, di tŏŏr′), n. **1.** a roundabout or circuitous way or course, esp. one used temporarily when the main route is closed. **—v.i. 2.** to make a detour; go by way of a detour. **—v.t. 3.** to cause to make a detour. **4.** to make a detour around.

de·tox·i·fi·ca·tion (dē tok′sə fi kā′shən) also **de·tox/i·ca/tion,** n. **1.** the metabolic process by which toxins are changed into less toxic or more readily excreted substances. **2.** the act of detoxifying. **3.** the state of being detoxified. **4.** the process of withdrawing a person from dependence on alcohol or another habituating drug.

de·tox·i·fy (dē tok′sə fī), v., **-fied, -fy·ing. —v.t. 1.** to rid of poison. **2.** to subject (a person) to detoxification. **—v.i. 3.** to undergo detoxification.

de·tract (di trakt′), v.i. **1.** to take away a part, as from value or reputation (usu. fol. by *from*). **—v.t. 2.** to divert; distract: *to detract attention from a problem.* **—de·trac/tor,** n.

de·trac·tion (di trak′shən), n. **1.** the act of disparaging or belittling

the reputation or worth of a person, work, etc. **2.** something that detracts.

de·train (dē trān′), v.i. **1.** to alight from a railroad train. **—v.t. 2.** to take from a railroad train. **—de·train/ment,** n.

de·trib·al·ize (dē trī′bə līz′), v.t., **-ized, -iz·ing.** to cause to lose tribal allegiances. **—de·trib/al·i·za/tion,** n.

det·ri·ment (de′trə mənt), n. **1.** loss, damage, disadvantage, or injury. **2.** a cause of loss or damage.

det·ri·men·tal (de′trə men′tl), adj. **1.** damaging; harmful. **—n. 2.** a detrimental person or thing. **—det/ri·men/tal·ly,** adv.

de·tri·tion (di trish′ən), n. the act of wearing away by rubbing.

de·tri·tus (di trī′təs), n. **1.** rock in small particles or other material worn or broken away from a mass, as by the action of water or glacial ice. **2.** any disintegrated material; debris. **—de·tri/tal,** adj.

De·troit (di troit′), n. **1.** a city in SE Michigan, on the Detroit River. 992,038. **2.** a river in SE Michigan, flowing S from Lake St. Clair to Lake Erie, forming part of the boundary between the U.S. and Canada. ab. 32 mi. (52 km) long.

de trop (də trō′), adj. **1.** too much; too many. **2.** in the way; not wanted.

de·tu·mes·cence (dē′tŏŏ mes′əns, -tyŏŏ-), n. subsidence of swelling or erection. **—de·tu·mes/cent,** adj.

deuce¹ (dŏŏs, dyŏŏs), n. **1.** a card having two pips. **2. a.** the face of a die having two pips. **b.** a cast or point of two in dice. **3.** a situation, as a tied score in a game, in which a player must score two successive points or games to win.

deuce² (dŏŏs, dyŏŏs), n. devil; dickens (used as a mild oath): *Where the deuce did they hide it?*

De·us (dē′əs, dā′-; *Lat.* de′ŏŏs), n. God. *Abbr.:* D. [< Latin: god]

de·us ex ma·chi·na (dā′əs eks mä′kə nə, dē′əs eks mak′ə nə), n. **1.** (in ancient Greek and Roman drama) a god introduced into a play to resolve the entanglements of the plot. **2.** any artificial or improbable device resolving the difficulties of a plot.

Deut., Deuteronomy.

deu·te·ri·um (dŏŏ tēr′ē əm, dyŏŏ-), n. an isotope of hydrogen. *Symbol:* D; *at. wt.:* 2.01; *at. no.:* 1.

deutero-, a combining form meaning "second": *deuterocanonical.* Also, *esp. before a vowel,* **deuter-.**

Deu·ter·on·o·my (dŏŏ′tə ron′ə mē, dyŏŏ′-), n. the fifth book of the Pentateuch.

deu·to·plasm (dŏŏ′tə plaz′əm, dyŏŏ′-), n. nutritive material, as yolk, in an egg or ovum. **—deu/to·plas/mic,** adj.

deut·zi·a (dŏŏt′sē ə, dyŏŏt′-, doit′-), n., pl. **-zi·as.** any of various small shrubs of the genus *Deutzia,* of the saxifrage family, having white or pink flowers.

De Va·le·ra (dev′ə lâr′ə, -lēr′ə), n. **Ea·mon** (ā′mən), 1882–1975, Irish political leader and statesman, born in the U.S.: prime minister of the Republic of Ireland 1932–48, 1951–54, 1957–59; president 1959–73.

de·val·u·a·tion (dē val′yŏŏ ā′shən), n. **1.** an official lowering of the exchange value of a country's currency relative to gold or other currencies. **2.** a reduction of a value, status, etc.

de·val·ue (dē val′yŏŏ), v., **-val·ued, -val·u·ing. —v.t. 1.** to set a lower exchange value on (a currency). **2.** to treat or cause to be treated as not valuable, desirable, etc. **—v.i. 3.** to undergo devaluation.

dev·as·tate (dev′ə stāt′), v.t., **-tat·ed, -tat·ing. 1.** to lay waste; render desolate: *The fire devastated the city.* **2.** to overwhelm, as with shock. **—dev·as/ta/tion,** n. **—dev/as·ta/tor,** n.

dev·as·tat·ing (dev′ə stā′ting), adj. **1.** tending or having the power to devastate. **2.** satirical, ironic, or caustic in an effective way: *a devastating portrayal of society.* **—dev/as·tat/ing·ly,** adv.

de Ve·ga (də vā′gə), n. Lope, (Lope Félix de Vega Carpio), 1562–1635, Spanish dramatist and poet.

de·vel·op (di vel′əp), v.t. **1.** to bring out the possibilities of; bring to a more advanced, effective, or usable state: *to develop one's talents; to develop natural resources.* **2.** to cause to grow or expand: *to develop one's biceps.* **3.** to bring into being or activity; produce: *to develop new techniques.* **4.** to generate or acquire, as by natural growth or internal processes: *to develop broad shoulders; to develop an allergy.* **5.** to elaborate or expand in detail: *to develop a theory.* **6.** to build on or otherwise change the use of (a piece of land), esp. so as to make more profitable. **7.** to cause to mature or evolve. **8.** to treat (an exposed film) with chemicals so as to render the latent image visible. **9.** to elaborate or transform the melodic, harmonic, and rhythmic characteristics of (musical themes or motifs). **10.** *Math.* to express in an extended form, as in a series. **11.** to bring (a chess piece) into effective play. **—v.i. 12.** to grow into a more mature state; advance; expand. **13.** to come gradually into existence or operation. **14. a.** to progress from an embryonic to an adult form. **b.** to progress from earlier to later stages of ontogeny or phylogeny. **c.** to reach sexual maturity. **15.** to be disclosed; become manifest: *The plot develops slowly.* **16.** to undergo developing, as a photographic film. **—de·vel/op·a·ble,** adj. **—de·vel/op·a·bil/i·ty,** n.

de·vel·op·er (di vel′ə pər), n. **1.** a person or thing that develops. **2.** a reducing agent or solution for developing a film or the like. **3.** a person who develops real estate, esp. by subdividing a piece of land and building houses, stores, or the like on it and selling them.

de·vel·op·ing (di vel′ə ping), adj. **1.** undergoing development; growing; evolving. **2.** (of a nation or geographical area) having living standards or industrial productivity well below the level possible with financial or technical aid; not yet highly industrialized.

de·vel·op·ment (di vel′əp mənt), *n.* **1.** the act or process of developing. **2.** a significant consequence or event. **3.** a developed state or form; maturity. **4.** the section of a musical composition in which themes or motifs are developed. **5.** a large group of dwellings, often of similar design and constructed as a community, esp. by a real-estate developer. **6.** the raising of funds, expansion of activities or opportunities, etc., esp. for an organization or foundation. —**de·vel′op·men′tal,** *adj.* —**de·vel′op·men′tal·ly,** *adv.*

de·vi·ant (dē′vē ənt), *adj.* **1.** deviating or departing from the norm; characterized by deviation. —*n.* **2.** a person or thing that deviates or departs markedly from the accepted norm.

de·vi·ate (*v.* dē′vē āt′; *adj., n.* -it), *v.,* **-at·ed, -at·ing,** *adj., n.* —*v.i.* **1.** to turn aside, as from a route, way, or course. **2.** to depart, as from an accepted procedure, standard, or course of action. **3.** to digress, as from a line of thought or reasoning. —*v.t.* **4.** to cause to swerve; turn aside. —*adj.* **5.** characterized by deviation or departure from an accepted norm or standard, as of behavior. —*n.* **6.** a person or thing that departs from the accepted norm or standard.

de·vi·a·tion (dē′vē ā′shən), *n.* **1.** departure from an accepted or established standard or norm. **2.** the difference between one of a set of statistical values and some fixed value, usu. the mean of the set. **3.** the error of a magnetic compass on a given heading as a result of local magnetism.

de·vice (di vīs′), *n.* **1.** a thing made for a particular purpose, esp. a mechanical, electric, or electronic invention. **2.** a plan, scheme, or procedure for effecting a purpose. **3.** a crafty scheme; trick. **4.** a word pattern, figure of speech, theatrical convention, etc., used in a literary or dramatic work to evoke a desired effect. **5.** something elaborately or fancifully designed. **6.** a representation or design used esp. as a heraldic charge or an emblem. **7.** a motto; slogan. —*Idiom.* **8.** **leave to one's own devices,** to allow (a person) to act according to desire or inclination.

dev·il (dev′əl), *n., v.,* **-iled, -il·ing** or (*esp. Brit.*) **-illed, -il·ling.** —*n.* **1. a.** (*sometimes cap.*) the supreme spirit of evil; Satan. **b.** a subordinate evil spirit at enmity with God. **2.** a wicked, cruel person. **3.** a clever or mischievous person. **4.** a person: *The lucky devil won the grand prize.* **5.** Also called **printer's devil.** a young worker below the level of apprentice in a printing office. **6.** any of various devices, often with projecting teeth. —*v.t.* **7.** to annoy; harass. **8.** to prepare with hot or savory seasonings: *to devil eggs.* —*Idiom.* **9. give the devil his due,** to acknowledge the accomplishments of someone otherwise considered unworthy. **10. go to the devil, a.** to become depraved. **b.** (used in the imperative to express anger, impatience, or rejection.) **11. let the devil take the hindmost,** to leave the least able or fortunate persons to suffer adverse consequences; leave behind or to one's fate: *They ran from the pursuing mob and let the devil take the hindmost.* **12. the devil to pay,** trouble to be faced as an aftermath; repercussions. —*Proverb.* **13. The devil can cite scripture for his own purpose,** Satan will distort anything, even a holy text. [< Latin < Greek *diábolos* Satan lit., slanderer]

dev·il·fish (dev′əl fish′), *n., pl.* (*esp. collectively*) **-fish,** (*esp. for kinds or species*) **-fish·es.** **1.** MANTA (def. 2). **2.** OCTOPUS.

dev·il·ish (dev′ə lish, dev′lish), *adj.* **1.** of, like, or befitting a devil. **2.** extreme; very great: *a devilish mess.* —*adv.* **3.** excessively; extremely. —**dev′il·ish·ly,** *adv.* —**dev′il·ish·ness,** *n.*

dev′il-may-care′, *adj.* reckless; careless; rollicking.

dev′il's ad′vocate, *n.* **1.** a person who advocates an opposing view, as for the sake of argument. **2.** an official of the Roman Catholic Church whose duty is to argue against a proposed beatification or canonization.

dev′il's food′ cake′, *n.* a rich, dark chocolate cake.

Dev′il's Is′land, *n.* a small island off the coast of French Guiana: former French penal colony. French, **Île du Diable.**

dev′il's-walk′ing-stick′, *n.* HERCULES-CLUB (def. 2).

dev·il·try (dev′əl trē), *n., pl.* **-tries. 1.** mischievous behavior. **2.** extreme or utter wickedness. **3.** an act or instance of mischievous or wicked behavior. **4.** diabolic magic or art.

dev·il·wood (dev′əl wŏŏd′), *n.* a small tree, *Osmanthus americanus,* of the olive family, of the SE U.S., yielding a hard wood.

de·vi·ous (dē′vē əs), *adj.* **1.** departing from the most direct way; circuitous; roundabout: *a devious course.* **2.** departing from the proper or accepted way: *a devious procedure.* **3.** not straightforward or sincere; shifty or underhand. **4.** without definite course: *a devious current.* —**de′vi·ous·ly,** *adv.* —**de′vi·ous·ness,** *n.*

de·vise (di vīz′), *v.,* **-vised, -vis·ing,** *n.* —*v.t.* **1.** to contrive, plan, or elaborate; invent from existing principles or ideas: *to devise a method.* **2.** to transmit (property) by will. —*v.i.* **3.** to form a plan; contrive. —*n.* **4. a.** the disposition of real property by will. **b.** a will or clause in a will disposing of property. **c.** the property so disposed of. —**de·vis′a·ble,** *adj.* —**de·vis′er,** *n.*

de·vi·tal·ize (dē vīt′l īz′), *v.t.,* **-ized, -iz·ing.** to deprive of vitality or vital properties; weaken. —**de·vi′tal·i·za′tion,** *n.*

de·vo·cal·ize (dē vō′kə līz′), *v.t.,* **-ized, -iz·ing.** to devoice. —**de·vo′cal·i·za′tion,** *n.*

de·voice (dē vois′), *v.,* **-voiced, -voic·ing.** —*v.t.* **1.** to pronounce (an ordinarily voiced speech sound) without or with reduced vibration of the vocal cords. —*v.i.* **2.** to devoice a speech sound.

de·void (di void′), *adj.* not possessing; totally lacking; destitute (usu. fol. by *of*).

de·voir (də vwär′, dev′wär), *n.* **1.** an act of civility or respect. **2. devoirs,** respects or compliments. **3.** responsibility; duty.

dev·o·lu·tion (dev′ə lōō′shən; *esp. Brit.* dē′və-), *n.* **1.** the act or fact of devolving; passage onward from stage to stage. **2.** the passing on to a successor of property or an unexercised right. **3.** disappearance or simplification of structure or function in the course of evolution. **4.** the transfer of power or authority from a central government to a local government. —**dev′o·lu′tion·ar′y,** *adj., n.,* —**dev′o·lu′tion·ist,** *n.*

de·volve (di volv′), *v.,* **-volved, -volv·ing.** —*v.t.* **1.** to transfer or delegate (a duty, responsibility, etc.) to or upon another; pass on. —*v.i.* **2.** to be transferred or passed on from one to another: *The responsibility devolved on me.* **3.** to become simpler or disappear, esp. in the process of evolution. —**de·volve′ment,** *n.*

De·vo·ni·an (də vō′nē ən), *adj.* **1.** noting or pertaining to a period of the Paleozoic Era, 405 million to 345 million years ago, characterized by the dominance of fishes and the advent of amphibians and ammonites. **2.** of or pertaining to Devonshire, England. —*n.* **3.** the Devonian Period or System.

Dev′onshire cream′, *n.* CLOTTED CREAM.

de·vote (di vōt′), *v.t.,* **-vot·ed, -vot·ing. 1.** to give up or apply to a particular pursuit, purpose, cause, etc.: *to devote one's time to study.* **2.** to set apart or dedicate by a solemn or formal act; consecrate: *to devote one's life to God.*

de·vot·ed (di vō′tid), *adj.* zealous or ardent in loyalty or affection: *a devoted friend.* —**de·vot′ed·ly,** *adv.* —**de·vot′ed·ness,** *n.*

dev·o·tee (dev′ə tē′, -tā′), *n.* a person who is greatly devoted to something; follower, enthusiast, or fan.

de·vo·tion (di vō′shən), *n.* **1.** earnest attachment to a cause, person, etc. **2.** profound dedication, esp. to religion; consecration. **3.** the act of devoting. **4.** Often, **devotions.** religious observance or worship; a form of prayer or worship for special use.

de·vo·tion·al (di vō′shə nl), *adj.* **1.** characterized by devotion. **2.** used in devotions: *devotional prayers.* —*n.* **3.** Often, **devotionals.** a short religious service. —**de·vo′tion·al·ly,** *adv.*

de·vour (di vour′), *v.t.* **1.** to swallow or eat up hungrily. **2.** to consume destructively; demolish: *Fire devoured the museum.* **3.** to take in greedily with the senses or intellect: *to devour a book.* **4.** to absorb or engross wholly: *a mind devoured by hatred.* —**de·vour′er,** *n.* —**de·vour′ing·ly,** *adv.*

de·vout (di vout′), *adj.* **1.** devoted to divine worship or service; pious; religious. **2.** expressing piety: *devout prayer.* **3.** earnest; fervent. —**de·vout′ly,** *adv.* —**de·vout′ness,** *n.*

dew (dōō, dyōō), *n.* **1.** moisture condensed from the atmosphere, esp. at night, and deposited in the form of small drops upon any cool surface. **2.** something compared to such drops of moisture, as in purity, delicacy, or refreshing quality. **3.** moisture in small drops on a surface, as tears or perspiration. —*v.t.* **4.** to wet with or as if with dew.

Dew′ar ves′sel (dōō′ər, dyōō′-), *n.* a kind of vacuum bottle used esp. to store liquefied gases. Also called **Dew′ar flask′.**

dew·ber·ry (dōō′ber′ē, -bə rē, dyōō′-), *n., pl.* **-ries.** the fruit of any of several trailing brambles or blackberries of the genus *Rubus.*

dew·claw (dōō′klô′, dyōō′-), *n.* **1.** a functionless claw on some dogs that does not reach the ground in walking. **2.** an analogous false hoof, as of deer. —**dew′clawed′,** *adj.*

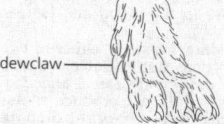

dewclaw—

dewclaw (def. 1)

dew·drop (dōō′drop′, dyōō′-), *n.* a drop of dew.

Dew·ey (dōō′ē, dyōō′ē), *n.* **1. George,** 1837–1917, U.S. admiral during the Spanish-American War. **2. John,** 1859–1952, U.S. philosopher and educator. **3. Mel·vil** (mel′vil), (*Melville Louis Kossuth Dewey*), 1851–1931, U.S. educator and innovator in library science.

Dew′ey dec′imal classifica′tion, *Trademark.* a system of library classification using three-digit numerals for major divisions and numerals following a decimal point for subdivisions: devised by Melvil Dewey. Also called **Dew′ey dec′imal sys′tem.**

dew·lap (dōō′lap′, dyōō′-), *n.* **1.** a pendulous fold of skin under the throat of a bovine animal. **2.** any similar part in other animals, as the wattle of fowl or the inflatable loose skin under the throat of some lizards. —**dew′lapped′,** *adj.*

DEW′ line′ (dōō, dyōō), *n.* a 3000-mi.(4800-km)-long network of radar stations north of the Arctic Circle, maintained by the U.S. and Canada to provide advance warning of the approach of hostile planes or missiles.

dew′ point′, *n.* the temperature to which air must be cooled, at a given pressure and water-vapor content, for it to reach saturation; temperature at which dew begins to form.

dew•y (dōō′ē, dyōō′ē), *adj.*, **-i•er, -i•est. 1.** moist with dew. **2.** DEWY-EYED. —**dew′i•ly**, *adv.* —**dew′i•ness**, *n.*

dew′y-eyed′, *adj.* romantically naive or credulous; innocent and trusting.

dex•ter (dek′stər), *adj.* **1.** on the right side; right. **2.** being or pertaining to the side of a heraldic shield to the right of the bearer. Compare SINISTER (def. 5).

dex•ter•i•ty (dek ster′i tē), *n.* **1.** skill or adroitness in using the body or esp. the hands. **2.** mental adroitness or skill; cleverness.

dex•ter•ous (dek′strəs, -stər əs), *adj.* **1.** skillful or adroit in the use of the hands or body; deft. **2.** having mental adroitness or skill; clever; quick. **3.** done with skill or adroitness. —**dex′ter•ous•ly**, *adv.* —**dex′ter•ous•ness**, *n.*

dex•tral (dek′strəl), *adj.* **1.** of, pertaining to, or on the right side; right. **2.** having a preference for using the right hand or side; right-handed. **3.** (of certain gastropod shells) coiling clockwise, as seen from the apex. Compare SINISTRAL. —**dex′tral•i•ty**, *n.* —**dex′tral•ly**, *adv.*

dextro-, a combining form representing DEXTROROTATORY, used esp. in the names of chemical compounds that in solution rotate polarized light in a clockwise direction: *dextroglucose.*

dex•tro•ro•ta•to•ry (dek′strō rō′tə tôr′ē, -tōr′ē) also **dex•tro•ro•ta•ry** (-rō′tə rē), *adj.* turning to the right, esp. rotating to the right of the plane of polarization of light: *dextrorotatory crystals.* Symbol: d- —**dex′tro•ro•ta′tion** (-tā′shən), *n.*

dex•trorse (dek′strôrs, dek strôrs′), *adj.* twining in a clockwise direction from the base. —**dex′trorse•ly**, *adv.*

dex•trose (dek′strōs), *n.* the dextrorotatory form of glucose, occurring in fruits and in animal tissues and commercially obtainable from starch by acid hydrolysis. Also called **corn sugar, grape sugar.**

dg, decigram.

DHA, docosahexaenoic acid: an omega-3 fatty acid present in fish oils.

Dha•ka or **Dac•ca** (dak′ə, dä′kə), *n.* the capital of Bangladesh, in the central part. 3,440,147.

dhar•ma (där′mə, dur′-), *n.* **1.** (in Hinduism and Buddhism) **a.** conformity to religious law, custom, duty, or to one's own character. **b.** the essential nature of the universe or one's own character. **2.** the doctrine or teaching of the Buddha. —**dhar′mic**, *adj.*

dho•ti (dō′tē), *n., pl.* **-tis.** a long loincloth worn by many Hindu men in India.

Dhu 'l-hij•jah (dōōl hij′ə), *n.* the 12th month of the Islamic calendar, in leap years containing one extra day.

Dhu 'l-Qa•da (dōōl kä′də), *n.* the 11th month of the Islamic calendar.

Dhu 'l-hij•jah (dōōl hij′ə), *n.* the twelfth month of the Muslim calendar, in leap year containing one extra day. Also, **Dhu 'l-hij′ja, Zu 'l-hijjah.**

Dhu 'l-Qa•da (dōōl kä′də), *n. Islam.* the eleventh month of the Muslim calendar. Also, **Zu 'l-kadah.**

dhur•rie or **dur•rie** (dûr′ē), *n.* a thick, nonpile cotton rug of India.

Di, *Chem. Symbol.* didymium.

di-, a combining form meaning "two," "double": *diamide; dicotyledon; dihedron.* Compare DIS-[2].

dia-, a prefix occurring orig. in loanwords from Greek, with the meanings "through, across, from point to point" (*diachronic; diameter; diarrhea*), "in different directions, apart, at an angle" (*dialysis; diastole; diatropism*), "completeness or thoroughness (of the action of the verb)" (*diagnosis*). Also, *esp. before a vowel,* **di-**.

di•a•be•tes (dī′ə bē′tis, -tēz), *n.* any of several disorders characterized by high levels of glucose in the blood and increased urine production, esp. diabetes mellitus.

diabe′tes mel′li•tus (mel′i təs), *n.* either of two chronic forms of diabetes in which insulin does not effectively transport glucose from the bloodstream: a rapidly developing form, affecting children and young adults, in which the body does not produce enough insulin and insulin must therefore be injected (**juvenile-onset diabetes**) or a slowly developing form in which the body's tissues become unable to use insulin effectively (**adult-onset diabetes**).

di•a•bet•ic (dī′ə bet′ik), *adj.* **1.** of, pertaining to, or having diabetes. —*n.* **2.** a person who has diabetes.

di•a•ble•rie (dē ä′blə rē, dī ab′lə-), *n.* **1.** diabolic magic or art; sorcery; witchcraft. **2.** the lore of devils; demonology. **3.** reckless mischief; deviltry.

di•a•bol•ic (dī′ə bol′ik) also **di′a•bol′i•cal**, *adj.* **1.** devilish; fiendish; outrageously wicked: *a diabolic plot.* **2.** pertaining to or actuated by a devil. —**di′a•bol′i•cal•ly**, *adv.*

di•ab•o•lism (dī ab′ə liz′əm), *n.* **1.** action aided or caused by the devil; sorcery; witchcraft. **2.** the character or condition of a devil. **3.** belief in or worship of devils. **4.** evil action; deviltry. —**di•ab′o•list**, *n.*

di•a•chron•ic (dī′ə kron′ik), *adj.* of or pertaining to the study of the changes in a language over a period of time: *diachronic linguistics.* Compare SYNCHRONIC. —**di′a•chron′i•cal•ly**, *adv.*

di•ac•o•nal (dī ak′ə nl), *adj.* pertaining to a deacon.

di•a•crit•ic (dī′ə krit′ik), *n.* **1.** Also called **diacrit′ical mark′.** a mark, point, or sign, as a cedilla, tilde, circumflex, or macron, added or attached to a letter or character, as to distinguish it from another of similar form, to give it a particular phonetic value, or to indicate stress. —*adj.* **2.** diacritical. **3.** diagnostic.

di•a•crit•i•cal (dī′ə krit′i kəl), *adj.* **1.** serving to distinguish; distinctive. **2.** capable of distinguishing. **3.** serving as a diacritic. —**di′a•crit′i•cal•ly**, *adv.*

di•a•dem (dī′ə dem′), *n.* **1.** CROWN (def. 1). **2.** an ornamental headband worn as a symbol of royalty. **3.** royal dignity or authority.

di•ad•ro•mous (dī ad′rə məs), *adj.* (of fish) migrating between fresh and salt waters.

Dia•ghi•lev (dē ä′gə lef′, -lif), *n.* **Sergei Pavlovich,** 1872–1929, Russian ballet producer.

di•ag•nose (dī′əg nōs′, -nōz′, dī′əg nōs′, -nōz′), *v.*, **-nosed, -nos•ing.** —*v.t.* **1.** to determine the identity of (a disease, illness, etc.) by a medical examination. **2.** to ascertain the cause or nature of (a disorder or problem) from the symptoms. —*v.i.* **3.** to make a diagnosis. —**di•ag•nos′a•ble**, *adj.*

di•ag•no•sis (dī′əg nō′sis), *n., pl.* **-ses** (-sēz). **1. a.** the process of determining by medical examination the nature and circumstances of a diseased condition. **b.** the decision reached from such an examination. **2.** an analysis of the cause or nature of a problem or situation. **3.** an answer or solution to a problematic situation. **4.** *Biol.* a precise description of a taxon.

di•ag•nos•tic (dī′əg nos′tik), *adj.* **1.** of, pertaining to, or used in diagnosis. **2.** serving to identify or characterize; being a precise indication. —*n.* **3.** DIAGNOSIS (def. 1). **4.** a symptom or characteristic of value in diagnosis. **5.** a device or substance used for the analysis or detection of diseases or other medical conditions. —**di′ag•nos′ti•cal•ly**, *adv.*

di•ag•nos•ti•cian (dī′əg no stish′ən), *n.* a specialist or expert in making diagnoses.

di•ag•nos•tics (dī′əg nos′tiks), *n.* (*used with a sing. v.*) the discipline or practice of diagnosis.

di•ag•o•nal (dī ag′ə nl, -ag′nl), *adj.* **1. a.** connecting two nonadjacent angles or vertices of a polygon or polyhedron: *a diagonal line.* **b.** extending from one edge of a solid figure to an opposite edge: *a diagonal plane.* **2.** having an oblique direction. **3.** having oblique lines, ridges, or markings. —*n.* **4.** a diagonal line or plane. **5.** VIRGULE. **6.** a diagonal row, part, or pattern. —**di•ag′o•nal•ly**, *adv.*

di•a•gram (dī′ə gram′), *n., v.,* **-gramed** or **-grammed, -gram•ing** or **-gram•ming.** —*n.* **1.** a drawing or plan that outlines and explains the parts or operation of something: *a diagram of an engine.* **2.** a figure, usu. consisting of a line drawing, made to accompany and illustrate a geometrical theorem, mathematical demonstration, etc. **3.** a chart or plan. —*v.t.* **4.** to represent by a diagram; make a diagram of. —**di′a•gram′ma•ble**, *adj.* —**di′a•gram•mat′ic** (-grə mat′ik), *adj.* —**di′a•gram•mat′i•cal•ly**, *adv.*

di•al (dī′əl, dīl), *n., v.,* **di•aled, di•al•ing** or (*esp. Brit.*) **di•alled, di•al•ling.** —*n.* **1.** a plate or disk on a clock, watch, or sundial, containing graduated markings or figures, upon which the time of day is indicated by hands, pointers, or shadows. **2.** a plate or disk with markings or figures for indicating or registering some measurement or number, usu. by means of a pointer. **3.** a rotatable plate, disk, or knob used for regulating a mechanism, making and breaking electrical connections, or the like, esp. one that tunes a radio or television. **4. a.** ROTARY DIAL. **b.** a set of numbered and lettered pushbuttons on a telephone that perform the function of a rotary dial. **5.** radio or television broadcasting: *a new personality on the morning dial.* —*v.t.* **6.** to indicate or register on or as if on a dial. **7.** to measure with or as if with a dial. **8.** to regulate or select by means of a dial. **9.** to make a telephone call to. —*v.i.* **10.** to dial a telephone. **11.** to tune in or regulate by means of a dial.

di•a•lect (dī′ə lekt′), *n.* **1.** a variety of a language distinguished from other varieties by features of phonology, grammar, and vocabulary and by its use by a group of speakers set off from others geographically or socially. **2.** a provincial, rural, or socially distinct variety of a language that differs from the standard language, esp. when considered as nonstandard. **3.** any special variety of a language: *the literary dialect.* **4.** a language considered as one of a group that have a common ancestor: *Persian, Latin, and English are Indo-European dialects.*

di•a•lec•tal (dī′ə lek′tl), *adj.* of, pertaining to, or characteristic of a dialect. —**di′a•lec′tal•ly**, *adv.*

di′alect at′las, *n.* LINGUISTIC ATLAS.

di•a•lec•tic (dī′ə lek′tik), *adj.* Also, **dialectical. 1.** pertaining to or of the nature of logical argumentation. **2.** DIALECTAL. —*n.* **3.** the art or practice of debate or conversation by which the truth of a theory or opinion is arrived at logically. **4.** logical argumentation. **5. dialectics,** (*often used with a sing. v.*) the arguments or bases of dialectical materialism, including the elevation of matter over mind and a constantly changing reality with a material basis. **6.** the juxtaposition or interaction of conflicting ideas, forces, etc. —**di′a•lec′ti•cal•ly**, *adv.*

dialec′tical mate′rialism, *n.* the Marxian system of thought that combines philosophical materialism with the Hegelian dialectic and forms the theoretical basis for Communism.

di•a•lec•tol•o•gy (dī′ə lek tol′ə jē), *n.* the study of dialects. —**di′a•lec′to•log′i•cal**, *adj.* —**di′a•lec•tol′o•gist**, *n.*

di′alog box′, *n. Computers.* (in a graphical user interface) a box, called up temporarily on the screen, that asks for user input.

di•a•logue or **di•a•log** (dī′ə lôg′, -log′), *n., v.,* **-logued, -logu•ing.** —*n.* **1.** conversation between two or more persons. **2.** the conversation between characters in a novel, drama, etc. **3.** an exchange of ideas or opinions on a particular issue esp. with a view to reaching an amicable agreement. **4.** a literary work in the form of a conversation. —*v.i.* **5.** to carry on a dialogue; converse. **6.** to discuss areas of disagreement frankly in order to resolve them. —*v.t.* **7.** to put into the form of a dialogue. —**di′a•logu′er,** *n.*

di′al tone′, *n.* a steady telephone tone indicating that the line is ready for dialing.

di•al•y•sis (dī al′ə sis), *n., pl.* **-ses** (-sēz′). **1.** the separation of crystalloids from colloids in a solution by diffusion through a membrane. **2.** the process, used in treating kidney disease, by which uric acid and urea are removed from circulating blood by means of a dialyzer.

di•a•lyze (dī′ə līz′), *v.,* **-lyzed, -lyz•ing.** —*v.t.* **1.** to subject to dialysis; separate or procure by dialysis. —*v.i.* **2.** to undergo dialysis. —**di′a•lyz′a•ble,** *adj.* —**di′a•lyz′a•bil′i•ty,** *n.* —**di′a•ly•za′tion,** *n.*

di•a•lyz•er (dī′ə lī′zər) also **di•al•y•za•tor** (dī al′i zā′tər), *n.* an apparatus containing a semipermeable membrane for dialysis.

di•a•man•té (dē′ə män tā′), *n.* **1.** glittery ornamentation, as of sequins. **2.** fabric covered with this.

di•am•e•ter (dī am′i tər), *n.* **1. a.** a straight line passing through the center of a circle or sphere and meeting the circumference or surface at each end. **b.** a straight line passing from side to side of any figure or body, through its center. **2.** the length of such a line. **3.** the width of a circular or cylindrical object. —**di•am′e•tral,** *adj.*

di•a•met•ri•cal (dī′ə me′tri kəl) also **di′a•met′ric,** *adj.* **1.** of, pertaining to, or along a diameter. **2.** being in direct opposition: *diametrical opinions.* —**di′a•met′ri•cal•ly,** *adv.*

dia•mond (dī′mənd, dī′ə-), *n.* **1.** a pure or nearly pure, extremely hard form of carbon crystallized in the isometric system. **2.** a piece of this substance. **3.** a transparent, flawless or almost flawless piece of this mineral, esp. when cut and polished, valued as a precious gem. **4.** a piece of jewelry containing a diamond. **5.** a piece of this mineral used in a drill or cutting tool. **6.** an equilateral quadrilateral, esp. as placed with its diagonals vertical and horizontal. **7.** a red rhombus-shaped figure on a playing card. **8.** a card bearing such figures. **9. diamonds,** (*used with a sing. or pl. v.*) the suit so marked. **10. a.** the infield in baseball. **b.** the entire playing field. —*adj.* **11.** made of or set with diamonds. **12.** having the shape of a diamond. **13.** indicating the 60th or 75th event of a series, as a wedding anniversary. —*v.t.* **14.** to adorn with or as if with diamonds. —***Idiom.*** **15. diamond in the rough,** a person or thing of inherent but uncultivated worth.

dia•mond•back (dī′mənd bak′, dī′ə-), *adj.* **1.** bearing diamond-shaped marks on the back. —*n.* **2.** either of two large venomous rattlesnakes of the genus *Crotalus* having diamond-shaped markings on the back, *C. adamanteus* of the southeastern U.S., and *C. atrox* of the western U.S. and Mexico.

dia′mondback ter′rapin, *n.* any turtle of the genus *Malaclemys,* of eastern and southern U.S. tidewaters.

dia′mond lane′, *n.* a highway or street lane for buses and passenger vans marked with a large diamond shape on the pavement.

di•an•thus (dī an′thəs), *n., pl.* **-thus•es.** any plant belonging to the genus *Dianthus,* of the pink family, having narrow leaves and flowers at the ends of stalks, as the carnation or sweet william.

di•a•pa•son (dī′ə pā′zən, -sən), *n.* **1.** a full, rich outpouring of melodious sound. **2.** the compass of a voice or instrument. **3.** a fixed standard of pitch. **4.** a principal stop of a pipe organ extending through the range of the instrument. **5.** TUNING FORK. —**di′a•pa′son•al,** *adj.*

di•a•pe•de•sis (dī′ə pi dē′sis), *n.* the passage of blood cells, esp. white blood cells, through intact blood vessel walls into the tissues. —**di′a•pe•det′ic** (-det′ik), *adj.*

dia•per (dī′pər, dī′ə pər), *n.* **1.** a piece of folded cloth or other absorbent material worn as underpants by a baby not yet toilet-trained. **2.** a fabric woven in a small, repeated, often geometric figure. **3.** the pattern itself. —*v.t.* **4.** to put a diaper on. **5.** to ornament with a diaperlike pattern.

di•aph•a•nous (dī af′ə nəs), *adj.* **1.** very sheer and light; nearly transparent. **2.** insubstantial; amorphous. —**di•aph′a•nous•ly,** *adv.* —**di•aph′a•nous•ness,** *n.*

di•a•pho•re•sis (dī′ə fə rē′sis), *n.* perspiration, esp. when artificially induced. —**di′a•pho•ret′ic** (-ret′ik), *adj., n.*

di•a•phragm (dī′ə fram′), *n.* **1.** a wall of muscle and connective tissue separating two cavities, esp. the partition separating the thoracic cavity from the abdominal cavity in mammals. **2. a.** a porous plate separating two liquids, as in a galvanic cell. **b.** a semipermeable membrane. **3.** a thin disk that vibrates when receiving or producing sound waves, as in a telephone or microphone. **4.** a thin, dome-shaped device usu. of rubber for wearing over the uterine cervix during sexual intercourse to prevent conception. **5.** a plate with a hole in the center or a ring that is placed on the axis of an optical instrument and that controls the amount of light entering the instrument. —*v.t.* **6.** to furnish with a diaphragm. —**di′a•phrag•mat′ic** (-frag mat′ik), *adj.* —**di′a•phrag•mat′i•cal•ly,** *adv.*

di•aph•y•sis (dī af′ə sis), *n., pl.* **-ses** (-sēz′). the shaft of a long bone. —**di′a•phys′i•al, di′a•phys′e•al** (-ə fiz′ē əl), *adj.*

di•a•pir (dī′ə pēr′), *n.* an anticline of rock the upper regions of which have been penetrated by material from below. —**di′a•pir′ic** (-pir′ik), *adj.*

di•a•rist (dī′ə rist), *n.* a person who keeps a diary.

di•ar•rhe•a or **di•ar•rhoe•a** (dī′ə rē′ə), *n.* an intestinal disorder characterized by frequent and fluid fecal evacuations.

di•a•ry (dī′ə rē), *n., pl.* **-ries.** **1.** a daily written record of one's experiences, observations, and feelings. **2.** a book for keeping such a record. **3.** a book for noting daily appointments and the like.

Di•as (dē′əs, -əsh), *n.* **Bartholomeu,** c1450–1500, Portuguese navigator: discovered Cape of Good Hope.

Di•as•po•ra (dī as′pər ə), *n.* **1.** the scattering of the Jews to countries outside of Palestine after the Babylonian captivity. **2.** (*often l.c.*) the body of Jews living in countries outside Palestine or modern Israel. **3.** such countries collectively. **4.** (*l.c.*) any group migration or flight from a country or region; dispersion. **5.** (*l.c.*) any group that has been dispersed outside its traditional homeland. [< Greek *diasporá* a dispersion]

di•a•ste•ma (dī′ə stē′mə), *n., pl.* **-ma•ta** (-mə tə). a gap between two adjacent teeth.

di•as•to•le (dī as′tl ē′, -tl ē), *n.* the normal rhythmical dilatation of the heart during which the chambers are filling with blood. Compare SYSTOLE (def. 1). —**di′as•tol′ic** (-ə stol′ik), *adj.*

di•as•tro•phism (dī as′trə fiz′əm), *n.* the action of the forces that cause the earth's crust to be deformed, producing continents, mountains, etc. —**di′a•stroph′ic** (-ə strof′ik, -strō′fik), *adj.* —**di′a•stroph′i•cal•ly,** *adv.*

di•a•tom (dī′ə təm, -tom′), *n.* any of numerous mostly marine algae of the class Bacillariophyceae (phylum Chrysophyta), each one-celled alga being enclosed in an intricately patterned double shell of silica, one shell fitting over the other like a box lid.

di′atoma′ceous earth′, *n.* a fine siliceous earth composed chiefly of the cell walls of diatoms and used in filtration. Also called **di•at•o•mite** (dī at′ə mīt′).

di•a•tom•ic (dī′ə tom′ik), *adj.* **1.** having two atoms in the molecule. **2.** containing two replaceable atoms or groups; binary. —**di′at•o•mic′i•ty** (-at ə mis′i tē), *n.*

di•a•ton•ic (dī′ə ton′ik), *adj.* of or pertaining to a major or minor musical scale containing five whole tones and two semitones or to music based on such a scale. —**di′a•ton′i•cal•ly,** *adv.*

di•a•tribe (dī′ə trīb′), *n.* a bitter, abusive denunciation or criticism.

di•az•e•pam (dī az′ə pam′), *n.* a benzodiazepine, $C_{16}H_{13}ClN_2O$, used chiefly as a muscle relaxant and to alleviate anxiety.

dib•ble (dib′əl), *n., v.,* **-bled, -bling.** —*n.* **1.** Also, **dib•ber** (dib′ər). a small, hand-held, pointed implement for making holes in soil, as for planting seedlings and bulbs. —*v.t.* **2.** to make holes (in soil) with a dibble. **3.** to plant with a dibble. —**dib′bler,** *n.*

dibs (dibz), *n. Informal.* **1.** money in small amounts. **2.** rights or claims regarding the use or possession of something: *I have dibs on the car when she brings it back.*

dice (dīs), *n.pl., sing.* **die,** *v.,* **diced, dic•ing.** —*n.* **1.** small cubes, marked on each side with one to six spots, usu. used in pairs in games or gambling. **2.** any of various games, esp. gambling games, played by shaking and throwing such cubes. **3.** any small cubes. —*v.t.* **4.** to cut into small cubes. **5.** to decorate with cubelike figures. **6.** to lose by gambling with dice (often fol. by *away*). —*v.i.* **7.** to play at dice. —***Idiom.*** **8. no dice, a.** of no use; ineffective. **b.** (used as a negative response to a request.) —**dic′er,** *n.*

di•ceph•a•lous (dī sef′ə ləs), *adj.* having two heads; two-headed. —**di•ceph′a•lism,** *n.*

dic•ey (dī′sē), *adj.,* **dic•i•er, dic•i•est.** unpredictable; risky; uncertain.

di•chlo•ride (dī klôr′īd, -id, -klōr′-), *n.* a compound in which two atoms of chlorine are combined with another element or group.

di•chon•dra (dī kon′drə), *n., pl.* **-dras.** any creeping vine of the genus *Dichondra,* of the morning glory family, often used as a ground cover.

di•chot•o•my (dī kot′ə mē), *n., pl.* **-mies.** **1.** division into two parts or kinds; subdivision into halves or pairs. **2.** division into two exclusive, opposed, or contradictory groups: *a dichotomy between thought and action.* **3.** a mode of branching by constant forking, as in some stems. **4.** the phase of the moon or of an inferior planet when half of its disk is visible. —**di′cho•tom′ic** (-kə tom′ik), *adj.* —**di′cho•tom′i•cal•ly,** *adv.* —**di•chot′o•mous,** *adj.*

di•chro•mat•ic (dī′krō mat′ik, -krə-), *adj.* **1.** having or showing two colors; dichromic. **2.** (of members of a species) exhibiting two color phases that are unrelated to age or sex. —**di•chro′ma•tism,** *n.*

di•chro•mic (dī krō′mik), *adj.* pertaining to or involving two colors only: *dichromic vision.*

dick•cis•sel (dik sis′əl), *n.* a bunting, *Spiza americana,* of the E and central U.S., having a brownish back streaked with black.

Dick•ens (dik′inz), *n.* **Charles (John Huf•fam)** (huf′əm), (*"Boz"*), 1812–70, English novelist. —**Dick•en•si•an** (di ken′zē ən), *adj.*

dick•er[1] (dik′ər), *v.i.* **1.** to bargain; haggle. —*n.* **2.** a petty bargain. **3.** a barter or swap.

dick•er[2] (dik′ər), *n.* the number or quantity ten, esp. of hides.

dick•ey or **dick•y** (dik′ē), *n., pl.* **dick•eys** or **dick•ies.** **1.** a garment that resembles the front or collar of a shirt and is worn as a separate piece under a jacket, dress, or the like. Compare VEST (def. 2). **2.** a small bird. **3.** a donkey, esp. a male. **4.** an outside seat on a carriage.

Dick•in•son (dik′in sən), *n.* **1. Emily (Elizabeth),** 1830–86, U.S. poet. **2. John,** 1732–1808, U.S. statesman and publicist.

di•cot•y•le•don (dī kot′l ēd′n, dī′kot l-), *n.* any flowering plant of the class Dicotyledones having two embryonic seed leaves and flower parts in fours or fives: includes most broad-leaved flowering trees and plants. —**di•cot′y•le′don•ous,** *adj.*

dic•ta (dik′tə), *n.* a pl. of DICTUM.

dic•tate (*v.* dik′tāt, dik tāt′; *n.* dik′tāt), *v.*, **-tat•ed, -tat•ing,** *n.* —*v.t.* **1.** to say or read aloud for a person to transcribe or for a machine to record. **2.** to prescribe authoritatively; command unconditionally: *to dictate peace terms to the enemy.* —*v.i.* **3.** to say or read aloud for transcription. **4.** to give orders. —*n.* **5.** an authoritative order or command. **6.** a guiding principle: *the dictates of conscience.*

dic′tat•ing machine′ (dik′tā ting), *n.* a machine for recording dictation, as on cassettes or disks, for subsequent transcription.

dic•ta•tion (dik tā′shən), *n.* **1.** the act or manner of dictating for reproduction in writing. **2.** the act or manner of transcribing words uttered by another. **3.** words that are dictated or that are reproduced from dictation. **4.** the playing or singing of music to be notated by a listener, esp. as a technique of training the ear. **5.** music notated from dictation. **6.** the act of commanding arbitrarily. **7.** something commanded. —**dic•ta′tion•al,** *adj.*

dic•ta•tor (dik′tā tər, dik tā′tər), *n.* **1.** a ruler exercising absolute power without hereditary right or the free consent of the people. **2.** a person who authoritatively prescribes conduct, usage, etc. **3.** a person who dictates, as to a secretary.

dic•ta•to•ri•al (dik′tə tôr′ē əl, -tōr′-), *adj.* **1.** of or pertaining to a dictator or dictatorship. **2.** appropriate to or characteristic of a dictator. **3.** inclined to dictate; imperious; overbearing: *a dictatorial attitude.* —**dic′ta•to′ri•al•ly,** *adv.* —**dic′ta•to′ri•al•ness,** *n.*

dic•ta•tor•ship (dik tā′tər ship′, dik′tā-), *n.* **1.** a country, government, or the form of government in which absolute power is exercised by a dictator. **2.** absolute, imperious, or overbearing power or control. **3.** the office or position held by a dictator.

dic•tion (dik′shən), *n.* **1.** style of speaking or writing as dependent upon choice of words. **2.** the accent, inflection, intonation, and speech-sound quality manifested by a speaker or singer; enunciation. —**dic′tion•al,** *adj.* —**dic′tion•al•ly,** *adv.*

dic•tion•ar•y (dik′shə ner′ē), *n., pl.* **-ar•ies. 1.** a book containing a selection of the words of a language, usu. arranged alphabetically, with information about their meanings, pronunciations, etymologies, inflected forms, etc. **2.** a book giving information on particular subjects or on a particular class of words, names, or facts, usu. arranged alphabetically: *a biographical dictionary; a dictionary of physics.* **3.** a list of words used by a word-processing program to check spellings in text.

dic•tum (dik′təm), *n., pl.* **-ta** (-tə), **-tums. 1.** an authoritative pronouncement; judicial assertion. **2.** a saying; maxim.

did (did), *v.* pt. of DO[1].

di•dact (dī′dakt), *n.* a didactic person.

di•dac•tic (dī dak′tik) also **di•dac′ti•cal,** *adj.* **1.** intended for instruction; instructive: *didactic poetry.* **2.** overinclined to lecture others: *a boring, didactic speaker.* **3.** teaching or intending to teach a moral lesson. **4. didactics,** (*used with a sing. v.*) the art or science of teaching. —**di•dac′ti•cal•ly,** *adv.* —**di•dac′ti•cism,** *n.*

did•dle[1] (did′l), *v.t.*, **-dled, -dling.** *Informal.* to cheat; swindle. —**did′dler,** *n.*

did•dle[2] (did′l), *v.*, **-dled, -dling.** —*v.i. Informal.* **1.** to toy; fool: *diddling with the controls.* **2.** to waste time (often fol. by *around*). **3.** to move back and forth with short rapid motions. —*v.t.* **4.** *Dial.* to move back and forth rapidly; jiggle. —**did′dler,** *n.*

did•dly (did′lē), *n. Slang.* the least amount: *not worth diddly.*

Di•de•rot (dē′də rō′), *n.* **Denis,** 1713–84, French encyclopedist.

di•do (dī′dō), *n., pl.* **-dos, -does.** Usu., **didos, didoes. 1.** a mischievous trick; prank; antic. **2.** a bauble or trifle.

Di•do (dī′dō), *n.* a legendary queen of Carthage who killed herself when abandoned by Aeneas.

di•dym•i•um (dī dim′ē əm, di-), *n.* a mixture of neodymium and praseodymium formerly thought to be an element. *Symbol:* Di

Did•y•mus (did′ə məs), *n.* the apostle Thomas. John 11:16; 20:24; 21:2.

die[1] (dī), *v.i.*, **died, dy•ing. 1.** to cease to live; undergo the complete and permanent cessation of vital functions; become dead. **2.** to cease to exist; vanish: *The happy look died on her face.* **3.** to lose force, strength, or active qualities. **4.** to cease to function; stop: *The engine died.* **5.** to pass gradually; fade or subside gradually (usu. fol. by *away, out,* or *down*). **6.** to faint or languish. **7.** to suffer as if fatally: *I'm dying of boredom!* **8.** to pine with desire, love, longing, etc. **9.** to desire keenly: *I'm dying for a cup of coffee.* **10.** *Theol.* to lose spiritual life. **11.** to be no longer subject; become indifferent: *to die to worldly matters.* **12. die away,** (of a sound) to become fainter and then cease altogether. **13. die down,** to become calm or quiet; subside. **14. die off,** to die one after another until the number is greatly reduced. **15. die out, a.** to cease to exist; become extinct. **b.** to die away; fade; subside. —***Idiom.*** **16. die hard,** to give way or cease to exist only slowly or after a bitter struggle: *Childhood beliefs die hard.*

die[2] (dī), *n., pl.* **dies** for 1, 2, 4; **dice** for 3; *v.*, **died, die•ing.** —*n.* **1. a.** any of various devices for cutting or forming material in a press or a stamping or forging machine. **b.** a hollow device of steel, often composed of several pieces to be fitted into a stock, for cutting the threads of bolts or the like. **c.** a steel block or plate with small conical holes through which wire, plastic rods, etc., are drawn. **2.** an engraved stamp for impressing a design upon some softer material, as in coining money. **3.** sing. of DICE. **4.** DADO (def. 1). —*v.t.* **5.** to impress, shape, or cut with a die. —***Idiom.*** **6. the die is cast,** the irrevocable decision has been made; fate has taken charge.

dief•fen•bach•i•a (dē′fən bak′ē ə, -bä′kē ə), *n., pl.* **-bach•i•as.** any tropical American plant of the genus *Dieffenbachia,* of the arum family, often cultivated as houseplants for their decorative foliage.

die′-hard′ or **die′hard′,** *n.* **1.** a person who vigorously resists change. —*adj.* **2.** resistant to change. —**die′-hard′ism,** *n.*

di•el (dī′əl, dē′-), *adj.* of or pertaining to a 24-hour period, esp. a regular daily cycle, as of the physiology or behavior of an organism.

di•e•lec•tric (dī′i lek′trik), *n.* **1.** a nonconductor of electricity; insulator. **2.** a substance in which an electric field can be maintained with a minimum loss of power. —*adj.* **3.** of or pertaining to a dielectric substance. —**di′e•lec′tri•cal•ly,** *adv.*

Dien Bien Phu (dyen′ byen′ fo͞o′), *n.* a town in NW Vietnam: site of defeat of French forces by Vietminh 1954, bringing to an end the French rule of Indochina.

di•en•ceph•a•lon (dī′en sef′ə lon′), *n., pl.* **-lons, -la** (-lə). the posterior section of the forebrain including the thalami and hypothalamus. —**di′en•ce•phal′ic** (-sə fal′ik), *adj.*

Di•eppe (dē ep′), *n.* a seaport in N France, on the English Channel. 26,111.

di•er•e•sis or **di•aer•e•sis** (dī er′ə sis), *n., pl.* **-ses** (-sēz′). **1.** a sign (¨) placed over the second of two adjacent vowels to indicate that it is to be pronounced separately, as in the spellings *naïve* and *coöperate.* **2.** the division made in a line or verse by coincidence of the end of a foot and the end of a word. —**di′e•ret′ic** (-ə ret′ik), *adj.*

die•sel (dē′zəl, -səl), *adj.* **1.** designating a machine or vehicle powered by a diesel engine: *diesel locomotive.* **2.** of or pertaining to a diesel engine: *diesel fuel.* —*n.* **3.** DIESEL ENGINE. **4.** a vehicle powered by a diesel engine. **5.** DIESEL FUEL. [after R. *Diesel* (1858–1913), German automotive engineer]

die′sel-elec′tric, *adj.* having an electric motor powered directly by a diesel-driven generator or by the batteries it charges.

die′sel en′gine, *n.* a compression-ignition engine in which fuel, introduced into air compressed to a temperature of approximately 1000° F (538° C), ignites at a virtually constant pressure.

die′sel fu′el, *n.* a combustible petroleum distillate used as fuel for diesel engines. Also called **die′sel oil′.**

Di•es I•rae (dē′ās ēr′ā), *n.* a Latin hymn on the Day of Judgment, commonly sung in a Requiem Mass. [Latin: day of wrath]

di•et[1] (dī′it), *n.* **1.** food and drink considered in terms of composition and effects on health. **2.** a particular selection of food, esp. for improving a person's physical condition or to prevent or treat disease: *a low-fat diet.* **3.** such a selection or a limitation on the amount a person eats for reducing weight: *to go on a diet.* **4.** the foods habitually eaten by a particular person, animal, or group. **5.** anything habitually provided or partaken of: *a steady diet of game shows and soap operas.* —*v.i.* **6.** to select or limit the food one eats, esp. to lose weight. **7.** to eat according to the requirements of a diet. —*v.t.* **8.** to regulate or limit the food of. **9.** to feed. —*adj.* **10.** suitable for consumption with a weight-reduction diet: *diet soft drinks.* —**di′et•er,** *n.*

di•et[2] (dī′it), *n.* **1.** the legislative body of certain countries, as Japan. **2.** the general assembly of the estates of the former Holy Roman Empire.

di•e•tar•y (dī′i ter′ē), *adj., n., pl.* **-tar•ies.** —*adj.* **1.** of or pertaining to diet. —*n.* **2.** an allowance of food. —**di′e•tar′i•ly,** *adv.*

di′etary law′, *n. Judaism.* any of the laws dealing with permitted foods, food preparation and combinations, and the utensils and dishes coming into contact with food. Compare KASHRUTH.

di•e•tet•ic (dī′i tet′ik), *adj.* Also, **di′e•tet′i•cal. 1.** pertaining to diet or to regulation of the use of food. **2.** prepared or suitable for special diets, esp. those requiring a restricted sugar or caloric intake. —*n.* **3. dietetics,** (*used with a sing. v.*) the science concerned with nutrition and food preparation.

di•eth•yl•stil•bes•trol (dī eth′əl stil bes′trôl, -trol), *n.* a synthetic estrogen, $C_{18}H_{20}O_2$, found to be carcinogenic to offspring when used to support pregnancy and now restricted in use. *Abbr.:* DES

di•e•ti•tian or **di•e•ti•cian** (dī′i tish′ən), *n.* a person who is an expert in nutrition or dietetics.

Dieu et mon droit (dyœ′ ā môn DRWA′), *French.* God and my right: motto on the royal arms of England.

dif•fer (dif′ər), *v.i.* **1.** to be unlike, dissimilar, or distinct in nature or qualities (often fol. by *from*). **2.** to disagree in opinion, belief, etc.; disagree (often fol. by *with* or *from*).

dif•fer•ence (dif′ər əns, dif′rəns), *n., v.*, **-enced, -enc•ing.** —*n.* **1.** the state or relation of being different; dissimilarity. **2.** an instance or point of unlikeness or dissimilarity: *the differences in their behavior.* **3.** a significant change in or effect on a situation: *It made no difference what I said; nothing could persuade him.* **4.** a distinguishing characteristic; distinctive quality, feature, etc. **5.** the degree to which one person or thing differs from another. **6.** the act of distinguishing; discrimination; distinction. **7.** a disagreement in opinion. **8.** a dispute or quarrel. **9.** *Math.* **a.** the amount by which one quantity is greater or less than another. **b.** (of a function f) an expression of the form $f(x + h) - f(x)$. **10.** a differentia. —*v.t.* **11.** to cause or constitute a difference in or between; make different. **12.** to perceive the difference in or between; discriminate.

dif•fer•ent (dif′ər ənt, dif′rənt), *adj.* **1.** not alike in character or quality; differing; dissimilar. **2.** not identical; separate or distinct: *three dif-*

ferent answers. **3.** various; several: *Different people told me the same story.* **4.** not ordinary; unusual. —**dif′fer•ent•ly,** *adv.* —**dif′fer•ent•ness,** *n.*

dif•fer•en•ti•a (dif′ə ren′shē ə, -shə), *n., pl.* **-ti•ae** (-shē ē′). **1.** the character or attribute by which one species is distinguished from all others of the same genus. **2.** the character or basic factor by which one entity is distinguished from another.

dif•fer•en•tial (dif′ə ren′shəl), *adj.* **1.** of or pertaining to difference or diversity. **2.** constituting a difference; distinguishing; distinctive. **3.** exhibiting or depending upon a difference or distinction. **4.** pertaining to or involving the difference of two or more motions, forces, etc. **5.** pertaining to or involving a mathematical derivative or derivatives. —*n.* **6.** a difference or the amount of difference, as in rate, cost, degree, or quality, between things that are comparable. **7.** DIFFERENTIAL GEAR. **8.** *Math.* **a.** a function of two variables that is obtained from a given function, $y = f(x)$, and that expresses the approximate increment in the given function as the derivative of the function times the increment in the independent variable, written as $dy = f'(x)dx$. **b.** any generalization of this function to higher dimensions. **9.** *Physics.* the quantitative difference between two or more forces, motions, etc.: *a pressure differential.* —**dif′fer•en′tial•ly,** *adv.*

dif′feren′tial cal′culus, *n.* the branch of mathematics that deals with differentials and derivatives.

dif′feren′tial gear′, *n.* an epicyclic train of gears designed to permit two or more shafts to rotate at different speeds.

dif•fer•en•ti•ate (dif′ə ren′shē āt′), *v.,* **-at•ed, -at•ing.** —*v.t.* **1.** to form or mark differently from other such things; distinguish. **2.** to perceive the difference in or between. **3.** to make different by modification, as a biological species. **4.** *Math.* to obtain the differential or the derivative of. —*v.i.* **5.** to become unlike or dissimilar. **6.** to make a distinction. **7.** (of cells or tissues) to change from relatively generalized to specialized kinds during development. —**dif′fer•en′ti•a•ble,** *adj.* —**dif′fer•en′ti•a′tion,** *n.* —**dif′fer•en′ti•a′tor,** *n.*

dif•fi•cult (dif′i kult′, -kəlt), *adj.* **1.** requiring special effort, skill, or planning; hard: *a difficult job.* **2.** hard to understand or solve: *a difficult problem.* **3.** hard to deal with or get on with: *a difficult pupil.* **4.** hard to please or satisfy. **5.** hard to persuade or induce; stubborn. **6.** disadvantageous; trying; hampering: *performed under difficult conditions.* **7.** fraught with hardship, esp. financial hardship: *difficult times.*

dif•fi•cul•ty (dif′i kul′tē, -kəl tē), *n., pl.* **-ties.** **1.** the fact or condition of being difficult. **2.** Often, **difficul•ties.** an embarrassing situation, esp. of financial affairs. **3.** a trouble or struggle. **4.** a cause of trouble, struggle, or embarrassment. **5.** a disagreement or dispute. **6.** reluctance; unwillingness. **7.** a demur; objection. **8.** something that is hard to do, understand, or surmount; impediment; obstacle.

dif•fi•dent (dif′i dənt), *adj.* **1.** lacking confidence in one's own ability, worth, or fitness; timid; shy. **2.** hesitant or tentative in manner; reserved. —**dif′fi•dence,** *n.* —**dif′fi•dent•ly,** *adv.*

dif•fract (di frakt′), *v.t.* to break up or bend by diffraction. —**dif•frac′tive,** *adj.*

dif•frac•tion (di frak′shən), *n.* a modulation of waves in response to an obstacle, as an object, slit, or grating, in the path of propagation, giving rise in light waves to a banded pattern or to a spectrum.

diffrac′tion grat′ing, *n.* a reflective surface etched with fine lines that is used to produce optical spectra by diffraction.

dif•fuse (*v.* di fyo͞oz′; *adj.* -fyo͞os′), *v.,* **-fused, -fusing,** *adj.* —*v.t.* **1.** to pour out and spread: *oil diffused over a surface.* **2.** to spread or scatter widely or thinly; disseminate. **3.** *Physics.* to spread or scatter by diffusion. —*v.i.* **4.** to spread. **5.** *Physics.* to intermingle by diffusion. —*adj.* **6.** characterized by great length or discursiveness in speech or writing; wordy. **7.** widely spread or scattered; dispersed. **8.** (of reflected light) scattered, as from a rough surface. —**dif•fuse′ly** (-fyo͞os′lē), *adv.* —**dif•fuse′ness,** *n.* —**dif•fus′i•ble** (-fyo͞o′zə bəl), *adj.* —**dif•fus′i•bil′i•ty,** *n.*

dif•fu•sion (di fyo͞o′zhən), *n.* **1.** the act of diffusing or the state of being diffused. **2.** prolixity of speech or writing. **3. a.** an intermingling of particles resulting from random thermal agitation, as in the dispersion of a vapor in air. **b.** a reflection or refraction of light or other radiation from an irregular surface or an erratic dispersion through a surface. **4.** a soft-focus effect in a photograph or film, achieved by placing a gelatin or silk plate in front of a light or lens or by the use of filters. **5.** the transmission of elements or features of one culture to another by nonviolent contact.

dif•fu•sion•ism (di fyo͞o′zhə niz′əm), *n.* any theory that attributes similarities between human culture traits to diffusion from one dominant culture or culture area. —**dif•fu′sion•ist,** *n., adj.*

dig[1] (dig), *v.,* **dug, dig•ging,** *n.* —*v.i.* **1.** to break up, turn over, or remove earth, sand, etc., as with a shovel, spade, bulldozer, or claw; make an excavation. **2.** to make one's way or work by or as if by removing or turning over material: *to dig through the files.* —*v.t.* **3.** to break up, turn over, or loosen (earth, sand, etc.), as with a shovel (often fol. by *up*). **4.** to form or excavate (a hole, tunnel, etc.) by removing material. **5.** to unearth, obtain, or remove by digging (often fol. by *up* or *out*). **6.** to find or discover by effort or search. **7.** to poke, thrust, or force: *He dug his heels into the ground.* **8. dig in, a.** to maintain one's opinion or position. **b.** *Informal.* to start eating. **9. dig into,** to involve oneself with vigorously. **10. dig out, a.** to hollow out by digging. **b.** to find by searching. **11. dig up, a.** to discover in the course of digging. **b.** to find or bring to light; locate. —*n.* **12.** a thrust; poke: *a dig in the ribs.* **13.** a cutting, sarcastic remark. **14.** an archaeological site undergoing excavation. **15. digs,** *Informal.* living quarters; lodgings.

dig[2] (dig), *v.,* **dug, dig•ging.** *Slang.* —*v.t.* **1.** to understand: *Can you dig what I'm saying?* **2.** to take notice of: *Dig those shoes he's wearing.* **3.** to like or enjoy. —*v.i.* **4.** to understand.

dig•a•my (dig′ə mē), *n., pl.* **-mies.** a second marriage after the death or divorce of the first spouse. Compare MONOGAMY (def. 3). —**dig′a•mous,** *adj.*

di•gest (*v.* di jest′, dī-; *n.* dī′jest), *v.t.* **1.** to convert (food) in the alimentary canal into a form that can be assimilated by the body. **2.** to promote the digestion of (food). **3.** to obtain ideas or meaning from; assimilate mentally: *to digest an article on nuclear energy.* **4.** to think over; ponder. **5.** to bear with patience; endure. **6.** to arrange in convenient or methodical order; reduce to a system; classify. **7.** to condense, abridge, or summarize. **8.** to soften or disintegrate (a substance), as by moisture, heat, or chemical action. —*v.i.* **9.** to digest food. **10.** to undergo digestion. —*n.* **11.** a collection or compendium, as of literary or scientific matter, esp. when classified or condensed. **12.** a systematic abstract of some body of law. —**di•gest′ed•ly,** *adv.* —**di•gest′ed•ness,** *n.*

di•ges•tion (di jes′chən, dī-), *n.* **1.** the process in the alimentary canal by which food is broken up physically, as by the action of the teeth, and chemically, as by the action of enzymes, and converted into a substance suitable for absorption and assimilation into the body. **2.** the function or power of digesting food. **3.** the act of digesting or the state of being digested. —**di•ges′tion•al,** *adj.*

di•ges•tive (di jes′tiv, dī-), *adj.* **1.** serving for or pertaining to digestion; having the function of digesting food: *the digestive tract.* **2.** promoting digestion. —*n.* **3.** a substance promoting digestion. —**di•ges′tive•ly,** *adv.*

diges′tive sys′tem, *n.* the system by which ingested food is acted upon by physical and chemical means to provide the body with absorbable nutrients and to excrete waste products: in mammals the system includes the alimentary canal extending from the mouth to the anus and the hormones and enzymes assisting in digestion.

dig•ger (dig′ər), *n.* **1.** a person or an animal that digs. **2.** a tool, part of a machine, etc., for digging. **3.** (*cap.*) Also called **Dig′ger In′dian.** a member of any of several Indian peoples of western North America, esp. of a tribe that dug roots for food. **4.** an Australian or New Zealand soldier of World War I. **5.** (*cap.*) *Eng. Hist.* a member of a group that advocated the abolition of private property and began in 1649 to cultivate certain common lands. **6.** *Slang.* a person hired by a scalper to buy tickets to a show or performance for resale by the scalper at inflated prices.

dig′ger wasp′, *n.* any of numerous solitary wasps of the family Sphecidae that excavate nests, as in soil, and provision them with prey paralyzed by stinging.

dig•it (dij′it), *n.* **1.** any of the Arabic numerals of 1 through 9 and 0. **2.** any symbol of other number systems, as 0 or 1 in the binary. **3.** a finger or toe. **4.** the breadth of a finger used as a unit of linear measure, usu. equal to ¾ of an inch (2 cm).

dig•it•al (dij′i tl), *adj.* **1.** of, pertaining to, or resembling a digit or finger. **2.** performed or manipulated with a finger: *a digital switch.* **3.** having digits or digitlike parts. **4.** of, pertaining to, or using data in the form of numerical digits: *a digital recording.* **5.** displaying a readout in numerical digits rather than by a pointer or hands on a dial: *a digital clock.* **6.** *Computers.* involving or using numerical digits expressed in a scale of notation to represent discretely all variables occurring in a problem. **7.** of, pertaining to, or using numerical calculations. —*n.* **8.** one of the keys or finger levers of keyboard instruments. **9.** a digital device, as a clock or watch. —**dig′it•al•ly,** *adv.*

dig′ital au′diotape, *n.* magnetic tape on which sound is digitally recorded with high fidelity for playback.

dig′ital comput′er, *n.* a computer that processes information in digital form. Compare ANALOG COMPUTER.

dig•i•tal•is (dij′i tal′is, -tā′lis), *n.* **1.** any plant of the genus *Digitalis,* of the figwort family, esp. the foxglove, *D. purpurea.* **2.** the dried leaves of the foxglove used as a heart stimulant.

digiti-, a combining form meaning "finger": *digitinervate.*

dig•i•tize (dij′i tīz′) also **digitalize,** *v.t.,* **-tized, -tiz•ing.** to convert (data) to digital form. —**dig′i•ti•za′tion,** *n.* —**dig′i•tiz′er,** *n.*

di•glos•si•a (dī glos′ē ə, -glô′sē ə), *n.* the use within a society of sharply divergent formal and informal varieties of a language for different social contexts or for performing different functions. —**di•glos′sic** (-glos′ik), *adj.*

di•glot (dī′glot), *adj.* **1.** bilingual. —*n.* **2.** a bilingual book or edition. —**di•glot′tic,** *adj.*

dig•ni•fied (dig′nə fīd′), *adj.* characterized by dignity of aspect or manner; stately; decorous. —**dig′ni•fied′ly** (-fīd′lē, -fī′id-), *adv.* —**dig′ni•fied′ness,** *n.*

dig•ni•fy (dig′nə fī′), *v.t.,* **-fied, -fy•ing.** **1.** to confer honor or dignity upon; honor. **2.** to give a grand title or name to; confer unmerited distinction upon: *to dignify pedantry by calling it scholarship.*

dig•ni•tar•y (dig′ni ter′ē), *n., pl.* **-tar•ies.** a person who holds a high rank or office, as in a government or church. —**dig′ni•tar′i•al** (-târ′ē əl), *adj.*

dig•ni•ty (dig′ni tē), *n., pl.* **-ties.** **1.** bearing, conduct, or manner indicative of self-respect, formality, or gravity. **2.** nobility or elevation of

D

character; worthiness. **3.** elevated rank, office, station, etc. **4.** relative standing; rank. **5.** a sign or token of respect: *a question unworthy of the dignity of a reply.*

di·gram (dī′gram), *n.* a sequence of two adjacent letters or other symbols.

di·graph (dī′graf, -gräf), *n.* a pair of letters representing a single speech sound, as *ea* in *meat* or *th* in *path.* —**di·graph′ic** (-graf′ik), *adj.* —**di·graph′i·cal·ly,** *adv.*

di·gress (di gres′, dī-), *v.i.* to wander away from the main topic or argument in speaking or writing. —**di·gress′er,** *n.* —**di·gress′ing·ly,** *adv.* —**digressive,** *adj.*

di·gres·sion (di gresh′ən, dī-), *n.* **1.** the act of digressing. **2.** a passage or section that deviates from the central theme in speech or writing. —**di·gres′sion·al, di·gres′sion·ar′y,** *adj.*

di·he·dral (dī hē′drəl), *adj.* **1.** having or formed by two planes. **2.** of or pertaining to a dihedron. —*n.* **3.** DIHEDRON. **4.** the angle at which the wings of an airplane are vertically inclined.

di·he·dron (dī hē′drən), *n.* a figure formed by two intersecting planes.

dike or **dyke** (dīk), *n., v.,* **diked, dik·ing.** —*n.* **1.** an embankment for controlling or holding back the waters of the sea or a river. **2.** DITCH. **3.** a bank of earth formed of material being excavated. **4.** CAUSEWAY. **5.** an obstacle; barrier. **6. a.** a long, narrow, cross-cutting mass of igneous rock intruded into a fissure in older rock. **b.** a similar mass of rock composed of other kinds of material, as sandstone. —*v.t.* **7.** to furnish or drain with a dike. **8.** to enclose, restrain, or protect by a dike. —**dik′er,** *n.*

dik·tat (dik tät′), *n.* a harsh settlement or decree imposed unilaterally, esp. on a defeated nation.

di·lap·i·date (di lap′i dāt′), *v.,* **-dat·ed, -dat·ing.** —*v.t.* **1.** to cause or allow to fall into a state of disrepair, as by misuse or neglect. —*v.i.* **2.** to decay. —**di·lap′i·da′tion,** *n.*

di·lap·i·dat·ed (di lap′i dā′tid), *adj.* fallen into partial ruin or decay, as from age, misuse, wear, or neglect.

di·lat·ant (di lā′nt, dī-), *adj.* **1.** dilating; expanding. **2.** exhibiting an increase in volume when changed in shape because of wider spacing between particles. **3.** (of rock) exhibiting an increase in volume because of recrystallization. —**di·lat′an·cy,** *n.*

dil·a·ta·tion (dil′ə tā′shən, dī′lə-) also **dilation.** **1.** a dilated formation or part. **2.** an abnormal enlargement of an organ, aperture, or canal of the body. **3. a.** an enlargement made in a body aperture or canal for surgical or medical treatment. **b.** a restoration to normal condition of an abnormally small body opening or passageway. —**dil′a·ta′tion·al,** *adj.*

di·late (dī lāt′, di-, dī′lāt), *v.,* **-lat·ed, -lat·ing.** —*v.t.* **1.** to make wider or larger; cause to expand: *to dilate the pupils of the eyes.* —*v.i.* **2.** to spread out; expand. **3.** to speak or write at length; expatiate (often fol. by *on* or *upon*). —**di·lat′a·ble,** *adj.* —**di·lat′a·bil′i·ty,** *n.* —**di·la′tive,** *adj.*

dil·a·to·ry (dil′ə tôr′ē, -tōr′ē), *adj.* **1.** tending to delay or procrastinate. **2.** intended to cause delay or gain time: *a dilatory strategy.* —**dil′a·to′ri·ly,** *adv.* —**dil′a·to′ri·ness,** *n.*

di·lem·ma (di lem′ə), *n., pl.* **-mas.** **1.** a situation requiring a choice between equally undesirable alternatives. **2.** any perplexing situation or problem. **3.** a form of syllogism in which the major premise is formed of two or more conditional propositions and the minor premise is a disjunctive proposition, as "If A, then B; if C then D. Either A or C. Therefore, either B or D." —**dil·em·mat′ic** (dil′ə mat′ik), *adj.* —**dil′em·mat′i·cal·ly,** *adv.*

dil·et·tante (dil′i tänt′, dil′i tänt′, -tän′tā, -tan′tē), *n., pl.* **-tantes, -tan·ti** (-tän′tē), *adj.* —*n.* **1.** a person who takes up an art, activity, or subject merely for amusement, esp. in a desultory or superficial way; dabbler. **2.** a lover of an art or science. —*adj.* **3.** of or characteristic of dilettantes. —**dil′et·tan′tish, dil′et·tan′te·ish,** *adj.*

dil·i·gence[1] (dil′i jəns), *n.* **1.** constant and earnest effort to accomplish what is undertaken. **2.** the degree of care and caution expected of a person, esp. as party to an agreement.

dil·i·gence[2] (dil′i jəns; *Fr.* dē lē zhäns′), *n., pl.* **-gen·ces** (-jən siz; *Fr.* -zhäns′). a public stagecoach, esp. as formerly used in France.

dil·i·gent (dil′i jənt), *adj.* **1.** constant and earnest in effort and application; attentive and persistent in doing something: *a diligent student.* **2.** done or pursued with persevering attention; painstaking: *a diligent search.* —**dil′i·gent·ly,** *adv.*

dill (dil), *n.* **1.** any plant of the genus *Anethum,* of the parsley family, esp. *A. graveolens,* having aromatic seeds and finely divided leaves used as a flavoring. **2.** the seeds or leaves. **3.** DILL PICKLE. —**dilled,** *adj.*

dill′ pick′le, *n.* a cucumber pickle flavored with dill.

dil·ly (dil′ē), *n., pl.* **-lies.** *Informal.* something or someone regarded as remarkable or unusual.

dil·ly·dal·ly (dil′ē dal′ē, -dal′-), *v.i.,* **-lied, -ly·ing.** to waste time, esp. by indecision.

di·lute (di lōōt′, dī-; *adj. also* dī′lōōt), *v.,* **-lut·ed, -lut·ing.** —*v.t.* **1.** to make (a liquid) thinner or weaker by the addition of water or the like. **2.** to make fainter, as a color. **3.** to reduce the strength, force, or efficiency of by admixture. —*v.i.* **4.** to become diluted. —*adj.* **5.** reduced in strength, as a chemical by admixture; weak. —**di·lut′er, di·lu′tor,** *n.* —**di·lu′tive,** *adj.*

di·lu·tion (di lōō′shən, dī-), *n.* **1.** the act of diluting or the state of being diluted. **2.** something diluted.

dim (dim), *adj.,* **dim·mer, dim·mest,** *v.,* **dimmed, dim·ming.** —*adj.* **1.** not bright; obscure from lack of light or weakness of emitted light: *a dim room; a dim light.* **2.** not seen or perceived clearly, distinctly, or in detail; indistinct; faint: *a dim outline.* **3.** not clear to the mind; vague: *a dim idea.* **4.** not brilliant; dull in luster: *a dim color.* **5.** not seeing clearly: *eyes dim with tears.* **6.** not likely to happen, succeed, or be favorable: *a dim chance of winning.* **7.** slow to understand; stupid; dimwitted. —*v.t.* **8.** to make dim or dimmer. **9.** to switch (the headlights of a vehicle) from the high to the low beam. —*v.i.* **10.** to become or grow dim or dimmer. —*Idiom.* **11. take a dim view of,** to regard with disapproval or skepticism. —**dim′ly,** *adv.* —**dim′ma·ble,** *adj.* —**dim′ness,** *n.*

Di·Mag·gi·o (də mä′jē ō′, -maj′ē ō′), *n.* **Joseph Paul** (*Joe*), born 1914, U.S. baseball player.

dime (dīm), *n.* **1.** a coin of the U.S. and Canada worth 10 cents. **2.** *Slang.* **a.** ten dollars. **b.** a 10-year prison sentence. —*Idiom.* **3. a dime a dozen,** abundant and thus of little value.

dime′ nov′el, *n.* a cheap melodramatic or sensational novel, usu. in paperback, esp. of the period c1850 to c1920.

di·men·sion (di men′shən, dī-), *n.* **1. a.** a property of space; extension in a given direction: *A straight line has one dimension, a parallelogram has two dimensions, and a parallelepiped has three dimensions.* **b.** the generalization of this property to spaces with curvilinear extension, as the surface of a sphere. **c.** a magnitude that serves to define the location of an element within a given set, as of a point on a line or an event in space-time. **2.** Usu., **dimensions. a.** measurement in length, width, and thickness. **b.** scope; importance: *the dimensions of a problem.* **3.** magnitude; size: *Matter has dimension.* **4.** an aspect or factor; side: *added a new dimension to their relationship.* **5. dimensions,** bodily measurements. —*v.t.* **6.** to shape or fashion to the desired dimensions. **7.** to indicate the dimensions on (a diagram or drawing). —**di·men′sion·al,** *adj.* —**di·men′sion·al′i·ty,** *n.* —**di·men′sion·al·ly,** *adv.* —**di·men′sion·less,** *adj.*

dim·e·ter (dim′i tər), *n.* a verse or line of two measures or feet.

di·meth·yl (dī meth′əl), *n.* ETHANE.

di·met·ro·don (dī me′trə don′), *n.* an extinct carnivorous mammal-like reptile of the North American Permian genus *Dimetrodon,* with high spines along the back.

di·min·ish (di min′ish), *v.t.* **1.** to make or cause to seem smaller, less, or less important; lessen; reduce. **2.** to reduce (a musical interval) by a half step less than a perfect or minor interval. **3.** to detract from the authority, honor, stature, or reputation of; disparage. **4.** to give a tapering form: *a diminished column.* —*v.i.* **5.** to lessen; decrease. —**di·min′ish·a·ble,** *adj.* —**di·min′ish·ment,** *n.*

dimin′ishing returns′, *n.* **1.** any rate of profit, production, benefits, etc., that beyond a certain point fails to increase proportionately with added investment, effort, or skill. **2.** the fact, often stated as a law or principle, that when any factor of production, as labor, is increased while other factors, as capital and land, are held constant, the output per unit of the variable factor will eventually diminish.

di·min·u·en·do (di min′yōō en′dō), *adj., adv., n., pl.* **-does.** *Music.* —*adj., adv.* **1.** gradually reducing in force or loudness; decrescendo (opposed to *crescendo*). —*n.* **2.** a gradual reduction of force or loudness. *Symbol:* >

dim·i·nu·tion (dim′ə nōō′shən, -nyōō′-), *n.* the act, fact, or process of diminishing; lessening; reduction.

di·min·u·tive (di min′yə tiv), *adj.* **1.** much smaller than the average or usual; tiny. **2.** pertaining to or productive of a form denoting smallness, familiarity, affection, or triviality, as the suffix *-let* in *droplet* from *drop.* —*n.* **3.** a diminutive element or formation. —**di·min′u·tive·ly,** *adv.*

di·mor·phism (dī môr′fiz əm), *n.* **1.** the occurrence of two forms distinct in structure, coloration, etc., among animals of the same species. **2.** the occurrence of two different forms of flowers, leaves, etc., on the same plant or on different plants of the same species. **3.** the property of some substances of crystallizing in two chemically identical but crystallographically distinct forms.

dim′-out′ or **dim′out′,** *n.* a reduction or concealment of night lighting, esp. in wartime to make the source less visible to an enemy.

dim·ple (dim′pəl), *n., v.,* **-pled, -pling.** —*n.* **1.** a small natural hollow, permanent or transient, on the surface of the human body, esp. one formed in the cheek in smiling. —*v.t.* **2.** to mark with or as if with dimples; produce dimples in: *A smile dimpled her face.* **3. a.** to dent (a metal sheet) so as to permit use of bolts or rivets with countersunk heads. **b.** to mark (a metal object) with a drill point as a guide for further drilling. —*v.i.* **4.** to form or show dimples. —**dim′ply,** *adj.*

dim sum (dim′ sum′), *n.* assorted small items of savory food, including small usu. steamed dumplings filled with meat, seafood, etc., served as a light Chinese meal.

dim·wit (dim′wit′), *n. Slang.* a stupid person. —**dim′wit′ted,** *adj.* —**dim′wit′ted·ly,** *adv.* —**dim′wit′ted·ness,** *n.*

din[1] (din), *n., v.,* **dinned, din·ning.** —*n.* **1.** a loud, confused noise; a continued tumultuous sound. —*v.t.* **2.** to assail with a din. **3.** to utter with clamor or persistent repetition. —*v.i.* **4.** to make a din.

din[2] (din), *n.* (*used with a pl. v.*) *Islam.* religion, esp. the religious observances of a Muslim. Compare IBADA, PILLARS OF ISLAM.

Di·nah (dī′nə), *n.* the daughter of Jacob and Leah. Gen. 30:21.

di·nar (di när′), *n.* **1.** the basic monetary unit of Algeria; of Bahrain, Iraq, Jordan, and Kuwait; of Libya; of Tunisia; and of Yugoslavia. **2.** a monetary unit of Iran.

dine (dīn), *v.,* **dined, din·ing,** —*v.i.* **1.** to eat the principal meal of the day; have dinner. **2.** to eat any meal. —*v.t.* **3.** to entertain at or provide with dinner. **4. dine out,** to eat a meal, esp. dinner, away from home.

din·er (dī′nər), *n.* **1.** a person who dines. **2.** a restaurant shaped like a dining car. **3.** an inexpensive restaurant.

di·nette (dī net′), *n.* **1.** a small space or alcove, often in or near the kitchen, serving as an informal dining area. Also called **dinette′ set′.** a table and set of chairs for such a space.

ding[1] (ding), *v.t.* **1.** to cause to make a ringing sound. **2.** to speak about insistently. —*v.i.* **3.** to make a ringing sound. **4.** to talk insistently. —*n.* **5.** a ringing sound.

ding[2] (ding), *Informal.* —*v.t.* **1.** to cause surface damage to: *to ding a fender.* **2.** to strike with force; hit. **3.** to reject or veto; blackball. **4.** to rebuke; reprimand. —*n.* **5.** a dent or scratch; nick. **6.** a blow or injury. **7.** a rejection.

ding·bat (ding′bat′), *n.* **1.** *Informal.* an eccentric or silly person. **2.** an ornamental piece of type for borders, separators, decorations, etc. **3.** an object, as a brick, serving as a missile.

ding-dong (ding′dông′, -dong′), *n.* **1.** the sound of a bell. **2.** any similar sound of repeated strokes. —*adj.* **3.** characterized by or resembling the sound of a bell. **4.** *Informal.* marked by rapid alternation of retaliatory action: *a ding-dong struggle.*

din·ghy (ding′gē), *n., pl.* **-ghies.** any small boat designed as a tender or lifeboat, either rowed, sailed, or driven by a motor. [< Hindi *diṅgī,* dim. of *diṅgā* boat]

din·go (ding′gō), *n., pl.* **-goes.** an Australian wild dog, *Canis dingo,* having a tawny coat.

ding·us (ding′əs), *n., pl.* **-us·es.** *Informal.* a gadget, device, or object whose name is unknown or forgotten.

din·gy (din′jē), *adj.,* **-gi·er, -gi·est. 1.** of a dark, dull, or dirty color or aspect; lacking brightness or freshness. **2.** shabby; dismal. —**din′gi·ly,** *adv.* —**din′gi·ness,** *n.*

dink (dingk), *n.* a softly hit ball in tennis or volleyball that falls just over the net.

dink·y (ding′kē), *adj.,* **-i·er, -i·est.** *Informal.* small and unimpressive: *a dinky old hotel.*

din·ner (din′ər), *n.* **1.** the main meal of the day, eaten in the evening or at midday. **2.** a formal meal in honor of some person or occasion. **3.** TABLE D'HÔTE. —**din′ner·less,** *adj.*

din′ner jack′et, *n.* TUXEDO (def. 1).

din′ner the′ater, *n.* **1.** a restaurant in which a stage production is performed usu. after dinner. **2.** stage productions performed in dinner theaters.

dino-, a combining form meaning "terrifying, frightful": *dinothere.*

di·no·saur (dī′nə sôr′), *n.* **1.** any herbivorous or carnivorous reptile of the extinct orders Saurischia and Ornithischia, of the Mesozoic Era: some were the largest known land animals. **2.** something that is unwieldy in size, anachronistically outmoded, or unable to adapt to change. [< New Latin < Greek *deino–* terrible + *saûros* lizard] —**di′no·sau′ri·an,** *adj.*

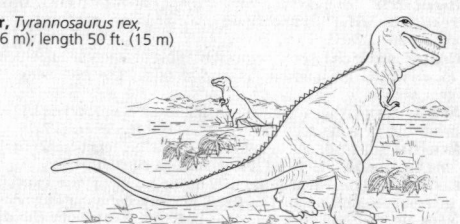

dinosaur, *Tyrannosaurus rex,*
height 20 ft. (6 m); length 50 ft. (15 m)

di·no·there (dī′nə thēr′), *n.* any extinct elephantlike mammal of the Late Tertiary genus *Deinotherium,* having large, inward-curving, lower tusks.

dint (dint), *n.* **1.** force; power: *to achieve success by dint of hard work.* **2.** a dent. —*v.t.* **3.** to make a dent in. **4.** to impress or drive in with force. —**dint′less,** *adj.*

di·o·cese (dī′ə sis, -sēz′, -sēs′), *n.* a district under the jurisdiction of a bishop. —**di·oc′e·san,** *adj.*

Di·o·cle·tian (dī′ə klē′shən), *n.* (*Gaius Aurelius Valerius Diocletianus*), A.D. 245–316, emperor of Rome 284–305.

di·ode (dī′ōd), *n.* a device, as a two-element electron tube or a semiconductor, through which current can pass freely in only one direction.

Di·og·e·nes (dī oj′ə nēz′), *n.* 412?–323 B.C., Greek Cynic philosopher. —**Di′o·gen′ic** (-ə jen′ik), **Di·og′e·ne′an,** *adj.*

Di·o·ny·si·a (dī′ə nish′ē ə, -nis′-), *n.pl.* the orgiastic and dramatic festivals held periodically in honor of Dionysus from which Greek comedy and tragedy developed.

Di·o·ny·sian (dī′ə nish′ən, -nis′ē ən, -nī′sē-) also **Di·o·nys·i·ac** (-nis′ē ak′, -nī′sē-), *adj.* **1.** pertaining to Dionysus or his worship; Bacchic. **2.** recklessly uninhibited; frenzied; orgiastic.

Di·o·ny·si·us (dī′ə nish′ē əs, -nis′-, -nish′əs, -nī′sē əs), *n.* **1.** ("*the Elder*"), 431?–367 B.C., Greek soldier: tyrant of Syracuse 405–367. **2.** **Saint,** died A.D. 268, pope 259–268.

Di·o·ny·sus or **Di·o·ny·sos** (dī′ə nī′səs), *n.* an ancient Greek and Roman fertility god, associated esp. with the vine and wine.

di·op·ter (dī op′tər), *n.* a unit of measure of the refractive power of a lens, having the dimension of the reciprocal of length and a unit equal to the reciprocal of one meter. *Abbr.:* D

di·op·tric (dī op′trik), *adj.* of or pertaining to refraction or refracted light. Also, **di·op′tri·cal.** —**di·op′tri·cal·ly,** *adv.*

di·o·ram·a (dī′ə ram′ə, -rä′mə), *n., pl.* **-ram·as. 1.** a scene in miniature reproduced in three dimensions by placing figures before a painted background. **2.** a life-size display representing a scene from nature, a historical event, or the like, using stuffed wildlife, wax figures, etc., in front of a painted or photographed background. **3.** a partly translucent picture viewed through an aperture. **4.** a building or room, often circular, for exhibiting such a scene or picture. —**di′o·ram′ic,** *adj.*

di·o·rite (dī′ə rīt′), *n.* a granular igneous rock consisting essentially of plagioclase feldspar and hornblende.

Di·os·cu·ri (dī′ə skyŏŏr′ī), *n.pl.* CASTOR AND POLLUX.

di·ox·ide (dī ok′sīd, -sid), *n.* an oxide containing two atoms of oxygen, each bonded directly to an atom of a second element.

di·ox·in (dī ok′sin), *n.* a general name for a family of chlorinated hydrocarbons, $C_{12}H_4Cl_4O_2$, esp. the isomer TCDD, a toxic by-product of pesticide and paper manufacture. Compare AGENT ORANGE.

dip (dip), *v.,* **dipped, dip·ping,** —*v.t.* **1.** to plunge temporarily into a liquid, so as to moisten, dye, or take up some of the liquid. **2.** to take up by bailing or ladling: *to dip water out of a boat.* **3.** to lower and raise: *to dip a flag in salutation.* **4.** to immerse in a solution containing an insecticide or pesticide. **5.** to make (a candle) by repeatedly plunging a wick into melted tallow or wax. —*v.i.* **6.** to plunge into a liquid and emerge quickly. **7.** to reach down into a liquid or container so as to remove something (usu. fol. by *into*). **8.** to withdraw something in small amounts: *to dip into one's savings.* **9.** to sink: *The sun dipped below the horizon.* **10.** to incline downward: *The road dips into a valley.* **11.** to decrease slightly or temporarily: *Stock-market prices often dip on Fridays.* **12.** to engage slightly in a subject: *to dip into astronomy.* **13.** to read here and there in a book or author's work (often fol. by *into*). —*n.* **14.** the act of dipping. **15.** something taken up by dipping. **16.** a scoop of ice cream. **17.** a substance into which something is dipped. **18.** a creamy mixture of seasoned foods for scooping with a cracker, potato chip, etc., served as an appetizer. **19.** a solution containing an insecticide or pesticide for use in dipping animals. **20.** a momentary lowering. **21.** a moderate or temporary decrease. **22.** a downward inclination, slope, or course. **23.** the amount of this. **24.** a hollow or depression in the land. **25.** a brief swim. **26.** the downward inclination of a mineral vein or stratum with reference to the horizontal. **27.** the angle that a freely rotating magnetic needle makes with the plane of the horizon. **28.** a short downward plunge, as of an airplane. —**dip′pa·ble,** *adj.*

di·phen·yl (dī fen′l, -fēn′l), *n.* BIPHENYL.

diph·the·ri·a (dif thēr′ē ə, dip-), *n.* a febrile infectious disease caused by the bacillus *Corynebacterium diphtheriae,* and characterized by the formation of a false membrane in the air passages, esp. the throat. —**diph·the′ri·al, diph·the·rit′ic** (-tha rit′ik), *adj.*

diph·the·roid (dif′thə roid′, dip′-), *adj.* **1.** resembling diphtheria, esp. in the formation of a false membrane in the throat. —*n.* **2.** any bacterium, esp. of the genus *Corynebacterium,* that resembles the diphtheria bacillus but does not produce diphtheria toxin.

diph·thong (dif′thông, -thong, dip′-), *n.* **1.** an unsegmentable, gliding speech sound varying continuously in phonetic quality but considered to be a single sound or phoneme, as the (oi) sound of *toy* or *boil.* —*v.t., v.i.* **2.** to diphthongize. —**diph·thon′gal,** *adj.*

diph·thong·ize (dif′thông īz′, -gīz′, -thong-, dip′-), *v.,* **-ized, -iz·ing.** —*v.t.* **1.** to change into or pronounce as a diphthong. —*v.i.* **2.** to become a diphthong. —**diph·thong·i·za′tion,** *n.*

diph·y·o·dont (dif′ē ə dont′), *adj.* having two successive sets of teeth, as most mammals.

diplo-, a combining form meaning "double," "in pairs": *diplococcus.*

di·plod·o·cus (di plod′ə kəs), *n., pl.* **-cus·es.** any North American sauropod dinosaur of the genus *Diplodocus:* it grew to a length of about 87 ft. (26.5 m).

dip·loid (dip′loid), *adj.* **1.** having two similar complements of chromosomes. —*n.* **2.** an organism or cell having double the basic haploid number of chromosomes. —**dip·loi′dic,** *adj.*

di·plo·ma (di plō′mə), *n., pl.* **-mas,** *Lat.* **-ma·ta** (-mə tə). **1.** a document given by an educational institution conferring a degree or certifying the successful completion of a course of study. **2.** a document conferring some honor or privilege. **3.** a public document, esp. one of historical interest.

di·plo·ma·cy (di plō′mə sē), *n.* **1.** the conduct by government officials of negotiations and other relations between nations. **2.** the art or science of conducting such negotiations. **3.** skill in managing negotiations, handling people, etc., so that there is little or no ill will; tact.

diplo′ma mill′, *n.* **1.** an unaccredited institution of higher learning that grants degrees without requiring proper qualifications. **2.** a college or university placing few academic demands on students.

D

dip·lo·mat (dip′lə mat′), *n.* **1.** a person appointed by a national government to conduct official negotiations and maintain political, economic, and social relations with other countries. **2.** a tactful person skilled in managing delicate situations.

dip·lo·mate (dip′lə māt′), *n.* a person, as a doctor or engineer, who has a diploma and has been certified as a specialist by a board in the appropriate field.

dip·lo·mat·ic (dip′lə mat′ik), *adj.* **1.** of, pertaining to, or engaged in diplomacy. **2.** skilled in dealing with sensitive matters or people; tactful. —**dip′lo·mat′i·cal·ly,** *adv.*

diplomat′ic corps′, *n.* the entire body of diplomats accredited to and resident at a court or capital.

diplomat′ic immu′nity, *n.* exemption from taxation, searches, arrest, etc., enjoyed by diplomatic officials and their dependents under international law.

dip·lo·pi·a (di plō′pē ə), *n.* a pathological condition of vision in which a single object appears double. Also called **double vision.** —**di·plop′ic** (-plop′ik, -plō′pik), *adj.*

dip·lo·pod (dip′lə pod′), *n.* any arthropod of the class Diplopoda, comprising the millipedes.

dip·no·an (dip′nō ən), *adj.* **1.** belonging or pertaining to the order Dipnoi, comprising the lungfishes. —*n.* **2.** a dipnoan fish.

di·pole (dī′pōl′), *n.* **1.** a pair of electric charges or magnetic poles of equal magnitude and opposite sign, set a finite distance apart. **2.** a polar molecule. **3.** Also called **di′pole anten′na.** an antenna of a transmitter or receiving set consisting of two equal rods extending in opposite direction from the connection to the lead-in wire. —**di·po′lar,** *adj.*

dip·per (dip′ər), *n.* **1.** a person or thing that dips. **2.** a cuplike container with a long handle, used for dipping. **3.** (*cap.*) **4.** Also called **water ouzel.** any small, stocky diving bird of the family Cinclidae, related to the thrushes, esp. *Cinclus aquaticus* of Europe and *C. mexicanus* of W North America, having dense oily plumage and frequenting rapid streams and rivers.

dip·so·ma·ni·a (dip′sə mā′nē ə, -sō-), *n.* an irresistible, typically periodic craving for alcoholic drink.

dip·stick (dip′stik′), *n.* a rod for measuring the depth of a liquid, esp. the level of crankcase oil in an automotive engine.

dip·ter·an (dip′tər ən), *n.* any insect of the order Diptera, including mosquitoes, gnats, and most flies, having one pair of wings for flying and a second pair reduced to small knobs for balancing. —**dip′ter·ous,** *adj.*

dip·tych (dip′tik), *n.* a pair of pictures on two panels, usu. hinged together.

dire (dī°r), *adj.*, **dir·er, dir·est. 1.** causing or involving great fear or suffering; terrible. **2.** indicating trouble, disaster, or the like: *dire predictions.* **3.** urgent; desperate: *in dire need.* —**dire′ly,** *adv.*

di·rect (di rekt′, dī-), *v.t.* **1.** to manage or guide by advice, instruction, etc. **2.** to regulate the course of; control. **3.** to administer; manage; supervise: *She directs the affairs of the estate.* **4.** to give authoritative instructions to; command; order or ordain: *I directed him to leave the room.* **5.** to serve as a director in the production or performance of (a musical work, play, motion picture, etc.). **6.** to tell or show (a person) the way to a place; guide. **7.** to aim or send toward a place or object: *to direct one's aim.* **8.** to channel or focus toward a given result, object, or end (often fol. by *to* or *toward*): *She directed her energies toward the work.* **9.** to address (words, a speech, etc.) to a person or persons. **10.** to address (a letter, package, etc.) to an intended recipient. —*v.i.* **11.** to act as a guide. **12.** to give commands or orders. **13.** to serve as the director of a play, film, orchestra, etc. —*adj.* **14.** proceeding in a straight line or by the shortest course; straight; not oblique: *a direct route.* **15.** proceeding in an unbroken line of descent: *a direct descendant.* **16.** without intermediary agents, conditions, etc.; immediate: *direct contact.* **17.** straightforward; frank; candid. **18.** absolute; exact: *the direct opposite.* **19.** consisting exactly of the words only used: *direct quotation.* **20.** *Math.* **a.** (of a proportion) containing terms of which an increase or decrease in one results in an increase or decrease in another. **b.** (of a function) being a function itself, in contrast to its inverse. **21.** of or by action of voters, which takes effect without any intervening agency. **22.** inevitable; consequential: *a direct result.* **23.** allocated for or arising from a particular known agency: *a direct cost.* **24.** of or pertaining to direct current. **25. a.** moving in an orbit in the same direction as the earth in its revolution around the sun. **b.** appearing to move on the celestial sphere in the direction of the natural order of the signs of the zodiac, from west to east. Compare RETROGRADE (def. 4). **26.** (of dye colors) substantive. —*adv.* **27.** in a direct manner; directly; straight: *Answer me direct.* —**di·rect′a·ble,** *adj.* —**di·rect′ness,** *n.*

direct′ cur′rent, *n.* an electric current of constant direction, having a magnitude that does not vary or varies only slightly. *Abbr.:* DC Compare ALTERNATING CURRENT. —**di·rect′-cur′rent,** *adj.*

direct′ depos′it, *n.* the electronic transfer of funds directly from the payer into the bank account of the recipient.

di·rect-di·al or **direct′ di′al,** *v.i., v.t.* to call by telephone without the assistance of an operator.

di·rect·ed (di rek′tid, dī-), *adj.* **1.** guided, regulated, or managed. **2.** subject to direction, guidance, etc. **3.** *Math.* having positive or negative direction or orientation assigned. —**di·rect′ed·ness,** *n.*

di·rec·tion (di rek′shən, dī-), *n.* **1.** an act or instance of directing. **2.** the line along which anything lies, faces, moves, etc., with reference to

the point or region toward which it is directed. **3.** the point or region itself: *The direction is north.* **4.** a position on a line extending from a specific point toward a point of the compass or toward the nadir or the zenith. **5.** a line of thought or action or a tendency or inclination: *the direction of contemporary thought.* **6.** Usu., **directions.** instruction or guidance for making, using, etc. **7.** order; command. **8.** management; control; supervision. **9.** the name and address of the intended recipient as written on a letter, package, etc. **10.** an instruction by a stage or film director, musical conductor, author, or composer regarding the interpretation of a work, the actions or objectives of performers, technical effects, etc. **11.** the technique, art, or business of giving such instruction; the work of a stage or film director or of a musical conductor. **12.** a purpose or orientation toward a goal that serves to guide or motivate; focus. —**di·rec′tion·al,** *adj.* —**di·rec′tion·less,** *adj.*

direc′tion find′er, *n.* a receiver with a loop antenna rotating on a vertical axis, used to ascertain the direction of incoming radio waves. —**direc′tion find′ing,** *n.*

di·rec·tive (di rek′tiv, dī-), *adj.* **1.** serving to direct; directing. —*n.* **2.** an authoritative instruction or direction; specific order.

direct′ light′ing, *n.* lighting in which most of the light is cast directly from the fixture or source to the illumined area.

di·rect·ly (di rekt′lē, dī-), *adv.* **1.** in a direct line, way, or manner; straight. **2.** at once; without delay. **3.** shortly; soon. **4.** exactly; precisely: *directly′ opposite the store.* **5.** openly or frankly; candidly: *to speak directly.* **6.** *Math.* in direct proportion. —*conj.* **7.** as soon as: *Directly he arrived, he sat down.*

direct′ mail′, *n.* mail, usu. consisting of advertising matter, appeals for donations, or the like, sent to large numbers of people. —**di·rect′-mail′,** *adj.*

direct′ mar′keting, *n.* marketing direct to the consumer, as by direct mail or coupon advertising.

direct′ ob′ject, *n.* a word or group of words representing the person or thing upon which the action of a verb is performed or toward which it is directed, as the pronoun *it* in *I saw it.*

di·rec·tor (di rek′tər, dī-), *n.* **1.** a person or thing that directs. **2.** one of a group of persons chosen to control or govern the affairs of a company or corporation. **3.** the person who interprets the script and supervises the development of a theater, film, television, or radio production. **4.** CONDUCTOR (def. 3). **5.** the manager or head of certain organized groups. —**di·rec·to′ri·al,** *adj.* —**di·rec′tor·ship′,** *n.*

direc′tor's chair′, *n.* a lightweight folding armchair with transversely crossed legs and a canvas seat and back panel traditionally used by motion-picture directors.

di·rec·to·ry (di rek′tə rē, -trē, dī-), *n., pl.* **-ries,** *adj.* —*n.* **1.** a book containing an alphabetical index of the names and addresses of persons in an area, organization, etc., or of a category of people. **2.** a board or tablet on a wall of a building listing the location of the occupants. **3.** a book of directions. **4. a.** a division in a hierarchical structure that organizes the storage of computer files on a disk. **b.** a listing of such stored files. **5. the Directory,** the body of five directors forming the executive power of France from 1795 to 1799. —*adj.* **6.** serving to direct; directive.

direct′ pri′mary, *n.* a primary in which members of a party nominate its candidates by direct vote.

di·rec·trix (di rek′triks, dī-), *n., pl.* **di·rec·trix·es, di·rec·tri·ces** (di rek′tri sēz′, dī-, dī′rek trī′sēz). a fixed line used in the description of a curve or surface.

direct′ speech′, *n.* a representation of speech in which the speaker's exact words are quoted, as in *She said, "I'm not going."* Compare INDIRECT SPEECH.

direct′ tax′, *n.* a tax, as an income or property tax, exacted directly from the persons who will bear the burden of it.

dire·ful (dī°r′fəl), *adj.* **1.** dreadful; awful; terrible. **2.** indicating trouble: *direful forecasts.* —**dire′ful·ly,** *adv.* —**dire′ful·ness,** *n.*

dirge (dûrj), *n.* **1.** a funeral song or tune, or one expressing mourning in commemoration of the dead. **2.** any composition resembling such a song or tune in character, as a poem of lament for the dead or solemn, mournful music. **3.** a mournful sound resembling a dirge. **4.** the office of the dead, or the funeral service as sung.

dir·i·gi·ble (dir′i jə bəl, di rij′ə-), *n.* **1.** AIRSHIP. —*adj.* **2.** able to be steered. —**dir′i·gi·bil′i·ty,** *n.*

dirn·dl (dûrn′dl), *n.* **1.** a dress with a close-fitting bodice and full skirt in Tyrolean style. **2.** a full, gathered skirt attached to a waistband or hip yoke.

dirt (dûrt), *n.* **1.** any foul or filthy substance, as mud, grime, dust, or excrement. **2.** earth or soil, esp. when loose. **3.** something or someone vile, mean, or worthless. **4.** moral filth; vileness; corruption. **5.** obscene or lewd language. **6.** gossip, esp. of a malicious nature. —*Idiom.* **7. do someone dirt,** to cause someone harm. **8. eat dirt,** to accept blame or insults humbly.

dirt′ bike′, *n.* TRAIL BIKE.

dirt′-cheap′, *adj.* **1.** very cheap. —*adv.* **2.** very cheaply.

dirt′ farm′er, *n.* a farmer who works the soil, distinguished from one who operates a farm with hired hands or tenants. —**dirt′ farm′ing,** *n.*

dirt′-poor′, *adj.* extremely impoverished.

dirt·y (dûr′tē), *adj.,* **dirt·i·er, dirt·i·est,** *v.,* **dirt·ied, dirt·y·ing,** *adv.* —*adj.* **1.** soiled with dirt; foul; unclean. **2.** spreading or imparting dirt;

soiling: *dirty smoke.* **3.** vile; mean; sordid; contemptible: *a dirty scoundrel.* **4.** obscene; pornographic; lewd. **5.** undesirable or unpleasant; thankless: *You left the dirty work for me.* **6.** very unfortunate or regrettable: *That's a dirty shame!* **7.** not fair or sportsmanlike; unscrupulous: *a dirty fighter.* **8.** hostile or resentful: *to give someone a dirty look.* **9.** (of a nuclear weapon) producing a relatively large amount of radioactive fallout. **10.** (of the weather) stormy. **11.** obtained through illegal or disreputable means: *dirty money.* **12.** appearing as if soiled; dingy; murky. **—*v.t., v.i.*** **13.** to make or become dirty. **—*adv.*** **14.** *Informal.* in a mean, unscrupulous, or underhand way. **15.** *Informal.* in a lewd manner: *to talk dirty.* —**dirt′i•ly,** *adv.* —**dirt′i•ness,** *n.*

dirt′y tricks′, *n.pl.* **1.** unethical or illegal activities directed against political opponents, esp. during a campaign. **2.** the covert activities of an intelligence agency.

dirt′y word′, *n.* **1.** a vulgar or taboo word; obscenity. **2.** any word, name, or concept considered loathsome or unmentionable: *"Lose" is a dirty word to this team.*

dis-, a prefix occurring orig. in loanwords from Latin with the meanings "apart, asunder" (*disperse; dissociate; dissolve*); now frequent in French loanwords and English coinages having a privative, negative, or reversing force relative to the base noun, verb, or adjective: *disability; disarm; disconnect; dishearten; dishonest; dislike; disobey.*

DIS, The Disney Channel (a cable television channel).

dis•a•bil•i•ty (dis′ə bil′i tē), *n., pl.* **-ties. 1.** lack of adequate strength or physical or mental ability; incapacity. **2.** a physical or mental handicap, esp. one that prevents a person from living a normal life or from holding a specific job. **3.** anything that disables or puts one at a disadvantage. **4.** the state or condition of being disabled. **5.** legal disqualification.

dis•a•ble (dis ā′bəl), *v.t.,* **-bled, -bling. 1.** to make unable or unfit; weaken or destroy the capability of; cripple. **2.** to make legally incapable; disqualify. —**dis•a′ble•ment,** *n.* —**dis•a′bler,** *n.*

dis•a•bled (dis ā′bəld), *adj.* handicapped; incapacitated.

dis•a•buse (dis′ə byo͞oz′), *v.t.,* **-bused, -bus•ing.** to free from deception or error. —**dis′a•bus′al,** *n.*

di•sac•cha•ride (dī sak′ə rīd′, -rid), *n.* any of a group of carbohydrates, as sucrose or lactose, that yield monosaccharides on hydrolysis.

dis•ac•cus•tom (dis′ə kus′təm), *v.t.* to free of a habit.

dis•ad•van•tage (dis′əd van′tij, -vän′-), *n., v.,* **-taged, -tag•ing. —*n.*** **1.** absence or deprivation of advantage or equality. **2.** the state or an instance of being in an unfavorable circumstance or condition. **3.** something that puts one in an unfavorable position or condition: *A bad temper is a disadvantage.* **4.** injury to interest, reputation, credit, profit, etc.; loss. **—*v.t.*** **5.** to subject to disadvantage.

dis•af•fect (dis′ə fekt′), *v.t.* to alienate the affection, sympathy, or support of; make discontented or disloyal. —**dis′af•fec′tion** (-shən), *n.*

dis•af•fil•i•ate (dis′ə fil′ē āt′), *v.,* **-at•ed, -at•ing. —*v.t.*** **1.** to dissociate. **—*v.i.*** **2.** to sever an affiliation. —**dis′af•fil′i•a′tion,** *n.*

dis•af•firm (dis′ə fûrm′), *v.t.* **1.** to deny; contradict. **2.** to annul or reverse. —**dis′af•fir•ma′tion** (-af ər mā′shən), *n.*

dis•a•gree (dis′ə grē′), *v.i.,* **-greed, -gree•ing. 1.** to fail to agree; differ: *The conclusions disagree with the facts.* **2.** to differ in opinion; dissent: *Three of the judges disagreed with the verdict.* **3.** to quarrel. **4.** to cause physical discomfort or ill effect (usu. fol. by *with*): *Oysters disagree with me.*

dis•a•gree•a•ble (dis′ə grē′ə bəl), *adj.* **1.** contrary to one's taste or liking; offensive; repugnant. **2.** unpleasant in manner or nature; surly; grouchy. —**dis′a•gree′a•ble•ness, dis′a•gree′a•bil′i•ty,** *n.* —**dis′a•gree′a•bly,** *adv.*

dis•a•gree•ment (dis′ə grē′mənt), *n.* **1.** the act or fact of disagreeing. **2.** lack of agreement; diversity; unlikeness. **3.** difference of opinion; dissent. **4.** a quarrel; argument.

dis•al•low (dis′ə lou′), *v.t.* **1.** to reject; veto. **2.** to refuse to admit the validity of. —**dis′al•low′a•ble,** *adj.* —**dis′al•low′ance,** *n.*

dis•am•big•u•ate (dis′am big′yo͞o āt′), *v.t.,* **-at•ed, -at•ing.** to remove the ambiguity from; make unambiguous. —**dis′am•big′u•a′tion,** *n.*

dis•ap•pear (dis′ə pēr′), *v.i.* **1.** to cease to be seen; vanish from sight. **2.** to cease to exist or be known; pass away. **—*v.t.*** **3.** to kidnap, imprison, or kill (someone, esp. an opponent of a right-wing Latin American government). —**dis′ap•pear′ance,** *n.*

dis•ap•point (dis′ə point′), *v.t.* **1.** to fail to fulfill the expectations or wishes of. **2.** to defeat the fulfillment of: *to disappoint hopes.* **—*v.i.*** **3.** to cause disappointment. —**dis′ap•point′er,** *n.*

dis•ap•point•ed (dis′ə poin′tid), *adj.* discouraged by the failure of one's hopes: *a disappointed applicant.* —**dis′ap•point′ed•ly,** *adv.*

dis•ap•point•ment (dis′ə point′mənt), *n.* **1.** the act or fact of disappointing. **2.** the state or feeling of being disappointed. **3.** a person or thing that disappoints.

dis•ap•pro•ba•tion (dis′ap rə bā′shən), *n.* condemnation.

dis•ap•prov•al (dis′ə pro͞o′vəl), *n.* the act or state of disapproving; a condemnatory feeling, look, or utterance; censure.

dis•ap•prove (dis′ə pro͞ov′), *v.,* **-proved, -prov•ing. —*v.t.*** **1.** to think (something) wrong or reprehensible; censure or condemn in opinion. **2.** to withhold approval from; decline to sanction. **—*v.i.*** **3.** to have an unfavorable opinion; express disapproval (usu. fol. by *of*). —**dis′ap•prov′er,** *n.* —**dis′ap•prov′ing•ly,** *adv.*

dis•arm (dis ärm′), *v.t.* **1.** to deprive of a weapon or weapons. **2.** to remove the fuze or other actuating device from: *to disarm a bomb.* **3.** to deprive of the means of attack or defense: *The lack of logic disarmed his argument.* **4.** to relieve of hostility, suspicion, etc.; win the affection or approval of; charm. **—*v.i.*** **5.** to lay down one's weapons. **6.** (of a country) to reduce or limit the size, equipment, armament, etc., of armed forces. —**dis•ar′ma•ment,** *n.* —**dis•arm′er,** *n.*

dis•arm•ing (dis är′ming), *adj.* removing or capable of removing hostility, suspicion, etc., as by being charming: *a disarming smile.* —**dis•arm′ing•ly,** *adv.*

dis•ar•range (dis′ə rānj′), *v.t.,* **-ranged, -rang•ing.** to disturb the arrangement of; disorder; unsettle. —**dis′ar•range′ment,** *n.*

dis•ar•ray (dis′ə rā′), *v.t.* **1.** to put out of array or order; throw into disorder. **2.** to undress. **—*n.*** **3.** disorder; confusion. **4.** disorder of apparel.

dis•ar•tic•u•late (dis′är tik′yə lāt′), *v.,* **-lat•ed, -lat•ing. —*v.t.*** **1.** to disjoint. **—*v.i.*** **2.** to become disjointed, as the bones of a body. —**dis′ar•tic′u•la′tion,** *n.*

dis•as•sem•ble (dis′ə sem′bəl), *v.,* **-bled, -bling. —*v.t.*** **1.** to take apart. **—*v.i.*** **2.** to come apart. —**dis′as•sem′bly,** *n.*

dis•as•so•ci•ate (*v.,* dis′ə sō′shē āt′, -sē-; *n.* -it, -āt′), *v.,* **-at•ed, -at•ing,** *n.* **—*v.t.*** **1.** to dissociate. **—*n.*** **2.** (among Jehovah's Witnesses) an apostate. —**dis′as•so′ci•a′tion,** *n.*

dis•as•ter (di zas′tər, -zä′stər), *n.* a calamitous event, esp. one occurring suddenly and causing great loss of life, damage, or hardship, as a flood, airplane crash, or business failure.

disas′ter ar′ea, *n.* a region affected by a major disaster, as a flood, and officially eligible for emergency governmental relief.

dis•as•trous (di zas′trəs, -zä′strəs), *adj.* causing great distress or injury; ruinous; very unfortunate; calamitous. —**dis•as′trous•ly,** *adv.* —**dis•as′trous•ness,** *n.*

dis•a•vow (dis′ə vou′), *v.t.* to disclaim knowledge of, connection with, or responsibility for; disown; repudiate. —**dis′a•vow′ed•ly,** *adv.* —**dis′a•vow′er,** *n.*

dis•band (dis band′), *v.t.* **1.** to break up or dissolve (an organization). **—*v.i.*** **2.** to disperse. —**dis•band′ment,** *n.*

dis•bar (dis bär′), *v.t.,* **-barred, -bar•ring.** to expel from the legal profession. —**dis•bar′ment,** *n.*

dis•be•lief (dis′bi lēf′), *n.* **1.** the inability or refusal to believe or to accept something as true. **2.** amazement; astonishment.

dis•be•lieve (dis′bi lēv′), *v.,* **-lieved, -liev•ing. —*v.t.*** **1.** to have no belief in; refuse or reject belief in. **—*v.i.*** **2.** to refuse or reject belief; have no belief. —**dis′be•liev′er,** *n.* —**dis′be•liev′ing•ly,** *adv.*

dis•burse (dis bûrs′), *v.t.,* **-bursed, -burs•ing. 1.** to pay out (money), esp. for expenses; expend. **2.** to distribute. —**dis•burs′a•ble,** *adj.* —**dis•burs′er,** *n.*

dis•burse•ment (dis bûrs′mənt), *n.* **1.** the act or an instance of disbursing. **2.** money paid out or spent.

disc (disk), *n.* **1.** Also, **disk.** a phonograph record. **2.** DISK (defs. 1, 2, 4–8).

dis•calced (dis kalst′) also **dis•cal•ce•ate** (-kal′sē it, -āt′), *adj.* barefoot: *discalced monks.*

dis•card (*v.* di skärd′; *n.* dis′kärd), *v.t.* **1.** to cast aside or dispose of; get rid of. **2. a.** to throw out (a playing card) from one's hand. **b.** to play (a card, not a trump, of a different suit from that of the card led). **—*v.i.*** **3.** to discard a playing card. **—*n.*** **4.** the act of discarding. **5.** a person or thing that is cast out or rejected. **6.** a card discarded. —**dis•card′a•ble,** *adj.* —**dis•card′er,** *n.*

disc′ cam′era, *n.* a camera that accepts a film cartridge in the form of a rotatable disc with film frames mounted around the outer edge.

dis•cern (di sûrn′, -zûrn′), *v.t.* **1.** to perceive by the sight or other sense or by the intellect; see, recognize, or apprehend. **2.** to distinguish mentally; recognize as distinct or different; discriminate: *to discern right from wrong.* **—*v.i.*** **3.** to distinguish or discriminate. —**dis•cern′er,** *n.* —**dis•cern′i•ble, dis•cern′a•ble,** *adj.*

dis•cern•ing (di sûr′ning, -zûr′-), *adj.* showing good judgment and understanding. —**dis•cern′ing•ly,** *adv.*

dis•cern•ment (di sûrn′mənt, -zûrn′-), *n.* **1.** the faculty of discerning; discrimination; acuteness of judgment and understanding. **2.** the act or an instance of discerning.

dis•charge (*v.* dis chärj′; *n.* dis′chärj, dis chärj′), *v.,* **-charged, -charg•ing,** *n.* **—*v.t.*** **1.** to relieve of a charge or load; unload: *to discharge a ship.* **2.** to remove or send forth: *They discharged the cargo at New York.* **3.** to fire or shoot (a firearm or missile). **4.** to pour forth; emit: *to discharge oil.* **5.** to relieve oneself of (an obligation, burden, etc.). **6.** to relieve of obligation, responsibility, etc. **7.** to fulfill, perform, or execute (a duty, function, etc.). **8.** to relieve or deprive of office, employment, etc.; dismiss from service. **9.** to release, send away, or allow to go (often fol. by *from*): *They discharged him from prison.* **10.** to pay (a debt). **11.** *Law.* **a.** to release (a defendant, esp. one under confinement). **b.** to release (a bankrupt) from former debts. **c.** to cancel (a contract). **12.** to order (a legislative committee) to cease further consideration of a bill so that it can be voted on. **13.** to rid (a battery, capacitor, etc.) of a charge of electricity. **14.** to release or remove (dye or color) from a textile, as by chemical bleaching. **—*v.i.*** **15.** to get rid of a burden or load. **16.** to deliver a charge or load. **17.** to pour forth. **18.** to go off or fire, as a firearm or missile. **19.** to blur or run, as a color or dye. **20.** to lose or

D

give up a charge of electricity. —*n.* **21.** the act of discharging a ship, load, etc. **22.** the act of firing a weapon, as a gun, by exploding the charge of powder. **23.** a sending or coming forth, as of water from a pipe; ejection; emission. **24.** the rate or amount of such issue. **25.** something sent forth or emitted. **26.** a relieving, ridding, or getting rid of something of the nature of a charge. **27.** *Law.* **a.** an acquittal or exoneration. **b.** an annulment, as of a court order. **c.** the freeing of one held under legal process. **28.** a relieving or being relieved of obligation or liability; fulfillment of an obligation. **29.** the payment of a debt. **30.** a release or dismissal, as from prison, an office, or employment. **31.** a certificate of such a release or a certificate of release from obligation or liability. **32. a.** the separation of a person from military service. **b.** a certificate of such separation. **33. a.** the removal or transference of an electric charge, as by the conversion of chemical energy to electrical energy. **b.** the equalization of a difference of potential, as between two terminals. —**dis•charge′a•ble,** *adj.* —**dis•charg′er,** *n.*

dis•ci•ple (di sī′pəl), *n.* **1.** any professed follower of Christ in His lifetime, esp. one of the 12 apostles. **2.** (*cap.*) a member of the Disciples of Christ. **3.** a pupil or an adherent of another; follower: *a disciple of Freud.* —**dis•ci′ple•like′,** *adj.* —**dis•ci′ple•ship′,** *n.*

Disci′ples of Christ′, *n.* Christian Church.

dis•ci•pli•nar•i•an (dis′ə plə nâr′ē ən), *n.* **1.** a person who enforces or advocates discipline. —*adj.* **2.** disciplinary.

dis•ci•pli•nar•y (dis′ə plə ner′ē), *adj.* of, for, or constituting discipline; enforcing, administering, or involving discipline.

dis•ci•pline (dis′ə plin), *n., v.,* **-plined, -plin•ing.** —*n.* **1.** training to act in accordance with rules; drill: *military discipline.* **2.** activity, exercise, or a regimen that develops or improves a skill; training. **3.** punishment inflicted by way of correction and training. **4.** the rigor or training effect of experience, adversity, etc. **5.** behavior in accord with rules of conduct: *good discipline in an army.* **6.** a branch of instruction or learning. **7.** a set or system of rules and regulations. **8.** the system of government regulating the practice of a church or order. —*v.t.* **9.** to train by instruction and exercise; drill. **10.** to bring to a state of order and obedience by training and control. **11.** to punish or penalize; correct; chastise. —**dis′ci•pli•nal** (-plə nl), *adj.* —**dis′ci•plin′er,** *n.*

disc′ (or **disk′**) **jock′ey,** *n.* a person who selects, plays, and often comments on records on a radio program or at a discotheque.

dis•claim (dis klām′), *v.t.* **1.** to deny or repudiate interest in or connection with; disavow; disown. **2.** to renounce a claim or right to. **3.** to reject the claims or authority of. —*v.i.* **4.** to renounce a claim or right.

dis•claim•er (dis klā′mər), *n.* **1.** the act of disclaiming; the repudiating or denying of a claim; disavowal. **2.** a person who disclaims. **3.** a statement, document, or the like that disclaims.

dis•close (di sklōz′), *v.t.,* **-closed, -clos•ing.** **1.** to make known; reveal. **2.** to lay open to view. —**dis•clos′er,** *n.*

dis•clos•ing (di sklō′zing), *adj.* revealing the presence of plaque on the teeth by staining them with a vegetable dye: *a disclosing tablet or liquid.*

dis•clo•sure (di sklō′zhər), *n.* **1.** the act or fact of disclosing something. **2.** something disclosed; a revelation.

dis•co (dis′kō), *n., pl.* **-cos,** *v.,* **-coed, -co•ing.** —*n.* **1.** a discotheque. **2.** a style of popular music for dancing with electronic instrumentation and a heavy, rhythmic beat. —*v.i.* **3.** to dance to disco, esp. at a discotheque.

dis•cog•ra•phy (di skog′rə fē), *n., pl.* **-phies.** **1.** a selective or complete list of phonograph recordings, typically of one composer, performer, or conductor. **2.** the analysis, history, or classification of phonograph recordings. —**dis•cog′ra•pher,** *n.*

dis•coid (dis′koid) also **dis•coi′dal,** *adj.* **1.** having the form of a disk; flat and circular. **2.** (of a composite flower) having a disk without rays.

dis•col•or (dis kul′ər), *v.t.* **1.** to change or spoil the color of; fade or stain. —*v.i.* **2.** to change color; become faded or stained.

dis•col•or•a•tion (dis kul′ə rā′shən) also **dis•col′or•ment,** *n.* **1.** the act or fact of discoloring or the state of being discolored. **2.** a discolored marking or area; stain.

dis•com•bob•u•late (dis′kəm bob′yə lāt′), *v.t.,* **-lat•ed, -lat•ing.** to confuse or disconcert; upset; frustrate. —**dis′com•bob′u•la′tion,** *n.*

dis•com•fit (dis kum′fit), *v.t.* **1.** to confuse and deject; disconcert. **2.** to frustrate the plans of; thwart; foil. —**dis•com′fit•er,** *n.*

dis•com•fi•ture (dis kum′fi chər), *n.* **1.** disconcertion; confusion; embarrassment. **2.** frustration of hopes or plans.

dis•com•fort (dis kum′fərt), *n.* **1.** an absence of comfort or ease; hardship or mild pain. **2.** anything that is disturbing to or interferes with comfort. —*v.t.* **3.** to disturb the comfort or happiness of; make uneasy. —**dis•com′fort•a•ble** (-fər tə bəl, -kumf′tə-), *adj.* —**dis•com′fort•ing•ly,** *adv.*

dis•con•cert (dis′kən sûrt′), *v.t.* **1.** to disturb the self-possession of; perturb; ruffle. **2.** to throw into disorder or confusion; disarrange. —**dis′con•cert′ing•ly,** *adv.* —**dis′con•cer′tion, dis′con•cert′ment,** *n.*

dis•con•nect (dis′kə nekt′), *v.t.* **1.** to sever or interrupt the connection of or between. —*v.i.* **2.** to sever a connection. **3.** to withdraw into one's private world. —*n.* **4.** an act or instance of disconnecting. —**dis′con•nect′er,** *n.* —**dis′con•nec′tion** (-shən), *n.*

dis•con•nect•ed (dis′kə nek′tid), *adj.* **1.** disjointed; broken. **2.** not coherent; seemingly irrational. —**dis′con•nect′ed•ly,** *adv.* —**dis′con•nect′ed•ness,** *n.*

dis•con•so•late (dis kon′sə lit), *adj.* **1.** without consolation or solace; hopelessly unhappy; inconsolable. **2.** characterized by or causing dejection; cheerless; gloomy. —**dis•con′so•late•ly,** *adv.* —**dis•con′so•la′tion, dis•con′so•late•ness,** *n.*

dis•con•tent (dis′kən tent′), *adj.* **1.** not content; dissatisfied; discontented. —*n.* **2.** Also, **dis′con•tent′ment.** lack of contentment. **3.** a restless craving for what one does not have. —*v.t.* **4.** to make discontent.

dis•con•tent•ed (dis′kən ten′tid), *adj.* dissatisfied; restlessly unhappy. —**dis′con•tent′ed•ly,** *adv.* —**dis′con•tent′ed•ness,** *n.*

dis•con•tin•u•ance (dis′kən tin′yo͞o əns), *n.* **1.** the act of discontinuing or the state of being discontinued; cessation. **2.** the termination of a lawsuit by some act of the plaintiff.

dis•con•tin•u•a•tion (dis′kən tin′yo͞o ā′shən), *n.* a breach or interruption of continuity or unity.

dis•con•tin•ue (dis′kən tin′yo͞o), *v.,* **-tin•ued, -tin•u•ing.** —*v.t.* **1.** to put an end to; stop; terminate. **2.** to cease using, producing, subscribing to, etc. **3.** to terminate or abandon (a lawsuit, claim, or the like). —*v.i.* **4.** to come to an end or stop; cease; desist. —**dis′con•tin′u•er,** *n.*

dis•con•ti•nu•i•ty (dis′kon tn o͞o′i tē, -yo͞o′-), *n., pl.* **-ties.** **1.** lack of continuity; irregularity. **2.** a break or gap. **3.** a point at which a mathematical function is not continuous.

dis•con•tin•u•ous (dis′kən tin′yo͞o əs), *adj.* **1.** not continuous; broken; interrupted; intermittent. **2.** *Math.* (of a function at a point) not continuous at the point. —**dis′con•tin′u•ous•ly,** *adv.* —**dis′con•tin′u•ous•ness,** *n.*

dis•cord (*n.* dis′kôrd; *v.* dis kôrd′), *n.* **1.** lack of concord or harmony between persons or things. **2.** disagreement; difference of opinion. **3.** strife; dispute; war. **4.** an inharmonious combination of musical tones sounded together. **5.** any confused or harsh noise; dissonance. —*v.i.* **6.** to disagree; be at variance.

dis•cord•ant (dis kôr′dnt), *adj.* **1.** being at variance; disagreeing; incongruous. **2.** disagreeable to the ear; dissonant; harsh. —**dis•cord′ant•ly,** *adv.*

dis•co•theque or **dis•co•thèque** (dis′kə tek′, dis′kə tek′), *n.* a nightclub for dancing to live or recorded music and often featuring sophisticated sound systems, elaborate lighting, and other effects. Also called **disco.**

dis•count (*v.* dis′kount, dis kount′; *n., adj.* dis′kount), *v.t.* **1.** to deduct a certain amount from (a bill, charge, etc.). **2.** to offer for sale or sell at a reduced price. **3.** to lend money on (commercial paper) after deducting interest. **4.** to buy or sell (a note, bill, etc.) discounted for the amount of interest yet to be paid. **5.** to leave out of account; disregard. **6.** to allow for exaggeration in (a statement, opinion, etc.). **7.** to take into account in advance, often so as to diminish the effect of. —*v.i.* **8.** to offer goods or services at a reduced price. —*n.* **9.** the act or an instance of discounting. **10.** an amount deducted from the usual list price. **11.** any deduction from the nominal value. **12.** a payment of interest in advance upon a loan of money. **13.** an allowance made for exaggeration or bias, as in a report or story. —*adj.* **14.** selling at less than the usual price. **15.** selling goods at a discount. —**dis′count•a•ble,** *adj.* —**dis′count•er,** *n.*

dis•coun•te•nance (dis koun′tn əns), *v.,* **-nanced, -nanc•ing,** *n.* —*v.t.* **1.** to disconcert, embarrass, or abash. **2.** to show disapproval of. —*n.* **3.** disapproval; disapprobation. —**dis•coun′te•nanc•er,** *n.*

dis•cour•age (di skûr′ij, -skur′-), *v.,* **-aged, -ag•ing.** —*v.t.* **1.** to deprive of courage, hope, or confidence; dishearten; dispirit. **2.** to dissuade (usu. fol. by *from*). **3.** to obstruct by opposition or difficulty; hinder. **4.** to express disapproval of; frown upon. —*v.i.* **5.** to become discouraged. —**dis•cour′age•ment,** *n.* —**dis•cour′ag•ing•ly,** *adv.*

dis•course (*n.* dis′kôrs, -kōrs, dis kôrs′, -kōrs′; *v.* dis kôrs′, -kōrs′), *n., v.,* **-coursed, -cours•ing.** —*n.* **1.** communication of thought by words; talk; conversation. **2.** a formal discussion of a subject in speech or writing, as a treatise or sermon. **3.** any unit of connected speech or writing longer than a sentence. —*v.i.* **4.** to communicate thoughts orally; talk; converse. **5.** to treat of a subject formally in speech or writing. —**dis•cours′er,** *n.*

dis•cour•te•ous (dis kûr′tē əs), *adj.* not courteous; impolite; rude. —**dis•cour′te•ous•ly,** *adv.* —**dis•cour′te•ous•ness,** *n.*

dis•cour•te•sy (dis kûr′tə sē), *n., pl.* **-sies.** **1.** lack or breach of courtesy; incivility; rudeness. **2.** a discourteous or impolite act.

dis•cov•er (di skuv′ər), *v.t.* **1.** to gain sight or knowledge of (something previously unseen or unknown). **2.** to notice or realize. —**dis•cov′er•a•ble,** *adj.* —**dis•cov′er•er,** *n.*

dis•cov•er•y (di skuv′ə rē), *n., pl.* **-er•ies.** **1.** the act or an instance of discovering. **2.** something discovered. **3.** *Law.* compulsory disclosure, as of facts or documents.

dis•cred•it (dis kred′it), *v.t.* **1.** to injure the credit or reputation of; defame. **2.** to destroy confidence in the reliability of: *Later research discredited that theory.* **3.** to give no credence to; disbelieve: *to discredit a witness.* —*n.* **4.** loss or lack of belief or confidence; distrust. **5.** loss or lack of repute or esteem; disrepute. **6.** something that damages a good reputation.

dis•creet (di skrēt′), *adj.* judicious in one's conduct or speech, esp. with regard to keeping silent about a delicate matter; prudent; circumspect; diplomatic. —**dis•creet′ly,** *adv.* —**dis•creet′ness,** *n.*

dis•crep•an•cy (di skrep′ən sē), *n., pl.* **-cies.** **1.** the state or quality of being discrepant; difference; inconsistency. **2.** an instance of difference or inconsistency.

dis·crep·ant (di skrep′ənt), *adj.* (usu. of two or more accounts, findings, etc.) differing; disagreeing; inconsistent. **—dis·crep′ant·ly,** *adv.*

dis·crete (di skrēt′), *adj.* **1.** apart or detached from others; separate; distinct. **2.** consisting of or characterized by distinct parts; discontinuous. **3.** *Math.* defined only for an isolated set of points: *a discrete variable.* **—dis·crete′ly,** *adv.* **—dis·crete′ness,** *n.*

dis·cre·tion (di kresh′ən), *n.* **1.** the power or right to decide or act according to one's own judgment. **2.** the quality of being discreet; prudence or decorum; tactfulness. **—Idiom. 3. at one's discretion,** in accordance with one's judgment or will. **—Proverb. 4. Discretion is the better part of valor,** caution should be the first priority.

dis·cre·tion·ar·y (di kresh′ə ner′ē), *adj.* subject or left to one's own discretion or control. **—dis·cre′tion·ar′i·ly,** *adv.*

dis·crim·i·nant (di skrim′ə nənt), *n.* a relatively simple mathematical expression that determines some of the properties, as the nature of the roots, of a given equation or function. **—dis·crim′i·nan′tal** (-nan′tl), *adj.*

dis·crim·i·nate (*v.* di skrim′ə nāt′; *adj.* -nit), *v.,* **-nat·ed, -nat·ing,** *adj.* **—v.i. 1.** to make a distinction in favor of or against a person or class to which the person belongs, rather than according to merit; show partiality. **2.** to note or observe a difference; distinguish accurately. **—v.t. 3.** to note or distinguish as different. **4.** to make or constitute a distinction in or between; differentiate. **—adj. 5.** marked by discrimination; making or evidencing nice distinctions. **—dis·crim′i·nate·ly,** *adv.* **—dis·crim′i·na′tor,** *n.*

dis·crim·i·nat·ing (di skrim′ə nā′ting), *adj.* **1.** analytical. **2.** discerning; perspicacious. **3.** having excellent taste or judgment. **4.** biased; discriminatory. **—dis·crim′i·nat′ing·ly,** *adv.*

dis·crim·i·na·tion (di skrim′ə nā′shən), *n.* **1.** an act or instance of discriminating. **2.** action or policies based on prejudice or partiality: *racial discrimination.* **3.** the power of making fine distinctions; discriminating judgment. **—dis·crim′i·na′tion·al,** *adj.*

dis·crim·i·na·to·ry (di skrim′ə nə tôr′ē, -tōr′ē), *adj.* characterized by or showing prejudice or partiality: *discriminatory practices in housing.* **—dis·crim′i·na·to′ri·ly,** *adv.*

dis·cur·sive (di skûr′siv), *adj.* **1.** passing aimlessly from one subject to another; digressive; rambling. **2.** proceeding by reasoning or argument rather than intuition. **—dis·cur′sive·ly,** *adv.* **—dis·cur′sive·ness,** *n.*

dis·cus (dis′kəs), *n., pl.* **dis·cus·es, dis·ci** (dis′ī). **1.** a circular disk, usu. wooden with a metal rim, for throwing in athletic competition. **2.** the sport of throwing this disk for distance.

dis·cuss (di skus′), *v.t.* to consider or examine by argument, comment, etc.; talk over or write about; debate. **—dis·cus′sion,** *n.*

dis·dain (dis dān′, di stān′), *v.t.* **1.** to look upon or treat with contempt; despise; scorn. **2.** to think unworthy of notice, response, etc.; consider beneath oneself: *to disdain replying to an insult.* **—n. 3.** a feeling of contempt for anything regarded as unworthy; haughty contempt; scorn. **—dis·dain′ful,** *adj.*

dis·ease (di zēz′), *n.* **1.** a disordered or abnormal condition of an organ or other part of an organism resulting from the effect of genetic or developmental errors, infection, nutritional deficiency, toxicity, or unfavorable environmental factors; illness; sickness. **2.** any harmful condition, as of society. **—dis·eased′,** *adj.* **—dis·eas′ed·ly,** *adv.* **—dis·eas′ed·ness,** *n.*

dis·em·bark (dis′em bärk′), *v.i.* **1.** to go ashore from a ship. **2.** to leave an aircraft or other vehicle. **—v.t. 3.** to remove or unload (cargo or passengers) from a ship, aircraft, or other vehicle. **—dis·em′bar·ka′tion,** *n.*

dis·em·bod·y (dis′em bod′ē), *v.t.,* **-bod·ied, -bod·y·ing.** to divest (a soul, spirit, etc.) of a body. **—dis′em·bod′i·ment,** *n.*

dis·em·bow·el (dis′em bou′əl), *v.t.,* **-eled, -el·ing** or (*esp. Brit.*) **-elled, -el·ling.** to remove the bowels or entrails from; eviscerate. **—dis′em·bow′el·ment,** *n.*

dis·en·chant (dis′en chant′, -chänt′), *v.t.* to rid of or free from enchantment, illusion, credulity, etc.; disillusion. **—dis′en·chant′ing,** *adj.* **—dis′en·chant′ment,** *n.*

dis·en·cum·ber (dis′en kum′bər), *v.t.* to free from a burden or other encumbrance; disburden.

dis·en·fran·chise (dis′en fran′chīz), *v.t.,* **-chised, -chis·ing.** to disfranchise. **—dis′en·fran′chise·ment** (-chīz mənt, -chiz-), *n.*

dis·en·gage (dis′en gāj′), *v.,* **-gaged, -gag·ing.** **—v.t. 1.** to release from attachment or connection: *to disengage a clutch.* **2.** to free (oneself) from an engagement, obligation, etc. **—v.i. 3.** to become disengaged. **—dis′en·gage′ed·ness,** *n.*

dis·en·tan·gle (dis′en tang′gəl), *v.,* **-gled, -gling.** **—v.t. 1.** to free from entanglement; untangle; extricate. **—v.i. 2.** to become disentangled. **—dis′en·tan′gle·ment,** *n.*

dis·en·thrall or **dis·en·thral** (dis′en thrôl′), *v.t.,* **-thralled, -thral·ling.** to free from bondage; liberate.

dis·e·qui·lib·ri·um (dis ē′kwə lib′rē əm, dis′ē-), *n.* lack of equilibrium; imbalance.

dis·es·tab·lish (dis′i stab′lish), *v.t.* **1.** to deprive of the character of being established; cancel; abolish. **2.** to withdraw exclusive state recognition or support from (a church). **—dis′es·tab′lish·ment,** *n.*

dis·es·tab·lish·men·tar·i·an (dis′i stab′lish mən târ′ē ən), *n.* **1.** a person who favors the separation of church and state, esp. the with-

drawal of special rights and support granted an established church by a state. **—adj. 2.** of or favoring the disestablishment of a state church. **—dis′es·tab′lish·men·tar′i·an·ism,** *n.*

dis·fa·vor (dis fā′vər), *n.* **1.** unfavorable regard; displeasure; dislike: *Everyone feared the king's disfavor.* **2.** the state of being regarded unfavorably; disrepute: *Short skirts are in disfavor this year.* **3.** a disadvantageous or detrimental act; disservice: *to do oneself a disfavor.* **—v.t. 4.** to regard or treat with disfavor. Also, *esp. Brit.,* **dis·fa′vour.** **—dis·fa′vor·er,** *n.*

dis·fel·low·ship (dis fel′ō ship′), *n., v.,* **-shiped, -ship·ing** or (*esp. Brit.*) **-shipped, -ship·ping.** **—n. 1.** (in some Protestant religions) the status of a member who, because of some serious infraction of church policy, has been denied the church's sacraments and any post of responsibility and is officially shunned by other members. **—v.t. 2.** to place in the status of disfellowship.

dis·fig·ure (dis fig′yər; *Brit.* -fig′ər), *v.t.,* **-ured, -ur·ing.** **1.** to mar the appearance or beauty of; deform; deface. **2.** to mar the effect or excellence of. **—dis·fig′ur·er,** *n.*

dis·fig·ure·ment (dis fig′yər mənt; *Brit.* -fig′ər-), *n.* **1.** an act or instance of disfiguring. **2.** a disfigured condition. **3.** something that disfigures, as a scar. Also called **dis·fig′ur·a′tion.**

dis·fran·chise (dis fran′chīz) also **disenfranchise,** *v.t.,* **-chised, -chis·ing.** **1.** to deprive (a person) of a right of citizenship, as of the right to vote. **2.** to deprive of a franchise, privilege, or right. **—dis·fran′chise·ment** (-chīz mənt, -chiz-), *n.*

discus

dis·gorge (dis gôrj′), *v.,* **-gorged, -gorg·ing.** **—v.t. 1.** to eject or throw out from the throat, mouth, or stomach; vomit forth. **2.** to surrender or yield (something, esp. something illicitly obtained). **3.** to discharge forcefully or as a result of force. **—v.i. 4.** to eject, yield, or discharge something. **—dis·gorge′ment,** *n.* **—dis·gorg′er,** *n.*

dis·grace (dis grās′), *n., v.,* **-graced, -grac·ing.** **—n. 1.** the loss of respect, honor, or esteem; ignominy; shame. **2.** a person, act, or thing that causes shame, reproach, or dishonor or is dishonorable or shameful. **3.** the state of being out of favor; exclusion from favor or trust: *courtiers and ministers in disgrace.* **—v.t. 4.** to bring or reflect shame or reproach upon. **5.** to dismiss with discredit; rebuke or humiliate: *to be disgraced at court.* **—dis·grace′ful,** *adj.*

dis·grun·tle (dis grun′tl), *v.t.,* **-tled, -tling.** to put into a state of sulky dissatisfaction; make discontent. **—dis·grun′tle·ment,** *n.*

dis·guise (dis gīz′, di skīz′), *v.,* **-guised, -guis·ing,** *n.* **—v.t. 1.** to change the appearance of so as to conceal identity or mislead, as with deceptive garb. **2.** to conceal the truth or actual character of by a counterfeit form or appearance; misrepresent: *to disguise one's intentions.* **—n. 3.** something that serves or is intended for disguising identity, character, or quality; a deceptive covering, condition, manner, etc. **4.** the makeup, mask, or costume of an entertainer. **5.** the act of disguising. **6.** the state of being disguised; masquerade. **—dis·guis′a·ble,** *adj.* **—dis·guis′ed·ly,** *adv.* **—dis·guis′er,** *n.*

dis·gust (dis gust′, di skust′), *v.t.* **1.** to cause loathing or nausea in. **2.** to offend the good taste, moral sense, etc., of. **—n. 3.** a strong distaste; nausea; loathing. **4.** repugnance caused by something offensive; strong aversion. **—dis·gust′ed·ly,** *adv.* **—dis·gust′ed·ness,** *n.* **—dis·gust′ing,** *adj.*

dish (dish), *n.* **1.** an open, relatively shallow container of pottery, glass, etc., used esp. for holding or serving food. **2.** any container used at table. **3.** the food served or contained in a dish. **4.** a particular article or preparation of food: *an easy dish to make.* **5.** the quantity held by a dish; dishful. **6.** something like a dish in form or use. **7.** concavity or the degree of concavity, as of a wheel. **8.** Also called **dish′ anten′na.** a dish-shaped reflector, used esp. for receiving satellite and microwave signals. **—v.t. 9.** to put into or serve in a dish, as food. **10.** to fashion like a dish; make concave. **11.** *Slang.* to gossip about in a disparaging manner. **—v.i. 12.** *Slang.* to gossip. **—Idiom. 13. dish it out,** *Informal.* to express one's opinions, reactions, etc., freely and aggressively. **14. dish out,** *Informal.* to deal out; distribute. [< Latin *discus* dish]

dis·ha·bille (dis′ə bēl′, -bē′) also **deshabille,** *n.* **1.** the state of being carelessly or partially dressed. **2.** a disorderly or disorganized state of mind or way of thinking.

dis·har·mo·ni·ous (dis′här mō′nē əs), *adj.* discordant.

dis·har·mo·ny (dis här′mə nē), *n., pl.* **-nies. 1.** lack of harmony; discord. **2.** something discordant.

dish·cloth (dish′klôth′, -kloth′), *n., pl.* **-cloths** (-klôthz′, -klothz′, -klôths′, -kloths′). a cloth for use in washing dishes.

dis·heart·en (dis här′tn), *v.t.* to depress the hope, courage, or spirits of; discourage. **—dis·heart′en·ing·ly,** *adv.* **—dis·heart′en·ment,** *n.*

dished (disht), *adj.* **1.** concave: *a dished face.* **2.** *Slang.* exhausted; worn out. **3.** (of a parallel pair of vehicle wheels) farther apart at the top than at the bottom.

di•shev•el (di shev′əl), *v.t.,* **-eled, -el•ing** or (*esp. Brit.*) **-elled, -el•ling.** **1.** to let down, as hair, or wear or let hang in loose disorder, as clothing. **2.** to cause untidiness and disarray in. —**di•shev′el•ment,** *n.*

di•shev•eled (di shev′əld), *adj.* unkempt; untidy; disarranged. Also, *esp. Brit.,* **di•shev′elled.**

dis•hon•est (dis on′ist), *adj.* **1.** not honest; disposed to lie, cheat, or steal; untrustworthy. **2.** proceeding from or exhibiting lack of honesty; fraudulent. —**dis•hon′est•ly,** *adv.*

dis•hon•es•ty (dis on′ə stē), *n., pl.* **-ties.** **1.** lack of honesty; a disposition to lie, cheat, or steal. **2.** a dishonest act; fraud.

dis•hon•or (dis on′ər), *n.* **1.** lack or loss of honor. **2.** disgrace; ignominy; shame. **3.** indignity; insult: *to do someone a dishonor.* **4.** a cause of shame or disgrace. —*v.t.* **5.** to deprive of honor; disgrace; bring reproach or shame on. **6.** to refuse to pay (a check, draft, etc.). **7.** to rape or seduce. —**dis•hon′or•er,** *n.*

dis•hon•or•a•ble (dis on′ər ə bəl), *adj.* **1.** showing lack of honor or integrity; ignoble; base; disgraceful; shameful. **2.** having no honor or good repute. —**dis•hon′or•a•bly,** *adv.*

dish•pan (dish′pan′), *n.* a large pan in which dishes, pots, etc., are washed.

dish•wash•er (dish′wosh′ər, -wô′shər), *n.* **1.** a person who washes dishes. **2.** a machine for washing dishes.

dish•wa•ter (dish′wô′tər, -wot′ər), *n.* **1.** water in which dishes are, or have been, washed. **2.** *Slang.* anything weak, dull, or inferior.

dis•il•lu•sion (dis′i lōō′zhən), *v.t.* **1.** to free from or deprive of illusion, belief, idealism, etc.; disenchant. —*n.* **2.** a freeing or a being freed from illusion or conviction; disenchantment. —**dis′il•lu′sion•ment,** *n.* —**dis′il•lu′sive** (-siv), *adj.*

dis•in•cline (dis′in klīn′), *v.t.,* **-clined, -clin•ing.** to make averse or unwilling.

dis•in•fect (dis′in fekt′), *v.t.* to cleanse of infection; destroy disease germs in. —**dis′in•fect′ant,** *n., adj.*

dis•in•for•ma•tion (dis in′fər mā′shən, dis′in-), *n.* false and misleading information publicly or secretly released by a government to the international news media or to rival intelligence agencies.

dis•in•gen•u•ous (dis′in jen′yōō əs), *adj.,* lacking in frankness, candor, or sincerity; insincere. —**dis′in•gen′u•ous•ly,** *adv.* —**dis′in•gen′u•ous•ness,** *n.*

dis•in•her•it (dis′in her′it), *v.t.* **1.** to exclude (an heir) from inheritance. **2.** to deprive of a heritage, country, right, privilege, etc. —**dis′in•her′i•tance,** *n.*

dis•in•te•grate (dis in′tə grāt′), *v.,* **-grat•ed, -grat•ing.** —*v.i.* **1.** to separate into parts or lose intactness or solidness; break up; deteriorate. **2.** *Physics.* **a.** to decay. **b.** (of a nucleus) to change into one or more different nuclei after being bombarded by high-energy particles, as gamma rays. —*v.t.* **3.** to reduce to particles, fragments, or parts; break up or destroy the cohesion of. —**dis•in′te•gra•ble** (-grə bəl), *adj.* —**dis•in′te•gra′tor,** *n.*

dis•in•ter (dis′in tûr′), *v.t.,* **-terred, -ter•ring.** **1.** to take out of the place of interment; exhume; unearth. **2.** to bring from obscurity into view. —**dis′in•ter′ment,** *n.*

dis•in•ter•est (dis in′tər ist, -trist), *n.* **1.** apathy; indifference. —*v.t.* **2.** to divest of interest.

dis•in•ter•est•ed (dis in′tə res′tid, -tri stid), *adj.* **1.** unbiased by personal interest or advantage; not influenced by selfish motives. **2.** not interested; indifferent. —**dis′in•ter′est•ed•ly,** *adv.* —**Usage.** DISINTERESTED was orig. used to mean "not interested, indifferent"; UNINTERESTED in its earliest use meant "impartial." By various developmental twists, DISINTERESTED is now used in both senses; UNINTERESTED, mainly in the sense "not interested, indifferent." Many object to the use of DISINTERESTED to mean "not interested" and continue to reserve the word strictly for the sense "impartial": *A disinterested observer is the best judge of behavior.* However, both senses are well established in all varieties of English.

dis•join (dis join′), *v.t.* **1.** to undo or prevent the junction or union of; disunite; separate. —*v.i.* **2.** to become disunited; separate. —**dis•join′a•ble,** *adj.*

dis•joint (dis joint′), *v.t.* **1.** to separate or disconnect the joints or joinings of. **2.** to put out of order; derange. —*v.i.* **3.** to come apart. **4.** to be dislocated; be out of joint. —*adj.* **5.** *Math.* **a.** (of two sets) having no common elements. **b.** (of a system of sets) having the property that every pair of sets is disjoint.

dis•joint•ed (dis join′tid), *adj.* **1.** having the joints or connections separated: *a disjointed fowl.* **2.** disconnected; incoherent: *a disjointed discourse.* —**dis•joint′ed•ly,** *adv.* —**dis•joint′ed•ness,** *n.*

dis•junc•tion (dis jungk′shən), *n.* **1.** the act of disjoining or the state of being disjoined: *a disjunction between thought and action.* **2. a.** a compound statement that is true only if at least one of a number of alternatives is true. **b.** the relationship between the components of such a proposition, expressed by the word "or."

dis•junc•tive (dis jungk′tiv), *adj.* **1.** serving or tending to disjoin. **2. a.** syntactically setting two or more expressions in opposition to each other, as *but* in *poor but happy,* or expressing an alternative, as *or* in *this or that.* **b.** not syntactically dependent upon some particular expression. **3. a.** characterizing logical propositions that include alternatives. **b.** (of a syllogism) containing at least one disjunctive proposition as a premise. —*n.* **4.** a disjunctive proposition. **5.** a disjunctive word. —**dis•junc′tive•ly,** *adv.*

disk (disk), *n.* **1.** any thin, flat, circular plate or object. **2.** any surface that is flat and round, or seemingly so: *the disk of the sun.* DISC (def. 1). **4.** any of several types of media for storing electronic data consisting of thin round plates of plastic or metal: *floppy disk; hard disk.* **5.** *Bot., Zool.* any of various roundish, flat structures or parts. **6.** INTERVERTEBRAL DISK. **7.** the central part of the flower head in composite plants, as the yellow center of the daisy. **8.** any of the circular steel blades of a disk harrow. Also, **disc** (for defs. 1, 2, 4–8). —**disk′like′,** *adj.*

disk′ drive′, *n.* a device in or attached to a computer that enables the user to read data from or store data on a disk.

disk•ette (di sket′), *n.* FLOPPY DISK.

disk′ flow′er, *n.* any of the tiny, closely clustered tubular florets that make up the disk of a composite flower. Also called **disk′ floret′.**

dis•like (dis līk′), *v.,* **-liked, -lik•ing,** *n.* —*v.t.* **1.** to regard with displeasure, antipathy, or aversion. —*n.* **2.** a feeling of aversion; antipathy. —**dis•lik′a•ble, dis•like′a•ble,** *adj.*

dis•lo•cate (dis′lō kāt′, dis lō′kāt), *v.t.,* **-cat•ed, -cat•ing.** **1.** to put out of place; put out of proper relative position. **2.** to put out of joint or out of position, as a limb or an organ. **3.** to throw out of order; upset; disorder: *Frequent strikes dislocated the economy.*

dis•lo•ca•tion (dis′lō kā′shən), *n.* **1.** an act or instance of dislocating. **2.** the state of being dislocated. **3.** (in a crystal lattice) a line about which there is a discontinuity in the lattice structure.

dis•lodge (dis loj′), *v.,* **-lodged, -lodg•ing.** —*v.t.* **1.** to remove or force out of a particular place. **2.** to drive out of a hiding place, a military position, etc. —*v.i.* **3.** to go from a lodging place. —**dis•lodg′ment, dis•lodge′ment,** *n.*

dis•loy•al (dis loi′əl), *adj.* false to one's obligations or allegiances; faithless. —**dis•loy′al•ist,** *n.* —**dis•loy′al•ly,** *adv.*

dis•loy•al•ty (dis loi′əl tē), *n., pl.* **-ties.** **1.** the quality of being disloyal; lack of loyalty; unfaithfulness. **2.** violation of allegiance or duty, as to a government. **3.** a disloyal act.

dis•mal (diz′məl), *adj.* **1.** causing gloom or dejection; dreary; cheerless. **2.** characterized by ineptness or lack of skill or interest. —*n.* **3.** *Southern U.S.* a tract of swampy land. —**dis′mal•ly,** *adv.* —**dis′mal•ness,** *n.*

dis•man•tle (dis man′tl), *v.t.,* **-tled, -tling.** **1.** to deprive or strip of apparatus, trappings, equipment, etc. **2.** to take apart. **3.** to divest of dress, covering, etc. —**dis•man′tle•ment,** *n.* —**dis•man′tler,** *n.*

dis•may (dis mā′), *v.,* **-mayed, -may•ing,** *n.* —*v.t.* **1.** to break down the courage of completely, as by sudden danger or trouble; daunt. **2.** to surprise in such a manner as to disillusion. **3.** to alarm; perturb. —*n.* **4.** sudden or complete loss of courage; utter disheartenment. **5.** sudden disillusionment. **6.** agitation of mind; perturbation.

dis•mem•ber (dis mem′bər), *v.t.* **1.** to deprive of limbs; divide limb from limb. **2.** to divide into parts; cut up. —**dis•mem′ber•er,** *n.* —**dis•mem′ber•ment,** *n.*

dis•miss (dis mis′), *v.t.* **1.** to direct or allow to leave: *dismissed the class.* **2.** to discharge from office or service: *to dismiss an employee.* **3.** to discard or reject; put aside from consideration: *to dismiss a story as rumor.* **4.** to remove from a court's consideration: *to dismiss all charges.* —**dis•miss′i•ble,** *adj.* —**dis•miss′ive,** *adj.*

dis•miss•al (dis mis′əl) also **dis•mis•sion** (-mish′ən), *n.* **1.** an act or instance of dismissing. **2.** the state of being dismissed. **3.** a spoken or written order of discharge as from employment.

dis•mount (*v.* dis mount′; *n. also* dis′mount′), *v.i.* **1.** to alight, as from a horse or bicycle. —*v.t.* **2.** to bring or throw down, as from a horse; unhorse; throw. **3.** to take (a mechanism) to pieces. —*n.* **4.** an act of dismounting. —**dis•mount′a•ble,** *adj.*

Dis•ney (diz′nē), *n.* **Walt(er E.),** 1901–66, U.S. creator and producer of animated cartoons, motion pictures, etc.

Dis•ney•land (diz′nē land′), **1.** *Trademark.* a large amusement park in Anaheim, Calif.: prototypical theme park. —*n.* **2.** any large, bustling place noted for its colorful attractions: *The new shopping center has become an after-hours Disneyland.* **3.** a land or place of make-believe; fantasyland.

dis•o•be•di•ence (dis′ə bē′dē əns), *n.* lack of obedience or refusal to comply; disregard or transgression.

dis•o•be•di•ent (dis′ə bē′dē ənt), *adj.* neglecting or refusing to obey; refractory. —**dis′o•be′di•ent•ly,** *adv.*

dis•o•bey (dis′ə bā′), *v.t., v.i.* to neglect or refuse to obey. —**dis′o•bey′er,** *n.*

dis•or•der (dis ôr′dər), *n.* **1.** lack of order or regular arrangement; confusion. **2.** an irregularity: *a disorder in legal proceedings.* **3.** breach of order; public disturbance. **4.** a disturbance in physical or mental health: *a mild stomach disorder.* —*v.t.* **5.** to destroy the order or regular arrangement of; disarrange. **6.** to derange the physical or mental health or functions of.

dis•or•dered (dis ôr′dərd), *adj.* **1.** lacking organization or regularity; in confusion; disarranged. **2.** afflicted with a physical or mental disorder. —**dis•or′dered•ly,** *adv.* —**dis•or′dered•ness,** *n.*

dis•or•der•ly (dis ôr′dər lē), *adj.* **1.** characterized by disorder; untidy. **2.** unruly; tumultuous. **3.** contrary to public order or morality. —**dis•or′der•li•ness,** *n.*

disor′derly con′duct, *n.* any of various petty misdemeanors, as breaches of the peace or offensive conduct in public.

dis•or•gan•i•za•tion (dis ôr′gə nə zā′shən), *n.* **1.** a breaking up of order or system; disunion or disruption of constituent parts. **2.** the absence of organization or orderly arrangement; disarrangement; disorder.

dis•or•gan•ize (dis ôr′gə nīz′), *v.t.*, **-ized, -iz•ing.** to destroy the organization, systematic arrangement, or orderly connection of; throw into confusion or disorder. **—dis•or′gan•iz′er,** *n.*

dis•o•ri•ent (dis ôr′ē ent′, -ōr′-), *v.t.* **1.** to cause to lose one's way. **2.** to confuse. **3.** to cause to lose perception of time, place, or one's personal identity.

dis•o•ri•en•tate (dis ôr′ē ən tāt′, -ōr′-), *v.t.*, **-tat•ed, -tat•ing.** to disorient. **—dis•o′ri•en•ta′tion,** *n.*

dis•own (dis ōn′), *v.t.* to refuse to acknowledge ownership of or responsibility for. **—dis•own′ment,** *n.*

dis•par•age (di spar′ij), *v.t.*, **-aged, -ag•ing. 1.** to speak of or treat slightingly; belittle. **2.** to bring reproach or discredit upon; lower the estimation of. **—dis•par′age•ment,** *n.*

dis•par•ag•ing (di spar′i jing), *adj.* tending to belittle or discredit. **—dis•par′ag•ing•ly,** *adv.*

dis•pa•rate (dis′pər it, di spar′-), *adj.* distinct in kind; essentially different; dissimilar; unlike. **—dis′pa•rate•ly,** *adv.* **—dis′pa•rate•ness,** *n.*

dis•par•i•ty (di spar′i tē), *n.*, *pl.* **-ties.** lack of similarity or equality; difference.

dis•pas•sion (dis pash′ən), *n.* the state or quality of being unemotional or uninvolved emotionally.

dis•pas•sion•ate (dis pash′ə nit), *adj.* free from or unaffected by passion; devoid of personal feeling or bias; impartial; calm. **—dis•pas′sion•ate•ly,** *adv.*

dis•patch (di spach′), *v.t.* **1.** to send off or away with speed, as a messenger, telegram, or body of troops. **2.** to put to death; kill. **3.** to transact or dispose of (a matter) promptly or speedily. **—***n.* **4.** the sending off of a messenger, letter, etc. **5.** the act of putting to death; execution. **6.** prompt or speedy action. **7.** a message or official communication sent with speed, esp. by special messenger. **8.** a news story transmitted to a newspaper by a reporter, wire service, etc.

dis•pel (di spel′), *v.t.*, **-pelled, -pel•ling. 1.** to drive off in various directions; disperse; dissipate. **2.** to cause to vanish; alleviate. **—dis•pel′la•ble,** *adj.* **—dis•pel′ler,** *n.*

dis•pen•sa•ble (di spen′sə bəl), *adj.* **1.** capable of being dispensed with or done without; not necessary or essential. **2.** capable of being dispensed or administered. **3.** *Rom. Cath. Ch.* capable of being permitted or forgiven, as an offense or sin. **—dis•pen′sa•bil′i•ty, dis•pen′sa•ble•ness,** *n.*

dis•pen•sa•ry (di spen′sə rē), *n.*, *pl.* **-ries. 1.** a place where something is dispensed, esp. medicines. **2.** a charitable or public facility where medicines are furnished and free or inexpensive medical advice is available.

dis•pen•sa•tion (dis′pən sā′shən, -pen-), *n.* **1.** an act or instance of dispensing; distribution. **2.** something that is distributed or given out. **3.** a certain order, system, or arrangement; administration or management. **4. a.** the divine ordering of the affairs of the world. **b.** a divinely appointed order or age. **5.** a dispensing with, doing away with, or doing without something. **6.** *Rom. Cath. Ch.* **a.** a relaxation of law granted by a competent superior. **b.** an official document authorizing this. **—dis′pen•sa′tion•al,** *adj.*

dis•pen•sa•tion•al•ism (dis′pən sā′shə nl iz′əm, -pen-), *n.* the interpreting of history as a series of divine dispensations.

dis•pense (di spens′), *v.*, **-pensed, -pens•ing,** *n.* **—***v.t.* **1.** to deal out; distribute. **2.** to administer: *to dispense the law without bias.* **3.** to make up and distribute (medicine), esp. on prescription. **4.** *Rom. Cath. Ch.* to grant a dispensation to. **—***v.i.* **5.** to grant dispensation. **6. dispense with, a.** to do without; forgo. **b.** to do away with; get rid of. **—dis•pens′er,** *n.*

dis•per•sal (di spûr′səl), *n.* DISPERSION.

dis•perse (di spûrs′), *v.*, **-persed, -pers•ing. —***v.t.* **1.** to drive or send off in various directions; scatter. **2.** to spread widely; disseminate. **3.** to dispel; cause to vanish: *The wind dispersed the fog.* **4.** to cause (particles) to separate uniformly throughout a solid, liquid, or gas. **5.** to subject (light) to dispersion. **—***v.i.* **6.** to separate and move apart in different directions without order or regularity; become scattered. **7.** to be dispelled; vanish. **—dis•pers′ed•ly,** *adv.* **—dis•pers′er,** *n.* **—dis•pers′i•bil′i•ty,** *n.* **—dis•pers′i•ble,** *adj.*

dis•per•sion (di spûr′zhən, -shən), *n.* **1.** Also, **dispersal.** an act or instance of dispersing or a state of being dispersed. **2. a.** the variation of the index of refraction of a transparent substance, as glass, with the wavelength of light. **b.** the separation of white or compound light into its respective colors, as in the formation of a spectrum by a prism. **3.** the scattering of values of a statistical variable around the mean or median of a distribution. **4.** Also called **disperse′ sys′tem.** a system of dispersed particles suspended in a solid, liquid, or gas. **5.** (*cap.*) DIASPORA (def. 1).

dis•pir•it (di spir′it), *v.t.* to deprive of spirit, hope, enthusiasm, etc.; discourage; dishearten.

dis•place (dis plās′), *v.t.*, **-placed, -plac•ing. 1.** to compel (a person or persons) to leave home, country, etc. **2.** to move or put out of the usual or proper place. **3.** to take the place of; replace; supplant. **4.** to remove from a position, office, or dignity. **—dis•place′a•ble,** *adj.* **—dis•plac′er,** *n.*

displaced′ per′son, *n.* a person driven or expelled from his or her homeland by war, famine, tyranny, etc. *Abbr.:* DP, D.P.

dis•place•ment (dis plās′mənt), *n.* **1.** the state of being displaced or the amount or degree to which something is displaced. **2. a.** the linear or angular distance in a given direction between a body or point and a reference position. **b.** the distance of an oscillating body from its equilibrium position. **3.** the volume of the space through which a piston travels during a single stroke in an engine, pump, or the like. **4.** the weight or the volume of fluid displaced by a floating or submerged body, as a ship. **5.** the offset of rocks caused by movement along a fault. **6.** the transfer of an emotion from its original focus to another object, person, or situation.

displace′ment ton′, *n.* a unit for measuring the displacement of a vessel, equal to a long ton of 2240 lb. (1016 kg) or 35 cu. ft. (1 cu. m) of seawater.

dis•play (di splā′), *v.t.* **1.** to show or exhibit; make visible. **2.** to reveal; betray: *to display fear.* **3.** to unfold; open out; spread out: *to display a sail.* **4.** to show ostentatiously; flaunt. **5.** to give special prominence to (words, captions, etc.) by choice and arrangement of type. **6.** to show (computer data) on a CRT or other screen. **—***v.i.* **7.** (of animals) to engage in a pattern of behavior designed to attract and arouse a mate. **—***n.* **8.** an act or instance of displaying; exhibition. **9. a.** the giving of prominence to particular words, sentences, etc., by the choice of types and position, as in an advertisement, headline, or news story. **b.** printed matter thus displayed. **10.** an arrangement, as of merchandise, designed to please the eye or attract buyers. **11. a.** the visual representation of the output of an electronic device. **b.** the portion of the device, as a screen, that shows this representation. **12.** a stereotyped pattern of animal behavior designed to attract and arouse a mate. **—dis•play′er,** *n.*

dis•please (dis plēz′), *v.*, **-pleased, -pleas•ing. —***v.t.* **1.** to incur the dissatisfaction or dislike of. **—***v.i.* **2.** to be unpleasant; cause displeasure. **—dis•pleas′ing•ly,** *adv.*

dis•pleas•ure (dis plezh′ər), *n.* **1.** dissatisfaction; disapproval. **2.** discomfort; uneasiness. **—dis•pleas′ure•a•ble,** *adj.*

dis•port (di spôrt′, -spōrt′), *v.t.* **1.** to divert or amuse (oneself). **2.** to display (oneself) in a sportive manner. **—***v.i.* **3.** to divert oneself; sport. **—***n.* **4.** diversion; amusement; play; sport. **—dis•port′ment,** *n.*

dis•pos•a•ble (di spō′zə bəl), *adj.* **1.** designed for or capable of being thrown away after being used or used up. **2.** free for use; available: *Every disposable vehicle was sent.* **—***n.* **3.** something disposable after use, as a paper cup or napkin. **—dis•pos′a•bil′i•ty,** *n.* **—dis•pos′a•bly,** *adv.*

dispos′able in′come, *n.* personal income that remains after taxes and expenses are paid.

dis•pos•al[1] (di spō′zəl), *n.* **1.** an act or instance of disposing; arrangement: *the disposal of the troops.* **2.** a disposing of or getting rid of something: *the disposal of wastes.* **3.** a disposing or allotting of, as by gift or sale; bestowal or assignment. **4.** power or right to dispose of a thing; control: *left at my disposal.*

dis•pos•al[2] (di spō′zəl), *n.* an electrical device in the drain of a sink, for grinding up garbage.

dis•pose (di spōz′), *v.*, **-posed, -pos•ing. —***v.t.* **1.** to give a tendency or inclination to; incline: *His temperament disposed him to argue readily with people.* **2.** to put in a particular or the proper order or arrangement; adjust by arranging the parts. **3.** to put in a particular or suitable place. **4.** to make fit or ready; prepare. **—***v.i.* **5.** to arrange or decide matters: *to do as God disposes.* **6. dispose of, a.** to deal with conclusively; settle. **b.** to get rid of; discard or destroy. **c.** to give away or sell. **—dis•pos′ing•ly,** *adv.*

dis•posed (di spōzd′), *adj.* having a certain inclination or disposition; inclined (usu. fol. by *to* or an infinitive). **—dis•pos′ed•ly,** *adv.*

dis•po•si•tion (dis′pə zish′ən), *n.* **1.** the predominant or prevailing tendency of one's spirits; characteristic attitude: *a girl with a pleasant disposition.* **2.** state of mind regarding something; inclination: *a disposition to gamble.* **3.** physical inclination or tendency: *the disposition of ice to melt when heated.* **4.** arrangement or placing, as of troops or buildings. **5.** final settlement of a matter. **6.** bestowal, as by gift or sale. **7.** power to dispose of a thing; control: *funds at one's disposition.* **8.** regulation; management; dispensation: *the disposition of God.* **—dis′po•si′tion•al,** *adj.*

dis•pos•sess (dis′pə zes′), *v.t.* to put (a person) out of possession or occupancy. **—dis′pos•ses′sion,** *n.* **—dis′pos•ses′sor,** *n.* **—dis′pos•ses′so•ry,** *adj.*

dis•pos•sessed (dis′pə zest′), *adj.* **1.** evicted, as from a dwelling or land; ousted. **2.** without property, status, etc., as wandering or displaced persons; rootless; disfranchised. **3.** having suffered the loss of prospects, relationships, etc.; disaffiliated; alienated.

dis•proof (dis pro͞of′), *n.* **1.** the act of disproving. **2.** proof to the contrary; refutation.

dis•pro•por•tion (dis′prə pôr′shən, -pōr′-), *n.* **1.** lack of proportion; lack of proper relationship in size, number, etc. **2.** something out of proportion. **—***v.t.* **3.** to make disproportionate. **—dis′pro•por′tion•a•ble,** *adj.* **—dis′pro•por′tion•a•bly,** *adv.*

dis•pro•por•tion•ate (dis′prə pôr′shə nit, -pōr′-), *adj.* not proportionate; out of proportion, as in size or number. **—dis′pro•por′tion•ate•ly,** *adv.*

dis•prove (dis pro͞ov′), *v.t.*, **-proved, -prov•ing.** to prove (an assertion, claim, etc.) to be false or wrong; refute; invalidate. **—dis•prov′a•ble,** *adj.* **—dis•prov′er,** *n.*

D

dis•pu•ta•tion (dis′pyŏŏ tā′shən), *n.* **1.** the act of disputing or debating; verbal controversy; discussion or debate. **2.** an academic exercise stressing the formal arguing of a thesis.

dis•pu•ta•tious (dis′pyŏŏ tā′shəs) also **dis•put•a•tive** (di spyŏŏ′tə-tiv), *adj.* fond of or given to disputation; argumentative; contentious. —**dis′pu•ta′tious•ly,** *adv.*

dis•pute (di spyōōt′), *v.,* **-put•ed, -put•ing,** *n.* —*v.i.* **1.** to engage in argument or debate. **2.** to argue vehemently; quarrel. —*v.t.* **3.** to argue or debate about. **4.** to argue against; call in question. **5.** to quarrel or fight about; contest. **6.** to strive against; oppose: *to dispute an advance of troops.* —*n.* **7.** a debate, controversy, or difference of opinion. **8.** a quarrel.

dis•qual•i•fi•ca•tion (dis kwol′ə fi kā′shən), *n.* **1.** an act or instance of disqualifying. **2.** the state of being disqualified. **3.** something that disqualifies.

dis•qual•i•fy (dis kwol′ə fī′), *v.t.,* **-fied, -fy•ing. 1.** to deprive of qualification or fitness; incapacitate. **2.** to deprive of legal, official, or other rights or privileges; declare ineligible or unqualified. **3.** to deprive of the right to participate in or win a contest because of a violation of the rules. —**dis•qual′i•fi′a•ble,** *adj.*

dis•qui•et (dis kwī′it), *n.* **1.** lack of calm, peace, or ease; anxiety; uneasiness. —*v.t.* **2.** to deprive of calm or peace. —**dis•qui′et•ly,** *adv.*

dis•qui•e•tude (dis kwī′i tōōd′, -tyōōd′), *n.* the state of disquiet; uneasiness.

dis•re•gard (dis′ri gärd′), *v.t.* **1.** to pay no attention to; leave out of consideration; ignore. **2.** to treat without due regard, respect, or attentiveness; slight. —*n.* **3.** lack of regard or attention; neglect. **4.** lack of due or respectful regard. —**dis′re•gard′a•ble,** *adj.* —**dis′re•gard′er,** *n.*

dis•re•pair (dis′ri pâr′), *n.* the condition of needing repair; an impaired or neglected state.

dis•rep•u•ta•ble (dis rep′yə tə bəl), *adj.* **1.** having a bad reputation. **2.** discreditable; dishonorable. **3.** shabby or shoddy. —**dis•rep′u•ta•ble•ness,** *n.* —**dis•rep′u•ta•bly,** *adv.*

dis•re•pute (dis′ri pyōōt′), *n.* bad repute; disfavor.

dis•re•spect (dis′ri spekt′), *n.* **1.** lack of respect; discourtesy; rudeness. —*v.t.* **2.** to regard or treat with contempt or rudeness; insult. —**dis′re•spect′ful,** *adj.*

dis•re•spect•a•ble (dis′ri spek′tə bəl), *adj.* not respectable. —**dis′re•spect′a•bil′i•ty,** *n.*

dis•robe (dis rōb′), *v.t., v.i.,* **-robed, -rob•ing.** to undress.

dis•rupt (dis rupt′), *v.t.* **1.** to cause disorder or turmoil in. **2.** to destroy, usu. temporarily, the normal continuance or unity of; interrupt: *to disrupt broadcasting.* **3.** to break apart: *to disrupt a connection.* —*adj.* **4.** broken apart; disrupted. —**dis•rupt′er, dis•rup′tor,** *n.*

dis•rup•tion (dis rup′shən), *n.* **1.** forcible separation or division into parts. **2.** a disrupted condition.

dis•rup•tive (dis rup′tiv), *adj.* tending to cause, or caused by disruption. —**dis•rup′tive•ly,** *adv.* —**dis•rup′tive•ness,** *n.*

dis•sat•is•fac•tion (dis′sat is fak′shən, dis sat′-), *n.* **1.** the state or attitude of not being satisfied; discontent; displeasure. **2.** a particular cause or feeling of displeasure or disappointment.

dis•sat•is•fy (dis sat′is fī′), *v.t.,* **-fied, -fy•ing.** to fail to satisfy; disappoint. —**dissatisfied,** *adj.*

dis•sect (di sekt′, dī-), *v.t.* **1.** to cut apart (an animal body, plant, etc.) to examine the structure and relation of parts. **2.** to examine minutely part by part; analyze. —**dis•sec′ti•ble,** *adj.* —**dis•sec′tor,** *n.*

dis•sect•ed (di sek′tid, dī-), *adj.* **1.** deeply divided into numerous segments, as a leaf. **2.** separated, by erosion, into many closely spaced crevices or gorges, as the surface of a plateau.

dis•sec•tion (di sek′shən, dī-), *n.* **1.** the act of dissecting. **2.** something that has been dissected. **3.** a detailed analysis.

dis•sem•blance (di sem′bləns), *n.* dissimulation.

dis•sem•ble (di sem′bəl), *v.,* **-bled, -bling.** —*v.t.* **1.** to give a false or misleading appearance to; conceal the real nature of. **2.** to put on the appearance of; feign. —*v.i.* **3.** to conceal one's true motives, thoughts, etc., by some pretense; speak or act hypocritically. —**dis•sem′bler,** *n.* —**dis•sem′bling•ly,** *adv.*

dis•sem•i•nate (di sem′ə nāt′), *v.t.,* **-nat•ed, -nat•ing.** to scatter or spread widely, as if sowing seed; promulgate extensively; broadcast; disperse. —**dis•sem′i•na′tion,** *n.* —**dis•sem′i•na′tive,** *adj.* —**dis•sem′i•na′tor,** *n.*

dis•sen•sion (di sen′shən), *n.* **1.** strong disagreement; a contention or quarrel; discord. **2.** difference in sentiment or opinion.

dis•sent (di sent′), *v.i.* **1.** to differ in sentiment or opinion, esp. from the majority (often fol. by *from*). **2.** to reject the doctrines or authority of an established church. —*n.* **3.** difference of sentiment or opinion. **4.** separation from an established church, esp. the Church of England; nonconformity. —**dis′si•dence,** *n.* —**dis′si•dent,** *n., adj.*

dis•sent•er (di sen′tər), *n.* **1.** a person who dissents, as from an established church or political party. **2.** (*sometimes cap.*) a person who dissents from the Church of England.

dis•sen•tient (di sen′shənt), *adj.* **1.** dissenting, esp. from the opinion of the majority. —*n.* **2.** a person who dissents. —**dis•sen′tience, dis•sen′tien•cy,** *n.* —**dis•sen′tient•ly,** *adv.*

dis•ser•tate (dis′ər tāt′), *v.i.,* **-tat•ed, -tat•ing.** to discuss a subject fully and learnedly; discourse. —**dis′ser•ta′tor,** *n.*

dis•ser•ta•tion (dis′ər tā′shən), *n.* **1.** an essay or thesis, esp. one written by a candidate for a doctorate. **2.** any formal discourse in speech or writing. —**dis′ser•ta′tion•al,** *adj.*

dis•serv•ice (dis sûr′vis), *n.* harmful or injurious service; an ill turn.

dis•sim•i•lar (di sim′ə lər, dis sim′-), *adj.* not similar; unlike; different. —**dis•sim′i•lar•ly,** *adv.*

dis•sim•i•lar•i•ty (di sim′ə lar′i tē, dis sim′-), *n., pl.* **-ties. 1.** unlikeness; difference. **2.** a point of difference.

dis•sim•i•late (di sim′ə lāt′), *v.,* **-lat•ed, -lat•ing.** —*v.t.* **1.** to modify (a sound) by dissimilation. —*v.i.* **2.** (of a sound) to become modified by dissimilation. —**dis•sim′i•la′tive,** *adj.* —**dis•sim′i•la•to′ry** (-lə tôr′ē, -tōr′ē), *adj.*

dis•sim•i•la•tion (di sim′ə lā′shən), *n.* **1.** the act of making or becoming unlike. **2.** the process by which a speech sound becomes different from a neighboring sound, as in *purple* from Old English *purpure,* or disappears because of an identical sound nearby, as in the pronunciation of *governor* as (guv′ə nər) instead of (guv′ər nər).

dis•si•mil•i•tude (dis′si mil′i tōōd′, -tyōōd′), *n.* **1.** unlikeness; difference; dissimilarity. **2.** a point of difference; dissimilarity.

dis•sim•u•late (di sim′yə lāt′), *v.,* **-lat•ed, -lat•ing.** —*v.t.* **1.** to disguise or conceal under a false appearance; dissemble. —*v.i.* **2.** to conceal one's true motives, thoughts, etc., by some pretense. —**dis•sim′u•la′tion,** *n.* —**dis•sim′u•la′tive,** *adj.* —**dis•sim′u•la′tor,** *n.*

dis•si•pate (dis′ə pāt′), *v.,* **-pat•ed, -pat•ing.** —*v.t.* **1.** to scatter in various directions; disperse; dispel. **2.** to spend or use wastefully or extravagantly; deplete. —*v.i.* **3.** to become scattered or dispersed. **4.** to indulge in extravagant, intemperate, or dissolute pleasure. —**dis′si•pat′er, dis′si•pa′tor,** *n.* —**dis′si•pa′tive,** *adj.*

dis•si•pat•ed (dis′ə pā′tid), *adj.* indulging in or characterized by excessive devotion to pleasure; dissolute. —**dis′si•pat′ed•ly,** *adv.* —**dis′si•pa′ted•ness,** *n.*

dis•si•pa•tion (dis′ə pā′shən), *n.* **1.** the act of dissipating. **2.** the state of being dissipated; dispersion; disintegration. **3.** a wasting by misuse: *the dissipation of a fortune.* **4.** amusement; diversion. **5.** dissolute way of living; intemperance. **6.** a process in which energy is used or lost without accomplishing useful work, as friction causing loss of mechanical energy.

dis•so•ci•ate (di sō′shē āt′, -sē-), *v.,* **-at•ed, -at•ing.** —*v.t.* **1.** to sever the association of; separate: *He tried to dissociate himself from his past.* **2.** to subject to dissociation. —*v.i.* **3.** to withdraw from association. **4.** to undergo dissociation. —**dis•so′ci•a′tive,** *adj.*

dis•so•ci•a•tion (di sō′sē ā′shən, -shē ā′-), *n.* **1.** an act or instance of dissociating. **2.** the state of being dissociated; disjunction; separation. **3.** the decomposition of a substance into simpler molecules or atoms with the addition of heat or energy. **4.** the splitting off of a group of mental processes from the main body of consciousness, as in amnesia or certain forms of hysteria.

dis•so•lute (dis′ə lōōt′), *adj.* indifferent to moral restraints; given to immoral or improper conduct; dissipated. —**dis′so•lute′ly,** *adv.* —**dis′so•lute′ness,** *n.*

dis•so•lu•tion (dis′ə lōō′shən), *n.* **1.** the act or process of resolving or dissolving into parts or elements. **2.** the resulting state. **3.** the undoing or breaking of a bond, partnership, etc. **4.** the breaking up of an assembly or organization; dismissal; dispersal. **5.** death; decease. **6.** a bringing or coming to an end; disintegration; termination. **7.** the process by which a solid, gas, or liquid is dispersed homogeneously in a gas, solid, or, esp., a liquid. —**dis′so•lu′tive,** *adj.*

dis•solve (di zolv′), *v.,* **-solved, -solv•ing,** *n.* —*v.t.* **1.** to make a solution of, as by mixing with a liquid; pass into solution: *to dissolve salt in water.* **2.** to melt; liquefy. **3.** to undo or break (a tie, union, etc.). **4.** to break up or order the termination of (an assembly or organization); dismiss. **5.** to bring to an end; terminate. **6.** to separate into parts or elements; disintegrate. **7.** to destroy the binding power or influence of: *to dissolve a spell.* **8.** to deprive of force; abrogate or annul: *to dissolve a marriage.* —*v.i.* **9.** to become dissolved, as in a solvent. **10.** to become melted or liquefied. **11.** to disintegrate or disperse. **12.** to lose intensity or strength. **13.** to break down emotionally; lose one's composure. **14.** to fade out one on-screen image while simultaneously fading in the next, overlapping the two during the process. —*n.* **15.** a transition from one on-screen image to the next made by dissolving. —**dis•solv′a•bil′i•ty,** *n.* —**dis•solv′a•ble,** *adj.* —**dis•solv′er,** *n.*

dis•so•nance (dis′ə nəns), *n.* **1.** inharmonious or harsh sound; discord; cacophony. **2.** an unresolved, discordant musical chord or interval. **3.** lack of harmony or agreement; incongruity.

dis•so•nant (dis′ə nənt), *adj.* **1.** disagreeing or harsh in sound; discordant. **2.** disagreeing or incongruous; at variance. **3.** harmonically unresolved. —**dis′so•nant•ly,** *adv.*

dis•suade (di swād′), *v.t.,* **-suad•ed, -suad•ing.** to deter by advice or persuasion; persuade not to do something (often fol. by *from*). —**dis•suad′a•ble,** *adj.* —**dis•suad′er,** *n.*

dis•sua•sion (di swā′zhən), *n.* an act or instance of dissuading.

dis•sua•sive (di swā′siv), *adj.* tending or liable to dissuade. —**dis•sua′sive•ly,** *adv.* —**dis•sua′sive•ness,** *n.*

dis•taff (dis′taf, -täf), *n.* **1.** a long staff for holding wool, flax, etc., from which the thread is drawn in spinning. —*adj.* **2.** pertaining to women, women's work, or the female line of descent.

dis•tal (dis′tl), *adj.* situated away from the point of origin or attachment, as of a limb or bone. Compare PROXIMAL (def. 1).

dis•tance (dis′təns), *n., v.,* **-tanced, -tanc•ing.** —*n.* **1.** the extent or amount of space between two things, points, lines, etc. **2.** the state or fact of being apart in space, as of one thing from another; remoteness. **3.** a linear extent of space: *to walk a distance.* **4.** an expanse; area: *A vast distance of water surrounded the ship.* **5.** the interval between two points of time; an extent of time. **6.** remoteness or difference in any respect. **7.** an amount of progress: *We've come a long distance on the project.* **8.** a distant point, place, or region. **9.** the distant part of a field of view: *a tree in the distance.* **10.** absence of warmth; reserve; coolness. **11.** (in a heat race) the space measured back from the winning post that a horse must reach by the time the winner passes the winning post or be eliminated from subsequent heats. —*v.t.* **12.** to leave behind at a distance, as at a race; surpass. **13.** to place at a distance. **14.** to cause to appear distant. —***Idiom.*** **15. go the distance, a.** (in horse racing) to run well in a long race. **b.** to complete something that requires sustained effort. **16. keep at a distance,** to treat with reserve. **17. keep one's distance,** to remain aloof.

dis•tant (dis′tənt), *adj.* **1.** far off or apart in space; remote. **2.** apart or far off in time. **3.** remote or far apart in any respect: *a distant relative.* **4.** reserved or aloof; not familiar or cordial. **5.** arriving from or going to a distance. —**dis′tant•ly,** *adv.*

dis•taste (dis tāst′), *n.* **1.** dislike; disinclination: *a distaste for household chores.* **2.** dislike for food or drink.

dis•taste•ful (dis tāst′fəl), *adj.* **1.** unpleasant, offensive, or causing dislike. **2.** unpleasant to the taste. **3.** showing distaste or dislike. —**dis•taste′ful•ly,** *adv.* —**dis•taste′ful•ness,** *n.*

dis•tem•per[1] (dis tem′pər), *n.* **1. a.** Also called **canine distemper.** an infectious disease chiefly of young dogs, caused by an unidentified virus and characterized by lethargy, fever, catarrh, and vomiting. **b.** an infectious disease of horses, caused by the bacillus *Streptococcus equi* and characterized by catarrh of the upper air passages and the formation of pus in the submaxillary and other lymphatic glands. **c.** Also called **feline distemper.** a usu. fatal viral disease of cats, characterized by fever, vomiting, and diarrhea, leading to severe dehydration. **2.** a deranged condition of mind or body; a disorder or disease: *a feverish distemper.* **3.** disorder or disturbance, esp. of a political nature.

dis•tem•per[2] (dis tem′pər), *n.* **1.** a technique of decorative painting in which glue or gum is used as a binder or medium to achieve a mat surface and rapid drying. **2.** a painting executed by this method. —*v.t.* **3.** to paint in distemper.

dis•tend (di stend′), *v.t., v.i.* **1.** to expand by stretching, as something hollow or elastic. **2.** to spread in all directions; expand; extend. —**dis•tend′er,** *n.*

dis•tend•ed (di sten′did), *adj.* **1.** increased, as in size or volume; expanded; dilated. **2.** swollen, by or as if by internal pressure, out of normal size or shape.

dis•till (di stil′), *v.t.* **1.** to subject to a process of vaporization and subsequent condensation, as for purification or concentration. **2.** to extract volatile components from or transform by distillation. **3.** to concentrate, purify, or separate by or as if by distillation. **4.** to extract the essential elements of. —*v.i.* **5.** to undergo or perform distillation. **6.** to drop, pass, or condense as a distillate. **7.** to fall in drops; trickle. —**dis•till′a•ble,** *adj.*

dis•til•late (dis′tl it, -āt′, di stil′it), *n.* the product obtained from the condensation of vapors in distillation.

dis•til•la•tion (dis′tl ā′shən), *n.* **1.** the process of heating, evaporating, and subsequently condensing a liquid. **2.** the purification or concentration of a substance or the separation of one substance from another by such a process. —**dis•til•la•to•ry** (di stil′ə tôr′ē, -tōr′ē), **dis•til′la•tive** (-tiv), *adj.*

dis•till•er (di stil′ər), *n.* **1.** an apparatus for distilling, as a condenser; still. **2.** a person or company whose business it is to extract alcoholic liquors by distillation. —**dis•till′er•y,** *n.*

dis•tinct (di stingkt′), *adj.* **1.** distinguished as not being the same; not identical; separate. **2.** different in nature or quality; dissimilar (sometimes fol. by *from*): *Gold is distinct from iron.* **3.** clear to the senses or intellect; plain; unmistakable: *a distinct shape.* **4.** unquestionably exceptional or notable: *a distinct honor.* —**dis•tinct′ly,** *adv.* —**dis•tinct′ness,** *n.*

dis•tinc•tion (di stingk′shən), *n.* **1.** a distinguishing as different. **2.** the recognizing of differences; discrimination: *to make a distinction between right and wrong.* **3.** a discrimination made between things as different: *Death comes to all without distinction.* **4.** the condition of being different; difference: *the distinction between talk and action.* **5.** a distinguishing quality or characteristic: *It has the distinction of being the oldest house in town.* **6.** a distinguishing or treating with special honor, attention, or favor. **7.** marked superiority; note; eminence. **8.** distinguished appearance.

dis•tinc•tive (di stingk′tiv), *adj.* **1.** serving to distinguish; characteristic; distinguishing: *the zebra's distinctive stripes.* **2.** having a special quality, style, attractiveness, etc.; notable. **3.** *Ling.* serving to distinguish meanings. —**dis•tinc′tive•ly,** *adv.*

dis•tin•gué (dē′stang gā′, di stang′gā), *adj.* having an air of distinction.

dis•tin•guée (dē′stang gā′, di stang′gā), *adj.* (of a woman) having an air of distinction.

dis•tin•guish (di sting′gwish), *v.t.* **1.** to mark off as different (often fol. by *from* or *by*): *His height distinguishes him from the other boys.* **2.** to recognize as distinct or different; recognize the individual features or characteristics of. **3.** to perceive clearly by sight or other sense; discern; recognize. **4.** to set apart as different; characterize: *Her Italian accent distinguishes her.* **5.** to make prominent or eminent: *to distinguish oneself in the arts.* **6.** to divide into classes; classify. —*v.i.* **7.** to indicate or show a difference (usu. fol. by *between*). **8.** to recognize or note differences; discriminate. —**dis•tin′guish•a•ble,** *adj.* —**dis•tin′guish•a•bil′i•ty,** *n.* —**dis•tin′guish•a•bly,** *adv.*

dis•tin•guished (di sting′gwisht), *adj.* **1.** made conspicuous by excellence; eminent; famous. **2.** having an air of distinction or dignity. **3.** conspicuous; marked. —**dis•tin′guished•ly,** *adv.*

dis•tort (di stôrt′), *v.t.* **1.** to twist awry or out of shape; alter the original or normal appearance of. **2.** to give a false, perverted, or disproportionate meaning to; misrepresent. **3.** to reproduce or amplify (an electronic signal) inaccurately. —**dis•tor′tive,** *adj.*

dis•tort•ed (di stôr′tid), *adj.* **1.** not truly or completely representing the facts or reality; misrepresented; false. **2.** twisted; deformed; misshapen. **3.** mentally or morally twisted, as with an aberration or bias. —**dis•tort′ed•ly,** *adv.* —**dis•tort′ed•ness,** *n.*

dis•tor•tion (di stôr′shən), *n.* **1.** an act of distorting. **2.** the state of being distorted. **3.** anything distorted, as an image or electronic signal. **4.** an aberration of a lens or system of lenses in which the magnification of the object varies with the lateral distance from the axis of the lens. —**dis•tor′tion•al, dis•tor′tion•ar′y,** *adj.*

D

dis•tract (di strakt′), *v.t.* **1.** to draw away or divert, as the mind or attention: *The music distracted us from our work.* **2.** to disturb or trouble greatly in mind; beset. **3.** to provide a pleasant diversion for; amuse; entertain. **4.** to separate or divide by dissension or strife. —**dis•tract′i•ble,** *adj.*

dis•tract•ed (di strak′tid), *adj.* **1.** having the attention diverted; not concentrating. **2.** rendered incapable of behaving, reacting, etc., in a normal manner, as by worry or remorse; disturbed. —**dis•tract′ed•ly,** *adv.* —**dis•tract′ed•ness,** *n.*

dis•trac•tion (di strak′shən), *n.* **1.** the act of distracting. **2.** the state of being distracted. **3.** mental distress or derangement. **4.** a person or thing that prevents concentration. **5.** something that amuses. —**dis•trac′tive,** *adj.*

dis•traught (di strôt′), *adj.* **1.** bewildered; deeply agitated. **2.** mentally deranged; crazed. —**dis•traught′ly,** *adv.*

dis•tress (di stres′), *n.* **1.** acute anxiety, pain, or sorrow. **2.** anything that causes anxiety, pain, or sorrow. **3.** a state of extreme necessity, trouble, or misfortune. **4.** the state of a ship or airplane requiring immediate assistance, as when on fire in transit. **5.** the legal seizure and detention of another's goods as security for debt, etc. —*v.t.* **6.** to afflict with pain, anxiety, or sorrow; trouble; worry. **7.** to subject to pressure or strain: *to be distressed by excessive work.* **8.** to compel by pain or force of circumstances. **9.** to scratch or stain (furniture, wood, etc.) so as to give an appearance of age. —**dis•tress′ing•ly,** *adv.*

dis•tressed (di strest′), *adj.* **1.** affected with or suffering from distress. **2.** (of merchandise or property for sale) damaged, out-of-date, or used. **3.** (of furniture or wood) purposely blemished or marred so as to give an antique appearance. **4.** (of fabric or clothing) processed or treated to appear faded or wrinkled, as if from long, steady use. **5.** DEPRESSED (def. 5). —**dis•tress′ed•ly,** *adv.*

dis•trib•u•tar•y (di strib′yo͞o ter′ē), *n., pl.* **-tar•ies.** an outflowing branch of a stream or river, typically found in a delta (opposed to *tributary*).

dis•trib•ute (di strib′yo͞ot), *v.t.,* **-ut•ed, -ut•ing. 1.** to divide and give out in shares; allot. **2.** to spread throughout a space or over an area; scatter. **3.** to pass out or deliver: *to distribute pamphlets.* **4.** to sell (merchandise) in a specified area. **5.** to divide into distinct phases or functions. **6.** to divide into classes. **7.** (in logic) to employ (a term) so as to refer to all individuals denoted by it. —**dis•trib′ut•a•ble,** *adj.*

dis•tri•bu•tion (dis′trə byo͞o′shən), *n.* **1.** an act or instance of distributing. **2.** the state or manner of being distributed. **3.** arrangement; classification. **4.** something that is distributed. **5.** the frequency of occurrence or the geographic range or place where any entity or category of entities occurs: *the distribution of coniferous forests.* **6.** placement; disposition. **7.** apportionment. **8.** the delivery of an item or items to the intended recipients, as mail or newspapers. **9.** the total number of an item delivered, sold, or given out. **10.** the marketing, transporting, and selling of goods. **11.** *Statistics.* a set of values or measurements of a set of elements, each measurement being associated with an element. —**dis′tri•bu′tion•al,** *adj.*

distribu′tion curve′, *n.* the curve or line of a graph in which cumulative frequencies are plotted as ordinates and values of the variate as abscissas.

dis•trib•u•tive (di strib′yə tiv), *adj.* **1.** serving to distribute, assign, or divide; characterized by or pertaining to distribution. **2.** referring to the members of a group individually, as the adjectives *each* and *every.* **3.** *Logic.* (of a term) distributed in a given logical proposition. **4. a.** (of a binary operation) having the property that terms in an expression may be expanded in a particular way to form an equivalent expression, as $a(b + c) = ab + ac$. **b.** having reference to this property: *the distributive law for multiplication over addition.* —*n.* **5.** a distributive word or expression. —**dis•trib′u•tive•ly,** *adv.*

dis•trib•u•tor (di strib′yə tər), *n.* **1.** a person or thing that distributes. **2.** a firm, esp. a wholesaler, that markets a line of merchandise gener-

ally or within a given territory. **3.** a device in a multicylinder engine that distributes the igniting voltage to the spark plugs.

dis•trict (dis′trikt), *n.* **1.** a division of territory, as of a country, state, or county, marked off for administrative, electoral, or other purposes. **2.** a region or locality. —*v.t.* **3.** to divide into districts.

dis′trict attor′ney, *n.* an officer who acts as attorney for the people or government within a specified district.

dis′trict court′, *n.* the federal trial court sitting in each district of the United States.

Dis′trict of Colum′bia, *n.* a federal area in the E United States, on the Potomac, coextensive with the federal capital, Washington. 543,213; 69 sq. mi. (179 sq. km). *Abbr.:* DC, D.C.

dis•trust (dis trust′), *v.t.* **1.** to regard with doubt or suspicion; have no trust in. —*n.* **2.** lack of trust; doubt; suspicion. —**dis•trust′er,** *n.*

dis•turb (di stûrb′), *v.t.* **1.** to interrupt the quiet, rest, or peace of; bother; unsettle. **2.** to interfere with; interrupt; hinder. **3.** to interfere with the arrangement or order of; disarrange: *to disturb the papers on a desk.* **4.** to perplex; trouble. —*v.i.* **5.** to cause disturbance to someone's sleep, rest, etc. —**dis•turb′er,** *n.*

dis•turb•ance (di stûr′bəns), *n.* **1.** the act of disturbing. **2.** the state of being disturbed. **3.** an instance of this; commotion. **4.** something that disturbs. **5.** an outbreak of disorder. **6.** any cyclonic storm or low-pressure area, usu. a small one.

dis•turbed (di stûrbd′), *adj.* **1.** marked by symptoms of mental illness. **2.** agitated or distressed; disrupted.

di•sul•fide (dī sul′fīd, -fid), *n.* **1.** (in inorganic chemistry) a sulfide containing two atoms of sulfur, as carbon disulfide, CS_2. **2.** (in organic chemistry) a sulfide containing the bivalent group $-SS-$, as diethyl disulfide, $C_4H_{10}S_2$.

dis•un•ion (dis yo͞on′yən), *n.* **1.** a severance of union; separation; disjunction. **2.** lack of unity; dissension.

dis•use (*n.* dis yo͞os′; *v.* -yo͞oz′), *n., v.,* **-used, -us•ing.** —*n.* **1.** discontinuance of use or practice. —*v.t.* **2.** to cease to use.

dit (dit), *n.* an echoic word, the referent of which is a click or brief tone interval, designating the dot of Morse code. Compare DAH.

ditch (dich), *n.* **1.** a long, narrow excavation in the ground, as for drainage or irrigation; trench. **2.** any natural channel or waterway. —*v.t.* **3.** to dig a ditch in or around. **4.** to derail or drive into a ditch. **5.** to crash-land on water and abandon (an aircraft). **6.** *Slang.* **a.** to get rid of. **b.** to escape from. —*v.i.* **7.** to dig a ditch. **8.** (of an aircraft or its crew) to crash-land on water.

di•the•ism (dī′thē iz′əm), *n.* **1.** the doctrine of or belief in two equally powerful gods. **2.** belief in the existence of two independent antagonistic principles, one good and the other evil. —**di′the•ist,** *n.* —**di′the•is′tic, di′the•is′ti•cal,** *adj.*

dith•er (dith′ər), *n.* **1.** a trembling; vibration. **2.** a state of flustered excitement or fear. —*v.i.* **3.** to act irresolutely; vacillate. —**dith′er•er,** *n.* —**dith′er•y,** *adj.*

dith•y•ramb (dith′ə ram′, -ramb′), *n.* **1.** a Greek choral song of vehement or wild character and usu. of irregular form. **2.** any wildly enthusiastic speech or writing. —**dith′y•ram′bic** (-bik), *adj.*

dit•ta•ny (dit′n ē), *n., pl.* **-nies. 1.** a Cretan plant, *Origanum dictamnus,* of the mint family, having spikes of purple flowers. **2.** a North American plant, *Cunila origanoides,* of the mint family, bearing clusters of purplish flowers.

dit•to (dit′ō), *n., pl.* **-tos,** *adv., v.,* **-toed, -to•ing.** —*n.* **1.** the aforesaid; the above; the same (used in accounts, lists, etc., to avoid repetition). Compare DITTO MARK. **2.** another of the same. **3.** *Informal.* a duplicate; copy. —*adv.* **4.** as already stated; likewise. —*v.t.* **5.** to make a copy of on a duplicating machine. **6.** to duplicate or repeat the action or statement of (another). [< Italian < Latin *dictus* said]

dit′to mark′, *n.* Often, **ditto marks.** two small marks (") indicating the repetition of something, usu. placed beneath the thing repeated.

dit•ty (dit′ē), *n., pl.* **-ties.** a short, simple song.

dit′ty bag′, *n.* a small bag used esp. by sailors to hold sewing implements, toiletries, etc.

di•u•ret•ic (dī′ə ret′ik), *adj.* **1.** increasing the volume of the urine excreted. —*n.* **2.** a diuretic medicine or agent, as a thiazide.

di•ur•nal (dī ûr′nl), *adj.* **1.** occurring each day; daily. **2.** of or belonging to the daytime. **3.** occurring in daily cycles: *the apparent diurnal motion of celestial bodies.* **4.** active by day, as certain birds and insects (opposed to *nocturnal*). **5.** opening by day and closing by night, as certain flowers. —**di•ur′nal•ly,** *adv.*

di•va (dē′və, -vä), *n., pl.* **-vas, -ve** (-ve). PRIMA DONNA (def. 1).

di•va•gate (dī′və gāt′), *v.i.,* **-gat•ed, -gat•ing. 1.** to wander; stray. **2.** to digress in speech. —**di′va•ga′tion,** *n.*

di•va•lent (dī vā′lənt), *adj.* having a valence of two. —**di•va′lence,** *n.*

di•van (di van′, -vän′, dī′van), *n.* a sofa or couch, usu. without arms or back, often usable as a bed.

di•var•i•cate (*v.* dī var′i kāt′, di-; *adj.* -kit, -kāt′), *v.,* **-cat•ed, -cat•ing,** *adj.* —*v.i.* **1.** to spread apart; branch; diverge. —*adj.* **2.** spread apart; widely divergent. —**di•var′i•cate•ly,** *adv.* —**di•var′i•cat′ing•ly,** *adv.* —**di•var′i•ca′tion,** *n.* —**di•var′i•ca′tor,** *n.*

dive (dīv), *v.,* **dived** or **dove, dived, div•ing,** *n.* —*v.i.* **1.** to plunge into water, esp. headfirst. **2.** to submerge, as a submarine. **3.** to plunge, fall, or descend through the air, into the earth, etc.: *The acrobats dived into nets.* **4.** (of an airplane) to descend rapidly. **5.** to penetrate suddenly into something, as with the hand: *to dive into one's purse.* **6.** to dart: *to dive into a doorway.* **7.** to enter deeply or plunge into a subject, activity, etc. —*v.t.* **8.** to cause to plunge, submerge, or descend. —*n.* **9.** an act or instance of diving. **10.** a jump or plunge into water, esp. in a prescribed way from a diving board. **11.** the steep, rapid descent of an airplane at a speed far exceeding that in level flight. **12.** a submerging, as of a submarine or skindiver. **13.** a dash, plunge, or lunge, as if throwing oneself at or into something. **14.** a sudden or sharp decline, as in stock prices. **15.** *Informal.* a dingy or disreputable bar or nightclub. **16.** (in boxing) a false show of being knocked out, usu. in a bout whose result has been prearranged. —**Usage.** Both DIVED and DOVE are standard as the past tense of DIVE. DIVED, the older form, is somewhat more common in edited writing, but DOVE occurs there so frequently that it also must be considered standard. DOVE is an Americanism that probably developed by analogy with alternations like *drive, drove* and *ride, rode.* It is the more common form in speech in the northern U.S. and in Canada, and its use seems to be spreading. The past participle of DIVE is always DIVED.

di•verge (di vûrj′, dī-), *v.,* **-verged, -verg•ing.** —*v.i.* **1.** to move, lie, or extend in different directions from a common point; branch off. **2.** to differ in opinion, character, form, etc.; deviate. **3.** *Math.* (of a sequence, series, etc.) to have no unique limit; to have infinity as a limit. **4.** to turn aside or deviate, as from a path, practice, or plan. —*v.t.* **5.** to deflect or turn aside.

di•ver•gence (di vûr′jəns, dī-), *n.* **1.** an act or instance of diverging. **2.** the degree or point of diverging. **3.** a difference of structure in related organisms caused by different environmental pressures. **4.** the net flow of air from a given region. —**di•ver′gent,** *adj.*

di•vers (dī′vərz), *adj.* several; various; sundry.

di•verse (di vûrs′, dī-, dī′vûrs), *adj.* **1.** of a different kind, form, character, etc.; unlike. **2.** of various kinds or forms; multiform. —**di•verse′ly,** *adv.* —**di•verse′ness,** *n.*

di•ver•si•fi•ca•tion (di vûr′sə fi kā′shən, dī-), *n.* **1.** the act or process of diversifying; state of being diversified. **2.** the practice of manufacturing a variety of products, investing in several kinds of securities, etc., esp. as protection in an economic slump.

di•ver•si•fied (di vûr′sə fīd′, dī-), *adj.* **1.** distinguished by various forms or by a variety of objects: *diversified activity.* **2.** distributed among or producing several types; varied: *diversified investments.*

di•ver•si•fy (di vûr′sə fī′, dī-), *v.,* **-fied, -fy•ing.** —*v.t.* **1.** to make diverse, as in form or character; give variety or diversity to; variegate. **2.** to distribute (investments) among different types of securities or industries. **3.** to expand (a business or product line) by manufacturing a larger variety of products. —*v.i.* **4.** to become diversified. —**di•ver′si•fi′a•ble,** *adj.* —**di•ver′si•fi′er,** *n.*

di•ver•sion (di vûr′zhən, -shən, dī-), *n.* **1.** the act of diverting or turning aside, as from a course or purpose: *a diversion of industry into the war effort.* **2.** a channel made to divert the flow of water from one course to another or to direct the flow of water draining from a piece of ground. **3.** distraction from business, care, etc.; recreation; a pastime. **4.** a military feint intended to draw off attention from the point of main attack.

di•ver•si•ty (di vûr′si tē, dī-), *n., pl.* **-ties. 1.** variety; multiformity. **2.** a point of difference.

di•vert (di vûrt′, dī-), *v.t.* **1.** to turn aside or from a path or course; deflect. **2.** to draw off to a different course, purpose, etc. **3.** to distract from serious occupation; entertain or amuse. —*v.i.* **4.** to turn aside; veer. —**di•vert′ed•ly,** *adv.* —**di•vert′i•ble,** *adj.*

di•ver•tic•u•li•tis (dī′vər tik′yə lī′tis), *n.* inflammation of one or more diverticula.

di•ver•tic•u•lo•sis (dī′vər tik′yə lō′sis), *n.* the presence of saclike herniations of the mucosal layer of the colon through the muscular wall.

di•ver•tic•u•lum (dī′vər tik′yə ləm), *n., pl.* **-la** (-lə). a blind, tubular sac or process branching off from a canal or cavity, esp. an abnormal, saclike herniation of the mucosal layer through the muscular wall of the colon. —**di′ver•tic′u•lar,** *adj.*

di•ver•tisse•ment (di vûr′tis mənt), *n.* **1.** a diversion or entertainment. **2.** a short ballet or other performance serving as an interlude in a play, opera, etc.

Di•ves (dī′vēz), *n.* **1.** the rich man of the parable in Luke 16:19–31. **2.** any rich man. [< Latin *dīves* rich, rich man]

di•vest (di vest′, dī-), *v.t.* **1.** to strip of clothing, ornament, etc. **2.** to strip or deprive (someone or something), esp. of property or rights; dispossess. **3.** to rid of or free from: *to divest oneself of responsibility for a decision.* **4.** to take away (property, legal rights, etc.). **5. a.** to sell off. **b.** to rid of through sale. —**di•ves′ti•ble,** *adj.*

di•vest•i•ture (di ves′ti chər, -cho͝or′, dī-), *n.* **1.** the act of divesting. **2.** the state of being divested. **3.** something, as property or investments, that has been divested. **4.** the sale of business holdings by government order.

di•vide (di vīd′), *v.,* **-vid•ed, -vid•ing,** *n.* —*v.t.* **1.** to separate into parts, groups, sections, etc. **2.** to separate or part from something else; sunder; cut off. **3.** to deal out in parts; distribute in shares; apportion. **4.** to cleave; part. **5.** to separate in opinion or feeling; cause to disagree: *The issue divided the senators.* **6.** to distinguish the kinds of; classify. **7. a.** to separate into equal parts by the process of mathematical division; apply the mathematical process of division to. **b.** to be a divisor of, without a remainder. **8.** to mark a uniform scale on (a ruler, thermometer, etc.). **9.** to separate (a legislature or other assembly) into two groups in ascertaining the vote on a question. —*v.i.* **10.** to become divided or separated. **11.** to share something with others. **12.** to diverge; branch; fork. **13.** to perform the mathematical process of division. **14.** to vote by separating into two groups. —*n.* **15.** a division: *a divide in the road.* **16.** the line or zone of higher ground between two adjacent streams or drainage basins. —**di•vid′a•ble,** *adj.*

di•vid•ed (di vī′did), *adj.* **1.** separated; separate. **2.** disunited. **3.** shared; apportioned. **4.** (of a leaf) cut into distinct portions by incisions extending to the midrib or base. —**di•vid′ed•ly,** *adv.* —**di•vid′ed•ness,** *n.*

div•i•dend (div′i dend′), *n.* **1.** a number that is to be divided by a divisor. **2. a.** a sum paid to shareholders out of company earnings. **b.** a pro-rata share of such a sum. **3.** a portion of an insurance premium returned to the policyholder as part of surplus funds. **4.** a share of anything divided. **5.** anything received in addition to or beyond what is expected; bonus.

di•vid•er (di vī′dər), *n.* **1.** a person or thing that divides. **2.** dividers, a pair of compasses, as used for dividing lines or measuring. **3.** a partition.

div•i•na•tion (div′ə nā′shən), *n.* **1.** the practice of seeking to foretell future events or discover hidden knowledge by occult or supernatural means. **2.** intuitive perception; instinctive foresight. —**di•vin•a•to•ry** (di vin′ə tôr′ē, -tōr′ē), *adj.*

di•vine (di vīn′), *adj.,* **-vin•er, -vin•est,** *n., v.,* **-vined, -vin•ing.** —*adj.* **1.** of, like, or from a god, esp. the Supreme Being. **2.** addressed or devoted to God or a god; religious; sacred: *divine worship.* **3.** heavenly; celestial: *the divine kingdom.* **4.** *Informal.* extremely good; unusually lovely. **5.** being a god; being God. **6.** of superhuman or surpassing excellence. —*n.* **7.** a theologian; scholar in religion. **8.** a priest or cleric. **9. the Divine, a.** God. **b.** the spiritual aspect in humans regarded as godly or godlike. —*v.t.* **10.** to discover or declare by divination; prophesy. **11.** to discover (water, metal, etc.) by means of a divining rod. **12.** to perceive by intuition or insight; conjecture. —*v.i.* **13.** to use or practice divination; prophesy. **14.** to have perception by intuition or insight; conjecture. [< Latin *dīvīnus,* der. of *dīvus* god] —**di•vin′a•ble,** *adj.* —**di•vine′ly,** *adv.*

Divine′ Com′edy, (Italian, *Divina Commedia*), a narrative epic poem (14th century) by Dante.

Divine′ Lit′urgy, *n.* See under LITURGY (def. 5).

Divine′ Mind′, *n. Christian Science.* MIND (def. 16).

divine′ of′fice, *n.* (*sometimes caps.*) OFFICE (def. 11c).

di•vin•er (di vī′nər), *n.* **1.** a person who divines; soothsayer; prophet. **2.** a person skilled in using a divining rod.

divine′ right′ of kings′, *n.* the right to rule derived directly from God, not from the consent of the people.

divine′ serv′ice, *n.* SERVICE[1] (def. 13).

div′ing duck′, *n.* any of numerous ducks that dive from the water's surface for their food (contrasted with *dabbling duck*).

div′ing suit′, *n.* any of various waterproof garments for underwater swimming or diving, esp. one that is weighted, hermetically sealed, and supplied with air under pressure.

divin′ing rod′, *n.* a rod, esp. a forked stick, supposedly useful in locating underground water or metal deposits.

di•vin•i•ty (di vin′i tē), *n., pl.* **-ties. 1.** the quality of being divine; divine nature. **2.** a divine being; God. **3. the Divinity,** (*sometimes l.c.*) the Deity. **4.** a being having divine attributes. **5.** the study or science of divine things; theology. **6.** godlike character; supreme excellence. **7.** a fluffy white fudge made with sugar, egg whites, and often nuts.

divin′ity school′, *n.* a Protestant seminary.

di•vis•i•ble (di viz′ə bəl), *adj.* **1.** capable of being divided. **2. a.** capable of being evenly divided, without remainder. **b.** of or pertaining to a group in which given any element and any integer, there is a second element that when raised to the integer equals the first element. —**di•vis′i•ble•ness,** *n.* —**di•vis′i•bly,** *adv.*

di•vi•sion (di vizh′ən), *n.* **1.** the act or process of dividing; state of being divided. **2.** the arithmetic operation inverse to multiplication; the process of ascertaining how many times one number or quantity is contained in another. **3.** something that divides or separates; partition. **4.** something that marks a division; dividing line or mark. **5.** one of the parts into which a thing is divided; section. **6.** separation by difference of opinion or feeling; disagreement; dissension. **7.** the separation of a legislature or other assembly into two groups in taking a vote. **8.** one of the parts into which a country or an organization is divided for political, judicial, military, or other purposes. **9. a.** (in the army) a major administrative and tactical unit, larger than a brigade and smaller than a corps. **b.** (in the navy) a tactical group of usu. four ships, part of a fleet or squadron. **10.** an administrative unit of an industrial enterprise, government bureau, university, etc. **11.** a category or grouping of sports teams or competitors according to standing, skill, weight, age, or the like. **12.** the primary subdivision in the classification of the plant kingdom; a plant phylum. **13.** a type of propagation in which new plants are grown from segments separated from the parent plant. —**di•vi′sion•al, di•vi′sion•ar′y,** *adj.* —**di•vi′sion•al•ly,** *adv.*

divi′sion sign′, *n.* the symbol (÷) or (/) placed between two expressions and denoting division of the first by the second.

di•vi•sive (di vī′siv), *adj.* **1.** forming or expressing division or distribu-

tion. **2.** creating dissension or discord. —**di•vi′sive•ly,** *adv.* —**di•vi′sive•ness,** *n.*

di•vi•sor (di vī′zər), *n.* **1.** a number by which another number, the dividend, is divided. **2.** a number contained in another given number a certain integral number of times, without a remainder.

di•vorce (di vôrs′, -vōrs′), *n., v.,* **-vorced, -vorc•ing.** —*n.* **1.** a judicial declaration dissolving a marriage and releasing both spouses from all matrimonial obligations. **2.** any formal separation of husband and wife according to established custom. **3.** total separation; disunion. —*v.t.* **4.** to separate by divorce: *The judge divorced the couple.* **5.** to break the marriage contract between oneself and (one's spouse) by divorce. **6.** to separate; cut off: *Life and art cannot be divorced.* —*v.i.* **7.** to get a divorce. —**di•vorce′a•ble,** *adj.* —**di•vorc′er,** *n.* —**di•vor′cive,** *adj.*

di•vor•cé (di vôr sā′, -vōr-, -vôr′sā, -vōr′-), *n.* a divorced man.

di•vor•cée or **di•vor•cee** (di vôr sā′, -sē′, -vōr-, -vôr′sā, -vōr′-), *n.* a divorced woman.

divorce′ mill′, *n. Informal.* a divorce court, esp. such a court in a state or country that does not impose difficult requirements, as a long period of residence or humiliating grounds, on those who wish to dissolve their marriage.

di•vulge (di vulj′, dī-), *v.t.,* **-vulged, -vulg•ing.** to disclose or reveal (something private, secret, or previously unknown). —**di•vulge′ment,** *n.* —**di•vulg′er,** *n.*

div•vy (div′ē), *v.,* **-vied, -vy•ing,** *n., pl.* **-vies.** *Informal.* —*v.t., v.i.* **1.** to divide; distribute (often fol. by *up*): *to divvy up loot.* —*n.* **2.** a distribution or sharing.

Dix (diks), *n.* **1. Dorothea Lynde** (*Dorothy*), 1802–87, U.S. educator and social reformer. **2. Otto,** 1891–1969, German painter and printmaker.

Dix•ie (dik′sē), *n.* the southern states of the United States, esp. those that were part of the Confederacy.

Dix•ie•crat (dik′sē krat′), *n.* a member of a faction of southern Democrats stressing states' rights and opposed to the civil-rights programs of the Democratic party, esp. a southern Democrat who bolted the party in 1948 and voted for the candidates of the States' Rights Democratic party. —**Dix′ie•crat′ic,** *adj.*

Dix′ie Cup′, 1. *Trademark.* a brand of disposable paper cup, as for beverages. **2.** *Navy Slang.* a round, white, brimmed hat worn by U.S. sailors.

Dix•ie•land (dik′sē land′), *n.* **1.** jazz marked by accented four-four rhythm and improvisatory solos and ensembles and played by a small band. **2.** Also, **Dix′ie Land.** DIXIE.

dix•it (dik′sit), *n.* an utterance.

diz•zy (diz′ē), *adj.,* **-zi•er, -zi•est,** *v.,* **-zied, -zy•ing.** —*adj.* **1.** having a sensation of whirling and a tendency to fall; giddy; vertiginous. **2.** bewildered; confused. **3.** causing giddiness or confusion: *a dizzy height.* **4.** heedless; thoughtless. **5.** *Informal.* foolish; silly. —*v.t.* **6.** to make dizzy. —**diz′zi•ly,** *adv.* —**diz′zi•ness,** *n.*

D.J., 1. Also, **DJ** (dē′jā′). disc jockey. **2.** District Judge. **3.** Doctor of Law. [< Latin *Doctor Jūris*]

Dji•bou•ti (ji bōō′tē), *n.* **1.** Formerly, **French Somaliland, French Territory of the Afars and Issas,** a republic in E Africa, on the Gulf of Aden: a former overseas territory of France; gained independence 1977. 434,116; 8960 sq. mi. (23,200 sq. km). **2.** the capital of this republic, in the SE part. 290,000. —**Dji•bou′ti•an,** *adj., n.*

dl, deciliter.

D layer, *n.* the lowest region of the ionosphere, at an altitude of ab. 50 mi. (80 km).

dm, decimeter.

D-mark or **D-Mark** (dē′märk′), *n.* a German mark; Deutsche mark.

D.M.D., Doctor of Dental Medicine.

DMSO, dimethyl sulfoxide: a liquid industrial solvent, C_2H_6OS, approved for topical use to reduce inflammation and diffuse drugs into the bloodstream.

DMZ, demilitarized zone.

DNA, deoxyribonucleic acid: an extremely long, double-stranded nucleic acid molecule arranged as a double helix that is the main constituent of the chromosome and that carries the genes as segments along its strands: found chiefly in the chromatin of cells and in many viruses.

DNA fingerprinting, *n.* the use of a DNA probe for the identification of an individual, as for the matching of genes from a forensic sample with those of a criminal suspect. Also called **genetic fingerprinting.** —**DNA fingerprint,** *n.*

DNA virus, *n.* any virus containing DNA.

Dnie•per or **Dne•pr** (nē′pər; *Russ.* dnyepʀ), *n.* a river rising in the W Russian Federation, flowing S through Belorussia and Ukraine to the Black Sea. 1400 mi. (2250 km) long.

DNR, do not resuscitate: used in hospitals to indicate a prior decision by the patient or the patient's family to avoid extraordinary means of prolonging life.

do[1] (dōō; *unstressed* dŏŏ, də), *v.* and *auxiliary v., pres. sing. 1st* and *2nd pers. do, 3rd* does, *pres. pl.* do; *past sing.* did and *pl. past part.* done; *pres. part.* do•ing; *n., pl.* dos, do's. —*v.t.* **1.** to perform (an act, duty, role, etc.). **2.** to execute (a piece or amount of work): *to do a hauling job.* **3.** to accomplish; finish: *He has already done it.* **4.** to put forth; exert: *Do your best.* **5.** to be the cause of (good, harm, credit, etc.); bring about; effect. **6.** to render, give, or pay (homage, justice, etc.). **7.** to deal with, fix, clean, arrange, etc., (anything) as the case may require:

D

to do the dishes. **8.** to travel; traverse: *We did 30 miles today.* **9.** to serve; suffice for: *This will do us for the present.* **10.** to condone or approve, as by custom or practice: *That sort of thing simply isn't done.* **11.** to travel at the rate of (a specified speed). **12.** to make or prepare: *I'll do the salad.* **13.** to serve (a term of time) in prison, or, sometimes, in office. **14.** to create or bring into being: *He does wonderful portraits.* **15.** to translate or change the form of: *They did the book into a movie.* **16.** to study or work at or in the field of: *I have to do my math tonight.* **17.** to explore or travel through as a sightseer: *They did Greece in 3 weeks.* **18.** to use (drugs), esp. habitually. **19.** *Slang.* to rob; steal from: *The law got him for doing banks.* —*v.i.* **20.** to act or conduct oneself; behave. **21.** to proceed: *to do wisely.* **22.** to get along; fare; manage: *to do without an automobile.* **23.** to be in a specified state of health: *Mother and child are doing fine.* **24.** to serve or be satisfactory, as for the purpose; be enough; suffice: *Will this do?* **25.** to finish or be finished. **26.** to happen; take place; transpire: *What's doing at the office?* **27.** (used as a substitute to avoid repetition of a verb or full verb expression): *I think as you do.* —*auxiliary v.* **28.** (used in interrogative, negative, and inverted constructions): *Do you like music? I don't care. Seldom does one see such greed.* **29.** (used to lend emphasis to a principal verb): *Do visit us!* **30. do away with, a.** to put an end to; abolish. **b.** to kill. **31. do for, a.** to cause the defeat, ruin, or death of. **b.** to keep house for; manage or provide for. **32. do in, a.** to kill; murder. **b.** to exhaust. **33. do out of,** *Informal.* to swindle; cheat. **34. do over,** to redecorate. **35. do up, a.** to wrap and tie up. **b.** to pin up or arrange (the hair). **c.** to renovate or clean. **d.** to fasten: *Do up your coat.* **e.** to dress: *The children were all done up in costumes.* **36. do with,** to benefit from; use. **37. do without,** to forgo; dispense with. —*n.* **38.** *Informal.* a burst of frenzied activity; action; commotion. **39.** *Informal.* a hairdo. **40.** a festive social gathering; party. —*Idiom.* **41. do or die,** to make a supreme effort. **42. dos and don'ts,** customs, rules, or regulations.

do² (dō), *n., pl.* **dos.** the musical syllable used for the first note of an ascending diatonic scale.

DOA or **D.O.A.,** dead on arrival.

do·a·ble (dōō′ə bəl), *adj.* capable of being done.

DOB or **D.O.B.** or **d.o.b.,** date of birth.

Do′ber·man pin′scher (dō′bər mən), *n.* one of a German breed of large, slender, muscular dogs having a short, usu. black or brown coat with rust markings. Also called **Do′ber·man.**

Do·bie (dō′bē), *n.* **(James) Frank,** 1888–1964, U.S. folklorist, educator, and author.

Do·bro (dō′brō), *pl.* **-bros** for 2. **1.** *Trademark.* a brand of acoustic guitar commonly used in country music, usually played on the lap and having a raised bridge and a metal resonator cone that produces a tremulous, moaning sound. —*n.* **2.** (*l.c.*) any guitar of this type.

dob·son·fly (dob′sən flī′), *n., pl.* **-flies.** a very large, soft-bodied neuropteran insect, *Corydalus cornutus,* commonly seen in fluttery flight above streams, noted for its abundant aquatic larvae.

doc (dok), *n. Informal.* **1.** doctor. **2.** a casual, impersonal term of address used to a man.

DOC, Department of Commerce.

doc., *pl.* **docs.** document.

do·cent (dō′sənt), *n.* **1.** a college or university lecturer. **2.** a knowledgeable guide, esp. one who conducts visitors through a museum. —**do′cent·ship,** *n.*

Do·ce·tism (dō sē′tiz əm, dō′si tiz′-), *n.* an early Christian heresy asserting that the sufferings of Christ were apparent and not real. —**Do·ce′tic,** *adj.* —**Do·ce′tist,** *n., adj.*

doc·ile (dos′əl; *Brit.* dō′sīl), *adj.* **1.** easily managed or handled; tractable. **2.** readily trained or taught; teachable. —**do·cil′i·ty** (-sil′i tē), *n.*

dock¹ (dok), *n.* **1.** a landing pier. **2.** the space or waterway between two piers or wharves, as for receiving a ship while in port. **3.** such a waterway, enclosed or open, together with the surrounding piers, wharves, etc. **4.** DRY DOCK. **5.** a platform for loading and unloading trucks, railway freight cars, etc. —*v.t.* **6.** to bring (a ship or boat) into a dock; lay up in a dock. **7.** to place in dry dock, as for repairs or painting. **8.** to join (an orbiting space vehicle) with another spacecraft or with a space station. —*v.i.* **9.** to come or go into a dock or dry dock. **10.** (of two space vehicles) to join together while in orbit.

dock² (dok), *n.* **1.** the solid or fleshy part of an animal's tail, as distinguished from the hair. **2.** the part of a tail left after cutting or clipping. —*v.t.* **3.** to cut off the end of; cut short: *to dock a tail.* **4.** to cut short the tail of. **5.** to deduct a part from (wages). **6.** to deduct from the wages of, usu. as a punishment. **7.** to deprive of something regularly enjoyed: *The campers were docked for disobeying their counselor.*

dock³ (dok), *n.* the place in a courtroom where a prisoner is placed during trial.

dock⁴ (dok), *n.* any of various weedy plants of the genus *Rumex,* buckwheat family, having a long taproot and clusters of small flowers.

dock·age¹ (dok′ij), *n.* **1.** a charge for the use of a dock. **2.** docking accommodations. **3.** the act of docking a ship.

dock·age² (dok′ij), *n.* **1.** a curtailment; deduction, as from wages. **2.** removable waste material in wheat and other grains.

dock·er (dok′ər), *n.* a person or device that docks tails.

dock·et (dok′it), *n.* **1.** a list of cases in court for trial, or the names of the parties who have cases pending. **2.** the list of business to be transacted by a board, council, legislative assembly, or the like. —*v.t.* **3.** to enter in the docket of the court. **4.** to abstract the heads of (a legal doc-

ument) and enter in a book. **5.** to endorse (a letter, document, etc.) with a memorandum.

dock·yard (dok′yärd′), *n.* **1.** a waterside area containing docks, workshops, warehouses, etc., for building and repairing ships, for storing naval supplies, etc. **2.** *Brit.* NAVY YARD.

doc·tor (dok′tər), *n.* **1.** a person licensed to practice medicine, as a physician, surgeon, dentist, or veterinarian. **2.** a person who has been awarded a doctor's degree. **3.** any of several artificial angling flies. **4.** an eminent scholar and teacher. **5.** a person skilled in repairing or improving something broken or flawed. —*v.t.* **6.** to give medical treatment to; act as a physician to. **7.** to treat (an ailment); apply remedies to. **8.** to restore to original or working condition; repair. **9.** to tamper with; falsify: *to doctor the birthdate on a passport.* **10.** to tamper with the ingredients of (a food or drink) in order to improve flavor. **11.** to revise, alter, or adapt for a specific purpose: *to doctor a play.* —*v.i.* **12.** to practice medicine. **13.** to take medicine; receive medical treatment. —*Idiom.* **14. just what the doctor ordered,** precisely what is required. [< Latin: teacher < *doc(ēre)* to teach] —**doc′tor·al, doc·to′ri·al** (-tôr′ē əl, -tōr′-), *adj.*

doc·tor·ate (dok′tər it), *n.* DOCTOR'S DEGREE (def. 1).

Doc′tor of Philos′ophy, *n.* **1.** a doctor's degree awarded for advanced studies in the humanities or the social, behavioral, or pure sciences. **2.** a person who has been awarded this degree. *Abbr.:* Ph.D.

Doc′tor of the Church′, *n.* a title conferred on an ecclesiastic for great learning and saintliness.

doc′tor's degree′, *n.* **1.** any of several academic degrees of the highest rank awarded by universities and some colleges, as the Ph.D. or Ed.D., or an honorary degree, as the LL.D. **2.** a degree awarded to a graduate of a school of medicine, dentistry, or veterinary science.

doc·tri·naire (dok′trə nâr′), *n.* **1.** a person who tries to apply some doctrine or theory without sufficient regard for practical considerations; an impractical theorist. —*adj.* **2.** dogmatic about one's ideas; fanatical: *a doctrinaire preacher.* **3.** merely theoretical; impractical. **4.** of, pertaining to, or characteristic of a doctrinaire.

doc·trine (dok′trin), *n.* **1.** a particular principle, position, or policy taught or advocated, as of a religion or government: *the Monroe Doctrine.* **2.** a body or system of teachings relating to a particular subject: *the doctrine of the Catholic Church.*

doc·u·dra·ma (dok′yə drä′mə, -dram′ə), *n.* a drama or story, esp. a television film, depicting current or historical events. [*docu(mentary)* + *drama*]

doc·u·ment (*n.* dok′yə mənt; *v.* -ment′), *n.* **1.** a written or printed paper furnishing information or evidence, as a passport, deed, bill of sale, or bill of lading; a legal or official paper. **2.** any written item, as a book, article, or letter, esp. of a factual or informative nature. **3.** a computer data file. —*v.t.* **4.** to furnish with documents. **5.** to furnish with references, citations, etc., in support of statements made. **6.** to support by documentary evidence: *to document a case.* **7.** to provide (a vessel) with a certificate giving particulars concerning nationality, ownership, tonnage, dimensions, etc. —**doc′u·ment′a·ble,** *adj.*

doc·u·men·ta·ry (dok′yə men′tə rē, -trē), *adj., n., pl.* **-ries.** —*adj.* **1.** Also, **doc·u·men·tal** (dok′yə men′tl). pertaining to, consisting of, or derived from documents. **2.** depicting an actual event, era, life story, etc., accurately and without fictional elements. —*n.* **3.** a documentary film, television program, etc. —**doc′u·men·tar′i·ly,** *adv.*

doc·u·men·ta·tion (dok′yə men tā′shən, -mən-), *n.* **1.** the use of documentary evidence. **2.** a furnishing with documents, as to substantiate a claim or the data in a book or article. **3.** instructional materials for computer software or hardware. —**doc′u·men·ta′tion·al,** *adj.*

DOD, Department of Defense.

dod·der¹ (dod′ər), *v.i.* to shake; tremble; totter. —**dod′der·er,** *n.*

dod·der² (dod′ər), *n.* a leafless parasitic plant, *Cuscuta gronovii,* of the morning glory family, having clusters of tiny white flowers on orange-yellow, twining stems.

dod·der·ing (dod′ər ing) also **dod·der·y** (-ə rē), *adj.* shaky or trembling, as from old age; tottering.

Dodd·ridge (dod′rij), *n.* **Philip,** 1702–51, English religious leader and hymn writer.

dodeca-, a combining form meaning "twelve": *dodecasyllabic.*

do·dec·a·he·dron (dō dek′ə hē′drən, dō′dek-), *n., pl.* **-drons, -dra** (-drə). a solid figure having 12 faces. —**do·dec′a·he′dral,** *adj.*

dodecahedron

rhombic   pentagonal

dodge (doj), *v.,* **dodged, dodg·ing,** *n.* —*v.t.* **1.** to elude or evade by a sudden shift of position or by strategy; avoid. **2.** (in printing a photograph) to shade (an area of a print) from exposure for a period while exposing the remainder of the print, in order to lighten or eliminate the area (sometimes fol. by *out*). —*v.i.* **3.** to move aside or change position suddenly, as to avoid a blow or get behind something. **4.** to use evasive methods; prevaricate. —*n.* **5.** a quick, evasive movement, as a sudden jump away to avoid a blow or the like. **6.** a shrewdly clever scheme, action, or contrivance to evade or deceive; shifty trick.

Dodge (doj), *n.* **Mary Elizabeth,** 1831–1905, U.S. editor and author of children's books.

dodge′ ball′, *n.* a game in which players are eliminated by being hit with an inflated ball.

Dodge′ Cit′y, *n.* a city in SW Kansas, on the Arkansas River: important frontier town and railhead on the old Santa Fe route. 18,001.

Dodg·son (doj′sən), *n.* **Charles Lutwidge** ("*Lewis Carroll*"), 1832–98, English mathematician and writer of children's books.

do·do (dō′dō), *n., pl.* **-dos, -does. 1.** a large, extinct, flightless bird, *Raphus cucullatus,* of the pigeon family, formerly inhabiting Mauritius. **2.** *Slang.* a dull-witted, slow-reacting person.

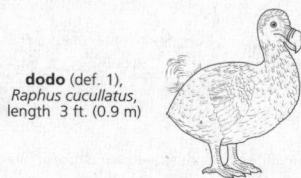

dodo (def. 1),
Raphus cucullatus,
length 3 ft. (0.9 m)

Do·do·ma (dō′dō mä, dō′də-), *n.* the capital of Tanzania, in the NE central part. 45,703.

doe (dō), *n., pl.* **does,** (*esp. collectively*) **doe.** the female of the deer, antelope, goat, rabbit, and certain other animals.

DOE, Department of Energy.

Do·eg (dō′eg), *n.* a servant of Saul who was ordered to put the priests of Nob to death. I Sam. 21:7; 22:9–19.

do·er (dōō′ər), *n.* **1.** a person or thing that does something, esp. a person who gets things done with vigor and efficiency. **2.** a person characterized by action, as distinguished from one given to contemplation.

does (duz), *v.* 3rd pers. sing. pres. indic. of DO¹.

doe·skin (dō′skin′), *n.* **1.** the skin of a doe. **2.** soft leather made from this or from sheepskin or lambskin, often used for gloves, jackets, etc. **3.** any of various fabrics with a napped, suedelike finish, used esp. for coats, suits, and sportswear.

doff (dof, dôf), *v.t.* **1.** to remove or take off, as clothing. **2.** to remove or tip (the hat), as in greeting. **3.** to throw off; get rid of.

dog (dôg, dog), *n., v.,* **dogged, dog·ging.** —*n.* **1.** a domesticated canid, *Canis familiaris,* bred in many varieties. **2.** any carnivore of the dog family Canidae, characterized in the wild state by a long muzzle, erect ears, and a long bushy tail; canid. **3.** the male of such an animal. **4.** a despicable man or youth. **5.** a fellow in general: *a lucky dog.* **6. dogs,** *Slang.* feet. **7.** *Slang.* **a.** something worthless or of extremely poor quality. **b.** an utter failure; flop. **8.** *Slang.* an unattractive person. **9. a.** any of various mechanical devices, as for gripping or holding something. **b.** a projection on a moving part for moving steadily or for tripping another part with which it engages. —*v.t.* **10.** to follow or track like a dog, esp. with hostile intent; hound. **11.** to drive or chase with a dog or dogs. —*Idiom.* **12. dog it,** *Informal.* to do something perfunctorily or not at all. **13. go to the dogs,** to deteriorate; degenerate. **14. lead a dog's life,** to have an unhappy existence. **15. let sleeping dogs lie,** to leave an existing situation alone rather than risk provoking something worse. **16. put on the dog,** *Informal.* to assume an attitude of wealth or importance. —*Proverb.* **17. The dog always returns to his vomit,** a criminal returns to the scene of the crime. Prov. 26:11. **18. You can't teach an old dog new tricks,** age makes it harder to learn. —*Saying.* **19. That dog won't hunt,** that idea or initiative won't work.

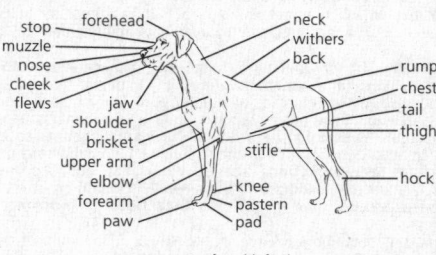

dog (def. 1)

dog·bane (dôg′bān′, dog′-), *n.* any of several plants of the genus *Apocynum,* with small white flowers, acrid milky juice, and a bitter root.

dog·ber·ry (dôg′ber′ē, -bə rē, dog′-), *n., pl.* **-ries. 1.** the berry or fruit of any of various plants, as the chokeberry, *Aronia arbutifolia,* or the mountain ash, *Sorbus americana.* **2.** the plant itself.

dog·catch·er (dôg′kach′ər, dog′-), *n.* a person employed by a munici-

pal pound, humane society, or the like, to find and impound stray or homeless dogs, cats, etc.

dog′ days′, *n.* **1.** the sultry part of summer when Sirius, the Dog Star, rises at the same time as the sun. **2.** a period marked by lethargy, inactivity, or indolence. —**dog′-day′,** *adj.*

doge (dōj), *n.* the chief magistrate in the former republics of Venice and Genoa. —**doge′dom,** *n.* —**doge′ship,** *n.*

dog′-ear′ or **dog′ear′,** *n.* **1.** (in a book) a corner of a page folded over like a dog's ear, as by careless use or to mark a place. —*v.t.* **2.** to fold down the corner of (a page in a book).

dog·fight (dôg′fīt′, dog′-), *n., v.,* **-fought, -fight·ing.** —*n.* **1.** a violent fight between dogs. **2.** combat between enemy aircraft. **3.** any rough-and-tumble physical battle. —*v.t.* **4.** to engage in a dogfight with. —*v.i.* **5.** to engage in a dogfight.

dog·fish (dôg′fish′, dog′-), *n., pl.* (*esp. collectively*) **-fish,** (*esp. for kinds or species*) **-fish·es. 1.** any of several small sharks, esp. of the genera *Mustelus* and *Squalus,* that are destructive to food fishes. **2.** any of various other fishes, as the bowfin.

dog·ged (dô′gid, dog′id), *adj.* persistent in effort; stubbornly tenacious. —**dog′ged·ly,** *adv.* —**dog′ged·ness,** *n.*

dog·ger·el (dô′gər əl, dog′ər-), *adj.* **1.** (of verse) **a.** comic or burlesque, and usu. loose or irregular in measure. **b.** crude; having no aesthetic value; poorly written. —*n.* **2.** doggerel verse.

dog·gone (dôg′gôn′, -gon′, dog′-), *v.t.,* **-goned, -goning,** *adj., superl.* **-gon·est,** *adv. Informal.* —*v.t.* **1.** to damn; confound. —*adj.* **2.** Also, **doggoned.** damned; confounded. —*adv.* **3.** Also, **doggoned.** damned: *a doggone poor sport.*

dog·gy¹ or **dog·gie** (dô′gē, dog′ē), *n., pl.* **-gies. 1.** a small dog or a puppy. **2.** a pet term for any dog.

dog·gy² or **dog·gie** (dô′gē, dog′ē), *adj.,* **-gi·er, -gi·est. 1.** of or pertaining to a dog. **2.** unusually fond of dogs. **3.** pretentious; ostentatious.

dog′gy bag′, *n.* a small bag or other container provided by a restaurant for a customer to take home leftovers.

dog·house (dôg′hous′, dog′-), *n., pl.* **-hous·es** (-hou′ziz). **1.** a small shelter for a dog. —*Idiom.* **2. in the doghouse,** in disfavor or disgrace.

do·gie or **do·gey** or **do·gy** (dō′gē), *n., pl.* **-gies** or **-geys.** *Western U.S.* a motherless calf.

dog·leg (dôg′leg′, dog′-), *n., v.,* **-legged, -leg·ging.** —*n.* **1.** a route or course that turns at a sharp angle. —*v.i.* **2.** to proceed around a sharp angle or along a zigzag course.

dog·ma (dôg′mə, dog′-), *n., pl.* **-mas, -ma·ta** (-mə tə). **1.** a system of principles or tenets, as of a church. **2.** a specific tenet or doctrine authoritatively put forth, as by a church. **3.** prescribed doctrine: *political dogma.* **4.** an established belief or principle.

dog·mat·ic (dôg mat′ik, dog-) also **dog·mat′i·cal,** *adj.* **1.** of the nature of a dogma; doctrinal. **2.** asserting opinions in a dictatorial manner; opinionated. —**dog·mat′i·cal·ly,** *adv.* —**dog·mat′i·cal·ness,** *n.*

dog·mat·ics (dôg mat′iks, dog-), *n.* (*used with a sing. v.*) the study of religious doctrines, esp. of the Christian church.

do′-good′ (dōō′), *adj.* of or befitting a do-gooder.

do-good·er (dōō′gŏŏd′ər, -gŏŏd′-), *n.* a well-intentioned but naive and sometimes ineffectual social reformer.

dog′ pad′dle, *n.* a rudimentary swimming stroke using a paddling of the arms and kicking of the feet in a somewhat crouching position. —**dog′-pad′dle,** *v.i.,* **-dled, -dling.**

dog′ rose′, *n.* an Old World wild rose, *Rosa canina,* having pink or white flowers.

dog·sled (dôg′sled′, dog′-), *n., v.,* **-sled·ded, -sled·ding.** —*n.* **1.** Also, **dog′ sledge′.** a sled pulled by dogs, esp. in the Arctic. —*v.i.* **2.** to travel by dogsled.

Dog′ Star′, *n.* **1.** the bright star Sirius in Canis Major. **2.** the bright star Procyon in Canis Minor.

dog′ tag′, *n.* **1.** a small disk attached to a dog's collar stating owner, address, etc. **2.** a metal identification tag worn or carried by armed forces personnel. **3.** *Informal.* any identification tag.

dog′-tired′, *adj.* utterly exhausted.

dog·tooth (dôg′tōōth′, dog′-), *n.* **1.** Also, **dog′ tooth′.** a canine tooth. **2.** one of a series of small pyramidal ornaments, usu. formed by a radiating arrangement of four sculptured leaves, used esp. in 13th-century English architecture.

dog′tooth vi′olet, *n.* any of several small lilies of the genus *Erythronium,* having two mottled leaves and a nodding yellow or purplish flower, esp. *E. americanum.* Also called **fawn lily, trout lily.**

dog′watch′ or **dog′ watch′,** *n.* **1.** either of two two-hour nautical watches, from 4 to 6 P.M. or from 6 to 8 P.M. **2.** *Informal.* any night shift, esp. the last or latest one.

dog·wood (dôg′wŏŏd′, dog′-), *n.* **1.** any tree or shrub of the genus *Cornus,* esp. *C. sanguinea,* of Europe, or *C. florida,* of America. **2.** the wood of any of these trees. —*adj.* **3.** made of such wood.

do·gy (dō′gē), *n., pl.* **-gies.** DOGIE.

Do·ha (dō′hä), *n.* the capital of Qatar, on the Persian Gulf. 217,294.

DOI, Department of the Interior.

doi·ly (doi′lē), *n., pl.* **-lies.** any small, ornamental mat, esp. one of embroidery or lace. [after a 17th-century London draper]

do·ing (dōō′ing), *n.* **1.** performance; execution. **2. doings,** deeds; proceedings; events.

do-it-your·self (dōō′i chər self′, -it yər-), *adj.* **1.** designed for use by amateurs without special training. —*n.* **2.** the practice or hobby of building or repairing things for oneself, usu. in one's own home. —**do′-it-your·self′er,** *n.*

DOJ, Department of Justice.

DOL, Department of Labor.

dol·ce (dōl′chä), *adj. Music.* sweet; soft.

dol·drums (dōl′drəmz, dol′-, dôl′-), *n.pl.* **1.** a state of inactivity or stagnation. **2.** a dull, depressed mood; low spirits. **3. the doldrums, a.** a belt of calms and light baffling winds N of the equator between the N and S trade winds in the Atlantic and Pacific oceans. **b.** the weather prevailing in this area.

dole (dōl), *n., v.,* **doled, dol·ing.** —*n.* **1.** an allotment of money, food, etc., as given at regular intervals by a charity. —*v.t.* **2.** to distribute in charity. **3.** to give out sparingly or in small quantities (usu. fol. by *out*): *to dole out water during a drought.* —*Idiom.* **4. on the dole,** *Chiefly Brit.* receiving relief payments from the government.

Dole (dōl), *n.* **Robert J(oseph),** born 1923, U.S. politician: senator 1969–96.

dole·ful (dōl′fəl), *adj.* sorrowful; mournful. —**dole′ful·ly,** *adv.* —**dole′ful·ness,** *n.*

dol·er·ite (dol′ə rīt′), *n.* any of various dark igneous rocks of basaltic composition. —**dol·er·it·ic** (-rit′ik), *adj.*

doll (dol), *n.* **1.** a small figure representing a baby or other human being, used esp. as a child's toy. **2.** *Slang.* **a.** a girl or woman. **b.** a pretty but expressionless or unintelligent woman. **c.** a physically attractive person. **d.** a generous or helpful person. **e.** (*sometimes cap.*) an affectionate or familiar term of address (sometimes offensive when used to strangers, subordinates, etc.). —*v.t., v.i.* **3. doll up, a.** to dress in fancy clothing, elaborate makeup, etc. **b.** to decorate: *to doll up a room for a party.* —**doll′·like′,** *adj.*

dol·lar (dol′ər), *n.* the basic monetary unit of various countries, including the U.S.

dol′lar av′eraging, *n.* a system of buying securities at regular intervals, using the same amount of cash for each purchase, over a considerable period of time regardless of the prevailing prices of the securities, resulting in having bought the total at an average cost. Also called **dol′lar cost′ av′eraging.**

dol′lar-a-year′ man′ (dol′ər ə yēr′), *n.* a federal appointee serving for a token annual salary, usually of one dollar.

dol′lar diplo′macy, *n.* **1.** a government policy of promoting the business interests of its citizens in other countries. **2.** diplomacy or foreign relations strengthened by well-publicized aid to a country, as in the form of food, machinery, and extensive credit.

dol·lar·fish (dol′ər fish′), *n., pl.* **-fish,** (*esp. collectively*) **-fish,** (*esp. for kinds or species*) **-fish·es. 1.** BUTTERFISH. **2.** MOONFISH.

dol′lar sign′, *n.* the symbol $ before a number indicating that the number represents dollars.

doll·house (dol′hous′), *n., pl.* **-hous·es** (-hou′ziz). **1.** a miniature house the scale of children's dolls. **2.** a cozy, diminutive house. Also, *esp. Brit.,* **doll′s′ house′.**

dol·lop (dol′əp), *n.* **1.** a lump or blob of some substance. **2.** a small amount: *a dollop of whipped cream.* —*v.t.* **3.** to dispense in dollops.

dol·ly (dol′ē), *n., pl.* **dol·lies,** *v.,* **dol·lied, dol·ly·ing.** —*n.* **1.** *Informal.* a doll. **2.** a low truck or cart with small wheels for moving heavy loads. **3.** a small wheeled platform, usu. having a short boom, on which a movie or television camera can be mounted for making moving shots. **4.** a tool for receiving and holding the head of a rivet while the other end is being headed. **5.** a small locomotive operating on narrow-gauge tracks, esp. in quarries or on construction sites. —*v.t.* **6.** to transport or convey (a camera) by means of a dolly. —*v.i.* **7.** to move a camera on a dolly, esp. toward or away from the subject being filmed or televised (often fol. by *in* or *out*): *to dolly in for a close-up.*

Dol·ly Var·den (dol′ē vär′dn), *n.* a red-speckled char, *Salvelinus malma,* of North American and E Asian streams.

dol·man (dōl′mən, dol′-), *n., pl.* **-mans. 1.** a woman's wrap with a loose, capelike back and sleeves in one piece with the body of the garment. **2.** a long outer robe worn by Turks.

dol′man sleeve′, *n.* a sleeve tapered from a very large armhole to fit closely at the wrist, usu. cut in one piece with the body of the garment.

dol·men (dōl′men, -mən, dol′-), *n.* a structure usu. regarded as a tomb, consisting of two or more large, upright stones set with a space between and capped by a horizontal stone. Compare CHAMBER TOMB. —**dol·men′ic,** *adj.*

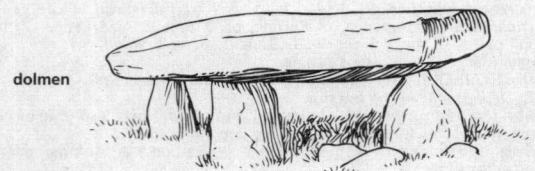

dolmen

do·lo·mite (dō′lə mīt′, dol′ə-), *n.* **1.** a very common mineral, calcium magnesium carbonate, $CaMg(CO_3)_2$, occurring in crystals and in masses. **2.** a rock consisting essentially or largely of this mineral. —**dol·o·mit·ic** (dol′ə mit′ik), *adj.*

do·lor (dō′lər), *n.* sorrow; grief. Also, *esp. Brit.,* **do′lour.**

do·lor·ous (dō′lər əs, dol′ər-), *adj.* full of or causing pain or sorrow; grievous; mournful. —**do′lor·ous·ly,** *adv.* —**do′lor·ous·ness,** *n.*

dol·phin (dol′fin, dôl′-), *n.* **1.** any small toothed cetacean of the family Delphinidae, esp. the species having a beaklike snout. Compare POR-POISE. **2.** Also called **dolphinfish, mahimahi.** either of two large, slender fishes, *Coryphaena hippurus* or *C. equisetis,* of warm and temperate seas. **3. a.** a pile, cluster of piles, or buoy to which a vessel may be moored. **b.** a cluster of piles used as a fender, as at the entrance to a dock. **4.** (*cap.*) the constellation Delphinus.

bottle-nosed dolphin,
Tursiops truncatus,
length 8 ½ ft. (2.6 m)

dolt (dōlt), *n.* a blockhead; dunce. —**dolt′ish,** *adj.* —**dolt′ish·ly,** *adv.* —**dolt′ish·ness,** *n.*

dom (dom), *n.* (*sometimes cap.*) a title of a monk in the Benedictine, Carthusian, Cistercian, and certain other monastic orders.

-dom, a suffix forming nouns that refer to domain (*kingdom*), collection of persons (*officialdom*), rank or station (*earldom*), or general condition (*freedom*).

do·main (dō mān′), *n.* **1.** a field of action, thought, influence, etc. **2.** the territory governed by a single ruler or government; realm. **3.** a region characterized by a specific feature, type of wildlife, etc. **4.** *Law.* land to which there is superior title and absolute ownership. **5.** *Math.* the set of values assigned to the independent variables of a function. **6.** one of many regions of magnetic polarity within a ferromagnetic body that collectively determine the magnetic properties of the body by their arrangement.

dome (dōm), *n., v.,* **domed, dom·ing.** —*n.* **1. a.** a vault, having a circular plan and usu. in the form of a portion of a sphere, so constructed as to exert an equal thrust in all directions. **b.** a domical roof or ceiling. **c.** a polygonal vault, ceiling, or roof. **2.** any covering or environment thought to resemble the hemispherical vault of a building or room. **3.** *Crystall.* a form having planes that intersect the vertical axis and are parallel to one of the lateral axes. **4.** *Geol.* a large-scale circular structural feature with flanks that slope gradually away from the center. **5.** a raised, glass-enclosed section of the roof of a railway passenger car, placed over an elevated section of seats to afford a full view of scenery. **6.** a mountain peak having a rounded summit. **7.** *Slang.* a person's head. —*v.t.* **8.** to cover with or as if with a dome. **9.** to shape like a dome. —*v.i.* **10.** to rise or swell as a dome. —**dom′al,** *adj.* —**dome′-like′,** *adj.*

Dome′ of the Rock′, *Islam.* a shrine in Jerusalem at the site from which Muhammad ascended through the seven heavens to the throne of God: built on the site of the Jewish Temple.

Domes′day (or **Dooms′day**) **Book′,** *n.* a record of a survey of the lands of England made by order of William the Conqueror about 1086, giving ownership, extent, value, etc., of the properties.

do·mes·tic (də mes′tik), *adj.* **1.** of or pertaining to the home, family, or household affairs. **2.** devoted to home life. **3.** tame; domesticated. **4.** of or pertaining to one's own or a particular country as apart from other countries: *domestic trade.* **5.** produced within one's own country; native. —*n.* **6.** a household servant. **7.** Usu., **domestics.** items produced in one's own country. **8. domestics,** household items made of cloth, as sheets and towels. —**do·mes′ti·cal·ly,** *adv.*

domes′tic an′imal, *n.* a relatively docile animal kept by humans for work or food or as a pet, esp. one of a breed notably different from the wild form.

do·mes·ti·cate (*v.* də mes′ti kāt′; *n.* -kit), *v.,* **-cat·ed, -cat·ing,** *n.* —*v.t.* **1.** to convert (animals, plants, etc.) to domestic uses. **2.** to tame (an animal), esp. by generations of breeding, to live in close association with human beings as a pet or work animal or for food, usu. compromising its ability to live in the wild. **3.** to adapt (a plant) so as to be cultivated by and beneficial to human beings. **4.** to accustom to household life. **5.** to take (something foreign, unfamiliar, etc.) for one's own use. —*v.i.* **6.** to adjust to domestic life. —*n.* **7.** something, as an animal, that has been domesticated. —**do·mes′ti·ca′tion,** *n.* —**do·mes′ti·ca′tor,** *n.*

do·mes·tic·i·ty (dō′me stis′i tē), *n., pl.* **-ties. 1.** the state of being domestic; home life. **2.** a domestic activity or duty.

domes′tic part′ner, *n.* either member of an unmarried, cohabiting, and esp. homosexual couple that seeks benefits usu. available only to spouses. —**domes′tic part′nership,** *n.*

domes′tic vi′olence, *n.* acts of violence against a person living in one's household, esp. a member of one's immediate family.

dom·i·cal (dō′mi kəl, dom′i-) also **dom′ic,** *adj.* **1.** domelike. **2.** having a dome. —**dom′i·cal·ly,** *adv.*

dom·i·cile (dom′ə sīl′, -səl, dō′mə-) also **dom·i·cil** (-səl), *n., v.,*

-ciled, -cil·ing. —*n.* **1.** a place of residence; house or home. **2.** a permanent legal residence. —*v.t.* **3.** to establish in a domicile.

dom·i·nance (dom′ə nəns), *n.* **1.** the condition of being dominant. **2.** control or ascendancy; rule. **3.** *Psychol.* the disposition of an individual to assert control in dealing with others. **4.** *Animal Behav.* **a.** high status in a social group, often as a result of aggressive behavior, involving prior access to food, mates, space, etc. **b.** hierarchical rank in a social group in terms of dominant and submissive behavior. **5.** the normal tendency for one side of the brain to be more important than the other in controlling certain functions. Sometimes, **dom′i·nan·cy.**

dom·i·nant (dom′ə nənt), *adj.* **1.** ruling or controlling; having or exerting authority. **2.** occupying a commanding or elevated position. **3.** predominant; chief or foremost. **4.** *Genetics.* **a.** of or pertaining to that allele of a gene pair that masks the effect of the other when both are present in the same cell or organism. **b.** of or pertaining to the hereditary trait determined by such an allele. **5.** pertaining to or based on the dominant in music. —*n.* **6.** *Genetics.* **a.** the dominant allele of a gene pair. **b.** the individual carrying such an allele. **c.** a dominant trait. Compare RECESSIVE (def. 3). **7.** the fifth tone of a diatonic scale. **8.** *Ecol.* any plant or sometimes animal that by virtue of its abundance, size, or habits exerts such an influence on the conditions of an area as to determine what other organisms can live there. —**dom′i·nant·ly,** *adv.*

dom·i·nate (dom′ə nāt′), *v.,* **-nat·ed, -nat·ing.** —*v.t.* **1.** to rule over; control. **2.** to tower above; overlook. **3.** to be the major factor or influence in. **4.** *Math.* (of a series, vector, etc.) to have terms or components greater in absolute value than the corresponding terms or components of a given series, vector, etc. —*v.i.* **5.** to exercise power or control; predominate; rule. **6.** to occupy a commanding or elevated position. —**dom′i·nat′ing·ly,** *adv.* —**dom′i·na′tion,** *n.* —**dom′i·na′tor,** *n.*

dom·i·neer (dom′ə nēr′), *v.i.* **1.** to exert dominance or control (usu. fol. by *over* or *above*). —*v.t.* **2.** to rule arbitrarily or despotically; dominate.

Dom·i·nic (dom′ə nik), *n.* **Saint,** 1170–1221, Spanish priest: founder of the Dominican order.

Dom·i·ni·ca (dom′ə nē′kə, də min′i kə), *n.* **Commonwealth of,** an island republic, one of the Windward Islands, in the E West Indies: a former British colony; gained independence 1978. 83,226; 290 sq. mi. (751 sq. km). *Cap.:* Roseau.

Do·min·i·can[1] (də min′i kən), *adj.* **1.** of or pertaining to St. Dominic or the Dominicans. —*n.* **2.** a member of one of the mendicant religious orders founded by St. Dominic.

Do·min·i·can[2] (də min′i kən *for 1, 3;* dom′ə nē′kən, də min′i- *for 2, 4*), *adj.* **1.** of or pertaining to the Dominican Republic. **2.** of or pertaining to the Commonwealth of Dominica. —*n.* **3.** a native or inhabitant of the Dominican Republic. **4.** a native or inhabitant of the Commonwealth of Dominica.

Domin′ican Repub′lic, *n.* a republic in the West Indies, occupying the E part of Hispaniola. 8,228,151; 19,129 sq. mi. (49,545 sq. km). *Cap.:* Santo Domingo. Formerly, **Santo Domingo, San Domingo.**

dom·i·nie (dom′ə nē, dō′mə-), *n.* **1.** *Chiefly Scot.* a schoolmaster. **2.** a pastor in the Dutch Reformed Church. **3.** *Chiefly Hudson Valley.* a pastor or minister.

do·min·ion (də min′yən), *n.* **1.** the power to govern; sovereign authority. **2.** the act or fact of ruling; domination. **3.** the territory subject to the control of a single ruler or government. **4.** (*often cap.*) any of the self-governing countries outside the United Kingdom belonging to the Commonwealth of Nations.

Dom·i·nique (dom′ə nēk′) also **Dom·i·nick** (dom′ə nik), *n.* an American breed of chicken with gray, barred plumage.

dom·i·no[1] (dom′ə nō′), *n., pl.* **-noes. 1.** a small, flat block, the face of which has two squares, each either blank or bearing pips or dots. **2.** **dominoes,** (*used with a sing. v.*) a game in which the ends of such pieces are matched.

dom·i·no[2] (dom′ə nō′), *n., pl.* **-noes, -nos. 1.** a loose, hooded cloak worn with a half mask by persons in masquerade. **2.** the mask. **3.** a person wearing such dress.

dom′i·no the′ory, *n.* **1.** a theory that if one country is taken over by communism, its neighbors will be taken over one after another. **2.** a theory that a particular event will precipitate similar ones elsewhere. Also called **dom′ino effect′, dom′ino reac′tion.**

Do·mi·nus (dō′mi nŏŏs′, dom′i-), *n. Latin.* God; the Lord.

Do·mi·nus vo·bis·cum (dō′mi nŏŏs′ vō bis′kŏŏm, dom′i-), *Latin.* the Lord be with you.

Do·mi·tian (də mish′ən, -ē ən), *n.* (*Titus Flavius Domitianus Augustus*), A.D. 51–96, Roman emperor 81–96.

don[1] (don; *Sp., It.* dôn), *n.* **1.** (*cap.*) Mr.; Sir: a Spanish title prefixed to a man's given name. **2.** (in Spanish-speaking countries) a lord or gentleman. **3.** (*cap.*) an Italian title of address, esp. for a priest. **4.** (in English universities) a head, fellow, or tutor of a college. **5.** the head of a Mafia family.

don[2] (don), *v.t.,* **donned, don·ning.** to put on or dress in: *to don one's gloves.*

do·nate (dō′nāt, dō nāt′), *v.,* **-nat·ed, -nat·ing.** —*v.t.* **1.** to present as a gift, esp. as a donation to a fund. —*v.i.* **2.** to make a contribution. —**do′na·tor,** *n.*

Don·a·tel·lo (don′ə tel′ō), *n.* (*Donato di Niccolo di Betto Bardi*), 1386?–1466, Italian sculptor.

do·na·tion (dō nā′shən), *n.* **1.** an act or instance of presenting a gift or contribution. **2.** a gift, as to a fund; contribution.

Don·a·tist (don′ə tist, dō′nə-), *n.* a member of a Christian sect that developed in N Africa in A.D. 311 and maintained that it alone constituted the whole and only true church.

Do·na·tus (dō nā′təs), *n.* **1.** early-4th-century bishop of Casae Nigrae in northern Africa: leader of a heretical Christian group. Compare DONATIST. **2. Aelius.** 4th century A.D., Roman grammarian.

done (dun), *v.* **1.** pp. of DO[1]. —*adj.* **2. a.** finished; completed; accomplished: *a done deal; Our work is done.* **b.** at a point of completion; through: *When you are done, turn out the lights.* **3.** cooked sufficiently. **4.** worn out, exhausted, or used up. **5.** in keeping with acceptable behavior or practice: *That sort of thing simply isn't done.* —*Idiom.* **6. be** or **have done with,** to break off relations with. **7. done for, a.** dead or dying. **b.** very tired; exhausted. **c.** doomed to failure. **8. done in,** very tired; exhausted. —*Usage.* Usage guides occasionally object to DONE in the adjectival senses "finished" and "through," but the meanings are standard. Originally, DONE was used attributively (*The argument between them was a done thing*). It is now more common as a complement, but the attributive use survives as the frozen locution *a done deal.*

do·nee (dō nē′), *n.* a person to whom a gift is made.

Do·netsk (də netsk′), *n.* a city in E Ukraine, in the Donets Basin. 1,110,000. Formerly, **Stalin, Stalino, Yuzovka.**

dong (dông, dong), *n.* a deep sound like that of a large bell.

Don·i·zet·ti (don′i zet′ē), *n.* **Gaetano,** 1797–1848, Italian composer.

Don Juan (don wän′ *or, Sp.,* dôn hwän′ *for 1, 2; esp. Brit.* don jōō′ən), *n.* **1.** a legendary Spanish nobleman famous for his many seductions and his dissolute life. **2.** a libertine; rake. **3.** a ladies' man or womanizer; romeo.

don·key (dong′kē, dông′-, dung′-), *n., pl.* **-keys,** *adj.* —*n.* **1.** a domesticated ass, *Equus asinus.* **2.** (since 1874) a representation of this animal as the emblem of the U.S. Democratic party. **3.** a stupid, silly, or obstinate person. —*adj.* **4.** auxiliary: *donkey engine; donkey pump.*

don′key work′ or **don′key·work′,** *n.* tedious, repetitious work; drudgery.

Donne (dun), *n.* **John,** 1573–1631, English poet and clergyman.

don·née (do nā′), *n.* a set of artistic or literary premises or assumptions.

Don′ner Pass′ (don′ər), *n.* a mountain pass in the Sierra Nevada, in E California. 7135 ft. (2175 m) high.

don·ny·brook (don′ē brŏŏk′), *n.* (*often cap.*) a brawl or free-for-all. Also called **Don′nybrook Fair′.**

do·nor (dō′nər), *n.* **1.** a person who gives or donates. **2.** a provider of blood, an organ, or other biological tissue for transfusion or transplantation. **3.** an atom that provides a pair of electrons to form a chemical bond. Compare ACCEPTOR (def. 3). —*adj.* **4.** of or pertaining to the biological tissue of a donor: *donor organ.* **5.** indicating, pertaining to, or for a giver of a donation, esp. a biological donation: *a donor card; donor records.* —**do′nor·ship′,** *n.*

do′-noth·ing (dōō), *n.* **1.** a lazy or shiftless person. —*adj.* **2.** characterized by inability or unwillingness to assume responsibility, work toward a goal, or the like.

Don Quix·o·te (don′ kē hō′tē, -tā, don kwik′sət), *n.* **1.** the hero of a novel by Cervantes who was inspired by lofty but impractical ideals. **2.** (*italics*) (*Don Quixote de la Mancha*) the novel itself (1605 and 1615).

Don′t′ Tread′ on Me′, —*Saying.* respect U.S. sovereignty: a motto inscribed on the first official American flag (1775).

doo·dle (dōōd′l), *v.,* **-dled, -dling,** *n.* —*v.i.* **1.** to draw or scribble idly. **2.** to engage in trifling activity. **3.** to play idly on a musical instrument. —*v.t.* **4.** to produce by doodling. **5.** to pass (time) idly (often fol. by *away*). —*n.* **6.** a figure produced by doodling.

doo·hick·ey (dōō′hik′ē), *n., pl.* **-eys.** *Informal.* a gadget; thingamajig.

doom (dōōm), *n.* **1.** fate or destiny, esp. adverse fate. **2.** ruin or death. —*v.t.* **3.** to destine, esp. to an adverse fate. **4.** to condemn to death. **5.** to ensure the failure of.

doom·say·er (dōōm′sā′ər), *n.* a person who predicts impending misfortune or disaster. —**doom′say′ing,** *adj., n.*

dooms·day (dōōmz′dā′), *n.* **1.** the day of the Last Judgment, the end of the world. **2.** nuclear destruction of the world.

Dooms′day Book′ (dōōmz′dā′), *n.* DOMESDAY BOOK.

dooms′day cult′, *n.* a religious cult that anticipates the imminent end of the world, esp. one that advocates collective suicide.

dooms′day machine′, *n.* a hypothetical computer of a national government that is programmed to trigger a nuclear war based on the actions of other nations.

door (dôr, dōr), *n.* **1.** a movable, usu. solid, barrier for opening and closing an entranceway, cupboard, cabinet, or the like, commonly turning on hinges or sliding in grooves. **2.** a doorway. **3.** a building, house, or the like as represented by its entrance: *two doors up the street.* **4.** any means of access: *the door to learning.* —*Idiom.* **5. lay at someone's door,** to hold someone accountable for. **6. lie at someone's door,** to be the responsibility of; be imputable to. **7. show someone the door,** to order someone to leave. —**door′less,** *adj.*

door·bell (dôr′bel′, dōr′-), *n.* a bell, chime, or buzzer connected with a door, rung by persons seeking admittance.

door′bell-ring′ing, *n.* political campaigning that takes a candidate from house to house.

door' chain', *n.* a short chain with a slide fitting, attached between the inside of a door and the doorjamb in such a way that the door will not open more than a few inches unless the chain is released.

do'-or-die' (dōō), *adj.* **1.** involving a desperate effort to succeed or face dire or even tragic consequences. **2.** involving an extreme emergency.

door•frame (dôr'frām', dōr'-), *n.* the frame of a doorway, including two jambs and a lintel, or head.

door•jamb (dôr'jam', dōr'-), *n.* either of the two sidepieces of a doorframe. Also called **doorpost.**

door•keep•er (dôr'kē'pər, dōr'-), *n.* **1.** a person who guards the entrance of a building. **2.** *Brit.* a janitor; hall porter.

door•knob (dôr'nob', dōr'-), *n.* the handle or knob by which a door is opened or closed.

door•man (dôr'man', -mən, dōr'-), *n., pl.* **-men** (-men', -mən). the door attendant of an apartment house, nightclub, etc., who assists those entering and departing.

door•nail (dôr'nāl', dōr'-), *n.* **1.** a large-headed nail formerly used for strengthening or ornamenting doors. —*Idiom.* **2. dead as a doornail,** unquestionably dead.

door' o'pener or **door'-o'pener,** *n.* something that is effective in leading to opportunity or success.

door•post (dôr'pōst', dōr'-), *n.* DOORJAMB.

door' prize', *n.* a prize awarded at a dance, party, or the like, often through a drawing.

door•step (dôr'step', dōr'-), *n.* a step in front of an outside door.

door•stop (dôr'stop', dōr'-), *n.* **1.** a weighted device or wedge for holding a door open. **2.** a device for preventing a door or doorknob from striking a wall, as a small rubber-tipped projection.

door'-to-door', *adj.* **1.** selling, canvassing, etc., at each house or apartment in an area. **2.** sent direct from the point of purchase to the point of delivery. —*adv.* **3.** in a door-to-door manner.

door•way (dôr'wā', dōr'-), *n.* **1.** the entryway providing access to a building, room, etc.; portal. **2.** a means of access: *the doorway to success.*

door•yard (dôr'yärd', dōr'-), *n.* a yard near the front door of a house.

doo-wop (dōō'wop'), *n.* a style of popular music for a singing group in which words and nonsense syllables are rhythmically chanted as support for a soloist.

do•pa (dō'pə), *n.* an amino acid, $C_9H_{11}NO_4$, formed from tyrosine in the liver during melanin and epinephrine biosynthesis. Compare L-DOPA.

do•pa•mine (dō'pə mēn'), *n.* a monoamine neurotransmitter that acts within certain brain cells to help regulate movement and emotion.

dope (dōp), *n., v.,* **doped, dop•ing,** *adj.* —*n.* **1.** any thick liquid preparation or paste, used in preparing a surface. **2.** a material used to absorb and hold a liquid, as in the manufacture of dynamite. **3. a.** any of various varnishlike products for coating a fabric, as of airplane wings, in order to strengthen it, make it waterproof, etc. **b.** a similar product used to coat the fabric of a balloon to reduce gas leakage. **4.** *Slang.* information; news. **5.** *Informal.* a stupid person. **6.** *Southeastern U.S.* soda pop, esp. cola-flavored. —*v.t.* —*v.i.* **7. dope out,** *Slang.* to figure out.

dop•ey or **dop•y** (dō'pē), *adj.,* **dop•i•er, dop•i•est.** *Informal.* **1.** stupid; inane. **2.** sluggish or befuddled, as from the use of narcotics or alcohol. —**dop'i•ness, dop'ey•ness,** *n.*

dop•ing (dō'ping), *n.* the use of a substance foreign to the body, or the use of a natural physiological substance taken in an abnormal quantity or by unnatural route of entry into the body, with the sole intention of artificially increasing performance in a competition.

dop•pel•gäng•er (dop'əl gang'ər; *Ger.* dô'pəl geng'ər), *n.* a ghostly double or counterpart of a living person.

Dop'pler effect' (dop'lər), *n.* a phenomenon characterized by a change (**Dop'pler shift'**) in the frequency of waves, as light or sound waves, observed when the wave source is moving relative to the observer.

dor (dôr), *n.* **1.** Also, **dor•bee•tle** (dôr'bēt'l). a common European dung beetle, *Geotrupes stercorarius.* **2.** any of several insects, as the June bug, that make a buzzing noise in flight.

Dor•cas (dôr'kəs), *n.* a Christian woman at Joppa who made clothing for the poor. Acts 9:36–41.

Do•ri•an (dôr'ē ən, dōr'-), *n.* **1.** a member of a Greek people or group of peoples who overran most of W Greece and the Peloponnesus in the 12th century B.C., bringing Mycenaean culture to an end. —*adj.* **2.** of or pertaining to the ancient Greek region of Doris or to the Dorians.

Dor•ic (dôr'ik, dor'-), *adj.* **1.** of or designating one of the five classical orders of architecture, characterized typically by a fluted column having as a capital a convex circular molding, or echinus, supporting a square slab, or abacus. **2.** DORIAN (def. 2). —*n.* **3.** a dialect of ancient Greek spoken in the S and E Peloponnesus and eastward from Crete through the islands of the S Aegean Sea to SW Asia Minor. **4.** rustic English speech.

dor•mant (dôr'mənt), *adj.* **1.** inactive, as in sleep; torpid. **2.** being in a state of minimal metabolic activity with cessation of growth. **3.** undeveloped, unasserted, or inactive; latent: *talents that lay dormant.* **4.** (of a volcano) not erupting. **5.** held in abeyance; temporarily inoperative. **6.** (of a pesticide) applied to a plant during a period of dormancy:

a dormant spray. **7.** (of a heraldic animal) lying with the head on the forepaws. —**dor'man•cy,** *n.*

dor•mer (dôr'mər), *n.* **1.** Also called **dor'mer win'dow.** a vertical window in a projection built out from a sloping roof. **2.** the entire projecting structure. —**dor'mered,** *adj.*

dormer

dor•mi•to•ry (dôr'mi tôr'ē, -tōr'ē), *n., pl.* **-ries,** *adj.* —*n.* **1.** a building, as at a college, containing rooms and facilities for residents. **2.** a large room, containing a number of beds and serving as communal sleeping quarters. —*adj.* **3.** of or designating a community inhabited mainly by commuters: *dormitory suburbs.*

dor•mouse (dôr'mous'), *n., pl.* **-mice** (-mīs'). any small usu. bushytailed Old World climbing rodent of the family Gliridae.

do•ron•i•cum (də ron'i kəm), *n.* any of various Eurasian composite plants of the genus *Doronicum,* cultivated for their showy yellow flowers.

dor•sal (dôr'səl), *adj.* **1.** of, pertaining to, or situated at the back, or dorsum. **2.** situated on or toward the upper side of the body, equivalent to the back, or posterior, in humans. **3.** *Bot.* ABAXIAL. —*n.* **4.** a dorsal structure. —**dor'sal•ly,** *adv.*

dor•si•ven•tral (dôr'sə ven'trəl), *adj.* **1.** *Bot.* having distinct dorsal and ventral sides, as most foliage leaves. **2.** *Zool.* dorsoventral. —**dor'si•ven•tral•i•ty,** *n.* —**dor'si•ven'tral•ly,** *adv.*

dor•so•ven•tral (dôr'sō ven'trəl), *adj.* **1.** *Zool.* pertaining to the dorsal and ventral aspects of the body; extending from the dorsal to the ventral side: *the dorsoventral axis.* **2.** *Bot.* dorsiventral. —**dor'so•ven'tral•i•ty,** *n.* —**dor'so•ven'tral•ly,** *adv.*

dor•sum (dôr'səm), *n., pl.* **-sa** (-sə). **1.** the back, as of the body. **2.** the back or outer surface of an organ, part, etc.

do•ry (dôr'ē, dōr'ē), *n., pl.* **-ries.** a small boat with a narrow, flat bottom, high bow, and flaring sides.

DOS (dôs, dos), *n.* an operating system for microcomputers.

DOS, Department of State.

dos•age (dō'sij), *n.* **1.** the administration of medicine in doses. **2.** the amount of medicine to be given. **3.** DOSE (def. 4). **4.** the process of adding a sugar solution to sparkling wine before corking.

dose (dōs), *n., v.,* **dosed, dos•ing.** —*n.* **1.** a quantity of medicine prescribed to be taken at one time. **2.** an intense and often disagreeable experience: *a dose of bad luck.* **3.** an amount of sugar solution added in the production of sparkling wine. **4.** the amount of radiation to which something has been exposed or the amount that has been absorbed by a given mass of material, esp. living tissue. —*v.t.* **5.** to give a dose of medicine to. **6.** to administer in doses. **7.** to add sugar to (wine) during production. —*v.i.* **8.** to take a dose of medicine. —*Idiom.* **9. get a dose of one's own medicine,** to receive back what was given out, esp. pain or punishment. —**dos'er,** *n.*

do-si-do (dō'sē dō'), *n., pl.* **-dos,** *v.,* **-doed, -do•ing.** —*n.* **1.** a figure in square dancing, in which two persons advance, pass around each other back to back, and return to their places. —*v.t.* **2.** to dance this figure around (one's partner). —*v.i.* **3.** to execute a do-si-do.

dos•sal or **dos•sel** (dos'əl), *n.* an ornamental hanging placed at the back of an altar or at the sides of the chancel.

dos•si•er (dos'ē ā', dô'sē ā'), *n.* a file of documents containing detailed information about a person or topic.

Dos•to•ev•sky or **Dos•to•yev•sky** (dos'tə yef'skē, dus'-), *n.* **Fyodor Mikhailovich,** 1821–81, Russian novelist.

dot[1] (dot), *n., v.,* **dot•ted, dot•ting.** —*n.* **1.** a small, roundish mark made with or as if with a pen. **2.** a small spot; speck. **3.** a small amount: *a dot of butter.* **4. a.** a point placed after a musical note or rest increasing the duration by one half the value. **b.** a point placed under or over a musical note indicating staccato. **5.** a signal of shorter duration than a dash, used in groups along with groups of dashes and spaces to represent letters, as in Morse code. **6.** an individual element in a halftone reproduction. —*v.t.* **7.** to mark with or as if with a dot or dots. **8.** to cover or sprinkle with or as if with dots: *trees dotting the landscape.* **9.** to form with dots. —*v.i.* **10.** to make a dot or dots. —*Idiom.* **11. dot one's i's and cross one's t's,** to be meticulous and precise. **12. on the dot,** precisely; exactly at the time specified. —**dot'like',** *adj.* —**dot'ter,** *n.*

dot[2] (dot, dôt), *n.* DOWRY (def. 1). —**do•tal** (dōt'l), *adj.*

DOT, Department of Transportation.

dot•age (dō'tij), *n.* **1.** a decline of mental faculties, esp. as associated with old age; senility. **2.** excessive or foolish affection.

dote (dōt), *v.,* **dot•ed, dot•ing,** *n.* —*v.i.* **1.** to bestow or express excessive fondness or love (usu. fol. by *on*). **2.** to be weak-minded or foolish, esp. associated with old age. —**dot'er,** *n.* —**dot'ing•ly,** *adv.*

dot'-ma'trix, *adj.* pertaining to the formation of characters and graphics with dots from a matrix, as by some computer printers.

dot·ter·el (dot′ər əl) also **dot·trel** (do′trəl), *n.* any of several plovers usu. inhabiting upland areas, esp. *Eudromias morinellus*, of Europe and Asia.

dot·ty[1] (dot′ē), *adj.,* **-ti·er, -ti·est.** *Informal.* **1.** crazy or eccentric. **2.** very enthusiastic or infatuated (usu. fol. by *about* or *over*). —**dot′ti·ly,** *adv.* —**dot′ti·ness,** *n.*

dot·ty[2] (dot′ē), *adj.,* **-ti·er, -ti·est.** marked with dots; dotted.

Dou′ay Bi′ble (dōō′ā), *n.* an English version of the Bible translated from the Vulgate by Roman Catholic scholars (New Testament 1582; Old Testament 1609). [after *Douay,* France]

dou·ble (dub′əl), *adj., n., v′.,* **-bled, -bling,** *adv.* —*adj.* **1.** twice as large, heavy, strong, etc.; twofold in size, amount, number, extent, etc. **2.** composed of two like parts or members; paired: *a double sink.* **3.** suitable for two persons: *a double room.* **4.** twofold in character or meaning; dual or ambiguous. **5.** marked by duplicity; deceitful; hypocritical: *a double life.* **6.** folded in two. **7.** (of a bed or bedclothes) full-size: *a double blanket.* **8.** (of flowers) having many more than the normal number of petals. —*n.* **9.** anything that is twice the usual size, quantity, strength, etc. **10.** a duplicate or counterpart. **11.** a person exactly or closely resembling another. **12.** a hotel room with two beds or a double bed, for occupancy by two people. **13.** a fold or plait. **14.** a sharp reversal, as of course. **15.** a trick or artifice, as of argument in a debate. **16. a.** an understudy. **b.** an actor who plays two or more parts in a play, usu. minor roles. **17.** a substitute who performs feats or actions in a movie or TV show too hazardous for a star. **18.** Also called **two-base hit.** a hit in baseball that enables the batter to reach second base safely. **19.** DOUBLE TIME. **20. doubles,** (*used with a sing. v.*) a game or match, as in tennis, in which there are two players on each side. **21.** (in bridge) a bid by an opponent indicating belief that the declarer's bid will not succeed or informing one's partner that one's hand is of a certain strength. —*v.t.* **22.** to make double or twice as great; add an equal amount of. **23.** to fold or bend with one part over another (often fol. by *over, up,* etc.). **24.** to clench: *to double one's fists.* **25.** to be twice as much as. **26.** to sail around (a projecting area of land). **27.** to pair; couple. **28.** (in bridge) to challenge (a declarer's bid) by calling "double." **29. a.** to be a double for (an actor). **b.** to perform (a role or roles) as an actor cast in more than one part. **30.** *Baseball.* **a.** to cause the advance of (a base runner) by a two-base hit. **b.** to cause (a run) to be scored by a two-base hit (often fol. by *in*). **c.** to put out (a base runner) as the second out of a double play. —*v.i.* **31.** to become double. **32.** to bend or fold (often fol. by *up* or *over*). **33.** to turn back on a course; reverse direction (often fol. by *back*). **34.** to serve in an additional capacity: *The director doubles as bit player.* **35.** to act as a double in a play, motion picture, or the like. **36.** to hit a double in baseball. **37.** to play an instrument besides one's regular instrument (usu. followed by *on*). **38.** to double-date. **39. double up, a.** to share quarters planned for only one person or family. **b.** to bend over, as from pain. —*adv.* **40.** to twice the amount, extent, etc.; twofold. **41.** two together: *to sleep double.* —*Idiom.* **42. double in brass,** to serve in more than one capacity. **43. double or nothing,** a bet in which one either wins twice as much as one has bet or gets nothing. **44. on the double, a.** without delay; rapidly. **b.** in double time, as marching troops.

dou′ble-act′ing, *adj.* **1.** accomplishing work or permitting movement in two directions. **2.** having twice the usual strength or effectiveness.

dou′ble-ac′tion, *adj.* (of a firearm) requiring only one pull of the trigger to cock and fire it.

dou′ble a′gent, *n.* a person who spies on a country while pretending to spy for it; a spy in the service of two rival countries.

dou′ble bar′, *n.* a double vertical line on a musical staff indicating the end of a piece of music or a principal section.

dou′ble-bar′reled, *adj.* **1.** (esp. of a shotgun) having two barrels mounted side by side. **2.** serving a double purpose or having two aspects.

dou′ble bass′ (bās), *n.* the largest instrument of the violin family, having three or, usu., four strings, rested vertically on the floor when played. —**dou′ble bass′ist,** *n.*

dou′ble-bill′, *v.t.,* **-billed, -bill·ing. 1.** to bill (different accounts) for the same charge. **2.** to present (a film) in a double feature.

dou′ble bind′, *n.* **1.** a situation in which a person is faced with contradictory demands such that to obey one is to disobey the other. **2.** DILEMMA (def. 1).

dou′ble-blind′, *adj.* pertaining to an experiment or clinical trial in which neither the researchers nor the subjects know which subjects are receiving the active treatment, medication, etc., so as to eliminate bias.

dou′ble boil′er, *n.* a utensil consisting of two pots, one of which fits partway into the other: water is boiled in the lower pot to cook or warm food in the upper.

dou′ble bond′, *n.* a chemical linkage consisting of two covalent bonds between two atoms of a molecule, represented in chemical formulas by two lines, two dots, or four dots, as $CH_2 = CH_2$; $CH_2:CH_2$; $CH_2::CH_2$.

dou′ble-book′, *v.t.* **1.** to make two reservations for (a hotel room, seat on a plane, etc.) so as to be certain of obtaining at least one. **2.** to overbook. —*v.i.* **3.** to make double reservations.

dou′ble-breast′ed, *adj.* **1.** (of a coat, jacket, etc.) having a front closure with a wide overlap that is secured at both the right and the left sides and typically shows two vertical rows of buttons when fastened.

2. (of a suit) having a coat or jacket that so overlaps. Compare SINGLE-BREASTED.

dou′ble-check′, *v.t., v.i.* **1.** to check again, as to verify; recheck. —*n.* **2.** a second examination or verification to assure accuracy, proper functioning, or the like.

dou′ble chin′, *n.* a fold of fat beneath the chin. —**dou′ble-chinned′,** *adj.*

dou′ble-click′, *v.i.* *Computers.* to click a mouse button twice in rapid succession, as to call up a program or select a file. —**dou′ble click′,** *n.*

dou′ble cross′, *n.* **1.** a betrayal or swindle of a friend or colleague. **2.** the act of winning or attempting to win a contest that one has agreed to lose. **3.** a genetic cross in which both parents are first-generation hybrids from single crosses.

dou′ble-cross′, *v.t.* to betray or swindle, esp. by an action contrary to an agreed upon course. —**dou′ble-cross′er,** *n.*

dou′ble dag′ger, *n.* a mark (‡) used for references, as for footnotes.

dou′ble date′, *n.* a date on which two couples go together. —**dou′ble-date′,** *v.i.,* **-dat·ed, -dat·ing.**

Dou·ble·day′ (dub′əl dā′), *n.* **Abner,** 1819–93, U.S. army officer: sometimes credited with inventing baseball.

dou′ble-deal′ing, *n.* **1.** deception or treachery; duplicity. —*adj.* **2.** using duplicity; treacherous.

dou′ble-deck′er, *n.* **1.** something with two decks, tiers, or the like. **2.** a sandwich of three slices of bread and two layers of filling.

dou′ble-dig′it, *adj.* of a percentage amounting to ten or more: *double-digit inflation.*

dou·ble-dip·ping (dub′əl dip′ing), *n.* the act or practice of receiving more than one form of compensation from the same employer or organization, as in earning a government salary while receiving a military retiree's pension. —**dou′ble-dip′,** *v.i.,* **-dipped, -dip·ping.** —**dou′ble-dip′per,** *n.*

dou′ble drib′ble, *n.* a basketball infraction in which a player stops and then resumes dribbling or dribbles using both hands. —**dou′ble-drib′ble,** *v.i.,* **-drib·bled, -drib·bling.**

dou′ble-edged′, *adj.* **1.** having two cutting edges, as an ax. **2.** capable of acting in two ways or having opposite effects or interpretations: *a double-edged remark.*

dou·ble en·ten·dre (dub′əl än tän′drə, -tänd′; *Fr.* dōō blän tän′dr°), *n., pl.* **dou·ble en·ten·dres** (dub′əl än tän′drəz, -tändz′; *Fr.* dōō blän-tän′dr°). **1.** a word or expression used so that it can be understood in two ways, esp. when one meaning is risqué. **2.** a double meaning; ambiguity.

dou′ble en′try, *n.* a bookkeeping method in which each transaction is entered twice in the ledger, once to the debit of one account and once to the credit of another. Compare SINGLE ENTRY.

dou′ble expo′sure, *n.* **1.** the act of exposing the same photographic film, plate, etc., twice. **2.** the picture resulting from this.

dou′ble fault′, *n.* (in tennis, squash, etc.) two faults in succession, resulting in the loss of the point, the loss of the serve, or both.

dou·ble-head·er (dub′əl hed′ər), *n.* **1.** two games, either between the same teams or different pairs of teams, played on the same day in immediate succession. **2.** two performances or events occurring one after the other. **3.** a railroad train pulled by two locomotives.

dou′ble he′lix, *n.* the spiral arrangement of the two complementary strands of DNA.

dou′ble-hung′, *adj.* (of a window) having two vertically sliding sashes, each closing a different part of the opening.

dou′ble jeop′ardy, *n.* the act of prosecuting a person a second time for the same offense: prohibited by the Fifth Amendment.

dou′ble-joint′ed, *adj.* having especially flexible joints that can bend in unusual ways or to an unusually great extent.

dou′ble knit′, *n.* a fabric knitted on a machine with two sets of needles and yarns, thereby having the same ribbing on both the face and the back.

dou′ble neg′ative, *n.* a syntactic construction in which two negative words are used in the same clause to express a single negation. —**Usage.** The DOUBLE NEGATIVE is universally considered nonstandard in Modern English: *They never paid me no money. He didn't have nothing to do with it.* In educated speech, *any* and *anything* would be substituted for *no* and *nothing.* Certain uses of double negation, to express an affirmative, are fully standard: *We cannot sit here and do nothing* (meaning we must do something). *In the not unlikely event that the bill passes, prices will rise* (meaning the event is likely). See also HARDLY.

dou′ble refrac′tion, *n.* the separation of a ray of light into two unequally refracted, plane-polarized rays of orthogonal polarizations, occurring in crystals in which the velocity of light rays is not the same in all directions.

dou·ble·speak (dub′əl spēk′), *n.* evasive, ambiguous, or high-flown language intended to deceive or confuse.

dou′ble stand′ard, *n.* **1.** any set of principles applied differently to one group of people than to another, as an unwritten code permitting men greater sexual freedom than women. **2.** BIMETALLISM.

dou′ble star′, *n.* two stars that appear together in the sky and usu. appear as one to the eye or through a low-power telescope.

dou·blet (dub′lit), *n.* **1.** a close-fitting jacket, sleeved or sleeveless, sometimes with a short skirt, worn by men in the Renaissance. **2.** a pair of like things; couple. **3.** one of a pair of like things; duplicate. **4.** a unit

D

composed of two closely or identically matched pieces, as an artificial gem. **5.** one of two or more words in a language that are derived from the same source, esp. through different routes, as *coy* and *quiet*, both taken from the same Latin word, *quiet* directly and *coy* by way of Old French. **6. doublets,** a throw of a pair of dice in which the same number of spots turns up on each die. **7.** a compound lens made of two thin lenses shaped so as to reduce chromatic and spherical aberrations.

dou•ble take′, *n.* a surprised delayed response, as to a person not recognized or a situation not grasped the first time.

dou′ble-talk′ or **dou•ble-talk′,** *n.* **1.** speech using nonsense syllables along with words in a rapid patter. **2.** deliberately evasive or ambiguous language. —*v.i.* **3.** to engage in double-talk. —*v.t.* **4.** to accomplish or persuade by double-talk. —**dou′ble-talk′er,** *n.*

dou′ble-team′, *v.t.* **1.** to defend against or block (an opposing player) by using two players, as in football. **2.** to use two people in the handling of: *to double-team a job.*

dou′ble time′, *n.* **1.** the fastest rate of marching troops, a slow jog at the rate of l80 paces per minute. **2.** a rate of overtime pay that is twice the regular wage rate.

dou′ble-time′, *v.i., v.t.,* **-timed, -tim•ing.** to move or cause to move in double time.

dou•ble-tree (dub′əl trē′), *n.* a pivoted bar with a whiffletree attached to each end, used in harnessing two horses abreast.

dou′ble vi′sion, *n.* DIPLOPIA.

doubt (dout), *v.t.* **1.** to be uncertain about; consider questionable or unlikely. **2.** to distrust. —*v.i.* **3.** to be uncertain. —*n.* **4.** a feeling of uncertainty. **5.** distrust or suspicion. **6.** a situation causing uncertainty. —*Idiom.* **7. beyond (a** or **the shadow of) a doubt,** with certainty; definitely. **8. in doubt,** in a state of uncertainty. **9. no doubt, a.** probably. **b.** certainly. **10. without doubt,** unquestionably; certainly. —**doubt′a•ble,** *adj.* —**doubt′er,** *n.* —**doubt′ing•ly,** *adv.*

doubt•ful (dout′fəl), *adj.* **1.** of uncertain outcome. **2.** uncertain. **3.** unsettled in opinion or belief; undecided; hesitant. **4.** of dubious character or value: *doubtful tactics.* **5.** unlikely; not probable. —**doubt′ful•ly,** *adv.* —**doubt′ful•ness,** *n.*

doubt′ing Thom′as, *n.* a person who refuses to believe without proof; skeptic. John 20:24–29.

doubt•less (dout′lis), *adv.* Also, **doubt′less•ly. 1.** without doubt; certainly. **2.** probably; presumably. —*adj.* **3.** certain; sure.

douche (d̅o̅o̅sh), *n., v.,* **douched, douch•ing.** —*n.* **1.** a jet or current of water, sometimes with a dissolved medicating or cleansing agent, applied to a body part, organ, or cavity for medicinal or hygienic purposes. **2.** an instrument, as a syringe, for administering it. —*v.t.* **3.** to apply a douche to. —*v.i.* **4.** to use a douche; undergo douching.

dough (dō), *n.* **1.** flour or meal combined with water, milk, etc. in a thick, pliable mass for baking into bread, pastry, etc. **2.** any similar soft, pasty mass. **3.** *Slang.* money. —**dough′like′,** *adj.*

dough•face (dō′fās′), *n.* (before and during the Civil War) a Northerner who sympathized with the South, or a Northern politician who was not opposed to slavery in the South.

dough•foot (dō′fŏŏt′), *n., pl.* **-feet** (-fēt′), **-foots.** *Informal.* an infantryman in the U.S. Army, esp. in World War II.

dough•nut or **do•nut** (dō′nət, -nut′), *n.* **1.** a small, usu. ring-shaped cake of sweetened dough fried in deep fat. **2.** a raised ball of deep-fried dough, filled with jelly, custard, etc. **3.** any thick, ring-shaped object.

dough•ty (dou′tē), *adj.,* **-ti•er, -ti•est.** courageous and resolute; valiant. —**dough′ti•ly,** *adv.* —**dough′ti•ness,** *n.*

dough•y (dō′ē), *adj.,* **dough•i•er, dough•i•est.** resembling dough, as in being soft, pale, or flabby. —**dough′i•ness,** *n.*

Doug•las (dug′ləs), *n.* **1. Kirk** (*Issur Danielovitch Demsky*), born 1916, U.S. actor. **2. Michael,** born 1944, U.S. actor and producer (son of Kirk Douglas). **3. Stephen A(rnold),** 1813–61, U.S. political leader. **4. William O(rville),** 1898–1980, Associate Justice of the U.S. Supreme Court 1939–75. **5.** the capital of the Isle of Man.

Doug′las fir′, *n.* a giant North American evergreen tree, *Pseudotsuga menziesii,* of the pine family, used for timber and as a Christmas tree. Also called **Doug′las pine′, Doug′las spruce′.**

Doug•lass (dug′ləs), *n.* **Frederick,** 1817–95, U.S. ex-slave, abolitionist, and orator.

Dou•kho•bor or **Du•kho•bor** (d̅o̅o̅′kō bôr′), *n.* a member of an independent religious sect originating in Russia in the 18th century, believing in the supreme authority of the inner voice and in the transmigration of souls, rejecting the divinity of Christ and the establishing of churches, and expressing opposition to civil authority by refusing to pay taxes, do military service, etc.

dour (d̅o̅o̅r, dou′ər, dou′ər), *adj.* **1.** sullen; gloomy. **2.** severe; stern. **3.** *Scot.* (of land) barren; rocky. —**dour′ly,** *adv.* —**dour′ness,** *n.*

douse or **dowse** (dous), *v.,* **doused** or **dowsed, dous•ing** or **dows•ing.** —*v.t.* **1.** to plunge into water or the like; drench. **2.** to throw water or other liquid on. **3.** to extinguish: *to douse a candle.* —*v.i.* **4.** to plunge or be plunged into a liquid. —**dous′er,** *n.*

dove¹ (duv), *n.* **1.** any bird of the family Columbidae, esp. the smaller species with pointed tails. Compare PIGEON (def. 1). **2.** a pure white member of this species, used as a symbol of innocence, gentleness, and peace. **3.** a person who advocates peace or a conciliatory national attitude. **4.** an innocent or gentle person. **5.** a warm gray color. —**dove′like′, dov′ish,** *adj.* —**dov′ish•ness,** *n.*

dove² (dōv), *v.* a pt. of DIVE.

dove•kie or **dove•key** (duv′kē), *n., pl.* **-kies** or **-keys.** a small short-billed black-and-white auk, *Alle alle,* of N Atlantic and Arctic oceans.

Do•ver (dō′vər), *n.* **1.** a seaport in E Kent, in SE England: point nearest the coast of France. 104,300. **2. Strait of.** French, **Pas de Calais.** a strait between England and France, connecting the English Channel and the North Sea: narrowest point 20 mi. (32 km). **3.** the capital of Delaware, in the central part. 23,512.

Do′ver sole′, *n.* **1.** a common European sole, *Solea solea,* esp. one caught in the English Channel: a choice food fish. **2.** a brownish speckled flatfish, *Microstomus pacificus,* of North American Pacific seas.

dove•tail (duv′tāl′), *n.* **1.** a tenon broader at its end than at its base; pin. **2.** a joint formed of one or more such tenons fitting tightly within corresponding mortises. —*v.t., v.i.* **3.** to join or fit together by means of a dovetail. **4.** to join or fit together compactly or harmoniously.

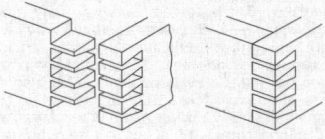

dovetail (def. 2)

dow•a•ger (dou′ə jər), *n.* **1.** a woman who holds some title or property from her deceased husband. **2.** an elderly woman of stately dignity. —*adj.* **3.** pertaining to or characteristic of a dowager. —**dow′a•ger•ism,** *n.*

dow•dy (dou′dē), *adj.,* **-di•er, -di•est,** *n., pl.* **-dies.** —*adj.* **1.** not stylish; drab; out-of-date: *dowdy clothes.* **2.** not neat; shabby. —*n.* **3.** a dowdy woman. —**dow′di•ly,** *adv.* —**dow′di•ness,** *n.* —**dow′dy•ish,** *adj.*

dow•el (dou′əl), *n., v.,* **-eled, -el•ing** or (*esp. Brit.*) **-elled, -el•ling.** —*n.* **1.** Also called **dow′el pin′.** a pin, usu. round, fitting into holes in two adjacent pieces to prevent their slipping or to align them. **2.** a round wooden rod of relatively small diameter. **3.** a peg, usu. of metal, set into the root canal of a natural tooth to support an artificial crown. —*v.t.* **4.** to reinforce or furnish with dowels.

dow•er (dou′ər), *n.* **1.** the portion of a deceased husband's real property allowed to his widow for life. **2.** DOWRY (def. 1). —*v.t.* **3.** to provide with a dower or dowry. —**dow′er•less,** *adj.*

dow•itch•er (dou′ich ər), *n.* any of several long-billed snipelike shorebirds of North America and Asia, esp. *Limnodromus griseus.*

Dow′ Jones′ Av′erage (dou), *Trademark.* any of the indexes published by Dow Jones & Company showing the average closing prices of the representative common stocks of 30 industrials, 20 transportation companies, and 15 utilities.

down¹ (doun), *adv.* **1.** from higher to lower; toward or into a lower position or level: *Tell him to come down.* **2.** on or to the ground, floor, or the like: *to fall down.* **3.** to or in a sitting or lying position. **4.** to an area or district considered lower from a geographical standpoint, esp. southward: *We drove down to San Diego.* **5.** to a lower value or rate: *Slow down.* **6.** to a lesser pitch or volume: *Turn down the radio.* **7.** in or to a calmer or less active state: *The wind died down.* **8.** from an earlier to a later time. **9.** from a greater to a lesser strength, amount, etc.: *to water down a drink.* **10.** earnestly: *to get down to work.* **11.** on paper: *Write this down.* **12.** thoroughly; fully; completely. **13.** in cash at the time of purchase: *$50 down and $20 a month.* **14.** to the point of defeat or submission: *to shout down the opposition.* **15.** to the source or actual position: *to track someone down.* **16.** into a condition of ill health. **17.** in or into a lower status or condition: *kept down by lack of education.* —*prep.* **18.** in a descending or more remote direction on or along: *They ran off down the street.* —*adj.* **19.** directed downward: *the down escalator.* **20.** being at a low position or on the ground, floor, or bottom. **21.** directed toward the south, a business district, etc. **22.** downcast; depressed. **23.** ailing or bedridden: *to be down with a bad cold.* **24.** *Football.* (of the ball) not in play. **25.** behind an opponent or opponents in points, games, etc. **26.** having lost the amount indicated, esp. at gambling: *to be down $10.* **27.** finished or taken care of: *five down and one to go.* **28.** out of order: *The computer is down again.* —*n.* **29.** a downward movement; descent. **30.** a turn for the worse; reverse. **31.** *Football.* one of a series of four plays during which a team must advance the ball at least 10 yd. (9 m) to keep possession of it. —*v.t.* **32.** to knock, throw, or bring down. **33.** to drink down, esp. quickly. **34.** to defeat in a game or contest. —*v.i.* **35.** to go down; fall. —*interj.* **36.** get down (used as a command or warning). —*Idiom.* **37. down cold** or **pat,** learned perfectly. **38. down in the mouth,** discouraged or depressed. **39. down on,** hostile or averse to. **40. down with,** to remove from power or do away with (used imperatively): *Down with the king!*

down² (doun), *n.* **1.** the soft first plumage of many young birds. **2.** the soft under plumage of birds. **3.** the under plumage of some birds, as geese and ducks, used for filling in quilts, clothing, etc., chiefly for warmth. **4.** a fine, soft pubescence on plants and some fruits. —*adj.* **5.** filled with down: *a down jacket.* —**down′less,** *adj.* —**down′like′,** *adj.*

down³ (doun), *n.* **1.** Often, **downs.** (esp. in southern England) open, rolling country usu. covered with grass. **2.** (*cap.*) any sheep of several breeds raised orig. in the downs of S England, as the Southdown, Suffolk, etc.

down′-and-dirt′y, *adj. Informal.* **1.** unscrupulous; nasty: *a down-and-dirty election campaign.* **2.** earthy; funky.

down-and-out (doun′ənd out′, -ən), *adj.* **1.** destitute; penniless. **2.** disabled; incapacitated. —*n.* **3.** Also, **down′-and-out′er.** a person who is down-and-out.

down·beat (doun′bēt′), *n.* **1.** the downward stroke of a conductor's arm or baton indicating the first or accented beat of a measure. **2.** the first beat of a measure. —*adj.* **3.** *Slang.* gloomy or depressing; pessimistic: *a movie with a downbeat ending.*

down·cast (doun′kast′, -käst′), *adj.* **1.** directed downward, as the eyes. **2.** dejected; depressed.

down·fall (doun′fôl′), *n.* **1.** overthrow; ruin. **2.** something causing this. **3.** a sudden fall of rain or snow. —**down′fall′en,** *adj.*

down·field (doun′fēld′), *adv., adj. Football.* past the line of scrimmage and toward the goal line of the defensive team.

down·grade (doun′grād′), *v.,* **-grad·ed, -grad·ing,** *n., adj., adv.* —*v.t.* **1.** to reassign to a lower level or status. **2.** to minimize the importance of. —*n.* **3.** a downward slope, esp. of a road. **4.** a lowering in status or importance; demotion or diminishment. —*adj., adv.* **5.** downhill. —*Idiom.* **6.** on the downgrade, in a decline: *a career on the downgrade.* —**down′grad′er,** *n.*

down·haul (doun′hôl′), *n.* any of various lines for pulling or holding down a sail or a yard.

down·heart·ed (doun′här′tid), *adj.* dejected; depressed. —**down′heart′ed·ly,** *adv.*

down·hill (*adv.* doun′hil′; *adj., n.* doun′hil′), *adv.* **1.** down the slope of a hill; downward. **2.** into a worse condition. —*adj.* **3.** going downward on or as if on a hill. **4.** free of obstacles; easy. **5.** of or pertaining to skiing downhill: *a downhill skier.* —*n.* **6.** a timed ski race down a steep trail. Compare SLALOM.

down′-home′, *adj.* characterized by the simple, informal, earthy qualities associated with rural people or rural areas, esp. of the southern U.S.: *down-home cooking.*

Down′ing Street′ (dou′ning), *n.* **1.** a street in W central London, England: government offices and residence of the prime minister. **2.** the British prime minister and cabinet.

down·link (doun′lingk′), *n.* **1.** a transmission path for data or other signals from a communications satellite or airborne platform to an earth station. —*adj.* **2.** pertaining to such transmission. Compare UPLINK.

down·load (doun′lōd′), *v.t.* to transfer (software or data) from a computer to a smaller computer or a peripheral device.

down·mar·ket (doun′mär′kit), *adj.* **1.** appealing or catering to lower-income consumers; widely affordable or accessible. —*adv.* **2.** in a down-market way.

down′ pay′ment, *n.* an initial amount given as partial payment at the time of purchase, as in installment buying.

down·play (doun′plā′), *v.t.* to represent as unimportant, insignificant, etc.; minimize; belittle.

down·pour (doun′pōr′, -pôr′), *n.* a heavy, drenching rain.

down·right (doun′rīt′), *adv.* **1.** completely; thoroughly: *downright angry.* —*adj.* **2.** thorough; absolute. **3.** frank; straightforward.

down·scale (doun′skāl′), *adj., v.,* **-scaled, -scal·ing.** —*adj.* **1.** located at or moving toward the lower end of a social or economic scale. **2.** plain, practical, or inexpensive. —*v.t.* **3.** DOWNSIZE (def. 1). **4.** to make less luxurious or expensive.

down·side (doun′sīd′), *n.* **1.** the lower or underneath side. **2.** a downward trend, esp. in stock prices.

down·size (doun′sīz′), *v.,* **-sized, -siz·ing,** *adj.* —*v.t.* **1.** to design or manufacture a smaller version of. **2.** to reduce in number; cut back. —*adj.* **3.** Also, **down′sized′.** being a smaller version: *a downsized car.*

down·spout (doun′spout′), *n.* a vertical pipe for conveying rainwater from a roof or gutter to the ground or to a drain; leader.

down·stage (*adv., n.* doun′stāj′; *adj.* doun′stāj′), *adv.* **1.** at or toward the front of the stage. —*adj.* **2.** of, pertaining to, or done at or toward the front of the stage: *a downstage exit.* —*n.* **3.** the front half of the stage.

down·stairs (*adv., n.* doun′stârz′; *adj.* -stârz′), *adv.* **1.** down the stairs. **2.** to or on a lower floor. —*adj.* **3.** Also, **down′stair′.** pertaining to or situated on a lower floor, esp. the ground floor. —*n.* **4.** (*used with a sing. v.*) the lower floor or floors of a building or their inhabited areas or furnishings: *Downstairs has been dusted.*

down·state (*n., adj.* doun′stāt′; *adv.* doun′stāt′), *n.* **1.** the S part of a U.S. state. —*adj.* **2.** located in or characteristic of this part. —*adv.* **3.** in or to the downstate area. —**down′stat′er,** *n.*

down·stream (doun′strēm′), *adv.* **1.** in the direction of the current of a stream. —*adj.* **2.** pertaining to the latter part of a process: *attempting to secure downstream financing.* **3.** *Genetics.* with or in the direction of transcription, translation, or synthesis of a DNA, RNA, or protein molecule.

down·swing (doun′swing′), *n.* **1.** a downward swing, as of a golf club. **2.** a downward trend, as of business.

Down′ (or **Down′s′**) **syn′drome,** *n.* a genetic disorder associated with the presence of an extra chromosome 21, characterized by mental retardation, weak muscle tone, and epicanthic folds at the eyelids. Formerly, **mongolism.** Also called **trisomy 21.** [after John L. H. *Down* (1828–96), British physician]

down′-the-line′, *adj.* **1.** unreserved; wholehearted: *a down-the-line endorsement.* —*adv.* **2.** wholeheartedly.

down·time (doun′tīm′), *n.* a time during a workshift when an employee is not working or a machine is not in operation.

down′-to-earth′, *adj.* practical and realistic.

down·town (doun′toun′), *adv.* **1.** to or in the main business section of a city. —*adj.* **2.** situated in the downtown section of a city. —*n.* **3.** the downtown section of a city. —**down′town′er,** *n.*

down·trod·den (doun′trod′n) also **down′trod′,** *adj.* tyrannized; oppressed. —**down′trod′den·ness,** *n.*

down·turn (doun′tûrn′), *n.* **1.** an act or instance of turning down, or the state of being turned down: *the downturn of a lower lip.* **2.** a downward trend; decline.

down′ un′der, *adv.* in or to Australia or New Zealand.

down·ward (doun′wərd), *adv.* **1.** Also, **down′wards.** from a higher to a lower level or condition. **2.** from a source or beginning. **3.** from a past time to the present. —*adj.* **4.** moving to a lower level or condition. **5.** descending from a source or beginning. —**down′ward·ly,** *adv.* —**down′ward·ness,** *n.*

down·wind (doun′wind′), *adv.* **1.** in the direction toward which the wind is blowing. **2.** on or toward the lee side: *The elephant stood downwind of us and caught our scent.* —*adj.* **3.** moving or situated downwind.

down·y (dou′nē), *adj.,* **down·i·er, down·i·est. 1.** of or like down; soft; fluffy. **2.** covered with down. —**down′i·ness,** *n.*

down′y mil′dew, *n.* **1.** any common fungus of the family Peronosporaceae, appearing on damp vegetable or animal matter as a white fuzzy mass of spores. **2.** a disease of plants caused by growth of downy mildew on the undersurface of the leaves, characterized by crumpling, yellowing, and death of the foliage.

down′y wood′peck·er, *n.* a small black-and-white North American woodpecker, *Picoides pubescens:* males have a red head patch.

dow·ry (dou′rē) also **dowery,** *n., pl.* **-ries. 1.** Also, **dower.** the money, goods, etc., that a wife brings to her husband at marriage. **2.** a natural gift; talent.

dox·ol·o·gy (dok sol′ə jē), *n., pl.* **-gies. 1.** a hymn or form of words containing an ascription of praise to God. **2. the Doxology,** the metrical formula beginning "Praise God from whom all blessings flow." —**dox′o·log′i·cal** (-sə log′i kəl), *adj.*

doy·en (doi en′, doi′ən; *Fr.* dwa yaN′), *n., pl.* **doy·ens** (doi enz′, doi′enz; *Fr.* dwa yaN′). the senior member, as in age or experience, of a group, profession, etc.

doy·enne (doi en′), *n.* a woman who is the senior member of a group, profession, etc.

Doyle (doil), *n.* **Sir Arthur Conan,** 1859–1930, British physician, novelist, and detective-story writer.

doze (dōz), *v.,* **dozed, doz·ing,** *n.* —*v.i.* **1.** to sleep lightly and briefly; nap. **2.** to fall into a light sleep unintentionally (often fol. by *off*): *to doze off during a lecture.* **3.** to be dull or half asleep. —*v.t.* **4.** to pass (time) in napping (often fol. by *away*): *to doze away the afternoon.* —*n.* **5.** a nap.

doz·en (duz′ən), *n., pl.* **doz·ens,** (*as after a numeral*) **doz·en,** *adj.* —*n.* **1.** a group of 12. **2. the dozens,** *Slang.* a ritualized game in which the players attempt to outdo each other in insults (usu. used in the phrase *play the dozens*). —*adj.* **3.** containing 12 parts.

DP or **D.P., 1.** data processing. **2.** displaced person.

dp, double play.

DPL, diplomat.

DPT or **DTP,** diphtheria, tetanus, pertussis: a mixed vaccine of inactivated diphtheria and tetanus toxoids and pertussis vaccine, used for primary immunization.

DR, *Real Estate.* dining room.

dr, 1. door. **2.** dram.

Dr., 1. Doctor. **2.** Drive (used in street names).

drab¹ (drab), *adj.,* **drab·ber, drab·best,** *n.* —*adj.* **1.** lacking in brightness, spirit, etc.; dull. **2.** of the color drab. —*n.* **3.** a brownish gray. **4.** any of several fabrics of this color, esp. of thick wool or cotton. —**drab′ly,** *adv.* —**drab′ness,** *n.*

drab² (drab), *n., v.,* **drabbed, drab·bing.** —*n.* **1.** a slatternly woman. **2.** a prostitute. —*v.i.* **3.** to associate with drabs.

dra·cae·na or **dra·ce·na** (drə sē′nə), *n., pl.* **-nas.** any of various plants of the genera *Cordyline* and *Dracaena,* of the agave family, cultivated for their decorative foliage.

drach·ma (drak′mə, dräk′-), *n., pl.* **-mas, -mae** (-mē). **1.** the basic monetary unit of modern Greece. **2.** any of various modern weights, esp. a dram.

Dra·co¹ (drā′kō), *n., gen.* **Dra·co·nis** (drā kō′nis, drə-). the Dragon, a northern circumpolar constellation between Ursa Major and Cepheus.

Dra·co² (drā′kō) also **Dra·con** (-kon), *n.* fl. late 7th century B.C., Athenian lawgiver: noted for the severity of his code of laws.

Dra·co·ni·an (drā kō′nē ən, drə-) also **Dra·con·ic** (-kon′ik), *adj.* **1.** of, pertaining to, or characteristic of Draco or his code of laws. **2.** (*often l.c.*) (esp. of punishment) unusually severe or cruel; harsh. —**Dra·co′ni·an·ism,** *n.* —**Dra·con′i·cal·ly,** *adv.*

Drac•u•la (drak′yə lə), *n.* **1.** (*italics*) a novel (1897) by Bram Stoker. **2. Count,** the central character in this novel: the archetype of a vampire. [< Low German *Dracol, Dracole, Dracle* a by-name of the Wallachian prince Vlad II, "the Impaler" (1431–76); orig. of the name is disputed, but it has long been popularly associated with Rumanian *dracul* the devil < Latin *dracō* dragon]

draft (draft, dräft), *n.* **1.** a drawing, sketch, or design. **2.** a preliminary form of any writing, subject to revision, refinement, etc. **3.** the act of drawing; delineation. **4.** a current of air in any enclosed space, esp. in a room or chimney. **5.** a device for regulating the current of air in a fireplace, etc. **6.** an act of drawing or pulling loads. **7.** something that is drawn or pulled; a haul. **8.** an animal or team of animals used to pull a load. **9.** the force required to pull a load. **10.** the taking of supplies, money, etc., from a given source. **11.** a selection of persons, as by lot, for military service, an athletic team, etc. **12.** the persons so selected. **13.** a bill of exchange. **14.** beer or ale drawn from a cask. **15.** an act of drinking or inhaling. **16.** something that is drunk or inhaled; a drink or dose. **17.** the depth to which a vessel is immersed when bearing a given load. **18.** a quantity of fish caught. **19.** *Metall.* the slight taper given to a pattern so that it may be drawn from the sand without injury to the mold. **20.** a line or border chiseled at the edge of a stone, to serve as a guide in leveling the surfaces. —*v.t.* **21.** to sketch. **22.** to compose. **23.** to draw or pull. **24.** to select by draft, as for military service. —*v.i.* **25.** to work as a draftsman. **26.** (in an automobile race) to drive close behind another car so as to benefit from the reduction in air pressure created in its wake. —*adj.* **27.** used for drawing loads: *a draft horse.* **28.** drawn from a cask rather than served from a bottle: *draft beer.* **29.** being a preliminary outline or sketch. —*Idiom.* **30. on draft,** available to be drawn from a cask: *beer on draft.* Also, *esp. Brit.,* **draught** (for defs. 1, 3–9, 14–23, 25, 27–30). —**draft′a•ble,** *adj.* —**draft′er,** *n.*

draft′ board′, *n.* a board of civilians charged with registering, classifying, and selecting persons for U.S. military service.

draft•ee (draf tē′, dräf-), *n.* a person who is drafted for military service. Compare ENLISTEE (def. 1).

drafts•man (drafts′mən, dräfts′-), *n., pl.* **-men. 1.** a person employed in making mechanical drawings. **2.** an artist exceptionally skilled in drawing: *Matisse was a superb draftsman.* **3.** a person who draws up documents. —**drafts′man•ship′,** *n.*

draft•y (draf′tē, dräf′-), *adj.,* **draft•i•er, draft•i•est.** characterized by or admitting unwanted or uncomfortable currents of air. Also, *esp. Brit.,* **draughty.** —**draft′i•ly,** *adv.* —**draft′i•ness,** *n.*

drag (drag), *v.,* **dragged, drag•ging,** *n.* —*v.t.* **1.** to draw slowly and with effort; haul. **2.** to search with a drag, grapnel, or the like: *to drag a lake for a gun.* **3.** to smooth (land) with a drag or harrow. **4.** to introduce or insert; inject: *He drags his war stories into every conversation.* **5.** to protract (something) tediously (often fol. by *out*): *They dragged the discussion out for three hours.* **6.** to pull (a graphical image) from one place to another on a computer display screen, esp. by using a mouse. —*v.i.* **7.** to be drawn or hauled along. **8.** to trail on the ground. **9.** to move heavily or slowly and with great effort. **10.** to feel listless or move in such a manner (often fol. by *around*): *This heat has everyone dragging around.* **11.** to lag behind. **12.** to take part in a drag race. **13.** to take a puff: *to drag on a cigarette.* —*n.* **14.** any device for dragging the bottom of a body of water to recover or detect objects. **15.** a heavy wooden or steel frame drawn over the ground to smooth it. **16.** a sledge for moving heavy objects. **17.** *Slang.* someone or something tedious; a bore. **18.** the aerodynamic force exerted on an airfoil, airplane, or other aerodynamic body that tends to reduce its forward motion. **19.** a metal shoe that serves as a brake for wagon wheels. **20.** an act of dragging. **21.** slow, laborious procedure. **22.** something that retards progress. **23.** a puff on a cigarette, pipe, etc. **24.** *Slang.* influence; clout. **25.** *Slang.* a dance, as at a high school or college. **26.** MAIN DRAG. —**drag′ger,** *n.*

drag•net (drag′net′), *n.* **1.** a net to be drawn along the bottom of a stream to catch fish, or along the ground for small game. **2.** an interlinked system for finding or catching someone, as a wanted criminal.

Dragnet, The, a parable of Jesus. Matt. 13:47–50.

drag•o•man (drag′ə mən), *n., pl.* **-mans, -men.** (in the Near East) a professional interpreter.

drag•on (drag′ən), *n.* **1.** a mythical monster generally represented as a huge winged reptile with a crested head, often spouting fire. **2.** a fierce, combative person. **3.** a very strict, protective woman. **4.** a soldier armed with such a musket. —**drag′on•like′,** *adj.*

drag•on•et (drag′ə net′, drag′ə nit), *n.* any fish of the genus *Callionymus,* the species of which are small and usu. brightly colored.

drag•on•fly (drag′ən flī′), *n., pl.* **-flies.** any nonstinging insect of the order Odonata (suborder Anisoptera), distinguished from the damselfly by having the wings open when at rest.

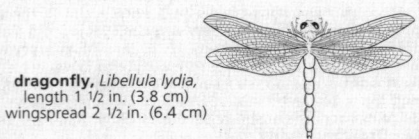

dragonfly, *Libellula lydia,* length 1 ½ in. (3.8 cm) wingspread 2 ½ in. (6.4 cm)

drag•on•head (drag′ən hed′) also **dragon's head,** *n.* any of several mints of the genus *Dracocephalum* having spikes of double-lipped flowers.

drag′on la′dy, *n.* (*often caps.*) a usu. glamorous woman who is perceived as exercising ruthless and corrupt power.

drag′on liz′ard, *n.* KOMODO DRAGON.

dra•goon (drə gōon′), *n.* **1.** a member of a unit of cavalry, orig. mounted infantry armed with short muskets, of a type common in European armies from c1600 to World War I. —*v.t.* **2.** to persecute by armed force; oppress. **3.** to force by oppressive measures; coerce. —**dra•goon′age,** *n.*

drag′ race′, *n.* a race between two or more automobiles starting from a standstill, the winner being the car that can accelerate the fastest. —**drag′ rac′er,** *n.* —**drag′ rac′ing,** *n.*

drag•ster (drag′stər), *n.* **1.** an automobile designed and built specifically for drag racing. **2.** a person who races such an automobile.

drain (drān), *v.t.* **1.** to draw off (a liquid) gradually; remove slowly, as by filtration. **2.** to empty by drawing off liquid: *to drain a crankcase.* **3.** to exhaust the resources of. —*v.i.* **4.** to flow off or empty gradually. —*n.* **5.** a pipe, conduit, etc., by which a liquid drains. **6.** an act of draining; gradual or continuous outflow. **7.** something that causes a large outflow or depletion. —*Idiom.* **8. go down the drain, a.** to become worthless or profitless; be wasted. **b.** to go out of existence; disappear. —**drain′a•ble,** *adj.* —**drain′er,** *n.*

drain•age (drā′nij), *n.* **1.** the act or process of draining. **2.** a system of drains. **3.** DRAINAGE BASIN. **4.** something that is drained off.

drain′age ba′sin, *n.* the area drained by a river and all its tributaries. Compare WATERSHED (def. 1).

drain•pipe (drān′pīp′), *n.* a large pipe that carries away the discharge of waste pipes, etc.

drake (drāk), *n.* a male duck. Compare DUCK¹ (def. 2).

Drake (drāk), *n.* **Sir Francis,** c1540–96, English admiral and explorer.

dram (dram), *n.* **1. a.** a unit of apothecaries' weight, equal to 60 grains, or ⅛ of an ounce (3.89 grams). **b.** ¹⁄₁₆ of an ounce in avoirdupois weight (27.34 grains; 1.77 grams). *Abbr.:* dr., dr **2.** FLUID DRAM. **3.** a small drink of liquor. **4.** a small amount of anything.

dra•ma (drä′mə, dram′ə), *n., pl.* **-mas. 1.** a prose or verse composition presenting in dialogue and action a story involving conflict or contrast of characters, intended to be performed on the stage; play. **2.** any event or series of events having vivid, conflicting elements that capture one's interest.

dra•mat•ic (drə mat′ik), *adj.* **1.** of or pertaining to the drama; theatrical. **2.** employing the form or style of the drama. **3.** involving conflict or contrast; vivid: *dramatic colors.* **4.** highly effective or compelling: *a dramatic silence.* —**dra•mat′i•cal•ly,** *adv.*

dramat′ic i′rony, *n.* irony derived from the audience's understanding of a speech or a situation not grasped by the characters in a dramatic piece.

dramat′ic mon′ologue, *n.* a literary form in which a character, addressing a silent auditor at a critical moment, reveals himself or herself and the dramatic situation.

dra•mat•ics (drə mat′iks), *n.* **1.** (*used with a sing. v.*) the art of producing or acting dramas. **2.** (*used with a pl. v.*) dramatic productions, esp. by amateurs. **3.** (*used with a pl. v.*) dramatic, overly emotional, or insincere behavior.

dram•a•tis per•so•nae (dram′ə tis pər sō′nē, drä′mə-), *n.* **1.** (*used with a pl. v.*) the characters in a play. **2.** (*used with a sing. v.*) a list of the characters of a play. [< Latin: characters of the play]

dram•a•tist (dram′ə tist, drä′mə-), *n.* a writer of dramas; playwright.

dram•a•ti•za•tion (dram′ə tə zā′shən, drä′mə-), *n.* **1.** the act of dramatizing. **2.** a dramatized version of a novel, historic incident, etc.

dram•a•tize (dram′ə tīz′, drä′mə-), *v.,* **-tized, -tiz•ing.** —*v.t.* **1.** to put into a form suitable for acting, as on a stage or in a film. **2.** to express or represent in a vivid or intense, often exaggerated manner. —*v.i.* **3.** to express oneself in a dramatic or exaggerated way. —**dram′a•tiz•a•ble,** *adj.* —**dram′a•tiz′er,** *n.*

drank (drangk), *v.* a pt. and pp. of DRINK.

drape (drāp), *v.,* **draped, drap•ing,** *n.* —*v.t.* **1.** to cover, surround, or hang with cloth or other fabric, esp. in graceful folds. **2.** to adjust (fabric, clothes, etc.) into graceful folds or attractive lines. **3.** to arrange, hang, or let fall carelessly: *to drape a towel on a doorknob.* —*v.i.* **4.** to hang, fall, or become arranged in folds, as drapery. —*n.* **5.** a curtain, usu. of heavy fabric and considerable length, esp. one of a pair drawn open and shut across or hung at the sides of a window. **6.** manner or style of hanging: *the drape of a skirt.* —**drap′a•ble, drape′a•ble,** *adj.*

dra•per•y (drā′pə rē), *n., pl.* **-per•ies. 1.** coverings, hangings, clothing, etc., of fabric, esp. as arranged in loose, graceful folds. **2.** Usu., **draperies.** long curtains, often of heavy fabric. **3.** the draping or arranging of hangings, clothing, etc., in graceful folds. **4.** cloths or textile fabrics collectively. **5.** *Brit.* **a.** DRY GOODS. **b.** the stock, shop, or business of a draper. —**dra′per•ied,** *adj.*

dras•tic (dras′tik), *adj.* **1.** acting with force or violence; violent. **2.** extremely severe or extensive: *drastic cuts in spending.* —**dras′ti•cal•ly,** *adv.*

drat (drat), *v.,* **drat•ted, drat•ting,** *interj.* —*v.t.* **1.** to damn; confound: *Drat your interference.* —*interj.* **2.** (used to express mild disgust, annoyance, or the like): *Drat, there goes the phone.*

Dra•vid•i•an (drə vid′ē ən), *n.* **1.** a language family of South Asia, spoken mainly in S India, and including Telugu and Tamil. **2.** a speaker of a language belonging to this family. —*adj.* **3.** of or pertaining to Dravidian or its speakers.

draw (drô), *v.*, **drew, drawn, draw•ing,** *n.* —*v.t.* **1.** to cause to move in a particular direction by or as if by a pulling force; pull; drag (often fol. by *along, away, in, out,* or *off*). **2.** to bring, take, or pull out, as from a receptacle or source: *to draw water from a well; to draw blood from a vein.* **3.** to bring toward oneself or itself, as by inherent force; attract: *The sale drew large crowds.* **4.** to sketch (someone or something) in lines or words; delineate; depict: *to draw a vase.* **5.** to compose or create (a picture) in lines. **6.** to mark or lay out; trace: *to draw perpendicular lines.* **7.** to frame or formulate: *to draw a distinction.* **8.** to write out in legal form (sometimes fol. by *up*): *Draw up the contract.* **9.** to inhale or suck in: *to draw liquid through a straw.* **10.** to derive or use, as from a source: *to draw strength from prayer.* **11.** to deduce; infer: *to draw a conclusion.* **12.** to get, take, or receive, as from a source: *to draw a salary of $600 a week.* **13.** to withdraw (funds) from an account. **14.** to write (a check) so as to take money from an account (often fol. by *on* or *against*). **15.** to produce; bring in: *The deposits draw interest.* **16.** to disembowel: *to draw a turkey.* **17.** to pull out to full or greater length; stretch: *to draw filaments of molten glass.* **18.** to bend (a bow) by pulling back the string in preparation for shooting an arrow. **19. a.** to choose or have assigned to one by or as if by lottery: *to draw kitchen duty.* **b.** to pick unseen or at random, as from among marked slips of paper or numbered tickets: *to draw straws to see who wins.* **20.** *Metalworking.* to form or reduce the sectional area of (a wire, tube, etc.) by pulling through a die. **21.** to wrinkle or shrink by contraction. **22.** *Med.* to cause to discharge: *to draw an abscess by a poultice.* **23.** (of a vessel) to need (a specific depth of water) to float. **24.** to finish (a contest) with neither side winning; tie. **25. a.** to take or be dealt (a playing card or cards) from the pack. **b.** (in bridge) to remove the outstanding cards in (a suit) by leading. **26.** (in billiards) to cause (a cue ball) to recoil after impact by administering a backward spin on the stroke. **27.** to steep (tea) in boiling water. —*v.i.* **28.** to exert a pulling, moving, or attracting force. **29.** to move or pass, esp. slowly or continuously, as under a pulling force: *The day draws near.* **30.** to take out a sword, pistol, etc., for action. **31.** to hold a drawing, lottery, or the like: *to draw for prizes.* **32.** to sketch or to trace figures; create a picture or depict an image by sketching. **33.** to be skilled in or practice the art of sketching. **34.** to shrink or contract (often fol. by *up*). **35.** to make a demand (usu. fol. by *on* or *upon*): *to draw on one's imagination.* **36. a.** to act as an irritant; cause blisters. **b.** to cause blood, pus, or the like to gather at a specific point. **37.** to produce or permit a draft, as a pipe or flue. **38.** to leave a contest undecided; tie. **39.** to attract customers, an audience, etc. **40.** to pull back the string of a bow in preparation for shooting an arrow. **41. draw away, a.** to move or begin to move away. **b.** to move farther ahead: *One runner drew away from the pack.* **42. draw in, a.** to cause to take part or enter, esp. unwittingly: *This is your fight; don't draw me in.* **b.** to make a sketch or drawing of: *to draw in a human figure against the landscape.* **43. draw off,** to move back or away. **44. draw on, a.** to come nearer; approach: *Winter was drawing on.* **b.** to clothe oneself in: *to draw on one's gloves.* **c.** to utilize or make use of, esp. as a source: *The article draws heavily on gossip.* **45. draw out, a.** to pull out; remove. **b.** to prolong; lengthen. **c.** to persuade to speak. **d.** to take (money) from a place of deposit. **46. draw up, a.** to draft, esp. in legal form or as a formal proposal. **b.** to put into position; arrange in order or formation. **c.** to bring or come to a stop; halt: *The bus drew up at the curb.* —*n.* **47.** an act of drawing. **48.** something that attracts customers, an audience, etc. **49.** something that is moved by being drawn, as the movable part of a drawbridge. **50.** something that is chosen or drawn at random, as a lot or chance. **51.** DRAWING (defs. 5, 6). **52.** a contest that ends in a tie. **53.** a football play in which the quarterback hands the ball to a back who is running toward the line of scrimmage. **54. a.** DRAW POKER. **b.** (in poker) a card or cards taken or dealt from the pack. **55. a.** a small, natural drainageway with a shallow bed; gully. **b.** the dry bed of a stream. **c.** *Chiefly Western U.S.* a coulee; ravine. **56.** the pull necessary to draw a bow to its full extent. —*Idiom.* **57. beat to the draw,** to react more quickly than (an opponent). **58. draw oneself up,** to assume an erect posture. **59. draw the curtain on** or **over, a.** to bring to a close: *to draw the curtain on a long career.* **b.** to keep secret. —**draw′a•ble,** *adj.*

draw•back (drô′bak′), *n.* **1.** an undesirable or objectionable feature; disadvantage. **2.** a refund of tariff or other tax, as when imported goods are reexported.

draw•bridge (drô′brij′), *n.* a bridge of which the whole or a section may be raised, lowered, or drawn aside, to prevent access or to leave a passage open for boats, barges, etc.

draw•er (drôr *for 1, 2;* drô′ər *for 3–5*), *n.* **1.** a sliding, lidless, horizontal compartment, as in a piece of furniture, that may be drawn out in order to gain access to it. **2. drawers,** (*used with a pl. v.*) a garment with legs that covers the lower half of the body, esp. an undergarment. **3.** a person or thing that draws. **4.** a person who draws a bill of exchange. **5.** a tapster.

draw•ing (drô′ing), *n.* **1.** the act of a person or thing that draws. **2.** a graphic representation by lines of an object or idea, as with a pencil. **3.** a sketch, plan, or design, esp. one made with pen, pencil, or crayon. **4.** the art or technique of making these. **5.** something decided by drawing lots; lottery. **6.** the selection, or time of selection, of the winning chance or chances sold by lottery or raffle.

draw′ing board′, *n.* **1.** a rectangular board on which paper is placed or mounted for drawing or drafting. —*Idiom.* **2. on the drawing board,** in the planning or design stage.

draw′ing card′, *n.* a person or thing that attracts attention or patrons.

draw′ing room′, *n.* **1.** a formal reception room, esp. in an apartment or private house. **2.** (in a railroad car) a private room for two or three passengers. **3.** *Brit.* a formal reception, esp. at court.

draw′ing ta′ble, *n.* a table having a surface consisting of a drawing board adjustable to various heights and angles.

draw•knife (drô′nīf′), *n., pl.* **-knives.** a carpenter's knife with a handle at each end at right angles to the blade, used by drawing over a surface.

drawl (drôl), *v.t., v.i.* **1.** to say or speak in a slow manner, usu. prolonging the vowels. —*n.* **2.** an act or utterance of a person who drawls. —**drawl′er,** *n.* —**drawl′ing•ly,** *adv.* —**drawl′y,** *adj.*

drawn (drôn), *v.* **1.** pp. of DRAW. —*adj.* **2.** tense; haggard. **3.** eviscerated, as a fowl.

drawn′ but′ter, *n.* melted butter, clarified and often seasoned with herbs or lemon juice.

draw′ pok′er, *n.* a variety of poker in which players may discard usu. up to three of the original five cards dealt to them and request replacements from the dealer.

draw′string′ or **draw′ string′,** *n.* a string or cord that closes, tightens, or gathers something, as the opening of a bag or garment or the panels of a curtain, when one or both of its ends are pulled.

dray (drā), *n.* **1.** a low strong cart without fixed sides, for carrying heavy loads. **2.** a sledge or sled. **3.** any vehicle, as a truck, used to haul goods, esp. one used for heavy loads. —*v.t.* **4.** to convey on a dray; haul. —*v.i.* **5.** to drive or operate a dray.

D.R.E., **1.** Director of Religious Education. **2.** Doctor of Religious Education.

dread (dred), *v.t.* **1.** to fear greatly: *to dread death.* **2.** to be very reluctant to do, meet, or experience. —*v.i.* **3.** to have fear or great reluctance. —*n.* **4.** terror or apprehension as to something in the future; great fear. **5.** a person or thing dreaded. —*adj.* **6.** greatly feared; frightful; terrible. **7.** held in awe or reverential fear.

dread•ful (dred′fəl), *adj.* **1.** causing great dread, fear, or terror; terrible: *a dreadful storm.* **2.** inspiring awe. **3.** extremely bad, unpleasant, or ugly: *a dreadful scandal.* —**dread′ful•ness,** *n.*

dread•locks (dred′loks′), *n.pl.* a hairstyle of many long ropelike locks.

dream (drēm), *n., v.,* **dreamed** or **dreamt, dream•ing,** *adj.* —*n.* **1.** a succession of images, thoughts, or emotions passing through the mind during sleep. **2.** a particular sequence of such images, thoughts, or feelings: *a recurring dream about a circus.* **3.** an involuntary vision occurring to a person when awake. **4.** a daydream or reverie. **5.** an aspiration; goal; aim. **6.** a wild or vain fancy. **7.** something of unreal or striking beauty, charm, or excellence. —*v.i.* **8.** to have a dream. **9.** to indulge in daydreams or reveries. **10.** to conceive of something in a very remote way (usu. fol. by *of*): *I wouldn't dream of leaving.* —*v.t.* **11.** to see or imagine in sleep or in a vision. **12.** to imagine as possible; fancy; conceive. **13.** to pass or spend (time) in dreaming (often fol. by *away*): *to dream away the afternoon.* **14. dream up,** to form in the imagination; devise. —*adj.* **15.** most desirable; ideal: *a dream vacation.* —**dream′ing•ly,** *adv.* —**dream′like′,** *adj.*

dream•er (drē′mər), *n.* **1.** a person who dreams. **2.** an impractical or unrealistic person. **3.** a person who has bold or highly speculative ideas or plans; visionary.

dream•land (drēm′land′), *n.* **1.** a pleasant, lovely land that exists only in dreams or the imagination; the region of reverie. **2.** a state of sleep.

dream•less (drēm′lis), *adj.* not marked, disturbed, or enhanced by dreams: *dreamless sleep.* —**dream′less•ly,** *adv.* —**dream′less•ness,** *n.*

dreamt (dremt), *v.* a pt. and pp. of DREAM.

dream′ team′, *n.* a number of persons of the highest ability associated in some joint action: *a dream team that should easily win the Olympics; a dream team of lawyers.*

dream′ tick′et, *n.* a pair of candidates for the office of president and vice president who are considered to appeal to most segments of the voting public.

dream′ world′ or **dream′world′,** *n.* the world of imagination or illusion rather than of objective reality.

dream•y (drē′mē), *adj.,* **dream•i•er, dream•i•est. 1.** of the nature of or typical of dreams; visionary. **2.** vague; dim. **3.** inducing dreams or a dreamlike mood, esp. pleasantly: *dreamy music.* **4.** given to daydreaming or reverie. **5.** abounding in dreams. **6.** wonderful; marvelous: *a dreamy new car.* —**dream′i•ly,** *adv.* —**dream′i•ness,** *n.*

drear•y (drēr′ē), *adj.,* **drear•i•er, drear•i•est. 1.** causing sadness or gloom; dismal. **2.** dull; boring; wearisome. **3.** sorrowful; sad; melancholy. —**drear′i•ly,** *adv.* —**drear′i•ness,** *n.*

dredge[1] (drej), *n., v.,* **dredged, dredg•ing.** —*n.* **1.** any of various powerful machines for dredging up or removing earth, as by means of a scoop or a series of buckets. **2.** a barge on which such a machine is mounted. **3.** a dragnet or other contrivance for gathering material or objects from the bottom of a river, bay, etc. —*v.t.* **4.** to clear out with a dredge: *to dredge a river.* **5.** to remove (sand, silt, etc.) from the bottom of a river or other body of water. —*v.i.* **6.** to use a dredge. **7. dredge up,** to discover and reveal; unearth.

dredge² (drej), *v.t.*, **dredged, dredg•ing.** to coat (food) with a powdery substance, as flour.

dreg (dreg), *n.* **1. dregs,** the sediment of liquids; lees; grounds. **2.** Usu., **dregs.** the least valuable part of anything: *the dregs of society.* **3.** a small remnant; any small quantity. —**dreg′gy,** *adj.* —**dreg′gi•ness,** *n.*

D region, *n.* D LAYER.

drei•del (drād′l), *n., pl.* **-dels, -del. 1.** a four-sided top bearing Hebrew letters, used in a children's game traditionally played on Hanukkah. **2.** the game itself.

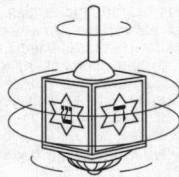

dreidel

Drei•ser (drī′sər, -zər), *n.* **Theodore,** 1871–1945, U.S. novelist.

drench (drench), *v.t.* **1.** to wet thoroughly; soak. **2.** to saturate by immersion in a liquid; steep. **3.** to cover or fill completely; bathe: *sunlight drenching the trees.* **4.** to administer a draft of medicine to (an animal), esp. by force. —*n.* **5.** a preparation for drenching or steeping. **6.** a draft of medicine, esp. one administered to an animal by force. —**drench′er,** *n.* —**drench′ing•ly,** *adv.*

Dres•den (drez′dən), *n.* the capital of Saxony in E Germany, on the Elbe River. 518,057.

Dres′den chi′na, *n.* porcelain ware produced at Meissen, Germany, near Dresden, after 1710.

dress (dres), *n.* **1.** an outer garment for women and girls, consisting of bodice and skirt cut or sewn as one piece. **2.** clothing; apparel; garb. **3.** formal attire. **4.** a particular form of appearance; guise. **5.** outer covering, as the plumage of birds. —*adj.* **6.** of or for a dress or dresses. **7.** of or for a formal occasion. **8.** requiring formal dress. —*v.t.* **9.** to put clothing upon; clothe. **10. a.** to decorate, esp. for display; trim: *to dress a store window.* **b.** to supply with accessories; adorn; embellish. **11.** to design clothing for or sell clothes to. **12.** to comb out and do up (hair). **13.** to trim and remove the feathers or skin, viscera, etc., of (fowl, game, etc.), esp. as preparation for cooking. **14.** to garnish with a dressing: *to dress a salad with oil and vinegar.* **15.** to prepare or finish (a raw or unfinished product) by various processes, as by tanning (skins) or shaping (stone). **16.** to apply medication or a dressing to (a wound or sore). **17.** to make straight; bring (troops) into line: *to dress ranks.* **18.** to cultivate (land, fields, etc.). **19.** to arrange or fill (a stage) by effectively placing properties, scenery, or oneself or others in the performing area. **20. a.** to prepare or bait (a fishhook) for use. **b.** to prepare (bait, esp. an artificial fly) for use. —*v.i.* **21.** to put on one's clothes. **22.** to put on or wear formal or fancy clothes: *to dress for dinner.* **23.** to come into line, as troops. **24.** to align oneself with the next soldier, marcher, dancer, etc., in line. **25. dress down, a.** to reprimand; scold. **b.** to dress informally or less formally. **26. dress up, a.** to put on one's best or fanciest clothing. **b.** to dress in costume or in the style of another person. **c.** to make more appealing or acceptable, as by omitting unpleasant features or details. —*Idiom.* **27. dress ship, a.** to decorate a ship by hoisting lines of flags running its full length. **b.** *U.S. Navy.* to display the national ensigns at each masthead and on the flagstaff.

dres•sage (drə säzh′, dre-), *n.* the art or method of training a horse in obedience and in precision of movement.

dress′ code′, *n.* a set of rules establishing the type of clothing to be worn in a given circumstance, as when on duty, or environment, as a church or a classroom.

dress•er¹ (dres′ər), *n.* **1.** a person who dresses. **2.** a person employed to dress actors, care for costumes, etc., at a theater, television studio, or the like. **3.** a person who dresses in a particular manner: *a fancy dresser.* **4.** any of several tools or devices used in dressing materials. **5. a.** a block, fitting into an anvil, on which pieces are forged. **b.** a mallet for shaping sheet metal.

dress•er² (dres′ər), *n.* **1.** a chest of drawers, usu. surmounted by a mirror; bureau. **2.** a sideboard or set of shelves for dishes and cooking utensils.

dress•ing (dres′ing), *n.* **1.** the act of a person or thing that dresses. **2.** a sauce, esp. for salad or other cold foods. **3.** stuffing for a fowl: *turkey dressing.* **4.** material used to dress or cover a wound. **5.** manure, compost, or other fertilizers.

dress′ing-down′, *n.* a severe reprimand; scolding.

dress′ing gown′, *n.* a robe worn while lounging, resting, applying makeup, etc.

dress′ing room′, *n.* a room in which to get dressed, esp. one for performers in a theater, television studio, or the like.

dress′ing ta′ble, *n.* a table or stand, usu. surmounted by a mirror, in front of which a person sits while dressing, applying makeup, etc.

dress′ rehears′al, *n.* a rehearsal of a play or the like using costumes,

scenery, properties, and lights as for a performance: often the final rehearsal.

dress′ shirt′, *n.* **1.** a man's shirt for formal or semiformal evening dress, usu. having French cuffs and a stiff or pleated front fastened by studs. **2.** a man's tailored shirt, with long or short sleeves, buttons down the front, and a soft or starched collar, worn with a tie.

dress•y (dres′ē), *adj.,* **dress•i•er, dress•i•est. 1.** appropriate to more formal or festive occasions: *This blouse is too dressy for the office.* **2.** fancy or stylish. —**dress′i•ly,** *adv.* —**dress′i•ness,** *n.*

Drey•fus (drā′fəs, drī′-), *n.* **Alfred,** 1859–1935, French army officer of Jewish descent: wrongfully convicted of treason; acquitted 1906.

drib (drib), *n.* a small or minute quantity; bit.

drib•ble (drib′əl), *v.,* **-bled, -bling,** *n.* —*v.i.* **1.** to fall or flow in drops or small quantities; trickle. **2.** to drivel; slaver. **3.** to advance a ball by bouncing it or a puck by giving it short, quick kicks or pushes. —*v.t.* **4.** to let fall in drops. **5. a.** (in basketball) to bounce (the ball), as in maneuvering for a pass or advancing for a score. **b.** (esp. in ice hockey and soccer) to move (the ball or puck) along by a rapid succession of short kicks or pushes. —*n.* **6.** a small trickling stream or a drop. **7.** a small quantity of anything: *a dribble of revenue.* —**drib′bler,** *n.*

dribs′ and drabs′, *n.pl.* small and usu. irregular amounts: *to repay a loan in dribs and drabs.*

dried (drīd), *v.* pt. and pp. of DRY.

dried′-up′, *adj.* **1.** depleted of water or moisture; gone dry. **2.** shriveled with age; wizened.

dri•er¹ (drī′ər), *n.* **1.** one that dries. **2.** any additive to speed the drying of paints, printing inks, etc. **3.** DRYER (def. 1).

dri•er² (drī′ər), *adj.* comparative of DRY.

dries (drīz), *n.* a pl. of DRY.

dri•est (drī′ist), *adj.* superlative of DRY.

drift (drift), *n.* **1.** a driving movement or action. **2.** (of a ship) the component of the movement that is due to the force of wind and currents. **3.** a broad, shallow ocean current that advances at the rate of 10 to 15 mi. (16 to 24 km) a day. **4.** the flow or the speed in knots of an ocean current. **5.** a gradual deviation from a natural or desirable position or course. **6.** the course along which something moves; tendency; aim: *a drift toward the political right.* **7.** a meaning; intent; purport: *the drift of a statement.* **8.** the state or process of being driven. **9.** something driven, as animals or rain. **10.** a heap of any matter driven together. **11.** a snowdrift. **12.** loose material, as gravel, sand, etc., transported and deposited by glacial ice or meltwater. **13.** CONTINENTAL DRIFT. **14.** a gradual change in some operating characteristic of a circuit, tube, or other electronic device, as an effect of warming up or of continued use. **15.** gradual change in the structure of a language. **16. a.** a round tapering piece of steel for enlarging holes in metal or for bringing holes in line to receive rivets or bolts. **b.** a flat tapered piece of steel used to drive tools with tapered shanks, as drill bits, from their holders. **17.** an approximately horizontal passageway in underground mining. **18.** the gradual deviation of a rocket or guided missile from its intended trajectory. —*v.i.* **19.** to be carried along, as by currents of water or by the force of circumstances. **20.** to wander aimlessly: *to drift from town to town.* **21.** to be driven into heaps, as by the wind. **22.** to deviate or vary, as from a proper position or set course. —*v.t.* **23.** to carry along: *The current drifted the boat to sea.* **24.** to drive into heaps. —**drift′ing•ly,** *adv.* —**drift′y,** *adj.,* **drift•i•er, drift•i•est.**

drift•er (drif′tər), *n.* **1.** a person or thing that drifts. **2.** a person who goes from one place, job, etc., to another but stays in each only briefly, esp. a hobo.

drift•wood (drift′wŏŏd′), *n.* **1.** wood floating on a body of water or cast ashore by it. **2.** such wood adapted for use in interior decoration. —*adj.* **3.** of, pertaining to, or made of driftwood.

drill¹ (dril), *n.* **1. a.** a shaftlike tool with two or more cutting edges for making holes in firm materials, esp. by rotation. **b.** a tool, esp. a hand tool, for holding and operating such a tool. **2.** *Mil.* **a.** training in formal marching or other precise military or naval movements. **b.** an exercise in such training: *gun drill.* **3. a.** any practice or exercise in marching. **b.** any strict, methodical, repetitive, or mechanical training, instruction, or exercise: *a spelling drill.* **4.** the correct or customary manner of proceeding. **5.** a gastropod mollusk, *Urosalpinx cinera,* that bores holes in bivalves. —*v.t.* **6.** to pierce or bore a hole in (something); penetrate or excavate with a drill. **7.** to make (a hole) by boring. **8. a.** to instruct and exercise (military trainees) in formation marching, in the carrying and handling of arms, etc. **b.** to train or rehearse (any group) in formation marching. **9.** to impart (knowledge) by strict training, discipline, or repetition. **10.** to train or rehearse (a person or group) in a subject, discipline, etc., by guided repetition, quizzing, and other techniques. —*v.i.* **11.** to pierce, bore, or excavate something with or as if with a drill. **12.** to penetrate deeply beneath the ground or the sea floor with specialized machinery to search for deposits or reservoirs of a natural substance: *to drill for oil.* **13.** to go through exercise in military or other training. —**drill′a•ble,** *adj.* —**drill′er,** *n.*

drill² (dril), *n.* **1.** a small furrow made in the soil in which to sow seeds. **2.** a row of seeds or plants thus sown. **3.** a machine for sowing in rows and for covering the seeds when sown. —*v.t.* **4.** to sow (seed) in drills. **5.** to sow or plant (soil, a plot of ground, etc.) in drills. —*v.i.* **6.** to sow seed in drills. —**drill′er,** *n.*

drill³ (dril), *n.* a strong twilled cotton fabric.

drill⁴ (dril), *n.* a large baboon, *Mandrillus leucophaeus,* of W Africa, smaller and less brightly colored than the closely related mandrill.

drill·mas·ter (dril′mas′tər, -mä′stər), *n.* **1.** a person who trains others in something, esp. routinely or mechanically. **2.** a person who instructs in military marching drill.

drill′ team′, *n.* a group trained, esp. for exhibition purposes, in precision marching, the manual of arms, etc.

dri·ly (drī′lē), *adv.* dryly.

drink (dringk), *v.,* **drank, drunk** or, often, **drank, drink·ing,** *n.* —*v.i.* **1.** to take water or other liquid into the mouth and swallow it; imbibe. **2.** to imbibe alcoholic drinks, esp. habitually or excessively; tipple. **3.** to show one's respect, affection, or good wishes for someone or something by a ceremonious swallow of wine or other drink (usu. fol. by *to*). —*v.t.* **4.** to take (a liquid) into the mouth and swallow. **5.** to take in (a liquid) in any manner; absorb. **6.** to take in through the senses, esp. with eagerness and pleasure (often fol. by *in*). **7.** to swallow the contents of (a cup, glass, etc.). **8.** to propose or participate in a toast to (a person or thing); toast: *to drink one's health.* —*n.* **9.** any liquid that is swallowed to quench thirst, for nourishment, etc.; beverage. **10.** liquor; alcohol. **11.** excessive indulgence in alcohol: *Drink was his downfall.* **12.** a swallow or draft of liquid; potion: *a drink of water.* **13. the drink,** a large body of water, as a lake or the ocean: *Her teammates threw her in the drink.*

drink·er (dring′kər), *n.* **1.** a person who drinks. **2.** a person who drinks alcohol habitually or to excess.

drink·ing (dring′king), *adj.* **1.** suitable for or used in drinking: *drinking water; a drinking glass.* **2.** of, pertaining to, or indulging in the drinking of alcohol, esp. to excess: *drinking companions; Is he a drinking man?* —*n.* **3.** habitual and excessive consumption of alcohol.

drink′ing foun′tain, *n.* a water fountain that ejects a jet of water for drinking without a cup.

drink′ing song′, *n.* a song of hearty character suitable for singing by a group engaged in convivial drinking.

drip (drip), *v.,* **dripped, drip·ping,** *n.* —*v.i.* **1.** to let drops fall; shed drops: *This faucet drips.* **2.** to fall in drops, as a liquid; dribble. —*v.t.* **3.** to let fall in drops. —*n.* **4.** an act of dripping. **5.** liquid that drips. **6.** the sound made by falling drops: *the irritating drip of a faucet.* **7.** *Slang.* a boring or colorless person. **8.** (in house painting) the accumulation of solidified drops of paint at the bottom of a painted surface. **9.** any device, as a molding, for shedding rainwater to keep it from running down a wall, falling onto the sill of an opening, etc. **10.** the continuous, slow introduction of a fluid into the body, usu. intravenously. —**drip′page,** *n.*

drip-dry (drip′drī′; *v. usu.* -drī′), *v.,* **-dried, -dry·ing,** *adj., n., pl.* **-dries.** —*v.i.* **1.** (of a garment or other, usu. cloth item) to dry unwrinkled and without losing shape when hung dripping wet, esp. after washing. —*v.t.* **2.** to hang so as to drip-dry: *to drip-dry a shirt.* —*adj.* **3.** able to be drip-dried: *drip-dry shirts.* —*n.* **4.** a garment or other item that can be drip-dried.

dript (dript), *v.* a pt. and pp. of DRIP.

drive (drīv), *v.,* **drove, driv·en, driv·ing,** *n.* —*v.t.* **1.** to send, expel, or otherwise cause to move by force or compulsion: *to drive away the flies.* **2.** to cause and guide the movement of (a vehicle, an animal, etc.): *to drive a car; to drive a mule.* **3.** to convey in a vehicle: *to drive someone home.* **4.** to force to work or act: *He drove the workers until they collapsed.* **5.** to impel; constrain; urge; compel. **6.** to carry (business, an agreement, etc.) vigorously through: *to drive a hard bargain.* **7.** to keep (machinery) going. **8.** (in baseball) **a.** to cause the advance of (a base runner) by a base hit or sacrifice fly. **b.** to cause (a run) to be scored by a base hit or sacrifice fly. **9.** to hit (a golf ball), esp. from the tee, as with a driver or driving iron. **10. a.** to hit, propel, or kick (a ball, shuttlecock, puck, etc.) with much force. **b.** (in football) to advance (the ball) aggressively by various strategies. **11. a.** to chase (game). **b.** to search (a district) for game. **12.** to float (logs) down a river or stream. **13.** (in mining, construction, etc.) to excavate. —*v.i.* **14.** to cause and guide the movement of a vehicle or animal. **15.** to go or travel in a driven vehicle. **16.** to hit a golf ball, esp. from the tee, as with a driver or driving iron. **17.** to strive vigorously toward a goal or objective. **18.** to go along before an impelling force; be impelled: *The ship drove before the wind.* **19.** to rush or dash violently. **20. drive at,** to intend to convey. —*n.* **21.** a trip in a vehicle. **22.** an impelling along, as of game, cattle, or floating logs, in a particular direction. **23.** the animals, logs, etc., thus driven. **24.** an inner urge that prompts activity directed toward the satisfaction of a basic, instinctive need: *hunger drive; sex drive.* **25.** a vigorous onset or onward course toward a goal or end. **26.** a strong military offensive. **27.** a united effort to accomplish some specific purpose, esp. to raise money, as for a charity. **28.** energy and initiative; motivation. **29.** vigorous pressure or effort, as in business. **30.** a road for vehicles, as a scenic route along a highway or a short roadway approaching a house. **31.** a driving mechanism, as of an automobile: *gear drive.* **32.** the point or points of power application to the roadway: *four-wheel drive.* **33. a.** an act driving a ball, puck, shuttlecock, or the like. **b.** the flight of a ball, puck, shuttlecock, or the like that has been driven with much force. **34.** a golf shot that is intended to carry a great distance. **35.** a hunt in which game is driven toward stationary hunters. —**driv′a·ble, drive′a·ble,** *adj.*

drive′-by′, *n., pl.* **-bys,** *adj.* —*n.* **1.** the action of driving by a specified locality, object, etc.: *a drive-by of Nelson's Monument.* **2.** a drive-by shooting: *The gang member was killed in a drive-by.* —*adj.* **3.** consisting of or featuring a drive-by: *We boarded the sightseeing bus for a drive-by tour of the nation's capital.* **4.** occurring while driving past a person, object, etc.: *a drive-by shooting.*

drive′-in′, *adj.* **1.** being, pertaining to, or using a facility or business designed to accommodate patrons in their automobiles: *a drive-in restaurant; drive-in customers.* —*n.* **2.** such a facility or business, esp. an outdoor motion-picture theater.

driv·el (driv′əl), *n., v.,* **-eled, -el·ing** or (*esp. Brit.*) **-elled, -el·ling.** —*n.* **1.** saliva flowing from the mouth, or mucus from the nose; slaver. **2.** childish, silly, or meaningless talk or thinking; nonsense; twaddle. —*v.i.* **3.** to let saliva flow from the mouth or mucus from the nose; slaver. **4.** to talk childishly or idiotically. —*v.t.* **5.** to utter childishly or idiotically. **6.** to waste foolishly. —**driv′el·er,** *n.* —**driv′el·ing·ly,** *adv.*

driv·en (driv′ən), *v.* **1.** pp. of DRIVE. —*adj.* **2.** being under compulsion, as to succeed or excel. —**driv′en·ness,** *n.*

driv·er (drī′vər), *n.* **1.** a person or thing that drives. **2.** a person who drives a vehicle; coachman, chauffeur, or the like. **3.** a person who drives animals, as a drover or cowboy. **4.** a golf club with a wooden head whose face has almost no slope, for hitting long low drives from the tee. **5. a.** a machine part that transmits force or motion. **b.** the member of a pair of connected pulleys, gears, etc., that is nearer to the power source. **6.** software that controls the interface between a computer and a peripheral device. **7.** the part of a loudspeaker that transforms the electrical signal into sound. —**driv′er·less,** *adj.*

driv′er's seat′, *n.* **1.** the seat from which a vehicle is operated. **2.** a position of power, dominance, or superiority.

drive′ shaft′, *n.* a shaft for imparting torque from a power source or prime mover to machinery.

drive′ train′, *n.* the power train of an automobile including the components between the engine and driving wheels, as the clutch and rear axle.

drive′-up′, *adj.* serving or accessible to customers who drive up in their cars: *a drive-up window at a bank.*

drive·way (drīv′wā′), *n.* **1.** a road, esp. a private one, leading from a street or other thoroughfare to a building, house, garage, etc. **2.** any road for driving on.

driv·ing (drī′ving), *adj.* **1.** having force and violence: *a driving storm.* **2.** vigorously active; energetic: *a driving young pop singer.* **3.** relaying or transmitting power. **4.** having, applying, or exercising pressure or momentum: *to dance with driving intensity.* **5.** used while operating a vehicle: *driving gloves.*

driv′ing range′, *n.* a tract of land for practicing long golf shots, esp. drives, with rentable clubs and balls.

driz·zle (driz′əl), *v.,* **-zled, -zling,** *n.* —*v.i.* **1.** to rain gently and steadily in fine drops; sprinkle. **2.** to fall in fine drops. —*v.t.* **3.** to let fall or pour in fine drops or a fine stream. **4.** to cover with or as if with fine drops. —*n.* **5.** a very light rain. **6.** *Meteorol.* precipitation consisting of numerous, minute droplets of water less than ¹⁄₅₀ in. (0.5 mm) in diameter. —**driz′zling·ly,** *adv.* —**driz′zly,** *adj.*

Dr. Jekyll and Mr. Hyde, (*The Strange Case of Dr. Jekyll and Mr. Hyde*) a novel (1886) by Robert Louis Stevenson.

droid (droid), *n.* android.

droll (drōl), *adj.* **1.** amusing in an odd way; whimsically humorous; waggish. —*n.* **2.** a droll person; jester; wag. —**droll′ness,** *n.* —**drol′ly,** *adv.*

-drome, a combining form meaning "course, racecourse" "an arena or building for holding races": *hippodrome; velodrome.*

drom·e·dar·y (drom′i der′ē, drum′-), *n., pl.* **-dar·ies.** the single-humped camel, *Camelus dromedarius,* of Arabia and N Africa. Compare BACTRIAN CAMEL. [< Late Latin *dromedārius* (*camēlus*) running (camel)]

dromedary, *Camelus dromedarius,*
6 ft. (1.8 m) high at shoulder;
length 9 ½ ft. (2.9 m)

drone¹ (drōn), *n.* **1.** the male of the honeybee and other bees that is stingless and makes no honey. **2.** a vehicle or craft operated by remote control, esp. a pilotless airplane guided by radio signals. **3.** a person who lives on the labor of others; parasitic loafer. **4.** a drudge.

drone² (drōn), *v.,* **droned, dron·ing,** *n.* —*v.i.* **1.** to make a continued, low, monotonous sound; hum; buzz. **2.** to speak in a monotonous tone. **3.** to proceed in a dull, monotonous manner (usu. fol. by *on*): *The meeting droned on for hours.* —*v.t.* **4.** to say in a dull, monotonous tone. —*n.* **5. a.** a musical instrument or one of its parts producing a continuous low tone, esp. a bagpipe. **b.** PEDAL POINT. **6.** a monotonous low tone; humming or buzzing sound. —**dron′er,** *n.* —**dron′ing·ly,** *adv.*

drool (drool), *v.i.* **1.** to water at the mouth, as in anticipation of food; salivate. **2.** to show excessive pleasure or anticipation of pleasure. **3.** to talk foolishly. —*n.* **4.** saliva running down from one's mouth; drivel.

droop (dro͞op), *v.i.* **1.** to sag, sink, bend, or hang down, as from exhaustion or lack of support. **2.** to fall into a weakened or dispirited state; flag; fade. **3.** to descend, as the sun; sink. —*v.t.* **4.** to let sink or drop: *an eagle drooping its wings.* —*n.* **5.** a sagging, sinking, or hanging down, as from exhaustion or lack of support. —**droop′ing•ly**, *adv.*

drop (drop), *n., v.,* **dropped, drop•ping.** —*n.* **1.** a small quantity of liquid that falls or is produced in a more or less spherical mass; liquid globule. **2.** the quantity of liquid contained in such a globule. **3.** a very small quantity of liquid: *to have a drop of tea.* **4.** a minute quantity of anything: *not even a drop of mercy.* **5.** Usu., **drops. a.** liquid medicine given in a dose or form of globules from a medicine dropper. **b.** a solution for dilating the pupils of the eyes, administered to the eyes in this manner. **6.** a limited amount of an alcoholic beverage: *He occasionally takes a drop after dinner.* **7.** an act or instance of dropping; fall; descent. **8.** the distance or depth to which anything drops: *a drop of ten feet.* **9.** a steep slope: *a short drop to the lake.* **10.** a decline in amount, degree, quality, value, etc. **11.** a small, usu. spherical, piece of candy; lozenge. **12.** a central depository where items are left or transmitted. **13.** a place where secret letters or packages can be left for picking up by another person without attracting attention. **14.** something resembling or likened to a liquid globule, as an ornament or jewel. **15.** a descent by parachute. **16.** an instance of dropping persons or supplies by parachute or the amount or number so dropped. **17.** the persons or supplies so dropped. **18.** something that drops or is used for dropping. **19.** TRAP-DOOR. **20.** a gallows. **21.** a slit or opening into which something can be dropped, as in a mailbox. **22.** the newborn young of an animal. —*v.i.* **23.** to fall in globules or small portions, as water or other liquid. **24.** to fall vertically; have an abrupt descent. **25.** to sink or fall to the ground, floor, or bottom as if inanimate. **26.** to fall lower in condition, degree, value, etc.; diminish or lessen; sink. **27.** to come to an end; cease; lapse: *There the matter dropped.* **28.** to fall or move to a position that is lower, farther back, inferior, etc.: *to drop back in line.* **29.** to withdraw; quit (often fol. by *out* or *from*): *to drop out of a race.* **30.** to pass or enter without effort into some condition, activity, or the like: *to drop into a reverie.* **31.** to make an unexpected or unannounced stop or visit at a place (usu. fol. by *in, by,* or *over*). **32.** to cease to appear or be seen; vanish: *to drop from sight.* **33.** to fall wounded, dead, etc.: *to drop in battle.* **34.** to move gently, as with the tide or a light wind (usu. fol. by *down*). **35.** *Slang.* to ingest an illicit drug orally; swallow. —*v.t.* **36.** to let fall in drops or small portions: *to drop cream into coffee.* **37.** to let or cause to fall. **38.** to cause or allow to sink to a lower position. **39.** to cause to decrease in value, amount, quality, etc.; reduce. **40.** to utter or express casually or incidentally: *to drop a hint.* **41.** to write and send: *Drop me a note.* **42.** to bring to the ground by a blow or shot. **43.** to set down or unload, as from a ship or car (often fol. by *off*): *Drop us at the corner.* **44.** to omit (a letter or syllable) in pronunciation or writing: *You drop your final r's.* **45.** to lower (the voice) in pitch or loudness. **46.** to abandon; forget: *to drop one's old friends.* **47.** to dismiss as an employee, member, etc.; remove: *to drop a consultant from the payroll.* **48.** to withdraw or cease to pursue: *The libel charges were eventually dropped.* **49.** to throw, shoot, hit, kick, or roll (a ball, puck, etc.) through or into a basket, hole, or other goal. **50.** to lose (a game, money, etc.) **51.** (of animals) to give birth to. **52.** to parachute (persons, supplies, etc.). **53.** to resew in a lower position: *to drop the hem of a skirt.* **54.** to lower (the wheels) into position for landing an airplane. **55.** to take (esp. an illicit drug) by swallowing; ingest: *to drop LSD.* **56. drop behind,** to fail to keep maintaining the necessary pace, quota of work, standard, etc. **57. drop off, a.** to fall asleep. **b.** to decrease; decline. **58. drop out, a.** to stop participating. **b.** to stop attending school or college. **c.** to abandon the conventions, customs, patterns, etc., of established society in favor of pursuing one's own lifestyle or goals. —*Idiom.* **59. at the drop of a hat,** at the slightest provocation or without delay: *to argue at the drop of a hat.* **60. drop in the bucket,** a small, inadequate amount. **61. get** or **have the drop on, a.** to aim and be ready to shoot a gun at (an antagonist) before the other person's gun can be drawn. **b.** to get or have at a disadvantage.

drop′ cloth′ or **drop′cloth′,** *n.* a sheet of cloth, plastic, or the like used by painters esp. to protect furniture or floors.

drop′-dead′, *adj.* inspiring awe, astonishment, or envy: *drop-dead elegance; a drop-dead beauty.*

drop′-in′, *n.* **1.** Also, **dropper-in.** a person or thing that pays an unexpected or uninvited visit. **2.** a social gathering to which guests pay a brief, informal visit. —*adj.* **3.** provided for short-term patronage: *a drop-in shelter for the homeless.* **4.** requiring only insertion to be ready for use: *a drop-in film cartridge.*

drop′ kick′, *n.* a kick made by dropping a ball to the ground and kicking it as it starts to bounce up. —**drop′-kick′,** *v.t., v.i.* —**drop′-kick′er, n.**

drop′ leaf′, *n.* a hinged leaf attached to a table that can be raised to extend the tabletop or folded vertically downward when not in use. —**drop′-leaf′,** *adj.*

drop′-off′, *n.* **1.** a vertical or very steep descent. **2.** a decline; decrease: *an unusual drop-off in sales.* **3.** a place where a person or thing can be left, received, accommodated, etc. —*adj.* **4.** of, for, or pertaining to a delivery or return of someone or something to a specified place, esp. to the return of a rented vehicle to a place other than the point of hire: *drop-off charges.*

drop′out′ or **drop′-out′,** *n.* **1.** a student, as in high school, who withdraws before completing a course of instruction. **2.** one who withdraws from established society, esp. to pursue an individualistic or unconventional lifestyle. **3.** a person who withdraws from a competition, job, task, etc.

drop•per (drop′ər), *n.* **1.** a person or thing that drops. **2.** a glass tube with a hollow rubber bulb at one end and a small opening at the other for drawing in a liquid and expelling it in drops; eyedropper.

drop•ping (drop′ing), *n.* **1.** the act of a person or thing that drops. **2.** something that drops or falls in drops. **3. droppings,** dung, esp. in the form of pellets.

drop′ seat′, *n.* **1.** a hinged seat, as in a taxicab, that can be pulled down for use. **2.** a rear panel in the bottom half of a one-piece garment that can be opened and lowered separately.

drop′ shot′, *n.* **1.** a ball or shuttlecock so softly hit that it falls to the playing surface just after clearing the net, as in tennis or badminton. **2.** a ball so softly hit that it falls suddenly to the ground just after striking the front wall, as in squash or handball.

dropt (dropt), *v.* a pt. and pp. of DROP.

drop•wort (drop′wûrt′, -wôrt′), *n.* a European plant, *Filipendula vulgaris,* of the rose family, bearing small scentless white or reddish flowers.

drop′ zone′, *n.* an area into which paratroopers, soldiers, or supplies are landed from aircraft for a military operation. *Abbr.:* DZ

dros•er•a (dros′ər ə), *n.* SUNDEW.

dro•soph•i•la (drō sof′ə lə, drə-), *n., pl.* **-las, -lae** (-lē′). FRUIT FLY (def. 2).

dross (drôs, dros), *n.* **1.** waste matter; refuse. **2.** a waste product taken off molten metal during smelting, essentially metallic in character.

drought (drout), *n.* **1.** a period of dry weather, esp. a long one that is injurious to crops. **2.** an extended shortage; scarcity; dearth. Sometimes, **drouth** (drouth). —**drought′y,** *adj.*

drove¹ (drōv), *v.* pt. of DRIVE.

drove² (drōv), *n., v.,* **droved, drov•ing.** —*n.* **1.** a number of oxen, sheep, or swine driven in a group; herd; flock. **2.** Usu., **droves.** a large crowd of human beings, esp. in motion. **3.** Also called **drove′ chis′el.** a chisel, from 2 to 4 in. (5 to 10 cm) broad at the edge, for dressing stones to an approximately true surface. —*v.t.* **4.** to dress (stone) with a drove.

drown (droun), *v.i.* **1.** to die of suffocation under water or other liquid. —*v.t.* **2.** to kill by submerging under water or other liquid. **3.** to destroy or get rid of by immersion: *to drown one's troubles in drink.* **4.** to flood or inundate with water or liquid; drench; soak. **5.** to overwhelm so as to render inaudible, as by a louder sound (often fol. by *out*). **6. drown in, a.** to be overwhelmed by. **b.** to be covered with or enveloped in. —**drown′er, n.**

drow•sy (drou′zē), *adj.,* **-si•er, -si•est. 1.** half-asleep; sleepy. **2.** marked by or resulting from sleepiness. **3.** dull; sluggish; listless. **4.** inducing lethargy or sleepiness: *drowsy spring weather.* —**drow′si•ly,** *adv.* —**drow′si•ness, n.**

drub (drub), *v.,* **drubbed, drub•bing,** *n.* —*v.t.* **1.** to beat with a stick or the like; flog; thrash. **2.** to defeat decisively, as in a game or contest. **3.** to drive as if by flogging: *Grammar was drubbed into our heads.* —*v.i.* **4.** to pound or drum. —*n.* **5.** a blow with a stick or the like. —**drub′ber, n.**

drudge (druj), *n., v.,* **drudged, drudg•ing.** —*n.* **1.** a person who does menial, distasteful, dull, or hard work. **2.** a person who works in a routine, unimaginative way. —*v.i.* **3.** to perform menial, distasteful, dull, or hard work; hack. —**drudg′er, n.** —**drudg′ing•ly,** *adv.*

drudg•er•y (druj′ə rē), *n., pl.* **-er•ies.** menial, distasteful, dull, or hard work.

drug (drug), *n., v.,* **drugged, drug•ging.** —*n.* **1.** a chemical substance used in the treatment, cure, prevention, or diagnosis of disease or to otherwise enhance physical or mental well-being. **2.** (in federal law) **a.** any substance listed in any of the recognized pharmacopoeias. **b.** any substance intended for use in the treatment or prevention of disease. **c.** any nonfood substance intended to affect any function of the body. **d.** any component of such a drug. **3.** a habit-forming medicinal or illicit substance. **4. drugs,** chemical substances prepared and sold as pharmaceutical items either by prescription or over the counter. —*v.t.* **5.** to administer a medicinal drug to. **6.** to stupefy or poison with a drug. **7.** to mix (food or drink) with a drug, esp. a stupefying, narcotic or poisonous drug. —*Idiom.* **8. drug on the market,** a commodity that is overabundant or not in demand in the market.

drug′ ad′dict, *n.* a person who is addicted to a narcotic.

drug•gist (drug′ist), *n.* **1.** PHARMACIST. **2.** the owner or operator of a drugstore.

drug′store′ or **drug′ store′,** *n.* the place of business of a druggist, usu. also selling toiletries, cosmetics, stationery, etc., and sometimes soft drinks and light meals.

Dru•id (dro͞o′id), *n.* (*often l.c.*) a member of a pre-Christian religious order among the ancient Celts of Gaul, Britain, and Ireland. [< Latin *druidae* (pl.) < French; cf. Old Irish *druid* wizard] —**dru•id′ic, dru•id′i•cal,** *adj.*

dru•id•ism (dro͞o′i diz′əm), *n.* **1.** the religion or rites of the Druids. **2.** a modern religion based on that of the druids.

drum (drum), *n., pl.* **drums,** (*esp. collectively for* 10) **drum,** *v.,* **drummed, drum•ming.** —*n.* **1.** a musical percussion instrument consisting of a hollow, usu. cylindrical body covered at one or both ends with a tightly stretched membrane, or head, which is struck with the hand, a stick, or a pair of sticks to produce a booming, tapping, or hollow sound. **2.** the sound produced by such an instrument, object, or device. **3.** any rumbling or deep booming sound. **4.** a natural organ by which an animal produces a loud or bass sound. **5.** EARDRUM. **6.** any cylindrical object with flat ends. **7.** a cylindrical part of a machine. **8.** a cylindrical box or receptacle, esp. a large, metal one for storing or transporting liquids. **9.** Also called **tambour. a.** any of several cylindrical stones laid one above the other to form a column or pier. **b.** a cylindrical or faceted construction supporting a dome. **10.** Also called **drumfish.** any of various croakers that produce a drumming sound. —*v.i.* **11.** to beat or play a drum. **12.** to beat on anything rhythmically. **13.** to make a sound like that of a drum; resound. **14.** (of ruffed grouse and other birds) to produce a sound resembling drumming. —*v.t.* **15.** to beat (a drum) rhythmically; perform by beating a drum. **16.** to call or summon by or as if by beating a drum. **17.** to drive or force by persistent repetition: *to drum an idea into someone.* **18.** to fill a drum with; store in a drum. **19. drum out, a.** to expel or dismiss from a military service in disgrace to the beat of a drum. **b.** to dismiss in disgrace. **20. drum up, a.** to call or summon by, or as if by, beating a drum. **b.** to obtain or create (trade, interest, etc.) through vigorous effort. **c.** to concoct; devise. —*Idiom.* **21. beat the drum for,** to publicize: *beating the drum for a new product.*

drum•fish (drum′fish′), *n., pl.* (*esp. collectively*) **-fish,** (*esp. for kinds or species*) **-fish•es.** DRUM (def. 10).

drum′ ma′jor, *n.* the leader of a marching band.

drum•mer (drum′ər), *n.* **1.** a person who plays a drum. **2.** a commercial traveler or traveling sales representative.

drum•roll (drum′rōl′), *n.* **1.** a roll on a drum. **2.** the sound of a drumroll.

drum•stick (drum′stik′), *n.* **1.** a stick for beating a drum. **2.** the meaty leg of a chicken, turkey, or other fowl.

drunk (drungk), *adj.* **1.** being in a temporary state in which one's physical and mental faculties are impaired by an excess of alcoholic drink; intoxicated. **2.** overcome or dominated by a strong feeling or emotion: *drunk with passion.* **3.** pertaining to or caused by intoxication or intoxicated persons. —*n.* **4. a.** an intoxicated person. **b.** DRUNKARD. **5.** a period of drinking alcohol heavily: *a week-long drunk.* —*v.* **6.** pp. and nonstandard pt. of DRINK.

drunk•ard (drung′kərd), *n.* a person who is habitually or frequently drunk.

drunk•en (drung′kən), *adj.* **1.** intoxicated; drunk. **2.** given to drunkenness. **3.** pertaining to, caused by, or marked by intoxication: *a drunken quarrel.* —**drunk′en•ly,** *adv.* —**drunk′en•ness,** *n.*

drunk•om•e•ter (drung kom′i tər, drung′kə mē′tər), *n.* a device for measuring the amount of alcohol in a person's breath to determine the amount of alcohol in the bloodstream.

drupe (droop), *n.* any fruit consisting of an outer skin, a usu. pulpy and succulent middle layer, and a hard and woody inner shell usu. enclosing a single seed, as a peach, cherry, or plum. —**dru•pa′ceous,** *adj.*

druse (drooz), *n.* an incrustation of small crystals on the surface of a rock or mineral.

Dru•sil•la (droo sil′ə), *n.* the daughter of Herod Agrippa and wife of Felix, who heard a discourse by the Apostle Paul. Acts 24:24–25.

druth•ers (druth′ərz), *n. Informal.* one's own way, choice, or preference: *If I had my druthers, I'd dance all night.*

Druze or **Druse** (drooz), *n. Islam.* a member of an independent religious sect living chiefly in Syria, Lebanon, and Israel, established in the 11th century as a branch of Isma'ili Shi'ism and containing elements of Christianity, Judaism, and Islam, and believing in the transmigration of souls and the ultimate perfection of humankind. —**Dru′ze•an, Dru′zi•an,** *adj.*

dry (drī), *adj.,* **dri•er, dri•est,** *v.,* **dried, dry•ing,** *n., pl.* **drys, dries.** —*adj.* **1.** free from moisture or excess moisture; not moist; not wet. **2.** having or characterized by little or no rain: *the dry season.* **3.** characterized by absence, deficiency, or failure of natural or ordinary moisture. **4.** not under, in, or on water: *to be on dry land.* **5.** not now containing or yielding water or other liquid; depleted or empty of liquid: *The well is dry.* **6.** not yielding milk: *a dry cow.* **7.** free from tears: *dry eyes.* **8.** drained or evaporated away: *a dry river.* **9.** desiring drink; thirsty. **10.** causing thirst: *dry work.* **11.** served or eaten without butter, jam, etc.: *dry toast.* **12.** (of bread, rolls, etc.) stale. **13.** of or pertaining to nonliquid substances or commodities: *dry measure; dry provisions.* **14.** dehydrated. **15.** (esp. of wines) not sweet. **16.** (of a cocktail) made with dry vermouth, esp. a relatively small amount. **17.** characterized by or favoring prohibition of the manufacture and sale of alcoholic liquors for use in beverages: *a dry state.* **18.** free from the use of alcoholic drink; sober. **19.** plain; bald; unadorned: *dry facts.* **20.** dull; uninteresting: *a dry subject.* **21.** expressed in a straight-faced, matter-of-fact way: *dry humor.* **22.** indifferent; cold; unemotional: *a dry answer.* **23.** unproductive: *The greatest of artists have dry years.* **24.** (of lumber) fully seasoned. **25. a.** (of masonry construction) built without fresh mortar or cement. **b.** (of a wall, ceiling, etc., in an interior) finished without the use of fresh plaster. —*v.t.* **26.** to make dry; free from moisture: *to dry the dishes.* —*v.i.* **27.** to become dry; lose moisture. **28. dry out, a.** to undergo detoxification after drug or alcohol abuse. **29. dry up, a.** to cease to exist; evaporate. **b.** *Informal.* to stop talking. **c.** (in acting) to forget

one's lines or part. —*n.* **30.** a prohibitionist. **31.** a dry area. —**dry′a•ble,** *adj.* —**dry′ly,** *adv.* —**dry′ness,** *n.*

dry•ad (drī′ad, -ad), *n., pl.* **-ads, -a•des** (-ə dēz′). (*often cap.*) a nymph of the woods. —**dry•ad′ic,** *adj.*

dry′-as-dust′, *adj.* dull; boring.

dry′ cell′, *n.* a cell in which the electrolyte exists in the form of a paste, is absorbed in a porous medium, or is otherwise restrained from flowing.

dry′ clean′ing, *n.* **1.** the cleaning of garments, fabrics, draperies, etc., with chemicals rather than with water. **2.** garments and other items for such cleaning. —**dry′-clean′,** *v.t.* —**dry′-clean′a•ble,** *adj.*

Dry•den (drīd′n), *n.* **John,** 1631–1700, English dramatist and critic.

dry′ dock′, *n.* a structure able to contain a ship, leaving all parts of the hull accessible for repairs, painting, or construction.

dry•er (drī′ər), *n.* **1.** Also, **drier.** a machine, appliance, or apparatus for removing moisture, as by forced ventilation or heat. **2.** DRIER¹ (defs. 1, 2).

dry′-eyed′, *adj.* not weeping; unmoved.

dry′ goods′, *n.pl.* textile fabrics and related merchandise, as distinguished esp. from groceries and hardware.

dry′ ice′, *n.* the solid form of carbon dioxide, which sublimes at −109.26°F (−78.48°C) and is used chiefly as a refrigerant.

dry′ing oil′, *n.* any of a group of oily, organic or synthetic liquids, as linseed oil, that when applied as a thin coating absorb atmospheric oxygen, forming a tough, elastic layer.

dry′land farm′ing (drī′land′), *n.* a mode of farming for regions of scant rainfall, relying on suitable crops and water-retentive tillage methods.

dry′ meas′ure, *n.* the system of volumetric units used in measuring dry commodities, as grain.

dry′ milk′, *n.* powdery milk from which about 95 percent of the moisture has been evaporated.

dry′-roast′ed or **dry′-roast′,** *adj.* roasted with little or no oil: *dry-roasted peanuts.*

dry′ rot′, *n.* **a.** a decay of seasoned timber, resulting in its becoming brittle and crumbling to a dry powder, caused by various fungi. **b.** any of various diseases of plants in which the rotted tissues are dry. **2.** any concealed or unsuspected inner decay.

dry′ run′, *n.* **1.** a rehearsal. **2.** practice in firing arms without using live ammunition. —**dry′-run′,** *adj.*

Dry′ Tor•tu′gas, *n.* a group of ten small islands at the entrance to the Gulf of Mexico W of Key West: a part of Florida; the site of Fort Jefferson.

dry′ wall′, *n.* **1.** Also, **dry′wall′. a.** an interior wall made of a prefabricated dry material. **b.** a material, as wallboard or plasterboard, used for such a wall. **2.** a masonry or stone wall laid up without mortar. —**dry′-wall′,** *v.t., adj.*

D.S., *Music.* from the sign. [< Italian *dal segno*]

DST or **D.S.T.,** daylight-saving time.

DTP, 1. diphtheria, tetanus, and pertussis. See DPT. **2.** desktop publishing.

d.t.'s or **D.T.'s** (dē′tēz′), *n.* DELIRIUM TREMENS.

du•ad (doo′ad, dyoo′-), *n.* a group of two; couple; pair.

du•al (doo′əl, dyoo′-), *adj.* **1.** of, pertaining to, or noting two. **2.** composed or consisting of two people, items, parts, etc., together; twofold; double: *dual ownership.* **3.** having a twofold, or double, character or nature. —**du′al•ly,** *adv.*

du′al cit′izenship, *n.* the status of a person who is a legal citizen of two or more countries.

du•al•ism (doo′ə liz′əm, dyoo′-), *n.* **1.** the state of being dual or consisting of two parts; division into two. **2. a.** (in metaphysics) any of various theories holding that reality is composed of two mutually irreducible substances. Compare MONISM (def. 1a), PLURALISM (def. 1a). **b.** (in epistemology) the view that substances are either material or mental. **3. a.** the theological doctrine that there are two eternal principles, one good and one evil. **b.** the belief that humans embody two parts, as body and soul. —**du′al•ist,** *n., adj.*

du•al•is•tic (doo′ə lis′tik, dyoo′-), *adj.* **1.** of, pertaining to, or of the nature of dualism. **2.** dual; twofold. —**du′al•is′ti•cal•ly,** *adv.*

du•al•i•ty (doo al′i tē, dyoo-), *n.* a dual state or quality; dualism.

du′al-pur′pose, *adj.* **1.** serving two functions. **2.** bred for two purposes, as to provide meat and milk or meat and eggs.

dub¹ (dub), *v.,* **dubbed, dub•bing,** —*v.t.* **1.** to invest with name, epithet, nickname, or title: *He was dubbed a hero.* **2.** to strike lightly with a sword in the ceremony of conferring knighthood; make or designate as a knight. **3.** to strike, cut, rub, or make smooth, as leather or timber. —**dub′ber,** *n.*

dub² (dub), *n. Slang.* an awkward, unskillful person.

dub³ (dub), *v.,* **dubbed, dub•bing,** *n.* —*v.t.* **1.** to thrust; poke. **2.** to hit (a golf ball) poorly; misplay (a shot). **3.** to execute poorly. —*v.i.* **4.** to thrust; poke. —*n.* **5.** a thrust; poke.

dub⁴ (dub), *v.,* **dubbed, dub•bing,** *n.* —*v.t.* **1.** to furnish (a film or tape) with a new sound track, as one recorded in the language of the country of import. **2.** to add (music, speech, etc.) to a film or tape recording (often fol. by *in*). **3.** to copy (a tape or disc). —*n.* **4.** the new sounds added to a film or tape. —**dub′ber,** *n.*

Du•bai (doo bī′), *n.* **1.** an emirate in the NE United Arab Emirates, on

the Persian Gulf. 419,104. **2.** the capital of the emirate of Dubai. 265,702.

Dub·ček (dōōb′chek; *Czech.* dōōp′chek), *n.* **Alexander,** 1921–92, Czechoslovakian political leader: first secretary of the Communist party 1968–69.

du·bi·e·ty (dōō bī′i tē, dyōō-) *n., pl.* **-ties. 1.** doubtfulness; doubt. **2.** a matter of doubt.

du·bi·ous (dōō′bē əs, dyōō′-), *adj.* **1.** marked by or occasioning doubt; equivocal: *a dubious reply.* **2.** of doubtful quality or propriety; questionable: *a dubious compliment.* **3.** of uncertain outcome. **4.** wavering in opinion; inclined to doubt; hesitant. —**du′bi·ous·ly,** *adv.* —**du′bi·ous·ness,** *n.*

du·bi·ta·ble (dōō′bi tə bəl, dyōō′-), *adj.* open to doubt; doubtful; uncertain. —**du′bi·ta·bly,** *adv.*

Dub·lin (dub′lin), *n.* **1.** the capital of the Republic of Ireland, in the E part, on the Irish Sea. 422,220. **2.** a county in E Republic of Ireland. 1,001,985; 356 sq. mi. (922 sq. km). *Co. seat:* Dublin. Irish, **Baile Àtha Cliath.**

Du Bois (dōō bois′), *n.* **W(illiam) E(dward) B(urghardt),** 1868–1963, U.S. educator and writer.

Du·bos (dōō bōs′), *n.* **Re·né Jules** (rə nā′), 1901–82, U.S. bacteriologist, born in France: early advocate of ecological concern.

du·cal (dōō′kəl, dyōō′-), *adj.* of or pertaining to a duke or dukedom.

du·ce (dōō′chä), *n., pl.* **-ces, -ci** (-chē). a leader or dictator.

duch·ess (duch′is), *n.* **1.** the wife or widow of a duke. **2.** a woman who holds the rank of a duke in her own right.

duch·y (duch′ē), *n., pl.* **duch·ies.** the territory ruled by a duke or duchess.

duck¹ (duk), *n., pl.* **ducks,** (*esp. collectively for 1, 2*) **duck. 1.** any of numerous relatively small and short-necked web-footed swimming birds of the family Anatidae, characterized by a broad, flat bill. **2.** the female of this bird, as distinguished from the male. Compare DRAKE¹. —*Idiom.* **3. like water off a duck's back,** with little or no apparent effect. —*Saying.* **4. If it looks like a duck, walks like a duck, and quacks like a duck, it's a duck,** all the available evidence adds up to one conclusion.

duck² (duk), *v.i.* **1.** to stoop or bend suddenly; bob. **2.** to avoid or evade a blow, unpleasant task, etc.; dodge. **3.** to plunge the whole body or the head momentarily under water. —*v.t.* **4.** to lower suddenly: *Duck your head down!* **5.** to avoid or evade (a blow, unpleasant task, etc.); dodge. **6.** to plunge or dip in water momentarily. —*n.* **7.** an act or instance of ducking. —**duck′er,** *n.*

duck³ (duk), *n.* **1.** a heavy plain-weave cotton fabric for tents, clothing, bags, etc. **2. ducks,** (*used with a pl. v.*) slacks or trousers made of this.

duck·bill (duk′bil′), *n.* PLATYPUS. Also called **duck′bill plat′ypus, duck′-billed plat′ypus.**

duck′-billed di′nosaur (duk′bild′), *n.* HADROSAUR.

duck′ boot′, *n.* a sturdy, shoelike waterproof boot.

duck′ing stool′, *n.* a former instrument of punishment consisting of a chair in which an offender was tied to be plunged into water.

duck·pins (duk′pinz′), *n.* **1.** (*used with a sing. v.*) a game like tenpins played with a short bowling pin of relatively large diameter. **2. duckpin,** a pin used in this game.

duck′ soup′, *n.* something that is easy to do or accomplish: *Fixing the car will be duck soup for anyone with the right tools.*

duck·weed (duk′wēd′), *n.* any plant of the family Lemnaceae, esp. of the genus *Lemna,* comprising minute aquatic plants that float free on still water.

duck·y (duk′ē), *adj.,* **duck·i·er, duck·i·est.** *Informal.* **1.** fine; excellent; wonderful. **2.** darling; charming; cute.

duct (dukt), *n.* **1.** any tube, canal, pipe, or conduit by which a liquid, air, or other substance is conducted or conveyed. **2.** a tube conveying bodily secretions or excretions. **3.** a conducting tube or tubule in plant tissues. **4.** a single enclosed runway for electrical conductors or cables. —**duct′less,** *adj.*

duc·tile (duk′tl, -til), *adj.* **1.** capable of being hammered out thin, as certain metals; malleable. **2.** capable of being drawn out into wire or threads, as gold. **3.** able to undergo change of form without breaking. **4.** capable of being molded or shaped; plastic. —**duc′tile·ly,** *adv.* —**duc·til′i·ty, duc′tile·ness,** *n.*

duct′ tape′, *n.* (duk, dukt), *n.* a strongly adhesive silver-gray cloth tape, used in plumbing, household repairs, etc.

duct·work (dukt′wûrk′), *n.* a system of ducts used for a particular purpose, as in a ventilation or heating system.

dud (dud), *n.* **1.** a device, person, or enterprise that proves to be a failure. **2.** a shell or missile that fails to explode after being fired.

dude (dōōd, dyōōd), *n.* **1.** a man excessively concerned with his clothes, grooming, and manners. **2.** *Slang.* a fellow. **3.** a person reared in a large city. **4.** *Western U.S.* an urban Easterner who vacations on a ranch.

dude′ ranch′, *n.* a ranch operated as a vacation resort.

dudg·eon (duj′ən), *n.* a feeling of offense or resentment; anger: *We left in high dudgeon.*

duds (dudz), *n.pl. Informal.* **1.** clothes, esp. a suit of clothes. **2.** belongings in general.

due (dōō, dyōō), *adj.* **1. a.** owing or owed: *This bill is due next month.* **b.** immediately owed: *This bill is due.* **2.** owing or observed as a moral

or natural right. **3.** rightful; proper; fitting: *in due time.* **4.** adequate; sufficient: *a due margin for delay.* **5.** expected to be ready, be present, or arrive; scheduled: *The plane is due at noon.* —*n.* **6.** something that is owed or naturally belongs to someone. **7.** Usu., **dues.** a regular fee payable at specific intervals, esp. to a group or organization: *membership dues.* —*adv.* **8.** directly or exactly: *a due east course.* —*Idiom.* **9. due to, a.** attributable to; ascribable to. **b.** because of; owing to: *absence from school due to illness.* **10. give someone his** or **her due, a.** to treat someone fairly. **b.** to acknowledge someone's unexpectedly positive behavior. **11. in due course,** in the natural order of events; eventually. **12. pay one's dues,** to earn respect by working hard and accumulating experience. —**due′ness,** *n.*

du·el (dōō′əl, dyōō′-), *n., v.,* **-eled, -el·ing** or (*esp. Brit.*) **-elled, -el·ling.** —*n.* **1.** a prearranged combat between two persons, fought with deadly weapons according to an accepted code of procedure. **2.** any contest between two persons or parties. —*v.t., v.i.* **3.** to fight in a duel. —**du′el·er, du′el·ist,** *n.*

due′ proc′ess of law′, *n.* the regular administration of a system of laws, which must conform to fundamental and generally accepted legal principles and be applied without favor or prejudice to all citizens. Also called **due′ proc′ess.**

du·et (dōō et′, dyōō-), *n., v.,* **-et·ted, -et·ting.** —*n.* **1.** a musical composition for two voices or instruments. —*v.i.* **2.** to perform a duet.

duff¹ (duf), *n. Slang.* the buttocks or rump.

duff² (duf), *n.* a boiled or steamed flour pudding, often containing currants, citron, etc.

duff³ (duf), *n.* organic matter in various stages of decomposition on the floor of the forest.

duf·fel or **duf·fle** (duf′əl), *n.* **1.** a camper's clothing and equipment. **2.** a coarse woolen cloth having a thick nap, used for coats, blankets, etc. **3.** DUFFEL BAG.

duf′fel bag′, *n.* a large, cylindrical bag, esp. of canvas, for personal belongings, orig. used by military personnel.

duff·er (duf′ər), *n.* **1.** *Informal.* **a.** a plodding, clumsy, incompetent person. **b.** a person inept or inexperienced at a specific sport, as golf. **2.** *Slang.* **a.** anything inferior, counterfeit, or useless. **b.** a peddler, esp. one who sells cheap, flashy goods.

Duf·field (duf′ēld), *n.* **George,** 1818–88, U.S. clergyman and hymn writer.

duf′fle (or **duf′fel) coat′,** *n.* a hooded overcoat of sturdy wool, usu. fastened with toggle buttons.

dug (dug), *v.* a pt. and pp. of DIG.

du·gong (dōō′gong, -gông), *n.* a plant-eating aquatic mammal, *Dugong dugon,* of Indian Ocean shores, having front flippers and a tail fin.

dug·out (dug′out′), *n.* **1.** a boat made by hollowing out a log. **2.** a roofed structure, usu. below ground level, in which baseball players sit when not on the field. **3.** a rough shelter formed by an excavation in the ground, or in the side of a hill, esp. one used by soldiers.

dui·ker (dī′kər), *n., pl.* **-kers,** (*esp. collectively*) **-ker.** any small African antelope of the genera *Cephalophus* and *Sylvicapra,* having short spikelike horns.

du jour (də zhŏŏr′, dōō) *adj.* as prepared or served on the particular day: *soup du jour.*

duke (dōōk, dyōōk), *n.* **1.** (in Continental Europe) the male ruler of a duchy, the sovereign of a small state. **2.** a British nobleman holding the highest hereditary title outside the royal family, ranking immediately below a prince and above a marquis. **3.** a nobleman of corresponding rank in certain other countries. **4.** a cultivated hybrid of the sweet and sour cherry. **5. dukes,** *Slang.* fists or hands. —*Idiom.* **6. duke it out,** to fight, esp. with the fists; do battle. [< Old French *duc* < Latin *dux* leader]

dul·cet (dul′sit), *adj.* **1.** pleasant to the ear; melodious. **2.** pleasant or agreeable to the eye or the feelings; soothing. —**dul′cet·ly,** *adv.* —**dul′cet·ness,** *n.*

dul·ci·fy (dul′sə fī′), *v.t.,* **-fied, -fy·ing. 1.** to make more agreeable; mollify; appease. **2.** to sweeten. —**dul′ci·fi·ca′tion,** *n.*

dul·ci·mer (dul′sə mər), *n.* **1.** a trapezoidal zither with metal strings that are struck with light hammers. **2.** a modern folk instrument with three or four strings plucked or strummed with the fingers.

dull (dul), *adj.* **1.** not sharp; blunt: *a dull knife.* **2.** causing boredom; tedious; uninteresting: *a dull sermon.* **3.** not lively or spirited; listless. **4.** not bright, intense, or clear; dim: *a dull day; a dull sound.* **5.** having very little depth of color; lacking in richness or intensity of color. **6.** slow in motion or action; not brisk; sluggish: *a dull day in the stock market.* **7.** mentally slow; somewhat stupid; obtuse. **8.** lacking keenness in the senses or feelings; insensible; unfeeling. **9.** not intense or acute: *a dull pain.* —*v.t., v.i.* **10.** to make or become dull. —**dull′ness, dull′ness,** *n.* —**dul′ly,** *adv.*

Dul·les (dul′əs), *n.* **John Foster,** 1888–1959, U.S. secretary of state 1953–59.

dulse (duls), *n.* a coarse edible red seaweed, *Rhodymenia palmata.*

du·ly (dōō′lē, dyōō′-), *adv.* **1.** in a due manner; properly; fittingly. **2.** in due season; punctually.

Du·mas (dōō mä′, dyōō-), *n.* **Alexandre** (*"Dumas père"*), 1802–70, and his son, **Alexandre** (*"Dumas fils"*), 1824–95, French dramatists and novelists.

dumb (dum), *adj.* **1.** lacking intelligence or good judgment; stupid; dull-witted. **2.** lacking the power of speech (often offensive when applied to humans): *a dumb animal.* **3.** temporarily unable to speak: *dumb with astonishment.* **4.** refraining from any or much speech; silent. **5.** made, done, etc., without speech. **6.** lacking some usual property, characteristic, etc. **7.** lacking electronic processing power of its own: *a dumb computer terminal.* Compare INTELLIGENT (def. 4). —*v.i.* **8. dumb down,** to reduce the intellectual level of: *to dumb down a textbook.*

Dum'bar·ton Oaks' (dum'bär tn), *n.* an estate in the District of Columbia: site of conferences held to discuss proposals for creation of the United Nations, August–October, 1944.

dumb·bell (dum'bel'), *n.* **1.** a hand weight for exercising, consisting of two heavy balls or disks connected by a graspable bar. **2.** *Slang.* a stupid person.

dumb' cane', *n.* a West Indian foliage plant, *Dieffenbachia seguine,* of the arum family, having yellow-blotched leaves that cause temporary speechlessness when chewed.

dumb·found (dum found', dum'found'), *v.t.* to make speechless with amazement; astonish.

dumb·struck (dum'struk') also **dumb·strick·en** (-strik'ən), *adj.* temporarily deprived of the power of speech, as by surprise or confusion; dumbfounded.

dumb·wait·er (dum'wā'tər), *n.* a small elevator, consisting typically of a box with shelves, used for moving food, garbage, etc., between floors, as in an apartment house or restaurant.

dum·dum (dum'dum'), *n.* a hollow-nosed or soft-nosed bullet that expands on impact, inflicting a severe wound.

dum·my (dum'ē), *n., pl.* **-mies,** *adj., v.,* **-mied, -my·ing.** —*n.* **1.** an imitation, representation, or copy of something, as for use in a display: *lipstick dummies of colored plastic.* **2.** a representation of a human figure, as for displaying clothes in store windows. **3.** *Informal.* a stupid person; dolt. **4.** a person who has nothing to say or who takes no active part in affairs. **5.** one put forward to act for others while ostensibly acting for oneself. **6.** *Slang.* a person who is characteristically and habitually silent. **7.** (in bridge) **a.** the declarer's partner, whose hand is exposed and played by the declarer. **b.** the hand of cards so exposed. **8.** sheets folded and made up to show the size, shape, sequence, and style of a contemplated piece of printing. **9.** a nonexplosive bomb used for practice exercises. —*adj.* **10.** noting or pertaining to an imitation, representation, or copy. **11.** counterfeit; sham; fictitious. **12.** put forward to act for others while ostensibly acting for oneself. —*v.t.* **13.** to prepare a printing dummy of (often fol. by *up*). **14.** to represent in a dummy (often fol. by *in*): *to dummy in an illustration.*

dump (dump), *v.t.* **1.** to drop or let fall in a mass; fling down or drop heavily or suddenly: *Dump the topsoil here.* **2.** to unload or empty out (a container), as by tilting or overturning. **3.** to empty out, as from a container. **4.** to be dismissed, fired, or released from a contract. **5.** to transfer or rid oneself of suddenly and irresponsibly: *Don't dump your troubles on me!* **6. a.** to put (goods or securities) on the market in large quantities and at a low price, esp. in an attempt to reduce losses. **b.** to sell (goods) into foreign markets below cost in an effort to destroy foreign competition. **7.** to output (computer data), often in binary or hexadecimal form, to diagnose a failure. —*v.i.* **8.** to fall or drop down suddenly. **9.** to throw away or discard garbage, refuse, etc. **10.** to release contents: *a sewage pipe that dumps in the ocean.* **11. dump on, a.** to criticize harshly; abuse. **b.** to unload one's problems onto (another person). —*n.* **12.** an accumulation of discarded garbage, refuse, etc. **13.** Also called **dumpsite, dumping-ground.** a place where garbage, refuse, etc., is deposited. **14.** a collection of ammunition, military stores, etc., deposited at some point, as near a battlefront, for distribution. **15.** the act of dumping. **16.** *Informal.* a place, house, or town that is dilapidated, dirty, or disreputable. **17.** a copy of dumped computer data.

dump·ish (dum'pish), *adj.* depressed; sad. —**dump'ish·ly,** *adv.* —**dump'ish·ness,** *n.*

dump·ling (dump'ling), *n.* **1.** a rounded mass of steamed and seasoned dough, often served in soups or stews. **2.** a wrapping of dough enclosing fruit or a savory filling, as of meat, and steamed, baked, or fried. **3.** a short, stout person.

dumps (dumps), *n.pl.* a depressed state of mind (usu. prec. by *in the*).

Dump·ster (dump'stər), *Trademark.* a brand of large metal bin for refuse, designed to be hoisted onto a truck for emptying.

dump·y¹ (dum'pē), *adj.,* **dump·i·er, dump·i·est.** dumpish; dejected; sulky.

dump·y² (dum'pē), *adj.,* **dump·i·er, dump·i·est.** short and stout; squat. —**dump'i·ly,** *adv.* —**dump'i·ness,** *n.*

dun¹ (dun), *v.,* **dunned, dun·ning,** *n.* —*v.t.* **1.** to make repeated demands upon, esp. for the payment of a debt. —*n.* **2.** a person, esp. a creditor, who duns another. **3.** a demand for payment; esp. a written one.

dun² (dun), *adj.* **1.** dull grayish brown or grayish yellow. **2.** dark; gloomy. —*n.* **3.** a dun color. **4.** a dun-colored horse with a black mane and tail. **5.** MAYFLY. —**dun'ness,** *n.*

Du·nant (dōō näN', dyōō-), *n.* **Jean Henri** (zhäN), 1828–1910, Swiss banker and philanthropist: founder of the Red Cross.

Dun·bar (dun'bär *for 1;* dun bär' *for 2, 3*), *n.* **1. Paul Laurence,** 1872–1906, U.S. poet. **2. William,** *c*1460–*c*1520, Scottish poet. **3.** a town in the Lothian region, in SE Scotland, at the mouth of the Firth of Forth: site of Cromwell's defeat of the Scots 1650. 4586.

Dun·can (dung'kən), *n.* **Isadora,** 1878–1927, U.S. dancer.

Dun·can Phyfe (dung'kən fīf'), *adj.* of, pertaining to, or resembling the furniture made by Duncan Phyfe, esp. the earlier pieces in the Sheraton and Directoire styles.

dunce (duns), *n.* a dull-witted, stupid, or ignorant person; dolt.

dunce' (or **dunce'·s) cap',** *n.* a tall cone-shaped hat formerly worn by slow or lazy students as a punishment. Also called **fool's cap.**

dun·der·head (dun'dər hed'), *n.* a dunce; blockhead; numbskull. Also called **dun·der·pate** (dun'dər pāt'). —**dun'der·head'ed,** *adj.*

dune (dōōn, dyōōn), *n.* a sand hill or sand ridge formed by the wind, usu. in desert regions or near lakes and oceans.

dune' bug'gy, *n.* a small, lightweight, open automotive vehicle equipped with oversize, low-pressure tires for traveling along sand beaches, over dunes, etc.

dung (dung), *n.* **1.** excrement, esp. of animals; manure. —*v.t.* **2.** to cover (ground) with or as if with dung. —**dung'y,** *adj.*

dun·ga·ree (dung'gə rē'), *n.* **1.** dungarees, **a.** work clothes, overalls, etc., of blue denim. **b.** BLUE JEANS. **2.** blue denim.

dung' bee'tle, *n.* any of various scarab beetles that feed on or breed in dung.

Dun'ge·ness crab' (dun'jə nes', dun'jə nes'), *n.* a crab, *Cancer magister,* of North American Pacific coastal waters.

dun·geon (dun'jən), *n.* **1.** a strong, dark prison or cell, usu. underground, as in a medieval castle. **2.** the keep or stronghold of a castle; donjon.

dung·hill (dung'hil'), *n.* **1.** a heap of dung. **2.** a repugnantly filthy or degraded place, abode, or situation.

dunk (dungk), *v.t.* **1.** to dip (a doughnut, cake, etc.) into coffee, milk, or the like, before eating. **2.** to submerge briefly in a liquid. **3.** to thrust (a basketball) downward through the basket. —*v.i.* **4.** to dip or submerge something, oneself, etc., in a liquid. **5.** to execute or attempt a dunk shot. —*n.* **6.** an act or instance of dunking. **7.** a liquid or creamy mixture into which food is dipped. **8.** DUNK SHOT. —**dunk'a·ble,** *adj., n.* —**dunk'er,** *n.*

Dunk·er (dung'kər) also **Dun·kard** (-kərd), *n.* a member of the Church of the Brethren, a denomination of Christians who practice trine immersion and are opposed to military service and the taking of oaths.

Dun·kirk (dun'kûrk), *n.* a seaport in N France: site of the evacuation of Allied forces under German fire 1940. 73,618. French, **Dun·kerque** (dœN kerk').

dunk' shot', *n.* a basketball shot whereby a player thrusts the ball downward through the basket.

dun·lin (dun'lin), *n.* a small sandpiper, *Calidris alpina,* that breeds in the N parts of the Northern Hemisphere.

dun·nage (dun'ij), *n.* **1.** baggage or personal effects. **2.** loose material laid beneath or wedged among objects carried by ship or rail to prevent injury from chafing or moisture or to provide ventilation.

Dunne (dun), *n.* **1. Finley Peter,** 1867–1936, U.S. humorist. **2. John Gregory,** born 1932, U.S. writer.

Duns Sco·tus (dunz skō'təs), *n.* **John** (*"Doctor Subtilis"*), 1265?–1308, Scottish scholastic theologian.

du·o (dōō'ō, dyōō'ō), *n., pl.* **du·os. 1.** DUET. **2.** two persons commonly associated with each other; couple. **3.** two things ordinarily placed or found together; a pair: *a duo of lovebirds.*

duo-, a combining form meaning "two": *duotone.*

du·o·dec·i·mal (dōō'ə des'ə məl, dyōō'-), *adj.* **1.** pertaining to twelfths or to the number 12. **2.** proceeding by twelves. —*n.* **3.** one of a system of numbers based on the number 12. **4.** one of 12 equal parts.

du·o·dec·i·mo (dōō'ə des'ə mō', dyōō'-), *n., pl.* **-mos,** *adj.* —*n.* Also called **twelvemo. 1.** a book size of about 5 × 7½ in. (13 × 19 cm), determined by printing on sheets folded to form 12 leaves or 24 pages. *Symbol:* 12 mo, 12° **2.** a book of this size. —*adj.* **3.** in duodecimo; twelvemo.

du·o·de·num (dōō'ə dē'nəm, dyōō'-; dōō od'n əm, dyōō'-), *n., pl.* **du·o·de·na** (dōō'ə dē'nə, dyōō'-; dōō od'n ə, dyōō'-), **du·o·de·nums.** the first portion of the small intestine, from the stomach to the jejunum.

dupe (dōōp, dyōōp), *n., v.,* **duped, dup·ing.** —*n.* **1.** a person who is easily deceived or fooled; gull. **2.** a person who unquestioningly or unwittingly serves a cause or another person. —*v.t.* **3.** to make a dupe of; deceive; delude; trick. —**dup'a·ble,** *adj.* —**dup'er,** *n.* —**dup'er·y,** *n.*

du·ple (dōō'pəl, dyōō'-), *adj.* **1.** having two parts; double; twofold. **2.** having two or sometimes a multiple of two beats in a measure: *duple meter.*

du·plex (dōō'pleks, dyōō'-), *n.* **1.** DUPLEX APARTMENT. **2.** DUPLEX HOUSE. **3.** a double-stranded region of DNA. —*adj.* **4.** having two parts; double; twofold. **5.** pertaining to or noting a telecommunications system, as most telephone systems, permitting the simultaneous transmission of two messages in opposite directions over one channel. —*v.t.* **6.** to make duplex; make or change into a duplex. —**du·plex'i·ty,** *n.*

du'plex apart'ment, *n.* an apartment with rooms on two connected floors.

du'plex house', *n.* a house having separate apartments for two families, esp. a two-story house with an apartment on each floor and two separate entrances.

du·pli·cate (*n., adj.* dōō'pli kit, dyōō'-; *v.* -kāt'), *n., v.,* **-cat·ed, -cat·ing,** *adj.* —*n.* **1.** a copy exactly like an original. **2.** anything corresponding in all respects to something else. —*v.t.* **3.** to make an exact copy of. **4.** to double; make twofold. **5.** to do or perform again; repeat: *to dupli-*

cate a performance. —*v.i.* **6.** to become duplicate. —*adj.* **7.** exactly like or corresponding to something else: *duplicate copies of a letter.* **8.** consisting of or existing in two identical or corresponding parts; double. **9.** noting a card game in which each team plays a series of identical hands, the winner being the team making the best total score: *duplicate bridge.* —*Idiom.* **10. in duplicate,** in two identical copies. —**dup/li·ca/tion,** *n.* —**du/pli·ca/tive,** *adj.*

du·pli·ca·tor (dōō/pli kā/tər, dyōō/-), *n.* a machine for making duplicates, as a mimeograph. Also called **du/plicating machine/.**

du·plic·i·ty (dōō plis/i tē, dyōō-), *n., pl.* **-ties. 1.** deceitfulness in speech or conduct; double-dealing. **2.** a twofold or double state or quality. —**du·plic/i·tous,** *adj.*

Du·Pont or **Du Pont** (dōō pont/, dyōō-, dōō/pont, dyōō/-), *n.* Eleuthère Irénée, 1771–1834, U.S. industrialist, born in France.

du·ra·ble (dōōr/ə bəl, dyōōr/-), *adj.* **1.** highly resistant to wear, decay, etc. **2.** capable of lasting; enduring. —*n.* **3. durables,** DURABLE GOODS. —**du/ra·bil/i·ty, du/ra·ble·ness,** *n.* —**du/ra·bly,** *adv.*

du/rable goods/, *n.pl.* goods, such as household appliances, that are not consumed in use and can be used for a period of time, usu. at least three years.

du·ral·u·min (dōō ral/yə min, dyōō-), *n.* a strong, lightweight alloy of aluminum, copper, and other metals, used in aircraft construction.

du·ra ma·ter (māˊtər), *n.* the tough, fibrous membrane forming the outermost of the three coverings of the brain and spinal cord. Also called **dura.** Compare ARACHNOID (def. 4), PIA MATER.

du·ra·men (dōō rāˊmin, dyōō-), *n.* HEARTWOOD.

Du·rant (də rant/), *n.* **Ariel,** 1898–1981, and her husband, **Will(iam James),** 1885–1981, U.S. historians.

du·ra·tion (dōō rāˊshən, dyōō-), *n.* **1.** the length of time something continues or exists. **2.** continuance in time. —**du·ra/tion·al,** *adj.*

Dur·ban (dûr/bən), *n.* a seaport in SE Natal, in the E Republic of South Africa. 982,075.

Dü·rer (dŏŏr/ər, dyŏŏr/-), *n.* **Albrecht,** 1471–1528, German painter and engraver.

du·ress (dōō res/, dyōō-, dōōr/is, dyōōr/-), *n.* **1.** compulsion by threat or force; coercion. **2.** constraint or coercion of a degree sufficient to void any legal agreement entered into or any act performed under its influence. **3.** forcible restraint, esp. imprisonment.

Dur·ham (dûr/əm, dur/-), *n.* **1.** a county in NE England. 598,700; 940 sq. mi. (2435 sq. km). **2.** a city in this county. 86,500. **3.** a city in N North Carolina. 143,439.

du·ri·an (dōōr/ē ən), *n.* **1.** the large edible fruit of a SE Asian tree, *Durio zibethinus,* of the bombax family, having a prickly rind and soft, nasty-smelling flesh. **2.** the tree itself.

dur·ing (dōōr/ing, dyōōr/-), *prep.* **1.** throughout the duration, continuance, or existence of: *He lived in Florida during the winter.* **2.** at some time or point in the course of: *They departed during the night.*

dur·mast (dûr/mast, -mäst/), *n.* any of several European oaks, esp. *Quercus petraea,* yielding a heavy elastic wood used for furniture and building.

Du·roc (dōōr/ok, dyōōr/-), *n.* one of an American breed of hardy red hogs having drooping ears. Also called **Du·roc-Jer·sey** (dōōr/ok jûr/zē, dyōōr/-).

dur·ra (dōōr/ə), *n.* a type of grain sorghum with slender stalks, cultivated in Asia and Africa and introduced into the U.S.

du/rum wheat/ (dōōr/əm, dyōōr/-), *n.* a wheat, *Triticum durum,* the grain of which yields flour used in making pasta. Also called **du/rum.**

Du·shan·be (dōō shän/bə, -shäm/-, dyōō-), *n.* the capital of Tajikistan, in the E part. 595,000.

dusk[1] (dusk), *n.* **1.** the state or period of partial darkness between day and night; the dark part of twilight. **2.** partial darkness; shade; gloom.

dusk[2] (dusk), *adj.* **1.** tending to darkness; dark. —*v.t., v.i.* **2.** to make or become dusk; darken. —**dusk/ish,** *adj.*

dusk·y (dus/kē), *adj.,* **dusk·i·er, dusk·i·est. 1.** somewhat dark; dimly lit; shadowy. **2.** having dark skin. **3.** of a dark color. **4.** gloomy; sad. —**dusk/i·ly,** *adv.* —**dusk/i·ness,** *n.*

dust (dust), *n.* **1.** earth or other matter in fine dry particles. **2.** a cloud of finely powdered earth or other matter in the air. **3.** any finely powdered substance, as sawdust. **4.** the ground; the earth's surface. **5.** the substance to which something, as the dead human body, is ultimately reduced by disintegration or decay. **6.** *Brit.* ashes, refuse, etc. **7.** a low or humble condition. **8.** anything worthless. **9.** disturbance; turmoil. **10.** GOLD DUST. **11.** the mortal body of a human being. **12.** a single particle or grain. —*v.t.* **13.** to wipe the dust from. **14.** to sprinkle with a powder or dust: *to dust crops with insecticide.* **15.** to strew or sprinkle (a powder, dust, or other fine particles): *to dust insecticide on a rosebush.* **16.** to soil with dust; make dusty. —*v.i.* **17.** to wipe dust from furniture, woodwork, etc. **18.** to become dusty. **19.** to apply dust or powder to a plant, one's body, etc. **20. dust off,** to prepare to use again, esp. after inactivity or storage. —*Idiom.* **21. bite the dust, a.** to die. **b.** to suffer defeat. **c.** to become ruined or unusable. **22. make the dust fly,** to work with vigor or speed. **23. throw dust in someone's eyes,** to mislead someone, esp. by distraction. —**dust/less,** *adj.*

Dust/ Bowl/, *n.* **1.** the region in the S central U.S. that suffered from dust storms in the 1930s. **2.** (*l.c.*) any region subject to dust storms.

dust/ dev/il, *n.* a small whirlwind 10–100 ft. (3–30 m) in diameter and

from several hundred to 1000 ft. (305 m) high, common in dry regions and made visible by the dust and debris it picks up from the ground.

dust·er (dus/tər), *n.* **1.** a person or thing that removes or applies dust. **2.** a cloth, brush, etc., for removing dust. **3.** a lightweight knee-length housecoat. **4.** an apparatus or device for sprinkling dust, powder, insecticide, or the like. **5.** a person employed in spreading insecticidal dusts on crops from a low-flying aircraft. **6. a.** a long lightweight overcoat, worn esp. in the early days of open automobiles to protect the clothing from dust. **b.** a loose-fitting lightweight coat for women.

dust/ storm/ or **dust/storm/,** *n.* a storm of strong winds and dust-filled air over normally arable land during a period of drought (disting. from *sandstorm*).

dust·up (dust/up/), *n.* a quarrel; argument; row.

dust·y (dus/tē), *adj.,* **dust·i·er, dust·i·est. 1.** filled, covered, or clouded with or as if with dust. **2.** of the nature of dust; powdery. **3.** of the color of dust; having a grayish cast.

dust/y mill/er, *n.* **1.** any of several plants having woolly foliage. **2.** ROSE CAMPION.

Dutch (duch), *adj.* **1.** of or pertaining to the Netherlands, its inhabitants, or their language. —*n.* **2.** (*used with a pl. v.*) the inhabitants of the Netherlands. **3.** the West Germanic language of the Netherlands and N and W Belgium. Compare FLEMISH.

Dutch/ door/, *n.* a door consisting of two units horizontally divided so that each half can be opened or closed separately.

dutch door

Dutch/ East/ In/dies, *n.* a former name of the Republic of INDONESIA.

Dutch/ elm/ disease/, *n.* a disease of elms characterized by wilting, yellowing, and falling of the leaves, caused by a fungus, *Ceratostomella ulmi,* transmitted by bark beetles.

Dutch/ Guian/a, *n.* former name of SURINAME.

Dutch/man's-breech/es, *n., pl.* **-breeches.** a plant, *Dicentra cucullaria,* of the fumitory family, having long clusters of pale-yellow two-spurred flowers.

Dutch/man's-pipe/, *n.* a climbing vine, *Aristolochia durior,* of the birthwort family, having large heart-shaped leaves and brownish-purple flowers of a curved form suggesting a tobacco pipe.

Dutch/ ov/en, *n.* **1.** a large heavy pot, as of cast iron, with a close-fitting lid, used for pot roasts, stews, etc. **2.** a metal utensil, open in front, for roasting before an open fire. **3.** a brick oven in which the walls are preheated for cooking.

Dutch/ Reformed/, *adj.* of or pertaining to a Protestant denomination (**Dutch/ Reformed/ Church/**), founded by Dutch settlers in New York in 1628 and renamed the Reformed Church in America in 1867.

Dutch/ treat/, *n.* a meal or entertainment for which each person pays his or her own way.

Dutch/ un/cle, *n.* a person, often a mentor or advisor, who criticizes or reproves with unsparing severity and frankness.

du·te·ous (dōō/tē əs, dyōō/-), *adj.* dutiful; obedient. —**du/te·ous·ly,** *adv.* —**du/te·ous·ness,** *n.*

du·ti·ful (dōō/tə fəl, dyōō/-), *adj.* **1.** performing the duties expected or required of one; respectful; obedient: *a dutiful child.* **2.** proceeding from or expressive of a sense of duty. —**du/ti·ful·ly,** *adv.*

du·ty (dōō/tē, dyōō/-), *n., pl.* **-ties. 1.** something that one is expected or required to do by moral or legal obligation. **2.** the binding force of something that is morally or legally right; moral or legal obligation. **3.** an action or task required by a person's position or occupation: *the duties of a clergyman.* **4.** the respectful and obedient conduct due a parent, elder, or superior. **5.** an act or expression of respect. **6.** a task or chore that one is expected to perform. **7. a.** an assigned military task, occupation, or place of service: *on radar duty.* **b.** the military service required of a citizen by a country. **8.** a specific or ad valorem tax imposed by law on the import or export of goods. **9.** a payment, service, etc., imposed and enforceable by law or custom. **10. a.** the amount of work done by an engine per unit amount of fuel consumed. **b.** the measure of effectiveness of any machine. **11.** the amount of water necessary to provide for a crop in a given area. —*Idiom.* **12. do duty as,** to serve the same function as; substitute for. **13. off duty,** not at one's post or work; at liberty. **14. on duty,** at one's post or work.

du/ty-free/, *adj.* **1.** free of customs duty. **2.** selling goods free of the usual customs duty: *the duty-free shop at an airport.* —*adv.* **3.** free of customs duty.

du·vet (dōō vā/, dyōō-), *n.* **1.** a usu. down-filled quilt; comforter. **2.** a decorative casing for such a quilt.

D.V.M. or **DVM,** Doctor of Veterinary Medicine.

dwarf (dwôrf), *n., pl.* **dwarfs, dwarves,** *adj., v.* —*n.* **1.** a person of abnormally small stature owing to a pathological condition, esp. a condition that produces short limbs or anatomical deformation. **2.** an animal or plant much smaller than the average of its kind or species. **3.** a diminutive being of folklore, often represented as a tiny old man, skilled as an artificer and having magical powers. **4.** DWARF STAR. —*adj.* **5.** of unusually small stature or size; diminutive. —*v.t.* **6.** to cause to seem small in size, character, etc., as by being much larger. **7.** to prevent the due development of; stunt. —*v.i.* **8.** to become stunted or smaller. —**dwarf′ish**, *adj.* —**dwarf′ism,** *n.* —**dwarf′like′,** *adj.*

dwarf′ star′, *n.* a star with relatively small mass and low or average luminosity, as the sun.

dwarves (dwôrvz), *n.* a pl. of DWARF.

dwell (dwel), *v.,* **dwelt** or **dwelled, dwell·ing,** *n.* —*v.i.* **1.** to live or stay as a permanent resident; reside. **2.** to exist or continue in a given condition or state. **3.** (of a moving tool or machine part) to be motionless for a certain interval during operation. **4. dwell on** or **upon,** to think, speak, or write about at length or with persistence; linger over. —*n.* **5.** a flat or cylindrical area on a cam for maintaining a follower in a certain position during part of a cycle. **6.** a period in a cycle in the operation of a machine or engine during which a given part remains motionless. —**dwell′er,** *n.*

dwelt (dwelt), *v.* a pt. and pp. of DWELL.

DWI, driving while intoxicated: often an official police abbreviation.

Dwight (dwīt), *n.* **Timothy,** 1826–1916, U.S. ecclesiastic: president of Yale University 1886–98.

dwin·dle (dwin′dl), *v.,* **-dled, -dling.** —*v.i.* **1.** to become smaller and smaller; shrink; diminish. **2.** to fall away, as in quality; degenerate. —*v.t.* **3.** to make smaller and smaller; cause to shrink.

Dy, *Chem. Symbol.* dysprosium.

dy·ad (dī′ad), *n.* **1.** a group of two; couple; pair. **2.** the double chromosomes resulting from the separation of the four chromatids of a tetrad. **3.** an element, atom, or group having a valence of two. **4.** *Math.* two vectors with no symbol connecting them, usu. considered as an operator. **5. a.** two people involved in an ongoing relationship or interaction. **b.** the relationship or interaction itself. —*adj.* **6.** of two parts. —**dy·ad′ic,** *adj.*

dyb·buk (dib′ək), *n.* (in Jewish folklore) a demon, or the soul of a dead person, that enters the body of a living person and directs the person's conduct, exorcism being possible only by a religious ceremony.

dye (dī), *n., v.,* **dyed, dye·ing.** —*n.* **1.** a coloring material or matter. **2.** a liquid containing coloring matter, for imparting a particular hue to cloth, paper, etc. **3.** color or hue, esp. as produced by dyeing. —*v.t.* **4.** to color (cloth, hair, etc.) with or as if with a dye: *to dye a dress green.* **5.** to impart (color) by means of a dye: *The coloring matter dyed green.* —*v.i.* **6.** to impart color, as a dye. **7.** to become colored when treated with a dye. —*Idiom.* **8. of the deepest** or **blackest dye,** of the most extreme or the worst sort. —**dy′a·ble, dye′a·ble,** *adj.* —**dy′er,** *n.*

dyed′-in-the-wool′, *adj.* **1.** through and through; complete: *a dyed-in-the-wool feminist.* **2.** dyed before weaving.

dy′er's-weed′, *n.* any of various plants yielding dyes, as the weld, *Reseda luteola* or the woad, *Isatis tinctoria.*

dye·stuff (dī′stuf′), *n.* a material yielding or used as a dye.

dy·ing (dī′ing), *adj.* **1.** about to die; approaching death. **2.** of or associated with death: *his dying hour.* **3.** given, uttered, or manifested just before death: *her dying words.* **4.** drawing to a close; ending: *the dying year.* —*n.* **5.** the act or process of ceasing to live, exist, or function; death; ending.

Dykes (dīks), *n.* **John B(acchus),** 1823–76, English musician and hymn writer.

Dyl·an (dil′ən), *n.* **Bob** (*Robert Zimmerman*), born 1941, U.S. folk-rock singer, guitarist, and composer.

dyna- or **dynamo-,** a combining form meaning "power": *dynamotor.*

dy·nam·ic (dī nam′ik), *adj.* Also, **dy·nam′i·cal. 1.** vigorously active or forceful; energetic. **2.** characterized by or producing change or progression: *a dynamic process.* **3. a.** of or pertaining to force or power. **b.** of or pertaining to force related to motion. **4.** of or pertaining to the science of dynamics. **5.** of or pertaining to the range of volume of musical sound. —*n.* **6.** a force producing change. **7.** DYNAMICS (def. 3). —**dy·nam′i·cal·ly,** *adv.*

dy·nam·ics (dī nam′iks), *n.* **1.** (*used with a sing. v.*) the branch of mechanics that deals with the motion and equilibrium of systems under the action of forces, usu. from outside the system. **2.** (*used with a pl. v.*) the motivating or driving forces in any field or system. **3.** (*used with a pl. v.*) the pattern or history of growth, change, and development in any field. **4.** (*used with a pl. v.*) variation and gradation in the volume of musical sound. **5.** (*used with a sing. or pl. v.*) psychodynamics.

dy·na·mism (dī′nə miz′əm), *n.* **1.** any of various theories or philosophical systems that seek to explain phenomena of nature by the action of force. Compare MECHANISM (def. 6), VITALISM (def. 1). **2.** great energy, force, or power; vigor. —**dy′na·mist,** *n.* —**dy′na·mis′tic,** *adj.*

dy·na·mite (dī′nə mīt′), *n., v.,* **-mit·ed, -mit·ing,** *adj.* —*n.* **1.** a high explosive, orig. consisting of nitroglycerin mixed with an absorbent substance, now with ammonium nitrate usu. replacing the nitroglycerin. **2.** any person or thing having a spectacular or potentially explosive effect. —*v.t.* **3.** to blow up, shatter, or destroy with dynamite. **4.** to mine or charge with dynamite. —*adj.* **5.** *Informal.* wonderful or exciting: *a dynamite idea.* —**dy′na·mit′er,** *n.* —**dy′na·mit′ic** (-mit′ik), *adj.*

dy·na·mo (dī′nə mō′), *n., pl.* **-mos. 1.** an electric generator, esp. for direct current. **2.** an energetic, hardworking, forceful person.

dy·na·mo·e·lec·tric (dī′nə mō i lek′trik) also **dy′na·mo·e·lec′tri·cal,** *adj.* pertaining to the conversion of mechanical energy into electric energy, or vice versa.

dy·na·mom·e·ter (dī′nə mom′i tər), *n.* **1.** a device for measuring mechanical force, as a balance. **2.** a device for measuring mechanical power, esp. one that measures the output or driving torque of a rotating machine. —**dy′na·mo·met′ric** (-mō me′trik), *adj.*

dy·na·mo·tor (dī′nə mō′tər), *n.* an electric machine for transforming direct current into alternating current or for altering the voltage of direct current.

dy·nas·ty (dī′nə stē; *Brit. also* din′ə stē), *n., pl.* **-ties. 1.** a sequence of rulers from the same family, stock, or group: *the Ming dynasty.* **2.** the rule of such a family or group. **3.** any succession of members of a powerful or influential family or group. —**dy·nas′tic** (-nas′tik), *adj.*

dyne (dīn), *n.* the standard centimeter-gram-second unit of force, equal to the force that produces an acceleration of one centimeter per second per second on a mass of one gram. *Abbr.:* dyn

dys-, a combining form meaning "ill," "bad," used esp. to form words denoting impaired or abnormal biological or mental processes: *dyslexia; dysplasia.*

dys·en·ter·y (dis′ən ter′ē), *n.* any infectious disease of the large intestines marked by hemorrhagic diarrhea with mucus and often blood in the feces. —**dys′en·ter′ic,** *adj.*

dys·func·tion (dis fungk′shən), *n.* **1.** impairment of function or malfunctioning, as of an organ or structure of the body. **2.** a consequence of a social activity or structure that undermines a social system. —**dys·func′tion·al,** *adj.*

dys·gen·ic (dis jen′ik), *adj.* pertaining to or causing degeneration in the type of offspring produced. Compare EUGENIC.

dys·gen·ics (dis jen′iks), *n.* (*used with a sing. v.*) the study of factors causing genetic deterioration in a population or species.

dys·lex·i·a (dis lek′sē ə), *n.* any of various reading disorders associated with impairment of the ability to interpret spatial relationships or to integrate auditory and visual information. —**dys·lex′ic,** *adj.*

dys·pep·sia (dis pep′shə, -sē ə) also **dys·pep′sy,** *n.* deranged or impaired digestion; indigestion (opposed to *eupepsia*).

dys·pep·tic (dis pep′tik), *adj.* Also, **dys·pep′ti·cal. 1.** pertaining to, subject to, or suffering from dyspepsia. **2.** gloomy and irritable. —*n.* **3.** a person subject to or suffering from dyspepsia.

dys·phe·mism (dis′fə miz′əm), *n.* **1.** the substitution of a harsh, disparaging, or unpleasant expression for a more neutral one. **2.** an expression so substituted. —**dys′phe·mis′tic,** *adj.*

dys·pla·sia (dis plā′zhə, -zhē ə, -zē ə), *n.* abnormal growth or development of cells, tissue, bone, or an organ. —**dys·plas′tic** (-plas′tik), *adj.*

dysp·ne·a (disp nē′ə), *n.* difficult or labored breathing. —**dysp·ne′al, dysp·ne′ic,** *adj.*

dys·pro·si·um (dis prō′sē əm, -shē-), *n.* a rare-earth element that is highly reactive and paramagnetic and used to absorb neutrons in nuclear reactors. *Symbol:* Dy; *at. wt.:* 162.50; *at. no.:* 66.

dys·troph·ic (di strof′ik, -strō′fik), *adj.* **1.** pertaining to or caused by dystrophy. **2.** (of a lake or pond) having brownish acidic water productive of vegetation along the shoreline and in shallow parts but poor in aquatic life.

dys·tro·phy (dis′trə fē) also **dys·tro·phi·a** (di strō′fē ə), *n.* **1.** faulty or inadequate nutrition or development. **2.** any of a number of disorders characterized by weakening, degeneration, or abnormal development of muscle.

dz., dozen.

E

E, e (ē), *n.*, *pl.* **Es** or **E's, es** or **e's. 1.** the fifth letter of the English alphabet, a vowel. **2.** any spoken sound represented by this letter. **3.** something having the shape of an E. **4.** a written or printed representation of the letter *E* or *e*.

E, *Symbol.* **1.** the fifth in order or in a series. **2.** a grade or mark indicating that a student's work is in need of improvement in order to be passing. **3. a.** the third note of the ascending C major scale. **b.** a tonality having E as the tonic. **4.** energy. **5.** *Biochem.* glutamic acid.

e, *Math. Symbol.* a transcendental constant equal to 2.7182818 ... , used as the base of natural logarithms; the limit of the expression $(1 + 1/n)^n$ as n approaches infinity.

each (ēch), *adj.* **1.** every one of two or more considered individually or one by one: *each stone in a wall; a door at each end.* —*pron.* **2.** every one individually; each one: *Each had a different solution to the problem.* —*adv.* **3.** to, from, or for each; apiece: *They cost a dollar each.* —**Usage.** When the adjective EACH follows a plural subject, the verb agrees with the subject: *The houses each have central heating.* When the pronoun, a singular form, is followed by an *of* phrase containing a plural noun or pronoun, strict usage requires the singular verb: *Each of the candidates has spoken on the issue.* Yet plural verbs tend to occur frequently even in edited writing. Usage guides also advise that EACH must be referred to by a singular pronoun. Again, actual usage does not always conform. Singular pronouns do occur in the most formal speech and writing: *Each club member had his own project.* But the use of plural pronouns has been increasing in the U.S., partially to avoid sexism: *Each club member had their own project.* These same general patterns of pronoun agreement are followed in the use of *anyone, anybody, everyone, everybody, no one, someone,* and *somebody.* See also THEY.

each' oth'er, *pron.* each the other; one another: *to love each other; to hold each other's hands; to talk to each other.*

ead., (in prescriptions) the same.

ea•ger (ē'gər), *adj.* **1.** characterized by keen or enthusiastic desire or interest; impatiently longing: *eager to try it.* **2.** characterized by or revealing earnestness or expectancy: *an eager look.* —**ea'ger•ly,** *adv.* —**ea'ger•ness,** *n.*

ea'ger bea'ver, *n.* a person who is excessively diligent or overly zealous.

ea•gle (ē'gəl), *n.* **1.** a robust, broad-winged bird of prey of the family Accipitridae, typically having a massive bill and talons. **2.** a figure of an eagle, much used as an emblem: *the Roman eagle.* **3.** a standard or seal bearing such a figure. **4.** one of a pair of silver military insignia in the shape of an eagle, worn by a colonel or, in the navy, by a captain. **5.** a former gold coin of the U.S., equal to ten dollars. **6.** (*cap.*) a U.S. gold coin, available in various denominations: first issued in 1986. **7.** a golf score of two below par for any single hole.

ea'gle eye', *n.* **1.** unusually sharp visual powers; keen ability to watch or observe. **2.** a person who has sharp vision or maintains a keen watchfulness. **3.** alert watchfulness. —**ea'gle-eyed',** *adj.*

ea'gle owl', *n.* any of several large owls of the genus *Bubo,* having prominent tufts of feathers on each side of the head.

ea'gle ray', *n.* any of several rays of the family Myliobatidae, found in tropical seas and noted for the soaring movements by which they propel themselves through the water.

ea'gle scout', *n.* (*often caps.*) a boy scout who has achieved the highest rank in U.S. scouting.

ea•glet (ē'glit), *n.* a young eagle.

Ea•kins (ā'kinz), *n.* **Thomas,** 1844–1916, U.S. painter.

ear¹ (ēr), *n.* **1.** the organ of hearing and equilibrium in vertebrates, in mammals consisting of an external ear and ear canal ending at the tympanic membrane, a middle ear with three ossicles for amplifying vibrations, and a liquid-filled inner ear with sensory nerve endings for hearing and balance. **2.** the sense of hearing: *sounds that are pleasing to the ear.* **3.** keen or sensitive perception of the differences of sound, esp. musical sounds. **4.** attention; heed: *to gain a person's ear.* **5.** any part that resembles or suggests an ear in position or form, as the handle of a teacup. —*Idiom.* **6. be all ears,** to be extremely attentive; listen

intently. **7. by ear,** without reference to musical notation; from memory. **8. fall on deaf ears,** to be disregarded; pass unheeded. **9. go in one ear and out the other,** to be heard but without understanding or effect. **10. have** or **keep one's ear to the ground,** to stay alert to current trends and viewpoints. **11. lend an** or **give ear,** to pay attention; listen carefully. **12. play it by ear,** to improvise, esp. in a situation filled with unknown factors. **13. set on one's ear,** to stir to excitement; amaze. **14. turn a deaf ear to,** to refuse to consider or deal with.

ear² (ēr), *n.* **1.** the spike of a cereal plant, containing the seed grains. —*v.i.* **2.** to form or put forth ears.

ear•ache (ēr'āk'), *n.* a pain or ache in the ear; otalgia.

ear' drops', *n.pl.* medicinal drops for use in the ears.

ear•drum (ēr'drum'), *n.* a membrane in the ear canal between the external ear and the middle ear; tympanic membrane.

eared' seal', *n.* any seal of the family Otariidae, comprising the sea lions and fur seals, having external ears and flexible hind flippers that are used when moving about on land.

ear•flap (ēr'flap'), *n.* a flap attached to a cap, for covering the ear in cold weather.

ear•ful (ēr'fŏŏl'), *n.*, *pl.* **-fuls. 1.** an outpouring of oral information or advice, esp. when given without solicitation. **2.** a sharp verbal rebuke; scolding.

Ear•hart (âr'härt), *n.* **Amelia (Mary),** 1897–1937, U.S. aviator.

earl (ûrl), *n.* a British nobleman of a rank below that of marquis and above that of viscount: called a count for a time after the Norman Conquest. The wife of an earl is a countess.

ear•less seal', *n.* any seal of the family Phocidae, lacking external ears and using the hind flippers only for swimming.

ear•lobe (ēr'lōb') or **ear' lobe',** *n.* the soft, pendulous lower part of the external ear.

ear•ly (ûr'lē), *adv.* and *adj.,* **-li•er, -li•est.** —*adv.* **1.** in or during the first part of a period of time, course of action, or series of events: *early in the year.* **2.** in the early part of the morning: *to get up early.* **3.** before the usual or appointed time; ahead of time. **4.** far back in time: *The Greeks early learned to navigate.* —*adj.* **5.** occurring in the first part of a period of time, course of action, or series of events: *an early hour of the day.* **6.** occurring before the usual or appointed time: *an early dinner.* **7.** belonging to a period far back in time. **8.** occurring in the near future: *I look forward to an early reply.* —*Idiom.* **9. early on,** not long after the beginning. —*Proverb.* **10. Early to bed and early to rise, makes a man healthy, wealthy, and wise,** moderation is a key to success: saying popularized by Benjamin Franklin in *Poor Richard's Almanac.* —**ear'li•ness,** *n.*

Ear'ly Amer'ican, *adj.* **1.** (of furniture, buildings, utensils, etc.) built or made in the U.S. in the colonial period or somewhat later. **2.** built or made in imitation of works of this period.

ear'ly bird', *n.* **1.** a person who rises at an early hour. **2.** a person who arrives before others. —*Proverb.* **3. The early bird catches the worm,** success depends on being active early or in the beginning stages of an undertaking.

ear'ly wood', *n.* SPRINGWOOD.

ear•mark (ēr'märk'), *n.* **1.** any identifying or distinguishing mark or characteristic: *all the earmarks of a conspiracy.* **2.** a mark of identification made on the ear of an animal to show ownership. —*v.t.* **3.** to set aside for a specific purpose, use, or recipient: *to earmark goods for export.* **4.** to mark with an earmark.

ear•muff (ēr'muf'), *n.* Usu., **earmuffs.** one of a pair of pads set on a headband and worn over the ears in cold weather.

earn (ûrn), *v.t.* **1.** to gain or get in return for one's labor or service: *to earn a living.* **2.** to merit as compensation; deserve: *to receive more than one has earned.* **3.** to acquire through merit: *to earn a reputation for honesty.* **4.** to gain as due return or profit: *Savings bonds earn interest.* **5.** to bring about or cause deservedly: *His fair dealing earned our confidence.* —*v.i.* **6.** to gain income. —**earn'er,** *n.*

earned' run', *n.* a run yielded by a baseball pitcher that is not the result of an error or passed ball.

earned' run' av'erage, *n.* a figure used to indicate the effectiveness of a baseball pitcher, obtained by calculating the average number of earned runs scored against the pitcher for every nine innings pitched. *Abbr.:* ERA, era

ear•nest¹ (ûr'nist), *adj.* **1.** serious in intention, purpose, or effort; sincerely zealous. **2.** showing depth and sincerity of feeling: *an earnest entreaty.* **3.** seriously important; grave. —*n.* **4.** full seriousness, as of intention or purpose: *to be in earnest.* —**ear'nest•ly,** *adv.* —**ear'nest•ness,** *n.*

ear•nest² (ûr'nist), *n.* **1.** a portion of something, given or done in advance as a pledge of the remainder. **2.** money given by a buyer to a seller to bind a contract. **3.** anything that gives pledge, promise, or indication of what is to follow.

earn•ings (ûr'ningz), *n.pl.* money earned; wages; profits.

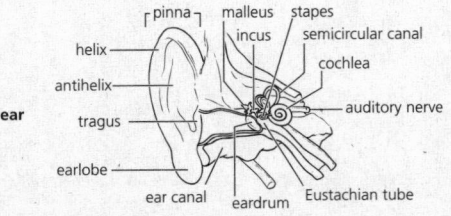

ear

Earp (ûrp), *n.* **Wyatt (Berry Stapp),** 1848–1929, U.S. law officer.

ear·phone (ēr′fōn′), *n.* **1.** a sound receiver, as of a radio or telephone, that fits in or over the ear. **2.** Usu., **earphones.** a headset.

ear·piece (ēr′pēs′), *n.* **1.** a piece that covers or passes over the ear, as on a cap or eyeglasses. **2.** an earphone.

ear·plug (ēr′plug′), *n.* a plug of soft, pliable material inserted into the opening of the outer ear, esp. to keep out water or noise.

ear·ring (ēr′ring′, ēr′ing), *n.* an ornament worn on or hanging from the lobe of the ear. —**ear′ringed,** *adj.*

ear·shot (ēr′shot′), *n.* the range or distance within which a sound, voice, etc., can be heard.

ear·split·ting (ēr′split′ing), *adj.* extremely loud or shrill in sound.

earth (ûrth), *n.* **1.** (*often cap.*) the planet third in order from the sun, having an equatorial diameter of 7926 mi. (12,755 km), a mean distance from the sun of 92.9 million mi. (149.6 million km), and a period of revolution of 365.26 days, and having one moon. **2.** the inhabitants of this planet: *The whole earth rejoiced.* **3.** this planet as the habitation of humans, often in contrast to heaven and hell. **4.** the surface of this planet: *to fall to earth.* **5.** the solid matter of this planet; dry land; ground. **6.** soil and dirt, as distinguished from rock and sand. **7.** the hole of a burrowing animal; lair. **8.** any of several metallic oxides that are difficult to reduce, as alumina, zirconia, and yttria. —*Idiom.* **9. on earth,** (used as an intensifier after interrogative pronouns): *Where on earth have you been?* **10. run to earth, a.** to chase (an animal) into its hole or burrow in hunting. **b.** to search out; track down.

earth·bound¹ (ûrth′bound′), *adj.* **1.** firmly set in or attached to the earth. **2.** limited to the earth or its surface. **3.** having only earthly interests. **4.** lacking in imaginative or distinctive quality: *earthbound prose.*

earth·bound² (ûrth′bound′), *adj.* headed for the earth: *an earthbound meteor.*

earth·en (ûr′thən), *adj.* **1.** composed of earth. **2.** made of baked clay. **3.** earthly; worldly.

earth·en·ware (ûr′thən wâr′), *n.* **1.** pottery of baked or hardened clay, esp. any of the coarse, opaque varieties. **2.** clay for making such pottery.

earth·ling (ûrth′ling), *n.* an inhabitant of earth; mortal.

earth′ lodge′ or **earth′lodge′,** *n.* a usu. dome-shaped dwelling of certain North American Indians, made of posts and beams covered with earth, grass, sod, etc., and having a central roof opening.

earth·ly (ûrth′lē), *adj.,* **-li·er, -li·est. 1.** of or pertaining to the earth, esp. as opposed to heaven; worldly. **2.** possible or conceivable: *an invention of no earthly use to anyone.* —**earth′li·ness,** *n.*

Earth′ly Par′adise, *n.* a paradise that, according to a popular medieval belief, existed somewhere on earth.

earth′ moth′er, *n.* (*often caps.*) **1.** the earth conceived of as the female principle of fertility and the source of all life. **2.** a female spirit or deity serving as a symbol of life or fertility. **3.** a sensuous, maternal woman.

earth·mov·er (ûrth′mōō′vər), *n.* a vehicle, as a bulldozer, for pushing or carrying excavated earth from place to place. —**earth′mov′ing,** *adj.*

earth·nut (ûrth′nut′), *n.* any of various roots, tubers, or underground growths, as the peanut or the truffle.

earth·quake (ûrth′kwāk′), *n.* **1.** a series of vibrations induced in the earth's crust by the abrupt rupture and rebound of rocks in which elastic strain has been slowly accumulating. **2.** something that is severely disruptive; upheaval.

earth·rise (ûrth′rīz′), *n.* the rising of the earth above the horizon of the moon or other celestial body.

earth′ sci′ence, *n.* any of various sciences, as geography, geology, or meteorology, that deal with the earth. Also called **geoscience.** —**earth′ sci′entist,** *n.*

earth·shak·ing (ûrth′shā′king), *adj.* imperiling, challenging, or significantly affecting basic beliefs, attitudes, relationships, etc. —**earth′shak′er,** *n.* —**earth′shak′ing·ly,** *adv.*

earth′-shat′tering, *adj.* EARTHSHAKING.

earth·shine (ûrth′shīn′), *n.* the faint illumination of the part of the moon not illuminated by sunlight, as during a crescent phase, caused by the reflection of light from the earth.

earth·star (ûrth′stär′), *n.* a fungus of the genus *Geaster,* having an outer covering that splits into the form of a star.

earth′ sta′tion, *n.* a facility equipped to receive, or receive and transmit, signals from or to communications satellites.

earth′ tone′, *n.* any of various warm, muted colors ranging from neutral to deep brown.

earth·ward (ûrth′wərd), *adv.* **1.** Also, **earth′wards.** toward the earth. —*adj.* **2.** directed toward the earth.

earth·work (ûrth′wûrk′), *n.* **1.** excavation and piling of earth in an engineering operation. **2.** a military construction formed chiefly of earth. **3.** an artistic work that consists of a large-scale modification of an area of land by an artist.

earth·worm (ûrth′wûrm′), *n.* any annelid worm that burrows in soil, esp. a worm of the genus *Lumbricus.*

earth·y (ûr′thē), *adj.,* **earth·i·er, earth·i·est. 1.** of the nature of or consisting of earth or soil. **2.** characteristic of earth: *an earthy smell.* **3.** realistic; practical. **4.** coarse or unrefined: *an earthy sense of humor.* **5.** robust; unaffected. —**earth′i·ness,** *n.*

ear′ trum′pet, *n.* a trumpet-shaped device held to the ear for amplifying sounds, formerly used as an aid to hearing.

ear·wax (ēr′waks′), *n.* a yellowish, waxlike secretion from certain glands in the external auditory canal; cerumen.

ear·wig (ēr′wig′), *n., v.,* **-wigged, -wig·ging.** —*n.* **1.** any of numerous dark and slender nocturnal insects of the order Dermaptera, having horny pincers at the rear that can rise up like a scorpion's. —*v.t.* **2.** to fill the mind of with prejudice by insinuations.

ease (ēz), *n., v.,* **eased, eas·ing.** —*n.* **1.** freedom from labor, pain, or physical annoyance; relaxation or comfort: *to enjoy one's ease.* **2.** freedom from concern, anxiety, or solicitude: *to be at ease about one's health.* **3.** freedom from difficulty; facility: *It can be done with ease.* **4.** freedom from financial need; plenty: *a life of ease.* **5.** freedom from stiffness, constraint, or formality; unaffectedness. —*v.t.* **6.** to free from anxiety or care: *to ease one's mind.* **7.** to mitigate, lighten, or lessen: *to ease pain.* **8.** to release from pressure or tension. **9.** to move or shift with great care: *to ease a car into a narrow parking space.* **10.** to render less difficult; facilitate. **11. a.** to bring (the helm or rudder of a vessel) slowly amidships. **b.** to bring the head of (a vessel) into the wind. —*v.i.* **12.** to abate in severity, pressure, tension, etc. (often fol. by *off* or *up*). **13.** to become less painful, burdensome, etc. **14.** to move, or be moved, with great care. **15. ease out,** to prevail upon tactfully to leave a job, etc. —*Idiom.* **16. at ease,** a position of rest in which soldiers standing in formation may relax but may not leave their places or talk.

ea·sel (ē′zəl), *n.* **1.** a stand or frame for supporting or displaying at an angle an artist's canvas, a blackboard, etc. **2.** a frame, often with adjustable masks, used to hold photographic paper flat and control borders when printing enlargements. —**ea′seled,** *adj.*

ease·ment (ēz′mənt), *n.* **1.** a right held by one property owner to make use of the land of another for a limited purpose, as right of passage. **2.** an easing; relief. **3.** something that gives ease; convenience.

eas·i·er (ē′zē ər), *adj.* comparative of EASY.

eas·i·est (ē′zē ist), *adj.* superlative of EASY.

eas·i·ly (ē′zə lē, ēz′lē), *adv.* **1.** in an easy manner; with ease; without trouble. **2.** beyond question; by far: *easily the best.* **3.** likely; well: *He may easily change his mind.*

eas·i·ness (ē′zē nis), *n.* **1.** the quality or condition of being easy. **2.** ease of manner.

east (ēst), *n.* **1.** a cardinal point of the compass, 90° to the right of north. *Abbr:* E **2.** the direction in which this point lies. **3.** (*usu. cap.*) a region or territory situated in this direction. **4. the East, a.** the continent of Asia and nearby islands; the Orient. **b.** the Far East. **c.** (formerly) the Soviet Union and its allies. **d.** the part of the U.S. east of the Mississippi River. **e.** the part of the U.S. east of the Allegheny Mountains, from Maryland to Maine. —*adj.* **5.** directed or proceeding toward the east. **6.** coming from the east: *an east wind.* **7.** lying toward or situated in the east: *the east side.* —*adv.* **8.** to, toward, or in the east: *heading east.*

East′ Bengal′, *n.* a part of the former Indian province of Bengal: now coextensive with Bangladesh. Compare BENGAL (def. 1).

east·bound (ēst′bound′), *adj.* proceeding or headed east: *an eastbound train.*

east′ by north′, *n.* a point on the compass 11°15′ north of east. *Abbr.:* EbN

east′ by south′, *n.* a point on the compass 11°15′ south of east. *Abbr.:* EbS

Eas·ter (ē′stər), *n.* an annual Christian festival in commemoration of the resurrection of Jesus Christ, observed on the first Sunday after the first full moon after the vernal equinox.

Eas′ter egg′, *n.* **1.** a dyed or painted hen's egg used as an Easter gift or decoration. **2.** an imitation of this, as an egg-shaped candy.

Eas′ter Is′land, *n.* an island in the S Pacific, ab. 2000 mi. (3180 km) W of and belonging to Chile: gigantic statues. 1867; ab. 45 sq. mi. (117 sq. km). Also called **Rapa Nui.** Spanish, **Isla de Pascua.**

Eas′ter lil′y, *n.* any of several white-flowered lilies that are artificially brought into bloom in early spring, esp. *Lilium longiflorum.*

east·er·ly (ē′stər lē), *adj., adv., n., pl.* **-lies.** —*adj.* **1.** moving, directed, or situated toward the east. **2.** (esp. of a wind) coming from the east. —*adv.* **3.** toward the east. **4.** from the east. —*n.* **5.** a wind that blows from the east. —**east′er·li·ness,** *n.*

Eas′ter Mon′day, *n.* the day after Easter, observed as a holiday in some places.

east·ern (ē′stərn), *adj.* **1.** lying toward or situated in the east. **2.** directed or proceeding toward the east. **3.** coming from the east: *an eastern wind.* **4.** (*often cap.*) of or pertaining to the East in the U.S. **5.** (*cap.*) of or pertaining to the Eastern Church or to any of the churches constituting it. **6.** (*usu. cap.*) of or pertaining to the East; Oriental. **7.** (*usu. cap.*) (formerly) of or pertaining to the Soviet Union and its allies.

East′ern Church′, *n.* **1.** any of the churches originating in countries formerly part of the Eastern Roman Empire, observing an Eastern rite and adhering to the Nicene Creed; Byzantine Church. **2.** ORTHODOX CHURCH (def. 2).

east·ern·er (ē′stər nər), *n.* (*often cap.*) a native or inhabitant of an eastern area, esp. the eastern U.S.

East′ern Estab′lishment, *n.* Americans living on the East Coast, esp. New Yorkers prominent in the legal, financial, and communications industries, and considered to have national political influence.

East′ern Hem′isphere, *n.* **1.** the part of the globe east of the Atlantic, including Asia, Africa, Australia, and Europe, their islands, and surrounding waters. **2.** that half of the earth traversed in passing eastward from the prime meridian to 180° longitude.
east•ern•ize (ē′stər nīz′), *v.t.*, **-ized, -iz•ing.** to influence with eastern ideas, customs, or practices. —**east′ern•i•za′tion,** *n.*
East′ern Or′thodox, *adj.* of or pertaining to the Orthodox Church.
East′ern Or′thodox Church′, *n.* ORTHODOX CHURCH (def. 1).
East′ern time′, *n.* See under STANDARD TIME. Also called **East′ern Stand′ard Time′.**
East′ In′dies, *n.pl.* (esp. formerly) **1.** the Malay Archipelago. **2.** SE Asia, including India, Indonesia, and the Malay Archipelago. Also called **East′ In′dia.** —**East′ In′dian,** *adj., n.*
East•man (ēst′mən), *n.* **George,** 1854–1932, U.S. philanthropist and inventor in the field of photography.
east′-northeast′, *n.* **1.** the point on a compass midway between east and northeast. —*adj.* **2.** coming from this point, as a wind. **3.** directed toward this point. —*adv.* **4.** toward this point. *Abbr.*: ENE
East′ Prus′sia, *n.* a former province in NE Germany: separated from Germany by the Polish Corridor; now divided between Poland and the Russian Federation. *Cap.*: Königsberg. —**East′ Prus′sian,** *adj., n.*
East′ Slav′ic, *n.* the branch of Slavic that includes Ukrainian, Belorussian, and Russian.
east′-southeast′, *n.* **1.** the point on a compass midway between east and southeast. —*adj.* **2.** coming from this point, as a wind. **3.** directed toward this point. —*adv.* **4.** toward this point. *Abbr.*: ESE
east•ward (ēst′wərd), *adv.* **1.** Also, **east′wards.** toward the east. —*adj.* **2.** moving, bearing, facing, or situated toward the east. —*n.* **3.** an eastward part, direction, or point. —**east′ward•ly,** *adj., adv.*
East•wood (ēst′wo͝od′), *n.* **Clint,** born 1930, U.S. actor and director.
eas•y (ē′zē), *adj.* and *adv.*, **eas•i•er, eas•i•est.** —*adj.* **1.** requiring no great effort; not difficult. **2.** free from pain, discomfort, worry, or care: *an easy mind.* **3.** providing or conducive to ease or comfort. **4.** easygoing; relaxed: *an easy disposition.* **5.** not harsh or strict; lenient. **6.** not burdensome or oppressive: *easy terms on a loan.* **7.** not difficult to influence or overcome; compliant: *easy prey.* **8.** free from formality or constraint: *an easy manner.* **9.** effortlessly clear and fluent: *an easy style of writing.* **10.** not constricting: *an easy fit.* **11.** not forced; moderate: *an easy pace.* **12.** not steep; gradual. **13.** not difficult to obtain; in plentiful supply and often weak in price. —*adv.* **14.** in an easy manner; easily; comfortably. —***Idiom.*** **15. easy come, easy go,** what is acquired without effort is just as easily lost. **16. take it** or **go easy on, a.** to act with moderation in using or consuming: *Take it easy on the popcorn.* **b.** to treat with clemency: *to go easy on a prisoner.*
eas′y chair′, *n.* an upholstered armchair for lounging.
eas•y•go•ing (ē′zē gō′ing), *adj.* **1.** not easily worried or angered; relaxed and rather casual; calm. **2.** unhurried.
eas′y mark′, *n.* one who is easily deceived or tricked.
eas′y street′, *n.* a state of wealth, financial independence, or ease.
eat (ēt), *v.*, **ate** (āt; *esp. Brit.* et), **eat•en** (ēt′n), **eat•ing,** *n.* —*v.t.* **1.** to take into the mouth and swallow for nourishment; chew and swallow (food). **2.** to consume gradually; wear away; corrode. **3.** to use up, esp. wastefully (often fol. by *away, into,* or *up*): *Unexpected expenses ate up their savings.* **4.** to make (a hole, passage, etc.), as by gnawing or corrosion. **5.** to ravage or devastate. **6.** to absorb or pay for: *The builder had to eat the cost of the repairs.* **7.** to cause anxiety or irritation in; worry; bother: *What's eating you now?* —*v.i.* **8.** to consume food; have a meal. **9.** to make a way, as by gnawing or corrosion: *Acid ate through the linoleum.* **10. eat in,** to eat or dine at home. **11. eat out,** to have a meal at a restaurant rather than at home. **12. eat up, a.** to consume wholly. **b.** to show enthusiasm for; take pleasure in. **c.** to believe without question. —***Idiom.*** **13. eat someone out of house and home,** to eat so much as to strain someone's resources of food or money. —***Proverb.*** **14. Eat, drink, and be merry,** enjoy life to the fullest. Is. 22:13; Eccl. 8:15. —**eat′a•ble,** *adj.* —**eat′er,** *n.*
eat•er•y (ē′tə rē), *n., pl.* **-er•ies.** *Informal.* a restaurant or other commercial establishment serving food.
eau de Co•logne (ō′ də kə lōn′), *n.* COLOGNE.
eau de toi•lette (ō′ də twä let′), *n.* TOILET WATER.
eave (ēv), *n.* Usu., **eaves.** the overhanging lower edge of a roof.
eaves•drop (ēvz′drop′), *v.i.*, **-dropped, -drop•ping.** to listen secretly to a private conversation. —**eaves′drop′per,** *n.*
E•bal (ē′bəl), *n.* a mountaintop altar set up by Moses and used by Joshua and other leaders of Israel. Deut. 27:4–5; Josh. 8:30.
ebb (eb), *n.* **1.** the flowing back of the tide as the water returns to the sea (opposed to *flood, flow*). **2.** a flowing backward or away; decline or decay. **3.** a point or state of decline: *His fortunes were at a low ebb.* —*v.i.* **4.** to flow back or away, as the water of a tide (opposed to *flow*). **5.** to decline or decay; fade away.
E•bed-Me•lech (ē′bed mē′lek), *n.* an Ethiopian who rescued the prophet Jeremiah from a cistern into which his enemies had thrown him. Jer. 38:7–13.
eb•on•y (eb′ə nē), *n., pl.* **-on•ies,** *adj.* —*n.* **1.** a hard, heavy, durable, dark wood from tropical trees of the African and Asian genus *Diospyros,* of the ebony family, used for cabinetry, ornamental objects, etc. **2.** any tree yielding such wood. **3.** a deep, lustrous black. —*adj.* **4.** made of ebony. **5.** of a deep, lustrous black.
e•bul•lient (i bul′yənt, i bo͝ol′-), *adj.* **1.** overflowing with enthusiasm, excitement, or vivacity; high-spirited; exuberant. **2.** bubbling up like a boiling liquid. —**e•bul′lience,** *n.* —**e•bul′lient•ly,** *adv.*
EC, European Community.
ec•ce ho•mo (ech′ā hō′mō, ek′ā *for 1;* ek′sē hō′mō, ek′ā *for 2*), *Latin.* **1.** "Behold the man!": the words with which Pilate presented Christ, crowned with thorns, to his accusers. John 19:5. —*n.* **2.** a painting, statue, or other representation of Christ crowned with thorns.
ec•cen•tric (ik sen′trik, ek-), *adj.* **1.** deviating from the accepted or customary character, practice, etc.; unconventional; peculiar; odd. **2.** not having the same center: used esp. of two circles or spheres at least one of which contains the centers of both. **3.** (of an axis, axle, etc.) not situated in the center. **4.** having the axis or support away from the center: *an eccentric wheel.* **5.** *Astron.* deviating from a circular form, as an elliptic orbit. —*n.* **6.** an eccentric person. **7.** something that is unusual, peculiar, or odd. **8.** a device for converting rotary motion to reciprocating motion, consisting of a disk with an off-center axis of revolution. —**ec•cen′tri•cal•ly,** *adv.*
ec•cen•tric•i•ty (ek′sən tris′i tē, ek′sen-), *n., pl.* **-ties.** **1.** an oddity or peculiarity, as of conduct. **2.** the quality of being eccentric. **3.** the amount by which something is eccentric. **4.** a mathematical constant expressed as the ratio of the distance from a point on a conic to a focus and the distance from the point to the directrix.
Eccl. or **Eccles.,** Ecclesiastes.
eccl. or **eccles.,** **1.** ecclesiastic. **2.** ecclesiastical.
ec•cle•si•a (i klē′zhē ə, -zē ə), *n., pl.* **-si•ae** (-zhē ē′, -zē ē′). **1.** an assembly, esp. the popular assembly of ancient Athens. **2.** a congregation; church. [< Latin < Greek *ekklēsía* assembly]
Ec•cle•si•as•tes (i klē′zē as′tēz), *n.* a book of the Bible, containing thoughts about life and its meaning. [Late Latin < Greek *ekklēsiastḗs* person addressing an assembly, der. of *ekklēsía* ECCLESIA]
ec•cle•si•as•tic (i klē′zē as′tik), *n.* **1.** a member of the clergy or other person in religious orders. —*adj.* **2.** ecclesiastical.
ec•cle•si•as•ti•cal (i klē′zē as′ti kəl), *adj.* of or pertaining to the church or the clergy; churchly; clerical; not secular.
Ec•cle•si•as•ti•cus (i klē′zē as′ti kəs), *n.* a book of the Apocrypha. Also called **Wisdom of Jesus, Son of Sirach.**
ec•crine (ek′rin, -rīn, -rēn), *adj.* of or pertaining to certain sweat glands, distributed over the entire body, that secrete a type of sweat important for regulating body heat (disting. from *apocrine*).
ec•dy•sis (ek′də sis), *n., pl.* **-ses** (-sēz′). the shedding or casting off of an outer coat or integument by snakes, crustaceans, etc. —**ec•dys′i•al** (-diz′ē əl, -dizh′əl), *adj.*
ECG, 1. electrocardiogram. **2.** electrocardiograph.
ech•e•lon (esh′ə lon′), *n.* **1.** a level of command, authority, or rank. **2.** a stepped formation, as of troops, ships, or planes, in which individuals or elements are arranged in parallel lines, each to the right or left of the one in front. **3.** one of the groups of a formation so arranged. —*v.t., v.i.* **4.** to form in an echelon.
ech•e•ve•ri•a (ech′ə və rē′ə), *n., pl.* **-ri•as.** any tropical American succulent plant of the genus *Echeveria,* having thick leaves that form rosettes.
e•chid•na (i kid′nə), *n., pl.* **-nas.** any long-snouted, spiny, insectivorous monotreme of the family Tachyglossidae, of Australia, Tasmania, and New Guinea. Also called **spiny anteater.**
e•chi•no•derm (i kī′nə dûrm′, ek′ə nə-), *n.* any marine invertebrate animal of the phylum Echinodermata, including starfishes, sea urchins, sea cucumbers, and sea lilies, characterized by a five-part radially symmetrical body and a calcareous endoskeleton.
e•chi•noid (i kī′noid, ek′ə noid′), *n.* **1.** any echinoderm of the class Echinoidea, comprising sea urchins and sand dollars, characterized by a rounded body and a rigid endoskeleton with movable spines. —*adj.* **2.** of, belonging to, or resembling the echinoids.
e•chi•nus (i kī′nəs), *n., pl.* **-ni** (-nī). **1.** SEA URCHIN. **2. a.** the prominent convex circular molding supporting the abacus of the capital of a Doric column. **b.** any similar ovolo molding, often carved with an egg-and-dart pattern, as one on an Ionic capital.
ech•o (ek′ō), *n., pl.* **ech•oes,** *v.*, **ech•oed, ech•o•ing.** —*n.* **1.** a repetition of sound produced by the reflection of sound waves from a wall, mountain, or other obstructing surface. **2.** a sound heard again near its source after being reflected. **3.** any repetition or close imitation, as of the ideas or words of another. **4.** a person who reflects or imitates another. **5.** a sympathetic or identical response, as to sentiments expressed. **6.** a lingering trace or effect. **7.** the reflection of a radio wave. —*v.i.* **8.** to emit an echo; resound with an echo: *The hall echoed with cheers.* **9.** to be repeated by or as if by an echo. —*v.t.* **10.** to repeat by or as if by an echo. **11.** to repeat or imitate the words, sentiments, etc., of (a person). **12.** to repeat or imitate (words, sentiments, etc.).
ech′o cham′ber, *n.* a room or studio with resonant walls for broadcasting or recording echoes or hollow sound effects.
ech•o•la•li•a (ek′ō lā′lē ə), *n.* the uncontrollable and immediate repetition of words spoken by another person, esp. as associated with mental disorder. —**ech′o•lal′ic** (-lal′ik, -lā′lik), *adj.*
ech•o•lo•ca•tion (ek′ō lō kā′shən), *n.* **1.** a method of locating objects by determining the time for an echo to return and the direction from which it returns, as by radar or sonar. **2.** the sonarlike system used by dolphins, bats, and other animals to detect objects by emitting usu.

high-pitched sounds that reflect off the object and return to the ears or other sensory receptors.

Eck·hart (ek′ärt), *n.* **Johannes,** (*"Meister Eckhart"*), c1260–1327?, Dominican theologian: founder of German mysticism.

é·clair (ā klâr′, i klâr′, ā′klâr), *n.* an elongated cream puff, filled with custard or whipped cream and usu. iced. [< French: lit., lightning]

ec·lamp·si·a (i klamp′sē ə), *n.* a form of toxemia of pregnancy, characterized by hypertension and convulsions.

é·clat (ā klä′), *n.* **1.** brilliance of success, reputation, etc. **2.** showy or elaborate display. **3.** acclamation; acclaim. [< French]

ec·lec·tic (i klek′tik), *adj.* **1.** selecting or choosing from various systems, methodologies, etc.; not following any one system. **2.** made up of elements selected from various sources: *an eclectic philosophy.* —*n.* **3.** Also, **ec·lec·ti·cist** (i klek′tə sist). a person who follows an eclectic method or mode. —**ec·lec′ti·cal·ly,** *adv.*

ec·lec·ti·cism (i klek′tə siz′əm), *n.* **1.** the use or advocacy of an eclectic method. **2.** an eclectic method or movement.

e·clipse (i klips′), *n., v.,* **e·clipsed, e·clips·ing.** —*n.* **1.** the obscuration of the light of the moon by the intervention of the earth between it and the sun **(lunar eclipse)** or the obscuration of the light of the sun by the intervention of the moon between it and a point on the earth **(solar eclipse). 2.** any obscuration of light. **3.** a reduction or loss of splendor, status, or reputation. —*v.t.* **4.** to cause to undergo eclipse: *The moon eclipsed the sun.* **5.** to make less outstanding or important by comparison; surpass. —**e·clips′er,** *n.*

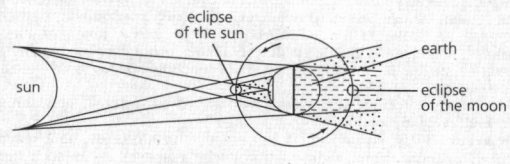

eclipse
of the sun

earth

sun

eclipse
of the moon

eclipse (def. 1a)

e·clip·tic (i klip′tik), *n.* **1.** the great circle formed by the intersection of the plane of the earth's orbit with the celestial sphere; the apparent annual path of the sun in the heavens. **2.** an analogous great circle on a terrestrial globe. —*adj.* Also, **e·clip′ti·cal. 3.** of or pertaining to an eclipse. **4.** of or pertaining to the ecliptic. —**e·clip′ti·cal·ly,** *adv.*

ec·logue (ek′lôg, -log), *n.* a pastoral poem, often in dialogue form.

ec·clo·sion (i klō′zhən), *n.* **1.** the emergence of an adult insect from its pupal case. **2.** the hatching of a larva from its egg.

ec·o·ca·tas·tro·phe (ek′ō kə tas′trə fē, ē′kō-), *n.* a widespread disaster caused by detrimental changes in the environment.

ec·o·cide (ek′ə sīd′, ē′kə-), *n.* the destruction of large areas of the natural environment by such activity as overexploitation of resources or dumping of harmful chemicals. —**ec′o·ci′dal,** *adj.*

e·col·o·gy (i kol′ə jē), *n.* **1.** the branch of biology dealing with the relations and interactions between organisms and their environment. **2.** the set of relationships existing between organisms and their environment. **3.** Also called **human ecology.** the branch of sociology concerned with the spacing and interdependence of people and institutions. **4.** the advocacy of protection of the air, water, and other natural resources from pollution or its effects; environmentalism. —**ec·o·log·i·cal** (ek′ə loj′i kəl, ē′kə-), **ec′o·log′ic,** *adj.* —**ec′o·log′i·cal·ly,** *adv.* —**e·col′o·gist,** *n.*

e·con·o·met·rics (i kon′ə me′triks), *n.* (*used with a sing. v.*) the application of statistical techniques to solving problems and testing theories in economics. —**e·con′o·met′ric, e·con′o·met′ri·cal,** *adj.* —**e·con′o·me·tri′cian** (-mi trish′ən), **e·con′o·met′rist,** *n.*

ec·o·nom·ic (ek′ə nom′ik, ē′kə-), *adj.* **1.** of or pertaining to the production, distribution, and use of income, wealth, and commodities. **2.** of or pertaining to the science of economics. **3.** involving one's personal resources of money. **4.** pertaining to use as a resource in the economy: *economic botany.* **5.** affecting or apt to affect the welfare of material resources: *weevils and other economic pests.* **6.** ECONOMICAL (def. 1).

ec·o·nom·i·cal (ek′ə nom′i kəl, ē′kə-), *adj.* **1.** avoiding waste or extravagance; involving the efficient use of wealth or resources; thrifty: *an economical meal; an economical use of space.* **2.** economic; pertaining to economics. —**ec′o·nom′i·cal·ly,** *adv.*

ec′onom′ic rent′, *n.* the return on a productive resource, as land or labor, that is greater than the amount necessary to keep the resource producing.

ec·o·nom·ics (ek′ə nom′iks, ē′kə-), *n.* **1.** (*used with a sing. v.*) the science that deals with the production, distribution, and consumption of goods and services, or human welfare. **2.** (*used with a pl. v.*) financial considerations; economically significant aspects.

e·con·o·mist (i kon′ə mist), *n.* a specialist in economics.

e·con·o·mize (i kon′ə mīz′), *v.,* **-mized, -miz·ing.** —*v.i.* **1.** to practice economy; avoid waste or extravagance. —*v.t.* **2.** to manage economically; use sparingly or frugally. —**e·con′o·miz′er,** *n.*

e·con·o·my (i kon′ə mē), *n., pl.* **-mies,** *adj.* —*n.* **1.** thrifty management; frugality in the expenditure or consumption of money, materials, etc. **2.** an act or means of thrifty saving: *Walking to work is one of my*

economies. **3.** the management of the resources of a community, country, etc., esp. with a view to its productivity. **4.** the prosperity or earnings of a place: *Inflation imperils the nation's economy.* **5.** the disposition or regulation of the parts or functions of any organic whole; an organized system. **6.** the efficient or sparing use of something: *economy of motion.* —*adj.* **7.** intended to save money: *an economy move.* **8.** costing less to make, buy, or operate: *an economy car.*

econ′omy class′, *n.* a low-priced class of travel accommodations, esp. on an airplane. —**econ′omy-class′,** *adj.*

econ′omy of scale′, *n.* the reduction in unit cost achieved by manufacturing an item on a large scale.

ec·o·sphere (ek′ō sfēr′, ē′kō-), *n.* **1.** the part of the atmosphere, from sea level to about 13,000 ft. (4000 m) above, in which it is possible to breathe normally without aid. **2.** BIOSPHERE.

ec·o·sys·tem (ek′ō sis′təm, ē′kō-), *n.* a system formed by the interaction of a community of organisms with its environment.

ec·o·type (ek′ə tīp′, ē′kə-), *n.* a subspecies or race that is esp. adapted to a particular set of environmental conditions. —**ec′o·typ′ic** (-tip′ik), *adj.* —**ec′o·typ′i·cal·ly,** *adv.*

ec·ru or **éc·ru** (ek′rōō, ā′krōō), *adj.* **1.** very light brown in color; beige. —*n.* **2.** an ecru color.

ec·sta·sy (ek′stə sē), *n., pl.* **-sies. 1.** rapturous delight. **2.** an overpowering emotion or exaltation; a state of sudden, intense feeling. **3.** the frenzy of poetic inspiration. **4.** mental transport or rapture from the contemplation of divine things. —**ec·stat·ic** (ek stat′ik), *adj.*

ec·to·derm (ek′tə dûrm′), *n.* the outer germ layer in the embryo of a metazoan. —**ec′to·der′mal, ec′to·der′mic,** *adj.*

ec·to·gen·e·sis (ek′tō jen′ə sis), *n.* development outside the body, as of an embryo in an artificial environment. —**ec′to·ge·net′ic** (-jə net′ik), *adj.*

ec·to·morph (ek′tə môrf′), *n.* a person of the ectomorphic type.

ec·to·mor·phic (ek′tə môr′fik), *adj.* having a thin body build, roughly characterized by the relative prominence of structures developed from the embryonic ectoderm (contrasted with *endomorphic, mesomorphic*). —**ec′to·morph′y,** *n.*

-ectomy, a combining form meaning "excision" of the organ or tissue specified by the initial element: *tonsillectomy.*

ectop′ic preg′nancy, *n.* the development of a fertilized ovum outside the uterus, as in a Fallopian tube.

ec·to·plasm (ek′tə plaz′əm), *n.* **1.** the outer portion of the cytoplasm of a cell. **2.** a viscous substance claimed by spiritualists to emanate from the body of a medium and then produce living forms. —**ec′to·plas′mic, ec′to·plas·mat′ic** (-mat′ik), *adj.*

ECU (ā kōō′ *or, sometimes,* ē′sē′yōō′), *n., pl.* **ECU's, ECUs.** a money of account of the European Economic Community.

Ec·ua·dor (ek′wə dôr′), *n.* a republic in NW South America. 11,690,535; 109,483 sq. mi. (283,561 sq. km). *Cap.:* Quito. —**Ec′ua·do′ran, Ec′ua·do′re·an, Ec′ua·do′ri·an,** *adj., n.*

ec·u·men·i·cal (ek′yōō men′i kəl; *esp. Brit.* ē′kyōō-) also **ec·u·men·ic,** *adj.* **1.** general; universal; worldwide. **2.** of or pertaining to the whole Christian church. **3.** promoting or fostering Christian unity throughout the world. **4.** interreligious or interdenominational. **5.** involving or containing a mixture of diverse, esp. international, elements. —**ec′u·men′i·cal·ly,** *adv.*

ec′umen′ical coun′cil or **Ec′umen′ical Coun′cil,** *n.* a solemn assembly in the Roman Catholic Church, convoked and presided over by the pope and composed of cardinals, bishops, and certain other prelates whose decrees, when confirmed by the pope, become binding.

ecumen′ical pa′triarch, *n.* the patriarch of Constantinople, the highest dignitary of the Greek Orthodox Church.

ec·u·me·nism (ek′yōō mə niz′əm, i kyōō′-; *esp. Brit.* ē′kyōō-), *n.* ecumenical principles, esp. as manifested in a movement promoting cooperation and unity among religious groups. —**ec′u·me·nist,** *n.*

ec·ze·ma (ek′sə mə, eg′zə-, ig zē′-), *n.* an inflammatory condition of the skin accompanied by itching and the exudation of serous matter. —**ec·zem′a·tous** (ig zem′ə təs, -zē′mə-), *adj.*

ed (ed), *n.* education: *driver's ed.*

ED, Department of Education.

ed., **1.** edited. **2.** *pl.* **eds.** edition. **3.** *pl.* **eds.** editor. **4.** education.

e·da·cious (i dā′shəs), *adj.* devouring; voracious; consuming.

e·dac·i·ty (i das′i tē), *n.* the state of being edacious; voraciousness; appetite.

E·dam (ē′dəm, ē′dam), *n.* a mild, hard, yellow cheese, produced in a round shape and coated with red wax.

ed·dy (ed′ē), *n., pl.* **-dies,** *v.,* **-died, -dy·ing.** —*n.* **1.** a current at variance with the main current in a stream of liquid or gas, esp. one having a rotary or whirling motion. **2.** a small whirlpool. **3.** any similar current, as of air, dust, or fog. **4.** a current or trend, as of opinion or events, running counter to the main current. —*v.t., v.i.* **5.** to move or whirl in eddies.

Ed·dy (ed′ē), *n.* **Mary (Morse) Baker** (*Mrs. Glover; Mrs. Patterson*), 1821–1910, U.S. founder of the Christian Science Church.

e·del·weiss (ād′l vīs′, -wīs′), *n.* a small composite plant, *Leontopodium alpinum,* having white woolly leaves and flowers, growing in the high altitudes of the Alps.

e·de·ma (i dē′mə), *n., pl.* **-mas, -ma·ta** (-mə tə). **1.** an abnormal accumulation of fluid in the tissue spaces, cavities, or joint capsules of the body, causing swelling of the area. **2.** a similar swelling in plants caused by excessive moisture.

E•den (ēd′n), *n.* **1.** Also called **Garden of Eden.** the place where Adam and Eve lived before the Fall. Gen. 2:8–24. **2.** any delightful region or abode; paradise. **3.** a state of perfect happiness; bliss. —**E•den•ic** (ē den′ik), *adj.*

e•den•tate (ē den′tāt), *adj.* **1.** belonging or pertaining to the Edentata, an order of New World mammals characterized by a reduced number of teeth and comprising armadillos, sloths, and anteaters. **2.** toothless. —*n.* **3.** an edentate mammal.

e•den•tu•lous (ē den′chə ləs), *adj.* lacking teeth; toothless.

E•des•sa (i des′ə), *n.* an ancient city in NW Mesopotamia, on the site of modern Urfa, in Turkey: an early center of Christianity.

edge (ej), *n., v.,* **edged, edg•ing.** —*n.* **1.** a line or border at which a surface terminates: *Grass grew along the edge of the road.* **2.** a brink or verge: *the edge of a cliff; the edge of disaster.* **3.** any of the narrow surfaces of a thin, flat object: *a book with gilt edges.* **4.** a line at which two surfaces of a solid object meet. **5.** the thin, sharp side of the blade of a cutting instrument or weapon. **6.** the sharpness proper to a blade: *The knife has lost its edge.* **7.** a quality of sharpness or keenness: *Her voice had an edge to it.* **8.** an improved position; advantage: *to have an edge on one's competitors.* **9.** (in cards) advantage, esp. the advantage gained by being on the dealer's left. —*v.t.* **10.** to provide with an edge or border. **11.** to put an edge on; sharpen. **12.** to make or force (one's way) gradually, esp. by moving sideways. —*v.i.* **13.** to move sideways. **14.** to advance gradually or cautiously: *a car edging up to the curb.* **15. edge in,** to work in or into, esp. in a limited period of time. **16. edge out,** to defeat (rivals or opponents) by a small margin. —*Idiom.* **17. on edge, a.** in a state of potential irritability; tense; nervous. **b.** eagerly impatient.

edged (ejd), *adj.* **1.** having an edge or edges (often used in combination): *a two-edged sword.* **2.** sarcastic; cutting: *an edged reply.*

edg•er (ej′ər), *n.* **1.** a person or thing that edges. **2.** a gardening tool for cutting a border around a lawn or flower bed.

edge•wise (ej′wīz′) also **edge•ways** (-wāz′), *adv.* **1.** with the edge forward; in the direction of the edge. **2.** sideways. —*Idiom.* **3. get a word in edgewise,** to succeed in participating in a conversation when someone else is constantly talking.

edg•ing (ej′ing), *n.* **1.** something that forms or is placed along an edge or border. **2.** the tilting of a ski to the side so that one edge cuts into the snow.

edg•y (ej′ē), *adj.,* **edg•i•er, edg•i•est.** **1.** nervously irritable; anxious; on edge. **2.** sharp-edged; sharply defined, as outlines. —**edg′i•ly,** *adv.* —**edg′i•ness,** *n.*

ed•i•ble (ed′ə bəl), *adj.* **1.** fit to be eaten as food; eatable. —*n.* **2.** Usu., **edibles.** edible substances; food. —**ed′i•bil′i•ty,** *n.*

e•dict (ē′dikt), *n.* **1.** a decree issued by a sovereign or other authority. **2.** any authoritative proclamation or command.

ed•i•fi•ca•tion (ed′ə fi kā′shən), *n.* **1.** an act of edifying. **2.** the state of being edified. **3.** moral improvement or guidance. —**e•dif•i•ca•to•ry** (i dif′i kə tôr′ē, -tōr′ē), *adj.*

ed•i•fice (ed′ə fis), *n.* **1.** a building, esp. one of large size or imposing appearance. **2.** any large, complex system or organization. —**ed′i•fi′cial** (-fish′əl), *adj.*

ed•i•fy (ed′ə fī), *v.t.,* **-fied, -fy•ing.** to instruct or benefit, esp. morally or spiritually; uplift; enlighten. —**ed′i•fi′er,** *n.* —**ed′i•fy′ing•ly,** *adv.*

Ed•in•burgh (ed′n bûr′ə, -bur′ə; *esp. Brit.* -brə), *n.* **1. Duke of,** PHILIP[1] (def. 3). **2.** the capital of Scotland, in the SE part, in the Lothian region. 470,085.

Ed•i•son (ed′ə sən), *n.* **1. Thomas Alva,** 1847–1931, U.S. inventor, esp. of electrical devices. **2.** a township in central New Jersey. 70,193.

ed•it (ed′it), *v.t.* **1.** to supervise or direct the preparation of (a publication); serve as editor of. **2.** to collect, prepare, and arrange (materials) for publication. **3.** to revise or correct, as a manuscript. **4.** to delete; eliminate (often fol. by *out*): *to edit out all references to his family.* **5.** to prepare (film, tape, etc.) by deleting, arranging, and splicing material. **6.** to alter the arrangement of (genes). **7.** to modify (computer data or text). —*n.* **8.** an instance or the process of editing. —**ed′it•a•ble,** *adj.*

e•di•tion (i dish′ən), *n.* **1.** one of a series of printings of a book, newspaper, etc., each issued at a different time and differing from another by alterations, additions, etc. **2.** the format in which a literary work is published: *a paperback edition.* **3.** the whole number of impressions or copies of a book, newspaper, etc., printed from one set of type at one time. **4.** a version, esp. of something presented to the public.

ed•i•tor (ed′i tər), *n.* **1.** a person responsible for the editorial part of a publishing firm or a publication. **2.** the supervisor of a department of a newspaper, magazine, etc. **3.** a person who edits material for publication, films, etc. **4.** a device for editing film or magnetic tape.

ed•i•to•ri•al (ed′i tôr′ē əl, -tōr′-), *n.* **1.** an article in a newspaper or other periodical presenting the opinion of the publishers or editors. **2.** a statement resembling this, as one broadcast on radio or television presenting the opinion of the station owners or managers. —*adj.* **3.** of or pertaining to an editor or editing. **4.** of, pertaining to, or resembling an editorial. —**ed′i•to′ri•al•ly,** *adv.*

ed•i•to•ri•al•ize (ed′i tôr′ē ə līz′, -tōr′-), *v.i.,* **-ized, -iz•ing.** **1.** to set forth one's position or opinion in or as if in an editorial. **2.** to inject personal interpretations or opinions into an otherwise factual account. —**ed′i•to′ri•al•i•za′tion,** *n.* —**ed′i•to′ri•al•iz′er,** *n.*

ed′itor in chief′, *n., pl.* **editors in chief.** the policy-making executive or principal editor of a publishing house, publication, or group of publications.

E•dom (ē′dəm), *n.* an ancient country between the Dead Sea and the Gulf of Aqaba, bordering ancient Palestine.

E•dom•ite (ē′də mīt′), *n.* a native or inhabitant of Edom, taken to be a descendant of Esau, or Edom, in the Bible. Gen. 36:9.

EDP, electronic data processing.

Ed•sel (ed′səl), *n.* **1.** an unpopular automobile produced by the Ford Motor Company between 1957 and 1962, named after the automaker Edsel Ford (1893–1943). **2.** *Informal.* any unpopular or untimely product.

EDT or **E.D.T.,** Eastern daylight-saving time.

ed•u•ca•ble (ej′o͝o kə bəl) also **ed•u•cat•a•ble** (-kā′tə bəl), *adj.* **1.** capable of being educated. **2.** of or designating mildly retarded individuals who may achieve self-sufficiency. —**ed′u•ca•bil′i•ty,** *n.*

ed•u•cate (ej′o͝o kāt′), *v.,* **-cat•ed, -cat•ing.** —*v.t.* **1.** to develop the faculties and powers of (a person) by instruction or schooling. **2.** to qualify by instruction or training for a particular calling or practice; train. **3.** to provide education for; send to school. **4.** to develop or train (the ear, taste, etc.). **5.** to impart knowledge to; provide with information: *to educate consumers.* —*v.i.* **6.** to educate a person or group.

ed•u•cat•ed (ej′o͝o kā′tid), *adj.* **1.** having undergone education. **2.** characterized by or displaying qualities of culture and learning. **3.** based on some information or experience: *an educated guess.*

ed•u•ca•tion (ej′o͝o kā′shən), *n.* **1.** the act or process of imparting or acquiring general knowledge and of developing the powers of reasoning and judgment. **2.** the act or process of imparting or acquiring particular knowledge or skills, as for a profession. **3.** a degree, level, or kind of schooling: *a college education.* **4.** the result produced by instruction, training, or study. **5.** the science or art of teaching; pedagogics. —**ed′u•ca′tion•al,** *adj.*

ed•u•ca•tive (ej′o͝o kā′tiv), *adj.* **1.** serving to educate. **2.** pertaining to or productive of education.

ed•u•ca•tor (ej′o͝o kā′tər), *n.* **1.** a person who educates, as a teacher, principal, or educational administrator. **2.** a specialist in educational theory and methods.

e•duce (i do͞os′, i dyo͞os′), *v.t.,* **e•duced, e•duc•ing.** **1.** to draw forth or bring out, as something potential or latent; elicit; develop. **2.** to infer or deduce. —**e•duc′i•ble,** *adj.* —**e•duc•tion** (i duk′shən), *n.*

Ed•ward[1] (ed′wərd), *n.* **1. Prince of Wales** and **Duke of Cornwall** (*"The Black Prince"*), 1330–76, English military leader (son of Edward III). **2. Lake,** a lake in central Africa, between Uganda and the Democratic Republic of the Congo: a source of the Nile. 830 sq. mi. (2150 sq. km).

Ed•ward[2] (ed′wərd), *n.* **1. Edward I,** (*"Edward Longshanks"*) 1239–1307, king of England 1272–1307 (son of Henry III). **2. Edward II,** 1284–1327, king of England 1307–27 (son of Edward I). **3. Edward III,** 1312–77, king of England 1327–77 (son of Edward II). **4. Edward IV,** 1442–83, king of England 1461–70, 1471–83: 1st king of the house of York. **5. Edward V,** 1470–83, king of England 1483 (son of Edward IV). **6. Edward VI,** 1537–53, king of England 1547–53 (son of Henry VIII and Jane Seymour). **7. Edward VII,** (*Albert Edward*) (*"the Peacemaker"*) 1841–1910, king of Great Britain and Ireland 1901–10 (son of Queen Victoria). **8. Edward VIII,** (*Duke of Windsor*) 1894–1972, king of Great Britain 1936: abdicated (son of George V; brother of George VI).

Ed•ward•i•an (ed wôr′dē ən, -wär′-), *adj.* **1.** of or pertaining to the reign of Edward VII or the styles of that period. **2.** reflecting the opulence characteristic of this reign. —*n.* **3.** a person who lived during the reign of Edward VII. —**Ed•ward′i•an•ism,** *n.*

Ed•wards (ed′wərdz), *n.* **Jonathan,** 1703–58, American theologian.

Ed′ward the Confes′sor, *n.* **Saint,** 1002?–66, English king 1042–66: founder of Westminster Abbey.

EEC, European Economic Community.

EEG, electroencephalogram.

eel (ēl), *n., pl.* (*esp. collectively*) **eel,** (*esp. for kinds or species*) **eels.** **1.** any of numerous elongated, snakelike marine or freshwater fishes of the order Apodes, having no ventral fins. **2.** any of several similar but unrelated fishes, as the lamprey.

eel•grass (ēl′gras′, -gräs′), *n.* a marine pondweed, *Zostera marina,* having ribbony, grasslike leaves.

eel•pout (ēl′pout′), *n.* **1.** any fish of the family Zoarcidae, esp. *Zoarces viviparus,* of Europe. **2.** BURBOT.

eel•worm (ēl′wûrm′), *n.* any small nematode worm of the family Anguillulidae, esp. one that is a parasite on plants.

EEOC, Equal Employment Opportunity Commission.

ee•rie or **ee•ry** (ēr′ē), *adj.,* **-ri•er, -ri•est.** uncanny, so as to inspire superstitious fear; strange and mysterious: *an eerie howl.* —**ee′ri•ly,** *adv.* —**ee′ri•ness,** *n.*

ef•fa•ble (ef′ə bəl), *adj.* utterable; expressible.

ef•face (i fās′), *v.t.,* **-faced, -fac•ing.** **1.** to wipe out; do away with; expunge: *to efface unhappy memories.* **2.** to rub out, erase, or obliterate (outlines, traces, inscriptions, etc.). **3.** to make (oneself) inconspicuous; withdraw (oneself) modestly or shyly. —**ef•face′a•ble,** *adj.* —**ef•face′ment,** *n.* —**ef•fac′er,** *n.*

ef•fect (i fekt′), *n.* **1.** something that is produced by an agency or cause; result; consequence. **2.** power to produce results; efficacy; force: *The protest had no effect.* **3.** the state of being effective or operative; operation or execution: *to bring a plan into effect.* **4.** a mental or emotional impression produced, as by a painting or speech. **5.** general meaning or purpose; intent: *I wrote a letter to that effect.* **6.** the making of a desired impression: *The expensive car was only for effect.* **7.** an illusory phenomenon: *a three-dimensional effect.* **8.** a scientific phenomenon (usu. named for its discoverer): *the Doppler effect.* —*v.t.* **9.** to produce as an effect; bring about; accomplish: *to effect a change.* —*Idiom.* **10. in effect, a.** virtually; implicitly. **b.** essentially; basically. **c.** operating or functioning; in force. **11. take effect, a.** to go into operation; begin to function. **b.** to produce a result. —**ef•fect′i•ble,** *adj.*

ef•fec•tive (i fek′tiv), *adj.* **1.** adequate to accomplish a purpose; producing the intended or expected result: *effective teaching methods.* **2.** in operation or in force; functioning; operative: *The law becomes effective at midnight.* **3.** producing a deep or vivid impression; striking: *an effective photograph.* **4.** prepared and available for service, esp. military service. —*n.* **5.** a member of the armed forces fit for duty or active service. —**ef•fec′tive•ly,** *adv.* —**ef•fec′tive•ness, ef•fec•tiv′i•ty,** *n.*

ef•fec•tor (i fek′tər), *n.* Also, **effecter.** a person or thing that effects something. **2. a.** an organ, cell, etc., that reacts to a nerve impulse, as a muscle by contracting or a gland by secreting. **b.** the part of a nerve that conveys such an impulse.

ef•fects (i fekts′), *n.pl.* **1.** goods; movables; personal property. **2.** SPECIAL EFFECTS.

ef•fec•tu•al (i fek′chōō əl), *adj.* **1.** capable of producing an intended effect; adequate. **2.** valid or binding, as an agreement or document. —**ef•fec′tu•al•ly,** *adv.* —**ef•fec′tu•al•ness, ef•fec′tu•al′i•ty,** *n.*

ef•fec•tu•ate (i fek′chōō āt′), *v.t.,* **-at•ed, -at•ing.** to bring about; effect. —**ef•fec′tu•a′tion,** *n.*

ef•fem•i•na•cy (i fem′ə nə sē), *n.* the state or quality of being effeminate.

ef•fem•i•nate (*adj.* i fem′ə nit; *v.* -nāt′), *adj., v.,* **-nat•ed, -nat•ing.** —*adj.* **1.** (of a man or boy) having traits, tastes, habits, etc., traditionally considered feminine, as softness or delicacy. **2.** characterized by softness, delicacy, weakness, or lack of vigor. —*v.t., v.i.* **3.** to make or become effeminate. —**ef•fem′i•nate•ly,** *adv.*

ef•fen•di (i fen′dē), *n., pl.* **-dis. 1.** a former Turkish title of respect, esp. for government officials. **2.** (in E Mediterranean countries) a man who is a member of the aristocracy.

ef•fer•ent (ef′ər ənt), *adj.* **1.** conveying or conducting away from an organ or part (opposed to *afferent*). —*n.* **2.** an efferent part, as a nerve or blood vessel. —**ef′fer•ent•ly,** *adv.*

ef•fer•vesce (ef′ər ves′), *v.i.,* **-vesced, -vesc•ing. 1.** to give off bubbles of gas, as a fermenting or carbonated liquid. **2.** to issue forth in bubbles. **3.** to show enthusiasm, excitement, or liveliness. —**ef′fer•ves′cence,** *n.* —**ef′fer•ves′cent,** *adj.*

ef•fete (i fēt′), *adj.* **1.** lacking in wholesome vigor; degenerate; decadent: *an effete, overrefined society.* **2.** exhausted of vigor or energy; worn out. **3.** unable to produce; sterile. —**ef•fete′ly,** *adv.* —**ef•fete′ness,** *n.*

ef•fi•ca•cious (ef′i kā′shəs), *adj.* capable of having the desired result or effect; effective as a means, measure, or remedy. —**ef′fi•ca′cious•ly,** *adv.* —**ef′fi•ca′cious•ness,** *n.*

ef•fi•ca•cy (ef′i kə sē), *n.* capacity for producing a desired result or effect; effectiveness.

ef•fi•cien•cy (i fish′ən sē), *n., pl.* **-cies. 1.** the state or quality of being efficient. **2.** accomplishment of or ability to accomplish a job with a minimum expenditure of time and effort. **3.** the ratio of the work done by a machine to the energy supplied to it, usu. expressed as a percentage. **4.** EFFICIENCY APARTMENT.

effi′ciency apart′ment, *n.* a small apartment consisting typically of a combined living room and bedroom, a bathroom, and a kitchenette.

effi′ciency ex′pert, *n.* a person who studies the methods, procedures, and job characteristics of a business or factory in order to devise ways to increase the efficiency of equipment and personnel. Also called **effi′ciency engineer′.**

ef•fi•cient (i fish′ənt), *adj.* **1.** performing or functioning effectively with the least waste of time and effort; competent; capable: *an efficient secretary.* **2.** satisfactory and economical to use: *a more efficient air conditioner.* **3.** producing an effect, as a cause; causative. **4.** using a given product or resource with maximum efficiency (used in combination): *a fuel-efficient engine.* —**ef•fi′cient•ly,** *adv.*

ef•fi•gy (ef′i jē), *n., pl.* **-gies. 1.** a representation or image, esp. sculptured, as on a monument. **2.** a crude representation of someone disliked, used for purposes of ridicule. —*Idiom.* **3. in effigy,** in public view in the form of an effigy: *a leader hanged in effigy by the mob.*

ef•flo•resce (ef′lə res′), *v.i.,* **-resced, -resc•ing. 1.** to burst into bloom; blossom. **2. a.** to change to a mealy or powdery substance upon exposure to air, as a crystalline substance through loss of water of crystallization. **b.** to become incrusted with crystals of salt or the like through evaporation or chemical change.

ef•flo•res•cence (ef′lə res′əns), *n.* **1.** the state or a period of flowering. **2.** an example or result of growth and development. **3. a.** the act or process of efflorescing. **b.** the resulting powdery substance or incrustation. **4.** a rash or eruption of the skin. —**ef′flo•res′cent,** *adj.*

ef•flu•ence (ef′lōō əns), *n.* **1.** the action or process of flowing out; efflux. **2.** something that flows out; emanation.

ef•flu•ent (ef′lōō ənt), *adj.* **1.** flowing out or forth. —*n.* **2.** something that flows out or forth; outflow; effluence. **3.** a stream flowing out of a

lake, reservoir, etc. **4.** sewage or other liquid waste that is discharged, as into a body of water.

ef•flu•vi•um (i flōō′vē əm), *n., pl.* **-vi•a** (-vē ə), **-vi•ums. 1.** a disagreeable or noxious exhalation, vapor, or odor. **2.** an invisible exhalation or vapor. —**ef•flu′vi•al,** *adj.*

ef•flux (ef′luks), *n.* **1.** outward flow, as of water. **2.** something that flows out; effluence. **3.** a passing or lapse of time. **4.** a passing away; expiration. Often, **ef•flux•ion** (i fluk′shən).

ef•fort (ef′ərt), *n.* **1.** exertion of physical or mental power. **2.** an earnest or strenuous attempt. **3.** something done by exertion or hard work. **4.** an achievement, as in literature or art: *The painting is one of her finest efforts.* **5.** action undertaken by a group for a specified purpose: *the war effort.* **6.** the force or energy that is applied to a machine for the accomplishment of useful work.

ef•fort•less (ef′ərt lis), *adj.* requiring or involving no effort; displaying no signs of effort; easy. —**ef′fort•less•ly,** *adv.* —**ef′fort•less•ness,** *n.*

ef•fron•ter•y (i frun′tə rē), *n., pl.* **-ter•ies. 1.** shameless or impudent boldness; barefaced audacity. **2.** an act or instance of this.

ef•ful•gent (i ful′jənt, i fōōl′-), *adj.* shining forth brilliantly; radiant. —**ef•ful′gence,** *n.* —**ef•ful′gent•ly,** *adv.*

ef•fuse (*v.* i fyōōz′; *adj.* i fyōōs′), *v.,* **-fused, -fus•ing,** *adj.* —*v.t.* **1.** to pour out or forth. —*v.i.* **2.** to exude; flow out. —*adj.* **3.** scattered; profuse. **4.** *Bot.* spread out loosely.

ef•fu•sive (i fyōō′siv), *adj.* **1.** extravagantly or unduly demonstrative; lacking reserve: *effusive greetings.* **2.** pouring out; overflowing. —**ef•fu′sive•ly,** *adv.* —**ef•fu′sive•ness,** *n.*

e.g., for example; for the sake of example; such as. [< Latin *exemplī grātiā*]

e•gal•i•tar•i•an (i gal′i târ′ē ən), *adj.* **1.** asserting, resulting from, or characterized by belief in the equality of all people, esp. in political, economic, or social life. —*n.* **2.** one who adheres to egalitarian beliefs. —**e•gal′i•tar′i•an•ism,** *n.*

Eg•bert (eg′bərt), *n.* A.D. 775?–839, king of the West Saxons 802–839; 1st king of the English 828–839.

e•gest (ē jest′, i jest′), *v.t.* to discharge from the body; excrete (opposed to *ingest*). —**e•ges′tion,** *n.* —**e•ges′tive,** *adj.*

e•ges•ta (ē jes′tə, i jes′-), *n.* (*used with a sing. or pl. v.*) matter egested from the body, as excrement or other waste.

egg¹ (eg), *n., v.,* **egged, egg•ing.** —*n.* **1.** the roundish reproductive body produced by the female of certain animals, as birds and most reptiles, consisting of an ovum and its envelope of albumen, jelly, membranes, egg case, or shell, according to species. **2.** such a body produced by a domestic bird, esp. the hen. **3.** the contents of an egg. **4.** something resembling a hen's egg. **5.** Also called **egg′ cell′.** the female gamete; ovum. **6.** *Informal.* a person: *He's a good egg.* —*v.t.* **7.** to prepare (food) by dipping in beaten egg. —*Idiom.* **8. egg on one's face,** conspicuous embarrassment caused by one's own indiscretion or faux pas. **9. lay an egg,** *Informal.* to fail wretchedly, esp. while trying to entertain. —*Saying.* **10. Don't put all your eggs in one basket,** don't venture all that you possess in a single enterprise. **11. walk on eggs,** to act with extreme caution. —**egg′less,** *adj.* —**egg′y,** *adj.*

egg² (eg), *v.t.,* **egged, egg•ing.** to incite or urge; encourage (usu. fol. by *on*).

egg•beat•er (eg′bē′tər), *n.* **1.** a small rotary beater for beating eggs, whipping cream, etc. **2.** *Slang.* a helicopter.

egg′ case′, *n.* OOTHECA.

egg′ cream′, *n.* a cold beverage made with milk, chocolate syrup, and soda water.

egg•cup (eg′kup′), *n.* a small cup for serving a boiled egg.

egg•head (eg′hed′), *n. Informal* (*often disparaging*). an intellectual.

egg•nog (eg′nog′), *n.* a thick drink made of eggs, milk or cream, sugar, and usu. rum, brandy, or whiskey.

egg•plant (eg′plant′, -plänt′), *n.* **1.** a plant, *Solanum melongena esculentum,* of the nightshade family, cultivated for its edible, usu. dark-purple fruit. **2.** the fruit of this plant used as a vegetable. **3.** a blackish purple color; aubergine.

egg′ roll′, *n.* a thin casing of egg dough rolled around a mixture of minced meat or shrimp, bamboo shoots, bean sprouts, etc., and fried in deep fat.

eggs′ Ben′edict, *n.* toasted halves of English muffin, each covered with a slice of ham and a poached egg and topped with hollandaise sauce.

egg•shell (eg′shel′), *n.* **1.** the shell of a bird's egg, consisting of keratin fibers and calcite crystals. **2.** a pale, yellowish-white color. —*adj.* **3.** like an eggshell, esp. in being thin and fragile. **4.** pale yellowish-white. **5.** (of paint) having little or no gloss.

egg′ tooth′, *n.* a calcareous prominence at the tip of the beak or upper jaw of an embryonic bird or reptile, used to break through the eggshell at hatching.

e•gis (ē′jis), *n.* AEGIS.

eg•lan•tine (eg′lən tīn′, -tēn′), *n.* the sweetbrier.

Eg•lon (eg′lon), *n.* a Moabite king who conquered and ruled the land of Israel and was killed by Ehud. Judg. 3:12–25.

e•go (ē′gō, eg′ō), *n., pl.* **e•gos. 1.** the "I" or self of any person; a thinking, feeling, and conscious being, able to distinguish itself from other selves. **2.** *Psychoanal.* the conscious, rational component of the psyche that experiences and reacts to the outside world and mediates between

E

the demands of the id and superego. **3.** egotism; self-importance. **4.** self-esteem or self-image. **5.** (*often cap.*) *Philos.* the enduring and conscious element that knows experience.

e•go•cen•tric (ē′gō sen′trik, eg′ō-), *adj.* **1.** regarding the self or the individual as the center of all things: *an egocentric view of the universe.* **2.** having little or no regard for interests or feelings other than one's own; self-centered. —*n.* **3.** an egocentric person. —**e′go•cen′tri•cal•ly,** *adv.* —**e′go•cen•tric′i•ty** (-tris′i tē), *n.* —**e′go•cen′trism,** *n.*

e•go•ism (ē′gō iz′əm, eg′ō-), *n.* **1.** the habit of valuing everything only in reference to one's personal interest (opposed to *altruism*). **2.** egotism or conceit. **3.** the view in ethics that morality ultimately rests on self-interest. —**e′go•ist,** *n.* —**e′go•is′tic, e•go•is′ti•cal,** *adj.* —**e′go•is′ti•cal•ly,** *adv.*

e•go•ma•ni•a (ē′gō mā′nē ə, -mān′yə, eg′ō-), *n.* psychologically abnormal egotism; extreme egocentrism. —**e′go•ma′ni•ac′,** *n.* —**e′go•ma•ni•a•cal** (ē′gō mə nī′i kəl, eg′ō-), *adj.*

e•go•tism (ē′gə tiz′əm, eg′ə-), *n.* **1.** excessive reference to oneself in conversation or writing; conceit; boastfulness. **2.** selfishness; self-centeredness; egoism. —**e′go•tist,** *n.*

e•go•tis•tic (ē′gə tis′tik, eg′ə-) also **e′go•tis′ti•cal,** *adj.* **1.** given to egotism. **2.** vain; boastful. **3.** indifferent to the well-being of others; selfish. —**e′go•tis′ti•cal•ly,** *adv.*

e•gre•gious (i grē′jəs, -jē əs), *adj.* extraordinary in some bad way; glaring; flagrant: *an egregious mistake; an egregious liar.* —**e•gre′gious•ly,** *adv.* —**e•gre′gious•ness,** *n.*

e•gress (*n.* ē′gres; *v.* i gres′), *n.* **1.** the act of going out or leaving. **2.** the right to go out. **3.** a means or place of going out; exit. **4.** the emergence of a heavenly body from an eclipse, transit, etc. —*v.i.* **5.** to go out; emerge. —**e•gres′sion,** *n.*

e•gret (ē′grit, eg′rit, ē gret′, ē′gret), *n.* **1.** any of several herons having long, graceful plumes during the breeding season. **2.** AIGRETTE.

E•gypt (ē′jipt), *n.* a country in NE Africa on the Mediterranean and Red seas. 64,791,891; 386,659 sq. mi. (1,001,449 sq. km). *Cap.:* Cairo. Arabic, **Misr.** Official name, **Arab Republic of Egypt.**

E•gyp•tian (i jip′shən), *n.* **1.** a native or inhabitant of Egypt. **2.** the extinct Afroasiatic language of Egypt under the Pharaohs. —*adj.* **3.** of or pertaining to ancient or modern Egypt, its people, or their language. —**E•gyp′tian•ism, E′gyp•tic′i•ty** (-tis′i tē), *n.*

Egyp′tian cot′ton, *n.* a variety of sea-island cotton having silky, strong fibers, grown chiefly in N Africa.

E•gyp•tol•o•gy (ē′jip tol′ə jē), *n.* the science or study of Egyptian antiquities. —**E•gyp′to•log′i•cal** (-tə loj′i kəl), *adj.* —**E′gyp•tol′o•gist,** *n.*

E•hud (ē′hud), *n.* a Benjamite judge of Israel who assassinated King Eglon. Judg. 3:15–4:1.

ei′co•sa•pen′ta•e•no′ic ac′id (ī′kō sə pen′tə i nō′ik, ī′kō sə pen′-), *n.* See EPA.

ei•der•down (ī′dər doun′), *n.* **1.** under plumage from the breast of the female eider duck. **2.** a heavy quilt, esp. one filled with eiderdown. **3.** a warm, lightweight knitted or woven fabric, napped on one or both sides.

ei′der duck′, *n.* any of several large diving ducks, esp. of the genus *Somateria,* of northern seas.

ei•det•ic (ī det′ik), *adj.* pertaining to or constituting visual impressions recalled vividly and readily reproducible with great accuracy: *eidetic imagery.*

ei•do•lon (ī dō′lən), *n., pl.* **-la** (-lə) **-lons. 1.** an unreal image; phantom; apparition. **2.** an ideal.

Eif′fel Tow′er (ī′fəl), *n.* a tower of skeletal iron construction in Paris, France: built for the exposition of 1889. 984 ft. (300 m) high. [after A. G. *Eiffel* (1832–1923), its engineer and principal designer]

eight (āt), *n.* **1.** a cardinal number, seven plus one. **2.** a symbol for this number, as 8 or VIII. **3.** a set of this many persons or things. **4.** an eight-cylinder engine. —*adj.* **5.** amounting to eight in number.

eight•ball (āt′bôl′), *n.* **1.** (in pool) **a.** a black ball bearing the number eight. **b.** a game in which one player or side must pocket all the solid or all the striped balls before pocketing the eightball. —*Idiom.* **2.** behind the eightball, in a difficult or unsolvable situation; stymied.

eight•een (ā′tēn′), *n.* **1.** a cardinal number, ten plus eight. **2.** a symbol for this number, as 18 or XVIII. **3.** a set of this many persons or things. —*adj.* **4.** amounting to 18 in number.

eight•eenth (ā′tēnth′), *adj.* **1.** next after the seventeenth; being the ordinal number for 18. **2.** being one of 18 equal parts. —*n.* **3.** an eighteenth part, esp. of one (¹⁄₁₈). **4.** the eighteenth member of a series.

Eight′eenth Amend′ment, *n.* an amendment to the U.S. Constitution, ratified in 1918, prohibiting the manufacture, sale, or transportation of alcoholic beverages for consumption: repealed in 1933.

eight•fold (āt′fōld′), *adj.* **1.** made up of eight parts or members. **2.** eight times as great or as much. —*adv.* **3.** in eightfold measure.

Eight′fold Path′, *n. Buddhism.* the eight pursuits of one seeking enlightenment, comprising right understanding, motives, speech, action, means of livelihood, effort, intellectual activity, and contemplation.

eighth (ātth, āth), *adj.* **1.** next after the seventh. **2.** being one of eight equal parts. —*n.* **3.** an eighth part, esp. of one (¹⁄₈). **4.** the eighth member of a series. —*adv.* **5.** in the eighth place; eighthly. —**eighth′ly,** *adv.*

Eighth′ Amend′ment, *n.* an amendment to the U.S. Constitution, ratified in 1791 as part of the Bill of Rights, guaranteeing reasonable bail, fines, and punishment.

Eighth′ Command′ment, *n.* "Thou shalt not steal": eighth of the Ten Commandments. Compare TEN COMMANDMENTS.

eighth′ note′, *n.* a musical note having one eighth the time value of a whole note.

eighth′ rest′, *n.* a musical rest equal in time value to an eighth note.

800 number, *n.* a toll-free telephone number preceded by the three-digit code "800," used esp. by a business to receive orders from distant customers.

eight•pen•ny (āt′pen′ē), *adj.* noting a nail 2½ in. (64 mm) long.

eight•y (ā′tē), *n., pl.* **eight•ies,** *adj.* —*n.* **1.** a cardinal number, ten times eight. **2.** a symbol for this number, as 80 or LXXX. **3.** a set of this many persons or things. —*adj.* **4.** amounting to 80 in number.

Ei•lat (ā lät′), *n.* ELAT.

ein•korn (īn′kôrn), *n.* a primitive form of wheat, *Triticum monococcum,* having a one-grained spikelet.

Ein•stein (īn′stīn), *n.* **Albert,** 1879–1955, German physicist, U.S. citizen from 1940: formulator of the theory of relativity. —**Ein•stein′i•an,** *adj.*

ein•stein•i•um (īn stī′nē əm), *n.* a transuranic element. *Symbol:* Es; *at. no.:* 99.

Eir•e (âr′ə, ī′rə, âr′ē, ī′rē), *n.* **1.** the Irish name of IRELAND. **2.** a former name of the Republic of IRELAND.

Ei•sen•how•er (ī′zən hou′ər), *n.* **Dwight David,** 1890–1969, U.S. general: 34th president of the U.S. 1953–61.

Ei′senhower Doc′trine, *n.* a foreign policy under Dwight D. Eisenhower that sought to prevent the spread of communism in the Middle East by means of containment.

Ei•sen•stein (ī′zən stīn′), *n.* **Sergei Mikhailovich,** 1898–1948, Russian theatrical and motion-picture director.

ei•ther (ē′thər, ī′thər), *adj.* **1.** one or the other of two: *You may sit at either end of the table.* **2.** each of two; the one and the other: *There are trees on either side of the river.* —*pron.* **3.** one or the other: *Either will do.* —*conj.* **4.** (a coordinating conjunction that, when used with *or,* indicates a choice): *Either call or write.* —*adv.* **5.** as well; likewise (used after negative clauses): *If you don't go, I won't either.* —**Usage.** When used as the subject, the pronoun EITHER takes a singular verb even when followed by a prepositional phrase with a plural object: *Either of the shrubs grows well in this soil.* As an adjective EITHER refers only to two of anything. As a pronoun EITHER sometimes occurs in reference to more than two (*either of the three children*), but ANY is more common (*any of the three children*). As a conjunction, EITHER often introduces a series of more than two: *pizza topped with either onions, peppers, or mushrooms.* Usage guides say that the verb used with subjects joined by the correlative conjunctions EITHER … OR (or NEITHER … NOR) is singular or plural depending on the number of the noun or pronoun nearer the verb: *Either the parents or the school determines the program. Either the school or the parents determine the program.* Practice varies, however, and often the presence of one plural, no matter where, results in a plural verb. See also NEITHER.

ei′ther-or′, *adj.* **1.** restricted in choice to two options: *an either-or situation.* —*n.* **2.** a choice having only two options.

e•jac•u•late (*v.* i jak′yə lāt′; *n.* -lit), *v.,* **-lat•ed, -lat•ing,** *n.* —*v.t.* **1.** to eject or discharge, esp. semen. **2.** to utter suddenly and briefly; exclaim. —*v.i.* **3.** to eject semen. —*n.* **4.** the semen emitted in an ejaculation. —**e•jac′u•la•to′ry** (-lə tôr′ē, -tōr′ē), *adj.*

e•jac•u•la•tion (i jak′yə lā′shən), *n.* **1.** an abrupt, exclamatory utterance. **2. a.** the act or process of ejaculating, esp. the discharge of semen by the reproductive organs. **b.** EJACULATE (def. 4).

e•ject (i jekt′), *v.t.* **1.** to drive or force out; expel. **2.** to dismiss, as from office. **3.** to evict. **4.** to throw out or throw off. —*v.i.* **5.** to propel oneself from a disabled airplane, esp. by an ejection seat. —**e•ject′a•ble,** *adj.*

e•jec•ta (i jek′tə), *n.* (*used with a sing. or pl. v.*) matter ejected, as from an erupting volcano.

e•jec•tion (i jek′shən), *n.* **1.** the act of ejecting, or the state of being ejected. **2.** something ejected, as lava.

ejec′tion seat′, *n.* an airplane seat that can be ejected together with the pilot in an emergency.

e•jec•tor (i jek′tər), *n.* **1.** a person or thing that ejects. **2.** (in a firearm or gun) the mechanism that, after firing, throws out the empty cartridge or shell.

eka-, a prefix used to form names for predicted chemical elements, added to the name of the next highest actually occurring element of the same group in the periodic table: *ekasilicon* (renamed *germanium* when actually discovered); *ekalead.*

eke (ēk), *v.t.,* **eked, ek•ing. eke out, 1.** to make (a living) or maintain (existence) meagerly and with great effort: *to eke out an income with odd jobs.* **2.** to supplement; add to. **3.** to mete out in small amounts: *eked out a supply.*

EKG, 1. electrocardiogram. **2.** electrocardiograph.

e•kis•tics (i kis′tiks), *n.* (*used with a sing. v.*) the scientific study of human settlements, drawing on diverse disciplines, including architecture, city planning, and behavioral science. —**e•kis′tic,** *adj.*

Ek•ron (ek′ron), *n.* the northernmost of the five chief Philistine cities, first inhabited by the tribe of Judah, then the tribe of Dan. Josh. 15:45–46; 19:40–43; I Sam. 17:52.

el¹ (el), *n.* an elevated railroad.

el² (el), *n.* ELL¹.

el³ (el), *n.* the letter *l*.

el·ab·o·rate (*adj.* i lab′ər it; *v.* -ə rāt′), *adj.*, *v.*, **-rat·ed, -rat·ing.** —*adj.* **1.** worked out in great detail; painstaking: *elaborate preparations.* **2.** ornate, showy, or gaudy: *an elaborate costume.* —*v.t.* **3.** to work out in minute detail. **4.** to develop or expand. **5.** to produce or develop by labor. —*v.i.* **6.** to add details or information; expand (usu. fol. by *on*): *to elaborate on an idea.* —**e·lab′o·rate·ly,** *adv.* —**e·lab′o·rate·ness,** *n.* —**e·lab′o·ra′tion,** *n.* —**e·lab′o·ra′tive,** *adj.*

E·laine (i lān′), *n.* any of several women in Arthurian romance, as the mother by Lancelot of Sir Galahad.

El A·la·mein (el ä′lä mān′, -ä′lə-), *n.* a town on the N coast of Egypt, ab. 70 mi. (113 km) W of Alexandria: decisive British victory in World War II, 1942. Also called **Alamein.**

E·lam (ē′ləm), *n.* an ancient kingdom E of Babylonia and N of the Persian Gulf. *Cap.:* Susa.

E·lam·ite (ē′lə mīt′), *n.* **1.** a native or inhabitant of ancient Elam. **2.** the extinct language of the Elamites, known principally from texts written in a cuneiform syllabary between the 13th and 5th centuries B.C. —*adj.* **3.** of or pertaining to Elam, its people, or their language.

é·lan (ā län′, ā lăn′), *n.* dash or vivacity; verve.

e·land (ē′lənd), *n.*, *pl.* **e·lands** (*esp. collectively*) **e·land.** either of two large African antelopes of the genus *Taurotragus,* having long, spirally twisted horns. [< Afrikaans]

é·lan vi·tal (Fr. ā län vē tal′), *n.* (esp. in Bergsonian philosophy) the vital or creative force in all organisms that is responsible for growth and evolution.

el·a·pid (el′ə pid), *n.* any venomous snake of the family Elapidae, having erect fangs in the upper jaw and including coral snakes and cobras.

e·lapse (i laps′), *v.*, **e·lapsed, e·laps·ing,** *n.* —*v.i.* **1.** (of time) to slip or pass by. —*n.* **2.** the passage of a period of time; lapse.

e·las·mo·branch (i las′mə brangk′, i laz′-), *adj.* **1.** belonging to the Elasmobranchii, the subclass of cartilaginous fishes comprising the sharks and rays. —*n.* **2.** an elasmobranch fish.

e·las·tic (i las′tik), *adj.* **1.** capable of returning to its original length or shape after being stretched. **2.** spontaneously expansive, as gases. **3.** flexible; adaptable: *elastic rules.* **4.** bouncy or springy: *an elastic step.* **5.** resilient, esp. after a setback; buoyant. **6.** noting a body having the property of elasticity. —*n.* **7.** fabric or material made elastic, as with strips of rubber. **8.** something made from this material, as a garter. **9.** RUBBER BAND. —**e·las′ti·cal·ly,** *adv.*

e·las·tic·i·ty (i la stis′i tē, ē′la stis′-), *n.* **1.** the state or quality of being elastic. **2.** flexibility; adaptability: *elasticity of meaning.* **3.** buoyancy; ability to overcome depression. **4.** the property of a substance that enables it to change its length, volume, or shape in direct response to a force effecting such a change and to recover its original form upon the removal of the force.

e·las·ti·cize (i las′tə sīz′), *v.t.*, **-cized, -ciz·ing.** to make elastic, as by inserting elastic cords or threads.

elas′tic tis′sue, *n.* connective tissue consisting chiefly of yellow, elastic fibers and composing certain ligaments and the walls of the arteries.

e·las·to·mer (i las′tə mər), *n.* an elastic substance occurring naturally, as natural rubber, or produced synthetically, as butyl rubber. —**e·las′to·mer′ic** (-mer′ik), *adj.*

E·lat or **Ei·lat** or **E·lath** (ā lät′), *n.* a seaport at the N tip of the Gulf of Aqaba, in S Israel: resort. 19,000.

e·late (i lāt′), *v.*, **e·lat·ed, e·lat·ing,** *adj.* —*v.t.* **1.** to make extremely happy; overjoy. —*adj.* **2.** elated.

e·lat·ed (i lā′tid), *adj.* jubilant; overjoyed. —**e·lat′ed·ly,** *adv.*

e·lat·er·id (i lat′ər id), *n.* **1.** CLICK BEETLE. —*adj.* **2.** belonging or pertaining to the click beetle family, Elateridae.

E·lath (ē′lath), *n.* a town at the head of the Gulf of Aqaba where King Solomon built a port. I Kings 9:26–28.

e·la·tion (i lā′shən), *n.* a feeling or state of great joy or pride; high spirits.

E layer, *n.* the radio-reflective ionospheric layer of maximum electron density, at an altitude of about 60 mi. (100 km).

El·ba (el′bə), *n.* an Italian island in the Mediterranean, between Corsica and Italy: site of Napoleon's first exile 1814–15. 26,830; 94 sq. mi. (243 sq. km).

El·be (el′bə, elb), *n.* a river in central Europe, flowing from the W Czech Republic NW through Germany to the North Sea. 725 mi. (1165 km) long. Czech, **Labe.**

el·bow (el′bō), *n.* **1.** the bend or joint of the human arm between the upper arm and forearm. **2.** the corresponding joint in the forelimb of a quadruped. **3.** something bent like an elbow, as a piece of pipe bent at an angle. **4.** Also called **ell, el.** a plumbing pipe or pipe connection having a right-angled bend. —*v.t.* **5.** to push aside with or as if with the elbow; jostle. **6.** to make (one's way) by so pushing. —*v.i.* **7.** to elbow one's way. —*Idiom.* **8.** at one's elbow, within easy reach; nearby. **9.** out at (the) elbows, **a.** poorly dressed; shabby. **b.** impoverished.

el′bow grease′, *n.* physical exertion; hard work.

el·bow·room (el′bō rōōm′, -rŏŏm′), *n.* **1.** space in which to move freely. **2.** scope; opportunity.

El·brus (el brōōs′), *n.* a mountain in the S Russian Federation in Europe, in the Caucasus: highest peak in Europe, 18,465 ft. (5628 m).

el·der¹ (el′dər), *adj. a compar. of* **old** *with* **eldest** *as superl.* **1.** of greater age; older. **2.** of higher rank; senior. **3.** of former times; earlier. —*n.* **4.** an older person: *a boy who respects his elders.* **5.** an aged person. **6.** an older, influential member of a tribe or community, often a chief or ruler. **7.** (in certain Protestant churches) a lay member who is a governing officer, often assisting the pastor in services.

el·der² (el′dər), *n.* any shrub or tree of the genus *Sambucus,* of the honeysuckle family, having divided leaves and clusters of small red, black, or yellow berries.

el·der·ber·ry (el′dər ber′ē, -bə rē), *n.*, *pl.* **-ries. 1.** the berries of the elder, used in making wine and jelly. **2.** ELDER².

eld·er·ly (el′dər lē), *adj.* **1.** approaching old age. **2.** of or pertaining to persons in later life. —*n.* **3. the elderly,** elderly persons collectively.

eld′er states′man, *n.* a respected older politician or political adviser.

eld·est (el′dist), *adj. a superl.* of **old** *with* **elder** *as compar.* oldest; first-born; of greatest age.

El Do·ra·do (el′ dō rä′dō, -rä′-), *n.* **1.** a legendary city of South America sought by the early Spanish explorers for its treasure, esp. gold. **2.** any place offering great wealth.

el·dritch (el′drich), *adj.* eerie; weird; spooky.

El·e·a·zar (el′ē ā′zər), *n.* a son of Aaron and his successor in the priesthood. Num. 20:28.

el·e·cam·pane (el′i kam pān′), *n.* a composite weed, *Inula helenium,* having yellow flowers and aromatic leaves and root.

e·lect (i lekt′), *v.t.* **1.** to choose or select by vote, as for an office: *to elect a mayor.* **2.** to determine in favor of (a method, course of action, etc.). **3.** to choose (a course of study). **4.** (of God) to select for divine mercy or favor, esp. for salvation. —*v.i.* **5.** to choose or select someone or something, as by voting. —*adj.* **6.** selected for an office, but not yet inducted (usu. used in combination): *the governor-elect.* **7.** select or choice: *an elect circle of artists.* **8.** chosen by God, esp. for eternal life. —*n.* **9. the elect** or **elected, a.** persons chosen or worthy to be chosen. **b.** a person or persons chosen by God, esp. for favor or salvation. [< Latin *ēlēctus* chosen] —**e·lect′a·ble,** *adj.* —**e·lect′a·bil′i·ty,** *n.* —**e·lec·tee** (i lek tē′), *n.*

e·lec·tion (i lek′shən), *n.* **1.** the selection by vote of a candidate for office. **2.** a public vote upon candidates, propositions, etc., submitted. **3.** the choice by God of individuals, as for favor or salvation.

Elec′tion Day′, *n.* **1.** the first Tuesday after the first Monday in November, on which national elections are held in the U.S. in even years. **2.** (often *l.c.*) any day designated for the election of public officials.

e·lec·tion·eer (i lek′shə nēr′), *v.i.* to work for the success of a particular candidate or party in an election.

e·lec·tive (i lek′tiv), *adj.* **1.** of or derived from the principle of electing to an office, position, etc. **2.** chosen by election, as an official. **3.** empowered to elect a candidate, as a body of persons. **4.** open to choice; optional: *elective surgery.* —*n.* **5.** a course that a student may select from among alternatives. —**e·lec′tive·ly,** *adv.*

e·lec·tor (i lek′tər), *n.* **1.** a person who elects, esp. a qualified voter. **2.** a member of the electoral college. —**e·lec′tor·al,** *adj.*

elec′toral col′lege, *n.* (often *caps.*) a body of electors chosen by the voters in each state to elect the president and vice-president of the U.S.

e·lec·tor·ate (i lek′tər it), *n.* the body of persons entitled to vote in an election.

E·lec·tra (i lek′trə), *n.* in Greek myth, the daughter of Agamemnon and Clytemnestra who incited Orestes to kill Clytemnestra and her lover.

Elec′tra com′plex, *n. Psychoanal.* an unresolved, unconscious libidinous desire of a daughter for her father. Compare OEDIPUS COMPLEX.

e·lec·tric (i lek′trik), *adj.* **1.** pertaining to, derived from, produced by, or involving electricity: *an electric shock.* **2.** producing, transmitting, or operated by electric currents: *an electric bell; electric cord.* **3.** thrilling; exciting. **4.** (of a musical instrument) **a.** ELECTRONIC (def. 3). **b.** amplified by electronic devices: *an electric guitar.* **5.** vivid; intense: *electric blue.* —*n.* **6.** something, as an appliance or toy, operated by electricity. —**e·lec′tri·cal,** *adj.*

elec′trical engineer′ing, *n.* the branch of engineering that deals with the practical application of the theory of electricity to the construction of machinery, power supplies, etc. —**elec′trical engineer′,** *n.*

elec′tric chair′, *n.* **1.** a chair used to electrocute criminals sentenced to death. **2.** the penalty of legal electrocution.

elec′tric charge′, *n.* the quantity of electricity in a substance, denoting esp. an excess or deficiency of electrons.

elec′tric eel′, *n.* a long eel-shaped South American freshwater fish, *Electrophorus electricus,* of the carp family, that can emit strong electric discharges.

elec′tric eye′, *n.* PHOTOCELL.

elec′tric field′, *n.* a region of space near a charged particle in which an electric force acts on other charged particles.

e·lec·tri·cian (i lek trish′ən, ē′lek-), *n.* a person who installs, operates, maintains, or repairs electric devices or electrical wiring.

e·lec·tric·i·ty (i lek tris′i tē, ē′lek-), *n.* **1.** a fundamental property of matter caused by the presence and motion of electrons, protons, or positrons, manifesting itself as attraction, repulsion, luminous and heating effects, and the like. **2.** electric current or power. **3.** the science dealing with electric charges and currents. **4.** a state or feeling of excitement, anticipation, or the like.

E

e·lec′tric ray′, *n.* any ray of the family Torpedinidae, capable of emitting strong electric discharges.

e·lec·tri·fy (i lek′trə fī′), *v.t.*, **-fied, -fy·ing. 1.** to charge with electricity. **2.** to supply (a region, community, etc.) with electric power. **3.** to equip for the use of electric power, as a railroad. **4.** to thrill, excite, or astonish. —**e·lec′tri·fi·ca′tion,** *n.* —**e·lec′tri·fi′er,** *n.*

electro-, a combining form representing ELECTRIC or ELECTRICITY: *electromagnetic.*

e·lec·tro·a·cous·tics (i lek′trō ə kōō′stiks), *n.* (*used with a sing. v.*) the branch of electronics that deals with the conversion of electricity into acoustical energy and vice versa.

e·lec·tro·car·di·o·gram (i lek′trō kär′dē ə gram′), *n.* the graphic record produced by an electrocardiograph. *Abbr.:* EKG, ECG Also called **cardiogram.**

e·lec·tro·car·di·o·graph (i lek′trō kär′dē ə graf′, -gräf′), *n.* a galvanometric device that detects variations in the electric potential that triggers the heartbeat, used to evaluate the heart's health. *Abbr.:* EKG, ECG —**e·lec′tro·car′di·o·graph′ic** (-graf′ik), *adj.* —**e·lec′tro·car′di·og′ra·phy** (-og′rə fē), *n.*

e·lec·tro·chem·is·try (i lek′trō kem′ə strē), *n.* the branch of chemistry that deals with the chemical changes produced by electricity and the production of electricity by chemical changes. —**e·lec′tro·chem′i·cal** (-i kəl), *adj.* —**e·lec′tro·chem′ist,** *n.*

e·lec·tro·con·vul·sive ther·a·py (i lek′trō kən vul′siv, i lek′-), *n.* the application of electric current to the head in order to induce a seizure, used to treat serious mental illnesses. *Abbr.:* ECT Also called **electroshock.**

e·lec·tro·cute (i lek′trə kyōōt′), *v.t.*, **-cut·ed, -cut·ing. 1.** to kill by electricity. **2.** to execute (a criminal) by electricity, as in an electric chair. —**e·lec′tro·cu′tion,** *n.*

e·lec·trode (i lek′trōd), *n.* a conductor through which an electric current enters or leaves a nonmetallic portion of a circuit, as a dielectric, an electrolyte, or a semiconductor.

e·lec·tro·di·al·y·sis (i lek′trō dī al′ə sis), *n.*, *pl.* **-ses** (sēz′). dialysis in which electrodes of opposite charge are placed on either side of a membrane to accelerate diffusion. —**e·lec′tro·di·a·lyt′ic** (-dī′ə lit′ik), *adj.* —**e·lec′tro·di·a·lyt′i·cal·ly,** *adv.*

e·lec·tro·dy·nam·ic (i lek′trō dī nam′ik) also **e·lec′tro·dy·nam′i·cal,** *adj.* **1.** pertaining to the force of electricity in motion. **2.** pertaining to electrodynamics.

e·lec·tro·dy·nam·ics (i lek′trō dī nam′iks), *n.* (*used with a sing. v.*) the branch of physics that deals with the interactions of electric, magnetic, and mechanical phenomena.

e·lec·tro·en·ceph·a·lo·gram (i lek′trō en sef′ə lə gram′), *n.* a graphic record produced by an electroencephalograph. *Abbr.:* EEG

e·lec·tro·en·ceph·a·lo·graph (i lek′trō en sef′ə lə graf′, -gräf′), *n.* an instrument for measuring and recording the electric activity of the brain. *Abbr.:* EEG —**e·lec′tro·en·ceph′a·lo·graph′ic** (-graf′ik), *adj.* —**e·lec′tro·en·ceph′a·log′ra·phy** (-log′rə fē), *n.*

e·lec·tro·jet (i lek′trə jet′), *n.* a current of ions in the upper atmosphere that moves with respect to the surface of the earth and causes various auroral phenomena.

e·lec·tro·ki·net·ics (i lek′trō ki net′iks, -kī-), *n.* (*used with a sing. v.*) the branch of physics that deals with electricity in motion. —**e·lec′tro·ki·net′ic,** *adj.*

e·lec·trol·o·gist (i lek trol′ə jist), *n.* a person trained to use electrolysis for removing moles, warts, or unwanted hair. —**e·lec·trol′o·gy,** *n.*

e·lec·trol·y·sis (i lek trol′ə sis), *n.* **1.** the passage of an electric current through an electrolyte with subsequent migration of charged ions to the negative and positive electrodes. **2.** the destruction of hair roots, tumors, etc., by an electric current.

e·lec·tro·lyte (i lek′trə līt′), *n.* **1.** any substance that dissociates into ions when melted or dissolved in a suitable medium and thus forms a conductor of electricity. **2.** a conducting medium in which the flow of current is accompanied by the movement of ions.

e·lec·tro·lyt·ic (i lek′trə lit′ik) also **e·lec′tro·lyt′i·cal,** *adj.* **1.** pertaining to or derived by electrolysis. **2.** pertaining to an electrolyte. —**e·lec′tro·lyt′i·cal·ly,** *adv.*

e·lec′tro·lyt′ic cell′, *n.* CELL (def. 6).

e·lec·tro·mag·net (i lek′trō mag′nit), *n.* a device consisting of an iron or steel core that is magnetized by electric current in a coil that surrounds it. —**e·lec′tro·mag·net′ic,** *adj.*

electromagnet′ic radia′tion, *n.* radiation consisting of electromagnetic waves, including radio waves, infrared, visible light, ultraviolet, x-rays, and gamma rays.

elec′tromagnet′ic spec′trum, *n.* the entire continuous spectrum of all forms of electromagnetic radiation, from gamma rays to long radio waves.

elec′tromagnet′ic u′nit, *n.* a unit, as an abampere, in the system of units derived from the magnetic effects of an electric current. *Abbr.:* EMU, emu

elec′tromagnet′ic wave′, *n.* a wave propagated at the speed of light by the periodic variations of electric and magnetic fields.

e·lec·tro·mag·net·ism (e lek′trō mag′ni tiz′əm), *n.* **1.** the phenomena associated with electric and magnetic fields and their interactions with each other and with electric charges and currents. **2.** the science

that studies these phenomena. —**e·lec·tro·mag·net′ic** (-mag net′ik), *adj.*

e·lec·tro·me·chan·i·cal (i lek′trō mə kan′i kəl), *adj.* of or pertaining to mechanical devices or systems electrically actuated.

e·lec·tro·met·al·lur·gy (i lek′trō met′l ûr′jē, -mə tal′ər jē), *n.* the science of the processing of metals by means of electricity. —**e·lec′tro·met′al·lur′gi·cal,** *adj.* —**e·lec′tro·met′al·lur′gist,** *n.*

e·lec·trom·e·ter (i lek trom′i tər, ē′lek-), *n.* a calibrated device used for measuring extremely low voltages. —**e·lec′tro·met′ric** (-me′trik), *adj.* **e·lec′tro·met′ri·cal,** *adj.* —**e·lec·trom′e·try,** *n.*

e·lec·tro·mo·tive (i lek′trə mō′tiv), *adj.* pertaining to, producing, or tending to produce a flow of electricity.

elec′tromo′tive force′, *n.* the energy available for conversion from nonelectric to electric form, or vice versa, per unit of charge passing through the source of the energy. *Abbr.:* emf

e·lec·tron (i lek′tron), *n.* an elementary particle that is a fundamental constituent of matter, having a negative charge of 1.602×10^{-19} coulombs, and existing independently or as the component outside the nucleus of an atom.

e·lec·tro·neg·a·tive (i lek′trō neg′ə tiv), *adj.* **1.** containing negative electricity; tending to migrate to the positive pole in electrolysis. **2.** assuming negative potential when in contact with a dissimilar substance. —**e·lec′tro·neg′a·tiv′i·ty,** *n.*

e·lec·tron·ic (i lek tron′ik, ē′lek-), *adj.* **1.** of or pertaining to electronics or to devices, circuits, or systems developed through electronics. **2.** of or pertaining to electrons or to an electron. **3.** (of a musical instrument) using electric or electronic means to produce or modify the sound. **4.** of, pertaining to, or controlled by computers. —**e·lec·tron′i·cal·ly,** *adv.*

electron′ic bank′ing, *n.* the use of computerized systems to conduct banking transactions, as the deposit or transfer of funds.

electron′ic flash′, *n.* a flash lamp, usu. attached to a camera or housed within the camera body, that produces brilliant flashes of light by the discharge of current through a gas-filled tube.

electron′ic mail′, *n.* a system for sending messages via telecommunications links between computers.

e·lec·tron·ics (i lik tron′iks, ē′lek-), *n.* **1.** (*used with a sing. v.*) the science dealing with the development and application of devices and systems involving the flow of electrons in a vacuum, in gaseous media, and in semiconductors. **2.** (*used with a pl. v.*) such devices considered as components of something: *the electronics of a garage-door opener; all the latest electronics.*

electron′ic surveil′lance, *n.* the gathering of information by surreptitious use of electronic devices, as in crime detection or espionage.

elec′tron mi′croscope, *n.* a microscope of extremely high power that uses beams of electrons focused by magnetic lenses instead of rays of light, the magnified image being formed on a fluorescent screen or recorded on a photographic plate.

elec′tron op′tics, *n.* (*used with a sing. v.*) the study and use of the physical and optical properties of beams of electrons under the influence of electric or magnetic fields.

elec′tron tube′, *n.* an electronic device that consists typically of a sealed glass bulb containing two or more electrodes, used to generate, amplify, and rectify electric oscillations and alternating currents.

elec′tron-volt′ or **elec′tron volt′,** *n.* a unit of energy, equal to the energy acquired by an electron accelerating through a potential difference of one volt and equivalent to 1.602×10^{-19} joules. *Abbr.:* eV, ev

e·lec·tro·op·tics or **e·lec·tro-op·tics** (i lek′trō op′tiks), *n.* (*used with a sing. v.*) the branch of physics dealing with the effects of electrical fields on optical phenomena. —**e·lec′tro-op′ti·cal,** —**e·lec′tro·op′ti·cal·ly,** *adv.*

e·lec·tro·phys·i·ol·o·gy (i lek′trō fiz′ē ol′ə jē), *n.* the branch of physiology dealing with the electric phenomena associated with the body and its functions. —**e·lec′tro·phys′i·o·log′i·cal** (-ə loj′i kəl), *adj.* —**e·lec′tro·phys′i·ol′o·gist,** *n.*

e·lec·tro·plate (i lek′trə plāt′), *v.*, **-plat·ed, -plat·ing.** *n.* —*v.t.* **1.** to plate or coat with a metal by electrolysis. —*n.* **2.** electroplated articles or ware. —**e·lec′tro·plat′er,** *n.*

e·lec·tro·pos·i·tive (i lek′trō poz′i tiv), *adj.* **1.** containing positive electricity; tending to migrate to the negative pole in electrolysis. **2.** assuming positive potential when in contact with a dissimilar substance. **3.** basic, as an element or group.

e·lec·tro·scope (i lek′trə skōp′), *n.* a device for detecting the presence and determining the sign of electric charges by means of electrostatic attraction and repulsion, often between two pieces of gold leaf enclosed in a glass-walled chamber. —**e·lec′tro·scop′ic** (-skop′ik), *adj.*

e·lec·tro·shock (i lek′trə shok′), *n.* ELECTROCONVULSIVE THERAPY.

e·lec·tro·stat·ic (i lek′trə stat′ik), *adj.* of or pertaining to static electricity or electrostatics. —**e·lec′tro·stat′i·cal·ly,** *adv.*

e·lec·tro·stat·ics (i lek′trə stat′iks), *n.* (*used with a sing. v.*) the branch of physics dealing with electric phenomena not associated with electricity in motion.

elec′trostat′ic u′nit, *n.* a unit in the system of electric units derived from the force of repulsion between two static charges.

e·lec·tro·ther·a·py (i lek′trō ther′ə pē), *n.* treatment of diseases by means of electricity.

e·lec·trot·o·nus (i lek trot′n əs, ē′lek-), *n.* the altered state of a nerve during the passage of an electric current through it. —**e·lec′tro·ton′ic** (-trə ton′ik), *adj.*

e·lec·tro·type (i lek′trə tīp′), *n., v.,* **-typed, -typ·ing.** —*n.* **1.** a facsimile, for use in printing, of a block of type, an engraving, etc., consisting of a thin copper or nickel shell deposited by electrolytic action in a wax, lead, or plastic mold of the original and backed with lead alloy. —*v.t.* **2.** to make an electrotype of. —**e·lec′tro·typ′er,** *n.* —**e·lec′tro·typ′ic** (-tip′ik), *adj.* —**e·lec′tro·typ′ist** (-tī′pist), *n.*

e·lec·tro·va·lence (i lek′trō vā′ləns) also **e·lec′tro·va′len·cy,** *n.* **1.** the valence of an ion, equal to the number of positive or negative charges acquired by an atom through a loss or gain of electrons. **2.** Also called **elec′trova′lent bond′.** IONIC BOND. —**e·lec′tro·va′lent,** *adj.* —**e·lec′tro·va′lent·ly,** *adv.*

e·lec·trum (i lek′trəm), *n.* **1.** an amber-colored alloy of gold and silver used in antiquity. **2.** German silver; nickel silver.

el·ee·mos·y·nar·y (el′ə mos′ə ner′ē, -moz′-, el′ē ə-), *adj.* involving charity or charitable donations.

el·e·gant (el′i gənt), *adj.* **1.** splendid or luxurious in dress, style, design, etc. **2.** polished and dignified, as in tastes, behavior, or literary style. **3.** graceful in form or movement. **4.** of superior quality; exceptional: *an elegant gift.* **5.** (of theories, solutions, computer programs, etc.) gracefully concise and simple; admirably succinct. —**el′e·gance,** *n.* —**el′e·gant·ly,** *adv.*

el·e·gi·ac (el′i jī′ək, -ak, i lē′jē ak′), *adj.* Also, **el′e·gi′a·cal. 1.** used in, suitable for, or resembling an elegy. **2.** expressing sorrow; mournful. **3.** (in classical prosody) noting a couplet, the first line of which is a dactylic hexameter and the second a pentameter. —*n.* **4.** an elegiac verse. **5.** a poem or poetry in such verses.

el·e·gy (el′i jē), *n., pl.* **-gies. 1.** a mournful, melancholy, or plaintive poem, esp. a lament for the dead. **2.** a poem written in elegiac meter. **3.** a mournful musical composition.

el·e·ment (el′ə mənt), *n.* **1.** a component or constituent of a whole or one of the parts into which a whole may be resolved by analysis. **2.** one of a class of substances that cannot be separated into simpler substances by chemical means. **3.** a natural habitat or environment. **4. elements, a.** atmospheric forces; weather. **b.** the rudimentary principles of an art or science. **c.** the bread and wine of the Eucharistic service. **5.** any group of people singled out, often with disapproval, as having identifiable behavior patterns, common goals, ethnic similarities, etc.: *the radical element.* **6.** one of the substances, usu. earth, air, fire, and water, formerly regarded as constituting the material universe. **7.** a component of a mechanical device: *a printing element on a typewriter.* **8.** *Math.* **a.** an infinitesimal part of a given quantity, similar in nature to it. **b.** an entity that satisfies all the conditions of belonging to a given set. **9.** one of the points, lines, planes, or other geometrical forms of which a figure is composed.

el·e·men·tal (el′ə men′tl), *adj.* **1.** being a fundamental constituent; uncompounded. **2.** pertaining to rudiments or first principles. **3.** starkly simple, primitive, or basic: *elemental emotions.* **4.** pertaining to the forces or phenomena of physical nature. **5.** pertaining to the four elements of earth, air, fire, and water, or any one of them. **6.** pertaining to chemical elements. —**el′e·men′tal·ly,** *adv.*

el·e·men·ta·ry (el′ə men′tə rē, -trē), *adj.* **1.** pertaining to rudiments or first principles. **2.** of or pertaining to an elementary school. **3.** of the nature of an ultimate constituent; simple or uncompounded: *an elementary part of matter.* **4.** pertaining to the four elements of earth, air, fire, and water, or to the great forces of nature. —**el′e·men·tar′i·ly** (-ter′ə lē), *adv.*

el′emen′tary par′ticle, *n.* any of the fundamental units of matter or radiation, including such particles or quanta as the leptons, the hadrons, and the photon.

elemen′tary school′, *n.* a school giving instructions in rudimentary subjects in six to eight grades, often with a kindergarten.

el·e·phant (el′ə fənt), *n., pl.* **-phants,** (*esp. collectively*) **-phant** for 1.

E

CHEMICAL ELEMENTS

Name	Symbol	Atomic No.	Atomic Mass*	Name	Symbol	Atomic No.	Atomic Mass*
Actinium	Ac	89	(227)	Neodymium	Nd	60	144.24
Aluminum	Al	13	26.98154	Neon	Ne	10	20.18
Americium	Am	95	(243)	Neptunium	Np	93	(237)
Antimony	Sb	51	121.75	Nickel	Ni	28	58.71
Argon	Ar	18	39.948	Niobium	Nb	41	92.9064
Arsenic	As	33	74.9216	Nitrogen	N	7	14.0067
Astatine	At	85	(210)	Nobelium	No	102	(256)
Barium	Ba	56	137.34	Osmium	Os	76	190.2
Berkelium	Bk	97	(247)	Oxygen	O	8	15.999
Beryllium	Be	4	9.01218	Palladium	Pd	46	106.4
Bismuth	Bi	83	208.9808	Phosphorus	P	15	30.97376
Boron	B	5	10.81	Platinum	Pt	78	195.09
Bromine	Br	35	79.904	Plutonium	Pu	94	(242)
Cadmium	Cd	48	112.41	Polonium	Po	84	(210)
Calcium	Ca	20	40.08	Potassium	K	19	39.098
Californium	Cf	98	(249)	Praseodymium	Pr	59	140.907
Carbon	C	6	12.011	Promethium	Pm	61	(147)
Cerium	Ce	58	140.12	Protactinium	Pa	91	(231)
Cesium	Cs	55	132.9054	Radium	Ra	88	(226)
Chlorine	Cl	17	35.453	Radon	Rn	86	(222)
Chromium	Cr	24	51.996	Rhenium	Re	75	186.2
Cobalt	Co	27	58.9332	Rhodium	Rh	45	102.9055
Copper	Cu	29	63.546	Rubidium	Rb	37	85.468
Curium	Cm	96	(247)	Ruthenium	Ru	44	101.07
Dysprosium	Dy	66	162.50	Samarium	Sm	62	150.4
Einsteinium	Es	99	(254)	Scandium	Sc	21	44.9559
Erbium	Er	68	167.26	Selenium	Se	34	78.96
Europium	Eu	63	151.96	Silicon	Si	14	28.086
Fermium	Fm	100	(253)	Silver	Ag	47	107.87
Fluorine	F	9	18.99840	Sodium	Na	11	22.9898
Francium	Fr	87	(223)	Strontium	Sr	38	87.62
Gadolinium	Gd	64	157.25	Sulfur	S	16	32.06
Gallium	Ga	31	69.72	Tantalum	Ta	73	180.948
Germanium	Ge	32	72.59	Technetium	Tc	43	(99)
Gold	Au	79	196.967	Tellurium	Te	52	127.60
Hafnium	Hf	72	178.49	Terbium	Tb	65	158.9254
Helium	He	2	4.00260	Thallium	Tl	81	204.37
Holmium	Ho	67	164.9304	Thorium	Th	90	232.0381
Hydrogen	H	1	1.0079	Thulium	Tm	69	168.9342
Indium	In	49	114.82	Tin	Sn	50	118.69
Iodine	I	53	126.9045	Titanium	Ti	22	47.9
Iridium	Ir	77	192.2	Tungsten	W	74	183.85
Iron	Fe	26	55.847	Unnilhexium	Unh	106	(263)
Krypton	Kr	36	83.80	Unnilpentium	Unp	105	(260)
Lanthanum	La	57	138.91	Unnilquadium	Unq	104	(257)
Lawrencium	Lr	103	(257)	Unnilseptium	Uns	107	(262)
Lead	Pb	82	207.2	Uranium	U	92	238.03
Lithium	Li	3	6.94	Vanadium	V	23	50.941
Luletium	Lu	71	174.97	Xenon	Xe	54	131.30
Magnesium	Mg	12	24.305	Ytterbium	Yb	70	173.04
Manganese	Mn	25	54.9380	Yttrium	Y	39	88.9059
Mendelevium	Md	101	(256)	Zinc	Zn	30	65.38
Mercury	Hg	50	200.59	Zirconium	Zr	40	91.22
Molybdenum	Mo	42	95.94				

*Approx. values for radioactive elements given in parentheses.

1. either of two very large five-toed mammals of the family Elephanti-dae, characterized by a long prehensile trunk and large tusks esp. in the males, including *Loxodonta africana* of Africa, with large flapping ears, and *Elephas maximus* of India, with smaller ears. 2. a representation of this animal, used in the U.S. since 1874 as the emblem of the Republican party.

elephant (Indian),
Elephas maximus,
9 ft. (2.7 m) high at shoulder;
tusks 4 to 5 ft. (1.2 m to 1.5 m)

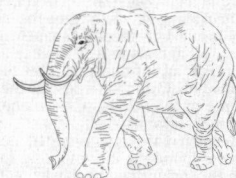

elephant (African),
Loxodonta africana,
11 ft. (3.4 m) high at shoulder;
tusks 6 to 8 ft. (1.8 m to 2.4 m)

el′ephant grass′, *n.* a cattail, *Typha elephantina,* of S Asia, used for making rope and baskets.
el•e•phan•ti•a•sis (el′ə fən tī′ə sis, -fan-), *n.* 1. a chronic disease characterized by marked enlargement of the legs, scrotum, and other parts due to obstruction of the lymphatic vessels, usu. caused by filariasis. 2. unchecked growth or development: *elephantiasis of the ego.*
el•e•phan•tine (el′ə fan′tēn, -tīn, -tin, el′ə fan tēn′, -tīn′), *adj.* 1. pertaining to or resembling an elephant. 2. of massive size; huge: *elephantine buildings.* 3. ponderous; clumsy: *elephantine humor.*
el′ephant seal′, *n.* either of two large seals of the genus *Mirounga,* of the Pacific coast of North America and the Antarctic Ocean, having a trunklike proboscis.
El•eu•sin•i•an mys′teries (el′yoo sin′ē ən), *n.pl.* the mysteries, celebrated annually at Eleusis and Athens in ancient times, in memory of the abduction and return of Persephone and in honor of Demeter and Dionysus.
el•e•vate (*v.* el′ə vāt′; *adj.* -vāt′, -vit), *v.,* **-vat•ed, -vat•ing,** *adj.* —*v.t.* 1. to raise to a higher place or position; lift up. 2. to raise to a higher state or rank; exalt; promote. 3. to raise to a higher intellectual or spiritual level. 4. to put in high spirits.
el′evated rail′road, *n.* a railroad system operating on an elevated structure, as over streets; el.
el•e•va•tion (el′ə vā′shən), *n.* 1. the height to which something is elevated or to which it rises. 2. the altitude of a place above sea level or ground level. 3. an elevated place; eminence. 4. a drawing that represents a building or other object as being projected geometrically on a vertical plane parallel to one of its sides. 5. *Surveying.* **a.** the angle between the line from an observer or instrument to an object above the observer or instrument and a horizontal line. **b.** the distance above a datum level. 6. the ability of a dancer to stay in the air while executing a step, or the height thus attained.
el•e•va•tor (el′ə vā′tər), *n.* 1. a person or thing that elevates or raises. 2. a moving platform or cage for carrying passengers or freight from one level to another, as in a building. 3. any of various mechanical devices for raising objects or materials. 4. a building in which grain is stored and handled by means of mechanical elevator and conveyor devices. 5. a hinged horizontal surface used on the wing of an aircraft to control its longitudinal inclination.
el′evator mu′sic, *n.* unintrusive background music of neutral character typically for broadcast in public areas.
e•lev•en (i lev′ən), *n.* 1. a cardinal number, ten plus one. 2. a symbol for this number, as 11 or XI. 3. a set of this many persons or things. —*adj.* 4. amounting to eleven in number.
e•lev•enth (i lev′ənth), *adj.* 1. next after the tenth; being the ordinal number for 11. 2. being one of 11 equal parts. —*n.* 3. an eleventh part, esp. of one (¹⁄₁₁). 4. the eleventh member of a series.
Elev′enth Amend′ment, *n.* an amendment to the U.S. Constitution, ratified in 1795, that prohibited an individual from suing a state government in the federal courts.
elev′enth hour′, *n.* the last possible moment for doing something: *a stay of execution at the eleventh hour.*
el•e•von (el′ə von′), *n.* (on an aircraft) a control surface functioning both as an elevator and as an aileron.
elf (elf), *n., pl.* **elves** (elvz). 1. a diminutive being in folklore given to mischievous interference in human affairs. 2. a small or mischievous person, esp. a child. —**elf′like′,** *adj.*
ELF or **elf,** EXTREMELY LOW FREQUENCY.
elf•in (el′fin), *adj.* 1. of or like an elf. 2. small and engagingly spritely or mischievous. 3. characterized by dwarfed plant growth: *elfin forest.* —*n.* 4. an elf.
elf•ish (el′fish), *adj.* elflike, esp. in being small and mischievous. —**elf′-ish•ly,** *adv.* —**elf′ish•ness,** *n.*
elf•lock (elf′lok′), *n.* Usu. **elflocks.** locks of hair tangled as if by elves.
El•gar (el′gər, -gär), *n.* **Sir Edward,** 1857–1934, English composer.

El Gre•co (el grek′ō, grā′kō), *n.* (*Domenikos Theotocopoulos*), 1541–1614, Spanish painter, born in Crete.
E•li (ē′lī), *n.* a Hebrew judge and priest. I Sam. 1–4.
e•lic•it (i lis′it), *v.t.* to draw or bring out or forth; evoke: *to elicit a response.*
e•lide (i līd′), *v.t.,* **e•lid•ed, e•lid•ing.** 1. to omit (a vowel, consonant, or syllable) in pronunciation. 2. to abridge. 3. to delete (a written word or passage). 4. to ignore; pass over.
el•i•gi•ble (el′i jə bəl), *adj.* 1. being a proper or worthy choice; desirable: *an eligible bachelor.* 2. meeting the stipulated requirements; qualified. 3. legally qualified to be elected or appointed to office: *eligible for the presidency.* —*n.* 4. a person or thing that is eligible. —**el′i•gi•bil′i•ty,** *n.* —**el′i•gi•bly,** *adv.*
E•li•hu (el′ə hyoo′, i lī′hyoo), *n.* a young man who entered into discourse with Job. Job. 32–37.
E•li•jah (i lī′jə), *n.* a Hebrew prophet of the 9th century B.C. I Kings 17; II Kings 2.
Eli′jah's chair′, *n.* a chair customarily set apart in honor of the prophet Elijah at the Jewish rite of circumcision.
Eli′jah's cup′, *n.* a cup of wine customarily set apart in honor of the prophet Elijah at the Jewish Passover Seder.
E•lim•e•lech (i lim′ə lek′), *n.* the father-in-law of Ruth and husband of Naomi. Ruth 1:1–3.
e•lim•i•nate (i lim′ə nāt′), *v.t.,* **-nat•ed, -nat•ing.** 1. to get rid of; eradicate. 2. to omit; leave out. 3. to defeat in a contest. 4. to kill; slaughter. 5. to void or expel, as waste, from the body. 6. to remove (a quantity) from an equation by elimination. [< Latin *ēlīmīnātus,* turned out of doors] —**e•lim′i•na′tive,** *adj.*
e•lim•i•na•tion (i lim′ə nā′shən), *n.* 1. the act of eliminating or the state of being eliminated. 2. (in a tournament) a contest in which an individual or team is eliminated after one defeat.
El•i•ot (el′ē ət, el′yət), *n.* 1. **Charles William,** 1834–1926, U.S. educator: president of Harvard University 1869–1909. 2. **George** (*Mary Ann Evans*), 1819–80, English novelist. 3. **John** ("*the Apostle of the Indians*"), 1604–90, American colonial missionary. 4. **T(homas) S(tearns)** (stûrnz), 1888–1965, British poet and critic, born in the U.S.
El•i•phaz (el′ə faz′), *n.* one of the three friends of Job who comforted him. Job 2:11; 4:1; 15:1.
E•lis•a•beth (i liz′ə bəth), *n.* the mother of John the Baptist. Luke 1:5–25.
E•li•sha (i lī′shə), *n.* a Hebrew prophet of the 9th century B.C., the successor of Elijah. II Kings 3–9.
e•li•sion (i lizh′ən), *n.* 1. the omission of a vowel, consonant, or syllable in pronunciation. 2. (in verse) the omission of a vowel at the end of one word when the next word begins with a vowel, as *th'orient.* 3. an act or instance of eliding or omitting something.
e•lite or **é•lite** (i lēt′, ā lēt′), *n.* 1. (*often used with a pl. v.*) the choice or best of a group, class, or the like. 2. (*used with a pl. v.*) persons of the wealthiest class. 3. a group of persons exercising authority within a larger group. 4. a 10-point type widely used in typewriters and having 12 characters to the inch. Compare PICA¹. —*adj.* 5. of the best or most select.
e•lit•ism (i lē′tiz əm, ā lē′-), *n.* 1. practice of or belief in rule by an elite. 2. consciousness of membership in or allegiance to a select group. —**e•lit′ist,** *n., adj.*
e•lix•ir (i lik′sər), *n.* 1. a sweetened aromatic solution of alcohol and water containing or used as a vehicle for medicinal substances. 2. Also called **elix′ir of life′.** an alchemic preparation formerly believed capable of prolonging life indefinitely. 3. an alchemic preparation formerly believed to be capable of transmuting base metals into gold. 4. QUINTESSENCE. 5. PANACEA.
E•liz•a•beth¹ (i liz′ə bəth), *n.* 1. (*Elizaveta Petrovna*) 1709–62, empress of Russia 1741–62 (daughter of Peter the Great). 2. (*Elizabeth Angela Marguerite Bowes-Lyon*) born 1900, queen consort of George VI of Great Britain (mother of Elizabeth II). 3. a city in NE New Jersey. 106,298.
E•liz•a•beth² (i liz′ə bəth), *n.* 1. **Elizabeth I,** (*Elizabeth Tudor*) 1533–1603, queen of England 1558–1603 (daughter of Henry VIII and Anne Boleyn). 2. **Elizabeth II,** (*Elizabeth Alexandra Mary Windsor*) born 1926, queen of Great Britain since 1952 (daughter of George VI).
E•liz•a•be•than (i liz′ə bē′thən, -beth′ən), *adj.* 1. of or pertaining to the reign of Elizabeth I, queen of England, or to her times: *Elizabethan drama.* —*n.* 2. a person who lived in England during the Elizabethan period, esp. a poet or dramatist.
elk (elk), *n., pl.* **elks,** (*esp. collectively*) **elk** for 1, 2. 1. Also called **wapiti.** a large North American deer, *Cervus canadensis.* 2. the moose, *Alces alces.* 3. pliable leather made from elk hide or from skin, as cowhide, tanned to resemble it. 4. (*cap.*) a member of a fraternal organization (Benevolent and Protective Order of Elks) that supports various charitable causes.
elk•hound (elk′hound′), *n.* NORWEGIAN ELKHOUND.
El•kin (el′kin), *n.* **Stanley,** 1930–95, U.S. novelist and short-story writer.
ell or **el** (el), *n.* 1. an extension usu. at right angles to one end of a building or room. 2. ELBOW (def. 4).
-elle, a noun suffix occurring in loanwords from French, where it orig. formed diminutives, now often with a derivative sense in which the di-

minutive force is lost (*bagatelle*; *rondelle*); also occurring in Anglicized forms of Latin words ending in *-ella* (*organelle*).

Elles'mere Is'land (elz'mēr) *n.* an island in the Arctic Ocean, NW of Greenland: a part of Canada. 76,600 sq. mi. (198,400 sq. km).

El'lice Is'lands (el'is), *n.pl.* a former name of TUVALU.

El·li·ott (el'ē ət, el'yət), *n.* **Charlotte,** 1789–1871, English hymn writer.

el·lipse (i lips'), *n.* a plane curve such that the sums of the distances of each point in its periphery from two fixed points, the foci, are equal; a conic section formed by the intersection of a right circular cone by a plane that cuts the axis and the surface of the cone.

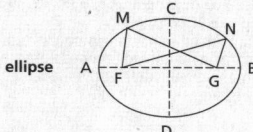

ellipse

el·lip·sis (i lip'sis), *n., pl.* **-ses** (-sēz). **1.** the omission from a sentence or other construction of one or more words understandable from the context that would complete or clarify the construction, as the omission of *been to Paris* from the second clause of *I've been to Paris but he hasn't.* **2.** a mark or marks, as ——, or ... , or * * *, to indicate an omission or suppression of letters or words.

el·lip·soid (i lip'soid), *n.* a solid figure whose plane sections are all ellipses or circles. —*adj.* **2.** ellipsoidal.

el·lip·soi·dal (i lip soid'l, el'ip-, ē'lip-), *adj.* pertaining to or having the form of an ellipsoid.

el·lip·ti·cal (i lip'ti kəl), *adj.* Also, **el·lip'tic. 1.** pertaining to or having the form of an ellipse. **2.** pertaining to or marked by grammatical ellipsis. **3. a.** characterized by extreme economy of expression in speech or writing. **b.** ambiguous; cryptic; obscure. —**el·lip'ti·cal·ly,** *adv.* —**el·lip'ti·cal·ness,** *n.*

El'lis Is'land, *n.* an island in upper New York Bay: a former U.S. immigrant examination station.

El·li·son (el'ə sən), *n.* **Ralph (Waldo),** 1914–94, U.S. novelist.

elm (elm), *n.* **1.** any tree of the genus *Ulmus*, as *U. procera*, characterized by the gradually spreading columnar manner of growth of its branches. Compare AMERICAN ELM. **2.** the wood of such a tree.

elm' bark' bee'tle, *n.* **1.** a shiny, dark reddish-brown European bark beetle, *Scolytus multistriatus*, now widespread in the U.S.: the primary vector of Dutch elm disease. **2.** a bark beetle, *Hylurgopinus opaculus*, of E North America, that also transmits Dutch elm disease.

elm' leaf' bee'tle, *n.* a leaf beetle, *Calerucella luteola*, of E North America, that feeds on the foliage of the elm.

El Mon·te (el mon'tē), *n.* a city in SW California, near Los Angeles. 104,661.

El Ni·ño (el nēn'yō), *n.* a warm ocean current of variable intensity that develops after late December along the coast of Ecuador and Peru and sometimes causes catastrophic weather conditions. [< Spanish: lit., the child, i.e., the Christ child, alluding to the appearance of the current near Christmas]

el·o·cu·tion (el'ə kyōō'shən), *n.* **1.** a style of speaking or reading aloud. **2.** the study and practice of public speaking. —**el'o·cu'tion·ar·y** (-shə ner'ē), *adj.* —**el'o·cu'tion·ist,** *n.*

E·lo·him (el'ō hēm', -him', e lō'him), *n.* God, esp. as used in the Hebrew text of the Old Testament. —**El'o·him'ic** (-him'ik), *adj.*

E·lo·hist (e lō'hist, el'ō-), *n.* a writer of one of the major sources of the Hexateuch, in which God is characteristically referred to as *Elohim* rather than *Yahweh*. Compare YAHWIST. —**El'o·his'tic,** *adj.*

e·lon·gate (el'ə kyōō'shən), *v.*, **-gat·ed, -gat·ing,** *adj.* —*v.t.* **1.** to lengthen or extend. —*v.i.* **2.** to increase in length. —*adj.* Also, **e·lon'gat·ed. 3.** extended; lengthened. **4.** long and thin. —**e'lon·ga'tive,** *adj.*

e·lon·ga·tion (i lông gā'shən, ē'lông-), *n.* **1.** the act of elongating or the state of being elongated. **2.** the angular distance, measured from the earth, between a planet or the moon and the sun or between a satellite and its primary.

e·lope (i lōp'), *v.i.*, **e·loped, e·lop·ing. 1.** to run off secretly to be married, usu. without the knowledge or consent of one's parents. **2.** to abandon one's spouse for a lover. **3.** to flee; escape. —**e·lope'ment,** *n.*

el·o·quent (el'ə kwənt), *adj.* **1.** skilled in fluent and forceful speech. **2.** exhibiting appropriate expression. **3.** (of actions, gestures, etc.) forcefully expressive. —**el'o·quence,** *n.* —**el'o·quent·ly,** *adv.*

El Pas·o (el pas'ō), *n.* a city in W Texas, on the Rio Grande. 579,307.

El Sal·va·dor (el sal'və dôr'), *n.* a republic in NW Central America. 5,661,827; 13,176 sq. mi. (34,125 sq. km). *Cap.:* San Salvador. Also called Salvador.

else (els), *adj.* **1.** other than those or that mentioned: *What else could I do?* **2.** in addition to those mentioned: *Who else was there?* **3.** other (used in the possessive following an indefinite pronoun): *someone else's money.* —*adv.* **4.** if not (usu. prec. by *or*): *It's a macaw, or else I don't know birds.* **5.** otherwise: *How else could I have acted?* **6.** at another place or time: *Where else should I look?* —*Idiom.* **7. or else,** or suffer

the consequences: *Do what I say, or else.* —**Usage.** The possessive forms of *somebody else, everybody else,* etc., are *somebody else's, everybody else's,* etc., the forms *somebody's else, everybody's else* now being considered nonstandard. One exception is the possessive for *who else,* occasionally formed as *whose else* (instead of *who else's*) when a noun does not immediately follow: *Is this book yours? Whose else could it be?*

else·where (els'hwâr', -wâr'), *adv.* somewhere else; in or to some other place: *You will have to look elsewhere for an answer.*

e·lu·ci·date (i lōō'si dāt'), *v.*, **-dat·ed, -dat·ing.** —*v.t.* **1.** to make lucid or clear; explain. —*v.i.* **2.** to provide clarification. —**e·lu·ci·da'tion,** *n.* —**e·lu'ci·da'tive,** *adj.* —**e·lu'ci·da'tor,** *n.*

e·lu·cu·brate (i lōō'kyōō brāt'), *v.t.*, **-brat·ed, -brat·ing.** to produce, as a literary work, by long and intensive effort. —**e·lu'cu·bra'tion,** *n.*

e·lude (i lōōd'), *v.t.*, **e·lud·ed, e·lud·ing. 1.** to avoid capture or escape detection by; evade. **2.** to escape the perception or comprehension of: *His popularity eludes me.* —**e·lud'er,** *n.*

E·lul (el'ōol), *n.* the twelfth month of the Jewish calendar.

e·lu·sion (i lōō'zhən), *n.* the act of eluding; escape or evasion.

e·lu·sive (i lōō'siv) also **e·lu·so·ry** (-sə rē, -zə-), *adj.* **1.** eluding one's clear perception; hard to express or define. **2.** skillfully evasive. —**e·lu'sive·ly,** *adv.* —**e·lu'sive·ness,** *n.*

e·lute (ē lōōt', i lōōt'), *v.t.*, **e·lut·ed, e·lut·ing.** to remove by dissolving, as absorbed material from an adsorbent. —**e·lu'tion,** *n.*

e·lu·vi·al (i lōō'vē əl), *adj.* of or pertaining to eluviation or eluvium.

e·lu·vi·a·tion (i lōō'vē ā'shən), *n.* the movement through the soil of materials brought into suspension or dissolved by the action of water.

e·lu·vi·um (i lōō'vē əm), *n., pl.* **-vi·a** (-vē ə). a deposit of soil, dust, etc., formed from the decomposition of rock and found in its place of origin.

el·ver (el'vər), *n.* a young eel, esp. one migrating up a stream from the ocean.

elves (elvz), *n.* pl. of ELF.

El·y·mas (el'ə məs), *n.* BAR-JESUS.

E·ly·si·um (i lizh'ē əm, i liz'-), *n.* **1.** the abode of the blessed after death in Greek religious belief. **2.** PARADISE (def. 4). —**E·ly'si·an,** *adj.*

em (em), *n., pl.* **ems. 1.** the letter *M, m.* **2. a.** the square of any size of type used as the unit of measurement for matter printed in that type size. **b.** (orig.) the portion of a line of type occupied by the letter *M* in type of the same size.

EM, electromagnetic.

em-[1], var. of EN-[1] before *b, p,* and sometimes *m: embalm.* Compare IM-[1].

em-[2], var. of EN-[2] before *b, m, p, ph: embolism; emphasis.*

e·ma·ci·ate (i mā'shē āt'), *v.t.*, **-at·ed, -at·ing.** to make abnormally thin by a gradual wasting away of flesh.

e·ma·ci·at·ed (i mā'shē ā'tid), *adj.* marked by emaciation.

e·ma·ci·a·tion (i mā'shē ā'shən, -sē-), *n.* **1.** abnormal thinness caused by starvation or by disease. **2.** the process of emaciating.

E-mail (ē'māl'), *n.* ELECTRONIC MAIL.

em·a·nate (em'ə nāt'), *v.*, **-nat·ed, -nat·ing.** —*v.i.* **1.** to flow out, issue forth; originate. —*v.t.* **2.** to send forth; emit. —**em'a·na'tive,** *adj.* —**em'a·na'tor,** *n.*

em·a·na·tion (em'ə nā'shən), *n.* **1.** an act or instance of emanating. **2.** something that emanates or is emanated. **3.** a gaseous product of radioactive disintegration. —**em'a·na'tion·al,** *adj.*

e·man·ci·pate (i man'sə pāt'), *v.t.*, **-pat·ed, -pat·ing. 1.** to free from restraint. **2.** to free (a slave) from bondage. —**e·man'ci·pa'tive,** *adj.* —**e·man'ci·pa'tor,** *n.*

e·man·ci·pa·tion (i man'sə pā'shən), *n.* **1.** the act of emancipating. **2.** the state or fact of being emancipated.

e·mas·cu·late (*v.* i mas'kyə lāt'; *adj.* -lit, -lāt'), *v.*, **-lat·ed, -lat·ing,** *adj.* —*v.t.* **1.** to castrate. **2.** to deprive of strength or vigor; weaken. —*adj.* **3.** deprived of strength or vigor. —**e·mas'cu·la'tion,** *n.*

em·balm (em bäm'), *v.t.* **1.** to treat (a dead body) so as to preserve it, as with chemicals, drugs, or balsams. **2.** to preserve from oblivion; keep in memory. **3.** to keep unchanged. **4.** to perfume. —**em·balm'er,** *n.*

em·bank·ment (em bangk'mənt), *n.* a bank, mound, dike, or the like, raised to hold back water, carry a roadway, etc.

em·bar·go (em bär'gō), *n., pl.* **-goes,** *v.,* **-goed, -go·ing.** —*n.* **1.** an order by a government prohibiting the movement of merchant ships into or out of its ports. **2.** an order from a government agency restricting or barring certain freight for shipment. **3.** any restriction imposed upon commerce by edict: *an embargo on munitions.* **4.** any restraint or prohibition. —*v.t.* **5.** to impose an embargo on. [< Spanish, der. of *embargar* to hinder, embarrass]

em·bark (em bärk'), *v.i.* **1.** to board a ship, aircraft, or other vehicle, as for a journey. **2.** to start or partake in an enterprise: *to embark on a business venture.* —*v.t.* **3.** to board (passengers) onto a ship, aircraft, or the like. **4.** to start up or invest in an enterprise. —**em·bark'ment,** *n.*

em·bar·ka·tion (em'bär kā'shən), *n.* the act or process of embarking. Sometimes, **embarcation.**

em·bar·rass (em bar'əs), *v.t.* **1.** to make ashamed or self-conscious; disconcert. **2.** to make difficult or intricate; complicate. **3.** to impede. **4.** to burden with debt. **5.** to become disconcerted or abashed. —**em·bar'rassed·ly,** *adv.* —**em·bar'rass·ing·ly,** *adv.*

em·bar·rass·ment (em bar'əs mənt), *n.* **1.** the state of being embarrassed; discomposure. **2.** an act of embarrassing. **3.** something or someone that embarrasses. **4.** an excess: *an embarrassment of riches.* **5.** fi-

E

nancial difficulty. **6.** *Med.* impairment of functioning associated with disease: *respiratory embarrassment.*

em·bas·sy (em/bə sē), *n., pl.* **-sies. 1.** the official headquarters of an ambassador. **2.** the function or office of an ambassador. **3.** a mission headed by an ambassador. **4.** a body of persons sent on a diplomatic mission.

em·bat·tle[1] (em bat/l), *v.t.,* **-tled, -tling. 1.** to arm or array for battle. **2.** to fortify (a town, camp, etc.).

em·bat·tle[2] (em bat/l), *v.t.,* **-tled, -tling.** to furnish with battlements.

em·bat·tled (em bat/ld), *adj.* **1.** disposed or prepared for battle. **2.** engaged in or beset by conflict or struggle.

em·bed (em bed/), *v.,* **-bed·ded, -bed·ding. —v.t. 1.** to fix into a surrounding mass: *to embed stones in cement.* **2.** to envelop or enclose. **3.** to contain or implant as an essential or characteristic part. **4.** to insert (a grammatical construction, as a phrase or clause) into a larger construction, as a clause or sentence. —*v.i.* **5.** to be fixed or incorporated into a surrounding mass.

em·bel·lish (em bel/ish), *v.t.* **1.** to beautify by or as if by ornamentation; adorn. **2.** to enhance with elaborative additions. —**em·bel/lish·ment,** *n.*

em·ber (em/bər), *n.* **1.** a small live piece of coal, wood, etc., as in a dying fire. **2. embers,** the smoldering remains of a fire.

Em/ber day/, *n.* any of the days in the quarterly three-day period of prayer and fasting (the Wednesday, Friday, and Saturday after the first Sunday in Lent, after Whitsunday, after Sept. 14, and after Dec. 13) observed in some Western churches. [Old English *ymbrendæg = ymbryne* recurrence (*ymb(e)* around + *ryne* a running) + *dæg* DAY]

em·bez·zle (em bez/əl), *v.t.,* **-zled, -zling.** to appropriate fraudulently to one's own use, as money entrusted to one's care. —**em·bez/zle·ment,** *n.* —**em·bez/zler,** *n.*

em·bit·ter (em bit/ər), *v.t.* **1.** to make bitter; cause to feel bitterness. **2.** to make bitter or more bitter in taste.

em·bla·zon (em blā/zən), *v.t.* **1.** to adorn with heraldic devices or emblems. **2.** to decorate brilliantly. **3.** to proclaim in celebration. —**em·bla/zon·er,** *n.* —**em·bla/zon·ment,** *n.*

em·blem (em/bləm), *n.* **1.** an object symbolizing a quality, state, etc.; symbol: *The olive branch is an emblem of peace.* **2.** a figure or design that identifies something: *the emblem of a school.* **3.** an allegorical picture, often inscribed with a motto, that embodies a moral principle. —*v.t.* **4.** to represent with an emblem. —**em·blem·at/ic,** *adj.*

em·bod·y (em bod/ē), *v.t.,* **-bod·ied, -bod·y·ing. 1.** to give a concrete form to; personify or exemplify: *works that embodied the spirit of the age.* **2.** to provide with a body; incarnate. **3.** to collect into a body; organize. **4.** to embrace or comprise. —**em·bod/i·ment,** *n.*

em·bold·en (em bōl/dən), *v.t.* to make bold; encourage.

em·bo·lism (em/bə liz/əm), *n.* **1.** the occlusion of a blood vessel by an embolus. **2.** intercalation, as of a day into a year.

em·bo·lus (em/bə ləs), *n., pl.* **-li** (-lī/). **1.** a formerly circulating clump of tissue, gas bubble, fat globule, etc., that has lodged in a blood vessel.

em·boss (em bôs/, -bos/), *v.t.* **1.** to raise (designs) from a surface; represent in relief. **2.** to decorate (a surface) with raised ornament. **3.** to raise a design on (a blank) with dies of similar pattern, one the negative of the other. —**em·boss/a·ble,** *adj.* —**em·boss/er,** *n.*

em·bou·chure (äm/bŏŏ shŏŏr/), *n.* **1.** the mouthpiece of a wind instrument. **2.** the adjustment of a player's mouth to an embouchure.

em·brace (em brās/), *v.,* **-braced, -brac·ing,** *n.* —*v.t.* **1.** to clasp in the arms; hug. **2.** to accept willingly: *to embrace an idea.* **3.** to adopt; accept: *to embrace a religion.* **4.** to include or contain. —*v.i.* **5.** to join in an embrace. —*n.* **6.** an encircling hug with the arms. —**em·brace/a·ble,** *adj.* —**em·brac/er,** *n.*

em·brac·er·y (em brā/sə rē), *n., pl.* **-er·ies.** an attempt to influence a judge or jury by corrupt means, as bribery or intimidation.

em·bra·sure (em brā/zhər), *n.* **1.** an opening in the wall of a fortification through which a cannon may be fired. **2.** a splayed enlargement of a door or window toward the inner face of a wall. —**em·bra/sured,** *adj.*

em·bro·cate (em/brō kāt/, -brə-), *v.t.,* **-cat·ed, -cat·ing.** to moisten and rub with a liniment or lotion.

em·bro·glio (em brōl/yō), *n., pl.* **-glios.** IMBROGLIO.

em·broi·der (em broi/dər), *v.t.* **1.** to decorate with embroidery. **2.** to form by or with embroidery. **3.** to embellish with ornate language, fictitious details, etc. —*v.i.* **4.** to do embroidery. **5.** to add elaborating details; embellish (often fol. by *on* or *upon*).

em·broi·der·y (em broi/də rē, -drē), *n., pl.* **-der·ies. 1.** the art or process of working ornamental designs upon cloth or other material with a needle and thread. **2. a.** embroidered work or ornamentation. **b.** an article containing embroidery. **3.** elaboration, as in telling a story.

em·broil (em broil/), *v.t.* **1.** to involve in conflict. **2.** to throw into confusion. —**em·broil/ment,** *n.*

em·bry·o (em/brē ō/), *n., pl.* **-os.** —*n.* **1.** an animal in the early stages of development in the womb or egg; in humans, the stage approximately from attachment of the fertilized egg to the uterine wall until about the eighth week of pregnancy. Compare FETUS, ZYGOTE. **2.** the rudimentary plant usu. contained in the seed. **3.** the beginning stage of anything. —**em·bry·on/ic** (-on/ik), *adj.*

em·bry·ol·o·gy (em/brē ol/ə jē), *n., pl.* **-gies. 1.** the study of embryonic formation and development. **2.** the origin, growth, and develop-

ment of an embryo: *the embryology of the chick.* —**em/bry·o·log/i·cal** (-ə loj/i kəl), **em/bry·o·log/ic,** *adj.* —**em/bry·o·log/i·cal·ly,** *adv.* —**em/bry·ol/o·gist,** *n.*

em/bry·o sac/, *n.* (in flowering plants) a large cell of the rudimentary seed, within which the embryo develops. Also called **megaspore.**

em·cee (em/sē/), *n., v.,* **-ceed, -cee·ing.** —*n.* **1.** master of ceremonies. —*v.i., v.t.* **2.** to serve or direct as master of ceremonies.

em/ dash/, *n. Print.* a dash one em long.

e·mend (i mend/), *v.t.* **1.** to edit or change (a text). **2.** to revise or correct. —**e·mend/a·ble,** *adj.* —**e/men·da/tion,** *n.*

em·er·ald (em/ər əld, em/rəld), *n.* **1.** a rare variety of beryl that is colored green by chromium and valued as a gem. **2.** EMERALD GREEN. —*adj.* **3.** having a clear, deep green color.

em/erald cut/, *n.* a cut used esp. on emeralds and diamonds in which the girdle has the form of a square or rectangle with truncated corners. Compare BRILLIANT CUT, MARQUISE (def. 3a).

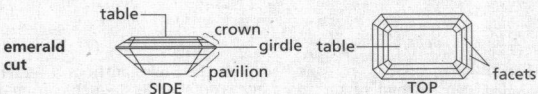

emerald cut — table · crown · girdle · table · pavilion · SIDE · TOP · facets

em/erald green/, *n.* a clear, deep green.

e·merge (i mûrj/), *v.i.,* **e·merged, e·merg·ing. 1.** to come forth into view, as from concealment. **2.** to rise or come forth from or as if from water. **3.** to arise, as a question. **4.** to come into existence; develop. **5.** to rise, as from an inferior state. —**e·mer/gence,** *n.* —**e·mer/gent,** *adj.*

e·mer·gen·cy (i mûr/jən sē), *n., pl.* **-cies,** *adj.* —*n.* **1.** a sudden, urgent, usu. unexpected occurrence requiring immediate action. **2.** a situation requiring help or relief, usu. created by an unexpected event: *a weather emergency.* —*adj.* **3.** required or used in an emergency: *emergency lights.*

emer/gency brake/, *n.* a hand- or pedal-operated brake used to prevent a motor vehicle from rolling, esp. after it has been parked. Also called **parking brake.**

emer/gency room/, *n.* a hospital area equipped and staffed for the prompt treatment of acute illness, trauma, or other medical emergencies. *Abbr.:* ER

e·mer·i·ta (i mer/i tə), *adj., n., pl.* **-tae** (-tē/). —*adj.* **1.** (of a woman) retired or honorably discharged from active professional duty but retaining the title of one's office or position: *professor emerita of music.* —*n.* **2.** a woman with such status.

e·mer·i·tus (i mer/i təs), *adj., n., pl.* **-ti** (-tī/, -tē/). —*adj.* **1.** retired or honorably discharged from active professional duty but retaining the title of one's office or position: *professor emeritus of history.* —*n.* **2.** an emeritus professor, minister, etc.

e·mersed (i mûrst/), *adj.* (of a plant) rising or standing out of water, surrounding leaves, etc.

Em·er·son (em/ər sən), *n.* **Ralph Waldo,** 1803–82, U.S. essayist and poet. —**Em/er·so/ni·an** (-sō/nē ən), *adj.*

em·er·y (em/ə rē, em/rē), *n.* a dark, impure, granular variety of corundum used for grinding and polishing.

em/ery board/, *n.* a small, stiff strip of paper or cardboard coated with powdered emery and used in manicuring.

e·met·ic (i met/ik), *adj.* **1.** causing vomiting, as a medicinal substance. —*n.* **2.** an emetic medicine or agent.

emf or **EMF,** or **E.M.F.,** or **e.m.f.,** electromotive force.

em·i·grant (em/i grənt), *n.* **1.** a person who emigrates from a native country or region. —*adj.* **2.** having left one country to settle in another.

em·i·grate (em/i grāt/), *v.i.,* **-grat·ed, -grat·ing.** to leave one country or region to settle in another; migrate. —**em/i·gra/tive,** *adj.*

em·i·gra·tion (em/i grā/shən), *n.* **1.** an act or instance of emigrating. **2.** a body of emigrants, or emigrants collectively. **3.** DIAPEDESIS. —**em/i·gra/tion·al,** *adj.*

é·mi·gré (em/i grā, em/i grā/), *n.* an emigrant, esp. a person who flees a native land because of political conditions.

em·i·nence (em/ə nəns), *n.* **1.** high station, rank, or repute. **2.** a high elevation; hill or height. **3.** (*cap.*) a title of honor, applied to cardinals (usu. prec. by *His* or *Your*). **4.** an anatomical projection, esp. on a bone.

em·i·nent (em/ə nənt), *adj.* **1.** high in station, rank, or repute; distinguished. **2.** greatest; utmost: *eminent fairness.* **3.** lofty; high. **4.** prominent; jutting: *an eminent nose.* —**em/i·nent·ly,** *adv.*

em/inent domain/, *n.* the power of the state to take private property for public use with payment of compensation to the owner.

e·mir (ə mēr/, ā mēr/), *n.* **1.** a chieftain, prince, commander, or head of state in some Islamic countries. **2.** a title of honor of the descendants of Muhammad.

em·ir·ate (em/ər it, ə mēr/it, -āt, ā mēr/-), *n.* **1.** the office or rank of an emir. **2.** the state or territory of an emir.

em·is·sar·y (em/ə ser/ē), *n., pl.* **-sar·ies,** *adj.* —*n.* **1.** a representative sent on a mission; delegate. **2.** an agent sent on a secret mission. —*adj.* **3.** pertaining to an emissary.

e·mis·sion (i mish/ən), *n.* **1.** an act or instance of emitting. **2.** something emitted. **3.** an official act of issuing, as paper money. **4.** a measure of the number of electrons emitted by the heated filament or cathode of a vacuum tube. **5.** an ejection or discharge of semen or other fluid from the body.

e·mit (i mit′), *v.t.*, **e·mit·ted, e·mit·ting. 1.** to send forth (liquid, light, particles, etc.); discharge. **2.** to utter (a sound): *to emit a cry.* **3.** to voice (opinions, etc.). **4.** to issue formally, as paper money.

Em·ma (em′ə), a novel (1815) by Jane Austen.

Em·man·u·el (i man′yōō əl), *n.* IMMANUEL.

Em·ma·us (ə mā′əs), *n.* a village near Jerusalem toward which two disciples were walking when they met the resurrected Jesus. Luke 24:13.

Em·men·tha·ler or **Em·men·ta·ler** (em′ən tä′lər), also **Em′men·thal′, Em′men·tal′,** *n.* a pale yellow Swiss cheese made from cow's milk and containing many large round holes.

em·mer (em′ər), *n.* a wheat, *Triticum dicoccum,* having a two-grained spikelet, grown as a forage crop.

Em·my (em′ē), *n., pl.* **-mys.** (*sometimes l.c.*) any of a group of awards given annually by the National Academy of Television Arts and Sciences for excellence in television programming, production, or performance.

e·mol·lient (i mol′yənt), *adj.* **1.** having the power to soften or soothe: *an emollient lotion for the skin.* —*n.* **2.** an emollient substance. —**e·mol′lience,** *n.*

e·mol·u·ment (i mol′yə mənt), *n.* compensation, as fees or tips, from employment; recompense.

e·mote (i mōt′), *v.i.,* **e·mot·ed, e·mot·ing. 1.** to show or pretend emotion. **2.** to portray emotion in acting, esp. exaggeratedly or ineptly. —**e·mot′er,** *n.*

e·mo·tion (i mō′shən), *n.* **1.** an affective state of consciousness in which joy, sorrow, fear, etc., is experienced, as distinguished from cognitive and volitional states of consciousness. **2.** any of the feelings of joy, sorrow, fear, hate, love, etc. **3.** a strong agitation of the feelings caused by experiencing love, hate, fear, etc. —**e·mo′tion·less,** *adj.*

e·mo·tion·al (i mō′shə nl), *adj.* **1.** pertaining to or involving the emotions. **2.** easily affected by emotion. **3.** attempting to sway the emotions: *an emotional plea for funds.* **4.** showing or describing very strong emotions. **5.** based on emotion rather than reason: *an emotional decision.* —**e·mo′tion·al·ly,** *adv.*

e·mo·tion·al·ism (i mō′shə nl iz′əm), *n.* **1.** a tendency to indulge in excessive, often morbid, emotion. **2.** conduct, policies, etc., that are based upon feelings rather than reason.

e·mo·tive (i mō′tiv), *adj.* **1.** pertaining to or showing emotion. **2.** directed toward or activating the emotions. —**e·mo′tive·ly,** *adv.* —**e·mo′tive·ness, e·mo·tiv·i·ty** (ē′mō tiv′i tē, i mō-), *n.*

em·pa·na·da (em′pə nä′də), *n.* a Latin American or Spanish turnover filled with ground meat, vegetables, fruit, etc., and baked or fried.

em·path·ic (em path′ik) also **em·pa·thet·ic** (em′pə thet′ik), *adj.* pertaining to or showing empathy: *an empathic response to another's suffering.* —**em·path′i·cal·ly, em′pa·thet′i·cal·ly,** *adv.*

em·pa·thize (em′pə thīz′), *v.i.,* **-thized, -thiz·ing.** to experience empathy (often fol. by *with*): *to empathize with another's grief.*

em·pa·thy (em′pə thē), *n.* **1.** the identification with or vicarious experiencing of the feelings, thoughts, etc., of another. **2.** the imaginative ascribing to an object of one's feelings or attitudes.

em·pen·nage (äm′pə näzh′, em′-), *n.* the rear part of an airplane or airship, usu. comprising the stabilizer, elevator, vertical fin, and rudder.

em·per·or (em′pər ər), *n.* **1.** the male sovereign or supreme ruler of an empire. —*Saying.* **2. The emperor has no clothes on,** the purported wealth, ability, accomplishments, and power of well-known figures may be a sham. [from a fairy tale by Hans Christian Andersen]

em′peror pen′guin, *n.* the largest penguin, *Aptenodytes forsteri,* of Antarctic coasts.

em·pha·sis (em′fə sis), *n., pl.* **-ses** (-sēz′). **1.** special stress or importance attached to something. **2.** something that is given special stress or importance. **3.** stress laid on particular words, by means of position, repetition, or other indication.

em·pha·size (em′fə sīz′), *v.t.,* **-sized, -siz·ing.** to give emphasis to; stress.

em·phat·ic (em fat′ik), *adj.* **1.** uttered with emphasis; strongly expressive. **2.** using emphasis in speech or action. **3.** forceful; insistent. **4.** clearly or boldly outlined. **5.** of or pertaining to a word or form used to add emphasis, as the stressed auxiliary *do* in affirmative statements, as in *I do like it.* —**em·phat′i·cal·ly,** *adv.*

em·phy·se·ma (em′fə sē′mə, -zē′-), *n.* **1.** a disease of the lungs characterized by difficulty in breathing due to abnormal enlargement and loss of elasticity of the air spaces. **2.** any abnormal distention of an organ or part of the body with air or other gas. —**em′phy·se′mic,** *adj.*

em·pire (em′pīⁿr; *for 7 also on* pēr′), *n.* **1.** a group of nations, states, or peoples ruled over by an emperor, empress, or other powerful sovereign, as the former British Empire. **2.** a government under an emperor or empress. **3.** (*often cap.*) the historical period during which a nation is under such a government: *French furniture of the Second Empire.* **4.** supreme power in governing; sovereignty; dominion. **5.** a large and powerful enterprise controlled by one person, family, or group: *a shipping empire.* **6.** (*cap.*) a variety of apple somewhat resembling the McIntosh. —*adj.* **7.** (*cap.*) characteristic of or developed during the first French Empire, 1804–15. [< Anglo-French, Old French < Latin *imperium*]

Em′pire State′, *n.* the state of New York (used as a nickname).

em·pir·ic (em pir′ik), *n.* **1.** a person who is guided primarily by experience. **2.** a quack; charlatan. —*adj.* **3.** empirical.

em·pir·i·cal (em pir′i kəl), *adj.* **1.** derived from experience or experiment. **2.** depending upon experience or observation alone, without using scientific method or theory, esp. in medicine. **3.** verifiable by experience or experiment. —**em·pir′i·cal·ly,** *adv.*

empir′ical for′mula, *n.* a chemical formula showing the elements of a compound and their relative proportions, as $(CH_2O)_n$ or H_2O.

em·pir·i·cism (em pir′ə siz′əm), *n.* **1.** empirical method or practice. **2.** the philosophic doctrine that all knowledge is derived from sense experience. Compare RATIONALISM (def. 2). **3.** undue reliance upon experience, as in medicine; quackery. **4.** a conclusion that is arrived at empirically. —**em·pir′i·cist,** *n., adj.*

em·place (em plās′), *v.t.,* **-placed, -plac·ing.** to put in place or position.

em·place·ment (em plās′mənt), *n.* **1.** a space prepared for the positioning of an artillery piece or other heavy weapon. **2.** a putting in place or position.

em·plane (em plān′), *v.i., v.t.,* **-planed, -plan·ing.** ENPLANE.

em·ploy (em ploi′), *v.,* **-ployed, -ploy·ing.** —*v.t.* **1.** to engage the services of (a person or persons); hire. **2.** to make use of for a specific task: *employed computers to solve the problem.* **3.** to devote (time, energies, etc.) to a particular activity. —*n.* **4.** employment; service. —**em·ploy′a·ble,** *adj.*

em·ploy·ee or **em·ploy·e** (em ploi′ē, em ploi ē′, em′ploi ē′), *n.* a person who has been hired to work for another.

em·ploy·er (em ploi′ər), *n.* a person or business that employs one or more people for wages or salary.

em·ploy·ment (em ploi′mənt), *n.* **1.** an act or instance of employing a person or thing. **2.** the state of being employed. **3.** work or business; occupation. **4.** an activity that occupies a person's time.

employ′ment a′gency, *n.* an agency that helps to find jobs for people or assists employers in filling vacant positions.

em·po·ri·um (em pôr′ē əm, -pōr′-), *n., pl.* **-po·ri·ums, -po·ri·a** (-pôr′ē ə, -pōr′-). **1.** a retail store selling a great variety of articles. **2.** a chief commercial center.

em·pow·er (em pou′ər), *v.t.* **1.** to give official or legal power or authority to. **2.** to endow with an ability; enable. —**em·pow′er·ment,** *n.*

em·press (em′pris), *n.* **1.** a female ruler of an empire. **2.** the consort of an emperor.

emp·ty (emp′tē), *adj.,* **-ti·er, -ti·est,** *v.,* **-tied, -ty·ing,** *n., pl.* **-ties.** —*adj.* **1.** containing nothing; devoid of contents. **2.** vacant; unoccupied. **3.** devoid of human activity. **4.** hollow; meaningless. **5.** unemployed; idle: *empty days.* **6.** *Math.* (of a set) containing no elements; null; void. **7.** hungry. **8.** frivolous; foolish. —*v.t.* **9.** to make empty. **10.** to discharge (contents). —*v.i.* **11.** to become empty. **12.** to debouch: *The river empties into the sea.* —*n.* **13.** an empty container. —*Idiom.* **14. running on empty,** having lost vitality, significance, or creative abilities. —**emp′ti·a·ble,** *adj.* —**emp′ti·ly,** *adv.* —**emp′ti·ness,** *n.*

emp′ty cal′orie, *n.* a calorie whose food source has little or no nutritional value.

emp′ty chair′, *n.* the refusal of a politician to debate during an electoral campaign.

emp′ty-hand′ed, *adj.* **1.** having nothing in the hands. **2.** having achieved nothing. **3.** bringing no gift, donation, etc.

emp′ty-head′ed, *adj.* foolish; brainless. —**emp′ty-head′ed·ness,** *n.*

emp′ty nest′ syn′drome, *n.* a depressed state felt by some parents after their children have grown up and left home.

em·pur·ple (em pûr′pəl), *v.,* **-pled, -pling.** —*v.t.* **1.** to color or tinge purple. —*v.i.* **2.** to become purple or deeply flushed.

em·py·re·al (em′pə rē′əl, -pī-, em pir′ē əl, -pī′rē-) also **empyrean,** *adj.* **1.** pertaining to the highest heaven in the cosmology of the ancients. **2.** pertaining to the sky; celestial. **3.** exalted; sublime.

em·py·re·an (em′pə rē′ən, -pī-, em pir′ē ən, -pī′rē-), *n.* **1.** the visible heavens; the firmament. —*adj.* **2.** EMPYREAL.

EMS, emergency medical service.

EMT, emergency medical technician.

e·mu (ē′myōō), *n., pl.* **e·mus.** a large, flightless, ratite bird, *Dromaius (Dromiceius) novaehollandiae,* of Australia, resembling the ostrich.

EMU or **emu,** electromagnetic unit.

em·u·late (*v.* em′yə lāt′; *adj.* -lit), *v.,* **-lat·ed, -lat·ing,** *adj.* —*v.t.* **1.** to imitate in an effort to equal or surpass. **2.** to rival with some degree of success. **3. a.** to imitate the functions of (another computer system) by means of software. **b.** to replace (software) with hardware to perform the same task. —**em′u·la·tive,** *adj.* —**em′u·la·tive·ly,** *adv.* —**em′u·la·tor,** *n.*

em·u·la·tion (em′yə lā′shən), *n.* effort or desire to equal or excel others.

e·mul·si·fy (i mul′sə fī′), *v.t., v.i.,* **-fied, -fy·ing.** to make into or become an emulsion. —**e·mul′si·fi′a·ble, e·mul′si·ble,** *adj.* —**e·mul′si·fi·ca′tion,** *n.* —**e·mul′si·fi′er,** *n.*

e·mul·sion (i mul′shən), *n.* **1.** any colloidal suspension of a liquid in another liquid. **2.** any liquid mixture containing medicine suspended in minute globules. **3.** a photosensitive layer of silver halide suspended in gelatin, thinly applied to one surface of a photographic film. —**e·mul′sive,** *adj.*

E

en (en), *n.* **1.** the letter *N*, *n.* **2.** a space that is half the width of an em.

en-[1], a prefix forming verbs that have the general sense "to cause (a person or thing) to be in" the place, condition, or state named by the stem; more specifically, "to confine in or place on" (*entomb*); "to cause to be in" (*enrich; enslave; entrust*); "to restrict," typically with the additional sense "on all sides, completely" (*encircle; enclose*). This prefix is also attached to verbs in order to make them transitive, or to give them a transitive marker if they are already transitive (*enkindle; enliven; enshield*). Also, *before labial consonants*, **em-.** Compare BE-, IN-[2].

en-[2], a prefix meaning "within, in," occurring in loanwords from Greek: *energy; enthusiasm.* Also, *before labial consonants*, **em-.**

en•a•ble (en ā′bəl), *v.t.*, **-bled, -bling. 1.** to make able; authorize or empower. **2.** to make possible or easy. —**en•a′bler,** *n.*

en•a•bling (en ā′bling), *adj.* conferring legal power or sanction, as by removing a disability: *an enabling act.*

en•act (en akt′), *v.t.* **1.** to make into an act or statute: *to enact a new tax law.* **2.** to represent in or as if in a play or the like; act the part of. —**en•act′a•ble,** *adj.* —**en•ac′tor,** *n.*

en•act•ment (en akt′mənt), *n.* **1.** the act or process of enacting. **2.** the state or fact of being enacted. **3.** something that is enacted; a law or statute.

e•nam•el (i nam′əl), *n., v.,* **-eled, -el•ing** or (*esp. Brit.*) **-elled, -el•ling.** —*n.* **1.** a glassy substance, usu. opaque, applied by fusion to the surface of metal, pottery, etc., as an ornament or for protection. **2.** ENAMELWARE. **3.** any of various varnishes, paints, coatings, etc., drying to a hard, glossy finish. **4.** an artistic work executed in enamel. **5.** the hard, glossy, calcareous covering of the crown of a tooth. —*v.t.* **6.** to inlay or overlay with enamel. —**e•nam′el•er,** *n.* —**e•nam′el•ist,** *n.* —**e•nam′el•work′,** *n.*

e•nam•el•ware (i nam′əl wâr′), *n.* metalware, as cooking utensils, covered with an enamel surface.

en•am•or (i nam′ər), *v.t.* to fill or inflame with love; charm; captivate (usu. used in the passive and fol. by *of*).

en•cae•nia (en sēn′yə, -sē′nē ə), *n.* **1.** (*used with a pl. v.*) festive ceremonies commemorating the founding of a city or the consecration of a church. **2.** (*cap.*) (*often used with a sing. v.*) ceremonies at Oxford University in honor of founders and benefactors.

en•camp (en kamp′), *v.i., v.t.* to lodge or settle in a camp.

en•camp•ment (en kamp′mənt), *n.* **1.** an act or instance of encamping. **2.** the place or quarters occupied in camping; camp.

en•cap•su•late (en kap′sə lāt′, -syōō-), *v.t.,* **-lat•ed, -lat•ing.** —*v.t.* **1.** to place in or as if in a capsule. **2.** to summarize or condense. —*v.i.* **3.** to become encapsulated. —**en•cap′su•la′tion,** *n.*

en•cap•sule (en kap′səl, -syōōl), *v.t., v.i.,* **-suled, -sul•ing.** to encapsulate.

en•case (en kās′), *v.t.,* **-cased, -cas•ing.** to enclose in or as if in a case. —**en•case′ment,** *n.*

en•caus•tic (en kô′stik), *adj.* **1.** painted with wax colors fixed with heat, or with any process in which colors are burned in. —*n.* **2.** a work of art produced by an encaustic process. —**en•caus′ti•cal•ly,** *adv.*

en•ceinte[1] (än sant′, -sant′, än-), *adj.* pregnant; with child.

en•ceinte[2] (än sant′, -sant′, än-), *n.* **1.** a ring of fortifications enclosing a place. **2.** the place enclosed.

en•ceph•a•li•tis (en sef′ə lī′tis), *n.* **1.** inflammation of the brain. **2.** SLEEPING SICKNESS (def. 2). —**en•ceph′a•lit′ic** (-lit′ik), *adj.*

encephalo-, a combining form meaning "brain": *encephalograph.*

en•ceph•a•lo•gram (en sef′ə lə gram′), *n.* an x-ray of the brain, usu. involving replacement of some cerebrospinal fluid by air or other gas that circulates to the brain's ventricular spaces and acts as a contrast medium.

en•ceph•a•lo•graph (en sef′ə lə graf′, -gräf′), *n.* **1.** an encephalogram. **2.** an electroencephalograph. —**en•ceph′a•lo•graph′ic** (-graf′ik), *adj.* —**en•ceph′a•lo•log′ra•phy** (-log′rə fē), *n.*

en•ceph•a•lon (en sef′ə lon′, -lən), *n., pl.* **-lons, -la** (-lə). the brain. —**en′ce•phal′ic** (-sə fal′ik), *adj.*

en•chant (en chant′, -chänt′), *v.t.* **1.** to subject to magical influence; place under a spell; bewitch. **2.** to delight utterly; captivate. **3.** to impart a magic quality or effect to. —**en•chant′er,** *n.* —**en•chant′ment,** *n.*

en•chant•ress (en chan′tris, -chän′-), *n.* **1.** a woman who practices magic; sorceress. **2.** an irresistibly charming woman.

en•chi•la•da (en′chə lä′də, -lad′ə), *n., pl.* **-das.** a tortilla rolled around a filling, as of meat or cheese, covered usu. with a chili-flavored sauce, and baked.

en•ci•na (en sē′nə), *n., pl.* **-nas.** CALIFORNIA LIVE OAK. —**en•ci′nal,** *adj.*

en•ci•pher (en sī′fər), *v.t.* to convert (a message) into cipher. —**en•ci′pher•er,** *n.*

en•cir•cle (en sûr′kəl), *v.t.,* **-cled, -cling. 1.** to form a circle around; surround; encompass. **2.** to make a circling movement around; make a circuit of. —**en•cir′cle•ment,** *n.*

en•clave (en′klāv, än′-), *n., v.,* **-claved, -clav•ing.** —*n.* **1.** a country or a portion of a country surrounded by foreign territory. **2.** any small, distinct area or group enclosed or isolated within a larger one. —*v.t.* **3.** to make an enclave of.

en•clit•ic (en klit′ik), *adj.* **1.** (of a word) closely connected in pronunciation with the preceding word and not having an independent accent

or phonological status. —*n.* **2.** an enclitic word, as the form of *are* in *we're.* —**en•clit′i•cal•ly,** *adv.*

en•close (en klōz′), *v.t.,* **-closed, -clos•ing. 1.** to close in on all sides; shut or hem in. **2.** to surround, as with a fence or wall: *to enclose land.* **3.** to insert in the same envelope, package, etc.: *to enclose a check.* **4.** to contain or hold. —**en•clos′a•ble,** *adj.*

en•clo•sure (en klō′zhər), *n.* **1.** something that encloses, as a fence or wall. **2.** an enclosed area, esp. a tract of land surrounded by a fence. **3.** something enclosed or included, as within a letter. **4.** an act or instance of enclosing; the state of being enclosed.

en•code (en kōd′), *v.t.,* **-cod•ed, -cod•ing.** to convert (information, a message, etc.) into code. —**en•cod′a•ble,** *adj.* —**en•cod′er,** *n.*

en•co•mi•ast (en kō′mē ast′, -əst), *n.* a person who utters or writes an encomium. —**en•co′mi•as′tic,** *adj.*

en•co•mi•um (en kō′mē əm), *n., pl.* **-mi•ums, -mi•a** (-mē ə). a usu. formal expression of high praise; eulogy.

en•com•pass (en kum′pəs), *v.t.* **1.** to form a circle about; encircle; surround. **2.** to enclose; envelop. **3.** to include comprehensively. **4.** to bring about; achieve. —**en•com′pass•ment,** *n.*

en•core (äng′kôr, -kōr, än′-), *interj., n., v.,* **-cored, -cor•ing.** —*interj.* **1.** again; once more (used by an audience in calling for a repetition or an additional performance). —*n.* **2.** a demand by an audience for a repetition of a song or act, performance of an additional piece, etc. **3.** the performance in response to such a demand. —*v.t.* **4.** to call for a repetition of. **5.** to call for an encore from (a performer).

en•coun•ter (en koun′tər), *v.t.* **1.** to come upon or meet with, esp. unexpectedly. **2.** to meet with or contend against (difficulties, opposition, etc.). **3.** to meet (a person, military force, etc.) in conflict. —*v.i.* **4.** to meet, esp. unexpectedly. —*n.* **5.** a meeting with a person or thing, esp. a casual, unexpected, or brief meeting. **6.** a meeting of people or groups that are in conflict; combat.

en•cour•age (en kûr′ij, -kur′-), *v.t.,* **-aged, -ag•ing. 1.** to inspire with courage, spirit, or confidence. **2.** to stimulate by guidance, approval, etc. **3.** to promote; foster. —**en•cour′ag•ing•ly,** *adv.* —**en•cour′age•ment,** *n.*

en•croach (en krōch′), *v.i.* **1.** to advance beyond established or proper limits; make gradual inroads. **2.** to trespass upon the property, domain, or rights of another, esp. gradually or stealthily. —**en•croach′er,** *n.* —**en•croach′ment,** *n.*

en•crust (en krust′), *v.t., v.i.* INCRUST.

en•crus•ta•tion (en′kru stā′shən), *n.* INCRUSTATION.

en•crypt (en kript′), *v.t.* to encipher or encode. —**en•cryp′tion, en′cryp•ta′tion,** *n.*

en•cul•tu•ra•tion (en kul′chə rā′shən), *n.* the process by which individuals adapt to their culture and assimilate its values. —**en•cul′tu•rate′,** *v.t.,* **-rat•ed, -rat•ing.**

en•cum•ber (en kum′bər), *v.t.* **1.** to impede or hinder; hamper. **2.** to block up or fill with superfluous or obstructive things. **3.** to weigh down; burden. **4.** to burden with obligations, debt, etc.

en•cum•brance (en kum′brəns), *n.* **1.** something that encumbers; a burden or hindrance. **2.** a child or other dependent. **3.** *Law.* a claim on property, as a mortgage.

en•cyc•li•cal (en sik′li kəl, -sī′kli-) also **en•cyc′lic,** *n.* **1.** a letter addressed by the pope to all the bishops of the church. —*adj.* **2.** (of a letter) intended for wide or general circulation; general.

en•cy•clo•pe•di•a or **en•cy•clo•pae•di•a** (en sī′klə pē′dē ə), *n.* a book or set of books containing articles on various topics, usu. in alphabetical arrangement, covering all branches of knowledge or all aspects of one subject. [< New Latin < Greek *enkyklopaidía* circular (i.e., well-rounded) education]

end (end), *n.* **1.** the last part, lengthwise, of anything that is longer than it is wide: *the end of a rope.* **2.** a point that indicates the full extent of something; limit; bounds. **3.** a part or place at or adjacent to an extremity: *the west end of town.* **4.** the most remote place or point. **5.** termination; conclusion. **6.** the concluding part. **7.** an intention or aim: *to gain one's ends.* **8.** the object for which a thing exists; purpose. **9.** an outcome or result. **10.** termination of existence; death. **11.** destruction or ruin, or a cause of this. **12.** a remnant or fragment. **13.** a share or part. **14.** a warp thread running vertically and interlaced with the filling yarn in the woven fabric. **15.** either of the linemen in football stationed farthest from the center. **16. the end,** *Slang.* someone or something incredibly good or bad; the limit. —*v.t.* **17.** to bring to an end; conclude; terminate. **18.** to form the end of. **19.** to kill. **20.** to surpass or epitomize (usu. in the infinitive): *the blunder to end all blunders.* —*v.i.* **21.** to come to an end; cease. **22.** to result (usu. fol. by *in*). **23.** to reach a final status or condition (often fol. by *up*). —*adj.* **24.** final or ultimate: *the end result.* —*Idiom.* **25. at the end of one's rope** or **tether,** at the end of one's resources, patience, or strength. **26. end to end,** in a row with ends touching. **27. go off the deep end, a.** to lose emotional control; become overwrought. **b.** to act in a reckless or impulsive manner. **28. in the end,** finally; after all. **29. keep** or **hold one's end up,** to perform one's part or share adequately. **30. make (both) ends meet,** to live within one's means. **31. no end,** very much or many: *to be pleased no end by the response.* **32. on end, a.** with one end down; upright. **b.** continuously. **33. put an end to,** to terminate; finish. —**end′er,** *n.*

en•dan•ger (en dān′jər), *v.t.* **1.** to expose to danger; imperil: *to endanger one's life.* **2.** to threaten with extinction. —**en•dan′ger•ment,** *n.*

endan'gered spe'cies, *n.* a species at risk of extinction because of human activity, changes in climate, changes in predator-prey ratios, etc., esp. when officially designated as such by a governmental or international agency.

en' dash', *n. Print.* a dash one en long.

end'-blown', *adj.* (of a flute) having a mouthpiece at the end of the tube through which the player's breath is directed. Compare TRANSVERSE (def. 2).

en•dear (en dēr'), *v.t.* to make dear, esteemed, or beloved: *He endeared himself to us with his gentle ways.* —**en•dear'ing•ly,** *adv.*

en•dear•ment (en dēr'mənt), *n.* an utterance or action expressing affection.

en•deav•or (en dev'ər), *v.i.* **1.** to exert oneself to do or effect something; make an effort; strive. —*v.t.* **2.** to attempt earnestly; try: *to endeavor to succeed.* —*n.* **3.** a strenuous effort; attempt.

en•dem•ic (en dem'ik), *adj.* Also, **en•dem'i•cal. 1.** natural to or characteristic of a particular place, people, etc.: *an endemic disease; endemic unemployment.* **2.** belonging exclusively or confined to a particular place: *a species of bat endemic to Mexico.* —*n.* **3.** an endemic organism or disease. —**en•dem'i•cal•ly,** *adv.*

end' game' or **end'game',** *n.* the final stage of a game of chess, usu. following the exchange of queens and the serious reduction of forces.

end•ing (en'ding), *n.* **1.** the final or concluding part; conclusion. **2.** a bringing or coming to an end; termination; close. **3.** death; destruction. **4. a.** a morpheme at the end of a word, esp. an inflection, as the *-s* in *cuts.* **b.** any final word part, as the *-ow* in *window.*

en•dive (en'dīv, än dēv'), *n.* **1.** a composite plant, *Cichorium endivia,* having a rosette of often curly-edged leaves used in salads. **2.** Also called **Belgian endive.** a young chicory plant deprived of light to form a narrow head of whitish leaves, eaten in salads or cooked.

end•less (end'lis), *adj.* **1.** having or seeming to have no end; boundless; infinite. **2.** interminable or incessant. **3.** made continuous, as by joining the two ends of a single length: *an endless chain.* —**end'less•ly,** *adv.* —**end'less•ness,** *n.*

end' line', *n.* **1.** the boundary line at either end of a court or playing field. **2.** a line at each end of a football field parallel to and 10 yds. (9 m) behind the goal line.

end•most (end'mōst'), *adj.* farthest; most distant; last.

end•note (end'nōt'), *n.* a note, as of explanation, emendation, or the like, added at the end of an article, chapter, etc.

en•do•blast (en'də blast'), *n.* **1.** ENDODERM (def. 1). **2.** HYPOBLAST (def. 2). —**en'do•blas'tic,** *adj.*

en•do•car•di•um (en'dō kär'dē əm), *n., pl.* **-di•a** (-dē ə). the serous membrane that lines the cavities of the heart.

en•do•carp (en'də kärp'), *n.* the inner layer of a pericarp, as the stone of certain fruits.

en•do•cra•ni•al cast' (en'dō krā'nē əl, en'-), *n.* a cast of the inside of the cranium, as of a fossil skull, used to determine brain size and shape.

en•do•crine (en'də krin, -krīn', -krēn'), *adj.* Also, **en•do•cri•nal** (en'də krīn'l, -krēn'l). **1.** secreting internally into the blood or lymph. **2.** of or pertaining to an endocrine gland or its secretion. —*n.* **3.** ENDOCRINE GLAND. Compare EXOCRINE.

en'docrine gland', *n.* any gland, as the thyroid, adrenal, or pituitary gland, that secretes hormones into the blood or lymph.

en•do•cri•nol•o•gy (en'dō krə nol'ə jē, -krī-), *n.* the study of the endocrine glands and their secretions, esp. in relation to their processes or functions. —**en'do•crin'o•log'ic** (-krin'l oj'ik, -krīn'-), **en'do•crin'o•log'i•cal,** *adj.* —**en'do•cri•nol'o•gist,** *n.*

en•do•derm (en'də dûrm'), *n.* **1.** Also called **endoblast.** the innermost cell layer of the embryo in its gastrula stage. **2.** the innermost body tissue that derives from this layer, as the gut lining. —**en'do•der'mal, en'do•der'mic,** *adj.*

en•do•der•mis (en'dō dûr'mis), *n.* a specialized tissue in the roots and stems of vascular plants.

en•do•don•tics (en'dō don'tiks) also **en•do•don•tia** (-don'shə, -shē ə), **en•do•don•tol•o•gy** (en'dō don tol'ə jē), *n.* (*used with a sing. v.*) the branch of dentistry dealing with the prevention, diagnosis, and treatment of diseases of the dental pulp and associated structures and tissues. Compare ROOT CANAL THERAPY (def. 1). —**en'do•don'tic,** *adj.* —**en'do•don'ti•cal•ly,** *adv.* —**en'do•don'tist,** *n.*

en•dog•a•my (en dog'ə mē), *n.* marriage within a specific tribe or similar social unit. Compare EXOGAMY (def. 1). —**en•dog'a•mous, en•dog'am•ic** (en'dō gam'ik), *adj.*

en•do•me•tri•um (en'dō mē'trē əm), *n., pl.* **-tri•a** (-trē ə). the membrane lining the uterus. —**en'do•me'tri•al,** *adj.*

en•do•morph (en'də môrf'), *n.* **1.** a mineral enclosed within another mineral. **2.** a person of the endomorphic type.

en•do•mor•phic (en'də môr'fik), *adj.* **1.** *Mineral.* **a.** occurring in the form of an endomorph. **b.** of or pertaining to endomorphs. **c.** taking place within a rock mass. **2.** having a heavy body build roughly characterized by the relative prominence of structures developed from the embryonic endoderm (contrasted with *ectomorphic, mesomorphic*). —**en'do•mor'phy,** *n.*

en•do•plasm (en'də plaz'əm), *n.* the inner portion of the cytoplasm of a cell. Compare ECTOPLASM (def. 1).

endoplas'mic retic'ulum, *n.* a network of tubular membranes within the cytoplasm of the cell, occurring either with a smooth surface (smooth endoplasmic reticulum) or studded with ribosomes (rough endoplasmic reticulum), involved in the transport of materials.

En•dor (en'dôr), *n.* a town where King Saul consulted a medium. I Sam. 28:7.

en•dor•phin (en dôr'fin), *n.* any of a group of peptides, resembling opiates, that are released in the body in response to stress or trauma and that react with the brain's opiate receptors to reduce the sensation of pain.

en•dorse (en dôrs'), *v.t.,* **-dorsed, -dors•ing. 1.** to express approval or support of, esp. publicly: *to endorse a political candidate.* **2.** to designate oneself as payee of (a check) by signing, usu. on the reverse side of the instrument. **3.** to sign one's name on (a commercial document or other instrument). **4.** to make over (a stated amount) to another as payee by one's endorsement. **5.** to write (something) on the back of a document, paper, etc. **6.** to acknowledge (payment) by placing one's signature on a bill, draft, etc. —**en•dors'a•ble,** *adj.* —**en•dors'er, en•dor'sor,** *n.*

en•dorse•ment (en dôrs'mənt), *n.* **1.** approval or sanction. **2.** the placing of one's signature, instructions, etc., on a document. **3.** a signature or instructions placed on the back of a check or other document, as for the purpose of assigning one's interest therein to another. **4.** a clause under which the stated coverage of an insurance policy may be altered.

en•do•scope (en'də skōp'), *n.* a slender, tubular optical instrument used for examining the interior of a body cavity or hollow organ. —**en'do•scop'ic** (-skop'ik), *adj.* —**en•dos'co•py,** *n.*

en•do•skel•e•ton (en'dō skel'i tn), *n.* the internal skeleton or framework of the body of an animal (opposed to *exoskeleton*). —**en'do•skel'e•tal,** *adj.*

en•do•sperm (en'də spûrm'), *n.* nutritive matter in seed-plant ovules, derived from the embryo sac.

en•do•spore (en'də spôr', -spōr'), *n.* **1.** the inner coat of a spore. Compare INTINE. **2.** a spore formed within a cell of a rod-shaped organism. —**en'do•spor'ous** (en dos'pər əs), *adj.*

en•do•the•li•um (en'dō thē'lē əm), *n., pl.* **-li•a** (-lē ə). a single layer of smooth tissue that lines the heart, blood vessels, lymphatic vessels, and serous cavities. —**en'do•the'li•al,** *adj.*

en•do•therm (en'də thûrm'), *n.* a warm-blooded animal.

en•do•ther•mic (en'dō thûr'mik) also **en•do•ther'mal,** *adj.* **1.** noting or pertaining to a chemical change that is accompanied by an absorption of heat (opposed to *exothermic*). **2.** WARM-BLOODED (def. 1). —**en'do•ther'mi•cal•ly,** *adv.* —**en'do•ther'my, en'do•ther'mism,** *n.*

en•dow (en dou'), *v.t.* **1.** to provide with a permanent fund or source of income, as by a donation: *to endow a college.* **2.** to furnish, as with some talent, faculty, or quality; equip. —**en•dow'er,** *n.*

en•dow•ment (en dou'mənt), *n.* **1.** the act of endowing. **2.** the property, funds, etc., with which an institution or person is endowed. **3.** Often, **endowments.** natural ability or talent.

end'pa•per or **end' pa•per,** *n.* a sheet of paper folded vertically once to form two leaves, one of which is pasted flat to the inside of the front or back cover of a book, with the other pasted to the inside edge of the first or last page to form a flyleaf. Also called **end' sheet'.**

end' point', *n.* **1.** a final goal or finishing point. **2.** the point in a titration usu. noting the completion of a chemical reaction and marked by some change, as in the color of an indicator. **3.** ENDPOINT.

end•point (end'point'), *n. Math.* the point on each side of an interval marking its extremity on that side. Also, **end point.**

end' prod'uct, *n.* the final or resulting product, as of an industry or a process of growth.

end' run', *n.* **1.** Also called **end' sweep'.** a running play in football in which the ballcarrier attempts to outflank the defensive end. **2.** an indirect or evasive and expedient maneuver.

end' ta'ble, *n.* a small table placed beside a chair or at the end of a sofa.

en•dur•a•ble (en dŏŏr'ə bəl, -dyŏŏr'-), *adj.* capable of being endured; bearable; tolerable. —**en•dur'a•bil'i•ty,** *n.* —**en•dur'a•bly,** *adv.*

en•dur•ance (en dŏŏr'əns, -dyŏŏr'-), *n.* **1.** the fact or power of bearing pain, hardship, or adversity. **2.** the ability to continue or last, esp. despite fatigue, stress, etc.; stamina. **3.** lasting quality; duration. **4.** something endured, as a hardship; trial.

en•dure (en dŏŏr', -dyŏŏr'), *v.,* **-dured, -dur•ing. —***v.t.* **1.** to hold out against; sustain without impairment or yielding; undergo: *to endure hardship.* **2.** to bear patiently or without resistance; tolerate. **3.** to admit of; allow; bear. —*v.i.* **4.** to continue to exist; last. **5.** to support adverse force or influence; suffer without yielding.

end' use' (yōōs), *n.* the ultimate use for which something is intended or to which it is put.

end•ways (end'wāz') also **end•wise** (-wīz'), *adv.* **1.** on end. **2.** with the end upward or forward. **3.** toward the ends or end; lengthwise. **4.** with ends touching; end to end.

end' zone', *n.* **1.** the area at either end of a football field between the goal line and the end line. **2.** the area at either end of an ice-hockey rink between the goal line and the closer of the two blue lines.

en•e•ma (en'ə mə), *n., pl.* **-mas. 1.** the injection of a fluid into the rec-

E

tum. **2.** the fluid injected. **3.** Also called **en′ema bag′.** a baglike device for administering an enema.

en•e•my (en′ə mē), *n., pl.* **-mies,** *adj.* —*n.* **1.** a person who hates, opposes, or fosters harmful designs against another; hostile opponent; adversary. **2.** an opposing military force; armed foe. **3.** a ship, aircraft, etc., of such a force. **4.** a hostile nation or state. **5.** a citizen of such a state. **6.** something harmful or prejudicial. **7. the Enemy,** the Devil; Satan. —*adj.* **8.** belonging to a hostile power or to any of its nationals: *enemy property.* —**Usage.** See COLLECTIVE NOUN.

en•e•my with•in′, *n.* someone who acts against the interests of a group or nation of which he or she is a part.

en•er•get•ic (en′ər jet′ik), *adj.* **1.** possessing or exhibiting energy, esp. in abundance; vigorous; active. **2.** powerful in action or effect; forceful; effective. —**en′er•get′i•cal•ly,** *adv.*

en•er•get•ics (en′ər jet′iks), *n. (used with a sing. v.)* the branch of physics that deals with energy. —**en′er•get′i•cist,** *n.* —**en′er•ge•tis′-tic** (-ji tis′tik), *adj.*

en•er•gize (en′ər jīz′), *v.,* **-gized, -giz•ing.** —*v.t.* **1.** to give energy to; rouse into activity. **2.** to supply electrical current to. —*v.i.* **3.** to be in operation; put forth energy. —**en′er•giz′er,** *n.*

en•er•gy (en′ər jē), *n., pl.* **-gies. 1.** the capacity for vigorous activity; available power. **2.** a feeling of having an adequate or abundant amount of such power. **3.** Often, **energies,** an exertion of such power; effort: *She threw all her energies into the job.* **4.** the habit of vigorous activity; vigor. **5.** the ability to act, lead others, or effect things forcefully. **6.** forcefulness of expression. **7.** *Physics.* the capacity to do work. *Symbol:* E **8.** any source of usable power, as fossil fuel, nuclear fission, electricity, or solar radiation.

en′ergy effi′ciency ra′tio, *n.* a measure of the efficiency of a heating or cooling system, equal to the ratio of the output in BTU per hour to the input in watts. *Abbr.:* EER

en′ergy lev′el, *n.* one of a quantized series of states in which matter may exist, each having constant energy and separated from others in the series by finite quantities of energy. Also called **en′ergy state′.**

En′ergy Star′ Pro′gram, *n.* a program of the U.S. Environmental Protection Agency encouraging the manufacture of personal computers that can reduce their energy consumption when left idle.

en•er•vate (*v.* en′ər vāt′; *adj.* i nûr′vit), *v.,* **-vat•ed, -vat•ing,** *adj.* —*v.t.* **1.** to deprive of force or strength; destroy the vigor of; weaken. —*adj.* **2.** lacking strength or vitality; enervated. —**en′er•va′tion,** *n.* —**en′er•va′tive,** *adj.* —**en′er•va′tor,** *n.*

en•fee•ble (en fē′bəl), *v.t.,* **-bled, -bling.** to make feeble; weaken. —**en•fee′ble•ment,** *n.* —**en•fee′bler,** *n.*

en•fi•lade (en′fə lād′, -läd′), *n., v.,* **-lad•ed, -lad•ing.** —*n.* **1.** sweeping gunfire from along the length of a line of troops, a battery, etc. **2.** an axial arrangement, as of doorways connecting a group of rooms, providing a long vista. —*v.t.* **3.** to attack with an enfilade.

en•fold (en fōld′), *v.t.* **1.** to wrap up; envelop. **2.** to surround with or as if with folds. **3.** to hug or clasp; embrace. **4.** to form into a fold or folds.

en•force (en fôrs′, -fōrs′), *v.t.,* **-forced, -forc•ing. 1.** to put or keep in force; compel obedience to: *to enforce a law.* **2.** to obtain by force or compulsion; compel: *to enforce obedience.* **3.** to impose (a course of action) upon a person. **4.** to support by force. **5.** to impress or urge forcibly. —**en•force′a•ble,** *adj.* —**en•force′a•bil′i•ty,** *n.* —**en•forc′ed•ly,** *adv.* —**en•force′ment,** *n.*

en•forc•er (en fôr′sər, -fōr′-), *n.* **1.** a person or thing that enforces. **2.** a member of a group, esp. a gang, charged with keeping dissident members obedient.

en•fran•chise (en fran′chīz), *v.t.,* **-chised, -chis•ing. 1.** to admit to citizenship, esp. to the right of voting. **2.** to endow (a city, constituency, etc.) with municipal or parliamentary rights. **3.** to set free; liberate, as from slavery. —**en•fran′chise•ment** (-chīz mənt, -chiz-), *n.* —**en•fran′chis•er,** *n.*

eng (eng), *n.* the symbol ŋ, used in phonetic alphabets to represent the sound (ng), as in *sing* (siŋ) or *sink* (siŋk).

ENG, electronic news gathering: a system of news reportage using portable television cameras and sound equipment.

en•gage (en gāj′), *v.,* **-gaged, -gag•ing.** —*v.t.* **1.** to occupy the attention or efforts of; involve: *He engaged her in conversation.* **2.** to secure for aid, employment, or use; hire: *to engage a caterer; to engage a room.* **3.** to attract and hold fast: *The book engaged my attention.* **4.** to attract or please. **5.** to bind, as by a pledge or promise; make liable. **6.** to bind by a pledge to marry; betroth (usu. used in the passive). **7.** to enter into conflict with: *Our army engaged the enemy.* **8.** to cause (gears or the like) to become interlocked; interlock with. **9.** to attach or secure. —*v.i.* **10.** to occupy oneself; become involved: *to engage in politics.* **11.** to take employment. **12.** to pledge one's word; assume an obligation. **13.** to cross weapons; enter into conflict. **14.** (of gears or the like) to interlock. —**en•gag′er,** *n.*

en•ga•gé (Fr. än gA zhā′), *adj.* involved in or committed to something, as a political cause.

en•gaged (en gājd′), *adj.* **1.** busy or occupied. **2.** pledged to be married; betrothed: *an engaged couple.* **3.** committed or involved. **4.** involved in conflict with. **5. a.** (of gears) interlocked. **b.** (of wheels) in gear with each other. **6.** built so as to be or appear to be attached to or partly embedded in a wall: *an engaged column.*

en•gage•ment (en gāj′mənt), *n.* **1.** the act of engaging or the state of

being engaged. **2.** an appointment or arrangement, esp. to be somewhere or do something at a particular time. **3.** an agreement to marry; betrothal. **4.** a pledge; an obligation or agreement. **5.** employment, or a period or post of employment. **6.** an encounter, conflict, or battle. **7.** the act or state of interlocking.

en•gag•ing (en gā′jing), *adj.* winning; attractive; pleasing: *an engaging smile.* —**en•gag′ing•ly,** *adv.*

en garde (än gärd′, än′), *interj.* (used as a direct call to fencers to assume the prescribed position preparatory to action.)

En•gels (eng′gəlz), *n.* **Friedrich,** 1820–95, German socialist in England: systematized Marxism with Karl Marx.

en•gen•der (en jen′dər), *v.t.* **1.** to produce, cause, or give rise to: *Hatred engendered violence.* **2.** to beget; procreate. —*v.i.* **3.** to be produced or caused; come into existence. —**en•gen′der•ment,** *n.*

en•gine (en′jən), *n.* **1.** a machine for converting thermal energy into mechanical energy or power to produce force and motion. **2.** a railroad locomotive. **3.** any mechanical contrivance. **4.** a machine or instrument used in warfare, as a battering ram, catapult, or piece of artillery. —**en′gined,** *adj.* —**en′gine•less,** *adj.*

en•gi•neer (en′jə nēr′), *n.* **1.** a person trained and skilled in any of various branches of engineering: *a civil engineer.* **2.** a person trained and skilled in the design, construction, and use of engines or machines. **3.** a person who operates or is in charge of an engine or locomotive. **4.** a member of an army, navy, or air force specially trained in engineering work. **5.** a skillful manager: *a political engineer.* —*v.t.* **6.** to plan, construct, or manage as an engineer. **7.** to alter or create by means of genetic engineering. **8.** to arrange, manage, or carry through by skillful or artful contrivance.

en•gi•neer•ing (en′jə nēr′ing), *n.* **1.** the practical application of science and mathematics, as in the design and construction of machines, vehicles, structures, roads, and systems. **2.** the action, work, or profession of an engineer. **3.** skillful or artful contrivance or manipulation.

Eng•lish (ing′glish), *n.* **1.** the West Germanic language of England: the official language of the United Kingdom and an official, standard, or auxiliary language in the U.S. and regions formerly under British or U.S. dominion **2.** *(used with a pl. v.)* **a.** the inhabitants of England. **b.** natives of England or persons of English ancestry living outside England. **3.** English language, composition, and literature as a course of study in school. **4.** simple, straightforward language. **5.** *(sometimes l.c.)* a spinning motion imparted to a ball, esp. in billiards. **6.** a 14-point printing type. **7.** a grade of calendered paper having a smooth matte finish. —*adj.* **8.** of or pertaining to England, its inhabitants, or the language English. —*v.t.* **9.** to translate into English. **10.** to adopt (a foreign word) into English; Anglicize. **11.** *(sometimes l.c.)* to impart English to (a ball).

Eng′lish break′fast, *n.* a hearty breakfast typically including eggs, bacon or ham, toast, and tea or coffee.

Eng′lish Chan′nel, *n.* an arm of the Atlantic between S England and N France, connected with the North Sea by the Strait of Dover. 350 mi. (565 km) long; 20–100 mi. (32–160 km) wide.

Eng′lish Civ′il War′, *n.* the war (1642–46) between the Parliamentarians and the Royalists, sometimes extended to include the events of the period 1646–48.

Eng′lish cock′er span′iel, *n.* one of an English breed of spaniels similar to the cocker spaniel but slightly larger.

Eng′lish dai′sy, *n.* the common European daisy, *Bellis perennis.*

Eng′lish horn′, *n.* a large oboe, a fifth lower in pitch than the ordinary oboe, having a pear-shaped bell and producing a mellow tone.

Eng•lish•man (ing′glish mən *or, often,* -lish-), *n., pl.* **-men.** a native or inhabitant of England.

Eng′lish muf′fin, *n.* a flat muffin made from yeast dough, usu. baked on a griddle, and then split and toasted before being eaten.

Eng′lish Revolu′tion, *n.* the events of 1688–89 by which James II was expelled and the sovereignty conferred on William and Mary. Also called **Bloodless Revolution, Glorious Revolution.**

Eng′lish sad′dle, *n.* a saddle having a steel cantle and pommel, no horn, full side flaps usu. set forward, and a well-padded leather seat.

Eng′lish set′ter, *n.* one of a breed of large setters having a long, flat coat, usu. white flecked with a darker color.

Eng′lish spar′row, *n.* HOUSE SPARROW.

Eng′lish spring′er span′iel, *n.* one of an English breed of springer spaniels having a medium-length, usu. black-and-white or liver-and-white coat.

Eng′lish wal′nut, *n.* **1.** a walnut tree, *Juglans regia.* **2.** the nut of this tree, widely used in cooking.

en•gorge (en gôrj′), *v.t., v.i.,* **-gorged, -gorg•ing. 1.** to swallow greedily; glut or gorge. **2.** to fill or congest with blood. —**en•gorge′ment,** *n.*

en•grave (en grāv′), *v.t.,* **-graved, -grav•ing. 1.** to cut or etch (letters, designs, etc.) into a hard surface, as of metal, stone, or the end grain of wood. **2.** to print from such a surface. **3.** to mark or ornament with incised letters, designs, etc.: *to engrave a ring with a floral pattern.* **4.** PHOTOENGRAVE. **5.** to impress deeply; infix: *That image is engraved on my mind.* —**en•grav′er,** *n.*

en•grav•ing (en grā′ving), *n.* **1.** the act or art of a person who engraves. **2.** the art of forming designs by cutting, etching with acids, a photographic process, etc., as on the surface of a metal plate or block of wood, from which impressions or prints of the design can be made. **3.**

the design engraved. **4.** an engraved plate or block. **5.** an impression or print from this.

en·gross (en grōs′), *v.t.* **1.** to occupy completely, as the mind or attention; absorb: *She is engrossed in her work.* **2.** to write or copy in a clear, attractive, large script or in a formal manner, as a public document or record: *to engross a deed.* **3.** to acquire large quantities of (a commodity) so as to control the market; monopolize.

en·gulf (en gulf′), *v.t.* **1.** to swallow up in or as if in a gulf; submerge: *The stormy sea engulfed the ship.* **2.** to overwhelm or envelop completely: *Grief engulfed him.* —**en·gulf′ment,** *n.*

en·hance (en hans′, -häns′), *v.t.,* **-hanced, -hanc·ing. 1.** to raise to a higher degree; intensify; magnify. **2.** to increase the value, attractiveness, or quality of; improve. **3.** to provide with more complex or sophisticated features. —**en·hance′ment,** *n.*

e·nig·ma (ə nig′mə), *n., pl.* **-mas, -ma·ta** (-mə tə). **1.** a puzzling or inexplicable occurrence or situation. **2.** a person of puzzling or contradictory character. **3.** a saying, picture, etc., containing a hidden meaning; riddle. —**en·ig·mat·ic** (en′ig mat′ik), *adj.*

en·join (en join′), *v.t.* **1.** to prescribe (a course of action) with authority or emphasis. **2.** to direct or order to do something; charge; bid. **3.** to prohibit or restrain by or as if by a legal injunction; proscribe; ban. —**en·join′er,** *n.* —**en·join′ment,** *n.*

en·join·der (en join′dər), *n.* **1.** a prohibition by injunction. **2.** an emphatic directive or order.

en·joy (en joi′), *v.t.* **1.** to take pleasure in; experience with joy. **2.** to have the benefit of; have and use with satisfaction: *to enjoy a six-percent rise in sales.* —*v.i.* **3.** *Informal.* to enjoy oneself. —*Idiom.* **4.** **enjoy oneself,** to experience pleasure; have a good time. —**en·joy′a·ble,** *adj.*

en·joy·ment (en joi′mənt), *n.* **1.** the act of enjoying. **2.** a feeling of pleasure and satisfaction; delight; gratification. **3.** the possession, use, or occupancy of something advantageous. **4.** a particular form or source of pleasure: *Bowling is his greatest enjoyment.* **5.** the exercise of a legal right: *the enjoyment of an estate.*

en·kin·dle (en kin′dl), *v.t., v.i.,* **-dled, -dling.** to kindle into flame, ardor, activity, etc. —**en·kin′dler,** *n.*

en·large (en lärj′), *v.,* **-larged, -larg·ing.** —*v.t.* **1.** to make larger; increase in extent, bulk, or quantity; add to: *to enlarge a house.* **2.** to increase the capacity or scope of; expand. **3.** to make (a photographic print) larger than the negative by projecting the negative's image through a lens onto sensitized paper. —*v.i.* **4.** to grow larger; increase; expand. **5.** to speak or write at length; expatiate: *to enlarge upon a point.* —**en·large′a·ble,** *adj.* —**en·larg′ed·ly,** *adv.* —**en·larg′er,** *n.*

en·large·ment (en lärj′mənt), *n.* **1.** an act of enlarging; increase, expansion, or amplification. **2.** an enlarged form of something. **3.** anything that enlarges something else; addition.

en·light·en (en līt′n), *v.t.* **1.** to give intellectual or spiritual understanding to; impart knowledge to; instruct: *to enlighten students.* **2.** to free of ignorance, false beliefs, or prejudice.

enlight′ened self′-in′terest, *n.* a belief that setting aside selfishness may eventually benefit an individual or institution.

en·light·en·ment (en līt′n mənt), *n.* **1.** the act of enlightening. **2.** the state of being enlightened. **3.** (*usu. cap.*) *Buddhism, Hinduism.* PRAJNA. **4. the Enlightenment,** a European philosophical movement of the 17th and 18th centuries, characterized by belief in the power of reason and by innovations in political, religious, and educational doctrine.

en·list (en list′), *v.i.* **1.** to enroll, usu. voluntarily, for military service. **2.** to enter into some cause or enterprise. —*v.t.* **3.** to engage for military service: *to enlist soldiers for the army.* **4.** to secure (a person, services, aid, etc.) for some cause or enterprise: *They enlisted our support.*

en·list·ed (en lis′tid), *adj.* of, pertaining to, or belonging to the part of the armed services ranking below commissioned officers or warrant officers: *enlisted personnel; enlisted seniority.*

en·list·ee (en lis′tē′), *n.* **1.** a person who enlists for military service. Compare DRAFTEE. **2.** an enlisted man or woman.

en·list·ment (en list′mənt), *n.* **1.** the act of enlisting; the state of being enlisted. **2.** the period of time for which one has enlisted.

en·liv·en (en lī′vən), *v.t.* **1.** to make vigorous, active, or lively; invigorate; animate. **2.** to make sprightly or cheerful; brighten; gladden.

en masse (än mas′, än′), *adv.* in a mass; all together; as a group: *The guests arrived en masse.*

en·mesh (en mesh′), *v.t.* to catch in or as if in a net; entangle.

en·mi·ty (en′mi tē), *n., pl.* **-ties.** a feeling or condition of hostility; hatred; ill will; animosity.

en·nui (än wē′), *n.* a feeling of utter weariness and discontent resulting from satiety or lack of interest; boredom.

E·noch (ē′nək), *n.* **1.** the father of Methuselah. Gen. 5:22. **2.** a son of Cain. Gen. 4:17.

e·no·ki (e nok′ē), *n.* a thin, long-stemmed and tiny-capped edible white mushroom, *Flamma velutipes,* native to Japan.

e·nor·mi·ty (i nôr′mi tē), *n., pl.* **-ties. 1.** outrageous or heinous character; atrociousness; monstrousness: *the enormity of the crime.* **2.** something outrageous or heinous, as an offense. **3.** greatness of size, scope, or extent; immensity: *The enormity of the task was overwhelming.*

e·nor·mous (i nôr′məs), *adj.* **1.** greatly exceeding the common size, extent, amount, or degree; huge; immense: *an enormous mansion.* **2.** outrageous: *enormous crimes.* —**e·nor′mous·ly,** *adv.*

E·nos (ē′nəs), *n.* the son of Seth. Gen. 5:6.

e·nough (i nuf′), *adj.* **1.** adequate for the want or need; sufficient for the purpose or to satisfy desire: *enough water; noise enough to wake the dead.* —*pron.* **2.** an adequate quantity or number; sufficiency: *Enough of us are here to begin.* —*adv.* **3.** in a quantity or degree that answers a purpose or satisfies a need or desire; sufficiently: *studied enough to pass the test.* **4.** fully or quite: *ready enough.* **5.** tolerably or passably: *He sings well enough.* —*interj.* **6.** (used to express impatience or exasperation.) **7. Enough is enough,** everything said or done already is more than sufficient.

e·nounce (i nouns′), *v.t.,* **e·nounced, e·nounc·ing. 1.** to utter or pronounce, as words; enunciate. **2.** to announce, declare, or proclaim. **3.** to state definitely, as a proposition.

en pas·sant (än′ pa sän′, än′), *adv.* **1.** in passing; by the way. —*n.* **2.** a method by which a chess pawn that is moved two squares can be captured by an opponent's pawn commanding the square that was passed.

en·plane (en plān′) also **emplane,** *v.i.,* **-planed, -plan·ing.** to board an airplane.

en prise (än′ prēz′, än′), *adj.* (of a chess piece) in line for capture; likely to be captured.

en·quire (en kwīr′), *v.i., v.t.,* **-quired, -quir·ing.** INQUIRE.

en·rage (en rāj′), *v.t.,* **-raged, -rag·ing.** to make extremely angry; put into a rage; infuriate. —**en·rag′ed·ly,** *adv.*

en rap·port (än′ ra pôr′), *adj.* in sympathy or accord; in agreement; congenial.

en·rap·ture (en rap′chər), *v.t.,* **-tured, -tur·ing.** to move to rapture; delight beyond measure. —**en·rap′tured·ly,** *adv.*

en·rich (en rich′), *v.t.* **1.** to supply with riches or wealth. **2.** to supply with abundance of anything desirable: *new words that have enriched the language.* **3.** to add greater value or significance to: *Art can enrich life.* **4.** to adorn or decorate. **5.** to improve in quality or productivity, as by adding desirable ingredients: *to enrich soil.* **6.** to increase the proportion of a valuable mineral or isotope in: *fuel enriched with uranium 235.* **7. a.** to restore to (a food) a nutrient lost in processing. **b.** to add vitamins and minerals to (food) to enhance its nutritive value. —**en·rich′er,** *n.* —**en·rich′ing·ly,** *adv.* —**en·rich′ment,** *n.*

en·roll or **en·rol** (en rōl′), *v.,* **-rolled, -roll·ing** or **-rol·ling.** —*v.t.* **1.** to write the name of (a person) in a roll or register; register. **2.** to make officially a member of a group. **3.** to enlist (oneself). **4.** to put in a record; record. **5.** to roll or wrap up. —*v.i.* **6.** to enroll oneself or become enrolled: *to enroll in college.* —**en·roll·ee′,** *n.*

en·roll·ment or **en·rol·ment** (en rōl′mənt), *n.* **1.** the act or process of enrolling. **2.** the state of being enrolled. **3.** the number of persons enrolled, as for a course or in a school.

en route (än rōōt′, en, än), *adv.* on or along the way. [< French]

en·sconce (en skons′), *v.t.,* **-sconced, -sconc·ing. 1.** to settle securely or snugly: *The kitten was ensconced in an armchair.* **2.** to cover or shelter; hide securely.

en·sem·ble (än säm′bəl, -sämb′, än-), *n.* **1.** all the parts of a thing taken together, so that each part is considered only in relation to the whole. **2.** the entire costume of an individual, esp. when all the parts are in harmony. **3.** a set of furniture. **4. a.** the united performance of an entire group of singers, musicians, etc. **b.** the group so performing: *a string ensemble.* **5.** a group of supporting entertainers, as actors, dancers, and singers, in a theatrical production.

ensem′ble act′ing, *n.* an approach to acting that emphasizes the unified work of the entire cast on behalf of the play rather than individual performances.

en·sheathe (en shēth′) also **en·sheath** (-shēth′), *v.t.,* **-sheathed, -sheath·ing.** to enclose in or as if in a sheath; sheathe.

en·shrine (en shrīn′), *v.t.,* **-shrined, -shrin·ing. 1.** to enclose in or as if in a shrine. **2.** to cherish as sacred. —**en·shrine′ment,** *n.*

en·shroud (en shroud′), *v.t.* to shroud; conceal.

en·si·form (en′sə fôrm′), *adj.* sword-shaped; xiphoid: *an ensiform leaf.*

en·sign (en′sən; *for 1–3 also* -sīn), *n.* **1.** a flag or banner, as a naval standard used to indicate nationality. **2.** a badge of office or authority, as heraldic arms. **3.** a sign, token, or emblem: *the dove, an ensign of peace.* **4.** the lowest commissioned officer in the navy or coast guard, ranking next below a lieutenant, junior grade.

en·si·lage (en′sə lij), *n., v.,* **-laged, -lag·ing.** —*n.* **1.** the preservation of green fodder in a silo or pit. **2.** the fodder preserved; silage. —*v.t.* **3.** ENSILE.

en·sile (en sīl′, en′sīl), *v.t.,* **-siled, -sil·ing.** to preserve (green fodder) in a silo. —**en·si′la·bil′i·ty,** *n.*

-ensis, a Latin adjectival suffix meaning "pertaining to," "originating in," used in modern Latin scientific coinages, esp. derivatives of place names: *canadensis; carolinensis.*

en·slave (en slāv′), *v.t.,* **-slaved, -slav·ing.** to make a slave or slaves of; reduce to or as if to slavery: *to enslave a people; enslaved by drugs.* —**en·slave′ment,** *n.* —**en·slav′er,** *n.*

en·snare (en snâr′), *v.t.,* **-snared, -snar·ing.** to capture in, or involve as if in, a snare; entrap: *ensnared by lies.* —**en·snare′ment,** *n.* —**en·snar′ing·ly,** *adv.*

en·sor·cell or **en·sor·cel** (en sôr′səl), *v.t.,* **-celled** or **-celed, -cell·ing** or **-cel·ing.** to bewitch. —**en·sor′cell·ment,** *n.*

E

en·sue (en sōō′), *v.i.*, **-sued, -su·ing. 1.** to follow in order; come afterward, esp. in immediate succession. **2.** to follow as a consequence; result. —**en·su′ing·ly**, *adv.*

en·sure (en shŏŏr′, -shûr′), *v.t.*, **-sured, -sur·ing. 1.** to secure or guarantee: *This letter will ensure you a hearing.* **2.** to make sure or certain. **3.** to make secure or safe, as from harm. **4.** INSURE (defs. 1–3). —**en·sur′er**, *n.*

en·tab·la·ture (en tab′lə chər, -chŏŏr′), *n.* (in classical architecture) the part of a temple or other building between the columns and the eaves, usu. composed of an architrave, a frieze, and a cornice.

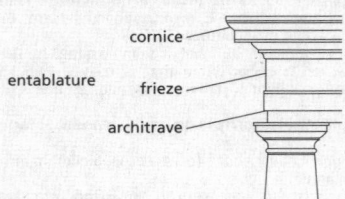

cornice
entablature
frieze
architrave

en·tail (*v.* en tāl′; *n. also* en′tāl), *v.t.* **1.** to cause or involve by necessity or as a consequence: *This project will entail a lot of work.* **2.** to limit the passage of (real property) to a specified line or category of heirs. **3.** to cause (anything) to descend to a fixed series of possessors. —*n.* **4.** the act of entailing. **5.** the state of being entailed. **6.** any predetermined order of succession, as to an office. **7.** something that is entailed, as an estate. **8.** the rule of descent settled for an estate. —**en·tail′ment**, *n.*

en·tan·gle (en tang′gəl), *v.t.*, **-gled, -gling. 1.** to make tangled; intertwine. **2.** to involve in or as if in a tangle; ensnare; enmesh: *to be entangled in intrigue.* **3.** to involve in difficulties. **4.** to confuse or perplex.

en·tan·gle·ment (en tang′gəl mənt), *n.* **1.** the act of entangling. **2.** the state of being entangled. **3.** something that entangles; snare; involvement; complication.

en·tente (än tänt′), *n.* **1.** an understanding between nations agreeing to follow a particular policy in international affairs. **2.** an alliance of parties to such an understanding.

en·tente cor·diale (än tänt′ kôr dyäl′, än tänt′), *n.* a friendly understanding, esp. between nations.

en·ter (en′tər), *v.t.* **1.** to come or go in or into: *to enter a room; The thought never entered my mind.* **2.** to penetrate or pierce: *The bullet entered the flesh.* **3.** to put in or insert. **4.** to become a member of; join. **5.** to cause to be admitted, as into a school or a competition: *to enter a horse in a race.* **6.** to begin upon; engage or become involved in: *to enter the medical profession.* **7.** to share in; have an intuitive understanding of: *able to enter the spirit of the work.* **8.** to make a record of; record or register. **9.** *Law.* **a.** to make a formal record of (a fact). **b.** to occupy or take possession of (lands), esp. under rightful claim. **10.** to put forward, submit, or register formally: *to enter an objection; to enter a bid.* —*v.i.* **11.** to come or go in. **12.** to be admitted, as into a school or competition. **13.** to make a beginning (often fol. by *on* or *upon*): *to enter upon a new phase in history.* **14.** to come upon the stage (used in stage directions, often as a 3rd person imperative): *The butler enters with a tray. Enter Othello.* **15. enter into, a.** to participate in; engage in. **b.** to investigate; consider. **c.** to sympathize with; share in. **d.** to form a constituent part or ingredient of.

en·ter·i·tis (en′tə rī′tis), *n.* **1.** inflammation of the intestines, esp. the small intestine. **2.** DISTEMPER[1] (def. 1c).

en·ter·o·bac·te·ri·a (en′tə rō bak tēr′ē ə), *n.pl., sing.* **-te·ri·um** (-tēr′ē əm). rod-shaped bacteria of the family Enterobacteriaceae, as those of the genera *Escherichia, Salmonella,* and *Shigella,* occurring normally or pathogenically in the intestines. —**en′ter·o·bac·te′ri·al**, *adj.*

en·ter·o·vi·rus (en′tə rō vī′rəs), *n., pl.* **-rus·es.** any of several picornaviruses of the genus *Enterovirus,* including poliovirus, that infect the human gastrointestinal tract and cause diseases of the nervous system. —**en′ter·o·vi′ral**, *adj.*

en·ter·prise (en′tər prīz′), *n.* **1.** a project undertaken, esp. one that is important or difficult or requires boldness or energy. **2.** a plan for such a project. **3.** participation or engagement in such projects. **4.** boldness or readiness in undertaking; adventurous spirit or ingenuity. **5.** a company organized for commercial purposes; business firm.

en·ter·pris·ing (en′tər prī′zing), *adj.* **1.** ready to undertake important, difficult, or new projects; energetic in carrying out an undertaking. **2.** characterized by imagination and initiative. —**en′ter·pris′ing·ly**, *adv.*

en·ter·tain (en′tər tān′), *v.t.* **1.** to hold the attention of pleasantly or agreeably; divert; amuse. **2.** to have as a guest; show hospitality to. **3.** to admit to the mind; consider: *I never entertained such an idea.* **4.** to hold in the mind; harbor; cherish: *to entertain thoughts of revenge.* —*v.i.* **5.** to exercise hospitality; provide entertainment for guests. —**en′ter·tain′er**, *n.*

en·ter·tain·ment (en′tər tān′mənt), *n.* **1.** the act of entertaining. **2.** diversion; amusement. **3.** something affording pleasure or amusement, esp. a performance. **4.** hospitable provision for the needs and wants of guests. **5.** a divertingly adventurous, comic, or picaresque novel.

en·thrall or **en·thral** (en thrôl′), *v.t.*, **-thralled, -thrall·ing** or **-thral·ling. 1.** to captivate or charm; spellbind. **2.** to put or hold in slavery; subjugate. —**en·thrall′ing·ly**, *adv.* —**en·thrall′ment**, *n.*

en·throne (en thrōn′), *v.t.*, **-throned, -thron·ing. 1.** to place on or as if on a throne. **2.** to invest with sovereign or episcopal authority. **3.** to exalt. —**en·throne′ment**, *n.*

en·thuse (en thōōz′), *v.*, **-thused, -thus·ing.** —*v.i.* **1.** to speak with or show enthusiasm. —*v.t.* **2.** to cause to become enthusiastic.

en·thu·si·asm (en thōō′zē az′əm), *n.* **1.** lively, absorbing interest; eager involvement. **2.** something in which such interest is shown: *Rock climbing is his latest enthusiasm.* **3.** any of various forms of extreme religious devotion, usu. associated with intense emotionalism and a break with orthodoxy.

en·thu·si·ast (en thōō′zē ast′, -ist), *n.* **1.** a person who is filled with enthusiasm for some principle, pursuit, etc.; devotee: *a sports enthusiast.* **2.** a religious visionary or fanatic.

en·thu·si·as·tic (en thōō′zē as′tik), *adj.* full of or characterized by enthusiasm; eager. —**en·thu′si·as′ti·cal·ly**, *adv.*

en·tice (en tīs′), *v.t.*, **-ticed, -tic·ing.** to lead on by exciting hope or desire; allure; tempt; inveigle. —**en·tic′ing·ly**, *adv.* —**en·tic′ing·ness**, *n.*

en·tice·ment (en tīs′mənt), *n.* **1.** the act or practice of enticing. **2.** something that entices; allurement.

en·tire (en tīər′), *adj.* **1.** having all the parts or elements; whole; complete. **2.** full or thorough. **3.** not broken, mutilated, or decayed; intact. **4.** unimpaired or undiminished. **5.** being wholly of one piece; undivided; continuous. **6.** without notches or indentations, as a leaf. **7.** not gelded. —*n.* **8.** an ungelded animal, esp. a stallion. —**en·tire′ness**, *n.*

en·tire·ly (en tīər′lē), *adv.* **1.** wholly or fully; completely or unreservedly. **2.** solely or exclusively.

en·tire·ty (en tīər′tē -tī′ri-), *n., pl.* **-ties. 1.** the state of being entire; completeness. **2.** something that is entire; the whole.

en·ti·tle (en tīt′l), *v.t.*, **-tled, -tling. 1.** to give a right or claim to something; qualify: *a position that entitles one to certain privileges.* **2.** to call by a particular title or name. **3.** to designate (a person) by an honorary title.

en·ti·tle·ment (en tī′tl mənt), *n.* **1.** the act of entitling. **2.** the state of being entitled. **3.** the right to guaranteed benefits under a government program.

en·ti·ty (en′ti tē), *n., pl.* **-ties. 1.** something that has a real existence; thing. **2.** something that exists as a distinct, independent, or self-contained unit. **3.** being or existence, esp. when considered as distinct, independent, or self-contained.

en·tomb (en tōōm′), *v.t.* **1.** to place in or as if in a tomb; bury; inter. **2.** to serve as a tomb for. —**en·tomb′ment**, *n.*

en·to·mol·o·gy (en′tə mol′ə jē), *n.* the branch of zoology dealing with insects. —**en′to·mo·log′i·cal** (-mə loj′i kəl), **en′to·mo·log′ic**, *adj.* —**en′to·mo·log′i·cal·ly**, *adv.* —**en′to·mol′o·gist**, *n.*

en·tou·rage (än′tōō räzh′), *n.* **1.** a group of attendants or associates, as of a person of rank or importance. **2.** surroundings; environment.

en·tr'acte (än trakt′, än-), *n.* **1.** the interval between two consecutive acts of a theatrical or operatic performance. **2.** a performance, as of music or dancing, given during such an interval. **3.** a piece of music or the like for such performance.

en·trails (en′trālz, -trəlz), *n.pl.* **1.** the inner organs of the body. **2.** the intestines. **3.** the internal parts of anything; insides.

en·train[1] (en trān′), *v.i.* **1.** to go aboard a train. —*v.t.* **2.** to put aboard a train. —**en·train′er**, *n.*

en·train[2] (en trān′), *v.t.* **1.** (of a substance, as a vapor) to carry along (a dissimilar substance, as drops of liquid) during a given process, as evaporation or distillation. **2.** (of a liquid) to trap (bubbles). —**en·train′ment**, *n.*

en·trance[1] (en′trans), *n.* **1.** the act of entering. **2.** a point or place of entering; an opening or passage for entering, as a doorway. **3.** the right, privilege, or permission to enter; admission: *college entrance exams.* **4.** the moment or place in a script at which an actor comes on the stage. **5.** the point in a musical score at which a particular voice or instrument joins the ensemble. **6.** a manner, means, or style of entering.

en·trance[2] (en trans′, -träns′), *v.t.*, **-tranced, -tranc·ing. 1.** to fill with delight or wonder; enrapture. **2.** to put into a trance. —**en·trance′ment**, *n.* —**en·tranc′ing·ly**, *adv.*

en·trant (en′trənt), *n.* **1.** a person who takes part in a competition or contest. **2.** a new member, as of an association or school. **3.** a person who enters.

en·trap (en trap′), *v.t.*, **-trapped, -trap·ping. 1.** to catch in or as if in a trap; ensnare. **2.** to bring unawares into difficulty or danger. **3.** to lure into performing an act or making a statement that is compromising or illegal. —**en·trap′ment**, *n.* —**en·trap′per**, *n.*

en·treat (en trēt′), *v.t.* **1.** to ask (a person) earnestly; beseech; implore; beg. **2.** to ask earnestly for (something). —*v.i.* **3.** to make an earnest request or petition. —**en·treat′ing·ly**, *adv.*

en·treat·y (en trē′tē), *n., pl.* **-treat·ies.** earnest request or petition; supplication; plea.

en·tre·chat (Fr. än trə shå′), *n., pl.* **-chats** (Fr. -shå′). a ballet jump in which the dancer crosses the feet repeatedly while in the air.

en·trée or **en·tree** (än′trā), *n.* **1.** a dish served as the main course of a meal. **2.** the privilege of entering; access. **3.** a means of obtaining entry. **4.** the act of entering; entrance.

en·trench (en trench′), *v.t.* **1.** to place in a position of strength; establish firmly or solidly. **2.** to dig trenches for defensive purposes around (oneself, a military position, etc.). —*v.i.* **3.** to encroach; trespass; infringe (usu. fol. by *on* or *upon*): *to entrench on the rights of another.* —**en·trench′ment,** *n.*

en·tre nous (än′trə nōō′, än′-), *adv.* between ourselves; confidentially.

en·tre·pôt or **en·tre·pot** (än′trə pō′, än′-), *n.* **1.** a warehouse. **2.** a center where goods are received for distribution, transshipment, or repackaging.

en·tre·pre·neur (än′trə prə nûr′), *n.* **1.** a person who organizes and manages an enterprise, esp. a business, usu. with considerable initiative and risk. —*v.t.* **2.** to deal with or initiate as an entrepreneur. —*v.i.* **3.** to act as an entrepreneur. —**en′tre·pre·neur′i·al,** *adj.* —**en′tre·pre·neur′ism,** *n.* —**en′tre·pre·neur′ship,** *n.*

en·tro·py (en′trə pē), *n.* **1.** a function of thermodynamic variables, as temperature or pressure, that is a measure of the energy that is not available for work in a thermodynamic process. *Symbol:* S **2.** (in data transmission and information theory) a measure of the loss of information in a transmitted signal or message. **3.** (in cosmology) a hypothetical tendency for the universe to attain a state of maximum homogeneity in. which all matter is at a uniform temperature. **4.** a state of disorder or disorganization or a hypothetical tendency toward such a state. —**en·tro·pic** (en trō′pik, -trop′ik), *adj.* —**en·tro′pi·cal·ly,** *adv.*

en·trust (en trust′), *v.t.* **1.** to give a trust or responsibility to (fol. by *with*). **2.** to place in trust for protection, care, or handling (fol. by *to*). —**en·trust′ment,** *n.*

en·try (en′trē), *n., pl.* **-tries. 1.** the act of entering; entrance. **2.** a place of entrance, esp. an entrance hall or vestibule. **3.** permission or right to enter; access. **4.** the act of entering or recording something, as in a book, register, or list. **5.** the statement, item, etc., so entered or recorded. **6.** a person or thing entered in a contest or competition. **7. a.** a word, phrase, abbreviation, etc., defined or explained in a dictionary or encyclopedia or listed for identification. **b.** such an item together with its definition or explanation. **8.** a record of a transaction in a bookkeeper's journal.

en′try-lev′el, *adj.* **1.** suitable for unskilled or inexperienced workers: *entry-level jobs.* **2.** being relatively simple in design and low in cost: *entry-level computers.*

en·try·way (en′trē wā′), *n.* a passage affording entrance.

en·twine (en twīn′), *v.t., v.i.,* **-twined, -twin·ing.** to twine about, around, or together. —**en·twine′ment,** *n.*

e·nu·cle·ate (*v.* i nōō′klē āt′, i nyōō′-; *adj.* -it, -āt′), *v.,* **-at·ed, -at·ing.** *adj.* —*v.t.* **1.** to deprive (a cell) of the nucleus. **2.** to remove (a kernel, tumor, eyeball, etc.) from its enveloping cover. —*adj.* **3.** having no nucleus. —**e·nu′cle·a′tion,** *n.*

e·nu·mer·a·ble (i nōō′mər ə bəl, i nyōō′-), *adj.* COUNTABLE (def. 2b). —**e·nu′mer·a·bly,** *adv.*

e·nu·mer·ate (i nōō′mə rāt′, i nyōō′-), *v.t.,* **-at·ed, -at·ing. 1.** to name one by one; specify as in a list: *to enumerate the flaws in a theory.* **2.** to ascertain the number of; count. —**e·nu′mer·a′tion,** *n.* —**e·nu′mer·a′tive** (-mə rā′tiv, -mər ə-), *adj.* —**e·nu′mer·a′tor,** *n.*

e·nun·ci·ate (i nun′sē āt′), *v.,* **-at·ed, -at·ing.** —*v.t.* **1.** to utter or pronounce, esp. in an articulate or a particular manner: *to enunciate the words clearly.* **2.** to state or declare definitely, as a theory. **3.** to announce or proclaim. —*v.i.* **4.** to pronounce words, esp. in an articulate manner. —**e·nun′ci·a′tion,** *n.*

en·u·re·sis (en′yə rē′sis), *n.* lack of control of urination; bed-wetting; urinary incontinence. —**en′u·ret′ic** (-ret′ik), *adj.*

en·vel·op (en vel′əp), *v.t.* **1.** to wrap up in or as if in a covering. **2.** to serve as a wrapping or covering for. **3.** to surround entirely. **4.** to attack (an enemy's flank). —**en·vel′op·ment,** *n.*

en·ve·lope (en′və lōp′, än′-), *n.* **1.** a flat paper container, as for a letter or thin package, usu. having a gummed flap or other means of closure. **2.** something that envelops; a wrapper or surrounding cover. **3.** a surrounding or enclosing part, as an integument or an outer membrane. **4.** *Geom.* a curve or surface tangent to each member of a set of curves or surfaces.

en·ven·om (en ven′əm), *v.t.* **1.** to impregnate with venom; make poisonous. **2.** to embitter.

en·vi·a·ble (en′vē ə bəl), *adj.* worthy of envy; very desirable. —**en′vi·a·ble·ness,** *n.* —**en′vi·a·bly,** *adv.*

en·vi·ron (en vī′rən, -vī′ərn), *v.t.* to form a circle or ring round; surround; envelop: *a house environed by pleasant grounds.*

en·vi·ron·ment (en vī′rən mənt, -vī′ərn-), *n.* **1.** the aggregate of surrounding things, conditions, or influences; surroundings; milieu. **2.** the air, water, minerals, organisms, and all other external factors surrounding and affecting a given organism at any time. **3.** the social and cultural forces that shape the life of a person or a population. **4.** the hardware or software configuration of a computer system. —**en·vi′ron·men′tal,** *adj.* —**en·vi′ron·men′tal·ly,** *adv.*

en·vi·ron·men·tal·ist (en vī′rən men′tl ist, -vī′ərn-), *n.* **1.** an expert on environmental problems. **2.** a person who advocates or works for protection of the air, water, animals, plants, and other natural resources from pollution or its effects. **3.** a person who believes that differences between individuals or groups, esp. in moral and intellectual attributes, are predominantly determined by environmental factors. —**en·vi′ron·men′tal·ism,** *n.*

Environmen′tal Protec′tion A′gency, *n.* EPA.

en·vi·rons (en vī′rənz, -vī′ərnz), *n.pl.* **1.** the surrounding parts or districts, as of a city; outskirts; suburbs. **2.** surroundings; environment. **3.** the nearby area or space; vicinity.

en·vis·age (en viz′ij), *v.t.,* **-aged, -ag·ing.** to contemplate; visualize; envision: *to envisage an era of great scientific discoveries.*

en·vi·sion (en vizh′ən), *v.t.* to picture mentally, esp. some future event or events.

en·voy¹ (en′voi, än′-), *n.* **1.** Also called **en′voy extraor′dinary and min′ister plenipoten′tiary.** a diplomatic representative ranking next below an ambassador. **2.** a diplomatic representative sent on a special or temporary mission. **3.** any accredited messenger or representative.

en·voy² or **en·voi** (en′voi, än′-), *n.* a short stanza concluding a poem, as a ballade, often containing a dedication or summary, or a similar postscript to a prose work.

en·vy (en′vē), *n., pl.* **-vies,** *v.,* **-vied, -vy·ing.** —*n.* **1.** a feeling of resentful discontent, begrudging admiration, or covetousness with regard to another's advantages, possessions, or attainments; desire for something possessed by another: one of the seven deadly sins. **2.** an object of envious feeling: *She was the envy of all her classmates.* —*v.t.* **3.** to regard with envy; be envious of. —**en′vy·ing·ly,** *adv.* —**en′vi·ous,** *adj.*

en·wind (en wīnd′), *v.t.,* **-wound, -wind·ing.** to wind or coil about; encircle.

en·wrap (en rap′), *v.t.,* **-wrapped, -wrap·ping. 1.** to wrap, envelop, or surround. **2.** to absorb or engross, as in thought.

en·zo·ot·ic (en′zō ot′ik), *adj.* **1.** (of a disease) prevailing among or afflicting animals in a particular locality. Compare EPIZOOTIC. —*n.* **2.** an enzootic disease.

en·zyme (en′zīm), *n.* any of various proteins, as pepsin and amylase, originating from living cells and capable of producing certain chemical changes in organic substances by catalytic action, as in digestion. —**en′zy·mat′ic,** *adj.*

en·zy·mol·o·gy (en′zī mol′ə jē, -zi-), *n.* the branch of biology that deals with the chemistry, biochemistry, and effects of enzymes. —**en′zy·mol′o·gist,** *n.*

E·o·cene (ē′ə sēn′), *adj.* **1.** noting or pertaining to an epoch of the Tertiary Period, occurring from 55 million to 40 million years ago, characterized by the advent of the modern mammalian orders. See table at GEOLOGIC TIME. —*n.* **2.** the Eocene Epoch or Series.

EOE, equal-opportunity employer.

e·o·hip·pus (ē′ō hip′əs), *n.* an extinct small horse of the North American Eocene, genus *Hyracotherium* (*Eohippus*), having four hoofed toes on the forefeet and three on the hind feet.

e·o·li·an (ē ō′lē ən), *adj.* of or pertaining to sand or rock material carried or arranged by the wind.

E·ol·ic (ē ol′ik), *n., adj.* AEOLIC.

e·o·lith (ē′ə lith), *n.* a chipped stone of the late Tertiary Period in Europe once thought to have been flaked by humans but now known to be the product of natural agencies. —**e′o·lith′ic,** *adj.*

e·on or **ae·on** (ē′ən, ē′on), *n.* **1.** an indefinitely long period of time; age. **2.** the largest division of geologic time, comprising two or more eras. **3.** one billion years.

EPA, 1. Environmental Protection Agency: an independent federal agency, created in 1970, that sets and enforces rules and standards that protect the environment and control pollution. **2.** eicosapentaenoic acid: an omega-3 fatty acid present in fish oils.

ep·au·let or **ep·au·lette** (ep′ə let′, -lit, ep′ə let′), *n.* **1.** an ornamental shoulder piece on dress and full-dress uniforms, chiefly of military officers. **2.** a usu. decorative strip or loop of fabric on the shoulder of a coat, dress, etc. [< French *épaulette = épaule* shoulder + *-ette*]

epaulet

epaulet (def. 1)

ep·a·zote (ep′ə zōt′), *n.* a goosefoot, *Chenopodium ambrosioides,* having strong-smelling leaves sometimes used medicinally or as flavoring.

é·pée or **e·pee** (ā pā′, ep′ā), *n.* **1.** a rapier with a three-sided blade and a guard over the tip. **2.** the art or sport of fencing with an épée, points being made by touching any part of the opponent's body with the tip of the weapon.

Eph., Ephesians.

e·phed·ra (i fed′rə, ef′i drə), *n., pl.* **-ras.** any desert gymnosperm plant of the genus *Ephedra,* of the family Gnetaceae, with leaves reduced to scales at stem joints.

e·phed·rine (i fed′rin, ef′i drēn′, -drin), *n.* a white, crystalline alkaloid, $C_{10}H_{15}N$, obtained from a species of *Ephedra* or synthesized: used in medicine chiefly for the treatment of asthma, hay fever, and colds.

e·phem·er·a (i fem′ər ə), *n., pl.* **-er·as** for 1. **1.** (*used with a sing. v.*) anything short-lived or transitory. **2.** (*used with a sing. or pl. v.*) such things collectively: *a writer of ephemera.* **3.** (*used with a pl. v.*) items, as pamphlets, notices, and tickets, orig. intended to be of use for only a short time, esp. when preserved as collectibles.

E

e•phem•er•al (i fem′ər əl), *adj.* **1.** lasting a very short time; short-lived; transitory. **2.** lasting but one day: *an ephemeral flower.* **—*n.* 3.** anything short-lived, as certain insects. —**e•phem′er•al•ly,** *adv.*
e•phem•er•id (i fem′ər id), *n.* MAYFLY.
e•phem•er•is (i fem′ər is), *n., pl.* **e•phe•mer•i•des** (ef′ə mer′i dēz′). **1.** a table showing the positions of a heavenly body on a number of dates in a regular sequence. **2.** an astronomical almanac containing such tables.
E•phe•sians (i fē′zhənz), *n. (used with a sing. v.)* a book of the New Testament, written by Paul.
Eph•e•sus (ef′ə səs), *n.* an ancient city in W Asia Minor, S of Smyrna (Izmir): famous temple of Artemis, or Diana; early Christian community, site of one of the seven churches of Asia (Rev. 1:11). —**E•phe•sian** (i fē′zhən), *adj., n.*
E•phra•im (ē′frē əm, ē′frəm), *n.* **1.** the younger son of Joseph. Gen. 41:52. **2.** one of the 12 tribes of Israel, traditionally descended from him. Gen. 48:1. **3.** the northern kingdom of Israel.
E•phra•im•ite (ē′frē ə mīt′, ē′frə-), *n.* **1.** a member of the tribe of Ephraim. **2.** an inhabitant of the northern kingdom of Israel.
epi-, a prefix occurring orig. in loanwords from Greek, with the following meanings: "on, upon, at" (*epicenter; epitaph*); "outer, exterior, or covering" (*epidermis; epithelium*); "extending generally" (*epicene; epidemic*); "accompanying, additional" (*epiphenomenon; episode*); "to, towards" (*epistle*); "following, succeeding" (*epigone*); "suddenness or forcefulness (of the action of the verb)" (*epilepsy; epiphany*). Also, *before a vowel or h,* **ep-.**
ep•i•ben•thos (ep′ə ben′thos), *n.* the aggregate of organisms living on the sea bottom between low tide and 100 fathoms (180 m).
ep•ic (ep′ik), *adj.* Also, **ep′i•cal. 1.** of or pertaining to a long poetic composition, usu. centered upon a hero, in which a series of great achievements or events is narrated in elevated style: *The* Iliad *is an epic poem.* **2.** resembling or suggesting such poetry: *an epic novel.* **3.** heroic; majestic; impressively great. **4.** of unusually great size or extent: *a crime wave of epic proportions.* **—*n.* 5.** an epic poem. **6.** epic poetry. **7.** a novel, film, etc., resembling or suggesting an epic. **8.** something worthy to form the subject of an epic. —**ep′i•cal•ly,** *adv.*
ep•i•can•thus (ep′i kan′thəs), *n., pl.* **-thi** (-thī, -thē). a fold of skin extending from the upper eyelid to or over the inner canthus of the eye, especially well developed in Asian peoples. Also called **ep′ican′thic fold′, eyefold.** —**ep′i•can′thic,** *adj.*
ep•i•car•di•um (ep′i kär′dē əm), *n., pl.* **-di•a** (-dē ə). the innermost layer of the pericardium. —**ep′i•car′di•al, ep′i•car′di•ac′,** *adj.*
ep•i•carp (ep′i kärp′), *n.* the outermost layer of a pericarp, as the rind or peel of certain fruits.
ep•i•cene (ep′i sēn′), *adj.* **1.** belonging to, or partaking of the characteristics of, both sexes. **2.** flaccid; feeble; weak: *epicene prose.* **3.** effeminate; unmasculine. **4.** (of a noun or pronoun) capable of referring to either sex, as *attendant, chairperson,* or *they.* **—*n.* 5.** an epicene person or thing. —**ep′i•cen′ism,** *n.*
ep•i•cen•ter (ep′ə sen′tər), *n.* **1.** a point, directly above the true center of disturbance, from which the shock waves of an earthquake apparently radiate. **2.** a focal point, as of activity; center. Also, *esp. Brit.,* **ep′i•cen′tre.** —**ep′i•cen′tral,** *adj.*
ep•i•cure (ep′i kyŏŏr′), *n.* a person who cultivates a refined taste, esp. in food and wine; connoisseur.
ep•i•cu•re•an (ep′i kyŏŏ rē′ən, -kyŏŏr′ē-), *adj.* **1.** having luxurious tastes or habits, esp. in eating and drinking. **2.** fit for an epicure. **3.** (*cap.*) of, pertaining to, or characteristic of Epicurus or Epicureanism. **—*n.* 4.** an epicure. **5.** (*cap.*) a disciple of Epicurus.
Ep•i•cu•re•an•ism (ep′i kyŏŏ rē′ə niz′əm, -kyŏŏr′ē-) also **Ep•i•cur•ism** (ep′i kyŏŏ riz′əm, ep′i kyŏŏr′iz əm), *n.* **1.** the philosophical system of Epicurus, holding that the world is a series of fortuitous combinations of atoms and that the highest good is pleasure, interpreted as freedom from disturbance or pain. **2.** (*l.c.*) epicurean indulgence, tastes, or habits.
Ep•i•cu•rus (ep′i kyŏŏr′əs), *n.* 342?–270 B.C., Greek philosopher.
ep•i•cy•cle (ep′ə sī′kəl), *n.* a circle whose center moves around in the circumference of a larger circle: used in Ptolemaic astronomy to account for irregularities in planetary motion. —**ep′i•cy′clic** (-sī′klik, -sik′lik), *adj.*
ep•i•dem•ic (ep′i dem′ik), *adj.* Also, **ep′i•dem′i•cal. 1.** (of a disease) affecting many individuals at the same time, and spreading from person to person in a locality where the disease is not permanently prevalent. **2.** extremely prevalent; widespread. **—*n.* 3.** a temporary prevalence of a disease. **4.** a rapid spread or increase in the occurrence of something. —**ep′i•dem′i•cal•ly,** *adv.* —**ep′i•de•mic′i•ty** (-də mis′i tē), *n.*
ep•i•de•mi•ol•o•gy (ep′i dē′mē ol′ə jē, -dem′ē-), *n.* **1.** the branch of medicine dealing with the incidence and prevalence of disease in large populations and with detection of the source and cause of epidemics. **2.** the factors contributing to the presence or absence of a disease. —**ep′i•de′mi•o•log′i•cal** (-ə loj′i kəl), *adj.* —**ep′i•de′mi•o•log′i•cal•ly,** *adv.* —**ep′i•de′mi•ol′o•gist,** *n.*
ep•i•den•drum (ep′i den′drəm), *n.* any of numerous tropical American orchids of the genus *Epidendrum,* having variously colored, often showy flowers.
ep•i•der•mis (ep′i dûr′mis), *n.* **1.** the outermost, nonvascular, nonsensitive layer of the skin, covering the dermis. **2.** the outer epithelial layer of animal tissue. **3.** a thin layer of cells forming the outer integument of seed plants and ferns. —**ep′i•der′mal, ep′i•der′mic,** *adj.* —**ep′i•der′mi•cal•ly,** *adv.*
ep•i•did•y•mis (ep′i did′ə mis), *n., pl.* **-di•dym•i•des** (-di dim′i dēz′, -did′ə mi-). an oval structure at the upper surface of each testicle, consisting of tightly convoluted sperm ducts. —**ep′i•did′y•mal,** *adj.*
ep•i•du•ral (ep′i dŏŏr′əl, -dyŏŏr′-), *adj.* **1.** situated on or outside the dura mater. **2.** of or pertaining to the insertion of an anesthetic into the lumbar spine in the space between the spinal cord and dura mater, which blocks sensation in the body from that point downward: *epidural anesthesia.* **—*n.* 3.** an epidural injection of anesthesia; spinal anesthesia.
ep•i•gas•tri•um (ep′i gas′trē əm), *n., pl.* **-tri•a** (-trē ə). the upper and median part of the abdomen, lying over the stomach.
ep•i•gen•e•sis (ep′i jen′ə sis), *n.* **1. a.** the approximately stepwise process by which genetic information, as modified by environmental influences, is translated into the substance and behavior of an organism. **b.** the theory that an embryo develops from the successive differentiation of an originally undifferentiated structure (opposed to *preformation*). **2.** ore deposition subsequent to the original formation of the enclosing country rock. —**ep′i•gen′e•sist, e•pig•e•nist** (i pij′ə nist), *n.* —**ep′i•ge•net′ic** (-jə net′ik), *adj.* —**ep′i•ge•net′i•cal•ly,** *adv.*
ep•i•glot•tis (ep′i glot′is), *n., pl.* **-glot•tis•es, -glot•ti•des** (-glot′i-dēz′). a flap of cartilage behind the tongue that helps close the opening to the windpipe during swallowing. —**ep′i•glot′tal,** *adj.*
ep•i•gram (ep′i gram′), *n.* **1.** a witty, ingenious, or pointed saying tersely expressed. **2.** epigrammatic expression: *a genius for epigram.* **3.** a short, concise poem, often satirical, displaying a witty or ingenious turn of thought. —**ep′i•gram•mat′ic** (-grə mat′ik), *adj.*
ep•i•graph (ep′i graf′, -gräf′), *n.* **1.** an inscription, esp. on a building, statue, or the like. **2.** an apposite quotation at the beginning of a book, chapter, etc.
ep•i•late (ep′ə lāt′), *v.t.,* **-lat•ed, -lat•ing.** to remove (hair) from by means of physical, chemical, or radiological agents; depilate. —**ep′i•la′tion,** *n.* —**ep′i•la′tor,** *n.*
ep•i•lep•sy (ep′ə lep′sē), *n.* a disorder of the nervous system, characterized either by mild, episodic loss of attention or sleepiness **(petit mal)** or by severe convulsions with loss of consciousness **(grand mal).** —**ep′i•lep′tic,** *adj., n.*
ep•i•logue or **ep•i•log** (ep′ə lôg′, -log′), *n.* **1.** a concluding part added to a literary work. **2.** a speech, usu. in verse, delivered by one of the actors after the conclusion of a play. **3.** the person speaking this.
ep•i•neph•rine or **ep•i•neph•rin** (ep′ə nef′rin), *n.* **1.** a hormone secreted by the adrenal medulla upon stimulation by the central nervous system in response to stress, as anger or fear, and acting to increase heart rate, blood pressure, cardiac output, and carbohydrate metabolism. **2.** a commercial preparation of this substance, used chiefly as a heart stimulant and antiasthmatic. Also called **adrenaline.**
Ep•i•pha•ni•a (ep′ə fə nī′ə), *n.* ancient name of the city HAMA.
e•piph•a•ny (i pif′ə nē), *n., pl.* **-nies. 1.** an appearance or manifestation, esp. of a deity. **2.** (*cap.*) a Christian festival, observed on Jan. 6, commemorating the manifestation of Christ to the gentiles in the persons of the Magi; Twelfth Day. **3.** a sudden, intuitive perception of or insight into reality or the essential meaning of something, often initiated by some simple, commonplace occurrence. **4.** a literary work or section of a work presenting such a moment of revelation and insight. —**ep•i•phan•ic** (ep′ə fan′ik), *adj.*
e•piph•y•sis (i pif′ə sis), *n., pl.* **-ses** (-sēz′). **1.** either of the ends of a long bone separated from the shaft by cartilage but later ossifying with it. **2.** PINEAL GLAND. —**e•piph′y•se′al** (-sē′əl, -zē′-), **ep•i•phys•i•al** (ep′-ə fiz′ē əl), *adj.*
ep•i•phyte (ep′ə fīt′), *n.* a plant that grows above the ground, supported nonparasitically by another plant or object, and deriving its nutrients and water from rain, the air, dust, etc.; air plant. —**ep′i•phyt′ic** (-fit′ik), *adj.*
e•pis•co•pa•cy (i pis′kə pə sē), *n., pl.* **-cies. 1.** government of the church by bishops. **2.** EPISCOPATE.
e•pis•co•pal (i pis′kə pəl), *adj.* **1.** of or pertaining to a bishop. **2.** based on or recognizing a governing order of bishops. **3.** (*cap.*) of or designating the Episcopal Church.
Epis′copal Church′, *n.* a church in the U.S. descended from the Church of England. Also called **Protestant Episcopal Church.**
E•pis•co•pa•lian (i pis′kə pāl′yən, -pā′lē ən), *adj.* **1.** pertaining or adhering to the Episcopal Church; Episcopal. **2.** (*l.c.*) pertaining or adhering to the episcopal form of church government. **—*n.* 3.** a member of the Episcopal Church. **4.** (*l.c.*) an adherent of episcopal church government. —**E•pis′co•pa′lian•ism,** *n.*
e•pis•co•pal•ism (i pis′kə pə liz′əm), *n.* the theory of church polity according to which the supreme authority is vested in the episcopal order as a whole, and not in any individual.
e•pis•co•pate (i pis′kə pit, -pāt′), *n.* **1.** the office, rank, or term of a bishop. **2.** the order or body of bishops. **3.** the diocese of a bishop. [< Late Latin *episcopātus.* See BISHOP.]
e•pi•si•ot•o•my (ə pē′zē ot′ə mē, ep′ə sī-), *n., pl.* **-mies.** a surgical incision into the perineum and vagina to allow sufficient clearance for childbirth.
ep•i•sode (ep′ə sōd′, -zōd′), *n.* **1.** an incident in the course of a series of events, in a person's life or experience, etc. **2.** an incident, scene, etc., within a narrative, usu. fully developed and either integrated within the main story or digressing from it. **3.** a digressive section in a

musical composition, as a fugue. **4. a.** any one of the separate productions that constitute a serial, as in motion pictures or radio. **b.** any one of the separate programs that constitute a television or radio series. **—ep′i•sod′ic** (-sod′ik, -zod′-), *adj.*

ep•i•stax•is (ep′ə stak′sis), *n.* NOSEBLEED.

ep•i•ste•mic (ep′ə stē′mik, -stem′ik), *adj.* of or pertaining to knowledge. **—ep′i•ste′mi•cal•ly,** *adv.*

e•pis•te•mol•o•gy (i pis′tə mol′ə jē), *n.* a branch of philosophy that investigates the origin, nature, methods, and limits of human knowledge. **—e•pis′te•mo•log′i•cal** (-mə loj′i kəl), *adj.*

e•pis•tle (i pis′əl), *n.* **1.** a letter, esp. a formal or didactic one. **2.** (*usu. cap.*) **a.** one of the apostolic letters in the New Testament. **b.** an extract read at the Eucharistic service in certain churches, usu. from the Epistles.

e•pis•to•lar•y (i pis′tl er′ē), *adj.* **1.** contained in or carried on by letters: *an epistolary friendship.* **2.** of, pertaining to, or consisting of letters. **3.** written in the form of a series of letters: *an epistolary novel.*

ep•i•taph (ep′i taf′, -täf′), *n.* **1.** a commemorative inscription on a tomb or mortuary monument about the person buried at that site. **2.** a brief composition in commemoration or praise of a deceased person.

ep•i•tha•la•mi•on (ep′ə thə lā′mē on′, -ən), *n., pl.* **-mi•a** (-mē ə). a song or poem in honor of a bride and bridegroom.

ep•i•the•li•al (ep′ə thē′lē əl), *adj.* of the epithelium.

ep•i•the•li•um (ep′ə thē′lē əm), *n., pl.* **-li•ums, -li•a** (-lē ə). any tissue layer covering body surfaces or lining the internal surfaces of body cavities, tubes, and hollow organs.

ep•i•thet (ep′ə thet′), *n.* **1.** a characterizing word or phrase added to or used in place of the name of a person or thing. **2.** a word, phrase, or expression used invectively as a term of abuse or contempt. **—ep′i•thet′ic, ep′i•thet′i•cal,** *adj.*

e•pit•o•me (i pit′ə mē), *n.* **1.** a person or thing that is typical of or possesses to a high degree the features of a whole class; embodiment: *She is the epitome of kindness.* **2.** a condensed account, as of a literary work; abstract. **—ep•i•tom•i•cal** (ep′i tom′i kəl), **ep′i•tom′ic,** *adj.*

e•pit•o•mize (i pit′ə mīz′), *v.t.*, **-mized, -miz•ing. 1.** to serve as a typical or perfect example of; typify. **2.** to make an epitome of; summarize. **—e•pit′o•mi•za′tion,** *n.* **—e•pit′o•miz′er,** *n.*

ep•i•zo•ot•ic (ep′ə zō ot′ik), *adj.* **1.** (of a disease) spreading quickly among animals. Compare ENZOOTIC (def. 1). **—***n.* **2.** an epizootic disease. **—ep′i•zo•ot′i•cal•ly,** *adv.*

e plu•ri•bus u•num (e plo͞o′ʀi bo͝os′ o͞o′no͝om; *Eng.* ē′ plo͝or′ə bəs yo͞o′-nəm), *Latin.* out of many, one: motto of the U.S.

ep•och (ep′ək; *esp. Brit.* ē′pok), *n.* **1.** a period of time marked by distinctive features, noteworthy events, changed conditions, etc.: *an epoch of peace.* **2.** the beginning of a distinctive period in the history of anything. **3.** a point of time distinguished by a particular event or state of affairs; a memorable date. **4.** any of several divisions of a geologic period during which a geologic series is formed. **5.** an arbitrarily fixed instant of time used as a reference in giving the elements of the orbit of a celestial body.

ep•och•al (ep′ə kəl; *esp. Brit.* ē′po-), *adj.* **1.** of, pertaining to, or of the nature of an epoch. **2.** extremely important, significant, or influential. **—ep′och•al•ly,** *adv.*

ep•o•nym (ep′ə nim), *n.* a person, real or imaginary, from whom something, as a tribe, nation, or place, takes or is said to take its name. **—ep•on•y•mous** (ə pon′ə məs), *adj.*

ep•ox•y (i pok′sē), *adj., n., pl.* **-ox•ies.,** *v.*, **-ox•ied, -ox•y•ing. —***adj.* **1.** (of an organic chemical) containing a group **(epox′y group′)** that consists of an oxygen atom bound to two already connected atoms, usu. carbon. **—***n.* **2.** Also called **epox′y res′in.** any of a class of resins derived by polymerization: used chiefly in adhesives, coatings, and castings. **—***v.t.* **3.** to bond (two materials) by means of an epoxy resin.

ep•si•lon (ep′sə lon′, -lən; *esp. Brit.* ep sī′lən), *n.* the fifth letter of the Greek alphabet (E, ε).

Ep′som salt′, *n.* Often, **Epsom salts.** hydrated magnesium sulfate, $MgSO_4 \cdot 7H_2O$, occurring as small colorless crystals: used in fertilizers, dyeing and tanning, and as a cathartic. [after their presence in the mineral water at *Epsom,* England]

Ep′stein-Barr′ vi′rus (ep′stīn bär′), *n.* a type of herpesvirus that causes infectious mononucleosis. *Abbr.:* EBV

eq•ua•ble (ek′wə bəl, ē′kwə-), *adj.* **1.** free from many changes or variations; uniform: *an equable climate.* **2.** not easily annoyed or disturbed; calm; even-tempered. **3.** uniform in operation or effect, as laws. **—eq′-ua•bil′i•ty, eq′ua•ble•ness,** *n.* **—eq′ua•bly,** *adv.*

e•qual (ē′kwəl), *adj., n., v.*, **e•qualed, e•qual•ing** or (*esp. Brit.*) **e•qualled, e•qual•ling. —***adj.* **1.** as great as; the same as (often fol. by *to* or *with*). **2.** like or alike in quantity, degree, value, etc. **3.** of the same rank, ability, merit, etc.: *two students of equal brilliance.* **4.** evenly proportioned or balanced: *an equal contest.* **5.** uniform in operation or effect: *equal laws.* **6.** adequate or sufficient in quantity or degree. **7.** having adequate powers, ability, or means; suited: *I felt equal to the task.* **8.** level, as a plain. **9.** tranquil or undisturbed. **10.** impartial or equitable. **—***n.* **11.** a person or thing that is equal. **—***v.t.* **12.** to be or become equal to; meet or match, as in value. **13.** to make or do something equal to: *to equal someone else's achievements.* **—e′qual•ly,** *adv.*

e′qual-ar′ea projec′tion, *n.* a map projection in which regions on the earth's surface that are of equal area are represented as equal.

E′qual Employ′ment Opportu′nity Commis′sion, *n.* an independent federal agency created under the Civil Rights Act of 1964, as amended, to police a program **(E′qual Employ′ment Opportu′nity)** to eliminate discrimination in employment based on race, color, age, sex, national origin, religion, or mental or physical handicap. *Abbr.:* EEOC

e•qual•i•ty (i kwol′i tē), *n., pl.* **-ties. 1.** the state or quality of being equal. **2.** uniform character, as of motion or surface. **3.** a statement that two quantities are equal; equation.

e•qual•ize (ē′kwə līz′), *v.t.*, **-ized, -iz•ing. 1.** to make equal. **2.** to make uniform. **3.** to balance the amplitude of an electronic circuit. **—e′-qual•i•za′tion,** *n.*

e•qual•iz•er (ē′kwə lī′zər), *n.* **1.** a person or thing that equalizes. **2.** any of various devices or appliances for equalizing strains, pressures, audio frequencies, etc. **3.** an electric network of inductance, capacitance, or resistance established between two points in a given network to secure some constant relation, as even attenuation, between the two points. **4.** *Slang.* a weapon, as a pistol.

e′qual opportu′nity, *n.* policies and practices, esp. in employment, that bar discrimination based on race, color, age, sex, religion, mental or physical handicap, or national origin. **—e′qual-opportu′nity,** *adj.*

E′qual Rights′ Amend′ment, *n.* a proposed amendment to the U.S. Constitution prohibiting discrimination on the basis of sex. *Abbr.:* ERA

e′qual sign′ or **e′quals sign′,** *n.* the symbol (=) used, esp. in a mathematical or logical expression, to indicate that the terms it separates are equal.

e′qual time′, *n.* an equal amount of time on the air, which radio and television licensees are required to offer to opposing candidates for public office and to those voicing diverging views on public referendums.

e•qua•nim•i•ty (ē′kwə nim′i tē, ek′wə-), *n.* composure, esp. under tension or strain; evenness of temper.

e•quate (i kwāt′), *v.t.*, **e•quat•ed, e•quat•ing. 1.** to regard, treat, or represent as equivalent or comparable: *to equate wealth with happiness.* **2.** to state the equality of or between; put in the form of an equation. **3.** to reduce to an average or to a common standard of comparison. **—e•quat′a•ble,** *adj.* **—e•quat′a•bil′i•ty,** *n.*

e•qua•tion (i kwā′zhən, -shən), *n.* **1.** the act of equating or making equal. **2.** the state of being equated or equal. **3.** equally balanced state; equilibrium. **4.** an expression or a proposition, often algebraic, asserting the equality of two quantities. **5.** a symbolic representation in chemistry showing the kind and amount of the starting materials and products of a reaction.

e•qua•tor (i kwā′tər), *n.* **1.** the great circle on a sphere or heavenly body whose plane is perpendicular to the axis and everywhere equidistant from the poles. **2.** the great circle of the earth that is equidistant from the North Pole and South Pole. **3.** a circle separating a surface into two congruent parts.

e•qua•to•ri•al (ē′kwə tôr′ē əl, -tōr′-, ek′wə-), *adj.* **1.** pertaining to an equator. **2.** typical of the regions at the earth's equator: *equatorial temperatures.* **—***n.* **3.** a telescope mounting having two axes of motion, one parallel to the earth's axis and one at right angles to it. **—e′qua•to′ri•al•ly,** *adv.*

E′quato′rial Guin′ea, *n.* a republic in W equatorial Africa: formerly a Spanish colony; gained independence 1968. 442,516; 10,824 sq. mi. (28,034 sq. km). *Cap.:* Malabo. Formerly, **Spanish Guinea.**

e•ques•tri•an (i kwes′trē ən), *adj.* **1.** of or pertaining to horseback riding. **2.** representing a person mounted on a horse: *an equestrian statue.* **3.** mounted on horseback. **—***n.* **4.** a person who rides horses. **—e•ques′tri•an•ism,** *n.*

e•ques•tri•enne (i kwes′trē en′), *n.* a woman who rides horses.

e•qui•dis•tant (ē′kwi dis′tənt, ek′wi-), *adj.* equally distant. **—e′qui•dis′tance,** *n.* **—e′qui•dis′tant•ly,** *adv.*

e•qui•lat•er•al (ē′kwə lat′ər əl, ek′wə-), *adj.* **1.** having all the sides equal: *an equilateral triangle.* **—***n.* **2.** a figure having all its sides equal. **3.** a side equivalent, or equal, to others. **—e′qui•lat′er•al•ly,** *adv.*

e•quil•i•brate (i kwil′ə brāt′, ē′kwə lī′brāt, ek′wə-), *v.*, **-brat•ed, -brat•ing. —***v.t.* **1.** to balance equally; keep in equipoise or equilibrium. **2.** to be in equilibrium with; counterpoise. **—***v.i.* **3.** to be in equilibrium; balance.

e•qui•lib•ri•um (ē′kwə lib′rē əm, ek′wə-), *n., pl.* **-ri•ums, -ri•a** (-rē ə). **1.** a state of rest or balance due to the equal action of opposing forces. **2.** equal balance between any powers, influences, etc.; equality of effect. **3.** mental or emotional balance; equanimity. **4.** a state or sense of steadiness and proper orientation of the body. **5.** the condition existing when a chemical reaction and its reverse reaction proceed at equal rates. **—e•quil′i•bra•to′ry** (i kwil′ə brə tôr′ē, -tōr′ē), *adj.*

e•quine (ē′kwīn, ek′wīn), *adj.* **1.** of, pertaining to, or resembling a horse. **—***n.* **2.** a horse.

e•qui•noc•tial (ē′kwə nok′shəl, ek′wə-), *adj.* **1.** pertaining to an equinox or the equinoxes, or to the equality of day and night. **2.** pertaining to the celestial equator. **3.** occurring at or about the time of an equinox. **—***n.* **4.** a violent rainstorm occurring at about the time of an equinox.

e•qui•nox (ē′kwə noks′, ek′wə-), *n.* the time when the sun crosses the plane of the earth's equator, making night and day of approximately equal length all over the earth and occurring about March 21 **(vernal equinox)** and Sept. 22 **(autumnal equinox).**

e•quip (i kwip′), *v.t.*, **e•quipped, e•quip•ping. 1.** to provide with what is needed for use or for an undertaking; fit out: *to equip an army.* **2.** to

E

dress; array. **3.** to furnish with intellectual or emotional resources; prepare. —**e·quip/per,** *n.*

eq·ui·page (ek/wə pij), *n.* **1.** a carriage. **2.** a carriage drawn by horses and attended by servants. **3.** outfit, as of a ship, army, or soldier; equipment.

e·quip·ment (i kwip/mənt), *n.* **1.** the articles, implements, etc., used or needed for a specific purpose or activity: *stereo equipment.* **2.** the act of equipping a person or thing. **3.** the state of being equipped. **4.** the knowledge and natural ability required for a task or occupation. **5.** the rolling stock of a railroad.

e·qui·poise (ē/kwə poiz/, ek/wə-), *n., v.,* **-poised, -pois·ing. —***n.* **1.** an equal distribution of weight; even balance; equilibrium. **2.** a counterpoise. —*v.t.* **3.** to equal or offset in weight; balance.

e·qui·po·ten·tial (ē/kwə pə ten/shəl, ek/wə-), *adj. Physics.* of the same or uniform potential at every point: *an equipotential surface.* —**e/·qui·po·ten/ti·al/i·ty,** *n.*

eq·ui·ta·ble (ek/wi tə bəl), *adj.* **1.** fair and impartial or reasonable; just and right: *equitable treatment of all citizens.* **2.** *Law.* **a.** pertaining to or valid in equity. **b.** pertaining to the system of equity, as distinguished from the common law. —**eq/ui·ta·bly,** *adv.*

eq·ui·ta·tion (ek/wi tā/shən), *n.* the act or art of riding on horseback.

eq·ui·ty (ek/wi tē), *n., pl.* **-ties. 1.** the quality of being fair or impartial; fairness; justice. **2.** something that is fair and just. **3.** *Law.* **a.** the application of the dictates of conscience or the principles of natural justice to the settlement of controversies. **b.** (in England and the U.S.) a system of jurisprudence serving to supplement and remedy the limitations and inflexibility of common law. **c.** an equitable right or claim. **4.** the monetary value of a property or business beyond any amounts owed on it in mortgages, claims, liens, etc. **5.** the interest of the owner of common stock in a corporation. **6.** (in a margin account) the excess of the market value of the securities over any indebtedness. **7.** ownership, esp. when considered as the right to share in future profits or appreciation in value.

eq/uity cap/ital, *n.* that portion of the capital of a business provided by the sale of stock.

eq/uity conver/sion, *n.* REVERSE-ANNUITY MORTGAGE.

e·quiv·a·lence (i kwiv/ə ləns or, for 3, ē/kwə vā/ləns), *n.* **1.** the state or fact of being equivalent; equality in value, force, significance, etc. **2.** an instance of this; an equivalent. **3.** the state of having equal chemical valence. **4.** *Logic.* **a.** the relation between two propositions such that they are either both true or both false. **b.** the relation between two propositions such that each logically implies the other. —*adj.* **5.** (of a logical or mathematical relationship) reflexive, symmetrical, and transitive.

e·quiv·a·lent (i kwiv/ə lənt or, for 6, ē/kwə vā/lənt), *adj.* **1.** equal in value, measure, force, effect, or significance: *His silence is equivalent to an admission of guilt.* **2.** corresponding in position, function, etc. **3.** having the same extent, as a triangle and a square of equal area. **4.** *Math.* (of two sets) able to be placed in one-to-one correspondence. **5.** *Logic.* having an equivalence relation, as two propositions. **6.** (of chemicals) having the same capacity to combine or react. —*n.* **7.** something equivalent.

e·quiv·o·cal (i kwiv/ə kəl), *adj.* **1.** allowing the possibility of more than one meaning or interpretation, esp. with intent to deceive or mislead; deliberately ambiguous: *an equivocal answer.* **2.** of doubtful nature or character; questionable; dubious; suspicious. **3.** of uncertain significance; not determined. —**e·quiv/o·cal/i·ty, e·quiv/o·ca·cy** (-kə sē), *n.* —**e·quiv/o·cal·ly,** *adv.*

e·quiv·o·cate (i kwiv/ə kāt/), *v.i.,* **-cat·ed, -cat·ing.** to use ambiguous or unclear expressions, usu. to mislead or to avoid commitment; hedge. —**e·quiv/o·cat/ing·ly,** *adv.* —**e·quiv/o·ca/tor,** *n.*

er (ə, ər), *interj.* (used to express or represent a pause, hesitation, uncertainty, etc.)

ER, emergency room.

Er, *Chem. Symbol.* erbium.

-er, a noun-forming suffix, added to nouns to form words designating persons from the object of their occupation or labor (*hatter; moonshiner; roofer*), or from their place of origin or abode (*Icelander; southerner*), or designating persons or things from some special characteristic or circumstance (*double-decker; fourth-grader; tanker; teenager*). When added to verbs, **-er** forms nouns denoting a person, animal, or thing that performs or is used in performing the action of the verb (*baker; eye-opener; fertilizer; pointer; teacher*).

e·ra (ēr/ə, er/ə), *n., pl.* **e·ras. 1.** a period of time marked by distinctive character, events, etc. **2.** the period of time to which anything belongs or is to be assigned. **3.** a system of chronologic notation reckoned from a given date. **4.** a point of time from which succeeding years are numbered, as at the beginning of a system of chronology. **5.** a date or an event forming the beginning of any distinctive period. **6.** a major division of geologic time composed of a number of periods.

ERA, **1.** Also, **era.** *Baseball.* earned run average. **2.** Equal Rights Amendment.

e·ra·di·ate (i rā/dē āt/), *v.i., v.t.,* **-at·ed, -at·ing.** to radiate. —**e·ra/di·a/tion,** *n.*

e·rad·i·cate (i rad/i kāt/), *v.t.,* **-cat·ed, -cat·ing. 1.** to remove or destroy utterly; extirpate: *to eradicate smallpox.* **2.** to erase by rubbing or by means of a chemical solvent. **3.** to pull up by the roots: *to eradicate weeds.* —**e·rad/i·ca·ble,** *adj.* —**e·rad/i·cant** (-kənt), *adj., n.* —**e·rad/i·ca/tion,** *n.* —**e·rad/i·ca/tive,** *adj.* —**e·rad/i·ca/tor,** *n.*

e·rase (i rās/), *v.,* **e·rased, e·ras·ing.** —*v.t.* **1.** to rub or scrape out, as letters or characters written, engraved, etc.; efface. **2.** to eliminate completely: *She couldn't erase the scene from her memory.* **3.** to obliterate (material recorded on magnetic tape or a magnetic disk). **4.** to obliterate recorded material from (a magnetic tape or disk): *to erase a computer disk.* —*v.i.* **5.** to give way to effacement readily or easily. **6.** to obliterate characters, markings, etc., from something. —**e·ras/a·ble,** *adj.* —**e·ra·sure** (i rā/shər), *n.*

e·ras·er (i rā/sər), *n.* **1.** a device, as a piece of rubber or cloth, for erasing marks of pencil, chalk, etc. **2.** one that erases.

E·ras·mus (i raz/məs), *n.* **Desiderius,** 1466?–1536, Dutch humanist, scholar, and theologian. —**E·ras/mi·an,** *adj.*

E·ras·tian·ism (i ras/chə niz/əm, -tē ə niz/-), *n.* the doctrine, advocated by Thomas Erastus, of the supremacy of the state over the church in ecclesiastical matters.

E·ras·tus (i ras/təs), *n.* **Thomas,** 1524–83, Swiss-German theologian. —**E·ras/ti·an,** *adj.*

er·bi·um (ûr/bē əm), *n.* a rare-earth element, having pink salts. *Symbol:* Er; *at. wt.:* 167.26; *at. no.:* 68.

ere (âr), *prep., conj.* before.

Er·e·bus (er/ə bəs), *n.* **1.** the underworld in ancient Greek belief. **2.** **Mount,** a volcano in Antarctica, on Ross Island. 13,202 ft. (4024 m).

e·rect (i rekt/), *adj.* **1.** upright and straight in position or posture: *to sit erect.* **2.** raised or directed upward or outward: *a dog with ears erect.* **3.** (of an organ or part) in a state of physiological erection. **4.** (of a plant part) vertical throughout: *an erect stem.* **5.** *Optics.* (of an image) having the same position as the object; not inverted. —*v.t.* **6.** to build; construct; raise. **7.** to raise and set in an upright or vertical position. **8.** to set up or establish, as a system or an institution; found. **9.** to bring about; cause to come into existence: *to erect barriers to progress.* **10.** *Geom.* to draw or construct (a line or figure) upon a given line, base, or the like. **11.** *Optics.* to change (an inverted image) to the normal position. —*v.i.* **12.** to become erect; stand up or out. —**e·rect/a·ble,** *adj.* —**e·rect/ly,** *adv.* —**e·rect/ness,** *n.*

e·rec·tile (i rek/tl, -til, -tīl), *adj.* **1.** capable of being distended with blood and becoming rigid, as tissue. **2.** capable of being erected or set upright. —**e·rec·til·i·ty** (i rek til/i tē, ē/rek-), *n.*

e·rec·tion (i rek/shən), *n.* **1.** something erected. **2. a.** a distended and rigid state of an organ or part containing erectile tissue, esp. the penis. **b.** an instance of this or a part or tissue in this state.

e·rec·tor (i rek/tər), *n.* **1.** Also, **e·rect/er.** a person or thing that erects. **2.** a muscle that erects a part of the body.

ere·long (âr/lông/, -long/), *adv.* before long; soon.

er·e·mite (er/ə mīt/), *n.* a hermit or recluse, esp. one under a religious vow. —**er/e·mit/ic** (-mit/ik), **er/e·mit/i·cal, er/e·mit/ish,** *adj.* —**er/e·mit/ism,** *n.*

erg¹ (ûrg), *n.* the centimeter-gram-second unit of work or energy, equal to the work done by a force of one dyne when its point of application moves through a distance of one centimeter in the direction of the force; 10^{-7} joule.

erg² (erg), *n.* any vast area covered with sand, as parts of the Sahara Desert.

er·ga·tive (ûr/gə tiv), *adj.* **1. a.** of or designating a grammatical case that indicates the subject of a transitive verb and is distinct from the case indicating the subject of an intransitive verb. **b.** similar to such a case in function or meaning, esp. in indicating an agent as subject. **2.** of or pertaining to a language that has an ergative case or in which the direct object of a transitive verb and the subject of an intransitive verb are paired grammatically by other means. —*n.* **3.** the ergative case. **4.** a word in the ergative case. —**er/ga·tiv/i·ty,** *n.*

er·go (ûr/gō, er/gō), *conj., adv.* therefore. [< Latin]

er·go·nom·ics (ûr/gə nom/iks), *n.* (*used with a sing. or pl. v.*) an applied science that coordinates the design of devices, systems, and physical working conditions with the capacities and requirements of the worker. Also called **human engineering.** —**er/go·nom/ic,** *adj.* —**er/go·nom/i·cal·ly,** *adv.*

er·got (ûr/gət, -got), *n.* **1. a.** a disease of rye and other cereal grasses, caused by a fungus of the genus *Claviceps,* esp. *C. purpurea,* which replaces the affected grain with a long, hard, blackish sclerotial body. **b.** the sclerotial body itself. **2.** the dried sclerotium of *C. purpurea,* developed on rye plants, from which various medicinal alkaloids are derived.

er·i·ca (er/i kə), *n., pl.* **-cas.** any low-growing evergreen shrub belonging to the genus *Erica,* of the heath family, including several species of heather. —**er/i·ca/ceous** (-kā/shəs), *adj.*

Er·ic·son or **Er·ics·son** (er/ik sən), *n.* **Leif,** fl. A.D. c1000, Norse mariner (son of Eric the Red).

Er/ic the Red/ (er/ik), *n.* born A.D. c950, Norse mariner: explorer and colonizer of Greenland c985.

E·rie (ēr/ē), *n., pl.* **E·ries,** (*esp. collectively*) **E·rie** for 3. **1. Lake,** a lake between the NE central United States and SE central Canada: the southernmost lake of the Great Lakes. 239 mi. (385 km) long; 9940 sq. mi. (25,745 sq. km). **2.** a port in NW Pennsylvania, on Lake Erie. 108,398. **3.** a member of an American Indian people, presumed to be Iroquoian-speaking, who lived S of Lake Erie in the 17th century.

E/rie Canal/, *n.* a canal in New York between Albany and Buffalo, connecting the Hudson River with Lake Erie: completed in 1825; now constitutes the major part of the New York State Barge Canal. 363 mi. (584 km) long.

E·rig·e·na (i rij′ə nə), *n.* **Johannes Scotus,** A.D. c810–c877, Irish philosopher and theologian.

e·rig·er·on (i rij′ə ron′, -ər ən), *n.* any composite plant of the genus *Erigeron,* having asterlike flower heads but with narrower and usu. more numerous white or purple rays.

Er·in (er′in), *n. Literary.* Ireland.

er·is·tic (e ris′tik), *adj.* **1.** Also, **er·is′ti·cal.** pertaining to controversy or disputation; controversial. —*n.* **2.** a person who engages in disputation; controversialist. **3.** the art of disputation. —**er·is′ti·cal·ly,** *adv.*

Er·i·tre·a (er′i trē′ə), *n.* a republic in NE Africa, on the Red Sea: Italian colony 1890–1941; province of Ethiopia 1962–93; independent since 1993. 3,589,687; 47,076 sq. mi. (121,927 sq. km). *Cap.:* Asmara. —**Er′i·tre′an,** *adj., n.*

er·mine (ûr′min), *n., pl.* **-mines,** (*esp. collectively*) **-mine** for 1, 2. **1.** a weasel of the Northern Hemisphere, *Mustela erminea,* having a white coat with a black-tipped tail in the winter. **2.** any of various weasels having a white winter coat. **3.** the white winter fur of the ermine, often including the black tail tip. **4.** the rank or position of a king, peer, or judge who wears a robe trimmed with ermine on official or state occasions. —**er′mined,** *adj.*

e·rode (i rōd′), *v.,* **e·rod·ed, e·rod·ing.** —*v.t.* **1.** to eat into or away; destroy by slow consumption or disintegration. **2.** to form (a gully, butte, etc.) by erosion. —*v.i.* **3.** to become eroded. —**e·rod′i·ble, e·rod′a·ble, e·ro·si·ble** (i rō′zə bəl, -sə-), *adj.* —**e·rod′i·bil′i·ty, e·rod′a·bil′i·ty,** *n.*

e·rog·e·nous (i roj′ə nəs) also **er·o·gen·ic** (er′ə jen′ik), *adj.* **1.** particularly sensitive to sexual stimulation, as certain areas of the body: *erogenous zones.* **2.** arousing or tending to arouse sexual desire. —**e·rog′e·ne′i·ty** (-nē′i tē), *n.*

E·ros (ēr′os, er′os), *n.* **1.** the ancient Greek god of carnal love. **2.** (*sometimes l.c.*) physical love; sexual desire. **3.** *Psychoanal.* **a.** the libido. **b.** instincts for self-preservation collectively.

e·ro·sion (i rō′zhən), *n.* **1.** the act or process of eroding. **2.** the state of being eroded. **3.** the process by which the surface of the earth is worn away by the action of water, glaciers, winds, waves, etc. —**e·ro′sion·al,** *adj.*

e·rot·ic (i rot′ik), *adj.* Also, **e·rot′i·cal.** **1.** of, pertaining to, or treating of sexual love. **2.** arousing or satisfying sexual desire. **3.** subject to or marked by strong sexual desire. —*n.* **4.** an erotic person. [< Greek *erōtikós* pertaining to Eros] —**e·rot′i·cal·ly,** *adv.*

e·rot·i·ca (i rot′i kə), *n.* (*used with a sing. or pl. v.*) literature or art dealing with sexual love.

e·rot·i·cism (i rot′ə siz′əm) also **er·o·tism** (er′ə tiz′əm), *n.* **1.** sexual or erotic quality or character. **2.** the use of erotic symbolism, themes, etc., as in art or literature. **3.** the condition of being sexually aroused or excited. **4.** sexual drive or tendency.

e·rot·i·cize (i rot′ə sīz′), *v.t.,* **-cized, -ciz·ing.** to render or make erotic. —**e·rot′i·ci·za′tion,** *n.*

err (ûr, er), *v.i.* **1.** to go astray in thought or belief; be mistaken or incorrect. **2.** to go astray morally; sin.

er·ran·cy (er′ən sē, ûr′-), *n., pl.* **-cies.** **1.** the state or an instance of erring. **2.** tendency to err.

er·rand (er′ənd), *n.* **1.** a short trip to accomplish a specific purpose, as to buy or deliver something or to convey a message, often for someone else. **2.** the purpose of such a trip. **3.** a special mission entrusted to a messenger; commission.

er·rant (er′ənt), *adj.* **1.** deviating from the regular or proper course; erring; straying. **2.** traveling, as a medieval knight in quest of adventure; roving adventurously. **3.** moving in an aimless or lightly changing manner: *an errant breeze.* —**er′rant·ly,** *adv.*

er·rant·ry (er′ən trē), *n., pl.* **-ries.** conduct or performance like that of a knight-errant.

er·ra·ta (i rä′tə, i rā′-, i rat′ə), *n., pl.* **-tas** for 2. **1.** pl. of ERRATUM. **2.** a list of errors and their corrections inserted, usu. on a separate page or slip of paper, in a book or other publication; corrigenda.

er·rat·ic (i rat′ik), *adj.* **1.** inconsistent or changeable in behavior; unpredictable. **2.** deviating from the usual or proper course; eccentric. **3.** having no certain or definite course; wandering; not fixed. **4.** (of a boulder, etc.) carried by glacial ice and deposited some distance from its place of origin. —*n.* **5.** an erratic or eccentric person. **6.** an erratic boulder or the like. —**er·rat′i·cal·ly,** *adv.* —**er·rat′i·cism,** *n.*

er·ra·tum (i rä′təm, i rā′-, i rat′əm), *n., pl.* **-ta** (-tə). **1.** an error in writing or printing. **2.** a statement of an error and its correction inserted, usu. on a separate page, in a book or other publication; corrigendum.

er·ro·ne·ous (ə rō′nē əs, e rō′-), *adj.* **1.** containing error; mistaken; incorrect. **2.** straying from what is right or proper. —**er·ro′ne·ous·ly,** *adv.* —**er·ro′ne·ous·ness,** *n.*

er·ror (er′ər), *n.* **1.** a deviation from accuracy or correctness; mistake. **2.** belief in something untrue; the holding of mistaken opinions. **3.** the condition of believing what is not true: *I was in error about the date.* **4.** a moral offense; wrongdoing; sin. **5.** a baseball misplay allowing a batter to reach base or a runner to advance. **6.** the difference between the observed or approximately determined value and the true value of a

quantity in mathematics or statistics. **7.** *Law.* a mistake in a matter of fact or law in a case tried in a court of record. **8.** a postage stamp distinguished by an imperfection, as in design. —**er′ror·less,** *adj.* —**er′ror·less·ly,** *adv.*

er·satz (er′zäts, -säts, er zäts′, -säts′), *adj.* **1.** serving as a substitute; synthetic; artificial: *ersatz coffee made from grain.* —*n.* **2.** an artificial substitute for something natural or genuine.

erst·while (ûrst′hwīl′, -wīl′), *adj.* former; of times past: *erstwhile friends.*

ERT, estrogen replacement therapy.

e·ru′cic ac′id (i rōō′sik), *n.* a solid fatty acid, a homologue of oleic acid, derived from oils of mustard seed and rapeseed.

e·ruct (i rukt′), *v.t., v.i.* **1.** to belch. **2.** to discharge violently; erupt. —**e·ruc·ta·tion** (i ruk tā′shən, ē′ruk-), *n.*

er·u·dite (er′yōō dīt′, er′ōō-), *adj.* characterized by great erudition; learned or scholarly. —**er′u·dite′ly,** *adv.* —**er′u·dite′ness,** *n.*

er·u·di·tion (er′yōō dish′ən, er′ōō-), *n.* knowledge acquired by study, research, etc.; learning; scholarship.

e·rupt (i rupt′), *v.i.* **1.** to burst forth: *Molten lava erupted from the volcano.* **2.** (of a volcano, geyser, etc.) to eject matter. **3.** to break out of a pent-up state, usu. in a sudden and violent manner: *Words of anger erupted from her.* **4.** to break out, as in a skin rash. **5.** (of teeth) to grow through surrounding hard and soft tissues and become visible in the mouth. —*v.t.* **6.** to release violently; burst forth with. **7.** (of a volcano, geyser, etc.) to eject (matter). —**e·rupt′i·ble,** *adj.*

e·rup·tion (i rup′shən), *n.* **1.** an issuing forth suddenly and violently; outburst; outbreak. **2.** the ejection of molten rock, steam, etc., as from a volcano or geyser. **3.** something that is erupted or ejected, as molten rock, volcanic ash, or steam. **4. a.** the breaking out of a rash or the like. **b.** the rash itself. **5.** the emergence of a growing tooth through the gum tissue.

e·rup·tive (i rup′tiv), *adj.* **1.** bursting forth, or tending to burst forth. **2.** pertaining to or of the nature of an eruption. **3.** noting a rock formed by the eruption of molten material. **4.** causing or accompanied by a rash or the like. —**e·rup′tive·ly,** *adv.*

er·vil (ûr′vil), *n.* a Eurasian vetch, *Vicia ervilia,* used for forage. Also called **ers.**

er·y·the·ma (er′ə thē′mə), *n.* abnormal redness of the skin due to local congestion, as in inflammation. —**er′y·them′a·tous** (-them′ə təs, -thē′mə-), **er′y·the′mic,** *adj.*

e·ryth·rism (i rith′riz əm, er′ə thriz′əm), *n.* abnormal redness, as of plumage or hair. —**er′y·thris′mal, er′y·thris′tic** (-thris′tik), *adj.*

e·ryth·ro·blast (i rith′rə blast′), *n.* a nucleated cell in the bone marrow from which a red blood cell develops. —**e·ryth′ro·blas′tic,** *adj.*

e·ryth·ro·cyte (i rith′rə sīt′), *n.* RED BLOOD CELL. —**e·ryth′ro·cyt′ic** (-sit′ik), *adj.*

e·ryth·ro·my·cin (i rith′rə mī′sin), *n.* an antibiotic, $C_{37}H_{67}NO_{13}$, produced by an actinomycete, *Streptomyces erythraeus,* used in the treatment of diseases caused by certain organisms.

e·ryth·ro·poi·e·sis (i rith′rō poi ē′sis), *n.* the production of red blood cells. —**e·ryth′ro·poi·et′ic** (-et′ik), *adj.*

Es, *Chem. Symbol.* einsteinium.

E·sar·had·don (ē′sär had′n), *n.* (*Assur-akh-iddin*), died 669 B.C., king of Assyria 681–669 B.C.

E·sau (ē′sô), *n.* a son of Isaac and Rebekah, older twin of Jacob, to whom he sold his birthright. Gen. 25:21–25.

es·ca·lade (es′kə lād′, -läd′, es′kə läd′, -läd′), *n., v.,* **-lad·ed, -lad·ing.** —*n.* **1.** a scaling or mounting by means of ladders, esp. in an assault upon a fortified place. —*v.t.* **2.** to mount, pass, or enter by means of ladders. —**es′ca·lad′er,** *n.*

es·ca·late (es′kə lāt′), *v.i., v.t.,* **-lat·ed, -lat·ing.** **1.** to increase in intensity, magnitude, etc.: *a time when prices escalate; to escalate a war.* **2.** to rise or raise on or as if on an escalator. —**es′ca·la′tion,** *n.* —**es′ca·la·to′ry** (-lə tôr′ē, -tōr′ē), *adj.*

es·ca·la·tor (es′kə lā′tər), *n.* **1.** a continuously moving stairway on an endless loop for carrying passengers up or down. **2.** a means of rising or descending or of increasing or decreasing, esp. by stages: *the social escalator.* **3.** ESCALATOR CLAUSE. —*adj.* **4.** of, pertaining to, or included in an escalator clause.

es′ca·la·tor clause′, *n.* a provision in a contract calling for adjustments, usu. increases, in charges, wages, or other payments, based on fluctuations in production costs, the cost of living, or other variables.

es·cal·lop or **es·cal·op** (e skol′əp, e skal′-), *v.,* **-loped, -lop·ing,** *n.* —*v.t.* **1.** to bake (food) in a sauce, milk, etc., often with breadcrumbs on top; scallop. —*n.* **2.** SCALLOP.

es·ca·pade (es′kə pād′, es′kə pād′), *n.* a reckless adventure or wild prank, esp. one contrary to usual or proper behavior.

es·cape (i skāp′), *v.,* **-caped, -cap·ing,** *n., adj.* —*v.i.* **1.** to slip or get away, as from confinement or restraint: *to escape from jail.* **2.** to avoid capture, punishment, or any threatened evil. **3.** to issue from a confining enclosure, as a gas or liquid. **4.** to slip away; fade. **5.** (of an orig. cultivated plant) to grow wild. —*v.t.* **6.** to slip away from or elude. **7.** to succeed in avoiding: *to escape capture.* **8.** to elude (one's memory, notice, search, etc.). **9.** (of a sound or utterance) to slip from or be expressed by inadvertently: *A sigh escaped her lips.* —*n.* **10.** an act or instance of escaping. **11.** the fact of having escaped. **12.** a means of escaping: *We used the tunnel as an escape.* **13.** avoidance of reality: *to* read mystery stories as an escape. **14.** leakage, as of water or gas, from a pipe or storage container. **15.** a plant that originated in cultivated stock and is now growing wild. **16.** a key on a microcomputer keyboard, often used to return to a previous program screen. —*adj.* **17.** for or providing an escape: *an escape hatch.* —**es•cap•ee′,** *n.*

escape′ art′ist, *n.* an entertainer adept in getting out of handcuffs or other confining devices.

escape′ clause′, *n.* a provision in a contract that enables a party to terminate contractual obligations in specified circumstances.

escape′ mech′anism, *n.* a means of avoiding an unpleasant life situation, as daydreaming.

es•cape•ment (i skāp′mənt), *n.* **1.** the portion of a watch or clock that measures beats and controls the speed of wheels in gear. **2.** a mechanism for regulating the motion of a typewriter carriage, consisting of pawls and a toothed wheel or rack. **3.** a mechanism in a piano that causes a hammer to fall back into rest position immediately after striking a string. **4.** an act of escaping. **5.** a way of escape; outlet.

escapement (def. 1)

escape′ veloc′ity, *n.* the minimum speed that an object at a given distance from a celestial body must have so that it will escape from orbit around the body.

es•cap•ism (i skā′piz əm), *n.* the avoidance of reality by absorption of the mind in entertainment or in an imaginative situation or activity. —**es•cap′ist,** *n.*

es•ca•role (es′kə rōl′), *n.* a broad-leaved form of *Cichorium endivia,* used in salads. Compare ENDIVE (def. 1).

es•carp (i skärp′), *n.* **1.** the inner slope or wall of the ditch surrounding a rampart. **2.** any similar steep slope.

es•carp•ment (i skärp′mənt), *n.* **1.** a long, precipitous, clifflike ridge of land, rock, or the like commonly formed by faulting or fracturing of the earth's crust. **2.** ground cut into an escarp around a fortification or defensive position.

es•cha•tol•o•gy (es′kə tol′ə jē), *n.* **1.** any system of religious doctrines concerning last or final matters, as death, judgment, or an afterlife. **2.** the branch of theology dealing with such matters. —**es•cha•to•log′i•cal** (es′kə tl oj′i kəl, e skat′l-), *adj.* —**es′cha•to•log′i•cal•ly,** *adv.* —**es′cha•tol′o•gist,** *n.*

es•cheat (es chēt′), *n. Law.* **1.** the reverting of property to the state when there are no legal heirs. **2.** the right to take property subject to escheat. —*v.i.* **3.** (of property) to revert by escheat. —*v.t.* **4.** to take or confiscate by escheat. —**es•cheat′a•ble,** *adj.* —**es•cheat′or,** *n.*

es•chew (es chōō′), *v.t.* to abstain or keep away from; shun; avoid. —**es•chew′al,** *n.* —**es•chew′er,** *n.*

Es•con•di•do (es′kən dē′dō), *n.* a city in SW California. 116,349.

es•cort (*n.* es′kôrt; *v.* i skôrt′), *n.* **1.** a person or persons accompanying another for protection, guidance, or courtesy. **2.** an armed or protective guard, as a body of soldiers or ships. **3.** a man who accompanies a woman in public, as to a social event. **4.** a man or woman hired to accompany another socially. **5.** protection, safeguard, or guidance on a journey. —*v.t.* **6.** to attend or accompany as an escort.

es•cri•toire (es′kri twär′), *n.* WRITING DESK (def. 1).

es•crow (es′krō, i skrō′), *n.* **1.** a deed, funds, or property deposited with a third party to be transferred to the grantee when certain conditions have been fulfilled. —*v.t.* **2.** to place in escrow. —*Idiom.* **3. in escrow,** held by a third party until certain conditions of an agreement are fulfilled: *an estate in escrow.*

es•cu•do (e skōō′dō), *n., pl.* **-dos. 1.** the basic monetary unit of Cape Verde and Portugal. **2.** any of various former gold or silver coins of Spain and Spanish America.

es•cu•lent (es′kyə lənt), *adj.* **1.** suitable for use as food; edible. —*n.* **2.** something edible, esp. a vegetable.

es•cutch•eon (i skuch′ən), *n.* **1.** a shield or shieldlike surface on which a coat of arms is depicted. **2.** an ornamental or protective plate around a keyhole, door handle, drawer pull, light switch, etc. **3.** a panel on the stern of a vessel bearing its name. —**es•cutch′eoned,** *adj.*

Esd., Esdras.

Es•dra•e•lon (es′drā ē′lon, -drə-, ez′-), *n.* a plain in N Israel, extending from the Mediterranean near Mt. Carmel to the Jordan River: scene of ancient battles. Also called **Plain of Jezreel.**

Es•dras (ez′drəs), *n.* **1.** either of the first two books of the Apocrypha, I Esdras or II Esdras. **2.** *Douay Bible.* **a.** EZRA (def. 1). **b.** either of two books, I Esdras or II Esdras, corresponding to the books of Ezra and Nehemiah, respectively, in the King James Version.

Es•dud (is dōōd′), *n.* Ashdod.

ESE or **E.S.E.,** east-southeast.

-ese, a suffix forming adjectival derivatives of place names, esp. countries or cities; frequently used nominally to denote the inhabitants of the place or their language: *Faroese; Japanese; Vietnamese; Viennese.* By analogy with such language names, **-ese** occurs in coinages denoting in a disparaging, often facetious way a characteristic jargon, style, or accent: *Brooklynese; bureaucratese; journalese; computerese.*

Esh•col (esh′kol), *n.* a valley north of Hebron, famous for fertility. Num. 13:24.

es•ker (es′kər), *n.* a serpentine ridge of gravelly and sandy drift, formed by glacial meltwater.

Es•ki•mo (es′kə mō′), *n., pl.* **-mos,** (*esp. collectively*) **-mo** for 1. **1.** a member of a people or group of peoples living on the coast and adjacent hinterland of arctic and subarctic regions from Greenland W through Canada and Alaska to extreme NE Siberia. **2.** the group of related languages spoken by the Eskimos, comprised of Inuit and the Yupik languages. —**Es′ki•mo′an,** *adj.* —**Es′ki•moid′,** *adj.* —**Usage.** The term ESKIMO has largely been supplanted by INUIT in Canada, and INUIT is used officially by the Canadian government. Many Inuit consider ESKIMO derogatory, in part because the word was, erroneously, long thought to mean "eater of raw meat." Nonetheless, ESKIMO continues in use in all parts of the world, esp. in historical, archaeological, and cultural contexts. The term *Native American* is sometimes used to include Eskimo and Aleut peoples. See also INDIAN.

Es′kimo cur′lew, *n.* a New World curlew, *Numenius borealis,* that breeds in N North America: possibly extinct.

Es′kimo dog′, *n.* **1.** one of a breed of strong, medium-sized dogs with a dense, coarse coat, used in arctic regions for hunting and pulling sleds. **2.** any dog of the arctic regions of North America used for pulling sleds. Also called **husky.**

ESL, English as a second language.

ESOP (ē′sop), *n.* a plan under which a company's capital stock is acquired by its employees or workers.

e•soph•a•gus (i sof′ə gəs, ē sof′-), *n., pl.* **-gi** (-jī′, -gī′). a muscular tube for the passage of food from the pharynx to the stomach; gullet. —**e•soph•a•ge•al** (i sof′ə jē′əl, ē′sə faj′ē əl), *adj.*

es•o•ter•ic (es′ə ter′ik), *adj.* **1.** understood by or meant for only the select few who have special knowledge or interest or for the initiates of a group; recondite. **2.** belonging to the select few. **3.** private; secret. —**es′o•ter′i•cal•ly,** *adv.*

es•o•ter•i•ca (es′ə ter′i kə), *n.pl.* esoteric facts or matters.

ESP, extrasensory perception: perception or communication outside of normal sensory capability, as in telepathy and clairvoyance.

es•pa•drille (es′pə dril′), *n.* a flat shoe with a cloth upper, a rope sole, and sometimes lacing around the ankle.

es•pal•ier (i spal′yər, -yā), *n.* **1.** a trellis or framework on which the trunk and branches of fruit trees or shrubs are trained to grow in one plane. **2.** a plant so trained. —*v.t.* **3.** to train on an espalier. **4.** to furnish with an espalier.

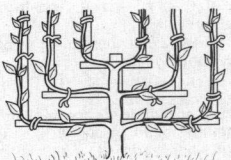

espalier (def. 1)

es•par•to (i spär′tō), *n., pl.* **-tos.** any of several grasses, esp. *Stipa tenacissima,* of S Europe and N Africa, used for making paper, cordage, etc. Also called **espar′to grass′.**

es•pe•cial (i spesh′əl), *adj.* **1.** special; exceptional: *of no especial importance; an especial friend.* **2.** of a particular kind, or peculiar to a particular one; particular: *your especial case.* —**es•pe′cial•ness,** *n.*

es•pe•cial•ly (i spesh′ə lē), *adv.* **1.** to an exceptional degree; particularly; markedly: *Be especially watchful.* **2.** in particular; above all. **3.** for a particular purpose; specifically: *designed especially for you.*

Es•pe•ran•to (es′pə rän′tō, -ran′-), *n.* an artificial language invented in 1887 for international use, based on word roots common to the major European languages. [orig. Esperanto pseudonym of the inventor, L. L. Zamenhof (1859–1917), Polish physician; lit., the hoping one] —**Es′pe•ran′tism,** *n.* —**Es′pe•ran′tist,** *n.*

es•pi•o•nage (es′pē ə näzh′, -nij, es′pē ə näzh′), *n.* **1.** the act or practice of spying. **2.** the use of spies by a government to discover the military and political secrets of other nations. **3.** the use of spies by a corporation or the like to acquire the plans or technical knowledge of a competitor: *industrial espionage.*

es•pla•nade (es′plə näd′, -nād′, es′plə näd′, -nād′), *n.* an open level space, esp. one serving for public walks or drives along a shore.

es•pous•al (i spou′zəl, -səl), *n.* **1.** adoption or advocacy, as of a cause or principle. **2.** Sometimes, **espousals. a.** a marriage ceremony. **b.** an engagement or betrothal celebration.

es•pouse (i spouz′, i spous′), *v.t.,* **-poused, -pous•ing. 1.** to adopt or embrace, as a cause; support. **2.** to marry. **3.** to give (a woman) in marriage. —**es•pous′er,** *n.*

es•pres•so (e spres′ō), *n.* a strong coffee prepared by forcing live steam through finely ground dark-roast coffee beans.

es•prit (e sprē′), *n.* **1.** sprightliness of spirit or wit; lively intelligence. **2.** ESPRIT DE CORPS.

es•prit de corps (e sprē′ də kôr′), *n.* a sense of unity and of common interests and responsibilities as developed among the members of a group. [< French]

es•py (i spī′), *v.t.,* **-pied, -py•ing.** to see at a distance; catch sight of.

es•quire (es′kwīᵊr, e skwīᵊr′), *n.* **1.** (*cap.*) a title of respect sometimes placed, esp. in its abbreviated form, after a man's surname in formal written address: in the U.S., chiefly applied to lawyers, women as well as men. *Abbr.:* Esq., Esqr. **2.** SQUIRE (def. 2). **3.** a man belonging to the order of English gentry ranking next below a knight.

ess (es), *n.* **1.** the letter *S, s.* **2.** something shaped like an S.

-ess, a suffix forming distinctively feminine nouns: *countess; goddess; lioness.* —**Usage.** Since at least the 14th century, English has borrowed nouns with this feminine suffix from French (French *-esse*) and also applied that ending to existing words, most frequently agent nouns in *-or* or *-er.* Some of the earliest borrowings—noble or religious titles—still flourish, as *princess, duchess, abbess,* and *prioress.* The use of -ESS words has declined sharply in the latter half of the 20th century. Among those words that are rarely used or are either rejected or discouraged in modern American English are *ambassadress, ancestress, authoress, poetess, proprietress, sculptress,* and *stewardess.* Some nouns in -ESS are still current: *actress* (but some women prefer *actor*); *adventuress; enchantress; governess* (only in its child-care sense); *heiress* (largely in journalistic writing); *hostess* (but women who conduct radio and television programs are *hosts*); *millionairess; mistress* (except in the sense of expert); *murderess; postmistress* (not in official U.S. government use); *seamstress; seductress; sorceress; temptress;* and *waitress.*

es•say (*n.* es′ā or, for 3, e sā′; *v.* e sā′), *n.* **1.** a short literary composition on a particular theme or subject, usu. in prose and generally analytic, speculative, or interpretative. **2.** anything resembling such a composition: *a picture essay.* **3.** an effort to perform or accomplish something; attempt. —*v.t.* **4.** to try; attempt. **5.** to put to the test; make trial of. —**es•say′er,** *n.*

es•say•ist (es′ā ist), *n.* a writer of essays.

es•sence (es′əns), *n.* **1.** the basic, real, and invariable nature of a thing; substance. **2.** a concentrated substance obtained from a plant, drug, or the like, by distillation, infusion, etc. **3.** an alcoholic solution of an essential oil; spirit. **4.** a perfume; scent. **5.** (in philosophy) the true nature or constitution of anything, as opposed to what is accidental, phenomenal, illusory, etc. **6.** something that exists, esp. a spiritual or immaterial entity. —*Idiom.* **7. in essence,** essentially; basically. **8. of the essence,** absolutely essential; crucial.

Es•sene (es′ēn, e sēn′), *n.* a member of a monastic Jewish sect that flourished in Palestine from the 2nd century B.C. to the 2nd century A.D. —**Es•se′ni•an, Es•sen•ic** (e sen′ik), *adj.*

es•sen•tial (ə sen′shəl), *adj.* **1.** absolutely necessary; indispensable. **2.** pertaining to or constituting the essence of a thing. **3.** noting or containing an essence of a plant, drug, etc. **4.** being such by its very nature or in the highest sense; natural; spontaneous: *essential happiness.* **5.** not associated with an underlying disease: *essential hypertension.* —*n.* **6.** a basic, indispensable, or necessary element; chief point. —**es•sen′tial•ly,** *adv.* —**es•sen′tial•ness,** *n.*

essen′tial ami′no ac′id, *n.* any amino acid that is required for life and growth but is not produced in the body, or is produced in insufficient amounts, and must be supplied by protein in the diet.

es•sen•tial•ism (ə sen′shə liz′əm), *n.* an educational doctrine advocating the teaching of culturally important concepts, ideals, and skills to all students, regardless of individual ability, needs, etc. Compare PROGRESSIVISM. —**es•sen′tial•ist,** *n., adj.*

essen′tial oil′, *n.* any of a class of volatile oils obtained from plants, possessing the odor and other characteristic properties of the plant: used in perfumes, flavors, and pharmaceuticals.

EST or **E.S.T.,** Eastern Standard Time.

-est¹, a suffix forming the superlative degree of adjectives and adverbs: *fastest; soonest; warmest.*

-est² or **-st,** an ending of the second person singular indicative of verbs, now occurring only in archaic forms or used in solemn or poetic language: *knowest; sayest; goest.*

est., **1.** established. **2.** estate. **3.** estimate. **4.** estimated. **5.** estuary.

es•tab•lish (i stab′lish), *v.t.* **1.** to bring into being on a firm or permanent basis; found; institute: *to establish a university.* **2.** to install or settle in a position, place, business, etc.: *to establish oneself in business.* **3.** to show to be valid or true; prove: *to establish the facts.* **4.** to ascertain; determine: *to establish the time of death.* **5.** to cause to be accepted or recognized: *to establish a custom.* **6.** to bring about: *to establish order.* **7.** to enact, appoint, or ordain on a permanent basis, as a law. **8.** to make (a church) a national or state institution. **9.** to obtain control of (a suit of cards) so that one can win all the subsequent tricks in it. —**es•tab′lish•a•ble,** *adj.* —**es•tab′lish•er,** *n.*

estab′lished church′, *n.* a church that is recognized by law, and sometimes financially supported, as the official church of a nation. Compare NATIONAL CHURCH.

es•tab•lish•ment (i stab′lish mənt), *n.* **1.** the act of establishing; the state or fact of being established. **2.** something established; a constituted order or system. **3. the Establishment,** the people and institutions constituting the existing power structure in society; institutional authority. **4.** (*often cap.*) the dominant or controlling group in a field of endeavor or organization: *the literary Establishment.* **5.** a household; place of residence including its furnishings, grounds, etc. **6.** a place of business together with its employees, merchandise, equipment, etc. **7.** a permanent civil, military, or other force or organization. **8.** an institution, as a school or hospital. **9.**

es•tab•lish•men•tar•i•an (i stab′lish mən târ′ē ən), *adj.* **1.** of or pertaining to an established church, esp. the Church of England, or the principle of state religion. **2.** (*cap.*) of, pertaining to, or favoring the Establishment. —*n.* **3.** a supporter or adherent of the principle of the establishment of a church by state law; an advocate of state religion. **4.** (*cap.*) a person who belongs to or favors the Establishment. —**es•tab′lish•men•tar′i•an•ism,** *n.*

es•tan•cia (e stän′sē ə), *n., pl.* **-cias.** (in Spanish America) a landed estate or a cattle ranch.

es•tate (i stāt′), *n.* **1.** a piece of landed property, esp. one of large extent with an elaborate house on it. **2.** *Law.* **a.** property or possessions. **b.** the amount, degree, or nature of a person's interest in land or other property. **c.** the property of a deceased person, a bankrupt, etc., viewed as an aggregate. **3.** a period or condition of life. **4.** condition or circumstances with reference to worldly prosperity, estimation, etc.; social status or rank. **5.** a major political or social group or class, esp. one once having specific political powers, as the clergy, nobles, and commons in France or the Lords Spiritual, Lords Temporal, and commons in England.

estate′ a′gent, *n. Brit.* **1.** a real-estate agent. **2.** the manager of a landed estate.

estate′ tax′, *n.* a tax imposed on the net worth of a decedent's property prior to distribution to the heirs. Also called **death tax.**

es•teem (i stēm′), *v.t.* **1.** to regard highly or favorably; regard with respect or admiration. **2.** to consider as of a certain value or a certain type; regard: *I would esteem it a great favor.* —*n.* **3.** favorable opinion or judgment; respect or regard: *to hold a person in esteem.*

es•ter (es′tər), *n.* a chemical compound produced by the reaction between an acid and an alcohol with the elimination of a molecule of water, as ethyl acetate, $C_4H_8O_2$, or methyl methacrylate, $C_5H_8O_2$.

Esth., Esther.

Es•ther (es′tər), *n.* **1.** the Jewish wife of Ahasuerus, who saved her people from destruction by Haman. **2.** a book of the Bible bearing her name.

es•thet•ic (es thet′ik), *adj., n.* AESTHETIC.

es•thet•ics (es thet′iks), *n.* (*used with a sing. v.*) AESTHETICS.

es•ti•ma•ble (es′tə mə bəl), *adj.* **1.** worthy of esteem; deserving respect or admiration. **2.** capable of being estimated. —**es′ti•ma•ble•ness,** *n.* —**es′ti•ma•bly,** *adv.*

es•ti•mate (*v.* es′tə māt′; *n.* -mit, -māt′), *v.,* **-mat•ed, -mat•ing,** *n.* —*v.t.* **1.** to form an approximate judgment or opinion regarding the worth, amount, size, weight, etc., of; calculate approximately: *to estimate costs.* **2.** to form an opinion of; judge. —*v.i.* **3.** to make an estimate. —*n.* **4.** an approximate judgment or calculation, as of the value, amount, time, size, or weight of something. **5.** a judgment or opinion, as of the qualities of a person or thing. **6.** a statement of the approximate charge for work to be done, submitted by a person or firm ready to undertake the work. —**es′ti•ma′tive,** *adj.* —**es′ti•ma′tor,** *n.*

es•ti•ma•tion (es′tə mā′shən), *n.* **1.** judgment or opinion. **2.** esteem; respect. **3.** approximate calculation; estimate.

es•ti•val (es′tə vəl, e stī′vəl), *adj.* pertaining or appropriate to summer.

es•ti•vate (es′tə vāt′), *v.i.,* **-vat•ed, -vat•ing. 1.** to spend the summer, as at a specific place or in a certain activity. **2.** (of an animal) to pass the summer in a torpid condition. —**es′ti•va′tor,** *n.*

Es•to•ni•a (e stō′nē ə, e stōn′yə), *n.* a republic in N Europe, on the Baltic, S of the Gulf of Finland: an independent republic 1918–40; annexed by the Soviet Union 1940; regained independence 1991. 1,444,721; 17,413 sq. mi. (45,100 sq. km). *Cap.:* Tallinn. —**Es•to′ni•an,** *adj., n.*

es•top•pel (e stop′əl), *n.* a legal bar that prevents a person from asserting a claim or fact that is inconsistent with a position that the person has previously taken.

es•trange (i strānj′), *v.t.,* **-tranged, -trang•ing. 1.** to alienate the feelings or affections of; make unfriendly or hostile. **2.** to remove to or keep at a distance. —**es•trange′ment,** *n.* —**es•trang′er,** *n.*

es•tro•gen (es′trə jən), *n.* any of several major female sex hormones produced primarily by ovarian follicles, capable of inducing estrus, producing secondary female sex characteristics, and preparing the uterus for the reception of a fertilized egg: synthesized and used in oral contraceptives and in various therapies.

es′trogen replace′ment ther′apy, *n.* the administration of estrogen, esp. in postmenopausal women, to reduce the chance of osteoporosis and heart disease. *Abbr.:* ERT

es′trous cy′cle, *n.* a series of physiological changes in sexual and other organs in female mammals, extending from one period of heat to the next.

es•trus (es′trəs), *n.* a recurring period of maximum sexual receptivity in most female mammals other than humans; heat.

es·tu·ar·y (es/chŏŏ er/ē), *n., pl.* **-ar·ies. 1.** that part of the mouth or lower course of a river in which the river's current meets the sea's tide. **2.** an arm or inlet of the sea at the lower end of a river. —**es/tu·ar/i·al** (-âr/ē əl), *adj.*

esu or **ESU,** electrostatic unit.

e·su·ri·ent (i sŏŏr/ē ənt), *adj.* hungry; greedy. —**e·su/ri·ence, e·su/ri·en·cy,** *n.* —**e·su/ri·ent·ly,** *adv.*

ET or **E.T.,** Eastern time.

ETA or **E.T.A.,** estimated time of arrival.

é·ta·gère or **e·ta·gere** (ā/tä zhâr/, ā/tə-), *n.* a stand with a series of open shelves for small objects, bric-a-brac, etc.

et al. (et al/, äl/, ôl/), **1.** and others. **2.** and elsewhere. [< Latin *alīī*]

etc., et cetera.

et cet·er·a (et set/ər ə, se/trə), *adv.* and others; and so forth; and so on (used to indicate that more of the same sort or class have been omitted for brevity). [< Latin] *Abbr.:* etc. —**Usage.** ET CETERA appears in English writing mostly in its abbreviated form, ETC. The expression *and et cetera* is redundant.

et-cet·er·a (et set/ər ə, -se/trə), *n., pl.* **-er·as. 1.** a number of other things or persons unspecified. **2.** etceteras, extras or sundries.

etch (ech), *v.t.* **1.** to engrave with an acid or the like, as to form a design in furrows that when charged with ink will give an impression on paper. **2.** to produce (a design, image, etc.) by this method, as on copper or glass. **3.** to outline clearly or sharply; delineate. **4.** to fix or imprint firmly: *His face is etched in my memory.* —*v.i.* **5.** to practice the art of etching.

etch·ing (ech/ing), *n.* **1.** the act or process of making designs or pictures on a metal plate, glass, etc., by the corrosive action of an acid. **2.** an impression, as on paper, taken from an etched plate. **3.** the design so produced. **4.** a metal plate bearing such a design.

e·ter·nal (i tûr/nl), *adj.* **1.** without beginning or end; lasting forever; always existing: *eternal life.* **2.** perpetual; ceaseless; endless: *eternal chatter.* **3.** enduring; immutable: *eternal principles.* **4.** existing outside all relations of time; not subject to change. —*n.* **5.** something that is eternal. **6. the Eternal,** GOD. —**e·ter·nal·i·ty** (ē/tûr nal/i tē), **e·ter/nal·ness,** *n.* —**e·ter/nal·ly,** *adv.*

Eter/nal Fa/ther, Strong/ to Save/, an American hymn (1860) with words by William Whiting.

e·ter·ni·ty (i tûr/ni tē), *n., pl.* **-ties. 1.** infinite time; duration without beginning or end. **2.** eternal existence, esp. as contrasted with mortal life. **3.** the timeless state into which the soul is believed to pass at death. **4.** a seemingly endless period of time. **5.** eternities, truths or realities regarded as timeless or eternal.

e·ter·nize (i tûr/nīz), *v.t.,* **-nized, -niz·ing. 1.** to make eternal; perpetuate. **2.** to immortalize. —**e·ter/ni·za/tion,** *n.*

eth·ane (eth/ān), *n.* a colorless, odorless, flammable gas, C₂H₆, of the methane series, present in natural gas, illuminating gas, and crude petroleum: used chiefly in organic synthesis and as a fuel gas.

E/than Frome/, a novel (1911) by Edith Wharton.

eth·a·nol (eth/ə nôl/, -nol/), *n.* ALCOHOL (def. 1).

eth·ene (eth/ēn), *n.* ETHYLENE.

e·ther (ē/thər), *n.* **1.** Also called **ethyl ether.** a colorless, highly volatile, flammable liquid, C₄H₁₀O, having an aromatic odor and sweet burning taste, used as a solvent and formerly as an inhalant anesthetic. **2.** upper regions of space; the clear sky; the heavens.

e·the·re·al (i thēr/ē əl), *adj.* **1.** light, airy, or tenuous. **2.** extremely delicate or refined: *ethereal beauty.* **3.** heavenly or celestial. **4.** of or pertaining to the upper regions of space. **5.** pertaining to, containing, or resembling ethyl ether. —**e·the/re·al·ly,** *adv.*

e·the·re·al·ize (i thēr/ē ə līz/), *v.t.,* **-ized, -iz·ing.** to make ethereal. —**e·the·re·al·i·za/tion,** *n.*

e·ther·ize (ē/thə rīz/), *v.t.,* **-ized, -iz·ing. 1.** to anesthetize with vaporized ether. **2.** to render groggy or numb, as if by an anesthetic. —**e/ther·i·za/tion,** *n.*

eth·ic (eth/ik), *n.* **1.** the body of moral principles or values held by or governing a culture, group, or individual: *the Christian ethic; a personal ethic.* **2.** a moral precept or rule of conduct.

eth·i·cal (eth/i kəl), *adj.* **1.** pertaining to or dealing with morals or the principles of morality; pertaining to ethics. **2.** being in accordance with the rules or standards for right conduct or practice, esp. the standards of a profession. **3.** (of drugs) sold only upon medical prescription. —**eth/i·cal·ly,** *adv.* —**eth/i·cal·ness, eth/i·cal/i·ty,** *n.*

eth·ics (eth/iks), *n.* **1.** (*used with a sing. or pl. v.*) a system or set of moral principles. **2.** (*used with a pl. v.*) the rules of conduct recognized in respect to a particular class of human actions or governing a particular group, culture, etc.: *medical ethics.* **3.** (*usu. used with a sing. v.*) the branch of philosophy dealing with values relating to human conduct, with respect to the rightness and wrongness of actions and the goodness and badness of motives and ends. **4.** (*used with a pl. v.*) moral principles, as of an individual: *His ethics forbade betrayal of a confidence.* —**eth·i·cist** (eth/ə sist), **e·thi·cian** (e thish/ən), *n.*

E·thi·o·pi·a (ē/thē ō/pē ə), *n.* a republic in E Africa: formerly a monarchy. 58,732,577; 424,724 sq. mi. (1,100,000 sq. km). *Cap.:* Addis Ababa. **2.** Also called **Abyssinia.** an ancient kingdom in NE Africa, bordering on Egypt and the Red Sea.

E·thi·o·pi·an (ē/thē ō/pē ən), *adj.* **1.** of or pertaining to Ethiopia or to its inhabitants. **2.** belonging to the part of Africa south of the equator.

3. belonging to a zoogeographical division comprising Africa south of the tropic of Cancer, the southern part of the Arabian Peninsula, and Madagascar. —*n.* **4.** a native or inhabitant of Ethiopia.

eth·moid (eth/moid), *adj.* **1.** Also, **eth·moi/dal.** of or pertaining to a cranial bone at the back of the nasal cavity, through which olfactory nerve processes pass into the nose. —*n.* **2.** the ethmoid bone.

eth·nic (eth/nik), *adj.* **1.** pertaining to or characteristic of a people, esp. a group (**eth/nic group/**) sharing a common and distinctive culture, religion, language, etc. **2.** being a member of an ethnic group, esp. a group that is a minority within a larger society: *ethnic Chinese in San Francisco.* **3.** belonging to or deriving from the cultural traditions of a people or country: *ethnic dances.* —*n.* **4.** a member of an ethnic group or minority. —**eth/ni·cal·ly,** *adv.*

eth·ni·cal (eth/ni kəl), *adj.* **1.** of, pertaining to, or concerned with ethnology. **2.** *Rare.* ETHNIC.

eth/nic cleans/ing, *n.* the elimination of an unwanted group from a society, as by genocide or forced migration.

eth·nic·i·ty (eth nis/i tē), *n.* ethnic traits, background, allegiance, or association.

ethno-, a combining form meaning "culture," "people," "ethnic group": *ethnography.*

eth·no·bot·a·ny (eth/nō bot/n ē), *n.* **1.** the plant lore and agricultural customs of a people. **2.** the systematic study of such lore and customs. —**eth/no·bot/a·nist,** *n.*

eth·no·cen·trism (eth/nō sen/triz əm), *n.* **1.** the belief in the inherent superiority of one's own ethnic group or culture. **2.** a tendency to view alien groups or cultures from the perspective of one's own. —**eth/no·cen/tric,** *adj.* —**eth/no·cen/tri·cal·ly,** *adv.*

eth·nog·ra·phy (eth nog/rə fē), *n.* the branch of anthropology dealing with the scientific description of individual cultures. —**eth·nog/ra·pher,** *n.* —**eth/no·graph/ic** (-nə graf/ik), **eth/no·graph/i·cal,** *adj.* —**eth/no·graph/i·cal·ly,** *adv.*

eth·no·his·to·ry (eth/nō his/tə rē), *n.* the anthropological study of cultures lacking a written history of their own, chiefly by examining their oral traditions and comparing them against whatever external evidence is available, as written accounts from other cultures of contact with these societies. —**eth/no·his·tor/i·cal** (-stôr/i kəl, -stor/-), **eth/no·his·tor/ic,** *adj.*

eth·nol·o·gy (eth nol/ə jē), *n.* **1.** a branch of anthropology that analyzes cultures, esp. in regard to their historical development and the similarities and dissimilarities between them. **2.** (formerly) **a.** ANTHROPOLOGY. **b.** a branch of anthropology dealing with racial origins, distribution, and characteristics. **3.** CULTURAL ANTHROPOLOGY. —**eth/no·log/i·cal** (-nə loj/i kəl), **eth/no·log/ic,** *adj.* —**eth/no·log/i·cal·ly,** *adv.* —**eth·nol/o·gist,** *n.*

eth·no·mu·si·col·o·gy (eth/nō myōō/zi kol/ə jē), *n.* the study of native music and its relationship to the society to which it belongs. —**eth/no·mu/si·col/o·gist,** *n.*

eth·no·nym (eth/nō nim), *n.* the name of a tribe, people, or ethnic group.

eth·no·phar·ma·col·o·gy (eth/nō fär/mə kol/ə jē), *n.* the scientific study of substances used medicinally, esp. folk remedies, by different ethnic or cultural groups.

eth·no·sci·ence (eth/nō sī/əns), *n.* the study of the systems of knowledge and classification of material objects and concepts in different cultures throughout the world.

e·thol·o·gy (ē thol/ə jē, i thol/-), *n.* the study of animal behavior with emphasis on the patterns that occur in natural environments. —**e·tho·log·i·cal** (ē/thə loj/i kəl, . eth/ə-), *adj.* —**e/tho·log/i·cal·ly,** *adv.* —**e·thol/o·gist,** *n.*

e·thos (ē/thos, ē/thōs, eth/os, -ōs), *n.* **1.** the fundamental character or spirit of a culture; the underlying sentiment that informs the beliefs, customs, or practices of a group or society. **2.** the distinguishing character or disposition of a community, group, person, etc. **3.** the moral element in dramatic literature that determines a character's action or behavior.

eth·yl (eth/əl), *n.* **1.** the univalent group C₂H₅–, derived from ethane. **2.** an antiknock fluid used in gasoline, containing tetraethyllead and other ingredients for a more even combustion.

eth/yl ac/etate, *n.* a colorless, volatile, flammable liquid, C₄H₈O₂, having a fragrant fruitlike odor: used in perfumes and flavorings and as a solvent for paints, varnishes, and lacquers.

eth/yl al/cohol, *n.* ALCOHOL (def. 1).

eth·yl·ene (eth/ə lēn/), *n.* a colorless, flammable gas, C₂H₄, used as an agent in the synthesis of organic compounds, in enhancing the color of citrus fruits, and in medicine chiefly as an inhalation anesthetic. —**eth/yl·e/nic** (-lē/nik, -len/ik), *adj.*

eth/ylene dichlo/ride, *n.* a colorless, heavy, oily, toxic liquid, C₂H₄Cl₂, having a chloroformlike odor: used in the synthesis of vinyl chloride and as a solvent for fats, waxes, resins, etc. Also called **eth/ylene chlo/ride.**

eth/ylene gly/col, *n.* GLYCOL (def. 1).

eth/yl e/ther, *n.* ETHER (def. 1).

e·ti·o·late (ē/tē ə lāt/), *v.,* **-lated, -lat·ing.** —*v.t.* **1.** to cause (a plant) to whiten or grow pale by excluding light. **2.** to cause to become weakened or sickly; drain of color or vigor. —*v.i.* **3.** (of plants) to whiten or grow pale through lack of light. —**e/ti·o·la/tion,** *n.*

e·ti·ol·o·gy (ē′tē ol′ə jē), *n., pl.* **-gies. 1. a.** the study of the causes of diseases. **b.** the cause or origin of a disease. **2. a.** any study of causes, causation, or causality. **b.** the cause postulated for something. —**e′ti·o·log′i·cal,** *adj.*

et·i·quette (et′i kit, -ket′), *n.* **1.** conventional requirements as to proper social behavior. **2.** a prescribed or accepted code of usage in matters of ceremony: *court etiquette.* **3.** the code of ethical behavior among the members of a profession: *medical etiquette.*

Et·na (et′nə), *n.* **Mount,** an active volcano in E Sicily. 10,758 (3280 m).

E·trus·can (i trus′kən), *n.* **1.** a member of a people inhabiting ancient Etruria, whose civilization flourished c700–400 B.C.: subsequently dominated and absorbed by the Romans. **2.** the extinct language of the Etruscans. —*adj.* **3.** of or pertaining to Etruria, the Etruscans, or their language. *Abbr.:* Etr.

et seq., and the following. [< Latin *et sequēns*]

é·tude (ā′tōōd, ā′tyōōd), *n.* **1.** a musical composition that practices some point of technique, but is also played for its artistic merit. **2.** STUDY (def. 12).

et·y·mol·o·gy (et′ə mol′ə jē), *n., pl.* **-gies. 1.** the history of a particular word or element of a word. **2.** an account of the origin and development of a word or word element. **3.** the study of historical linguistic change, esp. as manifested in individual words. —**et′y·mo·log′i·cal** (-mə loj′i kəl), *adj.* —**et′y·mo·log′i·cal·ly,** *adv.* —**et′y·mol′o·gist,** *n.*

Eu, *Chem. Symbol.* europium.

eu-, a combining form meaning "good," "well," occurring orig. in loanwords from Greek (*Eucharist; eudemon*); in scientific coinages, esp. taxonomic names, it often has the sense "true, genuine" (*eukaryote*).

eu·ca·lyp·tus (yōō′kə lip′təs), *n., pl.* **-ti** (-tī), **-tus·es.** any tree of the genus *Eucalyptus,* of the myrtle family, native to Australia and adjacent islands, having aromatic evergreen leaves. —**eu·ca·lyp′tic,** *adj.*

Eu·cha·rist (yōō′kə rist), *n.* **1.** the sacrament of Holy Communion; the sacrifice of the Mass; the Lord's Supper. **2.** the consecrated elements of the Holy Communion, esp. the bread. [< Greek *eucharistía* gratefulness, thanksgiving] —**Eu′cha·ris′tic, Eu′cha·ris′ti·cal,** *adj.*

eu·chre (yōō′kər), *n., v.,* **-chred, -chring.** —*n.* **1.** a card game for two, three, or four players, usu. played with the 32 highest cards in the deck. **2.** an instance of euchring or being euchred. —*v.t.* **3.** to get the better of (an opponent) in a hand at euchre by the opponent's failure to win the requisite tricks. **4.** *Slang.* to cheat; swindle: *The stockholders were euchred out of their investments.*

eu·clase (yōō′klās, -klāz), *n.* a rare green or blue mineral, beryllium aluminum silicate, BeAlSiO₄(OH), occurring in prismatic crystals: used as a gem.

Eu·clid (yōō′klid), *n.* **1.** fl. c300 B.C., Greek geometrician and educator at Alexandria. **2.** a city in NE Ohio, near Cleveland. 55,320.

Euclid′e·an geom′etry, *n.* geometry based upon the postulates of Euclid, esp. the postulate that only one line may be drawn through a given point parallel to a given line.

eu·de·mon or **eu·dae·mon** (yōō dē′mən), *n.* a good or benevolent demon or spirit.

eu·de·mon·ism or **eu·dae·mon·ism** (yōō dē′mə niz′əm), *n.* the doctrine in ethics that the basis of moral obligations is to be found in the tendency of right actions to produce happiness. —**eu·de′mon·is′tic,** *adj.*

Eu·gene (yōō jēn′), *n.* a city in W Oregon. 118,122.

Eu·gène (œ zhen′), *n.* **Prince** (*François Eugène de Savoie-Carignan*), 1663–1736, Austrian general, born in France.

eu·gen·ic (yōō jen′ik), *adj.* **1.** pertaining to or causing improvement in the type of offspring produced. Compare DYSGENIC. **2.** of or pertaining to eugenics. —**eu·gen′i·cal·ly,** *adv.*

eu·gen·ics (yōō jen′iks), *n.* (*used with a sing. v.*) a science concerned with improving a breed or species, esp. the human species, by such means as influencing or encouraging reproduction by persons presumed to have desirable genetic traits. —**eu·gen′i·cist** (-ə sist), *n.*

eu·gle·na (yōō glē′nə), *n., pl.* **-nas.** any freshwater protozoan of the genus *Euglena,* having a single flagellum.

eu·he·mer·ism (yōō hē′mə riz′əm, -hem′ə-), *n.* **1.** (*sometimes cap.*) the theory that the gods and the myths associated with them arose from the deification of great persons. **2.** any interpretation of myths that attributes their origin to historical persons. —**eu·he′mer·ist,** *n.* —**eu·he′mer·is′tic,** *adj.* —**eu·he′mer·is′ti·cal·ly,** *adv.* —**eu·he′mer·ize′,** *v.t., v.i.,* **-ized, -iz·ing.**

eu·kar·y·ote or **eu·car·y·ote** (yōō kar′ē ōt′, -ē ət), *n.* any organism with a fundamental cell type containing a distinct membrane-bound nucleus. Compare PROKARYOTE.

eu·lo·gi·a (yōō lō′jē ə; *for 2 also Greek* ev′lô yě′ä), *n., pl.* **-gi·as. 1.** blessed bread given to a congregation during vespers or at the end of the liturgy in the Eastern Church. **2.** a blessing in the Greek Orthodox Church.

eu·lo·gy (yōō′lə jē), *n., pl.* **-gies. 1.** a speech or writing in praise of a person or thing, esp. in honor of a deceased person. **2.** high praise or commendation. —**eu′lo·gize′** (-jīz′), *v.t.,* **-gized, -giz·ing.**

Eu·men·i·des (yōō men′i dēz′), *n.pl.* the Furies of Greek myth.

eu·nuch (yōō′nək), *n.* a castrated man, esp. one formerly employed by Oriental rulers as a harem guard or palace official. —**eu′nuch·ism,** *n.*

eu·on·y·mus (yōō on′ə məs), *n.* any shrub or vine of the genus *Euonymus,* of the staff-tree family, usu. having glossy evergreen leaves and clusters of orange or red fruits in open capsules. Also called **spindle tree.**

eu·pep·sia (yōō pep′shə, -sē ə), *n.* good digestion (opposed to *dyspepsia*). —**eu·pep′tic** (-tik), *adj.*

eu·phe·mism (yōō′fə miz′əm), *n.* **1.** the substitution of a mild, indirect, or vague expression for one thought to be offensive, harsh, or blunt. **2.** the expression so substituted: *"To pass away" is a euphemism for "to die."* —**eu′phe·mis′tic,** *adj.* —**eu′phe·mis′ti·cal·ly,** *adv.* —**eu′phe·mize′** (-mīz′), *v.t., v.i.,* **-mized, -miz·ing.**

eu·phen·ics (yōō fen′iks), *n.* (*used with a sing. v.*) a science concerned with improving human beings biologically after birth, as by genetic engineering. —**eu·phen′ic,** *adj.*

eu·pho·ni·um (yōō fō′nē əm), *n.* a brass musical instrument similar to but smaller than the tuba.

eu·pho·ny (yōō′fə nē), *n., pl.* **-nies.** agreeableness of sound; pleasing effect to the ear, esp. a pleasant sounding or harmonious combination or succession of words. —**eu·phon′ic** (-fon′ik), **eu·pho′ni·ous** (-fō′nē əs), *adj.*

eu·phor·bi·a (yōō fôr′bē ə), *n., pl.* **-bi·as.** any plant of the genus *Euphorbia,* comprising the spurges.

eu·pho·ri·a (yōō fôr′ē ə, -fōr′-), *n.* a strong feeling of happiness, confidence, or well-being. —**eu·phor′ic** (-fôr′ik, -for′-), *adj.* —**eu·phor′i·cal·ly,** *adv.*

eu·pho·tic (yōō fō′tik), *adj.* of or pertaining to the zone of a body of water extending from the surface to a depth at which enough light still penetrates for photosynthesis to occur.

Eu·phra·tes (yōō frā′tēz), *n.* a river in SW Asia, flowing from E Turkey through Syria and Iraq, joining the Tigris to form the Shatt-al-Arab near the Persian Gulf. 1700 mi. (2735 km) long. —**Eu·phra′te·an,** *adj.*

Eur·a·sia (yōō rā′zhə, -shə, yə-), *n.* Europe and Asia considered together as one continent.

Eur·a·sian (yōō rā′zhən, -shən, yə-), *adj.* **1.** of or pertaining to Eurasia. **2.** of mixed European and Asian descent. —*n.* **3.** a person of mixed European and Asian descent.

eu·re·ka (yōō rē′kə, yə-), *interj.* **1.** (used as an exclamation of triumph at a discovery.) **2.** (*cap.*) I have found (it): the reputed exclamation of Archimedes when he discovered a test, based on the principle of buoyancy, for the purity of gold. [< Greek *heúrēka* I have found (it)]

eu·rhyth·mic (yōō rith′mik, yə-) also **eu·rhyth′mi·cal,** *adj.* **1.** characterized by a pleasing rhythm; harmoniously ordered or proportioned. **2.** of or pertaining to eurhythmics. —**eu·ryth′mi·cal·ly,** *adv.*

eu·rhyth·mics (yōō rith′miks, yə-), *n.* (*used with a sing. or pl. v.*) the art of interpreting through bodily movement the rhythms of improvised music.

Eu·rip·i·des (yōō rip′i dēz′, yə-), *n.* c480–406? B.C., Greek dramatist. —**Eu·rip′i·de′an,** *adj.*

eu·ro (yōōr′ō, yûr′-), *n., pl.* **-ros.** the official common currency for countries that are members of the European Monetary Union.

Euro-, a combining form meaning "Europe," referring esp. to W Europe or the European Community: *Eurocentric; Eurocrat.*

Eu·ro·cur·ren·cy (yōōr′ō kûr′ən sē, -kur′-, yûr′-), *n., pl.* **-cies.** funds, esp. U.S. funds, deposited in a European bank and payable in the currency of that country.

Eu·rope (yōōr′əp, yûr′-), *n.* a continent in the W part of the landmass lying between the Atlantic and Pacific oceans, separated from Asia by the Ural Mountains on the E and the Caucasus Mountains and the Black and Caspian seas on the SE. In British usage, *Europe* sometimes contrasts with *England.* ab. 4,017,000 sq. mi. (10,404,000 sq. km).

Eu·ro·pe·an (yōōr′ə pē′ən, yûr′-), *n.* **1.** a native or inhabitant of Europe, or a person of European descent. **2.** a white person in a country with a largely nonwhite population. —*adj.* **3.** of or pertaining to Europe or its inhabitants. —**Eu′ro·pe′an·ly,** *adv.*

Europe′an Commu′nity, *n.* an association of W European countries that includes the European Atomic Energy Community (Euratom), the European Economic Community, the European Parliament, and allied organizations. *Abbr.:* EC **2.** EUROPEAN ECONOMIC COMMUNITY.

Europe′an Econom′ic Commu′nity, *n.* an association for economic cooperation established in 1957 by Belgium, France, Italy, Luxembourg, the Netherlands, and West Germany: later joined by the United Kingdom, the Republic of Ireland, Denmark, Greece, Spain, and Portugal; the Common Market. *Abbr.:* EEC

Eu′rope′an floun′der, *n.* See under FLOUNDER².

Europe′an plan′, *n.* (in hotels) a system of paying a fixed rate that covers lodging and service but not meals. Compare AMERICAN PLAN.

Europe′an Recov′ery Pro′gram, *n.* a plan for aiding the European nations in economic recovery after World War II, proposed by U.S. Secretary of State George C. Marshall. Also called **Marshall Plan.**

Europe′an red′ mite′, *n.* a red to red-brown mite, *Panonychus ulmi,* with white spots and dorsal spines: a widely distributed pest of fruit trees.

eu·ro·pi·um (yōō rō′pē əm, yə-), *n.* a rare-earth metallic element whose salts are light pink. *Symbol:* Eu; *at. wt.:* 151.96; *at. no.:* 63.

Eu·sta′chian tube′ (yōō stā′shən, -stā′kē ən), *n.* (*often l.c.*) a canal extending from the middle ear to the pharynx. [after B. *Eustachio* (1524?–74), Italian anatomist]

eu·sta·sy (yōō′stə sē), *n., pl.* **-sies.** any uniformly global change of sea level. —**eu·stat′ic** (-stat′ik), *adj.* —**eu·stat′i·cal·ly,** *adv.*

E

eu•tec•tic (yōō tek'tik), *adj.* **1.** of greatest fusibility: said of an alloy or mixture whose melting point is lower than that of any other alloy or mixture of the same ingredients. **2.** of or pertaining to such a mixture or its properties: *eutectic salts.* —*n.* **3.** a eutectic substance.

eu•tha•na•sia (yōō'thə nā'zhə, -zē ə, -zē ə), *n.* **1.** Also called **mercy killing.** the act of hastening the death of an incurably or terminally sick person, either by administering deadly drugs (**active euthanasia**) or by withholding treatment (**passive euthanasia**). **2.** an easy or painless death.

eu•tha•nize (yōō'thə nīz'), *v.t.* **-nized, -niz•ing.** to subject to euthanasia.

eu•then•ics (yōō then'iks), *n.* (*used with a sing. v.*) a science concerned with improving the human species through the improvement of its environment. —**eu•then•ist** (yōō then'ist, yōō'thə nist), *n.*

eu•the•ri•an (yōō thēr'ē ən), *adj.* **1.** belonging or pertaining to the group Eutheria, comprising the placental mammals. —*n.* **2.** a eutherian animal.

eu•troph•ic (yōō trof'ik, -trō'fik), *adj.* (of a lake) characterized by an abundant accumulation of nutrients that support a dense growth of algae and other organisms, the decay of which depletes the shallow waters of oxygen in summer. —**eu•troph'i•ca'tion,** *n.*

Eu•ty•chus (yōō'ti kəs), *n.* a young man whom the Apostle Paul restored to life. Acts 20:9–12.

eV or **ev,** electron-volt.

e•vac•u•ant (i vak'yōō ənt), *adj.* **1.** promoting evacuation from the bowels. —*n.* **2.** an evacuant medicine.

e•vac•u•ate (i vak'yōō āt'), *v.* **-at•ed, -at•ing.** —*v.t.* **1.** to leave empty; vacate. **2.** to remove (persons or things) from a place, esp. for reasons of safety. **3.** to remove persons from (a city, building, area, etc.), esp. for reasons of safety. **4. a.** to remove (troops, civilians, etc.) from a war zone, combat area, etc. **b.** to withdraw from (an occupied town, fort, etc.). **5.** to discharge or eject, esp. from the bowels. **6.** to produce a vacuum in (a vessel, electron tube, etc.). —*v.i.* **7.** to leave a place because of military or other dangers. **8.** to void; defecate. —**e•vac'u•a'tor,** *n.*

e•vac•u•a•tion (i vak'yōō ā'shən), *n.* **1.** the act or process of evacuating or the condition of being evacuated. **2.** discharge, as of waste matter, esp. from the bowels. **3.** something evacuated or discharged. **4.** the removal of persons or things from an endangered area. —**e•vac'u•a'tive** (-tiv), *adj.*

e•vac•u•ee (i vak'yōō ē', i vak'yōō ē'), *n.* a person who is withdrawn or removed from a place of danger.

e•vade (i vād'), *v.,* **e•vad•ed, e•vad•ing.** —*v.t.* **1.** to escape or avoid by speed or agility: *to evade one's pursuers.* **2.** to get around by cleverness or trickery: *to evade rules; to evade paying taxes.* **3.** to avoid doing or fulfilling: *to evade an obligation.* **4.** to avoid answering directly: *She evaded our questions by changing the subject.* **5.** to elude; escape: *The solution evaded him.* —*v.i.* **6.** to elude or get away by craft or slyness; escape.

e•val•u•ate (i val'yōō āt'), *v.t.,* **-at•ed, -at•ing. 1.** to determine or set the value or amount of; appraise: *to evaluate property.* **2.** to determine the significance or quality of; assess: *to evaluate the results.* **3.** to ascertain the numerical value of (a function, relation, etc.). —**e•val'u•a'tive,** *adj.* —**e•val'u•a'tor,** *n.*

e•val•u•a•tion (i val'yōō ā'shən), *n.* **1.** an act or instance of evaluating or appraising. **2.** a diagnosis or diagnostic study of a physical or mental condition.

ev•a•nesce (ev'ə nes'), *v.i.,* **-nesced, -nesc•ing.** to disappear gradually; fade away. —**ev'a•nes'cence,** *n.* —**ev'a•nes'cent,** *adj.*

e•van•gel[1] (i van'jəl), *n.* **1.** GOSPEL (def. 6). **2.** (*usu. cap.*) any of the four Gospels. **3.** a doctrine taken as a guide or regarded as of prime importance. **4.** good news or tidings.

e•van•gel[2] (i van'jəl), *n.* an evangelist.

e•van•gel•i•cal (ē'van jel'i kəl, ev'ən-), *adj.* Also, **e'van•gel'ic. 1.** pertaining to or in keeping with the Gospels and their teachings. **2.** belonging to or designating the Christian churches that emphasize the authority of the Scriptures, in opposition to the institutional authority of the church itself, and that stress personal conversion through faith in Christ. **3.** designating Christians, esp. since the 1970s, who hold to a conservative but not necessarily literal interpretation of the Bible. **4.** marked by ardent enthusiasm for a cause. —*n.* **5.** an adherent of evangelical doctrines. **6.** a person who belongs to an evangelical church or organization. —**e'van•gel'i•cal•ism,** *n.* —**e'van•gel'i•cal•ly,** *adv.*

e•van•ge•lism (i van'jə liz'əm), *n.* **1.** the preaching or promulgation of the Christian gospel; the work of an evangelist. **2.** missionary zeal, purpose, or activity.

e•van•ge•list (i van'jə list), *n.* **1.** a preacher of the Christian gospel, esp. a revivalist. **2.** (*cap.*) any of the writers (Matthew, Mark, Luke, and John) of the four Gospels. **3.** (*cap.*) a patriarch in the Mormon Church. —**e•van'ge•lis'tic,** *adj.* —**e•van'ge•lis'ti•cal•ly,** *adv.*

e•van•ge•lize (i van'jə līz'), *v.,* **-lized, -liz•ing.** —*v.t.* **1.** to preach the Christian gospel to. **2.** to convert to Christianity. —*v.i.* **3.** to preach the gospel; act as an evangelist. —**e•van'ge•li•za'tion,** *n.* —**e•van'ge•liz'er,** *n.*

Ev•ans (ev'ənz), *n.* **1. Sir Arthur John,** 1851–1941, English archaeologist. **2. Mary Ann,** ELIOT, George. **3. Maurice,** 1901–1989, U.S. actor and producer, born in England. **4. Walker,** 1903–75, U.S. photographer.

e•vap•o•rate (i vap'ə rāt'), *v.,* **-rat•ed, -rat•ing.** —*v.i.* **1.** to change from a liquid or solid state into vapor; pass off in vapor. **2.** to give off moisture. **3.** to disappear; vanish; fade: *His hopes evaporated.* —*v.t.* **4.** to convert into a gaseous state or vapor; drive off or extract in the form of vapor: *The sun evaporated the dew.* **5.** to extract moisture or liquid from, as by heat, so as to make dry or to reduce to a denser state: *to evaporate fruit.* **6.** to cause to disappear or fade; dissipate. —**e•vap'o•ra'tion,** *n.* —**e•vap'o•ra'tive** (-ə rā'tiv, -ər ə tiv), *adj.* —**e•vap'o•ra'tive•ly,** *adv.*

evap'orated milk', *n.* unsweetened milk concentrated and thickened by evaporation of water content to about half the original weight.

e•vap•o•rite (i vap'ə rīt'), *n.* any sedimentary rock, as gypsum or rock salt, formed by precipitation from evaporating seawater.

e•vap•o•tran•spi•ra•tion (i vap'ō tran'spə rā'shən), *n.* the transfer of moisture from the earth to the atmosphere by evaporation of water and transpiration from plants.

e•va•sion (i vā'zhən), *n.* **1.** an act or instance of escaping, avoiding, or shirking something: *evasion of one's duty; tax evasion.* **2.** the avoiding of an accusation, question, or the like, as by a subterfuge. **3.** a means of evading; subterfuge. —**e•va'sion•al,** *adj.*

e•va•sive (i vā'siv), *adj.* **1.** tending or seeking to evade; characterized by evasion: *an evasive answer.* **2.** elusive or evanescent. —**e•va'sive•ly,** *adv.* —**e•va'sive•ness,** *n.*

eve (ēv), *n.* **1.** (*sometimes cap.*) the evening or the day before a holiday, church festival, or any date or event: *Christmas Eve; the eve of an election.* **2.** the period preceding any event, crisis, etc.: *on the eve of the revolution.* **3.** the evening.

Eve (ēv), *n.* the first woman: wife of Adam and progenitor of the human race. Gen. 3:20.

e•ven (ē'vən), *adj.* **1.** level; flat; without surface irregularities; smooth: *an even road.* **2.** on the same level; in the same plane or line; parallel: *even with the ground.* **3.** free from variations or fluctuations; uniform; regular: constant: *even motion; an even color.* **4.** equal in measure or quantity: *even amounts of oil and vinegar.* **5.** divisible by two, as a number (opposed to *odd*). **6.** denoted by such a number: *the even pages of a book.* **7.** exactly expressible in integers, or in tens, hundreds, etc., without fractional parts: *an even seven miles.* **8.** (of a function) having a sign that remains the same when the sign of each independent variable is changed at the same time. **9.** equally balanced or divided; equal: *The scales are even.* **10.** leaving no balance of debt on either side; square. **11.** calm; placid; not easily excited or angered: *an even temper.* **12.** equitable, impartial, or fair: *an even bargain.* —*adv.* **13.** evenly: *The road ran even over the fields.* **14.** still; yet (used to emphasize a comparative): *even more suitable.* **15.** (used to suggest that some possibility constitutes an extreme case or an unlikely instance): *Even the slightest noise disturbs him. Even if she comes, she may not stay.* **16.** just (used to emphasize occurrence, coincidence, or simultaneousness of occurrences): *Even as help was coming, the troops surrendered.* **17.** fully or quite: *even to death.* **18.** indeed (used as an intensive for stressing the identity or truth of something): *He is willing, even eager, to do it.* **19.** exactly or precisely: *It was even so.* —*v.t.* **20.** to make even; level; smooth. **21.** to place in an even state as to claim or obligation; balance (often fol. by *up*): *to even up accounts.* —*v.i.* **22.** to become even: *The odds evened before the race.* —*Idiom.* **23. break even,** to have one's profits equal one's losses; neither gain nor lose. **24. get even,** to be revenged; retaliate. —**e'ven•ly,** *adv.* —**e'ven•ness,** *n.*

e•ven•fall (ē'vən fôl'), *n.* the beginning of evening.

e•ven•hand•ed (ē'vən han'did), *adj.* impartial; equitable. —**e'ven•hand'ed•ly,** *adv.* —**e'ven•hand'ed•ness,** *n.*

eve•ning (ēv'ning), *n.* **1.** the latter part of the day and early part of the night. **2.** the period from sunset to bedtime. **3.** any concluding or declining period: *the evening of life.* **4.** an evening's reception or entertainment: *Their evenings at home were widely attended.* —*adj.* **5.** of or pertaining to evening. **6.** occurring or seen in the evening.

eve'ning gown', *n.* a woman's formal dress, usu. having a floor-length skirt.

Eve'ning Prayer', *n.* EVENSONG.

eve'ning prim'rose, *n.* a plant, *Oenothera biennis*, having yellow flowers that open at nightfall.

eve'ning star', *n.* **1.** a bright planet, esp. Venus, seen in the western sky at or soon after sunset. **2.** any planet that rises before midnight.

e'ven mon'ey, *n.* equal odds in a wager.

E•ven•song (ē'vən sông', -song'), *n.* a form of worship said or sung in the evening in the Anglican Church.

e•vent (i vent'), *n.* **1.** something that happens or is regarded as happening; an occurrence, esp. one of some importance. **2.** something that occurs in a certain place during a particular interval of time. **3.** the outcome, issue, or result of anything; consequence. **4.** in the theory of relativity, an occurrence that is sharply localized at a single point in space and instant of time. **5.** a single sports contest within a scheduled program: *the figure-skating event.* —*Idiom.* **6. in any event,** regardless of what happens; in any case. Also, **at all events. 7. in the event of,** if there should be. **8. in the event that,** if it should happen that; in case.

e•ven-tem•pered (ē'vən tem'pərd), *adj.* not easily ruffled, annoyed, or disturbed; calm.

e•vent•ful (i vent'fəl), *adj.* **1.** full of events or incidents, esp. of a striking character. **2.** having important issues or results; momentous. —**e•vent'ful•ly,** *adv.* —**e•vent'ful•ness,** *n.*

event′ hori′zon, *n.* the boundary around a black hole on and within which no matter or radiation can escape.

e·ven·tide (ē′vən tīd′), *n.* evening.

e·ven·tu·al (i ven′chŏŏ əl), *adj.* happening at some indefinite future time or after a series of occurrences; ultimate: *His mistakes led to his eventual dismissal.*

e·ven·tu·al·i·ty (i ven′chŏŏ al′i tē), *n., pl.* **-ties.** a possible event, occurrence, or circumstance; contingency.

e·ven·tu·al·ly (i ven′chŏŏ ə lē), *adv.* finally; ultimately; at some later time.

e·ven·tu·ate (i ven′chŏŏ āt′), *v.i.* **-at·ed, -at·ing.** to be the issue or outcome; come about; result. —**e·ven′tu·a′tion,** *n.*

ev·er (ev′ər), *adv.* **1.** at any time: *Did you ever go skiing?* **2.** at all times; always: *an ever-present danger.* **3.** continuously: *ever since then.* **4.** in any possible case; by any chance; at all: *How did you ever manage to do it?* —**Idiom. 5. ever and again** or **anon,** now and then; from time to time. **6. ever so,** exceedingly; very: *I'm ever so sorry.*

Ev·er·est (ev′ər ist, ev′rist), *n.* **Mount,** a mountain in S Asia, on the boundary between Nepal and Tibet, in the Himalayas: the highest mountain in the world. 29,028 ft. (8848 m).

Ev·er·glades (ev′ər glādz′), *n.pl.* a partly forested marshland in S Florida, mostly S of Lake Okeechobee. Over 5000 sq. mi. (12,950 sq. km).

ev·er·green (ev′ər grēn′), *adj.* **1.** (of trees, shrubs, etc.) having green leaves throughout the year, the old foliage shedding only after the new has completely formed. —*n.* **2.** an evergreen plant. **3. evergreens,** evergreen twigs or branches used for decoration.

ev′ergreen oak′, *n.* any of several oaks, as the holm oak, having evergreen foliage.

ev·er·last·ing (ev′ər las′ting, -lä′sting), *adj.* **1.** lasting forever; eternal. **2.** lasting or continuing for an indefinitely long time: *the everlasting hills.* **3.** incessant; constantly recurring: *the everlasting changes of season.* **4.** wearisome; tedious: *his everlasting puns.* —*n.* **5. the,** eternal duration; eternity. **6. the Everlasting,** God. **7.** any of various plants that retain their shape or color when dried. —**ev′er·last′ing·ly,** *adv.*

ev·er·more (ev′ər môr′, -mōr′), *adv.* **1.** always; continually; forever. **2.** at all future times; henceforth.

Ev·ers (ev′ərz), *n.* **(James) Charles,** born 1922, and his brother **Med·gar (Wiley)** (med′gər), 1925–63, U.S. civil-rights leaders.

e·ver·sion (i vûr′zhən, -shən), *n.* a turning or being turned outward or inside out.

e·vert (i vûrt′), *v.t.* to turn outward or inside out.

eve·ry (ev′rē), *adj.* **1.** being one of a group or series taken collectively; each: *We go there every day.* **2.** all possible; the greatest possible degree of: *every prospect of success.* —**Idiom. 3. every now and then,** on occasion; from time to time. Also, **every once in a while, every so often. 4. every other,** every second; every alternate: *milk deliveries every other day.* **5. every which way,** in all directions; in disorganized fashion.

eve·ry·bod·y (ev′rē bod′ē, -bud′ē), *pron.* every person. —**Usage.** See EACH, ELSE.

eve·ry·day (ev′rē dā′; -dā′), *adj.* **1.** of or pertaining to every day; daily: *an everyday occurrence.* **2.** of or for ordinary days, as contrasted with Sundays, holidays, or special occasions: *everyday clothes.* **3.** such as is met with every day; ordinary; commonplace: *a placid, everyday scene.* —**eve′ry·day′ness,** *n.*

eve·ry·man (ev′rē man′), *n.* **1.** an ordinary person; the typical or average person. —*pron.* **2.** everybody; everyone.

eve·ry·one (ev′rē wun′, -wən), *pron.* **1.** every person; everybody. —**Proverb. 2. Everyone to whom much is given, of him will much be required,** one who has received blessings has great responsibilities. Luke 12:48. —**Usage.** See EACH.

eve·ry·place (ev′rē plās′), *adv.* everywhere.

eve·ry·thing (ev′rē thing′), *pron.* **1.** every single thing; every particular of an aggregate or total; all: *Put away everything on the floor.* **2.** something extremely important: *This news means everything to us.*

Ev′ery Time′ I′ Hear′ the Spir′it, a traditional American spiritual.

eve·ry·where (ev′rē hwâr′, -wâr′), *adv.* in every place or part; in all places. —**Usage.** See ANYPLACE.

eve·ry·wom·an (ev′rē wŏŏm′ən), *n., pl.* **-wom·en.** an ordinary woman; the typical or average woman.

e·vict (i vikt′), *v.t.* **1.** to expel (a person, esp. a tenant) from land, a building, etc., by legal process, as for nonpayment of rent. **2.** to recover (property, titles, etc.) by virtue of superior legal title. **3.** to throw or force out; eject; expel. —**e·vic′tion,** *n.*

ev·i·dence (ev′i dəns), *n., v.,* **-denced, -denc·ing.** —*n.* **1.** that which tends to prove or disprove something; ground for belief: *The play's long run on Broadway is evidence of its great popularity.* **2.** something that makes evident; an indication or sign: *His flushed look was evidence of his fever.* **3.** data presented to a court or jury to substantiate claims or allegations, including testimony, records, or objects. —*v.t.* **4.** to make evident or clear; show clearly; manifest: *to evidence one's approval.* **5.** to support by evidence: *She evidenced her accusation with incriminating letters.* —**Idiom. 6. in evidence,** plainly visible; conspicuous.

ev·i·dent (ev′i dənt), *adj.* plain or clear to the sight or understanding.

ev·i·den·tial (ev′i den′shəl), *adj.* noting, pertaining to, serving as, or based on evidence. —**ev′i·den′tial·ly,** *adv.*

ev·i·den·tia·ry (ev′i den′shə rē), *adj.* **1.** evidential. **2.** *Law.* constituting evidence.

ev·i·dent·ly (ev′i dənt lē, -dent′-; *for emphasis* ev′i dent′lē), *adv.* obviously; apparently.

e·vil (ē′vəl), *adj.* **1.** morally wrong or bad; immoral; wicked: *evil deeds; an evil life.* **2.** harmful; injurious: *evil laws.* **3.** characterized or accompanied by misfortune or suffering; unfortunate; disastrous: *to fall on evil days.* **4.** due to actual or imputed bad conduct or character: *an evil reputation.* **5.** marked by anger, irritability, irascibility, etc.: *an evil disposition.* —*n.* **6.** something evil; evil quality, intention, or conduct: *to choose the lesser of two evils.* **7.** the force in nature that governs and gives rise to wickedness and sin. **8.** the wicked or immoral part of someone or something. **9.** harm; mischief; misfortune: *to wish one evil.* **10.** anything causing injury or harm. **11.** a disease, as king's evil. —*adv.* **12.** in an evil manner; badly; ill: *It went evil with him.* —**Proverb. 13. Evil to him who evil thinks,** may one who thinks evil of others receive retribution. —**e′vil·ly,** *adv.* —**e′vil·ness,** *n.*

e·vil-do·er (ē′vəl dŏŏ′ər, ē′vəl dŏŏ′ər), *n.* a person who does evil or wrong. —**e′vil·do′ing,** *n.*

e′vil eye′, *n.* **1.** a look thought capable of inflicting injury or bad luck on someone. **2.** the power, superstitiously attributed to certain persons, of such a look. —**e′vil-eyed′,** *adj.*

E·vil-Me·ro·dach (ē′vil mi rō′dak), *n.* a king of Babylon who released Jehoiachin from prison. II Kings 25:27–30; Jer. 52:31–34.

e′vil-mind′ed, *adj.* **1.** having an evil disposition or harmful, malicious intentions. **2.** disposed to construe words, phrases, etc., in a lewd manner. —**e′vil-mind′ed·ly,** *adv.* —**e′vil-mind′ed·ness,** *n.*

Evil One, *n.* Satan, the devil. Matt. 13:19; John 17:15; Eph. 6:16; I John 2:13–14; 5:18–19.

e·vince (i vins′), *v.t.,* **e·vinced, e·vinc·ing. 1.** to show clearly; make evident or manifest; prove. **2.** to reveal the possession of (a quality, trait, etc.). —**e·vin′ci·ble,** *adj.* —**e·vin′cive,** *adj.*

e·vis·cer·ate (*v.* i vis′ə rāt′; *adj.* -ər it, -ə rāt′), *v.,* **-at·ed, -at·ing,** *adj.* —*v.t.* **1.** to remove the entrails from; disembowel. **2.** to deprive of vital or essential parts: *The censors eviscerated the book.* **3.** to remove the contents of (a body organ) by surgery. —*adj.* **4.** having had the entrails removed. —**e·vis′cer·a′tion,** *n.*

e·vi·ta·ble (ev′i tə bəl), *adj.* capable of being avoided; avoidable.

ev·o·ca·tion (ev′ə kā′shən, ē′vō kā′-), *n.* **1.** an act or instance of evoking; a calling forth: *the evocation of old memories.* **2.** the removal of a legal case to another court, esp. from a lower court for a complete review by a higher court, as in an appeal.

e·voc·a·tive (i vok′ə tiv, i vō′kə-), *adj.* tending to evoke: *perfume evocative of spring.* —**e·voc′a·tive·ly,** *adv.*

e·voke (i vōk′), *v.t.,* **e·voked, e·vok·ing. 1.** to call up or produce (memories, feelings, etc.). **2.** to elicit or draw forth: *His comment evoked many protests.* **3.** to produce or suggest through artistry and imagination: *a poem that evokes sounds and images of urban life.* **4.** to call up; cause to appear; summon: *to evoke a spirit from the dead.* —**e·vo′ca·ble,** *adj.*

ev·o·lu·tion (ev′ə lŏŏ′shən), *n.* **1.** any process of formation and growth; development: *the evolution of the theater.* **2.** a product of development; something evolved. **3.** *Biol.* **a.** the theory, proposed by Charles Darwin, that all existing organisms and species evolved from earlier, simpler forms by a series of gradual stages; Darwinism. **b.** the assumed mechanism by which, according to Darwin, organisms and species evolved from earlier, simpler forms. **4.** a motion incomplete in itself, but combining with coordinated motions to produce a single action, as in a machine. **5.** a pattern formed by or as if by a series of movements: *the evolutions of a figure skater.* **6.** an evolving or giving off of gas, heat, etc. **7.** *Math.* the extraction of a root from a quantity. **8.** a military training exercise. **9.** a movement executed by troops in formation.

ev·o·lu·tion·ist (ev′ə lŏŏ′shə nist), *n.* **1.** a person who believes in or supports the principles of evolution in biology. **2.** a person who supports a policy of gradual growth or development rather than sudden change or expansion. —*adj.* Also, **ev′o·lu′tion·is′tic. 3.** of or pertaining to evolution or evolutionists. **4.** believing in or supporting the principles of evolution in biology. —**ev′o·lu′tion·ism,** *n.*

e·volve (i volv′), *v.,* **e·volved, e·volv·ing.** —*v.t.* **1.** to develop gradually: *to evolve a scheme.* **2.** to give off or emit, as odors or vapors. —*v.i.* **3.** to come forth gradually into being; develop: *The whole idea evolved from a casual remark.* **4.** (of a species or population) to develop by a process of evolution. —**e·volv′a·ble,** *adj.* —**e·volve′ment,** *n.*

e·vulse (i vuls′), *v.t.,* **e·vulsed, e·vuls·ing.** to extract forcibly: *to evulse an infected molar.* —**e·vul′sion,** *n.*

ewe (yōō; *Dial.* yō), *n.* a female sheep, esp. when fully mature.

ew·er (yōō′ər), *n.* **1.** a pitcher or jug with a wide spout. **2.** a decorative vessel with a spout and handle, esp. a tall, slender one with a base.

ex¹ (eks), *prep.* **1.** without; not including: *ex dividend.* **2.** free of charges to the purchaser until removed from a specified place: *ex warehouse.*

ex² (eks), *n.* the letter *X, x.*

ex³ (eks), *n. Informal.* a former spouse; ex-wife or ex-husband.

ex-, **1.** a prefix occurring orig. in loanwords from Latin, meaning "out, out of, away, forth" (*egregious; exclude; exhale; exit; export; extract*), used also to signify that the action of a base verb has been carried to a conclusive point (*effect; exaggerate; excite; exhaust*), esp. in causative formations (*evacuate; exhilarate; expurgate*) or privative formations, including adjectives (*emasculate; enervate; exonerate*). Also, *before conso-*

E

nants other than c, f, p, q, s, *and* t *in Latin words,* **e-, ef-. 2.** a prefix meaning "former," "formerly having been": *ex-member; ex-wife.*

Ex., Exodus.

ex·ac·er·bate (ig zas′ər bāt′, ek sas′-), *v.t.,* **-bat·ed, -bat·ing. 1.** to increase the severity, bitterness, or violence of (disease, ill feeling, etc.); aggravate. **2.** to embitter the feelings of (a person); irritate; exasperate. **—ex·ac′er·ba′tion,** *n.*

ex·act (ig zakt′), *adj.* **1.** strictly accurate or correct: *an exact description.* **2.** precise, as opposed to approximate: *the exact date.* **3.** admitting of no deviation, as laws or discipline; strict or rigorous. **4.** capable of the greatest precision; characterized by or using strict accuracy: *an exact thinker.* **—v.t. 6.** to call for, demand, or require: *to exact respect.* **7.** to force or compel the payment, yielding, or performance of: *to exact tribute from a conquered people.* **—ex·act′ness,** *n.*

ex·act·a (ig zak′tə), *n., pl.* **-act·as.** a type of bet, esp. on horse races, in which the bettor must select the first- and second-place finishers in exact order.

ex·act·ing (ig zak′ting), *adj.* **1.** rigid or severe in demands or requirements: *an exacting teacher.* **2.** requiring close application or attention: *an exacting task.* **3.** given to or characterized by exaction; extortionate. **—ex·act′ing·ly,** *adv.*

ex·ac·tion (ig zak′shən), *n.* **1.** the act of exacting; extortion: *the exactions of usury.* **2.** an amount or sum exacted.

ex·ac·ti·tude (ig zak′ti to̅o̅d′, -tyo̅o̅d′), *n.* the quality of being exact; exactness; preciseness; accuracy.

ex·act·ly (ig zakt′lē), *adv.* **1.** in an exact manner; precisely; accurately. **2.** in every respect; just: *He will do exactly what he wants.* **3.** quite so; that's right.

ex·ag·ger·ate (ig zaj′ə rāt′), *v.,* **-at·ed, -at·ing. —v.t. 1.** to magnify beyond the limits of truth; overstate; represent disproportionately: *to exaggerate the difficulties of a situation.* **2.** to increase or enlarge abnormally: *That dress exaggerates my thinness.* **—v.i. 3.** to employ exaggeration, as in speech or writing.

ex·ag·ger·a·tion (ig zaj′ə rā′shən), *n.* **1.** the act of exaggerating. **2.** an instance of exaggerating; an overstatement.

ex·alt (ig zôlt′), *v.t.* **1.** to raise in rank, honor, power, character, quality, etc.; elevate. **2.** to praise highly; extol. **3.** to stimulate, as the imagination. **4.** to intensify, as a color.

ex·al·ta·tion (eg′zôl tā′shən, ek′sôl-), *n.* **1.** the act of exalting. **2.** the state of being exalted. **3.** elation of mind or feeling, sometimes abnormal or morbid in character; rapture. **4.** (in astrology) the sign or part of the zodiac in which the influence of a planet is most positive (opposed to *fall*). **5.** a flight of larks.

ex·alt·ed (ig zôl′tid), *adj.* **1.** raised or elevated, as in rank or character; of high station: *an exalted personage.* **2.** noble or elevated; lofty: *an exalted style of writing.* **3.** rapturously excited.

ex·am·i·na·tion (ig zam′ə nā′shən), *n.* **1.** the act of examining; inspection; inquiry; investigation. **2.** the state of being examined. **3.** the act or process of testing pupils, candidates, etc., as by questions. **4.** the test itself; the list of questions asked. **5.** the answers, statements, etc., made by one examined. **6.** formal legal interrogation.

ex·am·ine (ig zam′in), *v.t.,* **-ined, -in·ing. 1.** to inspect or scrutinize carefully: *to examine merchandise.* **2.** to observe, test, or investigate (a person's body or any part of it), esp. in order to evaluate general health or determine the cause of illness. **3.** to inquire into or investigate: *to examine one's motives.* **4.** to test the knowledge, reactions, or qualifications of (a pupil, candidate, etc.), as by questions. **5.** *Law.* to interrogate regarding conduct or knowledge of facts: *to examine a witness.* **—ex·am′in·er,** *n.*

ex·am·ple (ig zam′pəl, -zäm′-), *n., v.,* **-pled, -pling. —n. 1.** one of a number of things, or a part of something, taken to show the character of the whole. **2.** a pattern or model, as of something to be imitated or avoided: *to set a good example.* **3.** an instance serving for illustration; specimen. **4.** an instance illustrating a rule or method, as a mathematical problem proposed for solution. **5.** an instance, esp. of punishment, serving as a warning to others. **6.** a precedent; parallel case: *an action without example.* **—v.t. 7.** to give or be an example of; exemplify (used in the passive).

ex·an·i·mate (eg zan′ə mit, -māt′, ek san′-), *adj.* **1.** inanimate or lifeless. **2.** spiritless; disheartened.

ex·as·per·ate (*v.* ig zas′pə rāt′; *adj.* -pər it), *v.,* **-at·ed, -at·ing,** *adj.* **—v.t. 1.** to irritate or provoke to a high degree; annoy extremely. **—adj. 2.** *Bot.* having a rough, prickly surface. **—ex·as′per·at′ed·ly,** *adv.* **—ex·as′per·at′ing·ly,** *adv.* **—ex·as′per·a′tion,** *n.*

Ex·cal·i·bur (ek skal′ə bər), *n.* (in Arthurian legend) King Arthur's magic sword.

ex ca·the·dra (eks′ kə thē′drə, kath′i drə), *adv., adj.* from the seat of authority; with authority: used esp. of those papal pronouncements that are considered infallible.

ex·ca·vate (eks′kə vāt′), *v.t.,* **-vat·ed, -vat·ing. 1.** to make hollow by removing the inner part; make a hole or cavity in; form into a hollow, as by digging: *The ground was excavated for a foundation.* **2.** to make (a hole, tunnel, etc.) by removing material. **3.** to dig or scoop out (earth, sand, etc.). **4.** to expose or lay bare by or as if by digging; unearth. **—ex′ca·va′tor,** *n.*

ex·ca·va·tion (eks′kə vā′shən), *n.* **1.** a hole or cavity made by exca-

vating. **2.** the act of excavating. **3.** an area in which excavating has been done or is in progress, as an archaeological site.

ex·ceed (ik sēd′), *v.t.* **1.** to go beyond in quantity, degree, rate, etc.: *to exceed the speed limit.* **2.** to go beyond the bounds or limits of; overstep. **3.** to surpass; be superior to; excel. **—v.i. 4.** to be greater, as in quantity or degree. **5.** to surpass others; excel or be superior. **—ex·ceed′a·ble,** *adj.*

ex·ceed·ing (ik sē′ding), *adj.* extraordinary; exceptional. **—ex·ceed′ing·ly,** *adv.*

ex·cel (ik sel′), *v.,* **-celled, -cel·ling. —v.i. 1.** to surpass others or be superior in some respect or area; do extremely well: *to excel in math.* **—v.t. 2.** to surpass; be superior to; outdo.

Ex·cell (ik sel′), *n.* **Edwin,** 1851–1921, U.S. musician and hymn writer.

ex·cel·lence (ek′sə ləns), *n.* **1.** the fact or state of excelling; superiority; eminence: *excellence in physics.* **2.** an excellent quality or feature: *the many excellences of French cuisine.* **3.** (*cap.*) EXCELLENCY (def. 1).

Ex·cel·len·cy (ek′sə lən sē), *n., pl.* **-cies. 1.** Also, **Excellence.** a title of honor given to certain high officials, as governors, ambassadors, and Roman Catholic bishops and archbishops (prec. by *His, Her,* or *Your*). **2.** a person so entitled. **3.** (*l.c.*) Usu., **excellencies.** excellent qualities or features.

ex·cel·lent (ek′sə lənt), *adj.* possessing outstanding quality or superior merit; remarkably good. **—ex′cel·lent·ly,** *adv.*

ex·cept¹ (ik sept′), *prep.* **1.** with the exclusion of; excluding; save; but: *They were all there except me.* **—conj. 2.** only; with the exception (usu. fol. by *that*): *parallel cases except that one is younger than the other.* **3.** otherwise than; but (fol. by an *adv.,* phrase, or clause): *well fortified except here.* **—Idiom. 4. except for,** if it were not for: *She would travel more except for lack of money.*

ex·cept² (ik sept′), *v.t.* **1.** to exclude; leave out: *present company excepted.* **—v.i. 2.** to object (usu. fol. by *to* or *against*): *to except to a statement.* **—ex·cept′a·ble,** *adj.*

ex·cept·ing (ik sep′ting), *prep.* excluding; barring; saving; with the exception of; except.

ex·cep·tion (ik sep′shən), *n.* **1.** the act of excepting or the fact of being excepted. **2.** something excepted; an instance or case not conforming to the general rule. **3.** an adverse criticism, esp. on a particular point; opposition of opinion; objection; demurral. **4. a.** an objection, as to a ruling of the court during a trial. **b.** the notation in the court record of such an objection. **—Idiom. 5. take exception, a.** to make an objection; demur. **b.** to take offense.

ex·cep·tion·a·ble (ik sep′shə nə bəl), *adj.* liable to exception or objection; objectionable.

ex·cep·tion·al (ik sep′shə nl), *adj.* **1.** forming an exception or rare instance; unusual; extraordinary. **2.** unusually excellent; superior. **3.** (of a schoolchild) **a.** intellectually gifted. **b.** physically or esp. mentally handicapped to an extent that special schooling is required. **—ex·cep′tion·al·ly,** *adv.*

ex·cerpt (*n.* ek′sûrpt; *v.* ik sûrpt′, ek′sûrpt), *n.* **1.** a passage or quotation taken or selected from a book, document, film, or the like; extract. **—v.t. 2.** to take or select (a passage) from a book, film, or the like; extract. **3.** to take or select passages from (a book, film, or the like); abridge by choosing representative sections.

ex·cess (ik ses′, ek′ses), *n.* **1.** the fact of exceeding something else in amount or degree. **2.** the amount or degree by which one thing exceeds another. **3.** an extreme or excessive amount or degree; superabundance. **4.** a going beyond what is regarded as customary. **5.** immoderate indulgence; intemperance in eating, drinking, etc. **—adj. 6.** more than or above what is necessary, usual, or specified; extra: *excess profits.* **—v.t. 7.** to dismiss, demote, transfer, or furlough (an employee), esp. as part of a mass layoff.

ex·ces·sive (ik ses′iv), *adj.* going beyond the usual, necessary, or proper limit or degree; characterized by excess. **—ex·ces′sive·ly,** *adv.* **—ex·ces′sive·ness,** *n.*

ex·change (iks chānj′), *v.,* **-changed, -chang·ing,** *n.* **—v.t. 1.** to give up (something) for something else; part with for some equivalent or substitute. **2.** to replace (returned merchandise) with an equivalent or something else. **3.** to give and receive reciprocally; interchange: *to exchange blows; to exchange gifts.* **4.** to transfer for a recompense; barter: *to exchange goods with foreign countries.* **—v.i. 5.** to make an exchange; engage in bartering, replacing, or substituting one thing for another. **6.** to pass or be taken in exchange or as an equivalent. **—n. 7.** the act, process, or an instance of exchanging. **8.** something that is given or received as a replacement or substitution for something else: *The car was a fair exchange.* **9.** a place for buying and selling commodities, securities, etc., typically open only to members. **10.** a central office or central station: *a telephone exchange.* **11.** the settling of debits and credits by bills of exchange rather than by the actual transfer of money. **12.** the settling of financial obligations by the transfer of credits. **13.** the reciprocal transfer of equivalent sums of money, as in the currencies of two different countries. **14.** EXCHANGE RATE. **15. a.** the amount of the difference in value between two or more currencies. **b.** the difference in value of the same currency in two different places. **—ex·change′a·ble,** *adj.* **—ex·chang′er,** *n.*

exchange′ rate′, *n.* the ratio at which a unit of the currency of one country can be exchanged for that of another country.

exchange′ stu′dent, *n.* a student who studies at a foreign institution as part of a reciprocal program between two institutions or countries.

ex•cheq•uer (eks′chek ər, iks chek′ər), *n.* **1.** a treasury, as of a state or nation. **2.** (in Great Britain) **a.** (*often cap.*) the governmental department in charge of the public revenues. **b.** (formerly) an office administering the royal revenues and determining all cases affecting them. **c.** (*cap.*) an ancient common-law court trying cases affecting crown revenues: now merged with King's Bench. **3.** *Informal.* financial resources; funds.

ex•cise[1] (ek′sīz, -sīs; *v. also* ik sīz′), *n., v.,* **-cised, -cis•ing.** **—***n.* **1.** an internal tax or duty on certain commodities, as liquor or tobacco, levied on their manufacture, sale, or consumption within the country. **2.** a fee imposed for a license to pursue certain sports, occupations, etc. **—***v.t.* **3.** to impose an excise on. **—ex′cis•a•ble,** *adj.*

ex•cise[2] (ik sīz′), *v.t.,* **-cised, -cis•ing. 1.** to expunge, as a passage or sentence, from a text. **2.** to cut out or off, as a tumor.

ex•ci•sion (ek sizh′ən, ik-), *n.* **1.** the act of removal; an excising. **2.** the surgical removal of a foreign body or of tissue. **3.** EXCOMMUNICATION. **—ex•ci′sion•al,** *adj.*

ex•cit•a•ble (ik sī′tə bəl), *adj.* **1.** easily excited. **2.** *Physiol.* capable of responding to a stimulus; irritable. **—ex•cit′a•bil′i•ty, ex•cit′a•ble•ness,** *n.* **—ex•cit′a•bly,** *adv.*

ex•cit•ant (ik sīt′nt, ek′si tənt), *adj.* **1.** exciting; stimulating. **—***n.* **2.** *Physiol.* something that excites; stimulant.

ex•ci•ta•tion (ek′sī tā′shən, -si-), *n.* **1.** the act of exciting or the state of being excited. **2.** a process in which a molecule, atom, nucleus, or particle is excited.

ex•cite (ik sīt′), *v.t.,* **-cit•ed, -cit•ing. 1.** to arouse or stir up the emotions or feelings of: *to excite a person to anger.* **2.** to arouse or stir up (emotions or feelings); evoke; awaken: *to excite interest.* **3.** to stir to action; provoke or stir up: *to excite dogs to a frenzy.* **4.** *Physiol.* to stimulate: *to excite a nerve.* **5.** to raise (an atom, molecule, etc.) to an excited state. **6.** to supply with electricity for producing electric activity or a magnetic field: *to excite a dynamo.* **—ex•cite′ment,** *n.*

ex•cit•er (ik sī′tər), *n.* **1.** one that excites. **2.** an auxiliary generator that supplies energy for the excitation of another electric machine.

ex•ci•tor (ik sī′tər, -tôr), *n.* a nerve that increases the intensity of an action when stimulated.

ex•claim (ik sklām′), *v.i.* **1.** to cry out or speak suddenly and vehemently, as in surprise, strong emotion, or protest. **—***v.t.* **2.** to cry out; say loudly or vehemently. **—ex•cla•ma•tion** (ek′sklə mā′shən), *n.*

exclama′tion point′, *n.* the sign (!) used in writing after an exclamation or interjection, expressing strong emotion or astonishment, or to indicate a command. Also called **exclama′tion mark′.**

ex•clam•a•to•ry (ik sklam′ə tôr′ē, -tōr′ē), *adj.* **1.** using, containing, or expressing exclamation: *an exclamatory sentence.* **2.** pertaining to exclamation. **—ex•clam′a•to′ri•ly,** *adv.*

ex•clude (ik sklo͞od′), *v.t.,* **-clud•ed, -clud•ing. 1.** to shut or keep out; prevent the entrance of. **2.** to shut out from consideration, privilege, etc. **3.** to expel and keep out; thrust out; eject. **—ex•clu′sion,** *n.* **—ex•clu•so•ry** (ik sklo͞o′sə rē, -zə rē), *adj.*

ex•clu•sive (ik sklo͞o′siv, -ziv), *adj.* **1.** not admitting of something else; incompatible: *mutually exclusive plans of action.* **2.** omitting from consideration or account (often fol. by *of*): *a profit of ten percent, exclusive of taxes.* **3.** limited to that which is designated: *exclusive attention to business.* **4.** shutting out all others from a part or share: *an exclusive right to film the novel.* **5.** expensive or fashionable: *exclusive shops.* **6.** single or sole. **7.** disposed to resist the admission of outsiders to membership, association, intimacy, etc.: *an exclusive circle of friends.* **8.** excluding or tending to exclude, as from use or possession: *exclusive laws.* **9.** (of a first person plural pronoun) excluding the person addressed, as *we* in *We'll see you later.* Compare INCLUSIVE (def. 3). **—***n.* **10.** a news story obtained by a newspaper along with the privilege of using it first. **11.** an exclusive right or privilege. **—ex•clu′sive•ly,** *adv.* **—ex•clu′sive•ness, ex•clu•siv•i•ty** (eks′klo͞o siv′i tē), *n.*

ex•cog•i•tate (eks koj′i tāt′), *v.t.,* **-tat•ed, -tat•ing. 1.** to think out; devise; invent. **2.** to study intently and carefully in order to grasp or comprehend fully. **—ex•cog′i•ta•ble** (-tə bəl), *adj.* **—ex•cog′i•ta′tion,** *n.* **—ex•cog′i•ta′tive,** *adj.* **—ex•cog′i•ta′tor,** *n.*

ex•com•mu•ni•cate (*v.* eks′kə myo͞o′ni kāt′; *n., adj.* -kit, -kāt′), *v.,* **-cat•ed, -cat•ing,** *n., adj.* **—***v.t.* **1.** to cut off from communion or membership, esp. from the sacraments and fellowship of the church by ecclesiastical sentence. **—***n.* **2.** an excommunicated person. **—***adj.* **3.** excommunicated. **—ex′com•mu′ni•ca′tion,** *n.*

ex•co•ri•ate (ik skôr′ē āt′, -skōr′-), *v.t.,* **-at•ed, -at•ing. 1.** to denounce or berate severely; flay verbally: *He was excoriated for his mistakes.* **2.** to strip off or remove the skin from.

ex•cre•ment (ek′skrə mənt), *n.* waste matter discharged from the body, esp. feces. **—ex′cre•men′tous** (-men′təs), *adj.*

ex•cres•cent (ik skres′ənt), *adj.* **1.** growing abnormally out of something else; superfluous. **2.** (of a speech sound) inserted or added as a result of articulatory interaction or impetus, as the *t*-sound in *sense* (sents); intrusive; parasitic. **—ex•cres′cent•ly,** *adv.*

ex•cre•ta (ik skrē′tə), *n.pl.* excreted matter, as urine, feces, or sweat. **—ex•cre′tal,** *adj.*

ex•crete (ik skrēt′), *v.t.,* **-cret•ed, -cret•ing.** to separate and eliminate from an organic body; separate and expel from the blood or tissues, as waste or harmful matter. **—ex•cre′tion,** *n.* **—ex•cre′tive,** *adj.*

ex•cre•to•ry (ek′skri tôr′ē, -tōr′ē), *adj.* pertaining to or concerned in excretion; having the function of excreting: *excretory organs.*

ex•cru•ci•ate (ik skro͞o′shē āt′), *v.t.,* **-at•ed, -at•ing. 1.** to inflict severe pain upon; torture. **2.** to cause mental anguish to; irritate greatly.

ex•cru•ci•at•ing (ik skro͞o′shē ā′ting), *adj.* **1.** causing intense suffering; tormenting. **2.** intense or extreme: *excruciating pain.* **—ex•cru′ci•at′ing•ly,** *adv.*

ex•cul•pate (ek′skul pāt′, ik skul′pāt), *v.t.,* **-pat•ed, -pat•ing.** to clear from a charge of guilt or fault; free from blame; vindicate. **—ex•cul′pa•ble** (-pə bəl), *adj.* **—ex′cul•pa′tion,** *n.*

ex•cul•pa•to•ry (ik skul′pə tôr′ē, -tōr′ē), *adj.* tending to clear from a charge of fault or guilt.

ex•cur•rent (ik skûr′ənt, -skur′-), *adj.* **1.** running out or forth. **2.** giving passage outward: *the excurrent canal of certain sponges.* **3.** *Bot.* **a.** having the axis prolonged so as to form an undivided main stem or trunk, as the stem of the spruce. **b.** projecting beyond the apex, as the midrib in certain leaves.

ex•cur•sion (ik skûr′zhən, -shən), *n.* **1.** a short trip or outing to some place, usu. with the intention of a prompt return. **2.** the group of persons making such a trip. **3.** a trip on a train, ship, etc., at a reduced rate. **4.** a deviation or digression. **5.** the displacement of a body or a point from a mean position or neutral value, as in an oscillation. **6.** an accidental increase in the power level of a reactor, usu. forcing its emergency shutdown. **—ex•cur′sive,** *adj.*

ex•cur•sus (ek skûr′səs), *n., pl.* **-sus•es, -sus. 1.** a detailed discussion of some point in a book, esp. one added as an appendix. **2.** a digression or incidental excursion, as in a narrative.

ex•cuse (*v.* ik skyo͞oz′; *n.* -skyo͞os′), *v.,* **-cused, -cus•ing,** *n.* **—***v.t.* **1.** to regard or judge with indulgence; pardon or forgive; overlook (a fault, error, etc.). **2.** to offer an apology for; seek to remove the blame of: *He excused his absence by saying that he was ill.* **3.** to serve as an apology or justification for; justify: *Ignorance of the law excuses no one.* **4.** to release from an obligation or duty: *to be excused from jury duty.* **5.** to seek or obtain exemption or release for (oneself): *to excuse oneself from a meeting.* **6.** to refrain from exacting; remit; dispense with: *to excuse a debt.* **7.** to allow (someone) to leave: *If you'll excuse me, I have to make a telephone call.* **—***n.* **8.** an explanation offered as a reason for being excused; a plea offered in extenuation of a fault or for release from an obligation, promise, etc. **9.** a ground or reason for excusing or being excused: *Ignorance is no excuse.* **10.** the act of excusing someone or something. **11.** a pretext or subterfuge. **12.** an inferior or inadequate specimen of something specified: *His latest effort is a poor excuse for a poem.* **—ex•cus′a•ble,** *adj.* **—ex•cus′a•ble•ness,** *n.* **—ex•cus′a•bly,** *adv.* **—ex•cus′er,** *n.*

E

ex•e•cra•ble (ek′si krə bəl), *adj.* **1.** utterly detestable; abominable. **2.** very bad: *an execrable stage performance.* **—ex′e•cra•bly,** *adv.*

ex•e•crate (ek′si krāt′), *v.,* **-crat•ed, -crat•ing.** **—***v.t.* **1.** to detest utterly; abhor; abominate. **2.** to curse; imprecate evil upon; denounce. **—***v.i.* **3.** to utter curses.

ex•e•cute (ek′si kyo͞ot′), *v.t.,* **-cut•ed, -cut•ing. 1.** to carry out; accomplish: *to execute a plan.* **2.** to perform or do: *to execute a gymnastic feat.* **3.** to inflict capital punishment on; put to death according to law. **4.** to murder; assassinate. **5.** to produce in accordance with a plan or design. **6.** to perform or play (a piece of music). **7.** to give effect or force to, as a law. **8.** to carry out the terms of (a will). **9.** to complete and give validity to (a legal instrument) by fulfilling the legal requirements. **10.** to run (a computer program) or process (a command).

ex•e•cu•tion (ek′si kyo͞o′shən), *n.* **1.** the infliction of capital punishment or, formerly, of any legal punishment. **2.** the process of enforcing a court judgment. **3.** a mode or style of performance; technical skill, as in music. **—ex′e•cu′tion•al,** *adj.*

ex•e•cu•tion•er (ek′si kyo͞o′shə nər), *n.* **1.** an official who inflicts capital punishment in pursuance of a legal warrant. **2.** a person who executes an act, will, judgment, etc.

ex•ec•u•tive (ig zek′yə tiv), *n.* **1.** a person or group having administrative or supervisory authority in an organization. **2.** the person or group in whom the supreme executive power of a government is vested. **3.** the executive branch of a government. **—***adj.* **4.** of, pertaining to, or suited for carrying out plans, duties, etc.: *executive ability.* **5.** pertaining to or charged with the execution of laws or the administration of public affairs: *executive appointments.* **6.** designed for or used by executives.

exec′utive agree′ment, *n.* an agreement, usually pertaining to administrative matters and less formal than an international treaty, made between chiefs of state without senatorial approval.

exec′utive branch′, *n.* the branch of the U.S. government whose powers are vested in the president.

Exec′utive Man′sion, *n.* **1.** the official residence of the governor of a U.S. state. **2.** WHITE HOUSE (def. 1).

exec′utive of′ficer, *n.* **1.** the officer second in command of a military or naval organization. **2.** an officer charged with executive duties, as in a corporation.

exec′utive or′der, *n.* (*often caps.*) a rule or regulation issued by the president, governor, or other chief executive and having the force of law.

exec′utive priv′ilege, *n.* the discretionary right claimed by certain U.S. presidents to withhold information from Congress or the judiciary.

exec′utive sec′retary, *n.* a secretary with administrative responsibilities, esp. one who assists an executive in a business firm.

exec′utive ses′sion, *n.* a session of a legislative body or its leaders, generally closed to the public.

ex•ec•u•tor (ig zek′yə tər *or, for 1,* ek′si kyōō′-), *n.* **1.** a person who executes, carries out, or performs some duty, job, assignment, artistic work, etc. **2.** a person named in a decedent's will to carry out the provisions of that will. —**ex•ec′u•to′ri•al** (-tôr′ē əl, -tōr′-), *adj.* —**ex•ec′u•tor•ship′,** *n.*

ex•ec•u•trix (ig zek′yə triks), *n., pl.* **ex•ec•u•tri•ces** (ig zek′yə trī′sēz), **ex•ec•u•trix•es.** a woman named in a decedent's will to carry out the provisions of that will.

ex•e•ge•sis (ek′si jē′sis), *n., pl.* **-ses** (-sēz). critical explanation or interpretation, esp. of Scripture. —**ex′e•get′ic** (-jet′ik), **ex′e•get′i•cal,** *adj.* —**ex′e•get′i•cal•ly,** *adv.*

ex•e•gete (ek′si jēt′), *n.* a person skilled in exegesis.

ex•e•get•ics (ek′si jet′iks), *n.* (*used with a sing. v.*) the science of exegesis.

ex•em•pla (ig zem′plə), *n.* pl. of EXEMPLUM.

ex•em•plar (ig zem′plər, -plär), *n.* **1.** a model or pattern to be copied or imitated. **2.** a typical example or instance. **3.** an original or archetype. **4.** a copy of a book or text.

ex•em•pla•ry (ig zem′plə rē, eg′zəm pler′ē), *adj.* **1.** worthy of imitation; commendable: *exemplary conduct.* **2.** serving as a warning or deterrent: *The jury awarded exemplary damages.* **3.** serving as an illustration or specimen; typical. **4.** serving as a model or pattern. **5.** of, pertaining to, or composed of exempla: *the exemplary literature of the medieval period.* —**ex•em′pla•ri•ness,** *n.*

ex•em•pli•fi•ca•tion (ig zem′plə fi kā′shən), *n.* **1.** the act of exemplifying. **2.** something that exemplifies; an illustration or example. **3.** an attested copy of a document, under official seal.

ex•em•pli•fy (ig zem′plə fī′), *v.t.,* **-fied, -fy•ing.** **1.** to show or illustrate by example. **2.** to furnish or serve as an example of; typify. **3.** to make an attested copy of (a document) under seal. —**ex•em′pli•fi′a•ble,** *adj.* —**ex•em′pli•fi′er,** *n.*

ex•em•plum (ig zem′pləm), *n., pl.* **-pla** (-plə). **1.** an example or model. **2.** an anecdote that illustrates or supports a moral point, as in a medieval sermon.

ex•empt (ig zempt′), *v.t.* **1.** to free from an obligation or liability to which others are subject; release: *to exempt a student from an examination.* —*adj.* **2.** released from, or not subject to, an obligation, liability, etc.: *organizations exempt from taxes.* —*n.* **3.** a person who is exempt from an obligation. —**ex•empt′i•ble,** *adj.*

ex•emp•tion (ig zemp′shən), *n.* **1.** the circumstances of a taxpayer, as age or number of dependents, that permit certain deductions to be made from taxable income. **2.** the act of exempting. **3.** the state of being exempted; immunity. —**ex•emp′tive,** *adj.*

ex•e•quy (ek′si kwē), *n., pl.* **-quies.** **1.** Usu., **exequies.** funeral rites or ceremonies; obsequies. **2.** a funeral procession. —**ex•e•qui•al** (ek sē′kwē əl), *adj.*

ex•er•cise (ek′sər sīz′), *n., v.,* **-cised, -cis•ing.** —*n.* **1.** bodily or mental exertion, esp. for the sake of training or improvement. **2.** something done or performed as a means of practice or training. **3.** a putting into action, use, or effect: *the exercise of caution.* **4.** a written composition, musical piece, or artistic work executed for practice of technique. **5.** Often, **exercises.** a traditional ceremony: *graduation exercises.* **6.** a religious observance or service. —*v.t.* **7.** to put through exercises, or forms of practice or exertion, designed to train, develop, condition, etc. **8.** to put (faculties, rights, etc.) into action, practice, or use. **9.** to use or display in one's action or procedure: *to exercise judgment.* **10.** to make use of (one's privileges, powers, etc.). **11.** to discharge (a function); perform: *to exercise the duties of one's office.* **12.** to have as an effect: *to exercise an influence on someone.* **13.** to worry; make uneasy; annoy. —*v.i.* **14.** to go through exercises; take bodily exercise. —**ex′er•cis′a•ble,** *adj.* —**ex′er•cis′er,** *n.*

ex•ert (ig zûrt′), *v.t.* **1.** to put forth or into use, as power; exercise, as ability or influence; put into vigorous action. **2.** to put (oneself) into strenuous, vigorous action or effort. —**ex•er′tive,** *adj.*

ex•er•tion (ig zûr′shən), *n.* **1.** vigorous action or effort. **2.** an effort: *a great exertion to help others.* **3.** exercise, as of power or faculties. **4.** an instance of this.

ex•e•unt (ek′sē ənt, -ōōnt′), *v.i.* (they) go out (used as a stage direction): *Exeunt soldiers and townspeople.*

ex•fo•li•ate (eks fō′lē āt′), *v.,* **-at•ed, -at•ing.** —*v.t.* **1.** to throw off in scales, splinters, etc. **2.** to remove the surface of (a bone, the skin, etc.) in scales or laminae. —*v.i.* **3.** to throw off scales or flakes; peel off in thin fragments. **4. a.** to split or swell into a scaly aggregate, as certain minerals when heated. **b.** to separate into rudely concentric layers or sheets, as certain rocks during weathering. —**ex•fo′li•a′tion,** *n.* —**ex•fo′li•a′tive** (-ā′tiv, -ə tiv), *adj.*

ex•hal•ant (eks hā′lənt, ek sā′-), *adj.* **1.** exhaling; emitting. —*n.* **2.** something used for exhalation, as the ducts of certain mollusks.

ex•ha•la•tion (eks′hə lā′shən, ek′sə-), *n.* **1.** the act of exhaling. **2.** something that is exhaled; vapor; emanation.

ex•hale (eks hāl′, ek sāl′), *v.,* **-haled, -hal•ing.** —*v.i.* **1.** to emit breath or vapor; breathe out. **2.** to pass off as vapor; pass off as an effluence. —*v.t.* **3.** to breathe out; emit (air, vapor, sound, etc.). **4.** to give off as vapor. **5.** to draw out as a vapor or effluence; evaporate.

ex•haust (ig zôst′), *v.t.* **1.** to drain of strength or energy, wear out, or fatigue greatly, as a person: *I have exhausted myself working.* **2.** to use up or consume completely. **3.** to draw out all that is essential in (a subject, topic, etc.); treat or study thoroughly. **4.** to empty by drawing out the contents. **5.** to create a vacuum in. **6.** to draw out or drain off completely. **7.** to deprive wholly of useful or essential properties, possessions, resources, etc. **8.** to destroy the fertility of (soil), as by intensive cultivation. —*v.i.* **9.** to pass out or escape, as spent steam from the cylinder of an engine. —*n.* **10.** the escape of steam or gases from the cylinder of an engine. **11.** the steam or gases ejected. **12.** Also called **exhaust system.** the parts of an engine through which the exhaust is ejected. —**ex•haust′i•ble,** *adj.* —**ex•haus′tive,** *adj.*

ex•haus•tion (ig zôs′chən), *n.* **1.** extreme weakness or fatigue. **2.** the total consumption of something.

ex•hib•it (ig zib′it), *v.t.* **1.** to offer or expose to view; present for inspection: *to exhibit the latest models of cars.* **2.** to manifest or display: *to exhibit interest.* **3.** to place on show: *to exhibit paintings.* **4.** to make manifest; explain. **5.** to submit (a document, object, etc.) in evidence in a court of law. —*v.i.* **6.** to make or give an exhibition; present something to public view. —*n.* **7.** an act or instance of exhibiting; exhibition. **8.** something that is exhibited. **9.** an object or a collection of objects shown in an exhibition, fair, etc. **10.** a document or object exhibited in court and referred to and identified in written evidence. —**ex•hib′i•tor, ex•hib′it•er,** *n.*

ex•hi•bi•tion (ek′sə bish′ən), *n.* **1.** an exhibiting, showing, or presenting to view. **2.** a public display, as of artistic works, crafts, farm or factory products, performance skills, or objects of general interest. **3.** a large fair of extended duration, as a world's fair; an exposition.

ex•hi•bi•tion•ism (ek′sə bish′ə niz′əm), *n.* **1.** a tendency to display one's abilities or to behave in such a way as to attract attention. **2.** a psychiatric disorder characterized by a compulsion to exhibit the genitals. —**ex′hi•bi′tion•ist,** *n., adj.*

ex•hil•a•rate (ig zil′ə rāt′), *v.t.,* **-rat•ed, -rat•ing.** **1.** to enliven; invigorate; stimulate. **2.** to make cheerful or merry. —**ex•hil′a•rat′ing•ly,** *adv.* —**ex•hil′a•ra′tion,** *n.*

ex•hort (ig zôrt′), *v.t.* **1.** to urge, advise, or caution earnestly; admonish urgently. —*v.i.* **2.** to give urgent advice, recommendations, or warnings. —**ex•hort′er,** *n.* —**ex•hort′ing•ly,** *adv.*

ex•hor•ta•tion (eg′zôr tā′shən, ek′sôr-), *n.* **1.** the act or process of exhorting. **2.** an utterance, discourse, or address conveying urgent advice or recommendations.

ex•hume (ig zōōm′, -zyōōm′, eks hyōōm′), *v.t.,* **-humed, -hum•ing.** **1.** to dig (something buried, esp. a dead body) out of the earth; disinter. **2.** to revive or restore after neglect or a period of forgetting; bring to light. —**ex•hu•ma•tion** (eks′hyōō mā′shən), *n.*

ex•i•gen•cy (ek′si jən sē, ig zij′ən-), *n., pl.* **-cies.** **1.** exigent state or character; urgency. **2.** Usu., **exigencies.** the need, demand, or requirement intrinsic to a circumstance, condition, etc: *the exigencies of city life.* **3.** a case or situation which demands prompt action or remedy; emergency or plight. Often, **ex′i•gence.**

ex•i•gent (ek′si jənt), *adj.* **1.** requiring immediate action or aid; urgent; pressing. **2.** requiring a great deal, or more than is reasonable. —**ex′i•gent•ly,** *adv.*

ex•i•gi•ble (ek′si jə bəl), *adj.* liable to be exacted; requirable.

ex•ig•u•ous (ig zig′yōō əs, ik sig′-), *adj.* scanty; meager; small.

ex•ile (eg′zīl, ek′sīl), *n., v.,* **-iled, -il•ing.** —*n.* **1.** expulsion from one's native land or home by authoritative decree. **2.** the fact or state of such expulsion: *to live in exile.* **3.** prolonged separation from one's country or home, as by force of circumstances: *wartime exile.* **4.** a person banished or separated from his or her native land. **5. the Exile,** the Babylonian captivity of the Jews, 597–538 B.C. —*v.t.* **6.** to expel or banish (a person) from his or her country; expatriate. **7.** to separate from country, home, etc. —**ex′il•a•ble,** *adj.* —**ex′il•er,** *n.*

ex•il•ic (eg zil′ik, ek sil′-) also **ex•il′i•an,** *adj.* pertaining to exile, esp. that of the Jews in Babylonia.

ex•ist (ig zist′), *v.i.* **1.** to have actual being; be. **2.** to have life or animation; live. **3.** to continue to be or live: *Belief in magic still exists.* **4.** to have being in a specified place or under certain conditions; be found; occur. **5.** to achieve the basic needs of existence, as food and shelter. —**ex•ist′ent,** *adj.*

ex•ist•ence (ig zis′təns), *n.* **1.** continuance in being or life; life: *a struggle for existence.* **2.** mode of existing: *They were working for a better existence.* **3.** all that exists: *Existence shows a universal order.* **4.** something that exists; entity.

ex•is•ten•tial (eg′zi sten′shəl, ek′si-), *adj.* **1.** pertaining to existence. **2.** of, pertaining to, or characteristic of existentialism. —**ex′is•ten′tial•ly,** *adv.*

ex•is•ten•tial•ism (eg′zi sten′shə liz′əm, ek′si-), *n.* a philosophical movement, esp. of the 20th century, that stresses the individual's position as a self-determining agent responsible for his or her own choices. —**ex′is•ten′tial•ist,** *adj., n.*

ex•it[1] (eg′zit, ek′sit), *n.* **1.** a way or passage out. **2.** any of the marked ramps or spurs providing egress from a highway. **3.** a going out or away; departure: *to make one's exit.* **4.** a departure of an actor from the stage as part of the action of a play. —*v.i.* **5.** to go out; leave. —*v.t.* **6.** to leave; depart from: *to exit a building.* [< Latin *exitus* act or means of going out]

ex•it[2] (eg′zit, ek′sit), *v.i.* (he or she) goes offstage (used as a stage direction, often preceding the name of the character): *Exit Falstaff.*

ex′it poll′, *n.* a survey taken of a small percentage of voters as they leave the voting place, used esp. to forecast election results.

ex li•bris (eks lē′bris, lī′-), *adv., n., pl.* **-bris.** —*adv.* **1.** from the library of (a phrase inscribed in or on a book before the name of the owner). —*n.* **2.** BOOKPLATE.

exo-, a combining form meaning "outside," "outer," "external": *exocentric.*

ex•o•bi•ol•o•gy (ek′sō bī ol′ə jē), *n.* **1.** the study of potential life beyond the earth's atmosphere. **2.** the study of the effects of extraterrestrial conditions on living organisms from the planet Earth. —**ex′o•bi′o•log′i•cal** (-ə loj′i kəl), *adj.* —**ex′o•bi•ol′o•gist,** *n.*

ex•o•carp (ek′sō kärp′), *n.* EPICARP.

ex•o•crine (ek′sə krin, -krīn′), *adj.* **1.** secreting to an epithelial surface. **2.** of or pertaining to an exocrine gland or its secretion. —*n.* **3.** EXOCRINE GLAND.

ex′ocrine gland′, *n.* any gland, as a sweat gland or salivary gland, that secretes externally through a duct.

ex•o•dus (ek′sə dəs), *n.* **1.** a mass departure or emigration: *the summer exodus to the shore.* **2. the Exodus,** the departure of the Israelites from Egypt under Moses. **3.** (*cap.*) the second book of the Bible, containing an account of the Exodus.

ex of•fi•ci•o (eks′ ə fish′ē ō′), *adv., adj.* by virtue of office or official position. [< French]

ex•og•a•my (ek sog′ə mē), *n.* **1.** marriage outside a specific tribe or similar social unit. Compare ENDOGAMY. **2.** the union of gametes from parental organisms that are not closely related. **3.** CROSS-POLLINATION. —**ex•og′a•mous, ex′o•gam′ic** (-sə gam′ik), *adj.*

ex•og•e•nous (ek soj′ə nəs), *adj.* originating from outside; derived externally. —**ex•og′e•nism,** *n.* —**ex•og′e•nous•ly,** *adv.*

ex•on•er•ate (ig zon′ə rāt′), *v.t.,* **-at•ed, -at•ing.** **1.** to clear from accusation, guilt, or blame. **2.** to relieve from an obligation, duty, or task. —**ex•on′er•a′tion,** *n.* —**ex•on′er•a′tive,** *adj.*

ex•or•bi•tant (ig zôr′bi tənt), *adj.* exceeding the bounds of custom, propriety, or reason, esp. in amount or extent: *exorbitant prices; exorbitant luxury.* —**ex•or′bi•tance,** *n.* —**ex•or′bi•tant•ly,** *adv.*

ex•or•cise or **ex•or•cize** (ek′sôr sīz′, -sər-), *v.t.,* **-cised, -cis•ing** or **-cized, -ciz•ing.** **1.** to seek to expel (an evil spirit) by religious or solemn ceremonies. **2.** to free of evil spirits or malignant influences. —**ex′or•cise′ment,** *n.* —**ex′or•cis′er,** *n.*

ex•or•cism (ek′sôr siz′əm, -sər-), *n.* **1.** the act or process of exorcising. **2.** the ceremony or the formula used in exorcising. —**ex′or•cist,** *n.*

ex•or•di•um (ig zôr′dē əm, ik sôr′-), *n., pl.* **-di•ums, -di•a** (-dē ə). an introductory part, as of an oration or treatise. —**ex•or′di•al,** *adj.*

ex•o•skel•e•ton (ek′sō skel′i tn), *n.* an external covering or integument esp. when hard, as the shell of a crustacean (opposed to *endoskeleton*). —**ex′o•skel′e•tal,** *adj.*

ex•o•sphere (ek′sō sfēr′), *n.* the highest region of the atmosphere. —**ex′o•spher′ic,** *adj.*

ex•o•ter•ic (ek′sə ter′ik), *adj.* **1.** suitable for communication to the general public. **2.** not limited to the inner or select circle, as of disciples. **3.** pertaining to the outside; external. —**ex′o•ter′i•cal•ly,** *adv.*

ex•o•ther•mic (ek′sō thûr′mik) also **ex′o•ther′mal,** *adj.* noting or pertaining to a chemical change that is accompanied by a liberation of heat (opposed to *endothermic*). —**ex′o•ther′mi•cal•ly,** *adv.* —**ex′o•ther•mic′i•ty** (-thər mis′i tē), *n.*

ex•ot•ic (ig zot′ik), *adj.* **1.** not native; introduced from abroad; foreign: *exotic foods.* **2.** strikingly unusual or strange in effect, appearance, or nature: *exotic weapons.* —*n.* **3.** something exotic, as a bird or plant. —**ex•ot′i•cal•ly,** *adv.* —**ex•ot′ic•ness,** *n.*

ex•ot•i•ca (ig zot′i kə), *n.pl.* exotic things or objects.

ex•ot•i•cism (ig zot′ə siz′əm) also **ex•o•tism** (eg′zə tiz′əm, ek′sə-), *n.* **1.** exotic quality or character. **2.** something exotic, as a foreign word or idiom. —**ex•ot′i•cist,** *n.*

ex•pand (ik spand′), *v.t.* **1.** to increase in extent, size, scope, or volume. **2.** to stretch out; spread. **3.** to express in fuller form or greater detail; develop: *to expand a story into a novel.* **4. a.** to write (a mathematical expression) so as to show the products of its factors. **b.** to rewrite (a mathematical expression) as a sum, product, etc., of terms of a particular kind: *to expand a function in a power series.* —*v.i.* **5.** to increase in extent, size, scope, or volume. **6.** to spread out; unfold. **7.** to express something more fully (usu. fol. by *on* or *upon*). —**ex•pand′a•ble, ex•pand′i•ble,** *adj.* —**ex•pand′a•bil′i•ty, ex•pand′i•bil′i•ty,** *n.* —**ex•pand′er,** *n.*

ex•pand•ed (ik span′did), *adj.* **1.** increased in area, bulk, or volume; enlarged; extended: *an expanded version of a story.* **2.** (of a typeface) wider in proportion to its height. Compare CONDENSED (def. 4).

ex•panse (ik spans′), *n.* **1.** an uninterrupted space or area: *an expanse of water.* **2.** the arch of the sky; firmament.

ex•pan•sion (ik span′shən), *n.* **1.** the act or process of expanding. **2.** the state or quality of being expanded. **3.** the amount or degree of expanding. **4.** an expanded portion or form of a thing: *The book is an expansion of a series of articles.* **5.** EXPANSE. **6.** the development at length of an expression indicated in a contracted form, as $a^2 + 2ab + b^2$ for the expression $(a + b)^2$. **7.** an increase in economic and industrial activity (opposed to *contraction*).

ex•pan•sion•ism (ik span′shə niz′əm), *n.* a policy of expansion, as of territory or currency. —**ex•pan′sion•ist,** *n., adj.*

expan′sion slot′, *n.* a connection to which a new circuit board can be added to expand a computer's capabilities.

ex•pan•sive (ik span′siv), *adj.* **1.** having a wide range or extent; extensive. **2.** cordially welcoming; effusive: *an expansive host.* **3.** tending to expand or capable of expanding. **4.** causing expansion: *the expansive force of heat.* —**ex•pan′sive•ly,** *adv.* —**ex•pan′sive•ness,** *n.*

ex par•te (eks pär′tē), *adv.* **1.** from or on one side only of a dispute, as in a divorce action. —*adj.* **2.** one-sided; partial.

ex•pa•ti•ate (ik spā′shē āt′), *v.i.,* **-at•ed, -at•ing.** **1.** to elaborate in discourse or writing: *to expatiate upon a theme.* **2.** to move without restraint. —**ex•pa′ti•a′tion,** *n.* —**ex•pa′ti•a′tor,** *n.*

ex•pa•tri•ate (*v.* eks pā′trē āt′; *esp. Brit.* -pa′trē-; *adj., n.* -it, -āt′), *v.,* **-at•ed, -at•ing,** *adj., n.* —*v.t.* **1.** to banish; exile. **2.** to withdraw (oneself) from residence in or allegiance to one's native country. —*v.i.* **3.** to become an expatriate. —*adj.* **4.** dwelling in a foreign land; exiled. —*n.* **5.** an expatriated person. —**ex•pa′tri•a′tion,** *n.*

ex•pect (ik spekt′), *v.t.* **1.** to anticipate the occurrence or the coming of: *to expect guests.* **2.** to consider as reasonable, due, or justified: *We expect obedience.* **3.** *Informal.* to suppose; surmise. **4.** to anticipate the birth of (one's child). —***Idiom.*** **5. be expecting,** to be pregnant. —**ex•pect′an•cy,** *n.* —**ex•pect′ant,** *adj.*

ex•pec•ta•tion (ek′spek tā′shən), *n.* **1.** something expected. **2.** Often, **expectations.** a prospect of future benefit or fortune: *to have great expectations.* **3.** the degree of probability that something will occur: *There is little expectation that she will come.* **4.** the state of being expected. —**ex′pec•ta′tion•al,** *adj.*

ex•pec•to•rate (ik spek′tə rāt′), *v.,* **-rat•ed, -rat•ing.** —*v.i.* **1.** to expel matter from the throat or lungs by coughing or hawking and spitting. **2.** to spit. —*v.t.* **3.** to expel from the throat or lungs by coughing or hawking and spitting. **4.** to spit. —**ex•pec′to•rant,** *n.*

ex•pe•di•en•cy (ik spē′dē ən sē), *n., pl.* **-cies.** **1.** a regard for what is politic or advantageous rather than for what is right or just. **2.** something expedient. Often, **ex•pe′di•ence.**

ex•pe•di•ent (ik spē′dē ənt), *adj.* **1.** fit or suitable for the purpose; proper; advisable: *It is expedient that you go.* **2.** conducive to advantage; governed by self-interest; advantageous. —*n.* **3.** a handy means to an end. —**ex•pe′di•ent•ly,** *adv.*

ex•pe•dite (ek′spi dīt′), *v.t.,* **-dit•ed, -dit•ing.** **1.** to speed up the progress of. **2.** to perform promptly. **3.** to issue; dispatch. —**ex′pe•dit′er, ex′pe•di′tor,** *n.*

ex•pe•di•tion (ek′spi dish′ən), *n.* **1.** a journey or voyage made for a specific purpose, as exploration. **2.** the group of persons or vehicles engaged in such an activity. **3.** promptness or speed in accomplishing something. —**ex′pe•di′tion•ar•y,** *adj.*

ex•pe•di•tious (ek′spi dish′əs), *adj.* characterized by promptness; quick. —**ex′pe•di′tious•ly,** *adv.* —**ex′pe•di′tious•ness,** *n.*

ex•pel (ik spel′), *v.t.,* **-pelled, -pel•ling.** **1.** to drive or force out or away; discharge; eject. **2.** to cut off from membership: *to expel a student from a college.* —**ex•pel′la•ble,** *adj.* —**ex•pel′lant, ex•pel′lent,** *adj.*

ex•pend (ik spend′), *v.t.* **1.** to use up: *expended energy and time.* **2.** to pay out; spend. —**ex•pend′a•ble,** *adj.*

ex•pend•i•ture (ik spen′di chər), *n.* **1.** the act of expending something, esp. funds. **2.** something that is expended; expense.

ex•pense (ik spens′), *n., v.,* **-pensed, -pens•ing.** —*n.* **1.** cost; charge: *the expense of a good meal.* **2.** a cause or occasion of spending: *A car can be a great expense.* **3.** the act of expending; expenditure. **4. expenses, a.** charges incurred during a business assignment or trip. **b.** money paid as reimbursement for such charges. —*v.t.* **5.** to charge or write off as an expense. —***Idiom.*** **6. at the expense of,** at the sacrifice of; to the detriment of: *quantity at the expense of quality.*

ex•pen•sive (ik spen′siv), *adj.* **1.** entailing great expense: *an expensive party.* **2.** sold for a high price: *expensive clothes.* —**ex•pen′sive•ly,** *adv.* —**ex•pen′sive•ness,** *n.*

ex•pe•ri•ence (ik spēr′ē əns), *n., v.,* **-enced, -enc•ing.** —*n.* **1.** something personally lived through or encountered: *a frightening experience.* **2.** the observing, encountering, or undergoing of things generally as they occur in the course of time: *to learn from experience.* **3.** knowledge or practical wisdom gained from what one has observed, encountered, or undergone: *a person of experience.* —*v.t.* **4.** to have experience of; feel: *to experience pleasure.* —***Idiom.*** **5. experience religion,** to undergo a spiritual conversion by which one gains or regains faith in God. —***Saying.*** **6. Experience is the best teacher,** one learns best from one's own experience.

ex•pe•ri•en•tial (ik spēr′ē en′shəl), *adj.* pertaining to or derived from experience. —**ex•pe′ri•en′tial•ly,** *adv.*

ex•per•i•ment (*n.* ik sper′ə mənt; *v.* -ment′), *n.* **1.** a test, trial, or tentative procedure, esp. one for the purpose of discovering something unknown or of testing a principle, supposition, etc. **2.** the conducting of such operations. —*v.i.* **3.** to try or test esp. in order to discover or prove something: *to experiment with a new procedure.*

ex•per•i•men•tal (ik sper′ə men′tl), *adj.* **1.** pertaining to, derived from, or founded on experiment: *an experimental science.* **2.** tentative: *a program still in an experimental stage.* **3.** based on or derived from experience: *experimental knowledge.* —**ex•per′i•men′tal•ly,** *adv.*

ex•per•i•men•tal•ism (ik sper′ə men′tl iz′əm), *n.* **1.** the theory or practice of relying on experimentation; empiricism. **2.** fondness for experimenting or innovating. —**ex•per′i•men′tal•ist,** *n.*

ex•pert (ek′spûrt; *adj. also* ik spûrt′), *n.* **1.** a person who has special skill or knowledge in a particular field. —*adj.* **2.** possessing special skill

or knowledge; trained by practice. **3.** pertaining to or characteristic of an expert: *expert advice.* —**ex•pert′ly,** *adv.*
ex•per•tise (ek′spər tēz′), *n.* **1.** expert skill or knowledge. **2.** a written opinion by an expert.
ex′pert sys′tem, *n.* a computer program that imitates the functions of a human expert in a particular field, as in diagnosing a problem, by using logical operations to draw inferences from a stored body of specialized knowledge.
ex•pi•ate (ek′spē āt′), *v.t.,* **-at•ed, -at•ing.** to atone for; make amends or reparation for: *to expiate a crime.* —**ex′pi•a′tion,** *n.*
ex•pi•ra•tion (ek′spə rā′shən), *n.* **1.** termination; close: *the expiration of a contract.* **2.** the act of breathing out air from the lungs.
ex•pire (ik spīər′), *v.,* **-pired, -pir•ing.** —*v.i.* **1.** to come to an end; terminate. **2.** to emit the last breath; die. **3.** to breathe out. —*v.t.* **4.** to breathe out (air) from the lungs. —**ex•pir′er,** *n.*
ex•pi•ry (ik spīər′ē, ek′spə rē), *n., pl.* **-ries.** **1.** expiration of breath. **2.** a termination, as of life or a contract.
ex•plain (ik splān′), *v.t.* **1.** to make clear or intelligible. **2.** to make known in detail. **3.** to make clear the cause or reason of; account for: *I cannot explain his strange behavior.* —*v.i.* **4.** to give an explanation. **5.** **explain away,** to diminish the significance of through explanation; justify. —**ex•plain′a•ble,** *adj.*
ex•pla•na•tion (ek′splə nā′shən), *n.* **1.** the act or process of explaining. **2.** something that explains.
ex•plan•a•to•ry (ik splan′ə tôr′ē, -tōr′ē) also **ex•plan′a•tive,** *adj.* serving to explain: *an explanatory footnote.* —**ex•plan′a•to′ri•ly, ex•plan′a•tive•ly,** *adv.*
ex•ple•tive (ek′spli tiv), *n.* **1.** an interjectory word or expression, frequently profane; an exclamatory oath. **2.** a syllable, word, or phrase that serves to fill out a sentence, line of verse, etc., without conveying any meaning of its own, as the word *it* in *It is raining.* —*adj.* **3.** Also, **ex′ple•to′ry.** added merely to fill out a sentence or line, give emphasis, etc. —**ex′ple•tive•ly,** *adv.*
ex•pli•ca•ble (ek′spli kə bəl, ik splik′ə bəl), *adj.* capable of being explained. —**ex′pli•ca•bly,** *adv.*
ex•pli•cate (ek′spli kāt′), *v.t.,* **-cat•ed, -cat•ing.** to explain in detail. —**ex′pli•ca′tion,** *n.* —**ex′pli•ca′tor,** *n.*
ex•pli•ca•tive (ek′spli kā′tiv, ik splik′ə tiv) also **ex•pli•ca•to•ry** (ek′spli kə tôr′ē, -tōr′ē, ik splik′ə-), *adj.* explanatory; interpretive. —**ex′pli•ca′tive•ly,** *adv.*
ex•plic•it (ik splis′it), *adj.* **1.** fully and clearly expressed or demonstrated; leaving nothing implied: *explicit instructions.* **2.** clearly developed or formulated: *explicit intent.* **3.** unreserved in expression; outspoken: *explicit language.* —**ex•plic′it•ly,** *adv.*
ex•plode (ik splōd′), *v.,* **-plod•ed, -plod•ing.** —*v.i.* **1.** to expand with force and noise through rapid chemical change or decomposition, as gunpowder or nitroglycerine (opposed to *implode*). **2.** to burst violently, as a boiler from excessive pressure of steam. **3.** to erupt energetically: *to explode with laughter.* —*v.t.* **4.** to cause to explode. **5.** to discredit; disprove: *to explode a theory.*
explod′ed view′, *n.* a graphic representation that displays the parts of a mechanism separately while showing their spatial relationship.
ex•ploit[1] (ek′sploit, ik sploit′), *n.* a striking or notable deed; feat.
ex•ploit[2] (ik sploit′), *v.t.* **1.** to utilize, esp. for profit; turn to practical account: *to exploit a business opportunity.* **2.** to take advantage of; promote. **3.** to use selfishly for one's own ends. —**ex•ploit′a•tive, ex•ploit′ive,** *adj.* —**ex•ploit′er,** *n.*
ex•ploi•ta•tion (ek′sploi tā′shən), *n.* **1.** the use or working of something, esp. for profit: *exploitation of oil fields.* **2.** the use or manipulation of another person for one's own advantage. **3.** promotion; publicity. —**ex′ploi•ta′tion•al,** *adj.* —**ex′ploi•ta′tion•al•ly,** *adv.*
ex•plo•ra•tion (ek′splə rā′shən), *n.* **1.** an act or instance of exploring. **2.** the investigation of unknown regions.
ex•plor•a•to•ry (ik splôr′ə tôr′ē, -splōr′ə tōr′ē) also **ex•plor′a•tive,** *adj.* pertaining to or concerned with exploration: *exploratory surgery.*
ex•plore (ik splôr′, -splōr′), *v.,* **-plored, -plor•ing.** —*v.t.* **1.** to traverse or range over (a region, area, etc.) for the purpose of discovery: *to explore an island.* **2.** to look into closely; investigate: *explored the possibilities.* **3.** to examine, esp. mechanically, as with a surgical probe: *to explore a wound.* —*v.i.* **4.** to engage in exploration.
ex•plor•er (ik splôr′ər, -splōr′-), *n.* **1.** a person or thing that explores, esp. a person who investigates unknown regions. **2.** (*cap.*) Also called **Explor′er Scout′.** a person between the ages 14 and 20 who is in the exploring program sponsored by the Boy Scouts of America.
ex•plo•sion (ik splō′zhən), *n.* **1.** an act or instance of exploding; a violent expansion or bursting with noise (opposed to *implosion*). **2.** the noise of an explosion. **3.** a sudden, rapid, or great increase: *a population explosion.* **4.** PLOSION.
ex•plo•sive (ik splō′siv), *adj.* **1.** tending or serving to explode: *an explosive temper; an explosive gas.* **2.** pertaining to or of the nature of an explosion: *explosive violence.* **3.** likely to lead to violence or hostility: *an explosive issue.* **4.** PLOSIVE. —*n.* **5.** an explosive agent or substance. **6.** PLOSIVE. —**ex•plo′sive•ly,** *adv.* —**ex•plo′sive•ness,** *n.*
ex•po•nent (ik spō′nənt *or, esp. for 3,* ek′spō nənt), *n.* **1.** a person or thing that expounds or interprets. **2.** a person or thing that is a representative, advocate, or symbol. **3.** a symbol or number placed above and after another symbol or number to denote the power to which the latter is to be raised: *The exponents of the quantities* x^n, 2^m, y^4, *and* 3^5 *are, respectively,* n, m, 4, *and* 5.
ex•po•nen•tial (ek′spə nen′shəl), *adj.* **1.** of or pertaining to an exponent. **2. a.** of or pertaining to the constant *e.* **b.** (of an equation) having one or more unknown variables in one or more exponents. **3.** rising or expanding at a steady and usu. rapid rate: *exponential increases in manufacturing costs.* —*n.* **4. a.** the constant *e* raised to the power equal to a given expression, as e^{3x}, which is the exponential of $3x$. **b.** any positive constant raised to a power. —**ex′po•nen′tial•ly,** *adv.*
ex•po•nen•ti•a•tion (ek′spə nen′shē ā′shən), *n.* the raising of a number to any given power.
ex•port (*v.* ik spôrt′, ek′spôrt; *n., adj.* ek′spôrt, -spōrt), *v.t.* **1.** to ship (commodities) to other countries. **2.** to transmit abroad: *exporting political ideologies.* —*v.i.* **3.** to ship commodities to another country. —*n.* **4.** the act of exporting; exportation. **5.** something, as a commodity, that is exported. —*adj.* **6.** of or pertaining to the exportation of goods: *export duties.* —**ex•port′a•ble,** *adj.* —**ex•port′er,** *n.*
ex•por•ta•tion (ek′spôr tā′shən, -spōr-), *n.* **1.** the act of exporting. **2.** something exported.
ex•pose (ik spōz′), *v.t.,* **-posed, -pos•ing.** **1.** to lay open to danger: *to expose people to disease.* **2.** to uncover; bare: *to expose one's head to the rain.* **3.** to present to view; exhibit. **4.** to make known; reveal: *exposed her intentions.* **5.** to bring to light; unmask: *to expose a swindler.* **6.** to desert in an unsheltered place; abandon. **7.** to subject, as to the action of something: *to expose a photographic plate to light.*
ex•po•sé (ek′spō zā′), *n.* a public revelation, as of something discreditable: *a magazine exposé of political corruption.*
ex•posed (ik spōzd′), *adj.* **1.** being without shelter or protection. **2.** laid open to view.
ex•po•si•tion (ek′spə zish′ən), *n.* **1.** a large-scale public exhibition or show: *an automobile exposition.* **2.** the act of expounding, setting forth, or explaining. **3.** a detailed statement or explanation; explanatory treatise. **4.** the act of presenting to view; display. **5.** the first section of a fugue or a sonata form, in which the principal themes normally are introduced. —**ex′po•si′tion•al,** *adj.*
ex•pos•i•tor (ik spoz′i tər), *n.* a person who expounds or gives an exposition.
ex•pos•i•to•ry (ik spoz′i tôr′ē, -tōr′ē) also **ex•pos′i•tive,** *adj.* serving to expound, set forth, or explain: *expository writing.*
ex post fac•to (eks′ pōst′ fak′tō), *adv., adj.* **1.** after the fact; subsequently; retroactively. **2.** having retroactive force: *an ex post facto law.* [< Latin: from a thing done afterward]
ex•pos•tu•late (ik spos′chə lāt′), *v.i.,* **-lat•ed, -lat•ing.** to reason earnestly with someone by way of warning or rebuke. —**ex•pos′tu•lat′ing•ly,** *adv.* —**ex•pos′tu•la′tor,** *n.*
ex•pos•tu•la•tion (ik spos′chə lā′shən), *n.* an act or instance of expostulating. —**ex•pos′tu•la•to′ry** (-lə tôr′ē, -tōr′ē), **ex•pos′tu•la′tive** (-lā′tiv), *adj.*
ex•po•sure (ik spō′zhər), *n.* **1.** the act of exposing. **2.** the state of being exposed. **3.** disclosure, as of something private or secret. **4.** an act or instance of revealing or unmasking: *exposure of graft.* **5.** presentation to view: *His exposure of his anger shocked the company.* **6.** a laying open to the action or influence of something: *exposure to measles.* **7.** the condition of being exposed without protection to the effects of harsh weather: *suffering from exposure.* **8. a.** the act of presenting a photosensitive surface to light. **b.** a photographic image produced. **c.** the total amount of light received. **9.** situation with regard to sunlight or wind: *a southern exposure.* **10.** something exposed: *rock exposures.* **11.** public appearance, esp. on the mass media.
expo′sure me′ter, *n.* an instrument that measures the intensity of light in a certain place and indicates the proper photographic exposure setting. Also called **light meter.**
ex•pound (ik spound′), *v.t.* **1.** to set forth in detail: *to expound theories.* **2.** to explain; interpret. —*v.i.* **3.** to make a detailed statement (often fol. by *on*).
ex•press (ik spres′), *v.t.* **1.** to put into words: *to express an idea.* **2.** to show; reveal: *to express one's anger by a look.* **3.** to communicate the opinions or feelings of (oneself): *He expressed himself eloquently.* **4.** to convey or represent; depict. **5.** to represent by a symbol, character, figure, or formula. **6.** to send by express: *to express a package.* **7.** to squeeze out: *to express the juice of grapes.* **8.** to exude or emit (an odor, etc.) as if under pressure. **9.** (of a gene) to be active in the production of (a protein or a phenotype). —*adj.* **10.** clearly indicated; distinctly stated; explicit: *She defied my express command.* **11.** special; definite: *an express purpose.* **12.** direct or fast, esp. making few or no intermediate stops: *an express train.* **13.** used for direct or high-speed travel: *an express highway.* **14.** precise; exact: *an express image.* —*n.* **15.** an express vehicle. **16.** a system of sending freight, parcels, mail, etc., that is faster but more expensive than ordinary service. **17.** a company engaged in this business. **18.** something sent by express. —*adv.* **19.** by express: *to travel express.*
ex•pres•sion (ik spresh′ən), *n.* **1.** the act of expressing or setting forth in words: *the free expression of opinions.* **2.** a particular word, phrase, or form of words: *old-fashioned expressions.* **3.** the manner or form in which a thing is expressed: *delicacy of expression.* **4.** the power of expressing in words: *joy beyond expression.* **5.** outward indication of feeling or character. **6.** a facial look or vocal intonation expressing personal feeling. **7.** the quality or power of expressing an attitude, emotion, etc.:

a face that lacks expression. **8.** the act of expressing or representing, as by symbols. **9.** a mathematical symbol or combination of symbols representing a value, relation, or the like. **10.** the act or product of pressing out. **11. a.** the action of a gene in the production of a protein or a phenotype. **b.** EXPRESSIVITY (def. 2). —**ex•pres′sion•al,** *adj.* —**ex•pres′sion•less,** *adj.* —**ex•pres′sion•less•ly,** *adv.*

ex•pres•sion•ism (ik spresh′ə niz′əm), *n.* (*often cap.*) **1.** a style of art in which forms derived from nature are distorted and colors are intensified for expressive purposes. **2.** a style in literature and theater depicting the subjective aspect of experience esp. by using symbolism and nonnaturalistic settings. —**ex•pres′sion•ist,** *n., adj.* —**ex•pres′sion•is′tic,** *adj.* —**ex•pres′sion•is′ti•cal•ly,** *adv.*

ex•pres•sive (ik spres′iv), *adj.* **1.** full of expression; meaningful: *an expressive shrug.* **2.** serving to express: *a look expressive of gratitude.* **3.** of, pertaining to, or concerned with expression. **4.** of or pertaining to linguistic forms in which sounds denote a semantic field directly and nonarbitrarily through sound symbolism, as in onomatopoeia and emotionally charged words such as pejoratives. —**ex•pres′sive•ly,** *adv.* —**ex•pres′sive•ness,** *n.*

ex•pres•siv•i•ty (ek′spre siv′i tē), *n.* **1.** the quality or state of being expressive. **2.** the degree to which a particular gene produces its effect in an organism.

ex•press•ly (ik spres′lē), *adv.* **1.** for the specific purpose; specially: *I came expressly to see you.* **2.** in an express manner; explicitly: *She expressly demanded an apology.*

ex•pro•pri•ate (eks prō′prē āt′), *v.t.,* **-at•ed, -at•ing.** **1.** to take possession of, esp. for public use. **2.** to dispossess (a person) of ownership. **3.** to take from another and use as one's own: *expropriated original ideas.* —**ex•pro′pri•a′tor,** *n.*

ex•pul•sion (ik spul′shən), *n.* **1.** the act of expelling. **2.** the state of being expelled. —**ex•pul′sive** (-siv), *adj.*

ex•punc•tion (ik spungk′shən), *n.* the act of expunging or the state of being expunged.

ex•punge (ik spunj′), *v.t.,* **-punged, -pung•ing.** **1.** to strike or blot out; obliterate; erase. **2.** to eliminate completely; efface; destroy. —**ex•pung′er,** *n.*

ex•pur•gate (ek′spər gāt′), *v.t.,* **-gat•ed, -gat•ing.** **1.** to amend by removing objectionable words or passages. **2.** to purge or cleanse of something morally offensive. —**ex′pur•ga′tion,** *n.* —**ex′pur•ga′tor,** *n.* —**ex•pur•ga•to•ri•al** (ik spûr′gə tôr′ē əl, -tōr′-), **ex•pur′ga•to′ry,** *adj.*

ex•quis•ite (ik skwiz′it, ek′skwi zit), *adj.* **1.** of special beauty or charm or rare and appealing excellence: *exquisite flowers.* **2.** extraordinarily fine: *exquisite weather.* **3.** intense; acute: *exquisite pain.* **4.** of rare excellence of execution: *exquisite jewelry.* **5.** keenly or delicately sensitive or responsive: *an exquisite ear for music.* **6.** of particular refinement or elegance: *exquisite manners.* **7.** carefully sought out, chosen, or made: *exquisite distinctions.* —*n.* **8.** a person of fastidious standards in dress and grooming; dandy. —**ex•quis′ite•ly,** *adv.* —**Pronunciation.** The pronunciation of EXQUISITE has undergone a rapid change from (ek′skwi zit) to (ik skwiz′it). While the newer pronunciation is criticized by some, it is now more common in both the U.S. and England, and many younger educated speakers are not even aware of the older one. See also HARASS.

ex•sic•cate (ek′si kāt′), *v.t.,* **-cat•ed, -cat•ing.** to dry or remove the moisture from, as a substance. —**ex′sic•ca′tion,** *n.* —**ex′sic•ca′tive,** *adj.*

ex•tant (ek′stənt, ik stant′), *adj.* still existing; not destroyed or lost: *only three extant copies of the document.*

ex•tem•po•ra•ne•ous (ik stem′pə rā′nē əs), *adj.* **1.** done, spoken, or performed without preparation; impromptu: *an extemporaneous speech.* **2.** prepared in advance but delivered using few or no notes: *extemporaneous lectures.* **3.** performing with little or no advance preparation: *extemporaneous orators.* **4.** made for the occasion; improvised: *extemporaneous housing.* —**ex•tem′po•ra′ne•ous•ly,** *adv.*

ex•tem•po•rar•y (ik stem′pə rer′ē), *adj.* extemporaneous. —**ex•tem′po•rar′i•ly** (-râr′ə lē, -rer′-), *adv.* —**ex•tem′po•rar′i•ness,** *n.*

ex•tem•po•re (ik stem′pə rē), *adv.* in an extemporaneous manner: *performed extempore.* [< Latin: lit., out of time, at the moment]

ex•tem•po•rize (ik stem′pə rīz′), *v.,* **-rized, -riz•ing.** —*v.i.* **1.** to speak extemporaneously. **2.** to compose or perform extemporaneously. **3.** to do or manage something in a makeshift way. —*v.t.* **4.** to speak, perform, or devise extemporaneously. —**ex•tem′po•ri•za′tion,** *n.*

ex•tend (ik stend′), *v.t.* **1.** to stretch or draw out to full length: *extended the measuring tape.* **2.** to stretch or draw outward. **3.** to stretch forth; hold out: *to extend one's hand in greeting.* **4.** to make longer, as to reach a particular point: *to extend a highway to the next town.* **5.** to increase the duration of: *to extend a visit.* **6.** to enlarge the area, scope, or application of: *The military powers extended their authority abroad.* **7.** to grant or offer: *to extend aid to needy scholars.* **8.** to postpone the payment of (a debt) beyond the due date. **9.** to increase the bulk of, esp. by adding an inexpensive or plentiful substance. **10.** *Brit.* to seize (lands) by a writ of extent. **11.** to exert (oneself) to an unusual degree. —*v.i.* **12.** to be or become extended in length, duration, space, or scope. **13.** to reach, as to a particular point. —**ex•tend′i•ble, ex•tend′a•ble,** *adj.* —**ex•tend′i•bil′i•ty, ex•tend′a•bil′i•ty,** *n.*

ex•tend•ed (ik sten′did), *adj.* **1.** stretched or spread out. **2.** continued or prolonged: *an extended visit.* **3.** enlarged, as in scope or application: *extended insurance coverage.* **4.** extensive: *extended treatment of a subject.* **5.** EXPANDED (def. 2). **6.** of or pertaining to a meaning of a word other than its original or primary meaning.

extend′ed care′, *n.* generalized health or nursing care for convalescents or the disabled, when hospitalization is not required.

extend′ed fam′ily, *n.* a kinship group consisting of a married couple, their children, and various close relatives.

ex•ten•sion (ik sten′shən), *n.* **1.** an act or instance of extending. **2.** the state of being extended. **3.** that by which something is extended; an addition: *a four-room extension to a house.* **4.** an enlargement in scope or degree: *an extension of knowledge.* **5.** the total range of something; compass. **6.** an increase in length of time given one to meet an obligation, as the repayment of a debt. **7.** the property of a body by which it occupies space. **8. a.** the act of straightening a limb. **b.** the position that a limb assumes when it is straightened. **9.** an additional telephone that operates on a principal line. **10.** a program by which an institution, as a university, provides instruction or other services away from the regular location or outside regular hours. **11.** *Logic.* the class of things to which a term is applicable; denotation. Compare INTENSION (def. 5).

exten′sion lad′der, *n.* a ladder having two or more sections joined by a sliding mechanism that allows the ladder to be extended.

ex•ten•sive (ik sten′siv), *adj.* **1.** of great extent; wide; broad: *an extensive area.* **2.** covering a great area: *extensive travels.* **3.** comprehensive; far-reaching or thorough: *extensive knowledge.* **4.** great in amount, number, or degree: *extensive political influence.* **5.** of or having extension. **6.** of or pertaining to a system of farming in which large tracts of land are cultivated with minimum labor and expense (opposed to *intensive*). —**ex•ten′sive•ly,** *adv.*

ex•ten•sor (ik sten′sər, -sôr), *n.* a muscle that serves to extend or straighten a part of the body.

ex•tent (ik stent′), *n.* **1.** the space or degree to which a thing extends: *the extent of their property.* **2.** something having extension: *the limitless extent of the skies.* **3.** a writ by which a debtor's lands are valued and transferred to a creditor.

ex•ten•u•ate (ik sten′yo͞o āt′), *v.t.,* **-at•ed, -at•ing.** to make or try to make seem less serious esp. by offering excuses: *extenuating circumstances.*

ex•ten•u•a•tion (ik sten′yo͞o ā′shən), *n.* **1.** the act of extenuating; the state of being extenuated. **2.** a partial excuse.

ex•te•ri•or (ik stēr′ē ər), *adj.* **1.** being on the outer side: *exterior surfaces.* **2.** intended or suitable for outdoor use: *exterior paint.* **3.** situated or being outside: *exterior territories of a country.* —*n.* **4.** the outer surface or part; outside. **5.** outward form or appearance: *a placid exterior.*

exte′rior an′gle, *n.* **1.** an angle formed outside parallel lines by a third line that intersects them. **2.** an angle formed outside a polygon by one side and an extension of an adjacent side; the supplement of an interior angle of the polygon.

ex•ter•mi•nate (ik stûr′mə nāt′), *v.t.,* **-nat•ed, -nat•ing.** to get rid of by destroying: *to exterminate insect pests.* —**ex•ter′mi•na•ble** (-nə bəl), *adj.* —**ex•ter′mi•na′tion,** *n.*

ex•ter•mi•na•tor (ik stûr′mə nā′tər), *n.* **1.** a person or thing that exterminates. **2.** a person or business specializing in the extermination of vermin.

ex•tern (ek′stûrn), *n.* a person connected with an institution but not residing in it, as a doctor or medical student at a hospital.

ex•ter•nal (ik stûr′nl), *adj.* **1.** of or pertaining to the outside or outer part; outer: *an external surface.* **2.** to be applied to the outside of a body. **3.** situated or being outside something; acting or coming from without: *external influences.* **4.** pertaining to outward appearance: *external acts of worship.* **5.** pertaining to or concerned with foreign countries: *external affairs; external commerce.* **6.** of or pertaining to the world of things, considered as independent of the mind. —*n.* **7.** the outside; outer surface; exterior. **8. externals,** external features; outward appearance; superficialities. —**ex•ter′nal•ly,** *adv.*

exter′nal au′ditory mea′tus, *n.* the canal extending from the opening in the external ear to the tympanic membrane.

exter′nal-combus′tion en′gine, *n.* an engine, as a steam engine, in which fuel ignition takes place outside the cylinder or turbine.

exter′nal degree′, *n.* a college degree granted a person for study or work done off campus.

exter′nal ear′, *n.* the outer portion of the ear, consisting of the auricle and the external auditory meatus.

ex•ter•nal•ize (ik stûr′nl īz′), *v.t.,* **-ized, -iz•ing.** **1.** to make external; embody in an outward form. **2.** to attribute to external causes. **3.** to direct (the personality) outward in social relationships. —**ex•ter′nal•i•za′tion,** *n.*

ex•tern•ship (ek′stûrn ship′), *n.* a required period of supervised practice done off campus or away from one's affiliated institution.

ex•tinct (ik stingkt′), *adj.* **1.** no longer in existence: *an extinct species.* **2.** no longer in use: *an extinct custom.* **3.** no longer burning; extinguished. **4.** no longer active: *an extinct volcano.*

ex•tinc•tion (ik stingk′shən), *n.* **1.** the state of being extinguished or extinct. **2.** the act or process of becoming extinct: *the extinction of a species.* **3.** the reduction or loss of a conditioned response as a result of the absence or withdrawal of reinforcement. **4.** the darkness that results from rotation of a thin section to an angle **(extinc′tion an′gle)** at which plane-polarized light is absorbed by the polarizer.

ex•tin•guish (ik sting′gwish), *v.t.* **1.** to cause to stop burning; put out:

E

to extinguish a fire. **2.** to put an end to or bring to an end; wipe out of existence: *to extinguish hope.* **3.** to obscure or eclipse, as by superior brilliance. **4.** *Law.* to discharge (a debt), as by payment. —**ex•tin′guish•a•ble,** *adj.* —**ex•tin′guish•er,** *n.*

ex•tir•pate (ek′stər pāt′, ik stûr′pāt), *v.t.,* **-pat•ed, -pat•ing. 1.** to remove or destroy totally; exterminate. **2.** to pull up by or as if by the roots. —**ex′tir•pa′tion,** *n.* —**ex′tir•pa′tive,** *adj.* —**ex′tir•pa′tor,** *n.*

ex•tol or **ex•toll** (ik stōl′, -stol′), *v.t.,* **-tolled, -tol•ling.** to praise highly; laud.

ex•tort (ik stôrt′), *v.t.* **1.** to obtain by force, threat, intimidation, or abuse of authority. **2.** to elicit by cunning or persuasiveness.

ex•tor•tion (ik stôr′shən), *n.* **1.** the crime of obtaining money or some other thing of value by the abuse of one's office or authority. **2.** oppressive or illegal exaction of money. —**ex•tor′tion•ist, ex•tor′tion•er,** *n.*

ex•tor•tion•ate (ik stôr′shə nit), *adj.* **1.** excessive; exorbitant: *extortionate prices.* **2.** characterized by extortion: *extortionate moneylenders.* —**ex•tor′tion•ate•ly,** *adv.*

ex•tra (ek′strə), *adj., n., pl.* **-tras,** *adv.* —*adj.* **1.** beyond or more than what is usual, expected, or necessary; additional: *Make an extra copy.* **2.** superior to the usual: *extra comfort.* **3.** provided at an additional charge: *Home delivery is extra.* —*n.* **4.** an additional feature. **5.** an additional expense or charge. **6.** a special edition of a newspaper. **7.** an additional worker, esp. a person hired by the day to appear in the background action of a film. **8.** something of superior quality. —*adv.* **9.** in excess of the usual amount, size, or degree: *extra tall.*

extra-, a prefix meaning "outside of," "beyond the bounds of": *extragalactic; extralegal; extrasensory.*

ex•tra•cel•lu•lar (ek′strə sel′yə lər), *adj. Biol.* outside a cell or cells. —**ex′tra•cel′lu•lar•ly,** *adv.*

ex•tra•cor•po•re•al (ek′strə kôr pôr′ē əl, -pōr′-), *adj.* occurring or situated outside the body. —**ex′tra•cor•po′re•al•ly,** *adv.*

ex•tract (*v.* ik strakt′; *n.* ek′strakt), *v.t.* **1.** to pull or draw out, usu. with special effort: *to extract a tooth.* **2.** to draw forth; educe: *to extract information.* **3.** to derive; obtain: *extracted satisfaction from her success.* **4.** to take or copy out (excerpts), as from a book. **5.** to gain with determined effort: *to extract a secret from someone.* **6.** to separate or obtain from a mixture, as by pressure, distillation, or treatment with solvents. **7.** to determine (the root of a quantity). —*n.* **8.** something extracted. **9.** a passage taken from a written work; excerpt. **10.** a solid, viscid, or liquid substance containing the essence or active substance of a food, plant, or drug in concentrated form: *beef extract; vanilla extract.* —**ex•tract′a•ble, ex•tract′i•ble,** *adj.* —**ex•tract′a•bil′i•ty, ex•tract′i•bil′i•ty,** *n.*

ex•trac•tion (ik strak′shən), *n.* **1.** an act or instance of extracting something. **2.** descent; ancestry: *of foreign extraction.* **3.** something extracted; extract.

ex•trac•tive (ik strak′tiv), *adj.* **1.** serving to extract or based upon extraction: *oil and other extractive industries.* **2.** capable of being extracted: *extractive fuels.* **3.** of or of the nature of an extract. —*n.* **4.** something extracted or extractable.

ex•trac•tor (ik strak′tər), *n.* **1.** a person or thing that extracts. **2.** in a firearm or cannon) the mechanism that pulls the spent cartridge or shell case from the chamber. **3.** a centrifuge for spinning wet laundry so as to remove excess water.

ex•tra•cur•ric•u•lar (ek′strə kə rik′yə lər), *adj.* **1.** outside the regular curriculum or program of courses: *extracurricular activities.* **2.** outside one's regular work, responsibilities, or routine.

ex•tra•dite (ek′strə dīt′), *v.t.,* **-dit•ed, -dit•ing. 1.** to yield up to extradition. **2.** to obtain the extradition of.

ex•tra•di•tion (ek′strə dish′ən), *n.* the surrender of an alleged fugitive from justice or criminal by one state, nation, or authority to another.

ex•tra•dos (ek′strə dos′, -dōs′, ek strā′dos, -dōs), *n., pl.* **-dos** (-dōz′, -dōz), **-dos•es.** the exterior curve or surface of an arch or vault. Compare INTRADOS.

ex•tra•le•gal (ek′strə lē′gəl), *adj.* beyond the province or authority of law. —**ex′tra•le′gal•ly,** *adv.*

ex•tra•mar•i•tal (ek′strə mar′i tl), *adj.* pertaining to sexual relations with someone other than one's spouse: *extramarital affairs.*

ex•tra•mun•dane (ek′strə mun dān′), *adj.* of or pertaining to regions beyond the material world.

ex•tra•mu•ral (ek′strə myŏŏr′əl), *adj.* **1.** involving representatives of more than one school. **2.** occurring outside the walls or boundaries, as of a town or university: *extramural teaching.* Compare INTRAMURAL (defs. 1, 2). —**ex′tra•mu′ral•ly,** *adv.*

ex•tra•ne•ous (ik strā′nē əs), *adj.* **1.** introduced or coming from without; not forming an essential or proper part: *extraneous substances in our water.* **2.** not pertinent; irrelevant: *an extraneous remark.* —**ex•tra′ne•ous•ly,** *adv.* —**ex•tra′ne•ous•ness,** *n.*

ex•traor•di•nar•y (ik strôr′dn er′ē, ek′strə ôr′-), *adj.* **1.** being beyond what is usual, regular, or established: *extraordinary costs.* **2.** exceptional to a high degree; noteworthy; remarkable: *extraordinary speed.* **3.** having a special, often temporary task or responsibility: *minister extraordinary.* **4.** held for a special purpose: *an extraordinary meeting.* —**ex•traor′di•nar′i•ly,** *adv.*

ex•trap•o•late (ik strap′ə lāt′), *v.,* **-lat•ed, -lat•ing.** —*v.t.* **1.** to infer (an unknown) from something that is known; conjecture. **2.** to estimate (the value of a statistical variable) outside the tabulated or observed range. **3.** *Math.* to estimate (a function that is known over a range of values of its independent variable) to values outside the known range. —*v.i.* **4.** to perform extrapolation. —**ex•trap′o•la′tion,** *n.*

ex•tra•sen•so•ry (ek′strə sen′sə rē), *adj.* outside one's normal sense perception.

ex′trasen′sory percep′tion, *n.* See ESP.

ex•tra•ter•res•tri•al (ek′strə tə res′trē əl), *adj.* **1.** existing or originating outside the limits of the earth. —*n.* **2.** an extraterrestrial being. —**ex′tra•ter•res′tri•al•ly,** *adv.*

ex•trav•a•gance (ik strav′ə gəns), *n.* **1.** excessive or unnecessary outlay of money. **2.** unrestrained excess, as of actions or opinions. **3.** something extravagant.

ex•trav•a•gant (ik strav′ə gənt), *adj.* **1.** spending much more than is necessary or wise: *an extravagant shopper.* **2.** excessively high: *extravagant prices.* **3.** exceeding the bounds of reason or moderation: *extravagant demands.* **4.** going beyond what is deserved or justifiable: *extravagant praise.* —**ex•trav′a•gant•ly,** *adv.*

ex•trav•a•gan•za (ik strav′ə gan′zə), *n., pl.* **-zas. 1.** a production or entertainment, as a comic opera or musical comedy, with elaborate staging, costuming, and sensational effects. **2.** any lavish or opulent show or event.

ex•trav•a•sate (ik strav′ə sāt′), *v.,* **-sat•ed, -sat•ing,** *n.* —*v.t.* **1.** to force out, as blood, from the proper vessels, esp. so as to diffuse through the surrounding tissues. —*v.i.* **2.** to become extravasated. —*n.* **3.** extravasated material; extravasation.

ex•trav•a•sa•tion (ik strav′ə sā′shən), *n.* **1.** the act of extravasating. **2.** EXTRAVASATE.

ex•tra•vas•cu•lar (ek′strə vas′kyə lər), *adj.* situated outside the blood and lymph system.

ex•tra•ve•hic•u•lar (ek′strə vē hik′yə lər), *adj.* **1.** performed or occurring outside an orbiting spacecraft. **2.** of or pertaining to extravehicular activity.

ex•treme (ik strēm′), *adj.,* **-trem•er, -trem•est,** *n.* —*adj.* **1.** going well beyond the ordinary or average: *extreme measures.* **2.** exceedingly great in degree: *extreme joy.* **3.** farthest from the center or middle. **4.** utmost in direction or distance. **5.** immoderate; radical: *extreme fashions.* **6.** last; final: *extreme hopes.* **7.** *Chiefly Sports.* extremely dangerous or difficult: *extreme skiing.* —*n.* **8.** a very high degree: *cautious to an extreme.* **9.** one of two things as different from each other as possible: *the extremes of joy and grief.* **10.** an extreme act, measure, or condition: *the extreme of poverty.* **11.** *Math.* **a.** the first or the last term, as of a proportion or series. **b.** a relative maximum or relative minimum value of a function in a given region. **12.** the subject or the predicate of the conclusion of a syllogism. —**ex•treme′ly,** *adv.*

extreme′ly high′ fre′quency, *n.* any radio frequency between 30 and 300 gigahertz. *Abbr.:* EHF

extreme′ly low′ fre′quency, *n.* any radio frequency between 30 and 300 hertz. *Abbr.:* ELF

ex′treme unc′tion (ek′strēm, ik strēm′), *n.* ANOINTING OF THE SICK.

ex•trem•ism (ik strē′miz əm), *n.* a tendency to go to extremes or an instance of going to extremes, esp. in politics. —**ex•trem′ist,** *n.*

ex•trem•i•ty (ik strem′i tē), *n., pl.* **-ties. 1.** the extreme or terminal point, limit, or part of something. **2.** a limb of the body. **3.** Usu., **extremities.** the end part of a limb, as a hand or foot. **4.** Often, **extremities.** a condition of extreme need or danger: *the extremities of the poor.* **5.** an utmost degree: *the extremity of joy.* **6.** a drastic measure or effort: *to go to any extremity to succeed.* **7.** extreme character: *the extremity of his views.* **8.** a person's last moment before death.

ex•tri•cate (ek′stri kāt′), *v.t.,* **-cat•ed, -cat•ing.** to free or release from entanglement; disengage. —**ex′tri•ca•ble,** *adj.*

ex•trin•sic (ik strin′sik, -zik), *adj.* **1.** not essential or inherent; extraneous: *extrinsic facts.* **2.** being, operating, or coming from without: *extrinsic influences.* **3.** (of a muscle or nerve) originating outside the anatomical limits of a part. —**ex•trin′si•cal•ly,** *adv.*

extrin′sic fac′tor, *n.* VITAMIN B₁₂.

ex•tro•ver•sion or **ex•tra•ver•sion** (ek′strə vûr′zhən, -shən, ek′strə vûr′-), *n.* the act or state of being concerned primarily with the external environment rather than with one's own thoughts and feelings. Compare INTROVERSION.

ex•tro•vert (ek′strə vûrt′), *n.* **1.** an outgoing person; a person concerned primarily with the physical and social environment rather than with the self. —*adj.* **2.** Also, **ex′tro•vert′ed.** marked by extroversion; outgoing.

ex•trude (ik strŏŏd′), *v.,* **-trud•ed, -trud•ing.** —*v.t.* **1.** to force or press out: *extruding molten rock.* **2.** to shape (metal, plastic, etc.) by forcing through a die. —*v.i.* **3.** to become extruded.

ex•u•ber•ance (ig zōō′bər əns) also **ex•u•ber•an•cy,** *n., pl.* **-anc•es** also **-an•cies. 1.** the state of being exuberant. **2.** an exuberant act.

ex•u•ber•ant (ig zōō′bər ənt), *adj.* **1.** uninhibitedly enthusiastic or vigorous: *an exuberant welcome.* **2.** extremely good: *exuberant health.* **3.** profuse in growth or production: *exuberant vegetation.* —**ex•u′ber•ant•ly,** *adv.*

ex•ude (ig zōōd′, ik sōōd′), *v.i., v.t.,* **-ud•ed, -ud•ing. 1.** to ooze or cause to ooze out. **2.** to project abundantly; radiate.

ex•ult (ig zult′), *v.i.* to show or feel a lively or triumphant joy: *exulted over their victory.*

ex·ult·ant (ig zul′tnt), *adj.* highly elated; jubilant; triumphant. —**ex·ult′ant·ly,** *adv.*

ex·ul·ta·tion (eg′zul tā′shən, ek′sul-) also **ex·ult·an·cy** (ig zul′tn-sē), **ex·ult′ance,** *n.* the act of exulting or the state of being exultant.

ex·urb (ek′sûrb, eg′zûrb), *n.* a small, usu. prosperous community situated beyond the suburbs of a city. —**ex·ur·ban** (ek sûr′bən, eg zûr′-), *adj.* —**ex·ur′ban·ite′,** *n.*

ex·ur·bi·a (ek sûr′bē ə, eg zûr′-), *n.* a generalized area comprising the exurbs.

Eyck (īk), *n.* **Hubert van** or **Huybrecht van,** 1366–1426, and his brother **Jan van** (*Jan van Brugge*), 1385?–1440: Flemish painters.

eye (ī), *n., v.,* **eyed, ey·ing** or **eye·ing.** —*n.* **1.** the organ of sight; in vertebrates, one of a pair of spherical bodies contained in an orbit of the skull, along with its associated structures. **2.** sight; vision: *a sharp eye.* **3.** the power of seeing; appreciative or discriminating visual perception: *the eye of an artist.* **4.** a look, glance, or gaze: *to cast one's eye upon a scene.* **5.** an attentive look; observation: *under the eye of a guard.* **6.** regard, view, aim, or intention: *to have an eye to one's own advantage.* **7.** judgment; opinion: *in the eyes of the law.* **8.** a center; crux: *the eye of an issue.* **9.** something suggesting the eye in appearance, as the opening in the lens of a camera, a peephole, or a buttonhole. **10.** a bud, as of a potato or other tuber. **11.** a small, contrastingly colored part at the center of a flower. **12.** a usu. lean, muscular section of a cut of meat. **13.** a roundish spot, as on a tail feather of a peacock. **14.** the hole in a needle. **15.** a hole in a thing for the insertion of some object, as the handle of a tool: *the eye of an ax.* **16.** a metal or other ring through which something, as a rope or rod, is passed. **17.** the loop into which a hook is inserted. **18.** a photoelectric cell or similar device used to perform a function analogous to visual inspection. **19.** the region of lighter winds and fair weather at the center of a tropical cyclone. **20.** the direction from which a wind is blowing. —*v.t.* **21.** to look at; view: *to eye the wonders of nature.* **22.** to watch carefully: *eyed them with suspicion.* **23.** to make an eye in: *to eye a needle.* —*Idiom.* **24. be all eyes,** to be extremely attentive. **25. catch someone's eye,** to attract someone's attention. **26. give someone the eye,** to give someone a flirtatious or warning glance. **27. have an eye for,** to be discerning about. **28. have eyes for,** to be attracted to. **29. keep one's eyes open,** to be especially alert or observant. **30. make eyes,** to glance flirtatiously; ogle. **31. run one's eye over,** to examine hastily. **32. see eye to eye,** to agree. **33. with an eye to,** with the intention or consideration of. —*Proverb.* **34. An eye for an eye, a tooth for a tooth,** punishment should be equal to the crime. Ex. 21:23–24.

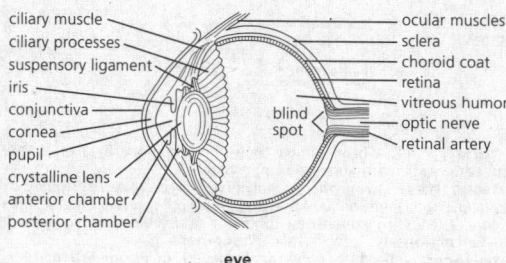

ciliary muscle
ciliary processes
suspensory ligament
iris
conjunctiva
cornea
pupil
crystalline lens
anterior chamber
posterior chamber
ocular muscles
sclera
choroid coat
retina
vitreous humor
optic nerve
retinal artery
blind spot

eye

eye·ball (ī′bôl′), *n.* **1.** the globe of the eye enclosed by the bony socket and eyelids. —*v.t.* **2.** *Informal.* to examine closely. —*Idiom.* **3. eyeball to eyeball,** aggressive and confrontational.

eye′ bank′, *n.* a place for the storage of corneas that have been removed from the eyes of people recently deceased, used for transplanting to the eyes of persons having corneal defects.

eye·bright (ī′brīt′), *n.* any plant of the genus *Euphrasia,* of the figwort family, formerly used for treating eye disorders.

eye·brow (ī′brou′), *n.* **1.** the bony arch or ridge forming the upper part of the orbit of the eye. **2.** the fringe of hair growing on this arch or ridge. **3.** a dormer having a roof that is an upwardly curved continuation of the main roof plane.

eye′-catch′er, *n.* a person or thing that attracts the attention. —**eye′-catch′ing,** *adj.*

eye′ chart′, *n.* a chart for testing vision, usu. containing letters in rows of decreasing size that are to be read at a fixed distance.

eye′ con′tact, *n.* direct visual interaction between two people.

eye·cup (ī′kup′), *n.* a device for applying eyewash to the eye, consisting of a cup with a rim shaped to fit snugly around the orbit of the eye.

eyed (īd), *adj.* **1.** having eyes of a specified kind (usu. used in combination): *a blue-eyed baby.* **2.** having eyelike spots.

eye·ful (ī′fŏol), *n., pl.* **-fuls. 1.** a thorough view: *to get an eyeful of city life.* **2.** *Informal.* a very good-looking person.

eye·glass (ī′glas′, ī′gläs′), *n.* **1. eyeglasses,** GLASS (def. 5). **2.** a single lens worn to aid vision; monocle. **3.** EYEPIECE.

eye·hole (ī′hōl′), *n.* **1.** PEEPHOLE. **2.** a circular opening for the insertion of a pin, hook, rope, etc.; eye.

eye·lash (ī′lash′), *n.* **1.** any of the short hairs growing as a fringe on the edge of an eyelid. **2.** Usu., **eyelashes.** the fringe formed by these hairs.

eye′ lens′, *n.* the lens of an eyepiece closest to the eye.

eye·let (ī′lit), *n.* **1.** a small hole for the passage of a cord or lace or for decoration. **2.** a lightweight fabric pierced by small holes finished with stitching, often arranged in flowerlike designs. **3.** a metal ring for lining a small hole; grommet.

eye·lid (ī′lid′), *n.* the movable lid of skin that covers and uncovers the eyeball.

eye·lin·er (ī′lī′nər), *n.* a cosmetic applied in a line along the eyelids, usu. next to the lashes, to accentuate the eyes.

eye·o·pen·er (ī′ō′pə nər), *n.* an experience or disclosure that provides sudden enlightenment. —**eye′o′pen·ing,** *adj.*

eye·piece (ī′pēs′), *n.* the lens or combination of lenses in an optical instrument through which the eye views the image formed by the objective lens or lenses; ocular.

eye′-pop′per, *n.* something causing astonishment or excitement. —**eye′-pop′ping,** *adj.*

eye′ shad′ow, *n.* a cosmetic coloring material applied to the eyelids.

eye·shot (ī′shot′), *n.* range of vision; view: *within eyeshot.*

eyes′-on′ly, *adj.* meant to be seen only by the addressee; confidential: *an eyes-only report.*

eye·sore (ī′sôr′, ī′sōr′), *n.* something unpleasant to look at.

eye·strain (ī′strān′), *n.* discomfort in the eyes produced by excessive or improper use.

eye·tooth (ī′tōoth′), *n., pl.* **-teeth** (-tēth′). a canine tooth of the upper jaw.

eye·wash (ī′wosh′, ī′wôsh′), *n.* **1.** a soothing solution applied locally to the eye. **2.** nonsense; bunk.

eye·wear (ī′wâr′), *n.* any of various devices, as spectacles or goggles, for aiding the vision or protecting the eyes.

eye·wit·ness (ī′wit′nis), *n.* **1.** a person who actually sees some act, occurrence, or the like, and can give a firsthand account of it. —*v.t.* **2.** to view as an eyewitness.

ey·rie or **ey·ry** (âr′ē, ēr′ē), *n., pl.* **-ries.** AERIE.

Ezek., Ezekiel.

E·ze·ki·el (i zē′kē əl), *n.* **1.** a Major Prophet of the 6th century B.C. **2.** a book of the Bible bearing his name. **3. Moses Jacob,** 1844–1917, U.S. sculptor.

Ez·ra (ez′rə), *n.* **1.** a Jewish scribe and prophet of the 5th century B.C. **2.** a book of the Bible bearing his name.

E

F

F, f (ef), *n., pl.* **Fs** or **F's, fs** or **f's.** **1.** the sixth letter of the English alphabet, a consonant. **2.** any spoken sound represented by this letter. **3.** something shaped like an F. **4.** a written or printed representation of the letter F or f.

F, *Symbol.* **1.** the sixth in order or in a series. **2.** (*sometimes l.c.*) (in some grading systems) a grade or mark that indicates academic work of the lowest quality; failure. **3. a.** the fourth note of the ascending C major scale. **b.** a tonality having F as the tonic. **4.** *Math.* **a.** field. **b.** function (of). **5.** Fahrenheit. **6.** farad. **7.** fluorine. **8.** (*sometimes l.c.*) *Physics.* **a.** force. **b.** frequency. **c.** fermi. **9.** phenylalanine.

f, *Symbol.* f-number.

fa (fä), *n.* the musical syllable used for the fourth tone of an ascending diatonic scale.

FAA, Federal Aviation Administration.

Fa•ber (fā′bər), *n.* **Frederick W(illiam),** 1814–63, English clergyman and hymn writer.

Fa′bian Soci′ety, *n.* an organization founded in England in 1884 to spread socialist principles gradually by peaceful means.

fa•ble (fā′bəl), *n., v.,* **-bled, -bling.** —*n.* **1.** a short tale used to teach a moral, often with animals as characters. **2.** a story not founded on fact. **3.** a legend or myth. **4.** lie; falsehood. —*v.t.* **5.** to describe as if actually so; talk about as if true: *She is fabled to be the daughter of a tycoon.*

fa•bled (fā′bəld), *adj.* **1.** celebrated in fables. **2.** having no real existence; fictitious: *fabled lands of everlasting plenty.* **3.** celebrated; famous; renowned: *a fabled beauty of stage and screen.*

fab•ric (fab′rik), *n.* **1.** a cloth made by weaving, knitting, or felting fibers. **2.** the texture of a cloth or material. **3.** framework; structure: *the fabric of society.* **4.** the spatial arrangement and orientation of the constituents of a rock. **5.** a building; edifice. **6.** the method of construction.

fab•ri•cate (fab′ri kāt′), *v.t.,* **-cat•ed, -cat•ing.** **1.** to make by art or skill and labor; construct. **2.** to make by assembling parts or sections. **3.** to devise; invent: *to fabricate an alibi.* **4.** to fake; forge (a document, signature, etc.). —**fab′ri•ca′tion,** *n.*

fab•u•list (fab′yə list), *n.* **1.** a person who invents or relates fables. **2.** a liar.

fab•u•lous (fab′yə ləs), *adj.* **1.** almost impossible to believe; incredible. **2.** exceptionally good or unusual; marvelous; superb. **3.** told about or known through fables or myths; purely imaginary. —**fab′u•lous•ly,** *adv.* —**fab′u•lous•ness,** *n.*

fa•cade or **fa•çade** (fə säd′, fa-), *n.* **1. a.** the front of a building, esp. an imposing or decorative one. **b.** any side of a building facing a public way or space and finished accordingly. **2.** a superficial appearance or illusion of something.

face (fās), *n., v.,* **faced, fac•ing.** —*n.* **1.** the front part of the head, from the forehead to the chin. **2.** a look or expression on this part: *a sad face.* **3.** an expression or look that indicates ridicule, disgust, etc.; grimace: *to make a face.* **4.** impudence; boldness. **5.** outward appearance. **6.** good reputation; dignity; prestige. **7.** the amount specified in a bill or note, exclusive of interest. **8.** the manifest sense or express terms, as of a document. **9.** the geographic characteristics or general appearance of a land surface. **10.** the surface: *the face of the earth.* **11.** the side, or part of a side, upon which the use of a thing depends: *the face of a playing card.* **12.** the most important or most frequently seen side; front. **13.** the outer or upper side of a fabric. **14.** the acting or working surface of an implement, tool, etc. **15.** any of the bounding surfaces of a solid figure: *a cube has six faces.* **16.** the front or end of a drift or excavation, where the material is being or was last mined. **17. a.** the working surface of a printer's type or plate, etc. **b.** Also called **typeface.** any design of type. **c.** Also called **typeface.** the general style or appearance of type: *broad or narrow face.* **18.** any of the plane surfaces of a crystal. —*v.t.* **19.** to look toward or in the direction of: *to face the light.* **20.** to have the front toward or permit a view of: *The building faces the street.* **21.** to confront directly: *to face the future.* **22.** to confront courageously or impudently (usu. fol. by *down* or *out*): *facing down an opponent.* **23.** to oppose or to meet defiantly: *to face fearful odds.* **24.** to cover or partly cover with a different material in front: *They faced the wooden house with brick.* **25.** to finish the edge of (a garment) with facing. **26.** to turn the face of (a playing card) upwards. **27.** to dress or smooth the surface of (a stone or the like). —*v.i.* **28.** to turn or be turned: *She faced toward the sea.* **29.** to be placed with the front in a certain direction: *The barn faces south.* **30.** to turn to the right, left, or in the opposite direction: *Left face!* **31. face off,** to confront, as in a contest. **32. face up to,** a. to admit. **b.** to meet courageously; confront. —*Idiom.* **33. face the music,** to accept the consequences of one's actions. **34. face to face, a.** opposite one another; facing. **b.** confronting one another. **c.** in dangerously close proximity: *face to face with death.* **35. in the face of, a.** in spite of; notwithstanding. **b.** when confronted with. **36. lose face,** to suffer humiliation. **37. on the face of it,** apparently; seemingly. **38. save face,** to escape from humiliation. **39. set one's face against,** to disapprove strongly of; oppose. **40. show one's face,** to be seen; make

an appearance. **41. to one's face,** in one's very presence; in direct confrontation. —**face′a•ble,** *adj.*

face′ card′, *n.* the king, queen, or jack of playing cards.

face•down (*adv.* fās′doun′; *n.* fās′doun′), *adv.* **1.** with the face or the front or upper surface downward. —*n.* **2.** Also, **face′-down′.** a direct confrontation; showdown.

face•less (fās′lis), *adj.* **1.** lacking a face. **2.** lacking personal distinction or identity: *a faceless mob.* **3.** unidentified or unidentifiable; concealing one's identity. —**face′less•ness,** *n.*

face′-lift′ or **face′ lift′,** *n.* **1.** plastic surgery on the face to eliminate sagging and wrinkles. **2.** a renovation or restyling, as of a room or building. —*v.t.* **3.** to perform a face-lift upon.

face′ mask′ or **face′mask′,** *n.* any of various devices to shield the face, sometimes attached to or forming part of a helmet, as that worn in a hazardous activity or a sport.

face′-off′, *n.* **1.** *Ice Hockey.* the act of putting the puck into play by dropping it between two players on opposing teams, as at the start of a game or period. **2.** a direct confrontation.

face•plate (fās′plāt′), *n.* **1.** a perforated disk mounted on a spindle of a lathe for holding work to be turned. **2.** the part of a protective headpiece, as a diver's or astronaut's helmet, that covers the upper portion of the face. **3.** the glass front of a cathode-ray tube upon which the image is displayed.

face′ pow′der, *n.* a cosmetic powder used to give a matte finish to the face.

fac•et (fas′it), *n., v.,* **-et•ed, -et•ing** or (*esp. Brit.*) **-et•ted, -et•ting.** —*n.* **1.** one of the small polished plane surfaces of a cut gem. **2.** a similar surface cut on a fragment of rock by the action of water, windblown sand, etc. **3.** aspect; phase: *all facets of production.* **4.** one of the corneal lenses of a compound arthropod eye. **5.** a small, smooth, flat area on a hard surface, esp. on a bone or a tooth. —*v.t.* **6.** to cut facets on.

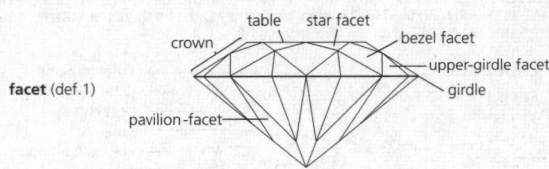

facet (def.1)

face′ time′, *n.* **1.** a brief appearance on television. **2.** a brief face-to-face meeting, esp. with someone important.

fa•ce•tious (fə sē′shəs), *adj.* **1.** not meant to be taken seriously or literally: *a facetious remark.* **2.** amusing; humorous. **3.** lacking serious intent; concerned with something amusing or frivolous: *a facetious person.* —**fa•ce′tious•ly,** *adv.* —**fa•ce′tious•ness,** *n.*

face′-to-face′, *adj.* **1.** having the fronts or faces toward or close to each other. **2.** involving close contact or direct opposition.

face•up (fās′up′), *adv.* with the face or the front or upper surface upward.

face val•ue (fās′ val′yōō *for 1;* fās′ val′yōō *for 2*), *n.* **1.** the value printed on the face of a stock, bond, etc. **2.** apparent value: *Do not accept promises at face value.*

fa•cial (fā′shəl), *adj.* **1.** of the face: *facial expression.* **2.** used to improve the condition of the face: *a facial cream.* —*n.* **3.** a treatment to beautify the face. —**fa′cial•ly,** *adv.*

fa′cial nerve′, *n.* either one of the seventh pair of cranial nerves, in mammals supplying facial muscles, the taste buds at the front of the tongue, the tear glands, and the salivary glands.

fa′cial tis′sue, *n.* a soft, disposable paper tissue esp. for cleansing the face or for use as a handkerchief.

fa•ci•es (fā′shē ēz′, -shēz), *n., pl.* **fa•ci•es.** **1.** general appearance, as of an animal or vegetable group. **2.** the appearance and characteristics of a rock formation, esp. as differentiated from contiguous deposits. **3.** a facial expression characteristic of a pathological condition. **4.** a distinctive phase of a prehistoric cultural tradition.

fac•ile (fas′il; *esp. Brit.* -īl), *adj.* **1.** quick in comprehension or action: *a facile mind.* **2.** superficial; shallow: *a facile answer to a hard question.* **3.** easily accomplished or attained: *a facile performance.* **4.** fluent; effortless: *a facile writing style.* —**fac′ile•ly,** *adv.* —**fac′ile•ness,** *n.*

fa•cil•i•tate (fə sil′i tāt′), *v.t.,* **-tat•ed, -tat•ing.** **1.** to make easier or less difficult; help forward: *Careful planning facilitates any kind of work.* **2.** to assist the progress of (a person). —**fa•cil′i•ta′tor,** *n.*

fa•cil•i•ty (fə sil′i tē), *n., pl.* **-ties.** **1.** Often, **facilities. a.** something designed, built, or installed to afford a specific convenience or service: *a new research facility.* **b.** Usu., **facilities.** something that permits the easier performance of an action, course of conduct, etc.: *a hotel with facili-*

ties for conferences. **2.** readiness or ease due to skill, aptitude, or practice; dexterity. **3.** an easy-flowing manner. **4.** the quality of being easily or conveniently done or performed. **5.** lack of difficulty; ease.

fac•ing (fā′sing), *n.* **1.** a covering in front, as an outer layer of stone on a brick wall. **2.** a lining applied along an edge of a garment for ornament or strengthening and sometimes turned outward, as on a cuff. **3. facings,** coverings of a different color applied on the collar, cuffs, etc., of a military coat.

fac•sim•i•le (fak sim′ə lē), *n., v.,* **-led, -le•ing.** **—***n.* **1.** an exact copy, as of a book, painting, or manuscript. **2.** FAX. **—***v.t.* **3.** to reproduce in facsimile; make a facsimile of. [< Latin *fac* make + *simile* similar]

fact (fakt), *n.* **1.** something that actually exists; reality; truth: *Your fears have no basis in fact.* **2.** something known to exist or to have happened. **3.** a truth known by actual experience or observation; something known to be true: *scientific facts about plant growth.* **4.** something said to be true or supposed to have happened. **5.** an actual or alleged event or circumstance, as distinguished from its legal effect or consequence. **—*Idiom.*** **6. in fact,** in truth; really; indeed: *They are, in fact, great patriots.* **—*Saying.*** **7. facts are facts,** one cannot avoid the truth.

fact′ find′er or **fact′-find′er,** *n.* a person who searches impartially for the actualities of a situtation, esp. an official investigator. **—fact′-find′ing,** *n., adj.*

fac•tion[1] (fak′shən), *n.* **1.** a group or clique within a larger group, party, government, organization, or the like. **2.** party strife and intrigue; discord; dissension. **—fac′tious,** *adj.*

fac•tion[2] (fak′shən), *n.* **1.** a form of writing or filmmaking that treats real people or events in a fictional account. **2.** a novel, play, or film in this form.

fac•ti•tious (fak tish′əs), *adj.* artificial or contrived; not spontaneous or natural. **—fac•ti′tious•ly,** *adv.* **—fac•ti′tious•ness,** *n.*

fac•ti•tive (fak′ti tiv), *adj.* of or pertaining to a verb that expresses the idea of rendering in a certain way and that takes a direct object and an additional word or phrase indicating the result of the process, as *made* in *They made him king.* **—fac′ti•tive•ly,** *adv.*

fac•tive (fak′tiv), *adj.* of or pertaining to a verb, adjective, or noun phrase that presupposes the truth of a following clause, as *realize* in *I didn't realize that he had left.*

fact′ of life′, *n.* **1.** any aspect of human existence that must be acknowledged or regarded as unalterable. **—*Idiom.*** **2. facts of life,** the facts concerning sex, reproduction, and birth.

fac•toid (fak′toid), *n.* something fictitious or unsubstantiated that is presented as fact, devised esp. to gain publicity, and accepted because of constant repetition. **—fac•toi′dal,** *adj.*

fac•tor (fak′tər), *n.* **1.** one of the elements contributing to a particular result or situation. **2.** one of two or more numbers, algebraic expressions, or the like, that when multiplied together produce a given product; a divisor: *6 and 3 are factors of 18.* **3.** any of certain substances necessary to a biochemical or physiological process, esp. those whose exact nature and function are unknown. **4.** a business organization that lends money on accounts receivable or buys and collects accounts receivable. **5.** a person who acts or transacts business for another; an agent. **6.** an agent or merchant earning a commission by selling goods belonging to others. **7.** a person or business organization that finances another's business. **—***v.t.* **8.** to express (a mathematical quantity) as a product of two or more quantities of like kind, as $30 = 2 \cdot 3 \cdot 5$, or $x^2 - y^2 = (x + y)(x - y)$. **9. factor in** or **into,** to include as a contributing element. **—fac′tor•a•ble,** *adj.* **—fac′tor•a•bil′i•ty,** *n.*

fac•tor•age (fak′tər ij), *n.* **1.** the work or business of a factor. **2.** the commission paid to a factor.

fac•to•ri•al (fak tôr′ē əl, -tōr′-), *n.* **1.** the product of a given positive integer multiplied by all lesser positive integers: The quantity four factorial $(4!) = 4 \cdot 3 \cdot 2 \cdot 1 = 24$. *Symbol: n!,* where *n* is the given integer. **—***adj.* **2.** of or pertaining to factors or factorials. **3.** of or pertaining to a factor or a factory. **—fac•to′ri•al•ly,** *adv.*

fac•tor•ing (fak′tər ing), *n.* **1.** the business of purchasing and collecting accounts receivable or of lending money on the basis of accounts receivable. **2.** the act or process of separating something, as an equation, formula, or cryptogram, into its component parts.

fac•to•ry (fak′tə rē, -trē), *n., pl.* **-ries.** **1.** a building or group of buildings with facilities for the manufacture of goods. **2.** (formerly) an establishment in a foreign country where factors carried on their business.

fac•to•tum (fak tō′təm), *n.* an assistant who takes on a wide range of tasks and responsibilities. [< Latin *fac* make, do + *tōtum* all]

fac•tu•al (fak′cho͞o əl), *adj.* **1.** of or pertaining to facts; concerning facts: *factual accuracy.* **2.** based on or restricted to facts: *a factual report.* **—fac′tu•al•ly,** *adv.* **—fac′tu•al′i•ty, fac′tu•al•ness,** *n.*

fac•ture (fak′chər), *n.* **1.** the act, process, or manner of making something; construction. **2.** the thing that is made.

fac•ul•ta•tive (fak′əl tā′tiv), *adj.* **1.** conferring a faculty, privilege, permission, or the power of doing or not doing something: *a facultative enactment.* **2.** being left to one's option or choice; optional. **3.** having the capacity to live under more than one specific set of environmental conditions, as a plant that can lead either a parasitic or a nonparasitic life (opposed to *obligate*). **4.** of or pertaining to the mental faculties. **5.** having the potential of taking place or assuming a specified character. **—fac′ul•ta′tive•ly,** *adv.*

fac•ul•ty (fak′əl tē), *n., pl.* **-ties.** **1.** an ability, natural or acquired, for a particular kind of action. **2.** one of the powers of the mind, as memory, reason, or speech. **3.** an inherent capability of the body. **4. a.** the entire teaching and administrative force of a university, etc. **b.** one of the departments of learning, as theology, medicine, or law, in a university. **5.** the members of a learned profession: *the medical faculty.*

fad (fad), *n.* a temporary fashion, manner of conduct, etc., esp. one followed enthusiastically by a group. **—fad′dish,** *adj.* **—fad′dist,** *n.*

fade (fād), *v.,* **fad•ed, fad•ing,** *n.* **—***v.i.* **1.** to lose brightness or vividness of color. **2.** to become dim, as light, or lose brightness of illumination. **3.** to lose freshness, vigor, strength, or health: *The tulips have faded.* **4.** to disappear or die gradually (often fol. by *away* or *out*): *His anger faded away.* **—***v.t.* **5.** to cause to fade or fade in or out. **6. fade in** (or **out**), **a.** (of a film or television image) to appear (or disappear) gradually. **b.** (of a recorded sound) to increase (or decrease) gradually in volume. **—***n.* **7.** an act or instance of fading. **8.** FADE-OUT (def. 1). **9.** a hairstyle in which the sides of the head are close-cropped and the top hair is shaped into an upright block.

fade•a•way (fād′ə wā′), *n.* **1.** SCREWBALL (def. 2). **2.** a slide in baseball made by a base runner to one side of the base. **3.** a jump shot made by a basketball player while falling away from the basket.

fade′-in′, *n.* **1.** a gradual increase in the visibility of a film or television scene. **2.** a gradual increase in the volume of recorded sound.

fade′-out′, *n.* **1.** a gradual decrease in the visibility of a film or television scene. **2.** a gradual decrease in the volume of broadcast or recorded sound. **3.** a gradual disappearance or reduction.

fa•er•ie or **fa•er•y** (fā′ə rē, fâr′ē), *n.* **1.** the imaginary land of the fairies; fairyland. **—***adj.* **2.** fairy.

fag (fag), *n., v.,* **fagged, fag•ging.** **—***n.* **1.** a drudge. **—***v.t.* **2.** to tire or weary by labor (often fol. by *out*).

fag′ end′, *n.* **1.** the last part or very end of something: *the fag end of a rope.* **2.** the unfinished end of a piece of cloth. **3.** a remnant or scrap, esp. of cloth at the end of a bolt.

fag•ot (fag′ət), *n.* **1.** a bundle of sticks, twigs, or branches bound together and used as fuel, a torch, etc. **2.** a bundle; bunch. **3.** a bundle of pieces of iron or steel to be welded, hammered, or rolled together at high temperature. **—***v.t.* **4.** to bind or make into a fagot. **5.** to ornament with fagoting.

fag•ot•ing (fag′ə ting), *n.* **1.** openwork embroidery in which some horizontal threads are drawn from the fabric and the remaining vertical threads are gathered into groups and tied at their midpoint. **2.** a decorative stitch in which thread is drawn in a ladderlike pattern across an opening between two edges of fabric.

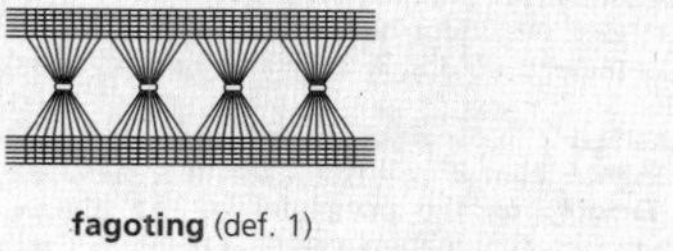

fagoting (def. 1)

Fahr•en•heit (far′ən hīt′), *adj.* noting, pertaining to, or measured according to a temperature scale **(Fahr′enheit scale′)** in which 32° represents the ice point and 212° the steam point. *Symbol:* F [after G. D. *Fahrenheit* (1686–1736), German physicist]

fa•ience or **fa•ïence** (fī äns′, -äɴs′, fā-), *n.* glazed earthenware or pottery, esp. a fine variety with highly colored designs.

fail (fāl), *v.i.* **1.** to fall short of success or achievement in something expected, attempted, desired, or approved: *The experiment failed.* **2.** to receive less than the passing grade or mark in an examination, class, or course of study. **3.** to be or become deficient or lacking; be insufficient or absent; fall short. **4.** to lose strength or vigor; become weak. **5.** to stop functioning or operating. **6.** to dwindle, pass, or die away. **7.** to become unable to meet or pay debts or business obligations; become insolvent or bankrupt. **8.** (of a building member, structure, machine part, etc.) to break, bend, or be otherwise destroyed or made useless because of an excessive load. **—***v.t.* **9.** to be unsuccessful in the performance or completion of: *He failed to do his duty.* **10.** (of some expected or usual resource) to prove of no use or help to: *His friends failed him.* **11.** to receive less than a passing grade or mark in. **12.** to declare (a person) unsuccessful in a test or course of study; give less than a passing grade to. **—*Idiom.*** **13. without fail,** with certainty; positively.

fail•ing (fā′ling), *n.* **1.** an act or instance of failing; failure. **2.** a defect or fault; shortcoming; weakness. **—***prep.* **3.** in the absence or default of: *Failing payment, we shall sue.*

faille (fīl, fāl), *n.* a soft transversely ribbed fabric of silk, rayon, or lightweight taffeta.

fail′-safe′, *adj.* **1.** pertaining to or noting a mechanism built into a system, as in an early warning system or a nuclear reactor, for ensuring safety should the system fail to operate properly. **2.** equipped with a secondary system that ensures continued operation even if the primary system fails. **3.** denoting a system of safeguards in which bombers may not proceed past a prearranged point or nuclear weapons may not be armed without direct orders. **4.** guaranteed to work; totally reliable. **—***n.* **5.** a fail-safe mechanism, system, or the like.

fail•ure (fāl′yər), *n.* **1.** an act or instance of failing or proving unsuccessful; lack of success. **2.** nonperformance of something due, required, or expected: *a failure to appear.* **3.** a subnormal quantity or quality; an insufficiency: *the failure of crops.* **4.** deterioration or decay, esp. of vigor or strength. **5.** a condition of being bankrupt by reason of insolvency. **6.** a becoming insolvent or bankrupt: *the failure of a bank.* **7.** a person or thing that proves unsuccessful.

fain (fān), *adv.* **1.** gladly; willingly: *He fain would accept.* —*adj.* **2.** content; willing. **3.** obliged. **4.** glad; pleased. **5.** desirous; eager.

faint (fānt), *adj.* **1.** lacking brightness, vividness, clearness, loudness, strength, etc. **2.** feeble or slight. **3.** feeling weak, dizzy, or exhausted; about to lose consciousness. **4.** lacking courage; cowardly; timorous. —*v.i.* **5.** to lose consciousness temporarily. **6.** to lose brightness. —*n.* **7.** a temporary loss of consciousness resulting from a decreased flow of blood to the brain; swoon. —**faint′ly,** *adv.* —**faint′ness,** *n.*

faint•heart•ed (fānt′här′tid), *adj.* lacking courage; cowardly; timorous. —**faint′heart′ed•ly,** *adv.*

fair¹ (fâr), *adj.* **1.** free from bias, dishonesty, or injustice. **2.** legitimately sought, done, given, etc.; proper under the rules: *a fair fight.* **3.** moderately large; ample: *a fair income.* **4.** neither excellent nor poor; moderately or tolerably good: *fair health.* **5. a.** (of the sky) bright; sunny; cloudless to half-cloudy. **b.** (of the weather) fine; with no prospect of rain, snow, or hail. **6.** of a light hue; not dark: *fair skin.* **7.** pleasing in appearance; attractive: *a fair young maiden.* **8.** (of a wind or tide) tending to aid the progress of a vessel. **9.** marked by favoring conditions; likely; promising: *in a fair way to succeed.* **10.** unobstructed; not blocked up. **11.** without irregularity or unevenness: *a fair surface.* **12.** free from blemish, imperfection, or anything that impairs the appearance, quality, or character. **13.** easy to read; clear: *fair handwriting.* **14.** courteous; civil: *fair words.* —*adv.* **15.** in a fair manner: *He doesn't play fair.* **16.** favorably; auspiciously. —*v.t.* **17.** to draw and adjust (the lines of a ship's hull being designed) to produce regular surfaces of the correct form. —*Idiom.* **18. bid fair,** to seem likely: *This entry bids fair to win first prize.* **19. fair and square, a.** honestly; justly; straightforwardly. **b.** honest; just; straightforward. **20. fair to middling,** only tolerably good; so-so. —**fair′ness,** *n.*

fair² (fâr), *n.* **1.** a usu. competitive exhibition of farm products, livestock, etc., often combined with entertainment. **2.** a periodic gathering of buyers and sellers in an appointed place. **3.** an exposition in which different exhibitors participate, often with the purpose of buying or selling or of familiarizing the public with the products: *a home-furnishings fair.* **4.** an exhibition and sale of articles to raise money, often for some charitable purpose.

fair′ ball′, *n.* a batted baseball that lands, rolls, or is caught within the foul lines or legal area of play.

Fair•banks (fâr′bangks′), *n.* **1. Charles Warren,** 1852–1918, political leader: vice president of the U.S. 1905–09. **2. Douglas,** 1883–1939, U.S. motion-picture actor. **3.** a city in central Alaska, on the Tanana River. 22,645.

fair′ catch′, *n.* a catch of a kicked football made after the receiving team signals that it will not attempt to advance the ball.

Fair′ Deal′, *n.* the principles of the liberal wing of the Democratic party under the leadership of President Harry S Truman, consisting largely of a continuation and development of the principles of the New Deal. Compare GREAT SOCIETY, NEW DEAL, NEW FRONTIER.

fair•ground (fâr′ground′), *n.* Often, **fairgrounds.** a place where fairs, horse races, etc., are held, esp. an area set aside by a county, city, or state for an annual fair and containing exhibition buildings.

fair′-haired′, *adj.* **1.** having light-colored hair. —*Idiom.* **2. fair-haired boy,** an up-and-coming person; favorite.

fair•ish (fâr′ish), *adj.* **1.** moderately good or large. **2.** moderately light in color.

fair•ly (fâr′lē), *adv.* **1.** in a fair manner; justly; impartially. **2.** moderately; tolerably: *a fairly heavy rain.* **3.** properly; legitimately: *a claim fairly made.* **4.** clearly; distinctly: *fairly seen.* **5.** so to speak; seemingly: *ears fairly steaming with rage.*

fair′ mar′ket price′, *n.* the price at which both a seller and a buyer are willing to do business.

fair′-mind′ed, *adj.* characterized by fair judgment; impartial; unprejudiced. —**fair′-mind′ed•ness,** *n.*

fair′ play′, *n.* just and honorable treatment, action, or conduct.

fair′ shake′, *n.* a just and equal opportunity or treatment.

fair•way (fâr′wā′), *n.* **1.** an unobstructed passage, way, or area. **2.** the part of a golf course where the grass is cut short between the tees and the putting greens, exclusive of the rough, trees, and hazards. **3.** the navigable portion of a waterway.

fair•y (fâr′ē), *n., pl.* **fair•ies,** *adj.* —*n.* **1.** (in folklore) one of a class of supernatural beings, generally conceived as having a diminutive human form and possessing magical powers. —*adj.* **2.** of or pertaining to fairies: *fairy magic.* **3.** of the nature of a fairy; fairylike. —**fair′y•hood′,** *n.*

fair•y•land (fâr′ē land′), *n.* **1.** the imaginary realm of fairies. **2.** an enchantingly beautiful region or place.

fair′y ring′, *n.* any of numerous mushrooms of meadows and open woods that spread in rings originating from mycelial growth, esp. the well-known *Marasmius oreades.*

fair′y shrimp′, *n.* any transparent branchiopod crustacean of the order Anostraca, of freshwater ponds.

fair′y tale′, *n.* **1.** a story, usu. for children, about elves, hobgoblins, dragons, fairies, or other magical creatures. **2.** an incredible or misleading statement or belief. Also called **fair′y sto′ry.**

faith (fāth), *n.* **1.** confidence or trust in a person or thing. **2.** belief that is not based on proof. **3.** belief in God or in the doctrines of religion: one of the three Christian virtues. **4.** belief in anything, as a code of ethics or standards of merit. **5.** a system of religious belief: *the Jewish faith.* **6.** the obligation of loyalty or fidelity to a person, promise, engagement, etc. **7.** the observance of this obligation; fidelity to one's promise, oath, allegiance, etc. **8.** the trust in God and in His promises as made through Christ and the Scriptures by which humans are justified or saved. —*Idiom.* **9. in faith,** in truth; indeed. [Middle English *feith* < Old French *feit* < Latin *fidēs* trust]

faith′ cure′, *n.* **1.** a method of attempting to cure disease by prayer and religious faith. **2.** a cure thus effected.

faith•ful (fāth′fəl), *adj.* **1.** steady in allegiance or affection; loyal; constant: *faithful friends.* **2.** reliable, trusted, or believed: *faithful assurances of help.* **3.** true to fact, a standard, or an original; accurate: *a faithful copy.* **4.** thorough in the performance of duty: *a faithful worker.* —*n.* **5. the faithful, a.** the believers in a faith, esp. the members of a Christian church or the adherents of Islam. **b.** the body of loyal members of any party or group. —**faith′ful•ly,** *adv.* —**faith′ful•ness,** *n.*

Faith′ful Serv′ant and the E′vil Serv′ant, The, a parable of Jesus. Luke 12:42–48.

faith′ group′, *n.* any group professing religious faith.

faith′ heal′ing, *n.* **1.** the use of religious faith or prayer to bring about healing. **2.** healing believed to have been brought about by this. —**faith′ heal′er,** *n.*

faith•less (fāth′lis), *adj.* **1.** not adhering to allegiance, promises, vows, or duty. **2.** not trustworthy; unreliable. **3.** lacking trust or belief, esp. without religious faith. —**faith′less•ly,** *adv.*

fa•ji•tas (fä hē′təz, fə-), *n.* (*used with a sing. or pl. v.*) a Tex-Mex dish of thin strips of grilled meat, served with tortillas, salsa, etc.

fake¹ (fāk), *v.,* **faked, fak•ing,** *n., adj.* —*v.t.* **1.** to create or render so as to mislead, deceive, or defraud others: *to fake a report showing nonexistent profits.* **2.** to pretend; simulate; feign: *to fake illness.* **3.** to imitate or concoct convincingly or acceptably; counterfeit: *to fake a person's signature.* **4.** to accomplish by trial and error or by improvising. **5.** to trick or deceive (an opponent) by making a fake (often fol. by *out*). **6.** to play jazz ad lib; improvise. —*v.i.* **7.** to fake something; pretend. **8.** to give a fake to an opponent. —*n.* **9.** anything that misleads, deceives, or defrauds others by seeming to be what it is not; a counterfeit; sham. **10.** a person who fakes; faker; fraud. **11.** a simulated play or move intended to deceive an opponent. —*adj.* **12.** designed to deceive or cheat; counterfeit. —**fak′er,** *n.*

fake² (fāk) also **flake,** *v.,* **faked, fak•ing,** *n.* —*v.t.* **1.** to lay (a rope) in a coil or series of long loops so as to allow to run freely without fouling or kinking (often fol. by *down*). —*n.* **2.** any complete turn of a rope that has been faked down. **3.** any of the various ways in which a rope may be faked down.

fak•er•y (fā′kə rē), *n., pl.* **-er•ies.** the practice or result of faking; deception.

fa•kir (fə kēr′, fā′kər) also **fa•keer′,** *n.* **1.** a Muslim or Hindu religious ascetic or mendicant monk commonly considered a wonderworker. **2.** a member of any Islamic religious order.

fa•la•fel (fə lä′fəl), *n.* a small deep-fried croquette of ground chickpeas or fava beans and spices.

Fa•la•sha (fä lä′shə, fə-), *n., pl.* **-shas,** (*esp. collectively*) **-sha.** a member of a historically Cushitic-speaking people of central Ethiopia who practice a form of Judaism.

fal•cate (fal′kāt) also **fal′cat•ed,** *adj.* curved like a scythe or sickle; hooked.

fal•con (fôl′kən, fal′-, fô′kən), *n.* **1.** any of various birds of prey of the family Falconidae, having long pointed wings and capable of swift, agile flight. **2. a.** the female gyrfalcon. **b.** the female peregrine falcon. Compare TERCEL. **3.** any bird of prey trained for use in falconry. **4.** a small light cannon in use from the 15th to the 17th centuries. —**fal•co•nine** (fôl′kə nīn′, -nin, fal′-, fô′kə-), *adj.* —**fal′co•noid′,** *adj.*

fal•con•er (fôl′kə nər, fal′-, fô′kə-), *n.* **1.** a person who hunts with falcons. **2.** a person who trains hawks for hunting.

fal•con•ry (fôl′kən rē, fal′-, fô′kən-), *n.* **1.** the sport of hunting with falcons or hawks. **2.** the art of training hawks to hunt.

fal•de•ral (fal′də ral′) also **fal•de•rol** (-rol′), **folderol,** *n.* **1.** mere nonsense; foolish talk or ideas. **2.** a trifle; gimcrack; gewgaw.

Falk′land Is′lands (fôk′lənd), *n.pl.* a group of islands in the S W Atlantic, E of Argentina, constituting a self-governing British colony. 2000; 4618 sq. mi. (11,961 sq. km). *Cap.:* Stanley. Spanish, **Islas Malvinas.**

fall (fôl), *v.,* **fell, fall•en, fall•ing,** *n.* —*v.i.* **1.** to drop or descend under the force of gravity, as to a lower place through loss or lack of support. **2.** to come or drop down suddenly to a lower position, esp. to leave a standing or erect position suddenly, whether voluntarily or not: *to fall on one's knees.* **3.** to become less or lower; become of a lower level, degree, amount, quality, value, number, etc.; decline: *The temperature fell rapidly.* **4.** to subside or abate. **5.** to hang down: *drapes falling in graceful folds.* **6.** to become lowered or directed downward, as the eyes. **7.** to become lower in pitch or volume, as the voice. **8.** to succumb to temptation or sin, esp. to become unchaste. **9.** to lose status, dignity, position, character, etc. **10.** to succumb to attack: *The city fell to the enemy.* **11.** to be overthrown, as a government. **12.** to drop down wounded or dead, esp. to be slain. **13.** to pass into some physical, mental, or emotional condition: *to fall into a coma; to fall in love.* **14.** to come or occur as if by dropping, as stillness or night. **15.** to issue forth: *Witty remarks fall easily from her lips.* **16.** to come by lot or chance: *The chore fell to me.* **17.** to come by chance into a particular position: *to fall among thieves.* **18.** to come to pass or occur at a certain time: *Christmas falls on a Monday this year.* **19.** to have its proper place: *The accent falls on the last syllable.* **20.** to come by right: *The inheritance fell to the only living relative.* **21.** to lose animation; appear disappointed or dismayed: *The child's face fell when the bird flew away.* **22.** to slope or extend in a downward direction: *The field falls gently to the river.* **23.** (of light) to shine; stream or beam: *Sunlight fell across the lawn.* **24.** (of the eyes or eyesight) to be drawn or directed, esp. unexpectedly or by chance: *My eyes fell upon a dish of candies.* **25.** to collapse, as through weakness, damage, poor construction, or the like. **26.** (of an animal, esp. a lamb) to be born. —*v.t.* **27.** to fell (a tree, animal, etc.). **28. fall away, a.** to withdraw support or allegiance. **b.** to become lean or thin; diminish; decline. **c.** to forsake one's faith, cause, or principles. **29. fall back,** to give way; recede; retreat. **30. fall back on** or **upon,** to have recourse to; rely on: *no savings to fall back on.* **31. fall behind, a.** to lag in pace or progress. **b.** to fail to pay one's debts on time. **32. fall down,** to perform disappointingly; disappoint; fail. **33. fall for,** *Slang.* **a.** to be deceived by: *to fall for an old trick.* **b.** to fall in love with. **34. fall in, a.** to fall to pieces toward the interior; sink inward. **b.** to take one's place in the ranks, as a soldier. **35. fall in with,** to start to associate with: *to fall in with bad company.* **36. fall off, a.** to decrease in number, amount, or intensity; diminish. **b.** *Naut.* to deviate from the heading; fall to leeward. **37. fall on** or **upon, a.** to assault. **b.** to become the obligation of. **c.** to experience or come upon. **38. fall out, a.** to quarrel; disagree. **b.** to happen; occur. **c.** to leave one's place in the ranks, as a soldier. **39. fall through,** to fail to be accomplished; collapse. **40. fall to, a.** to apply oneself; begin. **b.** to begin to eat. **41. fall under, a.** to be the concern or responsibility of. **b.** to be classified as; be included within. —*n.* **42.** an act or instance of falling or dropping from a higher to a lower place or position. **43.** that which falls or drops: *a heavy fall of rain.* **44.** the season of the year that comes after summer and before winter; autumn. **45.** a becoming less; a sinking to a lower level; decline: *the fall of the Roman Empire.* **46.** the distance through which anything falls: *a long fall to the ground from here.* **47.** Usu., **falls.** a cataract or waterfall. **48.** downward slope or declivity: *the gentle rise and fall of the meadow.* **49.** a falling from an erect position, as to the ground: *to have a bad fall.* **50.** a hanging down: *a fall of wild roses on a fence.* **51.** a succumbing to temptation; lapse into sin. **52. the Fall,** (*sometimes l.c.*) the lapse of human beings into a state of natural or innate sinfulness through the sin of Adam and Eve. **53.** surrender or capture, as of a city. **54.** proper place: *the fall of an accent on a syllable.* **55.** a hairpiece of long hair that is attached to the natural hair at the crown and usu. hangs freely down the back of the head. **56.** a decorative cascade of lace, ruffles, or the like. **57.** the flap opening at the front of some types of men's trousers. **58.** the part of a rolled collar that extends outward from where the collar folds over. **59.** the part of the rope of a tackle to which the power is applied in hoisting. **60.** the long soft hair that hangs over the forehead and eyes of certain terriers. **61.** (in astrology) the sign or part of the zodiac in which the influence of a planet is most negative (opposed to *exaltation*). —***Idiom.*** **62. fall (all) over oneself,** to behave with excessive deference; toady. **63. fall by the wayside, a.** to fall from grace. See GRACE (def. 16). Matt. 13:3–8; 18–23; Luke 8:5–15. **b.** to be defeated in an endeavor. **64. fall foul** or **afoul of, a.** to collide with, as ships. **b.** to quarrel or have a controversy with. **65. fall on stony ground,** to fail because of unfavorable conditions. Matt. 13:3–8, 18–23; Luke 8:5–15.

fal•la•cious (fə lā′shəs), *adj.* **1.** containing a fallacy; logically unsound: *fallacious arguments.* **2.** deceptive; misleading: *fallacious testimony.* **3.** disappointing; delusive: *a fallacious peace.* —**fal•la′cious•ly,** *adv.* —**fal•la′cious•ness,** *n.*

fal•la•cy (fal′ə sē), *n., pl.* **-cies. 1.** a deceptive, misleading, or false notion, belief, etc.; misconception. **2.** a misleading or unsound argument. **3.** deceptive, misleading, or false nature. **4.** any of various types of erroneous reasoning that render arguments logically unsound.

fall•back (fôl′bak′), *n.* **1.** an act or instance of falling back. **2.** something or someone to turn or return to, esp. for help or as an alternative. —*adj.* **3.** Also, **fall′-back′.** of or designating something kept in reserve or as an alternative: *a fallback plan.*

fall•en (fô′lən), *v.* **1.** pp. of FALL. —*adj.* **2.** having dropped or come down from a higher place, from an upright position, or from a higher level, amount, quality, number, etc. **3.** on the ground; prostrate; down flat: *Exhausted racers lay fallen by the road.* **4.** degraded or immoral. **5.** overthrown or conquered: *a fallen city.* **6.** dead: *fallen troops.*

fall′en an′gel, *n.* an angel who has rebelled against God and been cast out of heaven. Rev. 12:7–9.

fall•er (fô′lər), *n.* **1.** one that falls. **2.** a device that operates by falling. **3.** a logger hired to cut down trees; feller.

fall•fish (fôl′fish′), *n., pl.* **-fish•es,** (*esp. collectively*) **-fish.** a large minnow, *Semotilus corporalis,* of E North America.

fall′ guy′, *n. Slang.* **1.** an easy victim. **2.** a scapegoat. **3.** a person who agrees to serve as the scapegoat for or carry out a misdeed or crime, usu. for some reward.

fal•li•ble (fal′ə bəl), *adj.* **1.** liable to err, esp. in being deceived or mistaken. **2.** liable to be erroneous or false; not accurate: *fallible information.* —**fal′li•bil′i•ty,** *n.* —**fal′li•bly,** *adv.*

fall′ing-out′, *n., pl.* **fall•ings-out, fall•ing-outs.** a quarrel or estrangement between persons formerly in close association with one another.

fall′ing star′, *n.* a meteor; shooting star.

fall′ line′, *n.* **1.** the natural boundary between an upland and a lowland, as a piedmont and a coastal plain: marked, in temperate or humid areas, by waterfalls and rapids. **2.** (*caps.*) *Eastern U.S.* the imaginary line between the Piedmont and the Atlantic coastal plain. **3.** *Skiing.* the path of natural descent from one point on a slope to another.

fall•off (fôl′ôf′, -of′), *n.* a decline in quantity, vigor, etc.

fal•lo′pi•an (or **Fal•lo′pi•an**) **tube′** (fə lō′pē ən), *n.* either of a pair of long slender ducts in the female abdomen that transport ova from the ovary to the uterus and in fertilization transport sperm cells from the uterus to the released ova. [after Gabriello *Fallopio* (1523–62), Italian anatomist]

fall′out′ or **fall′-out′,** *n.* **1.** the settling to the ground of airborne particles ejected into the atmosphere from the earth by explosions, eruptions, forest fires, etc., esp. such settling from nuclear explosions. Compare RAINOUT (def. 2). **2.** an incidental effect, outcome, or product: *the psychological fallout of a divorce.*

fal•low¹ (fal′ō), *adj.* **1.** (of land) plowed and left unseeded for a season or more; uncultivated. **2.** not in use; inactive: *creative energies lying fallow.* —*n.* **3.** land that has undergone plowing and harrowing and has been left unseeded for one or more growing seasons. —*v.t.* **4.** to make (land) fallow for agricultural purposes. —**fal′low•ness,** *n.*

fal•low² (fal′ō), *adj.* pale yellow; light brown; dun.

fal′low deer′, *n.* a Eurasian deer, *Dama dama,* with a yellowish coat that is spotted in the summer.

false (fôls), *adj.,* **fals•er, fals•est,** *adv.* —*adj.* **1.** not true or correct; erroneous: *a false statement.* **2.** declaring what is untrue; lying: *a false witness.* **3.** not faithful or loyal; treacherous: *a false friend.* **4.** tending to deceive or mislead; deceptive: *a false impression.* **5.** not genuine; counterfeit; spurious: *a false passport.* **6.** based on mistaken impressions, ideas, or facts: *false pride.* **7.** used as a substitute or supplement, esp. temporarily: *false supports for a bridge.* **8.** *Biol.* having a superficial resemblance to something that properly bears the name: *the false acacia.* **9.** not accurately or honestly made, done, or adjusted: *a false balance.* **10.** inaccurate in pitch, as a musical note. —*adv.* **11.** dishonestly; faithlessly; treacherously. —***Idiom.*** **12. play someone false,** to betray or mislead someone. —**false′ly,** *adv.* —**false′ness,** *n.*

false′ alarm′, *n.* **1.** a false report of a fire to a fire department. **2.** something that excites unfounded alarm or expectation.

false′ arrest′, *n.* arrest or detention of a person that is contrary to or unauthorized by law.

false′ bot′tom, *n.* a horizontal partition above the actual bottom of a container, esp. one forming a secret compartment.

false′-heart′ed, *adj.* treacherous or deceitful; perfidious. —**false′-heart′ed•ly,** *adv.* —**false′-heart′ed•ness,** *n.*

false•hood (fôls′ho͝od), *n.* **1.** a false statement; lie. **2.** something false, as an untrue idea or belief. **3.** the act or practice of telling lies; mendacity. **4.** lack of conformity to truth or fact; falsity.

false′ impris′onment, *n.* the unlawful restraint of a person from exercising the right to freedom of movement.

false′ in′digo, *n.* any of several North American plants of the genus *Baptisia,* of the legume family.

false′-mem′o•ry syn′drome (fôls′mem′ə rē), *n.* a psychological condition in which a person believes that he or she remembers events that have not actually occurred.

false′ preg′nancy, *n.* the appearance of physiological signs of pregnancy without conception; pseudocyesis.

false′ pretense′, *n.* an illegal, deliberate misrepresentation of facts, as to obtain title to money or property.

false′ rib′, *n.* any of the lower five ribs on either side of the body, which are not directly attached to the sternum.

false′ start′, *n.* **1.** a premature start by a contestant in a race, as in a swimming or track event, necessitating calling the field back to start again. **2.** an unsuccessful launch of an undertaking.

false′ step′, *n.* **1.** a stumble. **2.** an unwise or blundering act.

fal•set•to (fôl set′ō), *n., pl.* **-tos,** *adj., adv.* —*n.* **1.** an unnaturally or artificially high-pitched voice or register, esp. in a man. **2.** a person, esp. a man, who sings with such a voice. —*adj.* **3.** of, noting, or having the quality and compass of such a voice. —*adv.* **4.** in a falsetto.

fal•si•fy (fôl′sə fī), *v.,* **-fied, -fy•ing.** —*v.t.* **1.** to make false or incorrect, esp. so as to deceive: *to falsify income-tax reports.* **2.** to fashion or alter fraudulently: *to falsify a signature.* **3.** to represent falsely: *to falsify one's family history.* **4.** to show or prove to be false; disprove; confute. —*v.i.* **5.** to make false statements. —**fal′si•fi′a•ble,** *adj.* —**fal′si•fi′a•bil′i•ty,** *n.* —**fal•si•fi•ca•tion** (fôl′sə fi kā′shən), *n.* —**fal′si•fi′er,** *n.*

fal•si•ty (fôl′si tē), *n., pl.* **-ties. 1.** the quality or condition of being false; incorrectness; untruthfulness; treachery. **2.** something false; a falsehood.

fal•ter (fôl′tər), *v.i.* **1.** to hesitate, waver, or fail in action, intent, endurance, etc.; give way: *courage that never faltered.* **2.** to speak hesitatingly. **3.** to move unsteadily; stumble. —*v.t.* **4.** to utter hesitatingly or brokenly: *to falter an apology.* —*n.* **5.** the act of faltering; an unsteadiness of gait, voice, etc. **6.** a faltering sound. —**fal′ter•ing•ly,** *adv.*

Fal•well (fôl′wel), *n.* **Jerry L.,** born 1933, U.S. clergyman, founder of

Moral Majority, now called the Liberty Foundation, and president since 1979.

FAM, The Family Channel (a cable television station).

fame (fām), *n.* **1.** widespread reputation, esp. of a favorable character; renown; public eminence. **2.** common estimation or opinion generally held of a person or thing; reputation. —***Saying.*** **3. have one's 15 minutes of fame,** to enjoy very brief celebrity.

fa•mil•ial (fə mil′yəl, -mil′ē əl), *adj.* of, pertaining to, or characteristic of a family: *familial ties.*

fa•mil•iar (fə mil′yər), *adj.* **1.** commonly or generally known or seen: *a familiar sight.* **2.** well-acquainted; thoroughly conversant: *to be familiar with a subject.* **3.** informal; easygoing; unceremonious: *to write in a familiar style.* **4.** closely intimate or personal: *to be on familiar terms.* **5.** unduly intimate; too personal: *The duchess complained of familiar servants.* **6.** domesticated; tame. **7.** of or pertaining to a family or household. —*n.* **8.** a familiar friend or associate. **9.** a supernatural spirit or demon supposed to attend a person or another demon, often in the form of an animal. **10. a.** an officer of the Inquisition, employed to arrest suspects. **b.** a domestic employed by a bishop, seminary, etc. —**fa•mil′iar•ly,** *adv.* —**fa•mil′iar•ness,** *n.*

fa•mil•i•ar•i•ty (fə mil′ē ar′i tē, -mil yar′-), *n., pl.* **-ties. 1.** thorough knowledge or mastery of a thing, subject, etc. **2.** the state of being familiar; friendly relationship; close acquaintance; intimacy. **3.** an absence of ceremony and formality; informality. **4.** freedom of behavior justified only by the closest relationship; undue intimacy; license. **5.** Often, **familiarities.** an instance of such freedom, as in action or speech. —***Proverb.*** **6. Familiarity breeds contempt,** one can grow bored with routine, unvarying exposure to the same people, things, events, etc.

fa•mil•iar•ize (fə mil′yə rīz′), *v.t.,* **-ized, -iz•ing. 1.** to make (oneself or another) well-acquainted or conversant with something; acquaint. **2.** to make (something) well-known; bring into common knowledge or use. —**fa•mil′iar•i•za′tion,** *n.* —**fa•mil′iar•iz′er,** *n.*

fam•i•ly (fam′ə lē, fam′lē), *n., pl.* **-lies,** *adj.* —*n.* **1.** parents and their children, considered as a group, whether dwelling together or not. **2.** the children of one person or one couple collectively: *We want a family of one girl and one boy.* **3.** the spouse and children of one person: *I'm taking the family on vacation next week.* **4.** any group of persons closely related by blood, as parents, children, uncles, aunts, and cousins. **5.** all those persons considered as descendants of a common progenitor. **6.** a group of persons who form a household, esp. under one head. **7.** the staff, or body of assistants, of an official: *the presidential family.* **8.** a group of related things or individuals: *the halogen family of elements.* **9.** a group of people who are generally not blood relations but who share common attitudes, interests, or goals. **10.** *Biol.* the usual major subdivision of an order or suborder in the classification of plants, animals, fungi, etc., usu. consisting of several genera. **11.** *Ling.* the largest category into which languages related by common origin can be classified with certainty: *the Indo-European and Sino-Tibetan families of languages.* Compare STOCK (def. 12), SUBFAMILY (def. 2). —*adj.* **12.** of, pertaining to, or characteristic of a family: *a family trait.* **13.** belonging to or used by a family: *the family automobile.* **14. a.** suitable or appropriate for adults and children: *a family amusement park.* **b.** not containing obscene language: *a family newspaper.* —***Idiom.*** **15. in a** or **the family way,** pregnant. —***Saying.*** **16. The family that prays together stays together,** a family that worships God together is likely to endure as a unit. —**Usage.** See COLLECTIVE NOUN.

fam′ily cir′cle, *n.* **1.** the closely related members of a family as a group. **2.** a section in a theater containing less expensive seats, as the topmost gallery.

fam′ily court′, *n.* COURT OF DOMESTIC RELATIONS.

fam′ily leave′, *n.* an unpaid leave of absence from work in order to have or take care of a baby or to care for an ailing family member.

fam′ily name′, *n.* **1.** the hereditary surname of a family. **2.** a given name frequently used in a family.

fam′ily plan′ning, *n.* **1.** a program for determining the size of families through the spacing or prevention of pregnancies. **2.** (loosely) birth control.

fam′ily prac′tice, *n.* medical specialization in general practice that requires additional training and leads to board certification. Also called **fam′ily med′icine.** —**fam′ily practi′tioner,** *n.*

fam′ily tree′, *n.* **1.** all the ancestors or descendants of a given family or group. **2.** a genealogical chart showing the ancestry, descent, and relationship of the members of a family or group.

fam′ily val′ues, *n.* the moral and ethical principles that are upheld and transmitted within a family, including such values as honesty, loyalty, industry, and religious faith: *Divorce rates, threatened neighborhoods and schools, and public scandal all create a hostile atmosphere that erodes family structure and family values* (1976 Republican Party Platform).

fam•ine (fam′in), *n.* **1.** extreme and general scarcity of food, esp. within a large geographical area. **2.** any extreme and general scarcity.

fam•ish (fam′ish), *v.t., v.i.* to suffer or cause to suffer extreme hunger.

fa•mous (fā′məs), *adj.* **1.** having a widespread reputation, usu. of a favorable nature; renowned; celebrated. **2.** first-rate; excellent. **3.** notorious: *a movie star famous for fights with directors.* —**fa′mous•ness,** *n.*

fa•mous•ly (fā′məs lē), *adv.* very well; excellently; in a splendid manner: *He's doing famously. They get on famously together.*

fan[1] (fan), *n., v.,* **fanned, fan•ning.** —*n.* **1.** a device for producing a current of air by the movement of one or more broad surfaces. **2.** an implement of feathers, leaves, paper, etc., often in the shape of a triangle or a semicircle, for waving lightly in the hand to create a cooling current of air about the body. **3.** anything resembling such an implement, as the tail of a bird. **4.** any of various electrical or mechanical devices consisting of vanes radiating from a central hub that revolves, producing a current of air. **5.** a series of revolving blades supplying air for winnowing or cleaning grain. —*v.t.* **6.** to move or agitate (the air) with or as if with a fan. **7.** to cause air to blow upon, as from a fan; cool or refresh with or as if with a fan. **8.** to stir to activity; incite: *to fan emotions.* **9.** to blow upon: *A cool breeze fanned the shore.* **10.** to spread out like a fan: *The dealer fanned the cards.* **11.** (of a baseball pitcher) to strike out (a batter). **12.** *Chiefly South Midland and Southern U.S.* to spank. —*v.i.* **13.** to strike, swing, or brush lightly at something. **14.** to spread out like a fan: *The forest fire fanned out in all directions.* **15.** (of a baseball batter) to strike out. [Old English *fann* < Latin *vannus* winnowing basket] —**fan′like′,** *adj.* —**fan′ner,** *n.*

fan[2] (fan), *n.* an enthusiastic devotee, follower, or admirer of a sport, pastime, celebrity, etc.; enthusiast. [short for *fanatic*]

fa•nat•ic (fə nat′ik), *n.* **1.** a person with an extreme and uncritical enthusiasm or zeal, as in religion or politics; zealot. —*adj.* **2.** fanatical.

fa•nat•i•cal (fə nat′i kəl), *adj.* motivated or characterized by an extreme, uncritical enthusiasm or zeal, as in religion or politics; rabid. —**fa•nat′i•cal•ly,** *adv.*

fa•nat•i•cism (fə nat′ə sīz′əm), *n.* fanatical character, spirit, or conduct.

fan′ belt′, *n.* (in automotive vehicles) a belt, driven by the crankshaft of an engine, that turns a fan for drawing cooling air through the radiator.

fan•cied (fan′sēd), *adj.* unreal; imaginary.

fan•ci•er (fan′sē ər), *n.* **1.** a person having a liking for or interest in something; enthusiast. **2.** a person who breeds animals, plants, etc., esp. to improve the strain.

fan•ci•ful (fan′si fəl), *adj.* **1.** characterized by or showing fancy; capricious or whimsical in appearance: *fanciful designs in lace.* **2.** suggested by fancy; imaginary; unreal: *fanciful lands of romance.* **3.** led by fancy rather than by reason and experience; whimsical: *a fanciful mind.* —**fan′ci•ful•ly,** *adv.* —**fan′ci•ful•ness,** *n.*

fan′ club′, *n.* a club enthusiastically devoted to a particular celebrity, sports team, etc.

fan•cy (fan′sē), *n., pl.* **-cies,** *adj.,* **-ci•er, -ci•est,** *v.,* **-cied, -cy•ing,** *interj.* —*n.* **1.** imagination or fantasy, esp. as exercised in a capricious manner. **2.** the artistic ability of creating unreal or whimsical imagery, decorative detail, etc., as in poetry or drawing. **3.** a mental image or conception; notion: *happy fancies of being famous.* **4.** an idea or opinion with little foundation; illusion. **5.** a caprice; whim; vagary. **6.** capricious preference; inclination; a liking: *to take a fancy to smoked oysters.* **7.** critical judgment; taste. **8.** amorous inclination; love. —*adj.* **9.** made, designed, grown, adapted, etc., to please the taste or fancy; of superfine quality or exceptional appeal: *fancy goods.* **10.** ornamental; decorative; not plain: *a cake with a fancy icing.* **11.** depending on imagination or caprice; whimsical; irregular: *a fancy conception of time.* **12.** much too costly; exorbitant: *a consultant who charges fancy fees.* —*v.t.* **13.** to picture to oneself; imagine: *Fancy yourself living with such an egotist!* **14.** to believe without being absolutely sure or certain: *I fancy you are my new neighbor.* **15.** to take a liking to; like. —*interj.* **16.** (used as an exclamation of mild surprise): *They invited you, too? Fancy!*

fan′cy-free′, *adj.* free from any emotional tie or influence, esp. that of love.

fan•cy•work (fan′sē wûrk′), *n.* ornamental needlework.

fan•dan•go (fan dang′gō), *n., pl.* **-gos.** a lively Spanish or Spanish-American dance in triple time, performed by a man and woman playing castanets.

fan•fare (fan′fâr), *n.* **1.** a flourish or short air played on trumpets or the like. **2.** an ostentatious display or flourish. **3.** publicity.

fan•fold (fan′fōld′), *n.* **1.** a pad or tablet of invoices, bills, blank sheets, etc., interleaved with carbon paper. —*adj.* **2.** made up in such a form: *a fanfold tablet.* **3.** designating continuous-form paper folded like a fan so that it will stack readily.

fang (fang), *n.* **1.** one of the long sharp hollow or grooved teeth of a venomous snake by which poison is injected. **2.** a long sharp projecting tooth, esp. a canine tooth. **3.** the root of a tooth or a pronglike segment of such a root. **4.** one of the chelicerae of a spider. **5.** a pointed tapering part of a thing. **6.** the tang of a tool.

fan′jet′ or **fan′ jet′,** *n.* **1.** Also called **turbofan.** a jet engine having a large impeller that takes in air for use partly for the combustion of fuel and partly as exhaust. **2.** an airplane having one or more such engines.

fan′ mail′, *n.* fan letters collectively.

Fan′nie Mae′ or **Fan′ny Mae′,** *n.* **1.** Federal National Mortgage Association. **2.** any of the publicly traded securities collateralized by a pool of mortgages backed by the Federal National Mortgage Association. Compare FREDDIE MAC, GINNIE MAE. [altered from *FNMA,* the association's initials]

fan•ny (fan′ē), *n., pl.* **-nies.** *Informal.* BUTTOCKS.

fan′ny pack′, *n.* a small zippered pouch suspended from a belt around the waist.

fan′ palm′, *n.* a palm having fan-shaped leaves, as the talipot.

fan•tail (fan′tāl′), *n.* **1.** a tail, end, or part shaped like a fan. **2.** a bird having a broad, upward-slanting tail, as one of a breed of domestic pigeon. **3.** FANTAIL GOLDFISH. **4. a.** the rounded overhang of the stern of some ships. **b.** the deck area within this. —*adj.* **5.** (of shrimp) shelled, split almost through, and flattened slightly before cooking. —**fan'-tailed',** *adj.*

fan'tail gold'fish, *n.* a variety of goldfish with a deeply cleft four-lobed tail held in line with the body.

fan·ta·sia (fan tā'zhə, -zhē ə, fan'tə zē'ə), *n., pl.* **-sias. 1.** a dramatic, somewhat fanciful musical work, as for piano, in idiosyncratic form. **2.** something unstructured to be unreal, weird, exotic, or grotesque.

fan·ta·sied (fan'tə sēd), *adj.* **1.** conceived of in or as a fantasy; imagined; storied. **2.** dreamt of or hoped for; longingly imagined.

fan·ta·sist (fan'tə sist, -zist), *n.* a person who writes or composes fantasies or fantasias in music, poetry, or the like.

fan·ta·size (fan'tə sīz'), *v.,* **-sized, -siz·ing.** —*v.i.* **1.** to conceive fanciful or extravagant notions, ideas, suppositions, or the like (often fol. by *about*). —*v.t.* **2.** to create in one's fancy, daydreams, or the like; imagine. —**fan'ta·siz'er,** *n.*

fan·tas·tic (fan tas'tik) also **fan·tas'ti·cal,** *adj.* **1.** conceived or seemingly conceived by an unrestrained imagination; odd and remarkable; bizarre; grotesque: *fantastic rock formations.* **2.** fanciful or capricious, as persons or their ideas or actions. **3.** not based on reality; imaginary or groundless; irrational: *fantastic fears.* **4.** extravagantly fanciful; marvelous. **5.** extremely great; lavish: *to earn a fantastic salary.* **6.** extraordinarily good: *a fantastic musical.* —**fan·tas'ti·cal·ly,** *adv.*

fan·ta·sy or **phan·ta·sy** (fan'tə sē, -zē), *n., pl.* **-sies,** *v.,* **-sied, -sy·ing.** —*n.* **1.** imagination, esp. when extravagant and unrestrained. **2.** the forming of mental images, esp. wondrous or strange fancies; imaginative conceptualizing. **3.** the succession of mental images thus formed. **4.** an imagined or conjured up sequence of events, esp. one provoked by an unfulfilled psychological need. **5.** an abnormal or bizarre sequence of mental images, as a hallucination. **6.** a supposition based on no solid foundation; visionary idea; illusion. **7.** caprice; whim. **8.** an imaginative or fanciful creation; intricate, elaborate, or whimsical design. **9.** a form or work of fiction based on highly imaginative or fanciful characters and premises. **10.** FANTASIA (def. 1). —*v.i.* **11.** to form mental images; imagine; fantasize. **12.** to write or play fantasias. —*v.t.* **13.** to form mental images of; create in the mind.

fan·ta·sy·land (fan'tə sē land', -zē-), *n.* a place or circumstance existing only in the imagination; dream world.

fan·tod (fan'tod), *n.* **1.** Usu., **fantods.** a state of extreme nervousness or restlessness; the willies; the fidgets (usu. prec. by *the*). **2.** Sometimes, **fantods.** a sudden outpouring of anger, outrage, or a similar intense emotion.

fan·wort (fan'wûrt', -wôrt'), *n.* any aquatic plant belonging to the genus *Cabomba,* of the water lily family, having very small flowers and submerged and floating leaves.

FAO, Food and Agriculture Organization.

far (fär), *adv., adj.,* **far·ther** or **fur·ther, far·thest** or **fur·thest.** —*adv.* **1.** at or to a great distance or remote point; a long way off: *far ahead of the fleet.* **2.** at or to a remote or advanced time: *to talk far into the night.* **3.** at or to a great, advanced, or definite point or degree of progress: *Having come this far, we might as well continue.* **4.** much or many: *I need far more time.* —*adj.* **5.** remote in time or place: *the far future.* **6.** extending to a great distance: *the far frontiers of empire.* **7.** more distant of the two: *the far corner.* —**Idiom. 8. a far cry,** quite some distance removed. **b.** very different. **9. by far, a.** by a great deal; very much: *too expensive by far.* **b.** plainly; obviously: *This melon is by far the ripest of all.* **10. far and away,** without doubt; to a large extent. **11. far and wide,** to great lengths; over great distances. Also, **far and near, near and far. 12. far be it from me,** I do not wish or dare (to interrupt, criticize, etc.): *Far be it from me to complain, but it's cold in here.* **13. go far,** to achieve a great deal. **14. how far,** to what distance, extent, or degree: *How far can the people be deceived?* **15. so far, a.** up to now. **b.** up to a certain point or extent. **16. the far side,** the farther or opposite side: *the far side of the moon.* **17. thus far,** so far.

far·ad (far'əd, -ad), *n.* the SI unit of capacitance, equal to that of a capacitor having a potential of 1 volt when charged with 1 coulomb of electricity. *Symbol:* F [after M. Faraday, (1791–1867), English physicist]

fa·rad·ic (fə rad'ik), *adj.* of or pertaining to a discontinuous, asymmetric, alternating electric current from the secondary winding of an induction coil.

far·a·dize (far'ə dīz'), *v.t.,* **-dized, -diz·ing.** to stimulate or treat (muscles or nerves) with induced alternating electric current. —**far'a·di·za'tion,** *n.* —**far'a·diz'er,** *n.* —**far'a·dism,** *n.*

far·a·way (fär'ə wā'), *adj.* **1.** distant; remote: *faraway lands.* **2.** dreamy; preoccupied: *a faraway look.*

farce (färs), *n., v.,* **farced, farc·ing.** —*n.* **1.** a comedy based on unlikely situations and exaggerated effects. **2.** humor of the type displayed in such works. **3.** a foolish or meaningless show; ridiculous sham; mockery. —*v.t.* **4.** to enliven (a speech or composition), esp. with witty material. —**far'ci·cal,** *adj.*

far·ceur (fär sûr'), *n.* **1.** a writer or director of an actor in farce. **2.** a joker; wag.

fare (fâr), *n., v.,* **fared, far·ing.** —*n.* **1.** the price of conveyance or passage in a bus, train, airplane, or other carrier. **2.** a person who pays to be conveyed in a vehicle; paying passenger. **3.** food; diet: *hearty fare.* **4.** something offered to the public, as for entertainment: *literary fare.*

—*v.i.* **5.** to experience good or bad fortune, treatment, etc.; get on: *I have fared well in my profession.* **6.** to go; turn out; happen (used impersonally): *It fared ill with them.* **7.** to go; travel. **8.** to eat and drink. —**far'er,** *n.*

Far' East', *n.* the countries of E Asia, including China, Japan, Korea, and sometimes adjacent areas.

Fa·rel (fə rel'), *n.* **Guillaume,** 1489–1565, Swiss religious leader.

fare'-thee-well', *n.* **1.** a state of perfection: *a meal done to a fare-thee-well.* **2.** the maximum effect; fullest measure or extent: *She played the scene to a fare-thee-well.*

fare·well (fâr'wel'), *interj.* **1.** good-bye; may you fare well: *Farewell, friends.* —*n.* **2.** an expression of good wishes at parting: *to make one's farewells.* **3.** leave-taking; departure: *a friendly farewell.* **4.** a party for a person who is about to retire from a job, depart on a trip, etc. —*adj.* **5.** parting; valedictory; final: *a farewell performance.*

farewell' address', *n.* **1.** (*caps.*) a statement that President George Washington published in a Philadelphia newspaper in 1796 to announce that he would not run for a third term and to give his views on foreign and domestic policy. **2.** a speech delivered by someone upon leaving a job, post, etc.

farewell'-to-spring', *n.* a W North American plant, *Clarkia amoena,* of the evening primrose family, with satiny, cup-shaped purple or pink flowers.

far'-fetched' or **far'fetched',** *adj.* improbable; not naturally pertinent; forced; strained: *a far-fetched excuse for being late.*

far'-flung', *adj.* **1.** extending over a great distance. **2.** widely disbursed or distributed.

fa·ri·na (fə rē'nə), *n.* flour or meal made from cereal grains and cooked as cereal, used in puddings, etc.

far·i·na·ceous (far'ə nā'shəs), *adj.* **1.** consisting or made of flour or meal, as food. **2.** containing starch, as seeds; starchy. **3.** MEALY (def. 1).

far·kle·ber·ry (fär'kəl ber'ē), *n., pl.* **-ries.** a shrub, *Vaccinium arboreum,* of the heath family, of the southern U.S., having small, waxy white flowers and black berries.

farm (färm), *n.* **1.** a tract of land, usu. with a house, barn, silo, etc., on which crops and often livestock are raised for livelihood. **2.** land or water devoted to the raising of animals, fish, plants, etc.: *a pig farm; an oyster farm.* **3.** the system, method, or act of collecting revenue by leasing a territory in districts. **4.** a country or district leased for the collection of revenue. **5.** a fixed yearly amount accepted from a person in view of local or district taxes that he or she is authorized to collect. —*v.t.* **6.** to cultivate (land). **7.** to take the proceeds or profits of (a tax, undertaking, etc.) on paying a fixed sum. **8.** to let or lease (taxes, revenues, an enterprise, etc.) to another for a fixed sum or a percentage (often fol. by *out*). **9.** to let or lease the labor or services of (a person) for hire. **10.** to contract for the maintenance of (a person, institution, etc.): *a county that farms its poor.* —*v.i.* **11.** to cultivate the soil; operate a farm. **12. farm out, a.** to assign or subcontract (work) to another, esp. to a smaller concern. **b.** to assign the care of (a child) to another. **c.** to assign (a baseball player) to a farm team. **d.** to exhaust (farmland) by overcropping. —**farm'a·ble,** *adj.*

farm·er (fär'mər), *n.* **1.** a person who operates a farm or cultivates land. **2.** an unsophisticated person from a rural area. **3.** a person who undertakes some service at a fixed price. **4.** a person who undertakes the collection of taxes, duties, etc., paying a fixed sum for the privilege of keeping what is collected.

Far·mer (fär'mər), *n.* **1. Fannie (Merritt),** 1857–1915, U.S. authority on cooking. **2. James (Leonard),** born 1920, U.S. civil-rights leader.

farm'er (or **farm'er's) cheese',** *n.* a cheese similar to dry cottage cheese, made by pressing together the soft white curds of whole or partly skimmed milk.

Farm'er-La'bor Par'ty (fär'mər lā'bər), *n.* **1.** a political party in Minnesota, founded in 1920 and merged with the Democratic party in 1944. **2.** a political party founded in Chicago in 1919 and dissolved in 1924.

Farm'ers' Alli'ance, *n.* an informal name for various regional political organizations that farmers established in the 1880s and that led to the formation of the Peoples' Party in 1891–92.

farm'hand' or **farm' hand',** *n.* a person who works on a farm, esp. a hired worker; hired hand.

farm·house (färm'hous'), *n., pl.* **-hous·es** (-hou'ziz). a house on a farm, esp. the farmer's residence.

farm·land (färm'land'), *n.* land capable of being cultivated.

farm·stead (färm'sted'), *n.* a farm with its buildings.

farm' team', *n.* a team, esp. a baseball team, in a minor league that is owned by or affiliated with a major-league team, for training or keeping players until ready or needed. Also called **farm' club'.**

farm·yard (färm'yärd'), *n.* a yard or enclosure surrounded by or connected with farm buildings.

far·o (fâr'ō), *n.* a gambling game in which players bet on cards as they are drawn from a box by the dealer.

far' piece', *n. Chiefly Midland and Southern U.S.* a considerable distance: *They moved a far piece from here.*

far·rag·i·nous (fə raj'ə nəs), *adj.* heterogeneous; mixed.

far·ra·go (fə rä'gō, -rā'-), *n., pl.* **-goes.** a confused mixture; hodgepodge; medley.

Far·ra·gut (far'ə gət), *n.* **David Glasgow,** 1801–70, U.S. admiral for the Union in the U.S. Civil War.

far′-reach′ing, *adj.* extending far in influence, effect, etc.: *The effect of the speech was far-reaching.* —**far′-reach′ing•ly,** *adv.*

far•row¹ (far′ō), *n.* **1.** a litter of pigs. —*v.t.* **2.** (of swine) to bring forth (young). —*v.i.* **3.** to produce a litter of pigs.

far•row² (far′ō), *adj.* (of a cow) not pregnant.

far•see•ing (fär′sē′ing), *adj.* **1.** having foresight; sagacious; discerning. **2.** able to see objects distinctly at a great distance.

Far•si (fär′sē), *n.* MODERN PERSIAN.

far•sight•ed (fär′sī′tid, -sī′tid), *adj.* **1.** seeing objects at a distance more clearly than those near at hand; hyperopic. **2.** seeing to a great distance. **3.** wise, as in foreseeing future developments; prescient. —**far′sight′ed•ly,** *adv.* —**far′sight′ed•ness,** *n.*

far•ther (fär′t͟hər), *adv., compar. of* **far** *with* **farthest** *as superl.* **1.** at or to a greater distance: *to run farther down the road.* **2.** at or to a more advanced point: *to go no farther in one's studies.* **3.** at or to a greater degree or extent: *The application of the law was extended farther.* —*adj., compar. of* **far** *with* **farthest** *as superl.* **4.** more distant or remote than something or some place nearer: *the farther side of the mountain.* **5.** extending or tending to a greater distance: *He made a still farther trip.* —**Usage.** Although some usage guides advise that only FARTHER can be used for physical distance (*We walked farther than we planned*), FARTHER and FURTHER have been used interchangeably in this and other senses throughout much of their histories. However, only FURTHER can be used in the adverbial sense "moreover" (*Further, you hurt my feelings*) and in the adjectival senses "more extended" (*no further comment*) and "additional" (*Further bulletins came in*).
The expression ALL THE FARTHER (or FURTHER) occurs chiefly in informal speech: *This is all the farther the train goes.* See also ALL.

far•thest (fär′t͟hist), *adj., superl. of* **far** *with* **farther** *as compar.* **1.** most distant or remote. **2.** most extended; longest. —*adv., superl. of* **far** *with* **farther** *as compar.* **3.** at or to the greatest distance or most advanced point. **4.** at or to the greatest degree or extent.

fas•ci•a (fash′ē ə), *n., pl.* **fas•ci•ae** (fash′ē ē′). **1.** any relatively broad, flat horizontal surface on a building, as the outer edge of a cornice. **2. a.** a band or sheath of connective tissue covering, supporting, or connecting the muscles or internal organs of the body. **b.** tissue of this kind. **3.** *Zool., Bot.* a distinctly marked band of color. —**fas′ci•al,** *adj.*

fas•ci•ate (fash′ē āt′, -ē it) also **fas′ci•at′ed,** *adj.* **1.** bound with a band, fillet, or bandage. **2.** *Bot.* abnormally compressed into a band or bundle, as stems grown together. **3.** *Zool.* **a.** composed of bundles. **b.** bound together in a bundle. **c.** marked with a band or bands.

fas•ci•a•tion (fash′ē ā′shən), *n.* **1.** the act of binding up or bandaging. **2.** the process of becoming fasciate. **3.** the resulting state. **4.** an abnormality in a plant, in which a stem enlarges into a flat, ribbonlike shape resembling several stems fused together.

fas•ci•cle (fas′i kəl), *n.* **1.** a section of a book or set of books being published in installments as separate pamphlets or volumes. **2.** a small bundle, tight cluster, or the like. **3.** a close cluster, as of flowers or leaves. **4.** a small bundle of nerve or muscle fibers.

fas•ci•nate (fas′ə nāt′), *v.*, **-nat•ed, -nat•ing.** —*v.t.* **1.** to attract and hold attentively or immovably by a unique power or some unusual or special quality; enthrall; spellbind; transfix. **2.** to arouse the interest or curiosity of; allure: *Ancient Egypt has always fascinated me.* —*v.i.* **3.** to capture the interest or grip the attention.

fas•ci•na•tion (fas′ə nā′shən), *n.* **1.** the power or action of fascinating. **2.** the state or an instance of being fascinated: *They watched in fascination.* **3.** a fascinating quality; powerful attraction; charm: *the fascination of foreign travel.*

fas•cism (fash′iz əm), *n.* **1.** (*sometimes cap.*) a totalitarian governmental system led by a dictator and emphasizing an aggressive nationalism, militarism, and often racism. **2.** (*sometimes cap.*) the philosophy, principles, or methods of fascism. **3.** (*cap.*) a movement toward or embodying fascism, esp. the one established by Mussolini in Italy 1922–43. [< Italian *fascismo* = *fasc(io)* bundle, political group + *-ismo* -ISM]

fas•cist (fash′ist), *n.* **1.** (*sometimes cap.*) a person who believes in fascism. **2.** (*cap.*) a member of a fascist movement or party. **3.** a person who is dictatorial or has extreme right-wing views. —*adj.* **4.** (*sometimes cap.*) Also, **fa•scis•tic** (fə shis′tik). of or like fascism or Italian Fascism. —**fa•scis′ti•cal•ly,** *adv.*

fash•ion (fash′ən), *n.* **1.** a prevailing custom or style of dress, etiquette, socializing, etc.; mode: *the latest fashion in boots.* **2.** conventional usage in dress, manners, etc., esp. of polite society, or conformity to it: *to be out of fashion.* **3.** manner; way; mode: *in a warlike fashion.* **4.** the make or form of anything; shape; pattern. —*v.t.* **5.** to give a particular shape or form to; make; construct. **6.** to adjust; adapt; fit. —***Idiom.*** **7. after** or **in a fashion,** to some minimal extent; in a rather poor way. —**fash′ion•er,** *n.*

fash•ion•a•ble (fash′ə nə bəl), *adj.* **1.** observant of or conforming to the fashion; stylish; modish. **2.** of, characteristic of, used, or patronized by the world of fashion: *a fashionable shop.* **3.** current; popular. —*n.* **4.** a fashionable person. —**fash′ion•a•bly,** *adv.*

fash′ion plate′, *n.* **1.** a person who always wears the latest style in dress. **2.** an illustration showing the current or new fashion in clothes.

fast¹ (fast, fäst), *adj.* **1.** moving or able to move, operate, function, or take effect quickly; quick; swift; rapid: *a fast horse; a fast typist.* **2.** done in or taking comparatively little time: *a fast race; fast work.* **3.** adapted to, allowing, productive of, or imparting rapid movement: *a hull with fast lines.* **4.** able to understand or respond quickly: *a fast mind.* **5. a.** (of a timepiece) indicating a time in advance of the correct time. **b.** noting or according to daylight-saving time. **6.** characterized by extreme energy and activity, esp. in the pursuit of pleasure: *leading a fast life.* **7.** resistant (often used in combination): *acid-fast.* **8.** firmly fixed in place; secure. **9.** held or caught firmly: **10.** firmly tied, as a knot. **11.** closed and made secure, as a door, gate, or shutter. **12.** such as to have securely: *to lay fast hold on a thing.* **13.** firm in adherence; loyal; devoted: *fast friends.* **14.** permanent, lasting, or unchangeable: *a fast color.* **15. a.** (of money, profits, etc.) made quickly or easily and sometimes deviously. **b.** cleverly quick and manipulative in making money: *a fast operator.* **16.** *Photog.* **a.** (of a lens) able to transmit a relatively large amount of light in a relatively short time. **b.** (of a film) requiring a relatively short exposure to attain a given density. **17.** *Horse Racing.* **a.** (of a track condition) completely dry. **b.** (of a track surface) very hard. —*adv.* **18.** quickly, swiftly, or rapidly. **19.** in quick succession: *Events followed fast upon one another.* **20.** tightly; firmly: *to hold fast.* **21.** soundly: *fast asleep.* **22.** in a wild or dissipated way; recklessly. **23.** ahead of the correct or announced time. —*n.* **24.** a fastening for a door, window, or the like. —***Idiom.*** **25. pull a fast one,** to engage in unexpectedly unfair or deceitful behavior to achieve one's goal.

fast² (fast, fäst), *v.i.* **1.** to abstain from all food. **2.** to eat only sparingly or of certain kinds of food, esp. as a religious observance. —*n.* **3.** an abstinence from food, or a limiting of one's food, esp. when voluntary and as a religious observance. **4.** a day or period of fasting.

fast³ (fast, fäst), *n.* a chain or rope for mooring a vessel.

fast•back (fast′bak′, fäst′-), *n.* **1.** a form of back for an automobile body consisting of a single, unbroken convex curve from the top to the rear bumper. **2.** an automobile having such a back.

fast•ball (fast′bôl′, fäst′-), *n.* a baseball pitch thrown at or near a pitcher's maximum velocity.

fast′ break′, *n.* (esp. in basketball) a play in which a team that has just regained the ball attempts to score quickly before their opponents reach the other end of the playing area.

fas•ten (fas′ən, fä′sən), *v.t.* **1.** to attach firmly or securely in place; fix securely to something else. **2.** to make secure, as an article of dress with buttons, clasps, etc., or a door with a lock, bolt, etc. **3.** to attach, associate, or connect: *to fasten a nickname on someone.* **4.** to direct (the eyes, thoughts, etc.) intently. —*v.i.* **5.** to become fixed or firm. **6.** to close firmly or securely; lock: *This clasp won't fasten.* **7.** to take a firm hold; seize (usu. fol. by *on* or *upon*): *to fasten on an idea.* **8.** to focus attention; concentrate (usu. fol. by *on* or *upon*): *His gaze fastened on the jewels.*

fast′-for′ward, *v.i.* (on a recording device or projector) to advance a tape or film rapidly using a function of the device. —**fast′-for′ward,** *n.*

fas•tid•i•ous (fa stid′ē əs, fə-), *adj.* **1.** excessively particular, critical, or demanding; hard to please: *a fastidious eater.* **2.** characterized by excessive care or delicacy; painstaking: *fastidious attention to detail.* —**fas•tid′i•ous•ly,** *adv.* —**fas•tid′i•ous•ness,** *n.*

fast′ lane′, *n.* **1.** the lane of a multilane roadway that is used by fast-moving vehicles, as when passing slower traffic. **2.** any activity or pursuit that is excessively high-pressured, competitive, and sometimes dissipated or dangerous.

fast•ness (fast′nis, fäst′-), *n.* **1.** a secure or fortified place; stronghold: *a mountain fastness.* **2.** the state of being fixed or firm. **3.** the state of being rapid.

fast′-talk′, *v.t.* to persuade with clever or facile argument, usu. so as to deceive or take advantage of.

fast track (fast′ trak′, fäst′ *for 1;* trak′ *for 2, 3*), *n.* **1.** a racetrack dry and hard enough for optimum speed. **2.** a railroad track for express trains. **3.** a career track in which a person advances more rapidly than usual: *an executive on the fast track.* —**fast′-track′,** *adj., v.i., v.t.*

fat (fat), *n., adj.,* **fat•ter, fat•test,** *v.,* **fat•ted, fat•ting.** —*n.* **1.** any of several oily solids or semisolids that are water-insoluble esters of glycerol with fatty acids and are the chief component of animal adipose tissue and many plant seeds: used in cookery and in the manufacture of soaps and other products. **2.** animal tissue containing much of this substance. **3.** obesity; corpulence. **4.** the richest or best part of anything: *the fat of the land.* **5.** an overabundance or excess; superfluity or reserve: *a budget without fat.* —*adj.* **6.** having too much flabby tissue; corpulent; obese: *a fat person.* **7.** plump; well-fed: *a fat chicken.* **8.** consisting of or containing fat; greasy; oily: *fat meat.* **9.** profitable; lucrative: *a fat job in government.* **10.** affording good opportunities, esp. for gain: *a fat recording contract.* **11.** wealthy; prosperous; rich: *to grow fat on bribes and graft.* **12.** big, broad, or extended; thick: *a fat roll of fifty-dollar bills.* **13.** plentiful; abundant: *a fat supply of food.* **14.** plentifully supplied: *a fat larder.* **15.** dull; stupid. **16.** abounding in a particular element: *Fat pine is rich in resin.* **17.** (of paint) having more oil than pigment. Compare LEAN² (def. 6). **18.** fertile, as land; productive. —*v.t., v.i.* **19.** to make or become fat. —***Idiom.*** **20. fat chance,** a very slight chance; small probability. **21. the fat is in the fire,** something has been done or started that cannot be reversed and will probably have dramatic or serious consequences. —**fat′ness,** *n.*

fa•tal (fāt′l), *adj.* **1.** causing or capable of causing death; mortal; deadly. **2.** causing destruction, misfortune, or ruin; calamitous: *The closing of the plant was fatal to the town.* **3.** decisively important; fateful: *The fatal hour was near.* **4.** proceeding from fate; inevitable: *a fatal series of events.* **5.** pertaining to or concerned with fate; fatalistic: *a fatal warning.*

fa·tal·ism (fāt′l iz′əm), *n.* **1.** the acceptance of all things and events as inevitable; submission to fate. **2.** the doctrine that all events are subject to fate or inevitable predetermination. —**fa′tal·ist,** *n.* —**fa′tal·is′tic,** *adj.* —**fa′tal·is′ti·cal·ly,** *adv.*

fa·tal·i·ty (fā tal′i tē, fə-), *n., pl.* **-ties. 1.** a death caused by a disaster: *a rise in highway fatalities.* **2.** the quality of causing death or disaster; deadliness. **3.** predetermined liability to disaster, misfortune, etc. **4.** the quality of being predetermined by or subject to fate. **5.** the fate or destiny of a person or thing. **6.** a fixed, unalterably predetermined course of things; inevitability.

fa·tal·ly (fāt′l ē), *adv.* **1.** in a manner leading to death or disaster. **2.** by a decree of fate or destiny; by inevitable predetermination.

fat·back (fat′bak′), *n.* **1.** *Chiefly South Midland and Southern U.S.* the fat and fat meat from the upper part of a side of pork, usu. cured by salt. **2.** a menhaden. **3.** the bluefish, *Pomatomus saltatrix.* **4.** a mullet.

fat′ cat′, *n. Slang.* **1.** a wealthy person from whom large political campaign contributions are expected. **2.** any wealthy person, esp. one who has become rich quickly through questionable dealings. **3.** an important, influential, or famous person.

fat′ cell′, *n.* a cell in loose connective tissue that is specialized for the synthesis and storage of fat.

fate (fāt), *n., v.,* **fat·ed, fat·ing. —***n.* **1.** something that unavoidably befalls a person; fortune; lot. **2.** the universal principle or ultimate agency by which the order of things is presumably prescribed; the decreed cause of events; time. **3.** that which is inevitably predetermined; destiny. **4.** ultimate outcome; final course or state: *the fate of a political campaign.* **5.** death, destruction, or ruin. **6. the Fates,** the three goddesses of destiny in Greek and Roman myth. —*v.t.* **7.** to predetermine, as by the decree of fate; destine (used in the passive): *a person who was fated to lead the country.*

fat·ed (fā′tid), *adj.* subject to, guided by, or predetermined by fate; destined.

fate·ful (fāt′fəl), *adj.* **1.** having momentous significance or consequences; decisively important; portentous: *a fateful meeting.* **2.** fatal, deadly, or disastrous. **3.** controlled or determined by destiny; inexorable. **4.** prophetic; ominous. —**fate′ful·ly,** *adv.*

fat′head min′now, *n.* a North American cyprinid fish, *Pimephales promelas,* having an enlarged soft head.

fa·ther (fä′t͟hər), *n.* **1.** a male parent; the begetter of a child; sire. **2.** a father-in-law, stepfather, or adoptive father. **3.** any male ancestor; forefather; progenitor. **4.** a man who gives paternal care to others; protector or provider. **5.** a person who has originated or established something. **6.** a precursor, prototype, or early form. **7.** one of the leading men in a city, town, etc. **8.** a priest or a title for a priest. **9.** (*cap.*) God, esp. the first person of the Trinity. **10.** a title of respect for an elderly man. —*v.t.* **11.** to beget. **12.** to be the creator, founder, or author of; originate. **13.** to act as a father toward. **14.** to take the responsibility for. **15.** to establish the paternity or source of. —*v.i.* **16.** to perform the tasks or duties of a male parent; act paternally. —**fa′ther·like′,** *adj.*

Fa′ther Christ′mas, *n. Brit.* SANTA CLAUS.

fa′ther fig′ure, *n.* a man who has or seems to have the qualities of an ideal male parent, inspiring in others the feelings, attitudes, and behavior typical of a child toward its father.

fa·ther·land (fä′t͟hər land′), *n.* **1.** one's native country. **2.** the land of one's ancestors.

Fa′ther of his Coun′try, *n.* epithet of George Washington.

Fa′ther of the Constitu′tion, *n.* one who attended the constitutional convention at Philadelphia in 1787, esp. James Madison.

Fa′ther's Day′, *n.* a day set aside in honor of fathers.

Fa′ther Time′, *n.* the personification of time as an old man, usu. having a white beard and carrying a scythe and an hourglass.

fath·om (fat͟h′əm), *n., pl.* **fath·oms,** (*esp. collectively*) **fath·om,** *n.* **1.** a nautical unit of length equal to 6 feet (1.8 m). *Abbr.:* f., fath, fm —*v.t.* **2.** to measure the depth of by means of a sounding line; sound. **3.** to penetrate to the truth of; comprehend; understand: *to fathom someone's motives.* —**fath′om·a·ble,** *adj.* —**fath′om·less,** *adj.*

fa·tigue (fə tēg′), *n., adj., v.,* **-tigued, -ti·guing. —***n.* **1.** weariness from bodily or mental exertion. **2.** a cause of weariness; labor; exertion. **3.** temporary diminution of the irritability or functioning of organs, tissues, or cells after excessive exertion or stimulation. **4.** the weakening or breakdown of material subjected to stress, esp. a repeated series of stresses: *metal fatigue.* **5.** Also called **fatigue′ du′ty. a.** nonmilitary labor by military personnel, as digging drainage ditches or raking leaves. **b.** the state of being engaged in such labor: *on fatigue.* **6. fatigues.** Also called **fatigue′ clothes′.** the military clothing worn for fatigue duty or field activity. —*adj.* **7.** of or pertaining to fatigues or clothing made to resemble them. —*v.t.* **8.** to weary with bodily or mental exertion; exhaust; enervate. —*v.i.* **9.** to become fatigued. —**fa·ti′guing·ly,** *adv.*

fat′ lip′, *n.* a swollen mouth or lip, as from a blow.

Fat′ Man′, *n.* the code name for the plutonium-core, implosion-type atom bomb the U.S. first tested and then dropped on Nagasaki in 1945. Compare LITTLE BOY.

fat′-sol′u·ble, *adj.* soluble in oils or fats.

fat·ten (fat′n), *v.t.* **1.** to make fat. **2.** to feed (animals) abundantly before slaughter. **3.** to enrich. —*v.i.* **4.** to grow fat. —**fat′ten·a·ble,** *adj.* —**fat′ten·er,** *n.*

fat·ty (fat′ē), *adj.,* **-ti·er, -ti·est. 1.** consisting of, containing, or resembling fat: *fatty tissue.* **2.** characterized by excessive accumulation of fat.

fat′ty ac′id, *n.* any of a class of aliphatic acids, esp. palmitic, stearic, or oleic acid, consisting of a long hydrocarbon chain ending in a carboxyl group that bonds to glycerol to form a fat.

fat·u·ous (fach′oo əs), *adj.* foolish or inane, esp. in an unconscious, complacent manner; silly. —**fat′u·ous·ly,** *adv.* —**fat′u·ous·ness,** *n.*

fau·ces (fô′sēz), *n., pl.* **-ces.** the cavity at the back of the mouth, leading into the pharynx. —**fau·cial** (fô′shəl), *adj.*

fau·cet (fô′sit), *n.* any device for controlling the flow of liquid from a pipe or the like by opening or closing an orifice; tap; cock.

Faulk·ner (fôk′nər), *n.* **William,** 1897–1962, U.S. novelist.

fault (fôlt), *n.* **1.** a defect or imperfection; failing. **2.** responsibility for failure or a wrongful act. **3.** an error or mistake. **4.** a misdeed or transgression. **5.** (in tennis, handball, etc.) **a.** a ball that when served does not land in the proper section of an opponent's court. **b.** a failure to serve the ball according to the rules, as from within a certain area. **6.** a break in the continuity of a body of rock or of a vein, with dislocation along the plane of the fracture. **7.** (of a horse jumping in a show) any of a number of improper executions in negotiating a jump, as a knockdown or refusal. —*v.i.* **8.** to commit a fault; blunder; err. —*v.t.* **9.** to accuse of error, misdeed, etc.; criticize, blame, or censure. —*Idiom.* **10. at fault, a.** open to censure; blameworthy: *at fault for lying.* **b.** in a dilemma; puzzled. **c.** (of hounds) unable to find the scent. **11. find fault,** to complain or be critical. **12. to a fault,** to an extreme degree; excessively: *generous to a fault.*

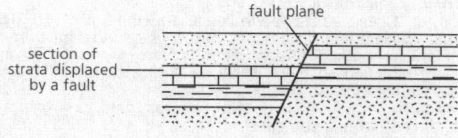

fault (def. 6)

fault·find·er (fôlt′fīn′dər), *n.* a person who habitually finds fault or criticizes, esp. in a petty way. —**fault′find′ing,** *n., adj.*

fault′ line′, *n.* the intersection of a geologic fault with the surface of the earth or other plane of reference.

fault·y (fôl′tē), *adj.,* **fault·i·er, fault·i·est.** having faults or defects; imperfect. —**fault′i·ly,** *adv.* —**fault′i·ness,** *n.*

faun (fôn), *n.* any of a class of ancient Roman deities of the countryside, identified with the satyrs of Greek myth. —**faun′like′,** *adj.*

fau·na (fô′nə), *n., pl.* **-nas, -nae** (-nē). **1.** (*used with a sing. or pl. v.*) the animals of a given region or period considered as a whole. **2.** a list of the animals of a given region or period. —**fau′nal,** *adj.*

Fau·ré (fô rā′, fō-), *n.* **Gabriel Urbain,** 1845–1924, French composer.

Faust (foust) also **Faus·tus** (fou′stəs, fô′-), *n.* **1.** a magician in medieval German legend who sold his soul to the devil in exchange for knowledge and power. **2.** (*italics*) a tragedy by Johann Wolfgang von Goethe (Part 1, 1808; Part 2, 1832).

Faus·ti·an (fou′stē ən), *adj.* **1.** of, pertaining to, or typical of Faust. **2.** sacrificing spiritual values for power, knowledge, or material gain.

Fauve (fōv), *n.* (*sometimes l.c.*) any of a group of French artists of the early 20th century whose works are characterized chiefly by the use of vivid colors in immediate juxtaposition and contours usu. in marked contrast to the color of the area defined. —**Fauv′ism,** *n.* —**Fauv′ist,** *n.*

faux (fō), *adj.* artificial or imitation; fake: *faux pearls.*

faux pas (fō pä′), *n., pl.* **faux pas** (fō päz′). a slip or blunder in etiquette, manners, or conduct; an embarrassing social error or indiscretion. [< French]

fa′va bean′, (fä′və), *n.* **1.** a bean, *Vicia faba,* of the Old World, bearing large pods containing edible seeds. **2.** the seed or pod of this plant. Also called **broad bean, horse bean.**

fa·vor (fā′vər), *n.* **1.** something done or granted out of goodwill, rather than from justice or for payment; a kind act. **2.** friendly or well-disposed regard; goodwill: *to win someone's favor.* **3.** popularity: *an athlete who enjoys great favor among the fans.* **4.** preferential treatment; partiality. **5.** a gift bestowed as a token of regard, love, etc., as formerly upon a knight by his lady. **6.** a ribbon, badge, etc., worn in evidence of goodwill or loyalty. **7.** a small gift or decorative item, as a noisemaker or paper hat, often distributed to guests at a party. —*v.t.* **8.** to regard with favor; approve; sanction. **9.** to prefer; treat with partiality. **10.** to show favor to; oblige; encourage: *Will you favor us with a reply?* **11.** to be favorable to; facilitate: *The wind favored their journey.* **12.** to treat or use gently: *to favor a sore wrist.* **13.** to aid or support: *They favored the party's cause with ample funds.* **14.** to bear a physical resemblance to: *to favor one's mother's family.* —*Idiom.* **15. find favor with,** to gain the approval of; be liked by. **16. in favor,** popular; widely accepted or enjoyed: *styles that are now in favor.* **17. in favor of, a.** on the side of; in support of. **b.** to the advantage of. **c.** (of a check, draft, etc.) payable to. **18. in one's favor,** to one's credit or advantage. **19. out of favor,** no longer liked or approved of. Also, *esp. Brit.,* **favour.**

F

fa•vor•a•ble (fā′vər ə bəl, fāv′rə-), *adj.* **1.** characterized by approval or support; positive: *a favorable report.* **2.** winning favor; pleasing: *a favorable impression.* **3.** affording advantage, opportunity, or convenience; advantageous: *a favorable position.* **4.** (of an answer) granting what is desired. **5.** boding well; propitious. —**fa′vor•a•bly,** *adv.*

fa•vored (fā′vərd), *adj.* **1.** regarded or treated with preference or partiality: *the favored child.* **2.** enjoying special advantages; privileged: *the favored classes.* **3.** of specified appearance (usu. used in combination): *ill-favored.*

fa•vor•ite (fā′vər it, fāv′rit), *n.* **1.** a person or thing regarded with special preference, pleasure, or approval. **2.** a competitor or contestant considered likely to win. **3.** a person treated with special or undue favor by a king, official, etc.: *favorites at the court.* —*adj.* **4.** regarded with particular favor or preference: *my favorite movie star.*

fa′vorite son′, *n.* **1.** a person nominated as a presidential candidate at a national political convention by the delegates from his or her home state. **2.** an eminent, successful man who is highly regarded in his hometown or state.

fa•vor•it•ism (fā′vər i tiz′əm, fāv′ri-), *n.* **1.** the favoring of one person or group over others with equal claims; partiality: *to show favoritism toward one's oldest child.* **2.** the state of being a favorite.

fawn[1] (fôn), *n.* **1.** a young deer, esp. an unweaned one. **2.** a light yellowish brown color. —*adj.* **3.** light yellowish brown. —*v.i.* **4.** (of a doe) to bring forth young. —**fawn′like′,** *adj.*

fawn[2] (fôn), *v.i.* **1.** to seek notice or favor by servile behavior; toady: *courtiers fawning over the king.* **2.** (esp. of a dog) to behave affectionately. —**fawn′er,** *n.* —**fawn′ing•ly,** *adv.*

fawn′ lil′y, *n.* DOGTOOTH VIOLET.

fax (faks), *n.* **1.** Also called **facsimile. a.** a method or device (**fax′ ma-chine′**) for transmitting documents, drawings, photographs, or the like by telephone or radio for exact reproduction elsewhere. **b.** an exact copy or reproduction so transmitted. —*v.t.* **2.** to transmit (documents, drawings, photographs, or the like) by fax.

fax′ mo′dem, *n.* a modem that can fax data, as documents or pictures, directly from a computer.

fay (fā), *n.* FAIRY (def. 1).

faze (fāz), *v.t.,* **fazed, faz•ing.** to cause to be disturbed or disconcerted; daunt; fluster.

FBI, Federal Bureau of Investigation: a bureau in the U.S. Department of Justice charged with conducting investigations for the Attorney General and with safeguarding national security.

FCC, Federal Communications Commission.

F clef, *n.* BASS CLEF.

FDA, Food and Drug Administration.

FDIC, Federal Deposit Insurance Corporation.

FDR, Franklin Delano Roosevelt.

Fe, *Chem. Symbol.* iron.

fe•al•ty (fē′əl tē), *n., pl.* **-ties. 1. a.** the fidelity of a feudal vassal to his lord or the pledge of such fidelity. **b.** a vassal's obligation to be faithful to his lord. **2.** fidelity; faithfulness; loyalty.

fear (fēr), *n.* **1.** a distressing emotion aroused by impending danger, evil, pain, etc., whether the threat is real or imagined; the feeling or condition of being afraid. **2.** a specific instance of or propensity for such a feeling: *a fear of heights.* **3.** concern or anxiety; solicitude: *a fear for someone's safety.* **4.** reverential awe, esp. toward God. **5.** something that causes fright or apprehension. —*v.t.* **6.** to regard with fear; be afraid of; dread: *to fear flying.* **7.** to be worried or afraid: *I fear that I'm going to fail the test.* **8.** to have reverential awe of. —*v.i.* **9.** to have fear; be afraid. —*Saying.* **10. The only thing we have to fear is fear itself,** being afraid can so immobilize you that you can't move to solve the very problems that are causing your fear: from Franklin D. Roosevelt's First Inaugural Address, March 4, 1933.

Fear (fēr), *n.* **1.** a river in SE North Carolina. 202 mi. (325 km) long. **2. Cape,** a cape at its mouth.

fear•ful (fēr′fəl), *adj.* **1.** causing or apt to cause fear; frightening: *a fearful blizzard.* **2.** feeling fear, dread, apprehension, or solicitude; apprehensive; anxious. **3.** full of awe. **4.** showing or caused by fear: *fearful behavior.* **5.** extreme in size, intensity, or badness: *fearful poverty.* —**fear′ful•ly,** *adv.* —**fear′ful•ness,** *n.*

fear•some (fēr′səm), *adj.* **1.** causing fear. **2.** afraid; timid: *a tiny, fearsome mouse.* **3.** inspiring awe or respect: *a fearsome intelligence.* —**fear′some•ly,** *adv.* —**fear′some•ness,** *n.*

fea•sance (fē′zəns), *n. Law.* the performance of some act, esp. a job or other duty.

fea•si•ble (fē′zə bəl), *adj.* **1.** capable of being done or accomplished: *a feasible plan.* **2.** probable; likely: *a feasible theory.* **3.** suitable: *a road feasible for travel.* —**fea′si•bil′i•ty,** *n.* —**fea′si•bly,** *adv.*

feast (fēst), *n.* **1.** any rich or abundant meal. **2.** a sumptuous entertainment or meal for many guests: *a wedding feast.* **3.** something highly agreeable or satisfying. **4.** a periodical celebration or time of celebration, usu. of a religious nature, commemorating an event, person, etc. —*v.i.* **5.** to partake of a feast; eat sumptuously. **6.** to dwell with gratification or delight, as on a picture or view. —*v.t.* **7.** to provide or entertain with a feast. —*Idiom.* **8. feast one's eyes,** to gaze with great joy, admiration, or relish. —*Proverb.* **9. After the feast comes the reckoning,** excessive pleasure exacts a toll.

Feast′ of Booths′, *n.* SUKKOTH.

Feast′ of Dedica′tion, *n.* HANUKKAH. Also called **Feast′ of Lights′.**

Feast′ of Lots′, *n.* PURIM.

Feast′ of Tab′ernacles, *n.* SUKKOTH.

Feast′ of Weeks′, *n.* SHAVUOTH.

feat (fēt), *n.* a noteworthy or extraordinary act or achievement, usu. displaying boldness, skill, etc.: *an athletic feat; a feat of heroism.*

feath•er (feth′ər), *n.* **1.** one of the horny epidermal structures that form the principal covering of birds, consisting of a hollow shaft bearing a series of slender barbs that interlock to form a flat surface on each side. **2.** kind; character; nature: *two boys of the same feather.* **3.** condition, as of health, spirits, etc.: *to be in fine feather after a vacation.* **4.** something like a feather, as a tuft or fringe of hair. **5.** something very light, small, or trivial. **6.** one of the vanes at the tail of an arrow or dart, for stabilization in flight. **7.** a spline for joining the grooved edges of two boards. **8.** a featherlike flaw, esp. in a precious stone. —*v.t.* **9.** to provide with feathers, as an arrow. **10.** to clothe or cover with or as if with feathers. **11.** to turn (an oar) after a stroke so that the blade becomes nearly horizontal, and hold it thus as it is moved back into position for the next stroke. **12. a.** to change the blade angle of (a propeller) so that the chords of the blades are approximately parallel to the line of flight. **b.** to turn off (an aircraft engine) while in flight. —*v.i.* **13.** to grow feathers. **14.** to be or become feathery in appearance. **15.** to feather an oar. —*Idiom.* **16. a feather in one's cap,** a praiseworthy achievement; honor. **17. feather one's nest,** to enrich oneself by exploiting one's favorable or privileged position.

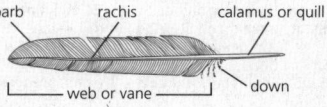

feather (def. 1)

feath′er bed′, *n.* a mattress or a bed cover, as a quilt, stuffed with soft feathers.

feath•er•bed•ding (feth′ər bed′ing), *n.* the practice by some unions of requiring an employer to hire more employees than are necessary or to limit production according to a union rule or a safety statute. —**feath′er•bed′,** *v.i., v.t.,* **-bed•ded, -bed•ding.**

feath•er•cut (feth′ər kut′), *n.* a woman's hairstyle in which the hair is cut short in layers and softly curled in a feathery effect.

feath•ered (feth′ərd), *adj.* covered, provided, or marked with or as if with feathers.

feath•er•ing (feth′ər ing), *n.* **1.** a covering of feathers; plumage. **2.** the arrangement of feathers on an arrow. **3.** a long fringe of hair, as on the legs, chest, or tail of a dog or the legs of a horse; feather.

feath•er•weight (feth′ər wāt′), *n.* **1.** any person or thing that is very light in weight. **2.** a boxer or weightlifter intermediate in weight between a bantamweight and a lightweight, esp. a professional boxer weighing up to 126 lb. (57 kg). **3.** an insignificant, shallow, or unintelligent person. —*adj.* **4.** belonging to the class of featherweights, esp. in boxing. **5.** extremely light in weight. **6.** unimportant; trifling; slight.

feath•er•y (feth′ə rē), *adj.* **1.** clothed or covered with feathers; feathered. **2.** resembling feathers; light; airy; unsubstantial.

fea•ture (fē′chər), *n., v.,* **-tured, -tur•ing.** —*n.* **1.** a prominent or conspicuous part or characteristic: *The best feature of the house is the sun porch.* **2.** something offered as a special or main attraction. **3.** Also called **fea′ture film′.** the main motion picture in a movie program. **4.** any part of the face, as the nose, chin, or eyes. **5. features,** the face; countenance. **6.** the form or cast of the face: *delicate of feature.* **7.** a column, cartoon, etc., appearing regularly in a newspaper or magazine. **8.** FEATURE STORY. —*v.t.* **9.** to make a feature of; give prominence to: *The magazine featured a story on the elections.* **10.** to have or present (a performer) in a lead role or a prominent supporting role. **11.** to be a feature or distinctive mark of. **12.** to delineate the main characteristics of; depict. **13.** *Informal.* to conceive of; imagine; fancy. —*v.i.* **14.** to play a major part. —*adj.* **15.** being or offered as a highlight; featured: *the feature attraction at the fair.* —**fea′ture•less,** *adj.*

fea•tured (fē′chərd), *adj.* **1.** made a feature or highlight; given prominence: *a featured actor.* **2.** having features or a certain kind of features (usu. used in combination): *a well-featured face.*

fea′ture-length′, *adj.* (of a motion picture, magazine story, etc.) long enough to serve as a feature; full-length.

fea′ture sto′ry, *n.* **1.** an article concerning a person, event, etc., usu. written with a personal slant. **2.** the most prominent story in a magazine, usu. the cover story.

febri-, a combining form meaning "fever": *febrific.*

fe•brile (fē′brəl, feb′rəl; *esp. Brit.* fē′brīl), *adj.* pertaining to or marked by fever; feverish. —**fe•bril•i•ty** (fi bril′i tē), *n.*

Feb•ru•ar•y (feb′rōō er′ē, feb′yōō-), *n., pl.* **-ar•ies.** the second month of the year, ordinarily containing 28 days, but containing 29 days in leap years. *Abbr.:* Feb. —*Pronunciation.* The second pronunciation shown above, with the first (r) replaced by (y), results both from dissimilation, the tendency of like sounds to become unlike when they follow each other closely, and from analogy with *January.* Although sometimes criticized, this dissimilated pronunciation of FEBRUARY is used by educated speakers and both (feb′ro͞o er′ē) and (feb′yo͞o er′ē) are considered standard.

fe•cal (fē′kəl), *adj.* of, pertaining to, or consisting of feces.

fe•ces (fē′sēz), *n.* (*used with a pl. v.*) waste matter discharged from the intestines through the anus; excrement.

feck•less (fek′lis), *adj.* **1.** ineffective; incompetent; futile. **2.** having no sense of responsibility; indifferent; lazy. —**feck′less•ly,** *adv.* —**feck′less•ness,** *n.*

fec•u•lent (fek′yə lənt), *adj.* full of dregs or fecal matter; foul, turbid, or muddy. —**fec′u•lence,** *n.*

fe•cund (fē′kund, -kənd, fek′und, -ənd), *adj.* **1.** producing or capable of producing offspring, fruit, vegetation, etc., in abundance; prolific. **2.** very productive or creative intellectually: *the fecund years of the Italian Renaissance.* —**fe•cun•di•ty** (fi kun′di tē), *n.*

fe•cun•date (fē′kən dāt′, fek′ən-), *v.t.*, **-dat•ed, -dat•ing. 1.** to make prolific or fruitful. **2.** to impregnate or fertilize. —**fe′cun•da′tion,** *n.*

fed (fed), *v.* **1.** pt. and pp. of FEED. —***Idiom.* 2. fed up,** impatient; disgusted; bored.

Fed (fed), *n.* **the Fed,** *Informal.* **1.** the Federal Reserve System. **2.** the Federal Reserve Board.

fed•er•a•cy (fed′ər ə sē), *n.*, *pl.* **-cies.** a confederacy.

fed•er•al (fed′ər əl), *adj.* **1.** pertaining to or of the nature of a union of states under a central government distinct from the individual governments of the separate states: *the federal government of the U.S.* **2.** of, pertaining to, or involving such a central government: *federal laws; federal troops.* **3.** (*cap.*) **a.** of, pertaining to, or supporting the Federalist Party or Federalism. **b.** pertaining to or supporting the Union government in the Civil War. **4.** of or pertaining to a compact or a league, esp. a league between nations or states. —*n.* **5.** an advocate of federation or federalism. **6.** (*cap.*) **a.** a federalist. **b.** a supporter of the Union, or a Union soldier in the Civil War.

Fed′eral Bu′reau of Investiga′tion, *n.* See FBI.

Fed′eral Communica′tions Commis′sion, *n.* a U.S. government agency charged with regulating interstate and foreign communications by radio, television, wire, and cable. *Abbr.:* FCC

Fed′eral Depos′it Insur′ance Corpora′tion, *n.* a public corporation that insures, up to a specified amount, all demand deposits of member banks. *Abbr.:* FDIC

Fed′eral Dis′trict, *n.* a district in which the national government of a country is located, esp. one in Latin America.

fed•er•al•ism (fed′ər ə liz′əm), *n.* **1. a.** the federal principle of government. **b.** advocacy of this principle. **2.** (*cap.*) the principles of the Federalist Party.

fed•er•al•ist (fed′ər ə list), *n.* **1.** an advocate of federalism. **2.** (*cap.*)a member or supporter of the Federalist party. **3.** (*italics*) a series of 85 essays (1787–88) by Alexander Hamilton, James Madison, and John Jay, written in support of the Constitution. —*adj.* **4.** Also, **fed′er•al•is′tic.** of federalism or the Federalists.

Fed′eralist (or **Fed′eral**) **Par′ty,** *n.* **1.** a political group that favored the adoption by the states of the Constitution. **2.** a political party in early U.S. history advocating a strong central government.

fed•er•al•ize (fed′ər ə līz′), *v.t.*, **-ized, -iz•ing. 1.** to bring under the control of a federal government. **2.** to bring together in a federal union, as different states. —**fed′er•al•i•za′tion,** *n.*

Fed′eral Land′ Bank′, *n.* a U.S. federal bank for making long-term loans to farmers.

Fed′eral Na′tional Mort′gage Associa′tion, *n.* a U.S. government-sponsored private corporation whose chief function is to supply funds for home mortgages through continuous purchases of mortgages from lending institutions. *Abbr.:* FNMA

Fed′eral Pow′er Commis′sion, *n.* FPC.

Fed′eral Reg′ister, *n.* a bulletin, published daily by the U.S. federal government, containing the schedule of hearings before Congressional and federal agency committees, together with orders, proclamations, etc., released by the executive branch of the government.

Fed′eral Repub′lic of Ger′many, *n.* official name of GERMANY.

Fed′eral Reserve′ note′, *n.* a form of paper money issued by a Federal Reserve Bank.

Fed′eral Reserve′ Sys′tem, *n.* a U.S. federal banking system that is under the control of a central board of governors **(Fed′eral Reserve′ Board′)** with a central bank **(Fed′eral Reserve′ Bank′)** in each of 12 districts and that has wide powers in controlling credit and the flow of money as well as in performing other functions, as regulating and supervising its member banks.

Fed′eral Sav′ings and Loan′ Insur′ance Corpora′tion, *n.* a public corporation, established in 1934, that insures, up to a specified amount, all deposits in member savings and loan associations. *Abbr.:* FSLIC

Fed′eral Trade′ Commis′sion, *n.* a U.S. government agency charged with investigating and enjoining illegal practices in interstate trade. *Abbr.:* FTC

fed•er•ate (*v.* fed′ə rāt′; *adj.* -ər it), *v.*, **-at•ed, -at•ing,** *adj.* —*v.t., v.i.* **1.** to unite in a federation. **2.** to organize on a federal basis. —*adj.* **3.** federated; allied. —**fed′er•a′tor,** *n.*

fed•er•a•tion (fed′ə rā′shən), *n.* **1.** the act of federating or uniting in a league. **2.** the formation of a political unity, with a central government, by a number of separate states, each of which retains control of its own internal affairs. **3.** a league or confederacy.

fe•do•ra (fi dôr′ə, -dōr′ə), *n.*, *pl.* **-ras.** a soft felt hat with a curved brim, worn with the crown creased lengthwise.

fee (fē), *n.*, *v.*, **feed, fee•ing.** —*n.* **1.** a sum charged or paid, as for professional services or for a privilege: *a doctor's fee; an admission fee.* **2.** *Law.* **a.** an estate of inheritance, either without limitation to a particular class of heirs or limited to one particular class of heirs. **b.** (in the Middle Ages) estate lands held of a feudal lord in return for services performed. **c.** a territory held in fee. —*v.t.* **3.** to give a gratuity to; tip. —***Idiom.* 4. in fee,** in full ownership: *an estate held in fee.*

fee•ble (fē′bəl), *adj.*, **-bler, -blest. 1.** physically weak; frail. **2.** weak intellectually or morally: *a feeble mind.* **3.** lacking in volume, brightness, distinctness, etc.: *feeble light.* **4.** lacking in substance or effectiveness: *feeble arguments.* —**fee′ble•ness,** *n.*

fee′ble-mind′ed, *adj.* **1.** lacking the normal mental powers. **2.** stupid; unintelligent: *feeble-minded remarks.* —**fee′ble-mind′ed•ly,** *adv.* —**fee′ble-mind′ed•ness,** *n.*

feed (fēd), *v.*, **fed, feed•ing,** *n.* —*v.t.* **1.** to give food to; supply with nourishment. **2.** to yield or serve as food for: *This land has fed ten generations.* **3.** to provide as food: *to feed breadcrumbs to pigeons.* **4.** to furnish for consumption. **5.** to satisfy; minister to; gratify. **6.** to supply, as for maintenance or operation: *to feed paper into a photocopier; to feed a printing press with paper.* **7.** to flow into or merge with so as to form or sustain: *streams that feed a river.* **8. a.** to provide lines, cues, or actions to (a performer). **b.** to supply (lines, cues, or actions) to a performer. **9.** to distribute (a local radio or television broadcast) via satellite or network. —*v.i.* **10.** (esp. of animals) to take food; eat. **11.** to be nourished or gratified; subsist: *to feed on fruit.* **12.** to flow, lead, or provide access: *The local roads feed into a state highway.* —*n.* **13.** food, esp. for farm animals. **14.** an allowance, portion, or supply of such food. **15.** a meal, esp. a lavish one. **16.** the act or process of feeding a furnace, machine, etc. **17.** the material, or the amount of it, so fed. **18.** a feeding mechanism. **19.** a local radio or television broadcast distributed by satellite or network to a much wider audience, esp. nationwide or international. —***Idiom.* 20. off one's feed,** *Slang.* without any appetite for food, esp. because of illness.

feed•back (fēd′bak′), *n.* **1.** the return of part of the output of a circuit, system, or device to the input, either purposely or unintentionally, as in the reflux of sound from a loudspeaker to a microphone in a public-address system. **2.** the furnishing of data concerning the operation or output of a machine to an automatic control device or to the machine itself, for monitoring or regulating operations. **3.** a reaction or response to a particular process or activity: *to get feedback from a speech.* **4.** information derived from such a reaction or response: *to use the feedback from an audience survey.* **5.** a self-regulatory biological system, as in the synthesis of some hormones, in which the output or response affects the input, either positively or negatively.

feed′ bag′ or **feed′bag′,** *n.* a bag for feeding horses, placed before the mouth and fastened around the head with straps.

feed•er (fē′dər), *n.* **1.** a person or thing that supplies food or feeds something. **2.** a bin or boxlike device from which farm animals may eat, esp. such a device allowing a number of chickens to feed simultaneously. **3.** a person or thing that takes food or nourishment. **4.** a person or device that feeds a machine. **5.** a tributary stream. **6. a.** a secondary road that feeds traffic to a major road. **b.** a branch of a main transportation line, as of railroad. **7.** an electric conductor, or group of conductors connecting primary equipment. **8.** STRAIGHT MAN.

feed′ing fren′zy, *n.* *Slang.* a ruthless attack on or exploitation of someone esp. by the media.

feed′lot′ or **feed′ lot′,** *n.* an area or establishment near a stockyard, where livestock are gathered to be fattened for market. Also called **feed′yard′.**

feel (fēl), *v.*, **felt, feel•ing,** *n.* —*v.t.* **1.** to perceive (something) by direct physical contact: *to feel the softness of fur; to feel a breeze.* **2.** to examine by touch: *to feel someone's forehead.* **3.** to have a physical sensation of: *to feel hunger.* **4.** to find or pursue (one's way) by touching, groping, or cautious moves. **5.** to be or become conscious of: *to feel pride.* **6.** to be emotionally affected by: *to feel profound grief.* **7.** to experience the effects of: *The whole region felt the storm.* **8.** to have a particular sensation or impression of (often used reflexively and usu. fol. by an adjunct or complement): *to feel oneself slighted; to feel hostility all around.* **9.** to have a general or thorough conviction of; think; believe: *I feel he's guilty.* —*v.i.* **10.** to have perception by touch or by any physical sensation other than those of sight, hearing, taste, and smell. **11.** to make examination by touch; grope: *She felt in her purse for a dime.* **12.** to perceive a state of mind or a condition of body: *to feel happy; to feel well.* **13.** to have a sensation of being: *to feel warm.* **14.** to make itself perceived or apparent; seem: *The ground feels icy underfoot.* **15. feel for,** to feel sympathy for or compassion toward; empathize with. **16. feel out,** to try to determine the mood or status of (a person or situation) by discreet, usu. informal or unofficial inquiries. —*n.* **17.** a quality of an object that is perceived by feeling or touching: *the feel of wool.* **18.** a sensation of something felt; vague mental impression or feeling: *a feel of sadness in the air.* **19.** the sense of touch: *soft to the feel.* **20.** native ability or acquired sensitivity: *to have a feel for teaching.* **21.** an act or instance of touching with the hand or fingers. —***Idiom.* 22. feel like,** to have a desire for; be favorably disposed toward. **23. feel (like) one-**

self, to be in one's normal healthy and happy state. **24. feel up to,** to feel able to, esp. to feel strong or healthy enough to.

feel•er (fē′lər), *n.* **1.** a person or thing that feels. **2.** a proposal, remark, hint, etc., designed to bring out the opinions or purposes of others. **3.** an organ of touch, as an antenna or a tentacle.

feel•ing (fē′ling), *n.* **1.** the function or the power of perceiving by touch or by any physical sensation not connected with sight, hearing, taste, or smell. **2.** a particular sensation of this kind: *a feeling of warmth.* **3.** the general state of consciousness considered independently of particular sensations, thoughts, etc. **4.** a consciousness or vague awareness: *a feeling of inferiority.* **5.** an emotion or emotional perception or attitude: *a feeling of joy.* **6.** capacity for emotion, esp. compassion. **7.** a sentiment; attitude; opinion: *The general feeling was in favor of the proposal.* **8. feelings,** sensibilities; susceptibilities: *to hurt one's feelings.* **9.** fine emotional endowment. **10. a.** emotion or sympathetic perception revealed by an artist in his or her work: *a poem without feeling.* **b.** the general impression conveyed by a work: *a painting with a romantic feeling.* **c.** sympathetic appreciation, as of music: *to play with feeling.* **—***adj.* **11.** sensitive; sentient. **12.** readily affected by emotion; sympathetic: *a feeling heart.* **13.** indicating or characterized by emotion: *a feeling reply to the charge.* —**feel′ing•ly,** *adv.* —**feel′ing•ness,** *n.*

feet (fēt), *n.* **1.** a pl. of FOOT. **—*Idiom.* 2. drag one's feet,** to act or proceed slowly or reluctantly. **3. get one's feet wet,** to take the first step in an activity, venture, etc. **4. have one's feet on the ground,** to have a realistic, sensible attitude or approach. **5. on one's feet, a.** in a standing position. **b.** in a secure, independent position or recovered state. **6. sit at the feet of,** to attend upon as a disciple or follower. **7. stand on one's own (two) feet, a.** to be financially self-supporting. **b.** to be independent. **8. sweep off one's feet,** to impress or overwhelm by ability, enthusiasm, or charm. **9. vote with one's feet,** to express dissatisfaction or discontent by leaving, esp. by fleeing a country.

feet•first (fēt′fûrst′), *adv.* with the feet foremost.

feet′ of clay′, *n.* **1.** a weakness or hidden flaw in the character of a greatly admired or respected person: *He was disillusioned to find that even Lincoln had feet of clay.* **2.** any unexpected or critical fault.

feign (fān), *v.t.* **1.** to represent fictitiously; put on an appearance of: *to feign sickness.* **2.** to invent fictitiously or deceptively, as a story or an excuse. **3.** to imitate deceptively: *to feign another's voice.* **—***v.i.* **4.** to make believe; pretend: *He is only feigning.*

feint (fānt), *n.* **1.** a movement made in order to deceive an adversary; an attack aimed at one place or point to distract from the real target. **2.** a feigned or assumed appearance. **—***v.i.* **3.** to make a feint: *The boxer feinted with his left.* **—***v.t.* **4.** to make a feint at; deceive with a feint. **5.** to make a false show of; simulate.

feist•y (fī′stē), *adj.,* **feist•i•er, feist•i•est. 1.** full of animation, energy, or courage; spirited; spunky; plucky. **2.** ill-tempered; pugnacious. —**feist′i•ly,** *adv.* —**feist′i•ness,** *n.*

feld•spar (feld′spär′, fel′-), *n.* any of a group of crystalline minerals, principally aluminosilicates of potassium, sodium, and calcium, characterized by two cleavages at nearly right angles: one of the most important constituents of igneous rocks.

fe•lic•i•tate (fi lis′i tāt′), *v.t.,* **-tat•ed, -tat•ing,** to compliment upon a happy event; congratulate. —**fe•lic′i•ta′tion,** *n.*

fe•lic•i•tous (fi lis′i təs), *adj.* **1.** well-suited for the occasion; apt; appropriate: *a felicitous speech of acceptance.* **2.** having a special ability for suitable manner or expression, as a person. **3.** enjoyable; pleasant: *a felicitous occasion.* —**fe•lic′i•tous•ly,** *adv.* —**fe•lic′i•tous•ness,** *n.*

fe•lic•i•ty (fi lis′i tē), *n., pl.* **-ties. 1.** the state of being happy, esp. in a high degree; bliss: *marital felicity.* **2.** an instance of this. **3.** a source of happiness. **4.** a skillful faculty or capacity: *felicity of expression.* **5.** an instance or display of this: *the many felicities of the poem.*

fe•line (fē′līn), *adj.* **1.** belonging or pertaining to the cat family, Felidae. **2.** catlike; characteristic of animals of the cat family: *feline agility.* **3.** sly, stealthy, or treacherous. **—***n.* **4.** an animal of the cat family; cat.

fe′line distem′per, *n.* DISTEMPER[1] (def. 1c).

fe′line leuke′mia vi′rus, *n.* a retrovirus, mainly affecting cats, that depresses the immune system and leads to opportunistic infections, lymphosarcoma, and other disorders. *Abbr.:* FeLV

Fe•lix (fē′liks), *n.* the husband of Drusilla who heard the Apostle Paul speak. Acts 24:24–25.

fell[1] (fel), *v.* pt. of FALL.

fell[2] (fel), *v.t.* **1.** to knock, strike, shoot, or cut down; cause to fall: *to fell a moose; to fell a tree.* **2.** (in sewing) to finish (a seam) by sewing the edge down flat. **—***n.* **3.** the amount of timber cut down.

fell[3] (fel), *adj.* **1.** fierce; cruel; dreadful; savage: *a fell beast.* **2.** destructive; deadly: *a fell blow; a fell disease.* **—*Idiom.* 3. at** or **in one fell swoop,** all at once or all together, as if by a single blow: *The tornado leveled the houses at one fell swoop.*

fell[4] (fel), *n.* the skin or hide of an animal; pelt.

fel•low (fel′ō), *n.* **1.** a man or boy: *a handsome fellow.* **2.** *Informal.* a beau; suitor. **3.** *Informal.* a person; one: *They don't treat a fellow very well here.* **4.** a companion; comrade; associate. **5.** a person belonging to the same rank or class; equal; peer. **6.** one of a pair; mate; match: *a shoe without its fellow.* **7. a.** a graduate student of a university or college to whom an allowance is granted for special study. **b.** a member of the corporation or board of trustees of certain universities or colleges. **8.** a member of any of certain learned societies: *a fellow of the British Academy.* **—***adj.* **9.** belonging to the same class or group; united by the same occupation, interests, circumstances, etc.: *fellow students.*

fel•low•ship (fel′ō ship′), *n.* **1.** the condition or relation of belonging to the same class or group: *the fellowship of humanity.* **2.** friendly relationship; companionship; camaraderie: *the fellowship among old friends.* **3.** community of interest, feeling, etc. **4.** friendliness. **5.** an association of persons having similar interests, occupations, enterprises, etc. **6. a.** the body of fellows in a college or university. **b.** the position or stipend of a fellow of a college or university. **c.** a foundation for the maintenance of a fellow in a college or university.

fel′low trav′eler, *n.* anyone who, although not a member, supports or sympathizes with some organization, movement, or the like. —**fel•low-trav•el•ing** (fel′ō trav′ə ling, -trav′ling), *adj.*

fel•on[1] (fel′ən), *n.* a person who has committed a felony.

fel•on[2] (fel′ən), *n.* an acute and painful inflammation of the tissues of a finger or toe, usu. near the nail. Also called **whitlow.**

fe•lo•ni•ous (fə lō′nē əs), *adj.* pertaining to or involving a felony: *felonious assult.* —**fe•lo′ni•ous•ly,** *adv.* —**fe•lo′ni•ous•ness,** *n.*

fel•o•ny (fel′ə nē), *n., pl.* **-nies.** an offense, as murder or burglary, of graver character than a misdemeanor and usu. punished by imprisonment for more than one year.

fel′ony mur′der, *n.* a killing treated as a murder because, though unintended, it occurred during the commission or attempted commission of a felony, as robbery.

fel•site (fel′sīt), *n.* a dense fine-grained igneous rock consisting typically of feldspar and quartz, both of which may appear as phenocrysts. —**fel•sit•ic** (fel sit′ik), *adj.*

felt[1] (felt), *v.* pt. and pp. of FEEL.

felt[2] (felt), *n.* **1.** a nonwoven fabric of wool, fur, or hair, matted together by heat, moisture, and great pressure. **2.** an article made of this fabric. **3.** any matted fabric or material, as of asbestos fibers or old paper, used for insulation and in construction. **4.** a heavily fulled woven fabric of cotton or wool in which the weave is virtually indiscernible. **—***adj.* **5.** pertaining to or made of felt. **—***v.t.* **6.** to make into felt; mat or press together. **7.** to cover with or as if with felt. **—***v.i.* **8.** to become matted together.

fe•luc•ca (fə luk′ə, -lo͞o′kə), *n., pl.* **-cas.** a sailing vessel, lateen-rigged on two masts, used esp. in the Mediterranean Sea.

fe•male (fē′māl), *n.* **1.** a person of the sex whose cell nuclei contain two X chromosomes and who is able to conceive and bear young; a girl or woman. **2.** any organism of the sex or sexual phase that normally produces egg cells. **3.** a plant having a pistil or pistils. **—***adj.* **4.** of, pertaining to, or being a female: *female organs; a female mammal.* **5.** of, pertaining to, or characteristic of a girl or woman; feminine: *female wisdom.* **6.** composed of females: *a female readership.* **7. a.** pertaining to a plant or the reproductive structure of a plant that produces or contains elements capable of being fertilized. **b.** (of seed plants) pistillate. **8.** being or having a recessed part into which a corresponding part fits: *a female plug.* Compare MALE (def. 8). —**fe′male•ness,** *n.*

fem•i•nine (fem′ə nin), *adj.* **1.** pertaining to or characteristic of women or girls: *feminine attire.* **2.** having qualities or characteristics traditionally ascribed to women, as sensitivity, delicacy, or prettiness. **3.** effeminate; womanish. **4.** belonging to the female sex; female: *a mostly feminine viewership.* **5.** of, pertaining to, or being the grammatical gender that has among its members most nouns referring to females, as well as other nouns. **—***n.* **6.** the feminine gender. **7.** a word or other form in or marking the feminine gender.

fem•i•nin•i•ty (fem′ə nin′i tē), *n.* **1.** the quality of being feminine; womanliness. **2.** women collectively. **3.** effeminacy. Sometimes, **fe•min•i•ty** (fi min′i tē).

fem•i•nism (fem′ə niz′əm), *n.* **1.** a doctrine advocating social, political, and economic rights for women equal to those of men. **2.** a movement for the attainment of such rights. **3.** feminine character. —**fem′i•nist,** *n., adj.* —**fem′i•nis′tic,** *adj.*

fem′inist theol′ogy, *n.* a form of theology that seeks to correct a perceived masculine bias in Christianity, and emphasizes that women are equal to men under God and must also be equal within the church.

femme fa•tale (fem′ fə tal′, -täl′, fā-), *n., pl.* **femmes fa•tales** (fem′ fə talz′, -tälz′, fā-). an irresistibly attractive woman, esp. one who leads men into danger or disaster; siren.

fem•o•ral (fem′ər əl), *adj.* of, pertaining to, or situated near the thigh or femur: *the femoral artery.*

fem•to•me•ter (fem′tə mē′tər), *n. Physics.* FERMI. *Symbol:* fm

fe•mur (fē′mər), *n., pl.* **fe•murs, fem•o•ra** (fem′ər ə). **1.** the long upper bone of the hind leg of vertebrates, extending from the pelvis to the knee; thighbone. **2.** the often enlarged third segment of an insect leg, between the trochanter and the tibia.

fen (fen), *n.* low land covered wholly or partially with water; boggy land; marsh.

fence (fens), *n., v.,* **fenced, fenc•ing. —***n.* **1.** a barrier enclosing or bordering a field, yard, etc., usu. made of posts and wire or wood, used to prevent entrance, confine a person or thing, or mark a boundary. **2.** a person who receives and disposes of stolen goods. **3.** the place of business of such a person. **—***v.t.* **4.** to enclose by a fence: *to fence a farm.* **5.** to separate by or as if by a fence or fences (often fol. by *in, off, out,* etc.): *to fence off a corner of a garden.* **6.** to prevent entry of by a fence; keep in or out. **7.** to sell (stolen goods) to a fence. **8.** to defend; protect; guard. **—***v.i.* **9.** to practice the art or sport of fencing. **10.** to parry arguments; strive to avoid giving direct answers; hedge. **—Idiom. 11. on the fence,** uncommitted; neutral; undecided. **—Saying. 12. Good fences make good neighbors,** relationships among acquaintances are smoother when people respect one another's privacy: popularized by Robert Frost in *Mending Wall* (1914). **—fence′like′,** *adj.*

fence′-mend′ing, *n.* the reestablishing or improving of contacts or relationships, esp. in politics, as after a dispute or estrangement.

fenc•er (fen′sər), *n.* **1.** a person who practices the art or sport of fencing. **2.** a horse trained to jump barriers, as for show or sport. **3.** a person who builds or repairs fences.

fence′-sit′ter, *n.* a person who remains neutral or undecided in a controversy. **—fence′-sit′ting,** *n.*

fenc•ing (fen′sing), *n.* **1.** the art, practice, or sport in which an épée, foil, or saber is used for defense and attack. **2.** a parrying of arguments; avoidance of direct answers: *political fencing on issues.* **3.** an enclosure or railing. **4.** fences collectively. **5.** material for fences.

fend′ (fend), *v.t.* **1.** to ward off (often fol. by *off*): *to fend off blows.* **—***v.i.* **2.** to resist or make defense: *to fend against poverty.* **3.** to provide; manage; shift: *to fend for oneself.*

fend•er (fen′dər), *n.* **1.** the part mounted over the road wheels of an automobile, bicycle, etc., to reduce the splashing of mud, water, and the like. **2.** a device on the front of a locomotive, etc., for clearing the track of obstructions. **3.** a mudguard or splash guard on a horse-drawn vehicle. **4.** a piece of timber, bundle of rope, or the like, hung over the side of a vessel to lessen shock or prevent chafing, as between the vessel and a dock. **5.** a low metal guard before an open fireplace to keep back falling coals. **6.** a person or thing that wards something off.

fend′er bend′er, *n. Informal.* a collision between motor vehicles involving only minor damage.

fe•nes•tra (fi nes′trə), *n., pl.* **-trae** (-trē). **1.** a small opening or perforation, as in a bone, esp. either of the two oval openings between the middle and inner ears. **2.** a transparent spot in an otherwise opaque surface, as in the wings of certain butterflies. **—fe•nes′tral,** *adj.*

fen•es•tra•tion (fen′ə strā′shən), *n.* **1.** the design and disposition of windows and other exterior openings of a building. **2. a.** an opening or perforation in an anatomical structure. **b.** surgery to effect such an opening, esp. into the inner ear.

fen•nec (fen′ek), *n.* a small large-eared desert fox, *Fennecus zerda*, of N Africa and Arabia.

fen•nel (fen′l), *n.* **1.** a plant, *Foeniculum vulgare*, of the parsley family, having aromatic feathery leaves and umbels of small yellow flowers. **2.** Also called **fen′nel seed′.** the aromatic aniselike fruit of this plant, used in cooking and medicine. **3.** FINOCHIO.

fen•u•greek (fen′yŏŏ grēk′, fen′ŏŏ-), *n.* an aromatic Eurasian plant, *Trigonella foenumgraecum*, of the legume family, cultivated chiefly for fodder.

-fer, a combining form meaning "that which carries" the thing specified by the initial element: *aquifer; conifer.*

fe•ral (fēr′əl), *adj.* **1.** existing in a wild state; not domesticated or cultivated. **2.** having reverted to the wild state. **3.** ferocious; savage.

fer-de-lance (fer′dl ans′, -äns′), *n.* a large pit viper, *Bothrops atrox*, of tropical America.

Fer•di•nand (fûr′dn and′), *n.* **1. Ferdinand I, a.** (*"Ferdinand the Great"*) died 1065, king of Castile 1033–65, king of Navarre and Leon 1037–65. **b.** 1503–64, Holy Roman emperor 1558–64 (brother of Emperor Charles V). **c.** (*Maximilian Karl Leopold Maria*) 1861–1948, king of Bulgaria 1908–18. **2. Ferdinand II, a.** (*"the Catholic"*) 1452–1516, king of Sicily 1468–1516, king of Aragon 1479–1516; as Ferdinand III, king of Naples 1504–16; as **King Ferdinand V,** joint sovereign (with Isabella I) of Castile 1474–1504. **b.** 1578–1637, Holy Roman emperor 1620–37. **3. Ferdinand III, a.** FERDINAND II (def. 2a). **b.** 1608–57, Holy Roman emperor 1637–57 (son of Ferdinand II).

fe•ri•a (fēr′ē ə), *n., pl.* **fe•ri•ae** (fēr′ē ē′), **fe•ri•as.** a weekday on which no church feast is celebrated. **—fe′ri•al,** *adj.*

fe•ria (fe′ryä), *n., pl.* **-rias** (-ryäs). *Spanish.* in Hispanic communities, a local festival or fair, usu. held in honor of a patron saint.

fer•ma•ta (fer mä′tə), *n., pl.* **-tas, -te** (-tā). *Music.* **1.** Also called **hold, pause.** the sustaining of a note, chord, or rest for a duration longer than the indicated time value, with the length of the extension at the performer's discretion. **2.** a symbol ⌢ placed over a note, chord, or rest indicating a fermata.

fer•ment (*n.* fûr′ment; *v.* fər ment′), *n.* **1.** any of a group of living organisms, as yeasts, molds, and certain bacteria, that cause fermentation. **2.** an enzyme that catalyzes the anaerobic breakdown of molecules that yield energy. **3.** FERMENTATION (def. 2). **4.** agitation or excitement; commotion: *artistic ferment; political ferment.* **—***v.t.* **5.** to act upon as a ferment. **6.** to cause to undergo fermentation. **7.** to inflame or excite; foment. **—***v.i.* **8.** to be fermented; undergo fermentation. **9.** to seethe with agitation or excitement. **—fer•ment′a•ble,** *adj.*

fer•men•ta•tion (fûr′men tā′shən), *n.* **1.** the act or process of fermenting. **2.** a chemical change brought about by a ferment, as the conversion of grape sugar into ethyl alcohol by yeast enzymes. **3.** agitation; excitement.

fer•mi (fûr′mē, fâr′-), *n. Physics.* a unit of length, 10^{-15} m, used in measuring nuclear distances. *Symbol:* F Also called **femtometer.** [after E. FERMI]

Fer•mi (fûr′mē, fâr′-), *n.* **Enrico,** 1901–54, Italian physicist, in the U.S. after 1939: Nobel prize 1938.

fer•mi•um (fûr′mē əm, fâr′-), *n.* a transuranic element, artificially produced from plutonium or uranium. *Symbol:* Fm; *at. no.:* 100. [after E. FERMI]

fern (fûrn), *n.* a nonflowering vascular plant of the class Filicinae, having fronds and reproducing by spores. **—fern′like′,** *adj.*

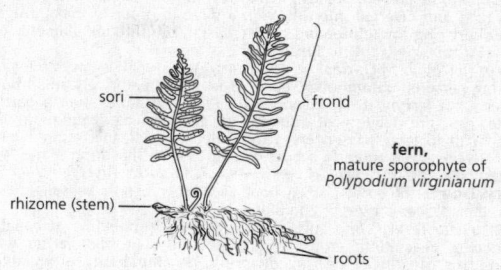

fern,
mature sporophyte of
Polypodium virginianum

fern′ seed′, *n.* the spores of ferns, formerly supposed to have the power to make persons invisible.

fe•ro•cious (fə rō′shəs), *adj.* **1.** savagely fierce or cruel; violently harsh; brutal: *a ferocious beating.* **2.** extreme or intense: *a ferocious thirst.* **—fe•ro′cious•ly,** *adv.* **—fe•ro′cious•ness,** *n.*

fe•roc•i•ty (fə ros′i tē), *n.* a ferocious quality or state; savage fierceness.

-ferous, a combining form meaning "carrying," "producing," "yielding" the thing specified by the initial element: *coniferous; pestiferous.* Compare -FER.

fer•re•dox•in (fer′ə dok′sin), *n.* any of a group of red-brown proteins containing iron and sulfur and acting as an electron carrier during photosynthesis, nitrogen fixation, or oxidation-reduction reactions.

fer•re•ous (fer′ē əs), *adj.* of, resembling, or containing iron: *a ferreous alloy.*

fer•ret¹ (fer′it), *n.* **1.** a domesticated variety of the polecat, used esp. in Europe for driving small mammals from their burrows. **2.** a North American prairie weasel, *Mustela nigripes*, with a black mask and black feet. **—***v.t.* **3.** to drive out by or as if by using a ferret (often fol. by *out*): *to ferret rabbits from their burrows; to ferret out enemies.* **4.** to hunt with ferrets. **5.** to hunt over with ferrets: *to ferret a field.* **6.** to search out: *to ferret out the facts.* **7.** to harry or worry; torment. **—***v.i.* **8.** to search about. **9.** to hunt with ferrets.

fer•ret² (fer′it), *n.* a narrow tape or ribbon, as of silk or cotton, used for trimming, etc. Also called **fer′ret•ing.**

fer•ric (fer′ik), *adj.* of or containing iron, esp. in the trivalent state.

fer′ric ox′ide, *n.* a red crystalline compound, Fe_2O_3, used as a pigment, mordant, and coating for magnetic tape.

Fer′ris wheel′ (fer′is), *n.* an amusement ride consisting of a large upright wheel rotating on a fixed stand and having seats suspended freely from its rim that remain right side up as they revolve. [G. W. G. *Ferris* (1859–96), U.S. engineer]

ferris wheel

fer•rite (fer′īt), *n.* **1.** a magnetic compound of ferric oxide with another metallic oxide, used in computer memory cores and other electronic equipment. **2.** the pure iron constituent of ferrous metals, as distinguished from the iron carbides.

fer•ro•mag•net•ic (fer′ō mag net′ik), *adj.* noting or pertaining to a substance, as iron, that below the Curie point can possess magnetization in the absence of an external magnetic field. **—fer′ro•mag′ne•tism** (-ni tiz′əm), *n.*

fer•ro•type (fer′ə tīp′), *v.*, **-typed, -typ•ing,** *n.* **—***v.t.* **1.** to put a glossy surface on (a photographic print) by pressing, while wet, on a metal sheet **(fer′rotype tin′)**. —*n.* **2.** Also called **tintype.** a positive photograph made on a sensitized sheet of enameled iron or tin.

fer•rous (fer′əs), *adj.* of or containing iron, esp. in the bivalent state.

fer•rule or **fer•ule** (fer′əl, -o͞ol), *n., v.,* **-ruled, -rul•ing.** —*n.* **1.** a ring, cap, or sleeve, usu. of metal, put around the end of a post, cane, tool, or the like, to prevent splitting. **2.** a bushing or adapter holding the end of a tube and inserted into a hole in a plate in order to make a tight fit. **3.** a short ring for reinforcing or decreasing the interior diameter of the end of a tube. —*v.t.* **4.** to furnish with a ferrule.

fer•ry (fer′ē), *n., pl.* **-ries,** *v.,* **-ried, -ry•ing.** —*n.* **1.** a service for transporting persons, automobiles, etc., across a comparatively small body of water. **2.** a ferryboat. **3.** a service for flying airplanes over a particular route, esp. the delivery of airplanes to an overseas destination. **4.** the legal right to ferry passengers, cargo, etc. —*v.t.* **5.** to convey back and forth over a fixed route in a boat or plane. **6.** to fly (an airplane) over a particular route, esp. for delivery. —*v.i.* **7.** to go in a ferry.

fer•ry•boat (fer′ē bōt′), *n.* a boat used to transport passengers, vehicles, etc., across a river or the like.

fer•tile (fûr′tl; *esp. Brit.* -tīl), *adj.* **1.** bearing, producing, or capable of producing vegetation, crops, etc., abundantly; prolific: *fertile soil.* **2.** bearing or capable of bearing offspring. **3.** abundantly productive; fecund: *a fertile imagination.* **4.** conducive to productiveness: *fertile showers.* **5. a.** fertilized, as a seed or egg. **b.** capable of developing, as a seed or egg. **c.** capable of producing reproductive structures or of causing fertilization. **6.** capable of being transmuted into a fissionable nuclide by irradiation with neutrons, as uranium 238. —**fer′tile•ly,** *adv.*

Fer′tile Cres′cent, *n.* a crescent-shaped agricultural region of the ancient Near East beginning at the Mediterranean Sea and extending between the Tigris and Euphrates rivers to the Persian Gulf.

fer•til•i•ty (fər til′i tē), *n.* **1.** the state or quality of being fertile. **2.** the ability to produce offspring; power of reproduction. **3.** the birthrate of a population.

fer•ti•li•za•tion (fûr′tl ə zā′shən), *n.* **1.** an act, process, or instance of fertilizing. **2.** the state of being fertilized. **3.** the union of male and female gametic nuclei. **4.** the enrichment of soil, as for the production of crops. —**fer′ti•li•za′tion•al,** *adj.*

fer•ti•lize (fûr′tl īz′), *v.t.,* **-lized, -liz•ing.** **1. a.** to render (the female gamete) capable of development by uniting it with the male gamete. **b.** to impregnate (an animal, plant, or other organism). **2.** to make fertile; enrich: *to fertilize farmland.* **3.** to make productive. —**fer′ti•liz′a•ble,** *adj.* —**fer′ti•liz′a•bil′i•ty,** *n.*

fer•ti•liz•er (fûr′tl ī′zər), *n.* **1.** any substance used to fertilize the soil, esp. a commercial or chemical manure. **2.** one that fertilizes.

fer•ule (fer′əl, -o͞ol), *n., v.,* **-uled, -ul•ing.** —*n.* **1.** a rod, cane, or flat piece of wood for punishing children. —*v.t.* **2.** to punish with a ferule.

fer•ven•cy (fûr′vən sē), *n.* warmth or intensity of feeling; fervor.

fer•vent (fûr′vənt), *adj.* **1.** having or showing very warm or intense spirit, feeling, enthusiasm, etc.; ardent; passionate: *a fervent admirer; a fervent plea.* **2.** hot; burning; glowing. —**fer′vent•ly,** *adv.*

fer•vid (fûr′vid), *adj.* **1.** heated or vehement in spirit, enthusiasm, etc.: *a fervid orator.* **2.** burning; glowing. —**fer•vid′i•ty, fer′vid•ness,** *n.* —**fer′vid•ly,** *adv.*

fer•vor (fûr′vər), *n.* **1.** great warmth and earnestness of feeling; passion; zeal: *to defend a cause with fervor.* **2.** intense heat. Also, *esp. Brit.,* **fer′vour.**

fes•cue (fes′kyo͞o), *n.* **1.** any grass of the genus *Festuca,* some species of which are cultivated for pasture or lawns. **2.** a pointer, as a straw or slender stick, used to point out the letters in teaching children to read.

fes•ter (fes′tər), *v.i.* **1.** to form pus; generate purulent matter; suppurate: *a festering wound.* **2.** to cause ulceration, as a foreign body in the flesh. **3.** to putrefy or rot. **4.** to rankle, as resentment or bitterness: *The desire for revenge festered in her heart.* —*v.t.* **5.** to cause to rankle: *envy festering the spirit.* —*n.* **6.** an ulcer; a rankling sore. **7.** a small, purulent, superficial sore.

fes•ti•val (fes′tə vəl), *n.* **1.** a day or time of religious or other celebration, marked by feasting, ceremonies, or other observances. **2.** a periodic commemoration, anniversary, or celebration: *an annual strawberry festival.* **3.** a period or program of festive activities, cultural events, or entertainment: *a music festival; a film festival.* **4.** gaiety; revelry; merrymaking. —*adj.* **5.** of, for, or marked by celebration.

fes•tive (fes′tiv), *adj.* **1.** pertaining to or suitable for a feast or festival: *festive decorations.* **2.** joyous; merry: *a festive mood.* —**fes′tive•ly,** *adv.* —**fes′tive•ness,** *n.* —**fes•tiv′i•ty,** *n.*

fes•toon (fe sto͞on′), *n.* **1.** a string or chain of flowers, foliage, ribbon, etc., suspended in a curve between two points. **2.** a decorative representation of this, as in architectural work or on pottery. —*v.t.* **3.** to adorn with or as if with festoons: *to festoon a hall.* **4.** to form into graceful curves or loops: *to festoon curtains.*

fest•schrift (fest′shrift′), *n., pl.* **-schrift•en** (-shrif′tən), **-schrifts.** (*often cap.*) a volume of scholarly articles contributed by many authors to honor a senior colleague or teacher.

Fes•tus (fes′təs), *n.* a governor of Judea at the time of the Apostle Paul. Acts 25–26.

fet•a (fet′ə), *n.* a soft, crumbly, white brine-cured Greek cheese usu. made from sheep's or goat's milk.

fe•tal or **foe•tal** (fēt′l), *adj.* of, pertaining to, or having the character of a fetus.

fe′tal al′cohol syn′drome, *n.* a variable cluster of birth defects that may include facial abnormalities, growth deficiency, mental retardation, and other impairments, caused by the mother's consumption of alcohol during pregnancy. *Abbr.:* FAS

fe′tal posi′tion, *n.* a posture resembling that of the fetus in the uterus, in which the body is curled with head and limbs drawn in.

fetch[1] (fech), *v.t.* **1.** to go and bring back; return with; get: *to fetch water from a well.* **2.** to cause to come; bring: *to fetch a doctor.* **3.** to sell for or bring (a price, financial return, etc.): *The horse fetched more money than it cost.* **4.** to attract; captivate. **5.** to take (a breath). **6.** to utter (a sigh, groan, etc.). **7.** to deal or deliver (a stroke, blow, etc.). **8.** to perform or execute (a movement, step, leap, etc.). **9.** to reach by sailing. **10.** (of a hunting dog) to retrieve (game). —*v.i.* **11.** to go and bring things. **12.** *Chiefly Naut.* to move or maneuver. **13.** to retrieve game (often used as a command to a hunting dog). **14.** to go by an indirect route (often fol. by *around* or *about*). —*n.* **15.** the distance of fetching: *a long fetch.* **16.** an area where ocean waves are being generated by the wind. **17.** the reach or stretch of a thing. **18.** a trick; dodge. —***Idiom.*** **19. fetch and carry,** to perform menial tasks. —**fetch′er,** *n.*

fetch[2] (fech), *n.* WRAITH (def. 1).

fetch•ing (fech′ing), *adj.* charming; captivating. —**fetch′ing•ly,** *adv.*

fete or **fête** (fāt, fet), *n., pl.* **fetes,** *v.,* **fet•ed, fet•ing.** —*n.* **1.** a festive celebration or entertainment. **2.** a day of celebration; holiday. **3.** a religious feast or festival. —*v.t.* **4.** to entertain at or honor with a fete.

fe•ti•cide (fē′tə sīd′), *n.* the act of destroying a fetus. —**fe′ti•cid′al,** *adj.*

fet•id (fet′id, fē′tid), *adj.* having an offensive odor; stinking; noisome. —**fet′id•ly,** *adv.* —**fet′id•ness, fe•tid′i•ty,** *n.*

fet•ish (fet′ish, fē′tish), *n.* **1.** an object regarded as having magical power; talisman. **2.** any object, idea, etc., eliciting unquestioning reverence or devotion: *to make a fetish of sports.* **3.** an object or nongenital part of the body, as a shoe, undergarment, or hank of hair, that is repeatedly preferred or exclusively used for achieving sexual excitement. —**fet′ish•ism,** *n.*

fet•ish•ism (fet′i shiz′əm, fē′ti-), *n.* **1.** belief in, preference for, or use of fetishes. **2.** excessive or blind devotion. Sometimes, **fet′ich•ism.** —**fet′ish•ist,** *n.* —**fet′ish•is′tic,** *adj.* —**fet′ish•is′ti•cal•ly,** *adv.*

fet•lock (fet′lok′), *n.* **1.** the projection of the leg of a horse behind the joint between the cannon bone and great pastern bone, bearing a tuft of hair. **2.** the tuft of hair itself. **3.** Also called **fet′lock joint′.** the joint at this point.

fe•tor (fē′tər), *n.* a strong, offensive smell; stench.

fet•ter (fet′ər), *n.* **1.** a chain or shackle placed on the feet. **2.** Usu., **fetters.** anything that confines or restrains. —*v.t.* **3.** to put fetters upon. **4.** to confine; restrain. —**fet′ter•er,** *n.*

fet•ter•bush (fet′ər bo͝osh′), *n.* an evergreen shrub, *Lyonia lucida,* of the heath family, native to the southern U.S., having clusters of fragrant white flowers.

fet•tle (fet′l), *n., v.,* **-tled, -tling.** —*n.* **1.** state; condition: *in fine fettle.* —*v.t.* **2. a.** to remove mold marks or sand from (a casting). **b.** to repair the hearth of (an open-hearth furnace).

fet•tuc•ci•ne or **fet•tuc•ci•ni** (fet′ə chē′nē), *n.* (*used with a sing. or pl. v.*) pasta cut in flat narrow strips.

fe•tus or **foe•tus** (fē′təs), *n., pl.* **-tus•es.** (used chiefly of viviparous mammals) the young of an animal in the womb or egg, esp. in the later stages of development, in humans being after the end of the second month of gestation. Compare EMBRYO (def. 1).

feud (fyo͞od), *n.* **1.** Also called **blood feud.** a bitter continuous hostility, esp. between families, clans, etc., lasting for many years or generations. **2.** a bitter quarrel or contention; argument. —*v.i.* **3.** to engage in a feud.

feu•dal (fyo͞od′l), *adj.* **1.** of, pertaining to, or like the feudal system. **2.** of or pertaining to the Middle Ages. **3.** of or pertaining to a fief or to the holding of a fief. —**feu′dal•ly,** *adv.*

feu•dal•ism (fyo͞od′l iz′əm), *n.* the feudal system.

feu′dal sys′tem, *n.* the political, military, and social system in the Middle Ages, based on the holding of lands in fief or fee and on the resulting relations between lord and vassal.

fe•ver (fē′vər), *n.* **1.** an abnormally high body temperature. **2.** any of various diseases in which high temperature is a prominent symptom, as scarlet fever or rheumatic fever. **3.** intense nervous excitement: *in a fever of anticipation.* —*v.t.* **4.** to affect with or as if with fever. —*v.i.* **5.** to become feverish; have or get a fever.

fe′ver blis′ter, *n.* a cold sore.

fe•ver•few (fē′vər fyo͞o′), *n.* a bushy plant, *Chrysanthemum parthenium,* bearing small white flowers formerly used as a fever remedy.

fe•ver•ish (fē′vər ish), *adj.* **1.** having fever. **2.** pertaining to, of the nature of, or resembling fever: *feverish excitement.* **3.** excited, restless, or uncontrolled, as if from fever. **4.** having a tendency to produce fever. —**fe′ver•ish•ly,** *adv.* —**fe′ver•ish•ness,** *n.*

fe′ver pitch′, *n.* a high degree of excitement.

fe•ver•weed (fē′vər wēd′), *n.* any of several plants belonging to the genus *Eryngium,* of the parsley family, esp. *E. foetidum,* of the West Indies, or *E. campestre,* of Europe.

fe•ver•wort (fē′vər wûrt′, -wôrt′), *n.* **1.** HORSE GENTIAN. **2.** BONESET.

few (fyo͞o), *adj.,* **-er, -est,** *n., pron.* —*adj.* **1.** not many but more than one: *Few artists live luxuriously.* —*n.* **2.** (*used with a pl. v.*) a small number or amount: *Send me a few.* **3. the few,** a special, limited number; the minority: *music that appeals to the few.* —*pron.* **4.** (used with a pl. v.) a small number of persons or things. —**Idiom. 5. few and far between,** not plentiful. **6. quite a few,** a fairly large number; many.

few·er (fyoo′ər), *adj.* **1.** of a smaller number: *fewer words and more action.* —*pron.* **2.** (used with a pl. v.) a smaller number: *Fewer have come than we hoped.*

fey (fā), *adj.* **1.** whimsical; strange: *a fey manner.* **2.** supernatural; enchanted: *elves and other fey creatures.* **3.** appearing to be under a spell; visionary. **4.** *Chiefly Scot.* doomed. **5.** being in an unnaturally excited state of mind, once thought to portend death.

fez (fez), *n., pl.* **fez·zes.** a felt cap, usu. red, shaped like a truncated cone and ornamented with a tassel, worn by men esp. in Egypt and formerly Turkey. [< Turkish, after *Fez,* city in Morocco where originally made]

fez

ff, 1. folios. **2.** (and the) following (pages, verses, etc.). **3.** *Music.* fortissimo.

f.g., field goal.

FHA, Federal Housing Administration.

FHLMC, Federal Home Loan Mortgage Corporation.

fi·an·cé (fē′än sā′, fē än′sā), *n.* a man engaged to be married; a man to whom a woman is engaged.

fi·an·cée (fē′än sā′, fē än′sā), *n.* a woman engaged to be married; a woman to whom a man is engaged.

fi·as·co (fē as′kō *or, esp. for 2,* -ä′skō), *n., pl.* **-cos, -coes. 1.** a complete and ignominious failure. **2.** a round-bottomed wine bottle, esp. one having a basketlike covering.

fi·at (fē′ät, -at; fī′at, -at), *n.* **1.** an authoritative decree, sanction, or order: *a royal fiat.* **2.** an arbitrary decree or pronouncement, esp. by a person or group of persons having absolute authority to enforce it: *to rule by fiat.* [< Latin: let it be done]

fib (fib), *n., v.,* **fibbed, fib·bing.** —*n.* **1.** a small or trivial lie; minor falsehood. —*v.i.* **2.** to tell a fib. —**fib′ber, fib′ster,** *n.*

fi·ber (fī′bər), *n.* **1.** a fine threadlike piece, as of cotton, jute, or asbestos. **2.** a slender filament: *a fiber of platinum.* **3.** filaments collectively. **4.** matter or material composed of filaments: *a plastic fiber.* **5.** something resembling a filament. **6.** an essential character, quality, or strength: *people of strong moral fiber.* **7. a.** filamentous matter from the bast tissue or other parts of plants, used for industrial purposes. **b.** ROOT HAIR. **8.** any of the filaments or elongated cells or structures that are combined in a bundle of tissue: *nerve fiber.* **9.** Also called **bulk, roughage.** the structural parts of plants, as cellulose, pectin, and lignin, that are wholly or partly indigestible, acting to increase intestinal bulk and peristalsis. Also, *esp. Brit.,* **fibre.** —**fi′ber·less,** *adj.*

fi·ber·board (fī′bər bôrd′, -bōrd′), *n.* a building material made of wood or other plant fibers compressed and cemented into rigid sheets.

fi·ber·fill (fī′bər fil′), *n.* synthetic fibers, as polyester, used as a filling or insulating material for pillows, quilts, garments, etc.

fi′ber·glass′ or **fi′ber glass′,** *n.* a material consisting of extremely fine filaments of glass that are combined in yarn and woven into fabrics, used in masses as a thermal and acoustical insulator, or embedded in various resins to make boat hulls, fishing rods, and the like.

fi′ber op′tics or **fi′ber·op′tics,** *n.* the technology of sending computer data, video and voice signals, etc., through laser-generated light carried in bundles of ultrapure, transparent fiber (**optical fiber**) whose refraction properties allow the light to be transmitted around curves. —**fi′ber·op′tic,** *adj.*

Fi·bo·nac′ci num′bers (fē′bō nä′chē), *n.pl.* the unending sequence 1, 1, 2, 3, 5, 8, 13, 21, ... where each term is defined as the sum of its two predecessors. Also called **Fibona′ci se′quence.**

fi·bril (fī′brəl, fib′rəl), *n.* **1.** a small or fine fiber or threadlike structure. **2.** ROOT HAIR. —**fi′bril·lar,** *adj.* —**fi′bril·lose′,** *adj.*

fi·bril·la·tion (fī′brə lā′shən, *or, esp. for 1,* fib′rə-), *n.* **1. a.** uncontrolled twitching or quivering of muscular fibrils. **b.** chaotic contractions across the atrium of the heart, causing fast and irregular ventricular activity; arrhythmia. **2.** the formation of fibrils.

fi·brin (fī′brin), *n.* **1.** the insoluble protein end product of blood coagulation, formed from fibrinogen by the action of thrombin. **2.** GLUTEN.

fi·bri·noid (fī′brə noid′, fib′rə-), *adj.* having the characteristics of fibrin.

fibro-, a combining form meaning "fiber": *fibrolite.*

fi·bro·blast (fī′brə blast′), *n.* a cell that contributes to the formation of connective tissue fibers. —**fi′bro·blas′tic,** *adj.*

fi·broid (fī′broid), *adj.* **1.** resembling fiber or fibrous tissue. **2.** composed of fibers. —*n.* **3.** FIBROMA.

fi·bro·ma (fī brō′mə), *n., pl.* **-mas, -ma·ta** (-mə tə). a tumor consisting essentially of fibrous tissue. —**fi·brom′a·tous** (fī brom′ə təs), *adj.*

fi·bro·sis (fī brō′sis), *n.* the development in an organ of excess fibrous connective tissue. —**fi·brot′ic** (-brot′ik), *adj.*

fi·brous (fī′brəs), *adj.* containing, consisting of, or resembling fibers. —**fi′brous·ly,** *adv.* —**fi′brous·ness,** *n.*

fib·u·la (fib′yə lə), *n., pl.* **-lae** (-lē′), **-las. 1.** the outer and thinner of the two bones extending from the knee to the ankle in primates. **2.** a corresponding bone of the leg or hind leg of other vertebrates, often rudimentary or ankylosed with the tibia. —**fib′u·lar,** *adj.*

-fic, a combining form meaning "making," "producing," "causing" the thing specified by the initial element: *honorific; pacific; prolific.*

FICA (fī′kə, fē′-) also **F.I.C.A.,** Federal Insurance Contributions Act.

fiche (fēsh), *n.* MICROFICHE.

fich·u (fish′oo, fē′shoo), *n., pl.* **fich·us.** a woman's sheer triangular scarf, worn over the shoulders or around the neck, often with the ends tucked into a low neckline.

fick·le (fik′əl), *adj.* **1.** not constant or loyal in affections. **2.** likely to change, esp. due to caprice, irresolution, or instability; casually changeable: *fickle weather.* —**fick′le·ness,** *n.*

fic·tion (fik′shən), *n.* **1.** the class of literature comprising works of imaginative narration, esp. in prose form. **2.** works of this class, as novels or short stories. **3.** something feigned, invented, or imagined, esp. a made-up story. **4.** the act of feigning, inventing, or imagining. **5.** an assumption that a fact exists, regardless of the truth of the matter, so that a legal principle can be applied on the basis of the existing facts. —**fic′tion·al,** *adj.* —**fic′tion·al·ize′,** *v.t.,* **-ized, -iz·ing.** —**fic′tion·al·ly,** *adv.*

fic·ti·tious (fik tish′əs), *adj.* **1.** created, taken, or assumed for the sake of concealment; not genuine; false: *fictitious names.* **2.** of, pertaining to, or consisting of fiction; created by the imagination: *a fictitious hero.* —**fic·ti′tious·ly,** *adv.* —**fic·ti′tious·ness,** *n.*

fic·tive (fik′tiv), *adj.* **1.** fictitious; imaginary. **2.** pertaining to the creation of fiction: *fictive inventiveness.* —**fic′tive·ly,** *adv.*

fi·cus (fī′kəs), *n., pl.* **fi·cus, fi·cus·es.** FIG[1] (def. 1).

fid·dle (fid′l), *n., v.,* **-dled, -dling.** —*n.* **1.** a musical instrument of the viol family. **2.** VIOLIN. **3.** a barrier to keep dishes, pots, utensils, etc., from sliding off a ship's table. **4.** *Informal.* a swindle; fraud. —*v.i.* **5.** to play the fiddle. **6.** to make trifling or fussing movements with the hands (often fol. by *with*). **7.** to touch or manipulate something, as to operate or adjust it; tinker (often fol. by *with*). **8.** to waste time; trifle; dally (often fol. by *around*). **9.** *Informal.* to cheat. —*v.t.* **10.** to play (a tune) on a fiddle. **11.** to trifle or waste (usu. used with *away*): *to fiddle time away.* **12.** *Informal.* **a.** to falsify (accounts). **b.** to contrive by cheating. —**Idiom. 13. (as) fit as a fiddle,** in perfect health; very fit. **14. fiddle while Rome burns,** to do something irresponsible during a crisis. —**fid′dler,** *n.*

fid·dle-fad·dle (fid′l fad′l), *n., v.,* **-dled, -dling.** —*n.* **1.** nonsense (often used as an interjection). **2.** something trivial. —*v.i.* **3.** to fuss with trifles.

fid·dle·head (fid′l hed′), *n.* **1.** the young coiled frond of a fern. **2.** an ornamental timber on a ship's bow, carved like the volute at the upper end of a violin.

fid′dler crab′, *n.* any small burrowing crab of the genus *Uca,* characterized by one greatly enlarged claw in the male.

fid·dling (fid′ling), *adj.* trifling; trivial: *a fiddling sum.*

fi·del·i·ty (fi del′i tē, fī-), *n., pl.* **-ties. 1.** strict observance of promises, duties, etc. **2.** LOYALTY. **3.** conjugal faithfulness. **4.** adherence to fact or detail. **5.** accuracy; exactness. **6.** the degree of accuracy with which sound or images are recorded or reproduced.

fidg·et (fij′it), *v.i.* **1.** to move about restlessly, nervously, or impatiently. —*v.t.* **2.** to cause to fidget; make uneasy. —*n.* **3.** Often, **fidgets.** the condition or an instance of being nervously restless, uneasy, or impatient.

fi·du·cial (fi doo′shəl, -dyoo′-), *adj.* **1.** accepted as a fixed basis of reference or comparison: *a fiducial point.* **2.** based on or having trust: *fiducial dependence upon God.* —**fi·du′cial·ly,** *adv.*

fi·du·ci·ar·y (fi doo′shē er′ē, -dyoo′-), *n., pl.* **-ar·ies,** *adj.* —*n.* **1.** *Law.* a person to whom property or power is entrusted for the benefit of another. —*adj.* **2.** *Law.* of or pertaining to the relation between a fiduciary and his or her principal. **3.** of, based on, or in the nature of trust: *fiduciary obligations of governments.* **4.** depending on public confidence for value or currency, as fiat money.

fie (fī), *interj.* (used to express mild disgust, annoyance, or disapproval.)

fief (fēf), *n.* **1.** a fee or feud held of a feudal lord; a tenure of land subject to feudal obligations. **2.** a territory held in fee. FIEFDOM (def. 2).

fief·dom (fēf′dəm), *n.* **1.** the estate or domain of a feudal lord. **2.** anything owned or controlled by one dominant person or group.

field (fēld), *n.* **1.** a piece of open or cleared land, esp. one suitable for pasture or tillage. **2. a.** a piece of ground devoted to sports or contests; playing field. **b.** an area in which field events are held. **3.** a sphere or branch of activity or interest: *the field of teaching.* **4.** the area drawn on or serviced by a business or profession; outlying areas where practical activities or operations are carried on: *our representatives in the field.* **5.** a job or research location away from regular workshop or study facilities, offices, etc. **6. a.** the scene of active military operations. **b.** a battleground. **c.** a battle. **7.** an expanse of anything: *a field of ice.* **8.** any region characterized by a particular feature, resource, activity, etc.: *an oil field.* **9.** the surface of a canvas, shield, flag, or coin on which something is portrayed: *a gold star on a field of blue.* **10.** all the competitors in a contest, or all the competitors except for the leader. **11.** (in betting) all the contestants or numbers that are grouped together as one. **12.** *Physics.* **a.** a region of space in which a force acts, as that around a magnet or a charged particle. **b.** the quantity defined by the force acting on a given object or particle at each point in such a region. **13.** the entire angular expanse visible through an optical instrument at a given time. **14.** the structure in a generator or motor that produces a magnetic field around a rotating armature. **15.** *Math.* a number system that has the same properties relative to the operations of addition, subtraction, multiplication, and division as the number system of all real numbers. **16.** the area of a photographic subject that is taken in by a lens at a particular diaphragm opening. **17.** the total complex of factors within which a psychological event occurs and is perceived as occurring. **18.** a unit of information, as a person's name, that combines with related fields, as an official title or company name, to form one complete record in a computerized database. **19.** one half of the scanning lines required to form a complete television frame. Compare FRAME (def. 9). —*v.t.* **20. a.** (in baseball) to catch or pick up (the ball) in play. **b.** to place (a player, group of players, or a team) in the field to play. **21.** to answer skillfully: *to field a difficult question.* **22.** to place in competition. **23.** to put into action. —*v.i.* **24.** to act as a fielder in baseball or cricket. —*adj.* **25.** *Sports.* **a.** of, taking place, or competed for on the field and not on the track, as the discus throw or shot put. **b.** of or pertaining to field events. **26.** of or pertaining to active combat service as distinguished from service in rear areas or at headquarters: *a field soldier.* **27.** of or pertaining to a field. **28.** working in the fields of a farm. **29.** working as a salesperson, representative, etc., in the field: *field agents.* **30.** grown or cultivated in a field. —**Idiom.** **31. keep the field,** to remain in competition or in battle; continue to contend. **32. play the field,** *Informal.* **a.** to engage in a broad range of activities. **b.** to date a number of persons during the same period of time. **33. take the field, a.** to begin to play, as in football or baseball; go into action. **b.** to go into battle.

Field (fēld), *n.* **1. Cyrus West,** 1819–92, U.S. financier. **2. Eugene,** 1850–95, U.S. poet and journalist. **3. Marshall,** 1834–1906, U.S. merchant and philanthropist.

field′ artil′lery, *n.* artillery mobile enough to accompany troops in the field.

field′ corn′, *n.* feed corn grown for stock.

field′ day′, *n.* **1.** a day devoted to athletic contests, as at a school. **2.** an outdoor gathering; outing; picnic. **3.** a day for military exercises and display. **4.** an occasion or opportunity for unrestricted activity, amusement, etc.: *The children had a field day with their new toys.*

field•er (fēl′dər), *n.* **1.** a baseball or cricket player who fields the ball. **2.** any of the baseball players of the infield or the outfield, esp. an outfielder.

field′er's choice′, *n.* a baseball fielder's attempt to put out a base runner rather than the batter when a play at first base would put out the batter.

field′ event′, *n.* an event in a track meet that involves throwing something, as a discus or javelin, or jumping and is not performed on the running track.

field•fare (fēld′fâr′), *n.* a European thrush, *Turdus pilaris,* having reddish brown plumage with an ashy head.

field′ goal′, *n.* **1.** a three-point goal made by place-kicking a football between the opponent's goalposts above the crossbar. **2.** a goal in basketball made while the ball is in play.

field′ hock′ey, *n.* a field game in which two teams of 11 players each use hockey sticks to try to drive a small ball into a netted goal.

field′ hos′pital, *n.* a temporary hospital established at isolated posts or in the field to support ground troops in combat.

field′ house′, *n.* **1.** a building housing the dressing facilities, storage spaces, etc., used in connection with an athletic field. **2.** a building used for indoor athletic events.

field′ lens′, *n.* the lens in an eyepiece that is farthest from the eye and that deviates rays toward the center of the eye lens.

field′ mag′net, *n.* a magnet for producing a magnetic field, as in a particle accelerator or an electric motor.

field′ mar′shal, *n.* an officer of the highest military rank in the British and certain other armies, and of the second highest rank in the French army.

field′ mouse′, *n.* any of various mice or voles inhabiting fields.

field′ of vi′sion, *n.* the entire view encompassed by the eye when it is trained in any particular direction.

field′ pea′, *n.* a variety of the common pea, *Pisum sativum arvense,* grown for forage and silage.

field′ pop′py, *n.* CORN POPPY.

Fields (fēldz), *n.* **W. C.** (*William Claude Dukenfield*), 1880–1946, U.S. vaudeville and motion-picture comedian.

field′ span′iel, *n.* one of a breed of spaniels having a flat or slightly wavy, usu. black coat, used for hunting and retrieving game.

field′ spar′row, *n.* a common North American finch, *Spizella pusilla,* of brushy pasturelands.

field•stone (fēld′stōn′), *n.* unfinished stone as found in fields, esp. when used for building purposes.

field′ stop′, *n.* the aperture that limits the field of view of a lens or system of lenses.

field′ the′ory, *n.* a detailed mathematical description of the distribution and movement of matter under the influence of one or more fields: *quantum field theory.*

field′ tri′al, *n.* **1.** a competition among sporting dogs under natural conditions in the field, with dogs judged on their performance in hunting. **2.** a trial of a new product or procedure to determine its usefulness or efficiency in actual performance.

field′ trip′, *n.* **1.** a school trip to gain firsthand knowledge away from the classroom, as to a museum or the outdoors. **2.** a trip by a researcher to gather data firsthand, as to a geological, archaeological, or other site.

field′ wind′ing (wīn′ding), *n.* the electrically conducting circuit, usu. a number of coils wound on individual poles and connected in series, that produces the magnetic field in a motor or generator.

field′work′ or **field′ work′,** *n.* work done in the field, as research, exploration, surveying, or interviewing. —**field′work′er,** *n.*

fiend (fēnd), *n.* **1.** Satan; the devil. **2.** any evil spirit; demon. **3.** a diabolically cruel or wicked person. **4.** a person or thing that causes mischief or annoyance. **5.** *Informal.* a person who is addicted or ardently attached to some habit, practice, condition, etc.: *an opium fiend; a fiend for neatness.* **6.** *Informal.* a person who is excessively interested in some game, sport, etc.; fan; buff. **7.** *Informal.* a person who is outstandingly gifted or skilled at something; whiz. —**fiend′ish,** *adj.*

fierce (fērs), *adj.,* **fierc•er, fierc•est.** **1.** menacingly wild, savage, or hostile. **2.** violent in force, intensity, etc. **3.** furiously eager or intense: *fierce competition.* **4.** *Informal.* extremely bad or severe: *a fierce cold.* [< Old French < Latin *ferus* wild] —**fierce′ly,** *adv.* —**fierce′ness,** *n.*

fier•y (fīˀrˀē, fīˀə rē), *adj.,* **fier•i•er, fier•i•est.** **1.** consisting of, attended with, characterized by, or containing fire. **2.** intensely hot. **3.** like or suggestive of fire: *a fiery red.* **4.** intensely ardent or passionate: *a fiery speech.* **5.** easily angered. **6.** causing a burning sensation, as certain condiments. **7.** inflamed, as a tumor or sore. —**fier′i•ness,** *n.*

fi•es•ta (fē es′tə), *n.* **1.** any festival or festive celebration. **2.** (in Spain and Latin America) a festive celebration of a religious holiday. [< Spanish < Latin *fēsta* feast]

fife (fīf), *n., v.,* **fifed, fif•ing.** —*n.* **1.** a high-pitched transverse flute used commonly in military and marching musical groups. —*v.i., v.t.* **2.** to play on a fife. —**fif′er,** *n.*

FIFO (fī′fō), *n.* **1.** FIRST-IN, FIRST-OUT (def. 1). **2.** a storage and retrieval technique, used mainly for computer data, in which the first item stored is the first item retrieved.

fif•teen (fif′tēn′), *n.* **1.** a cardinal number, ten plus five. **2.** a symbol for this number, as 15 or XV. **3.** a set of this many persons or things. —*adj.* **4.** amounting to 15 in number.

fif•teenth (fif′tēnth′), *adj.* **1.** next after the fourteenth; being the ordinal number for 15. **2.** being one of 15 equal parts. —*n.* **3.** a fifteenth part, esp. of one (¹/₁₅). **4.** the fifteenth member of a series.

Fif′teenth Amend′ment, *n.* an amendment to the U.S. Constitution, ratified in 1870, prohibiting the restriction of voting rights "on account of race, color, or previous condition of servitude."

fifth (fifth *or, often,* fith), *adj.* **1.** next after the fourth; being the ordinal number for five. **2.** being one of five equal parts. —*n.* **3.** a fifth part, esp. of one (¹/₅). **4.** the fifth member of a series. **5.** a fifth part of a gallon of liquor or spirits; ⁴/₅ of a quart (about 750 milliliters). **6. a.** a musical interval encompassing five diatonic degrees. **b.** a tone at this interval. **c.** the harmonic combination of two tones a fifth apart. —*adv.* **7.** in the fifth place; fifthly. —**fifth′ly,** *adv.*

Fifth′ Amend′ment, *n.* an amendment to the U.S. Constitution, providing chiefly that no person be required to testify against himself or herself in a criminal case or be subjected to double jeopardy.

fifth′ col′umn, *n.* **1.** a group of people who act traitorously and subversively out of a secret sympathy with an enemy of their country. **2.** (originally) Franco sympathizers in Madrid during the Spanish Civil War: so called in allusion to a statement in 1936 that the insurgents had four columns marching on Madrid and a fifth column of sympathizers in the city ready to rise and betray it. —**fifth′ col′umnist,** *n.*

Fifth′ Command′ment, *n.* "Honor thy father and thy mother, that thy days may be long upon the land which the Lord thy God giveth thee": fifth of the Ten Commandments. Compare TEN COMMANDMENTS.

fifth′ estate′, *n.* any class or group in society other than the nobility, the clergy, the middle class, and the press.

fifth′ wheel′, *n.* **1.** a horizontal ring or segment of a ring, consisting of two bands that slide on each other, placed above the front axle of a carriage and designed to support the forepart of the body while allowing it to turn freely in a horizontal plane. **2.** a superfluous or unwanted person or thing.

fif•ti•eth (fif′tē ith), *adj.* **1.** next after the forty-ninth; being the ordinal number for 50. **2.** being one of 50 equal parts. —*n.* **3.** a fiftieth part, esp. of one (¹/₅₀). **4.** the fiftieth member of a series.

fif•ty (fif′tē), *n., pl.* **-ties,** *adj.* —*n.* **1.** a cardinal number, ten times five. **2.** a symbol for this number, as 50 or L. **3.** a set of this many persons or things. **4. fifties,** the numbers from 50 through 59, as in referring to the years of a lifetime or of a century or to degrees of temperature. **5.** a fifty-dollar bill. —*adj.* **6.** amounting to 50 in number.

fifty-fif•ty or **50-50** (fif′tē fif′tē), *adj.* **1.** equally good and bad, likely and unlikely, favorable and unfavorable, etc.: *a fifty-fifty chance.* —*adv.*

2. in an evenly or equally divided way. **—*Idiom.* 3. go fifty-fifty (on),** to share equally in the cost, responsibility, or profits (of).

Fif′ty-four′-for′ty or Fight′, a slogan popular in 1846, esp. among Democrats, who asserted U.S. ownership of the entire Oregon country, including the part that Great Britain claimed between 49° and 54° 40′ N latitude.

fig (fig), *n.* **1.** any tree or shrub of the genus *Ficus,* of the mulberry family, bearing syconia as its fruit, esp. a small tree, *F. carica,* that yields the common edible fig. **2.** a contemptibly trifling amount; the least bit: *Their help wasn't worth a fig.* **3.** a gesture of contempt.

fight (fīt), *n., v.,* **fought, fight•ing. —*n.* 1.** a battle or combat. **2.** any contest or struggle. **3.** an angry argument or disagreement. **4.** a boxing bout. **5.** a game or diversion in which the participants hit or pelt each other with something harmless: *a pillow fight.* **6.** ability, will, or inclination to fight, strive, or resist. **—*v.i.* 7.** to engage in battle or in single combat; attempt to defend oneself against or to subdue, defeat, or destroy an adversary. **8.** to contend in any manner; strive vigorously for or against something. **—*v.t.* 9.** to contend with in battle or combat; war against. **10.** to contend with or against in any manner: *to fight despair.* **11.** to carry on (a battle, duel, etc.). **12.** to maintain (a cause, quarrel, etc.) by fighting or contending. **13.** to cause or set (a boxer, animal, etc.) to fight. **14.** to maneuver (troops, ships, etc.) in battle. **—*Idiom.* 15. fight it out,** to fight until a decision is reached. **16. fight shy of,** to keep away from; avoid.

fight•er (fī′tər), *n.* **1.** a boxer; pugilist. **2.** an aircraft designed to seek out and destroy enemy aircraft in the air and to protect bomber aircraft. **3.** a person who fights, struggles, etc. **4.** a person with the courage or disposition to fight, struggle, etc. **5.** an animal, as a dog, trained to fight or having the disposition to fight.

fight′ing chance′, *n.* a possibility of success following a struggle: *He barely has a fighting chance to get well.*

fight′ing fish′, *n.* any of several brightly colored labyrinth fishes of the genus *Betta,* native to SE Asia.

fig′ leaf′, *n.* **1.** the leaf of a fig tree. **2.** a representation of a fig leaf, esp. a cover for the genitalia on a statue or in a painting. **3.** something intended to conceal what may be considered indecorous or indecent.

fig′ mar′igold, *n.* any of various plants of the genus *Mesembryanthemum,* of the carpetweed family, having showy flowers of white, yellow, or pink.

fig•ment (fig′mənt), *n.* **1.** a mere product of mental invention; a fantastic notion. **2.** a feigned or invented story, theory, etc.

Fig′ Tree′, The, a parable of Jesus. Matt. 24:32–35; Mark 13:28–32; Luke 21:19–33.

fig•u•ra•tion (fig′yə rā′shən), *n.* **1.** the act of shaping into a particular figure. **2.** the resulting figure or shape: *emblematic figurations of the sun and the moon.* **3.** the act of representing figuratively. **4.** a figurative representation. **5.** the act of marking or adorning with a design. **6. a.** musical ornamentation used to embellish a melodic line. **b.** the figuring of a bass part.

fig•ur•a•tive (fig′yər ə tiv), *adj.* **1.** of the nature of or involving a figure of speech, esp. a metaphor; metaphorical; not literal. **2.** characterized by or abounding in figures of speech: *letters filled with figurative language.* **3.** representing by means of a figure or likeness, as in drawing or sculpture. **4.** representing by a figure or emblem; emblematic. **—fig′ur•a•tive•ly,** *adv.*

fig•ure (fig′yər; *esp. Brit.* fig′ər), *n., v.,* **-ured, -ur•ing. —*n.* 1.** a numerical symbol, esp. an Arabic numeral. **2.** an amount or value expressed in numbers. **3. figures,** the use of numbers in calculating; arithmetic. **4.** a written symbol other than a letter. **5.** the form or shape of something; outline. **6.** the bodily form or frame: *a graceful figure.* **7.** a character or personage, esp. one of distinction: *a well-known figure in society.* **8.** the appearance or impression made by a person or sometimes a thing. **9.** a representation, pictorial or sculptured, esp. of the human form. **10.** an emblem, type, or symbol: *The dove is a figure of peace.* **11.** a figure of speech. **12.** a textural pattern, as in cloth or wood. **13.** a distinct movement or division of a dance. **14.** a movement or series of movements in skating. **15.** a short succession of musical notes, as either a melody or a group of chords, that produces a single complete and distinct impression. **16.** a combination of geometric elements disposed in a plane shape or solid form, as a circle, polygon, or sphere. **17.** *Logic.* the form of a categorical syllogism with respect to the relative position of the middle term. **—*v.t.* 18.** to compute or calculate (often fol. by *up*): *to figure up a total.* **19.** to express in figures. **20.** to mark or adorn with a design or pattern. **21.** to represent or express by a figure of speech. **22.** to represent by a pictorial or sculptured figure, a diagram, or the like; picture or depict; trace (an outline, silhouette, etc.). **23.** *Informal.* to conclude, judge, reason, or think: *I figured that you wanted me to stay.* **24.** to notate (a musical bass line) with figures indicating the appropriate chords. **—*v.i.* 25.** to compute or work with numerical figures. **26.** to be or appear, esp. in a conspicuous or prominent way: *Your name figures importantly in my report.* **27.** *Informal.* (of a situation, act, request, etc.) to be logical, expected, or reasonable: *It figures: when I have the time to travel, I don't have the money.* **28. figure on, a.** to count or rely on. **b.** to take into consideration; plan on. **29. figure out, a.** to understand; solve. **b.** to calculate; compute.

fig•ured (fig′yərd), *adj.* **1.** ornamented with a device or pattern. **2.** formed or shaped: *figured stones.* **3.** represented by a pictorial or sculptured figure. **—fig•ured•ly** (fig′yərd lē, -yər id-), *adv.*

fig′ure eight′, *n.* a figure or form composed of two loops formed by a continuous line crossing itself, as in the figure 8, esp. as traced on ice in figure skating.

fig•ure•head (fig′yər hed′), *n.* **1.** a person who is head of a group, country, etc., in title but has no real authority or responsibility. **2.** a carved figure built into the bow of a sailing ship.

fig′ure of speech′, *n.* an expression in which words are used in a nonliteral sense, as in metaphor, or in an unusual construction, as in antithesis, or for their sounds, as in onomatopoeia, to suggest vivid images or to heighten effect.

fig′ure skat′ing, *n.* **1.** ice skating in which the skater traces intricate patterns on the ice and sometimes executes movements combining athleticism and dance. **2.** a competitive sport based on such ice skating. Compare SCHOOL FIGURE. **—fig′ure skat′er,** *n.*

fig•ur•ine (fig′yə rēn′), *n.* a small ornamental figure of pottery, metal, plastic, etc.; statuette.

fig′ wasp′, *n.* a chalcid wasp, *Blastophaga psenes,* that pollinates figs, usu. of the Smyrna variety.

fig•wort (fig′wûrt′, -wôrt′), *n.* any tall, usu. coarse woodland plant of the genus *Scrophularia,* having a terminal cluster of small flowers.

Fi•ji (fē′jē), *n.* a republic consisting of an archipelago of some 332 islands in the S Pacific, N of New Zealand, composed of the Fiji Islands and a smaller group to the NW: formerly a British colony. 792,441; 7078 sq. mi. (18,333 sq. km). *Cap.:* Suva.

fil•a•gree (fil′ə grē′), *n., adj., v.t.,* **-greed, -gree•ing.** FILIGREE.

fil•a•ment (fil′ə mənt), *n.* **1.** a very fine thread or threadlike structure; a fiber or fibril: *filaments of gold.* **2.** the stalklike portion of a stamen, supporting the anther. **3.** (in an incandescent lamp) the threadlike conductor, often of tungsten, that is heated to incandescence by the passage of current. **4.** the heating element (sometimes also acting as a cathode) of a vacuum tube, resembling the filament in an incandescent lamp. **—fil′a•ment•ed,** *adj.* **—fil′a•men′tous** (-men′təs), *adj.*

fi•lar•i•a (fi lâr′ē ə), *n., pl.* **-lar•i•ae** (-lâr′ē ē′). any threadlike roundworm of the superfamily Filarioidea, carried by mosquitoes and parasitic when adult in the blood or tissues of vertebrates. **—fi•lar′i•al,** *adj.*

fil•bert (fil′bərt), *n.* **1.** the thick-shelled edible nut of certain cultivated varieties of hazel, esp. of *Corylus avellana,* of Europe. **2.** a tree or shrub bearing such nuts. [< Anglo-French, alluding to St. *Philbert,* near whose feast day these nuts ripen]

F

filch (filch), *v.t.* to steal (esp. something of small value); pilfer; swipe. **—filch′er,** *n.* **—filch′ing•ly,** *adv.*

file[1] (fīl), *n., v.,* **filed, fil•ing. —*n.* 1.** a folder, cabinet, or other container in which papers, letters, etc., are arranged in convenient order. **2.** a collection of papers, records, etc., arranged in convenient order. **3.** a collection of related computer data or program records stored by name, as on a disk. **4.** a line of persons or things arranged one behind another (disting. from *rank*). **5.** a list or roll. **6.** one of the vertical lines of squares on a chessboard. **—*v.t.* 7.** to place in a file. **8.** to arrange (papers, records, etc.) in convenient order for storage or reference. **9.** to transmit (a news story), as by wire or telephone. **10.** to initiate (legal proceedings): *to file charges against someone.* **—*v.i.* 11.** to march in a file or line, one after another, as soldiers. **12.** to make application: *to file for a job.* **—*Idiom.* 13. on file,** held in a file or record; filed for easy retrieval or as evidence of something. **—file′a•ble,** *adj.* **—fil′er,** *n.*

file[2] (fīl), *n., v.,* **filed, fil•ing. —*n.* 1.** a metal tool, esp. of steel, having rough surfaces for reducing or smoothing metal, wood, etc. **2.** NAIL FILE. **—*v.t.* 3.** to reduce, smooth, or remove with or as if with a file. **—file′a•ble,** *adj.* **—fil′er,** *n.*

fi•lé (fi lā′, fē′lā), *n.* a powder made from the leaves of the sassafras tree, used as a thickener and flavoring, esp. in Creole soups and gumbos.

file′ clerk′, *n.* an office employee whose principal work is to file and retrieve papers, records, etc.

file•fish (fīl′fish′), *n., pl.* (*esp. collectively*) **-fish,** (*esp. for kinds or species*) **-fish•es.** any of several flattened marine fishes of the family Monacanthidae, having an elongated head with a small mouth and small spiny scales.

file′ foot′age, *n.* stock film footage, as scenes of crowds, cities, or events, kept for use in movies or on television.

file•name (fīl′nām′), *n.* an identifying name given to an electronically stored computer file, conforming to limitations imposed by the operating system, as in length or restricted choice of characters.

file′ serv′er, *n.* a computer that makes files available to workstations on a network. Compare SERVER.

fi•let (fi lā′, fil′ā), *n.* net or lace of square mesh.

fi•let mi•gnon (fi lā′ min yon′, -yôN′, min′yon), *n.* a small tender round of steak cut from the thick end of a beef tenderloin.

fil•i•al (fil′ē əl), *adj.* **1.** of, pertaining to, or befitting a son or daughter: *filial obedience.* **2.** having the relation of a child to a parent. **3.** *Genetics.* pertaining to the sequence of generations following the parental generation.

fil•i•a•tion (fil′ē ā′shən), *n.* **1.** the fact of being the child of a certain parent. **2.** descent as if from a parent; derivation. **3.** the judicial determination of the paternity of a child, esp. an illegitimate one. **4.** the relation of one thing to another from which it is derived. **5.** an affiliated branch, as of a society.

fil•i•bus•ter (fil′ə bus′tər), *n.* **1. a.** the use of obstructive tactics by a member of a legislative assembly to prevent the adoption of a measure. **b.** an exceptionally long speech used for this purpose. **c.** Also, **fil′i•bus′-ter•er.** a legislator who uses such tactics. **2.** an irregular military adventurer, esp. one who joins in fomenting or supporting a revolution in a foreign country. —*v.i.* **3.** to impede legislation by obstructive tactics. **4.** to act as an irregular military adventurer, esp. for revolutionary purposes. —*v.t.* **5.** to impede (legislation) by obstructive tactics.

fil•i•gree or **fil•a•gree** or **fil•la•gree** (fil′ə grē′), *n., adj., v.,* **-greed, -gree•ing.** —*n.* **1.** delicate ornamental work of fine silver, gold, or other metal wires, esp. lacy jewelers' work of scrolls and arabesques. **2.** anything very delicate or fanciful: *a filigree of frost.* —*adj.* **3.** composed of or resembling filigree. —*v.t.* **4.** to adorn with or form into filigree.

fil•ings (fī′lingz), *n.pl.* particles removed by a file.

Fil•i•pi•no (fil′ə pē′nō), *n., pl.* **-nos.** a native or inhabitant of the Philippines.

fill (fil), *v.t.* **1.** to make full; put as much as can be held into: *to fill a jar with water.* **2.** to occupy to the full capacity: *The crowd filled the hall.* **3.** to supply plentifully: *to fill a house with furniture.* **4.** to feed fully; satiate. **5.** to put into a receptacle: *to fill sand into a pail.* **6.** to be plentiful throughout: *Fish filled the rivers.* **7.** to pervade completely: *The odor filled the room.* **8.** to furnish (a vacancy or office) with an occupant. **9.** to occupy and perform the duties of (a position, post, etc.). **10.** to supply the requirements or contents of (an order for goods, a medical prescription, etc.); execute. **11.** to supply (a blank space) with written matter, decorative work, etc. **12.** to meet satisfactorily, as requirements: *to fill a need.* **13.** to stop up or close (a cavity, hole, etc.): *to fill a tooth.* **14.** to insert a filling into (a pastry or other food). **15. a.** to distend (a sail) by pressure of the wind so as to impart headway to a vessel. **b.** to brace (a yard) so that the sail will catch the wind on its after side. **16.** to adulterate: *to fill soaps with water.* **17.** to build up the level of (an area) with earth, stones, etc. —*v.i.* **18.** to become full. **19.** to become distended, as sails with the wind. **20. fill in, a.** to supply (missing information). **b.** to complete by adding detail, as a design or drawing, or by inserting required information into, as a document or form. **c.** to act as a substitute. **d.** to fill (a crack, hole, etc.) with a substance. **e.** to supply information to: *Fill us in on your work experience.* **21. fill out, a.** to complete (a document or form) by supplying required information. **b.** to become rounder and fuller, as the human face or figure. —*n.* **22.** a full supply; enough to satisfy want or desire: *to eat one's fill.* **23.** a quantity of earth, stones, etc., for building up the level of an area of ground. Compare BACKFILL. —**fill′a•ble,** *adj.*

fill•er (fil′ər), *n.* **1.** a person or thing that fills. **2.** a thing or substance used to fill a gap, cavity, or the like. **3.** a substance used to fill cracks, pores, etc., in a surface before painting or varnishing. **4.** a substance used to give solidity, bulk, etc., as sizing. **5.** journalistic material of secondary importance used to fill out a column or page. **6.** cotton or other material used to stuff an object, as a quilt or cloth toy. **7.** a plate, slab, etc., inserted between two parallel structural members to connect them.

fil•let (fil′it; *usually* fi lā′ *for 1, 7*), *n., v.,* **fil•let•ed** (fil′i tid) or, for 1, 7, **fil•leted** (fi lād′), **fil•let•ing.** —*n.* **1.** a boneless cut or slice of meat or fish, as the beef tenderloin. **2.** an ornamental ribbon for the head; headband. **3.** any narrow strip, as of wood, metal, or fabric. **4. a.** a decorative line impressed on a book cover, usu. at the top and bottom of the back. **b.** a rolling tool for impressing such lines. **5. a.** a narrow flat molding raised or sunk between larger moldings. **b.** the narrow flat raised strip between two flutes of a column. **6.** a raised rim or ridge, as a ring on the muzzle of a gun. —*v.t.* **7.** to cut or prepare (meat or fish) as a fillet. **8.** to bind or adorn with or as if with a fillet.

fill′-in′, *n.* **1.** a person or thing that fills in, as a substitute, replacement, or insertion. **2.** a brief summary; a rundown.

fill•ing (fil′ing), *n.* **1.** an act or instance of filling. **2.** something that is put in as a filler: *pie filling.* **3.** a substance such as cement, amalgam, gold, or the like, used to fill a cavity caused by decay in a tooth. **4.** Also called **weft, woof.** yarn carried by the shuttle and interlacing at right angles with the warp in woven cloth.

fil•lip (fil′əp), *v.t.* **1.** to strike with the nail of a finger snapped from the end of the thumb. **2.** to tap or strike smartly. **3.** to drive by or as if by a fillip. —*v.i.* **4.** to make a fillip with the fingers. —*n.* **5.** an act or instance of filliping; a smart tap or stroke. **6.** anything that tends to rouse, excite, or revive; a stimulus.

Fill•more (fil′môr, -mōr), *n.* **Millard,** 1800–74, 13th president of the United States 1850–53.

fil•ly (fil′ē), *n., pl.* **-lies. 1.** a young female horse. **2.** *Informal.* a girl or young woman.

film (film), *n.* **1.** a thin layer or coating: *a film of grease on a plate.* **2.** a thin sheet of any material: *a film of ice.* **3.** a thin skin or membrane. **4.** a delicate web of filaments or fine threads. **5.** a thin haze, blur, or mist. **6.** a cellulose nitrate or cellulose acetate composition made in thin sheets or strips and coated with a light-sensitive emulsion for taking photographs or motion pictures. **7.** MOTION PICTURE (defs. 1, 2). **8.** Often, **films. a.** motion pictures collectively. **b.** the motion-picture industry, or its productions, operations, etc. **c.** motion pictures, as a genre of art or entertainment: *experimental film.* —*v.t.* **9.** to cover with a film or thin skin. **10. a.** to photograph with a motion-picture camera. **b.** to reproduce in the form of a motion picture: *to film a novel.* —*v.i.* **11.** to become covered by a film. **12. a.** to be reproduced in a motion picture, esp. in a specified manner: *This story will film easily.* **b.** to direct, make, or otherwise engage in the production of motion pictures.

film′ clip′, *n.* a strip of motion-picture film, usu. depicting a brief scene from a longer film and often used for promotional purposes.

film•ic (fil′mik), *adj.* **1.** pertaining to or characteristic of motion pictures. **2.** containing characteristics resembling those of motion pictures. —**film′i•cal•ly,** *adv.*

film•mak•er (film′mā′kər), *n.* a producer or director of motion pictures. —**film′mak′ing,** *n.*

film′ noir′, *n.* **1.** a motion-picture genre marked by grim urban settings, hard-boiled, cynical, bleakly pessimistic characters, and starkly shadowed photography. **2.** a motion picture in this genre.

film•og•ra•phy (fil mog′rə fē), *n., pl.* **-phies.** a listing of motion pictures by actor, director, or the like, usu. including facts about the production of each film.

film•strip (film′strip′), *n.* a length of film containing a series of related transparencies for projection on a screen.

film•y (fil′mē), *adj.,* **film•i•er, film•i•est. 1.** thin and light; fine and gauzy: *a filmy material.* **2.** hazy or misty; glazed: *filmy eyes.* —**film′-i•ly,** *adv.* —**film′i•ness,** *n.*

fil•ter (fil′tər), *n.* **1.** any substance, as cloth, paper, porous porcelain, or charcoal, through which liquid or gas is passed to remove suspended impurities or to recover solids. **2.** any device, as a tank or tube, containing such a substance for filtering. **3.** any of various analogous devices, as for removing dust from air or impurities from tobacco smoke. **4.** *Informal.* a filter-tipped cigarette or cigar. **5.** a lens screen of dyed gelatin or glass used in photography to control the rendering of color or to diminish the intensity of light. **6.** an electronic circuit or device that passes certain frequencies and blocks others. —*v.t.* **7.** to remove by the action of a filter. **8.** to act as a filter for; to slow or partially obstruct the passage of. **9.** to pass through or as if through a filter. —*v.i.* **10.** to pass or slip through slowly, as through an obstruction or a filter; penetrate. —**fil′ter•a•ble,** *adj.*

filth (filth), *n.* **1.** offensive or disgusting dirt or refuse; foul matter. **2.** foul condition: *to live in filth.* **3.** moral impurity, corruption, or obscenity. **4.** vulgar or obscene language or thought.

filth•y (fil′thē), *adj.,* **filth•i•er, filth•i•est,** *v.,* **filth•ied, filth•y•ing,** *adv.* —*adj.* **1.** foul with, characterized by, or having the nature of filth; disgustingly or completely dirty. **2.** vulgar or obscene: *filthy language.* **3.** contemptibly offensive, vile, or objectionable. **4.** abundantly supplied (often fol. by *with*): *They're filthy with money.* —*v.t.* **5.** to make filthy; foul. —*adv.,* ***Idiom.*** **6. filthy rich,** extremely wealthy. —**filth′i•ly,** *adv.* —**filth′i•ness,** *n.*

fil•trate (fil′trāt), *v.,* **-trat•ed, -trat•ing,** *n.* —*v.t., v.i.* **1.** to filter. —*n.* **2.** liquid that has been passed through a filter. —**fil′trat•a•ble,** *adj.* —**fil•tra′tion,** *n.*

fin (fin), *n., v.,* **finned, fin•ning.** —*n.* **1.** a membranous, winglike or paddlelike organ attached to any of various parts of the body of fishes and certain other aquatic animals, used for propulsion, steering, or balancing. **2. a.** a winglike appendage to a hull, as one for controlling the dive of a submarine or for damping the roll of a surface vessel. **b.** FIN KEEL. **3.** any of certain small, subsidiary structures on an aircraft, designed to increase directional stability. **4.** any of a number of standing ridges, as on a radiator or engine cylinder, intended to maximize heat transfer to the surrounding air. **5.** any part, as of a mechanism, resembling a fin. **6.** (on an automobile body) a fin-shaped ornamental part, esp. on a rear fender **(tail fin). 7.** Usu., **fins.** FLIPPER (def. 2). —*v.t.* **8.** to cut off the fins from (a fish). **9.** to provide or equip with a fin. —*v.i.* **10.** to move the fins; lash the water with the fins. —**fin′like′,** *adj.*

fin•a•ble or **fine•a•ble** (fī′nə bəl), *adj.* subject to a fine; punishable by a fine. —**fin′a•ble•ness,** *n.*

fi•na•gle (fi nā′gəl), *v.,* **-gled, -gling.** —*v.t.* **1.** to trick, swindle, or cheat (a person) (often fol. by *out of*): *He finagled the backers out of a fortune.* **2.** to get or achieve (something) by guile, trickery, or manipulation: *to finagle an invitation.* —*v.i.* **3.** to practice deception or fraud; scheme. —**fi•na′gler,** *n.*

fi•nal (fīn′l), *adj.* **1.** pertaining to or coming at the end; last in place, order, or time. **2.** ultimate: *the final goal.* **3.** conclusive or decisive: *a final decision.* **4.** constituting the end or purpose: *a final result.* **5.** *Law.* precluding further controversy on the questions passed upon: *a final decree.* —*n.* **6.** something that is last or terminal. **7.** Often, **finals. a.** the last and decisive game, match, or round in a series, as in sports. **b.** the last, usu. comprehensive, examination in a course of study.

fi′nal cut′, *n.* the final edited version of a film, approved by the director and producer. Compare ROUGH CUT.

fi•na•le (fi nal′ē, -nä′lē), *n.* **1.** the last piece, division, or movement of a concert, opera, or composition. **2.** the concluding part of any performance, course of proceedings, etc.; end.

fi•nal•ist (fīn′l ist), *n.* a person entitled to participate in the final round of a contest, as in a musical or athletic competition.

fi•nal•i•ty (fī nal′i tē), *n., pl.* **-ties. 1.** the state, quality, or fact of being final; conclusiveness or decisiveness. **2.** something that is final; an ultimate act, utterance, belief, etc.

fi•na•lize (fīn′l īz′), *v.,* **-lized, -liz•ing.** —*v.t.* **1.** to put into final form; complete all the details of. —*v.i.* **2.** to complete an agreement; conclude negotiations. —**fi′na•li•za′tion,** *n.* —**fi′na•liz′er,** *n.*

Fi′nal Judg′ment, *n.* JUDGMENT (def. 8).

fi•nal•ly (fīn′l ē), *adv.* **1.** at the final point or moment. **2.** in a final manner; conclusively or decisively.

Fi′nal Solu′tion, *n.* the Nazi program of annihilating the Jews of Europe during the Third Reich. [trans. of German *endgültige Lösung*]

fi•nance (fi nans′, fī′nans), *n., v.,* **-nanced, -nanc•ing.** —*n.* **1.** the management of revenues, esp. those affecting the public, as in the fields of banking and investment. **2. finances,** the monetary resources, as of a company, individual, or government. —*v.t.* **3.** to supply with money or capital; obtain money or credit for. —*v.i.* **4.** to raise money or capital needed for financial operations. —**fi•nance′a•ble,** *adj.*

fi′nance com′pany, *n.* an institution engaged in such specialized forms of financing as lending money with property or goods as security, purchasing accounts receivable, and extending credit to manufacturers and retailers.

fi•nan•cial (fi nan′shəl, fī-), *adj.* **1.** pertaining or relating to money matters; pecuniary. **2.** of or pertaining to those commonly engaged in dealing with money and credit. —**fi•nan′cial•ly,** *adv.*

fin•an•cier (fin′ən sēr′, fī′nən-), *n.* **1.** a person skilled or engaged in managing large financial operations, whether public or corporate. —*v.t.* **2.** to finance. —*v.i.* **3.** to act as a financier.

fi•nanc•ing (fi nan′sing, fī′nan-), *n.* **1.** the act of obtaining or furnishing funds for a purchase or enterprise. **2.** the funds so obtained.

fin•back (fin′bak′), *n.* a whale of the genus *Balaenoptera,* esp. *B. physalus,* having a prominent dorsal fin; rorqual. Also called **fin′back whale′, fin whale.**

finch (finch), *n.* any of various small songbirds of the families Emberizidae, Fringillidae, and Estrildidae that have a short conical bill adapted for eating seeds.

find (fīnd), *v.,* **found, find•ing,** *n.* —*v.t.* **1.** to come upon by chance; meet with: *to find a dime in the street.* **2.** to locate, attain, or obtain by search or effort: *to find an apartment.* **3.** to recover (something lost). **4.** to discover or perceive after consideration: *to find something to be true.* **5.** to gain or regain the use of: *to find one's tongue.* **6.** to ascertain by study or calculation: *to find the sum of several numbers.* **7.** to feel; perceive: *He finds sorrow in the tale.* **8.** to become aware of (oneself), as being in a certain condition or place: *She awoke to find herself back home.* **9.** to discover. **10.** to encounter (a particular response): *I hope this finds favor with you.* **11. a.** to determine after judicial inquiry: *to find a person guilty.* **b.** to pronounce as an official act (an indictment, verdict, or judgment). —*v.i.* **12.** to determine an issue after judicial inquiry: *The jury found for the plaintiff.* **13. find out, a.** to discover, expose, or confirm. **b.** to uncover and expose the true nature of (someone): *You will be found out if you lie.* —*n.* **14.** an act of finding or discovering. **15.** something found, esp. a valuable or gratifying discovery. —***Idiom.*** **16. find oneself,** to discover and pursue one's genuine interests and talents. —**find′a•ble,** *adj.*

find•er (fīn′dər), *n.* **1.** a person or thing that finds. **2.** VIEWFINDER. **3.** a small wide-angle telescope attached to a larger one for locating objects to be studied. **4.** a person or firm that acts as agent in initiating a business transaction.

fin-de-siè•cle (*Fr.* faN də sye′klᵊ), *adj.* of, pertaining to, or characteristic of the final years of the 19th century, esp. in Europe, and to the rarefied aestheticism and world-weary, somewhat decadent sophistication of its society, art, and literature.

find•ing (fīn′ding), *n.* **1.** the act of a person or thing that finds; discovery. **2.** Often, **findings.** something that is found or ascertained. **3. a.** a decision or verdict after judicial inquiry. **b.** a U.S. presidential order authorizing an action. **4. findings,** small tools, components, etc., used by artisans.

fine¹ (fīn), *adj.,* **fin•er, fin•est,** *adv., v.,* **fined, fin•ing.** —*adj.* **1.** of superior or best quality; of high or highest grade; excellent: *fine wine.* **2.** consisting of minute particles: *fine sand.* **3.** very thin; slender: *fine thread.* **4.** keen; sharp, as a tool. **5.** delicate in texture or workmanship: *fine cotton.* **6.** highly skilled; accomplished: *a fine musician.* **7.** characterized by refinement or elegance; polished; refined: *fine manners.* **8.** affectedly ornate or elegant. **9.** delicate; subtle: *a fine distinction.* **10.** healthy; well: *In spite of her recent illness, she looks fine.* **11.** elegant in appearance; smart. **12.** good-looking; handsome: *a fine young man.* **13.** (of a precious metal or its alloy) free from impurities; containing a large amount of pure metal. —*adv.* **14.** *Informal.* excellently; very well: *You did fine on the test.* **15.** finely; delicately: *fine wrought lettering.* —*v.i.* **16.** to become fine or finer, as by refining. —*v.t.* **17.** to make fine or finer, esp. by refining or pulverizing. **18.** to reduce the size or proportions of (often used with *down* or *away*): *to fine down heavy features.* **19.** to clarify (wines or spirits) by filtration.

fine² (fīn), *n., v.,* **fined, fin•ing.** —*n.* **1.** a sum of money imposed as a penalty for an offense or dereliction: *a parking fine.* **2.** a fee paid by a feudal tenant to a landlord, as on the renewal of tenure. —*v.t.* **3.** to subject to a fine or pecuniary penalty; punish by a fine. —***Idiom.*** **4. in fine,** in short; briefly.

fi•ne³ (fē′nā), *n.* end (a musical direction indicating the end of a repeated section).

fine•a•ble (fī′nə bəl), *adj.* FINABLE.

fine′ art′ (fīn), *n.* a visual art created primarily for aesthetic purposes and valued for its beauty or expressiveness, specifically, painting, sculpture, drawing, watercolor, graphics, or architecture.

fine′-grain′, *adj.* (of a photographed image, developer or emulsion) having or permitting an inconspicuous or invisible grain.

fine′ print′ (fīn), *n.* the detailed wording of a contract, lease, or the like, often in type smaller than the main body of the document and including restrictions or qualifications that could be considered disadvantageous. Also called **small print.** —**fine′-print′,** *adj.*

fin•er•y (fī′nə rē), *n.* fine or showy dress, ornaments, etc.

fines herbes (fēn′ erb′, ûrb′), *n.pl.* finely chopped mixed herbs, as parsley, chervil, tarragon, and chives, used to flavor sauces, etc.

fine′spun′ or **fine′-spun′,** *adj.* **1.** spun or drawn out to a fine thread. **2.** highly or excessively refined or subtle.

fi•nesse (fi ness′), *n., v.,* **-nessed, -ness•ing.** —*n.* **1.** extreme delicacy or subtlety in performance, skill, discrimination, etc. **2.** skill and adroitness in handling a difficult or highly sensitive situation. **3.** a trick, artifice, or stratagem. **4.** an attempt to win a trick in bridge with a card lower than one in an opponent's hand. —*v.i.* **5.** to use finesse or artifice. **6.** to make a finesse at cards. —*v.t.* **7.** to bring about by finesse or artifice. **8.** to make a finesse with (a card). **9.** to force the playing of (a card) by a finesse.

fine′ struc′ture (fīn), *n.* **1.** a group of lines that are observed in the spectra of certain elements, as hydrogen. **2.** the aggregate of components of the cytoskeleton.

fine′-tooth′ (or **fine′-toothed′**) **comb′,** *n.* **1.** a comb having narrow, closely set teeth. —***Idiom.*** **2. go over** or **through with a fine-tooth comb,** to examine in close detail; search thoroughly.

fine′-tune′, *v.t.,* **-tuned, -tun•ing. 1.** to adjust (a radio or television receiver) for optimal reception. **2.** TUNE (def. 8). **3.** to make minor adjustments in so as to produce stability or improvement: *to fine-tune the nation's economy.* —**fine′-tun′er,** *n.*

fin′fish′ or **fin′ fish′,** *n., pl.* (*esp. collectively*) **-fish,** (*esp. for kinds or species*) **-fish•es.** a true fish, as disting. from a shellfish.

fin•ger (fing′gər), *n.* **1.** any of the jointed terminal members of the hand, esp. one other than the thumb. **2.** a part of a glove made to receive a finger. **3.** FINGERBREADTH. **4.** the length of a finger: approximately 4½ in. (11 cm). **5.** *Slang.* an informer or spy. **6.** something like a finger in form or use, as a projection or pointer. **7.** any of various projecting parts of machines. —*v.t.* **8.** to touch with the fingers; toy or meddle with; handle. **9. a.** to play on (an instrument) with the fingers. **b.** to perform or mark (a passage of music) with a certain fingering. **10.** *Slang.* **a.** to inform against or identify (a criminal) to the authorities. **b.** to designate as a victim, as of murder or other crime. —*v.i.* **11.** to touch or handle something with the fingers. —***Idiom.*** **12. have a finger in the pie, a.** to be involved in something; participate. **b.** to meddle in something. **13. keep one's fingers crossed,** to wish for good luck or success, esp. in a specific endeavor. **14. lay** or **put one's finger on, a.** to remember precisely. **b.** to locate exactly. **15. twist** or **wrap around one's (little) finger,** to exert complete control over, as through cajolery.

fin•ger•board (fing′gər bôrd′, -bōrd′), *n.* (of a violin, cello, etc.) the strip of wood on the neck against which the strings are stopped by the fingers.

fin•ger•breadth (fing′gər bredth′, -bretth′), *n.* the breadth of a finger: approximately ¾ in. (2 cm).

fin•gered (fing′gərd), *adj.* **1.** having fingers, esp. of a specified kind or number (usu. used in combination): *five-fingered.* **2.** spoiled or marred by handling, as merchandise.

fin•ger•ing (fing′gər ing), *n.* **1.** the action or method of using the fingers in playing on an instrument. **2.** the indication of the way the fingers are to be used in performing a piece of music.

fin•ger•ling (fing′gər ling), *n.* **1.** a young or small fish, esp. a very small salmon or trout. **2.** something very small.

fin′ger paint′, *n.* a jellylike paint used chiefly by children in painting with their fingers. —**fin′ger paint′ing,** *n.*

fin•ger-point•ing (fing′gər poin′ting), *n.* the imputation of blame or responsibility.

fin•ger•print (fing′gər print′), *n.* **1.** an impression of the markings of the inner surface of the last joint of the thumb or other finger, esp. when made for purposes of identification. **2.** any unique or distinctive pattern that presents unambiguous evidence of a specific person, substance, disease, etc. —*v.t.* **3.** to take or record the fingerprints of.

fin•ger•spell•ing (fing′gər spel′ing), *n.* communication in sign language by means of a manual alphabet.

fin•ger•tip (fing′gər tip′), *n.* **1.** the tip or end of a finger. **2.** a covering used to protect the end joint of a finger. —*adj.* **3.** extending to the fingertips, as a coat or veil. —***Idiom.*** **4. at one's fingertips,** immediately and easily available. **5. to one's fingertips,** thoroughly; completely.

fin•i•al (fin′ē əl, fī′nē-), *n.* **1.** a relatively small ornamental terminal feature at the top of a gable, spire, pinnacle, etc. **2.** a terminating ornament, as on the top of a post or a piece of furniture. **3.** a curve terminating the main stroke of the characters in some italic type fonts. —**fin′i•aled,** *adj.*

fin•ick•y or **fin•nick•y** (fin′i kē), also **fin•i•king** (fin′i king), *adj.,* **-ick•i•er, -ick•i•est.** excessively particular or fastidious; difficult to please; fussy.

fin•is (fin′is, fē nē′, fī′nis), *n.* end; conclusion.

fin•ish (fin′ish), *v.t.* **1.** to bring (something) to an end or to completion; complete. **2.** to come to the end of (a course, period of time, etc.): *to finish school.* **3.** to use completely (often fol. by *up* or *off*): *to finish up a can of paint.* **4.** to overcome completely; destroy or kill (often fol. by *off*): *This spray will finish off the cockroaches.* **5.** to complete and perfect in detail; put the final touches on (sometimes fol. by *up*): *She finished up a painting.* **6.** to put a finish on (wood, metal, etc.). **7.** to perfect (a person) in education, accomplishments, social graces, etc. **8.** to ready (livestock) for market by feeding a diet calculated to produce the desired weight. —*v.i.* **9.** to come to an end. **10.** to complete a course, project, etc. (sometimes fol. by *up*). **11.** (of livestock) to achieve the desired market weight. —*n.* **12.** the end or conclusion; the final part or last stage. **13.** the end of a hunt, race, etc.: *a close finish.* **14.** a decisive ending: *a fight to the finish.* **15.** the quality of being finished or completed with smoothness, elegance, etc. **16.** educational or social polish. **17.** the surface coating or texture of wood, metal, etc. **18.** something used or serving to finish, complete, or perfect a thing. **19.** Also called **fin'ish coat', fin'ishing coat'.** a final coat of plaster or paint. **20.** a material for application in finishing. **21.** the fat tissue of livestock. **22.** the flavor remaining in the mouth after a wine has been swallowed. —**fin'ish•er,** *n.*

fin•ished (fin'isht), *adj.* **1.** ended; completed; done. **2.** perfected in all details, as a product. **3.** polished to the highest degree of excellence. **4.** highly skilled; accomplished: *a finished violinist.* **5.** condemned, doomed, or in the process of extinction. **6.** (of livestock) fattened and ready for market.

fin'ishing nail', *n.* a slender nail with a small globular head that can easily be countersunk.

fin'ishing school', *n.* a private school, usu. a high school or junior college, that educates young women for life in society.

fin'ish line', *n.* a line marking the end of a race.

fi•nite (fī'nīt), *adj.* **1.** having bounds or limits; not infinite; measurable. **2. a.** (of a set of mathematical elements) capable of being completely counted. **b.** not infinite or infinitesimal. **c.** not zero. **3.** subject to limitations, as of space, time, circumstances, or the laws of nature. —*n.* **4.** something that is finite. —**fi'nite•ly,** *adv.* —**fi'nite•ness,** *n.*

fink (fingk), *Slang.* —*n.* **1.** a strikebreaker. **2.** a labor spy. **3.** an informer; stool pigeon. **4.** a contemptible or thoroughly unattractive person. —*v.i.* **5.** to inform to the police; squeal. **6.** to act as a strikebreaker; scab. **7. fink out,** to renege.

fin' keel', *n.* a finlike projection extending downward from the keel of a sailboat, preventing lateral motion and acting as ballast.

Fin•land (fin'lənd), *n.* **1.** Finnish, **Suomi.** a republic in N Europe: on the Baltic. 5,109,148; 130,119 sq. mi. (337,010 sq. km). *Cap.:* Helsinki. **2. Gulf of,** an arm of the Baltic, S of Finland.

fin•nan had•die (fin'ən had'ē), *n.* smoked haddock.

Fin•ney (fin'ē), *n.* **Charles Grandison,** 1792–1875, U.S. clergyman and educator.

Finn•ic (fin'ik), *n.* **1.** a branch of the Uralic language family that includes Finnish, Estonian, and a number of other languages of N and central European Russia. —*adj.* **2.** of or pertaining to Finnic or its speakers.

Finn•ish (fin'ish), *n.* **1.** the Finnic language of the Finns: an official language of Finland. —*adj.* **2.** of or pertaining to Finland, the Finns, or the language Finnish.

fi•no•chi•o or **fi•noc•chi•o** (fi nō'kē ō'), *n., pl.* **-chi•os.** a variety of fennel, *Foeniculum vulgare azoricum,* having celerylike stalks and enlarged edible leaf bases.

fin' whale', *n.* FINBACK.

fiord (fyôrd, fyōrd, fē ôrd', -ōrd'), *n.* FJORD.

fir (fûr), *n.* **1.** any evergreen tree of the genus *Abies,* of the pine family, having flat needles and erect cones. **2.** the wood of such a tree.

fire (fīʳr), *n., v.,* **fired, fir•ing.** —*n.* **1.** a state, process, or instance of combustion in which fuel or other material is ignited and combined with oxygen, giving off light, heat, and flame. **2.** a burning mass of material, as on a hearth or in a furnace. **3.** the destructive burning of a building, town, forest, etc.; conflagration. **4.** heat used for cooking, esp. the lighted burner of a stove: *Put the kettle on the fire.* **5.** brilliance, as of a gem. **6.** burning passion; ardor; excitement. **7.** liveliness of imagination. **8.** severe trial or trouble; ordeal. **9.** exposure to fire as a means of torture or ordeal. **10.** a spark or sparks. **11.** the discharge of firearms: *enemy fire.* **12.** a luminous object. —*v.t.* **13.** to set on fire. **14.** to supply with fuel; attend to the fire of. **15.** to subject to heat. **16.** to bake in a kiln. **17.** to heat very slowly for the purpose of drying, as tea. **18.** to inflame, as with passion; fill with ardor. **19.** to inspire. **20.** to light or cause to glow as if on fire. **21.** to discharge (a gun). **22.** to project (a bullet or the like) by or as if by discharging from a gun. **23.** to subject to explosion or explosive force, as a mine. **24.** to hurl; throw: to *fire a stone through a window.* **25.** to dismiss from a job. **26.** to drive out or away by or as if by fire. —*v.i.* **27.** to take fire; be kindled. **28.** to glow as if on fire. **29.** to become inflamed with passion; become excited. **30.** to shoot, as a gun. **31.** to discharge a gun. **32.** to hurl a projectile. **33.** (of plant leaves) to turn yellow or brown before the plant matures. —*Idiom.* **34. build a fire under,** *Informal.* to rouse or urge to take action, make a decision quickly, or work faster. **35. catch (on) fire,** to become ignited; burn. **36. fight fire with fire,** to use the same tactics as one's opponent. **37. on fire, a.** ignited; burning; afire. **b.** eager; ardent; zealous. **c.** highly feverish. **38. play with fire,** to trifle with a serious or dangerous matter. **39. take fire, a.** to become ignited; burn. **b.** to become inspired with enthusiasm or zeal. **40. under fire, a.** under attack, esp. by military forces. **b.** under censure or criticism. —*Proverb.* **41. A burnt child fears the fire,** experience teaches painful lessons that one is not likely to forget.

fire' ant', *n.* any of several omnivorous ants, as the migrant *Solenopsis geminata* of South America, having a burning sting.

fire•arm (fīʳr'ärm'), *n.* a weapon, as a rifle or pistol, from which a projectile is fired by gunpowder. —**fire'armed',** *adj.*

fire•ball (fīʳr'bôl'), *n.* **1.** a ball of fire, as the sun or a large burst of flame. **2.** a luminous meteor, sometimes exploding. **3.** lightning having the appearance of a globe of fire. **4.** the highly luminous central portion of a nuclear explosion. **5.** a projectile filled with explosive or combustible material. **6.** an exceptionally energetic or ambitious person.

fire•bird (fīʳr'bûrd'), *n.* any of several songbirds having bright red or orange plumage, as the Baltimore oriole.

fire' blight', *n.* a disease of fruit trees, esp. of pears and apples, that blackens the foliage and is caused by a bacterium, *Erwinia amylovora.*

fire•boat (fīʳr'bōt'), *n.* a powered vessel equipped to fight fires on boats, docks, shores, etc.

fire•bomb (fīʳr'bom'), *n.* **1.** an explosive device with incendiary effects. —*v.t.* **2.** to attack with firebombs.

fire•box (fīʳr'boks'), *n.* **1.** the box or chamber containing the fire of a steam boiler, furnace, etc. **2.** the furnace of a locomotive, where coal, oil, or other fuel is burned to generate steam. **3.** a box or panel with a device for notifying the fire station of an outbreak of fire.

fire•brat (fīʳr'brat'), *n.* a bristletail, *Thermobia domestica,* that lives in areas around furnaces, boilers, steampipes, etc.

fire•break (fīʳr'brāk'), *n.* a strip of plowed or cleared land made to check the spread of a prairie or forest fire.

fire•bug (fīʳr'bug'), *n.* arsonist; pyromaniac.

fire•bush (fīʳr'bŏŏsh'), *n.* any of several shrubs having bright red flowers or foliage, as the burning bush.

fire' com'pany, *n.* **1.** a company of firefighters. **2.** a company that insures against damage from fires.

fire' control', *n.* **1.** technical and sometimes automatic supervision of artillery or naval gunfire. **2.** the supervision or prevention of fires. —**fire'-con•trol',** *adj.*

fire•crack•er (fīʳr'krak'ər), *n.* a paper or cardboard cylinder filled with an explosive and having a fuse and discharged to make a noise, as during a celebration.

fire•damp (fīʳr'damp'), *n.* a combustible gas consisting chiefly of methane, formed esp. in coal mines, and dangerously explosive when mixed with certain proportions of atmospheric air.

fire' door', *n.* **1.** a door through which a boiler or furnace is fired or through which the fire is inspected. **2.** a fireproof or fire-resistant door in a building, intended to isolate an area from fire.

fire' drill', *n.* a practice drill of duties and procedures to be followed in case of fire.

fire'-eat'er, *n.* **1.** an entertainer who pretends to eat fire. **2.** an easily provoked, belligerent person. —**fire'-eat'ing,** *adj., n.*

fire' escape', *n.* a metal stairway down an outside wall for escaping from a burning building.

fire' extin'guisher, *n.* a portable container, usu. filled with special chemicals for putting out a fire.

fire'fight'er or **fire' fight'er,** *n.* a person who fights destructive fires. —**fire'fight'ing,** *n., adj.*

fire•fly (fīʳr'flī'), *n., pl.* **-flies.** any nocturnal beetle of the family Lampyridae having a light-producing organ at the rear of the abdomen. Also called **lightning bug.** Compare GLOWWORM.

fire•guard (fīʳr'gärd'), *n.* **1.** a protective framework of wire in front of a fireplace. **2.** *Western U.S.* a firebreak.

fire' i'rons, *n.pl.* the implements used for tending a fireplace.

fire•man (fīʳr'mən), *n., pl.* **-men.** **1.** a person employed to extinguish or prevent fires; firefighter. **2.** a person employed to tend fires; stoker. **3. a.** a person employed to fire and lubricate a steam locomotive. **b.** a person employed to assist the engineer of a diesel or electric locomotive. **4.** an enlisted person in the U.S. Navy assigned to the care and operation of a ship's machinery.

fire•place (fīʳr'plās'), *n.* **1.** the part of a chimney that opens into a room and in which fuel is burned; hearth. **2.** any open structure, usu. of masonry, for keeping a fire, as at a campsite.

fire'pow'er or **fire' pow'er,** *n.* the capability of a military force, unit, or weapons system measured in terms of the amount of effective fire that can be delivered to a target.

fire•proof (fīʳr'prŏŏf'), *adj.* **1.** resistant to destruction by fire. **2.** totally or almost totally unburnable. —*v.t.* **3.** to make fireproof.

fire' sale', *n.* a special sale of merchandise actually or supposedly damaged by fire. —**fire'-sale',** *adj.*

fire' screen', *n.* a screen placed in front of a fireplace for protection, esp. from sparks.

fire' ship', *n.* a vessel loaded with ignited combustibles and set adrift to destroy an enemy's ships or constructions.

fire'side chat', *n.* an informal address by a political leader over radio or television, esp. as given by President Franklin D. Roosevelt beginning in 1933.

fire'storm' or **fire' storm',** *n.* **1.** an atmospheric phenomenon, caused by a large fire, in which the rising column of air above the fire draws in strong winds often accompanied by rain. **2.** a vehemently intense and contagious response: *a firestorm of protest.*

fire•thorn (fīʳr'thôrn'), *n.* any thorny shrub of the genus *Pyracantha,* rose family, with evergreen foliage and orange berries.

fire' tow'er, *n.* a tower, as on a mountain, from which a watch for fires is kept.

fire•trap (fīᵊr′trap′), *n.* a building that, because of its age, material, structure, or the like, is esp. dangerous in case of fire.
fire′ wall′ or **fire′wall′,** *n.* **1.** a partition made of fireproof material to prevent the spread of a fire from one part of a building or ship to another or to isolate an engine compartment, as on a plane, automobile, etc. **2.** an integrated collection of security measures designed to prevent unauthorized electronic access to a networked computer system.
fire•wa•ter (fīᵊr′wô′tər, -wot′ər), *n.* alcoholic drink; liquor.
fire•weed (fīᵊr′wēd′), *n.* any of various plants, as the willow herb, appearing in recently burned clearings.
fire•work (fīᵊr′wûrk′), *n.* **1.** Often, **fireworks.** a combustible or explosive device for producing a striking display of light or a loud noise, used for signaling or as part of a celebration. **2. fireworks, a.** a pyrotechnic display. **b.** a display of violent temper or fierce activity.
fir•ing (fīᵊr′ing), *n.* **1.** the act of a person or thing that fires. **2.** material for a fire; fuel. **3.** the act of baking ceramics or glass.
fir′ing line′, *n.* **1. a.** the positions at which troops are stationed to fire upon the enemy or targets. **b.** the troops firing from this line. **2.** the forefront of any action or activity, esp. a controversy.
fir′ing pin′, *n.* a plunger in the firing mechanism of a firearm that strikes the cartridge primer, igniting the propelling charge.
fir′ing squad′, *n.* **1.** a military detachment assigned to execute a condemned person by shooting. **2.** a military detachment assigned to fire a salute at the burial of a person being honored.
fir•kin (fûr′kin), *n.* a small wooden vessel or tub for butter, lard, etc.
firm[1] (fûrm), *adj.* **1.** not soft or yielding when pressed; comparatively solid, hard, stiff, or rigid: *firm ground.* **2.** securely fixed in place. **3.** not shaking or trembling; steady: *a firm voice.* **4.** unyielding to change; fixed; steadfast; unalterable: *a firm belief.* **5.** indicating firmness or determination: *a firm expression.* **6.** not fluctuating much or falling, as prices, values, etc. **—***v.t., v.i.* **7.** to make or become firm (often fol. by *up*). **—***adv.* **8.** firmly. —**firm′ly,** *adv.* —**firm′ness,** *n.*
firm[2] (fûrm), *n.* **1.** a business. **2.** the name or title under which associated parties transact business: *the firm of Smith & Jones.*
fir•ma•ment (fûr′mə mənt), *n.* the arch or vault of heaven; sky. —**fir•ma•men•tal** (fûr′mə men′tl), *adj.*
fir′mer chis′el (fûr′mər), *n.* a narrow-bladed chisel for paring and mortising that is driven by hand pressure or with a mallet.
firm•ware (fûrm′wâr′), *n.* software stored permanently on a ROM chip.
first (fûrst), *adj.* **1.** being before all others with respect to time, order, rank, importance, etc., used as the ordinal number of *one.* **2.** highest or chief among several voices or instruments of the same class: *first alto; first horn.* **3.** LOW (def. 28). **—***adv.* **4.** before all others or anything else in time, order, rank, etc. **5.** before some other thing, event, etc.: *If you're going, phone first.* **6.** for the first time. **7.** in preference to something else; rather; sooner: *I'd die first.* **8.** in the first place; firstly. **—***n.* **9.** the person or thing that is first in time, order, rank, etc. **10.** the beginning. **11.** the first part; first member of a series. **12.** the voice or instrument that takes the highest or chief part in its class, esp. in an orchestra or chorus. **13.** low gear; first gear. **14.** the winning position or rank in a race or other competition. **15.** Usu., **firsts.** products of the highest quality or those produced without flaws. **—*Idiom.* 16. at first sight,** at the first glimpse; at once: *love at first sight.* **17. first and last,** everything considered; above all else; altogether. **18. first off,** at the outset; immediately. **19. first thing,** before anything else; at once; promptly. **—*Saying.* 20. First in war, first in peace, first in the hearts of his countrymen,** said of George Washington in a funeral oration by Gen. Henry Lee, December 1799. **21. First things first,** the most important things should be done first. —**first′ness,** *n.*
first′ aid′, *n.* emergency treatment given before regular medical services can be obtained. —**first′-aid′,** *adj.* —**first′-aid′er,** *n.*
First′ Amend′ment, *n.* an amendment to the U.S. Constitution, ratified in 1791 as part of the Bill of Rights, prohibiting Congress from interfering with freedom of religion, speech, assembly, or petition.
first′ base′, *n.* **1.** *Baseball.* **a.** the first in counterclockwise order of the bases from home plate. **b.** the position of the player covering the area of the infield near first base. **—*Idiom.* 2. get to first base,** to succeed in the initial phase of a plan or undertaking.
first′ base′man, *n.* the baseball player whose position is first base.
first•born (fûrst′bôrn′), *adj.* **1.** first in the order of birth; eldest. **—***n.* **2.** a firstborn child. **3.** a first result or product.
First′ Cause′, *n.* God.
first′-cause′ ar′gument, *n. Philos.* an argument for the existence of God, asserting the necessity of an uncaused cause of all subsequent series of causes, on the assumption that an infinite regress is impossible.
first′ class′, *n.* **1.** the best, finest, or highest class, grade, or rank. **2.** the most expensive and most luxurious class of accommodation on trains, ships, airplanes, etc. **3.** (in the U.S. Postal Service) the class of mail consisting of letters, postal cards, or the like, together with all mailable matter sealed against inspection.
first′-class′, *adj.* **1.** of the highest or best class or quality. **2.** best-equipped and most expensive. **3.** given or entitled to preferred treatment, handling, etc.: *first-class mail.* **—***adv.* **4.** by first-class conveyance.
First′ Command′ment, *n.* "I am the Lord thy God, who brought thee out of the land of Egypt, out of the house of bondage. Thou shalt have no other gods before me": first of the Ten Commandments. Compare TEN COMMANDMENTS.
first′ divi′sion, *n. Sports.* the half of a league comprising the teams having the best records at a particular time (opposed to *second division*).
first′ estate′, *n.* the first of the three estates: the clergy in France or the Lords Spiritual in England. Compare ESTATE (def. 5).
first′ fam′ily, *n.* **1.** a family having the highest or one of the highest social ranks in a given place. **2.** (*often caps.*) the family of the president of the U.S. or the family of the governor of a state.
first′ fruits′, *n.pl.* **1.** the earliest fruit of the season. **2.** the first products or results of anything.
first′-genera′tion, *adj.* **1.** being or belonging to the first generation of a family to be born in a particular country. **2.** being a naturalized citizen of a particular country. **3.** being the first model or version available to users: *a first-generation computer program.*
first′hand′ or **first′-hand′,** *adv.* **1.** from the first or original source; directly. **—***adj.* **2.** of or pertaining to the first or original source. **3.** direct from the original source: *firsthand knowledge of the riot.*
first′-in′, first′-out′, *n.* a method of handling inventory costs at the price paid most recently, assuming items purchased first will be sold first. *Abbr.:* FIFO Compare LAST-IN, FIRST-OUT.
first′ la′dy, *n.* **1.** (*often caps.*) the wife of the president of the U.S. or of the governor of a state. **2.** the wife of the head of any country. **3.** the foremost woman in any art, profession, or the like.
first′ lieuten′ant, *n.* a military officer ranking next above second lieutenant and next below a captain.
first′-line′, *adj.* **1.** available for immediate service, esp. combat service: *first-line troops.* **2.** of prime importance or quality.
first•ly (fûrst′lē), *adv.* in the first place; first.
first′ mate′, *n.* the officer of a merchant vessel ranking next below the captain. Also called **first officer, mate.**
First′ Na′tions, *n.pl.* the indigenous peoples of Canada.
first′ night′, *n.* **1.** the night on which a theatrical or other production is first performed in a place, esp. the night of the official opening. **2.** the performance itself.
first′-night′er, *n.* a person who attends the first night of a theatrical or other production.
First′ Nowell′, The, an English Christmas carol (1833).
first′ offend′er, *n.* a person convicted of an offense for the first time.
first′ of′ficer, *n.* FIRST MATE.
first′-past′-the-post′, *n.* a method of voting by which a candidate who has the largest number of votes in a constituency wins an election. Compare **proportional representation.**
first′ per′son, *n.* **1.** the grammatical person used by a speaker in statements referring to himself or herself or to a group including himself or herself. **2.** a pronoun or verb form in the first person, as *I, we,* or *am,* or a set of such forms.
first′-rate′, *adj.* **1.** excellent; superb. **2.** of the highest rank, rate, or class. **—***adv.* **3.** very well.
First′ Read′er, *n. Christian Science.* the elected official of a church or society who conducts the services and meetings and reads from the writings of Mary Baker Eddy and the Scriptures.
first′ ser′geant, *n.* **1.** (in the U.S. Army) **a.** a noncommissioned officer ranked above sergeant first class. **b.** the senior noncommissioned officer of a company, squadron, etc. **2.** a noncommissioned officer in the U.S. Marine Corps ranked above gunnery sergeant.
first′ strike′, *n.* the initial use of nuclear weapons in a conflict, in which the attacker tries to destroy the adversary's strategic nuclear forces.
first-string (fûrst′string′), *adj.* **1.** composed of regular members, participants, etc.: *the first-string team.* **2.** foremost; main: *first-string critics on a newspaper.* —**first′-string′er,** *n.*
First′ World′, *n.* the major industrialized non-Communist nations, including those in Western Europe, the United States, Canada, and Japan.
First′ World′ War′, *n.* WORLD WAR I.
firth (fûrth) also **frith,** *n.* an indentation of the seacoast.
fis•cal (fis′kəl), *adj.* **1.** of or pertaining to the public treasury or revenues: *fiscal policies.* **2.** of or pertaining to financial matters in general. **—***n.* **3.** (in some countries) a prosecuting attorney. **4.** a revenue stamp. —**fis′cal•ly,** *adv.*
fis′cal integ′rity, *n.* responsibility in the spending of public money, esp. a balanced budget.
fis′cal year′, *n.* any yearly period established for accounting purposes.
Fisch•er (fish′ər), *n.* **1. Robert James** (*"Bobby"*), born 1943, U.S. chess player. **2. William,** 1835–1912, U.S. musician and hymn writer.
fish (fish), *n., pl.* (*esp. collectively*) **fish,** (*esp. for kinds or species*) **fish•es,** *v.* **—***n.* **1.** any of various cold-blooded, aquatic vertebrates having gills, commonly fins, and typically an elongated body covered with scales: includes three unrelated classes. Compare JAWLESS FISH, CARTILAGINOUS FISH, BONY FISH. **2.** (loosely) any of various other aquatic animals. **3.** the flesh of fishes used as food. **4.** a symbol for Christ: from the Greek word *ichthys* and derived from the initials of the Greek words for "Jesus Christ, Son of God, Savior." **5.** a secret sign used by Christians to recognize one another during the days of persecution by the Romans. **6. Fishes,** PISCES (def. 1). **7.** *Informal.* a person: *an odd fish; a poor fish.* **8.** *Slang.* a new prison inmate. **9.** a long strip of wood, iron, etc., used

F

to strengthen a mast, joint, etc. —*v.t.* **10.** to go fishing for: *to fish trout.* **11.** to try to catch fish in (a stream, lake, etc.). **12.** to draw as if fishing (often fol. by *up* or *out*): *He fished a coin out of his pocket.* **13.** to reinforce (a mast or other spar) by fastening a spar, batten, metal bar, or the like, lengthwise over a weak place. —*v.i.* **14.** to catch or attempt to catch fish. **15.** to search carefully: *to fish through one's pockets.* **16.** to seek to obtain something indirectly or by artifice: *fishing for a compliment.* **17.** to search for or attempt to catch onto something under water, in mud, etc.: *to fish for mussels.* —*Idiom.* **18. fish in troubled waters,** to take advantage of uncertain conditions for personal profit. **19. fish out of water,** a person in a strange, uncomfortable environment. **20. neither fish nor fowl,** having no specific character or conviction; neither one thing nor the other. **21. other fish to fry,** other matters requiring attention. —**fish′a•ble,** *adj.*

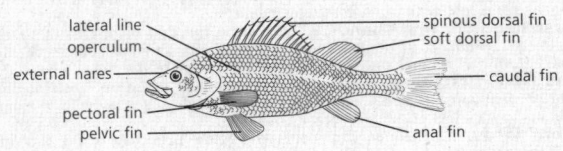

fish (def. 1)

Fish (fish), *n.* **Hamilton,** 1808–93, U.S. secretary of state 1869–77.
fish′ and chips′, *n.pl.* fried fish fillets and French fries.
fish′bowl′ or **fish′ bowl′,** *n.* **1.** a glass bowl for goldfish, snails, etc. **2.** a place, job, or condition in which one's activities are open to public view or scrutiny.
fish′ crow′, *n.* a crow, *Corvus ossifragus,* of the Atlantic and Gulf coasts of North America.
fish′ duck′, *n. Informal.* MERGANSER.
fish•er (fish′ər), *n.* **1.** a fisherman. **2.** a dark-furred North American marten, *Martes pennanti.* **3.** the fur of this animal.
fish•er•man (fish′ər mən), *n., pl.* **-men,** *adj.* —*n.* **1.** a person who fishes, whether for profit or pleasure. **2.** a ship used in fishing. —*adj.* **3.** Also, **fish′er•man's.** of or designating a knitting pattern primarily of cable-stitches usu. executed in thick, off-white yarn, or a garment made in this pattern and yarn.
fish•er•y (fish′ə rē), *n., pl.* **-er•ies. 1.** a place where fish are bred; fish hatchery. **2.** a place where fish or shellfish are caught. **3.** the occupation or industry of catching, processing, or selling fish or shellfish. **4.** the legal right to fish in certain waters or at certain times.
fish′ hawk′, *n.* OSPREY.
fish•hook (fish′hŏok′), *n.* a barbed hook for catching fish.

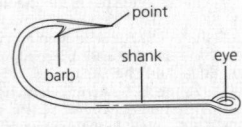

fishhook

fish′ing expedi′tion, *n.* **1.** a preliminary legal proceeding for examining an adversary's deposition, documents, etc. **2.** any inquiry carried on in the hope of discovering incriminating or exploitable information.
fish′ing pole′, *n.* a long, slender rod with a line and hook at one end for use in catching fish. Also called **fish pole.**
fish′ing rod′, *n.* a long slender flexible rod for use with a reel and line in catching fish. Compare FLY ROD.
fish′ lad′der, *n.* a series of ascending pools constructed to enable salmon or other fish to swim upstream around or over a dam.
fish•line (fish′līn′), *n.* a line with a fishhook attached for fishing.
fish′ meal′ or **fish′meal′,** *n.* dried fish ground for use as fertilizer, animal feed, or an ingredient in other foods.
fish•net (fish′net′), *n.* **1.** a net for catching fish. **2.** a fabric having an open mesh resembling a fishnet.
fish•plate (fish′plāt′), *n.* a metal or wooden plate or slab bolted to each of two members that have been butted or lapped together.
fish•pound (fish′pound′), *n.* a submerged net used in commercial fishing for capturing fish.
fish′ sto′ry, *n.* an exaggerated or incredible story.
fish•tail (fish′tāl′), *v.i.* **1.** to have the back end skid uncontrollably from side to side: *a car that fishtails at high speeds on wet roads.* **2.** to slow an airplane by causing its tail to move rapidly from side to side.
fish•wife (fish′wīf′), *n., pl.* **-wives. 1.** a woman who sells fish. **2.** a coarse-mannered, raucous woman.
fish•y (fish′ē), *adj.,* **fish•i•er, fish•i•est. 1.** like a fish esp. in smell or taste. **2.** consisting of or abounding in fish. **3.** of questionable character; dubious; suspicious: *That excuse sounds fishy.* **4.** dull and expressionless: *fishy eyes.* —**fish′i•ly,** *adv.* —**fish′i•ness,** *n.*

fis•sile (fis′əl), *adj.* **1.** capable of being split or divided; cleavable: *a fissile crystal.* **2.** fissionable.
fis•sion (fish′ən), *n.* **1.** the act of cleaving or splitting into parts. **2.** the splitting of the nucleus of an atom into nuclei of lighter atoms, accompanied by the release of energy. Compare FUSION (def. 4). **3.** the division of a biological organism into new organisms as a process of reproduction. —*v.t.* **4.** to cause (an atom) to undergo fission.
fis•sion•a•ble (fish′ə nə bəl), *adj.* capable of undergoing fission.
fis•sip•a•rous (fi sip′ər əs), *adj.* **1.** reproducing by fission. **2.** tending to split into factions or autonomous political units.
fis•sure (fish′ər), *n., v.,* **-sured, -sur•ing.** —*n.* **1.** a narrow opening produced by cleavage or separation of parts. **2.** CLEAVAGE (def. 2). **3.** a natural division or groove in an anatomical organ, as in the brain. —*v.t.* **4.** to make fissures in; cleave; split. —*v.i.* **5.** to open in fissures; become split. —**fis′su•ral,** *adj.* —**fis′sure•less,** *adj.*
fist (fist), *n.* **1.** the hand closed tightly with the fingers doubled into the palm and the thumb crossed over the fingers. **2.** INDEX (def. 5). —*v.t.* **3.** to clench into a fist. **4.** to grasp in the fist. —*Idiom.* **5. iron fist in a velvet glove,** ruthlessness and strength masked by courtesy.
fist•fight (fist′fīt′), *n.* a fight using bare fists.
fist•i•cuff (fis′ti kuf′), *n.* **1.** a cuff or blow with the fist. **2. fisticuffs,** combat with the fists. —*v.t., v.i.* **3.** to strike or fight with the fists.
fis•tu•la (fis′chŏo lə), *n., pl.* **-las, -lae** (-lē′). **1.** *Pathol.* a narrow passage or duct formed by disease or injury. **2.** a surgical opening into a hollow organ for drainage.
fis•tu•lous (fis′chŏo ləs) also **fis′tu•lar, fis•tu•late** (-lit), *adj.* **1.** pertaining to or resembling a fistula. **2.** tubelike; tubular. **3.** containing tubes or tubelike parts.
fit¹ (fit), *adj.,* **fit•ter, fit•test,** *v.,* **fit•ted** or **fit, fit•ting,** *n.* —*adj.* **1.** adapted or suited; appropriate: *This water isn't fit for drinking.* **2.** proper or becoming: *fit behavior.* **3.** prepared or ready: *crops fit for gathering.* **4.** in good physical condition; in good health. **5.** *Biol.* being adapted to the prevailing conditions and producing offspring that survive to reproductive age. —*v.t.* **6.** to be adapted to or suitable for (a purpose, object, occasion, etc.). **7.** to be proper or becoming for. **8.** to be of the right size or shape for: *The dress fitted her perfectly.* **9.** to make conform; adjust. **10.** to make qualified or competent. **11.** to prepare; make ready. **12.** to put with precise placement or adjustment: *He fitted the picture into the frame.* **13.** to provide; furnish; equip: *The car is fitted with radial tires.* —*v.i.* **14.** to be suitable or proper. **15.** to be of the right size or shape, as a garment for the wearer. **16. fit out** or **up,** to furnish with requisite supplies; equip. —*n.* **17.** the manner in which a thing fits: *The fit was perfect.* **18.** something that fits: *The coat is a poor fit.* **19.** the process of fitting. —*Idiom.* **20. fit to be tied,** extremely annoyed or angry. —**fit′ta•ble,** *adj.*
fit² (fit), *n.* **1.** a sudden acute attack or manifestation of a disease, esp. one marked by convulsions or unconsciousness: *a fit of epilepsy.* **2.** an onset or period of emotion, inclination, activity, etc.: *a fit of weeping.* —*Idiom.* **3. by** or **in fits and starts,** at irregular intervals; intermittently. **4. throw a fit,** to become extremely excited or angry.
fitch (fich) also **fitch•et** (fich′it), **fitch•ew** (-ŏo), *n.* **1.** the European polecat, *Mustela putorius.* **2.** the fur of the fitch.
fit•ful (fit′fəl), *adj.* having a spasmodic character; recurring irregularly: *fitful sleep.* —**fit′ful•ly,** *adv.* —**fit′ful•ness,** *n.*
fit•ness (fit′nis), *n.* **1.** HEALTH. **2.** the genetic contribution of an individual to the next generation's gene pool relative to the average for the population, usu. measured by the number of offspring or close kin that survive to reproductive age.
fit•ting (fit′ing), *adj.* **1.** suitable or appropriate; proper or becoming. —*n.* **2.** the act of a person or thing that fits. **3.** an act or instance of trying on clothes that are being made or altered. **4.** an item provided as standard equipment: *The various fittings needed to install an air conditioner.* —**fit′ting•ly,** *adv.* —**fit′ting•ness,** *n.*
Fitz•ger•ald (fits jer′əld), *n.* **1. Ella,** 1917–96, U.S. jazz singer. **2. F(rancis) Scott (Key),** 1896–1940, U.S. novelist.
five (fīv), *n.* **1.** a cardinal number, four plus one. **2.** a symbol for this number, as 5 or V. **3.** a set of this many persons or things. **4.** a five-dollar bill. —*adj.* **5.** amounting to five in number.
Five′ Civ′ilized Na′tions, *n.pl.* the collective name for the Cherokee, Creek, Choctaw, Chickasaw, and Seminole tribes of Indians who, in spite of their adaptation to European culture, were deported to the Indian Territory from 1830 to 1840. Also called **Five′ Civ′ilized Tribes′.**
five•fold (fīv′fōld′), *adj.* **1.** five times as great or as much. **2.** comprising five parts or members. —*adv.* **3.** in fivefold measure.
five′ hun′dred, *n.* a variety of euchre or rummy the object of which is to score 500 points first.
Five′ Na′tions, *n.pl.* the Iroquois Indian confederacy of New York, comprising the Mohawk, Oneida, Onondaga, Cayuga, and Seneca.
five′ o'clock′ shad′ow, *n.* a dark stubble on the jawline and cheeks of a man's face.
five•pen•ny (fīv′pen′ē), *adj.* **1.** noting a nail 1¾ in. (4.4 cm) long. **2.** worth five pence.
five′ sens′es, *n.pl.* the faculties of sight, hearing, smell, taste, and touch. Compare SIXTH SENSE.
five′-spot′, *n.* **1. a.** a playing card or the upward face of a die bearing five pips. **b.** a domino one half of which bears five pips. **2.** *Slang.* a five-dollar bill.

five′-star′, *adj.* **1.** designating a general of the army or a fleet admiral, as indicated by five stars on the insignia. **2.** indicating the highest rank or quality: *a five-star brandy.*

five W's, *n.pl. Journalism.* who, what, where, when, and why: the essential information in a lead paragraph of a news story.

fix (fiks), *v.t.* **1.** to repair; mend: *If it's not broken, don't try to fix it.* **2.** to put in order; adjust or arrange: *Fix your hair!* **3.** to make fast, firm, or stable. **4.** to place definitely and more or less permanently. **5.** to settle definitely; determine: *to fix a price.* **6.** to direct (the eyes, the attention, etc.) steadily. **7.** to attract and hold (the eye, the attention, etc.). **8.** to make set or rigid. **9.** to put into permanent form. **10.** to put or place (responsibility, blame, etc.) on a person. **11.** to assign or refer to: *to fix a time for the meeting.* **12.** to arrange or influence the outcome or action of, esp. privately or dishonestly: *to fix a game.* **13.** to get (a meal) ready; prepare (food). **14.** to put in a condition or position to make no further trouble. **15.** to get even with: *I'll fix you if you don't keep your promise.* **16.** to castrate or spay (an animal, esp. a pet). **17. a.** to make (a chemical) stable in consistency or condition; reduce from fluidity or volatility to a more stable state. **b.** to convert atmospheric nitrogen into a solid compound, as a nitrate fertilizer. **18.** to render (a photographic image) permanent by removing light-sensitive silver halides. **19.** to kill, make rigid, and preserve for microscopic study. —*v.i.* **20.** to become fixed. **21.** to become set; assume a rigid or solid form. **22.** to become stable or permanent. **23.** to settle down. **24. fix on** or **upon,** to decide on; determine. **25. fix up, a.** to make arrangements for. **b.** to provide with an introduction to someone for a date. **c.** to repair, cure, or resolve. —*n.* **26.** a position from which it is difficult to escape; predicament. **27.** a repair, adjustment, or solution, usu. of an immediate nature. **28.** a charted position of a vessel or aircraft, determined by two or more bearings taken on landmarks, heavenly bodies, etc. **29.** *Informal.* a clear determination: *Can you get a fix on the meaning of this paragraph?* **30.** *Slang.* an injection of heroin or other narcotic. **31.** *Slang.* an underhand or illegal arrangement. —**fix′a·ble,** *adj.* —**fix′a·bil′i·ty,** *n.* —**fix′er,** *n.*

fix·ate (fik′sāt), *v.,* **-at·ed, -at·ing.** —*v.t.* **1.** to fix; make stable or stationary. **2.** to concentrate one's attention on. —*v.i.* **3.** to concentrate one's attention (often followed by *on*). **4.** to develop a fixation.

fix·a·tion (fik sā′shən), *n.* **1.** the act of fixing or fixating or the state of being fixed or fixated. **2.** the process of rendering a photographic image permanent by removal of light-sensitive silver halides. **3.** a preoccupation with one subject, issue, etc.; obsession.

fix·a·tive (fik′sə tiv), *adj.* **1.** serving to fix; making fixed or permanent. —*n.* Also, **fix·a·tif** (fik′sə tiv, -tēf′). **2.** a fixative substance, as a spray that prevents blurring on a drawing or a solution that preserves microscopic specimens. **3.** a chemical substance, as sodium thiosulfate, used in photography to promote fixation.

fixed (fikst), *adj.* **1.** attached or placed so as to be firm and not readily movable; stationary. **2.** stable or permanent, as color. **3.** intent upon something; steadily directed: *a fixed stare.* **4.** definitely and permanently placed: *a fixed buoy.* **5.** not fluctuating or varying: *fixed income.* **6.** supplied with or having enough of something necessary or wanted, as money. **7.** coming each year on the same calendar date. **8.** put in order. **9.** arranged in advance privately or dishonestly: *a fixed race.* **10. a.** (of a chemical element) taken into a compound from its free state. **b.** nonvolatile, or not easily volatilized: *a fixed oil.* —**fix′ed·ly** (fik′sid lē, fikst′lē), *adv.*

fixed′ as′set, *n.* any long-term asset, as a building or tract of land.

fixed′ charge′, *n.* **1.** an expense that cannot be modified. **2.** a periodic obligation, as taxes or interest on bonds.

fixed′ oil′, *n.* a natural vegetable or animal oil that is nonvolatile, as lard oil or linseed oil.

fixed′-wing′, *adj.* (of an aircraft) having wings that are rigidly and permanently attached to the fuselage.

fix·i·ty (fik′si tē), *n., pl.* **-ties** for 2. **1.** the state or quality of being fixed; stability; permanence. **2.** something that is fixed, stable, or permanent.

fix·ture (fiks′chər), *n.* **1.** something securely and usu. permanently attached or appended, as to a building: *a light fixture.* **2.** a person or thing long established in the same place or position. **3.** a chattel that has been attached to property so that its removal would damage the property and may therefore be considered as part of the property. **4.** an event that takes place regularly.

fiz·gig (fiz′gig′), *n.* **1.** a type of firework that makes a loud hissing sound. **2.** a whirling toy that makes a whizzing noise.

fizz (fiz), *v.i.* **1.** to make a hissing or sputtering sound; effervesce. —*n.* **2.** a fizzing sound; effervescence. **3.** an effervescent beverage. —**fizz′er,** *n.*

fiz·zle (fiz′əl), *v.,* **-zled, -zling,** *n.* —*v.i.* **1.** to make a hissing or sputtering sound, esp. one that dies out weakly. **2.** to fail or expire feebly after a good start (often fol. by *out*). —*n.* **3.** a fizzling, hissing, or sputtering. **4.** a failure; fiasco.

fizz·y (fiz′ē), *adj.,* **fizz·i·er, fizz·i·est.** bubbly; fizzing.

fjeld (fyeld, fyel, fē eld′, -el′), *n.* a rocky barren plateau of the Scandinavian peninsula.

fjord or **fiord** (fyôrd, fyōrd, fē ôrd′, -ōrd′), *n.* **1.** a long narrow arm of the sea bordered by steep cliffs and usu. formed by glacial erosion. **2.** (in Scandinavia) a bay. —**fjord′ic,** *adj.*

FL, Florida.

Fla., Florida.

flab (flab), *n.* loose, excessive flesh.

flab·ber·gast (flab′ər gast′), *v.t.* to overcome with surprise and bewilderment; astound. —**flab′ber·gast′er,** *n.*

flab·by (flab′ē), *adj.,* **-bi·er, -bi·est. 1.** lacking firmness or tone; flaccid: *flabby muscles.* **2.** marked by flab: *a flabby stomach.* **3.** lacking determination; weak. —**flab′bi·ly,** *adv.* —**flab′bi·ness,** *n.*

flac·cid (flak′sid, flas′id), *adj.* **1.** soft and limp; not firm; flabby. **2.** lacking force; weak: *a flaccid defense.* —**flac·cid′i·ty, flac′cid·ness,** *n.*

flack¹ (flak), *Slang.* —*n.* **1.** PRESS AGENT. **2.** Also, **flack′er·y.** PUBLICITY. —*v.i.* **3.** to serve as a press agent or publicist.

flack² (flak), *n.* FLAK.

flac·on (flak′ən, fla kôⁿ′), *n.* a small bottle or flask with a stopper, esp. one used for perfume.

flag¹ (flag), *n., v.,* **flagged, flag·ging.** —*n.* **1.** a typically rectangular piece of cloth marked with distinctive colors or designs and used as a symbol, as of a nation or organization, or as a means of signaling. **2.** the tail of a deer or of a setter dog. **3.** *Journ.* NAMEPLATE (def. 2). **4.** a tab or tag attached as to a page or file card, to attract attention. **5.** any of the angled lines attached to a musical quarter note and to other notes of diminishing value. —*v.t.* **6.** to place a flag or flags over or on; decorate with flags. **7.** to signal or warn with or as if with a flag (sometimes fol. by *down*): *to flag a taxi; flag down a train.* **8.** to communicate (information) by or as if by a flag. **9.** to decoy, as game, by waving a flag or the like to excite attention or curiosity. **10.** to mark (a page, file, card, etc.) for attention, as by attaching protruding tabs. —**flag′ger,** *n.*

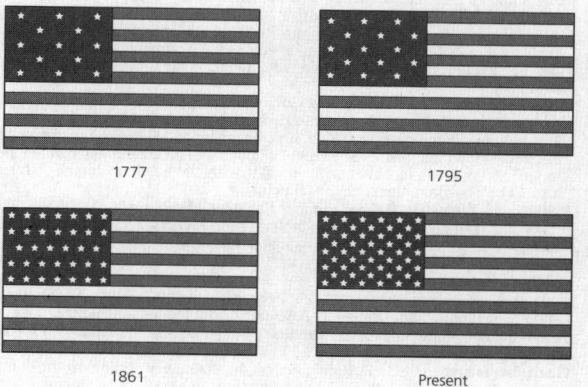

1777   1795

1861   Present

The American Flag

flag² (flag), *n.* **1.** any of various plants with long, sword-shaped leaves, as the sweet flag. **2.** the leaf of such a plant.

flag³ (flag), *v.i.,* **flagged, flag·ging. 1.** to fall off in vigor, energy, activity, interest, etc.: *Attendance flagged after the team lost.* **2.** to hang loosely or limply; droop.

flag⁴ (flag), *n., v.,* **flagged, flag·ging.** —*n.* **1.** FLAGSTONE. —*v.t.* **2.** to pave with flagstones. —**flag′ger,** *n.*

Flag′ Day′, *n.* June 14, the anniversary of the day (June 14, 1777) when Congress adopted the official U.S. flag.

fla·gel·la (fla jel′ə), *n.* a pl. of FLAGELLUM.

flag·el·lant (flaj′ə lənt, flə jel′ənt), *n.* **1.** a person who flagellates himself or herself for religious discipline. —*adj.* **2.** pertaining to flagellation. **3.** severely criticizing.

flag·el·late (*v.* flaj′ə lāt′; *adj., n.* -lit, -lāt′), *v.,* **-lat·ed, -lat·ing,** *adj., n.* —*v.t.* **1.** to whip; scourge. **2.** to punish or berate as if with a whip. —*adj.* **3.** Also, **flag′el·lat′ed.** *Biol.* having flagella. **4.** *Bot.* producing runners or runnerlike branches, as the strawberry. **5.** pertaining to or caused by flagellates. —*n.* **6.** any protozoan of the phylum Mastigophora, having one or more flagella.

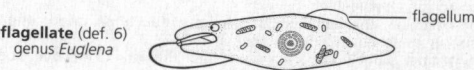

flagellate (def. 6)
genus *Euglena*

flagellum

fla·gel·lum (flə jel′əm), *n., pl.* **-gel·la** (-jel′ə), **-gel·lums. 1.** *Biol.* a long lashlike appendage serving as an organ of locomotion in protozoa, sperm cells, etc. **2.** *Bot.* a runner. **3.** the upper portion of the antenna of an insect. **4.** a whip or lash.

flag·ging¹ (flag′ing), *adj.* **1.** dwindling. **2.** weak, fatigued, or drooping. —**flag′ging·ly,** *adv.*

flag·ging² (flag′ing), *n.* **1.** flagstones collectively. **2.** a pavement or walk of flagstones.

fla·gi·tious (flə jish′əs), *adj.* **1.** shamefully wicked, as persons, actions, or times. **2.** heinous or flagrant, as a crime; infamous.

F

flag·man (flag′mən), *n., pl.* **-men. 1.** a person who signals with a flag or lantern, as at a railroad crossing. **2.** a person who has charge of or carries a flag.

flag·on (flag′ən), *n.* **1.** a large bottle for wine, liquors, etc. **2.** a container for holding liquids, as for use at table, esp. one with a handle, a spout, and usu. a cover.

flag·pole (flag′pōl′), *n.* **1.** Also called **flagstaff.** a staff or pole on which a flag is displayed. —*Idiom.* **2. run something up the flag-pole,** to announce (a proposal, plan, or idea) as a test to gauge reactions.

fla·grant (flā′grənt), *adj.* **1.** shockingly noticeable or evident; obvious; glaring: *a flagrant error.* **2.** notorious; scandalous: *a flagrant offender.* —**fla′gran·cy, fla′grance,** *n.* —**fla′grant·ly,** *adv.*

fla·gran·te de·lic·to (flə gran′tē di lik′tō), *adv.* in the very act of committing the offense.

flag·ship (flag′ship′), *n.* **1.** a ship carrying the commander of a fleet, squadron, or the like, and displaying the officer's commander's flag. **2.** the main vessel of a shipping line. **3.** the best or most important one of a group or system: *This store is the flagship of our chain.*

flag·staff (flag′staf′, -stäf′), *n.* FLAGPOLE.

Flag·staff (flag′staf′, -stäf′), *n.* a city in central Arizona. 34,743. ab. 6900 ft. (2100 m) high.

flag·stone (flag′stōn′), *n.* a flat stone slab used esp. for paving.

flag′-wav′ing, *n.* an ostentatiously emotional display of patriotism or factionalism. —**flag′-wav′er,** *n.*

flail (flāl), *n.* **1.** an instrument for threshing grain, consisting of a staff or handle to one end of which is attached a freely swinging stick or bar. —*v.t., v.i.* **2.** to beat or swing with or as if with a flail.

flair (flâr), *n.* **1.** a natural talent, aptitude, or ability; bent; knack: *a flair for comedy.* **2.** smartness of style or manner: *She dresses with great flair.*

flak or **flack** (flak), *n.* **1.** antiaircraft fire. **2.** critical or hostile reaction; strong opposition.

flake (flāk), *n., v.,* **flaked, flak·ing.** —*n.* **1.** a small, flat, thin piece, esp. one that has been or become detached from a larger piece or mass. **2.** any small piece or mass. **3.** a stratum or layer. **4.** *Slang.* an eccentric person; screwball. —*v.i.* **5.** to peel off or fall in flakes. —*v.t.* **6.** to remove in flakes. **7.** to cover with or as if with flakes. **8.** to break or form into flakes. —**flake′less,** *adj.* —**flak′er,** *n.*

flak·y or **flak·ey** (flā′kē), *adj.,* **flak·i·er, flak·i·est. 1.** of or like flakes. **2.** lying or cleaving off in flakes or layers. **3.** *Slang.* eccentric; wacky; dizzy. —**flak′i·ly,** *adv.* —**flak′i·ness,** *n.*

flam (flam), *n.* a drumbeat consisting of two notes in quick succession, with the accent on the second.

flam·bé (fläm bā′, flän-), *adj., v.,* **-béed, -bé·ing.** —*adj.* **1.** (of food) served in flaming liquor. —*v.t.* **2.** to pour liquor over and ignite.

flam·beau (flam′bō), *n., pl.* **-beaux** (-bōz), **-beaus. 1.** a flaming torch. **2.** a large ornamental candlestick.

flam·boy·ant (flam boi′ənt), *adj.* **1.** strikingly bold or brilliant; showy: *flamboyant clothes.* **2.** extravagantly dashing and colorful: *flamboyant behavior.* **3.** florid; ornate; elaborately styled. —**flam·boy′ance,** *n.* —**flam·boy′ant·ly,** *adv.*

flame (flām), *n., v.,* **flamed, flam·ing.** —*n.* **1.** a portion of burning gas or vapor, as from ignited wood or coal. **2.** Often, **flames.** the state or condition of blazing combustion. **3.** any flamelike condition; glow; inflamed condition. **4.** brilliant light; scintillating luster. **5.** bright coloring; a streak or patch of color. **6.** a bright reddish orange color. **7.** intense ardor, zeal, or passion. **8.** an object of one's passionate love; sweetheart. —*v.i.* **9.** to burn with a flame or flames; burst into flames; blaze. **10.** to glow like flame; shine brilliantly; flash. **11.** to burn or burst forth with strong emotion; break into open anger, indignation, etc. **12.** *Computers.* to send an e-mail message in which the writer makes a harsh and unwarranted personal attack on —*v.t.* **13.** to subject to the action of flame or fire. —**flam′er,** *n.* —**flame′less,** *adj.* —**flame′like′,** *adj.*

flame′ cell′, *n.* one of the hollow cells terminating the branches of the excretory tubules of certain invertebrates, having a tuft of continuously moving cilia.

fla·men·co (flə meng′kō, flə-), *n., pl.* **-cos,** *adj.* —*n.* **1. a.** a dance style characteristic of the Andalusian Gypsies that is marked by vigorous hand-clapping and stamping of the feet. **b.** a dance in this style. **2.** instrumental or vocal music suitable for accompanying flamenco. —*adj.* **3.** Also, **fla·men·can.** of or pertaining to flamenco. [< Spanish: pertaining to the Gypsies]

flame′-out′, *n.* the failure of a jet engine due to an interruption of the fuel supply or to faulty combustion.

flame·proof (flām′prōōf′), *adj.* resisting the effect of flames; not readily ignited or burned by flames.

flame′-retard′ant, *adj.* not subject to quick or easy burning esp. through chemical treatment: *flame-retardant curtains.*

flame·throw·er (flām′thrō′ər), *n.* a device, either mounted or portable, that sprays ignited incendiary fuel for some distance.

flame′ tree′, *n.* either of two Australian trees, *Brachychiton acerifolius* or *B. australis,* of the sterculia family, having lobed leaves and clusters of scarlet flowers.

flam·ing (flā′ming), *adj.* **1.** emitting flames; blazing; burning; fiery. **2.** like a flame in brilliance, heat, or shape. **3.** intensely ardent or passionate: *flaming youth.* —**flam′ing·ly,** *adv.*

fla·min·go (flə ming′gō), *n., pl.* **-gos, -goes.** any of several wading

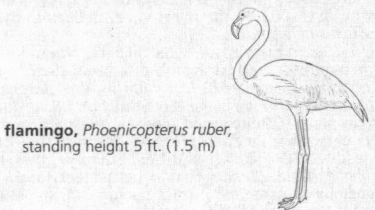

flamingo, *Phoenicopterus ruber,* standing height 5 ft. (1.5 m)

birds comprising the family Phoenicopteridae, having webbed feet, a bill bent downward at the tip, and pinkish to scarlet plumage.

flam·ma·ble (flam′ə bəl), *adj.* easily set on fire; combustible. —**flam′ma·bil′i·ty,** *n.*

flan (flan, flän; *for 2 also* flän), *n.* **1.** a Spanish dessert of baked sweetened egg custard with a caramel topping. **2.** an open, tartlike pastry, filled with cheese, custard, fruit, etc. **3.** a piece of metal shaped ready to form a coin but not yet stamped by the die.

Flan·a·gan (flan′ə gən), *n.* **Edward Joseph** (*"Father Flanagan"*), 1886–1948, U.S. Roman Catholic priest, born in Ireland.

Flan·ders (flan′dərz), *n.* a medieval country in W Europe, extending along the North Sea from the Strait of Dover to the Scheldt River: the corresponding modern regions include the provinces of East Flanders and West Flanders in W Belgium and the adjacent parts of N France and SW Netherlands.

flange (flanj), *n.* a rim, collar, ring, or pair of ridges projecting usu. at right angles from a shaft, pipe, machine housing, etc., as to strengthen it, provide support, or enable attachment of objects.

flank (flangk), *n.* **1.** the side of an animal or a person between the ribs and hip. **2.** the thin piece of flesh constituting this part. **3.** a cut of meat from the flank of an animal. **4.** the side of anything, as of a building. **5.** the extreme right or left side of an army or fleet. —*v.t.* **6.** to stand or be placed or posted at the flank or side of. **7.** to defend or guard at the flank. **8.** to menace or attack the flank of. **9.** to pass around or turn the flank of. —*v.i.* **10.** to occupy a position at the flank or side. **11.** to present the flank or side.

flank·er (flang′kər), *n.* **1.** a person or thing that flanks. **2.** *Football.* **a.** Also called **flank′er back′.** an offensive back who lines up outside of an end. **b.** SPLIT END.

flan·nel (flan′l), *n., v.,* **-neled, -nel·ing** or (*esp. Brit.*) **-nelled, -nel·ling.** —*n.* **1.** a soft, slightly napped fabric of wool or wool and another fiber, used for trousers, jackets, shirts, etc. **2.** a soft, warm, light fabric of cotton, thickly napped on one side, used for sleepwear, sheets, etc. **3.** **flannels. a.** an outer garment, esp. trousers, made of flannel. **b.** woolen undergarments. —*v.t.* **4.** to rub with flannel. —**flan′nel·ly,** *adj.*

flap (flap), *v.,* **flapped, flap·ping,** *n.* —*v.i.* **1.** to swing or sway back and forth loosely, esp. with noise. **2.** to move up and down, as wings or arms. **3.** to strike a blow with something broad and flexible. **4.** *Slang.* to talk in a foolish manner; babble. —*v.t.* **5.** to move (wings, arms, etc.) up and down. **6.** to cause to swing or sway loosely, esp. with noise. **7.** to strike with something broad and flat. **8.** to toss, fold, shut, etc., smartly, roughly, or noisily. —*n.* **9.** something flat and broad that is attached at one side only and hangs loosely or covers an opening. **10.** either of the two segments of a book jacket folding under the book's covers. **11.** one leaf of a folding door, shutter, or the like. **12.** a flapping motion. **13.** the noise produced by something that flaps. **14.** *Informal.* **a.** a state of nervous excitement. **b.** scandal; trouble. **15.** a movable surface used for increasing the lift or drag of an airplane.

flap·jack (flap′jak′), *n.* griddlecake; pancake.

flap·pa·ble (flap′ə bəl), *adj. Informal.* easily upset or confused, esp. under stress.

flap·per (flap′ər), *n.* **1.** something broad and flat used for striking or for making a noise by striking. **2.** a broad flat hinged or hanging piece; flap. **3.** a young woman flouting conventional behavior, esp. in the 1920s. **4.** a young bird just learning to fly.

flare (flâr), *v.,* **flared, flar·ing,** *n.* —*v.i.* **1.** to blaze with a sudden burst of flame (often fol. by up): *The fire flared up as the paper caught.* **2.** to burn with an unsteady, swaying flame. **3.** to burst out in sudden, fierce activity, passion, etc. (often fol. by up or out). **4.** to shine or glow. **5.** to spread gradually outward, as the end of a trumpet or the bottom of a wide skirt. —*v.t.* **6.** to cause to flare. **7.** to display conspicuously or ostentatiously. **8.** to signal by flares of fire or light. **9.** to discharge and burn (excess gas) at a well or refinery. **10. flare out** or **up,** to become suddenly enraged. —*n.* **11.** a flaring or swaying flame or light. **12.** a sudden blaze or burst of flame. **13. a.** a blaze of fire or light used as a signal, for illumination or guidance, etc. **b.** a device or substance producing such a blaze. **14.** a sudden burst, as of zeal or of anger. **15.** a gradual spread outward in form; outward curvature. **16.** something that spreads out. **17.** unwanted light reaching the image plane of an optical instrument, resulting from extraneous reflections, scattering by lenses, and the like. **18.** a fogged appearance given to an image by reflection within a camera lens or within the camera itself.

flare·up (flâr′up′), *n.* **1.** a sudden flaring up of flame or light. **2.** a sudden outburst of anger. **3.** a sudden outbreak of violence, disease, or other condition thought to be inactive.

flar•ing (flâr′ing), *adj.* **1.** blazing; flaming. **2.** glaringly bright or showy. **3.** spreading gradually outward in form: *a flaring skirt.*

flash (flash), *n.* **1.** a brief, sudden burst of bright light. **2.** a sudden, brief outburst or display, as of joy or wit. **3.** a very brief moment; instant. **4.** FLASHLIGHT (def. 1). **5.** gaudy or vulgar showiness; ostentatious display. **6.** a brief dispatch giving preliminary news of an important story. **7.** bright artificial light thrown briefly upon a subject during a photographic exposure. **8.** the sudden flame or intense heat produced by a bomb or other explosive device. **9.** a sudden thought, insight, or vision. **10. a.** a device, as a sluice, for confining and releasing water to send a vessel down a shallow stream. **b.** the rush of water thus produced. **11.** HOT FLASH. —*v.i.* **12.** to break forth into sudden flame or light, esp. transiently or intermittently. **13.** to gleam. **14.** to appear suddenly: *The answer flashed into his mind.* **15.** to move like a flash. **16.** to speak or behave with sudden anger, outrage, or the like (often fol. by *out*). **17.** to break into sudden action. —*v.t.* **18.** to emit or send forth (fire or light) in sudden flashes. **19.** to cause to flash, as powder by ignition or a sword by waving. **20.** to send forth like a flash. **21.** to communicate instantaneously, as by radio or telegraph. **22.** to make an ostentatious display of. **23.** to display suddenly and briefly: *She flashed her ID card at the guard.* **24.** to increase the flow of water in (a river, channel, etc.). **25. a.** to coat (glass or ceramics) with a layer of colored, opalescent, or white glass. **b.** to apply (such a layer). **c.** to color or make (glass) opaque by reheating. **26.** to protect (a roof, etc.) from leakage with flashing. —*adj.* **27.** sudden and brief: *a flash storm.* **28.** showy; ostentatious. **29.** counterfeit; sham. **30.** belonging to or connected with thieves, vagabonds, etc., or their cant or jargon. **31.** of or pertaining to followers of boxing, racing, etc. —*Idiom.* **32.** flash in the pan, **a.** a brief intense effort that produces negligible results. **b.** a person whose promise or success is transitory. **33.** flash on, *Slang.* to have a sudden vivid memory of or insight about.

flash•back (flash′bak′), *n.* **1.** the insertion of an earlier event into the chronological structure of a novel, motion picture, play, etc., or the scene so inserted. **2.** Also called **flash′back hallucino′sis.** *Psychiatry.* an abnormally vivid, often recurrent recollection of a disturbing past event, sometimes accompanied by hallucinations.

flash′bulb′ or **flash′ bulb′,** *n.* a glass bulb, filled with oxygen and aluminum or zirconium wire or foil, that when electrically ignited illuminates a photographic subject momentarily.

flash′card′ or **flash′ card′,** *n.* a card with words, numerals, etc., used as a teaching aid in rapid recognition drills.

flash′ flood′, *n.* a sudden and destructive rush of water down a narrow gully or over a sloping surface, caused by heavy rainfall.

flash′-for′ward, *n.* the insertion of a later event into the chronological structure of a novel, play, etc., or the scene so inserted.

flash•gun (flash′gun′), *n.* a device that simultaneously discharges a flashbulb or flashtube and operates a camera shutter.

flash•ing (flash′ing), *n.* pieces of sheet metal or the like used to cover and protect certain joints and angles, as where a roof comes in contact with a wall or chimney, esp. against leakage.

flash′ lamp′ or **flash′lamp′,** *n.* a lamp for providing momentary illumination of the subject of a photograph.

flash•light (flash′līt′), *n.* **1.** a small portable electric lamp powered by dry batteries or a tiny generator. **2.** a light that flashes, as a lighthouse beacon. **3.** any source of artificial light as used in flash photography.

flash′light fish′, *n.* a deep-sea fish, *Photoblepharon palpebratus,* of the lanterneye family, with luminous cheek organs that can be flashed on and off with a lid.

flash′ point′ or **flash′point′,** *n.* **1.** the lowest temperature at which a liquid in a specified apparatus will give off sufficient vapor to ignite momentarily on application of a flame. **2.** a point or stage at which an event or situation becomes critical. **3.** a situation or area having the potential of erupting in sudden violence.

flash•y (flash′ē), *adj.,* **flash•i•er, flash•i•est. 1.** briefly and superficially sparkling or brilliant: *a flashy performance.* **2.** ostentatious and tasteless; gaudy: *flashy clothes.* —**flash′i•ly,** *adv.* —**flash′i•ness,** *n.*

flask (flask, fläsk), *n.* **1.** a bottle, usu. of glass, having a rounded body and a narrow neck. **2.** a flat metal or glass bottle for carrying in the pocket: *a flask of brandy.* **3.** an iron container for shipping mercury, holding a standard commercial unit of 76 lb. (34 kg). **4.** a container into which sand is rammed around a pattern to form a mold.

flat¹ (flat), *adj.,* **flat•ter, flat•test,** *n., v.,* **flat•ted, flat•ting,** *adv.* —*adj.* **1.** horizontally level. **2.** level, even, or without unevenness of surface, as land or tabletops. **3.** having a surface that is without marked projections or depressions. **4.** lying horizontally and at full length. **5.** lying wholly on or against something. **6.** thrown down, laid low, or level with the ground, as fallen trees or buildings. **7.** having a generally level shape or appearance; not deep or thick. **8.** (of the heel of a shoe) low and broad. **9.** spread out, as an unrolled map or the open hand. **10.** deflated: *a flat tire.* **11.** absolute: *a flat denial.* **12.** lacking modification or variation: *a flat rate.* **13.** lacking vitality or animation; lifeless; dull. **14.** having lost its flavor, sharpness, or life; stale. **15.** (of a beverage) having lost its effervescence. **16.** lacking flavor or piquancy: *flat cooking.* **17.** pointless, as a joke. **18.** commercially inactive. **19.** (of a painting) not having the illusion of volume or depth. **20.** (of a photograph or painting) lacking contrast or gradations of tone or color. **21.** (of paint)

without gloss; not shiny. **22.** not clear, sharp, or ringing, as sound or a voice. **23.** lacking resonance and variation in pitch; monotonous. **24. a.** (of a tone) lowered a half step in pitch: *B flat.* **b.** below an intended pitch, as a note; too low (opposed to *sharp*). **25. flat a,** the *a*-sound (a) of *glad, bat,* or *act.* —*n.* **26.** something flat. **27.** a shoe, esp. a woman's shoe, with a flat heel or no heel. **28.** a flat surface, side, or part of anything. **29.** a flat area: *salt flats.* **30.** a marsh, shoal, or shallow. **31. a.** (in musical notation) the character ♭, which when attached to a note or to a staff degree lowers its significance one chromatic half step. **b.** a tone one chromatic half step below another. **32.** a piece of stage scenery consisting of a wooden frame, usu. rectangular, covered with lightweight board or fabric. **33.** a deflated automobile tire. **34.** an iron or steel bar of rectangular cross section. **35.** a shallow open box used for growing young plants or a closable one for shipping fruits and vegetables. **36.** the area of a football field immediately inside of or outside of an offensive end, close behind or at the line of scrimmage. —*v.t.* **37.** to make flat. **38.** to lower (a pitch), esp. one half step. —*v.i.* **39.** to become flat. —*adv.* **40.** in a flat position; horizontally; levelly. **41.** in a flat manner; positively; absolutely. **42.** completely; utterly: *flat broke.* **43.** exactly; precisely: *in two minutes flat.* **44.** below the true pitch: *to sing flat.* —*Idiom.* **45.** fall flat, to fail completely and noticeably. **46.** flat out, *Informal.* **a.** without hesitation; directly or openly. **b.** at full speed or with maximum effort. —**flat′ly,** *adv.* —**flat′ness,** *n.*

flat² (flat), *n.* a residential apartment.

flat•bed (flat′bed′), *n.* a truck or trailer having an open body in the form of a platform without sides or stakes. Also called **flat′bed trail′er, flat′bed truck′.**

flat′-bed′ press′, *n.* CYLINDER PRESS.

flat•car (flat′kär′), *n.* a railroad car consisting of a platform without sides or top.

flat′-coat′ed retriev′er, *n.* one of an English breed of sporting dogs with a fine, flat, dense black or liver-colored coat.

flat′-file′, *adj.* of or pertaining to a database system in which each database consists of a single file not linked to any other file.

flat•fish (flat′fish′), *n., pl.* (*esp. collectively*) **-fish,** (*esp. for kinds or species*) **-fish•es.** any of various bottom-dwelling fishes of the order *Pleuronectiformes,* including the flounders and soles, that have a greatly flattened, laterally oriented body with both eyes on the upper side.

flat•foot (flat′foot′ *or, for 1,* -foot′), *n., pl.* **-feet** for 1, **-foots** for 2. **1. a.** a condition in which the arch of the foot is flattened so that the entire sole rests upon the ground. **b.** Also, **flat′ foot′.** a foot with such an arch. **2.** *Slang.* a police officer; cop.

flat•foot•ed (flat′foot′id), *adj.* **1.** having flatfeet. **2.** firm and explicit; direct and uncompromising: *a flatfooted denial.* **3.** clumsy or plodding: *flatfooted writing.* —*Idiom.* **4. catch someone flatfooted,** to catch someone unprepared or in the midst of a transgression. —**flat′foot′ed•ly,** *adv.* —**flat′foot′ed•ness,** *n.*

flat′head cat′fish, *n.* a yellow and brown catfish, *Pylodictis olivaris,* common in the central U.S., having a flattened head and a projecting lower jaw. Also called **mudcat.**

flat•i•ron (flat′ī′ərn), *n.* a nonelectric iron with a flat bottom, for use in pressing clothes, cloth, etc.

flat′-out′, *adj. Informal.* **1.** using full speed or all of one's resources; all-out: *a flat-out effort.* **2.** downright; thoroughgoing: *a flat-out forgery.*

flat•ten (flat′n), *v.t.* **1.** to make flat (sometimes fol. by *out*). **2.** to knock down. —*v.i.* **3.** to become flat (sometimes fol. by *out*). **4. flatten out,** to fly (an aircraft) into a horizontal position, as after a dive.

flat•ter (flat′ər), *v.t.* **1.** to try to please by complimentary remarks or attention. **2.** to praise or compliment insincerely, effusively, or excessively. **3.** to represent favorably, esp. too favorably: *The portrait flatters her.* **4.** to show to advantage: *a hairstyle that flatters the face.* **5.** to play upon the vanity or susceptibilities of; cajole: *They flattered him into accepting the position.* **6.** to please or gratify by compliments or attentions: *I was flattered by the invitation.* **7.** to feel satisfaction with (oneself), sometimes mistakenly: *He flattered himself that the speech had gone well.* **8.** to beguile with hope; encourage prematurely, falsely, etc. —*v.i.* **9.** to use flattery. —**flat′ter•er,** *n.* —**flat′ter•ing•ly,** *adv.* —**flat′ter•y,** *n.*

flat•u•lent (flach′ə lənt), *adj.* **1.** having an accumulation of gas in the intestinal tract. **2.** generating such an accumulation of gas, as a food. **3.** having unsupported pretensions; inflated and empty; pompous; turgid. —**flat′u•lence, flat′u•len•cy,** *n.* —**flat′u•lent•ly,** *adv.*

fla•tus (flā′təs), *n., pl.* **-tus•es.** intestinal gas.

flat•ware (flat′wâr′), *n.* **1.** utensils, as knives, forks, and spoons, used at the table for serving and eating food. **2.** dishes for the table that are more or less flat, as plates and saucers.

flat•worm (flat′wûrm′), *n.* PLATYHELMINTH.

flaunt (flônt), *v.t.* **1.** to parade or display ostentatiously: *to flaunt one's wealth.* **2.** to ignore or treat with disdain; flout: *expelled for flaunting regulations.* —*v.i.* **3.** to parade or display oneself conspicuously, defiantly, or boldly. **4.** to wave conspicuously in the air. —**flaunt′ing•ly,** *adv.* —*Usage.* Usage guides object strongly to FLAUNT in the sense "to ignore or treat with disdain," advising that the proper word for this meaning is FLOUT. This use of FLAUNT has appeared in the speech and edited writing of well-educated, literate people. Nevertheless, many concerned speakers and writers avoid it.

flau•tist (flô′tist, flou′-), *n.* FLUTIST.

fla·vin (flā′vin), *n.* any of a group of yellow nitrogen-containing pigments, as riboflavin, that function as coenzymes.

fla·vor (flā′vər), *n.* **1.** taste, esp. the distinctive taste of something as it is experienced in the mouth. **2.** a substance or extract that provides a particular taste; flavoring. **3.** the characteristic quality of a thing: *to capture the flavor of an experience.* **4.** a particular quality noticeable in a thing: *language with a strong nautical flavor.* **5.** *Physics.* **a.** a property that distinguishes among the six kinds of quark: up, down, strange, charmed, bottom, and top. **b.** a property that distinguishes among the three kinds of lepton: electron, muon, and tauon. —*v.t.* **6.** to give flavor to (something). Also, *esp. Brit.,* **flavour.** —**fla′vor·less,** *adj.*

fla′vor of the month′, *n. Informal.* the subject of intense, usu. temporary interest; the current fashion.

flaw[1] (flô), *n.* **1.** a feature that mars the perfection of something; defect, weakness, or blemish: *a flaw in our plan.* **2.** a defect impairing legal soundness or validity. **3.** a crack, break, or breach. —*v.t.* **4.** to produce a flaw in. —*v.i.* **5.** to contract a flaw; become cracked or defective. —**flaw′less,** *adj.* —**flaw′less·ly,** *adv.* —**flaw′less·ness,** *n.*

flaw[2] (flô), *n.* **1.** a sudden, usu. brief windstorm or gust of wind. **2.** a short spell of rough weather. —**flaw′y,** *adj.*

flax (flaks), *n.* **1.** any plant of the genus *Linum*, family Linaceae, esp. *L. usitatissimum*, a slender annual with blue flowers that is cultivated for its fiber, used for making linen, and for its seeds, which yield linseed oil. **2.** the fiber of this plant. **3.** any of various plants resembling flax.

flax·en (flak′sən), *adj.* **1.** made of, pertaining to, or resembling flax. **2.** of the pale yellowish color of dressed flax.

flax·seed (flaks′sēd′), *n.* the seed of flax; linseed.

flay (flā), *v.t.,* **flayed, flay·ing. 1.** to strip off the skin or outer covering of, as by whipping. **2.** to criticize or scold with scathing severity. **3.** to strip of money or property. —**flay′er,** *n.*

F layer, *n.* the highest radio-reflective region of the ionosphere, at an altitude of ab. 80 mi. (130 km).

fl dr, fluid dram.

flea (flē), *n.* **1.** any small, flattened, wingless, bloodsucking insect of the order Siphonaptera, parasitic upon mammals and birds and noted for its ability to leap. **2.** any of various small beetles and crustaceans that leap like a flea, as the beach flea. —*Idiom.* **3. flea in one's ear, a.** a disconcerting rebuke or rebuff. **b.** a broad hint.

flea·bag (flē′bag′), *n. Slang.* **1.** a cheap, run-down hotel or rooming house. **2.** a flea-ridden or worthless animal.

flea·bane (flē′bān′), *n.* any of various composite plants, as *Erigeron philadelphicus,* reputed to destroy or drive away fleas.

flea′ bee′tle, any of numerous tiny leaf beetles of the subfamily Alticinae, having enlarged hind legs adapted for jumping.

flea·bite (flē′bīt′), *n.* **1.** the bite of a flea. **2.** the red spot caused by the bite of a flea. **3.** any petty annoyance or irritation.

flea′-bit′ten, *adj.* **1.** bitten by or infested with fleas. **2.** shabby; dilapidated; wretched. **3.** (of a horse) having a light-colored coat with small brown or reddish spots or streaks.

flea′ col′lar, *n.* a dog or cat collar impregnated with a chemical for repelling or killing fleas.

flea′ mar′ket, *n.* a market consisting of a number of stalls selling old or used articles, curios and antiques, cut-rate merchandise, etc.

flea·wort (flē′wûrt′, -wôrt′), *n.* a European plantain, *Plantago psyllium,* having seeds that are used in medicine.

fleck (flek), *n.* **1.** a speck; a small bit: *a fleck of dirt.* **2.** a spot or small patch of color, light, etc. —*v.t.* **3.** to mark with flecks; spot; dapple.

flec·tion (flek′shən), *n.* **1.** the act of bending. **2.** the state of being bent. **3.** a bent part; bend. **4.** FLEXION (def. 1). **5.** INFLECTION (def. 2).

fled (fled), *v.* pt. and pp. of FLEE.

fledge (flej), *v.,* **fledged, fledg·ing,** *adj.* —*v.t.* **1.** to bring up (a young bird) until it is able to fly. **2.** to furnish with or as if with feathers or plumage. **3.** to provide (an arrow) with feathers. —*v.i.* **4.** (of a young bird) to acquire the feathers necessary for flight. **5.** to acquire the characteristics of maturity.

fledg·ling (flej′ling), *n.* **1.** a young bird that has recently fledged and left the nest but is still dependent on parental care. **2.** an inexperienced person. —*adj.* **3.** young or inexperienced: *a fledgling diver.* Also, *esp. Brit.,* **fledge′ling.**

flee (flē), *v.,* **fled, flee·ing.** —*v.i.* **1.** to run away, as from danger or pursuers; take flight. **2.** to move or pass swiftly; fly; speed. —*v.t.* **3.** to run away from.

fleece (flēs), *n., v.,* **fleeced, fleec·ing.** —*n.* **1.** the coat of wool that covers a sheep or a similar animal. **2.** the wool shorn from a sheep at one shearing. **3.** something resembling a fleece. **4. a.** a fabric with a thick, fleecelike pile or nap, used for warmth, as in garments or linings. **b.** the nap or pile of such a fabric. —*v.t.* **5.** to deprive of money by fraud; swindle. **6.** to overcharge. **7.** to remove the fleece of (a sheep). **8.** to overspread or fleck with fleecelike masses. —**fleece′like′,** *adj.* —**fleec′er,** *n.*

fleet[1] (flēt), *n.* **1.** the largest organized unit of naval ships grouped for tactical or other purposes. **2.** the largest organization of warships under the command of a single officer. **3.** all the naval ships of a nation; navy. **4.** a large group of ships, airplanes, trucks, etc., under the same management or ownership: *a fleet of cabs.* **5.** a large group of ships, airplanes, automobiles, etc., moving or operating together.

fleet[2] (flēt), *adj.* **1.** swift; rapid: *to be fleet of foot; a fleet horse.* —*v.i.* **2.**

to move swiftly; fly. **3.** *Naut.* to change position; shift. —*v.t.* **4.** to cause (time) to pass lightly or swiftly. **5.** *Naut.* to move or change the position of. —**fleet′ly,** *adv.* —**fleet′ness,** *n.*

fleet′ ad′miral, *n.* the highest ranking officer in the U.S. Navy, ranking next above admiral.

fleet′-foot′ed, *adj.* able to run fast.

fleet·ing (flē′ting), *adj.* passing swiftly; vanishing quickly; transient: *a fleeting glance.* —**fleet′ing·ly,** *adv.* —**fleet′ing·ness,** *n.*

flei·shig (flā′shig, -shik), *adj. Judaism.* (in the dietary laws) consisting of, made from, or used only for meat or meat products. Compare MILCHIG, PAREVE.

Flem·ing[1] (flem′ing), *n.* **1.** a Flemish-speaking Belgian. **2.** a native or inhabitant of Flanders.

Flem·ing[2] (flem′ing), *n.* **1. Sir Alexander,** 1881–1955, Scottish bacteriologist: discoverer of penicillin. **2. Ian (Lancaster),** 1908–64, British writer. **3. Peggy (Gale),** born 1948, U.S. figure skater.

Flem·ish (flem′ish), *adj.* **1.** of or pertaining to Flanders, the Flemings, or their speech. —*n.* **2.** (*used with a pl. v.*) **a.** the Flemish-speaking inhabitants of Belgium; Flemings. **b.** the inhabitants of Flanders. **3.** the Dutch language as spoken in N and E Belgium and adjacent parts of France: one of the official languages of Belgium.

flesh (flesh), *n.* **1.** the soft substance of a vertebrate or other animal body between the skin and the skeleton, esp. muscular tissue. **2.** muscular and fatty tissue. **3.** this substance or tissue of animals as an article of food, usu. excluding fish and sometimes fowl; meat. **4.** excess fat; weight: *to put on flesh.* **5.** the body, esp. as distinguished from the spirit or soul: *The spirit is willing but the flesh is weak.* **6.** the physical or animal nature of humankind as distinguished from its moral or spiritual nature. **7.** living creatures generally. **8.** a person's family or relatives. **9.** the soft, pulpy portion of a fruit or vegetable. **10.** the surface of the human body; skin. —*v.t.* **11.** to feed (a hound or hawk) with flesh in order to make it more eager for the chase. **12.** to incite and accustom to bloodshed or battle by an initial experience. **13.** to inflame the ardor or passions of by a foretaste. **14.** to overlay or cover (a skeletal frame) with flesh or a fleshlike substance. **15.** to give dimension or substance to (often fol. by *out*): *The playwright fleshed out the characters.* **16.** to plunge (a weapon) into the flesh. **17.** to remove adhering flesh from (hides) in leather manufacture. —*v.i.* **18.** to become more fleshy or substantial (usu. fol. by *out*). —*Idiom.* **19. in the flesh,** present and alive before one's eyes; in person. **20. press the flesh,** *Informal.* to shake hands, as with voters during a political campaign. —**flesh′less,** *adj.*

flesh′ and blood′, *n.* **1.** offspring or relatives: *one's own flesh and blood.* **2.** the human body or nature: *more than flesh and blood can endure.* **3.** substance: *The concept lacks flesh and blood.*

flesh′ fly′, *n.* any fly of the family Sarcophagidae, comprising species that deposit their eggs or larvae in the flesh of animals.

flesh·ly (flesh′lē), *adj.,* **-li·er, -li·est. 1.** of or pertaining to the flesh or body; corporeal. **2.** carnal; sensual: *fleshly pleasures.* **3.** worldly, rather than spiritual. —**flesh′li·ness,** *n.*

flesh·pots (flesh′pots′), *n.pl.* places offering luxurious and unrestrained pleasure or amusement. [after Exodus 16:3]

flesh′ wound′ (woond), *n.* a wound that does not penetrate beyond the flesh; a slight or superficial wound.

flesh·y (flesh′ē), *adj.,* **flesh·i·er, flesh·i·est. 1.** having much flesh; plump. **2.** consisting of or resembling flesh. **3.** pulpy, as a fruit, or thick and tender, as a succulent leaf. —**flesh′i·ly,** *adv.* —**flesh′i·ness,** *n.*

fleur-de-lis or **fleur-de-lys** (flûr′dl ē′, dl ēs′, floor′-), *n., pl.* **fleurs-de-lis** or **fleurs-de-lys** (-dl ēz′). **1.** a stylized representation of an iris with three petals tied by a band, used ornamentally and as a heraldic device. **2.** the heraldic bearing of the royal family of France. **3.** a symbol for the Trinity. **4.** a symbol for the Mary, the mother of Jesus. **5.** the iris flower or plant.

fleur-de-lis

flew (floo), *v.* a pt. of FLY[1].

flex (fleks), *v.t.* **1.** to bend, as a part of the body. **2.** to tighten (a muscle) by contraction. —*v.i.* **3.** to bend. —*n.* **4.** the act of flexing.

flex·i·ble (flek′sə bəl), *adj.* **1.** capable of being bent, usu. without breaking; easily bent. **2.** susceptible to modification or adaptation; adaptable: *a flexible schedule.* **3.** willing or disposed to yield; pliable; tractable: *a flexible personality.* —**flex′i·bil′i·ty,** *n.* —**flex′i·bly,** *adv.*

flex·ile (flek′sil;), *adj.* flexible; pliant.

flex·ion (flek′shən), *n.* **1.** the act of bending a limb. **2.** the position that a limb assumes when it is bent.

flex·or (flek′sər), *n.* a muscle that serves to flex or bend a part of the body.

flex·time (fleks′tīm′) also **flex·i·time** (flek′si-), *n.* a system that allows an employee to choose the hours for starting and leaving work, according to guidelines specified by an employer. —**flex′tim′er,** *n.*

flex•u•ous (flek′sho͞o əs), *adj.* full of bends or curves; sinuous; winding. —**flex′u•os′i•ty** (-os′i tē), *n.* —**flex′u•ous•ly,** *adv.*

flex•ure (flek′shər), *n.* **1.** the act of flexing or bending. **2.** the state of being flexed or bent. **3.** bend; fold. —**flex′ur•al,** *adj.*

flib•ber•ti•gib•bet (flib′ər tē jib′it), *n.* a chattering or flighty, light-headed person. —**flib′ber•ti•gib′bet•y,** *adj.*

flick (flik), *n.* **1.** a sudden light blow or tap, as with a whip or the finger. **2.** the sound made by such a blow or tap. **3.** a light and rapid movement: *a flick of the wrist.* **4.** something thrown off with or as if with a jerk. —*v.t.* **5.** to strike with a sudden light, smart stroke. **6.** to remove with such a stroke: *to flick away a crumb.* **7.** to move, propel, or operate with a sudden stroke or jerk: *flicking the lights on and off.* —*v.i.* **8.** to move rapidly or jerkily. **9.** to flutter. **10.** to turn pages rapidly or idly (usu. fol. by *through*): *to flick through a magazine.*

flick•er¹ (flik′ər), *v.i.* **1.** to burn unsteadily; shine with a wavering light: *The candle flickered in the wind.* **2.** to move to and fro; vibrate or quiver. **3.** to flutter. —*v.t.* **4.** to cause to flicker. —*n.* **5.** an unsteady flame or light. **6.** a flickering movement. **7.** a brief appearance or feeling: *a flicker of interest.* **8.** the visual sensation of flickering that occurs when the interval between intermittent flashes of light is too long to permit fusion. —**flick′er•ing•ly,** *adv.* —**flick′er•y,** *adj.*

flick•er² (flik′ər), *n.* any of several North American woodpeckers of the genus *Colaptes,* having yellow or red underwings: now usu. considered a single species, *C. auratus.*

fli•er or **fly•er** (flī′ər), *n.* **1.** a person, animal, or thing that flies. **2.** an aviator or pilot. **3.** a person or thing that moves with great speed. **4.** a part of a machine having a rapid motion. **5.** a small handbill; circular. **6.** *Informal.* a flying jump or leap. **7.** *Informal.* a risky or speculative venture. **8.** one of the steps in a straight flight of stairs. Compare WINDER (def. 2). **9.** a trapeze artist; aerialist.

flight¹ (flīt), *n.* **1.** the act, manner, or power of flying. **2.** the distance covered or the course taken by a flying object: *a 500-mile flight; the flight of the ball.* **3.** a trip by an airplane, glider, etc., esp. a scheduled trip on an airline. **4.** an airplane making a scheduled trip. **5.** a number of beings flying in the air together: *a flight of geese.* **6.** the basic tactical unit of military air forces, consisting of two or more aircraft. **7.** the act, principles, or technique of flying an airplane: *flight training.* **8.** a journey into outer space. **9.** swift movement, transition, or progression. **10.** a transcending of the ordinary bounds of the mind: *a flight of fancy.* **11.** a series of steps between one floor or landing of a building and the next. —*v.i.* **12.** (of wild fowls) to fly in coordinated flocks.

flight² (flīt), *n.* **1.** an act or instance of fleeing or running away. —***Idiom.*** **2. put to flight,** to force to flee or run away; rout. **3. take flight,** to retreat; run away; flee.

flight′ control′, *n.* **1.** the direction of airplane movements, esp. take-offs and landings, by messages from the ground. **2.** the system or office providing this direction. **3.** the system of devices by which a pilot controls the movement of an airplane.

flight′ deck′, *n.* **1.** the upper deck of an aircraft carrier, designed for the landing and takeoff of aircraft. **2.** an elevated compartment in certain aircraft containing the instruments and controls used by the crew.

flight′ engineer′, *n.* a member of an aircraft crew responsible for the mechanical systems, fueling, and servicing of the craft.

flight′ line′, *n.* the area of an airfield used for the servicing and maintenance of airplanes.

flight′ path′, *n.* the trajectory of a moving aircraft or spacecraft relative to a fixed reference.

flight′ pay′, *n.* a pay supplement allowed by the U.S. Air Force to certain crew members who attain a minimum flight time per month.

flight′ plan′, *n.* an oral or written report to an air traffic control facility describing the route of a projected flight.

flight′ record′er, *n.* an electronic device aboard an aircraft that automatically records certain aspects of the aircraft's performance in flight; black box.

flight•y (flī′tē), *adj.,* **flight•i•er, flight•i•est.** **1.** frivolous and irresponsible. **2.** capricious; volatile. —**flight′i•ly,** *adv.* —**flight′i•ness,** *n.*

flim•flam (flim′flam′), *n., v.,* **-flammed, -flam•ming.** *Informal.* —*n.* **1.** a trick or deception, esp. a swindle. **2.** a piece of nonsense; twaddle. —*v.t.* **3.** to deceive, trick, or swindle. —**flim′flam′mer,** *n.* —**flim′flam′mer•y,** *n.*

flim•sy (flim′zē), *adj.,* **-si•er, -si•est,** *n., pl.* **-sies.** —*adj.* **1.** without material strength or solidity: *a flimsy fabric; a flimsy structure.* **2.** weak; inadequate; not effective or convincing: *a flimsy excuse.* —*n.* **3.** a thin paper, esp. for use in making several copies at a time. **4.** a copy made on such paper. —**flim′si•ly,** *adv.* —**flim′si•ness,** *n.*

flinch (flinch), *v.i.* **1.** to draw back or shrink, as from something dangerous, difficult, or unpleasant. **2.** to shrink or tense under pain; wince. —*n.* **3.** an act of flinching.

fling (fling), *v.,* **flung, fling•ing,** *n.* —*v.t.* **1.** to throw or cast with force, violence, or abandon. **2.** to move (oneself) violently or abruptly: *She flung herself angrily from the room.* **3.** to put or send suddenly or without preparation: *to fling someone into jail.* **4.** to project or speak sharply or aggressively: *He flung his answer at the questioner.* **5.** to involve (oneself) vigorously in an undertaking. **6.** to move, do, or say quickly. **7.** to throw aside or off. —*v.i.* **8.** to move with haste or violence. **9.** to fly into violent and irregular motions, as a horse. **10.** to speak harshly or abusively (usu. fol. by *out*). —*n.* **11.** an act or instance of flinging. **12.** a short period of unrestrained pursuit of one's desires: *to have one last fling before starting a new job.* **13.** an attempt at something: *to have a fling at playwriting.* **14.** Also called **Highland fling.** a lively Scottish dance characterized by flinging movements of the arms and legs.

flint (flint), *n.* **1.** a hard stone, a form of silica resembling chalcedony but more opaque, less pure, and less lustrous. **2.** a piece of this, esp. as used for striking fire. **3.** a chunk of this used as a primitive tool or as the core from which such a tool was struck. **4.** something very hard or unyielding. **5.** a small piece of metal alloy used to produce a spark in a cigarette lighter. —*v.t.* **6.** to furnish with flint. —**flint′like′,** *adj.*

Flint (flint), *n.* a city in SE Michigan. 138,164.

flint′ corn′, *n.* a variety of corn, *Zea mays indurata,* with very hard-skinned kernels.

flint•lock (flint′lok′), *n.* **1.** an outmoded gunlock in which a piece of flint striking against steel produces sparks that ignite the priming. **2.** a firearm with such a lock.

flip¹ (flip), *v.,* **flipped, flip•ping,** *n., adj.,* **flip•per, flip•pest.** —*v.t.* **1.** to toss, as with a snap of a finger and thumb, so as to cause to turn over in the air: *to flip a coin.* **2.** to toss, move, or activate with a sudden stroke or jerk: *to flip a switch.* **3.** to turn over, esp. with a short rapid gesture: *to flip pancakes with a spatula.* **4.** *Slang.* to make insane, irrational, angry, or highly excited (usu. fol. by *out*). **5.** to resell, esp. quickly, or refinance. —*v.i.* **6.** to make a flicking movement; strike at something smartly. **7.** to move oneself with or as if with flippers. **8.** to move jerkily. **9.** to turn over or perform a somersault. **10.** to read or look at rapidly or perfunctorily: *to flip through a magazine.* **11.** *Slang.* **a.** to react with excitement, astonishment, or delight. **b.** to become insane, irrational, or incensed (often fol. by *out*). —*n.* **12.** an act or instance of flipping. **13.** a somersault, esp. one performed in the air. **14.** *Informal.* FLIP SIDE. —*adj.* **15.** flippant; pert. —***Idiom.*** **16. flip one's lid** or **wig,** *Slang.* to lose control of one's temper; rage hysterically.

flip² (flip), *n.* a hot or cold mixed drink made with liquor or wine, sugar, beaten eggs, and nutmeg.

flip′ chart′, *n.* a set of sheets, as of cardboard, hinged at the top so that they can be flipped over to show information in sequence.

flip′-flop′, *n., v.,* **-flopped, -flop•ping,** *adv.* —*n.* **1.** a sudden or unexpected reversal, as of opinion or policy. **2.** a backward somersault. **3.** Also called **flip′-flop′ cir′cuit.** an electronic circuit having two stable conditions, each one corresponding to one of two alternative input signals. **4.** the sound or motion of something flapping. **5.** a flat backless shoe or slipper, esp. one of rubber with a thong between the first two toes. —*v.i.* **6.** to perform a flip-flop. —*adv.* **7.** with repeated sounds and motions as of something flapping. Also, **flip′-flap′** (for defs. 2, 4, 7), **flip′flop′** (for def. 5).

flip•pant (flip′ənt), *adj.* frivolously disrespectful, shallow, or lacking in seriousness. —**flip′pan•cy,** *n.* —**flip′pant•ly,** *adv.*

flip•per (flip′ər), *n.* **1.** a broad flat limb, as of a seal or whale, specially adapted for swimming. **2.** one of a pair of paddlelike devices, usu. of rubber, worn on the feet as an aid in scuba diving and swimming; fin. **3.** someone or something that flips.

flip′ side′, *n.* **1.** the reverse and usu. less popular side of a phonograph record. **2.** an opposite or reverse side.

flip′-top′, *adj.* **1.** having a hinged lid, cover, or top that can be flipped open. **2.** POP-TOP. —*n.* **3.** a flip-top item.

flirt (flûrt), *v.i.* **1.** to court playfully; act amorously, often without serious intentions. **2.** to trifle or toy, as with an idea. **3.** to move jerkily; dart about. —*v.t.* **4.** to give a sudden or brisk motion to; wave smartly. **5.** to propel with a toss or jerk; flick. —*n.* **6.** a person who is given to flirting. **7.** a sudden jerk or darting motion; a quick toss. —**flir•ta′tion,** *n.* —**flir•ta′tious,** *adj.*

flit (flit), *v.,* **flit•ted, flit•ting,** *n.* —*v.i.* **1.** to fly or move swiftly, lightly, or irregularly from one place or thing to another. **2.** to flutter, as a bird. **3.** to pass quickly: *A smile flitted across his face.* —*n.* **4.** a light, swift movement; flutter. —**flit′ting•ly,** *adv.*

float (flōt), *v.i.* **1.** to rest or remain on the surface of a liquid; be buoyant. **2.** to move gently on the surface of a liquid; drift along: *The canoe floated downstream.* **3.** to rest or move in a liquid, the air, etc.: *a balloon floating on high.* **4.** to move lightly and gracefully: *She floated down the stairs.* **5.** to move or hover before the eyes or in the mind. **6.** to pass from one person to another: *a rumor floating around town.* **7.** to be free from attachment or involvement. **8.** to move or drift about, esp. freely or aimlessly. **9.** (of a currency) to be allowed to fluctuate freely in the foreign-exchange market instead of being exchanged at a fixed rate. —*v.t.* **10.** to cause to float. **11.** to cover with water or other liquid; flood; irrigate. **12.** to launch (a company, scheme, etc.); set going. **13.** to issue (stocks, bonds, etc.) on the stock market in order to raise money. **14.** to let (a currency) fluctuate in the foreign-exchange market. **15.** to present for consideration, as an idea. **16.** to make smooth with a float, as the surface of plaster. —*n.* **17.** something that floats, as a raft. **18.** something for buoying up. **19.** an inflated bag to sustain a person in water; life preserver. **20.** (in a tank, cistern, etc.) a device, as a hollow ball, that through its buoyancy automatically regulates the level, supply, or outlet of a liquid. **21.** a floating platform attached to a wharf, bank, etc., and used as a landing. **22.** a hollow, boatlike structure under the wing or fuselage of a seaplane or flying boat that keeps it afloat in water. **23.** a piece of cork or other material supporting a baited fishing line in the water and indicating by its movement when a fish bites. **24.** an inflated organ that supports an animal in the water. **25.** a vehicle bearing a display, usu. an elaborate tableau, in a parade or procession. **26.** a drink with ice cream floating in it: *a root-beer float.* **27.** uncollected checks and commercial paper in process of transfer from bank to bank. **28.** a sum of money added to a salary, pension, etc., as to cover expenses. **29.** an act or instance of floating. **30. a.** a flat tool for spreading and smoothing plaster or stucco. **b.** a tool for polishing marble. **31.** a single-cut file of moderate smoothness. **32.** a loose-fitting, sometimes very full dress without a waistline. **33.** (in weaving and knitting) a length of yarn that extends over several rows or stitches without being interworked. **34.** a low-bodied dray for transporting heavy goods. —**float′a•ble,** *adj.* —**float′a•bil′i•ty,** *n.*

float•er (flō′tər), *n.* **1.** a person or thing that floats. **2.** a person who is continually changing his or her place of abode, employment, etc.; drifter. **3.** an employee without a fixed job assignment. **4.** a person who fraudulently votes, usu. for pay, in different places in the same election. **5.** a territorial animal that has been unable to claim a territory and is forced into marginal habitats. **6.** a speck or string that appears to be drifting across the eye just outside the line of vision; musca volitans. **7.** an insurance policy that covers movable personal property.

float•ing (flō′ting), *adj.* **1.** being buoyed up on water or other liquid. **2.** moving from one place to another: *a floating work force.* **3.** (of a body part or organ) away from its proper position, esp. in a downward direction: *a floating kidney.* **4. a.** in circulation or use, or not permanently invested, as capital. **b.** composed of sums due within a short time: *a floating debt.* **5.** *Mach.* **a.** having a soft suspension greatly reducing vibrations **b.** working smoothly.

float′ing point′, *n.* a decimal point whose location is not fixed.

float′ing rib′, *n.* any member of the two lowest pairs of ribs, not attached to the sternum or the cartilages of other ribs. Compare TRUE RIB.

float′ valve′, *n.* a valve that regulates the flow of liquid to or from a tank by means of a float.

flock[1] (flok), *n.* **1.** an assemblage of animals, esp. sheep, goats, or birds, that live, travel, or feed together. **2.** a large group of people or things: *flocks of sightseers.* **3. a.** the Christian church in relation to Christ. **b.** a single congregation in relation to its pastor. —*v.i.* **4.** to gather or go in a flock: *They flocked around the football hero.* —**flock′less,** *adj.* —**Usage.** See COLLECTIVE NOUN.

flock[2] (flok), *n.* **1.** a lock or tuft of wool, hair, cotton, etc. **2.** (*sometimes used with a pl. v.*) wool refuse, shearings of cloth, or old cloth torn to pieces, for upholstering furniture, stuffing mattresses, etc. **3.** Also called **flocking.** (*sometimes used with a pl. v.*) finely powdered wool, cloth, etc., used for producing a velvetlike pattern on wallpaper or cloth or for coating metal. —*v.t.* **4.** to stuff with flock. **5.** to decorate or coat with flock.

flock•ing (flok′ing), *n.* **1.** a velvetlike pattern produced on wallpaper or cloth decorated with flock. **2.** FLOCK[2] (def. 3).

floe (flō), *n.* **1.** a sheet of floating ice, chiefly on the surface of the sea, smaller than an ice field. **2.** a detached floating portion of such a sheet. Also called **ice floe.**

flog (flog, flôg), *v.t.,* **flogged, flog•ging.** **1.** to beat with a whip, stick, etc., esp. as punishment. **2.** *Slang.* **a.** to sell, esp. aggressively or vigorously. **b.** to promote; publicize.

flood (flud), *n.* **1.** a great flowing or overflowing of water, esp. over land not usu. submerged. **2.** any great outpouring or stream: *a flood of tears.* **3. the Flood,** a universal deluge mentioned in various ancient religions, esp. the deluge recorded in the Bible as having occurred in the time of Noah. Gen. 7. **4.** the rise or flowing in of the tide (opposed to *ebb*). **5.** a floodlight. —*v.t.* **6.** to cover with a flood; fill to overflowing. **7.** to cover or fill as if with a flood: *roads flooded with cars.* **8.** to overwhelm with an abundance of something: *to be flooded with mail.* **9.** to supply too much fuel to (the carburetor), so that the engine fails to start. **10.** to floodlight. —*v.i.* **11.** to flow or pour in or as if in a flood. **12.** to rise in a flood; overflow. **13.** to become flooded.

flood′ control′, *n.* the act or technique of controlling river flow with dams, dikes, artificial channels, etc., so as to minimize the occurrence of floods.

flood•gate (flud′gāt′), *n.* **1.** a gate designed to regulate the flow of water. **2.** anything serving to control the indiscriminate flow or passage of something.

flood′ lamp′, *n.* a floodlight.

flood•light (flud′līt′), *n., v.,* **-light•ed** or **-lit, -light•ing.** —*n.* **1.** a powerful artificial light so directed or diffused as to give a comparatively uniform illumination over a large area. **2.** a lamp or projector that produces such a light. —*v.t.* **3.** to illuminate with a floodlight.

flood′ plain′ or **flood′plain′,** *n.* a nearly flat plain along the course of a stream or river that is naturally subject to flooding.

flood′ tide′, *n.* the inflow of the tide; rising tide.

flood′ wall′, *n.* a wall built along a shore or bank to prevent floods by giving a raised, uniform freeboard.

flood•wa•ter (flud′wô′tər, -wot′ər), *n.* the water that overflows as the result of a flood.

flood•way (flud′wā′), *n.* the area under water during a flood, esp. a place to which waters are diverted by flood-control methods.

floor (flôr, flōr), *n.* **1.** the part of a room that forms its lower enclosing surface and upon which one walks. **2.** a continuous supporting surface extending horizontally throughout a building and constituting one level or stage in the structure; story. **3.** a level supporting surface in any structure: *the elevator floor.* **4.** one of two or more layers of material composing a floor. **5.** a platform or level area for a particular use: *a threshing floor.* **6.** the bottom of any more or less hollow place: *the floor of a tunnel.* **7.** a more or less flat extent of surface: *the floor of the ocean.* **8.** the part of a legislative chamber, meeting room, etc., where the members sit, and from which they speak. **9.** the right of one member to speak from such a place in preference to other members: *The senator from Alaska has the floor.* **10.** the area of a stock exchange, retail store, etc., where buying and selling or other business is conducted. **11.** a base or minimum level: *The government established price and wage floors.* —*v.t.* **12.** to cover or furnish with a floor. **13.** to bring down to the floor or ground; knock down. **14.** to overwhelm; defeat. **15.** to surprise and confound; nonplus. **16.** to push (the accelerator pedal) down to the floor of a vehicle, for maximum speed or power. —***Idiom.*** **17. mop** or **wipe the floor with,** *Informal.* to overwhelm completely; defeat. **18. take the floor,** to arise to address a meeting.

floor•board (flôr′bôrd′, flōr′bōrd′), *n.* **1.** any of the boards composing a floor. **2.** the floor of an automotive vehicle. —*v.t.* **3.** FLOOR (def. 16).

floor′ ex′ercise, *n.* a competitive gymnastics event in which each entrant performs a routine of acrobatic tumbling feats and balletic movements without using any apparatus.

floor′ fight′, *n.* a debate that takes place on the floor of a political convention rather than previously in a committee.

floor•ing (flôr′ing, flōr′-), *n.* **1.** a floor. **2.** floors collectively. **3.** materials for making floors.

floor′ lead′er, *n.* the leader of the majority or minority party in a legislature, as in the U.S. Congress, responsible for shaping the party's strategy and directing its activities on the floor.

floor′ man′ager, *n.* **1.** a person assigned to direct the proceedings on the floor of an assembly. **2.** the stage manager of a television program.

floor′ plan′, *n.* a diagram of a room, apartment, or floor of a building, usu. drawn to scale.

floor′ sam′ple, *n.* an appliance, piece of furniture, etc., that has been used for display or demonstration and is offered at a reduced price.

floor′ show′, *n.* a nightclub entertainment typically consisting of a series of singing, dancing, and often comedy acts.

flop (flop), *v.,* **flopped, flop•ping,** *n.* —*v.i.* **1.** to move around in a heavy, clumsy manner. **2.** to drop, fall, or turn in a heavy or negligent manner, often with a sudden bump or thud: *He flopped down on the couch.* **3.** to change suddenly, as from one side or party to another. **4.** to be a complete failure; fail: *The play flopped dismally.* **5.** *Informal.* to sleep or be lodged. —*v.t.* **6.** to drop with a sudden bump or thud. **7.** to move or swing loosely or clumsily; flap: *The buzzard flopped its wings.* **8.** to dispose (oneself) in a heavily negligent manner: *to flop oneself in a chair.* **9.** to invert (the negative of a photograph) so that the right and left sides are transposed. —*n.* **10.** an act of flopping. **11.** the sound of flopping; a thud. **12.** a complete failure: *The new comedy was a flop.* **13.** *Informal.* a place to sleep; temporary lodging.

flop′-eared′, *adj.* having long, drooping ears, as a hound.

flop•house (flop′hous′), *n., pl.* **-hous•es** (-hou′ziz). a cheap, rundown hotel or rooming house.

flop•py (flop′ē), *adj.,* **-pi•er, -pi•est,** *n., pl.* **-pies.** —*adj.* **1.** tending to flop: *a dog with floppy ears.* —*n.* **2.** FLOPPY DISK. —**flop′pi•ly,** *adv.*

flop′py disk′, *n.* a thin, usu. flexible plastic disk coated with magnetic material, for storing computer data and programs; diskette.

flops (flops), *n.* a measure of computer speed, equal to the number of floating-point operations the computer can perform per second (used esp. in combination with *mega-, giga-, tera-*).

flo•ra (flôr′ə, flōr′ə), *n., pl.* **flo•ras, flo•rae** (flôr′ē, flōr′ē) for 2. **1.** the plants of a particular region or period, listed by species and considered as a whole. **2.** a work systematically describing such plants. **3.** plants, as distinguished from fauna. **4.** the aggregate of bacteria, fungi, and other microorganisms occurring on or within the body: *intestinal flora.*

flo•ral (flôr′əl, flōr′-), *adj.* **1.** pertaining to or consisting of flowers: *a floral wreath.* **2.** of or pertaining to floras or a flora. —*n.* **3.** something having a floral pattern. —**flo′ral•ly,** *adv.*

Flor•ence (flôr′əns, flor′-), *n.* a city in Tuscany, in central Italy, on the Arno River. 421,299. Italian, **Firenze.**

Flor•en•tine (flôr′ən tēn′, -tīn′, flor′-), *adj.* **1.** of or pertaining to Florence, Italy. **2.** (of food) served or prepared with spinach: *eggs Florentine.* —*n.* **3.** a native or resident of Florence.

flo•res•cence (flô res′əns, flō-, flə-), *n.* the act, state, or period of flowering; bloom. —**flo•res′cent,** *adj.*

flo•ret (flôr′it, flōr′-), *n.* **1.** a small flower. **2.** one of the tightly clustered divisions of a head of broccoli or cauliflower.

flori-, a combining form meaning "flower": *floriferous.*

flo•ri•bun•da (flôr′ə bun′də, flōr′-), *n.* any of a class of roses characterized by a long blooming period and a profusion of large flowers.

flo•ri•cul•ture (flôr′i kul′chər, flōr′-), *n.* the cultivation of flowers or flowering plants, esp. for ornamental purposes. —**flo′ri•cul′tur•al,** *adj.* —**flo′ri•cul′tur•al•ly,** *adv.* —**flo′ri•cul′tur•ist,** *n.*

flor•id (flôr′id, flor′-), *adj.* **1.** reddish; ruddy; rosy: *a florid complexion.* **2.** flowery; excessively ornate; showy: *florid writing.* —**flo•rid•i•ty** (flô rid′i tē, flə-), **flor′id•ness,** *n.* —**flor′id•ly,** *adv.*

Flor•i•da (flôr′i də, flor′-), *n.* a state in the SE United States between the Atlantic and the Gulf of Mexico. 14,399,985; 58,560 sq. mi. (151,670 sq. km). *Cap.*: Tallahassee. *Abbr.*: FL, Fla. —**Flo•rid•i•an** (flə rid′ē ən), **Flor′i•dan**, *adj.*, *n.*

flor•in (flôr′in, flor′-), *n.* **1.** a former British coin, orig. of silver, equal to two shillings. **2.** the guilder of the Netherlands. **3.** a former gold coin of Florence, first issued in 1252. **4.** any of various former gold coins of Europe issued in imitation of this.

Flo•ri•o (flôr′ē ō′, flor′-), *n.* **John,** 1553?–1625, English lexicographer and translator.

flo•rist (flôr′ist, flōr′-, flor′-), *n.* **1.** a retailer of flowers and ornamental plants. **2.** a person who grows flowers. —**flo′ris•try,** *n.*

floss (flôs, flos), *n.* **1.** the cottony fiber yielded by the silk-cotton tree. **2. a.** short untwisted silk filaments, often used to make embroidery thread. **b.** embroidery thread of silk or fine cotton. **3.** any silky, filamentous matter, as the silk of corn. **4.** DENTAL FLOSS. —*v.i.* **5.** to use dental floss on the teeth. —*v.t.* **6.** to clean (the teeth) with dental floss.

floss•y (flô′sē, flos′ē), *adj.*, **floss•i•er, floss•i•est. 1.** made of or resembling floss; downy. **2.** showily stylish; fancy: *a flossy dress.*

flo•tage or **float•age** (flō′tij), *n.* **1.** the act or state of floating. **2.** floating power; buoyancy. **3.** something that floats; flotsam. **4.** the part of a ship above the water line.

flo•ta•tion or **floa•ta•tion** (flō tā′shən), *n.* **1.** the act or state of floating. **2.** the launching or financing of a commercial venture, bond issue, loan, etc. **3.** a process for separating the different minerals in a mass of powdered ore based on their tendency to sink in, or float on, a given liquid.

flo•til•la (flō til′ə), *n.* **1.** a group of small naval vessels, esp. a naval unit containing two or more squadrons. **2.** a group moving together: *a flotilla of cars.*

flot•sam (flot′səm), *n.* **1.** the part of the wreckage of a ship and its cargo found floating on the water. Compare JETSAM, LAGAN. **2.** refuse floating on water. **3.** useless or unimportant items; odds and ends. **4.** a vagrant population. Also called **flot′sam and jet′sam** (for defs. 3, 4).

flounce¹ (flouns), *v.*, **flounced, flounc•ing,** *n.* —*v.i.* **1.** to go with impatient or impetuous, exaggerated movements: *to flounce out of the room in a rage.* **2.** to move self-consciously and in a conspicuous manner: *The couple flounced around the ballroom.* **3.** to throw the body about spasmodically; flounder. —*n.* **4.** an act or instance of flouncing; a flouncing movement. —**flounc′y,** *adj.*, **flounc•i•er, flounc•i•est.**

flounce² (flouns), *n.*, *v.*, **flounced, flounc•ing.** —*n.* **1.** a strip of material gathered or pleated and attached along one edge, with the other edge left loose or hanging: used for trimming, as on the bottom of a skirt. —*v.t.* **2.** to trim with flounces.

floun•der¹ (floun′dər), *v.i.* **1.** to struggle with stumbling movements: *to flounder in the mud.* **2.** to struggle clumsily, helplessly, or falteringly: *I floundered for an excuse.* —**floun′der•ing•ly,** *adv.*

floun•der² (floun′dər), *n.*, *pl.* (*esp. collectively*) **-der,** (*esp. for kinds or species*) **-ders.** any of the flatfishes of the families Pleuronectidae and Bothidae, esp. those valued as food, as the North Atlantic *Platichthys flesus* (**European flounder**) and various plaices, soles, and turbots.

flour (flou′ər, flou′ər), *n.* **1.** the finely ground meal of grain, separated by bolting. **2.** a finely ground preparation of fish, bananas, dehydrated potatoes, etc. **3.** a fine, soft powder. —*v.t.* **4.** to make (grain) into flour. **5.** to coat with flour. —*v.i.* **6.** (of mercury) to form globules on the surface of an impure metal with which it cannot amalgamate. **7.** to disintegrate into minute particles.

flour•ish (flûr′ish, flur′-), *v.i.* **1.** to be in a vigorous state; thrive: *a period in which art flourished.* **2.** to be at the height of development, activity, influence, or fame; be in one's prime. **3.** to be successful; prosper. **4.** to grow luxuriantly or thrive in growth, as a plant. **5.** to make dramatic, sweeping gestures. **6.** to add embellishments and ornamental lines to writing, letters, etc. —*v.t.* **7.** to brandish dramatically; gesticulate with. —*n.* **8.** an act or instance of brandishing. **9.** an ostentatious or dramatic gesture or display. **10.** a decoration or embellishment, esp. in writing: *He added a few flourishes to his signature.* **11.** a parade of fine language; an expression used merely for effect. **12.** an elaborate musical passage; fanfare: *a flourish of trumpets.* **13.** a condition or period of thriving: *in full flourish.* —**flour′ish•ing•ly,** *adv.*

flout (flout), *v.t.* **1.** to treat with disdain or scorn; scoff at: *to flout the rules.* —*v.i.* **2.** to show disdain or scorn; scoff, mock, or gibe. —*n.* **3.** a disdainful or scornful remark or act; insult; gibe. —**Usage.** See FLAUNT.

flow (flō), *v.i.* **1.** to move along in a stream: *The river flows to the sea.* **2.** to circulate, as blood. **3.** to stream or well forth. **4.** to issue or proceed from a source: *Orders flowed from the office.* **5.** to come or go as in a stream: *Masses of people flowed by.* **6.** to proceed continuously and smoothly or easily: *The words flowed from his pen.* **7.** to hang loosely at full length: *hair flowing down her back.* **8.** to abound in something: *a land flowing with plentiful harvests.* **9.** to menstruate. **10.** to rise and advance, as the tide (opposed to *ebb*). —*v.t.* **11.** to cause or permit to flow. **12.** to cover with liquid; flood. —*n.* **13.** movement in or as if in a stream. **14.** the rate of flowing. **15.** the volume of fluid that flows through a passage during a given unit of time. **16.** stream. **17.** an outpouring or discharge of something: *a flow of blood.* **18.** MENSTRUATION. **19.** an overflowing; flood. **20.** the rise of the tide (opposed to *ebb*). **21.** the transference of energy: *heat flow.* —**Idiom. 22. go with the flow,** to follow prevailing trends.

flow′ chart′ or **flow′chart′,** *n.* a graphic representation, using symbols interconnected with lines, of the successive steps in a procedure or system. Also called **flow′ di′agram.**

flow•er (flou′ər), *n.* **1.** the blossom of a plant. Compare INFLORESCENCE. **2. a.** the part of a seed plant comprising the reproductive organs and their envelopes if any, esp. when such envelopes are more or less conspicuous in form and color. **b.** an analogous reproductive structure in other plants, as the mosses. **3.** a plant considered with reference to or cultivated for its blossom. **4.** a state of efflorescence or bloom: *Peonies were in flower.* **5.** an ornament representing a flower. **6.** an ornament or adornment. **7.** the finest or most flourishing period: *when knighthood was in flower.* **8.** the best or finest member, product, or example: *the flower of American youth.* **9. flowers,** (*used with a sing. v.*) a chemical substance in the form of a fine powder, esp. as obtained by sublimation. —*v.i.* **10.** to produce flowers; blossom; come to full bloom. **11.** to come out into full development; mature; flourish: *Her talent flowered early.* —*v.t.* **12.** to cover or deck with flowers. **13.** to decorate with a floral design. —**flow′er•less,** *adj.* —**flow′er•like′,** *adj.*

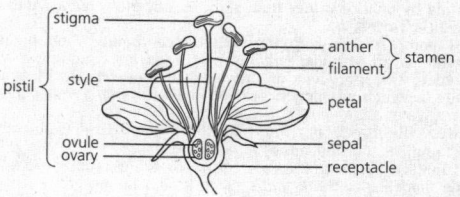

flower (in cross section)

flow′er bug′, *n.* any of several small speckled black bugs of the family Anthocoridae that feed on aphids and other plant pests.

flow′er child′, *n.* a hippie, esp. in the 1960s, advocating love, peace, and simple idealistic values.

flow′ering plant′, *n.* a plant that produces flowers, fruit, and seeds; angiosperm.

flow•er•y (flou′ə rē), *adj.*, **-er•i•er, -er•i•est. 1.** covered with or having many flowers. **2.** decorated with floral designs. **3.** rhetorically ornate or precious: *flowery language.* **4.** resembling a flower, as in fragrance. —**flow′er•i•ness,** *n.*

flown (flōn), *v.* a pp. of FLY¹.

fl. oz., fluid ounce.

flu (flōo), *n.* **1.** influenza. **2.** a specific variety of influenza, usu. named for its point of dissemination or its animal vector: *Hong Kong flu; swine flu.*

fluc•tu•ate (fluk′chōo āt′), *v.*, **-at•ed, -at•ing.** —*v.i.* **1.** to change continually; vary irregularly; rise and fall or up and down: *Prices fluctuated wildly.* **2.** to move in waves; undulate. —*v.t.* **3.** to cause to fluctuate. —**fluc′tu•ant,** *adj.* —**fluc′tu•a′tion,** *n.*

flue¹ (flōo), *n.* **1.** a passage or duct for smoke in a chimney. **2.** any duct or passage for air, gas, or the like. **3.** a tube, esp. a large one, in a fire-tube boiler. **4.** a narrow slit in the upper end of an organ pipe through which the air current is directed.

flue² (flōo), *n.* downy matter; fluff.

flue³ (flōo), *n.* a fishing net.

flu•ent (flōo′ənt), *adj.* **1.** spoken or written with ease: *fluent French.* **2.** able to speak or write smoothly, easily, or readily: *fluent in three languages.* **3.** smooth; easy; graceful: *fluent motion.* **4.** flowing or capable of flowing. —**flu′en•cy,** *n.* —**flu′ent•ly,** *adv.*

fluff (fluf), *n.* **1.** light downy particles, as of cotton. **2.** a soft light downy mass. **3.** something light or frivolous: *The book is pure fluff, but fun to read.* **4.** an error or blunder, esp. an actor's memory lapse in the delivery of lines. —*v.t.* **5.** to make fluffy; shake or puff out into a fluffy mass: *to fluff up the pillows.* **6.** to make a mistake in: *The leading man fluffed his lines.* —*v.i.* **7.** to become fluffy; move, float, or settle down like fluff. **8.** to make a mistake, esp. in performing.

fluff•y (fluf′ē), *adj.*, **fluff•i•er, fluff•i•est. 1.** of, resembling, or covered with fluff. **2.** light or airy: *a fluffy cake.* **3.** superficial or frivolous. —**fluff′i•ly,** *adv.* —**fluff′i•ness,** *n.*

flu•gel•horn or **flü•gel•horn** or **flue•gel•horn** (flōo′gəl hôrn′), *n.* a brass wind instrument with three valves, usu. pitched in B flat and used esp. in military bands. —**flu′gel•horn′ist,** *n.*

flu•id (flōo′id), *n.* **1.** a substance, as a liquid or gas, that is capable of flowing and that changes its shape at a steady rate when acted upon by a force. —*adj.* **2.** pertaining to a substance that easily changes its shape; capable of flowing. **3.** changing easily or readily; not fixed, stable, or rigid: *Our plans are fluid.* **4.** smooth and flowing: *fluid movements.* **5.** convertible into cash; liquid: *fluid assets.* —**flu•id′i•ty,** *n.*

flu′id dram′ (or **drachm′**), *n.* the eighth part of a fluid ounce. *Abbr.*: fl dr; *Symbol:* f

flu•id•ics (flōo id′iks), *n.* (*used with a sing. v.*) the technology dealing with the use of a flowing liquid or gas in various devices, esp. controls, to perform functions usu. performed by an electric current in electronic devices. Also called **fluerics.** —**flu•id′ic,** *adj.*

flu•id•i•ty (flōo id′i tē), *n.* **1.** the quality or state of being fluid. **2.** the ability of a substance to flow.

flu′id mechan′ics, *n.* an applied science dealing with the basic principles of gaseous and liquid matter.
flu′id ounce′, *n.* a measure of capacity equal to 1/16 pint or 1.8047 cubic inches (29.573 milliliters) in the U.S., and equal to 1/20 of an imperial pint or 1.7339 cubic inches (28.413 milliliters) in Great Britain. *Abbr.*: fl. oz.
fluke[1] (flo͞ok), *n.* **1.** the part of an anchor that catches in the ground, esp. the flat triangular piece at the end of each arm. **2.** the barbed head of a harpoon, spear, arrow, etc. **3.** either half of the triangular tail of a whale.
fluke[2] (flo͞ok), *n.* **1.** a stroke of good luck: *I got the job by a fluke.* **2.** a chance happening; accident. **3.** an accidentally successful stroke, as in billiards.
fluke[3] (flo͞ok), *n.* **1.** any of several American flounders of the genus *Paralichthys,* esp. *P. dentatus,* of the Atlantic Ocean. **2.** TREMATODE.
fluk•y or **fluk•ey** (flo͞o′kē), *adj.,* **fluk•i•er, fluk•i•est.** **1.** obtained or happening by chance rather than skill. **2.** uncertain, as a wind; changeable. —**fluk′i•ness,** *n.*
flume (flo͞om), *n.* **1.** a deep narrow defile containing a mountain stream or torrent. **2.** an artificial channel or trough for conducting water, as one used to transport logs or provide water power. **3.** an amusement park ride in which passengers are conveyed through a water-filled chute or over a water slide.
flum•mox (flum′əks), *v.t. Informal.* to bewilder; confound; confuse.
flung (flung), *v.* pt. and pp. of FLING.
flunk (flungk), *v.i.* **1.** to fail in a course or examination. —*v.t.* **2.** to get a failing mark in: *to flunk math.* **3.** to give a failing grade to. **4. flunk out,** to dismiss or be dismissed from a school because of failing grades: *to flunk out of college.* —*n.* **5.** a failure, as in a course or examination.
flunk•out (flungk′out′), *n.* a person who has flunked out of school.
flun•ky or **flun•key** (flung′kē), *n., pl.* **-kies** or **-keys.** **1.** a male servant in livery. **2.** an assistant who does menial work. **3.** a servile follower; toady; yes-man. —**flun′ky•ism,** *n.*
fluo•resce (flo͞o res′, flô-, flō-), *v.i.,* **-resced, -resc•ing.** to exhibit fluorescence. —**fluo•resc′er,** *n.*
fluo•res•cence (flo͞o res′əns, flô-, flō-), *n.* **1.** the emission of radiation, esp. of visible light, by a substance during exposure to external radiation, as light or x-rays. **2.** the property possessed by such a substance. **3.** the radiation so produced. —**fluo•res′cent,** *adj.*
fluores′cent lamp′, *n.* a tubular electric discharge lamp in which light is produced by the fluorescence of phosphors coating the inside of the tube.
fluor•i•date (flo͝or′i dāt′, flôr′-, flōr′-), *v.t.,* **-dat•ed, -dat•ing.** to introduce a fluoride into: *to fluoridate drinking water.*
fluor•i•da•tion (flo͝or′i dā′shən, flôr′-, flōr′-), *n.* the addition of fluorides to the public water supply to reduce the incidence of tooth decay.
fluor•ide (flo͝or′īd, flôr′-, flōr′-), *n.* a compound containing fluorine and another element or radical, as sodium fluoride, NaF.
fluor•i•nate (flo͝or′ə nāt′, flôr′-, flōr′-), *v.t.,* **-nat•ed, -nat•ing.** to treat or combine with fluorine. —**fluor′i•na′tion,** *n.*
fluor•ine (flo͝or′ēn, -in, flôr′-, flōr′-), *n.* the most reactive nonmetallic element, a pale yellow, corrosive, toxic gas that occurs combined, esp. in fluorite. *Symbol:* F; *at. wt.:* 18.9984; *at. no.:* 9.
fluo•rite (flo͝or′īt, flôr′-, flōr′-), *n.* a mineral, calcium fluoride, CaF_2, occurring in crystals and in masses: the chief source of fluorine.
fluoro-, **1.** a combining form meaning "fluorine" or "fluoride": *fluorocarbon.* **2.** a combining form meaning "fluorescence": *fluoroscope.*
fluor•o•car•bon (flo͝or′ō kär′bən, flôr′-, flōr′-), *n.* any of a class of compounds produced by substituting fluorine for hydrogen in a hydrocarbon and characterized by great chemical stability: used chiefly as a lubricant, refrigerant, fire-extinguishing agent, and insulator; banned as an aerosol propellant in the U.S. because of its apparent role in ozone layer depletion.
flur•ry (flûr′ē, flur′ē), *n., pl.* **-ries,** *v.,* **-ried, -ry•ing.** —*n.* **1.** a light, brief shower of snow. **2.** sudden commotion, excitement, confusion, or nervous hurry: *a flurry of activity before the party.* **3.** a brief rise or fall in prices or a brief period of heavy trading on the stock exchange. **4.** a sudden gust of wind. —*v.t.* **5.** to make confused or agitated; fluster. —*v.i.* **6.** (of snow) to fall or be blown in a flurry. **7.** to move in an excited or agitated manner. [b. FLUTTER and HURRY]
flush[1] (flush), *n.* **1.** a blush; rosy glow. **2.** a rushing or overspreading flow, as of water. **3.** a sudden rise of emotion: *a flush of anger.* **4.** glowing freshness or vigor: *the flush of youth.* **5.** a reddening of the skin, as from a fever, or a sensation of heat accompanying this. **6.** HOT FLASH. **7.** an act of cleansing by flushing. —*v.t.* **8.** to redden; cause to blush or glow. **9.** to flood or spray thoroughly with water, as for cleansing purposes. **10.** to flood or wash out by a sudden rush of water. **11.** to animate or excite; inflame: *flushed with success.* —*v.i.* **12.** to blush; redden. **13.** to flow with a rush; flow and spread suddenly. **14.** to be washed with a sudden rush of water.
flush[2] (flush), *adj.* **1.** even or level with a surface; forming the same plane: *The window frame is flush with the wall.* **2.** having direct contact; immediately adjacent: *The table was flush against the wall.* **3.** well-supplied, esp. with money; affluent; prosperous. **4.** abundant or plentiful, as money. **5.** having a ruddy or reddish color. **6.** full of vigor; lusty. **7.** full to overflowing. **8.** even or level with the right margin **(flush′ right′)** or the left margin **(flush′ left′)** of a type page; without an indention. —*adv.* **9.** on the same level or plane; evenly: *The door shuts flush with the wall.* **10.** in direct contact; squarely: *set flush against the edge.* —*v.t.* **11.** to make flush or even. —*v.i.* **12.** to send out shoots, as plants in spring. —*n.* **13.** a fresh growth, as of shoots and leaves.
flush[3] (flush), *v.t.* **1.** to rouse and cause to start up or fly off: *to flush a woodcock.* —*v.i.* **2.** to fly out or start up suddenly. —*n.* **3.** a flushed bird or flock of birds.
flush[4] (flush), *adj.* **1.** consisting entirely of cards of one suit: *a flush hand.* —*n.* **2.** a hand or set of cards all of one suit. Compare ROYAL FLUSH, STRAIGHT FLUSH.
flus•ter (flus′tər), *v.t.* **1.** to put into a state of nervous or agitated confusion: *to be flustered by an unexpected visitor.* **2.** to excite and confuse with drink. —*v.i.* **3.** to become nervously or agitatedly confused. —*n.* **4.** nervous excitement or confusion.
flute (flo͞ot), *n., v.,* **flut•ed, flut•ing.** —*n.* **1.** a wind instrument with a high range, consisting of a tube with a series of fingerholes or keys in which the wind is directed against a sharp edge, either directly or through a flue. **2.** one of a series of long, usu. rounded grooves, as on the shaft of a column. **3.** any groove or furrow, as in a ruffle of cloth or on a piecrust. **4.** a stemmed glass with a tall, slender bowl, used esp. for champagne. —*v.i.* **5.** to produce flutelike sounds. **6.** to play on a flute. —*v.t.* **7.** to utter in flutelike tones. **8.** to form flutes or furrows in.
flut•ing (flo͞o′ting), *n.* **1.** ornamentation with flutes, as on a column. **2.** a groove, furrow, or flute, or a series of these.
flut•ist (flo͞o′tist) also **flautist,** *n.* a flute player.
flut•ter (flut′ər), *v.i.* **1.** to wave or flap about: *Banners fluttered in the breeze.* **2.** to flap the wings rapidly or fly with flapping movements. **3.** to move in quick, irregular motions; vibrate. **4.** to beat rapidly, as the heart. **5.** to be tremulous or agitated. **6.** to go with irregular motions or aimless course. —*v.t.* **7.** to cause to flutter. **8.** to throw into nervous or tremulous excitement or agitation. —*n.* **9.** a fluttering movement. **10.** a state of nervous excitement or mental agitation: *a flutter of anticipation.* **11.** a stir; flurry. **12.** a variation in pitch resulting from rapid fluctuations in the speed of a sound recording. Compare WOW[2].
flut′ter kick′, *n.* a swimming kick in which the legs make rapid alternate up-and-down movements while the knees remain rigid, as in the crawl.
flu•vi•al (flo͞o′vē əl), *adj.* **1.** of or pertaining to a river. **2.** produced by or found in a river.
flux (fluks), *n.* **1.** a flowing or flow. **2.** the flowing in of the tide. **3.** continuous change or movement: *Our plans are in a state of flux.* **4. a.** the rate of flow of fluid, particles, or energy. **b.** a quantity expressing the strength of a field of force in a given area. **5. a.** a substance used to refine metals by combining with impurities to form a molten mixture that can be readily removed. **b.** a substance used to prevent oxidation of fused metal, as in soldering. **6.** an abnormal discharge of liquid matter from the bowels. —*v.t.* **7.** to melt; make fluid. **8.** to fuse by the use of flux. —*v.i.* **9.** to flow.
flux•ion (fluk′shən), *n.* **1.** an act of flowing; flow or flux. **2.** continuous change. **3.** *Math.* the derivative relative to the time.
fly[1] (flī), *v.,* **flew, flown, fly•ing,** *n., pl.* **flies.** —*v.i.* **1.** to move through the air using wings. **2.** to be carried through the air or through space by any force or agency. **3.** to float or flutter in the air: *flags flying in the breeze.* **4.** to travel in an aircraft or spacecraft. **5.** to operate an aircraft or spacecraft. **6.** to move suddenly and quickly; start unexpectedly: *He flew out of the room.* **7.** to change rapidly and unexpectedly from one state or position to another: *to fly into a rage; The door flew open.* **8.** to flee; escape. **9.** to move swiftly: *How time flies!* **10.** to move with an aggressive surge. **11.** to bat a fly ball in baseball. **12.** *Informal.* to be acceptable, believable, feasible, or successful: *It seemed like a good idea, but it just wouldn't fly.* —*v.t.* **13.** to make (something) float or move through the air: *to fly a kite.* **14.** to operate (an aircraft or spacecraft). **15.** to hoist aloft, as for display or signaling: *to fly a flag.* **16.** to operate an aircraft or spacecraft over: *to fly the Pacific.* **17.** to transport or convey by air. **18.** to escape from. **19. a.** to hang (scenery) above a stage by means of rigging. **b.** to raise (scenery) from the stage into the flies. **20. fly at,** to attack suddenly; lash out at. **21. fly out,** to make an out in baseball by hitting a fly ball that is caught by a player of the opposing team. —*n.* **22.** a strip of material sewn along one edge of a garment opening to conceal fasteners. **23.** a flap forming the door of a tent. **24.** the course of a flying object, as a ball. **25.** a regulating device for chime and striking mechanisms. **26. a.** the horizontal dimension of a flag as flown from a vertical staff. **b.** the end of the flag farther from the staff. Compare HOIST (def. 6). **27. flies.** Also called **fly loft.** the space above the stage used chiefly for storing scenery and equipment. —***Idiom.*** **28. fly high,** to be full of hope or elation. **29. fly in the face** or **teeth of,** to act in brazen defiance of: *to fly in the face of tradition.* **30. fly off the handle,** *Informal.* to become very angry, esp. without warning. **31. let fly, a.** to hurl or propel (an object). **b.** to give free rein to one's anger. **32. on the fly, a.** during flight. **b.** hurriedly; without pausing.
fly[2] (flī), *n., pl.* **flies.** **1.** any of numerous two-winged insects of the order Diptera, as the common housefly. **2.** any of various winged insects, as the mayfly or firefly. **3.** a fishhook dressed with feathers, silk, tinsel, etc., so as to resemble an insect or small fish, for use as a lure. —***Idiom.*** **4. fly in the ointment,** something that spoils an otherwise pleasant thing; detriment. Eccl. 10:1.
fly•a•way (flī′ə wā′), *adj.* **1.** fluttering or streaming in the wind; wind-

blown: *flyaway hair.* **2.** flighty; frivolous; giddy. **3.** ready for flight: *flyaway aircraft.*

fly′by′ or **fly′-by′,** *n., pl.* **-bys. 1.** the flight of a spacecraft close enough to a celestial object, as a planet, to gather scientific data. **2. a.** a low-altitude flight of an aircraft for the benefit of ground observers. **b.** FLYOVER (def. 1).

fly′-by-night′, *adj.* **1.** not reliable or well established, esp. in business, and primarily interested in making a quick profit: *a fly-by-night operation.* **2.** not lasting; impermanent; transitory. —*n.* Also, **fly′-by-night′er. 3.** a debtor who attempts to evade creditors. **4.** a fly-by-night person or business.

fly′-by-wire′, *adj.* (of an aircraft or spacecraft) actuated entirely by electronic controls.

fly′-cast′, *v.i.* to fish with a fly rod and an artificial fly as a lure, casting the fly with a whiplike motion of the rod and a length of line pulled from the reel before the cast.

fly•catch•er (flī′kach′ər), *n.* **1.** Also called **tyrant flycatcher.** any of numerous New World suboscine birds of the family Tyrannidae, that sally from perches to catch insects in the air. **2.** any of numerous similar Old World songbirds of the subfamily Muscicapinae.

fly•er (flī′ər), *n.* FLIER.

fly′-fish′, *v.i.* to fish with artificial flies as bait.

fly′-in′, *n.* **1.** a convention or other gathering at which participants arrive by air. —*adj.* **2.** of or for participants arriving by air: *a fly-in safari.* **3.** accessible only by air: *a remote fly-in fishing camp.*

fly•ing (flī′ing), *adj.* **1.** making flight or capable of making flight; passing through the air: *a flying insect.* **2.** floating, waving, or hanging in the air: *flying banners.* **3.** extending through the air. **4.** moving swiftly. **5.** made while moving swiftly: *a flying leap.* **6.** very hasty or brief; fleeting or transitory: *a flying visit.* **7.** designed or organized for swift movement or action. **8.** fleeing; running away. **9.** (of a sail) having none of its edges fastened to spars or stays. —*n.* **10.** the act of traveling in or operating an aircraft or spacecraft; flight. —*adv.* **11.** without being fastened to a yard, stay, or the like: *a sail set flying.*

fly′ing but′tress, *n.* an arch or segment of an arch projecting from a wall and transmitting the thrust of a roof or vault outward and downward to a solid buttress or pier.

fly′ing col′ors, *n.pl.* outstanding success; triumph: *He passed the test with flying colors.*

fly′ing drag′on, *n.* any arboreal lizard of the genus *Draco,* having an extensible membrane between elongated ribs for long, gliding leaps. Also called **flying lizard.**

fly′ing fish′, *n.* any of several warm-water marine fishes of the family Exocoetidae, noted for winglike fins that enable it to glide for some distance after leaping from the water.

fly′ing fox′, *n.* any large fruit bat of the genus *Pteropus,* principally of SE Asia, Australia, and oceanic islands.

fly′ing frog′, *n.* either of two East Indian frogs, *Rhacophorus nigrapalmatus* and *R. pardalis,* having webbed feet for long, gliding leaps.

fly′ing gur′nard, *n.* any marine fish of the family Dactylopteridae, esp. *Dactylopterus volitans,* having greatly enlarged, colorful pectoral fins that enable it to glide short distances through the air.

fly′ing le′mur, *n.* either of two lemurlike mammals of the SE Asian genus *Cynocephalus,* having broad folds of skin on both sides of the body to aid in gliding from tree to tree.

fly′ing liz′ard, *n.* FLYING DRAGON.

fly′ing phalan′ger, *n.* any of several phalangers having a fold of skin on each side of the body, permitting gliding leaps.

fly′ing sau′cer, *n.* any of various disk-shaped objects reportedly seen flying at high speeds and altitudes and alleged to come from outer space; UFO.

fly′ing squir′rel, *n.* any of various Old and New World nocturnal tree squirrels having extensible folds of skin along the body that permit long, gliding leaps.

fly′ing wedge′, *n.* a V-shaped formation, as of police, organized to penetrate a line of defense.

fly•leaf (flī′lēf′), *n., pl.* **-leaves.** a blank leaf in the front or the back of a book.

fly•o•ver (flī′ō′vər), *n.* **1.** a formation of aircraft flight for observation from the ground. **2.** a flight over a specified area.

fly•pa•per (flī′pā′pər), *n.* paper designed to destroy flies by catching them on its sticky surface or poisoning them on contact.

fly′ rod′, *n.* a light, flexible fishing rod used for fly-casting.

fly•speck (flī′spek′), *n.* **1.** a speck or tiny stain from the excrement of a fly. **2.** any minute spot. **3.** a minute detail or flaw. —*v.t.* **4.** to mark with flyspecks. **5.** to inspect for minute flaws.

fly•way (flī′wā′), *n.* a route between breeding and wintering areas taken by concentrations of migrating birds.

fly•weight (flī′wāt′), *n.* a boxer or weightlifter of the lightest competitive class.

fly•wheel (flī′hwēl′, -wēl′), *n.* a heavy disk or wheel rotating on a shaft so that its momentum gives almost uniform rotational speed to the shaft and to all connected machinery.

FM, 1. frequency modulation: a method of impressing a signal on a radio carrier wave by varying the frequency of the carrier wave. **2.** a system of radio broadcasting by means of frequency modulation. Compare AM.

Fm, *Chem. Symbol.* fermium.

FNMA, Federal National Mortgage Association.

f-number (ef′num′bər), *n.* a number corresponding to the ratio of the focal length to the diameter of a lens system, esp. a camera lens. *Symbol:* f/

foal (fōl), *n.* **1.** the nursing young of any mammal of the horse family. —*v.i., v.t.* **2.** to give birth to (a colt or filly).

foam (fōm), *n.* **1.** a collection of minute bubbles formed on the surface of a liquid by agitation, fermentation, etc. **2.** frothy perspiration on the skin, as of a horse. **3.** froth formed from saliva in the mouth, as in rabies. **4.** a thick, frothy substance, as shaving cream. **5.** (in firefighting) a substance that smothers the flames on a burning liquid by forming a layer of minute, stable, heat-resistant bubbles on the liquid's surface. **6.** a lightweight material in which gas bubbles are dispersed in a solid, as foam rubber. **7.** *Literary.* the sea. —*v.i.* **8.** to form or gather foam; emit foam; froth. —*v.t.* **9.** to cause to foam. **10.** to insulate or cover with foam. **11.** to make (plastic, metal, etc.) into a foam. —**Idiom. 12. foam at the mouth,** to be extremely or uncontrollably angry. —**foam′less,** *adj.* —**foam′like′,** *adj.* —**foam′y,** *adj.,* **-i•er, -i•est.**

foam•flow•er (fōm′flou′ər), *n.* a North American plant, *Tiarella cordifolia,* of the saxifrage family, having a cluster of small, usu. white flowers.

foam′ rub′ber, *n.* a light, spongy rubber, used for mattresses, etc.

fob[1] (fob), *n.* **1.** a watch pocket just below the waistline in trousers. **2.** a short chain or ribbon, usu. with a medallion or similar ornament, attached to a watch and worn hanging from a pocket. **3.** the medallion or ornament itself.

fob[2] (fob), *v.t.,* **fobbed, fob•bing. fob off, 1.** to induce someone to take (something inferior); palm off. **2.** to put (someone) off by deception or trickery: *She fobbed us off with phony excuses.*

fob or **f.o.b.** or **FOB** or **F.O.B.,** free on board: without charge to the buyer for goods placed on board a carrier at the point of shipment.

fo•cac•cia (fō kä′chə), *n., pl.* **-cias.** a large, round, flat Italian bread, sprinkled before baking with olive oil, salt, and often herbs.

fo•cal (fō′kəl), *adj.* of, pertaining to, or at a focus. —**fo′cal•ly,** *adv.*

fo•cal•ize (fō′kə līz′), *v.t., v.i.,* **-ized, -iz•ing. 1.** to bring or come to a focus. **2.** to localize. —**fo′cal•i•za′tion,** *n.*

fo′cal length′, *n.* the distance from a focal point of a lens or mirror to the corresponding principal plane. Also called **fo′cal dis′tance.**

fo′cal point′, *n.* **1.** either of two points on the axis of a mirror, lens, or other optical system, on which rays converge or from which they deviate. **2.** the center of activity or attention. **3.** the central or principal point of focus.

fo•ci (fō′sī, -kī), *n.* a pl. of FOCUS.

fo•cus (fō′kəs), *n., pl.* **-cus•es, -ci** (-sī, -kī), *v.,* **-cused, -cus•ing** or (*esp. Brit.*) **-cussed, -cus•sing.** —*n.* **1.** a central point, as of attraction, attention, or activity: *Prevention of war became the focus of diplomatic efforts.* **2.** a point at which rays of light, heat, or other radiation meet after being refracted or reflected. **3. a.** the focal point of a lens. **b.** the focal length of a lens. **c.** the clear and sharply defined condition of an image. **d.** the position of a viewed object or the adjustment of an optical device necessary to produce a clear image: *in focus; out of focus.* **4.** (of a conic section) a point having the property that the distances from any point on a curve to it and to a fixed line have a constant ratio for all points on the curve. **5.** the point of origin of an earthquake. **6.** the primary center from which a disease develops or in which it localizes. —*v.t.* **7.** to bring to a focus or into focus: *to focus the lens of a camera.* **8.** to concentrate: *to focus one's thoughts.* —*v.i.* **9.** to become focused.

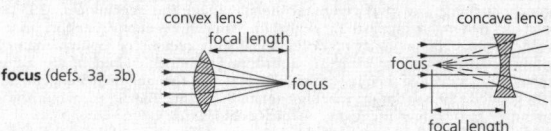

focus (defs. 3a, 3b)

fo′cus group′, *n.* a representative group of people questioned together about their opinions on issues of politics, product marketing, etc.

fod•der (fod′ər), *n.* **1.** coarse food for livestock. **2.** people considered as readily available and of little value: *cannon fodder.* **3.** raw material: *fodder for a comedian's routine.* —*v.t.* **4.** to feed with fodder.

foe (fō), *n.* **1.** a person who feels enmity, hatred, or malice toward another; enemy: *a bitter foe.* **2.** a military enemy. **3.** an opponent in a game or contest; adversary: *a political foe.* **4.** a person who is opposed in feeling, principle, etc., to something: *a foe to progress.* **5.** a thing that is harmful to or destructive of something.

fog (fog, fôg), *n., v.,* **fogged, fog•ging.** —*n.* **1.** a cloudlike mass or layer of minute water droplets or ice crystals near the surface of the earth, appreciably reducing visibility. **2.** any darkened state of the atmosphere, or the diffused substance that causes it. **3.** a state of mental confusion or unawareness; daze. **4.** a hazy effect on a developed photographic negative or positive. **5.** a mixture consisting of liquid particles dispersed in a gaseous medium. —*v.t.* **6.** to cover or envelop with or as if with fog: *The steam fogged his glasses.* **7.** to confuse or obscure: *The debate just fogged the issue.* **8.** to bewilder or perplex: *to fog the mind.* **9.** to produce fog on (a photographic negative or positive). —*v.i.* **10.** to become enveloped or obscured with or as if with fog. **11.** (of a photographic negative or positive) to become affected by fog. —**fog′less,** *adj.*

fog•bound (fog′bound′, fôg′-), *adj.* **1.** unable to sail or navigate because of heavy fog. **2.** enveloped or obscured by fog.

fog•ger (fog′ər, fô′gər), *n.* a device that spreads a chemical, as an insecticide, in the form of a fog.

fog•gy (fog′ē, fô′gē), *adj.*, **-gi•er, -gi•est.** **1.** thick with or having much fog; misty. **2.** covered or enveloped as if with fog: *a foggy mirror.* **3.** blurred or obscured; vague: *I haven't the foggiest notion of where she went.* **4.** bewildered; perplexed. **5.** (of a photographic negative or positive) affected by fog. —**fog′gi•ly,** *adv.* —**fog′gi•ness,** *n.*

Fog′gy Bot′tom, *n.* **1.** a low-lying area bordering the Potomac River in Washington, D.C. **2.** the U.S. Department of State, which has offices located in this area.

fog•horn (fog′hôrn′, fôg′-), *n.* **1.** a deep, loud horn for sounding warning signals to ships in foggy weather. **2.** a deep, loud voice.

fo•gy or **fo•gey** (fō′gē), *n., pl.* **-gies** or **-geys.** an extremely old-fashioned or conservative person (usu. prec. by *old*).

FOIA, Freedom of Information Act.

foi•ble (foi′bəl), *n.* **1.** a minor weakness or failing of character: *an all-too-human foible.* **2.** a quirk or eccentricity of character. **3.** the part of a sword or foil blade between the middle and the point, less strong than the forte.

foie gras (fwä grä′), *n.* the liver of specially fattened geese or ducks, used as a table delicacy, esp. in the form of a paste **(pâté de foie gras).**

foil[1] (foil), *v.t.* **1.** to prevent the success of; frustrate; thwart: *Loyal troops foiled the revolt.* **2.** to keep (a person) from succeeding in an enterprise, plan, etc. —**foil′a•ble,** *adj.*

foil[2] (foil), *n.* **1.** metal in the form of very thin sheets: *aluminum foil.* **2.** the metallic backing applied to glass to form a mirror. **3.** a thin layer of metal placed under a gem in a closed setting to improve its color or brilliancy. **4.** a person or thing that makes another seem better by contrast: *playing the foil for a comedian.* **5.** an arc or rounded space between cusps, as in Gothic window tracery. **6.** an airfoil or hydrofoil. —*v.t.* **7.** to cover or back with foil. **8.** to set off by contrast.

foil[3] (foil), *n.* **1.** a flexible four-sided rapier having a blunt point. **2. foils,** the art or practice of fencing with this weapon, points being made by touching the trunk of the opponent's body with the tip of the weapon.

foist (foist), *v.t.* **1.** to impose fraudulently or unjustifiably (usu. fol. by *off, on,* or *upon*): *to foist inferior goods on a customer.* **2.** to put or introduce surreptitiously or fraudulently (usu. fol. by *in* or *into*).

Fok•ker (fok′ər; *Du.* fok′əʀ), *n.* **1. An•tho•ny Her•man Ge•rard** (*Du.* än tō′nē heʀ′män gā′ʀäʀt), 1890–1939, Dutch airplane designer and builder. **2.** an aircraft designed or built by Fokker, esp. as used by Germany in World War I.

fold[1] (fōld), *v.t.* **1.** to bend (cloth, paper, etc.) over upon itself. **2.** to bring into a compact form by bending and laying parts together: *to fold up a map.* **3.** to bring together and intertwine or cross: *He folded his arms on his chest.* **4.** to bend or wind; entwine: *The child folded his arms around my neck.* **5.** to bring (the wings) close to the body, as a bird on alighting. **6.** to enclose; wrap; envelop: *to fold something in paper.* **7.** to embrace or clasp: *to fold someone in one's arms.* **8.** *Informal.* to bring to an end: *to fold a business.* —*v.i.* **9.** to be folded or be capable of folding. **10.** to place one's cards facedown so as to withdraw from the play. **11. a.** to fail, esp. to go out of business: *The magazine folded after a few years.* **b.** to end a run; close: *The show will fold next week.* **12. fold in,** to blend (a cooking ingredient) into a mixture by gently turning one part over another: *Fold in the egg whites.* **13. fold out** or **down,** to spread or open up; unfold. —*n.* **14.** a part that is folded; pleat; layer: *folds of cloth.* **15.** a line, crease, or hollow made by folding. **16.** a hollow place in undulating ground: *a fold of the mountains.* **17.** a coil of a serpent, string, etc. **18.** the act of folding or doubling over. **19.** a margin or ridge formed by the folding of a membrane or other flat body part; plica. —**fold′a•ble,** *adj.*

fold[2] (fōld), *n.* **1.** an enclosure for sheep. **2.** the sheep kept within it. **3.** a flock of sheep. **4.** a church or its members. **5.** a group sharing common beliefs, values, etc.: *to rejoin the fold.* —*v.t.* **6.** to confine (sheep or other domestic animals) in a fold.

-fold, a combining form meaning "having the number of kinds or parts" or "multiplied the number of times" specified by the initial element: *fourfold; manyfold.*

fold•a•way (fōld′ə wā′), *adj.* **1.** designed to be folded out of the way when not in use: *a foldaway bed.* —*n.* **2.** a foldaway item.

fold•er (fōl′dər), *n.* **1.** a folded sheet of light cardboard used to hold papers, as in a file. **2.** a printed sheet, as a circular or timetable, folded into a number of pagelike sections. **3.** one that folds.

fold′out′ or **fold′-out′,** *n.* **1.** a page larger than the trim size of a magazine or book, folded one or more times so as not to extend beyond the edges. —*adj.* **2.** designed to be unfolded for use, viewing, etc.

fold′up′ or **fold′-up′,** *n.* **1.** something, as a chair or bed, that can be folded up and stored away when not in use. **2.** a closing or failure, as of a business. **3.** a collapse or yielding; capitulation.

fo•li•a (fō′lē ə), *n.* pl. of FOLIUM.

fo•li•a•ceous (fō′lē ā′shəs), *adj.* **1.** of, like, or of the nature of a plant leaf; leaflike. **2.** bearing leaves or leaflike parts. **3.** consisting of leaflike plates or laminae; foliated. —**fo′li•a′ceous•ness,** *n.*

fo•li•age (fō′lē ij), *n.* **1.** the leaves of a plant, collectively; leafage. **2.** leaves in general. **3.** the ornamental representation of leaves, flowers, and branches, as in architecture. —**fo′li•aged,** *adj.*

fo•li•ate (*adj.* fō′lē it, -āt′; *v.* -āt′), *adj., v.,* **-at•ed, -at•ing.** —*adj.* **1.** covered with or having leaves. **2.** like a leaf. —*v.i.* **3.** to put forth leaves. **4.** to split into thin leaflike layers. —*v.t.* **5.** to shape like a leaf or leaves. **6.** to decorate with foils or foliage. **7.** to form into thin sheets. **8.** to spread over with a thin metallic backing. **9.** to number the folios or leaves of (a manuscript or book).

fo•li•a•tion (fō′lē ā′shən), *n.* **1.** the process of putting forth leaves. **2.** the arrangement of leaves within a bud. **3.** the consecutive numbering of the folios or leaves of a manuscript or book. **4.** a form of lamination produced in rocks by metamorphism. **5.** ornamentation with foliage. **6.** (in architecture) ornamentation with foils or with representations of foliage. **7.** formation into thin sheets. **8.** the application of foil to glass to make a mirror.

fo•lic (fō′lik, fol′ik), *adj.* of or derived from folic acid.

fo′lic ac′id, *n.* a water-soluble vitamin that is converted to a coenzyme essential to purine and thymine biosynthesis: deficiency causes a form of anemia.

fo•li•o (fō′lē ō′), *n., pl.* **-li•os,** *adj., v.,* **-li•oed, -li•o•ing.** —*n.* **1.** a sheet of paper folded once to make two leaves, or four pages, of a book or manuscript. **2.** a volume having pages of the largest size, formerly made from such a sheet. **3.** a leaf of a manuscript or book numbered only on the front side. **4. a.** (in a book) the number of each page. **b.** (in a newspaper) the number of each page together with the date and the name of the newspaper. **5.** *Law.* a certain number of words, in the U.S. generally 100, taken as a unit for computing the length of a document. —*adj.* **6.** pertaining to or having the format of a folio: *a folio volume.* —*v.t.* **7.** to number each leaf or page of.

fo•li•um (fō′lē əm), *n., pl.* **-li•a** (-lē ə). **1.** a thin leaflike stratum or layer; lamella. **2.** *Geom.* a loop; part of a curve terminated at both ends by the same node. Equation: $x^3 + y^3 = 3axy$.

folk (fōk), *n.* **1.** Usu., **folks.** (*used with a pl. v.*) people in general. **2.** Often, **folks.** (*used with a pl. v.*) people of a specified class or group: *country folk; poor folks.* **3.** (*used with a pl. v.*) people as the carriers of culture, esp. as representing a society's mores, customs, and traditions. **4. folks,** *Informal.* **a.** members of one's family; one's relatives. **b.** one's parents. —*adj.* **5.** of or originating among the common people: *folk beliefs; folk dances.* **6.** having unknown origins and reflecting the traditional forms of a society: *folk art.* —**folk′ish,** *adj.*

folk′ etymol′ogy, *n.* **1.** a modification of a linguistic form according either to a falsely assumed etymology, as *Welsh rarebit* from *Welsh rabbit,* or to a historically irrelevant analogy, as *bridegroom* from *bridegome.* **2.** a popular but false notion of the origin of a word.

folk•lore (fōk′lôr′, -lōr′), *n.* **1.** the traditional beliefs, legends, customs, etc., of a people; lore of a people. **2.** the study of such lore. **3.** a body of widely held but false or unsubstantiated beliefs. —**folk′lor′ic,** *adj.* —**folk′lor′ist,** *n.* —**folk′lor•is′tic,** *adj.*

folk′ mass′, *n.* a liturgical mass in which traditional music is replaced by folk music.

folk′ mu′sic, *n.* **1.** music, usu. of simple character and anonymous authorship, handed down among the common people by oral tradition. **2.** music by known composers that has become part of the folk tradition of a country or region.

folk′ song′, *n.* **1.** a song originating among the people of a country or area, passed by oral tradition from one singer or generation to the next, often existing in several versions, and marked generally by simple, modal melody and stanzaic, narrative verse. **2.** a song of similar character written by a known composer.

folk•sy (fōk′sē), *adj.,* **-si•er, -si•est.** **1.** friendly or neighborly; sociable. **2.** very informal; familiar; unceremonious: *The politician affected a folksy style.* —**folk′si•ness,** *n.*

folk′ tale′ or **folk′tale′,** *n.* a tale or legend originating and traditional among a people, esp. one forming part of an oral tradition.

folk•way (fōk′wā′), *n.* a traditional way of living, thinking, or acting in a particular social group; custom.

fol•li•cle (fol′i kəl), *n.* **1.** *Anat.* **a.** a small cavity, sac, or gland. **b.** one of the small ovarian sacs containing a maturing ovum. **2.** a dry seed pod consisting of a single carpel, splitting at maturity along the front of the seam.

fol•low (fol′ō), *v.* **1.** to come after in sequence, order of time, etc.; succeed: *The speech follows the dinner.* **2.** to go or come after; move behind in the same direction: *Drive ahead, and I'll follow you.* **3.** to accept as a guide or leader; accept the authority of. **4.** to conform to, comply with, or act in accordance with; obey: *to follow orders; to follow advice.* **5.** to imitate or copy: *to follow the latest fads.* **6.** to move forward along (a road, path, etc.). **7.** to come after as a result or consequence; result from: *Higher prices usually follow wage increases.* **8.** to go after or along with (a person) as companion. **9.** to go in pursuit of: *to follow an enemy.* **10.** to try for or attain to: *to follow an ideal.* **11.** to engage in or be concerned with as a pursuit: *to follow the sea as one's true calling.* **12.** to watch the movements, progress, or course of: *to follow a bird in flight.* **13.** to watch the development of or keep up with: *to follow the news.* **14.** to keep up with and understand (an argument, story, etc.): *Do you follow me?* —*v.i.* **15.** to come next after something else in sequence, order of time, etc. **16.** to happen or occur after something else; come next as an event. **17.** to result as an effect; occur as a consequence: *It follows then that they must be innocent.* **18. follow out,** to carry to a conclusion; execute. **19. follow through, a.** to carry out fully, as a stroke of a club in golf, a racket in tennis, etc. **b.** to continue an effort, plan, proposal, policy, etc., to its completion. **20. follow up, a.** to pursue closely and tenaciously. **b.** to increase the effectiveness of by further action or repetition. **c.** to pursue to a solution or conclusion.

fol•low•er (fol′ō ər), *n.* **1.** a person or thing that follows. **2.** a person who follows another in regard to his or her ideas or belief; disciple or adherent. **3.** a person who imitates, copies, or takes as a model or ideal: *a follower of current fashions.* **4.** an attendant, servant, or retainer. **5.** a mechanical part receiving motion from or following the movements of another part, esp. a cam.

fol•low•ing (fol′ō ing), *n.* **1.** a body of followers, attendants, adherents, etc. **2.** the body of admirers, attendants, patrons, etc., of someone or something: *That television show has a large following.* **3. the following,** that which comes immediately after, as pages or lines: *See the following for a list of exceptions.* **—***adj.* **4.** that comes after or next in order or time; ensuing: *the following day.* **5.** that is now to follow: *Check the following report for details.*

fol′low-through′, *n.* **1.** the completion of a motion, as in the stroke of a tennis racket. **2.** the portion of such a motion after the ball has been hit. **3.** the act of continuing a plan, project, scheme, or the like to its completion.

fol′low-up′, *n.* **1.** the act of following up. **2.** an action or thing that serves to increase the effectiveness of a previous one, as a second or subsequent letter, phone call, or visit. **3.** a news story providing additional information on a story or article previously published. **—***adj.* **4.** designed or serving to follow up, esp. to increase the effectiveness of a previous action: *a follow-up interview; follow-up care of a patient.*

fol•ly (fol′ē), *n., pl.* **-lies. 1.** the state or quality of being foolish; lack of understanding or sense. **2.** a foolish action, practice, idea, etc.; absurdity. **3.** a costly and foolish undertaking; unwise investment or expenditure. **4.** a whimsical or extravagant and often useless structure built to serve as a conversation piece, lend interest to a view, etc. **5. follies,** a theatrical revue.

Fo•mal•haut (fō′məl hôt′, -mə lō′), *n. Astron.* a star of the first magnitude and the brightest star in the constellation Piscis Austrinus.

fo•ment (fō ment′), *v.t.* **1.** to instigate or foster (discord, rebellion, etc.); promote the growth or development of: *to foment trouble.* **2.** to apply warm water or medicated liquid, ointments, etc., to (the surface of the body). **—fo′men•ta′tion,** *n.* **—fo•ment′er,** *n.*

fond[1] (fond), *adj.* **1.** having a liking or affection for (usu. fol. by *of*): *to be fond of animals.* **2.** loving; affectionate: *to give someone a fond look.* **3.** excessively tender or indulgent; doting: *a fond parent.* **4.** cherished with strong or unreasoning feeling: *to nourish fond hopes of becoming president.* **—fond′ly,** *adv.* **—fond′ness,** *n.*

fond[2] (fond; *Fr.* fôɴ), *n., pl.* **fonds** (fondz; *Fr.* fôɴ). background; foundation.

Fon•da (fon′də), *n.* **1. Henry,** 1905–82, U.S. actor. **2. Jane,** born 1937, U.S. actress (daughter of Henry Fonda).

fon•dant (fon′dənt), *n.* **1.** a thick, creamy sugar paste. **2.** a candy made of this paste.

fon•dle (fon′dl), *v.,* **-dled, -dling. —***v.t.* **1.** to handle or touch lovingly, affectionately, or tenderly; caress: *to fondle a precious object; to fondle one's baby.* **2.** to molest sexually by touching, stroking, etc. **—***v.i.* **3:** to show love or affection by caresses. **—fon′dler,** *n.*

fon•due (fon do͞o′, -dyo͞o′), *n.* **1.** a dish of Swiss origin consisting of melted cheese, white wine, seasonings, and often kirsch, served hot with pieces of bread for dipping. **2.** a dish of hot liquid in which small pieces of food are cooked or dipped: *beef fondue; chocolate fondue.*

font[1] (font), *n.* **1.** a receptacle for the water used in baptism. **2.** a receptacle for holy water; stoup. **3.** a productive source: *The book is a font of useful tips for travelers.* **4.** the reservoir for oil in a lamp.

font[2] (font), *n. Print.* a complete assortment of type of one style and size.

Fon•tan•a (fon tan′ə), *n.* a city in S California. 103,737.

fon•ta•nel or **fon•ta•nelle** (fon′tn el′), *n.* any of the spaces, covered by membrane, between the bones of a fetal or young skull.

Fon•teyn (fon tān′), *n.* **Dame Margot,** (*Margaret Hookham*), 1919–91, English ballerina.

fon•ti•na (fon tē′nə), *n.* a semisoft to firm pale yellow Italian cheese.

food (fo͞od), *n.* **1.** any nourishing substance taken into the body to sustain life, provide energy, promote growth, etc. **2.** more or less solid nourishment, as distinguished from liquids. **3.** a particular kind of solid nourishment: *a breakfast food; dog food.* **4.** whatever supplies nourishment to organisms: *plant food.* **5.** anything serving for consumption or use: *food for thought.*

Food′ and Ag′riculture Organiza′tion, *n.* the agency of the United Nations that institutes and administers programs, esp. in underdeveloped countries, for improving farming methods and increasing food production. *Abbr.:* FAO

Food′ and Drug′ Administra′tion, *n.* a division of the Department of Health and Human Services that protects the public against impure and unsafe foods, drugs, and cosmetics. *Abbr.:* FDA

food′ bank′, *n.* a nonprofit clearinghouse that receives donated food products and channels themto the needy.

food′ chain′, *n. Ecol.* a series of organisms interrelated in their feeding habits, the smallest being fed upon by a larger one, which in turn feeds a still larger one.

food′ court′, *n.* a space, as in a shopping mall, with a concentration of fast-food stalls and usu. a common eating area.

food′ cy′cle, *n.* FOOD WEB.

food′ poi′soning, *n.* **1.** any illness, as salmonellosis or botulism, caused by eating food contaminated with bacterial toxins and marked by severe intestinal symptoms. **2.** any illness caused by eating poisonous plants, fish, etc., or food containing chemical contaminants.

food′ proc′essor, *n.* an electric appliance with a closed container and interchangeable blades that can slice, chop, shred, purée, or otherwise process food at high speeds. **—food′ proc′essing,** *n.*

food′ pyr′amid, *n. Ecol.* the successive levels of predation in a food chain represented schematically as a pyramid because upper levels normally consist of decreasing numbers of larger predators.

food′ stamp′, *n.* a coupon that is redeemable for food, given to eligible needy persons under a federal program.

food•stuff (fo͞od′stuf′), *n.* a substance used as food.

food′ web′, *n.* the entirety of interrelated food chains in an ecological community. Also called **food cycle.**

fool[1] (fo͞ol), *n.* **1.** a silly or stupid person; one who lacks sense. **2.** a professional jester, formerly kept by a person of rank for amusement: *the court fool.* **3.** a person who has been tricked or deceived into appearing silly or stupid: *to make a fool of someone.* **4.** an ardent enthusiast who cannot resist an opportunity to indulge an enthusiasm (usu. prec. by a present participle): *a dancing fool.* **—***v.t.* **5.** to trick, deceive, or impose on: *They tried to fool us.* **—***v.i.* **6.** to act like a fool; joke; play. **7.** to jest; pretend; make believe: *I was only fooling.* **8. fool around, a.** to putter aimlessly; waste time. **b.** to trifle or flirt. **9. fool away,** to squander foolishly, as time or money. **10. fool with,** to handle or play with idly or carelessly. **—*Idiom.* 11. be nobody's fool,** to be wise or shrewd. [< Old French < Latin *follis* bellows, bag]

fool[2] (fo͞ol), *n.* an English dessert of crushed, cooked fruit mixed with cream or custard and served cold: *gooseberry fool.*

fool•har•dy (fo͞ol′här′dē), *adj.,* **-di•er, -di•est.** recklessly or thoughtlessly bold; foolishly rash or venturesome. **—fool′har′di•ly,** *adv.* **—fool′har′di•ness,** *n.*

fool•ish (fo͞o′lish), *adj.* **1.** resulting from or showing a lack of sense; unwise: *a foolish action.* **2.** lacking forethought or caution. **3.** trifling, insignificant, or paltry. **—fool′ish•ly,** *adv.* **—fool′ish•ness,** *n.*

fool•proof (fo͞ol′pro͞of′), *adj.* **1.** involving no risk or harm, even when tampered with. **2.** never-failing: *a foolproof method.*

fools•cap (fo͞olz′kap′), *n.* a type of inexpensive writing paper, esp. legal-size, lined, yellow sheets, bound in tablet form.

fool's′ cap′, *n.* **1.** a traditional jester's cap or hood, often multicolored and usu. having drooping peaks with bells. **2.** DUNCE CAP.

fool's′ gold′, *n.* iron or copper pyrites, sometimes mistaken for gold.

fool's′ par′adise, *n.* a state of enjoyment based on false beliefs or hopes; a state of illusory happiness.

foot (fo͝ot), *n., pl.* **feet** for 1–3, 5–8, 10–13, 16, 18; **foots** for 17; *v.* **—***n.* **1.** (in vertebrates) the terminal part of the leg, below the ankle joint, on which the body stands and moves. **2.** (in invertebrates) any part similar in position or function. **3.** a unit of length, orig. derived from the length of the human foot, that is divided into 12 inches and equal to 30.48 centimeters. *Abbr.:* ft., f. **4.** walking or running motion; pace: *swift of foot.* **5.** any part or thing resembling a foot, as in function, placement, or shape. **6.** a shaped or ornamented feature terminating the lower part of a leg or serving as the base of a piece of furniture. **7.** a rim, flange, or flaring part, often distinctively treated, serving as a base for a table furnishing or utensil, as a glass, teapot, or candlestick. **8.** the part of a stocking, sock, etc., covering the foot. **9.** an attachment on a sewing machine that holds and guides the fabric. **10.** the lowest part, or bottom, as of a hill, ladder, or page. **11.** a supporting part; base. **12.** the part of anything opposite the top or head: *the foot of a bed.* **13.** *Print.* the part of the type body that forms the sides of the groove, at the base. **14.** the last, as of a series. **15.** that which is written at the bottom, as the total of an account. **16.** a group of syllables constituting a metrical unit of a verse. **17.** Usu., **foots. a.** sediment or dregs. **b.** footlights. **18.** *Naut.* the lower edge of a sail. **—***v.i.* **19.** to walk; go on foot (often fol. by *it*): *We'll have to foot it.* **20.** to move the feet rhythmically, as to music or in dance (often fol. by *it*). **21.** (of a boat) to move forward; sail. **—***v.t.* **22.** to walk or dance on. **23.** to perform (a dance). **24.** to traverse on or as if on foot. **25.** to make or attach a foot to. **26.** to pay or settle: *to foot the bill.* **27.** to add (a column of figures) and set the sum at the foot. **28.** to seize with talons, as a hawk. **29.** to establish. **—*Idiom.* 30. get off on the right** (or **wrong**) **foot,** to begin well (or badly). **31. on foot,** by walking or running: *to travel on foot.* **32. put one's foot down,** to take a firm stand; be decisive or determined. **33. put one's foot in one's mouth,** to make an embarrassing blunder. **34. set foot on** or **in,** to go on or into; enter: *Don't set foot in this office again!* **35. under foot,** in the way.

foot•age (fo͝ot′ij), *n.* **1.** length or extent in feet: *the footage of lumber.* **2.** a motion-picture scene or scenes: *newsreel footage.*

foot′-and-mouth′ disease′, *n.* a contagious viral disease of cattle and other hoofed animals, characterized by blisters in the mouth and about the hoofs. Also called **hoof-and-mouth disease.**

foot•ball (fo͝ot′bôl′), *n.* **1.** any of several games in which each of two teams tries to get a ball across a goal, orig. by propelling it with the feet, esp. a game in which two opposing teams of 11 players each defend goals at opposite ends of a field, with points being scored chiefly by carrying the ball across the opponent's goal line or by place-kicking or drop-kicking the ball over the crossbar between the opponent's goal posts. **2.** the ball used in this game, an inflated oval with a bladder contained in a casing usu. made of leather. **3.** *Chiefly Brit.* RUGBY. **4.** *Chiefly Brit.* SOCCER. **5.** a problem or issue over which various individuals or groups debate or compete continually. **6.** (*cap.*) *Slang.* a briefcase containing the codes and options the president of the U.S. would use to launch a nuclear attack.

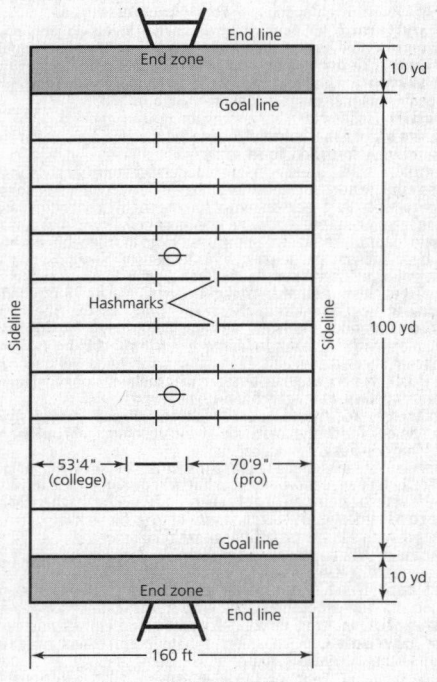

football field

Goal posts are 18'4" apart in professional football; 23'6" apart in college football.

foot•bridge (fo̅o̅t′brij′), *n.* a bridge intended for pedestrians only.

foot′-can′dle, *n.* a unit equivalent to the illumination produced by a source of one candle at a distance of one foot and equal to one lumen incident per square foot.

foot′-drag′ging or **foot′drag′ging**, *n.* reluctance or failure to proceed or act promptly.

foot•er (fo̅o̅t′ər), *n.* one or more lines of information repeated at the bottom of every page in a document. Compare HEADER (def. 7).

foot•fall (fo̅o̅t′fôl′), *n.* the sound of footsteps.

foot′ fault′, *n.* the failure of the server in tennis, volleyball, etc., to keep both feet behind the base line until the ball is hit or to keep at least one foot on the ground while hitting the ball.

foot•hill (fo̅o̅t′hil′), *n.* a low hill at the base of a mountain or mountain range.

foot•hold (fo̅o̅t′hōld′), *n.* **1.** a place or support for the feet; a place where a person may stand or walk securely. **2.** a secure position, esp. a firm basis for further progress or development.

foot•ing (fo̅o̅t′ing), *n.* **1.** the basis or foundation on which anything is established. **2.** a secure and established position. **3.** a place or support for the feet; foothold. **4.** a firm placing of the feet; stability: *to regain one's footing.* **5.** the part of a foundation bearing directly upon the earth. **6.** position or status assigned to a person, group, etc., in estimation or treatment. **7.** mutual standing; reciprocal relation: *to be on a friendly footing with someone.* **8.** entrance into a new position or relationship: *to gain a footing in society.* **9.** the act of adding a foot to something, as to a stocking. **10.** that which is added as a foot. **11.** the act of adding up a column of figures. **12.** the total of such a column.

foot′-in-mouth′ disease′, *n. Informal.* a tendency to use ill-chosen, badly timed, or embarrassing words.

foot′-lam′bert, *n.* a unit of luminance equal to the luminance of a surface emitting a luminous flux of one lumen per square foot.

foot•light (fo̅o̅t′līt′), *n.* **1.** Usu., **footlights.** the lights at the front of a

stage that are nearly on a level with the feet of the performers. **2.** the **footlights**, the stage; the acting profession.

foot•lock•er (fo̅o̅t′lok′ər), *n.* a small trunk kept at the foot of a bed, esp. to hold a soldier's or camper's personal effects.

foot•loose (fo̅o̅t′lo͞os′), *adj.* free to go or travel about; not confined by responsibilities.

foot•man (fo̅o̅t′mən), *n., pl.* **-men.** a liveried household servant who attends the door or carriage, waits on table, etc.

foot•note (fo̅o̅t′nōt′), *n., v.,* **-not•ed, -not•ing.** —*n.* **1.** an explanatory note or comment at the bottom of a page, referring to a specific part of the text on the page. **2.** a minor or tangential comment or event added or subordinated to a main statement or more important event: *That incident is a footnote to the history of art.* —*v.t.* **3.** to add a footnote or footnotes to (a text, statement, etc.); annotate.

foot•path (fo̅o̅t′path′, -päth′), *n., pl.* **-paths** (-pathz′, -päthz′, -paths′, -päths′). a path for people going on foot.

foot′-pound′, *n.* a unit of energy equal to the energy expended in raising one pound a distance of one foot. *Abbr.:* ft-lb

foot′-pound′al, *n.* a unit of energy equal to the energy expended by a one-pound weight accelerating at one foot per second as it moves a distance of one foot. *Abbr.:* ft-pdl

foot′-pound′-sec′ond, *adj.* of or pertaining to the system of units in which the foot, pound, and second are the principal units of length, mass, and time. *Abbr.:* fps

foot•print (fo̅o̅t′print′), *n.* **1.** a mark left by the foot, as in earth. **2.** an impression of the sole of a person's foot, esp. one taken for purposes of identification. **3.** the track of a tire, esp. on wet pavement. **4.** the area affected by an increase in the level of sound. **5.** the surface space occupied by something.

foot•rest (fo̅o̅t′rest′), *n.* a support for a person's feet.

foot•sie (fo̅o̅t′sē) also **footie**, *n. Informal.* **1.** Sometimes, **footsies.** the act of flirting or sharing a surreptitious intimacy. —*Idiom.* **2.** **play footsie(s) with, a.** to flirt with, esp. by furtively touching someone's foot or leg. **b.** to engage in clandestine or illicit relations with.

foot′ sol′dier, *n.* an infantryman.

foot•sore (fo̅o̅t′sôr′, -sōr′), *adj.* having sore or tender feet, as from much walking. —**foot′sore′ness**, *n.*

foot•step (fo̅o̅t′step′), *n.* **1.** the setting down of a foot, or the sound so produced; footfall; tread. **2.** the distance covered by a step in walking; pace. **3.** a footprint. **4.** a step by which to ascend or descend. —*Idiom.* **5.** **follow in someone's footsteps,** to succeed or imitate another person.

foot•stone (fo̅o̅t′stōn′), *n.* a stone set at the foot of a grave.

foot•stool (fo̅o̅t′sto͞ol′), *n.* a low stool upon which to rest one's feet when seated.

foot′-ton′, *n.* a unit of energy equal to the energy expended in raising a ton of 2240 pounds a distance of one foot.

foot•wear (fo̅o̅t′wâr′), *n.* articles to be worn on the feet.

foot•work (fo̅o̅t′wûrk′), *n.* **1.** the use of the feet, as in tennis, boxing, or dancing. **2.** travel from one place to another, as in fulfilling an assignment; legwork. **3.** the act of maneuvering, esp. in a skillful manner: *It took a bit of fancy footwork to avoid the issue.*

foo•zle (fo̅o̅′zal), *v.,* **-zled, -zling,** *n.* —*v.t., v.i.* **1.** to bungle; play clumsily: *to foozle a stroke in golf; to foozle on the last hole.* —*n.* **2.** an act of foozling, esp. a bad stroke in golf.

fop (fop), *n.* a vain man excessively concerned with his looks, clothes, and manners; dandy. —**fop′per•y**, *n.* —**fop′pish**, *adj.*

for (fôr; *unstressed* far), *prep.* **1.** with the object or purpose of: *to run for exercise.* **2.** intended to belong to or be used in connection with: *equipment for the army; a closet for dishes.* **3.** suiting the purposes or needs of: *medicine for the aged.* **4.** in order to obtain, gain, or acquire: *to work for wages.* **5.** (used to express a wish, as of something to be experienced or obtained): *O, for a cold drink!* **6.** sensitive or responsive to: *an eye for beauty.* **7.** desirous of: *a longing for adventure.* **8.** in consideration or payment of; in return for: *three for a dollar.* **9.** appropriate or adapted to: *a subject for speculation; clothes for winter.* **10.** with regard or respect to: *pressed for time.* **11.** during the continuance of: *for a long time.* **12.** in favor of; on the side of: *to be for honest government.* **13.** in place of; instead of: *a substitute for butter.* **14.** in the interest of; on behalf of: *to act for a client.* **15.** in exchange for; as an offset to: *blow for blow.* **16.** in punishment of: *payment for the crime.* **17.** in honor of: *to give a dinner for a person.* **18.** with the purpose of reaching: *to start for London.* **19.** contributive to: *for the advantage of everybody.* **20.** in order to save: *to flee for one's life.* **21.** in order to become: *to train recruits for soldiers.* **22.** in assignment or attribution to: *That's for you to decide.* **23.** such as to allow of or to require: *too many for separate mention.* **24.** such as results in: *my reason for going.* **25.** as affecting the interests or circumstances of: *bad for one's health.* **26.** in proportion or with reference to: *He is tall for his age.* **27.** in the character of; as being: *to know a thing for a fact.* **28.** by reason of; because of: *to shout for joy.* **29.** in spite of: *They're decent people for all that.* **30.** to the extent or amount of: *to walk for a mile.* **31.** (used to introduce a subject in an infinitive phrase): *It's time for me to go.* —*conj.* **32.** seeing that; since. **33.** because.

for-, a prefix meaning "away," "off," "to the uttermost," "extremely," "wrongly," or imparting a negative or privative force, occurring in verbs and nouns formed from verbs of Old or Middle English origin: *forbid; forget; forgo; forswear.*

fo·ra (fôr′ə, fōr′ə), *n.* a pl. of FORUM.

for·age (fôr′ij, for′-), *n., v.,* **-aged, -ag·ing.** —*n.* **1.** food for horses or cattle; fodder; provender. **2.** the seeking or obtaining of such food. **3.** the act of searching for provisions. —*v.i.* **4.** to wander or go in search of provisions. **5.** to search about; seek; rummage; hunt: *foraging in the pantry for a bread knife.* —*v.t.* **6.** to collect forage from; strip of supplies; plunder: *to forage the countryside for food.* **7.** to supply with forage. **8.** to obtain by foraging: *to forage berries for a pie.* —**for′ag·er,** *n.*

fo·ra·men (fə rā′mən), *n., pl.* **-ra·mens, -ram·i·na** (-ram′ə nə). a small opening, orifice, or perforation, as in a bone or in the ovule of a plant. —**fo·ram·i·nal** (fə ram′ə nl), *adj.*

fora′men mag′num (mag′nəm), *n.* the large opening in the base of the skull through which the spinal cord merges with the brain.

for·a·min·i·fer (fôr′ə min′ə fər, for′-), *n.* any chiefly marine protozoan of the sarcodinian order Foraminifera, typically having a linear, spiral, or concentric shell perforated by small holes or pores through which pseudopodia extend.

for·as·much as (fôr′əz much′ az′, əz, far-), *conj.* in view of the fact that.

for·ay (fôr′ā, for′ā), *n., v.,* **-ayed, -ay·ing.** —*n.* **1.** a quick raid or attack, usu. for the purpose of taking plunder; sortie. **2.** an initial venture outside one's customary range of activity: *a brief foray into real estate.* —*v.i.* **3.** to make a raid; pillage; maraud. **4.** to invade or make one's way, as for profit or adventure.

for·bade (fər bad′, -bād′, fôr-) (-bad′), *v.* pt. of FORBID.

for·bear (fôr bâr′), *v.,* **-bore, -borne, -bear·ing.** —*v.t.* **1.** to refrain or abstain from; desist from. —*v.i.* **2.** to refrain; hold back. **3.** to be patient or self-controlled when subject to annoyance or provocation. —**for·bear′ance,** *n.* —**for·bear′ing·ly,** *adv.*

for·bid (fər bid′, fôr-), *v.t.,* **-bade** or **-bad** or **-bid, -bid·den** or **-bid, -bid·ding.** **1.** to command (a person) not to do or have something or not to enter some place: *I forbid you entry to this house.* **2.** to prohibit (something); make a rule against: *to forbid smoking.* **3.** to make impossible; prevent; preclude: *Loyalty forbids any further comment.* —**for·bid′dance,** *n.*

Forbid′den Cit′y, *n.* a walled section of Beijing, built in the 15th century, containing the imperial palace.

forbid′den fruit′, *n.* **1.** the fruit of the tree of knowledge of good and evil, tasted by Adam and Eve against God's prohibition. Gen. 2:17; 3:3. **2.** any unlawful or immoral pleasure.

for·bid·ding (fər bid′ing, fôr-), *adj.* **1.** grim; sinister; threatening: *a forbidding scowl.* **2.** dauntingly steep or high: *forbidding cliffs.* **3.** disagreeably difficult: *a forbidding duty.* —**for·bid′ding·ly,** *adv.*

force (fôrs, fōrs), *n., v.,* **forced, forc·ing.** —*n.* **1.** physical power or strength: *to pull with all one's force.* **2.** strength exerted upon an object; physical coercion; violence: *to use force to open a door.* **3.** strength; energy; power: *the force of the waves; a personality of great force.* **4.** power to influence, affect, or control; efficacious power: *the force of circumstances.* **5.** *Law.* unlawful violence threatened or committed against persons or property. **6.** persuasive power; power to convince: *the force of an argument.* **7.** mental or moral strength: *force of character.* **8.** might, as of a ruler or realm; strength for war. **9.** Often, **forces.** the military or fighting strength, esp. of a nation. **10.** any body of persons combined for joint action: *a sales force.* **11.** intensity or strength of effect: *the force of her acting.* **12.** *Physics.* **a.** an influence on a body or system, producing or tending to produce a change in movement or shape or other effects. **b.** the intensity of such an influence. *Symbol:* F, f **13.** any influence or agency analogous to physical force: *social forces.* **14.** binding power, as of a contract. **15.** FORCE PLAY. **16.** value; significance; meaning. —*v.t.* **17.** to compel, constrain, or oblige (oneself or someone) to do something: *to force a suspect to confess.* **18.** to drive or propel against resistance: *to force one's way through a crowd; to force air into a tire.* **19.** to bring about or effect by force. **20.** to bring about of necessity or as a necessary result: *to force a smile.* **21.** to put or impose (something or someone) forcibly on or upon a person: *to force one's opinions on others.* **22.** to obtain or draw forth by or as if by force; extort: *to force a confession.* **23.** to enter or take by force; overpower: *They forced the town after a long siege.* **24.** to break open (a door, lock, etc.). **25.** to cause (plants, fruits, etc.) to grow or mature at an increased rate by artificial means. **26.** to press or urge (an animal, person, etc.) to violent effort or to the utmost. **27.** to use force upon. **28.** to rape. **29.** *Baseball.* **a.** to cause (a base runner) to be put out in a force play. **b.** to cause (a base runner or run) to score, as by walking a batter with the bases full (often fol. by *in*). **30.** (in cards) **a.** to compel (a player) to trump by leading a suit of which the player has no cards. **b.** to compel a player to play (a particular card). **c.** to compel (a player) to play so as to make known the strength of the hand. —*v.i.* **31.** to make one's way by force. —*Idiom.* **32. in force, a.** in operation; effective: *a rule no longer in force.* **b.** in large numbers; at full strength: *to attack in force.* —**force′a·ble,** *adj.* —**force′less,** *adj.* —**forc′er,** *n.*

forced (fôrst, fōrst), *adj.* **1.** enforced or compulsory: *forced labor.* **2.** strained, unnatural, or affected: *a forced laugh.* **3.** subjected to force. **4.** required by circumstances; emergency: *a forced landing of an airplane.* —**forc·ed·ly** (fôr′sid lē, fōrst′-), *adv.*

force′-feed′, *v.t.,* **-fed, -feed·ing. 1.** to compel to take food, esp. by means of a tube inserted into the throat. **2.** to compel to absorb or assimilate: *The recruits were force-fed military discipline.*

force·ful (fôrs′fəl, fōrs′-), *adj.* **1.** full of force; powerful; vigorous: *a*

forceful blow. **2.** effective; cogent; telling: *a forceful plea for justice.* —**force′ful·ly,** *adv.* —**force′ful·ness,** *n.*

force′ ma·jeure′ (ma zhŭr′, mä-), *n.* **1.** an overwhelming or irresistible force. **2.** an event or effect that may be considered impossible to control or anticipate.

force′ of hab′it, *n.* behavior occurring without thought and by virtue of constant repetition; habit.

force′-out′, *n. Baseball.* a put-out of a base runner on a force play.

force′ play′, *n. Baseball.* a play in which a base runner is forced to advance to the next base or to home plate in order to make room for another base runner, usu. resulting in an out for the first runner.

for·ceps (fôr′səps, -seps), *n., pl.* **-ceps, -ci·pes** (-sə pēz′). an instrument, as pincers or tongs, for seizing and holding objects firmly, as in surgical operations. —**for·cip·i·al** (fôr sip′ē əl), *adj.*

for·ci·ble (fôr′sə bəl, fōr′-), *adj.* **1.** done or effected by force: *forcible entry; forcible seizure.* **2.** having or producing force; powerfully effective. **3.** convincing, as reasoning: *a forcible theory.* —**for′ci·ble·ness, for′ci·bil′i·ty,** *n.* —**for′ci·bly,** *adv.*

ford (fôrd, fōrd), *n.* **1.** a place where a river or other body of water is shallow enough to be crossed by wading. —*v.t.* **2.** to cross (a river, stream, etc.) at a ford. —**ford′a·ble,** *adj.*

Ford (fôrd, fōrd), *n.* **1. Gerald R(udolph, Jr.)** (*Leslie Lynch King, Jr.*), born 1913, 38th president of the U.S. 1974–77. **2. Henry,** 1863–1947, U.S. automobile manufacturer. **3. John** (*Sean O'Feeney*), 1895–1973, U.S. film director.

fore¹ (fôr, fōr), *adj.* **1.** situated in front of something else. **2.** first in place, time, order, rank, etc.; forward; earlier. **3. a.** of or pertaining to a foremast. **b.** being a sail, yard, boom, etc., or any rigging belonging to a fore lower mast or to some upper mast of a foremast. **c.** situated at or toward the bow of a vessel; forward. —*adv.* **4.** at or toward the bow of a vessel. **5.** forward. —*n.* **6.** the forepart of anything; front. **7. the fore, the foremast. —*prep., conj.* **8.** Also, **'fore.** *Informal.* before. —*Idiom.* **9. fore and aft,** in, at, or to both ends of a ship. **10. to the fore,** into a conspicuous place or position; to or at the front.

fore² (fôr, fōr), *interj.* (used as a cry of warning on a golf course to persons who are in danger of being struck by a ball in flight.)

fore-, a prefix meaning "before" (in space, time, condition, etc.) (*forecast; foretaste; forewarn*), "front" (*forehead; forefront*), "preceding" (*forefather*), "superior" (*foreman*).

fore′-and-aft′, *Naut.* —*adj.* **1.** located along or parallel to a line from the stem to the stern. —*adv.* **2.** FORE¹ (def. 9).

fore·arm¹ (fôr′ärm′, fōr′-), *n.* **1.** the part of the arm between the elbow and the wrist. **2.** the corresponding part of the foreleg in certain quadrupeds.

fore·arm² (fôr ärm′, fōr′-), *v.t.* to arm or prepare beforehand, esp. for difficulties.

fore·bear or **for·bear** (fôr′bâr′, fōr′-), *n.* ancestor; forefather.

fore·bode (fôr bōd′, fōr-), *v.,* **-bod·ed, -bod·ing.** —*v.t.* **1.** to foretell or predict; be an omen of; portend: *clouds foreboding a storm.* **2.** to have a strong inner feeling or notion of (a future misfortune, evil, etc.); have a presentiment of. —*v.i.* **3.** to prophesy. **4.** to have a presentiment. —**fore·bod′er,** *n.*

fore·bod·ing (fôr bō′ding, fōr-), *n.* **1.** a prediction; portent. **2.** a strong inner feeling or notion of a future misfortune, evil, etc.; presentiment. —*adj.* **3.** of or indicating foreboding, esp. of evil. —**fore·bod′ing·ly,** *adv.* —**fore·bod′ing·ness,** *n.*

fore·brain (fôr′brān′, fōr′-), *n.* Also called **prosencephalon.** the anterior of the three embryonic divisions of the vertebrate brain, or the part of the adult brain derived from this tissue including the diencephalon and telencephalon.

fore·cast (fôr′kast′, -käst′, fōr′-), *v.,* **-cast** or **-cast·ed, -cast·ing,** *n.* —*v.t.* **1.** to predict (a future condition or occurrence); calculate in advance: *to forecast a heavy snowfall.* **2.** to serve as a prediction of; foreshadow. —*v.i.* **3.** to conjecture beforehand; make a prediction. —*n.* **4.** a prediction, esp. of future weather conditions. **5.** a conjecture as to something in the future. —**fore′cast·a·ble,** *adj.* —**fore′cast·er,** *n.*

fore·cas·tle (fōk′səl, fôr′kas′əl, -käs′əl, fōr′-) also **fo′c's'le,** *n.* **1.** a superstructure at or immediately aft of the bow of a vessel, used as a shelter for stores, machinery, etc., or as quarters for sailors. **2.** any sailors' quarters located in the forward part of a vessel, as a deckhouse. **3.** the forward part of the weather deck of a vessel, esp. the part forward of the foremast.

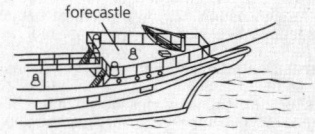

forecastle (def. 1)

fore′-check′, *v.i.* to obstruct or impede the movement or progress of an attacking opponent in the opponent's own defensive zone in ice hockey. Compare BACK-CHECK, CHECK (def. 13).

F

fore·close (fôr klōz', fōr-), v., **-closed, -clos·ing.** —v.t. **1. a.** to deprive (a mortgagor) of the right to redeem a property, esp. after defaulting on mortgage payments. **b.** to subject (a property) to foreclosure. **c.** to take away the right to redeem (a mortgage). **2.** to shut out; exclude. **3.** to hinder or prevent; preclude; forbid. **4.** to establish an exclusive claim to. **5.** to close, settle, or answer beforehand. —v.i. **6.** to foreclose a mortgage. —**fore·clos′a·ble,** adj. —**fore·clo′sure** (-klō′zhər), n.

fore·court (fôr′kôrt′, fōr′kōrt′), n. **1.** the part of either half of a tennis court that lies between the net and the line that marks the inbounds limit of a service. Compare BACKCOURT (def. 2). **2.** a courtyard before the entrance to a building or group of buildings.

fore·fa·ther (fôr′fä′thər, fōr′-), n. an ancestor; progenitor. —**fore′fa′ther·ly,** adj.

Fore′fathers′ Day′, n. the anniversary of the day (December 21, 1620, in Old Style December 11) on which the Pilgrims landed at Plymouth, Mass. Owing to an error in changing the date from the Old Style to the New, it is generally observed on December 22.

fore·fin·ger (fôr′fing′gər, fōr′-), n. the finger next to the thumb. Also called **index finger.**

fore·foot (fôr′foot′, fōr′-), n., pl. **-feet. 1.** one of the front feet esp. of a quadruped. **2. a.** the point at which the stem of a hull joins the keel. **b.** a curved member at this point in a wooden hull.

fore·front (fôr′frunt′, fōr′-), n. **1.** the foremost part or place. **2.** the position of greatest importance or prominence; vanguard.

fore·go¹ (fôr gō′, fōr-), v.t., v.i., **-went, -gone, -go·ing.** to go before; precede. —**fore·go′er,** n.

fore·go² (fôr gō′, fōr-), v.t., **-went, -gone, -go·ing.** FORGO.

fore·go·ing (fôr gō′ing, fōr-), adj. previously stated, written, or occurring; preceding: *the foregoing paragraph.*

fore·gone (fôr gôn′, -gon′, fōr-; fôr′gôn′, -gon′, fōr′-), adj. having gone before; previous; past.

fore′gone′ conclu′sion, n. **1.** an inevitable conclusion or result. **2.** a conclusion formed in advance of proper consideration of evidence, arguments, etc.

fore·ground (fôr′ground′, fōr′-), n. **1.** the ground or parts situated, or represented as situated, in the front; the portion of a scene nearest to the viewer (opposed to *background*). **2.** a prominent or important position; forefront.

fore·gut (fôr′gut′, fōr′-), n. **1. a.** the first portion of the vertebrate alimentary canal extending from the pharynx to the end of the stomach. **b.** the first portion of the alimentary canal in arthropods and annelids. **2.** the upper portion of the embryonic vertebrate alimentary canal from which the pharynx, esophagus, lungs, stomach, duodenum, liver, and pancreas develop. Compare HINDGUT, MIDGUT.

fore·hand (fôr′hand′, fōr′-), adj. **1.** (in tennis, squash, etc.) of, pertaining to, or being a stroke made with the palm of the hand facing the direction of movement. Compare BACKHAND (def. 5). **2.** being in front or ahead. **3.** done, given, or made in advance. —n. **4.** (in tennis, squash, etc.) a forehand stroke. **5.** the part of a horse in front of the rider. —adv. **6.** (in tennis, squash, etc.) with a forehand stroke.

fore·head (fôr′id, fōr′-; fôr′hed′, for′-), n. **1.** the part of the face above the eyebrows; brow. **2.** the fore or front part of something.

for·eign (fôr′in, for′-), adj. **1.** of or derived from another country or nation; not domestic or native: *foreign cars.* **2.** of or pertaining to dealings with other countries: *foreign relations.* **3.** external to one's own country or nation: *a foreign country.* **4.** carried on abroad, or with other countries: *foreign trade.* **5.** belonging to or coming from another place. **6. a.** of or pertaining to law outside the local jurisdiction. **b.** of or pertaining to the jurisdiction of another state, nation etc. **7.** not belonging to the place or body where found: *foreign matter in a chemical mixture.* **8.** not related to or connected with the thing under consideration: *That topic is foreign to our discussion.* **9.** alien in character; irrelevant or inappropriate. **10.** strange; unfamiliar. —**for′eign·ness,** n.

for′eign affairs′, n. activities and affairs of a nation arising from its dealings with other nations.

for′eign aid′, n. economic, technical, or military assistance given by one nation to another.

for′eign correspond′ent, n. a correspondent, as for a newspaper, assigned to send back news reports from a foreign country.

for·eign·er (fôr′ə nər, for′-), n. **1.** a person not native to or naturalized in the country or jurisdiction under consideration; alien. **2.** a person from outside one's community.

for′eign exchange′, n. **1.** commercial paper drawn on a person or corporation in a foreign nation. **2.** the process of balancing accounts in commercial transactions between businesses or individuals of different countries.

for′eign le′gion, n. a military unit made up of foreign volunteers in the service of a nation.

for′eign min′ister, n. (in countries other than the U.S.) a cabinet minister who conducts and supervises foreign and diplomatic relations with other states. —**for′eign min′istry,** n.

for′eign pol′icy, n. a policy pursued by a nation in its dealings with other nations, designed to achieve national objectives.

for′eign rela′tions, n.pl. **1.** the dealings and relationships between nations. **2.** the field of foreign affairs: *an expert in foreign relations.* **3.** the quality or character of foreign affairs as a consequence of foreign policy: *a deterioration in their foreign relations.*

for′eign serv′ice, n. (often caps.) a division of the U.S. Department of State or of a foreign office that supplies diplomatic and consular personnel.

fore·judge¹ (fôr juj′, fōr-), v.t., **-judged, -judg·ing.** to judge beforehand; prejudge. —**fore·judg′er,** n.

fore·judge² (fôr juj′, fōr-), v.t., **-judged, -judg·ing.** FORJUDGE.

fore·know (fôr nō′, fōr-), v.t., **-knew, -known, -knowing.** to know beforehand; foresee. —**fore·know′a·ble,** adj. —**fore·know′er,** n. —**fore·know′ing·ly,** adv.

fore·leg (fôr′leg′, fōr′-), n. one of the front legs esp. of a quadruped.

fore·limb (fôr′lim′, fōr′-), n. a front limb of an animal.

fore·man (fôr′mən, fōr′-), n., pl. **-men. 1.** a person in charge of a department or group of workers, as in a factory. **2.** the member of a jury who is selected to preside over and speak for all the jurors on the panel. —**fore′man·ship′,** n.

fore·mast (fôr′mast′, -mäst′, fōr′-; Naut. -məst), n. the mast nearest the bow in all vessels having two or more masts.

fore·most (fôr′mōst′, -məst, fōr′-), adj., adv. first in place, rank, importance, etc.: *the foremost surgeons; to put one's studies foremost.*

fore·moth·er (fôr′muth′ər, fōr′-), n. a female ancestor.

fore·name (fôr′nām′, fōr′-), n. a name that precedes the family name or surname; first name.

fore·noon (fôr′nōōn′, fōr′-), n. **1.** the period of daylight before noon. **2.** the latter part of the morning.

fo·ren·sic (fə ren′sik), adj. **1.** pertaining to or used in courts of law or in public debate. **2.** adapted or suited to argumentation; rhetorical. **3.** of, pertaining to, or involved with forensic medicine or forensic anthropology: *forensic laboratories.* —n. (used with a sing. v.) **4.** forensics, the art or study of argumentation and formal debate. **5.** forensics, a department of forensic medicine, as in a police laboratory.

foren′sic anthropol′ogy, n. the branch of physical anthropology concerned with identifying or characterizing skeletal or biological remains in questions of civil or criminal law.

foren′sic med′icine, n. the application of medical knowledge to questions of civil and criminal law, esp. in court proceedings.

fore·or·dain (fôr′ôr dān′, fōr′-), v.t. **1.** to ordain or appoint beforehand. **2.** to predestine; predetermine.

fore·run (fôr run′, fōr-), v.t., **-ran, -run, -run·ning. 1.** to come before; precede. **2.** to prefigure. **3.** to forestall.

fore·run·ner (fôr′run′ər, fōr′-, fôr run′ər, fōr-), n. **1.** predecessor; ancestor; forebear; precursor. **2.** an omen, sign, or indication of something to follow; portent. **3.** a person who appears in advance to announce the coming of someone or something else; herald; harbinger.

fore·see (fôr sē′, fōr-), v., **-saw, -seen, -see·ing.** —v.t. **1.** to see or know in advance; discern; foreknow. —v.i. **2.** to exercise foresight. —**fore·see′a·ble,** adj. —**fore·see′a·bil′i·ty,** n.

fore·shad·ow (fôr shad′ō, fōr-), v.t. to show or indicate beforehand; prefigure. —**fore·shad′ow·er,** n.

fore·shock (fôr′shok′, fōr′-), n. a relatively small earthquake that precedes a greater one by a few days or weeks and originates at or near the focus of the larger earthquake.

fore·short·en (fôr shôr′tən, fōr-), v.t. **1.** to reduce or distort (parts of a represented object that are not parallel to the picture plane) in order to convey the illusion of three-dimensional space. **2.** to abridge, reduce, or contract.

fore·sight (fôr′sīt′, fōr′-), n. **1.** care or provision for the future; provident care; prudence. **2.** the act or power of foreseeing; prevision; prescience. **3.** an act of looking forward. **4.** knowledge or insight of the future; foreknowledge. **5.** Surveying. **a.** a sight or reading taken on a forward point. **b.** (in leveling) a rod reading on a point the elevation of which is to be determined. —**fore′sight′ed,** adj. —**fore′sight′ed·ly,** adv. —**fore′sight′ed·ness,** n.

fore·skin (fôr′skin′, fōr′-), n. the prepuce of the penis.

for·est (fôr′ist, for′-), n. **1.** a large tract of land covered with trees and underbrush; woodland. **2.** (formerly, in England) a tract of land generally belonging to the sovereign and set apart for game. **3.** a thick cluster of vertical objects: *a forest of church spires.* —v.t. **4.** to supply or cover with trees; convert into a forest. —*Saying.* **5. not see the forest for the trees,** to fail to perceive the complete picture because of one's excessive attention to detail. —**for′est·al, fo·res·tial** (fə res′chəl), adj. —**for′est·ed,** adj.

fore·stall (fôr stôl′, fōr-), v.t. **1.** to prevent, hinder, or thwart by action in advance. **2.** to act beforehand with or get ahead of; anticipate. **3.** to buy up (goods) in advance in order to increase the price when resold. —**fore·stall′er,** n. —**fore·stall′ment,** n.

for·est·a·tion (fôr′ə stā′shən, for′-), n. the planting of forests.

for·est·er (fôr′ə stər, for′-), n. **1.** an expert in forestry. **2.** an officer having responsibility for the maintenance of a forest. **3.** an animal of the forest. **4.** any moth of the family Agaristidae, typically black with two yellowish or whitish spots on each wing.

for′est green′, n. LINCOLN GREEN.

for·est·land (fôr′ist land′, for′-), n. land containing or covered with forests.

for′est rang′er, n. an officer employed by the government to supervise the care and preservation of forests, esp. public forests.

for·est·ry (fôr′ə strē, for′-), n. **1.** the science of planting and taking care of trees and forests. **2.** the process of establishing and managing forests. **3.** forestland.

For·est Serv·ice, *n.* a division of the U.S. Department of Agriculture, created in 1905, that protects and develops the national forests and grasslands.

fore·swear (fôr swâr′, fōr-), *v.t., v.i.,* **-swore, -sworn, -swear·ing.** FORSWEAR.

fore·taste (*n.* fôr′tāst′, fōr′-; *v.* fôr tāst′, fōr-), *n., v.,* **-tast·ed, -tast·ing.** —*n.* **1.** a slight and partial experience, knowledge, or taste of something to come in the future; anticipation. —*v.t.* **2.** to have some advance experience or knowledge of (something to come).

fore·tell (fôr tel′, fōr-), *v.t.,* **-told, -tell·ing.** to tell of beforehand; predict; prophesy. —**fore·tell′er,** *n.*

fore·thought (fôr′thôt′, fōr′-), *n.* **1.** thoughtful provision beforehand; prudence. **2.** a thinking of something beforehand; previous consideration; anticipation. —**fore·thought′ful,** *adj.*

for·ev·er (fôr ev′ər, fər-), *adv.* **1.** without ever ending; eternally: *to last forever.* **2.** continually; incessantly; always: *forever complaining.* —*n.* **3.** an endless or seemingly endless period of time: *Don't spend forever on the phone.*

fore·warn (fôr wôrn′, fōr-), *v.t.* **1.** to warn in advance; alert. —*Proverb.* **2. Forewarned is forearmed,** advance awareness of problems can help to overcome them. —**fore·warn′ing·ly,** *adv.*

fore·went (fôr went′, fōr-), *v.* pt. of FOREGO.

fore·wing (fôr′wing′, fōr′-), *n.* either of the front smaller pair of wings of an insect having four wings.

fore·wom·an (fôr′wŏŏm′ən, fōr′-), *n., pl.* **-wom·en. 1.** a woman who supervises a department or group of workers. **2.** a woman on a jury who is selected to preside over and speak for all the jurors in the panel.

fore·word (fôr′wûrd′, -wərd, fōr′-), *n.* a short introductory statement in a published work, as a book, esp. when written by someone other than the author. Compare AFTERWORD.

for·feit (fôr′fit), *n.* **1.** a fine; penalty. **2.** an act of forfeiting; forfeiture. **3.** something to which the right is lost, as for commission of a crime or violation of a contract. **4.** an article deposited in a game because of a mistake and redeemable by a fine or penalty. **5. forfeits,** (*used with a sing. v.*) a game in which such articles are taken. —*v.t.* **6.** to subject to seizure as a forfeit. **7.** to lose or become liable to lose, as in consequence of crime or breach of engagement. —*adj.* **8.** lost or subject to loss by forfeiture. —**for′feit·a·ble,** *adj.* —**for′feit·er,** *n.* —**for′fei·ture** (-fi chər), *n.*

for·gath·er or **fore·gath·er** (fôr gath′ər), *v.i.* **1.** to gather together; convene; assemble. **2.** to encounter someone, esp. by chance.

for·gave (fər gāv′), *v.* pt. of FORGIVE.

forge¹ (fôrj, fōrj), *v.,* **forged, forg·ing,** *n.* —*v.t.* **1.** to form by heating and hammering; beat into shape. **2.** to form or make, esp. by concentrated effort: *to forge a treaty.* **3.** to imitate (handwriting, a signature, etc.) fraudulently; make a forgery of. —*v.i.* **4.** to commit forgery. **5.** to work at a forge. —*n.* **6.** a fireplace, hearth, or furnace in which metal is heated before shaping. **7.** the workshop of a blacksmith; smithy. —**forge′a·ble,** *adj.* —**forg′er,** *n.*

forge² (fôrj, fōrj), *v.i.,* **forged, forg·ing. 1.** to move ahead slowly; progress steadily: *to forge through dense underbrush.* **2.** to move ahead with increased speed and effectiveness (usu. fol. by *ahead*): *to forge ahead and finish the work quickly.*

for·ger·y (fôr′jə rē, fōr′-), *n., pl.* **-ger·ies. 1.** the crime of falsely making or altering a writing by which the legal rights or obligations of another person are apparently affected. **2.** a writing so made or altered, as a false document or signature. **3.** any spurious work that is claimed to be genuine, as a painting or coin; counterfeit. **4.** an act of producing something forged.

for·get (fər get′), *v.,* **-got, got·ten** or **-got, -get·ting.** —*v.t.* **1.** to cease to remember; be unable to recall: *to forget a name.* **2.** to omit or neglect unintentionally: *I forgot to lock the gate.* **3.** to leave behind unintentionally: *to forget one's keys.* **4.** to fail to think of; take no note of (often used imperatively): *Forget cooking, let's eat out tonight.* **5.** to neglect willfully or carelessly; disregard or slight. —*v.i.* **6.** to cease or omit to think of something. —*Idiom.* **7. forget oneself,** to say or do something improper.

for·get·ful (fər get′fəl), *adj.* **1.** apt to forget; absent-minded. **2.** heedless; neglectful (often fol. by *of*): *forgetful of others.* **3.** bringing on oblivion: *forgetful slumber.* —**for·get′ful·ly,** *adv.* —**for·get′ful·ness,** *n.*

forget′-me-not′, *n.* **1.** any of several Old World plants of the genus *Myosotis,* of the borage family, having light blue flowers. **2.** any similar or related plant.

forg·ing (fôr′jing, fōr′-), *n.* **1.** an act or instance of forging. **2.** something forged; a piece of forged work in metal.

for·give (fər giv′), *v.,* **-gave, -giv·en, -giv·ing.** —*v.t.* **1.** to grant pardon for or remission of (an offense, sin, etc.); absolve. **2.** to cancel or remit (a debt, obligation, etc.): *to forgive the interest owed on a loan.* **3.** to grant pardon to (a person). **4.** to cease to feel resentment against: *to forgive one's enemies.* —*v.i.* **5.** to pardon. —**for·giv′a·ble,** *adj.* —**for·give′ness,** *n.*

for·give·ness (fər giv′nis), *n.* **1.** the act of forgiving or the state of being forgiven; pardon. **2.** willingness to forgive.

for·giv·ing (fər giv′ing), *adj.* **1.** disposed to forgive or showing for-

giveness. **2.** offering the chance to recover from mistakes; tolerant: *This slope is forgiving of inexperienced skiers.* —**for·giv′ing·ly,** *adv.* —**for·giv′ing·ness,** *n.*

for·go or **fore·go** (fôr gō′), *v.t.,* **-went, -gone, -go·ing.** to abstain or refrain from; give up; renounce. —**for·go′er,** *n.*

for·got (fər got′), *v.* a pt. and pp. of FORGET.

for·got·ten (fər got′n), *v.* a pp. of FORGET.

forgot′ten man′, *n.* **1.** a person no longer in the mind of the general public. **2.** the average wage earner, regarded as economically deprived and forgotten by the federal government during the Great Depression.

for·judge or **fore·judge** (fôr juj′), *v.t.,* **-judged, -judg·ing.** *Law.* to exclude, expel, or deprive by a judgment. —**for·judg′ment,** *n.*

fork (fôrk), *n.* **1.** an instrument having two or more prongs or tines, for holding, lifting, etc., esp. an implement for handling food. **2.** a division into branches. **3.** the point or part at which a thing, as a river or a road, divides into branches. **4.** either of the branches into which a thing divides. **5.** a principal tributary of a river. —*v.t.* **6.** to pierce, raise, pitch, dig, etc., with a fork. **7.** to make into the form of a fork. **8.** to maneuver so as to place (two opposing chess pieces) under simultaneous attack by the same piece. —*v.i.* **9.** to divide into branches, as a road. **10.** to turn as indicated at a fork in a road, path, etc. **11.** *Informal.* **fork over, out,** or **up,** to deliver; pay; hand over. —**fork′less,** *adj.* —**fork′like′,** *adj.*

fork·ball (fôrk′bôl′), *n.* a baseball pitch thrown with the ball inserted between the index and middle fingers, causing it to dip sharply near home plate.

forked (fôrkt, fôr′kid), *adj.* **1.** having a fork or forklike branches. **2.** zigzag, as lightning. —*Idiom.* **3. to speak with** or **have a forked tongue,** to speak deceitfully; attempt to deceive.

fork·lift (fôrk′lift′), *n.* **1.** Also called **fork′lift truck′, fork′ truck′.** a small vehicle with two power-operated prongs at the front that can be slid under heavy loads in order to lift, carry, and stack them, as in warehouses. —*v.t.* **2.** to move or stack by forklift.

forklift (def. 1)

for·lorn (fôr lôrn′), *adj.* **1.** miserable, as in condition or appearance; dreary; wretched. **2.** lonely and sad; forsaken; desolate. **3.** expressive of hopelessness; despairing: *forlorn glances.* **4.** bereft; destitute: *forlorn of comfort.* —**for·lorn′ly,** *adv.*

form (fôrm), *n.* **1.** external appearance of a clearly defined area, as distinguished from color or material; configuration: *a triangular form.* **2.** the shape of a thing or person. **3.** a body, esp. that of a human being. **4.** a dummy having the same measurements as a human body, used for fitting or displaying clothing. **5.** something that gives or determines shape; a mold. **6.** a particular condition, character, or mode in which something appears: *water in the form of ice.* **7.** the manner or style of arranging and coordinating parts for a pleasing or effective result, as in literary or musical composition. **8.** the organization, placement, or relationship of basic elements, as lines and colors in a painting or volumes and voids in a sculpture, so as to produce a coherent image; the formal structure of a work of art. **9.** a particular kind, type, species, or variety, esp. of a zoological group. **10.** the combination of all the like faces possible on a crystal of given symmetry. **11.** due or proper shape; orderly arrangement of parts; good order. **12.** a set, prescribed, or customary order or method of doing something. **13.** a set order of words, as for use in religious ritual or in a legal document; formula. **14.** a document with blank spaces to be filled in with particulars before it is executed: *a tax form.* **15.** a typical document to be used as a guide in framing others for like cases: *a form for a deed.* **16.** a conventional method of procedure or behavior: *society's forms.* **17.** a formality or ceremony, often with implication of absence of real meaning. **18.** procedure according to a set order or method. **19.** conformity to the usages of society; formality; ceremony. **20.** procedure or conduct, as judged by social standards: *Good form demands that we go.* **21.** manner or method of performing something; technique: *The violinist displayed excellent form.* **22.** physical condition or fitness, as for performing: *a tennis player in peak form.* **23. a.** LINGUISTIC FORM. **b.** a particular shape of a word that occurs in more than one shape: *In I'm, 'm is a form of am.* **c.** a word with a particular inflectional ending or other modification: *Goes is a form of go.* **d.** the external shape or pattern of a word or other construction, as distinguished from its meaning, function, etc. **24.** temporary boarding or sheeting of plywood or metal for giving a desired shape to poured concrete, etc. **25.** a grade or class of pupils in a British secondary school or in certain U.S. private schools. **26.** a bench or long seat. **27.** an assemblage of printing types, leads, etc., secured in a chase to

F

print from. —*v.t.* **28.** to construct or frame. **29.** to make or produce. **30.** to serve to make up; compose; constitute: *Three citizens form the review board.* **31.** to place in order; arrange; organize. **32.** to frame (ideas, opinions, etc.) in the mind. **33.** to contract or develop (habits, friendships, etc.). **34.** to give form or shape to; shape; fashion. **35.** to give a particular form or shape to: *Form the dough into squares.* **36.** to mold or develop by discipline or instructions. **37.** to produce (a word or class of words) by adding an affix, combining elements, or changing the shape of the form: *to form the plural by adding -s.* —*v.i.* **38.** to take or assume form. **39.** to be formed or produced: *Ice began to form on the window.* **40.** to take a particular form or arrangement: *The ice formed in patches across the window.* —**form′a•ble,** *adj.* —**form′a•bly,** *adv.*

for•mal (fôr′məl), *adj.* **1.** being in accordance with the usual requirements, customs, etc.; conventional: *to pay one's formal respects.* **2.** marked by form or ceremony: *a formal occasion.* **3.** designed for wear or use at elaborate ceremonial or social events: *The invitation specified formal attire.* **4.** requiring dress suitable for elaborate social events: *a formal dance.* **5.** observant of conventional requirements of behavior, procedure, etc., as persons; punctilious. **6.** excessively ceremonious; prim; decorous. **7.** being a matter of form only; perfunctory: *formal courtesy.* **8.** made or done in accordance with procedures that ensure validity: *a formal authorization.* **9.** of, pertaining to, or emphasizing the organization or composition of the constituent elements in a work of art perceived separately from its subject matter: *the formal structure of a poem.* **10.** acquired in school; academic. **11.** symmetrical or highly organized: *a formal garden.* **12.** of or pertaining to language use typical of impersonal and official situations, characterized by adherence to traditional standards of correctness, often complex vocabulary and syntax, and the avoidance of contractions and colloquial expressions. **13.** pertaining to the form, shape, or mode of a thing, esp. as distinguished from the substance: *formal writing.* **14.** being such merely in appearance or name; nominal: *a formal head of state.* **15.** *Math.* **a.** (of a proof) in strict logical form with a justification for every step. **b.** (of a calculation) correct in form; made with strict justification for every step. —*n.* **16.** a dance, ball, or other social occasion that requires formal attire. **17.** an evening gown. —*adv.* **18.** in formal attire: *We're supposed to go formal.*

form•al•de•hyde (fôr mal′də hīd′, fər-), *n.* a toxic gas, CH_2O, used chiefly in aqueous solution as a disinfectant and preservative.

for•mal•ism (fôr′mə liz′əm), *n.* strict adherence to or observance of prescribed or traditional forms, as in music, poetry, and art. —**for′mal•ist,** *n., adj.* —**for′mal•is′tic,** *adj.*

for•mal•i•ty (fôr mal′i tē), *n., pl.* **-ties. 1.** condition or quality of being formal; accordance with required or traditional rules, procedures, etc.; conventionality. **2.** rigorously methodical character. **3.** strict adherence to established rules and procedures; rigidity. **4.** observance of form or ceremony. **5.** marked or excessive ceremoniousness. **6.** an established order or method of proceeding: *the formalities of judicial process.* **7.** a formal act or observance; ritual. **8.** something done merely or mainly for form's sake; a requirement of custom or etiquette.

for•mal•ize (fôr′mə līz′), *v.t.,* **-ized, -iz•ing. 1.** to make formal, esp. for the sake of official or authorized acceptance: *to formalize an agreement with a legal contract.* **2.** to give a definite form or shape to. —**for′mal•i•za′tion,** *n.* —**for′mal•iz′er,** *n.*

for′mal log′ic, *n.* the branch of logic concerned with the principles of deductive reasoning and with the form rather than the content of propositions.

for•mal•ly (fôr′mə lē), *adv.* **1.** in a formal manner. **2.** as regards form; in form: *a formally correct composition.*

for•mal•wear (fôr′məl wâr′), *n.* clothing designed for or customarily worn on formal occasions, as tuxedos and evening gowns.

for•mat (fôr′mat), *n., v.,* **-mat•ted, -mat•ting.** —*n.* **1.** the shape and size of a book as determined by the number of times the original sheet has been folded to form the leaves. Compare DUODECIMO, FOLIO (def. 2), OCTAVO, QUARTO. **2.** the general physical appearance of a book, magazine, or newspaper. **3.** the organization, plan, style, or type of something. **4.** the arrangement of data for computer input or output, as the number of fields in a database record or the margins in a report. **5.** the programming featured by a radio or television station: *a talk-show format.* —*v.t.* **6.** to plan or provide a format for. **7. a.** to set the format of (computer data input or output). **b.** to prepare (a computer disk) for writing and reading. —*v.i.* **8.** to devise a format. —**for′mat•ter,** *n.*

for•ma•tion (fôr mā′shən), *n.* **1.** the act or process of forming or the state of being formed: *the formation of ice.* **2.** the manner in which a thing is formed; disposition of parts; formal structure or arrangement. **3. a.** a particular arrangement or disposition of persons, as of troops or players on a team. **b.** any required assembling of the soldiers of a unit. **4. a.** a body of rocks classed as a stratigraphic unit for geologic mapping. Compare MEMBER (def. 8). **b.** the process of depositing rock or mineral of a particular composition or origin. —**for•ma′tion•al,** *adj.*

form•a•tive (fôr′mə tiv), *adj.* **1.** giving form or shape; forming; shaping; fashioning: *a formative process in manufacturing.* **2.** pertaining to formation or development: *a child's formative years.* **3. a.** capable of developing new cells or tissue by cell division and differentiation: *formative tissue.* **b.** concerned with the formation of an embryo, organ, or the like. **4.** pertaining to or used in the formation of words. —*n.* **5.** a derivational affix, esp. one that determines the part of speech of the derived word, as *-ness* in *loudness, hardness,* etc. **6.** (in a generative grammar) any minimal element of syntax, as a word or affix, that can be used in forming larger constructions. —**form′a•tive•ly,** *adv.*

form′ class′, *n.* a class of words or other forms in a language having one or more grammatical features in common, as all plural nouns or all nouns.

for•mer[1] (fôr′mər), *adj.* **1.** preceding in time; prior or earlier: *on a former occasion.* **2.** past, long past, or ancient: *in former times.* **3.** being the first mentioned of two (disting. from *latter*). **4.** having once or previously been; erstwhile: *a former president.*

form•er[2] (fôr′mər), *n.* a person or thing that forms or serves to form.

for•mer•ly (fôr′mər lē), *adv.* in time past; in an earlier period or age; previously.

form•fit•ting (fôrm′fit′ing), *adj.* designed to fit snugly around a given shape; close-fitting: *a formfitting blouse.*

for•mic (fôr′mik), *adj.* **1.** of or pertaining to ants. **2.** of or derived from formic acid.

for•mi•da•ble (fôr′mi də bəl *or, sometimes,* fər mid′ə-), *adj.* **1.** causing fear or apprehension: *a formidable opponent.* **2.** of discouraging or awesome size, difficulty, etc.; intimidating: *a formidable problem.* **3.** arousing feelings of awe or admiration: *formidable intelligence.* **4.** strong; forceful; powerful: *formidable opposition.* —**for′mi•da•bly,** *adv.*

form•less (fôrm′lis), *adj.* lacking a definite or regular form or shape; shapeless. —**form′less•ly,** *adv.* —**form′less•ness,** *n.*

form′ let′ter, *n.* a standardized letter that can be sent to any number of persons.

For•mo•sa (fôr mō′sə), *n.* TAIWAN.

for•mu•la (fôr′myə lə), *n., pl.* **-las, -lae** (-lē′). **1.** a set form of words, as for stating something authoritatively, for indicating procedure to be followed, or for prescribed use on some ceremonial occasion. **2.** any fixed or conventional method or approach: *popular novels produced by formula.* **3. a.** a mathematical rule or principle, frequently expressed in algebraic symbols. **b.** such a symbolic expression. **4.** an expression of the constituents of a compound by symbols and figures: *H_2O is the molecular formula for water.* **5.** a recipe or prescription. **6.** a special nutritive mixture, esp. of milk or milk substitute with other ingredients, in prescribed proportions for feeding a baby. **7.** a formal statement of religious doctrine.

for•mu•la•ic (fôr′myə lā′ik), *adj.* made according to a formula: *a formulaic plot.* —**for′mu•la′i•cal•ly,** *adv.*

for•mu•lar•y (fôr′myə ler′ē), *n., pl.* **-lar•ies,** *adj.* —*n.* **1.** a collection or system of formulas. **2.** a set form of words; formula. **3.** a book listing pharmaceutical substances and medicinal formulas. **4.** a book containing prescribed forms used in the service of a church. —*adj.* **5.** of or pertaining to a formula or formulas. **6.** of the nature of a formula.

for•mu•late (fôr′myə lāt′), *v.t.,* **-lat•ed, -lat•ing. 1.** to express in precise form; state definitely or systematically; *to formulate a theory.* **2.** to devise or develop, as a method or system. **3.** to reduce to or express in a formula. —**for•mu•la•ble** (fôr′myə lə bəl), *adj.* —**for′mu•la′tion,** *n.* —**for′mu•la′tor,** *n.*

for•ni•cate[1] (fôr′ni kāt′), *v.i.,* **-cat•ed, -cat•ing.** to commit fornication. —**for′ni•ca′tor,** *n.*

for•ni•cate[2] (fôr′ni kit, -kāt′) also **for′ni•cat′ed,** *adj. Biol.* arched or vaulted in form.

for•ni•ca•tion (fôr′ni kā′shən), *n.* **1.** voluntary sexual intercourse between two unmarried persons or two persons not married to each other. **2.** (in the Bible) **a.** adultery. **b.** idolatry. —**for•ni•ca•to•ry** (fôr′ni kə tôr′ē, -tōr′ē), *adj.*

For•rest (fôr′ist, for′-), *n.* **Nathan Bedford,** 1821–77, U.S. Confederate general.

for•sake (fôr sāk′), *v.t.,* **-sook, -sak•en, -sak•ing. 1.** to quit or leave entirely; abandon; desert: *to forsake one's family.* **2.** to give up or renounce (a habit, way of life, etc.); forgo. —**for•sak′er,** *n.*

for•sook (fôr so͝ok′), *v.* pt. of FORSAKE.

for•sooth (fôr so͞oth′), *adv.* (now used chiefly in derision or to express disbelief) in truth; in fact; indeed.

For•ster (fôr′stər), *n.* **E(dward) M(organ),** 1879–1970, English novelist.

for•swear (fôr swâr′), *v.,* **-swore, -sworn, -swearing.** —*v.t.* **1.** to renounce under oath; abjure: *to forswear one's sinful ways.* **2.** to deny vehemently or under oath. **3.** to perjure (oneself). —*v.i.* **4.** to swear falsely; commit perjury. —**for•swear′er,** *n.*

for•syth•i•a (fôr sith′ē ə, fər-; *esp. Brit.* -sī′thē ə), *n., pl.* **-syth•i•as.** any shrub of the genus *Forsythia,* of the olive family, having yellow flowers that blossom in early spring. [after William *Forsyth* (1737–1804), English horticulturist]

fort (fôrt, fōrt), *n.* **1.** a location occupied by troops and surrounded by defensive works, as walls and ditches. **2.** any permanent army post. **3.** (formerly) a trading post. —***Idiom.*** **4. hold the fort, a.** to defend one's position against attack or criticism. **b.** to maintain the existing state of affairs.

Fort-de-France (fôʀ də fräɴs′), *n.* the capital of Martinique, in the French West Indies. 97,000.

Fort′ Don′elson, *n.* a Confederate fort in NW Tennessee, on the Cumberland River: captured by Union forces in 1862.

forte[1] (fôrt, fōrt *or, for 1,* fôr′tā), *n.* **1.** a strong point, as of a person; an ability or role in which one excels; specialty. **2.** the part of a sword or foil blade between the hilt and the middle, stronger than the foible. —**Pronunciation.** In the sense of a person's strong point (*She draws* *well, but sculpture is her forte*), the older, historical pronunciation of FORTE is with one syllable: (fôrt) or (fōrt). Perhaps owing to confusion with the musical term *forte*, borrowed from Italian, a two-syllable pronunciation (fôr′tā) is increasingly heard, esp. from educated speakers, and is now also considered standard.

for•te² (fôr′tā), *Music.* —*adj.* **1.** loud; with force (opposed to *piano*). —*adv.* **2.** loudly. —*n.* **3.** a passage that is loud and forcible, or is intended to be so.

for•te•pi•a•no (fôr′tā pē ä′nō, -pyä′-), *adj., adv. Music.* loud and immediately soft.

for•te•pi•a•no (fôr′tə pē ä′nō, -pyä′-), *n., pl.* **-nos.** an early form of the grand piano having a wooden frame and less volume and resonance than a modern grand but greater clarity.

forth (fôrth, fōrth), *adv.* **1.** onward or outward in place or space; forward or away: *to go forth.* **2.** onward in time, in order, or in a series: *from that day forth.* **3.** out, as from concealment; into view or consideration: *Decency shines forth in his every action.*

forth•com•ing (fôrth′kum′ing, fōrth′-), *adj.* **1.** coming or about to come forth; approaching: *the forthcoming concert.* **2.** ready or available: *Help will be forthcoming whenever you ask.* **3.** frank and cooperative: *She will have to be more forthcoming in her testimony.* **4.** friendly and outgoing. —*n.* **5.** a coming forth; appearance.

forth•right (fôrth′rīt′, fōrth′-), *adj.* **1.** next after the thirty-ninth; being direct; outspoken: *a forthright answer.* —*adv.* Also, **forth′right′ly. 2. a.** in a direct course forward. **b.** in a straightforward manner; frankly. —**forth′right′ness,** *n.*

forth•with (fôrth′with′, -with′, fōrth′-), *adv.* immediately: *The action is suspended forthwith.*

for•ti•eth (fôr′tē ith), *adj.* **1.** next after the thirty-ninth; being the ordinal number for 40. **2.** being one of 40 equal parts. —*n.* **3.** a fortieth part, esp. of one (¹⁄₄₀). **4.** the fortieth member of a series.

for•ti•fi•ca•tion (fôr′tə fi kā′shən), *n.* **1.** the process or act of fortifying. **2.** something that fortifies or protects. **3.** Often, **fortifications.** military works constructed in order to defend or strengthen a position.

for•ti•fy (fôr′tə fī′), *v.,* **-fied, -fy•ing.** —*v.t.* **1.** to increase the defenses of: *to fortify a besieged town.* **2.** to furnish with a means of standing strain or wear: *to fortify cotton with nylon.* **3.** to impart strength or vigor to: *to fortify oneself with a good breakfast.* **4.** to increase the effectiveness of, as by additional ingredients: *to fortify a diet with vitamins.* **5.** to strengthen mentally or morally: *fortified by faith.* **6.** to confirm or corroborate: *to fortify an argument with facts.* —*v.i.* **7.** to set up fortifications. —**for′ti•fi′a•ble,** *adj.* —**for′ti•fi′er,** *n.* —**for′ti•fy′ing•ly,** *adv.*

for•tis•si•mo (fôr tis′ə mō′), *Music.* —*adj.* **1.** very loud. —*adv.* **2.** very loudly.

for•ti•tude (fôr′ti tōōd′, -tyōōd′), *n.* mental and emotional strength in facing adversity, danger, or temptation courageously. —**for′ti•tu′di•nous,** *adj.*

Fort′ Knox′, *n.* a military reservation in N Kentucky, SSW of Louisville: federal gold depository.

Fort′ Lar′amie, *n.* a former U.S. fort in SE Wyoming: important post on the Oregon Trail.

Fort′ Lau′der•dale, (lô′dər dāl′), *n.* a city in SE Florida: seashore resort. 162,842.

Fort′ Leav′enworth, *n.* a military reservation and U.S. Army training center in E Kansas adjoining Leavenworth, one of the oldest (1827) military posts W of the Mississippi and site of a federal penitentiary.

Fort′ McHen′ry, *n.* a fort in N Maryland, at the entrance to Baltimore harbor: Francis Scott Key wrote *The Star-Spangled Banner* during British bombardment in 1814.

Fort′ Moul′trie (mōōl′trē), *n.* a fort in the harbor of Charleston, S.C.: defended against British in the American Revolution by Col. William Moultrie (1730–1805); in the Civil War, played an important role in the bombardment of Fort Sumter and in Confederate defense.

fort•night (fôrt′nīt′, -nit), *n.* a period of fourteen nights and days; two weeks.

Fort′ Pulas′ki, *n.* a fort in E Georgia, at the mouth of the Savannah River: captured by Union forces in 1862; now a national monument.

FORTRAN (fôr′tran), *n.* a high-level programming language used mainly for solving problems in science and engineering. [*for(mula) tran(slator)*]

for•tress (fôr′tris), *n.* **1.** a fort or group of forts often including a town; citadel. **2.** any place of exceptional security; stronghold.

Fort′ Sum′ter, *n.* a fort in SE South Carolina, in the harbor of Charleston: its bombardment by the Confederates opened the Civil War on April 12, 1861.

for•tu•i•tous (fôr tōō′i təs, -tyōō′-), *adj.* **1.** happening or produced by chance; accidental. **2.** lucky; fortunate: *The money came at a most fortuitous moment.* —**for•tu′i•tous•ly,** *adv.* —**for•tu′i•tous•ness,** *n.*

for•tu•nate (fôr′chə nit), *adj.* **1.** receiving good from uncertain or unexpected sources; lucky. **2.** bringing or indicating good fortune: *a fortunate decision.* —**for′tu•nate•ly,** *adv.*

for•tune (fôr′chən), *n.* **1.** position in life as determined by wealth: *to make one's fortune.* **2.** wealth; riches: *lost a fortune.* **3.** an ample stock of material possessions: *inherited a fortune.* **4.** chance; luck: *had the bad fortune to go bankrupt.* **5. fortunes,** varied occurrences that happen or are to happen to a person in life. **6.** fate; destiny: *to tell someone's fortune.* **7.** (*cap.*) chance personified, commonly regarded as a mythical being distributing arbitrarily or capriciously the lots of life. —*Proverb.* **8. Fortune favors the brave,** people who act boldly often succeed. [< Latin *fortūna* chance, luck] —**for′tune•less,** *adj.*

for′tune cook′ie, *n.* a folded edible wafer containing a slip of paper with a printed maxim or prediction.

for′tune-tell′er, *n.* a person who claims the ability to predict the future. —**for′tune-tell′ing,** *n.*

Fort′ Wayne′, *n.* a city in NE Indiana. 183,359.

Fort′ Worth′, *n.* a city in N Texas. 451,814.

for•ty (fôr′tē), *n., pl.* **-ties,** *adj.* —*n.* **1.** a cardinal number, ten times four. **2.** a symbol for this number, as 40 or XL or XXXX. **3.** a set of this many persons or things. **4. forties,** the numbers from 40 through 49, as in referring to the years of a lifetime or of a century or to degrees of temperature. —*adj.* **5.** amounting to 40 in number. —**for′ty•ish,** *adj.*

for′ty-five′, *n.* **1.** a cardinal number, 40 plus 5. **2.** a symbol for this number, as 45 or XLV. **3.** a set of this many persons or things. **4.** a .45-caliber handgun or its cartridge. **5.** a 7-inch phonograph record played at 45 r.p.m.

for•ty-nin•er (fôr′tē nī′nər), *n.* a person participating in the California gold rush in 1849.

For′ty-ninth′ Par′allel, *n.* **1.** the line of latitude that marks the border between the United States and Canada from Lake of the Woods in Ontario and northen Minnesota to the Strait of Georgia in British Columbia. **2.** *Informal.* the Canada–U.S. border.

for′ty winks′, *n.* a short nap.

fo•rum (fôr′əm, fōr′əm), *n., pl.* **fo•rums, fo•ra** (fôr′ə, fōr′ə). **1.** the marketplace or public square of an ancient Roman city, the center of judicial and business affairs and place of assembly. **2.** a court; tribunal. **3. a.** a meeting place for discussion of matters of public interest or a means through which such discussion can be conducted, as a newspaper. **b.** a public meeting or assembly for such discussion. **c.** a discussion of a public issue or other serious topic by a select group, as of experts or specialists, esp. a radio or television broadcast for this purpose.

for•ward (fôr′wərd), *adv.* Also, **forwards. 1.** toward or to what is in front or in advance: *from this day forward; to step forward.* **2.** into view or consideration; forth: *brought forward a good suggestion.* —*adj.* **3.** directed toward a point in advance: *a forward motion.* **4.** being in a condition of advancement. **5.** ready; eager. **6.** presumptuous; bold: *a rude, forward child.* **7.** situated in the front: *the forward part of the ship.* **8.** of or for the future: *a forward price.* **9.** lying ahead: *Take the forward path.* **10.** radical or extreme. —*n.* **11. a.** a player stationed in advance of others on a team. **b.** either of two basketball players stationed in the forecourt. —*v.t.* **12.** to send onward; transmit, esp. to a new address: *to forward a letter.* **13.** to help onward; promote: *forwarding one's career.* **14.** to cause to advance: *to forward a tape on a VCR.* —**for′ward•a•ble,** *adj.* —**for′ward•er,** *n.* —**for′ward•ly,** *adv.*

for′ward-look′ing, *adj.* planning for or anticipating the future.

for•ward•ness (fôr′wərd nis), *n.* **1.** overreadiness to push oneself forward. **2.** the condition of being in advance.

for′ward pass′, *n.* a pass in football thrown from behind the line of scrimmage toward the opponent's goal. Compare LATERAL PASS.

for•wards (fôr′wərdz), *adv.* FORWARD.

for′ward-think′ing, *adj.* forward-looking.

for•went (fôr went′), *v.* pt. of FORGO.

Fos•dick (foz′dik), *n.* **Harry Emerson,** 1878–1969, U.S. preacher and author.

fos•sa (fos′ə), *n., pl.* **fos•sae** (fos′ē). a pit, cavity, or depression, as in a bone.

fosse or **foss** (fos, fôs), *n.* a moat or ditch, esp. in a fortification.

fos•sil (fos′əl), *n.* **1.** any preserved remains or imprint of a living organism, usu. of a former geologic age, as a bone, shell, or leaf impression. **2.** an outdated or old-fashioned person or thing. **3.** an obsolete or archaic word preserved in certain restricted contexts, as *nonce* in *for the nonce,* or a construction following a pattern no longer productive in the language, as *So be it.* —*adj.* **4.** of the nature of a fossil: *fossil insects.* **5.** formed from the remains of prehistoric life, as coal or oil: *fossil fuels; fossil resins.* **6.** belonging to a past epoch; antiquated: *a fossil approach to economics.* —**fos′sil•like′,** *adj.*

fos′sil fu′el, *n.* any combustible organic material, as oil, coal, or natural gas, derived from the remains of former life.

fos′sil gum′, *n.* any gum, found chiefly in the earth, that was yielded by a now fossilized tree. Compare AMBER.

fos•sil•ize (fos′ə līz′), *v.,* **-ized, -iz•ing.** —*v.t.* **1.** to convert into a fossil; replace organic matter with mineral substances in the remains of an organism. **2.** to cause to become outmoded or unchanging. —*v.i.* **3.** to become a fossil or fossillike.

fos•so•ri•al (fo sôr′ē əl), *adj.* **1.** digging or burrowing: *fossorial mammals.* **2.** adapted for burrowing, as the forepaws of the mole.

fos•ter (fô′stər, fos′tər), *v.t.* **1.** to promote the growth or development of: *to foster new ideas.* **2.** to bring up; rear: *to foster a child.* —*adj.* **3.** giving or receiving parental care though not kin by blood or related legally: *a foster parent.* —**fos′ter•age,** *n.*

Fos•ter (fô′stər, fos′tər), *n.* **Stephen (Collins),** 1826–64, U.S. songwriter.

fos'ter home', *n.* a household in which a child is given parental care by someone other than its birth parent or adoptive parent.

fought (fôt), *v.* pt. and pp. of FIGHT.

foul (foul), *adj.* **1.** grossly offensive to the senses; disgusting: *a foul smell.* **2.** marked by offensive matter or qualities: *foul air.* **3.** muddy; dirty, as a road. **4.** clogged or obstructed with foreign matter: *a foul gas jet.* **5.** stormy; inclement: *foul weather.* **6.** impeding navigation, as the wind or tide. **7.** morally offensive: *a foul deed.* **8.** profane; obscene: *foul language.* **9.** contrary to the rules or practices, as in a sport or game. **10.** obstructed; entangled: *a foul anchor.* **11.** marked with corrections and changes: *foul manuscripts.* —*adv.* **12.** in a foul manner. **13.** into foul territory; so as to be foul: *The ball went foul.* —*n.* **14.** a collision; entanglement: *a foul between racing sculls.* **15.** a violation of the rules of a sport or game. **16.** FOUL BALL. —*v.t.* **17.** to make foul; defile; soil. **18.** to clog; obstruct, as the bore of a gun. **19.** to collide with. **20.** to cause to become entangled or caught, as a rope. **21.** to dishonor; disgrace: *Scandal fouled his good name.* **22.** to hit (a pitched ball) foul. —*v.i.* **23.** to become foul. **24.** to come into collision. **25.** to become entangled or clogged. **26.** to commit a foul in a sport or game. **27.** to hit a foul ball. **28. foul out, a.** (of a baseball batter) to make an out by hitting a foul ball that is caught. **b.** to be expelled from a basketball game for having committed more fouls than are allowed. **29. foul up,** to make a mess; bungle or ruin things. —**foul'ly,** *adv.* —**foul'ness,** *n.*

fou·lard (fŏŏ lärd', fə-), *n.* **1.** a soft lightweight silk, rayon, or cotton fabric of twill or plain weave with a printed design, often of a small, even pattern. **2.** an article of clothing made of foulard.

foul' ball', *n.* a baseball hit outside the foul lines.

fouled'-up', *adj.* confused; disorganized.

foul' line', *n.* **1.** either of two lines on a baseball diamond connecting home plate with first and third base respectively, or their continuations to the end of the outfield. **2.** a line on a basketball court 15 ft. (4.6 m) from the backboard, from which foul shots are taken. **3.** a line on a bowling alley at right angles to the gutters and 60 ft. (18.3 m) from the center of the spot for the headpin, across which a bowler may not step.

foul·mouthed (foul'mouthd', -moutht'), *adj.* using obscene, profane, or scurrilous language.

foul' play', *n.* violent mischief, esp. murder.

foul' shot', *n.* a throw from the foul line given a basketball player after a foul has been called against an opponent.

foul' tip', *n.* a pitched baseball that glances off the bat into foul territory, usu. near the catcher.

foul'-up', *n.* **1.** a condition of disorder brought on by inefficiency or stupidity. **2.** failure of a mechanical part to operate correctly. **3.** *Slang.* a person who habitually makes mistakes.

found¹ (found), *v.* **1.** pt. and pp. of FIND. —*adj.* **2.** equipped; outfitted: *a new boat, fully found.* —*n.* **3.** free board and meals: *Maid wanted, good salary and found.*

found² (found), *v.t.* **1.** to establish on a firm basis or for enduring existence: *to found a new company.* **2.** to lay the lowest part of (a structure) firmly: *a house founded on solid rock.* **3.** to base; ground: *a story founded on fact.* **4.** to provide a basis for.

found³ (found), *v.t.* to melt and pour (metal, glass, etc.) into a mold.

foun·da·tion (foun dā'shən), *n.* **1.** the basis or groundwork of anything: *the moral foundation of both society and religion.* **2.** the natural or prepared ground or base on which some structure rests. **3.** the lowest division of a building, wall, or the like. **4.** the act of founding. **5.** the state of being founded. **6.** an institution financed by a donation or legacy, as to aid research, education, or the arts. **7.** an endowment for such an institution. **8.** a facial cosmetic used as the undercoating for other makeup; base.

found·er¹ (foun'dər), *n.* one who founds or establishes.

foun·der² (foun'dər), *v.i.* **1.** to fill with water and sink: *The ship foundered.* **2.** to sink; subside: *The building has foundered nearly ten feet.* **3.** to become wrecked; fail utterly: *The project foundered.* **4.** (of a horse) to suffer from laminitis. —*v.t.* **5.** to cause to suffer from laminitis. —*n.* **6.** LAMINITIS.

found·er³ (foun'dər), *n.* one who founds metal or type.

Found'ing Fa'ther, *n.* **1.** one of the framers of the U.S. Constitution. **2.** (*often l.c.*) a founder of an institution, company, etc.

found·ling (found'ling), *n.* an infant found abandoned; a child without a known parent or guardian.

found·ry (foun'drē), *n., pl.* **-ries. 1. a.** an establishment for producing castings from molten metal. **b.** an establishment where metal type is cast or melted down. **2.** the act or process of founding or casting metal. **3.** the category of metal objects made by founding; castings.

fount (fount), *n.* **1.** a spring of water; fountain. **2.** a source or origin: *a fount of ideas.*

foun·tain (foun'tn), *n.* **1.** a spring or source of water from the earth. **2.** the source or origin of anything. **3.** a jet or stream of water caused by mechanical means to spout from an opening. **4.** a structure for discharging such a jet. **5.** DRINKING FOUNTAIN. **6.** SODA FOUNTAIN. **7.** a reservoir for a liquid to be supplied continuously, as in a fountain pen.

foun·tain·head (foun'tn hed'), *n.* **1.** a spring from which a stream flows. **2.** a chief source: *a fountainhead of information.*

Foun'tain of Youth', *n.* a fabled spring whose waters were supposed to restore health and youth, sought in the Bahamas and Florida by Ponce de León and others.

foun'tain pen', *n.* a pen with a refillable reservoir that provides a continuous supply of ink to its point.

four (fôr, fōr), *n.* **1.** a cardinal number, three plus one. **2.** a symbol of this number, 4 or IV or IIII. **3.** a set of this many persons or things. **4. a.** an automobile powered by a four-cylinder engine. **b.** the engine itself. —*adj.* **5.** amounting to four in number.

four' bits', *n. Slang.* 50 cents. —**four'-bit'**, *adj.*

four'-chan'nel, *adj.* QUADRAPHONIC.

four·chette (fŏŏr shet'), *n.* **1.** the fold of skin that forms the posterior margin of the vulva. **2.** the wishbone of a bird.

four'-col'or proc'ess, *n.* a color printing process in which artwork is photographed through a succession of color filters to produce four plates, three of which are printed with colored inks and one with black.

four'-dimen'sional, *adj.* **1.** of or having four dimensions. **2.** of a space having points, or a set having elements, that require four coordinates for their unique determination.

four' flush', *n.* a hand in poker having four cards of one suit and one of another; an imperfect flush.

four'-flush', *v.i.* **1.** to bluff. **2.** to bluff in poker on the basis of a four flush.

four-flush·er (fôr'flush'ər, fōr'-), *n.* a person of unsubstantiated pretensions; bluffer.

four·fold (fôr'fōld', fōr'-), *adj.* **1.** comprising four parts or members. **2.** four times as great or as much. —*adv.* **3.** in fourfold measure.

four' free'doms, *n.* freedom of speech, freedom of worship, freedom from want, and freedom from fear: stated as goals of U.S. policy by President Franklin D. Roosevelt on January 6, 1941.

4-H Club (fôr'āch', fōr'-), *n.* an organization sponsored by the U.S. Department of Agriculture chiefly to instruct young people in modern farming methods and other useful skills. —**4-H**, *adj.* —**4-H'er**, *n.*

Four' Horse'men of the Apoc'alypse, *n.pl.* four horsemen symbolizing pestilence, war, famine, and death. Rev. 6:2–8.

Four' Hun'dred, *n.* the exclusive social set of a city or area. Also, **400.** [allegedly after the capacity of the ballroom in the mansion of Caroline Schermerhorn Astor, a leader of New York society in the late 19th century]

401(k) (fôr'ō'wun'kā', fōr'-), *n.* a savings plan that allows employees to contribute a fixed amount of income to a retirement account and to defer taxes until withdrawal.

Fou'rier se'ries, *n.* an infinite series that approximates a given function on a specified domain by using linear combinations of sines and cosines.

four'-in-hand', *n.* **1.** a long necktie to be tied in a slipknot with the ends left hanging. **2.** a vehicle drawn by four horses and driven by one person. **3.** a team of four horses.

four'-leaf' clo'ver, *n.* a clover leaf having four leaflets instead of the usual three, purported to bring good luck.

four'-let'ter word', *n.* a short word, typically of four letters, widely regarded as being obscene or scatological.

Four' No'ble Truths', *n.pl.* the doctrines of Buddha: all life is suffering, the cause of suffering is ignorant desire, this desire can be destroyed, the means to this is the Eightfold Path.

four'-o'clock', *n.* any plant of the genus *Mirabilis*, having tubular flowers that open in the late afternoon.

four'-pen'ny (fôr'pen'ē, -pə nē, fōr'-), *adj.* (of a nail) being 1½ in. (3.8 cm) long.

four'-post'er (fôr'pō'stər, fōr'-), *n.* a bed with four corner posts, as for supporting a canopy.

four·score (fôr'skôr', fōr'skōr'), *adj.* four times twenty; eighty.

four·some (fôr'səm, fōr'-), *n.* **1.** a company or set of four; two pairs. **2.** a golf match between two pairs of players.

four·square (fôr'skwâr', fōr'-), *adj.* **1.** consisting of four corners and four right angles; square. **2.** firm; forthright: *foursquare dedication.* —*adv.* **3.** without equivocation; forthrightly. —**four'square'ly**, *adv.* —**four'square'ness**, *n.*

four'-star', *adj.* **1.** designating a full general or admiral, as indicated by four stars on the insignia. **2.** rated or considered as being of the highest quality, esp. as indicated by four printed stars assigned in some rating systems: *a four-star restaurant.*

four·teen (fôr'tēn', fōr'-), *n.* **1.** a cardinal number, ten plus four. **2.** a symbol for this number, as 14 or XIV. **3.** a set of this many persons or things. —*adj.* **4.** amounting to 14 in number.

Four'teen Points', The, *n.* a statement of the war aims of the Allies, made by President Wilson on January 8, 1918.

four·teenth (fôr'tēnth', fōr'-), *adj.* **1.** next after the thirteenth; being the ordinal number for 14. **2.** being one of 14 equal parts. —*n.* **3.** a fourteenth part, esp. of one (¹/₁₄). **4.** the fourteenth member of a series.

Four'teenth Amend'ment, *n.* an amendment to the U.S. Constitution, ratified in 1868, defining national citizenship and forbidding the states to restrict the basic rights of citizens or other persons.

fourth (fôrth, fōrth), *adj.* **1.** next after the third; being the ordinal number for four. **2.** being one of four equal parts. **3.** pertaining to the gear transmission ratio at which the drive shaft speed is greater than that of third gear for a given engine crankshaft speed. —*n.* **4.** a fourth part, esp. of one (¼). **5.** the fourth member of a series. **6. a.** a musical interval encompassing four diatonic degrees. **b.** a tone at this interval. **c.** the harmonic combination of two tones a fourth apart. **7.** fourth gear. —*adv.* **8.** in the fourth place; fourthly. —**fourth′ly,** *adv.*

Fourth′ Amend′ment, *n.* an amendment to the U.S. Constitution, ratified in 1791 as part of the Bill of Rights, prohibiting unlawful search and seizure of personal property.

fourth′ class′, *n.* (in the U.S. Postal Service) the class of mail consisting of merchandise weighing one pound or more and not sealed against inspection.

fourth′-class′, *adj.* **1.** of, pertaining to, or designated as a class next below third. —*adv.* **2.** by fourth-class mail.

Fourth′ Command′ment, *n.* "Remember the sabbath day, to keep it holy": fourth of the Ten Commandments. Compare TEN COMMANDMENTS.

fourth′ dimen′sion, *n.* **1.** a dimension, usu. time, in addition to length, width, and depth, used to discuss phenomena that depend on four variables in geometrical language. **2.** something beyond scientific explanation. —**fourth′-di·men′sion·al,** *adj.*

fourth′ estate′, *n.* (*often caps.*) the journalistic profession or its members; the press.

Fourth′ of July′, *n.* INDEPENDENCE DAY.

Fourth′ Repub′lic, *n.* the republic established in France in 1945 and replaced by the Fifth Republic in 1958.

Fourth′ World′, *n.* the world's most poverty-stricken nations marked by very low GNP per capita and great dependence upon foreign aid.

four′-way′, *adj.* **1.** providing passage in four directions: *a four-way entrance.* **2.** applying to all four directions of traffic: *a four-way stop sign.* **3.** made up of four participants: *a four-way discussion.*

4WD, four-wheel drive.

four′-wheel′ drive′, *n.* a drive system in which engine power is transmitted to all four wheels of a vehicle for improved traction. —**four′-wheel′-drive′,** *adj.*

fowl (foul), *n., pl.* **fowls,** (*esp. collectively*) **fowl,** *v.* —*n.* **1.** any domestic hen or rooster; chicken. **2.** any of several other, usu. gallinaceous, birds, as turkeys or pheasants. **3.** a full-grown domestic fowl for food purposes, as distinguished from a chicken or young fowl. **4.** the flesh or meat of a domestic fowl. **5.** any bird (used chiefly in combination): *waterfowl; wildfowl.* —*v.i.* **6.** to hunt or take wildfowl.

fox (foks), *n., pl.* **fox·es,** (*esp. collectively*) **fox,** *v.* —*n.* **1.** any of several small carnivores of the dog family, Canidae, esp. those of the genus *Vulpes,* having a sharply pointed muzzle and a long bushy tail. **2.** the fur of this animal. **3.** a cunning or crafty person. **4.** *Bible.* a scavenger, perhaps the jackal. Ps. 63:10; Lam. 5:18. —*v.t.* **5.** to deceive or trick. **6.** to repair or finish (a shoe) with leather or other material on the upper front. —*Saying.* **7. let the fox guard the henhouse,** to give someone authority over a situation that he or she might exploit for personal gain. —**fox′like,** *adj.*

Fox¹ (foks), *n., pl.* **Fox·es,** (*esp. collectively*) **Fox. 1.** a member of an Native American people residing in Wisconsin at time of first contact, and later confined to a single settlement in E Iowa. **2.** the Algonquian language shared by the Fox, Sauk, and Kickapoo.

Fox² (foks), *n.* **George,** 1624–91, English religious leader: founder of the Society of Friends.

fox′fire′ or **fox′-fire′,** *n.* **1.** organic luminescence, esp. from certain fungi on decaying wood. **2.** any of various fungi causing luminescence in decaying wood.

fox·glove (foks′gluv′), *n.* a common plant, *Digitalis purpurea,* of the figwort family, with purple flowers on a tall spike: the leaves yield digitalis.

fox′ grape′, *n.* a grape, *Vitis labrusca,* chiefly of the northeastern U.S., bearing dark, sweet, musky fruit.

fox·hole (foks′hōl′), *n.* a pit for one or two soldiers dug as a shelter in a battle zone.

fox·hound (foks′hound′), *n.* any of several breeds and numerous strains of hounds trained to hunt foxes, typically medium-sized dogs with hanging ears, straight legs, and a short glossy coat of black, tan, and white.

fox·tail (foks′tāl′), *n.* **1.** the tail of a fox. **2.** any of various grasses having soft brushlike spikes of flowers.

fox′tail lil′y, *n.* any of various plants of the genus *Eremurus,* of the lily family, having tall spikes of showy flowers.

fox′ ter′rier, *n.* either of two English breeds of small terriers with a long, narrow head and a white coat usu. with black or tan, formerly used for driving foxes from their holes: one breed has a wiry coat and the other a smooth coat.

fox′ trot′, *n.* **1.** a ballroom dance in duple meter characterized by various combinations of slow and quick steps. **2.** a pace, as of a horse, consisting of a series of short steps.

fox·y (fok′sē), *adj.,* **fox·i·er, fox·i·est. 1.** slyly clever; cunning; crafty. **2.** yellowish brown or reddish brown. **3.** *Slang.* physically attractive, esp. in a sexually alluring way. **4.** brightly flavorful; brisk: *foxy wine.* —**fox′i·ly,** *adv.* —**fox′i·ness,** *n.*

foy·er (foi′ər, foi′ā, fwä yā′), *n.* **1.** the lobby of a theater, hotel, or apartment house. **2.** a vestibule or entrance hall in a house or apartment.

FPC, Federal Power Commission: a board of five members established chiefly to regulate the natural gas and electric power industries engaged in interstate commerce: replaced by the Federal Energy Regulatory Commission.

fpm or **ft/min,** feet per minute.

fps, 1. feet per second. **2.** foot-pound-second.

Fr, *Chem. Symbol.* francium.

fra·cas (frā′kəs, frak′əs), *n.* a noisy disorderly disturbance.

frac·tal (frak′tl), *n.* a geometrical structure that has a regular or an uneven shape repeated over all scales of measurement and that has a dimension (**frac′tal dimen′sion**), determined according to definite rules, that is greater than the spatial dimension of the structure.

frac·tion (frak′shən), *n.* **1. a.** a number usu. expressed in the form *a/b.* **b.** a ratio of algebraic quantities similarly expressed. **2.** a component in a volatile mixture whose range of boiling point temperatures allows it to be separated from other components by fractionation. **3.** a part of a whole: *Only a fraction of the members were present.* **4.** a small part or segment: *only a fraction of the cost.* **5.** a piece broken off; fragment. —*v.t., v.i.* **6.** to break into fractions.

frac·tion·al (frak′shə nl), *adj.* **1.** pertaining to fractions; comprising a part or the parts of a unit; constituting a fraction: *fractional numbers.* **2.** comparatively small; inconsiderable: *The profit was fractional.* **3.** of or pertaining to a process in which chemical mixtures are fractionated. —**frac′tion·al·ly,** *adv.*

frac·tion·ate (frak′shə nāt′), *v.t.,* **-at·ed, -at·ing. 1.** to separate or divide into component parts. **2.** to separate (a mixture) into ingredients or into portions having different properties, as by distillation or crystallization. —**frac′tion·a′tor,** *n.*

frac·tion·a·tion (frak′shə nā′shən), *n.* **1.** the act or process of fractionating. **2.** the state of being fractionated.

frac·tious (frak′shəs), *adj.* **1.** refractory; unruly: *a dangerous, fractious horse.* **2.** readily angered; quarrelsome. —**frac′tious·ly,** *adv.* —**frac′tious·ness,** *n.*

frac·ture (frak′chər), *n., v.,* **-tured, -tur·ing.** —*n.* **1.** the breaking of a bone, cartilage, or the like, or the resulting condition. Compare COMPOUND FRACTURE. **2.** a break; split. **3.** the characteristic manner of breaking. **4.** the characteristic appearance of a broken surface, as of a mineral. —*v.t.* **5.** to cause or to suffer a fracture in. **6.** to break; crack. **7.** *Slang.* to amuse highly. —*v.i.* **8.** to become fractured; break. —**frac′tur·a·ble,** *adj.* —**frac′tur·al,** *adj.*

frag·ile (fraj′əl), *adj.* **1.** easily broken or damaged; brittle: *a fragile vase; a fragile alliance.* **2.** vulnerably delicate in appearance: *fragile beauty.* **3.** lacking in substance or force; flimsy: *a fragile excuse.* —**frag′ile·ly,** *adv.* —**fra·gil·i·ty** (frə jil′i tē), *n.*

fragile X syndrome, *n.* a widespread form of mental retardation caused by a faulty gene on the X chromosome.

frag·ment (*n.* frag′mənt; *v.* frag′mənt, -ment, frag ment′), *n.* **1.** a part broken off or detached. **2.** an isolated part: *played a fragment of the symphony.* **3.** an odd piece; scrap. —*v.i.* **4.** to collapse or break into fragments. —*v.t.* **5.** to break (something) into pieces or fragments. **6.** to divide into fragments; disunify.

frag·men·tar·y (frag′mən ter′ē), *adj.* consisting of fragments; broken; incomplete: *fragmentary evidence; fragmentary remains.* —**frag′men·tar′i·ly,** *adv.* —**frag′men·tar′i·ness,** *n.*

frag·men·ta·tion (frag′mən tā′shən), *n.* **1.** the act or process of fragmenting or the state of being fragmented. —*adj.* **2.** of or designating an explosive device designed to scatter small metal fragments on detonation: *a fragmentation grenade; fragmentation bombs.*

Fra·go·nard (frA gô nAr′), *n.* **Jean Honoré,** 1732–1806, French painter.

fra·grance (frā′grəns), *n.* **1.** the quality of being fragrant. **2.** a sweet or pleasing scent. **3.** something, as a perfume, having a sweet or pleasing scent.

fra·grant (frā′grənt), *adj.* having a pleasing scent: *a fragrant rose.*

fraid·y-cat (frā′dē kat′), *n. Informal.* a timid, easily frightened person.

frail¹ (frāl), *adj.,* **-er, -est. 1.** having delicate health; weak. **2.** easily broken or damaged; fragile. **3.** morally weak; easily tempted. —**frail′ly,** *adv.* —**frail′ness,** *n.*

frail² (frāl), *n.* a basket made of rushes and used esp. for dried fruits.

frail·ty (frāl′tē, frā′əl-), *n., pl.* **-ties. 1.** the quality or state of being frail. **2.** a fault resulting from moral weakness.

frame (frām), *n., v.,* **framed, fram·ing.** —*n.* **1.** a border or case for enclosing a picture, mirror, etc. **2.** a rigid structure formed of joined pieces and used as a major support, as in buildings, machinery, and furniture. **3.** a body, esp. a human body, with reference to its size or build; physique: *a large frame.* **4.** a structure for admitting or enclosing something: *a window frame.* **5.** Usu., **frames.** the framework for a pair of eyeglasses. **6.** form, constitution, or structure in general. **7.** a particular state: *an unhappy frame of mind.* **8.** one of the successive pictures on a strip of film. **9.** a single traversal by the electron beam of all the scanning lines on a television screen. Compare FIELD (def. 19). **10. a.** one of the ten divisions of a bowling game. **b.** one of the squares on the scorecard in which the score for a given frame is recorded. **11.** RACK¹ (def. 4). **12.** a baseball inning. **13.** a machine or part of a machine supported by a framework, esp. as used in textile production: *a spinning frame.* **14.** one of the separate drawings in a comic strip, usu. set off by a frame. **15.** a rectangular portion of a page, often with enclosing lines, to set off printed matter in a newspaper, magazine, or the like. —*v.t.* **16.** to construct; shape. **17.** to devise; compose: *to frame a new constitution.* **18.** to conceive or imagine, as an idea. **19.** to incriminate (an innocent person) so as to ensure a verdict of guilty. **20.** to provide with or put into a frame, as a picture. **21.** to form (speech) carefully with the lips. **22.**

to prearrange fraudulently, as in a scheme or contest. **23.** to line up visually in a viewfinder or sight. —**fram′a•ble, frame′a•ble,** *adj.* —**frame′less,** *adj.* —**fram′er,** *n.*

frame′ of ref′erence, *n., pl.* **frames of reference.** a structure of concepts, values, customs, or views by means of which an individual or group evaluates data, communicates ideas, and regulates behavior.

frame′-up′, *n.* a fraudulent incrimination of an innocent person.

frame•work (frām′wûrk′), *n.* **1.** a skeletal structure designed to support or enclose something. **2.** a frame or structure composed of parts fitted together. **3.** FRAME OF REFERENCE.

franc (frangk), *n.* the basic monetary unit of Belgium, Burundi, Djibouti, France, Guinea, Luxembourg, Madagascar, Rwanda, and Switzerland.

France (frans, fräns), *n.* **1. Anatole** (*Jacques Anatole Thibault*), 1844–1924, French author. **2.** a republic in W Europe. 58,470,421; 212,736 sq. mi. (550,985 sq. km). *Cap.:* Paris.

Fran•ces•ca (fran ches′kə, frän-), *n.* **Piero della** (*Piero dei Franceschi*), c1420–92, Italian painter.

fran•chise (fran′chīz), *n., v.,* **-chised, -chis•ing.** —*n.* **1.** a privilege conferred on an individual, group, or company by a government: *a franchise to operate a bus system.* **2. a.** the right or license granted by a company to an individual or group to market its products or services in a specific territory. **b.** the right to own and operate a professional sports team as a member of a league. **3.** the right to vote. **4.** a legal immunity or exemption from a particular burden, exaction, or the like. —*v.t.* **5.** to grant a franchise to. —**fran′chis•a•ble,** *adj.* —**fran′chis•a•bil′i•ty,** *n.*

fran•chi•see (fran′chī zē′), *n., pl.* **-sees.** a person or company to whom a franchise is granted.

fran•chis•er (fran′chī zər), *n.* **1.** Also, **fran•chi•sor** (fran′chī zər, fran′chə zôr′). a person or company that grants a franchise. **2.** franchisee.

Fran•cis I (fran′sis), *n.* **1.** 1494–1547, king of France 1515–47. **2.** 1768–1835, first emperor of Austria 1804–35; as **Francis II,** last emperor of the Holy Roman Empire 1792–1806.

Fran•cis•can (fran sis′kən), *adj.* **1.** of or pertaining to St. Francis or the Franciscans. —*n.* **2.** a member of the mendicant order founded by St. Francis in the 13th century.

Fran′cis Fer′dinand, *n.* 1863–1914, archduke of Austria: his assassination precipitated the outbreak of World War I.

Francis Joseph I, *n.* 1830–1916, emperor of Austria 1848–1916; king of Hungary 1867–1916. German, **Franz Josef.**

Fran′cis of Assi′si, *n.* **Saint** (*Giovanni Francesco Bernardone*),1182?–1226, Italian friar: founder of the Franciscan order.

Fran′cis of Sales′ (sālz; *Fr.* sȧl), *n.* **Saint,** 1567–1622, French ecclesiastic and writer on theology: bishop of Geneva 1602–22.

fran•ci•um (fran′sē əm), *n.* a radioactive element of the alkali metal group. *Symbol:* Fr; *at. no.:* 87.

Fran•co (frang′kō), *n.* **Francisco** (*Francisco Paulino Hermenegildo Teódulo Franco-Bahamonde*), 1892–1975, Spanish dictator: head of Spain 1939–75. —**Fran′co•ist,** *n.*

Franco-, a combining form representing FRENCH or FRANCE: *Francophile; Franco-Prussian.*

fran•co•lin (frang′kə lin), *n.* any Eurasian or African partridge of the genus *Francolinus.*

Fran′co-Prus′sian War′ (frang′kō prush′ən), *n.* the war between France and Prussia, 1870–71.

fran•gi•ble (fran′jə bəl), *adj.* easily broken; breakable. —**fran′gi•bil′i•ty, fran′gi•ble•ness,** *n.*

fran•gi•pan•i (fran′jə pan′ē, -pä′nē), *n., pl.* **-pan•is, -pan•i.** **1.** a perfume prepared from or imitating the odor of the flower of a tropical American tree or shrub, *Plumeria rubra,* of the dogbane family. **2.** the tree or shrub itself.

frank[1] (frangk), *adj.* **1.** direct and unreserved in speech: *frank criticism.* **2.** lacking inhibition or subterfuge: *frank curiosity.* **3.** unmistakable; clinically evident: *frank blood.* —*n.* **4.** a stamp, printed marking, or signature on a piece of mail indicating that postal charges have been paid. —*v.t.* **5.** to mark (mail) for transmission by virtue of a frank. **6.** to enable to pass or go freely: *to frank a visitor through customs.* **7.** to facilitate the comings and goings of (a person). —**frank′ly,** *adv.* —**frank′ness,** *n.*

frank[2] (frangk), *n.* a frankfurter.

Frank[1] (frangk), *n.* **1.** a member of a confederation of Germanic peoples living on the right bank of the lower Rhine River in the 3rd century A.D. and by the 6th century ruling most of what is now France, the Low Countries, and W Germany. **2.** an inhabitant of any of the early medieval polities founded by the Franks and their descendants. **3.** (now in historical contexts) (in the Levant) any native of W Europe.

Frank[2] (frangk, frängk), *n.* **Anne,** 1929–45, German Jewish girl who died in Belsen concentration camp in Germany: her diaries about her family hiding from Nazis in Amsterdam (1942–44) published in 1947.

Frank•en•stein (frang′kən stīn′), *n.* **1.** a person who creates a monster or a destructive agency that cannot be controlled or that brings about the creator's ruin. **2.** Also called **Frank′enstein mon′ster.** the monster or destructive agency itself. [after a character in Mary Shelley's novel of the same name (1818)] —**Frank′en•stein′i•an,** *adj.*

Frank•fort (frangk′fərt), *n.* the capital of Kentucky, in the N part. 25,973.

Frank•furt (frangk′fûrt, frängk′fŏŏrt), *n.* **1.** Also called **Frank•furt am**

Main (frängk′fŏŏrt äm mīn′). a city in W Germany, on the Main River. 618,500. **2.** Also called **Frank•furt an der O•der** (frängk′fŏŏrt än dər ō′dər). a city in NE Germany, on the Oder River. 85,158.

frank•furt•er or **frank•fort•er** (frangk′fər tər), *n.* a cooked and smoked sausage usu. of beef or beef and pork.

frank•in•cense (frang′kin sens′), *n.* an aromatic gum resin from various Asian and African trees of the genus *Boswellia,* bursera family, used chiefly as an incense and in perfumery: one of three gifts, the other two being gold and myrrh, given by the Magi to the infant Jesus. Matt. 2:11.

Frank•lin (frangk′lin), *n.* **1. Aretha,** born 1942, U.S. soul, pop, and gospel singer. **2. Benjamin,** 1706–90, American statesman and inventor. **3.** a district in extreme N Canada, in the Northwest Territories, including the Boothia and Melville peninsulas, Baffin Island, and other Arctic islands. 549,253 sq. mi. (1,422,565 sq. km).

Frank′lin stove′, *n.* a cast-iron stove having the general form of a fireplace with the front open and often fitted with doors.

fran•tic (fran′tik), *adj.* **1.** desperate or wild with emotion; frenzied. **2.** marked by desperation; anxious: *a frantic effort.* —**fran′ti•cal•ly,** *adv.*

frappe (frap, fra pā′) also **frappé,** *n. Northeastern U.S.* a milk shake made with ice cream.

frap•pé (fra pā′), *n.* **1.** a fruit juice mixture frozen to a mush. **2.** a drink consisting of a liqueur poured over cracked or shaved ice. **3.** FRAPPE. —*adj.* **4.** chilled; iced; frozen.

fra•ter•nal (frə tûr′nl), *adj.* **1.** of or befitting a brother; brotherly. **2.** of or being a society of men associated in brotherly union, as for mutual aid or benefit. —**fra•ter′nal•ism,** *n.* —**fra•ter′nal•ly,** *adv.*

frater′nal twin′, *n.* one of a pair of twins, not necessarily resembling each other or of the same sex, that develop from two separately fertilized ova. Compare IDENTICAL TWIN.

fra•ter•ni•ty (frə tûr′ni tē), *n., pl.* **-ties.** **1.** a social organization of male students usu. with secret initiation and rites and a name composed of Greek letters. **2.** a group of persons associated by or as if by ties of brotherhood. **3.** any group or class of persons having common interests: *the medical fraternity.* **4.** an organization of laymen for religious or charitable purposes. **5.** brotherhood.

frat•er•nize (frat′ər nīz′), *v.i.,* **-nized, -niz•ing.** **1.** to associate in a friendly way. **2.** to associate cordially with members of a hostile group. —**frat′er•ni•za′tion,** *n.* —**frat′er•niz′er,** *n.*

frat•ri•cide (fra′tri sīd′, frā′-), *n.* **1.** the act of killing one's brother. **2.** a person who kills his or her brother. —**frat′ri•cid′al,** *adj.*

Frau (frou), *n., pl.* **Frau•en** (frou′ən), **Fraus.** the conventional German title of respect and term of address for a married woman.

fraud (frôd), *n.* **1.** deceit or trickery perpetrated for profit or to gain some unfair or dishonest advantage. **2.** a particular instance of such deceit or trickery: *mail fraud; election frauds.* **3.** something that is not what it pretends: *The relief program is a fraud.* **4.** an impostor.

fraud•u•lent (frô′jə lənt), *adj.* **1.** characterized by, involving, or proceeding from fraud. **2.** given to or using fraud; dishonest. —**fraud′u•lence, fraud′u•len•cy,** *n.* —**fraud′u•lent•ly,** *adv.*

fraught (frôt), *adj.* filled or attended (fol. by *with*): *an undertaking fraught with danger.*

Fräu•lein (froi′līn *or, often,* frô′-, frou′-), *n., pl.* **-leins, -lein.** the conventional German title of respect and term of address for an unmarried woman.

fray[1] (frā), *n.* **1.** a fight; skirmish; conflict. **2.** a noisy quarrel or debate.

fray[2] (frā), *v.t.* **1.** to wear (material) into loose threads at the edge or end: *to fray a cuff.* **2.** to wear out by rubbing. **3.** to cause strain on: *The argument frayed their nerves.* —*v.i.* **4.** to become frayed: *sweaters frayed at the elbows.* —*n.* **5.** a frayed part.

Fra•zer (frā′zər), *n.* **Sir James George,** 1854–1941, Scottish anthropologist.

fraz•zle (fraz′əl), *v.,* **-zled, -zling,** *n.* —*v.t., v.i.* **1.** to make or become physically or mentally fatigued. **2.** to wear to threads or shreds; fray. —*n.* **3.** a state of physical or nervous exhaustion: *worn to a frazzle.*

FRB or **F.R.B.,** **1.** Federal Reserve Bank. **2.** Federal Reserve Board.

freak[1] (frēk), *n.* **1.** an abnormal phenomenon or product or unusual object; anomaly; aberration. **2.** a person or animal on exhibition as an example of a strange deviation from nature. **3.** a sudden and apparently causeless change; caprice: *a freak of the weather.* **4.** a capricious notion. **5.** *Slang.* **a.** a habitual user or addict: *a drug freak; a heroin freak.* **b.** a devoted fan; enthusiast: *a baseball freak.* —*adj.* **6.** unusual; odd; irregular: *a freak epidemic.* —*v.t., v.i.* **7.** to make or become frightened, nervous, or excited. **8. freak out,** *Slang.* to lose or cause to lose emotional control, as from shock, fear, or joy.

freak[2] (frēk), *v.* **1.** to fleck, streak, or variegate: *great splashes of color freaking the sky.* —*n.* **2.** a fleck or streak of color.

freak•ish (frē′kish), *adj.* **1.** unusual; odd; grotesque: *a freakish appearance.* **2.** whimsical; capricious: *freakish changes.* —**freak′ish•ly,** *adv.* —**freak′ish•ness,** *n.*

freak′ of na′ture, *n.* a person or animal that is born or grows with abnormal physical features.

freak′-out′ or **freak′out′,** *n. Slang.* **1.** an act or instance of freaking out. **2.** a person who freaks out.

freak•y (frē′kē), *adj.,* **freak•i•er, freak•i•est.** **1.** FREAKISH. **2.** weird; strange. —**freak′i•ly,** *adv.* —**freak′i•ness,** *n.*

freck•le (frek′əl), *n., v.,* **-led, -ling.** —*n.* **1.** any of the small brownish spots on the skin that are caused by deposition of pigment and that increase in number and darken on exposure to sunlight; lentigo. —*v.t.* **2.** to cover with freckles. —*v.i.* **3.** to become freckled. —**freck′ly,** *adj.,* **-li•er, -li•est.**

Fred′die Mac′, *n.* **1.** See **Federal Home Loan Mortgage Corporation.** **2.** a publicly traded security that represents participation in a pool of mortgages guaranteed by the Federal Home Loan Mortgage Corporation. Compare FANNIE MAE, GINNIE MAE. [from the initials *FHLMC,* on the model of FANNIE MAE]

Fred•er•ick (fred′rik, -ər ik), *n.* **1. Frederick I, a.** (*"Frederick Barbarossa"*) 1123?–90, emperor of the Holy Roman Empire 1152–90. **b.** 1194–1250, king of Sicily 1198–1212: as Frederick II, emperor of the Holy Roman Empire 1215–50. **c.** 1657–1713, king of Prussia 1701–13 (son of Frederick William, the Great Elector). **2. Frederick II, a.** FREDERICK I (def. 1b). **b.** (*"Frederick the Great"*) 1712–86, king of Prussia 1740–86 (son of Frederick William I). **3. Frederick III, a.** 1415–93, emperor of the Holy Roman Empire 1452–93; as Frederick IV, king of Germany 1440–93. **b.** (*"the Wise"*) 1463–1525, elector of Saxony 1486–1525: protector of Martin Luther.

Fred•er•icks•burg (fred′riks bûrg′, fred′ər iks-), *n.* a city in NE Virginia: scene of a Confederate victory 1862. 15,322.

Fred′erick the Great′, *n.* FREDERICK II (def. 2b).

Fred′erick Wil′liam, *n.* **1.** (*"the Great Elector"*) 1620–88, elector of Brandenburg who increased the power and importance of Prussia. **2. Frederick William I,** 1688–1740, king of Prussia 1713–40. **3. Frederick William II,** 1744–97, king of Prussia 1786–97. **4. Frederick William III,** 1770–1840, king of Prussia 1797–1840. **5. Frederick William VI,** 1795–1861, king of Prussia 1840–61 (brother of William I of Prussia).

free (frē), *adj.,* **fre•er, fre•est,** *adv., v.,* **freed, free•ing.** —*adj.* **1.** enjoying personal rights or liberty, as one who is not in slavery or confinement. **2.** pertaining to or reserved for those who enjoy personal liberty: *living on free soil.* **3.** existing under, characterized by, or possessing civil and political liberties: *the free nations of the world.* **4.** enjoying political independence, as a people or country not under foreign rule. **5.** exempt from external authority, interference, or restriction; independent: *free choice.* **6.** able to do something at will: *free to act.* **7.** clear of obstructions or obstacles: *The highway is now free of fallen rock.* **8.** without engagements or obligations: *free time.* **9.** not occupied or in use: *The room is free now.* **10.** exempt or released; unburdened: *free from worry; free of taxes.* **11.** provided without a charge: *free parking.* **12.** unimpeded: *free movement.* **13.** loose; unattached: *to get one's arm free.* **14.** ready or generous in giving: *free with one's advice.* **15.** lavish; unstinted: *free spending.* **16.** frank and open; unconstrained. **17.** not subject to special regulations, restrictions, duties, etc.: *free passage.* **18.** of, pertaining to, or characterized by free enterprise: *a free economy.* **19.** open to all: *a free port.* **20.** not literal; loose: *a free translation.* **21.** not subject to rules or set forms: *free improvisation.* **22.** uncombined chemically: *free oxygen.* **23.** traveling under no force except gravity or inertia: *free flight.* **24.** (of a vowel) situated in an open syllable (opposed to *checked*). **25.** easily worked, as stone or land. **26.** (of a variable in logic) not occurring within the scope of a quantifier. Compare BOUND[1] (def. 11). **27.** (of a wind) blowing favorably nearly on the quarter. **28.** not containing a specified substance (often used in combination): *a sugar-free soft drink.* **29.** (of a linguistic form) capable of being used by itself as an independent word without combination with other forms: Fire *and* run *are free forms.* Compare BOUND[1] (def. 10). —*adv.* **30.** in a free manner; freely. **31.** away from the wind: *a sailboat running free.* —*v.t.* **32.** to set at liberty; release from bondage, imprisonment, or restraint. **33.** to exempt or deliver (usu. fol. by *from*). **34.** to relieve or rid (usu. fol. by *of*): *to free oneself of responsibility.* **35.** to disengage; clear (usu. fol. by *from* or *of*). **36. free up, a.** to release, as from restrictions. **b.** to disentangle. —*Idiom.* **37. for free,** without charge: *They mended my jacket for free.* **38. free and clear,** without any encumbrance, as a lien or mortgage. **39. free and easy, a.** casual; informal. **b.** inappropriately casual; presumptuous. **40. make free with, a.** to use as one's own. **b.** to treat with too much familiarity; take liberties with. **41. set free,** to release; liberate. **42. with a free hand,** generously. —**free′ly,** *adv.* —**free′ness,** *n.*

free′ a′gent, *n.* a professional athlete who is not under contract and is free to auction off his or her services to any team. —**free′ a′gency, free′ a′gentry,** *n.*

Free′ and Accept′ed Ma′sons, *n.* See under FREEMASON (def. 1).

free′ associa′tion, *n.* **1.** the uncensored expression of the ideas, impressions, etc., passing through the mind of a person undergoing psychoanalysis, a technique used to facilitate access to the unconscious. **2.** any process in which one idea, word, etc., suggests or elicits the next without following any logical order or conscious direction. —**free′-asso′ciate,** *v.i.,* **-at•ed, -at•ing.**

free′base′ or **free′-base′,** *v.,* **-based, -bas•ing,** *n.* —*v.t.* **1.** to purify (cocaine) by dissolving under heat with ether to remove salts and impurities. **2.** to smoke or inhale (freebased cocaine). —*v.i.* **3.** to freebase cocaine. —*n.* **4.** freebased cocaine. —**free′bas′er,** *n.*

free•bie or **free•bee** (frē′bē), *n. Informal.* something given or received without charge.

free•board (frē′bôrd′, -bōrd′), *n.* **1. a.** (on a cargo vessel) the distance between the uppermost deck considered fully watertight and the official load line. **b.** the portion of the side of a hull that is above the water. **2.** the height of the watertight portion of a building or other construction above a given level of water.

free•boot•er (frē′bo͞o′tər), *n.* pirate; buccaneer.

free•born (frē′bôrn′), *adj.* **1.** born free, rather than in slavery. **2.** pertaining to or befitting persons born free.

Freed′men's Bu′reau, *n.* an agency of the War Department set up in 1865 to assist freed slaves in obtaining relief, land, jobs, fair treatment, and education.

free•dom (frē′dəm), *n.* **1.** the state of being free or at liberty rather than in confinement or under physical restraint. **2.** exemption from external control. **3.** the power to determine action without restraint. **4.** political or national independence. **5.** personal liberty: *slaves who bought their freedom.* **6.** exemption; immunity: *freedom from fear.* **7.** the absence of or release from ties or obligations. **8.** ease or facility of movement or action. **9.** frankness of manner or speech. **10.** a liberty taken. **11.** civil liberty, as opposed to subjection to an arbitrary or despotic government. **12.** the right to enjoy all the privileges or special rights of citizenship, membership, etc., in a community or the like. **13.** the right to frequent, enjoy, or use at will.

free′dom march′ or **Free′dom March′,** *n.* an organized march protesting a government's restriction of or lack of support for civil rights, esp. such a march in support of racial integration in the U.S. in the 1960s. —**free′dom march′er,** *n.*

Free′dom of Informa′tion Act′, *n.* a law enacted in 1966 requiring that government records except those relating to national security, confidential financial data, and law enforcement be made available to the public on request. *Abbr.:* FOIA

free′dom of speech′, *n.* the right of people to express their opinions publicly without governmental interference, subject to the laws against libel, incitement to violence or rebellion, etc. Also called **free speech.**

free′dom of the press′, *n.* the right to publish information or opinions without governmental restriction, subject only to the laws of libel, obscenity, sedition, etc.

free′dom of the seas′, *n.* the doctrine that merchant ships may sail anywhere on the high seas without interference.

free′dom ride′ or **Free′dom Ride′,** *n.* (esp. in the 1960s) a bus trip made to parts of the southern U.S. by persons engaging in efforts to integrate racially segregated public facilities. —**free′dom rid′er,** *n.*

free′ en′terprise, *n.* **1.** the doctrine that a capitalist economy can regulate itself in a competitive market on the basis of supply and demand with a minimum of governmental regulation. **2.** the practice of or right to practice free enterprise.

free′ fall′, *n.* **1.** the hypothetical fall of a body such that the only force acting upon it is gravity. **2.** the part of a parachute jump that precedes the opening of the parachute.

free′ flight′, *n.* the flight of a rocket, missile, or aircraft without guidance or after fuel exhaustion or motor cutoff.

free′-float′ing, *adj.* **1.** lacking an apparent cause, focus, or object; generalized: *free-floating anxiety.* **2.** uncommitted; independent: *free-floating voters.* **3.** capable of relatively free movement.

free′-for-all′, *n.* **1.** a fight, argument, or contest open to everyone and usu. without rules. **2.** a disorderly fight or competitive situation involving various participants.

free′-form′ or **free′form′,** *adj.* **1.** characterized by asymmetrical or irregular form: *free-form sculpture.* **2.** functioning or evolving without advance planning or without following conventional structures; spontaneous: *free-form management.*

free′ hand′, *n.* unrestricted freedom or authority: *They gave the decorator a free hand.*

free•hand (frē′hand′), *adj.* **1.** drawn or executed by hand without guiding instruments, measurements, or other aids: *a freehand map.* —*adv.* **2.** in a freehand manner: *to draw freehand.*

free′-hand′ed, *adj.* **1.** generous; liberal. **2.** FREEHAND. —*adv.* **3.** FREEHAND. —**free′-hand′ed•ly,** *adv.* —**free′-hand′ed•ness,** *n.*

free′-heart′ed, *adj.* **1.** honest; frank. **2.** generous. —**free′-heart′ed•ly,** *adv.* —**free′-heart′ed•ness,** *n.*

free•hold (frē′hōld′), *n.* **1.** an estate in land, inherited or held for life. **2.** a form of tenure by which an estate is inherited or held for life. **3.** an estate held by freehold. —**free′hold′er,** *n.*

free′ kick′, *n.* an unhindered kick of a stationary soccer ball, usu. awarded to a player as the result of a foul committed by an opponent.

free′ lance′, *n.* **1.** a mercenary soldier of the Middle Ages who offered his services to any state or cause. **2.** FREELANCE (defs. 1, 2).

free•lance or **free-lance** (frē′lans′, -läns′, -lans′, -läns′), *n., v.,* **-lanced, -lanc•ing,** *adj., adv.* —*n.* **1.** Also, **free′lanc′er.** a person who sells work or services without working on a regular salary basis for one employer. **2.** a person who contends in causes without personal attachment or allegiance. —*v.i.* **3.** to act or work as a freelance. —*v.t.* **4.** to produce or sell as a freelance. —*adj.* **5.** of or pertaining to a freelance or the work of a freelance. —*adv.* **6.** in the manner of a freelance: *She works freelance.*

free•load (frē′lōd′, -lōd′), *Informal.* —*v.i.* **1.** to take advantage of the generosity of others without offering to help financially. —*v.t.* **2.** to get by freeloading: *to freeload meals.* —**free′load′er,** *n.*

free′ mar′ket, *n.* an economic market regulated by the forces of supply and demand.

free•mar•tin (frē′mär′tn), *n.* a female calf that is born as a twin with a male and is sterile as a result of exposure to masculinizing hormones produced by the male.

Free·ma·son (frē′mā′sən, frē′mā′-), *n.* **1.** a member of a widely distributed secret order (**Free′ and Accept′ed Ma′sons),** having for its object mutual assistance and the promotion of brotherly love among its members. **2.** (*l.c.*) **a.** one of a class of skilled stoneworkers of the Middle Ages, possessing secret signs and passwords. **b.** a member of a society composed of such workers, which also included honorary members not connected with the building trades. —**free′ma·son′ic** (-mə son′ik), *adj.*

free·ma·son·ry (frē′mā′sən rē), *n.* **1.** secret or tacit brotherhood; instinctive sympathy. **2.** (*cap.*) the principles, practices, etc., of Freemasons.

free′ port′, *n.* **1.** a port or special section of a port where goods may be unloaded, stored, and shipped without payment of customs duties. **2.** a port open under equal conditions to all traders.

Free′port Doc′trine, *n.* a policy advocated by Stephen Douglas in 1858 that would give a territorial legislature the right to bar slavery prior to the formation of a state constitution.

fre·er¹ (frē′ər), *n.* a person or thing that frees.

fre·er² (frē′ər), *adj.* comparative of FREE.

free′ rad′ical, *n.* a molecular fragment that bears one or more unpaired electrons and is therefore highly reactive, being capable of rapid oxidizing reactions that destabilize other molecules.

free′-range′, *adj.* **1.** (of livestock and domestic poultry) permitted to graze or forage for grain, etc., rather than being confined to a feedlot or a small enclosure: *a free-range pig.* **2.** of, pertaining to, or produced by free-range animals: *free-range eggs.*

free′ rein′, *n.* unhampered freedom of movement, choice, or action.

free′ ride′, *n.* **1.** *Informal.* something obtained without effort or cost: *The fact that you're the general's son doesn't mean you'll get a free ride in the army.* **2.** *Stud Poker.* a round of betting in which each player checks and therefore receives another card without having to contribute any chips to the pot.

free′ school′, *n.* a privately run school organized as an alternative to the traditional public or private school, usu. following a highly flexible approach to the curriculum and teaching methods.

free·si·a (frē′zhē ə, -zē ə, -zhə), *n., pl.* **-si·as.** any South African plant of the genus *Freesia,* of the iris family, having white, yellow, or pink tubular flowers.

free′ soil′, *n.* a region, esp. a U.S. territory, prohibiting slavery prior to the Civil War.

free′-soil′, *adj.* **1.** pertaining to or opposing the extension of slavery in the Territories. **2.** pertaining to or characteristic of the Free Soil party. —**free′-soil′ism,** *n.*

Free′ Soil′ Par′ty, *n.* a former political party (1845–54) that opposed the extension of slavery into U.S. territories.

fre·est (frē′ist), *adj.* superlative of FREE.

free·stand·ing (frē′stan′ding), *adj.* **1.** (of a sculpture, structure, etc.) unattached to a supporting unit or background; standing alone. **2.** not affiliated with others; autonomous: *a freestanding clinic.*

Free′ State′, *n.* (before the Civil War) a state in which slavery was prohibited.

free·stone (frē′stōn′), *n.* **1.** a peach or other fruit having a pit that does not cling to the pulp. **2.** the pit itself. **3.** a stone, as sandstone, that can be freely worked or quarried without splitting.

free·style (frē′stīl′), *n.* **1. a.** a swimming competition in which any of the standard strokes may be used, according to the swimmer's choice. **b.** the crawl. **2.** a performance or routine intended to demonstrate an individual's special skills or style, as in figure skating or gymnastics. —**free′styl′er,** *n.*

free·think·er (frē′thing′kər), *n.* a person who forms opinions on the basis of reason, independent of authority or tradition, esp. one whose religious opinions differ from established belief.

free′ thought′, *n.* thought unrestrained by deference to authority, tradition, or established belief, esp. in matters of religion.

free′ throw′, *n. Basketball.* FOUL SHOT.

free′ throw′ line′, *n. Basketball.* FOUL LINE (def. 2).

Free·town (frē′toun′), *n.* the capital of Sierra Leone, in W Africa. 469,776.

free′ trade′, *n.* international trade free from protective duties and quotas and subject only to such tariffs as are needed for revenue. —**free′-trade′,** *adj.*

free′ univer′sity, *n.* an institution run informally by and for college students, offering courses not usu. included in a traditional college curriculum.

free′ verse′, *n.* verse with no fixed metrical pattern.

free·ware (frē′wâr′), *n.* computer software distributed without charge. Compare SHAREWARE.

free·way (frē′wā′), *n.* an express highway with no intersections.

free·wheel (frē′hwēl′, -wēl′), *n.* **1.** a device in the transmission of a motor vehicle that automatically disengages the drive shaft whenever it begins to turn more rapidly than the engine. **2.** a rear bicycle wheel that has a device freeing it from the driving mechanism, as when the pedals are stopped in coasting. —*v.i.* **3.** (of a vehicle or its operator) to coast with the wheels disengaged from the driving mechanism. **4.** to move or function freely, independently, or irresponsibly. —**free′wheel′er,** *n.*

free·wheel·ing (frē′hwē′ling, -wē′-), *adj.* **1.** moving about freely. **2.** not concerned with or constrained by rules, conventions, or responsibil-

ities. **3.** (of remarks, actions, etc.) unrestrained; irresponsible: *Loose, freewheeling charges were traded during the trial.*

free′ will′, *n.* **1.** free and independent choice; voluntary decision. **2.** the doctrine that the conduct of human beings expresses personal choice and is not determined by physical or divine forces.

free·will (frē′wil′), *adj.* voluntary: *a freewill contribution.*

free′ world′, *n.* (*often caps.*) the nations of the world that are not under totalitarian control or influence.

freeze (frēz), *v.,* **froze, fro·zen, freez·ing,** *n.* —*v.i.* **1.** to become hardened into ice or into a solid body; change from the liquid to the solid state by loss of heat. **2.** to become hard or stiffened because of loss of heat: *Meat will freeze in a few hours.* **3.** to suffer the effects or sensation of intense cold: *We froze until the heat came on.* **4.** to be of the degree of cold at which water freezes: *It may freeze tonight.* **5.** to lose warmth of feeling: *My heart froze when I heard the news.* **6.** to become speechless or immobilized: *When in front of an audience he froze.* **7.** to stop suddenly and remain motionless: *I froze in my tracks.* **8.** to become obstructed by the formation of ice: *The water pipes froze.* **9.** to die or be injured because of frost or cold. **10.** to become fixed to something by or as if by the action of frost. **11.** to become unfriendly, secretive, or aloof (often fol. by *up*). —*v.t.* **12.** to change from a fluid to a solid form by loss of heat; congeal. **13.** to form ice on the surface of. **14.** to harden or stiffen (an object containing moisture) by cold. **15.** to quick-freeze. **16.** to subject to freezing temperature. **17.** to cause to suffer the effects of intense cold. **18.** to chill with fear. **19.** to immobilize with fright or alarm. **20.** to kill by frost or cold: *A late snow froze the buds.* **21.** to fix fast with ice: *a sled frozen to a sidewalk.* **22.** to obstruct or close by the formation of ice: *Cold had frozen the pipes.* **23.** to fix (rents, prices, etc.) at a specific amount, usu. by government order. **24.** to stop or limit production, use, or development of: *an agreement to freeze nuclear weapons.* **25.** to prevent (assets) from being liquidated or collected. **26.** to render (a part of the body) insensitive to pain or slower in its functioning by artificial means. **27.** to discourage by unfriendly or aloof behavior. **28.** to photograph (a moving subject) at a shutter speed fast enough to produce an unblurred, seemingly motionless image. **29.** to stop by means of a freeze-frame mechanism. **30.** to maintain possession of (a ball or puck) for as long as possible usu. without trying to score. **31. freeze out,** to exclude or compel to withdraw from participation, esp. by cold treatment or severe competition. **32. freeze over,** to become coated with ice. —*n.* **33.** a period of very cold weather, esp. an occurrence of temperatures below 32°F (0°C) persisting for at least several days. **34.** a legislative action to control prices, rents, production, etc. **35.** a decision by one or more nations to stop or limit production or development of weapons.

freeze′-dry′, *v.t.,* **-dried, -dry·ing.** to preserve (foods, blood plasma, antibiotics, etc.) by freezing the substance and then evaporating the moisture content in a high vacuum.

freeze′ frame′, *n.* an optical effect or technique in which a single frame of film is reprinted in a continuous series so as to give the effect of a still photograph when shown.

freez·er (frē′zər), *n.* **1.** a refrigerator, refrigerator compartment, cabinet, or room held at or below 32°F (0°C), used esp. for preserving and storing food. **2.** a machine containing a refrigerant for making ice cream, sherbet, or the like.

freez′er burn′, *n.* light-colored spots that appear on frozen food caused by loss of moisture due to faulty packaging or freezing methods.

freez·ing (frē′zing), *adj.* **1.** (of temperatures) approaching, at, or below the freezing point. **2.** extremely or uncomfortably cold.

freez′ing point′, *n.* the temperature at which a liquid freezes: *The freezing point of water is 32°F, or 0°C.*

freez′ing rain′, *n.* rain that falls as a liquid but freezes into glaze on contact with the ground.

freight (frāt), *n.* **1.** goods, cargo, or lading transported for pay. **2.** the ordinary means of transport of goods provided by common carriers. **3.** the charges for such transportation. —*v.t.* **4.** to load; burden: *freighted with private meaning.* **5.** to load with goods or merchandise for transportation. **6.** to transport as freight.

freight·er (frā′tər), *n.* **1.** a large ship or aircraft used mainly for carrying cargo. **2.** a person whose occupation it is to receive and forward freight.

freight′ ton′, *n.* TON¹ (def. 2).

freight′ train′, *n.* a train of freight cars.

Fre·ling·huy·sen (frē′ling hī′zən), *n.* **Theodore Jacob,** 1691–1747, Dutch Reformed clergyman in America.

Fre·mont (frē′mont), *n.* a city in W California, near San Francisco Bay. 183,575.

Fré·mont (frē′mont), *n.* **John Charles,** 1813–90, U.S. general and explorer: first Republican presidential candidate, 1856.

French¹ (french), *n.* **1.** a Romance language spoken in France, parts of Belgium and Switzerland, and present or former French or Belgian possessions. **2.** (*used with a pl. v.*) **a.** the inhabitants of France. **b.** natives of France or persons of French ancestry. —*adj.* **3.** of or pertaining to France or its inhabitants. **4.** of or pertaining to French or its speakers. —*v.t.* **5.** (*often l.c.*) to cut (snap beans) lengthwise into thin strips before cooking. **6.** (*often l.c.*) to trim the meat from the end of (a rib chop).

French² (french), *n.* **Daniel Chester,** 1850–1931, U.S. sculptor.

French′ and In′dian War′, *n.* the war in America in which France and its Indian allies opposed England 1754–60: treaty signed 1763.

French′ bread′, *n.* a yeast-raised white bread with a thick, crisp crust, typically made in long, slender loaves.

French′ bull′dog, *n.* one of a French breed of small, compact dogs with a large, square head and a short, sleek coat.

French′ Cana′dian, *n.* **1.** a Canadian whose first language is French, esp. a descendant of the colonists of New France. **2.** Also, **French′-Cana′dian.** of or pertaining to French Canadians or the French-speaking parts of Canada.

French′ cuff′, *n.* a double cuff formed by folding back a wide band at the end of a sleeve, usu. fastened by a cuff link.

French′ (or **french′**) **curve′,** *n.* a flat drafting instrument, usu. consisting of a sheet of clear plastic, the edges of which are cut into several scroll-like curves.

French′ dip′, *n.* a hot sandwich of sliced roast beef or other meat served on a roll with pan gravy.

French′ door′, *n.* a door having glass panes throughout its length, usu. hung in pairs.

French′ dress′ing, *n.* (*often l.c.*) **1.** salad dressing prepared chiefly from oil, vinegar, and seasonings; vinaigrette. **2.** a creamy and often sweet salad dressing, usu. orange in color.

French′ fries′, *n.pl.* strips of potato that have been deep-fried. Also called **French′-fried′ pota′toes.**

French′-fry′ or **french′-fry′,** *v.t.,* **-fried, -fry·ing.** to fry in deep fat: *to French-fry onion rings.*

French′ Gui·an′a (gē an′ə, -ä′nə), *n.* an overseas department of France, on the NE coast of South America: formerly a French colony. 73,012; 35,135 sq. mi. (91,000 sq. km). *Cap.:* Cayenne. **—French′ Guianese′, French′ Guian′an,** *adj., n.*

French′ horn′, *n.* a brass wind instrument with a long coiled tube having a conical bore and a flaring bell.

French′ Indochi′na, *n.* an area in SE Asia, formerly a French colonial federation: now comprising the three independent states of Vietnam, Cambodia, and Laos.

French′ leave′, *n.* a departure without ceremony, permission, or notice: *Taking French leave, he evaded his creditors.*

French′ Polyne′sia, *n.* a French overseas territory in the S Pacific, including the Society Islands, Marquesas Islands, and other scattered island groups. 191,400; 1544 sq. mi. (4000 sq. km). *Cap.:* Papeete.

French′ Revolu′tion, *n.* the revolution in France that began in 1789, overthrew the Bourbon monarchy, and ended with Napoleon's seizure of power in 1799.

French′ seam′, *n.* a seam stitched on both sides of the cloth, so as to cover the raw edges.

French′ toast′, *n.* bread dipped in a batter of egg and milk and sautéed until brown.

French′ West′ In′dies, *n.* the French islands in the Lesser Antilles of the West Indies, including Martinique and Guadeloupe and the five dependencies of Guadeloupe: administered as two overseas departments.

French′ win′dow, *n.* one of a pair of casement windows extending to the floor and giving access from a room to a porch, terrace, or garden.

fre·net·ic (frə net′ik), *adj.* frantic; frenzied.

fren·u·lum (fren′yə ləm), *n., pl.* **-la** (-lə). **1.** a small frenum. **2.** a strong spine or group of bristles on the hind wing of many butterflies and moths. **—fren′u·lar,** *adj.*

fre·num (frē′nəm), *n., pl.* **-na** (-nə). a fold of membrane, as on the underside of the tongue, that checks or restrains motion.

fren·zied (fren′zēd), *adj.* **1.** wildly excited or enthusiastic: *frenzied applause.* **2.** violently agitated; frantic; wild: *a frenzied search.* **—fren′zied·ly,** *adv.*

fren·zy (fren′zē), *n., pl.* **-zies,** *v.,* **-zied, -zy·ing.** **—n.** **1.** extreme mental agitation; wild or violent excitement. **2.** a fit or spell of mental derangement resembling or resulting from a mania. **3.** agitated or uncontrollable activity. **—v.t.** **4.** to drive to frenzy; make frantic.

fre·quen·cy (frē′kwən sē), *n., pl.* **-cies.** **1.** Also, **fre′quence.** the state or fact of being frequent; frequent occurrence. **2.** rate of occurrence. **3.** *Physics.* **a.** the number of periods or regularly occurring events of any given kind in a unit of time, usu. one second. **b.** the number of cycles or completed alternations per unit time of a wave or oscillation. *Symbol:* F; *Abbr.:* freq. **4.** *Math.* the number of times a value recurs in a unit change of the independent variable of a given function. **5.** *Statistics.* the number of items occurring in a given category.

fre′quency distribu′tion, *n.* the correspondence of a set of frequencies with the set of categories, intervals, or values into which a statistical population is classified.

fre′quency modula′tion, *n.* See FM.

fre·quent (*adj.* frē′kwənt; *v.* fri kwent′, frē′kwənt), *adj.* **1.** occurring at short intervals: *to make frequent trips to Japan.* **2.** constant, habitual, or regular: *a frequent guest.* **3.** located at short distances apart: *frequent towns along the shore.* **—v.t.** **4.** to visit often; go often to; be often in: *to frequent the art galleries.* **—fre·quent′er,** *n.* **—fre′quent·ly,** *adv.*

fre′quent fli′er, *n.* an airline passenger registered with a program that provides bonuses, as upgrades or free flights, based esp. on distance traveled. **—fre′quent-fli′er,** *adj.*

fres·co (fres′kō), *n., pl.* **-coes, -cos,** *v.,* **-coed, -co·ing.** **—n.** **1.** the art or technique of painting on a moist plaster surface with colors ground up in water or a limewater mixture. **2.** a picture or design so painted. **—v.t.** **3.** to paint in fresco.

fresh (fresh), *adj.* **1.** newly made or obtained: *fresh footprints.* **2.** recently arrived; just come: *fresh from school.* **3.** not previously known; new; novel: *to uncover fresh facts.* **4.** additional or further: *fresh supplies.* **5.** not salty, as water. **6.** not stale or spoiled: *Is the milk still fresh?* **7.** not preserved by freezing, canning, pickling, salting, drying, etc.: *fresh vegetables.* **8.** not tired or fatigued; brisk; vigorous: *She was still fresh after that long walk.* **9.** not faded, worn, obliterated, etc.: *fresh paint.* **10.** looking youthful and healthy: *a fresh beauty.* **11.** pure, cool, or refreshing, as air. **12.** (of wind) moderately strong or brisk. **13.** inexperienced; green; callow: *fresh recruits.* **14.** *Informal.* forward or presumptuous; impertinent. **15.** (of a cow) having recently given birth and begun a new milk flow. **—adv.** **16.** newly; recently; just now: *I am fresh out of ideas.* **—n.** **17.** the fresh part or time. **18.** a freshet. **—v.t., v.i.** **19.** to make or become fresh. **—fresh′ly,** *adv.* **—fresh′ness,** *n.*

fresh′ breeze′, *n.* a wind of 19–24 mph (9–11 m/sec).

fresh·en (fresh′ən), *v.* **1.** to refresh, revive, or renew. **2.** to remove saltiness from. **—v.i.** **3.** to become or grow fresh. **4.** (of a cow) to begin giving milk after calving. **5. freshen up,** to make oneself feel freshly clean, as by washing or changing clothes. **—fresh′en·er,** *n.*

fresh·et (fresh′it), *n.* **1.** a sudden rise in the level of a stream or a flooding caused by heavy rains or the rapid melting of snow and ice. **2.** a freshwater stream flowing into the sea.

fresh′ gale′, *n.* a wind of 39–46 mph (17–33 m/sec).

fresh·man (fresh′mən), *n., pl.* **-men,** *adj.* **—n.** **1.** a student in the first year at a university, college, or high school. **2.** a novice; beginner. **—adj.** **3.** of, pertaining to, or characteristic of a freshman. **4.** lacking seniority or experience; junior: *a freshman senator.* **5.** required of or suitable for freshmen: *freshman English.* **6.** initial; first: *This is my freshman year with the company.*

fresh′ wa′ter, *n.* **1.** water lacking a large amount of salt. **2.** inland water, as ponds, lakes, or streams, that is not salt.

fresh′wa′ter or **fresh′-wa′ter,** *adj.* **1.** of or living in water that is not salt: *freshwater fish.* **2.** accustomed only to fresh water: *a freshwater sailor.* **3.** small, provincial, or little known: *a freshwater college.*

Fres·no (frez′nō), *n.* a city in central California. 386,551.

fret[1] (fret), *v.,* **fret·ted, fret·ting.** **—v.i.** **1.** to feel or express worry, annoyance or discontent: *Fretting about the lost ring isn't going to help.* **2.** to cause corrosion; gnaw into something: *acids that fret at the strongest metals.* **3.** to make a way by gnawing, corrosion, wearing away, etc.: *The river frets at its banks until a new channel is formed.* **4.** to become eaten, worn, or corroded (often fol. by *away*). **5.** to move in agitation or commotion, as water. **—v.t.** **6.** to irritate, annoy, or vex; torment: *You mustn't fret yourself about that.* **7.** to wear away or consume by gnawing, friction, rust, corrosion, etc. **8.** to form or make by wearing away a substance. **9.** to agitate (water). **—n.** **10.** an irritated state of mind; annoyance; vexation. **11.** erosion; corrosion. **12.** a worn or eroded place.

fret

fret[2] (fret), *n., v.,* **fret·ted, fret·ting.** **—n.** **1.** an interlaced, angular design; fretwork. **2.** an angular design of bands within a border. **3.** a piece of decoratively pierced work placed in a clock case to deaden the sound of the mechanism. **—v.t.** **4.** to ornament with a fret or fretwork.

fret[3] (fret), *n., v.,* **fret·ted, fret·ting.** **—n.** **1.** any of the ridges of wood, metal, or string, set across the fingerboard of an instrument, as a guitar or lute, to help the fingers stop the strings at the correct points. **—v.t.** **2.** to provide with frets. **—fret′less,** *adj.*

fret·ful (fret′fəl), *adj.* disposed or quick to fret; irritable; peevish. **—fret′ful·ly,** *adv.* **—fret′ful·ness,** *n.*

fret′ saw′, *n.* a long narrow-bladed saw used to cut ornamental work from thin wood.

fret·work (fret′wûrk′), *n.* ornamental work consisting of interlacing parts, esp. work with the design formed by perforation.

Freud (froid), *n.* **1. Anna,** 1895–1982, British psychoanalyst, born in Austria (daughter of Sigmund Freud). **2. Lucian,** born 1932, British painter, born in Germany. **3. Sigmund,** 1856–1939, Austrian neurologist: founder of psychoanalysis.

Freud′ian slip′, *n.* an inadvertent mistake in speech or writing that supposedly reveals an unconscious motive, wish, attitude, etc.

fri·a·ble (frī′ə bəl), *adj.* easily crumbled or reduced to powder; crumbly: *friable rock.* **—fri′a·bil′i·ty, fri′a·ble·ness,** *n.*

fri·ar (frī′ər), *n.* a man who is a member of a Roman Catholic religious order, esp. the mendicant orders. [< Old French < Latin *frāter* brother] **—fri′ar·y,** *n., pl.* **-ar·ies.**

frib·ble (frib′əl), *v.,* **-bled, -bling,** *n.* **—v.i.** **1.** to act in a foolish or frivolous manner; trifle. **2.** to waste foolishly (often fol. by *away*): *to fribble away time.* **—n. 3.** a frivolous person or thing.

fric·as·see (frik′ə sē′), *n., v.,* **-seed, -see·ing.** **—n.** **1.** chicken or other meat cut in pieces, lightly sautéed, stewed, and served in a white sauce. **—v.t. 2.** to prepare as a fricassee.

fric·a·tive (frik′ə tiv), *n.* **1.** a consonant sound, as (th), (v), or (h), characterized by audible friction produced by forcing the breath through a constricted or partially obstructed passage in the vocal tract. —*adj.* **2.** of or pertaining to a fricative.

Frick (frik), *n.* Henry Clay, 1849–1919, U.S. industrialist and art patron.

fric•tion (frik′shən), *n.* **1.** surface resistance to relative motion, as of a body sliding or rolling. **2.** the rubbing of the surface of one body against that of another. **3.** dissension, as between persons or nations, because of differing views. —**fric′tion•al,** *adj.* —**fric′tion•less,** *adj.*

fric′tion tape′, *n.* a cloth or plastic adhesive tape impregnated with a moisture-resistant substance and used esp. to insulate and protect electrical wires and conductors.

Fri•day (frī′dā, -dē), *n.* the sixth day of the week, following Thursday.

fried•cake (frīd′kāk′), *n.* a small cake cooked in deep fat.

friend (frend), *n.* **1.** a person attached to another by feelings of affection or personal regard. **2.** a person who gives assistance; patron; supporter: *friends of the Boston Symphony.* **3.** a person who is on good terms with another; a person who is not hostile: *Who goes there? Friend or foe?* **4.** a member of the same nation, party, etc. **5.** (*cap.*) a member of the Society of Friends; Quaker. —*Idiom.* **6. fair-weather friend,** one who is unreliable when a friend needs help. **7. make friends with,** to enter into friendly relations with; become a friend to. —*Proverb.* **8. A friend in need is a friend indeed,** a true friend is one who helps no matter what the circumstances. —**friend′less,** *adj.*

friend•ly (frend′lē), *adj.,* **-li•er, -li•est,** *adv., n., pl.* **-lies.** —*adj.* **1.** characteristic of or befitting a friend: *a friendly greeting.* **2.** like a friend; kind; helpful. **3.** favorably disposed; inclined to approve, help, or support. **4.** not hostile or at variance; amicable. **5.** easy or pleasant to use, operate, understand, or experience (usu. used in combination): *visitor-friendly museums; viewer-friendly art; a friendly computer.* —*adv.* **6.** Also, **friend′li•ly.** in a friendly manner; like a friend. —*n.* **7.** a person who is friendly; one who shows no hostility. —**friend′li•ness,** *n.*

friend′ly fire′, *n.* fire, as by artillery, by one's own forces, that causes casualties to one's own troops.

Friend′ly Is′lands, *n.pl.* Tonga.

friend′ of the court′, *n. Law.* Amicus curiae.

friend•ship (frend′ship), *n.* **1.** the state of being a friend; association as friends: *to value a person's friendship.* **2.** a friendly relation or intimacy. **3.** friendly feeling or disposition.

Friend′ Who′ Came′ at Mid′night, The, a parable of Jesus. Luke 11:5–8.

fri•er (frī′ər), *n.* Fryer.

fries (frīz), *n.pl.* **1.** pl. of Fry¹. **2.** fried potatoes. —*v.* **3.** 3rd pers. sing. pres. indic. of Fry¹.

frieze¹ (frēz), *n.* **1.** the part of an entablature in classical architecture between the architrave and the cornice, often decorated with sculpture in low relief. **2.** a decorative, often carved band, as near the top of a wall or piece of furniture.

frieze² (frēz), *n.* **1.** a heavy, napped woolen cloth for coats. **2.** a heavy fabric with uncut pile loops, made of wool, mohair, cotton, or synthetic fibers and used for draperies and upholstery.

frig•ate (frig′it), *n.* **1.** a fast naval vessel of the late 18th and early 19th centuries, generally having a lofty ship rig and being heavily armed on one or two decks. **2.** a modern warship, ranging in size from a destroyer escort to a cruiser.

frig′ate bird′ or **frig′ate•bird′,** *n.* any of several long-winged, fork-tailed seabirds of the family Fregatidae, of tropical oceans, noted for snatching prey from other birds in flight. Also called **man-o′-war bird.**

fright (frīt), *n.* **1.** sudden and extreme fear; a sudden terror. **2.** a person or thing of shocking, grotesque, or ridiculous appearance.

fright•en (frīt′n), *v.t.* **1.** to make afraid or fearful; throw into a fright; terrify; scare. **2.** to drive by scaring (usu. fol. by *away, off,* etc.): *to frighten away pigeons from the roof.* —*v.i.* **3.** to become frightened: *a timid child who frightens easily.* —**fright′en•ing•ly,** *adv.*

fright•ful (frīt′fəl), *adj.* **1.** such as to cause fright; dreadful, terrible, or alarming: *a frightful explosion.* **2.** horrible, shocking, or revolting: *The storm did frightful damage.* **3.** *Informal.* unpleasant; disagreeable: *We had a frightful time.* **4.** *Informal.* very great; extreme: *That actor is a frightful ham.* —**fright′ful•ly,** *adv.* —**fright′ful•ness,** *n.*

frig•id (frij′id), *adj.* **1.** very cold in temperature: *a frigid climate.* **2. a.** without warmth of feeling; without ardor or enthusiasm: *a frigid reaction to the proposed law.* **b.** stiff or formal: *a polite but frigid welcome.* **3.** (of a woman) **a.** unable to experience an orgasm or sexual excitement during sexual intercourse. **b.** unresponsive to sexual advances or stimuli. **4.** unemotional or unimaginative: *a correct but frigid presentation.* —**fri•gid′i•ty,** *n.* —**frig′id•ly,** *adv.*

Frig•id•aire (frij′i dâr′), *Trademark.* a brand of electric refrigerator.

Frig′id Zone′, *n.* either of two regions, one between the Arctic Circle and the North Pole, or one between the Antarctic Circle and the South Pole.

fri•jol (frē hōl′) also **fri•jo•le** (-hō′lē), *n., pl.* **-jo•les** (-hō′lēz). any bean used for food, esp. the kidney bean.

frill (fril), *n.* **1.** a trimming, as a strip of cloth or lace, gathered at one edge and left loose at the other; ruffle. **2.** something resembling such a trimming, as the fringe of hair on the chest of some dogs or a flap of skin at the neck of certain lizards. **3.** affectation of manner, style, etc. **4.** something superfluous; luxury. —*v.t.* **5.** to trim with a frill or frills. **6.** to form into a frill. —**frill′i•ness,** *n.* —**frill′y,** *adj.,* **-i•er, -i•est.**

frilled′ liz′ard, *n.* an Australian lizard, *Chlamydosaurus kingi,* with a neck frill that enlarges in courtship or threat displays.

fringe (frinj), *n., v.,* **fringed, fring•ing.** —*n.* **1.** a decorative border of threads, cords, or the like, usu. hanging loosely from a raveled edge or separate strip. **2.** anything resembling or suggesting this; border; rim: *a fringe of grass.* **3.** an outer edge; margin; periphery: *on the fringe of the art world.* **4.** something regarded as peripheral, marginal, secondary, or extreme in relation to something else: *the lunatic fringe of a political party.* **5.** *Optics.* one of the alternate light and dark bands produced by diffraction or interference. **6.** Fringe benefit. —*v.t.* **7.** to furnish with or as if with a fringe. **8.** to serve as a fringe for, or to be arranged so as to suggest a fringe: *armed guards fringing the building.*

fringe′ ar′ea, *n.* an area in which radio or television reception is weak or distorted.

fringe′ ben′efit, *n.* a benefit, such as free life or health insurance or a pension, received by an employee in addition to regular pay.

fringed′ gen′tian, *n.* a gentian, *Gentianopsis crinita,* having a tubular blue corolla with four fringed petals.

fringed′ or′chis, *n.* any of several American orchids of the genus *Habenaria,* having a cut, fringed lip. Also called **fringed′ or′chid.**

fringe′ tree′, *n.* a small tree, *Chionanthus virginicus,* of the olive family, native to the southeastern U.S., bearing open clusters of long drooping white flowers.

frip•per•y (frip′ə rē), *n., pl.* **-per•ies. 1.** finery in dress, esp. when showy or gaudy. **2.** empty display; ostentation. **3.** gewgaws; trifles.

Fris•bee (friz′bē), *Trademark.* a brand of plastic concave disk, used for various catching games.

fri•sé (fri zā′), *n.* a rug or upholstery fabric having the pile in uncut loops or in a combination of cut and uncut loops.

Fri′sian Is′lands, *n.pl.* a chain of islands in the North Sea, extending along the coasts of the Netherlands, Germany, and Denmark: includes groups belonging to the Netherlands and to Germany and a group divided between Germany and Denmark.

frisk (frisk), *v.i.* **1.** to dance, leap, skip, or gambol; frolic: *The dogs and children frisked about on the lawn.* —*v.t.* **2.** to search (a person) for concealed weapons, contraband goods, etc., by feeling the person's clothing: *to frisk a crime suspect.* —*n.* **3.** a leap, skip, or caper. **4.** a frolic or gambol. **5.** the act of frisking a person.

frisk•y (fris′kē), *adj.,* **frisk•i•er, frisk•i•est.** lively; frolicsome; playful. —**frisk′i•ly,** *adv.* —**frisk′i•ness,** *n.*

frit or **fritt** (frit), *n., v.,* **frit•ted, frit•ting.** —*n.* **1.** a fused or partially fused material used as a basis for glazes or enamels. **2.** fused or calcined material prepared as part of the batch in glassmaking. —*v.t.* **3.** to fuse (materials) in making frit.

frit′ fly′, *n.* a minute European fly, *Oscinella frit,* the larvae of which are pests of grain.

frith (frith), *n.* Firth.

frit•il•lar•y (frit′l er′ē), *n., pl.* **-lar•ies. 1.** any of several orange-brown nymphalid butterflies having silvery spots on the undersides of the wings and often black borders and dots above. **2.** any of various bulbous plants of the genus *Fritillaria,* of the lily family, having bell-shaped flowers.

frit•ta•ta (fri tä′tə), *n., pl.* **-tas.** an unfolded omelet in which the eggs are mixed with vegetables, cheese, or other ingredients, cooked slowly over low heat, and then browned on top.

frit•ter¹ (frit′ər), *v.t.* **1.** to squander or disperse piecemeal; waste little by little (usu. fol. by *away*): *to fritter away one's money.* **2.** to break or tear into small pieces. —*v.i.* **3.** to dwindle, shrink, degenerate, etc. (often fol. by *away*): *to watch one's fortune fritter away.* **4.** to separate into fragments: *a plastic material having a tendency to fritter.* —*n.* **5.** a small piece, fragment, or shred.

frit•ter² (frit′ər), *n.* a small cake of fried batter, often containing corn, fruit, or other food.

fritz (frits), *n., Idiom.* **on the fritz,** *Informal.* not in working order: *Our TV went on the fritz last night.*

friv•o•lous (friv′ə ləs), *adj.* **1.** characterized by lack of seriousness or sense: *frivolous conduct.* **2.** (of a person) given to trifling or undue levity. **3.** of little or no weight, worth, or importance; not worthy of serious notice: *a frivolous suggestion.* —**fri•vol′i•ty** (fri vol′i tē), *n.* —**friv′o•lous•ly,** *adv.*

frizz (friz), *v.i., v.t.* **1.** to form into small crisp curls or little tufts. —*n.* **2.** something frizzed, as hair. —**friz′zy,** *adj.,* **-zi•er, -zi•est.**

friz•zle¹ (friz′əl), *v.,* **-zled, -zling,** *n.* —*v.t., v.i.* **1.** Frizz. —*n.* **2.** a short crisp curl. —**friz′zler,** *n.*

friz•zle² (friz′əl), *v.,* **-zled, -zling.** —*v.i.* **1.** to make a sizzling or sputtering noise in frying or the like: *bacon frizzling on the stove.* —*v.t.* **2.** to make (food) crisp by frying.

fro (frō), *adv.* from; back (used esp. in the phrase *to and fro*).

frock (frok), *n.* **1.** a gown or dress worn by a girl or woman. **2.** a smock worn by peasants and workers. **3.** a coarse outer garment with large sleeves, worn by monks. —*v.t.* **4.** to provide with, or clothe in, a frock. **5.** to invest with priestly or clerical office.

frog¹ (frog, frôg), *n., v.,* **frogged, frog•ging,** *adj.* —*n.* **1.** any tailless stout-bodied amphibian of the order Anura, including the smooth, moist-skinned frog species that live in a damp or semiaquatic habitat and the warty drier-skinned toad species that are mostly terrestrial as adults. **2.** any frog of the widespread family Ranidae, which are mostly semiaquatic and have smooth, moist skin and long hind legs used for leaping. **3.** a slight hoarseness: *a frog in the throat.* **4.** a small holder made of heavy material, placed in a bowl or vase to hold flower stems in position. **5.** the nut of a violin bow. —*v.i.* **6.** to hunt and catch frogs. —**frog′gy,** *adj.*

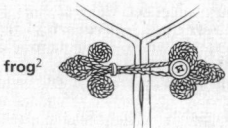

frog²

frog² (frog, frôg), *n.* **1.** an ornamental fastening for the front of a coat, consisting of a button and a loop through which it passes. **2.** a sheath suspended from a belt and supporting a scabbard.

frog³ (frog, frôg), *n.* a device at the intersection of two railroad tracks to permit the wheels and flanges on one track to cross or branch from the other.

frog⁴ (frog, frôg), *n.* a triangular mass of elastic horny substance in the middle of the sole of the foot of a horse or related animal.

frog·eye (frog′ī′, frôg′ī′), *n.*, *pl.* **-eyes** for 1. **1.** a small whitish leaf spot with a narrow darker border, produced by certain fungi. **2.** a plant disease so characterized. —**frog′eyed′,** *adj.*

frog·fish (frog′fish′, frôg′-), *n.*, *pl.* (*esp. collectively*) **-fish**, (*esp. for kinds or species*) **-fish·es.** **1.** any tropical marine fish of the family Antennariidae, having a wide froglike mouth and broad limblike pectoral fins. **2.** ANGLER (def. 3).

frog·hop·per (frog′hop′ər, frôg′-), *n.* any of several leaping homopterous insects of the family Cercopidae, which as a larva is surrounded by a frothy mass.

frog′ kick′, *n.* a swimming kick in which the legs are bent at the knees, extended outward, and then brought together forcefully.

frog·man (frog′man′, -mən, frôg′-), *n.*, *pl.* **-men** (-men′, -mən). a swimmer specially equipped with air tanks, wet suit, diving mask, etc., for underwater demolition, salvage, scientific exploration, etc.

frog·mouth (frog′mouth′, frôg′-), *n.*, *pl.* **-mouths** (-mouthz′, -mouths′). any of various large, very broad-mouthed nocturnal birds of the family Podargidae, of S and SE Asia and Australasia, akin to and resembling the goatsuckers.

frog's′-bit′ fam′ily, *n.* a family, Hydrocharitaceae, of aquatic plants with white flowers on long stalks and a berrylike fruit: includes elodea and tape grass.

Frois·sart (froi′särt; *Fr.* ᴿᴿwa sar′), *n.* **Jean** (zhän), 1333?–c1400, French chronicler.

frol·ic (frol′ik), *n.*, *v.*, **-icked, -ick·ing,** *adj.* —*n.* **1.** merry play; merriment; gaiety; fun. **2.** a merrymaking or party. **3.** playful behavior or action; prank. —*v.i.* **4.** to gambol merrily; to play in a frisky, light-spirited manner; romp: *The children were frolicking in the snow.* **5.** to have fun; engage in merrymaking; play merry pranks. —*adj.* **6.** merry; full of fun.

from (frum, from; *unstressed* frəm), *prep.* **1.** (used to specify a starting point in spatial movement): *a train running west from Chicago.* **2.** (used to specify a starting point in an expression of limits): *The number of stores will be increased from 25 to 30.* **3.** (used to express removal or separation, as in space, time, or order): *two miles from shore; 30 minutes from now; from one page to the next.* **4.** (used to express discrimination or distinction): *to be excluded from membership; to differ from one's father.* **5.** (used to indicate source or origin): *to come from the Midwest.* **6.** (used to indicate agent or instrumentality): *death from starvation.* **7.** (used to indicate cause or reason): *From the evidence, he must be guilty.*

From′ Green′land's I′cy Moun′tains, a Christian missionary hymn (1818) with words by Reginald Heber and music by Lowell Mason.

frond (frond), *n.* **1.** an often large, finely divided leaf, esp. as applied to the ferns and certain palms. **2.** a leaflike expansion not differentiated into stem and foliage, as in lichens. —**frond′ed,** *adj.*

frons (fronz), *n.*, *pl.* **fron·tes** (fron′tēz). the upper front portion of the head, esp. of an insect.

front (frunt), *n.* **1.** the foremost part or surface of anything. **2.** the part or side of anything that faces forward: *the front of a jacket.* **3.** the part or side of anything, as a building, that seems to look out or to be directed forward: *We sat in the front of the restaurant.* **4.** any side or face, as of a house. **5.** a facade, considered with respect to its architectural treatment or material: *a cast-iron front.* **6.** a property line along a street or the like: *a fifty-foot front.* **7.** a place or position directly before anything. **8.** a position of leadership in a particular endeavor or field: *She rose to the front of her profession.* **9. a.** the foremost line or part of an army. **b.** a line of battle. **c.** the place where combat operations are carried on. **10.** an area of activity, conflict, or competition: *news from the business front.* **11.** land facing a road, river, etc.; frontage. **12.** a distinguished person listed as an official of an organization for the sake of prestige but usu. inactive. **13.** a person or thing that serves as a cover for some other activity, esp. one of a secret, disreputable, or illegal nature; a blind: *The store was a front for gamblers.* **14.** outward impres-

sion of rank, position, or wealth. **15.** bearing or demeanor in confronting anything: *a calm front.* **16.** the forehead, or the entire face. **17.** a coalition or movement to achieve a particular end, usu. political: *the people's front.* **18.** an article of clothing worn over the breast, as a dickey. **19.** an interface or zone of transition between two dissimilar air masses. **20. a.** the auditorium of a theater. **b.** the business offices of a theater. **c.** the front of the stage; downstage. —*adj.* **21.** of or pertaining to the front. **22.** situated in or at the front: *front seats.* **23.** (of a speech sound) articulated with the tongue blade relatively far forward in the mouth, as either of the sounds of *tea.* —*v.t.* **24.** to have the front toward; face: *Our house fronts the lake.* **25.** to meet face to face; confront. **26.** to face in opposition, hostility, or defiance. **27.** to furnish or supply a front to: *to front a building with sandstone.* **28.** to serve as a front to: *A long, sloping lawn fronted their house.* **29.** to lead (a jazz or dance band). **30.** to articulate (a speech sound) at a position farther front in the mouth. —*v.i.* **31.** to have or turn the front in some specified direction: *Our house fronts on the lake.* **32.** to serve as a cover or disguise for another activity, esp. something of an illegal nature: *The shop fronts for a narcotics ring.* —*interj.* **33.** (used to call or command someone to come, look, etc., to the front, as in an order to troops on parade or in calling a hotel bellhop to the front desk). —*Idiom.* **34. in front,** in a forward place or position. **35. in front of, a.** ahead of. **b.** outside the entrance of. **c.** in the presence of. **36. out front, a.** outside the entrance. **b.** ahead of competitors. **c.** in or toward the theater audience or auditorium. **d.** *Informal.* candidly; frankly. **37. up front,** *Informal.* **a.** in advance; before anything else: *You'll have to make a payment of $5,000 up front.* **b.** frank; open; direct: *I want you to be up front with me.*

front·age (frun′tij), *n.* **1.** the front of a building or lot. **2.** the lineal extent of this front. **3.** the direction it faces. **4.** land abutting on a river, street, etc. **5.** the space lying between a building and the street, a body of water, etc.

fron·tal (frun′tl), *adj.* **1.** of, in, or at the front: *a frontal view; a frontal attack.* **2.** *Anat.* of, pertaining to, or situated near the forehead or the frontal bone. **3.** of or pertaining to the division between dissimilar air masses. **4.** of, pertaining to, or exhibiting frontality. —*n.* **5.** a movable cover or hanging for the front of an altar. **6.** FRONTLET (def. 1). —**front′al·ly,** *adv.*

fron′tal bone′, *n.* the broad front part of the skull, forming the forehead.

fron·tal·i·ty (frun tal′i tē, fron-), *n.* **1.** the representation of the front view of figures or objects in a work of art. **2.** the organization of planes parallel to the picture plane in the pictorial arts.

fron′tal lobe′, *n.* the anterior part of each cerebral hemisphere.

front′ burn′er, *n.* a condition or position of top priority: *to keep the issue of unemployment on the front burner.*

front′ court′, *n.* **1.** the section of the court nearest the front wall in certain games, as squash or handball. **2.** *Basketball.* **a.** a team's offensive half of the court. **b.** the players who play offensively in the front court, including the center and the two forwards.

fron·tier (frun tēr′, fron-), *n.* **1.** the part of a country that borders another country; boundary; border. **2.** land that forms the furthest extent of a country's settled or inhabited regions. **3.** Often, **frontiers.** the limit of knowledge or the most advanced achievement in a particular field. —*adj.* **4.** of, pertaining to, or located on the frontier: *a frontier town.*

fron·tiers·man (frun tērz′mən, fron-; *esp. Brit.* frun′tērz-), *n.*, *pl.* **-men.** a person who lives on a frontier.

fron·tis·piece (frun′tis pēs′, fron′-), *n.* **1.** an illustrated leaf preceding the title page of a book. **2.** a facade of a building, or a part of a facade, often highlighted by ornamentation.

front·lash (frunt′lash′), *n.* an action or opinion that is in reaction to a backlash.

front·let (frunt′lit), *n.* **1.** a decorative band, ribbon, etc., worn across the forehead. **2.** the forehead of a horse, deer, or similar mammal. **3.** the forehead of a bird when marked by a distinctive color or texture of the plumage. **4.** *Judaism.* the phylactery worn on the forehead.

front′ line′, *n.* **1.** FRONT (def. 9). **2.** the visible forefront in any action, activity, or field.

front′-line′, *adj.* **1.** located or designed to be used at a military front line: *a front-line helicopter.* **2.** of, pertaining to, or involving the forefront in any action, activity, or field: *front-line athletics.* **3.** highly proficient in the performance of one's duties.

front·man (frunt′man′), *n.*, *pl.* **-men** (-men′). **1.** a performer, as a singer, who leads a musical group. **2.** a person who serves as the nominal head of an organization and who represents it publicly. Also, *esp. for 2,* **front′ man′.**

front′ mat′ter, *n.* all material in a book that precedes the text proper.

front′ mon′ey, *n.* **1.** money paid in advance, as for goods or services. **2.** capital necessary to begin a business enterprise.

front′ of′fice, *n.* the executive or administrative officers of a company, organization, etc. —**front′-of′fice,** *adj.*

fron·ton (fron′ton), *n.* **1.** a building in which jai alai is played. **2.** JAI ALAI.

front′-page′, *adj.*, *v.*, **-paged, -pag·ing.** —*adj.* **1.** of major importance; worth putting on the first page of a newspaper. —*v.t.* **2.** to run (copy) on the front page of a newspaper.

front′-run′ner or **front′run′ner,** *n.* **1.** a person who leads in any competition. **2.** an entrant in a race who breaks to the front and establishes the pace. **3.** an entrant in a race who performs well only when ahead of the field. —**front′-run′ning,** *adj.*

front·ward (frunt′wərd) also **front′wards,** *adv.* in a direction toward the front.

front′-wheel′ drive′, *n.* an automotive drive system in which engine power is transmitted through the front wheels only.

frost (frôst, frost), *n.* **1.** a degree or state of coldness sufficient to cause the freezing of water. **2.** a covering of minute ice crystals, formed from the atmosphere at night upon the ground and exposed objects when they have cooled by radiation below the dew point. **3.** the act or process of freezing. **4.** coldness of manner or temperament. **5.** *Informal.* something that meets with lack of enthusiasm, as a theatrical performance or party; failure; flop. —*v.t.* **6.** to cover with frost. **7.** to give a frostlike surface to (glass, metal, etc.). **8.** to cover or decorate with frosting or icing; ice: *to frost a cake.* **9.** to bleach selected strands of (a person's hair). **10.** to kill or injure by frost. **11.** to make angry. —*v.i.* **12.** to become covered with frost or freeze (often fol. by *up* or *over*). **13.** (of varnish, paint, etc.) to dry with a film resembling frost. —**frost′like′,** *adj.*

Frost (frôst, frost), *n.* **Robert (Lee),** 1874–1963, U.S. poet.

frost·bite (frôst′bīt′, frost′-), *n., v.,* **-bit, -bit·ten, -bit·ing.** —*n.* **1.** injury to any part of the body after excessive exposure to extreme cold. —*v.t.* **2.** to injure by frost or extreme cold.

frost·ed (frô′stid, fros′tid), *adj.* **1.** covered with or having frost. **2.** made frostlike in appearance, as certain translucent glass. **3.** coated or decorated with frosting or icing. **4.** (of hair) highlighted, esp. by bleaching selected strands. **5.** quick-frozen. —*n.* **6.** a thick beverage of milk, ice cream, and flavoring.

frost′ heave′, *n.* an uplift in soil caused by the freezing of internal moisture.

frost·ing (frô′sting, fros′ting), *n.* **1.** a sweet, creamy mixture for coating or filling cakes, cookies, etc.; icing. **2.** a dull or lusterless finish, as on metal or glass. **3.** a process of highlighting the hair by bleaching selected strands. **4.** a material used for decorative work, as for signs and displays, made from flakes of powdered glass.

frost·line (frôst′līn′, frost′-), *n.* **1.** the maximum depth at which soil is frozen. **2.** the lower limit of permafrost.

frost·y (frô′stē, fros′tē), *adj.,* **frost·i·er, frost·i·est. 1.** characterized by or producing frost; freezing; very cold: *frosty weather.* **2.** consisting of or covered with a frost. **3.** lacking warmth of feeling; unfriendly: *a frosty greeting.* **4.** resembling frost; white or gray: *a wedding dress of frosty satin.* **5.** of or characteristic of old age: *a frosty brow.* —**frost′i·ly,** *adv.* —**frost′i·ness,** *n.* —**frost′less,** *adj.*

froth (frôth, froth), *n.* **1.** an aggregation of bubbles, as on an agitated liquid or at the mouth of a hard-driven horse; foam. **2.** a foam of saliva or fluid resulting from disease. **3.** something unsubstantial, trivial, or evanescent: *The play was a bit of froth.* —*v.t.* **4.** to cover with froth. **5.** to cause to foam. **6.** to emit like froth. —*v.i.* **7.** to give out froth; foam: *frothing at the mouth.* —**froth′y,** *adj.,* **-i·er, -i·est.**

frot·tage (frô täzh′), *n.* a technique in the visual arts of obtaining textural effects or images by rubbing lead, chalk, charcoal, etc., over paper laid on a granular or relieflike surface.

frou·frou (frōō′frōō′), *n., pl.* **-frous. 1.** elaborate decoration, esp. on women's clothing. **2.** a rustling, as of silk.

fro·ward (frō′wərd, frō′ərd), *adj.* willfully contrary; not easily managed. —**fro′ward·ly,** *adv.* —**fro′ward·ness,** *n.*

frown (froun), *v.i.* **1.** to contract the brow, as in displeasure or deep thought; scowl. **2.** to look displeased. **3.** to look disapprovingly (usu. fol. by *on* or *upon*): *to frown on a scheme.* —*v.t.* **4.** to express by a frown. **5.** to force or shame with a disapproving frown. —*n.* **6.** a frowning look; scowl. **7.** any expression or show of disapproval.

frowz·y (frou′zē), *adj.,* **frowz·i·er, frowz·i·est. 1.** dirty and untidy; slovenly. **2.** ill-smelling; musty. —**frowz′i·ly,** *adv.* —**frowz′i·ness,** *n.*

froze (frōz), *v.* pt. of FREEZE.

fro·zen (frō′zən), *v.* **1.** pp. of FREEZE. —*adj.* **2.** congealed by cold; turned into ice. **3.** covered with ice, as a stream. **4.** frigid; very cold. **5.** injured or killed by frost or cold. **6.** obstructed by ice, as pipes. **7.** chilly or cold in manner: *a frozen stare.* **8.** preserved by quick-freezing: *frozen foods.* **9.** (of food) prepared by chilling or freezing. **10.** (esp. of a drink) mixed with ice and puréed in an electric blender. **11.** (of an asset) not convertible into cash without substantial loss. **12.** not permitted to be changed or incapable of being altered; fixed: *frozen rents.*

FRS, Federal Reserve System.

frt., freight.

fructi-, a combining form meaning "fruit": *fructiferous.*

fruc·tif·er·ous (fruk tif′ər əs, frŏŏk-, frŏŏk-), *adj.* fruit-bearing; producing fruit. —**fruc·tif′er·ous·ly,** *adv.*

fruc·ti·fy (fruk′tə fī′, frŏŏk′-, frŏŏk′-), *v.,* **-fied, -fy·ing.** —*v.i.* **1.** to bear fruit. —*v.t.* **2.** to make fruitful or productive; fertilize.

fruc·tose (fruk′tōs, frŏŏk′-, frŏŏk′-), *n.* a crystalline, water-soluble, levorotatory ketose sugar, $C_6H_{12}O_6$, sweeter than sucrose, occurring in invert sugar, honey, and many fruits: chiefly used in foodstuffs.

fru·gal (frōō′gəl), *adj.* **1.** economical in use or expenditure; prudently saving or sparing; not wasteful: *a frugal manager.* **2.** entailing little expense; requiring few resources; meager; scanty: *a frugal meal.* —**fru·gal′i·ty, fru′gal·ness,** *n.* —**fru′gal·ly,** *adv.*

fruit (frōōt), *n., pl.* **fruits,** (*esp. collectively*) **fruit,** *v.* —*n.* **1.** the edible part of a plant developed from a flower and containing one or more seeds with any accessory tissues, as the peach, mulberry, or banana. **2.** the developed ovary of a seed plant with its contents and accessory parts, as the pea pod, nut, tomato, or pineapple. **3.** any product of plant growth useful to humans or animals. **4.** the spores and accessory organs of ferns, mosses, fungi, algae, or lichen. **5.** anything produced or accruing; product, result, or effect: *the fruits of one's labors.* —*v.i., v.t.* **6.** to bear or cause to bear fruit. —*Proverb.* **7. By their fruits shall ye know them,** people are known by their actions and accomplishments. Matt. 7:20. —**fruit′like′,** *adj.*

fruit′ bat′, *n.* any fruit-eating tropical Old World bat of the family Pteropodidae.

fruit·cake (frōōt′kāk′), *n.* **1.** a rich cake containing dried or candied fruit, nuts, spices, etc. **2.** *Slang.* a crazy or eccentric person.

fruit′ cup′, *n.* an assortment of fruits cut into pieces and served in a cup or glass as an appetizer or dessert.

fruit′ fly′, *n.* **1.** any of numerous small flies of the family Tephritidae, whose eggs are deposited in fruit for the larvae to feed on after hatching. **2.** Also called **drosophila.** any of numerous similar flies of the family Drosophilidae, which feed on the yeasts of fermenting fruit, esp. *D. melanogaster,* used in laboratory studies because of its large chromosomes and short life cycle.

fruit·ful (frōōt′fəl), *adj.* **1.** producing good results; beneficial; profitable. **2.** producing an abundant growth, as of fruit. —**fruit′ful·ly,** *adv.* —**fruit′ful·ness,** *n.*

fru·i·tion (frōō ish′ən), *n.* **1.** attainment of anything desired; realization; accomplishment: *to bring an idea to fruition.* **2.** enjoyment, as of something attained or realized. **3.** the state of bearing fruit.

fruit·less (frōōt′lis), *adj.* **1.** useless; unproductive; without results or success: *a fruitless search.* **2.** bearing no fruit; barren. —**fruit′less·ly,** *adv.* —**fruit′less·ness,** *n.*

fruit·let (frōōt′lit), *n.* a small fruit, esp. one of those forming an aggregate fruit.

fruit′ sug′ar, *n.* FRUCTOSE.

fruit·wood (frōōt′wŏŏd′), *n.* any of various woods from fruit-bearing trees, used for cabinetmaking and the like.

fruit·y (frōō′tē), *adj.,* **fruit·i·er, fruit·i·est. 1.** resembling fruit; having the taste or smell of fruit. **2.** rich in flavor. **3.** (of wine) having a grapelike taste. **4.** excessively sweet or mellifluous; cloying: *fruity prose; a fruity voice.* **5.** *Slang.* insane; crazy. —**fruit′i·ness,** *n.*

frum (frŏŏm), *adj. Yiddish.* religious; observant.

fru·men·ta·ceous (frōō′mən tā′shəs), *adj.* of the nature of or resembling wheat or other grain.

frump (frump), *n.* **1.** a woman who is dowdy, drab, and unattractive. **2.** a dull, old-fashioned person. —**frump′ish,** *adj.* —**frump′y,** *adj.,* **-i·er, -i·est.**

Frun·ze (frŏŏn′zə), *n.* former name (1926–91) of BISHKEK.

frus·trate (frus′trāt), *v.,* **-trat·ed, -trat·ing,** *adj.* —*v.t.* **1.** to make (plans, efforts, etc.) worthless or of no avail; defeat; nullify. **2.** to disappoint or thwart (a person). —*v.i.* **3.** to become frustrated. —*adj.* **4.** frustrated. —**frus′trat·ing·ly,** *adv.*

frus·trat·ed (frus′trā tid), *adj.* **1.** disappointed; thwarted: *a frustrated actor.* **2.** having a feeling of or filled with frustration; dissatisfied: *Her unresolved difficulty left her frustrated.*

frus·tra·tion (fru strā′shən), *n.* **1.** something that frustrates, as an unresolved problem. **2.** a feeling of dissatisfaction often accompanied by anxiety or depression, resulting from unfulfilled needs or unresolved problems.

frus·tum (frus′təm), *n., pl.* **-tums, -ta** (-tə). **1.** the part of a conical solid left after cutting off a top portion with a plane parallel to the base. **2.** the part of a solid, as a cone or pyramid, between two usu. parallel cutting planes.

fry¹ (frī), *v.,* **fried, fry·ing,** *n., pl.* **fries.** —*v.t.* **1. a.** to cook in fat or oil usu. over direct heat. **b.** to pan-broil: *to fry bacon.* —*v.i.* **2.** to undergo cooking in fat or oil. —*n.* **3.** a dish of fried food. **4.** a strip of French-fried potato. **5.** a gathering at which the chief food is fried, often outdoors: *a fish fry.* [< Old French < Latin *frīgere* to roast] —**fry′a·ble,** *adj.*

fry² (frī), *n., pl.* **fry. 1.** the young of fish. **2.** the young of various other animals, as frogs. **3.** people; individuals, esp. children: *games for the small fry.* [Middle English: seed, descendant]

Frye (frī), *n.* **(Herman) Northrop,** 1912–91, Canadian literary critic and educator.

fry·er or **fri·er** (frī′ər), *n.* **1.** a person or thing that fries. **2.** something, as a young chicken, to be cooked by frying. **3.** a pan for frying foods.

fry′ing pan′, *n.* **1.** a shallow long-handled pan in which food is fried. —*Idiom.* **2. out of the frying pan into the fire,** free of one predicament but immediately in a worse one. Sometimes, **fry′pan′.** Also called **skillet.**

f.s., foot-second.

FSH, follicle-stimulating hormone: an anterior pituitary peptide that stimulates the development of follicles in the female and spermatozoa in the male.

FSLIC, Federal Savings and Loan Insurance Corporation.

f-stop or **f stop** (ef′stop′), *n.* the setting of a camera lens aperture, as indicated by an f number.

ft., 1. feet. **2.** (in prescriptions) **a.** let it be made. **b.** let them be made. **3.** foot. **4.** fort. **5.** fortification.

FTC, Federal Trade Commission: a board, consisting of five members, charged with investigating and enjoining illegal practices in interstate trade, as price-fixing or fraudulent advertising.

ft-L, foot-lambert.

ft-lb, foot-pound.

FTP, 1. File Transfer Protocol: a software protocol for exchanging information between computers over a network. **2.** any program that implements this protocol.

ft-pdl, foot-poundal.

fuch·sia (fyōō'shə), *n., pl* **-sias. 1.** any shrubby plant of the genus *Fuchsia,* of the evening primrose family, with pink to purplish drooping flowers. **2.** a bright purplish red color. —*adj.* **3.** of the color fuchsia: *a fuchsia dress.*

fu·cus (fyōō'kəs), *n., pl.* **-ci** (-sī), **-cus·es.** any olive-brown seaweed of the genus *Fucus,* having branching fronds and air bladders.

fud·dle (fud'l), *v.,* **-dled, -dling,** *n.* —*v.t.* **1.** to muddle or confuse. **2.** to make drunk; intoxicate. —*v.i.* **3.** to tipple. —*n.* **4.** a confused state; muddle; jumble.

fud·dy-dud·dy (fud'ē dud'ē, -dud'ē), *n., pl.* **-dud·dies,** *adj.* —*n.* Also, **fud'dy. 1.** a person who is stuffy, old-fashioned, and conservative. **2.** a person who is fussy or picayune about details; fussbudget. —*adj.* **3.** stuffy, old-fashioned, and conservative. **4.** fussy; picayune.

fudge¹ (fuj), *n.* a soft candy made with sugar, butter, milk, and chocolate or other flavoring.

fudge² (fuj), *n., v.,* **fudged, fudg·ing.** —*n.* **1.** nonsense or foolishness (often used interjectionally). —*v.i.* **2.** to talk nonsense.

fudge³ (fuj), *v.,* **fudged, fudg·ing.** —*v.i.* **1.** to cheat (often fol. by *on*): *to fudge on an exam; to fudge on campaign promises.* **2.** to avoid coming to grips with something: *to fudge on an issue.* **3.** to exaggerate a cost, estimate, etc., in order to allow leeway for error. —*v.t.* **4.** to avoid coming to grips with (a subject, issue, etc.); evade; dodge: *to fudge a direct question.* **5.** to tamper with; fake: *to fudge data.*

fu·el (fyōō'əl), *n., v.,* **-eled, -el·ing** or (*esp. Brit.*) **-elled, -el·ling.** —*n.* **1.** combustible matter, as coal, wood, oil, or gas, used to maintain fire in order to create heat or power, or as an energy source for engines, power plants, or reactors. **2.** something that gives nourishment; food. **3.** something that sustains or encourages; stimulant: *fuel for debate.* —*v.t.* **4.** to supply with fuel. **5.** to encourage or stimulate: *to fuel suspicion.* —*v.i.* **6.** to obtain or replenish fuel. —**fu'el·er, fu'el·ler,** *n.*

fu'el cell', *n.* a device that produces a continuous electric current directly from the oxidation of a fuel, as that of hydrogen.

fu'el injec'tion, *n.* the spraying of liquid fuel into the cylinders or combustion chambers of an engine.

fu'el oil', *n.* an oil used for fuel, esp. one used as a substitute for coal, as crude petroleum.

fug (fug), *n.* stale air, esp. the humid, warm, ill-smelling air of a crowded room, kitchen, etc. —**fug'gy,** *adj.*

fu·ga·cious (fyōō gā'shəs), *adj.* **1.** fleeting; transitory. **2.** *Bot.* falling or fading early.

fu·gal (fyōō'gəl), *adj.* of or pertaining to a fugue, or composed in the style of a fugue. —**fu'gal·ly,** *adv.*

fu·gi·tive (fyōō'ji tiv), *n.* **1.** a person who is fleeing from prosecution, intolerable circumstances, etc.; a runaway. —*adj.* **2.** having taken flight, or run away: *a fugitive convict.* **3.** fleeting; transitory; elusive: *fugitive thoughts.* **4.** dealing with subjects of passing interest, as writings; ephemeral: *fugitive essays.* **5.** wandering, roving, or vagabond. —**fu'gi·tive·ly,** *adv.* —**fu'gi·tive·ness,** *n.*

fu·gu (fōō'gōō), *n., pl.* **-gus.** any of several species of puffer eaten as a delicacy after the removal of toxic parts.

fugue (fyōōg), *n.* **1.** a polyphonic composition based upon one, two, or more themes, which are enunciated by several voices or parts in turn. **2.** a period of amnesia during which the affected person seems to be conscious and to make rational decisions: upon recovery, the period is not remembered.

Füh·rer or **Fueh·rer** (fy'rər: *Eng.* fyŏŏr'ər), *n. German.* **1.** leader. **2.** **der Führer** (deʀ), the leader: title of Adolf Hitler.

Fu·ji (fōō'jē), *n.* a dormant volcano in central Japan, on Honshu island: highest mountain in Japan. 12,395 ft. (3778 m). Also called **Fu·ji·ya·ma** (fōō'jē yä'mə), **Fu·ji·san** (fōō'jē sän').

-ful, a suffix meaning "full of," "characterized by" (*beautiful; careful*); "tending to," "able to" (*harmful; wakeful*); "as much as will fill" (*spoonful*). —**Usage.** The plurals of nouns ending in -FUL are usu. formed by adding -*s* to the suffix: *two cupfuls.* Perhaps influenced by the phrase in which a noun is followed by the adjective FULL (*both arms full of packages*), some speakers and writers pluralize such nouns by adding -*s* before the suffix: *two cupsful.*

Ful·bright (fōōl'brīt'), *n.* **1. (James) William,** 1905–95, U.S. senator 1945–74. **2. a.** a grant awarded under the provisions of the Fulbright Act. **b.** a person who receives such a grant.

Ful'bright Act', *n.* an act of Congress (1946) that established funds for U.S. citizens to study or teach abroad as well as for foreigners to pursue similar activities in the U.S. [after J. W. FULBRIGHT]

ful·crum (fōōl'krəm, ful'-), *n., pl.* **-crums, -cra** (-krə). **1.** the support, or point of rest, on which a lever turns in moving a body. **2.** any prop

or support. **3.** any of various structures in an animal serving as a hinge or support.

ful·fill or **ful·fil** (fōōl fil'), *v.t.,* **-filled, -fill·ing. 1.** to carry out or bring to realization, as a prophecy or promise. **2.** to perform or do, as duty; obey or follow, as commands. **3.** to satisfy (requirements, obligations, etc.): *to fulfill a long-felt need.* **4.** to bring to an end; finish or complete, as a period of time. **5.** to develop the full potential of (usu. used reflexively): *to fulfill oneself in charitable work.* —**ful·fill'ment,** *n.*

ful·gent (ful'jənt), *adj.* shining brightly; dazzling; resplendent. —**ful'gent·ly,** *adv.* —**ful'gent·ness,** *n.*

ful·gu·rate (ful'gyə rāt'), *v.,* **-rat·ed, -rat·ing.** —*v.i.* **1.** to flash or dart like lightning. —*v.t.* **2.** *Med.* to destroy (esp. an abnormal growth) by electricity. —**ful'gu·ra'tion,** *n.*

fu·lig·i·nous (fyōō lij'ə nəs), *adj.* **1.** sooty; smoky. **2.** of the color of soot, as dark gray, dull brown, black, etc. —**fu·lig'i·nous·ly,** *adv.* —**fu·lig'i·nous·ness,** *n.*

full¹ (fōōl), *adj.* **1.** completely filled; containing all that can be held: *a full cup.* **2.** complete; entire; maximum: *a full supply of food.* **3.** of the maximum size, amount, extent, volume, etc.: *a full load of five tons; to receive full pay.* **4.** (of garments, drapery, etc.) wide, ample, or having ample folds. **5.** abundant; well-supplied: *a cabinet full of medicine.* **6.** filled or rounded out, as in form: *a full figure.* **7.** engrossed; occupied (usu. fol. by *of*): *She was full of her own anxieties.* **8.** of the highest rank: *a full professor.* **9.** of the same parents: *full brothers.* **10.** ample and complete in volume or richness of sound: *a full-toned voice.* **11.** (of wines) having considerable body. —*adv.* **12.** exactly or directly: *The blow struck him full in the face.* **13.** very: *You know full well what I mean.* **14.** fully, completely, or entirely; quite; at least: *It happened full 40 years ago.* —*v.t.* **15.** to make full by sewing, as by gathering or pleating. —*v.i.* **16.** (of the moon) to become full. —*n.* **17.** the highest or fullest state, condition, or degree: *The moon is at the full.* —**Idiom. 18. in full, a.** to or for the full or required amount. **b.** without abridgment. **19. to the full,** to the greatest extent; thoroughly. —**full'ness,** *n.*

full² (fōōl), *v.t.* **1.** to cleanse and thicken (cloth) by special processes in manufacture. —*v.i.* **2.** (of cloth) to become compacted or felted.

full·back (fōōl'bak'), *n.* **1.** (in football) a running back who lines up behind the quarterback and is farthest from the line of scrimmage. **2.** (in soccer, Rugby, and field hockey) a player stationed near the defended goal to carry out chiefly defensive duties.

full' blood', *n.* **1.** a person or animal of unmixed ancestry; one descended of a pure breed. Compare PUREBRED. **2.** relationship through both parents.

full'-blown', *adj.* **1.** completely developed: *an idea expanded into a full-blown book.* **2.** in full bloom: *a full-blown rose.*

full'-bod'ied, *adj.* of full strength, flavor, richness, etc.: *full-bodied wine; full-bodied writing.*

full'-court' press', *n.* a vigorous attack or offensive; strong pressure: *to stage a full-court press for tax reform.*

full' disclo'sure, *n.* complete release of information, esp. by a government.

full' dress', *n.* **1.** the formal attire customarily worn in the evening, as black tailcoats and white bow ties for men. **2.** a ceremonial style of dress.

full'-dress', *adj.* **1.** formal and complete in all details: *a full-dress uniform.* **2.** done or presented completely or thoroughly.

Ful·ler (fōōl'ər), *n.* **R(ichard) Buckminster,** 1895–1983, U.S. engineer, designer, and architect.

full'er's earth', *n.* an absorbent clay, used esp. for removing grease from fabrics, in fulling cloth, as a filter, and as a dusting powder.

Ful·ler·ton (fōōl'ər tən), *n.* a city in SW California, SE of Los Angeles. 109,740.

full'-fledged', *adj.* **1.** of full rank or standing: *a full-fledged professor.* **2.** fully developed.

full'-grown', *adj.* completely grown; mature.

full' house', *n.* a poker hand consisting of three of a kind and a pair. Also called **full' hand'.**

full'-length', *adj.* **1.** of standard or customary length: *a full-length motion picture.* **2.** showing or accommodating the full length or height of the human body: *a full-length mirror.*

full' moon', *n.* **1.** the moon when the whole of its disk is illuminated, occurring when in opposition to the sun. **2.** the phase of the moon at this time.

full' nel'son, *n.* a hold in which a wrestler, from behind the opponent, passes each arm under the corresponding arm of the opponent and locks the arms at the fingers or wrists on the back of the opponent's neck. Compare HALF NELSON.

full'-scale', *adj.* **1.** having the exact size or proportions of the original: *a full-scale replica.* **2.** using all possible means, facilities, etc.; complete: *a full-scale investigation; to begin full-scale operation.*

full'-serv'ice, *adj.* offering a wide range of services related to the basic line of business: *a full-service filling station.*

full'-size' or **full'-sized',** *adj.* **1.** of the usual or normal size of its kind: *a full-size kitchen.* **2.** (of a bed) 54 in. (137 cm) wide and 75 or 76 in. (191 or 193 cm) long; double. **3.** of or for a full-size bed: *full-size sheets.*

full' speed', *n.* **1.** the maximum speed. **2.** *Naut.* the speed normally maintained on a passage. —*adv.* **3.** at maximum speed.

F

full′-term′, *adj.* **1.** of or noting the entire duration of normal pregnancy. **2.** serving the complete designated term of office: *a full-term president.*

full′-time′, *adj.* **1.** working or operating the customary number of hours in each day, week, or month: *a full-time housekeeper; full-time production.* Compare PART-TIME. *—adv.* **2.** on a full-time basis: *to work full-time.* **—full′-tim′er,** *n.*

ful•mar (fo͝ol′mər), *n.* any of several gull-like pelagic birds akin to the shearwaters and petrels, esp. *Fulmarus glacialis,* of N oceans.

ful•mi•nant (ful′mə nənt), *adj.* **1.** occurring suddenly and with great intensity or severity; fulminating. **2.** *Pathol.* developing or progressing suddenly.

ful•mi•nate (ful′mə nāt′), *v.,* **-nat•ed, -nat•ing,** *n.* *—v.i.* **1.** to explode with a loud noise; detonate. **2.** to issue denunciations or the like (usu. fol. by *against*). *—v.t.* **3.** to cause to explode. **4.** to issue or pronounce with vehement denunciation, condemnation, or the like. *—n.* **5.** one of a group of unstable, explosive compounds derived from fulminic acid, esp. its mercury salt, used as a detonating agent. **—ful′mi•na′tor,** *n.* **—ful•mi•na•to•ry** (ful′mə nə tôr′ē, -tōr′ē), *adj.*

ful•some (fo͝ol′səm, ful′-), *adj.* **1.** offensive to good taste, esp. as being excessive; overdone: *fulsome décor.* **2.** disgusting; sickening; repulsive: *fulsome mounds of greasy foods.* **3.** excessively or insincerely lavish: *fulsome admiration.* **4.** encompassing all aspects; comprehensive: *a fulsome survey of homelessness in America.* **5.** abundant or copious. **—ful′some•ly,** *adv.* **—ful′some•ness,** *n.*

Ful•ton (fo͝ol′tn), *n.* **Robert,** 1765–1815, U.S. engineer and inventor: builder of the first profitable steamboat.

Fu′ Man•chu′ mus′tache (fo͞o′ man cho͞o′), *n.* a mustache whose ends droop to the chin. Also called **Fu′ Manchu′.** [after the mustache worn by *Fu Manchu,* an Oriental master criminal in films of the 1920s and '30s, based on novels by British author Sax Rohmer (1883–1959)]

fu•mar•ic (fyo͞o mar′ik), *adj.* of or derived from fumaric acid.

fumar′ic ac′id, *n.* a colorless, odorless solid, $C_4H_4O_4$, essential to cellular respiration in most eukaryotic organisms: used to make synthetic resins and as a replacement for tartaric acid in beverages and baking powders.

fu•ma•role (fyo͞o′mə rōl′), *n.* a hole in or near a volcano from which vapor rises. **—fu′ma•rol′ic** (-rol′ik), *adj.*

fum•ble (fum′bəl), *v.,* **-bled, -bling,** *n.* *—v.i.* **1.** to feel or grope about clumsily: *He fumbled in his pocket for the keys.* **2.** to fail to hold a ball after having touched it or carried it. **3.** to do something clumsily or unsuccessfully; blunder or fail. *—v.t.* **4.** to make, handle, etc., clumsily or ineffectively; botch: *to fumble an attempt.* **5.** to fail to hold (a ball) after having touched it or carried it. *—n.* **6.** the act of fumbling. **—fum′bler,** *n.* **—fum′bling•ly,** *adv.*

fume (fyo͞om), *n., v.,* **fumed, fum•ing.** *—n.* **1.** Often, **fumes.** any smokelike or vaporous exhalation from matter or substances, esp. of an odorous or harmful nature: *tobacco fumes; poisonous fumes of carbon monoxide.* **2.** an irritable or angry mood: *to be in a fume.* *—v.t.* **3.** to emit or exhale, as fumes or vapor. **4.** to treat with or expose to fumes. *—v.i.* **5.** to show fretful irritation or anger: *She always fumes when the mail is late.* **6.** to rise, or pass off, as fumes. **—fume′less,** *adj.* **—fume′like′,** *adj.* **—fum′ing•ly,** *adv.*

fu•mi•gate (fyo͞o′mi gāt′), *v.t.,* **-gat•ed, -gat•ing.** to expose to smoke or fumes, as in disinfecting or in exterminating vermin. **—fum′i•gant,** *n.* **—fu′mi•ga′tion,** *n.* **—fu•mi•ga•to•ry** (fyo͞o′mi gə tôr′ē, -tōr′ē, -gā′tə rē), *adj.*

fu•mi•ga•tor (fyo͞o′mi gā′tər), *n.* **1.** a person or thing that fumigates. **2.** a structure in which plants are fumigated to destroy insects.

fu•mi•to•ry (fyo͞o′mi tôr′ē, -tōr′ē), *n., pl.* **-ries.** any plant of the genus *Fumaria,* having grayish leaves and spikes of purplish flowers.

fun (fun), *n., v.,* **funned, fun•ning,** *adj.,* **fun•ner, fun•nest.** *—n.* **1.** something that provides mirth or amusement: *A picnic would be fun.* **2.** enjoyment or playfulness: *She's full of fun.* *—v.i., v.t.* **3.** *Informal.* to joke; kid. *—adj.* **4.** *Informal.* providing pleasure or amusement; enjoyable: *a fun thing to do; really a fun person.* **—*Idiom.*** **5. for** or **in fun,** as a joke; not seriously; playfully. **6. like fun,** *Informal.* certainly not; by no means: *Pay you double? Like fun!* **7. make fun of,** to make the object of ridicule; deride.

Fu•na•fu•ti (fo͞o′nə fo͞o′tē), *n.* the capital of Tuvalu. 1328.

fu•nam•bu•list (fyo͞o nam′byə list), *n.* a tightrope walker. **—fu•nam′bu•lism,** *n.*

func•tion (fungk′shən), *n.* **1.** the kind of action or activity proper to a person, thing, or institution; the purpose for which something is designed or exists; role. **2.** any ceremonious public or social gathering or occasion. **3.** a factor related to or dependent upon other factors: *Price is a function of supply and demand.* **4. a.** Also called **correspondence, map, mapping, transformation.** a relation between two sets in which one element of the second set is assigned to each element of the first set, as the expression $y = x^2$; operator. **b.** a formula expressing a relation between the angles of a triangle and its sides, as sine or cosine. **5.** the grammatical role a linguistic form has or the position it occupies in a particular construction. **6.** the contribution made by a social activity or structure to the maintenance of a social system. *—v.i.* **7.** to perform a specified action or activity; work; operate: *The computer isn't functioning now.* **8.** to have or exercise a function; serve: *In earlier English the present tense often functioned as a future.*

func•tion•al (fungk′shə nl), *adj.* **1.** of or pertaining to a function or functions. **2.** capable of operating or functioning: *When will the ventilating system be functional again?* **3.** having or serving a utilitarian purpose; capable of serving the purpose for which it was designed: *functional architecture; a chair that is functional as well as decorative.* **4.** (of a building or furnishing) constructed or made according to the principles of functionalism. **5.** of or pertaining to impaired function without known organic or structural cause: *a functional disorder.* **6.** pertaining to an algebraic operation: *a functional symbol.* **7.** (of linguistic analysis, language teaching, etc.) concerned with the communicative role of language rather than or in addition to its formal structure. **—func′tion•al•ly,** *adv.*

func′tional illit′erate, *n.* a person with some basic education who still falls short of a minimum standard of literacy or whose reading and writing skills are inadequate to everyday needs. **—func′tional illit′eracy,** *n.* **—func′tionally illit′erate,** *adj.*

func•tion•al•ism (fungk′shə nl iz′əm), *n.* **1.** (*often cap.*) **a.** a design movement evolved esp. in the early 20th century, advocating that form and design be determined by practical issues, as materials, construction, and purpose, with aesthetic effect subordinated to functionality. **b.** the doctrines and practices associated with this movement. **2.** a school of psychology that emphasizes the adaptiveness of mental and behavioral processes. **3.** *Sociol.* a theoretical orientation that views society as a system of interdependent parts whose functions contribute to the stability and survival of the system. **—func′tion•al•ist,** *n., adj.*

func•tion•ar•y (fungk′shə ner′ē), *n., pl.* **-ar•ies.** a person who functions in a specified capacity, esp. in government service; an official: *civil servants and other functionaries.*

func′tion key′, *n.* a key on a computer keyboard used alone or with other keys for operations.

fund (fund), *n.* **1.** a supply of money or monetary resources, as for some purpose: *a fund for a child's education; a retirement fund.* **2.** supply; stock: *a fund of knowledge.* **3. funds,** money immediately available; pecuniary resources. **4.** an organization created to manage the resources of a monetary fund. *—v.t.* **5.** to allocate or provide funds for (a program, project, etc.). **6.** to provide a fund to pay the interest or principal of (a debt).

fun•da•ment (fun′də mənt), *n.* **1.** the buttocks. **2.** the anus. **3.** a base or basic principle; underlying part; foundation.

fun•da•men•tal (fun′də men′tl), *adj.* **1.** serving as, or being an essential part of, a foundation or basis; basic; underlying: *fundamental principles.* **2.** of, pertaining to, or affecting the foundation or basis: *a fundamental revision.* **3.** being an original or primary source: *a fundamental idea.* *—n.* **4.** a basic principle, rule, law, or the like that serves as the groundwork of a system; essential part: *to master the fundamentals of a trade.* **5. a.** the root of a chord in music. **b.** the lowest component in a series of harmonics. **6.** *Physics.* the component of lowest frequency in a composite wave. **—fun′da•men•tal′i•ty, fun′da•men′tal•ness,** *n.* **—fun′da•men′tal•ly,** *adv.*

fun•da•men•tal•ism (fun′də men′tl iz′əm), *n.* **1.** (*sometimes cap.*) a movement in American Protestantism that arose in the early part of the 20th century in reaction to Modernism and that stresses the infallibility of the Bible not only in matters of faith and morals but also as a literal historical record. **2.** the beliefs held by those in this movement. **3.** strict adherence to any set of basic principles. **—fun′da•men′tal•ist,** *n., adj.*

fund′-rais′er or **fund′rais′er,** *n.* **1.** a person who solicits contributions or pledges. **2.** a social gathering held for such solicitation: *a fund-raiser to aid the community theater.*

fund′-rais′ing or **fund′rais′ing,** *n.* the act or process of raising funds by soliciting contributions or pledges, as for a nonprofit organization or a political cause.

fun•dus (fun′dəs), *n., pl.* **-di** (-dī). *Anat.* the base of a hollow organ, or the part furthest from the aperture. **—fun′dic,** *adj.*

fu•ner•al (fyo͞o′nər əl), *n.* **1.** the ceremonies for a dead person prior to burial or cremation; obsequies. **2.** a funeral procession. *—adj.* **3.** of or pertaining to a funeral: *funeral services; funeral expenses.* **—*Idiom.*** **4. be someone's funeral,** *Informal.* to have unpleasant consequences for someone.

fu′neral direc′tor, *n.* a person, usu. a licensed embalmer, who supervises or conducts the preparation of the dead for burial and directs or arranges funerals.

fu′neral home′, *n.* an establishment where the dead are prepared for burial or cremation, where the body may be viewed, and where funeral services are often held. Also called **fu′neral chap′el, fu′neral par′lor, mortuary.**

fu•ner•ar•y (fyo͞o′nə rer′ē), *adj.* of or pertaining to a funeral or burial: *a funerary urn.*

fu•ne•re•al (fyo͞o nēr′ē əl), *adj.* **1.** of or suitable for a funeral: *funereal black.* **2.** mournful; gloomy; dismal: *a funereal atmosphere.* **—fu•ne′re•al•ly,** *adv.*

fun•gi (fun′jī, fung′gī), *n.* a pl. of FUNGUS.

Fun•gi (fun′jī, fung′gī), *n.* (*used with a pl. v.*) a taxonomic kingdom, or in some classification schemes a division of the kingdom Plantae, comprising all the fungus groups and sometimes also the slime molds. Also called **Mycota.**

fun•gi•cide (fun′jə sīd′, fung′gə-), *n.* a substance or agent used for destroying fungi. **—fun′gi•cid′al,** *adj.* **—fun′gi•cid′al•ly,** *adv.*

Fun′gi Im•per•fec′ti (im′pər fek′tī), *n.* a class of fungi for which a sexually reproductive stage of the life cycle has not been found.

fun·gus (fung′gəs), *n., pl.* **fun·gi** (fun′jī, fung′gī), **fun·gus·es.** any member of the kingdom Fungi (or division Thallophyta of the kingdom Plantae), comprising single-celled or multinucleate organisms that live by decomposing and absorbing the organic material in which they grow: includes the mushrooms, molds, mildews, smuts, rusts, and yeasts. —**fun′gal,** *adj.* —**fun′gous,** *adj.*

fu·nic·u·lar (fyo͞o nik′yə lər), *adj.* **1.** of or pertaining to a rope or cord, or its tension. **2.** worked by a rope or the like.

fu·nic·u·lus (fyo͞o nik′yə ləs), *n., pl.* **-li** (-lī′). **1.** any cordlike structure, esp. certain nerve bundles. **2.** the stalk of an ovule.

funk[1] (fungk), *n.* **1.** cowering fear; state of great fright or terror. **2.** a dejected mood; depression. —*v.t.* **3.** to be afraid of. **4.** to frighten. **5.** to shrink from; try to shirk. —*v.i.* **6.** to shrink or quail in fear.

funk[2] (fungk), *n.* **1.** music having a funky quality. **2.** the state or quality of being funky. **3.** a strong smell; stench.

funk·y[1] (fung′kē), *adj.,* **funk·i·er, funk·i·est.** overcome with great fear; terrified.

funk·y[2] (fung′kē), *adj.,* **funk·i·er, funk·i·est. 1.** having an earthy, blues-based character: *funky jazz.* **2.** *Slang.* offbeat, odd, or quirky, as in appearance or style: *funky clothes.* **3.** having an offensive smell; foul-smelling. —**funk′i·ly,** *adv.* —**funk′i·ness,** *n.*

fun·nel (fun′l), *n., v.,* **-neled, -nel·ing** or (*esp. Brit.*) **-nelled, -nel·ling.** —*n.* **1.** a cone-shaped utensil with a tube at the apex for conducting liquid or other substance through a small opening, as into a bottle, jug, or the like. **2.** a smokestack, esp. of a steamship. **3.** a flue, tube, or shaft, as for ventilation. —*v.t.* **4.** to concentrate, channel, or focus: *They funneled their profits into research projects.* **5.** to pour through or as if through a funnel. —*v.i.* **6.** to pass through or as if through a funnel.

fun′nel cloud′, *n.* a rapidly rotating funnel-shaped cloud extending downward from the base of a cumulonimbus cloud, which, if it touches the surface of the earth, is a tornado or waterspout.

fun·ny (fun′ē), *adj.,* **-ni·er, -ni·est,** *n., pl.* **-nies,** *adv.* —*adj.* **1.** providing fun; amusing; comical: *a funny joke.* **2.** attempting to amuse; facetious. **3.** warranting suspicion; underhanded; deceitful: *There was something funny about those extra charges.* **4.** *Informal.* insolent; impertinent: *Don't get funny with me, mister.* **5.** curious; strange; peculiar; odd: *Her speech has a funny twang.* —*n.* **6.** *Informal.* a funny remark or story; joke: *to make a funny.* **7. funnies, a.** comic strips. **b.** Also called **funny paper.** the section of a newspaper reserved for comic strips, word games, etc. —*adv.* **8.** *Informal.* peculiarly: *a stranger who talked funny.* —**fun′ni·ly,** *adv.* —**fun′ni·ness,** *n.*

fun′ny bone′, *n.* **1.** the part of the elbow where the ulnar nerve passes close to the surface and which, when struck, causes a peculiar tingling sensation in the arm and hand. **2.** a sense of humor.

fun′ny mon′ey, *n. Slang.* **1.** counterfeit currency. **2.** currency of little value, as of a nation whose currency has been artificially inflated or recently devaluated.

fur (fûr), *n., adj., v.,* **furred, fur·ring.** —*n.* **1.** the fine, soft, thick, hairy coat of the skin of a mammal. **2.** the skin of certain animals, as minks or beavers, covered with this, used for garments, trimmings, etc. **3.** a garment made of fur. **4.** any coating resembling or suggesting fur, as certain matter on the tongue. —*adj.* **5.** of, pertaining to, or dealing in fur, animal skins, dressed pelts, etc.: *a fur coat; a fur trader.* —*v.t.* **6.** to line, face, or trim with fur. **7.** to apply furring to (a wall, ceiling, etc.). **8.** to clothe (a person) with fur. **9.** to coat with foul or deposited matter. —*Idiom.* **10. make the fur fly, a.** to cause a disturbance. **b.** to do something quickly. —**fur′less,** *adj.*

fu·ran (fyo͞or′an, fyo͞o ran′), *n.* a colorless, liquid, unsaturated, five-membered heterocyclic compound, C_4H_4O, obtained from furfural: used chiefly in organic synthesis. Also called **furfuran.**

fur·be·low (fûr′bə lō′), *n.* **1.** a ruffle or flounce, as on a woman's skirt or petticoat. **2.** any bit of showy trimming or finery. —*v.t.* **3.** to ornament with or as if with furbelows.

fur·bish (fûr′bish), *v.t.* **1.** to restore to freshness of appearance or good condition (often fol. by *up*). **2.** to polish.

Fur′bish louse′wort (fûr′bish), *n.* a lousewort, *Pedicularis furbishiae,* of Maine and SE Canada, with finely toothed leaves and a cluster of yellow flowers.

fur·cate (*adj.* fûr′kāt, -kit; *v.* -kāt), *adj., v.,* **-cat·ed, -cat·ing.** —*adj.* **1.** forked; branching. —*v.i.* **2.** to form a fork; branch.

fur·cu·la (fûr′kyə lə), *n., pl.* **-lae** (-lē′). a forked bone; wishbone. —**fur′cu·lar,** *adj.*

fur·fu·ra·ceous (fûr′fyə rā′shəs, -fə-), *adj.* **1.** of or containing bran. **2.** resembling bran. **3.** scaly; scurfy.

fur·fur·al (fûr′fyə ral′, -fə-), *n.* a colorless liquid, $C_5H_4O_2$, used in making plastics and refining oils.

fu·ri·ous (fyo͞or′ē əs), *adj.* **1.** full of fury, violent passion, or rage: *a furious letter of accusation.* **2.** intensely violent, as wind or storms. **3.** of unrestrained energy, speed, etc.: *furious activity.* —**fu′ri·ous·ly,** *adv.*

furl (fûrl), *v.t.* **1.** to gather into a roll and bind securely, as a sail against a spar or a flag against its staff. —*v.i.* **2.** to be furled. —*n.* **3.** something furled, as a roll.

fur·long (fûr′lông, -long), *n.* a unit of distance equal to 220 yards (201 m) or ¹⁄₈ of a mile (0.2 km). *Abbr.:* fur.

fur·lough (fûr′lō), *n.* **1.** a vacation or leave of absence, as one granted to a person in military service; leave. **2.** a usu. temporary layoff from work. **3.** a temporary leave of absence authorized for a prisoner from a

penitentiary. —*v.t.* **4.** to grant a furlough to. **5.** to lay (an employee or worker) off from work, usu. temporarily.

fur·nace (fûr′nis), *n.* **1.** a structure or apparatus in which heat may be generated, as for heating houses, smelting ores, or producing steam. **2.** a place characterized by intense heat.

fur·nish (fûr′nish), *v.t.* **1.** to supply (a house, room, etc.) with necessary appliances, esp. furniture. **2.** to provide or supply (often fol. by *with*): *The delay furnished me with the time I needed.*

fur·nish·ing (fûr′ni shing), *n.* **1. furnishings, a.** furniture, carpeting, etc., for a house or room. **b.** articles or accessories of dress: *men's furnishings.* **2.** that with which anything is furnished.

fur·ni·ture (fûr′ni chər), *n.* **1.** the movable articles, as tables, chairs, or cabinets, required for use or ornament in a house, office, or the like. **2.** fittings, apparatus, or necessary accessories for something. **3.** pieces of wood or metal for holding pages of type in place in a chase.

fu·ror (fyo͞or′ôr, -ər), *n.* **1.** a general outburst of enthusiasm, excitement, controversy, or the like. **2.** a prevailing fad, mania, or craze. **3.** fury; rage; madness.

fur·ri·er[1] (fûr′ē ər), *n.* a person who buys and sells furs, or one who makes, repairs, or cleans furs and fur garments; a fur dealer or fur dresser.

fur·ri·er[2] (fûr′ē ər), *adj.* comparative of FURRY.

fur·ring (fûr′ing), *n.* **1.** the act of lining, trimming, or clothing with fur. **2.** the fur used. **3.** the formation of a coating of matter on something, as on the tongue. **4. a.** the attaching of strips of wood or the like (**fur′ring strips′**) to a wall or other surface, as to provide an even support for lath or to provide an air space between the wall and plasterwork. **b.** material used for this purpose.

fur·row (fûr′ō, fur′ō), *n.* **1.** a narrow groove made in the ground, esp. by a plow. **2.** a narrow groovelike or trenchlike depression in any surface: *the furrows of a wrinkled face.* —*v.t.* **3.** to make a furrow or furrows in. **4.** to make wrinkles in (the face): *to furrow one's brow.* —*v.i.* **5.** to become furrowed.

fur·ry (fûr′ē), *adj.,* **fur·ri·er, fur·ri·est. 1.** consisting of or resembling fur. **2.** covered with fur; wearing fur: *furry animals.* **3.** obstructed or coated as if with fur. —**fur′ri·ly,** *adv.* —**fur′ri·ness,** *n.*

fur′ seal′, *n.* any of several eared seals, esp. of the genus *Callorhinus,* having a valuable plush underfur. Compare HAIR SEAL.

fur·ther (fûr′thər), *compar. adv. and adj. of* FAR *with superl.* **fur·thest,** *v.* —*adv.* **1.** at or to a greater distance; farther: *too tired to go further.* **2.** at or to a more advanced point; to a greater extent: *Let's not discuss it further.* **3.** in addition; moreover: *Further, he should be here any minute.* —*adj.* **4.** more distant or remote; farther: *The map shows it to be further than I thought.* **5.** more extended: *Does this mean a further delay?* **6.** additional: *Further meetings seem pointless.* —*v.t.* **7.** to help forward (an undertaking, cause, etc.); promote; advance; forward: *You can always count on her to further good causes.* —**Usage.** See FARTHER.

fur·ther·ance (fûr′thər əns), *n.* the act of furthering; promotion; advancement.

fur·ther·more (fûr′thər môr′, -mōr′), *adv.* moreover; besides; in addition.

fur·ther·most (fûr′thər mōst′), *adj.* most distant.

fur·thest (fûr′thist), *adj., adv. superl. of* FAR *with* **fur·ther** *as compar.* FARTHEST.

fur·tive (fûr′tiv), *adj.* **1.** taken, done, used, etc., surreptitiously or by stealth; secret: *a furtive glance.* **2.** sly; shifty: *a furtive manner.* —**fur′tive·ly,** *adv.* —**fur′tive·ness,** *n.*

fu·run·cle (fyo͞or′ung kəl), *n.* BOIL[2].

fu·ry (fyo͞or′ē), *n., pl.* **-ries. 1.** unrestrained or violent anger, rage, passion, or the like. **2.** violence; vehemence; fierceness: *the fury of a hurricane.* **3.** a fierce and violent person, esp. a woman. —*Idiom.* **4. like fury,** *Informal.* violently; intensely.

furze (fûrz), *n.* GORSE.

fu·sar·i·um (fyo͞o zâr′ē əm), *n., pl.* **-sar·i·a** (-zâr′ē ə). any fungus of the genus *Fusarium,* occurring primarily in temperate regions and causing wilt in plants and a variety of diseases in animals.

fuse[1] (fyo͞oz), *n., v.,* **fused, fus·ing.** —*n.* **1.** a tube, cord, or the like, filled or saturated with combustible matter, for igniting an explosive. **2.** FUZE (def. 1). —*v.t.* **3.** FUZE (def. 3). —*Idiom.* **4. have a short fuse,** *Informal.* to anger easily; have a quick temper.

plug fuse   cartridge fuse

fuse[2] (def. 1)

fuse[2] (fyo͞oz), *n., v.,* **fused, fus·ing.** —*n.* **1.** a device containing a conductor that melts when excess current runs through an electric circuit, opening and thereby protecting the circuit. —*v.t.* **2.** to combine or blend by melting together; melt. **3.** to unite or blend into a whole, as if by melting together: *The author skillfully fuses these fragments into a cohesive whole.* —*v.i.* **4.** to become liquid under the action of heat; melt. **5.** to become united or blended. —*Idiom.* **6. blow a fuse,** *Informal.* to lose one's temper; become enraged. —**fu′si·ble,** *adj.*

fu·se·lage (fyo͞o′sə läzh′, -lij, -zə-), *n.* the central structure of an airplane, containing passenger and cargo compartments, and to which are attached the tail assembly and wings.

fu•sil•lade (fyōō′sə lād′, -lād′, -zə-), *n., v.,* **-lad•ed, -lad•ing.** —*n.* **1.** a simultaneous or continuous discharge of firearms. **2.** a general discharge or outpouring of anything: *a fusillade of questions.* —*v.t.* **3.** to attack or shoot by a fusillade.

fu•sion (fyōō′zhən), *n.* **1.** the act or process of fusing or the state of being fused. **2.** that which is fused; the result of fusing: *A ballet production is the fusion of many talents.* **3.** a coalition of political parties or factions. **4.** the joining of atomic nuclei in a reaction to form nuclei of heavier atoms, as the combination of deuterium atoms to form helium atoms. Compare FISSION (def. 2). **5.** popular music that is a blend of two styles, esp. a combining of jazz with rock, classical music, or such ethnic elements as Brazilian or Japanese music.

fu′sion bomb′, *n.* HYDROGEN BOMB.

fuss (fus), *n.* **1.** an excessive display of attention or activity: *They made such a fuss over a little accident.* **2.** an argument or noisy dispute. **3.** a complaint or protest, esp. about something relatively unimportant. —*v.i.* **4.** to make much about trifles; pay excessive and needless attention: *to fuss over details.* **5.** to complain esp. about something relatively unimportant: *to fuss and fume about the delay.* —*v.t.* **6.** to disturb, esp. with trifles; annoy; bother. —**fuss′er,** *n.*

fuss•budg•et (fus′buj′it), *n.* a fussy or needlessly faultfinding person. —**fuss′budg′et•y,** *adj.*

fuss•y (fus′ē), *adj.,* **fuss•i•er, fuss•i•est. 1.** excessively busy with trifles; anxious or particular about petty details. **2.** hard to satisfy or please: *a fussy eater.* **3.** elaborately or ornately made, trimmed, or decorated: *a room with a fussy, cluttered look; a fussy hat.* **4.** full of details, esp. in excess. —**fuss′i•ly,** *adv.* —**fuss′i•ness,** *n.*

fus•tian (fus′chən), *n.* **1.** a stout fabric of cotton and flax. **2.** a fabric of stout twilled cotton or of cotton and low-quality wool, with a short nap or pile. **3.** inflated or turgid language: *Fustian can't disguise the story's meager plot.* —*adj.* **4.** made of fustian: *a fustian coat.* **5.** pompous or bombastic, as language. **6.** worthless; cheap.

fus•tic (fus′tik), *n.* **1.** the wood of a large, tropical American tree, *Chlorophora tinctoria,* of the mulberry family, yielding a light yellow dye. **2.** the tree itself. **3.** the dye. **4.** any of several other dyewoods.

fus•ti•gate (fus′ti gāt′), *v.t.,* **-gat•ed, -gat•ing. 1.** to cudgel; beat. **2.** to criticize harshly; castigate. —**fus′ti•ga′tion,** *n.* —**fus′ti•ga′tor,** *n.* —**fus•ti•ga•to•ry** (fus′ti gə tôr′ē, -tōr′ē), *adj.*

fus•ty (fus′tē), *adj.,* **-ti•er, -ti•est. 1.** having a stale smell; moldy; musty. **2.** old-fashioned or out-of-date, as architecture, furnishings, or the like. **3.** stubbornly conservative or old-fashioned; fogyish. —**fus′ti•ly,** *adv.* —**fus′ti•ness,** *n.*

fu•tile (fyōōt′l, fyōō′tīl), *adj.* **1.** incapable of producing any result; ineffective; useless; not successful: *Attempts to swim across the stormy channel were futile.* **2.** trifling; frivolous. —**fu′tile•ly,** *adv.* —**fu•til′i•ty,** *n.*

fu•ton (fōō′ton), *n.* a thin, quiltlike mattress placed on a floor for sleeping and folded and stored or used as seating at other times.

fu•ture (fyōō′chər), *n.* **1.** time that is to be or come hereafter. **2.** something that will exist or happen in time to come: *to foresee the future.* **3.** a condition, esp. of success or failure, to come: *to tell someone's future.* **4. a.** the future tense. **b.** a verb form or construction in the future tense. **5.** Usu., **futures.** commodities bought and sold speculatively for future delivery. —*adj.* **6.** being or coming hereafter: *future events.* **7.** pertaining to or connected with time to come: *one's future plans.* **8.** of, pertaining to, or being a verb tense, form, or construction that refers to events or states in time to come.

fu′ture life′, *n.* AFTERLIFE (def. 1). [1770–80]

fu′ture per′fect, *adj.* **1.** of or designating a verb tense or form indicating that the action or state expressed by the verb will be completed by or extend up to a time in the future. **2.** a form in this tense.

fu′ture shock′, *n.* physical and psychological disturbance caused by a person's inability to cope with very rapid social and technological change.

fu•tur•ism (fyōō′chə riz′əm), *n.* (*sometimes cap.*) a movement in the fine arts, developed orig. by a group of Italian artists about 1910, attempting to give artistic form to the dynamism and speed of industrial technology. —**fu′tur•ist,** *n.*

fu•tur•is•tic (fyōō′chə ris′tik), *adj.* **1.** of or pertaining to the future. **2.** ahead of the times; advanced: *futuristic technology.* **3.** (*sometimes cap.*) of or pertaining to futurism. —**fu′tur•is′ti•cal•ly,** *adv.*

fu•tu•ri•ty (fyōō tŏŏr′i tē, -tyŏŏr′-, -chŏŏr′-, -chûr′-), *n., pl.* **-ties. 1.** future time. **2.** future generations; posterity. **3.** the afterlife. **4.** a future state or condition; a future event, possibility, or prospect. **5.** the quality of being future. **6.** Also called **futu′rity race′,** a horse race, usu. for two-year-olds, in which the entrants are selected long before the race is run, sometimes before the birth of the foal.

fu•tur•ol•o•gy (fyōō′chə rol′ə jē), *n.* the study or forecasting of trends or developments in science, technology, political or social structure, etc.

fuze (fyōōz), *n., v.,* **fuzed, fuz•ing.** —*n.* **1.** a mechanical or electronic device to detonate an explosive charge. **2.** FUSE¹ (def. 1). —*v.t.* **3.** Also, **fuse.** to attach a fuze to (a bomb, mine, etc.).

fuzz¹ (fuz), *n.* **1.** loose, light, fibrous, or fluffy matter. **2.** a mass or coating of such matter: *the fuzz on a peach.* —*v.t., v.i.* **3.** to make or become fuzzy; make or become less clear, understandable, etc. (often fol. by *up*).

fuzz² (fuz), *n., pl.* **fuzz, fuzz•es** for 2. *Slang.* **1.** the police; police officers collectively. **2.** a police officer or detective.

fuzz•y (fuz′ē), *adj.,* **fuzz•i•er, fuzz•i•est. 1.** of the nature of or resembling fuzz. **2.** indistinct; blurred: *a fuzzy photograph.* **3.** muddleheaded or incoherent: *a fuzzy thinker.* —**fuzz′i•ly,** *adv.* —**fuzz′i•ness,** *n.*

FWD, 1. Also, **4WD** four-wheel drive. **2.** front-wheel drive.

-fy, a verbal suffix occurring in loanwords from Latin, with the meanings "to make, cause to be, render" (*clarify; purify*); "to become, be made" (*liquefy*). Compare -IFY.

FYI, for your information.

fyke (fīk), *n. Hudson and Delaware Valleys.* a bag-shaped fish trap.

G

G, g (jē), *n., pl.* **Gs** or **G's, gs** or **g's. 1.** the seventh letter of the English alphabet, a consonant. **2.** any spoken sound represented by this letter. **3.** something having the shape of a G. **4.** a written or printed representation of the letter *G* or *g*.

G, *pl.* **Gs** or **G's.** *Slang.* grand: a sum of one thousand dollars.

G, 1. gay. **2.** general: a motion-picture rating advising that the film is suitable for general audiences, or for children as well as adults. Compare NC-17, PG, PG-13, R (def. 4), X (def. 7). **3.** German. **4.** good.

G, *Symbol.* **1.** the seventh in order or in a series. **2. a.** the fifth note of the C major scale. **b.** a tonality having G as the tonic. **3.** conductance. **4.** constant of gravitation. **5.** gauss. **6.** *Biochem.* **a.** glycine. **b.** guanine.

g, *Symbol.* acceleration of gravity.

GA, 1. Gamblers Anonymous. **2.** general of the army. **3.** Georgia.

Ga, *Chem. Symbol.* gallium.

Ga., Georgia.

G.A., 1. General Agent. **2.** General Assembly.

gab (gab), *v.,* **gabbed, gab·bing,** *n. Informal.* —*v.i.* **1.** to talk or chat idly; chatter. —*n.* **2.** idle talk; chatter. —**gab′ber,** *n.*

gab·ar·dine (gab′ər dēn′, gab′ər dēn′), *n.* **1.** Also, **gaberdine.** a firm, tightly woven fabric of worsted, cotton, polyester, or other fiber, with a twill weave. **2.** GABERDINE (def. 1).

gab·ble (gab′əl), *v.,* **-bled, -bling,** *n.* —*v.i.* **1.** to speak or converse rapidly and unintelligibly; jabber. **2.** (of hens, geese, etc.) to cackle. —*v.t.* **3.** to utter rapidly and unintelligibly. —*n.* **4.** rapid, unintelligible talk. **5.** any quick succession of meaningless sounds. —**gab′bler,** *n.*

gab·by (gab′ē), *adj.,* **-bi·er, -bi·est.** talkative; garrulous. —**gab′bi·ness,** *n.*

gab·er·dine (gab′ər dēn′, gab′ər dēn′), *n.* **1.** Also, **gabardine.** a long, loose coat or frock for men, worn in the Middle Ages, esp. by Jews. **2.** GABARDINE (def. 1).

gab·fest (gab′fest′), *n. Informal.* **1.** a gathering at which there is a great deal of conversation. **2.** a long conversation.

ga·ble (gā′bəl), *n.* the portion of the front or side of a building, usu. triangular or nearly triangular in shape, enclosed by or masking the end of a roof that slopes downward from a central ridge. —**ga′bled,** *adj.* —**ga′ble·like′,** *adj.*

Ga·ble (gā′bəl), *n.* **(William) Clark,** 1901–60, U.S. film actor.

Ga·bon (gA bôn′) also **Gabun,** *n.* **1.** Official name, **Gab′onese Repub′lic.** a republic in W equatorial Africa: formerly a part of French Equatorial Africa; member of the French Community. 1,190,159; 102,290 sq. mi. (264,930 sq. km). *Cap.:* Libreville. **2.** an estuary in W Gabon. ab. 40 mi. (65 km) long. —**Gab·o·nese** (gab′ə nēz′, -nēs′, gä′bə-), *adj., n., pl.* **-nese.**

Ga·bo·ro·ne (gä′bə rō′ne, gab′ə-), *n.* the capital of Botswana, in the SE part. 110,973. Formerly, **Gaberones.**

Ga·bri·el (gā′brē əl), *n.* **1.** one of the archangels, appearing usu. as a divine messenger. Dan. 8:16, 9:21; Luke 1:19, 26. *Islam.* the angel of revelation and the intermediary between God and Muhammad. **3. Charles,** 1856–1932, U.S. musician and hymn writer.

gad[1] (gad), *v.i.,* **gad·ded, gad·ding.** to move aimlessly from one place to another in search of pleasure or amusement: *to gad about.*

gad[2] (gad), *n.* **1.** a goad for driving cattle. **2.** a pointed mining tool for breaking up rock, coal, etc.

Gad (gad), *n.* **1.** a son of Jacob and Zilpah. Gen. 30:11. **2.** one of the twelve tribes of Israel, traditionally descended from him. **3.** a Hebrew prophet and chronicler of the court of David. II Sam. 24:11–19.

gad·a·bout (gad′ə bout′), *n.* **1.** a person who moves about restlessly or aimlessly, esp. from one social activity to another. **2.** a person who travels often or to many different places, esp. for pleasure.

Gad·a·ra (gad′ər ə), *n.* a town on the Sea of Galilee where Jesus compelled demons to enter a herd of swine (the **Gad′arene swine′**). Mark 5:1–13. —**Gad·a·rene** (gad′ə rēn′, gad′ə rēn′), *adj.*

gad·fly (gad′flī′), *n., pl.* **-flies. 1.** any of various flies, as a horsefly or warble fly, that bite or annoy livestock. **2.** a person who persistently annoys or stirs up others, esp. with provocative criticism.

gadg·et (gaj′it), *n.* a usu. small mechanical or electronic contrivance or device; any ingenious article. —**gadg′et·y,** *adj.*

gadg·et·ry (gaj′i trē), *n.* mechanical or electronic contrivances; gadgets.

gad·o·lin·i·um (gad′l in′ē əm), *n.* a rare-earth metallic element. *Symbol:* Gd; *at. wt.:* 157.25; *at. no.:* 64. —**gad′o·lin′ic,** *adj.*

Gads·den (gadz′dən), *n.* **James,** 1788–1858, U.S. railroad promoter and diplomat.

Gads′den Pur′chase, *n.* a tract of 45,535 sq. mi. (117,935 sq. km), now contained in New Mexico and Arizona, purchased for $10,000,000 from Mexico in 1853, the treaty being negotiated by James Gadsden.

gad·wall (gad′wôl′), *n., pl.* **-walls,** (*esp. collectively*) **-wall.** a grayish brown North American dabbling duck, *Anas strepera.*

Gae·a (jē′ə), *n.* the ancient Greek goddess of the earth and mother of the Titans. [< Greek *gaîa* earth]

Gael (gāl), *n.* **1.** a native or inhabitant of the Highlands of Scotland, esp. one speaking Scottish Gaelic. **2.** any inhabitant of Scotland or Ireland speaking Irish or Scottish Gaelic, or a language ancestral to these.

Gael·ic (gā′lik), *n.* **1.** the Irish and Scottish Gaelic languages collectively. —*adj.* **2.** of or pertaining to Gaelic speakers or Gaelic.

gaff (gaf), *n.* **1.** an iron hook with a handle for landing large fish. **2.** the spur on a climbing iron, esp. as used by telephone linemen. **3.** a spar rising aft from a mast to support the head of a quadrilateral fore-and-aft sail. **4.** a metal spur for a gamecock. —*v.t.* **5.** to hook or land (a fish) with a gaff.

gaffe (gaf), *n.* a social blunder; faux pas.

gaf·fer (gaf′ər), *n.* **1.** the chief electrician on a motion-picture or television production. **2.** *Informal.* an old man.

gaff′ top′sail, *n.* a jib-headed fore-and-aft sail set above a gaff.

gag[1] (gag), *v.,* **gagged, gag·ging,** *n.* —*v.t.* **1.** to stop up the mouth of (a person) by putting something in it, thus preventing speech, shouts, etc. **2.** to restrain by force or authority from free speech. **3.** to hold open the jaws of, as in surgical operations. **4.** to cause to retch or choke. —*v.i.* **5.** to retch or choke. —*n.* **6.** something put into a person's mouth to prevent speech, shouting, etc. **7.** any forced or arbitrary suppression of free speech. **8.** a surgical instrument for holding the jaws open.

gag[2] (gag), *n., v.,* **gagged, gag·ging.** *Informal.* —*n.* **1.** a joke, esp. one introduced into a script or an actor's part. **2.** any contrived piece of wordplay or horseplay. —*v.i.* **3.** to tell jokes or make amusing remarks. **4.** to introduce gags into writing. **5.** to play on another's credulity, as by telling false stories. —*v.t.* **6.** to introduce gags into (a script, an actor's part, or the like) (usu. fol. by *up*).

ga·ga (gä′gä), *adj. Informal.* **1.** excessively and foolishly enthusiastic: *to go gaga over the new fashions.* **2.** ardently fond; infatuated. **3.** crazy; dotty. **4.** senile; mentally confused.

Ga·ga·rin (gä gär′in, gə-), *n.* **Yu·ri A·le·kse·ye·vich** (yŏŏr′ē al′ik sā′ə vich), 1934–68, Russian astronaut: first person to make an orbital space flight (1961).

gag·gle (gag′əl), *v.,* **-gled, -gling,** *n.* —*v.i.* **1.** to cackle. —*n.* **2.** a flock of geese when not flying. **3.** an often noisy or disorderly group or gathering; cluster: *a gaggle of sightseers.*

gag·man (gag′man′) also **gag·ster** (-star), *n., pl.* **-men. 1.** a person who writes gags for comedians. **2.** a comedian.

gag′ or′der, *n.* a court order banning reporters, attorneys, and other parties involved in a case before a court of law from reporting on or publicly disclosing anything relating to the case.

gag′ rule′, *n.* any rule restricting open discussion or debate concerning a given issue, esp. in a deliberative body.

gahn·ite (gä′nīt), *n.* a dark green to black mineral of the spinel group. [after J. G. *Gahn* (1745–1818), Swedish chemist]

Gai′a hypoth′esis (gā′ə), *n.* a model of the earth as a self-regulating organism, advanced as an alternative to a mechanistic model.

gai·e·ty (gā′i tē), *n., pl.* **-ties. 1.** the quality or state of being gay or cheerful; merriment. **2.** Often, **gaieties.** merrymaking or festivity: *the gaieties of the New Year season.* **3.** showiness; finery: *gaiety of dress.* Sometimes, **gayety.**

gai·jin (gī′jēn′; *Eng.* gī′jin), *n., pl.* **-jin** (-jēn; *Eng.* -jin). *Japanese.* an outsider; foreigner.

gail·lar·di·a (gā lär′dē ə), *n., pl.* **-di·as.** any composite plant of the genus *Gaillardia*, with yellow-rayed or red-rayed flower heads.

gai·ly (gā′lē), *adv.* **1.** merrily; cheerfully. **2.** brightly or showily.

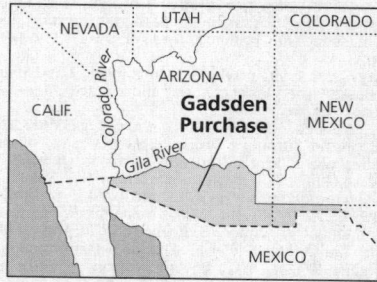

gain (gān), *v.t.* **1.** to get (something desired), esp. as a result of one's efforts; obtain; secure: *to gain possession of land; to gain permission to enter.* **2.** to acquire as an increase or addition: *to gain weight; to gain speed.* **3.** to obtain as a profit or advantage: *He didn't stand to gain much by the deal.* **4.** to win; get in competition: *to gain a prize.* **5.** to win (someone) to one's own side or point of view: *to gain supporters.* **6.** (of a watch or clock) to run fast by (a specified amount): *My watch gains six minutes a day.* **7.** to reach, esp. by effort; get to; arrive at: *to gain one's destination.* —*v.i.* **8.** to improve; make progress; advance: *to gain in health.* **9.** to get nearer, as in pursuit (usu. fol. by *on* or *upon*): *Our horse was gaining on the favorite.* **10.** to draw away from or farther ahead of one's competitors, pursuers, etc. (usu. fol. by *on* or *upon*). **11.** (of a watch or clock) to run fast. —*n.* **12.** profit or advantage: *I see no gain in this plan.* **13.** an increase or advance: *a gain in weight; a gain in power.* **14.** gains, profits or winnings. **15.** the act of gaining; acquisition. **16. a.** a measure of the increase in signal amplitude produced by an amplifier, expressed as the ratio of output to input. **b.** the effectiveness of a directional antenna as compared with a standard, nondirectional one. —*Proverb.* **17. No gain without pain,** success requires considerable effort. —**gain′a•ble,** *adj.*

gain•er (gā′nər), *n.* **1.** a person or thing that gains. **2.** a dive in which the diver takes off facing forward and performs a backward motion, executing either a complete somersault with entry feetfirst into the water (**full gainer**) or a half-somersault with entry headfirst (**half gainer**).

gain•ful (gān′fəl), *adj.* profitable; lucrative: *gainful employment.* —**gain′ful•ly,** *adv.* —**gain′ful•ness,** *n.*

gain•say (gān′sā′, gān sā′), *v.t.,* **-said, -say•ing. 1.** to deny; dispute; contradict. **2.** to speak or act against; oppose. —**gain′say′er,** *n.*

gait (gāt), *n.* **1.** a manner of walking, stepping, or running. **2.** any of the manners in which a horse moves, as a walk, trot, canter, gallop, or rack. —**gait′ed,** *adj.*

gait•er (gā′tər), *n.* **1.** a cloth or leather covering for the ankle and instep and sometimes also the shoe or boot, worn over the shoe or boot. **2.** a cloth or leather shoe with elastic insertions at the sides. **3.** an overshoe with a cloth top.

gal (gal), *n. Informal.* a girl or woman.

ga•la (gā′lə, gal′ə; *esp. Brit.* gä′lə), *adj.* **1.** marking or befitting a special occasion; festive; showy: *a gala affair.* —*n.* **2.** a festive occasion or celebration, often involving public entertainment.

ga•lac•tic (gə lak′tik), *adj.* **1. a.** of or pertaining to a galaxy. **b.** of or pertaining to the Milky Way. **2.** immense; vast: *a problem of galactic proportions.* **3.** pertaining to or stimulating the secretion of milk.

ga•lac•tose (gə lak′tōs), *n.* a white sugar, $C_6H_{12}O_6$, obtained from milk sugar and vegetable mucilage.

Gal•a•had (gal′ə had′), *n.* **1. Sir,** the noblest and purest knight of the Round Table, son of Lancelot and Elaine: gained the Holy Grail. **2.** a man showing devotion to the highest ideals.

Ga•lá•pa•gos Is′lands (gə lä′pə gōs′, -gəs, -lap′ə-), *n.pl.* an archipelago on the equator in the Pacific, ab. 600 mi. (965 km) W of and belonging to Ecuador: many unique species of animal life. 4058; 3029 sq. mi. (7845 sq. km).

Ga•la•te•a (gal′ə tē′ə), *n.* the woman brought to life by Aphrodite from the ivory statue carved by Pygmalion.

Ga•la•tia (gə lā′shə, -shē ə), *n.* an ancient country in central Asia Minor: later a Roman province; site of an early Christian community. —**Ga•la′tian,** *adj., n.*

Ga•la•tians (gə lā′shənz), *n.* (*used with a sing. v.*) a book of the New Testament, written to the Christians in Galatia.

gal•a•vant (gal′ə vant′, gal′ə vant′), *v.i.* GALLIVANT.

gal•ax•y (gal′ək sē), *n., pl.* **-ax•ies. 1. a.** a large system of stars held together by mutual gravitation and isolated from similar systems by vast regions of space. **b.** (*usu. cap.*) MILKY WAY. **2.** any large and brilliant or impressive assemblage of persons or things: *a galaxy of opera stars.* [≪ Greek *galaxías (kýklos)* the Milky (Way)]

Gal•braith (gal′brāth), *n.* **John Kenneth,** born 1908, U.S. economist, born in Canada.

gale (gāl), *n.* **1.** a very strong wind. **2.** a wind of 32–63 mph (14–28 m/sec): *a gale of laughter.*

Ga•len (gā′lən), *n.* **Claudius,** A.D. c130–c200, Greek physician and writer. Latin, **Ga•le•nus** (gə lē′nəs). —**Ga•len′ic** (-len′ik), *adj.*

ga•le•na (gə lē′nə) *also* **ga•le•nite** (-nīt), *n.* a common heavy mineral, lead sulfide, PbS, occurring in lead-gray crystals, usu. cubes, and cleavable masses: the principal ore of lead. —**ga•le′nic** (-lē′nik, -len′ik), *adj.*

gal′ Fri′day, *n.* a woman who acts as a general assistant in a business office and has a variety of secretarial and clerical duties. —*Usage.* See GIRL.

Ga•li•ci•a (gə lish′ə, -lish′ē ə; *for 2 also Sp.* gä lē′thyä, -syä), *n.* **1.** a region in E central Europe: a former crown land of Austria, included in S Poland after World War I, and now partly in Ukraine. ab. 30,500 sq. mi. (79,000 sq. km). **2.** a maritime region in NW Spain: a former kingdom, and later a province. 11,256 sq. mi. (29,153 sq. km).

Ga•li•le•an[1] (gal′ə lē′ən), *adj.* **1.** of or pertaining to Galilee. —*n.* **2.** a native or inhabitant of Galilee. **3.** a Christian. **4. the Galilean,** Jesus.

Ga•li•le•an[2] (gal′ə lā′ən, -lē′-), *adj.* of or pertaining to Galileo.

Gal•i•lee (gal′ə lē′), *n.* **1.** an ancient Roman province in what is now N Israel. **2. Sea of.** Also called **Lake Tiberias.** a lake in NE Israel through which the Jordan River flows. 14 mi. (23 km) long; 682 ft. (208 m) below sea level.

Gal•i•le•o (gal′ə lā′ō, -lē′ō), *n.* **1.** (*Galileo Galilei*), 1564–1642, Italian physicist and astronomer. **2.** a U.S. space probe to Jupiter, launched 1989.

gal•in•gale (gal′in gāl′, -ing-), *n.* any of numerous sedges of the genus *Cyperus,* esp. *C. langus,* having aromatic roots.

gal•i•pot or **gal•li•pot** (gal′ə pot′), *n.* a type of turpentine exuded on the stems of certain species of pine.

gall[1] (gôl), *n.* **1.** audacity; impudence; effrontery. **2.** BILE (def. 1). **3.** something bitter or severe. **4.** bitterness of spirit; rancor. —*Idiom.* **5. gall and wormwood,** bitterness of spirit; deep resentment.

gall[2] (gôl), *v.t.* **1.** to make sore by rubbing; chafe severely: *The saddle galled the horse's back.* **2.** to vex or irritate greatly: *An arrogant manner galls me.* —*v.i.* **3.** to be or become chafed. —*n.* **4.** a sore on the skin, esp. of a horse, due to rubbing. **5.** something very vexing or irritating. **6.** a state of vexation or irritation.

gall[3] (gôl), *n.* any abnormal outgrowth or swelling in a plant, as from viral damage, insect egg deposits, or chemical irritants.

gal•lant (*adj.* gal′ənt *for 1, 3, 4;* gə lant′, -länt′, gal′ənt *for 2, 5; n.* gə-lant′, -länt′, gal′ənt), *adj.* **1.** brave, spirited, or noble-minded: *a gallant knight; a gallant attempt.* **2.** exceptionally polite and attentive to women; chivalrous. **3.** stately; grand: *a gallant pageant.* **4.** showy, colorful, or stylish, as in dress. **5.** amorous; amatory. —*n.* **6.** a man exceptionally attentive to women. **7.** a stylish and dashing man. **8.** a suitor or lover. **9.** a paramour. **10.** a brave or noble-minded man. —**gal′lant•ly,** *adv.* —**gal′lant•ry,** *n., pl.* **-tries.**

gall′blad′der or **gall′ blad′der,** *n.* a membranous sac attached by ducts to the liver, in which bile is stored and concentrated.

gal•le•on (gal′ē ən, gal′yən), *n.* a large sailing vessel of the 15th to the 17th centuries used as a fighting or merchant ship, square-rigged on the foremast and mainmast and generally lateen-rigged on one or two after masts.

galleon

gal•le•ri•a (gal′ə rē′ə), *n., pl.* **-ri•as. 1.** a spacious passageway, court, or indoor mall, usu. having a high vaulted glass roof and containing commercial establishments. **2.** GALLERY (defs. 7, 9, 10).

gal•ler•y (gal′ə rē, gal′rē), *n., pl.* **-ler•ies. 1.** a raised area, often having a stepped or sloping floor, in a theater, church, or other public building to accommodate spectators, exhibits, etc. **2.** the uppermost of such areas in a theater, usu. containing the cheapest seats. **3.** the occupants of such an area in a theater. **4.** the general public, esp. when regarded as having popular or uncultivated tastes. **5.** any group of spectators or observers, as at a golf match or a legislative session. **6.** a room, series of rooms, or building devoted to the exhibition and often the sale of works of art. **7.** a long covered area, narrow and open at one or both sides, used esp. as a walk or corridor. **8.** *Chiefly South Atlantic States.* a long porch or portico; veranda. **9.** a long, relatively narrow room, esp. one for public use. **10.** a raised, balconylike platform or passageway running along the exterior wall of a building inside or outside. **11.** a large room or building used for photography, target practice, or other special purposes: *a shooting gallery.* **12.** a collection or group: *a gallery of misfits.* **13.** a projecting balcony or structure on the quarter or stern of a ship. **14.** an ornamental railing surrounding the top of a table, desk, etc. **15.** *Mining.* a level or drift. **16.** an underground passageway in a mine, earthwork, or fortification. **17.** a passageway made by an animal. —*Idiom.* **18. play to the gallery,** to act in a manner intended to appeal to or impress an undiscriminating public. —**gal′ler•ied,** *adj.*

gal•ley (gal′ē), *n., pl.* **-leys. 1. a.** the kitchen area of a ship, plane, or camper. **b.** any small narrow kitchen. **2.** a seagoing vessel propelled mainly by oars, used in ancient and medieval times, sometimes with the aid of sails. **b.** a long rowboat, as one used as a ship's boat by a warship or one used for dragging a seine. **3. a.** a long narrow tray, usu. of metal, for holding type that has been set. **b.** GALLEY PROOF.

gal′ley proof′, *n.* a proof, orig. one set from type in a galley, taken before the material has been made up into pages and usu. printed as a single column of type with wide margins for marking corrections.

gall•fly (gôl′flī′), *n., pl.* **-flies.** any of various insects that deposit their eggs in plants, causing the formation of galls.

gal•lic (gal′ik), *adj.* of or containing trivalent gallium.

Gal·lic (gal′ik), *adj.* **1.** of or pertaining to the French or France; characteristically French: *Gallic wit.* **2.** of or pertaining to the Gauls or Gaul. —**Gal′li·cal·ly,** *adv.*

Gal·li·can (gal′i kən), *adj.* **1.** of or pertaining to the Roman Catholic Church in France. **2.** of or pertaining to a school or party of French Roman Catholics, before 1870, advocating the restriction of papal authority. [< Medieval Latin *Gallicānus* French, Latin: of Gaul]

gal·li·mau·fry (gal′ə mô′frē), *n.*, *pl.* -**fries. 1.** a hodgepodge; jumble; confused medley. **2.** a ragout or hash.

gal·li·na·ceous (gal′ə nā′shəs), *adj.* belonging or pertaining to the order Galliformes, comprising ground-feeding domestic or game birds, as chickens, turkeys, grouse, quail, and pheasants.

gall·ing (gô′ling), *adj.* irritating; vexing. —**gall′ing·ly,** *adv.* —**gall′ing·ness,** *n.*

gal·li·nip·per (gal′ə nip′ər), *n. Informal.* any of various insects that sting or bite, esp. a large American mosquito, *Psorophora ciliata.*

gal·li·nule (gal′ə nōōl′, -nyōōl′), *n.* any of several typically brightly colored aquatic rails of the genera *Porphyrio, Porphyrula,* and *Gallinula,* having elongated, webless toes.

Gal·li·o (gal′ē ō′), *n.* a Roman proconsul of Achaia before whom the Apostle Paul appeared during his first mission to Corinth. Acts 18:12–17.

gal·li·um (gal′ē əm), *n.* a rare steel-gray metallic element used in high-temperature thermometers because of its high boiling point (1983°C) and low melting point (30°C). *Symbol:* Ga; *at. wt.:* 69.72; *at. no.:* 31; *sp. gr.:* 5.91 at 20°C.

gal·li·vant or **gal·a·vant** (gal′ə vant′, gal′ə vant′), *v.i.* **1.** to wander about, seeking pleasure or diversion; gad. **2.** to go about with members of the opposite sex. —**gal′li·vant′er,** *n.*

gal·lo·glass or **gal·low·glass** (gal′ō glas′, -gläs′), *n.* (formerly) a soldier owing allegiance to an Irish chief.

gal·lon (gal′ən), *n.* a common unit of capacity in English-speaking countries, equal to four quarts, the U.S. standard gallon being equal to 231 cubic inches (3.7853 liters), and the British imperial gallon to 277.42 cubic inches (4.546 liters). *Abbr.:* gal.

gal·lop·ing (gal′ə ping), *adj.* **1.** at a gallop; running or moving quickly. **2.** progressing rapidly, as a disease: *galloping pneumonia.* **3.** growing or spreading rapidly: *galloping inflation.*

gal·lows (gal′ōz, -əz), *n.*, *pl.* -**lows, -lows·es. 1.** a wooden frame consisting of two upright timbers with a crossbeam from which condemned persons are hanged. **2.** a similar structure from which something is suspended. **3.** execution by hanging: *a criminal sentenced to the gallows.*

gal′lows hu′mor, *n.* humor that treats serious, frightening, or painful subject matter in a light or satirical way.

gal′lows (or **gal′low**) **tree′,** *n.* GALLOWS (def. 1).

gall·stone (gôl′stōn′), *n.* an abnormal stony mass in the gallbladder or the bile passages, usu. composed of cholesterol.

Gal·lup (gal′əp), *n.* **George Horace,** 1901–84, U.S. statistician.

Gal′lup poll′, *n.* a representative sampling of public opinion or public awareness concerning a certain subject or issue. [after G. H. GALLUP]

ga·loot (gə lōōt′), *n. Slang.* an awkward, eccentric, or foolish person.

gal·op (gal′əp, ga lō′), *n.* **1.** a lively round dance in duple time. **2.** music suitable for a galop.

ga·lore (gə lôr′, -lōr′), *adv.* in abundance; in plentiful amounts (used postpositively): *food and drink galore.*

ga·losh (gə losh′), *n.* a waterproof overshoe, esp. a high one.

gals., gallons.

ga·lumph (gə lumf′), *v.i.* to move along heavily and clumsily.

galvan′ic bat′tery, *n.* BATTERY (def. 1a).

galvan′ic cell′, *n.* CELL (def. 5).

galvan′ic pile′, *n.* VOLTAIC PILE.

gal·va·nism (gal′və niz′əm), *n.* **1.** electricity, esp. as produced by chemical action. **2.** the therapeutic application of electricity to the body. —**gal·van′ic,** *adj.*

gal·va·nize (gal′və nīz′), *v.t.*, -**nized, -niz·ing. 1.** to stimulate by an electric current: *to galvanize muscles or nerves.* **2.** to stimulate; stir; startle into sudden activity: *to galvanize the public into action.* **3.** to coat (metal, esp. iron or steel) with zinc. —**gal′va·ni·za′tion,** *n.* —**gal′va·niz′er,** *n.*

gal′vanized i′ron, *n.* iron or steel, esp. in sheets, coated with zinc to prevent rust.

gam[1] (gam), *n. Slang.* a person's leg.

gam[2] (gam), *n.*, *v.*, **gammed, gam·ming. —***n.* **1.** a herd or school of whales. **2.** a social meeting or visit between whalers. —*v.i.* **3.** (of whales) to assemble into a herd or school. **4.** (of whalers) to participate in a gam.

Ga·ma (gam′ə, gä′mə), *n.* **Vasco da,** c1460–1524, Portuguese navigator: first to reach Europe from India.

Ga·ma·li·el (gə mā′lē əl, -māl′yəl), *n.* **1.** (*"the Elder"* or *"Gamaliel I"*), died A.D. 50?, the teacher of Paul (Acts 22:3); the grandson of Hillel. **2.** his grandson (*"the Younger"* or *"Gamaliel II"*), died A.D. 115?, leader of the Jews after the destruction of Jerusalem, A.D. 70.

Gam·bi·a (gam′bē ə), *n.* **1.** a river in W Africa, flowing W to the Atlantic. 500 mi. (800 km) long. **2. The,** a republic in W Africa: formerly a British crown colony and protectorate; gained independence 1965; member of the Commonwealth of Nations. 1,248,085; 4003 sq. mi. (10,368 sq. km). *Cap.:* Banjul. —**Gam′bi·an,** *adj.*, *n.*

gam·bit (gam′bit), *n.* **1.** an opening in chess in which a player seeks to obtain some advantage by sacrificing a pawn or piece. **2.** any maneuver by which one seeks to gain an advantage; ploy. **3.** a remark made to open or redirect a conversation.

gam·ble (gam′bəl), *v.*, -**bled, -bling,** *n. —v.i.* **1.** to play at a game of chance for money or other stakes. **2.** to stake or risk something of value, as money, on the outcome of something involving chance; bet. —*v.t.* **3.** to lose or squander by betting (usu. fol. by *away*): *He gambled all his hard-earned money away in one night.* **4.** to wager or risk (something of value); stake: *I'll gamble my life on his honesty.* **5.** to take a chance on. *We're gambling that our store will be a success.* —*n.* **6.** any matter or thing involving risk or hazardous uncertainty: **7.** a venture in a game of chance for stakes, esp. for high stakes. —**gam′bler,** *n.*

gam·boge (gam bōj′, -bōōzh′), *n.* **1.** a gum resin from various Asian trees of the genus *Garcinia,* family Guttiferae, esp. *G. hanburyi,* used as a yellow pigment. **2.** yellow or yellow-orange. —**gam·bo′gi·an,** *adj.*

gam·bol (gam′bəl), *v.*, -**boled, -bol·ing** or (*esp. Brit.*) -**bolled, -bol·ling,** *n. —v.i.* **1.** to skip about, as in dancing or playing; frolic. —*n.* **2.** a skipping or frisking about; frolic.

gam′brel roof′, *n.* a gable roof, each side of which has a shallower slope above a steeper one.

game[1] (gām), *n.*, *adj.*, **gam·er, gam·est,** *v.*, **gamed, gam·ing. —***n.* **1.** an amusement or pastime: *children's games; a card game.* **2.** the material or equipment used in playing certain games. **3.** a competitive activity involving skill, chance, or endurance and played according to a set of rules for the amusement of the players or spectators. **4.** a single occasion of such an activity or a division of one. **5.** the number of points required to win a game. **6.** the score at a particular stage in a game. **7.** a particular manner or style of playing a game. **8.** something resembling a game, as in requiring skill, endurance, or adherence to rules: *the game of diplomacy.* **9.** *Informal.* a business or profession: *He's in the real-estate game.* **10.** a trick or strategy: *to see through someone's game.* **11.** fun; sport; joke: *That's about enough of your games.* **12.** wild animals, including birds and fishes, such as are hunted for food or taken for sport or profit. **13.** the flesh of such wild animals or other game, used as food. **14.** any object of pursuit, attack, abuse, etc.: *to be fair game for practical jokers.* —*adj.* **15.** pertaining to or composed of animals hunted or taken as game or to their flesh. **16.** having a fighting spirit; plucky. **17.** having the required spirit or will (often fol. by *for* or an infinitive): *Who's game for a hike through the woods?* —*v.i.* **18.** to play games of chance for stakes; gamble. —*v.t.* **19.** to squander in gaming (usu. fol. by *away*). —**Idiom.** **20. make game of,** to make fun of; ridicule. **21. only game in town,** the only available choice. **22. play games,** to trifle with or manipulate others. **23. play the game,** to act in accordance with rules or standards, esp. to act honorably or justly. —**Saying.** **24. The game is not worth the candle,** the effort required is more than the results are worth. —**game′ly,** *adv.*

game[2] (gām), *adj.* lame: *a game leg.*

game′ bird′, *n.* any bird hunted chiefly for sport, as a quail or pheasant, esp. such a bird protected by game laws.

game·cock (gām′kok′), *n.* a rooster of a fighting breed or one bred and trained for fighting.

game′ fish′, *n.* a fish valued for the sport it gives the angler in its capture. Also called **sport fish.**

game·keep·er (gām′kē′pər), *n.* a person employed, as on an estate or game preserve, to prevent poaching and provide for the conservation of game. —**game′keep′ing,** *n.*

game′ law′, *n.* a law enacted for the preservation of game.

game′ of chance′, *n.* a game, as roulette, in which the outcome is determined by chance rather than by skill.

game′ plan′, *n.* **1.** a carefully planned strategy or course of action, as in politics or business. **2.** the strategy of an athletic team for winning a game.

game′ point′, *n.* **1.** (in tennis, squash, handball, etc.) a situation in which the next point scored could decide the winner of the game. **2.** the winning point itself.

game′ show′, *n.* a radio or television program in which contestants answer questions or play games in order to win prizes.

games·man·ship (gāmz′mən ship′), *n.* skill in manipulating people or events so as to gain an advantage or outwit one's opponents or competitors.

game·ster (gām′stər), *n.* a person who plays games, esp. a gambler.

gam·ete (gam′ēt, gə mēt′), *n.* a mature sexual reproductive cell, as a sperm or egg, that unites with another cell to form a new organism. —**ga·met·ic** (gə met′ik), **ga·me·tal** (gə mēt′l), *adj.* —**ga·met′i·cal·ly,** *adv.*

game′ the′ory, *n.* a mathematical theory that deals with strategies for maximizing gains and minimizing losses within prescribed constraints.

gam·ic (gam′ik), *adj.* requiring fertilization for reproduction; sexual. **2.** capable of developing only after fertilization.

gam·in (gam′in), *n.* **1.** a neglected boy left to run about the streets; street urchin. **2.** GAMINE.

gam·ine (gam′ēn, -in, ga mēn′), *n.* **1.** a neglected girl left to run about the streets. **2.** a diminutive girl, esp. one who is pert, impudent, or playfully mischievous. —*adj.* **3.** of or like a gamine: *a gamine personality; clothes for the gamine figure.*

gam·ing (gā′ming), *n.* **1.** gambling. **2.** the playing of games, esp. those developed to help solve problems, as in military or business situations.

gam·ma (gam′ə), *n., pl.* **-mas. 1.** the third letter of the Greek alphabet (Γ, γ). **2.** the third in a series of items. **3.** (*cap.*) a star that is usu. the third brightest of a constellation. **4.** a unit of weight equal to one microgram. **5.** a unit of magnetic field strength, equal to 10⁻⁵ gauss. **6.** a measure of the degree of development of a photographic negative or print.

gam′ma glob′u·lin, *n.* a protein fraction of blood plasma that responds to stimulation of antigens, as bacteria or viruses, by forming antibodies: used in the treatment of some viral diseases.

gam′ma ray′, *n.* **1.** a highly penetrating photon of high frequency, usu. 10¹⁹ Hz or more, emitted by an atomic nucleus. **2.** a stream of such photons.

gam·mon (gam′ən), *n.* a victory in backgammon in which the loser has not thrown off any pieces.

gam·o·gen·e·sis (gam′ə jen′ə sis), *n.* sexual reproduction. —**gam′o·ge·net′ic** (-ō jə net′ik), **gam′o·ge·net′i·cal,** *adj.* —**gam′o·ge·net′i·cal·ly,** *adv.*

-gamous or **-gamic,** a combining form meaning "having gametes or reproductive organs" of the kind specified by the initial element (*heterogamous*); also forming adjectives corresponding to nouns ending in -GAMY (*endogamous*).

gam·ut (gam′ət), *n.* **1.** the entire scale or range: *the gamut of dramatic emotion from grief to joy.* **2.** the whole series of recognized musical notes. [late Middle English < Medieval Latin; contr. of *gamma ut* = *gamma,* used to represent the first or lowest tone (G) in the medieval scale + *ut* (later *do*); the notes of the scale (*ut, re, mi, fa, sol, la, si*) being named from a Latin hymn to St. John the Baptist: *Ut* queant laxis *re*sonare fibris. *Mi*ra gestorum *fa*muli tuorum, *Sol*ve polluti *la*bii reatum, *S*ancte *I*ohannes]

gam·y or **gam·ey** (gā′mē), *adj.,* **gam·i·er, gam·i·est. 1.** having the tangy flavor of game, esp. game kept uncooked until slightly tainted: *the gamy taste of venison.* **2.** malodorous; smelly. **3.** plucky; spirited. **4.** lewd or suggestive; risqué. **5.** gross or squalid; unwholesome. —**gam′i·ly,** *adv.* —**gam′i·ness,** *n.*

-gamy, a combining form with the meanings "marriage" (*exogamy*), "union" (*syngamy*), "fertilization, pollination" (*autogamy*) of the kind specified by the initial element; also forming nouns corresponding to adjectives ending in -GAMOUS (*heterogamy*).

gan·der (gan′dər), *n.* **1.** the male of the goose. Compare GOOSE (def. 2). **2.** a silly person; goose. **3.** *Slang.* a look: *Take a gander at his new shoes.*

Gan·dhi (gän′dē, gan′-), *n.* **1. Indira,** 1917–84, prime minister of India 1966–77 and 1980–84 (daughter of Jawaharlal Nehru). **2. Mohandas Karamchand** ("*Mahatma*"), 1869–1948, Hindu religious leader, nationalist, and social reformer. **3. Rajiv,** 1944–91, prime minister of India 1984–1989 (son of Indira). —**Gan′dhi·an,** *adj.*

gang¹ (gang), *n.* **1.** a group or band: *a gang of cyclists; gangs of sightseers.* **2.** a group of youngsters or adolescents who associate closely, often exclusively, for social reasons, esp. such a group engaging in delinquent behavior. **3.** a group of people with compatible tastes or mutual interests who gather together for social reasons: *I'm throwing a party for the gang I bowl with.* **4.** a group of persons working together; squad; shift: *a gang of laborers.* **5.** a group of persons associated for some criminal or other antisocial purpose: *a gang of thieves.* **6.** a set of tools, electronic components or circuits, oars, etc., arranged to work together or simultaneously. **7.** a group of identical or related items. —*v.t.* **8.** to arrange in groups or sets; form into a gang: *to gang illustrations on one sheet.* **9.** to attack in a gang. —*v.i.* **10.** to form or act as a gang. **11. gang up on,** to set upon or attack as a group; combine against.

gang² (gang), *v.i. Chiefly Scot.* to go.

gang·bust·er (gang′bus′tər), *n. Informal.* **1.** a law-enforcement officer who specializes in breaking up gangs of criminals. **2.** someone or something having great impact, usu. in a positive way. **3. gangbusters,** an outstandingly successful state or situation. —*adj.* Often, **gangbusters. 4.** strikingly effective or successful: *a gangbusters year for compact cars.* **5.** enthusiastic: *to be gangbusters over an idea.* —**Idiom. 6.** like **gangbusters,** with vigor and speed.

Gan·ges (gan′jēz), *n.* a river flowing SE from the Himalayas in N India into the Bay of Bengal: sacred to Hindus. 1550 mi. (2495 km) long. —**Gan·get′ic** (-jet′ik), *adj.*

gang·land (gang′land′, -lənd), *n.* the world of organized crime.

gan·gle (gang′gəl), *v.i.,* **-gled, -gling.** to move awkwardly or ungracefully: *A tall, stiff-jointed man gangled past.*

gan·gli·ate (gang′glē āt′, -it) also **gan′gli·at′ed,** *adj.* having ganglia.

gan·gling (gang′gling) also **gangly,** *adj.* awkwardly tall and spindly; lank and loosely built.

gan·gli·on (gang′glē ən), *n., pl.* **-gli·a** (-glē ə), **-gli·ons. 1.** a concentrated mass of interconnected nerve cells. **2.** a cystic tumor formed on the sheath of a tendon. **3.** a center of intellectual or industrial force, activity, etc. —**gan′gli·al, gan′gli·ar,** or **gan·gli·on′ic** (-on′ik), *adj.*

gan·gly (gang′glē), *adj.,* **-gli·er, -gli·est.** GANGLING.

Gang′ of Four′, *n.* a group of four radical members of the Chinese Communist party who were leaders of the Cultural Revolution and who were purged and imprisoned after the death of Mao Zedong: Jiang Qing (widow of Mao), Wang Hongwen, Yao Wenyuan, and Zhang Chunqiao. Compare CULTURAL REVOLUTION, RED GUARD.

gang·plank (gang′plangk′), *n.* a flat plank or small movable structure for boarding or leaving a ship at a pier. Also called **gangway.**

gan·grene (gang′grēn, gang grēn′), *n.* necrosis or death of soft tissue due to obstructed circulation, usu. followed by decomposition and putrefaction. —**gan′gre·nous** (-grə nəs), *adj.*

gang′sta (or **gang′ster**) **rap′** (gang′stə), *n.* a type of rap music whose lyrics feature violence, sexual exploits, and the like.

gang·ster (gang′star), *n.* a member of a gang of criminals; mobster. —**gang′ster·ism,** *n.*

Gang·tok (gung′tok′), *n.* the capital of Sikkim, in NE India. 36,768.

gang·way (*n.* gang′wā′; *interj.* gang′wā′), *n.* **1.** a passageway or narrow walkway. **2. a.** an opening in the railing or bulwark of a ship, as that into which a gangplank fits. **b.** GANGPLANK. **3.** *Brit.* an aisle in the House of Commons separating the more influential members of the political parties from the younger, less influential members. **4.** a temporary path of planks, as at a building site. **5.** a main passage or level in a mine. —*interj.* **6.** (used to call for clear passage). —**gang′wayed′,** *adj.*

gan·net (gan′it), *n.* any of several large seabirds of the genus *Sula* (or *Morus*), of the booby family, inhabiting colder oceanic waters in both hemispheres.

gant·let (gant′lit, gônt′-), *n.* **1.** Also, **gauntlet.** a railroad track construction used in narrow places, in which two parallel tracks converge so that their inner rails cross, run parallel, and diverge again, thus allowing a train to remain on its own track at all times. **2.** GAUNTLET² (defs. 1, 2, 4).

gan·try (gan′trē) *n., pl.* **-tries. 1.** a framework spanning a railroad track or tracks for displaying signals. **2.** any of various spanning frameworks, as a bridgelike portion of certain cranes. **3.** a frame consisting of scaffolds on various levels used to erect vertically launched rockets and spacecraft. **4.** a framelike stand for supporting a barrel or cask.

GAO, General Accounting Office.

gap (gap), *n., v.,* **gapped, gap·ping.** —*n.* **1.** a break or opening, as in a fence, wall, or military line; breach. **2.** an empty space or interval; hiatus: *a gap in one's memory.* **3.** a wide divergence or difference; disparity: *a gap between expenses and income.* **4.** a difference or disparity in attitudes, perceptions, character, or development, or a lack of confidence or understanding, perceived as creating a problem: *the technology gap; a communications gap.* **5.** a deep sloping ravine or cleft through a mountain ridge. **6.** *Chiefly Midland and Southern U.S.* a mountain pass: *the Cumberland Gap.* —*v.t.* **7.** to make a gap, opening, or breach in. —*v.i.* **8.** to come open or apart; form or show a gap. —**gap′less,** *adj.*

gape (gāp, gap), *v.,* **gaped, gap·ing,** *n.* —*v.i.* **1.** to stare with open mouth, as in wonder. **2.** to open the mouth wide involuntarily as the result of hunger, sleepiness, or absorbed attention. **3.** to open as a gap; split or become open wide. —*n.* **4.** a wide opening; gap; breach. **5.** an act or instance of gaping. **6.** a stare, as in astonishment or with the mouth wide open. **7.** a yawn. **8.** *Zool.* the width of the open mouth. —**gap′ing·ly,** *adv.*

gapes (gāps, gaps), *n.* (*used with a sing. v.*) **1.** a parasitic disease of poultry and other birds, characterized by frequent gaping due to infestation of the trachea and bronchi with gapeworms. **2.** a fit of yawning. —**gap′y,** *adj.*

gar (gär), *n., pl.* (*esp. collectively*) **gar,** (*esp. for kinds or species*) **gars.** any long-jawed freshwater fish of the genus *Lepisosteus,* of North America. Also called **gar·fish** (gär′fish′).

G.A.R., Grand Army of the Republic.

ga·rage (gə räzh′, -räj′; *esp. Brit.* gar′ij, -äzh), *n., v.,* **-raged, -rag·ing.** —*n.* **1.** a building or indoor area for parking or storing motor vehicles. **2.** a commercial establishment for repairing and servicing motor vehicles. —*v.t.* **3.** to put or keep in a garage.

garage′ sale′, *n.* a sale of used or unwanted household goods or personal items, typically held in one's garage or yard. Also called **tag sale, yard sale.**

garb (gärb), *n.* **1.** a fashion or mode of dress, esp. of a distinctive, uniform kind: *the garb of a monk.* **2.** wearing apparel; clothes. **3.** outward appearance or form. —*v.t.* **4.** to dress; clothe.

gar·bage (gär′bij), *n.* **1.** discarded animal and vegetable matter, as from a kitchen; refuse. **2.** any matter that is no longer wanted or needed; trash. **3.** anything that is contemptibly worthless, inferior, or vile. **4.** worthless talk; lies; foolishness. **5.** meaningless or unwanted computer data, as caused by a bug.

gar·bage·man (gär′bij man′), *n., pl.* **-men.** a person employed to collect, haul away, and dispose of garbage.

gar·ban·zo (gär bän′zō), *n., pl.* **-zos.** CHICKPEA.

gar·ble (gär′bəl), *v.,* **-bled, -bling.** —*v.t.* **1.** to confuse unintentionally or ignorantly; jumble: *to garble instructions.* **2.** to make unfair or misleading selections from or arrangement of (fact, statements, writings, etc.); distort: *to garble a quotation.* —*n.* **3.** the act or process of garbling. **4.** an instance of garbling; a garbled phrase, literary passage, etc. —**gar′ble·a·ble,** *adj.* —**gar′bler,** *n.*

Gar·bo (gär′bō), *n.* **Greta** (*Greta Lovisa Gustaffson*), 1905–90, U.S. film actress, born in Sweden.

gar·bol·o·gy (gär bol′ə jē), *n.* the study of the material discarded by a society to learn what it reveals about cultural or social patterns. —**gar·bol′o·gist,** *n.*

gar·den (gär′dn), *n.* **1.** a plot of ground, usu. near a house, where flowers, shrubs, vegetables, fruits, or herbs are cultivated. **2.** a piece of ground or other space, commonly with ornamental plants, trees, etc., used as a park. **3.** a fertile and delightful spot or region. **4.** *Brit.* YARD² (def. 1). —*adj.* **5.** pertaining to, produced in, or suitable for cultivation or use in a garden: *fresh garden vegetables; garden furniture.* **6.** garden-variety. —*v.i.* **7.** to lay out, cultivate, or tend a garden. —*v.t.* **8.** to cultivate as a garden. —*Idiom.* **9. lead down** or **up the garden path,** to mislead through illusions of hope and reward; lead on; delude. [< Old French *jardin* < Germanic] —**gar′den·er,** *n.*

gar′den apart′ment, *n.* **1.** an apartment on the ground floor of an apartment building having direct access to a backyard or garden. **2.** a low-rise apartment building or building complex surrounded by lawns or gardens.

gar′den cress′, *n.* a peppergrass, *Lepidium sativum,* used in salad.

Gar′den Grove′, *n.* a city in SW California. 147,958.

gar′den he′liotrope, *n.* the cultivated valerian, *Valeriana officinalis.*

gar·de·nia (gär dē′nyə, -nē ə), *n., pl.* **-nias. 1.** any subtropical Old World evergreen tree or shrub of the genus *Gardenia,* of the madder family, having shiny leaves and fragrant white flowers. **2.** the flower of these plants.

Gar′den of E′den, *n.* EDEN.

gar′den-vari′ety, *adj.* common, usual, or ordinary; unexceptional.

Gard·ner (gärd′nər), *n.* **Erle Stanley,** 1889–1970, U.S. writer of detective stories.

Gar·field (gär′fēld′), *n.* **James Abram,** 1831–81, 20th president of the U.S., 1881.

gar·fish (gär′fish′), *n., pl.* (*esp. collectively*) **-fish,** (*esp. for kinds or species*) **-fish·es.** GAR.

gar·gan·tu·an (gär gan′chōō ən), *adj.* gigantic; enormous; colossal: *a gargantuan task.*

gar·gle (gär′gəl), *v.,* **-gled, -gling,** *n.* —*v.i.* **1.** to wash or rinse the throat or mouth with a liquid held in the throat and kept in motion by a stream of air from the lungs. —*v.t.* **2.** to gargle (the throat or mouth). **3.** to utter with a gargling sound. —*n.* **4.** any liquid used for gargling. **5.** a gargling sound. —**gar′gler,** *n.*

gar·goyle (gär′goil), *n.* **1.** a grotesquely carved figure of a human or animal. **2.** a spout, terminating in a grotesque representation of a human or animal figure with open mouth, projecting from the gutter of a building for throwing rainwater clear of the building.

gargoyle

gar·ish (gâr′ish, gar′-), *adj.* **1.** crudely or tastelessly colorful, showy, or elaborate, as clothes or decoration. **2.** excessively ornate or elaborate, as buildings or writings. **3.** dressed in or ornamented with bright colors. **4.** excessively bright; glaring. —**gar′ish·ly,** *adv.* —**gar′ish·ness,** *n.*

gar·land (gär′lənd), *n.* **1.** a wreath or festoon of flowers, leaves, or other material, worn for ornament or as an honor or hung on something as a decoration. **2.** a representation of such a wreath or festoon. **3.** a collection of short literary pieces, as poems and ballads; literary miscellany. **4.** *Naut.* a band, collar, or grommet, as of rope. —*v.t.* **5.** to crown with a garland; deck with garlands. —**gar′land·less,** *adj.* —**gar′land·like′,** *adj.*

Gar·land (gär′lənd), *n.* a city in NE Texas, near Dallas. 194,218.

gar·lic (gär′lik), *n.* **1.** a hardy plant, *Allium sativum,* of the amaryllis family, having a strongly pungent bulb. **2.** the bulb of this plant, consisting of smaller bulbs, or cloves, used in cooking. **3.** the flavor or smell of this bulb. —*adj.* **4.** cooked, flavored, or seasoned with garlic: *garlic bread; garlic salt.* —**gar′lick·y,** *adj.*

gar·ment (gär′mənt), *n.* **1.** any article of clothing. **2.** an outer covering or outward appearance. —*v.t.* **3.** to clothe, dress, or cover. —**gar′ment·less,** *adj.*

gar·ner (gär′nər), *v.t.* **1.** to gather or deposit in or as if in a granary or other storage place. **2.** to get; acquire; earn: *garnered a reputation as a financial expert.* **3.** to gather, collect, or hoard.

Gar·ner (gär′nər), *n.* **John Nance** (nans), 1868–1967, vice president of the U.S. 1933–41.

gar·net (gär′nit), *n.* **1.** any of a group of hard deep red, brownish, or green vitreous minerals, silicates of calcium, magnesium, iron, or manganese with aluminum or iron: several varieties are used as gems. **2.** a deep red color.

gar·nish (gär′nish), *v.t.* **1.** to provide or supply with something ornamental; adorn; decorate. **2.** to provide (a food) with something that adds flavor, decorative color, etc.: *garnished the punch with fruit and spices.* **3.** GARNISHEE. —*n.* **4.** something placed around or on a food or in a beverage to add flavor, decorative color, etc. **5.** adornment; decoration. —**gar′nish·a·ble,** *adj.* —**gar′nish·er,** *n.*

gar·nish·ee (gär′ni shē′), *v.,* **-nish·eed, -nish·ee·ing,** *n. Law.* —*v.t.* **1.**

to attach (money or property) by garnishment. **2.** to serve (a person) with a garnishment. —*n.* **3.** a person served with a garnishment.

gar·nish·ment (gär′nish mənt), *n.* **1.** *Law.* **a.** a warning served on a third party to hold wages, property, etc., belonging to a debtor. **b.** a summons to such a party to appear in court and give testimony in litigation between the debtor and a creditor. **2.** adornment or decoration.

ga·rote (gə rot′, -rōt′), *n., v.t.,* **-rot·ed, -rot·ing.** GARROTE.

gar·ret (gar′it), *n.* an attic, usu. a small, cramped one.

Gar·rick (gar′ik), *n.* **David,** 1717–79, English actor.

gar·ri·son (gar′ə sən), *n.* **1.** a body of troops stationed in a fortified place. **2.** any military post. —*v.t.* **3.** to provide with a garrison. **4.** to occupy (a fort, post, station, etc.) with troops. **5.** to put (troops) on duty in a fort, post, station, etc.

Gar·ri·son (gar′ə sən), *n.* **William Lloyd,** 1805–79, U.S. leader in the abolition movement.

Gar′rison fin′ish, *n.* the finish of a race, esp. a horse race, in which the winner comes from behind to win at the last moment.

gar·rote or **ga·rote** or **ga·rotte** or **gar·rotte** (gə rot′, -rōt′), *n., v.,* **-rot·ed, -rot·ing** or **-rot·ted, -rot·ting.** —*n.* **1.** a method of capital punishment of Spanish origin in which an iron collar is tightened around a condemned person's neck until death occurs by strangulation or by injury to the spinal column at the base of the brain. **2.** the collar-like instrument used for this method of execution. **3.** strangulation or throttling, esp. in the course of a robbery. **4.** an instrument, usu. a cord or wire with handles attached at the ends, used for strangling a victim. —*v.t.* **5.** to execute by the garrote. **6.** to strangle or throttle, esp. in the course of a robbery. —**gar·rot′er,** *n.*

gar·ru·lous (gar′ə ləs, gar′yə-), *adj.* **1.** excessively talkative in a rambling manner, esp. about trivial matters. **2.** wordy or diffuse. —**gar·ru·li·ty** (gə rōō′li tē), *n* —**gar′ru·lous·ly,** *adv.* —**gar′ru·lous·ness,** *n.*

gar·ter (gär′tər), *n.* **1.** a device for holding up a stocking or sock, usu. an elastic band worn around the leg or an elastic strap hanging from an undergarment. **2.** a similar band worn to hold up a shirt sleeve. **3.** *Brit.* (*cap.*) **a.** the badge of the Order of the Garter. **b.** the Order itself. —*v.t.* **4.** to fasten with a garter.

gar′ter belt′, *n.* an undergarment of cloth or elastic, with attached garters, worn by women to hold up stockings.

gar′ter snake′, *n.* any harmless snake of the genus *Thamnophis,* common in North and Central America, usu. with three longitudinal stripes on the back.

Gar·vey (gär′vē), *n.* **Marcus (Moziah),** 1887–1940, Jamaican black-rights activist in the U.S. (1916–27).

Gar·y (gâr′ē, gar′ē), *n.* a port in NW Indiana, on Lake Michigan. 114,256.

gas (gas), *n., pl.* **gas·es,** *v.,* **gassed, gas·sing.** —*n.* **1.** a fluid substance with the ability to expand indefinitely, as opposed to a solid or a liquid. **2.** any such fluid or mixture of fluids, used as a fuel, anesthetic, asphyxiating agent, etc. **3. a.** gasoline. **b.** the foot-operated accelerator of an automotive vehicle. **4.** FLATUS. **5.** an explosive mixture of firedamp with air. **6.** *Slang.* **a.** empty talk. **b.** a person or thing that is very entertaining, pleasing, or successful. —*v.t.* **7.** to supply with gas. **8.** to overcome, poison, or asphyxiate with gas or fumes. **9.** to singe (yarns or fabrics) with a gas flame to remove superfluous fibers. **10.** to treat or impregnate with gas. **11.** *Slang.* **a.** to talk nonsense or falsehood to. **b.** to amuse or affect strongly. —*v.i.* **12.** to give off gas, as a storage battery being charged. **13.** *Slang.* **a.** to indulge in idle, empty talk. **b.** to become drunk (often fol. by *up*). **14. gas up,** to fill the gasoline tank of an automobile, truck, or other vehicle. —*Idiom.* **15. step on the gas,** *Informal.* to increase one's speed; hurry.

gas·bag (gas′bag′), *n.* a bag for holding gas, as in a balloon or dirigible.

gas′ burn′er, *n.* **1.** the tip, jet, or nozzle from which gas issues, as on a stove. **2.** a stove or the like that burns gas as a fuel.

gas′ cham′ber, *n.* a room used for executing prisoners by poison gas.

gas·con·ade (gas′kə nād′), *n., v.,* **-ad·ed, -ad·ing.** —*n.* **1.** extravagant boasting; boastful talk. —*v.i.* **2.** to boast extravagantly; bluster. —**gas′con·ad′er,** *n.*

gas·e·ous (gas′ē əs, gash′əs), *adj.* **1.** existing in the state of a gas; not solid or liquid. **2.** pertaining to or having the characteristics of gas. **3.** *Informal.* lacking firmness or solidity; uncertain; not definite. **4.** GASSY (defs. 1, 3). —**gas′e·ous·ness,** *n.* —**gas·e′i·ty** (-i tē), *n.*

gas′-guz′zler or **gas′ guz′zler,** *n.* an automobile that has low fuel efficiency, getting relatively few miles per gallon. —**gas′-guz′zling,** *adj.*

gas′-guz′zler tax′, *n.* a tax imposed on the purchase price of an automobile not meeting fuel efficiency standards.

gash (gash), *n.* **1.** a long, deep wound or cut; slash. —*v.t.* **2.** to make a long, deep cut in; slash.

gas·i·fy (gas′ə fī′), *v.,* **-fied, -fy·ing.** —*v.t.* **1.** to convert into a gas. —*v.i.* **2.** to become a gas. —**gas′i·fi·ca′tion,** *n.* —**gas′i·fi′er,** *n.*

gas′ jet′, *n.* **1.** GAS BURNER (def. 1). **2.** a flame of illuminating gas.

gas·ket (gas′kit), *n.* **1.** a rubber, metal, or rope ring, for packing a piston or placing around a joint to make it watertight. **2.** a light line for securing a furled sail to a boom, gaff, or yard.

gas·light (gas′līt′), *n.* **1.** light produced by the combustion of illuminating gas. **2.** a gas burner or gas jet for producing this kind of light.

gas′ main′, *n.* a large pipe for conducting and distributing gas to smaller pipes or ducts.

G

gas′ mask′, *n.* a masklike device that filters air through charcoal and chemicals to protect the wearer against noxious gases.

gas′ me′ter, *n.* an apparatus for measuring and recording the amount of gas produced or consumed, esp. household gas.

gas•o•hol (gas′ə hôl′, -hol′), *n.* a mixture of gasoline and ethyl alcohol, generally containing no more than .10 percent alcohol, used as an automobile fuel. [*gas(oline)* + *(alc)ohol*]

gas•o•line (gas′ə lēn′, gas′ə lēn′), *n.* a volatile, flammable liquid mixture of hydrocarbons obtained from petroleum and used chiefly as fuel for internal-combustion engines. **—gas′o•lin′ic** (-lē′nik, -lin′ik), *adj.*

gasp (gasp, gäsp), *n.* **1.** a sudden, short intake of breath, as in shock or surprise. **2.** a convulsive effort to breathe. **3.** a short, convulsive utterance: *The words came out in gasps.* **—v.i. 4.** to catch one's breath. **5.** to struggle for breath with the mouth open; breathe convulsively. **6.** to desire or crave (usu. fol. by *for* or *after*). **—v.t. 7.** to utter with gasps (often fol. by *out, forth, away,* etc.). **8.** to breathe or emit with gasps (often fol. by *away*). **—Idiom. 9. last gasp,** final collapse; dying moments.

gas•ser (gas′ər), *n.* **1.** *Slang.* something very pleasing or successful, esp. a very funny joke. **2.** a person or thing that gasses.

gas′ sta′tion, *n.* SERVICE STATION (def. 1).

gas•sy (gas′ē), *adj.,* **-si•er, -si•est. 1.** full of or containing gas. **2.** resembling gas. **3.** flatulent. **4.** *Slang.* given to idle, empty talk. **—gas′si•ness,** *n.*

gas•tric (gas′trik), *adj.* pertaining to the stomach.

gas′tric juice′, *n.* the digestive fluid, containing pepsin and other enzymes, secreted by the glands of the stomach.

gas′tric ul′cer, *n.* an ulcer in the inner wall of the stomach.

gas•tri•tis (ga strī′tis), *n.* inflammation of the stomach, esp. of its mucous membrane. **—gas•trit•ic** (ga strit′ik), *adj.*

gastro-, a combining form meaning "stomach": *gastrology.* Also, *esp. before a vowel,* **gastr-.**

gas•tro•en•ter•i•tis (gas′trō en′tə rī′tis), *n.* inflammation of the stomach and intestines. **—gas•tro•en•ter•it′ic** (-rit′ik), *adj.*

gas•tro•en•ter•ol•o•gy (gas′trō en′tə rol′ə jē), *n.* the study of the structure, functions, and diseases of digestive organs. **—gas′tro•en′ter•o•log′ic, gas′tro•en′ter•o•log′i•cal,** *adj.* **—gas′tro•en′te•rol′o•gist,** *n.*

gas•tro•in•tes•ti•nal (gas′trō in tes′tə nl), *adj.* of, pertaining to, or affecting the stomach and intestines.

gas•tro•nome (gas′trə nōm′) also **gas•tron•o•mer** (ga stron′ə mər), **gas•tron′o•mist,** *n.* a connoisseur of good food; gourmet.

gas•tron•o•my (ga stron′ə mē), *n.* **1.** the art or science of good eating. **2.** a style of cooking or eating. **—gas•tro•nom•ic** (gas′trə nom′ik), **gas′tro•nom′i•cal,** *adj.* **—gas′tro•nom′i•cal•ly,** *adv.*

gas•tro•pod (gas′trə pod′), *n.* **1.** any of numerous mollusks of the class Gastropoda, as snails, whelks, and slugs, having a single shell, often coiled, reduced, or undeveloped, and moving by means of a wide muscular foot. **—adj. 2.** Also, **gas•trop•o•dous** (ga strop′ə dəs). belonging or pertaining to the gastropods.

gas•works (gas′wûrks′), *n., pl.* **-works.** (*used with a sing. v.*) a plant where heating and illuminating gas is manufactured and piped to consumers.

gate (gāt), *n.* **1.** a movable barrier, usu. on hinges, closing an opening in a fence, wall, or other enclosure. **2.** an opening permitting passage through an enclosure. **3.** a tower, architectural setting, etc., for defending or adorning such an opening or for providing a monumental entrance to a street, park, etc. **4.** any means of access or entrance: *the gate to success.* **5.** any movable barrier, as at a tollbooth or a railroad crossing. **6.** STARTING GATE. **7.** a gateway or passageway in a passenger terminal or pier that leads to a place for boarding a train, plane, or ship. **8.** a sliding barrier for regulating the passage of water, steam, or the like, as in a dam or pipe; valve. **9. a.** an obstacle in a slalom race, consisting of two upright poles anchored in the snow a certain distance apart. **b.** the opening between these poles, through which a competitor in a slalom race must ski. **10.** the total number of persons who pay for admission to an athletic contest, a performance, an exhibition, etc. **11.** the total receipts from such admissions. **12.** a temporary channel in a cell membrane through which substances diffuse into or out of a cell. **13. a.** a channel or opening in a mold through which molten metal is poured into the mold cavity. **b.** the waste metal left in such a channel after hardening. **14.** a circuit with one output that is actuated only by certain combinations of two or more inputs. **15. the gate,** rejection; dismissal: *to give a boyfriend the gate.*

-gate, a combining form extracted from WATERGATE, occurring as the final element in journalistic coinages, usu. nonce words, that name scandals resulting from concealed crime or other improprieties in government or business: *Irangate.*

gate′-crash′er, *n.* a person who attends a social function, performance, or sports event without an invitation or a ticket.

gate•keep•er (gāt′kē′pər), *n.* **1.** a person in charge of a gate, usu. to supervise the traffic or flow through it. **2.** guardian; monitor: *the gatekeepers of Western culture.*

gate′leg ta′ble (gāt′leg′) or **gate′-legged′ ta′ble,** *n.* a drop-leaf table having legs attached to a hinged frame that can be swung out to support the leaves.

gate•post (gāt′pōst′), *n.* the vertical post on which a gate is suspended by hinges, or the post against which the gate is closed.

Gates (gāts), *n.* **1. Horatio,** 1728-1806, American Revolutionary general, born in England. **2. William** (*Bill*), born 1956, U.S. entrepreneur.

gate•way (gāt′wā′), *n.* **1.** an entrance or passage that may be closed by a gate. **2.** a structure for enclosing such an opening or entrance. **3.** any passage by or point at which a region may be entered: *New York soon became the gateway to America.* **4.** software or hardware that links two computer networks.

gate′way drug′, *n.* any mood-altering drug, as a stimulant or tranquilizer, that does not cause physical dependence but may lead to the use of addictive drugs, as heroin.

Gath (gath), *n.* a Philistine city on the coast of Palestine, the home of Goliath. I Sam. 17:4.

gath•er (gath′ər), *v.t.* **1.** to bring together into one group, collection, or place; collect: *to gather firewood; to gather supporters.* **2.** to pick or harvest (any crop or natural yield) from its place of growth: *to gather fruit.* **3.** to pick up piece by piece: *Gather your toys from the floor.* **4.** to pick or scoop up: *She gathered the crying child in her arms.* **5.** to serve as a center of attention for; attract. **6.** to increase gradually and steadily: *The car gathered speed.* **7.** to take by selection from among other things; sort out; cull. **8.** to assemble or collect (one's energies or oneself) as for an effort (often fol. by *up*). **9.** to learn or conclude from observation; infer; deduce: *I gather that she is the real leader.* **10.** to wrap or draw around or close: *He gathered his scarf around his neck.* **11.** to contract (the brow) into wrinkles. **12.** to draw (cloth) up on a thread in fine folds or puckers by means of even stitches. **13.** to assemble (the printed sections of a book) in proper sequence for binding. **14.** to accumulate or collect (molten glass) at the end of a tube for blowing, shaping, etc. **—v.i. 15.** to come together around a central point; assemble. **16.** to collect or accumulate: *Clouds were gathering in the northeast.* **17.** to grow, as by accretion; increase. **18.** to become contracted into wrinkles, folds, or creases, as the brow or as cloth. **19.** to come to a head, as a sore in suppurating. **—n. 20.** a drawing together; contraction. **21.** Often, **gathers.** a fold or pucker, as in gathered cloth. **22.** an act or instance of gathering. **23.** an amount or number gathered, as during a harvest. **—Idiom. 24. be gathered to one's fathers,** to die. **—gath′er•a•ble,** *adj.* **—gath′er•er,** *n.*

gath•er•ing (gath′ər ing), *n.* **1.** an assembly; meeting. **2.** an assemblage of people; group; crowd. **3.** a collection, assemblage, or compilation of anything. **4.** the act of a person or thing that gathers. **5.** something that is gathered together. **6.** a gather or a series of gathers in cloth. **7.** an inflamed and suppurating swelling. **8.** a section in a book, usu. a sheet cut into several leaves.

Gat′ling gun′ (gat′ling), *n.* an early type of machine gun consisting of a cluster of barrels around an axis that is rotated by a hand crank, with each barrel being automatically loaded and fired once during each rotation.

ga•tor or **gat•er** or **'gat•er** (gā′tər), *n. Southern U.S. Informal.* an alligator.

GATT, General Agreement on Tariffs and Trade.

gauche (gōsh), *adj.* lacking social grace; awkward; tactless. **—gauche′ly,** *adv.* **—gauche′ness,** *n.*

gau•che•rie (gō′shə rē′, gō′shə rē′), *n.* **1.** lack of social grace; awkwardness; tactlessness. **2.** an act, movement, or comment that is gauche.

gau•cho (gou′chō), *n., pl.* **-chos.** a cowboy of the South American pampas.

gaud•y (gô′dē), *adj.,* **gaud•i•er, gaud•i•est. 1.** showy in a tasteless way; flashy; tawdry. **2.** ostentatiously ornamented; garish. **—gaud′i•ly,** *adv.* **—gaud′i•ness,** *n.*

gauge (gāj), *v.,* **gauged, gaug•ing,** *n.* **—v.t. 1.** to determine the exact dimensions, capacity, quantity, or force of; measure. **2.** to appraise, estimate, or judge. **3.** to make conformable to a standard. **4.** to mark or measure off; delineate. **5.** to chip or rub (bricks or stones) to a uniform size or shape. **—n. 6.** a standard of measure or measurement. **7.** a standard dimension, size, or quantity. **8.** any device or instrument for measuring, registering measurements, or testing something: *pressure gauge.* **9.** a means of estimating or judging; criterion; test. **10.** extent; scope; capacity. **11.** a unit of measure of the internal diameter of a shotgun barrel, equal to the number of lead bullets of such diameter required to make one pound. **12.** the distance between the inner edges of the heads of the rails in a track. **13.** the distance between a pair of wheels on an axle. **14.** the thickness or diameter of various, usu. thin, objects, as sheet metal or wire. **15.** the fineness of a knitted fabric as expressed in loops per every 1.5 in. (3.8 cm): *15 denier, 60 gauge stockings.* **16.** *Naut.* the position of one vessel as being to the windward or to the leeward of another vessel on an approximately parallel course. Also, *esp. in technical use,* **gage.**

Gau•guin (gō gaɴ′), *n.* (**Eugène Henri**) **Paul,** 1848-1903, French painter.

Gaul (gôl), *n.* **1.** an ancient region in W Europe, including the modern areas of N Italy, France, Belgium, and the S Netherlands: consisted of two main divisions, one part S of the Alps (**Cisalpine Gaul**) and another part N of the Alps (**Transalpine Gaul**). **2.** a province of the ancient Roman Empire, including the territory corresponding to modern France, Belgium, the S Netherlands, Switzerland, N Italy, and Germany W of the Rhine. **3.** a native or inhabitant of Gaul. **4.** a native or inhabitant of France. Latin, **Gallia** (for defs. 1, 2).

gaunt (gônt), *adj.* **1.** extremely thin and bony; haggard and drawn, as from hunger or weariness. **2.** bleak, desolate, or grim: *the gaunt landscape of the tundra.* —**gaunt′ly,** *adv.* —**gaunt′ness,** *n.*

gaunt•let[1] (gônt′lit, gänt′-), *n.* **1.** a mailed glove worn with a suit of armor to protect the hand. **2.** a glove with an extended cuff. **3.** the cuff itself. —*Idiom.* **4. take up the gauntlet,** to accept a challenge to fight. **5. throw down the gauntlet,** to challenge someone to fight.

gaunt•let[2] (gônt′lit, gänt′-), *n.* **1.** a former punishment, chiefly military, in which the offender was made to run between two rows of men who struck at him with switches or weapons as he passed. **2.** the two rows of men administering this punishment. **3.** an attack from two or all sides. **4.** a severe test; ordeal. **5.** GANTLET[1] (def. 1). —*Idiom.* **6. run the gauntlet,** to suffer severe criticism or tribulation. Also, **gantlet** (for defs. 1, 2, 4).

gauss (gous), *n.* the centimeter-gram-second unit of magnetic field strength, equal to 10[−4] tesla. *Symbol:* G

Gau•ta•ma (gō′tə mə, gou′-), *n.* BUDDHA. Also called **Gau′tama Bud′dha.**

gauze (gôz), *n.* **1.** thin and often transparent fabric made from any fiber in a plain or leno weave. **2.** a surgical dressing of loosely woven cotton. **3.** any material made of an open, meshlike weave, as of wire. **4.** a thin haze. —**gauz′i•ness,** *n.* —**gauz′y,** *adj.,* **-i•er, -i•est.**

gave (gāv), *v.* pt. of GIVE.

gav•el (gav′əl), *n., v.,* **-eled, -el•ing** or (*esp. Brit.*) **-elled, -el•ling.** —*n.* **1.** a small mallet used esp. by the presiding officer of a meeting or a judge usu. to signal for attention or order. **2.** a similar mallet used by an auctioneer to indicate acceptance of the final bid. —*v.t.* **3.** to begin or put into effect by striking a gavel: *to gavel the committee into session.* —*v.i.* **4.** to hammer or pound with a gavel: *to gavel for order.*

gav•el-to-gav•el (gav′əl tə gav′əl), *adj.* from the opening to the closing of a formal session or series of sessions: *gavel-to-gavel television coverage of the Congressional hearing.*

ga•vi•al (gā′vē əl), *n.* a large crocodilian, *Gavialis gangeticus,* of India and Pakistan, having elongated jaws. Also called **gharial.** —**ga′vi•al•oid′,** *adj.*

ga•votte (gə vot′), *n.* **1.** an old French dance in moderately quick quadruple meter. **2.** a piece of instrumental music in the rhythm of the gavotte.

gawk (gôk), *v.i.* **1.** to stare stupidly; gape. —*n.* **2.** an awkward, foolish person.

gawk•y (gô′kē) also **gawk′ish,** *adj.,* **gawk•i•er, gawk•i•est.** awkward; ungainly; clumsy. —**gawk′i•ly, gawk′ish•ly,** *adv.* —**gawk′i•ness, gawk′ish•ness,** *n.*

gay (gā), *adj.,* **-er, -est,** *n., adv.* —*adj.* **1.** having or showing a merry, lively mood: *gay spirits.* **2.** bright or showy: *gay colors.* **3.** given to or abounding in social or other pleasures: *a gay social season.* **4.** licentious; dissipated; wanton: *a wild, gay life.* **5.** homosexual. **6.** indicating or pertaining to homosexual interests or issues: *a gay organization.* —*n.* **7.** a homosexual person, esp. a male. —*adv.* **8.** in a gay manner. —**gay′ness,** *n.*

gay•e•ty (gā′i tē), *n., pl.* **-ties.** GAIETY.

gay•ly (gā′lē), *adv.* GAILY.

Ga•za (gä′zə, gaz′ə, gā′zə), *n.* a seaport on the Mediterranean Sea, in the Gaza Strip, adjacent to SW Israel. 118,300.

Ga′za Strip′, *n.* a coastal area on the E Mediterranean: formerly in the Palestine mandate, occupied by Israel 1967–94; since 1994 under Palestinian self-rule.

gaze (gāz), *v.,* **gazed, gaz•ing,** *n.* —*v.i.* **1.** to look steadily and intently, as with great interest or wonder. —*n.* **2.** a steady or intent look. —**gaz′er,** *n.*

ga•ze•bo (gə zā′bō, -zē′-), *n., pl.* **-bos, -boes. 1.** a structure, as an open or latticework pavilion or summerhouse, built on a site that provides an attractive view. **2.** a small roofed structure that is screened on all sides, used for outdoor entertaining and dining.

ga•zelle (gə zel′), *n., pl.* **-zelles,** (*esp. collectively*) **-zelle.** any of various small graceful antelopes of Africa and Asia, esp. of the genus *Gazella.* —**ga•zelle′like′,** *adj.*

ga•zette (gə zet′), *n., v.,* **-zet•ted, -zet•ting.** —*n.* **1.** a newspaper (now used chiefly in names): *The Phoenix Gazette.* **2.** *Brit.* a government journal listing appointments, promotions, etc. —*v.t.* **3.** *Brit.* to announce or list in a government journal.

gaz•et•teer (gaz′i tēr′), *n.* a geographical dictionary.

gaz•pa•cho (gə spä′chō, gä-), *n.* a cold soup made with oil and vinegar and chopped tomatoes, cucumbers, onions, and garlic.

Gc, gigacycle.

G clef, *n.* TREBLE CLEF.

Gd, *Chem. Symbol.* gadolinium.

Gdansk (gə dänsk′, -dansk′), *n.* a seaport in N Poland, on the Baltic Sea. 467,000. German, **Danzig.**

Ge, *Chem. Symbol.* germanium.

gear (gēr), *n.* **1. a.** a part, as a disk, wheel, or section of a shaft, having cut teeth of such form, size, and spacing that they mesh with teeth in another part to transmit or receive force and motion. **b.** an assembly of such parts. **2.** implements, tools, or apparatus, esp. as used for a particular occupation or activity; paraphernalia: *fishing gear.* **3.** portable

items of personal property, including clothing. **4.** wearing apparel; clothing. —*v.t.* **5.** to provide with or connect by gearing. **6.** to put in or into gear. **7.** to provide with gear; supply; equip. **8.** to prepare, adjust, or adapt to a particular situation, person, etc., in order to bring about satisfactory results: *The producers geared their output to seasonal demands.* —*v.i.* **9.** to fit exactly, as one part of gearing into another; come into or be in gear. **10. gear down, a.** to shift the transmission of a vehicle to a lower gear. **b.** to reduce in scope or intensity. **11. gear up, a.** to make or get ready for a future event or situation. **b.** to get or put on equipment or clothing for a particular purpose. **c.** to arouse or excite, as with enthusiasm or expectation. —*adj.* **12.** *Slang.* great; wonderful. —*Idiom.* **13. in** or **into high gear,** in or into a state of maximum speed and efficiency. **14. in gear, a.** in the state in which gears are connected or meshed: *The car is in gear.* **b.** in proper working order; functioning smoothly. **15. out of gear,** in the state in which gears are not connected or meshed: *The engine is out of gear.* **16. shift** or **switch gears,** to alter one's strategies in a significant way. —**gear′less,** *adj.*

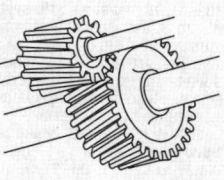

gear

gear′box′ or **gear′ box′,** *n.* a transmission, as of an automobile.

gear•ing (gēr′ing), *n.* **1.** an assembly of parts, esp. a train of gears, for transmitting and modifying motion and torque in a machine. **2.** the act or process of equipping with gears.

gear•shift (gēr′shift′), *n.* a lever for engaging and disengaging gears for a power-transmission system, esp. in a motor vehicle.

gear′wheel′ or **gear′ wheel′,** *n.* a wheel having teeth or cogs that engage with those of another wheel or part; cogwheel.

Geb (geb), *n. Egyptian Religion.* the god of the earth and the father of Osiris and Isis. Also, **Keb.**

geck•o (gek′ō), *n., pl.* **geck•os, geck•oes.** any small, mostly nocturnal tropical lizard of the family Gekkonidae, usu. having toe pads that can cling to smooth surfaces.

GED, general equivalency diploma.

Ged•a•li•ah (ged′l ī′ə, gi däl′yə), *n.* the governor of Judah after its conquest by Babylon. II Kings 25:22–26.

gee[1] (jē), *interj., v.,* **geed, gee•ing.** —*interj.* **1.** (used as a command to a horse or other draft animal to turn to the right or, esp. in the phrase *gee up,* to go faster.) —*v.t., v.i.* **2.** to turn or make a turn to the right. Compare HAW[2].

gee[2] (jē), *interj.* (used to express surprise, disappointment, enthusiasm, or simple emphasis.)

geek (gēk), *n. Slang.* any strange or eccentric person.

geese (gēs), *n.* a pl. of GOOSE.

gee•zer (gē′zər), *n. Slang.* an odd or eccentric man.

ge•fil′te fish′ (gə fil′tə), *n.* balls or cakes of chopped boned fish mixed with egg, matzo meal, etc., and simmered in a broth.

Ge•ha•zi (gē hā′zī), *n.* a servant of Elisha who corruptly sought rewards for his master. II Kings 4:8–37.

Ge•hen•na (gi hen′ə), *n.* **1.** the valley of Hinnom, near Jerusalem, where propitiatory sacrifices were made to Moloch. II Kings 23:10. **2.** HELL (def. 1). **3.** any place of extreme torment or suffering.

Geh•rig (ger′ig), *n.* Henry Louis (*"Lou"*), 1903–41, U.S. baseball player.

Gei′ger count′er (gī′gər), *n.* an instrument for detecting ionizing radiations, used chiefly to measure radioactivity. Also called **Gei′ger-Mül′ler count′er** (myoo′lər, mul′-).

Gei•sel (gī′zəl), *n.* Theodor Seuss (soos), (*"Dr. Seuss"*), 1904–91, U.S. humorist, illustrator, and author of children's books.

gei•sha (gā′shə, gē′-), *n., pl.* **-sha, -shas.** a Japanese woman trained as a professional singer, dancer, and companion for men.

gel (jel), *n., v.,* **gelled, gel•ling.** —*n.* **1.** a semirigid colloidal dispersion of a solid with a liquid or gas, as jelly or glue. **2.** GELATIN (def. 5). —*v.i.* **3.** to form or become a gel. **4.** JELL (def. 2).

ge•la•ti (jə lä′tē), *n.* a rich ice cream made with eggs.

gel•a•tin or **gel•a•tine** (jel′ə tn), *n.* **1.** a nearly transparent, glutinous substance, obtained by boiling the bones, ligaments, etc. of animals, and used in making jellies, glues, and the like. **2.** any of various similar substances, as vegetable gelatin. **3.** a preparation or product in which such a substance is the essential constituent. **4.** an edible jelly made of this substance. **5.** Also called **gel, gel′atin slide′.** a thin sheet of translucent, colored gelatin for placing over a stage light to produce lighting effects. [< French *gélatine* < Medieval Latin *gelātīna* < Latin *gelātus* frozen] —**ge•lat′i•nous,** *adj.*

ge•lat•i•nize (jə lat′n īz′, jel′ə tn-), *v.,* **-nized, -niz•ing.** —*v.t.* **1.** to

make gelatinous. **2.** to coat with gelatin, as paper. —*v.i.* **3.** to become gelatinous. —**ge·lat'i·ni·za'tion,** *n.* —**ge·lat'i·niz'er,** *n.*

ge·la·tion¹ (je lā'shən, jə-), *n.* solidification by cold; freezing.

ge·la·tion² (je lā'shən, jə-), *n.* the process of gelling.

geld (geld), *v.t.,* **geld·ed** or **gelt, geld·ing. 1.** to castrate: *to geld a stallion.* **2.** to deprive of something essential: *to be gelded of one's pride.*

geld·ing (gel'ding), *n.* a castrated male animal, esp. a horse.

gel·id (jel'id), *adj.* very cold; icy. —**ge·lid·i·ty** (jə lid'i tē), **gel'id·ness,** *n.* —**gel'id·ly,** *adv.*

gelt¹ (gelt), *v.* a pt. and past part. of GELD¹.

gelt² (gelt), *n. Slang.* money.

gem (jem), *n.* **1.** a mineral, pearl, or other natural substance valued for its rarity or inherent beauty and used in jewelry. **2.** something prized because of its beauty or worth. **3.** a person held in great esteem or affection. —*adj.* **4.** (of jewelry) noting perfection or very high quality: *gem color; a gem ruby.*

Ge·ma·ra (gə môr'ə, -mär'ä, -mä rä'), *n.* **1.** the section of the Talmud consisting essentially of commentary on the Mishnah. **2.** the Talmud.

ge·ma·tri·a (gə mä'trē ə), *n.* a cabbalistic system of interpretation of the Scriptures by substituting for a particular word another word whose letters give the same numerical sum.

ge·mein·schaft (gə mīn'shäft'), *n., pl.* **-schafts, -schaf·ten** (-shäf'-tən). (*often cap.*) a society or group characterized chiefly by a strong sense of common identity, close personal relationships, and an attachment to traditional and sentimental concerns.

gem·i·nate (jem'ə nāt'), *v.t., v.i.* to make or become doubled or paired. —**gem'i·na'tion,** *n.*

Gem·i·ni (jem'ə nī', -nē), *n., pl.* **1.** the Twins, a zodiacal constellation between Taurus and Cancer containing the bright stars Castor and Pollux. **2.** the third sign of the zodiac. [< Latin *geminī,* pl. of *geminus* twin]

gem·ol·o·gy or **gem·mol·o·gy** (je mol'ə jē), *n.* the science dealing with gemstones. —**gem·o·log·i·cal** (jem'ə loj'i kəl), *adj.* —**gem·ol'o·gist,** *n.*

gems·bok (gemz'bok'), *n., pl.* **-boks,** (*esp. collectively*) **-bok.** a large African antelope, *Oryx gazella,* having long, straight horns. Also called oryx.

gem·stone (jem'stōn'), *n.* a mineral or crystal that can be cut and polished for use as a gem.

ge·müt·lich or **ge·muet·lich** (gə mōōt'likh, -mōōt'-; *Ger.* -myt'-), *adj.* **1.** comfortable and pleasant; cozy. **2.** friendly; easygoing.

-gen, a combining form meaning "something that produces, stimulates the production of, or induces" the thing specified by the initial element: *antigen; carcinogen.* [< French *-gène* Greek *-genēs* born, produced; akin to *gignesthai* to beget, and to Latin *genus,* KIN]

Gen., **1.** General. **2.** Genesis.

gen., **1.** gender. **2.** genitive. **3.** genus.

gen·darme (zhän'därm; *Fr.* zhän DARM'), *n., pl.* **-darmes** (-därmz; *Fr.* -DARM'). **1.** a police officer in any of several European countries, esp. in France. **2.** a soldier, esp. in France, serving in an army group acting as armed police with authority over civilians.

gen·der (jen'dər), *n.* **1. a.** a set of grammatical categories applied to nouns, shown by the form of the noun itself or the choice of words that modify, replace, or refer to it, often correlated in part with sex or animateness, as in the choice of *he* to replace *the man, she* to replace *the woman,* or *it* to replace *the table,* but sometimes based on arbitrary assignment without regard to the referent of the noun, as in French *le livre* (masculine) "the book" or German *das Mädchen* (neuter) "the girl." **b.** one of the categories in such a set, as masculine, feminine, neuter, or common. **c.** meaning of a word or grammatical form in such a category. **2.** sex: *the feminine gender.* —**gen'der·less,** *adj.*

gen'der gap', *n.* the difference between women and men in regard to social, political, economic, or other attainments or attitudes, or the problem perceived to exist because of such difference.

gen'der-specif'ic, *adj.* for, characteristic of, or limited to either males or females: *gender-specific roles.*

gene (jēn), *n.* the basic physical unit of heredity; a linear sequence of nucleotides along a segment of DNA that provides the coded instructions for synthesis of RNA, which, when translated into protein, leads to the expression of hereditary character.

ge·ne·al·o·gy (jē'nē ol'ə jē, -al'ə-, jen'ē-), *n., pl.* **-gies. 1.** a record or account of the ancestry and descent of a person, family, group, etc. **2.** the study of family ancestries and histories. **3.** descent from an original form or progenitor; ancestry. —**ge'ne·a·log'i·cal** (-ə loj'i kəl), **ge'ne·a·log'ic,** *adj.* —**ge'ne·a·log'i·cal·ly,** *adv.* —**ge'ne·al'o·gist,** *n.*

gene' flow', *n.* changes in the frequency of alleles within a gene pool that occur as a result of interbreeding.

gene' map', *n.* GENETIC MAP.

gene' map'ping, *n.* the act or process of determining the precise location of a gene or genes on a particular chromosome.

gene' pool', *n.* the total genetic information in the gametes of all the individuals in a population.

gen·er·a (jen'ər ə), *n.* a pl. of GENUS.

gen·er·al (jen'ər əl), *adj.* **1.** of, pertaining to, or affecting all persons or things belonging to a group, category, or system: *a general meeting of union members; a general amnesty.* **2.** of, pertaining to, or true of such persons or things in the main; common to most; prevalent; usual: *the*

general mood of the people. **3.** not limited to one class, field, product, service, etc.; miscellaneous: *the general public.* **4.** considering or dealing with broad, universal, or important aspects, elements, etc.; not detailed: *general guidelines; a general description.* **5.** not specific or definite; approximate: *I had only a general idea of what was going on.* **6.** affecting the entire body: *general paralysis.* **7.** (of anesthesia or an anesthetic) causing loss of consciousness and abolishing sensitivity to pain throughout the body. **8.** having extended command or superior or chief rank: *the secretary general of the U.N.* —*n.* **9. a.** an army or air force officer ranking above a lieutenant general and below a general of the army or general of the air force. **b.** an army officer of any of the five highest ranks: brigadier general, major general, lieutenant general, general, or general of the army. **c.** an officer holding the highest rank in the U.S. Marine Corps. —*Idiom.* **10. in general, a.** with respect to the entirety; as a whole: *to like people in general.* **b.** as a rule; usually: *In general, the bus is on time.* —**gen'er·al·ness,** *n.*

gen'eral admis'sion, *n.* an admission charge for unreserved seats at a theatrical performance, sports event, etc.

Gen'eral Assem'bly, *n.* **1.** the legislature in some states of the U.S. **2.** the main deliberative body of the U.N., composed of delegations from member nations.

gen'eral deliv'ery, *n.* a postal service in which mail is held at a post office for pickup by the addressee.

gen'eral elec'tion, *n.* **1.** a final election of candidates for national, state, or local office, as opposed to a primary. **2.** a state or national election, as opposed to a local election.

gen·er·al·is·si·mo (jen'ər ə lis'ə mō'), *n., pl.* **-mos.** (in certain countries) the supreme commander of the armed forces.

gen·er·al·ist (jen'ər ə list), *n.* a person whose knowledge, aptitudes, and skills are applied to a field as a whole or to a variety of different fields (opposed to *specialist*).

gen·er·al·i·ty (jen'ə ral'i tē), *n., pl.* **-ties. 1.** an indefinite, unspecific, or undetailed statement: *to talk in generalities.* **2.** a general principle, rule, or law. **3.** the greater part or majority: *the generality of people.* **4.** the state or quality of being general.

gen·er·al·i·za·tion (jen'ər ə lə zā'shən), *n.* **1.** the act or process of generalizing. **2.** a result of this process; a general statement, idea, or principle. **3. a.** a proposition asserting something to be true either of all members of a certain class or of an indefinite part of that class. **b.** the process of obtaining such propositions. **4.** the act or process of responding to a stimulus similar to but distinct from a conditioned stimulus.

gen·er·al·ize (jen'ər ə līz'), *v.,* **-ized, -iz·ing.** —*v.t.* **1.** to infer (a general principle) from particular facts or instances. **2.** to form (a general opinion or conclusion) from only a few facts or cases. **3.** to give a broad or general character or form to. **4.** to bring into general use or knowledge. —*v.i.* **5.** to form general principles, opinions, etc. **6.** to deal, think, or speak in generalities. **7.** to make general inferences. —**gen'er·al·iz·a·ble,** *adj.* —**gen'er·al·iz'er,** *n.*

gen·er·al·ly (jen'ər ə lē), *adv.* **1.** usually; commonly; ordinarily. **2.** with respect to the larger part; for the most part: *a generally favorable outlook.* **3.** without reference to particular persons, situations, etc., that may be an exception: *generally speaking.*

gen'eral of'ficer, *n.* any military officer ranking above colonel.

gen'eral of the air' force', *n.* the highest ranking officer in the U.S. Air Force.

gen'eral of the ar'my, *n.* the highest ranking military officer; the next rank above general. Compare FLEET ADMIRAL.

gen'eral part'nership, *n.* a partnership in which each of the partners is fully liable for the firm's debts. Compare LIMITED PARTNERSHIP.

gen'eral post' of'fice, *n.* (in the U.S. postal system) the main post office of a city, county, etc., that also has branch post offices. *Abbr.:* G.P.O., GPO

gen'eral practi'tioner, *n.* a medical practitioner whose practice is not limited to any specific branch of medicine or class of diseases. *Abbr.:* G.P.

gen'eral-pur'pose, *adj.* useful in many ways; not limited in use or function: *general-purpose cattle.*

gen'eral relativ'ity, *n.* RELATIVITY (def. 2b).

gen'eral ses'sions, *n.* (in some states) a court of general jurisdiction in criminal cases.

gen·er·al·ship (jen'ər əl ship'), *n.* **1.** skill as commander of a large military force or unit. **2.** the rank or duties of a general. **3.** management or leadership.

gen'eral store', *n.* a store, usu. in a rural area, that sells a wide variety of merchandise, as clothing, food, and hardware, but is not divided into departments.

gen·er·ate (jen'ə rāt'), *v.,* **-at·ed, -at·ing.** —*v.t.* **1.** to bring into existence; originate; produce: *to generate ideas.* **2.** to create by a natural or chemical process: *to generate heat.* **3.** to be a source or cause of; inspire: *to generate enthusiasm.* **4.** to reproduce; procreate. **5.** *Math.* **a.** to trace (a figure) by the motion of a point, straight line, or curve. **b.** to act as base for all the elements of a given set: *The number 2 generates the set 2, 4, 8, 16.* **6.** to produce or specify (a grammatical construction or set of constructions) by the application of a rule or set of rules in a generative grammar. —*v.i.* **7.** to reproduce; propagate.

gen·er·a·tion (jen'ə rā'shən), *n.* **1.** the entire body of individuals born and living at about the same time: *the postwar generation.* **2.** the term of years, about 30 among human beings, accepted as the average period between the birth of parents and the birth of their offspring. **3.** a group of individuals, most of whom are the same approximate age, having similar ideas, problems, attitudes, etc. **4.** a group of individuals belonging to a specific category at the same time: *the generation of silent-screen stars.* **5.** a single step in natural descent, as of human beings, animals, or plants. **6.** a stage of technological development or production distinct from but based upon another stage: *a new generation of computers.* **7.** the offspring of a certain parent or couple, considered as a step in natural descent. **8.** the act or process of generating; procreation. **9.** the state of being generated. **10.** production by natural or artificial processes; evolution, as of heat or sound. **11. a.** one complete life cycle. **b.** one of the alternate phases that complete a life cycle having more than one phase: *the gametophyte generation.* **12.** the production of a geometrical figure by the motion of another figure. —**gen′er•a′tion•al,** *adj.* —**gen′er•a′tion•al•ly,** *adv.*

genera′tion gap′, *n.* a lack of communication between one generation and another, esp. between young people and their parents.

Generation X, *n.* the generation born in the United States after 1965. [after the novel of the same name (1991) by Doug Coupland]

gen•er•a•tive (jen′ər ə tiv, -ə rā′tiv), *adj.* **1.** capable of producing or creating. **2.** pertaining to the production of offspring. **3. a.** of or pertaining to generative grammar. **b.** using rules to generate surface linguistic forms from underlying, abstract forms. —**gen′er•a•tive•ly,** *adv.* —**gen′er•a•tive•ness,** *n.*

gen′erative gram′mar, *n.* **1.** a linguistic theory that attempts to describe the tacit knowledge a native speaker has of a language by establishing a set of formal rules that generate all the possible grammatical sentences of a language, while excluding all unacceptable sentences. Compare TRANSFORMATIONAL GRAMMAR. **2.** a set of such rules.

gen•er•a•tor (jen′ə rā′tər), *n.* **1.** a machine that converts one form of energy into another, esp. mechanical energy into electrical energy, as a dynamo. **2.** a person or thing that generates. **3.** an apparatus for producing a gas or vapor. **4.** an element or one of a set of elements from which a specified mathematical object can be formed by applying certain operations.

ge•ner•ic (jə ner′ik), *adj.* Also, **ge•ner′i•cal. 1.** of, pertaining to, or applicable to all the members of a genus, class, group, or kind. **2.** of, pertaining to, or constituting a genus. **3.** (of a word) applicable or referring to both men and women: *a generic pronoun.* **4.** not protected by trademark registration; nonproprietary: *a generic drug.* —*n.* **5.** a generic term. **6.** any product, as a food, drug, or cosmetic, that can be sold without a brand name. **7.** a wine made from two or more varieties of grapes, with no one grape constituting more than half the product (disting. from *varietal*). —**ge•ner′i•cal•ly,** *adv.* —**ge•ner′ic•ness,** *n.*

gen•er•os•i•ty (jen′ə ros′i tē), *n., pl.* **-ties. 1.** readiness or liberality in giving; munificence. **2.** freedom from meanness or pettiness; magnanimity. **3.** a generous act. **4.** largeness or fullness; amplitude.

gen•er•ous (jen′ər əs), *adj.* **1.** liberal in giving or sharing; unselfish. **2.** free from meanness or pettiness; magnanimous. **3.** large; abundant; ample: *a generous piece of pie.* **4.** rich or strong in flavor: *a generous wine.* **5.** fertile; prolific: *generous soil.* —**gen′er•ous•ly,** *adv.* —**gen′er•ous•ness,** *n.*

gen•e•sis (jen′ə sis), *n., pl.* **-ses** (-sēz′). an origin, creation, or beginning. [< Latin < Greek *génesis* origin, source, der. of *gígnesthai* to beget]

Gen•e•sis (jen′ə sis), *n.* the first book of the Bible, dealing with the Creation and the patriarchs.

gene′ splic′ing, *n.* the act or process of recombining genes from different sources to form new genetic combinations.

Ge•nêt (zhə nā′), *n.* **Edmond Charles Edouard** (*"Citizen Genêt"*), 1763–1834, French minister to the U.S. in 1793.

gene′ ther′apy, *n.* the treatment of a disease by replacing aberrant genes with normal ones, esp. through the use of viruses to transport the desired genes into the nuclei of blood cells.

ge•net•ic (jə net′ik) also **ge•net′i•cal,** *adj.* **1.** pertaining or according to genetics. **2.** of, pertaining to, or produced by genes; genic. **3.** of, pertaining to, or influenced by geneses or origins. —**ge•net′i•cal•ly,** *adv.*

-genetic, a combining form of adjectives corresponding to nouns ending in -GENESIS: *parthenogenetic.*

genet′ic code′, *n.* the biochemical instructions that translate the genetic information present as a linear sequence of nucleotide triplets in messenger RNA into the correct linear sequence of amino acids for the synthesis of a particular peptide chain or protein. Compare CODON, TRANSLATION (def. 6).

genet′ic coun′seling, *n.* the counseling of persons with established or potential genetic problems in regard to inheritance patterns and risks to future offspring.

genet′ic engineer′ing, *n.* **1.** the development and application of scientific methods, procedures, and technologies that permit direct manipulation of genetic material in order to alter the hereditary traits of a cell, organism, or population. **2.** a technique producing unlimited amounts of otherwise unavailable or scarce biological product by introducing DNA from certain living organisms into bacteria and then harvesting the product, as human insulin produced in bacteria by the human insulin gene. Also called **biogenetics.** —**genet′ic engineer′,** *n.*

genet′ic fin′gerprinting, *n.* DNA FINGERPRINTING. —**genet′ic fin′gerprint,** *n.*

genet′ic map′, *n.* an arrangement of genes on a chromosome.

ge•net•ics (jə net′iks), *n.* (*used with a sing. v.*) **1.** the branch of biology that deals with the principles and mechanisms of heredity and with the genetic contribution to similarities and differences among related organisms. **2.** the genetic properties or constitution of an organism or group. —**ge•net′i•cist,** *n.*

genet′ic screen′ing, *n.* assessment of an individual's genetic makeup to detect defects that may be transmitted to offspring or to try to predict genetic predisposition to certain illnesses.

Ge•ne•va (jə nē′və), *n.* **1.** the capital of the canton of Geneva, in SW Switzerland, on the Lake of Geneva: seat of the League of Nations 1920–46. 160,900. **2.** a canton in SW Switzerland. 365,200; 109 sq. mi. (282 sq. km). **3.** Lake of. Also called **Lake Leman.** a lake between SW Switzerland and France. 45 mi. (72 km) long; 225 sq. mi. (583 sq. km). French, **Genève** (for defs. 1, 2). German, **Genf** (for defs. 1, 2).

Gene′va Bi′ble, *n.* a Bible (1560) revised by English exiles in Geneva, the first to divide chapters into verses. Also called **Breeches Bible.**

Gene′va Conven′tion, *n.* one of a series of international agreements, first made in Geneva, Switzerland, in 1864, establishing rules for the humane treatment of prisoners of war and of the sick, the wounded, and the dead in battle.

Gene′va cross′, *n.* a red Greek cross on a white background, displayed to distinguish ambulances, hospitals, and persons belonging to the Red Cross Society.

Gen•ghis Khan (jeng′gis kän′ *or, often,* geng′-), *n.* 1162–1227, Mongol conqueror.

gen•ial (jēn′yəl, jē′nē əl), *adj.* **1.** warmly and pleasantly cheerful; cordial: *a genial disposition.* **2.** pleasantly warm; comfortably mild: *a genial climate.* **3.** characterized by genius. —**gen′ial•ly,** *adv.* —**ge′ni•al′i•ty** (-al′i tē), *n.* —**gen′ial•ness,** *n.*

-genic, a combining form often corresponding to nouns ending in -GEN or -GENY, with the following senses: "producing or causing" (*hallucinogenic*); "originating or developing in" (*neurogenic*); "pertaining to a gene or genes" (*polygenic*); "pertaining to suitability for reproduction by a medium" (*telegenic*). Compare -GENOUS.

ge•nie (jē′nē), *n.* **1.** JINN. **2.** a spirit, often appearing in human form, that when summoned by a person carries out the wishes of the summoner. —*Saying.* **3. let the genie out of the bottle,** to release an evil spirit or malign force.

ge•ni•i (jē′nē ī′), *n.* a pl. of GENIUS.

gen•i•tal (jen′i tl), *adj.* **1.** of or pertaining to reproduction. **2.** of or pertaining to the sexual organs. **3. a.** of, pertaining to, or characteristic of the phase of psychosexual development, from about ages three to five, during which the genitals become the focus of sexual pleasure. **b.** of or pertaining to the centering of sexual impulses and excitation on the genitalia.

gen•i•ta•li•a (jen′i tā′lē ə, -tāl′yə), *n.pl.* the organs of reproduction, esp. the external organs. —**gen′i•tal′ic** (-tal′ik), **gen′i•ta′li•al,** *adj.*

gen•i•tals (jen′i tlz), *n.pl.* GENITALIA.

gen′ital warts′, *n.pl.* warts occurring in the genital and anal areas and spread mainly by sexual contact, sometimes increasing the risk of cervical cancer in women.

gen•i•tive (jen′i tiv), *adj.* **1.** of or designating a grammatical case typically indicating possession, measure, origin, or other close association, as *painter's, week's, author's,* and *women's* in *the painter's brush, a week's pay, the author's book,* and *women's colleges.* **2.** pertaining to a construction similar to such a case in function or meaning, esp. in English a prepositional phrase with *of,* as in *the home of the mayor.* —*n.* **3.** the genitive case. **4.** a word or other form in the genitive case. **5.** a construction expressing a relationship usu. indicated by the genitive case. —**gen′i•ti′val** (-tī′val), *adj.* —**gen′i•ti′val•ly,** *adv.*

gen•i•to•u•ri•nar•y (jen′i tō yŏŏr′ə ner′ē), *adj.* of or pertaining to the genital and urinary organs.

gen•ius (jēn′yəs), *n., pl.* **gen•ius•es** for 2, 6, **gen•i•i** (jē′nē ī′) for 5. **1.** an exceptional natural capacity of intellect, esp. as shown in creative and original work in science, art, music, etc.: *the genius of Mozart.* **2.** a person having such capacity. **3.** natural ability or capacity; talent: *a genius for leadership.* **4.** distinctive character or spirit, as of a nation, period, or language. **5.** the guardian spirit of a place, person, institution, etc. **6.** a person who strongly influences for good or ill the character, conduct, or destiny of a person, place, or thing: *an evil genius.*

Gen•nes•a•ret (ge nes′ə ret′), *n.* Galilee. Luke 5:1.

Gen•o•a (jen′ō ə), *n.* a seaport in NW Italy, S of Milan. 762,895. Italian, **Genova.** —**Gen′o•ese′** (-ēz′, -ēs′), *n., pl.* **-ese,** *adj.*

gen•o•cide (jen′ə sīd′), *n.* the deliberate and systematic extermination of a national, racial, political, or cultural group. —**gen′o•cid′al,** *adj.*

gen•o•gram (jen′ə gram′, jē′nə-), *n.* a family tree depicting the histories, personalities, and relationships of family members, constructed esp. as a diagnostic or therapeutic aid.

gen•o•type (jen′ə tīp′, jē′nə-), *n.* **1.** the genetic makeup of an organism or group of organisms with reference to a single trait, set of traits, or an entire complex of traits. **2.** the sum total of genes transmitted from parent to offspring. Compare PHENOTYPE. —**gen′o•typ′ic** (-tip′ik), **gen′o•typ′i•cal** (-tip′i kəl), **gen′o•typ′i•cal•ly,** *adv.*

-genous, a combining form meaning "arising, developing, or growing" in the place or manner specified (*isogenous; myelogenous*); "giving rise to" the thing specified (*androgenous; erogenous*). Compare -GENY.

G

gen•re (zhän′rə; *Fr.* zhäN′R⁹), *n.*, *pl.* **-res** (-rəz; *Fr.* -R⁹), *adj.* —*n.* **1.** a class or category of artistic endeavor having a particular form, content, technique, or the like. **2.** painting in which scenes of everyday life form the subject matter and are usually done in a realistic style. **3.** genus; kind; sort; style. —**gen′re,** *adj.*

gens (jenz), *n.*, *pl.* **gen•tes** (jen′tēz). **1.** a group of families in ancient Rome claiming descent from a common ancestor and sharing the same nomen. **2.** a group of persons tracing common descent in the male line; clan.

gent (jent), *n.* a gentleman.

gen•teel (jen tēl′), *adj.* **1.** belonging or suited to polite society. **2.** well-bred or refined; polite; elegant. **3.** affectedly or pretentiously polite or delicate. —**gen•teel′ly,** *adv.* —**gen•teel′ness,** *n.*

gen•tian (jen′shən), *n.* **1.** any plant of the gentian family, esp. the genus *Gentiana,* having usu. blue but sometimes yellow, white, or red flowers. **2.** the root of a European species of gentian, *G. lutea,* used as a tonic.

gen′tian vi′olet, *n.* a dye derived from rosaniline, used as an indicator and as a fungicide.

gen•tile (jen′tīl), *adj.* (*sometimes cap.*) **1.** of or pertaining to any people not Jewish. **2.** Christian, as distinguished from Jewish. **3.** not Mormon. **4.** heathen or pagan. **5.** of or pertaining to a tribe, clan, nation, etc. —*n.* **6.** a person who is not Jewish, esp. a Christian. **7.** (among Mormons) a person who is not a Mormon. **8.** a heathen or pagan.

gen•til•i•ty (jen til′i tē), *n.* **1.** refinement. **2.** affected or pretentious politeness or elegance. **3.** the condition or status of belonging to the gentry. **4.** members of polite society collectively; the gentry.

gen•tle (jen′tl), *adj.,* **-tler, -tlest,** *v.,* **-tled, -tling.** —*adj.* **1.** kindly; amiable: *a gentle manner.* **2.** not severe, rough, or violent; mild; light: *a gentle tap on the arm.* **3.** moderate: *gentle heat.* **4.** not steep; gradual: *a gentle slope.* **5.** of good birth or family; wellborn. **6.** characteristic of good birth; honorable; respectable: *a gentle upbringing.* **7.** easily handled or managed; tractable: *a gentle animal.* **8.** soft or low: *a gentle sound.* **9.** polite; refined; courteous. —*v.t.* **10.** to tame; render tractable. **11.** to mollify; calm; pacify. **12.** to make gentle. **13.** to stroke; soothe by petting. **14.** to dignify. —**gen′tle•ness,** *n.* —**gen′tly,** *adv.*

gen′tle breeze′, *n.* a wind of 8–12 mph (4–5 m/sec).

gen•tle•man (jen′tl mən), *n.,* *pl.* **-men. 1.** a man of good family, breeding, or social position. **2.** (used as a polite term) a man: *the gentleman in the tweed suit.* **3.** gentlemen, (used as a form of address): *Gentlemen, please come this way.* **4.** a civilized, educated, sensitive, or well-mannered man. **5.** a male personal servant; valet. **6.** a male attendant upon a king, queen, or other royal person, who is himself of high birth or rank. **7.** a man with an independent income who does not work for a living. **8.** a male member of the U.S. Congress: *the gentleman from Massachusetts.* **9.** (formerly) a man above the rank of yeoman.

gen′tleman-at-arms′, *n.,* *pl.* **gentlemen-at-arms.** one of a guard of men who attend the British sovereign on state occasions.

gen′tleman-farm′er, *n.,* *pl.* **gentlemen-farmers.** a wealthy man who farms for pleasure rather than for basic income.

gen•tle•man•ly (jen′tl mən lē), *adj.* like, befitting, or characteristic of a gentleman. —**gen′tle•man•li•ness,** *n.*

gen′tlemen's (or **gen′tleman's**) **agree′ment,** *n.* an agreement

that, although unenforceable at law, is binding as a matter of personal honor.

gen•tle•per•son (jen′tl pûr′sən), *n.* a person of good family and position; gentleman or lady.

gen•tle•wom•an (jen′tl wŏŏm′ən), *n.,* *pl.* **-wom•en. 1.** a woman of good family, breeding, or social position. **2.** a civilized, educated, sensitive, or well-mannered woman; lady.

gen•tri•fi•ca•tion (jen′trə fi kā′shən), *n.* the upgrading of run-down urban neighborhoods by affluent people who buy and renovate the properties, thereby causing displacement of the resident poor.

gen•try (jen′trē), *n.* **1.** wellborn and well-bred people. **2.** (in England) the class below the nobility. **3.** an upper or ruling class; aristocracy. **4.** people, esp. considered as a specific group, class, or kind; folks: *the hockey gentry.*

gen•u•flect (jen′yŏŏ flekt′), *v.i.* **1.** to bend the knee or touch one knee to the floor in reverence or worship. **2.** to express a servile attitude; fawn. —**gen′u•flec′tion,** *n.* —**gen′u•flec′tor,** *n.*

gen•u•ine (jen′yŏŏ in *or, sometimes,* -īn′), *adj.* **1.** possessing the claimed character, quality, or origin; not counterfeit; authentic; real: *a genuine antique.* **2.** properly so called: *a genuine liberal.* **3.** free from pretense, or hypocrisy; sincere: *genuine admiration.* —**gen′u•ine•ly,** *adv.* —**gen′u•ine•ness,** *n.* —**Pronunciation.** The two pronunciations of GENUINE reflect a sharp social contrast. The first, (jen′yŏŏ in), is the usual educated pronunciation. The second, (jen′yŏŏ īn′), with the final syllable rhyming with *sign,* occurs chiefly among less educated speakers, esp. older ones. The latter pronunciation is sometimes used by educated speakers, as for emphasis or humorous effect.

ge•nus (jē′nəs), *n.,* *pl.* **gen•e•ra** (jen′ər ə), **ge•nus•es. 1.** the major subdivision of a biological family or subfamily in the classification of organisms, usu. consisting of more than one species. **2.** *Logic.* a class or group of individuals, or of species of individuals. **3.** a kind; class.

-geny, a combining form meaning "development," "formation," "growth" of the thing, or in the place or manner specified by the initial element: *phylogeny.*

geo-, a combining form meaning "the earth" (*geography*); "earth, ground" (*geoponics*); "geography" (*geopolitics*).

ge•o•bot•a•ny (jē′ō bot′n ē), *n.* PHYTOGEOGRAPHY. —**ge′o•bo•tan′i•cal** (-bə tan′i kəl), **ge′o•bo•tan′ic,** *adj.* —**ge′o•bot′a•nist,** *n.*

ge•o•cen•tric (jē′ō sen′trik), *adj.* **1.** having or representing the earth as a center: *a geocentric theory of the universe.* **2.** using the earth or earthly life as the only basis of evaluation. **3.** viewed or measured as from the center of the earth: *the geocentric position of the moon.* —**ge′o•cen′tri•cal•ly,** *adv.*

ge•o•chem•is•try (jē′ō kem′ə strē), *n.* **1.** the science dealing with the chemical changes in and the composition of the earth or other celestial bodies. **2.** the geological and chemical characteristics or features of any area: *the geochemistry of the lunar surface.* —**ge′o•chem′i•cal** (-i kəl), *adj.* —**ge′o•chem′i•cal•ly,** *adv.* —**ge′o•chem′ist,** *n.*

ge•o•chro•nol•o•gy (jē′ō krə nol′ə jē), *n.* the chronology of the earth, as based on both absolute and relative methods of age determination. —**ge′o•chron′o•log′ic** (-kron′l oj′ik), **ge′o•chron′o•log′i•cal,** *adj.* —**ge′o•chro•nol′o•gist,** *n.*

ge•ode (jē′ōd), *n.* **1.** a hollow concretionary or nodular stone often

GEOLOGIC TIME DIVISIONS

Era	Years Ago	Period	Epoch	Features and Events
	10,000	Quaternary	Recent	Modern humans
	2 million		Pleistocene	Widespread glacial ice (ice ages)
Cenozoic	10 million		Pliocene	Mountain uplift; cool climate; mammals increase in size and numbers
	25 million		Miocene	Widespread grasslands; grazing mammals; apes; whales
	40 million	Tertiary	Oligocene	Browsing mammals; sabertoothed tigers
	55 million		Eocene	Warm climate; modern birds and mammals; giant birds
	65 million		Paleocene	Mild to cool climate; age of mammals begins; primates
Mesozoic	140 million	Cretaceous		Last dinosaurs; modern insects; flowering plants
	190 million	Jurassic		Age of dinosaurs; first birds and mammals; flying reptiles
	230 million	Triassic		Active volcanoes; age of reptiles begins; first dinosaurs
Paleozoic	280 million	Permian		Conifer forests; extinction of many marine invertebrates
	310 million	Pennsylvanian (Carboniferous)		Warm climate; swamps and coal forests; first reptiles
	345 million	Mississippian (Carboniferous)		Shallow seas, low lands; fern forests: age of amphibians begins
	405 million	Devonian		Age of fishes; first amphibians, insects, land animals
	425 million	Silurian		Shellfish abundant; first land plants, modern fungi
	500 million	Ordovician		Primitive fishes; seaweeds; fungi
	570 million	Cambrian		Age of marine invertebrates begins: shellfish, echinoderms, etc.
Precambrian	2.5 billion	Proterozoic		Bacteria; algae; primitive multicellular life
	5 billion	Archeozoic		Earth's crust solidifies; earliest life forms; blue-green algae; free oxygen

lined with crystals. **2.** the hollow or cavity of this. —**ge·od′ic** (-od′ik), **ge·od′al** (-ōd′l), *adj.*

ge·o·des·ic (jē′ə des′ik, -dē′sik), *adj.* Also, **ge′o·des′i·cal. 1.** pertaining to the geometry of curved surfaces, in which geodesic lines take the place of the straight lines of plane geometry. **2.** pertaining to geodesy. —*n.* **3.** GEODESIC LINE.

ge′odes′ic dome′, *n.* a light domelike structure developed by R. Buckminster Fuller, consisting of a framework of straight members, usu. in tension, typically having the form of a projection upon a sphere of a grid of triangular or polygonal faces.

ge′odes′ic line′, *n.* the shortest line lying on a given surface and connecting two given points.

ge·od·e·sy (jē od′ə sē) also **ge·o·det·ics** (jē′ə det′iks), *n.* the branch of applied mathematics that deals with the measurement of the shape and area of large tracts of country, the exact position of geographical points, and the curvature, shape, and dimensions of the earth. —**ge·od′e·sist,** *n.*

ge·o·ec·o·nom·ics (jē′ō ek′ə nom′iks, -ē′kə-), *n.* (*used with a sing. v.*) the study of the influence of geography on economics. —**ge′o·ec′o·nom′ic, ge′o·ec′o·nom′i·cal,** *adj.* —**ge′o·e·con′o·mist** (-i kon′ə mist), *n.*

ge·og·ra·phy (jē og′rə fē), *n., pl.* **-phies. 1.** the science dealing with the areal differentiation of the earth's surface, as shown in the character, arrangement, and interrelations of such elements as climate, elevation, vegetation, population, and land use. **2.** the topographical features of a given region. **3.** a book dealing with geographical science or study, as a textbook. **4.** the arrangement of features of any complex entity: *the geography of the mind.* —**ge·og′raph·er,** *n.* —**ge·o·graph′ic, ge·o·graph′i·cal,** *adj.* —**ge·o·graph′i·cal·ly,** *adv.*

ge′olog′ic time′, *n.* the succession of eras, periods, and epochs as considered in historical geology.

ge·ol·o·gy (jē ol′ə jē), *n., pl.* **-gies. 1.** the science that deals with the dynamics and physical history of the earth, the rocks of which it is composed, and the physical, chemical, and biologic changes that the earth has undergone or is undergoing. **2.** the geologic features and processes occurring in a given area or region: *the geology of the Andes.* **3.** the study of the rocks and other physical features of the moon, planets, and other celestial bodies. **4.** a book dealing with geology, esp. a textbook. —**ge·o·log′ic, ge·o·log′i·cal,** *adj.* —**ge·o·log′i·cal·ly,** *adv.* —**ge·ol′o·gist,** *n.*

ge·o·mag·net·ism (jē′ō mag′ni tiz′əm), *n.* **1.** the earth's magnetic field and associated phenomena. **2.** the branch of geophysics that studies such phenomena. —**ge·o·mag·net′ic,** *adj.*

geomet′ric progres′sion, *n.* a sequence of terms in which the ratio between any two successive terms is the same, as the progression 1, 3, 9, 27, 81 or 144, 12, 1, $\frac{1}{12}$, $\frac{1}{144}$. Also called **geometric series.**

ge′omet′ric se′ries, *n.* an infinite series of the form, $c + cx + cx^2 + cx^3 + \ldots$, where c and x are real numbers. **2.** GEOMETRIC PROGRESSION.

ge·om·e·try (jē om′i trē), *n.* **1.** the branch of mathematics that deals with the deduction of the properties, measurement, and relationships of points, lines, angles, and figures in space by means of certain assumed properties of space. **2.** any specific system of this that operates in accordance with a specific set of assumptions: *Euclidean geometry.* **3.** a book on geometry, esp. a textbook. **4.** the shape or form of a surface or solid. **5.** a design or arrangement of objects in simple rectilinear or curvilinear form. —**ge′o·met′ric, ge′o·met′ri·cal,** *adj.* —**ge′o·met′ri·cal·ly,** *adv.*

ge·o·mor·phic (jē′ə môr′fik), *adj.* **1.** of, resembling, or pertaining to the form of the earth or of its surface features. **2.** of or pertaining to the form of any celestial body or of its features.

ge·o·mor·phol·o·gy (jē′ə môr fol′ə jē), *n.* the study of the characteristics, origin, and development of the form or surface features of the earth or other celestial bodies. —**ge′o·mor′pho·log′i·cal** (-fə loj′i kəl), **ge′o·mor′pho·log′ic,** *adj.* —**ge′o·mor·phol′o·gist,** *n.*

ge·oph·a·gy (jē of′ə jē) also **ge·o·pha·gia** (jē′ə fā′jə, -jē ə), *n.* the practice of eating earthy matter, esp. clay or chalk, as in famine-stricken areas. —**ge·oph′a·gous** (-gəs), *adj.*

ge·o·phys·ics (jē′ō fiz′iks), *n.* (*used with a sing. v.*) the branch of geology that deals with the physics of the earth and its atmosphere, including oceanography, seismology, volcanology, and geomagnetism. —**ge′o·phys′i·cal,** *adj.* —**ge·o·phys′i·cist,** *n.*

ge·o·pol·i·tics (jē′ō pol′i tiks), *n.* (*used with a sing. v.*) **1.** the study of the influence of physical geography on the politics, national power, or foreign policy of a state. **2.** the combination of geographic and political factors influencing or delineating a country or region. **3.** a national policy based on the interrelation of politics and geography. —**ge′o·po·lit′i·cal** (-pə lit′i kəl), *adj.* —**ge′o·pol′i·ti′cian** (-tish′ən), *n.*

ge·o·pon·ics (jē′ə pon′iks), *n.* (*used with a sing. v.*) **1.** the art or science of agriculture. **2.** gardening or farming in soil (contrasted with *hydroponics*).

George¹ (jôrj), *n.* **1. David Lloyd,** LLOYD GEORGE, David. **2. Henry,** 1839–97, U.S. economist. **3. Saint,** died A.D. 303?, Christian martyr: patron saint of England. **4. Lake,** a lake in E New York. 36 mi. (58 km) long.

George² (jôrj), *n.* **1. George I,** 1660–1727, king of England 1714–27. **2. George II,** 1683–1760, king of England 1727–60 (son of George I). **3. George III,** 1738–1820, king of England 1760–1820 (grandson of George

II). **4. George IV,** 1762–1830, king of England 1820–30 (son of George III). **5. George V,** 1865–1936, king of England 1910–36 (son of Edward VII). **6. George VI,** 1895–1952, king of England 1936–1952 (son of George V).

George·town (jôrj′toun′), *n.* **1.** Also, **George′ Town′.** the capital of the state of Penang, in NW Malaysia. 250,578. **2.** the capital of Guyana, at the mouth of the Demerara. 182,000. **3.** a residential section in the District of Columbia. **4.** the capital of the Cayman Islands, West Indies, on Grand Cayman. 12,000.

Geor·gia (jôr′jə), *n.* **1.** a state in the SE United States. 7,353,225; 58,876 sq. mi. (152,489 sq. km): *Cap.:* Atlanta. *Abbr.:* GA, Ga. **2.** Also called **Geor′gian Repub′lic.** Former official name, **Geor′gian So′viet So′cialist Repub′lic.** a republic in Transcaucasia, on the Black Sea, N of Turkey and Armenia: a former constituent republic of the U.S.S.R. 5,174,642; 26,872 sq. mi. (69,700 sq. km). *Cap.:* Tbilisi. **3. Strait of,** an inlet of the Pacific in SW Canada between Vancouver Island and the mainland. 150 mi. (240 km) long.

Geor·gian (jôr′jən), *adj.* **1.** of or pertaining to the period of British history from the accession of George I in 1714 to the death of George IV. **2.** of or pertaining to George V or his reign. **3.** of or designating the styles of architecture and furniture current in England esp. from 1714 to 1811. **4.** of or pertaining to the state of Georgia. **5.** of or pertaining to the Georgian Republic. —*n.* **6.** a person, esp. a writer, of either of the Georgian periods in England. **7.** a native or inhabitant of the state of Georgia. **8. a.** a native or inhabitant of the Georgian Republic. **b.** the Caucasian language of the Georgians.

Geor′gia pine′, *n.* LONGLEAF PINE.

ge·o·sci·ence (jē′ō sī′əns), *n.* EARTH SCIENCE.

ge·o·stat·ic (jē′ə stat′ik), *adj.* **1.** of or pertaining to pressure exerted by the weight of overlying rock. **2.** (of a construction) resistant to such pressure.

ge·o·sta·tion·ar·y (jē′ō stā′shə ner′ē), *adj.* of, pertaining to, or designating a satellite traveling in an orbit 22,300 mi. (35,900 km) above the earth's equator, at which the satellite's period of rotation matches the earth's and the satellite always remains in the same spot over the earth; geosynchronous.

ge·o·syn·cline (jē′ō sin′klīn), *n.* a portion of the earth's crust subjected to downward warping during a large span of geologic time. —**ge′o·syn·cli′nal,** *adj.*

ge·o·tec·ton·ic (jē′ō tek ton′ik), *adj.* TECTONIC (def. 2).

ge·o·ther·mal (jē′ō thûr′məl) also **ge·o·ther′mic,** *adj.* of or pertaining to the internal heat of the earth.

ge·o·trop·ic (jē′ō trop′ik, -trō′pik), *adj.* of, pertaining to, or exhibiting geotropism.

ge·ot·ro·pism (jē o′trə piz′əm), *n.* oriented movement or growth of an organism with respect to the force of gravity.

ge·ra·ni·um (ji rā′nē əm), *n.* **1.** Also called **crane's-bill.** any plant of the genus *Geranium*, having usu. pink or purplish flowers. **2.** Also called **stork's-bill.** any plant of the widely cultivated allied S African genus *Pelargonium*, having showy red, pink, or white flowers and sometimes fragrant leaves. **3.** a vivid red color.

ger·bil (jûr′bəl), *n.* any small burrowing cricetid rodent of the subfamily Gerbilinae, with long hind legs, popular as a pet.

ger·fal·con (jûr′fôl′kən, -fal′-, -fô′-), *n.* GYRFALCON.

ger·i·at·rics (jer′ē a′triks, jēr′-), *n.* (*used with a sing. v.*) **1.** the branch of medicine dealing with the diseases, debilities, and care of aged persons. **2.** the study of the physical processes and problems of aging; gerontology. —**ger·i·at′ric,** *adj., n.* —**ger′i·a·tri′cian** (-ə trish′ən) **ger′i·at′rist,** *n.*

germ (jûrm), *n.* **1.** a microorganism, esp. when disease-producing; microbe. **2.** a bud, offshoot, or seed. **3.** the rudiment of a living organism; an embryo in its early stages. **4.** the initial stage in development or evolution, as a germ cell or ancestral form. **5.** a source of development; origin; seed: *the germ of an idea.* [< Middle French < Latin *germen* shoot, sprout] —**germ′like′,** *adj.*

Ger·man (jûr′mən), *n.* **1.** a native or inhabitant of Germany. **2.** the West Germanic language of Germany, Austria, and most of Switzerland, historically comprising a broad range of dialects. *Abbr.:* G Compare HIGH GERMAN, LOW GERMAN. **3.** (*usu. l.c.*) an elaborate social dance resembling a cotillion. **4.** (*l.c.*) *New England and South Atlantic States.* a dancing party featuring the german. —*adj.* **5.** of or pertaining to Germany, its inhabitants, or their language.

Ger′man cock′roach, *n.* a common yellowish-brown cockroach, *Blatta germanica*, brought into the U.S. from Europe. Also called **cro·tonbug.**

Ger·man·ic (jər man′ik), *n.* **1.** a family of languages, a branch of the Indo-European family, that includes English, Dutch, German, the Scandinavian languages, and Gothic. *Abbr.:* Gmc **2.** an ancient Indo-European language, the immediate linguistic ancestor of the Germanic languages. *Abbr.:* Gmc —*adj.* **3.** of or pertaining to Germanic or its speakers. —**Ger·man′i·cal·ly,** *adv.*

ger·ma·ni·um (jər mā′nē əm), *n.* a hard, metallic, grayish white element, used chiefly as a semiconductor. *Symbol:* Ge; *at. wt.:* 72.59; *at. no.:* 32; *sp. gr.:* 5.36 at 20°C.

Ger′man mea′sles, *n.* RUBELLA.

Ger′man shep′herd, *n.* one of a breed of large dogs with erect ears, a bushy tail, and a thick, usu. gray or black-and-tan coat, often used in police work and as a guide dog.

G

Ger′man sil′ver, *n.* any of various alloys of copper, zinc, and nickel, usu. white and used for utensils and drawing instruments.

Ger•ma•ny (jûr′mə nē), *n.* a republic in central Europe: after World War II divided into four zones, British, French, U.S., and Soviet, and in 1949 into East Germany and West Germany; East and West Germany were reunited in 1990. 84,068,216; 137,852 sq. mi. (357,039 sq. km). *Cap.:* Berlin. Official name, **Federal Republic of Germany.** German **Deutschland.**

germ′ cell′, *n.* a sexual reproductive cell at any stage from the primordial cell to the mature gamete.

germ•free (jûrm′frē′, -frē′), *adj.* **1.** STERILE (def. 1). **2.** (of experimental animals) born and raised under sterile conditions.

ger•mi•cide (jûr′mə sīd′), *n.* an agent for killing germs or microorganisms. —**ger•mi•cid′al,** *adj.*

ger•mi•nal (jûr′mə nl), *adj.* **1.** being in the earliest stage of development: *germinal ideas.* **2.** of or pertaining to a germ or germs. —**ger′mi•nal•ly,** *adv.*

ger•mi•nate (jûr′mə nāt′), *v.,* **-nat•ed, -nat•ing.** —*v.i.* **1.** to begin to grow or develop. **2. a.** to develop into a plant or individual, as a seed, spore, or bulb. **b.** to put forth shoots; sprout. **3.** to come into existence; begin. —*v.t.* **4.** to cause to sprout or grow. **5.** to cause to come into existence; create. —**ger′mi•na′tion,** *n.* —**ger′mi•na′tor,** *n.*

germ′ plasm′, *n.* the substance of reproductive cells that contains chromosomes.

germ•proof (jûrm′prōof′), *adj.* not vulnerable to the action or penetration of germs.

germ′ the′ory, *n.* **1.** the theory that infectious diseases are due to the agency of germs or microorganisms. **2.** biogenesis.

germ′ war′fare, *n.* BIOLOGICAL WARFARE.

Ge•ron•i•mo (jə ron′ə mō′), *n.* (*Goyathlay*), 1829–1909, American Apache Indian chief.

ge•ron•tic (jə ron′tik), *adj.* of or pertaining to the last phase in the life cycle of an organism or in the life history of a species.

geronto-, a combining form meaning "old age": *gerontology.*

ger•on•toc•ra•cy (jer′ən tok′rə sē, jēr′-), *n., pl.* **-cies. 1.** government by a council of elders. **2.** a governing body consisting of old people.

ger•on•tol•o•gy (jer′ən tol′ə jē, jēr′-), *n.* the study of aging and the problems of aged people. —**ge•ron•to•log•i•cal** (jə ron′tl oj′i kəl), *adj.* —**ger′on•tol′o•gist,** *n.*

Ger•ry (ger′ē), *n.* **Elbridge,** 1744–1814, U.S. vice president 1813–14.

ger•ry•man•der (jer′i man′dər, ger′-), *v.* **1.** the dividing of a state, county, etc., into election districts so as to give one political party a majority in many districts while concentrating the voting strength of the other party into as few districts as possible. —*v.t.* **2.** to subject (a state, county, etc.) to a gerrymander. —**ger′ry•man′der•er,** *n.*

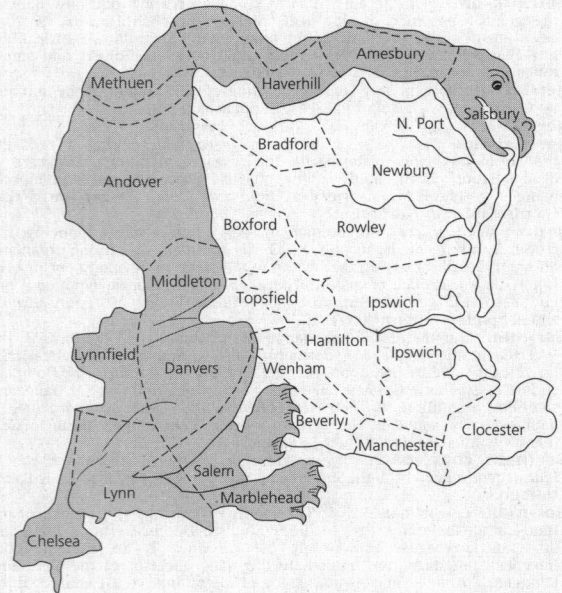

gerrymander

Ger•shom (gûr′shəm), *n.* the elder son of Moses and Zipporah. Ex. 18:3.

Gersh•win (gûrsh′win), *n.* **1. George,** 1898–1937, U.S. composer. **2.** his brother, **Ira,** 1896–1983, U.S. lyricist.

ger•und (jer′ənd), *n.* **1.** a form in Latin regularly derived from a verb and functioning as a noun, used in all cases but the nominative, as *dicendī* gen., *dicendō* dat., abl., etc., "saying." **2.** a form similar to the Latin gerund in meaning or function, as in English the *-ing* form of a verb when functioning as a noun, as *writing* in *Writing is easy.* —**ge•run•di•al** (jə run′dē əl), *adj.* —**ge•run′di•al•ly,** *adv.*

ges•so (jes′ō), *n., pl.* **-soes.** gypsum or plaster of Paris prepared with glue for use as a surface for painting. —**ges′soed,** *adj.*

ge•stalt (gə shtält′, -shtôlt′, -stält′, -stôlt′), *n., pl.* **-stalts, -stal•ten** (-shtäl′tn, -shtôl′-, -stäl′-, -stôl′-). *Psychol.* (*sometimes cap.*) a form or configuration having properties that cannot be derived by the summation of its component parts.

Gestalt′ psychol′ogy, *n.* the school or doctrine holding that behavioral and psychological phenomena cannot be fully explained by analysis of their component parts, as reflexes or sensations, but must be studied as wholes.

Ge•sta•po (gə stä′pō), *n.* the German secret police during the Nazi regime, notorious for its brutality. [< German (1933), acronym for *Ge(-heime) Sta(ats)po(lizei)* secret state police]

ges•tate (jes′tāt), *v.,* **-tat•ed, -tat•ing.** —*v.t.* **1.** to carry in the womb during the period from the initiation of the pregnancy to delivery. **2.** to think of and develop (an idea, opinion, or plan) slowly in the mind. —*v.i.* **3.** to experience the process of gestating offspring. **4.** to develop slowly. —**ges•ta′tion,** *n.* —**ges•ta′tion•al, ges•ta•tive** (jes′tə tiv, je stā′-), *adj.*

gesta′tional car′rier, *n.* SURROGATE MOTHER (def. 2a). Also called **gesta′tional moth′er.**

ges•tic•u•late (je stik′yə lāt′), *v.,* **-lat•ed, -lat•ing.** —*v.i.* **1.** to make or use gestures, esp. in an animated or excited manner with or instead of speech. —*v.t.* **2.** to express by gesturing. —**ges•tic′u•la′tion,** *n.* —**ges•tic′u•la′tive, ges•tic′u•la•to′ry** (-lə tôr′ē, -tōr′ē), *adj.*

ges•ture (jes′chər), *n., v.,* **-tured, -tur•ing.** —*n.* **1.** a movement or position of the hand, arm, body, head, or face that is expressive of an idea, opinion, emotion, etc.: *a threatening gesture.* **2.** the use of such movements to express thought, emotion, etc. **3.** any action, communication, etc., intended for effect or as a formality; considered expression; demonstration: *a gesture of friendship.* —*v.i.* **4.** to make or use a gesture or gestures. —*v.t.* **5.** to express by a gesture or gestures. —**ges′tur•al,** *adj.* —**ges′tur•er,** *n.*

ge•sund•heit (gə zŏŏnt′hīt), *interj.* (used to wish good health, esp. to a person who has just sneezed.)

get (get), *v.,* **got, got** or **got•ten, get•ting,** *n.* —*v.t.* **1.** to cause to be in one's possession or be available for one's use or enjoyment; obtain; acquire: *to get a good price for a house; to get information.* **2.** to earn: *to get the minimum wage.* **3.** to go after, take hold of, and bring (something) for oneself or another; fetch: *She got the trunk from the attic.* **4.** to cause or cause to become, to do, to move, etc., as specified: *to get one's hair cut; to get a fire to burn.* **5.** to communicate or establish communication with over a distance; reach: *to get someone by telephone.* **6.** to hear or hear clearly: *I didn't get your last name.* **7.** to acquire a mental grasp of; learn: *to get a lesson.* **8.** to capture; seize: *Get him before he escapes!* **9.** to receive as a punishment or sentence: *to get a spanking; to get a year in jail.* **10.** to prevail on; influence or persuade: *We'll get him to go with us.* **11.** to prepare; make ready: *to get dinner.* **12.** (esp. of animals) to beget. **13.** to affect emotionally: *Her tears got me.* **14.** to hit, strike, or wound: *The bullet got him in the leg.* **15.** to kill. **16.** to take vengeance on: *I'll get you yet!* **17.** to catch or be afflicted with: *to get malaria while in the tropics; to get butterflies before a performance.* **18.** to receive (one's deserts, esp. punishment) (fol. by *his, hers, theirs,* or *yours*): *You'll get yours!* **19.** to puzzle; irritate; annoy: *Their silly remarks get me.* **20.** to understand; comprehend: *to get a joke.* —*v.i.* **21.** to come to a specified place; arrive; reach: *to get home late.* **22.** to succeed, become enabled, or be permitted: *You get to meet a lot of interesting people.* **23.** to become or to cause oneself to become as specified; reach a certain condition: *to get ready; to get sick.* **24.** (used as an auxiliary verb fol. by a past participle to form the passive): *to get married; to get hit by a car.* **25.** to succeed in coming, going, arriving at, visiting, etc. (usu. fol. by *away, in, into, out, etc.*): *I don't get into town very often.* **26.** to bear, endure, or survive (usu. fol. by *through* or *over*): *Will he get through another bad winter?* **27.** to earn money; gain. **28.** to leave immediately: *He told us to get.* **29.** to start or enter upon the action of (fol. by a present participle expressing action): *to get moving.* **30. get about, a.** to move around physically from one place to another. **b.** to become known, as a rumor. **c.** to engage in social activities. **31. get across, a.** to succeed in communicating or explaining: *to get a message across.* **b.** to be or become clearly understood: *The message finally got across.* **32. get ahead,** to be successful, as in business or society. **33. get along, a.** to go away; leave. **b.** to get on. **34. get around, a.** to circumvent; outwit. **b.** to ingratiate oneself with (someone) by flattery or cajolery. **c.** to travel from place to place; circulate: *I don't get around much anymore.* **35. get at, a.** to reach; touch. **b.** to suggest, hint at, or imply; intimate: *What are you getting at?* **c.** to discover; determine: *to get at the root of a problem.* **36. get away, a.** to escape; flee. **b.** to start out; leave. **37. get away with,** to do or steal without consequent punishment. **38. get back, a.** to come back; return. **b.** to recover; regain. **c.** to be revenged. **39. get by, a.** to get beyond; pass. **b.** to escape the notice of. **c.** to survive or manage minimally. **d.** to expend little effort; be merely adequate. **40. get down, a.** to bring or come down; descend. **b.** to concentrate; attend. **c.** to depress; discourage; fatigue. **d.** to swallow. **e.** to relax and enjoy oneself completely. **41. get in, a.** to enter. **b.** to arrive at a destination. **c.** to enter into close association (usu. fol. by *with*): *getting in with the wrong crowd.* **d.** to be or cause to be elected to office or accepted into a group. **42. get off, a.** to dismount from or get out of. **b.** to begin a journey. **c.** to escape punishment. **d.** to help (someone) to escape punishment, esp. by providing legal assistance. **e.** to tell or write: *to get off a joke.* **f.** to have the effrontery: *Where does he get off telling me what to do?* **g.** to finish, as one's workday: *We get off at five o'clock.* **43. get on, a.** to make progress; proceed; advance. **b.** to have sufficient means to manage, survive, or fare. **c.** to be on good terms; agree: *She doesn't get on with her roommate.* **d.** to advance in age: *He is getting on in years.* **44. get out, a.** to leave (often fol. by *of*). **b.** to become publicly known. **c.** to withdraw or retire (often fol. by *of*). **d.** to produce or complete. **45. get over, a.** to recover from: *to get over an illness.* **b.** to get across. **46. get through, a.** to finish. **b.** to reach someone, as by telephone. **c.** to make oneself clearly understood. **47. get to, a.** to get in touch or into communication with; contact. **b.** to make an impression on; affect. **c.** to begin. **48. get together, a.** to accumulate; gather. **b.** to congregate; meet. **c.** to come to an accord; agree. **49. get up, a.** to sit up or stand; arise. **b.** to rise from bed. **c.** to ascend or mount. **d.** to prepare; arrange; organize: *to get up an exhibit.* **e.** to draw upon; marshal; rouse: *to get up one's courage.* **f.** (used as a command to a horse to start moving or go faster.) **g.** to dress up, as in a costume or by adding embellishments. —*n.* **50.** an offspring or the total of offspring, esp. of a male animal: *the get of a stallion.* **51.** a return of a ball, as in tennis, that would normally have resulted in a point for the opponent. —*Idiom.* **52. get it, a.** to be punished or reprimanded. **b.** to understand or grasp something. **53. get nowhere,** to fail despite much action and effort. **54. get off someone's back** or **case,** *Slang.* to cease to nag or criticize someone. **55. get somewhere,** to have success in life or in reaching a specific goal. **56. has** or **have got, a.** to possess or own; have: *Have you got the tickets?* **b.** must (fol. by an infinitive): *He's got to get to a doctor right away.* **c.** to suffer from: *Have you got a cold?* —**get/ta·ble, get/a·ble,** *adj.* —**Usage.** The use of GET rather than of forms of *to be* in the passive (*He won't get accepted with those grades*) is found today chiefly in informal speech and writing. In American English GOTTEN, although occasionally criticized, is an alternative standard past participle in most senses, esp. "to receive" and "to acquire": *I have gotten* (or *got*) *a dozen replies so far.* HAVE or HAS GOT meaning "must" has been in use since the early 19th century, often contracted: *You've got to carry your passport everywhere.* In the sense "to possess" this construction dates to the 15th century and is also often contracted: *She's got a master's degree in biology.* Occasionally condemned as redundant, these uses are nevertheless standard in all varieties of speech and writing. GOT without HAVE or HAS meaning "must" (*I got to buy a new suit*) is characteristic of the most relaxed, informal speech only. GOTTA is a pronunciation spelling representing this use. —**Pronunciation.** The pronunciation (git) for GET has existed since the 16th century. The same change is exhibited in (kin) for CAN and (yit) for YET. The pronunciation (git) is not regional and occurs in all parts of the country. It is most common as an unstressed syllable: *Let's get going!* (lets′ git gō′ing). In educated speech the pronunciation (git) in stressed syllables is rare and sometimes criticized. When GET is an imperative meaning "leave immediately," the pronunciation is usu. facetious: *Now get!* (nou′ git′).

get (get), *n., pl.* **git·tin** (gē tēn′, git′in), **gi·tim** (gē tēm′, git′im). *Hebrew.* **1.** a legal document, executed by a rabbi or Jewish court of law, dissolving the marriage bond between husband and wife. **2.** a divorce granted in accordance with Jewish law.

get·a·way (get′ə wā′), *n.* **1.** a getting away or fleeing; an escape. **2.** the start of a race. **3.** a place where one escapes for relaxation, vacation, etc., or a period of time for such recreation.

Geth·sem·a·ne (geth sem′ə nē), *n.* **1.** a garden E of Jerusalem, near the brook of Kidron: scene of Jesus' agony and betrayal. Matt. 26:36. **2.** (*l.c.*) a scene or occasion of suffering; calvary.

get′-togeth′er, *n.* **1.** an informal, usu. small social gathering. **2.** a meeting or conference.

Get·ty (get′ē), *n.* **J(ean) Paul,** 1892–1976, U.S. oil magnate.

Get·tys·burg (get′iz bûrg′), *n.* a borough in S Pennsylvania: Confederate forces defeated in a Civil War battle fought near here on July 1–3, 1863; national cemetery and military park. 7194.

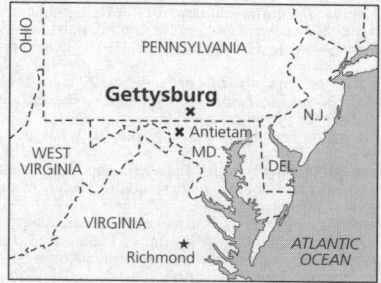

Get′tysburg Address′, *n.* the short speech made by President Lincoln on Nov. 19, 1863, at the dedication of the national cemetery at Gettysburg.

get′·up′ or **get′-up′,** *n. Informal.* **1.** costume; outfit. **2.** arrangement or format; style.

gew·gaw (gyōō′gô, gōō′-) *n.* something gaudy and useless; trinket; bauble. —**gew′gawed,** *adj.*

gey·ser (gī′zər, -sər *for 1;* gē′zər *for 2*), *n.* **1.** a hot spring that intermittently sends up fountainlike jets of water and steam into the air. **2.** *Brit.* a hot-water heater.

Ge·zer (gē′zər), *n.* an ancient Canaanite town, NW of Jerusalem.

Gha·na (gä′nə, gan′ə), *n.* **1.** a republic in W Africa comprising the former colonies of the Gold Coast and Ashanti, the protectorate of the Northern Territories, and the U.N. trusteeship of British Togoland: member of the Commonwealth of Nations since 1957. 18,100,703; 91,843 sq. mi. (237,873 sq. km). *Cap.:* Accra. **2. Kingdom of,** a medieval W African empire extending from near the Atlantic coast almost to Timbuktu; flourished about 9th–12th centuries. —**Gha′na·ian, Gha′ni·an,** *n., adj.*

ghast·ly (gast′lē, gäst′-), *adj., adv.* **1.** shockingly frightful or dreadful; horrible: *a ghastly murder.* **2.** resembling a ghost, esp. in being very pale; cadaverous. **3.** terrible; very bad: *a ghastly error.* —*adv.* **4.** Also, **ghast′li·ly, ghast′li·ly,** in a ghastly manner; horribly; terribly. **5.** with a deathlike quality. —**ghast′li·ness,** *n.*

ghee (gē), *n.* clarified butter made from the milk of cows or buffaloes.

gher·kin (gûr′kin), *n.* **1.** the small immature fruit of a variety of cucumber, used in pickling. **2. a.** the small spiny fruit of a tropical vine, *Cucumis anguria,* of the gourd family, used in pickling. **b.** the plant yielding this fruit. **3.** a small pickle, esp. one made from this fruit.

ghet·to (get′ō), *n., pl.* **-tos, -toes. 1.** a section of a city, esp. a thickly populated slum area, inhabited predominantly by members of a minority group. **2.** (formerly, in most European countries) a section of a city in which all Jews were required to live. **3.** a situation or environment to which a group has been relegated, as because of bias, or in which a group has segregated itself for various reasons: *female job ghettos; a suburban ghetto for millionaires.*

Ghib·el·line (gib′ə lin, -lēn′), *n.* **1.** a member of the aristocratic party in medieval Italy that supported the claims of the German emperors against the papacy: politically opposed to the Guelphs. —*adj.* **2.** of or pertaining to the Ghibellines. —**Ghib′el·lin·ism,** *n.*

ghost (gōst), *n.* **1.** the soul of a dead person, a disembodied spirit imagined as wandering, often in vague or evanescent form, among the living and sometimes haunting them; wraith. **2.** a mere shadow or semblance; trace: *She's a ghost of her former self.* **3.** a remote possibility: *not a ghost of a chance.* **4.** the principle of life; soul; spirit. **5.** GHOSTWRITER. **6.** a secondary, usu. faint or blurry image, as on a television screen or on a photographic negative or print. —*v.i.* **7.** to ghostwrite (a book, speech, etc.). —*v.i.* **8.** to ghostwrite. —*Idiom.* **9. give up the ghost, a.** to die. **b.** to cease to function or exist. —**ghost′ly,** *adj.*

ghost′ dance′, *n.* (*often caps.*) a ritual dance to call forth a vision of the afterlife: a central feature of a religious movement among American Indians in the late 19th century.

ghost′ town′, *n.* a town permanently abandoned by its inhabitants, as because of a business decline or because a nearby mine has been worked out.

ghost′writ′er or **ghost′ writ′er,** *n.* a person who writes a speech, book, article, etc., for another person who is named as or presumed to be the author. —**ghost′write′,** *v.t., v.i.,* **-wrote, -writ·ten, -writ·ing.**

ghoul (gōōl), *n.* **1.** an evil demon, orig. of Eastern legend, believed to rob graves, prey on corpses, etc. **2.** a grave robber. **3.** a person who revels in what is revolting.

ghoul·ish (gōō′lish), *adj.* **1.** strangely diabolical or cruel; monstrous. **2.** showing fascination with death or disease; morbid: *ghoulish curiosity.* **3.** of, pertaining to, or like a ghoul or ghouls. —**ghoul′ish·ly,** *adv.* —**ghoul′ish·ness,** *n.*

GHQ, *Mil.* general headquarters.

GHz, gigahertz.

gi or **gie** (gē), *n., pl.* **gis** or **gies.** a lightweight, usu. white costume consisting of loose-fitting pants and a jacket, worn for martial arts.

GI or **G.I.** (jē′ī′), *n., pl.* **GIs** or **GI's** or **G.I.'s,** *adj., v.,* **GI'd, GI'ing.** —*n.* **1.** a member or former member of the U.S. armed forces, esp. an enlisted soldier. —*adj.* **2.** rigidly adhering to military regulations and practices. **3.** of a standardized style or type issued or required by the U.S. armed forces: *GI shoes; a GI haircut.*

G.I. or **g.i., 1.** galvanized iron. **2.** gastrointestinal. **3.** general issue. **4.** government issue.

gi·ant (jī′ənt), *n.* **1.** (in folklore) a being with human form but superhuman size and strength. **2.** a person or thing of unusually great size or power. **3.** a person or thing of extraordinary importance, achievement, etc.: *one of the giants of aviation.* —*adj.* **4.** unusually large; gigantic; huge. **5.** of extraordinary power, importance, or achievement.

gi′ant·eat′er, *n.* a large tropical American anteater, *Myrmecophaga tridactyla,* with a long, bushy tail.

gi·ant·ess (jī′ən tis), *n.* **1.** (in folklore) a female being of human form but superhuman size and strength. **2.** any very large woman.

gi·ant·ism (jī′ən tiz′əm), *n.* **1.** GIGANTISM. **2.** the state or quality of being a giant.

gi′ant pan′da, *n.* PANDA (def. 1).

G

gi/ant sequoi/a, *n.* BIG TREE.

gi/ant sla/lom, *n.* a slalom race in which the course is longer and steeper and has wider turns than in a regular slalom.

gi/ant star/, *n.* a star having a diameter of from 10 to 100 times that of the sun, as Arcturus or Aldebaran.

gi/ant tor/toise, *n.* any of several large tortoises of the genus *Geochelone,* of the Galápagos Islands and islands near Madagascar.

gib•ber (jib′ər, gib′-), *v.i.* **1.** to speak inarticulately or meaninglessly. **2.** to speak foolishly; chatter. —*n.* **3.** gibbering utterance.

gib•ber•ish (jib′ər ish, gib′-), *n.* **1.** meaningless or unintelligible talk or writing; nonsense. **2.** talk or writing containing many obscure, pretentious, or technical words.

gib•bet (jib′it), *n.* **1.** a post with a projecting arm at the top, from which the bodies of executed criminals were formerly hung in chains for public display. **2.** a gallows. —*v.t.* **3.** to hang on a gibbet. **4.** to put to death by hanging on a gibbet. **5.** to hold up to public scorn.

gib•bon (gib′ən), *n.* any small, slender arboreal ape of the genera *Hylobates* or *Symphalangus,* of S Asia.

Gib•bon (gib′ən), *n.* **Edward,** 1737–94, English historian.

gib•bous (gib′əs) also **gib•bose** (-ōs), *adj.* (of a heavenly body) convex at both edges, as the moon when more than half full. —**gib′bous•ly,** *adv.* —**gib′bous•ness,** *n.*

gibbs•ite (gib′zīt), *n.* a mineral, hydrated aluminum oxide, Al_2O_3, $3H_2O$, occurring in whitish or grayish crystals and masses: an important constituent of bauxite ore.

gibe or **jibe** (jīb), *v.,* **gibed, gib•ing,** *n.* —*v.i.* **1.** to utter mocking or scoffing words; jeer. —*v.t.* **2.** to taunt; deride. —*n.* **3.** a taunting or sarcastic remark. —**gib′er,** *n.* —**gib′ing•ly,** *adv.*

Gib•e•on (gib′ē ən), *n.* a town in ancient Palestine, NW of Jerusalem. Josh. 9:3.

Gib•e•on•ite (gib′ē ə nīt′), *n.* one of the inhabitants of Gibeon, condemned by Joshua to be hewers of wood and drawers of water for the Israelites. Josh. 9.

GI Bill, *n.* any of various Congressional bills enacted to provide funds for college educations, home-buying loans, and other benefits for armed-services veterans. Also called **GI Bill of Rights.**

gib•let (jib′lit), *n.* Usu., **giblets.** the heart, liver, gizzard, or the like of a fowl.

Gi•bral•tar (ji brôl′tər), *n.* **1.** a British crown colony comprising a fortress and seaport located on a narrow promontory near the S tip of Spain. 29,934; 1⅞ sq. mi. (5 sq. km). **2. Rock of.** Ancient, **Calpe.** a long, precipitous mountain nearly coextensive with this colony: one of the Pillars of Hercules. 1396 ft. (426 m) high; 2½ mi. (4 km) long. **3. Strait of,** a strait between Europe and Africa at the Atlantic entrance to the Mediterranean. 8½–23 mi. (14–37 km) wide. **4.** any impregnable fortress or stronghold. —**Gi•bral•tar/i•an** (-târ′ē ən), *adj., n.*

Gib•son (gib′sən), *n.* **Charles Dana,** 1867–1944, U.S. artist and illustrator.

Gib′son girl/, *n.* **1.** the idealized American girl of the 1890s as represented in the illustrations of Charles Dana Gibson. **2.** of, indicating, or resembling the characteristic clothing of the Gibson girl, typically a high-necked, fitted blouse or bodice with full puff sleeves and a long skirt with a flared bottom and a tightly fitted waistline.

gid•dy (gid′ē), *adj.,* **-di•er, -di•est,** *v.,* **-died, -dy•ing.** —*adj.* **1.** affected with vertigo; dizzy. **2.** attended with or causing dizziness: *a giddy climb.* **3.** frivolous and lighthearted; flighty. —*v.t., v.i.* **4.** to make or become giddy. —**gid′di•ly,** *adv.* —**gid′di•ness,** *n.*

gid•dy•ap (gid′ē ap′, -up′) also **gid•dap** (gi dap′, -dup′), **gid•dy•up** (-up′), *interj.* (used as a command to a horse to speed up.)

Gid•e•on (gid′ē ən), *n.* a judge of Israel and conqueror of the Midianites. Judg. 6–8.

Gid′eons Interna′tional, *n.* an interdenominational lay society organized in 1899 to place Bibles in hotel rooms. Formerly, **Gid′eon Soci′ety.**

gift (gift), *n.* **1.** something given voluntarily without payment in return, as to honor a person or an occasion or to provide assistance; present. **2.** the act of giving. **3.** something bestowed or acquired without being sought or earned by the receiver. **4.** a special ability or capacity; natural endowment; talent: *a gift for music.* —*v.t.* **5.** to give some power, capacity, or talent to. **6.** to present (someone) with a gift: *just the thing to gift the newlyweds.*

gift′ certif′icate, *n.* a certificate entitling the bearer to select merchandise of a specified cash value from a store, usu. presented as a gift.

gift•ed (gif′tid), *adj.* **1.** having great special talent or ability: *a gifted storyteller.* **2.** having exceptionally high intelligence: *gifted children.* —**gift′ed•ly,** *adv.* —**gift′ed•ness,** *n.*

gift′ of gab/, *n.* an aptitude for speaking fluently, glibly, or persuasively.

Gift′ of the Ma′gi, *n.* one of three gifts—gold, frankincense, and myrrh—given by the Magi to the infant Jesus. Matt. 2:11.

gift′ of tongues/, *n.* SPEAKING IN TONGUES.

gift•ware (gift′wâr′), *n.* china, crystal, or other items suitable for gifts.

gift′-wrap/ or **gift/wrap/,** *v.,* **-wrapped, -wrap•ping.** —*v.t.* **1.** to wrap (something) with decorative paper, ribbon, etc., for presentation as a gift. —*n.* **2.** GIFTWRAPPING. —**gift′-wrap/per,** *n.*

gift•wrap•ping (gift′rap′ing), *n.* decorative paper, ribbon, etc., for wrapping items to be presented as gifts.

gig¹ (gig), *n., v.,* **gigged, gig•ging.** —*n.* **1.** a light, two-wheeled one-horse carriage. **2.** a light boat rowed with four, six, or eight long oars. **3.** something that whirls. —*v.i.* **4.** to ride in a gig.

gig² (gig), *n., v.,* **gigged, gig•ging.** —*n.* **1.** a device, commonly four hooks secured back to back, for dragging through a school of fish to hook them through the body. **2.** a spearlike device with a long, thick handle, used for spearing fish and frogs. —*v.t.* **3.** to catch or spear (a fish or frog) with a gig. —*v.i.* **4.** to catch fish or frogs with a gig.

gig³ (gig), *n., v.,* **gigged, gig•ing.** *Slang.* —*n.* **1.** a single professional engagement, usu. of short duration, as of jazz or rock musicians. **2.** any job, esp. one of short or uncertain duration. —*v.i.* **3.** to work as a musician, esp. in a single engagement.

giga-, a combining form used in the names of units of measure equal to one billion of the units denoted by the base word: *gigabyte.*

gig•a•byte (gig′ə bīt′, jig′-), *n.* a measure of data storage capacity equal to 1 billion (10^9) bytes.

gig•a•flops (gig′ə flops′, jig′-), *n.* a measure of computer speed, equal to one billion floating-point operations per second.

gi•gan•tic (jī gan′tik, ji-), *adj.* **1.** very large; huge: *a gigantic statue.* **2.** of, like, or befitting a giant. —**gi•gan′ti•cal•ly,** *adv.*

gi•gan•tism (jī gan′tiz əm, ji-, jī′gan tiz′əm), *n.* great overgrowth in size or stature of the body or developmentally related parts of the body.

gig•gle (gig′əl), *v.,* **-gled, -gling.** —*v.i.* **1.** to laugh in a silly, often high-pitched way, esp. with short, repeated gasps and titters, as from ill-concealed amusement or nervous embarrassment. —*n.* **2.** a silly, spasmodic laugh; titter; snicker. —**gig′gler,** *n.* —**gig′gly,** *adj.*

GIGO (gī′gō), *n.* the axiom that faulty data fed into a computer will result in distorted information. [*g(arbage) i(n) g(arbage) o(ut)*]

gig•o•lo (jig′ə lō′, zhig′-), *n., pl.* **-los.** a man living off the earnings or gifts of a woman, esp. a younger man supported by an older woman in return for his sexual attentions and companionship.

GI Joe, *n.* an enlisted soldier in the U.S. Army, esp. in World War II.

Gi′la mon′ster, *n.* a large, venomous lizard, *Heloderma suspectum,* of the SW United States and NW Mexico, covered with beadlike scales of yellow, orange, and black.

gil•bert (gil′bərt), *n.* the centimeter-gram-second unit of magnetomotive force, equal to 0.7958 ampere-turns.

Gil•bert (gil′bərt), *n.* **1. Sir Humphrey,** 1509?–83, English navigator and colonizer in America. **2. Sir William Schwenck** 1836–1911, English dramatist and poet: collaborator with Sir Arthur Sullivan.

Gil′bert Is′lands, *n.pl.* former name of KIRIBATI.

Gil•bo•a (gil bō′ə), *n.* a range of mountains between the plain of Jezreel and the Jordan Valley where Saul and his sons died while battling the Philistines. I Chron. 10:1–6.

gild (gild), *v.t.,* **gild•ed** or **gilt, gild•ing.** **1.** to coat with gold, gold leaf, or a gold-colored substance. **2.** to give a bright, pleasing, or specious aspect to. —*Idiom.* **3. gild the lily.** to add unnecessary refinements to something already exemplary. —**gild′a•ble,** *adj.* —**gild′er,** *n.*

Gil•e•ad (gil′ē əd), *n.* **1.** a district of ancient Palestine, E of the Jordan River, in present N Jordan. **2. Mount,** a mountain in NW Jordan. 3596 ft. (1096 m).

Gil•e•ad•ite (gil′ē ə dīt′), *n.* **1.** a member of a branch of the Israelite tribe descended from Manasseh. **2.** an inhabitant of ancient Gilead.

Gil•gal (gil′gal), *n.* the name of several places in ancient Palestine, esp. a site near Jericho where the Israelites encamped after crossing the Jordan. Josh. 4:19–24.

Gil•ga•mesh (gil′gə mesh′), *n.* a legendary Sumerian king, the hero of Sumerian and Babylonian epics.

gill¹ (gil), *n.* **1.** the respiratory organ of aquatic animals, as fish, that breathe oxygen dissolved in water. **2.** one of the radial plates that bear spores on the underside of the cap of certain mushrooms. —*Idiom.* **3. green** or **white around the gills,** somewhat pale, as from nausea or fright. **4. to the gills,** *Informal.* fully; completely; to capacity.

gill² (jil), *n.* a unit of liquid measure equal to ¼ of a pint (118.2937 ml).

gill³ (jil), *n.* a girl or young woman; sweetheart.

Gil•lette (ji let′), *n.* **King Camp,** 1855–1932, U.S. businessman: inventor of the safety razor.

gill′ fun′gus (gil), *n.* any mushroom of the order Agaricales, characterized by gills on the underside of the cap.

gil•ly•flow•er or **gil•li•flow•er** (jil′ē flou′ər), *n.* **1.** any of several pinks of the genus *Dianthus.* **2.** any of various other usu. fragrant flowers, esp. a stock, *Matthiola incana,* of the mustard family.

Gil•more (gil′môr, -mōr), *n.* **Joseph,** 1834–1918, U.S. clergyman and hymn writer.

gilt¹ (gilt), *v.* **1.** a pt. and pp. of GILD¹. —*adj.* **2.** coated with or as if with gold; gilded. **3.** gold in color; golden. —*n.* **4.** the thin layer of gold or other material applied in gilding.

gilt² (gilt), *n.* a young female swine, esp. one that has not produced a litter.

gilt′-edged/ or **gilt′-edge/,** *adj.* **1.** having the edge or edges gilded: *gilt-edged paper.* **2.** of the highest or best quality, kind, rating, etc.: *gilt-edged bonds.*

gim•bals (jim′bəlz, gim′-), *n.* (*used with a sing. v.*) Sometimes, **gimbal.** a contrivance, consisting of a ring or base on an axis, that permits an object, as a ship's compass, mounted in or on it to tilt freely in any direction. Also called **gim′bal ring/.**

gim·crack (jim′krak′), *n.* **1.** a showy, useless trifle; gewgaw; trinket. —*adj.* **2.** showy but useless.

gim·crack·er·y (jim′krak′ə rē), *n.* **1.** cheap, showy, useless ornaments, trinkets, etc. **2.** obvious or contrived effects, esp. in art, music, literature, etc.

gim·let (gim′lit), *n.* **1.** a small tool for boring holes, consisting of a shaft with a pointed screw at one end and a handle perpendicular to the shaft at the other. **2.** a cocktail of gin or vodka, lime juice, and sometimes sugar.

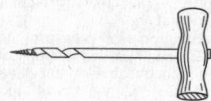

gimlet (def. 1)

gim·me (gim′ē), *n., pl.* -mes, -mies. **1.** *Pron. Spelling.* give me. —*n.* **2.** a final short putt in golf that a player is not required to take in informal play. **3. the gimmes** or **gimmies,** *Slang.* avarice; greed.

gim·mick (gim′ik), *n.* **1.** an ingenious or novel device or stratagem, esp. one used to draw attention or increase appeal; stunt; ploy. **2.** a concealed, usu. devious feature of something, as a plan or deal. **3.** a hidden mechanical device by which a magician works a trick or a gambler controls a game of chance. —**gim′mick·ry,** **gim′mick·e·ry,** *n.* —**gim′mick·y,** *adj.*

gimp (gimp), *n.* **1.** a limp. **2.** a person who limps; lame person. —*v.i.* **3.** to limp; walk in a halting manner. —**gimp′y,** *adj.*

gin¹ (jin), *n.* an alcoholic liquor distilled or redistilled with juniper berries, orange peel, or other flavorings.

gin² (jin), *n., v.,* ginned, gin·ning. —*n.* **1.** COTTON GIN. **2.** a trap or snare for game. **3.** any of various machines employing simple tackle or windlass mechanisms for hoisting. —*v.t.* **4.** to clear (cotton) of seeds with a gin. —**gin′ner,** *n.*

gin³ (jin), *n.* **1.** Also called **gin rummy.** a variety of rummy for two players, sometimes played with knocking. **2.** a hand in this game in which the cards are matched in sets, winning extra points.

gin′ and ton′ic (jin), *n.* a drink made with gin and quinine water, usu. garnished with a slice of lime or lemon.

gin·ger (jin′jər), *n.* **1.** a reedlike plant, *Zingiber officinale,* native to SE Asia but now cultivated in most tropical countries, having a pungent spicy rhizome used in cookery and medicine. **2.** any of various related or similar plants. **3.** piquancy; animation: *a dance performance with style and ginger.* **4.** a yellowish or reddish brown. —*v.t.* **5.** to treat or flavor with ginger. **6.** to enliven (usu. fol. by *up*): *to ginger up a talk with jokes.* —*adj.* **7.** flavored or made with ginger. —**gin′ger·y,** *adj.*

gin′ger ale′, *n.* a carbonated soft drink flavored with ginger extract.

gin′ger beer′, *n.* a soft drink similar to ginger ale but containing more ginger flavor.

gin·ger·bread (jin′jər bred′), *n.* **1.** a type of cake or fancifully shaped cookie flavored with ginger and molasses. **2.** elaborate, gaudy, or superfluous architectural ornamentation. —*adj.* **3.** heavily, gaudily, and superfluously ornamented: *a house with gingerbread trim.* —**gin′ger·bread′y,** *adj.*

gin·ger·ly (jin′jər lē), *adv.* **1.** with great care or caution; warily. —*adj.* **2.** cautious, careful, or wary. —**gin′ger·li·ness,** *n.*

gin·ger·snap (jin′jər snap′), *n.* a small, crisp cookie flavored with ginger and molasses.

ging·ham (ging′əm), *n.* yarn-dyed, plain-weave cotton fabric, usu. striped or checked. [< Dutch *gingang* < Malay *gaṇ gaṇ* striped]

gin·gi·va (jin jī′və, jin′jə-), *n., pl.* -gi·vae (-jī′vē, -jə vē′). GUM² (def. 1). —**gin·gi′val,** *adj.*

gin·gi·vec·to·my (jin′jə vek′tə mē), *n., pl.* -mies. surgical removal of gum tissue.

gin·gi·vi·tis (jin′jə vī′tis), *n.* inflammation of the gums.

Ging·rich (ging′grich), *n.* Newt(on), born 1943, U.S. politician.

gink·go or **ging·ko** (ging′kō, jing′-), *n., pl.* -goes or -koes. a cultivated shade tree, *Ginkgo biloba,* native to China, having fan-shaped leaves and fleshy seeds with edible kernels: the sole surviving member of the gymnosperm class Ginkgoatae.

gin′ mill′ (jin), *n. Slang.* a bar; saloon.

Gin′nie Mae′ (jin′ē), *n.* a bond or certificate sold by the Government National Mortgage Association. [from the initials *GNMA*]

gin′ rum′my, *n.* GIN³ (def. 1).

gin·seng (jin′seng), *n.* **1.** any plant of the genus *Panax,* having an aromatic root used medicinally. **2.** the root itself. **3.** a preparation, as tea or extract, made from the root.

Gior·gio·ne (jôr jō′nē), *n.* (*Giorgione de Castelfranco, Giorgio Barbarelli*) 1478?–1511, Italian painter.

Giot·to (jot′ō), *n.* (*Giotto di Bondone*) 1266?–1337, Florentine painter, sculptor, and architect.

gip (jip), *v.t., v.i.,* gipped, gip·ping, *n.* GYP¹. —**gip′per,** *n.*

gi·raffe (jə raf′; *esp. Brit.* -räf′), *n.* a tall, long-necked, spotted ruminant, *Giraffa camelopardalis,* of Africa: the tallest living quadruped animal. [< French < Italian < dial. Arabic *zirāfah*]

gird (gûrd), *v.t.,* gird·ed or girt, gird·ing. **1.** to encircle or bind with a belt or band. **2.** to surround; enclose; hem in. **3.** to prepare (oneself) for action; brace. **4.** to equip or invest, as with power or strength. —*Idiom.* **5.** **gird (up) one's loins,** to prepare oneself for something requiring strength or endurance.

gird·er (gûr′dər), *n.* **1.** a large beam, as of steel, reinforced concrete, or timber, for supporting masonry, joists, purlins, etc. **2.** a principal beam of wood, steel, etc., supporting the ends of joists.

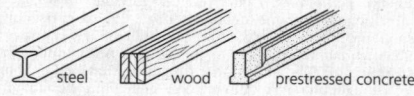

steel   wood   prestressed concrete

girders (def. 1)

gir·dle (gûr′dl), *n., v.,* -dled, -dling. —*n.* **1.** an undergarment, worn esp. by women, often boned or of elastic, for supporting and giving a slimmer appearance to the abdomen, hips, and buttocks. **2.** a belt, cord, sash, or the like, worn about the waist. **3.** anything that encircles, confines, or limits. **4.** the narrow edge or band between the upper and lower or front and back sections of a faceted gemstone. **5.** either of two bony encircling frameworks connecting the vertebrate limbs to the axial skeleton. **6.** a ring made around a tree trunk, branch, etc., by removing a band of bark. —*v.t.* **7.** to encircle with a belt; gird. **8.** to encompass; enclose; encircle. **9.** to move around (something or someone) in a circle. **10.** to cut away the bark and cambium in a ring around (a tree, branch, etc.). —**gir′dle·like′,** *adj.*

gir·dler (gûr′dlər), *n.* **1.** a person or thing that girdles. **2.** any of several insects, as a beetle, *Oncideres cingulata,* that cut a groove around the bark of a twig, stem, etc. **3.** a person who makes girdles.

girl (gûrl), *n.* **1.** a female child, from birth to full growth. **2.** a young, immature woman, esp., formerly, an unmarried one. **3.** a daughter: *My wife and I have two girls.* **4.** girlfriend; sweetheart. **5.** a female who is from a given place: *She's a Missouri girl.* **6. girls,** (used with a *sing.* or *pl. v.*) **a.** a range of sizes from 7 to 14, for garments made for girls. **b.** a garment in this size range. —**Usage.** Many women resent being called GIRLS or the less formal GALS. In business and professional offices, *the girl* or *my girl* in reference to one's secretary has decreased but not disappeared. Such terms as *the girls* for a group of women, GIRL or GAL FRIDAY for a female assistant, and BACHELOR GIRL for an unmarried woman are frequently regarded as offensive, and WORKING GIRL in the sense "a woman who works" is declining in use. See also LADY, WOMAN.

girl′ Fri′day, *n., pl.* girl Fridays. GAL FRIDAY. —**Usage.** See GIRL.

girl·friend (gûrl′frend′), *n.* **1.** a frequent or favorite companion; sweetheart. **2.** a female friend. **3.** a female lover.

girl·hood (gûrl′hŏŏd), *n.* **1.** the state or time of being a girl. **2.** girls collectively: *the nation's girlhood.*

girl·ish (gûr′lish), *adj.* of, like, or befitting a girl or girlhood. —**girl′ish·ly,** *adv.* —**girl′ish·ness,** *n.*

girl′ scout′, *n.* (*sometimes caps.*) a member of an organization of girls (**Girl′ Scouts′**) that seeks to develop character and citizenship, promote health, and foster skills.

Gi·ron·dist (jə ron′dist), *n.* **1.** a member of a French political party of moderate republicans (1791–93) whose leaders were from the department of Gironde. —*adj.* **2.** of or pertaining to the Girondists. —**Gi·ron′dism,** *n.*

girt¹ (gûrt), *v.* a pt. and pp. of GIRD.

girt² (gûrt), *v.t.* GIRD (def. 1).

girth (gûrth) also **girt,** *n.* **1.** the measure around a body or object; circumference. **2.** size; bulk. **3.** a band that passes underneath a horse or other animal to hold a saddle in place. **4.** something that encircles; a band or girdle.

GI series, *n.* gastrointestinal series: x-ray examination of the upper or lower gastrointestinal tract after barium sulfate is given orally or rectally as a contrast medium.

gis·mo or **giz·mo** (giz′mō), *n., pl.* -mos. *Informal.* a gadget or device.

gist (jist), *n.* **1.** the main or essential point of a matter: *the gist of a story.* **2.** the ground of a legal action.

Gi·ta (gē′tä), *n. Hinduism.* BHAGAVAD-GITA.

give (giv), *v.,* gave, giv·en, giv·ing, *n.* —*v.t.* **1.** to present voluntarily and without expecting compensation; bestow: *to give a birthday present to someone.* **2.** to hand to someone: *Give me that plate, please.* **3.** to place in someone's care: *I gave the folders to your assistant.* **4.** to grant (permission, opportunity, etc.) to someone: *Give me a chance.* **5.** to impart or communicate: *to give advice; to give a cold to someone.* **6.** to set forth or show; present; offer: *to give no reason for one's actions.* **7.** to pay or transfer possession to another in exchange for something: *They gave five dollars for the picture.* **8.** to furnish, provide, or proffer: *to give evidence.* **9.** to provide as an entertainment or social function: *to give a Halloween party.* **10.** to deal or administer: *to give medicine to a patient.* **11.** to put forth, emit, or utter; issue: *to give a cry.* **12.** to assign or admit as a basis of calculation or reasoning (usu. used passively): *These facts being given, the theory makes sense.* **13.** to produce, yield, or afford: *to give good results.* **14.** to make, do, or perform: *to give a lurch.* **15.** to perform or present publicly: *to give a concert.* **16.** to cause; be responsible for (usu. fol. by an infinitive): *They gave me to understand that you would be there.* **17.** to care about something to the value or extent of (something signifying "even a little bit"): *I don't give a hoot about their opinion. Frankly, I don't give a damn!* **18.** to relinquish or sacrifice: *to give one's life for a cause.* **19.** to convey or transmit: *Give Grandma my love.* **20.** to assign or allot: *They gave him the nickname "Scooter."* **21.** to bestow (the object of one's choice), as if by providence: *Give me the wide open spaces anytime.* **22.** to connect, as through a switchboard: *Give me 235-7522.* **23.** to present to an audience: *Ladies and gentlemen, I give you the governor of Texas.* **24.** to attribute or ascribe: *to give the devil his due.* **25.** to cause or occasion: *Strawberries give me a rash.* **26.** to apply fully or freely; devote: *to give one's attention to a problem.* **27.** to inflict as a punishment on another; impose a sentence of: *The judge gave him ten years.* **28.** to pledge, offer as a pledge, or execute and deliver: *She gave him her word. Can you give bond?* **29.** to concede or grant, as a point in an argument. —*v.i.* **30.** to make a gift or gifts;·contribute: *to give to the United Way.* **31.** to yield somewhat, as to influence or force; compromise: *Each side must give on some points.* **32.** to yield somewhat when subjected to weight, force, pressure, etc.: *A horsehair mattress doesn't give much.* **33.** to collapse; break down; fall apart: *The old chair gave when I sat on it.* **34.** to be warm and open in relationships with others: *a withdrawn person who doesn't know how to give.* **35.** *Informal.* to divulge information: *Okay now, give! What happened?* **36.** to afford a view or passage; face, open, or lead (usu. fol. by *on, onto,* etc.): *This door gives onto the hallway.* **37. give away, a.** to give as a present; bestow. **b.** to present (the bride) to the bridegroom in a marriage ceremony. **c.** to disclose, betray, or expose. **38. give back,** to return (something), as to the owner; restore. **39. give in, a.** to acknowledge defeat; yield. **b.** to hand in; deliver: *to give in one's timecard.* **40. give of,** to devote or contribute generously of: *to give of oneself.* **41. give off,** to put forth; emit: *The gardenia gives off a strong fragrance.* **42. give out, a.** to send out; emit. **b.** to make public; announce. **c.** to distribute; issue. **d.** to become exhausted or used up. **43. give over, a.** to put into the care or custody of; transfer. **b.** to submit fully: *She gave herself over to tears.* **c.** to devote to a specified activity: *The day was given over to relaxing.* **d.** to cease; stop: *to give over complaining.* **44. give up, a.** to abandon hope; despair. **b.** to desist from; renounce: *to give up smoking.* **c.** to surrender; relinquish. **d.** to devote (oneself) entirely to. —*n.* **45.** the quality or state of being resilient; springiness. —*Idiom.* **46. give and take, a.** to compromise in order to cooperate. **b.** to exchange ideas. **47. give it to,** *Informal.* to reprimand or punish. **48. give or take,** plus or minus a specified amount; more or less. —*Proverb.* **49. It is more blessed to give than to receive,** giving, rather than taking, brings spiritual rewards. Acts 20:35. —**giv′a·ble, give′a·ble,** *adj., n.* —**giv·ee′,** *n.* —**giv′er,** *n.*

give′-and-take′, *n.* **1.** the practice of dealing by compromise or mutual concession; cooperation. **2.** good-natured exchange of ideas, etc.

give·a·way (giv′ə wā′), *n.* **1.** an act or instance of giving something away. **2.** something that is given away, esp. as a gift or premium. **3.** an unintentional betrayal or disclosure. **4.** a radio or television program on which prizes are awarded to participants in contests, games, etc. —*adj.* **5.** constituting a giveaway: *a giveaway newspaper.*

give′back′ or **give′-back′,** *n.* **1.** (in union negotiations) a reduction in employee wages or benefits conceded by a union in exchange for other benefits or in recognition of depressed economic conditions. **2.** something returned, rebated, etc.

giv·en (giv′ən), *v.* **1.** pp. of GIVE. —*adj.* **2.** stated, fixed, or specified: *at a given time.* **3.** inclined; disposed; prone (often fol. by *to*): *given to making snide remarks.* **4.** bestowed as a gift; conferred. **5.** assigned as a basis of calculation or reasoning: *Given A and B, C follows.* —*n.* **6.** an established fact, condition, factor, etc.

giv′en name′, *n.* the name given to one, as distinguished from an inherited family name; first name.

giz·zard (giz′ərd), *n.* **1.** Also called **ventriculus.** the thick-walled, muscular lower stomach of many birds and reptiles that grinds partially digested food, often with the aid of ingested gravel. **2.** a similar structure in the foregut of arthropods and annelids, often lined with chitin and small teeth. **3.** the innards or viscera collectively, esp. the intestine and stomach.

Gk or **Gk.,** Greek.

gla·brous (glā′brəs), *adj. Biol.* having a surface devoid of hair or pubescence.

gla·cé (gla sā′), *adj.* **1.** candied, as fruits. **2.** frosted or iced, as cake. **3.** frozen. **4.** finished with a gloss, as kid or silk.

gla·cial (glā′shəl), *adj.* **1.** of or pertaining to glaciers or ice sheets. **2.** resulting from or associated with the action of ice or glaciers: *glacial terrain.* **3.** characterized by the presence of ice in extensive masses or glaciers. **4.** bitterly cold; icy: *a glacial winter wind.* **5.** happening or moving extremely slowly: *to work at a glacial pace.* **6.** icily unsympathetic or immovable: *a glacial stare.* **7.** of, pertaining to, or tending to develop into icelike crystals: *glacial phosphoric acid.* —**gla′cial·ly,** *adv.*

gla′cial ep′och, *n.* ICE AGE. Also called **gla′cial pe′riod.**

gla·ci·ate (glā′shē āt′, -sē-), *v.,* **-at·ed, -at·ing.** —*v.t.* **1.** to cover with ice or glaciers. **2.** to affect by glacial action. —*v.i.* **3.** to become frozen or covered with ice or glaciers. —**gla′ci·a′tion,** *n.*

gla·cier (glā′shər), *n.* an extended mass of ice formed from snow falling and accumulating over the years and moving very slowly, either descending from high mountains, as in valley glaciers, or moving outward from centers of accumulation, as in continental glaciers.

Gla′cier Bay′, *n.* a national park in SE Alaska, made up of large tidewater glaciers. 4381 sq. mi. (11,347 sq. km).

Gla′cier Na′tional Park′, *n.* a national park in NW Montana: glaciers; lakes; forest reserve. 1534 sq. mi. (3970 sq. km).

gla·ci·ol·o·gy (glā′shē ol′ə jē, -sē-), *n.* the branch of geology that deals with the nature, distribution, and action of glaciers and their effect on the earth's topography. —**gla′ci·o·log′i·cal** (-ə loj′i kəl), **gla′ci·o·log′ic,** *adj.* —**gla′ci·ol′o·gist,** *n.*

glad[1] (glad), *adj.* **1.** feeling joy or pleasure; delighted; pleased: *glad about the good news.* **2.** accompanied by or causing joy or pleasure: *glad tidings.* **3.** characterized by or showing cheerfulness, joy, or pleasure, as looks or utterances. **4.** very willing: *I'd be glad to help.* —**glad′ly,** *adv.* —**glad′ness,** *n.*

glad[2] (glad), *n.* GLADIOLUS (def. 1).

glad·den (glad′n), *v.t.* to make glad. —**glad′den·er,** *n.*

glade (glād), *n.* an open space in a forest.

glad′ hand′, *n.* a hearty welcome or enthusiastic reception, esp. one that is effusive or hypocritical. —**glad′-hand′,** *v.* —**glad′-hand′er,** *n.*

glad·i·a·tor (glad′ē ā′tər), *n.* **1.** (in ancient Rome) a man armed with a sword or other weapon and compelled to fight to the death in a public arena for the entertainment of spectators. **2.** someone who engages in a fight or controversy. **3.** a prizefighter. —**glad′i·a·to′ri·al** (-ə tôr′ē əl, -tōr′-), *adj.*

glad·i·o·la (glad′ē ō′lə), *n.* GLADIOLUS (def. 1). —**glad′i·o′lar,** *adj.*

glad·i·o·lus (glad′ē ō′ləs), *n., pl.* **-lus, -li** (-lī), **-lus·es** for 1; **-li** for 2. **1.** any plant of the genus *Gladiolus,* of the iris family, native esp. to Africa, having erect, sword-shaped leaves and spikes of flowers in a variety of colors. **2.** the middle segment of the sternum. [< Latin: small sword]

glad′ rags′, *n.pl. Informal.* dressy clothes, esp. for a party or other social event.

Glad·stone (glad′stōn′, -stən), *n.* **1. William Ew·art** (yōō′ərt), 1809–98, British prime minister four times between 1868 and 1894. **2.** GLADSTONE BAG.

Glad′stone bag′, *n.* a small rectangular suitcase hinged to open into two compartments of equal size.

glam (glam), *adj. Informal.* glamorous.

glam·or·ize or **glam·our·ize** (glam′ə rīz′), *v.t.,* **-ized, -iz·ing. 1.** to make glamorous. **2.** to glorify or romanticize: *a film that glamorizes war.* —**glam′or·i·za′tion,** *n.* —**glam′or·iz′er,** *n.*

glam·our or **glam·or** (glam′ər), *n.* **1.** the quality of fascinating, alluring, or attracting, esp. by a combination of charm and good looks. **2.** excitement, adventure, and unusual activity: *the glamour of being an explorer.* —*adj.* **3.** suggestive or full of glamour; glamorous: *a glamour job in television.* —**glam′or·ous, glam′our·ous,** *adj.* —**glam′or·ous·ly, glam′our·ous·ly,** *adv.*

glam′our stock′, *n.* a popular stock that rises quickly or continuously in price and attracts large numbers of investors.

glance (glans, gläns), *v.,* **glanced, glanc·ing,** *n.* —*v.i.* **1.** to look quickly or briefly. **2.** to gleam or flash; scintillate. **3.** to strike a surface or object obliquely, esp. so as to bounce off at an angle (often fol. by *off*): *The arrow glanced off his shield.* —*v.t.* **4.** to throw, hit, kick, or shoot (something) so as to cause an oblique bounce off a surface or object. —*n.* **5.** a quick or brief look. **6.** a gleam or flash, esp. of reflected light. **7.** a deflected movement or course; an oblique rebound. **8.** a passing reference or allusion.

glanc·ing (glan′sing, glän′-), *adj.* **1.** striking obliquely and bouncing off at an angle: *a glancing blow.* **2.** brief and indirect: *glancing references to a previous case.* —**glanc′ing·ly,** *adv.*

gland (gland), *n.* any organ or group of cells specialized for producing secretions, as insulin or sweat. Compare ENDOCRINE GLAND, EXOCRINE GLAND.

glan·du·lar (glan′jə lər), *adj.* **1.** consisting of, containing, or bearing glands. **2.** of, pertaining to, or resembling a gland: *a glandular disorder.* **3.** visceral; instinctive. —**glan′du·lar·ly,** *adv.*

glan′dular fe′ver, *n.* INFECTIOUS MONONUCLEOSIS.

glans (glanz), *n., pl.* **glan·des** (glan′dēz). the head of the penis (**glans pe′nis**) or of the clitoris (**glans′ clit′oris**).

glare[1] (glâr), *n., v.,* **glared, glar·ing.** —*n.* **1.** a very harsh, bright, dazzling light: *in the glare of sunlight.* **2.** a fiercely or angrily piercing stare. **3.** dazzling or showy appearance; showiness. —*v.i.* **4.** to shine with or reflect a very harsh, bright, dazzling light. **5.** to stare with a fiercely or angrily piercing look. —*v.t.* **6.** to express with a glare: *glaring their anger at each other.* —**glare′less,** *adj.*

glare[2] (glâr), *n.* a bright, smooth surface, as of ice.

glar·ing (glâr′ing), *adj.* **1.** shining with or reflecting a harshly bright light. **2.** very conspicuous or obvious; flagrant: *glaring errors.* **3.** marked by a fiercely or angrily piercing expression: *to cast a glaring eye on latecomers.* **4.** excessively or tastelessly showy or bright; garish. —**glar′ing·ly,** *adv.* —**glar′ing·ness,** *n.*

glar·y[1] (glâr′ē), *adj.,* **glar·i·er, glar·i·est.** harshly brilliant; glaring. —**glar′i·ness,** *n.*

glar·y[2] (glâr′ē), *adj.,* **glar·i·er, glar·i·est.** smooth and slippery, as ice.

Glas·gow (glas′gō, -kō; *for 2 also* glaz′gō), *n.* **1.** Ellen (Anderson Gholson), 1874–1945, U.S. novelist. **2.** a seaport in SW Scotland, on the Clyde River. 880,617.

glas·nost (glaz′nost, gläz′-), *n.* the declared public policy in the Soviet Union of openly and frankly discussing economic and political realities: initiated under Mikhail Gorbachev in 1985.

glass (glas, gläs), *n.* **1.** a hard, brittle, noncrystalline, more or less transparent substance, atomically a supercooled liquid, usu. produced by fusing silicates containing soda and lime, as in the ordinary variety used for windows and bottles. **2.** any artificial or natural substance having similar properties and composition, as fused borax or obsidian. **3.** something made of such a substance, as a windowpane. **4.** a tumbler or other comparatively tall, handleless drinking container. **5. glasses,** Also called **eyeglasses.** a device to compensate for defective vision or to protect the eyes from light, dust, etc., consisting usu. of two glass or plastic lenses set in a frame that includes two sidepieces extending over or around the ears (usu. used with *pair of*). **6.** a mirror. **7.** things made of glass, collectively; glassware: *to collect old glass.* **8.** a glassful. —*adj.* **9.** made of glass: *a glass tray.* **10.** furnished or fitted with panes of glass; glazed. —*Proverb.* **11. People who live in glass houses shouldn't throw stones,** those who attack others should make sure they are not themselves vulnerable.

glass·blow·ing (glas′blō′ing), *n.* the art or process of forming or shaping a mass of molten or heat-softened glass into ware by blowing air into it through a tube. —**glass′blow′er,** *n.*

glass′ ceil′ing, *n. Informal.* barriers to promotion for women and minority groups in a business or an institution.

glass′ cut′ter, *n.* **1.** a tool for cutting glass. **2.** a person who cuts glass into specified sizes. **3.** a person who etches or otherwise decorates the surface of glass. —**glass′ cut′ting,** *n.*

glass′ eel′, *n.* ELVER.

glass eye (glas′ ī′, gläs′ ī′ *for 1;* glas′ ī′, gläs′ ī′ *for 2*), *n.* **1.** an artificial eye made of glass or plastic. **2.** any of various fish, birds, etc., having eyes with a glassy or milky appearance.

glass·ful (glas′fŏŏl), *n., pl.* **-fuls.** an amount contained by or sufficient to fill a glass or tumbler. —**Usage.** See -FUL.

glass′ jaw′, *n.* a person's jaw, esp. that of a boxer, that is vulnerable to even a light blow.

glass·mak·ing (glas′mā′king, gläs′-), *n.* the art of making glass or glassware. —**glass′mak′er,** *n.*

glass′ snake′, *n.* any limbless, snakelike lizard of the genus *Ophisaurus,* of the Eastern U.S., Europe, and Asia, having the ability to regenerate its long fragile tail. Also called **glass′ liz′ard.**

glass·ware (glas′wâr′, gläs′-), *n.* articles of glass, esp. drinking glasses.

glass·work (glas′wûrk′, gläs′-), *n.* **1.** the manufacture of glass and glassware. **2.** articles of glass collectively; glassware. **3.** the fitting of glass; glazing. —**glass′work′er,** *n.*

glass·works (glas′wûrks′, gläs′-), *n., pl.* **-works.** a factory where glass is made.

glass·wort (glas′wûrt′, -wôrt′, gläs′-), *n.* any of several plants of the goosefoot family, having succulent stems with rudimentary leaves, formerly used in glassmaking. Also called **samphire.**

glass·y (glas′ē, gläs′ē), *adj.,* **glass·i·er, glass·i·est. 1.** resembling glass, as in transparency or smoothness. **2.** expressionless; dull: *glassy eyes; a glassy stare.* **3.** of the nature of glass; vitreous. —**glass′i·ly,** *adv.* —**glass′i·ness,** *n.*

Glas·ton·bur·y (glas′tən ber′ē, -bə rē), *n.* a borough of SW England: excavations of an important Iron Age lake village and ancient abbey; linked in folklore with King Arthur. 6773.

Glas·we·gian (gla swē′jən, -jē ən), *adj.* **1.** of or pertaining to Glasgow or its residents. —*n.* **2.** a native or resident of Glasgow.

glau·co·ma (glô kō′mə, glou-), *n.* a condition of elevated fluid pressure within the eyeball, caused by an abnormally narrow angle between the iris and cornea or by an obstruction within the canal through which the aqueous humor drains, causing damage to the eye and progressive loss of vision. —**glau·co′ma·tous** (-kō′mə təs, -kom′ə-), *adj.*

glaze (glāz), *v.,* **glazed, glaz·ing,** *n.* —*v.t.* **1.** to furnish or fill with glass: *to glaze a window.* **2.** to give a vitreous surface or coating to (a ceramic or the like), as by the application of a substance or by fusion of the body. **3.** to cover with a smooth, glossy surface or coating. **4.** to coat (a food) with a liquid substance that sets to form a smooth, glossy surface. **5.** to cover (a painting or parts of it) with a thin layer of transparent color in order to modify the tone. **6.** to give a glassy surface to, as by polishing. **7.** to give a coating of ice to, by or as if by dipping in water. —*v.i.* **8.** to become glazed or glassy: *Their eyes glazed over as the lecturer droned on.* —*n.* **9.** a smooth, glossy surface or coating. **10.** the substance for producing such a coating. **11. a.** a vitreous layer or coating on a piece of pottery. **b.** the substance of which such a layer or coating is made. **12.** a thin layer of transparent color spread over a painting. **13.** a smooth, lustrous surface on a fabric, produced by treating chemically and calendering. **14. a.** a substance, as sugar syrup, used to form a thin, glossy coating on food. **b.** stock cooked down to a thin paste. **15.** a thin coating of ice. —**glaz′er,** *n.* —**glaz′i·ly,** *adv.* —**glaz′i·ness,** *n.*

glazed (glāzd), *adj.* **1.** having a surface covered with a glaze; lustrous; smooth; glassy. **2.** fitted or set with glass. **3.** having a fixed, dazed, or lifeless expression.

gla·zier (glā′zhər), *n.* a person who fits windows or the like with glass or panes of glass. —**gla′zier·y,** *n.*

glaz·ing (glā′zing), *n.* **1.** the act of furnishing or fitting with glass; the work of a glazier. **2.** panes or sheets of glass set or made to be set in frames, as in windows, doors, or mirrors. **3.** the act of applying a glaze. **4.** a glazed surface.

gleam (glēm), *n.* **1.** a flash or beam of light: *the gleam of a lantern in the dark.* **2.** a subdued or reflected light. **3.** a brief or slight manifestation or occurrence; trace: *a gleam of hope.* —*v.i.* **4.** to send forth a gleam or gleams: *He polished the silver until it gleamed.* **5.** to appear suddenly and clearly like a flash of light. —**gleam′ing·ly,** *adv.* —**gleam′y,** *adj.* **gleam·i·er, gleam·i·est.**

glean (glēn), *v.t.* **1.** to gather, learn, or find out, usu. bit by bit or slowly and laboriously: *to glean information.* **2.** to gather (grain or the like) after the reapers or regular gatherers. —*v.i.* **3.** to collect or gather anything little by little or slowly. **4.** to gather what is left by reapers. —**glean′er,** *n.*

glean·ings (glē′ningz), *n.pl.* things found or acquired by gleaning.

glee (glē), *n.* **1.** open delight or pleasure; exultant joy; exultation. **2.** an unaccompanied part song for three or more voices, popular esp. in the 18th century.

glee′ club′, *n.* a chorus organized for singing usu. short pieces of choral music.

glee·ful (glē′fəl), *adj.* full of glee; merry; exultant. —**glee′ful·ly,** *adv.* —**glee′ful·ness,** *n.*

glen (glen), *n.* a small, narrow, secluded valley. —**glen′like′,** *adj.*

Glen·dale (glen′dāl′), *n.* **1.** a city in SW California, near Los Angeles. 178,481. **2.** a city in central Arizona, near Phoenix. 168,439.

Glenn (glen), *n.* **John (Herschel),** born 1921, U.S. astronaut and senator: first U.S. orbital spaceflight 1962.

Glen′ plaid′, *n.* **1.** a plaid pattern of muted colors or of black or gray and white, esp. one in which groups of both light and dark stripes alternate vertically and horizontally. **2.** a fabric having such a pattern. **3.** a garment made of such a fabric. Also called **Glen check.**

glib (glib), *adj.,* **glib·ber, glib·best. 1.** readily fluent, often thoughtlessly, superficially, or insincerely so: *a glib talker; glib answers.* **2.** easy or unconstrained: *glib manners.* —**glib′ly,** *adv.* —**glib′ness,** *n.*

glide (glīd), *v.,* **glid·ed, glid·ing,** *n.* —*v.i.* **1.** to move smoothly and continuously along, as if without effort or resistance. **2.** to pass by gradual or unobservable change (often fol. by *along, away, by,* etc.). **3.** to move quietly or stealthily or without being noticed (usu. fol. by *in, out, along,* etc.). **4. a.** to move in the air, esp. at an easy angle downward, with little or no engine power. **b.** to fly in a glider. **5.** to produce a glide sound. —*v.t.* **6.** to cause to glide. —*n.* **7.** a gliding movement, as in dancing. **8. a.** a transitional sound heard during the articulation linking two contiguous speech sounds, as the *y*-sound often heard between the *i* and *e* of *quiet.* **b.** a speech sound having the characteristics of both a consonant and a vowel; semivowel. **9.** an act or instance of gliding. **10.** a calm stretch of shallow, smoothly flowing water, as in a river. **11.** SLIP¹ (def. 36). **12.** a metal plate or plastic disk attached to the bottom of a furniture leg to facilitate moving and protect floors. **13.** a metal track in which a drawer, shelf, etc., moves in or out. —**glid′ing·ly,** *adv.*

glid·er (glī′dər), *n.* **1.** a motorless, heavier-than-air aircraft, launched by towing or by catapult. **2.** a person or thing that glides. **3.** a porch swing made of an upholstered seat suspended from a steel framework by links or springs.

glim·mer (glim′ər), *n.* **1.** a faint or unsteady light; gleam. **2.** a dim perception; faint glimpse or idea; inkling. —*v.i.* **3.** to shine faintly or unsteadily; twinkle, shimmer, or flicker. **4.** to appear faintly or dimly.

glim·mer·ing (glim′ər ing), *n.* **1.** GLIMMER. —*adj.* **2.** shining faintly or unsteadily. —**glim′mer·ing·ly,** *adv.*

glimpse (glimps), *n., v.,* **glimpsed, glimps·ing.** —*n.* **1.** a very brief passing look, sight, or view. **2.** a momentary or slight appearance. **3.** a vague idea; inkling. —*v.t.* **4.** to catch or take a glimpse of. —*v.i.* **5.** to look briefly; glance (usu. fol. by *at*). —**glimps′er,** *n.*

glint (glint), *n.* **1.** a tiny quick flash of light. **2.** gleaming brightness; luster. **3.** a brief or slight manifestation or occurrence; trace. —*v.i.* **4.** to shine with a glint. **5.** to move suddenly; dart. —*v.t.* **6.** to cause to glint; reflect.

glis·sade (gli säd′, -sād′), *n., v.,* **-sad·ed, -sad·ing.** —*n.* **1.** a skillful glide over snow or ice in descending a mountain, as on skis or a toboggan. **2.** a gliding or sliding step in ballet. —*v.i.* **3.** to perform a glissade.

glis·san·do (gli sän′dō), *adj., n., pl.* **-di** (-dē), **-dos.** —*adj.* **1.** performed with a gliding effect by sliding one or more fingers rapidly over the keys of a piano or strings of a harp. —*n.* **2.** a glissando passage.

glis·ten (glis′ən), *v.i.* **1.** to reflect a sparkling light or a faint intermittent glow, as a sleek or wet surface; shine lustrously. —*n.* **2.** a glistening; sparkle.

glitch (glich), *n.* **1.** *Informal.* a defect, error, or malfunction, as in a machine or plan. **2.** a brief or sudden interruption or surge in electric power.

glit·ter (glit′ər), *v.i.* **1.** to reflect light with a brilliant, sparkling luster; sparkle. **2.** to make a brilliant show. —*n.* **3.** a sparkling reflected light or luster. **4.** showy splendor. **5.** small glittering ornaments. —**glit′ter·ing·ly,** *adv.* —**glit′ter·y,** *adj.*

G

glit·te·ra·ti (glit′ə rä′tē), *n.pl.* ostentatiously wealthy, fashionable, or famous people.

glitz (glits), *n. Informal.* ostentatious glitter or glamour. —**glitz′i·ness**, *n.* —**glitz′y**, *adj.*, -i·er, -i·est.

gloat (glōt), *v.i.* **1.** to indulge in malicious or excessive satisfaction: *Our opponents gloated over our bad luck.* —*n.* **2.** an act or feeling of gloating. —**gloat′er**, *n.*

glob (glob), *n.* **1.** a drop or globule of a liquid. **2.** a usu. rounded quantity or lump of some plastic or moldable substance: *a glob of whipped cream.*

glob·al (glō′bəl), *adj.* **1.** pertaining to or involving the whole world; worldwide; universal. **2.** comprehensive. **3.** globular; globe-shaped. **4.** (of a computer operation, linguistic rule, etc.) operating on a group of similar strings, commands, etc., in a single step. —**glob′al·ly**, *adv.*

glob·al·ize (glō′bə līz′), *v.t.*, -ized, -iz·ing. to extend to other or all parts of the globe; make worldwide: *to globalize the auto industry.* —**glob′al·i·za′tion**, *n.*

glob′al vil′lage, *n.* the world, esp. considered as the home of all nations and peoples living interdependently.

glo′bal warm′ing, *n.* an increase in the earth's average atmospheric temperature that causes corresponding changes in climate and that may result from the greenhouse effect.

glo·bate (glō′bāt) also **glo′bat·ed**, *adj.* shaped like a globe.

globe (glōb), *n.* **1.** the planet Earth (usu. prec. by *the*). **2.** a planet or other celestial body. **3.** a sphere on which is depicted a map of the earth or of the heavens. **4.** a spherical body; sphere. **5.** anything more or less spherical, as a glass lampshade or fishbowl. —**globe′like′**, *adj.*

globe·fish (glōb′fish′), *n., pl.* (*esp. collectively*) -fish, (*esp. for kinds or species*) -fish·es. **1.** PUFFER (def. 2). **2.** OCEAN SUNFISH.

globe·flow·er (glōb′flou′ər), *n.* a plant of the genus *Trollius*, of the buttercup family, having spherical yellow flowers.

globe·trot·ter (glōb′trot′ər), *n.* a person who travels regularly to countries all over the world. —**globe′trot′ting**, *n., adj.*

glo·bose (glō′bōs, glō bōs′), *adj.* having the shape of a globe; globe-like.

glob·u·lar (glob′yə lər), *adj.* **1.** globe-shaped; spherical. **2.** composed of or having globules. **3.** worldwide; global. —**glob′u·lar′i·ty, glob′u·lar·ness**, *n.* —**glob′u·lar·ly**, *adv.*

glob·ule (glob′yōol), *n.* a small spherical body.

glob·u·lin (glob′yə lin), *n.* any of a group of plant and animal proteins that are soluble in salt solutions and coagulable by heat.

glock·en·spiel (glok′ən spēl′, -shpēl′), *n.* a musical instrument composed of a set of graduated steel bars mounted in a frame and struck with hammers, used esp. in bands. [< German, = *Glocken* bells + *Spiel* play]

glockenspiel

glom (glom), *v.*, **glommed, glom·ming**, *n. Slang.* —*v.t.* **1.** to steal. **2.** to catch or grab. **3.** to look at. **4. glom onto**, to grab; get hold of. —*n.* **5.** a look or glimpse.

gloom (glōom), *n.* **1.** total or partial darkness; dimness. **2.** a state of melancholy or depression; low spirits. **3.** a despondent or depressed look or expression. —**gloom′i·ly**, *adv.* —**gloom′i·ness**, *n.* —**gloom′y**, *adj.* -i·er, -i·est.

glop (glop), *n. Informal.* **1.** any gooey or gelatinous substance, esp. soft unappetizing food. **2.** sentimentality; mawkishness. —**glop′py**, *adj.*, -pi·er, -pi·est.

Glo·ri·a (glôr′ē ə, glōr′-), *n.* **1.** GLORIA IN EXCELSIS DEO. **2.** GLORIA PATRI.

Glo·ri·a in Ex·cel·sis De·o (glôr′ē ə in ek sel′sis dā′ō, glōr′-), *n.* the hymn beginning "Glory in the highest to God."

Glo·ri·a Pa·tri (glôr′ē ə pä′trē, glōr′-), *n.* the short hymn beginning "Glory be to the Father, and to the Son, and to the Holy Ghost."

glo·ri·fy (glôr′ə fī′, glōr′-), *v.t.*, -fied, -fy·ing. **1.** to cause to be or treat as being more splendid, excellent, etc., than would normally be considered: *to glorify military life.* **2.** to honor with praise, admiration, or worship; extol: *to glorify a hero.* **3.** to make glorious; invest with glory. **4.** to praise the glory of (God), esp. as an act of worship. —**glor′i·fi·ca′tion**, *n.*

glo·ri·ous (glôr′ē əs, glōr′-), *adj.* **1.** delightful; wonderful: *a glorious time.* **2.** conferring glory: *a glorious victory.* **3.** full of glory; entitled to great renown: *a glorious hero.* **4.** brilliantly beautiful or magnificent; splendid: *a glorious summer day.* —**glo′ri·ous·ly**, *adv.* —**glo′ri·ous·ness**, *n.*

Glo′rious Revolu′tion, *n.* ENGLISH REVOLUTION.

glo·ry (glôr′ē, glōr′ē), *n., pl.* -ries, *v.*, -ried, -ry·ing, *interj.* —*n.* **1.** very great praise, honor, or distinction bestowed by common consent; renown. **2.** something that is a source of honor, fame, or admiration; an

object of pride: *one of the glories of English poetry.* **3.** adoring praise or worshipful thanksgiving. **4.** resplendent beauty or magnificence: *the glory of autumn.* **5.** a state of great splendor or prosperity. **6.** a state of absolute happiness, gratification, etc.: *to be in one's glory.* **7.** the splendor and bliss of heaven; heaven. —*v.i.* **8.** to exult with triumph; rejoice proudly (usu. fol. by *in*): *Their parents gloried in their success.* —*interj.* **9.** Also, **glo′ry be**! Glory be to God (used to express surprise, elation, etc.). —*Idiom.* **10. go to (one's) glory**, to die.

gloss¹ (glos, glôs), *n.* **1.** a superficial luster or shine; glaze: *the gloss of satin.* **2.** a deceptively good appearance. **3.** a cosmetic that adds sheen or luster, esp. lip gloss. —*v.t.* **4.** to put a gloss upon. **5. gloss over**, to give a deceptively good appearance to; mask; cover up: *to gloss over someone's foibles.* —**gloss′er**, *n.*

gloss² (glos, glôs), *n.* **1.** an explanation or translation, by means of a marginal or interlinear note. **2.** a series of verbal interpretations of a text. —*v.t.* **3.** to insert glosses on; annotate. **4.** to place (a word) in a gloss. **5.** to give a misleading interpretation of; explain away (often fol. by *over* or *away*): *to gloss over a difficult text.* —*v.i.* **6.** to make glosses. —**gloss′ing·ly**, *adv.*

glos·sa (glos′ə, glô′sə), *n., pl.* **glos·sae** (glos′ē, glô′sē), **glos·sas. 1.** the tongue. **2.** one of a pair of median, sometimes fused lobes of the labium of an insect.

glos·sal (glos′əl, glô′səl), *adj.* of or pertaining to the tongue.

glos·sa·ry (glos′ə rē, glô′sə-), *n., pl.* -ries. a list of terms in a special subject, field, or area of usage, with accompanying definitions. —**glos·sar′i·al** (glo sâr′ē əl, glô-), *adj.* —**glos·sar′i·al·ly**, *adv.* —**glos′sa·rist**, *n.*

glosso- or **glotto-**, a combining form meaning "tongue" (*glossopharyngeal*), "speech" (*glossolalia*), "gloss" (*glossographer*).

gloss·y (glos′ē, glô′sē), *adj.*, **gloss·i·er, gloss·i·est**, *n., pl.* **gloss·ies.** —*adj.* **1.** having a shiny or lustrous surface. **2.** having a false or deceptive appearance or air, esp. of experience or sophistication; specious. —*n.* **3.** SLICK¹ (def. 9). **4.** a photograph printed on glossy paper. —**gloss′i·ly**, *adv.* —**gloss′i·ness**, *n.*

-glot, a combining form with the meaning "speaking, writing, or written in a language" of the number specified by the initial element: *polyglot.*

glot·tal (glot′l), *adj.* **1.** of or pertaining to the glottis. **2.** articulated or produced by or at the glottis: *a glottal sound.*

glot′tal stop′, *n.* a plosive consonant whose occlusion and release are accomplished chiefly at the glottis, as in the Scottish articulation of the *t*-sound of *little, bottle*, etc.

glot·tis (glot′is), *n., pl.* **glot·tis·es, glot·ti·des** (glot′i dēz′). the opening at the upper part of the larynx, between the vocal cords. —**glot′tal**, *adj.*

glot·to·chro·nol·o·gy (glot′ō krə nol′ə jē), *n.* the use of lexicostatistics to study the rate of change in vocabulary and the amount of vocabulary two presently distinct but related languages share, using this information to estimate how long ago the languages diverged. —**glot′to·chron′o·log′i·cal** (-kron′l oj′i kəl), *adj.*

glove (gluv), *n.* **1.** a covering for the hand made with a separate sheath for each finger and for the thumb. **2.** a similar covering made of padded leather and having a pocket in the area over the palm for catching baseballs. **3.** GAUNTLET¹ (def. 1). —*v.t.* **4.** to cover with or as if with a glove; provide with gloves. **5.** to serve as a glove for. —**glove′less**, *adj.* —**glove′like′**, *adj.*

glove′ box′, *n.* an enclosed compartment fitted with long gloves, used for handling contents without causing or incurring injury or contamination, as in a laboratory or hospital.

glove box

glove′ compart′ment, *n.* a compartment in the dashboard of an automobile for storing small items.

glow (glō), *n.* **1.** a light emitted by or as if by a substance heated to luminosity; incandescence: *the glow of coals in the fireplace.* **2.** brightness of color. **3.** a sensation or state of bodily heat. **4.** a warm, ruddy color of the cheeks. **5.** warmth of emotion or passion; ardor. —*v.i.* **6.** to emit bright light and heat without flame; become incandescent. **7.** (of the cheeks) to exhibit a healthy, ruddy color. **8.** to show emotion or elation: *to glow with pride.*

glow·er (glou′ər), *v.i.* **1.** to look or stare with sullen dislike, discontent, or anger. —*n.* **2.** a look of sullen dislike, discontent, or anger.

glow·ing (glō′ing), *adj.* **1.** incandescent. **2.** rich and warm in coloring:

glowing colors. **3.** showing the radiance of health, excitement, etc. **4.** warmly favorable or complimentary: *a glowing account of her work.* **—glow′ing•ly,** *adv.*

glow•worm (glō′wûrm′), *n.* the larva or wingless female of a beetle, *Lampyris noctiluca,* which emits a sustained greenish light. Compare FIREFLY.

glox•in•i•a (glok sin′ē ə), *n., pl.* **-i•as.** a cultivated tropical plant, *Sinningia speciosa,* of the gesneria family, with hairy leaves and bell-shaped flowers.

glu•cose (gloo͞′kōs), *n.* **1.** a simple sugar, $C_6H_{12}O_6$, that is a product of photosynthesis and is the principal source of energy for all living organisms: concentrated in fruits and honey or readily obtainable from starch, other carbohydrates, or glycogen. **2.** a syrup containing dextrose, maltose, and dextrine, obtained by the incomplete hydrolysis of starch. **—glu•cos′ic,** *adj.*

glue (gloo͞), *n., v.,* **glued, glu•ing.** **—***n.* **1.** a hard protein gelatin obtained by boiling skins, hoofs, and other animal substances in water and used as a strong adhesive. **2.** any of various preparations of this or a similar substance, used as an adhesive. **—***v.t.* **3.** to join or attach firmly with glue or as if with glue: *to glue a label on a package; to glue one's eyes to the TV set.*

glum (glum), *adj.,* **glum•mer, glum•mest.** sullenly or silently gloomy; dejected. **—glum′ly,** *adv.* **—glum′ness,** *n.*

glume (gloo͞m), *n.* one of a pair of chafflike bracts enclosing the floral parts of a spikelet in grasses.

glut (glut), *v.,* **glut•ted, glut•ting,** *n.* **—***v.t.* **1.** to feed or fill to satiety; sate: *to glut the appetite.* **2.** to feed or fill to excess; stuff: *to glut oneself with candy.* **3.** to flood (the market) with a particular item or service so that the supply greatly exceeds the demand. **4.** to choke up: *to glut a channel.* **—***v.i.* **5.** to eat to satiety or to excess. **—***n.* **6.** an excessive supply or amount; surfeit. **7.** an act of glutting or the state of being glutted. **—glut′ting•ly,** *adv.*

glu•ta•mate (gloo͞′tə māt′), *n.* a salt or ester of glutamic acid.

glu•tam′ic ac′id (gloo͞ tam′ik) also **glu′ta•min′ic ac′id** (gloo͞′tə-min′ik, gloo͞′-), *n.* a crystalline amino acid, $C_5H_9NO_4$, obtained by hydrolysis from wheat gluten and sugar-beet residues, used commercially as a flavor intensifier. *Abbr.:* Glu; *Symbol:* E

glu•ta•mine (gloo͞′tə mēn′, -min), *n.* a crystalline amino acid, $C_5H_{10}N_2O_3$, related to glutamic acid and found in many plant and animal proteins. *Abbr.:* Gln; *Symbol:* Q

glu•te•al (gloo͞′tē əl, gloo͞ tē′əl), *adj.* pertaining to the buttock muscles or the buttocks.

glu•ten (gloo͞t′n), *n.* a grayish, sticky component of wheat flour and other grain flours. [< Latin *glūten* glue] **—glu′ten•ous,** *adj.*

glu•te•us (gloo͞′tē əs, gloo͞ tē′-), *n., pl.* **-te•i** (-tē ī′, -tē′ī). any of the three muscles of each buttock, involved in the rotation and extension of the thigh, esp. the gluteus maximus.

glu′teus max′i•mus (mak′sə məs), *n., pl.* **glutei max•i•mi** (mak′sə-mī′). the broad, thick, outermost muscle of each buttock.

glu•ti•nous (gloo͞t′n əs), *adj.* gluey; viscid; sticky. **—glu′ti•nous•ly,** *adv.* **—glu′ti•nous•ness, glu′ti•nos′i•ty** (-os′i tē), *n.*

glut•ton (glut′n), *n.* **1.** a person who eats and drinks excessively or voraciously. **2.** a person with a remarkably great desire or capacity for something: *a glutton for work.*

glut•ton•y (glut′n ē), *n.* excessive eating and drinking: one of the seven deadly sins.

glyc•er•in (glis′ər in) also **glyc•er•ine** (-ər in, -ə rēn′), *n.* GLYCEROL.

glyc•er•ol (glis′ə rôl′, -rol′), *n.* a colorless liquid, $C_3H_8O_3$, used as a sweetener and preservative, and in suppositories and skin emollients.

gly•co•gen (glī′kə jən, -jen′), *n.* a polysaccharide, $(C_6H_{10}O_5)_n$, composed of glucose isomers, that is the principal carbohydrate stored by the animal body and is readily converted to glucose when needed for energy use.

gly•col (glī′kôl, -kol), *n.* **1.** a colorless, sweet liquid, $C_2H_6O_2$, used chiefly as an automobile antifreeze and as a solvent. **2.** any of a group of alcohols containing two hydroxyl groups. **—gly•col′ic** (-kol′ik), *adj.*

glyph (glif), *n.* **1.** a pictograph or hieroglyph. **2.** a sculptured figure or relief carving. **3.** an ornamental vertical channel or groove, esp. in Doric architecture. **4.** any symbol bearing information nonverbally, as a crossed-out cigarette on a no-smoking sign. **—glyph′ic,** *adj.*

GM or **G.M.,** **1.** General Manager. **2.** Grand Marshal. **3.** Grand Master.

G-man (jē′man′), *n., pl.* **G-men.** an agent for the FBI.

Gmc, Germanic.

GMT or **G.M.T.,** Greenwich Mean Time.

gnarl (närl), *n.* **1.** a knotty protuberance on a tree; knot. **—***v.t.* **2.** to twist into a knotted or distorted form.

gnarled (närld), *adj.* **1.** (of trees) full of or covered with gnarls; bent; twisted. **2.** having a rugged, weather-beaten appearance. **3.** crabby; cantankerous.

gnash (nash), *v.t.* **1.** to grind or strike (the teeth) together, esp. in rage or pain. **2.** to bite with grinding teeth. **—***v.i.* **3.** to gnash the teeth. **—gnash′ing•ly,** *adv.*

gnat (nat), *n.* any of certain small flies, esp. the biting gnats or punkies of the family Ceratopogonidae, the midges of the family Chironomidae, and the black flies of the family Simuliidae. **—gnat′like′,** *adj.* **—gnat′ty,** *adj.,* **-ti•er, -ti•est.**

gnat•catch•er (nat′kach′ər), *n.* any of various small, insect-eating New World songbirds of the genus *Polioptila* (subfamily Silviinae), having a long, mobile tail.

gnaw (nô), *v.,* **gnawed, gnawed** or **gnawn, gnaw•ing.** **—***v.t.* **1.** to bite or chew on, esp. persistently: *The kitten gnawed the slippers.* **2.** to wear away or remove by persistent biting. **3.** to form or make by gnawing: *to gnaw a hole.* **4.** to waste or wear away; erode. **5.** to trouble or torment by constant annoyance; vex; plague. **—***v.i.* **6.** to bite or chew persistently. **7.** to cause corrosion. **8.** to cause an effect resembling corrosion: *Her mistake gnawed at her conscience.* **—gnaw′er,** *n.*

gnaw•ing (nô′ing), *n.* **1.** the act of a person or thing that gnaws. **2.** Usu., **gnawings.** persistent, dull pains; pangs: *the gnawings of hunger.* **—gnaw′ing•ly,** *adv.*

gneiss (nīs), *n.* a metamorphic rock, generally made up of bands that differ in color and composition, some bands being rich in feldspar and quartz, others rich in hornblende or mica. **—gneiss′ic, gneiss′oid,** *adj.*

gnoc•chi (nok′ē, nyok′ē, nō′kē, nyō′-), *n.* (*used with a sing. or pl. v.*) small Italian dumplings made from potatoes, semolina, flour, or a combination of these.

gnome¹ (nōm), *n.* **1.** (originally in the writings of Paracelsus) any of a group of dwarflike beings inhabiting the interior of the earth. **2.** an expert in monetary or financial affairs; international banker or financier: *the gnomes of Zurich.* **—gnom′ish,** *adj.*

gnome² (nōm, nō′mē), *n.* a short, pithy expression of a general truth; aphorism.

gno•mic¹ (nō′mik, nom′ik), *adj.* of, pertaining to, or resembling a gnome.

gno•mic² (nō′mik, nom′ik) also **gno′mi•cal,** *adj.* **1.** like or containing gnomes or aphorisms. **2.** pertaining to or noting a writer of aphorisms, esp. any of certain Greek poets. **—gno′mi•cal•ly,** *adv.*

gno•sis (nō′sis), *n.* knowledge of spiritual matters; mystical knowledge.

gnos•tic (nos′tik), *adj.* Also, **gnos′ti•cal.** **1.** pertaining to knowledge. **2.** possessing knowledge, esp. esoteric knowledge of spiritual matters. **3.** (*cap.*) pertaining to or characteristic of the Gnostics. **—***n.* **4.** (*cap.*) a member of any of certain heretical early Christian mystical sects that claimed that matter was evil and denied that Christ had a natural corporeal existence. **—gnos′ti•cal•ly,** *adv.* **—Gnos′ti•cism** (-tə siz′əm), *n.*

GNP or **G.N.P.,** gross national product.

gnu (noo͞, nyoo͞), *n., pl.* **gnus,** (*esp. collectively*) **gnu.** either of two stocky, oxlike African antelopes, the silvery gray *Connochaetes taurinus* or the black *C. gnou.* Also called **wildebeest.**

go¹ (gō), *v.,* **went, gone, go•ing,** *n., pl.* **goes,** *adj.* **—***v.i.* **1.** to move or proceed, esp. to or from something: *to go home.* **2.** to leave a place; depart: *Go away!* **3.** to keep or be in motion; function or operate: *The engine is going now.* **4.** to become as specified: *to go mad.* **5.** to continue in a certain state or condition; be habitually: *to go barefoot.* **6.** to act as specified: *Go warily.* **7.** to act so as to come into a certain state or condition: *to go to sleep.* **8.** to be known: *to go by a false name.* **9.** to reach or give access to: *This door goes outside.* **10.** to pass or elapse: *The time went fast.* **11.** to be applied, allotted, etc., to a particular recipient or purpose: *My money goes for food and rent.* **12.** to be sold: *The house went for very little.* **13.** to be considered generally or usually: *He's tall, as jockeys go.* **14.** to tend: *This only goes to prove the point.* **15.** to result or end; turn out: *How did the game go?* **16.** to belong; have a place: *This book goes here.* **17.** (of colors, styles, etc.) to harmonize; be compatible; be suited. **18.** to fit or extend: *This belt won't go around my waist.* **19.** to be or become consumed, finished, etc.: *The cake went fast.* **20.** to be or become discarded, dismissed, etc.: *Those puns of yours have got to go!* **21.** to develop or proceed, esp. with reference to success or satisfaction: *How is your new job going?* **22.** to move or proceed with remarkable speed or energy: *Look at that airplane go!* **23.** to make a certain sound: *The gun goes bang.* **24.** to be phrased, written, or composed: *How does that song go?* **25.** to seek or have recourse; resort: *to go to court.* **26.** to become worn-out, weakened, etc. **27.** to die. **28.** to fail or give way: *The dike might go any minute.* **29.** to come into action; begin: *Go when you hear the bell.* **30.** to make up a quantity or content; be requisite: *Sixteen ounces go to the pound.* **31.** to be or be able to be divided: *Three goes into fifteen five times.* **32.** to contribute to an end result: *the items that go to make up the total.* **33.** to have as one's goal; intend (usu. fol. by an infinitive): *Their daughter is going to be a doctor.* **34.** to be permitted, approved, or the like: *Around here, anything goes.* **35.** to be authoritative; be the final word: *Whatever I say goes!* **36.** to subject oneself: *Don't go to any trouble.* **37.** *Informal.* to proceed (used as an intensifier): *He had to go ask for a loan. Go figure that out.* **38.** *Informal.* to urinate or defecate. **—***v.t.* **39.** to move or proceed with or according to; follow: *Going my way?* **40.** to share or participate in to the extent of: *to go halves.* **41.** *Informal.* to risk, pay, afford, bet, or bid: *I'll go fifty dollars for a ticket.* **42.** to yield, weigh, or grow to: *This field will go two bales of cotton.* **43.** to assume the obligation or function of: *His father went bail for him.* **44.** *Informal.* to say; remark (usu. used in recounting a conversation). **45.** *Informal.* to endure or tolerate: *I can't go his preaching.* **46. go about, a.** to occupy oneself with; perform. **b.** to change course at sea by tacking or wearing. **47. go after,** to attempt to obtain; strive for. **48. go against,** to be in conflict with or opposed to. **49. go ahead,** to proceed without hesitation or delay. **50. go along,** to agree; concur. **51. go around, a.** to be often in company. **b.** to be sufficient for all. **c.** to pass or circulate: *A rumor is going around.* **52. go at, a.** to assault; attack. **b.** to begin or proceed vigorously. **53. go by, a.** to pass: *Don't let this chance go by.* **b.** to be guided by. **54. go**

down, a. to decrease or subside, as in amount or size. **b.** to descend or sink. **c.** to suffer defeat. **d.** to be accepted or believed. **e.** to be remembered in history or by posterity. **f.** *Slang.* to happen; occur: *What's been going down since I've been away?* **g.** *Brit.* to leave a university, permanently or at the end of a term. **55. go for, a.** to make an attempt at; try for: *to go for a win.* **b.** to assault. **c.** to favor; like. **d.** to be used for the purpose of or be a substitute for: *material that goes for silk.* **56. go in for,** to adopt as one's particular interest; occupy oneself with. **57. go into, a.** to discuss or investigate. **b.** to undertake as one's study or work. **58. go in with,** to join in a partnership or union; combine with. **59. go off, a.** to explode. **b.** (of what has been expected or planned) to happen. **c.** to leave, esp. suddenly. **60. go on, a.** to happen or take place. **b.** to continue: *Go on working.* **c.** to behave; act. **d.** to talk effusively; chatter. **e.** (used to express disbelief): *Go on, you're kidding me.* **f.** to appear onstage in a theatrical performance. **61. go out, a.** to cease or fail to function: *The lights went out.* **b.** to participate in social activities. **c.** to take part in a strike. **62. go over, a.** to repeat; review. **b.** to be effective or successful: *The proposal didn't go over.* **c.** to examine. **d.** to read; scan. **63. go through, a.** to bear; experience. **b.** to examine or search carefully. **c.** to be accepted or approved. **d.** to use up; spend completely. **64. go through with,** to persevere with to the end; bring to completion. **65. go under, a.** to be overwhelmed or ruined; fail. **b.** (of a ship) to founder. **66. go up, a.** to be in the process of construction, as a building. **b.** to increase in cost, value, etc. **c.** *Brit.* to go to a university at the beginning of a term. —*n.* **67.** the act of going. **68.** energy or spirit: *She's got a lot of go.* **69.** a try at something; attempt: *to have a go at the puzzle.* **70.** a successful accomplishment; success. **71.** *Informal.* approval or permission, as to undertake something. **72.** a boxing bout: *the main go.* —*adj.* **73.** (esp. in aerospace) functioning properly; ready: *All systems are go.* —*Idiom.* **74. from the word go,** from the very start. **75. go all out,** to expend the greatest possible effort. **76. go and,** to be so thoughtless or unfortunate as to: *She had to go and lose her gloves.* **77. go it alone,** to act or proceed independently. **78. go (out) with,** *Informal.* to keep company with; court; date. **79. go the second mile,** to make an extra effort. **80. go together, a.** to be appropriately matched; be harmonious. **b.** to be romantically involved with one another; date steadily. **81. go to it,** to begin vigorously and at once. **82. go to the well,** to use funds for public expenditures. **83. let go, a.** to free; release (sometimes fol. by *of*). **b.** to cease to employ; dismiss. **c.** to abandon one's inhibitions. **d.** to dismiss; forget; discard. **84. let oneself go,** to free oneself of inhibitions or restraint. **85. no go,** *Informal.* **a.** futile; useless. **b.** canceled or aborted. **86. on the go,** very busy; active. **b.** while traveling. **87. to go,** for consumption off the premises where sold: *pizza to go.*

go² (gō), *n.* a Japanese board game for two in which black and white stones are placed on intersecting lines in such a way as to capture the opponent's stones and thereby control the board. Also called **I-go.**

G.O. or **g.o.**, **1.** general office. **2.** general order.

go•a (gō′ə), *n., pl.* **go•as.** a Tibetan gazelle, *Procapra picticaudata.*

Go•a (gō′ə), *n.* a state in SW India, on the Arabian Sea: formerly a part of Portuguese India; then part of the union territory of Goa, Daman, and Diu (1961–87). 1,007,749; 1429 sq. mi. (3702 sq. km). *Cap.:* Panaji.

Go′a, Daman′, and Di′u, *n.* a former territory of India, in the W part: now divided into the state of Goa, and the territory of Daman and Diu.

goad (gōd), *n.* **1.** a stick with a pointed or electrically charged end, for driving cattle, oxen, etc.; prod. **2.** anything that pricks, wounds, or urges on like such a stick; stimulus. —*v.t.* **3.** to prick or drive with, or as if with, a goad; prod; incite.

go′-a•head′, *n.* **1.** permission or a signal to proceed: *They got the go-ahead on the building project.* **2.** ambition, energy, or initiative; enterprise. —*adj.* **3.** signaling to proceed: *a go-ahead sign.* **4.** enterprising: *a go-ahead farmer.*

goal (gōl), *n.* **1.** the result or achievement toward which effort is directed; aim; end. **2.** the terminal point in a race. **3.** a pole, line, or other marker by which such a point is indicated. **4.** an area or point toward or into which players of various games attempt to propel a ball or puck to score points. **5.** the act of propelling a ball or puck toward or into such an area or object. **6.** the score made by achieving this.

goal•ie (gō′lē), *n.* GOALKEEPER.

goal•keep•er (gōl′kē′pər), *n.* (in ice hockey, field hockey, lacrosse, soccer, etc.) a player whose chief duty is to prevent the ball or puck from crossing or entering the goal. —**goal′keep′ing,** *n.*

goal′ line′, *n. Sports.* the line that bounds a goal, esp. the front line.

goal•mouth (gōl′mouth′), *n., pl.* **-mouths** (-mouthz′, mouths′). the area between the goalposts directly in front of the goal in certain games, as soccer, lacrosse, and hockey.

goal′post′ or **goal′ post′,** *n.* a post supporting a crossbar and, with it, forming the goal on a playing field in certain sports, as football.

goal•tend•er (gōl′ten′dər), *n.* GOALKEEPER.

goal•tend•ing (gōl′ten′ding), *n.* **1.** the act of defending the goal in various sports; goalkeeping. **2.** (in basketball) the illegal deflecting of the ball on its downward path toward the basket or while it is on the rim.

go•an•na (gō an′ə), *n., pl.* **-nas.** any Australian monitor lizard of the genus *Varanus.*

goat (gōt), *n.* **1.** any agile, hollow-horned ruminant of the Old World genus *Capra,* of the family Bovidae, closely related to sheep, usu. native to mountainous regions, and widely distributed in domesticated varieties. **2.** any of various related animals, as the Rocky Mountain goat. **3.** (*cap.*) CAPRICORN (def. 1). **4.** a scapegoat or victim. **5.** a lecherous man. —*Idiom.* **6. get someone's goat,** *Informal.* to anger, annoy, or frustrate a person.

goat•ee (gō tē′), *n.* a man's beard trimmed to a tuft or point on the chin. —**goat•eed′,** *adj.*

goat•fish (gōt′fish′), *n., pl.* **-fish•es,** (*esp. collectively*) **-fish.** any tropical reef fish of the family Mullidae, having a pair of long barbels below the mouth.

goats•beard (gōts′bērd′), *n.* **1.** any composite plant of the genus *Tragopogon,* having large solitary flower heads. **2.** a plant, *Aruncus dioicus,* of the rose family, having spikes of small white flowers.

goat•skin (gōt′skin′), *n.* **1.** the skin or hide of a goat. **2.** leather made from it.

gob (gob), *n.* **1.** a mass or lump. **2. gobs,** *Informal.* a large quantity: *gobs of money.*

gob•ble¹ (gob′əl), *v.,* **-bled, -bling.** —*v.t.* **1.** to swallow or eat hastily or hungrily in large pieces; gulp. **2.** to seize upon eagerly (often fol. by *up*): *He gobbled up all the news.* **3.** to take in hungrily; devour (often fol. by *up*): *to gobble up the books in the library.* —*v.i.* **4.** to eat hastily.

gob•ble² (gob′əl), *v.,* **-bled, -bling,** *n.* —*v.i.* **1.** to make the characteristic throaty cry of a male turkey. —*n.* **2.** the cry itself.

gob•ble•dy•gook or **gob•ble•de•gook** (gob′əl dē gook′), *n.* language characterized by circumlocution and jargon, usu. hard to understand: *the gobbledygook of some government reports.*

gob•bler (gob′lər), *n.* a male turkey.

go′-between′, *n.* a person who acts as an intermediary between persons or groups.

Go•bi (gō′bē), *n.* a desert in E Asia, mostly in Mongolia. ab. 500,000 sq. mi. (1,295,000 sq. km). —**Go′bi•an,** *adj.*

gob•let (gob′lit), *n.* **1.** a drinking glass with a foot and stem. **2.** a bowl-shaped drinking vessel in former use.

gob•lin (gob′lin), *n.* a grotesque sprite or elf that is mischievous or malicious toward people.

go′-by′, *n., pl.* **-bys.** *Informal.* a going by without notice; an intentional passing by; snub: *to give one the go-by.*

go•by (gō′bē), *n., pl.* (*esp. collectively*) **-by,** (*esp. for kinds or species*) **-bies.** any small marine or freshwater fish of the family Gobiidae, often having the pelvic fins united to form a suctorial disk.

go′-cart′, *n.* **1.** a small carriage for wheeling young children; stroller. **2.** a small, wheeled framework in which children learn to walk; walker. **3.** HANDCART. **4.** KART.

God (god), *n.* **1.** the creator and ruler of the universe; Supreme Being. **2.** (*l.c.*) **a.** one of several immortal powers, esp. one with male attributes, presiding over some portion of worldly affairs; deity. **b.** the image of such a deity; idol. **3.** (*l.c.*) any deified person or object. **4.** *Christian Science.* the Supreme Being considered with reference to the sum of His attributes. —*Proverb.* **5. God is in the details,** whatever one does should be done with care and thoroughness. **6. God's in his heaven, all's right with the world,** God blesses all, and all is well: popularized by Robert Browning in *Pippa Passes* (1841).

God′ and mam′mon, *n.* contrasted spiritual and material life. Matt. 6:24.

God′-aw′ful, *adj.* (*sometimes l.c.*) *Informal.* extremely dreadful or shocking.

God′ Be′ with′ You′ Till′ We′ Meet′ Again′, a Christian hymn (1882) with words by Jeremiah Rankin.

God′ Bless′ Amer′ica, a patriotic song (1938) by Irving Berlin.

god•child (god′chīld′), *n., pl.* **-chil•dren.** a child for whom a godparent serves as sponsor.

god•daugh•ter (god′dô′tər), *n.* a female godchild.

god•dess (god′is), *n.* **1.** a female god or deity. **2.** a greatly admired or adored woman. **3.** a woman of great beauty. —**god′dess•hood′, god′dess•ship′,** *n.*

Gö•del (gœd′l), *n.* **Kurt,** 1906–78, U.S. mathematician and logician, born in Czechoslovakia.

Gö′del's the′orem, *n.* the theorem that in a formal logical system incorporating the properties of the natural numbers, there exists at least one formula that can be neither proved nor disproved within the system. Also called **Gö′del's incomplete′ness the′orem.**

god•fa•ther (god′fä′thər), *n.* **1.** a man who serves as sponsor for a child, as at a baptism. **2.** the head of a Mafia family; don. —**god′fa′ther•ly,** *adj.*

God′-fear′ing, *adj.* **1.** deeply respectful or fearful of God. **2.** (*sometimes l.c.*) deeply religious; pious; devout.

god•for•sak•en (god′fər sā′kən, god′fər sā′-), *adj.* (*sometimes cap.*) **1.** desolate; remote; deserted: *They live in some godforsaken place.* **2.** wretched; neglected; pitiable.

God•head (god′hed′), *n.* **1. a.** the essential being of God; the Supreme Being. **b.** the Holy Trinity of God the Father, Christ the Son, and the Holy Ghost. **2.** (*l.c.*) divinity; godhood. **3.** (*l.c.*) *Rare.* a god or goddess; deity.

god•hood (god′hŏŏd), *n.* divine character or condition.

God′ Incar′nate, *n.* Jesus Christ.

God′ in Three′ Per′sons, *n.* the Trinity.

God′ Is′ Our′ Ref′uge and Strength′, a Christian hymn based on Psalm 46.

Go·di·va (gə dī′və), n. ("*Lady Godiva*"), died 1057, an English noblewoman who, according to legend, rode naked through the streets of Coventry to win relief for the people from a burdensome tax.

god·less (god′lis), adj. **1.** acknowledging no god or deity; atheistic. **2.** evil; sinful. —**god′less·ly,** adv. —**god′less·ness,** n.

god·like (god′līk′), adj. like or befitting God or a god; divine. —**god′-like′ness,** n.

god·ly (god′lē), adj., **-li·er, -li·est. 1.** obeying and revering God; devout; pious. **2.** coming from God; divine. —**god′li·ness,** n.

God-man (god′man′, -man′), n., pl. **-men** for 2. **1.** Jesus Christ. **2.** (*l.c.*) a being who possesses the combined attributes of a deity and of a human; demigod.

god·moth·er (god′muth′ər), n. a woman who serves as sponsor for a child, as at a baptism.

God′ Moves′ in a Myste′rious Way′, a Christian hymn (1774) with words by William Cowper.

God′ of Grace′ and God′ of Glo′ry, a Christian hymn (1930) with words by Harry Emerson Fosdick.

God′ of Our Fa′thers, a Christian and patriotic hymn (1876) with words by Daniel Roberts.

Go′ Down′, Mo′ses, a traditional American spiritual.

god·par·ent (god′pâr′ənt, -par′-), n. a godfather or godmother.

God′s′ coun′try, n. **1.** an area or region supposed to be favored by God, esp. a naturally beautiful rural area. **2.** an isolated rural area. **3.** one's native region.

god·send (god′send′), n. an unexpected thing or event that is particularly welcome and timely, as if sent by God.

god·son (god′sun′), n. a male godchild.

God·speed (god′spēd′), n. good fortune; success (used as a wish to a person starting on a journey, a new venture, etc.).

God′s′ plen′ty, n. an abundant or overabundant quantity.

God′s′ Word′, n. the Bible.

Godt·håb (gôt′hôp′, got′hop′), n. the capital of Greenland, in the SW part. 12,209.

God′ the Fa′ther, n. one of the three persons in the Trinity, the others being **God′ the Son′** and **God′ the Ho′ly Ghost′.**

God′ Understands′, a Christian hymn (1935) with words by Oswald Smith; often sung at funerals.

God′ Will′ Take′ Care′ of You′, a Christian hymn (1904) with words by Civilla Martin and music by Walter Stillman Martin.

god·wit (god′wit), n. any shorebird of the cosmopolitan genus *Limosa*, having a long bill that curves upward slightly.

Goeb·bels (gœ′bəlz, -bəls), n. **Joseph Paul,** 1897–1945, Nazi German offical: served as propaganda director.

go·er (gō′ər), n. **1.** a person or thing that goes. **2.** a person who attends frequently or habitually (usu. used in combination): *churchgoer; moviegoer.*

goes (gōz), v. **1.** 3rd pers. sing. pres. indic. of GO¹. —n. **2.** pl. of GO¹.

Goe·the (gœ′tə), n. **Johann Wolfgang von,** 1749–1832, German poet and dramatist. —**Goe·the·an, Goe′thi·an,** adj.

goe·thite (gō′thīt, gœ′tīt), n. a mineral, iron hydroxide, HFeO₂, occurring in yellow or brown earthy masses and in crystals: a common ore of iron.

go·fer or **go·fer** or **go·pher** (gō′fər), n. *Slang.* an employee whose chief duty is running errands.

Go·forth (gō′fôrth), n. **Jonathan,** 1859–1936, Canadian Christian missionary in China.

Gog and Ma·gog (gog′ ən mā′gog), n.pl. nations led by Satan at Armageddon against the kingdom of God. Rev. 20:8.

go′-get′ter, n. *Informal.* an enterprising, aggressive person. —**go′-get′ting,** adj.

gog·gle (gog′əl), n., v., **-gled, -gling,** adj. —n. **1. goggles,** large spectacles equipped with special lenses, protective rims, etc., to prevent injury to the eyes from strong wind, flying objects, blinding light, etc. **2.** a bulging or wide-open look of the eyes; stare. —v.i. **3.** to stare with bulging or wide-open eyes. **4.** (of the eyes) to bulge and be wide open in a stare. **5.** to roll the eyes. **6.** (of the eyes) to roll. —v.t. **7.** to roll (the eyes). —adj. **8.** (of the eyes) rolling, bulging, or staring.

Gogh (gō, gôкн; *Du.* кнôкн), n. **Vincent van,** van Gogh, Vincent.

go′-go′, adj. **1.** of or pertaining to the music and dancing performed at discotheques or nightclubs. **2.** performing at a discotheque or nightclub. **3.** *Informal.* full of vitality or daring: *the go-go generation.*

Go·gol (gō′gəl, -gôl), n. **Nikolai Vasilievich,** 1809–52, Russian writer.

go·ing (gō′ing), n. **1.** the act of leaving or departing; departure: *comings and goings.* **2.** the condition of surfaces, as those of roads, for walking or driving: *The going was bad.* **3.** progress; advancement: *slow going on the work.* **4.** Usu. **goings.** behavior; conduct; deportment. —adj. **5.** moving or working, as machinery. **6.** active, alive, or existing. **7.** continuing to operate or do business, esp. in a successful manner: *a going company.* **8.** current; prevalent; usual: *the going price of houses.* **9.** leaving; departing. —*Idiom.* **10. get going,** to begin; get started. **11. going away,** by a wide margin, esp. as established in the late stages of a sports contest. **12. going on,** nearly; almost: *It's going on four o'clock.*

go′ing-o′ver, n., pl. **go·ings-o·ver. 1.** a review, examination, or investigation. **2.** a severe, thorough scolding. **3.** a sound thrashing; beating.

go′ings-on′, n.pl. *Informal.* **1.** conduct or behavior, esp. when open to criticism. **2.** happenings; events.

goi·ter (goi′tər), n. an enlargement of the thyroid gland on the front and sides of the neck. Also, *esp. Brit.,* **goi′tre.** —**goi′trous** (-trəs), adj.

go′-kart′, n. KART.

Go′lan Heights′ (gō′lan, -län), n.pl. a range of hills in northern Israel, formerly belonging to Syria and occupied by Israel in 1967.

Gol·con·da (gol kon′də), n. **1.** a ruined city in S India, near Hyderabad. **2.** (*often l.c.*) a rich mine or other source of great wealth.

gold (gōld), n. **1.** a precious yellow metallic element, highly malleable and ductile, and not subject to oxidation or corrosion: one of three gifts, the other two being frankincense and myrrh, given by the Magi to the infant Jesus. Matt. 2:11. *Symbol:* Au; *at. wt.:* 196.967; *at. no.:* 79; *sp. gr.:* 19.3 at 20°C. **2.** a quantity of gold coins: *to pay in gold.* **3.** GOLD STANDARD. **4.** money; wealth; riches. **5.** something likened to gold in brightness, preciousness, superiority, etc.: *a heart of gold.* **6.** a bright, metallic yellow color, sometimes tending toward brown. **7.** GOLD MEDAL. —adj. **8.** consisting of gold. **9.** pertaining to gold. **10.** like gold. **11.** of the color of gold. **12.** (of a recording, compact disc, or cassette) having sold a minimum of 500,000 copies.

Gold·berg (gōld′bûrg), n. **1. Arthur Joseph,** 1908–90, U.S. jurist, statesman, and diplomat: associate justice of the U.S. Supreme Court 1962–65; ambassador to the U.N. 1965–68. **2. Reuben Lucius** ("*Rube*"), 1883–1970, U.S. cartoonist, whose work often depicts deviously complex and impractical inventions.

gold·brick (gōld′brik′), *Slang.* —n. **1.** Also, **gold′brick′er.** a person, esp. a soldier, who loafs on the job. —v.i. **2.** to shirk; loaf.

gold·bug (gōld′bug′), n. *Informal.* **1.** a person, esp. an economist or politician, who supports the gold standard. **2.** a person who believes in buying gold bullion as a personal investment.

gold′ certif′icate, n. a former paper currency issued by the U.S. government, redeemable for gold to a stated value.

gold′ dig′ger, n. **1.** a person who seeks or digs for gold in a gold field. **2.** *Informal.* a woman who associates with or marries a man chiefly for material gain. —**gold′ dig′ging,** n.

gold′ dust′, n. gold in fine particles.

gold·en (gōl′dən), adj. **1.** bright, metallic, or lustrous like gold; of the color of.gold: *golden hair.* **2.** made or consisting of gold: *golden earrings.* **3.** exceptionally valuable, advantageous, or fine: *a golden opportunity.* **4.** having glowing vitality: *golden youth.* **5.** full of happiness, prosperity, or vigor: *golden hours.* **6.** highly talented and favored: *television's golden boy.* **7.** richly soft and smooth: *a golden voice.* **8.** indicating the 50th event of a series, as a wedding anniversary.

gold′en age′, n. **1.** the most flourishing period in the history of a nation, literature, etc. **2.** (*sometimes cap.*) (in Greek and Roman myth) the first and best of several successive ages of the world, when humanity lived in peace and innocence. **3.** the period in life after middle age, traditionally characterized by wisdom, contentment, and useful leisure.

gold′en as′ter, n. any North American, asterlike, composite plant of the genus *Chrysopsis,* having bright, golden-yellow flower heads.

gold′en ban′tam corn′, n. a variety of sweet corn.

gold′en-brown′ al′gae, n.pl. a group of mostly marine, gold to yellow-brown algae of the phylum Chlorophyta, containing the pigments chlorophyll, carotene, and xanthophyll.

gold′en calf′, n. **1.** a golden idol set up by Aaron. Ex. 32. **2.** either of the two similar idols set up by Jeroboam. I Kings 12:28, 29. **3.** money or material goods.

gold′en ea′gle, n. a large, golden-brown eagle, *Aquila chrysaëtos,* of mountainous regions of the Northern Hemisphere.

Gold′en Fleece′, n. a fleece of gold, kept at Colchis by Aeëtes until its theft by Jason and the Argonauts.

Gold′en Gate′, n. a strait in W California, between San Francisco Bay and the Pacific. 2 mi. (3.2 km) wide.

gold′en goose′, n. a legendary goose that laid one golden egg a day and was killed by its impatient owner, who wanted all the gold immediately.

gold′en ham′ster, n. a light-colored hamster, *Mesocricetus auratus,* of Asia Minor, often kept as a laboratory animal or pet.

gold′en hand′shake, n. a special incentive, as generous severance pay, offered as an inducement to elect early retirement.

gold′en nem′atode, n. a yellowish European nematode, *Heterodera rostochiensis,* introduced in E North America as a parasite of potatoes and other nightshades.

gold′en old′ie, n. (*sometimes caps.*) something once popular and still regarded affectionately,as a popular song.

gold′en par′achute, n. an employment agreement guaranteeing an executive substantial compensation in the event of dismissal as a result of a merger or takeover.

gold′en pheas′ant, n. a pheasant, *Chrysolophus pictus,* orig. of W China and Tibet, having brilliant scarlet, orange, gold, green, and black plumage.

gold′en retriev′er, n. one of a British breed of medium-sized retrievers having a thick, flat or wavy golden coat with feathering on the neck, legs, and tail.

G

gold·en·rod (gōl/dən rod/), *n.* any composite plant of the genus *Solidago*, most species of which bear numerous small, yellow flower heads.

gold/en rule/, *n.* a rule of ethical conduct, usually phrased "Do unto others as you would have them do unto you," or, as in the Sermon on the Mount, "Whatsoever ye would that men should do to you, do ye even so unto them." Matt. 7:12; Luke 6:31: found in various wordings in most major religions.

gold·en·seal (gōl/dən sēl/), *n.* a plant, *Hydrastis canadensis*, of the buttercup family, having a thick yellow rootstock formerly used in medicine.

Gold/en Tem/ple, *n.* a religious complex in Amritsar, India, holy to Sikhs.

gold/en years/, *n.pl.* the years of retirement, normally after age 65.

gold/-filled/, *adj.* composed of a layer of gold backed with a base metal.

gold·finch (gōld/finch/), *n.* **1.** any of several New World finches of the genus *Carduelis*, esp. the widespread North American species *C. tristis*, the male of which has yellow body plumage in the summer. **2.** a related Old World finch, *Carduelis carduelis*, having a crimson face and wings marked with yellow.

gold·fish (gōld/fish/), *n.,* *pl.* (*esp. collectively*) **-fish,** (*esp. for kinds or species*) **-fish·es.** a small usu. yellow or orange cyprinid fish, *Carassius auratus*, native to China and bred in many varieties.

gold/ foil/, *n.* sheets of gold slightly thicker than gold leaf.

gold/ leaf/, *n.* gold in the form of very thin foil, as for gilding.

gold/ med/al, *n.* a medal, traditionally of gold, awarded to a person or team finishing first in a competition. Compare BRONZE MEDAL, SILVER MEDAL. —**gold/ med/alist.**

gold/ mine/, *n.* **1.** a mine yielding gold. **2.** a source of great wealth or profit. **3.** a copious source or reserve.

gold/ plate/, *n.* **1.** tableware or containers made of gold. **2.** a plating, esp. electroplating, of gold. —**gold/-plate,** *v.t.,* **-plat·ed, -plat·ing.**

gold/ reserve/, *n.* the stock of gold held, esp. by a government to back its currency or settle its debts.

gold/ rush/, *n.* a large-scale and hasty movement of people to a region where gold has been discovered, as to California in 1849.

gold/ stand/ard, *n.* a monetary system with gold of specified weight and fineness as the unit of value.

gold/ star/, *n.* a gold-colored star, as on a small banner, indicating that a member of one's family, organization, or the like was killed in military services, esp. during a war. —**gold/-star/,** *adj.*

Gold·wa·ter (gōld/wô/tər, -wot/ər), *n.* **Barry Morris,** born 1909, U.S. politician: U.S senator 1953–64 and 1968–87.

Gold·wyn (gōld/win), *n.* **Samuel** (*Samuel Goldfish*), 1882–1974, U.S. movie producer, born in Poland.

go·lem (gō/ləm, -lem), *n.* (in Jewish folklore) a figure artificially constructed in the form of a human being and endowed with life.

golf (golf, gôlf; *Brit. also* gof), *n.* **1.** a game in which clubs are used to hit a small ball into a series of holes, usu. 9 or 18, situated at various distances over a golf course, the object being to get the ball into each hole in as few strokes as possible. —*v.i.* **2.** to play golf. —**golf/er,** *n.*

golf/ ball/, *n.* **1.** a small dimpled ball with a tough cover and a resilient core of rubber, used in playing golf. **2.** a ball-shaped printing element on certain electric typewriters.

golf/ club/, *n.* **1.** any of various long-handled clubs with wooden or metal heads, for hitting the ball in golf. Compare IRON (def. 5), WOOD¹ (def. 6). **2.** an organization of golf players or the facilities used by such an organization.

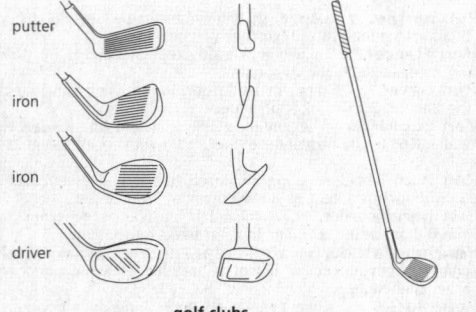

golf clubs

(labels: putter, iron, iron, driver)

golf/ course/, *n.* the usu. rolling 9- or 18-hole area of terrain, with greens and fairways, over which golf is played. Also called **golf/ links/.**

Gol·go·tha (gol/gə thə), *n.* CALVARY (defs. 1, 3). [< Late Latin < Greek *golgothâ* < Aramaic *gulgaltā,* akin to Hebrew *gulgōleth* skull]

Go·li·ath (gə lī/əth), *n.* the giant warrior of the Philistines whom David killed with a stone from a sling. I Sam. 17:48–51.

gol·ly (gol/ē), *interj.* (used as a mild exclamation expressing surprise, wonder, puzzlement, or the like.)

Go·mor·rah (gə môr/ə, -mor/ə), *n.* an ancient city destroyed because of its wickedness. Gen. 19:24, 25. —**Go·mor/re·an,** *adj.*

Gom·pers (gom/pərz), *n.* **Samuel,** 1850–1924, U.S. labor leader, born in England.

-gon, a combining form used in the names of geometrical figures having the number or sort of angles specified by the initial element: *isogon; polygon.*

go·nad (gō/nad, gon/ad), *n.* any organ or gland in which gametes are produced; an ovary or testis. —**go·nad/al, go·na/di·al** (-nā/dē əl), **go·nad/ic** (-nad/ik), *adj.*

gon·do·la (gon/dl ə *or, esp. for 1,* gon dō/lə), *n., pl.* **-las. 1.** a long, narrow, flat-bottomed boat, rowed by an oarsman at the stern: used on the canals in Venice, Italy. **2.** a passenger compartment suspended beneath a balloon or airship. Compare CAR (def. 3). **3.** an enclosed cabin suspended from an overhead cable, used to transport passengers, as up and down a ski slope. **4.** Also called **gon/dola car/.** an open railroad freight car with low sides, for transporting bulk freight and manufactured goods.

gondola (def. 1)

gon·do·lier (gon/dl ēr/), *n.* a person who rows or poles a gondola.

gone (gôn, gon), *v.* **1.** pp. of GO¹. —*adj.* **2.** departed; left. **3.** lost or hopeless. **4.** ruined. **5.** dead; deceased. **6.** past. **7.** weak and faint: *a gone feeling.* **8.** used up. **9.** *Slang.* **a.** pregnant: *two months gone.* **b.** great; outstanding. **c.** exhilarated; inspired. —*Idiom.* **10. far gone,** in an advanced state, as of love, exhaustion, or illness. **11. gone on,** *Informal.* infatuated with; in love with. —*Saying.* **12. gone but not forgotten,** remembered after death.

gon·er (gô/nər, gon/ər), *n. Informal.* a person or thing that is dead, lost, or past recovery.

Gone/ With the Wind/ (wind), a novel (1936) by Margaret Mitchell and a film (1939) starring Clark Gable and Vivien Leigh.

gong (gông, gong), *n.* **1.** a large bronze disk, of Asian origin, that produces a vibrant, hollow tone when struck. **2.** a shallow bell struck by an electrically or mechanically operated hammer. **3.** (in a clock or watch) a rod or wire, either straight or bent into a spiral, on which the time is struck. —**gong/like/,** *adj.*

-gonium, a combining form meaning "reproductive structure, esp. of plants," "group of cells that produce gametes or spores," "germ cell": *archegonium; oogonium.*

gon·na (gô/nə; *unstressed* gə nə), *Pron. Spelling.* going to (where *to* introduces an infinitive): *I'm gonna leave now.*

gon·o·coc·cus (gon/ə kok/əs), *n., pl.* **-coc·ci** (-kok/sī, -sē). the bacterium *Neisseria gonorrhoeae,* causing gonorrhea. —**gon/o·coc/cal, gon/o·coc/cic** (-kok/sik), *adj.* —**gon/o·coc/coid,** *adj.*

go/no-go or **go/-no/-go/** (gō/nō/gō/), *adj.* being or relating to a decision as to whether or not to proceed as planned, or to the time at which such a decision must be made.

gon·or·rhe·a (gon/ə rē/ə), *n.* a contagious, purulent inflammation of the urethra or the vagina, caused by the gonococcus. Also, *esp. Brit.* **gon/or·rhoe/a.** —**gon/or·rhe/al,** *adj.* —**gon/or·rhe/ic,** *adj.*

-gony, a combining form meaning "origin," "development": *cosmogony; merogony.*

gon·zo (gon/zō), *adj. Slang.* fiercely advocative or partial without regard for balance or objectivity.

goo (gōō), *n. Informal.* **1.** a thick or sticky substance. **2.** maudlin sentimentality.

goo·ber (gōō/bər), *n. South Midland and Southern U.S.* the peanut. Also called **goo/ber pea/.**

good (gŏŏd), *adj.,* **bet·ter, best,** *n., interj., adv.* —*adj.* **1.** morally excellent; virtuous; righteous: *a good man.* **2.** satisfactory in quality, quantity, or degree: *a good teacher; good health.* **3.** of high quality; excellent: *to wear good jewelry.* **4.** right; proper; fit: *It is good that you are here.* **5.** well-behaved: *a good child.* **6.** kind or friendly: *to do a good deed.* **7.** honorable or worthy: *a good name.* **8.** educated and refined: *a good background.* **9.** financially sound or safe: *His credit is good.* **10.** genuine; not counterfeit: *a good quarter.* **11.** sound or valid: *good judgment.* **12.** healthful; beneficial: *Fresh fruit is good for you.* **13.** in excellent condition; healthy: *good teeth.* **14.** not spoiled or tainted; edible; palatable. **15.** favorable; propitious: *good news.* **16.** cheerful; amiable: *in good spirits.* **17.** free of distress or pain; comfortable: *a patient in good condition.* **18.** agreeable; enjoyable: *Have a good time.* **19.** attractive: *She has a good figure.* **20.** (of the complexion) smooth; free from blemish. **21.** close; warm: *She's a good friend.* **22.** sufficient or ample: *a good supply.*

23. advantageous; satisfactory for the purpose: *a good day for fishing.* **24.** competent or skillful; clever: *good at arithmetic.* **25.** skillfully or expertly done: *a really good job.* **26.** conforming to rules of grammar, usage, etc.; correct: *good English.* **27.** socially proper: *good manners.* **28.** comparatively new or of relatively fine quality or condition: *good clothes.* **29.** full: *a good day's journey away.* **30.** fairly large or great: *a good amount.* **31.** free from precipitation or cloudiness: *good weather.* **32.** fertile; rich: *good soil.* **33.** loyal: *a good Democrat.* **34.** (of a return or service in tennis, handball, etc.) landing within the limits of a court or section of a court. **35.** (of the surface of a racetrack) drying after a rain so as to be still slightly sticky. **36.** designating the grade of meat, esp. lamb or veal, below choice. **37.** favorably regarded (used as an epithet): *the good ship Syrena.* —*n.* **38.** profit or advantage; worth; benefit: *What good will that do?* **39.** excellence or merit; kindness: *to do good.* **40.** moral righteousness; virtue: *to be a power for good.* **41. goods, a.** possessions, esp. movable effects or personal property. **b.** Sometimes, **good.** articles of trade; wares; merchandise: *linen goods.* **c.** *Informal.* what has been promised or is expected: *to deliver the goods.* **d.** *Informal.* evidence of guilt, as stolen articles: *caught with the goods.* **42. the good, a.** the ideal of goodness or morality. **b.** good things or persons collectively. —*interj.* **43.** (used as an expression of approval or satisfaction): *Good! Now we can all go home.* —*adv.* **44.** *Informal.* well. —*Idiom.* **45. come to no good,** to end in failure or as a failure. **46. for good,** finally and permanently; forever. **47. good and,** very (used as an intensifier): *The coffee is good and hot.* **48. good for, a.** certain to repay (money owed). **b.** the equivalent in value of: *This pass is good for two free seats.* **c.** serviceable or useful for (a specified length of time or distance). **49. no good,** without value or merit. **50. to the good, a.** generally advantageous: *That's all to the good, but what do I get out of it?* **b.** richer in profit or gain: *Afterwards, we were several thousand dollars to the good.* —*Proverb.* **51. A good man is hard to find,** a person who has the appropriate qualifications is rare. —**good′ish,** *adj.* —**Usage.** GOOD is common as an adverb in informal speech, esp. after forms of *do: He did good on the test.* In formal speech or edited writing the adverb WELL is used instead: *He did well on the test.* The adjective GOOD is standard after linking verbs like *taste, smell, look, feel, be,* and *seem: Everything tastes good. You're looking good today.* When used after *look* or *feel,* GOOD may refer to spirits as well as health. WELL as an adjective used after *look, feel,* or other linking verbs often refers to good health: *You're looking well; we missed you while you were in the hospital.* See also BAD[1].

Good′ Book′, *n.* the Bible.

good-by or **good-bye** (gŏŏd′bī′), *interj., n., pl.* **-bys.** GOOD-BYE.

good-bye or **good-bye** (gŏŏd′bī′), *interj., n., pl.* **-byes.** —*interj.* **1.** (a conventional expression used at parting.) —*n.* **2.** an act of saying good-bye; farewell or leave-taking. [contr. of *God be with ye*]

Good′ Con′duct Med′al, *n.* a medal awarded an enlisted person for meritorious behavior during the period of service.

good′ egg′, *n. Informal.* an agreeable or trustworthy person.

good′ faith′, *n.* accordance with standards of honesty, trust, sincerity, etc.: *to act in good faith.*

good′-fel′lowship, *n.* pleasant, convivial spirit; comradeship; geniality.

good-for-noth·ing (gŏŏd′fər nuth′ing, -nuth′-), *adj.* **1.** worthless; of no use. —*n.* **2.** a worthless or useless person.

Good′ Fri′day, *n.* the Friday before Easter, commemorating the Crucifixion of Jesus.

good′-heart′ed or **good′heart′ed,** *adj.* kind or generous; benevolent. —**good′-heart′ed·ly,** *adv.* —**good′-heart′ed·ness,** *n.*

good′ hu′mor, *n.* a cheerful or amiable mood. —**good′-hu′mored,** *adj.*

good·ie (gŏŏd′ē), *n., interj.* GOODY[1].

good′-look′ing, *adj.* having a pleasingly attractive appearance; handsome or beautiful.

good·ly (gŏŏd′lē), *adj.,* **-li·er, -li·est. 1.** of substantial size or amount: *a goodly sum.* **2.** of good or fine appearance. —**good′li·ness,** *n.*

Good·man (gŏŏd′mən), *n.* **Benjamin David** ("Benny"), 1909–86, U.S. jazz clarinetist and bandleader.

good′-na′tured, *adj.* having or showing a pleasant, kindly, agreeable disposition; amiable. —**good′-na′tured·ly,** *adv.* —**good′-na′tured·ness,** *n.*

Good′ Neigh′bor Pol′icy, *n.* a diplomatic policy of the U.S., first presented in 1933 by President Roosevelt, for the encouragement of friendly relations and mutual defense among the nations of the Western Hemisphere.

good·ness (gŏŏd′nis), *n.* **1.** the state or quality of being good. **2.** moral excellence; virtue. **3.** kindness; generosity. **4.** the best or most valuable part of anything; essence. **5.** a euphemism for God: *Thank goodness!* —*interj.* **6.** (used in expressions of surprise, alarm, etc.).

Good′ News′ Bi′ble, *n.* a Bible (1976) produced by the American Bible Society with language designed to be easily understood.

good′ old′ (or **ol′** or **ole′**) **boy′** (ōl), *n.* **1.** a man embodying the unsophisticated good fellowship and sometimes boisterous sociability regarded as characteristic of white males of the Southern U.S. **2.** a man, esp. a man, belonging to a network of friends and associates with close ties of loyalty and mutual support. —**good′ old′ boy′ism,** *n.*

good′ (or **Good′**) **Samar′itan,** *n.* a person who voluntarily gives help to those in distress or need: a parable of Jesus. Luke 10:30–37.

Good′ Shep′herd, *n.* Jesus Christ. John 10:11–14.

good′-sized′, *adj.* of ample or large size; rather large for its kind.

good′ sol′dier, *n.* one who is willing to place a cause or concern ahead of personal interest, esp. in politics.

Good·speed (gŏŏd′spēd′), *n.* **Edgar Johnson,** 1871–1962, U.S. Biblical scholar and translator.

good′-tem′pered, *adj.* good-natured; amiable. —**good′-tem′pered·ly,** *adv.* —**good′-tem′pered·ness,** *n.*

good′ time′, *n. Slang.* time deducted from an inmate's sentence for good behavior while in prison.

good′-time′ Char′lie (or **Char′ley**) (chär′lē), *n., pl.* **-lies** or **-leys.** *Informal.* an affable, sociable, pleasure-loving man.

good′will′ or **good′ will′,** *n.* **1.** friendly disposition; kindly regard; benevolence. **2.** cheerful acquiescence or consent. **3.** an intangible, salable asset arising from the reputation of a business and its relations with its customers.

good′ works′, *n.pl.* actions that are motivated by love of humanity.

good·y[1] or **good·ie** (gŏŏd′ē), *n., pl.* **good·ies,** *interj.* —*n.* Usu., **goodies. 1.** something pleasing to eat, as candy. **2.** something esp. desirable, attractive, or pleasing; something that causes delight. —*interj.* **3.** (used to express childish delight; sometimes used ironically).

good·y[2] (gŏŏd′ē), *n., pl.* **good·ies,** *adj.* GOODY-GOODY.

Good·year (gŏŏd′yēr′), *n.* **Charles,** 1800–60, U.S. inventor.

good′y-good′y, *n., pl.* **good·ies,** *adj.* —*n.* **1.** a person who is self-righteously, affectedly, or cloyingly good or virtuous. —*adj.* **2.** of or like a goody-goody.

good′y two′-shoes′ or **good′y-two′-shoes′,** *n., pl.* **-shoes,** *adj.* (*sometimes caps.*) GOODY-GOODY.

goo·ey (gŏŏ′ē), *adj.,* **goo·i·er, goo·i·est. 1.** like or covered with goo; sticky; viscid. **2.** extremely sentimental or emotionally effusive.

goof (gŏŏf), *Informal.* —*v.i.* **1.** to make an error, misjudgment, etc.; blunder. **2.** to waste or kill time; evade work or responsibility (often fol. by *off* or *around*). —*v.t.* **3.** to spoil or make a mess of; botch; bungle (often fol. by *up*). **4.** to tease or mock; kid (often fol. by *on*). —*n.* **5.** a foolish or stupid person. **6.** a mistake or blunder, esp. one due to carelessness. —**goof′y,** *adj.,* **-i·er, -i·est.**

goof·ball (gŏŏf′bôl′), *n. Slang.* **1.** an extremely incompetent, eccentric, or silly person. **2.** a pill containing a barbiturate or a tranquilizing drug.

goof′-off′, *n. Informal.* a person who habitually shirks work or responsibility; idler.

goof′-up′, *n. Informal.* a mistake, blunder, or malfunction.

goo·gol (gŏŏ′gəl), *n.* a number that is equal to 1 followed by 100 zeros, expressed as 10^{100}.

goon (gŏŏn), *n.* **1.** a hired hoodlum or thug. **2.** *Informal.* a stupid, foolish, or awkward person.

goon·y (gŏŏ′nē), *adj.,* **-i·er, -i·est,** *Informal.* weird; ridiculous; silly. —**goon′i·ly,** *adv.*

goop (gŏŏp), *n. Informal.* a viscous or sticky substance; goo. —**goop′y,** *adj.,* **goop·i·er, goop·i·est.**

goos·an·der (gŏŏ san′dər), *n.* MERGANSER.

goose (gŏŏs), *n., pl.* **geese** for 1, 2, 4, 8; **goos·es** for 5, 6; *v.,* **goosed, goos·ing.** —*n.* **1.** any of numerous wild or domesticated web-footed swimming birds of the family Anatidae, esp. of the genera *Anser* and *Branta,* most of which are larger and have a longer neck and legs than the ducks. **2.** the female of this bird (disting. from *gander*). **3.** the flesh of a goose, used as food. **4.** a silly or foolish person; simpleton. **5.** *Slang.* something that energizes or rouses; a prod. **6.** a tailor's smoothing iron with a curved handle. —*v.t. Slang.* **7. a.** to prod or urge to action or reaction. **b.** to add strength, vigor, numbers, etc., to (often fol. by *up*). **c.** to give a spurt of fuel to (a motor) to increase speed. —*Idiom.* **8. cook someone's goose,** *Informal.* to ruin someone's chances or future. —*Proverb.* **9. Don't kill the goose that laid the golden eggs,** don't destroy a sure source of future profit out of current greed.

goose·ber·ry (gŏŏs′ber′ē, -bə rē, gŏŏz′-), *n., pl.* **-ries. 1.** the sour, sometimes prickly fruit of certain shrubs of the genus *Ribes,* of the saxifrage family. **2.** any of these shrubs.

goose′ egg′, *n. Informal.* **1.** the numeral zero, esp. as a score in a game. **2.** a lump raised by a blow, esp. on the head.

goose′ flesh′ or **goose′flesh′,** *n.* a bristling of the hair on the skin, as from cold or fear. Also called **goose pimples, goose′ bumps/.**

goose·foot (gŏŏs′fŏŏt′), *n., pl.* **-foots.** any of numerous, often weedy plants of the genus *Chenopodium,* having inconspicuous greenish flowers.

goose′ grass′, *n.* CLEAVERS.

goose·neck (gŏŏs′nek′), *n.* a curved object resembling the neck of a goose, as a section of pipe or a long, flexible metal shaft on a desk lamp. —**goose′necked′,** *adj.*

goose′ pim′ples, *n.pl.* GOOSE FLESH. —**goose′-pim′ply,** *adj.*

goose′ step′, *n.* a marching step of some infantries in which the legs are swung high and kept straight and stiff. —**goose′-step′,** *v.i.,* **-stepped, -step·ping.** —**goose′-step′per,** *n.*

GOP or **G.O.P.,** Grand Old Party (an epithet of the Republican Party since 1880).

go·pher (gō′fər), *n.* **1.** Also called **pocket gopher.** any New World burrowing rodent of the family Geomyidae, having a stout body, a short

G

tail, and external cheek pouches. **2.** GROUND SQUIRREL. **3.** GOPHER TORTOISE. **4.** (*cap.*) a native or inhabitant of Minnesota (used as a nickname).

Go·pher (gō′fər), *n. Computers.* **1.** a protocol for a menu-based system of accessing documents on the Internet. **2.** any program that implements this protocol.

go′pher ball′, *n. Slang.* a pitched baseball hit for a home run.

go′pher snake′, *n.* a bullsnake, *Pituophis melanoleucus,* that preys on small burrowing mammals.

go′pher tor′toise, *n.* any North American burrowing land turtle of the genus *Gopherus.*

go′pher wood′, *n.* an unidentified wood used in building Noah's ark. Gen. 6:14.

go·pher·wood (gō′fər wŏŏd′), *n.* YELLOWWOOD.

Gor·ba·chev (gôr′bə chôf′, -chof′, gôr′bə chôf′, -chof′), *n.* **Mikhail S(ergeyevich),** born 1931, president of the Soviet Union 1988–91.

Gor′di·an knot′ (gôr′dē ən), *n.* **1.** a knot tied by Gordius, a legendary king of Phrygia, that, according to a prophecy, was to be undone only by the person who would rule Asia: Alexander the Great, not able to untie the knot, is said to have cut it with his sword. **2.** an intricate, seemingly insoluble problem. **—Idiom. 3. cut the Gordian knot,** to solve a problem boldly and decisively.

Gor·don (gôr′dn), *n.* **1. Adoniram Judson,** 1836–95, U.S. clergyman and evangelist. **2. Charles George** ("*Chinese Gordon*"; "*Gordon Pasha*"), 1833–85, British administrator in China and Egypt. **3. Mary (Catherine),** born 1949, U.S. novelist, short-story writer, and essayist.

Gor′don set′ter, *n.* one of a Scottish breed of large setters having a black-and-tan coat.

gore¹ (gôr, gōr), *n.* blood, esp. when clotted.

gore² (gôr, gōr), *v.t.,* **gored, gor·ing.** to pierce with or as if with a horn or tusk.

gore³ (gôr, gōr), *n., v.,* **gored, gor·ing. —n. 1.** a triangular piece of material inserted in a garment, sail, etc., to give it a desired shape. **2.** one of the panels, usu. tapered or shaped, making up a flaring skirt. **3.** a triangular tract of land, esp. one lying between larger divisions. **—v.t. 4.** to make or furnish with a gore or gores.

Gore (gôr, gōr), *n.* **Albert Arnold, Jr.** (*Al*), born 1948, vice president of the U.S. since 1993.

Gore-Tex (gôr′teks′, gōr′-), *Trademark.* a breathable, water-repellent fabric laminate used on clothing, shoes, etc.

Gor·gas (gôr′gəs), *n.* **William Crawford,** 1854–1920, U.S. physician and epidemiologist: chief sanitary officer of the Panama Canal 1904–13; surgeon general of the U.S. Army 1914–18.

gorge (gôrj), *n., v.,* **gorged, gorg·ing. —n. 1.** a narrow cleft with steep, rocky walls, esp. one through which a stream runs. **2.** a small canyon. **3.** a gluttonous meal. **4.** something that is swallowed; contents of the stomach. **5.** an obstructing mass: *an ice gorge.* **6.** the seam where the lapel joins the collar of a jacket or coat. **7.** the rear part of a bastion or similar outwork of a fortification. **8.** a primitive type of fishhook consisting of a sharply pointed piece of bone, antler, etc., that is attached to a line and becomes lodged in a fish's gills when swallowed. **9.** the throat; gullet. **10.** a feeling of strong disgust or anger: *Their cruelty made his gorge rise.* **—v.t. 11.** to stuff with food; glut: *to gorge oneself.* **12.** to swallow, esp. greedily. **13.** to fill or choke up. **—v.i. 14.** to eat greedily. **—gorg′er,** *n.*

gor·geous (gôr′jəs), *adj.* **1.** splendid or sumptuous in appearance, coloring, etc.; magnificent or beautiful. **2.** extremely pleasant or enjoyable: *I had a gorgeous time.* **—gor′geous·ly,** *adv.* **—gor′geous·ness,** *n.*

gor·get (gôr′jit), *n.* **1.** a patch on the throat of a bird or other animal, distinguished by its color, texture, etc. **2.** a piece of armor for the throat. **3.** a wimple of the Middle Ages, worn with the ends fastened in the hair. **4.** any of various coverings or trimmings for the neck or shoulders, as a collar or ruff, formerly worn by men and women. **—gor′get·ed,** *adj.*

Gor·gon (gôr′gən), *n.* **1.** any of three sister monsters of Greek myth, who had snakes for hair and whose appearance turned anyone looking at them into stone. **2.** (*l.c.*) a mean, ugly, or repulsive woman. **—Gor·go′ni·an** (-gō′nē ən), *adj.*

gor·go·ni·an (gôr gō′nē ən), *n.* **1.** any colonial coral of the order Gorgonacea, as the sea fan, forming a branching axial skeleton. **—adj. 2.** belonging or pertaining to the Gorgonacea.

Gor·gon·zo·la (gôr′gən zō′lə), *n.* a strong, semisoft Italian cheese veined with mold.

go·ril·la (gə ril′ə), *n., pl.* **-las. 1.** the largest anthropoid ape, *Gorilla gorilla,* of equatorial Africa, vegetarian and mainly terrestrial. **2.** an ugly or brutish person. **3.** a hoodlum or thug. **—go·ril′li·an, go·ril′line** (-īn, -in), *adj.* **—go·ril′loid,** *adj.*

Gö·ring or **Goe·ring** (gâr′ing, gûr′-), *n.* **Hermann Wilhelm,** 1893–1946, German field marshal and Nazi party leader.

gor·mand (gôr′mənd), *n.* GOURMAND.

gor·mand·ize (gôr′mən dīz′), *v.i., v.t.,* **-ized, -iz·ing.** to eat greedily or ravenously. **—gor′mand·iz′er,** *n.*

gorp (gôrp), *n.* a mixture of nuts, raisins, chocolate chips, etc., eaten as a high-energy snack, as by hikers.

gorse (gôrs), *n.* any spiny European evergreen shrub of the genus *Ulex,* of the legume family, having rudimentary leaves and yellow flowers. Also called **furze. —gors′y,** *adj.*

gosh (gosh), *interj.* (used as an exclamation of surprise or as a mild oath.)

gos·hawk (gos′hôk′), *n.* any of several robust short-winged hawks, esp. *Accipiter gentilis,* of North America and Eurasia.

Go·shen (gō′shən), *n.* a pastoral region in Lower Egypt, occupied by the Israelites before the Exodus. Gen. 45:10.

gos·ling (goz′ling), *n.* **1.** a young goose. **2.** a foolish, inexperienced person.

gos·pel (gos′pəl), *n.* **1.** the teachings of Jesus and the apostles; the Christian revelation. **2.** the story of Christ's life and teachings, esp. as contained in the first four books of the New Testament, namely Matthew, Mark, Luke, and John. **3.** (*usu. cap.*) any of these four books. **4.** Also called **gos′pel truth′.** something absolutely or unquestionably true. **5.** a doctrine regarded as of prime importance: *political gospel.* **6.** glad tidings, esp. concerning salvation and the kingdom of God. **7.** (*often cap.*) an extract from one of the four Gospels forming part of a church service. **8.** GOSPEL MUSIC. **—adj. 9.** of, pertaining to, or proclaiming the gospel or its teachings. **10.** in accordance with the gospel; evangelical. **11.** of, pertaining to, employing, or performing gospel music.

gos′pel mu′sic, *n.* impassioned rhythmic spiritual music influential in the development of soul music and rhythm and blues.

gos·sa·mer (gos′ə mər), *n.* **1.** a fine, filmy cobweb found on grass or bushes or floating in the air in calm weather. **2.** a thread or a web of this substance. **3.** any thin, light fabric, esp. one used for veils. **4.** something extremely light, flimsy, or delicate. **—adj. 5.** Also, **gos·sa·mer·y** (gos′ə mə rē). of or like gossamer; thin and light.

gos·sip (gos′əp), *n., v.,* **-siped** or **-sipped, -sip·ing** or **-sip·ping. —n. 1.** idle talk or rumor, esp. about the private affairs of others. **2.** light, familiar talk or writing. **3.** Also, **gos′sip·er, gos′sip·per.** a person given to tattling or idle talk. **—v.i. 4.** to talk idly, esp. about the affairs of others. **—gos′sip·y,** *adj.*

gos·sip·mon·ger (gos′əp mung′gər, -mong′-), *n.* a person given to gossiping.

got (got), *v.* **1.** a pt. and pp. of GET. **2.** *Informal.* have got. **—auxiliary verb. 3.** *Informal.* must; have got (fol. by an infinitive).

got·cha (goch′ə), *interj. Pron. Spelling.* got you (used to indicate comprehension, to exultingly point out a blunder, etc.).

Goth (goth), *n.* **1.** a member of a Germanic people settled N of the Black Sea in the 3rd century A.D., who, with the collapse of the Roman Empire, established kingdoms in Spain and Italy. Compare OSTROGOTH, VISIGOTH. **2.** a person of no refinement; barbarian.

Goth·am (goth′əm, gō′thəm), *n.* a nickname for New York City. **—Goth′am·ite′,** *n.*

goth·ic (goth′ik), *adj.* **1.** (*usu. cap.*) **a.** of or pertaining to a style of architecture prevalent in W Europe from the mid-12th to the 16th century, characterized by pointed arches, ribbed vaulting, flying buttresses, rich ornamentation, and a progressive lightening of structure. **b.** of or pertaining to a style of architecture reviving or imitating Gothic forms and motifs. **2.** (*cap.*) of or pertaining to the Goths or their language. **3.** (*usu. cap.*) of or pertaining to the Middle Ages; medieval. **4.** (*sometimes cap.*) barbarous or crude. **5.** (*often cap.*) of or pertaining to a style of literature characterized by a gloomy setting, mysterious, sinister, or violent events, and, in contemporary fiction, an imperiled heroine. **—n. 6.** (*usu. cap.*) the arts, crafts, or architecture of the Gothic period. **7.** (*cap.*) the extinct East Germanic language of the Goths, preserved esp. in Ulfilas' 4th-century translation of the Bible. *Abbr.:* Goth. **8.** (*often cap.*) a novel, play, film, etc., in the gothic style. **9.** (*often cap.*) **a.** a square-cut printing type without serifs or hairlines. **b.** BLACK LETTER. **—goth′i·cal·ly,** *adv.* **—goth′ic·ness, goth·ic·i·ty** (go this′i tē), *n.*

got·ta (got′ə), *Pron. Spelling.* got to.

got·ten (got′n), *v.* a pp. of GET.

Gou·da (gou′də, gōō′-), *n.* **1.** a city in the W Netherlands, NE of Rotterdam. 62,321. **2.** a semisoft to hard, yellowish Dutch cheese made from whole or partly skimmed cow's milk.

gouge (gouj), *n., v.,* **gouged, goug·ing. —n. 1.** a chisel having a partly cylindrical blade with the bevel on either the concave or the convex side. **2.** an act of gouging. **3.** a groove or hole made by gouging. **4.** an act of extortion; swindle. **—v.t. 5.** to scoop out or turn with or as if with a gouge. **6.** to dig or force out with or as if with a gouge (often fol. by *out*): *to gouge out an eye.* **7.** to make a gouge in: *to gouge one's leg.* **8.** to extort from, swindle, or overcharge. **—v.i. 9.** to engage in extortion or swindling. **—goug′er,** *n.*

gou·lash (gōō′läsh, -lash), *n.* **1.** a stew of beef or veal and vegetables, seasoned with paprika. **2.** a heterogeneous mixture; hodgepodge; jumble. [< Hungarian *gulyás,* short for *gulyáshús* herdsman's meat]

gou·ra·mi (gōō rä′mē), *n., pl.* (*esp. collectively*) **-mi,** (*esp. for kinds or species*) **-mis.** any of various tropical freshwater labyrinth fishes, of Asia and Africa, esp. *Osphronemus goramy,* a large Oriental food fish, and others popular for home aquariums.

gourd (gôrd, gōrd, gŏŏrd), *n.* **1.** the hard-shelled fruit of any plant belonging to the gourd family, esp. of the genus *Cucurbita.* **2.** a plant bearing such a fruit. **3.** a dried and excavated gourd shell used as a bottle, dipper, flask, etc. **—Idiom. 4. out of** or **off one's gourd,** *Slang.* out of one's mind; crazy.

gour·mand (gŏŏr mänd′, gŏŏr′mənd), *n.* **1.** one who is fond of good eating, often to excess. **2.** a gourmet; epicure. [< Old French *gormant* a glutton] **—gour′mand·ism,** *n.*

gour•man•dize (gŏŏr′mən dīz′), *v.i.*, **-dized, -diz•ing.** to enjoy good food and drink, esp. in lavish quantity. —**gour′man•diz′er,** *n.*

gour•met (gŏŏr mā′, gŏŏr′mā), *n.* **1.** a connoisseur of fine food and drink; epicure. —*adj.* **2.** of, characteristic of, or designed for gourmets. **3.** of or involving fancy or exotic foods.

gout (gout), *n.* **1.** a painful inflammation, esp. of the big toe, characterized by an excess of uric acid in the blood that leads to crystalline deposits in the small joints. **2.** a mass or splash, as of blood; spurt.

gov•ern (guv′ərn), *v.t.* **1.** to rule by right of authority, as a sovereign does: *to govern a nation.* **2.** to exercise a directing or restraining influence over; guide: *the motives governing a decision.* **3.** to hold in check; control: *to govern one's temper.* **4.** to serve as or constitute a law for: *the principles governing a case.* **5.** (of a word or class of words) to require the use of a particular form of (another word or class). **6.** to regulate the speed of (an engine) with a governor. —*v.i.* **7.** to exercise the function of government. **8.** to have predominating influence. —**gov′ern•a•ble,** *adj.* —**gov′ern•a•bil′i•ty, gov′ern•a•ble•ness,** *n.*

gov•ern•ance (guv′ər nəns), *n.* **1.** government; exercise of authority; control. **2.** a method or system of government or management.

gov•ern•ess (guv′ər nis), *n.* a woman employed in a private household to take charge of a child's upbringing and education. —**gov′er•ness•y,** *adj.*

gov•ern•ment (guv′ərn mənt, -ər mənt), *n.* **1.** the political direction and control exercised over the actions of the members, citizens, or inhabitants of communities, societies, and states; direction of the affairs of a state, community, etc. **2.** the form or system of rule by which a state, community, etc., is governed: *monarchical government.* **3.** the governing body of persons in a state, community, etc.; administration. **4.** a branch or service of the supreme authority of a state or nation, taken as representing the whole. **5.** (in some parliamentary systems, as that of the United Kingdom) **a.** the particular group of persons forming the cabinet at any given time: *The Prime Minister has formed a new government.* **b.** the parliament along with the cabinet. **6.** direction; control; management; rule. **7.** a district governed; province. **8.** POLITICAL SCIENCE. **9.** a relationship between two words in a sentence such that the use of one word requires the other to be of a particular form. —***Saying.*** **10. Government of the people, by the people, and for the people,** democracy: a saying made popular by Abraham Lincoln in the Gettysburg Address (1863). —**gov′ern•men′tal** (-men′tl), *adj.* —**gov′ern•men′tal•ly,** *adv.* —**Usage.** See COLLECTIVE NOUN.

gov•ern•ment-in-ex•ile (guv′ərn mənt in eg′zīl, -ek′sīl, -ər mənt-), *n.* a government temporarily moved to or formed in a foreign land by exiles who hope to establish that government in their native country after its liberation.

gov•er•nor (guv′ər nər, -ə nər), *n.* **1.** the executive head of a state in the U.S. **2.** a person charged with the direction or control of an institution, society, etc.: *the governors of a bank; the governor of a prison.* **3.** a ruler or chief magistrate appointed to govern a province, town, fort, or the like. **4.** a device for maintaining uniform speed (in a machine, engine, etc.) regardless of changes of load, as by regulating the supply of fuel or working fluid. —**gov′er•nor•ship′,** *n.*

Govt. or **govt.,** government.

gown (goun), *n.* **1.** a woman's dress or robe, esp. one that is full-length. **2.** a nightgown or similar garment. **3.** DRESSING GOWN. **4.** EVENING GOWN. **5.** a loose, flowing outer garment in any of various forms, worn by men and women as distinctive of office or profession. **6.** a protective overgarment, as one worn when performing surgery. **7.** the student and teaching body in a university or college town.

Go•ya (goi′ə), *n.* **Francisco de** (*Francisco José de Goya y Lucientes*), 1746–1828, Spanish painter.

gp. or **Gp.,** group.

GP or **G.P., 1.** General Practitioner. **2.** General Purpose. **3.** Gloria Patri. **4.** Graduate in Pharmacy. **5.** Grand Prix.

GPA, grade point average.

gpd or **GPD** or **g.p.d.,** gallons per day.

gph or **GPH** or **g.p.h.,** gallons per hour.

gpm or **GPM** or **g.p.m.,** gallons per minute.

GPO or **G.P.O., 1.** general post office. **2.** Government Printing Office.

gps or **GPS** or **g.p.s.,** gallons per second.

GPU or **G.P.U.** (gā′pā′ōō′, jē′pē′yōō′), *n.* the Soviet secret-police organization (1922–23).

GQ, General Quarters.

grab (grab), *v.,* **grabbed, grab•bing,** *n.* —*v.t.* **1.** to seize suddenly, eagerly, or roughly; snatch. **2.** to take illegal possession of; seize forcibly or unscrupulously: *to grab land.* **3.** to obtain and consume quickly: *Let's grab a sandwich.* **4.** *Informal.* **a.** to cause a reaction in; affect: *How does my idea grab you?* **b.** to arouse the interest or excitement of. —*v.i.* **5.** to make a grasping or clutching motion. **6.** (of brakes, a clutch, etc.) to take hold suddenly or with a jolting motion. —*n.* **7.** a sudden, eager grasp or snatch. **8.** seizure or acquisition by violent or unscrupulous means. **9.** something that is grabbed. **10.** a mechanical device for gripping objects. **11.** the capacity to hold or adhere. —***Idiom.*** **12. up for grabs,** available to whoever expends the necessary energy, money, or ingenuity first. —**grab′ber,** *n.*

grab′ bag′, *n.* **1.** a bag or container from which a person, as at a party, draws a gift without knowing what it is. **2.** any miscellaneous collection.

grab•by (grab′ē), *adj.,* **-bi•er, -bi•est. 1.** grasping; greedy. **2.** *Informal.* provoking immediate attention or interest; arresting. **3.** tending to grab or adhere.

grace (grās), *n., v.,* **graced, grac•ing.** —*n.* **1.** elegance or beauty of form, manner, motion, or action. **2.** attractive ease and smoothness of movement. **3.** a pleasing or attractive quality or endowment. **4.** favor or goodwill. **5.** a manifestation of favor, esp. by a superior. **6.** mercy; clemency; pardon. **7.** favor shown in granting a delay or temporary immunity. **8.** GRACE PERIOD. **9. a.** the freely given, unmerited favor and love of God. **b.** the influence or spirit of God operating in humans. **c.** a virtue or excellence of divine origin. **d.** the condition of being in God's favor or one of the elect. **10.** decency or propriety: *to have the grace to feel ashamed.* **11.** a short prayer before or after a meal, in which a blessing is asked and thanks are given. **12.** (*cap.*) a title used in addressing or mentioning a duke, duchess, or archbishop (usu. prec. by *Your, His,* etc.). **13. Graces,** the ancient Greek and Roman goddesses of beauty and kindness, usu. represented as three in number. —*v.t.* **14.** to lend or add grace to; adorn: *Many paintings graced the walls.* **15.** to favor or honor: *to grace an occasion with one's presence.* —***Idiom.*** **16. fall from grace, a.** to relapse into sin or disfavor. Gal. 5:4. **b.** to lose favor with those in power; become discredited. **17. in someone's good** (or **bad**) **graces,** regarded with favor (or disfavor) by someone. **18. with bad grace,** reluctantly; grudgingly. **19. with good grace,** willingly; ungrudgingly. —**grace′ful,** *adj.* —**grace′ful•ly,** *adv.* —**grace′ful•ness,** *n*

Grace′ Abound′ing to the Chief′ of Sin′ners, a spiritual autobiography (1666) by John Bunyan.

Grace•land (grās′lənd), *n.* a mansion and grounds in Nashville, Tenn., the former home of Elvis Presley.

grace•less (grās′lis), *adj.* **1.** lacking grace, pleasing elegance, or charm. **2.** without any sense of right or propriety. —**grace′less•ly,** *adv.* —**grace′less•ness,** *n.*

grace′ pe′riod, *n.* an allowance of time after a payment of a loan, insurance premium, etc., becomes due before one is subject to penalties or before the loan, policy, etc., is canceled.

gra•cious (grā′shəs), *adj.* **1.** pleasantly kind, benevolent, or courteous. **2.** characterized by good taste, comfort, ease, or luxury: *gracious suburban living.* **3.** indulgent or beneficent in a pleasantly condescending way, esp. to inferiors. **4.** merciful or compassionate: *our gracious king.* —*interj.* **5.** (used as an exclamation of surprise, relief, dismay, etc.) —**gra′cious•ly,** *adv.* —**gra′cious•ness,** *n.*

grack•le (grak′əl), *n.* **1.** any of several long-tailed New World blackbirds, esp. of the genus *Quiscalus,* as the common North American species *Q. quiscula,* having iridescent black plumage. **2.** any of several Old World birds of the family Sturnidae, esp. certain mynas.

grad (grad), *n. Informal.* a graduate.

grad•a•ble (grā′də bəl), *adj.* **1.** capable of being graded. **2.** (of an adjective or adverb) denoting a quality that can be present in varying degree and therefore capable of comparison or intensification, as *heavy* or *tall* but not *atomic* or *dental.* —**grad′a•bil′i•ty,** *n.*

gra•date (grā′dāt), *v.,* **-dat•ed, -dat•ing.** —*v.i.* **1.** to pass by gradual or imperceptible degrees, as one color into another. —*v.t.* **2.** to cause to gradate. **3.** to arrange in grades.

gra•da•tion (grā dā′shən), *n.* **1.** a process or change taking place through a series of stages, by degrees, or gradually. **2.** a stage, degree, or grade in such a series. **3.** the passing of one tint or shade of color to another, or one surface to another, by very small degrees. **4.** the act of grading. **5.** ABLAUT. **6.** the leveling of a land surface, resulting from the concerted action of erosion and deposition. —**gra•da′tion•al,** *adj.* —**gra•da′tion•al•ly,** *adv.*

grade (grād), *n., v.,* **grad•ed, grad•ing.** —*n.* **1.** a degree or step in a scale, as of rank, advancement, quality, value, or intensity. **2.** a class of persons or things of the same relative rank, quality, etc. **3.** a step or stage in a course or process. **4.** a single division of a school classified, usu. by year, according to the age or progress of the pupils. **5.** the pupils in such a division. **6. grades,** elementary school (usu. prec. by *the*). **7.** a letter, number, or other symbol indicating the relative quality of a student's work; mark. **8.** a classification or standard of food based on quality, size, etc.: *grade A milk.* **9.** inclination with the horizontal of a road, railroad, etc.; slope. **10.** the level at which the ground intersects the foundation of a building. **11.** an animal resulting from a cross between a parent of ordinary stock and one of a pure breed. —*v.t.* **12.** to arrange in a series of grades; class; sort: *a machine that grades eggs.* **13.** to determine the grade of. **14.** to assign a grade to (a student's work); mark. **15.** to cause to pass by degrees, as from one color or shade to another. **16.** to reduce to a level or to practicable degrees of inclination: *to grade a road.* **17.** to cross (an ordinary or low-grade animal) with an animal of a pure or superior breed. —*v.i.* **18.** to incline; slant or slope. **19.** to be of a particular grade or quality. **20.** to pass by degrees, as from one color or shade to another; blend. —***Idiom.*** **21. at grade,** on the same level: *a railroad crossing a highway at grade.* **22. make the grade,** to attain a specific goal; succeed. **23. up to grade,** of the desired or required quality.

-grade, a combining form meaning "walking, moving," in the manner or by the means specified by the initial element: *plantigrade.*

grade′ cross′ing, *n.* an intersection of a railroad track and another track, a road, etc., at the same level.

grade′ infla′tion, *n.* the awarding of higher grades than students deserve either to maintain a school's academic reputation or as a result of diminished teacher expectations.

grade′ point′, *n.* a numerical equivalent of a letter grade that is multiplied by the number of credits for the course taken.

grade′ point′ av′erage, *n.* a measure of scholastic attainment computed by dividing the total number of grade points received by the total number of credits taken.

grade′ school′, *n.* ELEMENTARY SCHOOL. —**grade′-school′er,** *n.*

gra·di·ent (grā′dē ənt), *n.* **1.** the degree of inclination of a highway, railroad, etc., or the rate of ascent or descent of a stream or river. **2.** an inclined surface; grade; ramp.

grad·u·al (graj′ʊ əl), *adj.* **1.** taking place, changing, moving, etc., by small degrees or little by little: *gradual improvement.* **2.** rising or descending at an even, moderate inclination: *a gradual slope.* —*n.* **3. a.** an antiphon sung between the Epistle and the Gospel in the Eucharistic service. **b.** a book containing the words and music of the parts of the liturgy that are sung by the choir. —**grad′u·al·ly,** *adv.* —**grad′u·al·ness,** *n.*

grad·u·al·ism (graj′ʊ ə liz′əm), *n.* **1.** the principle or policy of achieving some goal by gradual steps rather than by drastic change. **2.** a tenet of geology or evolutionary theory maintaining that change takes place gradually and continuously over long periods of geological time. —**grad′u·al·ist,** *n., adj.* —**grad′u·al·is′tic,** *adj.*

grad·u·ate (*n., adj.* graj′ʊ it, -āt′; *v.* -āt′), *n., adj., v.,* **-at·ed, -at·ing.** —*n.* **1.** a person who has received a degree or diploma on completing a course of study at a university, college, or school. **2.** a student who holds the bachelor's or the first professional degree and is studying for an advanced degree. —*adj.* **3.** of, pertaining to, or involved in academic study beyond the first or bachelor's degree: *a graduate student.* **4.** having an academic degree or diploma. —*v.i.* **5.** to receive a degree or diploma on completing a course of study: *to graduate from college.* **6.** to pass by degrees; change gradually. —*v.t.* **7.** to confer a degree upon or grant a diploma to. **8.** to receive a degree or diploma from: *to graduate college.* **9.** to arrange in grades or gradations; establish gradation in. —**grad′u·a′tor,** *n.* —**Usage.** GRADUATE followed by *from* is the most common construction today: *to graduate from Yale.* The passive form, once considered to be the only correct pattern, occurs infrequently today: *to be graduated from Yale.* Although condemned by some as nonstandard, the use of GRADUATE as a transitive verb meaning "to receive a degree or diploma from" is increasing in both speech and writing: *to graduate high school.*

grad·u·at·ed (graj′ʊ ā′tid), *adj.* characterized by or arranged in degrees, esp. successively, as according to height, depth, or difficulty. **2.** marked with divisions or units of measurement. **3.** (of a tax) increasing along with the taxable base: *a graduated income tax.*

grad′uate school′, *n.* a school, usu. a division of a university, offering courses leading to degrees more advanced than the bachelor's degree.

grad·u·a·tion (graj′ʊ ā′shən), *n.* **1.** an act of graduating or the state of being graduated. **2.** the ceremony of conferring degrees or diplomas, as at a college or school. **3.** arrangement in degrees, levels, or ranks. **4. a.** a mark on an instrument or vessel for indicating degree or quantity. **b.** such marks collectively.

graf·fi·ti (grə fē′tē), *n.* **1.** pl. of GRAFFITO. **2.** (*used with a pl. v.*) markings, as initials, slogans, or drawings, written or sketched on a sidewalk, wall, or the like. **3.** (*used with a sing. v.*) such markings as a whole or as constituting a particular group: *Not much graffiti appears there these days.* —**graf·fi′tist,** *n.*

graf·fi·to (grə fē′tō), *n., pl.* **-ti** (-tē). **1.** an ancient drawing or writing scratched on a wall or other surface. **2.** a single example of graffiti.

graft¹ (graft, gräft), *n.* **1. a.** a bud, shoot, or scion of a plant inserted in a groove, slit, or the like in a stem or trunk of another plant in which it continues to grow. **b.** the plant resulting from such an operation. **c.** the place where the scion is inserted **2.** a portion of living tissue surgically transplanted from one part of an individual to another, or from one individual to another, for its adhesion and growth. **3.** an act of grafting. —*v.t.* **4.** to insert (a graft) into a tree or other plant; insert a scion of (one plant) into another plant. **5.** to cause (a plant) to reproduce through grafting. **6.** to transplant (a portion of living tissue, as of skin or bone) as a graft. **7.** to attach as if by grafting. —*v.i.* **8.** to insert scions from one plant into another. —**graft′er,** *n.*

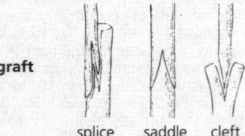

graft

splice   saddle   cleft

graft² (graft, gräft), *n.* **1.** the acquisition of money or advantage by dishonest or unfair means, esp. through the abuse of one's position or influence, as in politics. **2.** the gain or advantage acquired. —*v.t.* **3.** to obtain by graft. —*v.i.* **4.** to practice graft. —**graft′er,** *n.*

gra·ham (grā′əm, gram), *adj.* made of graham flour.

Gra·ham (grā′əm, gram), *n.* **1. Martha,** 1894–1991, U.S. dancer and choreographer. **2. William Franklin** (*"Billy"*), born 1918, U.S. evangelist.

gra′ham crack′er, *n.* a semisweet cracker made chiefly of whole-wheat flour.

Gra·hame (grā′əm), *n.* **Kenneth,** 1859–1932, Scottish writer.

grail (grāl), *n.* **1.** (*usu. cap.*) a cup or chalice that in medieval legend was associated with unusual powers and was much sought after by knights: identified with the cup used at the Last Supper and given to Joseph of Arimathea. **2.** (*sometimes cap.*) any greatly desired and sought-after objective. Also called **Holy Grail.**

grain (grān), *n.* **1.** a small, hard seed, esp. the seed of a food plant such as wheat, corn, rye, oats, rice, or millet. **2.** the gathered seed of food plants, esp. of cereal plants. **3.** such plants collectively. **4.** any small, hard particle, as of sand, gold, pepper, or gunpowder. **5.** the smallest unit of weight in the U.S. and British systems, equal to 0. 002285 ounce (0.0648 gram). **6.** the smallest possible amount of anything: *a grain of truth.* **7.** the arrangement or direction of the fibers in wood, meat, etc., or the pattern resulting from this. **8. a.** the side of leather from which the hair has been removed. **b.** the pattern or markings on this side. **9. a.** the fibers or yarn in a piece of fabric. **b.** the direction of threads in a woven fabric in relation to the selvage. **10.** the lamination or cleavage of stone, coal, etc. **11.** any of the individual crystalline particles composing a metal. **12.** a unit of weight equal to 50 milligrams or ¼ carat, used for pearls and sometimes diamonds. **13.** the size of constituent particles of any substance; texture. **14.** a granular texture or appearance: *a stone of coarse grain.* **15.** a state of crystallization: *boiled to the grain.* **16.** temper or natural character: *two brothers of similar grain.* —*v.t.* **17.** to form into grains; granulate. **18.** to give a granular appearance to. **19.** to paint in imitation of the grain of wood, stone, etc. **20.** to feed grain to (an animal). **21. a.** to remove the hair from (skins). **b.** to soften and raise the grain of (leather). —*Idiom.* **22. against the** or **one's grain,** in opposition to one's very nature; fundamentally displeasing to one.

grain′ al′cohol, *n.* ALCOHOL (def. 1).

grain′ el′evator, *n.* ELEVATOR (def. 4).

grain′ sor′ghum, *n.* any of several varieties of sorghum grown for grain and forage.

grain·y (grā′nē), *adj.,* **grain·i·er, grain·i·est. 1.** resembling grain; granular. **2.** full of grains or grain. **3.** (of a photographic negative or positive) having a granular appearance. —**grain′i·ness,** *n.*

gram¹ (gram), *n.* a metric unit of mass or weight equal to 15.432 grains; ¹/₁₀₀₀ of a kilogram. *Abbr.:* g, gr, gr.

gram² (gram), *n.* any of several beans, as the chickpea or mung bean, used as food.

-gram¹, a combining form meaning "something written, drawn, or plotted" (*diagram; epigram; histogram*); "a written or drawn symbol or sequence of symbols" (*ideogram; pentagram*); "a message" (*telegram*); "an image or graphic record made by an instrument or as part of a diagnostic procedure" (*electrocardiogram; spectrogram*). Compare -GRAPH.

-gram², a combining form of GRAM: *kilogram.*

-gram³, a combining form extracted from TELEGRAM, used in the titles of newsletters, direct-mail solicitations, etc. (*culturegram; electiongram*) or the names, sometimes humorous, of personally delivered messages or gifts (*Candygram*).

gram., **1.** grammar. **2.** grammatical.

gra·ma (grä′mə), *n.* any of various New World grasses of the genus *Bouteloua,* as *B. gracilis,* used as a pasture grass. Also called **gra′ma grass′.**

gra·ma·dan (grä mä′dän, grä′mä dän′, gräm dän′), *n.* the practice advocated by followers of Mahatma Gandhi in which village landowners in India transfer the title to and the management of their property to a village assembly that represents the interests of all the villagers. Also, **gram·dan** (gräm dän′).

gram′ at′om, *n.* the quantity of an element whose weight in grams is numerically equal to the atomic weight of the element. Also called **gram′-atom′ic weight′.**

gram′ cal′orie, *n.* CALORIE (def. 1a).

gram·mar (gram′ər), *n.* **1.** the study of the way the sentences of a language are constructed, esp. the study of morphology and syntax. **2.** these features or constructions themselves: *English grammar.* **3.** an account of these features or constructions: *a grammar of English.* **4.** (in generative grammar) a device, as a set of rules, whose output is all the sentences that are permissible in a given language, while excluding all those that are not permissible. **5.** the exposition or establishment of rules based on norms of correct and incorrect language usage; prescriptive grammar. **6.** knowledge or usage of the preferred or prescribed forms in speaking or writing: *She said his grammar was terrible.* **7.** a book treating such elements. —**gram·mar′i·an,** *n.*

gram′mar school′, *n.* **1.** an elementary school. **2.** *Brit.* a secondary school corresponding to a U.S. high school. **3.** a secondary school in which Latin and Greek are among the principal subjects taught.

gram·mat·i·cal (grə mat′i kəl), *adj.* **1.** of or pertaining to grammar. **2.** conforming to the rules of grammar or standard usage: *a grammatical sentence.* —**gram·mat′i·cal·ly,** *adv.*

gram·mat·i·cal·ize (grə mat′i kə līz′), *v.t.,* **-ized, -iz·ing.** to represent (semantic features) by grammatical means. —**gram·mat′i·cal·i·za′tion,** *n.*

grammat′ical mean′ing, *n.* the meaning expressed by an inflectional ending or some other grammatical device, as word order. Compare LEXICAL MEANING.

gram·ma·tol·o·gy (gram′ə tol′ə jē), *n.* the scientific study of systems of writing.

gram′ mol′ecule, *n.* MOLE⁴.

Gram·my (gram′ē), *n., pl.* **-mys, -mies.** one of a group of awards given annually by the National Academy of Recording Arts and Sciences for outstanding achievement in various technical and artistic categories.

gram·o·phone (gram′ə fōn′), *n. Chiefly Brit.* PHONOGRAPH. —**gram′o·phon′ic** (-fon′ik), **gram′o·phon′i·cal,** *adj.* —**gram′o·phon′i·cal·ly,** *adv.*

gram·pus (gram′pəs), *n., pl.* **-pus·es. 1.** a large dolphin, *Grampus griseus,* of northern seas. **2.** any of various other large dolphins, as the killer whale, *Orcinus (Orca) orca.* **3.** a giant whipscorpion, *Mastigoproctur giganteus,* of the southern U.S. and Mexico.

Gram′s′ meth′od (gramz), *n.* (*sometimes l.c.*) a method of characterizing bacteria that involves staining a slide of fixed specimens with gentian violet, washing with alcohol, and applying a counterstain.

Gra·na·da (grə nä′də), *n.* **1.** a medieval kingdom along the Mediterranean coast of S Spain. **2.** a city in S Spain: the capital of this former kingdom and last stronghold of the Moors in Spain; site of the Alhambra. 280,592. **3.** a city in SW Nicaragua, near Lake Nicaragua. 88,636.

gran·a·dil·la (gran′ə dil′ə), *n., pl.* **-las. 1.** the edible fruit of certain passionflowers, esp. *Passiflora quadrangularis,* of tropical America. **2.** any of the plants yielding these fruits.

gra·na·ry (grā′nə rē, gran′ə-), *n., pl.* **-ries. 1.** a storehouse or repository for grain. **2.** a region that produces great quantities of grain.

grand (grand), *adj.,* **grand·er, grand·est,** *n., pl.* **grands** for 10, **grand** for 11. —*adj.* **1.** impressive in size, appearance, or general effect: *grand mountain scenery.* **2.** stately; dignified: *a grand and regal manner.* **3.** highly ambitious or idealistic: *grand ideas for bettering the political situation.* **4.** esteemed; revered: *a grand old man.* **5.** high in rank or official dignity. **6.** of great importance, distinction, or pretension: *grand personages.* **7.** complete; comprehensive: *a grand total.* **8.** pretending to grandeur: *acting awfully grand since her promotion.* **9.** first-rate; splendid: *had a grand time.* —*n.* **10.** GRAND PIANO. **11.** *Informal.* a thousand dollars. —**grand′ly,** *adv.* —**grand′ness,** *n.*

grand-, a combining form used in kinship terms with the meaning "one generation more remote" than the relation denoted by the base word: *grandmother; grandnephew.*

Grand′ Ar′my of the Repub′lic, *n.* an organization, founded in 1866, composed of men who served in the Union forces during the Civil War. *Abbr.*: GAR, G.A.R.

grand·aunt (grand′ant′, -änt′), *n.* an aunt of one's father or mother; great-aunt.

grand·ba·by (gran′bā′bē, grand′-), *n., pl.* **-bies.** an infant grandchild.

Grand′ Banks′ (or **Bank′**), *n.* an extensive shoal SE of Newfoundland: fishing grounds. 350 mi. (565 km) long; 40,000 sq. mi. (104,000 sq. km).

Grand′ Canal′, *n.* **1.** a canal in E China, extending S from Tianjin to Hangzhou. 900 mi. (1450 km) long. **2.** a canal in Venice, Italy, forming the main city thoroughfare.

Grand′ Can′yon, *n.* a gorge of the Colorado River in N Arizona. over 200 mi. (320 km) long; 1 mi. (1.6 km) deep.

grand·child (gran′chīld′), *n., pl.* **-chil·dren.** a child of one's son or daughter.

grand·dad (gran′dad′), *n. Informal.* GRANDFATHER.

grand·dad·dy (gran′dad′ē), *n., pl.* **-dies.** *Informal.* GRANDFATHER.

grand·daugh·ter (gran′dô′tər), *n.* a daughter of one's son or daughter.

grand′ design′, *n.* a master plan or overall strategy.

grand′ duch′ess, *n.* **1.** the wife or widow of a grand duke. **2.** a woman who governs a grand duchy in her own right. **3.** a daughter of a czar or of a czar's son.

grand′ duch′y, *n.* a territory ruled by a grand duke or grand duchess.

grand′ duke′, *n.* **1.** the sovereign of a grand duchy, ranking next below a king. **2.** a son or grandson of a czar. —**grand′-du′cal,** *adj.*

grande dame (grän′ däm′, gränd′), *n., pl.* **grandes dames** (grän′ dämz′, gränd′). a usu. older woman of dignified bearing or great accomplishment.

gran·dee (gran dē′), *n.* a man of high social position or eminence, esp. a Spanish or Portuguese nobleman. —**gran·dee′ship,** *n.*

gran·deur (gran′jər, -jŏŏr), *n.* **1.** the quality or state of being grand: *the grandeur of the Rocky Mountains.* **2.** an instance of something that is grand.

grand·fa·ther (grand′fä′ᵗhər, gran′-), *n.* **1.** the father of one's father or mother. **2.** a forefather; ancestor. —**grand′fa′ther·ly,** *adj.*

grand′father clause′, *n.* **1.** a clause in the constitutions of some Southern states before 1915 intended to permit whites to vote while disfranchising blacks: it exempted the descendants of those who voted before 1867 from new rigid qualifications. **2.** any legal provision that exempts a business, class of persons, etc., from a new regulation that would affect prior rights and privileges.

grand·father (or **grand′father's)clock′,** *n.* a pendulum floor clock having a case as tall as or taller than a person; tall-case clock.

grand′ fina′le, *n.* an elaborate conclusion, as of a performance.

gran·di·flo·ra (gran′də flôr′ə, -flōr′ə), *n., pl.* **-ras.** any of several plant varieties or hybrids characterized by large showy flowers, as certain long-stemmed roses.

gran·dil·o·quence (gran dil′ə kwəns), *n.* speech that is lofty in tone and often pompous or bombastic. —**gran·dil′o·quent,** *adj.* —**gran·dil′o·quent·ly,** *adv.*

gran·di·ose (gran′dē ōs′), *adj.* **1.** affectedly grand; pompous: *grandiose words.* **2.** more complicated than necessary: *a grandiose scheme.* **3.** grand in an imposing way. **4.** *Psychiatry.* having an exaggerated belief in one's importance, sometimes reaching delusional proportions. —**gran·di·ose′ly,** *adv.* —**gran·di·ose′ness, gran·di·os′i·ty** (-os′i tē), *n.*

grand′ ju′ry, *n.* a jury designated to determine if a law has been violated and whether the evidence warrants prosecution. Compare PETTY JURY.

grand′ lar′ceny, *n.* larceny in which the value of the goods taken is above a certain legally specified amount. Compare PETTY LARCENY.

grand·ma (gran′mä′, -mô′, grand′-, gram′-), *n., pl.* **-mas.** *Informal.* GRANDMOTHER.

grand mal (gran′ mäl′, -mal′, grand′), *n.* severe epilepsy.

grand·moth·er (gran′muᵗh′ər, grand′-, gram′-), *n.* **1.** the mother of one's father or mother. **2.** a female ancestor. —**grand′moth′er·ly,** *adj.* —**grand′moth′er·li·ness,** *n.*

grand′mother (or **grand′mother's) clock′,** *n.* a pendulum clock similar to a grandfather clock but shorter.

grand·neph·ew (gran′nef′yōō, -nev′yōō, grand′-), *n.* a son of one's nephew or niece.

grand·niece (gran′nēs′, grand′-), *n.* a daughter of one's nephew or niece.

Grand′ Old′ Par′ty, *n.* See GOP.

Grand′ Ole′ Op′ry (ōl′ op′rē), a successful radio show from Nashville, Tenn., first broadcast on Nov. 28, 1925, noted for its playing of and continuing importance to country music.

grand′ op′era, *n.* a serious, usu. tragic, opera in which most of the text is set to music.

grand·pa (gran′pä′, -pô′, grand′-, gram′-), *n., pl.* **-pas.** *Informal.* GRANDFATHER.

grand·par·ent (gran′pâr′ənt, -par′-, grand′-), *n.* a parent of a parent; a grandmother or grandfather. —**grand′par′ent·ing,** *n.*

grand′ pian′o, *n.* a piano having the frame supported horizontally on three legs.

Grand′ Prai′rie, *n.* a city in NE Texas. 108,908

Grand′ Rap′ids, *n.* a city in SW Michigan. 190,395.

grand′ slam′, *n.* **1.** the winning of or bid for all thirteen tricks of a deal in bridge. **2.** a home run with three runners on base. **3.** the winning by a single player of several designated major championship contests in one season, as in golf or tennis.

grand·son (gran′sun′, grand′-), *n.* a son of one's son or daughter.

grand·stand (gran′stand′, grand′-), *n.* **1.** a main seating area, as of a stadium or racetrack. **2.** the people sitting in these seats. —*v.i.* **3.** to conduct oneself or perform showily to impress onlookers. —**grand′-stand′er,** *n.*

Grand′ Te′ton Na′tional Park′, *n.* a national park in NW Wyoming, including a portion of the Teton Range. 148 sq. mi. (383 sq. km).

grand′ tour′, *n.* **1.** an extended tour of Europe, formerly regarded as beneficial to young British gentlemen. **2.** an extended informative tour.

grand·un·cle (grand′ung′kəl), *n.* an uncle of one's father or mother; a great-uncle.

grange (grānj), *n.* **1.** a farm, with its nearby buildings. **2.** (*cap.*) the Patrons of Husbandry, a farmers' organization formed in 1867 for social and cultural purposes.

grang·er (grān′jər), *n.* **1.** *Northwestern U.S.* a farmer. **2.** (*cap.*) a member of the Grange.

gran·ite (gran′it), *n.* **1.** a coarse-grained igneous rock composed chiefly of feldspar and quartz, usu. with lesser amounts of one or more other minerals, as mica or hornblende. **2.** something of great hardness, firmness, or durability. —**gra·nit′ic** (grə nit′ik), *adj.*

gran·ite·ware (gran′it wâr′), *n.* **1.** ironware with a gray, stonelike enamel. **2.** pottery with a speckled appearance.

gran·ny or **gran·nie** (gran′ē), *n., pl.* **-nies,** *adj.* —*n.* **1.** *Informal.* GRANDMOTHER. **2.** an elderly woman. **3.** a fussy person. —*adj.* **4.** (of clothing for women) loose-fitted often with a high neckline, puff sleeves, and ruffles and lace trimmings: *a granny blouse.*

gran′ny glass′es, *n.* (*usu. with a pl. v.*) eyeglasses with wirelike metal frames that sometimes sit below the bridge of the nose and often have oval lenses (often used with *pair of*).

gran′ny knot′, *n.* an insecure version of a square knot in which the bights cross each other in the wrong direction next to the end.

Gran′ny Smith′, *n., pl.* **Granny Smiths.** a variety of green-skinned apple.

gra·no·la (grə nō′lə), *n.* a breakfast cereal of rolled oats, nuts, dried fruit, brown sugar, etc. [*orig. a trademark*]

grant (grant, gränt), *v.t.* **1.** to confer, esp. by a formal act: *to grant a charter.* **2.** to give; accord: *to grant permission.* **3.** to agree to: *to grant a request.* **4.** to accept for the sake of argument: *I grant that point.* **5.** to transfer or convey, esp. by deed or writing: *to grant property.* —*n.* **6.** something granted, as a privilege or right, a sum of money, or a tract of

G

land. **7.** the act of granting. **8.** a transfer of real property. **9.** a geographical unit in Vermont, Maine, and New Hampshire, orig. a grant of land to a person or group of people. —**Idiom. 10. take for granted, a.** to assume without question: *I take his honesty for granted.* **b.** to treat with careless indifference. —**grant′er,** *n.*

Grant (grant, gränt), *n.* **1.** Cary (*Archibald Leach*), 1904–86, U.S. actor, born in England. **2.** Ulysses S(impson), 1822–85, Union general: 18th president of the U.S. 1869–77.

gran·tee (gran tē′, grän-), *n.* the receiver of a grant.

grant′-in-aid′, *n., pl.* **grants-in-aid. 1.** a subsidy furnished by a central government to a local one to help finance a public project. **2.** a financial subsidy given to an individual or institution for research, educational, or cultural purposes.

gran·tor (gran′tər, grän′-, gran tôr′, grän-), *n.* a person or organization that makes a grant.

grants·man·ship (grants′mən ship′, gränts′-), *n.* skill in securing grants, as for research, from federal agencies, foundations, or the like.

gran·u·lar (gran′yə lər), *adj.* **1.** of the nature of granules; grainy. **2.** composed of or bearing granules or grains. **3.** showing a granulated structure. —**gran′u·lar′i·ty,** *n.* —**gran′u·lar·ly,** *adv.*

gran·u·late (gran′yə lāt′), *v.,* **-lat·ed, -lat·ing.** —*v.t.* **1.** to form into granules or grains. **2.** to make rough on the surface. —*v.i.* **3.** to become granular or grainy. —**gran′u·lat′er, gran′u·la′tor,** *n.* —**gran′u·la′tion,** *n.* —**gran′u·la′tive** (-lā′tiv, -lə tiv), *adj.*

gran′ulated sug′ar, *n.* a coarsely ground white sugar.

gran·ule (gran′yōōl), *n.* **1.** a little grain. **2.** a small particle; pellet.

grape (grāp), *n.* **1.** the edible smooth-skinned fruit that grows in clusters on vines of the genus *Vitis* and is fermented to make wine. **2.** GRAPEVINE. **3.** a dark purplish red color. **4. the grape,** WINE.

grape′ fern′, *n.* any of several ferns of the genus *Botrychium,* having grapelike clusters of sporangia.

grape·fruit (grāp′frōōt′), *n.* **1.** a large, roundish, yellow-skinned, edible citrus fruit having a juicy, acid pulp. **2.** the tropical or semitropical tree, *Citrus paradisi,* yielding this fruit.

grape′ hy′acinth, *n.* any plant belonging to the genus *Muscari,* of the lily family, having round blue grapelike flowers.

grape′ i′vy, *n.* a tropical American vine, *Cissus rhombifolia,* of the grape family, having glossy trifoliate leaves.

grape·shot (grāp′shot′), *n.* a cluster of small cast-iron balls formerly used as a charge for a cannon.

Grapes′ of Wrath′, The, a novel (1939) by John Steinbeck.

grape′ sug′ar, *n.* DEXTROSE.

grape·vine (grāp′vīn′), *n.* **1.** a vine that bears grapes. **2.** a person-to-person method of spreading gossip or information.

graph (graf, gräf), *n.* **1.** a diagram representing a system of connections or interrelations among two or more things, as by a number of distinctive dots or lines. **2.** *Math.* **a.** a series of discrete or continuous points, as in forming a curve or surface, each of which represents a value of a given function. **b.** a network of lines connecting points. **3.** a written symbol for an idea, a sound, or a linguistic expression. —*v.t.* **4.** to draw (a curve) as representing a given mathematical function. **5.** to represent by means of a graph.

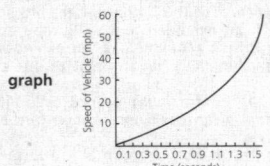

graph

-graph, a combining form meaning "something written, printed, drawn, or incised" (*autograph; lithograph; monograph; pictograph*); "an instrument that produces, transmits, or plays back a record, image, or message" (*phonograph; seismograph; telegraph*); "the image produced by a camera or similar apparatus" (*photograph; planigraph*); "a device or process for writing or printing" (*pantograph; stenograph*); "a graph or chart" (*hydrograph*); also used as a variant of -GRAM¹ (*holograph; ideograph*).

graph·eme (graf′ēm), *n.* **1.** a minimal unit of a writing system. **2.** a unit of a writing system consisting of all the written symbols or sequences of written symbols that are used to represent a single phoneme. —**gra·phe′mi·cal·ly,** *adv.*

gra·phe·mics (gra fē′miks), *n.* (*used with a sing. v.*) the study of writing systems and of their relation to speech.

-grapher, a combining form of agent nouns corresponding to nouns ending in -GRAPH or -GRAPHY: *calligrapher; geographer; photographer.*

graph·ic (graf′ik), *adj.* **1.** giving a clear and effective picture; vivid: *a graphic account of an earthquake.* **2.** pertaining to the use of diagrams, graphs, mathematical curves, or the like; diagrammatic. **3.** of, pertaining to, or expressed by writing: *graphic symbols.* **4.** formed by inscription or drawing. **5.** pertaining to the determination of mathematical values, solution of problems, etc., by direct measurement on diagrams instead of by ordinary calculations. **6.** of or pertaining to the graphic arts. —*n.* **7.**

a product of the graphic arts, as a drawing or print. **8.** a computer-generated image. Also, **graphical.** —**graph′i·cal·ly,** *adv.* —**graph′i·cal·ness, graph′ic·ness,** *n.*

-graphic, a combining form of adjectives corresponding to nouns ending in -GRAPH or -GRAPHY: *telegraphic.*

graph′ic arts′, *n.pl.* Also called **graphics.** the arts or techniques, as engraving, etching, woodcut, or lithography, by which copies of a design are printed from a plate, block, or the like. **2.** the arts of drawing, painting, and printmaking.

graph·ics (graf′iks), *n.* **1.** (*used with a sing. v.*) the art of drawing. **2.** (*used with a pl. v.*) GRAPHIC ARTS (def. 1). **3.** (*used with a pl. v.*) titles, credits, and other text shown on a motion picture or television screen before, after, or during a film or program. **4.** (*used with a sing. v.*) the science of calculating by diagrams. **5.** (*used with a sing. v.*) COMPUTER GRAPHICS.

graph·ite (graf′īt), *n.* a soft natural carbon occurring in black to dark gray foliated masses: used for pencil leads, as a lubricant, as a moderator in nuclear reactors, and for making crucibles and other refractories; plumbago. —**gra·phit·ic** (grə fit′ik), *adj.*

graph·ol·o·gy (gra fol′ə jē), *n.* **1.** the study of handwriting, esp. when regarded as yielding clues to the writer's character. **2.** GRAMMATOLOGY. —**graph·o·log·ic** (graf′ə loj′ik), **graph′o·log′i·cal,** *adj.* —**graph·ol′o·gist,** *n.*

graph′ pa′per, *n.* paper printed with a pattern of lines for plotting graphs.

-graphy, a combining form used in the names of processes or forms of writing, printing, representing, recording, or describing, or in the names of an art or science concerned with such processes: *biography; choreography; geography; orthography; photography.*

grap·nel (grap′nl), *n.* **1.** a device consisting of one or more hooks or clamps for grasping or holding; grapple; grappling iron. **2.** a small anchor with three or more flukes used for grappling or dragging or for anchoring a small boat.

grapnel (def. 2)

grap·ple (grap′əl), *v.,* **-pled, -pling,** *n.* —*v.i.* **1.** to hold or make fast to something, as with a grapple. **2.** to engage in a struggle or close encounter; come to grips: *wrestlers grappling.* **3.** to try to overcome or deal: *to grapple with a problem.* —*v.t.* **4.** to seize, hold, or fasten with or as if with a grapple. —*n.* **5.** GRAPNEL (def. 1). **6.** a seizing or gripping. **7.** a grip or close hold, as in wrestling. **8.** a hand-to-hand fight. —**grap′pler,** *n.*

grap′pling i′ron, *n.* GRAPNEL. Also called **grap′pling hook′.**

GRAS (gras), generally recognized as safe: a status label assigned by the FDA to a listing of substances (**GRAS′ list′**) not known to be hazardous to health.

grasp (grasp, gräsp), *v.t.* **1.** to seize and hold by or as if by clasping with the fingers or arms. **2.** to seize upon; hold firmly. **3.** to comprehend; understand: *I don't grasp your meaning.* —*v.i.* **4.** to make a motion of seizing: *grasped for the gun.* —*n.* **5.** the act of grasping. **6.** a hold or grip: *a firm grasp on a rope.* **7.** EMBRACE. **8.** reach; attainment: *to have a thing within one's grasp.* **9.** hold; possession; control. **10.** power to understand. **11.** thorough comprehension: *a good grasp of computer programming.* —**grasp′er,** *n.*

grasp·ing (gras′ping, gräs′-), *adj.* greedy; avaricious. —**grasp′ing·ly,** *adv.* —**grasp′ing·ness,** *n.*

grass (gras, gräs), *n.* **1.** any of various plants that have jointed stems and bladelike leaves and are cultivated for lawns, used as pasture, or cut for hay. **2.** such plants collectively. **3.** any of numerous related plants. **4.** grass-covered ground: *a picnic on the grass.* **5. grasses,** stalks or sprays of grass. —*v.t.* **6.** to cover with grass or turf. **7.** to feed with growing grass; pasture. —*v.i.* **8.** to produce grass; become covered with grass. —**Idiom. 9. go to grass,** to retire from one's occupation. **10. let the grass grow under one's feet,** to delay action. —**Proverb. 11. The grass is always greener on the other side of the fence,** conditions or circumstances different from our own seem more attractive. —**grass′like′,** *adj.* —**grass′y,** *adj.,* **-i·er, -i·est.**

grass′ carp′, *n.* a large weed-eating carp, *Ctenopharyngodon idella,* orig. native to China.

grass′ cloth′, *n.* a loosely woven fabric made from tough vegetable fibers, used for table linens, wall coverings, etc.

grass·hop·per (gras′hop′ər, gräs′-), *n.* **1.** any of numerous plant-eating orthopterous insects of the families Acrididae and Tettigoniidae, having enlarged upper hind legs adapted for leaping. **2.** a small light airplane used on low-flying missions, as for reconnaissance. **3.** a cocktail of light cream, green crème de menthe, and white crème de menthe or crème de cacao.

grass·land (gras′land′, gräs′-), *n.* **1.** an area, as a prairie, in which the natural vegetation consists largely of perennial grasses. **2.** land with grass growing on it, esp. farmland used for grazing or pasture.

grass′ roots′, *n.* (*used with a sing. or pl. v.*) **1.** ordinary citizens, esp. as contrasted with the leadership or elite. **2.** the agricultural and rural areas of a country. **3.** the people inhabiting these areas, esp. as a political, social, or economic group. **4.** the origin or basis of something. —**grass′-roots′,** *adj.*

grass′ snake′, *n.* any of various small slender snakes of North America, as the garter snake or green snake.

grass′ tree′, *n.* any Australian plant of the genus *Xanthorrhoea,* lily family, having a stout woody stem bearing a tuft of grasslike leaves.

grass′ wid′ow, *n.* **1.** a woman who is separated, divorced, or lives apart from her husband. **2.** a woman whose husband is often away from home, as on business or to pursue a sport or hobby. **3.** *Chiefly Dial.* **a.** a mistress who has been cast aside. **b.** a woman who has borne an illegitimate child. —**grass′wid′ow•hood′,** *n.*

grass′ wid′ower, *n.* **1.** a man who is separated, divorced, or lives apart from his wife. **2.** a man whose wife is away from home frequently or for a long time, as on business or to pursue a sport or hobby.

grate¹ (grāt), *n., v.,* **grat•ed, grat•ing.** —*n.* **1.** a frame of metal bars for holding fuel when burning, as in a fireplace, furnace, or stove. **2.** a framework of parallel or crossed bars used as a partition, guard, cover, or the like; grating. **3.** FIREPLACE. —*v.t.* **4.** to furnish with a grate or grates.

grate² (grāt), *v.,* **grat•ed, grat•ing.** —*v.i.* **1.** to have an irritating effect: *His chatter grates on my nerves.* **2.** to make a sound of rough scraping; rasp. **3.** to sound harshly; jar: *to grate on the ear.* **4.** to rub with rough or noisy friction. —*v.t.* **5.** to reduce to small particles by rubbing against a rough surface or a surface with many sharp-edged openings: *to grate a carrot.* **6.** to rub together with a harsh sound: *to grate one's teeth.* **7.** to irritate; annoy.

grate•ful (grāt′fəl), *adj.* **1.** deeply appreciative of kindness or benefits received; thankful: *grateful for your help.* **2.** expressing gratitude: *a grateful letter.* **3.** pleasing to the mind or senses: *a grateful breeze.* —**grate′ful•ly,** *adv.* —**grate′ful•ness,** *n.*

grat•er (grā′tər), *n.* **1.** a person or thing that grates. **2.** a kitchen device for grating food.

grat•i•fi•ca•tion (grat′ə fi kā′shən), *n.* **1.** the state of being gratified. **2.** something that gratifies; source of pleasure or satisfaction. **3.** the act of gratifying.

grat•i•fy (grat′ə fī′), *v.t.,* **-fied, -fy•ing. 1.** to give pleasure to (a person or persons) by satisfying desires or humoring inclinations or feelings: *Her praise gratified us all.* **2.** to satisfy; indulge: *to gratify one's appetites.* —**grat′i•fi′a•ble,** *adj.*

grat•in (grat′n, grät′-; *Fr.* GRA tan′), *n.* **1.** the crust formed on food cooked au gratin. **2.** a dish cooked au gratin: *potato gratin.*

gra•ti•né (grat′n ā′, grät′-; *Fr.* GRA tē nā′), *v.t.,* **-néed, -né•ing.** to bake or broil (food) in au gratin style.

grat•ing¹ (grā′ting), *n.* **1.** a fixed frame of bars or the like covering an opening to exclude persons, animals, coarse material, or objects while admitting light, air, or fine material. **2.** DIFFRACTION GRATING.

grat•ing² (grā′ting), *adj.* **1.** irritating; abrasive: *a grating personality.* **2.** (of sound) harsh; discordant. —**grat′ing•ly,** *adv.*

grat•is (grat′is, grā′tis), *adv., adj.* without charge or payment; free.

grat•i•tude (grat′i tōod′, -tyōod′), *n.* the quality or feeling of being grateful or thankful.

gra•tu•i•tous (grə tōo′i təs, -tyōo′-), *adj.* **1.** given, done, or obtained without charge; free; voluntary. **2.** being without apparent reason, cause, or justification: *a gratuitous insult.* **3.** *Law.* given without receiving any return value. —**gra•tu′i•tous•ly,** *adv.* —**gra•tu′i•tous•ness,** *n.*

gra•tu•i•ty (grə tōo′i tē, -tyōo′-), *n., pl.* **-ties. 1.** a gift of money over and above payment due for service; tip. **2.** something given without claim or demand.

gra•va•men (grə vā′mən), *n., pl.* **-vam•i•na** (-vam′ə nə). the part of an accusation weighing most heavily against the accused.

grave¹ (grāv), *n.* **1.** an excavation made in the earth in which to bury a dead body. **2.** any place of interment: *a watery grave.* **3.** the receptacle of what is dead, lost, or past: *the grave of unfulfilled ambitions.* **4.** death: *O grave, where is thy victory?* —**Idiom. 5.** have one foot in the grave, to be so frail, sick, or old that death appears imminent. **6.** make someone turn over in his or her grave, to do something that would have been unthinkably offensive to a specified person now dead. —**grave′less,** *adj.* —**grave′like′,** *adj.* —**grave′ward, grave′wards,** *adv., adj.*

grave² (grāv), *adj.,* **grav•er, grav•est. 1.** serious or solemn; sober: *grave thoughts of an uncertain future.* **2.** weighty; momentous: *grave responsibilities.* **3.** threatening a seriously bad outcome or involving serious issues; critical: *a grave situation.* —**grave′ly,** *adv.* —**grave′ness,** *n.*

grave³ (grāv), *v.t.,* **graved, grav•en** or **graved, grav•ing. 1.** to carve, sculpt, or engrave. **2.** to impress deeply: *graven on the mind.*

grave⁴ (grāv), *v.t.,* **graved, grav•ing.** to clean and apply a protective composition of tar to (the bottom of a ship).

gra•ve⁵ (grä′vā), *Music.* —*adj.* **1.** slow; solemn. —*adv.* **2.** slowly; solemnly.

grave′ ac′cent (grāv, gräv), *n.* a mark (`) placed over a vowel esp. to indicate that the vowel is open or lax, as French è, has distinct syllabic

value, as in English *belovèd*, or that the vowel or the syllable it is in has secondary stress or is pronounced with a low or falling pitch.

grave•dig•ger (grāv′dig′ər), *n.* a person whose occupation is digging graves.

grav•el (grav′əl), *n., v.,* **-eled, -el•ing** or (*esp. Brit.*) **-elled, -el•ling,** *adj.* —*n.* **1.** small stones and pebbles or a mixture of these with sand. —*v.t.* **2.** to cover with gravel. **3.** to perplex; puzzle. **4.** to irritate. —*adj.* **5.** GRAVELLY (def. 2). —**grav′el•ish,** *adj.*

grav•el•ly (grav′ə lē), *adj.* **1.** of, like, or abounding in gravel. **2.** harsh; raspy: *a gravelly voice.*

grav•en (grā′vən), *v.* **1.** a pp. of GRAVE³. —*adj.* **2.** deeply impressed; firmly fixed. **3.** carved; sculptured: *a graven idol.*

grav′en im′age, *n.* an idol carved from stone or wood.

grav•er (grā′vər), *n.* **1.** any of various tools for chasing, engraving, etc., as a burin. **2.** engraver; sculptor.

Graves (grāv), *n.* a dry red or white wine from the district of Graves in SW France.

Graves′ disease′ (grāvz), *n.* a disease characterized by an enlarged thyroid and increased basal metabolism due to excessive thyroid secretion.

grave•stone (grāv′stōn′), *n.* a stone, usu. inscribed, marking a grave.

grave•yard (grāv′yärd′), *n.* **1.** CEMETERY. **2.** a place in which obsolete or derelict objects are kept: *an automobile graveyard.*

grave′yard shift′, *n.* **1.** a work shift usu. beginning at about midnight and continuing for about eight hours. **2.** those who work this shift. Also called **grave′yard watch′.**

grav•id (grav′id), *adj.* pregnant. —**gra•vid•i•ty** (grə vid′i tē), **grav′id•ness,** *n.* —**grav′id•ly,** *adv.*

grav•i•da (grav′i də), *n., pl.* **-das, -dae** (-dē′). **1.** a woman's status regarding pregnancy: usu. followed by a Roman numeral designating the number of times the woman has been pregnant. **2.** a pregnant woman. Compare PARA³.

gra•vim•e•ter (grə vim′i tər), *n.* **1.** an instrument for measuring the specific gravity of a solid or liquid. **2.** an instrument for measuring variations in the gravitational field of the earth. —**grav•i•met•ric** (grav′ə me′trik), *adj.* —**grav•i•met′ri•cal•ly,** *adv.*

gra•vim•e•try (grə vim′i trē), *n.* the measurement of weight or density.

grav•i•tate (grav′i tāt′), *v.i.,* **-tat•ed, -tat•ing. 1.** to move under the influence of gravitational force. **2.** to tend toward the lowest level; sink. **3.** to be strongly attracted: *to gravitate toward one another.* —**grav′i•tat′er,** *n.*

grav•i•ta•tion (grav′i tā′shən), *n.* **1. a.** the force of attraction between any two masses. **b.** an act or process caused by this force. **2.** a sinking or falling. **3.** a movement or tendency toward something or someone: *the gravitation of people toward the suburbs.* —**grav′i•ta′tion•al,** *adj.* —**grav′i•ta′tion•al•ly,** *adv.*

grav•i•ty (grav′i tē), *n., pl.* **-ties. 1.** the force of attraction by which terrestrial bodies tend to fall toward the center of the earth. **2.** heaviness or weight. **3.** gravitation in general. **4.** ACCELERATION OF GRAVITY. **5.** serious or critical nature: *to ignore the gravity of one's illness.* **6.** serious or dignified behavior; dignity; solemnity: *to preserve one's gravity.* **7.** lowness in pitch, as of sounds.

grav•lax (gräv′läks), *n.* boned salmon cured in sugar, salt, pepper, and dill.

gra•vure (grə vyŏor′, grā′vyər), *n.* **1.** an intaglio process of photomechanical printing, such as photogravure or rotogravure. **2.** a print produced by gravure. **3.** the metal or wooden plate used in photogravure.

gra•vy (grā′vē), *n., pl.* **-vies. 1.** the fat and juices of cooked meat, often thickened and seasoned and used as a sauce. **2.** *Slang.* **a.** profit or money easily, unexpectedly, or illegally obtained. **b.** something advantageous or valuable obtained as a benefit beyond what is due or expected.

gray or **grey** (grā), *adj.,* **gray•er, gray•est** or **grey•er, grey•est,** *n., v.* —*adj.* **1.** of a color between white and black; having a neutral hue. **2.** dark, dismal, or gloomy: *gray skies.* **3.** dull, dreary, or monotonous. **4.** having gray hair. **5.** pertaining to old age; elderly: *gray households.* **6.** indeterminate and intermediate in character: *the gray area between realism and abstraction.* —*n.* **7.** any achromatic color; any color intermediate between white and black. **8.** something of this color. **9.** gray material or clothing: *to dress in gray.* **10.** (*often cap.*) a member of the Confederate army in the American Civil War, or the army itself. Compare BLUE (def. 5). **11.** a horse of a gray color. —*v.t., v.i.* **12.** to make or become gray. —**gray′ness,** *n.*

Gray (grā), *n.* **1.** James Martin, 1851–1935, U.S. clergyman. **2.** Thomas, 1716–71, English poet.

gray•back (grā′bak′), *n.* any of various marine and aquatic animals that are dark gray above and light-colored or white below, as the gray whale and certain sandpipers.

gray′ em′inence, *n.* a person who wields unofficial power, esp. through another person and often surreptitiously or privately. Also, **éminence grise.** [trans. of French *éminence grise*]

gray•fish (grā′fish′), *n., pl.* **-fish•es,** (*esp. collectively*) **-fish.** any of several American sharks, esp. the dogfishes of the genus *Squalus.*

gray•hound (grā′hound′), *n.* GREYHOUND.

gray•ish (grā′ish), *adj.* having a tinge of gray; slightly gray.

gray′ jay′, *n.* a deep-gray and white jay, *Perisoreus canadensis*, with no crest, common in North American coniferous forests.

G

gray·lag (grā′lag′), *n.* a gray Eurasian goose, *Anser anser,* that is the ancestor of most breeds of domestic goose.

gray·ling (grā′ling), *n.* any freshwater game fish of the genus *Thymallus,* related to the trout, with a large, brightly colored dorsal fin.

gray′ mar′ket, *n.* **1.** a market operating within the law in which scarce goods are sold at above-market prices. **2.** the selling of goods bought at a very large discount at prices substantially below the market price.

gray′ mat′ter, *n.* **1.** a reddish gray nerve tissue of the brain and spinal cord, consisting chiefly of nerve cell bodies, with few nerve fibers. Compare WHITE MATTER. **2.** *Informal.* brains or intellect.

gray′ par′rot, *n.* AFRICAN GRAY.

gray′ scale′, *n.* a scale of achromatic colors having equal gradations ranging from white to black.

gray′ squir′rel, *n.* any of various grayish squirrels of the genus *Sciurus,* esp. *S. carolinensis,* of E North America.

gray′ whale′, *n.* a grayish black whalebone whale, *Eschrichtius robustus,* of the N Pacific, growing to a length of 50 ft. (15.2 m).

gray′ wolf′, *n.* a large canid, *Canis lupus,* of the N Hemisphere, with a gray, blackish, or whitish coat, living and hunting in packs.

graze¹ (grāz), *v.,* **grazed, graz·ing.** —*v.i.* **1.** to feed on growing grass and herbage, as do cattle, sheep, etc. **2.** *Informal.* **a.** to eat small portions of food or snacks in place of regular meals. **b.** to sample small portions of a variety of foods at one meal. —*v.t.* **3.** to feed on (growing grass and herbage). **4.** to put cattle, sheep, etc., to feed on (grass, pastureland, etc.). **5.** to tend (grazing animals).

graze² (grāz), *v.,* **grazed, graz·ing,** *n.* —*v.t.* **1.** to touch or rub lightly in passing. **2.** to scrape the skin from; abrade: *The ball just grazed his shoulder.* —*v.i.* **3.** to touch or rub something lightly, or so as to produce slight abrasion, in passing: *to graze against a rough wall.* —*n.* **4.** a grazing; a touching or rubbing lightly in passing. **5.** a slight scratch or scrape made in passing; abrasion.

graz·ing (grā′zing), *n.* **1.** pastureland; a pasture. **2.** *Informal.* the act of eating snacks instead of regular meals, or of sampling small portions of a variety of foods. **3.** *Informal.* the act or practice of switching television channels frequently to watch several programs.

grease (*n.* grēs; *v.* grēs, grēz), *n.,* *v.,* **greased, greas·ing.** —*n.* **1.** the melted or rendered fat of animals, esp. when in a soft state. **2.** fatty or oily matter in general; lubricant. Also called **grease′ wool′.** wool, as shorn, before being cleansed of the oily matter. **4.** *Informal.* a bribe. —*v.t.* **5.** to put grease on; lubricate: *to grease the axle of a car.* **6.** to smear or cover with grease. **7.** to cause to occur easily; smooth the way. **8.** *Informal.* to bribe. —*Idiom.* **9.** grease someone's palm or hand, to give someone money as a bribe. —**grease′less,** *adj.* —**grease′less·ness,** *n.* —**grease′proof′,** *adj.*

grease′ mon′key, *n. Slang.* a mechanic, esp. one who works on automobiles or airplanes.

grease′paint′ or **grease′ paint′,** *n.* **1.** an oily mixture of melted tallow or grease and a pigment, used by actors, clowns, etc., for making up their faces. **2.** theatrical makeup.

grease′ pen′cil, *n.* a pencil of pigment and compressed grease used esp. for writing on glossy surfaces.

greas·er (grē′sər), *n.* **1.** a person or thing that greases. **2.** *Slang.* a swaggering young tough, esp. a member of a street gang.

grease·wood (grēs′wŏŏd), *n.* **1.** a shrub, *Sarcobatus vermiculatus,* of the goosefoot family, growing in the arid western U.S. **2.** any of various similar shrubs. **3.** *Western U.S.* MESQUITE.

greas·y (grē′sē, -zē), *adj.,* **greas·i·er, greas·i·est. 1.** smeared, covered, or soiled with grease. **2.** composed of or containing grease; oily: *greasy food.* **3.** greaselike in appearance or to the touch; slippery. **4.** insinuatingly unctuous in manner; repulsively slick; oily. —**greas′i·ly,** *adv.* —**greas′i·ness,** *n.*

greas′y spoon′, *n. Slang.* a cheap and rather unsanitary restaurant.

great (grāt), *adj.,* **great·er, great·est,** *adv., n., pl.* **greats,** (esp. collectively) **great,** *interj.* —*adj.* **1.** unusually or comparatively large in size or dimensions; big. **2.** large in number; numerous: *great herds of buffalo.* **3.** unusual or considerable in degree, power, intensity, etc.: *great pain.* **4.** first-rate; excellent: *to have a great time.* **5.** being such in an extreme or notable degree: *great friends.* **6.** notable; remarkable: *a great occasion.* **7.** important; highly significant or consequential: *the great issues in American history.* **8.** distinguished; famous: *a great inventor.* **9.** of noble or lofty character: *great thoughts.* **10.** chief or principal: *the great hall.* **11.** of high rank or social standing: *a great lady.* **12.** much in use or favor: *"Humor" was a great word with the old physiologists.* **13.** of extraordinary powers; having unusual merit; very admirable: *a great statesman.* **14.** of marked duration or length: *to wait a great while.* **15.** *Informal.* **a.** enthusiastic about some specified activity (usu. fol. by *on* or *for*): *He's great on poetry.* **b.** skillful; expert (usu. fol. by *at*): *She's great at golf.* **16.** being of one generation more remote from the family relative specified (used in combination): *a great-grandson.* —*adv.* **17.** *Informal.* very well: *Things have been going great for him.* —*n.* **18.** a person who has achieved importance or distinction in a field: *She is one of the theater's greats.* **19.** great persons, collectively: *England's literary great.* —*interj.* **20.** (used to express acceptance, appreciation, approval, admiration, etc.). **21.** (used ironically or facetiously to express disappointment, annoyance, distress, etc.): *Great! We just missed the last train home.* —**great′ly,** *adv.* —**great′ness,** *n.*

great′ ape′, *n.* any of the larger apes, including the gorilla, chimpanzee, and orangutan, but excluding the gibbon.

Great′ Attrac′tor, *n.* a vast concentration of matter whose gravitational pull alters the direction and speed of the Milky Way and other galaxies as they spread apart in the expanding universe posited by the big bang theory.

great′ auk′, *n.* a large flightless auk, *Pinguinus impennis,* of rocky islands off N Atlantic coasts: extinct since 1844.

great′-aunt′, *n.* GRANDAUNT.

Great′ Awak′ening, *n.* the series of religious revivals among Protestants in the American colonies, esp. in New England, lasting from about 1725 to 1770.

Great′ Bar′rier Reef′, *n.* a coral reef parallel to the coast of Queensland, in NE Australia. 1250 mi. (2010 km) long.

Great′ Ba′sin, *n.* a region in the western U.S. that has no drainage to the ocean: includes most of Nevada and parts of Utah, California, Oregon, Wyoming, and Idaho. 210,000 sq. mi. (544,000 sq. km).

Great′ Ba′sin Na′tional Park′, *n.* a national park in E Nevada: site of Lehman Caves. 120 sq. mi. (312 sq. km).

Great′ Bear′, *n.* the constellation Ursa Major.

Great′ Bi′ble, *n.* the English Bible (1539) sponsored by Thomas Cranmer and Thomas Cromwell in a revision by Miles Coverdale. Also called **Cromwell's Bible.**

great′ blue′ her′on, *n.* a large North American heron, *Ardea herodias,* having bluish gray plumage.

Great′ Brit′ain, *n.* an island of NW Europe, separated from the mainland by the English Channel and the North Sea: comprising England, Scotland, and Wales. 55,780,000; 88,790 sq. mi. (229,979 sq. km). Compare UNITED KINGDOM.

great′ cir′cle, *n.* **1.** a circle on a sphere such that the plane containing the circle passes through the center of the sphere. **2.** a circle of which a segment represents the shortest distance between two points on the surface of the earth.

great·coat (grāt′kōt′), *n.* a heavy overcoat.

Great′ Code′, The, a study (1982) of the Bible's influence by Northrop Frye.

Great′ Commis′sion, The, *n.* Christ's command to his disciples to go through the world teaching and baptizing. Matt. 28:18–20.

Great′ Com′moner, *n.* **1.** epithet of William Pitt the elder. **2.** epithet of Henry Clay. **3.** epithet of William Jennings Bryan.

Great′ Dane′, *n.* one of a breed of very large, powerful shorthaired dogs with a long, square muzzle.

Great′ Depres′sion, *n.* the economic crisis and period of low business activity in the U.S. and other countries, roughly beginning with the stock-market crash in October 1929 and continuing through most of the 1930s.

Great′ Divide′, *n.* **1.** CONTINENTAL DIVIDE (def. 2). **2.** the passage from life to death. **3.** an important division or difference.

Great′ Dog′, *n.* the constellation Canis Major.

Great·er (grā′tər), *adj.* designating a large city and its adjacent areas: *Greater New York; Greater Los Angeles.*

great′est show′ on earth′, *n.* epithet for the circus: coined by P.T. Barnum.

Great′ Expecta′tions, a novel (1861) by Charles Dickens.

Great′ Gats′by, The, (gats′bē), a novel (1925) by F. Scott Fitzgerald.

great′-grand′child, *n., pl.* **-grandchildren.** a grandchild of one's son or daughter.

great′-grand′daughter, *n.* a granddaughter of one's son or daughter.

great′-grand′father, *n.* a grandfather of one's father or mother.

great′-grand′mother, *n.* a grandmother of one's father or mother.

great′-grand′parent, *n.* a grandfather or grandmother of one's father or mother.

great′-grand′son, *n.* a grandson of one's son or daughter.

great′ guns′, *adv.* **1.** *Informal.* extremely well; very successfully: *The business is going great guns.* —*interj.* **2.** (used as an expression of surprise, astonishment, etc.).

great·heart·ed (grāt′här′tid), *adj.* **1.** having or showing a generous heart; magnanimous. **2.** high-spirited; courageous; fearless. —**great′heart′ed·ly,** *adv.* —**great′heart′ed·ness,** *n.*

great′ horned′ owl′, *n.* a large, brown-speckled New World owl, *Bubo virginianus,* having prominent ear tufts.

Great′ Lakes′, *n.pl.* a series of five lakes between the U.S. and Canada, comprising Lakes Erie, Huron, Michigan, Ontario, and Superior, connected with the Atlantic by the St. Lawrence River.

great′ lau′rel, *n.* a tall rhododendron, *Rhododendron maximum,* of E North America, with rose-pink flowers.

Great′ Mo′gul, *n.* **1.** any of the former Mogul emperors of India. **2.** (*l.c.*) an important or distinguished person.

Great′ Moth′er, The, *n.* a vaguely defined deity symbolizing maternity, the fertility of the earth, and femininity in general; the central figure in the religions of ancient Anatolia, the Near East, and the eastern Mediterranean, later sometimes taking the form of a specific goddess, as Cybele, Rhea, or Demeter. Also called **The Great′ God′dess.**

great′-neph′ew, *n.* a son of one's nephew or niece; grandnephew.

great′-niece′, *n.* a daughter of one's nephew or niece; grandniece.

Great′ Plains′, *n.* a semiarid region E of the Rocky Mountains, in the U.S. and Canada.

Great′ Pow′er, *n.* a nation that has exceptional military and economic strength, and consequently plays a major, often decisive, role in international affairs. —**Great′-Pow′er, great′-pow′er,** *adj.*

Great′ Rift′ Val′ley, *n.* a series of rift valleys running from the Jordan Valley in SW Asia to Mozambique in SE Africa.

Great′ Salt′ Lake′, *n.* a shallow salt lake in NW Utah. 2300 sq. mi. (5950 sq. km); 80 mi. (130 km) long; maximum depth 60 ft. (18 m).

Great′ Salt′ Lake′ Des′ert, *n.* an arid region in NW Utah, extending W from the Great Salt Lake to the Nevada border. 110 mi. (177 km) long; ab. 4000 sq. mi. (10,360 sq. km).

Great′ Schism′, *n.* a period of division in the Roman Catholic Church, 1378–1417, over papal succession, during which there were two, or sometimes three, claimants to the papal office.

great′ seal′, *n.* the principal seal of a government or state.

The Great Seal of The United States

Great′ Smok′y Moun′tains, *n.pl.* a range of the Appalachian Mountains in North Carolina and Tennessee; most of the range is included in Great Smoky Mountains National Park. 720 sq. mi. (1865 sq. km). Highest peak, Clingman's Dome, 6642 ft. (2024 m). Also called **Smoky Mountains, Great′ Smok′ies.**

Great′ Smo′ky Moun′tains Na′tional Park′, *n.* a national park in SE Tennessee and SW North Carolina, including most of the Great Smoky Mountains: hardwood forest. 808 sq. mi. (2092 sq. km).

Great′ Soci′ety, *n.* the goal of the Democratic party under the leadership of President Lyndon B. Johnson, chiefly to enact domestic programs to improve education, provide medical care for the aged, and eliminate poverty. Compare FAIR DEAL, NEW DEAL, NEW FRONTIER.

Great′ Spir′it, *n.* the chief deity in the religion of many North American Indian tribes.

Great′ Tribula′tion, the, *n.* a short period of great suffering at the end of time. Rev. 7:14.

great′-un′cle, *n.* GRANDUNCLE.

great′ unwashed′ or **Great′ Unwashed′,** *n.* the general public; the populace or masses.

Great′ Vow′el Shift′, *n.* a series of changes in the quality of the long vowels between Middle and Modern English as a result of which all were raised, while the high vowels (ē) and (o͞o), already at the upper limit, underwent breaking to become the diphthongs (ī) and (ou).

Great′ Wall′ of Chi′na, *n.* a system of fortified walls with a roadway along the top, constructed as a defense for China against the nomads of the regions that are now Mongolia and Manchuria: completed in the 3rd century B.C., but later repeatedly modified and rebuilt. 2000 mi. (3220 km).

Great′ War′, *n.* WORLD WAR I.

Great′ White′ Fa′ther, *n. Facetious.* **1.** the president of the U.S. **2.** any man who holds a position of great authority. [after the epithet supposedly used for the U.S. president by American Indians in the 19th century]

great′ white′ shark′, *n.* a large shark, *Carcharodon carcharias,* that occasionally attacks swimmers.

Great′ White′ Way′, *n.* the theater district along Broadway, near Times Square in New York City.

Great′ Zimbab′we, *n.* a complex of stone ruins discovered c1870 in Rhodesia, probably built by a Bantu people, and dating between the 9th and 15th centuries A.D.

grebe (grēb), *n.* any diving bird of the cosmopolitan order Podicipediformes, having a rudimentary tail and lobate toes.

Gre•cian (grē′shən), *adj.* **1.** Greek. —*n.* **2.** a Greek.

Greece (grēs), *n.* Ancient Greek, **Hellas.** Modern Greek, **Ellas.** a republic in S Europe at the S end of the Balkan Peninsula. 10,583,126; 50,147 sq. mi. (129,880 sq. km). *Cap.:* Athens.

greed (grēd), *n.* excessive or rapacious desire, esp. for wealth or possessions; avarice; covetousness. —**greed′i•ly,** *adv.* —**greed′i•ness,** *n.* —**greed′y,** *adj.,* **-i•er, -i•est.**

Greek (grēk), *adj.* **1.** of or pertaining to Greece, the Greeks, or their language. —*n.* **2.** a native or inhabitant of Greece. **3.** the Indo-European language of the Greeks. *Abbr.:* Gk **4.** *Informal.* anything unintelligible, as speech, writing, etc.: *This contract is Greek to me.* **5.** a person who belongs to a Greek-letter fraternity or sorority.

Greek′ cross′, *n.* a cross consisting of an upright crossed in the middle by a horizontal piece of the same length.

Greek′ Or′thodox Church′, *n.* the branch of the Orthodox Church constituting the national church of Greece.

Gree•ley (grē′lē), *n.* **1.** Horace, 1811–72, U.S. journalist, editor, and political leader. **2.** a city in N Colorado. 57,430.

green (grēn), *adj.* **1.** of the color of growing foliage, between yellow and blue in the spectrum: *green leaves.* **2.** covered with herbage or foliage; verdant: *green fields.* **3.** characterized by verdure: *a green Christmas.* **4.** made of green usu. leafy vegetables, as lettuce, spinach, or chicory: *a green salad.* **5.** not fully developed or matured; unripe: *green fruit.* **6.** unseasoned; not dried or cured: *green lumber.* **7.** immature in age or judgment; untrained; inexperienced: *green recruits.* **8.** simple; unsophisticated; gullible; naive. **9.** having a sickly or pale appearance: *to turn green with fear.* **10.** advocating or promoting environmentalism: *green politics; green consumers.* **11.** full of life and vigor; youthful: *a green old age.* **12.** fresh, recent, or new: *a green wound.* **13.** (of wine) having a flavor that is raw, harsh, and acid, due esp. to a lack of maturity. **14.** freshly slaughtered or raw: *green meat.* **15.** not fired, as bricks or pottery. **16.** (of cement or mortar) freshly set and not completely hardened. —*n.* **17.** a color intermediate in the spectrum between yellow and blue, an effect of light with a wavelength between 500 and 570 nm: found in nature as the color of most grasses and leaves while growing. **18.** a secondary color formed by the mixture of blue and yellow pigments. **19.** green coloring matter, as paint or dye. **20.** green material or clothing: *to be dressed in green.* **21. greens, a.** the leaves and stems of certain plants, as spinach, kale, or lettuce, eaten as a vegetable. **b.** fresh leaves or branches of trees, shrubs, etc., used for decoration; wreaths. **22.** grassy land; a plot of grassy ground. **23.** a piece of grassy ground constituting a town or village common. **24.** Also called **putting green.** the area of closely cropped grass surrounding each hole on a golf course. **25.** *Informal.* GREEN LIGHT (def. 1). **26.** *Slang.* money; greenbacks (usu. prec. by *the*). —*v.i., v.t.* **27.** to become or make green. —*Idiom.* **28.** green with envy, extremely jealous; green-eyed.

green′ al′gae, *n.pl.* grass-green algae of the phylum Chlorophyta, common on wet rocks, damp wood, and the surface of stagnant water.

green′ ano′le, *n.* ANOLE (def. 1).

Green•a•way (grēn′ə wā′), *n.* **Kate** (*Catherine*), 1846–1901, English painter and author and illustrator of children's books.

green•back (grēn′bak′), *n.* a U.S. legal-tender note, printed in green on the back; orig. issued against the credit of the country and not against gold or silver on deposit.

Green′back par′ty, *n.* a former U.S. political party, organized in 1874, opposed to the retirement or reduction of greenbacks and favoring their increase as the only paper currency. —**Green′back′er,** *n.*

Green′ Bay′, *n.* **1.** an arm of Lake Michigan, in NE Wisconsin. 120 mi. (195 km) long. **2.** a port in E Wisconsin at the S end of this bay. 102,708.

green′ bean′, *n.* the slender immature green pod of the kidney bean, eaten as a vegetable.

green•belt (grēn′belt′), *n.* **1.** an area of woods, parks, or open land surrounding a community. **2.** Also, **green′ belt′.** a strip of land on the edge of a desert that has been planted and irrigated to keep the desert from spreading.

Green′ Beret′, *n.* SPECIAL FORCES.

green•bri•er (grēn′brī′ər), *n.* CATBRIER.

green•bug (grēn′bug′), *n.* a pale green aphid, *Schizaphis graminum,* of North America, destructive of wheat, other grains, and alfalfa.

green′ card′, *n.* an official card, orig. green, issued by the U.S. government to foreign nationals permitting them to work in the U.S. —**green′-card′er,** *n.*

green′ corn′, *n.* the young tender ears of corn.

Greene (grēn), *n.* **1.** Graham, 1904–91, English novelist and journalist. **2. Nathanael,** 1742–86, American Revolutionary general. **3. Robert,** 1558–92, English dramatist and poet.

green•er•y (grē′nə rē), *n., pl.* **-er•ies. 1.** green foliage or vegetation; verdure. **2.** greens used for decoration. **3.** a place where green plants are grown.

green′-eyed′, *adj.* jealous; envious.

green′-eyed′ mon′ster, *n.* jealousy.

green•finch (grēn′finch′), *n.* a Eurasian finch, *Carduelis chloris,* having green and yellow plumage.

green•fly (grēn′flī′), *n., pl.* **-flies.** an aphid, *Coloradoa rufomaculata,* that is a common pest of chrysanthemums.

G

green·gage (grēn′gāj′), *n.* any of several varieties of light green plums.

green·gro·cer (grēn′grō′sər), *n.* a retailer of fresh vegetables and fruit. —**green′gro′cer·y,** *n., pl.* **-cer·ies.**

green·heart (grēn′härt′), *n.* **1.** a South American tree, *Ocotea* (or *Nectandra*) *rodiei,* of the laurel family, yielding a hard durable greenish wood. **2.** the wood itself.

green·horn (grēn′hôrn′), *n.* **1.** an untrained or inexperienced person. **2.** a naive or gullible person. **3.** a newly arrived immigrant; newcomer.

green·house (grēn′hous′), *n., pl.* **-hous·es** (-hou′ziz). a building, room, or area, usu. chiefly of glass, in which the temperature is maintained within a desired range, used for cultivating tender plants or growing plants out of season.

green′house effect′, *n.* heating of the atmosphere resulting from the absorption by certain gases, as carbon dioxide and water vapor, of solar energy that has been captured and reradiated by the earth's surface.

green′house gas′, *n.* any of the gases whose absorption of solar radiation is responsible for the greenhouse effect, including carbon dioxide, methane, ozone, and the fluorocarbons.

green·ing (grē′ning), *n.* **1.** any variety of apple whose skin is green when ripe. **2.** a restoration of youthful freshness and vigor; rejuvenation: *the greening of America.*

Green·land (grēn′land, -land′), *n.* a self-governing island belonging to Denmark located NE of North America: the largest island in the world. 53,733; ab. 840,000 sq. mi. (2,175,600 sq. km); over 700,000 sq. mi. (1,800,000 sq. km) icecapped. *Cap.:* Godthåb. —**Green′land·er,** *n.*

green′ light′, *n.* **1.** a green-colored traffic light used to signal permission to proceed. **2.** authorization or permission to proceed with an action or project.

green·mail (grēn′māl′), *n.* the practice of buying a large block of a company's stock so that the company is forced to repurchase the stock at inflated prices to avert a takeover. —**green′mail′er,** *n.*

Green′ Moun′tain Boys′, *n.pl.* the soldiers from Vermont in the American Revolution, orig. organized by Ethan Allen in 1775 to oppose the territorial claims of New York.

green′ on′ion, *n.* a young onion with a slender green stalk and a small bulb; scallion.

Green′ Par′ty, *n.* a liberal political party, esp. in Germany, focusing on environmental issues.

green′ pep′per, *n.* the mild-flavored, unripe fruit of the bell or sweet pepper, *Capsicum annuum grossum,* used as a vegetable.

Green′ Riv′er or′dinance, *n.* a local ordinance banning door-to-door selling. Also called **Green′ Riv′er law′.** [named after such an ordinance, passed in 1931 in Green River, Wyo.]

green·room (grēn′room′, -room′), *n.* a lounge in a theater, television studio, etc., for use by performers when they are not onstage or on the set.

Greens·bo·ro (grēnz′bûr′ō, -bur′ō), *n.* a city in N North Carolina. 196,167.

greens′ (or **green′**) **fee′,** *n.* a fee paid for playing on a golf course.

green′ snake′, *n.* any slender, green colubrine snake of the genus *Opheodrys,* of North America.

green′stick frac′ture (grēn′stik′), *n.* an incomplete fracture of a long bone, in which one side is broken and the other side is intact.

green·stone (grēn′stōn′), *n.* any of various altered basaltic rocks having a dark green color caused by the presence of chlorite, etc.

green′ sul′fur bacte′ria, *n.pl.* a group of green or brown bacteria of the families Chlorobiaceae and Chloroflexaceae that occur in aquatic sediments, sulfur springs, and hot springs and that utilize reduced sulfur compounds instead of oxygen.

green′ tea′, *n.* tea that is steamed to prevent fermentation and then rolled and dried.

green′ thumb′, *n.* an exceptional skill for gardening or for growing plants successfully. —**green′-thumbed′,** *adj.* —**green′-thumb′er,** *n.*

green′ tur′tle, *n.* a sea turtle, *Chelonia mydas,* common in tropical and subtropical seas, the flesh of which is used for turtle soup.

Green·wich (grin′ij, -ich, gren′- *for* 2), *n.* **1.** a borough in SE London, England: located on the prime meridian from which geographic longitude is measured; formerly the site of the Royal Greenwich Observatory. 216,600. **2.** a town in SW Connecticut. 59,578. **3.** *Informal.* GREENWICH TIME.

Green′wich Time′, *n.* the time as measured on the prime meridian running through Greenwich, England: used in England and as a standard of calculation elsewhere. Also called **Green′wich Mean′ Time′.**

Green′wich Vil′lage (gren′ich, grin′-), *n.* a section of New York City, in lower Manhattan: frequented esp. by artists and students.

green′-winged′ teal′, *n.* a dabbling duck, *Anas crecca,* of Eurasia and North America, having an iridescent green speculum in the wing.

greet (grēt), *v.t.* **1.** to address with some form of salutation; welcome. **2.** to meet or receive: *to greet a proposal with boos and hisses.* **3.** to manifest itself to: *Music greeted our ears.* —**greet′er,** *n.*

greet·ing (grē′ting), *n.* **1.** the act or words of one who greets; salutation. **2. greetings,** an expression of friendly or respectful regard.

greet′ing card′, *n.* a card, usu. folded, printed with a message of sentiment, and illustrated, for mailing or giving to a person on a special occasion, as a holiday or a birthday.

gre·gar·i·ous (gri gâr′ē əs), *adj.* **1.** fond of the company of others; so-

ciable. **2.** living in flocks or herds, as animals. **3.** *Bot.* growing in open clusters or colonies; not matted together. **4.** pertaining to a flock or crowd. —**gre·gar′i·ous·ly,** *adv.* —**gre·gar′i·ous·ness,** *n.*

Grego′rian cal′endar, *n.* the reformed Julian calendar now in use, according to which the ordinary year consists of 365 days, and a leap year of 366 days occurs in every year whose number is exactly divisible by 4 except centenary years whose numbers are not exactly divisible by 400, as 1700, 1800, and 1900. [after Pope Gregory XIII (1502-85)]

Grego′rian chant′, *n.* the plainsong used in the ritual of the Roman Catholic Church. [after Pope Gregory I]

Greg·o·ry¹ (greg′ə rē), *n.* Lady Augusta (*Isabella Augusta Persse*), 1852-1932, Irish dramatist.

Greg·o·ry² (greg′ə rē), *n.* **1. Gregory I, Saint** (*"Gregory the Great"*), A.D. c540-604, Italian pope 590-604. **2. Gregory VII, Saint** (*Hildebrand*) c1020-85, Italian pope 1073-85. **3. Gregory XIII,** (*Ugo Buoncompagni*) 1502-85, Italian pope 1572-85.

grem·lin (grem′lin), *n.* an imaginary, mischievous being humorously alleged to cause mechanical failures in aircraft or disruptions in any activity.

Gre·na·da (gri nā′də), *n.* **1.** one of the Windward Islands, in the E West Indies. **2.** an independent country comprising this island and the S Grenadines: a former British colony; gained independence 1974. 95,537; 133 sq. mi. (344 sq. km). *Cap.:* St. George's. —**Gre·na·di·an** (gri nā′dē ən), *adj., n.*

gre·nade (gri nād′), *n.* **1.** a small shell containing an explosive and thrown by hand or fired from a rifle or launching device. **2.** a similar missile containing a chemical, as for dispersing tear gas or fire-extinguishing substances.

gren·a·dier (gren′ə dēr′), *n.* **1.** a member of the first regiment of royal household infantry (**Gren′adier Guards′**) in the British Army. **2.** a foot soldier in certain former elite units, specially selected for strength and courage. **3.** (formerly) a soldier who threw grenades.

gren·a·dine (gren′ə dēn′, gren′ə dēn′), *n.* a sweet red syrup made from or tasting like pomegranate juice.

Gren·del (gren′dl), *n.* the monster killed by Beowulf in the Old English poem *Beowulf.*

Gresh·am (gresh′əm), *n.* **1. Sir Thomas,** 1519?-79, English financier. **2.** a town in NW Oregon. 58,130.

Gresh′am's law′, *n.* the tendency of the inferior of two forms of currency to circulate more freely than, or to the exclusion of, the superior, because of the hoarding of the latter. [after Sir T. Gresham]

grew (grōo), *v.* pt. of GROW.

grey (grā), *adj.* GRAY¹.

Grey (grā), *n.* **1. Charles, 2nd Earl,** 1764-1845, British prime minister 1830-34. **2. Lady Jane** (*Lady Jane Dudley*), 1537-54, descendant of Henry VII of England; executed as a rival to Mary I for the throne. **3. Zane** (zān), 1875-1939, U.S. novelist.

grey·hound or **gray·hound** (grā′hound′), *n.* one of a breed of tall, slender shorthaired dogs noted for their keen sight and swiftness.

grid (grid), *n.* **1.** a grating of crossed bars; gridiron. **2.** a network of horizontal and perpendicular lines, uniformly spaced, for locating points on a map, chart, building plan, or aerial photograph by means of a system of coordinates. **3.** any interconnecting network resembling this. **4.** a system of electrical distribution serving a large area, esp. by means of high-tension wires. **5.** a metallic framework in a storage cell or battery for conducting the electric current and supporting the active material. **6.** an electrode in a vacuum tube, usu. consisting of parallel wires, a coil of wire, or a screen, for controlling the flow of electrons between the other electrodes. **7.** *Survey.* a basic system of reference lines mapping a region, consisting of straight lines intersecting at right angles. **8.** Also, **gridiron.** a municipal road plan in which all or most thoroughfares cross at right angles. **9.** GRIDIRON (def. 1).

grid·der (grid′ər), *n. Informal.* a football player.

grid·dle (grid′l), *n., v.,* **-dled, -dling.** —*n.* **1.** a flat pan, rimless or with a slightly raised edge, for cooking pancakes, bacon, etc., over direct heat with little or no fat. **2.** any flat, heated surface, esp. on top of a stove, for cooking food. —*v.t.* **3.** to cook on a griddle.

grid·dle·cake (grid′l kāk′), *n.* a pancake.

grid·i·ron (grid′ī′ərn), *n.* **1.** a football field. **2.** a utensil consisting of parallel metal bars on which to broil meat or other food. **3.** any framework or network resembling a gridiron. **4.** a structure above the stage of a theater, from which hung scenery and the like are manipulated. **5.** GRID (def. 9). —*v.t.* **6.** to mark off into squares or design with a network of squares.

grid·lock (grid′lok′), *n.* **1.** a major traffic jam in which all vehicular movement comes to a stop because key intersections are blocked by traffic. **2.** a complete stoppage of normal activity: *a financial gridlock due to high interest rates.* —*v.t., v.i.* **3.** to cause or undergo a gridlock.

grief (grēf), *n.* **1.** keen mental suffering or distress over affliction or loss; sharp sorrow; painful regret. **2.** a cause or occasion of keen distress or sorrow. **3.** *Informal.* trouble; difficulty; annoyance: *Don't let his silly remark give you grief.* —*Idiom.* **4. come to grief,** to suffer misfortune. **5. good grief,** (used as an exclamation of dismay, surprise, or relief): *Good grief, it's started to rain again!*

grief′-strick′en, *adj.* overwhelmed by grief; deeply afflicted or sorrowful.

Grieg (grēg), *n.* **Edvard,** 1843-1907, Norwegian composer.

griev•ance (grē′vəns), *n.* **1.** a wrong considered as grounds for complaint. **2.** a complaint or resentment, as against an unjust act.

griev′ance commit′tee, *n.* a group of representatives chosen from a labor union or from both labor and management to consider and remedy workers' grievances.

griev•ant (grē′vənt), *n.* a person who submits a complaint for arbitration.

grieve (grēv), *v.,* **grieved, griev•ing.** —*v.i.* **1.** to feel grief or great sorrow. —*v.t.* **2.** to distress mentally; cause to feel grief or sorrow. —**griev′ed•ly,** *adv.* —**griev′er,** *n.* —**griev′ing•ly,** *adv.*

griev•ous (grē′vəs), *adj.* **1.** causing grief or great sorrow: *a grievous loss.* **2.** causing serious harm; flagrant; atrocious: *a grievous offense.* **3.** characterized by great pain or suffering: *arrested for causing grievous bodily harm.* **4.** burdensome or oppressive: *a grievous tax.* **5.** full of or expressing grief; sorrowful: *a grievous cry.* —**griev′ous•ly,** *adv.* —**griev′ous•ness,** *n.*

grif•fin (grif′in) also **griffon, gryphon,** *n.* a fabled monster, usu. having the head and wings of an eagle and the body of a lion. —**grif′fin•esque′,** *adj.*

griffin

Grif•fith (grif′ith), *n.* D(avid Lewelyn) W(ark), 1875–1948, U.S. film director and producer.

grif•fon¹ (grif′ən), *n.* **1.** a Belgian breed of toy dogs with upturned nose and wiry or smooth reddish brown coat. **2.** Also called **wirehaired pointing griffon.** a Dutch breed of medium-sized dogs having a coarse, wiry coat, usu. grayish with chestnut markings.

grif•fon² (grif′ən), *n.* GRIFFIN.

grift (grift), *n. Slang.* **1.** the practice of obtaining money by swindles, frauds, etc. **2.** money obtained from such practices. —**grift′er,** *n.*

grill (gril), *n.* **1.** an apparatus topped by a grated metal framework for cooking food over direct heat, as a gas or charcoal fire. **2.** a metal grate for broiling food over a fire; gridiron. **3.** a dish of grilled meat, fish, vegetables, etc. **4.** GRILLROOM. **5.** a group of small pyramidal marks, embossed or impressed in parallel rows on certain postage stamps to prevent erasure of cancellation marks. —*v.t.* **6.** to broil on a grill. **7.** to subject to severe and persistent cross-examination or questioning. **8.** to torment with heat. **9.** to mark with a series of parallel bars like those of a grill. —**grill′er,** *n.*

grille or **grill** (gril), *n.* **1.** a grating or openwork barrier, as for a gate, usu. of metal and often of decorative design. **2.** an opening covered by grillwork for admitting air to cool the engine of an automobile or the like. **3.** a perforated screen used to cover something, as a loudspeaker. **4.** a ticket window covered by a grating. —**grilled,** *adj.*

grill•room (gril′rōōm′, -rŏŏm′), *n.* a restaurant or dining room, as in a hotel, that specializes in serving grilled meat and fish.

grill•work (gril′wûrk′), *n.* material so formed as to function as or to have the appearance of a grille.

grilse (grils), *n., pl.* **grils•es,** (*esp. collectively*) **grilse.** an Atlantic salmon on its first return from the sea to fresh water.

grim (grim), *adj.,* **grim•mer, grim•mest.** **1.** stern and admitting of no compromise; harsh; unyielding: *grim determination.* **2.** of a sinister or ghastly character: *a grim joke.* **3.** having a harsh, forbidding, or morbid air: *a grim countenance.* **4.** fierce, savage, or cruel: *War is a grim business.* **5.** *Informal.* unpleasant. —**grim′ly,** *adv.* —**grim′ness,** *n.*

grim•ace (grim′əs, gri mās′), *n., v.,* **-aced, -ac•ing.** —*n.* **1.** a facial expression, often ugly or contorted, that indicates disapproval, pain, etc. —*v.i.* **2.** to make grimaces. —**grim′ac•er,** *n.*

gri•mal•kin (gri mal′kin, -môl′-), *n.* **1.** a cat. **2.** an old female cat. **3.** an ill-tempered old woman.

grime (grīm), *n., v.,* **grimed, grim•ing.** —*n.* **1.** dirt, soot, or other filthy matter, esp. adhering to or embedded in a surface. —*v.t.* **2.** to cover with dirt; make very dirty; soil. —**grim′i•ly,** *adv.* —**grim′i•ness** *n.* —**grim′y,** *adj.,* **-i•er, -i•est.**

Grimm (grim), *n.* **Jakob Ludwig Karl,** 1785–1863, and his brother **Wilhelm Karl,** 1786–1859, German philologists and folklorists.

Grim′ Reap′er, *n.* the personification of death as a man or cloaked skeleton holding a scythe.

grin (grin), *v.,* **grinned, grin•ning,** *n.* —*v.i.* **1.** to smile broadly, esp. as an indication of pleasure, amusement, or the like. **2.** to draw back the lips so as to show the teeth, as a snarling dog or a person in pain. —*v.t.* **3.** to express by grinning. —*n.* **4.** a broad smile. **5.** the act of producing a broad smile. **6.** the act of withdrawing the lips and showing the teeth, as in anger or pain. —**grin′ner,** *n.*

grind (grīnd), *v.,* **ground, grind•ing,** *n.* —*v.t.* **1.** to wear, smooth, or sharpen by abrasion or friction; whet: *to grind a lens.* **2.** to reduce to fine particles, as by pounding or crushing; pulverize. **3.** to oppress, torment, or crush: *ground by poverty.* **4.** to rub harshly or gratingly; grate

together; grit: *to grind one's teeth.* **5.** to operate by turning a crank: *to grind a hand organ.* **6.** to produce by crushing or abrasion: *to grind flour.* —*v.i.* **7.** to reduce something to fine particles. **8.** to rub harshly; grate. **9.** to be or become ground. **10.** to be polished or sharpened by friction. **11.** *Informal.* to work or study laboriously (often fol. by *away*). **12. grind out, a.** to produce in a routine or mechanical way. **b.** to extinguish (a cigarette or cigar) against a surface. —*n.* **13.** the act of grinding. **14.** a grinding sound. **15.** a grade of particle fineness into which a substance is ground: *coffee available in various grinds.* **16.** laborious, usu. uninteresting work. **17.** *Informal.* an excessively diligent student. —**grind′a•ble,** *adj.* —**grind′a•bil′i•ty,** *n.* —**grind′ing•ly,** *adv.*

grind•er (grīn′dər), *n.* **1.** a person or thing that grinds. **2.** a kitchen device or appliance for grinding food. **3.** a sharpener of tools. **4. a.** a molar tooth. **b. grinders,** *Slang.* the teeth. **5.** *Chiefly New Eng. and Inland North.* HERO SANDWICH.

grind′ing wheel′, *n.* a wheel composed of abrasive material, used for grinding.

grind•stone (grīnd′stōn′), *n.* **1.** a rotating solid stone wheel used for sharpening, shaping, etc. **2.** a millstone. —**Idiom.** **3. keep** or **put one's nose to the grindstone,** to work, study, or practice hard and steadily.

grip (grip), *n., v.,* **gripped, grip•ping.** —*n.* **1.** the act of grasping; seizing and holding fast; firm grasp. **2.** the power of gripping: *to have a strong grip.* **3.** a grasp, hold, or control: *in the grip of fear; Get a grip on yourself.* **4.** mental or intellectual hold: *to have a good grip on a problem.* **5.** competence or firmness in dealing with things: *to lose one's grip.* **6.** a special mode of clasping hands: *Members of the club use a secret grip.* **7.** something that seizes and holds, as a clutching device on a cable car. **8.** a handle or hilt. **9.** a sudden, sharp pain; spasm of pain. **10.** GRIPPE. **11.** *Older Use.* a small traveling bag. **12. a.** a stagehand. **b.** a general assistant on a film set for shifting scenery, moving furniture, etc. —*v.t.* **13.** to grasp or seize firmly; hold fast. **14.** to take hold on; hold the interest of: *to grip the mind.* **15.** to attach by a grip or clutch. —*v.i.* **16.** to take firm hold; hold fast. **17.** to take hold on the mind. —**Idiom.** **18. come to grips with,** to face and cope with.

gripe (grīp), *v.,* **griped, grip•ing,** *n.* —*v.i.* **1.** *Informal.* to complain naggingly or constantly; grumble. **2.** to suffer pain in the bowels. —*v.t.* **3.** to seize and hold firmly; grip; grasp; clutch. **4.** to produce pain in (the bowels) as if by constriction. **5.** to annoy or irritate: *His tone of voice gripes me.* **6.** to distress or oppress. —*n.* **7.** the act of gripping, grasping, or clutching. **8.** *Informal.* a nagging complaint. **9.** a firm hold; clutch. **10.** grasp; hold; control. **11.** something that grips or clutches; a claw or grip. **12.** a handle or hilt. **13.** Usu., **gripes.** an intermittent spasmodic pain in the bowels. —**grip′er,** *n.* —**grip′ing•ly,** *adv.*

grippe (grip), *n. Older Use.* INFLUENZA. —**grip′py,** *adj.,* **-pi•er, -pi•est.**

grip•ping (grip′ing), *adj.* holding the attention or interest intensely: *a gripping drama.*

gris•ly (griz′lē), *adj.,* **-li•er, -li•est.** **1.** causing a shudder or feeling of horror; gruesome: *a grisly murder.* **2.** formidable; grim. —**gris′li•ness,** *n.*

grist (grist), *n.* **1.** grain to be ground. **2.** ground grain; meal produced from grinding. **3.** a quantity of grain for grinding at one time; the amount of meal from one grinding. **4.** *Older Use.* a quantity or lot. —**Idiom.** **5. grist for** or **to one's mill,** something used to one's profit or advantage, esp. something seemingly unpromising. —**grist′er,** *n.*

gris•tle (gris′əl), *n.* cartilage, esp. in meat. —**grist′ly,** *adj.,* **-i•er, -i•est.**

grist•mill (grist′mil′), *n.* a mill for grinding grain, esp. the customer's own grain. —**grist′mill′er,** *n.*

grit (grit), *n., v.,* **grit•ted, grit•ting.** —*n.* **1.** hard, abrasive particles, as of sand, stone, or gravel. **2.** firmness of character; indomitable spirit; pluck. **3.** a coarse-grained siliceous rock, usu. with sharp, angular grains. **4.** the granular texture of stone, sandpaper, etc., with respect to coarseness or fineness. —*v.t.* **5.** to cause to grind or grate together. —*v.i.* **6.** to make a scratchy or slightly grating sound, as of sand being walked on; grate. —**Idiom.** **7. grit one's teeth,** to show tenseness, anger, or determination by clamping or grinding the teeth together. —**grit′ti•ly,** *adv.* —**grit′ti•ness,** *n.* —**grit′ty,** *adj.* **-ti•er, -ti•est.**

grits (grits), *n. (used with a sing. or pl. v.)* **1.** coarsely ground hominy, usu. boiled and served as a breakfast cereal or a side dish. **2.** grain hulled and coarsely ground.

griz•zle (griz′əl), *v.,* **-zled, -zling,** *adj., n.* —*v.i., v.t.* **1.** to make or become gray or partly gray. —*adj.* **2.** gray; grayish; devoid of hue. —*n.* **3.** gray or partly gray hair. **4.** a gray wig.

griz•zled (griz′əld), *adj.* **1.** having gray or partly gray hair. **2.** gray or partly gray.

griz•zly (griz′lē), *adj.,* **-zli•er, -zli•est,** *n., pl.* **-zlies.** —*adj.* **1.** somewhat gray; grayish. **2.** gray-haired. —*n.* **3.** GRIZZLY BEAR.

griz′zly bear′, *n.* a large North American brown bear, *Ursus arctos horribilis,* with coarse, gray-tipped fur: now restricted to interior Alaska, W Canada, and the N Rocky Mountains in the U.S.

groan (grōn), *n.* **1.** a low, mournful sound uttered in pain or grief. **2.** a deep, inarticulate sound uttered in derision, disapproval, etc. **3.** a deep grating or creaking sound due to a sudden or continued overburdening, as with a great weight. —*v.i.* **4.** to utter a deep, mournful sound expressive of pain or grief; moan. **5.** to make a deep, inarticulate sound expressive of derision, disapproval, etc. **6.** to make a sound resembling a groan; resound harshly: *The steps of the old house groaned under my*

G

weight. **7.** to be overburdened or overloaded. —*v.t.* **8.** to utter or express with groans. —**groan′er,** *n.*

gro•cer (grō′sər), *n.* the owner or operator of a store that sells general food supplies and certain nonedible articles of household use, as soaps and paper products. [< Old French *gross(i)er* wholesale merchant]

gro•cer•y (grō′sə rē, grōs′rē), *n., pl.* **-cer•ies.** **1.** Also called **gro′cery store′.** a grocer's store. **2.** Usu., **groceries.** food and other commodities sold by a grocer.

gro•dy (grō′dē), *adj.,* **-di•er, -di•est.** *Slang.* dirty or disgusting; sleazy; seedy. —**gro′di•ness,** *n.*

grog (grog), *n.* a mixture of rum and water, often flavored with lemon, sugar, and spices and sometimes served hot.

grog•gy (grog′ē), *adj.,* **-gi•er, -gi•est.** **1.** staggering, as from exhaustion or blows. **2.** dazed and weakened, as from lack of sleep. —**grog′gi•ly,** *adv.* —**grog′gi•ness,** *n.*

groin (groin), *n.* **1.** the fold or hollow where the thigh joins the abdomen. **2.** the general region of this fold or hollow.

grom•met (grom′it, grum′-) also **grummet,** *n.* **1.** any of various rings or washers, esp. one used as an insulator or gasket or as an eyelet protecting material where a rope passes. **2.** a ring of rope or wire used to secure sails, oars, etc. **3.** a washer or packing for sealing joints between sections of pipe. **4.** a metal-bound eyelet in cloth, sometimes used decoratively, as on a garment.

groom (gro͞om, gro͝om), *n.* **1.** BRIDEGROOM. **2.** a man or boy in charge of horses or a stable. **3.** any of several officers of the English royal household. —*v.t.* **4.** to tend carefully as to person and dress; make neat or tidy. **5.** to clean, brush, and otherwise tend (a horse, dog, etc.). **6.** to prepare for a position, election, etc.: *The mayor is being groomed for the presidency.* **7.** (of an animal) to tend (itself or another) by removing dirt or parasites from the fur, skin, feathers, etc.: often performed as a social act. [< Middle English *grom* boy, groom] —**groom′er,** *n.*

grooms•man (gro͞omz′mən, gro͝omz′-), *n., pl.* **-men.** a man who attends the bridegroom in a wedding ceremony.

Groot (*Du.* KHRōt; *Eng.* grōt), *n.* **Gerhard.** GROOTE, GERHARD.

Groote (*Du.* KHRō′tə; *Eng.* grōt), *n.* **Ger•hard** (*Du.* KHā′RäRt; *Eng.* gâr′härt), (*Gerardus Magnus*), 1340–84, Dutch religious reformer, educator, and author: founder of the order of Brethren of the Common Life. Also, **Groot, Groete.**

groove (gro͞ov), *n., v.,* **grooved, groov•ing.** —*n.* **1.** a long, narrow cut or indentation in a surface. **2.** a track or channel of a phonograph record for the needle or stylus. **3.** a fixed routine: *to get into a groove.* **4.** the furrow at the bottom of a piece of type. **5.** *Slang.* an enjoyable time or experience. —*v.t.* **6.** to cut a groove in; furrow. —*v.i.* **7.** *Slang.* **a.** to take great pleasure; enjoy oneself in a relaxed way: *grooving on the music.* **b.** to interact well; feel a rapport. **8.** to fix in a groove. —***Idiom.*** **9. in the groove,** *Slang.* **a.** in perfect form. **b.** in the popular fashion; up-to-date. —**groove′like′,** *adj.* —**groov′er,** *n.*

groov•y (gro͞o′vē), *adj.,* **groov•i•er, groov•i•est.** *Slang.* very pleasing; fashionably attractive; wonderful: *a groovy car.*

grope (grōp), *v.,* **groped, grop•ing,** *n.* —*v.i.* **1.** to feel about with the hands; feel one's way hesitantly: *to grope around in the darkness.* **2.** to search blindly or uncertainly: *to be groping for an answer.* —*v.t.* **3.** to seek by or as if by groping: *to grope one's way up the dark stairs.* —*n.* **4.** an act or instance of groping. —**grop′er,** *n.*

Gro•pi•us (grō′pē əs), *n.* **Walter,** 1883–1969, German architect, in the U.S. after 1937.

gros•beak (grōs′bēk′), *n.* any of various finches having a thick conical bill.

gros•grain (grō′grān′), *n.* a heavy corded ribbon or cloth of silk or rayon. —**gros′grained′,** *adj.*

gros point (grō′ point′), *n., pl.* **gros points.** **1.** a large stitch used in embroidery. **2.** a type of point lace with raised work and large designs.

gross (grōs), *adj.,* **gross•er, gross•est,** *n., pl.* **gross** for 11, **gross•es** for 12; *v.* —*adj.* **1.** without or before deductions; total (opposed to *net*): *gross earnings; gross sales.* **2.** flagrant and extreme; glaring: *gross injustice.* **3.** unqualified; rank. **4.** indelicate, indecent, obscene, or vulgar: *gross language.* **5.** lacking in refinement, good manners, education, etc.; unrefined. **6.** extremely or excessively fat. **7.** large, big, or bulky. **8.** of or concerning only the broadest or most general considerations, aspects, etc. **9.** *Slang.* extremely offensive or disgusting. **10.** thick; dense; heavy: *gross vegetation.* —*n.* **11.** a group of 12 dozen, or 144, things. *Abbr.:* gro. **12.** total income, profits, etc., before any deductions (opposed to *net*). —*v.t.* **13.** to have, make, or earn as a total before any deductions, as of taxes, expenses, etc.: *The company grossed over three million dollars last year.* **14. gross out,** *Slang.* to disgust or offend, esp. by crude language or behavior. —**gross′ly,** *adv.* —**gross′ness,** *n.*

gross•er (grō′sər), *n.* *Informal.* a motion picture or the like that grosses a certain amount of money: *a big box-office grosser.*

gross′ na′tional prod′uct, *n.* the total monetary value of all goods and services produced in a country during one year. *Abbr.:* GNP

gross′-out′, *n.* *Slang.* something disgusting or offensive.

gross′ ton′, *n.* *Chiefly Brit.* a long ton. See under TON[1] (def. 1).

gross′ weight′, *n.* total weight without deduction for tare or waste.

gro•tesque (grō tesk′), *adj.* **1.** odd or unnatural in shape, appearance, or character; fantastically ugly or absurd; bizarre. **2.** fantastic in the shaping and combination of forms, as in decorative work combining incongruous human and animal figures with scrolls, foliage, etc. —*n.* **3.** a grotesque object, design, person, or thing. —**gro•tesque′ly,** *adv.* —**gro•tesque′ness,** *n.*

Gro•ti•us (grō′shē əs), *n.* **Hugo** (*Huig De Groot*), 1583–1645, Dutch jurist and statesman.

grot•to (grot′ō), *n., pl.* **-toes, -tos.** **1.** a cave or cavern. **2.** an artificial cavernlike recess or structure. —**grot′toed,** *adj.*

grouch (grouch), *n.* **1.** a sulky, complaining, or morose person. **2.** a sulky, irritable, or morose mood. **3.** an ill-humored complaint. —*v.i.* **4.** to be sulky or morose; complain irritably. —**grouch′i•ly,** *adv.* —**grouch′i•ness,** *n.* —**grouch′y,** *adj.,* **-i•er, -i•est.**

grouch•y (grou′chē), *adj.,* **grouch•i•er, grouch•i•est.** sullenly discontented; sulky. —**grouch′i•ly,** *adv.* —**grouch′i•ness,** *n.*

ground[1] (ground), *n.* **1.** the solid surface of the earth; firm or dry land. **2.** earth or soil: *stony ground.* **3.** land having an indicated character: *rising ground.* **4.** Often, **grounds.** a tract of land appropriated to a special use: *picnic grounds; a hunting ground.* **5.** Often, **grounds.** the foundation or basis on which a belief or action rests; reason or cause: *grounds for dismissal.* **6.** subject for discussion; topic: *to go repeatedly over the same ground.* **7.** rational or factual support for one's position or attitude, as in a debate or argument: *on firm ground.* **8.** the main surface or background in painting, decorative work, lace, etc. **9.** the background in a visual field, contrasted with the figure. **10.** a coating of a substance serving as a surface to be worked on, as in painting or etching. **11. grounds,** dregs or sediment: *coffee grounds.* **12. grounds,** the gardens, lawn, etc., surrounding and belonging to a building. **13.** a conducting connection between an electric circuit or equipment and the earth or some other conducting body. **14.** the bottom of a body of water. **15.** the earth's solid or liquid surface; land or water. —*adj.* **16.** situated on, at, or near the surface of the earth: *a ground attack.* **17.** pertaining to the ground. **18.** operating on land: *ground forces.* —*v.t.* **19.** to lay or set on the ground. **20.** to place on a foundation; fix firmly; settle or establish; found. **21.** to instruct in elements or first principles: *to ground students in science.* **22.** to furnish with a ground or background, as on decorative work. **23.** to cover (wallpaper) with colors or other materials before printing. **24.** to establish a ground for (an electric circuit, device, etc.). **25.** to cause (a vessel) to run aground. **26.** to restrict (an aircraft or pilot) to the ground; prevent from flying. **27.** *Informal.* to restrict the activities, esp. the social activities, of, usu. as a punishment. —*v.i.* **28.** to come to or strike the ground. **29.** to hit a ground ball in baseball. **30. ground out,** *Baseball.* to be put out at first base after hitting a ground ball to the infield. —***Idiom.*** **31. break ground, a.** to plow. **b.** to begin excavation for a construction project. **c.** Also, **break new ground.** to do something original or innovative. **32. cover ground, a.** to travel over a certain area. **b.** to make some progress, as in dealing with a subject. **33. cut the ground from under,** to render ineffective or invalid by some anticipatory action. **34. from the ground up, a.** gradually from the most elementary level to the highest level. **b.** extensively; thoroughly. **35. gain ground, a.** to make progress; advance. **b.** to gain approval or acceptance. **36. give ground,** to yield to a superior force or forceful argument; retreat. **37. hold** or **stand one's ground,** to maintain one's position; be steadfast. **38. into the ground,** beyond a reasonable or necessary point: *to run an argument into the ground.* **39. lose ground, a.** to lose one's advantage; fail to advance. **b.** to suffer a reverse; lose popularity, strength, etc. **40. off the ground,** into action or well under way: *The play never got off the ground.* **41. on one's own ground,** in an area or situation that one knows well. **42. shift ground,** to change position in an argument or situation. **43. to ground, a.** into a den, burrow, shelter, or the like: *a fox gone to ground.* **b.** into concealment or hiding. —**ground′a•ble,** *adj.* —**ground′ward, ground′wards,** *adv., adj.*

ground[2] (ground), *v.* **1.** a pt. and pp. of GRIND. —*adj.* **2.** reduced to fine particles by grinding. **3.** having the surface abraded or roughened by or as if by grinding.

ground′ ball′, *n.* a batted baseball that rolls or bounces along the ground. Also called **grounder.**

ground′ bee′tle, *n.* any of numerous nocturnal, terrestrial beetles of the family Carabidae that feed chiefly on other insects.

ground•break•ing (ground′brā′king), *n.* **1.** the act or ceremony of breaking ground for a new construction. —*adj.* **2.** of or pertaining to a groundbreaking. **3.** originating or pioneering a new endeavor, field of inquiry, or the like. —**ground′break′er,** *n.*

ground′ cher′ry, *n.* **1.** any plant belonging to the genus *Physalis,* of the nightshade family, bearing an edible berry enclosed in an enlarged calyx. **2.** the fruit of any of these plants. Also called **husk tomato.**

ground′ control′, *n.* an airport facility that supervises the movement of aircraft and ground vehicles on ramps and taxiways. —**ground′ control′ler,** *n.*

ground′ cov′er, *n.* **1.** the herbaceous plants and low shrubs in a forest, considered as a whole. **2.** any of various low-growing plants and trailing vines used for covering the ground, esp. where grass is difficult to grow.

ground′ crew′, *n.* ground personnel responsible for the maintenance and repair of aircraft.

ground′-effect′ machine′, *n.* HOVERCRAFT.

ground•er (groun′dər), *n.* GROUND BALL.

ground′ floor′, *n.* **1.** the floor of a building at or nearest to ground level. **2.** *Informal.* an advantageous position or opportunity in a new enterprise.

ground′ glass′, *n.* **1.** glass that has had its polished surface removed by fine grinding and that is used to diffuse light. **2.** glass that has been ground into fine particles, esp. for use as an abrasive.

ground′ hem′lock, *n.* a prostrate yew, *Taxus canadensis*, of E North America, having flat needles and red berrylike fruit.

ground′hog′ or **ground′ hog′,** *n.* WOODCHUCK.

Ground′hog Day′, *n.* February 2, the day on which, according to folklore, the groundhog emerges from hibernation: if it sees its shadow, six more weeks of wintry weather are predicted.

ground′ i′vy, *n.* a creeping aromatic plant, *Glechoma hederacea*, of the mint family, having rounded leaves and clusters of small blue flowers.

ground·keep·er (ground′kē′pər), *n.* GROUNDSKEEPER.

ground·less (ground′lis), *adj.* without rational basis; unfounded: *groundless fears.* —**ground′less·ly,** *adv.* —**ground′less·ness,** *n.*

ground·ling (ground′ling), *n.* **1.** a plant or animal that lives on or close to the ground or at the bottom of the water. **2.** a person of unsophisticated or uncritical tastes. **3.** a person on the ground rather than in an aircraft. **4.** a member of a theater audience sitting in one of the cheaper seats or, in an Elizabethan theater, standing in the pit.

ground·mass (ground′mas′), *n.* the crystalline, granular, or glassy base or matrix of a porphyritic or other igneous rock, in which the more prominent crystals are embedded.

ground′ mer′istem, *n.* an area of primary growing tissue, at the stem tips of a plant, that develops into pith and cortex.

ground·nut (ground′nut′), *n.* **1.** a twining North American plant, *Apios tuberosa*, of the legume family, having clusters of fragrant brownish flowers and an edible tuber. **2.** *South Atlantic U.S., Brit.* PEANUT.

ground·out (ground′out′), *n.* a baseball play in which a batter is put out at first base after hitting a ground ball to the infield.

ground′ plan′, *n.* **1.** the plan of a floor of a building. **2.** a first or fundamental plan.

ground′ rule′, *n.* **1.** a basic or governing principle of conduct in a situation: *the ground rules of a debate.* **2.** any of certain sports rules adopted, as in baseball, for playing in a particular stadium or field.

grounds·keep·er (groundz′kē′pər) also **groundkeeper,** *n.* a person responsible for the care and maintenance of an estate, park, football field, or the like. —**ground′keep′ing,** *n.*

ground′speed′ or **ground′ speed′,** *n.* the speed of an aircraft with reference to the ground. Compare AIRSPEED.

ground′ squir′rel, *n.* any of various striped or variegated, mostly burrowing rodents of the squirrel family, esp. of the genus *Spermophilus* (or *Citellus*), that are widespread in North America and Eurasia and often do much damage to crops. Also called **gopher.**

ground′ stroke′, *n.* a tennis stroke made by hitting the ball after it has bounced from the ground.

ground′ sub′stance, *n.* **1.** Also called **matrix.** the substance in which tissue, cells, and intercellular structures are embedded or suspended. **2.** HYALOPLASM.

ground·swell (ground′swel′), *n.* **1.** a broad, deep swell or rolling of the sea, due to a distant storm or gale. **2.** a surge of feelings, esp. among the general public: *a groundswell of support for the governor.*

ground′-to-air′, *adj.* SURFACE-TO-AIR.

ground′wa′ter or **ground′ wa′ter,** *n.* the water beneath the surface of the ground, the source of spring and well water.

ground·work (ground′wûrk′), *n.* foundation or basis: *to lay the groundwork for an international conference.*

ground′ ze′ro, *n.* **1.** the point on the surface of the earth or water directly below, directly above, or at which an atomic or hydrogen bomb explodes. **2.** *Informal.* the very beginning or most elementary level.

group (grōōp), *n.* **1.** any collection or assemblage of persons or things; cluster; aggregation. **2.** a number of persons or things ranged or considered together as being related in some way. **3.** Also called **radical.** two or more atoms specifically arranged and usu. behaving as a single entity, as the hydroxyl group, –OH. **4.** any of the vertical columns of elements in the periodic table. **5.** a division of stratified rocks comprising two or more formations. **6. a.** an administrative and tactical unit of the U.S. Army consisting of two or more battalions and a headquarters. **b.** an administrative and operational unit of the U.S. Air Force subordinate to a wing, usu. composed of two or more squadrons. **7.** a section of an orchestra comprising the instruments of the same class. **8.** an algebraic system that is closed under an associative operation, as multiplication or addition, and in which there is an identity element that, on operating on another element, leaves the second element unchanged, and in which each element has corresponding to it a unique element that, on operating on the first, results in the identity element. —*v.t.* **9.** to place together in a group, as with others. **10.** to form into a group or groups. —*v.i.* **11.** to form a group. **12.** to be part of a group. —**group′wise,** *adv.* —Usage. See COLLECTIVE NOUN.

group′ dynam′ics, *n.* **1.** (*used with a pl. v.*) the interactions that influence the attitudes and behavior of people when they are grouped with others. **2.** (*used with a sing. v.*) the study of such interactions.

group·er[1] (grōō′pər), *n., pl.* (*esp. collectively*) **-er,** (*esp. for kinds or species*) **-ers.** any of various large warm-water sea basses, esp. of the genera *Epinephelus* and *Mycteroperca*.

group·er[2] (grōō′pər), *n.* **1.** a member of a group, as of tourists. **2.** *In-* *formal.* a member of a group of usu. single people who rent and share a house, as at a summer resort.

group·ie (grōō′pē), *n.* **1.** a young person, esp. a teenage girl, who is an ardent admirer of rock musicians and may follow them on tour. **2.** an ardent fan of a celebrity or of a particular activity: *a tennis groupie.*

group·ing (grōō′ping), *n.* **1.** an act or process of placing in groups. **2.** a set or arrangement of persons or things in a group.

group′ insur′ance, *n.* life, accident, or health insurance available to a group of persons, as the employees of a company, under a single contract.

group′ prac′tice, *n.* **1.** Also called **group′ med′icine.** the practice of medicine by an association of physicians and other health professionals who work together, usu. in one suite of offices. **2.** any similar practice by an association of professional persons. **3.** a system in which legal services are provided by a corporation retaining a number of lawyers.

group′ the′ory, *n.* the branch of mathematics that deals with the structure of mathematical groups and mappings between them.

group′ ther′apy, *n.* psychotherapy in which a group of patients, usu. led by a therapist, discuss, act out, or attempt to solve their problems.

group·think (grōōp′thingk′), *n.* the tendency of a decision-making group to strive for consensus and to avoid critical examination of alternatives.

group·ware (grōōp′wâr), *n.* software enabling a group to work together on common projects, share data, and synchronize schedules, esp. through networked computers.

grouse[1] (grous), *n., pl.* **grouse, grous·es.** any of various plump gallinaceous birds of the subfamily Tetraoninae, of the pheasant family, with a short bill and feathered legs. —**grouse′like′,** *adj.*

grouse[2] (grous), *v.,* **groused, grous·ing,** *n. Informal.* —*v.i.* **1.** to grumble; complain. —*n.* **2.** a complaint. —**grous′er,** *n.*

grout (grout), *n.* **1.** a thin, coarse mortar poured into narrow cavities, as masonry joints or rock fissures, to fill them and consolidate the adjoining objects into a solid mass. **2.** a coat of plaster for finishing a ceiling or interior wall. **3.** Usu., **grouts.** lees; grounds. —*v.t.* **4.** to fill or consolidate with grout. **5.** to use as grout. —**grout′er,** *n.*

grove (grōv), *n.* **1.** a small wood or forested area, usu. with no undergrowth. **2.** a small orchard or stand of fruit-bearing trees, esp. citrus trees.

grov·el (grov′əl, gruv′-), *v.i.,* **-eled, -el·ing** or (*esp. Brit.*) **-elled, -el·ling. 1.** to humble oneself or act in an abject manner. **2.** to lie or crawl with the face downward and the body prostrate, esp. in abject humility, fear, etc. **3.** to take pleasure in mean or base things. —**grov′el·er,** *esp. Brit.* **grov′el·ler,** *n.* —**grov′el·ing·ly,** *esp. Brit.* **grov′el·ling·ly,** *adv.*

Groves (grōvz), *n.* **Leslie Richard,** 1896–1970, U.S. general.

grow (grō), *v.,* **grew, grown, grow·ing.** —*v.i.* **1.** to increase in size by a natural process of development. **2.** to come into being and develop: *a plant that grows wild here.* **3.** to form and increase in size by a process of inorganic accretion, as by crystallization. **4.** to arise or issue as a natural development: *Our friendship grew from common interests.* **5.** to increase gradually in size, amount, etc.; expand: *Her influence has grown.* **6.** to become gradually attached or united by or as if by growth. **7.** to come to be by degrees; become: *to grow old.* —*v.t.* **8.** to cause to grow: *They grow corn.* **9.** to allow to grow: *to grow a beard.* **10.** to cover with a growth (used in the passive): *a field grown with corn.* **11. grow into, a.** to become large or tall enough to wear (an item of clothing). **b.** to become mature or experienced enough to handle. **12. grow on** or **upon, a.** to increase in influence or effect. **b.** to become gradually more liked or accepted by. **13. grow out of, a.** to become too large or mature for; outgrow. **b.** to originate in; develop from. **14. grow up, a.** to be or become fully grown; attain maturity. **b.** to come into existence; arise.

grow′ing pains′, *n.pl.* **1.** dull, quasi-rheumatic pains of varying degree in the limbs during childhood and adolescence, often popularly associated with the process of growing. **2.** emotional difficulties experienced during adolescence and preadulthood. **3.** difficulties attending a new project or rapid development of an existing project.

Grow′ing Seed′, The, a parable of Jesus. Mark 4:26–29.

growl (groul), *v.i.* **1.** to utter a deep guttural sound of anger or hostility, as a dog. **2.** to murmur or complain angrily; grumble. **3.** to rumble: *The thunder growled.* —*v.t.* **4.** to express by growling. —*n.* **5.** the act or sound of growling. —**growl′ing·ly,** *adv.* —**growl′y,** *adj.,* **growl·i·er, growl·i·est.**

grow′ light′, *n.* a fluorescent light bulb designed to emit light of a wavelength conducive to plant growth.

grown (grōn), *adj.* **1.** arrived at full growth or maturity; adult: *a grown man.* —*v.* **2.** pp. of GROW.

grown′-up′, *adj.* **1.** having reached the age of maturity. **2.** characteristic of or suitable for adults. —**grown′-up′ness,** *n.*

grown-up (grōn′up′), *n.* a mature, fully grown person; adult.

growth (grōth), *n.* **1.** the act or process or a manner of growing; development; gradual increase. **2.** size or stage of development: *to reach one's full growth.* **3.** completed development. **4.** development from a simpler to a more complex stage. **5.** development from another but related form or stage. **6.** something that has grown or developed: *a growth of weeds.* **7.** an abnormal increase in a mass of tissue, as a tumor. **8.** origin; source; production: *tobacco of domestic growth.* —*adj.* **9.** of or designating a business, industry, or equity security that grows or is expected to grow in value, earnings, etc., at a rate higher than average: *a growth industry; growth stocks.*

growth′ fund′, *n.* a mutual fund that invests primarily in growth stocks.

growth′ hor′mone, *n.* any substance that stimulates or controls the growth of an organism, esp. a species-specific hormone, as the human hormone somatotropin.

grub (grub), *n., v.,* **grubbed, grub·bing.** —*n.* **1.** the thick-bodied, sluggish larva of certain insects, esp. the beetle. **2.** an unkempt person. **3.** *Slang.* food; victuals. **4.** a dull, plodding person; drudge. —*v.t.* **5.** to dig; clear of roots, stumps, etc. **6.** *Slang.* to supply with food; feed. **7.** *Slang.* to scrounge: *to grub a cigarette.* —*v.i.* **8.** to dig; search by or as if by digging. **9.** to lead a laborious or groveling life; drudge. **10.** to engage in laborious study. —**grub′ber,** *n.*

grub·by (grub′ē), *adj.,* **-bi·er, -bi·est. 1.** dirty; slovenly. **2.** infested with grubs. **3.** contemptible; ignoble: *grubby tricks.* —**grub′bi·ly,** *adv.* —**grub′bi·ness,** *n.*

Gru·ber (grōō′bər), *n.* **Franz,** 1787–1863, German musician: composer of *Silent Night.*

grub·stake (grub′stāk′), *n., v.,* **-staked, -stak·ing.** —*n.* **1.** provisions, gear, etc., furnished to a prospector on condition of participating in the profits of any discoveries. **2.** money or other assistance furnished esp. to launch an enterprise. —*v.t.* **3.** to furnish with a grubstake. —**grub′-stak′er,** *n.*

Grub′ Street′, *n.* **1.** a street in London formerly inhabited by impoverished writers and literary hacks. **2.** literary hacks collectively.

grudge (gruj), *n., v.,* **grudged, grudg·ing.** —*n.* **1.** a feeling of ill will or resentment because of some real or fancied wrong. —*v.t.* **2.** to give or permit with reluctance: *They grudged us every day we were away.* **3.** to resent the good fortune of (another); begrudge. —**grudge′less,** *adj.* —**grudg′er,** *n.*

grudg·ing (gruj′ing), *adj.* displaying reluctance or unwillingness: *grudging acceptance.* —**grudg′ing·ly,** *adv.*

gru·el (grōō′əl), *n.* a thin cooked cereal made by boiling meal, esp. oatmeal, in water or milk.

gru·el·ing (grōō′ə ling, grōō′ling), *adj.* **1.** exhausting; very tiring; arduously severe: *a grueling marathon.* —*n.* **2.** any trying or exhausting procedure or experience. —**gru′el·ing·ly,** *adv.*

grue·some (grōō′səm), *adj.* **1.** causing horror and repugnance: *a gruesome murder.* **2.** full of or causing problems; distressing. —**grue′some·ly,** *adv.* —**grue′some·ness,** *n.*

gruff (gruf), *adj.* **1.** low and harsh; hoarse: *a gruff voice.* **2.** rough, brusque, or surly: *a gruff manner.* —**gruff′ish,** *adj.* —**gruff′ly,** *adv.* —**gruff′ness,** *n.*

grum·ble (grum′bəl), *v.,* **-bled, -bling,** *n.* —*v.i.* **1.** to murmur or mutter in discontent; complain sullenly. **2.** to utter low, indistinct sounds; growl. **3.** to rumble. —*v.t.* **4.** to express or utter with murmuring or complaining. —*n.* **5.** an expression of discontent; complaint. **6.** **grumbles,** a grumbling, discontented mood. **7.** a rumble. —**grum′bler,** *n.* —**grum′bly,** *adj.*

grum·met (grum′it), *n.* GROMMET.

grump (grump), *n.* **1.** a person given to complaining and ill humor. **2.** **the grumps,** a depressed or sulky mood. —*v.i.* **3.** to complain or sulk. —**grump′i·ly,** *adv.* —**grump′i·ness,** *n.* —**grump′y,** *adj.,* **-i·er, -i·est.**

Grun·dy (grun′dē), *n.* **Mrs.,** a narrow-minded, conventional person who is extremely critical of any breach of propriety. [after *Mrs. Grundy,* a character mentioned in the play *Speed the Plough* (1798) by Thomas Morton (1764?–1838), English playwright]

Grü·ne·wald (grōō′nə väld′), *n.* **Mathias,** (*Mathias Neithardt-Gothardt*), c1470–1528, German painter and architect.

grunge (grunj), *n. Slang.* **1.** dirt; filth; rubbish. **2.** something unpleasant or of inferior quality. —**grun′gi·ness,** *n.* —**grun′gy,** *adj.,* **-i·er, -i·est.**

grun·ion (grun′yən), *n.* a small silversides, *Leuresthes tenuis,* that lays its eggs on S California beaches.

grunt (grunt), *v.i.* **1.** to utter the deep, guttural sound characteristic of a hog. **2.** to utter a similar sound. **3.** to grumble, as in discontent. —*v.t.* **4.** to express with a grunt. —*n.* **5.** a sound of grunting. **6.** *Slang.* an infantryman. **7.** *Slang.* an unskilled worker; laborer. —**grunt′er,** *n.*

Gru·yère (grōō yâr′, gri-; *Fr.* grʏ yer′), *n.* a firm yellow cow's milk cheese, esp. of France and Switzerland, having small holes.

gryph·on (grif′ən), *n.* GRIFFIN.

GSA or **G.S.A., 1.** General Services Administration. **2.** Girl Scouts of America.

G-suit (jē′sōōt′), *n.* a garment designed to protect a pilot or astronaut from the effects of excessive acceleration forces.

GT, 1. an automobile in the style of a coupe, seating two or sometimes four, designed for comfort and high speed. **2.** a high-speed, two-door model of a four-door sedan.

gt., 1. gilt. **2.** great.

gtd., guaranteed.

GTO, Gran Turismo Omologato: conforming to specifications for a class of automobiles qualified to engage in various types of competitions.

GU, Guam.

gua·ca·mo·le (gwä kə mō′lē), *n.* a Mexican dip of mashed avocado mixed with lemon or lime juice, seasonings, and often tomato and onion.

gua·cha·ro (gwä′chə rō′), *n., pl.* **-ros.** OILBIRD.

gua·co (gwä′kō), *n., pl.* **-cos. 1.** a climbing composite plant, *Mikania guaco,* of tropical America. **2.** its leaves or a leaf extract, used locally for snakebite.

Gua·da·la·ja·ra (gwäd′l ə här′ə), *n.* the capital of Jalisco, in W Mexico. 2,244,715.

Gua·dal·ca·nal (gwäd′l kə nal′), *n.* the largest of the Solomon Islands, in the W central Pacific: U.S. victory over the Japanese 1942–43. 23,922; ab. 2500 sq. mi. (6475 sq. km).

Gua′dalupe Moun′tains Na′tional Park′, *n.* a national park E of El Paso, Texas: limestone fossil reef. 129 sq. mi. (334 sq. km).

Gua·de·loupe (gwäd′l ōōp′), *n.* two islands (**Basse-Terre** and **Grande-Terre**) separated by a narrow channel in the Leeward Islands of the West Indies: together with five dependencies they form an overseas department of France. 334,900; 687 sq. mi. (1179 sq. km). *Cap.:* Basse-Terre.

guai·ac (gwī′ak), *n.* a greenish brown resin obtained from the guaiacum tree, esp. from *Guaiacum officinale,* used in varnishes, as a food preservative, and as a medical test for the presence of blood in excreted matter. **2.** GUAIACUM (def. 2).

guai·a·cum (gwī′ə kəm), *n.* **1.** any of several tropical American trees or shrubs belonging to the genus *Guaiacum* of the caltrop family. **2.** the wood of this tree; lignum vitae. **3.** GUAIAC.

Guam (gwäm), *n.* an island in the W Pacific, the largest of the Mariana Islands: an unincorporated U.S. territory. 120,000; 212 sq. mi. (549 sq. km). *Cap.:* Agaña. *Abbr.:* GU —**Gua·ma′ni·an** (-mä′nē ən), *n., adj.*

guan (gwän), *n.* any of various long-tailed, typically arboreal gallinaceous birds of the family Cracidae, inhabiting New World tropical forests.

gua·na·co (gwä nä′kō), *n., pl.* **-cos.** a South American ruminant, *Lama guanicoe,* considered the wild ancestor of the domesticated llama and alpaca.

Guang·zhou or **Kwang·chow** or **Kuang·chou** (gwäng′jō′), *n.* the capital of Guangdong province, in SE China, on the Zhu Jiang. 3,290,000. Also called **Canton.**

guan·i·dine (gwan′i dēn′, -din, gwä′ni-), *n.* a crystalline, alkaline, water-soluble solid, CH_5N_3, used in making plastics, resins, and explosives.

gua·nine (gwä′nēn), *n.* a purine base, $C_5H_5N_5O$, that is a fundamental constituent of DNA and RNA, in which it forms base pairs with cytosine. *Symbol:* G

gua·no (gwä′nō), *n.* **1.** a natural manure composed chiefly of the excrement of sea birds, found esp. on islands near the Peruvian coast. **2.** any similar substance, as an artificial fertilizer made from fish.

gua·nyl′ic ac′id (gwä nil′ik), *n.* See GMP.

gua·ra·ni (gwär′ə nē′), *n., pl.* **-ni, -nis.** the basic monetary unit of Paraguay.

Gua·ra·ni or **Gua·ra·ní** (gwär′ə nē′), *n., pl.* **-nis, -nies,** (*esp. collectively*) **-ni. 1.** a member of any of a group of American Indian peoples of NE Paraguay and Brazil. **2.** the language of these peoples.

guar·an·tee (gar′ən tē′), *n., v.,* **-teed, -tee·ing.** —*n.* **1.** a promise or assurance, esp. one in writing, that something is of specified quality, content, benefit, etc., or will perform satisfactorily for a given length of time: *a money-back guarantee on a kitchen appliance.* **2.** GUARANTY (defs. 1, 2). **3.** something that assures a particular outcome or condition: *Wealth is no guarantee of happiness.* **4.** a person who gives a guarantee or guaranty; guarantor. **5.** a person to whom a guarantee is made. —*v.t.* **6.** to secure, as by giving or taking security. **7.** to make oneself answerable for (something) on behalf of someone else. **8.** to undertake to ensure for another, as rights or possessions. **9.** to serve as a warrant or guaranty for. **10.** to engage to protect or indemnify: *to guarantee a person against loss.* **11.** to engage (to do something). **12.** to promise (usu. fol. by a clause as object): *I guarantee that I'll be there.*

guar·an·tor (gar′ən tôr′, -tər), *n.* **1.** a person, group, system, etc., that guarantees. **2.** a person who makes or gives a guarantee, guaranty, warrant, etc.

guar·an·ty (gar′ən tē′), *n., pl.* **-ties. 1.** a warrant, pledge, or formal assurance given as security that another's debt or obligation will be fulfilled. **2.** something that is taken or presented as security. **3.** the act of giving security. **4.** a person who acts as a guarantor.

guard (gärd), *v.t.* **1.** to keep safe from harm or danger; protect; watch over. **2.** to keep under close watch in order to prevent escape, misconduct, etc. **3.** to keep under control as a matter of caution or prudence: *to guard one's temper.* **4.** to provide or equip with some safeguard or protective appliance, as to prevent loss, injury, etc. **5.** to position oneself in some sport so as to obstruct or impede the movement or progress of (an opponent on offense). **6.** to protect (a chess piece or a square) by placing a piece in a supportive or defensive position relative to it. —*v.i.* **7.** to take precautions (usu. fol. by *against*): *to guard against errors.* **8.** to give protection; keep watch; be watchful. —*n.* **9.** a person or group that guards, as one that keeps watch over prisoners or protects a place from disturbance, theft, etc. **10.** an act of guarding; a close watch, as over a prisoner or other person under restraint. **11.** a device, appliance, or attachment that prevents injury, loss, etc. **12.** something intended or serving to guard or protect; safeguard. **13.** a posture of defense or readiness, as in fencing, boxing, etc. **14. a.** either of the football linemen stationed between a tackle and the center. **b.** the position played by this lineman. **15.** either of the basketball players stationed in the backcourt. **16.** *Brit.* a railroad conductor. —**Idiom. 17. off (one's) guard,** unprepared; unwary. **18. on (one's) guard,** vigilant; wary. **19. stand guard over,** to watch over; protect. —**guard′er,** *n.*

guard′ dog′ or **guard′dog′,** *n.* a large aggressive dog trained to guard persons or property; watchdog.

guard′ du′ty, *n.* a military assignment involving watching over or protecting a person or place or supervising prisoners.

guard•ed (gär′did), *adj.* **1.** cautious; careful; prudent: *guarded comments.* **2.** protected, watched, or restrained, as by a guard. —**guard′ed•ly,** *adv.* —**guard′ed•ness,** *n.*

guard•house (gärd′hous′), *n.*, *pl.* **-hous•es** (-hou′ziz). a building used for housing military personnel on guard duty or for the temporary detention of prisoners.

guard•i•an (gär′dē ən), *n.* **1.** a person who guards, protects, or preserves. **2.** a person legally entrusted with the care of another's person or property, as that of a minor or someone legally incapacitated. —*adj.* **3.** guarding; protecting: *a guardian deity.* —**guard′i•an•ship,** *n.*

guard′ of hon′or, *n.* a guard specially designated for welcoming or escorting distinguished guests or for accompanying a casket in a military funeral. Also called **honor guard.**

guard•rail (gärd′rāl′) also **guard′rail′ing,** *n.* a protective railing, as along a road or stairway.

guards•man (gärdz′mən), *n.*, *pl.* **-men. 1.** a person who acts as a guard. **2.** a member of the U.S. National Guard.

Gua•te•ma•la (gwä′tə mä′lə), *n.* **1.** a republic in N Central America. 11,558,407; 42,042 sq. mi. (108,889 sq. km). **2.** Also called **Gua′tema′la Cit′y.** the capital of this republic. 1,500,000. —**Gua′te•ma′lan,** *adj., n.*

gua•va (gwä′və), *n.*, *pl.* **-vas. 1.** any tropical American tree or shrub of the genus *Psidium,* of the myrtle family, esp. *P. guajava.* **2.** the large yellow fruit of this tree used esp. for making jam.

gu•ber•na•to•ri•al (gōō′bər nə tôr′ē əl, -tōr′-, gyōō′-), *adj.* of or pertaining to a state governor or the office of state governor.

guck (guk, gŏŏk) also **gook,** *n. Slang.* **1.** slime or oozy dirt. **2.** any oozy or slimy substance.

gudg•eon (guj′ən), *n.* **1.** any small European cyprinid fish of the genus *Gobio* often used as bait. **2.** any of certain related fishes.

Guelph[1] or **Guelf** (gwelf), *n.* a member of the political party in medieval Italy that supported the sovereignty of the pope against the German emperors: opposed to the Ghibellines.

Guelph[2] (gwelf), *n.* a city in SE Ontario, in S Canada. 78,235.

gue•ril•la (gə ril′ə), *n.* See **GUERRILLA.**

Guern•sey (gûrn′zē), *n.*, *pl.* **-seys. 1. Isle of,** one of the Channel Islands, in the English Channel. 55,482; 25 sq. mi. (65 sq. km). **2.** one of a breed of tan and white dairy cattle orig. raised on this island.

guer•ril•la or **gue•ril•la** (gə ril′ə), *n.*, *pl.* **-las.** a member of a band of irregular soldiers engaged in guerrilla warfare. [< Spanish: band of guerillas, dim. of *guerra* war] —**guer•ril′la•ism,** *n.*

guerril′la war′fare, *n.* the use of surprise raids, sabotage, etc., by small, mobile groups of irregular forces operating in enemy-held territory.

guess (ges), *v.t.* **1.** to commit oneself to an opinion about (something) without sufficient evidence; hazard: *to guess a person's weight.* **2.** to estimate or conjecture about correctly: *I guessed that would be the answer.* **3.** to think, believe, or suppose: *I guess I can manage alone.* —*v.i.* **4.** to form an estimate or conjecture (often fol. by *at* or *about*): *to guess at the weight of a package.* —*n.* **5.** an opinion that one reaches on the basis of probability alone or in the absence of any evidence. **6.** the act of forming such an opinion: *to take a guess at someone's weight.* —*Saying.* **7. Your guess is as good as mine,** when unknowns predominate, anyone's answer may be correct. —**guess′er,** *n.*

guess•ti•mate or **gues•ti•mate** (*v.* ges′tə māt′; *n.* -mit, -māt′), *v.*, **-mat•ed, -mat•ing,** *n.* —*v.t.* **1.** to estimate without substantial basis in facts or statistics. —*n.* **2.** an estimate arrived at by guesswork.

guess•work (ges′wûrk′), *n.* work or procedure based on the making of guesses or conjectures.

guest (gest), *n.* **1.** a person who spends some time at another's home in a social activity, as a visit or party. **2.** a person who receives the hospitality of a club, a city, or the like. **3.** a person who patronizes a hotel, restaurant, etc., for what it provides. **4.** an often well-known person invited to appear in a regular program, series, etc., as a substitute for a regular member or as a special attraction. —*v.t.* **5.** to entertain as a guest. —*v.i.* **6.** to be a guest; make an appearance as a guest. —*adj.* **7.** provided for or done by a guest: *a guest towel.* **8.** participating or performing as a guest: *a guest conductor.*

Guest (gest), *n.* **Edgar A(lbert),** 1881–1959, U.S. journalist and writer of verse, born in England.

guest•house (gest′hous′), *n.*, *pl.* **-hous•es** (-hou′ziz). **1.** a building for guests separate from the main house on a large property. **2.** BED-AND-BREAKFAST.

gues•ti•mate (*v.* ges′tə māt′; *n.* -mit, -māt′), *v.t.*, **-mat•ed, -mat•ing,** *n.* GUESSTIMATE.

guest′ of hon′or, *n.* **1.** a person in whose honor a dinner, party, etc., is given. **2.** a distinguished person invited to a dinner, meeting, etc., esp. on some unique occasion.

guest′ room′ or **guest′room′,** *n.* a room for the lodging of guests.

guff (guf), *n.* **1.** empty or foolish talk; nonsense. **2.** insolent talk.

guf•faw (gu fô′, gə-), *n.* **1.** a loud, unrestrained burst of laughter. —*v.i.* **2.** to laugh loudly and boisterously.

Gug•gen•heim (gŏŏg′ən hīm′, gōō′gən-), *n.* **Daniel,** 1856–1930, U.S. industrialist and philanthropist.

Gui•an•a (gē an′ə, -ä′nə, gī an′ə), *n.* **1.** a vast tropical region in NE South America, bounded by the Orinoco, Negro, and Amazon rivers and the Atlantic. **2.** the coastal portion of this region, which includes Guyana, French Guiana, and Suriname. —**Gui•an′an, Gui•a•nese′** (-ə nēz′, -nēs′), *adj., n., pl.* **-nese.**

guid•ance (gīd′ns), *n.* **1.** the act or function of guiding; leadership; direction. **2.** advice or counseling, esp. for students on educational or vocational matters. **3.** something that guides. **4.** the process by which the flight of a missile or rocket may be altered by controls located either wholly in the projectile or partly at a ground base.

guide (gīd), *v.*, **guid•ed, guid•ing,** *n.* —*v.t.* **1.** to assist (a person) to travel through, or reach a destination in, an unfamiliar area, as by accompanying or giving directions to the person. **2.** to accompany (a sightseer) to show and comment upon points of interest. **3.** to force (a person, object, or animal) to move in a certain path. **4.** to supply (a person) with advice or counsel. **5.** to supervise (someone's actions or affairs) in an advisory capacity; manage. —*n.* **6.** a person who guides, esp. one hired to guide travelers, tourists, etc. **7.** a mark, tab, or the like to attract the eye and thus provide quick reference. **8.** a book, pamphlet, or the like with information, instructions, or advice; guidebook or handbook. **9.** a guidepost. **10.** a device that regulates or directs progressive motion or action: *a sewing-machine guide.* **11.** a spirit believed to direct the utterances of a medium. —**guid′er,** *n.*

guide•book (gīd′bŏŏk′), *n.* **1.** a book of directions, advice, and information for travelers or tourists. **2.** HANDBOOK (def. 1). —**guide′book′ish, guide′book′y,** *adj.*

guid′ed mis′sile, *n.* an aerial missile, as a rocket, steered during its flight by radio signals, clockwork controls, etc.

guide′ dog′, *n.* a dog that has been specially trained to lead or guide a blind person.

guide•line (gīd′līn′), *n.* **1.** any guide or indication of a future course of action: *guidelines on tax reform.* **2.** a lightly marked line used as a guide, as in composing a drawing or a typed page. **3.** a rope or cord that serves to guide one's steps, as over rocky or unfamiliar terrain.

Guide′ Me′, O′ Thou′ Great′ Jeho′vah, a Christian hymn (1745) with words by William Williams and music (1907) by John Hughes.

guide•post (gīd′pōst′), *n.* **1.** a post bearing a sign for the guidance of travelers, as at the intersection of two roads. **2.** anything serving as a guide; guideline.

guide′ rail′, *n.* a track or rail designed to control the movement of an object, as a door or window.

guild or **gild** (gild), *n.* **1.** an organization of persons with related interests, goals, etc., esp. one formed for mutual aid or protection. **2.** any of various medieval associations, as of merchants or artisans, organized for such purposes. **3.** a group of plants, as parasites, having a similar habit of growth and nutrition.

guil•der (gil′dər), *n.* the basic monetary unit of the Netherlands, Netherlands Antilles, and Suriname.

guild•hall or **gild•hall** (gild′hôl′), *n.* (in Britain) **1.** a hall built or used for a guild or corporation for its assemblies. **2.** the town hall.

guile (gīl), *n.* insidious cunning in attaining a goal; crafty or artful deception; duplicity.

guile•less (gīl′lis), *adj.* free from guile; sincere; straightforward. —**guile′less•ly,** *adv.* —**guile′less•ness,** *n.*

guil•le•mot (gil′ə mot′), *n.* a black or brown seabird of the genus *Cepphus,* of N seas, having a long, black bill, long neck, and red legs, as *C. grylle* and *C. columba.*

guil•lo•tine (gil′ə tēn′, gē′ə-; *esp. for v.* gil′ə tēn′, gē′ə-), *n., v.*, **-tined, -tin•ing.** —*n.* **1.** a device for beheading a person, consisting of a heavy blade that drops between two posts serving to guide its fall. **2.** any of various machines or instruments that cut powerfully and quickly, esp. one with a blade that drops vertically, as for trimming metal, paper, etc. —*v.t.* **3.** to behead by the guillotine. **4.** to cut with or as if with a guillotine. [< French, after J. I. *Guillotin* (1738–1814), French physician who urged its use as a humane method of execution]

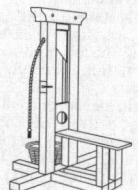

guillotine (def. 1)

guilt (gilt), *n.* **1.** the fact or state of having committed an offense, crime, violation, or wrong, esp. against moral or penal law; culpability: *to admit one's guilt in a robbery.* **2.** a feeling of responsibility or remorse for some offense, crime, wrong, etc., whether real or imagined.

3. conduct involving the commission of such crimes, wrongs, etc.; criminality: *to live a life of guilt.*

guilt′ by associa′tion, *n.* guilt implied by a person's association with another person who is in fact guilty.

guilt·less (gilt′lis), *adj.* **1.** free from guilt; innocent. **2.** having no knowledge or experience; innocent (usu. fol. by *of*). —**guilt′less·ly,** *adv.* —**guilt′less·ness,** *n.*

guilt·y (gil′tē), *adj.,* **i·er, i·est. 1.** having committed an offense, crime, violation, or wrong, esp. against moral or penal law; culpable: *to be found guilty of murder.* **2.** characterized by, connected with, or involving guilt; illicit: *guilty intent.* **3.** having or showing a sense of guilt, whether real or imagined: *a guilty conscience.* —**guilt′i·ly,** *adv.*

Guin·ea (gin′ē), *n., pl.* **-eas** for 4, 5. **1.** a coastal region in W Africa, extending from the Gambia River to the Gabon estuary. **2.** Formerly, **French Guinea.** an independent republic in W Africa, on the Atlantic coast. 7,405,375; ab. 96,900 sq. mi. (251,000 sq. km). *Cap.:* Conakry. **3. Gulf of,** a part of the Atlantic Ocean that projects into the W coast of Africa and extends from Ivory Coast to Gabon. **4.** (*l.c.*) a former money of account of the United Kingdom, equal to 21 shillings: still used in quoting fees or prices. **5.** (*l.c.*) a gold coin of Great Britain issued 1663–1813, worth 21 shillings. —**Guin′e·an,** *adj., n.*

Guin′ea-Bissau′, *n.* a republic on the W coast of Africa, between Guinea and Senegal: formerly a Portuguese overseas province; gained independence in 1974. 1,178,584; 13,948 sq. mi. (36,125 sq. km). *Cap.:* Bissau.

guin′ea fowl′ or **guin′ea·fowl′,** *n.* any of various large, plump gallinaceous birds of the family Numididae, orig. of Africa, esp. the domesticated species *Numida meleagris,* having spotted gray plumage and a bony casque on the head.

guin′ea hen′, *n.* **1.** the female of the guinea fowl. **2.** any guinea fowl.

guin′ea pig′, *n.* **1.** a cavy, esp. the stocky, tailless domesticated species *Cavia porcellus,* raised as a pet and for use in laboratories. **2.** the subject of any sort of test or experiment.

guin′ea (or **Guin′ea**) **worm′,** *n.* a long, slender roundworm, *Dracunculus medinensis,* parasitic under the skin of humans and other mammals, common in parts of India and Africa.

Guin·e·vere (gwin′ə vēr′), *n.* the wife of King Arthur and mistress of Lancelot.

gui·pure (gi pyŏŏr′; *Fr.* gē PYR′), *n., pl.* **-pures** (-pyŏŏrz′; *Fr.* -PYR′). **1.** any of various heavy laces made with tape, cords, wire, metallic thread, etc., esp. such a lace having bars instead of a net ground. **2.** any of various laces or trimmings having a large design without bars or a net ground.

gui·ro (gwēr′ō, gēr′ō), *n., pl.* **-ros.** a South American musical instrument consisting of a hollow gourd with a serrated surface that is scraped with a stick.

guise (gīz), *n., v.,* **guised, guis·ing.** —*n.* **1.** general external appearance; aspect; semblance. **2.** assumed appearance or mere semblance: *an intrusive question asked in the guise of friendship.* **3.** style of dress. —*v.t.* **4.** to dress; attire.

gui·tar (gi tär′), *n.* a stringed musical instrument with a long fretted neck, a flat, somewhat violinlike body, and typically six strings that are plucked with the fingers or with a plectrum. [< Spanish *guitarra*« Greek *kithára,* lyre-like instrument] —**gui·tar′ist,** *n.* —**Pronunciation.** See POLICE.

gui·tar·fish (gi tär′fish′), *n., pl.* (*esp. collectively*) **-fish,** (*esp. for kinds or species*) **-fish·es.** any sharklike ray of the family Rhinobatidae, of warm seas, resembling a guitar in shape when seen from above.

gu·lag (gōō′läg), *n.* (*sometimes cap.*) **1.** the system of forced-labor camps in the Soviet Union. **2.** a Soviet forced-labor camp. **3.** any prison or detention camp, esp. for political prisoners.

gulch (gulch), *n.* a deep, narrow ravine, esp. one marking the course of a stream or torrent.

gulf (gulf), *n.* **1.** a portion of an ocean or sea partly enclosed by land. **2.** a deep hollow; chasm or abyss. **3.** any wide gap or divergence, as between individuals in social status, opinion, etc., or between theory and practice. **4.** something that engulfs or swallows up. —*v.t.* **5.** to swallow up; engulf. —**gulf′like′,** *adj.*

Gulf′ States′, *n.pl.* **1.** the states of the U.S. bordering on the Gulf of Mexico: Florida, Alabama, Mississippi, Louisiana, and Texas. **2.** Also called **Persian Gulf States.** the oil-producing countries on or near the Persian Gulf: Bahrain, Iran, Iraq, Kuwait, Oman, Qatar, Saudi Arabia, and the United Arab Emirates.

Gulf′ Stream′, *n.* a warm ocean current flowing N from the Gulf of Mexico, along the E coast of the U.S., to an area off the SE coast of Newfoundland, where it becomes the western terminus of the North Atlantic Current.

Gulf′ War′, *n.* a conflict (Jan.–Feb. 1991) between Iraq and the United States and its allies to expel Iraq from Kuwait.

gulf·weed (gulf′wēd′), *n.* **1.** a coarse, olive-brown, branching seaweed, *Sargassum bacciferum,* common in the Gulf Stream and in tropical American seas, characterized by numerous berrylike air vessels. **2.** SARGASSUM (def. 1).

gull¹ (gul), *n.* any of various long-winged aquatic birds of the family Laridae, of worldwide distribution, typically white with gray or black upper wings and back.

gull² (gul), *v.t.* **1.** to deceive, trick, or cheat; hoodwink. —*n.* **2.** a person who is easily deceived or cheated; dupe.

Gul·lah (gul′ə), *n.* **1.** a member of a population of black Americans inhabiting the Sea Islands and the coastal regions of South Carolina, Georgia, and northeastern Florida. **2.** a creolized form of English spoken by the Gullahs, containing many words and grammatical features derived from African languages.

gul·let (gul′it), *n.* **1.** the esophagus. **2.** the throat or pharynx. **3.** a channel, ravine, or cut.

gul·li·ble (gul′ə bəl), *adj.* easily deceived or cheated; naive; credulous. Sometimes, **gul′la·ble.** —**gul′li·bil′i·ty,** *n.* —**gul′li·bly,** *adv.*

Gul′li·ver's Trav′els (gul′ə vərz), a social and political satire (1726) by Jonathan Swift, narrating the voyages of Lemuel Gulliver to four imaginary regions: Lilliput, Brobdingnag, Laputa, and the land of the Houyhnhnms.

gul·ly (gul′ē), *n., pl.* **-lies,** *v.,* **-lied, -ly·ing.** —*n.* Also, **gulley. 1.** a small valley or ravine orig. worn away by running water and serving as a drainageway after prolonged heavy rains; gulch. **2.** a ditch or gutter. —*v.t.* **3.** to make gullies in. **4.** to form (channels) by the action of water.

gulp (gulp), *v.i.* **1.** to gasp, as if taking large drafts of a liquid. —*v.t.* **2.** to swallow eagerly or hastily, or in large drafts or morsels (often fol. by *down*); gobble: *to gulp down lunch.* **3.** to suppress, subdue, or choke back as if by swallowing (often fol. by *down*): *to gulp down a sob.* —*n.* **4.** the act of gulping. **5.** the amount swallowed at one time; mouthful.

gum¹ (gum), *n., v.,* **gummed, gum·ming.** —*n.* **1.** any of various viscid, amorphous exudations from plants, hardening on exposure to air and soluble in or forming a viscid mass with water. **2.** any of various similar exudations, as resin. **3.** a sticky, adhesive preparation of such a plant substance, as for use in the arts or bookbinding. **4.** CHEWING GUM. **5.** GUM TREE. **6.** the adhesive by which a postage stamp is affixed. —*v.t.* **7.** to smear, stiffen, or stick together with gum. **8.** to clog with or as if with a gummy substance. —*v.i.* **9.** to exude or form gum. **10.** to become gummy. **11.** to become clogged with a gummy substance. **12. gum up,** *Slang.* to spoil or ruin.

gum² (gum), *n., v.,* **gummed, gum·ming.** —*n.* **1.** Often, **gums.** Also called **gingiva.** the firm, fleshy tissue covering the surfaces of the jaws and enveloping the necks of the teeth. —*v.t.* **2.** to masticate with toothless gums.

gum′ ammo′niac, *n.* an acrid gum resin derived from a W Asian plant, *Dorema ammoniacum,* of the parsley family, used chiefly in porcelain ceramics. Also called **ammoniac.**

gum′ ar′abic, *n.* a water-soluble gum obtained from the acacia tree, esp. *Acacia senegal,* used as an emulsifier or an adhesive, in inks, and in pharmaceuticals. Also called **acacia, gum′ aca′cia.**

gum·bo (gum′bō), *n., pl.* **-bos. 1.** a soup of chicken or seafood, greens, and seasonings, usu. thickened with okra. **2.** OKRA. **3.** soil that becomes sticky and nonporous when wet.

Gum·bo (gum′bō), *n.* (*sometimes l.c.*) LOUISIANA CREOLE.

gum·boil (gum′boil′), *n.* a small abscess on the gum originating in an abscess in the pulp of a tooth.

gum′bo-lim′bo, *n., pl.* **-lim·bos.** a tropical American tree, *Bursera simaruba,* of the bursera family, yielding an aromatic resin used in varnishes.

gum·boot (gum′bōōt′), *n.* a rubber boot usu. extending to the calf or knee.

gum′ dam′mar, *n.* DAMMAR.

gum·drop (gum′drop′), *n.* a small candy made of sweetened and flavored gum arabic, gelatin, or the like.

gum·my (gum′ē), *adj.,* **-mi·er, -mi·est. 1.** of, resembling, or of the consistency of gum; viscid; mucilaginous. **2.** covered with or clogged by gum or sticky matter. **3.** exuding gum. —**gum′mi·ness,** *n.*

gump·tion (gump′shən), *n.* **1.** initiative; resourcefulness. **2.** courage; spunk; guts. **3.** common sense; shrewdness. —**gump′tion·less,** *adj.* —**gump′tious,** *adj.*

gum′ res′in, *n.* a plant exudation consisting of a mixture of gum and resin.

gum·shoe (gum′shōō′), *n., v.,* **-shoed, -shoe·ing.** —*n.* **1.** *Slang.* a detective. **2.** a rubber overshoe. —*v.i.* **3.** *Slang.* to work as a detective.

gum′ tree′, *n.* any tree that exudes gum, as a eucalyptus, the sour gum, or the sweet gum.

gum·wood (gum′wŏŏd′), *n.* the wood of a gum tree, esp. of a eucalyptus or of the sweet gum.

gun (gun), *n., v.,* **gunned, gun·ning.** —*n.* **1.** a weapon consisting of a metal tube, with mechanical attachments, from which projectiles are shot by the force of an explosive; piece of ordnance. **2.** any portable firearm, as a rifle, shotgun, or revolver. **3.** a long-barreled cannon having a relatively flat trajectory. **4.** any device for shooting or ejecting something under pressure, as staples or paint. **5.** the firing of a weapon as a signal or salute; sound of a gunshot: *One runner started before the gun.* **6.** a person whose profession is killing; professional killer. —*v.t.* **7.** to shoot with a gun (often fol. by *down*). **8.** to cause (an engine or vehicle) to increase in speed very quickly by increasing the supply of fuel. —*v.i.* **9.** to shoot or hunt with a gun. **10. gun for, a.** to seek with intent to harm or kill. **b.** to seek; try earnestly to obtain: *to gun for a raise.* —**Idiom. 11. stick to** or **stand by one's guns,** to maintain one's position in the face of opposition. **12. under the gun,** under pressure, as to meet a deadline or solve a problem.

gun•boat (gun′bōt′), *n.* a small armed warship of light draft used in ports where the water is shallow.

gun′boat diplo′macy, *n.* diplomatic relations involving the use or threat of military force, esp. by a powerful nation against a weaker one.

gun•fight (gun′fīt′), *n.* a battle between two or more people or groups using guns. —**gun′fight′er,** *n.*

gun•fire (gun′fīr′), *n.* **1.** the firing of guns. **2.** the tactical use of firearms, esp. artillery, as distinguished from other weapons, as torpedoes or grenades.

gung-ho (gung′hō′), *Informal.* —*adj.* **1.** wholeheartedly enthusiastic and loyal; eager; zealous: *a gung-ho military outfit.* —*adv.* **2.** with overwhelming energy, enthusiasm, or success: *The business is going gung-ho.*

gunk (gungk), *n. Slang.* any sticky or greasy residue or accumulation. —**gunk′y,** *adj.,* **gunk•i•er, gunk•i•est.**

gun•lock (gun′lok′), *n.* the mechanism of a firearm by which the charge is exploded.

gun•man (gun′mən), *n., pl.* **-men. 1.** a person armed with or expert in the use of a gun, esp. one ready to use a gun unlawfully. **2.** a person who makes guns. —**gun′man•ship′,** *n.*

gun′met′al or **gun′ met′al,** *n.* **1.** any of various alloys or metallic substances with a dark gray or blackish color or finish, used for chains, belt buckles, etc. **2.** Also called **gun′metal gray′,** a dark gray with bluish or purplish tinge. **3.** a bronze formerly much used for cannon.

gun′ moll′, *n. Slang.* **1.** a female companion of a criminal. **2.** a female criminal. Also called **moll.**

gun•nel[1] (gun′l), *n.* any small eellike percoid fish of the family Pholidae, esp. *Pholis gunnellus,* of the N Atlantic.

gun•nel[2] (gun′l), *n.* GUNWALE.

gun•ner (gun′ər), *n.* **1.** a person who fires or assists in firing an artillery piece. **2.** a warrant officer in the U.S. Navy charged with the maintenance and firing of the ship's guns. **3.** a person who hunts with a gun. —**gun′ner•ship′,** *n.*

gun•ner•y (gun′ə rē), *n.* **1.** the art and science of constructing and operating guns, esp. large guns. **2.** the act of firing guns. **3.** guns collectively.

gun′nery ser′geant, *n.* a noncommissioned officer in the U.S. Marine Corps ranking above a staff sergeant.

gun•ny (gun′ē), *n., pl.* **-nies.** a strong coarse material made commonly from jute, esp. for bags or sacks; burlap.

gun•ny•sack (gun′ē sak′), *n.* a sack made of gunny or burlap. Also called **gun′ny•bag′.**

gun•play (gun′plā′), *n.* the exchange of gunshots, usu. with intent to wound or kill.

gun•point (gun′point′), *n.* **1.** the point or aim of a gun. —*Idiom.* **2. at gunpoint,** under threat of being shot.

gun•pow•der (gun′pou′dər), *n.* **1.** an explosive mixture, as of potassium nitrate, sulfur, and charcoal, used in shells and cartridges, in fireworks, and for blasting. **2.** Also called **gun′powder tea′.** a fine variety of green China tea, each leaf of which is rolled into a little ball.

Gun′powder Plot′, *n.* an unsuccessful plot to blow up King James I and the members of Parliament, November 5, 1605, in revenge for the laws against Roman Catholics. Compare GUY FAWKES DAY.

gun•run•ning (gun′run′ing), *n.* the smuggling of weapons into a country. —**gun′run′ner,** *n.*

gun•ship (gun′ship′), *n.* an armed helicopter or airplane used to provide close air support for combat troops.

gun•shot (gun′shot′), *n.* **1.** the shooting of a gun or the sound made by this. **2.** a bullet, projectile, or other shot fired from a gun. **3.** the range of a gun: *The bear was out of gunshot.* —*adj.* **4.** made by a gunshot.

gun′-shy′, *adj.* **1.** frightened by the sound of a gun firing. **2.** hesitant, wary, or distrustful, esp. because of previous unpleasant experience. —**gun′-shy′ness,** *n.*

gun•sling•er (gun′sling′ər), *n. Slang.* a gunfighter. —**gun′sling′ing,** *adj.*

gun•smith (gun′smith′), *n.* a person who makes or repairs firearms. —**gun′smith′ing,** *n.*

gun•wale or **gun•nel** (gun′l), *n.* the upper edge of the side or bulwark of a vessel.

gup•py (gup′ē), *n., pl.* **-pies.** a small freshwater livebearer, *Poecilia reticulata,* of the Caribbean region, often kept in aquariums.

gur•gi•ta•tion (gûr′ji tā′shən), *n.* a surging rise and fall; ebullient motion, as of water.

gur•gle (gûr′gəl), *v.,* **-gled, -gling,** *n.* —*v.i.* **1.** to flow in a broken, irregular, noisy current or course: *water gurgling from a bottle.* **2.** to make or emit a sound as of water doing this; babble. —*v.t.* **3.** to utter or express with a gurgling sound. —*n.* **4.** the act or noise of gurgling. —**gur′gling•ly,** *adv.*

Gur•ney (gûr′nē), *n.* **Dorothy B**(lomfield), 1858–1932, English hymn writer.

gu•ru (gŏōr′ŏō, gŏō rŏō′), *n., pl.* **-rus. 1.** a preceptor giving personal religious or spiritual instruction, esp. in Hinduism. **2.** any person who counsels or advises; mentor. **3.** a leader in a particular field: *the city's*

cultural gurus. [< Hindi *gurū* < Sanskrit *guru* venerable] —**gu′ru•ship′,** *n.*

gush (gush), *v.i.* **1.** to flow out or issue suddenly, copiously, or forcibly, as a fluid from confinement; pour. **2.** to express oneself extravagantly or emotionally; talk effusively. **3.** to have a sudden copious flow, as of blood or tears. —*v.t.* **4.** to emit suddenly, forcibly, or copiously; spurt. —*n.* **5.** a sudden copious outflow of a fluid. **6.** the fluid emitted. **7.** effusive and often insincere sentiment or enthusiasm.

gush•er (gush′ər), *n.* **1.** a person or thing that gushes. **2.** a flowing oil well, usu. of large capacity.

gush•y (gush′ē), *adj.,* **gush•i•er, gush•i•est.** given to or marked by excessively effusive or sentimental talk, behavior, etc. —**gush′i•ly,** *adv.* —**gush′i•ness,** *n.*

gus•set (gus′it), *n.* **1.** a small, triangular piece of material inserted into a shirt, shoe, etc., to improve the fit or for reinforcement. **2.** a plate for uniting structural members at a joint, as in a steel frame or truss.

gus•sy (gus′ē), *v.,* **-sied, -sy•ing.** *Informal.* —*v.t.* **1.** to adorn or decorate in a gimmicky, showy manner (usu. fol. by *up*): *to gussy up a room with mirrors and lights.* —*v.i.* **2.** to dress in one's best clothes (usu. fol. by *up*).

gust (gust), *n.* **1.** a sudden strong blast of wind. **2.** a sudden rush or burst of water, fire, smoke, sound, etc. **3.** an outburst of passionate feeling. —*v.i.* **4.** to blow or rush in gusts. —**gust′i•ly,** *adv.* —**gust′i•ness,** *n.* —**gust′y,** *adj.,* **gust•i•er, gust•i•est.**

gus•ta•to•ry (gus′tə tôr′ē, -tōr′ē), *adj.* of or pertaining to taste or tasting. —**gus′ta•to′ri•ly,** *adv.*

Gus•ta•vus (gu stā′vəs, -stä′-), *n.* **1. Gustavus I,** (*Gustavus Vasa*) 1496–1560, king of Sweden 1523–60. **2. Gustavus II,** (*Gustavus Adolphus*) ("*Lion of the North*") 1594–1632, king of Sweden 1611–32 (grandson of Gustavus I). **3. Gustavus III,** 1746–92, king of Sweden 1771–92. **4. Gustavus IV,** (*Gustavus Adolphus*) 1778–1837, king of Sweden 1792–1809 (son of Gustavus III). **5. Gustavus V** or **Gus•taf** or **Gus•tav V** (gus′täv), 1858–1950, king of Sweden 1907–50. **6. Gustavus VI** or **Gustav VI,** (*Gustaf Adolf*) 1882–1973, king of Sweden 1950–73 (son of Gustavus V).

gus•to (gus′tō), *n., pl.* **-toes. 1.** hearty or keen enjoyment, as in eating or drinking, or in action or speech in general; zest. **2.** individual taste or liking.

gut (gut), *n., v.,* **gut•ted, gut•ting,** *adj.* —*n.* **1.** the alimentary canal, esp. the intestine. Compare FOREGUT, MIDGUT, HINDGUT. **2. guts, a.** the bowels or entrails. **b.** courage and fortitude; nerve; determination. **c.** the inner working parts of a machine or device. **3.** the belly; stomach; abdomen. **4.** intestinal tissue or fiber. **5.** CATGUT. **6.** the silken substance taken from a silkworm when about to spin its cocoon. **7.** a narrow passage, as a channel of water or a defile between hills. —*v.t.* **8.** to take out the entrails of; disembowel: *to gut a fish.* **9.** to destroy the interior of: *Fire gutted the building.* **10.** to remove the vital or essential parts from. —*adj.* **11. a.** basic or essential: *to discuss the gut issues.* **b.** based on instincts or emotions: *a gut reaction.* —*Idiom.* **12. spill one's guts,** to tell everything; reveal one's innermost feelings.

Gu•ten•berg (gŏōt′n bûrg′), *n.* **Johannes,** (*Johann Gensfleisch*), c1400–68, German printer: first to print with movable type.

Gu′tenberg Bi′ble, *n.* an edition of the Vulgate printed at Mainz before 1456, ascribed to Gutenberg and others: probably the first large book printed with movable type.

gut•fight•er, (gut′fī′tər), *n.* one who is ruthless and aggressive, esp. in politics.

Guth•rie (guth′rē), *n.* **1. Sir (William) Tyrone,** 1900–71, English stage director and producer. **2. Woodrow Wilson** ("*Woody*"), 1912–67, U.S. folk singer.

gut•less (gut′lis), *adj.* lacking courage, substance, or vigor; weak or cowardly. —**gut′less•ness,** *n.*

guts•y (gut′sē), *adj.,* **guts•i•er, guts•i•est. 1.** daring or courageous; nervy: *a gutsy critic of the regime.* **2.** robust, vigorous, or earthy; lusty: *gutsy writing.* —**guts′i•ness,** *n.*

gut•ta (gut′ə), *n., pl.* **gut•tae** (gut′ē). one of a series of pendent ornaments, generally in the form of a frustum of a cone, attached to the undersides of the mutules of the Doric entablature.

gut•ta-per•cha (gut′ə pûr′chə), *n.* **1.** the milky juice, nearly white when pure, of various Malaysian trees of the sapodilla family, esp. *Palaquium gutta.* **2.** the tough rubberlike gum made from this: used as a dental cement, in golf balls, and for insulating electric wires.

gut•ter (gut′ər), *n.* **1.** a channel at the side or in the middle of a road or street, for leading off surface water. **2.** a channel at the eaves or on the roof of a building, for carrying off rain water. **3.** any channel, trough, or furrow for carrying off fluid. **4.** the sunken channel along either side of a bowling alley. **5.** the state or abode of those who live in degradation, squalor, etc.: *rose from the gutter to a position of prominence.* **6.** the white space formed by the inner margins of two facing pages in a bound book, magazine, or newspaper. —*v.i.* **7.** to flow in streams. **8.** (of a candle) to lose molten wax accumulated in a hollow space around the wick. **9.** (of a lamp or candle flame) to burn low or to be blown so as to be nearly extinguished. **10.** to form gutters, as water does. —*v.t.* **11.** to make gutters in; channel. **12.** to furnish with a gutter or gutters. —**gut′ter•like′,** *adj.*

gut•ter•snipe (gut′ər snīp′), *n.* **1.** a person belonging to or typical of the lowest or basest social group in a city. **2.** a street urchin. —**gut′ter•snip′ish,** *adj.*

G

gut·tur·al (gut′ər əl), *adj.* **1.** of or pertaining to the throat. **2.** harsh; throaty. **3.** pertaining to or characterized by a sound articulated in the back of the mouth, as the non-English velar fricative sound (кн). —*n.* **4.** a guttural sound. —**gut′tur·al·ly,** *adv.* —**gut′tur·al·ness, gut′tur·al′i·ty, gut′tur·al·ism,** *n.*

gut·ty (gut′ē), *adj.*, **-ti·er, -ti·est.** spirited and courageous; tough; gutsy.

guy¹ (gī), *n.* **1.** a man or boy; fellow. **2. guys,** persons of either sex; people. **3.** (*often cap.*) an effigy of Guy Fawkes burned in Britain on Guy Fawkes Day. **4.** *Chiefly Brit. Slang.* a grotesque person. —*v.t.* **5.** to ridicule.

guy² (gī), *n.* a rope, cable, or appliance used to guide and steady an object being hoisted or lowered, or to secure anything likely to shift its position.

Guy·a·na (gī an′ə, -ä′nə), *n.* an independent republic on the NE coast of South America: a former British protectorate; gained independence 1966; member of the Commonwealth of Nations. 706,116; 82,978 sq. mi. (214,913 sq. km). *Cap.:* Georgetown. Formerly, **British Guiana.** —**Guy′a·nese′** (-ə nēz′, -nēs′), *n., adj.*

Guy′ Fawkes′ Day′ (gī′ fôks′), *n.* (in Britain) November 5, celebrating the anniversary of the capture of Guy Fawkes. Compare Gunpowder Plot.

guy′ Fri′day, *n.* a man who does general secretarial and clerical duties in a business office.

guy·ot (gē ō′), *n.* a flat-topped seamount, found chiefly in the Pacific Ocean.

guz·zle (guz′əl), *v.i., v.t.,* **-zled, -zling.** to drink, or sometimes eat, greedily or excessively. —**guz′zler,** *n.*

gym (jim), *n.* **1.** a gymnasium. **2.** physical education. —*adj.* **3.** of, pertaining to, or used for athletics or physical education: *gym clothes.*

gym·kha·na (jim kä′nə), *n., pl.* **-nas. 1.** any of various special sporting or athletic events, as field day for equestrians or a gymnastics exhibition. **2.** a place where any such event is held. **3.** a competition in which sports cars are timed as they travel on a closed course that requires much maneuvering.

gym·na·si·ast (jim nä′zē ast′), *n.* a student in a gymnasium.

gym·na·si·um (jim nä′zē əm), *n., pl.* **-si·ums, -si·a** (-zē ə, -zhə). **1.** a building or room designed and equipped for indoor sports, exercise, or physical education. **2.** (in ancient Greece) a public facility for athletic training, usu. including a running track, exercise field, and palaestra. —**gym·na′si·al,** *adj.*

gym·nast (jim′nast, -nəst), *n.* a person trained and skilled in gymnastics.

gym·nas·tic (jim nas′tik), *adj.* of, pertaining to, or concerned with gymnastics. —**gym·nas′ti·cal·ly,** *adv.*

gym·nas·tics (jim nas′tiks), *n.* **1.** (*used with a pl. v.*) physical exercises that develop and demonstrate strength, balance, and agility, esp. such exercises performed mostly on special equipment. **2.** (*used with a sing. v.*) the practice, art, or competitive sport of such exercises. **3.** (*used with a pl. v.*) **a.** mental or creative feats of skill: *verbal gymnastics.* **b.** agile or strenuous physical maneuvers, as in having to move oneself along a difficult course.

gymno-, a combining form meaning "naked," "bare," "exposed": *gymnosperm.*

gym·no·sperm (jim′nə spûrm′), *n.* any nonflowering plant having seeds that are not enclosed in fruit at the time of pollination; any conifer, cycad, or ginkgo.

gy·nan·dro·morph (gī nan′drə môrf′, ji-), *n.* an individual having morphological characteristics of both sexes. —**gy·nan′dro·mor′phic, gy·nan′dro·mor′phous,** *adj.* —**gy·nan′dro·morph′ism, gy·nan′dro·mor′phy,** *n.*

gy·nan·drous (gī nan′drəs, ji-), *adj.* having stamens and pistils united in a column, as in orchids.

gy·ne·coc·ra·cy (gī′ni kok′rə sē, jin′i-), *n., pl.* **-cies.** government by women. —**gy·ne·co·crat′ic** (-kə krat′ik), *adj.*

gy·ne·coid (gī′ni koid′, jin′i-), *adj.* of or like a woman.

gy·ne·col·o·gy (gī′ni kol′ə jē, jin′i-), *n.* the branch of medicine that deals with the health maintenance and diseases of women, esp. of the reproductive organs. *Abbr.:* GYN, gyn —**gy′ne·co·log′ic** (-kə loj′ik), **gy′ne·co·log′i·cal,** *adj.* —**gy′ne·col′o·gist,** *n.*

gy·noe·ci·um (ji nē′sē əm, -shē-, gī-), *n., pl.* **-ci·a** (-sē ə, -shē ə). the pistil or pistils of a flower; the female parts of a flower.

-gynous, a combining form meaning "taking the attitude toward women" specified by the initial element (*misogynous*), "having wives" of the specified number (*polygynous*), "having the parts of a flower organized" in the position or manner specified (*epigynous*).

-gyny, a combining form occurring in nouns corresponding to adjectives ending in -gynous: *misogyny.*

gyp or **gip** (jip), *v.,* **gypped, gyp·ping,** *n. Informal.* —*v.t., v.i.* **1.** to defraud or rob by some sharp practice; swindle; cheat. —*n.* **2.** a swindle or fraud. **3.** Also, **gyp′per, gyp·ster** (jip′stər). a swindler or cheat.

gyp·sum (jip′səm), *n.* a soft mineral, hydrous calcium sulfate, $CaSO_4 \cdot 2H_2O$, occurring in massive or fibrous form and also as alabaster and selenite: used to make plaster of Paris and as a fertilizer.

gyp′sum board′, *n.* wallboard composed primarily of gypsum and often used as sheathing.

Gyp·sy (jip′sē), *n., pl.* **-sies,** *adj.* —*n.* **1.** a member of a traditionally itinerant people, orig. of N India, now residing mostly in permanent communities in many countries of the world. **2.** (*l.c.*) a person who resembles the stereotype of a Gypsy, as in appearance or itinerant way of life. **3.** (*l.c.*) *Informal.* an independent, usu. nonunion trucker, hauler, operator, etc. —*adj.* **4.** of or pertaining to the Gypsies. **5.** (*l.c.*) *Informal.* working independently or without a license: *gypsy truckers.* Also, *esp. Brit.,* **Gipsy, gipsy.** —**Gyp′sy·dom,** *n.* —**Gyp′sy·ish,** *adj.*

gyp′sy cab′, *n.* a taxicab that is licensed only to pick up passengers on call by telephone but often illegally cruises for passengers on the street.

gyp′sy moth′, *n.* a moth, *Porthetria dispar,* introduced into the U.S. from Europe, the larvae of which feed on the foliage of shade and other trees.

gy·rate (*v.* jī′rāt, jī rāt′; *adj.* jī′rāt), *v.,* **-rat·ed, -rat·ing,** *adj.* —*v.i.* **1.** to move in a circle or spiral or around a fixed point; whirl; revolve; rotate. —*adj.* **2.** *Zool.* having convolutions. —**gy·ra′tion,** *n.* —**gy·ra′tion·al,** *adj.* —**gy′ra·tor,** *n.*

gyre (jī°r), *n.* **1.** a ring or circle. **2.** a circular course or motion. **3.** a ringlike system of ocean currents rotating clockwise in the Northern Hemisphere and counterclockwise in the Southern Hemisphere.

gyr·fal·con (jûr′fôl′kən, -fal′-, -fô′kən), *n.* a large falcon, *Falco rusticolus,* of arctic and subarctic regions, having white to dark color phases.

gy·ro¹ (jī′rō), *n., pl.* **-ros. 1.** gyrocompass. **2.** gyroscope.

gy·ro² (jēr′ō, zhēr′ō; *Gk.* yē′rô), *n.* pressed beef or lamb roasted on a vertical spit, thinly sliced, and usu. served in a sandwich on pita bread.

gyro-, a combining form meaning "circle, rotation" (*gyromagnetic*), "gyroscope" (*gyrostabilizer*).

gy·ro·com·pass (jī′rō kum′pəs), *n.* a navigational compass containing a gyroscope rotor that registers the direction of true north along the surface of the earth.

gy·ro·mag·net·ic (jī′rō mag net′ik), *adj.* of or pertaining to the magnetic properties of a rotating charged particle.

gy·ro·pi·lot (jī′rə pī′lət), *n.* automatic pilot.

gy·ro·scope (jī′rə skōp′), *n.* an apparatus consisting of a rotating wheel so mounted that its axis can turn freely in certain or all directions, capable of maintaining the same absolute direction in space in spite of movements of the mountings: used to maintain equilibrium and to determine direction. —**gy′ro·scop′ic** (-skop′ik), *adj.* —**gy′ro·scop′i·cal·ly,** *adv.*

gy·rose (jī′rōs), *adj.* marked with wavy lines.

gy·ro·stat·ics (jī′rə stat′iks), *n.* (*used with a sing. v.*) the science dealing with the laws of rotating bodies. —**gy′ro·stat′ic,** *adj.* —**gy′ro·stat′i·cal·ly,** *adv.*

H

H, h (āch), *n., pl.* **Hs** or **H's, hs** or **h's. 1.** the eighth letter of the English alphabet, a consonant. **2.** any spoken sound represented by this letter. **3.** something shaped like an H. **4.** a written or printed representation of the letter *H* or *h.*

H, *Symbol.* **1.** the eighth in order or in a series. **2.** hydrogen.

h, *Physics Symbol.* PLANCK'S CONSTANT.

ha or **hah** (hä), *interj.* (used as an exclamation of surprise, interrogation, suspicion, triumph, etc.)

Ha, *Symbol.* hahnium.

Hab., Habakkuk.

Ha•bak•kuk (hə bak′ək, hab′ə kuk′, -kŏŏk′), *n.* **1.** a Minor Prophet of the 7th century B.C. **2.** a book of the Bible bearing his name.

ha•ba•ne•ro (hä′bə när′ō), *n., pl.* **-ros.** an extremely pungent small pepper, the fruit of a variety of *Capsicum chinense,* used in cooking.

ha•be•as cor•pus (hā′bē əs kôr′pəs), *n. Law.* **1.** a writ requiring a person to be brought before a judge or court, esp. to determine whether the person has been detained or imprisoned legally. **2.** the right to obtain such a writ as a protection against illegal detention or imprisonment. [< Latin: lit., have the body (first words of writ)]

hab•er•dash•er (hab′ər dash′ər), *n.* a retail dealer in men's furnishings.

hab•er•dash•er•y (hab′ər dash′ə rē), *n., pl.* **-er•ies.** a haberdasher's shop.

ha•bil•i•ment (hə bil′ə mənt), *n.* **1.** Usu., **habiliments. a.** clothes or clothing. **b.** clothes as worn in a particular profession, way of life, etc. **2. habiliments,** accouterments; trappings. **—ha•bil′i•men′tal** (-ə men′tl), **ha•bil′i•men′ta•ry,** *adj.* **—ha•bil′i•ment′ed,** *adj.*

ha•bil•i•tate (hə bil′i tāt′), *v.,* **-tat•ed, -tat•ing. —v.t. 1.** to clothe or dress. **2.** to make fit. **—v.i. 3.** to become fit. **—ha•bil′i•ta′tion,** *n.* **—ha•bil′i•ta′tive,** *adj.* **—ha•bil′i•ta′tor,** *n.*

hab•it (hab′it), *n.* **1.** an acquired pattern of behavior that has become almost involuntary as a result of frequent repetition. **2.** customary practice or use. **3.** a particular practice, custom, or usage: *the habit of shaking hands.* **4.** a dominant or regular character or tendency: *a habit of criticizing everyone.* **5.** addiction, esp. to narcotics (often prec. by *the*). **6.** mental character or disposition. **7.** characteristic bodily or physical condition. **8.** the characteristic crystalline form of a mineral. **9.** garb of a particular rank, profession, religious order, etc.; dress: *a monk's habit.* **10.** the special attire worn by a person for horseback riding, as the costume of jacket, shirt, breeches, boots, and hat worn in hunting. **—v.t. 11.** to clothe; array; attire. **—Saying. 12. Old habits die hard,** accustomed ways of doing things are difficult to change.

hab•it•a•ble (hab′i tə bəl), *adj.* capable of being inhabited. **—hab′it•a•bil′i•ty, hab′it•a•ble•ness,** *n.* **—hab′it•a•bly,** *adv.*

hab•it•ant¹ (hab′i tənt), *n.* an inhabitant.

ha•bi•tant² (hab′i tənt; *Fr.* A bē tän′), *n., pl.* **ha•bi•tants** (hab′i tənts; *Fr.* A bē tän′). a French Canadian, esp. a French-speaking inhabitant of rural Quebec.

hab•i•tat (hab′i tat′), *n.* **1.** the natural environment of an organism; place that is natural for the life and growth of an organism: *a jungle habitat.* **2.** the place where one is usu. found. **3.** a special environment for living in over an extended period, as an underwater research vessel. **4.** HABITATION (def. 1).

hab•i•ta•tion (hab′i tā′shən), *n.* **1.** a place of residence; dwelling; abode. **2.** the act of inhabiting; occupancy by inhabitants. **3.** a colony or settlement; community. **—hab′i•ta′tion•al,** *adj.*

hab′it-form′ing, *adj.* tending to cause addiction, esp. through physiological dependence.

ha•bit•u•al (hə bich′ŏŏ əl), *adj.* **1.** of the nature of a habit; fixed by or resulting from habit: *habitual courtesy.* **2.** being such by habit; confirmed: *a habitual gossip.* **3.** commonly used, followed, observed, etc., as by a particular person; customary. **—ha•bit′u•al•ly,** *adv.*

ha•bit•u•ate (hə bich′ŏŏ āt′), *v.,* **-at•ed, -at•ing.** to accustom (an individual) either physically or mentally to a particular situation; train.

hab•i•tude (hab′i tŏŏd′, -tyŏŏd′), *n.* **1.** customary condition or character. **2.** a habit or custom. **—hab′i•tu′di•nal,** *adj.*

ha•bit•u•é (hə bich′ŏŏ ā′, -bich′ŏŏ ā′), *n.* a frequent or habitual visitor to a place. [< French]

hab•i•tus (hab′i təs), *n., pl.* **-tus.** the physical characteristics and constitution of a person, esp. with regard to susceptibility to disease.

ha•ček or **há•ček** (hä′chek), *n.* a diacritical mark (ˇ) placed over a letter in some languages, as Czech and Lithuanian, and in some systems of phonetic transcription, esp. to indicate that a sound is palatalized.

ha•chure (ha shŏŏr′), *n., v.,* **-chured, -chur•ing. —n. 1.** one of a series of short parallel lines drawn on a map to indicate topographic relief. **2.** shading composed of such lines; hatching. **—v.t. 3.** to indicate or shade by hachures; hatch.

ha•ci•en•da (hä′sē en′də), *n., pl.* **-das.** (in Spanish America) **1.** a large landed estate, esp. one used for farming or ranching. **2.** the main house on such an estate.

hack¹ (hak), *v.t.* **1.** to cut, notch, slice, chop, or sever with irregular, often heavy blows (often fol. by *up* or *down*): *to hack down trees.* **2.** to clear (a road, path, etc.) by cutting away vines, trees, or other growth. **3.** to damage or injure by crude, harsh, or insensitive treatment, as a piece of writing. **4.** to reduce or cut ruthlessly; trim: *to hack a budget severely.* **5.** *Slang.* to deal or cope with; handle; tolerate: *I can't hack all this commuting.* **—v.i. 6.** to make rough cuts or notches; deal cutting blows. **7.** to cough harshly, usu. in short and repeated spasms. **8.** *Tennis.* **a.** to take an ineffective or awkward swing at the ball. **b.** to play at a mediocre level. **—n. 9.** a cut, gash, or notch. **10.** a tool for hacking, as an ax or pick. **11.** an act or instance of hacking; a cutting blow. **12.** a short, rasping dry cough. **—Idiom. 13. hack it,** *Slang.* to cope successfully with something.

hack² (hak), *n.* **1.** a person, esp. a professional, who surrenders individual independence, integrity, belief, etc., in return for money or other reward: *a political hack.* **2.** a writer whose services are for hire. **3.** a person who produces banal or mediocre work or who works at a dull or routine task. **4.** a horse kept for common hire or adapted for general work, esp. ordinary riding. **5.** a saddle horse. **6.** an old or worn-out horse; jade. **7.** a coach or carriage kept for hire; hackney. **8. a.** a taxicab. **b.** a cabdriver. **—v.t. 9.** to make a hack of; let out for hire. **10.** to make trite or stale by frequent use; hackney. **—v.i. 11.** to drive a taxi. **12.** to ride or drive on the road at an ordinary pace. **—adj. 13.** hired as a hack; of a hired sort: *a hack writer; hack work.* **14.** hackneyed; trite; banal: *hack writing.*

hack³ (hak), *n.* **1.** a rack for drying food, as fish. **2.** a rack for holding fodder for livestock. **—v.t. 3.** to place on a hack, as for drying or feeding.

hack•ber•ry (hak′ber′ē, -bə rē), *n., pl.* **-ries. 1.** any of several trees or shrubs of the genus *Celtis,* of the elm family, bearing cherrylike fruit. **2.** the sometimes edible fruit of such a tree. **3.** the wood of such a tree.

hack•er (hak′ər), *n.* **1.** a person or thing that hacks. **2.** a person who engages in an activity without talent or skill. **3.** *Slang.* **a.** a computer enthusiast who is especially proficient in programming. **b.** a computer user who attempts to gain unauthorized access to proprietary computer systems.

hack•ie (hak′ē), *n.* HACK² (def. 8b).

hack•le (hak′əl), *n., v.,* **-led, -ling. —n. 1.** the neck plumage of a male bird, as the domestic rooster. **2. hackles, a.** the erectile hair on the back of an animal's neck. **b.** anger, esp. when aroused in a challenging or challenged manner: *with one's hackles up.* **3.** *Angling.* **a.** the legs of an artificial fly made with feathers from the neck or saddle of a rooster or other such bird. **b.** one of the feathers in such a fly. **4.** a comb for dressing flax or hemp. **—v.t. 5.** to comb, as flax or hemp. **—Idiom. 6. raise one's hackles,** to arouse one's anger. Also, **heckle** (for defs 4, 5). **—hack′ler,** *n.*

hack•ney (hak′nē), *n.* **1.** a carriage for hire; cab. **2.** a horse used for ordinary riding or driving. **3.** (*cap.*) one of an English breed of horses having a high-stepping gait. **—adj. 4.** let out, employed, or done for hire. **—v.t. 5.** to make trite, common, or stale by frequent use. **6.** to use as a hackney. **—hack′ney•ism,** *n.*

hack•neyed (hak′nēd), *adj.* made commonplace or trite; stale; banal.

hack′saw′ or **hack′ saw′,** *n.* a saw for cutting metal, consisting typically of a narrow, fine-toothed blade fixed in a frame.

Hack′y Sack′ (hak′ē), *Trademark.* a small leather beanbag juggled with the feet as a game.

had (had), *v.* pt. and pp. of HAVE.

Ha•das•sah (hə dä′sə, hä-), *n.* a benevolent organization of Jewish women founded in New York City in 1912 by Henrietta Szold and concerned chiefly with bettering medical and educational facilities in Israel, forwarding Zionist activities in the U.S., and promoting world peace. [< Hebrew *hădassāh* lit., myrtle, the Hebrew name of Queen Esther; see Esther 2:7]

had•dock (had′ək), *n., pl.* (*esp. collectively*) **-dock,** (*esp. for kinds or species*) **-docks.** a food fish, *Melanogrammus aeglefinus,* of the cod family, of the N Atlantic.

Ha•des (hā′dēz), *n.* **1.** (in Greek myth) the underworld inhabited by the spirits of the dead. **2.** the ancient Greek god ruling over the underworld. **3.** (in the Revised Version of the New Testament) the abode or state of the dead. **4.** (*often l.c.*) hell. **—Ha•de•an** (hā dē′ən, hā′dē ən), *adj.*

hadj (haj), *n., pl.* **hadj•es.** hajj.

had•n't (had′nt), contraction of *had not.*

Ha•dri•an (hā′drē ən), *n.* (*Publius Aelius Hadrianus*) A.D. 76–138, Roman emperor 117–138.

had•ro•saur (had′rə sôr′), *n.* any chiefly bipedal herbivorous dinosaur of the family Hadrosauridae, of the Cretaceous Period, having a broad toothless beak. Also called **duck-billed dinosaur.** **—had′ro•sau′ri•an,** *adj.*

ha·fiz (hä′fiz), *n.* a title of respect for a Muslim who knows the Koran by heart.

haf·ni·um (haf′nē əm, häf′-), *n.* a toxic metallic element found in most zirconium minerals. *Symbol:* Hf; *at. wt.:* 178.49; *at. no.:* 72; *sp. gr.:* 12.1.

haft (haft, häft), *n.* a handle, esp. of a knife, sword, or dagger.

haf·ta·rah or **haph·ta·rah** (häf tôr′ə, -tōr′ə, häf′tä rä′), *n.*, *pl.* **-ta·rahs, -ta·roth, -ta·rot** (-tä rôt′). a portion of the Prophets read in the synagogue on the Sabbath and holy days immediately after the parashah.

hag (hag), *n.* **1.** an ugly or slatternly old woman. **2.** a witch or sorceress.

Hag., Haggai.

Ha·gar (hā′gär, -gər), *n.* the mother of Ishmael. Gen. 16.

hag·ga·dah or **hag·ga·da** (hə gô′də, hä′gä dä′), *n.*, *pl.* **-dahs** or **-das, -doth, -dot** (-dôt′). **1.** a book containing the story of the Exodus, used at the Seder service on Passover. **2.** (*cap.*) AGGADAH. —**hag·gad·ic** (hə gad′ik, -gä′dik), **hag·gad′i·cal**, *adj.*

Hag·ga·i (hag′ē ī′, hag′ī), *n.* **1.** a Minor Prophet of the 6th century B.C. **2.** a book of the Bible bearing his name.

hag·gard (hag′ərd), *adj.* **1.** gaunt, wasted, or exhausted in appearance, as from prolonged suffering or strain; worn: *the haggard faces of refugees.* **2.** wild; wild-looking. **3.** *Falconry.* (esp. of a hawk caught after it has acquired adult plumage) untamed. —*n.* **4.** a wild or untamed hawk caught after it has acquired adult plumage. —**hag′gard·ly**, *adv.*

hag·gis (hag′is), *n.* a traditional Scottish pudding made of the heart, liver, etc., of a sheep or calf, minced with suet and oatmeal, seasoned, and boiled in the stomach of the animal.

hag·gle (hag′əl), *v.*, **-gled, -gling**, *n.* —*v.i.* **1.** to bargain in a petty, quibbling, often contentious manner: *to haggle for a better price.* **2.** to dispute or cavil; wrangle: *to haggle over the use of a word.* —*v.t.* **3.** to mangle in cutting; hack. —*n.* **4.** the act of haggling; a wrangle or dispute. —**hag′gler**, *n.*

hag·i·oc·ra·cy (hag′ē ok′rə sē, hā′jē-), *n.*, *pl.* **-cies. 1.** government by a body of persons esteemed as holy. **2.** a state so governed.

Hag·i·og·ra·pha (hag′ē og′rə fə, hā′jē-), *n.* (*used with a sing. v.*) the third of the three Jewish divisions of the Old Testament, variously arranged, but usu. comprising the Psalms, Proverbs, Job, Song of Solomon, Ruth, Lamentations, Ecclesiastes, Esther, Daniel, Ezra, Nehemiah, and Chronicles. Also called **the Writings.** Compare PENTATEUCH, PROPHETS. [< Late Latin < Greek: sacred writings]

hag·i·og·ra·pher (hag′ē og′rə fər, hā′jē-) also **hag′i·og′ra·phist**, *n.* **1.** one of the writers of the Hagiographa. **2.** a writer of lives of the saints; hagiologist.

hag·i·og·ra·phy (hag′ē og′rə fē, hā′jē-), *n.*, *pl.* **-phies.** the writing and critical study of the lives of the saints. —**hag′i·o·graph′ic** (-ə graf′ik), **hag′i·o·graph′i·cal**, *adj.*

hag·i·ol·o·gy (hag′ē ol′ə jē, hā′jē-), *n.*, *pl.* **-gies. 1.** the branch of literature dealing with the lives and legends of the saints. **2. a.** a biography or narrative of a saint. **b.** a collection of such works. —**hag′i·o·log′ic** (-ə loj′ik), **hag′i·o·log′i·cal**, *adj.* —**hag′i·ol·o·gist**, *n.*

Hague (hāg), *n.* **The,** a city in the W Netherlands, near the North Sea: site of the government and the royal residence. 444,313. Dutch, **Den Haag, 's Gravenhage.** Compare AMSTERDAM.

hah (hä), *interj.* HA.

ha-ha (hä′hä′, hä′hä′), *interj.* (used as an exclamation or representation of laughter, as in expressing amusement or derision.)

hahn·i·um (hä′nē əm), *n.* UNNILPENTIUM. *Symbol:* Ha

hai·ku (hī′kōō), *n.*, *pl.* **-ku.** a Japanese poem or verse form, consisting of 17 syllables divided into 3 lines of 5, 7, and 5 syllables, often about nature or a season.

hail¹ (hāl), *v.t.* **1.** to cheer, salute, or greet; welcome: *to hail an old friend on the street.* **2.** to acclaim; approve enthusiastically: *We hail the new provisions for child care.* **3.** to call out to, as in order to stop or to attract the attention of: *to hail a cab; to hail the waiter.* —*v.i.* **4. hail from,** to have as one's place of birth or residence: *My roommate hails from Indiana.* —*n.* **5.** a shout or call to attract attention. **6.** a salutation or greeting. —*interj.* **7.** (used as a salutation, greeting, or acclamation.) —*Idiom.* **8. within hail,** within range of hearing; audible. —**hail′er**, *n.*

hail² (hāl), *n.* **1.** showery precipitation in the form of irregular pellets or balls of ice more than ⅕ in. (5 mm) in diameter, falling from a cumulonimbus cloud (disting. from *sleet*). **2.** a shower or storm of such precipitation. **3.** a shower of anything: *a hail of bullets.* —*v.i.* **4.** to pour down hail (often used impersonally with *it* as subject): *It hailed all afternoon.* **5.** to fall or shower like hail: *Arrows hailed on the troops.* —*v.t.* **6.** to pour down as or like hail: *The plane hailed leaflets on the city.*

Hai·le Se·las·sie I (hī′lē sə las′ē, -lä′sē), *n.* (*Ras Tafari*), 1891–1975, emperor of Ethiopia 1930–74: in exile 1936–41.

Hail′ Mar′y, *n.* **1.** AVE MARIA. **2.** Also called **Hail′ Mar′y pass′** (or **play′**), a long forward pass in football, esp. as a last-ditch attempt at the end of a game, where completion is considered unlikely.

hail·stone (hāl′stōn′), *n.* a pellet of hail.

hail·storm (hāl′stôrm′), *n.* a storm with hail.

Hail′ to the Chief′, the official song of the President of the United States, usu. played when the president appears at a formal public gathering: words taken from Sir Walter Scott's *Lady of the Lake* (1810), set to music by James Sanderson.

hair (hâr), *n.* **1.** any of the numerous fine, usu. cylindrical, keratinous filaments growing from the skin of mammals. **2.** an aggregate of such filaments, as that covering the human head or forming the coat of most mammals. **3.** any of various fine processes or bristles appearing on the surface of other animals or plants. **4.** HAIRCLOTH. **5.** a very small amount, degree, measure, magnitude, etc.; a fraction, as of time or space: *The falling rock missed him by a hair.* —*Idiom.* **6. get in someone's hair,** to pester or irritate someone. **7. hair of the dog (that bit one),** an alcoholic drink purporting to relieve a hangover. **8. let one's hair down, a.** to behave in a relaxed, informal, unrestrained manner. **b.** to speak candidly or frankly. **9. make someone's hair stand on end,** to strike or fill with horror; terrify. Job 4:13–15. **10. split hairs,** to make tiny, petty distinctions; nitpick. **11. tear one's hair (out),** to manifest extreme anxiety, grief, or anger. **12. to a hair,** perfect to the smallest detail. **13. turn a hair,** to show excitement, fear, or other response (usu. used in the negative): *to cut through heavy traffic without turning a hair.*

hair·ball (hâr′bôl′), *n.* a ball of hair accumulated in the stomach of a cat or other animal as a result of the animal's licking its coat.

hair·brained (hâr′brānd′), *adj.* HAREBRAINED.

hair·breadth (hâr′bredth′, -bretth′) also **hairsbreadth**, *n.* **1.** a very small space or distance: *to escape by a hairbreadth.* —*adj.* **2.** extremely narrow or close: *a hairbreadth escape.*

hair·brush (hâr′brush′), *n.* a brush for dressing the hair.

hair·cloth (hâr′klôth′, -kloth′), *n.* cloth woven with horsehair or camel's hair, used for upholstery and garments.

hair·cut (hâr′kut′), *n.* **1.** an act or instance of cutting the hair. **2.** the style in which the hair is cut and worn. —**hair′cut·ter**, *n.* —**hair′cut·ting**, *n.*, *adj.*

hair·do (hâr′dōō′), *n.*, *pl.* **-dos.** the style in which a person's hair is cut and arranged; coiffure.

hair·dress·er (hâr′dres′ər), *n.* a person who arranges or cuts hair.

hair′ fol′licle, *n.* a small cavity in the epidermis and dermis of the skin, from which a hair develops.

hair′ im′plant, *n.* the insertion of synthetic fibers or human hair into a bald area of the scalp. Compare HAIR TRANSPLANT.

hair·line (hâr′līn′), *n.* **1.** a very slender line. **2.** the border along which a growth of hair emerges or the contour formed by this, esp. at the upper forehead and the temples. **3. a.** a very fine line or stripe in fabric. **b.** a fabric, esp. a worsted, woven with this. **4.** *Print.* **a.** a very thin line on the face of a type. **b.** a thin rule for printing fine lines. —*adj.* **5.** narrow or fine as a hair: *a hairline fracture.*

hair′ net′, *n.* a cap of loose net, for holding the hair in place.

hair·piece (hâr′pēs′), *n.* a covering of false hair, as a toupee or fall, for concealing baldness or supplementing the existing hair.

hair·pin (hâr′pin′), *n.* **1.** a slender U-shaped piece of wire, shell, etc., used to fasten up the hair or hold a headdress. —*adj.* **2.** (of a road, curve in a road, etc.) sharply curved back, as in a U shape.

hair′-rais′er, *n.* a hair-raising story, experience, etc.

hair′-rais′ing, *adj.* terrifying or horrifying: *a hair-raising encounter with death.* —**hair′-rais′ing·ly**, *adv.*

hair′ seal′, *n.* any of various earless seals having coarse hair and no soft underfur. Compare FUR SEAL.

hair′ shirt′, *n.* a garment of coarse haircloth, worn next to the skin as a penance.

hair·split·ting (hâr′split′ing), *n.* **1.** the making of unnecessarily fine distinctions. —*adj.* **2.** characterized by such distinctions; quibbling: *hairsplitting arguments.* —**hair′split′ter**, *n.*

hair·spring (hâr′spring′), *n.* a fine, usu. spiral, spring used for oscillating the balance of a timepiece.

hair·streak (hâr′strēk′), *n.* any small, dark butterfly of the family Lycaenidae, having hairlike tails on the hind wings.

hair′style′ or **hair′ style′,** *n.* a style of cutting, arranging, or combing the hair; hairdo; coiffure.

hair′ trans′plant, *n.* the surgical transfer of clumps of skin with hair or of viable hair follicles to a bald area of the scalp. Compare HAIR IMPLANT.

hair·worm (hâr′wûrm′), *n.* any small, slender worm of the family Trichostrongylidae, parasitic in the alimentary canals of various animals.

hair·y (hâr′ē), *adj.*, **hair·i·er, hair·i·est. 1.** covered with hair; having much hair; hirsute. **2.** consisting of or resembling hair: *moss of a hairy texture.* **3.** *Slang.* difficult, frightening, or risky: *a hairy trip through the rapids; a hairy exam.* —**hair′i·ness**, *n.*

hair′y vetch′, *n.* a Eurasian vetch, *Vicia villosa*, having hairy stems and violet and white flowers: widely grown as forage.

Hai·ti (hā′tē), *n.* **1.** a republic in the West Indies occupying the W part of the island of Hispaniola. 6,611,407; 10,714 sq. mi. (27,750 sq. km). *Cap.:* Port-au-Prince. **2.** a former name of HISPANIOLA. —**Hai·tian** (hā′shən, -tē ən), *adj.*, *n.*

hajj (haj), *n.*, *pl.* **hajj·es.** the pilgrimage to Mecca, which every adult Muslim is supposed to make at least once in his or her lifetime: the fifth of the Pillars of Islam. Also, **hadj.**

haj·ji or **hadj·i** or **haj·i** (haj′ē), *n.*, *pl.* **haj·jis** or **hadj·is** or **haj·is.** a Muslim who has gone on a pilgrimage to Mecca. [< Arabic]

hake (hāk), *n.*, *pl.* (*esp. collectively*) **hake**, (*esp. for kinds or species*) **hakes.** any of various codlike marine food fishes of the genera *Merluccius* and *Urophycis.*

Hak·luyt (hak/lit), *n.* **Richard,** 1552?–1616, English geographer and editor of explorers' narratives.

ha·la·khah (hä lô/кнə, hä lä кнä/), *n.*, *pl.* **-la·khahs, -la·khoth, -la·khot** (-lä кнôt/). **1.** the body of Jewish law, comprising the oral law as transcribed in the Talmud and subsequent legal codes and rabbinical decisions. **2.** a law or tradition established by the halakhah. —**ha·la·khic** (hə lä/кнık, -lak/ık), *adj.*

ha·lal (hə läl/), *adj.* **1.** (of an animal or its meat) slaughtered or prepared in the manner prescribed by Islamic law. **2.** of or pertaining to halal meat: *a halal butcher.* —*n.* **3.** a halal animal or halal meat. [Arabic *halāl* lawful]

hal·berd (hal/bərd, hôl/-) also **hal·bert** (-bərt), *n.* a shafted weapon with an axlike cutting blade, beak, and apical spike, used esp. in the 15th and 16th centuries.

hal·cy·on (hal/sē ən), *adj.* **1.** calm; peaceful; tranquil: *halcyon weather.* **2.** prosperous: *halcyon years.* **3.** happy; joyful; carefree: *halcyon days of youth.* **4.** of or pertaining to the halcyon or kingfisher. —*n.* **5.** a bird of classical legend, identified with the kingfisher, that was said to magically calm the waves when it nested on the surface of the sea. **6.** any of various kingfishers, esp. of the genus *Halcyon.*

hale[1] (hāl), *adj.*, **hal·er, hal·est.** free from disease or infirmity. —**hale/ness,** *n.*

hale[2] (hāl), *v.t.*, **haled, hal·ing. 1.** to compel (someone) to go: *to hale a suspect into court.* **2.** to haul; pull. —**hal/er,** *n.*

Hale (hāl), *n.* **1. Edward Everett,** 1822–1909, U.S. clergyman and author. **2. George Ellery,** 1868–1938, U.S. astronomer. **3. Nathan,** 1755–76, American soldier hanged as a spy by the British during the American Revolution. **4. Sarah Jo·se·pha** (jō sē/fə), 1788–1879, U.S. editor and author.

Ha·leakala/ Na/tional Park/, *n.* a national park on Maui, Hawaii: site of 21-mi. (34-km) diameter volcanic crater. 43 sq. mi. (111 sq. km).

Ha·ley (hā/lē), *n.* **1. Alex,** 1921–92, U.S. writer. **2. William John Clifton,** ("Bill"), 1925–81, U.S. rock and roll musician.

half (haf, häf), *n.*, *pl.* **halves** (havz, hävz), *adj.*, *adv.* —*n.* **1.** one of two equal or approximately equal parts, as of an object, unit of measure or time, or other divisible whole; a part of a whole equal or almost equal to the remainder. **2.** a quantity or amount equal to such a part (½). **3.** either of two equal periods of play in a game, usu. with an intermission separating them. Compare QUARTER (def. 8). **4.** one of two; a part of a pair. **5.** a halfback. **6. a.** HALF DOLLAR. **b.** the sum of 50 cents. —*adj.* **7.** being one of two equal or approximately equal parts of a divisible whole: *a half quart.* **8.** being half or about half of anything in degree, amount, length, etc.: *at half speed; a half sleeve.* **9.** partial or incomplete: *half measures.* —*adv.* **10.** in or to the extent or measure of half: *half full.* **11.** in part; partly; incompletely: *half understood.* **12.** to some extent; almost: *half recovered.* —*Idiom.* **13. by half,** by a great deal; by far. **14. half again as much** or **as many,** 50 percent more: *This mug holds half again as much coffee as the smaller one.* **15. in half,** into halves or two approximately equal parts: *The vase broke in half.* **16. not (the) half of it,** a relatively minor part of the matter under discussion. —*Proverb.* **17. Half a loaf is better than none,** it is preferable to accept something rather than nothing.

half/-and-half/, *n.* **1.** a mixture of two things, esp. in equal or nearly equal proportions. **2.** milk and light cream combined in equal parts, esp. for table use. *Chiefly Brit.* a mixture of two malt liquors, esp. porter and ale. —*adj.* **4.** half one thing and half another. —*adv.* **5.** in two equal or nearly equal parts.

half·back (haf/bak/, häf/-), *n.* **1.** *Football.* **a.** one of two backs who typically line up on each side of the fullback. **b.** the position played by such a back. **2.** (in soccer, Rugby, field hockey, etc.) a player stationed near the forward line to carry out chiefly offensive duties.

half/-baked/, *adj.* **1.** insufficiently cooked. **2.** not completed; insufficiently planned or prepared: *a half-baked proposal.* **3.** lacking mature judgment or experience; unrealistic: *half-baked theorists.*

half/ bath/ or **half/-bath/,** *n.* a bathroom containing only a toilet and wash basin; powder room.

half/ blood/, *n.* the relation between persons having only one common parent.

half/-blood/, *n.* a person who has only one parent in common with another person, as a half sister or half brother. —**half/-blood/ed,** *adj.*

half/ broth/er, *n.* a male sibling related through one parent only.

half/-caste/, *n.* **1.** a person whose parents are of different races. —*adj.* **2.** of or pertaining to a half-caste.

half/ cock/, *n.* (on a firearm) the position of the hammer when held by the sear halfway between the firing and retracted positions so that the weapon cannot be fired.

half/-cocked/, *adj.* **1.** (of a firearm) held in the position of half cock. **2.** lacking mature consideration or enough preparation; ill-considered or ill-prepared; half-baked. —*Idiom.* **3. go off half-cocked,** to act or speak impulsively or thoughtlessly.

half/ dol/lar, *n.* a coin of the U.S. and Canada equal to 50 cents.

half/-doz/en, *n.* **1.** one half of a dozen; six. —*adj.* **2.** considering six as a unit; consisting of six.

half/ ea/gle, *n.* a gold coin of the U.S., discontinued in 1929, equal to five dollars.

half/ gain/er, *n.* See under GAINER (def. 2).

half/-gal/lon, *n.* **1.** half of a gallon, equal to 2 quarts (1.9 liters). —*adj.* **2.** holding or consisting of two quarts.

half/-glass/es, *n.* (*used with a pl. v.*) a pair of reading glasses, often shaped like the lower half of regular eyeglasses.

half/-heart/ed (haf/här/tid, häf/-), *adj.* having or showing little enthusiasm. —**half/heart/edly,** *adv.* —**half/heart/ed·ness,** *n.*

half/-hour/, *n.* **1.** a period of 30 minutes. **2.** the midpoint of an hour, as 12:30: *A clock struck the half-hour. Buses leave on the half-hour.* —*adj.* **3.** of, pertaining to, or consisting of a half-hour.

half/-life/ or **half/ life/,** *n.*, *pl.* **-lives** (-līvz/). **1.** the time required for one half the atoms of a given amount of a radioactive substance to decay. **2.** the time required for the activity of a substance taken into the body to lose one half its initial effectiveness.

half/-mast/, *n.* a position approximately halfway between the top of a mast, staff, etc., and its base.

half/-moon/, *n.* **1.** the moon when half its disk is illuminated. **2.** the phase of the moon at this time. **3.** something having the shape of a half-moon or crescent.

half/ nel/son, *n.* a hold in which a wrestler, from behind the opponent, passes one arm under the corresponding arm of the opponent and locks the hand on the back of the opponent's neck. Compare FULL NELSON.

half/ note/, *n.* a musical note equivalent in time value to half a whole note.

half·pen·ny (hā/pə nē, hāp/nē), *n.*, *pl.* **half·pen·nies** for 1; **half·pence** (hā/pəns) for 2. **1.** a former British coin equal to half a penny. **2.** the sum of half a penny.

half pint (haf/ pīnt/, häf/ *for 1;* haf/ pīnt/, häf/ *for 2*), *n.* **1.** half of a pint, equal to 8 fluid ounces (1 cup) or 16 tablespoons (0.2 liter). **2.** *Slang.* a very short person.

half/ rest/, *n.* a musical rest equal in time value to one half note.

half/ shell/, *n.* either of the halves of a double-shelled creature, as of an oyster, clam, or other bivalve mollusk.

half/ sis/ter, *n.* a female sibling related through one parent only.

half/ size/, *n.* any size in women's garments, usu. from 12½ to 24½, designed for a short-waisted, full figure.

half/-slip/, *n.* a woman's skirtlike undergarment, usu. of a straight or slightly flared shape and with a narrow elasticized waistband.

half/ step/, *n.* **1.** SEMITONE. **2.** *Mil.* a step 15 in. (38 cm) long in quick time and 18 in. (46 cm) long in double time.

half/time/ or **half/-time/,** *n.* **1.** the intermission or rest period between the two halves of a football, basketball, or other game. —*adj.* **2.** pertaining to or taking place during a halftime.

half·tone (haf/tōn/, häf/-), *n.* **1.** (in painting, drawing, graphics, photography, etc.) a value intermediate between light and dark. **2. a.** a printing process in which gradation of tone is obtained by a system of minute dots. **b.** the metal plate used in such a process. **c.** the print obtained in such a process. —**half/tone,** *adj.*

half/-track/ or **half/ track/,** *n.* **1.** a caterpillar tread that runs over and under the rear or driving wheels of a vehicle but is not connected with the forward wheels: used esp. on military vehicles. **2.** a motor vehicle with rear driving wheels on caterpillar treads. **3.** *Mil.* an armored vehicle equipped with half-tracks. —**half/-tracked/,** *adj.*

half/-truth/, *n.*, *pl.* **-truths.** a statement that is only partly true, esp. one intended to deceive, evade blame, or the like.

half/-turn/, *n.* a 180-degree turn; a direct reversal of direction or orientation, as from front to back or left to right.

half/ vol/ley, *n.* (in tennis, racquets, etc.) a stroke in which the ball is hit the moment it bounces from the ground. —**half/-vol/ley,** *v.t., v.i.*

half·way (haf/wā/, häf/-), *adv.* **1.** to half the distance; to midpoint: *to run halfway.* **2.** partially or nearly; almost: *He halfway surrendered to their demands.* —*adj.* **3.** midway, as between two places or points. **4.** going to or covering only half or part of the full extent: *halfway measures.* —*Idiom.* **5. meet halfway,** to compromise with; give in partially to.

half/way house/, *n.* **1.** an inn or stopping place situated approximately midway between two places on a road. **2.** any place considered as midway in a course. **3.** a residence for persons newly released from psychiatric hospitals, prisons, or other institutions that helps them to cope with their return to society.

half/-wit/, *n.* a person who lacks intelligence or good sense; feebleminded or foolish person; fool. —**half/-wit/ted,** *adj.* —**half/-wit/ted·ly,** *adv.* —**half/-wit/ted·ness,** *n.*

hal·i·but (hal/ə bət, hol/-), *n.*, *pl.* (*esp. collectively*) **-but,** (*esp. for kinds or species*) **-buts.** any of various large edible flounders, esp. of the genus *Hippoglossus.*

Hal·i·fax (hal/ə faks/), *n.* **1.** the capital of Nova Scotia, in SE Canada. 113,577. **2.** a city in West Yorkshire, in N central England. 91,171.

hal·ite (hal/īt, hā/līt), *n.* a soft grayish mineral, sodium chloride, NaCl, occurring as masses of interlocking cubic crystals; rock salt.

hal·i·to·sis (hal/ī tō/sis), *n.* a condition of having offensive-smelling breath; bad breath.

hall (hôl), *n.* **1.** a corridor or passageway in a building. **2.** the large entrance room of a house or building; vestibule. **3.** a large room or building for public gatherings; auditorium: *a concert hall.* **4.** a large building for residence, instruction, or other purposes at a college or university. **5.** a college that is part of a university. **6.** (in English colleges)

H

a. a large room in which the members and students dine. **b.** dinner in such a room. **7.** the chief room in a medieval castle or similar structure, used for eating, sleeping, and entertaining. **8.** the castle, house, or similar structure of a medieval chieftain or noble.

Hall (hôl), *n.* **1. A·saph** (ā′saf), 1829–1907, U.S. astronomer: discovered the satellites of Mars. **2. Charles Francis,** 1821–71, U.S. Arctic explorer. **3. Granville Stanley,** 1846–1924, U.S. psychologist and educator. **4. Prince,** 1748–1807, U.S. clergyman and abolitionist, born in Barbados: fought at Bunker Hill.

Hal·lel (hä′lāl, hä läl′), *n.* a Hebrew liturgical prayer consisting of all or part of Psalms 113–118, recited at the beginning of each new month of the Jewish calendar and on various festivals, as Passover and Hanukkah. [< Hebrew *hallēl* praise]

hal·le·lu·jah or **hal·le·lu·iah** (hal′ə lōō′yə), *interj.* **1.** Praise ye the Lord! —*n.* **2.** an exclamation of "hallelujah!" **3.** a shout of joy, praise, or gratitude. **4.** a musical composition wholly or principally based upon the word "hallelujah."

Hallelu′jah Cho′rus, a chorus in the *Messiah* by George Frideric Handel.

Hal′ley's com′et (hal′ēz *or, often,* hā′lēz), *n.* a comet with a period averaging 76 years: most recently visible in 1986.

hall·mark (hôl′märk′), *n.* **1.** an official mark or stamp indicating a standard of purity, used in marking gold and silver articles assayed by the Goldsmiths' Company of London; plate mark. **2.** any mark or special indication of genuineness, good quality, etc. **3.** any distinguishing feature or characteristic: *Accuracy is a hallmark of good scholarship.* —**hall′mark′er,** *n.*

hal·lo or **hol·lo** or **hol·loa** (hə lō′), *interj., n., pl.* **-los** or **-loas,** *v.,* **-loed, -lo·ing** or **-loaed, loa·ing.** —*interj.* **1.** (used to call or answer someone, or to incite dogs in hunting.) —*n.* **2.** the cry "hallo!" **3.** a shout of exultation. —*v.i.* **4.** to call with a loud voice; shout; cry, as after hunting dogs. —*v.t.* **5.** to incite or chase (something) with shouts and cries of "hallo!" **6.** to cry "hallo" to (someone). **7.** to shout (something).

Hall′ of Fame′, a national shrine in New York City commemorating the names of outstanding Americans. **2.** a number of individuals acclaimed as outstanding in a particular profession or activity.

hal·low (hal′ō), *v.t.* **1.** to make holy; sanctify; consecrate: *to hallow the name of the Lord.* **2.** to honor as holy; consider sacred; venerate: *to hallow a battlefield.* —**hal′low·er,** *n.*

hal·lowed (hal′ōd; *in liturgical use often* hal′ō id), *adj.* regarded as holy; venerated; sacred: *hallowed political institutions.* —**hal′lowed·ness,** *n.*

Hal·low·een or **Hal·low·e′en** (hal′ə wēn′, -ō ēn′, hol′-), *n.* the evening of Oct. 31; the eve of All Saints' Day: observed esp. by children, who dress in costume and play trick or treat. [(*All*)*hallow*(*s*) + *e*(*v*)*en* evening]

hall′ tree′, *n.* a clothes tree or hatrack.

hal·lu·ci·nate (hə lōō′sə nāt′), *v.,* **-nat·ed, -nat·ing.** —*v.i.* **1.** to have hallucinations. —*v.t.* **2.** to affect with hallucinations. **3.** to experience as a hallucination. —**hal·lu′ci·na′tor,** *n.*

hal·lu·ci·na·tion (hə lōō′sə nā′shən), *n.* **1.** a sensory experience of something that does not exist outside the mind, caused by various physical and mental disorders, or by reaction to certain toxic substances, and usu. manifested as visual or auditory images. **2.** the sensation caused by a hallucinatory condition or the object or scene visualized. **3.** a false notion, belief, or impression; illusion; delusion. —**hal·lu′ci·na′tion·al, hal·lu′ci·na′tive** (-nā′tiv, -nə tiv), *adj.*

hal·lu·ci·no·gen (hə lōō′sə nə jən), *n.* a substance that produces hallucinations. —**hal·lu′ci·no·gen′ic** (-jen′ik), *adj.*

hal·lux (hal′əks), *n., pl.* **hal·lu·ces** (hal′yə sēz′). the first or innermost digit of the foot of humans and of the hind foot of other vertebrates; big toe. —**hal′lu·cal** (-yə kəl), *adj.*

hall·way (hôl′wā′), *n.* **1.** a corridor, as in a building. **2.** an entrance hall.

ha·lo (hā′lō), *n., pl.* **-los, -loes,** *v.,* **-loed, -lo·ing.** —*n.* **1.** Also called **nimbus.** the representation, as in pictures or statuary, of a radiant light, usu. in the shape of a disk, ring, or rayed form, above or around the head of a divine, holy, or greatly exalted personage. **2.** something suggesting such a light or shape: *a halo of ringlets on a baby's head.* **3.** NIMBUS (def. 2). **4.** any of a variety of bright circles or arcs centered on the sun or moon, caused by the refraction or reflection of light by ice crystals suspended in the earth's atmosphere (disting. from *corona*). —*v.t.* **5.** to surround with a halo. —*v.i.* **6.** to form a halo.

ha′lo effect′, *n.* a potential inaccuracy in estimation or judgment, esp. of a person, due to a tendency to overgeneralize from a single salient feature or action, usu. in a favorable direction.

hal·o·gen (hal′ə jən, -jen′, hā′lə-), *n.* any of the nonmetallic elements, fluorine, chlorine, iodine, bromine, and astatine, that form binary salts by direct union with metals. —**ha·log·e·nous** (hə loj′ə nəs), *adj.*

hal′ogen lamp′, *n.* a gas-filled, high-intensity incandescent lamp containing a small amount of a halogen, as iodine.

hal·oid (hal′oid, hā′loid), *adj.* resembling or derived from a halogen.

hal·o·thane (hal′ə thān′), *n.* a colorless liquid, $C_2HBrClF_3$, used as an inhalant for general anesthesia.

halt[1] (hôlt), *v.i.* **1.** to stop; cease moving, operating: *The car halted in front of the house.* —*v.t.* **2.** to cause to stop; bring to a stop: *Production*

was halted during the strike. —*n.* **3.** a temporary or permanent stop; standstill: *to come to a halt.* —*interj.* **4.** (used as a command to stop and stand motionless, as to marching troops or to a fleeing suspect.) —**halt′er,** *n.*

halt[2] (hôlt), *v.i.* **1.** to falter, as in speech, reasoning, etc.; be hesitant; stumble. **2.** to be in doubt; waver between alternatives; vacillate. **3.** to be lame; limp. —*adj.* **4.** lame; limping: *an old, halt horse.* —*n.* **5.** lameness; a limp. **6. the halt,** lame people, esp. severely lamed ones: *the halt and the blind.* —**halt′er,** *n.*

hal·ter[1] (hôl′tər), *n.* **1.** a rope or strap with a noose or headstall for leading or restraining horses or cattle. **2.** a rope with a noose for hanging criminals; the hangman's noose. **3.** death by hanging. **4.** a woman's top, secured behind the neck and across the back, leaving the arms, shoulders, upper back, and often the midriff bare. —*v.t.* **5.** to put a halter on; restrain as by a halter. **6.** to hang (a person). —*adj.* **7.** being or having a neckline formed by straps that extend from the front of a backless, sleeveless bodice and are secured around the neck. —**hal′ter·like′,** *adj.*

hal·ter[2] (hal′tər), *n., pl.* **hal·te·res** (hal tēr′ēz). one of a pair of small knobbed appendages of dipterous flies, evolved from a second pair of wings and used for balance.

halt·ing (hôl′ting), *adj.* **1.** faltering or hesitating, esp. in speech. **2.** faulty or imperfect. **3.** limping or lame: *a halting gait.* —**halt′ing·ly,** *adv.*

halve (hav, häv), *v.t.,* **halved, halv·ing. 1.** to divide into two equal parts. **2.** to share equally. **3.** to reduce to half. **4.** *Golf.* to play (a hole, round, or match) in the same number of strokes as one's opponent.

halves (havz, hävz), *n.* **1.** pl. of HALF. —*Idiom.* **2. by halves,** incompletely or halfheartedly. **3. go halves,** to share equally; divide evenly.

ham[1] (ham), *n.* **1.** a cut of meat from a hog's hind quarter, between hip and hock; thigh. **2.** that part of a hog's hind leg. **3.** the part of the human leg behind the knee. **4.** Often, **hams.** the back of the thigh, or the thigh and the buttock together.

ham[2] (ham), *n., v.,* **hammed, ham·ming.** —*n.* **1.** an actor or performer who overacts. **2.** an operator of an amateur radio station. —*v.i., v.t.* **3.** to act with exaggerated expression of emotion; overact. —*Idiom.* **4. ham it up,** to overact; ham.

Ham (ham), *n.* the second son of Noah. Gen. 10:1.

Ha·ma (hä′mä, hä mä′), *n.* a city in W Syria, on the Orontes River. 137,589. Ancient, **Epiphania.** Biblical name, **Hamath.**

ham·a·dry′as baboon′ (ham′ə drī′əs), *n.* a N African and Arabian grayish baboon, *Comopithecus (Papio) hamadryas:* the male has a long dark mane. Also called **sacred baboon.**

Ha·man (hā′mən), *n.* the chief minister of King Ahasuerus and an enemy of the Jews. Esther 3–7.

ham·burg·er (ham′bûr′gər), *n.* **1.** a patty of ground beef. **2.** a sandwich consisting of such a patty fried or broiled and served on a bun or roll. **3.** ground beef.

ham′-hand′ed, *adj.* clumsy, inept, or heavy-handed: *a ham-handed apology.* —**ham′-hand′ed·ness,** *n.*

Ham·il·ton (ham′əl tən), *n.* **1. Alexander,** 1757–1804, first U.S. Secretary of the Treasury 1789–97. **2. Edith,** 1867–1963, U.S. classical scholar. **3. Lady Emma** (*Amy,* or *Emily, Lyon*), 1765?–1815, mistress of Viscount Nelson. **4.** former name of CHURCHILL RIVER. **5. Mount,** a mountain in W California, near San Jose: site of Lick Observatory. 4209 ft. (1283 m). **6.** a seaport in SE Ontario, in SE Canada, on Lake Ontario. 306,728. **7.** the capital of Bermuda. 3000.

Ham·il·to·ni·an (ham′əl tō′nē ən), *adj.* **1.** pertaining to or advocating Hamiltonianism. —*n.* **2.** a supporter of Alexander Hamilton or Hamiltonianism.

Ham·il·to·ni·an·ism (ham′əl tō′nē ə niz′əm), *n.* the political principles associated with Alexander Hamilton, esp. those stressing a strong central government and protective tariffs.

Ham·ite (ham′īt), *n.* a descendant of Ham. Gen. 10:1, 6–20.

ham·let (ham′lit), *n.* a small village.

Ham·let (ham′lit), *n.* the hero of a tragedy by Shakespeare, *Hamlet* (1603), a young prince who avenges the murder of his father.

Ham·lin (ham′lin), *n.* **Hannibal,** 1809–91, U.S. political leader: vice president of the U.S. 1861–65.

Ham·mar·skjöld (hä′mər shöld′, -shəld, ham′ər-), *n.* **Dag Hjalmar,** 1905–61, Swedish statesman: Secretary General of the United Nations 1953–61; Nobel peace prize 1961.

ham·mer (ham′ər), *n.* **1.** a tool consisting of a solid head, usu. of metal, set crosswise on a handle, used for driving nails, beating metals, etc. **2.** any of various instruments or devices resembling this in form, action, or use, as a gavel, a mallet for playing the xylophone, or one of the padded levers by which the strings of a piano are struck. **3.** the part of a lock of a firearm that strikes the primer or firing pin, explodes the percussion cap, etc., and causes the discharge; cock. **4.** a metal ball, usu. weighing 16 lb. (7.3 kg), attached to a steel wire at the end of which is a grip, for throwing in the hammer throw. —*v.t.* **5.** to beat or drive (a nail, peg, etc.) with a hammer. **6.** to fasten by using hammer and nails; nail (often fol. by *down, up,* etc.). **7.** to assemble or build with a hammer and nails (often fol. by *together*): *to hammer together a small crate.* **8.** to shape or ornament (metal or a metal object) by controlled blows of a hammer; beat out: *to hammer brass.* **9.** to form or construct by repeated, vigorous, or strenuous effort (often fol. by *out* or *together*): *to hammer out an agreement.* **10.** to pound or hit forcefully (often fol. by *out*): *to hammer out a tune on the piano.* **11.** to settle or resolve, as by strenuous or repeated effort (usu. fol. by *out*): *They hammered out their differences at last.* **12.** to present (points in an argument, an idea, etc.) forcefully or compellingly: *hammering home the need for action.* **13.** to impress (something) as if by hammer blows: *to hammer rules into someone's head.* —*v.i.* **14.** to strike blows with or as if with a hammer. **15.** to make persistent or laborious attempts to finish or perfect something (sometimes fol. by *away*): *She hammered away at her speech for days.* **16.** to reiterate; emphasize by repetition (often fol. by *away*): *The teacher likes to hammer away at the importance of punctuality.* —*Idiom.* **17. under the hammer,** for sale at public auction. —**ham′mer•er,** *n.*

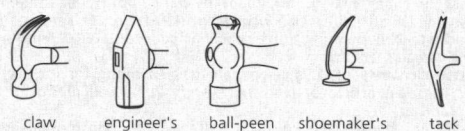

claw   engineer's   ball-peen   shoemaker's   tack

hammers

ham′mer and sick′le, *n.* **1.** the Communist emblem of the Soviet Union, consisting of a hammer with its handle across the blade of a sickle and a star above. **2.** a similar emblem used by Communist parties elsewhere.

ham•mered (ham′ərd), *adj.* shaped, formed, or ornamented by a metalworker's hammer: *hammered gold.*

ham•mer•head (ham′ər hed′), *n.* **1.** the part of a hammer designed for striking. **2.** any shark of the genus *Sphyrna*, having a mallet-shaped head with an eye at each end.

ham′mer•lock or **ham′mer lock′,** *n.* a wrestling hold in which one arm of an opponent is twisted and forced upward behind the opponent's back.

Ham•mer•stein (ham′ər stīn′), *n.* **1. Oscar,** 1847?–1919, U.S. theatrical manager, born in Germany. **2.** his grandson, **Oscar II,** 1895–1960, U.S. lyricist and librettist.

ham′mer throw′, *n.* a field event in which the hammer is thrown for distance. —**ham′mer throw′er,** *n.*

ham•mer•toe (ham′ər tō′), *n.* **1.** a deformity of a toe, usu. the second or third, in which there is a permanent angular flexion of the joints. **2.** a toe with such a deformity.

ham•mock[1] (ham′ək), *n.* a bed or couch of canvas, netted cord, or the like that hangs between two supports, to which it is attached by cords or springs. —**ham′mock•like′,** *adj.*

ham•mock[2] (ham′ək), *n.* HUMMOCK (def. 1).

Ham•mu•ra•bi (hä′mŏŏ rä′bē, ham′ŏŏ-) also **Ham•mu•ra•pi** (-rä′pē) *n.* 18th century B.C., king of Babylonia: instituted a legal code.

ham•my (ham′ē), *adj.,* **-mi•er, -mi•est.** characterized by a highly exaggerated, generally excessive or inappropriate show of emotions, responses, etc.: *a hammy actor; a hammy performance.* —**ham′mi•ly,** *adv.* —**ham′mi•ness,** *n.*

ham•per[1] (ham′pər), *v.t.* **1.** to hold back; hinder; impede: *Heavy rain hampered the flow of traffic.* **2.** to interfere with; curtail.

ham•per[2] (ham′pər), *n.* a large basket or wicker receptacle, usu. with a cover: *a clothes hamper; a picnic hamper.*

Hamp•ton (hamp′tən), *n.* **1. Lionel,** born 1913, U.S. jazz vibraphonist. **2. Wade,** 1818–1902, Confederate general: U.S. senator 1879–91. **3.** a city in SE Virginia, on Chesapeake Bay. 139,628.

ham•ster (ham′stər), *n.* any of several short-tailed, burrowing rodents of the family Cricetidae, of Eurasia, with large cheek pouches.

ham•string (ham′string′), *n., v.,* **-strung, -string•ing.** —*n.* **1.** (in humans) **a.** any of the tendons in the region behind the knee. **b.** ACHILLES TENDON. **2.** (in quadrupeds) the great tendon at the back of the hock. —*v.t.* **3.** to disable by cutting the hamstring or hamstrings; cripple. **4.** to render powerless, ineffective, etc.; thwart: *The attorneys were hamstrung by the judge's ruling.*

Han (hän), *n., pl.* **Hans,** (*esp. collectively*) **Han** for 3. **1.** a dynasty in China, 206 B.C.–A.D. 220, characterized by consolidation of the centralized state, territorial expansion, and cultural and scientific achievements. **2.** a river flowing from central China into the Chang Jiang at Wuhan. 900 mi. (1450 km) long. **3.** CHINESE (def. 3).

Han•cock (han′kok), *n.* **1. John,** 1737–93, American statesman: first signer of the Declaration of Independence. **2. Winfield Scott,** 1824–86, Union general in the Civil War.

hand (hand), *n.* **1.** the terminal, prehensile part of the arm in humans and higher primates, consisting of the wrist, metacarpals, fingers, and thumb. **2.** the corresponding part of the forelimb in any four-legged vertebrate. **3.** a terminal prehensile part, as the chela of a crustacean, or, in falconry, the foot of a falcon. **4.** something resembling a hand in shape or function: *the hands of a clock.* **5.** INDEX (def. 5). **6.** a person employed in manual labor or for general duty: *a ranch hand.* **7.** a person with great skill in or knowledge of something, esp. through long experience: *an old hand at fund-raising.* **8.** a person with reference to an ability or skill: *a poor hand at running a business.* **9.** skill; workmanship; characteristic touch: *The painting shows a master's hand.* **10.** Of-

ten, **hands.** possession or power; control, custody, or care: *My fate is in your hands.* **11.** a position, esp. one of control, used for bargaining, negotiating, etc. **12.** means; agency; instrumentality: *death by his own hand.* **13.** assistance; aid: *Give me a hand with this ladder.* **14.** side; direction: *no traffic on either hand of the road.* **15.** style of handwriting; penmanship. **16.** a person's signature: *to set one's hand to a document.* **17.** a round or outburst of applause for a performer. **18.** a promise or pledge, esp. in marriage. **19.** a linear measure equal to 4 inches (10.2 centimeters), used esp. in determining the height of horses. **20.** *Cards.* **a.** the cards dealt to or held by each player at one time. **b.** the person holding the cards. **c.** a single part of a game, in which all the cards dealt at one time are played. **21.** a bunch, cluster, or bundle of leaves, fruit, or the like. **22.** the deviation of a thread or tooth from the axial direction of a screw or gear, as seen from one end looking away toward the other. **23.** the properties of a fabric that can be sensed by touching it, as resilience and smoothness. —*v.t.* **24.** to deliver or pass with or as if with the hand. **25.** to help, assist, guide, etc., with the hand: *She handed the elderly woman across the street.* **26.** to give or provide with: *That handed me a laugh.* **27. hand down, a.** to deliver (the decision of a court). **b.** to transmit, esp. to a succeeding generation. **28. hand in,** to submit; present for acceptance. **29. hand off,** *Football.* to hand the ball to a member of one's team in the course of a play. **30. hand on,** to transmit; pass on to a successor, posterity, etc. **31. hand out,** to give or distribute; pass out. **32. hand over,** to deliver to another; surrender control of. —*adj.* **33.** of, belonging to, using, or used by the hand. **34.** made by hand. **35.** carried in or worn on the hand. **36.** operated by hand; manual. —*Idiom.* **37. at hand, a.** within reach; ready for use; accessible. **b.** about to happen. **38. at the hand(s) of,** by the action of; through the agency of. **39. by hand,** by using the hands, as opposed to machines; manually. **40. change hands,** to pass from one owner to another. **41. eat out of someone's hand,** to be totally submissive to another. **42. force someone's hand,** to compel a person to do or disclose something before he or she is ready to do so. **43. from hand to hand,** from one person to another; through successive ownership or possession. **44. from hand to mouth,** with nothing in reserve; precariously: *to live from hand to mouth.* **45. hand and foot, a.** with the arms and legs immobilized. **b.** with slavish attentiveness: *to wait on someone hand and foot.* **46. hand in** or **and glove,** in close association, esp. for nefarious purposes. **47. hand in hand, a.** alongside one another while holding hands. **b.** closely associated; in cooperation. **48. hand it to,** to give just respect to; pay respect to, as for an effort or achievement. **49. hand over fist,** speedily; increasingly: *making money hand over fist.* **50. hands down, a.** effortlessly; easily. **b.** indisputably; incontestably. **51. hand to hand,** in direct combat; at close quarters. **52. have a hand in,** to participate in. **53. have one's hands full,** to have as much work as one can handle; be excessively busy. **54. hold hands,** to join hands with another person, as in affection. **55. in hand, a.** under control. **b.** in one's possession. **c.** in the process of consideration or settlement. **56. join hands,** to unite in a common cause; combine. **57. keep one's hand in,** to continue to work at or practice so as not to lose one's skill or knowledge. **58. lay hands on, a.** to obtain; acquire. **b.** to seize, esp. in order to punish. **c.** to impose the hands on in a ceremonial fashion, as in ordination. **59. on one's hands,** under one's care or management; as one's responsibility. **60. on all hands** or **every hand,** everywhere or by everyone around: *sly remarks on all hands.* **61. on hand, a.** in one's possession; at one's disposal: *cash on hand.* **b.** present: *How many staff members are on hand?* **62. on the one hand,** from the first perspective; as the first argument. **63. on the other hand,** from the opposing perspective; conversely. **64. out of hand, a.** completely out of control. **b.** without delay or deliberation. **65. out of one's hands,** outside one's control. **66. show one's hand,** to disclose one's true motives. **67. sit on one's hands, a.** to fail to applaud. **b.** to fail to take appropriate action. **68. take in hand,** to undertake responsibility for; deal with. **69. the left hand doesn't know what the right hand is doing,** there is a lack of communication between the parts of an organization. **70. throw up one's hands,** to stop trying; admit to failure. **71. tie someone's hands,** to render someone powerless to act. **72. tip one's hand,** to reveal one's plans or intentions before the propitious time. **73. to hand, a.** within reach; accessible or nearby. **b.** into one's possession or view. **74. try one's hand at,** to undertake so as to test one's aptitude for. **75. turn** or **put one's hand to,** to set to work at; busy oneself with. **76. wash one's hands of,** to abandon any further responsibility for. Matt. 27:24. **77. with a heavy hand, a.** with severity; oppressively. **b.** in a clumsy manner; awkwardly; gracelessly. **78. Idle hands are the devil's tools,** idleness leads to mischief. —*Proverb.* **79. Never let your left hand know what your right hand is doing,** give freely to others without flaunting your generosity. Matt. 6:3.

Hand (hand), *n.* **Learn•ed** (lûr′nid), 1872–1961, U.S. jurist.

hand•bag (hand′bag′), *n.* **1.** a bag or case carried in the hand or by a handle or strap and commonly used by women to hold money, cosmetics, etc. **2.** VALISE.

hand•ball (hand′bôl′), *n.* **1.** a game, similar to squash, played by two or four persons who strike a ball against a wall or walls with the hand. **2.** the small, hard rubber ball used in this game. —**hand′ball′er,** *n.*

hand•bas•ket (hand′bas′kit, -bä′skit), *n.* **1.** a small basket with a handle for carrying by hand. —*Idiom.* **2. go to hell in a handbasket,** to degenerate quickly and decisively.

hand·bill (hand/bil/), *n.* a small printed notice, advertisement, or announcement, usu. for distribution by hand.

hand·book (hand/bŏŏk/), *n.* **1.** a book of instruction or guidance, as for an occupation; manual. **2.** a guidebook for travelers. **3.** a reference book in a particular field: *a medical handbook.*

hand/ brake/, *n.* **1.** a brake operated by a hand lever, as on a bicycle. **2.** (in an automobile) an emergency or parking brake operated by a hand lever.

hand·breadth (hand/bredth/, -bretth/) also **hand's-breadth,** *n.* a unit of linear measure that ranges from 2½ to 4 inches (6.4 to 10.2 cm).

hand·car (hand/kär/), *n.* a small railroad car or platform on four wheels propelled by a mechanism worked by hand, used for inspecting tracks, transporting workers, etc.

hand·cart (hand/kärt/), *n.* a small cart drawn or pushed by hand.

hand·clasp (hand/klasp/, -kläsp/), *n.* a gripping of hands by two or more people, as in greeting or parting.

hand·craft (hand/kraft/, -kräft/), *n.,* *v.t.* HANDICRAFT.

hand·cuff (hand/kuf/), *n.* **1.** a metal ring that can be locked around a prisoner's wrist, usu. one of a pair connected by a chain or bar; shackle. —*v.t.* **2.** to put handcuffs on. **3.** to restrain or thwart (someone).

hand·ed (han/did), *adj.* **1.** having or involving a hand or hands (usu. used in combination): *a two-handed backhand.* **2.** requiring a specified number of persons: *a four-handed game of poker.* **3.** preferring the use of a particular hand (usu. used in combination): *right-handed.*

hand·ed·ness (han/did nis), *n.* a tendency to use one hand more than the other.

Han·del (han/dl), *n.* **George Frideric** (*Georg Friedrich Händel*), 1685–1759, German composer in England after 1712. —**Han·del/i·an** (-dē/lē-ən), *adj.*

hand·ful (hand/fŏŏl), *n., pl.* **-fuls. 1.** the quantity or amount that the hand can hold. **2.** a small amount or quantity. **3.** *Informal.* a person or thing that is as much as one can manage or control.

hand/ grenade/, *n.* an explosive shell that is thrown by hand and exploded by impact or by means of a fuze.

hand·gun (hand/gun/), *n.* any firearm that can be held and fired with one hand; a revolver or a pistol.

hand·hold (hand/hōld/), *n.* **1.** a grip with the hand or hands. **2.** something to grip or take hold of, as a support or handle.

hand·hold·ing (hand/hōl/ding), *n.* constant reassurance, help, or instruction, as from a mentor.

hand·i·cap (han/dē kap/), *n., v.,* **-capped, -cap·ping.** —*n.* **1.** a race or other contest in which disadvantages or advantages of weight, distance, time, etc., are given to competitors to equalize their chances of winning. **2.** the disadvantage or advantage itself. **3.** any disadvantage that makes success more difficult. **4.** a physical or mental disability, esp. one that makes ordinary activities of daily living difficult. —*v.t.* **5.** to place at a disadvantage; disable or burden. **6.** to assign handicaps to (competitors). **7. a.** to attempt to predict the winner of (a contest, esp. a horse race), as by comparing past performances of the contestants. **b.** to assign odds for or against (any particular contestant).

hand·i·capped (han/dē kapt/), *adj.* **1.** physically or mentally disabled. **2.** (of a contestant) marked by being under, or having a handicap. —*n.* **3. the handicapped,** handicapped persons collectively.

hand·i·cap·per (han/dē kap/ər), *n.* **1.** an official who assigns handicaps to contestants, as in a horse race or golf tournament. **2.** a person employed, as by a newspaper, to make predictions on the outcomes of horse races.

hand·i·craft (han/dē kraft/, -kräft/), *n.* **1.** manual skill. **2.** an art, craft, or trade in which manual skill is required. **3.** the articles made by handicraft.

hand·i·ly (han/di lē, -dl ē), *adv.* **1.** in a handy manner; dexterously. **2.** easily: *to win handily.* **3.** conveniently; accessibly.

hand·i·work (han/dē wûrk/), *n.* **1.** work done by hand. **2.** the work of a particular person. **3.** the result of work done by hand.

hand·ker·chief (hang/kər chif, -chēf/), *n.* **1.** a small piece of fabric, usu. square, used for wiping the nose, eyes, etc., or worn as an accessory. **2.** a neckerchief or kerchief.

han·dle (han/dl), *n., v.,* **-dled, -dling.** —*n.* **1.** a part of a thing made specifically to be grasped or held by the hand. **2.** anything serving as or resembling a handle. **3.** *Slang.* a person's name, esp. the given name. **4.** the total amount bet on an event or game or during a time period, as at a racetrack or casino. **5.** HAND (def. 23). —*v.t.* **6.** to touch, pick up, carry, or feel with the hand or hands; use the hands on; take hold of. **7.** to manage, deal with, or be responsible for: *This computer handles all our billing.* **8.** to use or employ, esp. in a particular manner; manipulate: *to handle color expertly in painting.* **9.** to manage, direct, train, or control: *to handle troops.* **10.** to deal with (a subject, theme, etc.). **11.** to deal with or treat in a particular way: *to handle a person with tact.* **12.** to deal or trade in. —*v.i.* **13.** to behave or perform in a particular way when handled, directed, managed, etc: *The jet was handling poorly.* —*Idiom.* **14. get** or **have a handle on,** to acquire or possess a usable understanding of.

han·dle·bar (han/dl bär/), *n.* Usu., **handlebars.** the curved steering bar of a bicycle, motorcycle, etc., placed in front of the rider and gripped by the hands.

han/dlebar mustache/, *n.* a man's mustache having long, curved ends that resemble the handlebars of a bicycle.

han·dler (hand/lər), *n.* **1.** a person or thing that handles. **2.** a person who assists in the training of a boxer or is the boxer's second during a fight. **3.** a person who trains, exhibits, or directs an animal, as a dog in a show. **4.** a person who manages and represents a public figure, esp. a political candidate.

han·dling (hand/ling), *n.* **1.** a touching, grasping, or using with the hands. **2.** the manner of treating or dealing with something. **3.** the process by which something is packaged, transported, delivered, etc. —*adj.* **4.** of or pertaining to the process of transporting, delivering, etc.: *a 10 percent handling charge.*

hand·made (hand/mād/), *adj.* made by hand, not by machine.

hand·maid (hand/mād/) also **hand/maid/en,** *n.* **1.** a female servant or attendant. **2.** something subservient or subordinate: *Ceremony is but the handmaid of worship.*

hand/-me-down/, *n.* **1.** a used item passed along for further use by another, esp. an article of clothing. —*adj.* **2.** passed along for further use by another.

hand/-off/ or **hand/off/,** *n.* **1.** an offensive play in football in which a player, usu. a back, hands the ball to a teammate. **2.** the ball itself during the execution of such a transfer.

hand/ or/gan, *n.* a portable barrel organ played by means of a crank turned by hand.

hand·out (hand/out/), *n.* **1.** a portion of food or the like given to a needy person, as a beggar. **2.** a press release. **3.** any copy of a speech, fact sheet, etc., distributed at a meeting. **4.** anything given away for nothing, as a free sample of a product.

hand·pick (hand/pik/), *v.t.* **1.** to pick by hand. **2.** to select personally and with care.

hand/ pup/pet, *n.* a puppet designed to be fitted over the hand, which manipulates it.

hand·rail (hand/rāl/), *n.* a rail serving as a support or guard at the side of a stairway, platform, etc.

hand·saw (hand/sô/), *n.* any common saw with a handle at one end for manual operation with one hand.

hands/-down/, *adj.* **1.** easy: *a hands-down victory.* **2.** unchallenged; certain: *a hands-down bestseller.*

hand·set (*n.* hand/set/; *adj.* -set/, -set/), *n.* **1.** a telephone having a mouthpiece and earpiece mounted at opposite ends of a handle. —*adj.* **2.** (of type) set by hand.

hand·shake (hand/shāk/), *n.* **1.** a gripping and shaking of each other's hand, as to symbolize greeting, congratulation, agreement, or farewell. **2.** an exchange of signals in a computer system, ensuring synchronization whenever a connection, as with another device, is initially established.

hands/-off/, *adj.* characterized by nonintervention or noninterference.

hand·some (han/sam), *adj.,* **-som·er, -som·est. 1.** having an attractive, well-proportioned, and imposing appearance suggestive of health and strength; good-looking: *a handsome boy; a handsome couple.* **2.** having pleasing proportions or arrangements, as of shapes or colors; attractive: *a handsome interior.* **3.** considerable, ample, or liberal in amount: *a handsome fortune.* **4.** gracious; generous: *a handsome compliment.* **5.** adroit; graceful: *a handsome speech.* ——*Proverb.* **6.** Handsome is as handsome does, one's actions are more important than one's appearance. —**hand/some·ly,** *adv.* —**hand/some·ness,** *n.*

hands/-on/, *adj.* characterized by or involving active personal participation: *hands-on experience with computers.*

hand·spring (hand/spring/), *n.* an acrobatic movement in which the upright body wheels forward or backward in a complete circle, landing first on the hands and then on the feet.

hand·stand (hand/stand/), *n.* an act of supporting the body in a vertical position by balancing on the palms of the hands.

hand/-to-hand/, *adj.* close to one's adversary; at close quarters: *hand-to-hand combat.*

hand/-to-mouth/, *adj.* offering or providing the barest livelihood or sustenance; meager; precarious: *a hand-to-mouth existence.*

hand/ truck/, *n.* a two-wheeled, barrowlike conveyance for moving luggage, cartons, etc., consisting of a frame with a ledge at the bottom and handles at the top.

hand·work (hand/wûrk/), *n.* work done by hand, as distinguished from work done by machine. —**hand/ work/er,** *n.*

hand·wo·ven (hand/wō/vən), *adj.* woven by hand or on a hand-operated loom: *a handwoven sweater; a handwoven tapestry.*

hand·write (hand/rīt/), *v.t.,* **-wrote, -writ·ten, -writ·ing.** to write (something) by hand.

hand·writ·ing (hand/rī/ting), *n.* **1.** writing done with a pen or pencil in the hand. **2.** a style or manner of writing by hand, esp. that which characterizes a particular person. **3.** a handwritten document; manuscript. ——*Idiom.* **4.** handwriting on the wall, a premonition, portent, or clear indication, esp. of failure or disaster.

hand·y·man (han/dē man/), *n., pl.* **-men.** a person hired to do various small maintenance or repair jobs.

hang (hang), *v.,* **hung** or (*esp. for 4, 5, 13, 18*) **hanged, hang·ing,** *n.* —*v.t.* **1.** to fasten or attach (a thing) so that it is supported only from above or at a point near its own top; suspend. **2.** to attach or suspend so as to allow free movement: *to hang a door.* **3.** to place in position or fasten so as to allow easy or ready movement. **4.** to execute by suspending from a gallows, gibbet, yardarm, or the like: *to hang a convicted murderer.* **5.** to suspend by the neck until dead: *He committed suicide by hanging himself.* **6.** to furnish or decorate with something suspended: *to hang a room with pictures.* **7.** to fasten into position; fix at a proper angle: *to hang a scythe.* **8.** to fasten or attach (wallpaper, pictures, curtains, etc.) to a wall or the like. **9. a.** to exhibit (a painting or group of paintings). **b.** to put the paintings of (an art exhibition) on the wall of a gallery. **10.** to attach or annex as an addition: *to hang a rider on a bill.* **11.** to make (something) dependent on something else: *She hung the meaning of her puns on the current political scene.* **12.** to throw (a baseball pitch) so that it fails to break, as a curve. **13.** (used in mild curses and emphatic expressions, often as a euphemism for *damn*): *Well, I'll be hanged!* **14.** to keep (a jury) from rendering a verdict, as one juror by refusing to agree with the others. —*v.i.* **15.** to be suspended; dangle. **16.** to swing freely, as on a hinge. **17.** to incline downward, jut out, or lean over or forward. **18.** to be suspended by the neck, as from a gallows, and suffer death in this way. **19.** to be conditioned or contingent; be dependent: *Our future hangs on the outcome of their discussion.* **20.** to be doubtful or undecided; waver or hesitate. **21.** to remain unfinished or undecided; be delayed. **22.** to linger, remain, or persist. **23.** to float or hover in the air. **24.** to be oppressive, burdensome, or tedious: *guilt that hangs on one's conscience.* **25.** to fit or drape in graceful lines: *That coat hangs well in back.* **26. a.** to be exhibited: *Her works hang in this museum.* **b.** to have one's works on display: *Rembrandt hangs in the Metropolitan Museum of Art.* **27. hang around** or **about,** *Informal.* **a.** to spend time in a certain place or in certain company. **b.** to linger about; loiter. **28. hang back,** to hesitate or be reluctant to move forward or take action. **29. hang in (there),** *Informal.* to persevere or endure. **30. hang on, a.** to cling tightly. **b.** to persevere in doing something. **c.** to persist unremittingly, as an illness. **d.** to keep a telephone line open: *Hang on, I'll see if she's here.* **e.** to wait briefly; keep calm. **f.** to listen very attentively to: *They hung on his every word.* **31. hang out, a.** to lean out, suspend, or be suspended, as through an opening. **b.** *Informal.* to loiter idly; frequent a particular place. **c.** *Informal.* to associate in casual companionship. **32. hang over, a.** to remain unfinished or unsettled. **b.** to menace; overshadow. **33. hang up, a.** to suspend, as on a hook. **b.** to stop or delay the progress of. **c.** to end a telephone call by breaking the connection. —*n.* **34.** the way in which a thing hangs. **35.** *Informal.* the precise manner of doing, using, etc., something; knack. **36.** *Informal.* meaning or significance: *to get the hang of a subject.* **37.** the least degree of care, concern, etc. (used in mild curses and emphatic expressions as a euphemism for *damn*): *He doesn't give a hang about it.* —**Idiom. 38. hang a left** (or **right**), *Slang.* to make a left (or right) turn, as while driving an automobile. **39. hang fire, a.** (of a weapon) to be delayed in exploding or firing. **b.** to be kept in a state of delay. **40. hang five,** *Slang.* to ride a surfboard with the toes of the forward foot curled over the board's front. **41. hang in the balance,** to be in a precarious state or condition. **42. hang it up,** *Informal.* to quit; resign; give up. **43. hang loose,** *Slang.* to remain relaxed or calm. **44. hang one on,** *Slang.* **a.** to become extremely drunk. **b.** to hit (someone). **45. hang ten,** *Slang.* to ride a surfboard with the toes of both feet curled over the board's front edge. **46. hang together, a.** to be loyal to one another; remain united. **b.** to cohere. **c.** to be logical or consistent. **47. hang tough,** *Informal.* to remain unyielding or inflexible. —**Usage.** HANGED, the historically older form of the past tense and past participle, is rarely used except in the sense of putting to death, esp. legally: *to be hanged by the neck until dead.* But HUNG also occurs in this sense, except in legal documents, and is actually the more frequent form when legal execution is not meant: *The prisoner hung himself in his cell.*

hang·ar (hang′ər), *n.* **1.** a shed or shelter. **2.** any relatively wide structure used for housing airplanes or airships. [< French: shed, shelter]

hang·dog (hang′dôg′, -dog′), *adj.* **1.** browbeaten; defeated; abject: *a hangdog look.* **2.** shamefaced; guilty. **3.** suitable to a degraded or contemptible person; furtive.

hang·er (hang′ər), *n.* **1.** a shoulder-shaped frame with a hook at the top, usu. of wire, wood, or plastic, for draping and hanging a garment when not in use. **2.** a part of something by which it is hung, as a loop on a garment. **3.** a contrivance on which things are hung, as a hook. **4.** a person who hangs something.

hang′er-on′, *n., pl.* **hang·ers-on.** an unwanted person who remains in a place or with a group, another person, etc., in the hope of personal gain.

hang′ glid′er, *n.* a kitelike glider consisting of a V-shaped wing underneath which the pilot is strapped.

hang glider

hang′ glid′ing, *n.* the sport of launching oneself from a cliff or a steep incline and soaring through the air by means of a hang glider.

hang·ing (hang′ing), *n.* **1.** the act, an instance, or the form of capital punishment carried out by suspending a condemned criminal by the neck from a gallows, gibbet, or the like, until dead. **2.** something that hangs or is hung on a wall, as a drapery or tapestry. **3.** a suspending or temporary attaching, as of a painting. —*adj.* **4.** punishable by, deserving, or causing death by hanging: *a hanging crime.* **5.** inclined to inflict death by hanging: *a hanging jury.* **6.** suspended; pendent; overhanging. **7.** situated on a steep slope or at a height: *a hanging garden.* **8.** directed downward: *a hanging look.* **9.** made, holding, or suitable for a hanging object. —**hang′ing·ly,** *adv.*

hang·man (hang′mən), *n., pl.* **-men.** a person who hangs criminals who are condemned to death; public executioner.

hang′man's knot′, *n.* a slip noose for hanging a person.

hang·nail (hang′nāl′), *n.* a small piece of partly detached skin at the side or base of the fingernail.

hang·out (hang′out′), *n. Informal.* a place where a person frequently visits, esp. for socializing or recreation.

hang·o·ver (hang′ō′vər), *n.* **1.** the disagreeable physical aftereffects of drunkenness, usu. felt several hours after cessation of drinking. **2.** something remaining from a former period or state.

hang·tag (hang′tag′), *n.* a tag attached to a garment or other article giving information about its use, care, etc.

hang′-up′ or **hang′up′,** *n. Slang.* **1.** a preoccupation, fixation, or psychological block; complex. **2.** a source of annoying difficulty or burden; impediment; snag.

hank (hangk), *n.* **1.** SKEIN (def. 1). **2.** a specific length of thread or yarn according to the type of fiber, as 840 yards (768.1 m) for cotton or 300 yards (274.32 m) for linen. **3.** a coil, knot, or loop: *a hank of hair.* **4.** a ring, link, or shackle for securing the luff of a staysail or jib to its stay or the luff or head of a gaff sail to the mast or gaff.

han·ker (hang′kər), *v.i.* to have a restless or incessant longing (often fol. by *after, for,* or an infinitive). —**han′ker·er,** *n.*

han·ker·ing (hang′kər ing), *n.* a longing; craving. —**han′ker·ing·ly,** *adv.*

Han·key (hang′kē), *n.* **Katherine,** 1834–1911, English religious leader and hymn writer.

han·ky or **han·kie** (hang′kē), *n., pl.* **-kies.** a handkerchief.

han·ky-pan·ky or **han·key-pan·key** (hang′kē pang′kē), *n. Informal.* unethical behavior; mischief; deceit.

Han·na (han′ə), *n.* **Marcus Alonzo** ("Mark"), 1837–1904, U.S. merchant and politician.

Han·nah (han′ə), *n.* the mother of Samuel. I Sam. 1:20.

Han·ni·bal (han′ə bəl), *n.* **1.** 247–183 B.C., Carthaginian general who crossed the Alps and invaded Italy (son of Hamilcar Barca). **2.** a port in NE Missouri, on the Mississippi: Mark Twain's boyhood home. 18,811.

Ha·noi (ha noi′, hə-), *n.* the capital of Vietnam, in the N part, on the Songka River. 2,000,000.

Han·o·ver (han′ō vər), *n.* **1.** a member of the royal family that ruled Great Britain under that name from 1714 to 1901. **2.** a former province in NW Germany; now a district in Lower Saxony. **3.** the capital of Lower Saxony, in N central Germany. 495,300. German, **Han·no·ver** (hä nō′vər) (for defs. 2, 3).

Han′se·at′ic League′, *n.* a medieval league of towns of N Germany and adjacent countries for the promotion and protection of commerce.

Han′sen's disease′, *n.* LEPROSY. [after G. H. *Hansen* (1841–1912), Norwegian physician, discoverer of leprosy-causing bacterium]

han·som (han′səm), *n.* **1.** a low-hung, two-wheeled, covered vehicle drawn by one horse, for two passengers, with the driver being mounted on an elevated seat behind and the reins running over the roof. **2.** any similar horse-drawn vehicle. Also called **han′som cab′.** [after J. A. *Hansom* (1803–82), English architect who designed it]

hansom

hant or **ha'nt** (hant), *v.t., v.i., n. South Midland and Southern U.S.* HAUNT.

han·ta·vi·rus (hän′tə vī′rəs, han′-), *n., pl.* **-rus·es.** any of several viruses of the family Bunyaviridae, spread chiefly by wild rodents, that cause acute respiratory illness, kidney failure, and other syndromes. [after the *Hantaan* River in Korea, near which the virus first afflicted Westerners in the 1950s] —**han′ta·vi′ral,** *adj.*

Ha·nuk·kah or **Cha·nu·kah** (hä′nə kə, KHä′-), *n.* an eight-day Jewish festival starting on the 25th day of Kislev, commemorating the rededication of the Temple by the Maccabees following their victory over the Syrians and characterized chiefly by the lighting of the menorah. [< Hebrew *ḥănukkāh* lit., a dedicating]

hap·haz·ard (*adj., adv.* hap haz′ərd; *n.* hap′haz′-), *adj.* 1. characterized by lack of order or planning; irregular; chance; random. —*adv.* 2. haphazardly. —*n.* 3. mere chance; accident. —**hap·haz′ard·ly**, *adv.* —**hap·haz′ard·ness**, *n.*

hap·less (hap′lis), *adj.* unlucky; luckless; unfortunate. —**hap′less·ly**, *adv.* —**hap′less·ness**, *n.*

haplo-, a combining form meaning "single," "simple": *haplology.*

hap·loid (hap′loid), *adj.* Also, **hap·loi′dic.** 1. single; simple. 2. pertaining to a single set of chromosomes. —*n.* 3. an organism or cell having only one complete set of chromosomes, ordinarily half the normal diploid number.

hap·lol·o·gy (hap lol′ə jē), *n.* the omission of one of two similar adjacent syllables or sounds in a word, as in the pronunciation (prob′lē) for *probably.* —**hap′lo·log′ic** (-lə loj′ik), *adj.*

hap·pen (hap′ən), *v.i.* 1. to take place; come to pass; occur. 2. to come to pass by chance; occur without apparent reason or design. 3. to have the fortune or lot (to do or be as specified); chance: *I happened to see him on the street.* 4. to befall, as to a person or thing: *Don't worry; nothing happened to her.* 5. to meet or discover by chance (usu. fol. by *on* or *upon*): *to happen on a clue to a mystery.* 6. to be, come, go, etc., casually or by chance: *My friend happened along.*

hap·pen·ing (hap′ə ning), *n.* 1. an occurrence or event. 2. a spontaneous or unconventional performance or entertainment, often involving the audience. 3. any event considered worthwhile or unusual.

hap·pen·stance (hap′ən stans′), *n.* a chance happening or event.

hap·py (hap′ē), *adj.*, **-pi·er, -pi·est.** 1. delighted, pleased, or glad, as over a particular thing. 2. characterized by or indicative of pleasure, contentment, or joy: *a happy mood.* 3. favored by fortune; fortunate or lucky: *a happy, fruitful land.* 4. apt or felicitous, as actions, utterances, or ideas. 5. obsessed by or quick to use the item indicated (usu. used in combination): *a trigger-happy gangster.* —**hap′pi·ly**, *adv.* —**hap′pi·ness**, *n.*

hap′py cam′per, *n. Informal.* a person who is contented with a situation or circumstance.

hap′py-go-luck′y, *adj.* trusting cheerfully to luck; happily unworried or unconcerned.

hap′py hour′, *n.* a cocktail hour or period at a bar, when drinks are served at reduced prices or with free snacks.

hap′py hunt′ing ground′, *n.* the North American Indian heaven, conceived of as a paradise of hunting and feasting for warriors and hunters.

hap′py war′rior, *n.* 1. a person who is undiscouraged by difficulties or opposition. 2. (*cap.*) a nickname of Alfred E. Smith.

Haps·burg or **Habs·burg** (haps′bûrg), *n.* a German princely family, prominent since the 13th century, that has furnished sovereigns to the Holy Roman Empire, Austria, Spain, etc.

ha·ra-ki·ri (här′ə kēr′ē, har′ə-, har′ē-) also **hari-kari**, *n.* 1. ceremonial suicide by ripping open the abdomen with a dagger or knife: formerly practiced in Japan by members of the warrior class when disgraced or sentenced to death. 2. any suicidal action; a self-destructive act: *political hara-kiri.* [< Japanese = *hara* belly + *kiri* cut]

ha·rangue (hə rang′), *n., v.*, **-rangued, -rangu·ing.** —*n.* 1. a scolding or a verbal attack; diatribe. 2. a long, passionate, and vehement speech, esp. one delivered before a public gathering. 3. any long, pompous speech or writing of a tediously hortatory or didactic nature; sermonizing discourse. —*v.t.* 4. to address in a harangue. —*v.i.* 5. to deliver a harangue.

Ha·ra·re (hə rär′ā), *n.* the capital of Zimbabwe, in the NE part. 675,000. Formerly, **Salisbury.**

ha·rass (hə ras′, har′əs), *v.t.* 1. to disturb persistently; torment; pester; persecute. 2. to trouble by repeated attacks, incursions, etc., as in war or hostilities; harry; raid. —**ha·rass′a·ble**, *adj.* —**ha·rass′er**, *n.* —**ha·rass′ment**, *n.* —**Pronunciation.** HARASS, a 17th-century French borrowing, has traditionally been pronounced (har′əs). A newer pronunciation, (hə ras′), which has developed in North American but not British English, is sometimes criticized by older educated speakers. However, it is now the more common pronunciation among younger educated U.S. speakers, some of whom have only minimal familiarity with the older form. See also EXQUISITE.

har·bin·ger (här′bin jər), *n.* 1. one that announces or foreshadows the approach of someone or something; forerunner; herald. 2. a person sent in advance of troops, a royal train, etc., to provide or secure lodgings and other accommodations. —*v.t.* 3. to act as harbinger to; herald the coming of.

har·bor (här′bər), *n.* 1. a part of a body of water along the shore deep enough for anchoring a ship and so situated with respect to coastal features, whether natural or artificial, as to provide protection from winds, waves, and currents. 2. such a body of water having docks or port facilities. 3. any place of shelter or refuge. —*v.t.* 4. to give harbor to; offer refuge to: *to harbor refugees.* 5. to conceal; hide: *to harbor fugitives.* 6. to keep or hold in the mind; maintain; entertain: *to harbor suspicion.* 7. to house or contain. 8. to shelter (a vessel), as in a harbor. —*v.i.* 9. (of a vessel) to take shelter in a harbor. Also, *esp. Brit.,* **harbour.** —**har′bor·er**, *n.* —**har′bor·ous**, *adj.*

har′bor mas′ter, *n.* an official who supervises operations in a harbor area and administers its rules.

har′bor seal′, *n.* a spotted earless seal, *Phoca vitulina,* of the N Hemisphere.

hard (härd), *adj.* 1. not soft; solid and firm to the touch. 2. firmly formed; tight: *a hard knot.* 3. difficult to do or accomplish; fatiguing; troublesome: *a hard task.* 4. difficult or troublesome with respect to an action, situation, person, etc.: *hard to please.* 5. difficult to deal with, manage, control, overcome, or understand: *a hard problem.* 6. involving a great deal of effort, energy, or persistence: *hard labor.* 7. performing or carrying on work with great effort, energy, or persistence: *a hard worker.* 8. vigorous or violent in force; severe: *a hard fall.* 9. bad; unendurable; unbearable: *hard luck.* 10. oppressive; harsh; rough: *hard treatment.* 11. austere; severe: *a hard winter.* 12. harsh or severe in dealing with others: *a hard master.* 13. difficult to explain away; undeniable: *hard facts.* 14. factual, as distinguished from speculation or hearsay: *hard information.* 15. harsh or unfriendly; resentful; bitter: *hard feelings.* 16. of stern judgment or close examination; searching: *We took a hard look at our finances.* 17. lacking delicacy or softness; clear and distinct; sharp; harsh: *a hard line; hard features.* 18. severe or rigorous in terms: *a hard bargain.* 19. sternly realistic; dispassionate; unsentimental: *a hard view of life.* 20. incorrigible; disreputable; tough: *a hard character.* 21. (of the penis) erect. 22. (of water) containing mineral salts that interfere with the action of soap. 23. in coins or paper money as distinguished from checks, promissory notes, or the like: *hard cash.* 24. (of paper money) backed by gold reserves and readily convertible into foreign currency. 25. (of assets) having intrinsic value, as gold or diamonds. 26. (of alcoholic beverages) **a.** containing more than 22.5 percent alcohol by volume, as whiskey and brandy as opposed to beer and wine. **b.** strong because of fermentation; intoxicating: *hard cider.* 27. (of wine) tasting excessively of tannin. 28. (of an illicit narcotic or drug) known to be physically addictive, as opium, morphine, or cocaine. 29. (of a fabric) having relatively little nap; smooth. 30. (of the landing of a space vehicle) executed without decelerating. 31. (of a missile) capable of being launched from an underground silo. 32. (of a military installation) heavily reinforced. 33. (of wheat) having a high gluten content. 34. **a.** (of *c* and *g*) pronounced as (k) in *come* and (g) in *go.* **b.** (of consonants in Slavic languages) not palatalized. Compare SOFT (def. 19). —*adv.* 35. with great exertion; with vigor or violence; strenuously: *to work hard.* 36. earnestly, intently, or critically: *to look hard at a decision.* 37. harshly or severely. 38. so as to be solid, tight, or firm: *frozen hard.* 39. with strong force or impact: *to be hit hard.* 40. in a deeply affected manner; with genuine sorrow or remorse: *He took the news very hard.* 41. closely; immediately: *Defeat seemed hard at hand.* 42. to an unreasonable or extreme degree; excessively; immoderately. 43. *Naut.* closely, fully, or to the extreme limit: *hard aport.* —**Idiom.** 44. **be hard on,** to deal harshly or strictly with. 45. **hard by,** in close proximity to; near. 46. **hard put,** in great perplexity or difficulty; at a loss: *We are hard put to pay the rent now.* 47. **hard up,** *Informal.* **a.** urgently in need of money. **b.** feeling a lack or need.

hard′-and-fast′, *adj.* strongly binding; not to be set aside or violated: *hard-and-fast rules.* —**hard′-and-fast′ness,** *n.*

hard·back (härd′bak′), *n., adj.* HARDCOVER.

hard·ball (härd′bôl′), *n.* 1. baseball, as distinguished from softball. —*adj.* 2. tough or ruthless: *hardball politics.* 3. outspoken, challenging, or difficult: *hardball questions.* —**Idiom.** 4. **play hardball,** to be aggressive and ruthless in one's dealings.

hard′-bit′ten, *adj.* conditioned by battle or struggle; tough; stubborn.

hard′-boiled′, *adj.* 1. (of an egg) boiled in the shell long enough for the yolk and white to solidify. 2. unsentimental or realistic; tough: *a hard-boiled detective.*

hard·bound (härd′bound′), *adj.* (of a book) bound with a stiff cover, usu. of cloth or leather; casebound.

hard′ can′dy, *n.* candy made of boiled sugar and corn syrup, often fruit-flavored.

hard′ ci′der, *n.* See under CIDER.

hard′ coal′, *n.* ANTHRACITE.

hard′ cop′y, *n.* computer output printed on paper; printout. 2. copy that is finished and ready for the printer. —**hard′-cop′y,** *adj.*

hard′ core′, *n.* 1. the permanent, dedicated, and completely faithful nucleus of a group or movement, as of a political party. 2. the part of a group that is resistant to change. 3. those whose condition seems to be without hope of remedy or change.

hard′-core′, *adj.* 1. unswervingly committed; uncompromising: *a hard-core conservative.* 2. being so without apparent change or remedy; chronic: *hard-core unemployment.*

hard·cov·er (härd′kuv′ər), *n.* 1. a book bound in cloth, leather, or the like, over stiff material. —*adj.* 2. bound in cloth, leather, or the like, over stiff material. 3. noting or pertaining to such books: *hardcover sales.* Compare PAPERBACK. Also, **hardback.** —**hard′cov′ered,** *adj.*

hard′ disk′, *n.* a rigid disk coated with magnetic material, for storing computer programs and relatively large amounts of data.

hard·en (här′dn), *v.t.* 1. to make hard or harder. 2. to make pitiless or unfeeling: *to harden one's heart.* 3. to make rigid, hardy, or unyielding; reinforce; toughen. 4. to reinforce (a military or strategic installation) as protection against nuclear bombardment. —*v.i.* 5. to become hard or harder. 6. to become pitiless or unfeeling. 7. to become inured or unyielding; toughen.

hard·ened (här′dnd), *adj.* **1.** made or become hard or harder. **2.** pitiless; unfeeling. **3.** confirmed; inveterate: *a hardened criminal.* **4.** inured; toughened: *a hardened trooper.*

hard·hack (härd′hak′), *n.* a woolly-leaved North American shrub, *Spiraea tomentosa,* of the rose family, having short, spikelike clusters of rose-colored flowers. Also called **steeplebush.**

hard′ hat′ or **hard′hat′,** *n.* **1.** a protective helmet of metal or plastic, esp. as worn by construction or factory workers. **2.** a construction worker, esp. a member of a construction workers' union. **3.** *Informal.* a working-class conservative. —**hard′-hat′,** *adj.*

hard·head (härd′hed′), *n.* **1.** a shrewd, practical person. **2.** a blockhead.

hard′head′ed or **hard′-head′ed,** *adj.* **1.** not easily moved or deceived; practical; shrewd. **2.** obstinate; stubborn; willful. —**hard′head′ed·ly,** *adv.* —**hard′head′ed·ness,** *n.*

hard·heart·ed (härd′här′tid), *adj.* unfeeling; unmerciful; pitiless. —**hard′heart′ed·ly,** *adv.* —**hard′heart′ed·ness,** *n.*

hard′-hit′ting, *adj.* strikingly or effectively forceful: *a hard-hitting exposé.*

har·di·ness (här′dē nis), *n.* **1.** the capacity for enduring or sustaining hardship, privation, etc.; capability of surviving under unfavorable conditions. **2.** courage; boldness; audacity.

Har·ding (här′ding), *n.* **1. Chester,** 1792–1866, U.S. painter. **2. Warren G(amaliel),** 1865–1923, 29th president of the U.S. 1921–23.

hard′ knocks′, *n.pl. Informal.* adversity or hardships.

hard′ la′bor, *n.* compulsory labor imposed upon criminals in addition to imprisonment.

hard′ lens′, *n.* a contact lens of rigid plastic or silicon, exerting light pressure on the cornea of the eye. Compare SOFT LENS.

hard′ line′, *n.* an uncompromising or unyielding stand, esp. in politics. —**hard′-line′, hard′line′,** *adj.* —**hard′-lin′er,** *n.*

hard·ly (härd′lē), *adv.* **1.** only just; almost not; barely: *hardly any; hardly ever.* **2.** not at all; scarcely: *That report is hardly surprising.* —**Usage.** HARDLY, BARELY, SCARCELY all have a negative connotation, and the use of any of them with a supplementary negative (*I can't hardly remember*) is considered nonstandard except when done for humorous effect. See also DOUBLE NEGATIVE.

hard′ mon′ey, *n.* **1.** metallic currency. **2.** a slow expansion of the money supply.

hard·ness (härd′nis), *n.* **1.** the state or quality of being hard. **2.** that quality in water that is imparted by the presence of dissolved salts, esp. calcium sulfate or bicarbonate. **3.** the comparative ability of a substance to scratch or be scratched by another.

hard-nosed (härd′nōzd′), *adj. Informal.* hardheaded or tough; unsentimentally practical: *a hard-nosed leader.*

hard-of-hear·ing (härd′əv hēr′ing), *adj.* HEARING-IMPAIRED.

hard′ pal′ate, *n.* See under PALATE (def. 1).

hard-pressed (härd′prest′), *adj.* heavily burdened or oppressed; harried.

hard′ rock′, *n.* rock music dependent on a driving beat and amplified sound.

hard′ rub′ber, *n.* rubber vulcanized with a large amount of sulfur, usu. 25–35 percent, to render it stiff and comparatively inflexible.

hard·scrab·ble (härd′skrab′əl), *adj.* providing or yielding meagerly in return for much effort: *a hardscrabble existence.*

hard′ sell′, *n.* a method of advertising or selling that is aggressively insistent and direct (opposed to *soft sell*). —**hard′-sell′,** *v.t., v.i.,* **-sold, -sell·ing,** *adj.*

hard-set (härd′set′), *adj.* **1.** firmly or rigidly set; fixed. **2.** in a difficult position. **3.** determined; obstinate.

hard′-shell′, *adj.* Also, **hard′-shelled′. 1.** having a firm, hard shell, as a crab in its normal state; not having recently molted. **2.** rigid or uncompromising. —*n.* **3.** HARD-SHELL CRAB.

hard′-shell′ clam′, *n.* QUAHOG.

hard′-shell′ crab′, *n.* a crab, esp. an edible crab, that has not recently molted and has a hard shell.

hard·ship (härd′ship), *n.* **1.** a condition that is difficult to endure; suffering; deprivation; oppression. **2.** an instance or cause of this; something hard to bear.

hard·tack (härd′tak′), *n.* a hard, saltless biscuit, formerly much used aboard ships and for army rations.

hard·top (härd′top′), *n.* a style of car having a rigid metal top and no center posts between windows.

hard·ware (härd′wâr′), *n.* **1.** metalware, as tools, locks, hinges, or cutlery. **2.** the mechanical equipment necessary for conducting an activity, usu. distinguished from the theory and design that make the activity possible. **3.** weapons and combat equipment. **4.** the mechanical, magnetic, electronic, and electrical devices composing a computer system (disting. from *software*).

hard′ware plat′form, *n.* a group of compatible computers that can run the same software.

hard′-wired′ or **hard′wired′,** *adj.* **1. a.** built into a computer's hardware and thus not readily changed. **b.** (of a terminal) connected to a computer by a direct circuit rather than through a switching network. **2.** (of a behavior pattern) intrinsic and relatively unmodifiable.

hard·wood (härd′wŏŏd′), *n.* **1.** the hard, compact wood or timber of various trees, as the oak, cherry, maple, or mahogany. **2.** a tree yielding

such wood. —*adj.* **3.** made or constructed of hardwood: *a hardwood floor.*

har·dy (här′dē), *adj.,* **-di·er, -di·est. 1.** capable of enduring fatigue, hardship, exposure, etc.; sturdy; strong: *a hardy constitution.* **2.** (of plants) able to withstand the cold of winter in the open air. **3.** requiring great physical courage, vigor, or endurance: *the hardiest sports.* **4.** bold or daring; courageous: *hardy explorers.*

Har·dy (här′dē), *n.* **1. Oliver,** 1892–1957, U.S. motion-picture comedian. **2. Thomas,** 1840–1928, English novelist and poet.

hare (hâr), *n., pl.* **hares,** (*esp. collectively*) **hare.** any of several long-eared, hopping lagomorphs of the family Leporidae, esp. of the genus *Lepus,* closely related to the rabbits but usu. larger and characteristically bearing well-developed young. —**hare′like′,** *adj.*

hare·bell (hâr′bel′), *n.* a low plant, *Campanula rotundifolia,* of the bellflower family, having narrow leaves and blue, bell-shaped flowers.

hare·brained or **hair·brained** (hâr′brānd′), *adj.* giddy; reckless. —**hare′brained′ly,** *adv.* —**hare′brained′ness,** *n.*

Ha·re Krish·na (här′ē krish′nə, har′ē) **1.** a religious sect based on Vedic scriptures: founded in the U.S. in 1966. **2.** a member of this sect. [from chanted phrase *Hare Krishna!* < Hindi *harē kṛṣṇā* O Krishna!]

har·em (hâr′əm, har′-), *n.* **1.** the part of a Muslim palace or house reserved for the residence of women. **2.** the women in a Muslim household, including the mothers, sisters, wives, concubines, daughters, entertainers, and servants. **3.** a social group of female animals, as elephant seals, accompanied by a reproductive male who denies other males access to the group. [< Arabic *ḥarīm* harem, lit., forbidden]

har′em pants′, *n.* (*used with a pl. v.*) women's trousers usu. of soft fabric with full legs gathered at the ankle.

har·i·cot (har′ə kō′), *n.* **1.** any of various beans of the genus *Phaseolus,* esp. the kidney bean. **2.** the seed or unripe pod of any of these plants, eaten as a vegetable.

ha·ri·ka·ri (här′ē kär′ē, har′ē kar′ē), *n.* HARA-KIRI.

hark (härk), *v.i.* **1.** to listen attentively; hearken. —*v.t.* **2. hark back, a.** (of hounds) to return along the course in order to regain a lost scent. **b.** to recollect or recapitulate a previous event or topic.

hark·en (här′kən), *v.i., v.t.* HEARKEN.

Hark!′ the Her′ald An′gels Sing′, a Christmas hymn (1739) with words by Charles Wesley and music (1840) by Felix Mendelssohn.

Har·lem (här′ləm), *n.* **1.** a section of New York City, in the NE part of Manhattan. **2.** a tidal river in New York City, between the boroughs of Manhattan and the Bronx, which, with Spuyten Duyvil Creek, connects the Hudson and East rivers. 8 mi. (13 km) long. —**Har′lem·ite,** *n.*

Har′lem Ren′aissance, *n.* a renewal and flourishing of black literary and musical culture during the years after World War I in the Harlem section of New York City.

har·le·quin (här′lə kwin, -kin), *n.* **1.** (*often cap.*) a comic character in commedia dell'arte and the harlequinade, usu. masked, dressed in multicolored, diamond-patterned tights, and carrying a wooden sword or magic wand. **2.** a buffoon. —*adj.* **3.** fancifully colorful.

har·le·quin·ade (här′lə kwi nād′, -ki-), *n.* **1.** a pantomime, farce, or similar play in which Harlequin plays the principal part. **2.** buffoonery.

har′lequin bug′, *n.* a black stink bug, *Murgantia histrionica,* with red and yellow markings, that is a pest of cabbages and related plants.

har·lot (här′lət), *n.* a prostitute; whore. —**har′lot·ry,** *n.*

harm (härm), *n.* **1.** injury or damage; hurt: *to do someone bodily harm.* **2.** moral injury; evil; wrong. —*v.t.* **3.** to do or cause harm to; injure; damage; hurt: *to harm one's reputation.* —**Saying. 4.** First, do no harm, above all, do not prescribe a medical treatment that does more damage than good: said to be the first principle of Hippocrates. —**harm′ful,** *adj.* —**harm′ful·ly,** *adv.* —**harm′ful·ness,** *n.*

harm·less (härm′lis), *adj.* **1.** without the power or desire to do harm; innocuous: *a harmless prank.* **2.** without injury; unhurt; unharmed. —**harm′less·ly,** *adv.* —**harm′less·ness,** *n.*

har·mon·ic (här mon′ik), *adj.* **1.** pertaining to harmony, as distinguished from melody and rhythm. **2.** marked by harmony; in harmony; concordant; consonant. **3.** of, pertaining to, or noting a series of oscillations in which each oscillation has a frequency that is an integral multiple of the same basic frequency. **4.** *Math.* **a.** (of a set of values) related in a manner analogous to the frequencies of tones that are consonant. **b.** capable of being represented by sine and cosine functions. —*n.* **5.** OVERTONE (def. 1). **6.** a single oscillation whose frequency is an integral multiple of the fundamental frequency. —**har·mon′i·cal·ly,** *adv.* —**har·mon′i·cal·ness,** *n.*

har·mon·i·ca (här mon′i kə), *n., pl.* **-cas.** a musical wind instrument consisting of a small rectangular case containing a set of metal reeds connected to a row of holes, over which the player places the mouth and exhales and inhales to produce the tones. Also called **mouth organ.**

harmon′ic mo′tion, *n.* periodic motion consisting of one or more vibratory motions that are symmetric about a region of equilibrium, as the motion of a pendulum.

har·mon·ics (här mon′iks), *n.* **1.** (*used with a sing. v.*) the science of musical sounds. **2.** (*used with a pl. v.*) the partials or overtones of a fundamental tone. **3.** (*used with a pl. v.*) the flutelike tones of the strings of a stringed instrument, as the violin, made to vibrate so as to produce overtones.

har·mo·ni·ous (här mō′nē əs), *adj.* **1.** marked by agreement in feel-

H

ing, attitude, or action: *a harmonious group.* **2.** forming a pleasingly consistent whole; congruous: *harmonious colors.* **3.** pleasant to the ear; tuneful; melodious. **—har·mo′ni·ous·ly,** *adv.* **—har·mo′ni·ous·ness,** *n.*

har·mo·ni·um (här mō′nē əm), *n.* an organlike keyboard instrument with small metal reeds and pedal-operated bellows.

har·mo·nize (här′mə nīz′), *v.,* **-nized, -niz·ing.** **—v.t.** **1.** to bring into harmony or accord: *to harmonize one's views with the facts.* **2.** to accompany with appropriate harmony. **—v.i.** **3.** to be harmonious; be in accord; be congruous. **4.** to sing in harmony. **—har′mo·niz′a·ble,** *adj.* **—har′mo·ni·za′tion,** *n.* **—har′mo·niz′er,** *n.*

har·mo·ny (här′mə nē), *n., pl.* **-nies.** **1.** agreement; accord; harmonious relations. **2.** a consistent, orderly, or pleasing arrangement of parts; congruity. **3. a.** any simultaneous combination of tones. **b.** the simultaneous combination of tones, esp. when blended into chords pleasing to the ear; chordal structure, as distinguished from melody and rhythm. **c.** the science of the structure, relations, and practical combination of chords. [< Old French < Latin *harmonia* < Greek: joint, agreement, harmony]

Har·nack (här′näk), *n.* **Adolf von,** 1851–1930, German Protestant theologian, born in Estonia.

har·ness (här′nis), *n.* **1.** the combination of straps, bands, and other parts forming the working gear of a draft animal. Compare YOKE (def. 1). **—v.t. 2.** to put a harness on (a horse, donkey, dog, etc.); attach by a harness, as to a vehicle. **3.** to bring under conditions for effective use; gain control over for a particular end: *to harness water power.* **—Idiom. 4. in harness,** engaged in one's usual routine; working. **—har′ness·er,** *n.*

har′ness race′, *n.* a trotting or pacing race for standardbred horses harnessed to sulkies. **—har′ness rac′ing,** *n.*

harp (härp), *n.* **1.** a musical instrument consisting of a triangular frame formed by a soundbox, a pillar, and a curved neck, and having strings stretched between the soundbox and the neck that are plucked with the fingers. **2.** a harp-shaped implement or device. **3.** a vertical metal frame shaped to bend around the bulb in a standing lamp and used to support a lamp shade. **4.** *Informal.* HARMONICA. **—v.i. 5.** to play on a harp. **6. harp on** or **upon,** to repeat interminably and tediously. **—harp′er,** *n.* **—harp′ist,** *n.* **—harp′like′,** *adj.*

harp (def. 1)

Har′pers (or **Har′per's**) **Fer′ry** (här′pərz), *n.* a town in NE West Virginia at the confluence of the Shenandoah and Potomac rivers: site of John Brown's raid 1859. 361.

har·poon (här pōōn′), *n.* **1.** a barbed, spearlike missile attached to a rope, and thrown by hand or shot from a gun, used for killing and capturing whales and large fish. **—v.t. 2.** to strike, catch, or kill with or as if with a harpoon. **—har·poon′er,** *n.*

harp′ seal′, *n.* a N Atlantic earless seal, *Pagophilus groenlandicus.*

harp·si·chord (härp′si kôrd′), *n.* a keyboard instrument, precursor of the piano, in which the strings are plucked by leather or quill points connected with the keys, in common use from the 16th to the 18th century, and revived in the 20th. **—harp′si·chord′ist,** *n.*

Har·py (här′pē), *n., pl.* **-pies.** **1.** any of a group of winged supernatural beings of classical myth, two or three in number, portrayed by later authors as rapacious female monsters. **2.** (*l.c.*) a scolding, bad-tempered woman; shrew. **3.** (*l.c.*) a greedy, predatory person.

har·que·bus (här′kwə bəs) also **arquebus,** *n., pl.* **-bus·es.** any of several small-caliber long guns operated by a matchlock or wheel-lock mechanism, dating from about 1400.

har·ri·er¹ (har′ē ər), *n.* **1.** a person who or thing that harries. **2.** any of several short-winged hawks of the genus *Circus,* esp. *C. cyaneus,* of the N hemisphere, that typically hunt over treeless areas.

har·ri·er² (har′ē ər), *n.* **1.** one of a breed of medium-sized hounds sim-

ilar to a foxhound but smaller and used, usu. in packs, esp. in hunting hares. **2.** a cross-country runner.

Har·ri·man (har′ə mən), *n.* **1. Edward Henry,** 1848–1909, U.S. financier and railroad magnate. **2.** his son, **W(illiam) A·ve·rell** (ā′vər əl), 1891–1986, U.S. statesman.

Har·ris (har′is), *n.* **1. Frank,** 1856–1931, U.S. writer, born in Ireland. **2. Joel Chandler,** 1848–1908, U.S. writer. **3. Phil,** 1904–95, U.S. comedian and bandleader. **4. Roy,** 1898–1979, U.S. composer.

Har·ris·burg (har′is bûrg′), *n.* the capital of Pennsylvania, in the S part, on the Susquehanna River. 51,720.

Har·ri·son (har′ə sən), *n.* **1. Benjamin,** 1726?–91, American political leader (father of William Henry Harrison). **2. Benjamin,** 1833–1901, 23rd president of the U.S. 1889–93 (grandson of William Henry Harrison). **3. William Henry,** 1773–1841, 9th president of the U.S. 1841.

Har′ris Tweed′, *Trademark.* a brand of heavy, handwoven woolen fabric made in the Outer Hebrides.

har·row¹ (har′ō), *n.* **1.** an agricultural implement with spikelike teeth or upright disks, for leveling and breaking up clods in plowed land. **—v.t. 2.** to draw a harrow over (land). **3.** to disturb keenly or painfully; distress the mind, feelings, etc., of. **—har′row·er,** *n.*

har·row² (har′ō), *v.t. Archaic.* (of Christ) to descend into (hell) to free the righteous held captive.

har·rumph (hə rumf′), *v.i.* **1.** to clear the throat audibly in a self-important manner. **2.** to express oneself gruffly.

har·ry (har′ē), *v.,* **-ried, -ry·ing. —v.t. 1.** to harass; annoy; torment. **2.** to ravage (an area, town, etc.), as in war; devastate. **3.** to push (a person) along; hurry forcefully or tormentingly. **—v.i. 4.** to make harassing incursions.

harsh (härsh), *adj.* **1.** ungentle and unpleasant in action or effect: *harsh treatment.* **2.** grim or unpleasantly severe; stern; cruel; austere: *a harsh master.* **3.** physically uncomfortable; desolate; stark: *a harsh land.* **4.** unpleasant to the ear; grating; strident: *a harsh voice.* **5.** unpleasant or irritating to the body or the senses: *harsh detergents; harsh sunlight.* **—harsh′ly,** *adv.* **—harsh′ness,** *n.*

hart (härt), *n., pl.* **harts,** (*esp. collectively*) **hart.** a mature, fully antlered male European red deer.

Hart (härt), *n.* **1. Lo·renz** (lôr′ənts, lōr′-), 1895–1943, U.S. lyricist. **2. Moss,** 1904–61, U.S. playwright and librettist.

har·te·beest (här′tə bēst′, härt′bēst′), *n., pl.* **-beests,** (*esp. collectively*) **-beest.** any large African antelope of the genus *Alcelaphus,* having ringed horns that curve backward.

Hart·ford (härt′fərd), *n.* the capital of Connecticut, in the central part, on the Connecticut River. 124,196.

hart's′-tongue′ or **harts′-tongue′,** *n.* a bright green fern, *Phyllitis scolopendrium,* of the polypody family, having long, leathery, wavy-edged leaves.

har·um-scar·um (hâr′əm skâr′əm, har′əm skar′əm), *adj.* **1.** reckless; rash; irresponsible. **2.** disorganized; uncontrolled. **—adv. 3.** recklessly; wildly. **—n. 4.** a reckless person. **5.** reckless or unpredictable behavior or action. **—har′um-scar′um·ness,** *n.*

har·vest (här′vist), *n.* **1.** Also, **har′vest·ing.** the gathering of crops. **2.** the season when ripened crops are gathered. **3.** a crop or yield of one growing season. **4.** a supply of anything gathered at maturity and stored: *a harvest of wheat.* **5.** the result or consequence of any act, process, or event: *a harvest of memories.* **—v.t. 6.** to gather (a crop or the like); reap. **7.** to gather the crop from: *to harvest the fields.* **8.** to gain, win, etc. (a prize, product, etc.). **9.** to catch or take for use: *to harvest salmon from the river.* **—v.i. 10.** to gather a crop; reap. **—har′vest·a·ble,** *adj.* **—har′vest·a·bil′i·ty,** *n.* **—har′vest·er,** *n.*

har′vester ant′, *n.* any of several red or black ants, esp. of the genus *Pogonomyrmex,* of the southwestern U.S., that feed on and store the seeds of grasses.

har′vest fly′, *n.* CICADA.

har′vest mite′, *n.* CHIGGER (def. 1).

har′vest moon′, *n.* the moon at and about the period of fullness that is nearest to the autumnal equinox.

has (haz; *unstressed* həz, əz), *v.* a 3rd pers. sing. pres. indic. of HAVE.

has′-been′, *n.* a person or thing that is no longer effective, successful, popular, etc.

ha·sen·pfef·fer or **has·sen·pfef·fer** (hä′sən fef′ər), *n.* a highly seasoned stew of marinated rabbit meat.

hash (hash), *n.* **1.** diced cooked meat and potatoes or other vegetables browned together or reheated in gravy. **2.** a mess, jumble, or muddle. **3.** a reworking of old and familiar material. **—v.t. 4.** to chop into small pieces; make into hash; mince. **5.** to muddle or mess up. **6.** to discuss or review (something) thoroughly (often fol. by *out* or *over*). [< French *hacher* to cut up]

hash′ browns′, *n.pl.* diced or chopped boiled potatoes, often mixed with minced onion, fried until crisp.

Hash′e·mite King′dom of Jor′dan (hash′ə mīt′), *n.* official name of JORDAN.

hash′ house′, *n. Slang.* a cheap restaurant or diner.

Hash·i·mite (hash′ə mīt′), *n.* **1.** a member of any Arab dynasty in the Middle East founded by Husein ibn-Ali or his descendants. **—adj. 2.** of or pertaining to the Hashimites.

hash·ish or **hash·eesh** (hash′ēsh, hä shēsh′), *n.* **1.** the flowering tops and leaves of Indian hemp smoked, chewed, or drunk as a narcotic and

Ha·sid (hä′sid, ĸнä′-, ĸнô′-, ĸнä sēd′), n., pl. **Ha·sid·im** (hä sid′im, ĸнä-, ĸнä′sē dēm′). a member of a Jewish sect founded in Poland in the 18th century that emphasizes mysticism, ritual strictness, religious zeal, and joy. [< Hebrew *ḥāsīd* pious (person)] —**Ha·sid·ic** (hä sid′ik, hə-), *adj.* —**Has·i·dism** (has′i diz′əm, hä′si-), *n.*

Ha·ska·lah (hä skä′lä, hä′skä lä′), *n.* an 18th–19th-century movement among central and E European Jews, intended to modernize Jews and Judaism by encouraging adoption of secular European culture.

Has·mo·ne·an or **Has·mo·nae·an** (haz′mə nē′ən), *n.* a member of a Jewish priestly family in Judea in the 1st and 2nd centuries B.C. that included the Maccabees.

has·n't (haz′ənt), contraction of *has not.*

hasp (hasp), *n.* **1.** a clasp for a door, lid, etc., esp. one passing over a staple and fastened by a pin or a padlock. —*v.t.* **2.** to fasten with or as if with a hasp.

has·sle (has′əl), *n., v.,* **-sled, -sling.** *Informal.* —*n.* **1.** a disorderly dispute. **2.** a troublesome or trying situation; bother. —*v.i.* **3.** to dispute or quarrel. **4.** to be put to inconvenience, exertion, etc.: *to hassle with heat and heavy traffic.* —*v.t.* **5.** to bother or harass.

has·sock (has′ək), *n.* **1.** a thick, firm cushion used as a footstool or for kneeling. **2.** OTTOMAN (def. 3b). **3.** a thick tuft of coarse grass or sedge, as in a bog.

hast (hast), *v. Archaic.* 2nd pers. sing. pres. indic. of HAVE.

haste (hāst), *n.* **1.** swiftness of motion; speed. **2.** unnecessarily quick action; thoughtless, rash, or undue speed. **3.** urgent need of quick action; a hurry. —*Idiom.* **4. make haste,** to hasten; hurry. —*Proverb.* **5. Haste makes waste,** rushing through a task may result in errors. —*Saying.* **6. Make haste slowly,** to move quickly but carefully. —**haste′ful,** *adj.* —**haste′ful·ly,** *adv.*

has·ten (hā′sən), *v.i.* **1.** to move or act with haste; proceed with haste; hurry. —*v.t.* **2.** to cause to hasten; accelerate. —**has′ten·er,** *n.*

Has·tings (hā′stingz), *n.* **1. Thomas,** 1784–1872, U.S. musician and hymn writer. **2. Warren,** 1732–1818, first British governor general of India 1773–85. **3.** a seaport in E Sussex, in SE England: William the Conqueror defeated the Saxons near here 1066. 74,600.

hast·y (hā′stē), *adj.,* **hast·i·er, hast·i·est. 1.** moving or acting with haste; speedy; hurried. **2.** made or done with haste or speed: *a hasty visit.* **3.** unduly quick; precipitate; rash: *a hasty decision.* **4.** brief; fleeting; superficial: *a hasty glance.* **5.** easily irritated or angered; irascible. —**hast′i·ly,** *adv.* —**hast′i·ness,** *n.*

hast′y pud′ding, *n. New England.* cornmeal mush.

hat (hat), *n., v.,* **hat·ted, hat·ting.** —*n.* **1.** a shaped covering for the head, usu. with a crown and often a brim. **2. a.** the distinctive head covering of a Roman Catholic cardinal. **b.** the office or dignity of a cardinal. —*v.t.* **3.** to provide with a hat; put a hat on. —*Idiom.* **4. hat in hand,** humbly and respectfully, as in seeking help. **5. pass the hat,** to ask for contributions of money, as for charity. **6. take one's hat off to,** to express high regard for; praise. **7. talk through one's hat,** to make unsupported, absurd statements. **8. throw** or **toss one's hat in** or **into the ring,** to declare one's candidacy for political office. **9. under one's hat,** confidential; private; secret. **10. wear two** or **several hats,** to function in more than one capacity; fill two or more positions. —**hat′less,** *adj.* —**hat′less·ness,** *n.*

hat·band (hat′band′), *n.* a band or ribbon about the crown of a hat, just above the brim.

hatch¹ (hach), *v.t.* **1.** to bring forth (young) from the egg. **2.** to cause young to emerge from (the egg), as by brooding or incubating. **3.** to bring forth or produce; devise; plot. —*v.i.* **4.** to be hatched. **5.** to brood. —*n.* **6.** the act of hatching. **7.** something that is hatched, as a brood. —**hatch′a·ble,** *adj.* —**hatch′er,** *n.*

hatch² (hach), *n.* **1. a.** Also called **hatchway.** an opening in the deck of a vessel or in the floor or roof of a building, used as a passageway. **b.** the cover over such an opening. **2.** an opening or door in an aircraft. **3.** the lower half of a divided door. **4.** a small door, grated opening, or serving counter in or attached to a wall. —*Idiom.* **5. down the hatch,** (used as a toast).

hatch³ (hach), *v.t.* to mark with lines, esp. closely set parallel lines, as for shading in drawing or engraving.

hatch·back (hach′bak′), *n.* a style of automobile in which the rear deck lid and window lift open as a unit.

hat·check (hat′chek′), *adj.* **1.** engaged in the checking of hats, coats, etc., into temporary safekeeping: *a hatcheck girl.* **2.** used in checking hats, coats, etc.: *a hatcheck room.*

hatch·er·y (hach′ə rē), *n., pl.* **-er·ies.** a place for hatching eggs of hens, fish, etc.

hatch·et (hach′it), *n.* **1.** a small, short-handled ax having the end of the head opposite the blade in the form of a hammer, made to be used with one hand. **2.** tomahawk. —*v.t.* **3.** to cut, destroy, kill, etc., with a hatchet. **4.** to abridge, delete, excise, etc., as a text or portion of a text.

hatch′et job′, *n.* a maliciously or ruthlessly destructive critique or verbal attack.

hatch′et man′, *n.* **1.** a professional murderer. **2.** a writer or speaker who specializes in defamatory attacks, as on political candidates or public officials. **3.** a person whose job it is to execute unpleasant tasks for a superior, as dismissing employees.

hatch·ling (hach′ling), *n.* a young bird, reptile, or fish recently emerged from an egg.

hatch·way (hach′wā′), *n.* HATCH² (def. 1a).

hate (hāt), *v.,* **hat·ed, hat·ing.** —*v.t.* **1.** to dislike intensely or passionately; feel extreme aversion for or extreme hostility toward; detest. **2.** to be unwilling; dislike: *I hate to accept it.* —*v.i.* **3.** to feel hatred. —*n.* **4.** intense dislike; extreme aversion or hostility. **5.** the object of extreme aversion or hostility. —**hate′a·ble,** *adj.* —**hat′er,** *n.*

hate·ful (hāt′fəl), *adj.* **1.** arousing or deserving hate: *hateful oppression.* **2.** unpleasant; dislikable; distasteful: *hateful chores.* **3.** full of or expressing hate; malevolent: *a hateful speech.* —**hate′ful·ly,** *adv.* —**hate′ful·ness,** *n.*

hate·mon·ger (hāt′mung′gər, -mong′-), *n.* a person who kindles hatred, enmity, or prejudice in others. —**hate′mon′ger·ing,** *n.*

hate′ speech′, *n.* speech that attacks a person or group on the basis of race, religion, gender, or sexual orientation.

Hat′field-Mc·Coy′ Feud′ (hat′fēld′mə koi′), *n.* a blood feud between two mountain clans on the West Virginia–Kentucky border, the Hatfields of West Virginia and the McCoys of Kentucky, that grew out of their being on opposite sides during the Civil War and was especially violent from 1880 to 1890.

hath (hath), *v. Archaic.* 3rd pers. sing. pres. indic. of HAVE.

hath·a·yo·ga (hath′ə yō′gə, hut′ə-), *n.* a system of yoga based on physical exercises.

hat·pin (hat′pin′), *n.* a long pin, often with a decorative head, for securing a woman's hat to her hair.

hat·rack (hat′rak′), *n.* a frame, stand, or post with knobs or hooks for hanging hats.

ha·tred (hā′trid), *n.* the feeling of one who hates; intense dislike or extreme aversion or hostility.

hat·ter (hat′ər), *n.* a maker or seller of hats.

hat′ tree′, *n.* HALL TREE.

hat′ trick′, *n.* **1.** the knocking off by one bowler of three wickets with three successive pitches in a game of cricket. **2.** three goals or points scored by one player, as in a game of ice hockey or soccer. **3.** a clever or adroitly deceptive maneuver.

hau·berk (hô′bûrk), *n.* a medieval tunic of chain mail worn for defense.

haugh·ty (hô′tē), *adj.,* **-ti·er, -ti·est.** disdainfully proud; snobbish; arrogant. —**haugh′ti·ly,** *adv.* —**haugh′ti·ness,** *n.*

haul (hôl), *v.t.* **1.** to pull or draw with force; drag. **2.** to cart or transport; carry: *to haul freight.* **3.** to arrest or bring before a magistrate or other authority: *to haul someone into court.* —*v.i.* **4.** to pull or tug. **5.** to go or come to a place, esp. with effort: *to haul into town after a long drive.* **6.** to do carting or transport, or move freight commercially. **7. a.** to sail, as in a particular direction. **b.** (of the wind) to shift to a direction closer to the heading of a vessel (opposed to *veer*). **c.** (of the wind) to change direction, shift, or veer (often fol. by *round* or *to*). **8. haul off, a.** to withdraw; leave. **b.** *Informal.* to draw back the arm in order to strike. **9. haul up, a.** to bring before a superior for judgment or reprimand. **b.** to come to a halt; stop. **c.** (of a sailing vessel) to come closer to the wind. **d.** (of a vessel) to come to a halt. —*n.* **10.** an act or instance of hauling; strong pull or tug. **11.** something that is hauled. **12.** the load hauled at one time; quantity carried or transported. **13.** the distance or route over which anything is hauled. **14.** the quantity of fish taken at one draft of the net. **15.** the act of taking or acquiring something. **16.** something that is taken or acquired. —*Idiom.* **17. long** (or **short**) **haul, a.** a relatively great (or small) period of time. **b.** a relatively great (or little) distance. —**haul′er,** *n.*

haunch (hônch, hänch), *n.* **1.** the hip or the fleshy part of the body about the hip. **2.** a hindquarter of an animal. **3.** the leg and loin of an animal, used for food. **4. a.** either side of an arch, extending from the vertex or crown to the impost. **b.** the part of a beam projecting below a floor or roof slab. —**haunched,** *adj.*

haunt (hônt, hänt; *for 8 also* hant), *v.t.* **1.** to visit habitually or appear to frequently as a spirit or ghost: *to haunt a house; to haunt a person.* **2.** to recur persistently to the consciousness of; remain with: *Memories of love haunted me.* **3.** to visit frequently; go to often: *She haunted the art galleries.* **4.** to disturb or distress; cause to have anxiety: *His youthful escapades came back to haunt him.* —*v.i.* **5.** to reappear continually as a spirit or ghost. **6.** to remain persistently; stay; linger. —*n.* **7.** Often, **haunts.** a place frequently visited: *to return to one's old haunts.* **8.** *Chiefly Midland and Southern U.S.* a ghost. —**haunt′er,** *n.*

haunt·ed (hôn′tid, hän′-), *adj.* **1.** inhabited or frequented by ghosts: *a haunted castle.* **2.** showing the effects of persistent worry or misfortune: *the haunted look of a fugitive.*

haunt·ing (hôn′ting, hän′-), *adj.* **1.** remaining in the consciousness; not quickly forgotten: *a haunting melody.* —*n.* **2.** the act of a person or thing that haunts; visitation. —**haunt′ing·ly,** *adv.*

haus·frau (hous′frou′), *n., pl.* **-fraus, -frau·en** (-frou′ən). HOUSEWIFE.

haut·boy or **haut·bois** (hō′boi, ō′boi), *n., pl.* **-boys** or **-bois** (-boiz). OBOE. —**haut′boy·ist,** *n.*

haute (ōt) *also* **haut** (ō; *esp. before a vowel* ōt), *adj.* **1.** high-class; fancy: *an haute restaurant.* **2.** high; elevated; upper.

haute cou·ture (ōt′ ko͞o to͝or′), *n.* **1.** high fashion; the most fashionable, expensive, and exclusive designer clothing. **2.** the designers or dressmaking establishments that produce high fashion, collectively.

H

haute cui·sine (ōt′ kwi zēn′), *n.* **1.** gourmet cooking; food preparation as an art. **2.** fine food prepared in an elaborate manner.

hau·teur (hō tûr′, ō tûr′), *n.* haughty manner or spirit; arrogance.

haut monde (ō′ mond′) also **haute-monde** (ōt′mond′), *n.* high society.

Ha·van·a (hə van′ə), *n.* **1.** Spanish, **Habana.** the capital of Cuba, on the NW coast. 2,014,800. **2.** a cigar made in Cuba or of Cuban tobacco.

hav·da·lah (häv dô′lə, häv′dä lä′), *n.* a religious ceremony observed by Jews at the conclusion of the Sabbath or a festival. [< Hebrew *habhdālāh* lit., division, separation]

have (hav; *unstressed* həv, əv; *for 26 usually* haf), *v.* and *auxiliary v.*, *pres. sing. 1st* and *2nd pers.* **have,** *3rd* **has;** *pres. pl.* **have;** *past* and *past part.* **had;** *pres. part.* **hav·ing,** *n.* —*v.t.* **1.** to possess; own; hold for use; contain: *I have property. The work has an index.* **2.** to accept in some relation: *He wants to marry her, if she'll have him.* **3.** to get; receive; take: *to have a part in a play; to have news.* **4.** to experience, undergo, or endure: *Have a good time. He had a heart attack.* **5.** to hold in mind, sight, etc.: *to have doubts.* **6.** to cause to, as by command or invitation: *Have him come here at five.* **7.** to be in a certain relation to: *She has three cousins.* **8.** to show or exhibit in action or words: *She had the crust to refuse my invitation.* **9.** to be identified or distinguished by; possess the characteristic of: *This wood has a silky texture.* **10.** to engage in; carry on: *to have a talk; to have a fight.* **11.** to partake of; eat or drink: *We had cake for dessert.* **12.** to permit; allow: *I will not have any talking during the concert.* **13.** to assert or represent as being: *Rumor has it that she's moving.* **14.** to give birth to; beget: *to have a baby.* **15.** to hold an advantage over: *He has you there.* **16.** to outwit; deceive; cheat: *We realized we'd been had by a con artist.* **17.** to control or possess through bribery; bribe. **18.** to gain possession of: *There is none to be had at that price.* **19.** to hold or put in a certain position or situation: *The problem had me stumped.* **20.** to exercise; display: *Have pity on them.* **21.** to invite or cause to be present as a companion or guest: *We had Evelyn over for dinner.* **22.** to engage in sexual intercourse with. **23.** to know or be skilled in: *to have neither Latin nor Greek.* —*v.i.* **24.** to be in possession of money or wealth: *those who have and those who have not.* —*auxiliary verb.* **25.** (used with a past participle to form perfect tenses): *She has gone. I would have felt better if the hotel had cost less.* **26.** to be required, compelled, or under obligation (fol. by infinitival *to,* with or without a main verb): *I have to leave now.* **27.** **have at,** to attack with vigor. —*n.* **28.** Usu., **haves.** an individual or group that has wealth, social position, or other material benefits (contrasted with *have-not*). —*Idiom.* **29.** have done, to cease; finish. **30. have had it, a.** to be tired and disgusted: *I've had it with your excuses.* **b.** to be ready for discarding, as something shabby, old, or no longer useful or popular. **31. have it coming,** to deserve whatever good or ill fortune one receives. **32. have it in for,** to wish harm to. **33. have it out,** to reach an understanding through fighting or intense discussion. **34. have to do with, a.** to be connected or associated with: *Your ambition had a lot to do with your success.* **b.** to deal with; be concerned with. **35. to have and to hold,** to possess legally; have permanent possession of.

Ha·vel (hä′vel), *n.* **Vá·clav** (väts′läf′), born 1936, president of Czechoslovakia 1989–92, president of the Czech Republic since 1993.

ha·ven (hā′vən), *n.* **1.** a harbor; port. **2.** any place of shelter and safety; refuge; asylum.

have-not (hav′not′, -not′), *n.* Usu., **have-nots.** an individual or group that is without wealth, social position, or other material advantages (contrasted with *have*).

have·n't (hav′ənt), contraction of *have not.*

Hav·er·gal (hav′ər gəl), *n.* **Frances Ridley,** 1836–79, English hymn writer.

hav·er·sack (hav′ər sak′), *n.* a single-strapped bag worn over one shoulder and used for carrying supplies.

Ha·ver′sian canal′ (hə vûr′zhən), *n.* (*sometimes l.c.*) any of the channels in bone containing blood vessels and nerves.

hav·oc (hav′ək), *n.* **1.** great destruction or devastation; ruinous damage. —*Idiom.* **2. play havoc with, a.** to create confusion or disorder in. **b.** to destroy; ruin.

haw¹ (hô), *v.i.* **1.** to utter a sound representing a hesitation or pause in speech. —*n.* **2.** a hesitation; pause.

haw² (hô), *interj.* **1.** (used as a word of command to a horse or other draft animal, usu. directing it to turn to the left.) —*v.t., v.i.* **2.** to turn or make a turn to the left. Compare GEE¹.

Ha·wai·i (hə wī′ē, -wä′-, -wä′yə, hä vä′ē), *n.* **1.** a state of the United States comprising the Hawaiian Islands in the N Pacific: a U.S. territory 1900–59; admitted to the Union 1959. 1,183,723; 6424 sq. mi. (16,638 sq. km). *Cap.:* Honolulu. *Abbr.:* HI, Haw. **2.** the largest island of Hawaii, in the SE part. 63,468; 4021 sq. mi. (10,415 sq. km).

Ha·wai·ian (hə wī′ən, -wä′yən), *n.* **1. a.** a member of the Polynesian people who are the aboriginal inhabitants of the Hawaiian Islands. **b.** the Austronesian language of this people. **2.** any native or inhabitant of the Hawaiian Islands. —*adj.* **3.** of or pertaining to the Hawaiian Islands, their inhabitants, or the language Hawaiian.

Hawai′ian guitar′, *n.* a six-to-eight-string electric guitar fretted with a piece of metal or bone to produce a whining glissando sound. Also called **steel guitar.**

Hawai′ian hon′eycreeper, *n.* any of various finches of the subfamily Drepanidinae, native to the Hawaiian Islands, and including a number of very rare and extinct species.

Hawai′ian Is′lands, *n.pl.* a group of islands in the N Pacific; 2090 mi. (3370 km) SW of San Francisco: includes the islands of Hawaii, Maui, Oahu, Kauai, Molokai, Lanai, Niihau, Kahoolawe, and other islands and islets. Formerly, **Sandwich Islands.**

Hawai′ian shirt′, *n.* a short-sleeved sport shirt orig. of Hawaii, made of light fabric with colorful designs, esp. of birds and flowers.

Hawai′i time′, *n.* ALASKA-HAWAII TIME. Also called **Hawai′i Stand′ard Time′.**

Hawai′i Volca′noes Na′tional Park′, *n.* a large national park that includes the active volcanoes Kilauea and Mauna Loa on the island of Hawaii and the extinct crater Haleakala on Maui. 343 sq. mi. (890 sq. km).

haw·finch (hô′finch′), *n.* a common Eurasian finch, *Coccothraustes coccothraustes,* having black, golden brown, and white plumage and a large conical bill.

hawk¹ (hôk), *n.* **1.** any of various birds of prey of the family Accipitridae, having a short, hooked beak, broad wings, and curved talons. **2.** any of various other birds of prey, as falcons, or similar, unrelated birds, as nighthawks. **3.** a person who preys on others, as a sharper. **4.** a person, esp. one in public office, who advocates war or a belligerent national attitude. —*v.i.* **5.** to hunt on the wing like a hawk. **6.** to hunt using trained hawks.

hawk² (hôk), *v.t.* **1.** to peddle or offer for sale, esp. by calling aloud in public. **2.** to spread (rumors, news, etc.). —*v.i.* **3.** to carry wares about for sale; peddle.

hawk³ (hôk), *v.i.* **1.** to make an effort to raise phlegm from the throat; clear the throat noisily. —*v.t.* **2.** to raise by hawking: *to hawk phlegm up.* —*n.* **3.** a noisy effort to clear the throat.

hawk·er¹ (hô′kər), *n.* a person who hunts with hawks or other birds of prey.

hawk·er² (hô′kər), *n.* a person who offers goods for sale by shouting his or her wares in the street or going from door to door; peddler.

hawk′-eyed′, *adj.* having very keen sight.

hawk·ish (hô′kish), *adj.* **1.** resembling a hawk, as in appearance or behavior. **2.** advocating war or a belligerently threatening diplomatic policy. —**hawk′ish·ly,** *adv.* —**hawk′ish·ness,** *n.*

hawk′ moth′, *n.* any of numerous moths of the family Sphingidae, noted for their swift flight and ability to hover while sipping nectar from flowers. Also called **sphingid, sphinx moth.**

hawk′-nosed′, *adj.* having a nose curved like the bill of a hawk.

Hawks (hôks), *n.* **Annie,** 1835–1918, U.S. poet and hymn writer.

hawks′bill tur′tle (hôks′bil′), *n.* a sea turtle, *Eretmochelys imbricata,* the shell of which is the source of tortoise shell. Also called **hawks′-bill′.**

hawk′s′-eye′, *n.* a dark-blue chatoyant quartz formed by the silicification of crocidolite and used for ornamental purposes.

hawk·weed (hôk′wēd′), *n.* any weedy composite plant of the genus *Hieracium,* usu. bearing yellow or orange flower clusters.

haw·ser (hô′zər, -sər), *n.* a heavy rope for mooring or towing.

haw·thorn (hô′thôrn′), *n.* any of various small trees of the genus *Crataegus,* rose family, with stiff thorns and bright-colored fruit, often cultivated as hedges. —**haw′thorn′y,** *adj.*

Haw·thorne (hô′thôrn′), *n.* **1. Nathaniel,** 1804–64, U.S. writer. **2.** a city in SW California, SW of Los Angeles. 64,730.

hay (hā), *n.* **1.** herbage, as grass, clover, or alfalfa, cut and dried for use as forage. **2.** *Slang.* **a.** a small sum of money. **b.** money. —*v.t.* **3.** to convert (plant material) into hay. **4.** to feed with hay. —*v.i.* **5.** to cut grass, clover, or the like, and store for use as forage. —*Idiom.* **6. hit the hay,** *Informal.* to go to bed. —*Proverb.* **7. make hay while the sun shines,** to take advantage of favorable circumstances.

Hay (hā), *n.* **John Milton,** 1838–1905, U.S. statesman and author.

Hay·dn (hīd′n), *n.* **1. Franz Joseph,** 1732–1809, Austrian composer. **2. (Johann) Michael,** 1737–1806, Austrian composer (brother of Franz Joseph Haydn).

Hayes (hāz), *n.* **1. Helen** (*Helen Hayes Brown MacArthur*), 1900–93, U.S. actress. **2. Rutherford B(irchard),** 1822–93, 19th president of the U.S. 1877–81.

hay′ fe′ver, *n.* allergic rhinitis affecting the mucous membranes of the eyes and respiratory tract, caused by pollen of ragweed and certain other plants.

hay·loft (hā′lôft′, -loft′), *n.* a loft in a stable or barn for the storage of hay.

Hay′mar·ket Square′ (hā′mär′kit), *n.* a square in Chicago: scene of a riot (**Hay′market Ri′ot**) in 1886 between police and labor unionists.

Hay′-Paunce′fote Trea′ty (hā′pôns′fŏot), *n.* an agreement (1901) between the U.S. and Great Britain giving the U.S. the sole right to build a canal across Central America connecting the Atlantic and Pacific. Compare CLAYTON-BULWER TREATY. [named after J. M. HAY and Julian *Pauncefote* (1828–1902), English diplomat]

hay·rack (hā′rak′), *n.* **1.** a rack for holding hay for feeding horses or cattle. **2.** a rack or framework mounted on a wagon, for use in carrying hay, straw, or the like. **3.** the wagon and rack together.

hay·rick (hā′rik′), *n.* HAYSTACK.

hay·ride (hā′rīd′), *n.* a pleasure ride or outing, esp. at night, by a group in an open wagon or truck partly filled with hay.

hay·seed (hā′sēd′), *n.* **1.** grass seed, esp. that shaken out of hay. **2.**

small bits of the chaff, straw, etc., of hay. **3.** an unsophisticated person from a rural area; yokel; hick.

hay•stack (hā′stak′), *n.* a stack of hay with a conical or ridged top, built up in the open air for preservation.

Hay•ward (hā′wərd), *n.* a city in central California, SE of Oakland. 115,590.

hay•wire (hā′wīər′), *n.* **1.** wire used to bind bales of hay. **—*adj.* 2.** in disorder. **3.** out of control; disordered; crazy.

ha•zan or ***cha•zan*** (KHä′zən, KHä zän′), *n., pl.* ***ha•za•nim*** (KHä zô′nim, KHä′zä nēm′), *Eng.* **ha•zans.** *Hebrew.* a cantor of a synagogue.

haz•ard (haz′ərd), *n.* **1.** something causing danger, peril, risk, or difficulty: *the many hazards of the big city.* **2.** the absence or lack of predictability; chance; uncertainty. **3.** a bunker, sand trap, or the like, constituting an obstacle on a golf course. **4.** a game played with two dice, an earlier and more complicated form of craps. **5.** (in court tennis) any of the winning openings. **—*v.t.* 6.** to offer (a statement, conjecture, etc.) with the possibility of facing criticism, disapproval, failure, or the like; venture: *to hazard a guess.* **7.** to put to the risk of being lost; expose to risk. **8.** to take or run the risk of (a misfortune, penalty, etc.). **9.** to venture upon (anything of doubtful issue): *to hazard a dangerous encounter.* **—*Idiom.* 10. at hazard,** at risk. **—haz′ard•less,** *adj.* **—haz′ard•ous,** *adj.* **—haz′ard•ous•ness,** *n.*

haze[1] (hāz), *n., v.,* **hazed, haz•ing. —*n.* 1.** an aggregation in the atmosphere of very fine, widely dispersed, solid or liquid particles giving the air an opalescent appearance. **2.** vagueness or obscurity, as of the mind, perception, etc. **—*v.t., v.i.* 3.** to make or become hazy. **—haz′i•ly,** *adv.* **—haz′i•ness,** *n.* **—haz′y,** *adj.,* **-i•er, -i•est.**

haze[2] (hāz), *v.t.,* **hazed, haz•ing. 1.** to subject (freshmen, newcomers, etc.) to abusive or humiliating tricks and ridicule. **2.** to harass with unnecessary or disagreeable tasks. **—haz′er,** *n.*

ha•zel (hā′zəl), *n.* **1.** any small tree or shrub of the genus *Corylus,* of the birch family, having toothed ovate leaves and edible nuts. **2.** the wood of any of these trees. **3.** the hazelnut or filbert. **4.** a light golden- or greenish-brown color. **—*adj.* 5.** of or pertaining to the hazel. **6.** made of the wood of the hazel. **7.** of the color hazel.

ha•zel•nut (hā′zəl nut′), *n.* the nut of the hazel; filbert.

Ha•zor (hä zôr′, -zōr′), *n.* an ancient city in Israel, N of the Sea of Galilee: extensive excavations; capital of Canaanite kingdom. Josh. 11:1–13; 19:36.

h.b., *Football.* halfback.

H.B.M., Her Britannic Majesty; His Britannic Majesty.

HBO, *Trademark.* Home Box Office (a cable television channel).

H-bomb (āch′bom′), *n.* HYDROGEN BOMB.

HDL, high-density lipoprotein: a circulating lipoprotein that picks up cholesterol in the arteries and deposits it in the liver for reprocessing or excretion.

hdqrs., headquarters.

HDTV, high-definition television.

hdw. or **hdwe.,** hardware.

he (hē; *unstressed* ē), *pron., nom.* **he,** *poss.* **his,** *obj.* **him;** *pl. nom.* **they,** *poss.* **their** or **theirs,** *obj.* **them;** *n., pl.* **hes;** *adj.* **—*pron.* 1.** the male person or animal being discussed or last mentioned; that male. **2.** anyone (without reference to sex); that person: *He who hesitates is lost.* **—*n.* 3.** any male person or animal; a man: *hes and shes.* **—*adj.* 4.** male (usu. used in combination): *a he-goat.*

He, *Chem. Symbol.* helium.

head (hed), *n.* **1.** the anterior or upper part of the vertebrate body, containing the skull with mouth, eyes, ears, nose, and brain. **2.** the corresponding part of the body in invertebrates. **3.** the head considered as the center of the intellect; mind; brain: *a good head for mathematics.* **4.** the position or place of leadership, greatest authority, or honor. **5.** a person to whom others are subordinate, as the director of an institution; leader or chief. **6.** a person considered with reference to his or her mind, attributes, status, etc.: *wise heads; crowned heads.* **7.** the part of anything that forms or is regarded as forming the top or upper end: *head of a pin; head of a page.* **8.** the foremost part or front end of something or a forward projecting part: *head of a procession.* **9.** the part of a weapon, tool, etc., used for striking: *the head of a hammer.* **10.** a person or animal considered as one of a number, herd, or group: *a dinner at $20 a head; ten head of cattle.* **11.** the approximate length of a horse's head, as indicating a margin of victory in a race. **12.** a culminating point, usu. of a critical nature; crisis or climax: *to bring matters to a head.* **13.** froth or foam at the top of a liquid: *the head on beer.* **14. a.** any dense flower cluster or inflorescence. **b.** any other compact part of a plant, usu. at the top of the stem, as that composed of leaves in the cabbage. **15.** the maturated part of an abscess, boil, etc. **16.** a projecting point of a coast, esp. when high, as a cape, headland, or promontory. **17.** Also, **heads.** the obverse of a coin, as bearing a head or other principal figure (opposed to *tail*). **18.** one of the chief parts or points of a written or oral discourse. **19.** something resembling a head in form or a representation of a head, as a piece of sculpture. **20.** the source of a river or stream. **21. heads,** alcohol produced during the initial fermentation. **22.** HEADLINE. **23.** a toilet or lavatory, esp. on a boat or ship. **24. a.** the forepart of a vessel; bow. **b.** the upper edge of a quadrilateral sail. **c.** the upper corner of a jib-headed sail. **25.** *Gram.* **a.** a word or word group in a construction that can play the same grammatical role as the entire construction. **b.** the member of a construction upon which another member depends and to which it is subordinate. **26.** the stretched membrane covering the end of a drum or similar musical instrument. **27.** a level or road driven into solid coal for proving or working a mine. **28.** any of various devices on machine tools for holding, moving, indexing, or changing tools or work, as the turret of a lathe. **29.** (loosely) the pressure exerted by confined fluid: *a head of steam.* **30. a.** the vertical distance between two points in a liquid, as water, or some other fluid. **b.** the pressure differential resulting from this separation, expressed in terms of the vertical distance between the points. **31.** any of the parts of a tape recorder that record, play back, or erase magnetic signals on audiotape or videotape. **—*adj.* 32.** first in rank or position; chief; leading; principal: *a head official.* **33.** of or for the head (often used in combination): *head covering; headgear.* **34.** situated at the top, front, or head of anything (often used in combination): *headline; headboard.* **35.** moving or coming from a direction in front, as of a vessel: *head tide.* **36.** *Slang.* of or pertaining to drugs, drug paraphernalia, or drug users. **—*v.t.* 37.** to go at the head of or in front of; lead; precede: *to head a list.* **38.** to outdo or excel; take the lead in or over: *to head one's competitors in a field.* **39.** to be the head or chief of (sometimes fol. by *up*): *to head a school.* **40.** to direct the course of; turn the head or front of in a specified direction: *I'll head the boat for the shore.* **41.** to go around the head of (a stream). **42.** to furnish or fit with a head. **43.** to take the head off; decapitate; behead. **44.** to get in front of in order to stop, turn aside, attack, etc. **45.** HEADLINE (def. 4). **46.** to propel (a soccer ball) by striking it with the head, esp. with the forehead. **—*v.i.* 47.** to move forward toward a point specified; go in a certain direction: *to head toward town.* **48.** to form a head: *Cabbage heads quickly.* **49.** (of a river or stream) to have the head or source where specified. **50. head off,** to hinder the progress of; intercept. **—*Idiom.* 51. come to a head, a.** to suppurate, as a boil. **b.** to reach a crisis; culminate. **52. get one's head together,** to get oneself under control; become sensible. **53. give someone his** or **her head,** to allow someone freedom of choice. **54. go over someone's head,** to appeal to someone's official superior, as for redress of grievances. **55. go to one's head, a.** to overcome one with exhilaration, dizzyness, or intoxication. **b.** to fill one with conceit. **56. hang** or **hide one's head,** to manifest shame. **57. head and shoulders,** by an impressively great amount: *head and shoulders above the rest in talent.* **58. head over heels, a.** headlong, as in a somersault. **b.** intensely; completely: *head over heels in love.* **c.** impulsively; carelessly: *They plunged head over heels into the fighting.* **59. head to head,** in direct opposition or competition. **60. keep one's head,** to remain calm and effective. **61. keep one's head above water,** to remain financially solvent. **62. lay** or **put heads together,** to meet in order to discuss, consult, or scheme. **63. lose one's head,** to become uncontrolled or wildly excited. **64. make head,** to progress or advance, esp. despite opposition; make headway. **65. make head(s) or tail(s) of,** to understand or interpret to even a small extent (often used in the negative). **66. make heads roll,** to dismiss numbers of employees or subordinates. **67. one's head off,** extremely; excessively: *to laugh one's head off.* **68. on one's head,** as one's responsibility or fault. **69. out of one's head** or **mind, a.** insane; crazy. **b.** delirious; irrational. **70. over one's head,** beyond one's comprehension, ability, or resources. **71. take (it) into one's head,** to put together a plan. **72. turn someone's head, a.** to make someone smug or conceited. **b.** to confuse someone.

H

-head, a noun suffix of state or condition (*godhead; maidenhead*), occurring in words now mostly archaic or obsolete, many being superseded by forms in -HOOD.

head•ache (hed′āk′), *n.* **1.** a pain located in the head, as over the eyes, at the temples, or at the base of the skull. **2.** an annoying or bothersome person, situation, activity, etc. **—head′ach•y,** *adj.*

head•band (hed′band′), *n.* a band worn around the head.

head•board (hed′bôrd′, -bōrd′), *n.* a board forming the head of something, as a bed.

head•cheese (hed′chēz′), *n.* luncheon meat made of the edible parts of the head of a pig or calf and molded in its own aspic.

head′ cold′, *n.* a common cold characterized esp. by nasal congestion and sneezing.

head′ count′ or **head′count′,** *n.* an inventory of people in a group taken by counting individuals: *a head count of senators opposing the bill.*

head•dress (hed′dres′), *n.* a covering or decoration for the head: *a tribal headdress of feathers.*

head•ed (hed′id), *adj.* (usu. used in combination) **1.** having a head, mentality, or personality of the specified kind: *levelheaded; baldheaded.* **2.** having the specified number of heads: *a two-headed calf.*

head•er (hed′ər), *n.* **1.** a person or thing that removes or puts a head on something. **2.** a reaping machine that cuts off and gathers only the heads of the grain. **3.** a chamber where tubes are connected so that water or steam may pass freely among them. **4.** a manifold that channels exhaust gases from the engine cylinders. **5. a.** a brick or stone laid in a wall or the like so that its shorter ends are exposed or parallel to the surface. **b.** a framing member crossing and supporting the ends of

header

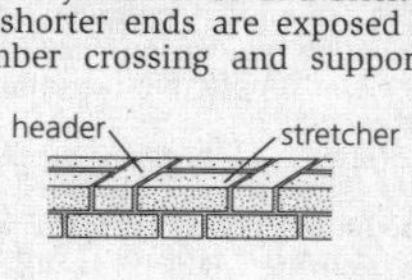

joists, studs, or rafters. **6.** a plunge or dive headfirst, as into water. **7.** a line of information placed at the top of a page for purposes of identification. Compare FOOTER.

head•first (hed′fûrst′), *adv.* **1.** with the head in front or bent forward: *to dive headfirst into the sea.* **2.** rashly; precipitately.

head•gear (hed′gēr′), *n.* **1.** a covering for the head, as a hat. **2.** a protective covering for the head, as a steel helmet. **3.** the parts of a harness about the animal's head. **4.** an orthodontic device worn on the head and attached to braces in the mouth, for exerting backward tension.

head•hunt•ing (hed′hun′ting), *n.* **1.** (among certain tribal peoples) the practice of hunting down and decapitating victims and preserving their heads as trophies. **2.** the search, esp. by professional recruiters, for executives to fill high-level positions. **3.** the act or practice of trying to destroy the power, position, or influence of one's competitors or foes. —**head′hunt′er**, *n.*

head•ing (hed′ing), *n.* **1.** something that serves as a head, top, or front. **2.** a title or caption of a page, chapter, etc. **3.** a section of the subject of a discourse. **4.** the compass direction toward which a traveler or vehicle is or should be moving; course. **5.** an active underground mining excavation. **6.** the angle between the axis from front to rear of an aircraft and some reference line, as magnetic north.

head•land (hed′land), *n.* **1.** a promontory extending into a large body of water. **2.** a strip of unplowed land at the ends of furrows or near a fence or border.

head•light (hed′līt′), *n.* a light or lamp, usu. equipped with a reflector, on the front of an automobile, locomotive, etc.

head•line (hed′līn′), *n.*, *v.*, **-lined, -lin•ing.** —*n.* Also called **head. 1.** a heading in a newspaper for any written material, sometimes for an illustration, to indicate subject matter. **2.** the largest such heading on the front page, usu. at the top. **3.** the line at the top of a page, containing the title, pagination, etc. —*v.t.* **4.** to furnish with a headline; head. **5.** to mention or name in a headline. **6.** to publicize, feature, or star (a specific performer, product, etc.). **7.** to be the star of (a show, nightclub act, etc.). —*v.i.* **8.** to be the star of an entertainment.

head•lin•er (hed′lī′nər), *n.* a performer whose name appears most prominently in a program or on a marquee; star.

head•lock (hed′lok′), *n.* a wrestling hold in which one arm is locked around the opponent's head.

head•long (hed′lông′, -long′), *adv.* **1.** with the head foremost; headfirst: *to plunge headlong into the water.* **2.** without delay; hastily. **3.** without deliberation; rashly. —*adj.* **4.** undertaken quickly and suddenly; made precipitately; hasty: *a headlong flight.* **5.** done or going with the head foremost. **6.** rash; impetuous.

head•mas•ter (hed′mas′tər, -mä′stər), *n.* the person in charge of a private school. —**head′mas′ter•ship′,** *n.*

head•mis•tress (hed′mis′tris), *n.* a woman in charge of a private school. —**head′mis′tress•ship′,** *n.*

head′-on′, *adj.* **1.** meeting with the fronts or heads foremost: *a head-on collision.* **2.** facing forward; frontal. **3.** characterized by direct opposition: *a head-on confrontation.* —*adv.* **4.** with the front or head foremost, esp. in a collision. **5.** in direct opposition.

head•phone (hed′fōn′), *n.* **1.** Usu., **headphones. 1.** a headset designed for use with a stereo system. **2.** any set of earphones.

head•piece (hed′pēs′), *n.* **1.** a piece of armor for the head; helmet. **2.** any covering for the head. **3.** a headset. **4.** intellect; judgment.

head•pin (hed′pin′), *n.* the pin standing nearest to the bowler when set up, at the head or front of the triangle; the number 1 pin.

head•quar•ter (hed′kwôr′tər, -kwô′-), *v.t.* **1.** to situate in headquarters. —*v.i.* **2.** to establish one's headquarters.

head•quar•ters (hed′kwôr′tərz, -kwô′-), *n.*, *pl.* **-ters.** (*used with a sing. or pl. v.*) a center of operations, as of the police, a military commander, or a business, from which orders are issued.

head•rest (hed′rest′), *n.* **1.** a rest or support of any kind for the head. **2.** a padded extension at the top of a seat back, esp. in an automobile for protection against whiplash.

head•room (hed′rōōm′, -rŏŏm′), *n.* **1.** the clear space between two decks on a vessel. **2.** Also called **headway.** clear vertical space, as between the head and sill of a doorway, esp. as to allow passage or comfortable occupancy. **3.** the additional power output capability of an amplifier when producing short-term peak signals.

heads (hedz), *adj.*, *adv.* **1.** (of a coin) with the top, or obverse, facing up. Compare TAILS. —*n.* **2.** HEAD (def. 17).

head•set (hed′set′), *n.* a device consisting of one or two earphones, and sometimes a microphone, attached to a headband.

head•stall (hed′stôl′), *n.* that part of a bridle or halter that encompasses the head of an animal.

head•stand (hed′stand′), *n.* an act or instance of supporting the body in a vertical position by balancing on the head, usu. with the aid of the hands.

head′ start′, *n.* **1.** an advantage given or acquired in any competition, endeavor, etc., as allowing one or more competitors in a race to start before the others. **2.** a productive beginning: *I'll get a head start on the paperwork this weekend.*

head•stone (hed′stōn′), *n.* a stone marker set at the head of a grave; gravestone.

head•stream (hed′strēm′), *n.* a stream that is a source of a river.

head•strong (hed′strông′, -strong′), *adj.* **1.** determined to have one's

own way; willful; stubborn; obstinate. **2.** proceeding from or exhibiting willfulness: *a headstrong course.* —**head′strong•ly,** *adv.* —**head′-strong′ness,** *n.*

heads-up (hedz′up′), *adj.* quick to grasp a situation and take advantage of opportunities; alert; resourceful.

head′-to-head′, *adj.* being or occurring in direct personal confrontation, encounter, or exchange.

head•wait•er (hed′wā′tər), *n.* a person in charge of waiters, busboys, etc., in a restaurant or dining car.

head•wa•ters (hed′wô′tərz, -wot′ərz), *n.pl.* the upper tributaries of a river.

head•way (hed′wā′), *n.* **1.** forward movement; progress in a forward direction: *The ship's headway was slowed by the storm.* **2.** progress in general: *to make headway in a career.* **3.** the time interval or distance between two vehicles or vessels traveling in the same direction over the same route.

head•wind (hed′wind′), *n.* a wind opposed to the course of a moving object, esp. an aircraft or other vehicle (opposed to *tailwind*).

head•word (hed′wûrd′), *n.* **1.** a word or phrase appearing as the heading of a chapter, dictionary or encyclopedia entry, etc. **2.** CATCHWORD (def. 2). **3.** a word that serves as the head of a grammatical construction.

head•y (hed′ē), *adj.,* **-i•er, -i•est. 1.** giddy; dizzy: *She felt heady with the triumph.* **2.** affecting the mind or senses greatly; intoxicating: *heady perfume.* **3.** exciting; exhilarating: *the heady news of victory.* **4.** rashly impetuous. —**head′i•ly,** *adv.* —**head′i•ness,** *n.*

heal (hēl), *v.t.* **1.** to make healthy, whole, or sound; restore to health; free from ailment. **2.** to repair or reconcile; settle: *to heal the rift between them.* **3.** to free from evil; cleanse; purify: *to heal the soul.* —*v.i.* **4.** to effect a cure. **5.** (of a wound, broken bone, etc.) to become whole or sound; mend (sometimes fol. by *up* or *over*). —**heal′er,** *n.*

health (helth), *n.* **1.** the general condition of the body or mind with reference to soundness and vigor: *in poor health.* **2.** soundness of body or mind; freedom from disease or ailment: *to lose one's health.* **3.** a polite or complimentary wish for a person's health, happiness, etc., esp. as a toast. **4.** vigor; vitality: *economic health.*

health′care′ or **health′ care′,** *n.* any field or enterprise concerned with supplying services, equipment, information, etc., for the maintenance or restoration of health.

health′ food′, *n.* any natural food popularly believed to promote or sustain good health, as through its vital nutrients.

health•ful (helth′fəl), *adj.* **1.** conducive to health; wholesome or salutary: *a healthful diet.* **2.** healthy. —**health′ful•ly,** *adv.* —**health′ful•ness,** *n.*

health′ insur′ance, *n.* insurance that compensates the insured for the medical expenses of an illness or hospitalization.

health′ main′tenance organiza′tion, *n.* a plan for comprehensive health services, prepaid by an individual or by a company for its employees, that provides treatment, preventive care, and hospitalization to each participating member in a central health center. *Abbr.:* HMO

health′ profes′sional, *n.* a person trained to work in any field of physical or mental health.

health•y (hel′thē), *adj.,* **-i•er, -i•est. 1.** possessing or enjoying good health or a sound and vigorous mentality. **2.** pertaining to or characteristic of good health, or a sound and vigorous mind: *a healthy appearance.* **3.** conducive to good health; healthful. **4.** prosperous or sound: *a healthy business.* **5.** fairly large: *I bought a healthy number of books.* —**health′i•ly,** *adv.* —**health′i•ness,** *n.*

heap (hēp), *n.* **1.** a group of things placed, thrown, or lying one on another; pile: *a heap of stones.* **2.** *Informal.* a great quantity or number; multitude. **3.** *Slang.* a dilapidated automobile. —*v.t.* **4.** to gather, put, or cast in a heap; pile. **5.** to accumulate; amass (often fol. by *up* or *together*): *to heap up riches.* **6.** to give, assign, or bestow in great quantity; load (often fol. by *on* or *upon*): *to heap blessings upon someone.* **7.** to load, supply, or fill abundantly: *to heap a plate with food.* —*v.i.* **8.** to become heaped or piled, as sand or snow; rise in a heap or heaps (often fol. by *up*). —**heap′er,** *n.* —**heap′y,** *adj.*

hear (hēr), *v.,* **heard** (hûrd), **hear•ing.** —*v.t.* **1.** to perceive by the ear: *to hear noises.* **2.** to learn by the ear or by being told; be informed of: *to hear news.* **3.** to listen to; give or pay attention to. **4.** to be among the audience at or of (something): *to hear a recital.* **5.** to give a formal, official, or judicial hearing to (something); consider officially, as a judge, sovereign, teacher, or assembly: *to hear a case.* **6.** to take or listen to the evidence or testimony of (someone): *to hear the defendant.* **7.** to listen to with favor, assent, or compliance. —*v.i.* **8.** to be capable of perceiving sound by the ear; have the faculty of perceiving sound vibrations. **9.** to receive information by the ear or otherwise: *to hear from a friend.* **10.** to listen with favor, assent, or compliance (often fol. by *of*): *I will not hear of your going.* **11.** (used interjectionally in the phrase *Hear! Hear!* to express approval, as of a speech.)

hear•ing (hēr′ing), *n.* **1.** the faculty or sense by which sound is perceived. **2.** the act of perceiving sound. **3.** opportunity to be heard: *to grant a hearing.* **4. a.** a preliminary legal examination of charges and evidence by a magistrate to determine whether prosecution is justified. **b.** a session in which testimony and arguments are presented, esp. before a judge, in a lawsuit. **5.** earshot.

hear′ing aid′, *n.* a compact electronic amplifier worn to improve one's hearing and usu. placed in or behind the ear.

hear·ing-ear′ dog′, *n.* a dog that has been trained to alert a hearing-impaired person to sounds, as a telephone ringing or dangerous noises.

hear·ing-impaired′, *adj.* having reduced or deficient hearing ability; hard-of-hearing.

heark·en or **hark·en** (här′kən), *v.i.* to give heed or attention to what is said; listen. —**heark′en·er,** *n.*

hear·say (hēr′sā′), *n.* unverified information acquired from another; rumor.

hear′say ev′idence, *n.* testimony in court based on what a witness has heard from another person rather than on personal knowledge.

hearse (hûrs), *n.* a vehicle for conveying a dead person to the place of burial.

Hearst (hûrst), *n.* **William Randolph,** 1863–1951, U.S. editor and publisher.

heart (härt), *n.* **1.** a muscular organ in vertebrates (four-chambered in mammals and birds, three-chambered in reptiles and amphibians, and two-chambered in fishes) that receives blood from the veins and pumps it through the arteries to oxygenate the blood during its circuit. **2.** any analogous contractile structure in invertebrate animals. **3.** the center of the total personality, esp. with reference to intuition, feeling, or emotion: *In your heart you know it's true.* **4.** the center of emotion, esp. as contrasted to the head as the center of the intellect. **5.** capacity for sympathy; feeling; affection: *His heart moved him to help the needy.* **6.** spirit, courage, or enthusiasm: *to lose heart.* **7.** the innermost or central part of anything: *in the heart of Paris.* **8.** the vital or essential part; core: *the heart of the matter.* **9.** the breast or bosom. **10.** a person (used esp. in expressions of praise or affection): *dear heart.* **11.** a conventional shape with rounded sides meeting in a point at the bottom and curving inward to a cusp at the top. **12.** a red figure or pip of this shape on a playing card. **13.** a card of the suit bearing such figures. **14. hearts, a.** (*used with a sing. or pl. v.*) the suit so marked. **b.** (*used with a sing. v.*) a game in which the players try to take all the hearts or to avoid taking tricks containing any of them. **15.** Also called **core.** a strand running through the center of a rope, the other strands being laid around it. —*Idiom.* **16. after one's own heart,** in accord with one's preference. **17. at heart,** in reality; fundamentally; basically. **18. break someone's heart,** to cause someone to be utterly devastated by sorrow or disappointment. **19. by heart,** entirely from memory. **20. eat one's heart out,** to grieve inconsolably. **21. from (the bottom of) one's heart,** with complete sincerity. Also, **from the heart. 22. have a heart,** to exhibit compassion and mercy. **23. have at heart,** to have as a fundamental motive. **24. have one's heart in one's mouth,** to be extremely anxious or fearful. **25. have one's heart in the right place,** to be well-intentioned. **26. in one's heart of hearts,** in one's private thoughts or feelings; deep within one. **27. lose one's heart to,** to fall in love with. **28. near** or **close to one's heart,** of great interest or concern to one. **29. set one's heart at rest,** to dismiss one's anxieties. **30. set one's heart on,** to wish for intensely; determine on. Also, **have one's heart set on. 31. take** or **lay to heart, a.** to consider seriously. **b.** to grieve over. **32. take heart,** to regain one's courage; become heartened. **33. to one's heart's content,** for as long as one wishes. **34. wear one's heart on one's sleeve,** to allow one's feelings, esp. of love, to show. **35. with all one's heart,** eagerly; cordially.

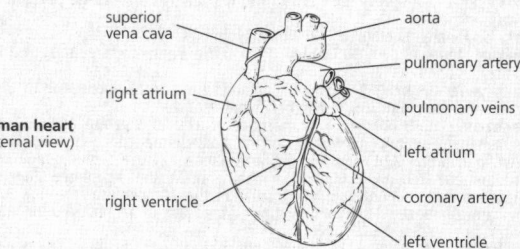

human heart
(external view)

superior vena cava
aorta
right atrium
pulmonary artery
pulmonary veins
left atrium
right ventricle
coronary artery
left ventricle

heart·ache (härt′āk′), *n.* emotional distress; sorrow; grief; anguish. —**heart′ach·ing,** *adj.*

heart′ attack′, *n.* **1.** any sudden insufficiency of oxygen supply to the heart that results in heart muscle damage; myocardial infarction. **2.** any sudden disruption of heart function.

heart·beat (härt′bēt′), *n.* a pulsation of the heart, including one complete systole and diastole.

heart′beat away′ from the pres′idency, *n.* a phrase used during presidential elections to indicate the importance of the vice president.

heart·break (härt′brāk′), *n.* great sorrow or anguish. —**heart′break·er,** *n.*

heart·bro·ken (härt′brō′kən), *adj.* crushed with sorrow or grief. —**heart′bro′ken·ly,** *adv.* —**heart′bro·ken·ness,** *n.*

heart·burn (härt′bûrn′), *n.* a burning sensation in the stomach, typically extending toward the esophagus, and sometimes associated with the eructation of an acid fluid; pyrosis.

heart·ed (här′tid), *adj.* having a specified kind of heart (used in combination): *hardhearted; sad-hearted.*

heart·en (här′tn), *v.t.* to give courage or confidence to; cheer. —**heart′en·er,** *n.* —**heart′en·ing·ly,** *adv.*

heart′ fail′ure, *n.* **1.** a condition in which the heart fatally ceases to function. **2.** a condition in which the heart pumps inadequate amounts of blood, characterized by edema, esp. of the lower legs, and shortness of breath.

heart·felt (härt′felt′), *adj.* deeply or sincerely felt: *heartfelt sympathy.*

hearth (härth), *n.* **1.** the floor of a fireplace, usu. of stone, brick, etc., often extending into a room. **2.** home; fireside. **3.** home and family life: *the joys of hearth and home.* **4. a.** the lower part of a blast furnace, cupola, etc., in which the molten metal collects and from which it is tapped out. **b.** the part of an open hearth upon which the charge is placed and melted down or refined. **5.** a brazier or chafing dish for burning charcoal. —**hearth′less,** *adj.*

hearth·side (härth′sīd′), *n.* FIRESIDE.

hearth·stone (härth′stōn′), *n.* **1.** a stone forming a hearth. **2.** home; hearth.

heart·land (härt′land′, -lənd), *n.* **1.** that part of a region considered essential to the viability of the whole, esp. a central land area relatively invulnerable to attack and capable of self-sufficiency. **2.** any central or vital area, as of a state, nation, or continent.

heart·less (härt′lis), *adj.* unfeeling; unkind; harsh; cruel. —**heart′less·ly,** *adv.* —**heart′less·ness,** *n.*

heart′-lung′ machine′, *n.* a pumping device through which diverted blood is oxygenated and returned to the body during heart surgery, temporarily functioning for the heart and lungs.

heart′ mur′mur, *n.* MURMUR (def. 3).

Heart′ of Dark′ness, a short novel (1902) by Joseph Conrad.

heart′ of palm′, *n.* the stripped terminal bud of a cabbage palm, eaten in salads or as a vegetable.

heart·rend·ing (härt′ren′ding), *adj.* causing or expressing intense grief, anguish, or distress. —**heart′rend′ing·ly,** *adv.*

hearts′ and flow′ers, *n.* (*used with a sing. or pl. v.*) maudlin sentimentality.

heart·sick (härt′sik′), *adj.* extremely depressed or unhappy; despondent. —**heart′sick·en·ing,** *adj.* —**heart′sick′ness,** *n.*

heart·stop·per (härt′stop′ər), *n.* something that overwhelms one with suspense or emotion.

heart·strings (härt′stringz′), *n.pl.* the deepest feelings; the strongest affections: *to tug at one's heartstrings.*

heart·throb (härt′throb′), *n.* **1.** a rapid beat or pulsation of the heart. **2.** a passionate or sentimental emotion. **3.** a person who inspires such emotion; sweetheart.

heart′-to-heart′, *adj.* **1.** frank; sincere and intimate: *a heart-to-heart talk.* —*n.* **2.** a frank talk, esp. between two people.

heart·warm·ing (härt′wôr′ming), *adj.* **1.** tenderly moving: *a heartwarming story.* **2.** gratifying; rewarding: *a heartwarming public response to the appeal.*

heart·wood (härt′wŏŏd′), *n.* the dense, dark, nonfunctioning older wood at the core of a tree trunk; duramen.

heart·worm (härt′wûrm′), *n.* **1.** a parasitic nematode, *Dirofilaria immitis*, transmitted by mosquitoes and invading the heart and pulmonary arteries of dogs and other canids. **2.** the disease caused by infection with heartworm.

heart·y (här′tē), *adj.*, **heart·i·er, heart·i·est. 1.** warm-hearted; cordial: *a hearty welcome.* **2.** genuine; sincere; heartfelt: *hearty dislike.* **3.** completely devoted; wholehearted: *hearty support.* **4.** exuberant; unrestrained: *hearty laughter.* **5.** forceful; violent: *a hearty push.* **6.** strong and well; vigorous: *hale and hearty.* **7.** substantial; abundant or nourishing: *a hearty meal.* **8.** enjoying or requiring abundant food: *a hearty appetite.* —**heart′i·ly,** *adv.* —**heart′i·ness,** *n.*

heat (hēt), *n.* **1.** the condition or quality of being hot; the state of a body having or generating a high degree of warmth. **2.** degree of hotness; temperature: *moderate heat.* **3.** the sensation of warmth or hotness. **4.** a bodily temperature higher than normal. **5.** a source of heat, as a stove burner or furnace. **6.** added or external energy that causes a rise in temperature, expansion, or other physical change. **7.** *Physics.* a nonmechanical energy transfer between regions of different temperature, as between a system and its surroundings or between two parts of the same system. *Symbol:* Q **8.** hot weather or climate. **9.** a period of hot weather. **10.** sharp, pungent flavor; spiciness. **11.** warmth or intensity of feeling; vehemence; passion. **12.** maximum intensity in an activity or condition; height: *the heat of battle; the heat of passion.* **13.** tension or strain, as from the pressure of events: *in the heat of a hasty departure.* **14.** *Slang.* **a.** pursuit or investigation by the police. **b.** intensified or coercive pressure: *to put the heat on someone.* **c.** censure; blame; hostile response. **d.** the police. **e.** a firearm; gun. **15.** a single intense effort or operation: *The painting was finished at a heat.* **16. a.** a single course in or division of a race or other contest. **b.** a race or other contest in which competitors attempt to qualify for entry in the final race or contest. **17. a.** a single operation of heating, as of metal in a furnace, in the treating and melting of metals. **b.** a quantity of metal produced by such an operation. **18. a.** sexual receptivity in animals, esp. females. **b.** the period or duration of such receptivity: *to be in heat.* **19.** an indication of high temperature, as by the color or condition of something. —*v.t.* **20.** to make hot or warm (often fol. by *up*). **21.** to excite emotionally; inflame; rouse. —*v.i.* **22.** to become hot or warm (often fol. by *up*). **23.** to become excited emotionally. **24. heat up,** to increase or become more active or intense. —*Proverb.* **25. If you can't stand the heat, get out of the kitchen,** don't stay around if you can't handle stress: a saying popularized by President Harry Truman. —**heat′a·ble,** *adj.* —**heat′less,** *adj.*

heat·ed (hē′tid), *adj.* excited or angry; impassioned; vehement: *a heated argument.* —**heat′ed·ly,** *adv.* —**heat′ed·ness,** *n.*

heat·er (hē′tər), *n.* **1.** an apparatus for heating, esp. one for heating water or the air in a room or other space. **2.** *Slang.* a firearm; gun.

heat′ exchang′er, *n.* a device for transferring the heat of one substance to another, as from the exhaust gases to the incoming air in a furnace.

heat′ exhaus′tion, *n.* a condition brought on by intense or prolonged exposure to heat, characterized by profuse sweating with loss of fluids and salts, pale and damp skin, rapid pulse, nausea, and dizziness, progressing to collapse. Compare HEATSTROKE.

hea·then (hē′thən), *n., pl.* **-thens, -then,** *adj.* —*n.* **1.** an unconverted individual of a people that do not acknowledge the God of the Bible or Koran; pagan. **2.** an irreligious, uncultured, or uncivilized person. —*adj.* **3.** of or pertaining to heathens; pagan. **4.** irreligious, uncultured, or uncivilized. —**hea′then·dom,** *n.* —**hea′then·ism,** *n.* —**hea′then·ize,** *v.t., v.i.,* **-ized, -iz·ing.** —**hea′then·ness,** *n.*

heath·er (heth′ər), *n.* any of various heaths, esp. *Calluna vulgaris,* of England and Scotland, having small pinkish purple flowers. —**heath′ered,** *adj.*

heat′ing pad′, *n.* a flexible fabric-covered pad containing insulated electrical heating elements for applying heat, esp. to the body.

heat′ light′ning, *n.* lightning too distant for thunder to be heard, observed as diffuse flashes near the horizon on summer evenings.

heat·proof (hēt′prŏŏf′), *adj.* resistant to the effects of heat; not readily damaged by heat: *a heatproof countertop.*

heat′ prostra′tion, *n.* HEAT EXHAUSTION.

heat′ pump′, *n.* a device that uses a compressible refrigerant to transfer heat in a reversible process from one body, as the ground, air, or water, to another body, as a building.

heat′ rash′, *n.* PRICKLY HEAT.

heat′ shield′, *n.* an exterior coating or structure that protects a spacecraft from excessive heating during reentry.

heat·stroke (hēt′strōk′), *n.* a disturbance of the temperature-regulating mechanisms of the body caused by overexposure to excessive heat, resulting in headache, fever, hot and dry skin, and rapid pulse, sometimes progressing to delirium and coma. Compare HEAT EXHAUSTION.

heat′ wave′, *n.* **1.** an air mass of high temperature covering an extended area and moving relatively slowly. **2.** a period of abnormally hot weather.

heave (hēv), *v.,* **heaved** or (*esp. Naut.*) **hove; heav·ing;** *n.* —*v.t.* **1.** to raise or lift with effort or force; hoist: *to heave a heavy ax.* **2.** to throw, esp. to lift and throw with effort or force: *to heave a stone through a window.* **3.** *Naut.* to move into a certain position or situation. **4.** to utter laboriously or painfully: *to heave a sigh.* **5.** to cause to rise and fall with a swelling motion: *to heave one's chest.* **6.** to vomit; throw up. **7.** to haul or pull on (a rope, cable, line, etc.). —*v.i.* **8.** to rise and fall in rhythmically alternate movements: *The ship heaved and rolled.* **9.** to breathe with effort; pant. **10.** to vomit; retch. **11.** to rise as if thrust up, as a hill; swell or bulge. **12.** to pull or haul on a rope, cable, etc. **13.** *Naut.* to move in a certain direction or into a certain position or situation: *The ship hove into sight.* **14. heave to, a.** to stop the headway of (a vessel), esp. by bringing the head to the wind and trimming the sails. **b.** to come to a halt. —*n.* **15.** an act or effort of heaving. **16.** a throw, toss, or cast. **17.** the horizontal component of the apparent displacement resulting from a geologic fault, measured in a vertical plane perpendicular to the strike. **18.** the rise and fall of the waves or swell of a sea. **19. heaves,** (*used with a sing. v.*) Also called **broken wind.** a disease of horses, similar to asthma in humans, characterized by difficult breathing. —*Idiom.* **20. heave ho!** (an exclamation used by sailors, as when heaving the anchor up.) —**heav′er,** *n.*

heave′-ho′, *n., pl.* **-hos.** *Informal.* an act of rejection, dismissal, or forcible ejection: *The bartender gave him the old heave-ho.*

heav·en (hev′ən), *n.* **1.** the abode of God, the angels, and the spirits of the righteous after death; the place or state of existence of the blessed after the mortal life. **2.** (*cap.*) Often, **Heavens.** the celestial powers; God. **3.** Often, **heavens.** God (used in expressions of emphasis, surprise, etc.): *For heaven's sake! Good heavens!* **4.** Usu., **heavens.** the sky, firmament, or expanse of space surrounding the earth. **5.** a place or state of supreme happiness. —**heav′en·ly,** *adj.*

Heav′enly Cit′y, *n.* NEW JERUSALEM.

heav′en-sent′, *adj.* providentially opportune.

heav′i·er-than-air′, *adj.* (of an aircraft) weighing more than the air it displaces, hence having to obtain lift by aerodynamic means.

heav·i·ly (hev′ə lē), *adv.* **1.** with a great weight: *heavily loaded.* **2.** ponderously; lumberingly: *to walk heavily.* **3.** oppressively: *Cares weigh heavily upon him.* **4.** severely; intensely: *to suffer heavily.* **5.** densely; thickly: *heavily wooded.* **6.** in large amounts: *to rain heavily.* **7.** without animation or vigor; in a dull manner; sluggishly.

heav·y (hev′ē), *adj.,* **heav·i·er, heav·i·est,** *n., pl.* **heav·ies,** *adv.* —*adj.* **1.** of great weight; hard to lift or carry: *a heavy load.* **2.** of great amount, quantity, or size: *a heavy vote; a heavy snowfall.* **3.** of great force, intensity, or turbulence: *heavy fighting; heavy seas.* **4.** of more than the usual or average weight: *a heavy person.* **5.** of high specific

gravity: *a heavy metal.* **6.** of major import; grave; serious: *a heavy offense.* **7.** deep or intense; profound: *a heavy slumber.* **8. a.** thickly armed or equipped with weapons of large size. **b.** (of guns) of the more powerful sizes: *heavy artillery.* **9.** hard to bear; burdensome; oppressive: *heavy taxes.* **10.** hard to cope with; trying; difficult: *a heavy schedule.* **11.** being as indicated to an unusual degree: *a heavy drinker.* **12.** broad, thick, or coarse: *heavy lines; heavy features.* **13.** weighted or laden: *air heavy with moisture.* **14.** fraught; loaded; charged: *words heavy with meaning.* **15.** depressed with trouble or sorrow; sad: *a heavy heart.* **16.** without vivacity or interest; ponderous; dull: *a heavy style.* **17.** slow or labored in movement or action; clumsy; lumbering: *a heavy walk.* **18.** loud and deep; sonorous: *heavy breathing.* **19.** overcast or cloudy; threatening rain. **20.** thick or dense: *heavy cream.* **21.** insufficiently raised or leavened: *heavy doughnuts.* **22.** (of food) not easily digested. **23.** having a large capacity or output; capable of doing rough work: *a heavy truck.* **24.** producing or refining basic materials, as steel or coal, used in manufacturing: *heavy industry.* **25.** *Informal.* possessing or using in large quantities: *heavy on the makeup.* **26.** sober, serious, or somber: *a heavy role.* **27. a.** of or pertaining to an isotope of greater atomic weight than the common isotope. **b.** of or pertaining to a compound containing such an element. **28.** (of a syllable in verse) **a.** stressed. **b.** long. **29.** *Slang.* **a.** excellent; remarkable. **b.** very serious or important. **c.** distressing or threatening. —*n.* **30. a.** a theatrical character or role that is tragic, unsympathetic, or villainous. **b.** an actor who plays this type of role, esp. the role of a villain. **31.** a gun of great weight or large caliber. **32.** *Slang.* **a.** a very important or influential person. **b.** a person employed to use violence or coercion. —*adv.* **33.** in a heavy manner; heavily. —*Idiom.* **34. heavy with child,** in a state of advanced pregnancy. Also, *of an animal,* **heavy with young.** —**heav′i·ness,** *n.*

heav′y-du′ty, *adj.* **1.** made to withstand great strain or use: *heavy-duty machinery.* **2.** very important, impressive, or serious: *heavy-duty competition.*

heav′y-foot′ed, *adj.* clumsy or ponderous. —**heav′y-foot′ed·ness,** *n.*

heav′y-hand′ed, *adj.* **1.** clumsy; graceless: *heavy-handed criticism.* **2.** oppressive; harsh: *a heavy-handed master.* —**heav′y-hand′ed·ly,** *adv.* —**heav′y-hand′ed·ness,** *n.*

heav′y-heart′ed, *adj.* sorrowful; melancholy; dejected. —**heav′y-heart′ed·ly,** *adv.* —**heav′y-heart′ed·ness,** *n.*

heav′y hit′ter, *n. Informal.* a very important or influential person; big shot.

heav′y met′al, *n.* aggressive, highly amplified, often harsh rock music with a heavy beat. —**heav′y-met′al,** *adj.*

heav·y·set (hev′ē set′), *adj.* **1.** having a large body build. **2.** stocky; stout.

heav′y wa′ter, *n.* water in which hydrogen atoms have been replaced by deuterium, used as a nuclear reactor coolant.

heav·y·weight (hev′ē wāt′), *adj.* **1.** heavy in weight. **2.** of more than average weight or thickness: *a coat of heavyweight material.* **3.** of or pertaining to heavyweights: *a heavyweight bout.* **4.** very powerful, influential, or important: *a team of heavyweight lawyers.* —*n.* **5.** a person of more than average weight. **6.** a boxer or weightlifter of the heaviest competitive class, esp. a professional boxer weighing more than 175 lb. (79.4 kg). **7.** a very powerful, influential, or important person, company, etc.

Heb or **Heb., 1.** Hebrew. **2.** *Bible.* Hebrews.

He·ber (hē′bər), *n.* **Reginald,** 1783–1826, English clergyman and hymn writer.

He·bra·ic (hi brā′ik), *adj.* of, pertaining to, or characteristic of the Hebrews or their culture. —**He·bra′i·cal·ly,** *adv.*

He·brew (hē′brōō), *n.* **1.** a member of any of a group of Semitic peoples who inhabited ancient Palestine and claimed descent from the Biblical patriarchs Abraham, Isaac, and Jacob. **2.** the Semitic language of the ancient Hebrews, retained as the liturgical and scholarly language of Judaism and revived as a vernacular in the 20th century. —*adj.* **3.** of or pertaining to the Hebrews or their language in its ancient or modern forms: *the Hebrew alphabet.*

He·brews (hē′brōōz), *n.* (*used with a sing. v.*) a book of the New Testament.

He′brew Scrip′tures, *n.pl.* BIBLE (def. 2). Also called **He′brew Bi′ble.**

He·bron (hē′brən), *n.* an ancient city of Palestine, formerly in W Jordan; occupied by Israel 1967–97; since 1997 under Palestinian self-rule. Arabic, **El Khalil.**

heck (hek), *n., interj.* (used as a mild expression of annoyance, rejection, disgust, etc., or as an intensive): *What the heck do you care? That was a heck of a good speech.*

heck·le (hek′əl), *v.,* **-led, -ling,** *n.* —*v.t.* **1.** to harass (a public speaker, performer, etc.) with impertinent questions, gibes, or the like. **2.** HACKLE¹ (def. 5). —*n.* **3.** HACKLE¹ (def. 4). —**heck′ler,** *n.*

hec·tare or **hek·tare** (hek′târ), *n.* a unit of surface or land measure equal to 100 ares, or 10,000 square meters (2.471 acres). *Abbr.:* ha

hec·tic (hek′tik), *adj.* **1.** characterized by agitation, excitement, or confused or hurried activity. **2.** of or designating a fevered condition, as in tuberculosis, attended by flushed cheeks, hot skin, and emaciation. **3.** affected with such fever; consumptive. **4.** flushed. —**hec′ti·cal·ly,** *adv.* —**hec′tic·ness,** *n.*

hec·to·gram or **hek·to·gram** (hek′tə gram′), *n.* a unit of mass or weight equal to 100 grams (3.527 ounces avoirdupois). *Abbr.:* hg

hec·to·li·ter or **hek·to·liter** (hek′tə lē′tər), *n.* a unit of capacity equal to 100 liters (2.8378 U.S. bushels or 26.418 U.S. gallons). *Abbr.:* hl

hec·to·me·ter or **hek·to·me·ter** (hek′tə mē′tər), *n.* a unit of length equal to 100 meters (328.08 ft.). *Abbr.:* hm

hec·tor (hek′tər), *v.t.* **1.** to harass or urge by bullying. —*v.i.* **2.** to act in a bullying way. —*n.* **3.** a bully.

Hec·tor (hek′tər), *n.* the eldest son of Priam and greatest Trojan hero in the Trojan War, in the course of which he was killed by Achilles.

he'd (hēd; *unstressed* ēd), **1.** contraction of *he had.* **2.** contraction of *he would.*

he·der (кнä′dər, hā′-) also **cheder,** *n.* (esp. formerly in E Europe) a private Jewish school for teaching young children the fundamentals of Judaism.

hedge (hej), *n., v.,* **hedged, hedg·ing.** —*n.* **1.** a row of bushes or small trees planted close together, esp. when forming a fence or boundary; hedgerow. **2.** any barrier or boundary. **3.** an act or means of hedging: *to buy gold as a hedge against inflation.* **4.** a qualifying or noncommittal statement. —*v.t.* **5.** to enclose with or separate by a hedge. **6.** to surround and confine or obstruct as if with a hedge: *I felt hedged in by the rules.* **7.** to mitigate a possible loss by counterbalancing (one's bets, investments, etc.). **8.** to evade or qualify so as to avoid commitment or allow for contingencies: *to hedge a question.* —*v.i.* **9.** to avoid commitment, esp. by qualifying or evasive statements. **10.** to prevent complete loss of a bet by betting an additional amount against the original bet. **11.** to enter transactions intended to protect against financial loss through a compensatory price movement. —**hedg′er,** *n.* —**hedg′y,** *adj.,* **hedg·i·er, hedg·i·est.**

hedge′ fund′, *n.* an open-end investment company organized as a limited partnership and using high-risk speculative methods to obtain large profits.

hedge·hog (hej′hog′, -hôg′), *n.* **1.** any Old World insectivore of the family Erinaceidae, esp. of the genus *Erinaceus,* having spiny hairs on the back and sides. **2.** the American porcupine.

hedge·hop (hej′hop′), *v.i.,* **-hopped, -hop·ping.** to fly an airplane at a very low altitude, as for spraying crops or for bombing. —**hedge′hop′per,** *n.*

hedge·row (hej′rō′), *n.* a row of bushes or trees forming a hedge.

he·don·ic (hē don′ik), *adj.* **1.** of or characterized by pleasure. **2.** pertaining to hedonism or hedonics. —**he·don′i·cal·ly,** *adv.*

he·don·ics (hē don′iks), *n.* (*used with a sing. v.*) the branch of psychology that deals with pleasurable and unpleasurable states of consciousness.

he·don·ism (hēd′n iz′əm), *n.* **1.** the doctrine that pleasure or happiness is the highest good. **2.** devotion to pleasure and self-gratification as a way of life. —**he′don·ist,** *n., adj.* —**he′don·is′tic,** *adj.* —**he′don·is′ti·cal·ly,** *adv.*

-hedral, a combining form used to form adjectives corresponding to nouns ending in -HEDRON: *polyhedral.*

-hedron, a combining form used in the names of geometrical solid figures having the form or number of faces specified by the initial element: *tetrahedron.*

hee·bie-jee·bies (hē′bē jē′bēz), *n.pl. Informal.* a condition of extreme nervousness; willies; jitters (usu. prec. by *the*).

heed (hēd), *v.t.* **1.** to give careful attention to: *to heed a warning.* —*v.i.* **2.** to give attention; have regard. —*n.* **3.** careful attention; notice (usu. with *give* or *take*). —**heed′er,** *n.* —**heed′ful,** *adj.* —**heed′ful·ly,** *adv.* —**heed′ful·ness,** *n.*

heed·less (hēd′lis), *adj.* careless; thoughtless; unmindful: *heedless of the danger.* —**heed′less·ly,** *adv.* —**heed′less·ness,** *n.*

hee·haw (hē′hô′), *n.* **1.** the braying sound made by a donkey. **2.** rude laughter. —*v.i.* **3.** to bray. **4.** to laugh rudely or raucously.

heel′-and-toe′, *adj.* of or designating a pace, as in race-walking contests, in which the heel of the front foot touches the ground before the toes of the rear one leave it.

heel′ bone′, *n.* CALCANEUS.

heeled (hēld), *adj.* **1.** provided with a heel or heels. **2.** provided with money (usu. used in combination): *well-heeled.* **3.** *Slang.* armed, esp. with a gun.

heft (heft), *n.* **1.** weight; heaviness. **2.** significance; importance. —*v.t.* **3.** to test the weight of by lifting and balancing: *He hefted the spear for a moment and then flung it.* **4.** to heave; hoist. —**heft′er,** *n.*

heft·y (hef′tē), *adj.,* **heft·i·er, heft·i·est.** **1.** heavy; weighty. **2.** big and strong; powerful; muscular. **3.** notably large or substantial: *a hefty increase in salary.* —**heft′i·ly,** *adv.* —**heft′i·ness,** *n.*

He·gel (hā′gəl), *n.* **Georg Wilhelm Friedrich,** 1770–1831, German philosopher.

he·gem·o·ny (hi jem′ə nē, hej′ə mō′nē), *n., pl.* **-nies.** leadership, predominant influence, or domination, esp. as exercised by one nation over others. —**heg·e·mon·ic** (hej′ə mon′ik), *adj.*

He·gi·ra (hi jī′rə, hej′ər ə), *n., pl.* **-ras. 1.** (*sometimes l.c.*) HIJRA. **2.** (*l.c.*) Also, **hejira.** any flight or journey to a more desirable or congenial place.

heh (hā), *n.* HE[2].

Hei·deg·ger (hī′deg ər, -di gər), *n.* **Martin,** 1889–1976, German philosopher.

heif·er (hef′ər), *n.* a young cow over one year old that has not produced a calf.

height (hīt), *n.* **1.** extent or distance upward: *The plane gained height rapidly.* **2.** distance upward from the lowest or a given level to a fixed point. **3.** the distance between the lowest and highest points of a person standing upright; stature. **4.** considerable or great altitude or elevation. **5.** Often, **heights. a.** a high place above a level; hill or mountain. **b.** the highest part; apex; summit: *to reach the heights in one's profession.* **6.** the highest or most intense point; utmost degree; peak: *the height of pleasure; the height of rush hour.*

height·en (hīt′n), *v.t.* **1.** to increase the degree or amount of; augment. **2.** to strengthen, deepen, or intensify: *to heighten one's awareness.* **3.** to increase the height of; make higher. **4.** to bring out the important features of, as in a drawing. —*v.i.* **5.** to increase: *The tension heightened.* **6.** to become brighter or more intense. —**height′en·er,** *n.*

Heim′lich maneu′ver (hīm′lik), *n.* an emergency procedure to aid a person choking on food or some other object by applying sudden pressure with an inward and upward thrust of the fist to the victim's upper abdomen in order to force the obstruction from the windpipe.

hei·nie (hī′nē), *n. Slang.* the buttocks.

hei·nous (hā′nəs), *adj.* utterly reprehensible or evil; odious; abominable: *a heinous offense.* —**hei′nous·ly,** *adv.* —**hei′nous·ness,** *n.*

heir (âr), *n.* **1.** a person who inherits or has a right of inheritance in the property of another following the latter's death. **2. a.** (in common law) a person who inherits all the property of a decedent, as by relationship or legal process. **b.** (in civil law) a person who succeeds to the place of a deceased person and assumes the rights and obligations of the deceased. **3.** a person who inherits or is entitled to inherit the rank, title, or position of another. **4.** a person or group considered as inheriting the tradition, talent, etc., of a predecessor. —**heir′less,** *adj.*

heir′ appar′ent, *n., pl.* **heirs apparent. 1.** an heir whose right is indefeasible, provided he or she survives the ancestor. **2.** a person whose succession to a position appears certain. —**heir′ appar′ency,** *n.*

heir·ess (âr′is), *n.* a woman who inherits or has a right of inheritance, esp. one who inherits great wealth.

heir·loom (âr′lōōm′), *n.* **1.** a family possession handed down from generation to generation. **2.** *Law.* property neither personal nor real that descends to the heir of an estate as part of the real property.

heir′ presump′tive, *n., pl.* **heirs presumptive.** a person who is expected to be the heir but whose expectations may be canceled by the birth of a nearer heir.

Hei·sen·berg (hī′zən bûrg′), *n.* **Werner Karl,** 1901–76, German physicist.

heist (hīst), *Slang.* —*n.* **1.** a robbery or holdup. —*v.t.* **2.** to take unlawfully, esp. in a robbery or holdup; steal. **3.** to rob or hold up. —**heist′er,** *n.*

he·ji·ra (hi jī′rə, hej′ər ə), *n., pl.* **-ras.** HEGIRA (def. 2).

held (held), *v.* pt. and pp. of HOLD[1].

hel·den·ten·or (hel′dn ten′ər; *Ger.* hel′dn tä nōr′), *n., pl.* **-ten·ors,** *Ger.* **-te·no·re** (-tā nō′rə). a tenor having a powerful voice suited to singing heroic roles, as in Wagnerian opera.

He′ Lead′eth Me′, a Christian hymn (1862) with words by Joseph Gilmore.

Hel·en (hel′ən), *n.* the beautiful daughter of Zeus and Leda and wife of Menelaus, whose abduction by Paris was the cause of the Trojan War. Also called **Hel′en of Troy′.**

Hel·e·na (hel′ə nə), *n.* the capital of Montana, in the W part. 23,938.

heli-, a combining form representing HELICOPTER: *helilift; heliport.*

he·li·a·cal (hi lī′ə kəl), *adj.* pertaining to or occurring near the sun, esp. applied to such risings and settings of a star as most nearly coincide with sunrise or sunset. —**he·li·a·cal·ly,** *adv.*

hel·i·borne (hel′ə bôrn′, -bōrn′), *adj.* transported by helicopter: *heliborne troops.*

hel·i·cal (hel′i kəl, hē′li-), *adj.* pertaining to or having the form of a helix; spiral. —**hel′i·cal·ly,** *adv.*

hel′ical gear′, *n.* a cylindrical gear wheel whose teeth follow the pitch surface in a helical manner.

hel·i·ces (hel′ə sēz′), *n.* a pl. of HELIX.

hel·i·coid (hel′i koid′, hē′li-), *adj.* **1.** coiled or curving like a spiral. —*n.* **2.** a warped geometric surface generated by a straight line moving so as to cut or touch a fixed helix. —**hel′i·coi′dal,** *adj.* —**hel′i·coi′dal·ly,** *adv.*

hel·i·con (hel′i kon′, -kən), *n.* a coiled tuba carried over the shoulder and used esp. in military bands.

hel·i·cop·ter (hel′i kop′tər, hē′li-), *n.* **1.** any of a class of heavier-than-air craft that are lifted and sustained in the air horizontally by rotating wings or blades turning on vertical axes through power supplied by an engine. —*v.i., v.t.* **2.** to fly or convey in a helicopter. [< French *hélicoptère* < Greek *hélix* spiral + *ptrrón* wing]

he·li·o·cen·tric (hē′lē ō sen′trik), *adj.* **1.** measured or considered as being seen from the center of the sun. **2.** having or representing the sun as a center: *a heliocentric concept of the universe.* —**he′li·o·cen′tri·cal·ly,** *adv.* —**he′li·o·cen·tric′i·ty** (-tris′i tē), **he′li·o·cen′tri·cism** (-trə siz′əm), *n.*

he·li·o·graph (hē′lē ə graf′, -gräf′), *n.* **1.** a device for signaling or sending messages by means of a movable mirror that reflects beams of light, esp. sunlight, over a distance. **2.** an instrument for photographing the sun, consisting of a camera and specially adapted telescope. —*v.t., v.i.* **3.** to communicate by heliograph. —**he·li·og′ra·pher** (-og′rə fər), *n.* —**he′li·o·graph′ic** (-graf′ik), *adj.* —**he′li·og′ra·phi·cal·ly**, *adv.* —**he′li·og′ra·phy**, *n.*

he·li·om·e·ter (hē′lē om′i tər), *n.* a telescope with a divided, adjustable objective, formerly used to measure small angular distances, as those between celestial bodies. —**he′li·o·met′ric** (-ə me′trik), **he′li·o·met′ri·cal**, *adj.* —**he′li·o·met′ri·cal·ly**, *adv.*

He·li·op·o·lis (hē′lē op′ə lis), *n.* **1.** Biblical name, **On.** an ancient ruined city in N Egypt, on the Nile delta. **2.** ancient Greek name of BAALBEK.

he·li·o·sphere (hē′lē ə sfēr′), *n.* the region around the sun over which the effect of the solar wind extends.

he·li·o·stat (hē′lē ə stat′), *n.* an instrument consisting of a mirror moved by clockwork, for reflecting the sun's rays in a fixed direction. —**he′li·o·stat′ic**, *adj.*

he·li·o·tax·is (hē′lē ō tak′sis), *n.* movement of an organism toward or away from sunlight. —**he′li·o·tac′tic** (-tik), *adj.*

he·li·o·ther·a·py (hē′lē ō ther′ə pē), *n.* treatment of disease by means of sunlight.

he·li·o·trope (hē′lē ə trōp′, hēl′yə-; *esp. Brit.* hel′yə-), *n.* any of numerous hairy plants of the genus *Heliotropium,* of the borage family, esp. *H. arborescens,* cultivated for its small, fragrant purple flowers.

hel·i·pad (hel′ə pad′, hēl′ə-), *n.* a takeoff and landing area for helicopters, usu. without commercial facilities.

hel·i·port (hel′ə pôrt′, -pōrt′, hēl′ə-), *n.* a takeoff and landing place for helicopters, often on the roof of a building.

hel·i·ski·ing (hel′ē skē′ing), *n.* skiing on remote mountains to which the participants are brought by helicopter.

he·li·um (hē′lē əm), *n.* an inert, gaseous element present in the sun's atmosphere and in natural gas, used as a substitute for flammable gases in dirigibles. *Symbol:* He; *at. wt.:* 4.0026; *at. no.:* 2; *density:* 0.1785 g/l at 0°C and 760 mm pressure. [< New Latin < Greek *hēli(os)* the sun]

He′ Lives,′ a Christian hymn (1933) with words and music by Alfred Ackley.

he·lix (hē′liks), *n., pl.* **hel·i·ces** (hel′ə sēz′), **he·lix·es. 1.** a spiral. **2.** the curve formed by a straight line drawn on a plane when that plane is wrapped around a cylindrical surface of any kind, esp. a right circular cylinder, as the curve of a screw. **3.** a spiral, scroll-like architectural ornament, as a volute on a Corinthian capital. **4.** the curved fold forming most of the rim of the external ear.

hell (hel), *n.* **1.** the place or state of punishment of the wicked after death; the abode of evil and condemned spirits. **2.** any place or state of torment or misery: *to make someone's life hell.* **3.** something that causes torment or misery. **4.** the powers of evil. **5.** the abode of the dead; Sheol or Hades. **6.** a box into which a printer throws discarded type. —*Idiom.* **7.** till hell freezes over, an impossibly long time; forever.

he′ll (hēl; *unstressed* ēl, hil, il), contraction of *he will.*

hell·bend·er (hel′ben′dər), *n.* a large, broad-headed salamander, *Cryptobranchus alleganiensis,* of rivers and streams in E North America.

hel·le·bore (hel′ə bôr′, -bōr′), *n.* **1.** any poisonous plant of the genus *Helleborus,* of the buttercup family, having basal leaves and clusters of flowers. **2.** any poisonous plant of the genus *Veratrum,* of the lily family. **3.** any of the poisonous or medicinal substances obtained from these plants.

Hel·len·ic (he len′ik, -lē′nik), *adj.* **1.** of or pertaining to the ancient Greeks or their language, culture, thought, etc., esp. from the 8th century B.C. to the death of Alexander the Great (323 B.C.). **2.** GREEK (def. 1). —*n.* **3.** GREEK (def. 3). —**Hel·len′i·cal·ly**, *adv.*

Hel·len·is·tic (hel′ə nis′tik), *adj.* **1.** of or pertaining to Greek civilization of the Mediterranean region and SW Asia from the death of Alexander the Great through the 1st century B.C., characterized by the blending of Greek and foreign cultures. **2.** of or pertaining to Hellenists. **3.** following or resembling Greek usage. —**Hel′len·is′ti·cal·ly**, *adv.*

Hel·les·pont (hel′ə spont′), *n.* ancient name of the DARDANELLES. —**Hel′les·pont′ine** (-spon′tin, -tīn), *adj.*

hell·fire (hel′fīr′), *n.* **1.** the fire of hell. **2.** punishment in hell.

hell·gram·mite (hel′grə mīt′), *n.* the aquatic larva of a dobsonfly, used as bait in fishing.

hel·lion (hel′yən), *n.* a disorderly, troublesome, rowdy, or mischievous person.

Hell·man (hel′mən), *n.* **Lillian Florence,** 1905–84, U.S. playwright.

hel·lo (he lō′, hə-, hel′ō), *interj., n., pl.* **-los. 1.** (used to express a greeting, answer a telephone, or attract attention.) **2.** (used as an exclamation of surprise, wonder, etc.) —*n.* **3.** an act or instance of saying "hello"; greeting. —*v.i.* **4.** to say or shout "hello."

helm (helm), *n.* **1. a.** a wheel or tiller by which a ship is steered. **b.** the entire steering apparatus of a ship. **2.** the place or post of control: *A stern taskmaster was at the helm of the company.* —*v.t.* **3.** to steer; direct. —**helm′less**, *adj.*

hel·met (hel′mit), *n.* **1.** any of various forms of protective, usu. rigid head covering worn by soldiers, firefighters, football players, cyclists, etc. **2.** a piece of medieval armor for the head; helm. **3.** anything resembling a helmet in form or position.

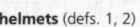

helmets (defs. 1, 2)

medieval   modern

hel′met shell′, *n.* **1.** a predatory marine gastropod of the family Cassidae, characterized by a thick heavy shell with a broadened outer lip. **2.** the shell of this animal, used for making cameos.

hel·minth (hel′minth), *n.* a worm, esp. a parasitic worm.

hel·min·thol·o·gy (hel′min thol′ə jē), *n.* the study of worms, esp. of parasitic worms. —**hel′min·thol′o·gist**, *n.*

helms·man (helmz′mən), *n., pl.* **-men.** a person who steers a ship. —**helms′man·ship′**, *n.*

hel·ot (hel′ət, hē′lət), *n.* a serf or slave.

help (help), *v.t.* **1.** to provide what is necessary to accomplish a task or satisfy a need; contribute strength, means, or effort; aid; assist: *He said he'd help me with my work. Let me help you with those packages.* **2.** to save; rescue; succor: *Help me, I'm falling!* **3.** to contribute to; facilitate or promote: *to help desegregation.* **4.** to be useful or profitable to: *Your knowledge of languages will help you in your career.* **5.** to refrain from; avoid (usu. prec. by *can* or *cannot*): *I can't help teasing him about it.* **6.** to prevent or stop (usu. prec. by *can* or *cannot*): *The disagreement could not be helped.* **7.** to make less unpleasant or monotonous; improve: *A new rug might help the room.* **8.** to relieve (someone) in need, sickness, pain, or distress: *to help the poor.* **9.** to alleviate; remedy: *Nothing seems to help my headache.* **10.** to serve food or drink to: *Help her to salad.* **11.** to serve or wait on (a customer), as in a store. —*v.i.* **12.** to give aid; be of service or advantage: *Every little bit helps.* **13. help out,** to assist, as during a time of need. —*n.* **14.** the act of helping; aid or assistance; relief or succor. **15.** a person or thing that helps: *You were a tremendous help after the fire.* **16.** a hired helper; employee. **17.** a body of such helpers. **18.** a domestic servant or a farm laborer. **19.** means of remedying, stopping, or preventing: *There is no help for it now.* **20.** *Older Use.* HELPING. —*interj.* **21.** (used as an exclamation to call for assistance or to attract attention.) —*Idiom.* **22. cannot** or **can't help but,** to be unable to refrain from or avoid; be obliged to: *Still, you can't help but admire her.* **23. help oneself to, a.** to serve oneself with: *Help yourself to the cake.* **b.** to take or use without asking permission; appropriate. **24. so help me (God),** I am speaking the truth; on my honor. —*Proverb.* **25. God helps those who help themselves,** one must make every effort to accomplish things on one's own. —**help′er**, *n.* —**help′ful**, *adj.* —**help′ful·ly**, *adv.* —**help′ful·ness**, *n.*

helper T cell, *n.* any of a group of T cells that activate the immune system either by enhancing the production of antibodies and other T cells or by mobilizing macrophages to engulf invading particles.

help·ing (hel′ping), *n.* a portion of food served to a person at one time.

help′ing verb′, *n.* AUXILIARY VERB.

help·less (help′lis), *adj.* **1.** unable to help oneself; weak or dependent. **2.** without aid or protection. **3.** deprived of strength or power; powerless; incapacitated: *helpless with laughter.* **4.** affording no help. —**help′less·ly**, *adv.* —**help′less·ness**, *n.*

help·mate (help′māt′), *n.* **1.** a companion and helper. **2.** a wife or husband.

Hel·sin·ki (hel′sing kē, hel sing′-), *n.* the capital of Finland, on the S coast. 490,034. Swedish, **Hel·sing·fors** (hel′sing fôrz′).

hel·ter-skel·ter (hel′tər skel′tər), *adv.* **1.** in headlong and disorderly haste: *running helter-skelter all over the house.* **2.** in a haphazard manner; without regard for order: *clothes scattered helter-skelter about the room.* —*adj.* **3.** carelessly hurried; confused. **4.** disorderly; haphazard. —*n.* **5.** tumultuous disorder; confusion.

helve (helv), *n., v.,* **helved, helv·ing.** —*n.* **1.** the handle of an ax, hatchet, hammer, or the like. —*v.t.* **2.** to furnish with a helve.

Hel·wys (hel′wis), *n.* **Thomas,** 1550–1616, English religious leader, founder of the first English Baptist church.

hem¹ (hem), *v.,* **hemmed, hem·ming,** *n.* —*v.t.* **1.** to fold back and sew down the edge of (cloth, a garment, etc.); form an edge or border on or around. **2.** to enclose or confine (usu. fol. by *in, around,* or *about*): *hemmed in by enemies.* —*n.* **3.** an edge made by folding back the margin of cloth and sewing it down. **4.** the bottom edge or border of a garment, drape, etc. —**hem′mer**, *n.*

hem² (hem), *interj., n., v.,* **hemmed, hem·ming.** —*interj.* **1.** (an utterance resembling a slight clearing of the throat, used esp. to attract attention or express doubt or hesitation.) —*n.* **2.** the utterance or sound of "hem." —*v.i.* **3.** to utter the sound "hem." **4.** to hesitate in speaking. —*Idiom.* **5. hem and haw, a.** to hesitate or falter while speaking. **b.** to avoid giving a direct answer.

he′-man′, *n., pl.* **-men.** *Informal.* a strong, tough, virile man.

he·mat·ic (hi mat′ik), *adj.* **1.** of or pertaining to blood; hemic. **2.** acting on the blood, as a medicine.

he•ma•tite (hē′mə tīt′), *n.* a mineral, ferric oxide, Fe_2O_3, occurring in brilliant black crystals and in earthy masses: the principal ore of iron. —**he′ma•tit′ic** (-tit′ik), *adj.*

he•ma•tog•e•nous (hē′mə toj′ə nəs), *adj.* **1.** originating in the blood. **2.** blood-producing. **3.** distributed or spread by way of the bloodstream, as in metastases of tumors or in infections; blood-borne.

he•ma•tol•o•gy (hē′mə tol′ə jē), *n.* the study of the nature, function, and diseases of the blood and of blood-forming organs. —**he′ma•to•log′ic** (-tl oj′ik), **he′ma•to•log′i•cal,** *adj.* —**he′ma•tol′o•gist,** *n.*

he•ma•to•ma (hē′mə tō′mə), *n., pl.* **-mas, -ma•ta** (-mə tə). a circumscribed collection of blood, usu. clotted, in a tissue or organ, caused by a break in a blood vessel.

Hem•ing•way (hem′ing wā′), *n.* **Ernest (Miller),** 1899–1961, U.S. novelist, short-story writer, and journalist.

hem•i•ple•gi•a (hem′i plē′jē ə, -jə), *n.* paralysis of one side of the body. —**hem′i•ple′gic,** *adj., n.*

he•mip•ter•an (hi mip′tər ən), *adj.* **1.** HEMIPTEROUS. —*n.* **2.** Also, **he•mip′ter•on′.** a true bug; hemipterous insect.

he•mip•ter•ous (hi mip′tər əs), *adj.* **1.** belonging or pertaining to the Hemiptera, an order of insects having forewings that are thickened and leathery at the base and membranous at the apex, comprising the true bugs. **2.** belonging or pertaining to the order Hemiptera, in some classifications comprising the heteropterous and homopterous insects.

hem•i•sphere (hem′i sfēr′), *n.* **1.** (*often cap.*) half of the terrestrial globe or celestial sphere, esp. one of the halves into which the earth is divided. Compare EASTERN HEMISPHERE, WESTERN HEMISPHERE, NORTHERN HEMISPHERE, SOUTHERN HEMISPHERE. **2.** a map or projection representing one of these halves. **3.** a half of a sphere. **4.** either of the lateral halves of the cerebrum. **5.** the area within which something occurs or dominates; sphere; realm.

hem•i•stich (hem′i stik′), *n.* **1.** half of a line of verse, esp. as divided by a caesura. **2.** an incomplete line of verse, or a line of less than the usual length. —**he•mis•ti•chal** (hə mis′ti kəl, hem′i stik′əl), *adj.*

hem•line (hem′līn′), *n.* the bottom edge of a coat, skirt, etc., esp. as expressed in inches from the floor.

hem•lock (hem′lok′), *n.* **1.** a poisonous plant, *Conium maculatum,* of the parsley family, having finely divided leaves and umbels of small white flowers. **2.** a poisonous drink made from this plant. **3.** any of various related plants, esp. of the genus *Cicuta,* as the water hemlock. **4.** Also called **hem′lock spruce′.** any of several tall coniferous trees of the genus *Tsuga,* of the pine family, having short, blunt needles and small cones. **5.** the soft, light wood of a hemlock tree, used in making paper and in construction.

he•mo•glo•bin (hē′mə glō′bin, hem′ə-), *n.* a conjugated protein in red blood cells that transports oxygen from the lungs to the tissues of the body. —**he′mo•glo′bic, he′mo•glo′bin•ous,** *adj.*

he•mo•phil•i•a (hē′mə fil′ē ə), *n.* any of several X-linked genetic disorders, symptomatic chiefly in males, in which excessive bleeding occurs from minor injuries owing to the absence or abnormality of a clotting factor in the blood. —**he′mo•phil′i•ac,** *n.*

he•mo•phil•ic (hē′mə fil′ik), *adj.* **1.** characteristic of or affected by hemophilia. **2.** (of bacteria) developing best in a culture containing blood, or in blood itself.

he•mop•ty•sis (hi mop′tə sis), *n.* the expectoration of blood or bloody mucus.

hem•or•rhage (hem′ər ij, hem′rij), *n., v.,* **-rhaged, -rhag•ing.** —*n.* **1.** a profuse discharge of blood. **2.** the loss of assets, esp. in large amounts. —*v.i.* **3.** to bleed profusely. **4.** to lose assets, esp. in large amounts. —*v.t.* **5.** to lose (assets): *The company was hemorrhaging cash.* —**hem′or•rhag′ic** (-ə raj′ik), *adj.*

hem•or•rhoid (hem′ə roid′, hem′roid), *n.* Usu., **hemorrhoids.** a varicose vein in the region of the anal sphincter, sometimes painful and bleeding. Also called **pile.** —**hem′or•rhoi′dal,** *adj.*

he•mo•sta•sis (hē′mə stā′sis) also **he•mo•sta•sia** (-stā′zhə, -zhē ə), *n.* **1.** the stoppage of bleeding. **2.** the stoppage of the circulation of blood in a part of the body. **3.** stagnation of blood in a part.

he•mo•stat (hē′mə stat′), *n.* an instrument or agent used to compress or treat bleeding vessels in order to arrest hemorrhage.

hemp (hemp), *n.* **1.** Also called **Indian hemp, marijuana.** a tall, coarse Asian plant, *Cannabis sativa,* of the family Cannabaceae, widely cultivated for its fiber and for its yield of intoxicating drugs. **2.** the tough fiber of this plant, used for making rope, coarse fabric, etc. **3.** any of various plants resembling hemp. **4.** any of various fibers similar to hemp. **5.** an intoxicating drug, as marijuana or hashish, prepared from the hemp plant.

hem•stitch (hem′stich′), *v.t.* **1.** to sew along a border from which threads have been drawn out, stitching the cross threads into little groups and usu. hemming the border as well. —*n.* **2.** the stitch used or the needlework done in hemstitching. —**hem′stitch′er,** *n.*

Hem•y (hem′ē), *n.* **Henri,** 1818–88, English musician and hymn writer.

hen (hen), *n.* **1.** the female of the domestic fowl. **2.** the female of any bird, esp. of a gallinaceous bird. **3.** the female of various crustaceans, as the lobster.

hen′-and-chick′ens, *n., pl.* **hens-and-chickens.** any of several succulent plants of the stonecrop family, esp. of the genus *Sempervivum,* that grow in clusters formed by runners or offshoots.

hen•bane (hen′bān′), *n.* an Old World plant, *Hyoscyamus niger,* of the

nightshade family, that has hairy foliage and greenish yellow flowers and possesses narcotic and poisonous properties.

hen•bit (hen′bit′), *n.* a weed, *Lamium amplexicaule,* of the mint family, having rounded leaves and small purplish flowers.

hence (hens), *adv.* **1.** as an inference from this fact; for this reason; therefore. **2.** from this time; from now: *a month hence.* **3.** from this source or origin.

hence•forth (hens′fôrth′, -fōrth′; hens′fôrth′, -fōrth′) also **hence•for•ward** (-fôr′wərd, -fōr′-), *adv.* from now on; from this point forward.

hench•man (hench′mən), *n., pl.* **-men. 1.** an unscrupulous and ruthless subordinate, esp. a member of a criminal gang. **2.** a political supporter or adherent, esp. one motivated by the hope of personal gain. **3.** a trusted attendant, supporter, or follower. —**hench′man•ship′,** *n.*

Hen•der•son (hen′dər sən), *n.* a city in SE Nevada, near Las Vegas. 101,997.

Hen•dricks (hen′driks), *n.* **Thomas Andrews,** 1819–85, vice president of the U.S. 1885.

henge (henj), *n.* a Neolithic monument of the British Isles, consisting of a circular area enclosed by a bank and ditch and often containing one or more circles of upright stone or wood pillars: probably used for ritual or astronomical purposes.

hen•na (hen′ə), *n., pl.* **-nas,** *v.* —*n.* **1.** an Asian shrub or small tree, *Lawsonia inermis,* of the loosestrife family, having elliptic leaves and fragrant flowers. **2.** a reddish orange dye made from the leaves of this plant, used esp. in coloring the hair. **3.** a color between red-brown and orange-brown. —*v.t.* **4.** to tint or dye with henna.

hen•ner•y (hen′ə rē), *n., pl.* **-ner•ies.** a place where poultry is kept or raised.

hen′ of the woods′ or **hen′-of-the-woods′,** *n.* a large grayish brown edible fungus, *Polyporus frondosus,* forming a mass of overlapping caps at the base of trees and somewhat resembling a hen.

hen•peck (hen′pek′), *v.t.* to nag, scold, or regularly find fault with (one's husband).

Hen•ry¹ (hen′rē), *n.* **1. Carl,** born 1913, U.S. clergyman and theologian. **2. Joseph,** 1797–1878, U.S. physicist. **3. O.,** pen name of William Sidney PORTER. **4. Patrick,** 1736–99, American patriot and orator. **5. Cape,** a cape in SE Virginia at the mouth of the Chesapeake Bay.

Hen•ry² (hen′rē), *n.* **1. Henry I, a.** 1068–1135, king of England 1100–35 (son of William the Conqueror). **b.** 1008–60, king of France 1031–60. **2. Henry II, a.** 1133–89, king of England 1154–89: first king of the Plantagenets. **b.** 1519–59, king of France 1547–59. **3. Henry III, a.** 1207–72, king of England 1216–72 (son of John). **b.** 1551–89, king of France 1574–89 (son of Henry II). **4. Henry IV, a.** (*Bolingbroke*) (*"Henry of Lancaster"*) 1367–1413, king of England 1399–1413 (son of John of Gaunt). **b.** (*"Henry of Navarre"*) 1553–1610, king of France 1589–1610: first of the Bourbon kings. **5. Henry V,** 1387–1422, king of England 1413–22 (son of Henry IV of Bolingbroke). **6. Henry VI,** 1421–71, king of England 1422–61, 1470–71 (son of Henry V). **7. Henry VII,** (*Henry Tudor*) 1457–1509, king of England 1485–1509: first king of the house of Tudor. **8. Henry VIII,** (*"Defender of the Faith"*) 1491–1547, king of England 1509–47 (son of Henry VII).

hen′ track′, *n. Slang.* Usu., **hen tracks.** an illegible or barely legible bit of handwriting. Also called **hen′ scratch′.**

hep¹ (hep), *adj. Older Slang.* HIP⁴.

hep² (hut, hup, hep), *interj.* one (used in counting cadence while marching).

he•pat•ic (hi pat′ik), *adj.* **1.** of, pertaining to, or acting on the liver. **2.** liver-colored; dark reddish brown. **3.** belonging or pertaining to the liverworts. —*n.* **4.** a liverwort.

he•pat•i•ca (hi pat′i kə), *n., pl.* **-cas.** any plant of the genus *Hepatica,* of the buttercup family, having heart-shaped leaves and delicate purplish or white flowers.

hep•a•ti•tis (hep′ə tī′tis), *n.* inflammation of the liver, caused by a virus or a toxin and characterized by jaundice, liver enlargement, and fever.

hepatitis A, *n.* a normally minor form of hepatitis caused by an RNA virus that does not persist in the blood: usu. transmitted by ingestion of contaminated food or water. Also called **infectious hepatitis.**

hepatitis B, *n.* a form of hepatitis caused by a DNA virus (**hepatitis B virus**) that persists in the blood and has a long incubation period: usu. transmitted by sexual contact or by injection or ingestion of infected blood or other bodily fluids.

hepatitis C, *n.* a form of hepatitis with clinical effects similar to those of hepatitis B, caused by a blood-borne retrovirus (**hepatitis C virus**) that may be of the hepatitis non-A, non-B type.

hepatitis non-A, non-B, *n.* a disease of the liver that is clinically indistinguishable from hepatitis B but is caused by a retrovirus or retroviruslike agent.

hep•a•to•cyte (hep′ə tə sīt′, hi pat′ə-), *n.* a cell of the main tissue of the liver; liver cell.

hep•cat (hep′kat′), *n. Older Slang.* **1.** a performer or admirer of jazz, esp. swing. **2.** HIPSTER¹ (def. 1).

He•phaes•tus (hi fes′təs), *n.* the ancient Greek god of fire, metalworking, and handicrafts, identified by the Romans with Vulcan.

Heph•zi•bah (hef′zə bə, -sə-), *n.* **1.** the wife of Hezekiah and the mother of Manasseh. II Kings 21:1. **2.** a name applied to Jerusalem,

H

possibly as denoting its prophesied restoration to the Jews after the Babylonian captivity. Is. 62:4.

hep·ta-, a combining form meaning "seven": *heptamerous.* Also, *esp. before a vowel,* **hept-.** [< Greek]

hep·ta·gon (hep′tə gon′), *n.* a polygon having seven angles and seven sides. **—hep·tag′o·nal** (-tag′ə nl), *adj.*

hep·tam·e·ter (hep tam′i tər), *n.* a verse of seven metrical feet. **—hep′ta·met′ri·cal** (-tə me′tri kəl), *adj.*

Hep·ta·teuch (hep′tə tōōk′, -tyōōk′), *n.* the first seven books of the Old Testament. [< Late Latin *Heptateuchos* < Late Greek *Heptáteuchos* the first seven books of the Old Testament = Greek *hepta-* HEPTA- + *teûchos* a book]

hep·tath·lon (hep tath′lən, -lon), *n.* an athletic contest for women comprising seven different track-and-field events and won by the contestant amassing the highest total score.

her (hûr; *unstressed* hər, ər), *pron.* **1.** the objective case of SHE, used as a direct or indirect object: *We saw her this morning. I gave her the message.* **2.** a form of the possessive case of SHE used as an attributive adjective: *Her coat is on the chair. I'm sorry about her leaving.* Compare HERS. **3.** (used instead of the pronoun *she* in the predicate after the verb *to be*): *It's her.* **—n. 4.** *Informal.* a female: *Is the new baby a her or a him?*

He·ra (hēr′ə, her′ə), *n.* an ancient Greek goddess, the wife and sister of Zeus: identified by the Romans with Juno.

Her·a·cli·tus (her′ə klī′təs), *n.* ("*the Obscure*") c540–c470 B.C., Greek philosopher. **—Her′a·cli′te·an** (-tē ən), *adj.*

her·ald (her′əld), *n.* **1.** a royal or official messenger, esp. one representing a monarch in an ambassadorial capacity during wartime. **2.** a person or thing that precedes or comes before; forerunner; harbinger: *the swallows, heralds of spring.* **3.** a person or thing that proclaims or announces. **4.** (in the Middle Ages) an officer who arranged tournaments and other functions, announced challenges, marshaled combatants, etc. **5.** an officer of a body concerned with armorial bearings, genealogies, etc., esp. an officer intermediate in rank between a king-of-arms and a pursuivant. **—v.t. 6.** to give tidings of; announce; proclaim; publicize. **7.** to signal the coming of; usher in.

he·ral·dic (he ral′dik, hə-), *adj.* of or pertaining to heralds or heraldry.

her·ald·ry (her′əl drē), *n., pl.* **-ries. 1.** the study of armorial bearings. **2.** the practice of blazoning and granting armorial bearings, tracing and recording genealogies, recording honors, and deciding precedence. **3.** a heraldic device or devices. **4.** ceremonial splendor; pageantry. **—her′ald·ist,** *n.*

herb (ûrb; *esp. Brit.* hûrb), *n.* **1.** a flowering plant whose stem above ground does not become woody and persistent. **2.** such a plant valued for its medicinal properties, flavor, or scent. **3.** Often, **the herb.** *Slang.* MARIJUANA. **—herb′al, herb′like′,** *adj.*

her·ba·ceous (hûr bā′shəs, ûr-), *adj.* **1. a.** (of a plant or plant part) not woody. **b.** having the texture, color, etc., of an ordinary foliage leaf. **2.** of or characteristic of an herb.

herb·age (ûr′bij, hûr′-), *n.* **1.** nonwoody vegetation. **2.** the succulent leaves and stems of herbaceous plants, esp. when used for grazing. **—herb′aged,** *adj.*

herb·al (ûr′bəl, hûr′-), *adj.* **1.** of, pertaining to, or consisting of herbs. **—n. 2.** a book about herbs or plants, usu. describing their medicinal properties. **3.** a herbarium.

herb·al·ist (hûr′bə list, ûr′-), *n.* **1.** a person who collects or deals in herbs, esp. medicinal herbs. **2.** HERB DOCTOR. **3.** an author of an herbal. **4.** (formerly) a botanist.

herb′al (or **herb′**) **tea′,** *n.* a tea made from dried herbs or spices and usu. containing no caffeine.

her·bar·i·um (hûr bâr′ē əm, ûr-), *n., pl.* **-bar·i·ums, -bar·i·a** (-bâr′ē ə). **1.** a collection of dried plants systematically arranged. **2.** a room or building in which such a collection is kept. **—her·bar′i·al,** *adj.*

herb′ doc′tor, *n.* a person who practices healing by the use of herbs; herbalist.

Her·bert (hûr′bərt), *n.* **1. George,** 1593–1633, English cleric and poet. **2. Matthew,** 1662–1714, English clergyman and Bible commentator. **3. Victor,** 1859–1924, U.S. composer, born in Ireland.

herb·i·cide (hûr′bə sīd′, ûr′-), *n.* a substance or preparation for killing plants, esp. weeds. **—her′bi·cid′al,** *adj.*

her·bi·vore (hûr′bə vôr′, -vōr′), *n.* a herbivorous animal.

her·biv·o·rous (hûr biv′ər əs, ûr-), *adj.* feeding on plants. **—her·biv′o·rous·ly,** *adv.*

herb′ Par′is, *n., pl.* **herbs Paris.** a European plant, *Paris quadrifolia,* of the lily family, formerly used in medicine.

herb′ Rob′ert, *n., pl.* **herbs Robert.** a wild geranium, *Geranium robertianum,* having fernlike, scented leaves and reddish purple flowers.

herb′ tea′, *n.* HERBAL TEA.

her·cu·le·an (hûr′kyə lē′ən, hûr kyōō′lē-), *adj.* **1.** requiring extraordinary strength or exertion: *a herculean task.* **2.** of enormous strength, courage, or size. **3.** (*cap.*) of or pertaining to Hercules.

Her·cu·les (hûr′kyə lēz′), *n., gen.* **-cu·lis** (-kyə lis) for 2. **1.** a hero of classical myth, the son of Zeus and Alcmene, who possessed exceptional strength and was renowned esp. for the 12 labors he performed to gain immortality. **2.** a northern constellation, between Lyra and Corona Borealis.

Her′cules-club′, *n.* **1.** a prickly tree, *Zanthoxylum clava-herculis,* of

the rue family, having a medicinal bark and berries. **2.** Also called **angelica tree, devil's-walking-stick.** a prickly shrub, *Aralia spinosa,* of the ginseng family, having a medicinal bark and root.

herd (hûrd), *n.* **1.** a number of animals feeding, traveling, or kept together; drove; flock: *a herd of zebras; a herd of sheep; a herd of cattle.* **2.** *Sometimes Disparaging.* a large group of people; crowd; mob: *a herd of autograph seekers.* **3. the herd,** the common people; masses: *to follow the herd.* **—v.i. 4.** to unite or move in a herd; assemble or associate as a herd. **—v.t. 5.** to gather into or as if into a herd. **—Idiom. 6. ride herd on,** to maintain control or discipline over. **—herd′er,** *n.*

herds·man (hûrdz′mən), *n., pl.* **-men. 1.** the keeper of a herd, esp. of cattle or sheep; herder. **2.** (*cap.*) the constellation Boötes.

here (hēr), *adv.* **1.** in or at this place (opposed to *there*): *Put the pen here.* **2.** to or toward this place; hither: *Come here.* **3.** at this point in an action, speech, etc.: *Here the speaker paused.* **4.** (used to call attention to some person or thing present, or to what the speaker has, offers, or discovers): *Here is your paycheck. Here she is!* **5.** present (used to answer a roll call). **6.** in the present life or existence: *We want but little here below.* **7.** in this instance or case; under consideration: *The matter here is of grave concern.* **—n. 8.** this place or point: *It's a long way from here.* **9.** this world; this life; the present. **—adj. 10.** (used for emphasis, esp. after a noun modified by a demonstrative adjective): *this package here.* **—interj. 11.** (used to command attention, give comfort, etc.) **—Idiom. 12. here and now,** without delay; immediately. **13. here and there,** in or to this place and that; in or to various places. **14. here goes,** (used to express resolution when beginning a bold or unpleasant action.) **15. here's to,** (used in offering a toast to someone or something.) **16. neither here nor there,** without relevance or importance; immaterial. **17. the here and now,** the immediate present. **—Usage.** See THERE.

here·af·ter (hēr af′tər, -äf′-), *adv.* **1.** after this in time or order; in the future; from now on. **2.** in the life or world to come. **3.** HEREINAFTER. **—n. 4.** a life or existence after death; the future beyond mortal existence. **5.** time to come; the future.

here·by (hēr bī′, hēr′bī′), *adv.* by this declaration, action, document, etc.; by means of this: *I hereby resign.*

her·ed·i·ta·ble (hə red′i tə bəl), *adj.* heritable.

her·ed·i·tar·y (hə red′i ter′ē), *adj.* **1.** passing, or capable of passing, naturally from parent to offspring through the genes. **2.** of or pertaining to inheritance or heredity. **3.** existing by reason of feelings or opinions held by predecessors; ancestral: *a hereditary enemy.* **4.** *Law.* **a.** descending by inheritance. **b.** transmitted or transmissible in the line of descent by force of law. **c.** holding title, rights, etc., by inheritance: *a hereditary proprietor.* **—he·red′i·tar′i·ly** (-târ′ə lē), *adv.* **—he·red′i·tar′i·ness,** *n.*

her·ed·i·ty (hə red′i tē), *n., pl.* **-ties. 1.** the passing on of characters or traits from parents to offspring as a result of the transmission of genes. **2.** the genetic characters so transmitted. **3.** the characteristics of an individual that are considered to have been passed on by the parents or ancestors.

Her·e·ford (hûr′fərd, her′ə- *for 1;* her′ə fərd *for 2, 3*), *n.* **1.** one of an English breed of beef cattle with a red coat and white face. **2.** a city in Hereford and Worcester, in W England. 47,300. **3.** HEREFORDSHIRE.

Her·e·ford·shire (hûr′ə fərd shēr′, -shər), *n.* a former county in W England, now part of Hereford and Worcester.

here·in (hēr in′), *adv.* **1.** in or into this place. **2.** in this fact, circumstance, etc.; in view of this.

here·in·af·ter (hēr′in af′tər, -äf′-) also **here·in·be·low** (-bi lō′), *adv.* afterward in this document, statement, etc.

here·of (hēr uv′, -ov′), *adv.* **1.** of this: *upon the receipt hereof.* **2.** concerning this: *more hereof later.*

here·on (hēr on′, -ôn′), *adv.* hereupon.

here's (hērz), contraction of *here is.*

her·e·sy (her′ə sē), *n., pl.* **-sies. 1.** religious opinion or doctrine at variance with the orthodox or accepted doctrine. **2.** the maintaining of such an opinion or doctrine. **3.** the willful and persistent rejection of any article of faith by a baptized member of the Roman Catholic church. **4.** any belief or theory that is strongly at variance with established beliefs, customs, etc.

her·e·tic (her′i tik), *n.* **1.** a professed believer who maintains religious opinions contrary to those accepted by his or her church. **2.** a baptized Roman Catholic who willfully and persistently rejects any article of faith. **3.** anyone who does not conform to an established view, doctrine, or principle.

he·ret·i·cal (hə ret′i kəl), *adj.* of, pertaining to, or characteristic of heretics or heresy. **—he·ret′i·cal·ly,** *adv.*

here·to·fore (hēr′tə fôr′, -fōr′), *adv.* before this time; until now.

here·un·der (hēr un′dər), *adv.* **1.** under or below this; subsequent to this. **2.** under authority of this.

here·up·on (hēr′ə pon′, -pôn′), *adv.* **1.** upon or on this. **2.** immediately following this.

here·with (hēr with′, -wiŧH′), *adv.* **1.** along with this. **2.** by means of this; hereby.

her·it·a·ble (her′i tə bəl), *adj.* **1.** capable of being inherited; inheritable; hereditary. **2.** capable of inheriting. **—her′it·a·bil′i·ty,** *n.* **—her′it·a·bly,** *adv.*

her·it·age (her′i tij), *n.* **1.** something that comes or belongs to one by reason of birth; an inherited lot or portion: *a heritage of democracy*. **2.** something reserved for one: *the heritage of the righteous*. **3.** *Law*. **a.** property, esp. land, that is passed on by inheritance. **b.** something inherited or inheritable by legal succession.

herk·y-jerk·y (hûr′kē jûr′kē), *adj.* progressing in a fitful or jerky manner: *a herky-jerky home movie*.

herm (hûrm), *n.* a monument consisting of a four-sided shaft tapering inward from top to bottom and bearing a head or bust. [< Greek *hermês* statue of Hermes]

her·maph·ro·dite (hûr maf′rə dīt′), *n.* **1.** an individual in which reproductive organs of both sexes are present. **2.** an organism, as an earthworm or plant, having normally both the male and female organs of generation. **3.** a person or thing in which two opposite qualities are combined. —*adj.* **4.** of or characteristic of a hermaphrodite. **5.** combining two opposite qualities. —**her·maph′ro·dism, her·maph′ro·dit· ism,** *n.* —**her·maph′ro·dit′ic** (-dit′ik), *adj.* —**her·maph′ro·dit′i· cal·ly,** *adv.*

her·me·neu·tics (hûr′mə nōō′tiks, -nyōō′-), *n.* (*used with a sing. v.*) **1.** the art or science of interpretation, esp. of the Scriptures. **2.** the branch of theology that deals with the principles of Biblical exegesis.

Her·mes (hûr′mēz), *n.* an ancient Greek god, the herald and messenger of the other gods, associated with commerce, invention, and cunning: identified by the Romans with Mercury.

her·met·ic (hûr met′ik) also **her·met′i·cal,** *adj.* **1.** made airtight by fusion or sealing. **2.** not affected by outward influence or power; isolated. **3.** (*sometimes cap.*) of, pertaining to, or characteristic of occult science, esp. alchemy. —**her·met′i·cal·ly,** *adv.*

her·mit (hûr′mit), *n.* **1.** a person who has withdrawn to a solitary place for a life of religious seclusion. **2.** any person living in seclusion; recluse. **3.** an animal of solitary habits. **4.** a spiced molasses cookie often containing raisins or nuts. —**her·mit′ic, her·mit′i·cal, her′mit·ish,** *adj.* —**her·mit′i·cal·ly,** *adv.* —**her′mit·ry,** *n.*

her·mit·age (hûr′mi tij), *n.* **1.** the habitation of a hermit. **2.** any secluded place of residence or habitation; retreat; hideaway.

her′mit crab′, *n.* any of various crabs, esp. of the genera *Pagurus* and *Eupagurus,* that insert their soft, usu. coiled abdomen into the empty shells of gastropod mollusks.

her′mit thrush′, *n.* a North American thrush, *Catharus guttatus,* noted for its complex and appealing song.

Her·mon (hûr′mən), *n.* **Mount,** a mountain in SW Syria, in the Anti-Lebanon range. 9232 ft. (2814 m).

her·ni·a (hûr′nē ə), *n., pl.* **-ni·as, -ni·ae** (-nē ē′). the protrusion of an organ or tissue through an opening in its surrounding walls, esp. in the abdominal region. —**her′ni·al,** *adj.*

her·ni·ate (hûr′nē āt′), *v.i.* **-at·ed, -at·ing.** to protrude abnormally so as to constitute a hernia. —**her′ni·a′tion,** *n.*

her′niated disk′, *n.* an abnormal protrusion of a spinal disk between vertebrae. Also called **ruptured disk, slipped disk.**

he·ro (hēr′ō), *n., pl.* **-roes;** for 5 also **-ros.** **1.** a man of distinguished courage or ability, admired for his brave deeds and noble qualities. **2.** any person who has heroic qualities or has performed a heroic act and is regarded as a model or ideal. **3.** the principal male character in a story, play, film, etc. **4.** (in antiquity) an individual possessing godlike prowess and beneficence who often came to be honored as a divinity. **5.** HERO SANDWICH.

He·ro (hēr′ō), *n.* **1.** a legendary priestess of Aphrodite and the lover of Leander. **2.** Also, **Heron.** (*Hero of Alexandria*) fl. 1st century A.D., Greek scientist.

Her·od (her′əd), *n.* (*"the Great"*) 73?–4 B.C., king of Judea 37–4.

Her′od A·grip′pa (ə grip′ə), *n.* (*Julius Agrippa*) c10 B.C.–A.D. 44, king of Judea 41–44 (grandson of Herod the Great).

Her′od An′ti·pas (an′ti pas′), *n.* died after A.D. 39, ruler of Galilee A.D. 4–39.

He·ro·di·as (hə rō′dē əs), *n.* the second wife of Herod Antipas; mother of Salome.

He·rod·o·tus (hə rod′ə təs), *n.* 484?–425? B.C., Greek historian.

he·ro·ic (hi rō′ik), *adj.* Also, **he·ro′i·cal.** **1.** of, pertaining to, or characteristic of a hero or heroine; daring; noble; intrepid: *a heroic explorer; heroic ambition.* **2.** having or involving recourse to daring or forceful action: *Heroic measures were taken to save the child's life.* **3.** dealing with the deeds, attributes, etc., of heroes and heroines, as in literature. **4.** larger than life-size: *a statue of heroic proportions.* —*n.* **5.** Usu. **heroics.** HEROIC VERSE. **6. heroics, a.** flamboyant or extravagant language, sentiment, or behavior, intended to seem heroic. **b.** heroic action or behavior. —**he·ro′i·cal·ly,** *adv.*

hero′ic age′, *n.* a period in the history of a nation when ancient heroes of myths and legends are supposed to have lived.

hero′ic po′em, *n.* a poem written in an epic style using lines of iambic pentameter.

hero′ic verse′, *n.* a form of verse adapted to the treatment of heroic or exalted themes: in classical poetry, dactylic hexameter; in English and German, iambic pentameter; and in French, the Alexandrine.

her·o·in (her′ō in), *n.* a white crystalline powder, $C_{21}H_{23}NO_5$, derived from morphine, that is narcotic and addictive: manufacture or importation is prohibited in the U.S. and many other nations.

her·o·ine (her′ō in), *n.* **1.** a woman of distinguished courage or ability,

admired for her brave deeds and noble qualities. **2.** the principal female character in a story, play, film, etc.

her·o·ism (her′ō iz′əm), *n.* **1.** the qualities or attributes of a hero or heroine; bravery. **2.** heroic conduct; courageous action.

her·on (her′ən), *n.* any of various long-legged, long-necked wading birds of the family Ardeidae, of worldwide distribution, usu. having a spearlike bill.

He·ron (hēr′on), *n.* HERO (def. 2).

he′ro sand′wich, *n.* a large sandwich consisting of a small loaf of bread filled with any of various ingredients, as cold cuts and cheese or sausage and peppers. Also called **hero.**

he′ro wor′ship, *n.* **1.** a profound reverence for great people or their memory. **2.** extravagant or excessive admiration for a personal hero. —**he′ro-wor′ship,** *v.t.,* **-shiped, -ship·ing** or (*esp. Brit.*) **-shipped, -ship·ping.**

her·pes (hûr′pēz), *n.* **1.** any of several diseases caused by herpesvirus, characterized by eruption of blisters on the skin or mucous membranes. **2.** HERPESVIRUS.

her′pes sim′plex (sim′pleks), *n.* a recurrent herpesvirus infection that produces clusters of small blisters on the mouth, lips, eyes, or genitalia.

her·pes·vi·rus (hûr′pēz vī′rəs), *n., pl.* **-rus·es.** any DNA-containing virus of the family Herpesviridae, members of which cause several kinds of diseases, as chickenpox and shingles.

her′pes zos′ter (zos′tər), *n.* SHINGLES.

her′pes zos′ter vi′rus, *n.* a type of herpesvirus that causes chickenpox and shingles. Also called **varicella zoster virus.**

her·pe·tol·o·gy (hûr′pi tol′ə jē), *n.* the branch of zoology dealing with reptiles and amphibians. —**her′pe·to·log′ic** (-tl oj′ik), **her′pe·to· log′i·cal,** *adj.* —**her′pe·to·log′i·cal·ly,** *adv.* —**her·pe·tol′o·gist,** *n.*

Herr (her; *Eng.* hâr), *n., pl.* **Her·ren** (her′ən; *Eng.* hâr′ən). the conventional German title and term of address for a man. [< German]

her·ring (her′ing), *n., pl.* (*esp. collectively*) **-ring,** (*esp. for kinds or species*) **-rings.** **1.** an important food fish, *Clupea harengus harengus,* found in enormous schools in the N Atlantic. **2.** a similar fish, *Clupea harengus pallasii,* of the N Pacific. **3.** any fish of the family Clupeidae, including herrings, shads, and sardines. —**her′ring·like′,** *adj.*

her·ring·bone (her′ing bōn′), *n.* **1.** a pattern consisting of adjoining vertical rows of slanting lines, any two contiguous lines suggesting either a V or an inverted V, used in masonry, textiles, etc. **2. a.** Also called **chevron, her′ringbone weave′,** a twill weave with this pattern. **b.** a fabric made with this weave. **c.** a garment made from such a fabric. **3.** a method of ascent by a skier requiring a V-shaped gait, or track, and placing weight on the inside of the ski. —*adj.* **4.** of herringbone weave or pattern: *herringbone tweed.*

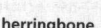
herringbone

her′ring gull′, *n.* a common large gull, *Larus argentatus,* of the Northern Hemisphere.

hers (hûrz), *pron.* **1.** a form of the possessive case of SHE used as a predicate adjective: *The red umbrella is hers. Are you a friend of hers?* **2.** that or those belonging to her: *Hers is the biggest garden on our street.*

Her·schel (hûr′shəl, hâr′-), *n.* **1. Sir John Frederick William,** 1792–1871, English astronomer. **2.** his father, **Sir William** (Friedrich Wilhelm Herschel), 1738–1822, English astronomer, born in Germany.

her·self (hər self′), *pron.* **1.** a reflexive form of HER (used as the direct or indirect object of a verb or the object of a preposition): *She supports herself. She bought herself a briefcase. She pulled the covers over herself.* **2.** (used as an intensive): *She herself wrote the letter.* **3.** (used in absolute constructions): *Herself only a child, she had to raise three younger brothers.* **4.** (used in place of SHE or HER in various compound and comparative constructions): *The producer and herself were not on speaking terms. The others were even more nervous than herself.* **5.** her normal or customary self: *After a few weeks of rest, she will be herself again.* **6.** *Irish Eng. and Scot.* a woman of importance, esp. the head of a household or family: *Herself has gone to market.*

her·sto·ry (hûr′stə rē, hûrs′trē), *n., pl.* **-ries.** history (used esp. in feminist literature and in women's studies as an alternative form to distinguish or emphasize the particular experience of women).

hertz (hûrts), *n., pl.* **hertz, hertz·es.** the SI unit of frequency, equal to one cycle per second. *Abbr.*: Hz

Her·zl (hûrt′səl, hârt′-), *n.* **Theodor,** 1860–1904, Hungarian-born Austrian Jewish writer and Zionist.

Her·zog (hert′sōk), *n.* **Johann Jakob,** 1805–82, German theologian.

he's (hēz; *unstressed* ēz), **1.** contraction of *he is.* **2.** contraction of *he has.*

He's′ Got′ the Whole′ World′ in′ His′ Hands′, a traditional American spiritual.

he/she (hē′shē′), a combined form used as a singular nominative pronoun to denote a person of either sex: *Each student may begin when he/she is ready.*

Hesh·van (hesh′vən, -vän, кhesh′-) also **Cheshvan**, *n.* the second month of the Jewish calendar.

He·si·od (hē′sē əd, hes′ē-), *n.* fl. 8th century B.C., Greek poet.

hes·i·tant (hez′i tənt), *adj.* **1.** hesitating; undecided, doubtful, or disinclined. **2.** lacking readiness of speech. —**hes′i·tan·cy**, *n.* —**hes′i·tant·ly**, *adv.*

hes·i·tate (hez′i tāt′), *v.,* **-tat·ed, -tat·ing.** —*v.i.* **1.** to be reluctant or wait to act because of fear, indecision, or disinclination; waver; vacillate: *She hesitated before taking the job.* **2.** to have scruples or doubts about something; have reservations. **3.** to stop for a moment; pause. **4.** to falter in speech; stammer. —*v.t.* **5.** to have scruples or doubts about (fol. by an infinitive): *He hesitated to break the law.* —**hes′i·tat′er, hes′i·ta′tor**, *n.* —**hes′i·tat′ing·ly**, *adv.* —**hes′i·ta′tion**, *n.*

Hess (hes), *n.* **1. Victor Francis,** 1883–1964, U.S. physicist, born in Austria. **2. Walter Rudolf,** 1881–1973, Swiss physiologist. **3. (Walther Richard) Rudolf,** 1894–1987, German Nazi official.

Hes·se (hes′ə *for 1;* hes *for 2),* *n.* **1. Hermann,** 1877–1962, German writer. **2. Hes·sen** (hes′ən). a state in central Germany. 5,508,000; 8150 sq. mi. (21,110 sq. km). *Cap.:* Wiesbaden.

Hes·sian (hesh′ən), *adj.* **1.** of or pertaining to Hesse or its inhabitants. —*n.* **2.** a native or inhabitant of Hesse. **3.** a Hessian mercenary used by England during the American Revolution. **4.** a hireling or ruffian.

Hes·ti·a (hes′tē ə), *n.* the ancient Greek goddess of the hearth.

hetero-, a combining form meaning "different," "other": *heterocyclic.* Also, *esp. before a vowel,* **heter-**.

het·er·o·clite (het′ər ə klīt′), *adj.* Also, **het′er·o·clit′ic** (-klit′ik), **het′·er·o·clit′i·cal. 1.** irregular or abnormal; anomalous. **2.** (of a word) irregular in inflection; having inflected forms belonging to more than one class of stems. —*n.* **3.** a person or thing that deviates from the ordinary rule or form. **4.** a heteroclite word.

het·er·o·cy·clic (het′ər ə sī′klik, -sik′lik), *adj.* **1.** of or pertaining to the branch of chemistry dealing with cyclic compounds in which at least one of the ring members is not a carbon atom. **2.** noting such compounds. —**het′er·o·cy′cle** (-sī′kəl), *n.*

het·er·o·dox (het′ər ə doks′), *adj.* **1.** not in accordance with established doctrines, esp. in theology. **2.** holding unorthodox doctrines or opinions. —**het′er·o·dox′ly**, *adv.* —**het′er·o·dox′y**, *n.*

het·er·o·ge·ne·ous (het′ər ə jē′nē əs, -jēn′yəs), *adj.* **1.** different in kind; unlike; incongruous. **2.** composed of parts of different kinds; having widely dissimilar elements or constituents; not homogeneous. **3.** (of a chemical mixture) composed of different substances or the same substance in different phases, as ice and water. —**het′er·o·ge·ne′i·ty** (-ə rō jə nē′i tē), **het′er·o·ge′ne·ous·ness**, *n.* —**het′er·o·ge′ne·ous·ly**, *adv.*

het·er·o·mor·phic (het′ər ə môr′fik), *adj.* **1.** *Biol.* dissimilar in shape, structure, or magnitude. **2.** *Entomol.* undergoing complete metamorphosis; possessing varying forms. —**het′er·o·mor′phism, het′er·o·mor′phy**, *n.*

het·er·on·o·mous (het′ə ron′ə məs), *adj.* **1.** subject to or involving different laws. **2.** *Biol.* subject to different laws of growth or specialization. —**het′er·on′o·mous·ly**, *adv.* —**het′er·on′o·my**, *n.*

het·er·o·nym (het′ər ə nim), *n.* a word spelled the same as another but having a different sound and meaning, as *lead* (to conduct) and *lead* (a metal). —**het′er·on′y·mous** (-ə ron′ə məs), *adj.* —**het′er·on′y·mous·ly**, *adv.*

het·er·op·ter·ous (het′ə rop′tər əs), *adj.* belonging or pertaining to the Heteroptera, in some classifications a suborder of hemipterous insects comprising the true bugs.

het·er·o·sex·ism (het′ər ə sek′siz əm), *n.* a prejudiced attitude or discriminatory practices against homosexuals by heterosexuals. —**het′·er·o·sex′ist**, *n., adj.*

het·er·o·sex·u·al (het′ər ə sek′shōō əl), *adj.* **1.** of, pertaining to, or exhibiting heterosexuality. **2.** pertaining to the opposite sex or to both sexes. —*n.* **3.** a heterosexual person.

het·er·o·sex·u·al·i·ty (het′ər ə sek′shōō al′i tē), *n.* sexual desire or behavior directed toward persons of the opposite sex.

het·er·o·sis (het′ə rō′sis), *n.* the increase in growth, size, yield, or other characters in hybrids over those of the parents. Also called **hybrid vigor.**

heu·land·ite (hyōō′lən dīt′), *n.* a usu. white or transparent zeolite, hydrous calcium-sodium aluminum silicate, occurring as crystals in basic volcanic rocks.

heu·ris·tic (hyōō ris′tik *or, often,* yōō-), *adj.* **1.** serving to indicate or point out; stimulating interest as a means of furthering investigation. **2.** encouraging a person to learn, discover, understand, or solve problems on his or her own, as by experimenting, evaluating possible answers or solutions, or by trial and error: *a heuristic teaching method.* —*n.* **3.** a heuristic method or argument. —**heu·ris′ti·cal·ly**, *adv.*

hew (hyōō *or, often,* yōō), *v.,* **hewed, hewed** *or* **hewn, hew·ing.** —*v.t.* **1.** to strike forcibly with an ax, sword, or other cutting instrument; chop. **2.** to make, shape, or smooth with or as if with cutting blows: *to hew a statue from marble.* **3.** to sever (a part) from a mass by means of cutting blows: *to hew branches from the tree.* **4.** to cut down; fell: *trees hewed down by the storm.* —*v.i.* **5.** to strike with cutting blows;

cut. **6.** to uphold, follow closely, or conform (usu. fol. by *to*): *to hew to the tenets of a political party.* —**hew′a·ble**, *adj.* —**hew′er**, *n.*

HEW, Department of Health, Education, and Welfare.

hew′ers of wood′ and draw′ers of wa′ter, *n.pl.* performers of menial tasks. Josh. 9:21.

He′ Who′ Would′ Val′iant Be′, a Christian hymn (1684) with words by John Bunyan.

hex (heks), *v.t.* **1.** to practice witchcraft on; bewitch. **2.** to bring bad luck to; jinx. —*n.* **3.** a spell; charm; jinx. **4.** a witch. —**hex′er**, *n.*

hexa-, a combining form meaning "six": *hexagon.* Also, *esp. before a vowel,* **hex-**.

hex·a·dec·i·mal (hek′sə des′ə məl), *adj.* **1.** of or pertaining to a numbering system that uses 16 as the radix and that represents digits greater than 9 with the letters A through F. **2.** relating to or encoded in such a system, esp. for use by computers.

hex·a·em·er·on (hek′sə em′ə ron′), *n.* the six days of Creation or the account of them in the Bible. Gen. 1. —**hex′a·em′er·ic**, *adj.*

hex·a·gon (hek′sə gon′, -gən), *n.* a polygon having six angles and six sides. —**hex·ag′o·nal** (-sag′ə nl), *adj.*

hex·a·gram (hek′sə gram′), *n.* a six-pointed starlike figure formed of two equilateral triangles placed concentrically with each side of a triangle parallel to a side of the other and on opposite sides of the center.

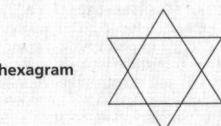
hexagram

hex·a·he·dron (hek′sə hē′drən), *n., pl.* **-drons, -dra** (-drə). a solid figure, as a cube, having six faces. —**hex′a·he′dral**, *adj.*

hex·am·e·ter (hek sam′i tər), *n.* **1.** a line of verse having six metrical feet. —*adj.* **2.** consisting of six metrical feet. —**hex·a·met′ric** (-sə me′trik), **hex′a·met′ri·cal, hex·am′e·tral**, *adj.*

hex·a·meth·yl·ene·tet·ra·mine (hek′sə meth′ə lēn te′trə mēn′), *n.* a white, crystalline, water-soluble powder, $C_6H_{12}N_4$, used esp. as a vulcanization accelerator and as a diuretic and urinary antiseptic. Also called **hex′a·mine** (-mēn′).

hex·ane (hek′sān), *n.* any of five isomeric hydrocarbons having the formula C_6H_{14}, of the alkane series, some of which are obtained from petroleum: used as solvents and in fuels.

hex·a·pod (hek′sə pod′), *n.* **1.** a six-legged arthropod of the class Insecta (formerly Hexapoda); an insect. —*adj.* **2.** of or pertaining to an insect. —**hex·ap′o·dous** (-sap′ə dəs), *adj.*

Hex·a·teuch (hek′sə tōōk′, -tyōōk′), *n.* the first six books of the Old Testament. —**Hex′a·teuch′al**, *adj.*

hex·ose (hek′sōs), *n.* any of a class of sugars, as glucose and fructose, containing six atoms of carbon.

hex′ sign′, *n.* any of various magical symbols of usu. stylized design, as those painted on barns by the Pennsylvania Dutch.

hex sign

hey (hā), *interj.* **1.** (used as an exclamation to call attention or to express pleasure, surprise, bewilderment, etc.) **2.** *Southern U.S. Informal.* hello: used as a greeting.

hey·day (hā′dā′), *n.* the stage or period of greatest vigor, strength, success, etc.; prime: *the heyday of the silent movies.* Sometimes, **hey′dey′.**

Hey·er·dahl (hā′ər däl′), *n.* **Thor,** born 1914, Norwegian ethnologist and author.

Hez·bol·lah or **Hiz·bal·lah** (*Arabic.* кhes′bä lä′), *n.* a radical Shi'ite Muslim organization in Lebanon engaged in guerrilla warfare against Israel.

Hez·e·ki·ah (hez′ə kī′ə), *n.* a king of Judah of the 7th and 8th centuries B.C. II Kings 18.

HF, 1. high frequency. **2.** Hispanic female.

Hf, *Symbol, Chem.* hafnium.

Hg, *Chem. Symbol.* mercury. [< New Latin *hydrargyrum*]

hgt., height.

hgwy., highway.

HHS, Department of Health and Human Services.

hi[1] (hī), *interj.* (used as a greeting.)

hi[2] (hī), *adj.* an informal, simplified spelling of HIGH: *hi fidelity.*

HI, Hawaii.

Hi•a•le•ah (hī′ə lē′ə), *n.* a city in SE Florida, near Miami: racetrack. 194,120.

hi•a•tus (hī ā′təs), *n., pl.* **-tus•es, -tus. 1.** a break or interruption in the continuity of a work, series, action, etc. **2.** a missing part; gap or lacuna. **3.** any gap or opening. **4.** the coming together, with or without a break or slight pause, of two adjacent vowels in different syllables, as in *see easily.* **5.** a natural fissure, cleft, or foramen in a bone or other structure. —**hi•a′tal,** *adj.*

hia′tus (or **hia′tal**) **her′ni•a,** *n.* protrusion of part of the stomach through the esophageal cleft of the diaphragm.

Hi•a•wath•a (hī′ə woth′ə, -wô′thə, hē′ə-), *n.* the central figure of Longfellow's poem *The Song of Hiawatha* (1855).

hi•ba•chi (hi bä′chē), *n., pl.* **-chis.** a small charcoal brazier covered with a grill. [< Japanese: fire pot]

hi•ber•nac•u•lum (hī′bər nak′yə ləm) also **hi•ber•nac•le** (hī′bər-nak′əl), *n., pl.* **-nac•u•la** (-nak′yə lə) also **-nac•les. 1.** a protective case or covering, esp. for winter, as of an animal or a plant bud. **2.** winter quarters, as of a hibernating animal.

hi•ber•nal (hī bûr′nl), *adj.* of or pertaining to winter; wintry.

hi•ber•nate (hī′bər nāt′), *v.i.,* **-nat•ed, -nat•ing. 1.** to spend the winter in close quarters in a dormant condition, as bears and certain other animals. **2.** to withdraw or be in seclusion; retire. **3.** to winter in a place with a milder climate. —**hi′ber•na′tion,** *n.* —**hi′ber•na′tor,** *n.*

Hi•ber•ni•a (hī bûr′nē ə), *n.* Latin name of IRELAND. —**Hi•ber′ni•an,** *adj., n.*

hi•bis•cus (hī bis′kəs, hi-), *n., pl.* **-cus•es. 1.** Also called **China rose.** a woody plant, *Hibiscus rosa-sinensis,* of the mallow family, having large, showy flowers. **2.** any of numerous other plants, shrubs, or trees of the genus *Hibiscus,* usu. having profuse blooms.

hic•cup or **hic•cough** (hik′up, -əp), *n., v.,* **-cuped** or **-cupped** or **-coughed, -cup•ing** or **-cup•ping** or **-cough•ing.** —*n.* **1.** a quick, involuntary inhalation that follows a spasm of the diaphragm and is suddenly checked by closure of the glottis, producing a short, relatively sharp sound. **2.** Usu., **hiccups.** the condition of having such spasms. —*v.i.* **3.** to make the sound of a hiccup: *The motor hiccuped as it started.* **4.** to have the hiccups.

hick (hik), *n.* **1.** an unsophisticated, provincial person; rube. —*adj.* **2.** unsophisticated or provincial: *hick ideas; a hick town.*

hick•ey or **hick•ie** (hik′ē), *n., pl.* **-eys** or **-ies. 1.** *Slang.* **a.** a pimple. **b.** a reddish mark left on the skin by a passionate kiss. **2.** any device or gadget whose name is forgotten or not known. **3.** a fitting used to mount a lighting fixture in an outlet box or on a pipe or stud. **4.** a tool used to bend tubes and pipes.

Hick•ok (hik′ok), *n.* **James Butler** ("*Wild Bill*"), 1837–76, U.S. frontiersman.

hick•o•ry (hik′ə rē, hik′rē), *n., pl.* **-ries. 1.** any North American tree of the genus *Carya,* of the walnut family: some bear edible nuts or yield a valuable wood. **2.** the wood of any of these trees. **3.** a switch or stick of this wood.

hid (hid), *v.* pt. and a pp. of HIDE[1].

hid•den (hid′n), *adj.* **1.** concealed; obscure; covert: *hidden meaning; hidden hostility.* —*v.* **2.** past part. of HIDE[1]. —**hid′den•ly,** *adv.* —**hid′den•ness,** *n.*

hid′den agen′da, *n.* an often duplicitously undisclosed plan or motive.

hid′den tax′, *n.* any tax paid by a manufacturer, supplier, or seller that is added to the consumer price.

Hid′den Treas′ure, The, a parable of Jesus. Matt. 13:44.

hide[1] (hīd), *v.,* **hid, hid•den** or **hid, hid•ing,** *n.* —*v.t.* **1.** to conceal from sight; prevent from being seen or discovered. **2.** to obstruct the view of; cover up: *The sun was hidden by the clouds.* **3.** to conceal from knowledge or exposure; keep secret: *to hide one's feelings.* —*v.i.* **4.** to conceal oneself; lie concealed: *I hid in the closet.* **5. hide out,** to go into or remain in hiding. —*n.* **6.** *Brit.* BLIND (def. 24). —*Proverb.* **7. Don't hide your light under a bushel,** don't conceal your talents and good works. Matt. 5:15. —**hid′a•ble,** *adj.* —**hid′a•bil′i•ty,** *n.* —**hid′er,** *n.*

hide[2] (hīd), *n., v.,* **hid•ed, hid•ing.** —*n.* **1.** the raw or dressed pelt or skin of a large animal, as a cow or horse. **2.** *Informal.* **a.** the skin of a human being: *You'll burn your hide in that hot sun.* **b.** safety or welfare: *trying to save the hides of fellow party members.* —*v.t.* **3.** *Informal.* to administer a beating to; thrash. —*Idiom.* **4. hide (n)or hair,** a trace or evidence, as of something missing. —**hide′less,** *adj.*

hide′-and-seek′, *n.* a children's game in which one player gives the other players a chance to hide and then tries to find them. Also called **hide′-and-go′-seek′.**

hide•a•way (hīd′ə wā′), *n.* **1.** a place to which a person can retreat; refuge: *a hideaway in the mountains.* —*adj.* **2.** hidden; concealed: *a hideaway bed.*

hide•bound (hīd′bound′), *adj.* **1.** narrow and rigid in opinion; inflexible. **2.** extremely conservative. —**hide′bound′ness,** *n.*

hid•e•ous (hid′ē əs), *adj.* **1.** horrible or frightful to the senses; repulsive; very ugly: *a hideous monster.* **2.** shocking or revolting to the moral sense: *a hideous crime.* **3.** distressing; appalling: *the hideous expense of moving to another city.* —**hid′e•ous•ly,** *adv.* —**hid′e•ous•ness, hid′e•os′i•ty** (-os′i tē), *n.*

hide′out′ or **hide′-out′,** *n.* a safe place for hiding, esp. from the law.

hie (hī), *v.,* **hied, hie•ing** or **hy•ing.** —*v.i.* **1.** to hasten; speed; go in haste. —*v.t.* **2.** to hasten (oneself).

hi•er•ar•chy (hī′ə rär′kē, hī′rär-), *n., pl.* **-chies. 1.** any system of persons or things ranked one above another. **2.** government by ecclesiastical rulers. —**hi′er•arch′,** *n.* —**hi′er•arch′i•cal, hi′er•arch′ic,** *adj.* —**hi′er•arch′i•cal•ly,** *adv.*

hi•er•at•ic (hī′ə rat′ik, hī rat′-), *adj.* **1.** Also, **hi′er•at′i•cal.** of or pertaining to priests or a priesthood; sacerdotal; priestly. **2.** of or designating a form of ancient Egyptian writing consisting of abridged forms of hieroglyphics, used by the priests in their records. **3.** fixed or formalized in style by tradition or convention: *hieratic sculptures.* —**hi′er•at′i•cal•ly,** *adv.*

hi•er•o•glyph•ic (hī′ər ə glif′ik, hī′rə-), *adj.* Also, **hi′er•o•glyph′i•cal. 1.** of or designating a pictographic script, as that of the ancient Egyptians, in which many of the symbols are conventionalized pictures of the things represented. **2.** inscribed with hieroglyphic symbols. **3.** hard to decipher; hard to read. —*n.* **4.** Also, **hi′er•o•glyph′.** a hieroglyphic symbol. **5.** Usu., **hieroglyphics.** hieroglyphic writing. **6.** a figure or symbol with a hidden meaning. **7. hieroglyphics,** characters or symbols that are difficult to decipher. —**hi′er•o•glyph′i•cal•ly,** *adv.*

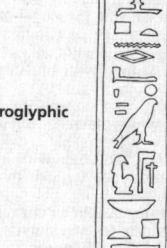

hieroglyphic

hi•er•ol•o•gy (hī′ə rol′ə jē, hī rol′-), *n.* **1.** literature or learning regarding sacred things. **2.** hagiological literature or learning. —**hi•er•o•log•ic** (hī′ər ə loj′ik, hī′rə-), **hi′er•o•log′i•cal,** *adj.* —**hi′er•ol′o•gist,** *n.*

Hi•er•on•y•mus (hī′ə ron′ə məs, hī ron′-), *n.* **Eusebius,** JEROME, Saint.

hi•fa•lu•tin or **hi•fa•lu•tin′** (hī′fə lōōt′n), *adj.* HIGHFALUTIN.

hi-fi (hī′fī′), *n., pl.* **-fis,** *adj.* —*n.* **1.** high fidelity. **2.** a phonograph, radio, or other sound-reproducing apparatus possessing high fidelity. —*adj.* **3.** of, pertaining to, or characteristic of such apparatus; high-fidelity.

hig•gle•dy-pig•gle•dy (hig′əl dē pig′əl dē), *adv.* **1.** in a jumbled, confused, or disorderly manner; helter-skelter. —*adj.* **2.** confused; jumbled.

high (hī), *adj.* **1.** having a great or considerable height; lofty; tall: *a high wall.* **2.** having a specified height: *The tree is now 20 feet high.* **3.** situated above the ground or some base; elevated: *a high ledge.* **4.** exceeding the common degree or measure; strong; intense: *high speed; high color.* **5.** expensive; costly; dear: *high prices; high rent.* **6.** exalted, as in rank, station, or eminence: *a high official.* **7.** elevated in pitch: *high notes.* **8.** extending to or from an elevation: *a high dive.* **9.** great in quantity, as number, degree, or force: *a high temperature; high cholesterol.* **10.** holding to High Church principles and practices. **11.** of great consequence; important; grave: *high crimes against humanity.* **12.** elated; merry or hilarious: *high spirits; a high old time.* **13.** rich; extravagant; luxurious: *to indulge in high living.* **14.** intoxicated or euphoric under the influence of alcohol or narcotics. **15.** remote: *high latitude; high antiquity.* **16.** extreme in opinion or doctrine, esp. in religion or politics: *a high Tory.* **17.** of or designating highland or inland regions. **18.** having considerable energy or potential power. **19.** pertaining to the gear transmission ratio at which the drive shaft speed and the speed of the engine crankshaft most closely correspond: *high gear.* **20.** (of a vowel) articulated with the upper surface of the tongue relatively close to the palate, as the vowels of *eat, it, boot,* and *put.* Compare LOW[1] (def. 27). **21.** (esp. of game) aged until verging on decomposition; slightly tainted. **22.** (of a pitched baseball) crossing the plate at a level above the batter's shoulders. **23.** (of a playing card) **a.** having greater value than other denominations or suits. **b.** able to take a trick; being a winning card. —*adv.* **24.** at or to a high point, place, or level. **25.** in or to a high rank or estimate: *to aim high in political ambition.* **26.** at or to a high amount or price. **27.** in or to a high degree. **28.** luxuriously; richly; extravagantly: *to live high.* **29.** *Naut.* as close to the wind as is possible while making headway with sails full. —*n.* **30.** high gear. **31.** an atmospheric pressure system characterized by relatively high pressure at its center. **32.** a high or the highest point, place, or level; peak: *a record high for unemployment.* **33. a.** an intoxicated or euphoric state induced by alcohol or narcotics. **b.** a period of sustained excitement, exhilaration, or the like. —*Idiom.* **34. high and dry, a.** (of a ship) grounded so as to be entirely above water at low tide. **b.** deserted; stranded: *to be left high and dry.* **35. high and low,** in every possible place; everywhere: *to search high and low.* **36. high on,** enthusiastic about; favorably disposed toward. **37. on high, a.** at or to a height; above. **b.** in heaven. **c.** having a high position, as one who makes important decisions: *the powers on high.* —**high′ly,** *adv.*

high′-and-might′y, *adj.* haughty; arrogant; domineering. —**high′-and-might′i•ness,** *n.*

high•ball (hī′bôl′), *n.* **1.** a drink of whiskey mixed with club soda or ginger ale and served with ice in a tall glass. **2. a.** a signal to start a train that is given with the hand or with a lamp. **b.** a signal for a train to move at full speed. —*v.i.* **3.** *Slang.* to move at full speed. —*v.t.* **4.** to signal to (the engineer of a train) to proceed.

high′ bar′, *n.* HORIZONTAL BAR.

high′ beam′, *n.* a bright headlight beam providing long-range illumination of a road, chiefly for use in nonurban areas.

high′ blood′ pres′sure, *n.* elevation of the arterial blood pressure or a condition resulting from it; hypertension.

high•born (hī′bôrn′), *adj.* of high rank by birth.

high•boy (hī′boi′), *n.* a tall chest of drawers on legs, usu. in two sections set one on top of the other.

high•bred (hī′bred′), *adj.* **1.** of superior breed. **2.** characteristic of superior breeding.

high•brow (hī′brou′), *n.* **1.** a person who has or affects superior intellectual or cultural interests and tastes. —*adj.* **2.** Also, **high′browed′.** of, pertaining to, or characteristic of a highbrow. —**high′brow•ism,** *n.*

high•bush blue′berry (hī′bŏŏsh′), *n.* a spreading, bushy blueberry shrub, *Vaccinium corymbosum,* with bluish black berries: the source of most cultivated blueberries.

high•bush cran′berry, *n.* a viburnum shrub, *Viburnum trilobum,* with broad clusters of white flowers and edible scarlet berries. Also called **cranberry bush.**

high•chair (hī′châr′), *n.* a tall chair with arms and very long legs and usu. a removable tray for food, for use by a very young child during meals.

High′ Church′, *adj.* (in the Anglican church) emphasizing the Catholic tradition, esp. in adherence to sacraments, rituals, and obedience to church authority. —**High′ Church′man,** *n.*

high′-class′, *adj.* of a type superior in quality or degree; first-rate: *high-class entertainment.*

high′ com′edy, *n.* comedy dealing with polite society, characterized by sophisticated, witty dialogue and an intricate plot. Compare LOW COMEDY.

high′ command′, *n.* **1.** the leadership or highest authority of a military command or other organization. **2.** the highest headquarters of a military force.

High′ Court′, *n.* **1.** SUPREME COURT. **2.** a superior court.

high′-defini′tion tel′evision, *n.* a television system having a high number of scanning lines per frame, producing a sharper image and greater picture detail. *Abbr.:* HDTV

high′-end′, *adj.* being the most expensive and technically sophisticated: *high-end stereo equipment.*

high′er crit′icism, *n.* the study of the Bible having as its object the establishment of such facts as authorship and date of composition, as well as determination of a basis for exegesis.

high′er educa′tion, *n.* education beyond high school, esp. that provided by colleges, graduate and professional schools.

High′er Ground′, a Christian hymn (1898) with words by Johnson Oatman, Jr.

high′er law′, *n.* an ethical or religious principle considered as taking precedence over the laws of society, and to which one may appeal in order to justify disobedience to a constitution or enacted law with which it conflicts.

high′er mathemat′ics, *n.* the advanced portions of mathematics, customarily considered as embracing all beyond ordinary arithmetic, geometry, algebra, and trigonometry.

high′er-up′, *n. Informal.* a person in a position of high authority in an organization; superior.

Highest, the, *n.* God. Luke 1:32,35.

high′ explo′sive, *n.* an explosive, as TNT, with a violent, swift reaction, used in shells and bombs. —**high′-ex•plo′sive,** *adj.*

high•fa•lu•tin (hī′fə lōōt′n) also **high•fa•lu•ting** (-lōō′ting, -lōōt′n), *adj. Informal.* pompous; haughty; pretentious.

high′ fidel′ity, *n.* sound reproduction over the full range of audible frequencies with very little distortion of the original signal. Also called **hi-fi.** —**high′-fi•del′i•ty,** *adj.*

high′-five′, *n., v.,* **-fived, -fiv•ing.** —*n.* **1.** a gesture of greeting, good-fellowship, or triumph in which one person slaps the upraised palm of the hand against that of another. —*v.t.* **2.** to greet with a high-five: *The two players high-fived each other.* —*v.i.* **3.** to do a high-five.

high•fli•er or **high•fly•er** (hī′flī′ər), *n.* **1.** one who is extravagant or extreme in ambition, pretensions, opinions, etc. **2.** a speculative stock whose price swings back and forth between high and low points. —**highflying, high-flying** *adj.*

high′-flown′, *adj.* **1.** extravagant in aims, pretensions, etc. **2.** pretentiously lofty; bombastic: *high-flown oratory.*

high′ fre′quency, *n.* the range of frequencies in the radio spectrum between 3 and 30 megahertz. —**high′-fre′quen•cy,** *adj.*

High′ Ger′man, *n.* the group of West Germanic dialects spoken in central and S Germany, Switzerland, and Austria, including standard literary German, which has combined features of several dialects.

high-grade (hī′grād′), *adj., v.,* **-grad•ed, -grad•ing.** —*adj.* **1.** of excellent or superior quality. **2.** (of ore) yielding a relatively large amount of the metal for which it is mined. —*v.t.* **3.** to steal (rich ore) from a mine. —**high′-grad′er,** *n.*

high′-hand′ed, *adj.* presumptuous; overbearing; arbitrary. —**high′-hand′ed•ly,** *adv.* —**high′-hand′ed•ness,** *n.*

high′ hat′, *n.* TOP HAT.

High′ Hol′idays, *n.pl.* the Jewish holidays of Rosh Hashanah and Yom Kippur. Also called **High′ Ho′ly Days′.**

high′ horse′, *n.* a haughty attitude; an arrogant or contemptuous manner: *to get off one's high horse and talk sense.*

high′ jinks′ or **hijinks,** *n.* (used with a pl. v.) boisterous celebration or merrymaking; unrestrained fun.

high′ jump′, *n.* **1.** an athletic field event in which competitors use a running start to jump for height over a crossbar. **2.** a jump for height made in this event. —**high′-jump′,** *v.i.,* —**high′-jump′er,** *n.*

high•land (hī′land), *n.* **1.** an elevated region; plateau. **2. highlands,** a mountainous region or elevated part of a country. —*adj.* **3.** of, pertaining to, or characteristic of highlands.

High•land•er (hī′lən dər), *n.* **1.** a native or inhabitant of the Highlands of Scotland. **2.** a soldier of a Highland regiment. **3.** (*l.c.*) an inhabitant of any highland region.

High′land fling′, *n.* FLING (def. 14).

high′-lev′el, *adj.* **1.** of or involving participants having high status: *a high-level meeting.* **2.** having senior authority or high status: *high-level personnel.* **3.** (of a programming language) based on a vocabulary of Englishlike statements for writing program code rather than the more abstract instructions typical of assembly language or machine language.

high•life (hī′līf′), *n.* **1.** an expensive, glamorous, or elegant style of living. **2.** a W African style of music and dance featuring traditional Yoruban drumming and syncopated guitar melodies.

high•light (hī′līt′), *v.t.* **1.** to emphasize or make prominent. **2.** to mark with a felt-tip highlighter: *to highlight passages of text.* **3.** to create highlights in. —*n.* **4. high′ light′.** an important, conspicuous, memorable, or enjoyable event, scene, part, or the like. **5.** an area of contrasting lightness or brightness, as on a glossy surface.

high•light•er (hī′lī′tər), *n.* **1.** a cosmetic used to emphasize some part of the face, as the eyes or the cheekbones. **2.** a felt-tip pen with a wide nib for highlighting passages of printed material in a soft, transparent color.

High′ Mass′, *n.* a Mass celebrated according to the complete rite, in which the liturgy is sung by the celebrant. Compare Low Mass.

high′-mind′ed, *adj.* having or showing exalted principles or feelings. —**high′-mind′ed•ly,** *adv.* —**high′-mind′ed•ness,** *n.*

high-muck-a-muck (hī′muk′ə muk′) also **high-muck•y-muck** (-muk′ē-), **high-muck•e•ty-muck** (-muk′i tē-), *n.* an important, influential, or high-ranking person, esp. one who is pompous or conceited.

high•ness (hī′nis), *n.* **1.** the quality or state of being high; loftiness. **2.** (*cap.*) a title of honor given to members of a royal family (usu. prec. by *His, Her, Your,* etc.).

high′ noon′, *n.* **1.** the exact moment of noon. **2.** the high point of a stage or period; peak. **3.** a crisis or confrontation.

high′-oc′cupancy ve′hicle lane′, *n.* DIAMOND LANE.

high′-oc′tane, *adj.* **1.** noting a gasoline with a relatively high octane number. **2.** dynamic; high-powered: *a high-octane performance of the concerto.*

high′-pitched′, *adj.* **1.** played or sung at a high pitch. **2.** emotionally intense: *a high-pitched argument.* **3.** (of a roof) having an almost vertical slope; steep.

high′ place′, *n.* (in ancient Semitic religions) a place of worship, usu. a temple or altar on a hilltop.

high′-pow′er, *adj.* **1.** (of a rifle) of a sufficiently high muzzle velocity and using a heavy enough bullet to kill large game. **2.** HIGH-POWERED.

high′-pow′ered, *adj.* **1.** of a forceful and driving character; very energetic or dynamic: *high-powered executives; high-powered selling methods.* **2.** capable of a high degree of magnification: *a high-powered microscope.*

high′-pres′sure, *adj., v.,* **-sured, -sur•ing.** —*adj.* **1.** having or involving a pressure above the normal. **2.** involving a high degree of stress; demanding: *a high-pressure job.* **3.** vigorous; persistent; aggressive: *high-pressure salesmanship.* —*v.t.* **4.** to use aggressively forceful sales tactics on: *high-pressured into buying a car.*

high′-priced′, *adj.* expensive; costly.

high′ pro′file, *n.* a deliberately conspicuous manner of conducting oneself or one's affairs: *to maintain a high profile in political life.* —**high′-pro′file,** *adj.*

high′-rise′ or **high′rise′,** *adj.* **1.** (of a building) having a comparatively large number of stories and equipped with elevators: *a high-rise apartment house.* **2.** of, pertaining to, characteristic of, or marked by high-rise buildings: *a high-rise urban cityscape.* —*n.* **3.** Also, **high′ rise′, high-rise.** a high-rise apartment or office building.

high·road (hī′rōd′), *n.* an easy or certain course: *the highroad to success.*

high′ roll′er or **high′roll′er,** *n.* **1.** a person who gambles for large stakes. **2.** a person or organization that spends money lavishly and sometimes recklessly. —**high′-roll′ing,** *adj.*

high′ school′, *n.* a school attended after elementary school or junior high school and usu. consisting of grades 9 or 10 through 12. —**high′-school′,** *adj.*

high′ sea′, *n.* Usu., **high seas.** the open sea or ocean, esp. beyond the three-mile limit or territorial waters of a country. —**high′-sea′,** *adj.*

high′ sign′, *n.* a gesture, glance, or facial expression used as a surreptitious signal to warn, admonish, or inform.

high′-speed′, *adj.* **1.** operating at, designed to operate at, or marked by high speed: *a high-speed drill; high-speed car chases.* **2.** suitable for minimum light exposure: *high-speed film.*

high′-spir′ited, *adj.* **1.** characterized by energetic enthusiasm, elation, vivacity, etc. **2.** boldly courageous; mettlesome. —**high′-spir′it·ed·ly,** *adv.* —**high′-spir′it·ed·ness,** *n.*

high′-step′ping, *adj.* **1.** seeking unrestrained pleasure; living a fast life. **2.** moving with the legs raised high: *a high-stepping horse.* —**high′-step′per,** *n.*

high′-strung′, *adj.* being highly sensitive or nervous in temperament.

high′ style′, *n.* style, as in clothes or behavior, marked by discrimination and trend-setting verve. —**high′-style,** *adj.*

high·tail (hī′tāl′), *v.i. Informal.* **1.** to go away or leave rapidly: *Last we saw of him, he was hightailing down the street.* —**Idiom. 2. hightail it,** to hurry.

high′ tea′, *n. Brit.* a late afternoon or early evening meal at which tea is served.

high′-tech′, *n.* **1.** high technology. **2.** a style of interior design using industrial and commercial fixtures, materials, etc., or incorporating elements having the stark, utilitarian appearance characteristic of industrial design. —*adj.* **3.** of, pertaining to, or suggesting high-tech or high technology.

high′ technol′ogy, *n.* technology that uses highly sophisticated equipment and advanced engineering techniques, as microelectronics, genetic engineering, or telecommunications. —**high′-tech·nol′o·gy,** *adj.*

high′-ten′sion, *adj.* subjected to or capable of operating under relatively high voltage: *high-tension wire.*

high′-test′, *adj.* (of gasoline) boiling at a relatively low temperature.

high′ tide′, *n.* **1.** the tide at its highest level of elevation. **2.** the time of high water. **3.** a culminating point.

high′ time′, *n.* the appropriate time or past the appropriate time: *It's high time you quit smoking.*

high′ top′, *n.* a sneaker that covers the ankle.

high′ trea′son, *n.* treason against the sovereign or state.

high′ wa′ter, *n.* **1.** water at its greatest elevation, as in a river. **2.** HIGH TIDE.

high′-wa′ter mark′, *n.* **1.** a mark showing the highest level reached by a body of water. **2.** the highest point of anything; acme.

high·way (hī′wā′), *n.* **1.** a main road, esp. one between towns or cities. **2.** any public road or waterway. **3.** any main or ordinary route, track, or course.

high·way·man (hī′wā′mən), *n., pl.* **-men.** a holdup man, esp. one on horseback, who robbed travelers along a public road.

high′way rob′bery, *n.* **1.** robbery committed on a highway against travelers, as by a highwayman. **2.** a price or fee that is unreasonably high; exorbitant charge. —**high′way rob′ber,** *n.*

high′ wire′, *n.* a tightrope stretched high above the ground.

H.I.H., Her Imperial Highness; His Imperial Highness.

hi·jack or **high·jack** (hī′jak′), *v.t.* **1.** to seize (an airplane or other vehicle) by threat or by force, esp. for ransom or political objectives. **2.** to steal (cargo) from a truck or other vehicle after forcing it to stop: *to hijack a load of whiskey.* **3.** to rob (a vehicle) after forcing it to stop: *They hijacked the truck outside the city.* —*n.* **4.** an act or instance of hijacking. —**hi′jack′er, high′jack′er,** *n.*

Hij·ra (hij′rə), *n.* (*sometimes l.c.*) *Islam.* **1.** the flight of Muhammad from Mecca to Medina to escape persecution A.D. 622: regarded as the beginning of the Muslim Era. **2.** the Muslim Era itself. Also, **Hegira, Hij′rah.**

hike (hīk), *v.,* **hiked, hik·ing,** *n.* —*v.i.* **1.** to walk or march a great distance, esp. through rural areas, for pleasure, exercise, military training, etc. **2.** to move up or rise, as out of place or position (often fol. by *up*): *My shirt hikes up if I don't wear a belt.* **3.** to hold oneself outboard on the windward side of a heeling sailboat to reduce the amount of heel. —*v.t.* **4.** to move or raise with a jerk (often fol. by *up*): *to hike up one's socks.* **5.** to increase, often sharply and unexpectedly: *to hike the price of milk.* —*n.* **6.** a long walk or march for recreational activity, military

training, or the like. **7.** an increase or rise, often sharp and unexpected: *a hike in wages.* —**hik′er,** *n.*

hi·lar·i·ous (hi lâr′ē əs, -lar′-, hī-), *adj.* **1.** arousing great merriment; extremely funny. **2.** boisterously merry or cheerful: *feeling hilarious from the champagne.* —**hi·lar′i·ous·ly,** *adv.* —**hi·lar′i·ty,** *n.*

hill (hil), *n.* **1.** a natural elevation of the earth's surface, smaller than a mountain. **2.** an incline, esp. in a road. **3.** an artificial heap, pile, or mound. **4. a.** a mound of earth raised about and above a plant or plant cluster. **b.** a cluster of plants within such a mound. **5. the Hill,** CAPITOL HILL. —*v.t.* **6.** to surround with hills. **7.** to form into a hill or heap. —**Idiom. 8. over the hill, a.** advanced in age; past one's prime. **b.** absent without permission from a military unit or prison. —**hill′i·ness,** *n.* —**hill′y,** *adj.,* **-i·er, -i·est.**

Hil·la·ry (hil′ə rē), *n.* **Sir Edmund P.,** born 1919, New Zealand mountain climber who scaled Mount Everest 1953.

hill·bil·ly (hil′bil′ē), *n., pl.* **-lies,** *adj.* —*n.* **1.** *Often Disparaging.* a person from a backwoods or other remote area, esp. from the mountains of the southern U.S. —*adj.* **2.** of, like, or pertaining to hillbillies: *hillbilly humor.* [*hill* + *Billy,* familiar form of William]

hill′billy mu′sic, *n.* COUNTRY MUSIC.

Hil·lel (hil′el, -āl, hi lāl′), *n.* c60 B.C.–A.D. 9?, Palestinian rabbi and interpreter of Biblical law.

hill·ock (hil′ək), *n.* a small hill.

hill·side (hil′sīd′), *n.* the side or slope of a hill.

hill·top (hil′top′), *n.* the top or summit of a hill.

hilt (hilt), *n.* **1.** the handle of a sword or dagger. **2.** the handle of any weapon or tool. —**Idiom. 3. to the hilt,** to the maximum extent or degree; completely; fully.

him (him), *pron.* **1.** the objective case of HE, used as a direct or indirect object: *I'll see him tomorrow. Give him the message.* **2.** (used instead of the pronoun *he* in the predicate after the verb *to be*): *It's him.* **3.** (used instead of the pronoun *his* before a gerund or present participle): *We were surprised by him wanting to leave.* —*n.* **4.** *Informal.* a male: *Is the new baby a her or a him?*

Him′ala′yan cat′, *n.* one of a breed of longhaired domestic cats developed by crossing the Persian cat and the Siamese and having the long coat and stocky body of the Persian and the coloring of the Siamese.

Him·a·la·yas (him′ə lā′əz, hi mäl′yəz), *n.pl.* **the,** a mountain range extending about 1500 mi. (2400 km) along the border between India and Tibet. Highest peak, Mt. Everest, 29,028 ft. (8848 m). Also called **Him′ala′ya Moun′tains.** —**Him′a·la′yan,** *adj., n.*

him·self (him self′; *medially often* im-), *pron.* **1.** a reflexive form of HIM (used as the direct or indirect object of a verb or as the object of a preposition): *He cut himself. He wrote himself a note. He felt a conflict within himself.* **2.** (used as an intensive): *He himself told me.* **3.** (used in absolute constructions): *Himself the soul of honor, he included many rascals among his intimates.* **4.** (used in place of HE or HIM in various compound and comparative constructions): *Only his son and himself were involved. His wife is as stingy as himself.* **5.** his normal or customary self: *He is himself again.* **6.** *Irish Eng. and Scot.* a man of importance: *Himself will be wanting an early dinner.*

Hi·na·ya·na (hē′nə yä′nə), *n.* the earlier of the two major schools of Buddhism, still prevalent in Sri Lanka, Burma, Thailand, and Cambodia, emphasizing personal salvation through one's own efforts. [< Sanskrit, = *hīna* lesser, inferior + *yāna* vehicle] —**Hi′na·ya′nist,** *n.*

hind[1] (hīnd), *adj.* situated in the rear or at the back; posterior: *the hind legs of an animal.*

hind[2] (hīnd), *n., pl.* **hinds,** (*esp. collectively*) **hind. 1.** the female of the European red deer in and after the third year. **2.** any of various groupers of the genus *Epinephelus,* of warm Atlantic seas, as the orange-speckled *E. adscensionis* (**rock hind**).

hind·brain (hīnd′brān′), *n.* the most posterior of the three embryonic divisions of the vertebrate brain or the parts derived from this tissue, including the medulla oblongata, the pons of mammals, and the cerebellum.

Hin·den·burg (hin′dən bûrg′), *n.* a giant German zeppelin that crashed and burned near Lakehurst, N.J., in 1937.

hin·der[1] (hin′dər), *v.t.* **1.** to cause delay, interruption, or difficulty in; hamper; impede. **2.** to prevent from doing, acting, or happening; stop. —*v.i.* **3.** to be an obstacle or impediment. —**hin′der·er,** *n.*

hind·er[2] (hīn′dər), *adj.* situated at the rear or back; posterior.

hind·gut (hīnd′gut′), *n.* **1. a.** the last portion of the vertebrate alimentary canal, between the cecum and the anus. **b.** the posterior part of the digestive tract of arthropods. **2.** the posterior part of the embryonic vertebrate alimentary canal, from which the colon develops. Compare FOREGUT, MIDGUT.

Hin·di (hin′dē), *n.* an Indo-Aryan language of N India, having equal status with English as an official language throughout India.

hind·most (hīnd′mōst′), *adj.* farthest behind or nearest the rear; last.

hind·quar·ter (hīnd′kwôr′tər, -kwô′-), *n.* **1.** hindquarters, the rear part of a quadruped. **2.** the posterior end of a halved carcass, as of a steer or lamb, sectioned usu. after the 12th rib.

hin·drance (hin′drəns), *n.* **1.** the act of hindering. **2.** the state of being hindered. **3.** a person or thing that hinders.

hind′ shank′, *n.* See under SHANK (def. 3).

H

hind·sight (hīnd′sīt′), *n.* recognition of the nature or requirements of a situation, event, etc., after its occurrence.

Hin·du (hin′dōō), *n., pl.* **-dus,** *adj.* —*n.* **1.** an adherent of Hinduism. —*adj.* **2.** of or pertaining to Hindus or Hinduism.

Hin·du·ism (hin′dōō iz′əm), *n.* the common religion of India, based upon the religion of the original Aryan settlers as expounded and evolved in the Vedas, Upanishads, Bhagavad-Gita, etc.

hind′ wing′, *n.* one of the second, or posterior, wings of an insect.

Hine (hīn), *n.* Stuart, born 1899, English clergyman and hymn writer.

hinge (hinj), *n., v.,* **hinged, hing·ing.** —*n.* **1.** a jointed device or flexible piece on which a door, gate, lid, or other attached part turns, swings, or moves. **2.** a natural anatomical joint at which motion occurs around a transverse axis, as that of the knee. **3.** that on which something is based or depends; pivotal consideration or factor. **4.** a gummed sticker, folded so as to form a hinge, for affixing a stamp to a page of an album. —*v.i.* **5.** to be dependent or contingent on, or as if on, a hinge (usu. fol. by *on* or *upon*): *Everything hinges on her decision.* —*v.t.* **6.** to attach by or as if by a hinge or hinges. **7.** to make or consider as dependent upon; predicate: *He hinged his action on future sales.*

hint (hint), *n.* **1.** an indirect, covert, or helpful suggestion; clue: *Give me a hint as to his identity.* **2.** a very slight or hardly noticeable amount: *a hint of garlic in the salad dressing.* **3.** a perceived indication or suggestion; note: *a hint of spring in the air.* —*v.t.* **4.** to give a hint of: *gray skies hinting a possible snowfall.* —*v.i.* **5.** to make indirect suggestion or allusion; subtly imply (usu. fol. by *at*): *The facts hinted at a solution to the problem.* —**hint′er,** *n.*

hin·ter·land (hin′tər land′), *n.* **1.** Often, **hinterlands.** the remote or less developed parts of a country; back country. **2.** the land lying behind a coastal region.

hip¹ (hip), *n.* **1.** the projecting part on each side of the body surrounding the hip joint; haunch. **2.** HIP JOINT.

hip² (hip), *n.* the fleshy fruit of a rose, often bright red.

hip³ (hip), *interj.* (used as a cheer or in signaling for cheers): *Hip, hip, hurrah!*

hip⁴ (hip), *adj.,* **hip·per, hip·pest,** *n. Slang.* —*adj.* **1.** familiar with or informed about the latest ideas, styles, developments, etc.; up-to-date; with-it. —*n.* **2.** the condition of being hip. —*Idiom.* **3. hip to,** aware of or attuned to; knowledgeable about: *to be hip to what's happening.* —**hip′ly,** *adv.* —**hip′ness,** *n.*

hip·bone (hip′bōn′), *n.* **1.** either of the two bones forming the sides of the pelvis, each consisting of three consolidated bones, the ilium, ischium, and pubis; innominate bone. **2.** ILIUM.

hip′ boot′, *n.* a hip-high boot, usu. of rubber, worn by fishermen, firefighters, etc.

hip-hop (hip′hop′), *n. Slang.* **1.** the popular subculture of usu. black urban youth, esp. the part concerned with rap music. **2.** RAP MUSIC.

hip·hug·ger (hip′hug′ər), *adj.* **1.** having a close-fitting waistline placed at the hip rather than at the natural waist: *hiphugger jeans.* —*n.* **2. hiphuggers,** hiphugger pants.

hip′ joint′, *n.* the ball-and-socket joint between the head of the femur and the innominate bone.

hip·pie or **hip·py** (hip′ē), *n., pl.* **-pies. 1.** a young person of the 1960s who rejected established social values, advocated spontaneity, free expression of love and the expanding of consciousness, often wore long hair and unconventional clothes, and used psychedelic drugs. **2.** any person resembling a hippie of the 1960s in attitude, dress, and behavior. —**hip′pie·dom,** *n.*

hip·po·cam·pus (hip′ə kam′pəs), *n., pl.* **-pi** (-pī, -pē). **1.** a sea horse of Greek myth having two forefeet and a body ending in the tail of a dolphin or fish. **2.** a curved ridge in the lateral ventricles of the mammalian brain: part of the limbic system. —**hip′po·cam′pal,** *adj.*

Hip·poc·ra·tes (hi pok′rə tēz′), (*"Father of Medicine"*) c460–c377 B.C., Greek physician. —**Hip·po·crat′ic** (hip′ə krat′ik), *adj.*

Hip·pocrat′ic oath′, *n.* an oath embodying the duties and obligations of physicians, usu. taken by those about to enter upon the practice of medicine.

hip·po·drome (hip′ə drōm′), *n.* **1.** an arena or structure for equestrian and other spectacles. **2.** (in ancient Greece and Rome) an oval track for horse and chariot races. —**hip′po·drom′ic** (-drom′ik), *adj.*

hip·po·pot·a·mus (hip′ə pot′ə məs), *n., pl.* **-mus·es, -mi** (-mī′). a large African mammal, *Hippopotamus amphibius,* with a hairless, thick body and short legs, living in and alongside rivers. [< Latin < Greek *hippopótamos* river horse] —**hip′po·po·tam′ic** (-pə tam′ik), **hip′po·po·ta′mi·an** (-tā′mē ən), *adj.*

hippopotamus, *Hippopotamus amphibius,* 4 ½ ft. (1.4 m) high at shoulder; length 13 ft. (4 m)

hip·py¹ (hip′ē), *adj.,* **-pi·er, -pi·est.** having big hips.
hip·py² (hip′ē), *n., pl.* **-pies.** HIPPIE.
hip·ster¹ (hip′stər), *n. Slang.* **1.** a person who is hip. **2.** HEPCAT (def. 1). **3.** BEATNIK.

hip·ster² (hip′stər), *n.* **1.** *Chiefly Brit.* HIPHUGGER (def. 2). **2.** Often, **hipsters.** hiphugger underpants.

hi·ra·ga·na (hēr′ə gä′nə), *n.* the cursive and more widely used of the two Japanese syllabaries. Compare KATAKANA.

Hi·ram (hī′rəm), *n.* a king of Tyre in the 10th century B.C. I Kings 5.

hir·cine (hûr′sīn, -sin), *adj.* **1.** of, pertaining to, or resembling a goat. **2.** having a goatish odor. **3.** lustful; libidinous.

hire (hīⁱr), *v.,* **hired, hir·ing.** —*v.t.* **1.** to engage the services of for wages or other payment: *to hire a clerk.* **2.** to engage the temporary use of at a set price; rent: *to hire a limousine.* **3. hire on,** to obtain employment; take a job: *They hired on as wranglers with the rodeo.* **4. hire out,** to offer or exchange one's services for payment: *He hired himself out as a handyman.* —*n.* **5.** the act of hiring. **6.** the condition of being hired. **7.** the price or compensation paid for the temporary use of something or for personal services or labor; pay. **8.** *Informal.* a person hired or to be hired. —*Idiom.* **9. for hire,** available for use or service in exchange for payment. Also, **on hire.** —**hir′a·bil′i·ty,** *n.* —**hir′a·ble, hire′a·ble,** *adj.* —**hir′er,** *n.*

hire·ling (hīⁱr′ling), *n.* **1.** a person who works only for pay, esp. in a menial or boring job, with little or no concern for the value of the work. —*adj.* **2.** serving for pay only. **3.** venal; mercenary.

Hi·ro·shi·ma (hēr′ō shē′mə, hi rō′shə mə), *n.* a seaport on SW Honshu, in SW Japan: first military use of atomic bomb Aug. 6, 1945. 1,034,000.

hir·sute (hûr′sōōt, hûr sōōt′), *adj.* **1.** hairy; shaggy. **2.** of, pertaining to, or characteristic of hair. —**hir′sute·ness,** *n.*

his (hiz; *unstressed* iz), *pron.* **1.** the possessive form of HE (used as an attributive or predicative adjective): *His coat is the brown one. This book is his. Do you mind his speaking first?* **2.** that or those belonging to him: *His was the strangest remark of all. I borrowed a tie of his.*

His·pan·ic (hi span′ik), *adj.* **1.** of or pertaining to Spain or Spanish-speaking countries. **2.** Also, **Hispan′ic-Amer′ican.** of or pertaining to Hispanics. —*n.* **3.** Also, **Hispan′ic Amer′ican.** a U.S. citizen or resident of Spanish or Latin-American descent. —**His·pan′i·cal·ly,** *adv.*

His·pan·io·la (his′pən yō′lə), *n.* an island in the West Indies, comprising Haiti and the Dominican Republic. 30,285 sq. mi. (78,460 sq. km).

hiss (his), *v.i.* **1.** to make or emit a sharp sound like that of the letter *s* when prolonged. **2.** to express disapproval or contempt by making this sound. —*v.t.* **3.** to express disapproval of by hissing. **4.** to silence or drive away by hissing (usu. fol. by *away, down,* etc.). **5.** to utter with a hiss. —*n.* **6.** a hissing sound, esp. one made in disapproval.

Hiss (his), *n.* Alger, born 1904, U.S. government official, accused of espionage 1948 and imprisoned for perjury 1950–54.

his·tol·o·gy (hi stol′ə jē), *n.* **1.** the branch of biology dealing with the study of tissues. **2.** the structure, esp. the microscopic structure, of organic tissues. —**his·to·log′i·cal** (his′tl oj′i kəl), **his′to·log′ic,** *adj.* —**his′to·log′i·cal·ly,** *adv.* —**his·tol′o·gist,** *n.*

his·to·pa·thol·o·gy (his′tō pə thol′ə jē), *n.* the branch of pathology dealing with the structure of abnormal or diseased tissue. —**his′to·path′o·log′ic** (-tə path′ə loj′ik), **his′to·path′o·log′i·cal,** *adj.* —**his′to·pa·thol′o·gist,** *n.*

his·to·phys·i·ol·o·gy (his′tə fiz′ē ol′ə jē), *n.* the branch of physiology dealing with tissues. —**his′to·phys′i·o·log′i·cal** (-ə loj′i kəl), *adj.*

his·to·ri·an (hi stôr′ē ən, -stōr′-), *n.* **1.** an expert in or authority on history. **2.** a writer of history; chronicler.

his·tor·ic (hi stôr′ik, -stor′-), *adj.* **1.** well-known or important in history: *a historic building.* **2.** HISTORICAL.

his·tor·i·cal (hi stôr′i kəl, -stor′-), *adj.* **1.** of, pertaining to, treating, or characteristic of history or past events: *historical records.* **2.** based on or suggested by history or documented material from the past: *a historical novel; a historical pageant.* **3.** having once existed or lived, as opposed to being part of legend, fiction, or religious belief: *a study of the historical Jesus.* **4.** narrated or mentioned in history; belonging to the past. **5.** noting or pertaining to analysis based on a comparison among several periods of development of a phenomenon, as in language or economics. **6.** HISTORIC (def. 1). —**his·tor′i·cal·ly,** *adv.* —**his·tor′i·cal·ness,** *n.*

histor′ical linguis′tics, *n.* the study of changes in a language or group of languages over a period of time.

his·tor·i·cism (hi stôr′ə siz′əm, -stor′-), *n.* **1.** a theory that history is determined by immutable laws and not by human agency. **2.** a theory that all cultural phenomena are historically determined and that historians must study each period without imposing any personal or absolute value system. **3.** a profound or excessive respect for historical institutions, as laws or traditions. —**his·tor′i·cist,** *n., adj.*

his·to·ri·og·ra·phy (hi stôr′ē og′rə fē, -stōr′-), *n., pl.* **-phies. 1.** the body of literature dealing with historical matters; histories collectively. **2.** the body of techniques, theories, and principles of historical research and presentation; methods of historical scholarship. **3.** the narrative presentation of history based on a critical examination, evaluation, and selection of material from primary and secondary sources and subject to scholarly criteria. **4.** an official history. —**his·to′ri·o·graph′ic** (-ə graf′ik), **his·to′ri·o·graph′i·cal,** *adj.* —**his·to′ri·o·graph′i·cal·ly,** *adv.*

his·to·ry (his′tə rē, his′trē), *n., pl.* **-ries. 1.** the branch of knowledge dealing with past events. **2.** a continuous, systematic narrative of past events as relating to a particular people, country, period, person, etc., usu. written as a chronological account. **3.** the aggregate of past events.

4. the record of past events and times, esp. in connection with the human race. **5.** a past notable for its important, unusual, or interesting events: *a ship with a history.* **6.** acts, ideas, or events that will or can shape the course of the future. **7.** a systematic account of any set of natural phenomena without reference to time. **8.** a drama representing historical events. **—*Idiom.* 9. be history,** to be no longer present, participating, or relevant: *If they lose this game, they're history.*

his•tri•on•ic (his′trē on′ik), *adj.* **1.** deliberately affected or self-consciously emotional; overly dramatic in behavior or speech. **2.** of or pertaining to actors or acting. **—his′tri•on′i•cal•ly,** *adv.*

his•tri•on•ics (his′trē on′iks), *n.* (*used with a sing. or pl. v.*) **1.** artificial behavior or speech for effect, as insincere or exaggerated expression of an emotion. **2.** dramatic representation; theatricals.

hit (hit), *v.,* **hit, hit•ting,** *n.* **—*v.t.* 1.** to deal a blow or stroke to: *Hit the nail with the hammer.* **2.** to come against with an impact: *The wheel hit the curb.* **3.** to reach with a missile, a weapon, a blow, or the like, as one throwing, shooting, or striking: *Did the arrow hit the target?* **4.** *Baseball.* **a.** to make (a base hit). **b.** BAT[1] (def. 10). **5.** to drive or propel by a stroke: *to hit a ball onto the green.* **6.** to have a marked effect or influence on; affect severely: *to be hit hard by inflation.* **7.** to request or demand of: *He hit me for a loan.* **8.** to reach or attain (a specified level or amount): *Prices hit a new high.* **9.** to be published in or released to; appear in: *The story hit the front page.* **10.** to land on or arrive in: *The troops hit the beach at dawn.* **11.** to give (someone) another playing card, drink, portion, etc. **12.** to come or light upon; meet with; find: *to hit the right answer.* **13.** to agree with; suit exactly: *to hit someone's fancy.* **14.** to succeed in representing or producing exactly: *to hit the right tone.* **15.** *Informal.* to begin to travel on: *Let's hit the road.* **16.** *Slang.* to kill; murder. **—*v.i.* 17.** to strike with a missile, a weapon, or the like; deal a blow or blows. **18.** to come into collision (often fol. by *against, on,* or *upon*). **19.** (of an internal-combustion engine) to ignite a mixture of air and fuel as intended. **20.** to come or light (usu. fol. by *upon* or *on*): *to hit on a new way.* **21. hit off, a.** to represent or describe precisely or aptly. **b.** to imitate, esp. in order to satirize. **22. hit on,** *Slang.* to make persistent sexual advances to. **23. hit out, a.** to deal a blow aimlessly. **b.** to make a violent verbal attack: *to hit out angrily at one's critics.* **—*n.* 24.** an impact or collision, as of one thing against another. **25.** a stroke that reaches an object; blow. **26.** a stroke of satire, censure, etc. **27.** BASE HIT. **28.** *Backgammon.* **a.** a game won by a player after the opponent has thrown off one or more men from the board. **b.** any winning game. **29.** a successful stroke, performance, or production; success: *The play is a hit.* **30.** *Slang.* a dose of a narcotic drug. **31.** *Slang.* a murder, esp. one carried out by criminal prearrangement. **—*Idiom.* 32. hit it off,** to be immediately compatible; get along. **33. hit or miss,** without concern for correctness or detail; haphazardly. **34. hit the books,** *Slang.* to study hard; cram. **35. hit the ceiling** or **roof,** *Informal.* to lose one's temper; become enraged. **36. hit the ground running,** to take action rapidly and fully equipped. **37. hit the hay** or **sack,** *Informal.* to go to bed; go to sleep. **38. hit the nail on the head,** to say or do exactly the right thing. **—hit′less,** *adj.* **—hit′ta•ble,** *adj.* **—hit′ter,** *n.*

hit′-and-miss′, *adj.* HIT-OR-MISS.

hit′-and-run′, *adj., v.,* **-ran, -run•ning.** **—*adj.* 1.** guilty of fleeing the scene of an accident one has caused, esp. a vehicular accident: *a hit-and-run driver.* **2.** involving or resulting from such action or conduct: *hit-and-run fatalities.* **3.** pertaining to or noting a baseball play in which a runner sprints toward the next base as the pitcher delivers the ball to the batter, who must try to hit it in order to protect the runner. **4.** marked by taking flight immediately after a quick, concentrated attack: *a hit-and-run raid.* **—*v.i.* 5.** to attempt or execute a hit-and-run play in baseball. **—hit′-and-run′ner,** *n.*

hitch[1] (hich), *v.t.* **1.** to fasten or tie, esp. temporarily, by means of a hook, rope, strap, etc.; tether: *to hitch a horse to a post.* **2.** to harness (an animal) to a vehicle (often fol. by *up*). **3.** to raise with jerks (usu. fol. by *up*); hike up: *to hitch up one's trousers.* **4.** to move or draw (something) with a jerk. **5.** *Slang.* to bind by marriage vows; unite in marriage; marry. **6.** to catch, as on a projection; snag. **—*v.i.* 7.** to stick, as when caught. **8.** to fasten oneself or itself to something (often fol. by *on*). **9.** to move roughly or jerkily: *The old buggy hitched along.* **10.** to hobble; limp. **—*n.* 11.** the act or fact of fastening, as to something, esp. temporarily. **12.** any of various knots or loops made to attach a rope to something in such a way as to be readily loosened. **13.** a period of military service. **14.** an unexpected difficulty, obstacle, delay, etc.: *a hitch in our plans for the picnic.* **15.** a hitching movement; jerk or pull. **16.** a hitching gait; a hobble or limp. **17.** a fastening that joins a movable tool to the mechanism that pulls it. **—hitch′er,** *n.*

hitch[2] (hich), *n. Informal.* hitchhike. **—hitch′er,** *n.*

Hitch•cock (hich′kok), *n.* **Sir Alfred (Joseph),** 1899–1980, U.S. film director, born in England.

hitch•hike (hich′hīk′), *v.,* **-hiked, -hik•ing,** *n.* **—*v.i.* 1.** to travel by standing on the side of the road and soliciting rides from passing vehicles. **—*v.t.* 2.** to ask for or get (a ride) by hitchhiking. **—*n.* 3.** an act of hitchhiking. **—hitch′hik′er,** *n.*

hi′-tech′, *n., adj.* HIGH-TECH.

hith•er (hith′ər), *adv.* **1.** to or toward this place: *to come hither.* **—*adj.* 2.** being on this or the closer side; nearer: *the hither side of the meadow.* **—*Idiom.* 3. hither and thither,** here and there. **4. hither and yon,** from here to a place at some distance; in many places.

hith•er•to (hith′ər to͞o′), *adv.* **1.** up to this time; until now: *a fact hitherto unknown.* **2.** to here.

Hit•ler (hit′lər), *n.* **Adolf,** (*"der Führer"*), 1889–1945, Nazi dictator of Germany, born in Austria: chancellor 1933–45; dictator 1934–45.

hit′ list′, *n. Informal.* **1.** a list of people singled out as targets for murder. **2.** a list of people, programs, etc., to be opposed.

hit′ man′ or **hit′man′,** *n. Slang.* **1.** a hired killer, esp. a professional killer from the underworld. **2.** HATCHET MAN (def. 3).

hit′-or-miss′, *adj.* careless; inattentive; haphazard.

hit′ parade′, *n.* **1.** a listing of popular songs ranked according to their popularity with listeners. **2.** any listing of popular or favorite persons or things.

hit′ squad′, *n. Slang.* **1.** a team of hit men. **2.** a group of political terrorists.

Hit•tite (hit′īt), *n.* **1.** a member of a people of central Anatolia who were a significant power in Anatolia and Syria from c1900 to c1200 B.C. **2.** their extinct Indo-European language, written in a cuneiform syllabary. **—*adj.* 3.** of the Hittites or their language.

HIV, *n.* AIDS VIRUS. [*h(uman) i(mmunodeficiency) v(irus)*]

hive (hīv), *n., v.,* **hived, hiv•ing.** **—*n.* 1.** a shelter constructed for housing a colony of honeybees; beehive. **2.** the colony of bees inhabiting a hive. **3.** something resembling a beehive in structure or use. **4.** a place swarming with busy occupants: *a hive of industry.* **5.** a swarming or teeming multitude. **—*v.t.* 6.** to gather into or cause to enter a hive. **7.** to store up in a hive. **8.** to store or lay away for future use or enjoyment. **—*v.i.* 9.** (of bees) to enter a hive. **10.** to live together in or as if in a hive. **11. hive off,** to separate or remove from a group.

hives (hīvz), *n.* (*used with a sing. or pl. v.*) a transient eruption of large, itchy wheals on the skin usu. caused by an allergic reaction; urticaria.

HM, Hispanic male.

H.M., **1.** Her Majesty. **2.** His Majesty.

HMO, health maintenance organization.

ho[1] (hō), *interj.* **1.** (used as a call to attract attention, sometimes specially used after a word denoting a destination): *Westward ho! Land ho!* **2.** (used as an exclamation of surprise or delight.)

ho[2] (hō), *interj.* (used as a command to a horse to stop.)

HO (hō), *n., pl.* **HOs, HO's.** (in police use) habitual offender.

Ho, *Chem. Symbol.* holmium.

hoa•gy or **hoa•gie** (hō′gē), *n., pl.* **-gies.** *New Jersey and Pennsylvania.* HERO SANDWICH.

hoar (hôr, hōr), *n.* **1.** hoarfrost; rime. **2.** a hoary coating or appearance. **—*adj.* 3.** hoary.

hoard (hôrd, hōrd), *n.* **1.** a supply or accumulation hidden or carefully guarded for preservation or future use: *a hoard of money; a hoard of food.* **—*v.t.* 2.** to accumulate a hoard of. **—*v.i.* 3.** to accumulate a hoard. **—hoard′er,** *n.*

hoard•ing[1] (hôr′ding, hōr′-), *n.* **1.** the act of a person who hoards. **2. hoardings,** things that are hoarded.

hoard•ing[2] (hôr′ding, hōr′-), *n.* **1.** a temporary fence enclosing a construction site. **2.** *Brit.* a billboard.

hoar•frost (hôr′frôst′, -frost′, hōr′-), *n.* FROST (def. 2).

hoarse (hôrs, hōrs), *adj.,* **hoars•er, hoars•est.** **1.** having a vocal tone characterized by weakness of intensity and excessive breathiness; husky. **2.** having a raucous voice. **3.** making a harsh, low sound. **—hoarse′ly,** *adv.* **—hoarse′ness,** *n.*

hoar•y (hôr′ē, hōr′ē), *adj.,* **–i•er, –i•est.** **1.** gray or white with age. **2.** ancient or venerable: *hoary myths.* **3.** tedious from familiarity; stale: *a hoary joke.* **—hoar′i•ly,** *adv.* **—hoar′i•ness,** *n.*

hoax (hōks), *n.* **1.** something intended to deceive or defraud. **—*v.t.* 2.** to deceive by a hoax; hoodwink. **—hoax′er,** *n.*

hob[1] (hob), *n.* **1.** a projection or shelf at the back or side of a fireplace, used for keeping food warm. **2.** a milling cutter for gear and sprocket teeth, splines, threads, etc., that is fed across the work as the work is rotated. **—*v.t., v.i.* 3.** to cut with a hob. **4.** to provide with hobnails. **—hob′ber,** *n.*

hob[2] (hob), *n.* **1.** a hobgoblin or elf. **—*Idiom.* 2. play hob with,** to do mischief or harm to. **3. raise hob,** to behave disruptively. **—hob′like′,** *adj.*

Ho•ban (hō′bən), *n.* **James,** c1762–1831, U.S. architect, born in Ireland: designed the White House.

Ho•bart (hō′bərt *or, for 1, 4,* -bärt; hō′bärt *for 2*), *n.* **1. Gar•ret Augus•tus** (gar′it), 1844–99, U.S. lawyer and politician: vice president of the U.S. 1897–99. **2.** a seaport on and the capital of Tasmania, SE of Australia. 128,603.

Hobbes (hobz), *n.* **Thomas,** 1588–1679, English philosopher and author. **—Hobbes′i•an,** *adj., n.*

hob•ble (hob′əl), *v.,* **-bled, -bling,** *n.* **—*v.i.* 1.** to walk lamely; limp. **2.** to proceed irregularly and haltingly. **—*v.t.* 3.** to cause to limp. **4.** to fasten together the legs of (a horse, mule, etc.) by short lengths of rope to prevent free motion. **5.** to impede; hamper the progress of. **—*n.* 6.** an act of hobbling; an uneven, halting gait. **7.** a rope, strap, etc., used to hobble an animal.

hob•ble•bush (hob′əl bo͝osh′), *n.* a NE North American viburnum, *Viburnum alnifolium,* with flat-topped clusters of small white flowers.

hob•by[1] (hob′ē), *n., pl.* **-bies.** **1.** an activity or interest pursued for pleasure or relaxation and not as a main occupation. **2.** a child's hobby-horse. **—hob′by•ist,** *n.*

hob•by² (hob′ē), *n., pl.* **-bies.** any of various small, very swift falcons, esp. *Falco subbuteo,* of Eurasia.

hob•by•horse (hob′ē hôrs′), *n.* **1.** a stick with a horse's head, or a rocking horse, ridden by children. **2.** a figure of a horse, attached at the waist of a performer in a morris dance, pantomime, etc. **3.** a pet idea or project.

hob•gob•lin (hob′gob′lin), *n.* **1.** something causing superstitious fear; bogy. **2.** a mischievous goblin.

hob•nail (hob′nāl′), *n.* **1.** a large-headed nail for protecting the soles of heavy boots and shoes. **2.** a small allover pattern consisting of small tufts, as on fabrics, or of small studs, as on glass. **—hob′nailed′,** *adj.*

hob•nob (hob′nob′), *v.,* **-nobbed, -nob•bing.** *n.* **—v.i.** **1.** to associate on very friendly terms: *to hobnob with royalty.* **—n.** **2.** a friendly, informal chat. **—hob′nob′ber,** *n.*

ho•bo (hō′bō), *n., pl.* **-bos, -boes. 1.** a tramp or vagrant. **2.** a migratory worker. **—ho′bo•ism,** *n.*

Hob′son's choice′ (hob′sənz), *n.* the choice of taking either that which is offered or nothing; the absence of a real alternative. [after Thomas *Hobson* (1544–1631), of Cambridge, England, who rented horses and gave his customer only one choice, that of the horse nearest the stable door]

Ho′ Chi′ Minh′ Cit′y, *n.* a seaport in S Vietnam. 4,000,000. Formerly, **Saigon.**

hock¹ (hok), *n.* **1.** the joint in the hind leg of a horse, cow, etc., above the fetlock joint, corresponding anatomically to the ankle in humans. **2.** a corresponding joint in a fowl. **—v.t. 3.** to hamstring.

hock² (hok), *v.t.* **1.** to pawn. **—n. 2.** the state of being deposited or held as security; pawn. **3.** the condition of owing; debt. **—hock′er,** *n.*

hock•ey (hok′ē), *n.* **1.** ICE HOCKEY. **2.** FIELD HOCKEY.

hock′ey stick′, *n.* the long, hooked stick used in field hockey or ice hockey.

hockey stick

ho•cus (hō′kəs), *v.t.,* **-cused, -cus•ing** or (*esp. Brit.*) **-cussed, -cus•sing. 1.** to play a trick on; hoax. **2.** to stupefy, as with drugged liquor. **3.** to infuse (liquor) with a drug.

ho•cus-po•cus (hō′kəs pō′kəs), *n., v.,* **-cused, -cus•ing** or (*esp. Brit.*) **-cussed, -cus•sing. —n. 1.** meaningless words used in conjuring. **2.** a juggler's trick; sleight of hand. **3.** mysterious or elaborate activity or talk, esp. for covering up a deception. **—v.t. 4.** to play tricks on or with. [pseudo-Latin rhyming formula used by magicians]

hod (hod), *n.* **1.** a portable trough fixed crosswise on top of a pole held against the shoulder and used for carrying bricks, mortar, etc. **2.** a coal scuttle.

hodge•podge (hoj′poj′), *n.* a heterogeneous mixture; jumble.

Hodg′kin's disease′, *n.* a malignant disorder characterized by enlargement of the lymph nodes and spleen and by lymphoid infiltration along the blood vessels.

hoe (hō), *n., v.,* **hoed, hoe•ing. —n. 1.** a long-handled implement with a thin, flat blade usu. set transversely, used esp. in breaking up the soil and in weeding. **2.** any of various implements of similar form, as for mixing plaster. **—v.t. 3.** to scrape, weed, or cultivate with a hoe. **—v.i. 4.** to use a hoe. **—ho′er,** *n.* **—hoe′like′,** *adj.*

scuffle hoe   draw hoe   weeding hoe   hoe

hoe

hoe•down (hō′doun′), *n.* **1.** a community dancing party typically featuring folk and square dances accompanied by lively hillbilly tunes played on the fiddle. **2.** the music typical of a hoedown.

Hof•fa (hof′ə), *n.* **James Riddle,** (*"Jimmy"*), 1913–75?, U.S. labor leader: president of the International Brotherhood of Teamsters 1957–71; disappeared 1975.

hog (hôg, hog), *n., v.,* **hogged, hog•ging. —n. 1.** a domesticated swine, *Sus scrofa;* pig. **2.** a domesticated swine weighing 120 lb. (54 kg) or more, raised for market. **3.** any of various hoofed, even-toed mammals of the Old World family Suidae, including the wild boar, warthog, and domesticated swine. **4.** a selfish, gluttonous, or filthy person. **5.** *Slang.* a large motorcycle. **6.** *Brit.* a sheep about one year old that has not been shorn. **—v.t. 7.** to appropriate selfishly; take more than one's share of. **8.** to arch (the back) upward like that of a hog. **9.** ROACH³ (def.

2). **—Idiom. 10. go (the) whole hog,** to do something thoroughly. **11. live** or **eat high off** or **on the hog,** to live prosperously and luxuriously. **—hog′ger,** *n.*

ho•gan (hō′gôn, -gən), *n.* a Navajo dwelling of rounded or angular shape constructed of logs and sticks covered with mud or sod.

hog•back (hôg′bak′, hog′-), *n.* a long, sharply crested ridge generally formed of steeply inclined strata that are especially resistant to erosion.

hog′ chol′era, *n.* an acute, usu. fatal, highly contagious disease of swine caused by an RNA virus of the genus *Pestivirus.* Also called **swine fever.**

hog•fish (hôg′fish′, hog′-), *n., pl.* (*esp. collectively*) **-fish,** (*esp. for kinds or species*) **-fish•es. 1.** a large, edible wrasse, *Lachnolaimus maximus,* of the W Atlantic. **2.** any of various other fishes having a fancied resemblance to a hog, as the pigfish.

hog•gish (hô′gish, hog′ish), *adj.* **1.** selfish or gluttonous. **2.** filthy. **—hog′gish•ly,** *adv.* **—hog′gish•ness,** *n.*

hog′-nosed′ skunk′, *n.* any naked-muzzled skunk of the genus *Conepatus,* found from the SW U.S. to Argentina. Also called **rooter skunk.**

hog′nose snake′ (hôg′nōz′, hog′-), *n.* any harmless North American snake of the genus *Heterodon* having an upturned snout.

hog′ pea′nut, *n.* a twining plant, *Amphicarpaea bracteata,* of the legume family, bearing pods that ripen in or on the ground.

hogs•head (hôgz′hed′, hogz′-), *n.* **1.** a large cask, esp. one containing from 63 to 140 gallons (238 to 530 liters). **2.** any of various units of liquid measure, esp. one equivalent to 63 gallons (238 liters). *Abbr.:* hhd

hog′ suck′er, *n.* any of several suckers of the genus *Hypentelium* inhabiting cool streams of E North America and characterized by a broad head that is concave above.

hog•tie (hôg′tī′, hog′-), *v.t.,* **-tied, -ty•ing. 1.** to tie (an animal) with all four feet together. **2.** to hamper; thwart: *Delays hogtied the investigation.*

hog•wash (hôg′wosh′, -wôsh′, hog′-), *n.* **1.** refuse given to hogs; swill. **2.** nonsense; bunk.

hog•weed (hôg′wēd′, hog′-), *n.* any coarse weed with composite flower heads, esp. the cow parsnip.

hog′-wild′, *adj.* wildly enthusiastic or excited.

Ho•hen•stau•fen (hō′ən shtou′fən), *n.* a member of the German princely family that ruled in Germany, Sicily, and the Holy Roman Empire in the 12th and 13th centuries.

Ho•hen•zol•lern (hō′ən zol′ərn), *n.* a member of the German royal family that ruled in Brandenburg, Prussia, and Germany 1415–1918.

ho-hum (hō′hum′, -hum′), *interj.* **1.** (an exclamation expressing boredom, weariness, or contempt.) **—adj. 2.** dull; routine: *a ho-hum performance.*

hoi pol•loi (hoi′ pə loi′), *n.* the common people; the masses (often preceded by *the*). [< Greek: the many]

hoi′sin sauce′ (hoi′sin, hoi sin′), *n.* a thick, sweet and spicy sauce made with soybeans, sugar, garlic, and chili peppers, used in Chinese cooking as a flavoring and as a condiment.

hoist (hoist *or, sometimes,* hīst), *v.t.* **1.** to raise or lift, esp. by some mechanical appliance: *to hoist the mainsail.* **2.** to raise to one's lips and drink: *to hoist a beer.* **—n. 3.** an apparatus for hoisting, as a block and tackle, a derrick, or a crane. **4.** the act of hoisting; a lift: *Give that sofa a hoist at your end.* **5.** the vertical dimension amidships of any sail that is hoisted with a yard. **6.** (on a flag) **a.** the vertical dimension as flown from a vertical staff. **b.** the edge running next to the staff. Compare FLY¹ (def. 26). **—hoist′er,** *n.*

hoi•ty-toi•ty (hoi′tē toi′tē), *adj.* **1.** pretentious; haughty. **2.** giddy; flighty. **—n. 3.** hoity-toity behavior.

hoke (hōk), *v.t.,* **hoked, hok•ing.** to alter or manipulate so as to give a deceptively or superficially improved quality (usu. fol. by *up*): *a speech hoked up with statistics.*

hok•ey (hō′kē), *adj.,* **-i•er, -i•est. 1.** cloyingly sentimental; mawkish. **2.** contrived in an obvious way. **—hok′ey•ness, hok′i•ness,** *n.*

ho•key-po•key (hō′kē pō′kē), *n.* **1.** hocus-pocus; trickery. **2.** a kind of ice cream formerly sold by street vendors.

ho•kum (hō′kəm), *n.* **1.** utter nonsense; bunkum. **2.** elements of low comedy or stale melodrama introduced into a play or story for laughter or effect.

Hol•bein (hōl′bīn), *n.* **1. Hans** (*"the Elder"*), 1465?–1524, German painter. **2.** his son, **Hans** (*"the Younger"*), 1497?–1543, German painter, chiefly in England.

hold¹ (hōld), *v.,* **held, hold•ing,** *n.* **—v.t. 1.** to have or keep in the hand; grasp: *to hold someone's hand.* **2.** to set aside; reserve or retain: *to hold a reservation.* **3.** to bear, sustain, or support with or as if with the hands or arms. **4.** to keep in a specified state: *The preacher held them spellbound.* **5.** to detain: *The police held her for questioning.* **6.** to conduct; carry on: *to hold a meeting.* **7.** to hinder; restrain: *Fear held me from acting.* **8.** to have the ownership or use of; possess or occupy: *to hold a position of authority.* **9.** to contain or be capable of containing: *This bottle holds a quart.* **10.** to make accountable: *We will hold you to your word.* **11.** to keep in the mind; believe: *held certain beliefs.* **12.** to regard; consider: *to hold a person responsible.* **13.** to keep forcibly: *Enemy forces held the hill.* **14.** to point; aim: *He held a gun on the prisoner.* **15.** to decide legally. **16.** to sustain (a musical note, chord, or rest). **17.** to omit, as from an order: *One burger hold the pickle.* **—v.i. 18.** to remain in a specified state: *Hold still.* **19.** to maintain a grasp; remain fast: *The clamp held.* **20.** to maintain one's position against opposition. **21.** to agree; sympathize: *She doesn't hold with new ideas.* **22.** to remain faithful: *to hold to one's purpose.* **23.** to remain valid: *The rule still holds.* **24.** to refrain; forbear (usu. used imperatively). **25. hold back, a.** to restrain; check: *to hold back tears.* **b.** to hinder the advancement of. **c.** to refrain from giving or revealing; withhold: *to hold back information.* **d.** to refrain from participating. **26. hold down, a.** to keep under control or at a low level: *to hold down interest rates.* **b.** to continue to function in: *to hold down a job.* **27. hold forth,** to speak at great length. **28. hold oneself in,** to exercise restraint. **29. hold off, a.** to keep at a distance; repel. **b.** to postpone action; defer. **30. hold on, a.** to keep a firm grip on something. **b.** to keep going; continue. **c.** to stop; halt (usu. used imperatively). **d.** to keep a telephone connection open. **31. hold out, a.** to present; offer. **b.** to continue to last: *Will the food hold out?* **c.** to refuse to yield. **d.** *Informal.* to withhold something expected or due: *Are you holding out on me?* **32. hold over, a.** to keep for future consideration or action. **b.** to keep beyond the arranged period: *to hold a movie over for an extra week.* **33. hold up, a.** to support; uphold. **b.** to delay; bring to a stop. **c.** to endure without losing effectiveness; persevere: *I'm tired but holding up.* **d.** to present for attention; display. **e.** to rob at gunpoint. **—*n.*** **34.** an act of holding fast with the hand or other physical means; grasp; grip: *a good hold on the rope.* **35.** something to hold a thing by; something to grasp, esp. for support. **36.** something that holds fast or supports something else. **37.** an order reserving something: *to put a hold on a library book.* **38.** a controlling force or dominating influence: *to have a hold on a person.* **39.** a wrestler's maneuver for seizing and controlling an opponent. **40.** FERMATA. **41.** a pause or delay. **42.** a prison cell. **43.** a receptacle: *a basket used as a hold for letters.* **44.** STRONGHOLD. **45.** a feature on a telephone that allows voice communication to be interrupted without breaking the connection. **—*Idiom.*** **46. get hold of, a.** to grasp; seize. **b.** to communicate with by telephone. **47. hold the fort,** to maintain a place or situation until someone else returns. **48. hold the line,** to maintain or restrain. **49. hold your horses,** to wait; be patient. **50. no holds barred,** without limits, rules, or restraints. **51. on hold, a.** into a state of interruption or suspension. **b.** into a state of being kept waiting incommunicado by a telephone hold. —**hold′a•ble,** *adj.*

hold² (hōld), *n.* **1.** the cargo space in the hull of a vessel, esp. between the lowermost deck and the bottom. **2.** the cargo compartment of an aircraft.

hold•all (hōld′ôl′), *n.* a container for holding odds and ends.

hold•er (hōl′dər), *n.* **1.** something that holds: *a pencil holder.* **2.** a person who has the ownership, possession, or use of something; owner; tenant. **3.** a person who has the legal right to enforce a negotiable instrument. —**hold′er•ship′,** *n.*

hold•fast (hōld′fast′, -fäst′), *n.* **1.** something used to hold or secure a thing in place. **2.** any of several rootlike or suckerlike parts of a plant or fungus serving for attachment.

hold•ing (hōl′ding), *n.* **1.** the act of a person or thing that holds. **2.** a section of land leased or otherwise tenanted, esp. for agricultural purposes. **3.** Often, **holdings.** legally owned property, as securities. **4. holdings,** the collection of books, periodicals, and other materials in a library. **5.** the illegal obstruction of an opponent, as in football, basketball, or ice hockey, by use of the hands, arms, or stick.

hold′ing com′pany, *n.* a company that controls other companies through stock ownership but that usu. does not engage directly in their productive operations.

hold′ing pat′tern, *n.* **1.** a traffic course held by aircraft at a specified location until cleared for landing. **2.** a condition of no progress or change.

Hold′ On′, a song of the Civil Rights movement, written by Alice Wine. Also called "Keep Your Eyes on the Prize."

hold•out (hōld′out′), *n.* **1.** an act of holding out. **2.** a person who declines to cooperate with others or to come to an agreement.

hold•o•ver (hōld′ō′vər), *n.* a person or thing remaining from a former period.

hold•up (hōld′up′), *n.* **1.** a robbery of a person at gunpoint. **2.** a delay in the progress of something. **3.** an instance of being charged excessively.

hole (hōl), *n., v.,* **holed, hol•ing.** **—*n.*** **1.** an opening through something; gap: *a hole in the roof.* **2.** a hollow place in a solid mass; cavity: *a hole in the ground.* **3.** the excavated habitation of an animal; burrow. **4.** a cramped or shabby place of habitation. **5.** a place of solitary confinement; dungeon. **6.** an embarrassing position or predicament. **7.** a small harbor; cove. **8.** a fault; flaw: *serious holes in your reasoning.* **9.** a deep, still place in a stream: *a swimming hole.* **10. a.** the circular opening in a golfing green into which the ball is to be played. **b.** a part of a golf course including fairway, rough, and hazards. **c.** the play on such a part considered as a unit of scoring. **11.** opening; slot: *We need someone to fill a hole in our department.* **12.** a mobile vacancy in the electronic structure of a semiconductor that acts as a positive charge carrier and has mass equivalent to the electron. **—*v.t.*** **13.** to make a hole in. **14.** to put or drive into a hole. **—*v.i.*** **15.** to make a hole in something. **16. hole out,** to strike a golf ball into a hole. **17. hole up, a.** to retire into a hole or cave for the winter. **b.** to hide from or as if from pursuers; take refuge. **—*Idiom.*** **18. hole in the wall,** a small or confining place, esp. one that is dingy or shabby. **19. in a** or **the hole, a.** in debt; in straitened circumstances. **b.** dealt facedown in the first round in a game of stud poker. **20. pick a hole** or **holes in,** to notice and point out flaws in. —**hole′less,** *adj.* —**hol′ey,** *adj.*

hole′ in one′, *n.* ACE (def. 5a).

-holic, var. of -AHOLIC: *chocoholic.*

hol•i•day (hol′i dā′), *n.* **1.** a day fixed by law or custom on which ordinary business is suspended in commemoration of some event or in honor of some person. **2.** any day of exemption from work. **3.** a period of exemption from burden: *a holiday from worry.* **4.** a religious festival; holy day. **5.** Sometimes, **holidays.** *Chiefly Brit.* VACATION. **—*adj.*** **6.** festive; joyous: *a holiday mood.* **7.** suitable for a holiday: *holiday attire.* **—*v.i.*** **8.** to vacation. —**hol′i•day′er,** *n.*

Hol•i•day (hol′i dā′), *n.* **Billie** (*"Lady Day"*), 1915–59, U.S. jazz singer.

ho′lier-than-thou′, *adj.* obnoxiously pious; sanctimonious.

ho•li•ness (hō′lē nis), *n.* **1.** the quality or state of being holy; sanctity. **2.** (*cap.*) a title of the pope (usu. prec. by *His* or *Your*).

ho′liness church′, *n.* one of several Christian groups emphasizing that a state of sinlessness, sanctification, or holiness follows conversion and is needed for salvation.

ho•lism (hō′liz əm), *n.* **1.** the theory that whole entities, as fundamental components of reality, have an existence other than as the mere sum of their parts. **2.** an approach to healing or health care, often involving therapies outside the mainstream of medicine, in which isolated symptoms or conditions are considered secondary to one's total physical and psychological state. **3.** any psychological system postulating that the human mind must be studied as a unit rather than as a sum of its individual parts. —**ho′list,** *n.*

ho•lis•tic (hō lis′tik), *adj.* **1.** incorporating or identifying with the principles of holism: *holistic psychology.* **2.** pertaining to or using therapies outside the mainstream of orthodox medicine, as chiropractic, homeopathy, or naturopathy. —**ho•lis′ti•cal•ly,** *adv.*

Hol•land (hol′ənd), *n.* **1. John Philip,** 1840–1914, Irish inventor in the U.S. **2.** the Netherlands. **3.** a medieval county and province on the North Sea, corresponding to the modern North and South Holland provinces of the Netherlands. **4.** (*often l.c.*) a cotton cloth with an opaque finish.

hol′lan•daise sauce′ (hol′ən dāz′, hol′ən dāz′), *n.* a sauce of egg yolks, butter, lemon juice, and seasonings.

hol•ler (hol′ər), *v.i.* **1.** to cry aloud; shout; yell. **—*v.t.*** **2.** to shout: *to holler insults.* **—*n.*** **3.** a loud cry; shout.

hol•low (hol′ō), *adj.* **1.** having a space or cavity inside; empty: *a hollow sphere.* **2.** having a depression or concavity: *a hollow surface.* **3.** sunken: *hollow cheeks.* **4.** not resonant: *a hollow voice.* **5.** lacking significance; meaningless: *a hollow victory.* **6.** insincere; false: *hollow compliments.* **—*n.*** **7.** an empty space within something; hole; cavity. **8.** a shallow valley. **—*v.t.*** **9.** to make hollow (often fol. by *out*): *to hollow out a log.* **10.** to form by hollowing action (often fol. by *out*): *to hollow a place in the sand.* **—*v.i.*** **11.** to become hollow. **—*adv.*** **12.** in a hollow manner: *The accusations rang hollow.* —**hol′low•ly,** *adv.* —**hol′low•ness,** *n.*

hol•ly (hol′ē), *n., pl.* **-lies.** **1.** any of numerous trees or shrubs of the genus *Ilex,* as *I. opaca* or *I. aquifolium,* with glossy leaves and red berries. **2.** the foliage and berries, used esp. for Christmas decoration.

hol•ly•hock (hol′ē hok′, -hôk′), *n.* a tall cultivated Asian plant, *Alcea rosea,* of the mallow family, having a long cluster of showy, variously colored flowers.

Hol•ly•wood (hol′ē wo͝od′), *n.* **1.** the NW part of Los Angeles, Calif.: center of the American motion-picture industry. **2.** a city in SE Florida near Miami. 124,992. —**Hol′ly•wood′ish,** *adj.*

Holmes (hōmz, hōlmz), *n.* **1. John Haynes,** 1879–1964, U.S. clergyman. **2. Oliver Wendell,** 1809–94, U.S. poet, essayist, and physician. **3.** his son, **Oliver Wendell,** 1841–1935, U.S. jurist.

hol•mi•um (hōl′mē əm), *n.* a rare-earth, trivalent element found in gadolinite. *Symbol:* Ho; *at. wt.:* 164.930; *at. no.:* 67.

holm′ oak′, *n.* an evergreen oak, *Quercus ilex,* of E Europe, having foliage resembling that of the holly.

holo-, a combining form meaning "whole," "entire": *holomorphic.* Also, *esp. before a vowel,* **hol-.**

hol•o•caust (hol′ə kôst′, hō′lə-), *n.* **1.** a great or complete devastation or destruction, esp. by fire. **2.** a sacrifice consumed by fire. **3. the Holocaust,** the systematic mass slaughter of European Jews in Nazi concentration camps during World War II. **4.** any reckless destruction of life. —**hol′o•caus′tal,** *adj.* —**hol′o•caus′tic,** *adj.*

hol•o•crine (hol′ə krin, -krīn′, hō′lə-), *adj.* **1.** (of a gland) releasing a secretion that is a product of disintegrating cells. **2.** (of a secretion) released by such a gland.

Hol•o•fer•nes (hol′ə fûr′nēz, hō′lə-), *n.* (in the Book of Judith) a general of Nebuchadnezzar killed by Judith.

hol•o•gram (hol′ə gram′, hō′lə-), *n.* a three-dimensional image of an object produced by recording on a photographic plate or film the patterns of interference formed by a split laser beam and then illuminating the pattern with usu. coherent light. Also called **holograph.**

hol•o•graph (hol′ə graf′, -gräf′, hō′lə-), *adj.* **1.** Also, **hol′o•graph′ic** (-graf′ik), **hol′o•graph′i•cal.** wholly written by the person in whose name it appears: *a holograph letter.* **—*n.*** **2.** a holograph writing, as a deed.

ho•log•ra•phy (hə log′rə fē), *n.* the process or technique of making holograms.

H

hol·o·phrase (hol′ə frāz′, hō′lə-), *n.* a single word expressing the ideas of a phrase or sentence. —**hol′o·phras′tic** (-fras′tik), *adj.*

hol·o·type (hol′ə tīp′, hō′lə-), *n.* the single specimen used as the basis for the original description of a species. —**hol′o·typ′ic** (-tip′ik), *adj.*

Hol·stein (hōl′stīn, -stēn) *n.* **1.** Also called **Hol′stein-Frie′sian.** one of a breed of large black-and-white dairy cattle originating in North Holland and Friesland. **2.** a region in N Germany, at the base of the peninsula of Jutland: a former duchy. Compare SCHLESWIG-HOLSTEIN.

hol·ster (hōl′stər), *n.* **1.** a sheathlike case for a firearm attached to a belt, shoulder sling, or saddle. —*v.t.* **2.** to put in a holster.

ho·ly (hō′lē), *adj.,* **-li·er, -li·est. 1.** recognized as or declared sacred by religious use or authority; consecrated: *holy ground.* **2.** dedicated or devoted to the service of God, the church, or religion. **3.** saintly; devout. **4.** having a spiritually pure quality: *a holy love.* **5.** venerated as or as if sacred: *a holy relic.* **6.** inspiring fear, awe, or distress: *He's a holy terror when he's angry.* —**ho′li·ly,** *adv.*

Ho′ly Ark′, *n.* a cabinet in a synagogue set into or against the wall that faces eastward toward Jerusalem, for keeping the scrolls of the Torah.

Ho′ly Bi′ble, *n.* BIBLE (def. 1).

ho′ly bread′, *n.* **1.** bread used in a Eucharistic service, both before and after consecration. **2.** *Eastern Ch.* eulogia (def. 1). **3.** *Gk. Orth. Ch.* antidoron (def. 1).

Ho′ly Cit′y, *n.* (*sometimes l.c.*) **1.** a city regarded as particularly sacred by the adherents of a religious faith, as Jerusalem by Jews and Christians, Mecca and Medina by Muslims, and Varanasi by Hindus. **2.** heaven. **3.** Jerusalem. Is. 51:1.

Ho′ly Commun′ion, *n.* COMMUNION (def. 1).

ho′ly day′, *n.* a consecrated day or religious festival.

Ho′ly Fam′ily, *n.* a representation in art of Mary, Joseph, and the infant Jesus.

Ho′ly Fa′ther, *n.* a title of the pope.

Ho′ly Ghost′, *n.* the third person of the Trinity. Also called **Holy Spirit.**

Ho′ly Grail′ or **ho′ly grail′,** *n.* GRAIL.

Ho′ly, Ho′ly, Ho′ly, a Christian hymn (1827) with words by Reginald Heber and music by John B. Dykes.

Ho′ly Land′, *n.* the S region of ancient Palestine; Judea.

Ho′ly Moth′er, *n.* honorific title of the Virgin Mary.

Ho′ly Of′fice, *n.* a Roman Catholic committee of ecclesiastics entrusted with matters pertaining to faith and morals.

ho′ly of ho′lies, *n.* **1.** a place of special sacredness. **2.** the innermost chamber of the Biblical tabernacle and the Temple in Jerusalem, in which the ark of the covenant was kept. **3.** *Eastern Ch.* the bema. [trans. of Late Latin *sanctum sanctōrum* (Vulgate), trans. of Greek *tò hágion tôn hagíon,* itself trans. of Hebrew *qōdesh haqqodāshīm*]

Ho′ly One′, *n.* **1.** God. Isa. 10:20. **2.** Jesus Christ, esp. as the Messiah. Mark 1:24; Acts 3:14.

ho′ly or′ders, *n.pl.* **1.** (*used with a sing. v.*) the rite of ordination. **2.** (*used with a sing. v.*) the rank or status of an ordained Christian minister. **3.** the degrees of the Christian ministry.

ho′ly pla′ces, *n.pl.* the places in the Holy Land, esp. Jerusalem, associated with the life, death, and resurrection of Christ.

Ho′ly Ro′man Em′pire, *n.* a Germanic empire located chiefly in central Europe, considered as beginning with the coronation of Charlemagne in A.D. 800 or of Otto the Great in A.D. 962 and lasting until the renunciation of the crown by Francis II in 1806.

Ho′ly Rood′, *n.* **1.** the cross on which Jesus died. **2.** (*l.c.*) a crucifix, esp. one above a rood screen.

Ho′ly Sat′urday, *n.* the Saturday preceding Easter.

Ho′ly Scrip′ture (or **Scrip′tures**), *n.* SCRIPTURE (def. 1).

Ho′ly See′, *n.* the see of the pope.

Ho′ly Sep′ulcher, *n.* the sepulcher in which the body of Jesus lay between His burial and His resurrection.

Ho′ly Spir′it, *n.* **1.** the spirit of God. **2.** HOLY GHOST.

Ho′ly Thurs′day, *n.* **1.** ASCENSION DAY. **2.** MAUNDY THURSDAY.

ho′ly war′, *n.* **1.** a war waged for what is supposed or proclaimed to be a holy purpose, as the defense of faith. **2.** any disagreement or argument between fanatical proponents of radically differing beliefs, opinions, etc.: *a holy war on the merits of computer operating systems; a holy war about welfare reform.*

ho′ly wa′ter, *n.* water blessed by a priest.

Ho′ly Week′, *n.* the week preceding Easter Sunday.

Ho′ly Writ′, *n.* SCRIPTURE (def. 1).

hom·age (hom′ij, om′-), *n.* **1.** respect; reverence: *to pay homage to one's forebears.* **2. a.** the formal acknowledgment by a feudal vassal of fealty to his lord. **b.** the relationship thus established between vassal and lord. **c.** something done or given in acknowledgment of vassalage. **3.** something acknowledging the worth of another: *a festschrift presented as an homage to a great teacher.*

hom·bre (om′brā, -brē), *n., pl.* **-bres.** man; fellow.

hom·burg (hom′bûrg), *n.* a man's felt hat with a soft crown dented lengthwise and a slightly rolled brim. [after *Homburg,* Germany, where it was first manufactured]

home (hōm), *n., adj., adv., v.,* **homed, hom·ing.** —*n.* **1.** a house, apartment, or other shelter that is the usual residence of a person, family, or household. **2.** the place in which one's domestic affections are centered. **3.** an institution for people with special needs: *a nursing home.* **4.** the dwelling place or retreat of an animal. **5.** the place or region where something is native or most common. **6.** any place of residence or refuge. **7.** a person's own country. **8.** headquarters: *The company's home is in Detroit.* **9.** (in games) the destination or goal. **10.** HOME PLATE. —*adj.* **11.** of or pertaining to one's home or country; domestic: *home products.* **12.** principal: *the corporation's home office.* **13.** reaching the mark aimed at: *a home thrust.* **14.** played in a team's own area. —*adv.* **15.** to, toward, or at home: *to go home.* **16.** deep; to the heart: *The truth struck home.* **17.** to the point aimed at: *He drove the nail home.* —*v.i.* **18.** to go or return home. **19.** to proceed toward a specified target (often fol. by *in* or *on*): *The missile homed in on the target.* —*v.t.* **20.** to send to or provide with a home. **21.** to direct, as toward an airport or target. —*Idiom.* **22. at home, a.** in one's own house or place of residence. **b.** prepared to receive social visits. **c.** comfortable; at ease: *Make yourself at home.* **d.** well-informed; proficient: *a scholar at home in the classics.* **23. bring home,** to make clearly evident. **24. home away from home,** a place with the comforts of home. **25. home free,** in a position assured of success or out of jeopardy.

home′ base′, *n.* **1.** HOME PLATE. **2.** HOME (def. 8).

home·bod·y (hōm′bod′ē), *n., pl.* **-bod·ies.** a person who prefers staying at home.

home·bound[1] (hōm′bound′), *adj.* going home: *homebound commuters.*

home·bound[2] (hōm′bound′), *adj.* confined to one's home, esp. because of illness.

home·boy (hōm′boi′), *n.* **1.** a person from the same locality as oneself. **2.** *Slang.* a close friend or fellow gang member.

home′ brew′, *n.* beer or other alcoholic beverage made at home. —**home′-brewed′,** *adj.*

home′-care′, *adj.* of, pertaining to, or designating care, esp. medical care, given or received at home.

home′ cen′ter, *n.* a store that specializes in materials and supplies for home improvements or repairs.

home·com·ing (hōm′kum′ing), *n.* **1.** a return to one's home. **2.** an annual event held by a college, university, or high school for visiting alumni. —**home′com′er,** *n.*

home′ comput′er, *n.* a microcomputer designed for use in the home, as with game and educational software or electronic on-line services, and typically less powerful and expensive than computers designed for business use.

home′ ec′ (ek), *n. Informal.* home economics.

home′ econom′ics, *n.* (*used with a sing. v.*) the study of nutrition, food, clothing, child development, family relationships, and household economics. —**home′ econ′omist,** *n.*

home′ entertain′ment, *n.* the equipment, as stereo systems, television, or computers, used for diversion in the home.

home′ fries′, *n.pl.* sliced boiled potatoes, fried in oil or butter. Also called **home′ fried′ pota′toes, cottage fries.**

home′ front′, *n.* the civilian sector of a nation at war when its armed forces are in combat abroad. —**home′-front′,** *adj.*

home·grown (hōm′grōn′), *adj.* **1.** grown or produced at home or in a particular region for local consumption: *homegrown tomatoes.* **2.** native to or characteristic of a region: *homegrown musicians.*

home·land (hōm′land′, -lənd), *n.* **1.** one's native land. **2.** a region created or considered as a state by or for a particular ethnic group: *the Palestinian homeland.* **3.** any of the racially and ethnically based regions

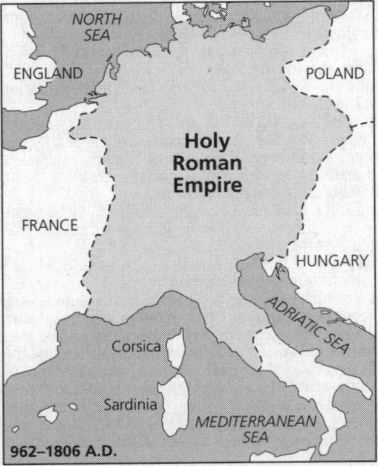

NORTH SEA

ENGLAND

POLAND

Holy Roman Empire

FRANCE

HUNGARY

ADRIATIC SEA

Corsica

Sardinia

MEDITERRANEAN SEA

962–1806 A.D.

created in South Africa by the government as nominally independent tribal states.

home·less (hōm′lis), *adj.* **1.** without a home: *a homeless child.* —*n.* **2. the homeless,** persons who lack permanent housing. —**home′less·ly,** *adv.* —**home′less·ness,** *n.*

home·ly (hōm′lē), *adj.,* **-li·er, -li·est. 1.** lacking in physical attractiveness; unattractive; plain. **2.** simple; unpretentious: *homely food.* **3.** commonly seen or known; familiar. —**home′li·ness,** *n.*

home·made (hōm′mād′), *adj.* **1.** made or prepared at home, locally, or on the premises: *All our pastry is homemade.* **2.** made in one's own country; domestic.

home·mak·er (hōm′mā′kər), *n.* **1.** a person who manages the household of his or her own family, esp. as a principal occupation. **2.** a person who manages a household for others, as for the sick or elderly. —**home′mak′ing,** *n., adj.* See HOUSEWIFE.

homeo- or **homoeo-** or **homoio-,** a combining form meaning "similar": *homeopathy.* [< Greek *homoio-,* comb. form of *hómoios* similar, like]

home′ of′fice, *n.* **1.** the main office of a company. **2.** (*caps.*) the governmental department in Great Britain dealing with domestic matters.

Home′ on the Range′, a song celebrating the open spaces of the American West.

ho·me·o·path·ic (hō′mē ə path′ik), *adj.* **1.** of, pertaining to, or according to the principles of homeopathy. **2.** practicing or advocating homeopathy. —**ho′me·o·path′i·cal·ly,** *adv.*

ho·me·op·a·thy (hō′mē op′ə thē), *n.* a method of treating disease by minute doses of drugs that in a healthy person would produce symptoms similar to those of the disease (opposed to *allopathy*). —**ho′me·o·path′** (-ə path′), **ho′me·op′a·thist,** *n.*

ho·me·o·sta·sis (hō′mē ə stā′sis), *n.* **1.** the tendency of a system, esp. the physiological system of higher animals, to maintain internal stability, owing to the coordinated response of its parts to any situation or stimulus tending to disturb its normal condition or function. **2.** a state of psychological equilibrium obtained when tension or a drive has been reduced or eliminated. —**ho′me·o·stat′ic** (-stat′ik), *adj.* —**ho′me·o·stat′i·cal·ly,** *adv.*

home·own·er (hōm′ō′nər), *n.* a person who owns a home.

home′ page′, *n. Computers.* the initial page of a site on the World Wide Web.

home′ plate′, *n.* the base in baseball at which the batter stands and which a base runner must reach safely in order to score a run, typically a slab of rubber set at the front corner of the diamond.

hom·er¹ (hō′mər), *n.* **1.** HOME RUN. **2.** HOMING PIGEON. —*v.i.* **3.** to hit a home run.

ho·mer² (hō′mər), *n.* an ancient Hebrew unit of capacity equal to ten baths in liquid measure or ten ephahs in dry measure. Also called **kor.**

Ho·mer (hō′mər), *n.* **1.** 9th-century B.C. Greek epic poet: reputed author of the *Iliad* and *Odyssey.* **2. Winslow,** 1836–1910, U.S. artist.

Ho·mer·ic (hō mer′ik), *adj.* **1.** of, pertaining to, or suggestive of Homer or his poetry. **2.** of heroic dimensions; grand: *Homeric feats of exploration.* —**Ho·mer′i·cal·ly,** *adv.*

home′room′ or **home′ room′,** *n.* a classroom in which a group of pupils in the same grade meet at the beginning of the day.

home′ rule′, *n.* self-government in local matters by a city, province, state, colony, or the like.

home′ run′, *n.* a hit in baseball allowing the batter to circle the bases and score a run.

home·school·ing (hōm′skoo′ling), *n.* the practice of teaching one's own children at home.

home·sick (hōm′sik′), *adj.* sad from a longing for home or family while away from them. —**home′sick′ness,** *n.*

home·spun (hōm′spun′), *adj.* **1.** spun or made at home: *homespun cloth.* **2.** made of homespun: *homespun clothing.* **3.** plain; simple: *homespun humor.* —*n.* **4.** a plain-weave cloth made at home or of homespun yarn. **5.** any cloth of similar appearance.

home·stead (hōm′sted, -stid), *n.* **1.** a dwelling with its land and buildings occupied by the owner as a home and exempted by a homestead law from seizure or sale for debt. **2.** any dwelling with its land and buildings where a family makes its home. —*v.t.* **3.** to acquire or settle on (land) as a homestead. —*v.i.* **4.** to acquire or settle on a homestead. —**home′stead·er,** *n.*

Home′stead Act′, *n.* a special act of Congress (1862) that made public lands in the West available to settlers without payment, usu. in lots of 160 acres, to be used as farms.

home′stead law′, *n.* **1.** any law exempting homesteads from seizure or sale for debt. **2.** any law making public lands available to settlers to be used as farms. **3.** any of various state laws granting special property tax exemptions or other privileges to homesteaders.

home·stretch (hōm′strech′), *n.* **1.** the straight part of a racetrack from the last turn to the finish line. Compare BACKSTRETCH. **2.** the final phase of any endeavor.

Home′, Sweet′ Home′, an American song by John Howard Payne.

home·town (hōm′toun′), *n.* the town or city in which one was born or lives or has one's principal residence.

home′ vid′eo, *n.* **1.** a videotape recorded by camcorder generally for noncommercial use, esp. for viewing at home. **2.** the business of renting or selling prerecorded videocassettes for viewing esp. at home.

home·ward (hōm′wərd), *adv.* **1.** Also, **home′wards.** toward home. —*adj.* **2.** directed toward home: *the homeward journey.*

home·work (hōm′wûrk′), *n.* **1.** schoolwork assigned to be done outside the classroom. **2.** thorough preparatory study of a subject: *to do one's homework for the next committee meeting.*

hom·ey (hō′mē), *adj.,* **hom·i·er, hom·i·est.** comfortably informal; cozy: *a homey inn.* —**hom′ey·ness, hom′i·ness,** *n.*

hom·i·cid·al (hom′ə sīd′l, hō′mə-), *adj.* **1.** of or pertaining to homicide. **2.** having an inclination to commit homicide. —**hom′i·cid′al·ly,** *adv.*

hom·i·cide (hom′ə sīd′, hō′mə-), *n.* **1.** the killing of one human being by another. **2.** a person who kills another; murderer.

hom·i·let·ic (hom′ə let′ik) also **hom′i·let′i·cal,** *adj.* **1.** of or pertaining to preaching or to a homily. **2.** of or pertaining to homiletics. —**hom′i·let′i·cal·ly,** *adv.*

hom·i·let·ics (hom′ə let′iks), *n.* (*used with a sing. v.*) the art of preaching.

hom·i·ly (hom′ə lē), *n., pl.* **-lies. 1.** a sermon typically on a scriptural topic. **2.** an admonitory or moralizing discourse. **3.** an inspirational saying or cliché.

hom·ing (hō′ming), *adj.* **1.** capable of returning home usu. over a great distance. **2.** guiding or directing to a destination or target, esp. by mechanical means: *a homing device.*

hom′ing pi′geon, *n.* a pigeon trained to carry messages and return home.

hom·i·nid (hom′ə nid), *n.* any of the modern or extinct bipedal primates of the family Hominidae, including all species of the genera *Homo* and *Australopithecus.*

hom·i·noid (hom′ə noid′), *n.* a member of the biological superfamily Hominoidea, including all modern great apes and humans and a number of their extinct ancestors and relatives.

hom·i·ny (hom′ə nē), *n.* whole or ground hulled corn from which the bran and germ have been removed by bleaching the whole kernels or by crushing and sifting.

hom′iny grits′, *n.* (*used with a sing. or pl. v.*) GRITS (def. 1).

Ho·mo (hō′mō), *n., pl.* **-mos. 1.** (*italics*) the genus of bipedal primates that includes modern humans and several extinct forms, as *H. erectus* and *H. habilis,* distinguished by their large brains and a dependence upon tools. **2.** (*sometimes l.c.*) **a.** a member of this genus. **b.** the species *Homo sapiens* or one of its members.

homo-, a combining form meaning "same, identical": *homogeneous; homology.* Also, *esp. before a vowel,* **hom-.**

ho·mog·e·nate (hə moj′ə nāt′, -nit, hō-), *n.* a mixture that has been homogenized.

ho·mo·ge·ne·ous (hō′mə jē′nē əs, -jēn′yəs, hom′ə-), *adj.* **1.** composed of parts or elements that are all of the same kind; not heterogeneous: *a homogeneous population.* **2.** of the same kind or nature; essentially alike. **3.** *Math.* **a.** having a common property throughout: *a homogeneous solid figure.* **b.** having all terms of the same degree: *a homogeneous equation.* —**ho′mo·ge·ne′i·ty** (-jə nē′i tē), **ho′mo·ge′ne·ous·ness,** *n.* —**ho′mo·ge′ne·ous·ly,** *adv.*

ho·mog·e·nize (hə moj′ə nīz′, hō-), *v.,* **-nized, -niz·ing.** —*v.t.* **1.** to form by blending unlike elements; make homogeneous. **2.** to emulsify the fat globules in (milk or cream), causing them to be equally distributed throughout. **3.** to make uniform or similar, as in composition or function: *to homogenize school systems.* —*v.i.* **4.** to become homogenized. —**ho·mog′e·ni·za′tion,** *n.* —**ho·mog′e·niz′er,** *n.*

ho·mog·e·nous (hə moj′ə nəs, hō-), *adj. Biol.* corresponding in structure because of a common origin. —**ho·mog′e·ny,** *n.*

hom·o·graph (hom′ə graf′, -gräf′, hō′mə-), *n.* a word of the same written form as another but of different meaning and usu. origin, whether pronounced the same way or not, as *bear¹* "to carry; support" and *bear²* "animal" or *lead¹* "to conduct" and *lead²* "metal." —**hom′o·graph′ic** (-graf′ik), *adj.*

Ho·moi·ou·si·an (hō′moi ōō′sē ən, -ou′-), *n.* **1.** a member of a 4th-century A.D. church party that maintained that the essence of the Son is similar to, but not the same as, that of the Father. —*adj.* **2.** pertaining to the Homoiousians or their doctrine. —**Ho′moi·ou′si·an·ism,** *n.*

ho·mol·o·gize (hə mol′ə jīz′, hō-), *v.,* **-gized, -giz·ing.** —*v.t.* **1.** to make or show to be homologous. —*v.i.* **2.** to be homologous; correspond. —**ho·mol′o·giz′er,** *n.*

ho·mol·o·gous (hə mol′ə gəs, hō-), *adj.* **1.** having the same or a similar relation; corresponding, as in relative position or structure. **2.** *Biol.* corresponding in structure and in evolutionary origin but not necessarily in function, as the wing of a bird and the foreleg of a horse (opposed to *analogous*). **3.** having the same alleles or genes in the same order of arrangement. **4.** of the same chemical type, but differing by a fixed increment of an atom or a constant group of atoms. **5.** pertaining to an antigen and its specific antibody.

hom·o·lo·graph·ic or **hom·a·lo·graph·ic** (hom′ə lə graf′ik), *adj.* representing parts with like proportions.

ho·mo·logue or **ho·mo·log** (hō′mə lôg′, -log′, hom′ə-), *n.* **1.** something homologous. **2.** any member of a homologous series of organic compounds: *Ethane is a homologue of the alkane series.*

ho·mol·o·gy (hə mol′ə jē, hō-), *n., pl.* **-gies. 1.** the state of being homologous. **2.** *Biol.* **a.** a fundamental similarity based on common descent. **b.** a structural similarity of two segments of one animal based on a common developmental origin. **3.** the similarity of organic compounds of a series in which each member differs from successive compounds by a fixed increment, as by CH$_2$. **4.** a classification of mathematical figures according to certain topological properties.

hom·o·nym (hom/ə nim/, *n.* **1.** HOMOPHONE (def. 1). **2.** a word the same as another in sound and spelling but different in meaning, as *chase* "to pursue" and *chase* "to ornament metal." **3.** HOMOGRAPH. **4.** a namesake. —**hom/o·nym/ic,** *adj.*

ho·mon·y·mous (hə mon/ə məs, hō-), *adj.* of the nature of homonyms; having the same name. —**ho·mon/y·mous·ly,** *adv.* —**ho·mon/y·my,** *n.*

hom·o·phone (hom/ə fōn/, hō/mə-), *n.* **1.** a word pronounced the same as another but differing in meaning, whether spelled the same way or not, as *heir* and *air.* **2.** a written element that represents the same spoken unit as another, as *ks,* a homophone of *x* in English.

ho·mop·ter·ous (hə mop/tər əs, hō-), *adj.* belonging or pertaining to the Homoptera, an order of sucking insects, including aphids, cicadas, leafhoppers, and scale insects, that have membranous forewings and hind wings.

Ho·mo sa·pi·ens (hō/mō sā/pē ənz), *n.* **1.** (*italics*) the species of bipedal primates to which modern humans belong, characterized by a brain capacity averaging 1400 cc (85 cu. in.) and by dependence upon language and the creation and utilization of complex tools. **2.** HUMANKIND.

ho·mo·sex·u·al (hō/mə sek/shōō əl), *adj.* **1.** attracted sexually to members of one's own sex. **2.** of or pertaining to homosexuality. —*n.* **3.** a homosexual person.

ho·mo·sex·u·al·i·ty (hō/mə sek/shōō al/i tē), *n.* **1.** sexual attraction toward members of one's own sex. **2.** sexual activity with another person of the same sex.

ho·mun·cu·lus (hə mung/kyə ləs, hō-), *n.,* *pl.* **-li** (-lī/). **1.** a fully formed, miniature human body believed, according to some medieval theories of the 16th and 17th centuries, to be contained in the spermatozoon. **2.** a graphic projection of the human image onto the surface of the motor cortex of the brain, depicting the extent of the area activating each part of the body subject to voluntary control. **3.** a diminutive human being. —**ho·mun/cu·lar,** *adj.*

hon (hun), *n. Informal.* HONEY (def. 6).

hon·cho (hon/chō), *n.,* *pl.* **-chos.** *Slang.* **1.** a leader, esp. an assertive leader; boss; chief. **2.** an important or influential person; bigshot.

Hon·du·ras (hon dōōr/əs, -dyōōr/-), *n.* **1.** a republic in NE Central America. 5,751,384; 43,277 sq. mi. (112,087 sq. km). *Cap.:* Tegucigalpa. **2. Gulf of,** an arm of the Caribbean Sea, bordered by Belize, Guatemala, and Honduras. —**Hon·du/ran,** *adj., n.*

hone (hōn), *n., v.,* **honed, hon·ing.** —*n.* **1.** a whetstone of fine, compact texture for sharpening razors and other cutting tools. —*v.t.* **2.** to sharpen on a hone. **3.** to enlarge or finish (a hole) with a hone. **4.** to make more acute or effective: *to hone one's skills.* —**hon/er,** *n.*

hon·est (on/ist), *adj.* **1.** honorable in principles, intentions, and actions; not disposed to lie, cheat, or steal; upright. **2.** showing uprightness and fairness: *honest dealings.* **3.** gained or obtained fairly: *to earn an honest living.* **4.** sincere; frank; open: *an honest face.* **5.** genuine or unadulterated: *honest goods.* **6.** respectable; having a good reputation: *an honest name.* **7.** truthful or creditable: *an honest account.* **8.** humble, plain, or unadorned. —**hon/est·ness,** *n.*

Hon/est Abe/, *n.* epithet of Abraham Lincoln.

hon·est·ly (on/ist lē), *adv.* **1.** in an honest manner. **2.** really; truly; genuinely: *I honestly don't know.* —*interj.* **3.** (used to express mild exasperation, disbelief, dismay, etc.): *Honestly! You're always on the phone.*

hon/est-to-good/ness or **hon/est-to-God/,** *adj.* **1.** real or genuine. —*adv.* **2.** really; truly; genuinely.

hon·es·ty (on/ə stē), *n., pl.* **-ties. 1.** uprightness; integrity; trustworthiness. **2.** truthfulness, sincerity, or frankness. **3.** freedom from deceit or fraud. **4.** a plant, *Lunaria annua,* of the mustard family, having clusters of purple flowers and semitransparent satiny pods. —***Proverb.* 5. Honesty is the best policy,** deception or withholding the truth ultimately has no benefit.

hone·wort (hōn/wûrt/, -wôrt/), *n.* any of several plants of the genus *Cryptotaenia,* of the parsley family, esp. *C. canadensis,* having clusters of small white flowers.

hon·ey (hun/ē), *n., pl.* **hon·eys,** *adj., v.,* **hon·eyed** or **hon·ied, hon·ey·ing.** —*n.* **1.** a sweet viscid fluid produced by bees from the nectar collected from flowers and stored in nests or hives as food. **2.** this substance as used in cooking or as a spread or sweetener. **3.** the nectar of flowers. **4.** any of various similarly sweet viscid products produced by insects or in other ways. **5.** something sweet, delicious, or delightful: *the honey of flattery.* **6.** *Informal.* **a.** sweetheart; darling. **b.** (*sometimes cap.*) an affectionate or familiar term of address (sometimes offensive when used to strangers, subordinates, etc.). **7.** *Informal.* something especially good of its kind: *a honey of a car.* —*adj.* **8.** of, like, or pertaining to honey; sweet. **9.** containing honey; flavored or sweetened with honey. —*v.t.* **10.** to talk flatteringly or endearingly to (often fol. by *up*). **11.** to sweeten or flavor with or as if with honey. —*v.i.* **12.** to use flattery, endearing terms, etc., in an effort to obtain something (often fol. by *up*). —***Proverb.* 13. You can catch more flies with honey than with vinegar,** pleasant words are more effective than harsh words. —**hon/ey·like/,** *adj.*

hon/ey bear/, *n.* KINKAJOU.

hon/ey·bee/ or **hon/ey bee/,** *n.* any bee that collects and stores honey, esp. *Apis mellifera.*

hon·ey·bunch (hun/ē bunch/) also **hon·ey·bun** (-bun/), *n. Informal.* HONEY (def. 6).

hon·ey·comb (hun/ē kōm/), *n.* **1.** a structure of rows of hexagonal wax cells, formed by bees in their hive for the storage of honey, pollen, and their eggs. **2.** anything resembling such a structure, esp. in containing many small units or holes. —*adj.* **3.** having the structure or appearance of a honeycomb. —*v.t.* **4.** to cause to be full of holes or cavities. **5.** to penetrate in all parts, esp. so as to undermine: *a city honeycombed with vice.*

hon·ey·creep·er (hun/ē krē/pər), *n.* **1.** any of several long-billed, brightly colored songbirds of the genera *Cyanerpes* and *Chlorophanes,* of the New World tropics, now usu. classed with the tanagers. **2.** HAWAIIAN HONEYCREEPER.

hon·ey·dew (hun/ē dōō/, -dyōō/), *n.* **1.** HONEYDEW MELON. **2.** the sweet material that exudes from the leaves of certain plants in hot weather. **3.** a sugary material secreted by aphids, leafhoppers, and other homopterous insects. —**hon/ey·dewed/,** *adj.*

hon/eydew mel/on, *n.* a variety of the winter melon, *Cucumis melo inodorus,* having a smooth, pale greenish rind and sweet, juicy, light green flesh.

hon/ey eat/er or **hon/ey·eat/er,** *n.* any of numerous chiefly Australasian songbirds of the family Meliphagidae, highly diverse in size, plumage, and habits, though typically having a tongue adapted for nectar-feeding.

hon·eyed or **hon·ied** (hun/ēd), *adj.* **1.** containing, consisting of, or resembling honey. **2.** flattering or ingratiating: *honeyed words.* **3.** pleasantly soft; dulcet or mellifluous: *honeyed tones.*

hon/ey guide/ or **hon/ey·guide/,** *n.* any of various small, drab-plumaged birds of the family Indicatoridae, of the Old World tropics: noted for their brood parasitism and the partiality of most species to honey, beeswax, and bee larvae.

hon/ey lo/cust, *n.* a thorny North American tree, *Gleditsia triacanthos,* of the legume family, having pinnate leaves and pods with a sweet pulp.

hon/ey mesquite/, *n.* a thorny drought-resistant tree, *Prosopis glandulosa,* of the legume family, native to the southwestern U.S.

hon·ey·moon (hun/ē mōōn/), *n.* **1.** a vacation or trip taken by a newly married couple. **2.** the month or so following a marriage. **3.** a period of blissful harmony. **4.** any new relationship characterized by an initial period of harmony and goodwill. —*v.i.* **5.** to spend one's honeymoon (usu. fol. by *in* or *at*). —**hon/ey·moon/er,** *n.*

hon/ey mush/room, *n.* the edible mushroom of the oak-root fungus, *Armillariella mellea.*

hon·ey·suck·le (hun/ē suk/əl), *n.* any upright or climbing shrub of the genus *Lonicera,* esp. *L. lonicera,* cultivated for its fragrant white, yellow, or red tubular flowers. —**hon/ey·suck/led,** *adj.*

Hong Kong (hong/ kong/), *n.* a former British crown colony comprising Hong Kong island (29 sq. mi.; 75 sq. km), Kowloon peninsula, nearby islands, and the adjacent mainland bordering SE China: reverted to Chinese sovereignty in 1997. 6,413,000; 404 sq. mi. (1046 sq. km). *Cap.:* Victoria. **2.** VICTORIA (def. 2). —**Hong/ Kong/er, Hong/kong/ite,** *n.*

Ho·ni·a·ra (hō/nē är/ə), *n.* the capital of the Solomon Islands, on N Guadalcanal. 26,000.

honk (hongk, hôngk), *n.* **1.** the cry of a goose. **2.** any similar sound, as of an automobile horn. —*v.i.* **3.** to emit a honk. **4.** to cause an automobile horn to sound. —*v.t.* **5.** to cause (an automobile horn) to sound. —**honk/er,** *n.*

honk·y-tonk (hong/kē tongk/, hông/kē tôngk/), *n.* **1.** a cheap, noisy, garish nightclub or dance hall. —*adj.* Also, **honk/y-tonk/y. 2.** of or characteristic of a honky-tonk. **3.** characterized by honky-tonks: *the honky-tonk part of town.* **4.** of or pertaining to ragtime music played on a tinny-sounding upright piano. —*v.i.* **5.** to visit honky-tonks. —**honk/y-tonk/er,** *n.*

Hon·o·lu·lu (hon/ə lōō/lōō), *n.* the capital of Hawaii, on S Oahu. 385,881.

hon·or (on/ər), *n.* **1.** honesty, fairness, or integrity in one's beliefs and actions: *a code of honor.* **2.** a source of credit or distinction: *to be an honor to one's country.* **3.** high respect, as for worth, merit, or rank: *to be held in great honor.* **4.** such respect manifested: *a memorial in honor of the dead; the place of honor at the table.* **5.** high public esteem; fame; glory: *to earn a position of honor.* **6.** the privilege of being associated with or receiving a favor from a respected person, group, etc.: *the honor of serving on a panel; I have the honor of introducing this evening's speaker.* **7.** Usu. **honors.** evidence, as a special ceremony, decoration, scroll, or title, of high rank or distinction: *military honors.* **8.** (*cap.*) a deferential title of respect, esp. for judges and mayors (prec. by *His, Her, Your,* etc.). **9. honors, a.** special rank or distinction conferred by a university, college, or school upon an outstanding student. **b.** a class or course for advanced students, usu. involving accelerated or independent work. **10.** chastity or purity in a woman. **11.** Also called **hon/or card/.** (in bridge) any of the five highest trump cards or any of the four aces in a no-trump contract. **12.** the privilege of teeing off in golf before the other player or side, given after the first hole to the player or side that won the previous hole. —*v.t.* **13.** to hold in honor or high respect; revere: *to honor one's ancestors.* **14.** to treat with honor. **15.** to confer honor or distinction upon. **16.** to show a courteous regard for: *to honor an invitation.* **17.** to accept or pay (a credit card, check, etc.). **18.** to accept as valid and conform to the request or demands of (an official document): *to honor a treaty.* **19.** (in square dancing) to meet or salute with a bow. —*adj.* **20.** of, pertaining to, or noting honor. —*Idiom.* **21. do honor to, a.** to show respect to. **b.** to be a credit to. **22. do the honors,** to act as host, as in serving at the dinner table. **23. on** or **upon one's honor, a.** accepting personal responsibility for one's actions. **b.** bound by one's word or good name. Also, *esp. Brit.,* **honour.** —*Proverb.* **24. Honor thy father and thy mother,** respect your parents: the Fifth Commandment. Ex. 20:12. —**hon′or•er,** *n.* —**hon′or•less,** *adj.*

hon•or•a•ble (on′ər ə bəl), *adj.* **1.** in accordance with or characterized by principles of honor; upright. **2.** worthy of honor and high respect; estimable; creditable. **3.** bringing honor or credit; consistent with honor or good reputation: *an honorable discharge from the army.* **4.** of high rank, dignity, or distinction. **5.** (*cap.*) (used as a title of respect for certain ranking government officials or as a title of courtesy for children of British peers ranking below a marquis.) *Abbr.:* Hon. —**hon′or•a•ble•ness,** *n.* —**hon′or•a•bly,** *adv.*

hon′orable men′tion, *n.* a citation conferred on a contestant, exhibit, etc., having exceptional merit though not winning a top honor or prize.

hon•o•rar•i•um (on′ə râr′ē əm), *n., pl.* **-rar•i•ums, -rar•i•a** (-râr′ē ə). **1.** a payment in recognition of acts or professional services for which custom or propriety forbids a price to be set. **2.** a fee for services rendered by a professional person.

hon•or•ar•y (on′ə rer′ē), *adj.* **1.** given for honor only, without the usual requirements or privileges: *an honorary degree.* **2.** holding a title or position conferred for honor only, without the usual compensation: *an honorary president.* **3.** (of an obligation) depending on one's honor for fulfillment. **4.** conferring or commemorating honor or distinction. **5.** given, made, or serving as a token of honor. —**hon′or•ar′i•ly** (-rârə-lē), *adv.*

hon•or•ee (on′ə rē′), *n.* a person who receives an honor, award, or special recognition.

hon′or guard′, *n.* GUARD OF HONOR.

hon•or•if•ic (on′ə rif′ik), *adj.* **1.** doing or conferring honor. **2.** conveying honor, as a title or a grammatical form used in speaking to or about a superior, elder, etc. —*n.* **3.** (in certain languages, as Chinese and Japanese) a class of forms used to show respect. **4.** a title or term of respect. —**hon′or•if′i•cal•ly,** *adv.*

hon′or roll′, *n.* **1.** a list of students who have earned grades above a specific average during a semester or school year. **2.** a list of names, usu. on a plaque in a public place, of local citizens who have served or died in the armed forces.

hon′or sys′tem, *n.* a system whereby the students at a school, the inmates in a prison, etc., are put on their honor to observe certain rules with a minimum of supervision.

hood[1] (hŏŏd), *n.* **1.** a soft or flexible covering for the head and neck, either separate or attached to a cloak, coat, etc. **2.** something resembling this, esp. in shape, as certain petals or sepals. **3.** the hinged movable part of an automobile body covering the engine. **4.** a metal canopy for a stove, ventilator, etc. **5.** an ornamental ruffle or fold on the back of the shoulders of an academic gown, jurist's robe, etc. —*v.t.* **6.** to furnish with a hood. **7.** to cover with or as if with a hood. —**hood′less,** *adj.* —**hood′like′,** *adj.*

hood[2] (hŏŏd), *n. Slang.* a hoodlum.

'hood (hŏŏd), *n. Slang.* neighborhood.

Hood (hŏŏd), *n.* **1. John Bell,** 1831–79, Confederate general. **2. Robin,** ROBIN HOOD. **3. Thomas,** 1799–1845, English poet and humorist. **4. Mount,** a volcanic peak in N Oregon, in the Cascade Range. 11,253 ft. (3430 m).

-hood, a noun suffix denoting state, condition, character, nature, etc., or a body of persons of a particular character or class: *childhood; likelihood; priesthood.*

hood•ed (hŏŏd′id), *adj.* **1.** having or covered with or as if with a hood: *hooded eyes.* **2.** hood-shaped. **3.** *Zool.* **a.** having on the head a hoodlike formation, crest, or the like. **b.** having a head that differs in color from the body. —**hood′ed•ness,** *n.*

hood′ed seal′, *n.* a large earless seal, *Cystophora cristata:* the male has a large, distensible, hoodlike sac on the head.

hood•lum (hŏŏd′ləm, hŏŏd′-), *n.* **1.** a thug or gangster. **2.** a young street ruffian, esp. one belonging to a gang. —**hood′lum•ish,** *adj.* —**hood′lum•ism,** *n.*

hoo•doo (hŏŏ′dŏŏ), *n., pl.* **-doos. 1.** VOODOO. **2.** bad luck. **3.** a person or thing that brings bad luck. **4.** a pillar of rock, usu. of fantastic shape, left by erosion. —*v.t.* **5.** to bring or cause bad luck to. —**hoo′doo•ism,** *n.*

hood•wink (hŏŏd′wingk′), *v.t.* to deceive or trick. —**hood′wink′a•ble,** *adj.* —**hood′wink′er,** *n.*

hoo•ey (hŏŏ′ē), *n., interj. Informal.* nonsense; bunk.

hoof (hŏŏf, hŏŏf), *n., pl.* **hoofs** or **hooves** for 1, 2, 4; **hoof** for 3, 7. **1.** the horny covering protecting the ends of the digits or encasing the foot in certain animals, as the ox and horse. **2.** the entire foot of a horse, donkey, etc. **3.** *Older Use.* a hoofed animal, esp. one of a herd. **4.** *Informal.* the human foot. —*v.t.* **5.** *Slang.* to walk (often fol. by *it*): *Let's*

hoof it. —*v.i.* **6.** *Slang.* to dance, esp. to tap-dance. —*Idiom.* **7. on the hoof,** (of livestock) not butchered; live. —**hoof′less,** *adj.*

hoof′-and-mouth′ disease′, *n.* FOOT-AND-MOUTH DISEASE.

hoof•beat (hŏŏf′bēt′, hŏŏf′-), *n.* the sound made by an animal's hoof in walking, running, etc.

hoof•er (hŏŏf′ər, hŏŏf′ər), *n. Slang.* a professional dancer, esp. a tap dancer.

hoo•ha or **hoo-hah** (*n.* hŏŏ′hä′; *interj.* hŏŏ′hä′), *n., pl.* **-ha** or **-has,** *interj. Informal.* —*n.* **1.** an uproarious commotion. —*interj.* **2.** (used to express mock surprise or excitement.)

hook (hŏŏk), *n.* **1.** a curved or angular piece of metal or other hard substance for catching, pulling, holding, or suspending something. **2.** a fishhook. **3.** anything that catches; snare; trap. **4.** something that attracts attention or entices: *a sales hook.* **5.** something, as a mark or symbol, having a sharp curve, bend, or angle at one end. **6.** a sharp curve or angle in the length or course of anything. **7.** a curved spit of land. **8.** a recurved and pointed organ or appendage of an animal or plant. **9.** a small curved catch inserted into a loop to form a clothes fastener. **10. a.** the path described by a ball, as in baseball, bowling, or golf, that curves in a direction opposite to the throwing hand or to the side of the ball from which it was struck. **b.** a ball describing such a path. **11.** (in boxing) a short circular punch delivered with the elbow bent. **12. hooks,** *Slang.* hands or fingers. —*v.t.* **13.** to seize, fasten, or catch hold of with or as if with a hook. **14.** to catch (fish) with a fishhook. **15.** *Slang.* to steal or seize by stealth. **16.** *Informal.* to catch or trick by artifice; snare. **17.** (of a bull or other horned animal) to catch on the horns or attack with the horns. **18.** to make (a rug, cushion, etc.) by drawing loops of yarn through cloth with or as if with a hook. **19.** to hit or throw (a ball) so that a hook results. **20.** to make hook-shaped; crook. —*v.i.* **21.** to become attached or fastened by or as if by a hook. **22.** to curve or bend like a hook. **23.** (of a ball) to describe a hook in course. **24. hook up, a.** to fasten with a hook or hooks. **b.** to assemble or connect, as components of a machine. **c.** to connect to a central source, as of power or water. **d.** *Informal.* to join or become associated with. —*Idiom.* **25. by hook or (by) crook,** by any means whatsoever. **26. get** (or **give**) **the hook,** *Informal.* to receive (or subject to) a dismissal. **27. hook, line, and sinker,** *Informal.* entirely; completely. **28. off the hook, a.** released from some difficulty or obligation. **b.** (of a telephone receiver) not resting on the cradle. **29. on one's own hook,** independently. —**hook′less,** *adj.* —**hook′like′,** *adj.*

hook•ah or **hook•a** (hŏŏk′ə), *n., pl.* **hook•ahs** or **hook•as.** a water pipe with a long flexible tube by which the smoke is drawn through a jar of water and thus cooled.

hook′ and eye′, *n.* a two-piece clothes fastener, consisting of a hook and a loop or bar caught by the hook.

hook′ and lad′der, *n.* a fire engine, usu. a tractor-trailer, fitted with long extensible ladders and other equipment. Also called **hook′-and-lad′der truck′.**

hooked (hŏŏkt), *adj.* **1.** bent like a hook; hook-shaped. **2.** having a hook or hooks. **3.** made by hooking: *a hooked rug.* **4.** *Informal.* **a.** addicted to narcotic drugs. **b.** very enthusiastic about or obsessed with something. **5.** *Slang.* married.

Hook•er (hŏŏk′ər), *n.* **1. Joseph,** 1814–79, Union general in the U.S. Civil War. **2. Richard,** 1554?–1600, English author and clergyman. **3. Thomas,** 1586?–1647, English Puritan: founder of Connecticut.

hook′ shot′, *n.* a one-handed basketball shot made with a sweeping arc of the arm over the head.

hook•up (hŏŏk′up′), *n.* **1.** an act or instance of hooking up. **2.** an assembly and connection of parts or apparatus into a circuit, network, machine, or system. **3.** the circuit, network, machine, or system so formed. **4.** a device or connection, as a plug, hose, or pipe, for conveying electricity, water, etc., from a source to a user. **5.** *Informal.* an association, alliance, or cooperative effort.

hook•worm (hŏŏk′wûrm′), *n.* **1.** any intestinal bloodsucking nematode worm with hooks around the mouth, belonging to the superfamily Ancylostomatoidea and parasitic in humans and other animals. **2.** a disease caused by hookworms, causing abdominal pain and, if untreated, severe anemia.

hook•y or **hook•ey** (hŏŏk′ē), *n.* unjustifiable absence from school or work (usu. in the phrase *play hooky*).

hoo•li•gan (hŏŏ′li gən), *n.* **1.** a ruffian or hoodlum. —*adj.* **2.** of or like hooligans. —**hoo′li•gan•ism,** *n.*

hoop (hŏŏp, hŏŏp), *n.* **1.** a rigid circular band or ring, as of metal or wood. **2.** such a band for holding together the staves of a cask, tub, etc. **3.** a large ring, as of metal or plastic, serving as a toy for a child to roll along the ground. **4.** a circular or ringlike object, part, or figure. **5.** the shank of a finger ring. **6.** a croquet wicket. **7. a.** a circular band of metal or other stiff material used to expand a woman's skirt. **b.** Usu. **hoops.** HOOP SKIRT (def. 1). **8. a.** the metal ring from which a basketball net is suspended, or the ring and net together. **b.** Often, **hoops.** the game of basketball. —*v.t.* **9.** to bind or fasten with or as if with a hoop. **10.** to encircle; surround. —**hoop′less,** *adj.* —**hoop′like′,** *adj.*

hoop•la (hŏŏp′lä), *n. Informal.* **1.** commotion; to-do. **2.** sensational publicity; ballyhoo. **3.** speech or writing intended to mislead or to obscure an issue.

hoo•poe (hŏŏ′pōō), *n.* an Old World bird with an erectile, fanlike crest, *Upupa epops,* comprising the sole member of the family Upupidae.

H

hoop′ skirt′, *n.* **1.** a framework of flexible, usu. horizontal hoops worn under a woman's full skirt to make it stand out. **2.** a full skirt suitable for wearing over this.

hoop′ snake′, *n.* any of several harmless snakes, as the mud snake, fabled to take the tail in the mouth and roll along like a hoop.

hoo·ray (hŏŏ rā′) also **hoo·rah** (-rä′), *interj., v.i.,* **-rayed, -ray·ing,** *n.* HURRAH.

Hoo·sier (hŏŏ′zhər), *n.* a native or inhabitant of Indiana (used as a nickname).

hoot (hŏŏt), *v.i.* **1.** to cry out or shout, esp. in disapproval or derision. **2.** to utter the cry characteristic of an owl. **3.** to utter a similar sound. —*v.t.* **4.** to assail with shouts of disapproval or derision: *The fans hooted the umpire.* **5.** to drive out, off, or away by hooting. —*n.* **6.** the cry of an owl. **7.** any similar sound, as an inarticulate shout. **8.** a cry or shout, esp. of disapproval or derision. **9.** *Informal.* the least bit of concern or interest; trifle: *I don't give a hoot.* **10.** *Slang.* an extremely funny person, situation, or event. —**hoot′er,** *n.* —**hoot′ing·ly,** *adv.*

hootch (hŏŏch), *n.* HOOCH.

hoot·en·an·ny (hŏŏt′n an′ē, hŏŏt′nan′-), *n., pl.* **-nies. 1.** an informal session or concert at which folk singers and instrumentalists perform for their own enjoyment, often with audience participation. **2.** *Older Use.* a thingumbob.

hoot′ owl′, *n.* any of various owls that hoot.

Hoo·ver (hŏŏ′vər), *n.* **1.** Herbert (Clark), 1874–1964, 31st president of the U.S. 1929–33. **2.** J(ohn) Edgar, 1895–1972, director of the U.S. FBI 1924–72.

Hoo′ver Dam′, *n.* official name of BOULDER DAM.

Hoo·ver·ville (hŏŏ′vər vil′), *n.* a collection of huts and shacks, as at the edge of a city, housing the unemployed during the 1930s. [H. HOO-VER + *-ville* < French: city]

hooves (hŏŏvz, hŏŏvz), *n.* a pl. of HOOF.

hop¹ (hop), *v.,* **hopped, hop·ping,** *n.* —*v.i.* **1.** to make a short, bouncing leap; move by leaping with all feet off the ground, as a rabbit. **2.** to leap on one foot. **3.** to make a short, quick trip, esp. in an airplane. **4.** to travel or move frequently from one place or situation to another (usu. used in combination): *to party-hop.* —*v.t.* **5.** to jump over; clear with a hop. **6.** to board or get onto (a vehicle): *to hop a plane.* **7.** to cross in an airplane. —*n.* **8.** a short leap, esp. on one foot. **9.** a journey, esp. a short trip by air. **10.** *Informal.* a dance or dancing party. **11.** a bounce or rebound, as of a ball. —**hop′ping·ly,** *adv.*

hop² (hop), *n., v.,* **hopped, hop·ping.** —*n.* **1.** any of several twining plants of the genus *Humulus,* of the hemp family, bearing male flowers in loose clusters and female flowers in small bract-covered spikes. **2. hops,** the dried ripe cones of the female flowers of this plant, used in brewing, medicine, etc. —*v.t.* **3.** to treat or flavor with hops. **4. hop up,** *Slang.* **a.** to excite; make enthusiastic. **b.** to add to the power of. **c.** to stimulate by narcotics.

hop′ clo′ver, *n.* a trefoil, *Trifolium campestre,* having yellow flowers that resemble hops when withered.

hope (hōp), *n., v.,* **hoped, hop·ing.** —*n.* **1.** the feeling that what is wanted can be had or that events will turn out well: one of the three Christian virtues. **2.** a particular instance of this feeling: *the hope of winning.* **3.** grounds for this feeling in a particular instance: *There is little hope of his recovery.* **4.** a person or thing in which expectations are centered: *The medicine was her last hope.* **5.** something that is hoped for. —*v.t.* **6.** to look forward to with desire and reasonable confidence. **7.** to believe, desire, or trust: *I hope you will be happy.* —*v.i.* **8.** to feel that something desired may happen: *We hope for an early spring.* —*Idiom.* **9. hope against hope,** to continue to hope when the situation appears bleak. —**hop′er,** *n.* —**hop′ing·ly,** *adv.*

hope′ chest′, *n.* a chest or the like used by a young woman for collecting clothing, linens, and other domestic or personal articles in anticipation of marriage.

hope·ful (hōp′fəl), *adj.* **1.** full of hope; expressing hope. **2.** exciting hope; promising advantage or success: *a hopeful prospect.* —*n.* **3.** a person who shows promise or aspires to success. —**hope′ful·ness,** *n.*

hope·ful·ly (hōp′fə lē), *adv.* **1.** in a hopeful manner. **2.** it is hoped; if all goes well: *Hopefully, we will get to the show on time.* —*Usage.* Although some strongly object to its use as a sentence modifier, HOPEFULLY meaning "it is hoped (that)" has been in use since the 1930s and is standard in all varieties of speech and writing. This use of HOPEFULLY parallels that of *certainly, curiously, frankly, regrettably,* and other sentence modifiers.

hope·less (hōp′lis), *adj.* **1.** providing no hope; beyond optimism or hope; desperate: *a hopeless medical condition.* **2.** without hope; despairing: *hopeless grief.* **3.** impossible to accomplish, solve, resolve, etc: *a hopeless misunderstanding.* **4.** not able to learn or act, perform, or work as desired; inadequate: *The new clerk is hopeless with figures.* —**hope′less·ly,** *adv.* —**hope′less·ness,** *n.*

hop′ horn′beam′, *n.* any of several Eurasian and North American trees of the genus *Ostrya,* of the birch family, esp. *O. virginiana,* bearing hoplike fruiting clusters.

Ho·pi (hō′pē), *n., pl.* **-pis,** (*esp. collectively*) **-pi. 1.** a member of a Pueblo Indian people of NE Arizona. **2.** the Uto-Aztecan language of the Hopi.

Hop·kins (hop′kinz), *n.* **1. Anthony,** born 1937, English actor, born in Wales. **2. Sir Frederick Gowland,** 1861–1947, English physician and biochemist. **3. Gerard Manley,** 1844–89, English poet. **4. Johns,** 1795–

1873, U.S. financier and philanthropist. **5. Mark,** 1802–87, U.S. educator.

Hop·kins·i·an·ism (hop kin′zē ə niz′əm), *n.* a modified Calvinism taught by Samuel Hopkins (1721–1803), that emphasized the sovereignty of God, the importance of His decrees, and the necessity of submitting to His will, accepting even damnation, if required, for His glory, and holding that ethics is merely disinterested benevolence. —**Hop·kin′si·an, Hop·kin·so·ni·an** (hop′kin sō′nē ən), *adj., n.*

hop·per (hop′ər), *n.* **1.** one that hops. **2.** any jumping insect, as a grasshopper. **3.** a funnel-shaped bin in which loose material, as grain or coal, is stored temporarily. **4.** a box into which a proposed legislative bill is dropped and thereby officially introduced.

Hop·per (hop′ər), *n.* **1. Edward,** 1882–1967, U.S. painter. **2. Grace Murray,** 1906–92, U.S. naval officer and computer scientist.

hop·ping (hop′ing), *adj.* **1.** active or busy. **2.** going from one place or situation to another of a similar specified type (usu. used in combination): *bar-hopping.* —*Idiom.* **3. hopping mad,** furious.

hop·sack·ing (hop′sak′ing), *n.* **1.** woven material for bags made chiefly of hemp and jute. **2.** Also, **hop·sack** (hop′sak′). a coarse fabric made of cotton, wool, or other fibers and similar to burlap, used in the manufacture of wearing apparel.

hop·scotch (hop′skoch′), *n.* **1.** a game in which a child hops around a diagram drawn on the ground or pavement to retrieve a small object, as a stone or stick, that was previously thrown down in one part of the diagram. —*v.i.* **2.** to jump or leap from one place to another: *small birds hopscotching on the lawn.* **3.** to move, pass, or journey quickly and directly, as from one place to another or through an area, subject, etc. —*v.t.* **4.** to jump, leap, or cross over in one continuous action. **5.** to travel through erratically or in a series of short trips.

hop′, skip′, and a jump′, *n.* a short distance. Also, **hop′, skip′, and jump′.**

Hor (hôr), *n.* **Mount,** the mountain where Aaron died and was buried. Num. 20:22–29; Deut. 32:50.

Hor·ace (hôr′is, hor′-), *n.* (*Quintus Horatius Flaccus*) 65–8 B.C., Roman poet and satirist.

Ho·ra·tian (hə rā′shən, hô-, hō-), *adj.* **1.** of or pertaining to Horace. **2. a.** of, pertaining to, or resembling the poetic style or diction of Horace. **b.** of or noting a Horatian ode.

Ho·ra′tio Al′ger (hə rā′shē ō′, hô-, hō-), *adj.* of or characteristic of the poor heroes in the novels of Horatio Alger, who achieve success and wealth through honesty and hard work.

horde (hôrd, hōrd), *n., v.,* **hord·ed, hord·ing.** —*n.* **1.** a large group, multitude, or number; crowd. **2.** a tribe or troop of Asian nomads. **3.** any nomadic group. **4.** a moving pack or swarm of animals. —*v.i.* **5.** to gather in a horde.

Ho·reb (hôr′eb, hōr′-), *n.* a mountain in the Bible sometimes identified with Mount Sinai. Ex. 3:1, 33:6.

hore·hound (hôr′hound′, hōr′-), *n.* **1.** an Old World plant, *Marrubium vulgare,* of the mint family, having downy leaves and containing a bitter juice used as an expectorant. **2.** any of various plants of the mint family. **3.** a lozenge flavored with horehound extract.

Ho·rite (hôr′īt, hōr′-), *n.* one of a people living on Mount Seir, displaced by the Israelites. Gen. 14:6; Deut. 2:12, 22.

ho·ri·zon (hə rī′zən), *n.* **1.** the line or circle that forms the apparent boundary between earth and sky. **2. a.** the small circle of the celestial sphere whose plane is tangent to the earth at the position of a given observer, or the plane of such a circle (**sensible horizon**). **b.** the great circle of the celestial sphere whose plane passes through the center of the earth and is parallel to the sensible horizon of a given position, or the plane of such a circle (**celestial horizon**). **3.** the limit or range of perception, knowledge, or the like. **4.** Usu. **horizons.** the scope of a person's interest, education, understanding, etc. [< Latin < Greek *horizōn* (*kýklos*) bounding (circle)] —**ho·ri′zon·less,** *adj.*

Hori′zon Club′, *n.* a division of Camp Fire, Inc., for members of high-school age.

hor·i·zon·tal (hôr′ə zon′tl, hor′-), *adj.* **1.** at right angles to the vertical; parallel to level ground. **2.** flat or level: *a horizontal position.* **3.** being in a prone or supine position; recumbent. **4.** near, on, or parallel to the horizon. **5.** measured or contained in a plane parallel to the horizon: *a horizontal distance.* **6.** of or pertaining to a position or individual of similar status: *horizontal mobility.* —*n.* **7.** anything horizontal, as a plane, direction, or object. —**hor′i·zon′tal·ly,** *adv.*

hor′izon′tal bar′, *n.* **1.** a bar fixed in a position parallel to the floor or ground, for use in chinning and other exercises. **2.** an event in gymnastics, judged on strength and grace while performing on such a bar. Also called **high bar.**

hor′izon′tal merg′er, *n.* the purchase by a company of a competitor or of a company dealing in similar products or services. Compare VERTICAL MERGER.

hor·mone (hôr′mōn), *n.* **1.** any of various internally secreted compounds formed in endocrine glands that affect the functions of specifically receptive organs or tissues when transported to them by the body fluids. **2.** a synthetic substance that acts like such a compound when introduced into the body. **3.** any of various plant compounds, as auxin or gibberellin, that control growth and differentiation of plant tissue. —**hor·mo′nal, hor·mon·ic** (-mon′ik, -mō′nik), *adj.*

horn (hôrn), *n.* **1.** one of the hard, keratinous, permanent, hollow, and usu. paired growths projecting from the head of certain ungulates, esp.

bovids. **2.** a similar growth, sometimes of compacted hair, as the median horn on a rhinoceros or the tusk of a narwhal. **3.** (not in technical use) antler. **4.** a process projecting from the head of an animal and suggestive of such a growth, as a feeler, tentacle, or crest. **5.** the keratinous substance of which horn growths are composed in vertebrates. **6.** any similar substance, as that forming tortoise shell, hoofs, nails, or corns. **7.** an article made of the material of an animal horn or like substance. **8.** any projection or extremity resembling the horn of an animal. **9.** something made from, resembling, or suggesting a hollowed-out animal horn: *a drinking horn.* **10.** a part resembling an animal horn attributed to deities, demons, etc.: *the devil's horn.* **11.** Usu., **horns,** the imaginary projections on a cuckold's brow. **12. a.** FRENCH HORN. **b.** HUNTING HORN. **c.** TRUMPET. **13.** an animal horn used as a wind instrument. **14.** an instrument for sounding a warning signal: *an automobile horn.* **15. a.** a tube of varying cross section used in some loudspeakers to couple the diaphragm to the sound-transmitting space. **b.** *Slang.* a loudspeaker. **16.** *Slang.* a telephone or radiotelephone: *I've been on the horn all morning.* **17.** a saddle pommel, esp. a high one. **18.** one of the curved extremities of a crescent, esp. of the crescent moon. **19.** a pyramidal mountain peak, esp. one having concave faces. **20.** a symbol of power or strength, as in the Bible: *a horn of salvation.* —*v.t.* **21.** to butt or gore with the horns. **22.** to cuckold. **23. horn in,** *Informal.* to thrust oneself forward obtrusively; intrude or interrupt. —*adj.* **24.** made of horn. —*Idiom.* **25. blow** or **toot one's own horn,** to boast about oneself. **26. draw** or **pull in one's horns,** to restrain oneself; become less belligerent. **27. on the horns of a dilemma,** confronted with two equally disagreeable choices. —**horn′less,** *adj.* —**horn′less•ness,** *n.* —**horn′like′,** *adj.*

horn•beam (hôrn′bēm′), *n.* any of various North American trees belonging to the genus *Carpinus,* of the birch family, yielding a hard heavy wood.

horn•bill (hôrn′bil′), *n.* any of various large birds of the family Bucerotidae, of the Old World tropics, having a massive, curved bill, usu. with a horny protuberance.

horn•blende (hôrn′blend′), *n.* a dark green to black mineral of the amphibole group, containing calcium, magnesium, iron, and aluminosilicates.

horn•book (hôrn′boŏk′), *n.* **1.** a leaf or page containing the alphabet, religious materials, etc., covered with a sheet of transparent horn and fixed in a frame with a handle, formerly used in teaching children to read. **2.** a primer or book of rudiments.

horned′ liz′ard, a flat-bodied iguanid lizard of the genus *Phrynosoma,* of W North America, having hornlike spines on the head. Also called **horned′ toad′.**

horned′ vi′per, a viper, *Cerastes cerastes,* of N African and extreme SW Asian deserts, having a hornlike spine above each eye. Also called **cerastes.**

hor•net (hôr′nit), *n.* any large stinging paper wasp of the family Vespidae, as *Vespa crabro,* introduced into the U.S. from Europe, or *Vespula maculata* of North America.

hor′net's nest′, *n.* a large amount of activity, trouble, hostility, or animosity.

horn•fels (hôrn′felz), *n.* a dark fine-grained metamorphic rock, the result of recrystallization of siliceous or argillaceous sediments by thermal metamorphism.

horn′ fly′, *n.* a small bloodsucking fly, *Haematobia irritans,* that is a pest, esp. of cattle.

horn′ of plen′ty, *n.* **1.** CORNUCOPIA. **2.** an edible trumpet-shaped chanterelle, *Craterellus cornucopiodes,* commonly found under certain trees of E North America and the Pacific coast.

horn•pipe (hôrn′pīp′), *n.* **1.** an English folk clarinet having one ox horn concealing the reed and another forming the bell. **2.** a lively jiglike dance, orig. to music played on a hornpipe, performed usu. by one person, and traditionally a favorite of sailors.

horn′-rims′, *n.pl.* eyeglasses with frames made of horn, tortoise shell, or plastic of a similar design. —**horn′-rimmed′,** *adj.*

horn•swog•gle (hôrn′swog′əl), *v.t.,* **-gled, -gling.** *Slang.* to swindle, cheat, hoodwink, or hoax.

horn•tail (hôrn′tāl′), *n.* any of various wasplike insects of the family Siricidae, the females of which have a hornlike ovipositor.

horn•worm (hôrn′wûrm′), *n.* the larva of any of several hawk moths, having a hornlike process at the rear of the abdomen.

horn•wort (hôrn′wûrt′, -wôrt′), *n.* any of several rootless aquatic herbs of the genus *Ceratophyllum,* having finely dissected, whorled leaves.

horn•y (hôr′nē), *adj.,* **horn•i•er, horn•i•est. 1.** consisting of a horn or a hornlike substance. **2.** having a horn or horns. **3.** hornlike through hardening; callous: *horny hands.* —**horn′i•ly,** *adv.* —**horn′i•ness,** *n.*

ho•rol•o•gist (hô rol′ə jist, hō-) also **ho•rol′o•ger,** *n.* **1.** an expert in horology. **2.** a person who makes clocks or watches.

ho•rol•o•gy (hô rol′ə jē, hō-), *n.* the art or science of making timepieces or of measuring time.

hor•o•scope (hôr′ə skōp′, hor′-), *n.* **1.** a diagram of the heavens, showing the relative position of planets and the signs of the zodiac, as at the moment of a person's birth, used esp. to predict events in a person's life. **2.** predictions or advice for the future, based on such a diagram. —**hor′o•scop′ic** (-skop′ik, -skō′pik), *adj.* —**ho•ros′co•py** (hô-ros′kə pē, hō-), *n.*

hor•ren•dous (hə ren′dəs), *adj.* shockingly dreadful; horrible: *a horrendous crime.* —**hor•ren′dous•ly,** *adv.*

hor•ri•ble (hôr′ə bəl, hor′-), *adj.* **1.** causing horror; shockingly dreadful. **2.** extremely unpleasant; deplorable; disgusting: *horrible living conditions.* —**hor′ri•ble•ness,** *n.* —**hor′ri•bly,** *adv.*

hor•rid (hôr′id, hor′-), *adj.* **1.** such as to cause horror; shockingly dreadful; abominable. **2.** extremely unpleasant or disagreeable; nasty. —**hor′rid•ly,** *adv.* —**hor′rid•ness,** *n.*

hor•rif•ic (hô rif′ik, ho-), *adj.* causing horror. —**hor•rif′i•cal•ly,** *adv.*

hor•ri•fy (hôr′ə fī′, hor′-), *v.t.,* **-fied, -fy•ing. 1.** to cause to feel horror. **2.** to distress greatly; shock or dismay. —**hor′ri•fi•ca′tion,** *n.* —**hor′ri•fy′ing•ly,** *adv.*

hor•ror (hôr′ər, hor′-), *n.* **1.** an overwhelming and painful feeling caused by something shocking, terrifying, or revolting; a shuddering fear: *to shrink back in horror.* **2.** anything that causes such a feeling. **3.** a strong aversion; abhorrence. **4.** *Informal.* something considered bad or tasteless: *That wallpaper is a horror.* **5. horrors,** *Informal.* **a.** DELIRIUM TREMENS. **b.** extreme depression. —*adj.* **6.** inspiring or creating horror or loathing: *a horror movie.* —*interj.* **7. horrors,** (used as a mild expression of dismay, surprise, disappointment, etc.)

hor′ror-struck′ or **hor′ror-strick′en,** *adj.* horrified; aghast.

hors d'oeuvre (ôr dûrv′), *n., pl.* **hors d'oeuvre** (ôr dûrv′), **hors d'oeuvres** (ôr dûrvz′, dûrv′). a small portion of food served as an appetizer before a meal or as a snack with cocktails. [< French]

horse (hôrs), *n., pl.* **hors•es,** (*esp. collectively*) **horse,** *v.,* **horsed, hors•ing,** *adj.* —*n.* **1.** a large, solid-hoofed, herbivorous mammal, *Equus caballus,* domesticated since prehistoric times, bred in numerous varieties, and used for carrying or pulling loads and for riding. **2.** a fully mature male animal of this type; stallion. **3.** something on which a person rides, sits, or exercises, as if astride the back of such an animal: *rocking horse.* **4.** Also called **trestle.** a frame or block, with legs, on which something is mounted or supported. **5. a.** VAULTING HORSE. **b.** POMMEL HORSE. **6.** Usu., **horses.** *Informal.* horsepower. **7.** *Slang.* an illicit aid to schoolwork, esp. a literal translation of a foreign-language text; pony; crib. —*v.t.* **8.** to provide with a horse or horses. **9.** to set on horseback. —*v.i.* **10.** to mount or go on a horse. **11.** (of a mare) to be in heat. **12. horse around,** *Informal.* to fool around; indulge in horseplay. —*adj.* **13.** of or for a horse or horses. **14.** drawn or powered by a horse or horses. **15.** unusually large. —*Idiom.* **16. from the horse's mouth,** from the original or a trustworthy source. **17. hold one's horses,** *Informal.* to be patient. **18. horse of another color,** something entirely different. Also, **horse of a different color.** —*Saying.* **19. look a gift horse in the mouth,** to be critical of a gift. —**horse′less,** *adj.* —**horse′like′,** *adj.*

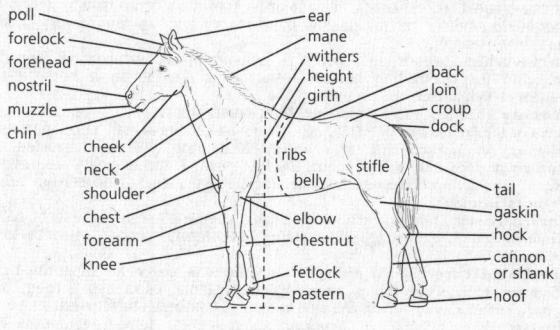

horse (def. 1)

horse′-and-bug′gy, *adj.* **1.** of or pertaining to the last few generations preceding the invention of the automobile. **2.** old-fashioned; outmoded.

horse•back (hôrs′bak′), *n.* **1.** the back of a horse. —*adv.* **2.** on horseback: *to ride horseback.*

horse′ chest′nut, *n.* **1.** any shrub or tree of the genus *Aesculus,* esp. *A. hippocastanum,* with large compound leaves and upright clusters of white flowers. **2.** the shiny brown nutlike seed of trees of the genus *Aesculus.*

horse•feath•ers (hôrs′feth′ərz), *Slang.* —*n.* **1.** rubbish; nonsense. —*interj.* **2.** (used to express contempt, annoyance, dismissal, etc.)

horse′ fly′ or **horse′fly′,** *n.* any bloodsucking, usu. large fly of the family Tabanidae, esp. of the genus *Tabanus,* a pest of horses, cattle, etc.

horse′ gen′tian, *n.* any weedy North American plant of the genus *Triosteum,* of the honeysuckle family, having leathery fruit.

horse′hair worm′, *n.* any long slender aquatic worm of the phylum Nematomorpha, developing parasitically on insects and crustaceans.

horse•hide (hôrs′hīd′), *n.* **1.** the hide of a horse. **2.** leather made from the hide of a horse. **3.** *Informal.* a baseball.

horse′ lat′itudes, *n.pl.* the latitudes, approximately 30° N and S, forming the edges of the trade-wind belt, characterized by high atmospheric pressure with calms and light variable winds.

horse•leech (hôrs′lēch′), *n.* a large leech, *Haemopis marmoratis*, that enters the mouth and nasal passages of horses.
horse′less car′riage (hôrs′lis), *n.* an automobile.
horse′ mack′erel, *n.* **1.** BLUEFIN TUNA. **2.** JACK MACKEREL.
horse•man (hôrs′mən), *n., pl.* **-men. 1.** a person who is skilled in riding a horse. **2.** a person on horseback. **3.** a person who owns, breeds, trains, or tends horses.
horse•man•ship (hôrs′mən ship′), *n.* **1.** the art, ability, skill, or manner of a horseman. **2.** EQUITATION.
horse•mint (hôrs′mint′), *n.* any of various wild mints, esp. a New World mint of the genus *Monarda*, with showy flowers.
horse′ mush′room, *n.* a very large North American agaric mushroom, *Agaricus arvensis*, of meadows and fields.
horse′ net′tle, *n.* a large prickly North American weed, *Solanum carolinense*, of the nightshade family, having clusters of violet to white flowers.
horse•play (hôrs′plā′), *n.* rough or boisterous play.
horse•pow•er (hôrs′pou′ər), *n.* **1.** a foot-pound-second unit of power, equivalent to 550 foot-pounds per second, or 745.7 watts. **2.** *Informal.* the capacity to achieve or produce; strength or talent.
horse•rad•ish (hôrs′rad′ish), *n.* **1.** a cultivated plant, *Armoracia rusticana*, of the mustard family, having small white flowers. **2.** the pungent root of this plant, grated and used as a condiment.
horse′ sense′, *n.* COMMON SENSE.
horse•shoe (hôrs′shōō′, hôrsh′-), *n., v.,* **-shoed, -shoe•ing. —n. 1.** a U-shaped metal plate, plain or with calks, nailed to a horse's hoof to protect it from being injured by hard or rough surfaces. **2.** something U-shaped, as a valley, river bend, or other natural feature. **3. horseshoes,** (*used with a sing. v.*) a game in which horseshoes or other U-shaped objects are tossed at an iron stake to encircle it or come as close to it as possible. **—v.t. 4.** to put a horseshoe or horseshoes on.
horse′shoe crab′, *n.* any of several large marine arthropods of the order Xiphosura, esp. *Limulus polyphemus*, of E North American shores, having a stiff tail and brown carapace curved like a horseshoe. Also called **king crab.**
horse′ show′, *n.* a competitive display of the capabilities and qualities of horses and their riders or handlers.
horse•tail (hôrs′tāl′), *n.* a nonflowering plant of the genus *Equisetum*, family Equisetaceae, with hollow jointed stems bearing scaly leaves and a spikelike cone bearing spores.
horse′ trade′, *n.* **1.** a shrewdly conducted exchange, as of favors or objects, usu. involving close bargaining. **2.** an exchanging or trading of horses. **—horse′-trade′,** *v.i.,* **-trad•ed, -trad•ing. —horse′-trad′er,** *n.*
horse•weed (hôrs′wēd′), *n.* a North American composite weed, *Erigeron canadensis*, having narrow hairy leaves and clusters of very small greenish flowers.
horse•whip (hôrs′hwip′, -wip′), *n., v.,* **-whipped, -whip•ping. —n. 1.** a whip for controlling horses. **—v.t. 2.** to beat with a horsewhip. **—horse′whip′per,** *n.*
hors•ey (hôr′sē), *adj.,* **hors•i•er, hors•i•est.** HORSY.
hors•y or **hors•ey** (hôr′sē), *adj.,* **hors•i•er, hors•i•est. 1.** of, pertaining to, or characteristic of a horse. **2.** dealing with or interested in horses or sports involving them: *the horsy set.* **3.** rather heavy and awkward in general appearance or facial structure. **—hors′i•ly,** *adv.* **—hors′i•ness,** *n.*
hor•ta•to•ry (hôr′tə tôr′ē, -tōr′ē), *adj.* urging to some course of conduct or action; exhorting; encouraging: *a hortatory speech.* **—hor′ta•to′ri•ly,** *adv.*
hor•ti•cul•ture (hôr′ti kul′chər), *n.* the science or art of cultivating flowers, fruits, vegetables or ornamental plants, esp. in a garden, orchard, or nursery. **—hor′ti•cul′tur•al,** *adj.* **—hor′ti•cul′tur•ist,** *n.*
Ho•rus (hôr′əs, hōr′-), *n. Egyptian Relig.* a solar deity, regarded as either the son or the brother of Isis and Osiris, and usually represented as a falcon or as a man with the head of a falcon.
Hos., Hosea.
ho•san•na (hō zan′ə), *interj., n., pl.* **-nas. 1.** (an exclamation used in praise of God or Christ.) **—n. 2.** a cry of "hosanna." **3.** a shout of praise or adoration; an acclamation. **—v.t. 4.** to praise, applaud, etc.
hose (hōz), *n., pl.* **hose** for 2, 3, **hos•es** for 1, *v.,* **hosed, hos•ing. —n. 1.** a flexible tube for conveying a liquid, as water, to a desired point: *a garden hose.* **2.** (*used with a pl. v.*) an article of clothing, or a pair of such articles, for the foot and some part of the leg; stocking or sock. **3.** (*used with a pl. v.*) **a.** men's tights, as were worn with and usu. attached to a doublet. **b.** BREECHES (def. 1). **—v.t. 4.** to water, wash, spray, or drench by means of a hose (often fol. by *down*). **—hose′like′,** *adj.*
Ho•se•a (hō zē′ə, -zā′ə), *n.* **1.** a Minor Prophet of the 8th century B.C. **2.** a book of the Bible bearing his name.
ho•sier•y (hō′zhə rē), *n.* **1.** stockings or socks of any kind. **2.** the business of a hosier.
hos•pice (hos′pis), *n.* **1.** a house of shelter or rest for pilgrims, strangers, etc., esp. one kept by a religious order. **2.** a health care facility, or a system of professional home visits and supervision, for supportive care of the terminally ill.
hos•pi•ta•ble (hos′pi tə bəl, ho spit′ə bəl), *adj.* **1.** receiving or treating guests or strangers warmly and generously: *a hospitable family.* **2.** characterized by or indicating warmth and generosity toward guests or strangers: *a hospitable smile.* **3.** favorably receptive or open (usu. fol. by *to*): *hospitable to new ideas.* **—hos′pi•ta•ble•ness,** *n.* **—hos′pi•ta•bly,** *adv.*
hos•pi•tal (hos′pi tl), *n.* **1.** an institution in which sick or injured persons are given medical or surgical treatment. **2.** a similar establishment for the care of animals. **3.** a repair shop for specific portable objects: *doll hospital.* **4.** *Brit.* a charitable institution for the needy.
hos•pi•tal•i•ty (hos′pi tal′i tē), *n., pl.* **-ties. 1.** the friendly reception and treatment of guests or strangers; an act or show of welcome. **2.** the quality of being hospitable and welcoming to guests or strangers.
hospital′ity suite′, *n.* a suite or room, as at a convention, where clients, potential customers, etc., may meet informally. Also called **hospital′ity room′.**
hos•pi•tal•ize (hos′pi tl īz′), *v.t.,* **-ized, -iz•ing.** to place in a hospital for medical care or observation. **—hos′pi•tal•i•za′tion,** *n.*
host¹ (hōst), *n.* **1.** a person who receives or entertains guests at home or elsewhere. **2.** an emcee, moderator, or interviewer for a television or radio program. **3.** a company, place, or the like that provides services or resources, as for a convention or sporting event. **4.** the landlord of an inn. **5.** a living animal or plant from which a parasite obtains nutrition. **6.** the recipient of a graft. **7.** HOST COMPUTER. **—v.t. 8.** to be the host at (a dinner, reception, etc.). **9.** to act as host to. **—v.i. 10.** to perform the duties or functions of a host. [< Latin *hospes* host, guest, stranger]
host² (hōst), *n.* **1.** a multitude or great number of persons or things: *a host of details.* **2.** an army.
Host (hōst), *n.* the bread or wafer consecrated in the celebration of the Eucharist. [< Middle French *oiste* < Late Latin *hostia* Eucharistic wafer (Latin: victim, sacrifice)]
hos•ta (hō′stə, hos′tə), *n., pl.* **-tas.** any of various plants belonging to the genus *Hosta*, of the lily family, as the plantain lily.
hos•tage (hos′tij), *n.* a person given or held as security for the fulfillment of certain conditions or terms, promises, etc., by another. **—hos′tage•ship′,** *n.*
host′ comput′er, *n.* the main computer in a network, which controls or performs certain functions for connected computers.
hos•tel (hos′tl), *n., v.* **-teled, -tel•ing** or (*esp. Brit.*) **-telled, -tel•ling. —n. 1.** Also called **youth hostel.** an inexpensive, supervised lodging place for young travelers. **2.** an inn. **—v.i. 3.** to travel, lodging each night at a hostel. [< Old French < Latin *hospitāle* guesthouse]
hos•tel•ry (hos′tl rē), *n., pl.* **-ries.** an inn or hotel.
host•ess (hō′stis), *n.* **1.** a woman who entertains guests in her own home or elsewhere. **2.** a woman employed in a restaurant or the like to seat patrons. **3.** a woman who acts as emcee, moderator, or interviewer for a television or radio program; host. **4.** a woman employed by an airline or other carrier to see that passengers are comfortable throughout a trip. **5.** a woman who manages a resort or hotel or who directs its social activities. **—v.t. 6.** to be or serve as hostess to or at. **—v.i. 7.** to perform the duties or functions of a hostess.
hos•tile (hos′tl; *esp. Brit.* -tīl), *adj.* **1.** of or pertaining to an enemy. **2.** opposed in feeling, action, or character; antagonistic: *hostile criticism.* **3.** not friendly or hospitable. **—n. 4.** a person or thing that is antagonistic or unfriendly; an enemy. **—hos′tile•ly,** *adv.*
hos•til•i•ty (ho stil′i tē), *n., pl.* **-ties. 1.** a hostile state, condition, or attitude; enmity; antagonism. **2.** a hostile act. **3.** opposition or resistance to an idea, plan, project, etc. **4. hostilities, a.** acts of warfare. **b.** war.
host′-specif′ic, *adj.* capable of living solely on or in one species of host.
hot (hot), *adj.,* **hot•ter, hot•test,** *adv., n.* **—adj. 1.** having or giving off heat; having a high temperature: *hot coffee.* **2.** having, attended with, or causing a sensation of great bodily heat. **3.** sharply peppery or pungent: *Is this mustard hot?* **4.** having or showing intense or violent feeling; ardent; vehement: *a hot temper.* **5.** violent, furious, or intense: *the hottest battle of the war.* **6.** strong or fresh, as a scent or trail. **7.** absolutely new; fresh: *hot off the press.* **8.** following very closely; close: *hot on the trail.* **9.** *Informal.* very good: *not so hot.* **10.** (of colors) extremely intense: *hot pink.* **11.** *Informal.* currently popular or in demand. **12.** *Slang.* extremely lucky or favorable. **13.** *Slang.* (in sports and games) playing well or winningly; scoring effectively. **14.** *Slang.* funny; absurd: *That's a hot one!* **15.** (in games) close to the object or answer being sought. **16.** *Informal.* extremely exciting or interesting; sensational: *hot news.* **17. a.** (of jazz) emotionally intense, propulsive, and marked by aggressive attack and warm, full tone. **b.** (of a musician) skilled in playing hot jazz. **18.** *Informal.* (of a vehicle) capable of attaining extremely high speeds. **19.** *Slang.* **a.** stolen recently or otherwise illegal and dangerous to possess. **b.** wanted by the police. **c.** dangerous. **20.** *Informal.* in a state of mind to perform exceedingly well or rapidly. **21.** actively conducting an electric current or containing a high voltage: *a hot wire.* **22.** RADIOACTIVE. **23.** noting any process involving plastic deformation of a metal at a temperature high enough to permit recrystallization: *hot working.* **—adv. 24.** in a hot manner; hotly. **25.** while hot. **26.** at a temperature high enough to permit recrystallization: *The wire was drawn hot.* **—n. —Idiom. 27. (all) hot and bothered,** *Informal.* excited or flustered. **28. hot and heavy,** *Informal.* in an intense, vehement, or passionate manner. **29. hot under the collar,** *Informal.* angry; excited; upset. **—hot′ly,** *adv.* **—hot′ness,** *n.*
hot′ air′, *n. Informal.* empty or exaggerated talk or writing.

hot·bed (hot′bed′), *n.* **1.** a boxlike glass structure covering a bed of earth that is heated by electric cables or fermenting manure, for growing plants out of season. **2.** a place or environment favoring rapid growth or spread, esp. of something unwanted.

hot′-blood′ed, *adj.* **1.** excitable; impetuous. **2.** ardent; passionate. —**hot′-blood′ed·ness,** *n.*

hot′-but′ton, *adj.* exciting strong feelings; highly charged; emotional: *hot-button issues.*

hot′ cake′ or **hot′cake′,** *n.* **1.** a pancake or griddlecake. —*Idiom.* **2. sell** or **go like hot cakes,** to be bought, taken, or disposed of very quickly, esp. in quantity.

hotch·pot (hoch′pot′), *n.* a gathering together of the property of a deceased person who has died intestate so that it can be divided equally among the decedent's legal heirs.

hot′ cor′ner, *n.* THIRD BASE (def. 2).

hot′ cross′ bun′, *n.* a bun with a cross of frosting on it, eaten chiefly during Lent.

hot′ dog′, *n.* **1.** a frankfurter. **2.** a sandwich of a frankfurter in a split roll. **3.** Also, **hot′dog′.** *Slang.* a person who hot-dogs; hot-dogger. —*interj.* **4.** (used to express great joy or delight.)

hot′-dog′ or **hot′dog′,** *v.,* **-dogged, -dog·ging,** *adj. Slang.* **1.** to perform intricate maneuvers in a sport, esp. surfing or skiing. **2.** to perform flamboyantly; show off. —*adj.* **3.** highly skillful. **4.** done for attention; showy or sensational. —**hot′dog′ger,** *n.*

hos·tel (ho tel′), *n.* a commercial establishment offering lodging to travelers and sometimes to permanent residents, and often having public restaurants, meeting rooms, or stores. [< French *hôtel,* Old French *hostel* HOSTEL]

ho·te·lier (ō′təl yā′, hōt′l ēr′, hō tel′yər), *n.* a manager or owner of a hotel or inn.

hot′ flash′, *n.* a sudden, temporary sensation of heat experienced by some women during menopause. Also called **hot′ flush′.**

hot·foot (hot′foot′), *n., pl.* **-foots. 1.** a practical joke in which a match is inserted surreptitiously in the victim's shoe and then lighted. —*v.i.* **2.** to go in great haste (often fol. by *it*): *to hotfoot it to the bank.* —*adv.* **3.** with great speed; in haste: *to run hotfoot to class.*

hot·head (hot′hed′), *n.* a short-tempered person. —**hot′head′ed,** *adj.* —**hot′head′ed·ly,** *adv.* —**hot′head′ed·ness,** *n.*

hot·house (hot′hous′), *n., pl.* **-hous·es** (-hou′ziz), *adj., v.,* **-housed, hous·ing.** —*n.* **1.** an artificially heated greenhouse for the cultivation of tender plants. **2.** a place favoring rapid growth; hotbed. —*adj.* **3.** of or pertaining to a plant grown in, or capable of being grown only in, a hothouse. **4.** overprotected, artificial, or unnaturally delicate. —*v.t.* **5.** to cultivate in a hothouse. **6.** to educate (children) at an unusually early age.

hot′ line′, *n.* **1.** a direct telecommunications link, as a telephone line or Teletype circuit, enabling immediate communication between heads of state in an international crisis. **2.** Also, **hot′line′.** a telephone number providing direct access to a company, professional service, or agency, as for information, the lodging of complaints, or counseling.

hot′ mon′ey, *n. Informal.* funds transferred frequently or hastily from one country to another chiefly to avoid depreciation in value or to take advantage of higher interest rates.

hot′ pep′per, *n.* any of various very pungent fruits of pepper plants of the genus *Capsicum.*

hot′ plate′, *n.* a portable appliance having an electrical unit for cooking.

hot′ pot′, *n. Chiefly Brit.* mutton or beef cooked with potatoes in a covered pot.

hot′ pota′to, *n. Informal.* a situation or issue that is difficult, unpleasant, or risky to deal with.

hot′ rod′, *n.* an automobile specially built or altered for fast acceleration and increased speed.

hot′-rod′, *v.i.,* **-rod·ded, -rod·ding. 1.** to drive a hot rod. **2.** *Informal.* to drive very fast. —**hot′rod′der,** *n.*

hot′ seat′, *n. Slang.* **1.** ELECTRIC CHAIR. **2.** a highly uncomfortable or embarrassing situation.

hot·shot (hot′shot′), *Slang.* —*adj.* **1.** highly successful and aggressive: *a hotshot sales manager.* **2.** displaying skill flamboyantly: *a hotshot ballplayer.* —*n.* **3.** Also, **hot′ shot′.** an impressively successful or skillful and often vain person. **4.** an express freight train.

hot′ spot′ or **hot′spot′,** *n.* **1.** a country or region where dangerous or difficult political situations exist or may develop. **2.** any area or place of known danger, instability, etc. **3.** *Informal.* a nightclub. **4.** a chromosome site or a section of DNA having a high frequency of mutation. **5.** a moist, raw sore on the skin of a dog or cat caused by constant licking of an irritation.

hot′ spring′, *n.* a thermal spring having water warmer than 98°F (37°C).

Hot′ Springs′, *n.* **1.** a city in central Arkansas: adjoins a national park (**Hot′ Springs′ Na′tional Park′**) noted for its thermal mineral springs. 35,166. **2.** a resort village in W Virginia: site of international conference (forerunner of Food and Agriculture Organization of the United Nations) in 1943 to aid agricultural and food supply adjustments after World War II.

hot′ stuff′, *n. Slang.* **1.** a person or thing of exceptional interest or merit. **2.** something unconventional, sensational, or daring.

hot·sy-tot·sy (hot′sē tot′sē), *adj. Slang.* about as right as can be; perfect: *Everything is just hotsy-totsy.*

hot′-tem′pered, *adj.* easily angered; short-tempered.

hot′ tub′, *n.* a wooden tub, usu. big enough to hold several persons, filled with hot water and often equipped with a whirlpool. —**hot′-tub′-ber,** *n.* —**hot′-tub′bing,** *n.*

hot′ wa′ter, *n. Informal.* trouble; a predicament.

hot′-wire′, *v.t.,* **-wired, -wir·ing.** to start the engine of (a motor vehicle) by short-circuiting the ignition.

Hou·di·ni (hoo dē′nē), *n.* **Harry** (*Erich Weiss*), 1874–1926, U.S. magician.

hound (hound), *n.* **1.** any of several breeds of dogs that pursue game either by sight or scent, esp. one having a long face and large drooping ears. **2.** any dog. **3.** a mean, contemptible person. **4.** an addict or devotee: *an autograph hound.* —*v.t.* **5.** to hunt or track with hounds, or as a hound does; pursue; dog. **6.** to annoy or persecute relentlessly; harass; badger. —*Idiom.* **7. follow the** or **ride to hounds,** to participate in a fox hunt. —**hound′er,** *n.* —**hound′ish, hound′y,** *adj.* —**hound′like′,** *adj.*

hound's′-tooth′, *adj.* patterned with hound's-tooth check: *a hound's-tooth jacket.*

hound's′-tooth′ (or **hounds′tooth′**) **check′,** *n.* a pattern of broken or jagged checks, used on a variety of fabrics.

hour (ou³r, ou′ər), *n.* **1.** a period of time equal to $\frac{1}{24}$ of a mean solar or civil day and equivalent to 60 minutes. **2.** any specific one of these 24 periods, usu. reckoned in two series of 12, one series from midnight to noon and the second from noon to midnight, but sometimes reckoned (esp. in military and non-U.S. usage) in one series of 24, from midnight to midnight: *He slept for the hour between 2 and 3* A.M. *The hour for the bombardment was between 1330 (1:30* P.M.*) and 1400 (2:00* P.M.*).* **3.** any specific time of day; the time indicated by a timepiece: *What is the hour?* **4.** a short or limited period of time: *to have one's hour of glory.* **5.** a particular or appointed time: *At what hour do you open?* **6.** a customary or usual time: *dinner hour.* **7.** the present time: *the issues of the hour.* **8. hours,** a. time spent at a workplace or in working, studying, etc.: *The doctor's hours were from 10 to 4.* **b.** customary time of going to bed and getting up: *to keep late hours.* **9.** the distance normally covered in an hour's traveling: *We live about an hour from the city.* **10.** a single period, as of instruction or therapy, usu. lasting from 40 to 55 minutes. **11.** CREDIT HOUR. —*Idiom.* **12. one's hour, a.** the time of one's death. **b.** any crucial moment or time. —**hour′less,** *adj.*

hour·glass (ou³r′glas′, -gläs′, ou′ər-), *n.* **1.** an instrument for measuring time, consisting of two bulbs of glass joined by a narrow passage through which a quantity of sand or mercury runs in just an hour. —*adj.* **2.** having or indicating the shape of this instrument: *a woman with an hourglass figure.*

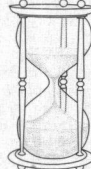

hourglass

hour′ hand′, *n.* the hand that indicates the hours on a clock or watch.

hour·long or **hour′-long′,** *adj.* lasting an hour.

hour·ly (ou³r′lē, ou′ər-), *adj.* **1.** of, pertaining to, occurring, or done each successive hour: *hourly news reports.* **2.** using an hour as a basic unit of reckoning: *hourly wages.* **3.** hired to work for wages by the hour: *hourly workers.* **4.** frequent; continual. —*adv.* **5.** at or during every hour; once an hour. **6.** frequently; continually.

house (*n., adj.* hous; *v.* houz), *n., pl.* **hous·es** (hou′ziz), *v.,* **housed, hous·ing,** *adj.* —*n.* **1.** a building in which people live; residence. **2.** a household. **3.** (*often cap.*) a family, including ancestors and descendants: *the House of Hapsburg.* **4.** a building, enclosure, or other construction for any of various purposes (usu. used in combination): *a clubhouse; a boathouse; a doghouse.* **5.** a theater, concert hall, or auditorium. **6.** the audience of a theater or the like. **7. a.** (*often cap.*) a legislative or official deliberative body, esp. one branch of a bicameral legislature: *the House of Representatives.* **b.** the building in which such a body meets. **c.** a quorum of such a body. **8.** (*often cap.*) a commercial establishment; business firm: *a publishing house.* **9.** a gambling casino or its management. **10.** a residential hall in a college or school; dormitory. **11.** the members or residents of any such residential hall. **12.** *Informal.* a brothel; whorehouse. **13.** Also called **parish.** the area enclosed by a circle 12 or 14 ft. (3.7 or 4.2 m) in diameter at each end of a curling rink, having the tee in the center. **14.** *Naut.* any enclosed shelter above the weather deck of a vessel: *bridge house.* **15.** *Astrol.* one of the 12 divisions of the celestial sphere, numbered counterclockwise from the point of the E horizon. **16.** HOUSE MUSIC. —*v.t.* **17.** to put or receive into a house, dwelling, or shelter; lodge or harbor: *to house students in* a dormitory; to house flood victims in a church. **18.** to provide with a place, as to work or study: This floor houses our executive staff. **19.** to be a receptacle or repository for; hold; contain: This casing houses the batteries. —v.i. **20.** to take shelter; dwell. —adj. **21.** of, pertaining to, or noting a house. **22.** suitable for or customarily used or kept in a house: house paint; house pets. **23.** (of a product) made by or for a specific retailer and often sold under the store's own label. **24.** served by a restaurant as its customary brand: the house wine. —Idiom. **25. bring down the house,** to inspire a live audience to break into prolonged, unrestrained laughter or applause over one's performance. **26. keep house,** to maintain a home; manage a household. **27. on the house,** as a gift from the management; free. **28. put** or **set one's house in order,** to settle one's affairs.

house′ arrest′, n. confinement of an arrested person to his or her home or to a public place, as a hospital, instead of a jail.

house•boat (hous′bōt′), n. a flat-bottomed bargelike boat fitted for use as a floating dwelling but not suited to rough water.

house•bound (hous′bound′), adj. restricted to the house, as by illness.

house•break (hous′brāk′), v.t., **-broke, -bro•ken, -break•ing. 1.** to train (a pet) to excrete outdoors or in a specific place. **2.** to train (a person) to adopt an appropriate or desirable mode of behavior; make tractable.

house•bro•ken (hous′brō′kən), adj. **1.** (of a pet) trained to avoid excreting inside the house or in improper places. **2.** (of a person) trained to behave in a socially appropriate manner; tractable.

house′ call′, n. a professional visit, as by a physician or sales representative, to the home of a patient or customer.

house•clean•ing (hous′klē′ning), n. **1.** the thorough cleaning of a house or apartment and its furnishings. **2.** the reforming of an organization, system, or the like by eliminating personnel or revising methods of operation. —house′clean′, v.t., v.i.

house•coat (hous′kōt′), n. a woman's robe or dresslike garment for casual wear about the house.

house′ crick′et, n. a common dark brown cricket, Acheta domesticus, that is sometimes an indoor pest.

house′ detec′tive, n. an employee, esp. of a department store or hotel, employed to prevent thefts, violations of regulations, or other misconduct by patrons.

House′ Divid′ed Against′ Itself′, a parable of Jesus. Matt. 12:25–28; Mark 3:23–26.

house•dress (hous′dres′), n. a relatively simple and inexpensive dress suitable for housework.

house′fly′ or **house′ fly′,** n., pl. **-flies.** a medium-sized, gray-striped fly, Musca domestica, common around human habitations in nearly all parts of the world.

house•guest (hous′gest′), n. a person staying with a household as a guest for one night or longer.

house•hold (hous′hōld′, -ōld′), n. **1.** the people of a house collectively; a family including any servants. —adj. **2.** of or pertaining to a household: household expenses. **3.** for use in the home, esp. for cooking, cleaning, or laundering: household bleach; household appliances. **4.** common; familiar: a household name in men's fashions.

house′hold effects′, n.pl. privately owned goods consisting chiefly of furniture, appliances, etc., for keeping house. Also called **house′hold goods′.**

house•hold•er (hous′hōl′dər, -ōl′-), n. **1.** a person who holds title to or occupies a house. **2.** the head of a family.

house′hold word′, n. a familiar name, phrase, or saying; byword.

house•hus•band (hous′huz′bənd), n. a married man who stays at home to manage the household while his wife goes out to work.

house•keep (hous′kēp′), v.i., **-kept, -keep•ing.** to keep or maintain a house.

house•keep•er (hous′kē′pər), n. **1.** a person, often hired, who does or directs the domestic work and planning necessary for a home, as housecleaning or buying food. **2.** an employee of a hotel, hospital, etc., who supervises the cleaning staff.

house•keep•ing (hous′kē′ping), n. **1.** the maintenance of a house or domestic establishment. **2.** the management of household affairs. **3.** the routine management, care, and servicing of any system.

house′keeping bill′, n. an act in a legislature that embodies a minor alteration to a law.

house•leek (hous′lēk′), n. a succulent plant, Sempervivum tectorum, of the stonecrop family, native to Europe, having reddish flowers and leaves forming dense basal rosettes.

house•maid (hous′mād′), n. a female servant employed in a home to do housework.

house′maid's knee′, n. inflammation of the bursa over the front of the kneecap.

house•mate (hous′māt′), n. a person with whom one shares a house or other dwelling.

house′ mouse′, n. an Old World mouse, Mus musculus, introduced worldwide.

house′ mu′sic, n. an up-tempo style of disco music characterized by deep bass rhythms, piano or synthesizer melodies, and soul-music singing, sometimes with elements of rap music.

House′ of Bur′gesses, n. the popular branch of the colonial legislature of Virginia or Maryland.

house′ of cards′, n. a structure or plan that is insubstantial and subject to imminent collapse.

House′ of Com′mons, n. the elective lower house of the Parliament of Great Britain, Canada, etc.

house′ of correc′tion, n. a place for the confinement and reform of persons convicted of minor offenses and not regarded as confirmed criminals.

house′ of God′, n. **1.** Also called **house′ of wor′ship, house′ of prayer′.** a building devoted to religious worship; a church, synagogue, temple, chapel, etc. **2.** Also, **House′ of God′.** Islam. Ka'ba.

House′ of Lords′, n. the nonelective upper house of the British Parliament.

House′ of Represen′tatives, n. the lower house of many national and state legislatures, as in the U.S., Mexico, and Japan.

house′ or′gan, n. a periodical issued by a business, institution, or the like for its employees, customers, etc., presenting news about the organization and its personnel.

house′ par′ty or **house′par′ty,** n. **1.** the entertainment of guests for one or more nights at one's home or at another place, as a fraternity or sorority house. **2.** the guests at such an affair or party.

house•plant (hous′plant′, -plänt′), n. an ornamental plant that is grown indoors.

house′-proud′, adj. proud of one's house and wishing to see it always at its best. —house′-pride′, n.

house′-rais′ing, n. a gathering of persons in a rural community to help one of its members build a house.

house′ rule′, n. a rule in a gambling game used only in a certain casino or among certain players.

house′sit′ or **house′-sit′,** v.i., **-sat, -sit•ting.** to take care of a residence while the regular occupant is away, esp. by living in it. —house′ sit′ter, house′-sit′ter, n.

house′ spar′row, n. a hardy brown and gray songbird, Passer domesticus, of the family Passeridae, native to Eurasia: now common in much of the world near human habitation. Also called **English sparrow.**

house′-to-house′, adj. **1.** conducted from one house to the next: a house-to-house survey. **2.** DOOR-TO-DOOR (def. 1).

house′ trail′er, n. a trailer fitted with accommodations for sleeping, eating, washing, etc. Compare MOBILE HOME.

House′ Un-Amer′ican Activ′ities Commit′tee, n. an investigative committee of the U.S. House of Representatives. Originally created in 1938 to inquire into subversive activities in the U.S., it was reestablished in 1945 as the Committee on Un-American Activities, renamed in 1969 as the Committee on Internal Security, and abolished in 1975. Abbr.: HUAC

house•wares (hous′wârz′), n.pl. articles of household equipment, as kitchen utensils or glassware.

house•warm•ing (hous′wôr′ming), n. a party to celebrate a person's or family's move to a new home.

house•wife (hous′wīf′ or, usu., huz′if for 2), n., pl. **-wives** (-wīvz′ or, usu., -ifs or -ivz for 2). **1.** a married woman who manages her own household, esp. as her principal occupation. **2.** Brit. a small case for sewing articles. —house′wif′ey, adj. —Usage. HOUSEWIFE is regarded by some as offensive, perhaps because it implies a lowly status or perhaps because it defines a woman's occupation in relation to a man. Homemaker is a common substitute.

house•work (hous′wûrk′), n. the work of cleaning, cooking, etc., to be done in housekeeping.

house•wreck•er (hous′rek′ər), n. WRECKER (def. 4).

hous•ing (hou′zing), n. **1.** any shelter, lodging, or dwelling place. **2.** houses collectively. **3.** the providing of houses or shelter. **4.** anything that covers or protects; casing. **5.** a fully enclosed case and support for a mechanism.

hous′ing proj′ect, n. a publicly built and operated housing development, usu. intended for low- or moderate-income tenants or senior citizens.

Hous•ton (hyōō′stən), n. **1.** Sam(uel), 1793–1863, U.S. soldier: president of the Republic of Texas 1836–38. **2.** a city in SE Texas: a port on a ship canal, connected with the Gulf of Mexico. 1,702,086. —Hous•to′ni•an (-stō′nē ən), adj., n.

Hou•yhn•hnm (hōō in′əm, hwin′əm, win′-), n. (in Jonathan Swift's Gulliver's Travels) one of a race of horses endowed with reason.

HOV, high-occupancy vehicle.

hove (hōv), v. a pt. and pp. of HEAVE.

hov•el (huv′əl, hov′-), n., v., **-eled, -el•ing** or (esp. Brit.) **-elled, -el•ling. —n. 1.** a small, very humble dwelling; wretched hut. **2.** any dirty, disorganized dwelling. **3.** an open shed, as for sheltering cattle or tools. —v.t. **4.** to shelter or lodge as in a hovel.

hov•er (huv′ər, hov′-), v.i. **1.** to hang fluttering or suspended in the air: a kite hovering over the yard. **2.** to keep lingering about; wait near at hand. **3.** to remain in an uncertain or irresolute state; waver: to hover between life and death. —hov′er•er, n. —hov′er•ing•ly, adv.

hov•er•craft (huv′ər kraft′, -kräft′, hov′-), n., pl. **-craft.** (sometimes cap.) a passenger craft that rides on a cushion of air, kept aloft by fans and driven forward by propellers.

how (hou), adv. **1.** in what way or manner; by what means?: How did *the fire start?* **2.** to what extent, degree, etc.?: *How difficult was the test?* **3.** in what state or condition?: *How is the baby?* **4.** for what reason; why?: *How can you talk such nonsense?* **5.** to what effect; with what meaning?: *How is one to interpret such actions?* **6.** at what amount or rate or in what measure or quantity?: *How much is this? How are these tomatoes sold?* **7.** what?: *How do you mean?* **8.** (used as an intensifier): *How seldom I go there!* **9.** by what title or name?: *How does one address the president?* **10.** in what form or shape?: *How does the demon appear in the first act?* —*conj.* **11.** the manner or way in which: *I couldn't figure out how to solve the problem.* **12.** about the manner or condition in which: *Be careful how you act.* **13.** in whatever manner or way; however: *You can dress how you please.* **14.** *Informal.* that: *She told us how he was honest and could be trusted.* —*n.* **15.** a question concerning the way or manner in which something is done, achieved, etc.: *a child's unending whys and hows.* **16.** a way or manner of doing something: *to consider all the hows and wherefores.* —*Idiom.* **17. and how!** *Informal.* certainly; you bet: *Am I happy? And how!* **18. here's how,** (used as a toast.) **19. how about,** what do you think or feel regarding? what is your response to?: *If they don't have pumpkin pie, how about apple?* **20. how come?** *Informal.* how is it that? why?: *How come you never visit us anymore?* **21. how so?** how does it happen to be so? why?: *You left early? How so?*

how•dah (hou′də), *n.* a seat or platform placed on the back of an elephant.

how′ do you do′, *interj.* (used as a conventional greeting.)

how-do-you-do (hou′də yə dōō′) also **how-de-do** (-dē-), *n., pl.* **-dos.** *Informal.* **1.** an act or instance of saying "how do you do" or a similar greeting; salutation. **2.** an awkward or unpleasant situation: *It's a fine how-do-you-do that they've refused to help us.*

how•dy (hou′dē), *interj.* (used as an expression of greeting.)

Howe (hou), *n.* **1. E(dgar) W(atson),** 1853–1937, U.S. novelist and editor. **2. Elias,** 1819–67, U.S. inventor of the sewing machine. **3. Irving,** 1920–93, U.S. social historian and literary critic. **4. Julia Ward,** 1819–1910, U.S. writer and reformer. **5. William, 5th Viscount,** 1729–1814, British general in the American Revolutionary War.

how•e′er (hou âr′), *adv., conj.* however.

How•ells (hou′əlz), *n.* **William Dean,** 1837–1920, U.S. author, critic, and editor.

how•ev•er (hou ev′ər), *adv.* **1.** nevertheless; yet; on the other hand; in spite of that: *We have not yet won; however, we shall keep trying.* **2.** to whatever extent or degree; no matter how: *However much you spend, I will reimburse you.* **3.** how?; how under the circumstances?: *However did you escape?* —*conj.* **4.** in whatever way, manner, or state: *Arrange your hours however you like.*

How′ Great′ Thou′ Art!′, a Christian hymn (1886) of Swedish origin with English words and music by Stuart K. Hine.

how•itz•er (hou′it sər), *n.* a cannon with a comparatively short barrel, used esp. for firing shells at an elevated angle.

howl (houl), *v.i.* **1.** (of a dog, wolf, or the like) to utter a characteristic loud, prolonged, mournful cry. **2.** (of a person or animal) to utter a similar cry, as in pain or rage; wail. **3.** to make a sound like an animal howling: *The wind howls through the trees.* **4.** to utter a loud laugh or scornful yell. —*v.t.* **5.** to utter with howls: *to howl the bad news.* **6.** to drive or force by howls (often fol. by *down*): *to howl down the opposition.* —*n.* **7.** the cry of a dog, wolf, or the like. **8.** a cry or wail, as of pain or rage. **9.** a sound like wailing: *the howl of the wind.* **10.** a loud laugh or scornful yell. **11.** something that causes a laugh or a scornful yell, as a joke or an embarrassing situation.

howl•er (hou′lər), *n.* **1.** one that howls. **2.** Also called **howl′er mon′key.** any large tropical American monkey of the genus *Alouatta,* the males of which make a howling noise. **3.** a mistake, esp. an embarrassing one in speech or writing, that evokes laughter.

howl•ing (hou′ling), *adj.* **1.** desolate, dismal, or dreary: *a howling wasteland.* **2.** very great; tremendous: *a howling triumph.* —**howl′ing•ly,** *adv.*

how′-to, *adj., n., pl.* **-tos.** —*adj.* **1.** giving basic instructions and directions to the layperson for doing or making something: *a how-to book on photography.* —*n.* **2.** the guidelines or detailed instructions for doing something. —**how′-to′er,** *n.*

How′ to Win′ Friends′ and In′fluence Peo′ple, a self-help book (1936) by Dale Carnegie.

hoy•den (hoid′n), *n.* a boisterous, bold, and carefree girl; tomboy. —**hoy′den•ish,** *adj.*

hp, horsepower.

H.P. or **h.p.** or **HP, 1.** high pressure. **2.** horsepower.

H.Q. or **h.q.** or **HQ,** headquarters.

HR, 1. home run. **2.** House of Representatives.

hr. or **h.,** hour.

h.r. or **hr** home run.

H.S., High School.

HT, 1. halftime. **2.** Also, **h.t.** at this time. **3.** under this title.

ht., height.

HTML, HyperText Markup Language: a set of standards, a variety of SGML, used to tag the elements of a hypertext document, the standard for documents on the World Wide Web.

Hts., Heights (used in place names).

hua•ra•che (wə rä′chē, -chä), *n., pl.* **-ches** (-chēz, -chäz). a Mexican sandal having the upper woven of leather strips.

hub (hub), *n.* **1.** the central part of a wheel, as that part into which the spokes are inserted. **2.** the central part or axle end from which blades or spokelike parts radiate on various devices, as on a fan or propeller. **3.** a center around which other things revolve or from which they radiate; a focus of activity, authority, commerce, etc.; core.

hub′-and-spoke′, *adj.* of or designating a system of air transportation by which local flights carry passengers to one major regional airport where they can board long-distance or other local flights for their final destinations.

Hub•bard (hub′ərd), *n.* **1. Elbert Green,** 1856–1915, U.S. author, editor, and printer. **2. L(afayette) Ron(ald),** 1911–86, U.S. science-fiction writer and religious leader.

Hub′bard squash′, *n.* a variety of winter squash having a green or yellow skin and yellow flesh.

Hub•ble (hub′əl), *n.* **Edwin Powell,** 1889–1953, U.S. astronomer: pioneer in extragalactic research.

hub•bub (hub′ub), *n.* **1.** a loud, confused noise, as of many voices. **2.** tumult; uproar; disorder.

hub•by (hub′ē), *n., pl.* **-bies.** *Informal.* husband.

hub•cap (hub′kap′), *n.* a removable cover for the center of the exposed side of an automobile wheel, covering the axle.

hu•bris (hyōō′bris, hōō′-), *n.* excessive pride or self-confidence; arrogance. —**hu•bris′tic,** *adj.*

huck•le•ber•ry (huk′əl ber′ē), *n., pl.* **-ries. 1.** the dark blue or black edible berry of any shrub belonging to the genus *Gaylussacia* of the heath family. **2.** a shrub bearing such fruit. **3.** BLUEBERRY (def. 1).

Huck′leberry Finn′ (fin), (*The Adventures of Huckleberry Finn*) a novel (1884) by Mark Twain.

huck•ster (huk′stər), *n.* **1.** an aggressive seller or promoter, esp. one who uses showy or dubious methods. **2.** a person whose business is advertising, esp. radio and television advertising. **3.** a peddler of small items, esp. fruits and vegetables; hawker. —*v.i.* **4.** to make petty bargains; haggle. **5.** to deal in small items; peddle. —*v.t.* **6.** to sell or promote, esp. in an aggressive and flashy manner. —**huck′ster•ism,** *n.* —**huck′ster•ish,** *adj.*

HUD (hud), *n.* Department of Housing and Urban Development.

hud•dle (hud′l), *v.,* **-dled, -dling,** *n.* —*v.i.* **1.** to gather or crowd together in a close mass: *They huddled around the stove to get warm.* **2.** to crouch, curl up, or draw oneself together. **3.** to confer or consult. —*v.t.* **4.** to heap or crowd together closely. **5.** to draw (oneself) closely together, as in crouching; nestle (often fol. by *up*). **6.** to put on (clothes) with careless haste (often fol. by *on*). —*n.* **7.** a closely gathered group, mass, or heap; bunch. **8.** a close gathering of football players behind the scrimmage line to hear instructions for the next play. **9.** a conference or consultation, esp. a private one about a serious matter. —**hud′dler,** *n.* —**hud′dling•ly,** *adv.*

Hud•son (hud′sən), *n.* **1. Henry,** died 1611?, English navigator and explorer. **2. William Henry,** 1841–1922, English naturalist and author. **3.** a river in E New York, flowing S to New York Bay. 306 mi. (495 km) long.

Hud′son Bay′, *n.* a large inland sea in N Canada. 850 mi. (1370 km) long; 600 mi. (965 km) wide; 400,000 sq. mi. (1,036,000 sq. km).

hue¹ (hyōō), *n.* **1.** a gradation or variety of a color; tint: *pale hues.* **2.** the property of light by which the color of an object is classified as red, blue, green, or yellow in reference to the spectrum. **3.** color: *all the hues of the rainbow.* **4.** form or appearance. **5.** COMPLEXION (def. 1).

hue² (hyōō), *n.* outcry, as of pursuers; clamor.

hue′ and cry′, *n.* **1.** public clamor, protest, or alarm. **2.** (formerly) the pursuit of a felon with loud outcries to give an alarm.

huff (huf), *n.* **1.** a mood of sulking anger; fit of resentment: *to walk out of a meeting in a huff.* —*v.t.* **2.** to give offense to; make angry. **3.** to treat with arrogance or contempt; bully. —*v.i.* **4.** to take offense; speak indignantly. **5.** to puff or blow; breathe heavily. **6.** to swell with pride or arrogance; bluster.

huff•y (huf′ē), *adj.,* **huff•i•er, huff•i•est. 1.** easily offended; touchy. **2.** offended; sulky; petulant: *a huffy mood.* **3.** snobbish; haughty. —**huff′i•ly,** *adv.* —**huff′i•ness,** *n.*

hug (hug), *v.,* **hugged, hug•ging,** *n.* —*v.t.* **1.** to clasp tightly in the arms, esp. with affection; embrace: *to hug one's child.* **2.** to cling firmly or fondly to; cherish: *to hug an opinion.* **3.** to keep close to, as in sailing or in moving along or alongside of: *a vessel hugging the shore; a car hugging the road.* —*v.i.* **4.** to cling together; lie close. —*n.* **5.** a tight clasp with the arms; embrace. —**hug′ger,** *n.* —**hug′ging•ly,** *adv.*

huge (hyōōj *or, often,* yōōj), *adj.,* **hug•er, hug•est. 1.** extraordinarily large in bulk, quantity, or area; gigantic: *a huge ship; a huge portion of ice cream.* **2.** very great; enormous: *The book was a huge success.* —**huge′ly,** *adv.* —**huge′ness,** *n.* —**Pronunciation.** See HUMAN.

Hü•gel (hyōō′gəl *or, often,* yōō′-), *n.* **Baron Friedrich von,** 1852–1925, English theologian and writer.

hug•ga•ble (hug′ə bəl), *adj.* inviting a close embrace; cuddly: *a huggable teddy bear.*

hug•ger-mug•ger (hug′ər mug′ər), *n.* **1.** disorder or confusion; muddle. **2.** secrecy; reticence. —*adj.* **3.** secret or clandestine. **4.** disorderly or confused. —*adv.* **5.** in a stealthy or disorderly manner; secretively or confusedly. —*v.t.* **6.** to keep secret or concealed; hush up. —*v.i.* **7.** to act secretly.

Hughes (hyōōz), *n.* **1. Charles Evans,** 1862–1948, Chief Justice of the U.S. 1930–41. **2. Howard (Robard),** 1905–76, U.S. businessman. **3. (James) Langston,** 1902–67, U.S. novelist and poet. **4. John,** 1873–1932, Welsh musician and hymn writer. **5. Ted,** born 1930, English poet: poet laureate since 1984.

Hu•go (hyōō′gō *or, often,* yōō′-), *n.* **Victor (Marie, Viscount)** 1802–85, French poet, novelist, and dramatist.

Hu•gue•not (hyōō′gə not′ *or, often,* yōō′-), *n.* a member of the Reformed or Calvinistic communion of France in the 16th and 17th centuries; French Protestant. —**Hu′gue•not′ic,** *adj.* —**Hu′gue•not•ism,** *n.*

huh (hu), *interj.* (used as an exclamation of surprise, disbelief, contempt, or interrogation.)

hu•la (hōō′lə), *n., pl.* **-las.** a sinuous Hawaiian native dance with intricate arm movements that tell a story in pantomime, usu. danced to rhythmic drumming and accompanied by chanting. Also called **hu′la-hu′la.**

Hu′la-Hoop′, *Trademark.* a large tubular plastic hoop rotated about the body by hip motion.

Hul•dah (hul′də), *n.* a prophet at the time of King Josiah. II Kings 22:14–20; II Chron. 34:22–28.

hulk (hulk), *n.* **1.** the body of an old or dismantled ship. **2.** a ship specially built to serve as a storehouse, prison, etc., and not for sea service. **3.** a clumsy-looking or unwieldy ship or boat. **4.** a bulky or unwieldy person, object, or mass. **5.** the shell of something wrecked, burned-out, or abandoned. —*v.i.* **6.** to appear as a large, massive bulk; loom (often fol. by *up*).

hulk•ing (hul′king), *adj.* heavy and clumsy; bulky.

hull¹ (hul), *n.* **1.** the husk, shell, or outer covering of a seed or fruit. **2.** the calyx of certain fruits, as the strawberry. —*v.t.* **3.** to remove the hull of; skin, peel, shell, or shuck. —**hull′er,** *n.*

hull² (hul), *n.* **1.** the hollow lowermost portion of a ship, floating partially submerged and supporting the remainder of the ship. **2. a.** the boatlike fuselage of a flying boat on which the plane lands or takes off. **b.** the cigar-shaped arrangement of girders enclosing the gasbag of a rigid dirigible. —*v.t.* **3.** to pierce (the hull of a ship), esp. below the water line. —*v.i.* **4.** to drift without power or sails. —**hull′-less,** *adj.*

hul•la•ba•loo (hul′ə bə lōō′), *n., pl.* **-loos.** a clamorous noise or disturbance; uproar.

hum (hum), *v.,* **hummed, hum•ming,** *n., interj.* —*v.i.* **1.** to make a low, continuous droning sound. **2.** to sing with closed lips, without articulating words. **3.** to give forth an indistinct sound of mingled voices or noises. **4.** to utter an indistinct sound in hesitation, embarrassment, or dissatisfaction; hem. **5.** to be in a state of busy activity; bustle: *a household humming with wedding preparations.* —*v.t.* **6.** to sound or utter by humming: *to hum a tune.* **7.** to bring, put, etc., by humming: *to hum a child to sleep.* —*n.* **8.** the act or sound of humming. —*interj.* **9.** (an inarticulate sound uttered in contemplation, hesitation, dissatisfaction, doubt, etc.)

hu•man (hyōō′mən *or, often,* yōō′-), *adj.* **1.** of, pertaining to, characteristic of, or having the nature of people: *human frailty.* **2.** consisting of people: *the human race.* **3.** of or pertaining to the social aspect of people: *human affairs.* **4.** sympathetic; humane: *a warmly human understanding.* —*n.* **5.** a human being. —**hu′man•like′,** *adj.* —**hu′man•ness,** *n.* —**Pronunciation.** Although they are sometimes criticized, pronunciations of words like HUMAN and HUGE as (yōō′mən) and (yōōj), with the initial (h) deleted, are heard from speakers at all social and educational levels.

hu′man be′ing, *n.* **1.** any individual of the genus *Homo,* esp. a member of the species *Homo sapiens.* **2.** a person, esp. as distinguished from other animals or as representing the human species: *conditions not fit for human beings; a delightful human being.*

hu•mane (hyōō mān′ *or, often,* yōō-), *adj.* **1.** characterized by tenderness, compassion, and sympathy for other beings, esp. for the suffering or distressed; merciful. **2.** of or pertaining to humanistic studies. —**hu•mane′ly,** *adv.* —**hu•mane′ness,** *n.*

hu′man ecol′ogy, *n.* ECOLOGY (def. 3).

hu′man engineer′ing, *n.* ERGONOMICS.

Hu′man Ge′nome Proj′ect, *n.* a federally funded U.S. scientific project to identify both the genes and the entire sequence of DNA base pairs that make up the human genome.

hu′man-in′terest, *adj.* (of a journalistic story) designed to arouse the reader's sympathy for the people and problems described.

hu•man•ism (hyōō′mə niz′əm; *often* yōō′-), *n.* **1.** (*often cap.*) any system or mode of thought or action in which human interests, values, and dignity predominate, esp. an ethical theory that often rejects the importance of a belief in God. **2.** devotion to or study of the humanities. **3.** (*sometimes cap.*) the studies, principles, or culture of the Renaissance humanists.

hu•man•ist (hyōō′mə nist; *often* yōō′-), *n.* **1.** a person with a strong concern for human welfare, values, and dignity. **2.** a person devoted to or versed in the humanities, esp. a classical scholar. **3.** a student of human nature or affairs. **4.** (*sometimes cap.*) any of the scholars in the Renaissance who pursued and promoted the study of the ancient Greek and Roman cultures, and emphasized secular, individualistic, and critical thought. **5.** (*often cap.*) a person who follows a form of scientific or philosophical humanism. —*adj.* **6.** of or pertaining to human nature,

affairs, or welfare. **7.** (*sometimes cap.*) of or pertaining to the humanities or classical scholarship, esp. that of the Renaissance humanists, or to philosophical or scientific humanism. —**hu′man•is′tic,** *adj.* —**hu′man•is′ti•cal•ly,** *adv.*

hu•man•i•tar•i•an (hyōō man′i târ′ē ən; *often* yōō-), *adj.* **1.** having concern for or helping to improve the welfare and happiness of people. **2.** of or pertaining to ethical or theological humanitarianism. —*n.* **3.** a person actively engaged in promoting human welfare and social reforms, as a philanthropist. **4.** a person who professes ethical humanitarianism.

hu•man•i•tar•i•an•ism (hyōō man′i târ′ē ə niz′əm; *often* yōō-), *n.* **1.** humanitarian principles or practices. **2. a.** the ethical doctrine that humanity's obligations are concerned wholly with the welfare of the human race. **b.** the doctrine that humankind may become perfect without divine aid. —**hu•man′i•tar′i•an•ist,** *n.*

hu•man•i•ty (hyōō man′i tē; *often* yōō-), *n., pl.* **-ties. 1.** all human beings collectively; the human race; humankind. **2.** the quality or condition of being human; human nature. **3.** the quality of being humane; kindness; benevolence; goodwill. **4. the humanities, a.** literature, languages, philosophy, art, etc., or their study: distinguished from the sciences. **b.** classical languages and classical literature, esp. as a field of study.

hu•man•ize (hyōō′mə nīz′; *often* yōō′-), *v.,* **-ized, -iz•ing.** —*v.t.* **1.** to make humane, kind, or gentle; civilize. **2.** to make human; give or attribute human character to. —*v.i.* **3.** to become human or humane. —**hu′man•i•za′tion,** *n.* —**hu′man•iz′er,** *n.*

hu•man•kind (hyōō′mən kīnd′, -kīnd′; *often* yōō′-), *n.* human beings collectively; the human race; humanity.

hu•man•ly (hyōō′mən lē; *often* yōō′-), *adv.* **1.** in the manner of human beings; according to human nature, esp. its weakness: *humanly resistant to change.* **2.** with regard to human needs or concerns; humanely: *to deal humanly with the homeless.* **3.** within the limits of human capability: *Is it humanly possible to know the future?* **4.** from or according to the viewpoint of humankind.

hu′man na′ture, *n.* **1.** the psychological and social qualities that characterize humankind. **2.** the character of human conduct, generally regarded as produced by living in primary groups.

hu′man rela′tions, *n.* (*usu. with a sing. v.*) the study of group behavior for the purpose of improving interpersonal relationships, as among employees.

hu′man re′sources, *n.* **1.** people, esp. the personnel employed by a given company, institution, or the like. **2.** (*used with a sing. v.*) HUMAN RESOURCES DEPARTMENT.

hu′man re′sources depart′ment, *n.* a department of an organization supervising matters of personnel.

hu′man rights′, *n.pl.* fundamental rights, esp. those believed to belong to an individual and in whose exercise a government may not interfere, as the rights to speak, associate, and work.

hum•ble (hum′bəl, um′-), *adj.,* **-bler, -blest,** *v.,* **-bled, -bling.** —*adj.* **1.** not proud or arrogant; modest. **2.** low in importance, status, or condition; lowly: *a humble home.* **3.** courteously respectful: *in my humble opinion.* **4.** insignificant; inferior; meek or submissive: *to feel humble in the presence of a great artist.* —*v.t.* **5.** to lower in condition, importance, or dignity; abase; mortify. **6.** to destroy the independence or will of; subdue. **7.** to make meek: *to humble one's heart.* —**hum′ble•ness,** *n.* —**hum′bler,** *n.* —**hum′bling•ly,** *adv.* —**hum′bly,** *adv.*

hum′ble pie′, *n.* **1.** humility forced upon someone; humiliation. —*Idiom.* **2. eat humble pie,** to be forced to apologize.

hum•bug (hum′bug′), *n., v.,* **-bugged, -bug•ging,** *interj.* —*n.* **1.** something intended to delude or deceive. **2.** a quality of falseness, deception, or hypocrisy. **3.** a person who is not what he or she claims to be; impostor. **4.** meaningless or empty talk; nonsense. —*v.t.* **5.** to delude; deceive; trick. —*v.i.* **6.** to practice deception. —*interj.* **7.** nonsense! —**hum′bug′ger,** *n.* —**hum′bug′ger•y,** *n.*

hum•ding•er (hum′ding′ər), *n. Informal.* a person or thing of remarkable excellence or effect.

hum•drum (hum′drum′), *adj.* **1.** lacking variety; boring; dull. —*n.* **2.** humdrum character or routine; monotony. **3.** a tedious or tiresome person or thing; bore. —**hum′drum′ness,** *n.*

hu•mer•al (hyōō′mər əl; *often* yōō′-), *adj.* **1.** of or pertaining to the humerus or brachium. **2.** of or pertaining to the shoulder.

hu•mer•us (hyōō′mər əs; *often* yōō′-), *n., pl.* **-mer•i** (-mə rī′). **1.** the long upper bone of the vertebrate arm or forelimb, extending from the shoulder to the elbow. **2.** BRACHIUM (def. 1).

hu•mid (hyōō′mid; *often* yōō′-), *adj.* containing a high amount of water or water vapor; noticeably moist: *humid air.* —**hu′mid•ly,** *adv.* —**hu′mid•ness,** *n.*

hu•mid•i•fi•er (hyōō mid′ə fī′ər; *often* yōō′-), *n.* any device for regulating moisture in the air indoors.

hu•mid•i•fy (hyōō mid′ə fī′; *often* yōō′-), *v.t.,* **-fied, -fy•ing.** to make humid. —**hu•mid′i•fi•ca′tion,** *n.*

hu•mid•i•ty (hyōō mid′i tē; *often* yōō′-), *n.* **1.** humid condition; moistness; dampness. **2.** RELATIVE HUMIDITY. **3.** an uncomfortably high amount of relative humidity.

hu•mi•dor (hyōō′mi dôr′; *often* yōō′-), *n.* a container specially fitted to keep cigars or other items of tobacco suitably moist.

hu•mil•i•ate (hyōō mil′ē āt′; *often* yōō′-), *v.t.,* **-at•ed, -at•ing.** to cause (a person) a painful loss of pride, self-respect, or dignity; mortify; abase. —**hu·mil/i·at/ing·ly,** *adv.*

hu·mil·i·a·tion (hyoo mil/ē ā/shən; *often* yoo-), *n.* **1.** an act or instance of humiliating or being humiliated. **2.** the state or feeling of being humiliated; mortification.

hu·mil·i·ty (hyoo mil/i tē; *often* yoo-), *n.* the quality or state of being humble; modest opinion of one's own importance or rank; meekness.

hum·ming·bird (hum/ing bûrd/), *n.* any of numerous tiny, usu. colorful New World birds of the family Trochilidae, having a long, slender bill for sipping nectar and narrow wings that beat very rapidly, enabling the bird to hover at a flower or dart in any direction.

hum·mock (hum/ək), *n.* **1.** Also, **hammock.** an elevated tract of land rising above the general level of a marshy region. **2.** a knoll or hillock. —**hum/mock·y,** *adj.*

hu·mon·gous (hyoo mung/gəs, -mong/-; *often* yoo-) also **humun·gous,** *adj. Slang.* extraordinarily large. [expressive coinage, perh. reflecting *huge* and *monstrous,* with stress pattern of *tremendous*]

hu·mor (hyoo/mər; *often* yoo/-), *n.* **1.** a comic, absurd, or incongruous quality causing amusement. **2.** the faculty of perceiving and expressing or appreciating what is amusing or comical: *a writer with humor and zest.* **3.** an instance of being or attempting to be comical or amusing; something humorous. **4.** comical writing or talk in general; comical books, skits, plays, etc. **5.** mental disposition or temperament. **6.** a temporary mood or frame of mind: *in a sulky humor today.* **7.** a capricious or freakish inclination; whim or caprice; odd trait. **8.** any animal or plant fluid. **9.** one of the body fluids once regarded as determining a person's constitution: blood, phlegm, black bile, or yellow bile. —*v.t.* **9.** to comply with the humor or mood of in order to soothe, cheer up, etc.: *to humor a child.* **10.** to adapt or accommodate oneself to: *I'll humor your whim for now.* —**Idiom. 11. out of humor,** dissatisfied; cross. Also, *esp. Brit.,* **humour.** —**hu/mor·less,** *adj.* —**hu/mor·less·ly,** *adv.* —**hu/mor·less·ness,** *n.*

hu·mor·esque (hyoo/mə resk/; *often* yoo/-), *n.* a musical composition of humorous or witty character. —**hu/mor·esque/ly,** *adv.*

hu·mor·ist (hyoo/mər ist; *often* yoo/-), *n.* a person with an active sense of humor, esp. one who uses humor skillfully, as in writing or talking. —**hu/mor·is/tic,** *adj.*

hu·mor·ous (hyoo/mər əs; *often* yoo/-), *adj.* **1.** characterized by humor; funny; comical: *a humorous anecdote.* **2.** having or showing the faculty of humor; droll; facetious: *a humorous person.* —**hu/mor·ous·ly,** *adv.* —**hu/mor·ous·ness,** *n.*

hump (hump), *n.* **1.** a rounded protuberance, esp. a fleshy protuberance on the back, as that due to abnormal curvature of the spine in humans, or that normally present in certain animals, as the camel or bison. **2. a.** a low, rounded rise of ground; hummock. **b.** a mountain or mountain range. —*v.t.* **3.** to raise (the back) in a hump; hunch. **4.** *Slang.* to exert (oneself) in a great effort. —*v.i.* **5.** to rise in a hump. **6.** *Slang.* to exert oneself; hustle. **b.** to hurry; rush. —**Idiom. 7. over the hump,** past the greatest difficulties or dangers.

hump·back (hump/bak/), *n.* **1.** a back that is humped in a convex position. **2.** KYPHOSIS. **3.** HUMPBACK WHALE.

hump/back salm/on, *n.* a pink salmon of N Pacific waters: a hump appears behind the head of spawning males.

hump/back whale/, *n.* a large whalebone whale, *Megaptera novaeangliae,* having long, narrow flippers.

humped (humpt), *adj.* having a hump.

humph (*an inarticulate expression resembling a snort or grunt; spelling pron.* humf), *interj.* **1.** (used to indicate disbelief, contempt, etc.) —*v.i.* **2.** to utter the sound "humph." —*v.t.* **3.** to say by or as if by expressing "humph."

Hum·phrey (hum/frē), *n.* **Hubert H(oratio),** 1911–78, U.S. vice president 1965–69.

Hump·ty Dump·ty (hump/tē dump/tē), *n.* **1.** an egg-shaped character in a Mother Goose nursery rhyme that fell off a wall and could not be put together again. **2.** (*sometimes l.c.*) something that has been damaged severely and usually irreparably.

hu·mun·gous (hyoo mung/gəs; *often* yoo-), *adj. Slang.* HUMONGOUS.

hu·mus (hyoo/məs; *often* yoo/-), *n.* the dark organic material in soils, produced by the decomposition of vegetable or animal matter.

Hun (hun), *n.* **1.** a member of a pastoral people of the Eurasian steppes, who in the late 4th century A.D. began a course of alternating conflict and alliance with their Iranian and Germanic neighbors and the Roman Empire: they reached the height of their power in Europe under Attila in the mid-5th century, and subsequently disappeared from history. **2.** (*often l.c.*) a barbarous, destructive person; vandal.

hunch (hunch), *v.t.* **1.** to thrust out or up in a hump; arch: *to hunch one's back.* **2.** to shove, push, or jostle. —*v.i.* **3.** to thrust oneself forward jerkily; lunge forward. **4.** to stand, sit, or walk in a bent posture. —*n.* **5.** a premonition or suspicion; guess; theory. **6.** a hump.

hunch·back (hunch/bak/), *n.* **1.** a person whose back is humped in a convex position because of abnormal spinal curvature. **2.** HUMPBACK (def. 1).

Hunch/back of No/tre Dame/, The, (French, *Notre Dame de Paris*), a novel (1831) by Victor Hugo.

hun·dred (hun/drid), *n., pl.* **-dreds,** (*as after a numeral*) **-dred. 1.** a cardinal number, ten times ten. **2.** a symbol for this number, as 100 or C. **3.** a set of this many persons or things. **4. hundreds, a.** a number

between 100 and 999, as in referring to an amount of money. **b.** a generally large number: *Hundreds came to the funeral.* **5.** a hundred-dollar bill. **6.** (formerly) an administrative division of an English county. **7.** a similar division in colonial Pennsylvania, Delaware, and Virginia, and in present-day Delaware. **8.** Also called **hun/dred's place/. a.** (in a mixed number) the position of the third digit to the left of the decimal point. **b.** (in a whole number) the position of the third digit from the right. —*adj.* **9.** amounting to 100 in number.

Hun/dred Days/, *n.* **1.** the period from March 20 to June 28, 1815, between the arrival of Napoleon in Paris, after his escape from Elba, and his abdication after the battle of Waterloo. **2.** a special session of Congress from March 9, 1933 to June 16, 1933, called by President Franklin D. Roosevelt, in which important social legislation was enacted.

hun·dred·fold (hun/drid fōld/), *adj.* **1.** a hundred times as great or as much. **2.** comprising a hundred parts or members. —*adv.* **3.** in a hundredfold measure.

hun·dredth (hun/dridth, -dritth), *adj.* **1.** next after the ninety-ninth; being the ordinal number for 100. **2.** being one of 100 equal parts. —*n.* **3.** a hundredth part, esp. of one (¹/₁₀₀). **4.** the hundredth member of a series. **5.** Also called **hun/dredth's place/.** (in decimal notation) the position of the second digit to the right of the decimal point.

hun·dred·weight (hun/drid wāt/), *n., pl.* **-weights,** (*as after a numeral*) **-weight.** a unit of avoirdupois weight commonly equivalent to 100 pounds (45.359 kilograms) in the U.S. *Abbr.:* cwt Also called **cental, quintal.**

Hun/dred Years/' War/, *n.* the series of wars between England and France, 1337–1453, in which England lost all its possessions in France except Calais.

hung (hung), *v.* **1.** pt. and past part. of HANG. —**Idiom. 2. hung over,** suffering the effects of a hangover. **3. hung up,** *Slang.* **a.** detained unavoidably. **b.** stymied or baffled by a problem. **c.** Also, **hung-up.** beset by psychological problems. **4. hung up on,** *Slang.* **a.** obsessed by: *a clerk hung up on petty details.* **b.** infatuated with. —**Usage.** See HANG.

Hun·gar·i·an (hung gâr/ē ən), *n.* **1.** a native or inhabitant of Hungary. **2. a.** a member of the ethnic group that comprises the overwhelming majority of the inhabitants of Hungary, and a significant minority in Transylvania, Slovakia, and adjacent parts of Yugoslavia. **b.** the Finno-Ugric language of this group. —*adj.* **3.** of or pertaining to Hungary or its inhabitants. **4.** of or pertaining to the Hungarians as an ethnic group, or to the language Hungarian.

Hun·ga·ry (hung/gə rē), *n.* a republic in central Europe. 9,935,774; 35,926 sq. mi. (93,050 sq. km). *Cap.:* Budapest. Hungarian, **Magyarország.**

hun·ger (hung/gər), *n.* **1.** a compelling need or desire for food. **2.** the painful sensation or state of weakness caused by the need of food: *to collapse from hunger.* **3.** a shortage of food; famine. **4.** a strong or compelling desire or craving; lust: *a hunger for power.* —*v.i.* **5.** to feel hunger; be hungry. **6.** to have a strong desire. —**hun/ger·ing·ly,** *adv.*

hun/ger strike/, *n.* a deliberate refusal to eat, undertaken in protest, as against imprisonment or social injustice. —**hun/ger-strike/,** *v.i.,* **-struck, strik·ing.** —**hun/ger strik/er,** *n.*

hung/ ju/ry, *n.* a jury that cannot agree on a verdict.

hun·gry (hung/grē), *adj.,* **-gri·er, -gri·est. 1.** having a desire, craving, or need for food; feeling hunger; ravenous. **2.** strongly or eagerly desirous: *hungry for success.* **3.** indicating or characterized by hunger or strong desire: *a hungry look in a person's eyes.* **4.** lacking needful or desirable elements; not fertile; poor: *hungry land.* **5.** marked by a scarcity of food: *the hungry years of the Great Depression.* —**hun/gri·ly,** *adv.* —**hun/gri·ness,** *n.*

hung/-up/, *adj.* HUNG (def. 3c).

hunk (hungk), *n.* **1.** a large piece or lump; chunk. **2.** *Slang.* a handsome man with a well-developed physique.

hun·ker (hung/kər), *v.i.* **1.** to squat on one's heels (often fol. by *down*). **2.** to hunch: *students hunkering over their books.* **3.** to hide, hide out, or take shelter (usu. fol. by *down*). **4.** to hold firmly or stubbornly to one's opinion, course, etc., as when criticized or thwarted (usu. fol. by *down*). —*n.* **5. hunkers,** the haunches.

Hun·ker (hung/kər), *n.* a member of the conservative faction in the Democratic party in New York State, 1845–48. Compare BARNBURNER. —**Hun/ker·ism,** *n.* —**Hun/ker·ous,** *adj.* —**Hun/ker·ous·ness,** *n.*

hunk·y-do·ry (hung/kē dôr/ē, -dōr/ē), *adj. Informal.* about as well as one could wish or expect; fine.

hunt (hunt), *v.t.* **1.** to chase or search for (game or other wild animals) for the purpose of catching or killing. **2.** to pursue (a person) aggressively in order to capture (often fol. by *down*): *to hunt down a kidnapper.* **3.** to search for; seek (often fol. by *up* or *out*): *to hunt out the perfect birthday gift.* **4.** to search thoroughly; scour. **5.** to pursue or take game in: *Poachers have been hunting the king's woods.* **6.** to use or direct (a horse, hound, etc.) in chasing game. —*v.i.* **7.** to engage in the pursuit, capture, or killing of wild animals for food or in sport. **8.** to make a search or quest (often fol. by *for* or *after*). —*n.* **9.** the act or practice of hunting game or other wild animals. **10.** a search or pursuit; a seeking to find. **11.** a group of persons associated or gathered for the purpose of hunting. —**hunt/a·ble,** *adj.*

hunt/-and-peck/, *n.* a method of typing whereby the typist looks for each key separately before striking it.

hunt·er (hun/tər), *n.* **1.** a person who hunts game or other wild animals for food or in sport. **2.** a searcher or seeker for something: *a treas-*

H

ure hunter. **3.** a horse specially trained for stamina and jumping ability in hunting. **4.** a dog trained to hunt game. **5.** (*cap.*) the constellation Orion. **6.** HUNTER GREEN. **—hunt′er•like′,** *adj.*

hunt•er-gath′er•er, *n.* a member of a group of people who subsist by hunting, fishing, or foraging in the wild.

hunt′er (or **hunt′er's**) **green′,** *n.* a dark-green color of yellowish cast.

hunt•ing (hun′ting), *n.* **1.** the act of a person, animal, or thing that hunts. **2.** the periodic oscillating of a rotating electromechanical system about a mean space position, as in a synchronous motor. **—adj. 3.** of, for, engaged in, or used while hunting: *a hunting cap.*

hunt′ing horn′, *n.* the earliest form of the modern horn, consisting of a conical tube coiled in a circle for carrying over the shoulder, and having a flaring bell and a trumpetlike mouthpiece.

hunt′ing knife′, *n.* a large sharp knife, usu. with a slightly curved blade, that is used to skin and cut up game, or sometimes to dispatch it.

Hun•ting•ton (hun′ting tən), *n.* **1. Collis Potter,** 1821–1900, U.S. railroad developer. **2. Samuel,** 1731–96, U.S. statesman: governor of Connecticut 1786–96. **3.** a city in W West Virginia, on the Ohio River. 56,300.

Hun′tington Beach′, *n.* a city in SW California, SE of Los Angeles. 189,220.

Hunts•ville (hunts′vil), *n.* a city in N Alabama. 160,325.

hur•dle (hûr′dl), *n., v.,* **-dled, -dling.** *—n.* **1.** a portable fencelike barrier over which contestants must leap in certain running races. **2. hurdles,** (*used with a sing. v.*) a track race in which contestants leap over a series of such barriers. **3.** any of various upright barriers over which horses must jump in certain turf races, as steeplechases, esp. an artificial barrier. **4.** a difficulty to be overcome; obstacle. **5.** *Chiefly Brit.* a movable rectangular frame of interlaced twigs, crossed bars, or the like, as for a temporary fence. **6.** a frame or sled on which criminals, esp. traitors, were formerly drawn to the place of execution. **—v.t. 7.** to leap over (a barrier), as in a race. **8.** to master (a difficulty, problem, etc.); overcome. **—hur′dler,** *n.*

hur•dy-gur•dy (hûr′dē gûr′dē, -gûr′-), *n., pl.* **-gur•dies. 1.** a barrel organ or similar musical instrument played by turning a crank. **2.** a lute- or guitar-shaped stringed musical instrument sounded by the revolution against the strings of a rosined wheel turned by a crank.

hurl (hûrl), *v.t.* **1.** to throw or fling with great force or vigor; cast. **2.** to throw or cast down. **3.** to utter with vehemence: *to hurl insults at the umpire.* *—v.i.* **4.** to throw a missile. *—n.* **5.** a forcible or violent throw; fling. **—hurl′er,** *n.*

Hurl•but (hûrl′bət, -but), *n.* **Jesse Lyman,** 1843–1930, U.S. clergyman and writer.

hurl•ing (hûr′ling), *n.* an Irish game resembling field hockey or lacrosse, played by two teams of 15 players each.

hurl•y (hûr′lē), *n., pl.* **hurl•ies.** commotion; hurly-burly.

hurl•y-burl•y (hûr′lē bûr′lē, -bûr′-), *n., pl.* **-burl•ies,** *adj.* *—n.* **1.** noisy disorder and confusion; commotion; uproar; tumult. *—adj.* **2.** full of commotion; tumultuous.

Hu•ron (hyŏŏr′ən, -on; *often* yŏŏr′-), *n., pl.* **-rons,** (*esp. collectively*) **-ron. 1.** a member of a confederacy of American Indian tribes formerly living E of Lake Huron: widely dispersed after 1649 as a result of Iroquois attacks. **2.** the extinct Iroquoian language of the Huron. **3. Lake,** a lake between the U.S. and Canada: second largest of the Great Lakes. 23,010 sq. mi. (59,595 sq. km).

hur•rah (hə rä′, -rô′) also **hur•ray** (-rā′), *interj.* **1.** (used as an exclamation of joy, exultation, appreciation, encouragement, or the like.) *—v.i.* **2.** to shout "hurrah." *—n.* **3.** an exclamation of "hurrah." **4.** hubbub; commotion; fanfare. **5.** a colorful or tumultuous event; spectacle or celebration. *—Idiom.* **6. last** or **final hurrah,** a final moment of glory; last notable achievement.

hur•ri•cane (hûr′i kān′, hur′-; *esp. Brit.* -kən), *n.* **1.** a violent, tropical, cyclonic storm, esp. of the W North Atlantic, having wind speeds of or in excess of 74 mph (33 m/sec). **2.** anything suggesting a violent storm. [< Spanish *huracán* < Taino (West Indian language)]

hur′ricane lamp′, *n.* a candlestick or oil lamp protected against drafts or winds by a glass chimney.

hur•ried (hûr′ēd, hur′-), *adj.* **1.** moving or working rapidly. **2.** done with hurry; hasty. **—hur′ried•ly,** *adv.* **—hur′ried•ness,** *n.*

hur•ry (hûr′ē, hur′ē), *v.,* **-ried, -ry•ing,** *n., pl.* **-ries.** *—v.i.* **1.** to move, proceed, or act with haste (often fol. by *up*). *—v.t.* **2.** to drive, carry, or cause to move with speed. **3.** to hasten; urge forward (often fol. by *up*). **4.** to impel or perform with undue haste; rush: *to hurry someone into a decision; to hurry a speech.* *—n.* **5.** a state of urgency or eagerness: *shoppers in a great hurry.* **6.** hurried movement or action; haste. **—hur′ry•ing•ly,** *adv.*

hur′ry-up′, *adj.* characterized by speed or the need for speed; quick: *a hurry-up phone call.*

hurt (hûrt), *v.,* **hurt, hurt•ing,** *n., adj.* *—v.t.* **1.** to cause bodily injury to; injure. **2.** to cause bodily pain to or in: *The old wound still hurts him.* **3.** to damage or impair (a material object) by rough use, improper care, etc.: *Stains can't hurt this fabric.* **4.** to affect adversely; harm: *to hurt one's reputation.* **5.** to offend or grieve: *to hurt one's feelings.* *—v.i.* **6.** to feel or suffer bodily or mental pain or distress; ache: *My back still hurts.* **7.** to cause bodily or mental pain or distress: *The blow to her pride hurt most.* **8.** to cause injury, damage, or harm. **9.** to suffer want or need. *—n.* **10.** a blow that inflicts a wound or the wound so in-

flicted. **11.** injury, damage, or harm. **12.** the cause of mental pain or offense, as a slight or insult. *—adj.* **13.** physically injured. **14.** offended; unfavorably affected: *hurt pride.* **15.** suggesting that one has been offended or is suffering in mind: *a hurt look on one's face.* **16.** damaged: *hurt merchandise.* **—hurt′a•ble,** *adj.* **—hurt′er,** *n.*

hurt•ful (hûrt′fəl), *adj.* causing hurt, distress, or injury; injurious. **—hurt′ful•ly,** *adv.* **—hurt′ful•ness,** *n.*

hur•tle (hûr′tl), *v.,* **-tled, -tling.** *—v.i.* **1.** to rush violently and often noisily or resoundingly; move with great speed. *—v.t.* **2.** to drive violently; fling; dash.

Hus (hŏŏs, hus), *n.* **Jan** (yän), 1369?–1415, Czech religious reformer and martyr.

hus•band (huz′bənd), *n.* **1.** a married man, esp. when considered in relation to his wife. *—v.t.* **2.** to manage, esp. with economy. **3.** to use frugally; conserve; store: *to husband one's resources.* **—hus′band•er,** *n.* **—hus′band•less,** *adj.* **—hus′band•ly,** *adj.*

hus•band•ry (huz′bən drē), *n.* **1.** the cultivation of crops and the raising of livestock. **2.** the application of scientific principles to farming. Compare ANIMAL HUSBANDRY. **3.** careful or thrifty management; frugality, thrift, or conservation.

hush (hush), *interj.* **1.** (used as a command to be silent or quiet.) *—v.i.* **2.** to become or be silent or quiet. *—v.t.* **3.** to make silent; silence. **4.** to suppress mention of; keep concealed (often fol. by *up*): *to hush up a scandal.* **5.** to calm, quiet, or allay: *to hush someone's fears.* *—n.* **6.** silence or quiet, esp. after noise; stillness.

hush•a•by (hush′ə bī′), *interj.* (used as a command to be silent): *Hushaby, baby.*

hush′-hush′, *adj.* highly secret or confidential.

hush′ mon′ey, *n.* a bribe to keep someone from revealing scandalous or damaging information.

hush′ pup′py, *n.* *Southern U.S.* a small deep-fried ball of cornmeal dough.

husk (husk), *n.* **1.** the dry external covering of certain fruits or seeds, esp. of an ear of corn. **2.** the enveloping or outer part of anything, esp. when dry or worthless. *—v.t.* **3.** to remove the husk from. **—husk′er,** *n.* **—husk′like′,** *adj.*

husk′ toma′to, *n.* GROUND CHERRY.

husk•y[1] (hus′kē), *adj.,* **husk•i•er, husk•i•est,** *n., pl.* **husk•ies.** *—adj.* **1.** big and strong; burly; brawny. **2.** (of the voice) somewhat hoarse, as when affected with a cold. **3.** like, covered with, or full of husks. *—n.* **4.** a size of garments for boys who are heavier than average. **5.** a garment in this size. **—husk′i•ly,** *adv.* **—husk′i•ness,** *n.*

husk•y[2] (hus′kē), *n., pl.* **husk•ies.** (*sometimes cap.*) **1.** ESKIMO DOG. **2.** SIBERIAN HUSKY.

Hus•sein (hŏŏ sān′), *n.* **Sad•dam** (sä′dəm, sə däm′), (*at-Takriti*), born 1937, president of Iraq since 1979.

Hussein I, *n.* born 1935, king of Jordan since 1953.

hus•sy (hus′ē, huz′ē), *n., pl.* **-sies. 1.** a brazen or disreputable woman. **2.** a mischievous or impudent girl.

hus•tings (hus′tingz), *n.* (*used with a sing. or pl. v.*) **1.** any place from which political campaign speeches are made. **2.** (before 1872) the temporary platform on which candidates for the British Parliament stood when nominated and from which they addressed the electors. **3.** the political campaign trail. **4.** Also called **hus′tings court′.** a local court in certain parts of Virginia.

hus•tle (hus′əl), *v.,* **-tled, -tling,** *n.* *—v.i.* **1.** to proceed or work rapidly or energetically. **2.** to push or force one's way; jostle or shove. **3.** to be aggressive, esp. in business or other financial dealings. **4.** *Slang.* to earn one's living by illicit or unethical means. *—v.t.* **5.** to convey or cause to move, esp. to leave, roughly or hurriedly. **6.** to pressure or coerce (a person) to buy or do something, esp. something illicit or ultimately unprofitable. **7.** to urge, prod, or speed up: *Hustle your work along.* **8.** to obtain by aggressive and often illicit means: *to hustle money from unsuspecting tourists.* **9.** to sell, promote, or publicize aggressively or vigorously. *—n.* **10.** energetic activity, as in work. **11.** discourteous shoving, pushing, or jostling. **12.** *Slang.* **a.** an inducing by pressure or deception to buy something, participate in a dishonest scheme, or the like. **b.** such a scheme, game, or trick. **—hus′tler,** *n.*

hut (hut), *n.* **1.** a small or humble dwelling of simple construction, esp. one made of natural materials, as logs or grass. **2.** a simple roofed shelter, often with one or two sides left open. *—v.t.* **3.** to furnish with a hut as temporary housing; billet. *—v.i.* **4.** to lodge or take shelter in a hut. **—hut′like′,** *adj.*

hutch (huch), *n.* **1.** a pen or enclosed coop for small animals: *a rabbit hutch.* **2.** a chestlike cabinet with doors or drawers, usu. with open shelves above. **3.** a chest, bin, etc., for storage. **4.** a small cottage, hut, or cabin.

Hutch•in•son (huch′in sən), *n.* **1. Anne Marbury,** 1591–1643, American religious liberal, born in England. **2. Thomas,** 1711–80, American colonial administrator of Massachusetts 1769–74.

Hut•ter•ite (hut′ə rīt′, hŏŏt′-), *n.* a member of an Anabaptist sect founded in Moravia that practices community of goods. [after Jacob Hutter (d. 1536), leader of the sect] **—Hut•ter•i•an** (hə tēr′ē ən, hŏŏ-), *adj., n.*

Hux•ley (huks′lē), *n.* **1. Aldous (Leonard),** 1894–1963, English novelist, essayist, and critic. **2. Sir Andrew Fielding,** born 1917, English physiologist (half brother of Aldous and Sir Julian Sorell). **3. Sir Julian**

Sorell, 1887–1975, English biologist and writer (brother of Aldous). **4. Thomas Henry,** 1825–95, English biologist and writer (grandfather of Aldous and Sir Julian Sorell).

huz·zah or **huz·za** (hə zä′), *interj.* **1.** (used as an exclamation of joy, applause, appreciation, etc.) —*n.* **2.** the exclamation "huzzah." **3.** an instance of giving praise or applause. —*v.i.* **4.** to shout "huzzah."

H.V. or **h.v.,** high velocity.

hwy or **hwy.,** highway.

hy·a·cinth (hī′ə sinth), *n.* **1.** a bulbous plant, *Hyacinthus orientalis*, of the lily family, cultivated for its cylindrical cluster of fragrant, colorful flowers. **2.** any similar or related plant, as the grape hyacinth or the water hyacinth. **3.** a plant fabled to have sprung from the blood of Hyacinthus and variously identified as an iris, gladiolus, larkspur, etc. **4.** a reddish orange zircon. **5.** a gem of the ancients, held to be the amethyst or sapphire. **6.** purplish blue. Also called **jacinth** (for defs. 3, 5). —**hy′a·cin′thine** (-sin′thin, -thīn), *adj.*

hy·a·line (*n.* hī′ə lēn′, -lin; *adj.* -lin, -līn′), *n.* **1.** Also, **hy·a·lin** (lin). a structureless, transparent substance found in cartilage, the eye, etc., resulting from the pathological degeneration of tissue. **2.** something glassy or transparent. —*adj.* **3.** of or pertaining to hyaline. **4.** glassy or transparent. **5.** of or pertaining to glass. **6.** amorphous; not crystalline.

hy·a·lite (hī′ə līt′), *n.* a colorless variety of opal, sometimes transparent like glass, and sometimes whitish and translucent.

hy′aloid mem′brane, *n.* the delicate, pellucid, and nearly structureless membrane enclosing the vitreous humor of the eye.

hy·al·o·plasm (hī al′ə plaz′əm, hī′ə lə-), *n.* the clear fluid portion of the cytoplasm, including the part surrounding the nucleus and various organelles. Also called **ground substance.** —**hy·al′o·plas′mic,** *adj.*

hy·brid (hī′brid), *n.* **1.** the offspring of two animals or plants of different breeds, varieties, or species, esp. as produced through human manipulation for specific genetic characteristics. **2.** a person produced by the interaction or crossbreeding of two unlike cultures, traditions, etc. **3.** anything derived from unlike sources, or composed of disparate or incongruous elements; composite. **4.** a word composed of elements orig. drawn from different languages, as *television*, whose components come from Greek and Latin. —*adj.* **5.** bred from two distinct races, breeds, varieties, or species. **6.** composite; formed or composed of heterogeneous elements. —**hy′brid·ism, hy·brid′i·ty** (-i tē), *n.*

hy·brid·ize (hī′bri dīz′), *v.,* **-ized, -iz·ing.** —*v.t.* **1.** to cause to produce hybrids; cross. **2.** to breed or cause the production of (a hybrid). —*v.i.* **3.** to produce hybrids. **4.** to cause the production of hybrids by crossing. **5.** to form a double-stranded nucleic acid of two single strands of DNA or RNA, or one of each, by allowing the base pairs of the separate strands to form complementary bonds. **6.** to fuse two cells of different genotypes into a hybrid cell. —**hy′brid·iz′a·ble,** *adj.* —**hy′brid·i·za′tion,** *n.* —**hy′brid·ist, hy′brid·iz′er,** *n.*

hy′brid perpet′ual, *n.* a cultivated rose bred from varieties having vigorous growth and more or less recurrent bloom.

hy′brid tea′, *n.* a cultivated rose orig. produced chiefly by crossing the tea rose and the hybrid perpetual.

hy′brid vig′or, *n.* HETEROSIS.

Hy·der·a·bad (hī′dər ə bäd′, -bad′), *n.* **1.** a former state in S India, now part of Andhra Pradesh. **2.** the capital of Andhra Pradesh, India, in the W part. 2,528,000. **3.** a city in SE Pakistan, on the Indus River. 795,000.

hydr-, var. of HYDRO-¹ before a vowel (*hydrangea*), used also as a base to which suffixes beginning in a vowel are added (*hydrant*).

hy·dra (hī′drə), *n., pl.* **-dras, -drae** (-drē) for 1–3, *gen.* **-drae** (-drē) for 4. **1.** (*often cap.*) a water monster of Greek myth having nine heads, each of which, if cut off, grew back as two. **2.** any freshwater polyp of the family Hydridae, having a cylindrical body with a ring of tentacles surrounding the mouth. **3.** a persistent or complex problem that presents new obstacles even as existing ones are overcome. **4.** (*cap.*) the Sea Serpent, a southern constellation extending through 90° of the sky, being the longest of all constellations.

hy′dra-head′ed, *adj.* **1.** containing many problems, difficulties, or obstacles. **2.** having many branches, divisions, facets, etc.

hy·dran·gea (hī drān′jə), *n., pl.* **-geas.** any shrub of the genus *Hydrangea*, of the saxifrage family, several of which are cultivated for their large flower clusters of white, pink, or blue.

hy·drant (hī′drənt), *n.* **1.** an upright pipe with a spout or nozzle, usu. in the street, for drawing water from a water main, esp. for fighting fires. **2.** a water faucet.

hy·drate (hī′drāt), *n., v.,* **-drat·ed, -drat·ing.** —*n.* **1.** any of a class of compounds containing chemically combined water. —*v.t., v.i.* **2.** to combine chemically with water. —**hy·dra′tion,** *n.* —**hy′dra·tor,** *n.*

hy·drau·lic (hī drô′lik, -drol′ik), *adj.* **1.** operated by, moved by, or pertaining to water or other liquids in motion. **2.** operated by the pressure created by forcing water, oil, or another liquid through a comparatively narrow pipe or orifice. **3.** of or pertaining to hydraulics. **4.** hardening under water, as a cement. —**hy·drau′li·cal·ly,** *adv.*

hydrau′lic brake′, *n.* a brake operated by fluid pressures in cylinders and connecting tubular lines.

hydrau′lic lift′, *n.* an elevator operated by fluid pressure, esp. one used for raising automobiles in service stations.

hy·drau·lics (hī drô′liks, -drol′iks), *n.* (*used with a sing. v.*) the sci-

ence that deals with the laws governing water or other liquids in motion and their applications in engineering.

hy·dra·zine (hī′drə zēn′), *n.* **1.** a colorless oily fuming liquid, N_2H_4, used as a reducing agent and a jet-propulsion fuel. **2.** a class of substances derived from this substance by replacing one or more hydrogen atoms by an organic group.

hy·dric¹ (hī′drik), *adj.* pertaining to or containing hydrogen.

hy·dric² (hī′drik), *adj.* of, pertaining to, or adapted to a wet or moist environment.

hy·dride (hī′drīd, -drid), *n.* a binary compound formed by hydrogen and another, usu. more electropositive element or group.

hy·dril·la (hī dril′ə), *n., pl.* **-las.** a submerged aquatic plant, *Hydrilla verticillata*, of the frog's-bit family, that has become a pest weed in lakes and waterways.

hy·dro (hī′drō), *n., pl.* **-dros,** *adj.* —*n.* **1.** hydroelectric power. —*adj.* **2.** of, pertaining to, or furnishing water, water power, or hydroelectricity.

hydro-¹, a combining form meaning "water": *hydroplane; hydrogen*. Also, *esp. before a vowel,* **hydr-.**

hydro-², a combining form representing HYDROGEN, used esp. in the names of chemical compounds in which hydrogen is combined with some negative element or radical: *hydrobromic*. Also, *esp. before a vowel,* **hydr-.**

hy·dro·bi·ol·o·gy (hī′drō bī ol′ə jē), *n.* the study of aquatic organisms. —**hy·dro·bi·o·log·i·cal** (hī′drə bī′ə loj′i kəl), **hy′dro·bi′o·log′ic,** *adj.* —**hy′dro·bi′o·log′i·cal·ly,** *adv.* —**hy′dro·bi′ol·o·gist,** *n.*

hy·dro·car·bon (hī′drə kär′bən, hī′drə kär′-), *n.* any of a class of aliphatic, cyclic, or aromatic compounds containing only hydrogen and carbon, as methane or benzene. —**hy′dro·car′bo·na′ceous,** *adj.*

hy·dro·ceph·a·lus (hī′drə sef′ə ləs) also **hy′dro·ceph′a·ly,** *n.* an accumulation of serous fluid within the cranium, esp. in infancy, due to obstruction of the movement of cerebrospinal fluid, often causing great enlargement of the head; water on the brain. —**hy·dro·ce·phal·ic** (hī′drō sə fal′ik), *adj., n.* —**hy′dro·ceph′a·lous,** *adj.*

hy′dro·chlo′ric ac′id (hī′drə klôr′ik, -klōr′-), *n.* a colorless corrosive fuming liquid, HCl, used in petrochemical and industrial processes.

hy·dro·chlo·ride (hī′drə klôr′īd, -id, -klōr′-), *n.* a salt, esp. of an alkaloid, formed by the direct union of hydrochloric acid with an organic base.

hy·dro·cor·ti·sone (hī′drə kôr′tə zōn′, -sōn′), *n.* a steroid hormone, $C_{21}H_{30}O_5$, of the adrenal cortex, active in carbohydrate and protein metabolism, similar to cortisone in effect.

hy′drocyan′ic ac′id, *n.* a colorless, highly poisonous liquid, HCN, an aqueous solution of hydrogen cyanide. Also called **prussic acid.**

hy·dro·dy·nam·ic (hī′drō dī nam′ik, -di-), *adj.* **1.** pertaining to forces in or motions of liquids. **2.** of or pertaining to hydrodynamics. —**hy′dro·dy·nam′i·cal·ly,** *adv.*

hy·dro·dy·nam·ics (hī′drō dī nam′iks, -di-), *n.* (*used with a sing. v.*) the branch of fluid dynamics that deals with liquids. —**hy′dro·dy·nam′i·cist** (-ə sist), *n.*

hy·dro·e·lec·tric (hī′drō i lek′trik), *adj.* pertaining to the generation and distribution of electricity derived from the energy of falling water or any other hydraulic source. —**hy′dro·e·lec·tric′i·ty** (-i lek tris′i tē, -ē′lek-), *n.*

hy·dro·foil (hī′drə foil′), *n.* **1.** a surface form creating a thrust against water in a direction perpendicular to the plane approximated by the surface. **2. a.** a winglike member having this form, designed to lift the hull of a moving vessel. **b.** a vessel equipped with hydrofoils.

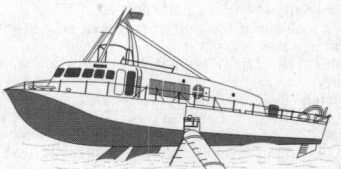

hydrofoil (def. 2b)

hy·dro·gen (hī′drə jən), *n.* a colorless, odorless, flammable gas, the lightest of the elements, that combines chemically with oxygen to form water. *Symbol:* H; *at. wt.:* 1.00797; *at. no.:* 1; *density:* 0.0899 g/l at 0°C and 760 mm pressure.

hy·dro·gen·ate (hī′drə jə nāt′, hī droj′ə-) also **hydrogenize,** *v.t.,* **-at·ed, -at·ing.** to combine or treat with hydrogen, esp. to add it to (an unsaturated organic compound). —**hy′dro·gen·a′tion,** *n.*

hy′drogen bomb′, *n.* a bomb, more powerful than an atomic bomb, that derives its explosive energy from the thermonuclear fusion reaction of hydrogen isotopes. Also called **H-bomb.**

hy′drogen chlo′ride, *n.* a colorless gas, HCl, having a pungent odor: the anhydride of hydrochloric acid.

hy′drogen i′on, *n.* ionized hydrogen of the form H⁺, found in aqueous solutions of all acids.

hy·dro·gen·ize (hī′drə jə nīz′, hī droj′ə-), *v.t.*, **-ized, -iz·ing.** HYDROGENATE. —**hy′dro·gen·i·za′tion,** *n.*

hy·drog·e·nous (hī droj′ə nəs), *adj.* of or containing hydrogen.

hy′drogen perox′ide, *n.* a colorless, unstable, oily liquid, H_2O_2, an aqueous solution of which is used chiefly as an antiseptic and a bleaching agent.

hy′drogen sul′fide, *n.* a colorless, flammable, water-soluble, poisonous gas, H_2S, having the odor of rotten eggs: used in the manufacture of chemicals, in metallurgy, and as a reagent.

hy·dro·ge·ol·o·gy (hī′drō jē ol′ə jē), *n.* the science dealing with the occurrence and distribution of underground water. —**hy·dro·ge·o·log·i·cal** (hī′drə jē′ə loj′i kəl), **hy·dro·ge′o·log′ic,** *adj.* —**hy·dro·ge·ol′o·gist,** *n.*

hy·drog·ra·phy (hī drog′rə fē), *n.* **1.** the science of the measurement, description, and mapping of the surface waters of the earth, esp. with reference to their use for navigation. **2.** those parts of a map collectively that represent surface waters. —**hy·drog′ra·pher,** *n.* —**hy·dro·graph·ic** (hī′drə graf′ik), **hy′dro·graph′i·cal,** *adj.* —**hy′dro·graph′i·cal·ly,** *adv.*

hy·droid (hī′droid), *adj.* **1.** of or pertaining to the hydrozoan order Hydroidea, including hydras and marine colonial forms. —*n.* **2.** the phase of hydrozoan development that consists of polyp forms.

hy·dro·ki·net·ics (hī′drō ki net′iks, -kī-), *n.* (*used with a sing. v.*) the branch of hydrodynamics that deals with the laws governing liquids or gases in motion.

hy′drolog′ic cy′cle, *n.* the natural sequence through which water passes into the atmosphere as water vapor, precipitates to earth, and returns to the atmosphere through evaporation.

hy·drol·o·gy (hī drol′ə jē), *n.* **1.** the science dealing with the occurrence, circulation, distribution, and properties of the waters of the earth and its atmosphere. **2.** HYDROGEOLOGY. —**hy·dro·log·ic** (hī′drə loj′ik), **hy′dro·log′i·cal,** *adv.* —**hy·drol′o·gist,** *n.*

hy·drol·y·sis (hī drol′ə sis), *n., pl.* **-ses** (-sēz′). chemical decomposition in which a compound is split into other compounds by reacting with water.

hy·dro·lyt·ic (hī′drə lit′ik), *adj.* of, producing, or resulting in hydrolysis.

hy·dro·lyze (hī′drə līz′), *v.t., v.i.,* **-lyzed, -lyz·ing.** to subject or be subjected to hydrolysis. —**hy′dro·lyz′a·ble,** *adj.* —**hy·dro·ly·za′tion,** *n.* —**hy′dro·lyz′er,** *n.*

hy′drolyzed veg′etable pro′tein, *n.* a vegetable protein broken down into amino acids and used as a food additive to enhance flavor.

hy·dro·met·al·lur·gy (hī′drə met′l ûr′jē), *n.* the process of extracting metals at ordinary temperatures by leaching ore with liquid solvents. —**hy·dro·met·al·lur′gi·cal,** *adj.*

hy·dro·me·te·or (hī′drə mē′tē ər, -ôr′), *n.* liquid water or ice in the atmosphere in various forms, as rain, ice crystals, hail, fog, or clouds.

hy·dro·me·te·or·ol·o·gy (hī′drə mē′tē ə rol′ə jē), *n.* the study of atmospheric water, esp. precipitation, as it affects agriculture, water supply, flood control, power generation, etc. —**hy·dro·me′te·or·o·log′i·cal** (-ər ə loj′i kəl), *adj.* —**hy·dro·me′te·or·ol′o·gist,** *n.*

hy·drom·e·ter (hī drom′i tər), *n.* an instrument for determining the specific gravity of a liquid, commonly consisting of a graduated tube weighted to float upright in the liquid. —**hy·dro·met·ric** (hī′drə me′trik), **hy′dro·met′ri·cal,** *adj.* —**hy·drom′e·try,** *n.*

hy·dro·naut (hī′drə nôt′, -not′), *n.* a person trained to work in deep-sea vessels for research and rescue purposes.

hy·drop·a·thy (hī drop′ə thē), *n.* a method of treating disease by immersing the body or body part in water, by taking water internally, or both. —**hy·dro·path·ic** (hī′drə path′ik), *adj.*

hy·dro·phil·ic (hī′drə fil′ik), *adj.* having a strong affinity for water; readily absorbing water.

hy·droph·i·lous (hī drof′ə ləs), *adj.* growing in water; hydrophytic. —**hy·droph′i·ly,** *n.*

hy·dro·pho·bi·a (hī′drə fō′bē ə), *n.* **1.** RABIES. **2.** an abnormal or unnatural dread of water. [< Late Latin < Greek: horror of water]

hy·dro·phyte (hī′drə fīt′), *n.* a plant that grows in water or very moist ground; an aquatic plant. —**hy·dro·phyt′ic** (-fit′ik), *adj.* —**hy′dro·phyt′ism,** *n.*

hy·dro·plane (hī′drə plān′), *n., v.,* **-planed, -plan·ing.** —*n.* **1.** a seaplane. **2.** an attachment to an airplane enabling it to glide on the water. **3.** a light, high-powered boat, esp. one with hydrofoils or a stepped bottom, designed to plane along the surface of the water at very high speeds. **4.** a horizontal rudder for submerging or elevating a submarine. —*v.i.* **5.** to skim over water in the manner of a hydroplane. **6.** to travel in or pilot a hydroplane. **7.** (of a vehicle or a tire) to ride on a film of water on a wet surface with a resulting decrease in braking and steering effectiveness. —**hy′dro·plan′er,** *n.*

hy·dro·pon·ics (hī′drə pon′iks), *n.* (*used with a sing. v.*) the cultivation of plants by placing the roots in liquid nutrient solutions rather than in soil; soilless growth of plants. —**hy·dro·pon′ic,** *adj.* —**hy′dro·pon′i·cal·ly,** *adv.*

hy·dro·pow·er (hī′drə pou′ər), *n.* hydroelectric power.

hy·dro·sphere (hī′drə sfēr′), *n.* the water on or surrounding the surface of the globe, including the water of the oceans and the water in the atmosphere.

hy·dro·stat (hī′drə stat′), *n.* **1.** an electrical device for detecting the

presence of water, as from overflow or leakage. **2.** a device for preventing damage to a steam boiler when its water sinks below a certain level.

hy·dro·stat·ics (hī′drə stat′iks), *n.* (*used with a sing. v.*) the branch of hydrodynamics that deals with the statics of fluids, esp. the equilibrium and pressure of liquids. —**hy′dro·stat′ic, hy′dro·stat′i·cal,** *adj.* —**hy′dro·stat′i·cal·ly,** *adv.*

hy·dro·ther·a·py (hī′drə ther′ə pē), *n.* the use of water in the treatment of disease or injury, as with soothing baths or sprays for wounds or heated pools for stiffened joints. —**hy′dro·ther′a·pist,** *n.*

hy·dro·ther·mal (hī′drə thûr′məl), *adj.* of or pertaining to the action of hot aqueous solutions or gases within or on the surface of the earth. —**hy·dro·ther′mal·ly,** *adv.*

hy·drous (hī′drəs), *adj.* **1.** containing water. **2.** containing water in some kind of chemical union, as in hydrates or hydroxides.

hy·drox·ide (hī drok′sīd, -sid), *n.* a chemical compound containing the hydroxyl group.

hydroxy-, a combining form used in the names of chemical compounds in which the hydroxyl group is present: *hydroxyketone.*

hy·drox·yl (hī drok′səl), *n.* the univalent group OH, found in both organic compounds, as ethyl alcohol, C_2H_5OH, and inorganic compounds, as sodium hydroxide, NaOH. —**hy′drox·yl′ic** (-sil′ik), *adj.*

hy·dro·zo·an (hī′drə zō′ən), *n.* **1.** any freshwater or marine cnidarian of the class Hydrozoa, including attached and free-swimming, often colonial, forms in which the medusa stage is reduced or lacking. —*adj.* **2.** belonging or pertaining to the hydrozoans.

hy·e·na (hī ē′nə), *n., pl.* **-nas.** a large carnivore of the family Hyaenidae, of Africa and S Asia, having a sloping back and large teeth and feeding chiefly on carrion, often in packs. —**hy·e′nic, hy·e′nine** (-nīn, -nin), *adj.*

hy·giene (hī′jēn), *n.* **1.** the application of scientific knowledge to the preservation of health and prevention of the spread of disease. **2.** a condition or practice conducive to the preservation of health, as cleanliness.

hy·gi·en·ic (hī′jē en′ik, hī jen′-, -jē′nik) also **hy′gi·en′i·cal,** *adj.* **1.** conducive to good health; healthful; sanitary. **2.** of or pertaining to hygiene. —**hy′gi·en′i·cal·ly,** *adv.*

hy·gi·en·ics (hī′jē en′iks, hī jen′-, -jē′niks), *n.* (*used with a sing. v.*) HYGIENE (def. 1).

hy·gien·ist (hī jē′nist, -jen′ist, hī′jē nist), *n.* **1.** an expert in hygiene. **2.** DENTAL HYGIENIST.

hy·grom·e·ter (hī grom′i tər), *n.* any instrument for measuring the water-vapor content of the atmosphere. —**hy·gro·met·ric** (hī′grə me′trik), *adj.* —**hy·grom′e·try,** *n.*

hy·ing (hī′ing), *v.* a pres. part. of HIE.

hy·men (hī′mən), *n.* a fold of mucous membrane partly closing the external orifice of the vagina in a virgin. —**hy′men·al,** *adj.*

hy·me·ne·al (hī′mə nē′əl), *adj.* of or pertaining to marriage.

hy·me·nop·ter·ous (hī′mə nop′tər əs), *adj.* belonging or pertaining to the Hymenoptera, an order of insects having, when winged, four membranous wings, and comprising the wasps, bees, ants, ichneumon flies, and sawflies.

hymn (him), *n.* **1.** a song or ode in praise or honor of God, a deity, a nation, etc. **2.** something resembling this, as a speech or essay in praise of someone or something. —*v.t.* **3.** to praise or celebrate in a hymn. **4.** to express in a hymn. —*v.i.* **5.** to sing hymns. —**hymn′like′,** *adj.*

hym·nal (him′nl), *n.* **1.** Also called **hymn·book** (-bŏŏk′). a book of hymns for use in a religious service. —*adj.* **2.** of or pertaining to hymns.

hym·no·dy (him′nə dē), *n.* **1.** the singing or composition of hymns or sacred songs. **2.** hymns collectively, esp. the hymns of a particular religion, place, or period.

hym·nol·o·gy (him nol′ə jē), *n.* **1.** the study of hymns, their history, classification, etc. **2.** HYMNODY. —**hym·nol′o·gist,** *n.*

hy·oid (hī′oid), *adj.* **1.** Also, **hy·oi′dal, hy·oi′de·an.** of or designating a bony or cartilaginous structure at the base of the vertebrate tongue, U-shaped in humans. —*n.* **2.** the hyoid bone or structure.

hyp·al·ge·si·a (hip′al jē′zē ə, -sē ə, hī′pal-) also **hy·pal·gia** (hī-pal′jə, -jē ə, hī-), *n.* decreased sensitivity to pain (opposed to *hyperalgesia*). —**hyp′al·ge′sic,** *adj.*

hype (hīp), *v.,* **hyped, hyp·ing,** *n. Informal.* —*v.t.* **1.** to stimulate, excite, or agitate (usu. fol. by *up*). **2.** to create interest in by flamboyant or dramatic methods; promote or publicize showily. **3.** to intensify or increase, often by questionable methods: *extra features added to cars to hype profits.* **4.** to trick; gull. —*n.* **5.** intensive or exaggerated publicity or promotion. **6.** a flamboyant or questionable claim, method, etc., used in advertising or publicity. **7.** a swindle, deception, or trick. —**hyp′er,** *n.*

hyped′-up′, *adj. Informal.* **1.** stimulated or excited, esp. excessively so. **2.** exaggerated; false.

hy·per (hī′pər), *adj. Informal.* **1.** very excitable or nervous; overexcited; keyed up. **2.** hyperactive. **3.** obsessively concerned; fanatical; rabid.

hyper-, a prefix meaning "excessive," "undue" (*hypercritical; hypersensitive*); "unusual, abnormal" (*hyperactive; hyperinflation*), used esp. in terms denoting conditions of the body in which substances or functions are at above-normal levels (*hyperglycemia; hypertension*), sometimes as a counterpart to a word formed with HYPO-; "greatly exceeding norms" (*hypervelocity*); "forming an analogue (to the thing named) in space of more than four dimensions" (*hyperspace*); "connecting in a nonsequential manner" (*hypertext*). Compare SUPER-.

hy·per·ac·tive (hī′pər ak′tiv), *adj.* **1.** unusually or abnormally active: *a hyperactive imagination.* **2.** (of children) displaying excessive physical activity sometimes associated with neurological or psychological causes. —**hy′per·ac′tion** (-ak′shən), *n.* —**hy′per·ac′tive·ly,** *adv.*

hy·per·ac·tiv·i·ty (hī′pər ak tiv′i tē), *n.* the condition of being hyperactive.

hy·per·al·ge·si·a (hī′pər al jē′zē ə, -sē ə) also **hy·per·al·gi·a** (-al′jē ə, -jə), *n.* an exaggerated sense of pain (opposed to *hypalgesia*). —**hy′per·al·ge′sic, hy·per·al·get′ic** (-jet′ik), *adj.*

hy·per·bar·ic (hī′pər bar′ik), *adj.* **1.** (of an anesthetic) having a specific gravity greater than that of cerebrospinal fluid. **2.** pertaining to or utilizing gaseous pressure greater than normal, esp. for administering oxygen in the treatment of certain diseases.

hy·per·bo·la (hī pûr′bə lə), *n., pl.* **-las.** the set of points in a plane whose distances to two fixed points in the plane have a constant difference; a curve consisting of two branches, formed by the intersection of a plane with a right circular cone when the plane makes a greater angle with the base than does the generator of the cone. *Equation:* $x^2/a^2 - y^2/b^2 = \pm 1$.

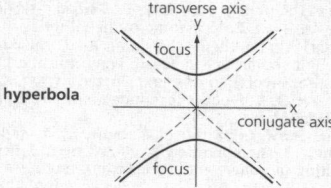

hy·per·bo·le (hī pûr′bə lē), *n., pl.* **-les. 1.** obvious and intentional exaggeration. **2.** an extravagant statement or figure of speech not intended to be taken literally, as "to wait an eternity." Compare LITOTES.

hy·per·bol·ic (hī′pər bol′ik) also **hy·per·bol′i·cal,** *adj.* **1.** of, having the nature of, or using hyperbole. **2.** of, pertaining to, or derived from a hyperbola. —**hy′per·bol′i·cal·ly,** *adv.*

hy·per·bo·lize (hī pûr′bə līz′), *v.,* **-lized, -liz·ing.** —*v.i.* **1.** to use hyperbole; exaggerate. —*v.t.* **2.** to represent or express with hyperbole or exaggeration.

hy·per·con·scious (hī′pər kon′shəs), *adj.* acutely aware. —**hy′per·con′scious·ly,** *adv.* —**hy′per·con′scious·ness,** *n.*

hy·per·cor·rect (hī′pər kə rekt′), *adj.* **1.** correct or excessively fastidious: *hypercorrect manners.* **2.** of or characterized by hypercorrection. —**hy′per·cor·rect′ly,** *adv.* —**hy′per·cor·rect′ness,** *n.*

hy·per·cor·rec·tion (hī′pər kə rek′shən), *n.* the use of an inappropriate pronunciation, grammatical form, or construction, as *between you and I,* resulting usu. from an effort to replace incorrect or seemingly incorrect forms with correct ones.

hy·per·e·mi·a (hī′pər ē′mē ə), *n.* an abnormally large amount of blood in any part of the body. —**hy′per·e′mic,** *adj.*

hy·per·ga·my (hī pûr′gə mē), *n.* marriage to a person of a social status higher than one's own; orig., esp. in India, the custom of allowing a woman to marry only into her own or a higher social group. —**hy·per′ga·mous,** *adj.*

hy·per·gly·ce·mi·a (hī′pər glī sē′mē ə), *n.* an abnormally high level of glucose in the blood. —**hy′per·gly·ce′mic,** *adj.*

hy·per·in·fla·tion (hī′pər in flā′shən), *n.* extreme, usu. rapid and uncontrolled economic inflation. —**hy′per·in·flate′,** *v.t.,* **-flat·ed, -flat·ing.**

hy·per·ki·ne·sia (hī′pər ki nē′zhə, -zhē ə, -zē ə, -kī-) also **hy·per·ki·ne·sis** (-nē′sis), *n.* **1.** an abnormal amount of uncontrolled muscular action; spasm. **2.** a hyperactive condition; hyperactivity. —**hy′per·ki·net′ic** (-net′ik), *adj.*

hy·per·mar·ket (hī′pər mär′kit), *n.* a very large self-service store that sells general merchandise and groceries.

hy·per·me·di·a (hī′pər mē′dē ə), *n.* (*usu. with a sing. v.*) a system in which various forms of information, as data, text, graphics, video, and audio, are linked together by a hypertext program.

hy·per·sen·si·tive (hī′pər sen′si tiv), *adj.* **1.** excessively sensitive: *hypersensitive to criticism.* **2.** allergic to a substance to which most people do not normally react. —**hy′per·sen′si·tive·ness, hy′per·sen′si·tiv′i·ty,** *n.*

hy·per·sen·si·tize (hī′pər sen′si tīz′), *v.t.,* **-tized, -tiz·ing.** to treat (a photographic film or emulsion) so as to increase its speed. —**hy′per·sen′si·ti·za′tion,** *n.*

hy·per·space (hī′pər spās′), *n.* **1.** space having more than three dimensions. **2.** (in science fiction) a non-Euclidean dimension that serves as a means of circumventing normal space-time relationships. —**hy′per·spa′tial** (-spā′shəl), *adj.*

hy·per·ten·sion (hī′pər ten′shən), *n.* **1. a.** elevation of the blood pressure, esp. the diastolic pressure. **b.** an arterial disease characterized by this condition. **2.** excessive or extreme nervous tension.

hy·per·ten·sive (hī′pər ten′siv), *adj.* **1.** characterized by or causing high blood pressure. —*n.* **2.** a person who has high blood pressure.

hy·per·text (hī′pər tekst′), *n.* a method of storing data through a computer program that allows a user to create and link fields of information at will and to retrieve the data nonsequentially.

hy·per·ther·mi·a (hī′pər thûr′mē ə) also **hy′per·ther′my,** *n.* **1.** abnormally high fever. **2.** treatment of disease by the induction of fever.

hy·per·thy·roid·ism (hī′pər thī′roi diz′əm), *n.* **1.** overactivity of the thyroid gland. **2.** a condition resulting from this, characterized by increased metabolism.

hy·per·to·ni·a (hī′pər tō′nē ə), *n.* increased rigidity, tension, and spasticity of the muscles.

hy·per·tro·phy (hī pûr′trə fē), *n., pl.* **-phies,** *v.,* **-phied, -phy·ing.** —*n.* **1.** abnormal enlargement of a part or organ due to an increase in the size of its cells; excessive growth. **2.** excessive growth or accumulation of any kind. —*v.t., v.i.* **3.** to affect with or undergo hypertrophy. —**hy·per·troph·ic** (hī′pər trof′ik, -trō′fik), *adj.*

hy·per·ven·ti·late (hī′pər ven′tl āt′), *v.,* **-lat·ed, -lat·ing.** —*v.i.* **1.** to be affected with hyperventilation; breathe abnormally fast and deep. **2.** to express excessive enthusiasm or excitement. —*v.t.* **3.** to cause (a patient) to breathe more rapidly and deeply than normal.

hy·per·ven·ti·la·tion (hī′pər ven′tl ā′shən), *n.* prolonged rapid or deep breathing, resulting in excessive oxygen levels in the blood often accompanying dizziness, chest pain, and tingling of extremities.

hy·pha (hī′fə), *n., pl.* **-phae** (-fē). (in a fungus) one of the threadlike elements of the mycelium.

hy·phen (hī′fən), *n.* **1.** a short line (-) used to connect the parts of a compound word or the parts of a word divided for any purpose. —*v.t.* **2.** to hyphenate. [< Late Latin < Greek *together*] —**hy·phen·ic** (hī-fen′ik), *adj.*

hy·phen·ate (*v.* hī′fə nāt′; *adj., n.* -nit, -nāt′), *v.,* **-at·ed, -at·ing,** *adj., n.* —*v.t.* **1.** to join by a hyphen. **2.** to write or divide with a hyphen. —*adj.* **3.** hyphenated. —*n.* **4.** a person working in more than one craft or occupation: *a hyphenate in the film industry who has gained fame as a writer-director-producer.* **5.** a person of mixed national origin or identity. —**hy′phen·a′tion,** *n.*

hy·phen·at·ed (hī′fə nā′tid), *adj.* **1.** of or designating a person or group of mixed national origin or identity: *an Irish-American club and other hyphenated organizations.* **2.** composed of distinct elements connected by or as if by a hyphen.

hyp·no·a·nal·y·sis (hip′nō ə nal′ə sis), *n.* psychoanalysis with the aid of hypnosis or hypnotic drugs. —**hyp′no·an′a·lyt′ic** (-an′l it′ik), *adj.*

hyp·no·gen·e·sis (hip′nə jen′ə sis), *n.* the induction of a hypnotic state. —**hyp′no·ge·net′ic** (-jə net′ik), *adj.*

hyp·nol·o·gy (hip nol′ə jē), *n.* the science dealing with the phenomena of sleep. —**hyp′no·log′ic** (-nl oj′ik), **hyp′no·log′i·cal,** *adj.* —**hyp·nol′o·gist,** *n.*

hyp·no·pe·di·a (hip′nə pē′dē ə), *n.* the act or process of learning during sleep, as by listening to recordings repeatedly.

hyp·no·sis (hip nō′sis), *n., pl.* **-ses** (-sēz). **1.** an artificially induced trance state resembling sleep, characterized by heightened susceptibility to suggestion. **2.** HYPNOTISM (defs. 1, 2).

hyp·no·ther·a·py (hip′nō ther′ə pē), *n.* treatment of a symptom, disease, or addiction by means of hypnotism. —**hyp′no·ther′a·pist,** *n.*

hyp·not·ic (hip not′ik), *adj.* **1.** of, pertaining to, or resembling hypnosis or hypnotism. **2.** inducing or like something that induces hypnosis. **3.** susceptible to hypnotism. **4.** inducing sleep. —*n.* **5.** an agent or drug that induces sleep; sedative. **6.** a person who is hypnotized or susceptible to hypnosis. —**hyp·not′i·cal·ly,** *adv.*

hyp·no·tism (hip′nə tiz′əm), *n.* **1.** the study or practice of inducing hypnosis. **2.** the act of hypnotizing. **3.** HYPNOSIS (def. 1). —**hyp′no·tist,** *n.*

hyp·no·tize (hip′nə tīz′), *v.,* **-tized, -tiz·ing.** —*v.t.* **1.** to put in a state of hypnosis. **2.** to influence or control by or as if by hypnotic suggestion. **3.** to transfix; spellbind; fascinate. —*v.t.* **4.** to practice hypnosis. —**hyp′no·tiz′a·ble,** *adj.* —**hyp′no·tiz′a·bil′i·ty,** *n.*

hy·po¹ (hī′pō), *n., pl.* **-pos.** *Informal.* **1.** a hypodermic syringe or injection. **2.** a stimulus or boost. —*v.t.* **3.** to stimulate by or as if by administering a hypodermic injection; boost: *to hypo a car by installing a bigger engine.*

hy·po² (hī′pō), *n.* sodium thiosulfate.

hy·po³ (hī′pō), *n., pl.* **-pos.** a hypochondriac.

hypo-, a prefix meaning "under, below," occurring esp. in words denoting an organ or location below a given body part (*hypodermic; hypothalamus*), or in terms denoting a body condition in which substances or functions are at below-normal levels (*hypothermia*), sometimes as a counterpart to a word formed with HYPER-; also used in the names of chemical compounds that are in a lower state of oxidation than a given compound (*hyposulfurous acid*). Also, *esp. before a vowel,* **hyp-.**

hy·po·al·ler·gen·ic (hī′pō al′ər jen′ik), *adj.* designed to minimize the likelihood of an allergic response, as by containing few or no potentially irritating substances: *hypoallergenic cosmetics.*

hy·po·blast (hī′pə blast′), *n.* **1.** the endoderm of an embryo. **2.** the cells entering into the inner layer of a young gastrula, capable of becoming endoderm and, to some extent, mesoderm. —**hy′po·blas′tic,** *adj.*

hy·po·chon·dri·a (hī′pə kon′drē ə) also **hy·po·chon·dri·a·sis** (-pō kən drī′ə sis), *n.* an excessive preoccupation with one's health, usu. focusing on some particular symptom, as cardiac or gastric problems; excessive worry or talk about one's health.

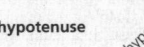
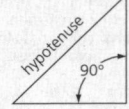

hypotenuse

90°

hy·po·chon·dri·ac (hī′pə kon′drē ak′), *adj.* **1.** Also, **hy′po·chon·dri′a·cal** (-kən drī′ə kəl). pertaining to, suffering from, or produced by hypochondria. **2.** of or pertaining to the hypochondrium. —*n.* **3.** a person suffering from or subject to hypochondria. —**hy′po·chon·dri′a·cal·ly,** *adv.*

hy·po·chon·dri·um (hī′pə kon′drē əm), *n., pl.* **-dri·a** (-drē ə). either of two regions of the upper abdomen, around the lower ribs. [< Greek *hypochóndrion* abdomen]

hy·poc·o·rism (hī pok′ə riz′əm), *n.* **1.** a pet name. **2.** the use of pet names. **3.** the use of forms imitative of baby talk.

hy·poc·ri·sy (hi pok′rə sē), *n., pl.* **-sies. 1.** the false profession of desirable or publicly approved qualities, beliefs, or feelings, esp. a pretense of having virtues, moral principles, or religious beliefs that one does not really possess. **2.** an act or instance of hypocrisy.

hyp·o·crite (hip′ə krit), *n.* a person who practices hypocrisy, esp. a person whose actions belie stated beliefs. —**hyp′o·crit′i·cal,** *adj.* —**hyp′o·crit′i·cal·ly,** *adv.*

hy·po·der·mic (hī′pə dûr′mik), *adj.* **1.** of or characterized by the introduction of medicine or drugs under the skin: *a hypodermic injection.* **2.** introduced under the skin: *a hypodermic medication.* **3.** pertaining to parts under the skin. **4.** stimulating; energizing. —*n.* **5.** a hypodermic injection. **6.** a hypodermic syringe or needle. —**hy′po·der′mi·cal·ly,** *adv.*

hypoder′mic syringe′, *n.* a small piston syringe having a detachable hollow needle **(hypoder′mic nee′dle)** for use in injecting solutions subcutaneously.

hy·po·der·mis (hī′pə dûr′mis) also **hy′po·derm′,** *n.* **1.** an underlayer of epithelial cells in arthropods and some other invertebrates that secretes the overlying cuticle or exoskeleton. **2.** *Bot.* a tissue or layer of cells beneath the epidermis. —**hy′po·der′mal,** *adj.*

hy·po·ge·al (hī′pə jē′əl) also **hy′po·ge′an, hy′po·ge′ous,** *adj.* existing, living, or growing underground.

hy·po·gly·ce·mi·a (hī′pō glī sē′mē ə), *n.* an abnormally low level of glucose in the blood. —**hy′po·gly·ce′mic,** *adj.*

hy·po·nym (hī′pə nim), *n.* a word that denotes a subcategory of a more general class: *Chair* and *table* are hyponyms of *furniture.* Compare SUPERORDINATE (def. 3). —**hy·pon′y·mous** (-pon′ə məs), *adj.* —**hy·pon′y·my,** *n.*

hy·po·sen·si·tize (hī′pə sen′si tīz′), *v.t.,* **-tized, -tiz·ing.** to cause (a person) to become less sensitive to (a substance producing an allergic reaction); desensitize. —**hy′po·sen′si·ti·za′tion,** *n.*

hy·pos·ta·sis (hī pos′tə sis, hi-), *n., pl.* **-ses** (-sēz′). **1.** (in philosophy) the underlying or essential part of anything, as distinguished from attributes; substance; essence. **2. a.** (in Christianity) one of the three real and distinct substances in the one undivided substance or essence of God. **b.** a person of the Trinity. **c.** the one personality of Christ in which two natures, human and divine, are united. **3. a.** the accumulation of blood or its solid components in parts of an organ or body due to poor circulation. **b.** sedimentation, as in a test tube. —**hy·po·stat·ic** (hī′pə stat′ik), **hy′po·stat′i·cal,** *adj.*

hy·pos·ta·tize (hī pos′tə tīz′, hi-), *v.t.,* **-tized, -tiz·ing.** to treat or regard (a concept) as a distinct substance or reality. —**hy·pos′ta·ti·za′tion,** *n.*

hy·po·ten·sion (hī′pə ten′shən), *n.* **1.** decreased or lowered blood pressure. **2.** a disease or condition characterized by this symptom.

hy·po·ten·sive (hī′pō ten′siv), *adj.* **1.** characterized by or causing low blood pressure, as shock. —*n.* **2.** a hypotensive person or agent.

hy·pot·e·nuse (hī pot′n ōōs′, -yōōs′), *n.* the side of a right triangle opposite the right angle.

hy·po·thal·a·mus (hī′pō thal′ə məs), *n., pl.* **-mi** (-mī′). a region of the diencephalon of the brain that is the regulating center for visceral functions, as sleep cycles, body temperature, and the activity of the pituitary gland. —**hy′po·tha·lam′ic** (-thə lam′ik), *adj.*

hy·poth·e·cate (hī poth′i kāt′), *v.t.,* **-cat·ed, -cat·ing.** to pledge to a creditor as security without delivering, as property or goods. —**hy·poth′e·ca′tion,** *n.* —**hy·poth′e·ca′tor,** *n.*

hy·po·ther·mal (hī′pə thûr′məl), *adj.* **1.** (of mineral deposits) formed at great depths and high temperatures. **2.** lukewarm; tepid.

hy·po·ther·mi·a (hī′pə thûr′mē ə), *n.* **1.** subnormal body temperature. **2.** the artificial reduction of body temperature to slow down metabolic processes, as for facilitating heart surgery. —**hy′po·ther′mic,** *adj.*

hy·poth·e·sis (hī poth′ə sis, hi-), *n., pl.* **-ses** (-sēz′). **1.** a provisional theory set forth to explain some class of phenomena, either accepted as a guide to future investigation **(working hypothesis)** or assumed for the sake of argument and testing. **2.** a proposition assumed as a premise in an argument. **3.** the antecedent of a conditional proposition. **4.** a mere assumption or guess. —**hy·poth′e·sist,** *n.*

hy·poth·e·size (hī poth′ə sīz′, hi-), *v.,* **-sized, -siz·ing.** —*v.i.* **1.** to form a hypothesis. —*v.t.* **2.** to assume by hypothesis.

hy·po·thet·i·cal (hī′pə thet′i kəl), *adj.* Also, **hy′po·thet′ic. 1.** assumed to exist by hypothesis; supposed; conjectural: *a hypothetical case.* **2.** of, pertaining to, involving, or characterized by hypothesis: *hypothetical reasoning.* —*n.* **3.** a hypothetical statement, situation, instance, etc. —**hy′po·thet′i·cal·ly,** *adv.*

hy·po·thy·roid·ism (hī′pə thī′roi diz′əm), *n.* **1.** deficient activity of the thyroid gland. **2.** the condition produced by a deficiency of thyroid secretion, resulting in goiter, and, in children, cretinism. —**hy′po·thy′-roid,** *adj.*

hyp·sog·ra·phy (hip sog′rə fē), *n.* **1.** a branch of geography that deals with the measurement and mapping of the topography of the earth above sea level. **2.** topographical relief, esp. as represented on a map. —**hyp′so·graph′ic** (-sə graf′ik), **hyp′so·graph′i·cal,** *adj.*

hy·rax (hī′raks), *n., pl.* **-rax·es, -ra·ces** (-rə sēz′). any small, short-legged mammal of the order Hyracoidea, of Africa and SW Asia, having hooflike nails on the toes.

hys·sop (his′əp), *n.* **1.** an aromatic plant, *Hyssopus officinalis,* of the mint family, native to Europe, having clusters of small blue flowers. **2.** any of various related or similar plants. **3.** an unidentified Biblical plant whose twigs were used in ceremonial sprinkling. Ex. 12:22; Ps. 51:7; John 19:29.

hyster-, var. of HYSTERO- before a vowel: *hysterectomy.*

hys·ter·ec·to·my (his′tə rek′tə mē), *n., pl.* **-mies.** surgical excision of the uterus. —**hys′ter·ec′to·mize,** *v.t.,* **-mized, -miz·ing.**

hys·te·ri·a (hi ster′ē ə, -stēr′-), *n.* **1.** a psychoneurotic disorder characterized by violent emotional outbreaks, disturbances of sensory and motor functions, and various abnormal effects due to autosuggestion. **2.** an uncontrollable emotional outburst, as from fear or grief, often characterized by irrationality, laughter, weeping, etc. **3.** a state of intense agitation, anxiety, or excitement, esp. as manifested by large groups or segments of society.

hys·ter·ic (hi ster′ik), *n.* **1.** Usu., **hysterics.** a fit of uncontrollable laughter or weeping; hysteria. **2.** a person subject to hysteria. —*adj.* **3.** hysterical.

hys·ter·i·cal (hi ster′i kəl), *adj.* **1.** of, pertaining to, characterized by, or suffering from hysteria. **2.** uncontrollably emotional or agitated. **3.** causing unrestrained laughter; very funny; hilarious: *a hysterical movie.* —**hys·ter′i·cal·ly,** *adv.*

hystero-, a combining form meaning "uterus": *hysterotomy.* Also, *esp. before a vowel,* **hyster-.**

hys·ter·ot·o·my (his′tə rot′ə mē), *n., pl.* **-mies.** the operation of cutting into the uterus, as in a Cesarean.

Hz, hertz.

I

I, i (ī), *n., pl.* **I's** or **Is, i's** or **is. 1.** the ninth letter of the English alphabet, a vowel. **2.** any spoken sound represented by this letter. **3.** something shaped like an I. **4.** a written or printed representation of the letter *I* or *i.*

I (ī), *pron., nom.* **I,** *poss.* **my** or **mine,** *obj.* **me;** *pl. nom.* **we,** *poss.* **our** or **ours,** *obj.* **us;** *n., pl.* **I's. —***pron.* **1.** the nominative singular pronoun used by a speaker or writer in referring to himself or herself. —*n.* **2.** (used to denote the narrator of a literary work written in the first person singular.) **3.** the ego; the self. —**Usage.** See ME.

I, interstate (used with a number to designate an interstate highway): *I-95.*

I, *Symbol.* **1.** the ninth in order or in a series. **2.** (*sometimes l.c.*) the Roman numeral for 1. Compare ROMAN NUMERALS. **3.** *Chem.* iodine. **4.** *Biochem.* isoleucine. **5.** *Elect.* current.

I, *Physics Symbol.* isotopic spin.

i, 1. *Math Symbol.* the imaginary number *A.* **2.** a unit vector on the *x*-axis of a coordinate system.

i-, var. of Y-.

-i-, the typical ending of the first element of compounds of Latin words, as -O- is of Greek words, but often used in English with a first element of any origin, if the second element is of Latin origin: *cuneiform; Frenchify.*

-ia, an ending of nouns borrowed from Greek and Latin, or coined in English or other languages on a Latin model, that denote esp. places (*Ethiopia; Georgia; Liberia*), states or conditions, esp. physical disorders (*insomnia; leukemia; phobia*), or plants (*fuchsia; zinnia*); also occurring in other nouns, often orig. or still plural (*bacteria; insignia; media*) or collective (*academia; militia*). The ending **-ia** has limited productivity as an English suffix, forming names of disorders (*hypoxia*) or plural or collective nouns (*militaria; suburbia*). Compare -Y².

IA or **Ia.,** Iowa.

i.a., in absentia.

-ial, var. of -AL¹: *insessorial; trucial.*

i•amb (ī'am, ī'amb), *n.* a prosodic foot of two syllables, a short followed by a long in quantitative meter, or an unstressed followed by a stressed in accentual meter, as in *Come live / with me / and be / my love.*

i•am•bic (ī am'bik), *adj.* **1.** pertaining to, consisting of, or employing iambs. **2.** of or designating Greek satirical poetry written in iambs. —*n.* **3. a.** an iamb. **b.** Usu., **iambics.** a verse or poem consisting of iambs. **4.** a satirical Greek poem in this meter. —**i•am'bi•cal•ly,** *adv.*

-ian, a suffix with the same meaning and properties as -AN¹; -**ian** is now the more productive of the two suffixes in recent coinages, esp. when the base noun ends in a consonant: *Orwellian; Washingtonian.*

-iana, var. of -ANA.

I' and Thou', a book of religious philosophy (1923) by Martin Buber.

i•at•ric (ī a'trik, ē a'-) also **i•at'ri•cal,** *adj.* of or pertaining to a physician or to medicine; medical.

-iatrics, a combining form occurring in words that have the general sense "healing, medical practice," with the initial element usu. denoting the type of person treated: *geriatrics; pediatrics.*

i•at•ro•gen•ic (ī a'trə jen'ik, ē a'-), *adj.* induced unintentionally by the medical treatment of a physician: *iatrogenic symptoms.* —**i•at'ro•gen'e•sis** (-ə sis), *n.* —**i•at'ro•gen•ic'i•ty** (-jə nis'i tē), *n.*

-iatry, a combining form occurring in words that have the general sense "healing, medical practice," with the initial element usu. denoting the area treated: *podiatry; psychiatry.*

ib., ibidem.

i•ba•da (ē bä'dä, -də), *n.* any of the religious duties of a Muslim, including the recital of the creed, the five daily recitals of prayers, the Ramadan fast, almsgiving, and the pilgrimage to Mecca.

I-beam (ī'bēm'), *n.* a rolled or extruded metal beam having a cross section resembling an I.

I•be•ri•a (ī bēr'ē ə), *n.* **1.** Also called **Ibe'rian Penin'sula.** a peninsula in SW Europe, comprising Spain and Portugal. **2.** an ancient region S of the Caucasus in what is now the Georgian Republic. —**I•be'ri•an,** *adj., n.*

i•bex (ī'beks), *n., pl.* **i•bex•es, ib•i•ces** (ib'ə sēz', ī'bə-), (*esp. collectively*) **i•bex.** any of several wild mountain goats of the genus *Capra,* of Eurasia and N Africa, having long recurved horns.

ibid. (ib'id), ibidem.

i•bi•dem (ib'i dəm, i bī'dəm, i bē'-), *adv.* in the same book, chapter, page, etc., previously cited. [< Latin]

-ibility, var. of -ABILITY: *reducibility.*

i•bis (ī'bis), *n., pl.* **i•bis•es,** (*esp. collectively*) **i•bis.** any of various large wading birds of the family Threskiornithidae, of warm regions, with a long, thin, downward-curved bill.

Ibi'zan hound', *n.* one of a breed of tall, slender hounds with a long, narrow head, large erect ears, and usu. a red and white coat.

-ible, var. of -ABLE, occurring in words borrowed from Latin (*credible; horrible; visible*), or modeled on the Latin type (*reducible*).

-ibly, var. of -ABLY: *credibly; visibly.*

i•bu•pro•fen (ī'byōō prō'fən), *n.* a nonsteroidal anti-inflammatory drug, $C_{13}H_{18}O_2$, used esp. for reducing local pain and swelling.

-ic, 1. a suffix forming adjectives from other parts of speech, occurring orig. in Greek and Latin loanwords (*metallic; poetic; archaic; public*) and, on this model, used as an adjective-forming suffix with the particular senses "having some characteristics of" (opposed to the simple attributive use of the base noun) (*balletic; sophomoric*); "in the style of" (*Byronic; Miltonic*); "pertaining to a family of peoples or languages" (*Finnic; Semitic; Turkic*). **2.** a suffix, specialized in opposition to -OUS, used to show the higher of two valences: *ferric chloride.* **3.** a noun suffix occurring chiefly in loanwords from Greek, where such words were orig. adjectival (*critic; magic; music*).

IC, 1. immediate constituent. **2.** integrated circuit. **3.** intensive care.

I.C., Jesus Christ.

-ical, a combination of -IC and -AL¹, used in forming adjectives from nouns (*rhetorical*); orig. it provided synonyms to adjectives ending in -IC (*poetical*), though certain of these formations are now different in meaning (*economical; historical*).

-ically, a suffix used to form adverbs from adjectives ending in -IC (*terrifically*) and -ICAL (*poetically; magically*).

Ic•a•rus (ik'ər əs), *n.* a youth of Greek myth, the son of Daedalus, who, attempting to escape from Crete with his father on wings of wax and feathers, flew so close to the sun that his wings melted and he plunged to his death in the sea.

ICBM or **I.C.B.M.,** intercontinental ballistic missile.

ice (īs), *n., v.,* **iced, ic•ing.** —*n.* **1.** the solid form of water, produced by freezing; frozen water. **2.** the frozen surface of a body of water. **3.** any substance resembling frozen water. **4.** a frozen dessert made of sweetened water and fruit juice. **5.** *Brit.* ICE CREAM. **6.** icing, as on a cake. **7.** reserve; formality; coldness. **8.** *Slang.* a diamond or diamonds. **9.** *Slang.* **a.** protection money paid to the police by the operator of an illicit business. **b.** a fee paid, as to a theater manager, to secure desirable tickets. **10.** *Slang.* methamphetamine prepared illicitly as crystals for smoking. —*v.t.* **11.** to cover with ice. **12.** to change into ice; freeze. **13.** to cool with ice: *Ice the sodas, please.* **14.** to cover with icing; frost: *to ice a cake.* **15.** to make cold, as if with ice. **16.** *Informal.* **a.** to make sure of; clinch; seal: *to ice a deal.* **b.** to assure success or victory in: *His second goal iced the game.* **17.** *Slang.* to kill; murder. —*v.i.* **18.** to change to ice; freeze. **19.** to become coated with ice (often fol. by *up*). —**Idiom.** **20. break the ice, a.** to overcome initial social awkwardness or formality. **b.** to make an effective beginning. **21. cut no ice,** to fail to impress or influence. **22. ice the puck,** to hit a hockey puck from one's own half of the rink to the far side of the opponent's half. **23. on ice, a.** assured of success or victory. **b.** in a state of abeyance or readiness. **24. (skating) on thin ice,** in a precarious or delicate situation.

ice' age', *n.* **1.** (*often caps.*) the geologically recent Pleistocene Epoch, during which much of the Northern Hemisphere was covered by great ice sheets. **2.** any one of the Permian, Carboniferous, Cambrian, or Precambrian glaciations. Also called **glacial epoch.**

ice' bag', *n.* a waterproof bag filled with ice and applied to a part of the body, as to reduce pain or swelling.

ice•berg (īs'bûrg), *n.* **1.** a large floating mass of ice detached from a glacier and carried out to sea. **2.** an emotionally cold person. —**Idiom.** **3. tip of the iceberg,** the first hint or revelation of a larger or more complex situation, problem, event, etc.

ice'berg let'tuce, *n.* a variety of lettuce having a cabbagelike head of crisp leaves.

ice•blink (īs'blingk'), *n.* a yellowish luminosity near the horizon or on the underside of a cloud caused by the reflection of light from sea ice.

ice•boat (īs'bōt'), *n.* **1.** a vehicle for rapid movement on ice, usu. consisting of a T-shaped frame on runners propelled by sails. **2.** ICEBREAKER (def. 1). —**ice'boat'er,** *n.* —**ice'boat'ing,** *n.*

ice•bound (īs'bound'), *adj.* **1.** held fast or hemmed in by ice: *an icebound ship.* **2.** obstructed or shut off by ice: *an icebound harbor.*

ice•box (īs'boks'), *n.* **1.** an insulated cabinet with a compartment for ice, used for preserving or cooling food and beverages. **2.** a refrigerator.

ice•break•er (īs'brā'kər), *n.* **1.** a ship specially built for breaking navigable passages through ice. **2.** something that eases tension or relieves formality. **3.** a tool or machine for chopping ice into small pieces.

ice•cap (īs'kap'), *n.* a thick cover of ice over an area, sloping in all directions from the center. —**ice'capped',** *adj.*

ice' chest', *n.* an insulated box that holds ice and is used for keeping food or beverages cold.

ice'-cold', *adj.* **1.** extremely cold. **2.** unemotional; passionless.

ice' cream', *n.* a frozen dessert made with cream or milk, sugar, flavoring, and sometimes eggs.

ice′-cream′ cone′, *n.* **1.** a thin, crisp, hollow conical wafer for holding ice cream. **2.** such a cone with ice cream in it.

ice′-cream so′cial, *n. Chiefly Northern, North Midland, and Western U.S.* a social gathering, usu. to raise money for a local church or school, where ice cream is the principal refreshment.

ice′ cube′, *n.* a small cube of ice, as one made in a special tray in a freezer.

ice′ danc′ing, *n.* a form of competitive skating in which a couple performs choreographed movements to music based on traditional ballroom dances and without the use of lifts.

ice·fall (īs′fôl′), *n.* **1.** a jumbled mass of ice in a glacier. **2.** a falling of ice from a glacier, iceberg, etc.

ice′ field′, *n.* a large sheet of floating ice, larger than an ice floe.

ice′ floe′, *n.* FLOE.

ice′ hock′ey, *n.* a game played on ice between two teams of six skaters each, the object being to score goals by shooting a puck into the opponents' cage using a stick with a wooden blade set at an obtuse angle to the shaft.

Ice·land (īs′lənd), *n.* **1.** a large island in the N Atlantic between Greenland and Scandinavia. 272,550 sq. mi. (102,820 sq. km). **2.** a republic including this island and several smaller islands: formerly Danish; independent since 1944. 247,357. *Cap.:* Reykjavik. **—Ice′land·er** (-lan′dər, -lən dər), *n.*

Ice·lan·dic (īs lan′dik), *adj.* **1.** of or pertaining to Iceland, its inhabitants, or their language. **—n. 2.** the North Germanic language of Iceland. *Abbr.:* Icel

Ice′land moss′, *n.* an edible lichen, *Cetraria islandica,* of arctic regions.

Ice′land spar′, *n.* a transparent variety of calcite that is double-refracting and is used as a polarizer.

ice′ milk′, *n.* a frozen dessert made with skim milk.

ice′ nee′dle, *n.* an acicular ice crystal afloat, in great numbers, in the atmosphere.

ice′ pack′, *n.* **1.** PACK ICE. **2.** ICE BAG.

ice′ pick′, *n.* a sharp-pointed tool for chipping ice.

ice′ plant′, *n.* a low-growing Old World plant, *Mesembryanthemum crystallinum,* of the carpetweed family, having tiny glistening sacs on its fleshy, edible leaves.

ice′ point′, *n.* the temperature at which a mixture of ice and air-saturated water at a pressure of one atmosphere is in equilibrium, represented by 32°F (0°C). Compare STEAM POINT.

ice′ sheet′, *n.* **1.** a thick sheet of ice covering an extensive area for a long period of time. **2.** a glacier covering a large fraction of a continent.

ice′ shelf′, *n.* an ice sheet projecting into coastal waters so that the end floats.

ice′ show′, *n.* an entertainment in which a company of ice skaters exhibit their skills to musical accompaniment.

ice′ skate′, *n.* **1.** a shoe fitted with a metal blade for skating on ice. **2.** SKATE¹ (def. 3). **—ice′-skate′,** *v.i.,* **-skat·ed, -skat·ing. —ice′ skat′er,** *n.*

ice′ storm′, *n.* a storm of freezing rain and widespread glaze formation.

ice′ wa′ter, *n.* **1.** ice-cold water. **2.** melted ice.

I Ching (ē′ jing′), *n.* an ancient Chinese book of divination, in which 64 pairs of trigrams are shown with various interpretations.

ich·neu·mon (ik nōō′mən, -nyōō′-), *n.* **1.** a slender, long-tailed mongoose, *Herpestes ichneumon,* of N Africa and S Europe, believed by the ancient Egyptians to devour crocodile eggs. **2.** ICHNEUMON FLY.

ichneu′mon fly′, *n.* any of numerous wasplike insects of the family Ichneumonidae, the larvae of which are parasites of the larvae and pupae of many insects, esp. moths and butterflies.

ich·nol·o·gy (ik nol′ə jē), *n.* the branch of paleontology dealing with the study of fossilized tracks, trails, burrows, and other trace fossils. **—ich′no·log′i·cal** (-nl oj′i kəl), *adj.*

ichthyo-, a combining form meaning "fish": *ichthyology.* Also, *esp. before a vowel,* **ichthy-.**

ich·thy·o·fau·na (ik′thē ə fô′nə), *n., pl.* **-nas, -nae** (-nē). (*used with a sing. or pl. v.*) the indigenous fishes of a region or habitat.

ich·thy·ol·o·gy (ik′thē ol′ə jē), *n.* the branch of zoology dealing with fishes. **—ich′thy·o·log′ic** (-ə loj′ik), ich′thy·o·log′i·cal,** *adj.* **—ich′thy·o·log′i·cal·ly,** *adv.* **—ich′thy·ol′o·gist,** *n.*

ich·thy·or·nis (ik′thē ôr′nis), *n.* any ternlike bird of the extinct Cretaceous genus *Ichthyornis,* having reptilelike vertebrae.

ich·thy·o·saur (ik′thē ə sôr′), *n.* any large fishlike reptile of the extinct order Ichthyosauria, having four flippers and a prominent caudal fin. **—ich′thy·o·sau′ri·an,** *adj.,* **n. —ich′thy·o·sau′roid,** *adj.*

-ician, a suffix forming nouns denoting occupations: *beautician.*

i·ci·cle (ī′si kəl), *n.* **1.** a pendent, tapering mass of ice formed by the freezing of dripping water. **2.** something resembling this, as a thin strip of silver foil used as a Christmas tree decoration. **3.** a cold, unemotional person. **—i′ci·cled,** *adj.*

i·ci·ly (ī′sə lē), *adv.* in an icy manner; coldly. **—i′ci·ness,** *n.*

ic·ing (ī′sing), *n.* **1.** a sweet mixture, as of sugar, liquid, butter, and flavoring, used as a creamy or hard coating on cakes, cookies, etc.; frosting. **2.** *Meteorol.* a coating of ice on a solid object. **3.** the freezing of atmospheric moisture on the surface of an aircraft. **4.** an infraction in ice

hockey called when the puck is iced and next touched by an opponent other than the goalkeeper.

ick (ik), *interj.* (used as an expression of distaste or repugnance.)

ick·y (ik′ē), *adj.,* **ick·i·er, ick·i·est.** *Informal.* **1.** repulsive or distasteful. **2.** excessively sweet or sentimental. **3.** unsophisticated or old-fashioned. **4.** sticky; viscid. **—ick′i·ness,** *n.*

i·con (ī′kon), *n.* **1.** a picture, image, or other representation. **2.** an image of Christ, a saint, etc., usu. painted on a wooden panel or done in mosaics and treated as sacred in the Eastern Church. **3.** a sign or representation that stands for something by virtue of a resemblance or analogy to it; symbol. **4.** a small graphic image on a computer screen representing a disk drive, a file, or a software command, as a wastebasket that can be used to delete a file. **—i·con′ic,** *adj.* **—i·con′i·cal·ly,** *adv.*

icono-, a combining form meaning "image," "likeness": *iconology.*

i·con·o·clast (ī kon′ə klast′), *n.* **1.** a person who attacks cherished beliefs or traditional institutions as being based on error or superstition. **2.** a breaker or destroyer of images, esp. those set up for religious veneration. **—i·con·o·clas′tic,** *adj.* **—i·con·o·clas′ti·cal·ly,** *adv.*

i·con·og·ra·phy (ī′kə nog′rə fē), *n., pl.* **-phies. 1.** symbolic representation, esp. the conventional meanings attached to an image. **2.** subject matter in the visual arts, esp. with reference to the conventions of treating a subject in artistic representation. **3.** the study or analysis of subject matter and its meaning in the visual arts; iconology. **4.** a representation or group of representations of a person, place, or thing. **—i′co·nog′ra·pher,** *n.* **—i·con′o·graph′ic** (ī kon′ə graf′ik), i·con′o·graph′i·cal,** *adj.* **—i·con′o·graph′i·cal·ly,** *adv.*

i·co·nol·o·gy (ī′kə nol′ə jē), *n.* **1.** the study of symbols or images and their significance. **2.** the study of icons or symbolic representations. **—i·con·o·log′i·cal** (ī kon′l oj′i kəl), *adj.* **—i·co·nol′o·gist,** *n.*

i·co·nos·ta·sis (ī′kə nos′tə sis), *n., pl.* **-ses** (-sēz′). a partition or screen on which icons are placed, separating the sanctuary from the main part of an Eastern church.

i·co·sa·he·dron (ī kō′sə hē′drən, ī kos′ə-), *n., pl.* **-drons, -dra** (-drə). a solid figure having 20 faces. **—i·co′sa·he′dral,** *adj.*

-ics, a suffix of nouns that denote a body of facts, knowledge, principles, etc., usu. corresponding to adjectives ending in -ic or -ical: *ethics; physics; politics; tactics.*

ICSH, interstitial-cell-stimulating hormone: a pituitary hormone that stimulates testosterone production in the interstitial cells of the testes: chemically identical with luteinizing hormone.

ic·ter·ic (ik ter′ik) also **ic·ter′i·cal,** *adj.* pertaining to or affected with icterus; jaundiced.

ic·ter·us (ik′tər əs), *n.* JAUNDICE (def. 1).

ic·tus (ik′təs), *n., pl.* **-tus·es, -tus. 1.** rhythmical or metrical stress in verse. **2. a.** an epileptic seizure. **b.** a stroke, esp. a cerebrovascular accident. **—ic′tic,** *adj.*

ICU, intensive care unit.

i·cy (ī′sē), *adj.,* **i·ci·er, i·ci·est. 1.** made of, full of, or covered with ice. **2.** resembling ice. **3.** very cold. **4.** lacking warmth of feeling; aloof.

id (id), *n. Psychoanal.* the part of the psyche that is the source of unconscious and instinctive impulses that seek satisfaction in accordance with the pleasure principle. Compare EGO (def. 2), SUPEREGO.

ID (ī′dē′), *n., pl.,* **ID's, IDs,** *v.,* **ID'd or IDed or ID'ed, ID'ing or ID·ing. 1.** a means of identification, as a document containing information regarding the bearer's identity. **—v.t. 2.** to identify. **3.** to issue an ID to: *Go to the admissions office if you haven't been ID'd yet.*

ID, Also, **Id.** Idaho.

I'd (īd), contraction of *I would* or *I had.*

-id¹, a suffix of nouns that have the general sense "offspring of, descendant of," occurring orig. in loanwords from Greek (*Atreid; Nereid*), and used in English on the Greek model, esp. in names of dynasties, with the dynasty's founder as the base noun (*Abbasid; Fatimid*), and in names of periodic meteor showers, with the base noun usu. denoting the constellation or other celestial object in which the shower appears (*Perseid*).

-id², a suffix occurring in English derivatives of modern Latin taxonomic names, esp. zoological families and classes; such derivatives are usu. nouns denoting a single member of the taxon or adjectives with the sense "pertaining to" the taxon: *arachnid; canid.*

-id³, var. of IDE: *lipid.*

-id⁴, a suffix occurring in descriptive adjectives borrowed from Latin, often corresponding to nouns ending in -or: *humid; pallid.* [< L -*idus*]

Id., Idaho.

id., idem.

I.D., 1. identification. **2.** identity. **3.** Intelligence Department.

-ida, a suffix of the names of zoological orders and classes: *Arachnida.*

-idae, a suffix of the names of zoological families: *Canidae.*

I·da·ho (ī′də hō′), *n.* a state in the NW United States. 1,189,251; 83,557 sq. mi. (216,415 sq. km). *Cap.:* Boise. *Abbr.:* ID, Ida.

ID bracelet, *n.* a bracelet, usu. of metal links, having an identification plate for the name of the wearer.

ID card, *n.* a card giving identifying data about a person, as name, age, hair color, etc., and often bearing a photograph.

-ide or **-id,** a suffix used in the names of chemical compounds: *bromide.*

i·de·a (ī dē′ə, ī dē′ə′), *n.* **1.** any conception existing in the mind as a result of mental understanding, awareness, or activity. **2.** a thought, conception, or notion. **3.** an impression: *Give me a general idea of what happened.* **4.** an opinion, view, or belief. **5.** a plan of action; intention: *with the idea of becoming an engineer.* **6.** a purpose or guiding principle: *What was the idea of that?* **7.** a groundless supposition; fantasy. **8.** *Philos.* **a.** a concept developed by the mind. **b.** a conception of what is desirable or ought to be; ideal. **c.** (*cap.*) *Platonism.* Also called **form.** an archetype or pattern of which the individual objects in any natural class are imperfect copies and from which they derive their being. **9.** a musical theme or figure. —**i•de′a•less,** *adj.*

i•de•al (ī dē′əl, ī dēl′), *n.* **1.** a conception of something in its perfection. **2.** a standard of perfection or excellence. **3.** a person or thing conceived as embodying such a conception or standard and taken as a model for imitation. **4.** an ultimate object or aim of endeavor, esp. one of high or noble character: *to compromise one's ideals.* **5.** something that exists only in the imagination. —*adj.* **6.** conceived as constituting a standard of perfection or excellence: *ideal beauty.* **7.** regarded as perfect of its kind: *an ideal spot for a home.* **8.** existing only in the imagination; not real or actual. **9.** advantageous; excellent; best: *It would be ideal if you could stay.* **10.** based upon an ideal or ideals: *the ideal theory of numbers.* **11.** *Philos.* **a.** pertaining to a possible state of affairs considered as highly desirable. **b.** pertaining to or of the nature of idealism.

i•de•al•ism (ī dē′ə liz′əm), *n.* **1.** the cherishing or pursuit of high or noble principles, purposes, or goals. **2.** the practice of idealizing. **3.** something idealized; an ideal representation. **4.** treatment of subject matter, as in art, in which a mental conception of beauty or form is stressed. **5.** any philosophical system or theory that maintains that the real is of the nature of thought or that the object of external perception consists of ideas.

i•de•al•ist (ī dē′ə list), *n.* **1.** a person who cherishes or pursues high or noble principles, purposes, or goals. **2.** a visionary or impractical person. **3.** a person who represents things as they might or should be rather than as they are. **4.** a writer or artist who treats subjects imaginatively. **5.** an adherent of the doctrines of idealism. —*adj.* **6.** idealistic.

i•de•al•is•tic (ī dē′ə lis′tik, ī′dē ə-), *adj.* of or pertaining to idealism or idealists. —**i•de′al•is′ti•cal•ly,** *adv.*

i•de•al•ize (ī dē′ə līz′), *v.*, **-ized, -iz•ing.** —*v.t.* **1.** to consider or represent as having qualities of ideal perfection or excellence. **2.** to represent in an ideal form or character. —*v.i.* **3.** to represent something in an ideal form. —**i•de′al•i•za′tion,** *n.* —**i•de′al•iz′er,** *n.*

i•de•al•ly (ī dē′ə lē), *adv.* **1.** in accordance with an ideal; perfectly. **2.** in theory or principle. **3.** in idea, thought, or imagination.

i•de•ate (ī′dē āt′), *v.*, **-at•ed, -at•ing.** —*v.t.* **1.** to form an idea, conception, or image of. —*v.i.* **2.** to form ideas or images; think. —**i•de′a•tive** (-ə tiv), *adj.* —**i′de•a′tion,** *n.*

i•de•a•tion•al (ī′dē ā′shə nl), *adj.* of or involving ideas or concepts. —**i′de•a′tion•al•ly,** *adv.*

i•dée fixe (ē dā fēks′), *n.*, *pl.* **i•dées fixes** (ē dā fēks′). a persistent or obsessing idea, often delusional, that in extreme form can be a symptom of psychosis. Also called **fixed idea.**

i•dem (ī′dem, id′em), *pron.*, *adj.* the same as previously given or mentioned. [< Latin]

i•den•ti•cal (ī den′ti kəl, i den′-), *adj.* **1.** similar or alike in every way. **2.** being the very same; selfsame. **3.** agreeing exactly: *identical opinions.* —**i•den′ti•cal•ly,** *adv.* —**i•den′ti•cal•ness,** *n.*

iden′tical twin′, *n.* one of a pair of twins who develop from a single fertilized ovum and therefore have the same genotype, are of the same sex, and usu. resemble each other closely. Compare FRATERNAL TWIN.

i•den•ti•fi•ca•tion (ī den′tə fi kā′shən, i den′-), *n.* **1.** an act or instance of identifying; the state of being identified. **2.** something, as a birth certificate or identity card, that identifies one. **3.** acceptance as one's own of the values and interests of a social group. **4.** **a.** a process by which one ascribes to oneself the qualities or characteristics of another person. **b.** perception of another as an extension of oneself.

identifica′tion brace′let, *n.* ID BRACELET.

identifica′tion card′, *n.* ID CARD.

i•den•ti•fy (ī den′tə fī′, i den′-), *v.*, **-fied, -fy•ing.** —*v.t.* **1.** to recognize or establish as being a particular person or thing; verify the identity of. **2.** to serve as a means of identification for. **3.** to regard or treat as the same or identical; make identical. **4.** to associate, as in name, interest, or action: *They identified him with the old regime.* **5.** to determine to what group (a given biological specimen) belongs. **6.** to associate (one or oneself) with another person or a group by identification. —*v.i.* **7.** to experience psychological identification: *The audience identified with the main character.* —**i•den′ti•fi′a•ble,** *adj.* —**i•den′ti•fi′er,** *n.*

i•den•ti•ty (ī den′ti tē, i den′-), *n.*, *pl.* **-ties.** **1.** the state or fact of remaining the same one, as under varying aspects or conditions. **2.** the condition of being oneself or itself, and not another: *He doubted his own identity.* **3.** condition or character as to who a person or what a thing is: *a case of mistaken identity.* **4.** the state or fact of being the same one as described. **5.** the sense of self, providing sameness and continuity in personality over time. **6.** exact likeness in nature or qualities: *an identity of interests.*

iden′tity cri′sis, *n.* **1.** a state or period of psychological distress, occurring esp. in adolescence, when a person seeks a clearer sense of self and an acceptable role in society. **2.** confusion as to goals and priorities: *The company is undergoing an identity crisis.*

id•e•o•gram (id′ē ə gram′, ī′dē-), *n.* a written symbol that represents an idea or object directly rather than a particular word or speech sound. Also **ideograph.**

i•de•ol•o•gist (ī′dē ol′ə jist, id′ē-), *n.* **1.** a specialist in ideology. **2.** a person who deals with systems of ideas. **3.** a person advocating a particular ideology. **4.** a visionary.

i•de•ol•o•gy (ī′dē ol′ə jē, id′ē-), *n.*, *pl.* **-gies.** **1.** the body of doctrine or thought that guides an individual, social movement, institution, or group. **2.** such a body of doctrine or thought forming a political or social program, along with the devices for putting it into operation. **3.** theorizing of a visionary or impractical nature. **4.** the study of the nature and origin of ideas. **5.** a philosophical system that derives ideas exclusively from sensation. —**i′de•o•log′ic** (-ə loj′ik), **i′de•o•log′i•cal,** *adj.* —**i′de•o•log′i•cal•ly,** *adv.*

i•de•o•mo•tor (ī′dē ə mō′tər, id′ē ə-), *adj.* of or pertaining to an involuntary body movement evoked by an idea or thought process rather than by sensory stimulation. —**i′de•o•mo′tion,** *n.*

ides (īdz), *n.* (*often cap.*) (*used with a sing. or pl. v.*) (in the ancient Roman calendar) the 15th day of March, May, July, or October, or the 13th day of the other months.

-idine, a suffix used to form names of organic chemical compounds, as amino derivatives (*toluidine; xylidine*) and nucleosides (*thymidine*).

idio-, a combining form meaning "proper to one," "peculiar": *idiomorphic.*

id•i•o•cy (id′ē ə sē), *n.*, *pl.* **-cies.** **1.** utterly senseless or foolish behavior; a stupid or foolish act or statement. **2.** the state of being an idiot; extreme mental deficiency.

id•i•o•lect (id′ē ə lekt′), *n.* a person's individual speech pattern. Compare DIALECT (def. 1). —**id′i•o•lec′tal,** *adj.*

id•i•om (id′ē əm), *n.* **1.** an expression whose meaning is not predictable from the usual grammatical rules of a language or from the usual meanings of its constituent elements, as *kick the bucket* "to die." **2.** a language, dialect, or style of speaking peculiar to a people.

id•i•o•mat•ic (id′ē ə mat′ik), *adj.* **1.** characteristic of a particular language; conforming to the usual manner of expression in a language. **2.** containing or using many idioms. **3.** having a distinct style or character, esp. in the arts: *an idiomatic composer.* —**id′i•o•mat′i•cal•ly,** *adv.* —**id′i•o•mat′i•cal•ness, id′i•o•ma•tic′i•ty** (-ō mə tis′i tē), *n.*

id•i•op•a•thy (id′ē op′ə thē), *n.*, *pl.* **-thies.** a disease not preceded or occasioned by any known morbid condition.

id•i•o•syn•cra•sy (id′ē ə sing′krə sē, -sin′-), *n.*, *pl.* **-sies.** **1.** a characteristic, habit, mannerism, etc., that is peculiar to or distinctive of an individual. **2.** the physical or mental constitution peculiar to an individual. **3.** a peculiarity of the physical or mental constitution, esp. a sensitivity to drugs, food, etc. —**id′i•o•syn•crat′ic** (-ō sin krat′ik, -sing-), *adj.* —**id′i•o•syn•crat′i•cal•ly,** *adv.*

id•i•ot (id′ē ət), *n.* **1.** an utterly stupid or foolish person. **2.** a person of the lowest order in a former classification of mental retardation.

id•i•ot•ic (id′ē ot′ik), *adj.* **1.** of or characteristic of an idiot. **2.** senselessly foolish or stupid. Sometimes, **id′i•ot′i•cal.** —**id′i•ot′i•cal•ly,** *adv.* —**id′i•ot′i•cal•ness,** *n.*

id•i•ot•ism (id′ē ə tiz′əm), *n.* IDIOCY.

id•i•ot sa•vant (id′ē ət sə vänt′, sa-; *Fr.* ē dyō SA VÄN′), *n.*, *pl.* **idiot savants,** *Fr.* **id•iots sa•vants** (ē dyō SA VÄN′). a mentally defective person with an exceptional skill or talent in a special field, as a highly developed ability to play music or to do arithmetic calculations.

i•dle (īd′l), *adj.*, **i•dler, i•dlest,** *v.*, **i•dled, i•dling,** *n.* —*adj.* **1.** not working or active; unemployed; doing nothing. **2.** not filled with activity: *idle hours.* **3.** not in use or operation: *idle machinery.* **4.** habitually doing nothing or avoiding work; lazy. **5.** of no real worth, importance, or purpose: *idle talk.* **6.** having no basis or reason; baseless; groundless: *idle fears.* **7.** frivolous; vain: *idle pleasures.* **8.** meaningless; senseless: *idle threats.* —*v.i.* **9.** to pass time doing nothing. **10.** to move or loiter aimlessly. **11.** (of a machine, engine, or mechanism) to operate at a low speed, disengaged from the load. —*v.t.* **12.** to pass (time) doing nothing (often fol. by *away*): *to idle away the afternoon.* **13.** to cause to be idle: *The strike idled many workers.* **14.** to cause (a machine, engine, or mechanism) to idle. —*n.* **15.** the state or quality of being idle. **16.** the state of a machine, engine, or mechanism that is idling: *an engine at idle.* —**i′dle•ness,** *n.* —**i′dler,** *n.* —**i′dly,** *adv.*

i′dle wheel′, *n.* a wheel for transmitting power and motion between a driving and a driven part, either by friction or by means of teeth.

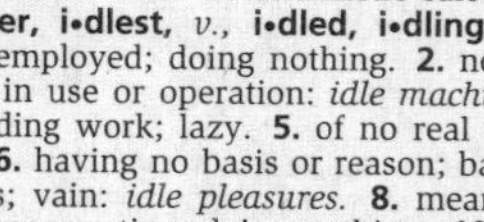

idle wheel

i•dol (īd′l), *n.* **1.** an image or other object representing a deity and worshiped as such. **2.** (in the Bible) a deity other than God. **3.** a person or thing devotedly or excessively admired. **4.** a mere image of something, visible but without substance. **5.** a false notion; fallacy.

i•dol•a•ter (ī dol′ə tər), *n.* **1.** a worshiper of idols. **2.** a person who is an immoderate admirer; devotee.

i•dol•a•trous (ī dol′ə trəs), *adj.* **1.** worshiping idols. **2.** given to excessive admiration or devotion. **3.** of or pertaining to idolatry. —**i·dol′a·trous·ly,** *adv.* —**i·dol′a·trous·ness,** *n.*

i·dol·a·try (ī dol′ə trē), *n., pl.* **-tries. 1.** the religious worship of idols. **2.** excessive admiration or devotion.

i·dol·ize (īd′l īz′), *v.,* **-ized, -iz·ing.** —*v.t.* **1.** to regard with adoration or devotion. **2.** to worship as a god. —*v.i.* **3.** to practice idolatry. —**i′·dol·i·za′tion,** *n.* —**i′dol·iz′er,** *n.*

Id·u·mae·a or **Id·u·me·a** (id′yŏŏ mē′ə), *n.* Greek name of EDOM. —**Id′u·mae′an,** *adj.*

i·dyll or **i·dyl** (īd′l), *n.* **1.** a poem or prose composition describing pastoral scenes or events or any charmingly simple episode or picturesque scene. **2.** material suitable for such a work. **3.** a long narrative poem on a major theme: *Tennyson's Idylls of the King.* **4.** an episode or scene of idyllic charm. **5.** a brief romantic affair.

i·dyl·lic (ī dil′ik), *adj.* **1.** charmingly simple or rustic; characterized by peaceful contentment. **2.** of or characteristic of an idyll. —**i·dyl′li·cal·ly,** *adv.*

IE or **I.E., 1.** Indo-European. **2.** Industrial Engineer.

i.e., that is. [< Latin *id est*]

-ier[1], var. of -ER[1], usu. in nouns designating trades: *collier; clothier; furrier; glazier.*

-ier[2], a noun suffix occurring mainly in loanwords from French, often similar in meaning to -EER, with which it is etymologically identical (*brigadier; financier*); it is also found in an older group of loanwords with stress on the initial syllable (*barrier; courier*) and in more recent borrowings without the final *r* sound (*dossier; hotelier*).

if (if), *conj.* **1.** in case that; granting or supposing that; on condition that: *I'll go if you do.* **2.** even though: *an enthusiastic if small audience.* **3.** whether: *She asked if I knew Spanish.* **4.** (used to introduce an exclamatory phrase): *If only Dad could see me now!* **5.** that: *I'm sorry if you don't agree.* **6.** a supposition; uncertain possibility. **7.** a condition or stipulation: *There are too many ifs in his agreement.* —**Idiom. 8. ifs, ands, or buts,** qualifications or excuses.

if or **IF,** intermediate frequency.

iff, *Math.* if and only if.

if·fy (if′ē), *adj.,* **-fi·er, -fi·est.** full of unresolved points or questions: *an iffy situation.* —**if′fi·ness,** *n.*

I formation (ī), *n.* a football offensive alignment in which the backs are positioned in line directly behind the quarterback.

-iformes, a combining form used in taxonomic names of animals, esp. orders of birds and fish, meaning "having the form of": *Beryciformes.*

-ify, a verbal suffix based on and having the same meanings as -FY, used in English derivatives and in loanwords from French formed in a parallel fashion: *classify; intensify; solidify.*

ig·loo (ig′lōō), *n., pl.* **-loos.** an Eskimo dwelling usu. built of blocks of hard snow and shaped like a dome.

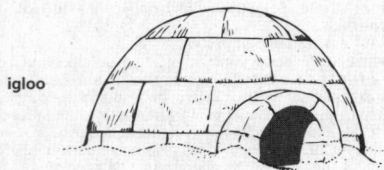

igloo

Igna′tius of Loyo′la, *n.* **Saint,** LOYOLA, Saint Ignatius.

ig·ne·ous (ig′nē əs), *adj.* **1.** produced under conditions involving intense heat, as rocks of volcanic origin or rocks crystallized from molten magma. **2.** of, pertaining to, or characteristic of fire.

ig·nis fat·u·us (ig′nis fach′ōō əs), *n., pl.* **ig·nes fat·u·i** (ig′nēz fach′ōō ī′). Also called **will-o'-the-wisp.** a flickering phosphorescent light seen at night chiefly over marshy ground and believed to be due to spontaneous combustion of gas from decomposed organic matter. **2.** something deluding or misleading.

ig·nite (ig nīt′), *v.,* **-nit·ed, -nit·ing.** —*v.t.* **1.** to set on fire; cause to burn. **2.** *Chem.* to heat intensely; roast. **3.** to arouse; kindle. —*v.i.* **4.** to catch fire; begin to burn. —**ig·nit′a·ble, ig·nit′i·ble,** *adj.* —**ig·nit′a·bil′i·ty, ig·nit′i·bil′i·ty,** *n.*

ig·ni·tion (ig nish′ən), *n.* **1.** the act of igniting or the state of being ignited. **2.** a means or device for igniting. **3.** (in an internal-combustion engine) the process, spark, or switch that ignites the fuel.

ig·no·ble (ig nō′bəl), *adj.* **1.** of low character; mean; base: *ignoble purposes.* **2.** of humble descent or rank. —**ig′no·bil′i·ty, ig·no′ble·ness,** *n.* —**ig·no′bly,** *adv.*

ig·no·min·i·ous (ig′nə min′ē əs), *adj.* **1.** marked by or attended with ignominy; discreditable; humiliating: *an ignominious retreat.* **2.** bearing or deserving ignominy; contemptible. —**ig′no·min′i·ous·ly,** *adv.* —**ig′no·min′i·ous·ness,** *n.*

ig·no·min·y (ig′nə min′ē, ig nom′ə nē), *n., pl.* **-min·ies. 1.** personal disgrace; dishonor. **2.** shameful or dishonorable quality or conduct.

ig·no·ra·mus (ig′nə rā′məs, -ram′əs), *n., pl.* **-mus·es.** an extremely ignorant person.

ig·no·rance (ig′nər əns), *n.* **1.** the state or fact of being ignorant; lack

of knowledge or learning. —**Saying. 2.** Ignorance of the law is no excuse, lack of knowledge of the law does not absolve one of guilt.

ig·no·rant (ig′nər ənt), *adj.* **1.** lacking in knowledge or training; unlearned. **2.** lacking special knowledge or information: *ignorant of physics.* **3.** uninformed; unaware. **4.** showing lack of knowledge or training. —**ig′no·rant·ly,** *adv.* —**ig′no·rant·ness,** *n.*

ig·nore (ig nôr′, -nōr′), *v.t.,* **-nored, -nor·ing. 1.** to refrain from noticing or recognizing: *to ignore insulting remarks.* **2.** (of a grand jury) to reject (a bill of indictment), esp. on grounds of insufficient evidence.

i·gua·na (i gwä′nə), *n., pl.* **-nas.** any lizard of the New World genus *Iguana,* esp. *I. iguana,* with a large stout body and a fringe from neck to tail.

i·gua·nid (i gwä′nid), *n.* **1.** any lizard of the family Iguanidae, typically with a long tail and, in the male, a bright expandable throat patch. —*adj.* **2.** belonging or pertaining to the iguanids.

i·guan·o·don (i gwä′nə don′, i gwan′ə-), *n.* a bipedal, plant-eating dinosaur, of the genus *Iguanodon,* that inhabited Europe in the early Cretaceous Period.

I′ have′ a dream′, a phrase in a speech by Martin Luther King, Jr. during a civil rights march on Washington on August 28, 1963, expressing hope for racial equality in the United States.

IHS, 1. Jesus. [< Late Latin < Greek: partial transliteration of the first three letters of *Iēsoûs* Jesus] **2.** Jesus Savior of Men. [< Medieval Latin *Iēsus Hominum Salvātor*] **3.** in this sign (the cross) shalt thou conquer. [< Latin *In Hōc Signō Vincēs*] **4.** in this (cross) is salvation. [< Latin *In Hōc Salūs*]

i·i·wi (ē ē′wē), *n., pl.* **-wis.** a Hawaiian honeycreeper, *Vestiaria coccinea,* having a red body and deeply curved bill.

Ike (īk), *n.* nickname for Dwight D. Eisenhower.

i·ke·ba·na (ik′ə bä′nə, ē′kä-), *n.* the Japanese art of arranging flowers.

IL, Illinois.

il-[1], var. of IN-[2] (by assimilation) before *l: illation.*

il-[2], var. of IN-[3] (by assimilation) before *l: illogical.*

-ile[1], var. of -ABLE in words borrowed from Latin, orig. suffixed to verb stems ending in a labial consonant (*labile; nubile*), later added to other verb stems (*agile; docile; facile; fragile*). Compare -TILE.

-ile[2], a suffix of adjectives borrowed from Latin, meaning "pertaining to or characteristic of" the class of persons named by the stem: *infantile; juvenile; puerile; virile.*

-ile[3], a suffix used to form words denoting the value of a statistical variable that divides a distribution into a given number of equal-sized groups, as specified by the initial element of the word: *decile; percentile.*

il·e·ac[1] (il′ē ak′), *adj.* of or pertaining to the ileum.

il·e·ac[2] (il′ē ak′), *adj.* of or pertaining to ileus.

ileo-, a combining form representing ILEUM: *ileostomy.*

il·e·um (il′ē əm), *n.* **1.** the third and lowest division of the small intestine, extending from the jejunum to the large intestine. **2.** the anterior portion of the arthropod hindgut. —**il′e·al,** *adj.*

il·e·us (il′ē əs), *n.* intestinal obstruction characterized by lack of peristalsis and leading to severe colicky pain and vomiting.

i·lex[1] (ī′leks), *n.* HOLM OAK.

i·lex[2] (ī′leks), *n.* HOLLY (def. 1).

Il·i·ad (il′ē əd), *n.* **1.** (*italics*) a Greek epic poem describing the siege of Troy, ascribed to Homer. **2.** (*often l.c.*) a long series of woes and travails.

I′ like′ Ike′, a political slogan in support of Dwight D. Eisenhower.

ilio-, a combining form representing ILIUM: *iliofemoral.*

il·i·um (il′ē əm), *n., pl.* **il·i·a** (il′ē ə). the uppermost of the three bones of each half of the vertebrate pelvic girdle; in humans, the broad upper portion of each hipbone.

Il·i·um (il′ē əm), *n.* Latin name of ancient TROY.

ilk[1] (ilk), *n.* **1.** family, class, or kind: *he and all his ilk.* —**Idiom. 2.** of that ilk, **a.** (in Scotland) of the same family name or place. **b.** of the same class or kind.

ilk[2] (ilk), *pron. Chiefly Scot.* each.

ill (il), *adj.,* **worse, worst,** *n., adv.* —*adj.* **1.** of unsound physical or mental health; unwell; sick. **2.** objectionable; faulty: *ill manners.* **3.** hostile; unkindly: *ill feeling.* **4.** evil; wicked: *of ill repute.* **5.** unfavorable; adverse: *ill fortune.* **6.** of inferior worth or ability: *an ill example of scholarship.* **7.** an unfavorable opinion or statement: *I can speak no ill of her.* **8.** harm or injury: *His remarks did much ill.* **9.** trouble; misfortune: *Many ills befell him.* **10.** evil: *the difference between good and ill.* **11.** sickness; disease. —*adv.* **12.** unsatisfactorily; poorly: *It ill befits a man to betray old friends.* **13.** in a hostile or unfriendly manner. **14.** unfavorably; unfortunately. **15.** with displeasure or offense. **16.** faultily; improperly. **17.** with difficulty or inconvenience: *an expense we can ill afford.* —**Idiom. 18. ill at ease,** uncomfortable; uneasy.

I′ll (īl), contraction of *I will.*

ill′-advised′, *adj.* acting or done without due consideration; imprudent: *an ill-advised remark.* —**ill′-advis′edly,** *adv.*

il·la·tion (i lā′shən), *n.* **1.** the act of inferring. **2.** an inference; conclusion.

ill′-bred′, *adj.* showing lack of good social breeding; unmannerly.

il·le·gal (i lē′gəl), *adj.* **1.** forbidden by law or statute. **2.** contrary to or forbidden by official rules or regulations. —*n.* **3.** an illegal immigrant. —**il·le·gal·ly,** *adv.*

il•le•gal•i•ty (il′ē gal′i tē), *n., pl.* **-ties. 1.** illegal condition or quality; unlawfulness. **2.** an illegal act.

il•leg•i•ble (i lej′ə bəl), *adj.* not legible; impossible or hard to read. —**il•leg′i•bil′i•ty, il•leg′i•ble•ness,** *n.* —**il•leg′i•bly,** *adv.*

il•le•git•i•ma•cy (il′i jit′ə mə sē), *n., pl.* **-cies.** the state or quality of being illegitimate.

il•le•git•i•mate (il′i jit′ə mit), *adj.* **1.** born of parents who are not married to each other. **2.** not sanctioned by usage or custom. **3.** unlawful; illegal. **4.** irregular; eccentric. —**il′le•git′i•mate•ly,** *adv.*

ill′-fat′ed, *adj.* **1.** destined to an unhappy fate: *an ill-fated voyage.* **2.** bringing bad fortune.

ill′-fa′vored, *adj.* **1.** unpleasant in appearance; homely or ugly. **2.** offensive; objectionable.

ill′-got′ten, *adj.* acquired by dishonest, improper, or evil means: *ill-gotten gains.*

ill′-hu′mor, *n.* a disagreeable or surly mood. —**ill′-hu′mored,** *adj.* —**ill′-hu′mored•ly,** *adv.* —**ill′-hu′mored•ness,** *n.*

il•lib•er•al (i lib′ər əl, i lib′rəl), *adj.* narrow-minded; bigoted. —**il•lib′er•al′i•ty, il•lib′er•al•ness, il•lib′er•al•ism,** *n.* —**il•lib′er•al•ly,** *adv.*

il•lic•it (i lis′it), *adj.* **1.** not legally permitted; unlawful. **2.** disapproved of or not permitted for moral or ethical reasons. —**il•lic′it•ly,** *adv.*

il•lim•it•a•ble (i lim′i tə bəl), *adj.* not limitable; boundless. —**il•lim′it•a•bil′i•ty, il•lim′it•a•ble•ness,** *n.* —**il•lim′it•a•bly,** *adv.*

Il•li•nois (il′ə noi′; *sometimes* -noiz′), *n.* **1.** a state in the central United States. 11,846,544; 56,400 sq. mi. (146,075 sq. km). *Cap.:* Springfield. *Abbr.:* IL, Ill. **2.** a river flowing SW from NE Illinois to the Mississippi River: connected by a canal with Lake Michigan. 273 mi. (440 km) long. **3. a.** (*used with a pl. v.*) the members of a group of American Indian tribes formerly occupying parts of Illinois and adjoining regions westward. **b.** the extinct Algonquian language of these people. —**Pronunciation.** The pronunciation of ILLINOIS with a final (z), which occurs chiefly among less educated speakers, is least common in Illinois itself, increasing in frequency with distance from the state.

il•lit•er•a•cy (i lit′ər ə sē), *n., pl.* **-cies. 1.** a lack of ability to read and write. **2.** the state of being illiterate. **3.** a mistake in writing or speaking.

il•lit•er•ate (i lit′ər it), *adj.* **1.** unable to read and write. **2.** having or demonstrating little education. **3.** showing lack of culture. **4.** displaying a marked lack of knowledge in a particular field: *musically illiterate.* —*n.* **5.** an illiterate person. —**il•lit′er•ate•ly,** *adv.*

ill′-man′nered, *adj.* having bad or poor manners; impolite.

ill′-na′tured, *adj.* having or showing an unpleasant disposition. —**ill′-na′tured•ly,** *adv.* —**ill′-na′tured•ness,** *n.*

ill•ness (il′nis), *n.* unhealthy condition; poor health; indisposition; sickness.

il•log•i•cal (i loj′i kəl), *adj.* not logical; contrary to or disregardful of the rules of logic; unreasoning: *an illogical reply.* —**il•log′i•cal•ness,** *n.* —**il•log′i•cal•ly,** *adv.*

ill′-treat′, *v.t.* to treat badly; maltreat; abuse. —**ill′-treat′ment,** *n.*

il•lume (i lo͞om′), *v.t.,* **-lumed, -lum•ing.** to illuminate.

il•lu•mi•nant (i lo͞o′mə nənt), *n.* an illuminating agent or material.

il•lu•mi•nate (i lo͞o′mə nāt′), *v.,* **-nat•ed, -nat•ing,** —*v.t.* **1.** to supply or brighten with light; light up. **2.** to make lucid; clarify. **3.** to decorate with lights. **4.** to enlighten. **5.** to make resplendent: *A smile illuminated her face.* **6.** to decorate (a manuscript or book) with colors and gold or silver. —*v.i.* **7.** to display lights, as in celebration. **8.** to become illuminated. —**il•lu′mi•nat′ing•ly,** *adv.*

il•lu•mi•na•ti (i lo͞o′mə nä′tē, -nā′tī), *n.pl., sing.* **-to** (-tō). **1.** persons claiming to possess superior enlightenment. **2.** (*cap.*) any of various religious sects claiming special enlightenment.

il•lu•mi•na•tion (i lo͞o′mə nā′shən), *n.* **1.** an act or instance of illuminating. **2.** the state of being illuminated. **3.** a decoration of lights. **4.** Sometimes, **illuminations.** a display using lights as a major decoration. **5.** intellectual or spiritual enlightenment. **6.** the intensity of light falling at a given place on a lighted surface; the luminous flux incident per unit area, expressed in lumens per unit of area. **7.** a supply of light. **8.** decoration of a manuscript or book with a painted design in color and gold or silver. **9.** a design used in such decoration.

il•lu•mine (i lo͞o′min), *v.t., v.i.,* **-mined, -min•ing.** to illuminate. —**il•lu′mi•na•ble,** *adj.*

ill-use (*v.* il′yo͞oz′; *n.* -yo͞os′), *v.,* **-used, -us•ing,** *n.* —*v.t.* **1.** to treat badly or unjustly. —*n.* **2.** Also, **ill′-us′age.** bad or unjust treatment.

il•lu•sion (i lo͞o′zhən), *n.* **1.** something that deceives by producing a false or misleading impression of reality. **2.** the state or condition of being deceived; misapprehension. **3.** an instance of being deceived. **4.** a perception, as of visual stimuli **(optical illusion),** that represents what is perceived in a way different from the way it is in reality. **5.** a delicate tulle of silk or nylon having a cobwebbed appearance, for trimmings, veilings, and the like. —**il•lu′sion•al, il•lu′sion•ar′y,** *adj.*

il•lu•sion•ism (i lo͞o′zhə niz′əm), *n.* a technique of using pictorial methods in order to deceive the eye. Compare TROMPE L'OEIL. —**il•lu′sion•is′tic,** *adj.*

il•lu•sion•ist (i lo͞o′zhə nist), *n.* a conjurer or magician who creates illusions, as by sleight of hand.

il•lu•sive (i lo͞o′siv), *adj.* illusory. —**il•lu′sive•ly,** *adv.* —**il•lu′sive•ness,** *n.*

il•lu•so•ry (i lo͞o′sə rē, -zə-), *adj.* **1.** causing illusion; deceptive; misleading. **2.** like an illusion; unreal. —**il•lu′so•ri•ly,** *adv.* —**il•lu′so•ri•ness,** *n.*

il•lus•trate (il′ə strāt′, i lus′trāt), *v.,* **-trat•ed, -trat•ing.** —*v.t.* **1.** to furnish with drawings, pictures, or other artwork: *to illustrate a book.* **2.** to make intelligible with examples or analogies; exemplify. —*v.i.* **3.** to clarify one's words with examples. —**il′lus•trat′a•ble,** *adj.*

il•lus•tra•tion (il′ə strā′shən), *n.* **1.** something that illustrates, as a picture in a book or magazine. **2.** a comparison or an example intended for explanation or corroboration. **3.** the act or process of illuminating. **4.** the act of clarifying or explaining; elucidation.

il•lus•tra•tive (i lus′trə tiv), *adj.* serving to illustrate; explanatory: *illustrative examples.* —**il•lus′tra•tive•ly,** *adv.*

il•lus•tra•tor (il′ə strā′tər, i lus′trā tər), *n.* an artist who makes illustrations: *an illustrator of children's books.*

il•lus•tri•ous (i lus′trē əs), *adj.* highly distinguished; renowned: *an illustrious leader.* —**il•lus′tri•ous•ly,** *adv.* —**il•lus′tri•ous•ness,** *n.*

il•lu•vi•a•tion (i lo͞o′vē ā′shən), *n.* the accumulation in one layer of soil of materials that have been leached out of another layer.

ill′ will′, *n.* hostile feeling; enmity. —**ill′-willed′,** *adj.*

Il•lyr•i•a (i lēr′ē ə), *n.* an ancient country along the E coast of the Adriatic. —**Il•lyr′i•an,** *adj., n.*

il•men•ite (il′mə nīt′), *n.* a common black mineral, iron titanate, $FeTiO_3$, an ore of titanium.

I′ Love′ to Tell′ the Sto′ry, a Christian children's hymn (1739) with words by Katherine Hankey.

I'm (īm), contraction of *I am.*

im-[1], var. of IN-[2] before *b, m, p: imbrute; immigrate; impassion.*

im-[2], var. of IN-[3] before *b, m, p: imbalance; immoral; imperishable.*

im-[3], var. of IN-[1] before *b, m, p: imbed; immure; impose.*

im•age (im′ij), *n., v.,* **-aged, -ag•ing.** —*n.* **1.** a physical likeness or representation of a person, animal, or thing, photographed, painted, sculptured, or otherwise made visible. **2.** an optical counterpart or appearance of an object, as is produced by reflection from a mirror, refraction by a lens, or the passage of luminous rays through a small aperture. **3.** a mental representation; idea; conception. **4.** *Psychol.* a mental representation of something previously perceived, in the absence of the original stimulus. **5.** form; appearance; semblance: *created in God's image.* **6.** counterpart; copy: *That child is the image of his mother.* **7.** a symbol; emblem. **8.** a general or public perception, as of a company, esp. when achieved by calculation aimed at creating goodwill. **9.** type; embodiment: *the image of frustration.* **10.** a description of something in speech or writing. **11.** a figure of speech, esp. a metaphor or a simile. **12.** an idol or representation of a deity: *They knelt down before graven images.* **13.** *Math.* the point or set of points in the range corresponding to a designated point in the domain of a given function. —*v.t.* **14.** to picture in the mind; imagine. **15.** to make an image of. **16.** to project (an image) on a surface. **17.** to reflect the likeness of; mirror. **18.** to describe in speech or writing. **19.** to symbolize; typify. —**im′age•a•ble,** *adj.* —**im′ag•er,** *n.*

im•age•mak•er (im′ij mā′kər), *n.* a person, as a publicist, who specializes in creating images, as for companies.

im•age•ry (im′ij rē, -i jə rē), *n., pl.* **-ries. 1.** mental images collectively, esp. those produced by the action of imagination. **2.** pictorial images. **3.** figurative description or illustration; rhetorical images collectively.

im•ag•i•na•ble (i maj′ə nə bəl), *adj.* capable of being imagined or conceived. —**i•mag′i•na•bly,** *adv.*

im•ag•i•nar•y (i maj′ə ner′ē), *adj.* existing only in the imagination or fancy; not real; fancied. —**im•ag′i•nar′i•ly,** *adv.*

imag′inary num′ber, *n.* a complex number having its real part equal to zero.

im•ag•i•na•tion (i maj′ə nā′shən), *n.* **1.** the action or faculty of forming mental images or concepts of what is not actually present to the senses. **2.** creative talent or ability. **3.** the product of imagining; a conception or mental creation. **4.** ability to face and resolve difficulties; resourcefulness: *a job that requires imagination.*

im•ag•i•na•tive (i maj′ə nə tiv, -nā′tiv), *adj.* **1.** characterized by or bearing evidence of imagination: *an imaginative tale.* **2.** of, pertaining to, or concerned with imagination. **3.** given to imagining. **4.** having exceptional powers of imagination. **5.** lacking truth; fanciful. —**i•mag′i•na•tive•ly,** *adv.* —**i•mag′i•na•tive•ness,** *n.*

im•ag•ine (i maj′in), *v.,* **-ined, -in•ing.** —*v.t.* **1.** to form a mental image of (something not actually present to the senses). **2.** to believe; fancy: *He imagined the house was haunted.* **3.** to assume; suppose: *I imagine they'll be here soon.* **4.** to conjecture; guess: *I cannot imagine what you mean.* —*v.i.* **5.** to form mental images of things not present to the senses; use the imagination. **6.** to suppose; think; conjecture. —**i•mag′in•er,** *n.*

im•ag•ing (im′ə jing), *n.* **1.** *Psychol.* a technique using mental images to control bodily processes and ease pain or to accomplish something one has visualized in advance. **2.** the use of computerized axial tomography, sonography, or other techniques and instruments to obtain pictures of the interior of the body.

i•ma•go (i mā′gō, i mä′-), *n., pl.* **-goes, -gi•nes** (-gə nēz′). **1.** an adult insect. **2.** *Psychoanal.* an idealized concept of a loved one, formed in childhood and retained unaltered in adult life.

i•mam (i mäm′), *n. Islam.* **1.** the officiating priest of a mosque. **2.** the title for a Muslim religious leader or chief. **3.** one of a succession of seven or twelve religious leaders, believed to be divinely inspired, of the Shi'ites. Also, **i·maum** (i mäm′, i môm′). —**i·mam′ship,** *n.*

I·ma′ri ware′ (i mär′ē), *n.* a fine Japanese porcelain with rich colors and floral underglaze.

im·bal·ance (im bal′əns), *n.* **1.** the state or condition of lacking balance, as in proportion or distribution. **2.** faulty muscular or glandular coordination.

im·be·cile (im′bə sil, -səl; *esp. Brit.* -sēl′), *n.* **1.** a person of the second order in a former classification of mental retardation, above the level of idiocy, having a mental age of seven or eight years and an intelligence quotient of 25 to 50. **2.** a stupid person; dolt. —*adj.* **3.** imbecilic. —**im′be·cile·ly,** *adv.*

im·bibe (im bīb′), *v.,* **-bibed, -bib·ing.** —*v.t.* **1.** to consume (liquids) by drinking; drink. **2.** to absorb or soak up: *Plants imbibe light from the sun.* **3.** to receive into the mind: *to imbibe a sermon.* —*v.i.* **4.** to drink, esp. alcoholic beverages. **5.** to absorb moisture. —**im·bib′er,** *n.*

im·bri·cate (*adj.* im′bri kit, -kāt′; *v.* -kāt′), *adj., v.,* **-cat·ed, -cat·ing.** —*adj.* **1.** overlapping in sequence, as tiles on a roof. **2.** overlapping like tiles, as scales or leaves. —*v.t., v.i.* **3.** to overlap. —**im′bri·cate·ly,** *adv.* —**im′bri·ca′tive,** *adj.*

im·bro·glio (im brōl′yō) also **embroglio,** *n., pl.* **-glios. 1.** a misunderstanding or disagreement of a complicated or bitter nature. **2.** an intricate and perplexing state of affairs. **3.** a confused heap.

im·brue (im brōō′) also **embrue,** *v.t.,* **-brued, -bru·ing.** to stain. —**im·brue′ment,** *n.*

im·bue (im byōō′), *v.t.,* **-bued, -bu·ing. 1.** to permeate or inspire profoundly: *imbued with patriotism.* **2.** to saturate deeply with moisture or color. **3.** to imbrue. —**im·bue′ment,** *n.*

IMF or **I.M.F.,** International Monetary Fund.

im·i·ta·ble (im′i tə bəl), *adj.* capable or worthy of being imitated. —**im·i·ta·bil′i·ty, im′i·ta·ble·ness,** *n.*

im·i·tate (im′i tāt′), *v.t.,* **-tat·ed, -tat·ing. 1.** to follow or endeavor to follow as a model or example: *to imitate an author's style.* **2.** to mimic; impersonate. **3.** to make a copy of; reproduce closely. **4.** to have or assume the appearance of; simulate. —**im′i·ta′tor,** *n.*

im·i·ta·tion (im′i tā′shən), *n.* **1.** a result or product of imitating. **2.** the act of imitating. **3.** a counterfeit; copy. **4.** a literary composition that imitates the manner or subject of another author or work. **5. a.** (in Aristotelian aesthetics) the representation of an object or an action as it ought to be. **b.** the representation of actuality in art or literature. **6.** the repetition of a melodic phrase at a different pitch or key from the original or in a different voice part. —*adj.* **7.** designed to imitate a genuine or superior article or thing: *imitation leather.* —*Proverb.* **8. Imitation is the sincerest form of flattery,** copying another's work, style, etc., compliments the originator. —**im′i·ta′tion·al,** *adj.*

im·i·ta·tive (im′i tā′tiv), *adj.* **1.** imitating; copying; given to imitation. **2.** of, pertaining to, or characterized by imitation. **3.** made in imitation of something; counterfeit. **4.** onomatopoeic. —**im′i·ta′tive·ly,** *adv.* —**im′i·ta′tive·ness,** *n.*

im·mac·u·late (i mak′yə lit), *adj.* **1.** free from spot or stain: *immaculate linen.* **2.** free from moral blemish or impurity; pure. **3.** free from errors: *an immaculate text.* —**im·mac·u·la·cy** (i mak′yə lə sē), **im·mac′u·late·ness,** *n.* —**im·mac′u·late·ly,** *adv.*

Immac′ulate Concep′tion, *n.* the Roman Catholic doctrine according to which the Virgin Mary was conceived in her mother's womb without the stain of original sin.

im·ma·nent (im′ə nənt), *adj.* **1.** remaining within; indwelling; inherent. **2.** *Philos.* (of a mental act) taking place within the mind of the subject and having no effect outside of it. **3.** (of the Deity) indwelling the universe, time, etc. Compare TRANSCENDENT (def. 3). —**im′ma·nence, im′ma·nen·cy,** *n.* —**im′ma·nent·ly,** *adv.*

im·ma·nent·ism (im′ə nən tiz′əm), *n.* a belief that the Deity indwells and operates directly within the universe or nature.

Im·man·u·el (i man′yōō əl), *n.* the name of the Messiah as prophesied by Isaiah, often represented in Christian exegesis as being Jesus Christ. Is. 7:14. [< Hebrew '*immānū′ēl* lit., God is with us]

im·ma·te·ri·al (im′ə tēr′ē əl), *adj.* **1.** of no essential consequence; not pertinent; unimportant. **2.** not material; incorporeal; spiritual. —**im′ma·te′ri·al·ly,** *adv.* —**im′ma·te′ri·al·ness,** *n.*

im·ma·ture (im′ə chōōr′, -tōōr′, -tyōōr′, -chûr′), *adj.* **1.** not mature or ripe. **2.** emotionally undeveloped; juvenile; childish. **3.** YOUTHFUL (def. 4). —**im′ma·ture′ly,** *adv.* —**im′ma·ture′ness,** *n.*

im·ma·tu·ri·ty (im′ə chōōr′i tē, -tōōr′-, -tyōōr′-, -chûr′-), *n., pl.* **-ties. 1.** a state or condition of being immature. **2.** an immature action or attitude.

im·meas·ur·a·ble (i mezh′ər ə bəl), *adj.* incapable of being measured; limitless. —**im·meas′ur·a·bil′i·ty, im·meas′ur·a·ble·ness,** *n.* —**im·meas′ur·a·bly,** *adv.*

im·me·di·a·cy (i mē′dē ə sē), *n., pl.* **-cies. 1.** the state, condition, or quality of being immediate. **2.** Often, **immediacies.** an immediate need: *the immediacies of everyday living.*

im·me·di·ate (i mē′dē it), *adj.* **1.** occurring or accomplished without delay; instant: *an immediate reply.* **2.** following or preceding without a lapse of time. **3.** having no object or space intervening: *in the immediate vicinity.* **4.** of or pertaining to the present time: *our immediate plans.* **5.** without intervening medium or agent; direct: *an immediate*

cause. **6.** having a direct bearing: *immediate considerations.* **7.** very close in relationship: *my immediate family.*

im·me·di·ate·ly (i mē′dē it lē), *adv.* **1.** without lapse of time; at once: *Please telephone immediately.* **2.** with no object or space intervening. **3.** closely: *immediately in the vicinity.* **4.** without intervening medium or agent. —*conj.* **5.** the moment that; as soon as.

im·me·mo·ri·al (im′ə môr′ē əl, -mōr′-), *adj.* extending back beyond memory, record, or knowledge: *from time immemorial.* —**im′me·mo′ri·al·ly,** *adv.*

im·mense (i mens′), *adj.* **1.** vast; immeasurable: *an immense territory.* **2.** splendid: *You did an immense job getting the project started.* —**im·mense′ly,** *adv.* —**im·mense′ness,** *n.*

im·men·si·ty (i men′si tē), *n.* **1.** enormous extent; vastness. **2.** the state or condition of being immense.

im·men·su·ra·ble (i men′shər ə bəl, -sər ə-), *adj.* immeasurable. —**im·men′su·ra·bil′i·ty, im·men′su·ra·ble·ness,** *n.*

im·merge (i mûrj′), *v.,* **-merged, -merg·ing.** to plunge or disappear into something. —**im·mer′gence,** *n.*

im·merse (i mûrs′), *v.t.,* **-mersed, -mers·ing. 1.** to plunge into or place under a liquid; dip; sink. **2.** to involve deeply; absorb: *immersed in her law practice.* **3.** to baptize by immersion. —**im·mers′i·ble,** *adj.*

im·mer·sion (i mûr′zhən, -shən), *n.* **1.** an act or instance of immersing. **2.** the state of being immersed. **3.** baptism in which the whole body of the person is submerged in the water. **4.** Also called **ingress.** the entrance of a heavenly body into an eclipse by another body, an occultation, or a transit.

im·mi·grant (im′i grənt), *n.* **1.** a person who migrates to another country, usu. for permanent residence. **2.** an organism found in a new habitat. —*adj.* **3.** of or pertaining to immigrants and immigration: *a department for immigrant affairs.*

im·mi·grate (im′i grāt′), *v.,* **-grat·ed, -grat·ing.** —*v.i.* **1.** to come to a country of which one is not a native, usu. for permanent residence. **2.** to pass or come into a new habitat or place, as an organism. —*v.t.* **3.** to introduce as settlers: *to immigrate cheap labor.* —**im′mi·gra′tor,** *n.*

im·mi·gra·tion (im′i grā′shən), *n.* **1.** the act of immigrating. **2.** a group or number of immigrants. —**im′mi·gra′tion·al, im′mi·gra·to′ry** (-grə tôr′ē, -tōr′ē), *adj.*

im·mi·nence (im′ə nəns), *n.* **1.** Also, **im′mi·nen·cy.** the state or condition of being imminent or impending: *the imminence of war.* **2.** something imminent, esp. an impending evil or danger.

im·mi·nent (im′ə nənt), *adj.* **1.** likely to occur at any moment; impending: *Her death is imminent.* **2.** projecting or leaning forward; overhanging. —**im′mi·nent·ly,** *adv.* —**im′mi·nent·ness,** *n.*

im·mix (i miks′), *v.t.,* **-mixed** or **-mixt, -mix·ing.** to mix in; mingle.

im·mo·bile (i mō′bəl, -bēl), *adj.* **1.** incapable of moving or being moved. **2.** not mobile or moving; motionless. —**im′mo·bil′i·ty,** *n.*

im·mo·bi·lize (i mō′bə līz′), *v.t.,* **-lized, -liz·ing. 1.** to make immobile or immovable; fix in place. **2.** to prevent the use, activity, or movement of: *The hurricane immobilized the airlines.* **3.** to prevent, restrict, or reduce normal movement in (the body, a limb, or a joint), as by a splint, cast, or prescribed bed rest. **4.** to render (an opponent's strategy) ineffective; stymie. —**im·mo′bi·li·za′tion,** *n.* —**im·mo′bi·liz′er,** *n.*

im·mod·er·ate (i mod′ər it), *adj.* exceeding just or reasonable limits; excessive; extreme. —**im·mod′er·ate·ly,** *adv.* —**im·mod′er·ate·ness,** *n.* —**im·mod′er·a′tion,** *n.*

im·mod·est (i mod′ist), *adj.* **1.** indecent; shameless. **2.** forward; impudent. —**im·mod′est·ly,** *adv.* —**im·mod′es·ty,** *n.*

im·mo·late (im′ə lāt′), *v.t.,* **-lat·ed, -lat·ing. 1.** to sacrifice. **2.** to kill as a sacrificial victim, as by fire; offer in sacrifice. **3.** to destroy by fire. —**im′mo·la′tor,** *n.*

im·mor·al (i môr′əl, i mor′-), *adj.* **1.** violating moral principles. **2.** licentious; lascivious. —**im·mor′al·ly,** *adv.*

im·mo·ral·i·ty (im′ə ral′i tē, im′ô-), *n., pl.* **-ties. 1.** immoral quality, character, or conduct. **2.** sexual misconduct. **3.** an immoral act.

im·mor·tal (i môr′tl), *adj.* **1.** not mortal; not liable or subject to death: *immortal souls.* **2.** not liable to perish or decay; everlasting: *immortal wisdom.* **3.** perpetual; constant: *an immortal enemy.* **4.** of or pertaining to immortal beings or immortality. **5.** (of a laboratory-cultured cell line) capable of dividing indefinitely. —*n.* **6.** an immortal being. **7.** a person of enduring fame. **8.** (*often cap.*) any of the gods of classical mythology. —**im·mor′tal·ly,** *adv.*

im·mor·tal·i·ty (im′ôr tal′i tē), *n.* **1.** immortal condition or quality; unending life. **2.** enduring fame.

im·mor·tal·ize (i môr′tl īz′), *v.t.,* **-ized, -iz·ing. 1.** to bestow unending fame upon; perpetuate. **2.** to make immortal; endow with immortality. —**im·mor′tal·i·za′tion,** *n.*

im·mo·tile (i mōt′l), *adj.* not able to move; not motile. —**im·mo·til·i·ty** (im′ō til′i tē), *n.*

im·mov·a·ble or **im·move·a·ble** (i mōō′və bəl), *adj.* **1.** incapable of being moved; fixed; stationary. **2.** unaffected by feeling: *an immovable heart.* **3.** implacable; unyielding. **4.** not moving; motionless. **5.** not changing from one date to another in different years: *Christmas is an immovable feast.* —*n.* **6.** something immovable. **7. immovables,** real property. —**im·mov′a·bil′i·ty,** *n.* —**im·mov′a·bly,** *adv.*

im·mune (i myōōn′), *adj.* **1.** protected from a disease or the like, as by inoculation. **2.** of or pertaining to the production of antibodies or lymphocytes that can react with a specific antigen: *immune reaction.* **3.** exempt; protected: *immune from punishment.* **4.** not responsive or susceptible: *immune to new ideas.* —*n.* **5.** an immune person.

im·mune′ response′, *n.* any of the body's immunologic reactions to an antigen.

im·mune′ sys′tem, *n.* a diffuse, complex network of interacting cells, cell products, and cell-forming tissues that protects the body from pathogens and other foreign substances, destroys infected and malignant cells, and removes cellular debris: the system includes the thymus, spleen, lymph nodes and lymph tissue, stem cells, white blood cells, antibodies, and lymphokines.

im·mu·ni·ty (i myōō′ni tē), *n., pl.* **-ties. 1.** the state of being immune from or insusceptible to a particular disease or the like. **2.** the condition that permits either natural or acquired resistance to disease. **3.** the ability of a cell to react immunologically in the presence of an antigen. **4.** exemption from any natural or usual liability. **5.** exemption from obligation, service, duty, liability, or prosecution.

immuno-, a combining form representing IMMUNE or IMMUNITY: *immunology.*

im·mu·no·as·say (im′yə nō ə sā′, -as′ā, i myōō′-), *n.* a laboratory method for detecting a substance by using an antibody reactive with it. —im′mu·no·as·say′a·ble, *adj.*

im·mu·no·bi·ol·o·gy (im′yə nō bī ol′ə jē, i myōō′-), *n.* the study of the immune response and the biological aspects of immunity to disease. —im′mu·no·bi′o·log′ic (-ə loj′ik), im′mu·no·bi′o·log′i·cal, *adj.* —im′mu·no·bi·ol′o·gist, *n.*

im·mu·no·chem·is·try (im′yə nō kem′ə strē, i myōō′-), *n.* the study of the chemistry of immunologic substances and reactions. —im′mu·no·chem′i·cal, *adj.* —im′mu·no·chem′i·cal·ly, *adv.* —im′mu·no·chem′ist, *n.*

im·mu·no·de·fi·cien·cy (im′yə nō di fish′ən sē, i myōō′-), *n., pl.* **-cies.** impairment of the immune response, predisposing to infection, certain chronic diseases, and cancer. —im′mu·no·de·fi′cient, *adj.*

im·mu·no·ge·net·ics (im′yə nō jə net′iks, i myōō′-), *n.* (*used with a sing. v.*) **1.** the branch of immunology dealing with the study of immunity in relation to genetic makeup. **2.** the study of genetic relationships among animals by comparison of immunologic reactions. —im′mu·no·ge·net′ic, im′mu·no·ge·net′i·cal, *adj.*

im·mu·no·gen·ic (im′yə nō jen′ik, i myōō′nə-), *adj.* causing or capable of producing an immune response. —im′mu·no·gen′i·cal·ly, *adv.* —im′mu·no·ge·nic′i·ty (-jə nis′i tē), *n.*

im·mu·no·he·ma·tol·o·gy (im′yə nō hē′mə tol′ə jē, i myōō′-), *n.* the study of blood and blood-forming tissue in relation to the immune response. —im′mu·no·he′ma·to·log′ic (-tl oj′ik), im′mu·no·he′ma·to·log′i·cal, *adj.*

im·mu·no·his·tol·o·gy (im′yə nō hi stol′ə jē, i myōō′-), *n.* the application of the methods of immunology to the study of tissues. —im′mu·no·his′to·log′ic (-tl oj′ik), im′mu·no·his′to·log′i·cal, *adj.* —im′mu·no·his′to·log′i·cal·ly, *adv.*

im·mu·nol·o·gy (im′yə nol′ə jē), *n.* the branch of science dealing with the components of the immune system, immunity from disease, the immune response, and immunologic techniques of analysis. —im′mu·no·log′ic (-nl oj′ik), im′mu·no·log′i·cal, *adj.* —im′mu·no·log′i·cal·ly, *adv.* —im′mu·nol′o·gist, *n.*

im·mu·no·pa·thol·o·gy (im′yə nō pə thol′ə jē, i myōō′-), *n.* the study of diseases having an immunologic or allergic basis. —im′mu·no·path′o·log′i·cal (-path′ə loj′i kəl), im′mu·no·path′o·log′ic, *adj.* —im′mu·no·path′o·log′i·cal·ly, *adv.* —im′mu·no·pa·thol′o·gist, *n.*

im·mu·no·ther·a·py (im′yə nō ther′ə pē, i myōō′-), *n., pl.* **-pies.** treatment designed to produce immunity to a disease or enhance the resistance of the immune system to an active disease process, as cancer. —im′mu·no·ther′a·peu′tic (-pyōō′tik), *adj.*

im·mure (i myōōr′), *v.t.,* **-mured, -mur·ing. 1.** to enclose within or as if within walls. **2.** to imprison. **3.** to build into or entomb in a wall. —im·mure′ment, im·mu·ra·tion (im′yə rā′shən), *n.*

im·mu·ta·ble (i myōō′tə bəl), *adj.* not mutable; unchangeable; changeless. —im·mu′ta·bil′i·ty, *n.* —im·mu′ta·bly, *adv.*

imp (imp), *n.* **1.** a small devil or demon. **2.** a mischievous child. —*v.t.* **3.** to repair or graft (a falcon's wing, tail, or feather) so as to improve powers of flight.

im·pact (*n.* im′pakt; *v.* im pakt′), *n.* **1.** the striking of one thing against another; collision. **2.** influence; effect: *the impact of Einstein on modern physics.* **3.** a forcible impinging: *the tremendous impact of the shot.* **4.** the force exerted by a new idea, concept, technology, or ideology: *the impact of the industrial revolution.* —*v.t.* **5.** to drive or press closely or firmly into something. **6.** to fill up; congest: *A vast crowd impacted St. Peter's Square.* **7.** to collide with: *a rocket designed to impact the planet Mars.* **8.** to have an impact or effect on; influence: *The decision may impact your whole career.* —*v.i.* **9.** to make contact forcefully. **10.** to have an impact: *Increased demand will impact on sales.*

im·pact·ed (im pak′tid), *adj.* **1.** (of a tooth) so confined or positioned in its socket as to be incapable of normal eruption. **2.** driven together; tightly packed. **3.** densely populated; overcrowded: *an impacted school district.*

im′pact print′er, *n.* a computer printer, as a dot-matrix or daisy-wheel printer, that forms characters by causing a printhead to strike at paper through an inked ribbon. Compare PAGE PRINTER.

im·pair (im pâr′), *v.t.* to make or cause to become worse; weaken;

damage: *habits that impair one's health.* —im·pair′a·ble, *adj.* —im·pair′er, *n.* —im·pair′ment, *n.*

im·pal·a (im pal′ə, -pä′lə), *n., pl.* **-pal·as,** (*esp. collectively*) **-pal·a.** an African antelope, *Aepyceros melampus,* the male of which has ringed, lyre-shaped horns.

im·pale (im pāl′), *v.t.,* **-paled, -pal·ing. 1.** to pierce or fix with or as if with something pointed. **2.** to pierce with a sharpened stake thrust up through the body, as for torture or punishment. **3.** to make helpless as if pierced through. **4.** to combine (coats of arms) on a shield with a pale dividing vertically. —im·pal′er, *n.* —im·pale′ment, *n.*

im·pal·pa·ble (im pal′pə bəl), *adj.* **1.** incapable of being perceived by the sense of touch; intangible. **2.** difficult for the mind to grasp readily. **3.** (of powder) so fine that when rubbed between the fingers no grit is felt. —im·pal′pa·bil′i·ty, *n.* —im·pal′pa·bly, *adv.*

im·pan·el (im pan′l) *v.t.,* **-eled, -el·ing** or (*esp. Brit.*) **-elled, -el·ling. 1.** to enter on a panel for jury duty. **2.** to select (a jury) from a panel. —im·pan′el·ment, *n.*

im·part (im pärt′), *v.t.* **1.** to make known; disclose: *to impart a secret.* **2.** to give; bestow: *to impart knowledge.* **3.** to grant a part or share of. —*v.i.* **4.** to grant a part or share; give. —im·part′a·ble, *adj.* —im·par·ta′tion, im·part′ment, *n.* —im·part′er, *n.*

im·par·tial (im pär′shəl), *adj.* not partial or biased; fair; just: *an impartial judge.* —im·par′ti·al′i·ty (-shē al′i tē), *n.* —im·par′tial·ly, *adv.*

im·pass·a·ble (im pas′ə bəl, -pä′sə-), *adj.* **1.** not allowing passage: *Snow made the roads impassable.* **2.** unable to be surmounted: *impassable differences.* —im·pass′a·bil′i·ty, *n.* —im·pass′a·bly, *adv.*

im·passe (im′pas, im pas′), *n.* **1.** a position or situation from which there is no escape; deadlock. **2.** a road or way that has no outlet; cul-de-sac.

im·pas·si·ble (im pas′ə bəl), *adj.* **1.** incapable of suffering pain. **2.** incapable of suffering harm. **3.** incapable of emotion; impassive. —im·pas′si·bil′i·ty, im·pas′si·ble·ness, *n.* —im·pas′si·bly, *adv.*

im·pas·sion (im pash′ən), *v.t.* to fill with intense feeling; inflame; excite.

im·pas·sioned (im pash′ənd), *adj.* filled with intense feeling or passion; passionate; ardent. —im·pas′sioned·ly, *adv.*

im·pas·sive (im pas′iv), *adj.* **1.** showing or feeling no emotion; unmoved. **2.** not subject to suffering. —im·pas′sive·ly, *adv.* —im·pas′sive·ness, im′pas·siv′i·ty, *n.*

im·pas·to (im pas′tō, -päs′stō), *n.* **1.** the laying on of paint thickly. **2.** the paint so laid on. **3.** enamel or slip applied to a ceramic object to form a decoration in low relief.

im·pa·tience (im pā′shəns), *n.* **1.** intolerance of anything that thwarts, delays, or hinders. **2.** eager desire for relief or change; restlessness.

im·pa·tiens (im pā′shənz), *n., pl.* **-tiens.** any of numerous plants belonging to the genus *Impatiens,* of the balsam family, having irregular, spurred flowers.

im·pa·tient (im pā′shənt), *adj.* **1.** not readily accepting interference; intolerant. **2.** indicating lack of patience: *an impatient answer.* **3.** restless in desire or expectation; eagerly desirous. —im·pa′tient·ly, *adv.* —im·pa′tient·ness, *n.*

im·peach (im pēch′), *v.t.* **1.** to accuse (a public official) of misconduct in office by bringing charges before an appropriate tribunal. **2.** to challenge the credibility of: *to impeach a witness.* **3.** to bring an accusation against. **4.** to cast an imputation upon: *to impeach a person's motives.* —im·peach′er, *n.*

im·peach·ment (im pēch′mənt), *n.* **1.** the act of impeaching; condition of being impeached. **2.** (in the U.S. Congress or a state legislature) the presentation of formal charges against a public official by the lower house, with trial to be before the upper house.

im·pec·ca·ble (im pek′ə bəl), *adj.* **1.** faultless; flawless: *impeccable manners.* **2.** not liable to sin; incapable of sin. —im·pec′ca·bil′i·ty, *n.* —im·pec′ca·bly, *adv.*

im·pe·cu·ni·ous (im′pi kyōō′nē əs), *adj.* having little or no money; penniless. —im′pe·cu′ni·ous·ly, *adv.* —im′pe·cu′ni·ous·ness, im′pe·cu′ni·os′i·ty (-os′i tē), *n.*

im·ped·ance (im pēd′ns), *n.* **1.** the total opposition to alternating current by an electric circuit, equal to the square root of the sum of the squares of the resistance and reactance of the circuit and usu. expressed in ohms. **2.** the ratio of the force on a system undergoing simple harmonic motion to the velocity of the particles in the system.

im·pede (im pēd′), *v.t.,* **-ped·ed, -ped·ing.** to retard in movement or progress by means of obstacles or hindrances; obstruct; hinder. —im·ped′er, *n.* —im·ped′i·bil′i·ty (-pē′də bil′i tē, -ped′ə-), *n.* —im·ped′i·ble, *adj.* —im·ped′ing·ly, *adv.*

im·ped·i·ment (im ped′ə mənt), *n.* **1.** obstruction; hindrance; obstacle. **2.** any physical defect that impedes normal or easy speech. **3.** a bar, usu. of blood or affinity, to marriage.

im·ped·i·men·ta (im ped′ə men′tə), *n.pl.* things that impede one; bulky equipment.

im·pel (im pel′), *v.t.,* **-pelled, -pel·ling. 1.** to drive or urge forward. **2.** to impart motion to.

im·pel·ler (im pel′ər), *n.* **1.** a person or thing that impels. **2.** a rotor for transmitting motion, as in a centrifugal pump, blower, turbine, or fluid coupling.

I

im•pend (im pend′), *v.i.* **1.** to be imminent; be about to happen. **2.** to threaten; menace: *He felt that danger impended.*

im•pen•e•tra•bil•i•ty (im pen′i trə bil′i tē, im′pen-), *n.* **1.** the state or quality of being impenetrable. **2.** the property of matter by which two bodies cannot occupy the same space simultaneously.

im•pen•e•tra•ble (im pen′i trə bəl), *adj.* **1.** incapable of being penetrated, pierced, or entered. **2.** unsympathetic to ideas or influences. **3.** incapable of being understood; unfathomable: *an impenetrable mystery.* **4.** possessing impenetrability. **—im•pen′e•tra•bly,** *adv.*

im•pen•i•tent (im pen′i tənt), *adj.* not feeling regret about one's sin or sins; obdurate. **—im•pen′i•tence, im•pen′i•ten•cy, im•pen′i•tent•ness,** *n.* **—im•pen′i•tent•ly,** *adv.*

im•per•a•tive (im per′ə tiv), *adj.* **1.** absolutely necessary or required: *It is imperative that we leave.* **2.** of the nature of or expressing a command. **3.** of or designating a grammatical mood used in commands, exhortations, etc., as in *Listen! Go!* Compare INDICATIVE (def. 2), SUBJUNCTIVE (def. 1). **—*n.*** **4.** a command; order. **5.** an unavoidable obligation or requirement: *the imperatives of leadership.* **6. a.** the imperative mood. **b.** a verb in this mood. **7.** an obligatory statement, principle, or the like. **—im•per′a•tive•ly,** *adv.* **—im•per′a•tive•ness,** *n.*

im•per•cep•ti•ble (im′pər sep′tə bəl), *adj.* **1.** very slight, gradual, or subtle: *the imperceptible slope of the road.* **2.** not perceived by or affecting the senses. **—im′per•cep′ti•bil′i•ty,** *n.* **—im′per•cep′ti•bly,** *adv.*

im•per•fect (im pûr′fikt), *adj.* **1.** of, pertaining to, or characterized by defects or weaknesses: *imperfect vision.* **2.** lacking completeness: *imperfect knowledge.* **3.** of or designating a verb tense or form typically indicating a habitual, repeated, or continuing action or state in the past or an action or state in progress at a point of reference in the past. **4.** not enforceable by law. **5.** (of a flower) having either stamens or pistils; unisexual. **—*n.*** **6.** the imperfect tense. **7.** a verb form in the imperfect tense. **—im•per′fect•ly,** *adv.*

im•per•fec•tion (im′pər fek′shən), *n.* **1.** fault; flaw. **2.** the quality or state of being imperfect.

im•per•fec•tive (im′pər fek′tiv), *adj.* **1.** of or noting an aspect of the verb, as in Russian, that indicates incompleteness or repetition of an action or state. **—*n.*** **2.** the imperfective aspect. **3.** a verb in this aspect.

im•pe•ri•al (im pēr′ē əl), *adj.* **1.** of, pertaining to, or characteristic of an empire or emperor. **2.** characterizing the rule or authority of a sovereign state over its dependencies. **3.** of a commanding quality, manner, or aspect. **4.** regal; imperious. **5.** of special or superior size or quality. **6.** (of weights and measures) conforming to the nonmetric standards legally established in Great Britain. **—*n.*** **7.** a member of an imperial party or of imperial troops. **—im•pe′ri•al•ly,** *adv.* **—im•pe′ri•al•ness,** *n.*

im•pe•ri•al•ism (im pēr′ē ə liz′əm), *n.* **1.** the policy of extending the rule or authority of an empire or nation over foreign countries, or of acquiring and holding colonies and dependencies. **2.** advocacy of imperial interests. **3.** an imperial system of government. **—im•pe′ri•al•ist,** *n., adj.* **—im•pe′ri•al•is′tic,** *adj.* **—im•pe′ri•al•is′ti•cal•ly,** *adv.*

impe′rial moth′, *n.* a yellow moth, *Eacles imperialis,* with purple bands.

impe′rial pres′idency, *n.* a presidency that wrongfully appropriates powers which are designated to other branches of government by the Constitution. [from a 1973 book of that name by Arthur M. Schlesinger]

im•per•il (im per′əl), *v.t.,* **-iled, -il•ing** or (*esp. Brit.*) **-illed, -il•ling.** to put in peril; endanger. **—im•per′il•ment,** *n.*

im•pe•ri•ous (im pēr′ē əs), *adj.* **1.** domineering in a haughty manner; dictatorial. **2.** urgent; imperative: *imperious need.* **—im•pe′ri•ous•ly,** *adv.* **—im•pe′ri•ous•ness,** *n.*

im•per•ish•a•ble (im per′i shə bəl), *adj.* not subject to decay; enduring. **—im•per′ish•a•bil′i•ty, im•per′ish•a•ble•ness,** *n.* **—im•per′ish•a•bly,** *adv.*

im•per•ma•nent (im pûr′mə nənt), *adj.* not permanent; transitory. **—im•per′ma•nence, im•per′ma•nen•cy,** *n.* **—im•per′ma•nent•ly,** *adv.*

im•per•me•a•ble (im pûr′mē ə bəl), *adj.* **1.** not permeable; impassable. **2.** (of porous substances, rocks, etc.) not permitting the passage of a fluid. **—im•per′me•a•bil′i•ty, im•per′me•a•ble•ness,** *n.* **—im•per′me•a•bly,** *adv.*

im•per•son•al (im pûr′sə nl), *adj.* **1.** lacking reference to a particular person: *an impersonal remark.* **2.** devoid of human character or traits: *an impersonal deity.* **3.** lacking human emotion or warmth. **4. a.** (of a verb) having only third person singular forms and used without an expressed subject, as Latin *pluit* "it is raining," or accompanied by an empty subject word, as the verb *rain* in *It is raining.* **b.** (of a pronoun) indefinite, as French *on* "one." **—im•per′son•al•ly,** *adv.*

im•per•son•al•ize (im pûr′sə nl īz′), *v.t.,* **-ized, -iz•ing.** to make impersonal. **—im•per′son•al•i•za′tion,** *n.*

im•per•son•ate (im pûr′sə nāt′), *v.,* **-at•ed, -at•ing.** **1.** to assume the character or appearance of; pretend to be: *He was arrested for impersonating a police officer.* **2.** to mimic the voice, mannerisms, etc., of (a person) in order to entertain. **—im•per′son•a′tion,** *n.* **—im•per′son•a′tor,** *n.*

im•per•ti•nence (im pûr′tn əns), *n.* **1.** unmannerly intrusion or presumption; insolence. **2.** impertinent quality or action. **3.** something impertinent. **4.** irrelevance; inappropriateness.

im•per•ti•nent (im pûr′tn ənt), *adj.* **1.** intrusively presumptuous; rude. **2.** not pertinent; irrelevant: *an impertinent detail.* **—im•per′ti•nent•ly,** *adv.* **—im•per′ti•nent•ness,** *n.*

im•per•turb•a•ble (im′pər tûr′bə bəl), *adj.* incapable of being upset or agitated; calm. **—im′per•turb′a•bil′i•ty,** *n.* **—im′per•turb′a•bly,** *adv.*

im•per•vi•ous (im pûr′vē əs), *adj.* **1.** not permitting penetration or passage: *The pelt is impervious to rain.* **2.** incapable of being injured or impaired: *impervious to wear and tear.* **3.** incapable of being influenced or affected: *impervious to reason.* **—im•per′vi•ous•ly,** *adv.* **—im•per′vi•ous•ness,** *n.*

im•pe•ti•go (im′pi tī′gō), *n.* a contagious skin infection, usu. streptococcal, characterized by pustules that erupt and form crusts. **—im′pe•tig′i•nous** (-tij′ə nəs), *adj.*

im•pet•u•ous (im pech′o͞o əs), *adj.* **1.** of, pertaining to, or characterized by sudden or rash action or emotion. **2.** moving with great force; violent: *impetuous winds.* **—im•pet′u•ous•ly,** *adv.* **—im•pet′u•ous•ness,** *n.*

im•pe•tus (im′pi təs), *n., pl.* **-tus•es.** **1.** a driving force; impulse; stimulus. **2.** the momentum of a moving body, esp. with reference to the cause of motion.

im•pi•e•ty (im pī′i tē), *n., pl.* **-ties.** **1.** the quality or state of being impious; irreverence. **2.** an impious act or practice.

im•pinge (im pinj′), *v.i.,* **-pinged, -ping•ing.** **1.** to encroach; infringe: *to impinge on another's rights.* **2.** to strike; collide: *light impinging on the lens.* **3.** to make an impression; have an effect: *ideas that impinge upon the imagination.* **—im•ping′ent,** *adj.* **—im•ping′er,** *n.* **—im•pinge′ment,** *n.*

im•pi•ous (im′pē əs, im pī′-), *adj.* **1.** not pious; lacking reverence, as for God or religious practice; irreligious. **2.** disrespectful. **—im′pi•ous•ly,** *adv.* **—im′pi•ous•ness,** *n.*

imp•ish (im′pish), *adj.* of, pertaining to, or befitting an imp; mischievous. **—imp′ish•ly,** *adv.* **—imp′ish•ness,** *n.*

im•plac•a•ble (im plak′ə bəl, -plā′kə-), *adj.* not to be appeased, mollified, or pacified; inexorable: *an implacable enemy.* **—im•plac′a•bil′i•ty, im•plac′a•ble•ness,** *n.* **—im•plac′a•bly,** *adv.*

im•plant (*v.* im plant′, -plänt′; *n.* im′plant′, -plänt′), *v.t.* **1.** to establish firmly in the mind: *to implant principles of behavior.* **2.** to plant securely: *to implant a post in the soil.* **3.** to insert or graft (a tissue, organ, or inert substance) into the body. **—*n.*** **4. a.** a device or material used for repairing or replacing part of the body. **b.** medication or radioactive material inserted into tissue for sustained therapy. **5. a.** a frame or support inserted permanently into the bone or soft tissue of the jaw to hold artificial teeth. **b.** an artificial tooth or bridge attached to such a device. **—im•plant′a•ble,** *adj.* **—im•plant′er,** *n.*

im•plan•ta•tion (im′plan tā′shən), *n.* **1.** the act of implanting. **2.** the state of being implanted. **3.** the attachment of the early embryo to the lining of the uterus.

im•plau•si•ble (im plô′zə bəl), *adj.* not plausible; causing disbelief: *an implausible alibi.* **—im•plau′si•bil′i•ty,** *n.* **—im•plau′si•bly,** *adv.*

im•ple•ment (*n.* im′plə mənt; *v. also* -ment′), *n.* **1.** an instrument, tool, or utensil for accomplishing work: *agricultural implements.* **2.** an article of equipment, as household furniture, clothing, or the like. **3.** a means; agent: *goodwill as an implement to peace.* **—*v.t.*** **4.** to fulfill; carry out: *implementing campaign promises.* **5.** to put into effect according to a definite plan or procedure. **6.** to provide with implements. **—im′ple•ment′a•ble,** *adj.* **—im′ple•men′tal,** *adj.* **—im′ple•men•ta′tion,** *n.* **—im′ple•ment′er, im′ple•men′tor,** *n.*

im•pli•cate (im′pli kāt′), *v.t.,* **-cat•ed, -cat•ing.** **1.** to show to be involved, usu. in an incriminating manner: *to be implicated in a crime.* **2.** to involve as a necessary circumstance; imply. **3.** to affect as a consequence: *Malfunctioning of one part of the nervous system implicates another part.*

im•pli•ca•tion (im′pli kā′shən), *n.* **1.** something implied or suggested as naturally to be inferred or understood: *an implication of dishonesty.* **2.** the act of implying. **3.** the state of being implied. **4.** the relation between two propositions such that the second is not false when the first is true. **5.** the act of implicating. **6.** the state of being implicated. **7.** a likely relationship: *the religious implications of ancient astrology.*

im•plic•it (im plis′it), *adj.* **1.** not expressly stated; implied: *implicit agreement.* **2.** unquestioning; absolute: *implicit trust.* **3.** potentially contained; inherent: *the drama implicit in the occasion.* **—im•plic′it•ly,** *adv.* **—im•plic′it•ness, im•plic′i•ty,** *n.*

im•plode (im plōd′), *v.,* **-plod•ed, -plod•ing.** **—*v.i.*** **1.** to burst inward (opposed to *explode*). **—*v.t.*** **2.** to pronounce (a consonant) with implosion.

im•plore (im plôr′, -plōr′), *v.,* **-plored, -plor•ing.** **—*v.t.*** **1.** to beg urgently or piteously; beseech: *They implored him to go.* **2.** to beg urgently or piteously for: *implore forgiveness.* **—*v.i.*** **3.** to make urgent or piteous supplication. **—im•plor′ing•ly,** *adv.*

im•plo•sion (im plō′zhən), *n.* **1.** the act of imploding; a bursting inward (opposed to *explosion*). **2.** the ingressive release of a suction stop. Compare PLOSION.

im•plo•sive (im plō′siv), *adj.* **1.** of or pertaining to a consonant characterized by a partial vacuum behind the point of closure. **—*n.*** **2.** an implosive consonant. **—im•plo′sive•ly,** *adv.*

im•ply (im plī′), *v.t.,* **-plied, -ply•ing.** **1.** to indicate or suggest without being explicitly stated: *His words implied a lack of faith.* **2.** to involve as a necessary circumstance: *Speech implies a speaker.* **—Usage.** See INFER.

im•po•lite (im′pə līt′), *adj.* not polite; rude. —**im′po•lite′ly,** *adv.* —**im′po•lite′ness,** *n.*

im•pon•der•a•ble (im pon′dər ə bəl), *adj.* **1.** not ponderable; not susceptible to precise measurement or evaluation. —*n.* **2.** something imponderable. —**im•pon′der•a•bil′i•ty, im•pon′der•a•ble•ness,** *n.* —**im•pon′der•a•bly,** *adv.*

im•port (*v.* im pôrt′, -pōrt′; *n.* im′pôrt, -pōrt), *v.t.* **1.** to bring in from a foreign country or other source: *to import goods for resale.* **2.** to bring or introduce from one use or connection into another: *foodstuffs imported from the farm.* **3.** to mean or signify: *Her words imported a change of attitude.* **4.** to involve as a necessary circumstance; imply. —*v.i.* **5.** to be of consequence or importance; matter. —*n.* **6.** something that is imported from abroad. **7.** the act of importing. **8.** consequence; importance: *matters of great import.* **9.** meaning; implication: *He felt the import of her words.* —**im•port′a•ble,** *adj.* —**im•port′a•bil′i•ty,** *n.* —**im•port′er,** *n.*

im•por•tance (im pôr′tns), *n.* the quality or state of being important; significance; consequence.

im•por•tant (im pôr′tnt), *adj.* **1.** of much or great significance or consequence: *an important event in world history.* **2.** of considerable distinction: *an important scientist.* **3.** self-important. —**im•por′tant•ly,** *adv.* —**Usage.** Both MORE IMPORTANT and MORE IMPORTANTLY occur at the beginning of a sentence in all varieties of Standard English: *More important* (or *More importantly*)*, her record as an administrator is unmatched.* Objections are raised against MORE IMPORTANTLY on the grounds that the phrase MORE IMPORTANT is an elliptical form of "What is more important," a construction in which the adverb IMPORTANTLY cannot occur. Nevertheless, MORE IMPORTANTLY is the more common expression, esp. in speech; it probably developed by analogy with other sentence-modifying adverbs, as *fortunately* and *regrettably.*

im•por•ta•tion (im′pôr tā′shən, -pōr-), *n.* **1.** the act of importing. **2.** something imported.

im•por•tu•nate (im pôr′chə nit), *adj.* **1.** overly urgent or persistent in solicitation. **2.** troublesome; annoying. —**im•por′tu•nate•ly,** *adv.* —**im•por′tu•nate•ness,** *n.*

im•por•tune (im′pôr to͞on′, -tyo͞on′, im pôr′chən), *v.,* **-tuned, -tun•ing,** *adj.* —*v.t.* **1.** to urge or press with excessive persistence. **2.** to trouble; annoy. —*v.i.* **3.** to make urgent or persistent solicitations. —*adj.* **4.** importunate. —**im′por•tune′ly,** *adv.* —**im′por•tun′er,** *n.*

im•por•tu•ni•ty (im′pôr to͞o′ni tē, -tyo͞o′-), *n., pl.* **-ties. 1.** the state or quality of being importunate. **2.** an importunate solicitation or demand.

im•pose (im pōz′), *v.,* **-posed, -pos•ing.** —*v.t.* **1.** to apply or establish by or as if by authority: *to impose taxes.* **2.** to thrust intrusively upon others: *to impose oneself uninvited.* **3.** to pass or palm off fraudulently or deceptively. **4.** to lay (type pages, plates, etc.) in proper order on an imposing stone or the like and secure in a chase for printing. **5.** to inflict, as a penalty. —*v.i.* **6.** to obtrude oneself or one's needs upon others: *Are you sure my request doesn't impose?* —**im•pos′a•ble,** *adj.*

im•pos•ing (im pō′zing), *adj.* impressive because of great size, stately appearance, dignity of bearing, etc. —**im•pos′ing•ly,** *adv.*

im•po•si•tion (im′pə zish′ən), *n.* **1.** the laying on of something as a burden or obligation. **2.** something imposed, as a burden or duty. **3.** the act of imposing by or as if by authority. **4.** deception; imposture. **5.** the arrangement of page plates in proper order on a press for printing a signature.

im•pos•si•bil•i•ty (im pos′ə bil′i tē, im′pos-), *n., pl.* **-ties. 1.** the quality or state of being impossible. **2.** something impossible.

im•pos•si•ble (im pos′ə bəl), *adj.* **1.** not possible; incapable of being or happening. **2.** unable to be performed or effected: *an impossible assignment.* **3.** difficult beyond reason or propriety: *an impossible situation.* **4.** utterly impracticable: *an impossible plan.* **5.** hopelessly unsuitable, undesirable, or objectionable: *an impossible person.* —**im•pos′si•ble•ness,** *n.* —**im•pos′si•bly,** *adv.*

im•post (im′pōst), *n.* **1.** a tax; duty; levy. **2.** the weight assigned to a horse in a race. —**im′post•er,** *n.*

im•pos•tor or **im•post•er** (im pos′tər), *n.* a person who practices deception under an assumed character, identity, or name.

im•pos•ture (im pos′chər), *n.* **1.** the action or practice of imposing fraudulently upon others. **2.** deception using an assumed character, identity, or name. **3.** an instance of fraudulent imposition. —**im•pos′trous** (-pos′trəs), **im•pos′tur•ous,** *adj.*

im•po•tence (im′pə təns) also **im′po•ten•cy,** *n.* the condition or quality of being impotent.

im•po•tent (im′pə tənt), *adj.* **1.** not potent; lacking power or ability. **2.** lacking force or effectiveness. **3.** (of a male) unable to attain or sustain a penile erection. **4.** (esp. of a male) sterile. —*n.* **5.** an impotent person. —**im′po•tent•ly,** *adv.*

im•pound (im pound′), *v.t.* **1.** to shut up in or as if in a pound; confine. **2.** to seize and retain in custody of the law: *to impound alien property.* —**im•pound′a•ble,** *adj.* —**im•pound′er,** *n.*

im•pov•er•ish (im pov′ər ish, -pov′rish), *v.t.* **1.** to reduce to poverty. **2.** to exhaust the strength or vitality of; deplete: *Excessive farming impoverished the soil.* —**im•pov′er•ish•er,** *n.* —**im•pov′er•ish•ment,** *n.*

im•pov•er•ished (im pov′ər isht, -pov′risht), *adj.* **1.** reduced to poverty. **2.** deprived of strength or vitality. **3.** (of a country or region) having few trees, flowers, birds, wild animals, etc.

im•prac•ti•ca•ble (im prak′ti kə bəl), *adj.* **1.** not practicable; incapable of being put into practice or use with the available means: *an impracticable plan.* **2.** impassable: *impracticable terrain.* —**im•prac′ti•ca•bil′i•ty,** *n.* —**im•prac′ti•ca•bly,** *adv.*

im•prac•ti•cal (im prak′ti kəl), *adj.* **1.** not practical or useful. **2.** incapable of dealing sensibly with practical matters. **3.** idealistic. **4.** impracticable. —**im•prac′ti•cal′i•ty, im•prac′ti•cal•ness,** *n.*

im•pre•cate (im′pri kāt′), *v.,* **-cat•ed, -cat•ing.** —*v.t.* **1.** to call down evil on; curse. —*v.i.* **2.** to invoke evil; utter curses. —**im′pre•ca′tor,** *n.* —**im′pre•ca•to′ry,** *adj.*

im•pre•cise (im′prə sīs′), *adj.* not precise; vague; inexact. —**im′pre•cise′ly,** *adv.* —**im′pre•ci′sion** (-sizh′ən), **im′pre•cise′ness,** *n.*

im•preg•na•ble (im preg′nə bəl), *adj.* **1.** strong enough to resist or withstand attack; unconquerable: *an impregnable fort.* **2.** irrefutable; unassailable. —**im•preg′na•bil′i•ty, im•preg′na•ble•ness,** *n.* —**im•preg′na•bly,** *adv.*

im•preg•nate (*v.* im preg′nāt; *adj.* -nit, -nāt), *v.,* **-nat•ed, -nat•ing,** *adj.* —*v.t.* **1.** to make pregnant. **2.** to fertilize. **3.** to cause to become permeated throughout: *to impregnate a handkerchief with perfume.* **4.** to fill interstices of with a substance. —*adj.* **5.** impregnated. —**im′preg•na′tion,** *n.* —**im•preg′na•tor,** *n.*

im•pre•sa•ri•o (im′prə sär′ē ō′, -sâr′-), *n., pl.* **-ri•os. 1.** a person who organizes or manages public entertainments, as operas or concerts. **2.** a manager; director.

im•press[1] (*v.* im pres′; *n.* im′pres), *v.t.* **1.** to affect deeply or strongly; influence: *He impressed us as sincere.* **2.** to establish firmly: *We impressed on her the importance of honesty.* **3.** to press (an object) into something. **4.** to produce (a mark) by pressure; imprint. **5.** to apply with pressure so as to leave an imprint. **6.** to furnish with a mark by or as if by stamping. **7.** to cause (a voltage) to appear or be produced on a conductor, circuit, etc. —*v.i.* **8.** to create a favorable impression: *behavior intended to impress.* —*n.* **9.** the act of impressing. **10.** a mark made by or as if by pressure. **11.** effect; impression. —**im•press′er,** *n.*

im•press[2] (*v.* im pres′; *n.* im′pres), *v.t.* **1.** to press or force into public service, esp. into the navy. **2.** to take for public use. **3.** to enlist into service by forceful argument: *impressed into helping the family move.*

im•pres•sion (im presh′ən), *n.* **1.** a strong effect produced on the intellect, feelings, or sense. **2.** the effect produced by an agency or influence. **3.** a somewhat vague awareness: *a general impression of distant voices.* **4.** a mark produced by pressure. **5.** an image in the mind caused by something external to it. **6.** the act of impressing or the state of being impressed. **7.** an imprint of the teeth or gums taken in plastic material that forms a mold in dentistry. **8.** a caricatured imitation of a usu. famous person by an entertainer. **9. a.** the process or result of printing from type, plates, an engraved block, etc. **b.** one of a number of printings made at different times from the same set of type. **c.** all the copies, as of a book, printed at one time from one setting of type or from one set of plates. —**im•pres′sion•al,** *adj.*

im•pres•sion•a•ble (im presh′ə nə bəl, -presh′nə-), *adj.* capable of being readily impressed. —**im•pres′sion•a•bil′i•ty, im•pres′sion•a•ble•ness,** *n.* —**im•pres′sion•a•bly,** *adv.*

im•pres•sion•ism (im presh′ə niz′əm), *n.* **1.** (*usu. cap.*) a style of late 19th-century painting characterized chiefly by short brush strokes of bright colors in immediate juxtaposition to represent the effect of light on objects. **2.** a style of literature that emphasizes mood and sensory impressions. **3.** a late 19th-century and early 20th-century style of musical composition in which subtle harmony, rhythm, and tonal color are used to evoke moods and impressions.

im•pres•sion•ist (im presh′ə nist), *n.* **1.** a painter, composer, or writer practicing impressionism. **2.** an entertainer who does impressions. —*adj.* **3.** of or pertaining to artistic impressionism. —**im•pres′sion•is′tic,** *adj.* —**im•pres′sion•is′ti•cal•ly,** *adv.*

im•pres•sive (im pres′iv), *adj.* arousing admiration or respect. —**im•pres′sive•ly,** *adv.* —**im•pres′sive•ness,** *n.*

im•press•ment (im pres′mənt), *n.* the act of impressing people or property into public service or use.

im•pri•ma•tur (im′pri mä′tər, -mā′-, im prim′ə to͝or′, -tyo͝or′), *n.* **1.** permission to print or publish a book, pamphlet, etc., granted by a bishop's authority after such work has received a censor's clearance. **2.** sanction; approval.

im•print (*n.* im′print; *v.* im print′), *n.* **1.** a mark or indentation impressed on something. **2.** any impression or impressed effect. **3. a.** the designation under which a publisher issues a given list of titles. **b.** a designation by which the books of a publisher are identified. —*v.t.* **4.** to mark by or as if by pressure. **5.** to produce (a mark) on something by pressure. **6.** to fix firmly on the mind. **7.** to acquire or establish by imprinting: *to imprint behavior.* —*v.i.* **8.** to experience imprinting.

im•print•ing (im prin′ting), *n.* rapid learning that occurs during a brief receptive period, typically in early life, and that establishes a long-lasting behavioral response to a specific individual, object, or category of stimuli, as attachment to a parent or preference for a type of habitat.

im•pris•on (im priz′ən), *v.t.* to confine in or as if in a prison. —**im•pris′on•a•ble,** *adj.* —**im•pris′on•er,** *n.* —**im•pris′on•ment,** *n.*

im•prob•a•bil•i•ty (im prob′ə bil′i tē, im′prob-), *n., pl.* **-ties. 1.** the quality or condition of being improbable. **2.** something improbable: *events once considered improbabilities.*

im•prob•a•ble (im prob′ə bəl), *adj.* not probable; unlikely to be true or to happen. —**im•prob′a•bly,** *adv.* —**im•prob′a•ble•ness,** *n.*

im•promp•tu (im promp′to͞o, -tyo͞o), *adj., adv., n., pl.* **-tus.** —*adj.* **1.** made or done without previous preparation: *an impromptu party.* **2.**

having the character of an improvisation. —*adv.* **3.** without preparation: *to deliver a speech impromptu.* —*n.* **4.** something impromptu. **5.** a piano work of improvisatory spirit.

im•prop•er (im prop′ər), *adj.* **1.** not proper; not strictly belonging, applicable, or correct: *drew improper conclusions.* **2.** not in accordance with propriety or regulations: *improper conduct.* **3.** abnormal; irregular: *improper functioning of the body.* —**im•prop′er•ly,** *adv.*

improp′er frac′tion, *n.* a fraction having the numerator greater than the denominator.

im•pro•pri•e•ty (im′prə prī′i tē), *n., pl.* **-ties. 1.** the quality or condition of being improper. **2.** inappropriateness; unsuitableness. **3.** unseemliness; indecorousness. **4.** an erroneous or unsuitable expression or act. **5.** an improper use of language.

im•prov (im′prov), *n.* IMPROVISATION.

im•prove (im prōōv′), *v.,* **-proved, -prov•ing.** —*v.t.* **1.** to bring into a more desirable or excellent condition; make better: *improving one's health.* **2.** to make (land) more useful, profitable, or valuable by enclosure, cultivation, etc. **3.** to increase the value of (real property) by betterments. —*v.i.* **4.** to increase in quality or value; become better. **5.** to make improvements. —**im•prov′a•ble,** *adj.* —**im•prov′a•bil′i•ty,** *n.* —**im•prov′a•bly,** *adv.* —**im•prov′ing•ly,** *adv.*

im•prove•ment (im prōōv′mənt), *n.* **1.** an act of improving or the state of being improved. **2.** a change or addition by which a thing is improved: *to make improvements on a house.*

im•prov•i•dent (im prov′i dənt), *adj.* not provident; neglecting to provide for future needs: *The improvident worker saved no money.* —**im•prov′i•dence,** *n.* —**im•prov′i•dent•ly,** *adv.*

im•prov•i•sa•tion (im prov′ə zā′shən, im′prə və-), *n.* **1.** an act of improvising. **2.** something improvised. —**im•prov′i•sa′tion•al,** *adj.*

im•pro•vise (im′prə vīz′), *v.,* **-vised, -vis•ing.** —*v.t.* **1.** to perform or deliver without previous preparation: *to improvise a sermon.* **2.** to compose (verse, music, etc.) on the spur of the moment. **3.** to make, provide, or arrange from whatever materials are readily available: *to improvise dinner.* —*v.i.* **4.** to compose, utter, execute, or arrange anything extemporaneously. —**im′pro•vis′er, im′pro•vi′sor,** *n.*

im•pru•dent (im prōōd′nt), *adj.* not prudent; lacking discretion; rash: *an imprudent remark.* —**im•pru′dence, im•pru′dent•ness, im•pru′den•cy,** *n.* —**im•pru′dent•ly,** *adv.*

im•pu•dence (im′pyə dəns), *n.* **1.** the quality or state of being impudent. **2.** impudent conduct or language.

im•pu•dent (im′pyə dənt), *adj.* of, pertaining to, or characterized by impertinence. —**im′pu•dent•ly,** *adv.*

im•pugn (im pyōōn′), *v.t.* to challenge as false; cast doubt upon: *The lawyer impugned the witness's story.* —**im•pugn′a•ble,** *adj.* —**im•pugn′a•bil′i•ty,** *n.* —**im•pugn′er,** *n.* —**im•pugn′ment,** *n.*

im•pulse (im′puls), *n.* **1.** the influence of a particular feeling, mental state, etc.: *a generous impulse.* **2.** sudden, involuntary inclination prompting to action: *swayed by impulse.* **3.** an instance of this: *an impulse to cry.* **4.** an impelling action or force driving onward or inducing motion. **5.** the effect of an impelling force. **6.** a progressive wave of excitation over a nerve or muscle fiber having a stimulating or inhibitory effect. **7.** the product of the average force acting upon a body and the time during which it acts, equivalent to the change in the momentum of the body produced by such a force. **8.** a single, usu. sudden, flow of electric current in one direction.

im•pul•sion (im pul′shən), *n.* **1.** the act of impelling. **2.** the resulting state or effect.

im•pul•sive (im pul′siv), *adj.* **1.** actuated or swayed by impulse: *an impulsive action.* **2.** characterized by impulsion: *impulsive forces.* —**im•pul′sive•ly,** *adv.* —**im•pul′sive•ness, im′pul•siv′i•ty,** *n.*

im•pu•ni•ty (im pyōō′ni tē), *n.* **1.** exemption from punishment. **2.** immunity from detrimental effects.

im•pure (im pyŏŏr′), *adj.* **1.** not pure; mixed with extraneous matter, esp. of an inferior nature: *impure water.* **2.** modified by admixture, as color. **3.** mixed or combined with something else: *an impure style of architecture.* **4.** regarded by a religion as unclean. **5.** not morally pure; unchaste. —**im•pure′ly,** *adv.* —**im•pure′ness,** *n.*

im•pu•ri•ty (im pyŏŏr′i tē), *n., pl.* **-ties. 1.** the quality or state of being impure. **2.** Often, **impurities.** something that is or makes impure: *to remove impurities from the air.*

im•pu•ta•tion (im′pyŏŏ tā′shən), *n.* **1.** the act of imputing. **2.** an attribution, as of fault or crime; accusation.

im•pute (im pyōōt′), *v.t.,* **-put•ed, -put•ing. 1.** to attribute or ascribe: *The children imputed magical powers to the old woman.* **2.** to attribute or ascribe (something discreditable) to someone or something. **3.** to attribute (righteousness, guilt, etc.) to a person or persons vicariously. **4.** to charge (a person) with fault. —**im•put′a•ble,** *adj.* —**im•put′a•tive,** *adj.* —**im•put′a•tive•ly,** *adv.* —**im•put′a•tive•ness,** *n.* —**im•put′ed•ly,** *adv.* —**im•put′er,** *n.*

in (in), *prep.* **1.** (used to indicate inclusion within space, a place, or limits): *walking in the park.* **2.** (used to indicate inclusion within something abstract or immaterial): *in politics; in the autumn.* **3.** (used to indicate inclusion within or occurrence during a period or limit of time): *in ancient times; a task done in ten minutes.* **4.** (used to indicate limitation or qualification, as of situation, condition, relation, manner, action, etc.): *to speak in a whisper.* **5.** (used to indicate means): *spoken in French.* **6.** (used to indicate motion or direction from outside to a point within) into: *Let's go in the house.* **7.** (used to indicate transition from one state to another): *to break in half.* **8.** (used to indicate object or purpose): *speaking in honor of the event.* —*adv.* **9.** in or into some place, position, state, relation, etc.: *Please come in.* **10.** on the inside; within. **11.** in one's house or office. **12.** in office or power. **13.** in possession or occupancy. **14.** having the turn to play, as in a game. **15.** *Baseball.* (of an infielder or outfielder) in a position closer to home plate than usual; short: *The third baseman played in.* **16.** on good terms; in favor: *in with his boss.* **17.** in vogue; in style: *Hats are in this year.* **18.** in season: *Watermelons will soon be in.* —*adj.* **19.** inner; internal: *the in part of a mechanism.* **20. a.** in favor with advanced or sophisticated people; fashionable; stylish: *the in place to dine.* **b.** comprehensible only to a special group: *an in joke.* **21.** included in a favored group. **22.** inbound: *an in train.* **23.** plentiful; available. **24.** being in power: *the in party.* —*n.* **25.** Usu., **ins.** persons who are in. **26.** pull or influence: *He's got an in with the senator.* **27.** a valid or playable return or service in sports. —***Idiom.*** **28. in for,** certain to undergo (a disagreeable experience). **29. in for it,** *Slang.* about to suffer punishment or unpleasant consequences. Also, *Brit.,* **for it. 30. in that,** because; inasmuch as.

IN, Indiana.

In, *Chem. Symbol.* indium.

in-[1], a prefix representing English *in* (*income; indwelling; inland*), used also as a verb-formative with transitive, intensive, or sometimes little apparent force (*intrust; inweave*). It often assumes the same forms as IN-[2], such as EN-[1], EM-[1], IM-[3].

in-[2], a prefix of Latin origin meaning primarily "in," but used also as a verb-formative with the same force as IN-[1] (*incarcerate; incantation*). Also, **il-, im-, ir-.** Compare EM-[1], EN-[1].

in-[3], a prefix of Latin origin, corresponding to English *un-*, having a negative or privative force, freely used as an English formative, esp. of adjectives and their derivatives and of nouns (*indefensible; inexpensive; invariable*). It has the same variants before consonants as IN-[2] (*immeasurable; illiterate; irregular,* etc.). Compare IL-[2], IM-[2], IR-[2].

-in[1], a noun suffix used in chemical nomenclature (*glycerin; acetin*). In spelling, usage wavers between *-in* and *-ine.* In chemistry a certain distinction of use is attempted, basic substances having the termination *-ine* rather than *-in* (*ammine; aniline*), and *-in* being restricted to certain neutral compounds, glycerides, glucosides, and proteids (*albumin; palmitin*), but this distinction is not always observed.

-in[2], a suffixal use of the adverb IN, extracted from SIT-IN, forming nouns, usu. from verbs, referring to organized protests through or in support of the named activity (*kneel-in; pray-in*) or, more generally, to any organized social or cultural activity (*cook-in; sing-in*).

in•a•bil•i•ty (in′ə bil′i tē), *n.* lack of ability.

in•ac•ces•si•ble (in′ək ses′ə bəl), *adj.* not accessible; unapproachable. —**in′ac•ces′si•bil′i•ty,** *n.* —**in′ac•ces′si•bly,** *adv.*

in•ac•cu•ra•cy (in ak′yər ə sē), *n., pl.* **-cies. 1.** something inaccurate; error. **2.** the quality or state of being inaccurate.

in•ac•cu•rate (in ak′yər it), *adj.* not accurate; incorrect or untrue. —**in•ac′cu•rate•ly,** *adv.*

in•ac•tion (in ak′shən), *n.* absence of action; idleness.

in•ac•ti•vate (in ak′tə vāt′), *v.t.,* **-vat•ed, -vat•ing.** to make inactive. —**in•ac′ti•va′tion,** *n.*

in•ac•tive (in ak′tiv), *adj.* **1.** not active: *an inactive volcano.* **2.** sedentary: *an inactive life.* **3.** sluggish; indolent. **4.** not on active military duty. **5. a.** chemically inert. **b.** having no effect on polarized light. —**in•ac′tive•ly,** *adv.* —**in′ac•tiv′i•ty,** *n.*

in•ad•e•qua•cy (in ad′i kwə sē), *n., pl.* **-cies. 1.** the state or condition of being inadequate. **2.** shortcoming; deficiency.

in•ad•e•quate (in ad′i kwit), *adj.* not adequate or sufficient. —**in•ad′e•quate•ly,** *adv.*

in•ad•mis•si•ble (in′əd mis′ə bəl), *adj.* not admissible; not allowable: *Such evidence would be inadmissible in any court.* —**in′ad•mis′si•bil′i•ty,** *n.* —**in′ad•mis′si•bly,** *adv.*

in•ad•vert•ence (in′əd vûr′tns), *n.* **1.** the quality or condition of being inadvertent; heedlessness. **2.** the act or effect of inattention; an oversight.

in•ad•vert•ent (in′əd vûr′tnt), *adj.* **1.** unintentional: *an inadvertent insult.* **2.** not attentive; heedless. **3.** of, pertaining to, or characterized by lack of attention. —**in′ad•vert′ent•ly,** *adv.*

in•ad•vis•a•ble (in′əd vī′zə bəl), *adj.* not advisable; unwise. —**in′ad•vis′a•bil′i•ty,** *n.* —**in′ad•vis′a•bly,** *adv.*

in•al•ien•a•ble (in āl′yə nə bəl, -ā′lē ə-), *adj.* not alienable; not transferable to another or capable of being repudiated: *inalienable rights.* —**in•al′ien•a•bil′i•ty,** *n.* —**in•al′ien•a•bly,** *adv.*

in•am•o•ra•ta (in am′ə rä′tə, in′am-), *n., pl.* **-tas.** a woman who loves or is loved; female sweetheart or lover.

in•am•o•ra•to (in am′ə rä′tō, in′am-), *n., pl.* **-tos.** a man who loves or is loved; male sweetheart or lover.

in′-and-out′, *adj.* **1.** alternately in and out of a particular situation, condition, venture, etc.; not continuous; irregular: *in-and-out work.* —*n.* **2.** *Manège.* an obstacle consisting of two fences placed too far apart to be cleared in one jump and too close together to allow more than one or two strides between.

in•ane (i nān′), *adj.* **1.** lacking sense, significance, or ideas; silly: *inane questions.* **2.** empty; void. —*n.* **3.** something that is empty or void, esp. the void of infinite space. —**in•ane′ly,** *adv.*

in•an•i•mate (in an′ə mit), *adj.* **1.** not animate; lifeless. **2.** spiritless;

sluggish; dull. **3.** (of a linguistic item) used with reference to objects, concepts, and beings regarded as lacking perception and volition (opposed to *animate*). **—in•an′i•mate•ly,** *adv.* **—in•an′i•mate•ness, in•an′i•ma′tion** (-mā′shən), *n.*

in•an•i•ty (i nan′i tē), *n., pl.* **-ties. 1.** lack of sense, significance, or ideas; silliness. **2.** something inane. **3.** shallowness; superficiality.

in•ap•pli•ca•ble (in ap′li kə bəl), *adj.* not applicable; unsuitable. **—in•ap′pli•ca•bil′i•ty,** *n.* **—in•ap′pli•ca•bly,** *adv.*

in•ap•pro•pri•ate (in′ə prō′prē it), *adj.* not appropriate; not proper or suitable: *an inappropriate dress for the occasion.* **—in′ap•pro′pri•ate•ly,** *adv.* **—in′ap•pro′pri•ate•ness,** *n.*

in•apt (in apt′), *adj.* **1.** not apt or fitting. **2.** without aptitude or capacity. **—in•apt′ly,** *adv.* **—in•apt′ness,** *n.*

in•ap•ti•tude (in ap′ti to͞od′, -tyo͞od′), *n.* **1.** lack of aptitude; unfitness. **2.** unskillfulness; lack of dexterity.

in•ar•tic•u•late (in′är tik′yə lit), *adj.* **1.** lacking the ability to express oneself, esp. in clear and effective speech: *an inarticulate speaker.* **2.** unable to use articulate speech: *inarticulate with rage.* **3.** not articulate; not uttered or emitted with expressive or intelligible modulations: *the baby's inarticulate sounds.* **4.** not fully expressed or expressible: *a voice choked with inarticulate agony.* **5.** *Anat., Zool.* not jointed; lacking joints. **—in′ar•tic′u•late•ly,** *adv.* **—in′ar•tic′u•late•ness,** *n.*

in•as•much as (in′əz much′ əz, az′), *conj.* **1.** in view of the fact that; seeing that; since. **2.** insofar as; to such a degree as.

in•at•ten•tion (in′ə ten′shən), *n.* **1.** lack of attention; negligence. **2.** an act of neglect.

in•at•ten•tive (in′ə ten′tiv), *adj.* not attentive; negligent. **—in′at•ten′tive•ly,** *adv.* **—in′at•ten′tive•ness,** *n.*

in•au•di•ble (in ô′də bəl), *adj.* not audible; incapable of being heard. **—in•au′di•bil′i•ty, in•au′di•ble•ness,** *n.* **—in•au′di•bly,** *adv.*

in•au•gu•ral (in ô′gyər əl, -gər əl), *adj.* **1.** of or pertaining to an inauguration. **2.** marking the beginning of a new venture, series, etc.: *the inaugural run of the pony express.* **—*n.* 3.** an address, as of a president, at the beginning of a term of office. **4.** an inaugural ceremony.

in•au•gu•rate (in ô′gyə rāt′, -gə-), *v.t.,* **-rat•ed, -rat•ing. 1.** to make a formal beginning of; commence; begin: *The end of World War II inaugurated the era of nuclear power.* **2.** to induct into office with formal ceremonies; install. **3.** to introduce into public use by some formal ceremony: *Airmail service between Washington, D.C., and New York City was inaugurated in 1918.* **—in•au′gu•ra′tion,** *n.* **—in•au′gu•ra′tor,** *n.*

Inaugura′tion Day′, *n.* the day on which the president of the U.S. is inaugurated, being the January 20 following the election.

in•aus•pi•cious (in′ô spish′əs), *adj.* not auspicious; boding ill; unfavorable. **—in′aus•pi′cious•ly,** *adv.* **—in′aus•pi′cious•ness,** *n.*

in′-between′, *n.* **1.** INTERMEDIARY. **—*adj.* 2.** intermediate. **—in′-be•tween′ness,** *n.*

in•board (in′bôrd′, -bōrd′), *adj.* **1.** located inside a hull or aircraft. **2.** located nearer the center, as of an airplane. **3.** (of a motorboat) having the motor inboard. **—*adv.* 4.** inside or toward the longitudinal axis or center of a hull, aircraft, machine, etc.

in•born (in′bôrn′), *adj.* naturally present at birth; innate.

in•bound (in′bound′), *adj.* inward bound: *inbound ships.*

in•bounds (in′boundz′), *adj.* **1.** being within the boundaries of a court or field. **2.** of or pertaining to passing a basketball onto the court from out of bounds.

in•bred (in′bred′), *adj.* **1.** naturally inherent; innate: *an inbred grace.* **2.** resulting from or involved in inbreeding.

in•breed (in′brēd′, in brēd′), *v.,* **-bred, -breed•ing. —*v.t.* 1.** to breed (individuals of a closely related group) repeatedly. **2.** to breed within; engender. **—*v.i.* 3.** to engage in or undergo such breeding.

In•ca (ing′kə), *n.* **1.** a member of any of the dominant groups of South American Indian peoples who established an empire in Peru prior to the Spanish conquest. **2.** a ruler or member of the royal family in the Incan empire. **—In•ca•ic** (ing kā′ik, in-), *adj.* **—In′can,** *n., adj.*

in•cal•cu•la•ble (in kal′kyə lə bəl), *adj.* **1.** unable to be calculated. **2.** very numerous or great. **3.** uncertain; undeterminable. **—in•cal′cu•la•bil′i•ty, in•cal′cu•la•ble•ness,** *n.* **—in•cal′cu•la•bly,** *adv.*

in•ca•les•cent (in′kə les′ənt), *adj.* increasing in heat or ardor. **—in′ca•les′cence,** *n.*

in•can•des•cence (in′kən des′əns), *n.* **1.** the emission of visible light by a body, caused by its high temperature. **2.** the light produced by such an emission.

in•can•des•cent (in′kən des′ənt), *adj.* **1.** glowing or white with heat. **2.** extremely bright or lucid; brilliant: *incandescent wit.* **3.** zestful; ardent. **—in′can•des′cent•ly,** *adv.*

in′candes′cent lamp′, *n.* a lamp in which a tungsten filament enclosed within an evacuated glass bulb glows as an electric current passes through it.

in•can•ta•tion (in′kan tā′shən), *n.* **1.** the chanting or uttering of words purporting to have magical power. **2.** the formula employed; spell. **3.** repetitious words used to heighten an effect. **—in′can•ta′tion•al, in•can′ta•to•ry** (-tə tôr′ē, -tōr′ē), *adj.* **—in′can•ta′tor,** *n.*

in•ca•pa•ble (in kā′pə bəl), *adj.* **1.** not having the necessary ability, qualification, or strength to perform some specified act or function. **2.** lacking ordinary capability; incompetent. **3.** legally unqualified. **—in•ca′pa•bil′i•ty, in•ca′pa•ble•ness,** *n.* **—in•ca′pa•bly,** *adv.*

in•ca•pac•i•tate (in′kə pas′i tāt′), *v.t.,* **-tat•ed, -tat•ing. 1.** to deprive of ability, qualification, or strength; disable. **2.** to deprive of legal power. **—in′ca•pac′i•ta′tion,** *n.*

in•ca•pac•i•ty (in′kə pas′i tē), *n.* **1.** lack of ability, qualification, or strength; incapability. **2.** lack of legal power to act.

in•car•cer•ate (in kär′sə rāt′), *v.t.,* **-at•ed, -at•ing. 1.** to imprison; confine. **2.** to enclose; constrict closely. **—in•car′cer•a′tion,** *n.* **—in•car′cer•a′tive,** *adj.* **—in•car′cer•a′tor,** *n.*

in•car•nate (*adj.* in kär′nit, -nāt; *v.* -nāt), *adj., v.,* **-nat•ed, -nat•ing. —*adj.* 1.** given a bodily, esp. a human, form: *a devil incarnate.* **2.** personified; typified: *chivalry incarnate.* **3.** red; crimson. **—*v.t.* 4.** to put into or represent in a concrete form. **5.** to be the embodiment or type of: *a woman who incarnates goodness.* **6.** to invest with a bodily, esp. a human, form.

in•car•na•tion (in′kär nā′shən), *n.* **1.** an incarnate being or form. **2.** a living being embodying a deity or spirit. **3. the Incarnation,** (*sometimes l.c.*) the doctrine that the second person of the Trinity assumed human form in the person of Jesus Christ. **4.** a person or thing regarded as embodying or exhibiting some quality, idea, or the like: *The dancer is the incarnation of grace.* **5.** the act of incarnating. **6.** state of being incarnated. **—in′car•na′tion•al,** *adj.*

in•cen•di•ar•y (in sen′dē er′ē), *adj., n., pl.* **-ar•ies. —*adj.* 1.** used or adapted for setting property on fire: *incendiary bombs.* **2.** of or pertaining to the criminal setting on fire of property. **3.** tending to arouse strife, sedition, etc.; inflammatory: *incendiary speeches.* **—*n.* 4.** a person who deliberately sets fire to property. **5.** a device containing napalm or the like, that burns with an intense heat. **6.** a person who stirs up strife; an agitator.

in•cense[1] (in′sens), *n., v.,* **-censed, -cens•ing. —*n.* 1.** an aromatic gum or other substance producing a sweet odor when burned. **2.** the perfume or smoke arising from incense. **3.** any pleasant fragrance. **4.** homage; adulation. **—*v.t.* 5.** to perfume with incense. **6.** to burn incense for.

in•cense[2] (in sens′), *v.t.,* **-censed, -cens•ing.** to arouse the wrath of; enrage. **—in•cense′ment,** *n.*

in′cense ce′dar, *n.* a tall, W North American coniferous tree, *Calocedrus decurrens,* of the cypress family.

in•cen•tive (in sen′tiv), *n.* **1.** something that incites or tends to incite to action or greater effort. **—*adj.* 2.** inciting, as to action. **—in•cen′tive•ly,** *adv.*

in•cep•tion (in sep′shən), *n.* beginning; commencement.

in•cep•tive (in sep′tiv), *adj.* **1.** beginning; initial. **2.** (of a verb form or aspect) expressing the beginning of the action indicated by the underlying verb, as Latin *calēscō* "become or begin to be hot" from *caleō* "be hot." **—*n.* 3.** the inceptive aspect. **4.** a verb in this aspect. **—in•cep′tive•ly,** *adv.*

in•cer•ti•tude (in sûr′ti to͞od′, -tyo͞od′), *n.* **1.** uncertainty; doubtfulness. **2.** instability; insecurity.

in•ces•sant (in ses′ənt), *adj.* continuing without interruption; unending: *an incessant noise.* **—in•ces′san•cy,** *n.* **—in•ces′sant•ly,** *adv.*

in•cest (in′sest), *n.* **1.** sexual relations between persons so closely related that they are forbidden by law or religion to marry. **2.** the crime of sexual relations, cohabitation, or marriage between such persons.

in•ces•tu•ous (in ses′cho͞o əs), *adj.* **1.** involving incest. **2.** guilty of incest. **3.** too closely interconnected: *an incestuous relationship between business and government.* **—in•ces′tu•ous•ly,** *adv.*

inch (inch), *n.* **1.** a unit of length, 1/12 of a foot, equivalent to 2.54 centimeters. **2.** a very small amount, degree, or distance: *averted disaster by an inch.* **—*v.t., v.i.* 3.** to move by small degrees: *We inched along the road.* **—*Idiom.* 4. every inch,** in every respect; completely. **5. within an inch of,** nearly; close to.

in•cho•ate (in kō′it, -āt; *esp. Brit.* in′kō āt′), *adj.* **1.** not yet completed or fully developed. **2.** just begun; incipient. **—in•cho′ate•ly,** *adv.* **—in•cho′ate•ness,** *n.*

inch•worm (inch′wûrm′), *n.* MEASURINGWORM.

in•ci•dence (in′si dəns), *n.* **1.** the rate or range of occurrence or influence of something: *a high incidence of flu.* **2.** occurrence; happening. **3. a.** the striking of a ray of light, beam of electrons, etc., on a surface, or the direction of striking. **b.** ANGLE OF INCIDENCE (def. 1).

in•ci•dent (in′si dənt), *n.* **1.** an occurrence or event. **2.** a distinct piece of action, as in a story. **3.** something that occurs casually in connection with something else. **4.** something appertaining or attaching to something else. **5.** a seemingly minor occurrence, esp. involving nations or factions, that can lead to serious consequences: *a border incident.* **—*adj.* 6.** likely to happen. **7.** naturally appertaining: *hardships incident to the life of an explorer.* **8.** conjoined, esp. as subordinate to a principal thing. **9.** falling or striking on something, as light rays.

in•ci•den•tal (in′si den′tl), *adj.* **1.** happening or likely to happen in an unplanned or subordinate conjunction with something else. **2.** incurred casually and in addition to the regular or main amount: *incidental expenses.* **—*n.* 3.** something incidental. **4. incidentals,** minor expenses. **—in′ci•den′tal•ness,** *n.*

in•ci•den•tal•ly (in′si den′tl ē *or, for 1,* -dent′lē), *adv.* **1.** apart or aside from the main subject; parenthetically. **2.** by chance.

in′ciden′tal mu′sic, *n.* music intended primarily to point up or accompany parts of the action of a play or to serve as transitional material between scenes.

in•cin•er•ate (in sin′ə rāt′), *v.t.,* **-at•ed, -at•ing.** to cause to burn to ashes; cremate. **—in•cin′er•a′tion,** *n.*

in•cin•er•a•tor (in sin′ə rā′tər), *n.* a furnace or apparatus for incinerating materials.

in•cip•i•ent (in sip′ē ənt), *adj.* beginning to exist or appear: *an incipient cold.* —**in•cip′i•ent•ly,** *adv.*

in•cise (in sīz′), *v.t.,* **-cised, -cis•ing. 1.** to cut into; cut marks or figures upon. **2.** to engrave with marks or figures.

in•cised (in sīzd′), *adj.* **1.** made by cutting; engraved: *an incised pattern.* **2.** made or cut cleanly: *an incised wound.* **3.** (of a leaf) sharply and irregularly notched.

in•ci•sion (in sizh′ən), *n.* **1.** a cut, gash, or notch. **2.** the act of incising. **3.** a surgical cut into a tissue or organ. **4.** incisiveness; keenness.

in•ci•sive (in sī′siv), *adj.* **1.** penetrating; cutting: *an incisive tone of voice.* **2.** clear and direct; keen: *an incisive commentary.* —**in•ci′sive•ly,** *adv.* —**in•ci′sive•ness,** *n.*

in•ci•sor (in sī′zər), *n.* any of the four anterior teeth in each jaw, used for cutting and gnawing.

in•cite (in sīt′), *v.t.,* **-cit•ed, -cit•ing.** to stimulate to action; urge on; stir up. —**in•cit′a•ble,** *adj.* —**in•cit′ant,** *adj., n.* —**in′ci•ta′tion** (-sī tā′shən, -si-), *n.* —**in•cit′er,** *n.* —**in•cit′ing•ly,** *adv.*

in•ci•vil•i•ty (in′sə vil′i tē), *n., pl.* **-ties. 1.** the quality or state of being uncivil **2.** an uncivil act. —**in•civ′il** (-siv′əl), *adj.*

in•clem•ent (in klem′ənt), *adj.* **1.** severe; stormy: *inclement weather.* **2.** not kind or merciful. —**in•clem′en•cy,** *n.* —**in•clem′ent•ly,** *adv.*

in•cli•na•tion (in′klə nā′shən), *n.* **1.** a special disposition of the mind or temperament; a liking or preference: *a great inclination for sports.* **2.** something to which one is inclined. **3.** the act of inclining or state of being inclined: *an inclination of the head.* **4.** a tendency toward a certain condition, action, etc. **5.** deviation or amount of deviation from a normal, esp. horizontal or vertical, direction or position. **6.** an inclined surface. **7. a.** the angle between two lines or two planes. **b.** the angle formed by the x-axis and a given line. —**in′cli•na′tion•al,** *adj.*

in•cline (*v.* in klīn′; *n.* in′klīn, in klīn′), *v.,* **-clined, -clin•ing,** *n.* —*v.i.* **1.** to deviate from the vertical or horizontal; slant. **2.** to have a mental tendency, preference, etc.; be disposed: *He inclines toward mysticism.* **3.** to approach; approximate: *The color inclines toward blue.* **4.** to tend in character or in course of action. **5.** to lean; bend. —*v.t.* **6.** to persuade; dispose: *Her attitude did not incline me to help her.* **7.** to bow; bend: *inclined his head in greeting.* **8.** to cause to lean or bend in a particular direction. —*n.* **9.** an inclined surface; slope; slant. —**in•clin′er,** *n.*

in•clined (in klīnd′), *adj.* **1.** deviating in direction from the horizontal or vertical; sloping. **2.** disposed; of a mind: *He was inclined to stay.* **3.** tending in a direction that makes an angle with a plane or line.

in•clude (in klo͞od′), *v.t.,* **-clud•ed, -clud•ing. 1.** to contain or encompass as part of a whole: *The meal includes dessert and coffee.* **2.** to place as part of a category. **3.** to enclose. —**in•clud′a•ble, in•clud′i•ble,** *adj.*

in•clu•sion (in klo͞o′zhən), *n.* **1.** the act of including or the state of being included. **2.** something that is included. **3.** a foreign body or inert structure within a cell. **4.** a solid, liquid, or gaseous body enclosed within a mineral or rock.

in•clu•sive (in klo͞o′siv), *adj.* **1.** including the limit or extremes in consideration or account: *from 6 to 37 inclusive.* **2.** including everything; comprehensive: *an inclusive fee.* **3.** (of a first person plural pronoun) including the person addressed, as *we* in *Shall we dance?* Compare EXCLUSIVE (def. 9). —***Idiom.* 4. inclusive of,** including: *Europe inclusive of Britain.* —**in•clu′sive•ly,** *adv.* —**in•clu′sive•ness,** *n.*

in•cog•i•tant (in koj′i tənt), *adj.* thoughtless; inconsiderate. —**in•cog′i•tant•ly,** *adv.*

in•cog•ni•ta (in′kog nē′tə, in kog′ni-), *adv., adj., n., pl.* **-tas.** —*adv., adj.* **1.** (of a woman or girl) with one's identity hidden or unknown. —*n.* **2.** a woman or girl who is incognita. **3.** the state or disguise of such a woman or girl.

in•cog•ni•to (in′kog nē′tō, in kog′ni tō′), *adv., adj., n., pl.* **-tos.** —*adv., adj.* **1.** with one's identity hidden or unknown. —*n.* **2.** a person who is incognito. **3.** the state or disguise of such a person.

in•cog•ni•zant (in kog′nə zənt), *adj.* lacking knowledge or awareness. —**in•cog′ni•zance,** *n.*

in•co•her•ence (in′kō hēr′əns, -her′-), *n.* **1.** the quality or state of being incoherent. **2.** something that is incoherent.

in•co•her•ent (in′kō hēr′ənt, -her′-), *adj.* **1.** lacking logical or meaningful connection: *incoherent thoughts.* **2.** inarticulate: *incoherent with rage.* **3.** lacking cohesion; loose; disjointed. —**in′co•her′ent•ly,** *adv.*

in•com•bus•ti•ble (in′kəm bus′tə bəl), *adj.* not combustible; incapable of being burned. —**in′com•bus′ti•bil′i•ty, in′com•bus′ti•ble•ness,** *n.* —**in′com•bus′ti•bly,** *adv.*

in•come (in′kum), *n.* **1.** the monetary payment received for goods or services, or from other sources, such as rents or investments; revenue; receipts: *an annual income of $25,000.* **2.** a coming in; influx. —**in′come•less,** *adj.*

in′comes pol′icy, *n.* a government policy to curb inflation that relies on voluntary compliance rather than on mandatory wage, price, or profit controls.

in′come tax′, *n.* a tax levied on the annual incomes of individuals and corporations.

in•com•ing (in′kum′ing), *adj.* **1.** coming in; arriving: *the incoming tide.* **2.** succeeding, as an officeholder: *the incoming mayor.* **3.** accruing, as profit. —*n.* **4.** the act of coming in; arrival.

in•com•men•su•ra•ble (in′kə men′sər ə bəl, -shər-), *adj.* not commensurable; having no common basis, measure, or standard of comparison. —**in′com•men′su•ra•bil′i•ty,** *n.* —**in′com•men′su•ra•bly,** *adv.*

in•com•men•su•rate (in′kə men′sər it, -shər-), *adj.* **1.** not commensurate; disproportionate; inadequate. **2.** incommensurable. —**in′com•men′su•rate•ly,** *adv.* —**in′com•men′su•rate•ness,** *n.*

in•com•mode (in′kə mōd′), *v.t.,* **-mod•ed, -mod•ing.** to inconvenience or discomfort; disturb; trouble.

in•com•mo•di•ous (in′kə mō′dē əs), *adj.* inconvenient; uncomfortable. —**in′com•mo′di•ous•ly,** *adv.* —**in′com•mo′di•ous•ness,** *n.*

in•com•mu•ni•ca•ble (in′kə myo͞o′ni kə bəl), *adj.* **1.** incapable of being communicated or imparted: *an incommunicable secret.* **2.** uncommunicative; taciturn. —**in′com•mu′ni•ca•bly,** *adv.*

in•com•mu•ni•ca•do (in′kə myo͞o′ni kä′dō), *adv., adj.* **1.** without means of communication with others: *to hold a spy incommunicado.* **2.** in solitary confinement.

in•com•mu•ni•ca•tive (in′kə myo͞o′ni kə tiv, -kā′-), *adj.* UNCOMMUNICATIVE. —**in′com•mu′ni•ca•tive•ly,** *adv.* —**in′com•mu′ni•ca•tive•ness,** *n.*

in•com•mut•a•ble (in′kə myo͞o′tə bəl), *adj.* **1.** unchangeable; immutable: *an incommutable law.* **2.** not exchangeable. —**in′com•mut′a•bil′i•ty, in′com•mut′a•ble•ness,** *n.* —**in′com•mut′a•bly,** *adv.*

in•com•pa•ra•ble (in kom′pər ə bəl, -prə bəl), *adj.* **1.** fine beyond comparison; matchless: *incomparable beauty.* **2.** not fit for comparison. —**in•com′pa•ra•bil′i•ty,** *n.* —**in•com′pa•ra•bly,** *adv.*

in•com•pat•i•ble (in′kəm pat′ə bəl), *adj.* **1.** unable to exist together in harmony: *incompatible roommates.* **2.** incongruous; discordant: *incompatible colors.* —**in′com•pat′i•bil′i•ty,** *n.* —**in′com•pat′i•bly,** *adv.*

in•com•pe•tence (in kom′pi təns) also **in•com′pe•ten•cy,** *n.* the quality or state of being incompetent.

in•com•pe•tent (in kom′pi tənt), *adj.* **1.** lacking qualification or ability; incapable. **2.** characterized by or showing incompetence. **3.** not legally qualified. —*n.* **4.** an incompetent person, as one who is mentally deficient. —**in•com′pe•tent•ly,** *adv.*

in•com•plete (in′kəm plēt′), *adj.* **1.** lacking some part. **2.** (of a forward pass) not completed. —**in′com•plete′ly,** *adv.* —**in′com•plete′ness,** *n.*

in•com•pre•hen•si•ble (in′kom pri hen′sə bəl, in kom′-), *adj.* impossible to comprehend; unintelligible. —**in′com•pre•hen′si•bil′i•ty, in′com•pre•hen′si•ble•ness,** *n.* —**in′com•pre•hen′si•bly,** *adv.*

in•com•put•a•ble (in′kəm pyo͞o′tə bəl), *adj.* incapable of being computed; incalculable. —**in′com•put′a•bly,** *adv.*

in•con•ceiv•a•ble (in′kən sē′və bəl), *adj.* **1.** not conceivable; unimaginable. **2.** unbelievable. —**in′con•ceiv′a•bil′i•ty, in′con•ceiv′a•ble•ness,** *n.* —**in′con•ceiv′a•bly,** *adv.*

in•con•clu•sive (in′kən klo͞o′siv), *adj.* leading to no clear result or answer. —**in′con•clu′sive•ly,** *adv.* —**in′con•clu′sive•ness,** *n.*

in•con•gru•ent (in kong′gro͞o ənt, in′kən gro͞o′-, -kəng-), *adj.* not congruent. —**in•con′gru•ence,** *n.* —**in•con′gru•ent•ly,** *adv.*

in•con•gru•i•ty (in′kən gro͞o′i tē, -kəng-), *n., pl.* **-ties. 1.** the quality or state of being incongruous. **2.** something incongruous.

in•con•gru•ous (in kong′gro͞o əs), *adj.* **1.** out of keeping or place; inappropriate. **2.** not harmonious in character. **3.** inconsistent: *an incongruous alibi.* —**in•con′gru•ous•ly,** *adv.* —**in•con′gru•ous•ness,** *n.*

in•con•se•quen•tial (in′kon si kwen′shəl, in kon′-), *adj.* **1.** having little importance; trivial. **2.** inconsequent; illogical. **3.** irrelevant. —**in′con•se•quen′ti•al′i•ty,** *n.* —**in′con•se•quen′tial•ly,** *adv.*

in•con•sid•er•a•ble (in′kən sid′ər ə bəl), *adj.* **1.** small, as in value, amount, or size. **2.** not worth consideration. —**in′con•sid′er•a•ble•ness,** *n.* —**in′con•sid′er•a•bly,** *adv.*

in•con•sid•er•ate (in′kən sid′ər it), *adj.* **1.** lacking regard for the rights or feelings of others. **2.** thoughtless; heedless. **3.** overhasty; rash. —**in′con•sid′er•ate•ly,** *adv.* —**in′con•sid′er•ate•ness, in′con•sid′er•a′tion,** *n.*

in•con•sist•en•cy (in′kən sis′tən sē), *n., pl.* **-cies. 1.** the quality or condition of being inconsistent. **2.** something that is inconsistent: *a report full of inconsistencies.* Often, **in′con•sist′ence.**

in•con•sist•ent (in′kən sis′tənt), *adj.* **1.** marked by incompatibility of elements: *an inconsistent story.* **2.** not in agreement with each other: *inconsistent claims.* **3.** not consistent in standards or behavior. —**in′con•sist′ent•ly,** *adv.*

in•con•sol•a•ble (in′kən sō′lə bəl), *adj.* not consolable. —**in′con•sol′a•bil′i•ty, in′con•sol′a•ble•ness,** *n.* —**in′con•sol′a•bly,** *adv.*

in•con•spic•u•ous (in′kən spik′yo͞o əs), *adj.* not conspicuous. —**in′con•spic′u•ous•ly,** *adv.* —**in′con•spic′u•ous•ness,** *n.*

in•con•stant (in kon′stənt), *adj.* not constant; changeable: *an inconstant breeze; an inconstant friend.* —**in•con′stan•cy,** *n.* —**in•con′stant•ly,** *adv.*

in•con•ti•nent (in kon′tn ənt), *adj.* **1.** unable to restrain natural discharges or evacuations of urine or feces. **2.** not being in control: *incontinent of temper.* **3.** lacking in moderation. —**in•con′ti•nence,** *n.*

in•con•tro•vert•i•ble (in′kon trə vûr′tə bəl, in kon′-), *adj.* not open to question; indisputable. —**in′con•tro•vert′i•bil′i•ty, in′con•tro•vert′i•ble•ness,** *n.* —**in′con•tro•vert′i•bly,** *adv.*

in•con•ven•ience (in′kən vēn′yəns), *n., v.,* **-ienced, -ienc•ing.** —*n.* **1.** the quality or state of being inconvenient. **2.** an inconvenient circumstance or thing. —*v.t.* **3.** to put to trouble; incommode.

in•con•ven•ient (in′kən vēn′yənt), *adj.* **1.** not easily accessible or at hand. **2.** inopportune; untimely. **3.** not suiting one's needs or purposes. —**in′con•ven′ient•ly,** *adv.*

in•cor•po•rate (*v.* in kôr′pə rāt′; *adj.* -pər it, -prit), *v.,* **-rat•ed, -rat•ing,** *adj.* —*v.t.* **1.** to form into a corporation. **2.** to introduce as an integral part: *to incorporate revisions into a text.* **3.** to include as a part: *His book incorporates his earlier essay.* **4.** to combine into one body or uniform substance. **5.** to embody: *It incorporates all her thinking on the subject.* **6.** to form into a society or organization. —*v.i.* **7.** to form a legal corporation. **8.** to combine so as to form one body. —*adj.* **9.** incorporated. —**in•cor′po•ra′tion,** *n.* —**in•cor′po•ra′tive,** *adj.*

in•cor•po•rat•ed (in kôr′pə rā′tid), *adj.* **1.** formed into a legal corporation. **2.** combined in one body.

in•cor•po•re•al (in′kôr pôr′ē əl, -pōr′-), *adj.* **1.** not corporeal or material; insubstantial. **2.** having no material value but giving evidence of value, as a franchise. —**in′cor•po′re•al′i•ty,** *n.* —**in′cor•po′re•al•ly,** *adv.*

in•cor•rect (in′kə rekt′), *adj.* **1.** not correct as to fact; inaccurate: *an incorrect answer on a test.* **2.** improper; inappropriate: *incorrect attire.* **3.** not correct in form, use, or manner. —**in′cor•rect′ly,** *adv.* —**in′cor•rect′ness,** *n.*

in•cor•ri•gi•ble (in kôr′i jə bəl, -kor′-), *adj.* **1.** bad beyond reform: *an incorrigible liar.* **2.** unruly; uncontrollable: *an incorrigible child.* **3.** firmly fixed; not easily changed: *an incorrigible habit.* **4.** not easily influenced: *an incorrigible optimist.* —**in•cor′ri•gi•bil′i•ty, in•cor′ri•gi•ble•ness,** *n.* —**in•cor′ri•gi•bly,** *adv.*

in•cor•rupt•i•ble (in′kə rup′tə bəl), *adj.* **1.** not corruptible; honest. **2.** not susceptible to decay. —**in′cor•rupt′i•bil′i•ty, in′cor•rupt′i•ble•ness,** *n.* —**in′cor•rupt′i•bly,** *adv.*

in•crease (*v.* in krēs′; *n.* in′krēs), *v.,* **-creased, -creas•ing,** *n.* —*v.t.* **1.** to make greater, as in number, size, strength, or quality; augment: *to increase one's knowledge.* —*v.i.* **2.** to become greater, as in number, size, strength, or quality. **3.** to multiply by propagation. —*n.* **4.** growth or augmentation in size, strength, or quality. **5.** the act or process of increasing. **6.** an amount by which something is increased. —**in•creas′a•ble,** *adj.* —**in•creas′ed•ly,** *adv.*

in•creas•ing•ly (in krē′sing lē), *adv.* to an increasing degree.

in•cred•i•ble (in kred′ə bəl), *adj.* **1.** so extraordinary as to seem impossible: *incredible speed.* **2.** hard to believe; unbelievable: *The book's plot is incredible.* —**in•cred′i•bil′i•ty,** *n.* —**in•cred′i•bly,** *adv.*

in•cre•du•li•ty (in′kri do͞o′li tē, -dyo͞o′-), *n.* the quality or state of being incredulous.

in•cred•u•lous (in krej′ə ləs), *adj.* **1.** disinclined or indisposed to believe; skeptical. **2.** indicating disbelief: *an incredulous look.* —**in•cred′u•lous•ly,** *adv.* —**in•cred′u•lous•ness,** *n.*

in•cre•ment (in′krə mənt, ing′-), *n.* **1.** something added or gained; addition; increase. **2.** the act or process of increasing. **3.** an amount by which something increases. **4.** one of a series of regular additions: *deposits in increments of $500.* **5. a.** the difference between two values of a variable; a change, positive, negative, or zero, in an independent variable. **b.** the increase of a function due to an increase in the independent variable. —**in′cre•men′tal** (-men′tl), *adj.* —**in′cre•men′tal•ly,** *adv.*

in•cres•cent (in kres′ənt), *adj.* waxing: *the increscent moon.* —**in•cres′cence,** *n.*

in•crim•i•nate (in krim′ə nāt′), *v.t.,* **-nat•ed, -nat•ing.** to accuse of or indicate involvement in a crime or fault: *The testimony of the defendant incriminated many others.* —**in•crim′i•na′tion,** *n.* —**in•crim′i•na′tor,** *n.* —**in•crim•i•na•to•ry** (-nə tôr′ē, -tōr′ē), *adj.*

in•crust (in krust′) also **encrust,** *v.t.* **1.** to cover or line with a crust or hard coating. **2.** to form into a crust. **3.** to deposit as a crust. —*v.i.* **4.** to form a crust. —**in•crust′ant,** *adj., n.*

in•crus•ta•tion (in′kru stā′shən) also **encrustation,** *n.* **1.** the act of incrusting or the state of being incrusted. **2.** a crust or hard coating. **3. a.** the inlaying or addition of enriching materials to a surface or an object. **b.** the materials used.

in•cu•bate (in′kyə bāt′, ing′-), *v.,* **-bat•ed, -bat•ing.** —*v.t.* **1.** to sit on (eggs) for the purpose of hatching. **2.** to hatch (eggs), as by sitting on them or by artificial heat. **3.** to maintain at a favorable temperature and in other conditions promoting development, as prematurely born infants. **4.** to develop as if by hatching: *pranksters incubating new schemes.* —*v.i.* **5.** to sit on eggs. **6.** to undergo incubation. —**in′cu•ba′tive,** *adj.*

in•cu•ba•tion (in′kyə bā′shən, ing′-), *n.* **1.** the act or process of incubating. **2.** the state of being incubated. **3.** the period between the initial infection and the appearance of symptoms of a disease. —**in′cu•ba′tion•al, in•cu•ba•to•ry** (in′kyə bə tôr′ē, -tōr′ē, ing′-), *adj.*

in•cu•ba•tor (in′kyə bā′tər, ing′-), *n.* **1.** an apparatus in which eggs are hatched artificially. **2.** an enclosed apparatus in which prematurely born infants are kept and cared for in controlled conditions. **3.** an apparatus in which media inoculated with microorganisms are cultivated at a constant temperature.

in•cu•bus (in′kyə bəs, ing′-), *n., pl.* **-bi** (-bī′), **-bus•es. 1.** NIGHTMARE. **2.** something that oppresses one like a nightmare.

in•cul•cate (in kul′kāt, in′kul kāt′), *v.t.,* **-cat•ed, -cat•ing. 1.** to implant by repeated statement or admonition: *to inculcate virtue in the young.* **2.** to cause to accept something, as an idea. —**in′cul•ca′tion,** *n.* —**in•cul′ca•tive** (-kə tiv), **in•cul′ca•to•ry** (-tôr′ē, -tōr′ē), *adj.* —**in•cul′ca•tor,** *n.*

in•cul•pa•ble (in kul′pə bəl), *adj.* not culpable; blameless. —**in•cul′pa•bil′i•ty, in•cul′pa•ble•ness,** *n.* —**in•cul′pa•bly,** *adv.*

in•cul•pate (in kul′pāt, in′kul pāt), *v.t.,* **-pat•ed, -pat•ing.** to incriminate. —**in′cul•pa′tion,** *n.* —**in•cul′pa•to′ry** (-pə tôr′ē, -tōr′ē), *adj.*

in•cum•ben•cy (in kum′bən sē), *n., pl.* **-cies. 1.** the quality or state of being incumbent. **2.** the position or term of an incumbent.

in•cum•bent (in kum′bənt), *adj.* **1.** currently holding an indicated office: *the incumbent president.* **2.** obligatory: *a duty incumbent upon me.* **3.** resting, lying, or pressing on something. —*n.* **4.** the holder of an office or an ecclesiastical benefice. —**in•cum′bent•ly,** *adv.*

in•cu•nab•u•la (in′kyo͞o nab′yə lə, ing′-), *n.pl., sing.* **-lum** (-ləm). **1.** books printed before 1501. **2.** the earliest stages or first traces of anything. —**in′cu•nab′u•lar,** *adj.*

in•cur (in kûr′), *v.t.,* **-curred, -cur•ring. 1.** to become liable for: *to incur debts.* **2.** to bring upon oneself: *incurred our displeasure.*

in•cur•a•ble (in kyo͝or′ə bəl), *adj.* **1.** not curable: *an incurable disease.* **2.** not susceptible to change: *incurable pessimism.* —**in•cur′a•bil′i•ty, in•cur′a•ble•ness,** *n.* —**in•cur′a•bly,** *adv.*

in•cur•sion (in kûr′zhən, -shən), *n.* **1.** a hostile entrance into or invasion of a place or territory; raid. **2.** an inroad; penetration.

in•cus (ing′kəs), *n., pl.* **in•cu•des** (in kyo͞o′dēz). the middle bone of the chain of three small bones in the middle ear of mammals. Also called **anvil.** —**in′cu•date′** (-kyə dāt′, -dit), **in′cu•dal,** *adj.*

in•cuse (in kyo͞oz′, -kyo͞os′), *adj.* hammered or stamped in, as a figure on a coin.

ind-, var. of INDO- before a vowel: *indamine.*

ind., 1. independent. **2.** index. **3.** indicative. **4.** industry.

in•debt•ed (in det′id), *adj.* **1.** obligated to repay money. **2.** obligated for favors or kindness received.

in•debt•ed•ness (in det′id nis), *n.* **1.** the state of being indebted. **2.** something owed.

in•de•cen•cy (in dē′sən sē), *n., pl.* **-cies. 1.** the quality or state of being indecent. **2.** an indecent act, remark, etc.

in•de•cent (in dē′sənt), *adj.* **1.** offending against standards of morality or propriety: *indecent language; indecent behavior.* **2.** unbecoming; unseemly: *indecent haste.* —**in•de′cent•ly,** *adv.*

inde′cent expo′sure, *n.* the intentional exposure of one's body, esp. the genitals, in a public place and in a manner offensive to the prevailing social standards of propriety.

in•de•ci•pher•a•ble (in′di sī′fər ə bəl), *adj.* incapable of being deciphered; impenetrable; incomprehensible. —**in′de•ci′pher•a•bil′i•ty, in′de•ci′pher•a•ble•ness,** *n.* —**in′de•ci′pher•a•bly,** *adv.*

in•de•ci•sion (in′di sizh′ən), *n.* inability to decide; vacillation.

in•de•ci•sive (in′di sī′siv), *adj.* **1.** characterized by indecision; irresolute. **2.** not clearly delineated; inconclusive. —**in′de•ci′sive•ly,** *adv.* —**in′de•ci′sive•ness,** *n.*

in•dec•o•rous (in dek′ər əs, in′di kôr′əs, -kōr′-), *adj.* not decorous; unseemly; unbecoming. —**in•dec′o•rous•ly,** *adv.* —**in•dec′o•rous•ness,** *n.*

in•de•co•rum (in′di kôr′əm, -kōr′-), *n.* **1.** indecorous behavior or character. **2.** something indecorous.

in•deed (in dēd′), *adv.* **1.** in fact; in truth (used for emphasis or confirmation): *It did indeed rain.* —*interj.* **2.** (used to express surprise or ironic skepticism): *That's a fine excuse indeed.*

in•de•fat•i•ga•ble (in′di fat′i gə bəl), *adj.* incapable of being tired out; untiring. —**in′de•fat′i•ga•bil′i•ty,** *n.* —**in′de•fat′i•ga•bly,** *adv.*

in•de•fen•si•ble (in′di fen′sə bəl), *adj.* **1.** not justifiable; inexcusable. **2.** incapable of being defended against physical attack. **3.** untenable: *indefensible arguments.* —**in′de•fen′si•bil′i•ty, in′de•fen′si•ble•ness,** *n.* —**in′de•fen′si•bly,** *adv.*

in•de•fin•a•ble (in′di fī′nə bəl), *adj.* not readily identified, described, analyzed, or determined. —**in′de•fin′a•ble•ness,** *n.* —**in′de•fin′a•bly,** *adv.*

in•def•i•nite (in def′ə nit), *adj.* **1.** having no fixed or specified limit: *an indefinite number.* **2.** not clearly defined or determined: *an indefinite boundary.* **3.** not firmly decided or committed; uncertain; vague: *She was indefinite about joining us for lunch.* —**in•def′i•nite•ly,** *adv.* —**in•def′i•nite•ness,** *n.*

indef′inite ar′ticle, *n.* an article, as English *a* or *an,* that denotes class membership of the noun it modifies without particularizing it.

indef′inite pro′noun, *n.* a pronoun, as English *some, any,* or *somebody,* that leaves unspecified the identity of its referent.

in•de•his•cent (in′di his′ənt), *adj.* not splitting open at maturity to discharge seeds or spores: *indehiscent fruit.* —**in′de•his′cence,** *n.*

in•del•i•ble (in del′ə bəl), *adj.* **1.** making marks that cannot be removed: *indelible pens.* **2.** not removable, as by washing or erasure: *indelible stains.* **3.** memorable; unforgettable: *indelible memories.* —**in•del′i•bil′i•ty, in•del′i•ble•ness,** *n.* —**in•del′i•bly,** *adv.*

in•del•i•cate (in del′i kit), *adj.* **1.** rather offensive to propriety or decency; improper: *indelicate language.* **2.** lacking sensitivity; tactless. —**in•del′i•cate•ly,** *adv.* —**in•del′i•ca•cy,** *n.*

in•dem•ni•fi•ca•tion (in dem′nə fi kā′shən), *n.* **1.** the act of indemnifying or the state of being indemnified. **2.** something that serves to indemnify. —**in′dem•nif′i•ca•to′ry** (-nif′i kə tôr′ē, -tōr′ē), *adj.*

in•dem•ni•fy (in dem′nə fī′), *v.t.,* **-fied, -fy•ing. 1.** to compensate for damage or loss sustained, expense incurred, etc. **2.** to secure against anticipated loss. —**in•dem′ni•fi′er,** *n.*

in•dem•ni•ty (in dem′ni tē), *n., pl.* **-ties.** **1.** protection or security against damage or loss. **2.** compensation for damage or loss sustained. **3.** legal exemption from penalties attaching to illegal actions.

in•dent[1] (*v.* in dent′; *n. also* in′dent), *v.t.* **1.** to form notches in the edge of: *Waves indented the beach.* **2.** to set in from the margin: *Indent the first line of a paragraph.* **3.** to sever (a document drawn up in duplicate) along an irregular line as a means of identification. **4.** to cut the edge of (copies of a document) in an irregular way. **5.** *Chiefly Brit.* to order by official requisition. *—v.i.* **6.** to form an indentation. *—n.* **7.** a toothlike notch or recess. **8.** an indention. **9.** a certificate issued by a state or the federal government at the close of the Revolutionary War for the principal or interest due on the public debt. **10.** *Brit.* a requisition for stores. **—in•dent′er, in•den′tor,** *n.*

in•dent[2] (*v.* in dent′; *n. also* in′dent), *v.t.* **1.** to press in so as to form a dent. **2.** to form a dent in. *—n.* **3.** DENT[1].

in•den•ta•tion (in′den tā′shən), *n.* **1.** a notch or recess. **2.** a series of notches: *the indentation of a maple leaf.* **3.** a notching or being notched. **4.** INDENTION (defs. 1, 2).

in•den•tion (in den′shən), *n.* **1.** the indenting of a written or printed line. **2.** the blank space left by indenting. **3.** the act of indenting or the state of being indented.

in•den•ture (in den′chər), *n., v.,* **-tured, -tur•ing.** *—n.* **1.** a deed or agreement executed in two or more copies with edges correspondingly indented. **2.** a contract by which a person, is bound to service. **3.** an official or formal document for use as a voucher. **4.** INDENTATION. *—v.t.* **5.** to bind by indenture, as an apprentice. **—in•den′ture•ship′,** *n.*

inden′tured serv′ant, *n.* a person who is bound to work for another for a specified period of time, esp. such a person who came to America during the colonial period.

in•de•pend•ence (in′di pen′dəns), *n.* the quality or state of being independent.

In•de•pend•ence (in′di pen′dəns), *n.* a city in W Missouri: starting point of the Santa Fe and Oregon trails. 111,669.

Independ′ence Day′, *n.* July 4, a U.S. holiday commemorating the adoption of the Declaration of Independence on July 4, 1776. Also called **Fourth of July.**

in•de•pend•en•cy (in′di pen′dən sē), *n., pl.* **-cies.** **1.** INDEPENDENCE (def. 1). **2.** a territory not under the control of any other power. **3.** (*cap.*) **a.** the principle that a congregation or church is autonomous, egalitarian, and free from external ecclesiastical control. **b.** the polity based on this principle.

in•de•pend•ent (in′di pen′dənt), *adj.* **1.** not influenced or controlled by others; thinking or acting for oneself. **2.** not depending or contingent upon something else. **3.** not relying on another for aid or support. **4.** refusing to be under obligation to others. **5.** possessing a competence: *financially independent.* **6.** sufficient to support one without the need to work: *an independent income.* **7.** executed or originating outside a given unit, agency, or business: *an independent inquiry.* **8.** free from party commitments: *independent voters.* **9.** (of a quantity or function) not depending upon another for its value. **10.** *Gram.* capable of standing syntactically as a complete sentence: *an independent clause.* Compare DEPENDENT (def. 4), MAIN (def. 2). **11.** (*cap.*) of or pertaining to religious Independency. *—n.* **12.** an independent person or thing. **13.** a small, privately owned business. **14.** (*sometimes cap.*) a person who votes without regard to the party affiliation of candidates. **15.** (*cap.*) an adherent of Independency. **—*Idiom.*** **16. independent of,** irrespective of; regardless of. **—in•de•pend′ent•ly,** *adv.*

in′-depth′, *adj.* intensive; thorough: *an in-depth study.*

in•de•scrib•a•ble (in′di skrī′bə bəl), *adj.* not describable; too extraordinary for description: *indescribable confusion.* **—in′de•scrib′a•bil′i•ty, in′de•scrib′a•ble•ness,** *n.* **—in′de•scrib′a•bly,** *adv.*

in•de•struct•i•ble (in′di struk′tə bəl), *adj.* not destructible. **—in′de•struct′i•bil′i•ty, in′de•struct′i•ble•ness,** *n.* **—in′de•struct′i•bly,** *adv.*

in•de•ter•mi•na•ble (in′di tûr′mə nə bəl), *adj.* **1.** incapable of being ascertained. **2.** incapable of being decided or settled. **—in′de•ter′mi•na•ble•ness,** *n.* **—in′de•ter′mi•na•bly,** *adv.*

in•de•ter•mi•nate (in′di tûr′mə nit), *adj.* **1.** not precisely fixed or determined; indefinite; vague. **2.** not settled in advance. **3.** *Math.* **a.** (of a quantity) undefined, as 0/0. **b.** (of an equation) able to be satisfied by more than one value for each unknown. **4.** (of an inflorescence) having the axis or axes not ending in a flower or bud. **—in′de•ter′mi•nate•ly,** *adv.* **—in′de•ter′mi•nate•ness,** *n.* **—in′de•ter′mi•na′tion** (-nā′shən), *n.*

in•dex (in′deks), *n., pl.* **-dex•es, -di•ces** (-də sēz′). **1.** (in a printed work) an alphabetical listing of names, places, and topics along with the numbers of the pages on which they are mentioned or discussed. **2.** a sequential arrangement of material, esp. in alphabetical or numerical order. **3.** something used or serving to point out; indication: *a true index of his character.* **4.** a pointer or indicator, as in a scientific instrument. **5.** Also called **fist.** a printed sign in the shape of a hand with extended index finger, used to point out a note or paragraph. **6.** a number or formula expressing a property or ratio: *index of growth; index of intelligence.* **7.** *Math.* **a.** EXPONENT (def. 3). **b.** the integer n in a radical $\sqrt[n]{\ }$ defining the n-th root: $\sqrt[3]{\ }$ *is a radical having index three.* **c.** a subscript or superscript indicating the position of an object in a series of similar objects, as the subscripts 1, 2, and 3 in the series x_1, x_2, x_3. **8.** (*usu. cap.*) any list of forbidden material deemed morally or politically harmful by authorities. *—v.t.* **9.** to provide with an index. **10.** to enter in an index. **11.** to serve to indicate. **12.** to adjust, as wages. **—in′dex•er,** *n.*

in•dex•a•tion (in′dek sā′shən), *n.* the automatic adjustment of wages, interest rates, etc., according to changes in the cost of living, esp. to compensate for inflation.

in′dex fin′ger, *n.* FOREFINGER.

in′dex fos′sil, *n.* a widely distributed fossil, of narrow range in time, regarded as characteristic of a given geological formation and used esp. in determining the age of related formations.

in′dex of refrac′tion, *n.* a number indicating the speed of light in a given medium, usu. as the ratio of the speed of light in a vacuum or in air to that in the given medium.

In•di•a (in′dē ə), *n.* **1.** a republic in S Asia: formerly a British colony; gained independence in 1947; became a republic within the Commonwealth of Nations in 1950. 967,612,804; 1,246,880 sq. mi. (3,229,419 sq. km). *Cap.:* New Delhi. **2.** a subcontinent in S Asia, S of the Himalayas, occupied by Bangladesh, Bhutan, India, Nepal, and Pakistan.

In′dia ink′, *n.* (*sometimes l.c.*) **1.** a black pigment consisting of lampblack mixed with glue or size. **2.** a fluid ink made from this pigment.

In•di•an (in′dē ən), *n.* **1.** AMERICAN INDIAN. **2.** any of the indigenous languages of the American Indians. **3.** a native, citizen, or inhabitant of the Republic of India. **4.** a native or inhabitant of the subcontinent of India. *—adj.* **5.** of or pertaining to the American Indians or their languages. **6.** of or pertaining to India or S Asia. **7.** ORIENTAL (def. 3). **8.** pertaining to a phytogeographical division comprising India S of the Himalayas, and Pakistan and Sri Lanka. **—Usage.** In modern times the term INDIAN may refer to a member of an aboriginal American people, to an inhabitant of the subcontinent of India, or to a citizen of the Republic of India. In the 18th century the term AMERICAN INDIAN came to be used for the aboriginal inhabitants of the U.S. and Canada; it now includes the aboriginal peoples of South America as well. AMERINDIAN and AMERIND developed in the next century in a further attempt to reduce ambiguity. The most recent designation, esp. in North America, is NATIVE AMERICAN. All these terms appear in edited writing. Whether one will gain ascendancy over the others remains to be seen. The only pre-European inhabitants of North America to whom INDIAN or terms using it usu. are not applied are the Eskimos and Aleuts. See also ESKIMO.

In•di•an•a (in′dē an′ə), *n.* a state in the central United States. 5,840,528; 36,291 sq. mi. (93,995 sq. km). *Cap.:* Indianapolis. *Abbr.:* IN, Ind. **—In′di•an′an, In′di•an′i•an,** *adj., n.*

In′dian′a bal′lot, *n.* a ballot on which the candidates are listed in separate columns by party. Also called PARTY-COLUMN BALLOT. Compare MASSACHUSETTS BALLOT, OFFICE-BLOCK BALLOT.

In•di•an•ap•o•lis (in′dē ə nap′ə lis), *n.* the capital of Indiana, in the central part. 752,279.

Indianapolis 500, *n.* a 500-mile oval-track race for rear-engine cars having particular specifications, held annually in Indianapolis, Ind.

In′dian corn′, *n.* **1.** CORN[1] (def. 1). **2.** any primitive corn with variegated kernels.

In′dian hemp′, *n.* **1.** a North American dogbane, *Apocynum cannabinum,* having a root with laxative and emetic properties. **2.** HEMP (def. 1).

In′dian O′cean, *n.* an ocean S of Asia, E of Africa, and W of Australia. 28,357,000 sq. mi. (73,444,630 sq. km).

In′dian paint′brush, *n.* any of several semiparasitic plants of the genus *Castilleja,* figwort family, with brightly colored, petallike bracts.

In′dian pud′ding, *n.* a sweet baked pudding made of cornmeal, molasses, milk, and various spices.

In′dian sum′mer, *n.* a period of mild, dry weather sometimes occurring in late October or early November.

In′dian Ter′ritory, *n.* a former territory of the U.S.: now in E Oklahoma. ab. 31,000 sq. mi. (80,000 sq. km).

In′dian wres′tling, *n.* **1.** a form of wrestling in which two opponents clasp each other's right or left hand and, placing the corresponding feet side by side, attempt to unbalance each other. **2.** a form of wrestling in which two opponents, lying side by side on their backs and in opposite directions, lock near arms and raise and lock corresponding legs, with each attempting to force the other's leg down until one opponent is unable to remain lying flat.

in•di•cate (in′di kāt′), *v.t.,* **-cat•ed, -cat•ing.** **1.** to be a sign of; evidence; show: *Snow indicates winter.* **2.** to point out or point to: *to indicate a place on a map.* **3.** to demonstrate the conditions of: *The thermometer indicates temperature.* **4.** to express minimally: *indicated his disapproval with a frown.* **5.** to show or suggest the suitability or necessity of: *The facts indicate a need for action.* **—in′di•cat′a•ble,** *adj.* **—in•dic′a•to′ry** (-dik′ə tôr′ē, -tōr′ē), *adj.*

in•di•ca•tion (in′di kā′shən), *n.* **1.** something serving to indicate; sign; token. **2.** something indicated as suitable or necessary. **3.** an act of indicating. **4.** the degree marked by an instrument.

in•dic•a•tive (in dik′ə tiv), *adj.* **1.** pointing out; expressive; suggestive: *behavior indicative of mental disorder.* **2.** of or designating the grammatical mood used for ordinary objective statements and questions, as the mood of the verb *plays* in *She plays tennis* or *were* in *Were they home?* Compare IMPERATIVE (def. 3), SUBJUNCTIVE (def. 1). *—n.* **3.** the indicative mood. **4.** a verb in the indicative. **—in•dic′a•tive•ly,** *adv.*

in•di•ca•tor (in′di kā′tər), *n.* **1.** a person or thing that indicates. **2.** a pointing or directing device, as a pointer on the dial of a measuring instrument. **3.** an instrument that indicates the condition of a machine in operation. **4. a.** a substance, as litmus, that indicates the presence or concentration of a certain constituent. **b.** a substance often used in a titration to indicate the point at which the reaction is complete. **5.** a plant or animal that indicates by its presence in a given area the existence of certain environmental conditions.

in•di•ces (in′də sēz′), *n.* a pl. of INDEX.

in•di•ci•a (in dish′ē ə), *n.pl., sing.* **-ci•um. 1.** the legends or stamplike devices printed on postal stationery or bulk mail to indicate that postage has been paid. **2.** distinctive marks.

in•dict (in dīt′), *v.t.* **1.** to charge with a crime: *The grand jury indicted him for rape.* **2.** to accuse of wrongdoing. **—in•dict•ee′,** *n.* **—in•dict′er, in•dict′or,** *n.*

in•dict•a•ble (in dī′tə bəl), *adj.* **1.** subject to being indicted. **2.** making a person liable to indictment: *an indictable offense.* **—in•dict′a•bil′i•ty,** *n.* **—in•dict′a•bly,** *adv.*

in•dict•ment (in dīt′mənt), *n.* **1.** an act of indicting. **2.** a formal accusation by a grand jury, initiating a criminal case. **3.** any charge, serious criticism, or cause for blame. **4.** the state of being indicted.

in•die (in′dē), *Informal.* **—n. 1.** an independently owned business or a self-employed person, esp. an independent producer of movies or records. **—***adj.* **2.** of, pertaining to, or being an indie.

in•dif•fer•ence (in dif′ər əns, -dif′rəns), *n.* **1.** lack of interest or concern. **2.** unimportance; little or no concern. **3.** the quality or condition of being indifferent. **4.** mediocrity.

in•dif•fer•ent (in dif′ər ənt, -dif′rənt), *adj.* **1.** without interest or concern; not caring; apathetic. **2.** having no bias or preference; impartial. **3.** neutral or average; routine: *an indifferent specimen.* **4.** not particularly good: *an indifferent performance.* **5.** of only moderate amount, extent, etc. **6.** immaterial or unimportant. **7.** not essential or obligatory, as an observance. **8.** neutral in chemical, electric, or magnetic quality. **9.** not differentiated or specialized, as cells or tissues. **—n. 10.** a person who is indifferent, esp. in matters of religion or politics. **—in•dif′fer•ent•ly,** *adv.*

in•dif•fer•ent•ism (in dif′ər ən tiz′əm, -dif′rən-), *n.* **1.** systematic indifference. **2.** the principle or opinion that differences of religious belief are unimportant. **—in•dif′fer•ent•ist,** *n.*

in•di•gence (in′di jəns), *n.* seriously impoverished condition; poverty.

in•dig•e•nous (in dij′ə nəs), *adj.* **1.** originating in and characteristic of a particular region or country; native (often fol. by *to*): *plants indigenous to Canada; indigenous peoples of southern Africa.* **2.** innate; inherent; natural (usu. fol. by *to*): *feelings indigenous to humans.* **—in•dig′e•nous•ly,** *adv.* **—in•dig′e•nous•ness, in′di•gen′i•ty** (-jen′i tē), *n.*

in•di•gent (in′di jənt), *adj.* **1.** lacking the necessities of life because of poverty; needy; poor; impoverished. **—n. 2.** a person who is indigent. **—in′di•gent•ly,** *adv.*

in•di•gest•i•ble (in′di jes′tə bəl, -dī-), *adj.* not digestible; not easily digested. **—in′di•gest′i•bil′i•ty,** *n.* **—in′di•gest′i•bly,** *adv.*

in•di•ges•tion (in′di jes′chən, -dī-), *n.* **1.** a feeling of discomfort after eating, as of heartburn, nausea, or bloating; dyspepsia. **2.** inadequate or abnormal digestion.

in•dig•nant (in dig′nənt), *adj.* feeling, characterized by, or expressing indignation. **—in•dig′nant•ly,** *adv.*

in•dig•na•tion (in′dig nā′shən), *n.* strong displeasure at something considered unjust, offensive, insulting, or base; righteous anger.

in•dig•ni•ty (in dig′ni tē), *n., pl.* **-ties.** an injury to a person's dignity; slighting or contemptuous treatment; a humiliating affront, insult, or injury.

in•di•go (in′di gō′), *n., pl.* **-gos, -goes,** *adj.* **—n. 1.** a blue dye, $C_{16}H_{10}N_2O_2$, obtained from various plants, esp. of the genus *Indigofera,* or manufactured synthetically. **2.** INDIGO BLUE (def. 2). **3.** any hairy plant of the genus *Indigofera,* having clusters of usu. red or purple flowers. **4.** a color ranging from a deep violet blue to a dark grayish blue. **—***adj.* **5.** of the color indigo.

in′digo blue′, *n.* **1.** INDIGO (def. 4). **2.** Also called **indigo, indigotin.** a dark blue, water-insoluble, crystalline powder, $C_{16}H_{10}N_2O_2$, the coloring principle of the dye indigo. **—in′di•go-blue′,** *adj.*

in•di•rect (in′də rekt′, -dī-), *adj.* **1.** deviating from a straight line, as a path. **2.** not resulting directly or immediately, as effects or consequences. **3.** not direct in action or procedure. **4.** devious; not straightforward. **5.** not direct in bearing, application, force, etc.: *indirect evidence.* **6.** of, pertaining to, or characteristic of indirect speech: *an indirect question.* **7.** not descending in a direct line of succession, as a title or inheritance. **—in′di•rect′ly,** *adv.* **—in′di•rect′ness,** *n.*

in′direct ev′idence, *n.* CIRCUMSTANTIAL EVIDENCE.

in′direct light′ing, *n.* reflected or diffused light, used esp. in interiors to avoid glare or shadows.

in′direct ob′ject, *n.* a word or group of words representing the person or thing with reference to which the action of a verb is performed, esp. as beneficiary of the action or receiver of the direct object, as *the boy* in *She gave the boy a book.*

in′direct speech′, *n.* the reporting of what a speaker said consisting not of the speaker's exact words but of a version transformed for grammatical inclusion in a larger sentence, as in *She said she wasn't going.* Compare DIRECT SPEECH.

in′direct tax′, *n.* a tax levied on a commodity that is paid by the consumer as part of the market price.

in•dis•cern•i•ble (in′di sûr′nə bəl, -zûr′-), *adj.* not discernible; not able to be seen or perceived clearly; imperceptible. **—in′dis•cern′i•ble•ness, in′dis•cern′i•bil′i•ty,** *n.* **—in′dis•cern′i•bly,** *adv.*

in•dis•creet (in′di skrēt′), *adj.* not discreet; lacking prudence, good judgment, or circumspection: *an indiscreet remark.* **—in′dis•creet′ly,** *adv.* **—in′dis•creet′ness,** *n.*

in•dis•crete (in′di skrēt′, in dis′krēt), *adj.* not discrete; not divided into parts.

in•dis•cre•tion (in′di skresh′ən), *n.* **1.** lack of discretion; imprudence. **2.** an indiscreet act, remark, etc. **—in′dis•cre′tion•ar′y,** *adj.*

in•dis•crim•i•nate (in′di skrim′ə nit), *adj.* **1.** not discriminating; lacking in care, judgment, selectivity, etc. **2.** not discriminate; haphazard. **3.** thrown together; jumbled. **—in′dis•crim′i•nate•ly,** *adv.* **—in′dis•crim′i•nate•ness, in′dis•crim′i•na′tion** (-nā′shən), *n.*

in•dis•pen•sa•ble (in′di spen′sə bəl), *adj.* **1.** absolutely necessary, essential, or requisite. **2.** incapable of being disregarded or neglected. **—n. 3.** a person or thing that is indispensable. **—in′dis•pen′sa•bil′i•ty, in′dis•pen′sa•ble•ness,** *n.* **—in′dis•pen′sa•bly,** *adv.*

in•dis•pose (in′di spōz′), *v.t.,* **-posed, -pos•ing. 1.** to make ill, esp. slightly. **2.** to make unfit; disqualify. **3.** to render averse or unwilling; disincline: *His anger indisposed him from helping.*

in•dis•posed (in′di spōzd′), *adj.* **1.** sick or ill, esp. slightly. **2.** disinclined or unwilling; averse: *indisposed to help.*

in•dis•put•a•ble (in′di spyōō′tə bəl, in dis′pyə-), *adj.* **1.** not disputable or deniable; uncontestable: *indisputable evidence.* **2.** unquestionably real, valid, true, etc. **—in′dis•put′a•bil′i•ty, in′dis•put′a•ble•ness,** *n.* **—in′dis•put′a•bly,** *adv.*

in•dis•tinct (in′di stingkt′), *adj.* **1.** not distinct; not clearly marked or defined: *indistinct markings.* **2.** not clearly distinguishable or perceptible. **3.** not distinguishing clearly: *indistinct vision.* **—in′dis•tinct′ly,** *adv.* **—in′dis•tinct′ness,** *n.*

in•dis•tin•guish•a•ble (in′di sting′gwi shə bəl), *adj.* **1.** not distinguishable. **2.** indiscernible; imperceptible. **—in′dis•tin′guish•a•ble•ness, in′dis•tin′guish•a•bil′i•ty,** *n.* **—in′dis•tin′guish•a•bly,** *adv.*

in•dite (in dīt′), *v.t.,* **-dit•ed, -dit•ing.** to compose or write (a speech, poem, etc.). **—in•dite′ment,** *n.* **—in•dit′er,** *n.*

in•di•um (in′dē əm), *n.* a rare metallic element that is soft, white, malleable, and easily fusible, is found combined in various ore minerals, and has two indigo-blue lines in its spectrum. *Symbol:* In; *at. wt.:* 114.82; *at. no.:* 49; *sp. gr.:* 7.3 at 20°C.

in•di•vid•u•al (in′də vij′ōō əl), *n.* **1.** a single human being, as distinguished from a group. **2.** PERSON. **3.** a distinct, indivisible entity. **4.** (in logic) an object referred to by a name or variable, as distinguished from a property or class. **—***adj.* **5.** single; particular; separate. **6.** intended for the use of one person only: *individual portions.* **7.** of or characteristic of a particular person or thing: *individual tastes.* **8.** distinguished by special or singular characteristics: *individual style.* **9.** existing as a distinct entity, or considered as such; discrete: *individual parts.*

in•di•vid•u•al•ism (in′də vij′ōō ə liz′əm), *n.* **1.** a social theory advocating the liberty, rights, or independent action of the individual. **2.** the principle or habit of independent thought or action. **3.** the pursuit of individual rather than common or collective interests; egoism. **4.** individual character; individuality. **5.** an individual peculiarity. **6.** *Philos.* **a.** the doctrine that only individual things are real. **b.** the doctrine or belief that all actions are determined by, or at least take place for, the benefit of the individual, not of society as a whole.

in•di•vid•u•al•ist (in′də vij′ōō ə list), *n.* **1.** a person who shows independence or individuality in thought or action. **2.** an advocate of individualism. **—in′di•vid′u•al•is′tic,** *adj.* **—in′di•vid′u•al•is′ti•cal•ly,** *adv.*

in•di•vid•u•al•i•ty (in′də vij′ōō al′i tē), *n., pl.* **-ties. 1.** the particular character, or aggregate of qualities, that distinguishes one person or thing from others. **2.** a person or thing of individual or distinctive character. **3.** the state or quality of being individual; existence as a distinct individual.

in•di•vid•u•al•ize (in′də vij′ōō ə līz′), *v.t.,* **-ized, -iz•ing. 1.** to make individual or distinctive; give an individual or distinctive character to. **2.** to mention, indicate, or consider individually; specify; particularize. **—in′di•vid′u•al•i•za′tion,** *n.* **—in′di•vid′u•al•iz′er,** *n.*

in•di•vid•u•al•ly (in′də vij′ōō ə lē), *adv.* **1.** one at a time; separately. **2.** personally: *Each of us is individually responsible.* **3.** in an individual or personally unique manner.

individ′ual retire′ment account′, *n.* a savings plan that permits an individual depositor to set aside savings that are tax-free until retirement or withdrawal. *Abbr.:* IRA Compare KEOGH PLAN.

in•di•vid•u•ate (in′də vij′ōō āt′), *v.t.,* **-at•ed, -at•ing. 1.** to form into an individual or distinct entity. **2.** to give an individual or distinctive character to; individualize. **—in′di•vid′u•a′tor,** *n.*

in•di•vis•i•ble (in′də viz′ə bəl), *adj.* **1.** not divisible; not separable into parts. **—n. 2.** something indivisible. **—in′di•vis′i•bil′i•ty, in′di•vis′i•ble•ness,** *n.* **—in′di•vis′i•bly,** *adv.*

indo-, a combining form representing INDIGO: *indophenol.* Also, *esp. before a vowel,* **ind-.**

Indo-, a combining form representing India: *Indo-European.*

In•do-Ar•y•an (in′dō âr′ē ən, -yən, -ar′; -är′yən), *n.* **1.** one of the two major divisions of the Indo-Iranian languages, including Sanskrit, Hindi, Bengali, Marathi, and other languages of India, Pakistan, Bangladesh, and Sri Lanka. **2. a.** a speaker of any of these languages. **b.** a speaker of the Indo-European language that was the ancestor of the ancient and modern Indo-Aryan languages. —*adj.* **3.** of or pertaining to these languages or their speakers.

In•do•chi•na (in′dō chī′nə), *n.* a peninsula in SE Asia, between the Bay of Bengal and the South China Sea, comprising Vietnam, Cambodia, Laos, Thailand, W Malaysia, and Burma. Compare FRENCH INDOCHINA. —**In′do•chi•nese′** (-nēz′, -nēs′), *adj., n., pl.* **-nese.**

in•doc•tri•nate (in dok′trə nāt′), *v.t.,* **-nat•ed, -nat•ing. 1.** to instruct in a doctrine or ideology, esp. dogmatically. **2.** to teach or inculcate. —**in•doc′tri•na′tion,** *n.* —**in•doc′tri•na′tor,** *n.*

In•do-Eu•ro•pe•an (in′dō yŏŏ r′ə pē′ən), *n.* **1.** a family of languages spoken or formerly spoken i n Europe and SW, central, and S Asia, and carried by colonization and conquest since c1500 to many other parts of the world: major branches of Indo-European are Anatolian, Indo-Iranian, Armenian, Greek, Slavic, Baltic, Albanian, Germanic, Tocharian, Italic, and Celtic. **2.** a member of any of the peoples speaking an Indo-European language. **3. a.** the language ancestral to the Indo-European languages; Proto-Indo-European. *Abbr.:* IE **b.** a speaker of this language. —*adj.* **4.** of or pertaining to Indo-European or its speakers.

In•do-I•ra•ni•an (in′dō i rā′nē ən, -i rä′-, -ī rā′-), *n.* a family of languages, a branch of the Indo-European family, that includes the Indo-Aryan and Iranian languages.

in•do•lent (in′dl ənt), *adj.* **1.** having or showing a disposition to avoid exertion; slothful. **2.** inactive or relatively benign: *indolent ulcer.* —**in′do•lence,** *n.* —**in′do•lent•ly,** *adv.*

in•dom•i•ta•ble (in dom′i tə bəl), *adj.* incapable of being subdued or overcome: *an indomitable fighter; indomitable courage.* —**in•dom′i•ta•bil′i•ty, in•dom′i•ta•ble•ness,** *n.* —**in•dom′i•ta•bly,** *adv.*

In•do•ne•sia (in′də nē′zhə, -shə), *n.* **Republic of,** a republic in the Malay Archipelago, consisting of Sumatra, Java, Bali, Sulawesi, the S part of Borneo, Irian Jaya, and about 13,000 small islands: won independence from the Netherlands in 1949. 209,774,138; ab. 741,100 sq. mi. (1,919,400 sq. km). *Cap.:* Jakarta. Formerly, **Netherlands East Indies, Dutch East Indies.**

In•do•ne•sian (in′də nē′zhən, -shən, -zē ən, -dō-), *n.* **1.** a native or inhabitant of Indonesia; a citizen of the Republic of Indonesia. **2.** a form of Malay that serves as an official language and lingua franca in Indonesia. —*adj.* **3.** of or pertaining to Indonesia, its inhabitants, or the language Indonesian.

in•door (in′dôr′, -dōr′), *adj.* located, used, or existing inside a building: *indoor plumbing; indoor games.*

in•doors (in dôrz′, -dōrz′), *adv.* in or into a building.

in•du•bi•ta•ble (in dōō′bi tə bəl, -dyōō′-), *adj.* not to be doubted; patently evident or certain; unquestionable. —**in•du′bi•ta•bil′i•ty, in•du′bi•ta•ble•ness,** *n.* —**in•du′bi•ta•bly,** *adv.*

in•duce (in dōōs′, -dyōōs′), *v.t.,* **-duced, -duc•ing. 1.** to lead or move by persuasion or influence, as to some action or state of mind: *Induce him to stay; induced them to forgiveness.* **2.** to cause: *It induces sleep.* **3.** to produce (an electric current) by induction. **4.** *Logic.* to assert or establish (a proposition about a class) on the basis of observations on a number of particular facts. **5.** *Genetics.* to increase expression of (a gene) by inactivating a negative control system or activating a positive control system; derepress. **6.** *Biochem.* to stimulate the synthesis of (a protein, esp. an enzyme) by increasing gene transcription. —**in•duc′i•ble,** *adj.*

in•duce•ment (in dōōs′mənt, -dyōōs′-), *n.* **1.** something that induces or persuades; incentive. **2.** the act of inducing. **3.** the state of being induced.

in•duct (in dukt′), *v.t.* **1.** to install in an office, benefice, position, etc., esp. with formal ceremonies. **2.** to introduce, esp. to something requiring special knowledge or experience; initiate (usu. fol. by *to* or *into*): *They inducted him into the mystic rites of the order.* **3.** to take (a draftee) into military service; draft. **4.** to bring in as a member.

in•duct•ance (in duk′təns), *n.* **1.** the property of a circuit by which a change in current induces, by electromagnetic induction, an electromotive force. **2.** INDUCTOR (def. 1).

in•duc•tee (in′duk tē′, in duk-), *n.* a person inducted into military service or some other organization.

in•duc•tion (in duk′shən), *n.* **1.** the act of inducing. **2.** formal installation in an office, benefice, or the like. **3.** (in logic) **a.** any form of reasoning in which the conclusion, though supported by the premises, does not follow from them necessarily. **b.** the process of estimating the validity of observations of part of a class of facts as evidence for a proposition about the whole class. **c.** a conclusion reached by this process. Compare DEDUCTION (def. 5). **4.** a presentation or bringing forward, as of facts or evidence. **5.** the process by which a body having electric or magnetic properties produces magnetism, an electric charge, or an electromotive force in a neighboring body without visible contact. **6.** the process or principle by which one part of an embryo influences the differentiation of another part. **7.** *Biochem.* the synthesis of an enzyme in response to an increased concentration of its substrate in the cell. —**in•duc′tion•less,** *adj.*

induc′tion heat′ing, *n.* a method of heating a conducting material, as metal in a furnace, by using electromagnetic induction to establish a current in the material.

in•duc•tive (in duk′tiv), *adj.* **1.** of, pertaining to, or involving electrical or magnetic induction. **2.** operating by induction: *an inductive machine.* **3.** of, pertaining to, or employing logical induction. **4.** capable of bringing about embryonic induction. **5.** serving to induce; leading or influencing. **6.** introductory. —**in•duc′tive•ly,** *adv.* —**in•duc′tive•ness,** *n.*

in•duc•tor (in duk′tər), *n.* **1.** a coil used to introduce inductance into an electric circuit. **2.** a person who inducts, as into office.

in•dulge (in dulj′), *v.,* **-dulged, -dulg•ing.** —*v.t.* **1.** to yield to or gratify (desires, feelings, etc.). **2.** to yield to the wishes or whims of; be lenient or permissive with. **3.** to allow to follow one's will or inclination: *to indulge oneself in reckless spending.* —*v.i.* **4.** to yield to an inclination or desire; indulge oneself (often fol. by *in*): *indulged in a bit of humor.* —**in•dulg′er,** *n.* —**in•dulg′ing•ly,** *adv.*

in•dul•gence (in dul′jəns), *n., v.,* **-genced, -genc•ing.** —*n.* **1.** the act or practice of indulging; humoring. **2.** the state of being indulgent. **3.** indulgent allowance or tolerance. **4.** something indulged in. **5.** (in Roman Catholicism) a partial remission of the temporal punishment that is still due for sin after absolution. **6.** (in the reigns of Charles II and James II) a royal dispensation to Protestant Dissenters and Roman Catholics granting them a certain amount of religious freedom. **7.** *Com.* an extension of time for payment or performance. —*v.t.* **8.** to provide with an ecclesiastical indulgence.

in•dul•gent (in dul′jənt), *adj.* characterized by or showing indulgence; benignly permissive. —**in•dul′gent•ly,** *adv.*

in•du•rate (*v.* in′dōō rāt′, -dyōō-; *adj.* in′dōō rit, -dyōō-; in dŏŏr′it, -dyŏŏr′-), *v.,* **-rat•ed, -rat•ing,** *adj.* —*v.t.* **1.** to make hard; harden: *Pressure and heat indurate the rock.* **2.** to make callous, stubborn, or unfeeling. **3.** to inure; accustom. **4.** to make enduring; establish. —*v.i.* **5.** to become hard. **6.** to become established. —*adj.* **7.** hardened; unfeeling.

in•du•ra•tion (in′dōō rā′shən, -dyōō-), *n.* **1.** the act of indurating. **2.** the state of being indurated. **3. a.** LITHIFICATION. **b.** hardening of rock by heat or pressure. **4.** an abnormal hardening of an area of the body. —**in′du•ra′tive,** *adj.*

In•dus (in′dəs), *n.* a river in S Asia, flowing from W Tibet through India and Pakistan to the Arabian Sea. 1900 mi. (3060 km) long.

indus., **1.** industrial. **2.** industry.

in•dus•tri•al (in dus′trē əl), *adj.* **1.** of or pertaining to a type of the nature of, or resulting from industry. **2.** having many and highly developed industries. **3.** engaged in an industry or industries. **4.** of or pertaining to the workers in industries. **5.** used or appropriate for use in industry. **6.** of or pertaining to a type of rock music characterized by heavy dissonant pounding. —*n.* **7.** an industrial product. **8. industrials,** stocks and bonds of industrial companies. —**in•dus′tri•al•ly,** *adv.* —**in•dus′tri•al•ness,** *n.*

indus′trial arts′, *n.pl.* the techniques of using tools and machinery, as taught in secondary and technical schools.

indus′trial engineer′ing, *n.* engineering applied to the planning, design, and control of industrial operations. —**indus′trial engineer′,** *n.*

in•dus•tri•al•ism (in dus′trē ə liz′əm), *n.* the economic organization of a society built largely on mechanized industry.

in•dus•tri•al•ist (in dus′trē ə list), *n.* **1.** a person who owns or manages an industrial enterprise. —*adj.* **2.** of, pertaining to, or characterized by industrialism.

in•dus•tri•al•ize (in dus′trē ə līz′), *v.,* **-ized, -iz•ing.** —*v.t.* **1.** to introduce industry into on a large scale: *They industrialized the entire valley.* —*v.i.* **2.** to undergo industrialization. —**in•dus′tri•al•i•za′tion,** *n.*

indus′trial park′, *n.* an industrial complex, typically in a suburban area and set in parklike surroundings.

indus′trial psychol′ogy, *n.* the application of psychological principles and techniques to business and industrial problems, as in the selection of personnel or development of training programs.

indus′trial revolu′tion, *n.* (*often caps.*) the complex of social and economic changes resulting from the mechanization of industry that began in England about 1760.

indus′trial-strength′ (in dus′trē əl strengkth′, -strength′, -strenth′), *adj.* **1.** unusually strong or effective; able to withstand great strain or use: *industrial-strength soap.* **2.** exceptionally powerful, potent, or the like: *an industrial-strength voice.*

in•dus•tri•ous (in dus′trē əs), *adj.* working energetically and devotedly; hard-working; diligent: *an industrious person.* —**in•dus′tri•ous•ly,** *adv.* —**in•dus′tri•ous•ness,** *n.*

in•dus•try (in′də strē), *n., pl.* **-tries. 1.** the aggregate of manufacturing enterprises in a particular field: *the steel industry.* **2.** any general business activity: *the tourist industry.* **3.** trade or manufacture in general. **4.** systematic work or labor. **5.** energetic, devoted activity at any work or task; diligence. **6.** *Archaeol.* an assemblage of artifacts regarded as unmistakably the work of a single prehistoric group.

in•dwell (in dwel′), *v.,* **-dwelt, -dwell•ing.** —*v.t.* **1.** to exist in as a moral principle or motivating force. —*v.i.* **2.** to abide within, as a guiding force, motivating principle, etc. (usu. fol. by *in*): *a divine spirit indwelling in nature.* —**in′dwell′er,** *n.*

-ine¹, an adjective-forming suffix meaning "of, pertaining to, or characteristic of," "of the nature of," "made of": *Alpine; equine; marine.*

-ine², a noun-forming suffix found in a diverse group of words primarily of Latin and Romance origin, including abstract nouns (*doctrine; famine; rapine*), agent nouns (*concubine; inquiline*), names of artifacts or workplaces (*fascine*), and diminutives (*figurine; tambourine*); in more recent coinages, this suffix occurs in names of prepared substances or commercial products (*brilliantine; gabardine; saltine*).

INDO-EUROPEAN LANGUAGES

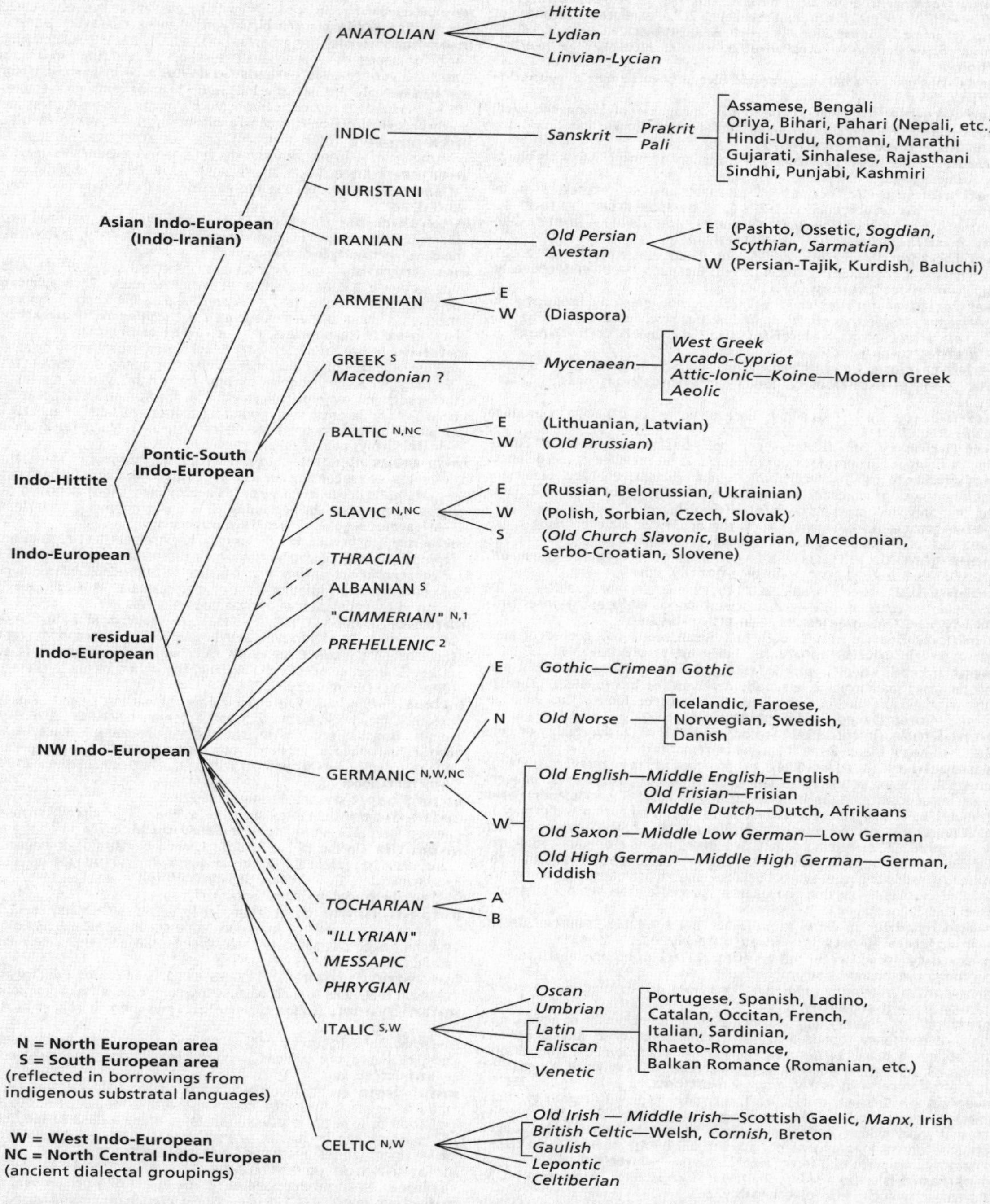

ANATOLIAN
- *Hittite*
- *Lydian*
- *Linvian-Lycian*

Asian Indo-European (Indo-Iranian)

INDIC — *Sanskrit* — *Prakrit* / *Pali*
- Assamese, Bengali
- Oriya, Bihari, Pahari (Nepali, etc.)
- Hindi-Urdu, Romani, Marathi
- Gujarati, Sinhalese, Rajasthani
- Sindhi, Punjabi, Kashmiri

NURISTANI

IRANIAN — *Old Persian* / *Avestan*
- E (Pashto, Ossetic, *Sogdian*, *Scythian*, *Sarmatian*)
- W (Persian-Tajik, Kurdish, Baluchi)

ARMENIAN
- E
- W (Diaspora)

GREEK [S] / *Macedonian* ? — *Mycenaean*
- *West Greek*
- *Arcado-Cypriot*
- *Attic-Ionic* — *Koine* — Modern Greek
- *Aeolic*

Pontic-South Indo-European

BALTIC [N,NC]
- E (Lithuanian, Latvian)
- W (*Old Prussian*)

SLAVIC [N,NC]
- E (Russian, Belorussian, Ukrainian)
- W (Polish, Sorbian, Czech, Slovak)
- S (*Old Church Slavonic*, Bulgarian, Macedonian, Serbo-Croatian, Slovene)

THRACIAN

ALBANIAN [S]

"CIMMERIAN" [N,1]

PREHELLENIC [2]

Indo-Hittite

Indo-European

residual Indo-European

NW Indo-European

GERMANIC [N,W,NC]
- E Gothic—Crimean Gothic
- N *Old Norse*
  - Icelandic, Faroese,
  - Norwegian, Swedish,
  - Danish
- W
  - *Old English*—*Middle English*—English
  - *Old Frisian*—Frisian
  - *Middle Dutch*—Dutch, Afrikaans
  - *Old Saxon*—*Middle Low German*—Low German
  - *Old High German*—*Middle High German*—German, Yiddish

TOCHARIAN
- A
- B

"ILLYRIAN"

MESSAPIC

PHRYGIAN

ITALIC [S,W]
- *Oscan*
- *Umbrian*
- *Latin* / *Faliscan*
  - Portugese, Spanish, Ladino,
  - Catalan, Occitan, French,
  - Italian, Sardinian,
  - Rhaeto-Romance,
  - Balkan Romance (Romanian, etc.)
- *Venetic*

CELTIC [N,W]
- *Old Irish* — *Middle Irish*—Scottish Gaelic, *Manx*, Irish
- *British Celtic*—Welsh, *Cornish*, Breton
- *Gaulish*
- *Lepontic*
- *Celtiberian*

N = North European area
S = South European area
(reflected in borrowings from indigenous substratal languages)

W = West Indo-European
NC = North Central Indo-European
(ancient dialectal groupings)

[1] hypothesized substratum language in proto-Baltic and Slavic area   [2] substratum language in Greek area (called by some "Pelasgian")

(The names of languages extinct as vernaculars have been italicized.)

I

in•e•bri•ant (in ē′brē ənt, i nē′-), *n.* **1.** an intoxicant. —*adj.* **2.** inebriating; intoxicating.

in•e•bri•ate (*v.* in ē′brē āt′, i nē′-; *n., adj.* -it), *v.,* **-at•ed, -at•ing,** *n., adj.* —*v.t.* **1.** to make drunk; intoxicate. **2.** to exhilarate, confuse, or stupefy mentally or emotionally. —*n.* **3.** an intoxicated person, esp. a drunkard. —*adj.* **4.** Also, **in•e′bri•at′ed.** drunk; intoxicated. —**in•e′bri•a′tion,** *n.*

in•ed•i•ble (in ed′ə bəl), *adj.* not edible; unfit to be eaten. —**in•ed′i•bil′i•ty,** *n.*

in•ed•u•ca•ble (in ej′o͝o kə bəl), *adj.* incapable of being educated, esp. because of some condition, as mental retardation or emotional disturbance. —**in•ed′u•ca•bil′i•ty,** *n.*

I′ Need′ Thee′ Eve′ry Hour′, a Christian hymn (1872) with words by Annie Hawks.

in•ef•fa•ble (in ef′ə bəl), *adj.* **1.** incapable of being expressed or described in words: *ineffable joy.* **2.** not to be spoken because of its sacredness; unutterable: *the ineffable name of the deity.* —**in•ef′fa•bil′i•ty, in•ef′fa•ble•ness,** *n.* —**in•ef′fa•bly,** *adv.*

in•ef•fec•tive (in′i fek′tiv), *adj.* **1.** not effective; not producing results; ineffectual. **2.** inefficient or incompetent; incapable. —**in′ef•fec′tive•ly,** *adv.* —**in′ef•fec′tive•ness,** *n.*

in•ef•fec•tu•al (in′i fek′cho͞o əl), *adj.* **1.** not effectual; producing no satisfactory or decisive effect: *an ineffectual remedy.* **2.** unavailing; futile: *ineffectual efforts.* —**in′ef•fec′tu•al′i•ty, in′ef•fec′tu•al•ness,** *n.* —**in′ef•fec′tu•al•ly,** *adv.*

in•ef•fi•ca•cious (in′ef i kā′shəs), *adj.* not able to produce the desired effect. —**in′ef•fi•ca′cious•ly,** *adv.* —**in′ef•fi•ca′cious•ness,** (-kas′i tē), *n.*

in•ef•fi•ca•cy (in ef′i kə sē), *n.* lack of power or capacity to produce the desired effect.

in•ef•fi•cien•cy (in′i fish′ən sē), *n., pl.* **-cies. 1.** the quality or condition of being inefficient; lack of efficiency. **2.** an instance of inefficiency.

in•ef•fi•cient (in′i fish′ənt), *adj.* **1.** not efficient; unable to effect or achieve the desired result with reasonable economy of means. **2.** lacking in ability; incompetent. —**in′ef•fi′cient•ly,** *adv.*

in•el•e•gance (in el′i gəns), *n.* **1.** the quality or state of being inelegant; lack of elegance. **2.** something that is inelegant.

in•el•e•gant (in el′i gənt), *adj.* not elegant; lacking in refinement, gracefulness, or good taste. —**in•el′e•gant•ly,** *adv.*

in•el•i•gi•ble (in el′i jə bəl), *adj.* **1.** not eligible; not qualified or fit: *ineligible for citizenship.* —*n.* **2.** a person who is ineligible. —**in•el′i•gi•bil′i•ty, in•el′i•gi•ble•ness,** *n.* —**in•el′i•gi•bly,** *adv.*

in•e•luc•ta•ble (in′i luk′tə bəl), *adj.* incapable of being evaded; inescapable. —**in′e•luc′ta•bil′i•ty,** *n.* —**in′e•luc′ta•bly,** *adv.*

in•ept (in ept′, i nept′), *adj.* **1.** lacking skill or aptitude, esp. for a particular task; maladroit. **2.** generally awkward or incompetent. **3.** inappropriate; unsuitable; out of place. **4.** absurd or foolish: *an inept remark.* —**in•ept′ly,** *adv.* —**in•ept′ness,** *n.*

in•ept•i•tude (in ep′ti to͞od′, -tyo͞od′, i nep′-), *n.* **1.** the quality or condition of being inept. **2.** an inept act or remark.

in•e•qual•i•ty (in′i kwol′i tē), *n., pl.* **-ties. 1.** the condition of being unequal; lack of equality; disparity. **2.** injustice; partiality. **3.** unevenness, as of surface. **4.** an instance of unevenness. **5.** variableness, as of climate. **6. a.** any component part of the departure from uniformity in astronomical phenomena, esp. in orbital motion. **b.** the amount of such a departure. **7.** a statement that two quantities are unequal, indicated by the symbol ≠; alternatively, by the symbol <, signifying that the quantity preceding the symbol is less than that following, or by the symbol >, signifying that the quantity preceding the symbol is greater than that following.

in•eq•ui•ta•ble (in ek′wi tə bəl), *adj.* not equitable; unjust or unfair. —**in•eq′ui•ta•ble•ness,** *n.* —**in•eq′ui•ta•bly,** *adv.*

in•eq•ui•ty (in ek′wi tē), *n., pl.* **-ties. 1.** lack of equity; unfairness. **2.** an unfair circumstance or proceeding.

in•er•rant (in er′ənt, -ûr′-), *adj.* free from error; infallible. —**in•er′ran•cy,** *n.* —**in•er′rant•ly,** *adv.*

in•ert (in ûrt′, i nûrt′), *adj.* **1.** having no inherent power of action, motion, or resistance (opposed to *active*): *inert matter.* **2.** having little or no ability to react, as nitrogen that occurs uncombined in the atmosphere. **3.** having no pharmacological action. **4.** inactive or sluggish by habit or nature. —**in•ert′ly,** *adv.* —**in•ert′ness,** *n.*

in•er•tia (in ûr′shə, i nûr′-), *n.* **1.** inertness, esp. with regard to effort, motion, action, and the like; inactivity; sluggishness. **2. a.** the property of matter by which it retains its state of rest or its velocity along a straight line so long as it is not acted upon by an external force. **b.** an analogous property of a force: *electric inertia.* —**in•er′tial,** *adj.*

in•es•cap•a•ble (in′ə skā′pə bəl), *adj.* incapable of being escaped, ignored, or avoided. —**in′es•cap′a•bly,** *adv.*

in•es•ti•ma•ble (in es′tə mə bəl), *adj.* **1.** incapable of being estimated or assessed; incalculable: *to do inestimable harm.* **2.** too precious to be estimated or appreciated; invaluable; priceless: *an inestimable champion of freedom.* —**in•es′ti•ma•bil′i•ty, in•es′ti•ma•ble•ness,** *n.* —**in•es′ti•ma•bly,** *adv.*

in•ev•i•ta•ble (in ev′i tə bəl), *adj.* **1.** unable to be avoided, evaded, or escaped; certain; necessary: *an inevitable conclusion.* —*n.* **2.** something that is unavoidable. —**in•ev′i•ta•bil′i•ty, in•ev′i•ta•ble•ness,** *n.* —**in•ev′i•ta•bly,** *adv.*

in•ex•act (in′ig zakt′), *adj.* not exact; not strictly precise or accurate: *an inexact calculation; an inexact science.* —**in′ex•act′i•tude′,** *n.* —**in′ex•act′ly,** *adv.* —**in′ex•act′ness,** *n.*

in•ex•cus•a•ble (in′ik skyo͞o′zə bəl), *adj.* incapable of being excused or justified. —**in′ex•cus′a•bil′i•ty,** *n.* —**in′ex•cus′a•bly,** *adv.*

in•ex•haust•i•ble (in′ig zô′stə bəl), *adj.* **1.** not exhaustible; incapable of being depleted: *an inexhaustible supply.* **2.** untiring; tireless: *an inexhaustible runner.* —**in′ex•haust′i•bil′i•ty,** *n.* —**in′ex•haust′i•bly,** *adv.*

in•ex•o•ra•ble (in ek′sər ə bəl), *adj.* **1.** unyielding; unalterable. **2.** not to be persuaded, moved, or affected by prayers or entreaties; merciless. —**in•ex′o•ra•bil′i•ty, in•ex′o•ra•ble•ness,** *n.* —**in•ex′o•ra•bly,** *adv.*

in•ex•pen•sive (in′ik spen′siv), *adj.* not expensive; not high in price; costing little. —**in′ex•pen′sive•ly,** *adv.* —**in′ex•pen′sive•ness,** *n.*

in•ex•pe•ri•ence (in′ik spēr′ē əns), *n.* **1.** lack of experience. **2.** lack of knowledge, skill, or wisdom gained from experience. —**in′ex•pe′ri•enced,** *adj.*

in•ex•pli•ca•ble (in ek′spli kə bəl, in′ik splik′ə-), *adj.* not explicable; incapable of being explained. —**in•ex′pli•ca•bil′i•ty, in•ex′pli•ca•ble•ness,** *n.* —**in•ex′pli•ca•bly,** *adv.*

in•ex•tri•ca•ble (in ek′stri kə bəl, in′ik strik′ə-), *adj.* **1.** from which one cannot extricate oneself: *an inextricable maze.* **2.** incapable of being disentangled, undone, or loosed: *an inextricable knot.* **3.** hopelessly intricate, involved, or perplexing: *an inextricable plot.* —**in•ex′tri•ca•bil′i•ty, in•ex′tri•ca•ble•ness,** *n.* —**in•ex′tri•ca•bly,** *adv.*

in•fal•li•ble (in fal′ə bəl), *adj.* **1.** absolutely trustworthy or sure: *an infallible rule.* **2.** unfailing in effectiveness or operation; certain: *an infallible remedy.* **3.** not fallible; exempt from liability to error, as persons, their judgment, or pronouncements. **4.** (in Roman Catholicism) immune from fallacy or error in expounding matters of faith or morals. —*n.* **5.** an infallible person or thing. —**in•fal′li•bil′i•ty, in•fal′li•ble•ness,** *n.* —**in•fal′li•bly,** *adv.*

in•fa•mous (in′fə məs), *adj.* **1.** having an extremely bad reputation. **2.** deserving of or causing an evil reputation; shamefully bad; detestable: *an infamous deed.* **3.** *Law.* **a.** (of a convicted felon) deprived of certain rights as a citizen. **b.** pertaining to offenses involving such deprivation. —**in′fa•mous•ly,** *adv.* —**in′fa•mous•ness,** *n.*

in•fa•my (in′fə mē), *n., pl.* **-mies. 1.** extremely bad reputation, public reproach, or strong condemnation as the result of a shameful, criminal, or outrageous act: *a time that will live in infamy.* **2.** infamous character or conduct. **3.** an infamous act or circumstance. **4.** *Law.* loss of rights, incurred by conviction of an infamous offense.

in•fan•cy (in′fən sē), *n., pl.* **-cies. 1.** the state or period of being an infant; very early childhood; babyhood. **2.** the corresponding period in the existence of anything; very early stage: *Space science is in its infancy.* **3.** infants collectively. **4.** *Law.* the period of life to the age of majority, usu. 18; minority.

in•fant (in′fənt), *n.* **1.** a child during the earliest period of its life, esp. before it can walk; baby. **2.** *Law.* a person below the age of majority; minor. **3.** a beginner, as in experience or learning; novice. **4.** anything in the first stage of existence or progress. —*adj.* **5.** of or pertaining to infants or infancy. **6.** being in infancy. **7.** being in the earliest stage. —**in′fant•hood′,** *n.*

in′fant bap′tism, *n.* See under BAPTISM.

in•fan•ti•cide (in fan′tə sīd′), *n.* **1.** the act of killing an infant. **2.** a person who kills an infant. —**in•fan′ti•cid′al,** *adj.*

in•fan•tile (in′fən tīl′, -til), *adj.* **1.** characteristic of or befitting an infant; babyish; childish. **2.** of or pertaining to infants or infancy. **3.** YOUTHFUL (def. 4). —**in′fan•til′i•ty** (-til′i tē), *n.*

in′fantile paral′ysis, *n.* POLIOMYELITIS.

in•fan•ti•lism (in′fən tl iz′əm, -tī liz′-, in fan′tl iz′əm), *n.* **1.** the persistence in an adult of markedly childish anatomical, physiological, or psychological characteristics. **2.** an infantile act, trait, etc., esp. in an adult.

in•fan•try (in′fən trē), *n., pl.* **-tries. 1.** soldiers or military units that fight on foot. **2.** a branch of an army composed of such soldiers.

in•fan•try•man (in′fən trē mən), *n., pl.* **-men.** a soldier of the infantry.

in•farct (in′färkt′, in färkt′), *n.* an area of tissue, as in the heart or kidney, that is dying or dead, having been deprived of its blood supply. —**in•farct′ed,** *adj.*

in•fat•u•ate (*v.* in fach′o͞o āt′; *adj., n.* -it, -āt′), *v.,* **-at•ed, -at•ing,** *adj., n.* —*v.t.* **1.** to inspire or possess with a foolish or unreasoning admiration or love. **2.** to affect with folly; make foolish or fatuous. —*adj.* **3.** characterized by foolish or irrational love or desire; infatuated. —*n.* **4.** a person who is infatuated. —**in•fat′u•a′tor,** *n.*

in•fat•u•a•tion (in fach′o͞o ā′shən), *n.* **1.** the state of being infatuated; foolish or all-absorbing passion. **2.** the object of a person's infatuation.

in•fect (in fekt′), *v.t.* **1.** to affect or contaminate with disease-producing germs. **2.** to taint or contaminate with any harmful substance: *to infect the air with poison gas.* **3.** to corrupt or affect morally. **4.** to imbue with some pernicious belief, opinion, etc. **5.** to affect so as to imbue with similar feeling: *His courage infected the others.* **6.** to affect with a computer virus. —**in•fect′ant,** *adj.* —**in•fec′tor, in•fect′er,** *n.*

in•fec•tion (in fek′shən), *n.* **1.** the act of infecting or the state of being infected. **2.** an infecting agency or influence. **3.** an infectious disease. **4.** the condition of suffering an infection. **5.** corruption of another's opinions, beliefs, etc. **6.** an influence or impulse passing from one to another and affecting feeling or action.

in•fec•tious (in fek′shəs), *adj.* **1.** communicable by infection, as from one person to another or from one part of the body to another. **2.** causing or communicating infection. **3.** tending to spread quickly and generally: *infectious laughter.* —**in•fec′tious•ly,** *adv.* —**in•fec′tious•ness,** *n.*

infec′tious hepati′tis, *n.* HEPATITIS A.

infec′tious mononucleo′sis, *n.* an acute infectious form of mononucleosis associated with Epstein-Barr virus and characterized by sudden fever and a benign swelling of lymph nodes. Also called **glandular fever.**

in•fe•lic•i•tous (in′fə lis′i təs), *adj.* not felicitous; inapt or inappropriate: *an infelicitous remark.* —**in′fe•lic′i•tous•ly,** *adv.*

in•fe•lic•i•ty (in′fə lis′i tē), *n., pl.* **-ties. 1.** the quality or state of being unhappy; unhappiness. **2.** misfortune; bad luck. **3.** an unfortunate circumstance. **4.** inaptness or inappropriateness, as of action or expression. **5.** something infelicitous: *infelicities of prose style.*

in•fer (in fûr′), *v.,* **-ferred, -fer•ring.** —*v.t.* **1.** to derive by reasoning; conclude or judge from premises or evidence. **2.** to guess; speculate; surmise. **3.** (of facts, circumstances, statements, etc.) to indicate or involve as a conclusion; lead to. **4.** to hint; imply; suggest. —*v.i.* **5.** to draw a conclusion, as by reasoning. —**in•fer′a•ble, in•fer′i•ble, in•fer′ri•ble,** *adj.* —**in•fer′a•bly,** *adv.* —**in•fer′rer,** *n.* —**Usage.** Most 20th-century usage guides condemn INFER when used to mean "to hint or suggest," as in *The next speaker rejected the proposal, inferring that it was made solely to embarrass the government.* The modern usage position is that the proper word for this meaning is IMPLY, and that to use INFER for it is to lose a valuable distinction. Many speakers and writers observe this claimed distinction scrupulously. Nevertheless, from its earliest appearance in English INFER has had the sense given in definition 3 above, a meaning that overlaps with the second definition of IMPLY when the subject is a condition, circumstance, or the like that leads inevitably to a certain conclusion or point.

in•fer•ence (in′fər əns, -frəns), *n.* **1.** the act or process of inferring. **2.** something that is inferred. **3.** *Logic.* **a.** the process of deriving from assumed premises either the strict logical conclusion or one that is to some degree probable. **b.** a proposition reached by a process of inference.

in•fer•en•tial (in′fə ren′shəl), *adj.* of, pertaining to, by, or dependent upon inference. —**in′fer•en′tial•ly,** *adv.*

in•fe•ri•or (in fēr′ē ər), *adj.* **1.** low or lower in station, rank, degree, or grade (often fol. by *to*). **2.** low or lower in place or position; closer to the bottom or base: *the inferior regions of the earth.* **3.** of comparatively low grade; poor in quality; substandard. **4.** *Bot.* **a.** situated below some other organ. **b.** (of a calyx) inserted below the ovary. **c.** (of an ovary) having a superior calyx. **5.** *Anat.* (of an organ or part) **a.** lower in place or position; situated beneath another. **b.** being toward the feet. Compare SUPERIOR (def. 9). **6.** *Astron.* **a.** (of a planet) having an orbit within that of the earth, as Mercury and Venus. **b.** (of a conjunction of an inferior planet) taking place between the sun and the earth. **7.** written or printed low on a line of text, as the "2" in H_2O; subscript. Compare SUPERIOR (def. 11). —*n.* **8.** a person inferior to another or others, as in rank or merit. **9.** SUBSCRIPT. —**in•fe•ri•or•i•ty** (in fēr′ē ôr′i tē, -or′-), *n.* —**in•fe′ri•or•ly,** *adv.*

inferior′ity com′plex, *n.* **1.** an intense feeling of inferiority, producing a personality characterized either by extreme reticence or, as a result of overcompensation, by extreme aggressiveness. **2.** lack of self-esteem or self-confidence.

in•fer•nal (in fûr′nl), *adj.* **1.** hellish; fiendish; diabolical: *an infernal plot.* **2.** extremely troublesome, annoying, etc.; outrageous: *an infernal nuisance.* **3.** of, inhabiting, or befitting hell or the underworld. —**in′fer•nal′i•ty,** *n.* —**in•fer′nal•ly,** *adv.*

in•fer•no (in fûr′nō), *n., pl.* **-nos. 1.** hell; the infernal regions. **2.** a place or region that resembles hell, esp. in intense heat.

in•fer•tile (in fûr′tl; *esp. Brit.* -tīl), *adj.* not fertile; unproductive; sterile; barren: *infertile soil.* —**in•fer′tile•ly,** *adv.* —**in′fer•til′i•ty, in•fer′tile•ness,** *n.*

in•fest (in fest′), *v.t.* **1.** to live in or overrun to an unwanted degree or in a troublesome manner: *mice infesting a farmhouse.* **2.** to cause to suffer a prevalence of: *a night infested with alarms.* —**in′fes•ta′tion,** *n.*

in•fi•del (in′fi dl, -del′), *n.* **1. a.** a person who does not accept a particular religion, esp. Christianity. **b.** (in Muslim use) a person who does not accept the Islamic faith; kaffir. **2.** a person who has no religious faith; an unbeliever. **3.** a person who disbelieves a particular theory, belief, etc. —*adj.* **4.** of or concerning infidels; heathen. **5.** without religious faith. **6.** Also, **in′fi•del′ic** (-del′ik). of, pertaining to, or characteristic of unbelievers or infidels.

in•fi•del•i•ty (in′fi del′i tē), *n., pl.* **-ties. 1.** marital unfaithfulness; adultery. **2.** disloyalty. **3.** a breach of trust; transgression.

in•field (in′fēld′), *n.* **1. a.** the area of a baseball field bounded by the base lines, usu. taken to also include the dirt area behind the bases. **b.** the positions played by the infielders, or the players themselves considered as a group (contrasted with *outfield*). **2.** the area enclosed by a racetrack or running track. **3.** the cultivated part of a farm nearest the farmhouse.

in•field•er (in′fēl′dər), *n.* any of the four defensive players, as first baseman, second baseman, shortstop, third baseman, stationed around the infield in baseball.

in•fight•ing (in′fī′ting), *n.* **1.** fighting at close range. **2.** fighting between rivals or people closely associated: *political infighting.* **3.** free-for-all fighting. —**in′fight′er,** *n.*

in•fil•trate (in fil′trāt, in′fil trāt′), *v.,* **-trat•ed, -trat•ing,** *n.* —*v.t.* **1.** to filter into or through; permeate. **2.** to cause to pass in by filtering. **3.** to move into (an organization, etc.) surreptitiously and with hostile intent: *to infiltrate enemy lines.* **4.** to pass a small number of (soldiers, spies, etc.) into a country or organization clandestinely and with hostile or subversive intent. —*v.i.* **5.** to pass into or through a substance, place, etc., by or as if by filtering. **6.** *Pathol.* to penetrate tissue spaces or cells. —*n.* **7.** something that infiltrates. **8.** *Pathol.* any substance penetrating tissues or cells and forming a morbid accumulation. —**in′fil•tra′tion,** *n.* —**in′fil•tra′tive,** *adj.* —**in′fil•tra′tor,** *n.*

in•fi•nite (in′fə nit), *adj.* **1.** immeasurably great: *infinite patience.* **2.** indefinitely or exceedingly great: *infinite sums of money.* **3.** unbounded or unlimited; boundless; endless: *God's infinite mercy.* **4.** *Math.* **a.** not finite. **b.** (of a set) having elements that can be put into one-to-one correspondence with a subset that is not the given set. —*n.* **5.** something that is infinite. **6.** the boundless regions of space. **7. the Infinite** or **the Infinite Being,** God. —**in′fi•nite•ly,** *adv.* —**in′fi•nite•ness,** *n.*

in•fin•i•tes•i•mal (in′fin i tes′ə məl), *adj.* **1.** indefinitely or exceedingly small; minute. **2.** immeasurably small; less than an assignable quantity: *to an infinitesimal degree.* **3.** of, pertaining to, or involving infinitesimals. —*n.* **4.** an infinitesimal quantity. **5.** *Math.* a variable having zero as a limit. —**in′fin•i•tes′i•mal•ly,** *adv.*

in•fin•i•tive (in fin′i tiv), *n.* **1.** a nonfinite verb form, in many languages the simple or basic form of the verb, that names the action or state without specifying the subject and that functions as a noun or is used with auxiliary verbs or, in English, after the word *to,* as *eat* in *I want to eat.* —*adj.* **2.** consisting of or containing an infinitive: *an infinitive clause. Abbr.:* infin. —**in′fin•i•ti′val** (-tī′vəl), *adj.* —**in•fin′i•tive•ly, in′fin•i•ti′val•ly,** *adv.*

in•fin•i•ty (in fin′i tē), *n., pl.* **-ties. 1.** the quality or state of being infinite. **2.** something that is infinite. **3.** infinite space, time, or quantity. **4.** an infinite extent, amount, or number. **5.** an indefinitely great amount or number. **6.** *Math.* **a.** the assumed limit of a sequence, series, etc., that increases without bound. **b.** infinite distance or an infinitely distant part of space. **7.** a distance setting of a camera lens beyond which everything is in focus.

in•firm (in fûrm′), *adj.* **1.** feeble or weak in body or health, esp. because of age. **2.** unsteadfast, faltering, or irresolute, as persons or the mind. **3.** not firm, solid, or strong. **4.** unsound or invalid, as an argument or a property title. —**in•firm′ly,** *adv.* —**in•firm′ness,** *n.*

in•fir•ma•ry (in fûr′mə rē), *n., pl.* **-ries.** a place for the care of the infirm, sick, or injured; hospital or facility serving as a hospital: *a school infirmary.*

in•fir•mi•ty (in fûr′mi tē), *n., pl.* **-ties. 1.** a physical weakness or ailment: *the infirmities of age.* **2.** the quality or state of being infirm; lack of strength. **3.** a moral weakness or failing.

in•fix (*v.* in fiks′, in′fiks′; *n.* in′fiks′), *v.t.* **1.** to fix, fasten, or drive in. **2.** to implant. **3.** to fix (a fact, idea, etc.) in the mind or memory; instill. **4.** to insert as an infix. —*n.* **5.** an affix that is inserted within a base or stem, as the *-m-* in Latin *-cumbere* "to lie down, assume a prone position," as compared with *cubāre* "to lie, be in a prone position." —**in′fix•a′tion, in•fix′ion** (-fik′shən), *n.*

in fla•gran•te de•lic•to (in flə gran′tē di lik′tō), *adv.* FLAGRANTE DELICTO.

in•flame (in flām′), *v.,* **-flamed, -flam•ing.** —*v.t.* **1.** to kindle or excite (passions, desires, etc.). **2.** to arouse to a high degree of passion or feeling; incite. **3.** to cause inflammation in. —*v.i.* **4.** to become excessively affected with inflammation. —**in•flam′er,** *n.* —**in•flam′ing•ly,** *adv.*

in•flam•ma•ble (in flam′ə bəl), *adj.* **1.** capable of being set on fire; combustible; flammable. **2.** easily aroused to passion or anger. —*n.* **3.** something inflammable. —**in•flam′ma•bil′i•ty, in•flam′ma•ble•ness,** *n.* —**in•flam′ma•bly,** *adv.* —**Usage.** INFLAMMABLE and FLAMMABLE both mean "combustible." INFLAMMABLE is the older by about 200 years. FLAMMABLE now has certain technical uses, particularly as a warning on vehicles carrying combustible materials, because of a belief that some might interpret the intensive prefix IN- of INFLAMMABLE as a negative prefix and thus think the word means "noncombustible." INFLAMMABLE is the word more usu. used in nontechnical and figurative contexts: *inflammable clothing; an inflammable temper.*

in•flam•ma•tion (in′flə mā′shən), *n.* **1.** redness, swelling, and fever in a local area of the body, often with pain and disturbed function, in reaction to an infection or to a physical or chemical injury. **2.** the act or fact of inflaming. **3.** the state of being inflamed.

in•flam•ma•to•ry (in flam′ə tôr′ē, -tōr′ē), *adj.* **1.** tending to arouse anger, hostility, passion, etc.: *inflammatory speeches.* **2.** of or caused by inflammation. —**in•flam′ma•to′ri•ly,** *adv.*

in•flat•a•ble (in flā′tə bəl), *adj.* **1.** capable of being inflated. —*n.* **2.** an inflatable object, esp. a small rubber boat inflated with air.

in•flate (in flāt′), *v.,* **-flat•ed, -flat•ing.** —*v.t.* **1.** to distend; swell or puff out; dilate. **2.** to expand or distend with air or gas: *to inflate a balloon.* **3.** to puff up with pride, satisfaction, etc. **4.** to increase unduly, as the level of prices or the amount of a currency or credit. —*v.i.* **5.** to become inflated. —**in•flat′er, in•fla′tor,** *n.*

in•flat•ed (in flā′tid), *adj.* **1.** distended with air or gas; swollen. **2.**

puffed up, as with pride. **3.** turgid or bombastic: *inflated prose.* **4.** unduly increased in level or amount: *inflated costs.*

in•fla•tion (in flā′shən), *n.* **1.** a steady rise in the level of prices related to an increased volume of money and credit and resulting in a loss of value of currency (opposed to *deflation*). **2.** the act of inflating. **3.** the state of being inflated.

in•fla•tion•ar•y (in flā′shə ner′ē), *adj.* of, pertaining to, characteristic of, or causing inflation: *inflationary prices.*

infla′tionary spi′ral, *n.* a cycle of worsening inflation as higher prices result in higher wages, increasing costs and resulting in still higher prices.

in•flect (in flekt′), *v.t.* **1.** to modulate (the voice). **2.** to change the form of (a word) by inflection; conjugate or decline. **3.** to bend; turn from a direct line or course. —*v.i.* **4.** to be characterized by grammatical inflection. —**in•flect′ed•ness,** *n.* —**in•flec′tive,** *adj.* —**in•flec′tor,** *n.*

in•flec•tion (in flek′shən), *n.* **1.** modulation of the voice; change in pitch or tone of voice. **2. a.** the process of adding affixes to or changing the shape of a base to give it a different syntactic function without changing its form class, as in forming *served* from *serve,* *sings* from *sing,* or *harder* from *hard* (contrasted with *derivation*). **b.** an affix added in this process, as the *-s* in *dogs* or the *-ed* in *played.* **c.** an inflected form of a word. **d.** the systematic description of the process of inflection in a language; accidence. **3.** a bend or angle. **4.** a change of curvature from convex to concave or vice versa. Also, *esp. Brit.,* **inflexion.**

in•flec•tion•al (in flek′shə nl), *adj.* of, pertaining to, characterized by, or used in inflection: *an inflectional language; an inflectional ending.* —**in•flec′tion•al•ly,** *adv.*

in•flex•i•ble (in flek′sə bəl), *adj.* **1.** not flexible; incapable of or resistant to being bent; rigid: *an inflexible plastic rod.* **2.** of an unyielding temper, purpose, will, etc.; immovable: *an inflexible determination.* **3.** not permitting change or variation; unalterable: *inflexible rules.* —**in•flex′i•bil′i•ty, in•flex′i•ble•ness,** *n.* —**in•flex′i•bly,** *adv.*

in•flict (in flikt′), *v.t.* **1.** to impose as something that must be borne or suffered: *to inflict punishment.* **2.** to impose (anything unwelcome): *to inflict a long visit on someone.* **3.** to deal or deliver, as a blow. —**in•flict′a•ble,** *adj.* —**in•flict′er,** *n.* —**in•flic′tor,** *n.* —**in•flic′tion,** *n.*

in′-flight′ or **in′flight′,** *adj.* done, served, or shown during flight in an aircraft: *an in-flight movie.*

in•flo•res•cence (in′flô res′əns, -flō-, -flə-), *n.* **1.** a flowering or blossoming. **2. a.** the arrangement of flowers on the axis or stem. **b.** the flowering part of a plant. **c.** a flower cluster. **d.** flowers collectively. —**in′flo•res′cent,** *adj.*

raceme of lily of the valley, *Convallaria majalis* — **spadix of** jack-in-the-pulpit, *Arisaema triphyllum* — **panicle of oats,** *Avena sativa*

inflorescence (def. 2a)

in•flow (in′flō′), *n.* **1.** an act of flowing in. **2.** something that flows in; influx.

in•flu•ence (in′flōō əns), *n., v.,* **-enced, -enc•ing.** —*n.* **1.** the capacity or power of persons or things to produce effects on others by intangible or indirect means. **2.** the action or process of producing such effects. **3.** a person or thing that exerts influence. **4.** the power to persuade or obtain advantages resulting from one's status, wealth, position, etc. **5.** *Astrol.* **a.** the supposed radiation of an ethereal fluid from the stars, regarded as affecting human actions and destinies. **b.** the exercise of occult power by the stars. —*v.t.* **6.** to exercise influence on; affect. **7.** to move or impel (a person) to some action; persuade. —*Idiom.* **8.** under the influence, *Law.* less than drunk but with one's nervous system impaired: *driving a car while under the influence.* —**in′flu•ence•a•ble,** *adj.* —**in′flu•enc•er,** *n.*

in•flu•en•tial (in′flōō en′shəl), *adj.* **1.** having or exerting great influence. —*n.* **2.** an influential person. —**in′flu•en′tial•ly,** *adv.*

in•flu•en•za (in′flōō en′zə), *n.* **1.** an acute, commonly epidemic disease occurring in several forms, caused by numerous rapidly mutating viral strains and characterized by respiratory symptoms and general prostration. **2.** any of various acute, contagious viral infections of domestic animals that affect the respiratory tract. —**in′flu•en′zal,** *adj.* —**in′flu•en′za•like′,** *adj.*

in•flux (in′fluks′), *n.* **1.** an act of flowing in; inflow. **2.** the arrival of people or things, esp. in large numbers: *an influx of tourists.* **3.** the place at which one stream flows into another or into the sea.

in•fo (in′fō), *n. Informal.* information.

in•fo•mer•cial (in′fō mûr′shəl), *n.* a program-length television commercial that is cast in a standard format, as a documentary or a talk show, so as to disguise the fact that it is an advertisement.

in•fo•pre•neur (in′f′ō prə nûr′, -nōōr′, -nyōōr′), *n.* a person whose business is gathering, processing, and providing information to advertising, marketing, and other firms.

in•form (in fôrm′), *v.t.* **1.** to give or impart knowledge of a fact or circumstance to: *We informed them of our arrival.* **2.** to supply (oneself) with knowledge of a matter or subject: *She informed herself of all the pertinent facts.* **3.** to pervade or permeate with manifest effect: *A love of nature informed his writing.* **4.** to animate or inspire. —*v.i.* **5.** to give information; supply knowledge or enlightenment. **6.** to furnish incriminating evidence about someone, as to the police (usu. fol. by *on* or *against*). —**in•form′a•ble,** *adj.* —**in•form′ing•ly,** *adv.*

in•for•mal (in fôr′məl), *adj.* **1.** without formality or ceremony; casual: *an informal visit.* **2.** not according to the prescribed, official, or customary way or manner; irregular; unofficial: *informal proceedings.* **3.** suitable to or characteristic of casual or familiar speech or writing. —**in•for′mal•ly,** *adv.*

in•for•mal•i•ty (in′fôr mal′i tē), *n., pl.* **-ties. 1.** the state of being informal; absence of formality. **2.** an informal act.

in•form•ant (in fôr′mənt), *n.* **1.** a person who informs or gives information; informer. **2.** a person who supplies social or cultural data in answer to the questions of an investigator. **3.** a native speaker of a language who supplies utterances or other data for one analyzing or learning the language.

in•for•mat•ics (in′fər mat′iks), *n.* (*used with a sing. v.*) INFORMATION SCIENCE.

in•for•ma•tion (in′fər mā′shən), *n.* **1.** knowledge communicated or received concerning a particular fact or circumstance; news. **2.** knowledge gained through study, communication, research, instruction, etc.; data; facts. **3.** the act or fact of informing. **4.** a service or employee whose function is to provide information to the public. **5.** *Law.* **a.** a formal criminal charge brought by a prosecuting officer rather than through the indictment of a grand jury. **b.** the document containing the depositions of witnesses against one accused of a crime. **6.** computer data at any stage of processing, as input, output, storage, or transmission. —**in′for•ma′tion•al,** *adj.*

informa′tion sci′ence, *n.* the study, collection, and management of information, using esp. computer storage and retrieval.

in′forma′tion su′perhighway, *n.* a large-scale communications network providing a variety of often interactive services, such as text databases, electronic mail, and audio and video materials, accessed through computers, television sets, etc. Also called **data highway.**

informa′tion the′ory, *n.* the mathematical theory concerned with the content, transmission, storage, and retrieval of information, usu. in the form of messages or data.

in•form•a•tive (in fôr′mə tiv) also **in•form•a•to•ry** (-tôr′ē, -tōr′ē), *adj.* giving information; instructive: *an informative book.* —**in•form′a•tive•ly,** *adv.* —**in•form′a•tive•ness,** *n.*

in•formed (in fôrmd′), *adj.* having or prepared with information or knowledge; educated. —**in•form′ed•ly,** *adv.*

informed′ consent′, *n.* a patient's consent to a medical or surgical procedure or to participation in a clinical study after being properly advised of the relevant medical facts and the risks involved.

in•form•er (in fôr′mər), *n.* **1.** a person who informs against another, esp. for money or other reward. **2.** a person who communicates information or news; informant.

in•fo•tain•ment (in′fō tān′mənt), *n.* broadcasting or publishing that strives to treat factual matter in an entertaining way, often by dramatically reenacting or fictionalizing real events.

in•fra (in′frə), *adv.* below, esp. when used in referring to parts of a text. Compare SUPRA.

infra-, a prefix meaning "below": *infrared; infrasonic.*

in•fract (in frakt′), *v.t.* to break or violate (a law, commitment, etc.); infringe. —**in•frac′tor,** *n.*

in•frac•tion (in frak′shən), *n.* breach; violation; infringement.

in•fra dig (in′frə dig′), *adj.* beneath one's dignity.

in•fra•lap•sar•i•an•ism (in′frə lap sâr′ē ə niz′əm), *n.* the doctrine that God decreed the election of a chosen number for redemption after the Fall (opposed to *supralapsarianism*). —**in′fra•lap•sar′i•an,** *n., adj.*

in•fran•gi•ble (in fran′jə bəl), *adj.* **1.** incapable of being broken or separated. **2.** inviolable. —**in•fran′gi•bil′i•ty,** *n.* —**in•fran′gi•bly,** *adv.*

in′fra•red′ or **in′fra-red′,** *n.* **1.** the part of the invisible spectrum that is contiguous to the red end of the visible spectrum and that comprises electromagnetic radiation of wavelengths from 800 nm to 1 mm. —*adj.* **2.** of, pertaining to, or using the infrared or its component rays: *infrared radiation.* Compare ULTRAVIOLET.

in•fra•struc•ture (in′frə struk′chər), *n.* **1.** the basic, underlying framework or features of a system or organization. **2.** the fundamental facilities serving a country, city, or area, as transportation and communication systems, power plants, and roads. **3.** the military installations of a country. —**in′fra•struc′tur•al,** *adj.*

in•fre•quent (in frē′kwənt), *adj.* **1.** happening or occurring at long intervals or rarely: *infrequent visits.* **2.** not constant, habitual, or regular: *an infrequent visitor.* **3.** not plentiful or many: *infrequent opportunities for advancement.* **4.** far apart in space. —**in•fre′quen•cy, in•fre′quence,** *n.* —**in•fre′quent•ly,** *adv.*

in•fringe (in frinj′), *v.,* **-fringed, -fring•ing.** —*v.t.* **1.** to commit a breach or infraction of; violate or transgress: *to infringe a copyright.* —*v.i.* **2.** to encroach or trespass (usu. fol. by *on* or *upon*): *to infringe on someone's privacy.* —**in•fring′er,** *n.*

in·fringe·ment (in frinj/mənt), *n.* **1.** a breach or infraction, as of a law or right; violation; transgression. **2.** an act of infringing.

in·fu·ri·ate (in fyŏŏr/ē āt/), *v.t.,* **-at·ed, -at·ing.** to make furious; enrage. —**in·fu/ri·at/ing·ly,** *adv.* —**in·fu/ri·a/tion,** *n.*

in·fuse (in fyŏŏz/), *v.,* **-fused, -fus·ing.** —*v.t.* **1.** to introduce, as if by pouring; cause to penetrate; instill (usu. fol. by *into*): *to infuse new life into a dying industry.* **2.** to imbue or inspire (usu. fol. by *with*): *The new coach infused the team with enthusiasm.* **3.** to steep or soak (leaves, bark, roots, etc.) in a liquid so as to extract the soluble properties or ingredients. —**in·fus/er,** *n.*

in·fu·sion (in fyŏŏ/zhən), *n.* **1.** the act or process of infusing. **2.** something that is infused. **3.** a liquid extract, as tea, prepared by steeping or soaking. **4. a.** the introduction of a saline or other solution into a vein. **b.** the solution used.

-ing[1], a suffix of nouns formed from verbs, expressing the action of the verb or its result, product, material, etc. (*the art of building; a new building; cotton wadding*). It is also used to form nouns from words other than verbs (*offing; shirting*). Compare -ING[2].

-ing[2], a suffix forming the present participle of verbs (*walking; thinking*), such participles being often used as participial adjectives: *warring factions.* Compare -ING[1].

in·gen·ious (in jēn/yəs), *adj.* **1.** characterized by cleverness or originality of invention: *an ingenious argument.* **2.** cleverly inventive; resourceful: *an ingenious mechanic.* —**in·gen/ious·ly,** *adv.* —**in·gen/ious·ness,** *n.* —**Usage.** INGENIOUS and INGENUOUS are now distinct from each other and are not synonyms. INGENIOUS means "characterized by cleverness" or "cleverly inventive," as in contriving new explanations or methods: *an ingenious device; ingenious designers.* INGENUOUS means "candid" or "innocent": *an ingenuous and sincere statement.*

in·gé·nue or **in·ge·nue** (an/zhə nŏŏ/, an /-), *n.* **1.** the role of an artless, innocent, unworldly girl or young woman, esp. as represented on the stage. **2.** an actress who plays such a role or specializes in playing such roles.

in·ge·nu·i·ty (in/jə nŏŏ/i tē, -nyŏŏ/-), *n., pl.* **-ties. 1.** the quality of being cleverly inventive or resourceful. **2.** cleverness or skillfulness of conception or design: *a device of great ingenuity.*

in·gen·u·ous (in jen/yŏŏ əs), *adj.* **1.** free from reserve, restraint, or dissimulation; candid; sincere. **2.** artless; innocent; naive. —**in·gen/u·ous·ly,** *adv.* —**in·gen/u·ous·ness,** *n.* —**Usage.** See INGENIOUS.

In·ger·soll (ing/gər sôl/, -sol/, -səl), *n.* **Robert Green,** 1833–99, U.S. lawyer, political leader, and orator.

in·gest (in jest/), *v.t.* to take into the body, as food or liquid (opposed to *egest*). —**in·gest/i·ble,** *adj.* —**in·ges/tion,** *n.*

in·glo·ri·ous (in glôr/ē əs, -glōr/-), *adj.* **1.** shameful; disgraceful: *inglorious retreat.* **2.** not famous or honored. —**in·glo/ri·ous·ly,** *adv.* —**in·glo/ri·ous·ness,** *n.*

In God/ We/ Trust/, 1. a motto appearing on U.S. currency. **2.** motto of Florida.

in·go·ing (in/gō/ing), *adj.* going in; entering.

in·got (ing/gət), *n.* a mass of metal cast in a convenient form for shaping, remelting, or refining.

in·grain (in grān/), *v.t.* to implant or fix deeply and firmly, as in the nature or mind.

in·grained (in grānd/, in/grānd/), *adj.* **1.** firmly fixed; deep-rooted; inveterate: *ingrained superstition.* **2.** wrought into or through the grain or fiber. —**in·grain·ed·ly** (in grā/nid lē, -grānd/-), *adv.*

in·grate (in/grāt), *n.* an ungrateful person.

in·gra·ti·ate (in grā/shē āt/), *v.t.,* **-at·ed, -at·ing.** to establish (oneself) in the favor or good graces of others, esp. by deliberate effort: *to ingratiate oneself with the boss.* —**in·gra/ti·at/ing·ly,** *adv.* —**in·gra/ti·a/tion,** *n.* —**in·gra/ti·a·to/ry** (-ə tôr/ē, -tōr/ē), *adj.*

in·grat·i·tude (in grat/i tŏŏd/, -tyŏŏd/), *n.* the state of being ungrateful; ungratefulness; unthankfulness.

in·gre·di·ent (in grē/dē ənt), *n.* **1.** something that enters as an element into a mixture: *the ingredients of a cake.* **2.** a constituent element of anything: *the ingredients of political success.*

In·gres (aN/grə), *n.* **Jean Auguste Dominique,** (zhäN), 1780–1867, French painter.

in·gress (in/gres), *n.* **1.** the act of going in or entering. **2.** the right to enter. **3.** a means or place of entering. **4.** IMMERSION (def. 4). —**in·gres·sion** (in gresh/ən), *n.*

in/-group/ or **in/group/,** *n.* a group of people sharing similar interests, attitudes, etc., and usu. considering those outside the group as inferior or alien. Compare OUT-GROUP.

in·grown (in/grōn/), *adj.* **1.** having grown into the flesh: *an ingrown toenail.* **2.** grown within or inward.

in·hab·it (in hab/it), *v.t.* **1.** to live or dwell in (a place), as people or animals. **2.** to exist or be situated within; dwell in: *Weird notions inhabit his mind.* —**in·hab/it·a·ble,** *adj.* —**in·hab/it·a·bil/i·ty,** *n.* —**in·hab/i·ta/tion,** *n.* —**in·hab/it·er,** *n.*

in·hab·it·ant (in hab/i tənt), *n.* a person or animal that inhabits a place, esp. as a permanent resident.

in·hab·it·ed (in hab/i tid), *adj.* having inhabitants: *an inhabited island.* —**in·hab/it·ed·ness,** *n.*

in·hal·ant (in hā/lənt), *n.* **1.** a volatile medicine or other substance that is inhaled for the effect of its vapor. —*adj.* **2.** used for inhaling.

in·ha·la·tion (in/hə lā/shən), *n.* **1.** an act or instance of inhaling. **2.** an inhalant.

in·ha·la·tor (in/hə lā/tər), *n.* **1.** an apparatus used to help inhale air, anesthetics, medicinal vapors, etc. **2.** an apparatus for giving artificial respiration; respirator.

in·hale (in hāl/), *v.,* **-haled, -hal·ing.** —*v.t.* **1.** to breathe in; draw in by breathing: *to inhale air.* **2.** *Informal.* to eat or drink rapidly or greedily. —*v.i.* **3.** to breathe in. **4.** to draw the smoke of cigarettes, cigars, etc., into the lungs.

in·hal·er (in hā/lər), *n.* **1.** an apparatus or device used in inhaling medicinal vapors, anesthetics, etc.; inhalator. **2.** a person who inhales.

in·here (in hēr/), *v.i.,* **-hered, -her·ing.** to belong intrinsically; be inherent.

in·her·ence (in hēr/əns, -her/-), *n.* the state or fact of inhering or being inherent.

in·her·ent (in hēr/ənt, -her/-), *adj.* existing in someone or something as a permanent and inseparable element, quality, or attribute; innate; ingrained. —**in·her/ent·ly,** *adv.*

in·her·it (in her/it), *v.t.* **1.** to take or receive (property, a right, a title, etc.) by succession or will, as an heir. **2.** to receive as if by succession from predecessors: *the problems inherited by the new administration.* **3.** to receive (a genetic character) by the transmission of hereditary factors. **4.** to succeed (a person) as heir. **5.** to receive as one's portion; come into possession of: *to inherit a sister's old clothes.* —*v.i.* **6.** to receive property or the like by inheritance.

in·her·it·a·ble (in her/i tə bəl), *adj.* **1.** capable of being inherited. **2.** capable of inheriting; qualified to inherit. —**in·her/it·a·bil/i·ty, in·her/it·a·ble·ness,** *n.* —**in·her/it·a·bly,** *adv.*

in·her·it·ance (in her/i təns), *n.* **1.** something that is or may be inherited; property passing at the owner's death to the heir or those entitled to succeed; legacy. **2.** the genetic characters transmitted from parent to offspring. **3.** something, as a quality or characteristic, received from progenitors or predecessors. **4.** the act or fact of inheriting. **5.** birthright; heritage.

inher/itance tax/, *n.* a tax levied on the value of property bequeathed to an heir.

in·her·i·tor (in her/i tər), *n.* a person who inherits; heir.

in·hib·it (in hib/it), *v.t.* **1.** to restrain, hinder, arrest, or check (an action, impulse, etc.). **2.** to prohibit; forbid. **3.** to suppress or restrain from free expression, as of psychologically or socially unacceptable behavior. —**in·hib/it·a·ble,** *adj.* —**in·hib/i·to/ry** (-tôr/ē, -tōr/ē), **in·hib/i·tive,** *adj.*

in·hib·it·ed (in hib/i tid), *adj.* **1.** overly restrained. **2.** suffering from psychological inhibition. —**in·hib/it·ed·ly,** *adv.* —**in·hib/it·ed·ness,** *n.*

in·hi·bi·tion (in/i bish/ən, in/hi-), *n.* **1.** the act of inhibiting. **2.** the state of being inhibited. **3.** something that inhibits; constraint. **4. a.** the conscious or unconscious restraint or suppression of behavior, impulses, etc., often due to guilt or fear produced by past punishment. **b.** the blocking or holding back of one psychological process by another. **5. a.** a restraining, arresting, or checking of the action of an organ or cell. **b.** the reduction of a reflex or other activity as the result of an antagonistic stimulation.

in hoc sig·no vin·ces (in hōk/ sig/nō wing/kās; *Eng.* in hok/ sig/nō vin/sēz), *Latin.* in this sign shalt thou conquer: motto used by Constantine the Great, from his vision, before battle, of a cross bearing these words.

in·hos·pi·ta·ble (in hos/pi tə bəl, in/ho spit/ə bəl), *adj.* **1.** not hospitable; unfriendly. **2.** (of a region, climate, etc.) not offering shelter, favorable conditions, etc.; barren: *an inhospitable rocky coast.* —**in·hos/pi·ta·ble·ness,** *n.* —**in·hos/pi·ta·bly,** *adv.*

in·hos·pi·tal·i·ty (in/hos pi tal/i tē, in hos/-), *n.* lack of hospitality; inhospitable treatment of visitors or guests.

in-house (*adj.* in/hous/; *adv.* -hous/), *adj., adv.* within, conducted within, or utilizing an organization's own staff or resources rather than external facilities: *in-house research; an ad created in-house.*

in·hu·man (in hyŏŏ/mən; *often* -yŏŏ/-), *adj.* **1.** lacking sympathy, pity, warmth, compassion, or the like; cruel; brutal; unfeeling: *an inhuman master.* **2.** not suited for human beings: *inhuman conditions.* **3.** not human: *inhuman forms.* —**in·hu/man·ly,** *adv.* —**in·hu/man·ness,** *n.*

in·hu·mane (in/hyŏŏ mān/; *often* -yŏŏ-), *adj.* not humane; lacking humanity, kindness, compassion, etc. —**in/hu·mane/ly,** *adv.*

in·hu·man·i·ty (in/hyŏŏ man/i tē; *often* -yŏŏ-), *n., pl.* **-ties. 1.** the state or quality of being inhuman or inhumane; cruelty. **2.** an inhuman or inhumane act.

in·hume (in hyŏŏm/; *often* -yŏŏm/), *v.t.,* **-humed, -hum·ing.** to bury; inter. —**in/hu·ma/tion,** *n.* —**in·hum/er,** *n.*

in·im·i·cal (i nim/i kəl), *adj.* **1.** adverse in tendency or effect; unfavorable; harmful: *conditions inimical to health.* **2.** unfriendly; hostile: *a cold, inimical gaze.* —**in·im/i·cal·ly,** *adv.* —**in·im/i·cal·ness, in·im/i·cal/i·ty,** *n.*

in·im·i·ta·ble (i nim/i tə bəl), *adj.* incapable of being imitated or copied; surpassing imitation; matchless. —**in·im/i·ta·bil/i·ty, in·im/i·ta·ble·ness,** *n.* —**in·im/i·ta·bly,** *adv.*

in·iq·ui·tous (i nik/wi təs), *adj.* characterized by iniquity; wicked; sinful. —**in·iq/ui·tous·ly,** *adv.* —**in·iq/ui·tous·ness,** *n.*

in•iq•ui•ty (i nik′wi tē), *n., pl.* **-ties. 1.** gross injustice or wickedness. **2.** a violation of right or duty; wicked act; sin.

in•i•tial (i nish′əl), *adj., n., v.,* **-tialed, -tial•ing** or (*esp. Brit.*) **-tialled, -tial•ling.** —*adj.* **1.** of, pertaining to, or occurring at the beginning; first: *the initial step in a process; the initial sound of a word.* —*n.* **2.** an initial letter, as of a word. **3.** the first letter of a proper name. **4.** a large, often ornamental letter used at the beginning of a chapter or other division of a book or manuscript. —*v.t.* **5.** to mark or sign with an initial or the initials of one's name, esp. as a token of approval. —**in•i′tial•ly,** *adv.*

in•i•tial•ism (i nish′ə liz′əm), *n.* an abbreviation or acronym formed from the initial letters of a group of words.

in•i•tial•ize (i nish′ə līz′), *v.t.,* **-ized, -iz•ing. 1.** to set (variables, counters, switches, etc.) to their starting values at the beginning of a computer program or subprogram. **2.** to prepare (a computer, printer, etc.) for reuse by clearing previous data from memory. **3.** to format (a disk). —**in•i′tial•i•za′tion,** *n.*

in•i•ti•ate (*v.* i nish′ē āt′; *adj., n.* -it, -āt′), *v.,* **-at•ed, -at•ing,** *adj., n.* —*v.t.* **1.** to begin, set going, or originate: *to initiate major social reforms.* **2.** to introduce into the knowledge of some art or subject. **3.** to admit into the membership of an organization or group, esp. with formal or secret rites. —*adj.* **4.** initiated; begun. **5.** admitted into an organization or group. **6.** introduced to the knowledge of a subject. —*n.* **7.** a person who has been initiated. —**in•i′ti•a′tor,** *n.*

in•i•ti•a•tion (i nish′ē ā′shən), *n.* **1.** formal admission or acceptance into an organization or group. **2.** the ceremonies or rites of admission. **3.** the act of initiating. **4.** the fact of being initiated.

in•i•ti•a•tive (i nish′ē ə tiv, i nish′ə-), *n.* **1.** an introductory act or step; leading action: *to take the initiative in making friends.* **2.** readiness and ability in initiating action; enterprise: *to lack initiative.* **3.** one's personal, responsible decision: *to act on one's own initiative.* **4. a.** a procedure by which a specified number of voters may propose a statute, constitutional amendment, or ordinance, and compel a popular vote on its adoption. **b.** the general right or ability to present a new bill or measure, as in a legislature. —*adj.* **5.** of or pertaining to initiation; serving to initiate; introductory: *initiative steps.* —**in•i′ti•a•tive•ly,** *adv.*

in•i•ti•a•to•ry (i nish′ē ə tôr′ē, -tōr′ē), *adj.* **1.** introductory; initial. **2.** serving to initiate. —**in•i′ti•a•to′ri•ly,** *adv.*

in•ject (in jekt′), *v.t.* **1.** to force (a fluid) into a passage, cavity, or tissue. **2.** to introduce (something new or different): *to inject humor into a situation.* **3.** to interject (a remark, suggestion, etc.), as into conversation. —**in•jec′tor,** *n.*

in•jec•tion (in jek′shən), *n.* **1.** the act of injecting. **2.** something that is injected. **3.** a liquid injected into the body, esp. for medicinal purposes. **4.** the process of putting a spacecraft into orbit or some other desired trajectory.

in′-joke′, *n.* a joke that can be understood or appreciated only by a limited group of people.

in•ju•di•cious (in′jo͞o dish′əs), *adj.* not judicious; unwise; imprudent; indiscreet. —**in′ju•di′cious•ly,** *adv.* —**in′ju•di′cious•ness,** *n.*

in•junc•tion (in jungk′shən), *n.* **1.** a judicial process or order requiring the person or persons to whom it is directed to do or refrain from doing a particular act. **2.** an act or instance of enjoining. **3.** a command; order; admonition. —**in•junc′tive,** *adj.* —**in•junc′tive•ly,** *adv.*

in•jure (in′jər), *v.t.,* **-jured, -jur•ing. 1.** to do or cause harm of any kind to; damage; hurt; impair: *to injure one's hand.* **2.** to wound or offend: *to injure a friend's feelings.* **3.** to treat unjustly or unfairly; wrong. —**in′jur•a•ble,** *adj.* —**in′jur•er,** *n.*

in•ju•ri•ous (in jo͝or′ē əs), *adj.* **1.** harmful, hurtful, or detrimental, as in effect: *injurious eating habits.* **2.** insulting; abusive; defamatory: *an injurious statement.* —**in•ju′ri•ous•ly,** *adv.* —**in•ju′ri•ous•ness,** *n.*

in•ju•ry (in′jə rē), *n., pl.* **-ju•ries. 1.** harm or damage done or sustained, esp. bodily harm: *to escape without injury.* **2.** a particular form or instance of harm: *an injury to one's shoulder; an injury to one's pride.* **3.** wrong or injustice done or suffered. **4.** *Law.* any violation of the rights, property, etc., of another for which damages may be sought.

in•jus•tice (in jus′tis), *n.* **1.** the quality or fact of being unjust; inequity. **2.** violation of the rights of others; unjust or unfair action or treatment. **3.** an unjust or unfair act; wrong.

ink (ingk), *n.* **1.** a fluid or viscous substance used for writing or printing. **2.** a dark protective fluid ejected by the cuttlefish and other cephalopods. —*v.t.* **3.** to mark, stain, cover, or smear with ink. **4.** to draw or re-trace with ink (often fol. by *in*). **5.** *Slang.* to sign one's name to: *to ink a contract.* —**ink′er,** *n.* —**ink′less,** *adj.*

ink•ber•ry (ingk′ber′ē, -bə rē), *n., pl.* **-ries. 1.** a holly bush, *Ilex glabra,* of E North America, with leathery leaves and black berries. **2.** the pokeweed. **3.** the berry of either plant.

ink•blot (ingk′blot′), *n.* a blot of ink, esp. one forming an irregular pattern and used in an inkblot test.

ink′blot test′, *n.* any psychological test in which patterns formed by inkblots are interpreted by the subject. Compare RORSCHACH TEST.

ink•horn (ingk′hôrn′), *n.* a small container of horn or other material, formerly used to hold writing ink.

ink′horn term′, *n.* an obscure, affectedly or ostentatiously erudite borrowing from another language, esp. Latin or Greek.

ink′-jet′ print′ing, *n.* a high-speed typing or printing process in which charged droplets of ink issuing from nozzles are directed onto paper under computer control. —**ink′-jet′ print′er,** *n.*

ink•ling (ingk′ling), *n.* **1.** a slight suggestion; hint; intimation: *They gave us no inkling of what was going to happen.* **2.** a vague idea or notion; slight understanding: *I don't have an inkling of how it works.*

ink•well (ingk′wel′), *n.* a small container for ink.

ink•wood (ingk′wo͝od′), *n.* a tropical tree, *Exothea paniculata,* of the soapberry family, yielding a hard reddish brown wood.

ink•y (ing′kē), *adj.,* **ink•i•er, ink•i•est. 1.** black as ink: *inky shadows.* **2.** resembling ink. **3.** stained with ink. **4.** of or pertaining to ink. **5.** consisting of or containing ink. **6.** written with ink. —**ink′i•ness,** *n.*

ink′y cap′, *n.* any mushroom of the genus *Coprinus,* esp. *C. atramentarius,* characterized by gills that disintegrate into blackish liquid after the spores mature.

in•laid (in′lād′, in lād′), *adj.* **1.** set into the surface of something: *an inlaid design on a chest.* **2.** decorated or made with a design set into the surface: *an inlaid table.*

in•land (*adj.* in′lənd; *adv., n.* -land′, -lənd), *adj.* **1.** pertaining to or situated in the interior part of a country or region: *inland cities.* **2.** *Chiefly Brit.* domestic or internal: *inland revenue.* —*adv.* **3.** in or toward the interior of a country. —*n.* **4.** the interior part of a country.

in′-law′, *n.* a relative by marriage.

in•lay (*v.* in′lā′, in′lā′; *n.* in′lā′), *v.,* **-laid, -lay•ing,** *n.* —*v.t.* **1.** to decorate (an object) with shaped pieces of contrasting material set in its surface. **2.** to insert or apply (pieces of wood, ivory, metal, etc.) in the surface of an object. —*n.* **3.** inlaid work. **4.** a layer of usu. fine material inserted in something else, esp. for ornament. **5.** a design or decoration made by inlaying. **6.** a tooth filling of metal, porcelain, or other durable material that is first shaped to fit a prepared cavity and then cemented into it. —**in′lay′er,** *n.*

in•let (in′let, -lit), *n.* **1.** an indentation of a shoreline, usu. long and narrow; small bay or arm. **2.** a narrow passage between islands.

in′-line skate′, *n.* a roller skate with typically four hard-rubber wheels in a straight line resembling the blade of an ice skate. —**in′-line skat′er,** *n.* —**in′-line skat′ing,** *n.*

in loc. cit., in the place cited.

in lo•co pa•ren•tis (in lō′kō pä ʀen′tēs; *Eng.* in lō′kō pə ren′tis), *adv. Latin.* in the place or role of a parent.

in•mate (in′māt′), *n.* a person who is confined in a prison, hospital, etc.

in me•mo•ri•am (in mə môr′ē əm, -mōr′-), *prep.* in memory (of); to the memory (of); as a memorial (to).

in•most (in′mōst′), *adj.* **1.** situated farthest within: *the inmost recesses of the forest.* **2.** most intimate: *one's inmost thoughts.*

inn (in), *n.* **1.** a commercial establishment that provides lodging and food for the public, esp. travelers; small hotel. **2.** a tavern. **3.** (*cap.*) any of several buildings in London formerly used as places of residence for students, esp. law students.

in•nards (in′ərdz), *n.pl.* **1.** the internal parts of the body; entrails or viscera. **2.** the internal mechanism, parts, structure, etc., of something: *an engine's innards.*

in•nate (i nāt′, in′āt), *adj.* **1.** existing in one from birth; inborn; native: *innate talents.* **2.** inherent in the character of something: *an innate defect in the hypothesis.* **3.** arising from the intellect or the constitution of the mind, rather than learned through experience: *an innate knowledge of good and evil.* —**in•nate′ly,** *adv.* —**in•nate′ness,** *n.*

in•ner (in′ər), *adj.* **1.** situated within or farther within; interior: *an inner room.* **2.** more intimate, private, or secret: *the inner workings of an organization.* **3.** of or pertaining to the mind or spirit; mental; spiritual: *the inner life.* **4.** not obvious; hidden or obscure: *an inner meaning.* —**in′ner•ly,** *adv., adj.* —**in′ner•ness,** *n.*

in′ner cir′cle, *n.* a small, intimate, and often influential group of people.

in′ner cit′y, *n.* a central and usu. older part of a city, densely populated, often deteriorating, and inhabited mainly by the poor.

in′ner-direct′ed, *adj.* guided by one's own set of values rather than by external pressures.

in′ner ear′, *n.* the inner, liquid-filled, membranous portion of the ear, involved in hearing and balance.

In′ner Light′, *n.* (in Quakerism) the light of Christ in the soul of every person, considered as a guiding force. Also called **In′ner Word′, Inward Light, Christ Within.**

in′ner man′, *n.* **1.** a person's spiritual or intellectual being. **2.** the stomach or appetite: *a hearty meal to satisfy the inner man.*

in′ner mis′sion, *n.* a movement, originating in the early 19th century within the evangelical churches of Germany and later spreading through Europe and America, that ministered chiefly to the material and spiritual needs of the poor and of social outcasts.

in•ner•most (in′ər mōst′), *adj.* **1.** farthest inward; inmost. **2.** most intimate or secret. —*n.* **3.** the innermost part.

in′ner tube′, *n.* a doughnut-shaped, flexible rubber tube inflated inside a tire to bear the weight of a vehicle.

in•ner•vate (i nûr′vāt, in′ər vāt′), *v.t.,* **-vat•ed, -vat•ing.** to furnish with nerves; grow nerves into. —**in′ner•va′tion,** *n.*

in•ning (in′ing), *n.* **1.** a division of a baseball game during which each team has an opportunity to score until three outs have been made against it. **2.** a similar opportunity to score in certain other games, as horseshoes. **3.** an opportunity for activity; a turn.

inn•keep•er (in′kē′pər), *n.* a person who owns or manages an inn or, sometimes, a hotel.

in•no•cence (in′ə səns), *n.* **1.** the quality or state of being innocent; freedom from sin or moral wrong. **2.** freedom from legal or specific wrong; guiltlessness. **3.** simplicity; absence of guile or cunning; naiveté. **4.** lack of knowledge or understanding. **5.** harmlessness; innocuousness. **6.** chastity. **7.** an innocent person or thing. **8.** BLUET (def. 1).

in•no•cent (in′ə sənt), *adj.* **1.** free from moral wrong; without sin; pure. **2.** free from legal or specific wrong; guiltless. **3.** not involving evil intent or motive: *an innocent misrepresentation.* **4.** not causing physical or moral injury; harmless: *innocent fun.* **5.** devoid (usu. fol. by *of*): *a law innocent of merit.* **6.** having or showing the simplicity or naiveté of an unworldly person; guileless; ingenuous. **7.** uninformed or unaware; ignorant. —*n.* **8.** an innocent person. **9.** a young child. **10.** a guileless person. **11.** a simpleton or idiot. [< Latin *in* + *nocēns,* der. of *nocēre* to harm] —**in′no•cent•ly,** *adv.*

In•no•cent (in′ə sənt), *n.* **1. Innocent I, Saint,** died A.D. 417, Italian pope 401–417. **2. Innocent II,** (*Gregorio Papareschi*) died 1143, Italian pope 1130–43. **3. Innocent III,** (*Giovanni Lotario de' Conti*) 1161?–1216, Italian pope 1198–1216. **4. Innocent IV,** (*Sinbaldo de Fieschi*) c1180–1254, Italian pope 1243–54. **5. Innocent XI,** (*Benedetto Odescalchi*) 1611–89, Italian pope 1676–89.

in•noc•u•ous (i nok′yo͞o əs), *adj.* **1.** not harmful or injurious; harmless: *an innocuous home remedy.* **2.** not likely to irritate or offend; inoffensive; *an innocuous remark.* —**in•noc′u•ous•ly,** *adv.* —**in•noc′u•ous•ness, in•no•cu•i•ty** (in′ə kyo͞o′i tē), *n.*

in•nom•i•nate (i nom′ə nit), *adj.* having no name; anonymous.

in•no•vate (in′ə vāt′), *v.,* **-vat•ed, -vat•ing.** —*v.i.* **1.** to introduce something new; make changes (often fol. by *on* or *in*): *to innovate on another's creation.* —*v.t.* **2.** to introduce (something new): *to innovate a computer operating system.* —**in′no•va′tor,** *n.* —**in′no•va•to′ry** (-və tôr′ē, -tōr′ē), *adj.*

in•no•va•tion (in′ə vā′shən), *n.* **1.** something new or different introduced. **2.** the act of innovating; introduction of new things or methods. —**in′no•va′tion•al,** *adj.*

in•no•va•tive (in′ə vā′tiv), *adj.* tending to innovate or characterized by innovation. —**in′no•va′tive•ly,** *adv.* —**in′no•va′tive•ness,** *n.*

in•nu•en•do (in′yo͞o en′dō), *n., pl.* **-dos, -does.** **1.** an indirect intimation about a person or thing, esp. of a disparaging or derogatory nature. **2.** *Law.* a parenthetic explanation or specification in a pleading.

in•nu•mer•a•ble (i no͞o′mər ə bəl, i nyo͞o′-), *adj.* **1.** very numerous. **2.** incapable of being counted; countless. Sometimes, **in•nu′mer•ous.** —**in•nu′mer•a•ble•ness, in•nu′mer•a•bil′i•ty,** *n.* —**in•nu′mer•a•bly,** *adv.*

in•nu•mer•ate (i no͞o′mər it, i nyo͞o′-), *adj.* **1.** unfamiliar with mathematical concepts and methods; ignorant in mathematics; not numerate. —*n.* **2.** an innumerate person. —**in•nu′mer•a•cy,** *n.*

-ino, a suffix used to form names of supersymmetric elementary particles in theoretical physics, usu. corresponding to names of elementary particles ending in -ON[1]: *gluino; gravitino; photino.*

in•ob•serv•ance (in′əb zûr′vəns), *n.* **1.** lack of attention; inattention. **2.** failure to observe a custom, rule, etc.; nonobservance. —**in′ob•serv′ant,** *adj.* —**in′ob•serv′ant•ly,** *adv.*

in•oc•u•la•ble (i nok′yə lə bəl), *adj.* capable of being inoculated. —**in•oc′u•la•bil′i•ty,** *n.*

in•oc•u•late (i nok′yə lāt′), *v.,* **-lat•ed, -lat•ing.** —*v.t.* **1.** to inject or implant (a vaccine, microorganism, antibody, or antigen) into the body in order to protect against, treat, or study a disease. **2.** to affect or treat (a person, animal, or plant) in this manner. **3.** to introduce (microorganisms) into surroundings suited to their growth, as a culture medium. **4.** to imbue (a person), as with ideas; indoctrinate. —*v.i.* **5.** to perform inoculation. —**in•oc′u•la′tive** (-lā′tiv, -lə-), *adj.* —**in•oc′u•la′tor,** *n.*

in•oc•u•la•tion (i nok′yə lā′shən), *n.* **1.** the act or process of inoculating. **2.** an instance of inoculating.

in•of•fen•sive (in′ə fen′siv), *adj.* **1.** causing no harm, trouble, or annoyance; innocuous. **2.** not objectionable, as to the senses: *an inoffensive odor.* —**in′of•fen′sive•ly,** *adv.* —**in′of•fen′sive•ness,** *n.*

in•op•er•a•ble (in op′ər ə bəl, -op′rə bəl), *adj.* **1.** not operable or practicable. **2.** not admitting of a surgical operation without undue risk; incapable of being treated or cured by surgery: *an inoperable tumor.*

in•op•er•a•tive (in op′ər ə tiv, -op′rə tiv, -op′ə rā′tiv), *adj.* **1.** not operative; not in operation. **2.** without effect: *inoperative remedies.* **3.** no longer in effect; void; canceled: *The earlier rule is now inoperative.* —**in•op′er•a•tive•ness,** *n.*

in•op•por•tune (in op′ər to͞on′, -tyo͞on′), *adj.* not opportune; inappropriate; inconvenient; untimely or unseasonable. —**in•op′por•tune′ly,** *adv.* —**in•op′por•tune′ness, in•op′por•tu′ni•ty,** *n.*

in•or•di•nate (in ôr′dn it), *adj.* **1.** not within proper limits; excessive: *to drink an inordinate amount of wine.* **2.** unrestrained in conduct, feelings, etc.: *an inordinate lover of antiques.* **3.** disorderly; uncontrolled. **4.** not regulated; irregular: *inordinate hours.* —**in•or′di•nate•ly,** *adv.* —**in•or′di•nate•ness,** *n.*

in•or•gan•ic (in′ôr gan′ik), *adj.* **1.** not having the structure or organization characteristic of living bodies. **2.** not characterized by vital processes. **3.** noting or pertaining to chemical compounds that are not hydrocarbons or their derivatives. **4.** not fundamental or related; extraneous. —**in′or•gan′i•cal•ly,** *adv.*

in′organ′ic chem′istry, *n.* the branch of chemistry dealing with inorganic compounds.

in•pa•tient (in′pā′shənt), *n.* a patient who stays in a hospital while receiving medical care or treatment.

in per•so•nam (in pər sō′nam), *adv., adj.* (of a legal proceeding or judgment) directed against a person or persons, rather than against property. Compare IN REM.

in•put (in′po͝ot′), *n., adj., v.,* **-put•ted** or **-put, -put•ting.** —*n.* **1.** something that is put in. **2.** the act or process of putting in. **3.** the power or energy supplied to a machine. **4.** the current or voltage applied to an electric or electronic circuit or device. **5. a.** data entered into a computer for processing. **b.** the process of introducing data into the internal storage of a computer. **6.** contribution of information, ideas, opinions, or the like: *Before making a decision we need your input.* **7.** the available data for solving a technical problem. —*adj.* **8.** of or pertaining to data or equipment used for input: *a computer's main input device.* —*v.t.* **9.** to enter (data) into a computer for processing. **10.** to contribute (ideas, information, or suggestions) to a project, discussion, etc.

in•put/out•put (in′po͝ot′out′po͝ot′), *n.* the combination of devices, channels, and techniques controlling the transfer of information between a CPU and its peripherals. *Abbr.:* I/O

in•quest (in′kwest), *n.* **1.** a legal or judicial inquiry, usu. before a jury, esp. one made by a coroner. **2.** the body of people appointed to hold such an inquiry, esp. a coroner's jury. **3.** the decision or finding based on such inquiry. **4.** an investigation or examination.

in•qui•e•tude (in kwī′i to͞od′, -tyo͞od′), *n.* restlessness or uneasiness; disquietude.

in•quire (in kwīər′) also **enquire,** *v.,* **-quired, -quir•ing.** —*v.i.* **1.** to seek information by questioning; ask: *to inquire about a person.* **2.** to make investigation (usu. fol. by *into*): *to inquire into the incident.* —*v.t.* **3.** to seek to learn by asking: *to inquire a person's name.* **4. inquire after,** to ask about the well-being of (someone not present). —**in•quir′a•ble,** *adj.* —**in•quir′er,** *n.* —**in•quir′ing•ly,** *adv.*

in•quir•y (in kwīər′ē, in′kwə rē) *n., pl.* **-quir•ies.** **1.** a seeking or request for truth, information, or knowledge. **2.** an investigation, as into an incident. **3.** a question; query.

in•qui•si•tion (in′kwə zish′ən, ing′-), *n.* **1.** an official investigation, esp. one of a political or religious nature, characterized by lack of regard for individual rights, prejudice on the part of the examiners, and recklessly cruel punishments. **2.** any harsh, difficult, or prolonged questioning. **3.** an investigation, or process of inquiry. **4.** (*cap.*) *Rom. Cath. Ch.* a former special tribunal, engaged chiefly in combating and punishing heresy. —**in′qui•si′tion•al,** *adj.*

in•quis•i•tive (in kwiz′i tiv), *adj.* **1.** given to inquiry or research; eager for knowledge; curious. **2.** unduly curious; prying. —**in•quis′i•tive•ly,** *adv.* —**in•quis′i•tive•ness,** *n.*

in•quis•i•tor (in kwiz′i tər), *n.* **1.** a person who makes an inquisition. **2.** a questioner, esp. an unduly curious or harsh one. **3.** a member of the Inquisition.

in re (in rē′, rā′), *prep.* in the matter of.

in rem (in rem′), *adv., adj.* (of a legal proceeding or judgment) directed against a thing, rather than against a person, as a legal proceeding for the recovery of property. Compare IN PERSONAM.

in′-res′idence, *adj.* having a special post or assignment at an institution, usu. with residential privileges (usu. used in combination): *a poet-in-residence at the university.*

I.N.R.I., Jesus of Nazareth, King of the Jews. [< Late Latin *Iēsūs Nazarēnus, Rēx Iūdaeōrum*]

in•road (in′rōd′), *n.* **1.** a damaging or serious encroachment: *inroads on our savings.* **2.** a sudden hostile incursion; raid; foray.

in•rush (in′rush′), *n.* a rushing or pouring in.

INS or **I.N.S.,** Immigration and Naturalization Service.

in•sa•lu•bri•ous (in′sə lo͞o′brē əs), *adj.* unfavorable to health; unwholesome. —**in′sa•lu′bri•ous•ly,** *adv.* —**in′sa•lu′bri•ty** (-bri tē), *n.*

ins′ and outs′, *n.pl.* intricacies; particulars; peculiarities: *the ins and outs of the tax laws.*

in•sane (in sān′), *adj.* **1.** (*not in technical use*) mentally unsound or deranged; demented; mad. **2.** of, characteristic of, or for persons who are mentally deranged: *insane actions; an insane asylum.* **3.** utterly senseless; irrational: *an insane plan.* —**in•sane′ly,** *adv.* —**in•sane′ness,** *n.*

in•san•i•tar•y (in san′i ter′ē), *adj.* not sanitary; unclean; likely to cause disease. —**in•san′i•tar′i•ness,** *n.*

in•san•i•ty (in san′i tē), *n., pl.* **-ties.** **1.** (*not in technical use*) the condition of being insane; mental illness or disorder. **2.** *Law.* such unsoundness of mind as affects legal responsibility or capacity. **3.** extreme folly; senselessness; foolhardiness.

in•sa•tia•ble (in sā′shə bəl, -shē ə-), *adj.* not satiable; incapable of being satisfied: *insatiable hunger; insatiable ambition.* —**in•sa′tia•bil′i•ty, in•sa′tia•ble•ness,** *n.* —**in•sa′tia•bly,** *adv.*

in•scribe (in skrīb′), *v.t.,* **-scribed, -scrib•ing.** **1.** to address or dedicate (a book, photograph, etc.) to a person, esp. by writing a brief personal note in or on it. **2.** to mark (a surface) with words, characters, etc., esp. in a durable or conspicuous way. **3.** to write, print, mark, or engrave (words, characters, etc.). **4.** to enroll, as on an official list. **5.** *Geom.* to draw (one figure) within another figure so that the inner lies entirely within the boundary of the outer, touching it at as many points as possible: *to inscribe a circle in a square.* **6.** *Brit.* **a.** to issue (a loan) in the form of shares with registered stockholders. **b.** to buy or sell (stocks). —**in•scrib′a•ble,** *adj.* —**in•scrib′er,** *n.*

in·scrip·tion (in skrip′shən), *n.* **1.** something inscribed, as a word or words carved on stone or other hard surface. **2.** a brief dedication or other note written and signed by hand in a book, on a photograph, etc. **3.** the act of inscribing. **4.** *Brit.* **a.** an issue of securities or stocks. **b.** a block of shares in a stock, as bought or sold by one person. **5.** the lettering running across the field of a coin, medal, etc. Compare LEGEND (def. 5). —**in·scrip′tion·al**, *adj.* —**in·scrip′tion·less**, *adj.*

in·scrip·tive (in skrip′tiv), *adj.* of, pertaining to, or of the nature of an inscription. —**in·scrip′tive·ly**, *adv.*

in·scru·ta·ble (in skrōō′tə bəl), *adj.* **1.** incapable of being investigated, analyzed, or scrutinized. **2.** not easily understood; mysterious; unfathomable: *an inscrutable smile.* —**in·scru′ta·bil′i·ty, in·scru′ta·ble·ness**, *n.* —**in·scru′ta·bly**, *adv.*

in·seam (in′sēm′), *n.* an inside or inner seam of a garment, esp. the seam of a trouser leg that runs from the crotch down to the bottom of the leg.

in·sect (in′sekt), *n.* **1.** any animal of the class Insecta, comprising small, air-breathing arthropods having the body divided into three parts (head, thorax, and abdomen), and having two antennae, three pairs of legs, and usu. two pairs of wings. **2.** any small arthropod, such as a spider, tick, or centipede, having a superficial, general similarity to members of the class Insecta. **3.** a contemptible or unimportant person. —*adj.* **4.** of, pertaining to, like, or used for or against insects: *an insect bite; insect powder.* —**in′sec·ti·val** (-tī′vəl), *adj.*

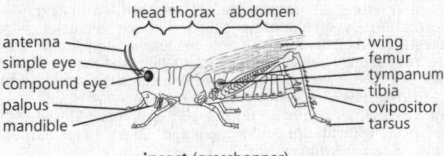

insect (grasshopper)

in·sec·ti·cide (in sek′tə sīd′), *n.* a substance or preparation used for killing insects. —**in·sec′ti·cid′al**, *adj.*

in·sec·ti·vore (in sek′tə vôr′, -vōr′), *n.* an insectivorous animal or plant.

in·sec·tiv·o·rous (in′sek tiv′ər əs), *adj.* feeding chiefly on insects.

in·se·cure (in′si kyŏŏr′), *adj.* **1.** subject to fears, doubts, etc.; not confident or assured: *an insecure person.* **2.** not safe; exposed or liable to risk or danger: *insecure borders.* **3.** not firmly or reliably placed or fastened: *an insecure ladder.* —**in′se·cure′ly**, *adv.* —**in′se·cure′ness**, *n.* —**in′se·cu′ri·ty**, *n., pl.* **-ties.**

in·sem·i·nate (in sem′ə nāt′), *v.t.,* **-nat·ed, -nat·ing. 1.** to inject semen into (the female reproductive tract); impregnate. **2.** to sow; implant seed into. —**in·sem′i·na′tion**, *n.*

in·sen·sate (in sen′sāt, -sit), *adj.* **1.** not endowed with sensation; inanimate. **2.** without feeling or sensitivity; cold; cruel. **3.** without sense, understanding, or judgment; foolish. —**in·sen′sate·ly**, *adv.* —**in·sen′sate·ness**, *n.*

in·sen·si·ble (in sen′sə bəl), *adj.* **1.** incapable of feeling or perceiving; deprived of sensation; unconscious. **2.** not subject to a particular feeling or sensation: *insensible to shame; insensible to the cold.* **3.** unaware; unconscious: *We are not insensible of your kindness.* **4.** not perceptible by the senses; imperceptible: *insensible transitions.* **5.** unresponsive in feeling; apathetic. —**in·sen′si·bly**, *adv.* —**in·sen′si·bil′i·ty**, *n.*

in·sen·si·tive (in sen′si tiv), *adj.* **1.** not emotionally sensitive or sympathetic; unfeeling; callous: *an insensitive nature; insensitive to the needs of the poor.* **2.** not physically sensitive: *insensitive skin.* **3.** not affected by physical or chemical agencies or influences: *insensitive to light.* —**in·sen′si·tive·ness, in·sen′si·tiv′i·ty**, *n.*

in·sen·ti·ent (in sen′shē ənt, -shənt), *adj.* not sentient; without sensation or feeling. —**in·sen′ti·ence, in·sen′ti·en·cy**, *n.*

in·sep·a·ra·ble (in sep′ər ə bəl, -sep′rə-), *adj.* **1.** incapable of being separated, parted, or disjoined. —*n.* **2.** Usu., **inseparables.** inseparable objects, qualities, etc. —**in·sep′a·ra·bil′i·ty, in·sep′a·ra·ble·ness**, *n.* —**in·sep′a·ra·bly**, *adv.*

in·sert (*v.* in sûrt′; *n.* in′sûrt), *v.t.* **1.** to put or place in: *to insert a key in a lock.* **2.** to introduce into the body of something: *to insert a new paragraph in an article.* —*n.* **3.** something inserted or to be inserted. **4.** an extra leaf or section, as an advertisement, printed independently, for binding or tipping into a book or periodical. —**in·sert′a·ble**, *adj.* —**in·sert′er**, *n.*

in·ser·tion (in sûr′shən), *n.* **1.** the act of inserting. **2.** something inserted. **3.** *Bot., Zool.* **a.** the place or manner of attachment, as of a muscle to the part it moves or a leaf to a stem. **b.** the part of the structure that is attached. **4.** lace, embroidery, or the like, to be sewn between parts of other material. **5.** INJECTION (def. 4). —**in·ser′tion·al**, *adj.*

in·serv·ice (in sûr′vis, in′sûr′-), *adj.* taking place while one is employed: *an in-service training program.*

in·ses·so·ri·al (in′sə sôr′ē əl, -sōr′-), *adj.* adapted for perching, as a bird's foot.

in·set (*n.* in′set′; *v.* in set′), *n., v.,* **-set, -set·ting.** —*n.* **1.** something inserted; insert. **2.** a small picture, map, etc., inserted within the border of a larger one. **3.** a piece of cloth set into a garment, usu. as an ornamental panel. **4.** an inflow, esp. of water. —*v.t.* **5.** to set in or insert: *to inset a panel in a dress.* —**in′set′ter**, *n.*

in·shore (in′shôr′, -shōr′), *adj.* **1.** situated or carried on close to the shore: *inshore waters.* —*adv.* **2.** toward the shore.

in·side (in′sīd′, in′sīd′), *prep.* **1.** on the inner side or part of; within: *inside the circle.* **2.** prior to; within: *to arrive inside an hour.* —*adv.* **3.** in or into the inner part: *Look inside.* **4.** indoors: *to play inside on rainy days.* **5.** by true nature; basically: *Inside, she's really very shy.* **6.** *Slang.* in prison. —*n.* **7.** the inner part; interior: *the inside of the house.* **8.** the inner side or surface: *the inside of the hand.* **9.** **insides,** *Informal.* the inner parts of the body, esp. the stomach and intestines. **10.** a position within a select circle of power, prestige, etc.: *to be on the inside in the administration.* **11.** the part closest to a specified point, as the part of an oval track closest to the inner rail. **12.** inward nature, thoughts, feelings, etc. **13.** confidential or private information: *to have an inside on the new plans.* —*adj.* **14.** situated or being on or in the inside; interior; internal: *an inside seat.* **15.** private; confidential; restricted: *inside information.* **16.** *Baseball.* (of a pitched ball) passing between home plate and the batter. —*Idiom.* **17. inside of,** within the space or period of. **18. inside out, a.** with the inner side reversed to face the outside. **b.** thoroughly; completely.

in′side job′, *n.* a crime committed by or in collusion with a person or persons closely associated with the victim.

in·sid·er (in′sī′dər), *n.* **1.** a person who is a member of a group, organization, society, etc. **2.** a person belonging to a select circle of power, prestige, etc., esp. one who is privy to confidential information. **3.** a person who has some special advantage or influence.

in′sid·er trad′ing, *n.* the illegal buying and selling of securities by persons acting on privileged information. —**in′sid·er trad′er**, *n.*

in′side track′, *n.* **1.** the inner, or shorter, track of a racecourse. **2.** an advantageous position in a competitive situation.

in·sid·i·ous (in sid′ē əs), *adj.* **1.** intended to entrap or beguile: *an insidious plan.* **2.** stealthily treacherous or deceitful: *an insidious enemy.* **3.** operating or proceeding inconspicuously but with grave effect: *an insidious disease.* —**in·sid′i·ous·ly**, *adv.* —**in·sid′i·ous·ness**, *n.*

in·sight (in′sīt′), *n.* **1.** an instance of apprehending the true nature of a thing, esp. through intuitive understanding. **2.** penetrating mental vision or discernment. **3.** *Psychol.* **a.** an understanding of the motivations behind one's thoughts or behavior. **b.** (in psychotherapy) a recognition of the sources of one's emotional or mental problem.

in·sight·ful (in′sīt′fəl), *adj.* characterized by or displaying insight; perceptive. —**in·sight′ful·ly**, *adv.* —**in·sight′ful·ness**, *n.*

in·sig·ni·a (in sig′nē ə), *n., formally a pl. of* **insigne,** *but usu. used as a sing. with pl.* **-ni·a** *or* **-ni·as. 1.** a badge or distinguishing mark of office or honor: *military insignia.* **2.** a distinguishing mark or sign of anything: *an insignia of mourning.* Sometimes, **insigne.**

insignia

| Lieutenant General | First Sergeant (E-8) | Corps of Engineers | Military Police | Women's Army Corps | Third Infantry Division |

in·sig·nif·i·cance (in′sig nif′i kəns), *n.* the quality or condition of being insignificant; lack of importance or consequence.

in·sig·nif·i·cant (in′sig nif′i kənt), *adj.* **1.** unimportant, trifling, or petty: *Omit the insignificant details.* **2.** too small to be important: *an insignificant sum.* **3.** without weight, influence, or distinction; contemptible: *an insignificant fellow.* **4.** without meaning; meaningless: *insignificant sounds.* —**in′sig·nif′i·cant·ly**, *adv.*

in·sin·cere (in′sin sēr′), *adj.* not sincere; not honest in the expression of actual feeling; hypocritical. —**in′sin·cere′ly**, *adv.*

in·sin·cer·i·ty (in′sin ser′i tē), *n., pl.* **-ties. 1.** the quality of being insincere; lack of sincerity. **2.** an instance of being insincere.

in·sin·u·ate (in sin′yōō āt′), *v.,* **-at·ed, -at·ing.** —*v.t.* **1.** to suggest or hint slyly: *He insinuated that they were lying.* **2.** to instill or infuse subtly or artfully, as into the mind: *to insinuate doubt.* **3.** to bring or introduce into a position or relation by indirect or artful methods: *to insinuate oneself into favor.* —*v.i.* **4.** to make insinuations. —**in·sin′u·a′tive** (-sin′yōō ā′tiv, -yōō ə-), **in·sin′u·a·to·ry** (-tôr′ē, -tōr′ē), *adj.* —**in·sin′u·a′tive·ly**, *adv.* —**in·sin′u·a′tor**, *n.*

in·sin·u·at·ing (in sin′yōō ā′ting), *adj.* **1.** tending to instill doubts, distrust, etc.; suggestive: *an insinuating letter.* **2.** gaining favor or winning confidence by artful means: *an insinuating manner.* —**in·sin′u·at′ing·ly**, *adv.*

in·sin·u·a·tion (in sin′yōō ā′shən), *n.* **1.** an indirect or covert suggestion or hint, esp. of a derogatory nature. **2.** the art or power of stealing into the affections and pleasing; ingratiation. **3.** an act or instance of insinuating.

in·sip·id (in sip′id), *adj.* **1.** without distinctive, interesting, or stimulating qualities; vapid: *an insipid personality.* **2.** without sufficient taste to be pleasing, as food or drink; bland: *a rather insipid soup.* —**in′si·pid′i·ty, in·sip′id·ness**, *n.* —**in·sip′id·ly**, *adv.*

in·sist (in sist′), *v.i.* **1.** to be emphatic, firm, or resolute; dwell with earnestness or emphasis (usu. fol. by *on* or *upon*): *to insist on a point;*

to insist on checking every fact. —*v.t.* **2.** to assert or demand firmly or persistently: *I insist that you go.* —**in•sist′er,** *n.* —**in•sist′ing•ly,** *adv.*

in•sist•ence (in sis′təns), *n.* **1.** the act or fact of insisting. **2.** the quality of being insistent.

in•sist•ent (in sis′tənt), *adj.* **1.** emphatic in dwelling upon or maintaining something; persistent. **2.** compelling attention or notice: *an insistent tone.* —**in•sist′ent•ly,** *adv.*

in si•tu (in sī′to͞o, -tyo͞o, sē′-, sit′o͞o), *adv., adj.* situated in its original or natural place or position.

in•so•bri•e•ty (in′sə brī′i tē), *n.* lack of sobriety or moderation; intemperance; drunkenness.

in•so•far (in′sə fär′, -sō-), *adv.* to such an extent (usu. fol. by *as*): *I will do the work insofar as I am able.*

in•sole (in′sōl′), *n.* **1.** the inner sole of a shoe or boot. **2.** a thickness of material laid as an inner sole within a shoe, esp. for comfort.

in•so•lent (in′sə lənt), *adj.* **1.** boldly rude or disrespectful; contemptuously impertinent; insulting: *an insolent reply.* —*n.* **2.** an insolent person. —**in′so•lence,** *n.* —**in′so•lent•ly,** *adv.*

in•sol•u•ble (in sol′yə bəl), *adj.* **1.** incapable of being dissolved: *insoluble salts.* **2.** incapable of being solved: *an insoluble problem.* —**in•sol′u•bil′i•ty, in•sol′u•ble•ness,** *n.* —**in•sol′u•bly,** *adv.*

in•solv•a•ble (in sol′və bəl), *adj.* incapable of being solved; insoluble. —**in•solv′a•bil′i•ty,** *n.* —**in•solv′a•bly,** *adv.*

in•sol•ven•cy (in sol′vən sē), *n.* the condition of being insolvent; bankruptcy.

in•sol•vent (in sol′vənt), *adj.* **1.** not solvent; unable to satisfy creditors or discharge liabilities. **2.** pertaining to bankrupt persons or bankruptcy. —*n.* **3.** a person who is insolvent.

in•som•ni•a (in som′nē ə), *n.* difficulty in falling or staying asleep, esp. when chronic. —**in•som′ni•ac′,** *n., adj.* —**in•som′ni•ous,** *adj.*

in•so•much (in′sə much′, -sō-), *adv.* **1.** to such an extent or degree; so (usu. fol. by *that*). **2.** inasmuch (usu. fol. by *as*).

in•sou•ci•ance (in so͞o′sē əns; *Fr.* aɴ so͞o syäɴs′), *n.* the quality of being insouciant; lack of care or concern; indifference.

in•sou•ci•ant (in so͞o′sē ənt; *Fr.* aɴ so͞o syäɴ′), *adj.* free from concern, worry, or anxiety; carefree; nonchalant. —**in•sou′ci•ant•ly,** *adv.*

in•spect (in spekt′), *v.t.* **1.** to look carefully at or over: *to inspect every part of a motor.* **2.** to view or examine formally or officially: *to inspect troops.* —**in•spect′a•ble,** *adj.* —**in•spect′a•bil′i•ty,** *n.*

in•spec•tion (in spek′shən), *n.* **1.** the act of inspecting. **2.** formal or official viewing or examination. —**in•spec′tion•al,** *adj.*

in•spec•tor (in spek′tər), *n.* **1.** a person who inspects. **2.** an officer appointed to inspect. **3.** a police officer usu. ranking next below a superintendent. —**in•spec′to•ral, in′spec•to′ri•al** (-tôr′ē əl, -tōr′-), *adj.* —**in•spec′tor•ship′,** *n.*

in•spi•ra•tion (in′spə rā′shən), *n.* **1.** an inspiring or animating influence. **2.** something inspired, as an idea. **3.** a result of inspired activity. **4.** a thing or person that inspires. **5.** *Theol.* a divine influence directly and immediately exerted upon the mind or soul. **6.** the drawing of air into the lungs; inhalation. **7.** the act of inspiring. **8.** the quality or state of being inspired. —**in′spi•ra′tion•al,** *adj.* —**in′spi•ra′tion•al•ly,** *adv.*

in•spire (in spīər′), *v.,* **-spired, -spir•ing.** —*v.t.* **1.** to fill with an animating, quickening, or exalting influence: *Her courage inspired her followers.* **2.** to produce or arouse (a feeling, thought, etc.): *to inspire confidence.* **3.** to fill or affect with a feeling, thought, etc.: *to inspire a person with distrust.* **4.** to influence or impel: *Competition inspired them to greater efforts.* **5.** to communicate or suggest by a divine or supernatural influence. **6.** to guide or control by divine influence. **7.** to give rise to, bring about, cause, etc.: *a philosophy that inspired a revolution.* **8.** to take (air, gases, etc.) into the lungs in breathing; inhale. —*v.i.* **9.** to give inspiration. **10.** to inhale. —**in•spir•a•tive** (in spīər′ə tiv, in′spi rā′-tiv), *adj.* —**in•spir′ed•ly,** *adv.* —**in•spir′er,** *n.* —**in•spir′ing•ly,** *adv.*

in•sta•bil•i•ty (in′stə bil′i tē), *n.* **1.** the quality or state of being unstable; lack of stability. **2.** the tendency to behave in an unpredictable, changeable, or erratic manner: *emotional instability.*

in•stall or **in•stal** (in stôl′), *v.t.,* **-stalled, -stall•ing** or **-stal•ling.** **1.** to place in position or connect for use: *to install a heating system.* **2.** to establish in an office, position, or place: *to install oneself in new quarters.* **3.** to induct into an office or the like with ceremonies or formalities. —**in•stall′er,** *n.*

in•stal•la•tion (in′stə lā′shən), *n.* **1.** something installed, as machinery or apparatus placed in position or connected for use. **2.** the act of installing. **3.** the fact of being installed. **4.** any more or less permanent military post, camp, base, or the like.

in•stall•ment¹ or **in•stal•ment** (in stôl′mənt), *n.* **1.** any of several parts into which a debt or other sum is divided for payment at successive fixed times. **2.** a single portion of something issued in parts at successive times: *a magazine serial in six installments.*

in•stall•ment² or **in•stal•ment** (in stôl′mənt), *n.* **1.** the act of installing. **2.** the fact of being installed; installation.

install′ment plan′, *n.* a system for paying for an item in fixed amounts at specified intervals.

in•stance (in′stəns), *n.* **1.** a case or occurrence of something: *fresh instances of oppression.* **2.** an example put forth in proof or illustration: *to cite a few instances.* **3.** the institution and prosecution of a legal case. —*v.t.* **4.** to cite as an instance or example. **5.** to exemplify by an instance. —*v.i.* **6.** to cite an instance. —***Idiom.*** **7. at the instance of,** at the urging or suggestion of. **8. for instance,** for example.

in•stan•cy (in′stən sē), *n.* **1.** the quality of being instant; urgency; pressing nature. **2.** immediateness.

in•stant (in′stənt), *n.* **1.** an infinitesimal or very short space of time; moment. **2.** the point of time now present: *Come here this instant!* **3.** a particular moment: *at the instant of contact.* **4.** an instant beverage or other product, esp. instant coffee. —*adj.* **5.** succeeding without any interval of time; immediate: *instant relief.* **6.** pressing or urgent: *instant need.* **7.** (of a food or beverage) processed so as to require minimal time and effort to prepare, as just the addition of water: *instant coffee.* **8.** produced, occurring, or appearing rapidly and with little or no preparation or effort: *instant answers.* **9.** designed to act or produce results quickly or immediately: *an instant lottery.* **10.** present; current: *the instant case before the court.* —*adv.* **11.** instantly.

in•stan•ta•ne•ous (in′stən tā′nē əs), *adj.* **1.** occurring, done, or completed in an instant; immediate: *an instantaneous response.* **2.** existing at or pertaining to a particular instant. —**in′stan•ta′ne•ous•ly,** *adv.* —**in′stan•ta′ne•ous•ness, in′stan•ta•ne′i•ty** (-tn ē′i tē), *n.*

in′stant cam′era, *n.* a usu. portable camera that produces a finished picture shortly after each exposure.

in•stan•ter (in stan′tər), *adv.* immediately; at once.

in•stan•ti•ate (in stan′shē āt′), *v.t.,* **-at•ed, -at•ing.** to provide an instance of or concrete evidence in support of (a theory, claim, etc.). —**in•stan′ti•a′tion,** *n.* —**in•stan′ti•a′tive,** *adj.*

in•stant•ly (in′stənt lē), *adv.* **1.** immediately; at once. **2.** urgently.

in′stant re′play, *n.* **1. a.** the recording and immediate rebroadcasting of a segment of a live television broadcast, esp. of a sports event. **b.** the segment recorded and immediately rebroadcast. **2.** any immediate repetition, review, or reenactment.

in•state (in stāt′), *v.t.,* **-stat•ed, -stat•ing.** to place in a state, position, or office; install. —**in•state′ment,** *n.*

in•stead (in sted′), *adv.* **1.** as a substitute or replacement; in the place or stead of someone or something. **2.** as a preferred or accepted alternative; in preference. —***Idiom.*** **3. instead of,** in place of.

in•step (in′step′), *n.* **1.** the arched upper surface of the human foot between the toes and the ankle. **2.** the part of a shoe, stocking, etc., covering this surface. **3.** the front of the hind leg of a horse, cow, etc., between the hock and the pastern joint; cannon.

in•sti•gate (in′sti gāt′), *v.t.,* **-gat•ed, -gat•ing.** **1.** to cause by incitement; foment: *to instigate a quarrel.* **2.** to urge, provoke, or incite to some action or course: *to instigate people to revolt.* —**in′sti•gat′ing•ly,** *adv.* —**in′sti•ga′tion,** *n.* —**in′sti•ga′tive,** *adj.* —**in′sti•ga′tor,** *n.*

in•still or **in•stil** (in stil′), *v.t.,* **-stilled, -still•ing** or **-stil•ling.** **1.** to infuse slowly or gradually, as into the mind or feelings: *to instill courtesy in a child.* **2.** to put in drop by drop. —**in′stil•la′tion,** *n.* —**in•still′er,** *n.* —**in•still′ment,** *n.*

in•stinct¹ (in′stingkt), *n.* **1.** an inborn pattern of activity or tendency to action common to a given biological species. **2.** a natural or innate impulse, inclination, or tendency. **3.** a natural aptitude or gift: *an instinct for making money.* **4.** natural intuitive power.

in•stinct² (in stingkt′), *adj.* filled or infused with some animating principle (usu. fol. by *with*): *instinct with life.*

in•stinc•tive (in stingk′tiv) also **in•stinc•tu•al** (-cho͞o əl), *adj.* **1.** pertaining to or of the nature of instinct. **2.** prompted by or resulting from or as if from instinct; natural; unlearned. —**in•stinc′tive•ly, in•stinc′tu•al•ly,** *adv.*

in•sti•tute (in′sti to͞ot′, -tyo͞ot′), *v.,* **-tut•ed, -tut•ing,** *n.* —*v.t.* **1.** to set up; establish; organize. **2.** to inaugurate; initiate; start. **3.** to set in operation: *to institute a lawsuit.* **4.** to establish in an office or position. **5.** to invest with the spiritual charge of a church or parish. —*n.* **6.** a society or organization for carrying on a particular work, as of a literary, scientific, or educational character. **7.** the building occupied by such a society. **8. a.** a college devoted to instruction in technical subjects. **b.** a unit within a university organized for advanced instruction and research in a relatively narrow field. **c.** a short instructional program in some specialized activity. **9.** an established principle, law, custom, or organization. **10. institutes,** an elementary treatise on law. **11.** something instituted. —**in′sti•tut′er, in′sti•tu′tor,** *adj.*

in•sti•tu•tion (in′sti to͞o′shən, -tyo͞o′-), *n.* **1.** an organization or establishment devoted to the promotion of a cause or program, esp. one of an educational or charitable character. **2.** the building devoted to such work. **3.** a place for the care or confinement of people, as mental patients. **4.** a well-established and structured pattern of behavior or of relationships that is a fundamental part of a culture: *the institution of marriage.* **5.** any established law, custom, etc. **6.** any familiar, long-established person, thing, or practice; fixture. **7.** the act of instituting.

in•sti•tu•tion•al (in′sti to͞o′shə nl, -tyo͞o′-), *adj.* **1.** of, pertaining to, or of the nature of an institution. **2.** characterized by the drabness, and impersonality attributed to large institutions: *institutional food.* **3.** (of advertising) having as the primary object the establishment of goodwill and a favorable reputation rather than immediate sales. **4.** pertaining to institutes or principles, esp. of jurisprudence. —**in′sti•tu′tion•al•ly,** *adv.*

in•sti•tu•tion•al•ism (in′sti to͞o′shə nl iz′əm, -tyo͞o′-), *n.* **1.** the system or advocacy of institutions devoted to public, charitable, or other purposes. **2.** strong attachment to established institutions, as of religion. **3.** the policy

I

or practice of using public institutions to house people considered incapable of caring for themselves. —**in′sti•tu′tion•al•ist,** *n.*

in•sti•tu•tion•al•ize (in′sti to͞o′shə nl īz′, -tyo͞o′-), *v.t.,* **-ized, -iz•ing.** **1.** to make institutional. **2.** to make into or treat as an institution: *the danger of institutionalizing racism.* **3.** to place or confine in an institution. —**in′sti•tu′tion•al•i•za′tion,** *n.*

in•struct (in strukt′), *v.t.* **1.** to furnish with knowledge, esp. by a systematic method; teach; educate. **2.** to furnish with orders or directions; direct; order; command. **3.** to furnish with information; inform; apprise. **4.** (of a judge) to guide (a jury) by outlining the legal principles involved in the case under consideration. —**in•struct′i•ble,** *adj.*

in•struc•tion (in struk′shən), *n.* **1.** the act or practice of instructing or teaching; education. **2.** knowledge or information imparted. **3.** an item of such knowledge or information. **4.** Usu., **instructions.** orders or directions. **5.** the act of furnishing with authoritative directions. **6.** a computer command. —**in•struc′tion•al,** *adj.*

in•struc•tive (in struk′tiv), *adj.* serving to instruct or inform. —**in•struc′tive•ly,** *adv.* —**in•struc′tive•ness,** *n.*

in•struc•tor (in struk′tər), *n.* **1.** a person who instructs; teacher. **2.** a teacher in a college or university who ranks below an assistant professor. —**in•struc′tor•ship′,** *n.*

in•stru•ment (in′strə mənt), *n.* **1.** a mechanical tool or implement, esp. one used for delicate or precision work: *surgical instruments.* **2.** a device for producing musical sounds. **3.** a means by which something is effected or done; agency: *an instrument of government.* **4.** a device for measuring the present value of a quantity under observation. **5.** a mechanical or electronic device for monitoring, measuring, or controlling, esp. one used in navigation of aircraft. **6.** a formal legal document, as a draft or bond: *negotiable instruments.* **7.** a person used by another as a means to some private end; tool. —*v.t.* **8.** to equip with instruments. **9.** to arrange (a composition) for musical instruments; orchestrate.

in•stru•men•tal (in′strə men′tl), *adj.* **1.** serving or acting as an instrument or means; useful; helpful. **2.** performed on or written for a musical instrument or instruments. **3.** of or pertaining to an instrument or tool. **4.** of or designating a grammatical case or form typically indicating means or agency. —*n.* **5.** **a.** the instrumental case. **b.** a word in the instrumental case. **6.** a piece of music played by an instrument or a group of instruments. —**in′stru•men′tal•ly,** *adv.*

in•stru•men•tal•ist (in′strə men′tl ist), *n.* a person who plays a musical instrument.

in•stru•men•ta•tion (in′strə men tā′shən), *n.* **1.** the arranging of music for instruments, esp. for an orchestra. **2.** the list of instruments for which a composition is scored. **3.** the use of, or work done by, instruments. **4.** instrumental agency. **5.** the process of developing, manufacturing, and using instruments, esp. in science and industry.

in′strument fly′ing, *n.* the control and navigation of an aircraft by reference to its gauges and electronics, with little or no visual reference outside the cockpit.

in′strument land′ing, *n.* a landing accomplished by use of an aircraft's gauges and ground-based electronics.

in′strument pan′el, *n.* **1.** a panel on which are mounted an array of dials, lights, and gauges that monitor the performance of an airplane, boat, or machine. **2.** DASHBOARD (def. 1).

in•sub•or•di•nate (in′sə bôr′dn it), *adj.* **1.** not submitting to authority; disobedient. —*n.* **2.** a person who is insubordinate. —**in′sub•or′di•nate•ly,** *adv.* —**in′sub•or′di•na′tion,** *n.*

in•sub•stan•tial (in′səb stan′shəl), *adj.* **1.** not substantial or real; lacking substance. **2.** not solid or firm; weak; flimsy. **3.** not substantial in amount or size; inconsiderable. —**in′sub•stan′ti•al′i•ty,** *n.* —**in′sub•stan′tial•ly,** *adv.*

in•suf•fer•a•ble (in suf′ər ə bəl), *adj.* not to be endured; intolerable. —**in•suf′fer•a•ble•ness,** *n.* —**in•suf′fer•a•bly,** *adv.*

in•suf•fi•cien•cy (in′sə fish′ən sē), *n., pl.* **-cies.** **1.** deficiency in amount, force, power, competence, or fitness; inadequacy. **2.** an instance of this. **3.** inability of an organ or other body part to function normally: *cardiac insufficiency.* Sometimes, **in′suf•fi′cience.**

in•suf•fi•cient (in′sə fish′ənt), *adj.* **1.** not sufficient; lacking in what is required: *an insufficient answer.* **2.** deficient in force, quality, or amount; inadequate: *insufficient protection.* —**in′suf•fi′cient•ly,** *adv.*

in•su•lar (in′sə lər, ins′yə-), *adj.* **1.** of or pertaining to an island or islands: *insular possessions.* **2.** dwelling or situated on an island. **3.** forming an island: *insular rocks.* **4.** detached; standing alone; isolated. **5.** of or characteristic of islanders. **6.** narrow-minded or illiberal; provincial: *insular attitudes.* **7.** *Pathol.* characterized by isolated spots or patches. **8.** *Anat.* of or pertaining to islands of tissue, as the islets of Langerhans. —**in′su•lar•ism,** *n.* —**in′su•lar′i•ty,** *n.* —**in′su•lar•ly,** *adv.*

in•su•late (in′sə lāt′, ins′yə-), *v.t.,* **-lat•ed, -lat•ing.** **1.** to cover, line, or separate with a material that prevents or reduces the passage, transfer, or leakage of heat, electricity, or sound. **2.** to place in an isolated or protected situation. —**in′su•la′tive,** *adj.*

in•su•la•tion (in′sə lā′shən, ins′yə-), *n.* **1.** material used for insulating. **2.** the act of insulating. **3.** the state of being insulated.

in•su•la•tor (in′sə lā′tər, ins′yə-), *n.* **1.** **a.** a material of such low conductivity that the flow of electric current through it is negligible. **b.** a device made of such material, as glass or porcelain, for supporting a charged conductor and electrically isolating it. **2.** a person or thing that insulates.

in•su•lin (in′sə lin, ins′yə-), *n.* **1.** a hormone, produced by the beta cells of the islets of Langerhans of the pancreas, that regulates the metabolism of glucose and other nutrients. **2.** any of several commercial preparations of this substance, each absorbed into the body at a particular rate: used for treating diabetes.

in′sulin shock′, *n.* a state of collapse caused by a decrease in blood sugar resulting from the administration of excessive insulin.

in•sult (*v.* in sult′; *n.* in′sult), *v.t.* **1.** to treat or speak to insolently or with contemptuous rudeness; affront. **2.** to offend or demean. —*n.* **3.** an insolent or contemptuously rude action or remark. **4.** something having the effect of an affront: *That book is an insult to one's intelligence.* **5.** *Med.* **a.** an injury or trauma. **b.** an agent that inflicts this. —***Saying.*** **6.** **add insult to injury,** to inflict additional harm on a person who has already been hurt. —**in•sult′a•ble,** *adj.* —**in•sult′ing•ly,** *adv.*

in•su•per•a•ble (in so͞o′pər ə bəl), *adj.* incapable of being passed over, overcome, or surmounted. —**in•su′per•a•bly,** *adv.*

in•sup•port•a•ble (in′sə pôr′tə bəl, -pōr′-), *adj.* **1.** not endurable; unbearable; insufferable. **2.** incapable of being supported or justified, as by evidence: *an insupportable accusation.* —**in′sup•port′a•bly,** *adv.*

in•sup•press•i•ble (in′sə pres′ə bəl), *adj.* incapable of being suppressed; irrepressible. —**in′sup•press′i•bly,** *adv.*

in•sur•ance (in sho͝or′əns, -shûr′-), *n.* **1.** the act, system, or business of insuring property, life, one's person, etc., against loss or harm arising in specified contingencies, in return for payment. **2.** coverage by contract in which one party agrees to indemnify or reimburse another for loss that occurs under the terms of the contract. **3.** the contract itself, set forth in a written agreement or policy. **4.** the amount for which anything is insured. **5.** any means of guaranteeing against loss or harm: *to take vitamin C as insurance against colds.*

in•sure (in sho͝or′, -shûr′), *v.,* **-sured, -sur•ing.** —*v.t.* **1.** to guarantee against loss or harm. **2.** to secure indemnity to or on, in case of loss, damage, or death. **3.** to issue or procure an insurance policy on or for. **4.** ENSURE (defs. 1–3). —**in•sur′a•bil′i•ty,** *n.*

in•sured (in sho͝ord′, -shûrd′), *n.* a person whose life or property is covered by an insurance policy.

in•sur•er (in sho͝or′ər, -shûr′-), *n.* a person or company that contracts to indemnify another in the event of loss or damage; underwriter.

in•sur•gence (in sûr′jəns), *n.* an act of rebellion; insurrection.

in•sur•gen•cy (in sûr′jən sē), *n., pl.* **-cies.** **1.** the state or condition of being insurgent. **2.** rebellion against an existing government by a group not recognized as a belligerent. **3.** rebellion within a group, as by members against leaders.

in•sur•gent (in sûr′jənt), *n.* **1.** a person who takes part in forcible opposition or armed resistance to an established government or authority; rebel. **2.** a member of a group who revolts against the policies of the leadership. —*adj.* **3.** rising in revolt; rebellious.

in•sur•mount•a•ble (in′sər moun′tə bəl), *adj.* incapable of being surmounted or overcome; insuperable. —**in′sur•mount′a•bil′i•ty, in′sur•mount′a•ble•ness,** *n.* —**in′sur•mount′a•bly,** *adv.*

in•sur•rec•tion (in′sə rek′shən), *n.* an act or instance of rising in arms or open rebellion against an established government or authority. —**in′sur•rec′tion•al,** *adj.* —**in′sur•rec′tion•ar′y,** *adj., n., pl.* **-ar•ies.** —**in′sur•rec′tion•ism,** *n.* —**in′sur•rec′tion•ist,** *n.*

in•sus•cep•ti•ble (in′sə sep′tə bəl), *adj.* not susceptible; not readily influenced or affected (usu. fol. by *of* or *to*). —**in′sus•cep′ti•bil′i•ty,** *n.* —**in′sus•cep′ti•bly,** *adv.*

in•tact (in takt′), *adj.* **1.** not altered, broken, impaired, or diminished; remaining uninjured, sound, or whole. **2.** complete or whole, esp. not castrated. **3.** having the hymen unbroken; virginal. —**in•tact′ly,** *adv.* —**in•tact′ness,** *n.*

in•tagl•io (in tal′yō, -täl′-), *n., pl.* **-tagl•ios, -ta•gli** (-tal′yē, -täl′-), *v.,* **-tagl•ioed, -tagl•io•ing.** —*n.* **1.** incised carving, as opposed to carving in relief. **2.** ornamentation with a figure or design sunk below the surface. **3.** a figure or design so produced. **4.** a gem, seal, piece of jewelry, etc., cut with an incised or sunken design. **5.** an incised or countersunk die. **6.** a printing process in which a design or text is recessed below the surface of a plate so that when ink is applied and the excess wiped off, ink remains in the grooves for transfer to paper. —*v.t.* **7.** to incise or display in intaglio.

in•take (in′tāk′), *n.* **1.** the place or opening at which a fluid is taken into a channel, pipe, etc. **2.** an act or instance of taking in. **3.** a thing or a quantity taken in. **4.** a narrowing; contraction.

in•tan•gi•ble (in tan′jə bəl), *adj.* **1.** not tangible; not corporeal or material; impalpable. **2.** not definite or clear to the mind; vague; elusive. —*n.* **3.** something intangible, esp. an intangible asset, as goodwill. —**in•tan′gi•bil′i•ty, in•tan′gi•ble•ness,** *n.* —**in•tan′gi•bly,** *adv.*

in•te•ger (in′ti jər), *n.* **1.** one of the positive or negative numbers 1, 2, 3, etc., or zero. **2.** a complete entity.

in•te•gra•ble (in′ti grə bəl), *adj.* capable of being integrated, as a mathematical function or differential equation. —**in′te•gra•bil′i•ty,** *n.*

in•te•gral (in′ti grəl, in teg′rəl), *adj.* **1.** of or belonging as an essential part of the whole; necessary to completeness; constituent: *an integral part.* **2.** composed of parts that together constitute a whole. **3.** entire; complete; whole. **4.** pertaining to or being an integer; not fractional. **5.** pertaining to or involving mathematical integrals. —*n.* **6.** an integral whole. **7.** *Math.* **a.** the numerical measure of the area bounded above by the graph of a given function, below by the *x*-axis, and on the sides by ordinates drawn at the endpoints of a specified interval. **b.** a primitive. **c.** any of several analogous quantities. —**in′te•gral•ly,** *adv.*

in′tegral cal′culus, *n.* the branch of mathematics that deals with integrals, esp. the methods of ascertaining indefinite integrals and applying them to the solution of differential equations and the determining of areas, volumes, and lengths.

in•te•grate (in′ti grāt′), *v.,* **-grat•ed, -grat•ing.** —*v.t.* **1.** to bring together or incorporate into a unified, harmonious, or interrelated whole or system. **2.** to combine to produce a whole or a larger unit. **3.** to make part of a larger unit or a group: *to integrate an individual into society.* **4.** to give equal opportunity and consideration to (a racial or other ethnic group). **5.** to make (a school, restaurant, neighborhood, etc.) accessible or available to all racial and other ethnic groups. —*v.i.* **6.** to become integrated. **7.** to meld with and become part of the dominant culture. —**in′te•gra′tive,** *adj.*

in′tegrated cir′cuit, *n.* a circuit of transistors, resistors, and capacitors constructed on a single semiconductor wafer or chip, in which the components are interconnected to perform a given function; microcircuit. *Abbr.:* IC

in•te•gra•tion (in′ti grā′shən), *n.* **1.** an act or instance of incorporating or combining into a whole. **2.** an act or instance of integrating a racial or other ethnic group. **3.** an act or instance of integrating a school, organization, etc. **4.** *Math.* the operation of finding the integral of a function or equation, esp. solving a differential equation. **5.** behavior that is in harmony with the environment. **6.** *Psychol.* the organization of the constituent elements of the personality into a coordinated, harmonious whole. **7.** COADAPTATION (def. 2). —**in•te•gra′tion•ist,** *n.*

in•teg•ri•ty (in teg′ri tē), *n.* **1.** uncompromising adherence to moral and ethical principles; soundness of moral character; honesty. **2.** the state of being whole or entire: *to preserve the integrity of the empire.* **3.** a sound or unimpaired condition.

in•teg•u•ment (in teg′yə mənt), *n.* **1.** a natural covering, as a skin, shell, or rind. **2.** any covering, coating, or enclosure. —**in•teg′u•men′ta•ry** (-men′tə rē), *adj.*

in•tel•lect (in′tl ekt′), *n.* **1.** the faculty of the mind by which one knows or understands, as distinguished from that by which one feels or wills; capacity for thinking and acquiring knowledge. **2.** capacity for thinking and acquiring knowledge of a high or complex order. **3.** a particular mind or intelligence, esp. of a high order. **4.** a person possessing a great capacity for thought and knowledge. **5.** minds collectively. —**in′tel•lec′tive,** *adj.* —**in′tel•lec′tive•ly,** *adv.*

in•tel•lec•tu•al (in′tl ek′cho͞o əl), *adj.* **1.** appealing to or engaging the intellect: *intellectual pursuits.* **2.** of, pertaining to, or requiring the intellect or its use. **3.** placing a high value on or pursuing things of interest to the intellect, esp. the higher or more abstract forms of knowledge. **4.** developed by or relying on the intellect rather than emotions or feelings; rational. **5.** possessing or showing mental capacity to a high degree; of superior intellect. —*n.* **6.** a person who values or pursues intellectual interests. **7.** a person professionally engaged in mental labor. **8.** a person of superior intellect. —**in′tel•lec′tu•al•ly,** *adv.*

in•tel•lec•tu•al•ism (in′tl ek′cho͞o ə liz′əm), *n.* **1.** devotion to intellectual pursuits. **2.** the exercise of the intellect. **3.** excessive emphasis on abstract or intellectual matters, esp. with a lack of proper consideration for emotions. —**in′tel•lec′tu•al•ist,** *n.* —**in′tel•lec′tu•al•is′tic,** *adj.* —**in′tel•lec′tu•al•is′ti•cal•ly,** *adv.*

in•tel•lec•tu•al•ize (in′tl ek′cho͞o ə līz′), *v.,* **-ized, -iz•ing.** —*v.t.* **1.** to make intellectual; analyze intellectually or rationally. **2.** to ignore the emotional or psychological significance of (an action, feeling, etc.) by an excessively intellectual or abstract explanation. —*v.i.* **3.** to talk or write intellectually; reason; philosophize. —**in′tel•lec′tu•al•i•za′tion,** *n.*

in•tel•li•gence (in tel′i jəns), *n.* **1.** capacity for learning, reasoning, and understanding; aptitude in grasping truths, relationships, facts, meanings, etc. **2.** mental alertness or quickness of understanding. **3.** manifestation of a high mental capacity: *He writes with intelligence and wit.* **4.** the faculty or act of understanding. **5.** information received or imparted; news. **6. a.** secret information, esp. about an enemy. **b.** the gathering or distribution of such information. **c.** the evaluated conclusions drawn from such information. **d.** an organization engaged in gathering such information: *military intelligence.* **7.** (*often cap.*) an intelligent being or spirit, esp. an incorporeal one, as an angel.

intel′ligence quo′tient, *n.* an intelligence test score that is obtained by dividing mental age, which reflects the age-graded level of performance as derived from population norms, by chronological age and multiplying by 100: a score of 100 thus indicates a performance at exactly the normal level for that age group. *Abbr.:* IQ

in•tel•li•genc•er (in tel′i jən sər), *n.* **1.** a person or thing that conveys information. **2.** an informer; spy.

intel′ligence test′, *n.* any of various tests designed to measure the relative intellectual capacity of a person.

in•tel•li•gent (in tel′i jənt), *adj.* **1.** having good understanding or a high mental capacity; quick to comprehend. **2.** displaying quickness of understanding, sound thought, or good judgment: *an intelligent reply.* **3.** having the faculty of reasoning and understanding; possessing intelligence: *intelligent beings on other planets.* **4.** (of an electronic device) containing built-in processing power; smart: *an intelligent terminal.* —**in•tel′li•gen′tial** (-jen′shəl), *adj.* —**in•tel′li•gent•ly,** *adv.*

in•tel•li•gent•si•a (in tel′i jent′sē ə, -gent′-), *n.pl.* intellectuals considered as a group or class, esp. as a cultural, social, or political elite.

in•tel•li•gi•ble (in tel′i jə bəl), *adj.* **1.** capable of being understood; comprehensible. **2.** *Philos.* able to be apprehended by the mind only; conceptual. —**in•tel′li•gi•bil′i•ty,** *n.* —**in•tel′li•gi•bly,** *adv.*

in•tem•per•ance (in tem′pər əns, -prəns), *n.* **1.** immoderate indulgence in alcoholic beverages. **2.** excessive indulgence of appetite or passion. **3.** lack of moderation or restraint.

in•tem•per•ate (in tem′pər it, -prit), *adj.* **1.** given to or characterized by excessive or immoderate indulgence in alcoholic beverages. **2.** immoderate in indulgence of appetite or passion. **3.** showing lack of moderation or due restraint, as in action or speech; unrestrained; unbridled. **4.** extreme in temperature, as climate. —**in•tem′per•ate•ly,** *adv.* —**in•tem′per•ate•ness,** *n.*

in•tend (in tend′), *v.t.* **1.** to have in mind as something to be done or brought about; plan: *We intend to leave in a month.* **2.** to design or mean for a particular purpose, use, or recipient: *a fund intended for emergency use only.* **3.** to design to express or indicate, as by one's words; refer to. **4.** (of words, terms, statements, etc.) to mean or signify. —*v.i.* **5.** to have a purpose or design. —**in•tend′er,** *n.*

in•tend•ed (in ten′did), *adj.* **1.** purposed; intentional: *an intended snub.* **2.** prospective: *his intended wife.* —*n.* **3.** *Informal.* the person one plans to marry; one's fiancé or fiancée.

in•tense (in tens′), *adj.* **1.** existing or occurring in a high or extreme degree; great in force, strength, severity, or amount: *intense heat.* **2.** acute, strong, or vehement in feeling; ardent: *intense dislike.* **3.** having a characteristic quality in a high degree: *blindingly intense sunlight.* **4.** concentrated and strenuous or earnest; intensive: *intense thought.* **5.** (of color) very deep: *intense red.* —**in•tense′ly,** *adv.* —**in•tense′ness,** *n.*

in•ten•si•fi•er (in ten′sə fī′ər), *n.* **1.** a person or thing that intensifies. **2.** a linguistic element, esp. an adverb, that indicates and usu. increases the degree of emphasis or force to be given to the item it modifies, as *very* or *somewhat;* intensive.

in•ten•si•fy (in ten′sə fī′), *v.,* **-fied, -fy•ing.** —*v.t.* **1.** to make intense or more intense. **2.** to increase the density and contrast of (a photographic negative) chemically. —*v.i.* **3.** to become intense or more intense. —**in•ten′si•fi•ca′tion,** *n.*

in•ten•sion (in ten′shən), *n.* **1.** intensification; increase in degree. **2.** intensity; high degree. **3.** relative intensity; degree. **4.** exertion of the mind; determination. **5.** *Logic.* the set of attributes belonging to all and only those things to which a given term is correctly applied; connotation. Compare EXTENSION (def. 11). —**in•ten′sion•al,** *adj.* —**in•ten′sion•al•ly,** *adv.*

in•ten•si•ty (in ten′si tē), *n., pl.* **-ties. 1.** the quality or condition of being intense. **2.** great energy, strength, concentration, or vehemence, as of activity, thought, or feeling. **3.** a high or extreme degree, as of cold or heat. **4.** the degree or extent to which something is intense. **5.** a high degree of emotional excitement; depth of feeling: *The poem lacked intensity.* **6.** the strength or sharpness of a color due esp. to its degree of freedom from admixture with its complementary color. **7.** *Physics.* magnitude, as of energy or a force per unit of area, volume, time, etc.

in•ten•sive (in ten′siv), *adj.* **1.** of or characterized by intensity: *intensive questioning.* **2.** tending to intensify; intensifying. **3.** of or pertaining to a system of farming in which large amounts of labor and often capital are expended to gain high yields on small tracts of land (opposed to *extensive*). **4.** requiring or having a high concentration of a specified quality or element (used in combination): *a labor-intensive industry.* **5.** (of a grammatical form or construction) indicating increased emphasis or force: *Certainly* is an intensive adverb. *Myself* in *I did it myself* is an intensive pronoun. —*n.* **6.** something that intensifies. **7.** an intensive form or construction. —**in•ten′sive•ly,** *adv.*

inten′sive care′, *n.* the use of specialized equipment and personnel for continuous monitoring and care of the critically ill, usu. in a special center in a hospital **(inten′sive care′ u′nit).**

in•tent[1] (in tent′), *n.* **1.** something that is intended; purpose; design; intention: *The original intent was to raise funds.* **2.** the act or fact of intending, as to do something: *criminal intent.* **3.** *Law.* the state of a person's mind that directs his or her actions toward an objective. **4.** meaning or significance. —***Idiom.*** **5. to** or **for all intents and purposes,** for all practical purposes; practically speaking; virtually.

in•tent[2] (in tent′), *adj.* **1.** firmly or steadfastly fixed or directed: *an intent stare.* **2.** having the attention sharply focused on something: *intent on one's work.* **3.** determined or resolved; having the mind or will fixed on some goal: *intent on revenge.* —**in•tent′ly,** *adv.* —**in•tent′ness,** *n.*

in•ten•tion (in ten′shən), *n.* **1.** an act or instance of determining mentally upon some action or result. **2.** the end or object intended; purpose. **3. intentions, a.** purpose or attitude toward the effect of one's actions or conduct: *a bungler with good intentions.* **b.** purpose or attitude with respect to marriage: *Are his intentions serious?* **4.** the act or fact of intending. **5.** *Logic.* reference by signs, concepts, etc., to concrete things, their properties, classes, or the relationships among them. **6.** meaning or significance. **7.** the person or thing meant to benefit from a prayer.

in•ter (in tûr′), *v.t.,* **-terred, -ter•ring.** to place (a dead body) in a grave or tomb; bury.

inter-, a prefix meaning "between, among," "mutually, reciprocally": *intercity; interdepartmental; intermarry; interweave.*

in•ter•act (in′tər akt′), *v.i.* to act upon one another. —**in′ter•ac′tant,** *n.*

in•ter•ac•tion (in′tər ak′shən), *n.* reciprocal action, effect, or influence. —**in′ter•ac′tion•al,** *adj.*

in·ter·ac·tive (in'tər ak'tiv), *adj.* **1.** acting upon one another. **2.** (of a computer or program) characterized by or allowing immediate two-way communication between a source of information and a user, who can initiate or respond to queries. **—in'ter·ac'tive·ly,** *adv.*

in'terac'tive fic'tion, *n.* an adventure or mystery story, in the form of a video game or book, in which the player or reader is given choices as to how the story line is to develop.

in·ter·breed (in'tər brēd'), *v.,* **-bred, -breed·ing.** *—v.t.* **1.** to crossbreed (a plant or animal). **2.** to cause to breed together. **—v.i. 3.** to crossbreed; hybridize. **4.** to breed or mate with a closely related individual, as in a small, closed population.

in·ter·ca·lar·y (in tûr'kə ler'ē, in'tər kal'ə rē), *adj.* **1.** interpolated; interposed. **2.** inserted or interpolated in the calendar, as an extra day or month. **3.** (of a year) having such an inserted day, month, etc. **—in·ter'ca·lar'i·ly,** *adv.*

in·ter·ca·late (in tûr'kə lāt'), *v.t.,* **-lat·ed, -lat·ing. 1.** to interpolate or insert; interpose. **2.** to insert (an extra day, month, etc.) in the calendar. **—in·ter'ca·la'tion,** *n.* **—in·ter'ca·la'tive,** *adj.*

in·ter·cede (in'tər sēd'), *v.i.,* **-ced·ed, -ced·ing. 1.** to interpose in behalf of someone, as by pleading or petition: *to intercede with the governor for a condemned man.* **2.** to attempt to reconcile differences between two people or groups; mediate. **—in'ter·ced'er,** *n.*

in·ter·cept (*v.* in'tər sept'; *n.* in'tər sept'), *v.t.* **1.** to take, seize, or halt (someone or something on the way from one place to another); cut off from an intended destination: *to intercept a messenger.* **2.** to secretly listen to or record (a transmitted communication). **3.** to stop or interrupt the course, progress, or transmission of. **4.** to take possession of (a ball or puck) during an attempted pass by an opposing team. **5.** to stop or check (passage, travel, etc.): *to intercept an escape.* **6.** to catch up to and destroy (an aircraft or missile). **7.** *Math.* to mark off or include, as between two points or lines. **8.** to intersect. **—n. 9.** INTERCEPTION. **10.** an intercepted communication. **11.** *Math.* **a.** an intercepted segment of a line. **b.** (in a coordinate system) the distance from the origin to the point at which a curve or line intersects an axis. **—in'ter·cep'tive,** *adj.*

in·ter·cep·tion (in'tər sep'shən), *n.* **1.** an act or instance of intercepting. **2.** the state or fact of being intercepted.

in·ter·cep·tor or **in·ter·cept·er** (in'tər sep'tər), *n.* **1.** a person or thing that intercepts. **2.** a fighter airplane capable of speedily intercepting hostile aircraft.

in·ter·ces·sion (in'tər sesh'ən), *n.* **1.** an act or instance of interceding. **2.** an interposing or pleading on behalf of another person. **3.** a prayer to God on behalf of another. **—in'ter·ces'so·ry,** *adj.*

in·ter·change (*v.* in'tər chānj'; *n.* in'tər chānj'), *v.,* **-changed, -chang·ing,** *n.* **—v.t. 1.** to put each in the place of the other; cause (one thing) to change places with another: *to interchange pieces of modular furniture.* **2.** to give and receive (things) reciprocally; exchange. **3.** to cause to follow one another alternately. **—v.i. 4.** to occur by turns or in succession; alternate. **5.** to change places, as one with another. **—n. 6.** an act or instance of interchanging. **7.** a multilevel highway intersection arranged so that vehicles may move from one road to another without crossing the streams of traffic. **—in'ter·chang'er,** *n.*

in·ter·change·a·ble (in'tər chān'jə bəl), *adj.* **1.** (of two things) capable of being put or used in the place of each other: *interchangeable symbols.* **2.** (of one thing) capable of replacing or changing places with something else: *an interchangeable part.* **—in'ter·change'a·bil'i·ty, in'ter·change'a·ble·ness,** *n.* **—in'ter·change'a·bly,** *adv.*

in·ter·col·le·giate (in'tər kə lē'jit, -jē it), *adj.* **1.** taking place between or participating in activities between different colleges: *intercollegiate athletics.* **2.** of or representative of two or more colleges.

in·ter·com (in'tər kom'), *n.* a communication system within a building, airplane, etc., with a loudspeaker or receiver for listening and a microphone for speaking at each of two or more points.

in·ter·com·mu·ni·cate (in'tər kə myōō'ni kāt'), *v.,* **-cat·ed, -cat·ing.** *—v.i.* **1.** to communicate mutually, as people. **2.** to afford passage from one to another, as rooms. *—v.t.* **3.** to exchange (messages or communications) with one another. **—in'ter·com·mu'ni·ca'tion,** *n.* **—in'ter·com·mu'ni·ca'tive** (-kā'tiv, -kə-), *adj.*

in·ter·com·mun·ion (in'tər kə myōōn'yən), *n.* **1.** mutual communion, association, or relations. **2.** a communion service among members of different denominations.

in·ter·com·mu·ni·ty (in'tər kə myōō'ni tē), *n., pl.* **-ties,** *adj.* **—n. 1.** common ownership, use, participation, etc. **—adj. 2.** of or between communities.

in·ter·con·nect (in'tər kə nekt'), *v.t.* **1.** to connect with one another. **—v.i. 2.** to be or become connected or interrelated. **—adj. 3.** of or pertaining to privately owned telecommunications equipment that interconnects with the public telephone network. **—in'ter·con·nect'ed·ness,** *n.* **—in'ter·con·nec'tion,** *n.*

in·ter·con·ti·nen·tal (in'tər kon'tn en'tl), *adj.* **1.** between or among continents; involving two or more continents. **2.** traveling or capable of traveling between continents.

intercontinen'tal ballis'tic mis'sile, *n.* any supersonic missile that has a range of at least 3500 nautical mi. (6500 km) and follows a ballistic trajectory after a powered, guided launching. *Abbr.:* ICBM

in·ter·course (in'tər kôrs', -kōrs'), *n.* **1.** dealings or communication between individuals, groups, countries, etc. **2.** sexual relations or a sexual coupling, esp. coitus.

in·ter·de·nom·i·na·tion·al (in'tər di nom'ə nā'shə nl), *adj.* occurring between, involving, or common to different religious denominations. **—in'ter·de·nom'i·na'tion·al·ism,** *n.*

in·ter·de·part·men·tal (in'tər dē'pärt men'tl, -di pärt-), *adj.* involving or existing between two or more departments: *interdepartmental rivalry.* **—in'ter·de'part·men'tal·ly,** *adv.*

in·ter·de·pend·ent (in'tər di pen'dənt), *adj.* mutually dependent; depending on each other. **—in'ter·de·pend'ence, in'ter·de·pend'en·cy,** *n.* **—in'ter·de·pend'ent·ly,** *adv.*

in·ter·dict (*n.* in'tər dikt'; *v.* in'tər dikt'), *n.* **1.** any prohibitory act or decree of a court or an administrative officer. **2.** a punishment by which the faithful, remaining in communion with the Roman Catholic Church, are forbidden certain sacraments and prohibited from participation in certain sacred acts. *—v.t.* **3.** to forbid; prohibit. **4.** to cut off authoritatively from certain ecclesiastical functions and privileges. **5. a.** to impede the flow of (troops, supplies, etc.) or hinder the use of (a road, airfield, etc.) by steady ground fire or bombing. **b.** to impede the shipment of (supplies, contraband, etc.) by military operations or other aggressive measures. **—in'ter·dic'tion,** *n.*

in·ter·dis·ci·pli·nar·y (in'tər dis'ə plə ner'ē), *adj.* involving two or more disciplines or fields.

in·ter·est (in'tər ist, -trist), *n.* **1.** a feeling of having one's attention, concern, or curiosity particularly engaged by something: *She has an interest in architecture.* **2.** something that arouses such feelings; something in which one is interested: *Chess is his only interest.* **3.** the power to excite such feelings; quality of being interesting: *a subject that holds little interest for me.* **4.** concern or importance: *a matter of primary interest.* **5.** a business, cause, etc., in which a person has a share, concern, or responsibility. **6.** a legal share, right, or title, as in the ownership of property or in a business undertaking. **7.** participation in a cause or in advantage or responsibility. **8.** Often, **interests.** a group exerting influence on and often financially involved in an enterprise, industry, or sphere of activity. **9.** the state of being affected by something in respect to advantage or detriment. **10.** Often, **interests.** benefit; advantage: *We have your best interests in mind.* **11.** regard for one's own advantage or profit; self-interest. **12.** influence due to personal importance or capability. **13. a.** a sum paid or charged for the use of money or for borrowing money. **b.** such a sum expressed as a percentage of the amount borrowed to be paid over a given period, usu. one year. **14.** something added or thrown in above an exact equivalent: *He returned the insult with interest.* *—v.t.* **15.** to engage or excite the attention or curiosity of. **16.** to concern (a person, nation, etc.) in something; involve. **17.** to cause to take a personal concern or share; induce to participate. **—Idiom. 18. in the interest(s) of,** for the sake of; on behalf of.

in·ter·est·ed (in'tər ə stid, -trə stid, -tə res'tid), *adj.* **1.** having an interest or share; concerned. **2.** having the attention or curiosity engaged. **3.** influenced by personal or selfish motives: *an interested witness.* **—in'ter·est·ed·ly,** *adv.* **—in'ter·est·ed·ness,** *n.*

in'terest group', *n.* a group of people drawn or acting together because of a common interest, concern, or purpose.

in·ter·est·ing (in'tər ə sting, -trə sting, -tə res'ting), *adj.* engaging or exciting and holding the attention or curiosity: *an interesting book.* **—in'ter·est·ing·ly,** *adv.* **—in'ter·est·ing·ness,** *n.*

in·ter·face (*n.* in'tər fās'; *v. also* in'tər fās'), *n., v.,* **-faced, -fac·ing.** **—n. 1.** a surface regarded as the common boundary of two bodies, spaces, or phases. **2.** the area shared by or linking two or more disciplines or fields of study. **3.** a common boundary or interconnection between systems, equipment, concepts, or people. **4.** something that enables separate and sometimes incompatible elements to coordinate or

---

in'ter·a'gen·cy, *adj.*
in'ter·al·li'ance, *n.*
in'ter·as·so'ci·a'tion, *n.*
in'ter·as'tral, *adj.*
in'ter·ax'i·al, *adj.*
in'ter·bank', *adj.*
in'ter·bor'ough, *adj.*
in'ter·branch', *adj.*
in'ter·busi'ness, *adj.*
in'ter·church', *adj.*
in'ter·cir'cu·late', *v.,* -lat·ed, -lat·ing.

in'ter·cit'y, *adj.*
in'ter·coast'al, *adj.*
in'ter·col'lege, *adj.*
in'ter·com'pa·ny, *adj.*
in'ter·com·plex'i·ty, *n., pl.* -ties.
in'ter·cor'po·rate, *adj.*
in'ter·cor're·la'tion, *n.*
in'ter·coun'ty, *adj.*
in'ter·cra'ni·al, *adj.*
in'ter·crys'tal·line, *adj.*
in'ter·di·vi'sion·al, *adj.;* -ly, *adv.*
in'ter·fac'tion·al, *adj.*

in'ter·fa·mil'ial, *adj.*
in'ter·fed'er·a'tion, *n.*
in'ter·fra·ter'nal, *adj.;* -ly, *adv.*
in'ter·gen'er·a'tion, *n.*
in'ter·li'brar·y, *adj.*
in'ter·loop', *n.*
in'ter·mar'gi·nal, *adj.*
in'ter·mem'brane, *adj.*
in'ter·mu·nic'i·pal, *adj.*
in'ter·mus'cu·lar, *adj.;* -ly, *adv.*
in'ter·mu·se'um, *adj.*
in'ter·nu'cle·on'ic, *adj.*

in'ter·o'ce·an'ic, *adj.*
in'ter·op'er·a·tive, *n., adj.*
in'ter·or'gan, *adj.*
in'ter·par'ish, *adj.*
in'ter·par'ty, *adj.*
in'ter·po'lar, *adj.*
in'ter·re'gion·al, *adj.*
in'ter·so·ci'e·tal, *adj.*
in'ter·tan'gle, *v.t.,* -gled, -gling.
in'ter·ter'ri·to'ri·al, *adj.*
in'ter·trib'al, *adj.*
in'ter·u'ni·ver'si·ty, *adj.*

communicate. **5.** communication or interaction. **6.** computer hardware or software designed to communicate information between hardware devices, between software programs, between devices and programs, or between a computer and a user. *—v.t.* **7.** to bring into an interface. **8.** to bring together; connect or mesh. *—v.i.* **9.** to be in an interface. **10.** to function as an interface. **11.** to meet or communicate directly; interact.

in•ter•faith (in′tər fāth′), *adj.* occurring between or involving persons belonging to different religions.

in•ter•fere (in′tər fēr′), *v.i.*, **-fered, -fer•ing. 1.** to come into opposition or collision so as to hamper, hinder, or obstruct someone or something: *Constant distractions interfere with work.* **2.** to take part in the affairs of others; meddle: *to interfere in someone's life.* **3.** to interpose or intervene for a particular purpose. **4.** to strike one foot or leg against another in moving, as a horse. **5. a.** (in a game or sport) to obstruct the action of an opposing player in a way barred by the rules. **b.** (in football) to run interference for a teammate carrying the ball. **6.** to come into collision; be in opposition; clash. **7.** *Physics.* to cause interference.

in•ter•fer•ence (in′tər fēr′əns), *n.* **1.** an act, fact, or instance of interfering. **2.** something that interferes. **3.** the process in which waves, as of light or sound, of the same frequency combine to reinforce or cancel each other, the amplitude of the resulting wave being equal to the sum of the amplitudes of the combining waves. **4. a.** a jumbling of radio signals, caused by the reception of undesired ones. **b.** the signals or device producing the incoherence. **5.** *Football.* **a.** the act of a teammate or of teammates legally running ahead of a ballcarrier and blocking prospective tacklers: *to run interference for the halfback.* **b.** the act of illegally hindering an opponent from catching a forward pass or a kick. **6.** the distorting or inhibiting effect of previously learned behavior on subsequent learning. **—in′ter•fe•ren′tial** (-fə ren′shəl), *adj.*

in•ter•fer•on (in′tər fēr′on), *n.* any of various proteins, produced by virus-infected cells, that inhibit reproduction of the invading virus and induce resistance to further infection.

in•ter•ga•lac•tic (in′tər gə lak′tik), *adj.* of, existing, or occurring in the space between galaxies.

in•ter•gla•cial (in′tər glā′shəl), *adj.* **1.** occurring or formed between times of glacial action. *—n.* **2.** an interglacial period.

in•ter•gov•ern•men•tal (in′tər guv′ərn men′tl, -ər men′-), *adj.* involving two or more governments or levels of government.

in•ter•im (in′tər əm), *n.* **1.** an intervening time; interval; meantime: *in the interim.* **2.** a temporary or provisional arrangement. *—adj.* **3.** for, during, or connected with an intervening period of time; temporary; provisional: *an interim order.*

in•te•ri•or (in tēr′ē ər), *adj.* **1.** situated or being within or inside; internal; inner: *an interior room of a house.* **2.** of or pertaining to that which is within: *an interior view.* **3.** situated well inland from the coast or border. **4.** domestic: *interior trade.* **5.** private or hidden. **6.** of the mind or soul; mental or spiritual: *the interior life.* *—n.* **7.** the internal or inner part; space or regions within; inside. **8.** the inside of a building, apartment, or room. **9.** a pictorial representation of the inside of a room or building. **10.** the inland parts of a region, country, etc. **11.** the domestic affairs of a country as distinguished from its foreign affairs: *the Department of the Interior.* **12.** the inner or inward nature or character of anything. **—in•te′ri•or′i•ty** (-ôr′i tē, -or′-), *n.* **—in•te′ri•or•ly,** *adv.*

inte′rior an′gle, *n.* **1.** an angle formed between parallel lines by a third line that intersects them. **2.** an angle formed within a polygon by two adjacent sides.

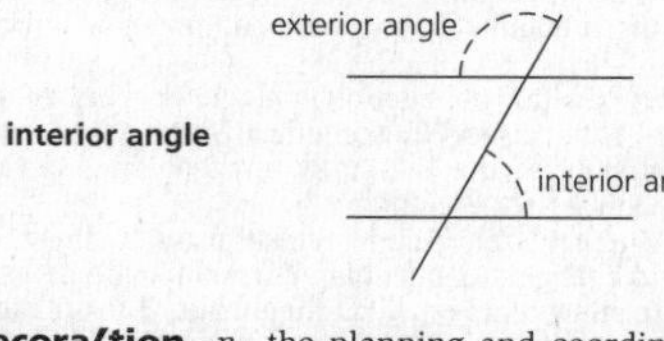

inte′rior decora′tion, *n.* the planning and coordination of the color schemes, furnishings, and other decorative elements of the interior of a house, apartment, office, etc. **—inte′rior dec′orator,** *n.*

inte′rior design′, *n.* the design and coordination of the decorative and usu. architectural features of the interior of a house, apartment, office, etc. **—inte′rior design′er,** *n.*

inte′rior mon′ologue, *n.* a form of stream-of-consciousness writing that represents the inner thoughts of a character.

in•ter•ject (in′tər jekt′), *v.t.* to insert, often abruptly, between other things; interpolate: *to interject a remark.* **—in′ter•jec′tor,** *n.*

in•ter•jec•tion (in′tər jek′shən), *n.* **1.** the act of interjecting. **2.** something interjected, as a remark. **3.** the utterance of a word or phrase expressive of emotion; the uttering of an exclamation. **4. a.** a member of a class of words typically used in grammatical isolation to express emotion, as *Hey! Oh! Ouch! Ugh!* **b.** any other word or expression so used, as *Good grief! Indeed! Abbr.:* interj. **—in′ter•jec′tion•al, in′ter•jec′to•ry** (-tə rē), *adj.* **—in′ter•jec′tion•al•ly,** *adv.*

in•ter•lace (in′tər lās′, in′tər lās′), *v.*, **-laced, -lac•ing.** *—v.i.* **1.** to cross one another as if woven together; intertwine: *Their hands interlaced.* *—v.t.* **2.** to unite or arrange (threads, strips, parts, etc.) so as to intercross one another, passing alternately over and under; intertwine. **3.** to mingle; blend. **4.** to diversify by intermingling: intersperse: *She interlaced her lecture on Schubert with some of his songs.*

in•ter•lay (in′tər lā′), *v.t.*, **-laid, -lay•ing. 1.** to lay between; interpose. **2.** to diversify with something laid between or inserted: *to interlay silver with gold.*

in•ter•leaf (in′tər lēf′), *n., pl.* **-leaves** (-lēvz′). an additional leaf, usu. blank, inserted between or bound with the printed leaves of a book, as to separate chapters or provide room for a reader's notes.

in•ter•leave (in′tər lēv′), *v.t.*, **-leaved, -leav•ing. 1.** to provide with interleaves. **2.** to insert blank leaves between (the regular leaves). **3.** to insert something alternately and regularly between the parts of.

in•ter•leav•ing (in′tər lē′ving), *n.* a method for making data retrieval more efficient by rearranging or renumbering the sectors on a hard disk or by splitting a computer's main memory into sections so that the sectors or sections can be read in alternating cycles.

in•ter•lin•gual (in′tər ling′gwəl), *adj.* pertaining to or using two or more languages: *an interlingual dictionary.* **—in′ter•lin′gual•ism,** *n.*

in•ter•lock (*v.* in′tər lok′; *n.* in′tər lok′), *v.i.* **1.** to fit into each other, as parts of machinery, so that all action is synchronized. **2.** to interweave, interlace, or interrelate, one with another: *The branches of the trees interlock to form an archway.* *—v.t.* **3.** to lock one with another. **4.** to fit (parts) together to ensure coordinated action. *—n.* **5.** the condition of being interlocked. **6.** a device for preventing a mechanism from operating when another mechanism is in such a position that the two operating simultaneously might produce undesirable results. **7.** a stretch fabric made with a circular knitting machine having two alternating sets of long and short needles. **—in′ter•lock′er,** *n.*

in•ter•lo•cu•tion (in′tər lə kyo͞o′shən), *n.* conversation; dialogue.

in•ter•loc•u•tor (in′tər lok′yə tər), *n.* **1.** a person who takes part in a conversation or dialogue. **2.** a person who questions; interrogator.

in•ter•loc•u•to•ry (in′tər lok′yə tôr′ē, -tōr′ē), *adj.* **1.** of the nature of, pertaining to, or occurring in conversation. **2.** interjected into the main course of speech. **3.** *Law.* (of a decision, decree, etc.) not finally decisive of a case; provisional. **—in′ter•loc′u•to′ri•ly,** *adv.*

in•ter•lope (in′tər lōp′, in′tər lōp′), *v.i.*, **-loped, -lop•ing. 1.** to thrust oneself into the domain or affairs of others. **2.** to intrude into some region or field of trade without a proper license. **—in′ter•lop′er,** *n.*

in•ter•lude (in′tər lo͞od′), *n.* **1.** an intervening episode, period, or space. **2. a.** an early English comedic sketch performed between the parts of a play or other entertainment. **b.** a play, esp. a comedy or farce, derived from this. **c.** a morality play of the 14th to 16th centuries, typically containing farcical or comic elements. **3.** any intermediate performance or entertainment, as between the acts of a play. **4.** an instrumental passage or a piece of music rendered between the parts of a song, church service, drama, etc. **—in′ter•lu′di•al,** *adj.*

in•ter•lu•nar (in′tər lo͞o′nər), *adj.* pertaining to the moon's monthly period of invisibility between the old moon and the new.

in•ter•mar•riage (in′tər mar′ij), *n.* **1.** marriage between a man and woman of different groups, as races, religions, ethnic groups, or tribes. **2.** marriage between a man and woman within a specific group, as required by custom or law; endogamy. **3.** marriage between close blood relatives.

in•ter•mar•ry (in′tər mar′ē), *v.i.*, **-ried, -ry•ing. 1.** to become connected by marriage, as two families, tribes, etc. **2.** to marry within one's family. **3.** to marry outside one's religion, ethnic group, etc.

in•ter•me•di•ar•y (in′tər mē′dē er′ē), *n., pl.* **-ar•ies,** *adj.* *—n.* **1.** an intermediate agent or agency; a go-between or mediator. **2.** a medium or means. **3.** an intermediate form or stage. *—adj.* **4.** being between; intermediate. **5.** acting as an intermediary between persons or parties.

in•ter•me•di•ate (in′tər mē′dē it), *adj.* **1.** being, situated, or acting between two points, stages, things, persons, etc.: *the intermediate steps in a procedure.* **2.** of or pertaining to an intermediate school. **3.** (of an automobile) mid-size. *—n.* **4.** a person who acts between others; intermediary; mediator. **5.** something intermediate, as a form or class. **6.** a substance formed during a chemical reaction but before the end product is formed: *a dye intermediate.* **—in′ter•me′di•ate•ly,** *adv.*

interme′diate school′, *n.* **1.** a school for grades 4 through 6. **2.** a junior high school.

in•ter•ment (in tûr′mənt), *n.* the act or ceremony of interring; burial.

in•ter•mez•zo (in′tər met′sō, -med′zō), *n., pl.* **-mez•zos, -mez•zi** (-met′sē, -med′zē). **1.** a short dramatic, musical, or other entertainment of light character introduced between the acts of a drama or opera. **2.** a short musical composition between main divisions of an extended musical work. **3.** a short independent musical composition.

in•ter•mi•na•ble (in tûr′mə nə bəl), *adj.* **1.** having no apparent limit or end; unending: *an interminable job.* **2.** monotonously or annoyingly protracted or continued; incessant: *interminable talk.* **—in•ter′mi•na•ble•ness, in•ter′mi•na•bil′i•ty,** *n.* **—in•ter′mi•na•bly,** *adv.*

in•ter•min•gle (in′tər ming′gəl), *v.t., v.i.*, **-gled, -gling.** to mingle, one with another; intermix. **—in′ter•min′gle•ment,** *n.*

in•ter•mis•sion (in′tər mish′ən), *n.* **1.** a short interval allowing a rest between the acts of a play or parts of a performance. **2.** a period during which action temporarily ceases; an interval between periods of activity. **—in′ter•mis′sive** (-mis′iv), *adj.*

in•ter•mit (in′tər mit′), *v.*, **-mit•ted, -mit•ting.** *—v.t.* **1.** to discontinue temporarily; suspend. *—v.i.* **2.** to stop or pause at intervals; be intermittent. **3.** to cease or break off operations for a time.

in·ter·mit·tent (in′tər mit′nt), *adj.* stopping or ceasing for a time; alternately ceasing and beginning again: *an intermittent pain.* —**in′ter·mit′tence,** *n.* —**in′ter·mit′tent·ly,** *adv.*

in·ter·mix (in′tər miks′), *v.t., v.i.* to mix together; intermingle.

in·tern[1] (*v.* in tûrn′; *n.* in′tûrn), *v.t.* **1.** to confine within prescribed limits, as prisoners of war or enemy aliens. **2.** to impound until the termination of a war, as a ship of a belligerent.

in·tern[2] (in′tûrn), *n.* Also, **interne.** **1.** a resident member of the medical staff of a hospital, usu. a recent medical school graduate serving under supervision. **2.** STUDENT TEACHER. **3.** someone, as a student or recent graduate, working as an apprentice or trainee to gain practical experience in an occupation. —*v.i.* **4.** to serve as an intern.

in·ter·nal (in tûr′nl), *adj.* **1.** situated or existing in the interior of something; interior. **2.** of or pertaining to the inside or inner part. **3.** acting or coming from within. **4.** existing, occurring, or found within the limits or scope of something; intrinsic: *internal logic.* **5.** of or pertaining to the domestic affairs of a country. **6.** of or produced by the psyche or inner recesses of the mind; subjective. **7.** present or occurring within an organism or one of its parts. **8.** to be taken inside the body, esp. orally. **9.** away from the surface or closer to the center of the body or of a part; inner. —*n.* **10.** Usu., **internals.** entrails; innards. **11.** an inner or intrinsic attribute. —**in·ter′nal·ly,** *adv.*

inter′nal-combus′tion en′gine, *n.* an engine of one or more working cylinders in which combustion takes place within the cylinders.

inter′nal gear′, *n.* a gear having teeth cut on an inner cylindrical surface.

in·ter·nal·ize (in tûr′nl īz′), *v.t.,* **-ized, -iz·ing.** **1.** to incorporate within oneself (cultural values, mores, etc.) through learning, socialization, or identification. **2.** to make subjective or give a subjective character to. **3.** to acquire (a linguistic rule, structure, etc.) as part of one's language competence. —**in·ter′nal·i·za′tion,** *n.*

inter′nal med′icine, *n.* the branch of medicine dealing with the diagnosis and nonsurgical treatment of diseases.

inter′nal rev′enue, *n.* the revenue of a government from any domestic source, usu. any source other than customs.

Inter′nal Rev′enue Serv′ice, *n.* the division of the U.S. Department of the Treasury that collects internal revenue, including income taxes and excise taxes, and enforces revenue laws. *Abbr:* IRS

in·ter·na·tion·al (in′tər nash′ə nl), *adj.* **1.** between or among nations; involving two or more nations: *international trade.* **2.** of or pertaining to two or more nations or their citizens: *a matter of international concern.* **3.** pertaining to the relations between nations: *international law.* **4.** having members or activities in several nations. **5.** transcending national boundaries or viewpoints. —*n.* **6.** (*cap.*) any of several international socialist or communist organizations formed in the 19th and 20th centuries. **7.** an organization, business enterprise, or group having branches, dealings, or members in several countries. **8.** a member or employee of such an organization or enterprise, esp. an employee working in a foreign country. —**in′ter·na′tion·al·ly,** *adv.*

Interna′tional Bi′ble Bap′tist Fel′lowship, *n.* a Christian fundamentalist denomination, the fifth-largest Baptist group in the United States.

In′terna′tional Court′ of Jus′tice, *n.* the chief judicial agency of the United Nations, established in 1945 to decide disputes arising between nations. Also called **World Court.**

In′terna′tional Date′ Line′, *n.* a theoretical line following approximately the 180th meridian, the regions to the east of which are counted as being one day earlier in their calendar dates than the regions to the west.

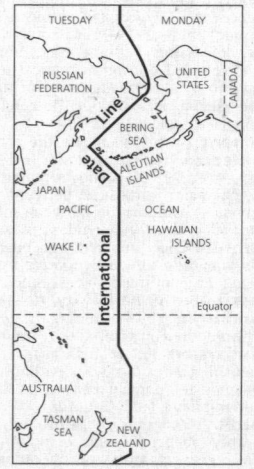

International Date Line

in·ter·na·tion·al·ism (in′tər nash′ə nl iz′əm), *n.* **1.** the principle of cooperation among nations for the promotion of their common good. **2.** international character, relations, cooperation, or control. **3.** (*cap.*) the principles or methods of a communist or socialist International.

in′terna′tional law′, *n.* the body of rules that nations generally recognize as binding in their conduct toward one another.

In′terna′tional Mon′etary Fund′, *n.* a specialized agency of the United Nations that promotes the stabilization of the world's currencies and maintains a monetary pool from which member nations can draw to correct deficits in their balance of payments. *Abbr.:* IMF

in′terna′tional Morse′ code′, *n.* a form of Morse code used in international radiotelegraphy. Also called **continental code.**

in′terna′tional nau′tical mile′, *n.* a unit of distance at sea or in the air equal to 1.852 kilometers.

Interna′tional Phonet′ic Al′phabet, *n.* a set of symbols and modifying signs devised by the International Phonetic Association to provide a consistent and universally understood system for transcribing the speech sounds of any language. *Abbr.:* IPA

interna′tional rela′tions, *n.* a branch of political science dealing with the relations between nations.

Interna′tional Stan′dard Book′ Num′ber, *n.* a unique, internationally utilized number code assigned to a book for the purposes of identification and inventory control. *Abbr.:* ISBN

Interna′tional Stand′ard Se′rial Num′ber, *n.* a unique, internationally utilized number code assigned to a serial publication for the purposes of identification and inventory control. *Abbr.:* ISSN

Interna′tional Sys′tem of U′nits, *n.* an internationally accepted system of physical units, using the meter, kilogram, second, ampere, kelvin, mole, and candela as the basic units of length, mass, time, electric current, temperature, amount of substance, and luminous intensity. *Abbr.:* SI

in·ter·ne·cine (in′tər nē′sēn, -sīn, -nes′ēn, -nes′īn), *adj.* **1.** of or pertaining to conflict or struggle within a group: *an internecine feud.* **2.** mutually destructive. **3.** characterized by great slaughter; deadly.

in·tern·ist (in′tûr nist, in tûr′nist), *n.* a physician specializing in the diagnosis and nonsurgical treatment of diseases, esp. of adults.

in·ter·of·fice (in′tər ô′fis, -of′is), *adj.* functioning or communicating between the offices of a company or organization: *an interoffice memo.*

in·ter·plan·e·tar·y (in′tər plan′i ter′ē), *adj.* being or occurring between the planets or between a planet and the sun.

in·ter·play (*n.* in′tər plā′; *v.* in′tər plā′, in′tər plā′), *n.* **1.** reciprocal relationship, action, or influence. —*v.i.* **2.** to exert influence on each other.

in·ter·po·late (in tûr′pə lāt′), *v.,* **-lat·ed, -lat·ing.** —*v.t.* **1.** to introduce (something additional or extraneous) between other things or parts; interject; interpose. **2.** to insert, estimate, or find an intermediate term in (a mathematical sequence). **3. a.** to alter (a text) by the insertion of new matter, esp. deceptively or without authorization. **b.** to insert (new or spurious matter) in this manner. —*v.i.* **4.** to make an interpolation. —**in·ter′po·lat′er, in·ter′po·la′tor,** *n.* —**in·ter′po·la′tion,** *n.* —**in·ter′po·la′tive,** *adj.*

in·ter·pose (in′tər pōz′), *v.,* **-posed, -pos·ing.** —*v.t.* **1.** to place between; cause to intervene: *to interpose an opaque body between a light and the eye.* **2.** to put in (a remark, question, etc.) in the midst of a conversation or discourse. **3.** to bring (influence, action, etc.) to bear between parties or on behalf of a party. —*v.i.* **4.** to come between other things; assume an intervening position or relation. **5.** to step in between parties at variance; mediate. **6.** to put in or make a remark by way of interruption.

in·ter·po·si·tion (in′tər pə zish′ən), *n.* **1.** the act of interposing or the state of being interposed. **2.** something interposed. **3.** the doctrine that an individual state of the U.S. may oppose any federal action it believes encroaches on its sovereignty.

in·ter·pret (in tûr′prit), *v.t.* **1.** to give or provide the meaning of; explain; elucidate: *to interpret a parable.* **2.** to construe or understand in a particular way: *to interpret a reply as favorable.* **3.** to translate orally. **4.** to bring out the meaning of (a dramatic work, music, etc.) by performance or execution. **5.** to perform (a song, role in a play, etc.) according to one's own understanding or sensitivity. —*v.i.* **6.** to translate what is said in a foreign language. **7.** to explain something; give an explanation. —**in·ter′pret·a·ble,** *adj.*

in·ter·pre·ta·tion (in tûr′pri tā′shən), *n.* **1.** the act of interpreting; elucidation; explication. **2.** the meaning assigned to another's creative work, action, behavior, etc. **3.** oral translation. **4.** the performing of a dramatic part, music, etc., so as to bring out the meaning or to demonstrate one's conception of it. **5.** the assignment of meaning to abstract symbols in a logical system. —**in·ter′pre·ta′tion·al,** *adj.*

in·ter·pret·er (in tûr′pri tər), *n.* **1.** a person who interprets, esp. a person who translates orally for speakers of different languages. **2.** computer hardware or software that transforms a program instruction written in a high-level language into machine language and executes it before proceeding to the next instruction. Compare COMPILER (def. 2).

in·ter·pre·tive (in tûr′pri tiv), *adj.* Also **interpretative.** of, pertaining to, or serving to interpret; explanatory. —**in·ter′pre·tive·ly,** *adv.*

in·ter·ra·cial (in′tər rā′shəl), *adj.* of, involving, or for members of different races: *interracial amity.* —**in′ter·ra′cial·ly,** *adv.*

in·ter·reg·num (in′tər reg′nəm), *n., pl.* **-nums, -na** (-nə). **1.** an interval of time between the close of a sovereign's reign and the accession of the normal or legitimate successor. **2.** any period during which a state is without a permanent ruler. **3.** any pause or interruption in continuity. —**in′ter·reg′nal,** *adj.*

in·ter·re·late (in′tər ri lāt′), *v.t., v.i.,* **-lat·ed, -lat·ing.** to bring or enter into reciprocal relation.

in·ter·re·lat·ed (in′tər ri lā′tid), *adj.* reciprocally or mutually related. —**in′ter·re·lat′ed·ly,** *adv.* —**in′ter·re·lat′ed·ness,** *n.*

in·ter·ro·bang (in ter′ə bang′), *n.* a printed punctuation mark (‽), designed to combine the question mark (?) and the exclamation point (!), indicating a mixture of query and interjection.

in·ter·ro·gate (in ter′ə gāt′), *v.,* **-gat·ed, -gat·ing.** —*v.t.* **1.** to ask questions of (a person), esp. formally and thoroughly. —*v.i.* **2.** to ask questions of someone. —**in′ter′ro·ga′tor,** *n.*

in·ter·ro·ga·tion (in ter′ə gā′shən), *n.* **1.** an act of interrogating; questioning. **2.** an instance of being interrogated. **3.** a question; inquiry. —**in′ter′ro·ga′tion·al,** *adj.*

interroga′tion point′, *n.* QUESTION MARK. Also called **interroga′tion mark′.**

in·ter·rog·a·tive (in′tə rog′ə tiv), *adj.* **1.** of, pertaining to, or conveying a question. **2.** forming, constituting, or used in or to form a question: *an interrogative pronoun; an interrogative sentence.* —*n.* **3.** an interrogative word, particle, or construction, as *who?* or *what?* —**in′ter·rog′a·tive·ly,** *adv.*

in·ter·rog·a·to·ry (in′tə rog′ə tôr′ē, -tōr′ē), *adj., n., pl.* **-to·ries.** —*adj.* **1.** conveying or expressing a question; interrogative. —*n.* **2.** a question; inquiry. **3.** (in law) a formal or written question.

in·ter·rupt (*v.* in′tə rupt′; *n.* in′tə rupt′), *v.t.* **1.** to cause or make a break in the continuity or uniformity of (a course, process, condition, etc.). **2.** to break off or cause to cease, as in the middle of something: *He interrupted his work to answer the bell.* **3.** to stop (a person) in the midst of something, esp. by an interjected remark. —*v.i.* **4.** to interfere with action or speech, esp. by interjecting a remark: *Please don't interrupt.* —*n.* **5.** a hardware or software signal that temporarily stops program execution in a computer so that another procedure can be carried out. —**in′ter·rupt′i·ble,** *adj.* —**in′ter·rup′tive,** *adj.*

in·ter·rupt·er or **in·ter·rup·tor** (in′tə rup′tər), *n.* **1.** a person or thing that interrupts. **2.** a device for interrupting or periodically opening and closing a circuit, as in a doorbell.

in·ter·rup·tion (in′tə rup′shən), *n.* **1.** an act or instance of interrupting. **2.** the state of being interrupted. **3.** something that interrupts. **4.** cessation; intermission.

in·ter·scho·las·tic (in′tər skə las′tik), *adj.* existing or occurring between schools, or representative of different schools.

in·ter·sect (in′tər sekt′), *v.t.* **1.** to cut or divide by passing through or across: *The highway intersects the town.* —*v.i.* **2.** to cross, as lines or wires. **3.** *Geom.* to have one or more points in common: *intersecting lines.*

in·ter·sec·tion (in′tər sek′shən), *n.* **1.** a place where two or more roads meet; junction. **2.** any place of intersection or the act or fact of intersecting. **3.** *Math.* **a.** Also called **product.** the set of elements that two or more sets have in common. *Symbol:* ∋ **b.** the greatest lower bound of two elements in a lattice. —**in′ter·sec′tion·al,** *adj.*

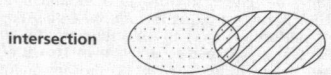

intersection

in·ter·space (*n.* in′tər spās′; *v.* in′tər spās′), *n., v.,* **-spaced, -spac·ing.** —*n.* **1.** a space between things; interval. —*v.t.* **2.** to put a space between. **3.** to occupy or fill the space between. —**in·ter·spa·tial** (in′tər-spā′shəl), *adj.* —**in′ter·spa′tial·ly,** *adv.*

in·ter·sperse (in′tər spûrs′), *v.t.,* **-spersed, -spers·ing. 1.** to scatter here and there or place at intervals among other things: *to intersperse flowers among shrubs.* **2.** to diversify with something placed or scattered at intervals: *to intersperse a speech with anecdotes.* —**in′ter·spers′ed·ly,** *adv.* —**in′ter·sper′sion, in′ter·sper′sal,** *n.*

in·ter·state (*adj.* in′tər stāt′; *n.* in′tər stāt′), *adj.* **1.** connecting or involving different states. —*n.* **2.** (*sometimes cap.*) a highway that is part of the nationwide U.S. Interstate Highway System.

in·ter·stel·lar (in′tər stel′ər), *adj.* situated or occurring between the stars: *interstellar dust.*

in·ter·stice (in tûr′stis), *n., pl.* **-stic·es** (-stə sēz′, -stə siz′). **1.** a small or narrow space or interval between things or parts: *the interstices between the slats of a fence.* **2.** an interval of time. —**in·ter′sticed,** *adj.*

in·ter·sti·tial (in′tər stish′əl), *adj.* **1.** pertaining to, situated in, or forming interstices. **2.** situated in the interstices of a tissue or organ. —*n.* **3.** an imperfection in a crystal caused by the presence of an extra atom in an otherwise complete lattice. Compare VACANCY (def. 6). —**in′ter·sti′tial·ly,** *adv.*

in·ter·tid·al (in′tər tīd′l), *adj.* of or pertaining to the littoral region that is above the low-water mark and below the high-water mark.

in·ter·twine (in′tər twīn′), *v.t., v.i.,* **-twined, -twin·ing.** to twine together. —**in′ter·twine′ment,** *n.* —**in′ter·twin′ing·ly,** *adv.*

in·ter·val (in′tər vəl), *n.* **1.** an intervening period of time: *an interval of 50 years.* **2.** a period of temporary cessation; pause. **3.** a space be-

tween things, points, limits, etc.: *an interval of ten feet between posts.* **4.** *Math.* **a.** the totality of points on a line between two designated points or endpoints that may or may not be included. **b.** any generalization of this to higher dimensions, as a rectangle with sides parallel to the coordinate axes. **5.** the space between soldiers or units in military formation. **6.** the difference in pitch between two tones sounded simultaneously or successively. **7.** *Brit.* INTERMISSION (def. 1). —**Idiom.** **8.** **at intervals. a.** now and then. **b.** here and there. —**in·ter·val·ic** (in′tər val′ik), **in·ter·val′ic** (in′tər val′ik), *adj.*

in·ter·vene (in′tər vēn′), *v.i.,* **-vened, -ven·ing. 1.** to come between disputing people, groups, etc.; intercede; mediate. **2.** to occur or be between two things. **3.** to occur between other events or periods: *Nothing important has intervened.* **4.** to occur incidentally so as to modify or hinder: *We enjoyed the picnic until the rain intervened.* **5.** to interfere with force or a threat of force: *to intervene in the affairs of another country.* **6.** to become a party to a legal suit pending between other parties, esp. in an attempt to protect one's personal interests. —**in′ter·ven′ient,** *adj.* —**in′ter·ve′nor, in′ter·ven′er,** *n.*

in·ter·ven·tion (in′tər ven′shən), *n.* **1.** the act or fact of intervening. **2.** interposition or interference of one state in the affairs of another. —**in′ter·ven′tion·al, in′ter·ven′tion·ar′y,** *adj.*

in′terver′tebral disk′, *n.* the plate of fibrocartilage between the bodies of adjacent vertebrae.

in·ter·view (in′tər vyōō′), *n.* **1.** a formal meeting in which one or more persons question, consult, or evaluate another person: *a job interview.* **2. a.** a conversation or meeting in which a writer or reporter obtains information from one or more persons for a news story, broadcast, etc. **b.** the report of such a conversation. —*v.t.* **3.** to have an interview with. —*v.i.* **4.** to have an interview; be interviewed (sometimes fol. by *with*). **5.** to give or conduct an interview. —**in′ter·view′a·ble,** *adj.*

in·ter·weave (*v.* in′tər wēv′; *n.* in′tər wēv′), *v.,* **-wove** or **-weaved, -wo·ven** or **-wove** or **-weaved, -weav·ing.** —*v.t.* **1.** to weave together, as threads or branches. **2.** to intermingle or combine as if by weaving: *to interweave truth with fiction.* —*v.i.* **3.** to become woven together; interlace; intermingle. —*n.* **4.** the act of interweaving or the state of being interwoven; blend. —**in′ter·weave′ment,** *n.* —**in′ter·weav′er,** *n.* —**in′ter·weav′ing·ly,** *adv.*

in·tes·ta·cy (in tes′tə sē), *n.* the state or fact of being intestate at death.

in·tes·tate (in tes′tāt, -tit), *adj.* **1.** not having made a will: *to die intestate.* **2.** not disposed of by will: *Her property remains intestate.* —*n.* **3.** a person who dies intestate.

in·tes·ti·nal (in tes′tə nl; *Brit.* in′tes tīn′l), *adj.* of, pertaining to, or affecting the intestines: *intestinal obstruction.* —**in·tes′ti·nal·ly,** *adv.*

intes′tinal for′titude, *n.* courage; resoluteness; endurance; guts.

in·tes·tine (in tes′tin), *n.* **1.** Usu., **intestines.** the lower part of the alimentary canal, extending from the pylorus to the anus. **2.** Also called **small intestine.** the narrow, longer part of the intestines, comprising the duodenum, jejunum, and ileum, that serves to digest and absorb nutrients. **3.** Also called **large intestine.** the broad, shorter part of the intestines, comprising the cecum, colon, and rectum, that absorbs water from and eliminates the residues of digestion. —*adj.* **4.** internal; domestic; civil: *intestine strife.*

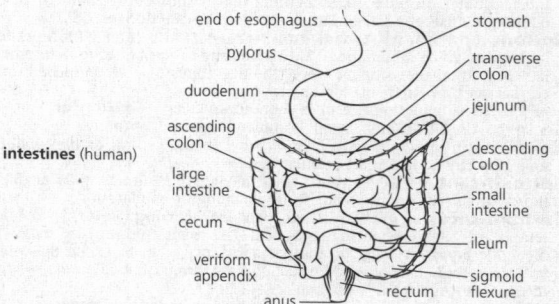

intestines (human)

Labels: end of esophagus; stomach; pylorus; transverse colon; duodenum; jejunum; ascending colon; descending colon; large intestine; small intestine; cecum; ileum; veriform appendix; sigmoid flexure; anus; rectum

In′ the Bleak′ Midwin′ter, a Christmas hymn (1872) with words by Christina Rossetti.

In′ the Gar′den, a Christian hymn (1912) with words and music by Austin Miles.

in·ti·fa·da (in′tə fä′də), *n.* (*sometimes cap.*) a revolt begun in December 1987 by Palestinian Arabs to protest Israel's occupation of the West Bank and Gaza Strip.

in·ti·ma·cy (in′tə mə sē), *n., pl.* **-cies. 1.** the state of being intimate. **2.** a close, familiar, and affectionate personal relationship. **3.** a close association with or deep understanding of a place, subject, etc. **4.** an act or expression serving as a token of familiarity or affection: *the intimacy of using first names.* **5.** privacy, esp. as suitable to the telling of a secret: *in the intimacy of his studio.*

in·ti·mate[1] (in′tə mit), *adj.* **1.** associated in close personal relations: *an intimate friend.* **2.** characterized by or involving warm friendship or a familiar association or feeling: *an intimate greeting.* **3.** private; closely personal: *one's intimate affairs.* **4.** characterized by or suggesting privacy or intimacy; cozy: *an intimate café.* **5.** (of an association, knowledge, understanding, etc.) arising from close personal connection or familiar experience. **6.** (of apparel) worn next to the skin. **7.** showing a close union or combination of particles or elements: *an intimate mixture.* **8.** inmost; personal: *intimate secrets.* **9.** of, pertaining to, or characteristic of the inmost or essential nature; intrinsic: *the intimate structure of an organism.* **—***n.* **10.** an intimate friend or associate. **—in′ti•mate•ly,** *adv.*

in•ti•mate[2] (in′tə māt′), *v.t.,* **-mat•ed, -mat•ing.** to indicate or make known indirectly; hint; imply; suggest. **—in′ti•mat′er,** *n.* **—in′ti•ma′tion,** *n.*

in•tim•i•date (in tim′i dāt′), *v.t.,* **-dat•ed, -dat•ing. 1.** to make timid; fill with fear. **2.** to overawe or cow, as through the force of one's personality or by display of wealth, talent, etc. **3.** to force into or deter from some action by inducing fear. **—in•tim′i•da′tion,** *n.* **—in•tim′i•da′tor,** *n.*

in•tinc•tion (in tingk′shən), *n.* (in a communion service) the act of steeping the bread or wafer in the wine, enabling the communicant to receive the two elements conjointly.

in•tine (in′tēn, -tīn), *n.* the inner coat of a spore, as a pollen grain.

intl. or **intnl.,** international.

in•to (in′to͞o; *unstressed* -to͞o, -tə), *prep.* **1.** to the inside of; in toward: *He walked into the room.* **2.** toward or in the direction of: *going into town.* **3.** to a point of contact with; against: *backed into a parked car.* **4.** (used to indicate insertion or immersion in): *plugged into the socket.* **5.** (used to indicate entry, inclusion, or introduction in a place or condition): *received into the church.* **6.** to the state, condition, or form assumed or brought about: *lapsed into disrepair; translated into another language.* **7.** to the occupation, action, possession, circumstance, or acceptance of: *went into banking; coerced into complying.* **8.** (used to indicate a continuing extent in time or space): *lasted into the night; far into the distance.* **9.** (used to indicate the number to be divided by another number): *2 into 20 equals 10.* **10.** *Informal.* interested or absorbed in, esp. obsessively: *She's into yoga.*

in•tol•er•a•ble (in tol′ər ə bəl), *adj.* **1.** not tolerable; unendurable; insufferable: *intolerable pain.* **2.** excessive. **—in•tol′er•a•bil′i•ty, in•tol′er•a•ble•ness,** *n.* **—in•tol′er•a•bly,** *adv.*

in•tol•er•ance (in tol′ər əns), *n.* **1.** lack of toleration; unwillingness or refusal to tolerate or respect contrary opinions or beliefs, persons of different races or backgrounds, etc. **2.** abnormal sensitivity or allergy, as to heat or to a food or drug.

in•tol•er•ant (in tol′ər ənt), *adj.* **1.** not tolerating or respecting beliefs, opinions, usages, manners, etc., different from one's own, as in political or religious matters. **2.** unable or unwilling to tolerate or endure (usu. fol. by *of*): *intolerant of heat.* **—in•tol′er•ant•ly,** *adv.*

in•to•nate (in′tō nāt′, -tə-), *v.t.,* **-nat•ed, -nat•ing. 1.** to utter with a particular tone or modulation of voice. **2.** to intone; chant; recite.

in•to•na•tion (in′tō nā′shən, -tə-), *n.* **1.** the pattern or melody of pitch changes in connected speech, esp. the pitch pattern of a sentence, which distinguishes kinds of sentences or speakers of different language cultures. **2.** the act or manner of intonating. **3.** the ability to produce musical tones on pitch. **4.** something that is intoned or chanted. **5.** the opening phrase of a Gregorian chant. **—in′to•na′tion•al,** *adj.*

in•tone (in tōn′), *v.,* **-toned, -ton•ing. —***v.t.* **1.** to utter with a particular tone or voice modulation. **2.** to give tone or variety of tone to; vocalize. **3.** to utter in a singing voice (the first tones of a section in a liturgical service). **4.** to recite or chant in monotone. **—***v.i.* **5.** to speak or recite in a singing voice, esp. in monotone; chant. **—in•ton′er,** *n.*

in to•to (in tō′tō), *adv.* in all; completely; entirely; wholly.

in•town (in′toun′, in toun′), *adj.* being in the central or metropolitan area of a city or town: *an intown motel.*

in•tox•i•cant (in tok′si kənt), *n.* **1.** an intoxicating agent, as alcoholic liquor or certain drugs. **—***adj.* **2.** intoxicating or exhilarating.

in•tox•i•cate (in tok′si kāt′), *v.,* **-cat•ed, -cat•ing. —***v.t.* **1.** to affect temporarily with diminished physical and mental control by means of alcoholic liquor, a drug, or another substance, esp. to excite or stupefy with liquor. **2.** to make enthusiastic; elate strongly; exhilarate. **—***v.i.* **3.** to cause or produce intoxication.

in•tox•i•ca•tion (in tok′si kā′shən), *n.* **1.** inebriation; drunkenness. **2.** an act or instance of intoxicating. **3.** overpowering exhilaration or excitement of the mind or emotions. **4.** *Pathol.* poisoning.

intra-, a prefix meaning "within": *intramural.* Compare INTRO-.

In′tra•coast′al Wa′terway (in′trə kō′stəl, in′-), *n.* a system of canals and naturally sheltered bays and channels, extending 2666 mi. (4300 km) along the Atlantic and Gulf coasts of the U.S.: maintained to protect small craft from the open sea.

in•trac•ta•ble (in trak′tə bəl), *adj.* **1.** not docile or manageable; stubborn. **2.** hard to treat, relieve, or cure. **—in•trac′ta•bil′i•ty, in•trac′ta•ble•ness,** *n.* **—in•trac′ta•bly,** *adv.*

in•tra•dos (in′trə dos′, -dōs′, in trā′dos, -dōs), *n., pl.* **-dos** (-dōz′, -dōz), **-dos•es.** the interior curve or surface of an arch or vault. Compare EXTRADOS.

in•tra•mu•ral (in′trə myo͝or′əl), *adj.* **1.** involving only students at the same school or college. **2.** being or occurring within the walls, boundaries, or confines, as of an institution or organization. Compare EXTRAMURAL. **3.** being inside the wall surrounding an anatomical organ or cavity. **—in′tra•mu′ral•ly,** *adv.*

in•tran•si•gent or **in•tran•si•geant** (in tran′si jənt), *adj.* **1.** refusing to agree or compromise; uncompromising; inflexible. **—***n.* **2.** an intransigent person, as in politics. **—in•tran′si•gence, in•tran′si•gen•cy,** *n.* **—in•tran′si•gent•ly,** *adv.*

in•tran•si•tive (in tran′si tiv), *adj.* of or being a verb that indicates a complete action without being accompanied by a direct object, as *sit* or *lie,* and that in English does not form a passive. **—in•tran′si•tive•ly,** *adv.* **—in•tran′si•tive•ness, in•tran′si•tiv′i•ty,** *n.*

in•tra•pre•neur (in′trə prə nûr′, -no͝or′, -nyo͝or′), *n.* an employee of a corporation allowed to exercise some independent entrepreneurial initiative. **—in′tra•pre•neur′i•al,** *adj.* **—in′tra•pre•neur′ship,** *n.*

in•tra•state (in′trə stāt′), *adj.* existing or occurring within the boundaries of a state, esp. of the U.S.: *intrastate commerce.*

in•tra•u•ter•ine (in′trə yo͞o′tər in, -tə rīn′), *adj.* located or occurring within the uterus.

intrau′terine device′, *n.* any of various contrivances, as a loop or coil, for insertion into the uterus as a contraceptive. *Abbr.:* IUD

in•tra•ve•nous (in′trə vē′nəs), *adj.* **1.** being or occurring within a vein. **2.** of, pertaining to, employed in, or administered by injection into a vein. *Abbr.:* IV **—in′tra•ve′nous•ly,** *adv.*

in•trep•id (in trep′id), *adj.* fearless; dauntless: *an intrepid explorer.* **—in′tre•pid′i•ty, in•trep′id•ness,** *n.* **—in•trep′id•ly,** *adv.*

in•tri•ca•cy (in′tri kə sē), *n., pl.* **-cies. 1.** intricate character or state. **2.** an intricate part, action, etc.

in•tri•cate (in′tri kit), *adj.* **1.** having many interrelated parts or facets; entangled or involved. **2.** hard to understand, work, or make; complex. **—in′tri•cate•ly,** *adv.* **—in′tri•cate•ness,** *n.*

in•trigue (*v.* in trēg′; *n. also* in′trēg), *v.,* **-trigued, -tri•guing,** *n.* **—***v.t.* **1.** to arouse the curiosity or interest of by unusual, new, or otherwise fascinating qualities. **2.** to accomplish or force by crafty plotting or underhand machinations. **—***v.i.* **3.** to plot craftily or underhandedly. **4.** to carry on a secret or illicit love affair. **—***n.* **5.** the use of underhand machinations or deceitful stratagems. **6.** such a machination or stratagem or a series of them; a plot or crafty dealing: *political intrigues.* **7.** a secret or illicit love affair. **—in•tri′guer,** *n.* **—in•tri′guing•ly,** *adv.*

in•trin•sic (in trin′sik, -zik) also **in•trin′si•cal,** *adj.* **1.** belonging to a thing by its very nature: *intrinsic value.* **2.** (of certain muscles, nerves, etc.) belonging to or lying within a given part. **—in•trin′si•cal•ly,** *adv.*

in•tro (in′trō), *n., pl.* **-tros.** *Informal.* an introduction.

intro-, a prefix meaning "inside," "within": *introduce; introversion.* Compare INTRA-.

in•tro•duce (in′trə do͞os′, -dyo͞os′), *v.t.,* **-duced, -duc•ing. 1.** to present (a person) to another so as to make acquainted. **2.** to acquaint (two or more persons) with each other personally: *Will you introduce us?* **3.** to present (a person, product, etc.) to a group or to the general public for or as if for the first time by a formal act, announcement, etc.: *to introduce a debutante to society.* **4.** to bring (a person) to first knowledge or experience of something: *He introduced me to skiing.* **5.** to create, propose, bring into notice, use, etc., for the first time; institute: *to introduce a new procedure.* **6.** to present for official consideration or action, as a legislative bill. **7.** to begin; preface: *to introduce a speech with an anecdote.* **8.** to put or place into something for the first time; insert: *to introduce a figure into a design.* **9.** to bring in or establish, as something foreign, alien, or not native: *a plant introduced into America.* **10.** to present (a speaker, performer, etc.) to an audience. **11.** to present (a person) at a royal court. **—in′tro•duc′er,** *n.* **—in′tro•duc′i•ble,** *adj.*

in•tro•duc•tion (in′trə duk′shən), *n.* **1.** the act of introducing or the state of being introduced. **2.** a formal personal presentation of one person to another or others. **3.** a preliminary part, as of a book, musical composition, or the like, leading up to the main part. **4.** an elementary treatise. **5.** an act or instance of inserting. **6.** something introduced.

in•tro•duc•to•ry (in′trə duk′tə rē) also **in′tro•duc′tive,** *adj.* serving or used to introduce; preliminary. **—in′tro•duc′to•ri•ly,** *adv.* **—in′tro•duc′to•ri•ness,** *n.*

in•tro•it (in′trō it, -troit), *n.* **1.** a part of a psalm with antiphon recited by the celebrant at the beginning of the Roman Catholic mass. **2.** (in the Anglican or Lutheran Church) a psalm or anthem sung as the celebrant of the Holy Communion enters the sanctuary. **3.** a choral response sung at the beginning of a religious service.

in•tro•spect (in′trə spekt′), *v.i.* **1.** to practice introspection; consider one's own internal state or feelings. **—***v.t.* **2.** to look into or examine (one's own mind, feelings, etc.). **—in′tro•spec′tive,** *adj.* **—in′tro•spec′tive•ly,** *adv.* **—in′tro•spec′tive•ness,** *n.*

in•tro•spec•tion (in′trə spek′shən), *n.* **1.** observation or examination of one's own mental and emotional state, mental processes, etc. **2.** the tendency or disposition to do this. **—in′tro•spec′tion•al,** *adj.* **—in′tro•spec′tion•ist,** *n., adj.*

in•tro•ver•sion (in′trə vûr′zhən, -shən, in′trə vûr′-), *n.* **1.** the act of directing one's interest inward or to things within the self. **2.** the state of being concerned primarily with one's own thoughts and feelings rather than with the external environment. Compare EXTROVERSION. **—in′tro•ver′sive, in′tro•ver′tive,** *adj.*

in•tro•vert (in′trə vûrt′), *n.* a shy person; a person concerned primarily with inner thoughts and feelings rather than with the physical or social environment.

in•trude (in tro͞od′), *v.,* **-trud•ed, -trud•ing. —***v.t.* **1.** to thrust or bring in without invitation, permission, or welcome. **2.** *Geol.* to thrust or force into. —*v.i.* **3.** to come in without permission or welcome. **4.** *Geol.* to enter as an intrusion. —**in•trud′er,** *n.* —**in•trud′ing•ly,** *adv.*

in•tru•sion (in tro͞o′zhən), *n.* **1.** an act or instance of intruding. **2.** the state of being intruded. **3.** an illegal act of entering or taking possession of another's property. **4. a.** emplacement of molten rock in preexisting rock. **b.** rock emplaced in this manner. **c.** a process analogous to magmatic intrusion, as the injection of a plug of salt into sedimentary rocks. **d.** the matter forced in. —**in•tru′sion•al,** *adj.*

in•tru•sive (in tro͞o′siv), *adj.* **1.** tending or apt to intrude; annoying: *intrusive memories of loss.* **2.** characterized by or involving intrusion. **3.** intruding; thrusting in. **4. a.** (of a rock) having been forced between preexisting rocks or rock layers while in a molten or plastic condition. **b.** of or pertaining to such rocks. **5.** of or designating a speech sound inserted in connected speech where it is not present in the spelling, as an *r*-sound inserted by some speakers before *-ing* in the word *drawing;* excrescent. —**in•tru′sive•ly,** *adv.* —**in•tru′sive•ness,** *n.*

in•tu•bate (in′to͞o bāt′, -tyo͞o-), *v.t.,* **-bat•ed, -bat•ing.** to insert a tube into (a hollow anatomical structure, as the larynx), esp. for admitting air or a fluid. —**in′tu•ba′tion,** *n.*

in•tu•it (in to͞o′it, -tyo͞o′-), *v.t., v.i.* to know or understand by intuition. —**in•tu′it•a•ble,** *adj.*

in•tu•i•tion (in′to͞o ish′ən, -tyo͞o-), *n.* **1.** direct perception of truth, fact, etc., independent of any reasoning process; immediate apprehension. **2.** a fact, truth, etc., perceived in this way. **3.** a keen and quick insight. **4.** the quality or ability of having such direct perception or quick insight. —**in′tu•i′tion•al,** *adj.* —**in′tu•i′tion•al•ly,** *adv.*

in•tu•i•tive (in to͞o′i tiv, -tyo͞o′-), *adj.* **1.** perceiving by intuition. **2.** perceived by, resulting from, or involving intuition: *intuitive knowledge.* **3.** having or possessing intuition. **4.** capable of being perceived or known by intuition. —**in•tu′i•tive•ly,** *adv.* —**in•tu′i•tive•ness,** *n.*

in•tu•mesce (in′to͞o mes′, -tyo͞o-), *v.i.,* **-mesced, -mesc•ing.** **1.** to swell up, as with heat; become tumid. **2.** to bubble up.

in•tu•mes•cence (in′to͞o mes′əns, -tyo͞o-), *n.* **1.** a swelling up, as with congestion. **2.** a swollen mass. —**in′tu•mes′cent,** *adj.*

in•tus•sus•cept (in′təs sə sept′), *v.t.* to take within, as one part of the intestine into an adjacent part; invaginate. —**in′tus•sus•cep′tive,** *adj.*

in•tus•sus•cep•tion (in′təs sə sep′shən), *n.* **1.** a taking within. **2.** Also called **invagination.** the slipping of one part within another, as of the intestine.

In•u•it or **In•nu•it** (in′o͞o it, -yo͞o-), *n., pl.* **-its,** (*esp. collectively*) **-it.** **1. a.** a member of any of the Eskimo groups inhabiting an area extending from Greenland to W arctic Canada. **b.** Eskimo (def. 1). **2.** Also called **In′uit-Inu′piaq.** the speech of all the Eskimo groups from Greenland to NW Alaska. —**Usage.** See Eskimo, Indian.

I•nuk•ti•tut (i no͝ok′ti to͞ot′, i nyo͝ok′-), *n.* the group of Inuit dialects spoken by Eskimos of central and E arctic Canada.

in•un•dant (in un′dənt), *adj.* flooding or overflowing; inundating.

in•un•date (in′ən dāt′, -un-), *v.t.,* **-dat•ed, -dat•ing.** **1.** to flood; overspread with water; deluge. **2.** to overwhelm: *inundated with letters of protest.* —**in′un•da′tion,** *n.* —**in′un•da′tor,** *n.*

in•ure (in yo͝or′, i no͝or′), *v.,* **-ured, -ur•ing.** —*v.t.* **1.** to toughen or harden by use or exposure; accustom; habituate (usu. fol. by *to*): *inured to cold.* —*v.i.* **2.** to come into use; take or have effect. **3.** to become beneficial or advantageous. —**in•ure′ment,** *n.*

in•urn (in ûrn′), *v.t.* **1.** to put, as ashes from a cremation, into an urn. **2.** to bury; inter. —**in•urn′ment,** *n.*

in u•ter•o (in yo͞o′tə rō′), *adv., adj.* in the uterus; unborn.

in•u•tile (in yo͞o′til), *adj.* of no use or service. —**in•u′tile•ly,** *adv.*

in•vade (in vād′), *v.,* **-vad•ed, -vad•ing.** —*v.t.* **1.** to enter forcefully as an enemy; go into with hostile intent. **2.** to enter as if to take possession: *to invade a neighbor's home.* **3.** to enter and affect injuriously or destructively: *viruses that invade the bloodstream.* **4.** to intrude upon: *to invade someone's privacy.* **5.** to encroach or infringe upon: *to invade the rights of citizens.* **6.** to penetrate; spread into or over: *City dwellers invaded the suburbs.* —*v.i.* **7.** to make an invasion. —**in•vad′er,** *n.*

in•vag•i•nate (*v.* in vaj′ə nāt′; *adj.* -nit, -nāt′), *v.,* **-nat•ed, -nat•ing,** *adj.* —*v.t.* **1.** to insert or receive, as into a sheath; sheathe. **2.** to fold or draw (a tubular anatomical structure) back within itself; intussuscept. —*v.i.* **3.** to become invaginated; undergo invagination. **4.** to form a pocket by turning in. —*adj.* **5.** folded or turned back upon itself. **6.** sheathed.

in•va•lid[1] (in′və lid; *Brit.* -lēd′), *n.* **1.** an infirm or sickly person, esp. one who is too sick or weak to care for himself or herself. —*adj.* **2.** unable to care for oneself due to infirmity or disability. **3.** of or for invalids. —*v.t.* **4.** to make an invalid. **5.** *Chiefly Brit.* to evacuate (military personnel) from a theater of operations because of injury or illness.

in•val•id[2] (in val′id), *adj.* **1.** not valid; without force or foundation; indefensible. **2.** deficient in substance or cogency; weak. **3.** void or without legal force, as a contract. —**in•val′id•ly,** *adv.* —**in•val′id•ness,** *n.*

in•val•i•date (in val′i dāt′), *v.t.,* **-dat•ed, -dat•ing.** **1.** to render invalid; discredit. **2.** to deprive of legal force or efficacy; nullify. —**in•val′i•da′tion,** *n.* —**in•val′i•da′tor,** *n.*

in•val•u•a•ble (in val′yo͞o ə bəl), *adj.* beyond calculable value; of inestimable worth; priceless. —**in•val′u•a•bly,** *adv.*

in•var•i•a•ble (in vâr′ē ə bəl), *adj.* **1.** not variable or capable of being changed; static. —*n.* **2.** something that is invariable; a constant. —**in•var′i•a•bil′i•ty, in•var′i•a•ble•ness,** *n.* —**in•var′i•a•bly,** *adv.*

in•var•i•ant (in vâr′ē ənt), *adj.* **1.** invariable; constant. —*n.* **2.** a mathematical quantity or expression that is constant throughout a certain range of conditions. —**in•var′i•ant•ly,** *adv.*

in•va•sion (in vā′zhən), *n.* **1.** an act or instance of invading, esp. by an army. **2.** the entrance or advent of anything troublesome or harmful, as disease. **3.** entrance as if to take possession or overrun: *the annual invasion of tourists.* **4.** infringement by intrusion: *invasion of privacy.*

in•va•sive (in vā′siv), *adj.* **1.** characterized by or involving invasion; offensive. **2.** invading, or tending to invade; intrusive. **3.** requiring the entry of a needle, catheter, or other medical instrument into a part of the body.

in•vec•tive (in vek′tiv), *n.* **1.** vehement denunciation, censure, or reproach; vituperation. **2.** an insulting or abusive word or expression. —*adj.* **3.** vituperative; denunciatory; censoriously abusive. —**in•vec′tive•ly,** *adv.* —**in•vec′tive•ness,** *n.*

in•veigh (in vā′), *v.i.* to protest strongly or attack vehemently with words; rail (usu. fol. by *against*): *to inveigh against isolationism.* —**in•veigh′er,** *n.*

in•vei•gle (in vā′gəl, -vē′-), *v.t.,* **-gled, -gling.** **1.** to entice or lure by artful talk or inducements. **2.** to acquire by beguiling talk or methods: *to inveigle a door pass from the usher.* —**in•vei′gle•ment,** *n.* —**in•vei′gler,** *n.*

in•vent (in vent′), *v.t.* **1.** to originate as a product of one's own ingenuity, experimentation, or contrivance: *to invent a better mousetrap.* **2.** to produce or create with the imagination: *to invent a story.* **3.** to make up or fabricate (something fictitious or false): *to invent excuses.* —**in•vent′i•ble,** *adj.*

in•ven•tion (in ven′shən), *n.* **1.** the act of inventing. **2.** *U.S. Patent Law.* a new process, machine, improvement, etc., that is recognized as the product of some unique intuition or genius. **3.** anything invented or devised. **4.** the power or faculty of inventing or originating. **5.** an act or instance of creating by exercise of the imagination, esp. in art, music, etc. **6.** something fabricated, as a false statement. **7.** a short contrapuntal musical composition for keyboard instrument. —**in•ven′tion•al,** *adj.*

in•ven•tive (in ven′tiv), *adj.* **1.** apt at inventing, devising, or contriving. **2.** apt at creating with the imagination. **3.** having the function of inventing. **4.** pertaining to, involving, or showing invention. —**in•ven′tive•ly,** *adv.* —**in•ven′tive•ness,** *n.*

in•ven•tor (in ven′tər), *n.* a person who invents, esp. one who devises some new process, appliance, machine, or article; one who makes inventions. Sometimes, **in•vent′er.**

in•ven•to•ry (in′vən tôr′ē, -tōr′ē), *n., pl.* **-to•ries,** *v.,* **-to•ried, -to•ry•ing.** —*n.* **1.** a complete listing of merchandise or stock on hand, work in progress, raw materials, etc., made each year by a business. **2.** the items represented on such a list, as a merchant's stock of goods. **3.** the aggregate value of a stock of goods. **4.** a detailed, often descriptive list of articles, giving the code number, quantity, and value of each; catalog. **5.** a formal list of the property of a person or estate. **6.** a tally of one's personality traits, aptitudes, skills, etc., for use in counseling and guidance. **7.** a catalog of natural resources. **8.** the act of making a catalog or detailed listing. —*v.t.* **9.** to make an inventory of; enter in an inventory; catalog. **10.** to evaluate or summarize. **11.** to keep an available supply of (merchandise); stock. —*v.i.* **12.** to have value as shown by an inventory: *stock that inventories at two million dollars.* —**in′ven•to′ri•a•ble,** *adj.* —**in′ven•to′ri•al,** *adj.* —**in′ven•to′ri•al•ly,** *adv.*

in•verse (in vûrs′, in′vûrs), *adj.* **1.** reversed in position, order, direction, or tendency. **2.** (of a proportion) containing terms of which an increase in one results in a decrease in another. **3.** inverted; turned upside down. —*n.* **4.** an inverted state or condition. **5.** something that is inverse; the direct opposite. **6.** inverse function. —*v.t.* **7.** to invert. —**in•verse′ly,** *adv.*

in′verse func′tion, *n. Math.* the function that replaces another function when the dependent and independent variables of the first function are interchanged for an appropriate set of values of the dependent variable.

in•ver•sion (in vûr′zhən, -shən), *n.* **1.** an act or instance of inverting. **2.** the state of being inverted. **3.** anything that is inverted. **4.** anastrophe. **5.** a reversal of the usual order of words, as in the placement of the subject after an auxiliary verb in a question. **6.** the turning inward of an anatomical part, as the foot. **7.** a hydrolysis of certain carbohydrates, as cane sugar, that results in a reversal of direction of the rotatory power of the carbohydrate solution. **8. a.** the process or result of transposing the musical tones of an interval or chord so that the original bass becomes an upper voice. **b.** (in counterpoint) the transposition of the upper voice part below the lower, and vice versa. **c.** presentation of a melody in contrary motion to its original form. **9.** a reversal of the linear order of genes on a chromosome. **10.** a reversal in the normal atmospheric lapse rate, the temperature rising at higher altitudes rather than falling. **11.** a conversion of direct current into alternating current. **12.** the operation of forming the inverse of a point, curve, function, etc. —**in•ver′sive,** *adj.*

in•vert (*v.* in vûrt′; *adj., n.* in′vûrt), *v.t.* **1.** to turn upside down. **2.** to reverse in position, order, direction, or relationship. **3.** to turn inward or back upon itself. **4.** to turn inside out. **5.** to subject to chemical inversion. **6.** to subject to musical inversion. —*v.i.* **7.** to become chemically inverted. —*adj.* **8.** subjected to chemical inversion. —*n.* **9.** a postage stamp with all or part of the central design printed upside down. —**in•vert′i•ble,** *adj.* —**in•vert′i•bil′i•ty,** *n.*

in•ver•te•brate (in vûr′tə brit, -brāt′), *adj.* **1. a.** without a backbone or spinal column; not vertebrate. **b.** of or pertaining to creatures without a backbone. **2.** without strength of character. —*n.* **3.** an invertebrate animal. **4.** a person who lacks strength of character. —**in•ver′te•bra•cy** (-brə sē), **in•ver′te•brate•ness,** *n.*

invert′ed pleat′, *n.* a reverse box pleat having the flat fold turned in.

in•vest (in vest′), *v.t.* **1.** to put (money) to use, by purchase or expenditure, in something offering potential profitable returns. **2.** to use (money), as in accumulating something: *to invest large sums in books.* **3.** to use, give, or devote (time, talent, etc.), as to achieve something. **4.** to furnish with power, authority, or rank. **5.** to endow with a power, right, etc.; vest: *Feudalism invested the lords with authority over their vassals.* **6.** to endow with a quality or characteristic: *to invest a friend with every virtue.* **7.** to infuse or belong to, as a quality or characteristic: *Goodness invests his every action.* **8.** to install in an office or position. **9.** to clothe or attire. **10.** to cover, adorn, or envelop: *Spring invests the trees with leaves.* —*v.i.* **11.** to make financial investments. —**in•vest′a•ble, in•vest′i•ble,** *adj.* —**in•ves′tor,** *n.*

in•ves•ti•gate (in ves′ti gāt′), *v.,* **-gat•ed, -gat•ing.** —*v.t.* **1.** to search or examine into the particulars of; examine in detail. **2.** to examine the particulars of so as to learn about something hidden, unique, or complex, esp. in an attempt to find a motive, cause, or culprit: *to investigate a murder.* —*v.i.* **3.** to make inquiry, examination, or investigation. —**in•ves′ti•ga•ble,** *adj.* —**in•ves′ti•ga•tive, in•ves′ti•ga•to•ry** (-gə tôr′ē, -tōr′ē), *adj.* —**in•ves′ti•ga′tor,** *n.*

in•ves•ti•ga•tion (in ves′ti gā′shən), *n.* **1.** the act or process of investigating or the condition of being investigated. **2.** a searching inquiry for ascertaining facts; detailed or careful examination. —**in•ves′ti•ga′tion•al,** *adj.*

inves′tigative new′ drug′, *n.* an unproven drug that is approved by the Food and Drug Administration for restricted use in clinical trials. *Abbr.:* IND

in•ves•ti•ture (in ves′ti chər, -chŏŏr′), *n.* the act or process of investing, as with a rank, office, or title.

in•vest•ment (in vest′mənt), *n.* **1.** the investing of money or capital for profitable returns. **2.** a particular instance or mode of investing. **3.** a thing invested in, as a business. **4.** something that is invested; sum invested. **5.** the act or fact of investing or state of being invested, as with a garment. **6.** a devoting, using, or giving of time, talent, emotional energy, etc., as to achieve something.

invest′ment com′pany, *n.* a company that invests its funds in other companies and issues its own securities against these investments. Also called **invest′ment trust′.**

in•vet•er•ate (in vet′ər it), *adj.* **1.** confirmed in a habit, practice, feeling, or the like: *an inveterate gambler.* **2.** firmly established by long continuance, as a disease; chronic. —**in•vet′er•a•cy** (-ə sē), *n.* —**in•vet′er•ate•ly,** *adv.* —**in•vet′er•ate•ness,** *n.*

in•vid•i•ous (in vid′ē əs), *adj.* **1.** calculated to create ill will; causing resentment or envy. **2.** offensively or unfairly discriminating; injurious: *invidious comparisons.* —**in•vid′i•ous•ly,** *adv.* —**in•vid′i•ous•ness,** *n.*

in•vig•or•ate (in vig′ə rāt′), *v.t.,* **-at•ed, -at•ing.** to give vigor to; fill with life and energy; energize. —**in•vig′or•at′ing•ly,** *adv.* —**in•vig′or•a′tive,** *adj.* —**in•vig′or•a′tive•ly,** *adv.* —**in•vig′or•a′tor,** *n.*

in•vin•ci•ble (in vin′sə bəl), *adj.* **1.** incapable of being conquered, defeated, or subdued. **2.** insuperable; insurmountable: *invincible difficulties.* —**in•vin′ci•bil′i•ty, in•vin′ci•ble•ness,** *n.* —**in•vin′ci•bly,** *adv.*

in•vi•o•la•ble (in vī′ə lə bəl), *adj.* **1.** prohibiting violation; secure from destruction, violence, infringement, or desecration: *an inviolable sanctuary.* **2.** incapable of being violated; unassailable: *inviolable secrecy.* —**in•vi′o•la•bil′i•ty, in•vi′o•la•ble•ness,** *n.* —**in•vi′o•la•bly,** *adv.*

in•vi•o•late (in vī′ə lit, -lāt′), *adj.* **1.** free from violation, injury, desecration, or outrage. **2.** undisturbed. **3.** unbroken. **4.** not infringed. —**in•vi′o•la•cy** (in vī′ə lə sē), **in•vi′o•late•ness,** *n.* —**in•vi′o•late•ly,** *adv.*

in•vis•i•ble (in viz′ə bəl), *adj.* **1.** not visible; not perceptible by the eye. **2.** out of sight; hidden: *an invisible seam.* **3.** not perceptible or discernible by the mind: *invisible differences.* **4.** not ordinarily found in financial statements or reflected in statistics or a listing: *Goodwill is an invisible asset to a business.* **5.** concealed from public knowledge. —*n.* **6.** an invisible thing or being. **7. the invisible,** the unseen or spiritual world. —**in•vis′i•bil′i•ty, in•vis′i•ble•ness,** *n.* —**in•vis′i•bly,** *adv.*

invis′ible gov′ernment, *n.* a group that creates public policy without being responsible to the electorate.

invis′ible ink′, *n.* a writing fluid that is invisible until treated, as by heat or chemicals.

Invis′ible Man′, The, **1.** a novel (1897) by H.G. Wells. **2.** a novel (1952) by Ralph Ellison.

in•vi•ta•tion (in′vi tā′shən), *n.* **1.** the act of inviting. **2.** the written or spoken form with which a person is invited. **3.** attraction or incentive; allurement. **4.** a provocation: *The speech was an invitation to rebellion.*

in•vi•ta•tion•al (in′vi tā′shə nl), *adj.* restricted to participants who have been invited.

in•vite (*v.* in vīt′; *n.* in′vīt), *v.,* **-vit•ed, -vit•ing,** *n.* —*v.t.* **1.** to request the presence or participation of in a kindly or courteous way: *to invite friends to dinner.* **2.** to request politely or formally: *to invite donations.* **3.** to act so as to bring on or render probable: *to invite trouble.* **4.** to call forth or give occasion for: *Those big shoes invite laughter.* **5.** to at-

tract, allure, entice, or tempt. —*v.i.* **6.** to give invitation; offer attractions or allurements. —*n.* —**in•vi•tee** (in′vi tē′, -vī-), *n.* —**in•vit′er, in•vi′tor,** *n.*

in•vit•ing (in vī′ting), *adj.* attractive, alluring, or tempting: *an inviting offer.* —**in•vit′ing•ly,** *adv.* —**in•vit′ing•ness,** *n.*

in vi•tro (in vē′trō), *adj.* (of a biological entity or process) developed or maintained in a controlled, nonliving environment, as a laboratory vessel. Compare IN VIVO.

in vi′tro fertiliza′tion, *n.* a technique by which an ovum is fertilized with sperm in a laboratory dish and subsequently implanted in a uterus for gestation. *Abbr.:* IVF

in vi•vo (in vē′vō), *adj.* (of a biological entity or process) being or occurring within a living organism or in a natural setting. Compare IN VITRO.

in•vo•ca•tion (in′və kā′shən), *n.* **1.** the act of invoking or calling upon a deity, spirit, etc., for aid, protection, inspiration, or the like; supplication. **2.** any petitioning or supplication for help or aid. **3.** a form of prayer invoking God's presence, said at the beginning of a public or religious ceremony. **4.** an entreaty for guidance from a Muse, deity, etc., at the beginning of an epic poem. **5.** an incantation. **6.** the act of referring to something, as a concept or document, for support and justification. **7.** the enforcing or use of a legal or moral precept or right. —**in•voc′a•to•ry** (-vok′ə tôr′ē, -tōr′ē), *adj.*

in•voice (in′vois), *n., v.,* **-voiced, -voic•ing.** —*n.* **1.** an itemized bill for goods sold or services provided, containing prices, the total charge, and the terms. **2.** the merchandise or shipment itself. —*v.t.* **3.** to present an invoice to or for.

in•voke (in vōk′), *v.t.,* **-voked, -vok•ing. 1.** to call for with earnest desire; make supplication or pray for: *to invoke God's mercy.* **2.** to call on (a deity, Muse, etc.), as in prayer or supplication. **3.** to declare to be binding or in effect: *to invoke the law.* **4.** to appeal to, as for confirmation. **5.** to petition or call on for help or aid. **6.** to call forth or upon (a spirit) by incantation. **7.** to cause, call forth, or bring about. —**in•vo′ca•ble,** *adj.* —**in•vok′er,** *n.*

in•vol•un•tar•y (in vol′ən ter′ē), *adj.* **1.** not voluntary; independent of one's will: *an involuntary listener.* **2.** unintentional; unconscious: *an involuntary gesture.* **3.** *Physiol.* acting or functioning without volition: *involuntary muscles.* —**in•vol•un•tar•i•ly** (in vol′ən ter′ə lē, -vol′ən târ′-), *adv.* —**in•vol′un•tar′i•ness,** *n.*

in•vo•lute (*adj.* in′və lōōt′; *v.* in′və lōōt′), *adj., v.,* **-lut•ed, -lut•ing.** —*adj.* **1.** intricate; complex. **2.** curled or curved inward or spirally: *a gear with involute teeth.* **3.** rolled inward from the edge, as a leaf. **4.** (of shells) having the whorls closely wound. —*v.i.* **5.** to become involute. **6.** to return to a normal shape, size, or state. —**in′vo•lute′ly,** *adv.*

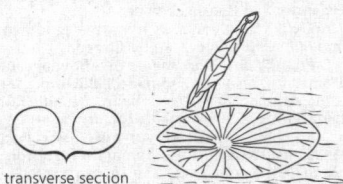

transverse section

involute leaves of white lotus, *Nymphaea lotus*

in•vo•lu•tion (in′və lōō′shən), *n.* **1.** an act or instance of involving or entangling; involvement. **2.** the state of being involved. **3.** something complicated. **4.** *Biol.* retrogression; restoration of a former state. **5.** *Physiol.* the regressive changes in the body occurring with old age. **6.** a complex grammatical construction in which the subject is separated from its predicate by intervening clauses or phrases. **7.** a mathematical function that is its own inverse. —**in•vo•lu′tion•al,** *adj.*

in•volve (in volv′), *v.t.,* **-volved, -volv•ing. 1.** to include as a necessary circumstance, condition, or consequence; imply; entail: *This job involves long hours.* **2.** to include within itself or its scope. **3.** to bring into an intricate or complicated form or condition. **4.** to cause to be troublesomely associated, as in something embarrassing or unfavorable: *Don't involve me in your quarrel!* **5.** to combine inextricably (usu. fol. by *with*). **6.** to implicate, as in guilt or crime, or in any matter or affair. **7.** to engage the interests or emotions or commitment of. **8.** to envelop or enfold, as if with a wrapping. —**in•volve′ment,** *n.*

in•volved (in volvd′), *adj.* **1.** intricate or complex. **2.** implicated: *involved in crime.* **3.** concerned in some affair, esp. in a way likely to cause danger or unpleasantness. **4.** committed or engaged: *politically involved.*

in•vul•ner•a•ble (in vul′nər ə bəl), *adj.* **1.** incapable of being wounded, hurt, or damaged. **2.** proof against or immune to attack: *an invulnerable fortress.* —**in•vul′ner•a•bil′i•ty, in•vul′ner•a•ble•ness,** *n.* —**in•vul′ner•a•bly,** *adv.*

in•ward (in′wərd), *adv.* Also, **in′wards. 1.** toward the inside, interior, or center, as of a place, space, or body. **2.** into or toward the mind or soul: *Let us turn our thoughts inward.* —*adj.* **3.** proceeding or directed toward the inside or interior. **4.** situated within or in or on the inside;

inner. **5.** pertaining to the inside or inner part. **6.** located within the body. **7.** inland: *inward passage.* **8.** mental or spiritual; inner. **9.** closely personal; intimate. —*n.* **10.** the inward or internal part; inside. **11. inwards,** the inward parts of the body; innards.

In′ward Light′, *n.* INNER LIGHT.

in•ward•ly (in′wərd lē), *adv.* **1.** in or on the inside or inner part; internally. **2.** privately; secretly: *Inwardly, he disliked his guest.* **3.** within the self; mentally or spiritually: *to stay inwardly calm.* **4.** in low or soft tones; not aloud. **5.** toward the inside, interior, or center.

in′-your′-face′, *adj. Informal.* involving confrontation; defiant; provocative.

I/O, *Computers.* input/output.

I.O. or **i.o.,** indirect object.

IOC or **I.O.C.,** International Olympic Committee.

i•o•dine (ī′ə dīn′, -din; *in Chem. also* -dēn′) also **i•o•din** (-din), *n.* a nonmetallic halogen element occurring as a grayish-black crystalline solid that sublimes to a dense violet vapor when heated: used as an antiseptic, as a nutritional supplement, and in radiolabeling. Compare RADIOIODINE. Symbol: I; *at. wt.:* 126.904; *at. no.:* 53; *sp. gr.:* (solid) 4.93 at 20°C.

i•o•dize (ī′ə dīz′), *v.t.,* **-dized, -diz•ing.** to treat, impregnate, or affect with iodine or an iodide. —**i′o•di•za′tion,** *n.* —**i′o•diz′er,** *n.*

I′o moth′, *n.* a large North American moth, *Automeris io,* with an eyelike spot on each hind wing.

i•on (ī′ən, ī′on), *n.* **1.** an atom or atom group electrically charged by the loss or gain of electrons, represented by a plus or a minus sign, as a cation (Na⁺, Ca⁺⁺) or anion (Cl⁻). **2.** one of the electrically charged particles formed in a gas by electric discharge. —**i•on′ic,** *adj.*

-ion, a suffix, appearing in words of Latin origin, denoting action or condition, used to form nouns from stems of adjectives (*communion; union*) and verbs (*legion; opinion; suspicion*). Compare -TION.

I•o•na (ī ō′nə), *n.* an island in the Hebrides, off the W coast of Scotland: center of early Celtic Christianity.

I•o•ni•an (ī ō′nē ən), *n.* **1.** a member of the ancient Greek people or group of peoples, principally migrants from Attica and Euboea, who colonized Ionia c1050–1000 B.C. **2.** a native or inhabitant of Ionia. —*adj.* **3.** of or pertaining to Ionia or the Ionians.

I•on•ic (ī on′ik), *adj.* of or designating one of the five classical orders of architecture, characterized by a fluted column with a molded base and a capital composed of two pairs of connected volutes.

ion′ic bond′, *n.* the electrostatic bond between two ions formed through the transfer of one or more electrons.

ioniza′tion cham′ber, *n.* an apparatus for detecting and analyzing ionizing radiation by measuring current between electrodes in a vessel filled with a gas at normal or lower than normal pressure.

i•on•ize (ī′ə nīz′), *v.,* **-ized, -iz•ing.** —*v.t.* **1.** to separate or change into ions. **2.** to produce ions in. —*v.i.* **3.** to become changed into the form of ions, as by dissolving. —**i′on•iz′a•ble,** *adj.* —**i′on•i•za′tion,** *n.*

i•on•o•sphere (ī on′ə sfēr′), *n.* the region of the earth's atmosphere between the stratosphere and the exosphere, consisting of several ionized layers and extending from about 50 to 250 mi. (80 to 400 km) above the surface of the earth. —**i•on′o•spher′ic** (-sfer′ik), *adj.*

i•o•ta (ī ō′tə), *n., pl.* **-tas.** **1.** a very small quantity; jot; whit. **2.** the ninth letter of the Greek alphabet (I, ι).

IOU or **I.O.U.,** *n., pl.* **IOUs, IOU's,** or **I.O.U.'s.** a written acknowledgment of a debt, esp. an informal one consisting only of the letters *IOU,* the sum owed, and the debtor's signature.

-ious, variant of -ous, often with corresponding nouns ending in -ITY: *facetious; hilarious.*

I•o•wa (ī′ə wə), *n.* **1.** a state in the central United States. 2,851,792; 56,290 sq. mi. (145,790 sq. km). *Cap.:* Des Moines. *Abbr.:* IA, Ia., Io. **2.** a river flowing SE from N Iowa to the Mississippi River. 291 mi. (470 km) long. —**I′o•wan,** *adj., n.*

IPA, International Phonetic Alphabet.

ip•e•cac (ip′i kak′), *n.* **1.** a tropical South American shrubby plant, *Cephaelis ipecacuanha,* of the madder family. **2.** the dried root of this plant, used as an emetic. Also called **ip•e•cac•u•an•ha** (ip′i kak′yōō an′ə).

ipr or **i.p.r.,** inches per revolution.

ips or **i.p.s.,** inches per second.

ip•se dix•it (ip′sē dik′sit), *n.* an assertion without proof.

ip•si•lat•er•al (ip′sə lat′ər əl), *adj.* pertaining to, situated on, or affecting the same side of the body. —**ip′si•lat′er•al•ly,** *adv.*

ip•so fac•to (ip′sō fak′tō), *adv.* by the fact itself; by the very nature of the deed: *to be condemned ipso facto.* [< Latin]

IQ, intelligence quotient.

IR, infrared.

Ir, *Chem. Symbol.* iridium.

ir-¹, var. of IN-² (by assimilation) before *r: irradiate.*

ir-², var. of IN-³ (by assimilation) before *r: irreducible.*

IRA or **I.R.A.,** **1.** individual retirement account. **2.** Irish Republican Army.

I•ran (i ran′, i rän′, ī ran′), *n.* **1.** Formerly (until 1935), **Persia.** a republic in SW Asia: an Islamic republic since 1979. 67,540,002; ab. 635,000 sq. mi. (1,644,650 sq. km). *Cap.:* Teheran. **2. Plateau of,** a plateau in SW Asia, mostly in Iran and Afghanistan, extending from the Tigris to the Indus rivers.

Iran., Iranian.

Iran′-Con′tra Affair′, *n.* a secret initiative by members of the National Security Council and the Central Intelligence Agency, revealed in 1986 and 1987, to sell arms to Iran in exchange for hostages held there from 1979 to 1981, the revenue diverted to buy military assistance for the Contras in Nicaragua.

I•ra•ni•an (i rā′nē ən, i rä′-, ī rā′-), *adj.* **1.** of or pertaining to Iran or its inhabitants. **2.** of, pertaining to, or denoting one of the two major branches of the Indo-Iranian languages, including Persian, Kurdish, Baluchi, and Pashto. —*n.* **3.** the Iranian languages. **4.** a native or inhabitant of Iran.

I•raq (i rak′, i räk′), *n.* a republic in SW Asia, N of Saudi Arabia and W of Iran, centering in the Tigris-Euphrates basin of Mesopotamia. 22,219,289; 172,000 sq. mi. (445,480 sq. km). *Cap.:* Baghdad. —**I•ra′qi,** *adj., n.*

i•ras•ci•ble (i ras′ə bəl), *adj.* **1.** easily provoked to anger; very irritable. **2.** characterized or produced by anger: *an irascible response.* —**i•ras′ci•bil′i•ty, i•ras′ci•ble•ness,** *n.* —**i•ras′ci•bly,** *adv.*

i•rate (ī rāt′, ī′rāt), *adj.* **1.** angry or enraged. **2.** arising from or characterized by anger: *an irate letter.* —**i•rate′ly,** *adv.* —**i•rate′ness,** *n.*

ire (ī͞er), *n.* intense anger; wrath. —**ire′ful,** *adj.* —**ire′ful•ly,** *adv.* —**ire′ful•ness,** *n.*

Ire•land (ī͞er′lənd), *n.* **1.** Latin, **Hibernia.** an island of the British Isles, W of Great Britain, comprising Northern Ireland and the Republic of Ireland. 32,375 sq. mi. (83,850 sq. km). **2. Republic of.** Formerly, **Irish Free State** (1922–37), **Eire** (1937–49). a republic occupying most of the island of Ireland. 3,555,500; 27,137 sq. mi. (70,285 sq. km). *Cap.:* Dublin. Irish, **Eire.** —**Ire′land•er,** *n.*

i•ren•ic (ī ren′ik, ī rē′nik) also **i•ren′i•cal,** *adj.* tending to promote peace or reconciliation; peaceful or conciliatory. —**i•ren′i•cal•ly,** *adv.*

ir•i•des•cent (ir′i des′ənt), *adj.* displaying a play of lustrous changing colors like those of the rainbow. —**ir′i•des′cence,** *n.* —**ir′i•des′cent•ly,** *adv.*

i•rid•i•um (i rid′ē əm), *n.* a precious metallic element resembling platinum: used in alloys. Symbol: Ir; *at. wt.:* 192.2; *at. no.:* 77; *sp. gr.:* 22.4 at 20°C.

I•ri•jah (ī rī′jə), *n.* a soldier who arrested Jeremiah while the Babylonians were besieging Jerusalem. Jer. 37:11–14.

i•ris (ī′ris), *n., pl.* **i•ris•es;** *esp. for 1* **ir•i•des** (ir′i dēz′, ī′ri-); *for 2, 3* **i•ris. 1.** the contractile, circular diaphragm forming the colored portion of the eye and containing an opening, the pupil, in its center. **2.** any plant of the genus *Iris,* having flowers with three upright petals and three drooping, petallike sepals. **3.** a flower of this plant. **4.** (*cap.*) an ancient Greek goddess of the rainbow and messenger of the gods. **5.** a rainbow. **6.** an iris-in or iris-out.

I•rish (ī′rish), *n.* **1.** (*used with a pl. v.*) **a.** the inhabitants of Ireland. **b.** natives of Ireland or persons of Irish ancestry living outside Ireland. **2.** the Celtic language of Ireland, now largely supplanted as a vernacular by English. *Abbr.:* Ir —*adj.* **3.** of or pertaining to Ireland, its inhabitants, or the language Irish. —*Idiom.* **4. get one's Irish up,** *Informal.* to become angry or outraged. —**I′rish•ly,** *adv.*

I′rish Chris′tian Broth′er, *n.* BROTHER OF THE CHRISTIAN SCHOOLS (def. 2).

I′rish cof′fee, *n.* a mixture of hot coffee and Irish whiskey, sweetened and topped with whipped cream.

I′rish Free′ State′, *n.* a former name of the Republic of IRELAND.

I′rish pota′to, *n.* POTATO (def. 1).

I′rish Repub′lican Ar′my, *n.* an underground Irish nationalist organization founded to work for Irish independence from England: its Provisional wing follows a policy of terrorism. *Abbr.:* IRA, I.R.A.

I′rish set′ter, *n.* one of an Irish breed of large setters having a moderately long, silky mahogany-red coat.

I′rish stew′, *n.* a stew, esp. of lamb, with potatoes, onions, etc.

I′rish ter′rier, *n.* one of an Irish breed of medium-sized terriers having a dense, wiry reddish coat and a short beard.

I′rish wa′ter span′iel, *n.* one of an Irish breed of large water spaniels having a thick, curly liver-colored coat, a curly topknot, and short hair on the face and thin, tapering tail.

I′rish whis′key, *n.* any whiskey made in Ireland, characteristically a product of barley.

I′rish wolf′hound, *n.* one of an Irish breed of large, very tall dogs with a rough, wiry coat.

i•ri•tis (ī rī′tis), *n.* inflammation of the iris of the eye. —**i•rit•ic** (ī rit′ik), *adj.*

irk (ûrk), *v.t.* to irritate, annoy, or exasperate.

irk•some (ûrk′səm), *adj.* annoying; irritating; exasperating; tiresome: *irksome restrictions.* —**irk′some•ly,** *adv.* —**irk′some•ness,** *n.*

i•ron (ī′ərn), *n.* **1.** a ductile, malleable, silver-white metallic element, used in its impure carbon-containing forms for making tools, implements, machinery, etc. Symbol: Fe; *at. wt.:* 55.847; *at. no.:* 26; *sp. gr.:* 7.86 at 20°C. **2.** something hard, strong, unyielding, or the like: *hearts of iron.* **3.** an instrument, utensil, weapon, etc., made of iron. **4.** an appliance with a flat metal bottom, used when heated, as by electricity, to press or smooth clothes, linens, etc. **5.** any of a series of nine ironheaded golf clubs having progressively sloped-back faces, used for driving or lofting the ball. Compare WOOD¹ (def. 6). **6.** a branding iron. **7.** a harpoon. **8. irons,** shackles or fetters. **9.** a sword. —*adj.* **10.** of, con-

I

taining, or made of iron. **11.** resembling iron in firmness, strength, color, etc. **12.** stern; harsh; cruel. **13.** inflexible; unrelenting. **14.** strong; robust; healthy. **15.** holding or binding strongly: *an iron grip.* —*v.t.* **16.** to smooth or press with a heated iron, as clothes or linens. **17.** to shackle or fetter with irons. —*v.i.* **18.** to press clothes, linens, etc., with an iron. **19. iron out,** to clear away (difficulties). —*Idiom.* **20. in irons, a.** (of a sailing vessel) unable to maneuver because of the position of the sails with relation to the direction of the wind. **b.** Also, **into irons.** in shackles or fetters. **21. irons in the fire,** undertakings; projects. —**i′ron•like′,** *adj.*

I′ron Age′, *n.* **1.** the period in the history of humankind, following the Stone Age and the Bronze Age, marked by the use of implements and weapons made of iron: in Europe generally regarded as extending from the first millennium B.C. to the early first century A.D.. **2.** (*often l.c.*) (in Greek and Roman myth) the last and worst of the ages of the human race, characterized by danger, corruption, and toil.

i•ron•clad (*adj.* ī′ərn klad′; *n.* -klad′), *adj.* **1.** covered or cased with iron plates, as a vessel; armor-plated. **2.** very rigid or exacting; inflexible; unbreakable: *an ironclad contract.* —*n.* **3.** a wooden warship of the middle or late 19th century having iron or steel armor plating.

I′ron cur′tain, *n.* (*sometimes caps.*) a barrier to understanding and the exchange of information created by the hostility of one country toward another, esp. such a barrier between the Soviet Union or its allies and other countries.

I′ron Duke′, *n.* epithet of the first Duke of Wellington.

i•ron•fist•ed (ī′ərn fis′tid), *adj.* ruthless and tyrannical.

i′ron hand′, *n.* strict or harsh control. —**i′ron-hand′ed,** *adj.*

i′ron horse′, *n.* Older Use. a locomotive.

i•ron•ic (ī ron′ik) also **i•ron′i•cal,** *adj.* **1.** of, pertaining to, containing, or characterized by irony or mockery: *an ironic smile.* **2.** using or prone to irony. —**i•ron′i•cal•ly,** *adv.* —**i•ron′i•cal•ness,** *n.*

i•ron•ing (ī′ər ning), *n.* **1.** the act or process of smoothing or pressing clothes, linens, etc., with a heated iron. **2.** articles of clothing or the like that have been or are to be ironed.

i′roning board′, *n.* a flat, cloth-covered board on which clothing, linens, or similar articles are ironed.

I′ron La′dy, *n.* epithet of Margaret Thatcher.

i′ron lung′, *n.* a rigid respirator that encloses the whole body except the head and in which alternate pulsations of high and low pressure induce normal breathing movements or force air into and out of the lungs.

i′ron man′, *n.* a person of great physical endurance who can perform a given task or job tirelessly.

i′ron-on′, *adj.* designed to be applied with heat and pressure, as by an iron: *an iron-on patch for pants.*

i′ron ox′ide, *n.* FERRIC OXIDE.

i′ron pyri′tes or **py′rite),** *n.* PYRITE.

i•ron•side (ī′ərn sīd′), *n.* a strong person with great power of endurance or resistance.

I•ron•side (ī′ərn sīd′), *n.* Henry Allan, 1876–1951, U.S. clergyman and writer.

i′ron•smith (ī′ərn smith′), *n.* a worker in iron; blacksmith.

i•ron•stone (ī′ərn stōn′), *n.* **1.** any iron-bearing mineral or rock with siliceous impurities. **2.** Also called **i′ronstone chi′na.** a hard white stoneware.

i•ron•ware (ī′ərn wâr′), *n.* articles of iron, as pots, kettles, or tools; hardware.

i•ron•weed (ī′ərn wēd′), *n.* any North American composite plant of the genus *Vernonia* having tubular, chiefly purple or red disk flowers.

i•ron•wood (ī′ərn wŏŏd′), *n.* any of various trees, as the hornbeam, yielding a hard, heavy wood.

i•ron•work (ī′ərn wûrk′), *n.* objects or parts of objects made of iron: *ornamental ironwork.*

i•ron•works (ī′ərn wûrks′), *n., pl.* **-works.** (*used with a sing. or pl. v.*) a place where iron is smelted or where it is cast or wrought.

i•ro•ny (ī′rə nē, ī′ər-), *n., pl.* **-nies. 1.** the use of words to convey a meaning that is the opposite of its literal meaning. **2.** an outcome of events contrary to what was, or might have been, expected. **3.** the incongruity of this.

Ir•o•quoi•an (ir′ə kwoi′ən), *n.* **1.** a family of American Indian languages, including Huron, the languages of the Iroquois Five Nations, and Cherokee, spoken or formerly spoken in the E Great Lakes region and parts of the eastern U.S. **2.** a member of an Iroquoian-speaking people. —*adj.* **3.** of or pertaining to the Iroquois or the language family Iroquoian.

Ir•o•quois (ir′ə kwoi′, -kwoiz′), *n., pl.* **-quois.** a member of any of the American Indian peoples, orig. centered in New York, that comprise the Five Nations confederacy: surviving Iroquois live primarily in New York, Wisconsin, Oklahoma, Ontario, and Quebec.

ir•ra•di•ance (i rā′dē əns), *n.* incident flux of radiant energy per unit area.

ir•ra•di•ate (i rā′dē āt′), *v.*, **-at•ed, -at•ing. 1.** to shed rays of light upon; illuminate. **2.** to illumine intellectually or spiritually. **3.** to radiate (light, illumination, etc.). **4.** to heat with radiant energy. **5.** to expose to radiation, as for medical treatment. —**ir•ra′di•at′ing•ly,** *adv.* —**ir•ra′di•a′tive,** *adj.* —**ir•ra′di•a′tor,** *n.*

ir•ra•di•a•tion (i rā′dē ā′shən), *n.* **1.** the act of irradiating. **2.** the

state of being irradiated. **3.** a ray of light; beam. **4.** *Optics.* the apparent enlargement of an object when seen against a dark background. **5.** the use of x-rays or other forms of radiation for treatment of disease, manufacture of vitamin D, etc. **6.** exposure to x-rays or other radiation. **7.** IRRADIANCE. **8.** intellectual or spiritual enlightenment.

ir•ra•tion•al (i rash′ə nl), *adj.* **1.** lacking the faculty of reason; deprived of reason. **2.** lacking sound judgment or logic: *irrational arguments.* **3.** not controlled or governed by reason: *irrational behavior.* **4. a.** (of a number) not capable of being expressed exactly as a ratio of two integers. **b.** (of a function) not capable of being expressed exactly as a ratio of two polynomials. **c.** (of an equation) having an unknown under a radical sign or, alternately, with a fractional exponent. **5. a.** of or pertaining to a syllable in Greek or Latin prosody whose quantity does not fit the meter. **b.** noting a foot containing such a syllable. —*n.* **6.** IRRATIONAL NUMBER. —**ir•ra′tion•al•ly,** *adv.* —**ir•ra′tion•al•ness,** *n.*

irra′tional num′ber, *n.* a number that cannot be exactly expressed as a ratio of two integers.

ir•rec•on•cil•a•ble (i rek′ən sī′lə bəl, i rek′ən sī′-), *adj.* **1.** incapable of being brought into harmony or agreement; incompatible. **2.** incapable of being made to acquiesce or compromise; implacably opposed: *irreconcilable enemies.* —*n.* **3.** a person or thing that is irreconcilable. **4.** a person who is opposed to agreement or compromise. —**ir•rec′on•cil′a•bil′i•ty, ir•rec′on•cil′a•ble•ness,** *n.* —**ir•rec′on•cil′a•bly,** *adv.*

ir•re•cu•sa•ble (ir′i kyōō′zə bəl), *adj.* not subject to objection to or rejection. —**ir′re•cu′sa•bly,** *adv.*

ir•re•deem•a•ble (ir′i dē′mə bəl), *adj.* **1.** not redeemable; incapable of being bought back or paid off. **2.** irremediable; irreparable; hopeless. **3.** being beyond redemption: *an irredeemable villain.* **4.** (of paper money) not convertible into gold or silver. —**ir′re•deem′a•bly,** *adv.*

ir•re•den•ta (ir′i den′tə), *n.* a region under the political jurisdiction of one nation but related to another through cultural, historical, or ethnic ties.

ir•re•duc•i•ble (ir′i dōō′sə bəl, -dyōō′-), *adj.* **1.** not reducible; incapable of being reduced, diminished, or further simplified. **2.** incapable of being brought into a different condition or form. —**ir′re•duc′i•bil′i•ty, ir′re•duc′i•ble•ness,** *n.* —**ir′re•duc′i•bly,** *adv.*

ir•ref•ra•ga•ble (i ref′rə gə bəl), *adj.* not to be disputed or contested. —**ir•ref′ra•ga•bil′i•ty,** *n.* —**ir•ref′ra•ga•bly,** *adv.*

ir•re•fran•gi•ble (ir′i fran′jə bəl), *adj.* **1.** not to be broken or violated. **2.** incapable of being refracted. —**ir′re•fran′gi•bil′i•ty, ir′re•fran′gi•ble•ness,** *n.* —**ir′re•fran′gi•bly,** *adv.*

ir•ref•u•ta•ble (i ref′yə tə bəl, ir′i fyōō′tə bəl), *adj.* not refutable; incontrovertible: *an irrefutable argument.* —**ir•ref′u•ta•bil′i•ty, ir•ref′u•ta•ble•ness,** *n.* —**ir•ref′u•ta•bly,** *adv.*

ir•re•gard•less (ir′i gärd′lis), *adv.* Nonstandard. regardless. —**Usage.** IRREGARDLESS is considered nonstandard because of the two negative elements *ir-* and *-less.* Those who use the word, including on occasion educated speakers, may do so from a desire to add emphasis. IRREGARDLESS first appeared in the early 20th century and was perhaps popularized by its use in a comic radio program of the 1930s.

ir•reg•u•lar (i reg′yə lər), *adj.* **1.** lacking symmetry, even shape, formal arrangement, etc.: *an irregular pattern.* **2.** variable in timing or rhythm; erratic: *irregular intervals.* **3.** not conforming to established rules, etiquette, etc. **4.** not according to rule or to the accepted principle, method, course, order, etc. **5.** not conforming to the prevalent pattern of formation, inflection, etc., in a language, as English verbs that do not form the past tense by adding *-ed:* the irregular verbs keep and see. **6.** flawed, damaged, or failing to meet a specific standard of manufacture: *a sale of irregular shirts.* —*n.* **7.** a person or thing that is irregular. **8.** a product or material that does not meet specifications or standards of the manufacturer, as one having imperfections in its pattern.

ir•reg•u•lar•i•ty (i reg′yə lar′i tē), *n., pl.* **-ties. 1.** the quality or state of being irregular. **2.** something irregular. **3.** a breach of rules, customs, etc. **4.** occasional mild constipation.

ir•rel•e•vance (i rel′ə vəns), *n.* **1.** the quality or condition of being irrelevant. **2.** an irrelevant thing, act, etc.

ir•rel•e•van•cy (i rel′ə vən sē), *n., pl.* **-cies.** IRRELEVANCE.

ir•rel•e•vant (i rel′ə vənt), *adj.* not relevant; not applicable or pertinent. —**ir•rel′e•vant•ly,** *adv.* —**Pronunciation.** The pronunciation of IRRELEVANT as (i rev′ə lənt), as if spelled *irrevelant,* is the result of metathesis, the transposition of two sounds, in this case, the (l) and the (v). RELEVANT, the base word, is occasionally subject to the same process. Analogy with words like *prevalent* and *equivalent* may play a role.

ir•re•li•gion (ir′i lij′ən), *n.* **1.** lack of religion. **2.** hostility or indifference to religion; impiety. —**ir′re•li′gion•ist,** *n.*

ir•re•li•gious (ir′i lij′əs), *adj.* **1.** not religious; not practicing a religion and feeling no religious impulses. **2.** showing or characterized by a lack of religion. **3.** showing indifference or hostility to religion.

ir•re•me•di•a•ble (ir′i mē′dē ə bəl), *adj.* not admitting of remedy, cure, or repair. —**ir′re•me′di•a•ble•ness,** *n.* —**ir′re•me′di•a•bly,** *adv.*

ir•rep•a•ra•ble (i rep′ər ə bəl), *adj.* not reparable; incapable of being rectified, remedied, or made good: *an irreparable mistake.* —**ir•rep′a•ra•bil′i•ty, ir•rep′a•ra•ble•ness,** *n.* —**ir•rep′a•ra•bly,** *adv.*

ir•re•place•a•ble (ir′i plā′sə bəl), *adj.* incapable of being replaced; unique: *an irreplaceable vase.* —**ir′re•place′a•bly,** *adv.*

ir•re•press•i•ble (ir′i pres′ə bəl), *adj.* incapable of being repressed or restrained; uncontrollable: *irrepressible laughter.* —**ir′re·press′i·bil′i·ty,** **ir′re·press′i·ble·ness,** *n.* —**ir′re·press′i·bly,** *adv.*

ir·re·sist·i·ble (ir′i zis′tə bəl), *adj.* **1.** not resistible; incapable of being resisted or withstood: *an irresistible impulse.* **2.** enticing; alluring; tempting to possess: *an irresistible necklace.* —**ir′re·sist′i·bil′i·ty, ir′re·sist′i·ble·ness,** *n.* —**ir′re·sist′i·bly,** *adv.*

ir·res·o·lute (i rez′ə loot′), *adj.* not resolute; doubtful; infirm of purpose; vacillating. —**ir·res′o·lute′ly,** *adv.* —**ir·res′o·lute′ness, ir·res′o·lu′tion,** *n.*

ir·re·spec·tive (ir′i spek′tiv), *adj.* without regard to; ignoring or discounting (usu. fol. by *of*): *Irrespective of the weather, I should go.* —**ir′re·spec′tive·ly,** *adv.*

ir·re·spon·si·ble (ir′i spon′sə bəl), *adj.* **1.** said, done, or characterized by a lack of a sense of responsibility. **2.** not capable of or qualified for responsibility. **3.** not responsible, answerable, or accountable to higher authority. **4.** an irresponsible person. —**ir′re·spon′si·bil′i·ty, ir′re·spon′si·ble·ness,** *n.* —**ir′re·spon′si·bly,** *adv.*

ir·re·spon·sive (ir′i spon′siv), *adj.* not responsive; not responding or ready to respond. —**ir′re·spon′sive·ness,** *n.*

ir·rev·er·ence (i rev′ər əns), *n.* **1.** the quality of being irreverent; lack of reverence or respect. **2.** an irreverent act or statement. **3.** the condition of not being venerated or respected. —**ir·rev′er·ent,** *adj.* —**ir·rev′er·ent·ly,** *adv.*

ir·re·vers·i·ble (ir′i vûr′sə bəl), *adj.* not reversible; incapable of being changed: *His refusal is irreversible.* —**ir′re·vers′i·bil′i·ty, ir′re·vers′i·ble·ness,** *n.* —**ir′re·vers′i·bly,** *adv.*

ir·rev·o·ca·ble (i rev′ə kə bəl), *adj.* not to be revoked or recalled; unalterable: *an irrevocable commitment to quality.* —**ir·rev′o·ca·bil′i·ty, ir·rev′o·ca·ble·ness,** *n.* —**ir·rev′o·ca·bly,** *adv.*

ir·ri·gate (ir′i gāt′), *v.t.,* **-gat·ed, -gat·ing.** **1.** to supply (land) with water by artificial means, as by diverting streams, flooding, or spraying. **2.** to supply or wash (an orifice, wound, etc.) with a spray or a flow of some liquid. **3.** to moisten; wet. —**ir′ri·ga·ble,** *adj.* —**ir′ri·ga·bly,** *adv.* —**ir′ri·ga′tion,** *n.* —**ir′ri·ga′tion·al,** *adj.* —**ir′ri·ga′tive,** *adj.* —**ir′ri·ga′tor,** *n.*

ir·ri·ta·ble (ir′i tə bəl), *adj.* **1.** easily irritated or annoyed; readily excited to impatience or anger. **2.** *Biol.* able to be excited to a characteristic action or function by the application of a stimulus. **3.** *Pathol.* abnormally excitable or sensitive to stimulation. —**ir′ri·ta·bil′i·ty, ir′ri·ta·ble·ness,** *n.* —**ir′ri·ta·bly,** *adv.*

ir·ri·tant (ir′i tnt), *adj.* **1.** tending to cause irritation; irritating. —*n.* **2.** anything that irritates. **3.** a biological, chemical, or physical agent that stimulates a characteristic function or elicits a response, esp. an inflammatory response. —**ir′ri·tan·cy,** *n.*

ir·ri·tate (ir′i tāt′), *v.,* **-tat·ed, -tat·ing.** —*v.t.* **1.** to excite to impatience or anger; annoy. **2.** *Physiol., Biol.* to excite (a living system) to some characteristic action or function. **3.** *Pathol.* to bring (a body part) to an abnormally excited or sensitive condition. —*v.i.* **4.** to cause irritation or become irritated. —**ir′ri·ta′tor,** *n.*

ir·ri·ta·tion (ir′i tā′shən), *n.* **1.** the act of irritating or the state of being irritated. **2.** something that irritates. **3.** *Physiol., Pathol.* **a.** the bringing of a bodily part or organ to an abnormally excited or sensitive condition. **b.** the condition itself.

ir·rupt (i rupt′), *v.i.* **1.** to break or burst in suddenly. **2.** to manifest violent activity or emotion, as a group of persons. **3.** (of animals) to increase suddenly in numbers through a lessening of the number of deaths. —**ir·rup′tion,** *n.* —**ir·rup′tive,** *adj.* —**ir·rup′tive·ly,** *adv.*

IRS, Internal Revenue Service.

Ir·vine (ûr′vīn), *n.* a city in SW California. 125,624.

Ir·ving (ûr′ving), *n.* **1. Washington,** 1783–1859, U.S. essayist, story writer, and historian. **2.** a city in NE Texas, near Dallas. 164,617.

is (iz), *v.* 3rd pers. sing. pres. indic. of BE.

Is., **1.** Isaiah. **2.** island. **3.** isle.

I·saac (ī′zək), *n.* a son of Abraham and Sarah, and father of Jacob. Gen. 21:1–4.

I·sa·iah (ī zā′ə; *esp. Brit.* ī zī′ə), *n.* **1.** a Major Prophet of the 8th century B.C. **2.** a book of the Bible bearing his name.

-isation, *Chiefly Brit.* var. of -IZATION.

ISBN, International Standard Book Number.

Is·car·i·ot (i skar′ē ət), *n.* the surname of Judas, the betrayer of Jesus. Mark 3:19; 14:10, 11. [< Late Latin *Iscariōta* < Greek *Iskariṓtēs* < Hebrew *īsh-qərīyōth* man of *Kerioth* a village in Palestine].

is·chi·um (is′kē əm), *n., pl.* **-chi·a** (-kē ə). **1.** the backward-facing lower bone of each half of the vertebrate pelvis; the lower portion of either innominate bone in humans. **2.** either of the bones on which the body rests when sitting. —**is′chi·ad′ic, is′chi·at′ic, is′chi·al,** *adj.*

-ise, *Chiefly Brit.* var. of -IZE.

I·seult or **Y·seult** (i soolt′), *n.* a heroine of Arthurian legend, the wife of King Mark of Cornwall and the lover of Tristram.

-ish[1], **1.** a suffix forming adjectives from nouns, with the meanings "pertaining to" (*British; Spanish*); "after the manner of," "having the characteristics of," "like" (*babyish; girlish; mulish*); "addicted to," "inclined or tending to" (*bookish; freakish*); "near or about" (*fiftyish; sevenish*). **2.** a suffix forming adjectives from other adjectives, with the meanings "somewhat," "rather" (*oldish; reddish; sweetish*).

-ish[2], a formative occurring in verbs borrowed from French (*nourish; perish*), used rarely to form verbs in English from Latin bases (*extinguish*).

Ish-bo·sheth (ish bō′shith), *n.* a son and successor of Saul. II Sam. 2–4.

Ish·ma·el (ish′mē əl, -mā-), *n.* **1.** the son of Abraham and Hagar: both he and Hagar were cast out of Abraham's family by Sarah. Gen. 16:11, 12. **2.** outcast; pariah.

Ish·ma·el·ite (ish′mē ə līt′, -mā ə-, -mə-), *n.* **1.** a member of a Biblical people descended from Ishmael, who is regarded in Muslim tradition as the progenitor of the Arabs. **2.** ISHMAEL (def. 2).

Ish·tar (ish′tär), *n.* the Assyrian and Babylonian goddess of love and war, identified with the Phoenician Astarte and the Semitic Ashtoreth.

I·sis (ī′sis), *n.* an Egyptian goddess of fertility, the sister and wife of Osiris and mother of Horus, and usually represented as a woman with a cow's horns with the solar disk between them: later worshiped in the Greek and Roman empires.

Is·lam (is läm′, -lam′, iz-, is′ləm, iz′-), *n.* **1.** the religion of the Muslims, as set forth in the Koran, that teaches that there is only one God, Allah, and that Muhammad is His prophet. **2.** the whole body of Muslim believers, their civilization, and the countries in which theirs is the dominant religion. —**Is·lam′ic, Is/lam·it′ic** (-lə mit′ik), *adj.*

Is·lam·a·bad (is lä′mə bäd′, -lam′ə bad′), *n.* the capital of Pakistan, in the N part, near Rawalpindi. 201,000.

Islam′ic cal′endar, *n.* the lunar calendar used by Muslims and reckoned from A.D. 622: the calendar year consists of 354 days and contains 12 months.

is·land (ī′lənd), *n.* **1.** a tract of land completely surrounded by water and not large enough to be called a continent. **2.** something resembling an island, esp. in being isolated. **3.** a freestanding unit with a counter or work surface on top, situated in the middle area of a room so as to permit access from all sides. **4.** a clump of woodland in a prairie. **5.** an isolated hill. **6.** an isolated portion of anatomical tissue differing in structure from the surrounding tissue. —*v.t.* **7.** to make into an island. **8.** to dot with islands. **9.** to place on an island; isolate. —*Proverb.* **10. No man is an island,** everyone is an interdependent part of society. John Donne, *Meditation XVII.*

is·land·er (ī′lən dər), *n.* a native or inhabitant of an island.

isle (īl), *n., v.,* **isled, isl·ing.** —*n.* **1.** a small island. **2.** any island. —*v.t.* **3.** to make into or as if into an isle. **4.** to place on or as if on an isle.

is·let (ī′lit), *n.* a very small island. —**is′let·ed,** *adj.*

is′let of Lang′er·hans (läng′ər häns′, -hänz′), *n.* any of the clusters

I

LARGEST ISLANDS OF THE WORLD

Name	Location (Sovereignty)	Area sq. mi.	Area sq. km	Leading City
Greenland	N Atlantic (Danish)	840,000	2,175,000	Godthab
New Guinea	SW Pacific (Papua New Guinean and Indonesian)	316,000	818,000	Port Moresby; Jayapura
Borneo	SW Pacific (Indonesian, Malaysian, and Bruneian)	290,000	750,000	Banjermasin; Kuching; Bandar Seri Begawan
Madagascar	W Indian Ocean (Malagasy)	227,800	590,000	Antananarivo
Baffin Island	Canadian Arctic (Canadian)	190,000	492,000	Frobisher Bay
Sumatra	E Indian Ocean (Indonesian)	164,147	425,141	Medan
Honshu	NW Pacific (Japanese)	88,851	230,124	Tokyo
Ellesmere Island	Canadian Arctic (Canadian)	82,119	212,688	
Victoria Island	Canadian Arctic (Canadian)	81,930	212,119	-
Sulawesi	SW Pacific (Indonesian)	72,986	189,034	Ujung Pandang
South Island	SW Pacific (New Zealand)	58,093	150,460	Christchurch
Java	E Indian Ocean (Indonesian)	51,032	132,173	Jakarta
North Island	SW Pacific (New Zealand)	44,281	114,690	Wellington
Cuba	Caribbean (Cuban)	44,218	114,525	Havana
Newfoundland	NW Atlantic (Canadian)	42,734	110,680	St. John's
Luzon	W mid-Pacific (Philippine)	40,420	104,688	Manila
Iceland	N Atlantic (Iceland)	39,698	102,820	Reykjavik
Mindanao	W mid-Pacific (Philippine)	36,537	94,631	Davao
Novaya Zemlya	Russian Arctic (Russian)	35,000	90,650	-

of endocrine cells in the pancreas that are specialized to secrete insulin. Also called **is′land of Lang′erhans.**

isls., islands.

ism (iz′əm), *n.* a distinctive doctrine, theory, system, or practice: *capitalism, socialism, and other isms.*

-ism, a suffix appearing in loanwords from Greek, where it was used to form action nouns from verbs (*baptism*); on this model, used as a suffix in the formation of nouns denoting action or practice, condition, principles, doctrines, a usage or characteristic, devotion, etc.: *Darwinism; despotism; plagiarism; realism; witticism.* Compare -IST, -IZE.

Is•ma•i•li•a or **Is•ma′i•li•ya** (is′mä ə lē′ə, -mī ə-), *n.* a seaport at the midpoint of the Suez Canal, in NE Egypt. 236,300.

Is•ma′i•li•ya (is′mä ə lē′ə, -mī ə-), *n.* **1.** a Shi′ite sect having an esoteric philosophy. **2.** ISMAILIA. —**Is•ma•il′i** (-il′ē) **Is•ma•il′i•an** (-il′ē-ən), *n., adj.*

isn′t (iz′ənt), contraction of *is not.*

i•so•bar (ī′sə bär′), *n.* a line drawn on a weather map or chart that connects points at which the barometric pressure is the same. —**i′so•bar′ic** (-bar′-), *adj.* —**i′so•bar•ism** (-bär′-), *n.*

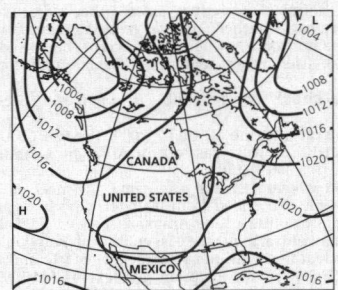

isobar

i•so•late (ī′sə lāt′, is′ə-), *v.t.,* **-lat•ed, -lat•ing.** **1.** to set or place apart; detach or separate so as to be alone. **2.** to keep (an infected person) from contact with noninfected persons; quarantine. —**i′so•la′tion,** *n.*

i•so•la•tion•ism (ī′sə lā′shə niz′əm, is′ə-), *n.* the policy or doctrine that peace and economic advancement can best be achieved by isolating one′s country from alliances and commitments with other countries. —**i′so•la′tion•ist,** *n., adj.*

i•so•mer (ī′sə mər), *n.* a chemical compound or nuclide that displays isomerism.

i•som•er•ism (ī som′ə riz′əm), *n.* **1.** the relation of two or more compounds, radicals, or ions that are composed of the same kinds and numbers of atoms but differ from each other in structural or spatial arrangement. **2.** the relation of two or more nuclides that have the same atomic number and mass number but different energy levels and half-lives. **3.** the state or condition of being isomerous. —**i•so•mer•ic** (ī′sə mer′ik), *adj.* —**i′so•mer′i•cal•ly,** *adv.*

i•som•er•ous (ī som′ər əs), *adj.* **1.** having an equal number of parts, markings, etc. **2.** (of a flower) having the same number of members in each whorl.

i•so•met•ric (ī′sə me′trik), *adj.* Also, **i′so•met′ri•cal.** **1.** of, pertaining to, or having equality of measure. **2.** of or pertaining to isometric exercise. **3.** noting or pertaining to a system of crystallization that is characterized by three equal axes at right angles to one another. **4.** designating a method of projection (**isomet′ric projec′tion**) in which a three-dimensional object is represented by a drawing (**i′somet′ric draw′ing**) having the horizontal edges of the object drawn usu. at a 30° angle and all verticals projected perpendicularly from a horizontal base. —*n.* **5.** **isometrics,** ISOMETRIC EXERCISE (def. 1). **6.** an isometric drawing. —**i′so•met′ri•cal•ly,** *adv.*

i′so•met′ric ex′ercise, *n.* **1.** a program of exercises in which a muscle group is tensed against another muscle group or an immovable object so that the muscles may contract without shortening. **2.** any specific exercise of this type.

i•so•mor•phic (ī′sə môr′fik), *adj.* **1.** *Biol.* having the same form or appearance. **2.** ISOMORPHOUS. **3.** *Math.* pertaining to two sets related by an isomorphism.

i•so•mor•phism (ī′sə môr′fiz əm), *n.* **1.** the state or property of being isomorphous or isomorphic. **2.** *Math.* a one-to-one relation onto the map between two sets, which preserves the relations existing between elements in its domain.

i•so•mor•phous (ī′sə môr′fəs), *adj.* (of a chemical compound or mineral) capable of crystallizing in a form similar to that of another compound or mineral.

i•so•pod (ī′sə pod′), *n.* **1.** any flattened crustacean of the order Isopoda, having seven pairs of similar legs, as wood lice and various aquatic forms. —*adj.* **2.** of or pertaining to the Isopoda. —**i•sop•o•dan** (ī sop′ə dn), *adj.,* *n.* —**i•sop′o•dous,** *adj.*

i•so•pro•pyl (ī′sə prō′pil), *n.* the univalent group C_3H_7, an isomer of the propyl group.

i′sopro′pyl al′cohol, *n.* a colorless, flammable liquid, C_3H_8O, used in antifreeze and rubbing alcohol and as a solvent.

i•sos•ce•les (ī sos′ə lēz′), *adj.* (of a straight-sided plane figure) having two sides equal: *an isosceles triangle; an isosceles trapezoid.*

i•sos•ta•sy or **i•sos•ta•cy** (ī sos′tə sē), *n.* **1.** the equilibrium of the earth′s crust, a condition in which the forces tending to elevate balance those tending to depress. **2.** the state in which pressures from every side are equal. —**i•so•stat•ic** (ī′sə stat′ik), *adj.*

i•so•ster•ic (ī′sə ster′ik), *adj.* having the same number of valence electrons in the same configuration but differing in the kinds and numbers of atoms.

i•so•therm (ī′sə thûrm′), *n.* **1.** a line on a weather map or chart connecting points having equal temperature. **2.** a curve representing changes in volume and pressure while at the same temperature.

i•so•ther•mal (ī′sə thûr′məl) also **i′so•ther′mic,** *adj.* **1.** occurring at constant temperature. **2.** pertaining to an isotherm. —**i′so•ther′mal•ly,** *adv.*

i•so•ton•ic (ī′sə ton′ik), *adj.* **1.** of or pertaining to solutions with equal osmotic pressure. **2.** *Physiol.* **a.** of or pertaining to a muscular contraction in which the muscle shortens while tension increases, as in continuous lifting. **b.** of or pertaining to a solution containing the same salt concentration as mammalian blood. —**i′so•to•nic′i•ty** (-tə nis′i tē), *n.*

i•so•tope (ī′sə tōp′), *n.* one of two or more forms of a chemical element having the same number of protons, or the same atomic number, but having different numbers of neutrons, or different atomic weights. —**i′so•top′ic** (-top′ik), *adj.* —**i′so•top′i•cal•ly,** *adv.* —**i•sot•o•py** (ī sot′ə pē, ī′sə tō′pē), *n.*

i•so•trop•ic (ī′sə trop′ik, -trō′pik) also **i•sot•ro•pous** (ī so′trə pəs), *adj.* having physical properties, as elasticity or transmissivity, that are the same in measurement along all axes or directions. —**i•sot′ro•py,** *n.*

Is•ra•el (iz′rē əl, -rā-), *n.* **1.** a republic in SW Asia, on the Mediterranean: formed as a Jewish state in 1948. 5,534,672; 7984 sq. mi. (20,679 sq. km). *Cap.:* Jerusalem. **2.** the people traditionally descended from Jacob; the Jewish people. **3.** a name given to Jacob after he had wrestled with the angel. Gen. 32:28. **4.** the northern kingdom of the Hebrews, including 10 of the 12 tribes. Compare JUDAH (def. 3). **5.** a group considered by its members or by others as God′s chosen people. [< Latin *Isrāēl* < Greek *Isrāēl* < Hebrew *Yisrā′ēl* lit., God perseveres]

Is•rae•li (iz rā′lē), *n., pl.* **-lis,** (*esp. collectively*) **-li,** *adj.* —*n.* **1.** a native or inhabitant of modern Israel. —*adj.* **2.** of or pertaining to modern Israel or its inhabitants.

Is•ra•el•ite (iz′rē ə līt′, -rā-), *n.* **1.** a descendant of Jacob, esp. a member of the Hebrew people who inhabited the ancient kingdom of Israel. **2.** one of a group considered as God′s chosen people. —*adj.* **3.** of or pertaining to ancient Israel or its people.

Is•sa•char (is′ə kär′), *n.* **1.** a son of Jacob and Leah. Gen. 30:18. **2.** one of the 12 tribes of Israel, traditionally descended from him.

Is•sei (ēs′sā′), *n., pl.* **-sei.** (*sometimes l.c.*) a Japanese immigrant to North America, esp. one who came to the U.S. prior to World War II and was ineligible for citizenship before 1952. Compare KIBEI, NISEI, SANSEI.

is•su•a•ble (ish′ōō ə bəl), *adj.* **1.** able to be issued or to issue. **2.** forthcoming; receivable. **3.** open to debate or contest; litigable. —**is′su•a•bly,** *adv.*

is•su•ance (ish′ōō əns), *n.* the act of issuing.

is•su•ant (ish′ōō ənt), *adj.* (of a heraldic animal) rising with only the forepart visible.

is•sue (ish′ōō; *esp. Brit.* is′yōō), *n., v.,* **-sued, -su•ing.** —*n.* **1.** the act of sending out or putting forth; promulgation; distribution. **2.** a series of things or one of a series of things that is printed, published, or distributed at one time: *a new bond issue; the latest issue of a magazine.* **3.** a point in question or a matter that is in dispute. **4.** a matter or dispute, the decision of which is of special or public importance. **5.** a point at which a matter is ready for decision: *to bring a case to an issue.* **6.** something proceeding from any source, as a product, result, or consequence. **7.** the result or outcome of a proceeding, affair, etc. **8.** offspring; progeny: *to die without issue.* **9.** a going, coming, passing, or flowing out. **10.** a place or means of egress; outlet or exit. **11.** something that comes out, as an outflowing stream. **12.** a distribution of food rations, clothing, or equipment to military personnel. **13. a.** a discharge of blood, pus, or the like. **b.** an incision, ulcer, or the like, emitting such a discharge. **14. issues,** (in English law) the profits from land or other property. —*v.t.* **15.** to deliver for use, sale, etc.; put into circulation. **16.** to mint, print, or publish for sale or distribution. **17.** to distribute (food, clothing, etc.) to military personnel. **18.** to send out; discharge; emit. —*v.i.* **19.** to go, pass, or flow out; emerge: *to issue forth to battle.* **20.** to be sent, put forth, or distributed publicly. **21.** to be printed or published. **22.** to originate or proceed from any source. **23.** to arise as a result or consequence; result. **24.** to be born or descended. **25.** to come as a yield or profit, as from land. —*Idiom.* **26. at issue,** being disputed; as yet undecided. **27. join issue, a.** to enter into controversy. **b.** to submit an issue jointly for legal decision. **28. take issue,** to disagree; dispute. —**is′sue•less,** *adj.* —**is′su•er,** *n.*

-ist, a suffix of nouns, often corresponding to verbs ending in *-ize* or nouns ending in *-ism,* that denote a person who practices or is concerned with something, or holds certain principles, doctrines, etc.: *apologist; machinist; novelist; socialist; Thomist.* Compare -ISM, -ISTIC, -IZE.

Is•tan•bul (is′tän bōōl′, -tan-, -täm-), *n.* a seaport in NW Turkey, on both sides of the Bosporus: site of capital of Byzantine and Ottoman empires. 5,494,900. Formerly (A.D. 330–1930), **Constantinople.**

isth•mus (is′məs), *n., pl.* **-mus•es, -mi** (-mī). **1.** a narrow strip of land, bordered on both sides by water, connecting two larger bodies of land. **2.** a relatively narrow passage or strip of tissue joining two cavities or parts of an organ. —**isth′moid,** *adj.*

-istic, a suffix having some of the meanings of -IC (*characteristic; futuristic; simplistic*), often forming adjectives corresponding to nouns ending in -IST or -ISM (*antagonistic; artistic; linguistic; realistic*).

is•tle (ist′lē) also **ixtle,** *n.* a fiber from any of several tropical American agave or yucca plants, used in making material for bags, carpets, etc.

it (it), *pron., nom.* **it,** *poss.* **its,** *obj.* **it,** *pl. nom.* **they,** *poss.* **their** or **theirs,** *obj.* **them,** *n.* —*pron.* **1.** (used to represent an inanimate thing understood, previously mentioned, about to be mentioned, or present in the immediate context): *It was broken. You can't tell a book by its cover.* **2.** (used to represent a person or animal understood, previously mentioned, or about to be mentioned whose gender is unknown or disregarded): *Who was it? It was John.* **3.** (used to represent a group understood or previously mentioned): *The judge told the jury it could recess.* **4.** (used to represent a concept or abstract idea understood or previously stated): *It all started with Adam and Eve.* **5.** (used to represent an action or activity understood, previously mentioned, or about to be mentioned): *Since you don't like it, you don't have to go skiing.* **6.** (used as the impersonal subject of the verb *to be*, esp. to refer to time, distance, or the weather): *It is six o'clock. It was foggy.* **7.** (used in statements expressing an action, condition, fact, circumstance, or situation without reference to an agent): *If it weren't for Edna, I wouldn't go.* **8.** (used in referring to something as the origin or cause of pain, pleasure, etc.): *Where does it hurt?* **9.** (used in referring to a source not specifically named or described): *It is said that love is blind.* **10.** (used in referring to the general state of affairs or life in general): *How's it going with you?* **11.** (used as an anticipatory subject or object to make a sentence more eloquent or suspenseful or to shift emphasis): *It is necessary that you do your duty. It was a gun that he was carrying.* **12.** (used in referring to a critical event that has finally happened or is about to happen): *The lights went out. We thought, this is it!* **13.** *Informal.* (used instead of the pronoun *its* before a gerund or present participle): *It having rained for only one hour didn't help the crops.* —*n.* **14.** (in children's games) the player who is to perform some task, as, in tag, the one who must catch the others. —**Usage.** See ME.

I•tal•ian (i tal′yən), *n.* **1.** a native or inhabitant of Italy. **2.** a Romance language spoken in Italy, Corsica, and the canton of Ticino in Switzerland. *Abbr.:* It —*adj.* **3.** of or pertaining to Italy, its people, or their language. —**Pronunciation.** The pronunciation of ITALIAN with an initial (ī) sound (pronounced like *eye*) is heard primarily from uneducated speakers. It is sometimes used facetiously or disparagingly and is usu. considered offensive.

i•tal•ic (i tal′ik, ī tal′-), *adj.* **1.** designating or pertaining to a style of printing types in which the letters usu. slope to the right, used for emphasis, to separate different kinds of information, etc. **2.** Often, **italics.** italic type.

i•tal•i•cize (i tal′ə sīz′, ī tal′-), *v.,* **-cized, -ciz•ing.** —*v.t.* **1.** to print in italic type. **2.** to underscore (a word, sentence, or the like) with a single line, as in indicating italics. —*v.i.* **3.** to use italics.

It•a•ly (it′l ē), *n.* a republic in S Europe, comprising a peninsula S of the Alps, and Sicily, Sardinia, Elba, and other smaller islands: a kingdom 1870–1946. 57,534,088; 116,294 sq. mi. (301,200 sq. km). *Cap.:* Rome. Italian, **Italia.**

It′ Came′ upon′ the Mid′night Clear′, a Christmas hymn (1846) with words by Edmund H. Sears.

itch (ich), *v.i.* **1.** to have or feel a peculiar tingling or uneasy irritation of the skin that causes a desire to scratch the part affected. **2.** to cause such a feeling: *This shirt itches.* **3.** *Informal.* to scratch a part that itches. **4.** to have a desire to do or get something: *to itch after fame.* —*v.t.* **5.** to cause to have an itch. **6.** *Informal.* to scratch (a part that itches). **7.** to annoy; vex; irritate. —*n.* **8.** the sensation of itching. **9.** a restless desire or longing: *an itch for excitement.* **10.** the itch, SCABIES.

itch•y (ich′ē), *adj.,* **itch•i•er, itch•i•est. 1.** having or causing an itching sensation. **2.** characterized by itching. —**itch′i•ness,** *n.*

it′d (it′əd), **1.** contraction of *it would.* **2.** contraction of *it had.*

-ite[1], a suffix of nouns denoting esp. persons associated with a place, tribe, leader, doctrine, system, etc. (*Campbellite; Israelite; laborite*); minerals and fossils (*ammonite; anthracite*); explosives (*cordite; dynamite*); chemical compounds, esp. salts of acids whose names end in *-ous* (*phosphite; sulfite*); pharmaceutical and commercial products (*vulcanite*); a member or component of a part of the body (*somite*).

-ite[2], a suffix occurring orig. in loanwords form Latin, forming adjectives from nouns of Latin origin: *crinite; ratite.*

i•tem (*n., v.* ī′təm; *adv.* ī′tem), *n.* **1.** a separate article or particular: *50 items on the list.* **2.** a piece of information or news. **3.** *Slang.* a topic of gossip. —*adv.* **4.** also; likewise (used esp. to introduce each article or statement in a list or series).

i•tem•ize (ī′tə mīz′), *v.,* **-ized, -iz•ing.** —*v.t.* **1.** to state or present by items; give the particulars of: *to itemize an account.* **2.** to list as an item. —*v.i.* **3.** to list separately all allowable deductions in computing income tax. —**i′tem•i•za′tion,** *n.* —**i′tem•iz′er,** *n.*

i′tem ve′to, *n.* the power, as of a state governor, to veto particular

items of a bill without having to veto the entire bill. Also called **line-item veto.**

it•er•ate (it′ə rāt′), *v.t.,* **-at•ed, -at•ing.** to utter or do again or repeatedly. —**it′er•ance,** *n.*

it•er•a•tion (it′ə rā′shən), *n.* **1.** the act of repeating; a repetition. **2.** a problem-solving or computational method in which a succession of approximations, each building on the one preceding, is used to achieve a desired degree of accuracy.

it•er•a•tive (it′ə rā′tiv, -ər ə tiv), *adj.* repeating; making repetition; repetitious. —**it′er•a′tive•ly,** *adv.* —**it′er•a′tive•ness,** *n.*

i•tin•er•an•cy (ī tin′ər ən sē, i tin′-) also **i•tin•er•a•cy** (-ə sē), *n.* **1.** the act of traveling from place to place, esp. in the discharge of duty or the conducting of business. **2.** the system of rotation governing the ministry of the Methodist Church.

i•tin•er•ant (ī tin′ər ənt, i tin′-), *adj.* **1.** traveling from place to place, esp. on a circuit, as a minister or judge. **2.** working in one place for a comparatively short time and then moving on to another place, as a physical or outdoor laborer. —*n.* **3.** a person who alternates between working and wandering. **4.** a person who travels from place to place, esp. for duty or business. —**i•tin′er•ant•ly,** *adv.*

i•tin•er•ar•y (ī tin′ə rer′ē, i tin′-), *n., pl.* **-ar•ies. 1.** a detailed plan for a journey, esp. a list of places to visit. **2.** a line of travel; route. **3.** an account of a journey. **4.** a guidebook for travelers.

i•tin•er•ate (ī tin′ə rāt′, i tin′-), *v.i.,* **-at•ed, -at•ing.** to go from place to place, esp. in a regular circuit, as a preacher or judge.

-itis, a suffix occurring in words that denote an inflammation or disease affecting a given part of the body (*appendicitis; bronchitis; phlebitis*); also forming nouns, often nonce words, that denote an obsessive state of mind or tendency facetiously compared to a disease (*electionitis; telephonitis*).

it′ll (it′l), a contraction of *it will.*

its (its), *pron.* the possessive form of IT (used as an attributive adjective): *The book has lost its jacket. I'm sorry about its being so late.*

it's (its), **1.** contraction of *it is: It's starting to rain.* **2.** contraction of *it has: It's been a long time.*

it•self (it self′), *pron.* **1.** a reflexive form of IT (used as the direct or indirect object of a verb or as the object of a preposition): *The battery recharges itself. The bird built a nest for itself.* **2.** (used as an intensive of IT, a nonpersonal pronoun or a noun): *which itself is a fact; The land itself was not for sale.* **3.** (used in place of IT in absolute constructions): *Itself open to question, the jury resigned.* **4.** its normal or usual self: *The injured cat was never quite itself again.* —**Usage.** See MYSELF.

it•ty-bit•ty (it′ē bit′ē) also **it•sy-bit•sy** (it′sē bit′sē), *adj. Informal.* very small; tiny.

-ity, a noun suffix based on and having the same function as -TY[2], used in English derivatives and in loanwords from French formed in a parallel fashion: *femininity; jollity; oddity; technicality.*

IU, 1. immunizing unit. **2.** Also, **I.U.** international unit.

IUD, intrauterine device.

IV (ī′vē′), *n., pl.* **IVs, IV's.** an apparatus for intravenous delivery of electrolyte solutions, medicines, and nutrients.

I've (īv), contraction of *I have.*

-ive, a suffix of adjectives (and nouns of adjectival origin) expressing tendency, disposition, function, connection, etc.: *active; detective.*

Ives (īvz), *n.* **1. Burl,** 1909–95, U.S. folk singer and actor. **2. Charles Edward,** 1874–1954, U.S. composer. **3. James Merritt,** 1824–95, U.S. lithographer. Compare CURRIER.

i•vo•ry (ī′və rē, ī′vrē), *n., pl.* **-ries,** *adj.* —*n.* **1.** the hard white substance, a variety of dentine, composing the main part of the tusks of the elephant, walrus, etc. **2.** this substance when taken from a dead animal and used to make articles and objects. **3.** an article made of this substance, as a carving. **4.** a material resembling or imitating this substance, esp. vegetable ivory. **5.** the tusk of an elephant, walrus, or other animal. **6. ivories,** *Slang.* **a.** the keys of a piano or similar instrument. **b.** dice. **7.** a creamy or yellowish white. —*adj.* **8.** consisting or made of ivory. **9.** of the color ivory. —**i′vo•ry•like′,** *adj.*

i′vory-billed′ wood′pecker, *n.* a large black-and-white woodpecker, *Campephilus principalis,* of the southern U.S. and Cuba: close to extinction. Also called **i′vory-bill′.**

I′vory Coast′, *n.* a republic in W Africa: formerly part of French West Africa; gained independence 1960. 11,630,000; 124,504 sq. mi. (322,463 sq. km). *Cap.:* Yamoussoukro. French, **Côte d'Ivoire.** —**I•vo•ri•an** (ī vôr′ē ən, ī vōr′-), *adj., n.*

i′vory nut′, *n.* the seed of a low South American palm, *Phytelephas macrocarpa,* yielding vegetable ivory.

i′vory tow′er, *n.* **1.** a place or situation remote from worldly or practical affairs: *the university as an ivory tower.* **2.** an attitude of aloofness from or disregard for worldly or affairs. —**i′vory-tow′ered,** *adj.*

i•vy (ī′vē), *n., pl.* **i•vies,** *adj.* —*n.* **1.** a climbing vine, *Hedera helix,* of the ginseng family, native to Eurasia and N Africa, having smooth, shiny evergreen leaves: widely cultivated. —*adj.* **2.** (often *cap.*) IVY LEAGUE. —**i′vy•like′,** *adj.*

I′vy League′, *n.* **1.** a group of colleges and universities in the northeastern U.S., consisting of Yale, Harvard, Princeton, Columbia, Dartmouth, Cornell, the University of Pennsylvania, and Brown, having a reputation for high scholastic achievement and social prestige. **2.** of,

pertaining to, or characteristic of Ivy League colleges or their students and graduates. —**I′vy Lea′guer,** *n.*

I′ Will′ Sing′ the Won′drous Sto′ry, a Christian hymn (1886) with words by Francis Rowley and music by Peter Bilhorn.

I•wo Ji•ma (ē′wə jē′mə, ē′wō), *n.* one of the Volcano Islands, in the N Pacific, S of Japan: under U.S. administration after 1945; returned to Japan 1968.

Ix•tac•ci•huatl or **Iz•tac•ci•huatl** (ēs′täk sē′wät′l), also **Ix•ta•ci• huatl** (-tä sē′-), *n.* an extinct volcano in S central Mexico, SE of Mexico City. 17,342 ft. (5286 m).

I•yar or **Iy•yar** (ē yär′, ē′yär), *n.* the eighth month of the Jewish calendar.

-ize, a verb-forming suffix occurring orig. in loanwords from Greek that have entered English through Latin or French (*baptize; barbarize; catechize*); within English, **-ize** is added to adjectives and nouns to form transitive verbs with the general senses "to render, make" (*fossilize; sterilize; Americanize*), "to convert into, give a specified character or form to" (*computerize; dramatize;*), "to subject to (as a process, sometimes named after its originator)" (*hospitalize; terrorize; galvanize; oxidize; winterize*). Also formed with **-ize** are a more heterogeneous group of verbs, usu. intransitive, denoting a change of state (*crystallize*), kinds or instances of behavior (*apologize; tyrannize*), or activities (*economize; philosophize*). Also, *esp. Brit.,* **-ise**[1]. Compare -ISM, -IST.

Iz•mir (iz′mēr), *n.* **1.** Formerly, **Smyrna.** a seaport in W Turkey on the Gulf of Izmir: important city of Asia Minor from ancient times. 1,489,817. **2. Gulf of.** Formerly, **Gulf of Smyrna.** an arm of the Aegean Sea in W Turkey. 35 mi. (56 km) long; 14 mi. (23 km) wide.

J

J, j (jā), *n., pl.* **Js** or **J's, js** or **j's. 1.** the tenth letter of the English alphabet, a consonant. **2.** any spoken sound represented by this letter. **3.** something having the shape of a J. **4.** a written or printed representation of the letter *J* or *j*.

J, *Symbol.* the tenth in order or in a series.

j, *Math Symbol.* **1.** a unit vector on the *y*-axis of a coordinate system. **2.** the imaginary number $\sqrt{-1}$.

JA or **J.A., 1.** joint account. **2.** Joint Agent. **3.** Judge Advocate.

jab (jab), *v.,* **jabbed, jab•bing,** *n.* —*v.t.* **1.** to poke sharply or abruptly, as with an end or point: *This pin is jabbing my neck.* **2.** to thrust abruptly: *to jab an elbow into someone's ribs.* **3.** to punch, esp. with a short, quick blow. —*v.i.* **4.** to poke or punch with short, quick blows: *to jab at a fire with a stick; The boxer jabbed instead of swinging.* —*n.* **5.** a poke with the end or point of something; sharp, quick thrust. **6.** a short, quick punch. —**jab′bing•ly,** *adv.*

Ja•bal (jā′bəl), *n.* a son of Lamech, and the progenitor of nomadic shepherds. Gen. 4:20.

jab•ber (jab′ər), *v.i., v.t.* **1.** to speak rapidly, indistinctly, incoherently, or nonsensically; chatter. —*n.* **2.** rapid, indistinct, or nonsensical talk; gibberish. —**jab′ber•er,** *n.* —**jab′ber•ing•ly,** *adv.*

jab•ber•wock•y (jab′ər wok′ē), *n., pl.* **-wock•ies.** (*sometimes cap.*) writing or speech with nonsensical words.

Jab•bok (jab′ək), *n.* a tributary of the Jordan River, near where Jacob wrestled with God. Gen. 32:22.

ja•bot (zha bō′, ja-; *esp. Brit.* zhab′ō, jab′ō), *n.* a decorative ruffle at the neckline and extending down the front of a woman's blouse or dress or, formerly, of a man's shirt.

jac•a•ran•da (jak′ə ran′də, -ran dä′), *n., pl.* **-das.** any of various tropical trees belonging to the genus *Jacaranda,* of the catalpa family, having showy clusters of usu. purplish flowers.

ja•cinth (jā′sinth, jas′inth), *n.* **1. a.** a reddish brown variety of zircon. **b.** any of various other gemstones of this color or color variety, as spinel. **2.** HYACINTH (defs. 3, 5).

jack (jak), *n.* **1.** any of various portable devices for raising or lifting heavy objects short heights, using various mechanical, pneumatic, or hydraulic methods: *an automobile jack.* **2.** Also called **knave.** a playing card bearing the picture of a soldier or servant. **3.** a connecting device in an electrical circuit designed for the insertion of a plug: *a telephone jack.* **4.** (*cap.*) *Informal.* fellow; buddy; man (usu. used in addressing a stranger). **5. a.** one of a set of small, six-pointed metal objects or pebbles used in the game of jacks. **b. jacks,** (*used with a sing. v.*) a children's game in which these objects are tossed and gathered, usu. while bouncing a rubber ball. **6.** any of several carangid fishes, esp. of the genus *Caranx,* as *C. hippos* (**jack crevalle**), of the W Atlantic Ocean. **7.** a small flag flown at the bow of a vessel, usu. symbolizing its nationality. **8.** (*cap.*) a sailor. **9.** LUMBERJACK. **10.** a device for turning a spit. **11.** a small, usu. white bowl or ball used as a mark for lawn bowlers to aim at. **12.** a premigratory young male salmon. **13.** *Falconry.* the male of a kestrel, hobby, or esp. of a merlin. —*v.t.* **14.** to lift or move (something) with or as if with a jack (usu. fol. by *up*): *to jack up a car.* **15.** to increase, raise, or accelerate (prices, wages, speed, etc.) (usu. fol. by *up*): *to jack up rents.* **16.** to boost the morale of; encourage (usu. fol. by *up*). **17.** to hunt or fish for with a jacklight. —*v.i.* **18.** to hunt or fish with a jacklight. —*adj.* **19.** *Carpentry.* having a height or length less than that of most of the others in a structure: *jack rafter; jack truss.* —*Saying.* **20. jack of all trades and master of none,** one who can do many things fairly well but none of them expertly.

jack•al (jak′əl, -ôl), *n.* **1.** any of several nocturnal wild dogs of the genus *Canis,* esp. *C. aureus,* of Asia and Africa, that scavenge or hunt in packs. **2.** a person who performs dishonest or base deeds as the accomplice of another. **3.** a person who performs menial or degrading tasks for another.

jack•a•napes (jak′ə nāps′), *n.* **1.** an impertinent, presumptuous fellow. **2.** an impudent, mischievous child.

jack•ass (jak′as′), *n.* **1.** a male donkey. **2.** a contemptibly foolish or stupid person; dolt; blockhead; ass. —**jack′ass′er•y,** *n.*

jack′ bean′, *n.* a bushy tropical plant, *Canavalia ensiformis,* of the legume family, grown esp. for forage.

jack′ cheese′, *n.* MONTEREY JACK.

jack•daw (jak′dô′), *n.* a small Eurasian crow with a gray nape, *Corvus monedula,* that nests in chimneys and rock cavities.

jack•et (jak′it), *n.* **1.** a short coat, in any of various forms, usu. opening down the front. **2.** a garmentlike article designed to be placed around the body for some use other than as clothing. Compare LIFE JACKET, STRAITJACKET. **3.** a protective outer covering. **4.** the skin of a potato, esp. when it has been cooked. **5.** a removable paper cover for protecting the binding of a bound book, usu. bearing the title and author's name. **6.** the cover of a paperbound book, usu. bearing an illustration. **7.** an envelope, holder, or cover of cardboard or paper, as for a phonograph record or a document. **8.** a metal casing, as the steel covering around the barrel of a gun or the core of a bullet. —*v.t.* **9.** to put a jacket on. —**jack′et•ed,** *adj.* —**jack′et•less, —jack′et•like′,** *adj.*

jack•fish (jak′fish′), *n., pl.* (*esp. collectively*) **-fish,** (*esp. for kinds or species*) **-fish•es. 1.** any of several pikes, esp. the northern pike. **2.** the sauger.

Jack′ Frost′, *n.* frost or freezing cold personified.

jack•fruit (jak′frōōt′), *n.* **1.** a large, tropical tree, *Artocarpus heterophyllus,* of the mulberry family, with glossy leaves. **2.** the knobby, yellow, edible fruit of this plant, reaching the size of a watermelon.

jack•ham•mer (jak′ham′ər), *n.* a portable drill operated by compressed air and used to drill rock, break up pavement, etc.

jack′-in-the-box′ or **jack′-in-a-box′,** *n., pl.* **-box•es.** a toy consisting of a box from which an enclosed figure springs up when the lid is opened.

jack′-in-the-pul′pit, *n., pl.* **-pul•pits.** any North American plant of the genus *Arisaema,* of the arum family, having an upright spadix arched over by a spathe.

jack-in-the-pulpit, *Arisaema triphyllum*

jack•knife (jak′nīf′), *n., pl.* **-knives,** *v.,* **-knifed, -knif•ing.** —*n.* **1.** a large pocketknife. **2.** a dive in which the diver bends in midair to touch the toes, keeping the legs straight, and then straightens out. —*v.i.* **3.** to bend over from or at the middle; double over like a jackknife. **4.** (of a trailer truck) to have the cab and trailer swivel at the linkage until they form a V shape, as the result of an abrupt stop or accident. **5.** (in diving) to perform a jackknife. —*v.t.* **6.** to cause to jackknife. **7.** to cut with a jackknife.

jack•light (jak′līt′), *n.* a portable light used as a lure in hunting or fishing at night.

jack′ mack′erel, *n.* an edible carangid fish, *Trachurus symmetricus,* of the Pacific North American coast, resembling a mackerel. Also called **horse mackerel.**

jack′-of-all′-trades′, *n., pl.* **jacks-of-all-trades.** a person who is adept at many different kinds of work.

jack-o'-lan•tern (jak′ə lan′tərn), *n.* **1.** a hollowed pumpkin with openings cut to represent a human face, traditionally displayed at Halloween, often with a candle or other light inside. **2.** any phenomenon of light, as a corona discharge or an ignis fatuus. **3.** a poisonous luminescent orange fungus, *Omphalotus olearius,* that grows in clusters at the base of tree stumps.

jack′ pine′, *n.* a scrubby pine, *Pinus banksiana,* growing on poor, rocky land in Canada and the northern U.S.

jack′ plane′, *n.* a carpenter's plane for rough surfacing.

jack•pot (jak′pot′), *n.* **1.** the chief prize or the cumulative stakes in a game, lottery, or the like. **2.** (in draw poker) a pot that accumulates until a player opens the betting with a pair of predetermined denomination, usu. jacks or better. **3.** an outstanding reward or success. —*Idiom.* **4. hit the jackpot, a.** to achieve sudden success. **b.** to win a jackpot.

jack′ rab′bit, *n.* any of various large hares of W North America, having long hind legs and long ears.

jack•rab•bit (jak′rab′it), *adj.* **1.** resembling a jack rabbit, as in suddenness or rapidity of movement. —*v.i.* **2.** to go or start forward in a rapid, sudden movement.

Jack′ Rus′sell ter′rier (jak), *n.* one of an English breed of small, short-legged terriers with a white coat with tan or black markings.

jack′ salm′on, *n.* **1.** WALLEYE (def. 1). **2.** COHO.

jack•smelt (jak′smelt′), *n., pl.* **-smelts,** (*esp. collectively*) **-smelt.** a silversides, *Atherinopsis californiensis,* of Californian shores.

jack•snipe (jak′snīp′), *n., pl.* (*esp. collectively*) **-snipe,** (*esp. for kinds or species*) **-snipes. 1.** a short-billed Eurasian snipe, *Limnocryptes minimus.* **2.** any of several related snipes.

Jack•son (jak′sən), *n.* **1. Andrew** (*"Old Hickory"*), 1767–1845, U.S. general: 7th president of the U.S. 1829–37. **2. Helen Hunt** (*Helen Maria Fiske*), 1830–85, U.S. novelist and poet. **3. Jesse L(ouis),** born 1941, U.S. Baptist minister and civil-rights and political activist. **4. Mahalia,** 1911–72, U.S. gospel singer. **5. Thomas Jonathan** (*"Stonewall Jackson"*), 1824–63, Confederate general in the American Civil War. **6.** the capital of Mississippi, in the central part. 193,097.

Jack•so•ni•an (jak sō′nē ən), *adj.* **1.** of or pertaining to Andrew Jackson, his ideas, the period of his presidency, or the political principles or social values associated with him: *Jacksonian democracy.* —*n.* **2.** a follower of Andrew Jackson.

Jack•son•ville (jak′sən vil′), *n.* a seaport in NE Florida, on the St. John's River. 665,070.

jack•straw (jak′strô′), *n.* **1.** one of the thin strips of wood or other material used in jackstraws. **2. jackstraws,** (*used with a sing. v.*) a game in which piled jackstraws must be picked up, one by one, without disturbing the heap.

Ja•cob (jā′kəb), *n.* a son of Isaac and Rebekah, younger twin of Esau, and father of the 12 patriarchs. Gen. 24:24–34.

Jac•o•be•an (jak′ə bē′ən), *adj.* **1.** of or pertaining to James I of England or to his period. **2.** of or pertaining to the style of literature and drama produced during the early 17th century. —*n.* **3.** a writer, statesman, or other personage of the Jacobean period.

Jac•o•be′an lil′y, *n.* a bulbous plant, *Sprekelia formosissima,* of the amaryllis family, native to Mexico, bearing a large, bright red flower.

Jac•o•bin (jak′ə bin), *n.* **1.** (in the French Revolution) a member of a radical political club that instituted the Reign of Terror. **2.** an extreme radical, esp. in politics. **3.** a Dominican friar. —**Jac′o•bin′ic, Jac′o•bin′i•cal,** *adj.* —**Jac′o•bin•ism,** *n.*

Ja′cob's lad′der, *n.* **1.** a ladder seen by Jacob in a dream, reaching from the earth to heaven. Gen. 28:12. **2.** *Naut.* a hanging ladder having ropes or chains supporting wooden or metal rungs or steps.

Ja′cob's-lad′der, *n.* any plant of the genus *Polemonium,* of the phlox family, with cup-shaped blue flowers and paired leaflets in a ladderlike arrangement.

Ja′cob's well′, *n.* a well where Jesus spoke to a Samaritan woman. John 4:1–26.

jac•quard (jak′ärd, jə kärd′), *n.* (*often cap.*) **1.** a fabric with an elaborately woven pattern produced on a Jacquard loom. **2.** JACQUARD LOOM.

Jac′quard or **jac′quard) loom′,** *n.* a loom for producing elaborate designs in an intricate weave **(Jac′quard weave′** or **jac′quard weave′)** constructed from a variety of basic weaves.

Ja•cuz•zi (jə kōō′zē), *Trademark.* a brand name for a device for a whirlpool bath and related products.

jade¹ (jād), *n.* **1.** either of two minerals, jadeite or nephrite, sometimes green, highly esteemed as an ornamental stone for carvings, jewelry, etc. **2.** an object, as a carving, made from either mineral. **3.** Also called **jade′ green′.** green, varying from bluish green to yellowish green.

jade² (jād), *n., v.,* **jad•ed, jad•ing.** —*n.* **1.** a worn-out, broken-down, worthless, or vicious horse. **2.** a disreputable, ill-tempered, or indiscreet woman. —*v.t., v.i.* **3.** to make or become dull, worn-out, or weary, as from overwork or overuse.

jad•ed (jā′did), *adj.* **1.** dulled or dissipated by overindulgence: *a jaded appetite.* **2.** worn-out, as by overwork or overuse. —**jad′ed•ly,** *adv.*

jade•ite (jā′dīt), *n.* the most precious type of jade; a colorless, green, or black pyroxene, sodium aluminum silicate, NaAlSi₂O₆.

jade′ plant′, *n.* a succulent S African shrub, *Cassula argentea,* of the stonecrop family, with small oval leaves.

Ja•el (jā′əl), *n.* a woman who killed Sisera by hammering a tent pin into his head as he slept. Judg. 4:17–22.

Jaf•fa (jaf′ə, jä′fə; *locally* yä′fä) also **Yafo,** *n.* a former seaport in W Israel, part of Tel Aviv-Jaffa since 1950: ancient Biblical town. Ancient, Joppa.

jag¹ (jag), *n., v.,* **jagged, jag•ging.** —*n.* **1.** a sharp projection on an edge or surface. —*v.t.* **2.** to cut or slash, esp. in points or pendants along the edge. —*v.i.* **3.** to move with a jerk; jog. —**jag′less,** *adj.*

jag² (jag), *n.* **1.** a period of unrestrained indulgence in an activity; spree; binge: *a crying jag.* **2.** a state of intoxication from liquor.

jag•ged (jag′id), *adj.* **1.** raggedly notched; sharply irregular on the surface or at the borders. **2.** having a harsh, rough, or uneven quality. —**jag′ged•ly,** *adv.* —**jag′ged•ness,** *n.*

jag•uar (jag′wär, -yŏō är′; *esp. Brit.* jag′yŏō ər), *n.* a large, powerful cat, *Panthera onca,* of tropical America, having a tawny coat with black rosettes.

jaguar, *Panthera onca,*
head and body 5 ft. (1.5 m);
tail 2 ½ ft. (0.8 m)

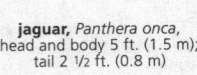

ja•gua•run•di (jä′gwə run′dē, -gyŏō ə-, jag′wə-, -yŏō ə-), *n., pl.* **-dis.** a mainly tropical American wildcat, *Felis yagouaroundi,* with a long body and tail.

jai a•lai (hī′ lī′, hī′ ə lī′, hī′ ə lī′), *n.* a game resembling handball, played on a three-walled court by two, four, or six players who use a long, curved wicker basket strapped to the wrist to catch and throw a small, hard ball against the front wall. Compare FRONTON.

jail (jāl), *n.* **1.** a prison, esp. one for the detention of persons awaiting trial or convicted of minor offenses. —*v.t.* **2.** to take into or hold in lawful custody; imprison. —**jail′a•ble,** *adj.*

jail•bird (jāl′bûrd′), *n.* a person confined in jail; convict.

jail•break (jāl′brāk′), *n.* an escape from prison, esp. by forcible means.

jail•er or **jail•or** (jā′lər), *n.* **1.** a person in charge of a jail or section of a jail. **2.** a person who forcibly confines another.

jail•house (jāl′hous′), *n., pl.* **-hous•es** (-hou′ziz). a jail or building used as a jail.

Jain (jīn) also **Jai•na** (jī′nə), **Jain′ist,** *n.* an adherent of Jainism.

Jain•ism (jī′niz əm), *n.* a dualistic religion founded in the 6th century B.C. as a revolt against current Hinduism and emphasizing asceticism and nonviolence toward all living creatures.

Ja•kar•ta or **Dja•kar•ta** (jə kär′tə), *n.* the capital of Indonesia, on the NW coast of Java. 6,503,449. Formerly, **Batavia.**

Ja′kob-Creutz′feldt disease′ (yä′kôb) *n.* CREUTZFELDT-JAKOB DISEASE.

ja•la•pe•ño or **ja•la•pe•no** (hä′lə pān′yō), *n., pl.* **-ños** or **-nos.** a hot green or orange-red pepper, the fruit of a variety of *Capsicum annuum,* used esp. in Mexican cooking. Also called **ja′lape′ño pep′per.**

ja•lop•y (jə lop′ē), *n., pl.* **-lop•ies.** an old, decrepit, or unpretentious automobile.

jal•ou•sie (jal′ə sē′), *n.* **1.** a blind or shutter made with horizontal slats that can be adjusted to admit light and air but exclude rain and sun. **2.** a window made of glass slats or louvers of a similar nature.

jam¹ (jam), *v.,* **jammed, jam•ming,** *n.* —*v.t.* **1.** to press, squeeze, or wedge into a confined space: *to jam socks into a drawer.* **2.** to bruise or crush by squeezing: *to jam one's hand in a door.* **3.** to fill tightly; cram. **4.** to push or thrust violently on or against something: *Jam your foot on the brake.* **5.** to block up by crowding: *Crowds jammed the doors.* **6.** to put or place in position with a violent gesture (often fol. by *on*): *He jammed on his hat and stalked out.* **7.** to make (something) unworkable by causing parts to become stuck, displaced, etc.: *to jam a lock.* **8. a.** to interfere with (radio signals or the like) by sending out other signals of approximately the same frequency. **b.** (of radio signals or the like) to interfere with (other signals). —*v.i.* **9.** to become stuck, wedged, fixed, blocked, etc.: *This door jams easily.* **10.** to press or push, often violently, as into a confined space or against one another: *They jammed into the elevator.* **11.** (of a machine, part, etc.) to become unworkable, as through the wedging or displacement of a part. **12.** to participate in a jam session. —*n.* **13.** the act of jamming or the state of being jammed. **14.** a mass of objects, vehicles, etc., crammed together in such a way as to stop or severely impede movement: *a traffic jam.* **15.** *Informal.* a difficult or embarrassing situation: *Their lying got them into a jam.*

jam² (jam), *n.* a preserve of slightly crushed fruit boiled with sugar. —**jam′like′, jam′my,** *adj.*

Ja•mai•ca (jə mā′kə), *n.* **1.** an island in the West Indies, S of Cuba. 4413 sq. mi. (11,430 sq. km). **2.** a republic coextensive with this island: formerly a British colony; became independent in 1962; a member of the Commonwealth of Nations. 2,615,582. *Cap.:* Kingston. —**Ja•mai′can,** *adj., n.*

Jamai′ca gin′ger, *n.* **1.** an alcoholic extract of ginger used as a flavoring. **2.** powdered ginger root used medicinally.

Jamai′ca rum′, *n.* a heavy, pungent, slowly fermented rum made in Jamaica.

jamb (jam), *n.* **1.** either of the vertical sides of a doorway, window, or other opening. **2.** either of two members forming the sidepieces for the frame of an opening.

jam•ba•lay•a (jum′bə lī′ə), *n.* **1.** a Creole dish of rice, ham, sausage, shellfish, etc., usu. cooked with tomatoes, onions, peppers, and spices. **2.** any mixture or jumble; hodgepodge.

jam•bo•ree (jam′bə rē′), *n.* **1.** a carousal; any noisy merrymaking. **2.** a festive gathering, often including speeches and entertainment. **3.** a large national or international gathering of the Boy Scouts or Girl Scouts (disting. from *camporee*).

James¹ (jāmz), *n.* **1.** Also called **James′ the Great′.** one of the 12 apostles, the son of Zebedee and brother of the apostle John. Matt. 4:21. **2. a.** the person identified in Gal. 1:19 as a brother of Jesus. **b.** one of the books or epistles of the New Testament ascribed to him. **3.** Also called **James′ the Less′.** (*"James the son of Alphaeus"*) one of the 12 apostles. Matt. 10:3; Mark 3:18; Luke 6:15. **4. Henry,** 1811–82, U.S. philosopher (father of Henry and William James). **5. Henry,** 1843–1916, U.S. writer in England. **6. Jesse (Woodson),** 1847–82, U.S. outlaw and legendary figure. **7. William,** 1842–1910, U.S. psychologist and pragmatist philosopher. **8.** a river flowing E from the W part of Virginia to Chesapeake Bay. 340 mi. (547 km) long. **9.** a river flowing S from central North Dakota to the Missouri River. 710 mi. (1143 km) long.

James² (jāmz), *n.* **1. James I,** 1566–1625, king of England and Ireland 1603–25; as **James VI,** king of Scotland 1567–1625 (son of Mary Stuart). **2. James II,** 1633–1701, king of England, Ireland, and Scotland 1685–88 (son of Charles I of England). **3. James III,** STUART, James Francis Edward.

James•town (jāmz′toun′), *n.* **1.** a village in E Virginia: first permanent English settlement in North America 1607; restored 1957. **2.** the capital of St. Helena, in the S Atlantic Ocean. 1516.

jam′-pack′, *v.t.* to fill or pack as tightly or fully as possible.

jam′ ses′sion, *n.* a meeting of a group of musicians, esp. jazz musicians, to play for their own enjoyment.

jam′-up, *n.* JAM¹ (def. 14).

Jane′ Doe′ (jān′ dō′), *n.* a fictitious name used in legal proceedings for a female party whose true name is not known. Compare JOHN DOE.

Jane Eyre (jān′ âr′), a novel (1847) by Charlotte Brontë.

jan·gle (jang′gəl), *v.,* **-gled, -gling,** *n.* —*v.i.* **1.** to produce a harsh, discordant sound: *coins jangling together.* **2.** to speak angrily; wrangle. —*v.t.* **3.** to cause to make a harsh, discordant, usu. metallic sound. **4.** to cause to become irritated or upset: *loud noise that jangles the nerves.* —*n.* **5.** a harsh or discordant sound. **6.** an argument, dispute, or quarrel. —**jan′gler,** *n.* —**jan′gly,** *adj.*

jan·i·tor (jan′i tər), *n.* a person employed in an apartment house, office building, school, etc., to keep the public areas clean and do minor repairs; caretaker. —**jan′i·to′ri·al** (-tôr′ē əl, -tōr′-), *adj.*

Jan·sen (jan′sən, yän′-), *n.* **Cornelis Otto** (*Cornelius Jansenius*), 1585–1638, Dutch Roman Catholic theologian.

Jan·sen·ism (jan′sə niz′əm), *n.* the doctrinal system of Cornelis Jansen, denying free will and maintaining that human nature is corrupt and that Christ died for the elect and not for all people: condemned as heretical by the Catholic Church. —**Jan′sen·ist,** *n.*

Jan·u·ar·y (jan′yōō er′ē), *n., pl.* **-ar·ies.** the first month of the year, containing 31 days. *Abbr.:* Jan.

Ja·nus (jā′nəs), *n.* a Roman god of doorways and beginnings, usu. represented as having a head with two faces looking in opposite directions. [< Latin, special use of *jānus* doorway, archway, arcade]

ja·pan (jə pan′), *n., adj., v.,* **-panned, -pan·ning.** —*n.* **1.** any of various durable black varnishes, orig. from Japan, for coating metal or other surfaces. **2.** work varnished and figured in the Japanese manner. —*adj.* **3.** of or pertaining to japan. —*v.t.* **4.** to varnish with japan or japanlike material; lacquer. —**ja·pan′ner,** *n.*

Ja·pan (jə pan′), *n.* a constitutional monarchy on a chain of islands off the E coast of Asia: main islands, Hokkaido, Honshu, Kyushu, and Shikoku. 125,716,637; 141,529 sq. mi. (366,560 sq. km). *Cap.:* Tokyo. Japanese, **Nihon, Nippon. 2. Sea of,** the part of the Pacific Ocean between Japan and mainland Asia.

Japan′ clo′ver, *n.* a drought-resistant lespedeza, *Lespedeza striata,* native to Asia, used for pasturage and hay.

Jap·a·nese (jap′ə nēz′, -nēs′), *n., pl.* **-nese,** *adj.* —*n.* **1.** a native or inhabitant of Japan. **2.** a member of a people constituting the overwhelming majority of the inhabitants of Japan and the Ryukyu Islands. **3.** the language of this people, affiliated by some with the Altaic languages. *Abbr.:* Japn, Japn. —*adj.* **4.** of or pertaining to Japan, the Japanese, or their language.

Jap′anese′ androm′eda, *n.* an Asian evergreen shrub, *Pieris japonica,* of the heath family, having broad, glossy leaves and drooping clusters of whitish blossoms.

Jap′anese bee′tle, *n.* an iridescent green beetle, *Popillia japonica,* of the scarab family, native to Japan, established esp. in E North America as a crop and garden pest.

Jap′anese ce′dar, *n.* a Japanese evergreen tree, *Cryptomeria japonica,* of the bald cypress family, valued for its wood.

Jap′anese chin′ (chin), *n.* one of an Asian breed of toy dogs having a long, silky, black-and-white or red-and-white coat, a short nose, and a plumed tail carried over the back.

Jap′anese i′ris, *n.* a plant, *Iris kaempferi,* native to Japan, having broad, showy flowers in a variety of colors.

Jap′anese ma′ple, *n.* a small maple tree, *Acer palmatum,* of Korea and Japan, having bright red foliage in autumn.

Jap′anese′ persim′mon, *n.* **1.** the soft, orange or reddish, edible fruit of an Asian tree, *Diospyros kaki.* **2.** the tree itself.

Jap′anese plum′, *n.* a small tree, *Prunus salicina,* native to China, bearing edible yellowish fruit.

Jap′anese quince′, *n.* a flowering quince, *Chaenomeles speciosa,* of Japan, having scarlet flowers and pear-shaped fruit.

Jap′anese spurge′, *n.* a low Japanese plant, *Pachysandra terminalis,* grown as a ground cover.

Japan′ wax′, *n.* a pale yellow, waxy, water-insoluble solid obtained from the fruit of certain sumacs, as *Rhus succedanea,* native to Japan and China: used chiefly in candles, polishes, and waxes.

jape (jāp), *v.,* **japed, jap·ing.** *n.* —*v.i.* **1.** to jest; joke; gibe. —*v.t.* **2.** to mock or make fun of. —*n.* **3.** a joke; jest; quip. **4.** a trick or practical joke. —**jap′er,** *n.* —**jap′er·y,** *n.* —**jap′ing·ly,** *adv.*

Ja·pheth (jā′fith), *n.* a son of Noah. *Gen.* 5:32.

ja·pon·i·ca (jə pon′i kə), *n.* **1.** CAMELLIA. **2.** JAPANESE QUINCE.

jar¹ (jär), *n.* **1.** a broad-mouthed container, usu. cylindrical and of glass or earthenware. **2.** the quantity such a container can hold.

jar² (jär), *v.,* **jarred, jar·ring.** —*v.t.* **1.** to have a sudden and unpleasant effect on: *The sudden noise jarred me.* **2.** to cause to vibrate or shake: *The explosion jarred several buildings.* **3.** to cause to sound discordantly. —*v.i.* **4.** to have a harshly unpleasant or perturbing effect on one's nerves, feelings, etc. **5.** to produce a harsh, grating sound; sound discordantly. **6.** to conflict, clash, or disagree. —*n.* **7.** a jolt or shake, as from concussion. **8.** a sudden unpleasant effect upon the mind, feelings, or senses; shock. **9.** a harsh or discordant sound or combination of sounds. —**jar′ring·ly,** *adv.*

jar·di·niere (jär′dn ēr′, zhär′dn yâr′), *n.* **1.** an ornamental receptacle or stand for holding plants or flowers. **2.** diced and boiled vegetables, used esp. as a garnish.

jar·gon (jär′gən, -gon), *n.* **1.** the vocabulary, peculiar to a particular trade, profession, or group: *medical jargon.* **2.** unintelligible talk or writing; gibberish; babble. **3.** language that is characterized by uncommon vocabulary and convoluted syntax and is often vague in meaning.

jas·mine (jaz′min, jas′-) also **jessamine,** *n.* any of numerous shrubs or vines belonging to the genus *Jasminum,* of the olive family, having fragrant flowers used in perfumes and teas.

Ja·son (jā′sən), *n.* a legendary Greek hero, the leader of the Argonauts, who retrieved the Golden Fleece from King Aeëtes of Colchis with the help of Medea.

jas·per (jas′pər), *n.* **1.** an opaque variety of quartz, usu. red or brown: often used in decorative carvings. **2.** Also called **jas′per·ware′.** a fine colored stoneware with raised designs in white.

Jas·pers (yäs′pərs), *n.* **Karl** (kärl), 1883–1969, German philosopher.

jaun·dice (jôn′dis, jän′-), *n., v.,* **-diced, -dic·ing.** —*n.* **1.** Also called **icterus.** yellow discoloration of the skin, whites of the eyes, etc., due to an increase of bile pigments in the blood. **2.** a state of feeling in which views are prejudiced or judgment is distorted, as by envy or resentment. —*v.t.* **3.** to distort or prejudice, as by resentment or envy.

jaun·diced (jôn′dist, jän′-), *adj.* **1.** affected with or colored by or as if by jaundice: *jaundiced skin.* **2.** affected with or exhibiting prejudice or distorted judgment: *a jaundiced viewpoint.*

jaunt (jônt, jänt), *n.* **1.** a short journey, esp. one taken for pleasure. —*v.i.* **2.** to make a short journey.

jaun·ty (jôn′tē, jän′-), *adj.,* **-ti·er, -ti·est. 1.** easy and sprightly in manner or bearing: *to walk with a jaunty step.* **2.** smartly trim, as clothing: *a jaunty hat.* —**jaun′ti·ly,** *adv.* —**jaun′ti·ness,** *n.*

Ja·va (jä′və; *esp. for 2* jav′ə), *n.* **1.** the main island of Indonesia. 91,269,528 (with Madura); 51,032 sq. mi. (132,173 sq. km). **2.** (*usu. l.c.*) *Slang.* coffee: *a cup of java.*

Ja′va man′, *n.* the fossil remains of a form of *Homo erectus* found in Java.

jave·lin (jav′lin, jav′ə-), *n.* **1.** a light spear, usu. thrown by hand. **2.** a spearlike shaft about 8½ ft. (2.7 m) long and usu. made of wood, used in throwing for distance as a field event.

jaw (jô), *n.* **1.** either of two tooth-bearing bones or bony structures, the mandible or maxilla, forming the framework of the vertebrate mouth. **2.** the part of the face covering these bones. **3. jaws,** anything resembling a pair of jaws in shape or in power to grasp or hold. **4.** one of two or more parts, as of a machine, that grasp or hold something or that attach to similar parts. —*v.i.* **5.** *Slang.* to chat; gossip.

jaw·bone (jô′bōn′), *n., v.,* **-boned, -bon·ing.** —*n.* **1.** any bone of a jaw, esp. a mandible. —*v.t.* **2.** to influence by persuasion, esp. by public appeal, rather than by exertion of force or one's authority. —**jaw′bon′ing,** *n., adj.*

jaw·break·er (jô′brā′kər), *n.* **1.** a word that is hard to pronounce. **2.** a very hard, usu. round, candy.

jaw′less fish′, *n.* any fish of the class Agnatha (and order Cyclostomata), including the hagfishes and lampreys, characterized by a circular sucking mouth that lacks jaws.

Jaws′ of Life′, *Trademark.* a heavy-duty tool that can cut through metal or pry apart sections of it: used esp. to free people trapped in wrecked vehicles.

jay (jā), *n.* **1.** any of various typically noisy, gregarious songbirds of the family Corvidae, mostly of the Northern Hemisphere, having blue or gray plumage. **2.** *Slang.* **a.** a talkative person; chatterer. **b.** a fop.

Jay (jā), *n.* **John,** 1745–1829, first Chief Justice of the U.S. 1789–95.

jay·bird (jā′bûrd′), *n.* JAY.

Jay·cee (jā′sē′), *n.* a member of the Junior Chamber of Commerce, a civic group for young business and community leaders.

Jay·hawk·er (jā′hô′kər), *n.* **1.** a native or inhabitant of Kansas (used as a nickname). **2.** (*sometimes l.c.*) a plundering marauder, esp. one of the antislavery guerrillas in Kansas and Missouri before and during the Civil War.

Jay′s′ Trea′ty, *n.* a treaty (1794) between the U.S. and Great Britain that resolved lingering disputes. [after John JAY]

jay·vee (jā′vē′), *n.* **1.** JUNIOR VARSITY. **2.** a player on a junior varsity team.

jay·walk (jā′wôk′), *v.i.* to cross a street heedlessly or at a place other than a regular crossing. —**jay′walk′er,** *n.*

jazz (jaz), *n.* **1.** music originating in New Orleans around the beginning of the 20th century and subsequently developing through various increasingly complex styles, generally marked by intricate, propulsive rhythms, polyphonic ensemble playing, improvisatory, virtuosic solos, melodic freedom, and a harmonic idiom ranging from simple diatonicism through chromaticism to atonality. **2.** a style of dance music marked by some of the features of jazz. **3.** *Slang.* liveliness; spirit; excitement. **4.** *Slang.* insincere or pretentious talk. —*v.t.* **5.** to play (music) in the manner of jazz. **6.** *Slang.* **a.** to excite or enliven. **b.** to accelerate. —*v.i.* **7.** *Slang.* to act or proceed with great energy or liveliness. **8. jazz up,** *Slang.* **a.** to enliven. **b.** to embellish. —**jazz′er,** *n.*

Jazz′ Age′, *n.* the period in the U.S. extending from the end of World War I through the 1920s, characterized by prosperity, unconventional social behavior, and the rise of jazz.

J

jazz·er·cise (jaz′ər sīz′), *n.* vigorous dancing done to jazz dance music as an exercise for physical fitness.

jazz·man (jaz′man′, -mən), *n.*, *pl.* **-men** (-men′, -mən). a musician who plays jazz.

jazz′-rock′, *n.* music that combines elements of both jazz and rock and is usu. performed on amplified electric instruments.

jazz·y (jaz′ē), *adj.*, **jazz·i·er**, **jazz·i·est.** **1.** pertaining to or suggestive of jazz music. **2.** *Slang.* active or lively. **3.** *Slang.* fancy or flashy: *a jazzy sweater.* —**jazz′i·ly**, *adv.* —**jazz′i·ness**, *n.*

JC, junior college.

J.C., **1.** Jesus Christ. **2.** Julius Caesar.

JD, juvenile delinquent.

J.D., **1.** Doctor of Jurisprudence; Doctor of Law. [< New Latin *Jūris Doctor*] **2.** Doctor of Laws. [< New Latin *Jūrum Doctor*] **3.** Justice Department.

jeal·ous (jel′əs), *adj.* **1.** resentful and envious, as of someone's success, achievements, advantages, etc.: *to be jealous of a rich brother.* **2.** proceeding from suspicious fears or envious resentment: *a jealous rage.* **3.** inclined to suspicions or fears of rivalry, unfaithfulness, etc., as in love: *a jealous husband.* **4.** watchful in guarding something: *to be jealous of one's independence.* **5.** intolerant of unfaithfulness or rivalry: *The Lord is a jealous God.* —**jeal′ous·ly**, *adv.* —**jeal′ous·ness**, *n.*

jeal·ous·y (jel′ə sē), *n.*, *pl.* **-ous·ies.** **1.** the quality or state of being jealous. **2.** an instance of being jealous; a jealous feeling, disposition, state, or mood: *petty jealousies.*

jean (jēn), *n.* **1.** Sometimes, **jeans.** a sturdy twilled fabric, usu. of cotton. **2. jeans,** (*used with a pl. v.*) **a.** BLUE JEANS. **b.** trousers of various fabrics, styled or constructed like blue jeans.

Je·bus (jē′bəs), *n.* an ancient Canaanite city taken by David: it later became Jerusalem. Judges 19:10.

Jeb·u·site (jeb′yə sīt′), *n.* a member of an ancient Canaanite people that lived in Jebus. Gen. 15:21; Ex. 3:8. —**Jeb′u·sit′ic** (-sit′ik), **Jeb′u·sit′i·cal**, *adj.*

Jeep (jēp), *Trademark.* a small, rugged utility vehicle with four-wheel drive, orig. developed for military use.

jee·pers (jē′pərz), *interj.* (used as a mild exclamation of surprise or emotion.) Often, **jee′pers cree′pers** (krē′pərz).

jeer (jēr), *v.i.* **1.** to speak or shout derisively; scoff or gibe rudely. —*v.t.* **2.** to speak or shout derisively at; taunt; mock. **3.** to drive away by derisive shouts (fol. by *out of, off,* etc.): *to jeer an actor off the stage.* —*n.* **4.** a jeering utterance; derisive or rude gibe. —**jeer′er**, *n.* —**jeer′ing·ly**, *adv.*

Jef·fers (jef′ərz), *n.* **(John) Robinson**, 1887–1962, U.S. poet.

Jef·fer·son (jef′ər sən), *n.* **Thomas**, 1743–1826, 3rd president of the U.S. 1801–09.

Jef′ferson Cit′y, *n.* the capital of Missouri, in the central part, on the Missouri River. 33,619.

Jef′ferson Da′vis's Birth′day, *n.* June 3 or the first Monday in June, observed as a legal holiday in some Southern states.

Jef′ferson Day′, *n.* April 13, Thomas Jefferson's birthday, a legal holiday in Alabama, sometimes celebrated by the Democratic party by the holding of fund-raising dinners.

Jef·fer·so·ni·an (jef′ər sō′nē ən), *adj.* **1.** pertaining to or advocating the political principles and doctrines of Thomas Jefferson, esp. those stressing minimum control by the central government, the inalienable rights of the individual, and the superiority of an agrarian economy and rural society. —*n.* **2.** a supporter of Thomas Jefferson or Jeffersonianism. —**Jef′fer·so′ni·an·ism**, *n.*

Jef′frey pine′, *n.* a long-needled pine tree, *Pinus jeffreyi*, of high mountains in W North America.

je·had (ji häd′), *n.* JIHAD.

Je·ho·a·haz (jē hō′ə haz′), *n.* **1.** a king of Israel, the son of Jehu. II Kings 10:35. **2.** a ruler of Judah, son of Josiah. II Kings 23:30–34.

Je·hoi·a·chin (jē hoi′ə kin), *n.* a king of Judah who was imprisoned by Nebuchadnezzar and later released by Evil-Merodach. II Kings 24:8–16; 25:27–30.

Je·ho·ram (jē hôr′am, -hōr′-), *n.* JORAM.

Je·hosh·a·phat (ji hosh′ə fat′, -hos′-), *n.* a king of Judah who reigned in the 9th century B.C. I Kings 22:41–50.

Je·ho·vah (ji hō′və), *n.* **1.** a name of God in the Old Testament, a rendering of the ineffable name, JHVH, in the Hebrew Scriptures. **2.** (in modern Christian use) God. —**Je·ho′vic**, *adj.*

Jeho′vah's Wit′nesses, a Christian sect, founded in the U.S. in the late 19th century, that believes in the imminent destruction of the world's wickedness and the establishment of a theocracy under God's rule.

Je·hu (jē′hyoo *or, often,* -hoo), *n.*, *pl.* **-hus.** **1.** a king of Israel noted for his furious chariot attacks. II Kings 9. **2.** (*l.c.*) **a.** the driver of a cab or coach. **b.** a fast driver.

je·june (ji joon′), *adj.* **1.** lacking interest or significance; insipid: *a jejune novel.* **2.** lacking maturity; childish: *jejune behavior.* **3.** lacking nutritive elements: *a jejune diet.* —**je·june′ly**, *adv.* —**je·june′ness**, *n.*

je·ju·num (ji joo′nəm), *n.* the middle portion of the small intestine, between the duodenum and the ileum. —**je·ju′nal**, *adj.*

Jek′yll and Hyde′ (jek′əl, jē′kal), *n.* a person marked by dual personality, one aspect of which is good and the other bad.

jell (jel), *v.i.* **1.** to congeal; become jellylike in consistency. **2.** to become clear, substantial, or definite; crystallize. —*v.t.* **3.** to cause to jell.

jel·lied (jel′ēd), *adj.* **1.** congealed or brought to the consistency of jelly: *jellied consommé.* **2.** containing or spread over with jelly or syrup.

Jell-O (jel′ō), *Trademark.* a dessert made from a mixture of gelatin, sugar, and fruit flavoring.

jel·ly (jel′ē), *n.*, *pl.* **-lies**, *v.*, **-lied**, **-ly·ing**, *adj.* —*n.* **1.** a sweet spread of fruit juice boiled with sugar and sometimes pectin, then cooled to a soft, sticky consistency. **2.** any substance having such consistency. —*v.t.* **3.** to make into jelly; bring to the consistency of jelly. —*v.i.* **4.** to come to the consistency of jelly. —*adj.* **5.** containing or made, spread, or coated with jelly or syrup.

jel·ly·bean (jel′ē bēn′), *n.* a small, bean-shaped, chewy candy.

jel′ly dough′nut, *n.* a raised doughnut filled with jelly and often sprinkled with powdered sugar.

jel·ly·fish (jel′ē fish′), *n.*, *pl.* (*esp. collectively*) **-fish**, (*esp. for kinds or species*) **-fish·es.** **1.** any stinging, jellylike marine cnidarian of the class Scyphozoa, living in the developmental stage as a tiny attached polyp and in the adult stage as a large free-floating medusa with trailing tentacles. **2.** an indecisive or weak person.

jel′ly roll′, *n.* a thin, rectangular layer of sponge cake spread with fruit jelly and rolled up.

jen·net (jen′it), *n.* **1.** a female donkey. **2.** a small Spanish horse.

jen·ny (jen′ē), *n.*, *pl.* **-nies.** **1.** SPINNING JENNY. **2.** the female of certain animals, esp. a female donkey or a female bird.

jeop·ard·ize (jep′ər dīz′), *v.t.*, **-ized**, **-iz·ing.** to put in jeopardy; hazard; risk; imperil.

jeop·ard·y (jep′ər dē), *n.*, *pl.* **-dies.** **1.** risk of or exposure to loss, harm, death, or injury; hazard; danger: *to put one's life in jeopardy.* **2.** *Law.* the hazard that a defendant will suffer punishment when found guilty in a criminal proceeding. —**jeop′ard·ous**, *adj.*

Jeph·thah (jef′thə), *n.* a judge of Israel. Judg. 11, 12.

Jer., **1.** *Bible.* Jeremiah. **2.** Jersey.

jer·e·mi·ad (jer′ə mī′əd, -ad), *n.* a prolonged lament; complaint.

Jer·e·mi·ah (jer′ə mī′ə), *n.* **1.** a Major Prophet of the 6th and 7th centuries B.C. **2.** a book of the Bible bearing his name. *Abbr.*: Jer. —**Jer′e·mi′an**, **Jer′e·mi·an′ic** (-mī an′ik), *adj.*

Jer·i·cho (jer′i kō′), *n.* an ancient city of Palestine, N of the Dead Sea, formerly in W Jordan; occupied by Israel 1967–94; since 1994 under Palestinian self-rule.

jerk¹ (jûrk), *n.* **1.** a quick, sharp pull, thrust, throw, or the like; sudden, abrupt movement: *The train started with a jerk.* **2.** a sudden involuntary muscle contraction, as of a reflex. **3.** *Slang.* a contemptibly naive, stupid, or insignificant person. **4. the jerks,** involuntary, spasmodic muscular movements, as from emotional tension or excitement. —*v.t.* **5.** to pull, twist, move, thrust, or throw with a quick, suddenly arrested motion: *She jerked the child by the hand.* —*v.i.* **6.** to give a jerk or jerks. **7.** to move with a quick, sharp motion; move spasmodically. —**jerk′er**, *n.*

jerk² (jûrk), *v.t.* to preserve (meat, esp. beef) by cutting in strips and drying in the sun.

jerk·y¹ (jûr′kē), *adj.*, **jerk·i·er**, **jerk·i·est.** **1.** characterized by jerks or sudden starts; spasmodic. **2.** *Slang.* silly; foolish; stupid; ridiculous. —**jerk′i·ly**, *adv.* —**jerk′i·ness**, *n.*

jerk·y² (jûr′kē), *n.* jerked meat.

Jer·o·bo·am (jer′ə bō′əm), *n.* **1.** the first king of the Biblical kingdom of the Hebrews in N Palestine. I Kings 11:26–40; 14:20. **2.** (*l.c.*) a large wine bottle having a capacity of about four ordinary bottles or 3 liters (3.3 qt.).

Je·rome (jə rōm′), *n.* **Saint** (*Eusebius Hieronymus*), A.D. c340–420, Christian ascetic and Biblical scholar: chief preparer of the Vulgate.

jer′ry-built′, *adj.* **1.** built cheaply and flimsily; shoddy. **2.** contrived or developed in a haphazard fashion. —**jer′ry-build′**, *v.t.*, **-built**, **-building.** —**jer′ry-build′er**, *n.*

jer·sey (jûr′zē), *n.*, *pl.* **-seys.** **1.** a plain-knit, machine-made fabric of wool, silk, nylon, etc., characteristically soft and elastic, used for garments. **2.** a close-fitting knitted sweater or shirt. **3.** (*cap.*) one of a breed of dairy cattle, raised orig. on the island of Jersey.

Jer·sey (jûr′zē), *n.* **1.** a British island in the English Channel: the largest of the Channel Islands. 88,510; 44 sq. mi. (116 sq. km). *Cap.*: St. Helier. **2.** NEW JERSEY. —**Jer′sey·an**, *n.*, *adj.* —**Jer′sey·ite′**, *n.*

Jer′sey Cit′y, *n.* a seaport in NE New Jersey, opposite New York City. 226,022.

Jer·ub·baal (jer′ə bāl′, jer′ə bā′əl, -bāl′), *n.* Gideon.

Je·ru·sa·lem (ji roo′sə ləm, -zə-), *n.* an ancient holy city for Jews, Christians, and Muslims; divided between Israel and Jordan 1948–67; Jordanian sector annexed by Israel 1967; capital of Israel since 1950. 482,700. —**Je·ru′sa·lem·ite′**, *adj.*, *n.*

Jeru′salem ar′tichoke, *n.* **1.** a sunflower, *Helianthus tuberosus*, having edible, tuberous underground rootstocks. **2.** the tuber itself.

Jeru′salem Bi′ble, *n.* a translation (1966) of the Bible, designed for Roman Catholics.

Jeru′salem cher′ry, *n.* an Old World plant, *Solanum pseudocapsicum*, of the nightshade family, having white flowers and cherrylike fruits.

Jeru′salem crick′et, *n.* a reddish brown cricket, *Stenopelmatus* *fuscus,* of arid areas in W North America, with a banded abdomen and short spiny legs.

Jeru'salem, My' Hap'py Home', a 16th-century Christian hymn which portrays a vision of heaven.

Jeru'salem thorn', *n.* **1.** a Christ's-thorn. **2.** a spiny tropical American tree, *Parkinsonia aculeata,* of the legume family, having long clusters of large yellow flowers.

Jes·se (jes'ē), *n.* the father of David. I Sam. 16.

jest (jest), *n.* **1.** a joke or witty remark; witticism; quip. **2.** a jeer or taunt, often of a playful or teasing nature. **3.** sport or fun: *to speak half in jest, half in earnest.* **4.** the object of laughter; laughingstock. —*v.i.* **5.** to speak in a humorous or playfully teasing way. **6.** to speak derisively; gibe or scoff.

jest·er (jes'tər), *n.* **1.** a person who is given to jesting. **2.** a professional fool or clown, esp. at a medieval court.

Je·su (jē'zōō, jā'-, yā'-), *n.* Jesus (def. 1). [Middle English < Latin *Iēsu,* form of *Iēsus* < Greek *Iēsoû;* see Jesus]

Jes·u·it (jezh'ōō it, -yōō it, jez'-), *n.* **1.** a member of a Roman Catholic religious order for men **(Society of Jesus)** founded by Ignatius of Loyola in 1534. **2.** *(often l.c.)* a crafty, intriguing, or equivocating person. —Jes/u·it'i·cal, *adj.* —Jes/u·it'i·cal·ly, *adv.* —Jes/u·it·ry, *n.*

Je·sus (jē'zəs, -zəz), *n.* **1.** Also called **Je'sus Christ', Je'sus of Naz'areth.** born 4? B.C., crucified A.D. 29?, the source of the Christian religion. **2.** ("the Son of Sirach") the author of the Apocryphal book of Ecclesiasticus, who lived in the 3rd century B.C. **3.** *Christian Science.* the supreme example of God's nature expressed through human beings. [Middle English < Latin *Iēsus* < Greek *Iēsoûs* < Hebrew *Yēshūa',* var. of *Yəhōshūa'* God is help]

Je'sus Loves' Me', a Christian children's hymn (1860) with words by Anna B. Warner and music by William B. Bradbury.

jet¹ (jet), *n., v.,* **jet·ted, jet·ting,** *adj.* —*n.* **1.** a stream of a liquid, gas, or small solid particles forcefully shooting forth from a nozzle, orifice, etc. **2.** something that issues in such a stream, as water or gas. **3.** a spout or nozzle for emitting liquid or gas. **4.** JET PLANE. **5.** JET ENGINE. —*v.i.* **6.** to move or travel by jet propulsion or jet-propelled craft. **7.** to be shot forth in a stream. —*v.t.* **8.** to transport by jet plane. **9.** to shoot (something) forth in a stream; spout. —*adj.* **10.** pertaining to, associated with, or involving a jet, jet engine, or jet plane. **11.** in the form of or producing a jet or jet propulsion: *a jet nozzle.*

jet² (jet), *n.* **1.** a hard black coal, susceptible of a high polish, sometimes used in jewelry. **2.** a deep black. —*adj.*

jet'-black', *adj.* deep black: *jet-black hair.*

je·té (zhə tā'), *n., pl.* **-tés.** any of various jumps in ballet with one leg thrown outward and forward.

jet' en'gine, *n.* an engine, as of an aircraft, that produces forward motion by the rearward exhaust of a jet of fluid or heated air and gases.

Jeth·ro (jeth'rō), *n.* the father-in-law of Moses. Ex. 3:1. Also called **Reuel.** Ex. 2:18.

jet' lag' or **jet'lag',** *n.* a temporary disruption of the body's normal biological rhythms after high-speed air travel through several time zones. —**jet'-lagged',** *adj.*

jet·lin·er (jet'lī'nər), *n.* a jet airliner for passengers.

jet' plane', *n.* an airplane moved by jet propulsion.

jet'-propelled', *adj.* **1.** propelled by a jet engine or engines. **2.** suggesting a jet engine in force or speed; powerful or very fast.

jet' propul'sion, *n.* the propulsion of a body by its reaction to a force ejecting a gas or a liquid from it.

jet·sam or **jet·som** (jet'səm), *n.* goods that are cast overboard deliberately, as to lighten or stabilize a vessel in an emergency, and that sink where jettisoned or are washed ashore. Compare FLOTSAM.

jet' set', *n.* an international social set of wealthy people who travel frequently by jetliner to parties and resorts. —**jet'-set'ter,** *n.*

jet' stream', *n.* **1.** strong, generally westerly winds concentrated in a relatively narrow and shallow stream in the upper troposphere of the earth. **2.** similar strong winds in the atmosphere of another planet. **3.** the exhaust of a jet or rocket engine.

jet·ti·son (jet'ə sən, -zən), *v.t.* **1.** to cast (cargo, supplies, etc.) overboard or out so as to lighten or stabilize a vessel or aircraft in an emergency. **2.** to throw off (something) as an obstacle or burden; discard. —*n.* **3.** the act of casting goods from a vessel or aircraft to lighten or stabilize it. **4.** JETSAM.

jet·ty¹ (jet'ē), *n., pl.* **-ties,** *v.,* **-tied, -ty·ing.** —*n.* **1.** a pier or structure of stones, piles, or the like, projecting into the sea or other body of water to protect a harbor, deflect the current, etc. **2.** a wharf or landing pier. **3.** the piles or wooden structure protecting a pier. **4.** an overhanging upper story of a building. —*v.i.* **5.** to project or overhang; jut.

jet·ty² (jet'ē), *adj.* deep black.

Jew (jōō), *n.* **1.** a member of a people now living in many countries of the world who trace their descent from the Israelites of the Bible, or from postexilic adherents of Judaism. **2.** a person whose religion is Judaism. **3.** a subject of the ancient kingdom of Judah.

jew·el (jōō'əl), *n., v.,* **-eled, -el·ing** or *(esp. Brit.)* **-elled, -el·ling.** —*n.* **1.** a cut and polished precious stone; gem. **2.** a fashioned ornament for personal adornment, esp. of a precious metal set with gems. **3.** a person or thing that is treasured, esteemed, or indispensable. **4.** a durable bearing used in fine timepieces and other delicate instruments, made of nat-

ural or synthetic precious stone or other very hard material. —*v.t.* **5.** to set or adorn with jewels. —**jew'el·like',** *adj.*

jew·el·er (jōō'ə lar), *n.* a person who designs, makes, sells, or repairs jewelry, watches, etc. Also, *esp. Brit.,* **jew'el·ler.**

jew·el·fish (jōō'əl fish'), *n., pl.* **-fish·es,** *(esp. collectively)* **-fish.** a brightly colored cichlid fish, *Hemichromis bimaculatus,* native to Africa.

jew·el·ry (jōō'əl rē), *n.* objects of personal adornment, as necklaces, rings or bracelets, esp. when made of precious metals, gemstones, pearls, or other organic elements and distinguished by very fine design and craft. Compare COSTUME JEWELRY. Also, *esp. Brit.,* **jew'el·ler·y.**

jew·el·weed (jōō'əl wēd'), *n.* any of several plants belonging to the genus *Impatiens,* of the balsam family, having yellow spurred flowers and a seedpod that bursts to the touch when ripe.

jew·fish (jōō'fish'), *n., pl. (esp. collectively)* **-fish,** *(esp. for kinds or species)* **-fish·es.** any of several large groupers, esp. *Epinephelus itajara,* of warm Atlantic seas.

Jew·ish (jōō'ish), *adj.* **1.** of, pertaining to, or characteristic of Jews or Judaism. —*n.* **2.** *Informal.* Yiddish. —**Jew'ish·ness,** *n.*

Jew'ish cal'endar, *n.* a calendar used by Jews, as for determining religious holidays, that is reckoned from the traditional date of the Creation (corresponding to 3761 B.C.).

Jew·ry (jōō'rē), *n., pl.* **-ries. 1.** the Jewish people collectively. **2.** a district inhabited mainly by Jews; ghetto.

Jew's' (or **Jews'')** **harp',** *n. (sometimes l.c.)* a small, simple musical instrument consisting of a lyre-shaped metal frame containing a metal tongue, which is plucked while the frame is held in the teeth, the vibrations causing twanging tones.

Jez·e·bel (jez'ə bel', -bəl), *n.* **1.** the wife of Ahab, king of Israel. I Kings 16:31. **2.** *(often l.c.)* a wicked, shameless woman.

Jez·re·el (jez'rē əl, -el'), *n.* Plain of, ESDRAELON. —**Jez're·el·ite',** *n.*

JF, Jewish female.

JFK, John Fitzgerald Kennedy.

J.H.S., junior high school.

jib¹ or **jibb** (jib), *n.* **1.** any of various triangular sails set forward of a mast. —**Idiom. 2.** cut of one's jib, one's general appearance.

jib² (jib), *n.* **1.** the projecting arm of a crane. **2.** the boom of a derrick.

jibe¹ (jīb), *v.i., v.t.,* **jibed, jib·ing,** *n.* GIBE.

jibe² (jīb), *v.i., v.t.,* **jibed, jib·ing.** to be in harmony or accord; agree; correspond.

ji·ca·ma (hē'kə mə, hik'ə-), *n., pl.* **-mas. 1.** the large tuberous root of a tropical American twining plant, *Exogonium bracteotum,* of the legume family, eaten raw or cooked. **2.** the plant itself.

jif·fy (jif'ē) also **jiff** (jif), *n., pl.* **jif·fies** also **jiffs.** *Informal.* a very short time; moment; instant: *to get dressed in a jiffy.*

jig¹ (jig), *n., v.,* **jigged, jig·ging.** —*n.* **1.** a plate, box, or open frame for holding work and for guiding a machine tool to the work. **2.** any of several devices that are jerked up and down in or pulled through the water to attract fish to a line. **3.** an apparatus for washing coal or separating ore from worthless matter by shaking and washing. **4.** a cloth-dyeing machine in which a roll of fabric is unwound, passed through a vat of dye, and then wound onto another cylinder. —*v.t.* **5.** to treat, cut, produce, etc., with a jig. —*v.i.* **6.** to use a jig. **7.** to fish with a jig.

jig² (jig), *n., v.,* **jigged, jig·ging.** —*n.* **1.** a rapid, lively, springy, irregular dance for one or more persons, usu. in triple meter. **2.** a piece of music for such a dance. —*v.t.* **3.** to dance (a jig or any lively dance). **4.** to sing or play in the time or rhythm of a jig: *to jig a tune.* **5.** to cause to move with quick, jerky or bobbing motions. —*v.i.* **6.** to dance or play a jig. **7.** to move with a quick, jerky motion; hop; bob. —**Idiom. 8.** in jig time, with dispatch; rapidly. —**jig'like', jig'gish,** *adj.*

jig·ger¹ (jig'ər), *n.* **1.** a person or thing that jigs. **2.** any of various sails. **3.** any of various mechanical devices, many of which have a jerky or jolting motion. **4.** some contrivance, article, or part that one cannot or does not name more precisely. **5. a.** a measure of 1½ oz. (45 ml) used in cocktail recipes. **b.** a small whiskey glass holding this amount. **6.** a machine for forming ceramic plates or the like in a plaster mold rotating beneath a template. **7.** JIG¹ (def. 2).

jig·ger² (jig'ər), *n.* **1.** Also called **jig'ger flea'.** CHIGOE. **2.** CHIGGER (def. 1).

jig·ger³ (jig'ər), *v.t.* **1.** to jerk rapidly; jig. **2.** to manipulate or alter, esp. for illegal or unethical purposes.

jig·gle (jig'əl), *v.,* **-gled, -gling,** *n.* —*v.t., v.i.* **1.** to move up and down or to and fro with short, quick jerks. —*n.* **2.** a jiggling movement. —**jig'gler,** *n.* —**jig'gly, -gli·er, -gli·est.**

jig·saw (jig'sô'), *n., v.,* **-sawed, -sawed** or **-sawn, -saw·ing,** *adj.* —*n.* **1.** Also, **jig' saw'.** an electric machine saw with a narrow, vertically mounted blade, for cutting curves, complex patterns, etc. —*v.t.* **2.** to cut or form with or as if with a jigsaw. —*adj.* **3.** formed by or as if by a jigsaw: *jigsaw ornamentation.*

jig'saw puz'zle, *n.* **1.** a set of irregularly cut pieces of pasteboard, wood, or the like that form a picture or design when fitted together. **2.** a complex, confusing situation, condition, or item.

ji·had or **je·had** (ji häd'), *n.* **1.** a holy war undertaken as a sacred duty by Muslims. **2.** any vigorous crusade for a principle.

jil·lion (jil'yən), *n., pl.* **-lions,** *(as after a numeral)* **-lion.** *Informal.* an indefinitely vast number; zillion.

jilt (jilt), *v.t.* **1.** to reject or cast aside (a lover or sweetheart), esp. abruptly or unfeelingly. —*n.* **2.** a woman who jilts a lover. —**jilt'er,** *n.*

J

Jim′ Crow′ (jim), *n.* (*sometimes l.c.*) a practice or policy of segregating or discriminating against blacks. Also called **Jim′ Crow′ism, jim′ crow′ism.** [so called from the name of a song sung by Thomas Rice (1808–60) in a minstrel show] —**Jim′-Crow′,** *adj.*

jim′-dan′dy, *adj., n., pl.* **-dies.** *Informal.* —*adj.* **1.** of superior quality; excellent. —*n.* **2.** something of outstanding quality or excellence.

jim•my (jim′ē), *n., pl.* **-mies,** *v.,* **-mied, -my•ing.** —*n.* **1.** a short crowbar. **2.** a large male crab, esp. of Chesapeake Bay. —*v.t.* **3.** to force open with or as if with a jimmy.

jim•son•weed (jim′sən wēd′), *n.* a coarse, rank weed, *Datura stramonium,* of the nightshade family, with poisonous oaklike leaves, tubular flowers, and prickly fruit. Compare THORN APPLE.

jin•gle (jing′gəl), *v.,* **-gled, -gling,** *n.* —*v.i.* **1.** to make clinking or tinkling sounds: *sleighbells jingling.* **2.** to move or proceed with such sounds. **3.** to sound or rhyme in a light, repetitious manner. —*v.t.* **4.** to cause to jingle. —*n.* **5.** a tinkling or clinking sound. **6.** something that makes such a sound. **7.** a catchy succession of repetitious sounds, as in verse. **8.** a piece of verse or a short song with these catchy sounds, usu. of a light or humorous character: *an advertising jingle.* —**jin′gler,** *n.* —**jin′gling•ly,** *adv.* —**jin′gly,** *adj.*

jin•go (jing′gō), *n., pl.* **-goes.** a person who professes belligerent patriotism and favors an aggressive foreign policy.

jin•go•ism (jing′gō iz′əm), *n.* the spirit, policy, or practice of jingoes; bellicose chauvinism. —**jin′go•ist,** *n., adj.*

jinn (jin) also **jin•ni** (ji nē′, jin′ē), *n., pl.* **jinns** also **jin•nis,** (*esp. collectively*) **jinn** also **jin•ni.** (in Islamic myth) any of a class of spirits, lower than the angels, capable of appearing in human and animal forms and influencing humankind.

jin•rik•i•sha or **jin•rik•sha** (jin rik′shô, -shä), *n., pl.* **-shas.** a small, two-wheeled, cartlike passenger vehicle with a fold-down top, pulled by one person, formerly used widely in Japan and China. Also called **ricksha, rickshaw.**

jinx (jingks), *n.* **1.** one thought to bring bad luck. **2.** a condition or spell of misfortune. —*v.t.* **3.** to bring bad luck to.

jit•ter (jit′ər), *n.* **1.** the act or the condition of a person or thing that jitters. **2. jitters,** a feeling of fright or uneasiness (usu. prec. by *the*): *to get the jitters in an empty house.* **3.** fluctuating movement, as in an image on a television screen. —*v.i.* **4.** to make a series of quick, shivering or jumping movements. **5.** to behave nervously.

jit•ter•bug (jit′ər bug′), *n., v.,* **-bugged, -bug•ging.** —*n.* **1.** a strenuously acrobatic jazz dance marked by standardized steps along with twirls, splits, and somersaults. **2.** a person who dances the jitterbug. —*v.i.* **3.** to dance the jitterbug. —**jit′ter•bug′ger,** *n.*

jit•ter•y (jit′ə rē), *adj.,* **-ter•i•er, -ter•i•est. 1.** extremely tense and nervous; jumpy. **2.** having a jitter; marked by quick, jumping movements. —**jit′ter•i•ness,** *n.*

jiu•jit•su (jo͞o jit′so͞o) also **jiu•jut•su** (-jut′-, -jo͞ot′-), *n.* JUJITSU.

jive (jīv), *n., v.,* **jived, jiv•ing,** *adj.* —*n.* **1.** swing music or early jazz. **2.** the jargon associated with swing music and early jazz. **3.** *Slang.* deceptive, exaggerated, or meaningless talk. —*v.i.* **4.** to play jive. **5.** to dance to jive; jitterbug. **6.** *Slang.* to engage in kidding, teasing, or exaggeration. —*v.t.* **7.** *Slang.* to tease; fool; kid. —*adj.* **8.** *Slang.* insincere or deceptive. —**jiv′er,** *n.* —**jiv′ey,** *adj.,* **jiv•i•er, jiv•i•est.**

JM, Jewish male.

Jo•ab (jō′ab), *n.* a commander of David's army and the slayer of Absalom. II Sam. 3:27; 18:14.

Jo•an•na (jō an′ə), *n.* a member of the household of Herod Antipas, who gave money to Jesus and his disciples, and witnessed the empty tomb after Jesus' resurrection. Luke 24:1–10.

Joan of Arc (jōn′ əv ärk′), *n.* **Saint** (*"the Maid of Orléans"*), 1412?–31, French martyr who raised the siege of Orléans. French, **Jeanne d'Arc.**

Jo•ash (jō′ash), *n.* a king of Judah, reigned 837?–800? B.C., successor of Athaliah. II Kings 13:10–13.

job (job), *n., v.,* **jobbed, job•bing,** *adj.* —*n.* **1.** a piece of work, esp. a specific task done as part of one's occupation or for an agreed price. **2.** a post of employment; position. **3.** any task or project. **4.** a responsibility; duty: *It is your job to be on time.* **5.** the execution or performance of a task: *to do a good job.* **6.** the material or item being worked upon. **7.** a state of affairs; matter: *to make the best of a bad job.* **8.** a difficult task: *We had a job getting him to agree.* **9.** *Informal.* an example of a specific type: *That little sports job is a great car.* **10.** *Slang.* a theft or similar crime. **11.** a public or official act or decision done for improper private gain. **12.** a unit of work for a computer. —*v.i.* **13.** to work at jobs or odd pieces of work; work by the piece. **14.** to do business as a jobber. **15.** to turn public business improperly to private gain. —*v.t.* **16.** to assign (work, a contract for work, etc.) in separate portions, as to different contractors or workers (often fol. by *out*). **17.** to buy in large quantities from wholesalers or manufacturers and sell to dealers in smaller quantities. **18.** to swindle or trick. **19.** to carry on (public business) for improper private gain. —*adj.* **20.** of or for a particular job or transaction. **21.** bought, sold, or handled together: *to buy in job quantities.* —***Idiom.*** **22. do a job on, a.** to damage or destroy. **b.** to deceive; snow. **23. on the job, a.** while working; at work. **b.** on the alert.

Job (jōb), *n.* **1.** the central figure in an Old Testament parable of the righteous sufferer. **2.** a book of the Bible bearing his name.

job′ ac′tion, *n.* a work slowdown or other organized action used by employees as a means of protest or to compel an employer to accede to demands.

job′ bank′, *n.* a usu. computerized collection of information on available jobs, for use by those seeking employment.

job•ber (job′ər), *n.* **1.** a wholesale merchant, esp. one selling to retailers. **2.** a pieceworker. **3.** (formerly) a merchant dealing in special, odd, or job lots. **4.** a person who practices jobbery.

job′-hop′, *v.i.,* **-hopped, -hop•ping.** to change jobs frequently. —**job′-hop′per,** *n.*

job′-hunt′, *v.i.* to seek employment; look for a job. —**job′-hunt′er,** *n.*

job′ lot′, *n.* **1.** a large, often assorted quantity of goods sold or handled as a single transaction. **2.** a miscellaneous collection; quantity of odds and ends.

Job's′ com′forter (jōbz), *n.* a person who unwittingly or maliciously depresses or discourages someone while attempting to be consoling.

Job's-tears (jōbz′tērz′), *n.* **1.** (*used with a pl. v.*) the hard, nearly spherical bracts that surround the female flowers of an Asian grass, *Coix lacryma-jobi,* used as beads. **2.** (*used with a sing. v.*) the grass itself.

Jo•cas•ta (jō kas′tə), *n.* a legendary queen of Thebes who was both the mother and wife of Oedipus.

Joch•e•bed (jok′ə bed′), *n.* the mother of Aaron and Moses. Ex. 6:20.

jock¹ (jok), *n.* **1.** a jockstrap. **2.** *Informal.* a person who enjoys or is good at sports; athlete. **3.** *Informal.* an enthusiast: *a computer jock; science jocks.*

jock² (jok), *n.* a jockey.

jock•ey (jok′ē), *n.* **1.** a person who rides horses professionally in races. **2.** DISC JOCKEY. **3.** *Informal.* a person who pilots, operates, or guides the movement of something, as a vehicle. —*v.t.* **4.** to ride (a horse) as a jockey. **5.** *Informal.* to operate or guide the movement of; pilot; drive. **6.** to move by skillful maneuvering. **7.** to manipulate cleverly or trickily. —*v.i.* **8.** to aim at an advantage by skillful maneuvering. **9.** to act trickily; seek an advantage by trickery.

Jock′ey shorts′, *Trademark.* short, close-fitting underpants for men with an elastic band around the waist; briefs.

jock′ itch′, *n.* a ringworm of the groin area, caused by any of several fungi.

jock•strap (jok′strap′), *n.* an elasticized belt with a pouch for supporting the genitals, worn as an undergarment by men esp. while participating in athletics. Also called **athletic supporter.**

jo•cose (jō kōs′, jə-), *adj.* given to or characterized by joking; playful. —**jo•cose′ly,** *adv.* —**jo•cos′i•ty** (-kos′i tē), **jo•cose′ness,** *n.*

joc•u•lar (jok′yə lər), *adj.* given to or characterized by joking or jesting; waggish; facetious: *jocular remarks.* —**joc′u•lar′i•ty,** *n.* —**joc′u•lar•ly,** *adv.*

joc•und (jok′ənd, jō′kənd), *adj.* cheerful; merry; jolly. —**jo•cun•di•ty** (jō kun′di tē), *n.* —**joc′und•ly,** *adv.*

joe (jō), *n. Slang.* coffee.

Joe (jō), *n. Informal.* a typical male representative of an occupation, trait, or state of being usu. expressed by a mock surname: *Joe College; Joe Six-Pack.*

Jo•el (jō′əl), *n.* **1.** a Minor Prophet of the postexilic period. **2.** a book of the Bible bearing his name.

jo•ey (jō′ē), *n., pl.* **-eys.** *Australian.* a young animal, esp. a kangaroo.

jog¹ (jog), *v.,* **jogged, jog•ging,** *n.* —*v.t.* **1.** to move with a push or jerk. **2.** to stir into activity or alertness, as by a reminder: *to jog one's memory.* **3.** to cause (a horse) to go at a steady trot. **4.** to align the edges of (a stack of sheets of paper of the same size) by gently tapping. —*v.i.* **5.** to run at a slow, steady pace. **6.** to ride at a steady trot. —*n.* **7.** a shake; slight push; nudge. **8.** a steady trot, as of a horse. **9.** an act or instance of jogging: *to go for a jog.* **10.** a jogging pace. —**jog′ger,** *n.*

jog² (jog), *n., v.,* **jogged, jog•ging.** —*n.* **1.** an irregularity of line or surface; projection; notch. **2.** a bend or turn. —*v.i.* **3.** to bend or turn: *The road jogs to the left there.*

jog•gle (jog′əl), *v.,* **-gled, -gling,** *n.* —*v.t.* **1.** to shake slightly; move to and fro, as by repeated jerks; jiggle. **2.** to join or fasten by fitting a projection into a recess. **3.** to fit or fasten with dowels. —*v.i.* **4.** to move irregularly, with a jogging or jolting motion; shake. —*n.* **5.** the act of joggling. **6.** a slight shake or jolt. **7.** a projection on one of two joining objects that fits into a corresponding recess in the other to prevent slipping. **8.** an enlarged area, as on a post, for supporting the foot of a strut, brace, etc. —**jog′gler,** *n.*

Jo•han•nes•burg (jō han′is bûrg′, -hä′nis-, yō-), *n.* a city in S Transvaal, in the NE Republic of South Africa. 1,609,408.

Jo•han•nine (jō han′in, -īn), *adj.* of or pertaining to the apostle John or to the books in the New Testament attributed to him.

john (jon), *n. Informal.* a toilet or bathroom.

John¹ (jon), *n.* **1.** the apostle John, believed to be the author of the fourth Gospel, three Epistles, and the book of Revelation. **2.** the fourth Gospel. **3.** any of the three Epistles of John; I, II, or III John. **4.** JOHN THE BAPTIST. **5.** (*John Lackland*) 1167?–1216, king of England 1199–1216: signer of the Magna Carta 1215 (son of Henry II). **6. Elton** (*Reginald Kenneth Dwight*), born 1947, English rock singer, pianist, and songwriter.

John² (jon), **1. John III,** (*John Sobieski*) 1624–96, king of Poland 1674–96. **2. John XXIII,** (*Angelo Giuseppe Roncalli*) 1881–1963, Italian ecclesiastic: pope 1958–63.

John′ Birch′ Soci′ety, *n.* an ultraconservative organization, founded in December 1958 by Robert Welch, Jr., chiefly to combat alleged Communist activities in the U.S.

John′ Brown′s′ Bod′y, a long narrative poem (1928) by Stephen Vincent Benét, about the U.S. Civil War.

John′ Bull′, *n.* **1.** England; the English people. **2.** the typical Englishman. [after *John Bull*, chief character in Arbuthnot's allegory *The History of John Bull* (1712)] —**John′ Bull′ish,** *adj.*

John′ Doe′ (dō), *n.* **1.** an anonymous, average man. **2.** a fictitious name used in legal proceedings for a male party whose true name is not known. Compare JANE DOE.

John′ Han′cock, *n.* a person's signature.

John′ Hen′ry, *n., pl.* **John Henries. 1.** a person's signature. **2.** a black man of U.S. folklore possessing exceptional strength.

John•ny or **John•nie** (jon′ē), *n., pl.* **-nies.** (*sometimes l.c.*) **1.** a familiar term of address for a man or boy. **2.** a short, collarless gown fastened in back, worn by medical patients, as in a hospital.

john•ny•cake (jon′ē kāk′), *n. Northern U.S.* a flat cake or bread made with cornmeal, usu. cooked on a griddle.

John′ny-come′-late′ly, *n., pl.* **Johnny-come-latelies** or **-latelys,** **Johnnies-come-lately.** a late arrival or participant; newcomer.

John′ny-jump′-up′, *n., pl.* **Johnny-jump-ups. 1.** any of various American violets, esp. *Viola pedunculata.* **2.** a small form of the pansy, *Viola tricolor.*

John′ny Reb′ (reb), *n.* a Confederate soldier; Rebel.

John′ of Damas′cus, *n.* **Saint,** A.D. c675–749, priest, theologian, and scholar of the Eastern Church, born in Damascus.

John′ of the Cross′, *n.* **Saint** (*Juan de Yepis y Álvarez*), 1542–91, Spanish mystic, writer, and theologian: cofounder with Saint Theresa of the order of Discalced Carmelites. Spanish, **San Juan de la Cruz.**

John′ Paul′, **1. John Paul I,** (*Albino Luciani*) 1912–78, Italian ecclesiastic: pope 1978. **2. John Paul II,** (*Karol Wojtyła*) born 1920, Polish ecclesiastic: pope since 1978.

John Q. Public, *n.* the average or typical U.S. citizen.

John•son (jon′sən), *n.* **1. Andrew,** 1808–75, 17th president of the U.S. 1865–69. **2. Earvin** (*"Magic"*), born 1959, U.S. basketball player. **3. James Price,** 1891–1955, U.S. pianist and jazz composer. **4. James Weldon,** 1871–1938, U.S. poet, essayist, editor, and social reformer. **5. J(ohn) Rosamond,** U.S. composer (brother of James Weldon Johnson). **6. Lyndon Baines,** 1908–73, 36th president of the U.S. 1963–69. **7. Richard Mentor,** 1780–1850, vice president of the U.S. 1837–41. **8. Samuel** (*"Dr. Johnson"*), 1709–84, English lexicographer and writer. **9. Torrey,** born 1909, U.S. clergyman, founder of Youth for Christ.

John′son grass′, *n.* a sorghum, *Sorghum halepense,* that spreads by creeping rhizomes, grown for fodder.

John•ston (jon′stən, -sən), *n.* **1. Albert Sidney,** 1803–62, Confederate general in the U.S. Civil War. **2. Joseph Eggleston,** 1807–91, Confederate general in the U.S. Civil War.

Johns′town Flood′ (jonz′toun′), *n.* a disastrous flood (1889) that killed 2,200 people in Johnstown, Pa., after a dam burst.

John′ the Bap′tist, *n.* the forerunner and baptizer of Jesus. Matt. 3.

join (join), *v.t.* **1.** to bring or put together or in contact; connect: *to join hands.* **2.** to come into contact or union with: *The brook joins the river.* **3.** to bring together in a particular relation or for a specific purpose; unite: *to join forces.* **4.** to become a member of: *to join a club.* **5.** to enlist in: *to join the Navy.* **6.** to come into the company of; meet or accompany: *I'll join you later.* **7.** to participate with in some act or activity. **8.** to unite in marriage. **9.** to meet or engage in (battle or conflict). **10.** to adjoin; meet. **11.** to draw a curve or straight line between: *to join two points on a graph.* —*v.i.* **12.** to come into or be in contact or connection. **13.** to become united, associated, or allied (usu. fol. by *with*): *Join with us in our campaign.* **14.** to take part with others (often fol. by *in*). **15.** to be contiguous or close; adjoin. **16.** to enlist in one of the armed forces (often fol. by *up*). **17.** to meet in battle or conflict. —*n.* **18.** a joining. **19.** a place or line of joining; seam. —**join′a•ble,** *adj.*

join•er (joi′nər), *n.* **1.** a person or thing that joins. **2.** a carpenter, esp. one who constructs doors, window sashes, paneling, and other permanent woodwork. **3.** a person given to joining groups.

joint (joint), *n.* **1.** the place at which two things, or separate parts of one thing, are joined or united, either rigidly or so as to permit motion. **2.** a connection between pieces of wood, metal, etc., often reinforced with nails, screws, or glue. **3. a.** the place of union between two bones or elements of a skeleton, whether fixed or permitting movement. **b.** the mechanical form of such a union: *the ball-and-socket joint of the hip; the hinge joint of the elbow.* **c.** the structural components, as the adjacent bone edges and their attachments. **4.** the place of articulation between two parts or segments of an insect, crustacean, or other arthropod. **5.** the node of a plant stem where a leaf or branch emerges, esp. when bent at an angle. **6.** a large piece of meat, usu. with a bone, esp. a piece suitable for roasting. **7.** *Slang.* **a.** a disreputable place of public entertainment. **b.** a dwelling or establishment; place. **c.** prison. **8.** a fracture plane in crystalline or sedimentary rock, commonly arranged in intersecting sets. **9.** *Math.* NODE (def. 6). —*adj.* **10.** shared by or common to two or more: *joint custody.* **11.** undertaken or produced by two or more in conjunction or in common: *a joint effort.* **12.** sharing or acting in common: *joint authorship.* **13.** joined or associated, as in relation, interest, or action: *joint owners.* **14.** *Law.* joined together in obligation or ownership. **15.** of or pertaining to both branches of a bicameral legislature: *a joint session of Congress.* —*v.t.* **16.** to unite by a joint. **17.** to form or provide with joints. **18.** to cut (meat, fowl, etc.) at the joints so as to separate into pieces: *to joint a chicken.* **19.** to prepare (a board or the like) for fitting in a joint, as by truing the edge. —*v.i.* **20.** to fit together by or as if by joints. —*Idiom.* **21. out of joint, a.** dislocated, as a bone. **b.** in an unfavorable or disordered state. —**joint′less,** *adj.*

Joint′ Chiefs′ of Staff′, *n.pl.* the chief military advisory body to the President of the U.S., consisting of the Chiefs of Staff of the Army and the Air Force, the commandant of the Marine Corps, the Chief of Naval Operations, and a chairperson drawn from one of the armed forces.

joint•ly (joint′lē), *adv.* in combination or partnership.

joint′ resolu′tion, *n.* a resolution adopted by both branches of a legislature that becomes law if signed by the chief executive.

joint′ ven′ture, *n.* a business enterprise in which two or more companies enter a temporary partnership. —**joint′ ven′turer,** *n.*

joist (joist), *n.* one of a number of small parallel beams of timber, steel, or reinforced concrete that support a floor or ceiling.

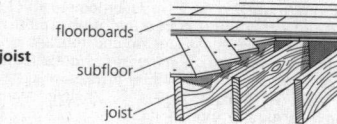

joist — floorboards — subfloor — joist

jo•jo•ba (hō hō′bə), *n., pl.* **-bas.** a shrub, *Simmondsia chinensis* (or *S. californica*), of the southwest U.S. and Mexico, bearing seeds that are the source of an oil (**jojo′ba oil′**) used in cosmetics and as a lubricant.

joke (jōk), *n., v.,* **joked, jok•ing.** —*n.* **1.** a short humorous anecdote with a punch line. **2.** anything said or done to provoke laughter or cause amusement. **3.** something amusing or ridiculous: *I don't see the joke in that.* **4.** an object of laughter or ridicule, esp. because of being inadequate or sham. **5.** a matter not of great seriousness; trifling matter: *The loss was no joke.* **6.** something not presenting an expected challenge; something very easy: *The test was a joke.* **7.** PRACTICAL JOKE. —*v.i.* **8.** to speak or act in a playful or merry way. **9.** to say something in fun or teasing rather than in earnest: *I was only joking.* —*v.t.* **10.** to subject to jokes; make fun of; tease. —**joke′less,** *adj.* —**jok′ing•ly,** *adv.*

jok•er (jō′kər), *n.* **1.** a person who jokes. **2.** one of two extra playing cards in a pack, usu. imprinted with the figure of a jester, used in some games as the highest card or as a wild card. **3.** a seemingly minor clause or expression inserted in a legal document, legislative bill, etc., to change its effect or defeat its purpose. **4.** an unexpected or final element that completely changes or reverses a situation or result. **5.** an expedient for getting the better of someone. **6.** *Informal.* a person considered unworthy of respect. **7.** a prankster or wise guy.

Jo•liot-Cu•rie (zhōl yō′kyŏŏr′ē, -kyŏŏ rē′), *n.* **1. Irène,** (*Irène Curie*), 1897–1956, French nuclear physicist (daughter of Pierre and Marie Curie). **2.** her husband, **(Jean) Frédéric** (zhän), (*Jean Frédéric Joliot*), 1900–58, French nuclear physicist.

jol•li•ty (jol′i tē), *n., pl.* **-ties. 1.** a jolly or merry mood, condition, or activity; gaiety. **2. jollities,** jolly festivities.

jol•ly (jol′ē), *adj.,* **-li•er, -li•est,** *v.,* **-lied, -ly•ing,** *n., pl.* **-lies,** *adv.* —*adj.* **1.** being in good spirits; merry. **2.** cheerfully festive: *a jolly party.* **3.** delightful; charming. —*v.t.* **4.** to try to keep (a person) in good humor, esp. to gain a desired end (usu. fol. by *along*). **5.** to tease, esp. good-naturedly. —*n.* **6.** Usu., **jollies.** *Informal.* pleasurable excitement; kicks; fun. —*adv.* **7.** *Brit.* very: *jolly good.* —**jol′li•ness,** *n.*

Jol′ly Rog′er (roj′ər), *n.* a flag flown by pirates, having a white skull and crossbones on a black field.

Jolly Roger

jolt (jōlt), *v.t.* **1.** to cause to move by or as if by sudden rough jerks or bumps; shake up roughly. **2.** to knock sharply so as to move or dislodge; jar. **3.** to shock or startle. **4.** to bring to a specified state sharply or abruptly: *to jolt someone into awareness.* **5.** to interfere with, esp. in a rough manner; interrupt disturbingly. —*v.i.* **6.** to move with a sharp jerk or a series of sharp jerks. —*n.* **7.** a jolting movement or blow. **8.** a psychological shock. **9.** a sudden, unexpected setback. **10.** a bracing dose of something: *a jolt of whiskey.* —**jolt′er,** *n.* —**jolt′ing•ly,** *adv.*

Jo•nah (jō′nə), *n.* **1.** a Minor Prophet who, for his impiety, was thrown overboard from his ship and swallowed by a large fish, remaining in its belly for three days before being cast up onto the shore un-

J

harmed. **2.** a book of the Bible bearing his name. **3.** a person or thing regarded as bringing bad luck. —**Jo′nah·esque′**, *adj.*

Jon·a·than[1] (jon′ə thən), *n.* a son of Saul and friend of David. I Sam. 18–20.

Jon·a·than[2] (jon′ə thən), *n.* a variety of red apple. [after *Jonathan Hasbrouck* (d. 1846), U.S. jurist]

Jones (jōnz), *n.* **1. Anson,** 1798–1858, president of the Republic of Texas. **2. Casey** (*John Luther Jones*), 1864–1900, U.S. locomotive engineer: folk hero of ballads, stories, and plays. **3. Inigo,** 1573–1652, English architect. **4. John Paul** (*John Paul*), 1747–92, American naval commander in the Revolutionary War, born in Scotland. **5. Mary Harris** (*"Mother Jones"*), 1830–1930, U.S. labor leader, born in Ireland. **6. Robert Tyre** (*"Bobby"*), 1902–71, U.S. golfer. **7. Rufus Matthew,** 1863–1948, U.S. Quaker, teacher, author, and humanitarian. **8. Sam(uel Porter),** 1847–1906, U.S. evangelist.

Jones·es (jōn′ziz), *n.pl.* —*Idiom.* **keep up with the Joneses,** to compete socially with one's neighbors or associates, esp. by buying the things they have.

Jones·town (jōnz′toun′), *n.* a former settlement in N Guyana, NW of Georgetown: site of agricultural commune of an American religious cult called the People's Temple; mass suicide and murder 1978.

jon·quil (jong′kwil, jon′-), *n.* a narcissus, *Narcissus jonquilla,* having long, narrow leaves and yellow or white flowers.

Jon·son (jon′sən), *n.* **Ben,** 1573?–1637, English dramatist and poet. —**Jon·so′ni·an** (-sō′nē ən), *adj.*

Jop·lin (jop′lin), *n.* **1. Scott,** 1868–1917, U.S. ragtime pianist and composer. **2.** a city in SW Missouri. 38,893.

Jop·pa (jop′ə), *n.* ancient name of JAFFA.

Jo·ram (jôr′am, jōr′-) also **Jehoram,** *n.* **1.** a king of Judah, the son of Jehoshaphat. II Kings 8:16–24. **2.** a king of Israel, son of Ahab and Jezebel; slain by Jehu. II Kings 3:1–6; 9:14–26.

Jor·dan (jôr′dn), *n.* **1. Barbara Charline,** 1936–96, U.S. political leader and educator. **2. June,** born 1936, U.S. poet, novelist, and essayist. **3. Michael,** born 1963, U.S. basketball player. **4.** Official name, **Hashemite Kingdom of Jordan.** a kingdom in SW Asia, consisting of the former Transjordan and a part of Palestine that, since 1967, has been occupied by Israel. 4,324,638; 37,264 sq. mi. (96,514 sq. km). *Cap.*: Amman. **5.** a river in SW Asia, flowing from S Lebanon through the Sea of Galilee, then S between Israel and Jordan through W Jordan into the Dead Sea. 200 mi. (320 km) long. —**Jor·da′ni·an** (-dā′nē ən), *n., adj.*

Jo·seph (jō′zəf, -səf), *n.* **1.** a son of Jacob and Rachel who was sold into slavery by his jealous brothers. Gen. 30:22–24; 37. **2.** the husband of Mary, the mother of Jesus. Matt. 1:16–25. **3.** (*Hinmaton-yalaktit*) c1840–1904, leader of the Nez Percé. **4.** (*l.c.*) a woman's riding coat popular in colonial America.

Jo′seph of Ar·i·ma·thae′a (ar′ə mə thē′ə), *n.* a member of the Sanhedrin who placed the body of Jesus in the tomb. Matt. 27:57–60; Mark 15:43.

Jo·se·phus (jō sē′fəs), *n.* **Flavius,** A.D. 37?–c100, Jewish historian.

josh (josh), *v.t., v.i.* to tease in a bantering way: chaff. —**josh′er,** *n.*

Josh·u·a (josh′ōō ə), *n.* **1.** the successor of Moses as leader of the Israelites. Deut. 31:14, 23; 34:9. **2.** a book of the Bible bearing his name.

Josh′ua tree′, an evergreen tree, *Yucca brevifolia,* with long, twisted branches, growing in arid regions of the southwestern U.S.

Jo·si·ah (jō sī′ə), *n.* a king of Judah, reigned 640?–609? B.C. II Kings 22.

jos·tle (jos′əl), *v.,* **-tled, -tling,** *n.* —*v.t.* **1.** to bump against, push, or elbow roughly or rudely. **2.** to drive or force by or as if by pushing or shoving. **3.** to contend with: *rivals jostling each other for advantage.* **4.** to exist in close contact or proximity with. —*v.i.* **5.** to bump or brush against others, as in a crowd; push or shove. **6.** to make one's way by pushing or shoving. **7.** to exist in close contact or proximity. **8.** to compete; contend. —*n.* **9.** the act of jostling; a rough bump or push. —**jos′tle·ment,** *n.* —**jos′tler,** *n.*

jot (jot), *v.,* **jot·ted, jot·ting,** *n.* —*v.t.* **1.** to write or mark down quickly or briefly (usu. fol. by *down*): *Jot down the license number.* —*n.* **2.** the least amount; a little bit: *I don't care a jot.* —**jot′ter,** *n.*

Jo·tham (jō′thəm), *n.* a son of Gideon. Judg. 9:5–21.

joule (jōōl, joul), *n.* the SI unit of work or energy, equal to the work done by a force of one newton when its point of application moves through a distance of one meter in the direction of the force. *Abbr.*: J, j

jounce (jouns), *v.,* **jounced, jounc·ing,** *n.* —*v.t., v.i.* **1.** to move joltingly or roughly up and down; bounce. —*n.* **2.** a jouncing movement. —**jounc′y,** *adj.,* **jounc·i·er, jounc·i·est.**

jour·nal (jûr′nl), *n.* **1.** a daily record, as of occurrences, experiences, or observations. **2.** a newspaper, esp. a daily one. **3.** a periodical or magazine, esp. one published for a group, learned society, or profession. **4.** a record, usu. daily, of the proceedings and transactions of a legislative body or an organization. **5.** (in double-entry bookkeeping) a book into which all transactions are entered before being posted into the ledger. **6.** a log or logbook. **7.** the portion of a shaft or axle contained by a plain bearing. —*v.t.* **8.** to enter in a journal.

jour·nal·ese (jûr′nl ēz′, -ēs′), *n.* a style of writing regarded as typical of newspapers and magazines.

jour·nal·ism (jûr′nl iz′əm), *n.* **1.** the occupation of gathering, writing, editing, and publishing or broadcasting news. **2.** newspapers and magazines; the press. **3.** a course of study for a career in journalism. **4.** material written for a newspaper or magazine. **5.** writing marked by a popular slant.

jour·nal·ist (jûr′nl ist), *n.* **1.** a person whose profession is journalism. **2.** a person who keeps a journal.

jour·nal·is·tic (jûr′nl is′tik), *adj.* of or characteristic of journalism or journalists. —**jour′nal·is′ti·cal·ly,** *adv.*

jour·ney (jûr′nē), *n., pl.* **-neys.** **1.** a traveling from one place to another, usu. taking a rather long time; trip. **2.** a distance or course traveled. **3.** a period of travel: *a week's journey.* **4.** passage or progress from one stage to another: *the journey to success.* —*v.i.* **5.** to make a journey; travel. —**jour′ney·er,** *n.*

jour·ney·man (jûr′nē mən), *n., pl.* **-men.** **1.** a person who has served an apprenticeship at a trade or handicraft and is certified to work at it under another person. **2.** a competent but routine worker or performer. **3.** a person hired to do work for another, usu. by the day.

joust (joust, just, jōōst), *n.* **1.** a combat in which two mounted knights armed with lances attempted to unhorse each other, esp. as part of a tournament. **2.** a personal competition or struggle. —*v.i.* **3.** to engage in a joust. **4.** to contend or compete. —**joust′er,** *n.*

jo·vi·al (jō′vē əl), *adj.* endowed with or characterized by hearty, joyous humor or a spirit of good-fellowship. —**jo′vi·al·ly,** *adv.*

jowl[1] (joul; *sometimes* jōl), *n.* **1.** a jaw, esp. the lower jaw. **2.** the cheek. **3.** the meat of the cheek of a hog. —**jowled,** *adj.*

jowl[2] (joul; *sometimes* jōl), *n.* a fold of flesh hanging from the jaw, as of a person who is fat.

joy (joi), *n.* **1.** a feeling or state of great delight or happiness, as caused by something exceptionally good or satisfying; keen pleasure; elation. **2.** a source or cause of keen pleasure or delight: *a book that was a joy to read.* **3.** the expression or display of glad feeling; gaiety.

Joyce (jois), *n.* **James (Augustine Aloysius),** 1882–1941, Irish writer. —**Joyc′e·an,** *adj., n.*

joy·ful (joi′fəl), *adj.* **1.** full of joy; glad; delighted. **2.** showing or expressing joy: *a joyful look.* **3.** causing or bringing joy; delightful: *a joyful event.* —**joy′ful·ly,** *adv.* —**joy′ful·ness,** *n.*

Joy′ful, Joy′ful, We′ Adore′ Thee′, a Christian hymn with words (1907) by Henry van Dyke and music by Ludwig van Beethoven.

joy·less (joi′lis), *adj.* affording or causing no joy or pleasure. —**joy′less·ly,** *adv.* —**joy′less·ness,** *n.*

joy·ous (joi′əs), *adj.* joyful; happy; jubilant: *a joyous shout.* —**joy′ous·ly,** *adv.* —**joy′ous·ness,** *n.*

joy·ride (joi′rīd′), *n., v.,* **-rode, -rid·den, -rid·ing.** —*n.* **1.** a pleasure ride in an automobile, esp. when the vehicle is driven recklessly or used without the owner's permission. **2.** a brief exciting or reckless interlude. —*v.i.* **3.** to go on a joyride. —**joy′rid′er,** *n.*

joy·stick (joi′stik′), *n.* **1.** *Informal.* the control stick of an airplane, tank, or other vehicle. **2.** a lever used to control the movement of a cursor or other graphic element, as in a video game.

Joy′ to′ the World′, a Christmas hymn with words (1719) by Isaac Watts and music by George Frideric Handel, adapted by Lowell Mason.

JP or **J.P.,** Justice of the Peace.

Jr. or **jr.,** Junior.

Juá·rez (wär′ez, hwär′-), *n.* **1. Benito (Pablo),** 1806–72, president of Mexico 1857–72. **2. Ciudad,** CIUDAD JUÁREZ.

Ju·bal (jōō′bəl), *n.* a descendant of Cain: the progenitor of musicians and those who produce musical instruments. Gen. 4:21.

ju·bi·lant (jōō′bə lənt), *adj.* showing great joy, satisfaction, or triumph; exultant. —**ju′bi·lance, ju′bi·lan·cy,** *n.* —**ju′bi·lant·ly,** *adv.*

ju·bi·la·tion (jōō′bə lā′shən), *n.* **1.** a feeling of or the expression of joy or exultation. **2.** the act of rejoicing or jubilating. **3.** a joyful or festive celebration.

ju·bi·lee (jōō′bə lē′, jōō′bə lē′), *n.* **1.** the celebration of any of certain anniversaries, as the 25th, 50th, 60th, or 75th. **2.** the completion of 50 years of existence, activity, or the like. **3.** any season or occasion of rejoicing or festivity. **4.** rejoicing or jubilation. **5.** (in the Roman Catholic Church) **a.** Also called **ju′bilee year′.** an appointed year or other period, ordinarily every 25 years, in which a plenary indulgence is granted upon repentance and the performance of certain acts. **b.** the plenary indulgence granted. **6.** a yearlong period observed by Jews in ancient times every 50 years, during which Jewish slaves were freed, alienated lands restored to the original owner, and the fields left untilled. Lev. 25. Compare SABBATICAL YEAR (def. 2). **7.** an African-American folk song concerned with future happiness or deliverance from tribulation. —*adj.* **8.** flambé: *cherries jubilee.*

Jud., **1.** Judges. **2.** Judith (Apocrypha).

jud., **1.** Judge. **2.** judgment. **3.** judicial. **4.** judiciary.

Ju·dah (jōō′də), *n.* **1.** the fourth son of Jacob and Leah. Gen. 29:35. **2.** one of the 12 tribes of Israel, traditionally descended from him. **3.** the Biblical kingdom of the Hebrews in S Palestine, including the tribes of Judah and Benjamin. Compare ISRAEL (def. 4).

Ju·da·ic (jōō dā′ik) also **Ju·da′i·cal,** *adj.* of or pertaining to Judaism or the Jews; Jewish. —**Ju·da′i·cal·ly,** *adv.*

Ju·da·i·ca (jōō dā′i kə), *n.pl.* things pertaining to Jewish life and customs, esp. when of a historical, literary, or artistic nature, as books or ritual objects.

Ju·da·ism (jōō′dē iz′əm, -də-), *n.* **1.** the monotheistic religion of the Jews, based on the precepts of the Old Testament and the teachings and commentaries of the rabbis as found chiefly in the Talmud. **2.** belief in and conformity to this religion, its practices, and ceremonies. **3.** this religion considered as forming the basis of the cultural and social identity of the Jews. **4.** Jews collectively. —**Ju′da•ist,** *n.* —**Ju′da•is′tic,** *adj.*

Ju•da•ize (jo͞o′dē īz′, -də-), *v.,* **-ized, -iz•ing.** —*v.i.* **1.** to conform to the spirit, character, principles, or practices of Judaism. —*v.t.* **2.** to bring into conformity with Judaism. —**Ju′da•i•za′tion,** *n.*

Ju•das (jo͞o′dəs), *n.* **1.** Judas Iscariot, the disciple who betrayed Jesus. Mark 3:19. **2.** a person treacherous enough to betray a friend; traitor. **3.** Also called **Saint Judas** or **Saint Jude.** one of the 12 apostles (not Judas Iscariot). Luke 6:16; Acts 1:13; John 14:22. **4.** a brother of James and possibly of Jesus. Matt. 13:55; Mark 6:3. **5.** (*usu. l.c.*) Also called **ju′das hole′.** a peephole, as in the door of a prison cell. —*adj.* **6.** used as a decoy to lead other animals to slaughter: *a Judas goat.*

Ju′das Maccabae′us, *n.* Maccabaeus, Judas.

Ju′das tree′, *n.* **1.** a purple-flowered Eurasian tree, *Cercis siliquastrum,* of the legume family, supposed to be the kind of tree upon which Judas hanged himself. **2.** any of various other trees of the same genus, as the redbud.

Jude (jo͞od), *n.* **1.** a book of the New Testament. **2.** the author of this book, sometimes identified with Judas, the brother of James.

Ju•de•a (jo͞o dē′ə), *n.* the S region of ancient Palestine: existed under Persian, Greek, and Roman rule; divided between Israel and Jordan in 1948; occupied by Israel since 1967. —**Ju•de′an,** *adj., n.*

Judeo- or **Judaeo-,** a combining form representing Judaic or Judaism: *Judeo-Christian.*

Ju•de•o-Chris•tian (jo͞o dā′ō kris′chən, -dē′-), *adj.* of or pertaining to the religious writings, beliefs, values, or traditions held in common by Judaism and Christianity.

Ju•dez•mo (jo͞o dez′mō), *n.* a language based on Old Spanish and written in Hebrew script, spoken by descendants of Sephardic Jews expelled from Spain in the 15th century.

Judg., Judges.

judge (juj), *n., v.,* **judged, judg•ing.** —*n.* **1.** a public officer authorized to hear and decide cases in a court of law. **2.** a person appointed to decide in a competition, contest, or matter at issue. **3.** a person qualified to pass critical judgment: *a good judge of horses.* **4.** an administrative head of Israel in the period between the death of Joshua and the accession to the throne by Saul. —*v.t.* **5.** to pass legal judgment on: *The court judged him not guilty.* **6.** to hear evidence or legal arguments in (a case) in order to pass judgment; try. **7.** to form a judgment or opinion of; decide upon critically: *to judge a book by its cover.* **8.** to decide or settle authoritatively; adjudge: *The censor judged the book obscene.* **9.** to infer, think, or hold as an opinion. **10.** to make a careful guess about; estimate: *I judged the distance to be about two miles.* **11.** to act as a judge in (a contest or competition). **12.** (of the ancient Hebrew judges) to govern. —*v.i.* **13.** to act as a judge; pass judgment. **14.** to form an opinion or estimate. —***Proverb.*** **15. Judge not according to appearances,** examine things and people carefully; things are not always what they seem. John 7:24. **16. Judge not, that ye be not judged,** remember that you are likely to be measured by the same criteria you apply to others. Matt. 7:1. —**judg′er,** *n.* —**judge′ship,** *n.*

Judg•es (juj′iz), *n.* (*used with a sing. v.*) a book of the Bible containing the history of Israel under the judges, covering the period from the death of Joshua to the accession of Saul.

judg•ment (juj′mənt), *n.* **1.** an act or instance of judging. **2.** the ability to judge, make a decision, or form an opinion objectively or wisely, esp. in matters affecting action; good sense; discernment. **3.** the demonstration or exercise of such capacity. **4.** the forming of an opinion, estimate, notion, or conclusion, as from circumstances presented to the mind. **5.** the opinion formed. **6. a.** a judicial decision given by a judge or court. **b.** the obligation, esp. a debt, arising from a judicial decision. **c.** the certificate embodying such a decision. **7.** a misfortune regarded as inflicted by divine sentence, as for sin. **8.** Also called **Last Judgment, Final Judgment.** the final trial of all people, both the living and the dead, at the end of the world. Also, *esp. Brit.,* **judge′ment.**

judg•men•tal (juj men′tl), *adj.* **1.** involving the exercise of judgment. **2.** tending to make judgments, esp. moral judgments.

judg′ment call′, *n.* **1.** a decision made by a referee or umpire in a sporting event that is based on personal observation of a disputed play. **2.** any subjective or debatable determination.

Judg′ment Day′, *n.* the day of the Last Judgment; doomsday.

ju•di•ca•to•ry (jo͞o′di kə tôr′ē, -tōr′ē), *n., pl.* **-to•ries,** *adj.* —*n.* **1.** a court of law and justice; tribunal; judiciary. **2.** the administration of justice. —*adj.* **3.** of or pertaining to the administration of justice; judiciary.

ju•di•ca•ture (jo͞o′di kā′chər, -kə cho͝or′), *n.* **1.** the administration of justice, as by judges or courts. **2.** the office, function, or authority of a judge. **3.** the jurisdiction of a judge or court. **4.** a body of judges. **5.** the power of administering justice by legal trial and determination.

ju•di•cial (jo͞o dish′əl), *adj.* **1.** pertaining to judgment in courts of justice or to the administration of justice: *judicial proceedings.* **2.** pertaining to courts of law or to judges; judiciary: *judicial functions.* **3.** proper to the character of a judge, esp. fair and impartial. **4.** inclined to make or give judgments; critical; discriminating. **5.** decreed, sanctioned, or enforced by a court: *a judicial decision.* **6.** giving or seeking judgment, as in a dispute or contest. **7.** inflicted by God as a judgment or punishment. —**ju•di′cial•ly,** *adv.* —**ju•di′cial•ness,** *n.*

judi′cial branch′, *n.* the branch of the U.S. government whose powers are vested in the Supreme Court and the federal court system.

judi′cial review′, *n.* the power of a court to adjudicate the constitutionality of laws or acts of a government official.

ju•di•ci•ar•y (jo͞o dish′ē er′ē, -dish′ə rē), *n., pl.* **-ar•ies,** *adj.* —*n.* **1.** the judicial branch of government. **2.** the system of courts of justice in a country. **3.** judges collectively. —*adj.* **4.** pertaining to the judicial branch or system or to judges.

ju•di•cious (jo͞o dish′əs), *adj.* having, exercising, or characterized by good or discriminating judgment; discreet, prudent, balanced, or wise: *judicious use of one's money; a judicious selection.* —**ju•di′cious•ly,** *adv.* —**ju•di′cious•ness,** *n.*

Ju•dith (jo͞o′dith), *n.* **1.** a Jewish woman who saved her town from the besieging Assyrian army by cutting off the head of its commander, Holofernes, while he slept. **2.** a book of the Apocrypha and Douay Bible bearing her name.

ju•do (jo͞o′dō), *n.* a martial art based on jujitsu but differing from it in banning dangerous throws and blows and stressing the athletic or sport element. —**ju′do•ist,** *n.*

Jud•son (jud′sən), *n.* **Adoniram,** 1788–1850, U.S. missionary.

jug (jug), *n.* **1.** a large container usu. of earthenware, metal, or glass, commonly having a handle and a narrow neck, sometimes with a cap or cork. **2.** the contents of such a container; jugful. **3.** *Slang.* jail; prison. —*v.t.* **4.** to put into a jug. **5.** *Slang.* to put in jail; imprison.

jug′ band′, *n.* a small band that plays chiefly blues or folk music on very simple instruments, as washboards, harmonicas, kazoos, and empty jugs, the latter being played by blowing across the openings.

Jug•ger•naut (jug′ər nôt′, -not′), *n.* **1.** (*often l.c.*) any large, overpowering, destructive force or object. **2.** (*often l.c.*) anything requiring blind devotion or cruel sacrifice.

jug•gle (jug′əl), *v.,* **-gled, -gling,** *n.* —*v.t.* **1.** to keep (several objects, as balls) in continuous motion in the air simultaneously by tossing and catching. **2.** to hold, catch, or balance precariously. **3.** to alter or manipulate in order to deceive, as by subterfuge or trickery: *to juggle the accounts.* **4.** to manage or alternate the requirements of (two or more activities) so as to handle each adequately: *to juggle the obligations of work and school.* —*v.i.* **5.** to perform feats of dexterity, as tossing up and keeping in continuous motion a number of balls, plates, knives, etc.

jug•gler (jug′lər), *n.* **1.** a person who performs juggling feats, as with balls or knives. **2.** a person who deceives by trickery; trickster. —**jug′gler•y,** *n.*

Ju•go•sla•vi•a (yo͞o′gō slä′vē ə), *n.* Yugoslavia. —**Ju′go•sla′vi•an,** *adj., n.* —**Ju′go•slav′ic,** *adj.*

jug•u•lar (jug′yə lər, jo͞o′gyə-), *adj.* **1.** of or pertaining to the throat or neck. **2.** of or designating any of several veins of the neck that convey blood from the head to the heart. —*n.* **3.** a jugular vein. **4.** a vital part or area that is particularly vulnerable to attack: *to go for the jugular.*

juice (jo͞os), *n., v.,* **juiced, juic•ing.** —*n.* **1.** the natural fluid that can be extracted from a plant or one of its parts, esp. a fruit: *orange juice.* **2.** the liquid part or contents of a plant or animal substance. **3.** the natural fluids of an animal body: *gastric juices.* **4.** any extracted liquid. **5.** essence; spirit. **6.** strength or vitality; force; vigor. **7.** *Slang.* **a.** electricity. **b.** gasoline or fuel oil. **8.** *Slang.* **a.** money obtained by extortion. **b.** money loaned at exorbitant interest rates. **c.** the interest rate itself. **9.** *Slang.* influence; power. **10.** *Informal.* gossip or scandal. —*v.t.* **11.** to extract juice from. —*v.i.* **12. juice up, a.** to add power, energy, or speed to; strengthen. **b.** to add excitement to. —**juice′less,** *adj.*

juic•er (jo͞o′sər), *n.* a kitchen appliance for extracting juice from fruits and vegetables.

juic•y (jo͞o′sē), *adj.,* **juic•i•er, juic•i•est.** **1.** full of juice; succulent: *a juicy pear.* **2.** very profitable, satisfying, or substantive: *a juicy contract; a juicy part in a movie.* **3.** very interesting or colorful, esp. when slightly scandalous or improper: *a juicy bit of gossip.* —**juic′i•ly,** *adv.* —**juic′i•ness,** *n.*

ju•jit•su (jo͞o jit′so͞o) also **ju•jut•su** (-jut′-, -jo͝ot′-), *n.* a Japanese method of defending oneself without weapons by using the strength and weight of one's adversary to disable him or her.

ju•ju (jo͞o′jo͞o), *n., pl.* **-jus.** **1.** a fetish or amulet used by some West African peoples. **2.** the magical power attributed to such an object. **3.** a ban or interdiction effected by it. **4.** a style of Nigerian popular music using electric guitars, traditional drums, and call-and-response singing. —**ju′ju•ism,** *n.* —**ju′ju•ist,** *n.*

ju•jube (jo͞o′jo͞ob; *for 1 also* jo͞o′jo͞o bē′), *n.* **1.** a small, chewy fruit-flavored candy or lozenge. **2.** Chinese date.

juke[1] (jo͞ok), *v.,* **juked, juk•ing,** *n.* —*v.t.* **1.** to make a move intended to deceive (an opponent) in football. —*n.* **2.** a fake or feint usu. intended to deceive a defensive player.

juke[2] (jo͞ok), *n.* a jukebox.

juke•box (jo͞ok′boks′), *n.* a coin-operated phonograph, typically in an illuminated cabinet, having a variety of records that can be selected by push button.

ju•lep (jo͞o′lip), *n.* **1.** mint julep. **2.** a preparation of water and a flavored syrup, often medicated and used as a tonic.

Jul•ian[1] (jo͞ol′yən), *n.* (*Flavius Claudius Julianus*) (*"the Apostate"*) A.D. 331–363, Roman emperor 361–363.

Jul•ian[2] (jo͞ol′yən), *adj.* of or pertaining to Julius Caesar.

Jul′ian cal′endar, *n.* the calendar established by Julius Caesar in 46 B.C., fixing the length of the year at 365 days and at 366 days every fourth year. There are 12 months of 30 or 31 days, except for February,

J

which has 28 days with the exception of every fourth year, or leap year, when it has 29 days. Compare GREGORIAN CALENDAR.

Jul′ian of Nor′wich *n.* c1342–c1413, English mystic.

ju•li•enne (jo͞o′lē en′), *adj.* **1.** Also, **ju′li•enned′.** (of food, esp. vegetables) cut into thin strips or small, matchlike pieces. —*n.* **2.** julienne vegetables used as a garnish. **3.** a clear soup garnished with julienne vegetables.

Ju•ly (jo͞o lī′, jə-), *n., pl.* **-lies.** the seventh month of the year, containing 31 days. *Abbr.:* Jul.

Ju•ma•da (jo͞o mä′dä), *n.* either of two successive months of the Muslim year, the fifth **(Jumada I)** or the sixth **(Jumada II).**

jum•ble (jum′bəl), *v.,* **-bled, -bling,** *n.* —*v.t.* **1.** to mix in a confused mass; put or throw together without order. **2.** to confuse mentally; muddle. —*v.i.* **3.** to be mixed together in a disorderly heap or mass. **4.** to meet or come together confusedly. —*n.* **5.** a disordered heap or mass. **6.** a confused mixture; medley. **7.** a state of confusion or disorder.

jum•bo (jum′bō), *n., pl.* **-bos,** *adj.* —*n.* **1.** a person, animal, or thing very large of its kind. —*adj.* **2.** very large: *the jumbo box of cereal.*

jum′bo jet′, *n.* a widebody jet airliner.

jump (jump), *v.i.* **1.** to spring clear of the ground or other support by a sudden muscular effort; leap. **2.** to move suddenly or quickly: *to jump out of bed.* **3.** to move or jerk involuntarily, as from shock: *I jumped when the firecracker exploded.* **4.** to obey or respond quickly and energetically: *The waiter was told to jump when the captain signaled.* **5.** *Informal.* to be full of activity; bustle: *The town is jumping with excitement.* **6.** to rise suddenly in amount: *Prices jumped this quarter.* **7.** to proceed abruptly, ignoring intervening steps or deliberation: *to jump to a conclusion.* **8.** to move or change haphazardly, aimlessly, abruptly, or after a short period: *to jump from one job to another.* **9.** to omit letters, numbers, etc.; skip: *This typewriter jumps.* **10.** to parachute from an airplane. **11.** to take eagerly; seize (often fol. by *at*): *We jumped at the offer.* **12.** to enter into something with vigor (usu. fol. by *in* or *into*): *She jumped right into the discussion.* **13.** to advance rapidly or abruptly, esp. in rank: *to jump from clerk to manager in six months.* **14.** to start a campaign, program, military attack, etc. (usu. fol. by *off*). **15.** (in checkers) to move from one side of an opponent's piece to a vacant square on the opposite side, thus capturing the piece. **16.** to make a jump bid in bridge. **17.** (of newspaper copy) to continue on a subsequent page, following intervening copy. —*v.t.* **18.** to leap or spring over: *to jump a stream.* **19.** to cause to leap: *to jump a horse over a fence.* **20.** to skip or pass over; bypass. **21.** to elevate, esp. in rank, by causing to skip or pass rapidly through intermediate stages. **22.** to move past or start before (a signal); anticipate: *The car jumped the red light.* **23.** to increase sharply. **24.** to capture (an opponent's piece in checkers) by leaping over. **25.** to attack or pounce upon without warning, as from ambush: *The gang jumped him in a dark alley.* **26.** to raise (the bid in bridge) by more than necessary to reach the next bidding level. **27.** to flee from; skip: *to jump town.* **28.** (of trains, trolleys, etc.) to spring off or leave (the track). **29.** to get on board hastily or with little preparation: *He jumped a plane for Chicago.* **30.** to seize or occupy illegally or forcibly (a mining claim or the like). **31.** to continue (a newspaper story) from one page to another over intervening copy. **32.** to connect (a dead battery) to a live battery by attaching booster cables between the respective terminals. **33. jump on,** to berate suddenly and severely. —*n.* **34.** an act or instance of jumping; leap. **35.** a space, obstacle, or apparatus that is cleared or to be cleared in a leap. **36.** a short or hurried journey. **37.** a descent by parachute from an airplane. **38.** a sudden rise in amount, price, etc. **39.** a sudden upward or other movement of an inanimate object. **40.** an abrupt transition from one point or thing to another, with omission of what intervenes. **41.** a move or one of a series of moves: *to stay one jump ahead of the police.* **42.** an athletic contest that features a leap or jump. Compare HIGH JUMP, LONG JUMP. **43.** a sudden start as from nervous excitement. **44.** the act of taking an opponent's piece in checkers by leaping over it to an unoccupied square. **45. the jumps,** *Informal.* restlessness; anxiety. —***Idiom.* 46. get** or **have the jump on,** to have an initial advantage over. **47. jump from the frying pan into the fire,** to go from a bad situation to a worse one. **48. jump ship, a.** to escape from a ship, esp. one in a foreign port. **b.** to desert or defect, as from a group or organization.

jump′ ball′, *n.* a basketball tossed into the air above and between two opposing players by the referee in putting the ball into play.

jump•er[1] (jum′pər), *n.* **1.** a person or thing that jumps. **2.** a participant in a jumping event, as in track or skiing. **3.** a horse trained to jump obstacles. **4.** JUMP SHOT. **5.** a boring tool or device worked with a jumping motion. **6.** a short length of conductor used to make an electrical connection, usu. temporary, between terminals of a circuit or to bypass a circuit. **7.** Also called **jump′er ca′ble.** BOOSTER CABLE. **8.** a kind of sled. **9.** any of various fishes that leap from the water.

jump•er[2] (jum′pər), *n.* **1.** a sleeveless dress, or a skirt with a bib and straps or with an open-sided bodice, usu. worn over a blouse. **2.** a loose outer jacket worn esp. by workers and sailors. **3.** *Brit.* a pullover sweater.

jump′ing bean′, *n.* the seed of any of certain Mexican plants of the genera *Sebastiania* and *Sapium,* of the spurge family: the movements of a moth larva inside the seed cause it to move about or jump.

jump′ing jack′, *n.* **1.** a toy consisting of a jointed figure that is made to jump, move, or dance by pulling a string or stick attached to it. **2.** an exercise in which one starts from a standing position with legs together and arms at the sides, then jumps to a position with the legs spread apart and the arms brought together over the head, and then jumps back into the starting position.

jump′ing mouse′, *n.* any mouselike rodent of the subfamily Zapodinae, having hind legs modified for jumping.

jump′ing-off′ place′, *n.* **1.** a place used as a starting point, as for a trip or enterprise. **2.** an out-of-the-way place; the farthest limit of anything settled or civilized. Also called **jump′ing-off′ point′.**

jump′ing spi′der, *n.* any of several small, hairy spiders of the family Salticidae, that stalk and jump upon their prey.

jump′-off′, *n.* **1.** a place for jumping off. **2.** a point or time of departure, as of a race or a military attack. **3.** a supplementary contest among horses tied in a jumping contest.

jump rope (*n.* jump′ rōp′; *v.* rōp′), *n.* **1.** an exercise or children's game in which a rope is swung over and under a jumper who must leap over it each time it reaches the feet. **2.** the rope used. —*v.i.* **3.** to play this game or do this exercise.

jump′ seat′, *n.* a movable or folding seat, as between the front and back seats in a taxicab, used as an extra seat.

jump′ shot′, *n.* a basketball shot made by releasing the ball at the peak of a vertical leap.

jump′-start′, *n.* **1.** the starting, by means of booster cables, of an internal-combustion engine that has a discharged or weak battery. —*v.t.* **2.** to give a jump-start to: *to jump-start the car's engine.* **3.** to enliven or revive: *to jump-start a sluggish economy.*

jump•suit (jump′so͞ot′), *n.* **1.** a one-piece suit worn by parachutists for jumping. **2.** a garment fashioned after it, usu. combining a shirt with shorts or trousers in one piece.

jump•y (jum′pē), *adj.,* **jump•i•er, jump•i•est. 1.** nervous or apprehensive; jittery. **2.** characterized by sudden starts, jerks, or jumps. —**jump′i•ly,** *adv.* —**jump′i•ness,** *n.*

jun•co (jung′kō), *n., pl.* **-cos.** any of several small, gray or gray and brown North American finches of the genus *Junco,* esp. *J. hyemalis,* a common winter resident of the U.S. Also called **snowbird.**

junc•tion (jungk′shən), *n.* **1.** an act of joining or the state of being joined. **2.** a place or point where two or more things meet, converge, or are joined. **3.** a place or station where railroad lines meet, cross, or diverge. **4.** an intersection of roads. **5.** something that joins other things together. —**junc′tion•al,** *adj.*

junc•ture (jungk′chər), *n.* **1.** a point of time, esp. one made critical by a concurrence of circumstances: *At this juncture, we must decide whether to continue negotiations.* **2.** a serious state of affairs; crisis. **3.** the line or point at which two bodies are joined; joint or articulation; seam. **4.** an act of joining or the state of being joined. **5.** something by which two things are joined. **6. a.** a transition between successive speech sounds or between a speech sound and silence, as at the boundary of a morpheme, word, or clause, marked by a break in articulatory continuity: *Juncture distinguishes words such as* night rate *and* nitrate. **b.** the feature marking such a transition. —**junc′tur•al,** *adj.*

June (jo͞on), *n.* the sixth month of the year, containing 30 days.

Ju•neau (jo͞o′nō), *n.* the capital of Alaska, in the SE part. 19,528.

June′ bug′ or **June′bug′,** *n.* any of several large brown beetles of the genus *Phyllophaga,* of the scarab family, appearing in late spring and early summer.

Jung (yo͝ong), *n.* **Carl Gustav,** 1875–1961, Swiss psychiatrist and psychologist. —**Jung′i•an,** *adj., n.*

Jung•frau (yo͝ong′frou′), *n.* a mountain in S Switzerland, in the Bernese Alps. 13,668 ft. (4166 m).

jun•gle (jung′gəl), *n.* **1.** wild land overgrown with dense vegetation, often nearly impenetrable, esp. tropical vegetation. **2.** any confused mass or agglomeration of objects; jumble. **3.** something that baffles or perplexes; maze: *a jungle of rules and regulations.* **4.** a place or scene of violence, struggle for survival, or ruthless competition: *The city was a concrete jungle.* **5.** *Slang.* a hobo camp. —**jun′gled,** *adj.* —**jun′gly,** *adj.*

jun′gle fe′ver, *n.* a severe variety of malaria common in the East Indies.

jun′gle fowl′, *n.* any of several S or SE Asian forest birds of the genus *Gallus,* of the pheasant family, esp. *G. gallus,* considered to be ancestral to domestic chickens.

jun•gle•gym (jung′gəl jim′, -jim′), *n.* a playground apparatus consisting of a framework of horizontal and vertical bars on which children can climb.

jun•ior (jo͞on′yər), *adj.* **1.** younger (typically designating a son named after his father; often written as *Jr.* following the name): *the junior Mr. Hansen; Edward Hansen, Jr.* **2.** of more recent election, appointment, or admission: *a junior member of the club; the junior Senator from Michigan.* **3.** of lower rank or standing: *a junior partner.* **4.** of or pertaining to juniors in school or college. **5.** of later date; subsequent to. **6.** composed of younger members: *the junior division.* **7.** being smaller than the usual size. —*n.* **8.** a person who is younger than another. **9.** a person who is newer or of lower rank, as in a profession; subordinate. **10.** a student in the next to the last year at a high school, college, or university. **11. a.** Often, **juniors.** a range of odd-numbered sizes, chiefly 3–15, for garments for women with short waists and narrow shoulders. **b.** a garment in this size range. **12.** a boy; youth; son.

jun′ior col′lege, *n.* a collegiate institution offering courses only through the first two years of college instruction and granting an associate's degree or a certificate of title.

jun′ior high′ school′, *n.* a school attended after elementary school and usu. consisting of grades seven through nine.

Jun′ior League′, *n.* any local branch of a women's organization, the Association of the Junior Leagues of America, Inc., whose members engage in volunteer welfare work and civic affairs. **—Jun′ior Lea′guer,** *n.*

jun′ior var′sity, *n.* a university, college, or school team that competes at a level below that of the varsity.

ju·ni·per (jo͞o′nə pər), *n.* **1.** any of several evergreen shrubs or trees of the genus *Juniperus,* of the cypress family, having scaly leaves and berrylike cones that yield an oil used in flavoring gin. **2.** a tree mentioned in the Old Testament, thought to be the retem.

ju′niper ber′ry, *n.* the berrylike cone of a juniper.

junk¹ (jungk), *n.* **1.** old or discarded material or objects, as metal, paper, or rags, some of which may be reusable: *junk accumulating in the attic.* **2.** something regarded as worthless, meaningless, or contemptible; trash. **3.** old cable or cordage used when untwisted for making gaskets, swabs, oakum, etc. **—v.t. 4.** to cast aside as junk; discard as no longer of use; scrap. **—adj. 5.** cheap, worthless, unwanted, or trashy: *junk jewelry.* **—junk′y,** *adj.,* **-i·er, -i·est.**

junk² (jungk), *n.* a seagoing ship used primarily in Chinese waters, having square sails spread by battens, a high stern, and usu. a flat bottom.

junk²

junk′ bond′, *n.* a corporate bond with a low rating and a high yield, often involving high risk.

jun·ket (jung′kit), *n.* **1.** a custardlike dessert of flavored milk curdled with rennet. **2.** a pleasure excursion: *a junket down the Mississippi.* **3.** a trip taken by a government official at public expense, ostensibly for the purpose of obtaining information. **—v.i. 4.** to go on a junket: *Congressmen junketing in Asia.* **—v.t. 5.** to entertain; feast; regale.

junk′ food′, *n.* **1.** food, as potato chips or candy, that is high in calories but of little nutritional value. **2.** anything that is attractive or diverting but of negligible substance. **—junk′-food′,** *adj.*

junk·ie or **junk·y** (jung′kē), *n., pl.* **junk·ies.** *Informal.* **1.** a drug addict, esp. one addicted to heroin. **2.** a person with an insatiable craving for something: *a chocolate junkie.* **3.** an enthusiastic follower; devotee: *a baseball junkie.*

junk′ mail′, *n.* unsolicited commercial material, as advertisements and requests for donations, mailed in bulk.

junk·man (jungk′man′), *n., pl.* **-men.** a dealer in resalable used metal, paper, rags, and other junk.

junk·yard (jungk′yärd′), *n.* a yard for the collection, storage, and resale of junk.

Ju·no (jo͞o′nō), *n.* a Roman goddess associated with women and childbirth, and identified with the Greek goddess Hera.

jun·ta (ho͞on′tə, jun′-, hun′-), *n., pl.* **-tas.** **1.** a small group ruling a country, esp. immediately after a coup d'état and before a legally constituted government has been instituted. **2.** a deliberative or administrative council, esp. in Spain and Latin America. **3.** JUNTO.

jun·to (jun′tō), *n., pl.* **-tos.** a self-appointed committee, esp. with political aims; cabal.

Ju·pi·ter (jo͞o′pi tər), *n.* **1.** the supreme deity of the ancient Romans, associated with the sky and rain: identified with the Greek god Zeus. **2.** the planet fifth in order from the sun, having an equatorial diameter of 88,729 mi. (142,796 km), a mean distance from the sun of 483.6 million mi. (778.3 million km), a period of revolution of 11.86 years, and at least 14 moons. It is the largest planet in the solar system, encircled by a series of rings similar to but smaller than those of Saturn.

ju·ra (jo͞or′ə, yo͞or′ə), *n.* pl. of JUS.

ju·ral (jo͞or′əl), *adj.* **1.** pertaining to law; legal. **2.** of or pertaining to rights and obligations. **—ju′ral·ly,** *adv.*

Ju·ras·sic (jo͞o ras′ik), *adj.* **1.** of or pertaining to a geologic period of the Mesozoic Era, from 190 million to 140 million years ago, characterized by the presence of dinosaurs and the advent of birds and mammals. **—n. 2.** the Jurassic Period or System.

ju·ris·dic·tion (jo͞or′is dik′shən), *n.* **1.** the right, power, or authority to administer justice by hearing and determining controversies. **2.** power; authority; control: *to have military jurisdiction over the occupied territories.* **3.** the extent or range of judicial, law-enforcement, or other authority: *a case under the jurisdiction of the local police.* **4.** the territory

over which authority is exercised. **—ju·ris·dic′tion·al,** *adj.* **—ju′ris·dic′tion·al·ly,** *adv.* **—ju′ris·dic′tive,** *adj.*

ju·ris·pru·dence (jo͞or′is pro͞od′ns), *n.* **1.** the science or philosophy of law. **2.** a body or system of laws. **—ju′ris·pru·den′tial** (-pro͞o den′shəl), *adj.* **—ju′ris·pru·den′tial·ly,** *adv.*

ju·rist (jo͞or′ist), *n.* a person versed in the law, as a judge, lawyer, or legal scholar.

ju·ror (jo͞or′ər, -ôr), *n.* **1.** a member of a jury. **2.** a member of the panel from which a jury is selected.

ju·ry¹ (jo͞or′ē), *n., pl.* **-ries,** *v.,* **-ried, -ry·ing. —n. 1.** a group of persons sworn to render a verdict or true answer on a question or questions submitted to them, esp. such a group selected by law and sworn to examine the evidence in a case and render a verdict to a court. **2.** a group of persons chosen to adjudge prizes, awards, etc., as in a competition. **—v.t. 3.** to select or evaluate (entries), as by means of a jury. **—Usage.** See COLLECTIVE NOUN.

ju·ry² (jo͞or′ē), *adj.* makeshift or temporary, as for an emergency: *a jury mast; a jury rig.*

ju′ry-rig′, *v.t.,* **-rigged, -rig·ging.** to assemble hastily or from whatever is at hand, esp. for temporary use: *to jury-rig stage lights using car headlights.*

jus (jus, yo͞os), *n., pl.* **ju·ra** (jo͞or′ə, yo͞or′ə). **1.** a legal right. **2.** law as a system or in the abstract. [< Latin *jūs* law, right]

just¹ (just), *adv.* **1.** within a brief preceding time; but a moment before: *The sun just came out.* **2.** exactly or precisely: *That's just what I mean.* **3.** by a narrow margin; barely: *just over six feet tall; It just missed the target.* **4.** only or merely: *I was just a child. Don't just sit there.* **5.** at this moment: *The movie is just ending.* **6.** simply: *We'll just have to wait and see.* **7.** quite; really; positively: *The weather is just glorious.* **—adj. 8.** guided by reason, justice, and fairness. **9.** done or made according to principle; equitable; proper: *a just reply.* **10.** based on right; rightful; lawful: *a just claim.* **11.** in keeping with truth or fact; true; correct: *a just analysis.* **12.** given or awarded rightly; deserved: *a just punishment; a just reward.* **13.** in accordance with standards or requirements; proper or right: *just proportions.* **14.** (esp. in Biblical use) righteous. **15.** actual, real, or genuine. **—just′ly,** *adv.* **—just′ness,** *n.*

just² (just), *n., v.i.* JOUST. **—just′er,** *n.*

Just′ as I′ Am′, a Christian hymn (1836) with words by Charlotte Elliott.

jus·tice (jus′tis), *n.* **1.** the quality of being just; righteousness, equitableness, or moral rightness. **2.** rightfulness or lawfulness, as of a claim: *to complain with justice.* **3.** justness of ground or reason. **4.** the quality of being true or correct. **5.** the moral principle determining just conduct. **6.** conformity to this principle, as manifested in conduct; just dealing or treatment: *to seek justice.* **7.** the administering of deserved punishment or reward. **8.** the maintenance or administration of what is just according to law: *a court of justice.* **9.** judgment of individuals or causes by judicial process: *to administer justice.* **10.** a judicial officer; a judge or magistrate. **—Idiom. 11. bring to justice,** to cause to come before a court for trial or to receive punishment for one's misdeeds. **12. do justice to, a.** to act fairly toward. **b.** to appreciate properly. **c.** to reflect or express the worth of properly. **—Proverb. 13. Justice is blind,** the law should be impartial. **—jus′tice·less,** *adj.*

jus′tice of the peace′, *n.* a local public officer having authority to try minor civil and criminal cases, administer oaths, solemnize marriages, etc.

jus·tice·ship (jus′tis ship′), *n.* the office of a justice.

jus·ti·fi·a·ble (jus′tə fī′ə bəl, jus′tə fī′-), *adj.* capable of being justified; defensible: *justifiable homicide.* **—jus′ti·fi′a·bil′i·ty, jus′ti·fi′a·ble·ness,** *n.* **—jus′ti·fi′a·bly,** *adv.*

jus·ti·fi·ca·tion (jus′tə fi kā′shən), *n.* **1.** a reason, fact, circumstance, or explanation that justifies. **2.** an act of justifying. **3.** the state of being justified. **4.** the act of God whereby humankind is absolved of guilt or sin. **5.** the act or result of justifying a line or lines of type.

jus·ti·fy (jus′tə fī′), *v.,* **-fied, -fy·ing. —v.t. 1.** to show or prove to be just, right, or reasonable: *The pleasure we get from these paintings justifies their high cost.* **2.** to defend or uphold as warranted or well-grounded: *Don't try to justify his rudeness.* **3.** to declare innocent or guiltless; absolve; acquit. **4.** to space out words or characters in (one or more lines of type), esp. to produce an even margin. **—v.i. 5. a.** to show that what was done was legally warranted. **b.** to qualify as bail or surety. **6.** (of a line of type) to fit exactly into a desired length. **—jus′ti·fi′er,** *n.* **—jus′ti·fy′ing·ly,** *adv.*

jut (jut), *v.,* **jut·ted, jut·ting,** *n.* **—v.i. 1.** to extend beyond the main body or line; project; protrude: *a strip of land jutting out into the bay.* **—n. 2.** something that juts out; a projecting or protruding point.

jute (jo͞ot), *n.* **1.** a strong, coarse fiber used for making burlap, gunny, cordage, etc., obtained from two East Indian plants, *Corchorus capsularis* and *C. olitorius,* of the linden family. **2.** either of these plants.

Jut·land (jut′lənd), *n.* a peninsula comprising the continental portion of Denmark. 11,441 sq. mi. (29,630 sq. km). Danish, **Jylland. —Jut′land·er,** *n.* **—Jut′land·ish,** *adj.*

ju·ve·nile (jo͞o′və nl, -nīl′), *adj.* **1.** of, characteristic of, or suitable for children or young people: *juvenile interests; juvenile books.* **2.** young; youthful. **3.** immature; childish; infantile: *juvenile tantrums.* **—n. 4.** a young person; youth. **5. a.** a youthful male or female theatrical role. **b.** an actor or actress who plays such parts. **6.** a book for children. **7.** a

J

young bird when first fully feathered and before reaching maturity. **8.** a two-year-old racehorse. —**ju′ve•nile•ly,** *adv.*

ju′venile court′, *n.* a law court having jurisdiction over youths, generally those of less than 18 years.

ju′venile delin′quency, *n.* illegal or antisocial behavior by a minor, constituting a matter for action by the juvenile courts.

ju′venile delin′quent, *n.* a minor who cannot be controlled by parental authority and commits antisocial or criminal acts, as vandalism or violence.

ju′venile-on′set diabe′tes, *n.* See under DIABETES MELLITUS.

jux•ta•pose (juk′stə pōz′, juk′stə pōz′), *v.t.,* **-posed, -pos•ing.** to place close together or side by side, esp. for comparison or contrast.

jux•ta•po•si•tion (juk′stə pə zish′ən), *n.* **1.** an act or instance of placing close together or side by side, esp. for comparison or contrast. **2.** the state of being close together or side by side. —**jux′ta•po•si′-tion•al,** *adj.*

JV or **J.V., 1.** joint venture. **2.** junior varsity.

Jy., July.

K, k (kā), *n., pl.* **Ks** or **K's, ks** or **k's. 1.** the 11th letter of the English alphabet, a consonant. **2.** any spoken sound represented by this letter. **3.** something shaped like a K. **4.** a written or printed representation of the letter K or k.

K, 1. Kelvin. **2.** *Computers.* **a.** the number 1024 or 2¹⁰: *A binary 32K memory has 32,768 positions.* **b.** kilobyte. **3.** the number 1000: *a $20K salary.* **4.** kindergarten.

K, *Symbol.* **1.** the 11th in order or in a series. **2.** potassium. [< New Latin *kalium*] **3.** strikeout.

K2 (kā′tōō′), *n.* a mountain in N Kashmir, in the Karakoram range: second highest peak in the world. 28,250 ft. (8611 m).

kab (kab), *n.* CAB².

Ka·'ba or **Ka·'bah** or **Ka·'a·bah** (kä′bə, kä′ə bə), *n.* a small cubical building in the courtyard of the central mosque in Mecca, containing a sacred black stone: the chief object of Muslim pilgrimages.

kab·a·la or **kab·ba·la** (kab′ə lə, kə bä′-), *n., pl.* **-las.** CABALA. —**kab′a·lism,** *n.* —**kab′a·list,** *n.* —**kab′a·lis′tic,** *adj.*

ka·bob (kə bob′), *n.* KEBAB.

ka·bu·ki (kə bōō′kē, kä′bōō kē′), *n.* a popular drama of Japan characterized by elaborate costuming, stylized acting, and the performance of all roles by male actors. Compare Nō. [< Japanese: song-and-dance-art]

Ka·bul (kä′bōol, -bal, kə bōōl′), *n.* **1.** the capital of Afghanistan, in the NE part. 913,164. **2.** a river flowing E from NE Afghanistan to the Indus River in Pakistan. 360 mi. (580 km) long.

ka·chi·na or **ka·tchi·na** (kə chē′nə), *n., pl.* **-nas. 1.** any of a class of supernatural beings who play a role in the religious beliefs of Pueblo Indian peoples. **2.** a masked dancer impersonating such a being. **3.** a carved wooden doll representing a kachina.

kad·dish (kä′dish), *n., pl.* **kad·di·shim** (kä dish′im). *Judaism. (often cap.)* **1.** a liturgical prayer glorifying God that is recited during each of the daily services. **2.** a form of this prayer recited by mourners. [< Aramaic *qaddīsh* holy (one)]

kaf·fee·klatsch or **kaf·fee klatsch** (kä′fē kläch′, -klach′, kô′-), also **coffee klatsch,** *n.* a social gathering for informal conversation at which coffee is served.

Kaf·ka (käf′kä, -kə), *n.* **Franz,** 1883–1924, Austrian writer, born in Prague.

kaf·tan (kaf′tan, kaf tan′), *n.* CAFTAN.

ka·hu·na (kə hōō′nə), *n., pl.* **-nas.** a native Hawaiian priest, healer, or sorcerer.

kai·ser (kī′zər), *n.* **1.** a German emperor: the title used from 1871 to 1918. **2.** an Austrian emperor. **3.** a ruler of the Holy Roman Empire.

kale (kāl), *n.* a cabbagelike cultivated plant, *Brassica oleracea acephala,* of the mustard family, having leaves used as a vegetable.

ka·lei·do·scope (kə lī′də skōp′), *n.* **1.** a tubular optical instrument in which loose bits of colored glass at the end of the tube are reflected in mirrors so as to display ever-changing symmetrical patterns as the tube is rotated. **2.** a continually shifting pattern, scene, or the like. —**ka·lei′do·scop′ic** (-skop′ik), *adj.* —**ka·lei′do·scop′i·cal·ly,** *adv.*

ka·mi·ka·ze (kä′mi kä′zē), *n., pl.* **-zes,** *adj.* —*n.* **1.** (during World War II) a member of a special corps in the Japanese air force charged with suicidal missions against U.S. warships. **2.** an airplane filled with explosives and flown by a kamikaze. —*adj.* **3.** of or resembling a kamikaze; wildly reckless; suicidal.

Kam·pa·la (käm pä′lə, kam-), *n.* the capital of Uganda, in the S part. 458,423.

Kam·pu·che·a (kam′pōō chē′ə), *n.* **People's Republic of,** a former official name of CAMBODIA. —**Kam′pu·che′an,** *adj., n.*

ka·na (kä′nə), *n.* a Japanese syllabic script consisting of 71 symbols and having two written varieties. Compare HIRAGANA, KATAKANA.

Ka·nak·a (kə nak′ə, -nä′kə, kan′ə kə), *n., pl.* **-nak·as.** *(sometimes l.c.)* **1.** HAWAIIAN (def. 1a). **2.** (esp. formerly) a member of any people indigenous to the islands of the S Pacific. [< Hawaiian: person]

Kan·chen·jun·ga (kän′chən jŏŏng′gə), *n.* a mountain in S Asia, between NE India and Nepal, in the E Himalayas: third highest in the world. 28,146 ft. (8579 m).

kan·ga·roo (kang′gə rōō′), *n., pl.* **-roos,** *(esp. collectively)* **-roo.** any herbivorous leaping marsupial of the family Macropodidae, of Australia

great gray kangaroo, *Macropus giganteus,*
head and body 4 ft. (1.2 m);
tail 3 ½ ft. (1 m)

and adjacent islands, having short forelimbs, powerful hind legs, and a long, thick tail.

kan′garoo court′, *n.* **1.** a self-appointed tribunal that disregards or parodies existing principles of law or human rights, esp. such a court in a frontier area or among criminals in prison. **2.** any crudely or irregularly operated court, esp. one so controlled as to render a fair trial impossible.

kangaroo′ rat′, *n.* any of various small jumping rodents of the genus *Dipodomys,* of Mexico and W North America.

Kan·sas (kan′zəs), *n.* **1.** a state in the central United States. 2,572,150; 82,276 sq. mi. (213,094 sq. km). *Cap.:* Topeka. *Abbr.:* KS, Kans., Kan., Kas. **2.** a river in NE Kansas, flowing E to the Missouri River. 169 mi. (270 km) long. —**Kan′san,** *adj., n.*

Kan′sas Cit′y, *n.* **1.** a city in W Missouri, at the confluence of the Kansas and Missouri rivers. 443,878. **2.** a city in NE Kansas, adjacent to Kansas City, Mo. 142,630.

Kan′sas-Nebras′ka Act′, *n.* an act of Congress (1854) annulling the Missouri Compromise, providing for the organization of the territories of Kansas and Nebraska, and permitting these territories self-determination on the question of slavery.

Kant (kant, känt), *n.* **Immanuel,** 1724–1804, German philosopher. —**Kant′i·an,** *adj., n.* —**Kant′i·an·ism,** *n.*

ka·o·lin or **ka·o·line** (kā′ə lin), *n.* a fine white clay used in the manufacture of porcelain. —**ka′o·lin′ic,** *adj.*

ka·o·lin·ite (kā′ə lə nīt′), *n.* a mineral, hydrated aluminum disilicate, $Al_2Si_2O_5(OH)_4$, the most common constituent of kaolin.

ka·pok (kā′pok), *n.* the silky down that invests the seeds of a tropical silk-cotton tree (**ka′pok tree′**), *Ceiba pentandra:* used for stuffing pillows, life jackets, etc., and for acoustical insulation.

ka·put (kä pŏŏt′, -pōŏt′, kə-), *adj. Slang.* **1.** ruined; done for; demolished. **2.** unable to operate or continue; broken: *The TV went kaput.*

Ka·ra·chi (kə rä′chē), *n.* a seaport in S Pakistan, near the Indus delta: former national capital; now capital of Sind province. 5,208,170.

Kar·a·ite (kâr′ə īt′), *n.* a member of a Jewish sect, founded in Persia in the 8th century, that rejected the Talmud and rabbinical teachings in favor of adherence to the Bible. —**Kar′a·ism,** *n.*

ka·ra·o·ke (kar′ē ō′kē), *n.* an act of singing along to a music video, esp. one from which the original vocals have been electronically eliminated. [< Japanese, = *kara* empty + *oke* orchestra]

kar·at or **car·at** (kar′ət), *n.* a unit for measuring the fineness of gold, pure gold being 24 karats fine. *Abbr.:* k., kt.

ka·ra·te (kə rä′tē), *n.* a Japanese method of self-defense using fast, hard blows with the hands, elbows, knees, or feet. [< Japanese, = *kara* empty + *te* hand(s)]

kar·ma (kär′mə), *n.* **1.** (in Hinduism and Buddhism) action seen as bringing upon oneself inevitable results, either in this life or in a reincarnation. **2.** (in Theosophy) the cosmic principle of rewards and punishments for the acts performed in a previous incarnation. **3.** the good or bad emanations felt to be generated by someone or something. —**kar′mic,** *adj.*

karst (kärst), *n.* an area of limestone terrane characterized by sinks, ravines, and underground streams. —**karst′ic,** *adj.*

kart (kärt), *n.* a small, light, low-slung four-wheeled vehicle, powered by a gasoline engine.

Kas·bah or **Cas·bah** (kaz′bä, käz′-), *n.* the older, native Arab quarter of a North African city, esp. Algiers.

kash·mir (kazh′mēr, kash′-), *n.* CASHMERE.

Kash·mir (kash′mēr, kazh′-, kash mēr′, kazh-), *n.* **1.** Also, **Cashmere.** a region in SW Asia, in N India: sovereignty in dispute between India and Pakistan since 1947. **2.** Official name, **Jammu and Kashmir.** the part of this region occupied by India, forming a state in the Indian union. 5,981,600; ab. 53,500 sq. mi. (138,000 sq. km). *Cap.:* Srinagar (summer); Jammu (winter).

Kash′mir (or **Cash′mere**) **goat′,** *n.* any of a long-haired breed of goat raised in Tibet, India, Afghanistan, and Turkey for its meat, milk, and cashmere wool.

kash·ruth or **kash·rut** (käsh rŏŏt′, käsh′rŏŏt), *n.* **1.** the Jewish dietary laws. **2.** fitness for use with respect to Jewish law.

ka·ta·ka·na (kä′tə kä′nə), *n.* the more angular, less commonly used of the two Japanese syllabaries. Compare HIRAGANA.

Kat·mai (kat′mī), *n.* **1. Mount,** an active volcano in SW Alaska. 7500 ft. (2286 m). **2.** a national monument including Mt. Katmai and the Valley of Ten Thousand Smokes. 4215 sq. mi. (10,915 sq. km).

Kat·man·du or **Kath·man·du** (kät′män dōō′, kat′man-), *n.* the capital of Nepal, in the central part. 235,160.

ka·ty·did (kā′tē did), *n.* any of several large, usu. green, long-horned American grasshoppers, the males of which produce a characteristic strident song.

katz·en·jam·mer (kat′sən jam′ər), *n.* **1.** the unpleasant aftereffects of excessive drinking; hangover. **2.** uneasiness; anguish; distress. **3.** an uproar; clamor.

kau·ri (kou′rē), *n., pl.* **-ris. 1.** Also called **kau′ri pine′.** a tall New Zealand evergreen tree, *Agathis australis,* of the araucaria family, yielding timber and a resin (**kau′ri res′in** or **kau′ri gum′**) used in varnishes and linoleum. **2.** the wood or resin of this tree.

ka·va (kä′və), *n., pl.* **-vas. 1.** a Polynesian shrub, *Piper methysticum,* of the pepper family: the aromatic roots are used to make an intoxicating beverage. **2.** the beverage made from kava.

kay·ak (kī′ak), *n.* **1.** an Eskimo canoe with a skin cover on a light framework, made watertight by flexible closure around the waist of the occupant and propelled with a double-bladed paddle. **2.** a small boat resembling this used in sports. —*v.i.* **3.** to go or travel by kayak. —**kay′ak·er,** *n.*

kay·o (kā′ō′, kā′ō′), *n., pl.* **kay·os,** *v.t.,* **kay·oed, kay·o·ing.** See KO.

Ka·zakh·stan (kä′zäk stän′), *n.* a republic in central Asia, NE of the Caspian Sea and W of China. 16,898,572; 1,049,155 sq. mi. (2,717,300 sq. km). *Cap.:* Akmola. Former official name, **Kazakh′ So′viet So′cialist Repub′lic.**

Ka·zan (kə zan′, -zän′), *n.* **Elia,** born 1909, U.S. film and stage director and novelist, born in Turkey.

ka·zoo (kə zōō′), *n., pl.* **-zoos.** a musical toy consisting of a tube that is open at both ends and has a hole in the side covered with parchment or membrane, which produces a buzzing sound when the performer hums into one end.

KB, kilobyte.

Kb, kilobit.

kb, kilobar.

kc, 1. kilocycle. **2.** kilocurie.

kCi, kilocurie.

Kea·ton (kēt′n), *n.* **Buster** (*Joseph Francis Keaton*), 1895–1966, U.S. film comedian and director.

Keats (kēts), *n.* **John,** 1795–1821, English poet. —**Keats′i·an,** *adj.*

Keb (keb), *n. Egyptian Religion.* GEB.

ke·bab or **ka·bob** or **ke·bob** (kə bob′), *n.* small pieces of meat or seafood seasoned or marinated and broiled, often with peppers, onions, or other vegetables, on a skewer.

Ke·ble (kē′bəl), *n.* **John,** 1792–1866, English clergyman and poet.

Ke·dar (kē′dər), *n.* the second son of Ishmael. Gen. 25:13.

Ke·dron (kē′drən), *n.* KIDRON.

keel (kēl), *n.* **1.** a central fore-and-aft structural member in the bottom of a ship's hull extending from the stem to the sternpost. **2. keel over, a.** to capsize or overturn. **b.** to fall in or as if in a faint. —*Idiom.* **3. on an even keel,** in a steady, stable, or calm state.

keen[1] (kēn), *adj.* **1.** finely sharpened; so shaped as to cut or pierce readily: *a keen razor.* **2.** sharp, piercing, or biting: *a keen wind.* **3.** acutely or finely perceptive; extremely sensitive, responsive, or alert: *keen ears; a keen mind.* **4.** having great acumen; shrewdly intelligent; astute: *a keen observer of human nature.* **5.** animated by strong feeling or desire: *keen competition.* **6.** intense, as feeling or desire. **7.** eager; interested; enthusiastic (often fol. by *about,* on, etc., or an infinitive): *I was keen to go swimming.* **8.** *Slang.* great; wonderful; marvelous. —**keen′ly,** *adv.* —**keen′ness,** *n.*

keen[2] (kēn), *n.* **1.** a wailing lament for the dead. —*v.i.* **2.** to wail in lamentation for the dead. —*v.t.* **3.** to bewail or lament by or with keening. —**keen′er,** *n.*

keep (kēp), *v.,* **kept, keep·ing,** *n.* —*v.t.* **1.** to hold or retain in one's possession, either permanently or temporarily. **2.** to hold in a given place; put or store: *to keep mints in a dish.* **3.** to maintain (some action), as in accordance with duty: *to keep watch.* **4.** to cause to continue in a given position, state, course, or action: *to keep a light burning.* **5.** to maintain in condition or order: *to keep a lawn mowed.* **6.** to maintain in usable or edible condition; preserve: *to keep meat by freezing it.* **7.** to hold in custody or under guard, as a prisoner. **8.** to cause to stay in a particular place; detain: *The work kept me at the office.* **9.** to have readily available for use or sale: *to keep machine parts in stock.* **10.** to maintain in one's service or for one's use: *to keep a car and chauffeur.* **11.** to associate with: *to keep bad company.* **12.** to have the care, charge, or custody of: *She keeps my dog when I travel.* **13.** to refrain from disclosing: *to keep a secret.* **14.** to withhold, as from use; reserve; save: *to keep the best wine for guests.* **15.** to restrain or prevent, as from an action: *to keep a pipe from leaking.* **16.** to control; regulate: *to keep one's temper.* **17.** to maintain by writing: *to keep a diary.* **18.** to record regularly or consistently: *to keep attendance figures.* **19.** to observe; obey or fulfill (a law, rule, promise, etc.). **20.** to observe (a season, festival, etc.) with formalities or rites. **21.** to raise and provide for the care of as owner: *to keep goats.* **22.** to remain in (a place, spot, etc.): *Please keep your seats.* **23.** to maintain one's position in or on: *to keep a job.* **24.** to continue to follow (a path, course, etc.). —*v.i.* **25.** to continue in an action, course, position, or state: *to keep going; to keep calm.* **26.** to remain in a particular place: *to keep indoors.* **27.** to continue without damage or spoilage: *Will the milk keep for another day?* **28.** to admit of being reserved for a future occasion: *The rest of the story will keep.* **29.** to stay as specified (fol. by *away, back, off, out,* etc.): *Keep off the grass.* **30.** to restrain oneself; refrain (usu. fol. by *from*): *Try to keep from smiling.* **31. keep at,** to persevere in. **32. keep back, a.** to hold in check; restrain. **b.** to stay away from. **33. keep down, a.** to maintain at an acceptable level; control. **b.** to prevent from advancing or flourishing. **c.** to avoid regurgi-

tation of. **34. keep on,** to persevere. **35. keep to, a.** to adhere to; conform to: *to keep to the rules.* **b.** to confine oneself to: *to keep to one's bed.* **36. keep up, a.** to perform as swiftly or successfully as others. **b.** to persevere; continue. **c.** to maintain in good condition or repair. **d.** to stay informed. —*n.* **37.** board and lodging; subsistence; support. **38.** the innermost and strongest structure or central tower of a medieval castle; dungeon. —*Idiom.* **39. for keeps, a.** with the understanding that winnings are retained by the winner. **b.** with serious intent or purpose. **c.** permanently; forever. **40. keep to oneself, a.** to remain aloof from the society of others. **b.** to hold (something) as secret or confidential.

keep·er (kē′pər), *n.* **1.** a person who guards or watches, as a prison warden. **2.** a person who assumes responsibility for another; guardian. **3.** a person who owns or operates a business (usu. used in combination): *a hotelkeeper.* **4.** a person responsible for the maintenance of something (often used in combination): *a zookeeper.* **5.** a person responsible for the preservation and conservation of something valuable, as a curator or game warden. **6.** a person who abides by a requirement. **7.** a fish large enough to be caught and retained lawfully. **8.** a football play in which the quarterback runs with the ball, usu. after a faked hand-off. **9.** something that serves to hold in place, retain, etc. —**keep′er·less,** *adj.* —**keep′er·ship′,** *n.*

keep·ing (kē′ping), *n.* **1.** agreement or conformity in things or elements associated together: *actions in keeping with one's words.* **2.** the act of a person or thing that keeps; observance, custody, or care.

keep·sake (kēp′sāk′), *n.* anything kept, or given to be kept, as a token of friendship or affection; remembrance.

Keep′ Your′ Eyes′ on′ the Prize′, HOLD ON.

kees·hond (kās′hond′, kēs′-), *n., pl.* **-hon·den** (-hon′dən). any of a Dutch breed of medium-sized dogs with a thick black-tipped gray coat, a foxlike head, and a tail carried over the back.

kees·ter (kē′stər), *n.* KEISTER.

keet (kēt), *n.* a young guinea fowl.

ke·fir (kə fēr′), *n.* a tart-tasting drink orig. of the Caucasus, made from cow's or sometimes goat's milk to which the bacteria *Streptococcus* and *Lactobacillus* have been added.

keg (keg), *n.* **1.** a small cask or barrel holding from 5 to 10 gallons (19 to 38 liters). **2.** a unit of weight equal to 100 pounds (45 kg), used for nails.

keg·ler (keg′lər), *n.* a participant in a bowling game.

keg·ling (keg′ling), *n.* the sport of bowling.

keis·ter or **kees·ter** (kē′stər), *n. Slang.* the buttocks; rump.

Kel·ler (kel′ər), *n.* **Helen (Adams),** 1880–1968, U.S. lecturer and author: blind and deaf from infancy.

Kel·logg (kel′ôg, -og), *n.* **1. Frank Billings,** 1856–1937, U.S. statesman: Secretary of State 1925–29; Nobel peace prize 1929. **2. W(ill) K(eith),** 1860–1951, U.S. manufacturer of prepared cereals and philanthropist.

Kel′logg-Bri·and′ Pact′ (kel′ôg brē änd′, -än′, -og-), *n.* a treaty renouncing war as an instrument of national policy and urging peaceful means for the settlement of international disputes, orig. signed in 1928 by 15 nations, later joined by 49 others. Also called **Kel′logg Peace′ Pact′.** [named after F. B. KELLOGG and A. BRIAND]

Kel·ly (kel′ē), *n.* **1. Gene** (*Eugene Curran*), 1912–96, U.S. dancer, choreographer, actor, and director. **2. Walt,** 1913–73, U.S. cartoonist.

kel′ly green′ (kel′ē), *n.* a strong yellow-green.

ke·loid (kē′loid), *n.* an abnormal proliferation of scar tissue, as on the site of a surgical incision. —**ke·loi′dal,** *adj.*

kelp (kelp), *n.* **1.** any large, brown, cold-water seaweed of the family Laminariaceae, used as food and in manufacturing processes. **2.** a bed or mass of such seaweeds. **3.** the ashes of these seaweeds, a source of iodine.

kelp′ bass′ (bas), *n.* a sea bass, *Paralabrax clathratus,* of S California coastal waters, valued as a food and game fish.

kel·pie[1] or **kel·py** (kel′pē), *n., pl.* **-pies.** a water spirit of Scottish folklore reputed to cause drownings.

kel·pie[2] *n.* any of an Australian breed of medium-sized sheep-herding dogs with a short, harsh, straight coat and erect ears.

Kelt (kelt), *n.* CELT. —**Kelt′ic,** *n., adj.*

Kel·vin (kel′vin), *n.* **1. William Thomson, 1st Baron,** 1824–1907, English physicist and mathematician. **2.** (*l.c.*) the base SI unit of temperature, defined to be $1/273.16$ of the triple point of water. *Symbol:* K —*adj.* **3.** of or pertaining to an absolute scale of temperature (**Kel′vin scale′**) based on the kelvin in which the degree intervals are equal to those of the Celsius scale.

Ke·mal A·ta·türk (kə mäl′ at′ə tûrk′, ä′tä-), *n.* (*Mustafa Kemal*) (*"Kemal Pasha"*) 1881–1938, Turkish general: president of Turkey 1923–38.

Kem·pis (kem′pis), *n.* **Thomas à,** 1379?–1471, German ecclesiastic.

kempt (kempt), *adj.* neatly or tidily kept: *a kempt little cottage; kempt hair.*

Ken (ken), *n.* **Thomas,** 1631–1711, English clergyman and hymn writer.

ken·do (ken′dō), *n.* a Japanese form of fencing using bamboo foils or wooden swords grasped with both hands.

Ke·nite (kē′nīt), *n.* one of a nomadic tribe who fought the Israelites. Num. 24:21–22.

Ken·nan (ken′ən), *n.* **George Frost,** born 1904, U.S. author and diplomat.

Ken·ne·dy (ken′i dē), *n.* **1. Anthony M.,** born 1936, associate justice of the U.S. Supreme Court since 1988. **2. John Fitzgerald,** 1917–63, 35th president of the U.S. 1961–63. **3. Joseph Patrick,** 1888–1969, U.S. financier and diplomat (father of John Fitzgerald and Robert Francis). **4. Robert Francis,** 1925–68, U.S. political leader and government official. **5. Cape,** former name (1963–73) of Cape CANAVERAL.

ken·nel (ken′l), *n., v.,* **-neled, -nel·ing** or (*esp. Brit.*) **-nelled, -nel·ling.** —*n.* **1.** a house or shelter for a dog or a cat. **2.** Often, **kennels.** an establishment where dogs or cats are bred, trained, or boarded. —*v.t.* **3.** to put or keep in or as if in a kennel.

ken′nel club′, *n.* an association that establishes standards for dog breeds, records pedigrees, and sets rules for dog shows.

Ken′ne·saw Moun′tain (ken′ə sô′), *n.* a mountain in N Georgia, near Atlanta: battle 1864. 1809 ft. (551 m).

ke·no (kē′nō), *n.* a game of chance, adapted from lotto for gambling purposes.

ke·no·sis (ki nō′sis), *n.* the doctrine that Christ relinquished His divine attributes so as to experience human suffering. —**ke·not′ic** (-not′ik), *adj.*

Kent (kent), *n.* **1. James,** 1763–1847, U.S. jurist. **2. Rockwell,** 1882–1971, U.S. illustrator and painter. **3.** a county in SE England. 1,445,400; 1442 sq. mi. (3735 sq. km).

Ken·tuck·y (kən tuk′ē), *n.* **1.** a state in the E central United States. 3,883,723; 40,395 sq. mi. (104,625 sq. km). *Cap.:* Frankfort. *Abbr.:* KY, Ken., Ky. **2.** a river flowing NW from E Kentucky to the Ohio River. 259 mi. (415 km) long. —**Ken·tuck′i·an,** *adj., n.*

Kentuck′y blue′grass, *n.* a grass, *Poa pratensis,* of the Mississippi valley, used for pasturage and lawns.

Kentuck′y Der′by, *n.* a horse race for three-year-olds run annually in May at Churchill Downs, Louisville, Ky.

Kentuck′y ri′fle, *n.* a long-barreled muzzleloading flintlock rifle developed near Lancaster, Pa., in the early 18th century and widely used on the frontier. Also called **Pennsylvania rifle.**

Ken·ya (ken′yə, kēn′-), *n.* **1.** a republic in E Africa: a member of the Commonwealth of Nations and formerly a British crown colony and protectorate. 28,803,085; 223,478 sq. mi. (578,808 sq. km). *Cap.:* Nairobi. **2. Mount,** an extinct volcano in central Kenya. 17,040 ft. (5194 m). —**Ken′yan,** *adj., n.*

Ken·yat·ta (ken yä′tə), *n.* **Jomo,** 1893?–1978, president of Kenya 1964–78.

Ke′ogh plan′ (kē′ō), *n.* a pension plan for a self-employed person or an unincorporated business.

Kep·ler (kep′lər), *n.* **Johann,** 1571–1630, German astronomer.

kept (kept), *v.* pt. and pp. of KEEP.

ker-, an unstressed syllable prefixed to onomatopoeic and other expressive words, usu. forming adverbs or interjections: *kerflop; kerplunk; kersplosh.* Compare CA-.

ker·a·tin (ker′ə tin), *n.* a tough, insoluble protein that is the main constituent of hair, nails, horn, hoofs, etc., and of the outermost layer of skin. —**ker′a·tin·i·za′tion,** or —**ke·rat·i·nous** (kə rat′n əs), *adj.*

kerb (kûrb), *n., v.t. Brit.* CURB (defs. 1, 5, 9).

ker·chief (kûr′chif, -chēf), *n.* **1.** a woman's square scarf worn as a covering for the head or sometimes the shoulders. **2.** HANDKERCHIEF.

Ker·man (kər män′, ker-), *n.* **1.** a city in SE Iran. 257,284. **2.** KIRMAN.

Kern (kûrn), *n.* **Jerome (David),** 1885–1945, U.S. composer.

ker·nel (kûr′nl), *n., v.,* **-neled, -nel·ing** or (*esp. Brit.*) **-nelled, -nel·ling.** —*n.* **1.** the softer, usu. edible part contained in the shell of a nut or the stone of a fruit. **2.** the body of a seed within its husk or integuments. **3.** the central or most important part of anything; essence; gist; core. —*v.t.* **4.** to enclose in or as if in a kernel. —**ker′nel·less,** *adj.*

kern·ing (kûr′ning), *n.* the typesetting of two adjacent letters closer together than is usual.

ker·o·sene or **ker·o·sine** (ker′ə sēn′, ker′ə sēn′, kar′-), *n.* a mixture of liquid hydrocarbons obtained by distilling petroleum, bituminous shale, or the like and widely used as a fuel and cleaning solvent.

ker·plunk (kər plungk′), *adv.* with or as if with a sudden muffled thud: *The rock hit the water kerplunk.*

Ker′ry blue′ ter′rier, *n.* one of an Irish breed of medium-sized terriers having a long head with face whiskers and a soft, wavy, bluish-gray coat.

ke·ryg·ma (ki rig′mə), *n.* the preaching of the gospel of Christ, esp. in the manner of the early church. [< Greek *kḗrygma* proclamation, preaching] —**ker·yg·mat·ic** (ker′ig mat′ik), *adj.*

kes·trel (kes′trəl), *n.* any of various small falcons that hover as they hunt, esp. *Falco sparverius,* of North America, and *F. tinnunculus,* of Eurasia.

ketch (kech), *n.* a sailing vessel rigged fore and aft on two masts, the larger, forward one being the mainmast and the after one, stepped forward of the rudderpost, being the mizzen or jigger. Compare YAWL (def. 2).

ketch·up (kech′əp, kach′-) also **catsup,** *n.* a condiment consisting usu. of puréed tomatoes, onions, vinegar, sugar, and spices. [< Malay *kachap* fish sauce, perh. < dial. Chinese]

ke·tone (kē′tōn), *n.* any of a class of organic compounds containing a carbonyl group, CO, attached to two alkyl groups, as CH_3COCH_3. —**ke·ton·ic** (-ton′ik), *adj.*

ket·tle (ket′l), *n.* **1.** a container, usu. of metal, in which to boil liquids, cook foods, etc.; pot. **2.** TEAKETTLE. **3.** KETTLEDRUM. **4.** KETTLE HOLE. **5.** a

gathering of soaring birds, as vultures, utilizing circular updrafts of warm air to gain elevation.

ket·tle·drum (ket′l drum′), *n.* a drum consisting of a hollow hemisphere of brass, copper, or fiberglass over which is stretched a skin, the tension of which can be modified by screws or foot pedals to vary the pitch. Compare TIMPANI. —**ket′tle·drum′mer,** *n.*

ket′tle hole′, *n.* **1.** a deep, kettle-shaped depression in glacial drift. **2.** POTHOLE (def. 2).

Ke·tur·ah (ki tŏŏr′ə), *n.* the second wife of Abraham. Gen. 25:1.

keV or **kev,** kiloelectron volt.

Kew·pie (kyōō′pē), *Trademark.* a small, plump doll with a topknot.

key[1] (kē), *n.* **1.** a small metal instrument specially cut to fit into a lock and move its bolt. **2.** any of various devices resembling or functioning as a key: *the key of a clock.* **3.** something that affords a means to achieve, master, or understand something else: *the key to happiness; the key to training a dog.* **4.** something that secures or controls entrance to a place: *Gibraltar is the key to the Mediterranean.* **5.** a book or other text containing the solutions to material given elsewhere, as testing exercises. **6.** a systematic explanation of abbreviations, symbols, and the like used in a dictionary, map, etc.: *pronunciation key.* Compare LEGEND (def. 4). **7.** the system, method, pattern, etc., used to decode or decipher a cryptogram. **8.** one of the buttons on the keyboard of a typewriter, computer, or the like that are pressed to operate the device, as while inputting data. **9. a.** (in a keyboard instrument) one of the levers that when depressed by the performer sets in motion the playing mechanism. **b.** (on a woodwind instrument) a metal lever that opens and closes a vent. **c.** the relationship perceived between all tones in a given unit of music and a single tone or a keynote; tonality. **d.** the principal tonality of a composition: *a symphony in the key of C minor.* **e.** the keynote or tonic of a scale. **10.** tone or pitch, as of voice: *to speak in a high key.* **11.** mood or characteristic style, as of expression or thought: *He writes in a melancholy key.* **12.** degree of intensity, as of feeling or action. **13.** a pin, bolt, wedge, or other piece inserted in a space to lock or hold parts of a mechanism or structure together; cotter. **14.** a small piece of steel inserted between the hub of a wheel or the like and its shaft so that torque is transmitted between them. **15.** a contrivance for grasping and turning a bolt, nut, etc. **16.** a group of characters that identifies a record in a database or other computer file. **17. a.** a device for opening and closing electrical contacts, as a lever used to produce signals in telegraphy. **b.** a hand-operated switching device capable of switching one or more parts of a circuit. **18.** *Biol.* a systematic tabular classification of the significant characteristics of the members of a group of organisms to facilitate identification and comparison. **19.** *Archit.* a keystone or boss. **20.** a wedge, as for tightening a joint or splitting a stone or timber. **21.** KEYHOLE (def. 2). **22.** the dominant tonal value of a photograph, high key being light tonal value with minimal contrast and low key being generally dark with minimal contrast. **23.** *Bot.* a samara. —*adj.* **24.** chief; major; essential; fundamental; pivotal: *a key industry.* —*v.t.* **25.** to regulate or adjust (actions, thoughts, speech, etc.) to a particular state or activity; bring into conformity. **26.** to coordinate; harmonize. **27.** to regulate the musical pitch of. **28.** to provide with a key. **29.** to mark or set (a text, layout, diagram, etc.) with symbols, letters, etc., as to show where certain matter should be inserted or to indicate where more detailed information can be found. **30.** to lock with or as if with a key. **31.** to provide (an arch or vault) with a keystone. **32.** to keyboard (data) into a computer (sometimes fol. by *in*). —*v.i.* **33.** to use a key. **34.** to keyboard. **35. key (in) on,** to single out as important. **36. key up,** to increase tension in; stimulate. —**key′less,** *adj.*

key[2] (kē), *n.* a reef or low island; cay.

Key (kē), *n.* **Francis Scott,** 1780–1843, U.S. lawyer: author of *The Star-Spangled Banner.*

key·board (kē′bôrd′, -bōrd′), *n.* **1.** the row or set of keys on a piano, organ, or the like. **2.** a set of keys, usu. arranged in tiers, for operating a typewriter, typesetting machine, computer terminal, or the like. **3.** any of various musical instruments played by means of a pianolike keyboard, esp. an electric piano or organ. —*v.t.* **4.** to enter (data) into a computer by means of a keyboard. **5.** to set (text) in type, using a machine operated by a keyboard. —*v.i.* **6.** to enter data or typeset text using a keyboard. —**key′board′er,** *n.*

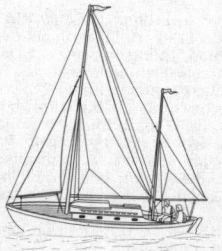

ketch

key′ card′, *n.* a small plastic card containing data on an embedded magnetized strip that can electronically unlock a door, actuate a machine, etc.

key•hole (kē′hōl′), *n.* **1.** a hole for inserting a key in a lock, esp. one in the shape of a circle with a narrow rectangle beneath it. **2.** an area at each end of a basketball court that is bounded by two lines extending from the end line parallel to and equidistant from the sidelines and terminating in a circle around the foul line.

Key′ Lar′go (lär′gō), *n.* the largest island of the Florida Keys. 30 mi. (48 km) long; 2 mi. (3.2 km) wide.

Key′ lime′, *n.* a yellow lime with a bitter rather than sour taste.

Key′ lime′ pie′, *n.* a custardlike pie made with lime juice, condensed milk, and eggs and served in a pastry shell.

Keynes (kānz), *n.* **John Maynard, 1st Baron,** 1883–1946, English economist and writer.

Keynes•i•an (kān′zē ən), *adj.* **1.** pertaining to the economic theories of Keynes, esp. that the level of national income and employment both depend on consumption and investment spending. —*n.* **2.** an advocate of the theories of Keynes. **—Keynes′i•an•ism,** *n.*

key•note (kē′nōt′), *n., v.,* **-not•ed, -not•ing.** —*n.* **1.** the note or tone on which a key or system of tones is founded; tonic. **2.** the central idea, principle, policy, or the like of a speech, program, thought, political campaign, etc. **3.** KEYNOTE ADDRESS. —*v.t.* **4.** to deliver a keynote address at. **5.** to serve as the keynote for. —*v.i.* **6.** to provide a keynote, esp. a keynote statement. **—key′not′er,** *n.*

key′note address′, *n.* a speech, as at a political convention, that presents important issues, principles, policies, etc. Also called **key′note speech′.**

key•pad (kē′pad′), *n.* a small panel of numeric and other special keys, as on a computer keyboard.

key•punch (kē′punch′), *n.* **1.** a machine, operated by a keyboard, for coding information by punching holes in cards or paper tape in specified patterns. —*v.t.* **2.** to punch holes in (a card or paper tape) using a keypunch. **3.** to insert (data) into a computer by means of a keypunch. **—key′punch′er,** *n.*

key′ ring′, *n.* a ring, usu. metal, for holding keys.

key•stone (kē′stōn′), *n.* **1.** the wedge-shaped piece at the summit of an arch, regarded as holding the other pieces in place. **2.** something on which associated things depend; foundation: *the keystone of one's philosophy.*

Key′stone Kop′ (kop), *n.* **1.** Usu., **Keystone Kops.** (in early silent movies) a team of comic policemen noted for their slapstick routines. **2.** Also, **Key′stone Cop′.** a person noted for bungling inefficiency: *a backfield of Keystone Kops.*

key•stroke (kē′strōk′), *n.* one stroke of any key on a machine operated by a keyboard, as a typewriter or computer terminal.

Key′ West′, *n.* **1.** the westernmost island of the Florida Keys, in the Gulf of Mexico. 4 mi. (6.4 km) long; 2 mi. (3.2 km) wide. **2.** a seaport on this island: the southernmost city in the U.S. 24,292.

key′word′ or **key′ word′,** *n.* a word that serves as a key, as to the meaning of another word, a sentence, or a passage.

kg, **1.** keg. **2.** kilogram.

KGB or **K.G.B.,** the Soviet secret police responsible for intelligence and internal security, formed in 1954. [< Russian, for *K(omitét) g(osudárstvennoi) b(ezopásnosti)* Committee for State Security]

kgf, kilogram-force.

kg-m, kilogram-meter.

khak•i (kak′ē, kä′kē), *n., pl.* **khak•is,** *adj.* —*n.* **1.** dull yellowish brown. **2.** a stout, usu. twilled fabric of this color, used esp. in making uniforms. **3.** Usu., **khakis. a.** a uniform made of this cloth, esp. a military uniform. **b.** a garment made of this cloth, esp. trousers. —*adj.* **4.** of the color khaki. **5.** made of khaki. [< Urdu < Persian *khākī* dusty]

Khar•toum or **Khar•tum** (kär tōōm′), *n.* the capital of the Sudan, at the junction of the White and Blue Nile rivers. 476,218.

Khir•bet Qum•ran (kēr′bet kōōm′rän), *n.* an archaeological site in W Jordan, near the Dead Sea: Dead Sea Scrolls found here 1947.

Khmer Rouge (kmâr′ rōōzh′, kə mâr′), *pl.* **Khmers Rouges** (kmâr′ rōōzh′, kə mâr′) for 2. **1.** a Cambodian guerrilla and rebel force, orig. Communist and Communist-backed. **2.** a member or supporter of this force.

kHz, kilohertz.

KIA, 1. Also, **K.I.A.** killed in action. **2.** *n., pl.* **KIA's, KIAs.** a member of the military services who has been killed in action.

kib•ble (kib′əl), *v.,* **-bled, -bling,** *n.* —*v.t.* **1.** to grind or divide into particles or pellets, as coarse-ground meal or prepared dry dog food. —*n.* **2.** the grains or pellets resulting from this.

kib•butz (ki bōōts′, -bōōts′), *n., pl.* **-but•zim** (-bōōt sēm′). (in Israel) a community settlement, usu. agricultural, organized under collectivist principles. [< Modern Hebrew *qibbūṣ* lit., gathering]

kib•butz•nik (ki bōōts′nik, -bōōts′-), *n.* a member of a kibbutz.

Ki•bei (kē′bā′), *n., pl.* **-bei.** (*sometimes l.c.*) a person of Japanese descent, born in North America but educated mainly in Japan. Compare ISSEI, NISEI, SANSEI.

kib•itz (kib′its), *v.i. Informal.* —*v.i.* **1.** to act as a kibitzer. —*v.t.* **2.** to offer advice or criticism to as a kibitzer.

kib•itz•er (kib′it sər), *n. Informal.* **1.** a spectator at a card game who reads the players' cards over their shoulders, often giving unsolicited

advice. **2.** a giver of unsolicited advice; busybody; meddler. **3.** a person who jokes or chitchats, esp. while others are trying to work.

ki•bosh (kī′bosh, ki bosh′), *n. Slang.* **1.** nonsense. —*Idiom.* **2. put the kibosh on,** to put an end to; squelch; check.

kick (kik), *v.t.* **1.** to strike with the foot or feet: *to kick a ball.* **2.** to drive, force, thrust, etc., by or as if by kicks. **3.** *Football.* to score (a field goal or a conversion) by place-kicking the ball. **4.** *Informal.* to make (a car) increase in speed, esp. in auto racing. **5.** *Slang.* to give up or break (a drug addiction): *He kicked the habit.* —*v.i.* **6.** to make a rapid, forceful thrust with the foot, feet, leg, or legs; strike with the feet or legs: *to kick at a ball.* **7.** to resist, object, or complain. **8.** to recoil, as a firearm when fired. **9.** to be actively or vigorously involved: *alive and kicking.* **10. kick around** or **about, a.** to treat harshly. **b.** to speculate about; discuss. **c.** to move frequently from place to place; roam; wander. **d.** to linger or remain for a long interval without being used, noticed, or resolved. **11. kick back, a.** to recoil, esp. vigorously or unexpectedly. **b.** to give someone a kickback. **12. kick in, a.** to contribute one's share, esp. in money. **b.** to go into effect; become operational. **13. kick off, a.** *Football.* to begin or resume play by a kickoff. **b.** *Slang.* to die. **c.** to initiate (an undertaking). **14. kick on,** to switch on; turn on. **15. kick out,** to eject; get rid of. **16. kick over, a.** (of an internalcombustion engine) to begin ignition; turn over. **17. kick up, a.** to drive or force upward by kicking. **b.** to stir up (trouble); make or cause (a disturbance, scene, etc.). **c.** (esp. of a machine part) to move rapidly upward: *The lever kicks up, engaging the gear.* —*n.* **18.** the act of kicking; a blow or thrust with the foot, feet, leg, or legs. **19.** power or disposition to kick: *a horse with a mean kick.* **20.** an objection or complaint. **21. a.** thrill; pleasurable excitement. **b.** a strong but temporary interest, often an activity: *Photography is her latest kick.* **22.** a stimulating or intoxicating quality in alcoholic drink or certain drugs. **b.** vim, vigor, or energy. **23.** *Football.* **a.** an instance of kicking the ball. **b.** any method of kicking the ball: *a place kick.* **c.** a kicked ball. **d.** the distance such a ball travels. **24.** a recoil, as of a gun. **—kick′a•ble,** *adj.* **—kick′less,** *adj.*

Kick•a•poo (kik′ə pōō′), *n., pl.* **-poos,** (*esp. collectively*) **-poo. 1.** a member of an American Indian people that formerly lived in the upper Midwest and now reside in Kansas, Oklahoma, and the state of Coahuila in Mexico. **2.** the dialect of the Fox language spoken by the Kickapoo.

kick•back (kik′bak′), *n.* **1.** a portion of profit given to someone as payment for having made the income possible, esp. as in an underhand or illegal scheme involving the use of political or professional influence. **2.** a sudden, uncontrolled movement of a machine, tool, weapon, or other device, as on starting or in striking an obstruction.

kick′ box′ing, *n.* a form of boxing in which the gloved combatants may also kick with bare feet.

kick•er (kik′ər), *n.* **1.** a person or thing that kicks. **2.** *Slang.* **a.** a disadvantageous point or circumstance, usu. concealed or unnoticed. **b.** a surprising change or turn of events.

kick′off′ or **kick′-off′,** *n.* **1.** *Football.* a place kick from the 40-yard line of the team kicking at the beginning of the first and third periods or after the team kicking has scored a touchdown or field goal. **2.** *Soccer.* a kick that puts a stationary ball into play from the center line of the field at the start of a quarter or after a goal has been scored. **3.** the initial stage of something; start; beginning.

kick′ pleat′, *n.* an inverted pleat extending upward a short distance from the hemline at the back of a narrow skirt, to allow freedom in walking.

kick•stand (kik′stand′), *n.* a device for supporting a bicycle or motorcycle when not in use, pivoted to the rear axle in such a way that it can be kicked down from a horizontal to a vertical position.

kick′-start′ or **kick′start′,** *v.t.* **1.** to start by means of a device (**kick′start′er**) that operates by a downward kick on a pedal: *to kick-start a motorcycle.* **2.** JUMP-START (def. 3).

kick•y (kik′ē), *adj.,* **kick•i•er, kick•i•est.** *Slang.* pleasurably amusing or exciting: *a kicky tune.*

kid¹ (kid), *n., v.,* **kid•ed, kid•ing,** *adj.* —*n.* **1.** *Informal.* **a.** a child or young person. **b.** (used as a familiar form of address.) **2.** a young goat. **3.** leather made from the skin of a kid or goat, used esp. for shoes and gloves. **4.** an article made from this leather. —*v.t.* **5.** (of a goat) to give birth to (young). —*adj.* **6.** made of kidskin. **7.** *Informal.* younger: *my kid sister.* **—kid′dish,** *adj.* **—kid′dish•ness,** *n.* **—kid′like′,** *adj.*

kid² (kid), *v.,* **kid•ded, kid•ding.** *Informal.* —*v.t.* **1.** to talk or deal jokingly with; tease; jest with. **2.** to fool; deceive; humbug. —*v.i.* **3.** to speak or act deceptively in jest; jest. **—kid′der,** *n.* **—kid′ding•ly,** *adv.*

kid•die or **kid•dy** (kid′ē), *n., pl.* **-dies.** *Informal.* a child; youngster; tot.

kid•do (kid′ō), *n., pl.* **-dos, -does.** *Informal.* (used as a familiar form of address.)

Kid•dush (kid′əsh, ki dōōsh′), *n. Judaism.* a blessing recited over a cup of wine or over bread on the Sabbath or on a festival. [< Hebrew *qiddūsh* lit., sanctification]

kid′ glove′, *n.* a glove made of kid leather. **—Idiom. 2. handle with kid gloves,** to treat with extreme tact or gentleness.

kid•nap (kid′nap), *v.t.,* **-napped** or **-naped, -nap•ping** or **-nap•ing.** to carry off (a person) by force or fraud, esp. for use as a hostage or to extract ransom; abduct. **—kid′nap•pee′, kid′nap•ee′,** *n.* **—kid′nap•per, kid′nap•er,** *n.*

kid·ney (kid′nē), *n.* **1.** one of a pair of organs in the rear of the upper abdominal cavity of vertebrates that filter waste from the blood, excrete uric acid or urea, and maintain water and electrolyte balance. **2.** any similar structure in invertebrates. **3.** the meat of an animal's kidney used as food. **4.** constitution or temperament. **5.** kind; sort: *to associate only with people of one's own kidney.*

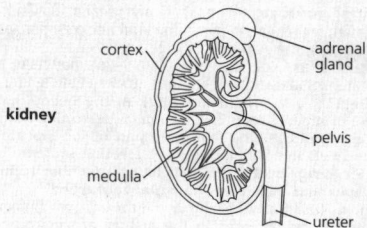

kidney

cortex
adrenal gland
pelvis
medulla
ureter

kid′ney bean′, *n.* **1.** a bean plant, *Phaseolus vulgaris,* cultivated in many varieties for its edible seeds and pods. **2.** its mature seed, esp. the dark red, kidney-shaped seed of some varieties.

kid′ney stone′, *n.* a stony mineral concretion formed abnormally in the kidney.

Ki·dron (kē′drən, kid′rən), *n.* a ravine E of Jerusalem, leading to the Mount of Olives: traditionally identified by Jewish, Christian, and Muslim religions as the Valley of Decision, the place of final judgment. Joel 3:2, 12. Also, **Kedron.**

kid·skin (kid′skin′), *n.* leather made from the skin of a young goat; kid.

kid′ stuff′, *n.* **1.** something appropriate only for children. **2.** something very easy or simple.

kiel·ba·sa (kil bä′sə, kēl-), *n., pl.* **-sas, -sy** (-sē) a smoked sausage of coarsely chopped beef and pork, flavored with garlic and spices.

Kier·ke·gaard (kēr′ki gärd′, -gär′, -gôr′), *n.* Sö·ren Aa·bye (sœ′rən ô′by), 1813–55, Danish philosopher and theologian. —**Kier′ke·gaard′i·an,** *adj.*

Ki·ev (kē′ef, -ev), *n.* the capital of Ukraine, on the Dnieper River. 2,587,000. —**Ki′ev·an,** *adj., n.*

Ki·ga·li (kē gä′lē), *n.* the capital of Rwanda, in the central part. 156,650.

Ki·kon·go (kē kong′gō), *n.* Kongo (def. 3).

Kil·i·man·ja·ro (kil′ə mən jär′ō), *n.* a volcanic mountain in NE Tanzania: highest peak in Africa. 19,321 ft. (5889 m).

kill¹ (kil), *v.t.* **1.** to deprive of life; cause the death of; slay. **2.** to destroy; do away with; extinguish. **3.** to neutralize the active qualities of: *to kill an odor.* **4.** to spoil the effect of: *His extra brushwork killed the painting.* **5.** to cause (time) to pass with a minimum of boredom. **6.** to spend (time) unprofitably. **7.** *Informal.* to overcome completely or with irresistible effect: *That comedian kills me.* **8.** *Informal.* to cause distress or discomfort to. **9.** *Informal.* to tire completely; exhaust. **10.** to defeat or veto (a legislative bill, etc.). **11.** to turn off; switch off: *to kill the lights; to kill an engine.* —*v.i.* **12.** to inflict or cause death. **13.** to commit murder. **14.** to overcome completely; produce an irresistible effect: *dressed to kill.* **15.** kill off, to destroy completely. —*n.* **16.** the act of killing, esp. game. **17.** an animal or animals killed.

kill² (kil), *n. Chiefly New York State.* a channel; creek; stream; river: used esp. in place names.

kill·deer (kil′dēr′), *n., pl.* **-deers, -deer.** a common New World plover of farmland and meadows, *Charadrius vociferus,* having two black bands around the upper breast.

kill·er (kil′ər), *n.* **1.** a person or thing that kills. **2.** *Slang.* something or someone having a formidable impact, devastating effect, etc. —*adj.* **3.** severe; powerful: *a killer cold.*

kill′er bee′, *n.* **1.** African honeybee. **2.** Africanized honeybee.

kill′er cell′, *n.* any of several types of lymphocyte or leukocyte capable of destroying cells that have acquired foreign characteristics.

kill′er in′stinct, *n.* a willingness to quickly or forcibly capitalize on another's weakness or vulnerability.

kill′er whale′, *n.* a large, predatory, black-and-white dolphin, *Orcinus orca.*

kill·ing (kil′ing), *n.* **1.** the act of a person or thing that kills. **2.** the total game killed on a hunt. **3.** a quick and unusually large profit or financial gain. —*adj.* **4.** fatal or destructive. **5.** exhausting: *a killing pace.* **6.** *Informal.* irresistibly funny. —**kill′ing·ly,** *adv.*

kill·joy′ or **kill′joy′,** *n.* a person who spoils the joy or pleasure of others; spoilsport.

kiln (kil, kiln), *n.* a furnace or oven for burning, baking, or drying something, esp. one for firing pottery, calcining limestone, or baking bricks.

ki·lo (kē′lō, kil′ō), *n., pl.* **-los. 1.** a kilogram. **2.** a kilometer.

kil·o·bit (kil′ə bit′), *n. Computers.* **1.** 1024 (2¹⁰) bits. **2.** (loosely) 1000 bits. *Symbol:* Kb

kil·o·byte (kil′ə bīt′), *n. Computers.* **1.** 1024 (2¹⁰) bytes. **2.** (loosely) 1000 bytes. *Symbol:* K, KB

kil·o·cal·o·rie (kil′ə kal′ə rē), *n.* 1000 small calories. *Abbr.:* kcal

kil·o·cu·rie (kil′ə kyŏŏr′ē, -kyŏŏ rē′), *n.* a unit of radioactivity, equal to 1000 curies. *Abbr.:* kCi

kil·o·cy·cle (kil′ə sī′kəl), *n.* kilohertz: no longer in technical use. *Abbr.:* kc

kil′o·e·lec′tron volt′ (kil′ō i lek′tron), *n.* a unit of energy, equal to 1000 electron-volts. *Abbr.:* keV, kev

kil·o·gram (kil′ə gram′), *n.* **1.** a unit of mass equal to 1000 grams: the base SI unit of mass; its international prototype, a platinum-iridium cylinder, is kept in Sèvres, France. *Abbr.:* kg **2.** a unit of force, equal to the force that produces an acceleration of 9.80665 meters per second per second when acting on a mass of one kilogram. *Abbr.:* kg Also, *esp. Brit.,* **kil′o·gramme′.**

kil·o·hertz (kil′ə hûrts′), *n., pl.* **-hertz, -hertz·es.** a unit of frequency, equal to 1000 cycles per second. *Abbr.:* kHz Formerly, **kilocycle.**

kil·o·li·ter (kil′ə lē′tər), *n.* a unit of volume, equal to 1000 liters; a cubic meter. *Abbr.:* kl Also, *esp. Brit.,* **kil′o·li′tre.**

kil·o·me·ter (ki lom′i tər, kil′ə mē′-), *n.* a unit of length, the common measure of distances equal to 1000 meters (3280.8 feet or 0.621 mile). *Abbr.:* km Also, *esp. Brit.,* **kil′o·me′tre.** —**kil·o·met·ric** (kil′ə me′trik), *adj.*

kil·o·ton (kil′ə tun′), *n.* **1.** a unit of weight, equal to 1000 tons. **2.** an explosive force equal to that of 1000 tons of TNT.

kil·o·volt (kil′ə vōlt′), *n.* a unit of electromotive force, equal to 1000 volts. *Abbr.:* kV, kv

kil·o·watt (kil′ə wot′), *n.* a unit of power, equal to 1000 watts. *Abbr.:* kW, kw

kil′owatt-hour′, *n.* a unit of energy, equivalent to the energy transferred or expended in one hour by one kilowatt of power; approximately 1.34 horsepower-hours. *Abbr.:* kWh, kwh

kilt (kilt), *n.* a pleated, knee-length tartan skirt worn by Scotsmen in the Highlands or in some military regiments.

kil·ter (kil′tər), *n.* good condition; order: *The engine was out of kilter.*

kilt·ie (kil′tē), *n.* **1.** a person who wears a kilt, esp. a member of a regiment in which the kilt is worn as part of the dress uniform. **2.** a sports shoe with a fringed tongue that flaps over the lacing. **3.** the tongue of such a shoe.

ki·mo·no (kə mō′nə, -nō), *n., pl.* **-nos. 1.** a loose, wide-sleeved Japanese robe, fastened at the waist with a broad sash. **2.** a loose dressing gown, esp. for women. —**ki·mo′noed,** *adj.*

kin (kin), *n.* **1.** all of a person's relatives; kindred. **2.** a relative or kinsman. **3.** a group of persons tracing or claiming descent from a common ancestor, or constituting a family, clan, tribe, or race. **4.** someone or something of the same or similar kind. **5.** family relationship or kinship. —*adj.* **6.** of the same family; related; akin. **7.** of the same kind or nature; having affinity. —**Idiom. 8.** of kin, related; akin. —**kin′less,** *adj.*

-kin, a diminutive suffix of nouns: *lambkin.*

ki·nase (kī′nās, -nāz, kin′ās, -āz), *n.* an enzyme that effects the transfer of a phosphate group from ATP to another molecule.

kind¹ (kīnd), *adj.* **1.** of a good or benevolent nature or disposition, as a person; compassionate. **2.** having, showing, or proceeding from benevolence: *kind words.* **3.** considerate or helpful; humane (often fol. by *to*): *to be kind to animals.*

kind² (kīnd), *n.* **1.** a class or group of animals, people, objects, etc., classified on the basis of common traits; category. **2.** nature or character: *to differ in degree rather than in kind.* **3.** an example of something; variety; sort. **4.** a more or less adequate example of something: *The vines formed a kind of roof.* —**Idiom. 5.** in kind, **a.** in the same way; with something of the same kind as that received. **b.** in goods, commodities, or services rather than money: *payment in kind.* **6.** kind of, *Informal.* to some extent; somewhat; rather: *It's kind of dark.* **7.** of a kind, of the same class, nature, character, etc.: *two of a kind.* —**Usage.** The phrase THESE (or THOSE) KIND OF, followed by a plural noun (*these kind of flowers; those kind of people*) is frequently condemned as ungrammatical because it is said to combine a plural demonstrative (*these; those*) with a singular noun, KIND. Historically, KIND is an unchanged or unmarked plural noun like *deer, folk, sheep,* and *swine,* and the construction KIND OF is an old one, occurring in the writings of Shakespeare, Swift, Jane Austen, and, in modern times, Winston Churchill and Jimmy Carter. KIND has also developed the plural KINDS, evidently because of the feeling that the old pattern was incorrect. THESE KIND OF nevertheless persists in use, esp. in less formal speech and writing. In edited, more formal prose, THIS KIND OF and THESE KINDS OF are more common. SORT OF has been influenced by the use of KIND as an unchanged plural: *these sort of books.* This construction too is often considered incorrect and appears mainly in less formal speech and writing. KIND (or SORT) OF as an adverbial modifier meaning "somewhat" occurs in informal speech and writing: *Sales have been kind (or sort) of slow these last few weeks.*

kin·der·gar·ten (kin′dər gär′tn, -dn), *n.* a class or school for young children, usu. five-year-olds. —**kin′der·gart′ner, kin′der·gar′ten·er** (-gärt′nər, -gärd′-), *n.*

kind·heart·ed (kīnd′här′tid), *adj.* having or showing sympathy or kindness. —**kind′heart′ed·ly,** *adv.* —**kind′heart′ed·ness,** *n.*

kin·dle (kin′dl), *v.,* **-dled, -dling.** —*v.t.* **1.** to start (a fire); cause (a flame or blaze) to begin burning. **2.** to set fire to or ignite (fuel or any combustible matter). **3.** to excite or arouse; stir up; set going. **4.** to light up or make bright. —*v.i.* **5.** to begin to burn. **6.** to become aroused or animated. **7.** to become bright or glowing. —**kin′dler,** *n.*

K

kind·li·ness (kīnd′lē nis), *n.* **1.** the state or quality of being kindly; benevolence. **2.** a kindly deed.

kin·dling (kind′ling), *n.* **1.** material that can be readily ignited, used in starting a fire. **2.** the act of a person who kindles.

kind·ly (kīnd′lē), *adj.,* **-li·er, -li·est,** *adv.* —*adj.* **1.** having, showing, or proceeding from a kind disposition: *kindly people.* **2.** gentle or mild; benign. **3.** pleasant or beneficial. —*adv.* **4.** in a kind manner. **5.** cordially or heartily: *We thank you kindly.* **6.** obligingly; please: *Kindly close the door.* **7.** with liking; favorably: *to take kindly to an idea.*

kind·ness (kīnd′nis), *n.* **1.** the state or quality of being kind. **2.** a kind act; favor. **3.** kind behavior. **4.** friendly feeling; liking.

kin·dred (kin′drid), *n.* **1.** a person's relatives: kin; kinfolk. **2.** relationship by birth or descent, or sometimes by marriage; kinship. —*adj.* **3.** having the same belief, attitude, or feeling. **4.** associated by origin, nature, qualities, etc. **5.** related by birth or descent; having kinship.

kin·e·mat·ics (kin′ə mat′iks, kī′nə-), *n.* (*used with a sing. v.*) the branch of mechanics that deals with pure motion, without reference to the masses or forces involved in it. —**kin′e·mat′ic, kin′e·mat′i·cal,** *adj.* —**kin′e·mat′i·cal·ly,** *adv.*

kin·e·scope (kin′ə skōp′, kī′nə-), *n.* **1.** a cathode-ray tube with a fluorescent screen on which an image is reproduced by a directed beam of electrons. **2.** a film record of a television program.

ki·ne·sics (ki nē′siks, -ziks, kī-), *n.* (*used with a sing. v.*) the study of body movements, gestures, facial expressions, etc., as a means of communication. —**ki·ne′sic,** *adj.* —**ki·ne′si·cal·ly,** *adv.*

ki·ne·si·ol·o·gy (ki nē′sē ol′ə jē, -zē-, kī-), *n.* the study of the anatomy and physiology of body movement, esp. in relation to physical education or therapy. —**ki·ne′si·ol′o·gist,** *n.*

ki·net·ic (ki net′ik, kī-), *adj.* **1.** pertaining to or caused by motion. **2.** characterized by movement. —**ki·net′i·cal·ly,** *adv.*

kinet′ic en′ergy, *n.* the energy of a body with respect to its motion. Compare POTENTIAL ENERGY.

ki·net·ics (ki net′iks, kī-), *n.* (*used with a sing. v.*) the branch of mechanics that studies the actions of forces in producing or changing the motion of masses.

kin·folk (kin′fōk′), *n.pl.* relatives or kindred. Sometimes, **kin′folks′, kinsfolk.**

king (king), *n.* **1.** a male sovereign or monarch; a man who holds by life tenure, and usu. by hereditary right, the chief authority over a country and people. **2.** a person or thing preeminent in its class: *the king of actors.* **3.** a playing card bearing a picture of a king. **4.** the chief chess piece of each color, whose checkmating is the object of the game: moved one square at a time in any direction. **5.** a checker piece that has been moved entirely across the board and has been crowned, thus allowing it to be moved in any direction. —*v.t.* **6.** to make a king of; crown. —*adj.* **7.** large; king-size. **8.** preeminent.

King (king), *n.* **1. Martin Luther, Jr.,** 1929–68, U.S. Baptist minister; civil-rights leader. **2. William Lyon Mackenzie,** 1874–1950, prime minister of Canada 1921–26, 1926–30, 1935–48. **3. William Rufus DeVane,** 1786–1853, vice president of the U.S. 1853.

King′ and I′, The, a musical (1951) by Richard Rodgers and Oscar Hammerstein.

King′ Cot′ton, *n.* cotton and cotton-growing considered, in the pre-Civil War South, as a vital commodity, the major factor not only in the economy but also in politics.

king′ crab′, *n.* **1.** HORSESHOE CRAB. **2.** Also called **Alaskan king crab.** a large, edible crab, *Paralithodes camtschatica,* of cold North Pacific waters, esp. abundant along the coasts of Alaska and Japan.

king·dom (king′dəm), *n.* **1.** a state or government having a king or queen as its head. **2.** anything constituting an independent realm; domain: *the kingdom of thought.* **3.** a realm of nature, esp. one of the three broad divisions of natural objects: *the animal, vegetable, and mineral kingdoms.*

King′dom Hall′, *n.* a meeting place of Jehovah's Witnesses for religious services.

king·fish (king′fish′), *n., pl.* (*esp. collectively*) **-fish,** (*esp. for kinds or species*) **-fish·es. 1.** any of various large edible croakers, esp. of the genus *Menticirrhus,* of North American coastal waters. **2.** KING MACKEREL. **3.** *Informal.* a person regarded as a leader or authority.

king·fish·er (king′fish′ər), *n.* any of various usu. brightly colored birds of the family Alcedinidae, of worldwide distribution, with large heads and robust bills: many dive for fish.

King′ George′'s War′, *n.* a war (1744–48) waged by England and its colonies against France, constituting the North American phase of the War of the Austrian Succession.

King′ Go′ing to War′, The, a parable of Jesus. Luke 14:31–32.

King′ James′ Ver′sion, *n.* an English version of the Bible prepared in England under James I and published in 1611. Also called the **Authorized Version.**

King′ Lear′ (lēr′), a tragedy (1606) by William Shakespeare.

king·let (king′lit), *n.* **1.** a king ruling over a small country or territory. **2.** any of several very small songbirds of the genus *Regulus,* of the Northern Hemisphere, having a patch of bright color on the crown of the head.

king·ly (king′lē), *adj.,* **-li·er, -li·est,** *adv.* —*adj.* **1.** pertaining to, suggesting, or befitting a king; regal. **2.** having the rank of king. —*adv.* **3.** in the manner of a king; regally. —**king′li·ness,** *n.*

king′ mack′erel, *n.* a game fish, *Scomberomorus cavalla,* of the W Atlantic Ocean.

king·mak·er (king′mā′kər), *n.* a person who has great power and influence in the choice of a ruler, candidate for public office, business leader, or the like. —**king′mak′ing,** *n., adj.*

king′ of beasts′, *n.* the lion.

king′ of kings′, *n.* a king having other kings subject to him.

King′ of kings′ (or **Kings′**), *n.* Christ; Jesus. **2.** God; Jehovah.

king′ pen′guin, *n.* a large penguin, *Aptenodytes patagonicus,* found on islands bordering the Antarctic Circle.

King′ Phil′ip's War′, *n.* the war (1675–76) between New England colonists and a confederation of Indians under their leader, King Philip.

king·pin (king′pin′), *n.* **1.** (in bowling) **a.** the headpin. **b.** the pin at the center; the number 5 pin. **2.** *Informal.* a person or thing of chief importance. **3.** either of the pins that are a part of the mechanism for turning the front wheels in some automotive steering systems.

king′ post′ or **king′post′,** *n.* a structural member running vertically between the apex and base of a triangular roof truss.

Kings (kingz), *n.* (*used with a sing. v.*) either of two books of the Bible, I Kings or II Kings, which contain the history of the kings of Israel and Judah.

king′ salm′on, *n.* CHINOOK SALMON.

Kings′ Can′yon Na′tional Park′, *n.* a national park in E California: deep granite gorges; giant sequoias; mountains. 708 sq. mi. (1835 sq. km).

king's′ Eng′lish, *n.* standard, educated, or correct English speech or usage, esp. of England. Also called, *when a queen is sovereign,* **queen's English.**

king's′ e′vil, *n.* scrofula: so called because it was supposed to be curable by the touch of the reigning sovereign.

king·ship (king′ship), *n.* **1.** the state, office, or dignity of a king. **2.** rule by a king; monarchy. **3.** aptitude for kingly duties.

king′-size′ or **king′-sized′,** *adj.* **1.** larger or longer than the usual size. **2.** (of a bed) extra large, usu. 76–78 in. (193–198 cm) wide and 80–84 in. (203–213 cm) long. **3.** of or for a king-size bed.

Kings′ Moun′tain, *n.* a ridge in N South Carolina: American victory over the British 1780.

king′ snake′ or **king′snake′,** *n.* any of several harmless New World snakes of the genus *Lampropeltis,* that often feed on other snakes.

Kings·ton (kingz′tən, king′stən), *n.* **1. Maxine Hong,** born 1940, U.S. novelist. **2.** the capital of Jamaica. 600,000. **3.** a port in SE Ontario, in SE Canada, on Lake Ontario. 55,050.

Kings·town (kingz′toun′), *n.* the capital of St. Vincent and the Grenadines, on SW St. Vincent island. 28,942.

kink (kingk), *n.* **1.** a twist or curl, as in a thread, rope, wire, or hair. **2.** a muscular stiffness or soreness, as in the neck or back. **3.** a flaw or imperfection likely to hinder the operation of something, as a machine or plan. **4.** an eccentricity or quirk. —*v.t., v.i.* **5.** to form or cause to form a kink or kinks, as a rope.

Kinkaid′ Act′, *n.* an act of Congress (1904) providing for the granting of 640-acre homesteads to settlers in western Nebraska. [named after Moses *Kinkaid* (1854–1922), American Congressman]

kin·ka·jou (king′kə jōō′), *n., pl.* **-jous.** a brownish arboreal mammal, *Potos flavus,* of the raccoon family, of tropical America, having a prehensile tail.

kink·y (king′kē), *adj.,* **kink·i·er, kink·i·est.** full of kinks; closely twisted or curled: *kinky hair.* —**kink′i·ly,** *adv.* —**kink′i·ness,** *n.*

Kin·sha·sa (kin shä′sə, kin′shä sə), *n.* the capital of the Democratic Republic of the Congo, in the NW part, on the Zaire (Congo) River. 2,653,558. Formerly, **Léopoldville.**

kins·man (kinz′mən), *n., pl.* **-men. 1.** a relative, esp. a male. **2.** a person of the same nationality or ethnic group, esp. a male.

kins·wom·an (kinz′wŏŏm′ən), *n., pl.* **-wom·en. 1.** a female relative. **2.** a woman of the same nationality or ethnic group.

ki·osk (kē′osk, kē osk′), *n.* **1.** a small building or structure open on one or more sides, used as a newsstand, refreshment stand, etc. **2.** a thick, columnlike structure on which notices and advertisements are posted. **3.** an open pavilion or summerhouse common in Turkey and Iran. **4.** *Brit.* a telephone booth. [< French *kiosque* stand in a public park < Turkish *köşk* < Persian *kūshk* palace, villa]

Ki·o·wa (kī′ə wä, -wä′, -wə′), *n., pl.* **-was,** (*esp. collectively*) **-wa. 1.** a member of a Plains Indian people living between the Arkansas and Red rivers in the mid-19th century: later confined to a reservation in the Indian Territory. **2.** the language of the Kiowa, akin to the Tanoan languages.

kip¹ (kip), *n.* **1.** the hide of a young or small beast. **2.** a bundle or set of such hides.

kip² (kip), *n.* a unit of weight equal to 1000 pounds (453.6 kg).

kip·per (kip′ər), *n.* **1.** a fish, esp. a herring, that has been cured by splitting, salting, drying, and smoking. **2.** a male salmon during or after the spawning season. —*v.t.* **3.** to cure (herring, salmon, etc.) by splitting, salting, drying, and smoking.

kir (kēr), *n.* (*sometimes cap.*) an apéritif of white wine or sometimes champagne flavored with cassis.

Kir·ghi·zia (kir gē′zhə, -zhē ə), *n.* former name of **Kyrgyzstan.** Former official name, **Kirghiz′ So′viet So′cialist Repub′lic.**

Ki·ri·ba·ti (kēr′ē bä′tē, kēr′ə bas′), *n.* a republic in the central Pacific

Ocean, on the equator, comprising 33 islands. 66,250; 263 sq. mi. (681 sq. km). *Cap.:* Tarawa. Formerly, **Gilbert Islands.**

Kir·jath Ar·ba (kėr′jath är′bə), *n.* **1.** Hebron. Gen. 23:2. **2.** an Israeli settlement near Hebron.

kirk (kûrk, kirk), *n.* **1.** *Chiefly Scot.* a church. **2. the Kirk,** the Church of Scotland (Presbyterian), as distinguished from the Church of England or the Scottish Episcopal Church. —**kirk′man,** *n., pl.* **-men.**

Kirk·pat·rick (kûrk pa′trik), *n.* **1. Jeane (Jordan)** (jēn), born 1926, U.S. diplomat: ambassador to the U.N. 1981–85. **2. Mount,** a mountain in Antarctica, near Ross Ice Shelf. ab. 14,855 ft. (4528 m).

Kir′li·an photog′raphy (kėr′lē ən), *n.* a photographic process that purportedly records electrical discharges naturally emanating from living objects in the form of an auralike glow.

Kir·man (kir män′, kər-) also **Kerman,** *n.* a Persian rug marked by ornate flowing designs and light, muted colors.

Kirt′land's war′bler (kûrt′ləndz), *n.* a gray-and-yellow wood warbler, *Dendroica kirtlandii,* that breeds only in north-central Michigan.

ki·ruv (kē′ʀŏŏv), *n. Hebrew.* the act or practice of bringing secularized Jews closer to Judaism, esp. Orthodox Judaism, as through seminars, meetings, and religious rituals.

Kish (kish), *n.* an ancient Sumerian and Akkadian city: its site is 8 mi. (13 km) east of the site of Babylon in S Iraq.

Ki·shi·nev (kish′ə nef′, -nôf′, -nof′), *n.* the Russian name of **Chişinău.**

Kis·lev (kis′lav, kēs lev′), *n.* the third month of the Jewish calendar. [< Hebrew *kislēw*]

kis·met (kiz′mit, -met, kis′-), *n.* fate; destiny.

kiss (kis), *v.t.* **1.** to touch or press with the lips slightly pursed in token of affection, greeting, reverence, etc. **2.** to touch gently or lightly: *The breeze kissed her face.* **3.** to put, bring, take, or express by kissing: *She kissed the baby's tears away. They kissed each other good-bye.* **4.** (of a billiard ball) to make slight contact with or brush (another ball). —*v.i.* **5.** to join lips, as in affection, love, or passion; touch or caress one another with the lips. **6.** to touch lightly or gently. **7. kiss off,** *Slang.* to reject or dismiss bluntly or coarsely. —*n.* **8.** an act or instance of kissing. **9.** a slight touch or contact. **10.** a small baked meringue. **11.** a small, sometimes conical, bite-size chocolate candy. —**kiss′a·ble,** *adj.*

kiss′-and-tell′, *adj.* disclosing secrets or confidences; gossipy: *a kiss-and-tell memoir.*

kiss·er (kis′ər), *n.* **1.** a person who kisses. **2.** *Slang.* **a.** the face. **b.** the mouth.

kiss′ing cous′in, *n.* **1.** See under KISSING KIN. **2.** something closely related or very similar.

Kis·sin·ger (kis′ən jər), *n.* **Henry A(lfred),** born 1923, U.S. secretary of state 1973–77, born in Germany.

kiss′ing kin′, *n.* any more or less distant kin familiar enough to be greeted with a kiss, as a cousin (**kissing cousin).**

kiss′ of death′, *n.* a fatal or destructive relationship or action: *The support of the outlawed group was the kiss of death to the candidate.*

kiss′-off′, *n. Slang.* an unceremonious or rude dismissal.

kiss′ of peace′, *n.* **1.** a ceremonial greeting or embrace given as a token of Christian love and unity. **2.** a ceremonial kiss formerly given, esp. at a baptism or Eucharistic service, as a token of Christian love and unity. Also called **pax.**

Kist·na (kist′nə), *n.* former name of KRISHNA (def. 2).

kit (kit), *n.* **1.** a set of tools, supplies, or materials for a specific purpose: *a first-aid kit; a sales kit.* **2.** a case or container for these. **3.** a set of materials or parts from which something can be assembled: *a model airplane kit.* —*Idiom.* **4. the whole kit and caboodle,** all the persons or things concerned.

kit′ bag′ or **kit′bag′,** *n.* a small bag or knapsack, as for a soldier.

kitch·en (kich′ən), *n.* **1.** a room or place equipped for cooking or preparing food. **2.** culinary department. **3.** the staff or equipment of a kitchen. —*adj.* **4.** of or resembling a pidginized language, esp. as used for communication between employers and employees who do not speak the same language. —**kitch′en·like′,** *adj.* —**kitch′en·y,** *adj.*

kitch′en cab′inet, *n.* a group of unofficial advisers on whom a head of government appears to rely heavily.

kitch·en·ette or **kitch·en·et** (kich′ə net′), *n.* a very small, compact kitchen.

kitch′en gar′den, *n.* a garden where vegetables, herbs, and fruit are grown for one's own use. —**kitch′en gar′dener,** *n.*

kitch′en mid′den, *n.* a mound consisting of shells of edible mollusks and other refuse, marking the site of a prehistoric human habitation.

kitch′en police′, *n.* See KP.

kitch′en-sink′, *adj.* marked by an indiscriminate and omnivorous use of elements: *a kitchen-sink approach to moviemaking.*

kitch·en·ware (kich′ən wâr′), *n.* cooking equipment or utensils.

kite (kīt), *n., v.,* **kit·ed, kit·ing.** —*n.* **1.** a light frame covered with some thin material, to be flown in the wind at the end of a long string. **2.** any of various slim, graceful hawks, as of the New World genera *Elanoides* and *Ictinia* and the Old World genus *Milvus,* with long, pointed wings and usu. a notched or forked tail. **3.** a worthless or fraudulently written instrument of credit, esp. a check written for an amount greater than that on deposit and covered with another bogus check drawn on a different bank. **4.** a person who preys on others; sharper. —*v.i.* **5.** to fly or move with a rapid or easy motion like that of

a kite. **6.** to obtain money or credit through kites. —*v.t.* **7.** to write (a bad check) to obtain money or credit. —**kit′er,** *n.* —**kite′like′,** *adj.*

kith (kith), *n.* **1.** acquaintances, friends, neighbors, or the like. —*Idiom.* **2. kith and kin,** relatives or acquaintances and relatives together.

kith·a·ra (kith′ər ə) also **cithara,** *n., pl.* **-ras.** a lyrelike musical instrument of ancient Greece having a wooden soundbox.

kitsch (kich), *n.* something of tawdry design, appearance, or content created to appeal to popular or undiscriminating taste. —**kitsch′y,** *adj.*

kit·ten (kit′n), *n.* a young cat. —*v.i.* **2.** (of a cat) to give birth.

kit·ten·ish (kit′n ish), *adj.* **1.** coyly playful. **2.** like or in the manner of a kitten. —**kit′ten·ish·ly,** *adv.* —**kit′ten·ish·ness,** *n.*

kit·ti·wake (kit′ē wāk′), *n.* either of two small cliff-nesting gulls of the genus *Rissa,* of northern seas.

kit·ty[1] (kit′ē), *n., pl.* **-ties.** **1.** a kitten. **2.** a pet name for a cat.

kit·ty[2] (kit′ē), *n., pl.* **-ties.** **1.** a pool or reserve of money, often collected from a number of people or sources and designated for a particular purpose. **2. a.** a pool into which players in a card game put some of their winnings, as to pay for refreshments. **b.** (in poker) the pot.

kit′ty-cor′nered or **kit′ty-cor′ner,** *adj., adv.* CATER-CORNERED.

Kit′ty Hawk′, *n.* a village in NE North Carolina: Wright brothers' airplane flight 1903.

ki·va (kē′və), *n., pl.* **-vas.** a large chamber in a Pueblo Indian village, often wholly or partly underground, used for religious ceremonies and other purposes.

Ki·wa·nis (ki wä′nis), *n.* an organization founded in 1915 for the promulgation of higher ideals in business and professional life. —**Ki·wa′ni·an,** *n.*

ki·wi (kē′wē), *n., pl.* **-wis.** **1.** any of several flightless, nocturnal birds comprising the order Apterygiformes, of New Zealand. **2.** Also called **ki′wi·fruit′** (-frōōt′). the egg-sized edible berry of the Chinese gooseberry, having fuzzy brownish skin and green flesh. **3.** *Informal.* a New Zealander.

kiwi (def. 1) *Apteryx australis,* length to 28 in. (71 cm); bill 6 in. (15 cm)

K.J.V., King James Version.

KKK or **K.K.K.,** Ku Klux Klan.

Klam′ath weed′, *n.* the St.-John's-wort, *Hypericum perforatum.*

klatsch or **klatch** (kläch, klach), *n.* a casual gathering, as for conversation.

klax·on (klak′sən), *n.* a loud electric horn often used as a warning signal.

Kleen·ex (klē′neks), *Trademark.* a brand of facial tissue.

Klein′ bot′tle (klīn), *n.* a one-sided figure consisting of a tapered tube whose narrow end is bent back, run through the side of the tube, and flared to join the wide end, allowing any two points on the figure to be joined by an unbroken line.

klep·to·ma·ni·a (klep′tə mā′nē ə, -mān′yə), *n.* a compulsion to steal having no relation to need or the monetary value of the object. —**klep′to·ma′ni·ac′** (-nē ak′), *n., adj.*

klieg′ light′, *n.* a powerful type of arc light once widely used in motion-picture studios.

Klimt (klimt), *n.* **Gustav,** 1862–1918, Austrian painter.

klip·spring·er (klip′spring′ər), *n.* a small African antelope, *Oreotragus oreotragus,* of mountainous regions.

Klon·dike (klon′dīk), *n.* **1.** a region of the Yukon territory in NW Canada: gold rush 1897–98. **2.** a river in this region, flowing into the Yukon. 90 mi. (145 km) long. **3.** (*l.c.*) a variety of solitaire.

kludge (klōōj), *n. Slang.* an inelegant but successful solution to a problem in computer hardware or software.

klutz (kluts), *n. Slang.* **1.** a clumsy, awkward person. **2.** a stupid or inept person; blockhead. —**klutz′y,** *adj.,* **klutz·i·er, klutz·i·est.** —**klutz′i·ness,** *n.*

km, kilometer.

km/sec, kilometers per second.

knack (nak), *n.* **1.** a special skill, talent, or aptitude. **2.** a clever or adroit way of doing something.

knack·wurst (näk′wûrst, -wŏŏrst) also **knockwurst,** *n.* a short, thick, highly seasoned sausage.

Knapp (nap), *n.* **Phoebe,** 1839–1908, U.S. musician and hymn writer.

knap·sack (nap′sak′), *n.* a canvas, nylon, or leather bag for clothes or other supplies, carried on the back by soldiers, hikers, etc.

knar (när), *n.* a knot on a tree or in wood. —**knarred, knar′ry,** *adj.*

knave (nāv), *n.* **1.** an unprincipled, untrustworthy, or dishonest person. **2.** (in cards) the jack.

knav·er·y (nā′və rē), *n., pl.* **-er·ies.** **1.** unprincipled or dishonest dealing; trickery. **2.** a knavish act or practice.

knav·ish (nā′vish), *adj.* like or befitting a knave; untrustworthy; dishonest. —**knav′ish·ly,** *adv.* —**knav′ish·ness,** *n.*

knead (nēd), *v.t.* **1.** to work (dough, clay, etc.) into a uniform mixture by pressing, folding, and stretching. **2.** to manipulate by similar movements, as the body in a massage. **3.** to make by kneading: *to knead bread.* —**knead′er,** *n.*

knee (nē), *n., v.,* **kneed, knee•ing.** —*n.* **1.** the joint of the human leg that allows for movement between the femur and tibia and is covered by the patella; the central area of the leg between the thigh and the lower leg. **2.** a joint superficially similar to but not anatomically homologous with the human knee, as the tarsal joint of a bird or the carpal joint in the forelimb of a horse or cow. **3.** the part of a garment covering the knee. **4.** something resembling a bent knee, as a rigid or braced angle between two framing members. **5.** a woody growth projecting from the roots of certain swamp-growing trees, as the bald cypress. —*v.t.* **6.** to strike or touch with the knee. —***Idiom.*** **7. bring someone to his** or **her knees,** to force someone into submission or compliance.

knee•cap (nē′kap′), *n.* **1.** the patella. **2.** a protective covering for the knee. —*v.t.* **3.** to cripple (a person) by shooting in the knee. —**knee′cap′per,** *n.*

knee′-deep′, *adj.* **1.** reaching the knees: *knee-deep mud.* **2.** submerged or covered up to the knees: *knee-deep in water.* **3.** deeply embroiled; enmeshed; involved: *knee-deep in trouble.*

knee′-high′, *adj.* **1.** as high as the knees. —*n.* **2.** Also, **knee′-hi′.** a sock or stocking that reaches to just below the knees.

knee′ jerk′, *n.* a reflex extension of the leg resulting from a sharp tap on the patellar tendon.

knee′-jerk′, *adj. Informal.* reacting in an automatic, habitual manner; unthinking: *a knee-jerk liberal.*

knee′-jerk′ lib′eral, *n. Slang.* a political liberal with unthinking reactions to policies or leaders.

kneel (nēl), *v.i.,* **knelt** or **kneeled, kneel•ing.** to go down or rest on the knees or a knee.

kneel•er (nē′lər), *n.* **1.** a person or thing that kneels. **2.** a bench, pad, or the like, to kneel on.

knell (nel), *n.* **1.** the sound made by a bell rung slowly, esp. for a death or a funeral. **2.** a sound or sign announcing someone's death or the end or failure of something. **3.** any mournful sound. —*v.i.* **4.** (of a bell) to sound, as at a funeral. **5.** to give forth a mournful, ominous, or warning sound. —*v.t.* **6.** to proclaim or summon by or as if by a bell.

knelt (nelt), *v.* a pt. and pp. of KNEEL.

Knes•set (knes′et, kə nes′-), *n.* the unicameral parliament of Israel.

knew (no͞o, nyo͞o), *v.* pt. of KNOW.

Knick•er•bock•er (nik′ər bok′ər), *n.* **1.** a resident of the state of New York. **2.** a descendant of the Dutch settlers of New York. **3. knickerbockers,** KNICKERS (def. 1). [generalized from Diedrich *Knickerbocker,* fictitious author of Washington Irving's *History of New York* (1809)]

knick•ers (nik′ərz), *n.* (*used with a pl. v.*) **1.** loose-fitting short trousers gathered in at the knees. **2.** *Brit.* women's underpants. —***Idiom.*** **3. get one's knickers in a twist,** *Brit. Slang.* to get flustered or agitated.

knick•knack (nik′nak′), *n.* an ornamental trinket.

knife (nīf), *n., pl.* **knives** (nīvz), *v.,* **knifed, knif•ing.** —*n.* **1.** an instrument for cutting, consisting of a sharp-edged metal blade fitted with a handle. **2.** a knifelike weapon; dagger or short sword. **3.** any blade for cutting, as in a tool or machine. —*v.t.* **4.** to apply a knife to; cut, stab, etc., with a knife. **5.** to attempt to defeat or undermine in a secret or underhanded way. —*v.i.* **6.** to move or cleave through something with or as if with a knife: *The ship knifed through the sea.* —***Idiom.*** **7. under the knife,** undergoing surgery. —**knif′er,** *n.*

knight (nīt), *n.* **1.** (in the Middle Ages) **a.** a mounted soldier serving under a feudal superior. **b.** a man, usu. of noble birth, who after serving as page and squire was raised to honorable military rank and bound to chivalrous conduct. **2.** any person of a rank similar to that of the medieval knight. **3.** a man upon whom nonhereditary knighthood is conferred by a sovereign, in Great Britain ranking next below a baronet. **4.** a member of any order or association that designates its members as knights. **5.** a chess piece shaped like a horse's head, moved one square vertically and then two squares horizontally or one square horizontally and two squares vertically. —*v.t.* **6.** to dub or make (a man) a knight.

knight′-er′rant, *n., pl.* **knights-errant.** a knight who traveled in search of adventures, to exhibit military skill, to engage in chivalrous deeds, etc.

knight•hood (nīt′ho͝od), *n.* **1.** the rank, dignity, or vocation of a knight. **2.** knightly character or qualities. **3.** the body of knights.

knight•ly (nīt′lē), *adj.* **1.** of, resembling, or characteristic of a knight. **2.** composed of knights. —**knight′li•ness,** *n.*

Knights′ of Colum′bus, *n.* an international fraternal and benevolent organization of Roman Catholic men, founded in 1882.

Knight′ Tem′plar, *n., pl.* **Knights Templars, Knights Templar. 1.** a member of a religious and military order founded by Crusaders in Jerusalem about 1118 and suppressed in 1312. **2.** a member of a Masonic order in the U.S. claiming descent from the medieval order.

knish (knish), *n.* a baked turnover filled usu. with potatoes or meat.

knit (nit), *v.,* **knit•ted** or **knit, knit•ting,** *n.* —*v.t.* **1.** to make (a garment, fabric, etc.) by interlocking loops of yarn by hand with knitting needles or by machine. **2.** to join closely and firmly, as members or parts. **3.** to contract into folds or wrinkles: *to knit the brow.* —*v.i.* **4.** to become closely and firmly joined together; grow together, as broken bones. **5.** to contract into folds or wrinkles, as the brow. **6.** to do knitting. —*n.* **7.** a fabric or garment produced by knitting. **8.** the basic stitch in knitting, formed by pulling a loop of the working yarn forward through an existing stitch and then slipping that stitch off the needle. Compare PURL[1] (def. 1). —**knit′ta•ble,** *adj.* —**knit′ter,** *n.*

knit•ting (nit′ing), *n.* **1.** the act of one that knits, esp. the act of forming a fabric by looping a continuous yarn on knitting needles. **2.** knitted work.

knit′ting nee′dle, *n.* **1.** either of two instruments used for hand knitting: a straight rod of steel, wood, plastic, etc., pointed at one or both ends, used in pairs, or a single curved, flexible rod with two pointed ends. **2.** any of various needlelike devices used in machine knitting.

knob (nob), *n.* **1.** a projecting part, usu. rounded, forming a handle, as on a door or drawer, or a control device, as on a radio. **2.** a rounded lump or protuberance on the surface or at the end of something.

knob•by (nob′ē), *adj.,* **-bi•er, -bi•est. 1.** full of rounded lumps or protuberances. **2.** shaped like a knob. —**knob′bi•ness,** *n.*

knock (nok), *v.i.* **1.** to strike a sounding blow, as in seeking admittance, calling attention, or giving a signal. **2.** to strike in collision; bump: *to knock into a table.* **3.** to make a pounding noise: *The car's engine is knocking badly.* **4.** *Informal.* to find fault. **5.** to end a card game, as in gin rummy, by laying down a hand in which those cards not included in sets total less than a specific amount. —*v.t.* **6.** to give a sounding or forcible blow to; hit; strike; beat. **7.** to drive, force, or render by striking: *to knock a man senseless.* **8.** to make by striking a blow or blows: *to knock a hole in the wall.* **9.** to strike (a thing) against something else. **10.** *Informal.* to criticize, esp. in a carping manner. **11. knock around** or **about, a.** to wander, esp. living briefly in one place after another. **b.** to mistreat; manhandle. **12. knock back,** *Slang.* to drink (a beverage), esp. quickly and heartily. **13. knock down, a.** to cause to fall by striking. **b.** to dismantle for ease of handling. **c.** to lower the price of. **d.** to sell at auction, as through a blow of the auctioneer's hammer. **14. knock off, a.** to cease an activity, esp. the day's work. **b.** to cease (work). **c.** *Informal.* to do, produce, or dispose of quickly, hurriedly, or with ease: *to knock off a couple of stories in a day.* **d.** *Slang.* to murder. **e.** to reduce a price by the amount of. **f.** *Slang.* to disable or defeat. **g.** *Slang.* to rob; burglarize. **h.** to copy or plagiarize. **15. knock out, a.** to defeat (an opponent) in a boxing match by striking such a blow that the opponent is unable to rise within the specified time. **b.** to make unconscious. **c.** to make tired or exhausted. **d.** *Informal.* to produce quickly; knock off. **e.** to damage or destroy: *to knock out the power lines.* **f.** *Slang.* to impress greatly; overwhelm with amazed delight. **16. knock over, a.** to strike (someone or something) from an erect to a prone position. **b.** to distress; overcome. **c.** *Slang.* to rob, burglarize, or hijack. **17. knock together,** to make or construct in a hurry or with little attention to detail. —*n.* **18.** an act or instance of knocking. **19.** the sound of knocking, esp. a rap, as at a door. **20.** a blow or thump. **21.** *Informal.* an adverse criticism. **22.** the noise resulting from faulty combustion or incorrect functioning within an internal-combustion engine. **23.** (in cricket) an inning. —***Idiom.*** **24. knock it off,** to cease doing or saying something. **25. knock out (of the box),** to cause (a baseball pitcher) to be replaced by getting several hits. **26. knock the** or **one's socks off,** *Informal.* to have an overwhelming effect on: *The song knocked the socks off the audience.* **27. knock on wood,** (used, often while actually knocking on something made of wood, to ward off ill luck when one has just mentioned one's good fortune, health, happiness, or the like.) —**knock′less,** *adj.*

knock•a•bout (nok′ə bout′), *n.* **1.** a small fore-and-aft–rigged sailboat with a mainsail and a jib but no bowsprit. **2.** something designed or suitable for rough or casual use, as a sturdy jacket or old car. —*adj.* **3.** suitable for rough use, as a garment. **4.** rough; boisterous. **5.** slapstick: *knockabout comedy.* **6.** shiftless; aimless.

knock•down (nok′doun′), *adj.* **1.** capable of knocking something down; overwhelming; irresistible: *a knockdown blow.* **2.** constructed of parts that can readily be disassembled and assembled: *knockdown furniture.* **3.** offered or acquired for less than the prevailing rate: *knockdown prices.* —*n.* **4.** a knockdown object. **5.** an act or instance of knocking down, esp. by a blow. **6.** something that fells or overwhelms. **7.** a reduction or lowering, as in price or number.

knock′-down′-drag′-out′, *adj.* marked by unrelenting violence: *a knock-down-drag-out fight.*

knock′-knee′, *n.* **1.** inward curvature of the legs, causing the knees to knock together in walking. **2. knock-knees,** the knees of a person whose legs have such curvature. —**knock′-kneed′,** *adj.*

knock′off′ or **knock′-off′,** *n.* an unlicensed, cheap copy of something, esp. fashion clothing.

knock•out (nok′out′), *n.* **1.** an act or instance of knocking out. **2.** the state or fact of being knocked out. **3.** a knockout blow. **4.** *Informal.* a person or thing overwhelmingly attractive, appealing, or successful. —*adj.* **5.** serving to knock out: *the knockout punch.*

knock•wurst (nok′wûrst, -wo͝orst), *n.* KNACKWURST.

knoll[1] (nōl), *n.* a small, rounded hill or mound. —**knoll′y,** *adj.*

knoll[2] (nōl), *v.t.* **1.** to ring or toll a bell for; announce by tolling. **2.** to ring or toll (a bell). —*v.i.* **3.** to sound, as a bell; ring. **4.** to sound a knell. —**knoll′er,** *n.*

Knos•sos or **Cnos•sus** (nos′əs), *n.* a ruined city in N central Crete: capital of the ancient Minoan civilization. —**Knos′si•an,** *adj.*

knot (not), *n., v.,* **knot•ted, knot•ting.** —*n.* **1.** an interlacing, looping, etc., of a cord, rope, or the like, drawn tight into a knob, for fastening two cords together or a cord to something else. **2.** a tangled mass; snarl. **3.** an ornamental piece of ribbon or similar material tied or folded upon itself. **4.** a group or cluster of persons or things. **5.** the hard, cross-grained mass of wood at the place where a branch joins a tree trunk. **6.** a part of this mass showing in a piece of lumber. **7.** a small lump or swelling. **8.** a constriction or cramping, as of a muscle. **9.** any of various fungal diseases of trees forming a gnarl. **10.** an intricate or difficult matter; complicated problem. **11. a.** a unit of speed equal to one nautical mile or about 1.15 statute miles per hour. **b.** a unit of 47 feet 3 inches (13.79 m) on a line, marked off in knots, formerly used to measure distance. **c.** a nautical mile. **12.** a bond or tie: *the knot of matrimony.* **13.** *Math.* NODE (def. 6). —*v.t.* **14.** to tie in a knot; form a knot in. **15.** to secure or fasten by a knot. **16.** to form protuberances or knobs in; make knotty. —*v.i.* **17.** to become tied or tangled in a knot. **18.** to form knots or joints. —**knot′less,** *adj.* —**knot′like′,** *adj.*

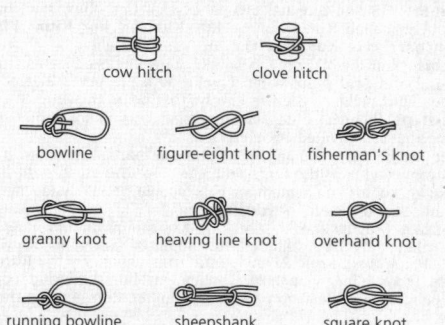

cow hitch   clove hitch

bowline   figure-eight knot   fisherman's knot

granny knot   heaving line knot   overhand knot

running bowline   sheepshank   square knot

knots (def. 1)

knot•hole (not′hōl′), *n.* a hole in a board or plank formed by the falling out of a knot or a portion of a knot.
knot•ty (not′ē), *adj.,* **-ti•er, -ti•est. 1.** having or full of knots. **2.** involved, intricate, or difficult. —**knot′ti•ly,** *adv.* —**knot′ti•ness,** *n.*
know (nō), *v.,* **knew, known, know•ing,** *n.* —*v.t.* **1.** to perceive or understand as fact or truth; apprehend clearly and with certainty. **2.** to have established or fixed in the mind or memory: *to know a poem by heart.* **3.** to be cognizant or aware of: *I know it.* **4.** to be acquainted or familiar with (a thing, place, person, etc.): *I know the mayor well.* **5.** to understand from experience or practice: *to know how to make gingerbread.* **6.** to be able to distinguish, as one from another: *to know right from wrong.* **7.** to recognize: *I'd know her if I saw her again.* **8.** *Archaic.* to have sexual intercourse with. Gen. 4:1. —*v.i.* **9.** to have knowledge or clear and certain perception, as of fact or truth. **10.** to be cognizant or aware, as of some circumstance or occurrence; have information. —*n.* **11.** the fact or state of knowing; knowledge. —*Idiom.* **12. in the know,** privy to information. —**know′a•ble,** *adj.* —**know′er,** *n.*
know′-how′, *n.* knowledge of how to do something; expertise.
know•ing (nō′ing), *adj.* **1.** affecting or revealing shrewd knowledge of secret or private information: *a knowing glance.* **2.** having knowledge or information; intelligent. **3.** shrewd, sharp, or astute. **4.** conscious; intentional; deliberate. —**know′ing•ly,** *adv.* —**know′ing•ness,** *n.*
know′-it-all′, *n.* a person who acts as though he or she had better knowledge or understanding than anyone else.
knowl•edge (nol′ij), *n.* **1.** acquaintance with facts, truths, or principles; general erudition. **2.** familiarity or conversance, as by study or experience: *a knowlege of human nature.* **3.** the fact or state of knowing; clear and certain mental apprehension. **4.** awareness, as of a fact or circumstance. **5.** something that is or may be known; information. **6.** the body of truths or facts accumulated in the course of time. **7.** the sum of what is known: *Knowledge of the situation is limited.* —*Idiom.* **8. to one's knowledge,** according to the information available to one: *To my knowledge, he never worked here.*
knowl•edge•a•ble or **knowl•edg•a•ble** (nol′i jə bəl), *adj.* possessing or exhibiting knowledge, insight, or understanding; well-informed; perceptive. —**knowl′edge•a•bly,** *adv.*
known (nōn), *v.* **1.** pp. of KNOW. —*n.* **2.** a known quantity.
know′-noth′ing, *n.* **1.** an ignorant or totally uninformed person; ignoramus. **2.** (*caps.*) a member of a U.S. political party of the 1850s, whose aim was to exclude Catholics and the foreign-born from political participation: so called because members professed ignorance of the party's activities. **3.** a person whose anti-intellectualism, xenophobia, and other political attitudes recall the Know-Nothings. —*adj.* **4.** grossly ignorant; totally uninformed. **5.** (*caps.*) of or pertaining to the Know-Nothings. **6.** of or pertaining to a political know-nothing.
Knox (noks), *n.* **1. Henry,** 1750–1806, American Revolutionary general. **2. John,** c1510–72, Scottish religious reformer and historian. **3. Ronald,** 1888–1957, English Roman Catholic priest and Bible translator.
Knox•ville (noks′vil), *n.* a city in E Tennessee, on the Tennessee River. 169,311.

knuck•le (nuk′əl), *n., v.,* **-led, -ling.** —*n.* **1.** any joint of a finger, esp. one of the articulations of a metacarpal with a phalanx. **2.** the rounded prominence of such a joint when the finger is bent. **3.** BRASS KNUCKLES. —*v.t.* **4.** to rub or press with the knuckles. **5. knuckle down, a.** to apply oneself vigorously and earnestly; become serious. **b.** Also, **knuckle under.** to submit; yield. —**knuck′ly,** *adj.,* **-li•er, -li•est.**
knuck′le ball′ or **knuck′le•ball′,** *n.* a slow baseball pitch that moves erratically toward home plate, delivered by holding the ball between the thumb and the knuckles or fingertips. Also called **knuck•ler** (nuk′lər). —**knuck′le•ball′er,** *n.*
knuck•le•head (nuk′əl hed′), *n. Informal.* a stupid, bumbling, inept person. —**knuck′le•head′ed,** *adj.*
KO (*n.* kā′ō′, kā′ō′; *v.* kā′ō′), *n., pl.* **KOs** or **KO's,** *v.,* **KO'd, KO'•ing.** —*n.* **1.** a knockout in boxing. —*v.t.* **2.** to knock unconscious in boxing; knock out. Often, **K.O., k.o.**
ko•a•la (kō ä′lə), *n., pl.* **-las.** a gray, tree-dwelling Australian marsupial, *Phascolarctos cinereus,* resembling a teddy bear.

koalas, *Phascolarctos cinereus,*
length 2 1/2 ft. (0.8 m)

Ko•be (kō′bē, -bā), *n.* a seaport on S Honshu, in S Japan. 1,413,000.
Ko•dak (kō′dak), *Trademark.* a portable roll-film camera introduced by George Eastman in 1888.
Ko′diak bear′, *n.* a large brown bear, *Ursus arctos middendorffi,* inhabiting coastal areas of Alaska and British Columbia.
Koest•ler (kest′lər, kes′lər), *n.* **Arthur,** 1905–83, British novelist, critic, and journalist; born in Hungary.
kohl•ra•bi (kōl rä′bē, -rab′ē), *n., pl.* **-bies.** a cultivated cabbage, *Brassica oleracea gongylodes,* of the mustard family, with an edible bulblike stem.
Kok•ka (kôk′kä), *adj.* of or pertaining to the branch of Shinto recognized as the official state religion of Japan. Cf. **Shuha.**
Kol Ni•dre (kôl′ nē drä′, kōl′ nid′rə, -rä), *n.* a Jewish prayer recited on the eve of Yom Kippur, asking that all unfulfilled vows to God be nullified. [< Aramaic *kōlnidhrē* all vows]
Ko•mo′do drag′on (kə mō′dō), *n.* a monitor lizard, *Varanus komodoensis,* of certain Indonesian islands: the largest lizard in the world. Also called **Komo′do liz′ard.**
Kon•go (kong′gō), *n.* **1.** Also, **Congo, Kakongo.** a major historic kingdom of W central Africa, whose rulers, Christianized under Portuguese influence in the late 15th century, exercised largely nominal authority after 1710. **2.** Also, **Bakongo.** (*used with a pl. v.*) the members of a group of modern African peoples of the S Congo Republic, W Zaire, and NW Angola. **3.** Also, **Kikongo.** the Bantu language or languages of these peoples, a creolized form of which serves as a lingua franca in the lower Congo River basin.
kook (kōōk), *n. Slang.* an eccentric, strange, or crazy person.
kook•a•bur•ra (kōōk′ə bûr′ə, -bur′ə), *n., pl.* **-ras.** any of several Australian and Papuan birds of the genus *Dacelo,* of the kingfisher family, esp. *D. gigas,* having a loud call that resembles laughter.
kook•y or **kook•ie** (kōō′kē), *adj.,* **kook•i•er, kook•i•est.** *Slang.* of or like a kook; eccentric, strange, or crazy.
ko•peck or **ko•pek** (kō′pek), *n.* a monetary unit of Russia, the Soviet Union, and its successor states, equal to $1/100$ of the ruble.
kor (kôr, kōr), *n.* HOMER[2].
Ko•rah (kôr′ə, kōr′ə), *n.* a Levite who led a rebellion against Moses and Aaron. Num. 16. Also, **Core.**
Ko•ran (kə rän′, -ran′, kô-, kō-), *n.* the sacred text of Islam, divided into 114 chapters, or suras: revered as the word of God, dictated to Muhammad by the archangel Gabriel, and accepted as the foundation of Islamic law, religion, culture, and politics. Often, **Qur'an.** [< Arabic *qur'ān* book, akin to *qara'a* to read] —**Ko•ran′ic,** *adj.* —**Ko•ran′i•cal•ly,** *adv.*
Ko•re•a (kə rē′ə), *n.* **1.** a former country in E Asia, on a peninsula SE of Manchuria and between the Sea of Japan and the Yellow Sea: a kingdom prior to 1910; under Japanese rule 1910–45. **2. Democratic People's Republic of,** official name of NORTH KOREA. **3. Republic of,** official name of SOUTH KOREA.
Ko•re•an (kə rē′ən), *n.* **1.** a native or inhabitant of Korea. **2.** the language of this people, affiliated by some with the Altaic languages. —*adj.* **3.** of or pertaining to Korea, the Koreans, or their language.
Kore′an War′, *n.* the war (1950–53) between North Korea, aided by Communist China, and South Korea, aided by the U.S. and other United Nations members forming an armed force.
Kos•ci•us•ko (kos′kē us′kō, kos′ē-; *for 1 also* kosh chōōsh′-), *n.* **1. Thaddeus** (*Tadeusz Andrzej Bonawentura Kościuszko*), 1746–1817, Polish patriot: general in the American Revolutionary army. **2. Mount,** the

highest mountain in Australia, in SE New South Wales. 7316 ft. (2230 m).

ko·sher (kō′shər), *adj.* **1. a.** fit or allowed to be eaten or used, according to the dietary or ceremonial laws of Judaism. **b.** adhering to these laws. **2.** *Informal.* proper; legitimate. —*n.* **3.** *Informal.* kosher food. —*v.t.* **4.** to make kosher. [< Hebrew *kāshēr* right, fit]

ko′sher-style′, *adj.* featuring traditional Jewish dishes but not adhering to the dietary laws: *a kosher-style restaurant.*

kow·tow (kou′tou′, -tou′, kō′-), *v.i.* **1.** to act in an obsequious manner; show servile deference. **2.** to touch the forehead to the ground while kneeling, as an act of worship, respect, etc., esp. in former Chinese custom. —*n.* **3.** the act of kowtowing. [< Chinese *kòutóu* lit., knock (one's) head] —**kow′tow′er,** *n.*

KP (kā′pē′), *n., pl.* **KPs, KP's** for 2. **1.** military duty as a kitchen helper: *assigned to KP.* **2.** a soldier detailed to work as kitchen help. [*k(itchen) p(olice)*]

kph or **k.p.h.,** kilometers per hour.

Kr, *Chem. Symbol.* krypton.

kraal (kräl), *n.* **1.** an enclosure for cattle and other domestic animals in S Africa. **2. a.** a village of the native peoples of South Africa. **b.** such a village as a social unit. **3.** an enclosure where wild animals are exhibited, as in a zoo. —*v.t.* **4.** to shut up in a kraal, as cattle.

kraft (kraft, kräft), *n.* a strong, usu. brown paper processed from wood pulp, used chiefly for bags and as wrapping paper.

krait (krīt), *n.* any nocturnal venomous S Asian elapid snake of the genus *Bungarus,* having broad black-and-white or black-and-yellow bands.

Kra·ka·tau or **Kra·ka·tao** (krak′ə tou′, krä′kə-), also **Kra·ka·to·a** (-tō′ə), *n.* a volcano and small island in Indonesia, between Java and Sumatra: violent eruption 1883.

kra·ter or **cra·ter** (krā′tər), *n.* (in ancient Greece and Rome) a bowl in which water and wine were mixed.

K ration, *n.* an emergency military field ration for use under combat conditions, consisting of three separate packaged meals. Compare C RATION.

kraut (krout), *n. Informal.* sauerkraut.

Krem·lin (krem′lin), *n.* **1. the Kremlin,** the government of Russia or of the Soviet Union. **2.** the citadel of Moscow, housing the offices of the Russian and, formerly, of the Soviet government.

Krish·na (krish′nə), *n.* **1.** an avatar of Vishnu and one of the most popular of Hindu deities. **2.** Formerly, **Kistna.** a river in S India, flowing E from the Western Ghats to the Bay of Bengal. 800 mi. (1290 km) long.

Kriss Krin·gle (kris′ kring′gəl), *n.* SANTA CLAUS. [alter., by folk etym., of German *Christkindl* little Christ child = *Christ* CHRIST + *kind* CHILD]

Krupp (krup), *n.* **Alfred,** 1812–87, German industrialist and manufacturer of armaments.

kryp·ton (krip′ton), *n.* an inert monatomic gaseous element, present in very small amounts in the atmosphere. *Symbol:* Kr; *at. wt.:* 83.80; *at. no.:* 36.

KS, Kansas.

kt., **1.** karat. **2.** kiloton. **3.** knot.

K.T., **1.** Knights Templars. **2.** Knight of the Order of the Thistle.

Kua·la Lum·pur (kwä′lə loom poor′), *n.* the capital of Malaysia, in the SW Malay Peninsula. 937,875.

Ku·blai Khan (koo′blī kän′) also **Ku′bla Khan′** (koo′blə), *n.* 1216–94, khan c1260–94: founder of the Mongol dynasty in China (grandson of Genghis Khan).

Ku·brick (kyoo′brik), *n.* **Stanley,** born 1928, U.S. film director.

ku·do (koo′dō, kyoo′-), *n., pl.* **-dos.** a statement of praise or approval; accolade; compliment. ——**Usage.** See KUDOS[1].

ku·dos (koo′dōz, -dōs, -dos, kyoo′-), *n.* (*used with a sing. v.*) honor; glory; acclaim. ——**Usage.** KUDOS entered English in the 19th century as a singular noun, a transliteration of a Greek singular noun meaning "praise or renown." Used largely in university circles, it became popular among journalists in the 1920s, esp. for headlines: *Playwright receives kudos.* Because such contexts often do not reveal whether the term is singular or plural, and because the word ends in -s, the marker of the regular English plural, KUDOS eventually came to be treated as a plural meaning "accolades." The singular form KUDO has been produced from this supposed plural by back formation and has developed the meaning "statement of praise, accolade." Usage guides generally advise against using KUDO (with plural KUDOS), and sometimes even reject the singular word KUDOS.

kud·zu (kood′zoo), *n., pl.* **-zus.** a fast-growing vine, *Pueraria lobata,* of the legume family, planted esp. for fodder and to retain soil.

Ku Klux Klan (koo′ kluks′ klan′), *n.* **1.** a secret organization in the southern U.S., active for several years after the Civil War, that aimed to suppress the newly acquired rights of blacks. **2.** Official name, **Knights of the Ku Klux Klan.** a secret organization inspired by the former, founded in 1915 and directed against blacks, Catholics, Jews, and other groups. Also called **Ku′ Klux′.** —**Ku′ Klux′er, Ku′ Klux′ Klans′man** (or **Klan′ner**), *n.* —**Ku′ Klux′ism,** *n.*

kum·quat (kum′kwot), *n.* **1.** a small, orange-colored citrus fruit with a sweet rind and acid pulp, eaten chiefly as a preserve. **2.** any shrub of the genus *Fortunella,* of the rue family, that bears this fruit.

kun·da·li·ni (koon′dl ē′nē), *n.* (in yoga) a vital force at the base of the spine that is activated by exercises.

kung fu (kung′ foo′, koong′), *n.* a Chinese martial art based on the use of fluid movements of the arms and legs. [< Chinese *gōngfú* lit., skill]

Kurd (kûrd, koord), *n.* a member of a people of SW Asia, the principal inhabitants of Kurdistan. —**Kurd′ish,** *adj.*

Kur·di·stan (kûr′də stan′, -stän′), *n.* **1.** a mountain and plateau region in SE Turkey, NW Iran, and N Iraq, inhabited largely by Kurds. 74,000 sq. mi. (191,660 sq. km). **2.** any of the rugs woven by the Kurds.

kur·gan (koor gän′, -gan′), *n.* an ancient burial mound constructed over a pit grave: earliest occurrence 4th millennium B.C., in the Russian Steppes.

Ku·wait (koo wāt′), *n.* **1.** a sovereign monarchy in NE Arabia, on the NW coast of the Persian Gulf: formerly a British protectorate. 2,076,805; ab. 8000 sq. mi. (20,720 sq. km). **2.** the capital of this monarchy. 167,750. —**Ku·wai′ti** (-wä′tē), *n., pl.* **-tis,** *adj.*

Kuy·per (kī′pər, koi′-), *n.* **Abraham,** 1837–1920, Dutch theologian.

kvetch (kvech), *Slang.* —*v.i.* **1.** to complain, esp. chronically. —*n.* **2.** Also, **kvetch′er.** a person who kvetches.

kW or **kw,** kilowatt.

kWh or **kwhr** or **K.W.H.,** kilowatt-hour.

KY or **Ky.,** Kentucky.

ky·ack (kī′ak), *n.* a type of packsack that consists of two connected sacks and is hung on either side of a packsaddle.

ky·a·nite (kī′ə nīt′), *n.* a mineral, aluminum silicate, Al_2SiO_5, occurring in bluish bladed crystals or in masses, used as a refractory.

Kyo·to (kē ō′tō, kyō′-), *n.* a city on S Honshu, in central Japan: the capital of Japan. 794–1868. 1,472,993.

ky·pho·sis (kī fō′sis), *n.* an abnormal convex curvature of the spine, with a resultant bulge at the upper back. —**ky·phot′ic** (-fot′ik), *adj.*

Kyr·gyz·stan (kir′gi stän′, -stan′), *n.* a republic in central Asia, S of Kazakhstan and N of Tajikistan: a former constituent republic of the U.S.S.R. 4,540,185; 76,641 sq. mi. (198,500 sq. km.). *Cap.:* Bishkek. Formerly **Kirghizia.**

Kyr·i·e e·le·i·son (*Rom. Cath. Ch.,* Angl. Ch. kēr′ē ā′ e lā′ə sôn′, -son′, -sən; *Gk. Orth. Ch.* kēr′kē e e le′ē sôn), *n.* **1.** (*italics*) the brief petition "Lord, have mercy," used in various offices of the Greek Orthodox Church and of the Roman Catholic Church. **2.** the brief response or petition in services in the Anglican Church, beginning with the words, "Lord, have mercy upon us." **3.** Also called **Kyr′i·e′.** a musical setting of either of these. [< Late Greek *Kýrie eléēson* Lord, have mercy]

L

L, l (el), *n., pl.* **Ls** or **L's, ls** or **l's. 1.** the 12th letter of the English alphabet, a consonant. **2.** any spoken sound represented by this letter. **3.** something shaped like an L. **4.** a written or printed representation of the letter *L* or *l*.

L (el), *n., pl.* **L's** or **Ls.** *Informal.* an elevated railroad.

L (el), *n., pl.* **L's** or **Ls.** ell.

L, *Symbol.* **1.** the 12th in order or in a series. **2.** (*sometimes l.c.*) the Roman numeral for 50. Compare ROMAN NUMERALS. **3.** leucine.

L-, *Biochem. Symbol.* (of a molecule) having a configuration resembling the levorotatory isomer of glyceraldehyde: printed as a small capital, roman character (disting. from D-).

l-, *Symbol.* levorotatory; levo- (disting. from *d*-).

L-, levo-.

la (lä), *n.* the musical syllable used for the sixth tone in the ascending diatonic scale.

LA, 1. Louisiana. **2.** light alcohol. **3.** low alcohol.

La, *Chem. Symbol.* lanthanum.

La., Louisiana.

lab (lab), *n.* laboratory.

La·ban (lā′bən), *n.* the father of Leah and Rachel and the father-in-law of Jacob. Gen. 24:29; 29:16–30.

la·bel (lā′bəl), *n., v.,* **-beled, -bel·ing** or (*esp. Brit.*) **-belled, -bel·ling.** —*n.* **1.** an inscribed slip of paper, cloth, or other material, for attachment to something to indicate its manufacturer, nature, ownership, destination, etc. **2.** a short word or phrase descriptive of a person, group, intellectual movement, etc. **3.** a word or phrase indicating that what follows belongs in a particular category or classification, as the word *Physics* before a dictionary definition. **4.** a brand or trademark, esp. of a manufacturer of phonograph records, tape cassettes, etc. **5.** the manufacturer using such a label. **6.** a molding over a door or window. **7.** a radioactive or heavy isotope incorporated into a molecule for use as a tracer. **8.** a narrow horizontal heraldic band with downward extensions. —*v.t.* **9.** to affix a label to; mark with a label. **10.** to designate or describe by or on a label: *The bottle was labeled poison.* **11.** to put in a certain class; classify. **12.** to incorporate a radioactive or heavy isotope into (a molecule) in order to make traceable. —**la′bel·er,** *n.*

La Belle Dame Sans Mer·ci (*Fr.* lA bel dAm sän mer sē′), a ballad (1819) by John Keats.

la·bi·a (lā′bē ə), *n. pl.* of LABIUM.

la·bi·al (lā′bē əl), *adj.* **1.** of, pertaining to, or resembling a labium. **2.** of or pertaining to the lips. **3.** (of a speech sound) articulated using one or both lips, as the sounds (p), (v), (m), (w), or (ōo). **4.** of or designating the surface of a tooth facing the lips. Compare BUCCAL (def. 3), LINGUAL (def. 4). —*n.* **5.** a labial speech sound, esp. a consonant. —**la′bi·al′i·ty,** *n.* —**la′bi·al·ly,** *adv.*

la·bi·a ma·jo·ra (lā′bē ə mə jôr′ə, -jōr′ə), *n.pl., sing.* **la·bi·um ma·jus** (lā′bē əm mā′jəs). the outer folds of skin of the external female genitalia.

la·bi·a mi·no·ra (lā′bē ə mi nôr′ə, -nōr′ə), *n.pl., sing.* **la·bi·um mi·nus** (lā′bē əm mī′nəs). the inner folds of skin of the external female genitalia.

la·bi·ate (lā′bē it, -āt′), *adj.* **1.** having parts that are shaped or arranged like lips; lipped. **2.** pertaining or belonging to the mint family. —*n.* **3.** a labiate plant.

la·bile (lā′bəl, -bīl), *adj.* **1.** apt or likely to change. **2.** (of a chemical compound) capable of changing state or becoming inactive when subjected to heat or radiation. —**la·bil·i·ty** (lə bil′i tē, lā-), *n.*

labio-, a combining form meaning "lip": *labiodental.*

la·bi·um (lā′bē əm), *n., pl.* **-bi·a** (-bē ə). **1.** a lip or liplike structure or part. **2.** any of the folds of skin bordering the vulva. **3.** the lower petal of a labiate flower. **4.** the lower or rearmost unpaired mouthpart of an insect or other arthropod.

la·bor (lā′bər), *n.* **1.** productive activity, esp. for the sake of economic gain. **2.** the body of persons engaged in such activity, esp. those working for wages. **3.** this body of persons considered as a class (distinguished from *management*). **4.** physical or mental work, esp. of a hard or fatiguing kind; toil. **5.** a job or task done or to be done. **6. a.** the uterine contractions of childbirth. **b.** the interval from the onset of these contractions to childbirth. —*v.i.* **7.** to perform labor; work; toil. **8.** to strive, as toward a goal; work hard (often fol. by *for*): *to labor for peace.* **9.** to move slowly and with effort. **10.** to function at a disadvantage (usu. fol. by *under*): *to labor under a misapprehension.* **11.** to undergo childbirth. **12.** to roll or pitch heavily, as a ship. —*v.t.* **13.** to develop or dwell on in excessive detail: *Don't labor the point.* **14.** to burden or tire. —*adj.* **15.** of or pertaining to workers, their associations, or working conditions: *labor reforms.* Also, *esp. Brit.,* **labour.** —*Idiom.* **16. labor of love, a.** a task done for satisfaction rather than for profit. **b.** labor done out of the love of God. I Thess. 1:3.

lab·o·ra·to·ry (lab′rə tôr′ē, -tōr′ē, lab′ər ə-; *Brit.* lə bor′ə tə rē, -ə trē), *n., pl.* **-ries,** *adj.* —*n.* **1.** a place equipped to conduct scientific

experiments or tests or to manufacture chemicals, medicines, etc. **2.** any place, situation, set of conditions, or the like, conducive to experimentation, investigation, and observation. —*adj.* **3.** relating to techniques of work in a laboratory: *laboratory methods; laboratory research.*

la′bor camp′, *n.* **1.** a penal colony where inmates are forced to work. **2.** a camp for the shelter of migratory farm workers.

La′bor Day′, *n.* a legal holiday in the U.S. and Canada observed on the first Monday in September in honor of labor.

la·bored (lā′bərd), *adj.* **1.** done or made with difficulty; heavy: *labored breathing.* **2.** showing the effects of great effort; strained: *labored writing.* —**la′bored·ly,** *adv.*

la·bor·er (lā′bər ər), *n.* a worker, esp. a person engaged in work that requires bodily strength rather than skill or training.

la′bor force′, *n.* WORK FORCE.

la·bo·ri·ous (lə bôr′ē əs, -bōr′-), *adj.* **1.** requiring much work, exertion, or perseverance: *a laborious undertaking.* **2.** characterized by or exhibiting excessive effort; labored. —**la·bo′ri·ous·ly,** *adv.* —**la·bo′ri·ous·ness,** *n.*

la′bor·sav′ing or **la′bor-sav′ing,** *adj.* designed to reduce human labor: *The dishwasher is a laborsaving device.*

la′bor un′ion, *n.* an organization of wage earners or salaried employees for mutual aid and protection and for dealing collectively with employers; trade union.

la·bour (lā′bər), *n., v.i., v.t. adj. Chiefly Brit.* LABOR.

La′bour Par′ty, *n.* a political party in Great Britain, formed in 1900 and characterized by the promotion of labor interests, nationalization, and social reforms.

Lab′rador retriev′er, *n.* one of a breed of solidly-built retrievers with a short, dense black, yellow, or chocolate coat and a thick, tapering tail, raised orig. in Newfoundland.

la·brum (lā′brəm, lab′rəm), *n., pl.* **la·bra** (lā′brə, lab′rə). **1.** a lip or liplike part. **2. a.** the upper or foremost unpaired mouthpart of an insect or other arthropod. **b.** the outer margin of the aperture of a shell of a gastropod.

la·bur·num (lə bûr′nəm), *n.* any poisonous tree or shrub of the genus *Laburnum,* of the legume family, with drooping clusters of bright yellow flowers.

lab·y·rinth (lab′ə rinth), *n.* **1.** an intricate combination of paths or passages in which it is difficult to find one's way or to reach the exit. **2.** a maze of paths bordered by high hedges, as in a park or garden. **3.** a complicated or tortuous arrangement or state of things or events; a bewildering complex. **4. a.** the bony cavity or membranous part of the inner ear. **b.** the aggregate of air chambers in the ethmoid bone, between the eye and the upper part of the nose.

labyrinth

lab′yrinth fish′, *n.* any freshwater fish of the family Anabantidae, of SE Asia and Africa, having a labyrinthine structure above each gill chamber enabling it to breathe air.

lab·y·rin·thine (lab′ə rin′thin, -thēn) also **lab·y·rin·thi·an** (-thē ən), **lab′y·rin′thic,** *adj.* **1.** of, pertaining to, or resembling a labyrinth. **2.** complicated; tortuous: *labyrinthine reasoning.*

lac (lak), *n.* a resinous deposit secreted on certain trees by a female scale insect, *Laccifer lacca,* of S Asia, and used chiefly in varnishes. Compare SHELLAC.

lace (lās), *n., v.,* **laced, lac·ing.** —*n.* **1.** a netlike ornamental fabric made of threads by hand or machine. **2.** a cord or string for holding or drawing together, as when passed through holes in opposite edges. **3.** ornamental cord or braid, esp. of gold or silver, used to decorate uniforms, hats, etc. —*v.t.* **4.** to fasten, draw together, or compress by or as if by means of a lace. **5.** to pass (a cord, leather strip, etc.), as through holes. **6.** to interlace; intertwine. **7.** to adorn or trim with lace. **8.** to add a small amount of alcoholic liquor or other substance to: *coffee laced with brandy.* **9.** to beat; thrash. **10.** to compress the waist of (a person) by drawing tight the laces of a corset, or the like. **11.** to mark or streak, as with color. —*v.i.* **12.** to be fastened with a lace. **13.** to attack physically or verbally (usu. fol. by *into*). —**lace′like′,** *adj.*

L

Lac·e·dae·mon (las/i dē/mən), *n.* SPARTA. —**Lac/e·dae·mo/ni·an** (-di mō/nē ən), *adj., n.*

lac·er·ate (*v.* las/ə rāt/; *adj.* -ə rāt/, -ər it), *v.*, **-at·ed, -at·ing,** *adj.* —*v.t.* **1.** to tear roughly; mangle. **2.** to distress or torture mentally or emotionally; wound deeply; pain greatly. —*adj.* **3.** LACERATED. —**lac/er·a·ble,** *adj.* —**lac/er·a·bil/i·ty,** *n.* —**lac/er·a/tive,** *adj.*

lac·er·at·ed (las/ə rā/tid), *adj.* **1.** mangled; torn. **2.** pained; distressed. **3.** *Biol.* having jagged edges, as certain leaves.

lac·er·a·tion (las/ə rā/shən), *n.* **1.** the result of lacerating; a rough, jagged tear or wound. **2.** the act of lacerating.

lace·wing (lās/wing/), *n.* any of several slender green neuropteran insects of the family Chrysopidae, with delicate transparent wings: the larvae prey upon aphids and other plant pests.

lace·work (lās/wûrk/), *n.* LACE (def. 1).

La·chish (lā/kish), *n.* a Canaanite city captured by Joshua: now an archaeological site in Israel. Josh. 10:31–34.

lach·ry·mal (lak/rə məl), *adj.* **1.** of, pertaining to, or characterized by tears. **2.** LACRIMAL.

lach·ry·mose (lak/rə mōs/), *adj.* **1.** suggestive of or tending to cause tears; mournful. **2.** given to shedding tears readily; tearful. —**lach/ry·mose/ly,** *adv.* —**lach/ry·mos/i·ty** (-mos/i tē), *n.*

lac·ing (lā/sing), *n.* **1.** the act of a person or thing that laces. **2.** a beating; thrashing. **3.** a small amount of alcoholic liquor or any other substance added to food or drink. **4.** a lace used for fastening, as in a shoe or corset.

lack (lak), *n.* **1.** deficiency or absence of something needed or desirable: *lack of money; lack of skill.* **2.** something missing or wanted: *After he left, they really felt the lack.* —*v.t.* **3.** to be without; have need of: *You lack common sense.* **4.** to fall short in respect of: *He lacks three votes to win.* —*v.i.* **5.** to be absent or missing: *Nothing lacks but their full agreement.* **6.** to have a scarcity of something: *She will never lack for friends.*

lack·a·dai·si·cal (lak/ə dā/zi kəl), *adj.* **1.** being without vigor or spirit; listless. **2.** lazy; indolent. —**lack/a·dai/si·cal·ly,** *adv.* —**lack/a·dai/si·cal·ness,** *n.*

lack·ey (lak/ē), *n.* **1.** a servile follower; toady. **2.** a liveried manservant; footman. —*v.t.* **3.** to serve obsequiously.

lack·lus·ter (lak/lus/tər), *adj.* **1.** lacking brilliance or radiance; dull: *lackluster eyes.* **2.** lacking liveliness or vitality: *a lackluster performance.* —*n.* **3.** a lack of brilliance or vitality. Also, *esp. Brit.,* **lack/lus/tre.**

la·con·ic (lə kon/ik), *adj.* using few words; terse; concise: *a laconic reply.* —**la·con/i·cal·ly,** *adv.*

lac·quer (lak/ər), *n.* **1.** a protective coating consisting of a resin, cellulose ester, or both, dissolved in a volatile solvent sometimes with pigment added. **2.** any of various resinous varnishes, esp. one obtained from a Japanese tree, *Rhus verniciflua,* used to produce a highly polished, lustrous surface on wood. **3.** Also called **lac/quer·ware/.** ware, esp. of wood, coated with such a varnish and often inlaid. —*v.t.* **4.** to coat with lacquer. **5.** to cover, as with facile or fluent words or explanations cleverly worded, etc.; obscure the faults of; gloss (often fol. by *over*): *The speech tended to lacquer over the terrible conditions.*

lac·ri·mal (lak/rə məl), *adj.* Also, **lachrymal.** of, pertaining to, situated near, or constituting the glands that secrete tears.

lac/rimal gland/, *n.* either of two tear-secreting glands situated in the outer angle of the orbit in mammals.

lac·ri·ma·tion (lak/rə mā/shən), *n.* the secretion of tears, esp. in abnormal abundance.

La Crosse (lə krôs/, kros/), *n.* a city in W Wisconsin, on the Mississippi River. 48,347.

la·crosse (lə krôs/, -kros/), *n.* a game, originated by Indians of North America, in which two 10-member teams try to send a ball into each other's goal, each player using a crosse or stick at the end of which is a netted pocket for catching, carrying, or throwing the ball. [< Canadian French: lit., the crook]

lact-, var. of LACTO- before a vowel: *lactalbumin.*

lac·tase (lak/tās, -tāz/), *n.* an enzyme capable of breaking down lactose into glucose and galactose.

lac·tate[1] (lak/tāt), *v.i.,* **-tat·ed, -tat·ing.** to secrete milk.

lac·tate[2] (lak/tāt), *n.* an ester or salt of lactic acid.

lac·ta·tion (lak tā/shən), *n.* **1.** the secretion of milk. **2.** the period of milk production. —**lac·ta/tion·al,** *adj.* —**lac·ta/tion·al·ly,** *adv.*

lac·te·al (lak/tē əl), *adj.* pertaining to, consisting of, or resembling milk; milky. —**lac/te·al·ly,** *adv.*

lac·tic (lak/tik), *adj.* of, pertaining to, or obtained from milk.

lac/tic ac/id, *n.* a syrupy liquid, $C_3H_6O_3$, produced by anaerobic metabolism, as in the fermentation of milk or carbohydrates.

lacto-, a combining form meaning "milk" (*lactometer*) or "lactic acid" (*lactobacillus*). Also, **lacti-;** *esp. before a vowel,* **lact-.**

lac·tose (lak/tōs), *n.* **1.** a disaccharide, $C_{12}H_{22}O_{11}$, present in milk, that upon hydrolysis yields glucose and galactose. **2.** a white, crystalline, sweet, water-soluble commercial form of this compound obtained from whey and used in infant feedings, in confections and other foods, and in bacteriological media. Also called **milk sugar.**

la·cu·na (lə kyōō/nə), *n., pl.* **-nae** (-nē) **-nas. 1.** a gap or missing part, as in a manuscript; hiatus. **2.** *Anat.* any minute cavity, as in the substance of bone. —**la·cu/nal,** *adj.*

la·cus·trine (lə kus/trin), *adj.* **1.** of, pertaining to, living or growing in lakes: *lacustrine organisms.* **2.** formed at the bottom or along the shore of lakes: *lacustrine geological deposits.*

lad (lad), *n.* a boy or youth; young man.

lad·der (lad/ər), *n.* **1.** a structure of wood, metal, or rope commonly consisting of two sidepieces between which a series of rungs are set at suitable distances to provide a means of climbing up or down. **2.** a means of rising, as to eminence: *the ladder of success.* **3.** a graded series of stages or levels in status: *high on the political ladder.* **4.** *Chiefly Brit.* a run in a stocking. —**lad/der·less,** *adj.* —**lad/der·like/,** *adj.*

lad/der-back/, *n.* a chair back having a number of horizontal slats between uprights.

lade (lād), *v.,* **lad·ed, lad·en** or **lad·ed, lad·ing.** —*v.t.* **1.** to put a burden or load on or in; load: *to lade a cargo ship.* **2.** to put as a load: *to lade coal on a barge.* **3.** to load oppressively; burden: *laden with responsibilities.* **4.** to fill or cover abundantly: *trees laden with fruit.* **5.** to ladle. —*v.i.* **6.** to take on a load. **7.** to ladle a liquid. —**lad/er,** *n.*

lad·en (lād/n), *adj.* **1.** burdened. —*v.t.* **2.** to lade.

la-di-da or **la-de-da** or **lah-di-dah** (lä/dē dä/), *Informal.* —*interj.* **1.** (used as an expression of derision directed at affected gentility or pretentious refinement.) —*adj.* **2.** affected; pretentious; foppish: *a la-di-da manner.* —*n.* **3.** behavior or speech characterized by affected or exaggerated gentility.

La/dies' Day/, *n.* (*often l.c.*) a day on which women can participate in a certain activity at a reduced fee or at no cost.

la/dies' (or **la/dy's**) **man/,** *n.* a man who strives to please women and to attract their attention and admiration.

la/dies' room/, *n.* a public lavatory for women.

lad·ing (lā/ding), *n.* **1.** the act of loading cargo, freight, or the like. **2.** load; cargo.

La·di·no (lə dē/nō), *n., pl.* **-nos** for 2. **1.** JUDEZMO. **2.** (in Spanish America) a mestizo.

la·dle (lād/l), *n., v.,* **-dled, -dling.** —*n.* **1.** a long-handled utensil with a cup-shaped bowl for dipping or conveying liquids. **2.** a bucketlike, refractory-lined container for transferring molten metal. —*v.t.* **3.** to dip or convey with or as if with a ladle: *to ladle soup into bowls.* —**la/dler,** *n.*

la·dy (lā/dē), *n., pl.* **-dies,** *adj.* —*n.* **1.** a woman who is refined, polite, and well-spoken. **2.** a woman of high social position or economic class. **3.** any woman; female (sometimes used in combination): *the lady who answered the phone; a saleslady.* **4.** (used in direct address: often offensive in the singular): *Ladies and gentlemen, welcome. Lady, you're in my way.* **5.** wife: *The ambassador and his lady arrived late.* **6.** *Slang.* a female lover or steady companion. **7.** (*cap.*) (in Great Britain) the proper title of any woman whose husband is higher in rank than baronet or knight, or who is the daughter of a nobleman not lower than an earl, often given by courtesy to the wife of a baronet or knight. **8.** a woman who has proprietary rights or authority, as over a manor; female feudal superior. Compare LORD (def. 4). **9, 10.** a woman who is the object of chivalrous devotion. **11.** (*usu. cap.*) an attribute or abstraction personified as a woman: *Lady Fortune; Lady Virtue.* —*adj.* —**Usage.** In the meanings "refined, polite woman" and "woman of high social position" the noun LADY is the parallel of *gentleman.* As forms of address, both nouns are used in the plural (*Ladies and gentlemen, thank you for your cooperation*), but only LADY occurs in the singular. Except in chivalrous, literary, or similar contexts (*Lady, spurn me not*), this singular is now usu. perceived as rude or at least insensitive: *Where do you want the new air conditioner, lady?* Other uses that are commonly disliked include LADY in compounds or phrases referring to occupation or position (*cleaning lady; forelady; saleslady*) and as a modifier (*lady artist; lady doctor*). Increasingly, sex-neutral terms replace LADY (*cleaner; supervisor; salesperson* or *salesclerk*). When it is relevant to specify the sex of the performer or practitioner, *woman* rather than LADY is used, the parallel term being *man: Men doctors outnumber women doctors on the hospital staff by three to one.* See also -PERSON, -WOMAN.

la/dy·bee/tle or **la/dy bee/tle,** *n.* LADYBUG.

la/dy·bird bee/tle (lā/dē bûrd/), *n.* LADYBUG. Also called **la/dy·bird/.**

la·dy·bug (lā/dē bug/), *n.* any of numerous small, round, often brightly colored and spotted beetles of the family Coccinellidae, feeding chiefly on aphids and other small insects but including several forms that feed on plants.

la·dy·fin·ger (lā/dē fing/gər), *n.* a small finger-shaped sponge cake.

la·dy·fish (lā/dē fish/), *n., pl.* (*esp. collectively*) **-fish,** (*esp. for kinds or species*) **-fish·es.** BONEFISH.

la·dy-in-wait·ing (lā/dē), *n., pl.* **la·dies-in-wait·ing.** a lady who is in attendance upon a queen or princess.

la/dy-kill/er, *n. Informal.* a man who is irresistible to women or has the reputation for being so. —**la/dy-kill/ing,** *n., adj.*

la·dy·like (lā/dē līk/), *adj.* of, pertaining to, or befitting a lady; well-bred; proper: *ladylike good manners.* —**la/dy·like/ness,** *n.*

la·dy·ship (lā/dē ship/), *n.* **1.** (*often cap.*) the form used in speaking of or to a woman having the title of *Lady* (usu. prec. by *her* or *your*). **2.** the rank of a lady.

la/dy's maid/, *n.* a woman's personal attendant.

la/dy's man/, *n.* LADIES' MAN.

la/dy's-slip/per or **la/dy-slip/per,** *n.* any of several orchids, esp. of the genus *Cypripedium,* that have a slipper-shaped flower lip.

La/dy with/ the Lamp/, *n.* epithet of Florence Nightingale.

la·e·trile (lā′i tril), *n.* a controversial drug prepared chiefly from apricot pits and purported to cure cancer.

La·fa·yette (laf′ē et′, laf′ā-, lä′fē-, -fā-), *n.* **1. Marie Joseph Paul Yves Roch Gilbert du Motier, Marquis de,** 1757–1834, French statesman and general. **2.** a city in S Louisiana. 102,281.

Lafayette′ Escadrille′, *n.* a contingent of American aviators who in 1916 served as volunteers **(Escadrille Américaine)** in the French air force and in 1918 became the 103rd Pursuit Squadron of the U.S. Army.

Laf′fer curve′ (laf′ər), *n. Econ.* a relationship postulated between tax rates and tax receipts indicating that rates above a certain level actually produce less revenue because they discourage taxable endeavors and vice versa. [named after Arthur *Laffer* (born 1940), U.S. economist, who postulated it]

La Fol·lette (lə fol′it), *n.* **Robert Marion,** 1855–1925, U.S. politician.

La Fon·taine (lä′ fon ten′, -tän′), *n.* **Jean de** (zhän), 1621–95, French poet and fabulist.

lag (lag), *v.,* **lagged, lag·ging,** *n.* —*v.i.* **1.** to fail to maintain a desired pace or speed: *Some in the race began lagging; to lag behind in production.* **2.** to linger; delay. **3.** to decrease gradually; flag: *Interest lagged as the meeting went on.* —*v.t.* **4.** to fail to keep up with: *The industry still lags the national economy.* —*n.* **5.** a lagging or falling behind; retardation. **6.** a person who lags behind **7.** an interval of time: *a lag of ten minutes.* **8.** *Mech.* the amount of retardation of some motion.

lag·an (lag′ən), *n.* goods thrown or sunk in the sea but attached to a buoy so that they may be recovered.

Lag b'O·mer (läg bō′mər, bə ō′mer), *n.* a Jewish festival celebrated on the 33rd day of the Omer and commemorating the end of the plague among Rabbi Akiba's students.

la·ger (lä′gər, lô′-), *n.* a light beer aged at low temperatures from six weeks to six months. Also called **la′ger beer′.**

lag·gard (lag′ərd), *n.* **1.** a person or thing that lags; lingerer; loiterer. —*adj.* **2.** moving, developing, or responding slowly; sluggish. —**lag′gard·ly,** *adj., adv.* —**lag′gard·ness,** *n.*

la·gniappe or **la·gnappe** (lan yap′, lan′yap), *n.* **1.** a small gift given by a merchant to a customer for making a purchase; bonus. **2.** a gratuity; tip.

lag·o·morph (lag′ə môrf′), *n.* any member of the order Lagomorpha, comprising the hares, rabbits, and pikas and resembling the rodents but having two pairs of upper incisors. —**lag′o·mor′phic, lag′o·mor′phous,** *adj.*

la·goon (lə gōōn′), *n.* **1.** an area of shallow water separated from the sea by low sandy dunes. **2.** any small, pondlike body of water, esp. one connected with a larger body of water. **3.** an artificial pool for storage and treatment of polluted or very hot sewage, industrial waste, etc.

La·gos (lā′gōs, lä′gos), *n.* a seaport in SW Nigeria: former capital. 1,097,000.

La·hore (lə hôr′, -hōr′), *n.* a city in NE Pakistan: the capital of Punjab province. 2,922,000.

la·ic (lā′ik), *adj.* **1.** Also, **la′i·cal.** lay; secular. —*n.* **2.** one of the laity.

laid (lād), *v.* pt. and pp. of LAY[1].

laid′-back′, *adj. Informal.* relaxed; easygoing; carefree: *a laid-back way of living.*

lain (lān), *v.* pp. of LIE[2].

lair (lâr), *n.* **1.** a den or resting place of a wild animal. **2.** a secret retreat or base of operations; hideout: *a pirate's lair.*

lais·sez faire or **lais·ser faire** (les′ā fâr′), *n.* **1.** the theory or system of government that upholds the autonomous character of the economic order, believing that government should intervene as little as possible in the direction of economic affairs. **2.** the practice or doctrine of noninterference in the affairs of others, esp. with reference to individual conduct or freedom of action. [< French: lit., allow to act] —**lais′sez-faire′, lais′ser-faire′,** *adj.*

la·i·ty (lā′i tē), *n.* **1.** the body of religious worshipers, as distinguished from the clergy. **2.** the people outside of a particular profession, as distinguished from those belonging to it.

La·ius (lā′əs, lā′ē əs), *n.* a legendary king of Thebes, the husband of Jocasta and father of Oedipus.

lake (lāk), *n.* **1.** a body of fresh or salt water of considerable size, surrounded by land. **2.** any similar body or pool of other liquid, as oil.

lake·front (lāk′frunt′), *n.* the land along the edge of a lake.

lake′ her′ring, *n.* a cisco or whitefish, esp. *Coregonus artedii,* of the Great Lakes.

Lake′ of the Woods′, *n.* a lake in S Canada and the N United States, between N Minnesota and Ontario and Manitoba provinces. 1485 sq. mi. (3845 sq. km).

lake·shore (lāk′shôr′, -shōr′), *n.* LAKEFRONT.

lake′ stur′geon, *n.* a sturgeon, *Acipenser fulvescens,* of the Great Lakes and the Mississippi and St. Lawrence rivers.

lake′ trout′, *n.* a large, fork-tailed char, *Salvelinus namaycush,* of N North American lakes.

Lake·wood (lāk′wŏŏd′), *n.* a city in central Colorado, near Denver. 126,031.

La·ko·ta or **La·kho·ta** (lə kō′tə), *n., pl.* **-tas,** (*esp. collectively*) **-ta. 1.** a member of a Plains Indian people, the westernmost branch of the Dakota. **2.** the dialect of Dakota spoken by the Lakotas.

lal·ly·gag (lä′lē gag′, lal′ē-) also **lollygag,** *v.i.,* **-gagged, -gag·ging.** *Informal.* to spend time idly; loaf.

lam (lam), *n., v.,* **lammed, lam·ming.** *Slang.* —*n.* **1.** a hasty escape. —*v.i.* **2.** to escape. **3.** to thrash —*v.t.* **4.** to thrash. —*Idiom.* **5. on the lam,** *Slang.* hiding or in flight from the police.

Lam., Lamentations.

la·ma (lä′mə), *n., pl.* **-mas.** a Lamaist monk.

La·ma·ism (lä′mə iz′əm), *n.* the Mahayana Buddhism of Tibet and Mongolia, having a hierarchical monastic organization. —**La′ma·ist,** *n.* —**La′ma·is′tic,** *adj.*

La·marck (lə märk′, lä-), *n.* **Jean Baptiste Pierre Antoine de Monet de,** 1744–1829, French naturalist.

la·ma·ser·y (lä′mə ser′ē), *n., pl.* **-ser·ies.** a monastery of lamas.

La·maze′ meth′od (lə mäz′), *n.* a method by which an expectant mother is prepared for childbirth by education, psychological and physical conditioning, and breathing exercises.

lamb (lam), *n.* **1.** a young sheep. **2.** the meat of a young sheep. **3.** a person who is gentle or innocent. **4.** a person who is easily outsmarted. **5. the Lamb,** JESUS CHRIST. —*v.i.* **6.** to give birth to a lamb.

Lamb (lam), *n.* **1. Charles** ("*Elia*"), 1775–1834, English essayist and

LARGEST LAKES OF THE WORLD

Lake	Country or Countries	Locality	Area sq. mi.	Area sq. km
Caspian Sea	Iran-Azerbaijan-Russian Federation-Kazakhstan-Turkmenistan	W Asia	169,000	438,000
Superior	Canada-United States	Great Lakes, between Ontario and Michigan	31,820	82,415
Victoria	Kenya-Tanzania-Uganda	E central Africa	26,828	69,485
Aral Sea	Kazakhstan-Uzbekistan	Central Asia	26,166	67,770
Huron	Canada-United States	Great Lakes, between Ontario and Michigan	23,010	59,595
Michigan	United States	Great Lakes, between Michigan and Wisconsin	22,400	58,015
Baikal	Russian Federation	S Siberia	13,200	34,188
Tanganyika	Zaire-Tanzania	E central Africa	12,700	32,893
Great Bear Lake	Canada	W Northwest Territories	12,275	31,792
Great Slave Lake	Canada	S Northwest Territories	11,172	28,935
Nyasa	Malawi-Mozambique-Tanzania	SE Africa	11,000	28,500
Chad	Chad-Niger-Nigeria	NW central Africa	10,000	26,000
Erie	Canada-United States	Great Lakes, between Ontario and Ohio	9940	25,745
Winnipeg	Canada	S Manitoba	9300	24,085
Ontario	Canada-United States	Great Lakes, between Ontario and New York	7540	19,530
Balkhash	Kazakhstan	SE Kazakhstan	7115	18,430
Ladoga	Russian Federation	NW Russian Federation	7000	18,000
Maracaibo	Venezuela	Along coast of NW Venezuela	6300	16,320
Onega	Russian Federation	NW Russian Federation	3764	9750
Turkana	Kenya-Ethiopia	NW Kenya	3500	9100
Eyre	Australia	NE South Australia	3420	8885
Titicaca	Bolivia-Peru	Altiplano, Andes Mts.	3200	8290
Nicaragua	Nicaragua	SW Nicaragua	3060	7925
Athabaska	Canada	NE Alberta and NW Saskatchewan	3000	7800
Reindeer Lake	Canada	N part of Manitoba-Saskatchewan boundary	2444	6330
Torrens	Australia	E South Australia	2400	6220
Urmia	Iran	NW Iran	2317	6000
Great Salt Lake	United States	NW Utah	2300	5950
Qing Hai	China	NE Qinghai	2300	5950
Issyk-Kul	Kyrgyzstan	NE Kyrgyzstan	2250	5830
Vanern	Sweden	SW Sweden	2141	5545

critic. **2. Mary Ann,** 1764–1847, English author who wrote in collaboration with her brother Charles Lamb.

lam·ba·da (läm bä′də, -dä), *n., pl.* **-das. 1.** a Brazilian ballroom dance for couples, with gyrating movements and close interlocking of the partners. **2.** music for this dance.

lam·baste or **lam·bast** (lam bäst′, -bast′), *v.t.,* **-bast·ed, -bast·ing.** *Informal.* **1.** to beat or whip severely. **2.** to reprimand harshly; berate.

lam·ben·cy (lam′bən sē), *n., pl.* **-cies. 1.** the quality of being lambent. **2.** something that is lambent.

lam·bent (lam′bənt), *adj.* **1.** running or moving lightly over a surface: *lambent tongues of flame.* **2.** dealing lightly and gracefully with a subject: *lambent wit.* **3.** softly bright or radiant: *a lambent light.* **—lam′bent·ly,** *adv.*

lamb·kin (lam′kin), *n.* **1.** a little lamb. **2.** LAMB (def. 3).

lamb·like (lam′līk′), *adj.* passive; gentle; meek.

Lamb′ of God′, *n.* Jesus Christ. John 1:29, 36.

lamb·skin (lam′skin′), *n.* **1.** the skin of a lamb, esp. when dressed with its wool, and used for clothing. **2.** leather made from such skin. **3.** parchment made from such skin.

lamb's′-quar′ters, *n., pl.* **-ters.** a pigweed, *Chenopodium album.*

lame·brain (lām′brān′), *n. Informal.* a stupid person; dunce; fool. **—lame′brained′,** *adj.*

lame′ duck′, *n.* **1.** an elected official or group continuing in office in the period between an election defeat and a successor's assumption of office. **2.** a president who is completing a term of office and chooses not to run or is ineligible to run for reelection. **3.** anyone or anything soon to be supplanted by another. **4.** a person or thing that is disabled, ineffective, or inefficient. **—lame′-duck′,** *adj.*

Lame′ Duck′ Amend′ment, *n.* TWENTIETH AMENDMENT.

lame′-duck′ ses′sion (lām′duk′), *n.* (formerly) the December to March session of those members of the U.S. Congress who were defeated for reelection the previous November.

la·mel·la (lə mel′ə), *n., pl.* **-mel·lae** (-mel′ē), **-mel·las.** a thin plate, scale, membrane, or layer, as a scale of horny tissue or a mushroom gill.

la·ment (lə ment′), *v.t.* **1.** to express often vocal mourning or grief for or over: *lamented the death of their leader.* **2.** to be very sorry for; regret. **—v.i. 3.** to mourn deeply and often vocally. **—n. 4.** an often vocal expression of grief or mourning. **5.** elegy; dirge. **—la·ment′er,** *n.*

la·men·ta·ble (lə men′tə bəl, lam′ən tə-), *adj.* **1.** fit to be lamented; regrettable: *a lamentable decision.* **2.** mournful; sorrowful. **—la·men′ta·ble·ness,** *n.* **—la·men′ta·bly,** *adv.*

lam·en·ta·tion (lam′ən tā′shən), *n.* the act of or instance of lamenting; lament.

Lam·en·ta·tions (lam′ən tā′shənz), *n.* (*used with a sing. v.*) a book of the Bible, traditionally ascribed to Jeremiah.

la·ment·ed (lə men′tid), *adj.* mourned for: *our late lamented friend.* **—la·ment′ed·ly,** *adv.*

lam·i·na (lam′ə nə), *n., pl.* **-nae** (-nē′), **-nas. 1.** a thin plate, scale, or layer. **2.** a thin layer or coating lying over another, as in certain minerals. **3.** the blade or expanded portion of a leaf.

lam·i·nal¹ (lam′ə nl), *adj.* **1.** (of a speech sound) articulated with the blade of the tongue. **—n. 2.** a laminal speech sound.

lam·i·nal² (lam′ə nl), *adj.* LAMINAR.

lam·i·nar (lam′ə nər) also **lam·i·nar·y** (lam′ə ner′ē), *adj.* composed of, or arranged in, laminae.

lam·i·nar·i·a (lam′ə nâr′ē ə), *n., pl.* **-nar·i·as.** any of various often very large kelps of the genus *Laminaria,* some species of which are the source of algins used as thickening or stabilizing agents in foodstuffs and other products.

lam·i·nate (*v.* lam′ə nāt′; *adj., n.* -nāt′, -nit), *v.,* **-nat·ed, -nat·ing,** *adj., n.* **—v.t. 1.** to separate or split into thin layers. **2.** to form (metal) into a thin plate, as by beating or rolling. **3.** to construct from layers of material bonded together. **4.** to cover or overlay with laminae. **—v.i. 5.** to split into thin layers. **—adj. 6.** composed of or having laminae. **—n. 7.** a laminated product; lamination. **—lam′i·na′tor,** *n.*

lam·i·nat·ed (lam′ə nā′tid), *adj.* **1.** formed of thin layers or laminae. **2.** constructed of layers of material bonded together: *laminated wood.*

lam·i·na·tion (lam′ə nā′shən), *n.* **1.** the act of laminating or the state of being laminated. **2.** arrangement in thin layers. **3.** LAMINA.

lam·i·ni·tis (lam′ə nī′tis), *n.* inflammation of the laminae in the hoof of a horse.

lamino-, a combining form representing LAMINAL¹: *lamino-alveolar.*

Lam·mas (lam′əs), *n.* **1.** a former festival in England, held on August 1, in which bread made from the first harvest of corn was blessed. **2.** a festival observed by Roman Catholics on August 1, in memory of St. Peter's imprisonment and his miraculous deliverance. Also called **Lam′mas Day′.**

lam·mer·gei·er or **lam·mer·gey·er** or **lam·mer·geir** (lam′ər gī′ər, -gīr′), *n.* a large, eaglelike Eurasian vulture, *Gypaëtus barbatus,* with a tuft of bristlelike feathers below the bill.

lamp (lamp), *n.* **1.** any of various devices furnishing artificial light, as by electricity or gas. **2.** a container for burning an inflammable liquid, as oil, at a wick for illumination. **3.** a source of intellectual or spiritual light: *the lamp of learning.* **4.** any of various devices furnishing heat, ultraviolet, or other radiation: *an infrared lamp.* **5.** a celestial body that gives off light. **6. lamps,** *Slang.* the eyes. **—lamp′less,** *adj.*

Lamp′ and the Lamp′stand, The (lamp′stand′), a parable of Jesus. Matt. 5:15–16; Mark 4:21; Luke 8:16.

lamp·black (lamp′blak′), *n.* a fine black pigment consisting of almost pure carbon collected as soot from the smoke of burning carbonaceous materials.

lamp′per eel′ (lam′pər), *n.* LAMPREY.

lamp·light (lamp′līt′), *n.* the light cast by a lamp.

lam·poon (lam pōōn′), *n.* **1.** a broad, often harsh satire directed against an individual or institution. **—v.t. 2.** to ridicule in a lampoon. **—lam·poon′er, lam·poon′ist,** *n.* **—lam·poon′er·y,** *n.*

lamp·post (lamp′pōst′), *n.* a post supporting a lamp that lights an outdoor area.

lam·prey (lam′prē), *n.* any parasitic eellike jawless fish of the family Petromyzonidae, that attaches to other fishes with its round, sucking mouth lined with rasping teeth.

lamp·shade (lamp′shād′), *n.* a shade for shielding the glare of a lighted lamp.

lamp′ shell′ or **lamp′shell′,** *n.* BRACHIOPOD.

LAN (lan), *n.* LOCAL-AREA NETWORK.

la·nate (lā′nāt) also **lanose,** *adj.* covered with something resembling wool; woolly.

Lan·ca·shire (lang′kə shēr′, -shər), *n.* a county in NW England. 1,381,300; 1174 sq. mi. (3040 sq. km). Also called **Lancaster.**

Lan·cas·ter (lang′kə stər; *for 2, 3 also* -kas tər), *n.* **1.** a member of the English royal family that reigned 1399–1461, descended from John of Gaunt, Duke of Lancaster. **2.** a city in Lancashire, in NW England. 130,400. **3.** a city in SE Pennsylvania. 58,980. **4.** a town in S California. 119,186. **5.** LANCASHIRE.

lance (lans, läns), *n., v.,* **lanced, lanc·ing. —n. 1.** a long wooden shaft with a pointed metal head used esp. by a knight as a weapon in charging. **2.** an implement resembling a lance, as a spear for killing a harpooned whale. **3.** LANCET. **—v.t. 4.** to open with or as if with a lancet. **5.** to pierce with or as if with a lance.

Lan·ce·lot (lan′sə lət, -lot′, län′-), *n.* **Sir,** the greatest of King Arthur's knights and the lover of Queen Guinevere.

lan·cet (lan′sit, län′-), *n.* a sharp-pointed surgical instrument, usu. with two edges, for making small incisions.

land (land), *n.* **1.** any part of the earth's surface, as a continent or an island, not covered by a body of water. **2.** an area of ground with reference to its nature or composition: *arable land.* **3.** an area of ground with specific boundaries: *to buy land in Florida.* **4.** rural or farming areas, as contrasted with urban areas: *They left the land for the city.* **5.** *Law.* any part of the earth's surface that can be owned as property, and everything annexed to it, whether by nature or by the human hand. **6.** a part of the earth's surface marked off by natural or political boundaries or the like; a region or country: *They came from many lands.* **7.** a realm or domain: *the land of the living.* **8.** a surface between furrows, as on a millstone or on the interior of a rifle barrel. **—v.t. 9.** to bring to or set on land. **10.** to bring into or cause to arrive in a particular place, position, or condition: *His behavior will land him in jail.* **11.** *Informal.* to catch or capture; gain; win: *to land a job.* **12.** to bring (a fish) onto land or into a boat, as with a hook or a net. **—v.i. 13.** to come to land or shore: *The boat lands at Cherbourg.* **14.** to go or come ashore from a ship or boat. **15.** to alight upon or strike a surface, as the ground or a body of water: *The plane landed on time.* **16.** to come to rest or arrive in a particular place, position, or condition (sometimes fol. by *up*): *to land in trouble; to land up 40 miles from home.*

lan·dau (lan′dô, -dou), *n.* **1.** a four-wheeled, two-seated carriage with a top made in two parts that may be let down or folded back. **2.** a sedanlike automobile with a short convertible back.

land′ bridge′ or **land′bridge′,** *n.* an actual or hypothetical strip of land that connects adjacent continental landmasses and serves as a route of dispersal for plants and animals.

land·ed (lan′did), *adj.* **1.** owning land, esp. an estate: *landed gentry.* **2.** consisting of land: *landed property.*

land·er (lan′dər), *n.* a space probe designed to land on a planet or other solid celestial body. Compare ORBITER.

land·fall (land′fôl′), *n.* **1.** an approach to or sighting of land. **2.** the land sighted or reached. **3.** a landslide.

land·fill (land′fil′), *n.* **1.** Also called **sanitary landfill.** a low area of land that is built up from deposits of solid refuse in layers covered by soil. **2.** the solid refuse itself. **—v.i. 3.** to create more usable land by this means. **—v.t. 4.** to build up (land) by means of a landfill.

land·form (land′fôrm′), *n.* a specific geomorphic feature on the surface of the earth, ranging from large-scale features such as plains and mountains to minor features such as hills and valleys.

land′ grant′, *n.* a tract of land given by the government, as for colleges or railroads.

land′-grant′ col′lege, *n.* a college or university (**land′-grant′ univer′sity**) originally granted land and funds from the federal government provided that it teach agriculture and engineering; now mostly state supported. Compare MORRILL ACT.

land·ing (lan′ding), *n.* **1.** the act of a person or thing that lands. **2.** a place where persons or goods are landed. **3.** the level floor between flights of stairs or at the head or foot of a flight of stairs.

land′ing craft′, *n.* any of various flat-bottomed naval vessels designed to move troops and equipment close to shore.

land'ing gear', *n.* the wheels, floats, etc., of an aircraft, upon which it lands and moves on ground or water.

land'ing strip', *n.* AIRSTRIP.

Lan·dis (lan'dis), *n.* **Ken·e·saw Mountain** (ken'ə sô'), 1866–1944, U.S. jurist: first commissioner of baseball 1920–44.

land·la·dy (land'lā'dē), *n., pl.* **-dies. 1.** a woman who owns and leases apartments, houses, land, etc., to others. **2.** a woman who owns or runs an inn, rooming house, or boardinghouse.

land·locked (land'lokt'), *adj.* **1.** shut in completely, or almost completely, by land: *a landlocked bay.* **2.** having no access to the sea: *a landlocked country.* **3.** living in waters shut off from the sea, as some fish.

land·lord (land'lôrd'), *n.* **1.** a person or organization that owns and leases apartments to others. **2.** a person who owns and leases land, buildings, etc. **3.** a person who owns or runs an inn, rooming house, etc. **4.** a landowner. —**land'lord'ly**, *adj.*

land·lub·ber (land'lub'ər), *n.* an unseasoned sailor or someone unfamiliar with the sea.

land·mark (land'märk'), *n.* **1.** a prominent or conspicuous object on land that serves as a guide, esp. to ships at sea or to travelers on a road; a distinguishing landscape feature marking a site or location. **2.** something used to mark the boundary of land. **3.** a building or other place of outstanding historical, aesthetic, or cultural importance. **4.** a significant or historic event, juncture, achievement, etc.: *The court decision stands as a landmark in constitutional law.* —*v.t.* **5.** to declare (a building, site, etc.) a landmark.

land·mass (land'mas'), *n.* a part of the continental crust above sea level having a distinct identity, as a continent or large island.

Land' of Beu'lah, *n.* (in Bunyan's *Pilgrim's Progress*) the peaceful land in which the pilgrim awaits the call to the Celestial City.

land' of milk' and hon'ey or **Land' of Milk' and Hon'ey**, *n.* **1.** a land of fertility and abundance. **2.** the blessings of heaven. **3.** the Promised Land: *a land flowing with milk and honey.* Ex. 3:8.

land' of Nod' (nod), *n.* the mythical land of sleep.

Land' of Oz', *n.* an unreal, otherworldly, or magical place. Also called **Oz.** [after the magical place created by L. Frank Baum in *The Wonderful Wizard of Oz* (1900) and other fantasy novels]

Land' of the Mid'night Sun', *n.* **1.** any of those countries containing land within the Arctic Circle where there is a midnight sun in midsummer, esp. Norway, Sweden, or Finland. **2.** LAPLAND.

Land' of the Ris'ing Sun', *n.* JAPAN.

Lan·don (lan'dən), *n.* **Alfred** ("*Alf*") **Mossman**, 1887–1987, U.S. politician.

land·own·er (land'ō'nər), *n.* an owner or proprietor of land. —**land'own'er·ship**, *n.* —**land'own'ing**, *n., adj.*

land' reform', *n.* any governmental program involving the redistribution of agricultural land among the peasants or farmers.

Lan·drum-Grif'fin Act' (lan'drəm grif'in), *n.* an act of Congress (1959) outlawing secondary boycotts, requiring public disclosure of the financial records of unions, and guaranteeing the use of secret ballots in union voting.

Land·sat (land'sat'), *n.* a U.S. scientific satellite that studies and photographs the earth's surface by using remote-sensing techniques.

land·scape (land'skāp'), *n., v.,* **-scaped, -scap·ing**, *adj.* —*n.* **1.** a section or expanse of natural scenery, usu. extensive, that can be seen from a single viewpoint. **2.** a picture representing natural inland or coastal scenery. **3.** the art of depicting such scenery. **4.** a sphere of activity; arena; scene: *the political landscape.* —*v.t.* **5.** to improve the appearance of (an area of land, a highway, etc.), as by planting trees, shrubs, or grass, or altering the contours of the ground. —*v.i.* **6.** to do landscape gardening or landscape architecture as a profession. —*adj.* **7.** pertaining to, designating, or producing horizontal, sideways orientation of computer output, with lines of data parallel to the two longer sides of a page (contrasted with *portrait*).

land·scap·er (land'skā'pər), *n.* a gardener who does landscape gardening.

land·scap·ist (land'skā'pist), *n.* an artist who paints landscapes.

land·side (land'sīd'), *n.* the part of a plow consisting of a sidepiece opposite the moldboard, for guiding the plow and resisting the side pressure caused by the turning of the furrow.

land·slide (land'slīd'), *n., v.,* **-slid, -slid** or **-slid·den, -slid·ing.** —*n.* **1.** the falling or sliding of a mass of soil, detritus, or rock on or from a steep slope. **2.** the mass itself. **3.** an election in which a particular candidate or party receives an overwhelming mass or majority of votes. **4.** any overwhelming victory. —*v.i.* **5.** to come down in or as if in a landslide. **6.** to win an election by an overwhelming majority. Also called, *esp. Brit.,* **land·slip** (land'slip') (for defs. 1, 2).

lands·man[1] (landz'mən), *n., pl.* **-men. 1.** Also, **landman.** a person who lives or works on land. **2.** an inexperienced sailor or one who has not been to sea before.

lands·man[2] (länts'mən), *n., pl.* **-men.** a fellow countryman.

land'-to-land', *adj.* **1.** designed for launching or traveling from a base on land to a target or destination on land: *a land-to-land missile.* —*adv.* **2.** from a base on land to a target on land.

land·ward (land'wərd), *adv.* **1.** Also, **land'wards.** toward the land or interior. —*adj.* **2.** lying, facing, or tending toward the land or away from the coast. **3.** being in the direction of the land: *a landward breeze.*

lane (lān), *n.* **1.** a narrow way or passage between hedges, fences, walls, or houses. **2.** any narrow or well-defined passage, track, channel, or course. **3.** a longitudinally defined part of a highway wide enough to accommodate one vehicle, often set off from adjacent lanes by painted lines. **4.** a fixed route followed by ocean steamers or airplanes: *shipping lanes.* **5.** (in a running or swimming race) the marked-off space or path within which a competitor must remain. **6.** BOWLING ALLEY (def. 1).

Lang·land (lang'lənd), *n.* **William**, 1332?–c1400, English poet. Also called **Langley.**

Lang·ley (lang'lē), *n.* **1. Edmund of**, YORK, Edmund of Langley, 1st Duke of. **2. Samuel Pierpont**, 1834–1906, U.S. astronomer, physicist, and pioneer in aeronautics. **3. William**, LANGLAND, William.

lang·ley (lang'lē), *n.* a unit of incident solar radiation, equal to one calorie per square centimeter. [after S. P. LANGLEY]

lan·gous·tine (lang'gə stēn'), *n.* a large prawn, *Nephrops norvegicus,* used for food.

lang·syne or **lang syne** (lang'zīn', -sīn'), *Scot.* —*adv.* **1.** long since; long ago. —*n.* **2.** time long past.

lan·guage (lang'gwij), *n.* **1.** a body of words and the systems for their use common to a people of the same community or nation, the same geographical area, or the same cultural tradition: *the French language.* **2. a.** communication using a system of arbitrary vocal sounds, written symbols, signs, or gestures in conventional ways with conventional meanings: *spoken language; sign language.* **b.** the ability to communicate in this way. **3.** the system of linguistic signs or symbols considered in the abstract. **4.** any set or system of formalized symbols, signs, sounds, or gestures used or conceived as a means of communicating: *the language of mathematics.* **5.** the means of communication used by animals: *the language of birds.* **6.** communication of thought, feeling, etc., through a nonverbal medium: *body language; the language of flowers.* **7.** the study of language; linguistics. **8.** the vocabulary or phraseology used by a particular group, profession, etc. **9.** a particular manner of verbal expression: *flowery language.* **10.** choice of words or style of writing; diction: *the language of poetry.* **11.** a set of symbols and syntactic rules for their combination and use, by means of which a computer can be given directions. [< Anglo-French < Latin *lingua* language, tongue]

lan'guage arts', *n.pl.* verbal and written skills taught in elementary and secondary schools to improve proficiency in using language.

lan'guage lab'oratory, *n.* a room with sound-reproducing and recording equipment by means of which students practice listening to and speaking a foreign language. Also called **lan'guage lab'.**

lan·guid (lang'gwid), *adj.* **1.** lacking in vigor or vitality; slack or slow: *a languid manner.* **2.** lacking in spirit or interest; listless. **3.** drooping or flagging from weakness or fatigue; faint. —**lan'guid·ly**, *adv.*

lan·guish (lang'gwish), *v.i.* **1.** to be or become weak or feeble; droop; fade. **2.** to lose vigor and vitality. **3.** to suffer neglect, distress, or hardship: *to languish in prison.* **4.** to pine with desire or longing. **5.** to assume an expression of tender, sentimental melancholy. —*n.* **6.** the act or state of languishing. **7.** a tender, melancholy look or expression. —**lan'guish·er**, *n.* —**lan'guish·ment**, *n.*

lan·guish·ing (lang'gwi shing), *adj.* **1.** becoming languid, in any way. **2.** expressive of languor; indicating tender, sentimental melancholy. **3.** lingering: *a languishing death.* —**lan'guish·ing·ly**, *adv.*

lan·guor (lang'gər), *n.* **1.** lack of energy or vitality; sluggishness. **2.** lack of spirit or interest; listlessness; stagnation.

lan·guor·ous (lang'gər əs), *adj.* **1.** characterized by languor; languid. **2.** inducing languor: *languorous fragrance.* —**lan'guor·ous·ly**, *adv.* —**lan'guor·ous·ness**, *n.*

lan·gur (lung gŏŏr'), *n.* any slender, long-tailed, leaf-eating monkey of the genus *Presbytis,* of S Asia.

lan·iard (lan'yərd), *n.* LANYARD.

lank (langk), *adj.* **1.** (of hair) straight and limp; without spring or curl. **2.** unduly long and slender: *lank grass.* **3.** lean; gaunt; thin. —**lank'ly**, *adv.* —**lank'ness**, *n.*

lank·y (lang'kē), *adj.,* **lank·i·er, lank·i·est.** ungracefully tall and thin: *a lanky boy.* —**lank'i·ly**, *adv.* —**lank'i·ness**, *n.*

lan·o·lin (lan'l in), *n.* a fatty substance, extracted from wool, used in ointments, cosmetics, waterproof coatings, etc. Sometimes, **lan·o·line** (-in, -ēn'). Also called **wool fat.** —**lan'o·lat'ed** (-ā'tid), *adj.*

Lan·sing (lan'sing), *n.* the capital of Michigan, in the S part. 119,590.

lan·ta·na (lan tan'ə), *n., pl.* **-nas.** any of numerous tropical shrubs of the genus *Lantana,* of the verbena family, cultivated for their bright and aromatic flowers.

lan·tern (lan'tərn), *n.* a transparent or translucent, usu. portable, case for enclosing a light and protecting it from the wind, rain, etc.

lan·tha·num (lan'thə nəm), *n.* a rare-earth, trivalent, metallic element, allied to aluminum, found in certain minerals, as monazite. *Symbol:* La; *at. wt.:* 138.91; *at. no.:* 57; *sp. gr.:* 6.15 at 20°C.

lan·yard or **lan·iard** (lan'yərd), *n.* **1.** a short rope or wire used on board ships to secure riggings. **2.** a small cord or rope for securing or suspending a small object, as a whistle about the neck. **3.** a cord with a small hook at one end, used in firing certain kinds of cannon. **4.** a cord worn around the left shoulder by a member of a decorated military unit. **5.** a white cord worn around the right shoulder by military police and secured to a pistol.

L

Lao (lou), *n., pl.* **Laos** (louz), (*esp. collectively*) **Lao. 1.** a member of a people of Laos and N Thailand. **2.** the Tai language of the Laos.

La•od•i•ce•a (lā od′ə sē′ə, lā′ə də-), *n.* ancient name of LATAKIA: the site of one of the seven churches of Asia (Rev. 1:11).

La•os (lä′ōs, lous, lā′os), *n.* a country in SE Asia: formerly part of French Indochina. 5,116,959; 91,500 sq. mi. (236,985 sq. km). *Cap.:* Vientiane.

La•o•tian (lā ō′shən, lou′shən), *n.* **1.** a native or inhabitant of Laos. **2.** LAO. **—*adj.* 3.** of or pertaining to Laos or its inhabitants.

Lao-tzu or **Lao-tse** or **Lao•zi** (lou′dzu′), *n.* (*Li Erh, Li Er*) 6th-century B.C. Chinese philosopher: reputed founder of Taoism.

lap[1] (lap), *n.* **1.** the front part of the human body from the waist to the knees when in a sitting position. **2.** the part of the clothing that covers this part of the body. **3.** a place, environment, or situation of rest or nurture: *the lap of luxury.* **4.** an area of responsibility, care, charge, or control: *They dropped the problem right in my lap.* **5.** a hollow place, as a hollow among hills. **6.** a part of a garment that extends over another: *the lap of a coat.* **7.** a loose border or fold.

lap[2] (lap), *v.,* **lapped, lap•ping,** *n.* **—*v.t.* 1.** to fold over or around something; wrap or wind. **2.** to enwrap in something; wrap up; clothe. **3.** to envelop or enfold: *lapped in luxury.* **4.** to lay (something) partly over something underneath. **5.** to lie partly over (something underneath); overlap. **6.** to get a lap or more ahead of (a competitor) in racing. **7.** to cut or polish with a lap. **8.** to join, as by scarfing, to form a single piece with the same dimensions throughout. **—*v.i.* 9.** to fold or wind around something. **10.** to lie partly over or alongside of something else. **11.** to lie upon and extend beyond a thing; overlap. **12.** to extend beyond a limit. **—*n.* 13.** the act of lapping. **14.** the amount of material required to go around a thing once. **15.** a complete circuit of a course in racing or in walking for exercise. **16.** one stage of a long trip, undertaking, etc. **17.** an overlapping part. **18.** the extent or amount of overlapping. **19.** a rotating wheel or disk holding an abrasive or polishing powder on its surface, used for gems, cutlery, etc.

lap[3] (lap), *v.,* **lapped, lap•ping,** *n.* **—*v.t.* 1.** (of water) to wash against or beat upon (something) with a light, slapping or splashing sound. **2.** to take in (liquid) with the tongue; lick in. **—*v.i.* 3.** to wash or move in small waves with a light, slapping or splashing sound: *The water lapped gently against the mooring.* **4.** to take up liquid with the tongue; lick up a liquid. **5. lap up, a.** to take up (liquid) with the tongue, esp. eagerly. **b.** to receive enthusiastically: *to lap up applause.* **c.** to be persuaded about gullibly. **—*n.* 6.** the act of lapping liquid. **7.** the lapping of water against something. **8.** the sound of this: *the quiet lap of the sea on the rocks.* **9.** something lapped up, as liquid food for dogs. **—lap′per,** *n.*

laparo-, a combining form meaning "abdominal wall": *laparotomy.*

lap•a•ro•scope (lap′ər ə skōp′), *n.* an endoscope equipped for viewing the abdominal cavity through a small incision and for performing local surgery. **—lap′a•ro•scop′ic** (-skop′ik), *adj.* **—lap′a•ros′co•pist** (-ə ros′kə pist), *n.* **—lap′a•ros′co•py,** *n., pl.* **-pies.**

lap•a•rot•o•my (lap′ə rot′ə mē), *n., pl.* **-mies.** a surgical incision through the abdominal wall.

La Paz (lə päz′, päs′), *n.* **1.** the administrative capital of Bolivia, in the W part; Sucre is the official capital. 992,592; ab. 12,000 ft. (3660 m) above sea level. **2.** the capital of Baja California Sur, in NW Mexico. 75,000.

lap′ belt′, *n.* (in a motor vehicle) a seat belt fastening across the lap of a driver or a passenger.

lap•board (lap′bôrd′, -bōrd′), *n.* a thin, flat board to be held on the lap for use as a table or writing surface.

la•pel (lə pel′), *n.* the front part of a garment, as a coat or shirt, that is folded back on the chest and is joined to a collar or forms one continuous piece with it. **—la•pelled′,** *adj.*

lap•i•dar•y (lap′i der′ē), *n., pl.* **-dar•ies,** *adj.* **—*n.* 1.** Also, **lap′i•dist.** a worker who cuts, polishes, and engraves precious stones. **2.** Also, **la•pid•ar•ist** (lə pid′ər ist). an expert in precious stones and the art or techniques used in cutting and engraving them. **3.** the art of cutting, polishing, and engraving precious stones. **4.** an old book on the lore of gems. **—*adj.*** Also, **lap•i•dar•i•an** (lap′i dâr′ē ən). **5.** pertaining to the cutting or engraving of precious stones. **6.** characterized by an exactitude and extreme refinement that suggests gem cutting: *a lapidary style.* **7.** pertaining to, or suggestive of inscriptions on stone monuments.

lap•in (lap′in), *n.* **1.** a rabbit. **2.** rabbit fur.

lap•is (lap′is, lā′pis), *n., pl.* **lap•i•des** (lap′i dēz′). LAPIS LAZULI.

lap•is laz•u•li (lap′is laz′o͝o lē, -lī′, laz′yo͝o-, lazh′o͝o-), *n.* **1.** a deep blue semiprecious gemstone composed mainly of lazurite with smaller quantities of other minerals. **2.** a sky-blue color. Also called **lapis.**

lap′ robe′, *n.* a blanket used to cover one's lap or legs, as when sitting outdoors or riding in an open vehicle.

lapse (laps), *n., v.,* **lapsed, laps•ing. —*n.* 1.** an accidental or temporary decline or deviation from an expected or accepted condition or state: *a lapse of justice.* **2.** a slip or error, often of a trivial sort; failure: *a lapse of memory.* **3.** an interval or passage of time; elapsed period. **4.** a moral fall, as from rectitude or virtue. **5.** a fall or decline to a lower grade, condition, or degree: *a lapse into savagery.* **6.** the act of falling, slipping, sliding, etc., slowly or by degrees. **7.** a falling into disuse. **8.** termination of an insurance policy, due to nonpayment of a premium. **9.** *Law.* the termination of a right or privilege through neglect to exercise it or through failure of some contingency. **10.** LAPSE RATE. **—*v.i.* 11.** to fall or deviate from a previous standard; fail to maintain a normative level: *The author often lapsed into bad prose.* **12.** to come to an end; stop: *We let our subscription lapse.* **13.** to fall, slip, or sink; subside: *to lapse into silence.* **14.** to fall into disuse: *The custom lapsed after a period of time.* **15.** to deviate or abandon principles, beliefs, etc.: *to lapse into heresy.* **16.** to fall spiritually, as an apostate: *to lapse from grace.* **17.** to pass away, as time; elapse. **18.** (of an insurance policy) to cease being in force; terminate. **19.** *Law.* to become void, as a legacy to someone who dies before the testator. **—laps′a•ble, laps′i•ble,** *adj.* **—laps′er,** *n.*

lapse′ rate′, *n.* the rate of decrease of atmospheric temperature with increase of elevation vertically above a given location.

lap•top (lap′top′), *n.* a portable, usu. battery-powered microcomputer small enough to rest on the lap.

lap•wing (lap′wing′), *n.* any of several large plovers of the genus *Vanellus,* esp. *V. vanellus,* of Eurasia and N Africa, having a long, upcurved crest, an erratic, flopping flight, and a shrill cry.

lar•ce•ny (lär′sə nē), *n., pl.* **-nies.** *Law.* the wrongful taking of the personal goods of another with intent to convert them to the taker's own use. **—lar′ce•nist,** *n.* **—lar′ce•nous,** *adj.* **—lar′ce•nous•ly,** *adv.*

larch (lärch), *n.* **1.** any deciduous conifer of the genus *Larix,* yielding a tough durable wood. **2.** the wood of such a tree. **—larch′en,** *adj.*

lard (lärd), *n.* **1.** the rendered fat of hogs, esp. the internal fat of the abdomen. **—*v.t.* 2.** to apply lard or grease to. **3.** to insert strips of fat in (lean meat) before cooking. **4.** to enrich for improvement or ornamentation: *a literary work larded with mythological allusions.*

lar•der (lär′dər), *n.* **1.** a room or place where food is kept; pantry. **2.** a supply of food.

Lard•ner (lärd′nər), *n.* **Ring(gold Wilmer),** 1885–1933, U.S. short-story writer and journalist.

La•re•do (lə rā′dō), *n.* a city in S Texas, on the Rio Grande. 149,914.

lar′es and pena′tes, *n.pl.* **1. Lares and Penates,** *Rom. Religion.* the benevolent spirits and gods of the household. **2.** the cherished possessions of a family or household.

large (lärj), *adj.,* **larg•er, larg•est,** *n., adv.* **—*adj.* 1.** of more than average size, quantity, degree, etc.; big; great: *a large house.* **2.** on a great scale: *a large producer of kitchen equipment.* **3.** of great scope or range; extensive; broad: *a large variety of interests.* **4.** grand or pompous: *large talk.* **5.** *Naut.* FREE (def. 29). **—*n.* 6. a.** a size of garments for persons who are heavier or broader than average. **b.** a garment in this size. **—*adv.* 7.** *Naut.* with the wind free or abaft the beam so that all sails draw fully. **—*Idiom.* 8. at large, a.** not incarcerated; free. **b.** broadly and inclusively; at length. **c.** as a whole; in general. **d.** Also **at-large.** representing the whole of a political division or similar body rather than one part of it. **—large′ness,** *n.*

large′ intes′tine, *n.* INTESTINE (def. 3).

large•ly (lärj′lē), *adv.* **1.** to a great extent; in great part; generally; chiefly. **2.** in great quantity; much.

large′mouth′ bass′ or **large′-mouth′ bass′** (bas), *n.* a North American freshwater game fish, *Micropterus salmoides,* having a large mouth extending behind the eye.

large′-print′ or **large′ print′,** *adj.* set in a type size larger than normal for use by persons with impaired vision: *large-print newspapers.*

larg′er-than-life′, *adj.* exceedingly imposing or impressive.

large′-scale′, *adj.* **1.** very extensive; of great scope: *a large-scale business plan.* **2.** made to a large scale: *a large-scale map.*

lar•gess or **lar•gesse** (lär jes′, lär′jis), *n.* **1.** generous bestowal of gifts. **2.** the gift or gifts, as of money, so bestowed.

lar•i•at (lar′ē ət), *n.* a long, noosed rope used to catch horses, cattle, or other livestock; lasso.

lark[1] (lärk), *n.* **1.** any of numerous chiefly Old World songbirds of the family Alaudidae, of open country, typically having drab plumage and a long hind claw. **2.** any of various similar birds of other families, as the meadowlark and titlark.

lark[2] (lärk), *n.* **1.** a merry, carefree adventure; frolic; escapade. **2.** innocent or good-natured mischief; a prank. **—*v.i.* 3.** to have fun; frolic; romp. **4.** to behave mischievously; play pranks.

lark•spur (lärk′spûr′), *n.* any of several plants belonging to the genus *Delphinium,* of the buttercup family, characterized by the spur-shaped formation of the calyx and petals.

lar•va (lär′və), *n., pl.* **-vae** (-vē). the immature, wingless, feeding stage of an insect that undergoes complete metamorphosis. **—lar′val,** *adj.*

la•ryn•ge•al (lə rin′jē əl, lar′ən jē′əl) also **la•ryn•gal** (lə ring′gəl), *adj.* **1.** of, pertaining to, or located in the larynx. **2.** (of a speech sound) articulated in the larynx; glottal. **—*n.* 3.** a laryngeal speech sound. **4.** any of several reconstructed consonant phonemes of Proto-Indo-European, evident principally from their manifestation as vowels or effect on contiguous vowels in extant Indo-European languages. **—la•ryn′ge•al•ly,** *adv.*

lar•yn•gi•tis (lar′ən jī′tis), *n.* inflammation of the larynx, often with accompanying sore throat, hoarseness or loss of voice, and dry cough. **—lar′yn•git′ic** (-jit′ik), *adj.*

laryngo-, a combining form representing LARYNX: *laryngoscope.* Also, *esp. before a vowel,* **laryng-.**

lar•yn•gol•o•gy (lar′ing gol′ə jē), *n.* the branch of medicine dealing with the larynx. **—la•ryn•go•log•i•cal** (lə ring′gə loj′i kəl), **la•ryn′go•log′ic,** *adj.* **—lar′yn•gol′o•gist,** *n.*

lar•ynx (lar′ingks), *n., pl.* **la•ryn•ges** (lə rin′jēz), **lar•ynx•es.** a muscu-

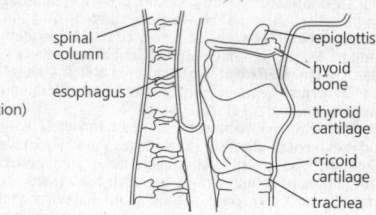

human larynx (side section)

spinal column • esophagus • epiglottis • hyoid bone • thyroid cartilage • cricoid cartilage • trachea

lar and cartilaginous structure at the upper part of the vertebrate trachea, in which the vocal cords are located.

la·sa·gna or **la·sa·gne** (lə zän′yə, lä-), *n.* **1.** large, rectangular strips of pasta. **2.** a baked dish consisting of layers of this pasta, cheese, tomato sauce, and usu. ground meat.

las·civ·i·ous (lə siv′ē əs), *adj.* **1.** inclined to lustfulness; wanton; lewd. **2.** expressive of lust or lewdness. —**las·civ′i·ous·ly,** *adv.* —**las·civ′i·ous·ness,** *n.*

lase (lāz), *v.i.,* **lased, las·ing.** to give off the coherent light of a laser; act as a laser.

la·ser (lā′zər), *n.* a device that produces a nearly parallel, nearly monochromatic, and coherent beam of light by exciting atoms and causing them to radiate their energy in phase. Compare MASER. [*l*(*ightwave*) *a*(*mplification by*) *s*(*timulated*) *e*(*mission of*) *r*(*adiation*)]

la′ser disc′, *n.* OPTICAL DISC.

la′ser print′er, *n.* a high-speed, high-resolution computer printer that uses a laser to form dot-matrix patterns and an electrostatic process to print a page at a time. —**la′ser print′ing,** *n.*

la′ser vid′eodisc, *n.* VIDEODISC.

lash¹ (lash), *n.* **1.** the flexible section of cord or the like forming the extremity of a whip. **2.** a swift stroke or blow, with a whip or the like, given as a punishment. **3.** something that goads or pains in a manner compared to the action of a whip. **4.** a swift, whiplike movement, as of an animal's tail. **5.** a violent beating or impact, as of waves or rain, against something. **6.** an eyelash. —*v.t.* **7.** to strike or beat, as with a whip or something similarly slender and flexible. **8.** to beat violently or sharply against. **9.** to drive by or as if by strokes of a whip. **10.** to attack, scold, or punish severely with words. **11.** to dash, fling, or switch suddenly and swiftly. —*v.i.* **12.** to strike vigorously at someone or something, as with a weapon or whip (often fol. by *out*): *He lashed wildly at his attackers.* **13.** to attack someone or something with harsh words (often fol. by *out*): *to lash out at injustice.* **14.** to move suddenly and swiftly; rush, dash, or flash: *The coiled snake lashed suddenly.*

lash² (lash), *v.t.* to bind or fasten with a rope, cord, etc.

lashed (lasht), *adj.* having eyelashes, esp. of a specified kind or description (usu. used in combination): *long-lashed blue eyes.*

lash·ing¹ (lash′ing), *n.* **1.** the act of one that lashes. **2.** a whipping with or as if with a lash. **3.** a severe scolding; tongue-lashing.

lash·ing² (lash′ing), *n.* **1.** a binding or fastening with a rope or the like. **2.** the rope or the like used.

lass (las), *n.* **1.** a girl or young woman, esp. one who is unmarried. **2.** a female sweetheart.

Las′sa fe′ver (lä′sə), *n.* an infectious, often fatal disease characterized by fever and pharyngitis, caused by an arenavirus.

Las′sen Volcan′ic Na′tional Park′, *n.* a national park in N California, in the S Cascade Range, including Lassen Peak. 163 sq. mi. (422 sq. km).

las·sie (las′ē), *n.* a young girl; lass.

las·si·tude (las′i tōōd′, -tyōōd′), *n.* **1.** weariness of body or mind from strain, oppressive climate, etc.; listlessness; languor. **2.** a condition of indolent indifference.

las·so (las′ō, la sōō′), *n., pl.* **-sos, -soes. 1.** a long rope or line of hide or other material with a running noose at one end, used for roping horses, cattle, etc. —*v.t.* **2.** to catch with or as if with a lasso.

last¹ (last, läst), *adj., a superl. of* **late** *with* **later** *as compar.* **1.** occurring or coming after all others, as in time, order, or place: *the last line on a page.* **2.** most recent; next before the present: *last week.* **3.** being the only one remaining: *my last dollar.* **4.** final: *in her last hours.* **5.** ultimate or conclusive; definitive. **6.** lowest in prestige or importance: *last prize.* **7.** coming after all others in one's expectations, considerations, etc.: *the last person we'd want to represent us.* **8.** individual; single: *every last person.* —*adv.* **9.** after all others; latest: *I arrived last.* **10.** on the most recent occasion: *when last seen.* **11.** in the end; finally; in conclusion. —*n.* **12.** a person or thing that is last. **13.** a final appearance or mention: *That's the last we'll hear of it.* **14.** the end or conclusion: *going on vacation the last of September.* —*Idiom.* **15.** at (long) last, after considerable delay; finally. **16.** breathe one's last, to die.

last² (last, läst), *v.i.* **1.** to go on or continue in time: *The festival lasted three weeks.* **2.** to continue unexpended or unexhausted; be enough: *Enjoy it while the money lasts.* **3.** to continue in force, vigor, effectiveness, etc. **4.** to continue or remain in usable condition: *The gloves didn't last.* —*v.t.* **5.** to continue to survive for the duration of (often fol. by *out*).

last³ (last, läst), *n.* **1.** a wooden or metal form in the shape of the hu-

man foot on which boots or shoes are shaped or repaired. —*v.t.* **2.** to shape on or fit to a last. —**last′er,** *n.*

last′-ditch′, *adj.* constituting a final, desperate effort: *a last-ditch attempt to avert war.*

last′ hurrah′, *n.* **1.** a politician's final campaign. **2.** any final attempt, competition, performance, success, or the like: *his last hurrah as a college football star.* [from *The Last Hurrah,* a novel (1956) by U.S. author Edwin O'Connor (1918–68)]

last′-in′, first′-out′, *n.* **1.** a method of handling inventory costs at the price of the earliest items, assuming that items purchased last will be sold first. *Abbr.:* LIFO   Compare FIRST-IN, FIRST-OUT. **2.** LIFO (def. 2).

last·ing (las′ting, lä′sting), *adj.* continuing or enduring a long time; permanent; durable. —**last′ing·ly,** *adv.* —**last′ing·ness,** *n.*

Last′ Judg′ment, *n.* JUDGMENT (def. 8).

last·ly (last′lē, läst′-), *adv.* in conclusion; finally.

last′ min′ute (min′it), *n.* the time just preceding a deadline or other conclusive event. —**last′-min′ute,** *adj.*

last′ name′, *n.* SURNAME (def. 1).

Last′ of the Mohi′cans, The, a historical novel (1826) by James Fenimore Cooper. Compare *Leather-Stocking Tales.*

last′ rites′, *n.pl.* religious rites performed for the dying or the dead.

last′ straw′, *n.* the last of a succession of irritations or troubles that leads to a loss of patience, a disaster, etc.

Last′ Sup′per, *n.* **1.** the supper of Jesus and His disciples on the eve of His Crucifixion. Compare LORD'S SUPPER (def. 1). **2.** a work of art representing this. **3.** (*italics.*) *The,* a mural (1495–98) by Leonardo da Vinci.

Last′ Things′, *n.pl.* the subjects of eschatology: the second coming of Christ, the end of history, and the final destiny of the individual and humankind as a whole.

last′ word′, *n.* **1.** the closing remark or comment, as in an argument. **2.** a final or definitive work, statement, etc.: *This book is the last word on the topic.* **3.** the latest, most modern thing: *the last word in hairdos this season.*

Las Ve·gas (läs vā′gəs), *n.* a city in SE Nevada. 327,878.

Lat·a·ki·a (lat′ə kē′ə *or, esp. for 1,* lä′tä kē′ä), *n.* **1.** Ancient, **Laodicea.** a seaport in NW Syria, on the Mediterranean. 191,329. **2.** a coastal district in Syria, in the W part. 389,552.

latch (lach), *n.* **1.** a device for holding a door, gate, or the like closed, consisting basically of a bar falling or sliding into a catch, groove, hole, etc. —*v.t.* **2.** to close or fasten with a latch. —*v.i.* **3.** to close tightly so that the latch is secured. **4. latch on,** to grab hold. **5. latch onto, a.** to obtain. **b.** to attach oneself to.

latch·key (lach′kē′), *n., pl.* **-keys.** a key for releasing a latch or springlock, esp. on an outer door.

latch′key child′, *n.* a child who must spend part of the day alone and unsupervised, as when the parents are away at work.

late (lāt), *adj.,* **lat·er** or **lat·ter, lat·est** or **last,** *adv.,* **lat·er, lat·est.** —*adj.* **1.** occurring after the usual or proper time: *a late spring.* **2.** continued until after the usual time or hour; protracted: *a late business meeting.* **3.** near or at the end of the day or well into the night: *a late hour.* **4.** most recent: *a late news bulletin.* **5.** immediately preceding the present one; former: *the late attorney general.* **6.** recently deceased: *the late Mr. Phipps.* **7.** occurring at an advanced stage in life: *a late marriage.* **8.** belonging to an advanced period or stage in the history or development of something: *the late phase of feudalism.* —*adv.* **9.** after the usual or proper time, or after delay: *to arrive late.* **10.** until after the usual time or hour; until an advanced hour, esp. of the night: *to work late.* **11.** at or to an advanced time. **12.** recently but no longer; lately. —*Idiom.* **13. of late,** lately; recently. —**late′ness,** *n.*

late·com·er (lāt′kum′ər), *n.* one that arrives late.

la·teen (la tēn′, lə-), *adj.* pertaining to or having a lateen sail or sails.

lateen′ sail′, *n.* a triangular sail set on a long sloping yard, used esp. on the Mediterranean Sea.

late·ly (lāt′lē), *adv.* of late; recently; not long since.

la·ten·cy (lāt′n sē), *n., pl.* **-cies. 1.** the state of being latent. **2.** LATENT PERIOD.

la′tency pe′riod, *n.* **1.** the stage of personality development, extending from about four or five years of age to the beginning of puberty, during which sexual urges appear to lie dormant. **2.** LATENT PERIOD (def. 1).

la·ten·si·fy (lā ten′sə fī′), *v.t.,* **-fied, -fy·ing.** to increase the developability of (the latent image on a film or plate) after exposure. —**la·ten′si·fi·ca′tion,** *n.*

la·tent (lāt′nt), *adj.* **1.** present but not visible, apparent, or actualized; existing as potential: *latent ability.* **2.** (of an infectious agent or disease) remaining in an inactive or hidden phase; dormant. —**la′tent·ly,** *adv.*

la′tent heat′, *n.* heat absorbed or radiated during a change of phase at constant temperature and pressure.

la′tent pe′riod, *n.* **1.** Also, **latency period.** the interval between exposure to a carcinogen, toxin, or disease-causing organism and development of a consequent disease. **2.** the interval between a stimulus and response. Also called **latency.**

lat·er (lā′tər), *adj., adv.* a compar. of LATE.

lat·er·al (lat′ər əl), *adj.* **1.** of or pertaining to the side; situated at, proceeding from, or directed to a side: *a lateral view.* **2.** pertaining to or entailing a new but generally equivalent position, office, etc., as distin-

L

guished from a promotion or demotion: *a lateral move.* **3.** (of a speech sound) articulated so that the breath passes on either or both sides of the tongue, as the sound (l). —*n.* **4.** a lateral part or extension, as a branch or shoot. **5.** a lateral speech sound. **6.** LATERAL PASS. —*v.i.* **7.** to throw a lateral pass. **8.** to move laterally or sideways: *migrating birds lateraling down into Cape May.* —*v.t.* **9.** to throw (the ball) in a lateral pass. —**lat•er•al•ly,** *adv.*

lat•er•al•i•ty (lat′ə ral′i tē), *n.* **1.** the use of one hand in preference to the other. Compare HANDEDNESS. **2.** the dominance or superior development of one side of the body or brain.

lat•er•al•i•za•tion (lat′ər ə lə zā′shən), *n.* functional specialization of the brain, with some skills, as language, occurring primarily in the left hemisphere and others, as the perception of visual and spatial relationships, occurring primarily in the right hemisphere.

lat′eral line′, *n.* a linear array of sensory structures along the sides of fish and amphibians.

lat′eral pass′, *n.* a pass in football thrown parallel to the line of scrimmage or backward from the position of the passer.

Lat•er•an (lat′ər ən), *n.* the church of St. John Lateran, the cathedral church of the city of Rome; the church of the pope as bishop of Rome.

lat•est (lā′tist), *adj., adv. a superl. of* **late** *with* **later** *as compar.* **1.** most recent; current: *latest fashions.* **2.** last. —*n.* **3. the latest,** the most recent news, development, disclosure, etc.: *the latest in personal computers.* —*Idiom.* **4. at the latest,** not any later than (a specified time): *by noon at the latest.*

la•tex (lā′teks), *n., pl.* **lat•i•ces** (lat′ə sēz′), **la•tex•es.** **1.** a milky liquid in certain plants, as milkweeds, euphorbias, poppies, or the plants yielding rubber, that coagulates on exposure to air. **2.** any emulsion in water of finely divided particles of synthetic rubber or plastic, used esp. in adhesives and paints.

lath (lath, lä th), *n., pl.* **laths** (lathz, laths, lä thz, lä ths). **1.** a thin, narrow strip of wood, used with other strips to form latticework, a backing for plaster or stucco, a support for slates and other roofing materials, etc. **2.** wire mesh or the like used in place of wooden laths as a backing for plasterwork. —**lath′like′,** *adj.*

lathe (lā th), *n., v.,* **lathed, lath•ing.** —*n.* **1.** a machine for use in working a piece of wood, metal, etc., by holding and rotating it about a horizontal axis against a tool that shapes it. —*v.t.* **2.** to cut, shape, or treat on a lathe.

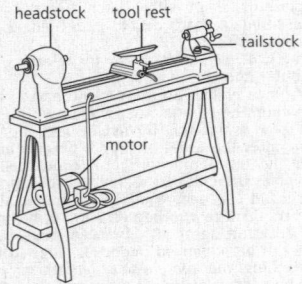

woodworking lathe (def. 1)

lath•er (lath′ər), *n.* **1.** foam or froth made by a detergent, esp. soap, stirred or rubbed in water. **2.** foam or froth formed in profuse sweating, as on a horse. **3.** *Informal.* a state of excitement, agitation, or the like. —*v.i.* **4.** to form a lather: *a soap that lathers well.* **5.** to become covered with lather, as a horse. —*v.t.* **6.** to apply lather to; cover with lather. **7.** *Informal.* to beat or whip. —**lath′er•er,** *n.*

lath•ing (lath′ə riz′əm, lä′thing), *n.* **1.** the act or process of applying lath. **2.** a quantity of lath in place.

lath•y•rism (lath′ə riz′əm), *n.* a painful disorder esp. of domestic animals caused by ingestion of a poison found in legumes of the genus *Lathyrus* and marked by spastic paralysis. —**lath′y•rit′ic** (-rit′ik), *adj.*

lat•i•go (lat′i gō′), *n., pl.* **-gos, -goes.** *n.* a leather strap on the saddletree of a Western saddle used to tighten and secure the cinch.

Lat•i•mer (lat′ə mər), *n.* **Hugh,** c1470–1555, English Protestant Reformation bishop, reformer, and martyr.

Lat•in (lat′n), *n.* **1.** the Italic language of ancient Rome, maintained through the Middle Ages and into modern times as the liturgical language of Western Christianity and an international language of learned discourse. *Abbr.:* L **2. a.** a member of any people speaking a language descended from Latin. **b.** a native or inhabitant of any country in Latin America; Latin American. **3.** a native or inhabitant of Latium. —*adj.* **4. a.** Latin-American. **b.** of or pertaining to any of the peoples of Europe or the New World speaking languages descended from Latin. **5.** of or pertaining to Latium or its inhabitants. **6.** of or pertaining to the Latin alphabet.

Lat′in al′phabet, *n.* the alphabetical script derived from the Greek alphabet through Etruscan, used for the writing of Latin and adopted,

with modifications and additions, by the languages of W Europe, including English. Also called **Roman alphabet.**

Lat′in Amer′ica, *n.* the part of the American continents south of the United States in which Spanish, Portuguese, or French is officially spoken. —**Lat′in-Amer′ican,** *adj.* —**Lat′in A•mer′i•can,** *n.*

Lat′in cross′, *n.* an upright or vertical bar crossed near the top by a shorter horizontal bar.

lat•ish (lā′tish), *adj.* somewhat or rather late.

la•tis•si•mus dor•si (lə tis′ə məs dôr′sī), *n., pl.* **la•tis•si•mi dorsi** (lə tis′ə mī′). a broad, flat muscle on each side of the middle of the back, the action of which draws the arm backward and downward.

lat•i•tude (lat′i tōōd′, -tyōōd′), *n.* **1. a.** the angular distance, measured north or south from the equator, of a point on the earth's surface, expressed in degrees. **b.** a place or region as marked by this distance: *tropical latitudes.* **2.** freedom from narrow restrictions; freedom of action, opinion, etc.: *They allow their children latitude in choosing friends.* **3.** the angular distance from the ecliptic of a point on the celestial sphere. **4.** the ability of a photographic emulsion to record the brightness values of a subject in their true proportion to one another.

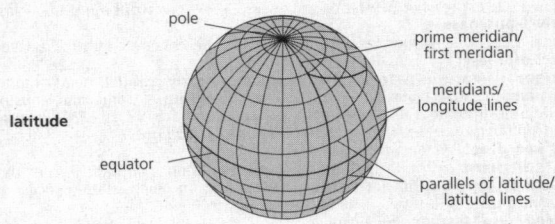

latitude

lat•i•tu•di•nal (lat′i tōōd′n l, -tyōōd′-), *adj.* of or pertaining to latitude. —**lat′i•tu′di•nal•ly,** *adv.*

La•ti•um (lā′shē əm), *n.* a country in ancient Italy, SE of Rome.

lat•ke (lät′kə), *n., pl.* **-kes.** a pancake made of grated potato.

la•trine (lə trēn′), *n.* a toilet or something used as a toilet, esp. in a military installation.

lat•ter (lat′ər), *adj.* **1.** being the second mentioned of two (disting. from *former*): *Of the two versions of the story, I prefer the latter.* **2.** more advanced in time; later: *in these latter days of human progress.* **3.** near or comparatively near to the end: *the latter part of the century.*

lat′ter-day′, *adj.* **1.** of a later or following period: *latter-day pioneers.* **2.** of the present period or time; modern.

Lat′ter-day Saint′, *n.* a Mormon.

lat•tice (lat′is), *n., v.,* **-ticed, -tic•ing.** —*n.* **1.** a structure of crossed wooden or metal strips usu. arranged to form a diagonal pattern of open spaces between the strips. **2.** a window, gate, or the like consisting of such a structure. **3.** an arrangement in space of isolated points in a regular pattern, showing the positions of atoms, molecules, or ions in the structure of a crystal. **4.** a partially ordered set in which every subset containing exactly two elements has a greatest lower bound or intersection and a least upper bound or union. —*v.t.* **5.** to furnish with a lattice or latticework. **6.** to form into a lattice. —**lat′tice•like′,** *adj.*

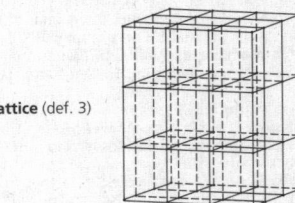

lattice (def. 3)

lat•tice•work (lat′is wûrk′), *n.* **1.** work consisting of crossed strips usu. arranged in a diagonal pattern of open spaces. **2.** a lattice.

Lat•vi•a (lat′vē ə, lät′-), *n.* a republic in N Europe, on the Baltic, S of Estonia; an independent state 1918–40; annexed by the Soviet Union 1940; regained independence 1991. 2,437,649; 25,395 sq. mi. (65,773 sq. km). *Cap.:* Riga. —**Lat′vi•an,** *adj., n.*

laud (lôd), *v.t.* **1.** to praise; extol. —*n.* **2.** a song or hymn of praise. —**laud′er, lau′da•tor** (-dā′tər), *n.*

laud•a•ble (lô′də bəl), *adj.* deserving praise; praiseworthy; commendable: *a laudable idea.* —**laud′a•bly,** *adv.*

laud•a•to•ry (lô′də tôr′ē, -tōr′ē) also **laud′a•tive,** *adj.* containing or expressing praise. —**laud′a•to′ri•ly,** *adv.*

laugh (laf, läf), *v.i.* **1.** to express mirth, pleasure, derision, or nervousness with an audible, vocal expulsion of air from the lungs that can range from a loud burst of sound to a series of quiet chuckles and is usu. accompanied by characteristic facial and bodily movements. **2.** to feel the emotion so expressed: *She laughed inwardly at the scene.* **3.** to make a sound resembling laughter: *A coyote laughed in the dark.* —*v.t.* **4.** to drive, put, bring, etc., by or with laughter (often fol. by *out, down,* etc.): *They laughed him out of town.* **5.** to utter with laughter: *He laughed his consent.* **6. laugh at,** **a.** to ridicule; deride. **b.** to find amusing. **7. laugh off,** to dismiss as trivial. —*n.* **8.** the act or sound of laughing; laughter. **9.** an expression of mirth, derision, etc., by laughing. **10.** a person or thing that provokes laughter, amusement, or ridicule: *That physics exam was a laugh.* **11. laughs,** *Informal.* fun; amusement. —*Idiom.* **12.** **have the last laugh,** to prove successful despite the doubts of others. **13. laugh out of the other side of one's mouth** or **face,** to become regretful or chastened after initial joy or boastfulness. **14. laugh up** or **in one's sleeve,** to be secretly derisive or amused.

laugh•a•ble (laf′ə bəl, lä′fə-), *adj.* such as to cause laughter; funny; amusing. —**laugh′a•ble•ness,** *n.* —**laugh′a•bly,** *adv.*

laugh•ing (laf′ing, lä′fing), *adj.* **1.** uttering sounds like laughter, as some birds. **2.** laughable: *That mistake is no laughing matter.* —*n.* **3.** LAUGHTER. —**laugh′ing•ly,** *adv.*

laugh′ing gas′, *n.* NITROUS OXIDE.

laugh′ing gull′, *n.* a small, black-headed gull of New World coastlines, *Larus atricilla,* having a laughlike cry.

laugh′ing hye′na, *n.* SPOTTED HYENA.

laugh′ing jack′ass, *n.* KOOKABURRA.

laugh•ing•stock (laf′ing stok′, lä′fing-), *n.* an object of ridicule; the butt of a joke or the like.

laugh′ line′, *n.* CROW'S-FOOT (def. 1).

laugh•ter (laf′tər, läf′-), *n.* **1.** the action or sound of laughing. **2.** an experiencing of the emotion expressed by laughing. **3.** an expression or appearance of merriment or amusement. —*Saying.* **4. Laughter is the best medicine,** laughter can provide a respite from one's troubles.

Laugh•ton (lôt′n), *n.* **Charles,** 1899–1962, U.S. actor, born in England.

laugh′ track′, *n.* prerecorded laughter added to a recorded radio or television program to feign or enhance audience response.

launch[1] (lônch, länch), *v.t.* **1.** to set (a boat or ship) in the water. **2.** to float (a newly constructed ship) usu. by allowing it to slide down an incline into the water. **3.** to send forth or release: *to launch a spacecraft; The submarine launched its torpedoes.* **4.** to start (a person) on a course, career, etc. **5.** to start; initiate: *to launch a scheme; to launch a new product.* **6.** to throw; hurl. —*v.i.* **7.** to burst out or plunge boldly or directly into action, speech, etc. **8.** to start out or forth; push out or put forth on the water. —*n.* **9.** the act of launching. —**launch′a•ble,** *adj.*

launch[2] (lônch, länch), *n.* **1.** a heavy open or half-decked boat propelled by oars or by an engine. **2.** a large utility boat carried by a warship.

launch•er (lôn′chər, län′-), *n.* **1.** a person or thing that launches. **2.** a structural device designed to support and hold a rocket, missile, etc., in position for firing.

launch′ (or **launch′ing**) **pad′** or **launch′pad′,** *n.* **1.** the platform on which a rocket, missile, etc., is launched. **2.** something that serves to launch or initiate.

launch′ ve′hicle, *n.* a rocket used to launch a spacecraft or satellite into orbit or a probe into space.

launch′ win′dow, *n.* the time period when a spacecraft must be launched if it is to achieve its mission.

laun•der (lôn′dər, län′-), *v.t.* **1.** to wash (clothes, linens, etc.). **2.** to wash and iron (clothes). **3.** *Informal.* **a.** to disguise the source of (illegal or secret funds or profits), usu. by transmittal through a foreign bank or a complex network of intermediaries. **b.** to disguise the true nature of (a transaction, operation, or the like) by routing money or goods through one or more intermediaries. **4.** to remove embarrassing or unpleasant elements from in order to make more acceptable: *to launder one's image before running for office.* —*v.i.* **5.** to wash laundry. **6.** to undergo washing and ironing: *The shirt didn't launder well.* —**laun′der•a•ble,** *adj.* —**laun′der•er,** *n.*

laun•der•ette (lôn′də ret′, län′-) also **laun•drette** (-dret′), *n.* a self-service laundry having coin-operated washers, driers, etc.

laun•dress (lôn′dris, län′-), *n.* a woman whose work is the washing and ironing of clothes, linens, etc.

Laun•dro•mat (lôn′drə mat′, län′-), *Trademark.* a type of launderette.

laun•dry (lôn′drē, län′-), *n., pl.* **-dries.** **1.** articles of clothing, linens, etc., that have been or are to be washed. **2.** a business establishment where clothes, linens, etc., are laundered. **3.** a room or area, as in a home or apartment building, reserved for doing the family wash.

laun′dry list′, *n.* a lengthy, esp. random list of items: *a laundry list of new products; a laundry list of requests.*

Laur•a•sia (lô rā′zhə, -shə), *n.* a hypothetical landmass in the Northern Hemisphere that separated near the end of the Paleozoic Era to form North America and Eurasia.

lau•re•ate (lôr′ē it, lor′-), *n.* **1.** a person who has been honored for achieving distinction in a particular field or with a particular award: *a Nobel laureate.* **2.** POET LAUREATE. —*adj.* **3.** deserving or having special recognition for achievement (often used immediately after the noun that is modified): *novelist laureate; conjurer laureate.* **4.** crowned or decked with laurel as a mark of honor. —**lau′re•ate•ship,** *n.*

lau•rel (lôr′əl, lor′-), *n.* **1.** Also called **bay, sweet bay.** a small European evergreen tree, *Laurus nobilis,* of the laurel family, having dark, glossy green leaves. **2.** any tree of the genus *Laurus.* **3.** any of various similar trees or shrubs, as the mountain laurel or the California laurel. **4.** the foliage of the laurel as an emblem of victory or distinction. **5.**

Usu., **laurels.** honor won, as for achievement in a field or activity. —*Idiom.* **6. look to one's laurels,** to be on guard against rivals. **7. rest on one's laurels,** to cease to strive for further successes or accolades.

Lau•ren•tian (lô ren′shən), *adj.* **1.** of or pertaining to the St. Lawrence River. **2.** pertaining to the granite intrusions and orogeny in Canada around the Great Lakes during Archeozoic time.

Lauren′tian Moun′tains, *n.pl.* a range of low mountains in E Canada, between the St. Lawrence River and Hudson Bay. Also called **Lau•ren′tians.**

lau′ric ac′id (lôr′ik, lor′-), *n.* a white, crystalline, fatty acid, $C_{12}H_{24}O_2$, occurring in many vegetable fats, esp. coconut oil.

Lau•sanne (lō zan′), *n.* the capital of Vaud, in W Switzerland, on the Lake of Geneva. 123,700.

la•va (lä′və, lav′ə), *n.* **1.** the molten, fluid rock that issues from a volcano or volcanic vent. **2.** the rock formed when this solidifies, occurring in many structurally different varieties. [< Italian: avalanche < Latin *lābēs* a sliding down]

la•va•bo (lə vā′bō, -vä′-), *n., pl.* **-boes.** **1. a.** the ritual washing of the celebrant's hands after the offertory in the mass. **b.** the passage recited at this time. **c.** the small towel or basin used. **2.** a stone basin or trough used for washing, as in a medieval monastery. **3.** a washbowl with a spigot-equipped water tank above, both mounted on a wall: now often used for decoration or as a planter.

la•vage (lə väzh′, lav′ij), *n.* **1.** a washing. **2.** the cleansing of a bodily organ, as the stomach, by irrigation.

lav•a•liere or **lav•a•lier** or **la•val•lière** (lav′ə lēr′, lä′və-), *n.* an ornamental pendant, usu. jeweled, worn on a chain around the neck.

lavaliere′ mi′crophone, *n.* a small microphone that hangs around the neck of a performer or speaker.

lav•a•to•ry (lav′ə tôr′ē, -tōr′ē), *n., pl.* **-ries.** **1.** a room fitted with equipment for washing the hands and face and usu. with flush toilet facilities. **2.** a flush toilet; water closet. **3.** a bowl or basin with running water for washing or bathing purposes; washbowl.

lave (lāv), *v.t.,* **laved, lav•ing.** **1.** to wash; bathe. **2.** (of a river, sea, etc.) to flow along, against, or past; wash.

lav•en•der (lav′ən dər), *n.* **1.** a pale bluish purple. **2.** any Old World plant of the genus *Lavandula,* of the mint family, esp. *L. officinalis,* having spikes of fragrant, pale purple flowers that yield an essential oil used in perfumery. **3.** the dried flowers or other parts of this plant placed among linen, clothes, etc., for scent or as a preservative. **4.** Also called **lav′ender wa′ter.** toilet water, shaving lotion, etc., made with a solution of oil of lavender.

lav•ish (lav′ish), *adj.* **1.** expended, bestowed, or occurring in abundance: *a lavish serving of food.* **2.** using or giving in great amounts; prodigal: *to be lavish with one's time or money; to be lavish of affection.* —*v.t.* **3.** to expend or give in great amounts or without limit: *to lavish gifts on a person.* —**lav′ish•er,** *n.* —**lav′ish•ly,** *adv.* —**lav′ish•ness,** *n.*

La•voi•sier (läv′wäz yā′, ləv wäz′-), *n.* **Antoine Laurent,** 1743–94, French chemist.

law (lô), *n.* **1.** the principles and regulations established by a government or other authority and applicable to a people, whether by legislation or by custom enforced by judicial decision. **2.** any written or positive rule or collection of rules prescribed under the authority of the state or nation, as by the people in its constitution. **3.** a system or collection of such rules. **4.** the condition of society brought about by observance of such rules: *maintaining law and order.* **5.** the field of knowledge concerned with these rules; jurisprudence: *to study law.* **6.** the body of such rules concerned with a particular subject: *commercial law; tax law.* **7.** an act of the highest legislative body of a state or nation. **8.** the profession that deals with law and legal procedure: *to practice law.* **9.** legal action; litigation: *to go to law.* **10.** an agent that enforces the law, esp. the police: *The law arrived to quell the riot.* **11.** any rule or injunction that must be obeyed. **12.** a rule of proper conduct sanctioned by conscience, concepts of natural justice, or the will of a deity: *a moral law.* **13.** a rule or manner of behavior that is instinctive or spontaneous: *the law of self-preservation.* **14.** (in philosophy, science, etc.) **a.** a statement of a relation or sequence of phenomena invariable under the same conditions. **b.** a mathematical rule. **15.** a principle based on the predictable consequences of an act, condition, etc.: *the law of supply and demand.* **16.** a rule, principle, or convention regarded as governing the structure or the relationship of an element in the structure of something, as of a language or work of art: *the laws of playwriting; the laws of grammar.* **17.** a commandment or a revelation from God. **18.** (*sometimes cap.*) a divinely appointed order or system. **19. the Law,** LAW OF MOSES. **20.** the part of the Bible, esp. of the New Testament, that expresses precepts, in contradistinction to its promises: *the law of Christ.* —*v.i.* **21.** to institute legal action; bring suit; sue. —*v.t.* **22.** *Chiefly Dial.* to sue or prosecute. —*Idiom.* **23. be a law to** or **unto oneself,** to act independently or unconventionally, esp. without regard for established mores. **24. lay down the law, a.** to issue orders imperiously. **b.**

Law (lô), *n.* **William,** 1686–1761, English clergyman and devotional writer.

law′-abid′ing, *adj.* abiding by or keeping the law; obedient to law: *law-abiding citizens.* —**law′-abid′ingness,** *n.*

law′ and or′der, *n.* strict control of crime and repression of violence, sometimes involving the possible restriction of civil rights.

L

law•break•er (lô′brā′kər), *n.* a person who breaks or violates the law. —**law′break′ing,** *n., adj.*

law•ful (lô′fəl), *adj.* **1.** allowed by law: *a lawful enterprise.* **2.** sanctioned by law; legitimate: *a lawful heir.* **3.** appointed or recognized by law; legally qualified: *a lawful king.* **4.** acting or living according to the law; law-abiding. —**law′ful•ly,** *adv.* —**law′ful•ness,** *n.*

law•giv•er (lô′giv′ər), *n.* a person who promulgates a law or a code of laws. —**law′giv′ing,** *n., adj.*

law•less (lô′lis), *adj.* **1.** contrary to or without regard for the law: *lawless violence.* **2.** uncontrolled by law; unruly; disorderly: *a lawless crew.* **3.** uncontrollable; unbridled: *lawless passion.* **4.** illegal: *lawless activities.* —**law′less•ly,** *adv.* —**law′less•ness,** *n.*

law•mak•er (lô′mā′kər), *n.* a person who makes or enacts law; legislator. —**law′mak′ing,** *n., adj.*

law•man (lô′man′, -mən), *n., pl.* **-men** (-men′, -mən). an officer of the law, as a sheriff or police officer.

lawn[1] (lôn), *n.* a stretch of open, grass-covered land, esp. one closely mowed, as near a house, on an estate, or in a park. —**lawn′y,** *adj.*

lawn[2] (lôn), *n.* a sheer, plain-weave linen or cotton fabric, bleached, dyed, or printed. —**lawn′y,** *adj.*

lawn′ bowl′ing, *n.* a game played with wooden balls on a level, closely mowed green having a slight bias, the object being to roll one's ball as near as possible to a smaller white ball at the other end of the green. Also called **bowls.** —**lawn′ bowl′er,** *n.*

lawn′ mow′er, *n.* a hand-operated or motor-driven machine for cutting the grass of a lawn.

lawn′ ten′nis, *n.* tennis, esp. when played on a grass court.

law′ of av′erages, *n.* **1.** a statistical principle formulated by Jakob Bernoulli to show a more or less predictable ratio between the number of random trials of an event and the outcomes that result. **2.** the principle that, in the long run, probability as naively conceived will operate and influence any one occurrence.

Law′ of Mo′ses, *n.* **1.** the ancient law of the Hebrews, ascribed to Moses and contained in the Pentateuch. **2.** the Pentateuch, forming the first of the three Jewish divisions of the Old Testament.

Law•rence (lôr′əns, lor′-), *n.* **1. D(avid) H(erbert),** 1885–1930, English novelist. **2. Ernest O(rlando),** 1901–58, U.S. physicist. **3. Gertrude,** 1901?–52, English actress. **4. Saint,** died A.D. 258?, early church martyr. **5. T(homas) E(dward)** (*T. E. Shaw*) (*"Lawrence of Arabia"*), 1888–1935, English soldier and writer.

law•ren•ci•um (lô ren′sē əm), *n.* a synthetic, radioactive, metallic element, the last of the actinide series. *Symbol:* Lr; *at. no.:* 103.

law•suit (lô′so͞ot′), *n.* a case in a court of law involving a claim, complaint, etc., by one party against another; suit at law.

law•yer (lô′yər, loi′ər), *n.* a person whose profession is to represent clients in a court of law or to advise or act for them in other legal matters. —**law′yer•like′, law′yer•ly,** *adj.*

law•yer•ing (lô′yər ing, loi′ər-), *n.* the practice of law; the duties, functions, or skills of a lawyer.

lax (laks), *adj.* **1.** not strict or severe; careless or negligent: *lax morals.* **2.** loose or slack; not tense, rigid, or firm: *a lax rope.* **3.** not rigidly exact or precise; vague: *lax ideas.* **4.** loose, open, or not retentive, as the bowels. **5.** having the bowels loose or open. **6.** open or not compact; having a loosely cohering structure; porous: *lax texture.* **7.** (of a vowel) articulated with relatively relaxed tongue muscles. Compare TENSE[1] (def. 4). —**lax′ly,** *adv.* —**lax′ness,** *n.*

lax•a•tive (lak′sə tiv), *n.* **1.** a medicine or agent for relieving constipation. —*adj.* **2.** of, pertaining to, or constituting a laxative; purgative.

lax•i•ty (lak′si tē), *n.* the state or quality of being lax; looseness.

lay[1] (lā), *v.,* **laid, lay•ing,** *n.* —*v.t.* **1.** to put or place in a horizontal position or position of rest; set down: *to lay a book on a desk.* **2.** to knock or beat down, as from an erect position; strike or throw to the ground: *One punch laid him low.* **3.** to put or place in a particular position: *The dog laid its ears back.* **4.** to cause to be in a particular state or condition: *Their motives were laid bare; We laid their doubts at rest.* **5.** to set, place, or apply (often fol. by *to* or *on*): *to lay a hand on someone.* **6.** to dispose or place in proper position or in an orderly fashion: *to lay bricks.* **7.** to place on, along, or under a surface: *to lay a pipeline.* **8.** to establish as a basis; set up: *to lay the foundations for further negotiations.* **9.** to present or submit for notice or consideration: *I laid my case before the commission.* **10.** to present, bring forward, or make, as a claim or charge. **11.** to impute, attribute, or ascribe: *to lay blame on the inspector.* **12.** to bury: *They laid him in the old churchyard.* **13.** to bring forth and deposit (an egg or eggs). **14.** to impose as a burden, duty, penalty, or the like: *to lay an embargo on oil shipments.* **15.** to place dinner service on (a table); set. **16.** to place on or over a surface, as paint; cover or spread with something else. **17.** to devise or arrange, as a plan. **18.** to deposit as a wager; stake: *He laid $10 on the horse.* **19.** to bet (someone): *I'll lay you ten to one that we win.* **20.** to set (a trap). **21.** to place, set, or locate: *The scene is laid in France.* **22.** to smooth down or make even: *to lay the nap of cloth.* **23.** to quiet or make vanish: *to lay a ghost.* **24.** to cause to subside: *A light rain layed the dust.* **25.** to bring (a stick, lash, etc.) down, as on a person, in inflicting punishment. **26.** to form by twisting strands together, as a rope. **27.** to move or turn (a sailing vessel) into a certain position or direction. **28.** to put (dogs) on a scent. —*v.i.* **29.** to lay eggs. **30.** to wager or bet. **31.** to apply oneself vigorously. **32.** to deal or aim blows vigorously (usu. fol. by *on, at, about,* etc.). **33.** *Nonstandard.* LIE[2]. **34.** *South Midland U.S.* to plan or scheme (often fol. by *out*). **35.** *Naut.* to take up a specified position, direction, etc.: *to lay close to the wind.* **36. lay aboard,** (formerly, of a fighting ship) to come alongside (another fighting ship) in order to board. **37. lay aside, a.** to abandon; reject. **b.** to save for use at a later time; store. **38. lay away, a.** to reserve for later use; save. **b.** to hold merchandise pending final payment or request for delivery: *to lay away a winter coat.* **c.** to bury (someone). **39. lay by,** to put away for future use; store; save: *She had managed to lay by money for college.* **40. lay down, a.** to give up; hand over; yield. **b.** to assert firmly; state authoritatively. **c.** to stock; store: *to lay down wine.* **41. lay for,** to wait for in hiding in order to ambush. **42. lay in,** to store away for future use. **43. lay into,** to attack physically or verbally. **44. lay off, a.** to dismiss (an employee), esp. temporarily because of slack business. **b.** *Informal.* to cease or quit. **c.** *Slang.* to stop annoying or teasing. **d.** *Informal.* to stop work. **e.** to mark off; measure; plot. **f.** to transfer (blame or responsibility) to another. **45. lay on, a.** to cover with; apply: *to lay on a coat of wax.* **b.** to strike blows; attack violently. **46. lay open, a.** to cut open. **b.** to expose; reveal. **c.** to expose or make vulnerable, as to blame, suspicion, or criticism. **47. lay out, a.** to extend at length. **b.** to spread out in order; arrange; prepare. **c.** to plan; plot; design. **d.** to ready (a corpse) for burial. **e.** *Informal.* to spend or contribute (money). **f.** *Slang.* to knock (someone) down or unconscious. **g.** *Slang.* to scold vehemently; reprimand. **h.** to make a layout of. **48. lay over, a.** to postpone. **b.** to make a stopover. **49. lay to, a.** to check the motion of (a ship). **b.** to put (a ship) in a dock or other place of safety. **c.** to attack vigorously. **d.** to put forth effort; apply oneself. **50. lay up, a.** to put away for future use; store up. **b.** to cause to be confined to bed or kept indoors; disable. **c.** to construct (a masonry structure). **d.** to apply (alternate layers of a material and a binder) to form a bonded material. —*n.* **51.** the way or position in which a thing is laid or lies: *the lay of the south pasture.* **52.** the quality of a fiber rope characterized by the degree of twist, the angles formed by the strands, and the fibers in the strands. **53.** a share of the profits or the catch of a whaling or fishing voyage, distributed to officers and crew. —***Idiom.*** **54. lay about one,** to strike or aim blows in every direction. **55. lay it on (thick),** to flatter someone or boast extravagantly; exaggerate. —**Usage.** LAY and LIE are often confused. LAY is most commonly a transitive verb and takes an object. Its forms are regular. If "place" or "put" can be substituted in a sentence, a form of LAY is called for: *Lay the folders on the desk. She laid the baby in the crib.* LAY also has several intransitive senses, among them "to lay eggs," and it forms many phrasal verbs, such as LAY OFF and LAY OVER.

LIE, with the overall senses "to be in a horizontal position, recline" and "to rest, remain, be situated, etc.," is intransitive and takes no object. Its forms are irregular; its past tense form is identical with the present tense or infinitive form of LAY: *Lie down, children. Abandoned cars were lying along the road. The dog lay in the shade and watched the kittens play. The folders have lain on the desk since yesterday.* Although forms of LIE and LAY occur interchangeably in all but the most careful, formal speech, the following constructions are generally considered nonstandard and appear rarely in edited written English: *Lay down, children. The dog laid in the shade. Abandoned cars were laying along the road. The folders have laid on the desk since yesterday.*

lay[2] (lā), *v.* pt. of LIE[2].

lay[3] (lā), *adj.* **1.** belonging to, involving, or performed by the laity, as distinguished from the clergy: *a lay sermon.* **2.** not belonging to, connected with, or proceeding from a profession, esp. the law or medicine: *a lay opinion on a legal case.*

lay[4] (lā), *n.* **1.** a short narrative or other poem. **2.** a song.

lay•a•bout (lā′ə bout′), *n.* a lazy or idle person; loafer.

Lay•a•mon (lā′ə mən, lä′yə-), *n.* fl. c1200, English poet and chronicler.

lay′a•way plan′ (lā′ə wā′), *n.* a method of purchasing by which an item is reserved by the store until the customer has completed payments, usu. made monthly. Also called **will-call.**

lay′ broth′er, *n.* a man who has taken religious vows and habit but is employed by his order chiefly in manual labor.

lay•er (lā′ər), *n.* **1.** a thickness of some material laid on or spread over a surface: *a layer of soot on the window sill; two layers of paint.* **2.** bed; stratum: *alternating layers of basalt and sandstone.* **3.** a person or thing that lays: *a carpet layer.* **4.** a hen kept for egg production. **5.** one of several items of clothing worn one on top of the other. **6.** a shoot or twig that is induced to root while still attached to the living stock, as by bending and covering with soil. **7.** a person or thing that lays. —*v.t.* **8.** to make a layer of. **9.** to form or arrange in layers. **10.** to arrange or wear (clothing) in layers: *to layer a vest over a blouse.* **11.** to propagate by layering. —*v.i.* **12.** to separate into or form layers. **13.** (of a garment) to permit of wearing in layers; be used in layering.

lay′er cake′, *n.* a cake made in layers, with a cream, jelly, or other filling between them.

lay•er•ing (lā′ər ing), *n.* **1.** the wearing of lightweight or unconstructed garments one upon the other, as for style or warmth. **2.** a method of propagating plants by causing their shoots to take root while still attached to the parent plant.

lay•ette (lā et′), *n.* an outfit of clothing, etc., for a newborn baby.

lay′ing on′ of hands′, *n.* **1.** a rite in which a cleric's hands touch the person to be ordained, healed, etc. **2.** the placing of the hands, as of a faith healer, upon a person to be cured.

lay•man (lā′mən), *n., pl.* **-men. 1.** a person who is not a member of the clergy; one of the laity. **2.** a person who is not a member of a given profession, as law or medicine.

lay•off (lā′ôf′, -of′), *n.* **1.** the act of dismissing employees, esp. temporarily. **2.** a period of enforced unemployment or inactivity.

lay′ of the land′, *n.* the general state or condition of affairs under consideration; the facts of a situation.

lay•out (lā′out′), *n.* **1.** an arrangement or plan: *We objected to the layout of the house.* **2.** the act of laying or spreading out. **3.** a plan or sketch showing the arrangement of copy and artwork in an advertisement, newspaper or magazine page, etc. **4.** (in advertising, publishing, etc.) the technique, process, or occupation of making layouts. **5.** SPREAD (def. 24). **6.** *Informal.* a place, as of residence or business, and the features that go with it; a setup: *a fancy layout with a swimming pool and a tennis court.* **7.** *Informal.* a display or spread, as of dishes at a meal. **8.** a collection or set of tools, implements, or the like. **9.** an arrangement of cards dealt according to a given pattern, as in solitaire.

lay•o•ver (lā′ō′vər), *n.* STOPOVER.

lay•per•son (lā′pûr′sən), *n.* **1.** a person who is not a member of the clergy; one of the laity. **2.** a person who is not a member of a given profession, as law or medicine.

lay′ read′er, *n.* a layperson authorized by an Anglican bishop to conduct parts of a service.

lay′-up′ or **lay′up′,** *n.* a basketball shot made close to the basket and often angled off the backboard.

lay•wom•an (lā′wo͝om′ən), *n., pl.* **-wom•en. 1.** a woman who is not a member of the clergy. **2.** a woman who is not a member of a given profession, as law or medicine.

Laz•a•rus (laz′ər əs), *n.* **1.** the diseased beggar in the parable of the rich man and the beggar. Luke 16:19–31. **2.** a brother of Mary and Martha whom Jesus raised from the dead. John 11:1–44; 12:1–18. **3. Emma,** 1849–87, U.S. poet.

laze (lāz), *v.,* **lazed, laz•ing.** —*v.i.* **1.** to idle or lounge lazily (often fol. by *around*). —*v.t.* **2.** to pass (time, life, etc.) lazily (usu. fol. by *away*).

laz•u•lite (laz′ə līt′, lazh′ə-), *n.* an azure-blue mineral, hydrous magnesium iron aluminum phosphate, $(FeMg)Al_2P_2O_8(OH)_2$.

laz•u•rite (laz′ə rīt′, lazh′ə-), *n.* a deep blue mineral, sodium calcium silicate with sulfate, formerly ground into a pigment.

la•zy (lā′zē), *adj.,* **-zi•er, -zi•est,** *v.,* **-zied, -zy•ing.** —*adj.* **1.** averse or disinclined to work, activity, or exertion; indolent. **2.** causing idleness or indolence: *a hot, lazy afternoon.* **3.** slow-moving; sluggish: *a lazy stream.* **4.** (of a livestock brand) placed on its side instead of upright. —*v.i.* **5.** to laze. —**la′zi•ly,** *adv.* —**la′zi•ness,** *n.* —**la′zy•ish,** *adj.*

la•zy•bones (lā′zē bōnz′), *n.* (*usu. with a sing. v.*) *Informal.* a lazy person.

la′zy Su′san (or **su′san**) or **La′zy Su′san,** *n.* **1.** a revolving tray for foods, condiments, etc., placed usu. at the center of a dining table. **2.** any similar structure, as a shelf or tabletop, designed to revolve so that whatever it holds can be seen or reached easily.

la′zy tongs′, *n.* extensible tongs for grasping objects at a distance, consisting of a series of pairs of crossing pieces, each pair pivoted together in the middle and connected with the next pair at the extremities.

lb., *pl.* **lbs., lb.** pound. [< Latin *lībra*]

LBJ, Lyndon Baines Johnson.

L.C., Library of Congress.

l.c., **1.** left center. **2.** letter of credit. **3.** in the place cited. **4.** lowercase.

LCD, *pl.* **LCDs, LCD's.** liquid-crystal display: a display of information, as on digital watches, portable computers, and calculators, using a liquid-crystal film that changes its optical properties when a voltage is applied.

L.C.D. or **l.c.d.,** lowest common denominator.

L.C.F. or **l.c.f.,** lowest common factor.

l'cha•im (lə ᴋʜä′yim, lə ᴋʜä yēm′), *interj. Hebrew.* (used as a drinking toast.) [*ləḥayyīm* lit., to life]

L.C.M. or **l.c.m.,** least common multiple; lowest common multiple.

LD, long distance (telephone call).

L-do•pa (el′dō′pə), *n.* the levorotatory isomer of dopa, converted in the brain to dopamine: used in synthetic form chiefly for treating parkinsonism. Also called **levodopa**.

lea (lē, lā) also **ley,** *n.* a tract of open ground, esp. grassland; meadow.

leach (lēch), *v.t.* **1.** to dissolve out soluble constituents from (ashes, soil, etc.) by percolation. **2.** to cause (water or other liquid) to percolate through something. —*v.i.* **3.** (of ashes, soil, etc.) to undergo the action of percolating water. **4.** to percolate, as water. —*n.* **5.** a leaching. **6.** the material leached. **7.** a vessel for use in leaching. —**leach′a•ble,** *adj.* —**leach′a•bil′i•ty,** *n.* —**leach′er,** *n.*

lead[1] (lēd), *v.t.* **1.** to go before or with to show the way; conduct or escort; guide: *to lead a group on a hike.* **2.** to conduct by holding and guiding: *to lead a horse by a rope.* **3.** to influence or induce; cause: *What led her to change her mind?* **4.** to guide in direction, course, action, opinion, etc.; bring: *You can lead him around to your point of view.* **5.** to go through or pass (time, life, etc.): *to lead a full life.* **6.** to conduct or bring (water, wire, etc.) in a particular course. **7.** (of a road, passage, etc.) to serve to bring (a person) to a place: *The next street will lead you to the post office.* **8.** to take or bring: *The visitors were led into the senator's office.* **9.** to be in control or command of; direct: *He led the British forces during the war.* **10.** to go at the head of or in advance of (a procession, list, etc.); proceed first in: *The mayor will lead the parade.* **11.** to be superior to; have the advantage over: *The first baseman leads his teammates in runs batted in.* **12.** to have top position or first place in: *Iowa leads the nation in corn production.* **13.** to have the directing or principal part in: *Who is going to lead the discussion?* **14.** to act as leader of (an orchestra, band, etc.); conduct. **15.** to begin a hand in a card game with (a card or suit specified). —*v.i.* **16.** to act as a guide; show the way. **17.** to afford passage to a place: *That path leads directly to the house.* **18.** to go first; be in advance. **19.** to result in; (usu. fol. by *to*): *The incident led to her resignation.* **20.** to take the directing or principal part. **21.** to take the offensive. **22.** to make the first play in a card game. **23.** to be led, as a horse. **24.** (of a runner in baseball) to leave a base before the delivery of a pitch (often fol. by *away*). **25. lead off, a.** to begin; start. **b.** *Baseball.* to be the first player in the batting order or the first batter in an inning. **26. lead on,** to mislead. —*n.* **27.** the first or foremost place; position in advance of others: *to take the lead in the race.* **28.** the extent of such an advance position. **29.** a person or thing that leads. **30.** a leash. **31.** a suggestion or piece of information that helps to direct or guide; tip; clue. **32.** a guide or indication of a road, course, method, etc., to follow. **33.** precedence; example; leadership. **34. a.** the principal part in a play. **b.** the person who plays it. **35. a.** the act or right of playing first in a card game. **b.** the card, suit, etc., so played. **36.** the opening paragraph of a newspaper story, serving as a summary. **37.** an often flexible and insulated single conductor, as a wire, used in electrical connections. **38.** the act of taking the offensive. **39.** *Naut.* **a.** the direction of a rope, wire, or chain. **b.** Also called **leader.** any of various devices for guiding a running rope. **40.** an open channel through a field of ice. **41.** the act of aiming a weapon ahead of a moving target. **42.** the distance ahead of a moving target that a weapon must be aimed in order to hit it. **43.** the first of a series of boxing punches. —*adj.* **44.** most important; principal; leading; first: *a lead editorial.* **45.** (of a runner in baseball) nearest to scoring. —***Idiom.*** **46. lead someone on a (merry) chase** or **dance,** to entice someone into difficulty and confusion by behaving unpredictably. **47. lead up to, a.** to prepare the way for. **b.** to approach (something) gradually.

lead[2] (led), *n.* **1.** a heavy, comparatively soft, malleable, bluish-gray metal, sometimes found in its natural state but usu. combined as a sulfide, esp. in galena. *Symbol:* Pb; *at. wt.:* 207.19; *at. no.:* 82; *sp. gr.:* 11.34 at 20°C. **2.** something made of this metal or of one of its alloys. **3.** a plummet or mass of lead suspended by a line, as for taking soundings. **4.** bullets collectively; shot. **5.** black lead or graphite. **6.** a small stick of graphite, as used in pencils. **7.** Also, **leading.** a thin strip of type metal or brass less than type-high, used for increasing the space between lines of type. **8.** a grooved bar of lead in which sections of glass are set, as in stained-glass windows. **9. leads,** *Brit.* a flat lead roof. **10.** WHITE LEAD. —*v.t.* **11.** to cover, line, weight, treat, or impregnate with lead or one of its compounds. **12.** to insert leading between lines of type. **13.** to fix (window glass) in position with leads.

lead•ed (led′id), *adj.* (of gasoline) containing tetraethyllead.

lead•en (led′n), *adj.* **1.** heavy like lead; hard to lift or move: *leaden feet.* **2.** dull, spiritless, or gloomy: *leaden prose.* **3.** of a dull gray color: *leaden skies.* **4.** oppressive; heavy: *a leaden silence.* **5.** sluggish; listless: *a leaden pace.* **6.** of poor quality or little value. **7.** made or consisting of lead. —*v.t.* **8.** to make leaden or sluggish. —**lead′en•ly,** *adv.*

lead•er (lē′dər), *n.* **1.** a person or thing that leads. **2.** a guiding or directing head, as of an army, movement, or political group. **3. a.** CONDUCTOR (def. 3). **b.** the principal musical performer in a group. **4.** a featured article of trade, esp. one offered at a low price to attract customers. Compare LOSS LEADER. **5.** *Brit.* a newspaper editorial. **6.** blank film or tape at the beginning of a length of film or magnetic tape, used for threading a motion-picture camera, tape recorder, etc. Compare TRAILER (def. 6). **7.** a length of line or wire to which a fishing lure or hook is attached. **8.** DOWNSPOUT. **9.** a horse harnessed at the front of a team. **10. leaders,** a row of dots or a short line to lead a reader's eye across a page. **11.** LEAD[1] (def. 40b). —**lead′er•less,** *adj.*

lead•er•ship (lē′dər ship′), *n.* **1.** the position or function of a leader. **2.** ability to lead. **3.** an act or instance of leading; guidance; direction. **4.** the leaders of a group.

lead•foot (led′fo͝ot′), *n., pl.* **-foots, -feet.** *Informal.* a person who drives a motor vehicle too fast, esp. habitually.

lead′-free′ (led), *adj.* UNLEADED (def. 1).

lead′ glass′ (led), *n.* glass containing lead oxide.

lead′-in′ (lēd), *n.* **1.** something that leads in or introduces; introduction; opening. **2.** the connection between an antenna and a transmitter or receiving set. **3.** the portion of a television or radio broadcast that precedes a commercial. —*adj.* **4.** (of a conductor) carrying input to an electric or electronic device or circuit, esp. from an antenna.

lead•ing[1] (lē′ding), *adj.* **1.** principal; most important; foremost: *a leading medical authority.* **2.** coming in advance of others; first: *We rode in the leading car.* **3.** directing, guiding. —*n.* **4.** the act of a person or thing that leads. —**lead′ing•ly,** *adv.*

lead•ing[2] (led′ing), *n.* **1.** a covering or framing of lead: *the leading of a stained-glass window.* **2. a.** LEAD[2] (def. 7). **b.** the spacing between lines of type, esp. in computer-generated typeset output.

lead′ing edge′ (lē′ding), *n.* **1.** the edge of an airfoil or propeller blade facing the direction of motion. **2.** the forward edge of an air mass. **3.** forefront; vanguard. —**lead′ing-edge′,** *adj.*

lead·ing la′dy (lē′ding), *n.* an actress who plays the principal female role in a motion picture or play.

lead′ing man′ (lē′ding), *n.* an actor who plays the principal male role in a motion picture or play.

lead′ing ques′tion (lē′ding), *n.* a question so worded as to suggest the proper or desired answer.

Lead′, Kind′ly Light′, a Christian hymn (1833) with words by John Henry Newman.

lead′ line′ (led), *n.* a line by which a lead is lowered into the water to take soundings.

lead′-off′ (led), *adj.* leading off or beginning: *the lead-off item on the agenda.*

lead-off (lēd′ôf′, -of′), *n.* **1.** an act that starts something; start; beginning. —*adj.* **2.** of or denoting the first baseball player in the batting order or the first player to bat in an inning: *the leadoff hitter.*

lead′ pen′cil (led), *n.* a pencil made of graphite in a wooden or metal holder.

lead′ poi′soning (led), *n.* a toxic condition produced by ingestion, inhalation, or skin absorption of lead or lead compounds, resulting in various dose-related symptoms including anemia, nausea, muscle weakness, confusion, blindness, and coma.

lead′ time′ (led), *n.* the period of time between the initial phase of a process and the emergence of results, as between the planning and completed manufacture of a product.

lead′-up′ (led), *n.* something that provides an approach to or preparation for an event or situation.

leaf (lēf), *n., pl.* **leaves** (lēvz). **1.** one of the expanded, usu. green organs borne by the stem of a plant. **2.** any similar or corresponding lateral outgrowth of a stem. **3.** leaves collectively; foliage. **4.** a sheet of paper or other writing material, esp. as part of a document, one side of each sheet constituting a page. **5.** a thin sheet of metal: *silver leaf.* **6.** a lamina or layer. **7.** a sliding, hinged, or detachable flat part, as of a door or tabletop. —*v.i.* **8.** to put forth leaves. **9.** to turn pages, esp. quickly (usu. fol. by *through*): *to leaf through a book.* —*v.t.* **10.** to thumb or turn, as the pages of a book or magazine, in a casual or cursory inspection of the contents. —*Idiom.* **11. in leaf,** covered with foliage; having leaves. **12. take a leaf out of** or **from someone's book,** to use someone as an exemplar. **13. turn over a new leaf,** to begin anew; make a fresh start. —**leaf′less,** *adj.* —**leaf′like′,** *adj.*

leaf·age (lē′fij), *n.* FOLIAGE.

leaf·hop·per (lēf′hop′ər), *n.* any of numerous slender, sap-sucking homopterous insects, of the family Cicadellidae, that leap from leaf to leaf, sometimes spreading plant diseases.

leaf′ in′sect, *n.* any of several orthopterous insects of the family Phillidae, of S Asia and the Malay Archipelago, having a body that resembles a leaf in color and form. Also called **walking leaf.**

leaf·let (lēf′lit), *n., v.,* **-let·ed** or **-let·ted, -let·ing** or **-let·ting.** —*n.* **1.** a small flat or folded sheet of printed matter, as an advertisement or notice, usu. intended for free distribution. **2.** one of the separate blades or divisions of a compound leaf. **3.** a small leaflike part or structure. —*v.t.* **4.** to distribute leaflets or handbills to or among. —*v.i.* **5.** to distribute leaflets. —**leaf′let·eer′** (-li tēr′), **leaf′let·er,** *n.*

leaf′ min′er, *n.* any of various insect larvae, including small caterpillars, that tunnel into leaves and stems, leaving winding trails or broad blotches of pale tissue.

leaf′ spot′, *n.* any of various plant diseases characterized by the formation of spots on the leaves.

leaf·stalk (lēf′stôk′), *n.* PETIOLE (def. 1).

leaf·y (lē′fē), *adj.,* **leaf·i·er, leaf·i·est. 1.** having, abounding in, or covered with leaves or foliage: *the leafy woods.* **2.** having broad leaves or consisting mainly of leaves: *leafy vegetables.* **3.** leaflike; foliaceous. —**leaf′i·ness,** *n.*

league¹ (lēg), *n., v.,* **leagued, lea·guing.** —*n.* **1.** a covenant or compact made between persons, parties, states, etc., for the promotion or maintenance of common interests or for mutual assistance or service. **2.** the aggregation of persons, parties, states, etc., associated in such a covenant or compact; confederacy. **3.** an association of individuals having a common goal. **4.** a group of athletic teams organized to compete chiefly among themselves: *a bowling league.* **5.** group; class; category: *As a pianist he simply isn't in your league.* —*v.t., v.i.* **6.** to unite in a league; combine. —*Idiom.* **7. in league,** working together, esp. clandestinely; conspiring.

league² (lēg), *n.* a unit of distance, varying at different periods and in different countries, in English-speaking countries usu. estimated roughly at 3 miles (4.8 kilometers).

League′ of Na′tions, *n.* an international organization created in 1919 to promote world peace and cooperation: dissolved in 1946.

Le·ah (lē′ə), *n.* the first wife of Jacob. Gen. 29:23–26.

leak (lēk), *n.* **1.** an unintended hole, crack, or the like, through which liquid, gas, light, etc., enters or escapes: *a leak in the roof.* **2.** an act or instance of leaking. **3.** any means of unintended entrance or escape. **4.** the loss of electric current from a conductor, usu. resulting from poor insulation. **5.** a disclosure of secret, esp. official, information, as to the news media, by an unnamed source. —*v.i.* **6.** to let a liquid, gas, light, etc., enter or escape, as through an unintended hole or crack: *The boat leaks.* **7.** to pass in or out in this manner, as liquid, gas, or light: *gas leaking from a pipe.* **8.** to become known unintentionally (usu. fol. by *out*): *The news leaked out.* —*v.t.* **9.** to let (liquid, gas, light, etc.) enter or escape: *This camera leaks light.* **10.** to allow to become known, as information given out covertly. —**leak′er,** *n.*

leak·age (lē′kij), *n.* **1.** an act of leaking; leak. **2.** something that leaks in or out. **3.** the amount that leaks in or out.

leak·proof (lēk′proof′), *adj.* designed to prevent leaking: *a leakproof container.*

leak·y (lē′kē), *adj.,* **leak·i·er, leak·i·est.** allowing liquid, gas, etc., to enter or escape. —**leak′i·ness,** *n.*

lean¹ (lēn), *v.,* **leaned** or (*esp. Brit.*) **leant, lean·ing,** *n.* —*v.i.* **1.** to incline or bend from a vertical position: *to lean out the window.* **2.** to incline, as in a particular direction; slant: *The post leans to the left.* **3.** to incline in feeling, opinion, action, etc.: *to lean toward socialism.* **4.** to rest or lie for support: *to lean against a wall.* **5.** to depend or rely (usu. fol. by *on* or *upon*): *someone to lean on in an emergency.* —*v.t.* **6.** to incline or bend: *He leaned his head forward.* **7.** to cause to lean or rest; prop: *to lean a chair against a railing.* **8. lean on,** *Informal.* to pressure or threaten. —*n.* **9.** the act or state of leaning; inclination. —**lean′er,** *n.*

lean² (lēn), *adj.* **1.** (of persons or animals) without much flesh or fat; not plump or fat; thin: *lean cattle.* **2.** (of meat) containing little or no fat. **3.** lacking in richness, fullness, etc.; poor: *a lean diet; lean years.* **4.** spare; economical. **5.** (of a mixture in a fuel system) having a relatively low ratio of fuel to air (contrasted with *rich*). **6.** (of paint) having more pigment than oil. Compare FAT (def. 17). **7.** (of ore) having a low mineral content; low-grade. —*n.* **8.** the part of flesh that consists of muscle rather than fat. **9.** the lean part of anything. —**lean′ness,** *n.*

Le·an·der (lē an′dər), *n.* a legendary Greek youth, the lover of Hero, who swam the Hellespont every night to visit her until he was drowned in a storm.

lean·ing (lē′ning), *n.* inclination; tendency: *literary leanings.*

lean′-to′, *n., pl.* **-tos. 1.** a shed supported at one side by trees or posts and having an inclined roof. **2.** a roof of a single pitch with the higher end abutting a wall or larger building. **3.** a structure with such a roof.

leap (lēp), *v.,* **leaped** or **leapt** (lept, lēpt), **leap·ing,** *n.* —*v.i.* **1.** to spring through the air from one point to another; jump: *to leap over a ditch.* **2.** to move or act quickly or suddenly: *to leap aside; to leap at an opportunity.* **3.** to pass, come, rise, etc., as if with a jump: *an idea leaped to mind.* —*v.t.* **4.** to pass over by or as if by jumping: *to leap a fence.* **5.** to cause to leap: *to leap a horse.* —*n.* **6.** a spring, jump, or bound; light, springing movement. **7.** the distance covered in a leap. **8.**

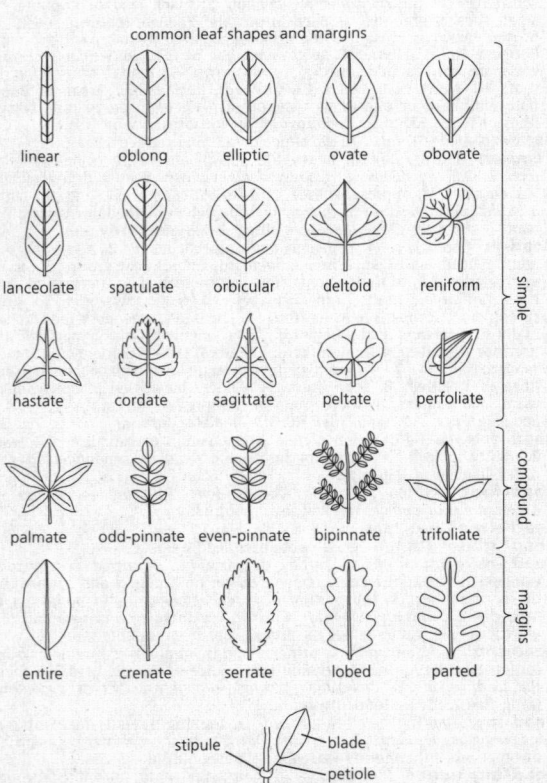

common leaf shapes and margins

linear   oblong   elliptic   ovate   obovate

lanceolate   spatulate   orbicular   deltoid   reniform

hastate   cordate   sagittate   peltate   perfoliate

simple

palmate   odd-pinnate   even-pinnate   bipinnate   trifoliate

compound

entire   crenate   serrate   lobed   parted

margins

stipule   blade   petiole

leaf parts

a place leaped or to be leaped over or from. **9.** an abrupt transition: *a successful leap to stardom.* **10.** a sudden and decisive increase: *a leap in profits.* **—*Idiom.*** **11. by leaps and bounds,** very rapidly. **12. leap in the dark,** an action that risks unpredictable consequences. —**leap′er,** *n.*

leap•frog (lēp′frog′, -frôg′), *n., v.,* **-frogged, -frog•ging.** —*n.* **1.** a game in which players take turns in leaping over another player bent over from the waist. —*v.t.* **2.** to jump over (a person or thing) in or as if in leapfrog. **3.** to cause to move as if in leapfrog: *manufacturers leapfrogging prices because of the cost of raw materials.* —*v.i.* **4.** to move or advance in or as if in leapfrog. —**leap′frog′ger,** *n.*

leap′ year′, *n.* **1.** (in the Gregorian calendar) a year that contains 366 days, with February 29 as an additional day: occurring in years whose last two digits are evenly divisible by four, except for centenary years not divisible by 400. **2.** a year containing an extra day in any calendar. Compare COMMON YEAR.

learn (lûrn), *v.,* **learned** (lûrnd) or **learnt, learn•ing.** —*v.t.* **1.** to acquire knowledge of or skill in by study, instruction, or experience: *to learn a new language.* **2.** to become informed of or acquainted with; ascertain: *to learn the truth.* **3.** to memorize: *He learned the poem in ten minutes.* **4.** to gain (a habit, mannerism, etc.) by experience, exposure to example, or the like; acquire: *She learned patience from her father.* **5.** (of a device or machine, esp. a computer) to perform an analogue of human learning using artificial intelligence. **6.** *Nonstandard.* to instruct in; teach. —*v.i.* **7.** to acquire knowledge or skill: *to learn rapidly.* **8.** to become informed (often fol. by *of* or *about*): *to learn of an accident.* **—*Proverb.*** **9. You have to learn to crawl before you can walk,** skills must be acquired before more advanced ones are possible. —**learn′a•ble,** *adj.* —**learn′er,** *n.*

learn•ed (lûr′nid *for 1–3;* lûrnd *for 4*), *adj.* **1.** having much knowledge; scholarly; erudite: *learned professors.* **2.** connected or involved with the pursuit of knowledge, esp. of a scholarly nature: *a learned journal.* **3.** of or showing learning or knowledge; well-informed: *learned in the ways of the world.* **4.** acquired by experience, study, etc.: *learned behavior.* —**learn′ed•ly,** *adv.* —**learn′ed•ness,** *n.*

learn•ing (lûr′ning), *n.* **1.** knowledge acquired by systematic study in any field of scholarly application. **2.** the act or process of acquiring knowledge or skill. **3.** *Psychol.* the modification of behavior through practice, training, or experience. **—*Proverb.*** **4. A little learning** (or **knowledge**) **is a dangerous thing,** partial knowledge of a subject is sometimes worse than ignorance.

learn′ing curve′, *n.* **1.** a graphic representation of progress in learning measured against the time required to achieve mastery. **2.** the process of learning upon which such a representation is based.

learn′ing disabil′ity, *n.* any of several conditions characterized in school-aged children by difficulty in accomplishing specific tasks, esp. reading and writing, and associated with impaired development of a part of the central nervous system.

learn′ing-disa′bled, *adj.* pertaining to or having a learning disability: *a learning-disabled child.*

lease (lēs), *n., v.,* **leased, leas•ing.** —*n.* **1.** a contract conveying land, renting property, etc., to another for a specified period in consideration of rent or other compensation. **2.** the property leased. **3.** the period of time for which a lease is made: *a five-year lease.* —*v.t.* **4.** to grant the temporary possession or use of (lands, tenements, etc.) to another, usu. for compensation at a fixed rate; let: *to lease one's apartment to a friend.* **5.** to take or hold by lease: *He leased the farm from the sheriff.* —*v.i.* **6.** to grant a lease; let or rent: *to lease at a lower rental.* **—*Idiom.*** **7. a new lease on life,** a chance to improve one's situation or to live longer or more happily. —**leas′er,** *n.*

lease•back (lēs′bak′), *n.* the sale of property to a buyer who then leases it back to the seller, who often becomes the principal tenant, thus providing substantial tax savings for both.

lease•hold (lēs′hōld′), *n.* **1.** property acquired under a lease. **2.** a tenure under a lease. —*adj.* **3.** held by lease.

lease•hold•er (lēs′hōl′dər), *n.* a tenant under a lease.

leash (lēsh), *n.* **1.** a chain, strap, etc., for controlling or leading a dog or other animal; lead. **2.** control; restraint: *to keep one's temper in leash.* **3.** a brace and a half, as of foxes or hounds; set of three animals. —*v.t.* **4.** to secure or control by or as if by a leash: *to leash the energy of the atom.* **5.** to bind together by or as if by a leash; connect; link.

least (lēst), *adj., a superl. of* **little** *with* **less** *or* **lesser** *as compar.* **1.** smallest in size, amount, degree, etc.; slightest: *to pay the least amount of attention.* **2.** lowest in consideration, position, or importance. —*n.* **3.** something that is least; the least amount, quantity, degree, etc. —*adv.* **4.** *superl. of* **little** *with* **less** *as compar.* to the smallest extent, amount, or degree: *That's the least important question of all.* **—*Idiom.*** **5. at least, a.** at the lowest estimate or figure. **b.** at any rate; in any case. **6. not in the least,** not in the smallest degree; not at all: *not in the least concerned.* **—*Proverb.*** **7. Least said, soonest mended,** apologies and discussion may only worsen a mistake.

least′ com′mon denom′inator, *n.* the smallest number that is a common denominator of a given set of fractions. Also called **lowest common denominator.**

least′ com′mon mul′tiple, *n.* LOWEST COMMON MULTIPLE.

leath•er (leth′ər), *n.* **1.** the skin of an animal with the hair removed and prepared by tanning or a similar process to preserve it and make it pliable or supple when dry. **2.** an article made of this material. —*adj.* **3.** pertaining to, made of, or resembling leather.

leath′er•back tur′tle (leth′ər bak′), *n.* a large sea turtle, *Dermochelys coriacea,* having the shell covered by a leathery skin: the largest living sea turtle. Also called **leath′er•back′.**

leath•er•ette (leth′ə ret′), *n.* a material constructed and finished to simulate leather.

leath•er•neck (leth′ər nek′), *n. Informal.* a U.S. marine. [from the leather-lined collar that was formerly part of the uniform]

Leath′er-Stock•ing Tales′ (leth′ər stok′ing), a series of historical novels by James Fenimore Cooper, comprising *The Pioneers, The Last of the Mohicans, The Prairie, The Pathfinder,* and *The Deerslayer.*

leath•er•y (leth′ə rē), *adj.* like leather in appearance or texture; tough and flexible. —**leath′er•i•ness,** *n.*

leave[1] (lēv), *v.,* **left, leav•ing.** —*v.t.* **1.** to go out of or away from, as a place: *to leave the house.* **2.** to depart from permanently; quit: *to leave a job.* **3.** to let remain behind: *The bear left tracks in the snow.* **4.** to let stay or be as specified: *to leave a motor running.* **5.** to let (a person or animal) remain in a position to do something without interference: *We left him to his work.* **6.** to let (a thing) remain for another's action or decision: *We left the details to the lawyer.* **7.** to give in charge; deposit; entrust: *Leave the package with my neighbor.* **8.** to give up: *She left music to study engineering.* **9.** to turn aside from; abandon or disregard: *We will leave this subject for now.* **10.** to give for use after one's death or departure: *to leave all one's money to charity.* **11.** to have remaining after death: *He leaves a wife and three children.* **12.** to have as a remainder after subtraction: *2 from 4 leaves 2.* **13.** *Nonstandard.* LET[1] (defs. 1, 2, 4). —*v.i.* **14.** to go away, depart, or set out: *We leave for Europe tomorrow.* **15. leave off, a.** to stop; cease; discontinue. **b.** to stop using or wearing. **c.** to omit. **16. leave out,** to omit; exclude. **—Usage.** LEAVE is interchangeable with LET when followed by ALONE with the sense "to refrain from annoying or interfering with": *Leave* (or *Let*) *him alone and he will assemble the apparatus properly.* The use of LEAVE ALONE for LET ALONE in the sense "not to mention" is nonstandard: *There wasn't even standing room, let* (not *leave*) *alone a seat.* Other substitutions of LEAVE for LET are generally regarded as nonstandard: *Let* (not *Leave*) *us sit down and talk this over. Let* (not *Leave*) *her do it her own way. The police wouldn't let* (not *leave*) *us cross the barriers.* See also LET[1].

leave[2] (lēv), *n.* **1.** permission to do something: *to beg leave to go.* **2.** permission to be absent, as from work or military duty: *to get leave after basic training.* **3.** the time this permission lasts: *30 days' leave.* **4.** the bowling pin or pins in upright position after the bowl of the first ball. **—*Idiom.*** **5. take leave of,** to part or separate from: *Have you taken leave of your senses?* **6. take one's leave,** to depart, as after a formal good-bye: *We should take our leave before the speeches begin.*

leave[3] (lēv), *v.i.,* **leaved, leav•ing.** to put forth leaves; leaf.

leav•en (lev′ən), *n.* **1.** a substance, as yeast or baking powder, that causes fermentation and expansion of dough or batter. **2.** fermented dough reserved for producing fermentation in a new batch of dough. **3.** an element that produces an altering or transforming influence. —*v.t.* **4.** to add leaven to (dough or batter) and cause to rise. **5.** to permeate with an altering or transforming element.

leav•en•ing (lev′ə ning), *n.* **1.** Also called **leav′ening a′gent.** a substance used to produce fermentation in dough or batter; leaven. **2.** the process of causing fermentation by leaven. **3.** LEAVEN (def. 3).

Leav•en, The (lev′ən), a parable of Jesus. Matt. 13:33; Luke 13:20–21.

leave′ of ab′sence, *n.* **1.** permission to be absent from duty, employment, service, etc.; leave. **2.** the length of time granted in such permission: *a two-year leave of absence.*

leaves (lēvz), *n.* pl. of LEAF.

leave′-tak′ing, *n.* a saying farewell; a parting or good-bye; departure: *Their leave-taking was brief.*

leav•ing (lē′ving), *n.* **1.** something that is left; residue. **2. leavings,** leftovers or remains; refuse.

Leb•a•non (leb′ə nən, -non′), *n.* a republic at the E end of the Mediterranean, N of Israel. 3,858,736; 3927 sq. mi. (10,170 sq. km). *Cap.:* Beirut. —**Leb′a•nese′** (-nēz′, -nēs′), *adj., n., pl.* **-nese.**

Le•bens•raum (lā′bəns roum′, -bənz-), *n.* (*often l.c.*) **1.** additional territory considered, esp. by Nazi Germany, to be necessary for national survival or for expansion of trade. **2.** any additional space needed in order to act, function, etc. [< German: living space]

lech•er (lech′ər), *n.* a man given to excessive sexual indulgence; lascivious or licentious man.

lech•er•ous (lech′ər əs), *adj.* **1.** given to or characterized by lechery; lustful. **2.** erotically suggestive; inciting to lust. —**lech′er•ous•ly,** *adv.* —**lech′er•ous•ness,** *n.*

lech•er•y (lech′ə rē), *n., pl.* **-er•ies. 1.** unrestrained indulgence of sexual desire. **2.** a lecherous act.

lec•i•thin (les′ə thin), *n.* **1.** any of a group of phospholipids, containing choline and fatty acids, that are a component of cell membranes and are abundant in nerve tissue and egg yolk. **2.** a commercial form of this substance, obtained chiefly from soybeans, corn, and egg yolk, used in foods, cosmetics, and inks.

lec•tern (lek′tərn), *n.* **1.** a reading desk in a church from which the Bible lessons are read during the service. **2.** a stand with a slanted top, used to hold a book, speech, etc., at the proper height for a standing reader or speaker.

lec•tin (lek'tin), *n.* any of a group of proteins that bind to specific carbohydrates and act as an agglutinin.

lec•tion (lek'shən), *n.* **1.** a version of a passage in a particular copy or edition of a text. **2.** a sacred writing read in a divine service.

lec•tion•ar•y (lek'shə ner'ē), *n., pl.* **-ar•ies.** a book or a list of lections for reading in a divine service.

lec•tor (lek'tər), *n.* a lecturer in a college or university. —**lec'tor•ate** (-tər it, -tə rāt'), **lec'tor•ship',** *n.*

lec•ture (lek'chər), *n., v.,* **-tured, -tur•ing.** —*n.* **1.** a discourse read or delivered before an audience or class, esp. for instruction or to set forth some subject: *a lecture on modern art.* **2.** a speech of warning or reproof as to conduct; long, tedious reprimand. —*v.i.* **3.** to give a lecture or series of lectures: *She spent the year lecturing to student groups.* —*v.t.* **4.** to deliver a lecture to or before; instruct by lectures. **5.** to rebuke or reprimand at some length.

lec•tur•er (lek'chər ər), *n.* **1.** a person who lectures. **2.** an academic rank given in universities to a teacher ranking below assistant professor.

led (led), *v.* pt. and pp. of LEAD¹.

LED, *pl.* **LEDs, LED's.** light-emitting diode: a semiconductor diode that emits light when conducting current, used in electronic equipment, esp. for displaying readings on digital watches, calculators, etc.

Led•bet•ter (led'bet ər), *n.* **Huddie** ("*Leadbelly*"), 1888–1954, U.S. folksinger and composer.

le•der•ho•sen (lā'dər hō'zən), *n.pl.* leather shorts, usu. with suspenders, worn esp. in Bavaria.

ledge (lej), *n.* **1.** a relatively narrow, projecting part, as a horizontal, shelflike projection on a wall or a raised edge on a tray. **2.** a more or less flat shelf of rock protruding from a cliff or slope. **3.** a reef, ridge, or line of rocks in the sea or other body of water. **4.** *Mining.* **a.** a layer or mass of rock underground. **b.** a lode or vein. —**ledge'less,** *adj.*

ledg•er (lej'ər), *n.* **1.** an account book of final entry, in which business transactions are recorded. **2.** a flat slab of stone laid over a grave.

ledg'er line', *n.* a short line added above or below a musical staff to accommodate an increase in range.

lee¹ (lē), *n.* **1.** protective shelter: *the lee of a rock in a storm.* **2.** the side or part that is sheltered or turned away from the wind: *huts erected under the lee of the mountain.* **3.** *Chiefly Naut.* the quarter or region toward which the wind blows.

lee² (lē), *n.* Usu., **lees.** the insoluble matter that settles from a liquid, esp. from wine; sediment; dregs.

Lee (lē), *n.* **1. Ann,** 1736–84, British mystic: founder of Shaker sect in U.S. **2. Charles,** 1731–82, American Revolutionary general, born in England. **3. Francis Lightfoot,** 1734–97, American Revolutionary statesman. **4. Gypsy Rose** (*Rose Louise Hovick*), 1914–70, U.S. entertainer. **5. Henry** ("*Light-Horse Harry*"), 1756–1818, American Revolutionary general (father of Robert E. Lee). **6. Richard Henry,** 1732–94, American Revolutionary statesman (brother of Francis L. Lee). **7. Robert E(dward),** 1807–70, Confederate general in the Civil War (son of Henry Lee). **8. Sir Sidney,** 1859–1926, English biographer and critic. **9. Tsung-Dao,** born 1926, Chinese physicist.

leech (lēch), *n.* **1.** any bloodsucking annelid worm of the class Hirudinea, as the European *Hirudo medicinalis,* once used widely for bloodletting. **2.** a person who clings to another for personal gain, esp. without giving anything in return; parasite. —*v.t.* **3.** to apply leeches to, so as to bleed. **4.** to cling to and feed upon or drain, as a leech does; exhaust; deplete. —*v.i.* **5.** to hang on to a person in the manner of a leech. —**leech'like',** *adj.*

leek (lēk), *n.* a plant, *Allium ampeloprasum,* of the amaryllis family, allied to the onion, having a cylindrical bulb and leaves used in cookery.

leer (lēr), *v.i.* **1.** to look with a sideways glance, esp. suggestive of lascivious interest or sly and malicious intention. —*n.* **2.** a lascivious or sly look. —**leer'ing•ly,** *adv.*

leer•y (lēr'ē), *adj.,* **leer•i•er, leer•i•est.** wary; suspicious (usu. fol. by *of*): *I'm leery of his financial advice.* —**leer'i•ly,** *adv.* —**leer'i•ness,** *n.*

lee•ward (lē'wərd; *Naut.* lōō'ərd), *adj.* **1.** pertaining to, in, or moving toward the quarter toward which the wind blows (opposed to *windward*). —*n.* **2.** the lee side; point or quarter toward which the wind blows. —*adv.* **3.** toward the lee. —**lee'ward•ly,** *adv.*

Lee'ward Is'lands (lē'wərd), *n.pl.* a group of islands in the Lesser Antilles of the West Indies, near Puerto Rico.

lee•way (lē'wā'), *n.* **1.** extra time, space, materials, etc., within which to act; margin: *to have ten minutes' leeway to catch a train.* **2.** a degree of freedom of action or thought: *The instructions give us plenty of leeway.* **3.** the drift of a ship leeward from its heading. **4.** the amount an aircraft is blown off its normal course by crosswinds.

left¹ (left), *adj.* **1.** of, pertaining to, or located on or near the side of a person or thing that is turned toward the west when the subject is facing north (opposed to *right*). **2.** (*often cap.*) of or belonging to the political Left; having liberal or radical views in politics. —*n.* **3.** the left side, or something that is on the left side. **4.** a turn toward the left: *Make a left at the next corner.* **5. the Left, a.** those individuals or organized groups advocating liberal reform or revolutionary change in the social, political, or economic order. **b.** the liberal position held by these people. **6.** (*usu. cap.*) **a.** the part of a legislative assembly, esp. in continental Europe, that is situated to the left of the presiding officer. **b.** the more liberal members of such an assembly, who customarily sit in this part. **7.** STAGE LEFT. **8.** a boxing blow delivered by the left hand. —*adv.* **9.** toward the left.

left² (left), *v.* pt. and pp. of LEAVE¹.

left' brain', *n.* the left cerebral hemisphere, controlling activity on the right side of the body: in humans, usu. showing some degree of specialization for language and calculation. Compare RIGHT BRAIN.

left' field', *n.* **1.** (in baseball) **a.** the area of the outfield to the left of center field, as viewed from home plate. **b.** the position of the player covering this area. **2.** a position or circumstance that is remote from an ordinary or general trend. —*Idiom.* **3. (out) in left field,** extraordinarily wrong. —**left' field'er,** *n.*

left'-hand', *adj.* **1.** on or to the left: *a left-hand turn.* **2.** of, for, or with the left hand.

left'-hand'ed, *adj.* **1.** having the left hand more dominant or effective than the right; preferably using the left hand: *a left-handed pitcher.* **2.** adapted to or performed by the left hand: *a left-handed tool; a left-handed tennis serve.* **3. a.** rotating counterclockwise. **b.** (of a gear tooth or screw thread) twisting counterclockwise as it recedes from an observer. **4.** ambiguous or doubtful and often unfavorable or derogatory by implication: *a left-handed compliment.* **5.** clumsy or awkward. **6.** of, pertaining to, or issuing from a morganatic marriage: so called from the custom, in morganatic marriage ceremonies, of having the bridegroom give his left hand to the bride. —*adv.* **7.** with the left hand: *to write left-handed.* **8.** toward the left hand; in a counterclockwise direction: *The strands of the rope are laid left-handed.* —**left'-hand'ed•ly,** *adv.* —**left'-hand'ed•ness,** *n.*

left'-hand'er, *n.* **1.** a person who is left-handed, esp. a baseball pitcher who throws with the left hand. **2.** *Informal.* a slap or punch delivered with the left hand.

left•ist (lef'tist), *n.* (*sometimes cap.*) **1.** a member of the political Left; liberal or radical. —*adj.* **2.** of, pertaining to, characteristic of, or advocated by the political Left. —**left'ism,** *n.*

left•o•ver (left'ō'vər), *n.* **1.** Usu., **leftovers.** food remaining uneaten at the end of a meal, esp. when saved for later use. **2.** anything left or remaining from a larger amount; remainder. —*adj.* **3.** being left or remaining, as an unused portion or amount: *leftover meatloaf.*

left•ward (left'wərd), *adv.* **1.** Also, **left'wards.** toward or on the left. —*adj.* **2.** situated on the left. **3.** directed toward the left. —**left'ward•ly,** *adv.*

left' wing', *n.* the liberal or radical element in a political party or other organization. —**left'-wing',** *adj.* —**left'-wing'er,** *n.*

left•y¹ or **left•ie** (lef'tē), *n., pl.* **left•ies.** *Informal.* a left-handed person.

left•y² (lef'tē), *Informal.* —*adj.* **1.** LEFT-HANDED. **2.** LEFTIST. —*adv.* **3.** with the left hand: *He bats lefty.*

leg (leg), *n., v.,* **legged, leg•ging.** —*n.* **1.** either of the two lower limbs of a biped, as a human being, or any of the paired limbs of an animal, that support and move the body. **2.** the lower limb of a human being from the knee to the ankle. **3.** something resembling or suggesting a leg in use, position, or appearance. **4.** the part of a garment, boot, or the like that covers the leg. **5.** one of usu. several relatively slender supports for a piece of furniture. **6.** one of the sides of a forked object, as of a compass or pair of dividers. **7.** one of the sides of a triangle other than a base or hypotenuse. **8.** one of the distinct sections of any course: *the last leg of a trip.* **9. a.** one of a designated number of contests that must be completed successfully before a winner can be determined. **b.** one of the stretches or sections of a relay race. **10. a.** the part of a cricket field to the left of and behind the batsman as he faces the bowler or to the right of and behind him if he is left-handed. **b.** the fielder playing this part of the field. **c.** the position of this fielder. **11. legs,** *Slang.* **a.** (of a motion picture) the capacity to draw large audiences steadily over a long period. **b.** staying power: *The intended bestseller turned out to have no legs.* —*v.t.* **12.** to move or propel (a boat) with the legs. —*Idiom.* **13. a leg to stand on,** factual support for one's claims or arguments. **14. a leg up,** an added advantage, help, or means of encouragement. **15. leg it,** to walk rapidly or run. **16. on one's** or **its last legs,** just short of exhaustion, breakdown, failure, etc. **17. stretch one's legs,** to move or walk around after prolonged sitting.

leg•a•cy (leg'ə sē), *n., pl.* **-cies,** *adj.* **1.** (in a will) a gift of property, esp. personal property, as money; bequest. **2.** anything handed down from the past, as from an ancestor or predecessor. —*adj.* **3.** *Computers.* of or pertaining to data that was created on obsolescent software or hardware.

le•gal (lē'gəl), *adj.* **1.** permitted by law; lawful: *Such acts are not legal.* **2.** of or pertaining to law; connected with the law or its administration: *the legal profession.* **3.** appointed, established, or authorized by law; deriving authority from law. **4.** recognized by law rather than by equity. **5.** of, pertaining to, or characteristic of the profession of law or of lawyers: *a legal mind.* —*n.* **6.** a person who acts in a legal manner or with legal authority. **7.** a person whose status is protected by or in accordance with law. **8. legals,** authorized investments that may be made by fiduciaries, as savings banks or trustees. —**le'gal•ly,** *adv.*

le'gal age', *n.* the age, 18 in most states, at which a person is legally responsible and may enter into contracts, execute deeds, etc.

le'gal aid', *n.* free legal service to persons unable to pay for a lawyer.

le'gal ea'gle, *n.* Often Disparaging. a lawyer.

le•gal•ese (lē'gə lēz', -lēs'), *n.* language containing an excessive amount of legal terminology or of legal jargon.

le'gal hol'iday, *n.* a public holiday established by law, during which certain work, government business, etc., is restricted.

le•gal•ism (lē′gə liz′əm), *n.* **1.** strict adherence to law or prescription, esp. to the letter rather than the spirit. **2.** the theological doctrine that salvation is gained through good works. —**le′gal•ist,** *n.* —**le′gal•is′tic,** *adj.* —**le′gal•is′ti•cal•ly,** *adv.*

le•gal•i•ty (lē gal′i tē), *n., pl.* **-ties. 1.** the state or quality of being in conformity with the law; lawfulness. **2.** attachment to or observance of law. **3.** Usu., **legalities.** a duty or obligation imposed by law.

le•gal•ize (lē′gə līz′), *v.t.,* **-ized, -iz•ing.** to make legal; authorize. —**le′gal•i•za′tion,** *n.*

le′gal pad′, *n.* a ruled writing tablet, usu. of yellow, legal-size paper.

le′gal-size′ or **le′gal-sized′,** *adj.* **1.** (of paper) measuring approximately 8½ × 14 in. (22 × 36 cm). **2.** (of office supplies and equipment) made for holding legal-size sheets of paper. Compare LETTER-SIZE.

le′gal ten′der, *n.* currency that may be lawfully tendered in payment of money debts and that may not be refused by creditors.

le′gal weight′, *n.* the weight of merchandise itself plus that of its immediate wrapping material but not of the outside shipping container: used esp. in some Latin American countries in assessing import duties.

leg•ate (leg′it), *n.* **1.** an ecclesiastic delegated by the pope as his representative. **2.** (in ancient Rome) **a.** an assistant to a general or to the governor of a province. **b.** a provincial governor appointed by the emperor. **3.** an envoy or emissary. —**leg′ate•ship′,** *n.*

leg•a•tee (leg′ə tē′), *n.* a person to whom a legacy is bequeathed.

le•ga•tion (li gā′shən), *n.* **1.** a diplomatic minister and staff in a foreign mission. **2.** the official headquarters of a diplomatic minister. **3.** the office or position of a legate; mission. —**le•ga′tion•ar′y,** *adj.*

le•ga•to (lə gä′tō), *adj., adv. Music.* smooth and connected; without breaks between the successive tones. Compare STACCATO.

leg•end (lej′ənd), *n.* **1.** a nonhistorical or unverifiable story handed down by tradition from earlier times and popularly accepted as historical. **2.** the body of stories of this kind, esp. as they relate to a particular people, group, or clan: *the winning of the West in American legend.* **3.** an inscription, esp. on a coat of arms, a monument, a picture, or the like. **4.** a table on a map, chart, or the like, listing and explaining the symbols used. Compare KEY[1] (def. 6). **5.** the lettering running around the field of a coin, medal, etc. Compare INSCRIPTION (def. 5). **6.** a collection of stories about an admirable person. **7.** a person who is the center of such stories: *to become a legend in one's own lifetime.*

leg•end•ar•y (lej′ən der′ē), *adj., n., pl.* **-ar•ies.** —*adj.* **1.** of, pertaining to, or of the nature of a legend. **2.** celebrated or described in legend: *a legendary hero.* —*n.* **3.** a collection of legends. —**leg′end•ar′i•ly,** *adv.*

leg•er•de•main (lej′ər də mān′), *n.* **1.** sleight of hand. **2.** trickery; deception. **3.** any artful trick.

leg•ged (leg′id, legd), *adj.* having a specified number or kind of legs (often used in combination): *two-legged; long-legged.*

leg•ging (leg′ing), *n.* **1.** Also, **leg•gin** (leg′in). a covering, as of leather or canvas, for the leg, usu. from ankle to knee, worn by soldiers, riders, workers, etc. **2. leggings,** (*used with a pl. v.*) close-fitting trousers worn outdoors in the winter. —**leg′ginged,** *adj.*

leg•gy (leg′ē), *adj.,* **-gi•er, -gi•est. 1.** having awkwardly long legs. **2.** having long, attractively shaped legs: *leggy dancers.* **3.** pertaining to or characterized by the showing of the legs: *a leggy stage show.* **4.** (of plants) long and thin; spindly. —**leg′gi•ness,** *n.*

Leg•horn (leg′hôrn′ *for 1, 2;* -ərn, -hôrn′ *for 3*), *n.* **1.** (*l.c.*) a fine, smooth, plaited straw. **2.** (*l.c.*) a hat made of such straw, often having a broad, soft brim. **3.** one of a breed of chickens that are prolific layers of white-shelled eggs.

leg•i•ble (lej′ə bəl), *adj.* **1.** capable of being read or deciphered, esp. with ease, as writing or printing; easily readable. **2.** capable of being discerned or distinguished: *Anger was legible in his behavior.* —**leg′i•bil′i•ty, leg′i•ble•ness,** *n.* —**leg′i•bly,** *adv.*

le•gion (lē′jən), *n.* **1.** the largest unit of the Roman army, comprising at different periods from about 4000 to 6000 foot soldiers, with a much smaller complement of cavalry. **2.** a military or semimilitary unit. **3. the Legion. a.** AMERICAN LEGION. **b.** FOREIGN LEGION. **4.** any large group of armed men. **5.** any great number of persons or things; multitude; throng. Mark 5:9. —*adj.* **6.** very great in number: *The holy man's followers were legion.*

le•gion•ar•y (lē′jə ner′ē), *adj., n., pl.* **-ar•ies.** —*adj.* **1.** of, pertaining to, or belonging to a legion. **2.** constituting a legion or legions. —*n.* **3.** a soldier of a legion. **4.** LEGIONNAIRE (def. 2).

le•gion•naire (lē′jə nâr′), *n.* **1.** (*often cap.*) a member of the American Legion. **2.** a member of any legion; legionary.

legionnaires′ disease′, *n.* a form of pneumonia caused by bacteria of the genus *Legionella,* esp. *L. pneumophila,* typically acquired by inhaling airborne droplets from a contaminated water supply.

leg•is•late (lej′is lāt′), *v.,* **-lat•ed, -lat•ing.** —*v.i.* **1.** to make or enact laws. —*v.t.* **2.** to create or control by legislation: *attempts to legislate morality.*

leg•is•la•tion (lej′is lā′shən), *n.* **1.** the act of making or enacting laws. **2.** a law or a body of laws enacted.

leg•is•la•tive (lej′is lā′tiv), *adj.* **1.** having the function of making laws: *a legislative body.* **2.** of or pertaining to the enactment of laws: *legislative proceedings.* **3.** pertaining to a legislature: *a legislative recess.* **4.** enacted or ordained by legislation or a legislature: *a legislative ruling.* —**leg′is•la′tive•ly,** *adv.*

leg′islative branch′, *n.* the branch of the U.S. government whose powers are vested in the Congress.

leg•is•la•tor (lej′is lā′tər), *n.* **1.** a person who gives or makes laws. **2.** a member of a legislative body. —**leg′is•la•to′ri•al** (-lə tôr′ē əl, -tōr′-), *adj.* —**leg′is•la′tor•ship′,** *n.*

leg•is•la•ture (lej′is lā′chər), *n.* a deliberative body of persons, usu. elective, who are empowered to make, change, or repeal the laws of a country or state; the branch of government having the power to make laws, as distinguished from the executive and judiciary.

le•git (lə jit′), *adj. Informal.* legitimate.

le•git•i•ma•cy (li jit′ə mə sē), *n.* the state of being legitimate.

le•git•i•mate (*adj., n.* li jit′ə mit; *v.* -māt′), *adj., v.,* **-mat•ed, -mat•ing,** *n.* —*adj.* **1.** according to law; lawful: *the property's legitimate owner.* **2.** in accordance with established rules, principles, or standards. **3.** born of legally married parents: *legitimate children.* **4.** in accordance with the laws of reasoning; valid; logical: *a legitimate conclusion.* **5.** resting on or ruling by the principle of hereditary right: *a legitimate sovereign.* **6.** justified; genuine: *a legitimate complaint.* **7.** of the normal or regular type or kind. **8.** of or pertaining to professionally produced stage plays, as distinguished from burlesque, vaudeville, etc. —*v.t.* **9.** to make lawful or legal; pronounce as lawful: *Parliament legitimated her accession to the throne.* **10.** to confer legitimacy upon (a bastard). **11.** to show or declare to be legitimate or proper. **12.** to justify; sanction or authorize. —*n.* **13.** a person who is established as being legitimate. —**le•git′i•mate•ly,** *adv.* —**le•git′i•mate•ness,** *n.* —**le•git′i•ma′tion,** *n.*

le•git•i•mize (li jit′ə mīz′), *v.t.,* **-mized, -miz•ing.** LEGITIMATE. —**le•git′i•mi•za′tion,** *n.*

leg•man (leg′man′, -mən), *n., pl.* **-men** (-men′, -mən). **1.** a person employed as an assistant to gather information, run errands, etc. **2.** a reporter who gathers news firsthand.

Le•gree (li grē′), *n.* **Simon,** SIMON LEGREE.

leg•room (leg′rōōm′, -rŏŏm′), *n.* space sufficient for keeping one's legs in a comfortable position, as in an automobile.

leg•ume (leg′yōōm, li gyōōm′), *n.* **1.** any plant of the legume family, esp. one used for feed, food, or as a soil-improving crop. **2.** the pod, bean, or pea of such a plant, often used for food.

le•gu•mi•nous (li gyōō′mə nəs), *adj.* **1.** pertaining to, of the nature of, or bearing legumes. **2.** belonging to the legume family.

leg′ warm′er, *n.* a footless, stockinglike knitted covering for the leg, orig. worn by ballet dancers to keep the leg muscles warm in class or rehearsal.

leg•work (leg′wûrk′), *n.* **1.** work or research involving extensive walking or traveling about, usu. away from one's workplace. **2.** action of the legs as executed by an athlete, dancer, etc.

lei (lā, lā′ē), *n., pl.* **leis.** (in Hawaii) a wreath of flowers, leaves, etc., worn around the neck.

Leib•niz or **Leib•nitz** (līb′nits, līp′-), *n.* **Gottfried Wilhelm von,** 1646–1716, German philosopher and mathematician. —**Leib•niz′i•an, Leib•nitz′i•an,** *adj., n.*

Leices•ter (les′tər), *n.* **1. 1st Earl of,** DUDLEY, Robert. **2.** a city in Leicestershire, in central England. 290,600. **3.** LEICESTERSHIRE. **4.** one of an English breed of large sheep, noted for its coarse, long wool and large yield of mutton.

Leices•ter•shire (les′tər shēr′, -shər), *n.* a county in central England. 836,500; 986 sq. mi. (2555 sq. km). Also called **Leicester.**

Leigh (lē), *n.* **Vivien** (*Vivien Hartley*), 1913–67, English actress.

lei•sure (lē′zhər, lezh′ər), *n.* **1.** freedom from the demands of work or duty: *a life of leisure.* **2.** time free from the demands of work or duty: *the leisure to pursue hobbies.* **3.** unhurried ease: *a work written with leisure.* —*adj.* **4.** free or unoccupied: *leisure hours.* **5.** having leisure; not required to work for a living: *the leisure class.* **6.** designed for recreational use: *video games and other leisure products.* —***Idiom.* 7. at leisure, a.** with free or unrestricted time. **b.** without haste or pressure; slowly. **c.** out of work; unemployed. **8. at one's leisure,** when one has free time; at one's convenience. —**lei′sure•less,** *adj.*

lei•sure•ly (lē′zhər lē, lezh′ər-), *adj.* **1.** acting, proceeding, or done without haste; unhurried; deliberate: *a leisurely conversation.* **2.** showing or suggesting ample leisure; unhurried: *a leisurely manner.* —*adv.* **3.** in a leisurely manner; without haste: *to travel leisurely.*

lei′sure suit′, *n.* a man's casual suit, consisting of trousers and a matching jacket styled like a shirt.

leit•mo•tif (līt′mō tēf′), *n.* a motif or theme associated throughout a music drama with a particular person, situation, or idea.

lek (lek), *n., v.,* **lekked, lek•king.** *Animal Behav.* —*n.* **1.** a place where males assemble during the mating season and engage in competitive displays that attract females. —*v.i.* **2.** (of a male) to assemble in a lek and engage in competitive displays.

LEM (lem), *n., pl.* **LEMs, LEM's.** lunar excursion module: the portion of the Apollo spacecraft in which astronauts landed on the moon from another orbiting module.

Le•man (lē′mən), *n.* **Lake,** GENEVA, Lake of.

lem•ma[1] (lem′ə), *n., pl.* **lem•mas, lem•ma•ta** (lem′ə tə). **1.** a subsidiary proposition introduced in proving some other proposition; a helping theorem. **2.** an argument, theme, or subject, esp. when indicated in a heading. **3.** a word or phrase that is glossed; headword.

lem•ma[2] (lem′ə), *n., pl.* **lem•mas.** the tough, sometimes leathery lower bract surrounding the floral parts in a grass spikelet.

lem·ma·tize (lem′ə tīz′), *v.t.*, **-tized, -tiz·ing.** to sort (words in a list or text) in order to determine the headwords, under which related words, as inflected forms, are then listed. —**lem′ma·ti·za′tion,** *n.*

lem·ming (lem′ing), *n.* any of various small, mainly arctic, cricetid rodents esp. of the genus *Lemmus,* noted for periodic mass migrations that sometimes result in mass drownings.

lem·nis·cus (lem nis′kəs), *n., pl.* **-nis·ci** (-nis′ī, -nis′kē). a band of sensory nerve fibers in the brain.

lem·on (lem′ən), *n.* **1.** the yellowish, acid fruit of a subtropical citrus tree, *Citrus limon.* **2.** LEMON YELLOW. **3.** *Informal.* a person or thing that proves to be defective, imperfect, or unsatisfactory; dud: *Our car turned out to be a lemon.* —*adj.* **4.** made of or with lemon. **5.** having the color, taste, or odor of lemon. —**lem′on·like′, lem′on·y,** *adj.*

lem·on·ade (lem′ə nād′, lem′ə nād′), *n.* a beverage consisting of lemon juice, sweetener, and water, sometimes carbonated.

lem′on balm′, *n.* a mint, *Melissa officinalis,* with small white or pale yellow flowers and lemon-scented leaves used as a flavoring.

lem′on drop′, *n.* a lemon-flavored lozenge.

lem′on grass′, *n.* any of several lemon-scented grasses of the genus *Cymbopogon,* esp. *C. citratus,* of tropical regions, used in cooking and as the source of an aromatic oil used esp. in perfumery.

lem′on law′, *n.* a law that requires manufacturers to replace, repair, or refund the cost of automobiles that prove to be defective.

lem′on oil′, *n.* a fragrant yellow essential oil obtained from the rinds of lemons or manufactured synthetically, used as a flavoring and in perfumery, furniture polish, etc.

lem′on squash′, *n. Brit.* a soft drink made with sweetened lemon juice and water.

lem′on verbe′na, *n.* a South American plant, *Aloysia triphylla,* having long, slender leaves with a lemonlike fragrance.

lem′on yel′low, *n.* a clear, light yellow to greenish yellow color.

Lem·u·el (lem′yŏŏ əl), *n.* a Hebrew king whose mother's teachings are recorded in Proverbs 31.

le·mur (lē′mər), *n.* any small, arboreal, chiefly nocturnal prosimian primate of the family Lemuridae, of Madagascar and the Comoro Islands, having large eyes and a foxlike face. —**le′mur·like′,** *adj.*

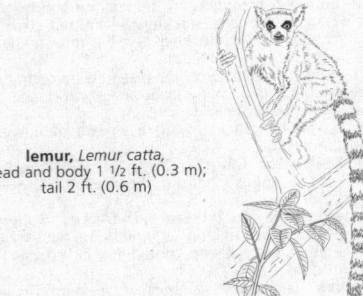

lemur, *Lemur catta,*
head and body 1 ½ ft. (0.3 m);
tail 2 ft. (0.6 m)

lend (lend), *v.,* **lent, lend·ing.** —*v.t.* **1.** to grant the use of (something) on condition that it or its equivalent will be returned. **2.** to give (money) on condition that it is returned and that interest is paid for its temporary use. **3.** (of a library) to allow the use of (books and other materials) outside library premises for a specified period. **4.** to give or contribute obligingly or helpfully: *to lend one's support to a cause.* **5.** to adapt (itself or oneself) to something; be suitable for: *The building lends itself to inexpensive remodeling.* **6.** to furnish or impart: *Distance lends enchantment to the view.* —*v.i.* **7.** to make a loan. —*Idiom.* **8. lend a hand,** to give help; aid. —**lend′a·ble,** *adj.* —**lend′er,** *n.*

lend′ing li′brary, *n.* **1.** a library whose books and other materials can be borrowed. **2.** a commercial library that rents materials for a fee.

lend′-lease′, *n., v.,* **-leased, -leas·ing.** —*n.* **1.** the matériel and services supplied by the U.S. to its allies during World War II under an act of Congress (**Lend′-Lease′ Act′**) passed in 1941. **2.** the system by which such aid was supplied. —*v.t.* **3.** to supply (matériel or services) by the lend-lease system.

L'En·fant (län fän′), *n.* **Pierre Charles,** 1754–1825, U.S. engineer and architect, born in France: designer of Washington, D.C.

L'En·gle (leng′gəl), *n.* **Madeleine,** born 1918, U.S. novelist and Christian essayist.

length (lengkth, length, lenth), *n.* **1.** the longest extent of anything as measured from end to end: *the length of a river.* **2.** the measure of the greatest dimension of a plane or solid figure. **3.** extent from beginning to end of a series, enumeration, account, book, etc.: *a report 300 pages in length.* **4.** extent in time; duration: *the length of a visit.* **5.** a distance determined by the extent of something specified: *Hold the picture at arm's length.* **6.** a piece or portion of a certain or a known extent: *a length of rope.* **7.** the quality or state of being long rather than short: *a journey remarkable for its length.* **8.** Usu., **lengths.** the extent to which a desired end is pursued: *to go to great lengths to get what one wants.* **9.**

a large extent or expanse of something. **10.** the measure from end to end of a horse, boat, etc., as a unit of distance in racing: *The horse won by two lengths.* **11.** the extent of a garment related to a point it reaches on the wearer's body or on a garment used as a standard of measurement (usu. used in combination): *an ankle-length gown; a three-quarter-length coat.* **12.** the relative duration of time involved in pronouncing a sound, esp. a vowel, or syllable; quantity. —*Idiom.* **13. at length, a.** after a considerable time; finally. **b.** fully; in detail. **14. go to any length(s),** to do anything required to accomplish one's purpose.

length·en (lengk′thən, leng′-, len′-), *v.t., v.i.* to make or become greater in length; make or grow longer. —**length′en·er,** *n.*

length·wise (lengk′thwīz′, length′-, lenth′-) also **length·ways** (-wāz′), *adv., adj.* in the direction of the length.

length·y (lengk′thē, leng′-, len′-), *adj.,* **length·i·er, length·i·est. 1.** of great length; very long: *a lengthy journey.* **2.** excessively long: *a lengthy explanation.* —**length′i·ly,** *adv.* —**length′i·ness,** *n.*

le·ni·en·cy (lē′nē ən sē, lēn′yən-) also **le′ni·ence,** *n., pl.* **-en·cies** also **-enc·es. 1.** the quality or state of being lenient. **2.** a lenient act.

le·ni·ent (lē′nē ənt, lēn′yənt), *adj.* agreeably tolerant; not strict or severe; indulgent: *to be lenient toward the children.* —**le′ni·ent·ly,** *adv.*

Le·nin (len′in), *n.* **V(ladimir) I(lyich)** (*Vladimir Ilyich Ulyanov*) (*"N. Lenin"*), 1870–1924, Russian revolutionary leader: Soviet premier 1918–24.

Le·nin·grad (len′in grad′), *n.* a former name (1924–91) of ST. PETERSBURG (def. 1).

Le·nin·ism (len′ə niz′əm), *n.* a modification of Marxism as taught by Lenin, with emphasis on the need for a well-trained party of professional revolutionaries. —**Le′nin·ist,** *n., adj.*

len·i·tive (len′i tiv), *adj.* **1.** softening, soothing, or mitigating, as medicines or applications. **2.** mildly laxative. —*n.* **3.** a lenitive medicine or application.

lens (lenz), *n., pl.* **lens·es,** *v.* —*n.* **1.** a piece of transparent substance, usu. glass, having two opposite surfaces either both curved or one curved and one plane, used in optical devices for changing the convergence of light rays, as for magnification, or in correcting defects of vision. **2.** a combination of such pieces. **3.** some analogous device, as for affecting sound waves, electromagnetic radiation, or streams of electrons. **4.** Also called **crystalline lens.** a doubly convex, transparent body in the eye, behind the pupil, that focuses incident light on the retina. **5.** a body of rock or ore that is thick in the middle and thinner toward the edges, similar in shape to a biconvex lens. —*v.t.*

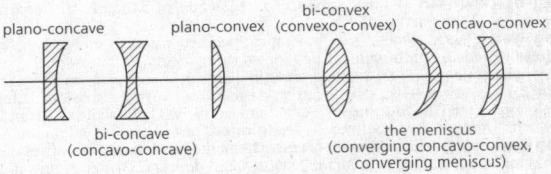

lenses (def. 1)

Lent (lent), *n.* (in the Christian religion) an annual season of fasting and penitence in preparation for Easter, beginning on Ash Wednesday and lasting 40 weekdays to Easter.

Lent·en also **lent·en** (len′tn), *adj.* **1.** of, pertaining to, or suitable for Lent. **2.** suggesting Lent, as in austerity; meager.

len·ti·cel (len′tə sel′), *n.* a corky slash or spot appearing on plant bark, above the epidermal stoma, that allows for the exchange of gases between the atmosphere and inner tissue. —**len′ti·cel·late** (-it), *adj.*

len·tic·u·lar (len tik′yə lər), *adj.* **1.** of or pertaining to a lens. **2.** biconvex. **3.** resembling the seed of a lentil in form; lentil-shaped. —**len·tic′u·lar·ly,** *adv.*

len·ti·go (len tī′gō), *n., pl.* **-tig·i·nes** (-tij′ə nēz′). a freckle or other pigmented spot.

len·til (len′til, -tl), *n.* **1.** a plant, *Lens culinaris,* of the legume family, having flattened, biconvex seeds used as food. **2.** the seed itself.

len·to (len′tō), *Music.* —*adj.* **1.** slow. —*adv.* **2.** slowly.

Le·o¹ (lē′ō), *n.* **1.** the Lion, a zodiacal constellation between Cancer and Virgo, containing the bright star Regulus. **2.** the fifth sign of the zodiac. [< Latin: lion]

Le·o² (lē′ō, lā′ō), *n.* **1. Leo I, Saint** (*"Leo the Great"*), A.D. c390–461, Italian ecclesiastic: pope 440–461. **2. Leo III, Saint,** A.D. c750–816, Italian ecclesiastic: pope 795–816. **3. Leo X** (*Giovanni de'Medici*), 1475–1521, Italian ecclesiastic: pope 1513–21 (son of Lorenzo de'Medici). **4. Leo XIII** (*Giovanni Vincenzo Pecci*), 1810–1903, Italian ecclesiastic: pope 1878–1903.

Le·o·nar·do da Vin·ci (lē′ə när′dō də vin′chē, dä vin′-, lā′-), *n.* 1452–1519, Italian artist, architect, and engineer.

Le·on·i·das (lē on′i dəs), *n.* died 480 B.C., Greek hero: king of Sparta 489?–480.

le·o·nine (lē′ə nīn′), *adj.* **1.** of or pertaining to a lion. **2.** resembling or suggestive of a lion. **3.** (*cap.*) of or pertaining to any of the popes named Leo.

leop•ard (lep′ərd), *n.* **1.** a large, powerful, spotted Asian or African cat, *Panthera pardus,* usu. tawny with black markings; the Old World panther. **2.** the fur or pelt of this animal. **3.** any similar cat, as the snow leopard. **—*Proverb.* 4. A leopard can't change its spots,** someone's intrinsic nature can't be altered. Jer. 13:23.

leop′ard frog′, *n.* **1.** a common North American green frog, *Rana pipiens,* having white-edged dark oval spots on its back. **2.** any of several similar North American frogs.

Lé•o•pold•ville (lē′ə pōld vil′, lā′-), *n.* former name of KINSHASA.

le•o•tard (lē′ə tärd′), *n.* a skintight one-piece garment for the torso, having a high or low neck, long or short sleeves, and a lower portion resembling either briefs or tights, worn by acrobats, dancers, etc. Compare TIGHTS.

lep•er (lep′ər), *n.* **1.** a person who has leprosy. **2.** a person rejected or ostracized for unacceptable behavior, opinions, character, or the like; outcast.

lepido-, a combining form meaning "scale": *lepidopteron.*

lep•i•dop•ter•an (lep′i dop′tər ən), *adj.* **1.** LEPIDOPTEROUS. **—*n.* 2.** a lepidopterous insect.

lep•i•dop•ter•ol•o•gy (lep′i dop′tə rol′ə jē), *n.* the branch of zoology dealing with butterflies and moths. **—lep′i•dop′ter•ist,** *n.*

lep•i•dop•ter•on (lep′i dop′tər ən), *n., pl.* **-ter•a** (-tər ə). a lepidopteran.

lep•i•dop•ter•ous (lep′i dop′tər əs) also **lep′i•dop′ter•al,** *adj.* belonging or pertaining to the Lepidoptera, an order of insects comprising the butterflies, moths, and skippers, in the adult state having four membranous wings more or less covered with small scales.

lep•o•rine (lep′ə rīn′, -rin), *adj.* of or resembling a rabbit or hare.

lep•re•chaun (lep′rə kôn′, -kon′), *n.* a dwarf or sprite of Irish folklore, often represented as a little old man who will reveal the location of a crock of gold to anyone who catches him.

lep•ro•sy (lep′rə sē), *n.* a chronic, slowly progressing, usu. mildly infectious disease caused by the bacillus *Mycobacterium leprae,* marked by destruction of tissue and loss of sensation and characterized in persons with poor resistance by numerous inflamed skin nodules and in persons with better resistance by local areas of firm, dry patches. Also called **Hansen's disease. —lep•rot•ic** (le prot′ik), *adj.*

lep•rous (lep′rəs), *adj.* **1.** affected with leprosy. **2.** of or resembling leprosy. **3.** *Biol.* covered with scales. **—lep′rous•ly,** *adv.* **—lep′rous•ness,** *n.*

lepto-, a combining form meaning "thin," "fine," "slight": *leptotene.*

lep•ton (lep′ton), *n., pl.* **-tons.** any of a class of weakly interacting elementary particles with spin of ½, as the electron and muon. **—lep•ton′ic,** *adj.*

Ler•ner (lûr′nər), *n.* **Alan Jay,** 1918–86, U.S. lyricist and librettist.

les•bi•an (lez′bē ən), *n.* **1.** a female homosexual. **2.** (*cap.*) a native or inhabitant of Lesbos. **—*adj.* 3.** of, pertaining to, or characterized by female homosexuality. **4.** (*cap.*) of or pertaining to Lesbos.

lese′ (or **lèse′**) **maj′esty** (lēz), *n.* **1. a.** a crime, esp. high treason, committed against a monarch or government. **b.** an offense that violates the dignity of a ruler. **2.** an attack on any custom, institution, belief, etc., held sacred or revered.

le•sion (lē′zhən), *n.* **1.** an injury; hurt; wound. **2.** any localized area of diseased or injured tissue or of abnormal structural change.

Le•so•tho (lə so͞o′to͞o, -sō′tō), *n.* a monarchy in S Africa: formerly a British protectorate; gained independence 1966; member of the Commonwealth of Nations. 2,007,814; 11,716 sq. mi. (30,344 sq. km). *Cap.:* Maseru. Formerly, **Basutoland.**

less (les), *adv., a compar. of* **little** *with* **least** *as superl.* **1.** to a smaller extent, amount, or degree: *less exact.* **2.** most certainly not (often prec. by *much* or *still*): *I could barely pay for my own meal, much less for hers.* **3.** in any way different; other: *He's nothing less than a thief.* **—*adj., a compar. of* little** *with* **least** *as superl.* **4.** smaller in size, amount, degree, etc.; not so large, great, or much: *less money; less speed.* **5.** lower in consideration, rank, or importance: *no less a person than the mayor.* **6.** fewer: *less than ten.* **—*n.* 7.** a smaller amount or quantity: *She eats less every day.* **8.** something inferior or not as important: *People have been imprisoned for less.* **—*prep.* 9.** minus; without: *a year less two days.* **—*Idiom.* 10. less and less,** to a decreasing extent or degree. **—*Saying.* 11. Less is more,** simplicity in art, fashion, etc., is more effective than excess. **—Usage.** Many modern usage guides say that FEWER must be used before plural nouns specifying individuals or readily distinguishable units: *fewer words; no fewer than 31 of the 50 states.* LESS, the guides maintain, should modify only singular mass nouns (*less sugar; less money*) and singular abstract nouns (*less doubt; less power*). It should modify plural nouns only when they suggest combination into a unit, group, or aggregation: *less than $50* (a sum of money); *less than three miles* (a unit of distance). Standard English practice does not consistently reflect these distinctions. When followed by *than,* LESS occurs at least as often as FEWER in modifying plural nouns that refer to countable persons or things, and the use of LESS in this construction is increasing in all varieties of English: *less than eight million people; no less than 31 of the 50 states.* When not followed by *than,* FEWER is more frequent in written English, although the use of LESS is increasing: *As compared with last month's record, we did more work with less people.*

-less, an adjective-forming suffix meaning "without," "not having" that specified by the noun base (*careless; shameless*); added to verbs, it is equivalent to "un-" plus the present participle of the verb, or "un-" plus the verb plus "-able" (*quenchless; tireless*).

les•see (le sē′), *n.* a person to whom a lease is granted. **—les•see′-ship,** *n.*

less•en (les′ən), *v.i.* **1.** to become less. **—*v.t.* 2.** to make less; reduce.

Les•seps (les′əps), *n.* **Ferdinand Marie, Vicomte de,** 1805–94, French engineer and diplomat: promoter of the Suez Canal.

less•er (les′ər), *adj., a compar. of* **little** *with* **least** *as superl.* **1.** smaller, as in size, value, or importance: *a lesser evil.* **—*adv., a compar. of* little** *with* **least** *as superl.* **2.** less.

less′er ape′, *n.* any of several arboreal apes of the family Hylobatidae, including the gibbon and siamang.

les•son (les′ən), *n.* **1.** a section into which a course of study is divided, esp. a single, continuous session of instruction in a subject or skill: *to take driving lessons.* **2.** a unit of a book, an exercise, etc., that is assigned to a student for study. **3.** something to be learned or studied: *the lessons of the past.* **4.** a useful piece of practical wisdom acquired by experience or study: *The accident taught him a lesson.* **5.** an instructive example: *Her faith should serve as a lesson to all of us.* **6.** a reproof or punishment intended to teach one better ways. **7.** a portion of Scripture read at a divine service; lection; pericope.

les•sor (les′ôr, le sôr′), *n.* a person who grants a lease.

lest (lest), *conj.* **1.** for fear that; so that (one) should not: *I used notes lest faulty memory should lead me astray.* **2.** that (used after words expressing fear, danger, etc.): *We worried lest the plan become known.*

let¹ (let), *v.,* **let, let•ting. —*v.t.* 1.** to allow or permit: *to let one's hair grow.* **2.** to allow to pass, go, or come: *He let us into the house.* **3.** to cause to; make: *to let her know the truth.* **4.** (used in the imperative as an auxiliary expressive of a request, command, warning, suggestion, etc.): *Let me see. Let's go. Just let them try it!* **5.** to grant the occupancy or use of for rent or hire: *to let rooms.* **6.** to contract or assign for performance: *to let work to a carpenter.* **—*v.i.* 7.** to admit of being leased: *an apartment to let for $200 a week.* **8. let down, a.** to disappoint or betray; fail. **b.** to lower. **c.** to make (a garment) longer. **d.** (of an airplane) to descend to a lower altitude for landing. **9. let in,** to admit. **10. let in on,** to allow to share in: *I'll let you in on a secret.* **11. let off, a.** to release explosively: *to let off steam.* **b.** to excuse from work or responsibility. **c.** to release with little or no punishment. **12. let on, a.** to reveal, as information or one's true feelings. **b.** to pretend. **13. let out, a.** to make known. **b.** to release from confinement, restraint, etc. **c.** to alter (a garment) so as to make larger or looser. **d.** to be finished or dismissed: *School lets out in May.* **14. let up, a.** to abate; diminish. **b.** to cease; stop. **15. let up on,** to become more lenient with. **—*n.* 16.** *Brit.* a housing rental. **—*Idiom.* 17. let be,** to refrain from interfering with or bothering. **18. let someone have it,** *Informal.* to attack or assault. **—Usage.** Perhaps because LET'S has come to be felt as a word in its own right rather than as the contraction of LET US, it often occurs in informal speech and writing with redundant or appositional pronouns: *Let's us plan a picnic. Let's you and I* (or *me*) *get together tomorrow.* Usage guides suggest avoiding *let's us* in formal speech and writing. Both *let's you and me* and *let's you and I* occur in the relaxed speech of educated speakers. The former conforms to the traditional rules of grammar; the latter, nonetheless, occurs more frequently. See also LEAVE¹.

let² (let), *n.* **1.** (in tennis, badminton, etc.) any shot or action that must be replayed, esp. an otherwise valid serve that has hit the top of the net. **2.** *Chiefly Law.* an impediment or obstacle: *to act without let or hindrance.*

-let, a diminutive suffix attached to nouns (*booklet; piglet*), and, by extraction from BRACELET, a suffix denoting a band, ornament, or article of clothing worn on the part of the body specified by the noun (*anklet*).

let•down (let′doun′), *n.* **1.** a disillusionment or disappointment: *The news was a letdown.* **2.** depression; deflation: *I felt a terrible letdown after the party.* **3.** a decrease in volume, force, energy, etc. **4.** the descent of an aircraft preparatory to a landing approach.

le•thal (lē′thəl), *adj.* **1.** of or causing death; deadly; fatal: *a lethal weapon; a lethal dose.* **2.** made to cause death: *a lethal injection.* **3.** causing great harm; disastrous: *The disclosures were lethal to his candidacy.* **—le•thal′i•ty, le′thal•ness,** *n.* **—le′thal•ly,** *adv.*

le′thal gene′, *n.* a gene that under certain conditions causes the death of an organism. Also called **le′thal fac′tor, le′thal muta′tion.**

le•thar•gic (lə thär′jik) also **le•thar′gi•cal,** *adj.* **1.** of or affected with lethargy; drowsy; sluggish. **2.** producing lethargy. **—le•thar′gi•cal•ly,** *adv.*

leth•ar•gy (leth′ər jē), *n., pl.* **-gies.** the quality or state of being drowsy and dull or listless and unenergetic; apathetic or sluggish inactivity.

Le•the (lē′thē), *n.* **1.** a river in the ancient Greek underworld whose water caused those who drank it to forget their past. **2.** (*usu. l.c.*) forgetfulness; oblivion. [< Greek *lḗthē* lit., forgetfulness, der. of *lanthánesthai* to forget] **—Le•the•an** (li thē′ən, lē′thē ən), *adj.*

let's (lets), contraction of *let us.*

let•ted (let′id), *v.* a pt. and pp. of LET².

let•ter (let′ər), *n.* **1.** a written or printed communication addressed to a person or organization and usu. transmitted by mail. **2.** a symbol or character that is conventionally used in writing and printing to represent a speech sound and is part of an alphabet. **3.** a piece of printing type bearing such a symbol or character. **4.** a particular style of type. **5.** Often, **letters.** a formal document granting a right or privilege. **6.** actual wording; literal meaning, as distinct from implied meaning or intent (opposed to *spirit*): *the letter of the law.* **7. letters,** (*used with a sing. or pl. v.*) **a.** literature in general. **b.** the profession of literature. **c.** learning; knowledge, esp. of literature. **8.** an emblem consisting of the initial of a school, awarded to a student for accomplishment, esp. in athletics. —*v.t.* **9.** to mark or write with letters; inscribe. —*v.i.* **10.** to earn a letter in a school activity, esp. a sport. —***Idiom.*** **11. to the letter,** to the last particular; precisely: *I followed your instructions to the letter.*

let′ter bomb′, *n.* an envelope containing an explosive device designed to detonate when the envelope is opened by the recipient.

let′ter box′, *n.* a public or private mailbox.

let′ter car′rier, *n.* MAIL CARRIER.

let•tered (let′ərd), *adj.* **1.** educated or learned. **2.** literate. **3.** of or characterized by learning or literary culture. **4.** marked with or as if with letters.

let•ter•head (let′ər hed′), *n.* **1.** a printed heading on stationery, esp. one giving the name and address of a person, business concern, institution, etc. **2.** a sheet of paper with such a heading.

let•ter•ing (let′ər ing), *n.* **1.** the act or process of inscribing with or forming letters. **2.** the letters inscribed.

let′ter of cred′it, *n.* **1.** a document issued by a banker to one or more correspondents allowing the person named to draw money to a specified amount. **2.** a letter from a bank notifying a person that drafts on the issuer have been authorized up to a specified amount.

let′ter-per′fect, *adj.* **1.** knowing one's part, lesson, or the like, perfectly. **2.** precise or exact in every detail.

let•ter•press (let′ər pres′), *n.* **1.** the process of printing from letters or type in relief, rather than from intaglio plates or planographically. **2.** matter printed in such a manner. **3.** *Chiefly Brit.* printed text. —*adj.* **4.** set in letterpress: *letterpress work.*

let′ter-qual′i•ty, *adj.* designating or producing type equal in sharpness and resolution to that produced by an electric typewriter: *a letter-quality computer printer. Abbr.:* LQ

let′ter-size′, *adj.* **1.** (of paper) measuring approximately 8½ × 11 in. (22 × 28 cm). **2.** (of office supplies and equipment) made for holding letter-size sheets of paper. Compare LEGAL-SIZE.

let′ters testamen′tary, *n.pl.* an instrument issued by a court or public official authorizing an executor to take control of and dispose of the estate of a deceased person.

let•tuce (let′is), *n.* **1.** a cultivated composite plant, *Lactuca sativa,* occurring in many varieties and having succulent leaves used for salads. **2.** the leaves of this plant. **3.** any species of *Lactuca.* **4.** *Slang.* paper money; cash.

let•up (let′up′), *n.* cessation; pause; relief.

leu•ke•mi•a (lo͞o kē′mē ə), *n.* any of several cancers of the bone marrow characterized by an abnormal increase of white blood cells in the tissues, resulting in anemia, increased susceptibility to infection, and impaired blood clotting. —**leu•ke′mic,** *adj.*

leu•ko•cyte or **leu•co•cyte** (lo͞o′kə sīt′), *n.* WHITE BLOOD CELL. —**leu′ko•cyt′ic** (-sit′ik), *adj.*

lev (lef), *n., pl.* **lev•a** (lev′ə). the basic monetary unit of Bulgaria.

Lev., Leviticus.

Le•vant (li vant′), *n.* the lands bordering the E shores of the Mediterranean Sea. —**Levantine,** *adj., n.*

lev•ee[1] (lev′ē), *n.* **1.** an embankment designed to prevent the flooding of a river. **2.** a natural deposit of sand or mud built up along the side of a river or stream. **3.** one of the small continuous ridges surrounding fields that are to be irrigated. **4.** a landing place for ships; quay. —*v.t.* **5.** to furnish with a levee.

lev•ee[2] (lev′ē, le vē′), *n.* **1.** (in Great Britain) a public court assembly, held in the early afternoon, at which men only are received. **2.** a reception, usu. in someone's honor. **3.** (formerly) a reception of visitors held on rising from bed, as by a royal or other personage.

lev•el (lev′əl), *adj., n., v.,* **-eled, -el•ing** or (*esp. Brit.*) **-elled, -el•ling.** —*adj.* **1.** having no part higher than another; having a flat or even surface. **2.** being in a plane parallel to the plane of the horizon; horizontal. **3.** equal, as in height, condition, status, or advancement. **4.** even, equable, or uniform: *to speak in a level voice.* **5.** filled to a height even with the rim of a container: *a level teaspoon of salt.* **6.** mentally well-balanced; sensible; rational: *to keep a level head in a crisis.* **7.** of or pertaining to a particular rank or involving members of such a rank (usu. used in combination): *high-level discussions.* —*n.* **8.** the horizontal line or plane in which anything is situated, with regard to its elevation: *a shelf built at eye level.* **9.** a position with respect to a given or specified height: *The water rose to a level of 30 feet.* **10.** a position or plane in a graded scale of values: *an average level of skill.* **11.** rank or status, as in a hierarchy: *the top levels of government.* **12.** stratum or sphere: *levels of meaning; elections on a local level.* **13.** an extent, measure, or degree of intensity, concentration, quantity, etc.: *low levels of radiation; to increase levels of production.* **14.** a horizontal surface, as a floor in a building or other structure: *the upper level of the bridge.* **15.** a device used for determining or adjusting something to a horizontal surface. **16. a.** a surveying instrument consisting of a spirit level mounted on a frame with a telescopic sight, used for establishing a horizontal. **b.** an observation made with this instrument. **17.** an imaginary line or surface everywhere at right angles to the plumb line. **18.** a horizontal position or condition. **19.** a level or flat surface, as an extent of land approximately horizontal and unbroken by irregularities. **20.** the interconnected horizontal mine workings at a particular elevation or depth: *the 1500-foot level.* —*v.t.* **21.** to make (a surface) level, even, or flat; make horizontal. **22.** to raise or lower to a particular level or position. **23.** to bring (something) to the level of the ground: *to level trees.* **24.** *Informal.* to knock down (a person). **25.** to make equal, as in status or condition. **26.** to make even or uniform, as coloring. **27.** to aim or point (a weapon, criticism, etc.) at a mark or objective. **28.** to find the relative elevation of different points in (land), as with a surveyor's level. —*v.i.* **29.** to bring things or persons to a common level. **30.** to aim a weapon, criticism, etc., at a mark or objective. **31.** to speak truthfully and openly (often fol. by *with*). **32. a.** to take a level in surveying. **b.** to use a leveling instrument. **33. level off, a.** (of an aircraft) to maintain a constant altitude after a climb or descent. **b.** to become stable; reach a constant or limit. **c.** to make even or smooth. —***Idiom.*** **34. find one's (own) level,** to attain a position or status that matches one's ability. **35. one's level best,** one's very best; one's utmost. **36. on the level,** honest; sincere; reliable. —**lev′el•ly,** *adv.* —**lev′el•ness,** *n.*

lev•el•er (lev′ə lər), *n.* **1.** a person or thing that levels. **2.** a person or thing that promotes the abolition of inequalities or other distinctions between people. Also, *esp. Brit.,* **leveller.**

lev•el•head•ed (lev′əl hed′id), *adj.* having common sense and sound judgment. —**lev′el•head′ed•ly,** *adv.* —**lev′el•head′ed•ness,** *n.*

lev′el play′ing field′, *n.* a state of equality; an equal opportunity.

lev•er (lev′ər, lē′vər), *n.* **1.** a rigid bar that pivots about one point and that is used to move an object at a second point by a force applied at a third. **2.** a means or agency of persuading or of achieving an end. —*v.t.* **3.** to move or lift with or as if with a lever. —*v.i.* **4.** to use a lever.

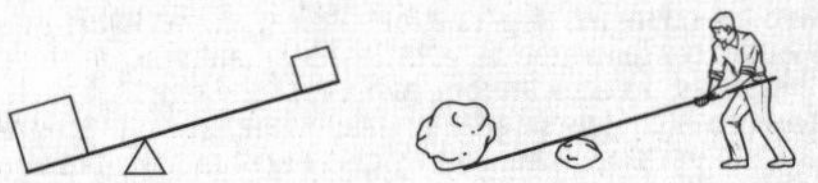

levers (def. 1)

lev•er•age (lev′ər ij, lev′rij; lē′vər ij, -vrij), *n., v.,* **-aged, -ag•ing.** —*n.* **1.** the action of a lever. **2.** the mechanical advantage or power gained by using a lever. **3.** power or ability to act effectively or to influence people. **4.** the use of a small initial investment to gain a relatively high return, as in using borrowed money at a fixed rate to buy controlling interest in a company. —*v.t.* **5.** to exert influence on. **6.** to provide with leverage. **7.** to speculate in (invested funds) by using leverage.

lev′eraged buy′out, *n.* the purchase of a company with borrowed money, using the company's assets as collateral, and often discharging the debt and realizing a profit by liquidating the company. *Abbr.:* LBO

Le•vi (lē′vī, lā′vē), *n.* **1.** a son of Jacob and Leah. Gen. 29:34. **2.** one of the 12 tribes of Israel, traditionally descended from him. **3.** original name of MATTHEW (def. 1). **4.** a Levite.

lev•i•a•ble (lev′ē ə bəl), *adj.* **1.** capable of being levied. **2.** liable or subject to a levy.

le•vi•a•than (li vī′ə thən), *n.* **1.** (*often cap.*) (in the Bible) a sea monster. Ps. 104:26 **2.** any huge marine animal, as the whale. **3.** something of immense size or power. **4.** (*cap., italics*) a philosophical work (1651) by Thomas Hobbes dealing with the political organization of society. [< Late Latin ≪ Hebrew *liwyāthān*]

lev•i•gate (lev′i gāt′), *v.t.,* **-gat•ed, -gat•ing.** to rub, grind, or reduce to a fine powder, with or without the addition of a liquid.

lev•i•rate (lev′ər it, -ə rāt′, lē′vər it, -və rāt′), *n. Judaism.* the custom of marriage between a man and his brother's widow, required in Biblical law under certain circumstances. Deut. 25:5–10. —**lev•i•rat•ic** (lev′ə rat′ik, lē′və-), **lev′i•rat′i•cal,** *adj.*

Le•vi's (lē′vīz), (*used with a pl. v.*) *Trademark.* a brand of jeans, esp. blue jeans.

lev•i•tate (lev′i tāt′), *v.,* **-tat•ed, -tat•ing.** —*v.i.* **1.** to rise or float in the air, esp. as a result of a supernatural power. —*v.t.* **2.** to cause to rise or float in the air. —**lev′i•ta′tion,** *n.* —**lev′i•ta′tion•al,** *adj.*

Le•vite (lē′vīt), *n.* **1.** a member of the tribe of Levi, esp. one appointed to assist the Temple priests. **2.** a descendant of the tribe of Levi, having honorific religious duties.

Le•vit•i•cal (li vit′i kəl), *adj.* **1.** of or pertaining to the Levites. **2.** of or pertaining to Leviticus or the law **(Levit′ical law′)** contained in Leviticus. —**Le•vit′i•cal•ly,** *adv.*

Le•vit•i•cus (li vit′i kəs), *n.* the third book of the Bible, containing laws chiefly concerning the priests and Jewish ceremonial observance. [< Late Latin *Lēviticus* (*liber*) Levitical (book) < Greek *Leuïtikós.* See LEVITE]

lev•i•ty (lev′i tē), *n., pl.* **-ties.** **1.** lightness of mind, character, or behavior, esp. lack of appropriate seriousness or earnestness. **2.** an instance or exhibition of this. **3.** fickleness.

lev•y (lev′ē), *n., pl.* **lev•ies,** *v.,* **lev•ied, lev•y•ing.** —*n.* **1.** an imposing or collecting, as of a tax, by authority or force. **2.** the amount owed or collected. **3.** the conscription of troops. **4.** the troops conscripted. —*v.t.* **5.** to impose (a tax, fine, etc.): *to levy a duty on imports.* **6.** to conscript (troops). **7.** to start or wage (war). —*v.i.* **8.** to seize or attach property by judicial order.

lewd (lo͞od), *adj.* **1.** inclined to, characterized by, or inciting to lust or lechery; lascivious. **2.** obscene or indecent, as language; salacious. —**lewd′ly,** *adv.* —**lewd′ness,** *n.*

Lew·is (lōō′is), *n.* **1. C(ecil) Day, Day-Lewis, Cecil. 2. C(live) S(taples)** (*"Clive Hamilton"*), 1898–1963, English novelist, literary historian, and Christian essayist. **3. (Harry) Sinclair,** 1885–1951, U.S. writer. **4. John L(lewellyn),** 1880–1969, U.S. labor leader. **5. Meriwether,** 1774–1809, U.S. explorer: leader of the Lewis and Clark expedition 1804–06.

lew·is·ite (lōō′ə sīt′), *n.* a pale yellow, odorless compound, $C_2H_2AsCl_3$, used as a vesicant in World War I.

lex·eme (lek′sēm), *n.* a minimal lexical unit in a language, as a word or idiomatic phrase, esp. an abstract form underlying any inflected forms.

lex·i·cal (lek′si kəl), *adj.* **1.** of or pertaining to the words or vocabulary of a language, esp. as distinguished from its grammatical and syntactic aspects. **2.** of, pertaining to, or of the nature of a lexicon. **—lex′i·cal·i·ty,** *n.* **—lex′i·cal·ly,** *adv.*

lex·i·cal·ize (lek′si kə līz′), *v.t.,* **-ized, -iz·ing. 1.** to make (an affix, phrase, etc.) a lexical item in the vocabulary of a language. **2.** to represent (a set of semantic features) by a lexical item.

lex′ical mean′ing, *n.* the meaning of a base morpheme or word, independent of its use within a construction. Compare GRAMMATICAL MEANING.

lex·i·cog·ra·pher (lek′si kog′rə fər), *n.* a writer, editor, or compiler of a dictionary.

lex·i·cog·ra·phy (lek′si kog′rə fē), *n.* **1.** the writing, editing, or compiling of dictionaries. **2.** the principles and procedures involved in writing, editing, or compiling dictionaries. **—lex′i·co·graph′ic** (-kə graf′ik), **lex′i·co·graph′i·cal, lex′i·co·graph′i·cal·ly,** *adv.*

lex·i·col·o·gy (lek′si kol′ə jē), *n.* the study of the formation, meaning, and use of words. **—lex′i·co·log′i·cal** (-kə loj′i kəl), **lex′i·co·log′ic,** *adj.* **—lex′i·col′o·gist,** *n.*

lex·i·con (lek′si kon′, -kən), *n., pl.* **-ca** (-kə), **-cons. 1.** a wordbook or dictionary, esp. of Greek, Latin, or Hebrew. **2.** the vocabulary of a particular language, field, social class, person, etc. **3.** inventory or record: *the lexicon of human relations.* **4.** the total inventory of words or morphemes in a given language.

lex·i·co·sta·tis·tics (lek′si kō stə tis′tiks), *n.* (*used with a sing. v.*) the statistical study of the vocabulary of a language or languages for historical purposes. Compare GLOTTOCHRONOLOGY. **—lex′i·co·sta·tis′tic, lex′i·co·sta·tis′ti·cal,** *adj.*

Lex·ing·ton (lek′sing tən), *n.* **1.** a town in E Massachusetts, NW of Boston: first battle of American Revolution fought here April 19, 1775. 29,479. **2.** a city in N Kentucky. 204,165.

lex·is (lek′sis), *n.* the vocabulary of a language, esp. as distinguished from its grammar; the total stock of words in a language; lexicon.

ley¹ (lā, lē), *n.* LEA.

ley² (lā), *n.* a pewter containing about 80 percent tin and 20 percent lead.

LF, low frequency.

lg. tn., long ton.

Lha·sa (lä′sə, -sä, las′ə), *n.* the capital of Tibet, in SW China: sacred city of Lamaism. 310,000.

Lha′sa ap′so (ap′sō), *n., pl.* **-sos.** one of a Tibetan breed of small dogs with a long, heavy, straight coat that falls over the face and a tail carried over the back.

Li, *Chem. Symbol.* lithium.

li·a·bil·i·ty (lī′ə bil′i tē), *n., pl.* **-ties. 1.** liabilities, **a.** moneys owed; debts or pecuniary obligations (opposed to *assets*). **b.** liabilities as detailed on a balance sheet, esp. in relation to assets and capital. **2.** something disadvantageous: *His lack of education is his biggest liability.* **3.** Also, **li′a·ble·ness.** the state or quality of being liable.

li·a·ble (lī′ə bəl), *adj.* **1.** legally responsible: *You are liable for the damage caused by your action.* **2.** subject or susceptible: *to be liable to heart disease.* **3.** likely or apt: *She's liable to get angry.*

li·aise (lē āz′), *v.i.,* **-aised, -ais·ing.** to form a liaison.

li·ai·son (lē ā′zən, lē′ā zôn′; lē′ə zon′ *or, often,* lā′ə-), *n.* **1.** the contact or connection maintained by communications between units of the armed forces or of any other organization in order to ensure concerted action, cooperation, etc. **2.** a person who initiates and maintains such a contact or connection. **3.** an illicit sexual relationship. **4.** a speech-sound redistribution, occurring esp. in French, in which an otherwise silent final consonant is articulated as the initial sound of a following word that begins with a vowel or silent *h,* as in *Je suis un homme* (zhə swē zœ nôm′).

li·a·na (lē ä′nə, -an′ə), *n., pl.* **-nas.** any of various usu. woody vines that may climb as high as the tree canopy in a tropical forest. Also, **li·ane** (lē än′). **—li·a′noid,** *adj.*

li·ar (lī′ər), *n.* a person who tells lies.

lib (lib), *n. Informal.* liberation: *women's lib; men's lib.*

li·ba·tion (lī bā′shən), *n.* **1.** a pouring out of wine or other liquid in honor of a deity. **2.** the liquid poured out. **3.** *Often Facetious.* **a.** an intoxicating beverage, as wine. **b.** an act or instance of drinking such a beverage. **—li·ba′tion·al, li·ba′tion·ar′y,** *adj.*

lib·ber (lib′ər), *n. Informal.* an advocate or member of a social liberation movement: *a women's libber.*

li·bel (lī′bəl), *n., v.,* **-beled, -bel·ing** *or* (*esp. Brit.*) **-belled, -bel·ling. —n. 1. a.** defamation by written or printed words, pictures, or the like, rather than by spoken words. **b.** the crime of publishing such matter. **2.** anything that is defamatory or that maliciously or damagingly misrepre-

sents. **—v.t. 3.** to publish a libel against. **4.** to misrepresent damagingly. **5.** to institute suit against by a libel, as in an admiralty court.

li·bel·er (lī′bə lər), *n.* a person who libels; a person who publishes a libel assailing another. Also, *esp. Brit.,* **li′bel·ler.**

li·bel·ous (lī′bə ləs), *adj.* containing, constituting, or involving a libel; maliciously or damagingly defamatory. Also, *esp. Brit.,* **li′bel·lous. —li′bel·ous·ly;** *esp. Brit.,* **li′bel·lous·ly,** *adv.*

lib·er·al (lib′ər əl, lib′rəl), *adj.* **1.** favorable to progress or reform, as in political or religious affairs. **2.** (*often cap.*) designating or pertaining to a political party advocating measures of progressive political reform. **3.** pertaining to, based on, or having views or policies advocating individual freedom of action and expression. **4.** of or pertaining to representational forms of government rather than aristocracies and monarchies. **5.** free from prejudice or bigotry; tolerant. **6.** free of or not bound by traditional or conventional ideas, values, etc.; open-minded. **7.** characterized by generosity and willingness to give in large amounts. **8.** given freely or abundantly; generous. **9.** not strict or rigorous; free; not literal: *a liberal interpretation of a rule.* **10.** of, pertaining to, or based on the liberal arts: *a liberal education.* **—n. 11.** a person of liberal principles or views. **12.** (*often cap.*) a member of a liberal political party, esp. the Liberal Party in Great Britain. **—lib′er·al·ly,** *adv.* **—lib′er·al·ness,** *n.*

lib′eral arts′, *n.pl.* **1.** academic college courses providing general knowledge and comprising the arts, humanities, natural sciences, and social sciences. **2.** (during the Middle Ages) studies comprising the quadrivium and trivium.

lib·er·al·ism (lib′ər ə liz′əm, lib′rə-), *n.* **1.** the quality or state of being liberal, as in behavior or attitude. **2.** a political and social philosophy advocating individual freedom, representational forms of government, progress and reform, and protection of civil liberties. **3.** (*sometimes cap.*) the principles and practices of a liberal party in politics. **4.** a movement in modern Protestantism that emphasizes freedom from tradition and authority in matters of belief.

Lib′eral Par′ty, *n.* **1.** a British political party formed in the 1830's as successor to the Whigs; dominant until World War I. **2.** any other political party advocating liberal policies.

lib·er·ate (lib′ə rāt′), *v.t.,* **-at·ed, -at·ing. 1.** to set free, as from imprisonment or bondage. **2.** to free (a nation or area) from control by a foreign or oppressive government. **3.** to free (a group or individual) from social or economic constraints or discrimination, esp. arising from traditional role expectations or bias. **4.** to disengage; set free from combination, as a gas. **5.** *Informal.* to steal or take over illegally: *The prisoners liberated a consignment of chocolates.* **—lib′er·a′tor,** *n.*

lib·er·a·tion (lib′ə rā′shən), *n.* **1.** the act of liberating or the state of being liberated. **2.** the gaining of equal rights or full social or economic opportunities for a particular group: *gay liberation.* **3.** the gaining of protection from abuse or exploitation: *animal liberation; children's liberation.* **—lib′er·a′tion·ist,** *n., adj.*

libera′tion theol′ogy, *n.* a modern Christian theology stressing liberation from racial, economic, and political oppression. **—libera′tion theolo′gian,** *n.*

Li·be·ri·a (lī bēr′ē ə), *n.* a republic in W Africa: founded by freed American slaves 1822. 2,602,068; ab. 43,000 sq. mi. (111,370 sq. km). *Cap.:* Monrovia. **—Li·be′ri·an,** *adj., n.*

Liberia

lib·er·tar·i·an (lib′ər târ′ē ən), *n.* **1.** a person who advocates liberty, esp. with regard to thought or conduct. **2.** a person who maintains the doctrine of free will (disting. from *necessitarian*). **—adj. 3.** advocating liberty or conforming to principles of liberty. **4.** maintaining the doctrine of free will. **—lib′er·tar′i·an·ism,** *n.*

lib·er·tine (lib′ər tēn′, -tin), *n.* **1.** a person who is morally or sexually unrestrained, esp. a dissolute man; a profligate; rake. **2.** a freethinker in religious matters. **3.** a person freed from slavery in ancient Rome. **—adj. 4.** free of moral, esp. sexual, restraint; dissolute; licentious. **5.** freethinking in religious matters.

lib·er·ty (lib′ər tē), *n., pl.* **-ties. 1.** freedom from arbitrary or despotic government or control. **2.** freedom from external or foreign rule; independence. **3.** freedom from control, interference, obligation, restriction, etc.; power or right of acting according to choice. **4.** freedom from captivity, confinement, or physical restraint. **5. a.** permission granted to a sailor to go ashore, usu. for less than 24 hours. **b.** the time spent ashore. **6.** freedom to frequent or use a place: *The visitors were given the liberty of the city.* **7.** unwarranted or impertinent freedom in action or speech, or a form or instance of it: *to take liberties.* **8.** a female figure personifying freedom from despotism. **—*Idiom.*** **9. at liberty, a.** free from captivity or restraint. **b.** unemployed; out of work. **c.** free to do or be as specified. **—*Saying.*** **10. Give me liberty or give me death!** death is preferable to tyranny: a statement (1775) by Patrick Henry.

Lib′erty Bell′, *n.* the bell of Independence Hall in Philadelphia, rung on July 8, 1776 to proclaim the adoption of the Declaration of Independence: moved behind Independence Hall in 1976.

Lib′erty Founda′tion, *n.* a political action group formed mainly of Protestant fundamentalists to further strict conservative aims, as strong antiabortion laws, the restoration of school prayer, the teaching of creationism in public schools, and the curbing of books and television programs considered antireligious or immoral. Formerly, **Moral Majority.**

lib′erty pole′, *n.* **1.** Also called **lib′erty tree′.** a pole or tree, often with a liberty cap or a banner at the top, usu. located on a village green or in a market square, used by the Sons of Liberty in many colonial towns as a symbol of protest against British rule and around which anti-British rallies were held. **2.** a tall flagpole, traditionally with a liberty cap at the top, serving as a symbol of liberty.

Lib′erty ship′, *n.* a slow cargo ship built in large numbers for the U.S. merchant marine during World War II and having a capacity of about 11,000 deadweight tons.

li•bid•i•nous (li bid′n əs), *adj.* **1.** full of lust; lustful; lewd; lascivious. **2.** of, pertaining to, or characteristic of the libido. **—li•bid′i•nous•ly,** *adv.* **—li•bid′i•nous•ness,** *n.*

li•bi•do (li bē′dō), *n., pl.* **-dos. 1.** *Psychoanal.* all of the instinctual energies and desires that are derived from the id. **2.** sexual instinct or drive. **—li•bid′i•nal** (-bid′n l), *adj.* **—li•bid′i•nal•ly,** *adv.*

Li•bra (lē′brə, lī′-), *n.* **1.** the Balance, a zodiacal constellation between Virgo and Scorpius. **2.** the seventh sign of the zodiac. [< Latin: pair of scales]

li•brar•i•an (lī brâr′ē ən), *n.* **1.** a person engaged in library work who has professional training in library science. **2. a.** the chief administrative officer of a library. **b.** any person in charge of a library. **3.** a person in charge of any specialized body of information, as a collection of musical scores. **—li•brar′i•an•ship′,** *n.*

li•brar•y (lī′brer′ē, -brə rē, -brē), *n., pl.* **-brar•ies. 1. a.** a place, as a building or set of rooms, containing books, recordings, or other reading, viewing, or listening materials arranged and cataloged in a fixed way. **b.** such a place together with the staff maintaining it, as a public facility funded by a government, as part of a school, business, etc., or as a private establishment. **2.** any collection of books, or the space containing them. **3.** any set of items resembling a library in appearance, organization, or purpose: *a library of computer software.* **4.** a series of books of similar character or alike in size, binding, etc., issued by a single publishing house. **5.** *Biol.* a collection of standard materials or formulations by which specimens are identified. **6.** CANON[1] (def. 8). **—Pronunciation.** LIBRARY, with two barely separated *r*-sounds, is particularly vulnerable to dissimilation—the tendency for neighboring like sounds to become unlike, or for one of them to disappear altogether. The pronunciation (lī′brer ē), therefore, while still the most common, is frequently reduced to the dissimilated (lī′bə rē) or (lī′brē). A third dissimilated form (lī′ber ē) is more likely to be heard from less educated or very young speakers and is often criticized. See COLONEL, FEBRUARY.

li′brary bind′ing, *n.* a tough, durable cloth binding for books.

li′brary card′, *n.* a card issued by a library that allows the holder to borrow books and other materials.

Li′brary of Con′gress, *n.* the national library of the U.S. in Washington, D.C.

li′brary sci′ence, *n.* the study of the organization and operation of a library.

li•bret•to (li bret′ō), *n., pl.* **-bret•tos, -bret•ti** (-bret′ē). **1.** the text of an opera or similar work. **2.** a book or booklet containing such a text. **—li•bret′tist,** *n.*

Li•bre•ville (*Fr.* lē brə vēl′), *n.* the capital of Gabon, in the W part, on the Gulf of Guinea. 350,000.

Lib•y•a (lib′ē ə), *n.* **1.** an ancient name of the part of N Africa W of Egypt. **2.** a republic in N Africa between Tunisia and Egypt: formerly a monarchy 1951–69. 5,648,359; 679,400 sq. mi. (1,759,646 sq. km). *Cap.:* Tripoli.

lice (līs), *n.* pl. of LOUSE.

li•cense (lī′səns), *n., v.,* **-censed, -cens•ing. —***n.* **1.** formal permission from a governmental or other constituted authority to do something, as to carry on some business or profession. **2.** a certificate, tag, plate, etc., giving proof of such permission; official permit: *a driver's license.* **3.** permission to do or not to do something. **4.** intentional deviation from rule, convention, or fact, as for the sake of literary or artistic effect: *poetic license.* **5.** exceptional freedom allowed in a special situation. **6.** excessive freedom or liberty. **—***v.t.* **7.** to issue or grant a license to. **8.** to give permission to; authorize. **—li′cens•a•ble,** *adj.* **—li′cens•er;** *esp. Law,* **li•cen•sor** (lī′sən sər, lī′sən sôr′), *n.*

li′censed prac′tical nurse′, *n.* a person who has completed a program in nursing and is licensed to provide basic nursing care under the supervision of a physician or registered nurse. *Abbr.:* LPN

li•cen•see or **li•cen•cee** (lī′sən sē′), *n.* a person, company, etc., to whom a license is granted or issued.

li′cense plate′, *n.* a plate or tag, usu. of metal, bearing evidence of official registration and permission, as for the use of a motor vehicle.

li•cen•ti•ate (lī sen′shē it, -āt′), *n.* a person who has received a license, as from a university, to practice an art or profession. **—li•cen′ti•ate•ship′,** *n.* **—li•cen′ti•a′tion,** *n.*

li•cen•tious (lī sen′shəs), *adj.* **1.** sexually unrestrained; lascivious; libertine; lewd. **2.** unrestrained by law or general morality; lawless; immoral. **3.** going beyond customary or proper bounds or limits; disregarding rules. **—li•cen′tious•ly,** *adv.* **—li•cen′tious•ness,** *n.*

li•chee (lē′chē), *n.* LITCHI.

li•chen (lī′kən), *n.* any complex organism of the group Lichenes, composed of a fungus in symbiotic union with an alga, most commonly forming crusty patches on rocks and trees.

lic•it (lis′it), *adj.* legal; lawful; legitimate. **—lic′it•ly,** *adv.*

lick (lik), *v.t.* **1.** to pass the tongue over the surface of, as to moisten, taste, or eat (often fol. by *up, off, from,* etc.): *to lick a postage stamp; to lick an ice-cream cone.* **2.** to make, or cause to become, by stroking with the tongue: *to lick a spoon clean.* **3.** (of waves, flames, etc.) to pass or play lightly over. **4.** *Informal.* **a.** to hit or beat, esp. as a punishment; thrash; whip. **b.** to defeat, as in a fight, or contest. **c.** to outdo or surpass. **—***v.i.* **5.** to move quickly or lightly. **6. lick up,** to lap up; devour greedily. **—***n.* **7.** a stroke of the tongue over something. **8.** as much as can be taken up by one stroke of the tongue. **9.** SALT LICK. **10.** *Informal.* **a.** a blow. **b.** a brief, brisk burst of activity or energy. **c.** a quick pace or clip; speed. **d.** a small amount: *I haven't done a lick of work all week.* **11.** Usu., **licks.** a musical phrase, as by a jazz soloist in improvising. **—*Idiom.*** **12. last licks,** a final turn or opportunity. **13. lick and a promise,** a hasty and perfunctory performance of a chore. **14. lick into shape,** *Informal.* to bring to completion or perfection through discipline, hard work, etc. **15. lick one's wounds,** to attempt to heal or soothe oneself after injury or defeat.

lick′e•ty-split′ (lik′i tē), *adv. Informal.* at great speed; rapidly: *to travel lickety-split.*

lick•ing (lik′ing), *n.* **1.** *Informal.* **a.** a beating. **b.** a reversal or disappointment; defeat or setback. **2.** the act of a person or thing that licks.

lick•spit•tle (lik′spit′l) also **lick′spit′,** *n.* a contemptible, fawning person; a servile flatterer or toady.

lic•o•rice (lik′ər ish, lik′rish, lik′ə ris), *n.* **1.** a Eurasian plant, *Glycyrrhiza glabra,* of the legume family. **2.** the sweet-tasting, dried root of this plant or an extract made from it, used in medicine, confectionery, etc. **3.** a candy flavored with licorice root.

lid (lid), *n., v.,* **lid•ded, lid•ding. —***n.* **1.** a removable or hinged cover for closing the opening, usu. at the top, of a pot, jar, trunk, etc.; a movable cover. **2.** an eyelid. **3.** a restraint, ceiling, or curb, as on prices or news. **—***v.t.* **4.** to supply or cover with a lid.

Li•di•ce (lē′də chā′, -tsā′, lid′ə sē), *n.* a village in the W Czech Republic: destroyed by the Nazis in 1942 in reprisal for the assassination of a high Nazi official. 509.

li•do•caine (lī′də kān′), *n.* a synthetic crystalline powder, $C_{14}H_{22}N_2O$, used as a local anesthetic and to treat certain arrhythmias.

lie[1] (lī), *n., v.,* **lied, ly•ing. —***n.* **1.** a false statement made with deliberate intent to deceive; a falsehood. **2.** something intended or serving to convey a false impression; imposture. **3.** the charge or accusation of lying: *He flung the lie back at his accusers.* **—***v.i.* **4.** to speak falsely or utter untruth knowingly, as with intent to deceive. **5.** to express what is false; convey a false impression. **—***v.t.* **6.** to bring about or affect by lying (often used reflexively): *to lie one's way out of a difficulty.* **—*Idiom.*** **7. give the lie to, a.** to accuse of lying. **b.** to prove the untruthfulness of; belie. **8. lie through one's teeth,** to tell a brazen, vicious lie. **—*Saying.*** **9. I cannot tell a lie,** I am unable to lie, a statement attributed to George Washington as a boy.

lie[2] (lī), *v.,* **lay, lain, ly•ing,** *n.* **—***v.i.* **1.** to be in or assume a horizontal, recumbent, or prostrate position, as on a bed or the ground; recline (often fol. by *down*). **2.** (of objects) to rest in a horizontal or flat position: *The book lies on the table.* **3.** to be or remain in a position or state of inactivity, restraint, concealment, etc.: *to lie in ambush.* **4.** to rest, press, or weigh (usu. fol. by *on* or *upon*): *These things lie upon my mind.* **5.** to be placed or situated: *land lying along the coast.* **6.** to be stretched out or extended: *the broad plain that lies before us.* **7.** to be in or have a specified direction; extend: *The trail from here lies to the west.* **8.** to be found or located in a particular area or place: *The fault lies here.* **9.** to consist or be grounded (usu. fol. by *in*): *The real remedy lies in education.* **10.** to be buried in a particular spot. **11.** *Law.* to be sustainable or admissible, as an action or appeal. **12. lie in,** to be confined to bed in childbirth. **13. lie over,** to be or become postponed. **14. lie to,** (of a ship) to lie comparatively stationary, usu. with the head as near the wind as possible. **15. lie up,** to lie at rest; stay in bed. **16. lie with,** to be the duty or function of. **—***n.* **17.** the manner, relative position, or direction in which something lies. **18.** the haunt or covert of an animal. **19.** *Golf.* the position of the ball relative to how easy or how difficult it is to play. **—*Idiom.*** **20. lie down on the job,** *Informal.* to do less than one could or should do; shirk one's obligations. **21. take lying down,** to accept or capitulate to without remonstrance.

Lieb•frau•milch (lēb′frou milk′, lēp′-; *Ger.* lēp′frou milkн′), *n.* a white wine produced chiefly in the region of Hesse in Germany.

Liech•ten•stein (lik′tən stīn′, likн′-), *n.* a small principality in central

Europe between Austria and Switzerland. 31,461; 65 sq. mi. (168 sq. km). *Cap.*: Vaduz. —**Liech′ten•stein′er,** *n.*

lied (lēd), *v.* pt. and pp. of LIE¹.

Lie•der•kranz (lē′dər kränts′, -krants′), *Trademark.* a strong, soft cheese with a creamy center, made in small rectangular blocks.

lie′ detec′tor, *n.* an instrument that produces a record of the changes in certain body activities, as blood pressure, pulse, breathing, and perspiration, which may be interpreted to indicate the truth of a person's answers under questioning. Also called **polygraph.**

liege (lēj, lēzh), *n.* **1.** a feudal lord entitled to allegiance and service. **2.** a feudal vassal or subject. —*adj.* **3.** entitled to or owing feudal allegiance and service. **4.** pertaining to the relation between a feudal vassal and lord.

lien (lēn, lē′ən), *n.* the legal right to hold another's property or to have it sold or applied for payment of a claim, esp. to satisfy a debt.

lieu (lōō), *n.* **1.** place; stead. —*Idiom.* **2. in lieu of,** in place of; instead of: *He gave us an IOU in lieu of cash.*

lieu•ten•ant (lōō ten′ənt; *in Brit. use, except in the navy,* lef ten′ənt), *n.* **1. a.** FIRST LIEUTENANT. **b.** SECOND LIEUTENANT. **2.** a commissioned officer in the U.S. Navy or Coast Guard ranking above a lieutenant junior grade. **3.** a person who holds an office, civil or military, in subordination to a superior for whom he or she acts: *If she can't attend, she will send her lieutenant.* —**lieu•ten′an•cy,** *n., pl.* **-cies.**

lieuten′ant colo′nel, *n.* a commissioned army or air force officer ranking above a major.

lieuten′ant comman′der, *n.* a commissioned officer in the U.S. Navy or Coast Guard ranking above a lieutenant.

lieuten′ant gen′eral, *n.* a commissioned army or air force officer ranking above a major general.

lieuten′ant gov′ernor, *n.* **1.** an official next in rank to the governor of a state. **2.** the chief executive of a Canadian province, appointed by the governor general. —**lieuten′ant gov′ernorship,** *n.*

lieuten′ant jun′ior grade′, *n.* a commissioned officer in the U.S. Navy or Coast Guard ranking above an ensign.

life (līf), *n., pl.* **lives** (līvz), *adj.* —*n.* **1.** the general condition that distinguishes organisms from inorganic objects and dead organisms, being manifested by growth through metabolism, a means of reproduction, and internal regulation in response to the environment. **2.** the animate existence or period of animate existence of an individual: *to risk one's life; a long life.* **3.** a corresponding state, existence, or principle of existence conceived of as belonging to the soul: *eternal life.* **4.** the general or universal condition of human existence: *Life is like that.* **5.** any specified period of animate existence: *a couple in middle life.* **6.** the period of existence, activity, or effectiveness of something inanimate, as a machine, lease, or play. **7.** a living being: *Several lives were lost in the fire.* **8.** living things collectively: *insect life.* **9.** a particular aspect of existence: *an active physical life.* **10.** the course of existence or sum of experiences and actions that constitute a person's existence. **11.** a biography: *a life of Willa Cather.* **12.** animation; liveliness; spirit: *The party was full of life.* **13.** resilience; elasticity. **14.** the force that makes or keeps something alive; the vivifying or quickening principle. **15.** a mode or manner of existence, as in the world of affairs or society. **16.** LIFE SENTENCE. **17.** anything or anyone considered to be as precious as life: *She was his life.* **18.** a person or thing that enlivens: *the life of the party.* **19.** effervescence or sparkle, as of wines. **20.** pungency or strong, sharp flavor, as of substances when fresh or in good condition. **21.** nature or any of the forms of nature as the model or subject of a work of art: *drawn from life.* **22.** (*cap.*) Jesus. John 14:6. —*adj.* **23.** for or lasting a lifetime; lifelong: *a life membership in a club; life imprisonment.* **24.** of or pertaining to animate existence: *life functions.* **25.** working from nature or using a living model: *a life drawing.* —*Idiom.* **26. bring to life, a.** to restore to consciousness. **b.** to make animated. **27. come to life, a.** to recover consciousness. **b.** to become animated. **c.** to appear lifelike. **28. for dear life,** with the most desperate effort possible. **29. for the life of one,** even with the utmost effort. **30. not on your life,** absolutely not. **31. take one's life in one's hands,** to risk death knowingly. **32. to the life,** in perfect imitation; exactly. —**life′less,** *adj.* —**life′less•ly,** *adv.* —**life′less•ness,** *n.* —**life′like,** *adj.*

life′-and-death′ also **life-or-death,** *adj.* involving possible loss of life; mortal; crucially important: *a life-and-death struggle.*

life•blood (līf′blud′), *n.* **1.** the blood, considered as essential to maintain life. **2.** a life-giving, vital, or animating element: *Agriculture is the lifeblood of the country.*

life•boat (līf′bōt′), *n.* a ship's boat, designed to be readily able to rescue and maintain persons from a sinking vessel.

life′ bu′oy, *n.* any of various buoyant devices for supporting a person fallen into the water.

life′-care′ or **life′care′,** *adj.* designed to provide for the basic needs of elderly residents, usu. in return for an initial fee and monthly service payments: *a life-care facility; life-care communities.*

life′ cy′cle, *n.* **1.** the sequence of developmental changes undergone by an organism from one primary form, as a gamete, to the recurrence of the same form in the next generation. **2.** a series of stages, as childhood and middle age, that characterize the course of existence of an individual, group, or culture.

life′ expect′ancy, *n.* the number of years an individual is expected to live, according to statistical estimates taking into account sex, physical condition, occupation, etc.

life′ force′, *n.* ÉLAN VITAL.

life•guard (līf′gärd′), *n.* **1.** an expert swimmer employed, as at a beach or pool, to protect bathers from drowning or other accidents and dangers. —*v.i.* **2.** to work as a lifeguard.

life′ his′tory, *n.* **1.** the history of developmental changes undergone by an organism from inception to death. **2.** LIFE CYCLE (def. 1).

life′ insur′ance, *n.* insurance providing for payment of a sum of money to a named beneficiary upon the death of the policyholder.

life′ jack′et, *n.* a life preserver in the form of a sleeveless jacket. Also called **life vest.**

Life′, lib′erty, and the pursuit′ of hap′piness, inalienable rights of human beings, as stated in the U.S. Declaration of Independence (1776).

life•line (līf′līn′), *n.* **1.** a line or rope for saving life, as one attached to a lifeboat. **2.** any of various lines running above the decks, spars, etc., of a ship or boat to give sailors something to grasp when there is danger of falling or being washed away. **3.** the line by which a diver is lowered and raised. **4.** any of several anchored lines used by swimmers for support. **5.** a route over which supplies must be sent to sustain an area or group of persons otherwise isolated.

life•long (līf′lông′, -long′), *adj.* lasting or continuing through all or much of one's life: *lifelong regret.*

life′ net′, *n.* a strong net or the like held by firefighters or others to catch persons jumping from a burning building.

life′ of Ri′ley, *n. Informal.* a carefree, comfortable life.

life′-or-death′, *adj.* LIFE-AND-DEATH.

life′ preserv′er, *n.* a buoyant jacket, belt, or other like device for keeping a person afloat.

lif•er (līf′ər), *n. Informal.* **1.** a person sentenced to or serving a term of life imprisonment. **2.** a person who has devoted a lifetime to a profession, occupation, or pursuit.

life′ raft′, *n.* a raft, often inflatable, for use in emergencies, as when a ship must be abandoned.

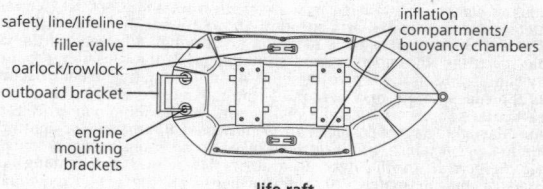

life raft

life•sav•er (līf′sā′vər), *n.* **1.** one who rescues another from danger of death, esp. from drowning. **2.** one that saves a person, as from a difficult situation or critical moment. —**life′sav′ing,** *adj., n.*

life′ sci′ence, *n.* any science that deals with living organisms, their life processes, and their interrelationships, as genetics, botany, and ecology. —**life′ sci′entist,** *n.*

life′ sen′tence, *n.* a sentence condemning a convicted felon to spend the rest of life in prison.

life′-size′ or **life′-sized′,** *adj.* of the natural size of an object, person, etc., in life: *a life-size statue.*

life′ span′, *n.* **1.** the longest period over which the life of any organism or species may extend. **2.** the longevity of an individual.

life′ style′ or **life′-style′,** *n.* the typical way of living, reflecting attitudes, preferences, etc., of an individual or group.

life′-support′, *adj.* of or pertaining to equipment or measures that sustain or artificially substitute for essential body functions, as breathing, or that allow humans to function within a hostile environment, as outer space or ocean depths.

life•time (līf′tīm′), *n.* **1.** the time that the life of someone or something continues; the term of a life: *peace within our lifetime.* —*adj.* **2.** for the duration of a person's life: *a lifetime membership.*

life′ vest′, *n.* LIFE JACKET.

life•work (līf′wûrk′), *n.* the complete or principal work, labor, or task of a lifetime.

LIFO (lī′fō), *n.* **1.** LAST-IN, FIRST-OUT (def. 1). **2.** a data storage and retrieval technique, usu. implemented using a queue, in which the last item stored is the first item retrieved.

lift (lift), *v.t.* **1.** to move or bring (something) upward from the ground or other support to a higher position; hoist. **2.** to raise or direct upward: *to lift one's head.* **3.** to remove or rescind by an official act, as a ban, curfew, or tax. **4.** to stop or put an end to (a boycott, blockade, etc.). **5.** to hold up or display on high. **6.** to raise in rank, condition, estimation, etc.; elevate or exalt. **7.** to make louder, as the voice or something voiced. **8.** *Informal.* to steal. **9.** AIRLIFT (def. 3). **10.** to remove (plants and tubers) from the ground, as after harvest or for transplanting. **11.** to pay off (a mortgage, promissory note, etc.). **12.** to cease temporarily from directing (fire or bombardment) on an objective or area. —*v.i.* **13.** to go up; yield to upward pressure: *The balloon lifted.* **14.** to pull or strain upward in the effort to raise something. **15.** to move upward or rise; rise and disperse, as clouds or fog. **16.** (of rain) to stop temporarily. **17.** to rise to view above the horizon when approached, as land seen from the sea. —*n.* **18.** the act of lifting, raising, or rising. **19.** the distance that anything rises or is raised. **20.** a lifting or raising force. **21.** the weight, load, or quantity lifted. **22.** an act or instance of lifting to climb or mount. **23.** a ride in a vehicle, esp. one given to a pedestrian. **24.** a feeling of exaltation or uplift. **25.** assistance or aid. **26.** a device or apparatus for lifting: *a hydraulic lift.* **27.** a movement in which a dancer, skater, etc., lifts up a partner. **28. a.** SKI LIFT. **b.** CHAIR LIFT. **29.** *Brit.* ELEVATOR (def. 2). **30.** *Informal.* a theft. **31.** a rise or elevation of ground. **32.** the component of force exerted by air on an airfoil in a direction perpendicular to the forward motion and opposite to the pull of gravity. **33.** the replaceable bottom layer of material on the heel of a boot or shoe. **34.** AIRLIFT (defs. 1, 2). —*Idiom.* **35. lift a finger** or **hand,** to exert any effort at all.

Lift′ Ev′ery Voice and Sing′, a hymn (1900) with words by James Weldon Johnson and music by J. Rosamund Johnson. Also called "The Black National Anthem."

lift′off′ or **lift′-off′,** *n.* **1.** the action of an aircraft in becoming airborne or of a rocket in rising from its launching site under its own power. **2.** the instant when such action occurs.

lig•a•ment (lig′ə mənt), *n.* a band of strong connective tissue serving to connect bones or hold organs in place.

li•gand (lī′gənd, lig′ənd), *n.* **1.** a molecule, as an antibody, hormone, or drug, that binds to a receptor. **2.** a molecule, ion, or atom that is bonded to the central metal atom of a coordination compound.

lig•a•ture (lig′ə chər, -chŏŏr′), *n., v.,* **-tured, -tur•ing.** —*n.* **1.** the act of binding or tying up. **2.** anything that serves for binding or tying up, as a band, bandage, or cord. **3.** a tie or bond. **4.** a stroke or bar connecting two letters. **5.** a character or type combining two or more letters, as *fl* and *ffl.* **6.** a group of musical notes connected by a slur. **7.** a thread or wire for surgical constriction of blood vessels or for removing tumors by strangulation. —*v.t.* **8.** to bind with a ligature; tie up.

light¹ (līt), *n., adj.,* **light•er, light•est,** *v.,* **light•ed** or **lit, light•ing.** —*n.* **1.** something that makes things visible or affords illumination: *All colors depend on light.* **2.** electromagnetic radiation to which the organs of sight react, ranging in wavelength from about 400 to 700 nanometers and propagated at about 186,282 miles per second (299,972 km/sec). **b.** electromagnetic radiation just beyond either end of the visible spectrum; ultraviolet or infrared radiation. **3.** the sensation produced by stimulation of the organs of sight. **4.** an illuminating agent or source, as the sun, a lamp, or a beacon. **5.** the radiance or illumination from a particular source, as a candle or the sun. **6.** the illumination from the sun; daylight, daybreak, or dawn. **7.** daytime. **8.** a particular light or illumination in which an object seen takes on a certain appearance: *viewing the portrait in dim light.* **9.** a device for or means of igniting, as a spark, flame, or match. **10.** a traffic light. **11.** the aspect in which a thing appears or is regarded: *Try to look at the situation in a better light.* **12.** *Art.* **a.** the effect of light falling on an object or scene as represented in a picture. **b.** one of the brightest parts of a picture. **13.** a gleam or sparkle, as in the eyes. **14.** illumination. **15.** spiritual illumination or awareness; enlightenment. **16.** a window, or a pane or compartment of a window. **17.** mental insight; understanding. **18. lights,** the information, ideas, or mental capacities possessed: *to act according to one's lights.* **19.** a lighthouse. —*adj.* **20.** having light or illumination; bright; well-lighted. **21.** pale, whitish, or not deep or dark in color: *a light blue.* **22.** (of coffee or tea) containing enough milk or cream to produce a light color. —*v.t.* **23.** to set burning, as a candle, lamp, fire, match, or cigarette; kindle; ignite. **24.** to turn on or switch on (an electric light): *to light the lamp.* **25.** to give light to; furnish with light or illumination: *to light a room.* **26.** to make (an area or object) bright with or as if with light (often fol. by *up*). **27.** to cause (the face, surroundings, etc.) to brighten, esp. with joy, animation, or the like (often fol. by *up*): *A smile lit up her face.* **28.** to guide or conduct with a light. —*v.i.* **29.** to take fire or become kindled. **30.** to ignite a cigar, cigarette, or pipe for purposes of smoking (usu. fol. by *up*). **31.** to become illuminated when switched on: *This table lamp won't light.* **32.** to become bright, as with light or color (often fol. by *up*): *The sky lights up at sunrise.* **33.** to brighten with animation or joy, as the face or eyes (often fol. by *up*). —*Idiom.* **34. bring to light,** to discover or reveal. **35. come to light,** to be discovered or revealed. **36. in a good** (or **bad**) **light,** under favorable (or unfavorable) circumstances. **37. in (the) light of,** taking into account; because of; considering. **38. light at the end of the tunnel,** a prospect of success, relief, or redemption. **39. see the light, a.** to come into existence or prominence. **b.** to understand mentally at last. **40. shed** or **throw light on,** to clarify. —*Proverb.* **41. Better to light one little candle than to curse the darkness,** even small actions help to dispel the wrongs of the world. **42. Let there be light,** God's command to create the universe out of the void. Gen. 1:3.

light² (līt), *adj.* **1.** of little weight; not heavy: *a light load.* **2.** of little weight in proportion to bulk; of low specific gravity: *a light metal.* **3.** of less than the usual or average weight: *light clothing.* **4.** weighing less than the proper or standard amount: *a light rain; light sleep.* **6.** using or applying little or slight pressure or force. **7.** not distinct; faint. **8.** easy to endure, deal with, or perform; not difficult or burdensome: *light duties.* **9.** not very profound or serious; amusing or entertaining: *light reading.* **10.** of little importance or consequence; trivial: *The loss of a job is no light matter.* **11.** easily digested: *light food.* **12.** not rich or heavy: *a light snack.* **13.** (of alcoholic beverages) **a.** not heavy or strong: *a light apéritif.* **b.** (esp. of

beer and wine) having fewer calories and usu. a lower alcohol content than the standard product. **14.** spongy or well-leavened, as cake. **15.** (of soil) containing much sand; porous or crumbly. **16.** slender or delicate in form or appearance. **17.** airy or buoyant in movement; nimble or agile: *light on one's feet.* **18.** free from trouble, sorrow, or worry; cheerful; carefree: *a light heart.* **19.** characterized by lack of proper seriousness; frivolous. **20.** easily swayed; changeable; volatile. **21.** dizzy; slightly delirious. **22.** (of soldiers) lightly armed or equipped: *light cavalry.* **23.** having little or no cargo, encumbrance, or the like; not burdened: *a light freighter.* **24.** adapted by small weight or slight build for small loads or swift movement: *a light truck.* **25.** using small-scale machinery primarily for the production of consumer goods: *light industry.* **26.** (of a syllable) **a.** unstressed. **b.** short. —*adv.* **27.** without much or extra baggage: *to travel light.* **28.** LIGHTLY.

light³ (līt), *v.i.,* **light•ed** or **lit, light•ing.** **1.** to get down or descend, as from a horse or a vehicle. **2.** to come to rest, as on a spot or thing; fall or settle upon; land: *The bird lighted on the branch. My eye lighted on some friends in the crowd.* **3. light into,** to attack physically or verbally. **4. light out,** *Informal.* to depart quickly.

light′ adapta′tion, *n.* the reflex adjustment of the eye to bright light, consisting of a constriction of the pupil, an increase in the number of functioning cones, and a decrease in the number of functioning rods. —**light′-a•dapt′ed,** *adj.*

light′ breeze′, *n.* a wind of 4–7 miles per hour (2–3 m/sec).

light′ bulb′, *n.* an electric light bulb; incandescent lamp.

light′ cream′, *n.* sweet cream with less butterfat than heavy cream.

light′-du′ty, *adj.* adapted or designed to withstand comparatively moderate loads, use, or stress: *light-duty trucks.* Compare HEAVY-DUTY.

light′-emit′ting di′ode, *n.* LED.

light•en¹ (līt′n), *v.i.* **1.** to become lighter or less dark; brighten. **2.** to brighten or light up, as the eyes or features. **3.** to flash as or like lightning. —*v.t.* **4.** to give light to; illuminate. **5.** to brighten (the eyes, features, etc.). **6.** to make lighter or less dark. —**light′en•er,** *n.*

light•en² (līt′n), *v.t.* **1.** to make lighter in weight. **2.** to lessen the load of or upon. **3.** to make less burdensome or oppressive; mitigate: *to lighten taxes.* **4.** to cheer or gladden: *Such news lightens my heart.* —*v.i.* **5.** to become less severe, stringent, or harsh; ease up. **6.** to become less heavy, burdensome, or oppressive. **7.** to become less gloomy; perk up. **8. lighten up,** to become less serious or earnest.

light′er-than-air′, *adj.* **1.** (of an aircraft) weighing less than the air it displaces, hence obtaining lift from aerostatic buoyancy. **2.** of or pertaining to lighter-than-air craft.

light•face (līt′fās′), *n.* **1.** a printing type characterized by thin, light lines. —*adj.* **2.** Also, **light′-faced′.** (of printed matter) set in lightface. Compare BOLDFACE.

Light•foot (līt′fŏŏt′), *n.* **Joseph Barber,** 1828–89, English clergyman and Bible scholar.

light′-foot′ed, *adj.* stepping lightly or nimbly; light of foot; nimble. —**light′-foot′ed•ly,** *adv.* —**light′-foot′ed•ness,** *n.*

light•head•ed (līt′hed′id), *adj.* **1.** giddy, dizzy, or delirious. **2.** having or showing a frivolous or volatile disposition; thoughtless. —**light′-head′ed•ly,** *adv.* —**light′head′ed•ness,** *n.*

light•heart•ed (līt′här′tid), *adj.* carefree; cheerful; gay. —**light′-heart′ed•ly,** *adv.* —**light′heart′ed•ness,** *n.*

light′ heav′yweight, *n.* a boxer intermediate in weight between a middleweight and a heavyweight, esp. a professional boxer weighing up to 175 lb. (80 kg).

light•house (līt′hous′), *n., pl.* **-hous•es** (-hou′ziz). a tower or other structure displaying a light or lights for the guidance of mariners.

lighthouse

light•ing (lī′ting), *n.* **1.** the act of igniting or illuminating. **2.** the arrangement of lights to achieve particular effects. **3.** an effect achieved by the arrangement of lights. **4.** the way light falls upon a face, object, etc., esp. in a picture.

light•ly (līt′lē), *adv.* **1.** with little weight, force, intensity, etc.; gently. **2.** to only a small amount or degree; slightly: *lightly fried eggs.* **3.** nimbly; quickly. **4.** with a lack of concern; indifferently. **5.** cheerfully; without complaining: *to take bad news lightly.* **6.** without due consideration or reason (often used negatively): *an offer not to be refused lightly.* **7.** easily; without trouble or effort: *His success did not come lightly.* **8.** frivolously; flippantly. **9.** airily; buoyantly.

light′ me′ter, *n.* EXPOSURE METER.

light•ness[1] (līt′nis), *n.* **1.** the state or quality of being light or illuminated. **2.** a thin or pale coloration.

light•ness[2] (līt′nis), *n.* **1.** the state or quality of being light in weight. **2.** the quality of being agile, nimble, or graceful. **3.** lack of pressure or burdensomeness. **4.** lack of seriousness; levity in actions, thoughts, or speech. **5.** gaiety of manner, speech, style, etc.

light•ning (līt′ning), *n.* **1.** a brilliant electric spark discharge in the atmosphere, occurring within a thundercloud, between clouds, or between a cloud and the ground. —*v.i.* **2.** to emit a flash or flashes of lightning (often used impersonally with *it* as subject): *Go inside if it starts to lightning.* —*adj.* **3.** of, pertaining to, or resembling lightning, esp. in regard to speed of movement: *lightning flashes; lightning speed.* —***Saying.*** **4. Lightning never strikes twice in the same place,** events are unique in their timing and circumstances.

light′ning arrest′er, *n.* a device for preventing damage to radio, telephonic, or other electric equipment from lightning or other high-voltage currents.

light′ning bug′, *n.* FIREFLY.

light′ning rod′, *n.* **1.** a rodlike metallic conductor installed to divert lightning away from a structure by providing a direct path to the ground. **2.** a person or thing that attracts negative feelings, opinions, etc., thereby diverting them from other targets.

Light′ of the World′, *n.* Jesus Christ. John 8:12; 9:5; 12:46.

light′ op′era, *n.* OPERETTA.

light′ pen′, *n.* a hand-held light-sensitive input device used for drawing on a computer display screen or for pointing at characters or objects, as when choosing options from a menu.

light•plane (līt′plān′), *n.* a lightweight passenger airplane with relatively limited performance capability.

light′ show′, *n.* an entertainment consisting of changing patterns of light and color, often accompanied by music and sound effects.

lights′ out′, *n.* **1.** an order, usu. by bugle, that all camp or barrack lights are to be extinguished immediately. **2.** bedtime.

light•weight (līt′wāt′), *adj.* **1.** light in weight: *a lightweight topcoat.* **2.** without seriousness of purpose; trivial or trifling. **3.** of or pertaining to a lightweight: *the new lightweight contender.* —*n.* **4.** a person of less than average weight. **5.** *Informal.* a person who is of little influence, importance, or effect. **6.** a boxer intermediate in weight between a featherweight and a welterweight, esp. a professional boxer weighing up to 135 lb. (61 kg). **7.** a weightlifter intermediate in weight between a featherweight and a middleweight.

light′-year′, *n.* **1.** the distance traversed by light in one mean solar year, about 5.88 trillion mi. (9.46 trillion km): used as a unit in measuring stellar distances. **2. light-years, a.** a very great distance, esp. in development or progress: *Today's computers are light-years ahead of older ones.* **b.** a very long time.

lig•ne•ous (lig′nē əs), *adj.* of the nature of or resembling wood; woody.

lig•ni•form (lig′nə fôrm′), *adj.* having the form of wood; resembling wood.

lig•ni•fy (lig′nə fī′), *v.*, **-fied, -fy•ing.** —*v.t.* **1.** to convert into wood; cause to become woody. —*v.i.* **2.** to become wood or woody. —**lig′ni•fi•ca′tion,** *n.*

lig•nite (lig′nīt), *n.* a soft coal, usu. dark brown, often having a distinct woodlike texture, and intermediate in density and carbon content between peat and bituminous coal. —**lig•nit′ic** (-nit′ik), *adj.*

lig•ure (lig′yŏŏr), *n.* a precious stone, possibly an orange zircon. Ex. 28:19.

Ligu′rian Sea′, *n.* a part of the Mediterranean between Corsica and the NW coast of Italy.

lik•a•ble or **like•a•ble** (lī′kə bəl), *adj.* readily or easily liked; pleasing. —**lik′a•ble•ness, lik′a•bil′i•ty,** *n.*

like[1] (līk), *adj.*, (*Poetic*) **lik•er, lik•est,** *prep., adv., conj., n., interj.* —*adj.* **1.** of the same form, appearance, kind, character, amount, etc.: *I cannot remember a like instance.* **2.** corresponding or agreeing in general or in some noticeable respect; similar; analogous: *drawing, painting, and like arts.* **3.** bearing resemblance. **4.** *Dial.* likely. —*prep.* **5.** similarly to; in the manner characteristic of: *She works like a beaver.* **6.** resembling; similar to: *Your necklace is like mine.* **7.** characteristic of: *It would be like him to forget our appointment.* **8.** as if there is promise of; indicative of: *It looks like rain.* **9.** disposed or inclined to (usu. prec. by *feel*): *to feel like going to bed.* **10.** (used correlatively to indicate similarity through relationship): *like father, like son.* **11.** (used to establish an intensifying, often facetious, comparison): *ran like hell; sleeps like a log.* —*adv.* **12.** nearly; approximately: *The house is more like 40 years old.* **13.** *Informal.* likely or probably: *Like enough he'll come with us.* —*conj.* **14.** in the same way as; just as; as: *It happened like you said it would.* **15.** as if: *He acted like he was afraid.* —*n.* **16.** a similar or comparable person or thing, or persons or things; counterpart, match, or equal (usu. prec. by a possessive adjective or *the*): *No one has seen her like in a long time.* **17.** kind; sort; type; ilk (usu. prec. by a possessive adjective): *I despise toadies and their like.* **18. the like,** something of a similar nature: *They grow oranges, lemons, and the like.* —*interj.* **19.** *Informal.* (used preceding a WH-word, an answer to a question, or other information in a sentence on which the speaker wishes to focus attention): *Like, why didn't you write to me? The music was, like, really great.* **20.** *Chiefly Brit. Informal.* (used following an adjective, phrase, or clause, usu. implying that the description or evaluation therein is the speaker's own characterization of the matter): *standing against the wall, looking very tough, like.* —***Idiom.*** **21. like anything, blazes, crazy,** or **mad,** *Informal.* extremely; extensively: *I ran like crazy.* **22. like to** or **liked to,** *Nonstandard.* was on the verge of or came close to (doing something): *The poor kid like to froze.* **23. something like,** approximately the same as. **24. the like** or **likes of,** the equal of. —**lik′er,** *n.* —**Usage.** LIKE[1] as a conjunction meaning "as, in the same way as" (*Many shoppers study the food ads like brokers study market reports*) or "as if" (*It looks like it will rain*) has been used for nearly 500 years and by many distinguished literary and intellectual figures. Since the mid-19th century there have been objections to these uses. Nevertheless, such uses are almost universal today in all but the most formal speech and writing, in which *as, as if,* and *as though* are more commonly used than LIKE: *The general accepted full responsibility for the incident, as any professional soldier would. Many of the bohemians lived as if* (or *as though*) *there were no tomorrow.* The strong strictures against the use of LIKE as a conjunction have resulted in the occasional hypercorrect use of *as* as a preposition where LIKE is idiomatic: *She looks as a sympathetic person.* See also AS.

like[2] (līk), *v.*, **liked, lik•ing,** *n.* —*v.t.* **1.** to take pleasure in; find agreeable or congenial to one's taste: *to like opera.* **2.** to regard with favor; have a kindly or friendly feeling for (a person, group, etc.). **3.** to wish or want: *I'd like a piece of cake.* —*v.i.* **4.** to feel inclined; wish: *Stay if you like.* —*n.* **5.** Usu., **likes.** the things a person likes.

-like, a suffixal use of LIKE[1] in the formation of adjectives: *childlike; lifelike.*

like•a•ble (lī′kə bəl), *adj.* LIKABLE.

like•ly (līk′lē), *adj.*, **-li•er, -li•est,** *adv.* —*adj.* **1.** probably or apparently destined (usu. fol. by an infinitive): *something not likely to happen.* **2.** seeming like truth, fact, or certainty; believable: *a likely story.* **3.** seeming to fulfill requirements or expectations; apparently suitable: *a likely place to live.* **4.** showing promise of achievement or excellence; promising. —*adv.* **5.** probably: *We will most likely stay home this evening.* —**like′li•hood′, like′li•ness,** *n.*

like′-mind′ed, *adj.* having a similar or identical opinion, disposition, etc. —**like′-mind′ed•ly,** *adv.* —**like′-mind′ed•ness,** *n.*

lik•en (lī′kən), *v.t.* to represent as similar or like; compare: *to liken someone to a weasel.*

like•ness (līk′nis), *n.* **1.** a portrait; copy. **2.** the state or fact of being like or similar. **3.** the semblance or appearance of something; guise.

like•wise (līk′wīz′), *adv.* **1.** moreover; in addition; also; too. **2.** in like manner; in the same way; similarly: *I'm tempted to do likewise.*

lik•ing (lī′king), *n.* **1.** preference, inclination, or favor: *a liking for popular music.* **2.** pleasure or taste: *much to our liking.* **3.** the state or feeling of a person who likes.

li•lac (lī′lək, -läk, -lak), *n.* **1.** any shrub of the genus *Syringa,* of the olive family, as *S. vulgaris,* having large clusters of fragrant purple or white flowers. **2.** pale reddish purple. —*adj.* **3.** having the color lilac.

Lil•li•put (lil′i put′, -pət), *n.* an imaginary country inhabited by people about 6 in. (15 cm) tall, described in Swift's *Gulliver's Travels* (1726).

Lil•li•pu•tian (lil′i pyōō′shən), *adj.* **1.** extremely small; tiny. **2.** petty. —*n.* **3.** an inhabitant of Lilliput. **4.** a very small person.

Li•long•we (li lông′wā), *n.* the capital of Malawi, in the SW part. 186,800.

lilt (lilt), *n.* **1.** rhythmic swing or cadence. **2.** a lilting song or tune. —*v.i., v.t.* **3.** to sing or play in a light, or rhythmic manner. —**lilt′ing•ly,** *adv.*

lil•y (lil′ē), *n., pl.* **lil•ies,** *adj.* —*n.* **1.** any scaly-bulbed plant of the genus *Lilium,* having showy, funnel-shaped or bell-shaped flowers. **2.** the flower or the bulb of such a plant. **3.** any of various related or similar plants or their flowers, as the mariposa lily or the calla lily. **4.** FLEUR-DE-LIS (def. 1). —*adj.* **5.** white as a lily: *her lily hands.*

lil′y-liv′ered, *adj.* weak or lacking in courage; cowardly.

lil′y of the val′ley, *n., pl.* **lilies of the valley. 1.** a plant, *Convallaria majalis,* of the lily family, having an elongated cluster of small, drooping, bell-shaped, fragrant white flowers. **2.** a plant mentioned in the Bible. Song of Solomon 2:10.

lil′y pad′, *n.* the large, floating leaf of a water lily.

lil′y-white′, *adj.* **1.** white as a lily. **2.** pure; untouched by corruption or imperfection. **3.** designating or pertaining to any faction or group opposing the inclusion of blacks in political or social life.

Li•ma (lē′mə), *n.* the capital of Peru, near the Pacific coast. 4,605,043.

li′ma bean′ (lī′mə), *n.* **1.** a bean, *Phaseolus limensis,* having a broad, flat, edible seed. **2.** the seed.

limb (lim), *n.* **1.** one of the paired bodily appendages of animals, used esp. for moving or grasping; a leg, arm, or wing. **2.** a large or main branch of a tree. —***Idiom.*** **3. out on a limb,** in a risky or vulnerable situation. —**limb′less,** *adj.*

lim•ber (lim′bər), *adj.* **1.** characterized by ease in bending the body; supple; lithe. **2.** bending readily; flexible; pliant. —*v.i.* **3.** to make oneself limber (usu. fol. by *up*): *to limber up before the game.* —*v.t.* **4.** to make (something) limber (usu. fol. by *up*). —**lim′ber•ness,** *n.*

lim′bic sys′tem, *n.* a group of structures in the brain that include the hippocampus, olfactory bulbs, hypothalamus, and amygdala and are associated with emotion and homeostasis.

lim•bo[1] (lim′bō), *n., pl.* **-bos. 1.** (*often cap.*) a region on the border of hell or heaven in Roman Catholic teaching, serving as the abode after death of unbaptized infants and of the righteous who died before the coming of Christ. **2.** a place or state of oblivion for persons or things cast aside, forgotten, or out of date. **3.** an intermediate, transitional, or midway state or place. **4.** a place or state of imprisonment or confinement. [< Medieval Latin *in limbō* on hell's border (Latin: on the edge)]

lim•bo² (lim′bō), *n., pl.* **-bos.** a dance from the West Indies in which the dancer bends backward from the knees and moves with a shuffling step under a horizontal bar that is lowered after each successive pass. [cf. Jamaican English *limba* limber]

lime¹ (līm), *n., v.,* **limed, lim•ing.** *—n.* **1.** a white or grayish white, odorless, lumpy, very slightly water-soluble solid, CaO, used chiefly in mortars, plasters, and cements, in bleaching powder, and in the manufacture of steel, paper, glass, and various chemicals of calcium. **2.** a calcium compound for improving crops grown in soils deficient in lime. **3.** BIRDLIME. *—v.t.* **4.** to treat (soil) with lime or compounds of calcium. **5.** to smear (twigs, branches, etc.) with birdlime. **6.** to catch with or as if with birdlime. **7.** to paint or cover (a surface) with a composition of lime and water; whitewash. —**lim′i•ness,** *n.* —**lim′y,** *adj.,* **-i•er, -i•est.**

lime² (līm), *n.* **1.** the small, greenish yellow, acid fruit of a citrus tree, *Citrus aurantifolia,* allied to the lemon. **2.** the tree that bears this fruit. **3.** a greenish yellow. *—adj.* **4.** of the color lime. **5.** of or made with limes.

lime³ (līm), *n.* the European linden, *Tilia europaea.*

lime•ade (līm′ād′, līm′ād′), *n.* a beverage of lime juice, sugar, and water.

lime•light (līm′līt′), *n.* **1.** a position at the center of public attention, interest, observation, or notoriety: *an artist in the limelight.* **2.** (formerly) a spotlight unit for the stage, using a flame of mixed gases directed at a cylinder of lime and a special lens to concentrate the light in a strong beam. —**lime′light′er,** *n.*

lime•stone (līm′stōn′), *n.* a sedimentary rock consisting predominantly of calcium carbonate, varieties of which are formed from the skeletons of marine microorganisms and coral: used as a building stone and in the manufacture of lime.

lime•wood (līm′wo͝od′), *n.* the wood of a linden.

lim•it (lim′it), *n.* **1.** the final, utmost, or furthest boundary or point as to extent, amount, continuance, etc. **2.** a boundary or bound, as of a country or district. **3. limits,** the premises or region enclosed within boundaries. **4.** *Math.* a number such that the value of a given function remains arbitrarily close to this number when the independent variable is sufficiently close to a specified point or is sufficiently large. **5.** the maximum sum by which a bet may be raised at any one time. **6. the limit,** *Informal.* something or someone that exasperates, delights, etc., to an extreme degree. *—v.t.* **7.** to restrict by or as if by establishing limits: *Please limit answers to 25 words.* **8.** to confine or keep within limits: *to limit expenditures.* —**lim′it•a•ble,** *adj.* —**lim′i•ta′tion,** *n.*

lim•it•ed (lim′i tid), *adj.* **1.** confined within limits; restricted or circumscribed. **2.** restricted in governing powers by limitations prescribed in laws and in a constitution: *a limited monarchy.* **3.** unimaginative; lacking originality. **4.** *Chiefly Brit.* (*usu. cap.*) incorporated; Inc. *Abbr.:* Ltd. **5.** (of trains, buses, etc.) making only a limited number of stops en route. *—n.* **6.** a limited train, bus, etc. —**lim′it•ed•ly,** *adv.*

lim′ited edi′tion, *n.* an edition, as of a book or lithograph, limited to a specified small number of copies.

lim′ited part′nership, *n.* a partnership in which the liability of at least one of the partners is limited to the amount that partner has invested. Compare GENERAL PARTNERSHIP.

lim′ited war′, *n.* a war conducted with deliberately restricted aims and resources by at least one of the belligerents.

lim•it•ing (lim′i ting), *adj.* **1.** serving to restrict or restrain; restrictive; confining. **2.** (of an adjective or other modifier) serving to restrict, rather than describe, the word it modifies, as *this* in *this room* or *certain* in *a certain person.* Compare DESCRIPTIVE (def. 2a).

limn (lim), *v.t.* **1.** to represent in drawing or painting. **2.** to outline; delineate. **3.** to portray in words; describe.

lim•o (lim′ō), *n., pl.* **lim•os.** *Informal.* a limousine.

li•mo•nite (lī′mə nīt′), *n.* a brown-to-yellow mineral mixture, mostly noncrystalline iron hydroxide with hematite and goethite: an ore of iron. —**li′mo•nit′ic** (-nit′ik), *adj.*

lim•ou•sine (lim′ə zēn′, lim′ə zēn′), *n.* **1.** any large, luxurious automobile, esp. one driven by a chauffeur. **2.** a large sedan or small bus for transporting passengers to and from an airport, train station, etc.

lim′ousine lib′eral, *n.* *Informal.* one who espouses the cause of the poor or underprivileged without practical understanding of their lives.

limp¹ (limp), *v.i.* **1.** to walk with a labored movement, as when lame. **2.** to proceed in a lame, faltering, or labored manner. **3.** to progress with great difficulty; make little or no advance. *—n.* **4.** a lame movement or gait. —**limp′er,** *n.* —**limp′ing•ly,** *adv.*

limp² (limp), *adj.* **1.** lacking stiffness or rigidity, as of substance or structure: *a limp body.* **2.** weary; tired; fatigued. —**limp′ly,** *adv.* —**limp′ness,** *n.*

lim•pet (lim′pit), *n.* any of various marine gastropods with a low conical shell open beneath, usu. adhering to rocks.

lim•pid (lim′pid), *adj.* **1.** clear, transparent, or pellucid, as water, crystal, or air. **2.** free from obscurity; lucid; clear: *limpid prose.* **3.** completely calm. —**lim•pid′i•ty, lim′pid•ness,** *n.* —**lim′pid•ly,** *adv.*

linch•pin (linch′pin′), *n.* **1.** a pin inserted through the end of an axletree to keep the wheel on. **2.** something that holds the various elements of a complicated structure together.

Lin•coln (ling′kən), *n.* **1. Abraham,** 1809–65, 16th president of the U.S. 1861–65. **2.** the capital of Nebraska, in the SE part. 203,076. **3.** a city in Lincolnshire, in E central England. 73,200. **4.** LINCOLNSHIRE. **5.** one of an English breed of large mutton sheep noted for their heavy fleece of coarse, long wool.

Lin•coln•esque (ling′kə nesk′), *adj.* like or characteristic of Abraham Lincoln.

Lin′coln green′, *n.* an olive-green color.

Lin′coln's Birth′day, *n.* **1.** February 12, a legal holiday in some states of the U.S., in honor of the birth of Abraham Lincoln. **2.** PRESIDENTS' DAY.

Lin•coln•shire (ling′kən shēr′, -shər), *n.* a county in E England. 574,600; 2272 sq. mi. (5885 sq. km). Also called **Lincoln.**

Lin′coln's Sec′ond Inau′gural Address′, *n.* a speech given by Abraham Lincoln on March 4, 1865, during which he urged that the nation should deal with the aftermath of the Civil War "with malice toward none, with charity for all."

Lind•bergh (lind′bûrg, lin′-), *n.* **1. Anne (Spencer) Morrow,** born 1906, U.S. writer (wife of Charles Augustus Lindbergh). **2. Charles Augustus,** 1902–74, U.S. aviator: made the first solo nonstop transatlantic flight in 1927.

lin•den (lin′dən), *n.* **1.** any tree of the genus *Tilia,* of the linden family, as *T. americana,* of North America, or *T. europaea,* of Europe, having fragrant yellowish white flowers and heart-shaped toothed leaves. **2.** the soft, light, white wood of any of these trees. Compare BASSWOOD.

line¹ (līn), *n., v.,* **lined, lin•ing.** *—n.* **1.** a long mark of very slight breadth, made with a pen, pencil, tool, etc., on a surface. **2.** a continuous extent of length, straight or curved, without breadth or thickness; the trace of a moving point. **3.** something arranged along a line, esp. a straight line; a row: *a line of trees.* **4.** a number of persons standing one behind the other and waiting their turns at or for something; queue. **5.** something resembling a traced line, as a seam or furrow: *lines of stratification in rock.* **6.** a furrow or wrinkle on the face, neck, etc. **7.** an indication of demarcation; boundary; limit: *the county line; a fine line between right and wrong.* **8.** a row of written or printed letters, words, etc. **9.** a unit in the metrical structure of a poem or lyric, composed of feet. **10.** Usu., **lines.** the words of an actor's part in a drama, musical comedy, etc. **11.** a short written message: *Drop me a line when you're on vacation.* **12.** a system of public conveyances, as buses or trains, plying regularly over a fixed route. **13.** a transportation company: *a steamship line.* **14.** a course of direction; route: *the line of march.* **15.** a course of action, procedure, thought, policy, etc.: *That newspaper follows a conservative line.* **16.** a piece of pertinent or useful information: *I've got a line on a good used car.* **17.** a series of generations of persons, animals, or plants descended from a common ancestor: *a line of kings.* **18.** a person's occupation or business: *What line are you in?* **19.** *Informal.* a mode of conversation intended to impress or influence: *He handed us a line about his rich relatives.* **20.** outline or contour: *a ship of fine lines.* **21. lines,** a plan of construction, action, or procedure: *two books written along the same lines.* **22.** a circle of the terrestrial or celestial sphere: *the equinoctial line.* **23.** *Art.* **a.** a mark made by a pencil, brush, or the like, that defines the contour of a shape, forms hatching, etc. **b.** the edge of a shape. **24. a.** a telephone connection: *Please hold the line.* **b.** a wire circuit connecting two or more pieces of electric apparatus, esp. the circuit connecting points or stations in a telegraph or telephone system or the system itself. **25.** a stock of goods of the same general class but having a range of styles, sizes, prices, or quality. **26.** an assembly line. **27.** *Law.* a limit defining one estate from another; the outline or boundary of a piece of real estate. **28.** (in bridge) a line on a score sheet below which points are scored toward game and above which bonus points are scored. **29.** *Music.* any of the straight, horizontal, parallel strokes of the staff, or one placed above or below the staff. **30. a.** a series of fortifications: *the Maginot line.* **b.** Often, **lines.** a distribution of troops, ships, etc., arranged for defense or drawn up for battle: *behind enemy lines.* **c.** the combatant forces of an army or navy, or their officers. **31.** a body or formation of troops or ships drawn up abreast (disting. from *column*). **32.** a thread, string, cord, rope, etc. **33.** a clothesline. **34.** a cord, wire, etc., used for measuring or as a guide. **35.** a pipe or hose: *a steam line.* **36.** a rope or cable used at sea. **37.** a cord or string with a hook, sinker, float, etc., for catching fish. **38. a.** either of the two front rows of opposing football players lined up opposite each other on the line of scrimmage. **b.** LINE OF SCRIMMAGE. **39.** the betting odds established by bookmakers for events not covered by pari-mutuel betting, esp. sporting events, as football or basketball. **40.** the two wings and center that comprise an ice hockey team's offensive unit. *—v.i.* **41.** to take a position in a line; range (often fol. by *up*). **42.** *Baseball.* **a.** to hit a line drive. **b.** to line out. *—v.t.* **43.** to bring into a line, or into line with others (often fol. by *up*): *to line up troops.* **44.** to mark with a line or lines. **45.** to form a line along: *Rocks lined the drive.* **46.** to apply liner to (the eyes). **47.** to delineate with or as if with lines; draw: *to line a silhouette.* **48. line out, a.** *Baseball.* to be put out by hitting a line drive caught on the fly by a player of the opposing team. **b.** *Informal.* to execute or perform: *to line out a song.* **49. line up,** to secure; make available. *—Idiom.* **50. down the line, a.** in every way; thoroughly. **b.** in the future. **51. draw the line,** to impose a restriction or limit. **52. hold the line,** to maintain the status quo, esp. in order to forestall unfavorable developments. **53. in line, a.** in alignment; straight. **b.** in conformity, agreement, or proportion. **c.** (of behavior) under control; appropriate. **d.** arranged one behind the other. **54. in (the) line of duty,** in the execution of one's duties, esp. with regard to the responsibility for life and death: *a police officer wounded in the line of duty.* **55. into line, a.** into a straight row. **b.** into conformity or proportion: *to bring manufacturing prices into line.* **56. lay it on the line,** *Informal.* **a.** to pay the money required; pay up. **b.** to impart information directly and frankly. **57. off line, a.** occurring or functioning away from the central work location, as an assembly line. **b.** not in operation; not functioning. **c.** not actively linked to a computer or central computer. **58. on line, a.** on or part of an assembly line. **b.** in or into operation. **c.** actively linked to a computer. **59. on the line, a.** in a vulnerable position. **b.** during the transaction; immediately: *to pay cash on the line.* **60. out of line, a.** not in a straight line. **b.** not in conformity; inappropriate. **c.** disrespectful; presumptuous. —**lin′a•ble, line′a•ble,** *adj.*

line² (līn), *v.t.*, **lined, lin•ing. 1.** to cover the inner side or surface of: *to line a coat with blue silk.* **2.** to cover: *Bookcases lined the walls of the room.* **3.** to furnish or fill: *to line shelves with provisions.* **4.** to reinforce (the back of a book) with glued fabric, paper, vellum, etc. —*n.* **5.** a thickness of glue, as between two veneers in a sheet of plywood.

lin•e•age (lin′ē ij), *n.* **1.** lineal descent from an ancestor; ancestry. **2.** the line of descendants of a particular ancestor; family; race.

lin•e•al (lin′ē əl), *adj.* **1.** being in the direct line, as a descendant or ancestor, or in a direct line, as descent or succession. **2.** of or transmitted by lineal descent. —**lin′e•al•ly,** *adv.*

lin•e•a•ment (lin′ē ə mənt), *n.* **1.** Often, **lineaments.** a feature or detail of a face, body, or figure, considered with respect to its outline or contour. **2.** Usu., **lineaments.** distinguishing features. **3.** a linear topographic feature of regional extent that is believed to reflect underlying crustal structure.

lin•e•ar (lin′ē ər), *adj.* **1.** of, consisting of, or using lines: *linear design.* **2.** pertaining to or represented by lines: *linear dimensions.* **3.** extended or arranged in a line: *a linear series.* **4.** involving measurement in one dimension only. **5.** of or pertaining to the characteristics of a work of art in which forms and rhythms are defined chiefly in terms of line. **6.** having the form of or resembling a line: *linear nebulae.* **7.** *Math.* **a.** consisting of, involving, or describable by terms of the first degree. **b.** having the same effect on a sum as on each part of a sum: *a linear operation.* **8.** narrow and elongated: *a linear leaf.* —**lin′e•ar′i•ty,** *n.* —**lin′e•ar•ly,** *adv.*

Linear A, *n.* an ancient system of writing, not yet deciphered, inscribed on clay tablets, pottery, and other objects found at Minoan sites on Crete and other Greek islands.

Linear B, *n.* an ancient system of writing used for Mycenaean Greek, deciphered chiefly from clay tablets found at Knossos and Pylos.

lin′ear equa′tion, *n.* a first-order equation involving two variables: its graph is a straight line in the Cartesian coordinate system.

lin′ear meas′ure, *n.* any system for measuring length, or any unit used in such a system.

lin′ear perspec′tive, *n.* a graphic system for representing depth and volume on a flat surface by means of lines converging at a point or points on a horizon.

line′ art′, *n.* graphic material that consists of lines or areas of pure black and pure white and requires no screening for reproduction. Compare HALFTONE (def. 2).

lin•e•ate (lin′ē it, -āt′) also **lin′e•at′ed,** *adj.* marked with lines, esp. parallel lengthwise lines; striped.

lin•e•a•tion (lin′ē ā′shən), *n.* **1.** an act or instance of marking with or tracing by lines. **2.** a division into lines. **3.** an outline or delineation. **4.** an arrangement or group of lines.

line•back•er (līn′bak′ər), *n.* a football player on defense who takes a position close behind the linemen.

line′ draw′ing, *n.* a drawing done exclusively in line, providing gradations in tone entirely through variations in width and density.

line′ drive′, *n.* a batted baseball that travels low, fast, and straight. Also called **liner.**

line′-i′tem ve′to, *n.* ITEM VETO.

line•man (līn′mən), *n., pl.* **-men. 1.** a person who installs or repairs telephone, telegraph, or other wires. **2.** one of the players in the defensive line of a football team, as a center, guard, tackle, or end.

lin•en (lin′ən), *n.* **1.** fabric woven from flax yarns. **2.** Often, **linens.** bedding, tablecloths, shirts, etc., made of linen cloth or a more common substitute, as cotton. **3.** yarn or thread made from flax. —*adj.* **4.** made of linen: *a linen jacket.* —***Idiom.*** **5. wash** or **air one's dirty linen in public,** to reveal one's personal secrets or shame to outsiders.

lin′en clos′et, *n.* a closet in which sheets, towels, etc., are kept.

line′ of cred′it, *n.* CREDIT LINE (def. 2).

line′ of fire′, *n.* a horizontal line from the muzzle of a weapon in the direction of the axis of the bore, just prior to firing.

line′ of scrim′mage, *n.* an imaginary line on a football field, parallel to the goal lines, along which opposing teams face each other at the beginning of each play.

line′ of sight′, *n.* **1.** Also called **line′ of sight′ing.** an imaginary straight line running through the aligned sights of a firearm, surveying equipment, etc. **2.** Also called **line′ of vi′sion.** an imaginary straight line that connects the center of the eye with the point focused on.

line′ print′er, *n.* an impact printer that produces a full line of computer output at a time.

lin•er¹ (lī′nər), *n.* **1.** a ship or airplane operated by a transportation or conveyance company. **2.** EYELINER. **3.** LINE DRIVE. **4.** a person or thing that traces by or marks with lines.

lin•er² (lī′nər), *n.* **1.** something serving as a lining. **2.** a protective covering, usu. of cardboard, for a phonograph record; jacket. **3.** a person who fits or provides linings.

lines•man (līnz′mən), *n., pl.* **-men. 1.** an official in tennis and soccer who indicates when the ball goes out of bounds. **2.** an official in football who marks the distances gained or lost on a play. **3.** an official in hockey who calls icing and offside violations and conducts face-offs.

line•up (līn′up′), *n.* **1.** an orderly arrangement of persons or things in or as if in a line. **2.** the persons or things themselves. **3.** (in police investigations) a group of persons, including suspects in a crime, lined up to allow identification by the victim of the crime. **4.** a list of the participating players in a game, as of baseball, together with their positions. **5.** an organization of people or groups for some common purpose: *a lineup of support for the new tax bill.* **6.** a schedule of programs, events, etc.: *the fall lineup of TV programs.* **7.** a list of products or services offered by a company; line.

-ling¹, a suffix of nouns, often pejorative, denoting one concerned with (*hireling; underling*) or forming a diminutive (*princeling; duckling*).

-ling², an adverbial suffix expressing direction, position, or state: *darkling; sideling.*

lin•ger (ling′gər), *v.i.* **1.** to remain or stay on in a place longer than is usual or expected, as if from reluctance to leave. **2.** to remain alive or in use, though with diminishing vitality. **3.** to dwell in contemplation, thought, or enjoyment: *to linger over the beauty of a painting.* **4.** to be tardy in action; delay; dawdle. **5.** to walk slowly; saunter along. —*v.t.* **6.** to pass (time) in a leisurely or a tedious manner (usu. fol. by *away* or *out*). —**lin′ger•er,** *n.* —**lin′ger•ing•ly,** *adv.*

lin•ge•rie (län′zhə rā′, -rē′, lan′-, lan′zhə rē′, -jə-), *n.* underwear, sleepwear, and other items of intimate apparel worn by women.

lin•go (ling′gō), *n., pl.* **-goes. 1.** the language or vocabulary, esp. the jargon or slang, of a particular field, group, or individual. **2.** language or speech, esp. if strange or foreign.

ling•on•ber•ry (ling′ən ber′ē), *n., pl.* **-ries.** MOUNTAIN CRANBERRY.

lin•gua (ling′gwə), *n., pl.* **-guae** (-gwē). the tongue or a part like a tongue.

lin′gua fran′ca (frang′kə), *n., pl.* **lingua fran•cas, lin•guae fran•cae** (ling′gwē fran′sē, frang′kē). **1.** any language that is widely used as a means of communication among speakers of other languages. **2.** (*caps.*) a pidgin with a lexicon drawn largely from Italian spoken in Mediterranean ports from the late Middle Ages to the early 20th century.

lin•gual (ling′gwəl), *adj.* **1.** of or pertaining to the tongue. **2.** pertaining to languages. **3.** articulated with the aid of the tongue, esp. the tip of the tongue, as the sound (d) or (n). **4.** of or designating the surface of a tooth facing the tongue. Compare BUCCAL (def. 3), LABIAL (def. 4). —*n.* **5.** a lingual speech sound. —**lin′gual•ly,** *adv.*

lin•gui•ne or **lin•gui•ni** (ling gwē′nē), *n.* (*used with a sing. or pl. v.*) a type of pasta in long, slender, flat strips.

lin•guist (ling′gwist), *n.* **1.** a specialist in linguistics. **2.** a person who is skilled in several languages; polyglot.

lin•guis•tic (ling gwis′tik), *adj.* **1.** of or pertaining to language. **2.** of or pertaining to linguistics. —**lin•guis′ti•cal•ly,** *adv.*

linguis′tic at′las, *n.* a collection of maps showing the distribution of various linguistic features and forms in the speech of a given area. Also called **dialect atlas.**

linguis′tic form′, *n.* any meaningful unit of speech, as a sentence, phrase, word, or morpheme.

linguis′tic geog′raphy, *n.* the study of regional variation in a language or dialect. —**linguis′tic geog′rapher,** *n.*

lin•guis•tics (ling gwis′tiks), *n.* (*used with a sing. v.*) the study of language, including phonetics, phonology, morphology, syntax, semantics, pragmatics, and historical linguistics.

lin•i•ment (lin′ə mənt), *n.* a liquid or semiliquid, usu. medicated preparation for rubbing on the skin, esp. to relieve soreness, inflammation, or sprain.

lin•ing (lī′ning), *n.* **1.** something that is used to line another thing; a layer of material on the inner side or surface of something. **2.** the material used to strengthen the back of a book after the sheets have been folded, backed, and sewed. **3.** the act or process of lining something.

link (lingk), *n.* **1.** one of the rings or separate pieces of which a chain is composed. **2.** anything serving to connect one part or thing with another; a bond or tie: *The locket was a link with the past.* **3.** a unit in a communications system, as a radio relay station or a television booster station. **4.** any of a number of connected sausages. **5.** CUFF LINK. **6.** a ring, loop, or the like: *a link of hair.* **7. a.** (in a surveyor's chain) a unit of length equal to 7.92 inches (20.12 centimeters). **b.** one of 100 rods or loops of equal length forming a surveyor's or engineer's chain. **8.** BOND¹ (def. 14). **9.** a rigid, movable piece or rod, connected with other parts by means of pivots or the like, for the purpose of transmitting motion. —*v.t., v.i.* **10.** to join by or as if by a link or links; unite (often fol. by up): *The new bridge will link the island to the mainland. The company will soon link up with a hotel chain.* —**link′er,** *n.*

link•age (ling′kij), *n.* **1.** the act of linking, or the state or manner of being linked. **2.** a system of links. **3.** an association of two or more genes, usu. on the same chromosome, that tend to be inherited as a unit (**link′age group′**) and to express a set of characteristic traits. **4.** an assembly of four or more rods for transmitting motion, usu. in the same plane or in parallel planes. **5.** a factor or relationship that connects or ties one thing to another; link: *Administration officials sought to establish a linkage between tax cuts and investment levels.* **6.** a measure of the voltage induced in a circuit, equal to the product of the magnetic flux and the number of turns in the surrounding coil.

linked (lingkt), *adj.* **1.** connected by or as if by links. **2.** (of a gene) exhibiting linkage.

link′ing verb′, *n.* COPULA (def. 2).

links (lingks), *n.pl.* GOLF COURSE.

link•up (lingk′up′), *n.* **1.** a contact or linkage established, as between military units or two spacecraft. **2.** something serving as a linking element or system; a connection or hookup.

Lin•nae•us (li nē′əs), *n.* **Carolus** (*Carl von Linné*), 1707–78, Swedish botanist. —**Lin•nae′an, Lin•ne′an,** *adj.*

li•no•le•um (li nō′lē əm), *n.* a hard, washable floor covering formed by coating burlap or canvas with linseed oil, powdered cork, and rosin, and adding pigments to create the desired colors and patterns. [< Latin *līn(um)* flax, linen + *oleum* oil]

Lin•o•type (lī′nə tīp′), *Trademark.* a typesetting machine that casts solid lines of type from brass dies or matrices, selected automatically by a keyboard.

lin•seed (lin′sēd′), *n.* FLAXSEED.

lin′seed oil′, *n.* a drying oil obtained by pressing flaxseed, used in making paints, printing inks, linoleum, etc.

lint (lint), *n.* **1.** minute shreds or ravelings of yarn; bits of thread. **2.** staple cotton fiber used to make yarn. —**lint′y,** *adj.,* **lint•i•er, lint•i•est.**

lin•tel (lin′tl), *n.* a horizontal architectural member supporting the weight above an opening, as a window or a door.

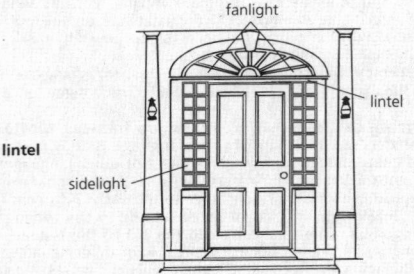

lint•er (lin′tər), *n.* **1. linters,** short cotton fibers that stick to seeds after a first ginning. **2.** a machine for removing lint.

li•on (lī′ən), *n.* **1.** a large, usu. tawny-yellow cat, *Panthera leo,* of Africa and S Asia, having a tufted tail and, in the male, a large mane. **2.** a person of great strength or courage. **3.** a prominent or influential person who is sought after as a celebrity: *a literary lion.* **4.** (*cap.*) LEO¹. **5.** (*cap.*) a member of a Lions Club. —**Proverb. 6. The lion shall lie down with the lamb,** there shall be peace among enemies (based on Is. 11:6). —**li′on•esque′,** *adj.* —**li′on•like′,** *adj.*

li•on•ess (lī′ə nis), *n.* a female lion.

li•on•fish (lī′ən fish′), *n., pl.* **-fish•es,** (*esp. collectively*) **-fish.** any of several long-finned, brightly striped scorpionfishes, esp. of the genus *Pterois.*

li•on•heart•ed (lī′ən här′tid), *adj.* exceptionally courageous or brave. —**li′on•heart′ed•ness,** *n.*

li•on•ize (lī′ə nīz′), *v.t.,* **-ized, -iz•ing.** to treat (a person) as a celebrity. —**li′on•i•za′tion,** *n.* —**li′on•iz′er,** *n.*

Li′ons Club′, *n.* a local club of business and professional people belonging to a worldwide organization of similar clubs (**Li′ons Club′ Interna′tional**) founded in 1917.

li′on's share′, *n.* the largest part, esp. an unreasonably large portion.

lip (lip), *n., adj., v.,* **lipped, lip•ping.** —*n.* **1.** either of the two fleshy parts or folds forming the margins of the mouth. **2.** Usu., **lips.** these parts as organs of speech: *I heard it from his own lips.* **3.** a projecting edge on a container or other hollow object: *the lip of a pitcher.* **4.** any edge or rim. **5.** the edge of an opening or cavity, as of a canyon or a wound. **6.** *Slang.* impudent talk; back talk. **7.** a liplike anatomical part or structure; labium. **8.** *Bot.* a labium or labellum. **9.** the position and arrangement of lips and tongue in playing a wind instrument; embouchure. —*adj.* **10.** of or for the lips: *lip ointment.* **11.** made with the lips: *to read lip movements.* **12.** superficial or insincere: *to offer lip praise.* —*v.t.* **13.** to touch with the lips. **14.** to utter, esp. softly. **15.** to kiss. **16.** to hit a golf ball over the rim of (the hole). —*v.i.* **17.** to use the lips in playing a wind instrument. —**Idiom. 18. keep a stiff upper lip, a.** to

face misfortune bravely and resolutely. **b.** to suppress the display of any emotion. **19. smack one's lips,** to indicate one's keen enjoyment or pleasurable anticipation.

li•pase (lī′pās, lip′ās), *n.* any of a class of enzymes that break down fats, produced by the liver, pancreas, and other digestive organs or by certain plants.

lip•ec•to•my (li pek′tə mē, lī-), *n., pl.* **-mies.** the surgical removal of fatty tissue. Compare LIPOSUCTION.

Li Peng (lē′ pung′), *n.* born 1929, Chinese Communist leader: premier since 1987.

lip′ gloss′ or **lip′-gloss′,** *n.* cosmetic gloss for the lips.

lip•id (lip′id, lī′pid) also **lip•ide** (-īd, -id; -pīd, -pid), *n.* any of a group of organic compounds comprising fats, waxes, and similar substances that are greasy, insoluble in water, and soluble in alcohol: one of the chief structural components of the living cell.

Lip•iz•za•ner or **Lip•pi•za•ner** (lip′it sä′nər, -ə zä′-), also **Lip′iz•zan′,** *n.* one of an Austrian breed of compact, usu. gray or white horses trained esp. at the Spanish Riding School in Vienna and used in dressage exhibitions.

lip•o•chrome (lip′ə krōm′, lī′pə-), *n.* any of the naturally occurring pigments that contain a lipid, as carotene. —**lip′o•chro′mic,** *adj.*

lip•o•cyte (lip′ə sīt′, lī′pə-), *n.* FAT CELL.

lip•o•fill•ing (lip′ə fil′ing, lī′pə-), *n.* the surgical transfer of fat removed by liposuction to areas of the body that need filling out.

lip•oid (lip′oid, lī′poid), *adj.* **1.** Also, **lip•oi′dal.** fatty; resembling fat. —*n.* **2.** a fat or fatlike substance, as lecithin or wax. **3.** LIPID.

li•pol•y•sis (li pol′ə sis, lī-), *n.* the hydrolysis of fats into fatty acids and glycerol, as by lipase. —**lip•o•lit•ic** (lip′ə lit′ik, lī′pə-), *adj.*

lip•o•pro•tein (lip′ə prō′tēn, -tē in, lī′pə-), *n.* any of the class of proteins that contain a lipid combined with a simple protein.

lip•o•some (lip′ə sōm′, lī′pə-), *n.* an artificial vesicle composed of a phospholipid outer layer and an inner core of a drug or other matter to be transported into a cell. —**lip′o•so′mal,** *adj.*

lip•o•suc•tion (lip′ə suk′shən, lī′pə-), *n.* the surgical withdrawal of excess fat from local areas under the skin by means of a small incision and vacuum suctioning.

Lipp•mann (lip′mən; *also* lēp män′ *for*), *n.* **Walter,** 1889–1974, U.S. journalist.

lip•read•ing (lip′rē′ding), *n.* a method, as by a deaf person, of understanding spoken words by interpreting the movements of a speaker's lips without hearing the sounds made. —**lip′read′,** *v.* —**lip′read′er,** *n.*

lip′ serv′ice, *n.* insincere profession of friendship, admiration, support, etc.; service by words only: *He paid only lip service to the dictator.*

lip•stick (lip′stik′), *n.* a crayonlike oil-based cosmetic for coloring the lips, usu. packaged in a tube. —**lip′sticked′,** *adj.*

lip′-sync′ or **lip′-synch′,** *v.,* **-synced, -sync•ing** or **-synched, -synch•ing.** —*v.t.* **1.** to synchronize (recorded sound) with lip movements, as of an actor in a film. **2.** to match lip movements with (recorded speech or singing). —*v.i.* **3.** to synchronize or match lip movements and recorded sound.

liq•ue•fa•cient (lik′wə fā′shənt), *n.* something that liquefies or promotes liquefaction.

liq•ue•fac•tion (lik′wə fak′shən), *n.* **1.** the act or process of liquefying. **2.** the state of being liquefied. —**liq′ue•fac′tive,** *adj.*

liq′uefied petro′leum gas′, *n.* a gas liquefied by compression, consisting of flammable hydrocarbons, as propane and butane: used chiefly as a domestic or industrial fuel, and in organic synthesis, esp. of synthetic rubber. *Abbrev.:* LPG Also called **bottled gas.**

liq•ue•fy (lik′wə fī′), *v.t., v.i.,* **-fied, -fy•ing.** to make or become liquid. —**liq′ue•fi′a•ble,** *adj.* —**liq′ue•fi′er,** *n.*

li•queur (li kûr′, -kyŏŏr′), *n.* any of a class of alcoholic liquors, usu. strong, sweet, and highly flavored, as Chartreuse or curaçao; cordial.

liq•uid (lik′wid), *adj.* **1.** composed of molecules that move freely among themselves but do not tend to separate like those of gases; neither gaseous nor solid. **2.** of, pertaining to, or consisting of liquids: *a liquid diet.* **3.** flowing like water. **4.** in cash or readily convertible into cash without significant loss of principal: *liquid assets.* —*n.* **5.** a liquid substance. —**liq′uid•ly,** *adv.* —**liq′uid•ness,** *n.*

liq•ui•date (lik′wi dāt′), *v.,* **-dat•ed, -dat•ing.** —*v.t.* **1.** to settle or pay (a debt): *to liquidate a claim.* **2.** to reduce (accounts) to order; determine the amount of (indebtedness or damages). **3.** to dissolve (a business or estate) by apportioning the assets to offset the liabilities. **4.** to convert (inventory, securities, or other assets) into cash. **5.** to get rid of, esp. by killing. —*v.i.* **6.** to liquidate debts or accounts; go into liquidation. —**liq′ui•da′tion,** *n.* —**liq′ui•da′tor,** *n.*

liq′uid crys′tal, *n.* a liquid having certain crystalline characteristics, esp. different optical properties in different directions when exposed to an electric field, used in electronic displays.

li•quid•i•ty (li kwid′i tē), *n.* **1.** a liquid state or quality. **2.** the ability or ease with which assets can be converted into cash.

liq′uid meas′ure, *n.* the system of volumetric units ordinarily used in measuring liquid commodities, as milk or oil.

liq•uor (lik′ər *or, for 3,* -wôr), *n.* **1.** a distilled beverage, as brandy or whiskey, as distinguished from a fermented beverage, as wine or beer. **2.** any liquid substance, as broth from cooked meats or vegetables. **3.** a solution of a medicinal substance in water or other liquid. **4.** a usu.

concentrated solution of a substance for use in the industrial arts. —*v.i.* **5.** *Informal.* to drink large quantities of liquor (often fol. by *up*).

li•ra (lēr′ə), *n., pl.* **li•re** (lēr′ā), **li•ras.** the basic monetary units of Italy, Malta, and Turkey.

Lis•bon (liz′bən), *n.* the capital of Portugal, in the SW part, on the Tagus estuary. 807,937. Portuguese, **Lis•bo•a** (lēzh bô′ə).

lisp (lisp), *n.* **1.** a speech defect consisting in pronouncing *s* and *z* like or nearly like the *th*-sounds of *thin* and *this,* respectively. **2.** any unconventional articulation of the sibilants, as the pronunciation of (s) and (z) with the tongue raised so that the breath is emitted laterally. **3.** the act, habit, or sound of lisping. —*v.t., v.i.* **4.** to pronounce or speak with a lisp. **5.** to speak imperfectly, esp. in a childish manner. —**lisp′er,** *n.* —**lisp′ing•ly,** *adv.*

LISP (lisp), *n.* a high-level programming language that processes data in the form of lists: widely used in artificial-intelligence applications.

lis•some or **lis•som** (lis′əm), *adj.* **1.** lithe and graceful; supple; lithesome. **2.** agile, nimble, or active. —**lis′some•ness,** *n.*

list[1] (list), *n.* **1.** a series of names or other items written or printed together in a meaningful grouping or sequence so as to constitute a record: *a list of members.* **2.** all of the books of a publisher that are available for sale. **3.** LIST PRICE. —*v.t.* **4.** to set down together in a list; make a list of. **5.** to enter in a list, directory, catalog, etc.: *to list him among the members.* **6.** to register (a security) on a stock exchange so that it may be traded there. —*v.i.* **7.** to be offered for sale, as in a catalog, at a specified price: *This radio lists at $49.95.* —**list′a•ble,** *adj.*

list[2] (list), *n.* **1.** a strip of cloth or other material. **2.** a selvage or selvages collectively. **3.** a strip or band of any kind. **4.** a stripe of color. **5.** a division of the hair or beard. **6.** one of the ridges or furrows of earth made by a lister. **7.** a strip of material, as bark or sapwood, to be trimmed from a board. —*adj.* **8.** made of selvages or strips of cloth. —*v.t.* **9.** to produce furrows and ridges on (land) with a lister. **10.** to prepare (ground) for planting by making ridges and furrows. **11.** to cut away a narrow strip of wood from the edge of (a stave, plank, etc.).

list[3] (list), *n.* **1.** a leaning to one side, as of a ship. —*v.i.* **2.** (of a ship or boat) to incline to one side; careen. —*v.t.* **3.** to cause (a vessel) to incline to one side.

list•ed (lis′tid), *adj.* **1.** (of a security) admitted to trading privileges on a stock exchange. **2.** (of a telephone number or telephone subscriber) represented in a telephone directory.

lis•ten (lis′ən), *v.i.* **1.** to give attention with the ear; attend closely for the purpose of hearing. **2.** to heed; obey (often fol. by *to*): *Children don't always listen to their parents.* **3.** to wait attentively to perceive a sound or signal (usu. fol. by *for*): *to listen for footsteps.* —*v.t.* **4. listen in, a.** to listen to a broadcast, as on the radio: *Listen in tomorrow for the conclusion.* **b.** to listen to a conversation without joining it. **c.** to eavesdrop (often fol. by *on* or *to*): *Someone was listening in on our phone call.* —**lis′ten•er,** *n.*

lis•ten•er•ship (lis′ə nər ship′, lis′nər-), *n.* the people or number of people who listen to a radio station, type of music, etc.

lis′tening post′, *n.* any position or location for obtaining secret information about an enemy.

list•er (lis′tər), *n.* **1.** Also called **list′er plow′.** a plow with a double moldboard, used to prepare the ground for planting by producing furrows and ridges. **2.** Also called **list′er plant′er, list′er drill′.** a lister plow fitted with attachments for dropping and covering seeds.

Lis•ter (lis′tər), *n.* **Joseph, 1st Baron Lister of Lyme Regis,** 1827–1912, English surgeon: founder of modern antiseptic surgery.

list•ing (lis′ting), *n.* **1.** a list. **2.** the act of compiling a list. **3.** something listed or included in a list: *a listing in the telephone directory.*

list•less (list′lis), *adj.* having or showing little or no interest in anything; languid; spiritless. —**list′less•ly,** *adv.* —**list′less•ness,** *n.*

list′ price′, *n.* the price at which a product is usu. sold to the public, from which a trade discount is computed by a wholesaler.

list′ serv′er, *n. Computers.* any program that distributes messages to a mailing list.

Liszt (list), *n.* **Franz,** 1811–86, Hungarian composer and pianist.

lit[1] (lit), *v.* **1.** a pt. and pp. of LIGHT[1]. —*adj.* **2.** *Slang.* under the influence of liquor or narcotics; intoxicated (often fol. by *up*).

lit[2] (lit), *v.* a pt. and pp. of LIGHT[3].

lit[3] (lit), *n.* literature: *a course in English lit.*

lit•a•ny (lit′n ē), *n., pl.* **-nies. 1.** a ceremonial or liturgical form of prayer consisting of a series of invocations or supplications with responses that are the same for a number in succession. **2. the Litany,** the supplication in this form in the *Book of Common Prayer.* **3.** a recitation or recital that resembles a litany. **4.** a prolonged or tedious account: *a whole litany of complaints.*

Lit.B., Bachelor of Letters; Bachelor of Literature.

li•tchi or **li•chee** (lē′chē), *n., pl.* **-tchis** or **-chees. 1.** the fruit of a Chinese tree, *Litchi chinensis,* of the soapberry family, consisting of a thin, brittle shell enclosing a sweet, jellylike pulp and a single seed. **2.** the tree itself.

Lit.D., Doctor of Letters; Doctor of Literature.

lite (līt), *adj.* an informal, simplified spelling of LIGHT[2], used esp. in labeling, naming, or advertising commercial products. —**lite′ness,** *n.*

-lite or **-lyte,** a combining form used in the names of minerals or fossils: *aerolite.* Compare -LITH.

li•ter (lē′tər), *n.* a unit of liquid capacity equal to the volume of one kilogram of distilled water at 4°C and equivalent to 1.0567 U.S. liquid quarts. *Abbr.:* l Also, *esp. Brit.,* **litre.**

lit•er•a•cy (lit′ər ə sē), *n.* **1.** the quality or state of being literate, esp. the ability to read and write. **2.** possession of education; culture: *to question someone's literacy.* **3.** a person's knowledge of a particular subject or field: *to acquire computer literacy.*

lit•er•al (lit′ər əl), *adj.* **1.** in accordance with, involving, or being the primary or strict meaning of a word or words; not figurative or metaphorical: *the literal meaning of a word.* **2.** following the words of the original very closely and exactly: *a literal translation.* **3.** true to fact; unembellished; actual or factual: *a literal description of conditions.* **4.** being actually such, without exaggeration or inaccuracy: *the literal extermination of a city.* **5.** tending to construe words in the strict sense or in an unimaginative way. —**lit′er•al•ly,** *adv.* —**lit′er•al•ness,** *n.*

lit•er•al•ly (lit′ər ə lē), *adv.* **1.** in the literal or strict sense: *What does the word mean literally?* **2.** in a literal manner; word for word: *to translate literally.* **3.** actually; without exaggeration or inaccuracy: *The city was literally destroyed.* **4.** in effect; in substance; very nearly; virtually.

lit′eral-mind′ed, *adj.* unimaginative; prosaic.

lit•er•ar•y (lit′ə rer′ē), *adj.* **1.** pertaining to or of the nature of books and writings, esp. those classed as literature: *literary history.* **2.** pertaining to authorship: *literary style.* **3.** versed in or acquainted with literature; well-read. **4.** engaged in or having the profession of literature or writing: *a literary man.* **5.** preferring books to actual experience; bookish. —**lit′er•ar′i•ly,** *adv.* —**lit′er•ar′i•ness,** *n.*

lit•er•ate (lit′ər it), *adj.* **1.** able to read and write. **2.** having or showing knowledge of literature, writing, etc.; literary; well-read. **3.** characterized by skill, lucidity, polish, or the like: *literate writing.* **4.** having knowledge or skill in a specified field: *literate in computers.* **5.** having an education; educated. —*n.* **6.** a person who can read and write. **7.** a learned person. —**lit′er•ate•ly,** *adv.*

lit•e•ra•ti (lit′ə rä′tē, -rā′-), *n.pl., sing.* **-ra•tus** (-rä′təs, -rā′-). persons of scholarly or literary attainments; intellectuals.

lit•er•a•ture (lit′ər ə chər, -cho͝or′, li′trə-), *n.* **1.** writing in prose or verse regarded as having permanent worth through its intrinsic excellence. **2.** the entire body of writings of a specific language, period, people, etc. **3.** the writings dealing with a particular subject: *the literature of ornithology.* **4.** the profession of a writer or author. **5.** literary work or production. **6.** any kind of printed material, as circulars, leaflets, or handbills: *literature describing company products.*

lithe (līth), *adj.,* **lith•er, lith•est.** bending readily; pliant; limber; supple; flexible. —**lithe′ly,** *adv.* —**lithe′ness,** *n.*

lithe•some (līth′səm), *adj.* lithe; lissome. —**lithe′some•ly,** *adv.* —**lithe′some•ness,** *n.*

lith•ic (lith′ik), *adj.* **1.** pertaining to or consisting of stone. **2.** pertaining to clastic rocks, either sedimentary or volcanic, containing a large proportion of debris from previously formed rocks. **3.** of, pertaining to, or containing lithium. —*n.* **4.** a stone artifact. —**lith′i•cal•ly,** *adv.*

-lithic, a combining form used in the names of cultural phases in archaeology characterized by the use of a particular type of tool: *Neolithic.*

lith•i•fi•ca•tion (lith′ə fi kā′shən), *n.* the process or processes by which unconsolidated materials are converted into coherent solid rock, as by compaction or cementation.

lith•i•um (lith′ē əm), *n.* **1.** a soft, silver-white metallic element, the lightest of all metals, occurring combined in certain minerals. *Symbol:* Li; *at. wt.:* 6.939; *at. no.:* 3; *sp. gr.:* 0.53 at 20°C. **2.** LITHIUM CARBONATE.

lith′ium car′bonate, *n.* a colorless crystalline compound, Li_2CO_3, slightly soluble in water: used in paints and glazes and in medicine for treating bipolar disorder or mania.

lith•o (lith′ō), *n., pl.* **lith•os,** *adj., v.,* **lith•oed, lith•o•ing.** —*n.* **1.** lithography. **2.** lithograph. —*adj.* **3.** lithographic. —*v.t.* **4.** to lithograph.

litho-, a combining form meaning "stone," "calculus": *lithography.* Also, *esp. before a vowel,* **lith-.**

lith•o•graph (lith′ə graf′, -gräf′), *n.* **1.** a print produced by lithography. —*v.t.* **2.** to produce or copy by lithography. —**li•thog′ra•pher** (-thog′rə fər), *n.*

li•thog•ra•phy (li thog′rə fē), *n.* a printing technique by which the image to be printed is fixed on a stone or metal plate with a combination of ink-absorbent and ink-repellent vehicles. —**lith•o•graph** (lith′ə-graf′), *n.* —**li•thog′ra•pher,** *n.* —**lith′o•graph′ic,** *adj.*

lith•o•sphere (lith′ə sfēr′), *n.* the crust and upper mantle of the earth. —**lith′o•spher′ic** (-sfer′ik), *adj.*

Lith•u•a•ni•a (lith′o͞o ā′nē ə), *n.* a republic in N Europe, on the Baltic, S of Latvia: an independent state 1918–40; annexed by the Soviet Union 1940; regained independence 1991. 3,635,932; 25,174 sq. mi. (65,200 sq. km). *Cap.:* Vilnius. Lithuanian, **Lietuva.**

lit•i•ga•ble (lit′i gə bəl), *adj.* triable in a court of law; subject to litigation.

lit•i•gant (lit′i gənt), *n.* a person engaged in a lawsuit.

lit•i•gate (lit′i gāt′), *v.,* **-gat•ed, -gat•ing.** —*v.t.* **1.** to make the subject of a lawsuit; contest at law. —*v.i.* **2.** to carry on a lawsuit. —**litigation,** *n.* —**lit′i•ga′tive,** *adj.* —**lit′i•ga′tor,** *n.*

li•ti•gious (li tij′əs), *adj.* **1.** of or pertaining to litigation. **2.** subject or open to litigation. **3.** inclined to litigate: *a litigious person.* **4.** inclined to dispute or disagree; argumentative. —**li•ti′gious•ly,** *adv.* —**li•ti′gious•ness, li•ti′gi•os′i•ty** (-tij′ē os′i tē), *n.*

lit•mus (lit′məs), *n.* a blue coloring matter obtained from certain lichens, esp. *Roccella tinctoria*, that turns blue in alkaline solution and red in acid solution: widely used as a chemical indicator.

lit′mus pa′per, *n.* a strip of paper impregnated with litmus, used as a chemical indicator.

lit′mus test′, *n.* **1.** a test using litmus paper or solution to indicate the acidity or alkalinity of a solution. **2.** a crucial test using a single issue or factor as the basis for judgment.

li•to•tes (līʹtə tēz′, litʹə-, lī tōʹtēz), *n., pl.* **-tes.** understatement, esp. that in which an affirmative is expressed by the negative of its contrary, as in "not bad at all." Compare HYPERBOLE.

lit•ter (litʹər), *n.* **1.** objects strewn or scattered about; scattered rubbish. **2.** a condition of disorder or untidiness: *We were appalled at the litter of the room.* **3.** a number of young brought forth by a multiparous animal at one birth: *a litter of six kittens.* **4.** a framework of cloth stretched between two parallel bars, for the transportation of a sick or wounded person; stretcher. **5.** a vehicle carried by people or animals, consisting of a bed or couch, often covered and curtained, suspended between shafts. **6.** straw, hay, or the like, used as bedding for animals or as protection for plants. **7.** the layer of slightly decomposed organic material on the surface of the floor of the forest. **8.** any of various absorbent materials, esp. pellets of clay, used for lining a box **(litʹter box′)** in which a cat can eliminate waste. —*v.t.* **9.** to strew (a place) with scattered objects, rubbish, etc.: *to be fined for littering the sidewalk.* **10.** to scatter (objects) in disorder: *They littered their toys from one end of the playroom to the other.* **11.** to be strewn about (a place) in disorder (often fol. by *up*): *Bits of paper littered the floor.* **12.** to give birth to (young), as a multiparous animal. **13.** to supply (an animal) with litter for a bed. **14.** to use (straw, hay, etc.) for litter. **15.** to cover (a floor or other area) with straw, hay, etc., for litter. —*v.i.* **16.** to give birth to a litter. **17.** to strew objects about: *If you litter, you may be fined.*

lit•té•ra•teur also **lit•te•ra•teur** (litʹər ə tûr′, -tŏŏr′), *n.* a literary person, esp. a writer of literary works.

lit•ter•bag (litʹər bag′), *n.* a small paper or plastic bag for trash or rubbish, as one carried in an automobile.

lit•ter•bug (litʹər bug′), *n.* a person who litters public places with trash. —**litʹter•bug′ging,** *n.*

lit•tle (litʹl), *adj.*, **litʹtler** or **less** or **lessʹer, litʹtlest** or **least**, *adv.*, **less, least,** *n.* —*adj.* **1.** small in size; not big; tiny: *a little desk in the corner of the room.* **2.** short in duration or extent; brief: *a little while.* **3.** small in number: *a little group of scientists.* **4.** small in amount or degree; not much: *little hope.* **5.** of a certain amount; appreciable (usu. prec. by *a*): *We're having a little difficulty.* **6.** being such on a small scale: *little farmers.* **7.** younger or youngest: *my little brother.* **8.** not strong, forceful, or loud; weak: *a little voice.* **9.** minor; unimportant: *life's little discomforts.* **10.** small in influence, position, affluence, etc.: *tax reductions to help the little wage earner.* **11.** mean, narrow, or illiberal: *a little mind.* **12.** endearingly small or so considered: *Bless your little heart!* **13.** contemptibly small, petty, mean, etc.: *filthy little tricks.* —*adv.* **14.** not at all (used before a verb): *He little knows what awaits him.* **15.** in only a small amount or degree; not much; slightly: *a little known work of art; little better than before.* **16.** seldom; rarely; infrequently: *We see each other very little.* —*n.* **17.** a small amount, quantity, or degree: *They did little to make us comfortable. Save a little for me.* **18.** a short distance: *It's down the road a little.* **19.** a short time: *Stay here for a little.* —*Idiom.* **20. little by little,** by small degrees; gradually. **21. not a little,** to a great extent; very much; considerably. **22. too little, too late,** belated and inadequate.

Lit′tle Amer′ica, *n.* a base in the Antarctic, on the Bay of Whales, S of the Ross Sea: established by Adm. Richard E. Byrd of the U.S. Navy in 1929; used for later Antarctic expeditions.

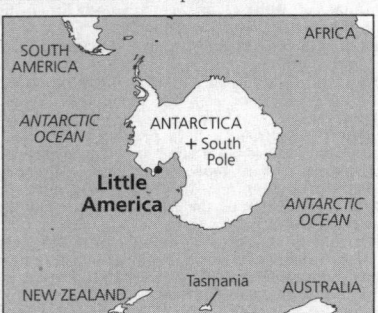

Lit′tle Big′horn (or **Horn**), *n.* a river flowing N from N Wyoming to S Montana into the Bighorn River: General Custer and troops defeated near its juncture by Indians 1876. 80 mi. (130 km) long.

lit′tle-bit′ty, *adj. Informal.* extremely small; tiny.

Lit′tle Boy′, *n.* the code name for the uranium-fueled atomic bomb dropped by the U.S. on Hiroshima in 1945. Compare FAT MAN.

Lit′tle Cor′poral, *n.* epithet of Napoleon I.

Lit′tle Dip′per, *n.* the group of seven bright stars in Ursa Minor resembling a dipper in outline.

Lit′tle Dog′, *n.* the constellation Canis Minor.

Lit′tle Gi′ant, *n.* epithet of Stephen Douglas.

Lit′tle League′, *n.* a baseball league for players ages 8 to 12, usu. sponsored by a business or other organization. —**Lit′tle Lea′guer,** *n.*

Lit′tle Lord′ Faunt′le•roy (fônt′lə roi′), **1.** (*italics*) a children's novel (1886) by Frances H. Burnett. **2.** a pampered or excessively well-behaved young boy resembling the hero of this book.

lit′tle magazine′, *n.* a magazine, usu. small in format and of limited circulation, that publishes literary works.

lit′tle man′, *n.* (*sometimes caps.*) **1.** the common or ordinary person. **2.** the ordinary investor, as opposed to big investment institutions.

lit•tle•neck (litʹl nek′), *n.* the quahog clam, *Mercenaria mercenaria*, when young and small.

Lit′tle Nell′, *n.* the child heroine of Charles Dickens's novel *The Old Curiosity Shop* (1840–41).

lit′tle peo′ple, *n.pl.* **1.** (in folklore) small, imaginary beings, as elves, fairies, or leprechauns. **2.** the common people, esp. workers, small merchants, or the like, who lead conventional, presumably unremarkable lives. **3.** small children. **4.** midgets or dwarfs.

Lit′tle Prin′cess, The, a children's novel (1905) by Frances H. Burnett.

Lit′tle Prince′, The, a fairy tale (1943) by Antoine de Saint-Exupéry.

Lit′tle Rock′, *n.* the capital of Arkansas, in the central part, on the Arkansas River. 178,136.

lit′tle the′ater, *n.* **1.** noncommercial or amateur theater, produced and acted by members of a local community. **2.** (in the U.S.) the movement, 1910–25, that generated such theater, orig. intended to include experimental drama.

lit′tle toe′, *n.* the fifth, outermost, and smallest digit of the foot.

Lit′tle Wom′en, a novel (1868) by Louisa May Alcott.

lit•to•ral (litʹər əl), *adj.* **1.** of or pertaining to the shore of a lake, sea, or ocean. **2.** (on ocean shores) of or pertaining to the biogeographic region between the sublittoral zone and the high-water line. **3.** of or pertaining to the region of freshwater lake beds from the sublittoral zone up to and including damp areas on shore. Compare INTERTIDAL. —*n.* **4.** a littoral region.

li•tur•gi•cal (li tûr′ji kəl) also **li•tur′gic,** *adj.* **1.** of or pertaining to formal public worship or liturgies. **2.** of or pertaining to the liturgy or Eucharistic service. **3.** of or pertaining to liturgics. —**li•tur′gi•cal•ly,** *adv.*

li•tur•gics (li tûr′jiks), *n.* **1.** (*used with a sing. v.*) the science or art of conducting public worship. **2.** the study of liturgies.

lit•ur•gist (litʹər jist), *n.* **1.** an authority on liturgies. **2.** a compiler of a liturgy or liturgies. **3.** a person who uses or favors the use of a liturgy.

lit•ur•gy (litʹər jē), *n., pl.* **-gies. 1.** a form of public worship; ritual. **2.** a collection of formularies for public worship. **3.** a particular arrangement of services. **4.** a particular form or type of the Eucharistic service. **5.** the service of the Eucharist, esp. this service **(Divine Liturgy)** in the Eastern Church.

Lit•vak (litʹväk), *n.* a Jew from Lithuania or a neighboring country or region.

liv•a•ble or **live•a•ble** (livʹə bəl), *adj.* **1.** suitable for living in; habitable; comfortable: *to make an old house livable.* **2.** worth living; endurable: *something to make life more livable.*

live¹ (liv), *v.,* **lived** (livd), **liv•ing.** —*v.i.* **1.** to be alive. **2.** to continue to have life; remain alive: *to live to a ripe old age.* **3.** to continue in existence, operation, memory, etc.; last: *a book that lives in my memory.* **4.** to maintain or support one's existence; provide for oneself: *to live on one's income.* **5.** to feed or subsist (usu. fol. by *on* or *upon*): *to live on rice and bananas.* **6.** to dwell or reside: *to live in a cottage.* **7.** to pass life in a specified manner: *They lived happily ever after.* **8.** to direct or regulate one's life: *to live by the golden rule.* **9.** to experience or enjoy life to the full: *At 50 she was just beginning to live.* **10.** to cohabit (usu. fol. by *with*). —*v.t.* **11.** to pass (life): *to live a life of ease.* **12.** to practice, represent, or exhibit in one's life: *to live one's philosophy.* **13. live down,** to cause (a mistake, disgrace, etc.) to be forgotten or forgiven through one's subsequent blameless behavior. **14. live in** (or **out**), to reside at (or away from) the place of one's employment, esp. as a domestic servant. **15. live up to,** to behave so as to satisfy or represent (ideals, standards, etc.). —*Idiom.* **16. live it up,** *Informal.* to live in an extravagant or wild manner; pursue pleasure. —*Proverb.* **17. Live and learn,** to learn from experience. **18. Live and let live,** to be tolerant of others.

live² (līv), *adj.,* **liv•er, liv•est** for 4–7, 13–15, *adv.* —*adj.* **1.** being alive; living: *live animals.* **2.** of, pertaining to, or during the life of a living being: *the animal's live weight.* **3.** characterized by or indicating the presence of living creatures: *the live sounds of the forest.* **4.** *Informal.* (of a person) energetic; alert; lively: *The club members are a really live bunch.* **5.** full of life, energy, or activity: *His approach is live and fresh.* **6.** burning or glowing: *live coals.* **7.** having resilience or bounce: *a live tennis ball.* **8.** being in play, as a baseball or football. **9.** loaded or unexploded, as a cartridge or shell: *live ammunition.* **10.** made up of people who are actually present: *to perform before a live audience.* **11.** broadcast while happening or being performed; not prerecorded or taped: *a live telecast.* **12.** being highly resonant or reverberant, as an auditorium or concert hall. **13.** vivid or bright, as color. **14.** of current interest or importance; unsettled: *live issues.* **15.** moving or imparting motion; powered: *the live head on a lathe.* **16.** still in use, or to be used, as type set up or copy for printing. **17.** electrically connected to a source of potential difference, or electrically charged so as to have a potential different from that of earth: *a live wire.* **—*adv.*** **18.** by transmission at the actual moment of occurrence or performance: *a program broadcast live.*

lived (līvd, livd), *adj.* having life, a life, or lives, as specified (usu. in combination): *long-lived.* **—Pronunciation.** The adjective LIVED is not derived from the verb *live* (liv), but from the noun *life* (līf), to which the suffix -ED[3] has been added. The original pronunciation, therefore, retains the vowel (ī) of *life.* Since the *f* of *life* changes to *v* when *-ed* is added, as when *leaf* becomes *leaved,* this LIVED is identical in spelling to the past and past participle *lived,* which is pronounced (livd). Conflation of the two words has led to the increasing use of the latter pronunciation for the adjective in such combinations as *long-lived* and *short-lived.* Both pronunciations (līvd, livd) are now considered standard.

live′-in′ (liv), *adj.* **1.** residing at the place of one's employment: *a live-in maid.* **2.** living in a cohabitant relationship.

live•li•hood (līv′lē ho͝od′), *n.* a means of supporting one's existence, esp. financially or vocationally; living.

live•long (liv′lông′, -long′), *adj.* (of time) whole or entire, esp. when tediously long, slow in passing, etc.: *to fret the livelong day.*

live•ly (līv′lē), *adj.* and *adv.,* **-li•er, -li•est.** **—*adj.*** **1.** full or suggestive of life or vital energy; active, vigorous, or brisk: *a lively discussion.* **2.** animated; spirited, vivacious, or sprightly: *a lively tune; a lively wit.* **3.** eventful, stirring, or exciting: *The opposition gave us a lively time.* **4.** bustling with activity; astir: *The marketplace was lively with vendors.* **5.** strong, keen, or distinct; vivid: *a lively recollection.* **6.** striking, telling, or effective, as an expression or instance. **7.** vivid or bright, as color or light: *a lively pink.* **8.** sparkling, as wines. **9.** fresh or invigorating, as air: *a lively breeze.* **10.** rebounding quickly; springing back; resilient: *a lively tennis ball.* **—*adv.*** **11.** with briskness, vigor, or animation; briskly: *to step lively.* **—live′li•ly,** *adv.* **—live′li•ness,** *n.*

liv•en (lī′vən), *v.t.* **1.** to put life or spirit into; enliven (often fol. by *up*): *What can we do to liven up the party?* **—*v.i.*** **2.** to become more lively (usu. fol. by *up*).

live′ oak′ (līv), *n.* **1.** an evergreen oak, *Quercus virginiana,* of the southern U.S., having a short, broad trunk and shiny, oblong leaves. **2.** the hard, durable wood of this tree.

live′-out′, *adj.* residing away from the place of one's employment: *a live-out cook.*

liv•er[1] (liv′ər), *n.* **1.** a large, reddish brown, glandular organ in vertebrates, located in the upper abdominal cavity and functioning in the secretion of bile and in essential metabolic processes. **2.** this organ of an animal, as a calf, chicken, or goose, used as food. **3.** a diseased condition of the liver; biliousness: *a touch of liver.* **4.** a reddish brown color. **—*v.i.*** **5.** (of paint, ink, etc.) to undergo irreversible thickening.

liv•er[2] (liv′ər), *n.* **1.** a person who lives in a manner specified: *an extravagant liver.* **2.** a dweller; inhabitant.

liv•er•ish (liv′ər ish), *adj.* **1.** resembling liver, esp. in color. **2.** having a liver disorder; bilious. **3.** disagreeable; crabbed; melancholy: *a liverish disposition.* **—liv′er•ish•ness,** *n.*

liv•er•leaf (liv′ər lēf′), *n., pl.* **-leaves.** HEPATICA.

liv′er sau′sage (liv′ər), *n.* LIVERWURST.

liv′er spots′ (liv′ər), *n.pl.* CHLOASMA.

liv•er•wort (liv′ər wûrt′, -wôrt′), *n.* any mosslike bryophyte of the class Hepaticae, growing chiefly on damp ground, rocks, or tree trunks.

liv•er•wurst (liv′ər wûrst′, -wo͝orst′, -wo͝osht′), *n.* a cooked sausage containing a large percentage of liver, esp. one made with pork liver and pork meat.

liv•er•y[1] (liv′ə rē, liv′rē), *n., pl.* **-er•ies.** **1.** a distinctive uniform, badge, or device formerly provided by someone of rank or title for his or her retainers, as in time of war. **2.** a uniform worn by servants. **3.** distinctive attire worn by an official, a member of a company or guild, etc. **4.** Also called **liv′ery com′pany.** any of various companies of the City of London descended from medieval trade and craft guilds and formerly characterized by such livery. **5.** characteristic dress, garb, or outward appearance: *the green livery of summer.* **6.** the care, feeding, stabling, etc., of horses for pay. **7.** LIVERY STABLE. **8.** a company that rents out automobiles, boats, etc. **9.** *Law.* an ancient method of conveying a freehold by formal delivery of possession.

liv•er•y[2] (liv′ə rē), *adj.* LIVERISH.

liv•er•y•man (liv′ə rē mən, liv′rē-), *n., pl.* **-men.** **1.** an owner of or an employee in a livery stable. **2.** a member of a livery company.

liv′ery sta′ble, *n.* a stable where horses and vehicles are cared for or rented out for pay.

lives (līvz), *n.* pl. of LIFE.

live•stock (līv′stok′), *n.* (*used with a sing. or pl. v.*) the horses, cattle, sheep, and other useful animals kept or raised on a farm or ranch.

live•trap (līv′trap′), *n., v.,* **-trapped, -trap•ping.** **—*n.*** **1.** a trap for capturing a wild animal alive and without injury. **—*v.t.*** **2.** to capture (a wild animal) in a livetrap.

live′ wire′ (līv), *n. Informal.* an energetic, keenly alert person.

liv•id (liv′id), *adj.* **1.** having a discolored, bluish appearance caused by a bruise, congestion of blood vessels, strangulation, etc. **2.** dull blue; dark, grayish blue. **3.** enraged; furiously angry: *Carelessness makes me absolutely livid.* **4.** reddish or flushed. **5.** deathly pale; pallid; ashen: *Fear turned his cheeks livid.* **—liv′id•ly,** *adv.* **—li•vid′i•ty,** *n.*

liv•ing (liv′ing), *adj.* **1.** having life; being alive; not dead. **2.** in actual existence or use; extant: *living languages.* **3.** active or thriving; vigorous; strong: *a living faith.* **4.** pertaining to or suitable for human activity or existence: *living conditions; living space.* **5.** of or pertaining to living persons: *within living memory.* **6.** lifelike; true to life: *The statue is the living image of the general.* **7.** being in its natural state or place: *living rock; a living brook.* **8.** burning or glowing; live. **9.** very; absolute (used as an intensifier): *to scare the living daylights out of someone.* **—*n.*** **10.** the act or condition of a person or thing that lives. **11.** the means of maintaining life; livelihood: *to earn a living.* **12.** a particular manner, state, or status of life: *luxurious living.* **13. the living,** living persons collectively. **14.** *Brit.* the benefice of a cleric. **—liv′ing•ly,** *adv.*

Liv′ing Bi′ble, *n.* a U.S. Bible paraphrase (New Testament 1962, Bible 1971).

liv′ing fos′sil, *n.* an organism that is a living, virtually unchanged example of an otherwise extinct group.

liv′ing room′, *n.* **1.** a room in a home used by the members of the household for leisure activities, entertaining guests, etc.; parlor. **2.** LEBENSRAUM.

liv′ing stand′ard, *n.* STANDARD OF LIVING.

Liv•ing•stone (liv′ing stən), *n.* **1. David,** 1813–73, Scottish missionary and explorer in Africa. **2.** a town in SW Zambia, on the Zambezi River, near Victoria Falls: the former capital. 94,637.

liv′ing wage′, *n.* a wage on which it is possible for a wage earner or an individual and his or her family to live at least according to minimum customary standards.

liv′ing will′, *n.* a document in which a person stipulates that no extraordinary measures are to be used to prolong his or her life in the event of a terminal illness.

Li•vo•ni•a (li vō′nē ə), *n.* **1.** a former Russian province on the Baltic: now part of Latvia and Estonia. **2.** a city in SE Michigan, near Detroit. 101,415. **—Li•vo′ni•an,** *adj., n.*

liz•ard (liz′ərd), *n.* **1.** any scaly reptile of the suborder Lacertilia (Sauria), order Squamata, typically having a long body, long tail, and four legs, as the chameleon, iguana, or gecko. **2.** leather made from the skin of a lizard, used for shoes, purses, etc. **3.** LOUNGE LIZARD.

Lju•blja•na (lo͞o′blē ä′nə, -nä), *n.* the capital of Slovenia, in the central part. 305,211.

Lk., Luke.

′ll, **1.** a contraction of *shall* or *will: I'll answer the phone. She'll pay the check. What'll we do?* **2.** contraction of *till*[1] (used when the preceding word ends in *t*): *Wait'll the children see this!*

ll., lines.

lla•ma (lä′mə, yä′-), *n., pl.* **-mas.** **1.** a woolly-haired South American ruminant of the genus *Lama,* related to the camel, believed to be a domesticated variety of the guanaco. **2.** cloth made from the soft fleece of the llama, often combined with wool.

lla•no (lä′nō, yä′-), *n., pl.* **-nos.** (in the southwestern U.S. and Spanish America) an extensive grassy plain with few trees.

Lloyd′ George′ (loid), *n.* **David, 1st Earl of Dwy•for** (do͞o′vôr), 1863–1945, British prime minister 1916–22.

Lloyd′ Web′ber (web′ər), *n.* **Sir Andrew,** born 1948, English composer of musicals.

LM (*often* lem), lunar module.

lo[1] (lō), *interj.* look! see! (now usu. used as an expression of surprise in the phrase *lo and behold*).

lo[2] (lō), *adj.* an informal, simplified spelling of LOW[1], used esp. in labeling or advertising commercial products: *lo calorie.*

loach (lōch), *n.* any slender freshwater fish of the family Cobitidae, having barbels around the mouth.

load (lōd), *n.* **1.** anything put in or on something for conveyance or transportation; freight; cargo: *a truck with a load of watermelons.* **2.** the quantity that can be or usu. is carried at one time, as in a cart. **3.** this quantity taken as a unit of measure or weight (usu. used in combination): *carload; wagonload.* **4.** the quantity borne or sustained by something; burden: *a tree weighed down by its load of fruit.* **5.** the weight supported by a structure or part. **6.** the amount of work assigned to or to be done by a person, team, department, machine, or mechanical system: *a reasonable load of work.* **7.** something that weighs down or oppresses like a burden; onus: *That's a load off my mind.* **8. loads,** *Informal.* a great quantity or number: *loads of fun; loads of people.* **9.** the charge for a firearm. **10.** a commission charged to buyers of mutual-fund shares. **11.** any of the unmoving and unvarying forces that a structure is designed to oppose, as stress from wind or earthquake. **12. a.** the power delivered by a generator, motor, power station, or transformer. **b.** a device that receives power. **13.** the external resistance overcome by an engine, dynamo, or the like, under given conditions, measured and expressed in terms of the power required. **—*v.t.*** **14.** to put a load on or in; fill: *to load a ship.* **15.** to supply abundantly, lavishly, or excessively with something (often fol. by *down*): *They loaded us down with gifts.* **16.** to weigh down, burden, or oppress (often fol. by *down*): *to load oneself down with obligations.* **17.** to insert a charge, projectile, etc., into (a firearm). **18.** to place (film, tape, etc.) into a camera or other device. **19.** to place film, tape, etc., into (a camera or other device). **20.** to take on as a load: *a ship loading coal.* **21.** to add to the weight of, sometimes fraudulently: *The silver candlesticks were loaded with lead.* **22.** to increase (the net premium of an insurance policy) by adding charges, as for expenses. **23.** to overcharge (a word, expression, etc.) with extraneous values of emotion, sentiment, or the like. **24.** to add additional or prejudicial meaning to (a statement, question, etc.): *The attorney kept loading his questions in the hope of getting the reply he wanted.* **25.** *Baseball.* to have or put runners at (first, second, and third bases): *to load the bases with two out in the eighth inning.* **26. a.** to bring (a program or data) into a computer's RAM, as from a disk, so as to make it available for processing. **b.** to place (an input/output medium) into an appropriate device, as by inserting a disk into a disk drive. **27.** to add (a power-absorbing device) to an electric circuit. **—*v.i.* 28.** to put on or take on a load, as of passengers or goods: *All trucks load at the platform.* **29.** to load a firearm. **30.** to enter a conveyance: *The students loaded quickly into the buses.* **31.** to become filled or occupied. **—*adv.* 32. loads,** *Informal.* very much; a great deal: *It would help loads if you could send some money.* **—*Idiom.* 33. get a load of,** *Slang.* to look at or listen to; notice.

load•ed (lō′did), *adj.* **1.** bearing or having a load; full: *a loaded bus.* **2.** containing ammunition or an explosive charge: *a loaded rifle.* **3.** (of a word, statement, or argument) charged with emotions or associations that prevent rational or unprejudiced communication. **4.** *Slang.* having a great deal of money; rich. **5.** (of dice) fraudulently weighted so as to increase the chances that certain combinations will appear face up when the dice are thrown. **6.** (of a product, building, etc.) including many extra features, accessories, luxuries, or the like.

load•er (lō′dər), *n.* **1.** a person or thing that loads. **2.** a self-propelled machine with a shovel or bucket at the end of articulated arms, used to raise earth or other material and load it into a dump truck.

load′ fac′tor, *n.* the percentage of available seats, space, or carrying weight paid for and used by passengers, shippers, etc.

load•ing (lō′ding), *n.* **1.** the act of a person or thing that loads. **2.** that with which something is loaded; load, burden, or charge. **3.** the ratio of the gross weight of an airplane to engine power, wing span, or wing area. **4.** an addition to the net premium of an insurance policy, to cover expenses and allow a margin for contingencies and profit.

loaf[1] (lōf), *n., pl.* **loaves** (lōvz). **1.** a portion of bread or cake usu. baked in an oblong mass with a rounded top. **2.** a shaped or molded mass of food, as of chopped meat: *a veal loaf.*

loaf[2] (lōf), *v.i.* **1.** to idle away time. **2.** to lounge or saunter lazily and idly. **—*v.t.* 3.** to pass idly (usu. fol. by *away*): *to loaf one's life away.*

loaf•er (lō′fər), *n.* a person who loafs; lazy person; idler.

Loaf•er (lō′fər), *Trademark.* a moccasinlike slip-on shoe.

loam (lōm), *n.* **1.** a rich, friable soil containing a relatively equal mixture of sand and silt and a somewhat smaller proportion of clay. **2.** a mixture of clay, sand, straw, etc., used in making molds for founding and in plastering walls, stopping holes, etc. **3.** earth or soil. **—*v.t.* 4.** to cover or stop with loam. **—loam′i•ness,** *n.* **—loam′y,** *adj.*

Lo-Am•mi (lō am′ī), *n.* a name given by the prophet Hosea to his son. Hos. 1:9.

loan (lōn), *n.* **1.** the act of lending; a grant of the temporary use of something: *the loan of a book.* **2.** something lent or furnished on condition of being returned, esp. a sum of money lent at interest. **—*v.t.* 3.** to make a loan of; lend: *Will you loan me your umbrella?* **4.** to lend (money) at interest. **—*v.i.* 5.** to make a loan or loans; lend. **—*Idiom.* 6. on loan,** loaned or borrowed for temporary use or employment. **—loan′a•ble,** *adj.*

loan•er (lō′nər), *n.* **1.** one that loans. **2.** something, as a car or appliance, that is lent, esp. to replace an item being serviced or repaired.

loan′ shark′, *n. Informal.* a person who lends money at excessively high rates of interest; usurer.

loan•word (lōn′wûrd′), *n.* a word in one language that has been borrowed from another language and usu. naturalized, as *wine,* taken into Old English from Latin *vinum,* or *macho,* taken into Modern English from Spanish.

loath or **loth** (lōth, lōth), *adj.* unwilling; reluctant: *to be loath to admit a mistake.* **—loath′ly,** *adv.* **—loath′ness,** *n.*

loathe (lōth), *v.t.,* **loathed, loath•ing.** to feel disgust or intense aversion for; abhor. **—loath′er,** *n.*

loath•ing (lō′thing), *n.* strong dislike or disgust; intense aversion. **—loath′ing•ly,** *adv.*

loath•some (lōth′səm, lōth′-), *adj.* causing feelings of loathing; disgusting; revolting; repulsive: *a loathsome skin disease.* **—loath′some•ly,** *adv.* **—loath′some•ness,** *n.*

loaves (lōvz), *n.* pl. of LOAF[1].

lob (lob), *v.,* **lobbed, lob•bing,** *n.* **—*v.t.* 1.** to hit (a ball) in a high arc to the back of the opponent's court in tennis. **2.** to fire (a missile) in a high trajectory so that it drops onto a target. **3.** to bowl (the ball) with a slow underhand motion in cricket. **4.** to throw (something) slowly in an arc. **—*v.i.* 5.** to lob a ball. **—*n.* 6.** a lobbed ball. **—lob′ber,** *n.*

lob•by (lob′ē), *n., pl.* **-bies,** *v.,* **-bied, -by•ing.** **—*n.* 1.** an entrance hall, corridor, or vestibule, as in a public building, often serving as an anteroom; foyer. **2.** a public room or hall adjacent to a legislative chamber. **3.** a group of persons who try to influence legislators or other public officials to vote or act in favor of a special interest. **—*v.i.* 4.** to try to influence legislation or administrative decisions. **—*v.t.* 5.** to try to influence the actions or votes of (public officials). **6.** to urge or procure the passage of (legislation) by lobbying. **—lob′by•ist,** *n.*

lobe (lōb), *n.* **1.** a roundish projection or division, as of an organ or a leaf. **2.** EARLOBE.

lo•bec•to•my (lō bek′tə mē), *n., pl.* **-mies.** the surgical removal of a lobe, esp. of the lung.

lobed (lōbd), *adj.* **1.** having a lobe or lobes. **2.** (of a leaf) having lobes or divisions extending less than halfway to the middle of the base.

lobe′fin fish′ (lōb′fin′) also **lobe′finned fish′,** *n.* CROSSOPTERYGIAN.

lo•bel•ia (lō bēl′yə), *n., pl.* **-ias.** any tall nonwoody plant of the genus *Lobelia,* having long terminal clusters of showy two-petaled flowers.

lob•lol•ly (lob′lol′ē), *n., pl.* **-lies. 1.** *South Midland and Southern U.S.* a mire; mudhole. **2.** a thick gruel.

lob′lolly pine′, *n.* **1.** a coniferous tree, *Pinus taeda,* of the southeastern U.S., having bundles of stout, often twisted needles and blackish gray bark. **2.** the wood of this tree, used for timber and pulpwood.

lo•bo (lō′bō), *n., pl.* **-bos.** the gray or timber wolf of the western U.S.

lo•bot•o•my (lə bot′ə mē, lō-), *n., pl.* **-mies.** a surgical incision into or across a lobe, esp. the prefrontal lobe, of the brain to sever nerves for the purpose of relieving a mental disorder or treating psychotic behavior. **—lo•bot′o•mize′,** *v.t.,* **-mized, -miz•ing.**

lob•ster (lob′stər), *n., pl.* (*esp. collectively*) **-ster,** (*esp. for kinds or species*) **-sters. 1.** any of various large, edible, marine, stalk-eyed decapod crustaceans, esp. of the genus *Homarus,* having large, asymmetrical pincers. **2.** any of various similar crustaceans, as certain crayfishes. **3.** the edible meat of these animals.

lob′ster pot′, *n.* a trap for catching lobsters, typically a box made of wooden slats with a funnellike entrance to the bait. Also called **lob′ster trap′.**

lob′ster shift′, *n. Informal.* a late night work shift, esp. at a newspaper office. Also called **lob′ster trick′.**

lob′ster ther′midor (or **Ther′midor**), *n.* a dish of cooked lobster meat placed back in the shell with a cream sauce, sprinkled with grated cheese, and browned in the oven.

lo•cal (lō′kəl), *adj.* **1.** pertaining to or characterized by place or position in space; spatial. **2.** pertaining to, characteristic of, or restricted to a particular place: *a local custom.* **3.** pertaining to a city, town, or small district rather than an entire state or country: *local transportation.* **4.** stopping at most or all stations: *a local train.* **5.** pertaining to or affecting a particular part or particular parts, as of a physical system or organism: *a local disease.* **6.** (of anesthesia or an anesthetic) affecting only a particular part or area of the body without concomitant loss of consciousness. **—*n.* 7.** a local train, bus, etc. **8.** a newspaper item of local interest. **9.** a local branch of a union, fraternity, etc. **10.** a local anesthetic. **11.** Often, **locals. a.** a local person or resident. **b.** a local athletic team. **—*v.i.* 12.** *Informal.* to travel by or take a local train or the like. **—lo′cal•ly,** *adv.*

lo-cal (lō′kal′, -kal′), *adj.* LOW-CAL.

lo′cal-ar′ea net′work, *n.* **1.** a system for linking private telecommunications equipment, as in a building or cluster of buildings. **2.** a computer network confined to a limited area, linking esp. personal computers so that programs, data, peripheral devices, and processing tasks can be shared. Compare MULTIUSER SYSTEM. Also called **LAN.**

lo′cal col′or, *n.* distinctive, sometimes picturesque characteristics or peculiarities of a place or period as represented in literature or drama, or as observed in reality.

lo•cale (lō kal′, -käl′), *n.* **1.** a place or locality, esp. with reference to events or circumstances connected with it: *to move to a warmer locale.* **2.** the scene or setting, as of a novel, play, or motion picture.

lo′cal gov′ernment, *n.* **1.** the administration of the local affairs of a city, town, or other district by its inhabitants. **2.** the governing body of such a district.

lo•cal•i•ty (lō kal′i tē), *n., pl.* **-ties. 1.** a specific place or area; location: *They moved to another locality.* **2.** the state or fact of having a location: *the locality that every material object must have.*

lo•cal•ize (lō′kə līz′), *v.,* **-ized, -iz•ing.** **—*v.t.* 1.** to make local; confine or restrict to a particular place. **—*v.i.* 2.** to gather, collect, or concentrate in one locality. **—lo′cal•iz′a•ble,** *adj.* **—lo′cal•i•za′tion,** *n.*

lo•cate (lō′kāt, lō kāt′), *v.,* **-cat•ed, -cat•ing.** **—*v.t.* 1.** to identify or discover the place or location of: *to locate a missing book.* **2.** to establish in a position, situation, or locality; place; settle. **3.** to assign or ascribe a particular location to (something), as by knowledge or opinion: *Some scholars locate the Garden of Eden in Babylonia.* **4.** to survey and enter a claim to a tract of land; take possession of land. **—*v.i.* 5.** to establish one's business or residence in a place; settle. **—lo•cat′a•ble,** *adj.* **—lo′cat•er,** *n.*

lo•ca•tion (lō kā′shən), *n.* **1.** a place or situation occupied. **2.** a place of settlement, activity, or residence: *a good location for a young doctor.* **3.** a tract of land of designated situation or limits: *a mining location.* **4.** a site outside a movie studio used for shooting all or part of a film. **5.** the act of locating or state of being located. **—*Idiom.* 6. on location,** engaged in filming at a place away from the studio, esp. one that is or is like the setting of the screenplay: *on location in Rome.* **—lo•ca′tion•al,** *adj.* **—lo•ca′tion•al•ly,** *adv.*

loc•a•tive (lok′ə tiv), *adj.* **1.** of or designating a grammatical case that typically indicates place in or at which, as Latin *domī* "at home." **—*n.* 2.** the locative case. **3.** a word or other form in the locative case.

lo•ca•tor (lō′kā tər, lō kā′tər), *n.* a person who determines or establishes the boundaries of land or a mining claim.

loc. cit. (lok′ sit′), in the place cited. [< Latin *locō citātō*]

loch (lok, lokh), *n. Scot.* **1.** a lake. **2.** a partially landlocked or protected bay; a narrow arm of the sea.

Loch′ Ness′ mon′ster, *n.* a large aquatic animal resembling a serpent or a plesiosaurlike reptile, reported to have been seen in the waters of Loch Ness, Scotland, but not proved to exist.

lo·ci (lō′sī, -kē, -kī), *n.* pl. of LOCUS.

lock[1] (lok), *n.* **1.** a device for securing a door, gate, lid, drawer, or the like when closed, consisting of a bolt or system of bolts propelled and withdrawn by a mechanism operated by a key, dial, etc. **2.** any contrivance for fastening or securing something. **3.** (in a firearm) the mechanism that explodes the charge; gunlock. **4.** an enclosed chamber in a canal, dam, etc., with gates at each end, for raising or lowering vessels from one level to another by admitting or releasing water. **5.** an air lock or decompression chamber. **6.** complete and unchallenged control; an unbreakable hold: *to have a lock on the senatorial nomination.* **7.** *Slang.* someone or something certain of success; sure thing. **8.** any of various wrestling holds, esp. a hold secured on the arm, leg, or head. —*v.t.* **9.** to fasten or secure (a door, window, building, etc.) by the operation of a lock or locks. **10.** to shut in by or as if by means of a lock, as for security or restraint. **11.** to make fast or immovable by or as if by a lock: *to lock the steering wheel on a car.* **12.** to join or unite firmly by interlinking or intertwining: *to lock arms.* **13.** to hold fast in an embrace. **14.** to move (a ship) by means of a lock or locks, as in a canal. **15.** to furnish with locks, as a canal. —*v.i.* **16.** to become locked: *This door locks with a key.* **17.** to become fastened, fixed, or interlocked: *gears that lock into place.* **18.** to go or pass by means of a lock or locks, as a vessel. **19. lock in, a.** to commit to unalterably. **b.** (of an investor) to be unable or unwilling to sell or shift securities. **20. lock out, a.** to keep out by or as if by a lock. **b.** to subject (employees) to a lockout. **21. lock up, a.** to imprison for a crime. **b.** to make (type) immovable in a chase by securing the quoins. **c.** to fasten or secure with a lock or locks. **d.** to lock the doors of a house, automobile, etc. **e.** to fasten or fix firmly, as by engaging parts. —*Idiom.* **22. lock horns,** to come into conflict; clash. **23. lock, stock, and barrel,** with every part or item included; completely. **24. under lock and key,** securely locked up. —**lock′a·ble,** *adj.* —**lock′less,** *adj.*

lock[2] (lok), *n.* **1.** a tress, curl, or ringlet of hair. **2. locks,** the hair of the head.

lock·box (lok′boks′), *n.* **1.** a strongbox. **2.** a rented post-office box equipped with a lock. **3.** Also called **lockout box.** an electronic device that unscrambles cable television pictures for subscribers only.

lock·down (lok′doun′), *n.* the confining of prisoners to their cells, as following a riot or other disturbance.

Locke (lok), *n.* **John,** 1632–1704, English philosopher.

lock·er (lok′ər), *n.* **1.** a chest, compartment, or closet in which clothing and valuables may be locked for safekeeping. **2.** a large, typically room-size compartment, as in a cold-storage plant, for keeping frozen foods. **3.** a person or thing that locks.

lock′er loop′, *n.* a loop of fabric at the back of a garment near the neckline, used to hang the garment on a hook.

lock′er room′, *n.* a room containing lockers, as in a gymnasium, factory, or school, for changing clothes and for the storage of personal belongings.

lock′er-room′, *adj.* of, characteristic of, or suitable to conversation in a locker room; earthy or bawdy: *locker-room humor.*

lock·et (lok′it), *n.* a small case for a miniature portrait, a lock of hair, or other keepsake, usu. worn on a necklace.

lock′-in′, *n.* **1.** an act or instance of becoming unalterable, unmovable, or rigid. **2.** commitment, binding, or restriction.

lock′ing pli′ers, *n.* (used with a sing. or pl. v.) pliers whose jaws are connected at a sliding pivot, permitting them to be temporarily locked in a fixed position for ease in grasping and turning nuts.

lock·jaw (lok′jô′), *n.* tetanus in which the jaws become firmly locked together.

lock′ nut′, *n.* **1.** a nut specially constructed to prevent its coming loose, usu. having a means of providing extra friction between itself and the screw. **2.** a thin supplementary nut screwed down upon a regular nut to prevent its loosening.

lock·out (lok′out′), *n.* the temporary closing of a business or the refusal by an employer to allow employees to come to work until they accept the employer's terms.

lock′out box′, *n.* LOCKBOX (def. 3).

lock·smith (lok′smith′), *n.* a person who makes or repairs locks and keys. —**lock′smith′er·y,** *n.* —**lock′smith′ing,** *n.*

lock·step (lok′step′), *n.* **1.** a way of marching in very close file, in which the leg of each person moves with and closely behind the corresponding leg of the person ahead. **2.** a rigidly inflexible pattern or process. —*adj.* **3.** rigidly inflexible: *a lockstep educational curriculum.*

lock·up (lok′up′), *n.* **1.** a jail, esp. a local one for temporary detention. **2.** the act of locking up or the state of being locked up. **3.** a temporary imprisonment or detention.

Lock·wood (lok′wŏŏd′), *n.* **Belva Ann Bennett,** 1830–1917, U.S. lawyer and women's-rights activist.

lo·co (lō′kō), *n.,* *pl.* **-cos.** **1.** LOCOWEED. **2.** *Slang.* an insane person. —*adj.* **3.** *Slang.* out of one's mind; insane; crazy.

lo·co·ism (lō′kō iz′əm), *n.* a disease chiefly of sheep, horses, and cattle, caused by the eating of locoweed and characterized by weakness, impaired vision, irregular behavior, and paralysis.

lo·co·mo·tion (lō′kə mō′shən), *n.* the act or power of moving from place to place.

lo·co·mo·tive (lō′kə mō′tiv), *n.* **1.** a self-propelled, vehicular engine for pulling or, sometimes, pushing a train or individual railroad cars. **2.** an organized group cheer, as at an athletic contest, that progressively increases in speed. —*adj.* **3.** of or pertaining to locomotives. **4.** of, pertaining to, or aiding in locomotion. **5.** moving or traveling by means of its own mechanism or powers. **6.** serving to produce such movement; adapted for or used in locomotion: *locomotive organs.* —**lo′co·mo′tive·ly,** *adv.* —**lo′co·mo′tive·ness, lo′co·mo·tiv′i·ty,** *n.*

lo·co·mo·tor (lō′kə mō′tər), *adj.* **1.** Also, **lo′co·mo′to·ry.** of, pertaining to, or affecting locomotion. —*n.* **2.** a person or thing that is capable of locomotion.

lo·co·weed (lō′kō wēd′), *n.* any of various leguminous plants of the genera *Astragalus* and *Oxytropis,* of the southwestern U.S. and Mexico, causing locoism in sheep, horses, etc.

loc·ule (lok′yool), *n.* a small compartment or chamber, as the pollen-containing cavity within an anther.

lo·cus (lō′kəs), *n.,* *pl.* **-ci** (-sī, -kē, -kī). **1.** a place; locality. **2.** a center or source, as of activities or power: *locus of control.* **3.** *Math.* the set of all points, lines, or surfaces that satisfy a given requirement. **4.** the position of a gene on a chromosome.

lo·cust (lō′kəst), *n.* **1.** Also called **short-horned grasshopper.** any of several grasshoppers of the family Acrididae, having short antennae and commonly migrating in swarms that strip the vegetation from large areas. **2.** any of various cicadas, as the seventeen-year locust. **3.** any North American tree of the genus *Robinia,* of the legume family, esp. *R. pseudoacacia,* having pinnate leaves and clusters of fragrant white flowers. **4.** the durable wood of this tree. **5.** any of various other trees, as the carob and the honey locust.

lo′cust bean′, *n.* CAROB.

lo·cu·tion (lō kyōō′shən), *n.* **1.** a particular form of expression; a word, phrase, or expression, esp. as used by a particular person, group, etc. **2.** a style of speech or verbal expression; phraseology.

lo·cu·tion·ar·y, *adj.* of or pertaining to the act of conveying semantic content in an utterance, considered as independent of the interaction between the speaker and the listener.

lode (lōd), *n.* **1.** a veinlike deposit, usu. metalliferous. **2.** a rich supply or source.

lo·den (lōd′n), *n.* **1.** a sturdy, water-repellent cloth, usu. of coarse wool, used for coats and jackets. **2.** Also called **lo′den green′.** the deep olive-green color of this fabric.

lode·star or **load·star** (lōd′stär′), *n.* **1.** a star that shows the way. **2.** POLARIS. **3.** something that serves as a guide or on which the attention is fixed.

lode·stone or **load·stone** (lōd′stōn′), *n.* **1.** a variety of magnetite that possesses magnetic polarity and attracts iron. **2.** a piece of this serving as a magnet. **3.** something that attracts strongly.

lodge (loj), *n.,* *v.,* **lodged, lodg·ing.** —*n.* **1.** a makeshift or rough shelter or habitation; cabin or hut. **2.** a house used as a temporary residence, as in the hunting season. **3.** a house or cottage, as in a park or on an estate, occupied by a gatekeeper, caretaker, gardener, or other employee. **4.** a resort hotel, motel, or inn. **5.** the main building of a camp, resort hotel, or the like. **6.** the meeting place of a branch of certain fraternal organizations. **7.** the members composing the branch. **8.** any of various North American Indian dwellings, as a wigwam or long house. **9.** the people who live in such a dwelling or a family or unit of North American Indians. **10.** the den of an animal or group of animals, esp. beavers. —*v.i.* **11.** to have a habitation or quarters, esp. temporarily, as in a hotel, motel, or inn: *We lodged in a guest house.* **12.** to live in rented quarters in another's house. **13.** to be fixed, implanted, or caught in a place or position; come to rest; stick: *The bullet lodged in the wall.* —*v.t.* **14.** to furnish with a habitation or quarters, esp. temporarily; accommodate. **15.** to furnish with a room or rooms in one's house for payment; have as a lodger. **16.** to serve as a residence, shelter, or dwelling for; shelter. **17.** to put, store, or deposit for storage or keeping; stow. **18.** to bring or send into a particular place or position. **19.** to house or contain. **20.** to vest (power, authority, etc.). **21.** to put or bring (information, a complaint, etc.) before a court or other authority. **22.** to beat down or lay flat, as vegetation in a storm. **23.** to track (a deer) to its lair.

Lodge (loj), *n.* **1. Henry Cabot,** 1850–1924, U.S. senator 1893–1924. **2.** his grandson, **Henry Cabot, Jr.,** 1902–85, U.S. statesman.

lodge′pole pine′, *n.* **1.** a tall pine, *Pinus contorta,* of W North America, having one type of cone that opens and drops its seeds every second year and another, resin-covered cone that opens only when a fire burns off the resin. **2.** the wood of this tree, used as timber.

lodg·er (loj′ər), *n.* a person who lives in rented quarters in another's house; roomer.

lodg·ing (loj′ing), *n.* **1.** accommodation in a house, esp. in rooms for rent: *to furnish board and lodging.* **2.** a temporary place to stay; temporary quarters. **3. lodgings,** a room or rooms rented for residence in another's house.

Loes (lōz), *n.* **Harry Dixon,** 1892–1965, U.S. musician and hymn writer.

lo·ess (lō′es, les, lus), *n.* a loamy, usu. yellowish and calcareous deposit formed by wind, common in the Mississippi Valley and in Europe and Asia. —**lo·ess′i·al,** *adj.*

Loewe (lō), *n.* **Frederick,** born 1904, U.S. composer, born in Austria.

loft (lôft, loft), *n.* **1.** a room, storage area, or the like within a sloping roof; attic; garret. **2.** a gallery or upper level in a church, hall, etc., for a special purpose: *a choir loft.* **3.** HAYLOFT. **4.** an upper story of a business building, warehouse, or factory, typically consisting of open, unpartitioned floor area. **5.** such an upper story converted or adapted to any of various uses, as quarters for living, studios for artists or dancers, exhibition galleries, or theater space. **6.** Also called **loft′ bed′.** a balcony or platform built over a living area and used for sleeping. **7.** *Golf.* **a.** the slope of the face of the head of a club backward from the vertical, tending to drive the ball upward. **b.** the act of lofting. **c.** a lofting stroke. **8.** the resiliency of fabric or yarn, esp. wool. **9.** the thickness of a fabric or of insulation used in a garment, as a down-filled jacket. —*v.t.* **10.** to hit or throw aloft: *He lofted a fly ball into center field.* **11.** *Golf.* **a.** to slant the face of (a club). **b.** to hit (a golf ball) into the air or over an obstacle. **c.** to clear (an obstacle) in this manner. **12.** to store in a loft. —*v.i.* **13.** to hit or throw something, esp. a ball, aloft. **14.** to go high into the air when hit, as a ball.

loft•y (lôf′tē, lof′-), *adj.,* **loft•i•er, loft•i•est. 1.** extending high in the air; of imposing height; towering: *lofty mountains.* **2.** exalted in rank, dignity, or character; eminent. **3.** elevated in style, tone, or sentiment, as writings or speech. **4.** arrogantly or condescendingly superior in manner; haughty. **5.** noting a rig of a sailing ship having extraordinarily high masts. —**loft′i•ly,** *adv.* —**loft′i•ness,** *n.*

log¹ (lôg, log), *n., v.,* **logged, log•ging.** —*n.* **1.** a portion or length of the trunk or of a large limb of a felled tree. **2.** something inert, heavy, or not sentient. **3.** a record concerning details of the trip of a ship or aircraft. **4.** a register of the operation of a machine. **5.** any of various detailed, usu. sequential records, as of the progress of an activity. **6.** a written account of everything transmitted by a radio or television station or network. **7.** any of various devices for determining the speed of a ship. —*v.t.* **8.** to cut (trees) into logs. **9.** to cut down the trees or timber on (land). **10.** to enter in a log; compile. **11.** to make a (certain speed), as a ship or airplane: *to log 18 knots.* **12.** to travel for (a certain distance or a certain amount of time), according to the record of a log: *He has logged 10,000 hours flying time.* —*v.i.* **13.** to cut down trees and get out logs from the forest for timber. **14. log in** or **on,** to gain access to a secured computer system or on-line service by keying in personal identification information. **15. log off** or **out,** to terminate a session on such a system or service. —**log′gish,** *adj.*

log² (lôg, log), *n.* LOGARITHM.

lo•gan•ber•ry (lō′gən ber′ē), *n., pl.* **-ries. 1.** a dark red, tart, elongated berry of a hybrid blackberry bush, *Rubus loganobaccus,* of the rose family. **2.** the plant itself.

log•a•rithm (lô′gə rith′əm, -rith′-, log′ə-), *n.* the exponent of the power to which a base number must be raised to equal a given number; log: *2 is the logarithm of 100 to the base 10 (2 = log₁₀ 100).* —**log′a•rith′mic,** *adj.*

log•book (lôg′bŏŏk′, log′-), *n.* a book in which details of a trip made by a ship or aircraft are recorded; log.

loge (lōzh), *n.* **1.** (in a theater) the front section of the lowest balcony, separated from the back section by an aisle or railing or both. **2.** a box in a theater or opera house. **3.** any small enclosure; booth.

log•ger (lô′gər, log′ər), *n.* **1.** a person whose work is logging; lumberjack. **2.** a tractor used in logging.

log•ger•head (lô′gər hed′, log′ər-), *n.* **1.** a thick-headed or stupid person; blockhead. **2.** LOGGERHEAD TURTLE. **3.** LOGGERHEAD SHRIKE. **4.** a ball or bulb of iron with a long handle, used, after being heated, to melt tar, heat liquids, etc. —*Idiom.* **5. at loggerheads,** in conflict; quarreling. —**log′ger•head′ed,** *adj.*

log′gerhead shrike′, *n.* a North American shrike, *Lanius ludovicianus,* gray above and white below with black wings, tail, and mask.

log′gerhead tur′tle, *n.* a large sea turtle, *Caretta caretta,* having a large head and a rounded carapace.

log•gi•a (lō′jē ə, loj′ə), *n., pl.* **-gi•as, -gie** (-jä, -jē). a gallery or arcade open to the air on at least one side.

loggia

log•ging (lô′ging, log′ing), *n.* the process, work, or business of cutting down trees and transporting the logs to sawmills.

log•ic (loj′ik), *n.* **1.** the science that investigates the principles governing correct or reliable inference. **2.** SYMBOLIC LOGIC. **3.** a particular method of reasoning or argumentation. **4.** the system or principles of reasoning applicable to any branch of knowledge or study. **5.** reason or sound judgment, as in utterances or actions. —**log′ic•less,** *adj.*

log•i•cal (loj′i kal), *adj.* **1.** according to or agreeing with the principles of logic: *a logical inference.* **2.** reasoning in accordance with the principles of logic. **3.** reasonable; to be expected: *the logical consequence*

of such threats. **4.** of or pertaining to logic. —**log′i•cal′i•ty, log′i•cal•ness,** *n.* —**log′i•cal•ly,** *adv.*

lo•gis•tics (lō jis′tiks, lə-), *n.* (*used with a sing. or pl. v.*) **1.** the branch of military science dealing with the procurement of equipment, movement of personnel, provision of facilities, etc. **2.** the planning, implementation, and coordination of the details of any operation. —**lo•gis′tic, lo•gis′ti•cal,** *adj.* —**lo•gis′ti•cal•ly,** *adv.*

log•jam (lôg′jam′, log′-), *n.* **1.** an immovable pileup or tangle of logs, as in a river, causing a blockage. **2.** any blockage or massive accumulation: *a logjam of bills before Congress.*

lo•go (lō′gō), *n., pl.* **-gos. 1.** Also called **logotype.** a graphic representation or symbol of a company name, trademark, abbreviation, etc., often uniquely designed for ready recognition. **2.** LOGOTYPE (def. 1)

LOGO (lō′gō), *n.* a high-level programming language used to teach children how to use computers. [< Greek *lógos* word]

logo-, a combining form meaning "word" (*logogram*), "speech" (*logorrhea*), "ratio" (*logarithm*). Also, *esp. before a vowel,* **log-.**

log•o•gram (lô′gə gram′, log′ə-), *n.* a conventional, abbreviated symbol for a frequently recurring word or phrase, as the symbol & for the word *and.* Also called **log′o•graph′** (-graf′, -gräf′). —**log′o•gram• mat′ic** (-grə mat′ik), *adj.* —**log′o•gram•mat′i•cal•ly,** *adv.*

log•o•griph (lô′gə grif, log′ə-), *n.* an anagram or other word puzzle. —**log′o•griph′ic,** *adj.*

lo•gom•a•chy (lō gom′ə kē), *n., pl.* **-chies. 1.** a dispute about or concerning words. **2.** an argument or debate marked by the reckless or incorrect use of words. —**log•o•mach′ic** (lô′gə mak′ik, log′ə-), **log′o• mach′i•cal,** *adj.* —**log•om′a•chist, log′o•mach′,** *n.*

log•o•phile (lô′gə fīl′, log′ə-), *n.* a lover of words.

log•or•rhe•a (lô′gə rē′ə, log′ə-), *n.* **1.** pathologically incoherent, repetitious speech. **2.** incessant or compulsive talkativeness; wearisome volubility. —**log′or•rhe′ic,** *adj.*

lo•gos (lō′gos, -gōs, log′os), *n.* **1.** (in Greek philosophy) the rational principle that governs and develops the universe. **2.** (in Christian theology) the divine word or reason incarnate in Jesus Christ. John 1:1–14.

log•o•type (lô′gə tīp′, log′ə-), *n.* **1.** Also called **logo.** a single piece of type bearing two or more uncombined letters, a syllable, or a word. **2.** LOGO (def. 2). —**log′o•typ′y,** *n.*

log•roll•ing (lôg′rō′ling, log′-), *n.* **1.** the exchange of support or favors, esp. by legislators for mutual political gain. **2.** cronyism or mutual favoritism among writers, editors, or critics, as in the form of reciprocal flattering reviews. **3.** the action of rolling logs to a particular place. **4.** the action of rotating a log rapidly in the water by treading upon it, esp. as a competitive sport; birling.

lo•gy (lō′gē), *adj.,* **-gi•er, -gi•est.** lacking physical or mental energy or vitality; sluggish; dull; lethargic. —**lo′gi•ly,** *adv.* —**lo′gi•ness,** *n.*

-logy, a combining form meaning "field of scientific study, discipline," used also to denote the body of principles, theories, data, etc., produced by learned endeavor (*archaeology; pathology; theology*); "set of abstract notions" (*ideology; methodology*); "set of texts" (*trilogy*); "systematic listing" (*genealogy*); "linguistic usage" (*tautology; phraseology*).

loin (loin), *n.* **1.** Usu., **loins.** the parts of the vertebrate body that lie on either side of the spine between the ribs and the hipbones. **2.** a cut of meat from this region, esp. a portion including the vertebrae of such parts. **3. loins, a.** the parts of the human body between the hips and the lower ribs, esp. regarded as the seat of physical strength and generative power. **b.** the genital and pubic area; genitalia.

loin•cloth (loin′klôth′, -kloth′), *n., pl.* **-cloths** (-klôthz′, -klothz′, -klôths′, -kloths′). a cloth worn around the loins or hips, esp. in tropical regions as the only clothing.

Lo•is (lō′is), *n.* a Christian woman, the grandmother of Timothy. II Tim. 1:5.

loi•ter (loi′tər), *v.i.* **1.** to linger aimlessly or as if aimlessly in or about a place. **2.** to move in a slow, idle manner. **3.** to waste time or dawdle over work. —*v.t.* **4.** to pass (time) in an idle or aimless manner (usu. fol. by *away*): *to loiter away the afternoon in daydreaming.* —**loi′ter•er,** *n.* —**loi′ter•ing•ly,** *adv.*

loll (lol), *v.i.* **1.** to recline or lean in a relaxed, lazy, or indolent manner; lounge: *to loll on a sofa.* **2.** to hang loosely; droop; dangle. —*v.t.* **3.** to allow to hang, droop, or dangle. —**loll′er,** *n.* —**loll′ing•ly,** *adv.*

lol•la•pa•loo•za or **lol•la•pa•loo•sa** (lol′ə pə lōō′zə), *n., pl.* **-zas** or **-sas.** *Slang.* an extraordinary or unusual thing, person, or event; an exceptional example or instance.

Lol•lard (lol′ərd), *n.* an English or Scottish follower of the religious teachings of John Wycliffe. [late Middle English < Middle Dutch *lollaert* mumbler (of prayers)] —**Lol′lard•y, Lol′lard•ry, Lol′lard•ism,** *n.*

lol•li•pop or **lol•ly•pop** (lol′ē pop′), *n.* a piece of hard candy attached to the end of a small stick that is held in the hand while the candy is licked.

lol•ly•gag (lol′ē gag′), *v.i.,* **-gagged, -gag•ging.** LALLYGAG.

Lo•mé (lô mā′), *n.* the capital of Togo, on the Gulf of Guinea. 366,476.

Lon•don (lun′dən), *n.* **1. Jack,** 1876–1916, U.S. writer. **2.** a metropolis in SE England, on the Thames: capital of the United Kingdom. **3. City of,** an old city in the central part of the former county of London: the ancient nucleus of the modern metropolis. 4700; 1 sq. mi. (3 sq. km). **4. County of,** a former administrative county comprising the City of London and 28 metropolitan boroughs, now part of Greater London. **5. Greater,** an urban area comprising the city of London and 32 metropolitan boroughs. 6,770,400; 609 sq. mi. (1575 sq. km). **6.** a city in S Ontario, in SE Canada. 269,140.

Lon′don broil′, *n.* a flank steak or similar cut of beef, usu. broiled and served in thin, crosscut slices.

Lon·don·der·ry (lun′dən der′ē), *n.* **1.** a county in N Northern Ireland. 130,889; 804 sq. mi. (2082 sq. km). **2.** its county seat, a seaport. 62,697. Also called **Derry.**

lone (lōn), *adj.* **1.** being alone; solitary; unaccompanied: *a lone traveler.* **2.** standing by itself or apart; isolated: *a lone house in the valley.* **3.** sole; single; only: *our lone competitor in the field.* **4.** unfrequented. **5.** lonesome; lonely. **6.** unmarried or widowed. —**lone′ness,** *n.*

lone·ly (lōn′lē), *adj.,* **-li·er, -li·est. 1.** affected with or causing a depressing feeling of being alone. **2.** destitute of friendly companionship, support, etc.: *a lonely exile.* **3.** lone; solitary; without company. **4.** remote from places of human habitation; desolate; unfrequented: *a lonely road.* **5.** standing apart; isolated: *a lonely tower.* —**lone′li·ness,** *n.*

lon·er (lō′nər), *n.* a person who is or prefers to be alone, esp. one who avoids the company of others.

lone·some (lōn′səm), *adj.* **1.** depressed or sad because of the lack of friends or companionship; lonely. **2.** attended with or causing such a feeling: *a lonesome evening at home.* **3.** lonely in situation; remote, desolate, or isolated. —*Idiom.* **4.** on or by one's lonesome, *Informal.* alone. —**lone′some·ly,** *adv.* —**lone′some·ness,** *n.*

Lone′ Star′ State′, *n.* Texas (used as a nickname).

lone′ wolf′, *n. Informal.* a person who prefers to live, act, or work alone or independent of others.

long¹ (lông, long), *adj.,* **long·er** (lông′gər, long′-), **long·est** (lông′gist, long′-), *n., adv.* —*adj.* **1.** having considerable or greater than usual linear extent in space. **2.** having considerable or greater than usual duration in time. **3.** extending, lasting, or totaling a number of specified units: *eight miles long; eight hours long.* **4.** containing many items or units: *a long list.* **5.** requiring a considerable time to relate, read, etc.: *a long story.* **6.** extending beyond normal, moderate, or desired limits: *to work long hours; The sleeves are long on me.* **7.** experienced as passing slowly, as because of tedium. **8.** reaching well into the past: *a long memory.* **9.** the longer of two or the longest of several: *the long way home; a brick with the long side exposed.* **10.** taking a long time; slow: *to be long in getting here.* **11.** forward-looking or considering all aspects; broad: *to take a long view.* **12.** intense, thorough, or critical; seriously appraising: *a long look at one's mistakes.* **13.** having an ample supply or endowment (often fol. by *on*): *long on brains.* **14.** extending relatively far: *a long reach.* **15.** being higher or taller than usual. **16.** being against great odds; unlikely: *a long chance.* **17. a.** (of a speech sound) lasting a relatively long time. **b.** having the sound of the English vowels in *mate, meet, mite, mote, moot,* and *mute,* historically descended from vowels that were long in duration. Compare SHORT (def. 13). **18. a.** (of a syllable in quantitative verse) lasting a longer time than a short syllable. **b.** stressed. **19.** having a considerable time to run, as a promissory note. **20.** holding or accumulating securities or commodities in the expectation that prices will rise: *a long position in hog futures.* **21.** marked by a large difference in the numbers of a given betting ratio or in the amounts wagered: *long odds.* —*n.* **22.** a comparatively long time: *They haven't been gone for long.* **23.** a long sound or syllable. **24. a.** a size of garments for men who are taller than average. **b.** a garment in this size. —*adv.* **25.** for or through a great extent of space or, esp., time: *a reform long advocated.* **26.** for or throughout a specified extent, esp. of time: *How long did he stay?* **27.** (used elliptically in referring to the length of an absence, delay, etc.): *Will she be long?* **28.** throughout a specified period of time: *It's been muggy all summer long.* **29.** at a point of time far distant from the time indicated: *long before.* —*Idiom.* **30. as long as, a.** provided that. **b.** seeing that; since: *As long as you're going, I'll go too.* **c.** Also, **so long as.** during the time that; while. **31. before long,** soon. **32. the long and (the) short of,** the essential point or result of: *The long and short of it is that they'll have to sell the house.*

long² (lông, long), *v.i.* to have an earnest or strong desire or craving; yearn: *to long for spring; to long to return home.*

Long (lông, long), *n.* **1. Crawford Williamson,** 1815–78, U.S. surgeon: first to use ether as an anesthetic. **2. Huey Pierce,** 1893–1935, U.S. politician.

long′-a·go′, *adj.* of or pertaining to the distant past.

Long′ Beach′, *n.* a city in SW California, S of Los Angeles. 433,852.

long·boat (lông′bōt′, long′-), *n.* the largest boat carried by a sailing ship.

long·bow (lông′bō′, long′-), *n.* a large bow drawn by hand, as that used by English archers from the 12th to the 16th centuries. —**long′bow′man,** *n., pl.* **-men.**

long′ dis′tance, *n.* telephone service between distant places.

long′-dis′tance, *adj.* **1.** of, from, or between distant places: *a long-distance phone call.* **2.** for, over, or covering long distances: *a long-distance runner.* —*adv.* **3.** by long-distance telephone service: *to call someone long-distance.*

long′ divi′sion, *n.* division, usu. by a number of two or more digits, in which each step of the process is written down.

long′-drawn′-out′, *adj.* lasting a very long time; protracted; drawn-out: *a long-drawn-out story.* Often, **long′-drawn′.**

lon·gev·i·ty (lon jev′i tē, lôn-), *n.* **1.** long life; great duration of individual life: *a family known for longevity.* **2.** length of life: *research in*

longevity. **3.** length of service, tenure, etc.; seniority: *promotions based on longevity.*

Long·fel·low (lông′fel′ō, long′-), *n.* **Henry Wadsworth** (wodz′-wərth), 1807–82, U.S. poet.

long·hair (lông′hâr′, long′-), *Informal.* —*n.* **1.** *Sometimes Disparaging.* an intellectual. **2.** a person devoted to the arts, esp. a lover of classical music. **3.** a person having long hair, esp. a hippie. **4.** a domestic cat having long fur. —*adj.* Also, **long′haired′. 5.** having long hair: *a longhair cat.* **6.** of or characteristic of longhairs or their tastes.

long·hand (lông′hand′, long′-), *n.* **1.** writing of the ordinary kind, in which words are written out in full. —*adj.* **2.** written in longhand.

long′ haul′, *n.* HAUL (def. 17).

long′-haul′, *adj.* pertaining to or engaged in the transport of freight over long distances: *long-haul trucking.*

long′-horned′ bee′tle, *n.* any of numerous, often brightly colored beetles of the family Cerambycidae, usu. with long antennae, the larva of which bores into the wood of trees.

long′-horned′ grass′hopper, *n.* any of numerous insects of the family Tettigoniidae, having long, threadlike antennae.

long′ house′, *n.* a communal structure, mainly of the Iroquois, orig. consisting of a wooden, bark-covered framework often as much as 100 ft. (30.5 m) in length: formerly used as a dwelling.

long·ing (lông′ing, long′-), *n.* **1.** strong, persistent desire or craving, esp. for something unattainable or distant: *filled with longing for home.* **2.** an instance of this: *a sudden longing to see old friends.* —*adj.* **3.** characterized by earnest desire: *a longing look.* —**long′ing·ly,** *adv.*

long·ish (lông′ish, long′-), *adj.* somewhat long.

Long′ Is′land, *n.* an island in SE New York: the New York City boroughs of Brooklyn and Queens are at its W end. 118 mi. (190 km) long.

lon·gi·tude (lon′ji tōōd′, -tyōōd′), *n.* angular distance east or west on the earth's surface, as measured, usu. in degrees, from the meridian of some particular place to the prime meridian at Greenwich, England. —**lon′gi·tu′di·nal,** *adj.* —**lon′gi·tu′di·nal·ly,** *adv.*

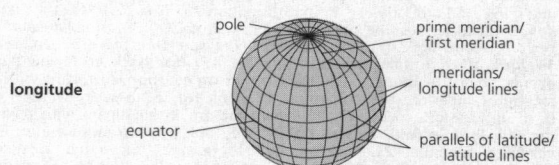

longitude

pole / prime meridian/ first meridian / meridians/ longitude lines / equator / parallels of latitude/ latitude lines

long′ johns′, *n.pl.* LONG UNDERWEAR.

long′ jump′, *n.* **1.** a jump for distance from a running start. **2.** an athletic field event featuring competition in the long jump. Also called **broad jump.** —**long′jump′,** *v.i.* —**long′ jump′er,** *n.*

long′-last′ing, *adj.* **1.** enduring or existing for a long period of time: *a long-lasting friendship.* **2.** effective for a relatively long period of time: *a long-lasting pain reliever.*

long′leaf pine′ (lông′lēf′, long′-), *n.* **1.** an American pine, *Pinus palustris,* valued as a source of turpentine and for its timber. **2.** the wood of this tree. Also called **Georgia pine.**

long′-lived′ (-līvd′, -livd′), *adj.* **1.** having a long life or duration: *a long-lived animal; long-lived fame.* **2.** lasting or functioning a long time: *a long-lived battery.* —**long′-lived′ness,** *n.*

Long′ Par′liament, *n.* the English Parliament that assembled in 1640, was dismissed by Cromwell in 1653, reconvened in 1659, and was dissolved in 1660.

long′-play′ing, *adj.* of or pertaining to microgroove phonograph records devised to be played at 33⅓ revolutions per minute.

long′-range′, *adj.* **1.** considering or extending into the future: *a long-range forecast; long-range plans.* **2.** designed to cover or operate over a long distance: *long-range rockets.*

long′-run′, *adj.* happening or presented over a long period of time: *a long-run hit play.*

long·shore (lông′shôr′, -shōr′, long′-), *adj.* existing, found, or employed along the shore or at a seaport.

long·shore·man (lông′shôr′mən, -shōr′-, long′-), *n., pl.* **-men.** a person employed on the wharves of a port, as in loading and unloading vessels.

long′ shot′, *n.* **1.** a horse, team, etc., that has little chance of winning and carries long odds. **2.** an attempt or undertaking that offers much but in which there is little chance for success. **3.** an attempt or project that is unlikely to be successful. **4.** a movie or television shot that gives a broad or full view of a scene or subject from a relatively great distance. Compare CLOSEUP (def. 2). —*Idiom.* **5. by a long shot,** by any means: *You aren't finished by a long shot.*

long′-sight′ed, *adj.* **1.** farsighted. **2.** having great foresight. —**long′-sight′ed·ness,** *n.*

Longs′ Peak′ (lôngz, longz), *n.* a peak in N central Colorado, in Rocky Mountain National Park. 14,255 ft. (4345 m).

long·spur (lông′spûr′, long′-), *n.* any of several songbirds of the genus *Calcarius* (subfamily Emberizinae), inhabiting tundra or prairies of the Northern Hemisphere, having a long hind claw on each foot.

long·stand·ing (lông′stan′ding, long′-), *adj.* existing for a long time: *a longstanding disagreement.*

long′-suf′fering, *adj.* **1.** enduring injury, trouble, or provocation long and patiently. —*n.* **2.** long and patient endurance of injury or trouble. —**long′-suf′feringly,** *adv.*

long′ suit′, *n.* **1.** the suit in which the most cards are held in a hand. **2.** the quality, activity, or endeavor in which one excels: *Diligence is not his long suit.*

long′-term′, *adj.* **1.** covering or involving a relatively long period of time: *long-term memory.* **2.** maturing after a relatively long period of time: *a long-term bond.*

long·time (lông′tīm′, long′-), *adj.* existing or continuing as such for a long period of time; longstanding: *longtime friends.*

long′ un′derwear, *n.* a close-fitting, usu. knitted undergarment with legs reaching to the ankles, worn as protection against cold.

long·ways (lông′wāz′, long′-), *adv., adj.* LENGTHWISE.

long′-wind′ed, *adj.* **1.** talking or writing at tedious length: *long-winded speakers.* **2.** (of speech or writing) continued to a tedious length. —**long′-wind′ed·ly,** *adv.* —**long′-wind′ed·ness,** *n.*

long·wise (lông′wīz′, long′-), *adv., adj.* LENGTHWISE.

loo·fah or **loo·fa** (lōo′fə), also **luffa,** *n., pl.* **-fahs** or **-fas. 1. a.** any of several tropical vines of the genus *Luffa,* of the gourd family, bearing large elongated fruit. **b.** the fruit of such a vine. **2.** the dried fibrous interior of this fruit, used as a sponge.

look (lŏok), *v.i.* **1.** to turn one's eyes toward something or in some direction in order to see. **2.** to use one's sight in seeking, searching, examining, watching, etc.: *to look through the papers.* **3.** to glance or gaze in a manner specified: *to look questioningly at a person.* **4.** to appear to the eye as specified: *to look pale.* **5.** to appear to the mind; seem: *The case looks promising.* **6.** to direct attention or consideration: *Let's look at the facts.* **7.** to face or afford a view: *The room looks out on the garden.* **8.** to tend, as in bearing or significance: *Conditions look toward war.* —*v.t.* **9.** to give (someone) a look: *Can you look me in the eye and say that?* **10.** to have an appearance appropriate to or befitting: *to look one's age.* **11.** to observe or pay attention to: *Now look what you've done!* **12.** to express or suggest by looks: *to look one's annoyance at a person.* **13.** to appear to be; look like: *I'm sure I looked a perfect fool.* **14. look after,** to take care of; attend to. **15. look back,** to review past events; return in thought. **16. look down on** or **upon,** to regard with a feeling of superiority or contempt. **17. look for, a.** to seek; search for. **b.** to anticipate; expect. **18. look forward to,** to anticipate with pleasure. **19. look in (on),** to visit briefly. **20. look into,** to inquire into; investigate; examine. **21. look on, a.** to be a spectator; watch. **b.** Also, **look upon.** to consider; regard. **22. look out,** to be alert to danger; be careful. **23. look out for,** to take watchful care of. **24. look over,** to examine, esp. briefly. **25. look to, a.** to pay attention to. **b.** to direct one's expectations or hopes to; depend on. **c.** to expect or anticipate. **26. look up, a.** to become better or more prosperous; improve. **b.** to search for, as an item of information, in a reference book or the like. **c.** to seek out, esp. to visit: *to look up an old friend.* **27. look up to,** to regard with admiration or respect; esteem. —*n.* **28.** the act of looking. **29.** a visual search or examination. **30.** the way in which a person or thing appears; aspect: *the look of an honest man.* **31.** an expressive glance: *to give someone a sharp look.* **32.** fashion; style: *the latest look in furniture.* **33. looks, a.** general aspect; appearance: *to like the looks of a place.* **b.** attractive, pleasing appearance. —*Proverb.* **34. Look before you leap,** consider matters carefully before taking action.

look′-alike′ or **look′a·like′,** *n.* **1.** a person or thing that looks like or closely resembles another; double. —*adj.* **2.** being or characteristic of a look-alike.

look·er (lŏok′ər), *n.* **1.** a person who looks. **2.** *Informal.* a very attractive person.

look′er-on′, *n., pl.* **look·ers-on.** a person who looks on; onlooker; spectator.

look′ing glass′, *n.* **1.** a mirror. **2.** the glass used in a mirror.

look·out (lŏok′out′), *n.* **1.** the act of looking out or keeping watch. **2.** a watch kept, as for something that may come or happen. **3.** a person or group keeping a watch. **4.** a station or place from which a watch is kept. **5.** an object of care or concern: *That's not my lookout.* **6.** view; prospect; outlook.

look′-see′, *n. Informal.* a usu. quick visual inspection or survey; look: *to have a look-see.*

look′up′ or **look′-up′,** *n.* an act or instance of looking something up, as information in a reference book or an on-line database.

loom[1] (lōom), *n.* a hand-operated or power-driven apparatus for weaving fabrics, containing harnesses, reed, shuttles, treadles, etc.

loom[2] (lōom), *v.i.* **1.** to come into view in indistinct and enlarged form: *The island loomed through the mist.* **2.** to rise before or overhang with an appearance of great or portentous size: *Suddenly a police officer loomed over him.* **3.** to assume form as an impending event: *A battle looms at the convention.* —*n.* **4.** a looming appearance, as of something seen indistinctly at a distance or through a fog.

loon[1] (lōon), *n.* any of several large, ducklike diving birds of the order Gaviiformes, nesting along fresh water in colder regions of the Northern Hemisphere.

loon[2] (lōon), *n.* a crazy or simple-minded person.

loon·y or **loon·ey** (lōo′nē), *adj.,* **loon·i·er, loon·i·est,** *n., pl.* **loon·ies**

or **loon·eys.** *Informal.* —*adj.* **1.** lunatic; insane. **2.** extremely or senselessly foolish. —*n.* **3.** a lunatic. —**loon′i·ness,** *n.*

loon′y bin′, *n. Informal.* an insane asylum or the psychiatric ward of a hospital.

loon′y tunes′, *adj., n., pl.* **loony tunes.** *Informal.* LOONY.

loop (lōop), *n.* **1.** a portion of a cord, ribbon, etc., folded or doubled upon itself so as to leave an opening between the parts. **2.** anything shaped more or less like a loop. **3.** a curved piece or a ring used for the insertion of something or as a handle. **4.** a circular area at the end of a trolley line, railroad line, etc., where cars turn around. **5.** an arm of a cloverleaf where traffic may turn off or onto a main road or highway. **6.** a maneuver executed by an airplane in such a manner that the airplane describes a closed curve in a vertical plane. **7.** a closed electric or magnetic circuit. **8.** the reiteration of a set of instructions in a computer routine or program. **9.** a piece of magnetic tape or film with the ends joined to form an endless strip so that the same material is continuously replayed. **10.** ANTINODE. —*v.t.* **11.** to form into a loop. **12.** to make a loop in. **13.** to enfold or encircle in or with something arranged in a loop. **14.** to fasten by forming into a loop or by means of a loop: *to loop up the draperies.* **15.** to cause (a missile or projectile) to trace a looping or looplike trajectory through the air. **16.** to fly (an airplane) in a loop or series of loops. **17.** to complete or alter (a film or film segment) by recording new or more dialogue or other sound onto the existing soundtrack. —*v.i.* **18.** to make or form a loop: *The river loops around the two counties.* **19.** to move by forming loops, as a measuringworm, or by tracing a looplike path. **20.** to perform a loop or series of loops in an airplane. **21.** to record dialogue, sound effects, etc., onto an existing film track or soundtrack. —*Idiom.* **22. out of the loop,** excluded from the circle of people having power or receiving important information. **23. throw** or **knock for a loop,** to overwhelm with surprise or confusion.

looped (lōopt), *adj.* **1.** having or consisting of loops; loopy. **2.** *Slang.* **a.** drunk; inebriated. **b.** eccentric; loopy. **c.** enthusiastic; keen: *These days he's looped on rodeos.*

loop·hole (lōop′hōl′), *n.* **1.** a narrow opening in the wall of a fortification for observation, the admission of light or air, or the discharge of weapons. **2.** a means of escape or evasion, esp. a means or opportunity of evading a law, contract, etc.

loop′ knot′, *n.* a knot made by doubling over a line at its end and tying both thicknesses into a square knot in such a way as to leave a loop.

loop′-the-loop′, *n.* **1.** an airplane maneuver in which a plane, starting upward, makes one complete vertical loop. **2.** a ride in an amusement park that simulates this maneuver.

loop·y (lōo′pē), *adj.,* **loop·i·er, loop·i·est. 1.** full of loops. **2.** *Slang.* **a.** eccentric; crazy; dotty. **b.** befuddled or confused.

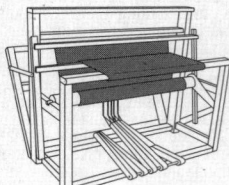

loom[1] (def. 1)

loose (lōos), *adj.,* **loos·er, loos·est,** *adv., v.,* **loosed, loos·ing.** —*adj.* **1.** free or released from fastening or attachment: *a loose end.* **2.** not firmly fixed or attached: *a loose tooth; a loose board in a floor.* **3.** free from confinement or restraint; unfettered: *loose cats prowling around.* **4.** not bound together: *loose papers; to wear one's hair loose.* **5.** not put up in a package or other container: *loose mushrooms.* **6.** not fitting closely or tightly: *a loose sweater.* **7.** not firm, taut, or rigid: *a loose rein.* **8.** relaxed or limber in nature: *to run with a loose, open stride.* **9.** not close or compact in structure or arrangement: *a loose weave.* **10.** imposing few restraints; allowing freedom for independent action: *a loose federation of city-states.* **11.** not strict, exact, or precise: *a loose translation.* **12.** available for disposal; unappropriated: *loose funds.* **13.** lacking in reticence or power of restraint: *a loose tongue.* **14.** (of the bowels) lax. **15.** lacking moral restraint or integrity: *loose character.* **16.** uncombined, as a chemical element. —*adv.* **17.** in a loose manner; loosely (often used in combination): *loose-fitting.* —*v.t.* **18.** to let loose; free from bonds or restraint. **19.** to release, as from constraint, obligation, or penalty. **20.** to set free from fastening or attachment: *to loose a boat from its moorings.* **21.** to unfasten, undo, or untie, as a bond or knot. **22.** to shoot; discharge; let fly: *to loose missiles at the invaders.* **23.** to make less tight; slacken; relax. —*v.i.* **24.** to let go a hold. **25.** to hoist anchor; get under way. **26.** to shoot or let fly an arrow, bullet, etc. (often fol. by *off*). —*Idiom.* **27. break loose,** to free oneself; escape. **28. cast loose,** to unfasten; set adrift; free. **29. cut loose, a.** to release or be released from domination. **b.** to behave wildly; revel; carouse. **30. hang** or **stay loose,** *Informal.* to remain relaxed and unperturbed. **31. let loose, a.** to free or become free. **b.** to yield; give way. **c.** to speak or act with unrestricted freedom: *to let loose with a few swear words.* **32. on the loose, a.** free; unconfined. **b.** behaving in a free or unrestrained way. **33. turn** or **set loose,** to free from confinement. —**loose′ly,** *adv.* —**loose′ness,** *n.*

loose′ can′non, *n.* a person whose reckless behavior endangers the efforts or welfare of others.

loose′ construc′tionist, *n.* one who interprets the Constitution broadly. Compare STRICT CONSTRUCTIONIST.

loose′ end′, *n.* **1.** Usu., **loose ends.** an unsettled or unfinished detail. —***Idiom.*** **2. at loose ends,** in an uncertain or unsettled situation or position; without an occupation or plans.

loose′-joint′ed, *adj.* **1.** having or marked by easy, free movement; limber. **2.** having loose joints. —**loose′-joint′ed•ness,** *n.*

loose′-leaf′, *adj.* **1.** having individual leaves held in a binder **(loose′-leaf′ bind′er),** as by rings that open and close, in such a way as to allow their removal or replacement without tearing: *a loose-leaf notebook.* **2.** of or for use with a loose-leaf binder: *loose-leaf paper.*

loos•en (lo͞o′sən), *v.t.* **1.** to make less tight: *to loosen a belt; to loosen one's grasp.* **2.** to make less firmly fixed in place: *to loosen a tooth.* **3.** to unfasten or undo, as a bond or fetter. **4.** to set free from restraint or constraint. **5.** to make less compact or dense: *to loosen the soil.* **6.** to relax in strictness or severity. **7.** to relieve (the bowels) of constipation. —*v.i.* **8.** to become loose or looser (sometimes fol. by *up*). **9. loosen up,** to become less tense or formal; relax. —**loos′en•er,** *n.*

loose•strife (lo͞os′strīf′), *n.* **1.** any of various plants belonging to the genus *Lysimachia,* of the primrose family, having clusters of usu. yellow flowers. **2.** any of several plants belonging to the genus *Lythrum,* of the loosestrife family. Compare PURPLE LOOSESTRIFE.

loose′-tongued′, *adj.* unrestrained or irresponsible in speech; given to gossiping.

loot (lo͞ot), *n.* **1.** spoils or plunder taken by pillaging, as in war. **2.** anything taken by dishonesty, force, stealth, etc.: *a burglar's loot.* **3.** a collection of gifts or purchases. **4.** *Slang.* money. **5.** the act of looting. —*v.t.* **6.** to carry off or take (something) as loot: *to loot a nation's art treasures.* **7.** to plunder or pillage (a place), as in war; despoil. **8.** to rob, as by burglary or corrupt activity in public office: *to loot the public treasury.* —*v.i.* **9.** to take loot; plunder. —**loot′er,** *n.*

lop[1] (lop), *v.,* **lopped, lop•ping,** *n.* —*v.t.* **1.** to cut off (branches, twigs, etc.) from a tree or other plant. **2.** to cut off (a limb or part) from a person, animal, etc. **3.** to cut off the branches, twigs, etc., of (a tree or other plant). **4.** to eliminate as unnecessary or excessive: *We had to lop off whole pages of the report.* —*v.i.* **5.** to remove parts by or as if by cutting. —*n.* **6.** parts or a part lopped off. —**lop′per,** *n.*

lop[2] (lop), *v.,* **lopped, lop•ping,** *adj.* —*v.i.* **1.** to hang loosely or limply; droop. **2.** to move in a drooping or heavy, awkward way. —*adj.* **3.** hanging down limply or droopingly: *lop ears.*

lope (lōp), *v.,* **loped, lop•ing,** *n.* —*v.i.* **1.** to move or run with bounding steps, as a quadruped, or with a long, easy stride, as a person. **2.** to canter leisurely with a long, easy stride, as a horse. —*v.t.* **3.** to cause to lope. —*n.* **4.** the act or gait of loping; a long, easy stride. —**lop′er,** *n.*

lop•sid•ed (lop′sī′did), *adj.* **1.** heavier, larger, or more developed on one side than the other; unevenly balanced; unsymmetrical. **2.** leaning to one side. —**lop′sid′ed•ly,** *adv.* —**lop′sid′ed•ness,** *n.*

lo•qua•cious (lō kwā′shəs), *adj.* **1.** talking or tending to talk much or freely; talkative; garrulous: *a loquacious dinner guest.* **2.** characterized by excessive talk; wordy. —**lo•qua′cious•ly,** *adv.* —**lo•qua′cious•ness, lo•quac′i•ty** (-kwas′i tē), *n.*

lo•quat (lō′kwot, -kwat), *n.* **1.** a small evergreen tree, *Eriobotrya japonica,* native to China and Japan, cultivated as an ornamental and for its yellow, plumlike fruit. **2.** the fruit itself.

lo•ran (lôr′an, lōr′-), *n.* (*sometimes cap.*) a navigational system for locating one's position by determining the time displacement between radio signals from two known stations.

lord (lôrd), *n.* **1.** a person who has authority, control, or power over others; master or ruler. **2.** a person who exercises authority from property rights; an owner of land, houses, etc. **3.** a person who has great influence in a profession: *the great lords of banking.* **4.** a feudal superior; the proprietor of a manor. **5.** a titled nobleman or peer; a person whose ordinary appellation contains by courtesy the title *Lord* or some higher title. **6. Lords,** the Lords Spiritual and Lords Temporal comprising the House of Lords. **7.** (*cap.*) (in Great Britain) **a.** the title of certain high officials: *Lord Mayor of London.* **b.** the formally polite title of a bishop: *Lord Bishop of Durham.* **c.** the title informally substituted for marquis, earl, viscount, etc. **8.** (*cap.*) the Supreme Being; God. **9.** (*cap.*) Jesus Christ. —*interj.* **10.** (*often cap.*) (used in exclamatory phrases to express surprise, delight, dismay, etc.): *Lord, what a beautiful day!* —***Idiom.*** **11. lord it,** to behave arrogantly or imperiously: *to lord it over one's friends.* —***Proverb.*** **12. The Lord gives and the Lord takes away,** the will of God is paramount. Job 1:21. —**lord′ly,** *adj.,* **-li•er, -li•est.**

Lord′ of hosts′ (or **Hosts′**), *n.* Jehovah; God. I Sam. 1:3; 17:45; Ps. 24:10.

Lord′ Protec′tor, *n.* PROTECTOR (def. 2).

Lord's′ day′ (or **Day′**), *n.* **the,** Sunday.

lord•ship (lôrd′ship), *n.* (*often cap.*) (in Great Britain) a term of respect used when speaking of or to judges or certain noblemen (usu. prec. by *his* or *your*).

Lord's′ My′ Shep′herd, The, a Christian hymn based on Psalm 23, which begins "The Lord is my shepherd; I shall not want."

Lord's′ Prayer′ (prâr), *n.* **the,** the prayer given by Jesus to His disciples, and beginning with the words *Our Father.* Matt. 6:9–13; Luke 11:2–4.

Lord's′ Sup′per, *n.* **the, 1.** EUCHARIST. **2.** LAST SUPPER.

lore (lôr, lōr), *n.* **1.** the body of knowledge, esp. of a traditional, anecdotal, or popular nature, on a particular subject: *nature lore; local lore.* **2.** learning, knowledge, or erudition. —**lore′less,** *adj.*

Lo•renz (lôr′ənz, -ents, lōr′-), *n.* **Konrad (Zacharias),** 1903–89, Austrian ethologist.

lo-res (lō′rez′), *adj.* low-resolution.

lor•gnette (lôrn yet′), *n.* a pair of eyeglasses or opera glasses mounted on a handle.

lor•gnon (*Fr.* lôR nyôɴ′), *n., pl.* **-gnons** (*Fr.* -nyôɴ′). LORGNETTE.

Los Al•a•mos (lôs al′ə mōs′, los), *n.* a town in central New Mexico, NW of Sante Fe: atomic research center. 11,039.

Los An•ge•les (lôs an′jə ləs, los), *n.* a seaport in SW California: second largest city in the U.S. 3,448,613; with suburbs 6,997,000.

lose (lo͞oz), *v.,* **lost, los•ing.** —*v.t.* **1.** to come to be without, as through accident: *They lost all their belongings in the storm.* **2.** to fail inadvertently to retain, usu. temporarily: *I just lost a dime under this sofa.* **3.** to suffer the deprivation of: *to lose one's job.* **4.** to be bereaved of by death: *to lose a sister.* **5.** to fail to preserve or maintain: *to lose one's balance.* **6.** (of a timepiece) to run slower by: *The watch loses three minutes a day.* **7.** to forfeit the possession of: *to lose a fortune by gambling.* **8.** to get rid of: *to lose weight.* **9.** to bring to destruction: *Ship and crew were lost.* **10.** to damn: *to lose one's soul.* **11.** to have slip from sight or awareness: *We lost him in the crowd.* **12.** to stray from: *to lose one's way.* **13.** to leave far behind: *She managed to lose the other runners.* **14.** to use to no purpose; waste: *to lose time in waiting.* **15.** to fail to gain or win: *to lose a bargain; to lose a bet.* **16.** to be defeated in: *They lost four games in five.* **17.** to cause the loss of: *The delay lost the battle for them.* **18.** to let go astray: *We lost ourselves in the woods.* **19.** to allow (oneself) to become engrossed in something: *I had lost myself in thought.* **20.** (of a physician) to fail to preserve the life of (a patient). **21.** (of a woman) to fail to be delivered of (a live baby). —*v.i.* **22.** to suffer loss: *to lose on a contract.* **23.** to suffer defeat. **24.** to depreciate in effectiveness: *a classic that loses in translation.* **25.** (of a timepiece) to run slow. **26. lose out,** to suffer defeat or loss. —***Idiom.*** **27. lose it,** to fail to maintain composure or control. —***Proverb.*** **28. I only regret that I have but one life to lose for my country,** the last words (1776) of the American patriot Nathan Hale.

los•er (lo͞o′zər), *n.* **1.** a person or group that loses. **2. a.** a person who has failed significantly at something: *a loser at marriage.* **b.** someone or something that disappoints. **3.** *Slang.* MISFIT (def. 3).

loss (lôs, los), *n.* **1.** the act of losing possession of something. **2.** disadvantage or deprivation from separation or loss: *bearing the loss of a robbery.* **3.** something that is lost. **4.** an amount or number lost: *The loss of life increased each day.* **5.** an instance of losing: *the loss of old friends.* **6.** deprivation through death: *to mourn the loss of a grandparent.* **7.** a losing by defeat. **8.** failure to preserve or maintain: *loss of engine speed.* **9.** destruction; ruin. **10.** Often, **losses.** the number of soldiers lost through death or capture. **11.** an event, as death or property damage, for which an insurer must make indemnity under the terms of a policy. **12.** a measure of the power lost in an electrical system, as by conversion to heat, expressed as a relation between power input and power output, as the ratio of or difference between the two quantities. —***Idiom.*** **13. at a loss, a.** at less than cost. **b.** in a state of bewilderment or uncertainty.

lost (lôst, lost), *adj.* **1.** no longer possessed: *lost friends.* **2.** no longer to be found: *lost articles.* **3.** having gone astray: *lost children.* **4.** not used to good purpose: *a lost advantage.* **5.** not won: *a lost prize.* **6.** attended with defeat: *a lost battle.* **7.** destroyed; ruined: *lost ships.* **8.** preoccupied; rapt: *lost in thought.* **9.** distracted; distraught: *the lost look of a man trapped.* —*v.* **10.** pt. and pp. of LOSE. —***Idiom.*** **11. lost to, a.** no longer belonging to. **b.** no longer possible or open to: *The opportunity was lost to us.* **c.** insensible to: *lost to all sense of duty.*

Lost′ Coin′, The, a parable of Jesus. Luke 15:8–10.

Lost′ Col′ony, *n.* a settlement of British colonists whom Walter Raleigh sent to Roanoke Island (now part of North Carolina) in 1587 and of whom no trace was found after 1591.

Lost′ Genera′tion, *n.* **1.** the generation of men and women who came of age during or immediately following World War I: viewed, as a result of their war experiences and the social upheaval of the time, as cynical, disillusioned, and without cultural or emotional stability. **2.** a group of American writers of this generation, including Ernest Hemingway, F. Scott Fitzgerald, and John Dos Passos.

Lost′ Sheep′, The, a parable of Jesus. Matt. 18:10–14; Luke 15:1–7.

lost′ tribes′, *n.pl.* the members of the 10 tribes of ancient Israel taken into captivity in 722 B.C. by Sargon II and believed never to have returned to Palestine.

lot (lot), *n., v.,* **lot•ted, lot•ting.** —*n.* **1.** one of a set of objects, as straws or pebbles, drawn or thrown from a container to decide a question or choice by chance. **2.** the casting or drawing of such objects: *to choose a person by lot.* **3.** the decision or choice made by such a method. **4.** allotted share; portion. **5.** fate; fortune; destiny: *Her lot was not a happy one.* **6.** a distinct piece of land: *a building lot.* **7.** a piece of land forming a part of a district, city, or other community. **8.** a piece of land having a specified use: *a parking lot.* **9.** a motion-picture studio and its surrounding property. **10.** a distinct parcel, as of merchandise: *furniture auctioned off in 20 lots.* **11.** a number of things or persons: *There's one more, and that's the lot.* **12.** kind; sort: *He's a bad lot.* **13.** a great·many or a great deal: *a lot of books; lots of money.* —*v.t.* **14.** to divide or distribute by lot. **15.** to divide, as land, into lots. —**Idiom. 16.** **a lot,** to a notable degree; much: *I feel a lot better.* **17. draw** or **cast lots,** to settle a question by the use of lots. —**lot′ter,** *n.*

Lot (lot), *n.* Abraham's nephew, whose wife was changed into a pillar of salt for looking back during their flight from Sodom. Gen. 13:1–12, 19.

lo·tion (lō′shən), *n.* a liquid preparation containing insoluble material in suspension or emulsion for medicinal, cleansing, protective, or soothing application to the skin.

lots (lots), *adv.* much; a great deal: *That's lots better.*

lot·ter·y (lot′ə rē), *n., pl.* **-ter·ies. 1.** a gambling game or method of raising money in which a large number of tickets are sold and a drawing is held for prizes. **2.** a drawing of lots. **3.** any happening or process that is or appears to be determined by chance: *Life is a lottery.*

lot·to (lot′ō), *n., pl.* **-tos. 1.** a game of chance that is similar to bingo. **2.** a lottery, esp. one operated by a state government, in which players choose numbers that are matched against those of the official drawing.

lo·tus (lō′təs), *n., pl.* **-tus·es. 1.** a plant believed to be a jujube or elm and referred to in Greek legend as yielding a fruit that induced a state of dreamy and contented forgetfulness in those who ate it. **2.** the fruit of this plant. **3.** any aquatic plant of the genus *Nelumbo,* of the water lily family, having shieldlike leaves and showy, solitary flowers usu. projecting above the water. **4.** any of several water lilies of the genus *Nymphaea.* **5.** a decorative motif derived from such a plant and used widely in ancient art, as on the capitals of Egyptian columns. **6.** any shrubby plant of the genus *Lotus,* of the legume family, having red, pink, yellow, or white flowers.

lo′tus posi′tion, *n.* a standard seated posture for yoga with legs intertwined, left foot over right thigh and right foot over left thigh.

loud (loud), *adj.* **1.** having exceptional volume or intensity: *loud talking; loud thunder.* **2.** making or uttering strongly audible sounds: *a quartet of loud trombones.* **3.** clamorous; noisy: *a loud party.* **4.** emphatic; insistent: *loud in one's praises.* **5.** garish; ostentatious: *a loud necktie.* **6.** obtrusively vulgar; coarse. **7.** strong or offensive in smell. —*adv.* **8.** in a loud manner; loudly: *Don't talk so loud.* —**Idiom. 9. out loud,** aloud; audibly. —**loud′ly,** *adv.* —**loud′ness,** *n.*

loud·mouthed (loud′mou⁴hd′, -mouth′), *adj.* given to loud or indiscreet talk. —**loud′mouth′,** *n.*

loud·speak·er (loud′spē′kər), *n.* **1.** any of various devices that convert amplified electronic signals into audible sound. **2.** Also called **speaker.** a transducer that performs this function in an audio system, typically mounted in a box-like enclosure.

Lou′ Gehr′ig's disease′ (lōō), *n.* AMYOTROPHIC LATERAL SCLEROSIS.

Lou·is¹ (lōō′is), *n.* Joe (*Joseph Louis Barrow*), 1914–81, U.S. boxer: world heavyweight champion 1937–49.

Lou·is² (lōō′ē; *Fr.* lwē), *n.* **1.** Louis I (*"the Pious"*), A.D. 778–840, emperor of the Holy Roman Empire 814–840 (son of Charlemagne). **2. Louis IX, Saint,** 1214?–70, king of France 1226–70. **3. Louis XI,** 1423–83, king of France 1461–83 (son of Charles VII). **4. Louis XII** (*"the Father of the People"*), 1462–1515, king of France 1498–1515. **5. Louis XIII,** 1601–43, king of France 1610–43 (son of Henry IV of Navarre). **6. Louis XIV** (*"the Great"; "the Sun King"*), 1638–1715, king of France 1643–1715 (son of Louis XIII). **7. Louis XV,** 1710–74, king of France 1715–74 (great- grandson of Louis XIV). **8. Louis XVI,** 1754–93, king of France 1774–92 (grandson of Louis XV). **9. Louis XVII** (*"Louis Charles of France"*), 1785–95, titular king of France 1793–95 (son of Louis XVI). **10. Louis XVIII** (*Louis Xavier Stanislas*), 1755–1824, king of France 1814–15, 1815–24 (brother of Louis XVI).

Lou·i·si·an·a (lōō ē′zē an′ə, lōō′ə zē–, lōō′ē–), *n.* a state in the S United States. 4,350,579; 48,522 sq. mi. (125,672 sq. km). *Cap.:* Baton Rouge. *Abbr.:* LA, La. —**Lou·i′si·an′an, Lou·i′si·an′i·an,** *adj., n.*

Loui′sian′a Cre′ole, *n.* a French-based creole spoken in some black communities of Louisiana.

Loui′sian′a Pur′chase, *n.* the territory that the U.S. purchased from France in 1803 for $15,000,000, extending from the Mississippi River to the Rocky Mountains and from the Gulf of Mexico to Canada.

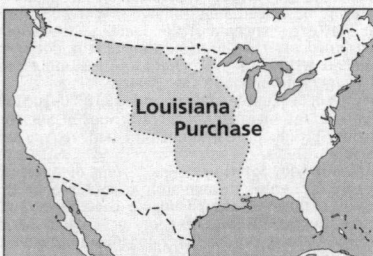

Louisiana Purchase

Lou·is·ville (lōō′ē vil′, -ə vəl), *n.* a port in N Kentucky, on the Ohio River: Kentucky Derby. 270,308. —**Lou′is·vill′ian,** *n.*

lounge (lounj), *v.,* **lounged, loung·ing,** *n.* —*v.i.* **1.** to pass time indolently. **2.** to rest or recline indolently; loll. **3.** to go or move in a leisurely manner. —*v.t.* **4.** to pass (time) indolently: *to lounge the afternoon away.* —*n.* **5.** an often backless sofa having a headrest at one end. **6.** a usu. public room for relaxing or waiting. **7.** a section on a train, plane, or ship for socializing.

lounge′ car′, *n.* CLUB CAR.

lounge′ chair′, *n.* a chair, as a recliner, designed for lounging.

lounge·wear (lounj′wâr′), *n.* clothing suitable for wear during leisure time, esp. at home.

loupe (lōōp), *n.* a magnifying glass used by jewelers and watchmakers, esp. one designed to fit in the eye socket.

Lourdes (lōōrd, lōōrdz; *Fr.* lōōrd), *n.* a city in SW France: Roman Catholic shrine famed for miraculous cures. 18,096.

louse (*n.* lous; *v. also* louz), *n., pl.* **lice** (līs) for 1–3, **lous·es** for 4, *v.,* **loused, lous·ing.** —*n.* **1.** any of various small, flat, wingless insects of the order Anoplura, with sucking mouthparts, that are parasitic on humans and other mammals, as *Pediculus humanus capitis* (**head louse**) and *P. humanus corporis* (**body louse**). **2.** any similar insect of the order Mallophaga, with biting mouthparts, parasitic on birds and some mammals. **3.** APHID. **4.** *Slang.* a contemptible person. —*v.t.* **5.** to delouse. **6. louse up,** *Slang.* to spoil; botch.

lous·y (lou′zē), *adj.,* **lous·i·er, lous·i·est. 1.** infested with lice. **2.** *Informal.* **a.** mean; contemptible: *That was a lousy thing to do.* **b.** wretchedly bad; miserable: *a lousy job of repainting.* —**Idiom. 3. lousy with,** *Slang.* well supplied with: *lousy with money.* —**lous′i·ly,** *adv.*

lout (lout), *n.* a clumsy, boorish person; oaf. —**lout′ish,** *adj.* —**lout′ish·ly,** *adv.* —**lout′ish·ness,** *n.*

lou·ver or **lou·vre** (lōō′vər), *n.* **1.** any of a series of narrow openings framed at their longer edges with slanting, overlapping fins or slats, adjustable for admitting light and air while shutting out rain. **2.** a fin or slat framing such an opening. **3.** a ventilating turret or lantern, as on the roof of a medieval building. **4.** any of a system of slits, as in the hood of an automobile, for ventilation. —**lou′vered,** *adj.*

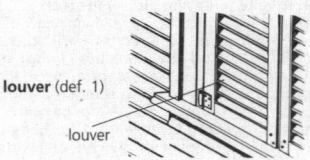

louver (def. 1)

louver

love (luv), *n., v.,* **loved, lov·ing.** —*n.* **1.** a profoundly tender, passionate affection for another person. **2.** a feeling of warm personal attachment or deep affection. **3.** a person toward whom love is felt. **4.** a love affair. **5.** affectionate concern for the well-being of others: *love of one's neighbor.* **6.** a strong predilection, enthusiasm, or liking: *a love of books.* **7.** the object of such liking or enthusiasm: *The theater was her great love.* **8.** the benevolent affection of God for His creatures, or the reverent affection due from them to God. **9.** a score of zero, as in tennis. —*v.t.* **10.** to have love or affection for. **11.** to have a strong liking for: *to love music.* **12.** to need or require: *Plants love sunlight.* **13.** to embrace and kiss as a lover. —*v.i.* **14.** to feel the emotion of love. —**Idiom. 15. in love (with),** infused with or feeling deep affection or passion (for); enamored (of). **16. make love, a.** to have sexual relations. **b.** to neck; pet. **c.** to court; woo. —**Proverb. 17. Love thy neighbor as thyself,** put the common interest above selfishness. Lev. 19:18. —**lov′a·ble, love′a·ble,** *adj.* —**love′less,** *adj.*

love′ affair′, *n.* **1.** a romantic relationship or episode between lovers; an amour. **2.** an active enthusiasm for something: *my love affair with sailing.*

love′ ap′ple, *n.* TOMATO.

love·bird (luv′bûrd′), *n.* **1.** any of various small parrots, esp. of the genus *Agapornis,* of Africa, noted for the affection shown between mates. **2. lovebirds,** a pair of lovers.

love′ child′, *n.* a child born out of wedlock.

love′ feast′, *n.* **1.** (among the early Christians) a meal eaten in token of brotherly love and charity; agape. **2.** a rite in imitation of this, practiced by a number of modern denominations; a fellowship meal. **3.** a banquet or gathering of persons to promote good feeling, restore friendly relations, honor a special guest, etc.

love′ han′dles, *n.pl. Informal.* bulges of fat at the sides of the waist.

Lov·ell (luv′əl), *n.* Sir Alfred Charles Bernard, born 1931, English astronomer.

love·lorn (luv′lôrn′), *adj.* being without love or a lover.

love·ly (luv′lē), *adj.,* **-li·er, -li·est. 1.** having a beauty that appeals to the heart or mind as well as to the eye; charmingly or gracefully beautiful. **2.** highly pleasing; delightful: *We had a lovely time.* **3.** of a great moral or spiritual beauty: *a lovely character.* —**love′li·ly,** *adv.* —**love′li·ness,** *n.*

love·mak·ing (luv′mā′king), *n.* **1.** the act of courting. **2.** sexual activity.

love′ po′tion, *n.* a magical potion believed to arouse love.

lov·er (luv′ər), *n.* **1.** a person who is in love with another. **2.** a person who has a sexual or romantic relationship with another. **3.** PARAMOUR (def. 1). **4.** a devotee of something: *a lover of music.* —**lov′er·less,** *adj.* —**lov′er·like′,** *adj.*

love′ seat′, *n.* a chair or small upholstered sofa for two persons.

love·sick (luv′sik′), *adj.* **1.** languishing with love: *a lovesick adolescent.* **2.** expressing passionate yearning: *a lovesick note.* —**love′sick′ness,** *n.*

love·y-dove·y (luv′ē duv′ē), *adj.* amorously affectionate.

lov′ing (luv′ing), *adj.* warmly affectionate. —**lov′ing·ly,** *adv.*

lov′ing cup′, *n.* a large drinking cup with two or more handles given as a prize or token of esteem.

low¹ (lō), *adj.* **1.** situated, placed, or occurring not far above the ground, floor, or base: *a low shelf.* **2.** of small extent upward: *a low fence.* **3.** not far above the horizon: *The moon was low in the sky.* **4.** lying below the general level: *low ground.* **5.** being near sea level and esp. near the sea: *low country.* **6.** bending downward; deep: *a low bow.* **7.** décolleté or low: *a low neckline.* **8.** rising but slightly from a surface: *low relief on a frieze.* **9.** of less than average or normal height or depth: *The river is low this time of year.* **10.** near the first of a series: *a low number.* **11.** ranked near the beginning or bottom on a scale of measurement: *a low income bracket.* **12.** most discouraging or debased: *the low point in his life.* **13.** lacking strength or vigor; listless. **14.** depressed or dejected. **15.** of small number, amount, degree, force, or intensity: *low visibility; a generator with a low output.* **16.** indicated or represented by a low number: *a low latitude.* **17.** soft; subdued; not loud: *a low murmur.* **18.** deep in pitch. **19.** assigning or attributing little value: *a low estimate of a new book.* **20.** containing a relatively small amount or number (sometimes used in combination): *a diet low in starches; low-calorie foods.* **21.** nearing depletion: *low on funds.* **22.** humble: *of low birth.* **23.** of inferior quality: *a low grade of fabric.* **24.** base; disreputable: *low companions.* **25.** coarse; vulgar: *entertainment of a low sort.* **26.** *Biol.* having a relatively simple structure; primitive. **27.** (of a vowel) articulated with a relatively large opening above the tongue, as the vowels of *hat, hot,* and *ought.* Compare HIGH (def. 20). **28.** pertaining to the gear transmission ratio at which the drive shaft moves at the lowest speed with relation to the speed of the engine crankshaft; first. **29.** (of a pitched ball) passing the plate at a level below that of the batter's knees: *a low curve.* **30.** holding to Low Church principles and practices. —*adv.* **31.** in or to a low position, point, or degree: *crouched low in the bushes.* **32.** near the ground, floor, or base: *The plane flew low.* **33.** in or to a humble or abject state: *swore to bring him low.* **34.** in or to a condition of depletion. **35.** at comparatively small cost: *to buy something low and sell it high.* **36.** at or to a low pitch, volume, or intensity. —*n.* **37.** something that is low; a low or the lowest point, place, or level: *recent lows in the stock market.* **38.** a low transmission gear. **39.** an atmospheric low-pressure system; cyclone. —*Idiom.* **40.** lay low, **a.** to overpower or kill: *to lay one's attackers low.* **b.** to knock down. **c.** *Informal.* to lie low. **41.** lie low, **a.** to hide oneself. **b.** to wait quietly before acting. —**low′ish,** *adj.* —**low′ness,** *n.*

low² (lō), *v.i.* **1.** to utter the deep sound characteristic of cattle; moo. —*v.t.* **2.** to utter by or as if by lowing. —*n.* **3.** the act or sound of lowing.

low·ball (lō′bôl′), *v.t.* **1.** to deliberately estimate a lower price than one intends to charge: *to lowball the cost of a shipment.* **2.** to give a false estimate or bid for.

low′ beam′, *n.* an automobile headlight beam providing short-range illumination, used chiefly in urban areas.

low′ blood′ pres′sure, *n.* HYPOTENSION.

low′ blow′, *n.* **1.** an illegal blow below an opponent's waist in boxing. **2.** an unfair or unsportsmanlike criticism or attack.

low·brow (lō′brou′), *n.* **1.** a person with little interest in matters of intellect or culture. —*adj.* **2.** characteristic of or being a lowbrow. —**low′brow′ism,** *n.*

low′-budg′et, *adj.* made or done on a small budget; costing relatively little: *a low-budget film.*

low-cal (lō′kal′, -kal′), *adj.* containing fewer calories than usual or standard: *a low-cal diet.*

Low′ Church′, *adj.* pertaining to the view or practice in the Anglican Church that emphasizes evangelicalism over the sacraments, church rituals, and church authority. Compare HIGH CHURCH, BROAD CHURCH. —**Low′ Church′man,** *n.*

low′ com′edy, *n.* comedy based on slapstick, physical action, broadly humorous or farcical situations, and often bawdy jokes. Compare HIGH COMEDY. —**low′ come′dian,** *n.*

Low′ Coun′tries, *n.pl.* the lowland region near the North Sea, forming the lower basin of the Rhine, Meuse, and Scheldt rivers, divided in the Middle Ages into numerous small states: corresponding to modern Belgium, Luxembourg, and the Netherlands.

low′ coun′try, *n.* a low-lying region or area, as the coastal plains of the Carolinas and Georgia.

low·down (*n.* lō′doun′; *adj.* -doun′), *n.* **1.** the real and unadorned facts: *Give me the lowdown on the situation.* —*adj.* **2.** contemptible; base; mean: *a lowdown trick.* **3.** FUNKY² (def. 1).

Low·ell (lō′əl), *n.* **1.** Amy, 1874–1925, U.S. poet and critic. **2.** James Russell, 1819–91, U.S. poet, essayist, and diplomat. **3.** Percival, 1855–1916, U.S. astronomer (brother of Amy Lowell). **4.** Robert, 1917–77, U.S. poet.

low′-end′, *adj.* relatively inexpensive: *low-end stereo equipment.*

low·er¹ (lō′ər), *v.t.* **1.** to cause to descend; let or put down: *to lower a flag.* **2.** to make lower in height or level: *to lower the water in a canal.* **3.** to reduce in amount, price, degree, or force. **4.** to make less loud or lower in pitch. **5.** to bring down in rank or estimation. **6.** to alter the articulation of (a vowel) by increasing the distance of the tongue downward from the palate. —*v.i.* **7.** to become lower, grow less, or diminish. **8.** to descend; sink: *the sun lowering in the west.* —*adj.* **9.** comparative of LOW¹. **10.** of or pertaining to the parts of a river farthest from the source. **11.** (*often cap.*) of or pertaining to an early division of a geologic period, system, or the like: *the Lower Devonian.* —*n.* **12.** Usu. **lowers.** a denture for the lower jaw. **13.** a lower berth.

low·er² (lou′ər, lou³r) also **lour,** *v.i.* **1.** to be dark and threatening. **2.** to look sullen; scowl; glower. —*n.* **3.** a dark, threatening appearance. **4.** a frown; scowl.

low·er·case (lō′ər kās′), *adj., v.,* **-cased, -cas·ing,** *n.* —*adj.* **1.** (of an alphabetical letter) of a particular form often different from and smaller than its corresponding capital letter, as a, b, q, r. —*v.t.* **2.** to print or write with a lowercase letter or letters. —*n.* **3.** a lowercase letter.

low′er cham′ber (lō′ər), *n.* LOWER HOUSE.

low′er class′ (lō′ər), *n.* a class of people below the middle class in social standing and generally characterized by low income and lack of education. —**low′er-class′,** *adj.*

low·er·class·man (lō′ər klas′mən, -kläs′-), *n., pl.* **-men.** UNDERCLASSMAN.

low′er crit′icism (lō′ər), *n.* Biblical criticism having as its purpose the reconstruction of the original texts of the books of the Bible. Also called **textual criticism.** Compare HIGHER CRITICISM.

low′er house′ (lō′ər), *n.* one of two branches of a legislature, generally larger and more representative than the upper branch.

Low·er Slob·bo·vi·a (lō′ər slə bō′vē ə, slo-), *n.* any place considered to be remote, poor, or unenlightened. [after an imaginary country of that name in the comic strip *Li'l Abner* by Al Capp]

low′est com′mon denom′inator, *n.* LEAST COMMON DENOMINATOR.

low′est com′mon mul′tiple, *n.* the smallest number that is a common multiple of a given set of numbers. Also called **least common multiple.**

low′ fre′quency, *n.* a radio frequency between 30 and 300 kilohertz. *Abbr.:* LF —**low′-fre′quen·cy,** *adj.*

Low′ Ger′man, *n.* the West Germanic dialects of N Germany, forming with Dutch a single dialect complex distinct from the High German dialects. *Abbr.:* LG

low′-grade′, *adj.* **1.** of inferior grade or quality: *low-grade silver ore.* **2.** being close to the low end of a range of measurement: *a low-grade fever.*

low′-key′ or **low′-keyed′,** *adj.* of reduced intensity; restrained; understated.

low·land (lō′lənd), *n.* **1.** land that is low or level in comparison with the adjacent country. **the Lowlands,** a low, level region in S, central, and E Scotland. —*adj.* **3.** of, pertaining to, or characteristic of a lowland or lowlands.

Low·land·er (lō′lən dər, -lan′-), *n.* **1.** a native or inhabitant of the Lowlands of Scotland. **2.** (*l.c.*) an inhabitant of any lowland region.

low′-lev′el, *adj.* **1.** undertaken by or composed of members having a low status: *a low-level meeting.* **2.** having low status or rank: *low-level personnel.* **3.** undertaken at or from a low altitude: *low-level bombing.*

low·life (lō′līf′), *n., pl.* **-lifes. 1.** a disreputable or degenerate person. **2.** a stratum of society composed of lowlifes. —**low′-life′,** *adj.*

low·ly (lō′lē), *adj.,* **-li·er, -li·est. 1.** humble in station, condition, or nature: *a lowly cottage.* **2.** humble in attitude, behavior, or spirit; meek. —**low′li·ly,** *adv.* —**low′li·ness,** *n.*

low′-ly′ing, *adj.* lying near sea level or the ground surface: *low-lying land.*

Low′ Mass′, *n.* a Mass that is said, and not sung, by the celebrant, who is assisted by one server, and which has less ceremonial form than a High Mass, using no music or choir. Compare HIGH MASS.

low′-mind′ed, *adj.* having or showing coarse or vulgar taste or interests. —**low′-mind′ed·ly,** *adv.* —**low′-mind′ed·ness,** *n.*

low′-pitched′, *adj.* **1.** relatively deep in pitch or soft in sound: *a low-pitched whistle.* **2.** (of a roof) having a low proportion of vertical to lateral dimensions; gently sloping.

low′-pres′sure, *adj.* **1.** having, involving, or operating under a low or below normal pressure. **2.** relaxed; easygoing.

low′ pro′file, *n.* a deliberately inconspicuous or anonymous manner. —**low′-pro′file,** *adj.*

low′-rent′, *adj. Informal.* second-rate; bargain-basement.

low·rid·er (lō′rī′dər), *n.* **1.** a customized car fitted with hydraulic jacks that permit lowering of the chassis nearly to the road. **2.** a person who drives such a car.

low′-rise′, *adj.* **1.** having few stories and usu. no elevator: *low-rise apartment buildings.* —*n.* **2.** a low-rise building.

low′ road′, *n.* a course of action that is merely expedient.

Low·ry (lou′rē, lou′ə-), *n.* **Robert,** 1826–99, U.S. clergyman, musician, and hymn writer.

low′-tech′, *adj.* LOW-TECHNOLOGY.

low′ technol′ogy, *n.* technology utilizing equipment and production techniques that are relatively unsophisticated. Compare HIGH TECHNOLOGY. —**low′-tech′nol′o•gy,** adj.

low•ten′sion, adj. subjected to or capable of operating under relatively low voltage: low-tension wire.

low′-tick′et, adj. having a relatively low price: low-ticket products.

low′ tide′, n. **1.** the tide at the point of maximum ebb. **2.** the lowest point: Her spirits were at low tide.

low′-wa′ter mark′, n. **1.** the lowest point reached by a low tide. **2.** the lowest or least admirable level.

lox (loks), n. salmon brine-cured with either salt or sugar.

loy•al (loi′əl), adj. **1.** faithful to one's sovereign, government, or state: a loyal subject. **2.** faithful to one's oath or obligations: loyal to a vow. **3.** faithful to any person or thing conceived as deserving fidelity: a loyal friend. **4.** characterized by or showing faithfulness: loyal conduct. —**loy′al•ly,** adv.

loy•al•ist (loi′ə list), n. **1.** a person who remains loyal, esp. to a sovereign or existing government. **2.** (sometimes cap.) a person who remained loyal to the British during the American Revolution; Tory. —**loy′al•ism,** n.

loy′al opposi′tion, n. a political opposition whose action is consistent with patriotism or loyalty to the nation.

Loy′al Or′der of Moose′, n. MOOSE (def. 2).

loy•al•ty (loi′əl tē), n., pl. **-ties. 1.** the state or quality of being loyal. **2.** a feeling of faithfulness or allegiance: a man of fierce loyalties.

loy′alty oath′, n. a pledge of fealty to, and promise to avoid subversion against, a group, esp. a government.

Loy•o•la (loi ō′lə), n. **Saint Ignatius of** (Iñigo López de Loyola), 1491–1556, Spanish ecclesiastic: founder of the Society of Jesus.

loz•enge (loz′inj), n. a small flavored tablet made from sugar or syrup and often medicated.

LP, pl. **LPs, LP's.** a phonograph record played at 33⅓ r.p.m.; long-playing record.

LPGA, Ladies Professional Golf Association.

lpm or **LPM,** lines per minute: a measure of the speed of a computer printer.

LPN, licensed practical nurse.

Lr, Chem. Symbol. lawrencium.

LSD (el′es′dē′), n. lysergic acid diethylamide: a crystalline solid, $C_{20}H_{25}N_3O$, the diethyl amide of lysergic acid, a powerful psychedelic drug that produces temporary hallucinations and a psychotic state.

Lt., lieutenant.

Lt. Col., Lieutenant Colonel. Often, **LTC**

Lt. Comdr. or **Lt. Com.,** Lieutenant Commander.

Ltd. or **ltd.,** limited.

Lt. Gen., Lieutenant General. Often, **LTG**

Lu, Chem. Symbol. lutetium.

Lu•an•da (loo an′də, -än′-), n. the capital of Angola, in SW Africa. 1,200,000.

lu•au (loo′ou), n., pl. **-aus.** an outdoor feast of Hawaiian food, usu. with entertainment.

Lu•ba•vitch•er (loo′bə vich′ər, loo bä′vi chər), n. **1.** a member of a missionary Hasidic movement founded in the 1700s by Rabbi Shneour Zalman of Lyady. —adj. **2.** of or pertaining to the Lubavitchers or their movement. [< Yiddish lubavitsher, after Lubavitsh (< Byelorussian Lyubavichi) a town that was the center of the movement, 1813–1915]

lub•ber (lub′ər), n. **1.** a big, clumsy, stupid person; lout. **2.** an awkward or unskillful sailor; landlubber. —**lub′ber•ly,** adj., adv.

Lub•bock (lub′ək), n. a city in NW Texas. 188,090.

lube (loob), n., v., **lubed, lub•ing.** Informal. —n. **1.** lubricant. **2.** an application of a lubricant to a vehicle. —v.t. **3.** to lubricate: to lube a bicycle chain.

lu•bri•cant (loo′bri kənt), n. **1.** a substance, as oil or grease, for lessening friction, esp. in the working parts of a mechanism. **2.** something that increases ease of functioning. —adj. **3.** used in lubricating.

lu•bri•cate (loo′bri kāt′), v., **-cat•ed, -cat•ing.** —v.t. **1.** to apply an oily or greasy substance to in order to diminish friction; make slippery. **2.** to cause to run smoother; ease: to lubricate relations between enemies. **3.** Slang. to provide with liquor. **4.** Slang. to bribe. —v.i. **5.** to act as a lubricant. **6.** to apply a lubricant to something. —**lu′bri•ca′tion,** n. —**lu′bri•ca′tion•al,** adj. —**lu′bri•ca′tive,** adj. —**lu′bri•ca′tor,** n.

lu•bri•cious (loo brish′əs), adj. **1.** arousing or expressive of sexual desire; lustful; lecherous. **2.** smooth and slippery. —**lu•bri′cious•ly,** adv. —**lu•bric′i•ty** (-bris′i tē), n.

lu•bri•cous (loo′bri kəs), adj. **1.** having an oily smoothness; slippery. **2.** salacious; lubricious.

Lu•cas (loo′kəs), n. **George,** born 1945, U.S. film director.

Luce (loos), n. **1. Clare Boothe,** born 1903, U.S. writer, politician, and diplomat. **2. Henry Robinson,** 1898–1967, U.S. publisher and editor (husband of Clare Boothe Luce).

lu•cent (loo′sənt), adj. **1.** shining with light. **2.** translucent; clear. —**lu′cen•cy,** n. —**lu′cent•ly,** adv.

lu•ces (loo′sēz), n. pl. of LUX.

lu•cid (loo′sid), adj. **1.** easily understood; intelligible: a lucid explanation. **2.** rational; sane: a lucid moment in his madness. **3.** glowing with light; luminous. **4.** clear; pellucid; transparent. —**lu•cid′i•ty, lu′cid•ness,** n. —**lu′cid•ly,** adv.

Lu•ci•fer (loo′sə fər), n. **1.** a proud rebellious archangel, identified with

Satan, who fell from heaven. **2.** the planet Venus when appearing as the morning star. **3.** (l.c.) Also called **lu′cifer match′.** MATCH¹ (def. 1). [< Latin: morning star, lit., light-bringing]

lu•cif•er•ous (loo sif′ər əs), adj. **1.** bringing or providing light. **2.** providing insight or enlightenment.

Lu•cite (loo′sīt), Trademark. a transparent or translucent plastic, any of a class of methyl methacrylate ester polymers.

luck (luk), n. **1.** the force that seems to operate for good or ill in a person's life, as in shaping events or opportunities: With my luck I'll probably be too late. **2.** good fortune; success: to have luck finding work. **3.** some object on which good fortune is supposed to depend: This rabbit's foot is my luck. —v. Informal. **4. luck into** or **onto,** to meet or acquire through accidental good fortune. **5. luck out,** to have an occasion or run of exceptionally good luck. —Idiom. **6. down on one's luck,** in unfortunate circumstances; unlucky. **7. in luck,** lucky; fortunate. **8. out of luck,** unlucky; unfortunate. **9. push** or **crowd one's luck,** to jeopardize success by taking further risks; go too far. —**luck′less,** adj.

luck•y (luk′ē), adj., **-i•er, -i•est. 1.** having or marked by good luck; fortunate: That was my lucky day. **2.** happening fortunately: a lucky accident. **3.** believed to bring good luck: a lucky penny. —**luck′i•ly,** adv.

lu•cra•tive (loo′krə tiv), adj. profitable; moneymaking; remunerative: a lucrative business. —**lu′cra•tive•ly,** adv. —**lu′cra•tive•ness,** n.

lu•cre (loo′kər), n. monetary reward or gain; money.

Lu•cre•tius (loo krē′shəs), n. (Titus Lucretius Carus) 97?–54 B.C., Roman poet and philosopher. —**Lu•cre′tian,** adj.

lu•cu•brate (loo′kyoo brāt′), v.i., **-brat•ed, -brat•ing. 1.** to work, write, or study laboriously, esp. at night. **2.** to write learnedly. —**lu′cu•bra′tion,** n. —**lu′cu•bra•to′ry** (-kyoo′brə tôr′ē, -tōr′ē), adj.

Lu′cy Ston′er (stō′nər), n. a person who advocates the retention of the maiden name by married women. [after Lucy STONE]

Lud•dite (lud′īt), n. **1.** a member of any of various bands of workers in England (1811–16) who destroyed industrial machinery in the belief that its use diminished employment. **2.** any opponent of new technologies or of technological change. [after Ned Ludd, 18th-cent. Leicestershire worker who originated the idea]

lu•di•crous (loo′di krəs), adj. causing or deserving laughter because of absurdity; ridiculous; laughable: a ludicrous lack of efficiency. —**lu′di•crous•ly,** adv. —**lu′di•crous•ness,** n.

lug¹ (lug), v., **lugged, lug•ging.** —v.t. **1.** to pull or carry with force or effort: to lug a heavy suitcase upstairs. **2.** to introduce or interject inappropriately or irrelevantly: to lug personalities into a discussion of philosophy. **3.** (of a sailing ship) to carry an excessive amount of (sail) for the conditions prevailing. —v.i. **4.** to pull or tug laboriously. **5.** (of an engine or machine) to jerk, hesitate, or strain. —n. **6.** an act or instance of lugging; a forcible pull; haul. **7.** a wooden box for transporting fruit or vegetables. **8.** Slang. a request for or exaction of money, as for political purposes: They put the lug on him at the office.

lug² (lug), n. **1.** a projecting piece by which anything is held or supported. **2.** a ridge or welt that helps to provide traction, as on a tire or the sole of a shoe. **3.** a leather loop hanging down from a saddle, through which a shaft is passed for support. **4.** Slang. **a.** an awkward, clumsy fellow. **b.** a blockhead. **c.** a man; guy.

luge (loozh), n., v., **luged, lug•ing.** —n. **1.** a one- or two-person sled for coasting or racing down a chute, used esp. in Europe. —v.i. **2.** to go or race on a luge. —**lug′er,** n.

lug•gage (lug′ij), n. suitcases, trunks, etc.; baggage.

lug′ nut′, n. a large nut fitting on a heavy bolt, used esp. in attaching a wheel to a motor vehicle.

lu•gu•bri•ous (loo goo′brē əs, -gyoo′-), adj. mournful, dismal, or gloomy, esp. in an affected, exaggerated, or unrelieved manner: lugubrious songs of lost love. —**lu•gu′bri•ous•ly,** adv. —**lu•gu′bri•ous•ness, lu•gu•bri•os•i•ty** (lə goo′brē os′i tē, -gyoo′-), n.

Luke (look), n. **1.** an early Christian disciple and companion of Paul, a physician and probably a gentile: traditionally believed to be the author of the third Gospel and the Acts. **2.** the third Gospel.

luke•warm (look′wôrm′), adj. **1.** moderately warm; tepid. **2.** having or showing little enthusiasm; indifferent: lukewarm applause.

lull (lul), v.t. **1.** to put to sleep or rest by soothing means: to lull a child to sleep with singing. **2.** to soothe or quiet. **3.** to give or lead to feel a false sense of safety. —v.i. **4.** to quiet down; let up; subside: furious activity that finally lulled. —n. **5.** a temporary calm, quiet, or stillness; a lull in a storm. **6.** a soothing sound: the lull of falling waters. —**lull′er,** n. —**lull′ing•ly,** adv.

lull•a•by (lul′ə bī′), n., pl. **-bies,** v., **-bied, -by•ing.** —n. **1.** a song used to lull a child to sleep. **2.** any lulling song. —v.t. **3.** to lull with or as if with a lullaby.

lu•lu (loo′loo), n., pl. **-lus.** Slang. any remarkable or outstanding person or thing: That black eye is a lulu.

lum•ba•go (lum bā′gō), n. chronic or recurrent pain in the lumbar region of the back.

lum•bar (lum′bər, -bär), adj. **1.** of or pertaining to the loin or loins. —n. **2.** a lumbar vertebra, artery, or the like.

lum•ber¹ (lum′bər), n. **1.** timber sawed or split into planks, boards, etc. **2.** miscellaneous useless articles that are stored away. —v.i. **3.** to cut timber and prepare it for market. —v.t. **4.** to convert (a specified amount, area, etc.) into lumber. **5.** to heap together in disorder. **6.** to fill up or obstruct with miscellaneous useless articles; encumber.

lum·ber² (lum′bər), *v.i.* to move clumsily or heavily, esp. from great or ponderous bulk.

lum·ber·jack (lum′bər jak′), *n.* a person who works at lumbering; logger.

lum·ber·mill (lum′bər mil′), *n.* a mill for dressing logs and lumber.

lum·ber·yard (lum′bər yärd′), *n.* a yard where lumber is stored for sale.

lu·men (lōō′mən), *n.*, *pl.* **-mens, -mi·na** (-mə nə). **1.** the unit of luminous flux, equal to the luminous flux emitted in a unit solid angle by a point source of one candle intensity. *Abbr.:* lm **2.** *Anat.* the canal, duct, or cavity of a tubular organ.

lu·mi·nance (lōō′mə nəns), *n.* **1.** the state or quality of being luminous. **2.** the quality or condition of radiating or reflecting light: *the blinding luminance of the sun.* **3.** the quantitative measure of brightness of a light source or an illuminated surface, equal to luminous flux per unit solid angle emitted per unit projected area of the source or surface.

lu·mi·nar·i·a (lōō′mə när′ē ə), *n.*, *pl.* **-nar·i·as.** a Mexican Christmas lantern consisting of a lighted candle set in sand inside a paper bag.

lu·mi·nar·y (lōō′mə ner′ē), *n.*, *pl.* **-nar·ies.** **1.** a celestial body, as the sun or moon. **2.** a body, object, etc., that gives light. **3.** a person who has attained eminence in a field or is an inspiration to others.

lu·mi·nes·cence (lōō′mə nes′əns), *n.* **1.** the emission of light not caused by incandescence and occurring at a temperature below that of incandescent bodies. **2.** the light produced by such an emission. **—lu′·mi·nes′cent,** *adj.*

lu·mi·nous (lōō′mə nəs), *adj.* **1.** radiating or reflecting light; shining; bright. **2.** lighted up or illuminated; well-lighted: *the luminous ballroom.* **3.** brilliant intellectually; enlightened or enlightening, as a writer or a writer's works. **4.** clear; readily intelligible: *a concise, luminous report.* **—lu′mi·nos′i·ty,** *n.* **—lu′mi·nous·ly,** *adv.* **—lu′mi·nous·ness,** *n.*

lum·mox (lum′əks), *n. Informal.* a clumsy, stupid person.

lump¹ (lump), *n.* **1.** a piece or mass of solid matter without regular shape or of no particular shape: *a lump of coal.* **2.** a protuberance or swelling: *a blow that raised a lump on his head.* **3.** an aggregation, collection, or mass; clump: *All the articles were piled in a great lump.* **4.** a small block of granulated sugar, for sweetening hot coffee, tea, etc. **5.** majority; plurality; multitude: *The great lump of voters are still undecided.* **6. lumps,** *Informal.* harsh criticism, punishment, or defeat. **7.** *Informal.* a heavy, clumsy, and usu. stupid person. **—adj. 8.** in the form of a lump or lumps: *lump sugar.* **9.** made up of a number of items taken together; not divided: *to pay a debt in a lump sum.* **—v.t. 10.** to unite into one aggregation, collection, or mass (often fol. by *together*): *We lumped the reds and blues together.* **11.** to deal with, consider, etc., in the lump or mass. **—v.i. 12.** to form a lump or lumps. **13.** to move heavily and awkwardly. **—Idiom. 14. get** or **take one's lumps,** to receive or endure hardship, punishment, criticism, etc. **—lump′y,** *adj.,* **-i·er, -i·est. —lump′i·ly,** *adv.* **—lump′i·ness,** *n.*

lump² (lump), *v.t. Informal.* to put up with; resign oneself to; accept and endure: *If you don't like it, you can lump it.*

lump·ec·to·my (lum pek′tə mē), *n.*, *pl.* **-mies.** the surgical removal of a breast cyst or tumor.

lump·fish (lump′fish′), *n.*, *pl.* (*esp. collectively*) **-fish,** (*esp. for kinds or species*) **-fish·es.** any thick-bodied, knobby-skinned fish of the family Cyclopteridae, having pelvic fins united to form a sucking disc.

lu·na·cy (lōō′nə sē), *n.*, *pl.* **-cies. 1.** insanity; mental disorder. **2.** intermittent insanity, formerly believed to be related to phases of the moon. **3.** extreme foolishness or an instance of it: *The decision to resign was sheer lunacy.* **4.** *Law.* unsoundness of mind sufficient to incapacitate one for legal transactions.

lu′na moth′, *n.* a pale green saturniid moth, *Actias luna,* with crescent spots and long tails on the hind wings.

lu·nar (lōō′nər), *adj.* **1.** of or pertaining to the moon: *the lunar orbit.* **2.** measured by the moon's revolutions: *a lunar month.* **3.** resembling the moon; round or crescent-shaped.

lu′nar eclipse′, *n.* See under ECLIPSE (def. 1a).

lu′nar month′, *n.* MONTH (def. 4b).

lu′nar year′, *n.* YEAR (def. 4a).

lu·na·tic (lōō′nə tik), *n.* **1.** an insane person. **2.** a person whose actions and manner are marked by extreme eccentricity or recklessness. **3.** *Law.* a person legally declared to be of unsound mind and who therefore is not held legally responsible or capable. **—adj. 4.** insane; demented; crazy. **5.** wildly or recklessly foolish. **6.** designated for or used by the insane: *a lunatic asylum.* [< Old French *lunatique* < Late Latin *lūnāticus* moonstruck] **—lu·nat′i·cal·ly,** *adv.*

lu′natic fringe′, *n.* members on the periphery of any group, as in politics or religion, who hold extreme or fanatical views.

lunch (lunch), *n.* **1.** a light midday meal between breakfast and dinner; luncheon. **2.** any light meal or snack. **—v.i. 3.** to eat lunch. **4. out to lunch,** *Slang.* in a daze; inattentive or unaware. **—Saying. 5. There's no such thing as a free lunch,** everything has a cost.

lunch·box (lunch′boks′), *n.* a small container, usu. with a handle, for carrying one's lunch to school or work. Also called **lunchpail, lunch′buck′et** (-buk′it).

lunch′ count′er, *n.* **1.** a counter, as in a store or restaurant, where light meals and snacks are served. **2.** a luncheonette.

lunch·eon (lun′chən), *n.* lunch, esp. a formal lunch held in connection with a meeting or other special occasion. **—lunch′eon·less,** *adj.*

lunch·eon·ette (lun′chə net′), *n.* a small restaurant where light meals are served; lunchroom; lunch counter.

lunch′eon meat′, *n.* any of various sausages or molded loaf meats, usu. sliced and served cold, as in sandwiches.

lunch·meat (lunch′mēt′), *n.* LUNCHEON MEAT.

lunch·pail (lunch′pāl′), *n.* LUNCHBOX.

lunch·room (lunch′rōōm′, -rŏŏm′), *n.* **1.** a room, as in a school or workplace, where light meals or snacks can be bought or where food brought from home may be eaten. **2.** a luncheonette.

lunch·time (lunch′tīm′), *n.* a period set aside for eating lunch or the period of an hour or so, beginning roughly at noon, during which lunch is commonly eaten.

lung (lung), *n.* either of the two saclike respiratory organs in the thorax of humans and other air-breathing vertebrates.

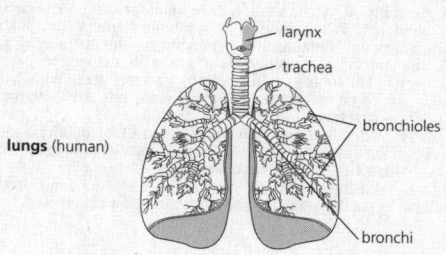

lungs (human)

larynx
trachea
bronchioles
bronchi

lunge (lunj), *n.*, *v.*, **lunged, lung·ing. —n. 1.** a sudden forward thrust, as with a sword or knife; stab. **2.** any sudden forward movement; plunge. **—v.i. 3.** to make a lunge or thrust; move with a lunge. **—lung′er,** *n.*

lung·fish (lung′fish′), *n.*, *pl.* (*esp. collectively*) **-fish,** (*esp. for kinds or species*) **-fish·es.** any fleshy-finned fish, related to the ancient crossopterygians, having lungs as well as gills, including three surviving genera: *Neoceratodus* of Australia, *Protopterus* of Africa, and *Lepidosiren* of South America.

lung·wort (lung′wûrt′, -wôrt′), *n.* any of several plants once believed to cure pulmonary disorders, esp. a European plant, *Pulmonaria officinalis,* of the borage family, having large spotted leaves and blue flowers.

luni-, a combining form meaning "moon": *lunitidal.*

lu·pine¹ (lōō′pin), *n.* any plant of the genus *Lupinus,* of the legume family, esp. *L. perennis,* having tall, dense clusters of blue, pink, or white flowers.

lu·pine² (lōō′pīn), *adj.* **1.** pertaining to, characteristic of, or resembling the wolf. **2.** savage; ravenous; predatory.

lu·pus (lōō′pəs), *n.* SYSTEMIC LUPUS ERYTHEMATOSUS. **—lu′pous,** *adj.*

lu′pus er·y·the·ma·to′sus (er′ə thē′mə tō′səs, -them′ə-), *n.* any of several autoimmune diseases, esp. systemic lupus erythematosus, characterized by red, scaly skin patches.

lurch¹ (lûrch), *n.* **1.** an act or instance of swaying abruptly. **2.** a sudden tip or roll to one side, as of a ship or a staggering person. **3.** an awkward, swaying or staggering motion or gait. **—v.i. 4.** (of a ship) to roll or pitch suddenly. **5.** to stagger or sway. **—lurch′ing·ly,** *adv.*

lurch² (lûrch), *n.* **1.** a situation at the close of various games in which the loser scores nothing or is far behind the opponent. **—Idiom. 2. leave in the lurch,** to desert when help is needed most.

lure (lŏŏr), *n.*, *v.*, **lured, lur·ing. —n. 1.** anything that attracts, entices, or allures. **2.** the power of attracting or enticing. **3.** a decoy; live or esp. artificial bait used in fishing or trapping. **4.** a feathered decoy used in falconry to recall a hawk. **5.** a flap or tassel dangling from the dorsal fin of pediculate fishes, as the angler, that attracts prey to the mouth region. **—v.t. 6.** to attract, entice, or tempt; allure. **7.** to draw or recall, as by a lure or decoy. **—lur′ing·ly,** *adv.*

lu·rid (lŏŏr′id), *adj.* **1.** gruesome; horrible: *the lurid details of an accident.* **2.** wildly dramatic or sensational; shocking: *the lurid tales of pulp magazines.* **3.** shining with an unnatural, fiery glow; garishly red: *a lurid sunset.* **4.** wan, pallid, or ghastly in hue; livid. **—lu′rid·ly,** *adv.* **—lu′rid·ness,** *n.*

lurk (lûrk), *v.i.* **1.** to lie or wait in concealment, as a person in ambush; remain in or around a place secretly or furtively. **2.** to go furtively; slink. **3.** to exist unperceived or unsuspected. **—lurk′er,** *n.* **—lurk′ing·ly,** *adv.*

Lu·sa·ka (lōō sä′kə), *n.* the capital of Zambia, in the S central part. 818,994.

lus·cious (lush′əs), *adj.* **1.** highly pleasing to the taste or smell: *luscious peaches.* **2.** richly satisfying to the senses or the mind: *the luscious style of his poetry.* **3.** richly adorned; luxurious: *luscious furnishings.* **4.** arousing physical or sexual desire; voluptuous. **5.** sweet to excess; cloying. **—lus′cious·ly,** *adv.* **—lus′cious·ness,** *n.*

lush (lush), *adj.* **1.** (of vegetation) growing abundantly; luxuriant. **2.** succulent; tender and juicy. **3.** characterized by luxuriant vegetation: *a lush valley.* **4.** characterized by abundance, luxuriousness, opulence, etc.: *the lush surroundings of an estate.* **—lush′ly,** *adv.* **—lush′ness,** *n.*

Lu·si·ta·ni·a (lōō′si tā′nē ə), n. 1. (*italics*) a British luxury liner sunk by a German submarine in the North Atlantic on May 7, 1915: one of the events leading to U.S. entry into World War I. 2. an ancient region and Roman province in the Iberian Peninsula, corresponding generally to modern Portugal. —**Lu′si·ta′ni·an**, *adj.*, *n.*

lust (lust), n. 1. intense sexual desire. 2. uncontrolled or illicit sexual desire: one of the seven deadly sins. 3. a passionate or overwhelming desire or craving (usu. fol. by *for*): *a lust for power*. 4. ardent enthusiasm; zest: *a lust for life*. —*v.i.* 5. to have intense sexual desire. 6. to have a passionate yearning or desire (often fol. by *for* or *after*).

lus·ter (lus′tər), n. 1. the state or quality of shining by reflecting light; sheen or gloss: *the luster of satin*. 2. a substance, as a coating or polish, used to impart sheen or gloss. 3. radiant or luminous brightness; brilliance; radiance. 4. radiance of beauty, excellence, distinction, or glory: *achievements that add luster to one's name*. 5. a shining ornament, as a cut-glass pendant. 6. a chandelier, candleholder, etc., ornamented with cut-glass pendants. 7. any natural or synthetic fabric with a lustrous finish. 8. an iridescent metallic film produced on the surface of a ceramic glaze. 9. the nature of a mineral surface with respect to its reflective qualities. —*v.t.* 10. to finish (fur, cloth, pottery, etc.) with a luster or gloss. —*v.i.* 11. to be or become lustrous. Also, *esp. Brit.*, **lustre**. —**lus′ter·less**, *adj.* —**lus′trous**, *adj.*

lust·y (lus′tē), *adj.*, **lust·i·er**, **lust·i·est**. 1. full of or characterized by healthy vigor. 2. hearty, as a meal. 3. spirited; enthusiastic. 4. lustful; lecherous. —**lust′i·ly**, *adv.* —**lust′i·ness**, *n.*

lute (lōōt), n. a stringed musical instrument having a long, fretted neck and a hollow, typically pear-shaped body with a vaulted back.

lute

lu·te·ti·um (lōō tē′shē əm), n. a trivalent rare-earth element. *Symbol:* Lu; *at. wt.:* 174.97; *at. no.:* 71.

Lu·ther (lōō′thər), n. **Martin**, 1483–1546, German leader of the Protestant Reformation.

Lu·ther·an (lōō′thər ən), *adj.* 1. of or pertaining to Luther, adhering to his doctrines, or belonging to one of the Protestant churches that bear his name. —*n.* 2. a follower of Luther or an adherent of his doctrines; a member of the Lutheran Church. —**Lu′ther·an·ism**, *n.*

Lu′theran Church′ in Amer′ica, n. a Christian denomination founded in 1962, the largest Lutheran group in the United States.

Lu′theran Church′, Missour′i Syn′od, n. a Christian denomination founded in Missouri in 1847, the second-largest Lutheran group in the United States.

luv (luv), n. *Eye Dialect.* love.

lux (luks), n., pl. **lu·ces** (lōō′sēz). a unit of illumination, equivalent to 0.0929 foot-candle and equal to the illumination produced by luminous flux of one lumen falling perpendicularly on a surface one meter square. *Symbol:* lx Also called **meter-candle**.

Lux., Luxembourg.

Lux·em·bourg (luk′səm bûrg′), n. 1. a grand duchy surrounded by Germany, France, and Belgium. 422,474; 999 sq. mi. (2585 sq. km). 2. the capital of this grand duchy. 76,640. 3. a province in SE Belgium: formerly a part of the grand duchy of Luxembourg. 226,452; 1706 sq. mi. (4420 sq. km). Also, **Luxemburg** (for defs. 1, 2).

lux·u·ri·ant (lug zhŏŏr′ē ənt, luk shŏŏr′-), *adj.* 1. abundant in growth, as vegetation; lush. 2. producing abundantly, as soil; fertile. 3. richly abundant, profuse, or superabundant. 4. florid, as imagery or ornamentation; lacking in restraint. —**lux·u′ri·ance**, *n.* —**lux·u′ri·ant·ly**, *adv.*

lux·u·ri·ate (lug zhŏŏr′ē āt′, luk shŏŏr′-), *v.i.*, **-at·ed**, **-at·ing**. 1. to enjoy oneself without stint; indulge in luxury. 2. to grow fully or abundantly; thrive. 3. to take great delight; revel. —**lux·u′ri·a′tion**, *n.*

lux·u·ry (luk′shə rē, lug′zhə-), n., pl. **-ries**, *adj.* —*n.* 1. a material object, service, etc., conducive to physical comfort or sumptuous living, but usu. not a necessity of life. 2. free indulgence in the comforts and pleasures afforded by such things: *a life of luxury*. 3. a means of ministering to indulgence: *This travel plan gives you the luxury of choosing which countries you can visit*. 4. a pleasure out of the ordinary allowed to oneself: *the luxury of an extra piece of cake*. 5. a foolish or worthless form of self-indulgence: *the luxury of self-pity*. —*adj.* 6. of, pertaining to, or providing luxury: *a luxury hotel*. —**lux·u′ri·ous**, *adj.* —**lux·u′ri·ous·ly**, *adv.* —**lux·u′ri·ous·ness**, *n.*

LWV or **L.W.V.**, League of Women Voters.

-ly, 1. a suffix forming adverbs from adjectives: *gladly; gradually; secondly*. 2. a suffix meaning "every," attached to nouns denoting units of time: *hourly; daily*. 3. an adjective suffix meaning "-like": *saintly; cowardly*.

ly·can·thro·py (lī kan′thrə pē), n. 1. a delusion in which one imagi-

nes oneself to be a wolf or other wild animal. 2. the supposed or fabled assumption by a human being of the appearance of a wolf. —**ly·can·throp·ic** (lī′kən throp′ik), *adj.*

Lyc·a·o·ni·a (lik′ā ō′nē ə, -ōn′yə, lī′kā-), n. an ancient country in S Asia Minor: later a Roman province.

ly·cée (lē sā′), n., pl. **-cées** (-sāz′; *Fr.* -sā′). a secondary school, esp. in France, maintained by the government.

ly·ce·um (lī sē′əm), n. 1. an institution for popular education, providing discussions, lectures, concerts, etc. 2. a building for such activities. 3. (*cap.*) a gymnasium near ancient Athens, where Aristotle established a school. 4. LYCÉE.

Ly·cra (lī′krə), *Trademark.* a brand of spandex.

Lyd·i·a (lid′ē ə), n. an ancient kingdom in W Asia Minor: under Croesus, a wealthy empire including most of Asia Minor. *Cap.*: Sardis.

lye (lī), n. 1. a highly concentrated, aqueous solution of potassium hydroxide or sodium hydroxide. 2. any solution resulting from leaching, percolation, or the like.

ly·ing[1] (lī′ing), n. 1. the telling of lies. —*adj.* 2. telling or containing lies; deliberately untruthful. —**ly′ing·ly**, *adv.*

ly·ing[2] (lī′ing), *v.* pres. part. of LIE[2]. —**ly′ing·ly**, *adv.*

ly′ing-in′, n., pl. **ly·ings-in**, **ly·ing-ins**, *adj.* —*n.* 1. the state of being in childbed; confinement. 2. pertaining to or providing facilities for childbirth: *a lying-in hospital*.

Lyme′ disease′ (līm), n. a chronic, recurrent infectious disease characterized by joint pains, fatigue, and sometimes neurological disturbances, caused by a tick-borne spirochete, *Borrelia burgdorferi*, that often induces a transient bull's-eye reddening of the skin at the site of infection.

lymph (limf), n. a clear, yellowish, coagulable fluid, circulated by the lymphatic system, that resembles blood plasma but contains mainly lymphocytes and fats.

lymph-, var. of LYMPHO- before a vowel: *lymphadenitis*.

lym·phat·ic (lim fat′ik), *adj.* 1. pertaining to, containing, or conveying lymph. 2. (of persons) having the characteristics, as flabbiness or sluggishness, formerly believed to be due to an excess of lymph in the system. —*n.* 3. a lymphatic vessel. —**lym·phat′i·cal·ly**, *adv.*

lymphat′ic sys′tem, n. the system of glands, tissues, and passages involved in generating lymphocytes and circulating them through the body in the medium of lymph: includes the lymph vessels, lymph nodes, thymus, and spleen.

lymph′ node′, n. any of the glandlike masses of tissue in the lymph vessels containing cells that become lymphocytes. Also called **lymph′ gland′**.

lympho-, a combining form representing LYMPH: *lymphocyte*. Also, *esp. before a vowel*, **lymph-**.

lym·pho·cyte (lim′fə sīt′), n. a type of nongranular white blood cell important in the production of antibodies. Compare B CELL (def. 1), T CELL. —**lym′pho·cyt′ic** (-sit′ik), *adj.*

lym·phoid (lim′foid), *adj.* 1. of, pertaining to, or resembling lymph. 2. of or pertaining to the tissue (**lym′phoid tis′sue**) that occurs in the lymph nodes, thymus, tonsils, and spleen and produces lymphocytes.

lym·pho·ma (lim fō′mə), n., pl. **-mas**, **-ma·ta** (-mə tə). a tumor arising from any of the cellular elements of lymph nodes. —**lym·pho′ma·toid′**, *adj.*

lym·pho·sar·co·ma (lim′fō sär kō′mə), n. a malignant tumor in lymphoid tissue, caused by the growth of abnormal lymphocytes.

lymph′ sys′tem, n. LYMPHATIC SYSTEM.

lynch (linch), *v.t.* to put to death, esp. by hanging, by mob action and without legal authority. [shortening of *lynch law*, after the self-instituted tribunals presided over by William *Lynch* (1742–1820) of Virginia]

lynch′ law′, n. the administration of summary punishment, esp. death, upon a presumed offender by a mob acting without legal process or authority.

lynch·pin (linch′pin′), n. LINCHPIN.

lynx (lingks), n., pl. **lynx·es**, (*esp. collectively*) **lynx**. any of several wildcats of the genus *Lynx*, having long limbs, a short tail, and usu. tufted ears.

Ly·ons (lē ôn′, lī′ənz), n. a city in E France at the confluence of the Rhone and Saône rivers. 418,476. French, **Lyon**.

Ly·ra (lī′rə), n., *gen.* **-rae** (-rē). the Lyre, a northern constellation between Cygnus and Hercules, containing the bright star Vega.

lyre (līər), n. 1. a small harplike musical instrument of ancient Greece used esp. to accompany singing and recitation. 2. (*cap.*) the constellation Lyra. —**lyr′ist**, *n.*

lyre (def. 1)

lyre·bird (līʳr′bûrd′), *n.* either of two large passerine birds of the genus *Menura,* of E Australia, the males of which have long tails that are lyre-shaped when spread.

lyr·ic (lir′ik), *adj.* Also, **lyr′i·cal. 1.** (of a poem) having the form and general effect of a song, esp. one expressing the writer's feelings. **2.** pertaining to or writing lyric poetry. **3.** characterized by or expressing strong, spontaneous feeling: *lyric writing.* **4.** pertaining to, rendered by, or employing singing. **5.** (of a voice) relatively light of volume and modest in range: *a lyric soprano.* **6.** pertaining, adapted, or sung to the lyre, or composing poems to be sung to the lyre: *ancient Greek lyric odes.* —*n.* **7.** a lyric poem. **8.** Usu., **lyrics.** the words of a song. —**lyr′i·cal·ly,** *adv.* —**lyr′i·cism** (-ə siz′əm), *n.*

lyr·i·cist (lir′ə sist), *n.* **1.** a person who writes the lyrics for songs. **2.** a lyric poet.

lys·er′gic ac′id (lī sûr′jik, li-), *n.* a crystalline solid, $C_{16}H_{16}N_2O_2$: used in the synthesis of LSD.

lyser′gic ac′id di·eth·yl·am′ide (dī eth′ə lam′īd, -eth′ə lə mīd′), *n.* See LSD.

ly·sin (lī′sin), *n.* an antibody causing the disintegration of erythrocytes or bacterial cells.

ly·sine (lī′sēn, -sin), *n.* a crystalline, basic, essential amino acid, $H_2N(CH_2)_4CH(NH_2)COOH$, produced chiefly from many proteins by hydrolysis. *Abbr.:* Lys; *Symbol:* K

ly·sis (lī′sis), *n.* **1.** the dissolution or destruction of cells by lysins. **2.** the gradual recession of a disease. Compare CRISIS (def. 4).

-lysis, a combining form with the meanings "breakdown," "decomposition" of or by means of the thing specified by the initial element: *cytolysis; hydrolysis; photolysis.*

lyso- or **lysi-,** a combining form meaning "lysis," "decomposition": *lysocline; lysogenic.*

ly·so·some (lī′sə sōm′), *n.* a cell organelle containing enzymes that break down proteins and other large molecules into smaller constituents and that disintegrate the cell itself after its death. —**ly′so·so′mal,** *adj.*

ly·so·zyme (lī′sə zīm′), *n.* an enzyme that is destructive of bacteria and functions as an antiseptic, found in tears, leukocytes, mucus, egg albumin, and certain plants.

Lys·tra (lis′trə), *n.* a city in Lycaonia, home of Timothy and the place where the Apostle Paul cured a lame man and was attacked with stones. Acts 16:1–2; 14:6–19.

Lyte (līt), *n.* **Henry,** 1793–1847, English clergyman and hymn writer.

lyt·ic (lit′ik), *adj.* of, noting, or pertaining to lysis or a lysin.

-lytic, a combining form meaning "breaking down," "opposing the effects of," occurring esp. in adjectives that correspond to nouns ending in -LYSIS: *cytolytic; hydrolytic.*

-lyze, a combining form occurring in verbs that correspond to nouns ending in -LYSIS: *hydrolyze.* Also, *esp. Brit.,* **-lyse.**

L

M

M, m (em), *n., pl.* **Ms** or **M's, ms** or **m's. 1.** the 13th letter of the English alphabet, a consonant. **2.** any spoken sound represented by this letter. **3.** something shaped like an M. **4.** a written or printed representation of the letter *M* or *m*.

M, *Symbol.* **1.** the 13th in order or in a series. **2.** the Roman numeral for 1000. **3.** magnetization. **4.** methionine. **5.** minim. **6.** mach.

m, 1. mass. **2.** medieval. **3.** medium. **4.** meter. **5.** middle. **6.** minor.

M-1 (em′wun′), *n., pl.* **M-1's.** a semiautomatic, gas-operated, .30 caliber, clip-fed rifle.

M-14 (em′fôr′tēn′, -fôr′-), *n., pl.* **M-14's.** a fully automatic, gas-operated, .30 caliber rifle.

M-16 (em′siks′tēn′), *n., pl.* **M-16's.** a lightweight, magazine-fed rifle operating either automatically or semiautomatically.

ma (mä), *n., pl.* **mas.** *Informal.* mother.

MA, Massachusetts.

M.A., Master of Arts. [< Latin *Magister Artium*]

ma'am (mam, mäm; *unstressed* məm), *n.* (*often cap.*) MADAM (def. 1).

ma′-and-pa′, *adj.* MOM-AND-POP.

mabe′ pearl′ (mäb, mä′bē), *n.* a smooth cultured pearl with one flat and one convex surface.

Mac- or **Mc-** or **M'-** or **M'-,** a prefix found in family names of Irish or Scottish Gaelic origin.

Mac., Maccabees.

ma·ca·bre (mə kä′brə, -käb′, -kä′bər), *adj.* **1.** gruesome in character; ghastly. **2.** of, dealing with, or representing death. Sometimes, **ma·ca·ber** (mə kä′bər).

mac·ad·am (mə kad′əm), *n.* **1.** a macadamized road or pavement. **2.** the broken stone used for macadamizing.

mac·a·da′mi·a nut′ (mak′ə dā′mē ə), *n.* the round, hard-shelled nut of an Australian tree, *Macadamia ternifolia,* of the protea family, cultivated in Hawaii.

mac·ad·am·ize (mə kad′ə mīz′), *v.t.,* **-ized, -iz·ing.** to pave by compacting broken stone, often with asphalt or tar.

Ma·cao (mə kou′), *n.* **1.** a Portuguese territory in S China; a peninsula in the Zhu Jiang delta and two adjacent islands. 426,400; 6 sq. mi. (16 sq. km). **2.** the capital of this territory. Portuguese, **Macáu.**

ma·caque (mə kak′, -käk′), *n.* any monkey of the genus *Macaca,* chiefly of Asia, characterized by cheek pouches and usu. a short tail.

mac·a·ro·ni (mak′ə rō′nē), *n., pl.* **-nis, -nies. 1.** small tubular pasta made of wheat flour. **2.** an English dandy of the 18th century affecting Continental ways.

mac·a·roon (mak′ə rōōn′), *n.* a cookie made of beaten egg whites, sugar, and almond paste or ground coconut.

Mac·Ar·thur (mə kär′thər), *n.* **Douglas,** 1880–1964, U.S. general.

Ma·cau·lay (mə kô′lē), *n.* **1. Dame Rose,** c1885–1958, English novelist. **2. Thomas Babington, 1st Baron,** 1800–59, English historian and statesman.

ma·caw (mə kô′), *n.* any of various extremely large, long-tailed parrots of the genera *Ara* and *Anodorhynchus,* of the New World tropics, noted for their brilliant plumage and harsh voice.

Mac·beth (mək beth′, mak-), *n.* **1.** died 1057, king of Scotland 1040–57. **2.** (*italics*) a tragedy (1606?) by William Shakespeare.

Mac·ca·bae·us (mak′ə bē′əs), *n.* **Judas** or **Judah** (*"the Hammer"*), died 160 B.C., Judean patriot.

Mac·ca·be·an (mak′ə bē′ən), *adj.* of or pertaining to the Maccabees or to Judas Maccabaeus.

Mac·ca·bees (mak′ə bēz′), *n.* **1.** (*used with a plural v.*) a priestly Jewish family who ruled Judea in the 1st and 2nd centuries B.C., esp. Judas Maccabaeus and his brothers, who defeated the Syrians in 165? and re-dedicated the Temple. **2.** (*used with a sing. v.*) either of two books of the Apocrypha, I Maccabees or II Maccabees, that contain the history of the Maccabees.

Mac·don·ald (mək don′əld), *n.* **Sir John Alexander,** 1815–91, Canadian statesman, born in Scotland.

Mac·Don·ald (mək don′əld), *n.* **James Ramsay,** 1866–1937, British prime minister 1924, 1929–35.

mace¹ (mās), *n.* **1.** a clublike armor-breaking weapon, often with a spiked metal head, used chiefly in the Middle Ages. **2.** a ceremonial staff symbolic of office.

mace² (mās), *n.* a spice made from the inner husk of the nutmeg.

Mace (mās), *Trademark.* **1.** a chemical spray that causes severe eye and skin irritation: used to incapacitate rioters, assailants, etc. —*v.t.,* **Maced, Mac·ing. 2.** (*sometimes l.c.*) to spray with Mace.

Mac·e·do·ni·a (mas′i dō′nē ə, -dōn′yə), *n.* **1.** Also, **Mac·e·don** (mas′i don′). an ancient kingdom in the Balkan Peninsula, in SE Europe: now a region in N Greece, SW Bulgaria, and the Republic of Macedonia. **2.** a republic in S Europe: formerly (1945–92) a constituent republic of Yugoslavia. 2,113,866; 9928 sq. mi. (25,713 sq. km). *Cap.:* Skopje. —**Mac·e·do′ni·an,** *adj., n.*

mac·er·ate (mas′ə rāt′), *v.,* **-at·ed, -at·ing.** —*v.t.* **1.** to soften or separate into parts by steeping in a liquid. **2.** to cause to grow thin or waste away. —*v.i.* **3.** to become macerated. —**mac′er·a′tion,** *n.* —**mac′er·a′tive,** *adj.* —**mac′er·a′tor,** *n.*

mach or **Mach** (mäk), *n.* a number indicating the ratio of the speed of an object to the speed of sound in the medium through which the object is moving. *Abbr.:* M

mache or **mâche** (mäsh), *n.* CORN SALAD.

ma·chet·e (mə shet′ē, -chet′ē), *n., pl.* **-chet·es.** a heavy swordlike knife used as a cutting implement and weapon.

Mach·i·a·vel·li (mak′ē ə vel′ē), *n.* **Niccolò di Bernardo,** 1469–1527, Italian political philosopher. —**Mach′i·a·vel′li·an,** *adj., n.*

mach·i·na·tion (mak′ə nā′shən), *n.* Usu., **machinations.** a crafty scheme or maneuver; an intrigue.

ma·chine (mə shēn′), *n., v.,* **-chined, -chin·ing.** —*n.* **1.** an apparatus consisting of interrelated parts with separate functions, used in the performance of some kind of work: *a sewing machine.* **2. a.** a device that transmits or modifies force or motion. **b.** Also called **simple machine.** any of several elementary mechanisms, as the lever, wheel and axle, pulley, screw, wedge, or inclined plane. **c.** a combination of simple machines. **3.** an automobile or airplane. **4.** any of various apparatus, devices, etc., that dispense things, esp. a vending machine. **5.** any complex agency or operating system: *the machine of government.* **6.** a group of persons that conducts or controls a political party or organization. **7.** a person or thing that acts in a mechanical or automatic manner. **8.** a mechanical contrivance formerly used for producing stage effects. **9.** a literary contrivance introduced for special effect. —*v.t.* **10.** to make, prepare, or finish with a machine or machine tool.

machine′ gun′, *n.* a firearm capable of shooting a continuous stream of bullets. —**ma·chine′-gun′,** *v.t.,* **-gunned, -gun·ning.**

machine′ lan′guage, *n.* a usu. numerical coding system specific to the hardware of a given computer model, into which any high-level or assembly program must be translated before being run.

machine′-read′able, *adj.* (of data) in a form suitable for direct acceptance and processing by computer, as an electronic file on a magnetic disk.

ma·chin·er·y (mə shē′nə rē), *n., pl.* **-er·ies. 1.** an assemblage of machines. **2.** the parts of a machine collectively. **3.** a system by which action is maintained or by which some result is obtained.

machin′ery of gov′ernment, *n.* the complex procedures and processes by which a government functions.

machine′ shop′, *n.* a workshop in which metal and other substances are cut, shaped, etc., by machine tools.

ma·chin·ist (mə shē′nist), *n.* **1.** a person who operates machinery, esp. an operator of machine tools. **2.** a person who makes or repairs machines. **3.** a warrant officer who assists the engineering officer in the engine room.

ma·chis·mo (mä chēz′mō, -chiz′-, mə-), *n.* an exaggerated sense of manliness; an attitude that virility, aggressiveness, strength, or right to dominate are concomitants of masculinity.

mach′ (or **Mach′**) **num′ber,** *n.* MACH.

ma·cho (mä′chō), *adj.* having or characterized by machismo.

Mach·pe·lah (mak pē′lä), *n.* the site of a cave, probably in the ancient city of Hebron, where Abraham, Sarah, Rebekah, Isaac, Jacob, and Leah were buried. Gen. 23:19; 25:9; 49:30; 50:13.

Ma·chu Pic·chu (mä′chōō pēk′chōō, pē′chōō), *n.* the site of an ancient Incan city in the Andes, in S central Peru.

mack·er·el (mak′ər əl, mak′rəl), *n., pl.* (*esp. collectively*) **-el,** (*esp. for kinds or species*) **-els. 1.** any of various scombrid fishes, esp. a food fish, *Scomber scombrus,* of the N Atlantic, having wavy cross markings on the back. **2.** SPANISH MACKEREL.

mack′erel shark′, *n.* any of various fierce sharks of the family Lamnidae, including the great white shark and the mako.

mack·i·naw (mak′ə nô′), *n.* **1.** a heavy woolen fabric with a shaggy nap on both sides, often woven in a plaid pattern. **2.** a short, double-breasted coat of this or a similar material. —**mack′i·nawed′,** *adj.*

Mack′inaw trout′, *n.* LAKE TROUT.

Mac·lar·en (mə klar′ən), *n.* **Alexander,** 1826–1910, English clergyman and Bible scholar.

Mac·mil·lan (mək mil′ən), *n.* **Harold,** 1894–1986, British prime minister 1957–63.

Mac·Mil·lan (mək mil′ən), *n.* **Donald Baxter,** 1874–1970, U.S. arctic explorer.

Ma·con (mā′kən), *n.* a city in central Georgia. 109,191.

Mâ·con (mä kôn′), *n.* a city in E central France. 38,404.

mac·ra·mé or **mac·ra·me** (mak′rə mā′), *n.* **1.** Also called **mac′ramé lace′.** lacelike webbing made of knotted cord or yarn. **2.** the technique of producing macramé.

mac·ro (mak′rō), *adj., n., pl.* **-ros.** —*adj.* **1.** very large in scale or capability. **2.** of or pertaining to macroeconomics. —*n.* **3.** a single instruction, for use in a computer program, that represents a sequence of instructions or keystrokes.

macro-, a combining form meaning "large, esp. in comparison with others of its kind" (*macromolecule*), "abnormally large" (*macrocyte*), "major, significant" (*macroevolution*), "not local, extending over a broad area" (*macroclimate*), "visible to the naked eye" (*macrophyte*); often contrasting with MICRO- (*macrocosm*).

mac·ro·bi·ot·ics (mak′rō bī ot′iks), *n.* (*used with a sing. v.*) a program emphasizing harmony with nature, esp. through a restricted, primarily vegetarian diet.

mac·ro·cli·mate (mak′rə klī′mit), *n.* the general climate of a large area, as that of a continent or country. Compare MICROCLIMATE. —**mac′ro·cli·mat′ic** (-rō klī mat′ik), *adj.* —**mac′ro·cli·mat′i·cal·ly**, *adv.*

mac·ro·cosm (mak′rə koz′əm), *n.* the universe considered as a whole (opposed to *microcosm*). —**mac′ro·cos′mic**, *adj.* —**mac′ro·cos′mi·cal·ly**, *adv.*

mac·ro·ec·o·nom·ics (mak′rō ek′ə nom′iks, -ē′kə-), *n.* (*used with a sing. v.*) the study of large economic systems comprised of different sectors, as that of a nation. Compare MICROECONOMICS. —**mac′ro·ec′o·nom′ic**, *adj.* —**mac′ro·e·con′o·mist** (-i kon′ə mist), *n.*

mac·ro·ev·o·lu·tion (mak′rō ev′ə lo̅o̅′shən; *esp. Brit.* -ē′və-), *n.* major evolutionary change of species and taxa. —**mac′ro·ev′o·lu′tion·ar′y**, *adj.*

mac′ro lens′, *n.* a lens used to bring into focus objects very close to the camera.

ma·cron (mā′kron, mak′ron), *n.* **1.** a horizontal line used over a vowel to show that it is long or has a specific pronunciation, as (ā) in *fate* (fāt). **2.** this symbol used in prosody to indicate a long or stressed syllable.

mac·ro·nu·tri·ent (mak′rō no̅o̅′trē ənt, -nyo̅o̅′-), *n.* **1.** any of the nutritional components required in relatively large amounts: protein, carbohydrate, fat, and the essential minerals. **2.** any of the chemical elements required by plants in relatively large amounts: nitrogen, phosphorus, and potassium.

mac·ro·phage (mak′rə fāj′), *n.* a large white blood cell, occurring principally in connective tissue and in the bloodstream, that ingests foreign particles and infectious microorganisms by phagocytosis. —**mac′ro·phag′ic** (-faj′ik), *adj.*

mac·ro·scop·ic (mak′rə skop′ik) also **mac′ro·scop′i·cal**, *adj.* **1.** visible to the naked eye. Compare MICROSCOPIC (def. 1). **2.** pertaining to large units; comprehensive. —**mac′ro·scop′i·cal·ly**, *adv.*

mac·ro·struc·ture (mak′rō struk′chər), *n.* an overall structure or organizational scheme.

mac·ro·vil·lus (mak′rō vil′əs), *n., pl.* **-vil·li** (-vil′ī). any of the fingerlike extensions of the surface of epithelial tissue, as the tubules of the kidney, functioning to increase the biologically active membrane area.

mac·u·la (mak′yə lə), *n., pl.* **-lae** (-lē′), **-las.** a spot, esp. on the skin. **2. a.** an opaque spot on the cornea. **b.** Also, **yellow spot.** an irregularly oval, yellow-pigmented area on the central retina containing color-sensitive rods and the sharpest point of vision. —**mac′u·lar**, *adj.*

mac′ular degenera′tion, *n.* degeneration of the central portion of the retina, resulting in a loss of sharp vision.

mac·u·late (mak′yə lit), *adj.* **1.** spotted; stained. **2.** defiled; impure. —**mac′u·la′tion** (-lā′shən), *n.*

mad (mad), *adj.*, **mad·der, mad·dest**, *n., v.*, **mad·ded, mad·ing** —*adj.* **1.** mentally disturbed; deranged. **2.** greatly provoked or irritated; enraged. **3.** affected with rabies; rabid: *a mad dog.* **4.** extremely foolish or illogical; imprudent or irrational: *a mad scheme.* **5.** impetuous: frantic: *mad haste.* **6.** brimming with enthusiasm; infatuated: *mad about opera.* **7.** wildly frivolous; hilarious: *had a mad time at the party.* —*n.* **8.** an angry period or mood. —*v.t., v.i.* **9.** to madden. —*Idiom.* **10. like mad,** at a furious pace: *rushing around like mad.* —**mad′ly**, *adv.* —**mad′ness**, *n.*

Mad·a·gas·car (mad′ə gas′kər), *n.* an island republic in the Indian Ocean, about 240 mi. (385 km) off the SE coast of Africa: formerly a French colony; gained independence 1960. 14,061,627; 226,657 sq. mi. (587,041 sq. km). *Cap.:* Antananarivo. Formerly, **Malagasy Republic.** —**Mad′a·gas′can**, *n., adj.*

mad·am (mad′əm), *n., pl.* **mes·dames** (mā dam′, -däm′) for 1; **madams** for 2. **1.** (*often cap.*) a respectful term of address to a woman. **2.** a woman in charge of a household. [< Old French, orig. *ma dame* my lady]

mad·ame (mad′əm, mə dam′, -däm′, ma-), *n., pl.* **mes·dames** (mā dam′, -däm′). (*often cap.*) **1.** a French title equivalent to Mrs.: *Madame Curie.* **2.** a title for a woman, esp. one who comes from a non-English-speaking country. *Abbr.:* Mme.

mad·cap (mad′kap′), *adj.* **1.** recklessly impulsive; rash: *madcap schemes.* —*n.* **2.** a madcap person.

MADD (mad), *n.* Mothers Against Drunk Driving.

mad·den (mad′n), *v.t.* **1.** to anger intensely; infuriate. **2.** to make insane. —*v.i.* **3.** to become mad.

mad·den·ing (mad′n ing), *adj.* **1.** driving to madness: *maddening thirst.* **2.** exasperating: *maddening apathy.* —**mad′den·ing·ly**, *adv.*

mad·der¹ (mad′ər), *n.* **1.** any plant of the genus *Rubia*, esp. the climbing *R. tinctorum*, of Europe, having open clusters of small yellowish flowers. **2.** the root of this plant, formerly used in dyeing. **3.** a reddish dye derived from madder.

mad·der² (mad′ər), *adj.* comparative of MAD.

mad·dest (mad′ist), *adj.* superlative of MAD.

mad·ding (mad′ing), *adj.* tumultuous: *the madding crowd.*

made (mād), *v.* **1.** pt. and pp. of MAKE. —*adj.* **2.** produced (often used in combination): *machine-made clothes.* **3.** artificially produced; not originating in nature: *made fur.* **4.** invented; concocted: *a made story.* **5.** prepared from several ingredients: *a made dish.* **6.** assured of success: *a made man.* —*Idiom.* **7. have it made,** *Informal.* to be confident or possessed of success.

Ma·dei·ra (mə dēr′ə, -dâr′ə), *n.* **1.** a group of eight islands off the NW coast of Africa belonging to Portugal. 258,000; 308 sq. mi. (798 sq. km). *Cap.:* Funchal. **2.** the chief island of this group. 286 sq. mi. (741 sq. km). **3.** (*often l.c.*) a fortified amber-colored wine from Madeira. **4.** a river in W Brazil flowing NE to the Amazon: chief tributary of the Amazon. 2100 mi. (3380 km) long.

mad·e·leine (mad′l in, mad′l ān′, -en′), *n.* a small shell-shaped cake.

mad·e·moi·selle (mad′ə mə zel′, mad′mwə-, mam zel′), *n., pl.* **mademoiselles, mes·de·moi·selles** (mā′də mə zel′, -zelz′, mād′mwə-). **1.** (*often cap.*) a French title equivalent to Miss. *Abbr.:* Mlle. **2.** a French governess. **3.** SILVER PERCH (def. 1).

made′-to-or′der, *adj.* **1.** made to individual specifications or requirements. **2.** perfectly suited.

made′-up′, *adj.* **1.** falsely fabricated; concocted: *a made-up story.* **2.** wearing facial makeup. **3.** put together; finished.

mad·house (mad′hous′), *n., pl.* **-hous·es** (-hou′ziz). **1.** a hospital for the mentally disturbed. **2.** a disorderly, often noisy place.

Mad·i·son (mad′ə sən), *n.* **1.** Dolly or Dolley (*Dorothea Payne*), 1768–1849, wife of James Madison. **2.** James, 1751–1836, 4th president of the U.S. 1809–17. **3.** the capital of Wisconsin, in the S part. 194,586.

Mad′ison Av′enue, *n.* **1.** an avenue in New York City, once the principal location for advertising firms. **2.** the U.S. advertising industry.

mad·man (mad′man′, -mən), *n., pl.* **-men** (-men′, -mən). a person who is or appears to be insane.

mad′ mon′ey, *n.* **1.** a small sum of money kept in reserve for emergencies or minor purchases. **2.** carfare carried by a woman on a date to enable her to get home in case she and her escort quarrel.

Ma·don·na¹ (mə don′ə), *n.* **1.** the Virgin Mary. **2.** a picture or statue representing the Virgin Mary. [< Italian: my lady]

Ma·don·na² (mə don′ə), *n.* (*Madonna Louise Veronica Ciccone*), born 1958, U.S. pop singer and actress.

mad·ras (mad′rəs, mə dras′, -dräs′), *n.* **1.** a light cotton fabric of various weaves, esp. one in multicolored plaid or stripes. **2.** a thin curtain fabric of a gauzelike weave with figures of heavier yarns. **3.** a large brightly colored silk or cotton kerchief often used for turbans.

Ma·dras (mə dras′, -dräs′), *n.* **1.** the capital of Tamil Nadu state, in SE India, on the Bay of Bengal. 4,277,000. **2.** former name of TAMIL NADU.

Ma·drid (mə drid′), *n.* the capital of Spain, in the central part. 3,123,713. —**Mad·ri·le·ni·an** (mad′rə lē′nē ən, -lēn′yən), *n., adj.*

mad·ri·gal (mad′ri gəl), *n.* **1.** an unaccompanied polyphonic secular vocal composition, esp. of the 16th and 17th centuries. **2.** part song; glee. —**mad′ri·gal·ist**, *n.*

ma·dro·ne or **ma·dro·na** (mə drō′nə), also **ma·dro·ño** (-drōn′yō), *n., pl.* **-nes** or **-nas**, also **-ños.** an evergreen tree, *Arbutus menziesii*, of the heath family, native to W North America, having red flaky bark and bearing edible reddish berries.

mad·tom (mad′tom′), *n.* any of several small North American freshwater catfishes of the genus *Noturus*, having a poisonous pectoral spine.

mad·wo·man (mad′wo̅o̅m′ən), *n., pl.* **-wom·en.** a woman who is or appears to be insane.

mad·wort (mad′wûrt′, -wôrt′), *n.* a mat-forming plant, *Aurinia saxatilis* (or *Alyssum saxatille*), of the mustard family, having spatulate leaves and open clusters of pale yellow flowers.

mael·strom (māl′strəm), *n.* **1.** a powerful whirlpool often hazardous to approach. **2.** a tumultuous state of affairs. **3.** (*cap.*) a powerful current off the NW coast of Norway.

maes·tro (mī′strō), *n., pl.* **-tros.** **1.** an eminent composer, teacher, or conductor of music. **2.** a master of any art.

Ma·fi·a (mä′fē ə, maf′ē ə), *n.* **1.** a secret organization allegedly engaged in criminal activities in the U.S., Italy, and elsewhere. **2.** (in Sicily) **a.** (*l.c.*) a spirit of hostility to the law. **b.** a 19th-century secret society that acted in this spirit. **3.** (*l.c.*) any influential clique.

ma·fi·o·so (mä′fē ō′sō), *n., pl.* **-si** (-sē), **-sos.** (*often cap.*) a member of the Mafia.

mag (mag), *n.* magazine.

mag·a·zine (mag′ə zēn′, mag′ə zēn′), *n.* **1.** a periodical publication, usu. paperbound, that typically contains essays, stories, poems, and often illustrations. **2.** a television program that combines interviews, commentary, and entertainment. **3.** a room for keeping gunpowder and other explosives. **4.** a military depot for arms or provisions. **5.** a receptacle on a gun for holding cartridges. **6.** CARTRIDGE (def. 4).

Mag·da·la (mag′də lə), *n.* an ancient town in Palestine, W of the Sea of Galilee: supposed home of Mary Magdalene.

Mag·da·lene (mag′də lēn′, -lən, mag′də lē′nē), *n.* **the**, MARY MAGDALENE.

Ma·gel·lan (mə jel′ən), *n.* **1. Ferdinand**, c1480–1521, Portuguese navigator. **2. Strait of**, a strait near the S tip of South America between the

(M)

mainland of Chile and Tierra del Fuego, connecting the Atlantic and the Pacific. 360 mi. (580 km) long.

Ma•gen Da•vid (mä′gən dä′vid, mä gen′ dä vēd′), *n.* STAR OF DAVID. [< Hebrew *māghen dāwīd* lit., shield of David]

ma•gen•ta (mə jen′tə), *n.* a purplish red.

mag•got (mag′ət), *n.* a soft-bodied, legless larva of certain flies. —**mag′got•y,** *adj.*

Ma•gi (mā′jī), *n.pl., sing.* **-gus** (-gəs). **1.** (*sometimes l.c.*) the wise men, three by tradition, who paid homage to the infant Jesus, bringing him gifts of gold, frankincense, and myrrh. Matt. 2:1–12. **2.** (*sometimes l.c.*) a class of Zoroastrian priests in ancient Media and Persia. [see MAGUS] —**Ma′gi•an** (-jē ən), *n., adj.*

mag•ic (maj′ik), *n.* **1.** the art of producing illusions, as by sleight of hand. **2.** the practice of using various techniques, as incantation, to exert control over the supernatural or the forces of nature. **3.** a result of such practice. **4.** power or influence exerted through this practice. **5.** any extraordinary influence or power: *the magic of fame.* —*adj.* **6.** done by or employed in magic: *a magic trick.* **7.** mysteriously enchanting, skillful, or effective. —**mag′i•cal,** *adj.* —**mag′i•cal•ly,** *adv.*

ma•gi•cian (mə jish′ən), *n.* **1.** a person who performs sleight-of-hand tricks or other illusions. **2.** a sorcerer.

Ma′gi•not line′ (mazh′ə nō′), *n.* a zone of fortifications erected by France before World War II, but outflanked by a German invasion in 1940. [after André *Maginot*, French minister of war]

mag•is•te•ri•al (maj′ə stēr′ē əl), *adj.* **1.** of, pertaining to, or befitting a master; authoritative. **2.** imperious; domineering: *a magisterial tone.* —**mag′is•te′ri•al•ly,** *adv.*

mag•is•trate (maj′ə strāt′, -strit), *n.* **1.** a civil officer charged with the administration of the law. **2.** a minor judicial officer, as a justice of the peace or the judge of a police court, having jurisdiction to try minor criminal cases and to conduct preliminary examinations of persons charged with serious crimes. —**mag′is•trate′ship,** *n.* —**mag′is•trat′i•cal** (-strat′i kəl), *adj.* —**mag′is•trat′i•cal•ly,** *adv.*

mag•lev (mag′lev′), *n.* (*often cap.*) a high-speed railway system in which the train is suspended just above or below a guide rail by a powerful magnetic field and propelled by a linear induction motor.

mag•ma (mag′mə), *n., pl.* **-mas, -ma•ta** (-mə tə). **1.** molten material beneath or within the earth's crust, from which igneous rock is formed. **2.** a mixture or suspension of mineral or organic matter. —**mag•mat′ic** (-mat′ik), *adj.*

Mag•na Car•ta (or **Char•ta**) (mag′nə kär′tə), *n.* **1.** the charter of liberties forced from King John by the English barons at Runnymede, June 15, 1215. **2.** any basic law guaranteeing liberties. [< Medieval Latin: lit., great charter]

mag•na cum lau•de (mäg′nə kŏŏm lou′dā, -də, -dē; mag′nə kum lō′dē), *adv.* with great praise: used in diplomas to designate the next-to-highest of three honors for grades above the average. Compare CUM LAUDE, SUMMA CUM LAUDE.

mag•nan•i•mous (mag nan′ə məs), *adj.* **1.** generous in forgiving an insult or injury; free from pettiness. **2.** noble; high-minded. —**mag′na•nim′i•ty** (-nə nim′i tē), *n.* —**mag•nan′i•mous•ly,** *adv.*

mag•nate (mag′nāt, -nit), *n.* a person of great influence, importance, or standing in a particular field.

mag•ne•si•um (mag nē′zē əm, -zhəm, -shē əm), *n.* a light, ductile, silver-white metallic element that burns with a dazzling light, used in alloys, fireworks, and flashbulbs. *Symbol:* Mg; *at. wt.:* 24.312; *at. no.:* 12; *sp. gr.:* 1.74 at 20°C.

mag•net (mag′nit), *n.* **1.** a body, as a piece of iron or steel, that possesses the property of attracting certain substances, as iron. **2.** LODESTONE (defs. 1, 2). **3.** a thing or person that attracts.

mag•net•ic (mag net′ik), *adj.* **1.** of or pertaining to a magnet or magnetism. **2.** having the properties of a magnet. **3.** capable of being magnetized or attracted by a magnet. **4.** of, pertaining to, or being a medium created with magnetically sensitive material for storing electronic data, as a magnetic card or disk, and usu. allowing erasure and reuse. **5.** pertaining to the magnetic field of the earth: *the magnetic equator.* **6.** exerting a strong attractive power or charm: *a magnetic personality.* **7.** pertaining to various bearings and measurements as indicated by a magnetic compass: *magnetic amplitude.* —**mag•net′i•cal•ly,** *adv.*

magnet′ic disk′, *n.* **1.** HARD DISK. **2.** FLOPPY DISK.

magnet′ic field′, *n.* **1.** a region of space near a magnet, electric current, or moving charged particle in which a magnetic force acts on any other magnet, electric current, or moving charged particle. **2.** a vector quantity defined by the force exerted on a given object at each point in such a region.

magnet′ic induc′tion, *n.* **1.** Also called **magnet′ic flux′ den′sity.** a vector quantity used as a measure of the strength of a magnetic field. *Symbol:* B **2.** magnetization induced by proximity to a magnetic field.

magnet′ic nee′dle, *n.* a slender magnetized steel rod that when adjusted to swing in a horizontal plane, as in a compass, indicates the direction of the earth's magnetic fields.

magnet′ic north′, *n.* north as indicated by a magnetic compass, differing in most places from true north.

magnet′ic pole′, *n.* **1.** the region of a magnet toward which the lines of magnetic induction converge (**south pole**) or from which the lines of induction diverge (**north pole**). **2.** either of the two points on the earth's surface where the dipping needle of a compass stands vertical, one in the arctic, the other in the antarctic.

magnet′ic res′onance im′aging, *n.* a process of producing images of the body regardless of intervening bone by means of a strong magnetic field and low-energy radio waves. *Abbr.:* MRI

magnet′ic storm′, *n.* a temporary disturbance of the earth's magnetic field induced by radiation and streams of charged particles from the sun.

magnet′ic tape′, *n.* a ribbon of material coated with a substance sensitive to electromagnetic impulses and used to record sound, images, or data. Compare AUDIOTAPE, VIDEOTAPE.

mag•net•ism (mag′ni tiz′əm), *n.* **1.** the properties of attraction possessed by magnets; the molecular properties common to magnets. **2.** the agency producing magnetic phenomena. **3.** the science dealing with magnetic phenomena. **4.** strong attractive power or charm.

mag′net is′sue, *n.* a political issue that can attract wide and varied support from voters.

mag•net•ite (mag′ni tīt′), *n.* a common black mineral, ferrous and ferric iron oxide, $FeFe_2O_4$, that is the most magnetic mineral and an important iron ore.

mag•net•ize (mag′ni tīz′), *v.t.* **-ized, -iz•ing. 1.** to make a magnet of; impart the properties of a magnet to. **2.** to exert an attracting or compelling influence upon. —**mag′ne•tiz′a•ble,** *adj.* —**mag′net•i•za′tion,** *n.* —**mag′net•iz′er,** *n.*

mag•ne•to (mag nē′tō), *n., pl.* **-tos.** a small electric generator in which permanent magnets provide the magnetic field.

magneto-, a combining form representing MAGNETIC or MAGNETISM in compound words: *magnetometer.*

mag•ne•tom•e•ter (mag′ni tom′i tər), *n.* **1.** an instrument for measuring the intensity of a magnetic field. **2.** an instrument for detecting the presence of ferrous or magnetic materials, as in concealed weapons. —**mag′ne•to•met′ric** (-nē′tə me′trik), *adj.* —**mag′ne•tom′e•try,** *n.*

mag•ne•to•pause (mag nē′tō pôz′), *n.* **1.** the boundary between the earth's magnetosphere and interplanetary space, ab. 40,000 mi. (65,000 km) above the earth, marked by an abrupt decrease in the earth's magnetic induction. **2.** a similar feature of another planet.

mag•ne•to•sphere (mag nē′tə sfēr′), *n.* **1.** the outer region of the earth's ionosphere where the earth's magnetic field controls the motion of charged particles, as in the Van Allen belts. **2.** such a region of another planet. —**mag′ne•to•spher′ic** (-sfer′ik), *adj.*

mag•ne•to•stric•tion (mag nē′tō strik′shən), *n.* a change in dimensions exhibited by ferromagnetic materials when subjected to a magnetic field. —**mag′ne•to•stric′tive** (-tə strik′tiv), *adj.*

mag•ne•tron (mag′ni tron′), *n.* a two-element vacuum tube used to generate microwaves, as in a microwave oven.

mag′net school′, *n.* a public school with a specialized program designed to draw students from throughout a community.

Mag•nif•i•cat (mag nif′i kat′, -kät′; mäg nif′i kät′, män yif′-), *n.* **1.** the canticle of the Virgin Mary in Luke 1:46–55. **2.** a musical setting for this. [< Latin: (it) magnifies (the first word of the hymn)]

mag•ni•fi•ca•tion (mag′nə fi kā′shən), *n.* **1.** the act of magnifying or the state of being magnified. **2.** the power to magnify. Compare POWER (def. 19a). **3.** a magnified image.

mag•nif•i•cent (mag nif′ə sənt), *adj.* **1.** splendid or impressive in appearance: *a magnificent palace.* **2.** very fine; superb: *magnificent weather.* **3.** noble; sublime. **4.** (*usu. cap.*) (formerly used as a title) great: *Lorenzo the Magnificent.* **5.** lavish: *a magnificent feast.* —**mag•nif′i•cence,** *n.* —**mag•nif′i•cent•ly,** *adv.*

mag•ni•fy (mag′nə fī′), *v.,* **-fied, -fy•ing.** —*v.t.* **1.** to increase the apparent size of. **2.** to make greater in actual size; enlarge. **3.** to exaggerate; overstate: *to magnify one's difficulties.* **4.** to intensify; heighten. —*v.i.* **5.** to increase or be able to increase the apparent or actual size of an object. —**mag′ni•fi′a•ble,** *adj.* —**mag′ni•fi′er,** *n.*

mag′nifying glass′, *n.* a lens that makes an object appear larger.

mag•nil•o•quent (mag nil′ə kwənt), *adj.* speaking or expressed in a lofty or grandiose style; bombastic. —**mag•nil′o•quence,** *n.* —**mag•nil′o•quent•ly,** *adv.*

mag•ni•tude (mag′ni tōōd′, -tyōōd′), *n.* **1.** size; extent; dimensions. **2.** great importance: *affairs of magnitude.* **3.** greatness of size or amount. **4. a.** the brightness of a celestial body as expressed on a logarithmic scale where an increase of 1 equals a reduction in brightness by a factor of 2.512, the sixth magnitude being the dimmest observable with the naked eye. **b.** ABSOLUTE MAGNITUDE. **5.** a number characteristic of a quantity and forming a basis for comparison with similar quantities, as length. —*Idiom.* **6. of the first magnitude,** of greatest significance.

mag•no•lia (mag nōl′yə, -nō′lē ə), *n., pl.* **-lias. 1.** any shrub or tree of the genus *Magnolia*, of the magnolia family, having large usu. fragrant flowers, much cultivated for ornament. **2.** the blossom of any such shrub or tree, as of the evergreen magnolia tree.

mag•num (mag′nəm), *n.* **1.** a large wine bottle having a capacity of two ordinary bottles, or 1.5 liters (1.6 quarts). **2.** a magnum cartridge or firearm. —*adj.* **3.** (of a cartridge) equipped with a larger charge than other cartridges of the same size. **4.** (of a firearm) using such a cartridge.

mag′num o′pus, *n.* a great work, esp. the chief work of a writer or artist.

Ma•gog (mā′gog), *n.* GOG AND MAGOG.

mag·pie (mag′pī′), *n.* **1.** any of various birds of the genus *Pica*, of the jay family, having long, graduated tails, black-and-white plumage, and noisy habits. **2.** an incessantly talkative person. **3.** a person who collects or hoards things.

mag·uey (mag′wā, mə gā′), *n.* **1.** any of several plants of the agave family, esp. the cantala, *Agave cantala.* **2.** any of various fibers related to or resembling cantala.

Ma·gus (mā′gəs), *n., pl.* **-gi** (-jī). **1.** (*sometimes l.c.*) one of the Magi. **2.** (*l.c.*) a magician; sorcerer. **3.** (*sometimes l.c.*) a Zoroastrian priest. [< Latin < Greek *mágos* < Old Persian *maguš*]

mag′ wheel′, *n.* a motor vehicle wheel made of lightweight magnesium steel.

Ma·ha·na·im (mā′hə nā′im), *n.* a town in Gilead east of the Jordan River, headquarters for David during the rebellion of Absalom. II Sam. 17:24.

ma·ha·ra·jah or **ma·ha·ra·ja** (mä′hə rä′jə, -zhə), *n., pl.* **-jahs** or **-jas.** a former ruling prince in India, esp. of one of the major states.

ma·ha·ra·nee or **ma·ha·ra·ni** (mä′hə rä′nē), *n., pl.* **-nees** or **-nis.** **1.** the wife of a maharajah. **2.** a former Indian princess being sovereign in her own right.

ma·ha·ri·shi (mä hə rē′shē, mə här′ə-), *n., pl.* **-shis.** a Hindu religious sage.

ma·hat·ma (mə hät′mə, -hat′-), *n., pl.* **-mas.** (*sometimes cap.*) **1.** a Brahman sage. **2.** (esp. in India) a person who is held in the highest esteem for wisdom and saintliness.

Ma·ha·ya·na (mä′hə yä′nə), *n.* one of the two major schools of Buddhism, characterized by a belief in a common search for salvation. Compare HINAYANA. [< Sanskrit = *mahā-* great + *yāna* vehicle] **—Ma′ha·ya′nist,** *n.*

Ma·hi·can (mə hē′kən), *n., pl.* **-cans,** (*esp. collectively*) **-can. 1.** a member of an American Indian people who lived in the middle and upper Hudson River valley in the 17th century. **2.** the extinct Eastern Algonquian language of the Mahican.

ma·hi-ma·hi (mä′hē mä′hē), *n., pl.* **-hi.** the dolphin, genus *Coryphaena,* used for food; dolphinfish.

mah-jongg or **mah·jong** (mä′jông′, -jong′, -zhông′, -zhong′), *n.* a game of Chinese origin usu. played by four persons with 144 dominolike tiles marked in suits.

Mah·ler (mä′lər), *n.* Gustav, 1860–1911, Austrian composer.

ma·hog·a·ny (mə hog′ə nē), *n., pl.* **-nies. 1.** any of several tropical American trees of the genus *Swietenia,* esp. *S. mahogoni* and *S. macrophylla,* yielding hard, reddish brown wood used for making furniture. **2.** the wood itself. **3.** any of various related or similar trees or their wood. **4.** a reddish brown color.

mah·zor (mäKH zôr′; *Eng.* mäKH′zər), *n., pl.* **mah·zo·rim** (mäKH zô-RēM′), *Eng.* **mah·zors.** *Hebrew.* a Jewish prayer book designed for use on festivals and holy days.

maid (mād), *n.* **1.** a female servant. **2.** a girl or young unmarried woman, esp. a virgin. **—maid′ish,** *adj.*

maid·en (mād′n), *n.* **1.** a girl or young unmarried woman; maid. **2.** a horse that has never won a race. **3.** an instrument resembling the guillotine, formerly used in Scotland. **—adj. 4.** of, pertaining to, or befitting a maiden. **5. a.** unmarried: *a maiden aunt.* **b.** virgin. **6.** first: *a maiden flight.* **7.** (of a horse) never having won a race. **—maid′en·ly,** *adj.*

maid·en·hair (mād′n hâr′), *n.* any of numerous ferns of the genus *Adiantum,* of the polypody family, having slender glossy stalks and finely divided fronds. Also called **maid′enhair fern′.**

maid′enhair tree′, *n.* GINKGO.

maid′en name′, *n.* a woman's surname before marriage.

maid′-in-wait′ing, *n., pl.* **maids-in-wait·ing.** an unmarried woman who serves as an attendant to a queen or princess.

maid′ of hon′or, *n.* **1.** an unmarried woman who is the chief attendant of a bride. Compare MATRON OF HONOR. **2.** an unmarried woman, usu. of noble birth, attendant on a queen or princess.

maid·serv·ant (mād′sûr′vənt), *n.* a female servant.

mail[1] (māl), *n.* **1.** letters, packages, etc., that are sent or delivered by means of the postal service. **2.** a single collection or delivery of such postal matter. **3.** Also, **mails.** the system, usu. operated by the government, for sending or delivering such postal matter. **4.** a conveyance used as a carrier of mail. **—adj. 5.** of or pertaining to mail. **—v.t. 6.** to send by mail.

mail[2] (māl), *n.* flexible armor of metal rings or plates.

mail′bag (māl′bag′), *n.* **1.** a mail carrier's bag. **2.** a sack for shipping mail.

mail′ bomb′, *n.* LETTER BOMB.

mail·box (māl′boks′), *n.* **1.** a public box in which mail is placed for pickup and delivery. **2.** a private box into which mail is delivered. **3.** a file in a computer for the storage of electronic mail.

mail′ car′rier, *n.* a person employed to deliver mail.

mail′ drop′, *n.* **1.** a receptacle or slot into which incoming mail is placed for pickup. **2.** DROP (def. 13).

mail·ing (mā′ling), *n.* a batch of mail sent at one time.

mail′ing list′, *n.* **1.** a list of addresses to which mail, esp. advertisements, can be sent. **2.** a list of E-mail addresses to which messages, usually on a specific topic, are sent; a discussion group whose messages are distributed through E-mail: *I'm on the early American history mailing list on the Internet.* Compare LIST SERVER.

mail·lot (mä yō′, ma-), *n.* **1.** a close-fitting, one-piece bathing suit for women. **2.** tights for dancers, acrobats, etc. **3.** a close-fitting knitted shirt, esp. a pullover.

mail·man (māl′man′), *n., pl.* **-men.** MAIL CARRIER.

mail′ or′der, *n.* an order for goods received or shipped through the mail. **—mail′-or′der,** *adj., v.t.*

mail′-or′der house′, *n.* a retail firm doing its business by mail.

maim (mām), *v.t.* **1.** to deprive of the use of some part of the body, esp. by wounding. **2.** to impair; disfigure. **—maim′er,** *n.*

Mai·mon·i·des (mī mon′i dēz′), *n.* (*Moses ben Maimon*) ("*RaMBaM*"), 1135–1204, Jewish philosopher and jurist.

main (mān), *adj.* **1.** chief in size, extent, or importance; principal; leading. **2.** syntactically independent. **3.** pertaining to or connected to a mainmast or mainsail. **4.** sheer; utmost: *by main strength.* **—n. 5.** a principal pipe or duct in a system used to distribute water, gas, etc. **6.** physical strength or force: *might and main.* **7.** the chief part or point: *in the main, a good plan.* **8.** the open ocean: *the bounding main.* **9.** MAINLAND. **—main′ly,** *adv.*

main′ clause′, *n.* a clause that can stand alone as a sentence, containing a subject and a predicate with a finite verb, as *I was there in the sentence I was there when he arrived;* independent clause. Compare SUBORDINATE CLAUSE.

main′ deck′, *n.* the uppermost weatherproof deck, running the full length of a ship.

main′ drag′, *n. Slang.* the main street of a town.

Maine (mān), *n.* **1.** a state in the NE United States, on the Atlantic coast. 1,243,316; 33,215 sq. mi. (86,027 sq. km). *Cap.:* Augusta. *Abbr.:* ME, Me. **2.** a historical region and former province in NW France. **3.** (*italics*) a U.S. battleship blown up in the harbor of Havana, Cuba, on February 15, 1898: this incident stimulated popular support in the U.S. for the Spanish-American War.

Maine′ coon′ cat′, *n.* one of an American breed of large semilonghaired domestic cats with a shaggy ruff and a long, bushy tail. Also called **Maine′ coon′.**

main·frame (mān′frām′), *n.* a large computer, often the hub of a system serving many users. Compare MICROCOMPUTER, MINICOMPUTER.

main·land (mān′land′, -lənd), *n.* the principal land of a country, region, etc., as distinguished from adjacent islands or a peninsula. **—main′land′er,** *n.*

main′ line′, *n.* a principal highway or railway line.

main·spring (mān′spring′), *n.* **1.** the principal spring in a mechanism, as in a watch. **2.** the chief motive power; the impelling cause.

main·stay (mān′stā′), *n.* **1.** a person or thing that acts as a chief support or part. **2.** the stay that secures the mainmast forward.

main·stream (mān′strēm′), *n.* **1.** the principal or dominant course, tendency, or trend. **2.** a river having tributaries. **—adj. 3.** belonging to or characteristic of a principal or widely accepted group, movement, style, etc. **4.** of, pertaining to, or characteristic of jazz falling historically between Dixieland and modern jazz, esp. swing music. **—v.t. 5.** to send into the mainstream. **6.** to place in regular school classes: *to mainstream handicapped children.*

main′ street′, *n.* **1.** the principal thoroughfare in a small town. **2.** (*caps.*) the outlook, environment, or life of a small town.

main·tain (mān tān′), *v.t.* **1.** to keep in existence or continuance; preserve. **2.** to keep in due condition, operation, or force. **3.** to keep in a specified state, position, etc. **4.** to affirm; assert; declare. **5.** to provide for the upkeep or support of. **—main·tain′a·ble,** *adj.* **—main·tain′er,** *n.* **—main′te·nance** (-tə nəns), *n.*

main′ verb′, *n.* a word used as the final verb in a verb phrase, expressing the lexical meaning of the verb phrase, as *drink* in *I don't drink, going* in *I am going,* or *spoken* in *We have spoken.*

Mairzy Doats, (mâr′zē dōts′), a popular nonsense song (1943), whose first line is "Mairzy doats and dozy doats and liddle lamzy divey" ("Mares eat oats and does eat oats and little lambs eat ivy").

mai·tre (or **mai·tre**) **d′** (mā′tər dē′, mā′trə, met′rə), *n., pl.* **maitre** (or **maitre**) **d′s.** MAÎTRE D'HÔTEL.

mai·tre d'hô·tel (mā′trə dō tel′; *Fr.* me tR³ dō tel′), *n., pl.* **mai·tres d'hôtel** (mā′traz; *Fr.* me tR³). **1.** a headwaiter. **2.** a steward or butler. **3.** the owner or manager of a hotel.

maize (māz), *n.* **1.** CORN[1] (def. 1). **2.** a pale yellow resembling the color of corn.

maj·es·ty (maj′ə stē), *n., pl.* **-ties. 1.** regal, lofty, or stately dignity; imposing character; grandeur. **2.** supreme greatness or authority; sovereignty. **3.** (*usu. cap.*) a title of a sovereign (usu. prec. by *his, her,* or *your*). **—ma·jes′tic,** *adj.* **—ma·jes′ti·cal·ly,** *adv.*

Maj. Gen., Major General.

ma·jor (mā′jər), *n.* **1.** a commissioned military officer ranking below a lieutenant colonel and above a captain. **2.** one of superior rank, ability, or power in a specified class. **3. a.** field of study in which a student specializes. **b.** a student specializing in such a field: *a history major.* **4.** a person of full legal age. **5.** a major musical interval, chord, or scale. **6. the majors,** the major leagues. **—adj. 7.** greater in size, extent, or amount: *a major part.* **8.** greater in rank or importance: *a major talent.* **9.** of great risk; serious: *a major operation.* **10.** of or pertaining to a majority. **11.** of full legal age. **12.** *Music.* **a.** (of an interval) being between the tonic and the second, third, sixth, or seventh degrees of a major scale: *a major third.* **b.** (of a chord) having a major third between the

Ⓜ

root and the note next above it. **c.** based on a major scale: *a major key.* **13.** pertaining to the subject in which a student specializes. *—v.i.* **14.** to follow an academic major: *majoring in physics.*

Ma•jor (mā′jər), *n.* **John,** born 1943, British prime minister 1990–97.

ma′jor ax′is, *n.* the axis of an ellipse that passes through the two foci.

Ma•jor•ca (mə jôr′kə, -yôr′-), *n.* a Spanish island in the W Mediterranean: the largest of the Balearic Islands. 534,511; 1405 sq. mi. (3640 sq. km). *Cap.:* Palma. Spanish, **Mallorca.** —**Ma•jor′can,** *adj., n.*

ma•jor-do•mo (mā′jər dō′mō), *n., pl.* **-mos. 1.** a man in charge of a great household, as that of a sovereign. **2.** a steward; butler. **3.** a person who makes arrangements for another.

ma•jor•ette (mā′jə ret′), *n.* **1.** a girl or woman who twirls a baton with a marching band. **2.** a girl or woman who leads a marching band. Also called **drum majorette.**

ma′jor gen′eral, *n.* a military officer ranking below a lieutenant general and above a brigadier general.

ma•jor•i•ty (mə jôr′i tē, -jor′-), *n., pl.* **-ties. 1.** the greater part or number; a number larger than half the total. **2.** the amount by which the greater number surpasses the remainder (disting. from *plurality*). **3.** the party or faction with the majority vote. **4.** the state of being of full legal age: *to attain one's majority.* **5.** the military rank or office of a major.

major′ity lead′er, *n.* the floor leader of the majority party in a legislature.

ma′jor league′, *n.* **1.** either of the two main professional baseball leagues in the U.S. **2.** a league of like stature in other sports. **3.** BIG LEAGUE (def. 2). —**ma′jor-league′,** *adj.* —**ma′jor-lea′guer,** *n.*

Ma′jor Proph′et, *n.* any of a group of Old Testament prophets, including Isaiah, Jeremiah, and Ezekiel. Compare MINOR PROPHET.

ma′jor scale′, *n.* a musical scale consisting of a series of whole steps except for half steps between the third and fourth and seventh and eighth degrees.

ma′jor suit′, *n.* hearts or spades, esp. with reference to their higher point values in bridge. Compare MINOR SUIT.

ma•jus•cule (mə jus′kyo͞ol, maj′ə skyo͞ol′), *adj.* **1.** written in capital letters or uncials (opposed to *minuscule*). —*n.* **2.** a capital letter or uncial.

Ma•kah (mə kô′), *n., pl.* **-kahs,** (*esp. collectively*) **-kah. 1.** a member of an American Indian people of the Olympic Peninsula in northwest Washington. **2.** the Wakashan language of the Makah.

make (māk), *v.,* **made, mak•ing,** *n.* *—v.t.* **1.** to bring into existence by shaping, changing, or combining material: *to make a dress.* **2.** to cause to exist or happen: *to make trouble.* **3.** to cause to become: *to make someone happy.* **4.** to appoint; name: *made her chairwoman.* **5.** to put in the proper condition or state, as for use; prepare: *to make a bed; made dinner.* **6.** to transform: *making a vice into a virtue.* **7.** to induce; compel: *to make them do it.* **8.** to produce, earn, or win for oneself: *to make a good salary.* **9.** to write; compose: *to make a poem.* **10.** to draw up; draft: *to make a will.* **11.** to agree upon; arrange: *to make a deal.* **12.** to establish; enact: *to make laws.* **13.** to become; develop into: *You'll make a good lawyer.* **14.** to form in the mind: *to make a decision.* **15.** to judge as to the truth, nature, or meaning of: *What do you make of that remark?* **16.** to estimate; reckon: *I make the value at $1000.* **17.** to put together; form: *to make a matched set.* **18.** to amount to; total: *Two plus two makes four.* **19.** to provide: *That book makes good reading.* **20.** to be sufficient to constitute: *One story does not make a writer.* **21.** to be adequate or suitable for: *This table will make a good lectern.* **22.** to assure the success or fame of: *to make someone's reputation.* **23.** to deliver; utter: *to make a stirring speech.* **24.** to move at a particular speed: *to make 60 miles an hour.* **25.** to reach; attain: *didn't quite make 79 before dying.* **26.** to arrive in time for; catch: *just made the last plane.* **27.** to attain a position in or on: *The novel made the bestseller list.* **28.** to receive notice in or on: *It made the evening news.* **29. a.** to take a trick with (a card). **b.** to fulfill (a contract or bid) in bridge. **30.** to score: *She made 40 points.* **31.** to close (an electric circuit). *—v.i.* **32.** to act so as to be what is specified: *to make sure.* **33.** to be made, as specified: *This fabric makes into beautiful drapery.* **34.** to move or proceed in a particular direction: *to make after the thief.* **35. make away with, a.** to carry off; steal. **b.** to destroy; kill. **36. make for, a.** to move toward. **b.** to promote, result in, or sustain: *Calm makes for fewer arguments.* **37. make off,** to run away. **38. make off with,** to carry away; steal. **39. make out, a.** to write out or complete, as a bill or check. **b.** to perceive the meaning of; fathom. **c.** to decipher; discern. **d.** to suggest or impute: *He made me out to be a liar.* **e.** to manage; succeed: *How are you making out in school?* **40. make over, a.** to remodel; alter. **b.** to transfer the title of (property). **41. make up, a.** to constitute; compose. **b.** to put together; compile. **c.** to concoct; invent. **d.** to compensate: *This will make up for your trouble.* **e.** to complete. **f.** to put in order; arrange: *made up the bed.* **g.** to settle; decide: *Make up your mind.* **h.** to settle amicably. **i.** to become reconciled. **j.** to dress in costume and makeup. **k.** to apply cosmetics. **l.** to make good on (something deficient). **m.** to arrange typeset and graphic matter for: *making up newspaper pages.* **42. make up to,** to behave ingratiatingly toward. **43. make with,** *Informal.* to employ; use: *Stop making with the jokes.* *—n.* **44.** the style or manner in which something is made; form. **45.** brand: *a foreign make of car.* **46.** disposition; character. **47.** the act or process of making. **48.** quantity made; output. **49.** *Slang.* identification; description: *to get a make on the crook.* —***Idiom.*** **50. make as if** or **as though,** *Informal.* to act as if; pretend. **51. make believe,** to pretend; imagine. **52. make do,** to manage with whatever is available. **53. make good, a.** to succeed. **b.** to provide payment or redress for. **c.** to accomplish successfully. **d.** Also, **make good on.** to fulfill, as a promise. **54. make it,** to achieve success. **55. make light of,** to treat as insignificant. **56. make like,** *Informal.* to pretend to be or to be like: *to make like a clown.* **57. make much of, a.** to treat as significant. **b.** to be attentive to. **58. make or break,** to succeed or fail. **59. make short work of,** to finish or dispose of quickly. **60. on the make,** in pursuit of social, professional, or financial gain. —**mak′a•ble,** *adj.*

make′-believe′, *n.* **1.** pretense, esp. of an innocent or playful kind; feigning. —*adj.* **2.** pretended; feigned; imaginary.

make′-do′, *adj., n., pl.* **-dos.** —*adj.* **1.** used as a substitute; makeshift. —*n.* **2.** something makeshift.

make•fast (māk′fast′, -fäst′), *n.* a structure to which a ship is tied up, as a bollard or buoy.

Ma•kem•ie (mə kem′ē, -kā′mē), *n.* **Francis,** 1658–1708, the Irish founder of the Presbyterian Church in America.

make′-or-break′, *adj.* either successful or ruinous.

make•o•ver (māk′ō′vər), *n.* **1.** renovation; restoration. **2.** cosmetic treatment and hair styling, usu. to change one's customary look.

mak•er (mā′kər), *n.* **1.** a person or thing that makes. **2.** a manufacturer. **3.** (*cap.*) God. **4.** the party executing a legal instrument, esp. a promissory note. **5.** the card player who first names the successful bid. —***Idiom.*** **6. go to** or **meet one's Maker,** to die.

Ma•ker (mā′kər), *n.* **Frederick C(harles),** 1844–1927, English musician and hymn writer.

make′-read′y, *n.* the process of preparing a form for printing by overlays or underlays to equalize the impression.

make•shift (māk′shift′), *n.* **1.** a temporary expedient or substitute. —*adj.* **2.** being or serving as a makeshift.

make′up′ or **make′-up′,** *n.* **1.** cosmetics for the face or some part of it: *eye makeup.* **2.** a lotion, cream, or the like applied to the skin, esp. of the face, as to enhance or disguise its color. **3.** the application of cosmetics. **4.** the total ensemble of cosmetics, costumes, etc., used by a theatrical performer. **5.** the manner of being put together; composition. **6.** physical or mental constitution: *the makeup of a criminal.* **7. a.** the act or process of arranging the type, illustrations, etc., on each page of a publication. **b.** the appearance of a page, as a result of such arrangement. **8.** an examination, assignment, or the like given to offset a student's previous absence or failure.

make′-work′, *n.* work created to keep a person from being idle or unemployed.

mak•ing (mā′king), *n.* **1.** the act of a person or thing that makes. **2.** structure; constitution; makeup. **3.** the means or cause of success or advancement. **4.** Usu., **makings.** capacity; potential: *He has the makings of a first-rate officer.* **5. makings,** material of which something may be made. **6.** something made. **7.** a quantity made; batch.

ma•ko (mā′kō, mä′-), *n., pl.* **-kos.** a powerful mackerel shark, *Isurus oxyrinchus.*

mal-, a combining form meaning "bad," "wrongful," "ill," occurring orig. in loanwords from French (*maladroit*); on this model, used in the formation of other words (*malcontent; malfunction*). Compare MALE-.

Mal., Malachi.

Ma•la•bo (mə lä′bō), *n.* the capital of Equatorial Guinea, on N Bioko island. 40,000. Formerly, **Santa Isabel.**

Mal•a•chi (mal′ə kī′), *n.* **1.** a Minor Prophet of the 5th century B.C. **2.** the book of the Bible bearing his name.

mal•a•chite (mal′ə kīt′), *n.* a green mineral, basic copper carbonate, $Cu_2CO_3(OH)_2$, an ore of copper, used for making ornamental articles.

mal•ad•just•ed (mal′ə jus′tid), *adj.* badly adjusted, esp. to one's social circumstances, environment, etc. —**mal′ad•just′ment,** *n.*

mal•a•droit (mal′ə droit′), *adj.* lacking in adroitness; awkward. —**mal′a•droit′ly,** *adv.* —**mal′a•droit′ness,** *n.*

mal•a•dy (mal′ə dē), *n., pl.* **-dies. 1.** a disorder or disease of the body. **2.** any unhealthy condition or disorder.

Malagas′y Repub′lic, *n.* former name of MADAGASCAR.

ma•laise (ma lāz′, -lez′, mə-), *n.* **1.** a condition of general bodily weakness or discomfort, often marking the onset of a disease. **2.** a vague feeling of unease. **3.** an unhealthy or disordered condition.

mal•a•mute or **mal•e•mute** (mal′ə myo͞ot′), *n.* ALASKAN MALAMUTE.

Mal•a•prop (mal′ə prop′), *n.* **Mrs.,** a character in Richard Sheridan's *The Rivals* (1775), noted for her misapplication of words.

mal•a•prop•ism (mal′ə prop iz′əm), *n.* **1.** a confused use of words in which an appropriate word is replaced by one with similar sound but ludicrously inappropriate meaning. **2.** an instance of this, as in "Lead the way and we'll precede."

mal•ap•ro•pos (mal′ap rə pō′), *adj.* **1.** inappropriate; inopportune: *a malapropos remark.* —*adv.* **2.** inappropriately; inopportunely.

ma•lar•i•a (mə lâr′ē ə), *n.* any of a group of usu. intermittent or remittent diseases characterized by attacks of chills, fever, and sweating and caused by a parasitic protozoan transferred to the human bloodstream by an anopheles mosquito. [< Italian, contr. of *mala aria* bad air] —**ma•lar′i•al, ma•lar′i•an, ma•lar′i•ous,** *adj.*

ma•lar•key (mə lär′kē), *n.* *Informal.* speech or writing designed to obscure, mislead, or impress; bunkum.

Ma•la•wi (mə lä′wē), *n., pl.* **-wis,** (*esp. collectively*) **-wi. 1.** Formerly,

Nyasaland. a republic in SE Africa, on Lake Malawi: formerly a British protectorate; became an independent member of the Commonwealth of Nations in 1964; a republic since 1966. 9,609,081; 45,747 sq. mi. (118,484 sq. km). *Cap.:* Lilongwe. **2. Lake.** Formerly, **Nyasa,** a lake in SE Africa, between Malawi, Tanzania, and Mozambique. 11,000 sq. mi. (28,500 sq. km). **—Ma·la'wi·an,** *adj., n.*

Ma·lay (mā'lā, mə lā'), *n.* **1.** a member of a people of Southeast Asia comprising the principal inhabitants of the Malay Peninsula, adjacent parts of E Sumatra, and the intervening islands and living in many coastal settlements on Borneo, Sumatra, and other islands of the Indonesian archipelago. **2.** the Austronesian language of the Malays.

Ma·lay·a (mə lā'ə), *n.* **1.** MALAY PENINSULA. **2. Federation of,** a former federation of states in the S Malay Peninsula: a former British protectorate; now part of Malaysia. 50,690 sq. mi. (131,287 sq. km). **—Ma·lay'an,** *adj., n.*

Ma'lay Archipel'ago, *n.* an extensive island group in the Indian and Pacific oceans, SE of Asia, including the Sunda Islands, the Moluccas, and the Philippines. Also called **Malaysia.**

Ma'lay Penin'sula, *n.* a peninsula in SE Asia, consisting of W (mainland) Malaysia and the S part of Thailand. Also called **Malaya.**

Ma·lay·sia (mə lā'zhə, -shə), *n.* **1.** a constitutional monarchy in SE Asia: a federation, comprising Malaya, Sabah, and Sarawak. 20,376,235; 127,317 sq. mi. (329,759 sq. km). *Cap.:* Kuala Lumpur. **2.** MALAY ARCHIPELAGO. **—Ma·lay'sian,** *adj., n.*

Mal·chus (mal'kəs), *n.* a high priest's servant whose ear was cut off by Peter in the Garden of Gethsemane. John 18:10.

Mal·colm X (mal'kəm eks'), *n.* (*Malcolm Little*), 1925–65, U.S. civilrights activist and religious leader.

mal·con·tent (mal'kən tent'), *adj.* **1.** not satisfied with current conditions. **2.** dissatisfied with the existing government. **—n. 3.** a malcontent person.

Mal·dives (môl'dēvz, mal'dīvz), *n.* **Republic of,** a republic in the Indian Ocean, SW of Sri Lanka, consisting of about 1200 islands: British protectorate 1887–1965. 280,391; 115 sq. mi. (298 sq. km). *Cap.:* Male. **—Mal·div'i·an** (-div'ē ən), *adj., n.*

male (māl), *n.* **1.** a person bearing an X and Y chromosome pair in the cell nuclei and normally having a penis, scrotum, and testicles and developing hair on the face at adolescence; a boy or man. **2.** an organism of the sex or sexual phase that normally produces a sperm cell or male gamete. **3.** a plant having a stamen or stamens. **—adj. 4.** of, pertaining to, or being a male: *the male skeleton; a male squirrel.* **5.** of, pertaining to, or characteristic of a boy or man; masculine: *the male ego.* **6.** composed of males: *a male choir.* **7. a.** of or pertaining to a plant or its reproductive structure producing or containing microspores. **b.** (of seed plants) staminate. **8.** made to fit into a corresponding open or recessed part: *a male plug.* Compare FEMALE (def. 8). **—male'ness,** *n.*

Ma·lé (mä'lā, -lē), *n.* the capital of the Maldives. 46,334.

male-, a combining form meaning "evil," occurring in loanwords from Latin: *malediction.* Compare MAL-.

male' chau'vinist, *n.* a male who patronizes, disparages, or discriminates against females in the belief that they are inferior to males. **—male' chau'vinism,** *n.*

mal·e·dic·tion (mal'i dik'shən), *n.* a curse; imprecation. **—mal'e·dic'tive, mal'e·dic'to·ry** (-tə rē) *adj.*

mal·e·fac·tor (mal'ə fak'tər), *n.* **1.** a person who violates the law; criminal. **2.** a person who does evil. **—mal'e·fac'tion,** *n.*

ma·lef·ic (mə lef'ik), *adj.* producing evil; harmful: *a malefic spell.*

ma·lef·i·cent (mə lef'ə sənt), *adj.* evil or harmful; malicious. **—ma·lef'i·cence,** *n.*

mal·e·mute (mal'ə myōōt'), *n.* ALASKAN MALAMUTE.

ma·lev·o·lent (mə lev'ə lənt), *adj.* **1.** wishing evil or harm to others; malicious. **2.** producing harm or evil; injurious. **—ma·lev'o·lence,** *n.* **—ma·lev'o·lent·ly,** *adv.*

mal·fea·sance (mal fē'zəns), *n.* misconduct or wrongdoing, esp. by a public official. Compare MISFEASANCE. **—mal·fea'sant,** *adj., n.*

mal·for·ma·tion (mal'fôr mā'shən, -fər-), *n.* faulty or anomalous formation or structure: *malformation of the teeth.*

mal·formed (mal fôrmd'), *adj.* faultily or anomalously formed.

mal·func·tion (mal fungk'shən), *n.* **1.** failure to function properly. **—v.i. 2.** to fail to function properly.

Ma·li (mä'lē), *n.* **Republic of,** a republic in W Africa: formerly a territory of France; gained independence 1960. 9,945,383; 478,821 sq. mi. (1,240,140 sq. km). *Cap.:* Bamako. Formerly, **French Sudan. —Ma'li·an,** *adj., n.*

mal·ice (mal'is), *n.* **1.** a desire to inflict harm or suffering on another. **2.** harmful intent on the part of a person who commits an unlawful act injurious to another. **—ma·li·cious** (mə lish'əs), *adj.* **—ma·li'cious·ly,** *adv.* **—ma·li'cious·ness,** *n.*

mal'ice afore'thought, *n.* a predetermination to commit an unlawful act without just cause or provocation (applied chiefly to cases of first-degree murder).

ma·lign (mə līn'), *v.t.* to speak harmful untruths about; slander; defame. **—ma·lign'er,** *n.* **—ma·lign'ly,** *adv.*

ma·lig·nant (mə lig'nənt), *adj.* **1.** inclined to cause harm, suffering, or distress. **2.** very dangerous or harmful in influence or effect. **3. a.** tending to produce death, as bubonic plague. **b.** (of a tumor) characterized

by uncontrolled growth; cancerous, invasive, or metastatic. **—ma·lig'nan·cy,** *n., pl.* **-cies. —ma·lig'nant·ly,** *adv.*

ma·lin·ger (mə ling'gər), *v.i.* to pretend illness, esp. in order to shirk duty or work. **—ma·lin'ger·er,** *n.*

Ma·lin·ke (mə ling'kā, -kē), *n., pl.* **-kes,** (*esp. collectively*) **-ke. 1.** a member of an African people of Senegambia, Guinea, Guinea-Bissau, the Ivory Coast, and Mali. **2.** a group of dialects, varying in mutual intelligibility, of the Mande language shared by the Malinke, Bambara, and other peoples.

mall (môl), *n.* **1.** a large retail complex containing stores and restaurants in adjacent buildings or in a single large building. **2.** an urban street lined with shops and closed off to motor vehicles. **3.** a large area with shade trees used as a public walk or promenade.

mal·lard (mal'ərd), *n., pl.* **-lards,** (*esp. collectively*) **-lard.** a common, almost cosmopolitan, wild duck, *Anas platyrhynchos,* from which the domestic ducks are descended.

mal·le·a·ble (mal'ē ə bəl), *adj.* **1.** capable of being extended or shaped by hammering or pressure from rollers. **2.** adaptable; tractable: *a malleable personality.* **—mal'le·a·bly,** *adv.* **—mal'le·a·bil'i·ty,** *n.*

mal·let (mal'it), *n.* **1.** a hammerlike tool with an enlarged head, typically of wood, used for driving another tool, as a chisel, or for striking a surface without causing damage. **2.** a light hammer used in playing a vibraphone, xylophone, etc. **3.** the wooden implement used to strike a ball in croquet or polo.

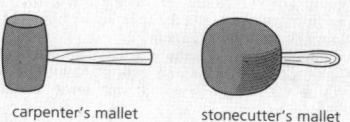

carpenter's mallet   stonecutter's mallet

mallets (def. 1)

mall·ing (mô'ling), *n.* **1.** the overbuilding of shopping malls in a region: *the malling of America.* **2.** the practice of frequenting malls to socialize or shop.

mal·low (mal'ō), *n.* any of various plants of the genus *Malva,* of the mallow family, as the musk mallow.

mall' rat', *n. Slang.* a person, esp. a teenager, who frequents shopping malls to socialize, window-shop, etc.

mal·nour·ished (mal nûr'isht, -nur'-), *adj.* poorly or improperly nourished; suffering from malnutrition.

mal·nu·tri·tion (mal'nōō trish'ən, -nyōō-), *n.* lack of proper nutrition; inadequate or unbalanced nutrition.

mal·oc·clu·sion (mal'ə klōō'zhən), *n.* irregular contact of opposing teeth in the upper and lower jaws. **—mal'oc·clud'ed,** *adj.*

mal·o·dor·ous (mal ō'dər əs), *adj.* **1.** having a foul odor. **2.** disreputable; scandalous. **—mal·o'dor·ous·ly,** *adv.* **—mal·o'dor·ous·ness,** *n.*

mal·prac·tice (mal prak'tis), *n.* **1.** dereliction of professional duty, as by a physician or lawyer, through reprehensible ignorance or negligence or through criminal intent, esp. when injury or loss follows. **2.** any improper, negligent practice. **—mal'prac·ti'tion·er** (-tish'ə nər), *n.*

malt (môlt), *n.* **1.** germinated grain used in brewing and distilling. **2.** an alcoholic beverage, as beer, fermented from malt. **3.** MALTED MILK (def. 2). **—v.t. 4.** to convert (grain) into malt by soaking in water and allowing to germinate. **5.** to mix with malt or extract of malt. **—v.i. 6.** to become malt. **7.** to produce malt from grain. **—malt'i·ness,** *n.* **—malt'y,** *adj.,* **malt·i·er, malt·i·est.**

Mal·ta (môl'tə), *n.* **1.** an island in the Mediterranean south of Sicily. 95 sq. mi. (246 sq. km). **2.** a republic consisting of this island and two adjacent islands: a former British colony; now a member of the Commonwealth of Nations. 379,365; 122 sq. mi. (316 sq. km). *Cap.:* Valletta. **—Maltese,** *adj., n.*

malt·ase (môl'tās, -tāz), *n.* an enzyme that converts maltose to glucose.

malt·ed (môl'tid), *n.* MALTED MILK.

malt'ed milk', *n.* **1.** a soluble powder made of dehydrated milk and malted cereals. **2.** a beverage made by dissolving malted milk in milk and usu. adding ice cream and flavoring.

malt' liq'uor, *n.* beer having a relatively high alcohol content.

malt·ose (môl'tōs), *n.* a white, crystalline, water-soluble sugar, $C_{12}H_{22}O_{11}·H_2O$, formed by the action of diastase, esp. from malt, on starch: used chiefly as a nutrient or sweetener, and in culture media. Also called **malt' sug'ar.**

mal·treat (mal trēt'), *v.t.* to treat or handle badly or roughly; abuse. **—mal·treat'er,** *n.* **—mal·treat'ment,** *n.*

ma·ma or **mam·ma** (mä'mə, mə mä'), *n., pl.* **-mas.** MOTHER[1] (defs 1,2). [nursery word, with parallels in other European languages]

ma'ma's boy', *n.* a boy or man excessively dependent on his mother.

mam·ba (mäm'bä), *n., pl.* **-bas.** any of several long slender tree snakes of the genus *Dendroaspis,* of central and S Africa, the bite of which is often fatal.

mam·bo (mäm'bō), *n., pl.* **-bos,** *v.,* **-boed, -bo·ing. —n. 1.** a ballroom dance of Caribbean origin similar to the rumba and cha-cha. **—v.i. 2.** to dance the mambo.

Ⓜ

Mam·e·luke (mam′ə lōōk′) also **Mamluk,** *n.* **1.** a member of an Egyptian military class, originally slaves, in power from about 1250 to 1517 and influential until 1811. **2.** (*l.c.*) (in Muslim countries) a slave.

mam·ma[1] (mä′mə, mə mä′), *n.* MAMA.

mam·ma[2] (mam′ə), *n., pl.* **mam·mae** (mam′ē). a structure of mammals comprising one or more mammary glands with an associated nipple or teat, activated for the secretion of milk in the female after the birth of young.

mam·mal (mam′əl), *n.* any warm-blooded vertebrate of the class Mammalia, characterized by a covering of hair on some or most of the body, a four-chambered heart, and nourishment of the newborn with milk from maternal mammary glands. —**mam·ma·li·an** (mə mā′lē ən), *adj., n.*

mam·mal·o·gy (mə mal′ə jē), *n.* the branch of zoology that deals with mammals. —**mam·mal·o·gist,** *n.*

mam·ma·ry (mam′ə rē), *adj.* of or pertaining to mammae or mammary glands.

mam′mary gland′, *n.* any of the accessory reproductive organs of female mammals that occur in pairs on the chest or ventral surface and contain milk-producing lobes with ducts that empty into a nipple.

mam·mo·gram (mam′ə gram′), *n.* an x-ray photograph obtained by mammography.

mam·mog·ra·phy (ma mog′rə fē), *n.* x-ray photography of a breast, esp. for detection of tumors.

mam·mon (mam′ən), *n.* riches or material wealth, esp. as an influence for evil or immorality. Matt. 6:24; Luke 16:9, 11, 13. [< Late Latin < Greek < Aramaic *māmōnā* riches]

mam·moth (mam′əth), *n.* **1.** any extinct true elephant of the family Elephantidae, esp. of the Pleistocene genus *Mammuthus.* Compare MASTODON. **2.** anything very large. —*adj.* **3.** very large; enormous.

wooly mammoth, *Mammuthus primigenius*,
9 ft. (2.7 m) high at shoulder;
tusks to 16 ft. (4.9 m)

Mam′moth Cave′ Na′tional Park′, *n.* a national park in central Kentucky: limestone caverns. 79 sq. mi. (205 sq. km).

mam·zer (mom′zər), *n. Slang.* **1.** a bastard. **2.** a rascal.

man (man), *n., pl.* **men,** *interj., v.,* **manned, man·ning.** —*n.* **1.** an adult male person, as distinguished from a boy or a woman. **2.** a member of the species *Homo sapiens* or all the members of this species collectively, without regard to sex. **3.** the human individual as representing the species, without reference to sex; the human race; humankind: *Man hopes for peace.* **4.** a human being; person: *every man for himself.* **5.** a husband. **6.** a male lover or sweetheart. **7.** a male having qualities considered appropriately masculine: *made a man of him.* **8.** a male servant or attendant. **9.** a feudal tenant; vassal. **10.** *Slang.* male friend; ally: *my main man.* **11.** *Slang.* a term of familiar address: *Man, take it easy.* **12.** a playing piece used in certain games, as chess or checkers. **13. the man** also **the Man,** *Slang.* **a.** an authoritative or controlling person or group. **b.** (among blacks) white persons collectively; white society. —*interj.* **14.** (used to express astonishment or delight): *Man, what a car!* —*v.t.* **15.** to supply with people, as for service: *to man the ship.* **16.** to take one's place at, as to defend or operate: *to man the ramparts; to man the phones.* **17.** to strengthen; fortify: *to man yourself for danger.* —*Idiom.* **18. a man after one's own heart,** a person with whom one enthusiastically agrees. I Sam. 13:14. **19. man and boy,** ever since childhood: *He's been working, man and boy, for 50 years.* **20. one's own man,** free from restrictions or influences; independent. **21. to a man,** including everyone. —**man′ful,** *adj.* —**man′ful·ly,** *adv.* —**man′ful·ness,** *n.* —**man′less·ly,** *adv.* —*Usage.* The use of generic MAN ("human being"), alone and in compounds such as *mankind,* is declining. Critics of generic MAN maintain that its use is sometimes ambiguous and often slighting of women. Although some editors and writers dismiss these objections, many now choose instead such terms as *human being(s), human race, humankind, people,* or, when necessary, *men and women* or *women and men.* See also -MAN, -PERSON, -WOMAN.

Man (man), *n.* **Isle of,** an island of the British Isles, in the Irish Sea. 64,282; 227 sq. mi. (588 sq. km). *Cap.:* Douglas.

-man, a combining form of MAN: *layman; postman.* —*Usage.* The use of -MAN as the last element in compounds referring to a person of either sex who performs some function (*anchorman; chairman; spokesman*) has declined in recent years. In some instances the sex-neutral *-person* is substituted for -MAN (*anchorperson; chairperson; spokesperson*), and sometimes a form with no suffix at all is used (*anchor; chair*). Terms ending in -MAN that designate specific occupations (*foreman; mailman; policeman,* etc.) have been dropped by the U.S. government in favor of neutral terms, and many industries and business firms have done likewise. The compounds *freshman, lowerclassman, underclassman,* and *upperclassman* are still generally used in schools, *freshman* in Congress also, and they are applied to both sexes. As a modifier, *freshman* is used with both singular and plural nouns: *a freshman athlete; freshman legislators.* See also MAN, -PERSON, -WOMAN.

man·a·cle (man′ə kəl), *n., v.,* **-cled, -cling.** —*n.* **1.** a shackle for the hand; handcuff. **2.** Usu. **manacles.** restraints; checks. —*v.t.* **3.** to handcuff; fetter. **4.** to hamper; restrain.

man·age (man′ij), *v.,* **-aged, -ag·ing.** —*v.t.* **1.** to bring about or succeed in accomplishing; contrive: *They managed to see the governor.* **2. a.** to take charge of; supervise: *to manage a business; managing investments.* **b.** to handle the career or functioning of: *to manage a performer.* **3.** to dominate or influence by tact, flattery, or artifice: *to manage a difficult child.* **4.** to control in action or use: *managing a boat in a storm.* —*v.i.* **5.** to be in charge or control of an enterprise, business, etc. **6.** to function; get along: *to manage without a car.* —**man′age·a·ble,** *adj.* —**man′age·a·bil′i·ty, man′age·a·ble·ness,** *n.* —**man′age·a·bly,** *adv.*

man′aged cur′rency, *n.* a currency whose value is established and maintained by deliberate governmental action working through national and international financial institutions, in contrast to the quasi-automatic gold standard.

man′aged news′, *n.* news that is manipulated to serve the interests of a government.

man·age·ment (man′ij mənt), *n.* **1.** the act or process of managing. **2.** skill in managing; executive ability. **3.** the persons controlling and directing an enterprise; executives. **4.** such persons considered as a class (disting. from *labor*).

man′agement informa′tion sys′tem, *n.* a computerized information-processing force offering management support to a company. *Abbr.:* MIS

man·ag·er (man′i jər), *n.* **1.** a person who manages an enterprise or one of its parts. **2. a.** a person who directs the activities of an athlete or team. **b.** a student in a high school or college who assists an athletic coach by keeping a team's records, caring for equipment, and the like. **3.** a person who manages another's career. —**man′a·ge′ri·al** (-jēr′ē-əl), *adj.* —**man′a·ge′ri·al·ly,** *adv.*

man′aging ed′itor, *n.* an editor who supervises the editorial processes of a publication or publishing house.

Ma·na·gua (mə nä′gwä), *n.* **1. Lake,** a lake in W Nicaragua. 390 sq. mi. (1010 sq. km). **2.** the capital of Nicaragua, in the W part. 682,111.

Ma·na·ma (mə nam′ə), *n.* the capital of Bahrain. 151,500.

ma·ña·na (mä nyä′nä; *Eng.* mə nyä′nə), *Spanish.* —*n.* **1.** tomorrow; the (indefinite) future. —*adv.* **2.** tomorrow; in the (indefinite) future.

Ma·nas·sas (mə nas′əs), *n.* a town in NE Virginia, near which the first and second Battles of Bull Run (known in the South as the **Battle of Manassas**) were fought in 1861 and 1862.

Ma·nas·seh (mə nas′ə), *n.* **1.** the first son of Joseph. Gen. 41:51. **2.** one of the 12 tribes of Israel, traditionally descended from him. Gen. 48:14–19. **3.** a king of Judah of the 7th century B.C. II Kings 21.

man·a·tee (man′ə tē′, man′ə tē′), *n., pl.* **-tees.** any plant-eating aquatic mammal of the genus *Trichechus,* of Caribbean and W Africa waters, having front flippers and a broad spoon-shaped tail.

Man·ches·ter (man′ches′tər, -chə stər), *n.* **1.** a city in NW England. 451,000. **2.** a city in S New Hampshire. 98,320.

Man′chester ter′rier, *n.* one of a breed of slender terriers with a long, narrow head and a short, glossy black-and-tan coat, raised orig. in Manchester, England.

man′-child′, *n., pl.* **men-chil·dren.** a male child; boy; son.

Man·chu (man chōō′), *n., pl.* **-chus,** (*esp. collectively*) **-chu. 1.** a member of a Tungusic people of Manchuria who conquered China in the 17th century and established a dynasty (**Manchu′ dy′nasty** or **Ch′ing** 1644–1912). **2.** the Tungusic language of the Manchus.

Man·chu·ri·a (man chōōr′ē ə), *n.* a historic region in NE China. ab. 413,000 sq. mi. (1,070,000 sq. km). —**Man·chu′ri·an,** *adj., n.*

-mancy, a combining form meaning "divination," of the kind specified by the initial element: *necromancy.*

Man·dae·an or **Man·de·an** (man dē′ən), *n.* **1.** a member of a Gnostic sect with modern adherents in SE Iraq and Khuzistan in Iran. **2.** Also, **Man·da′ic** (-dā′ik). a form of Aramaic used in sacred texts of the Mandaeans. —*adj.* **3.** of or pertaining to the Mandaeans.

man·da·la (mun′dl ə), *n., pl.* **-las.** a schematized representation of the cosmos in Hindu and Buddhist iconography, usu. a concentric configuration of geometric shapes each of which contains an image or attribute of a deity.

man·da·rin (man′də rin), *n.* **1.** (in the Chinese Empire) a member of any of the nine ranks of public officials. **2.** (*cap.*) **a.** a more or less uniform spoken form of the Chinese language based loosely on the dialect of Beijing and used by officials in late imperial China. **b.** the group of closely related Chinese dialects, including Mandarin and the modern standard language, spoken in SW, central, and N China and in Manchuria. **3. a.** a small spiny citrus tree, *Citrus reticulata,* native to China, bearing flattish orange-yellow to deep orange loose-skinned fruit. **b.** this fruit, some hybrid varieties of which are called tangerines. **4.** an influential or powerful government official or bureaucrat. **5.** a member of an elite or powerful group or class. —*adj.* **6.** of or pertaining to a mandarin or mandarins. **7.** elegantly refined, as in language or taste.

man′darin col′lar, *n.* a narrow stand-up collar not quite meeting at the front.

man′darin duck′, *n.* a crested Asian duck, *Aix galericulata,* having variegated purple, green, chestnut, and white plumage.

man·darin or′ange, *n.* MANDARIN (def. 3).

man·date (man′dāt) *n., v.,* **-dat·ed, -dat·ing.** —*n.* **1.** a command or authorization to act in a particular way given by the electorate to its representative. **2.** any authoritative order or command: *a royal mandate.* **3.** (in the League of Nations) a commission given to a nation to administer the government and affairs of a former Turkish territory or German colony. **4.** such a territory or colony. **5.** a command from a superior court or official to a lower one. —*v.t.* **6.** to authorize or decree (a particular action). **7.** to make mandatory. **8.** to consign (a territory) under a mandate. —**man′da·to′ri·ly,** *adv.* —**man′da·to′ry,** *adj.*

Man·de (män′dā), *n., pl.* **-des,** (*esp. collectively*) **-de. 1.** a language family of W Africa, a branch of the Niger-Congo family, primarily spoken in Mali, Guinea, Sierra Leone, Liberia, and the Ivory Coast. **2.** a member of any of the peoples who speak these languages.

Man·de·la (man del′ə), *n.* **Nelson (Rolihlahla),** born 1918, president of South Africa since 1994.

man·di·ble (man′də bəl), *n.* **1.** the bone or bony composite comprising the lower jaw of vertebrates. **2.** (in birds) **a.** the lower part of the bill. **b. mandibles,** the upper and lower parts of the bill. **3.** (in arthropods) one of the first pair of mouthpart appendages, typically a biting organ. —**man·dib′u·lar** (-dib′yə lər), **man·dib′u·late,** *adj.*

Man·din·go (man ding′gō), *n., pl.* **-gos** or **-goes,** (*esp. collectively*) **-go. 1.** MALINKE. **2. a.** (esp. formerly) MANDE. **b.** a member of a subgroup of Mande-speaking peoples, including the Malinke and Bambara.

man·do·lin (man′dl in, man′dl ĭn′), *n.* a stringed musical instrument with a pear-shaped body and a fretted neck. —**man′do·lin′ist,** *n.*

mandolin

man·drake (man′drāk, -drik), *n.* a narcotic, short-stemmed European plant, *Mandragora officinarum,* of the nightshade family, having a fleshy, often forked root somewhat resembling a human form.

man·drel or **man·dril** (man′drəl), *n.* **1.** a shaft or bar inserted into a workpiece to hold it during machining. **2.** a spindle on which a circular saw or grinding wheel rotates.

man·drill (man′dril), *n.* a large W African baboon, *Mandrillus sphinx:* the male has a ribbed, blue and scarlet muzzle.

mane (mān), *n.* **1.** the long thick hair around or at the back of the neck of some animals, as the horse or lion. **2.** long luxuriant hair on the head of a person. —**maned,** *adj.* —**mane′less,** *adj.*

man′-eat′er, *n.* **1.** an animal that eats or is said to eat human flesh. **2.** MAN-EATING SHARK. **3.** a cannibal. —**man′-eat′ing,** *adj.*

man′-eat′ing shark′, *n.* any shark known to attack human beings, esp. the great white shark.

maned′ wolf′, *n.* a South American wild dog, *Chrysocyon brachyurus,* having a shaggy reddish coat.

ma·nège or **ma·nege** (ma nezh′, -nāzh′), *n.* **1.** the art of training and riding horses. **2.** the action, movements, or paces of a trained horse. **3.** a school for training horses and teaching horsemanship.

ma·nes (mā′nēz; *Lat.* mä′nes), *n.* (*sometimes cap.*) **1.** (*used with a pl. v.*) the spirits of the dead in ancient Roman belief to whom graves were dedicated. **2.** (*used with a sing. v.*) the spirit or shade of a particular dead person.

Ma·net (ma nā′), *n.* **Édouard,** 1832–83, French painter.

ma·neu·ver (mə nōō′vər), *n., v.,* **-vered, -ver·ing.** —*n.* **1.** a planned movement of troops, warships, etc. **2. maneuvers,** a series of tactical exercises simulating the conditions of war, carried out by large bodies of military or naval personnel, sometimes together. **3.** an act or instance of changing the direction of a moving vehicle. **4.** a physical movement or procedure, esp. when skillful. **5.** a clever or crafty tactic; ploy. —*v.t.* **6.** to change the position of by a maneuver. **7.** to position, manipulate, or make by maneuvers: *to maneuver one's way across rocks.* **8.** to steer as required. —*v.i.* **9.** to perform a maneuver or maneuvers. **10.** to scheme; intrigue. Also, *esp. Brit.,* **manoeuvre.** [< French < Latin *manū operārī* to work with the hands] —**ma·neu′ver·a·ble,** *adj.* —**ma·neu′ver·a·bil′i·ty,** *n.* —**ma·neu′ver·er,** *n.*

man′ Fri′day, *n., pl.* **men Friday** (or **Fridays**). a reliable male assistant; right-hand man.

man·ga·nese (mang′gə nēs′, -nēz′), *n.* a hard, brittle, grayish white, metallic element, an oxide of which, MnO₂, is a valuable oxidizing agent: used chiefly as an alloying agent in strengthening steel. *Symbol:* Mn; *at. wt.:* 54.938; *at. no.:* 25; *sp. gr.:* 7.2 at 20°C.

mange (mānj), *n.* any of various skin diseases caused by parasitic

mites, affecting animals and sometimes humans and characterized by loss of hair and scabby eruptions.

man·ger (mān′jər), *n.* a box or trough in a stable or barn from which livestock eat.

man·gle¹ (mang′gəl), *v.t.,* **-gled, -gling. 1.** to injure severely, disfigure, or mutilate by cutting, slashing, or crushing: *A sleeve was mangled in the machinery.* **2.** to spoil; ruin; mar badly: *to mangle a text by careless typesetting.* —**man′gler,** *n.*

man·gle² (mang′gəl), *n., v.,* **-gled, -gling.** —*n.* **1.** a machine for pressing laundry by passing it between heated rollers. —*v.t.* **2.** to press with a mangle.

man·go (mang′gō), *n., pl.* **-goes, -gos. 1. a.** the oblong sweet fruit of a tropical tree, *Mangifera indica,* of the cashew family. **b.** the tree itself. **2.** *Chiefly Midland U.S.* SWEET PEPPER.

man·go·steen (mang′gə stēn′), *n.* **1.** the juicy, edible fruit of an East Indian tree, *Garcinia mangostana.* **2.** the tree itself.

man·grove (mang′grōv, man′-), *n.* **1.** any tropical tree or shrub belonging to the genus *Rhizophora,* of the family Rhizophoraceae, the species of which are mostly low trees growing in marshes or tidal shores, noted for interlacing above-ground roots. **2.** any similar plant.

man·gy (mān′jē), *adj.,* **-gi·er, -gi·est. 1.** having, caused by, or like mange. **2.** squalid; shabby: *a mangy little suburb.* —**man′gi·ly,** *adv.* —**man′gi·ness,** *n.*

man·han·dle (man′han′dl, man han′dl), *v.t.,* **-dled, -dling. 1.** to handle roughly. **2.** to move by human strength alone.

Man·hat·tan (man hat′n, mən-), *n.* **1.** Also called **Manhat′tan Is′land.** an island in New York City surrounded by the Hudson, East, and Harlem rivers. 13½ mi. (22 km) long. **2.** a borough of New York City approximately coextensive with Manhattan Island. 1,427,533. **3.** (*often l.c.*) a cocktail of rye, vermouth, and bitters. —**Man·hat′tan·ite′,** *n.*

Manhat′tan clam′ chow′der, *n.* a chowder made from clams, tomatoes, and other vegetables.

Manhat′tan Proj′ect, *n.* the unofficial designation for the U.S. War Department's secret program, organized in 1942, to explore the isolation of radioactive isotopes and the production of an atomic bomb: initial research was conducted at Columbia University in Manhattan.

man·hole (man′hōl′), *n.* a hole, usu. with a cover, giving access to a sewer, drain, steam boiler, etc.

man·hood (man′hŏŏd′), *n.* **1.** the state or time of being a man. **2.** traditional manly qualities. **3.** the male genitalia. **4.** men collectively.

man·hunt (man′hunt′), *n.* an intensive, usu. organized search for a person, esp. a criminal, fugitive, or person charged with a crime. —**man′-hunt′er,** *n.*

ma·ni·a (mā′nē ə, mān′yə), *n., pl.* **-ni·as. 1.** excessive excitement or enthusiasm; craze. **2.** a pathological state characterized by euphoric mood, excessive activity and talkativeness, impaired judgment, and sometimes psychotic symptoms. —**man·ic** (man′ik), *adj.*

-mania, a combining form of MANIA (*megalomania*); extended to mean "enthusiasm, often of an extreme and transient nature," for that specified by the initial element (*bibliomania*).

ma·ni·ac (mā′nē ak′), *n.* **1.** an insane person; lunatic. **2.** an overly zealous or enthusiastic person. —**ma·ni·a·cal** (mə nī′ə kəl), *adj.* —**ma·ni′a·cal·ly,** *adv.*

man′ic-depres′sive, *adj.* **1.** suffering from bipolar disorder. —*n.* **2.** a manic-depressive person.

man′ic disor′der, *n.* an affective disorder characterized by euphoric mood, excessive activity and talkativeness, impaired judgment, and sometimes psychotic symptoms, as grandiose delusions.

Man·i·che·an or **Man·i·chae·an** (man′i kē′ən), *n.* **1.** Also, **Man·i·chee** (man′i kē′). an adherent of a religious dualism that originated in Persia in the 3rd century A.D., combining elements of Gnostic Christianity, Buddhism, and Zoroastrianism. —*adj.* **2.** of or pertaining to the Manicheans or their doctrines. [< Late Latin *Manichaeus* < Late Greek *Manichaîos* Mani (A.D. 216–276), the founder of the religion] —**Man′i·che′an·ism,** **Man′i·chae′an·ism,** *n.*

ma·ni·cot·ti (man′i kot′ē), *n.* (*used with a sing. or pl. v.*) large tubular noodles usu. stuffed with cheese and baked in a tomato sauce.

man·i·cure (man′i kyŏŏr′), *n., v.,* **-cured, -cur·ing.** —*n.* **1.** a cosmetic treatment of the hands or fingernails, esp. the cleaning, trimming, and polishing of the nails and the removal of cuticle. —*v.t.* **2.** to apply manicure treatment to (the hands or fingernails). **3.** to trim or cut meticulously: *to manicure a lawn.* —**man′i·cur′ist,** *n.*

man·i·fest (man′ə fest′), *adj.* **1.** readily perceived by the eye or the understanding; evident: *a manifest error.* —*v.t.* **2.** to make clear or evident to the eye or the understanding: *to manifest disapproval.* —*n.* **3.** a list of the cargo or passengers carried by a ship, plane, truck, or train. —**man′i·fest′a·ble,** *adj.* —**man′i·fest′ly,** *adv.*

man·i·fes·ta·tion (man′ə fe stā′shən, -fe-), *n.* **1.** an act of manifesting. **2.** the state of being manifested. **3.** outward or perceptible indication; materialization: *a clear manifestation of the disease.* **4.** a public demonstration, as for political effect.

Man′ifest Des′tiny, *n.* the 19th-century belief that it was inevitable for the U.S. to expand to the Pacific coast.

man·i·fes·to (man′ə fes′tō), *n., pl.* **-tos, -toes.** a public declaration of intentions, opinions, or purposes.

man·i·fold (man′ə fōld′), *adj.* **1.** of many kinds; numerous and varied: *manifold duties.* **2.** having numerous different parts, features, or

(M)

forms: *a manifold social program.* **3.** using or operating similar or identical devices at the same time. **4.** being such for many reasons: *a manifold enemy.* —*n.* **5.** something having many different parts or features. **6.** a carbon copy; facsimile. **7.** a pipe or fitting with several openings for funneling the flow of liquids or gasses, as in the exhaust system of an automobile engine. **8.** a set of elements having in common a number of topologic properties. —*adv.* **9.** very much; in great measure: *to multiply burdens manifold.* —*v.t.* **10.** to make copies of, as with carbon paper. —**man′i·fold′ly**, *adv.* —**man′i·fold′ness**, *n.*

man·i·kin or **man·ni·kin** (man′i kin), *n.* **1.** a little man; dwarf; pygmy. **2.** MANNEQUIN.

Ma·nil·a (mə nil′ə), *n.* **1.** the capital of the Philippines, on W central Luzon. 1,630,485. **2.** (*sometimes l.c.*) MANILA PAPER.

Manil′a hemp′, *n.* ABACA (def. 2).

Manil′a (or **manil′a**) **pa′per**, *n.* strong, light brown or buff paper orig. made from abaca fiber but now also from wood pulp substitutes or other fibers.

man′ in the street′, *n.* the ordinary person; the average citizen: *the political opinions of the man in the street.*

ma·nip·u·late (mə nip′yə lāt′), *v.t.*, **-lat·ed, -lat·ing. 1.** to manage or influence skillfully and often unfairly: *to manipulate people's feelings.* **2.** to handle or use, esp. with skill: *to manipulate a large tractor.* **3.** to adapt or change (accounts, figures, etc.) to suit one's purpose or advantage. —**ma·nip′u·la·ble, ma·nip′u·la·bil′i·ty**, *n.* —**ma·nip′u·la′tion**, *n.* —**ma·nip′u·la·tive, adj.** —**ma·nip′u·la·tive·ly**, *adv.*

Man·i·to·ba (man′i tō′bə), *n.* **1.** a province in central Canada. 1,063,016; 250,946 sq. mi. (649,046 sq. km). *Abbr.:* Man. *Cap.:* Winnipeg. **2. Lake,** a lake in the S part of this province. 120 mi. (195 km) long; 1817 sq. mi. (4705 sq. km). —**Man′i·to′ban**, *adj., n.*

man·i·tou or **man·i·tu** (man′i tōō), also **man·i·to** (-tō′), *n., pl.* **-tous** or **-tus,** also **-tos.** (among Algonquian Indian peoples) any of a number of spirits residing in objects and phenomena of the natural world, as in animals, trees, water, the earth, and the sky.

man·kind (man′kīnd′ *for 1;* man′kīnd′ *for 2*), *n.* **1.** human beings collectively without reference to sex; humankind. **2.** men as distinguished from women. —**Usage.** See MAN.

man·ly (man′lē), *adj.,* **-li·er, -li·est,** *adv.* —*adj.* **1.** having qualities traditionally ascribed to men; virile; not feminine or boyish. **2.** pertaining to or suitable for males: *manly sports.* —*adv.* **3.** in the manner of, or befitting, a man. —**man′li·ness**, *n.*

man′-made′, *adj.* produced, formed, or made by humans; not resulting from natural processes.

Mann (man *for 1;* män, män *for 2*), *n.* **1. Horace,** 1796–1859, U.S. educational reformer. **2. Thomas,** 1875–1955, German novelist, in the U.S. 1938–52.

man·na (man′ə), *n., pl.* **-nas** *for 4.* **1.** the food miraculously supplied to the Israelites in the wilderness. Ex. 16:14–36. **2.** spiritual sustenance of divine origin. **3.** a sudden or unexpected source of help or gratification. **4.** any of several crusty edible lichens of the genus *Lecanora,* common in Arabian and African deserts. **5.** the exudation of the ash *Fraxinus ornus* and related plants; a source of mannitol.

Mann′ Act′ (man), *n.* an act of Congress (1910) making it a federal offense to participate in the interstate transportation of a woman for immoral purposes.

manned (mand), *adj.* carrying or operated by one or more persons: *a manned spacecraft.*

man·ne·quin or **man·i·kin** or **man·ni·kin** (man′i kin), *n.* **1.** a three-dimensional representation of the human form used in window displays, for making or fitting clothes, etc.; dummy. **2.** a person employed to model clothing.

man·ner (man′ər), *n.* **1.** a way of doing, being done, or happening; mode of action: *In what manner were you notified?* **2. manners, a.** the prevailing customs; ways of living of a people, class, or period: *Victorian manners.* **b.** ways of behaving with reference to polite standards: *good manners.* **3.** a person's outward bearing: *a charming manner.* **4.** characteristic or customary way of doing or making; fashion: *built in the 19th-century manner.* **5.** an air of distinction. **6.** (*used with a sing. or pl. v.*) kind; sort: *What manner of man is he? All manner of things were happening.* **7.** characteristic style in art or literature: *verses in the manner of Spenser.* —**Idiom. 8. to the manner born,** accustomed by birth to a high position: *a gentleman to the manner born.*

man·nered (man′ərd), *adj.* **1.** having manners of a specified kind (usu. used in combination): *ill-mannered.* **2.** having distinctive mannerisms; affected: *a mannered walk.*

man·ner·ism (man′ə riz′əm), *n.* **1.** a habitual or characteristic manner or way of doing something. **2.** marked or excessive adherence to an unusual or a particular manner esp. when affected. **3.** (*often cap.*) a style of art of 16th-century Europe marked by complex perspective and elongation of forms. —**man′ner·ist**, *n.* —**man′ner·is′tic**, *adj.*

man·ner·ly (man′ər lē), *adj.* **1.** having or showing good manners; courteous. —*adv.* **2.** courteously; politely. —**man′ner·li·ness**, *n.*

man·ni·kin (man′i kin), *n.* MANIKIN.

man·nish (man′ish), *adj.* being typical or suggestive of a man rather than a woman. —**man′nish·ly**, *adv.* —**man′nish·ness**, *n.*

ma·no (mä′nō), *n., pl.* **-nos.** the upper or hand-held stone used when grinding maize or other grains on a metate.

Ma·no·ah (mə nō′ə), *n.* the father of Samson. Judges 13.

Man′ of Gal′ilee, *n.* Jesus.

man′ of God′, *n.* CLERGYMAN.

man′ of let′ters, *n.* a man engaged in literary or scholarly pursuits.

Man′ of Sor′rows, *n.* (in Christian exegesis) an appellation of Jesus as the suffering Savior. Is. 53:3.

man′ of the cloth′, *n.* CLERGYMAN.

man′ of the house′, *n.* the male head of a household.

man′-of-war′, *n., pl.* **men-of-war. 1.** WARSHIP. **2.** PORTUGUESE MAN-OF-WAR.

man′ on horse′back, *n.* **1.** a military leader who has the potential to become dictator. **2.** DICTATOR (def. 1).

man·or (man′ər), *n.* **1.** a feudal estate, consisting of a lord's house and adjoining lands over which he exercises control. **2.** (in England) the house of a lord with the land belonging to it; a landed estate. **3.** the main house or mansion on an estate, plantation, etc. —**ma·no·ri·al** (mə nôr′ē əl, -nōr′-), *adj.*

man′-o′-war′ bird′ (man′ə wôr′), *n.* FRIGATE BIRD.

man′ pow′er, *n.* **1.** the power supplied by human physical exertions. **2.** a unit of power assumed to be equal to the rate at which a person can do mechanical work and commonly taken as $^{1}/_{10}$ horsepower. **3.** MANPOWER.

man·pow·er (man′pou′ər), *n.* power in terms of people available or required for work or military service.

man·qué (mäng kā′, män-), *adj.* unsuccessful; unfulfilled (used postpositively): *a poet manqué.* [< French]

man·sard (man′särd, -sərd), *n.* **1.** Also called **man′sard roof′**. a roof with four sloping sides, each of which has a steeper lower part and a shallower upper part. **2.** the story under such a roof.

manse (mans), *n.* **1.** the house occupied by a minister or parson. **2.** a stately residence; mansion.

man·serv·ant (man′sûr′vənt), *n., pl.* **men·serv·ants.** a male servant.

Mans·field (manz′fēld′), *n.* **1. Katherine** (*Kathleen Beauchamp Murry*), 1888–1923, English short-story writer. **2. Mount,** a mountain in N Vermont: highest peak of the Green Mountains, 4393 ft. (1339 m). **3.** a city in W Nottinghamshire, in central England. 100,000. **4.** a city in N Ohio. 51,640.

-manship, a combination of -MAN and -SHIP, used with the meaning "skill in a particular activity, esp. of a competitive nature": *brinkmanship; one-upmanship.*

man·sion (man′shən), *n.* **1.** a very large or stately residence. **2.** MANOR. **3.** *Astrol.* **a.** HOUSE (def. 15). **b.** each of 28 divisions of the sky occupied by the moon on successive days.

man′-sized′ or **man′-size′**, *adj.* **1.** big; generous: *a man-sized sandwich.* **2.** formidable: *a man-sized undertaking.*

man·slaugh·ter (man′slô′tər), *n.* the unlawful killing of a human being without malice aforethought.

man·sue·tude (man′swi tōōd′, -tyōōd′), *n.* mildness; gentleness.

man·ta (man′tə, män′-), *n., pl.* **-tas. 1.** (in Spain and Spanish America) a cloak or wrap. **2.** Also called **man′ta ray′, devilfish.** any warm-water ray of the family Mobulidae, esp. of the genus *Manta,* measuring up to 24 ft. (7.3 m) across.

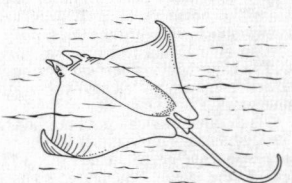

manta (def. 2),
Manta hamiltoni,
18 ft. (5.5 m) across "wing tips";
total length 20 ft. (6 m); tail 6 ft. (1.8 m)

man′-tai′lored, *adj.* (of women's clothing) tailored in the general style of men's clothing.

man·tel or **man·tle** (man′tl), *n.* **1.** a construction framing the opening of a fireplace and usu. covering part of the chimney breast in a decorative manner. **2.** Also called **mantelshelf.** a shelf above a fireplace opening. Also called **man′tel·piece′, man′tle·piece′** (-pēs′).

man·tic (man′tik), *adj.* **1.** of or pertaining to divination. **2.** having the power of divination. —**man′ti·cal·ly**, *adv.*

-mantic, a combining form used in the formation of adjectives corresponding to nouns ending in -MANCY: *necromantic.*

man·tid (man′tid), *n.* MANTIS.

man·til·la (man til′ə, -tē′ə), *n., pl.* **-las. 1.** a silk or lace head scarf arranged over a high comb to fall over the back and shoulders, worn esp. by women in Spain or Latin America. **2.** a short mantle or light cape.

man·tis (man′tis) also **mantid,** *n., pl.* **-tis·es, -tes** (-tēz) also **-tids.** a predaceous insect of the family Mantidae, having a long prothorax and typically holding the forelegs in an upraised position as if in prayer.

man·tis·sa (man tis′ə), *n., pl.* **-sas.** the decimal part of a common logarithm. Compare CHARACTERISTIC (def. 3a).

man′tis shrimp′, *n.* any of numerous shrimplike crustaceans of the order Stomatopoda having a greatly enlarged second pair of grasping forelimbs somewhat resembling those of a mantis.

man·tle (man′tl), *n., v.,* **-tled, -tling.** —*n.* **1.** a long, loose, capelike garment; sleeveless cloak. **2.** something that covers, envelops, or conceals: *the mantle of darkness.* **3.** the portion of the earth, about 1800 mi. (2900 km) thick, between the crust and the core. **4.** an outgrowth of the body wall in mollusks and brachiopods that lines the inner surface of the shell valves and secretes a shell-forming substance. **5.** an incombustible hood that becomes incandescent and gives off a brilliant light when placed around a flame. **6.** the back, scapular, and inner wing plumage of a bird. **7.** MANTEL. —*v.t.* **8.** to cover with or as if with a mantle; envelop; conceal. —*v.i.* **9.** to overspread a surface. **10.** to flush; blush. **11.** to become covered with a coating, as foam.

Man·tle (man′tl), *n.* **Mickey (Charles)**, 1931–95, U.S. baseball player.

man·tle·piece (man′tl pēs′), *n.* MANTEL.

man′-to-man′, *adj.* characterized by directness and openness; frank: *a man-to-man talk.*

man′-to-man′ de/fense, *n.* (esp. in basketball and football) a method of defense in which each defensive player guards a specific offensive player. Compare ZONE DEFENSE.

man·tra (man′trə, män′-) also **man·tram** (-trəm), *n., pl.* **-tras** also **-trams. 1.** (in Hinduism and Buddhism) a sacred word or formula repeated as an incantation. **2.** any often repeated word, formula, or stock phrase; slogan. —**man′tric**, *adj.*

man·u·al (man′yōō əl), *adj.* **1.** operated by hand rather than mechanically or automatically: *a manual gearshift.* **2.** involving or requiring human effort; physical: *manual labor.* **3.** of or pertaining to the hands. —*n.* **4.** a book easily held in the hand, esp. one giving information or instructions. **5.** a typewriter whose keys and carriage are powered solely by the typist's hands. **6.** the prescribed drill in handling a rifle: *military manual of arms.* **7.** a musical keyboard, esp. one of several belonging to a pipe organ. —**man′u·al·ly**, *adv.*

man′ual al′phabet, *n.* a set of finger configurations corresponding to the letters of the alphabet, used by the deaf in fingerspelling.

man·u·fac·ture (man′yə fak′chər), *v.,* **-tured, -tur·ing,** *n.* —*v.t.* **1.** to make or produce by hand or machinery, esp. on a large scale. **2.** to work up (material) into form for use: *to manufacture cotton.* **3.** to fabricate; concoct: *to manufacture an excuse.* **4.** to produce in a mechanical way: *manufactured a daily quota of poetry.* —*n.* **5.** the making of goods or wares by manual labor or by machinery, esp. on a large scale: *the manufacture of cars.* **6.** the making or producing of something; generation: *the manufacture of body cells.* **7.** the thing manufactured. —**man′u·fac′tur·a·ble**, *adj.* —**man′u·fac′tur·al**, *adj.* —**man′u·fac′tur·er**, *n.*

man·u·mit (man′yə mit′), *v.t.,* **-mit·ted, -mit·ting.** to release from slavery or servitude. —**man′u·mis′sion**, *n.* —**man′u·mit′ter**, *n.*

ma·nure (mə nōōr′, -nyōōr′), *n., v.,* **-nured, -nur·ing.** —*n.* **1.** excrement, esp. of animals, used as fertilizer. **2.** any natural or artificial substance for fertilizing the soil. —*v.t.* **3.** to treat (land) with fertilizing matter. —**ma·nur′er**, *n.* —**ma·nu′ri·al**, *adj.* —**ma·nu′ri·al·ly**, *adv.*

man·u·script (man′yə skript′), *n.* **1.** a written, typewritten, or computer-produced text before being set in type. **2.** writing as distinguished from print. —*adj.* **3.** written by hand or using a typewriter or word processor: *manuscript documents.* —**man′u·script′al**, *adj.*

Manx (mangks), *n.* **1.** (*used with a pl. v.*) the inhabitants of the Isle of Man. **2.** the extinct Celtic language of the Isle of Man, closely related to Irish and Scottish Gaelic. —*adj.* **3.** of or pertaining to the Isle of Man, its inhabitants, or their language.

Manx′ cat′, *n.* one of a breed of shorthaired, tailless domestic cats.

man·y (men′ē), *adj.,* **more, most,** *n., pron.* —*adj.* **1.** constituting or forming a large number; numerous: *many people.* **2.** noting each one of a large number (usu. fol. by *a* or *an*): *For many a day it rained.* —*n.* **3.** a large or considerable number of persons or things: *A good many of the beggars were blind.* **4. the many,** the greater part of humankind. —*pron.* **5.** many persons or things: *Many were unable to attend.* —*Idiom.* **6. many a time,** again and again; frequently. —*Proverb.* **7. Many are called, but few are chosen,** only the most qualified people will be selected (to do God's work). Matt. 22:11–14.

man′y-sid′ed, *adj.* **1.** having many sides or aspects: *a many-sided question.* **2.** having many interests or talents; versatile: *a many-sided person.* —**man′y-sid′ed·ness**, *n.*

man·za·nil·la (man′zə nēl′yə, -nē′ə), *n., pl.* **-las.** a pale, very dry sherry from Spain.

man·za·ni·ta (man′zə nē′tə), *n., pl.* **-tas.** any of several W North American shrubs or small trees belonging to the genus *Arctostaphylos,* of the heath family.

Mao·ism (mou′iz əm), *n.* the theories and policies of Mao Zedong, esp. his strategy for revolution. —**Mao′ist**, *adj., n.*

mao-tai or **mao tai** (mou′tī′), *n.* a strong liquor of China distilled from sorghum.

Mao Ze·dong (mou′ zə dông′, dzə-) also **Mao Tse-tung** (mou′ tsə-tōōng′, dzə dōōng′), *n.* 1893–1976, chairman of the People's Republic of China 1949–59 and of the Chinese Communist party 1943–76.

map (map), *n., v.,* **mapped, map·ping.** —*n.* **1.** a representation, usu. on a flat surface, of selected features of all or a part of the earth or a portion of the heavens, shown in their respective relationships according to some convention of representation. **2.** any maplike delineation or representation. **3.** FUNCTION (def. 4a). —*v.t.* **4.** to represent or delineate on or as if on a map. **5.** to sketch or plan (often fol. by *out*): *to map out a new career.* —*Idiom.* **6. off the map,** out of existence; into oblivion: *Cities were wiped off the map.* **7. on the map,** in or into a position of prominence or renown: *The casino put our town on the map.* —**map′pa·ble**, *adj.* —**map′per**, *n.*

ma·ple (mā′pəl), *n.* **1.** any of numerous trees or shrubs of the genus *Acer,* grown for shade or ornament, for timber, or for sap. **2.** the wood of any of these. **3.** the flavor of maple syrup or maple sugar. —**ma′ple·like′**, *adj.*

ma′ple sug′ar, *n.* a yellowish brown sugar produced by boiling down maple syrup.

ma′ple syr′up, *n.* a syrup produced by partially boiling down the sap of the sugar maple or other maple tree.

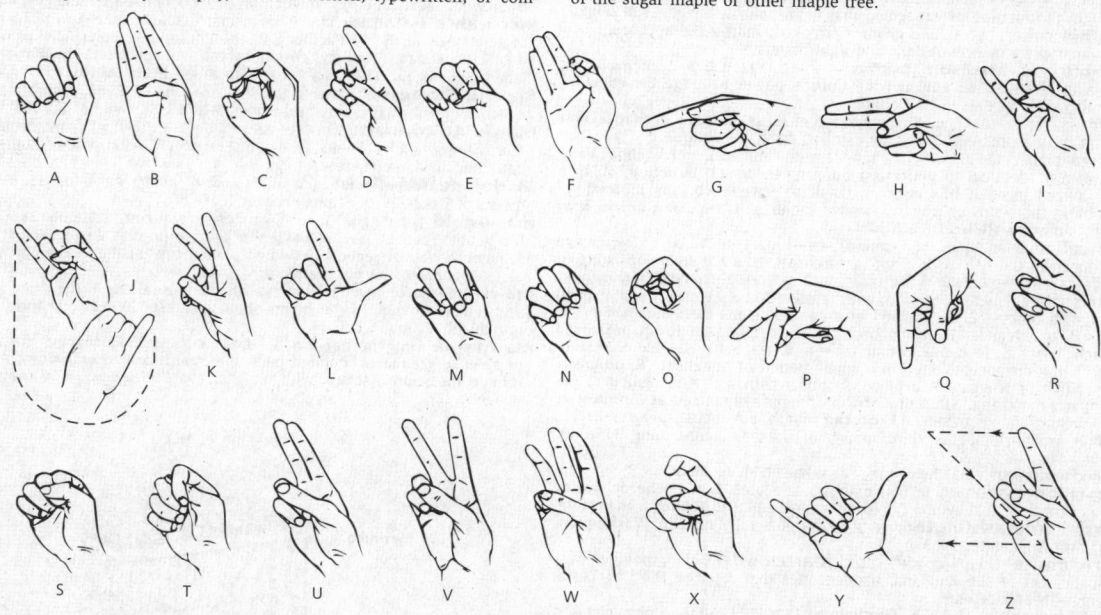

manual alphabet

M

map•mak•er (map′mā′kər), *n.* a person or firm that makes maps; cartographer.

map•ping (map′ing), *n.* **1.** the act or operation of making maps. **2.** FUNCTION (def. 4a).

Ma•pu•to (mə pōō′tō), *n.* the capital of Mozambique, on Delagoa Bay. 491,800. Formerly, **Lourenço Marques.**

ma•qui•la•do•ra (mə kē′lə dôr′ə), *n., pl.* **-ras.** a factory run by a U.S. company in Mexico to take advantage of cheap labor and lax regulation.

ma•quil•lage (mak′ē äzh′), *n.* MAKEUP (defs. 1, 4).

ma•quis (mä kē′, ma-), *n., pl.* **-quis** (-kēz′, -kē′). **1.** (*often cap.*) a French underground movement resisting the Nazi occupation of France in World War II. **2.** a member of this movement.

mar (mär), *v.t.,* **marred, mar•ring.** to damage the attractiveness or appeal of; impair.

mar•a•bou (mar′ə bōō′) also **marabout,** *n., pl.* **-bous, -bouts. 1.** any of several naked-headed, carrion-eating storks of the genus *Leptoptilus,* esp. *L. crumeniferus,* of sub-Saharan Africa. **2.** material made from the feathers of marabous and used to trim women's hats and clothing. **3. a.** thrown silk that can be dyed without being scoured. **b.** a fabric made of such silk.

ma•rac•a (mə rä′kə, -rak′ə), *n., pl.* **-rac•as.** a gourd-shaped rattle filled with seeds or pebbles and used as a rhythm instrument.

Mar•a•can•da (mar′ə kan′də), *n.* ancient name of SAMARKAND.

Ma•rah (mâr′ə), *n.* a pool or well that was the first place the Israelites stopped after crossing the Red Sea. Num. 33:8–9.

mar•a•schi•no (mar′ə skē′nō, -shē′-), *n.* a cordial distilled from marasca cherries.

maraschino cher′ry, *n.* a cherry preserved in maraschino or imitation maraschino.

ma•ras•mus (mə raz′məs), *n.* malnutrition occurring in infants and young children, caused by insufficient intake of calories or protein and characterized by thinness, dry skin, poor muscle development, and irritability. **—ma•ras′mic, —ma•ras′moid,** *adj.*

mar•a•thon (mar′ə thon′, -thən), *n.* **1.** a foot race over a course measuring 26 mi. 385 yd. (42 km 352 m). **2.** any long-distance race. **3.** an extended contest or event requiring great endurance: *a dance marathon.* **—mar′a•thon′er,** *n.*

ma•raud (mə rôd′), *v.i.* **1.** to rove in quest of plunder; raid for booty. **—v.t. 2.** to raid; plunder. **—ma•raud′er,** *n.*

Ma•ra•vi (mə rä′vē), *n., pl.* **-vis,** (*esp. collectively*) **-vi.** a member of any of a group of African peoples living mainly between the W and S shores of Lake Malawi and the lower Zambezi River.

mar•ble (mär′bəl), *n., adj., v.,* **-bled, -bling. —n. 1.** metamorphosed limestone that consists chiefly of recrystallized calcite or dolomite, occurs in a wide range of colors and variegations, takes a high polish, and is used esp. in sculpture and architecture. **2.** a little ball usu. made of glass or agate for use in games. **3. marbles,** (*used with a sing. v.*) any of various games for children played with marbles on a marked area of the ground. **4. marbles,** *Slang.* wits; common sense: *to lose one's marbles.* **—adj. 5.** consisting of or resembling marble. **—v.t. 6.** to color or stain in imitation of variegated marble: *to marble the edges of a book.*

mar′ble cake′, *n.* a cake given a streaked, marblelike appearance by the incomplete mixing of dark and light batters.

Mar•bur•y v. Madison (mär′ber ē, -bə rē), *n.* a U.S. Supreme Court decision of 1803 that affirmed the Court's power to judge the constitutionality of laws passed by Congress.

marc (märk; *Fr.* MAR), *n.* **1.** the residue of skins and pips of grapes after the juice is expressed. **2.** brandy distilled from this residue.

mar•ca•site (mär′kə sīt′), *n.* **1.** a common mineral, iron sulfide, FeS₂, chemically identical to pyrite but differing in crystal structure. **2. a.** a crystallized form of this mineral, used for jewelry. **b.** any mineral resembling this form or any substance imitating it, esp. as used in jewelry. **—mar′ca•sit′i•cal** (-sit′i kəl), *adj.*

mar•cel (mär sel′), *n., v.,* **-celled, -cel•ling. —n. 1. a.** a deep wave produced in the hair with a hot curling iron. **b.** a hairstyle consisting of such waves. **—v.t. 2.** to wave (hair) in a marcel. **—mar•cel′ler,** *n.*

march (märch), *v.i.* **1.** to walk with regular and measured tread, esp. in step with others. **2.** to proceed in a deliberate manner: *marched off to bed.* **3.** to advance: *Time marches on.* **4.** to take part in an organized march. **—v.t. 5.** to cause to march. **—n. 6.** the act or course of marching. **7.** the distance covered in a single period of marching. **8.** progress: *the march of science.* **9.** a piece of music with a rhythm suited to accompany marching. **10.** a procession of people organized as a protest or demonstration. **—Idiom. 11. on the march,** advancing; progressing.

March (märch), *n.* the third month of the year, containing 31 days. *Abbr.:* Mar.

Mar•chesh•van (mär hesh′vən, -vän, -ᴋʜesh′-), *n.* HESHVAN.

mar•chion•ess (mär′shə nis, mär′shə nes′), *n.* **1.** the wife or widow of a marquess. **2.** a woman holding a rank equal to that of a marquess.

March′ on Wash′ington, *n.* a civil-rights rally held in Washington, D.C., on August 28, 1963.

Mar•cion•ite (mär′shə nīt′) also **Mar′cion•ist,** *n.* a member of a Gnostic sect of the 2nd and 3th centuries that rejected the Old Testament. **—Mar′cion•ism,** *n.*

Mar•co•ni (mär kō′nē), *n.* **Guglielmo,** 1874–1937, Italian physicist and inventor in the field of wireless telegraphy.

Mar•co Po•lo (mär′kō pō′lō), *n.* POLO, Marco.

Mar•cus Au•re•li•us (mär′kəs ô rē′lē əs, ô rēl′yəs), *n.* A.D. 121–180, Stoic philosopher: emperor of Rome 161–180. Also called **Mar′cus Aure′lius An•to•ni′nus** (an′tə nī′nəs).

Mar•di Gras (mär′dē grä′, grä′), *n.* **1.** the day before Lent celebrated, as in New Orleans, as a day of carnival; Shrove Tuesday. **2.** a pre-Lenten carnival period climaxing on this day. [< French: lit., fat Tuesday]

mare¹ (mâr), *n.* a fully mature female horse or other equine animal.

ma•re² (mär′ā, mâr′ē), *n., pl.* **ma•ri•a** (mär′ē ə, mâr′-). any of several large dark plains on the moon and Mars.

mare's′-nest′, *n.* **1.** a discovery that proves to be a delusion or a hoax. **2.** a very confused or disordered place or situation.

mare's′-tail′, *n.* **1.** a long narrow cirrus cloud with a flowing appearance. **2.** an erect aquatic Old World plant, *Hippuris vulgaris,* of the family Hippuridaceae, with crowded whorls of narrow hairlike leaves.

mar•ga•rine (mär′jər in, -jə rēn′, märj′rin), *n.* a butterlike product made of refined vegetable oils blended sometimes with animal fats and emulsified usu. with water or milk.

mar•gay (mär′gā), *n.* a small spotted cat, *Felis wiedii,* of the southwestern U.S. and tropical America.

mar•gin (mär′jin), *n.* **1.** the space around the printed or written matter on a page. **2.** a border; edge. **3.** an amount allowed or available beyond what is necessary: *margin for error.* **4.** a limit beyond or below which something ceases to exist or to be desirable or possible: *the margin of endurance.* **5.** an amount or degree of difference: *to win by a margin of three votes.* **6. a.** security, usu. a percentage of a transaction, that a client deposits with a broker as a provision against loss. **b.** the amount representing the client's investment or equity in such an account. **7.** the difference between the amount of a loan and the market value of the collateral pledged as security for it. **8.** the difference between the cost of merchandise and the net sales. **9.** the point at which the return from economic activity barely covers the cost of production and below which production is unprofitable. **—v.t. 10.** to provide with a margin or border. **11.** to enter in the margin, as of a book. **12. a.** to deposit a margin upon: *to margin an account.* **b.** to purchase (securities) on margin.

mar•gin•al (mär′jə nl), *adj.* **1.** pertaining to a margin. **2.** situated on a border, edge, or fringe. **3.** at the lower limits; minimal for requirements: *marginal ability.* **4.** written or printed in the margin of a page. **5.** insignificant; minor: *a marginal improvement.* **6.** having contact with two or more cultural groups but not fully accepted in any of them. **7. a.** selling goods at a price that just equals the additional cost of producing the last unit supplied. **b.** of or pertaining to goods produced and marketed at margin: *marginal profits.* **—mar′gin•al′i•ty,** *n.* **—mar′gin•al•ly,** *adv.*

mar•gi•na•li•a (mär′jə nā′lē ə, -näl′yə), *n.pl.* marginal notes, as in a manuscript.

mar•gue•rite (mär′gə rēt′), *n.* **1.** the European daisy, *Bellis perennis.* **2.** any of several daisylike chrysanthemums, esp. *Chrysanthemum frutescens.*

ma•ri•a•chi (mär′ē ä′chē), *n., pl.* **-chis. 1.** a Mexican band composed typically of itinerant street musicians. **2.** a member of a mariachi. **3.** the traditional Mexican dance music played by a mariachi.

Mar′i•an′a Is′lands (mâr′ē an′ə, mar′-, mâr′-, mar′-), *n.pl.* a group of 15 islands in the W Pacific, E of the Philippines: comprised of Guam, a U.S. possession, and the commonwealth of the Northern Mariana Islands. 396 sq. mi. (1026 sq. km). Also called **Mar′i•an′as.**

Ma•ri•a The•re•sa (mə rē′ə tə rā′sə, -zə), *n.* 1717–80, archduchess of Austria; queen of Hungary and Bohemia 1740–80 (wife of Francis II).

Ma•rie An•toi•nette (mə rē′ an′twə net′, an′tə-), *n.* (*Josèphe Jeanne Marie Antoinette*) 1755–93, queen of France 1774–93: wife of Louis XVI; daughter of Maria Theresa.

Marie′ de Mé•di•cis′ (də mā′də sēs′, med′i chē), *n.* 1573–1642, queen of Henry IV of France: regent 1610–17.

mar•i•gold (mar′i gōld′), *n.* **1.** any of several composite plants, esp. of the genus *Tagetes,* having golden or orange flowers and strong-scented foliage. **2.** any of several unrelated plants, esp. of the genus *Calendula,* as *C. officinalis,* the pot marigold.

ma•ri•jua•na or **ma•ri•hua•na** (mar′ə wä′nə), *n.* **1.** the dried leaves and female flowers of the hemp plant used esp. in cigarette form as an intoxicant. **2.** HEMP (def. 1).

ma•rim•ba (mə rim′bə), *n., pl.* **-bas.** a musical instrument consisting of a set of graduated wooden bars, often with resonators beneath to reinforce the sound, struck with mallets. [< Portuguese < a Bantu language]

marimba

Mar•in (mär′in), *n.* **John,** 1870–1953, U.S. painter and etcher.

ma•ri•na (mə rē′nə), *n., pl.* **-nas.** a boat basin offering dockage and services for small craft.

mar•i•nade (*n.* mar′ə nād′; *v.* mar′ə nād′), *n., v.,* **-nad•ed, -nad•ing.** —*n.* **1.** a liquid mixture, as of vinegar or wine, oil, herbs, and spices, in which food is steeped before cooking. —*v.t.* **2.** MARINATE.

ma•ri•na•ra (mär′ə när′ə, mar′ə nar′ə), *n.* **1.** a spicy tomato, onion, and garlic sauce. —*adj.* **2.** served with such a sauce: *shrimp marinara.*

mar•i•nate (mar′ə nāt′), *v.t.,* **-nat•ed, -nat•ing.** to steep (food) in a marinade. —**mar′i•na′tion,** *n.*

ma•rine (mə rēn′), *adj.* **1.** of or pertaining to the sea: *marine vegetation.* **2.** adapted for use at sea: *a marine barometer.* **3.** pertaining to navigation or shipping; nautical; maritime. **4.** of or pertaining to marines. —*n.* **5.** a member of the U.S. Marine Corps. **6.** one of a class of naval troops serving both on shipboard and on land. **7.** seagoing ships, esp. with reference to nationality or class. **8.** a picture with a marine subject; seascape. **9.** a department of naval affairs, as in France.

Marine′ Corps′, *n.* a branch of the U.S. armed forces trained for sea-launched assaults on land targets.

mar•i•ner (mar′ə nər), *n.* a person who directs or assists in the navigation of a ship; sailor.

Mar•i•ol•o•gy (mâr′ē ol′ə jē), *n.* the study of and beliefs concerning the Virgin Mary. —**Mar′i•ol′o•gist,** *n.*

mar•i•on•ette (mar′ē ə net′), *n.* a puppet manipulated from above by strings attached to its jointed limbs.

mar•i•po′sa lil′y (mar′ə pō′sə, -zə), *n.* any lily of the genus *Calochortus,* of the western U.S. and Mexico, having showy tuliplike flowers. Also called **mar′i•po′sa, maripo′sa tu′lip.**

Mar•ist (mâr′ist, mar′-), *n.* a member of a Roman Catholic religious order founded in Lyons, France, in 1816 for missionary and educational work in the name of the Virgin Mary.

mar•i•tal (mar′i tl), *adj.* **1.** of or pertaining to marriage: *marital vows.* **2.** of or pertaining to a husband. —**mar′i•tal•ly,** *adv.*

mar•i•time (mar′i tīm′), *adj.* **1.** pertaining to navigation or shipping on the sea. **2.** of or pertaining to the sea: *maritime weather.* **3.** bordering on the sea: *a maritime state.* **4.** living near or in the sea: *maritime plants.* **5.** characteristic of sailors; nautical.

mar•jo•ram (mär′jər əm), *n.* any of several aromatic herbs of the mint family, esp. *Origanum majorana* **(sweet marjoram),** having leaves used as a seasoning.

mark[1] (märk), *n.* **1.** a visible impression on a surface, as a line, spot, scratch, dent, or stain. **2.** a symbol used in writing or printing: *a punctuation mark.* **3.** a token or indication; sign: *to bow as a mark of respect.* **4.** a noticeable or lasting effect; imprint: *The experience had left its mark on her.* **5.** a distinctive or characteristic trait: *a mark of nobility.* **6.** a device or symbol serving to identify, indicate origin or ownership, etc. **7.** TRADEMARK. **8.** a sign, usu. a cross, made instead of a signature. **9. a.** a symbol used in rating a student's achievement; grade. **b.** Often, **marks.** any evaluative rating: *gave him high marks for trying.* **10.** an object or sign serving to indicate position. **11.** a point reached, as on a scale or in a process: *the halfway mark.* **12.** a recognized or required standard of merit: *work that's not up to the mark.* **13.** a target; goal: *to miss the mark.* **14.** distinction; note: *a man of mark.* **15. a.** an object of derision or abuse: *an easy mark for bullies.* **b.** the victim of a swindle. **16.** (*cap.*) (used with a numeral to designate a model of an item of manufacture, as a weapon or car.) **17.** the starting line in a race. **18.** any of the points marked at intervals on a sounding line to indicate depth. **19.** a tract of land held in common by a medieval Germanic community. —*v.t.* **20.** to be a distinguishing feature of: *a day marked by sadness.* **21.** to put a mark or marks on. **22.** to evaluate with an academic mark; grade: *to mark exams.* **23.** to label with indications of price or quality: *to mark merchandise.* **24.** to trace or form by or as if by marks: *to mark out a plan of attack.* **25.** to designate by or as if by marks: *to mark passages to be memorized.* **26.** to single out; destine: *marked for greatness.* **27.** to record, as a score. **28.** to make manifest: *to mark approval with a nod.* **29.** to give heed to: *Mark my words.* **30.** to observe: *marked a change in the weather.* **31.** to deposit a scent mark on. —*v.i.* **32.** to take notice; give attention; consider. **33.** to make a mark or marks. **34. mark down, a.** to reduce the price of. **b.** to note in writing. **35. mark off,** to mark the dimensions or boundaries of. **36. mark up, a.** to mar or deface with marks. **b.** to mark with notations or symbols. **c.** to raise the price of. —***Idiom.*** **37. beside the mark,** not pertinent; irrelevant. **38. make one's mark,** to achieve success. **39. mark time, a.** to function in an unproductive way. **b.** to move the feet alternately as if marching but without advancing. **40. wide of the mark,** far from the target or objective.

mark[2] (märk), *n.* **1.** the basic monetary unit of Germany. **2.** a former European unit of weight, esp. for gold and silver, generally equal to 8 ounces (249 grams).

Mark (märk), *n.* **1.** one of the four Evangelists: traditionally believed to be the author of the second Gospel. **2.** the second Gospel. **3. King,** a king of Cornwall in Arthurian legend: the husband of Iseult and uncle of Tristram.

Mark An•to•ny (märk an′tə nē), *n.* ANTONY, Mark.

mark•down (märk′doun′), *n.* **1.** a reduction in the price of an item. **2.** the amount by which a price is reduced.

marked (märkt), *adj.* **1.** striking; conspicuous: *marked success.* **2.** watched as an object of suspicion or vengeance: *a marked man.* **3.** having a mark or marks: *strikingly marked birds.* **4.** (of a linguistic form) **a.** characterized by the presence of a distinctive feature, grammatical marker, or element of meaning not present in a similar or related item: The word *drake,* which specifies "male," is marked, in contrast to *duck,* which does not specify sex. **b.** occurring less typically than an alternative form. —**mark′ed•ly,** *adv.* —**mark′ed•ness,** *n.*

mark•er (mär′kər), *n.* **1.** a person or thing that marks. **2.** something used to mark location. **3.** a counter used in card playing. **4.** something, as a scent, that establishes territorial possession. **5.** a linguistic element, as an affix or word, that indicates the category or function of the form it accompanies: *the plural marker* -s.

mar•ket (mär′kit), *n.* **1.** an open place or a building where buyers and sellers convene for the sale of goods. **2.** a store for the sale of food. **3.** a meeting of people for buying and selling. **4.** the people assembled. **5.** trade in a particular commodity: *the cotton market.* **6.** demand for a commodity: *a dwindling market for leather goods.* **7.** the body of existing or potential buyers for specific goods or services: *the health-food market.* **8.** a region in which goods and services are bought or used: *the foreign market.* **9.** an economic situation in which supply and demand interact through the activity of buyers and sellers: *market forces; a market economy.* **10.** STOCK MARKET. —*v.i.* **11.** to deal commercially in a market. **12.** to buy provisions for the home. —*v.t.* **13.** to offer in a market for sale. **14.** to sell. —***Idiom.*** **15. in the market for,** interested in buying. **16. on the market,** for sale; available. —**mar′ket•a•ble,** *adj.* —**mar′ket•a•bil′ity, mar′ket•a•ble•ness,** *n.* —**mar′ket•er,** *n.*

mar•ket•eer (mär′ki tēr′), *n.* a person who sells goods or services in or to a market.

mar′ket gar′den, *n.* a garden or farm for growing vegetables for market. —**mar′ket gar′dener,** *n.* —**mar′ket gar′dening,** *n.*

mar•ket•ing (mär′ki ting), *n.* **1.** the act of buying or selling in a market. **2.** the activities, as advertising, packaging, and selling, involved in transferring goods from the producer to the consumer.

mar•ket•place (mär′kit plās′), *n.* **1.** an open area where a market is held. **2.** the world of business, trade, and economics. **3.** any sphere in which things, as ideas or artistic creations, compete for recognition.

mar′ket price′, *n.* the price at which a commodity, security, or service is selling in the open market.

mar′ket re′search, *n.* the gathering and studying of data relating to consumer preferences, purchasing power, etc., usu. done prior to marketing a new product.

mar′ket share′, *n.* the percentage of sales of a particular product achieved by a single company in a given period of time.

mar′ket val′ue, *n.* the value of a business, property, etc., in terms of what it can be sold for on the open market.

mark•ing (mär′king), *n.* **1.** a mark or marks. **2.** a pattern of marks or colorations, as on a plant or animal. **3.** the act of one that marks.

mark•ka (märk′kä), *n., pl.* **-kaa** (-kä). the basic monetary unit of Finland.

mark′ of the beast′, *n.* **1.** the mark put on the forehead of those who worship the beast, the symbol of opposition to God. **2.** the stain of apostasy, regarded as both indelible and inescapable. Rev. 13:16.

marks•man (märks′mən), *n., pl.* **-men.** a person who demonstrates skill in shooting at an object or target; a person who shoots well. —**marks′man•ship′,** *n.*

marks•wom•an (märks′wo͝om′ən), *n., pl.* **-wom•en.** a woman skilled in shooting at an object or target.

mark•up (märk′up′), *n.* **1.** an increase in the price of an item. **2. a.** the amount added to the cost of goods to fix a selling price. **b.** the difference between cost and selling price, usu. stated as a percentage. **3.** the putting of a legislative bill into final form. **4.** a set of instructions on a manuscript or tags in an electronic document to determine styles of type, makeup of pages, and the like.

marl (märl), *n.* **1.** a friable earthy deposit consisting of clay and calcium carbonate, used esp. as a fertilizer for soils deficient in lime. —*v.t.* **2.** to fertilize with marl. —**marl′y,** *adj.*

Marl•bor•ough (märl′bûr ō, -bur ō -brə, môl′-), *n.* **John Churchill, 1st Duke of,** CHURCHILL, John.

mar•lin (mär′lin), *n., pl.* (*esp. collectively*) **-lin,** (*esp. for kinds or species*) **-lins.** any large saltwater game fish of the genera *Makaira* and *Tetrapturus,* with a spearlike upper jaw.

Mar•lowe (mär′lō), *n.* **Christopher,** 1564–93, English dramatist.

mar•ma•lade (mär′mə lād′, mär′mə lād′), *n.* a jellylike preserve containing small pieces of citrus fruit and rind, as of oranges.

Mar•ma•ra (mär′mər ə), *n.* **Sea of,** a sea in NW Turkey connected with the Black Sea by the Bosporus, and with the Aegean by the Dardanelles. 4300 sq. mi. (11,135 sq. km).

mar•mo•re•al (mär môr′ē əl, -mōr′-) also **mar•mo′re•an,** *adj.* of or like marble. —**mar•mo′re•al•ly,** *adv.*

mar•mo•set (mär′mə zet′, -set′), *n.* any squirrel-sized South and Central American monkey of the family Callithricidae, having soft fur and a long nonprehensile tail.

mar•mot (mär′mət), *n.* any stocky burrowing rodent of the genus *Marmota,* as the woodchuck.

Marne (märn; *Fr.* MARN), *n.* a river in NE France, flowing W to the Seine near Paris: battles 1914, 1918, 1944. 325 mi. (525 km) long.

Mar•o•nite (mar′ə nīt′), *n.* a member of a body of Uniates living chiefly in Lebanon, who maintain a Syriac liturgy and a married clergy, and who are governed by the patriarch of Antioch.

ma·roon[1] (mə rōōn′), *n.* **1.** a dark brownish red color. —*adj.* **2.** of the color maroon.

ma·roon[2] (mə rōōn′), *v.t.* **1.** to put ashore and abandon on a desolate island or coast. **2.** to isolate without aid or resources. —*n.* **3.** (*often cap.*) a member of any of a number of black communities in the West Indies and Guiana formed by fugitive slaves in the 17th and 18th centuries. **4.** a person who is marooned.

mar·quee (mär kē′), *n.* **1.** a projecting structure over the entrance to a building, as a theater or hotel. **2.** a large outdoor tent for sheltering a party or reception.

mar·quess (mär′kwis), *n.* **1.** a British nobleman ranking below a duke and above an earl. **2.** MARQUIS. —**mar′quess·ate,** *n.*

mar·que·try or **mar·que·te·rie** (mär′ki trē), *n.* inlaid work of variously colored woods or other materials forming a picture or pattern, esp. in furniture.

Mar·quette (mär ket′), *n.* **Jacques** (*"Père Marquette"*), 1637–75, French Jesuit missionary and explorer in America.

mar·quis (mär′kwis, mär kē′), *n., pl.* **-quis·es, -quis** (-kēz′). a European nobleman ranking below a duke and above a count. —**mar′quis·ate** (-kwə zit), *n.*

mar·quise (mär kēz′), *n., pl.* **-quis·es. 1.** the wife or widow of a marquis. **2.** a woman holding a rank equal to that of a marquis. **3. a.** Also called **marquise′ cut′.** a gem cut, esp. for a diamond, yielding a low pointed oval usu. with 58 facets. Compare BRILLIANT CUT, EMERALD CUT. **b.** a gem cut in this style. **4.** MARQUEE.

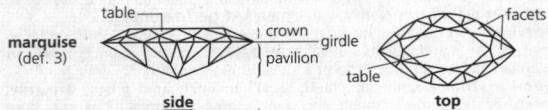

marquise (def. 3)

table — crown girdle — facets — pavilion — table

side   **top**

Mar·ra·no (mə rä′nō), *n., pl.* **-nos.** a Spanish or Portuguese Jew forced to convert to Christianity during the late Middle Ages. [< Spanish: lit., pig, from the Jewish law forbidding the eating of pork]

mar·riage (mar′ij), *n.* **1.** the social institution under which a man and woman live as husband and wife by legal or religious commitments. **2.** the state, condition, or relationship of being married. **3.** the legal or religious ceremony that formalizes marriage. **4.** an intimate living arrangement without legal sanction: *a trial marriage.* **5.** any intimate association or union. **6.** a blending of different elements or components. —**mar′riage·a·ble,** *adj.* —**mar′riage·a·bil′i·ty,** *n.*

mar′riage of conven′ience, *n.* a marriage entered into chiefly for social, political, or economic advantage, usu. without love.

mar·ried (mar′ēd), *adj.* **1.** united in marriage. **2.** of or pertaining to marriage or married persons. **3.** joined; united. —*n.* **4.** Usu., **marrieds.** married people.

mar·row (mar′ō), *n.* **1.** the soft fatty vascular tissue in the cavities of bones; a major site of blood cell production. **2.** the inmost or essential part. **3.** strength; vitality. —**mar′row·y,** *adj.*

mar′row squash′, *n.* any of several squashes having a smooth surface, oblong shape, and hard rind.

mar·ry (mar′ē), *v.,* **-ried, -ry·ing.** —*v.t.* **1.** to take as a husband or wife; take in marriage. **2.** to perform the marriage ceremony for; join in wedlock. **3.** to give in marriage; arrange the marriage of: *married off all their children.* **4.** to join or unite intimately. **5.** to gain through marriage: *to marry money.* —*v.i.* **6.** to take a husband or wife; wed. **7.** to unite closely or agreeably; blend: *This wine and cheese marry well.*

Mars (märz), *n.* **1.** the ancient Roman god of war and agriculture, identified with the Greek god Ares. **2.** the planet fourth in order from the sun, having a diameter of 4222 mi. (6794 km), a mean distance from the sun of 141.6 million mi. (227.9 million km), a period of revolution of 686.95 days, and two moons.

mar·seilles (mär sālz′), *n.* (*sometimes cap.*) a thick cotton fabric woven with an embossed effect.

Mar·seilles (mär sā′), *n.* a seaport in SE France, on the Gulf of Lions. 1,110,511. French, **Mar·seille** (mAR se′yə).

marsh (märsh), *n.* a tract of waterlogged soil, typically treeless and covered with emersed rushes, cattails, and other tall grasses. —**marsh′y,** *adj.,* **-i·er, -i·est.** —**marsh′i·ness,** *n.*

mar·shal (mär′shəl), *n., v.,* **-shaled, -shal·ing** or (*esp. Brit.*) **-shalled, -shal·ling.** —*n.* **1.** an administrative officer of a U.S. judicial district with duties similar to those of a sheriff. **2.** the chief of a police or fire department. **3.** a police officer. **4.** an official who leads special ceremonies, as a parade. **5.** an army officer of the highest rank, as in France. Compare FIELD MARSHAL. **6.** a high officer of a royal household or court. —*v.t.* **7.** to arrange in proper or effective order: *to marshal facts.* **8.** to array, as for battle. —**mar′shal·cy, mar′shal·ship′,** *n.* —**mar′shal·er;** *esp. Brit.,* **mar′shal·ler,** *n.*

Mar·shall (mär′shəl), *n.* **1. George C(atlett),** 1880–1959, U.S. general and statesman. **2. John,** 1755–1835, Chief Justice of the U.S. 1801–35. **3. Peter,** 1902–49, U.S. clergyman, chaplain of the Senate. **4. Thomas Riley,** 1854–1925, vice president of the U.S. 1913–21. **5. Thurgood,** 1908–93, associate justice of the U.S. Supreme Court 1967–91.

Mar′shall Is′lands, *n.pl.* a group of 34 atolls in the W central Pacific: formerly a part of the Trust Territory of the Pacific Islands; since 1986 a self-governing area associated with the U.S. 60,652; 70 sq. mi. (181 sq. km). —**Mar′shall·ese′** (-sha lēz′, -lēs′), *n., pl.* **-ese,** *adj.*

Mar′shall Plan′, *n.* EUROPEAN RECOVERY PROGRAM.

marsh′ el′der, *n.* any of various composite plants of the genus *Iva* that grow in salt marshes.

marsh′ gas′, *n.* a gaseous decomposition product of organic matter, consisting primarily of methane. Also called **swamp gas.**

marsh′ hawk′, *n.* a common harrier of North America, *Circus cyaneus hudsonius.*

marsh′ hen′, *n.* any of various rails or raillike birds.

marsh·land (märsh′land′), *n.* a habitat that is dominated by marshes, swamps, bogs, and the like.

marsh′ mal′low, *n.* an Old World mallow, *Althaea officinalis,* having pink flowers, found in marshy places.

marsh·mal·low (märsh′mel′ō, -mal′ō), *n.* **1.** a spongy confection of gelatin, sugar, corn syrup, and flavoring. **2.** a sweetened paste made from the root of the marsh mallow. —**marsh′mal′low·y,** *adj.*

marsh′ mar′igold, *n.* a yellow-flowered plant, *Caltha palustris,* of the buttercup family, growing in marshes and meadows; cowslip.

mar·su·pi·al (mär sōō′pē əl), *n.* **1.** any animal of the order Marsupialia, comprising mammals having no placenta and bearing immature young that complete their development in a pouch on the mother's abdomen: examples include opossums, kangaroos, phalangers, and dasyures. —*adj.* **2.** pertaining to, resembling, or having a marsupium. **3.** of or relating to marsupials. [< New Latin *marsupiālis* pertaining to a pouch]

marsu′pial mouse′, *n.* any of various mouse-sized carnivorous dasyurids, of Australia and neighboring islands.

mar·su·pi·um (mär sōō′pē əm), *n., pl.* **-pi·a** (-pē ə). the pouch or fold of skin on the abdomen of a female marsupial.

mart (märt), *n.* **1.** market; trading center. **2.** a building, center, or exposition for the sale of goods, as by wholesalers to retailers.

mar·ten (mär′tn), *n., pl.* **-tens,** (*esp. collectively*) **-ten. 1.** any of several mainly arboreal carnivores of the genus *Martes,* of the weasel family, inhabiting northern forests, prized for its soft, glossy fur. **2.** the fur of such an animal.

Mar·tha (mär′thə), *n.* the sister of Mary and Lazarus. Luke 10:38–42; John 11:1–44.

mar·tial (mär′shəl), *adj.* **1.** inclined or disposed to war; warlike. **2.** pertaining to or suitable for war or the armed forces: *martial music.* **3.** characteristic of or befitting a warrior: *a martial stride.* —**mar′tial·ism,** *n.* —**mar′tial·ist,** *n.* —**mar′tial·ly,** *adv.*

mar′tial art′, *n.* Usu., **martial arts.** any of the traditional forms of East Asian self-defense or combat utilizing physical skill and coordination, as karate or judo, often practiced as a sport. —**mar′tial art′ist,** *n.*

mar′tial law′, *n.* **1.** law temporarily imposed by state military forces, esp. when civil authority has broken down. **2.** law imposed in occupied territory by the military forces of the occupying power.

Mar·tian (mär′shən), *adj.* **1.** of, pertaining to, or like the planet Mars or its hypothetical inhabitants. —*n.* **2.** a supposed inhabitant of the planet Mars.

mar·tin (mär′tn), *n.* any of various swallows having a wedge-shaped or notched tail. [presumably generic use of the personal name traditionally by assoc. with March (Latin *Mārtius*), when the bird arrives, and Martinmas, when it leaves]

Mar·tin (mär′tn), *n.* **1. Civilla,** 1869–1948, U.S. hymn writer. **2. Homer Dodge,** 1836–97, U.S. painter. **3. Saint,** A.D. 316?–397, French prelate: bishop of Tours 370?–397. **4. W(alter) Stillman,** 1862–1935, U.S. clergyman and hymn writer (husband of Civilla Martin).

mar·ti·net (mär′tn et′, mär′tn et′), *n.* **1.** a strict disciplinarian, esp. a military one. **2.** someone who stubbornly adheres to methods or rules. —**mar′ti·net′ism,** *n.*

mar·tin·gale (mär′tn gāl′), *n.* **1.** part of the tack or harness of a horse, consisting of a strap that fastens to the girth, passes between the forelegs, and fastens to the noseband or reins: used to steady or hold down the horse's head. **2.** a stay for a jib boom or bowsprit. **3.** a system of gambling in which the stakes are doubled or otherwise raised after each loss.

mar·ti·ni (mär tē′nē), *n., pl.* **-nis.** a cocktail made with gin or vodka and dry vermouth.

Mar·ti·nique (mär′tn ēk′), *n.* an island in the E West Indies; an overseas department of France. 336,000; 425 sq. mi. (1100 sq. km). *Cap.:* Fort-de-France. —**Mar′ti·ni′can,** *adj., n.*

Mar′tin Lu′ther King′ Day′, *n.* the third Monday in January, a legal holiday in some states of the U.S., commemorating the birthday (Jan. 15) of Martin Luther King, Jr.

Mar·tin·mas (mär′tn məs), *n.* a church festival, November 11, in honor of St. Martin.

mar·tyr (mär′tər), *n.* **1.** a person who willingly suffers death rather than renounce his or her religion. **2.** a person who is put to death or suffers on behalf of a cause. **3.** a person who undergoes severe or constant suffering. —*v.t.* **4.** to make a martyr of, esp. by putting to death. **5.** to torment; torture. —**mar′tyr·dom,** *n.*

mar·vel (mär′vəl), *n., v.,* **-veled, -vel·ing** or (*esp. Brit.*) **-velled, -vel·ling.** —*n.* **1.** something that arouses wonder, admiration, or astonishment: *an engineering marvel.* **2.** a feeling of wonder. —*v.t.* **3.** to wonder at: *I marvel that you won.* —*v.i.* **4.** to be filled with wonder.

Mar•vell (mär′vəl), *n.* Andrew, 1621–78, English poet.

mar•vel•ous (mär′və ləs), *adj.* **1.** superbly fine: *a marvelous show.* **2.** tending to arouse wonder, admiration, or astonishment. **3.** preternatural. Also, *esp. Brit.,* **mar′vel•lous.** —**mar′vel•ous•ly,** *adv.*

Marx (märks), *n.* **Karl (Heinrich),** 1818–83, German economist, philosopher, and socialist.

Marx′ Broth′ers, *n.* a family of U.S. comedians, including **Julius Henry** (*"Groucho"*), 1890–1977, **Arthur** (*Adolph Marx*) (*"Harpo"*), 1888–1964, **Leonard** (*"Chico"*), 1887–1961, and **Herbert** (*"Zeppo"*), 1901–79.

Marx•ism (märk′siz əm) also **Marx•i•an•ism** (-sē ə niz′əm), *n.* the system of thought developed by Karl Marx and Friedrich Engels, esp. the doctrines that class struggle has been the main agency of historical change and that capitalism will inevitably be superseded by a socialist order and classless society. —**Marx′ist, Marx′i•an,** *n., adj.*

Mar•y¹ (mâr′ē), *n.* **1.** Also called **Virgin Mary.** the mother of Jesus. **2.** the sister of Lazarus and Martha. John 2. **3.** the mother of James. Mark 15:40. **4.** the wife of Clopas. John 19:25. **5.** **MARY, QUEEN OF SCOTS. 6.** (*Princess Victoria Mary of Teck*) 1867–1953, queen of England 1910–36 (wife of George V).

Mar•y² (mâr′ē), *n.* **1. Mary I,** (*Mary Tudor*) (*"Bloody Mary"*) 1516–58, queen of England 1553–58 (wife of Philip II of Spain; daughter of Henry VIII). **2. Mary II,** 1662–94, queen of England 1689–94: joint ruler with her husband William III (daughter of James II).

Mar•y•knoll (mâr′ē nōl′), *n.* a community of Roman Catholic priests (the **Mar′yknoll Fa′thers**) near Ossining, N.Y., founded in 1911, where foreign missionaries are trained.

Mar•y•land (mer′ə lənd), *n.* a state in the E United States, on the Atlantic coast. 5,071,604; 10,577 sq. mi. (27,395 sq. km). *Cap.*: Annapolis. *Abbr.*: MD, Md. —**Mar′y•land•er,** *n.*

Mar′y Mag′dalene, *n.* Mary of Magdala: traditionally identified with the repentant woman whom Jesus forgave. Luke 7:37–50.

Mar′y, Queen′ of Scots′, *n.* (*Mary Stuart*) 1542–87, queen of Scotland 1542–67.

mar•zi•pan (mär′zə pan′), *n.* a confection made of almond paste and sugar molded into various shapes.

Ma•sa•da (mə sä′də), *n.* an ancient fortress in Israel on the SW shore of the Dead Sea.

Ma•sai (mä sī′, mä′sī), *n., pl.* **-sais,** (*esp. collectively*) **-sai.** **1.** a member of a traditionally pastoral African people of the upland steppes of S Kenya and NE Tanzania. **2.** the Nilotic language of the Masai.

mas•car•a (ma skar′ə; *Brit.* -skär′ə), *n.* **1.** a cosmetic applied to lengthen or darken the eyelashes. —*v.t.* **2.** to apply mascara to.

mas•cot (mas′kot, -kət), *n.* an animal, person, or thing adopted by a group as its symbol and bringer of good luck.

mas•cu•line (mas′kyə lin), *adj.* **1.** pertaining to or characteristic of a man or men. **2.** having qualities traditionally ascribed to men, as strength and boldness. **3.** of, pertaining to, or being the grammatical gender that is among its members most nouns referring to males, as well as other nouns, as Spanish *dedo* "finger" or German *Bleistift* "pencil." **4.** (of a woman) mannish. —*n.* **5.** the masculine gender. **6.** a word or other form in or marking the masculine gender. —**mas′cu•line•ly,** *adv.* —**mas′cu•lin′i•ty, mas′cu•line•ness,** *n.*

ma•ser (mā′zər), *n.* a device for producing or amplifying electromagnetic waves by exciting atoms and causing them to radiate their energy in phase. Compare LASER.

Ma•se•ru (mä′sə rōō′, maz′ə rōō′), *n.* the capital of Lesotho, in the NW part. 109,382.

mash (mash), *v.t.* **1.** to reduce to a pulpy mass by beating or pressure: *to mash turnips.* **2.** to crush. **3.** to mix (crushed malt or meal of grain) with hot water to form wort. —*n.* **4.** a soft pulpy mass. **5.** a pulpy condition. **6.** a mixture of boiled grain, bran, meal, etc., fed to livestock. **7.** crushed malt or grain meal mixed with hot water to form wort.

MASH (mash), *n.* mobile army surgical hospital.

mash•er (mash′ər), *n.* a thing or person that mashes: *a potato masher.*

Mash•had (mash had′) also **Meshed,** *n.* a city in NE Iran: Muslim shrine. 1,463,508.

mask (mask, mäsk), *n.* **1.** a covering for all or part of the face, worn to conceal one's identity. **2.** a grotesque or humorous false face: *party masks.* **3.** anything that disguises or conceals: *His politeness is a mask for anger.* **4.** a covering, as of wire or gauze, worn over all or part of the face for protection, as from dust, a pitched ball, or the spread of infection. **5.** a device worn over the mouth and nose, as to facilitate breathing. **6.** a likeness of a face. **7.** a molded or carved covering for the face of an actor, representing the character portrayed, as in Greek drama. **8.** a protective shield, as of paper or plastic, used for covering an area of something, as of a photograph. **9.** a cosmetic preparation applied to the face to tighten, cleanse, or refresh the skin. **10.** an often grotesque representation of a face or head used as a decorative device. **11.** the dark shading on the muzzle of certain dogs. **12.** the face or head, as of a fox. **13.** a stencil applied to the surface of a semiconductor to permit selective etching or deposition. **14.** MASQUE. —*v.t.* **15.** to disguise; conceal: *to mask one's intentions.* **16.** to cover, conceal, or shield with a mask. **17.** to hinder, as an army, from conducting an operation. —*v.i.* **18.** to put on a mask; disguise oneself. —**mask′like′,** *adj.*

masked (maskt, mäskt), *adj.* **1.** using or wearing a mask. **2.** disguised; hidden: *masked treachery.* **3.** having facial markings that resemble a mask, as a raccoon.

masked′ ball′, *n.* a ball at which masks are worn.

mask′ing tape′, *n.* adhesive tape used esp. for protecting surfaces.

mas•och•ism (mas′ə kiz′əm, maz′-), *n.* **1.** the tendency to find pleasure in self-denial, submissiveness, etc. **2.** the act of turning one's destructive tendencies inward or upon oneself. —**mas′och•ist,** *n.* —**mas′och•is′tic,** *adj.* —**mas′och•is′ti•cal•ly,** *adv.*

ma•son (mā′sən), *n.* **1.** a person whose trade is building with firm units, as stones or bricks. **2.** a person who dresses stones or bricks. **3.** (*cap.*) FREEMASON. —*v.t.* **4.** to construct of or strengthen with masonry.

Ma•son (mā′sən), *n.* **1. George,** 1725–92, American statesman. **2. Lowell,** 1792–1872, U.S. musician and hymn writer.

ma′son bee′, *n.* any of numerous solitary bees, as of the family Megachilidae, that construct nests of clay.

Ma′son-Dix′on line′ or **Ma′son and Dix′on line′,** *n.* the boundary between Pennsylvania and Maryland surveyed (1763–67) by Charles Mason and Jeremiah Dixon, regarded as separating North from South.

Ma•son•ic (mə son′ik), *adj.* pertaining to or characteristic of Freemasons or Freemasonry. —**Ma•son′i•cal•ly,** *adv.*

ma•son•ry (mā′sən rē), *n., pl.* **-ries. 1.** work constructed by a mason, esp. stonework. **2.** the craft or occupation of a mason. **3.** (*cap.*) FREEMASONRY (def. 2).

ma′son wasp′, *n.* any of several solitary wasps, as *Rygchium dorsale,* that construct nests of mud or clay.

Ma•so•rah or **Ma•so•ra** (mə sôr′ə, -sōr′ə), *n.* a body of scribal notes that form a textual guide to the Hebrew Old Testament, compiled from the 7th to 10th centuries A.D. —**Mas•o•ret′ic** (mas′ə ret′ik), *adj.*

masque or **mask** (mask, mäsk), *n.* **1.** an elaborate court entertainment in England in the 16th and 17th centuries combining pantomime, dialogue, music, singing, dancing, and mechanical effects. **2.** a dramatic composition for such entertainment. **3.** MASKED BALL.

mas•quer•ade (mas′kə rād′), *n., v.,* **-ad•ed, -ad•ing.** —*n.* **1.** a festive gathering of people wearing masks and costumes. **2.** a costume worn at such a gathering. **3.** false outward show; pretense. —*v.i.* **4.** to represent oneself falsely. **5.** to disguise oneself. **6.** to take part in a masquerade. —**mas′quer•ad′er,** *n.*

mass¹ (mas), *n.* **1.** a body of coherent matter, usu. of indefinite shape: *a mass of dough.* **2.** a collection of incoherent particles, parts, or objects regarded as forming one body: *a mass of sand.* **3.** aggregate; whole: *People, in the mass, mean well.* **4.** a considerable number or quantity: *a mass of errors.* **5.** bulk; massiveness: *towers of great mass and strength.* **6.** the greater part of something: *the great mass of American films.* **7.** *Physics.* the quantity of matter as determined from its weight or from Newton's second law of motion. *Abbr.:* m **8. the masses,** the ordinary or common people as a whole. —*adj.* **9.** pertaining to, involving, or affecting a large number of people: *mass unemployment.* **10.** participated in or performed by a large number of people: *mass demonstrations.* **11.** involving or characteristic of the mass of the people: *a mass audience.* **12.** designed to reach a large number of people: *mass communications.* **13.** done on a large scale: *mass destruction.* —*v.i.* **14.** to come together in or form a mass: *clouds massing in the west.* —*v.t.* **15.** to assemble or distribute in a mass: *houses massed in blocks.*

mass² (mas), *n.* **1.** (*often cap.*) the liturgy of the Eucharist. Compare HIGH MASS, LOW MASS. **2.** (*often cap.*) the celebration of the Eucharist. **3.** a musical setting of the mass.

Mas•sa•chu•sett or **Mas•sa•chu•set** (mas′ə chōō′sit), *n., pl.* **-setts** or **-sets,** (*esp. collectively*) **-sett** or **-set. 1.** a member of an American Indian people of E Massachusetts. **2.** the extinct Eastern Algonquian language of the Massachusetts.

Mas•sa•chu•setts (mas′ə chōō′sits), *n.* a state in the NE United States, on the Atlantic coast. 6,092,352; 8257 sq. mi. (21,385 sq. km). *Cap.*: Boston. *Abbr.*: MA, Mass.

Mas′sachu′setts bal′lot, *n.* a ballot on which the candidates, with their party designations, are listed alphabetically in columns under the office for which they were nominated. Compare INDIANA BALLOT, OFFICE-BLOCK BALLOT.

Mas′sachu′setts Bay′ Com′pany, *n.* a company, chartered in England in 1629 to establish a colony on Massachusetts Bay, that founded Boston in 1630.

mas•sa•cre (mas′ə kər), *n., v.,* **-cred, -cring.** —*n.* **1.** the wanton killing of a large number of esp. unresisting human beings. **2.** a general slaughter of animals. **3.** the inflicting of great damage or defeat. —*v.t.* **4.** to kill in a massacre; slaughter. **5.** to injure thoroughly.

mas•sage (mə säzh′, -säj′; *esp. Brit.* mas′äzh), *n., v.,* **-saged, -sag•ing.** —*n.* **1.** the act or skill of treating the body by rubbing, kneading, patting, or the like, as to stimulate circulation or relieve tension. —*v.t.* **2.** to treat by massage. **3.** to cajole; flatter. **4.** to manipulate so as to produce a desired result: *to massage data.* —**mas•sag′er, mas•sag′ist,** *n.*

mas•sa•sau•ga (mas′ə sô′gə), *n., pl.* **-gas.** a small rattlesnake, *Sistrurus catenatus,* found from the Great Lakes to the Mexican border.

mass′-en′ergy equa′tion, *n.* the equation, $E = mc^2$, formulated by Albert Einstein, expressing the equivalence of mass and energy, where E is energy, m is mass, and c is the velocity of light.

mas•seur (mə sûr′, -sōōr′), *n.* a man who provides massage as a profession or occupation. [< French]

(M)

mas·seuse (mə sōōs′, -sōōz′, -sœz′), *n.* a woman who provides massage as a profession or occupation. [< French]

mas·sif (ma sēf′, mas′if), *n.* **1.** a compact portion of a mountain range, containing one or more summits. **2.** a band or zone of the earth's crust raised or depressed as a unit and bounded by faults.

mas·sive (mas′iv), *adj.* **1.** consisting of or forming a large mass; bulky and heavy: *massive columns.* **2.** imposingly large or prominent: *a massive forehead.* **3.** large in scale, amount, or degree: *a massive dose.* **4.** great in extent or profundity. **5.** having no outward crystal form although sometimes crystalline in internal structure. —**mas′sive·ly,** *adv.*

mass′ mar′keting, *n.* the production and distribution of a product intended to be sold to a relatively high proportion of the population. —**mass′-mar′ket,** *v.t.* —**mass′-mar′keter,** *n.*

mass′ me′dia, *n.pl.* the means of communication, as television and newspapers, used to reach great numbers of people.

mass′ noun′, *n.* a noun, as *water, electricity,* or *happiness,* that typically refers to an indefinitely divisible substance or an abstract notion and that in English cannot be used, in such a sense, with the indefinite article or in the plural. Compare COUNT NOUN.

mass′ num′ber, *n.* the number of nucleons in an atomic or isotopic nucleus. *Symbol:* A

mass′-produce′, *v.t.,* **-duced, -duc·ing.** to produce (goods) in large quantities, esp. by machinery. —**mass′-produc′er,** *n.* —**mass′-produc′ible,** *adj.* —**mass′ produc′tion,** *n.*

mass′ spectrom′eter, *n.* a device that uses deflection of ions in an electromagnetic field as a basis for identifying the kinds of particles present in a substance. —**mass′ spectrom′etry,** *n.*

mass′ trans′it, *n.* a large-scale public transportation system in a metropolitan area, usu. including buses, subways, and elevated trains.

mast (mast, mäst), *n.* **1.** a spar or structure rising above the hull and upper portions of a ship to hold sails, spars, rigging, etc. **2.** any upright pole, as a support for an aerial, a post in certain cranes, etc. —*v.t.* **3.** to provide with a mast. —*Idiom.* **4. before the mast,** as a seagoing sailor. —**mast′less,** *adj.* —**mast′like′,** *adj.*

mas·tec·to·my (ma stek′tə mē), *n., pl.* **-mies.** the surgical removal of all or part of the breast or mamma.

mas·ter (mas′tər, mä′stər), *n.* **1.** a person with the ability or power to control: *master of one's fate.* **2.** an owner of a slave or animal. **3.** an employer, esp. of servants. **4.** the male head of a household. **5.** a person preeminent in a discipline, as an art or science: *the great masters of modern art.* **6.** an esteemed religious leader: *a Zen master.* **7.** Chiefly *Brit.* a male teacher. **8.** a worker qualified to teach apprentices. **9.** a bridge or chess player who has won or placed in a designated number of tournaments. **10.** a person who commands a merchant ship. **11.** a victor; conqueror. **12.** an officer of the court who assists a judge by taking testimony and making a report to the court. **13.** a person who has been awarded a master's degree. **14.** a boy or young man (used chiefly as a term of address). **15.** an original document, drawing, manuscript, etc., from which copies are made. **16.** a tape or disk from which duplicates may be made. **17.** a device for controlling another device operating in a similar way. Compare SLAVE (def. 4). —*adj.* **18.** being master; exercising mastery; dominant. **19.** chief; principal: *a master list.* **20.** controlling others of its type: *master switch.* **21.** being a master from which copies can be made: *a master tape.* **22.** eminently skilled: *master designer.* **23.** to make oneself master of: *to master a language.* **24.** to conquer; overcome. **25.** to rule or direct as master. **26.** to produce a master tape, disk, or record of. —**mas′ter·less,** *adj.*

mas′ter bed′room, *n.* a principal bedroom in a dwelling.

mas·ter·ful (mas′tər fəl, mä′stər-), *adj.* **1.** having or showing the qualities of a master; authoritative. **2.** dominating; imperious. **3.** showing mastery; masterly. —**mas′ter·ful·ly,** *adv.* —**mas′ter·ful·ness,** *n.*

mas′ter key′, *n.* a key that will open a number of different locks, the proper keys of which are not interchangeable.

mas·ter·mind (mas′tər mīnd′, mä′stər-), *v.t.* **1.** to plan and direct skillfully. —*n.* **2.** a person who originates or is primarily responsible for the execution of a project.

Mas′ter of Arts′, *n.* **1.** a master's degree given in the humanities. **2.** a recipient of this degree. *Abbr.:* M.A., A.M.

Mas′ter of cer′emonies, *n.* a person who conducts events, as at a formal occasion or television broadcast, acting as host and introducing the speakers or performers. *Abbr.:* MC

Mas′ter of Sci′ence, *n.* **1.** a master's degree given in the sciences. **2.** a recipient of this degree. *Abbr.:* M.S., M.Sc., S.M., Sc.M.

mas·ter·piece (mas′tə rē pēs′, mä′stər-), *n.* **1.** a person's greatest piece of work, as in an art. **2.** a fine example of skill or excellence: *a masterpiece of improvisation.* **3.** a piece made by a person aspiring to the rank of master in a medieval guild.

mas′ter plan′, *n.* a general plan for achieving an objective.

mas′ter ser′geant, *n.* **1.** a noncommissioned officer in the army ranking above a sergeant first class. **2.** a noncommissioned officer in the air force ranking above a technical sergeant. **3.** a noncommissioned officer in the marines ranking above a gunnery sergeant.

mas·ter·stroke (mas′tər strōk′, mä′stər-), *n.* an extremely skillful or effective action.

mas·ter·y (mas′tə rē, mä′stə-), *n., pl.* **-ter·ies. 1.** command; grasp: *a mastery of Italian.* **2.** superiority; dominance: *mastery over one's enemies.* **3.** expert skill or knowledge. **4.** possession of skillful technique.

mast·head (mast′hed′, mäst′-), *n.* **1.** a box or column, usu. on the editorial page of a newspaper or magazine, giving the names of the owners, staff members, etc. **2.** NAMEPLATE (def. 2). **3. a.** the head of a mast. **b.** the uppermost point of a mast.

mas·tic (mas′tik), *n.* **1.** a small Mediterranean tree, *Pistacia lentiscus,* of the cashew family, that is the source of an aromatic resin used in making varnish and adhesives. **2.** resin obtained from the mastic or a related tree. **3. a.** any of various preparations containing bituminous materials and used as an adhesive or seal. **b.** a pasty form of cement used for filling holes in masonry or plaster.

mas·ti·cate (mas′ti kāt′), *v.,* **-cat·ed, -cat·ing.** —*v.t.* **1.** to chew (food). **2.** to reduce to a pulp by crushing or kneading. —*v.i.* **3.** to chew. —**mas′ti·ca·ble** (-kə bəl), *adj.* —**mas′ti·ca′tion,** *n.* —**mas′ti·ca′tor,** *n.* —**mas′ti·ca·to′ry** (-kə tôr′ē, -tōr′ē), *adj.*

mas·tiff (mas′tif, mä′stif), *n.* one of a breed of large, powerful short-haired dogs with a fawn, apricot, or brindled coat and dark muzzle.

mas·to·don (mas′tə don′), *n.* any of numerous extinct elephantlike mammals of the Oligocene through Pleistocene epochs, esp. of the genus *Mastodon* (formerly *Mammut*), distinguished from elephants by their tooth structure. Compare MAMMOTH (def. 1). —**mas′to·don′ic,** *adj.*

mastodon,
Mammut americanum,
7 to 9½ ft. (2.1 to 2.9 m)
high at shoulder

mas·toid (mas′toid), *adj.* **1.** of or pertaining to the mastoid process. **2.** resembling a breast or nipple. —*n.* **3.** the mastoid process.

mas′toid proc′ess, *n.* a large bony prominence on the base of the skull behind the ear containing air spaces that connect with the middle ear cavity.

mas·tur·ba·tion (mas′tər bā′shən), *n.* **1.** the stimulation or manipulation of one's own genitals, esp. to orgasm. **2.** the stimulation, by manual or other means exclusive of coitus, of another's genitals. —**mas′tur·bate′,** *v.i., v.t.,* **-bat·ed, -bat·ing.**

mat¹ (mat), *n., v.,* **mat·ted, mat·ting.** —*n.* **1.** a piece of fabric, as of plaited or woven fiber, used on a floor or other surface as a covering. **2.** a smaller piece of material set under an object, as a dish. **3.** a thick pad placed on a floor to protect wrestlers, tumblers, and gymnasts. **4.** a thick tangled mass, as of hair or weeds. —*v.t.* **5.** to cover with or as if with mats or matting. **6.** to form into a mat, as by interweaving. —*v.i.* **7.** to form tangled masses. —*Idiom.* **8. go to the mat,** to support or defend a person or cause with vigor and determination.

mat² (mat), *n., v.,* **mat·ted, mat·ting.** —*n.* **1.** material serving as a frame or border for a picture. —*v.t.* **2.** to provide (a picture) with a mat.

mat·a·dor (mat′ə dôr′), *n.* the bullfighter in a bullfight who traditionally kills the bull.

Ma·ta Ha·ri (mä′tə här′ē, mat′ə har′ē), *n.* (*Gertrud Margarete Zelle*) 1876–1917, Dutch dancer in France: executed as a spy by the French.

match¹ (mach), *n.* a slender piece of wood or other flammable material tipped with a chemical substance that produces fire when rubbed on a rough or chemically prepared surface.

match² (mach), *n.* **1.** a person or thing that equals or resembles another in some respect. **2.** a person or thing able to deal with another as an equal: *to meet one's match.* **3.** a person or thing that is an exact counterpart of another. **4.** a corresponding, suitably associated, or harmonious pair. **5. a.** a game or contest in which two or more contestants or teams oppose each other. **b.** a contest consisting of a specific number of sets: *a tennis match.* **6.** any contest or competition that resembles a sports match: *a shouting match.* **7.** a person considered with regard to suitability as a partner in marriage: *a good match.* **8.** a matrimonial union; marriage. **9.** to equal: *to match his score.* **10.** to be the match or counterpart of: *The skirt matches the jacket perfectly.* **11.** to cause to correspond: *to match actions and beliefs.* **12.** to fit together. **13.** to place in opposition or conflict. **14.** to provide with an adversary or competitor of equal power: *The teams were well matched.* **15.** to encounter as an adversary with equal power. **16.** to prove a match for. **17.** to unite in marriage; procure a matrimonial alliance for. **18. a.** to toss (coins) into the air and then compare the matching or contrasting sides that land facing up. **b.** to match coins with. —*v.i.* **19.** to be equal or suitable. **20.** to correspond: *These gloves do not match.* —**match′a·ble,** *adj.* —**match′er,** *n.*

match·book (mach′bŏŏk′), *n.* a small folder into which matches are stapled or glued.

match·box (mach′boks′), *n.* a small box for matches.

match·less (mach′lis), *adj.* having no equal; peerless: *matchless courage.* —**match′less·ly,** *adv.* —**match′less·ness,** *n.*

match·mak·er (mach′mā′kər), *n.* **1.** a person who arranges marriages by introducing possible mates. **2.** a person who arranges potential alliances. —**match′make′,** *v.i.* —**match′mak′ing,** *n., adj.*

match′ play′, *n.* golf competition in which the score is reckoned by counting the holes won by each side. —**match′ play′er,** *n.*

match′ point′, *n.* **1.** (in tennis, squash, handball, etc.) a situation in which the next point scored could decide the winner of the match. **2.** the winning point itself.

match•stick (mach′stik′), *n.* **1.** a short piece of wood used in making matches. **2.** something suggesting a matchstick in thinness or fragility.

match′-up′ or **match′up′,** *n.* MATCH[2].

mate[1] (māt), *n., v.,* **mat•ed, mat•ing.** —*n.* **1.** a husband or wife; spouse. **2.** one member of a pair of mated animals. **3.** one of a pair: *a mate of a glove.* **4.** COUNTERPART. **5.** an associate or companion. **6. a.** FIRST MATE. **b.** an assistant to a warrant officer or other functionary on a ship. **7.** an aide, as to a skilled worker. —*v.t.* **8.** to join as mates. **9.** to bring (animals) together for breeding. **10.** to join or associate suitably; couple. **11.** to treat as comparable. —*v.i.* **12.** to become mated. **13.** to copulate. **14.** to marry. —**mate′less,** *adj.*

mate[2] (māt), *n., v.t.,* **mat•ed, mat•ing,** *interj.* CHECKMATE (defs. 1, 3, 5).

ma•té or **ma•te** (mä′tā, mat′ā, mä tā′), *n., pl.* **-tés** or **-tes. 1.** a South American holly tree, *Ilex paraguariensis.* **2.** the dried leaves of this tree. **3.** a tealike South American beverage made from these leaves. Also called **yerba maté.**

ma•ter•fa•mil•i•as (mā′tər fə mil′ē əs), *n.* the mother of a family.

ma•te•ri•al (mə tēr′ē əl), *n.* **1.** the substance of which something is made or composed. **2.** something that serves as crude or raw matter to be used or developed. **3.** a constituent element. **4.** a textile fabric. **5.** ideas or facts that can provide the basis for or be incorporated into some work: *to gather material for a book.* **6. materials,** the articles or apparatus needed to make or do something: *writing materials.* **7.** a person considered as suited to a particular sphere of activity: *college material.* —*adj.* **8.** formed or consisting of matter; physical; corporeal: *the material world.* **9.** relating to, concerned with, or involving matter: *material forces.* **10.** pertaining to the physical rather than the spiritual or intellectual aspect of things: *material comforts.* **11.** worldly; unspiritual. **12.** of substantial import; important: *to make a material difference.* **13.** pertinent; essential: *a material question.* **14.** likely to influence the determination of a case: *material evidence.* **15.** of or pertaining to matter as distinguished from form. —**ma•te′ri•al•ly,** *adv.*

ma•te•ri•al•ism (mə tēr′ē ə liz′əm), *n.* **1.** preoccupation with or emphasis on material objects, comforts, and considerations, as opposed to spiritual or intellectual values. **2.** the philosophical theory that regards matter and its motions as constituting the universe, and all phenomena, including those of mind, as due to material agencies. —**ma•te′ri•a•list,** *n., adj.* —**ma•te′ri•al•is′tic,** *adj.* —**ma•te′ri•al•is′ti•cal•ly,** *adv.*

ma•te•ri•al•ize (mə tēr′ē ə līz′), *v.,* **-ized, -iz•ing.** —*v.i.* **1.** to become realized: *Our plans never materialized.* **2.** to come into perceptible existence; appear. **3.** to assume material form. —*v.t.* **4.** to give material form to; realize. **5.** to invest with material attributes. **6.** to make physically perceptible. **7.** to cause to be materialistic. —**ma•te′ri•al•i•za′tion,** *n.*

ma•té•ri•el or **ma•te•ri•el** (mə tēr′ē el′), *n.* the aggregate of equipment and supplies used by an organization, as the military. Compare PERSONNEL.

ma•ter•nal (mə tûr′nl), *adj.* **1.** of, pertaining to, having the qualities of, or befitting a mother. **2.** related through a mother: *his maternal aunt.* **3.** derived or inherited from a mother. —**ma•ter′nal•ism,** *n.* —**ma•ter′nal•is′tic,** *adj.* —**ma•ter′nal•ly,** *adv.*

ma•ter•ni•ty (mə tûr′ni tē), *n.* **1.** the state of motherhood. **2.** motherly quality; motherliness. **3.** a section of a hospital devoted to the care of women at childbirth and of their newborn infants. —*adj.* **4.** applicable for mothers before, during, and after childbirth: *maternity leave.* **5.** suitable for wear by pregnant women: *maternity clothes.*

math (math), *n.* mathematics.

math•e•mat•i•cal (math′ə mat′i kəl) also **math′e•mat′ic,** *adj.* **1.** of, pertaining to, or of the nature of mathematics: *mathematical truth.* **2.** employed in the operations of mathematics: *mathematical instruments.* **3.** having the exactness, precision, or certainty of mathematics. —**math′e•mat′i•cal•ly,** *adv.*

math•e•ma•ti•cian (math′ə mə tish′ən), *n.* an expert or specialist in mathematics.

math•e•mat•ics (math′ə mat′iks), *n.* **1.** (*used with a sing. v.*) the systematic treatment of magnitude and relationships between figures, forms, and quantities expressed symbolically. **2.** (*used with a sing. or pl. v.*) mathematical procedures, operations, or properties.

Math•er (math′ər, math′-), *n.* **1. Cotton,** 1663–1728, American clergyman and author. **2.** his father, **Increase,** 1639–1723, American clergyman.

Ma•thi•as (mə thī′əs), *n.* **Robert Bruce** (*Bob*), born 1930, U.S. track-and-field athlete.

mat•in (mat′n), *n.* **1.** (*often cap.*) **matins,** (*used with a sing. v.*) **a.** the first of the seven canonical hours, beginning at midnight or daybreak, in conjunction with lauds. **b.** Also called **Morning Prayer.** the service of morning liturgical prayer in the Anglican communion. —*adj.* **2.** Also, **mat′in•al.** pertaining to the early morning or to matins. [< Old French *matin* < Latin *mātūtīnus* of the morning]

mat•i•née or **mat•i•nee** (mat′n ā′; *esp. Brit.* mat′n ā′), *n.* a dramatic or musical performance held in the daytime, usu. in the afternoon. [< French: morning]

matinée′ i′dol, *n.* a handsome male actor.

matri-, a combining form meaning "mother": *matrilineal.*

ma•tri•arch (mā′trē ärk′), *n.* **1.** the female head of a family or tribal line. **2.** a woman who is the founder or dominant member of a group. —**ma′tri•ar′chal, ma′tri•ar′chic,** *adj.* —**ma′tri•ar′chal•ism,** *n.*

ma•tri•ar•chy (mā′trē är′kē), *n., pl.* **-chies. 1.** a family, society, or state governed by women. **2.** a form of social organization in which the mother is head of the family and descent is reckoned in the female line.

ma•tri•ces (mā′tri sēz′, ma′tri-), *n.* a pl. of MATRIX.

mat•ri•cide (ma′tri sīd′, mā′-), *n.* **1.** the act of killing one's mother. **2.** a person who kills his or her mother. —**mat′ri•cid′al,** *adj.*

ma•tric•u•late (mə trik′yə lāt′), *v.,* **-lat•ed, -lat•ing.** —*v.t.* **1.** to enroll as a student in a college or university. —*v.i.* **2.** to become matriculated. —**ma•tric′u•lant,** *n.* —**ma•tric′u•la′tion,** *n.* —**ma•tric′u•la′tor,** *n.*

mat•ri•lin•e•al (ma′trə lin′ē əl, mā′-) also **mat′ri•lin′e•ar,** *adj.* tracing, signifying, or based upon descent through the female line. Compare PATRILINEAL. —**mat′ri•lin′e•al•ly, mat′ri•lin′e•ar•ly,** *adv.*

mat•ri•mo•ny (ma′trə mō′nē), *n., pl.* **-nies. 1.** the state of being married; marriage. **2.** the rite, ceremony, or sacrament of marriage. —**mat′ri•mo′ni•al,** *adj.* —**mat′ri•mo′ni•al•ly,** *adv.*

ma•trix (mā′triks, ma′-), *n., pl.* **ma•tri•ces** (mā′tri sēz′, ma′-), **ma•trix•es. 1.** something that constitutes the place or point from which something else originates. **2.** a formative tissue, as the epithelium from which nails grow. **3. a.** the intercellular substance of a tissue. **b.** GROUND SUBSTANCE (def. 1). **4.** the fine-grained portion of a rock in which coarser crystals or rock fragments are embedded. **5.** a crystalline phase in an alloy in which other phases are embedded. **6.** a mold for casting typefaces. **7.** (in a press or stamping machine) a multiple die or perforated block on which the material to be formed is placed. **8.** a rectangular array of numbers, algebraic symbols, or mathematical functions, esp. when such arrays are added and multiplied according to certain rules. **9.** a similar rectangular array consisting of rows and columns of numbers, symbols, etc., used in displaying statistical variables, linguistic features, or other data.

ma•tron (mā′trən), *n.* **1.** a married woman, esp. one who is mature and dignified. **2.** a woman who has charge of the domestic affairs of a hospital or other institution. **3.** a woman officer, as in a prison for women. —**ma′tron•hood′,** *n.* —**ma′tron•ly,** *adj.*

ma′tron of hon′or, *n.* a married woman acting as the principal attendant of the bride at a wedding. Compare MAID OF HONOR (def. 1).

Matt., Matthew.

Mat•ta•thi•as (mat′ə thī′əs), *n.* died 167? B.C., Jewish priest in Judea (father of Judas Maccabaeus).

matte or **mat** or **matt** (mat), *adj., n., v.,* **mat•ted** or **matt•ed, mat•ting** or **matt•ing.** —*adj.* **1.** having a dull or lusterless surface: *matte paint.* —*n.* **2.** a dull surface, as on metals, paint, paper, or glass. **3.** a tool for producing such a surface. **4.** an unfinished metallic product of the smelting of certain sulfide ores, as copper. —*v.t.* **5.** to finish with a matte surface.

mat•ter (mat′ər), *n.* **1.** the substance of which any physical object consists or is composed. **2.** physical or corporeal substance in general, whether solid, liquid, or gaseous, esp. as distinguished from incorporeal substance, as spirit or mind, or from qualities, actions, and the like. **3.** something that occupies space. **4.** a particular kind of substance: *coloring matter.* **5.** a situation; affair: *a trivial matter.* **6.** an amount or extent reckoned approximately: *a matter of 10 miles.* **7.** importance; significance: *decisions of little matter.* **8.** reason; cause: *a matter for complaint.* **9.** the substance of discourse or writing. **10.** something written or printed: *reading matter.* **11.** things sent by mail: *postal matter.* **12.** a substance discharged by a living body, esp. pus. **13.** that which relates to form as potentiality does to actuality. **14.** *Law.* statement or allegation. **15.** *Print.* **a.** material for work; copy. **b.** type set up. **16.** *Christian Science.* the concept of substance shaped by the limitations of the human mind. **17. a matter of life and death,** something of vital or crucial importance. —*v.i.* **18.** to be of importance; signify: *It matters to me.* **19.** to suppurate. —***Idiom.*** **20. as a matter of fact,** in reality; actually. **21. for that matter,** as far as that is concerned; as for that. **22. no matter, a.** regardless or irrespective of: *no matter how we try.* **b.** it is unimportant; it makes no difference: *No matter, this string will do as well as any other.* **23. to be the matter,** to be a source of concern; be amiss or awry: *What's the matter? Something's the matter.*

Mat•ter•horn (mat′ər hôrn′), *n.* a mountain on the border of Switzerland and Italy, in the Pennine Alps. 14,780 ft. (4505 m). French, **Mont Cervin.**

mat′ter of course′, *n.* something that follows logically or naturally.

mat′ter-of-fact′, *adj.* **1.** adhering strictly to fact. **2.** nonchalant. —**mat′ter-of-fact′ly,** *adv.* —**mat′ter-of-fact′ness,** *n.*

Mat•thew (math′yo͞o), *n.* **1.** one of the four Evangelists; one of the 12 apostles. **2.** the first Gospel.

Mat′thew's Bi′ble, *n.* a revision of Tyndale's version of the Bible, printed in Antwerp in 1537: basis of the Great Bible.

Mat•thi•as (mə thī′əs), *n.* a disciple chosen to take the place of Judas Iscariot as one of the apostles. Acts 1:23–26.

mat•ting[1] (mat′ing), *n.* **1.** MAT[1] (def. 1). **2.** material for mats. **3.** mats collectively.

mat•ting[2] (mat′ing), *n.* a dull, slightly roughened surface.

mat·tock (mat′ək), *n.* a digging tool shaped like a pickax with one end broad instead of pointed.

mat·tress (ma′tris), *n.* **1.** a large pad used as or on a bed and consisting of a cloth case filled with straw, cotton, foam rubber, or similar supporting material. **2.** AIR MATTRESS. **3.** a mat woven of brush, poles, or similar material, used to prevent erosion of dikes, jetties, etc. **4.** a layer of any material used to cushion or protect.

mat·u·ra·tion (mach′ə rā′shən), *n.* the act or process of maturing. —**mat′u·ra′tion·al,** *adj.*

ma·ture (mə tŏŏr′, -tyŏŏr′, -chŏŏr′, -chûr′), *adj.,* **-tur·er, -tur·est,** *v.,* **-tured, -tur·ing.** —*adj.* **1.** fully developed in body or mind. **2.** complete in natural growth or development: *mature plants.* **3. a.** ripe: *mature peaches.* **b.** fully aged: *mature wine.* **4.** expressive of maturity: *a mature appearance.* **5.** completed: *mature plans.* **6.** no longer developing or expanding: *mature technologies.* **7.** intended for adults: *mature movies.* **8.** composed of adults: *mature audiences.* **9.** payable; due: *a mature bond.* —*v.t.* **10.** to make ripe, as fruit. **11.** to bring to full development: *Experience has matured him.* —*v.i.* **12.** to become mature; ripen. **13.** to come to full development. **14.** to become due. —**ma·ture′ly,** *adv.* —**ma·tur′er,** *n.* —**ma·tu′ri·ty,** *n.*

mat·zo or **mat·zoh** (mät′sə), *n., pl.* **-zos** or **-zohs** (-səz), **-zoth, -zot, -zos** (-sōt, -sōs). unleavened bread in the form of large wafers, eaten by Jews during Passover.

mat′zo ball′, *n.* a dumpling made from matzo meal.

maud·lin (môd′lin), *adj.* **1.** embarrassingly sentimental: *a maudlin story about a lost dog.* **2.** mawkishly foolish from drink.

Maugham (môm), *n.* **W(illiam) Somerset,** 1874–1965, English writer.

maul (môl), *n.* **1.** a heavy hammer often with a wooden head used esp. for driving stakes or wedges. —*v.t.* **2.** to handle or use roughly; manhandle. **3.** to injure by rough treatment; bruise. —**maul′er,** *n.*

Maul·din (môl′dən), *n.* **William Henry (Bill),** born 1921, U.S. political cartoonist.

Mau·na Ke·a (mou′nə kā′ə, mô′nə kē′ə), *n.* a dormant volcano on the island of Hawaii. 13,784 ft. (4201 m).

mau·na lo·a (mou′nə lō′ə, mô′nə), *n., pl.* **mauna lo·as.** a vine, *Canavalia microcarpa,* of the legume family, naturalized in Hawaii, having pink or lavender flowers used in leis. [after MAUNA LOA]

Mau′na Lo′a (lō′ə), *n.* an active volcano on the island of Hawaii, in Hawaii Volcanoes National Park. 13,680 ft. (4170 m).

maun·der (môn′dər), *v.i.* to talk ramblingly or unintelligibly.

Maun′dy Thurs′day (môn′dē), *n.* the Thursday of Holy Week, commemorating Jesus' Last Supper.

Mau·re·ta·ni·a or **Mau·ri·ta·ni·a** (môr′i tā′nē ə), *n.* an ancient kingdom in NW Africa: it included the territory that is modern Morocco and part of Algeria. —**Mau′re·ta′ni·an,** *adj., n.*

Mau·ri·ta·ni·a (môr′i tā′nē ə), *n.* **1.** Official name, **Islamic Republic of Mauritania,** a republic in NW Africa: formerly a French colony; independent 1960. 2,411,317; 397,955 sq. mi. (1,030,700 sq. km). *Cap.:* Nouakchott. **2.** MAURETANIA. —**Mau′ri·ta′ni·an,** *adj., n.*

Mau·ri·tius (mô rish′əs, -rish′ē əs), *n.* **1.** an island in the Indian Ocean, E of Madagascar. 720 sq. mi. (1865 sq. km). **2.** a republic consisting of this and several other islands: a former British colony. 1,154,272; 788 sq. mi. (2040 sq. km). *Cap.:* Port Louis. —**Mau·ri′tian,** *adj., n.*

mau·so·le·um (mô′sə lē′əm, -zə-), *n., pl.* **-le·ums, -le·a** (-lē′ə). **1.** a stately tomb. **2.** a burial place for the remains of many individuals. **3.** a large oppressive building or room. —**mau′so·le′an,** *adj.*

mauve (mōv, môv), *n.* a pale bluish purple.

ma·ven or **ma·vin** (mā′vən), *n.* expert; connoisseur. [< Yiddish < Hebrew]

mav·er·ick (mav′ər ik, mav′rik), *n.* **1.** an unbranded animal, esp. a motherless calf. **2.** a person who takes an independent stand in a group.

mawk·ish (mô′kish), *adj.* **1.** sentimental; maudlin. **2.** mildly sickening in flavor. —**mawk′ish·ly,** *adv.* —**mawk′ish·ness,** *n.*

max (maks), *n. Slang.* **1.** maximum. —*Idiom.* **2. to the max,** to the greatest or furthest degree; totally.

max·i (mak′sē), *n., pl.* **max·is. 1.** MAXISKIRT. **2.** a garment having a maxiskirt, as a coat.

maxi-, a combining form with the meanings "very large in comparison with others of its kind" (*maxi-budget; maxi-taxi*); "of great scope or intensity" (*maxi-devaluation; maxi-service*); (of clothing) "long, nearly ankle-length" (*maxiskirt*).

max·il·la (mak sil′ə), *n., pl.* **max·il·lae** (mak sil′ē). **1.** an upper jaw or jawbone. **2.** one of the paired appendages immediately behind the mandibles of arthropods.

max·il·lar·y (mak′sə ler′ē, mak sil′ə rē), *adj., n., pl.* **-lar·ies.** —*adj.* **1.** of or pertaining to a maxilla. —*n.* **2.** one of a pair of bones constituting the upper jaw.

max·il·lo·fa·cial (mak sil′ō fā′shəl), *adj.* of, pertaining to, or affecting the jaws and the face.

max·im (mak′sim), *n.* **1.** an expression of a general truth or principle, esp. an aphoristic or sententious one. **2.** a principle or rule of conduct.

Max·im (mak′sim), *n.* **1. Hiram Percy,** 1869–1936, U.S. inventor. **2. Sir Hiram Stevens,** 1840–1916, English inventor, born in the U.S. **3.** his brother, **Hudson,** 1853–1927, U.S. inventor.

max·i·ma (mak′sə mə), *n.* a pl. of MAXIMUM.

max·i·mal (mak′sə məl), *adj.* of or being a maximum; greatest possible; highest. —**max′i·mal·ly,** *adv.*

max·i·mal·ist (mak′sə mə list), *n.* a person who favors a radical and immediate approach to the achievement of a set of goals or the completion of a program.

Max·i·mil·ian[1] (mak′sə mil′yən), *n.* 1832–67, archduke of Austria: emperor of Mexico 1864–67.

Max·i·mil·ian[2] (mak′sə mil′yən), *n.* **1. Maximilian I,** 1459–1519, emperor of the Holy Roman Empire 1493–1519. **2. Maximilian II,** 1527–76, emperor of the Holy Roman Empire 1564–76.

max·i·mize (mak′sə mīz′), *v.t.,* **-mized, -miz·ing. 1.** to increase to the greatest possible amount or degree: *to maximize profits.* **2.** to give the highest estimate to. **3.** to make fullest use of. —**max′i·mi·za′tion,** **max′i·miz′er,** *n.* —**max′i·miz′er,** *n.*

max·i·mum (mak′sə məm), *n., pl.* **-mums, -ma** (-mə), *adj.* —*n.* **1.** the highest amount, value, or degree attained or attainable. **2.** an upper limit allowed by law or regulation. **3. a.** the value of a mathematical function at a certain point in its domain, which is greater than or equal to the values at all other points in the immediate vicinity of the point. **b.** the point in the domain at which a maximum occurs. —*adj.* **4.** being the greatest or highest attainable or attained. —**max′i·mum·ly,** *adv.*

max·i·skirt (mak′sē skûrt′), *n.* a long skirt ending below the calf, usu. nearer the ankle.

max·well (maks′wel, -wəl), *n.* the centimeter-gram-second unit of magnetic flux, equal to the magnetic flux through one square centimeter normal to a magnetic field of one gauss. [after J. C. MAXWELL]

Max·well (maks′wel, -wəl), *n.* **James Clerk** (klärk), 1831–79, Scottish physicist.

may (mā), *auxiliary v., pres.* **may;** *past* **might;** *imperative, infinitive, and participles lacking.* **1.** (used to express possibility): *It may rain. You may have been right.* **2.** (used to express opportunity or permission): *You may enter.* **3.** (used to express contingency, esp. in clauses indicating condition, concession, purpose, result, etc.): *strange as it may seem; Let us concur so that we may live in peace.* **4.** (used to express wish or prayer): *Long may you live!*

May[1] (mā), *n., v.,* **Mayed, May·ing.** —*n.* **1.** the fifth month of the year, containing 31 days. **2.** (*often l.c.*) the early flourishing part of life; prime. **3.** the festive activities of May Day. —*v.i.* **4.** (*l.c.*) to gather flowers in May.

May[2] (mā), *n.* **Cape,** a cape at the SE tip of New Jersey, on Delaware Bay.

ma·ya (mä′yä, -yə), *n.* (in Vedantic philosophy) the illusion of the reality of sensory experience and of the experienced qualities and attributes of oneself. —**ma′yan,** *adj.*

Ma·ya (mä′yə), *n., pl.* **-yas,** (esp. collectively) **-ya. 1.** a member of any of a group of American Indian peoples of Mexico, Guatemala, Honduras, and Belize: builders of a major pre-Columbian civilization that flourished c300 B.C.–A.D. 900. **2.** a member of a modern American Indian people of southern Mexico, Guatemala, and parts of Honduras who are the descendants of this ancient civilization. **3.** any of the Mayan languages. —**Ma′yan,** *adj., n.*

may·be (mā′bē), *adv., n., pl.* **-bes.** —*adv.* **1.** perhaps; possibly: *Maybe I'll go too.* —*n.* **2.** a possibility or uncertainty.

May′ Day′, *n.* the first day of May variously celebrated with festivities and observances.

May·day (mā′dā′), *n.* an international radiotelephone distress call. [< French (*venez*) *m'aider* (come) help me!]

may·flow·er (mā′flou′ər), *n.* **1.** any of various plants that blossom in May, as the hepatica. **2.** (*cap., italics*) the ship on which the Pilgrims sailed from England to the New World in 1620.

May′flower com′pact, *n.* an agreement to establish a government, entered into by the Pilgrims on the *Mayflower* on November 11, 1620.

may·fly (mā′flī′), *n., pl.* **-flies.** any of numerous insects of the family Ephemeridae, with large transparent forewings and threadlike tails, living for a relatively long period as an aquatic nymph and only for two days or less as an adult.

may·hem (mā′hem, mā′əm), *n.* **1.** the crime of willfully inflicting an injury on another so as to cripple or mutilate. **2.** random or deliberate violence or damage. **3.** rowdy disorder.

may·n't (mā′ənt, mānt), contraction of *may not.*

may·o (mā′ō), *n.* mayonnaise. [by shortening; cf. -o]

May·o (mā′ō), *n.* **1. Charles Horace,** 1865–1939, and his brother **William James,** 1861–1939, U.S. surgeons. **2.** a county in NW Connaught province, in the NW Republic of Ireland. 115,016; 2084 sq. mi. (5400 sq. km).

may·on·naise (mā′ə nāz′, mā′ə nāz′), *n.* a thick dressing of egg yolks, vinegar or lemon juice, oil, and seasonings.

may·or (mā′ər, mâr), *n.* the chief executive official of a municipality. —**may′or·al,** *adj.*

may·or·al·ty (mā′ər əl tē, mâr′əl-), *n., pl.* **-ties.** the office or tenure of a mayor.

May·pole (mā′pōl′), *n.* (*often l.c.*) a pole, decorated with flowers and ribbons, around which people dance on May Day.

may·pop (mā′pop′), *n.* **1.** the edible fruit of a passion flower. **2.** PASSION FLOWER.

may·weed (mā′wēd′), *n.* a composite plant, *Anthemis cotula,* native to Europe and Asia but naturalized in North America, having rank-smelling foliage and flower heads with a yellow disk and white rays.

maze (māz), *n., v.,* **mazed, maz·ing.** —*n.* **1.** a confusing network of paths; labyrinth. **2.** an intricate system that daunts or perplexes. **3.** *Chiefly Dial.* a state of bewilderment. —*v.t.* **4.** *Chiefly Dial.* to daze; stupefy. —**mazed·ly** (māzd′lē, mā′zid-), *adv.* —**maze′like′,** *adj.*

ma·zel tov (mä′zəl tôv′, tôf′, tōv′), *interj.* (used to express congratulations.) [< Hebrew *mazzāl tōbh* good luck]

ma·zur·ka (mə zûr′kə, -zŏŏr′-), *n., pl.* **-kas. 1.** a lively Polish dance in quick triple meter. **2.** music for or in the rhythm of this dance.

maz·zard (maz′ərd), *n.* a wild sweet cherry, *Prunus avium,* used as a rootstock for cultivated varieties of cherries.

MB, 1. Manitoba, Canada. **2.** *Computers.* megabyte; megabytes.

Mb, *Computers.* megabit; megabits.

mb, *Physics.* **1.** millibar; millibars. **2.** millibarn; millibarns.

MBA or **M.B.A.,** Master of Business Administration.

Mba·bane (bä bän′, -bä′nē, əm bä-), *n.* the capital of Swaziland, in the NW part. 38,290.

mba·qan·ga (bä käng′gə, əm bä-), *n.* a rhythmic style of South African popular music derived from Zulu music, jazz, and rock and played on electric guitar, bass, and drums.

M.B.E., Member of the Order of the British Empire.

MC, 1. Marine Corps. **2.** master of ceremonies. **3.** Medical Corps. **4.** Member of Congress.

Mc·Al·len (mə kal′ən), *n.* a city in S Texas, on the Rio Grande. 87,270.

Mc·Bain (mək bān′), *n.* **Ed** (*Evan Hunter*), born 1926, U.S. mystery writer.

Mc·Car′ran-Wal′ter Act′ (mə kar′ən wôl′tər), *n.* the Immigration and Nationality Act enacted by the U.S. Congress in 1952 that removed racial barriers to immigration and empowered the Department of Justice to deport immigrants or naturalized citizens engaging in subversive activities.

Mc·Car·thy (mə kär′thē), *n.* **1. Joseph R(aymond),** 1909–57, U.S. politician. **2. Mary (Therese),** 1912–89, U.S. novelist.

Mc·Car·thy·ism (mə kär′thē iz′əm), *n.* the use of unsubstantiated accusations or unfair investigative techniques in an attempt to expose disloyalty or subversion. [after J. R. McCARTHY] —**Mc·Car′thy·ite′,** *n.*

Mc·Clel·lan (mə klel′ən), *n.* **George Brinton,** 1826–85, Union general in the American Civil War.

Mc·Cor·mack (mə kôr′mik), *n.* **1. John,** 1884–1945, U.S. tenor, born in Ireland. **2. John William,** 1891–1980, U.S. politician.

Mc·Cor·mick (mə kôr′mik), *n.* **Cyrus Hall,** 1809–84, U.S. inventor.

Mc·Coy (mə koi′), *n.* the genuine thing or person as promised, stated, or implied (usually prec. by *the* or *the real*): *Those other paintings are copies, but this one is the real McCoy.*

Mc·Cul·lers (mə kul′ərz), *n.* **Carson,** 1917–67, U.S. author.

Mc·Cul·loch v. Maryland (mə kul′ək, -əкн), *n.* a U.S. Supreme Court decision in 1819 that asserted the authority of the federal government over the states.

Mc·Guf·fey (mə guf′ē), *n.* **William Holmes,** 1800–73, U.S. educator.

Mc·In·tosh (mak′in tosh′), *n.* a variety of red eating apple. [after John McIntosh of Ontario, who first cultivated it (1796)]

McJob (mək job′), *n.* an unstimulating, low-wage job with few benefits, esp. in a service industry. [coined by Douglas Coupland (b. 1961) in the novel *Generation X*]

Mc·Kin·ley (mə kin′lē), *n.* **1. William,** 1843–1901, 25th president of the U.S. 1897–1901. **2.** Also called **Denali. Mount,** a mountain in central Alaska, in Denali National Park; highest peak in North America, 20,320 ft. (6194 m).

Mc·Pher·son (mək fûr′sən, -fēr′-), *n.* **Aimee Semple,** 1890–1944, U.S. evangelist, born in Canada.

MD, 1. Maryland. **2.** Doctor of Medicine. [< New Latin *Medicīnae Doctor*]

Md, *Chem. Symbol.* mendelevium.

Md., Maryland.

M.Div., Master in Divinity.

MDR, 1. minimum daily requirement. **2.** minimum dietary requirement.

mdse., merchandise.

me (mē), *pron.* **1.** the objective case of *I,* used as a direct or indirect object: *They asked me to the party. Give me your hand.* **2.** (used instead of the pronoun *I* in the predicate after the verb *to be*): *It's me.* **3.** (used instead of the pronoun *my* before a gerund or present participle): *Did you hear about me getting promoted?* —*adj.* **4.** of or involving an obsessive interest in one's own satisfaction: *the me decade.* —**Usage.** The traditional rule is that personal pronouns after the verb *be* take the nominative case (*I; she; he; we; they*). Some 400 years ago, ME and other objective pronouns (*him; her; us; them*) began to replace the subjective forms after *be.* Today, such constructions—*It's me. That's him. It must be them*—are almost universal in informal speech. In formal speech and in edited writing, however, the subjective forms are used: *It must be they. The figure at the window had been she, not her husband.* The objective forms have also replaced the subjective forms in speech in such constructions as *Me neither. Who, them?* and frequently in comparisons after *as* or *than: She's no faster than him at climbing.* Another traditional rule is that gerunds, being verb forms functioning as nouns, must be preceded by the possessive pronoun (*my; your; her; its; their;* etc.):

The landlord objected to my (not *me*) *having a dog.* In practice, however, both objective and possessive forms appear before gerunds, the possessive being more common in formal, edited writing, the objective more common in informal writing and speech. See also THAN.

ME, 1. Maine. **2.** Middle East.

Me., Maine.

me·a cul·pa (mē′ä kŏŏl′pä; *Eng.* mā′ə kul′pə), *Latin.* through my fault (used as an acknowledgment of personal error).

mead (mēd), *n.* an alcoholic drink of fermented honey and water.

Mead (mēd), *n.* **1. Margaret,** 1901–78, U.S. anthropologist. **2. Lake,** a lake in NW Arizona and SE Nevada, formed by Hoover Dam on the Colorado River. 227 sq. mi. (588 sq. km).

Meade (mēd), *n.* **George Gordon,** 1815–72, Union general in the American Civil War.

mead·ow (med′ō), *n.* **1.** a limited, relatively flat area of low vegetation dominated by grasses. **2.** a tract of grassland in an upland area near the timberline. —**mead′ow·less,** *adj.* —**mead′ow·y,** *adj.*

mead′ow beau′ty, *n.* any of several North American plants of the genus *Rhexia,* family Melastomataceae, with rose-pink flowers and large yellow stamens.

mead′ow fes′cue, *n.* a European fescue, *Festuca pratensis,* of the grass family, grown for pasture in North America.

mead′ow grass′, *n.* any grass of the genus *Poa,* esp. *P. pratensis,* the Kentucky bluegrass.

mead·ow·land (med′ō land′), *n.* land that is kept as meadow.

mead·ow·lark (med′ō lärk′), *n.* either of two grassland-dwelling North American songbirds of the genus *Sturnella,* of the oriole subfamily, having a brown-streaked back and a yellow breast.

mead′ow mouse′, *n.* any of numerous short-tailed rodents of the genus *Microtus* and allied genera, chiefly of fields and meadows.

mead′ow mush′room, *n.* an edible white mushroom of the genus *Agaricus,* esp. *A. campestris,* cultivated for commerce.

mead′ow rue′, *n.* any of several plants belonging to the genus *Thalictrum,* of the buttercup family.

mead′ow saf′fron, *n.* AUTUMN CROCUS.

mead·ow·sweet (med′ō swēt′), *n.* **1.** any plant of the genus *Spiraea,* of the rose family, esp. *S. latifolia,* having white or pink flowers. **2.** any plant of the closely related genus *Filipendula* (or *Ulmaria*).

mea·ger (mē′gər), *adj.* **1.** deficient in quantity or quality; scanty: *a meager salary; meager fare.* **2.** having little flesh; lean. Also, *esp. Brit.,* **mea′gre.** —**mea′ger·ly,** *adv.* —**mea′ger·ness,** *n.*

meal[1] (mēl), *n.* **1.** the food served and eaten at one time or occasion. **2.** one such regular time or occasion for eating. —**meal′less,** *adj.*

meal[2] (mēl), *n.* **1.** a coarse, unsifted powder ground from the edible seeds of any grain: *barley meal.* **2.** any ground or powdery substance, as of nuts or seeds.

meals′ on wheels′, *n.* (*sometimes cap.*) a program, usually one supported or subsidized by a charitable, social, or government agency, for delivering hot meals regularly to elderly, disabled, or convalescing persons who are housebound and cannot cook for themselves.

meal′ tick′et, *n.* **1.** a ticket that entitles the bearer to meals. **2.** someone or something necessary for one's livelihood: *Her voice was her meal ticket.*

meal·time (mēl′tīm′), *n.* the usual time for a meal.

meal·worm (mēl′wûrm′), *n.* the larva of any of several darkling beetles of the genus *Tenebrio,* that infests granaries and is used as food for birds and animals.

meal·y (mē′lē), *adj.,* **meal·i·er, meal·i·est. 1.** having the qualities of meal; powdery. **2.** of or containing meal. **3.** covered with or as if with meal or powder. **4.** flecked as if with meal; spotty. **5.** pale; sallow: *a mealy complexion.* **6.** mealy-mouthed. —**meal′i·ness,** *n.*

meal·y·bug (mē′lē bug′), *n.* any of several scalelike homopterous insects of the families Pseudococcidae and Eriococcidae that are covered with a powdery wax secretion and feed on plants.

meal′y-mouthed′ or **meal′y-mouthed′,** *adj.* avoiding the use of plain or honest language; deceitful.

mean[1] (mēn), *v.,* **meant, mean·ing.** —*v.t.* **1.** to have in mind as one's purpose or intention; intend. **2.** to intend for a particular destiny: *They were meant for each other.* **3.** to intend to express or indicate: *What do you mean by "perfect"?* **4.** to have as its sense or signification; signify. **5.** to bring, cause, or produce as a result: *Prosperity means peace.* **6.** to have the value of: *Money means everything to them.* —*v.i.* **7.** to have specified intentions: *We meant well.*

mean[2] (mēn), *adj.,* **-er, -est. 1.** uncharitable; malicious: *a mean remark.* **2.** small-minded; ignoble: *mean motives.* **3.** stingy; miserly. **4.** inferior in quality or character. **5.** low in status: *mean servants.* **6.** bad-tempered: *a mean old horse.* **7.** excellent; topnotch: *plays a mean game of tennis.* —**mean′ly,** *adv.* —**mean′ness,** *n.*

mean[3] (mēn), *n.* **1.** Usu., **means.** (*used with a sing. or pl. v.*) an agency, instrument, or method used to attain an end. **2. means, a.** available resources, esp. money. **b.** considerable financial resources: *a person of means.* **3.** something midway between two extremes. —*Idiom.* **4. by all means,** certainly: *Try it, by all means.* **5. by any means,** in any way; at all. **6. by means of,** by the agency of; through. **7. by no means,** not at all.

mean·ing (mē′ning), *n.* **1.** what is intended to be or actually is expressed or indicated; import: *the three meanings of a word.* **2.** the end,

purpose, or significance of something. —**mean′ing·ful,** *adj.* —**mean′-**
ing·ful·ly, *adv.* —**mean′ing·less,** *adj.* —**mean′ing·less·ly,** *adv.*

mean′ so′lar day′, *n.* DAY (def. 3a).

mean·spir·it·ed (mēn′spir′i tid), *adj.* petty; small-minded; ungenerous. —**mean′spir′it·ed·ly,** *adv.* —**mean′spir′it·ed·ness,** *n.*

mean′ square′, *n.* the mean of the squares of a set of numbers.

means′ test′, *n.* an investigation into the finances of a person applying for public assistance.

means′-test′, *v.t.* **1.** to subject (a person or a specific benefit) to a
means test: *Government proposes to means-test Medicare.* —*v.i.* **2.** to
perform a means test: *fair and responsible means-testing.*

mean′ sun′, *n.* an imaginary sun moving uniformly in the celestial
equator and taking the same time to make its annual circuit as the true
sun does in the ecliptic.

meant (ment), *v.* pt. and pp. of MEAN[1].

mean·time (mēn′tīm′), *n.* **1.** the intervening time. —*adv.* **2.** MEAN-
WHILE.

mean·while (mēn′hwīl′, -wīl′), *n.* **1.** MEANTIME. —*adv.* **2.** in the intervening time; during the interval. **3.** at the same time.

Mean·y (mē′nē), *n.* **George,** 1894–1980, U.S. labor leader.

mea·sles (mē′zəlz), *n.* (*used with a sing. or pl. v.*) **1.** an acute infectious disease caused by a paramyxovirus, characterized by small red
spots, fever, and coldlike symptoms, usu. occurring in childhood; rube-
ola. **2.** any of certain other eruptive diseases, esp. rubella.

mea·sly (mē′zlē), *adj.,* **-sli·er, -sli·est. 1.** contemptibly small: *a measly
salary.* **2.** infected with measles.

meas·ure (mezh′ər), *n., v.,* **-ured, -ur·ing.** —*n.* **1.** a unit or standard
of measurement. **2.** a system of measurement. **3.** an instrument, as a
graduated rod or a container of standard capacity, for measuring. **4.** the
extent, dimensions, quantity, etc., of something, ascertained esp. by
comparison with a standard. **5.** the act or process of ascertaining the
extent, dimensions, or quantity of something; measurement. **6.** a definite or known quantity measured out: *a measure of wine.* **7.** any standard of comparison, estimation, or judgment. **8.** a quantity, degree, or
proportion. **9.** a moderate amount. **10.** reasonable bounds or limits:
spending without measure. **11.** a legislative bill or enactment. **12.** Usu.,
measures. actions or procedures intended as a means to an end:
measures to avert suspicion. **13.** a short rhythmical movement or arrangement, as in poetry or music. **14.** a particular kind of such arrangement. **15.** the music contained between two bar lines; bar. **16.** a metrical unit. **17.** an air or melody. **18.** a slow, dignified dance. **19.**
measures, *Geol.* beds; strata. —*v.t.* **20.** to ascertain the extent,
dimensions, quantity, capacity, etc., of, esp. by comparison with a
standard. **21.** to mark off or deal out by way of measurement (often fol.
by *off* or *out*): *to measure out a cup of flour.* **22.** to estimate the relative
amount, value, etc., of, by comparison with some standard. **23.** to
judge or appraise by comparison with something or someone else. **24.**
to serve as the measure of. **25.** to adjust or proportion. **26.** to travel
over; traverse. —*v.i.* **27.** to take measurements. **28.** to admit of measurement. **29.** to be of a specified measure. **30. measure up, a.** to attain
equality: *The exhibition didn't measure up to last year's.* **b.** to have the
right qualifications: *He didn't quite measure up.* —*Idiom.* **31. beyond**
or **above measure,** too great or too much to be reckoned. **32. for good**
measure, as an extra: *In addition to dessert, they served chocolates for
good measure.* **33. have** or **take someone's measure,** to assess someone's merit or worth. **34. in a** or **some measure,** to some extent.
—**meas′ur·a·ble,** *adj.* —**meas′ur·a·bil′i·ty, measurableness,** *n.*
—**meas′ur·a·bly,** *adv.* —**meas′ure·ment,** *n.* —**meas′ur·er,** *n.*

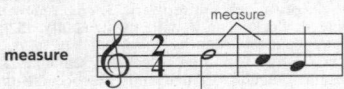

measure

meas·ured (mezh′ərd), *adj.* **1.** ascertained or apportioned by measure.
2. accurately regulated or proportioned. **3.** regular or uniform, as in
movement; rhythmical. **4.** deliberate and restrained: *measured terms.*
—**meas′ured·ly,** *adv.*

meas′ured response′, *n.* a restrained military response to an act of
aggression or confrontation.

meas·ure·less (mezh′ər lis), *adj.* too great to be measured; limitless.
—**meas′ure·less·ly,** *adv.* —**meas′ure·less·ness,** *n.*

meas′ur·ing·worm′ or **meas′uring worm′,** *n.* a geometrid moth
larva that progresses by bringing the rear end of the body forward and
then advancing the front end. Also called **inchworm.**

meat (mēt), *n.* **1.** the flesh of animals, used for food. **2.** the edible part
of anything, as a nut. **3.** the essential point or part; gist. **4.** substantial
content. —*Proverb.* **5.** One man's meat is another man's poison,
tastes differ. —**meat′less,** *adj.* —**meat′y,** *adj.,* **-i·er, -i·est.**

meat′ and pota′toes, *n. Informal.* the essential or basic part: *Community service is the meat and potatoes of this program.*

meat′-and-pota′toes, *adj. Informal.* fundamental; down-to-earth; basic: *What are the meat-and-potatoes issues of the election?* Also,
meat′-and-po·ta′to.

meat·ball (mēt′bôl′), *n.* **1.** a small ball of seasoned ground meat. **2.**
Slang. a clumsy or ineffectual person.

meat·head (mēt′hed′), *n. Slang.* BLOCKHEAD.

meat′ loaf′, *n.* a dish of ground meat baked in the shape of a loaf.

Mec·ca (mek′ə), *n.* **1.** a city in W Saudi Arabia: birthplace of Muhammad; spiritual center of Islam. 550,000. **2.** (*often l.c.*) a place that attracts many people with interests in common. —**Mec′can,** *adj., n.*

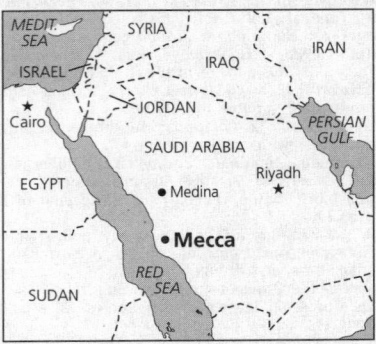

me·chan·ic (mə kan′ik), *n.* **1.** a person who repairs machinery. **2.** a
worker skilled in the use of tools and equipment.

me·chan·i·cal (mə kan′i kəl), *adj.* **1.** of or pertaining to machinery or
tools. **2.** operated by machinery. **3.** caused by or derived from machinery. **4.** using machine parts only. **5.** lacking spontaneity; routine. —**me·**
chan′i·cal·ly, *adv.* —**me·chan′i·cal·ness,** *n.*

mechan′ical draw′ing, *n.* drawing, as of machinery, done with the
aid of rulers, scales, compasses, etc.

mechan′ical engineer′ing, *n.* the branch of engineering dealing
with the design and production of machinery. —**mechan′ical engine-**
er′, *n.*

me·chan·ics (mə kan′iks), *n.* **1.** (*used with a sing. v.*) the branch of
physics that deals with the action of forces on bodies and with motion,
comprising kinetics, statics, and kinematics. **2.** (*used with a sing. v.*) the
theoretical and practical application of this science to machinery and
mechanical appliances. **3.** (*usu. with a pl. v.*) the technical aspect or
working part; mechanism; structure. **4.** (*usu. with a pl. v.*) routine or
basic methods, procedures, techniques, or details.

mech·a·nism (mek′ə niz′əm), *n.* **1.** an assembly of moving parts performing a complete functional motion. **2.** the agency or means by
which an effect is produced or a purpose is accomplished. **3.** machinery; mechanical appliances. **4.** the structure or arrangement of parts of
a machine or similar device. **5.** routine methods or procedures. **6.** the
theory that everything in the universe is produced by matter in motion.
Compare DYNAMISM (def. 1), VITALISM (def. 1). **7.** a mode of behavior that
helps an individual deal with the physical or psychological environment.
Compare DEFENSE MECHANISM, ESCAPE MECHANISM. —**mech′a·nis′mic,** *adj.*

mech·a·nis·tic (mek′ə nis′tik), *adj.* **1.** of or pertaining to the theory of
mechanism or to mechanists. **2.** of or pertaining to mechanics. —**mech′-**
a·nis′ti·cal·ly, *adv.*

mech·a·nize (mek′ə nīz′), *v.t.,* **-nized, -niz·ing. 1.** to make mechanical. **2.** to operate or perform by or as if by machinery. **3.** to introduce
machinery into, esp. in order to replace manual labor. **4.** to equip with
tanks and other armored vehicles. —**mech′a·ni·za′tion,** *n.*

med·al (med′l), *n.* **1.** a flat piece of metal, often a disk, bearing an inscription or design and issued as a token of commemoration or as a reward for bravery, merit, or the like. **2.** a similar object bearing a religious image, as of a saint.

Med′al for Mer′it, *n.* a medal awarded by the U.S. to a civilian for
distinguished service to the country: discontinued after World War II.

med·al·ist (med′l ist), *n.* **1.** a person to whom a medal has been
awarded. **2.** a designer, engraver, or maker of medals. Also, *esp. Brit.,*
med′al·list.

me·dal·lion (mə dal′yən), *n.* **1.** a large medal. **2.** something resembling a medal. **3.** a round or oval portion of food, as meat.

Med′al of Free′dom, *n.* an award by the president of the U.S. for
outstanding achievement: the highest civilian decoration.

Med′al of Hon′or, *n.* a Congressional award for exceptional gallantry
and bravery in combat: the highest U.S. military decoration.

med·dle (med′l), *v.i.,* **-dled, -dling.** to involve oneself in a matter
without invitation; interfere. —**med′dler,** *n.* —**med′dling·ly,** *adv.*

med·dle·some (med′l səm), *adj.* given to meddling; intrusive.
—**med′dle·some·ly,** *adv.* —**med′dle·some·ness,** *n.*

Mede (mēd), *n.* a member of an Iranian people of Media, united with
the Persians after c550 B.C.

med·e·vac (med′ə vak′), *adj.* of, pertaining to, or being aircraft for
evacuating wounded personnel from battle.

med·fly or **Med·fly** (med′flī′), *n., pl.* **-flies.** MEDITERRANEAN FRUIT FLY.

me·di·a (mē′dē ə), *n.* **1.** a pl. of MEDIUM. **2.** (*usu. with a pl. v.*) the
means of communication, as radio, television, newspapers, and magazines, with wide reach and influence. —*adj.* **3.** pertaining to or concerned with the media: *media research.* —**Usage.** MEDIA, like *data,* is

Originally introduced in France after the Revolution of 1789, the metric system has been modified somewhat as it has come into nearly universal acceptance. Although use of the metric system has been legal in the United States since 1966, the United States is the only industrialized nation that still prefers the customary English units, except in scientific and technical usage. Scientists the world over now use the standards codified in 1981 by the International Standardization Organization (ISO). The International System of Units are known as SI units, after Systéme Internationale, the French spelling.

SI BASE UNITS

Quantity	Unit	Symbol*
length	metre*	m
mass	kilogram	kg
time	second	s
electric current	ampere	A
thermodynamic temperature	kelvin	K
amount of substance	mole	mol
luminous intensity	candela	cd

SI SUPPLEMENTARY UNITS

plane angle	radian	rad
solid angle	steradian	sr

*metre and litre are spelled meter and liter in the U.S.

SI DECIMAL PREFIXES

SI units are decimal: they are derived from multiples of the number ten. By scientific convention, the following set of prefixes is used when referring to multiples or fractions, thus a kilogram would be 1000 grams; a millimeter would be 1/1000 of a meter; and a picofarad would be one trillionth of a farad.

Value and Equivalent	Unit	Symbol
$1\ 000\ 000\ 000\ 000\ 000\ 000 = 10^{18}$	exa-	E
$1\ 000\ 000\ 000\ 000\ 000 = 10^{15}$	peta-	P
$1\ 000\ 000\ 000\ 000 = 10^{12}$	tera-	T
$1\ 000\ 000\ 000 = 10^{9}$	giga-	G
$1\ 000\ 000 = 10^{6}$	mega-	M
$1\ 000 = 10^{3}$	kilo-	K
$100 = 10^{2}$	*hecto-	h
$10 = 10^{1}$	*deka- or deca-	da
$1 = 10^{0}$	(unprefixed)	–
$0.1 = 10^{-1}$	*deci-	d
$0.01 = 10^{-2}$	*centi-	c
$0.001 = 10^{-3}$	milli-	m
$0.000\ 001 = 10^{-6}$	micro-	μ
$0.000\ 000\ 001 = 10^{-9}$	nano-	n
$0.000\ 000\ 000\ 001 = 10^{-12}$	pico-	p
$0.000\ 000\ 000\ 000\ 001 = 10^{-15}$	femto-	f
$0.000\ 000\ 000\ 000\ 000\ 001 = 10^{-18}$	atto-	a

*to be avoided in technical use

METRIC AND U.S. EQUIVALENTS

LINEAR MEASURE

U.S. Customary	Metric
1 inch	25.4 millimeters (mm)
	2.54 centimeters (cm)
1 foot (12 in.)	304.8 millimeters (mm)
	30.48 centimeters (cm)
	0.3048 meter (m)
1 yard (36 in.; 3 ft.)	0.9144 meter (m)
1 rod (16.5 ft.; 5.5 yds.)	5.029 meters (m)
1 statute mile (5280 ft.; 1760 yds.)	1609.3 meters (m)
	1.6093 kilometers (km)

Metric U.S.	Customary
1 millimeter (mm)	0.03937 in.
1 centimeter (cm)	0.3937 in.
1 meter (m)	39.37 in.
	3.2808 ft.
	1.0936 yds.
1 kilometer (km)	3280.8 ft.
	1093.6 yds.
	0.62137 mi.

LIQUID MEASURE

U.S. Customary	Metric
1 fluid ounce (fl. oz.)	29.573 milliliters (ml)
1 pint (16 fl. oz.)	0.473 (liter) (l)
1 quart (2 pints; 32 fl. oz.)	9.4635 deciliters (dl)
	0.94635 liter (l)
1 gallon (4 quarts; 128 fl. oz.)	3.7854 liters (l)

Metric U.S.	Customary
1 milliliter (ml)	0.033814 fl. oz.
1 deciliter (dl)	3.3814 fl. oz.
1 liter (l)	33.814 fl. oz.
	1.0567 qts.
	0.26417 gal.

AREA MEASURE

U.S. Customary	Metric
square inch (0.007 sq. ft.)	6.452 square centimeters (cm²)
	645.16 square millimeters (mm²)
square foot (144 sq. in.)	929.03 square centimeters (cm²)
	0.092903 square meter (m²)
square yard (9 sq. ft.)	0.83613 square meter (m²)
square rod (30.25 sq. yd.)	
square mile (640 acres)	2.59 square kilometers (km²)

Metric U.S.	Customary
1 square millimeter (mm²)	0.00155 square inch (sq. in.)
1 square centimeter (cm²)	0.155 square inch (sq. in.)
1 centiare	10.764 square feet (sq. ft.)
1 square kilometer (km²)	0.38608 square mile (sq. mi.)

CAPACITY

U.S. Customary	Metric
cubic inch (0.00058 cu. ft.)	16.387 cubic centimeters (cc; cm³)
	0.016387 liter (l)
cubic foot (1728 cu. in.)	0.028317 cubic meter (m³)
cubic yard (27 cu. ft.)	0.76455 cubic meter (m³)
cubic mile (cu. mi.)	4.16818 cubic kilometers (k³)

Metric U.S.	Customary
1 cubic centimeter (cc; cm³)	0.061023 cubic inch (cu. in.)
1 cubic meter (m³)	35.135 cubic feet (1.3079 cu. yd.)
1 cubic kilometer (km³)	0.23990 cubic mile

AVOIRDUPOIS WEIGHTS

U.S. Customary	Metric
1 grain	0.064799 gram (g)
1 ounce (437.5 grains)	28.350 grams (g)
1 pound (16 oz.)	0.45359 kilograms (kg)
1 short ton (2000 lb.)	907.18 kilograms (kg)
	0.90718 metric ton
1 long ton (2240 lb.)	1016 kilograms (kg)
	1.016 metric tons

METRIC UNITS

EASY ESTIMATION GUIDE (rounded off for rule-of-thumb estimations).

Prefix Metric Unit			U.S. Equivalents		
milli- = 1/1000	1 millimeter =	0.039 inch			
centi- = 1/100	1 centimeter =	0.39 inch			
deci- = 1/10	1 decimeter =	3.937 inches =	0.32 foot		
	1 meter =	39.37 inches =	3.2 feet =	1.1 yard	
deka- = 10	1 dekameter =	393.7 inches =	32 feet =	10 yards	
hecto- = 100	1 hectometer =	3937 inches =	328 feet =	109 yards	
kilo- = 1000	1 kilometer =	39300 inches =	3280 feet =	1090 yards	

METRIC CONVERSION TABLES

Metric to U.S.			U.S. to Metric		
Length					
millimeters × 0.04 = inches			inches × 25.4 = millimeters		
centimeters × 0.39 = inches			inches × 2.54 = centimeters		
meters × 3.28 = feet			feet × .304 = meters		
meters × 1.09 = yards			yards × 0.91 = meters		
kilometers × 0.6 = miles			miles × 1.6 = kilometers		
Volume					
milliliters × 0.03 = fluid ounces			teaspoons × 5 = milliliters		
milliliters × 0.06 = cubic inches			tablespoons × 15 = milliliters		
liters × 2.1 = pints			cubic inches × 16 = milliliters		
liters × 1.06 = quarts			fluid ounces × 30 = milliliters		
liters × 0.26 = gallons			cups × 0.24 = liters		
cubic meters × 35.3 = cubic feet			pints × 0.47 = liters		
cubic meters × 1.3 = cubic yards			quarts × 0.95 = liters		
			gallons × 3.8 = liters		
			cubic feet × 0.03 = cubic meters		
			cubic yards × 0.76 = cubic meters		
Mass					
grams × 0.035 = ounces			ounces × 28 = grams		
kilograms × 2.2 = pounds			pounds × 0.45 = kilograms		
short tons × 0.9 = metric tons			metric tons × 1.1 = short tons		
Area					
Metric to U.S.					
square centimeters × 0.16 = square inches					
square meters × 1.2 = square yards					
square kilometers × 0.4 = square miles					
hectares (ha) × 2.5 = acres					
U.S. to Metric					
square inches × 6.5 = square centimeters					
square feet × 0.09 = square meters					
square yards × 0.8 = square meters					
square miles × 2.6 = square kilometers					
acres × 0.4 = hectares					
(the hectare is not an official SI unit, but is permitted)					
Temperature					
degrees Fahrenheit – 32 × 5/9 = degrees Celsius					
degrees Celsius × 9/5 + 32 = degrees Fahrenheit					

(M)

the plural form of a word borrowed directly from Latin. The singular, MEDIUM, early developed the meaning "an intervening agency, means, etc.," and was first applied to newspapers two centuries ago. In the 1920s MEDIA began to appear as a singular collective noun. This singular is now common in the fields of mass communication and advertising but is usu. not found outside them.

me′dia event′, *n.* an event staged or exploited for its news value.

me•di•al (mē′dē əl), *adj.* **1.** in or pertaining to the middle. **2.** pertaining to a mean; average. **3.** (of a sound or letter) occurring within a word, syllable, or other linguistic unit, as the sounds (i) and (t) in *city;* not initial or final. —*n.* **4.** a medial sound or letter. —**me′di•al•ly,** *adv.*

me•di•an (mē′dē ən), *adj.* **1.** pertaining to a plane that divides something into two equal parts, esp. one that divides an animal into right and left halves. **2.** situated in or pertaining to the middle; medial. —*n.* **3.** the middle number in a given sequence of numbers, or the average of the middle two numbers when the sequence has an even number of numbers: *4 is the median of 1, 3, 4, 8, 9.* **4.** a straight line from a vertex of a triangle to the midpoint of the opposite side. **5.** Also called **midpoint.** a vertical line that divides a histogram into two equal parts. **6.** Also called **me′dian strip′.** a paved or landscaped strip set in the middle of a highway to separate opposing lanes of traffic.

me•di•ate (mē′dē āt′), *v.*, **-at•ed, -at•ing.** —*v.t.* **1.** to settle (a dispute) as an intermediary. **2.** to bring about by serving as intermediary: *to mediate a settlement.* **3.** to convey by or as if by an intermediary. —*v.i.* **4.** to act between parties to effect an agreement. **5.** to reconcile disagreements. —**me′di•a′tion,** *n.* —**me′di•a′tor,** *n.*

med•ic (med′ik), *n.* **1.** a military medical corpsman. **2.** a doctor; intern.

Med•i•caid (med′i kād′), *n.* (*sometimes l.c.*) a federal and state program of medical insurance for persons with very low incomes.

med•i•cal (med′i kəl), *adj.* **1.** pertaining to the science or practice of medicine. **2.** curative; medicinal; *medical properties.* **3.** pertaining to or requiring treatment by other than surgical means. **4.** pertaining to or indicating the state of one's health: *a medical leave.* —**med′i•cal•ly,** *adv.*

med′ical exam′iner, *n.* a government official who performs postmortem examinations of bodies to determine the cause of death.

Med•i•care (med′i kâr′), *n.* (*sometimes l.c.*) a U.S. government program of medical insurance for aged or disabled persons.

med•i•cate (med′i kāt′), *v.t.*, **-cat•ed, -cat•ing.** **1.** to treat with medicine or medicaments. **2.** to impregnate with a medicine: *medicated cough drops.* —**med′i•ca′tion,** *n.*

Med•i•ci (med′i chē), *n.* **1. Catherine de′.** CATHERINE DE MÉDICIS. **2. Cosmo** or **Cosimo de′** (*"the Elder"*), 1389–1464, Italian banker and statesman. **3. Cosmo** or **Cosimo de′** (*"the Great"*), 1519–74, first grand duke of Tuscany. **4. Giovanni de′,** LEO X. **5. Giulio de′,** CLEMENT VII. **6. Lorenzo de′** (*"the Magnificent"*), 1449–92, ruler of Florence 1478–92. **7. Maria de′,** MARIE DE MÉDICIS. —**Med′i•ce′an** (-sē′ən, -chē′ən), *adj.*

me•dic•i•nal (mə dis′ə nl), *adj.* **1.** of, pertaining to, or having the properties of a medicine; curative; remedial. **2.** disagreeably suggestive of medicine: *a medicinal taste.* —**me•dic′i•nal•ly,** *adv.*

med•i•cine (med′ə sin; *esp. Brit.* med′sən), *n.*, *v.*, **-cined, -cin•ing.** —*n.* **1.** any substance used in treating disease or illness. **2.** the art, science, or profession of preserving health and of curing or alleviating disease. **3. a.** the art or science of treating disease by nonsurgical means. **b.** the branch of the medical profession concerned with this. **4.** (among North American Indians) any object or practice regarded as having magical powers. —*v.t.* **5.** to administer medicine to. —***Idiom.*** **6. take one's medicine,** to submit bravely or resignedly to punishment, esp. when deserved.

med′icine ball′, *n.* a solid, heavy, leather-covered ball tossed for exercise.

med′icine man′, *n.* a person believed to possess magical powers, esp. among North American Indians; shaman.

med′icine show′, *n.* a traveling troupe, esp. in the late 1800s, offering entertainment in order to attract customers for the patent medicines offered for sale.

me•di•e•val or **me•di•ae•val** (mē′dē ē′vəl, med′ē-, mid′ē-, mid ē′vəl), *adj.* of, pertaining to, or characteristic of the Middle Ages. —**me′di•e′val•ist,** *n.* —**me′di•e′val•ly,** *adv.*

med•i•gap (med′i gap′), *n.* (*sometimes cap.*) a supplemental health insurance that provides coverage for people whose government insurance benefits are insufficient.

Me•di•na (mə dē′nə), *n.* a city in W Saudi Arabia, where Muhammad was first accepted as the Prophet and where his tomb is located. 198,196.

me•di•o•cre (mē′dē ō′kər), *adj.* of only ordinary or moderate quality; barely adequate. —**me′di•oc′ri•ty** (-ok′ri tē), *n.*

med•i•tate (med′i tāt′), *v.*, **-tat•ed, -tat•ing.** —*v.i.* **1.** to engage in thought or contemplation; reflect. —*v.t.* **2.** to plan in the mind; intend: *to meditate revenge.* —**med′i•ta′tion,** *n.* —**med′i•ta′tor,** *n.*

med•i•ta•tive (med′i tā′tiv), *adj.* given to, characterized by, or indicative of meditation; contemplative. —**med′i•ta′tive•ly,** *adv.* —**med′i•ta′tive•ness,** *n.*

Med•i•ter•ra•ne•an (med′i tə rā′nē ən), *n.* **1.** MEDITERRANEAN SEA. **2.** a person whose physical characteristics are considered typical of the peoples native to the Mediterranean area. **3. the,** the islands and countries of the Mediterranean Sea collectively. —*adj.* **4.** pertaining to, situated on or near, or dwelling about the Mediterranean Sea. **5.** of or pertaining to the peoples native to the lands along or near the Mediterranean Sea. **6.** (*l.c.*) surrounded or nearly surrounded by land. [< Latin *mediterrāneus* midland, inland]

Med′iterra′nean fruit′ fly′, *n.* a small, black-and-white, two-winged fly, *Ceratitis capitata,* of many warm regions that implants eggs that hatch into maggots within ripening fruit. Also called **medfly, Medfly.**

Med′iterra′nean Sea′, *n.* a sea surrounded by Africa, Europe, and Asia. 2400 mi. (3865 km) long; 1,145,000 sq. mi. (2,965,550 sq. km). Also called **Mediterranean.**

me•di•um (mē′dē əm), *n.*, *pl.* **-di•a** (-dē ə) for 1–9, 12, **-di•ums** for 1–12, *adj.* —*n.* **1.** a middle state or condition; mean. **2.** something intermediate in nature or degree. **3.** an intervening substance, as air, through which a force acts or an effect is produced. **4.** the element that is the natural habitat of an organism. **5.** surrounding objects, conditions, or influences; environment. **6.** an intervening agency, means, or instrument by which something is conveyed or accomplished: *Words are a medium of expression.* **7.** one of the means or channels of general communication, information, or entertainment in society, as newspapers, radio, or television. **8.** the substance in which specimens are displayed or preserved. **9.** Also called **culture medium.** a nutrient material suitable for the cultivation of microorganisms, tissues, etc. **10.** a person through whom the spirits of the dead are alleged to be able to contact the living. **11. a.** a size, as of garments, to fit the average figure. **b.** an item in this size. **12.** the material or technique with which an artist works. —*adj.* **13.** about halfway between extremes in degree, quantity, position, or quality.

me′dium fre′quency, *n.* any radio frequency between 300 and 3000 kHz. *Abbr.:* MF

me′dium-sized′ or **me′dium-size′,** *adj.* neither very large nor very small.

med•lar (med′lər), *n.* a small tree, *Mespilus germanica,* of the rose family, the fruit of which resembles a crab apple and is not edible until the early stages of decay.

med•ley (med′lē), *n.*, *pl.* **-leys.** **1.** a mixture, esp. of heterogeneous elements; jumble. **2.** a piece of music combining passages from various sources. —*adj.* **3.** mixed; mingled.

med′ley re′lay, *n.* **1.** a track relay race in which individual members of a team usu. run unequal segments. **2.** a swimming relay race in which each member of a team uses a different stroke.

me•dul•la (mə dul′ə), *n.*, *pl.* **-dul•las, -dul•lae** (-dul′ē). **1. a.** bone marrow. **b.** the soft marrowlike center of an organ, as the kidney or adrenal gland. **c.** MEDULLA OBLONGATA. **2.** the pith of plants. —**med•ul•lar•y** (med′l er′ē, mej′ə ler′ē, mə dul′ə rē), *adj.*

medul′la ob•long•a′ta (ob′lông gä′tə, -long-), *n.*, *pl.* **medulla oblongatas.** the lowest or hindmost part of the vertebrate brain, continuous with the spinal cord.

me•du•sa (mə do͞o′sə, -zə, -dyo͞o′-), *n.*, *pl.* **-sas, -sae** (-sē, -zē). the free-swimming body form in the life cycle of a jellyfish or other coelenterate, usu. dome-shaped with tentacles. —**me•du′soid,** *adj.*

Me•du•sa (mə do͞o′sə, -zə, -dyo͞o′-), *n.* the only mortal of the three Gorgons: decapitated by Perseus.

meek (mēk), *adj.*, **-er, -est.** **1.** humbly patient or docile, as under provocation from others. **2.** overly submissive or compliant; spiritless; tame. —***Proverb.*** **3. The meek shall inherit the earth,** the humble shall be rewarded at the end. Matt. 5:5. —**meek′ly,** *adv.* —**meek′ness,** *n.*

meer•kat (mēr′kat), *n.* SURICATE.

meer•schaum (mēr′shəm, -shôm), *n.* **1.** a mineral, hydrous magnesium silicate, $H_4Mg_2Si_3O_{10}$, occurring in white, claylike masses, used esp. for pipe bowls. **2.** a tobacco pipe with a bowl made of meerschaum. [< German, = *Meer* sea + *Schaum* foam]

meet[1] (mēt), *v.*, **met, meet•ing,** *n.* —*v.t.* **1.** to come into the presence of; encounter: *I met him on the street yesterday.* **2.** to become acquainted with; be introduced to: *I've never met your cousin.* **3.** to join at an agreed or designated place or time: *Meet me at noon.* **4.** to be present at the arrival of: *to meet a train.* **5.** to come to the apprehension of: *A strange sight met my eyes.* **6.** to enter into dealings or conference with. **7.** to come into physical contact with: *The car met the bus head-on.* **8.** to encounter in opposition, conflict, or contest: *The rival teams meet each other next week.* **9.** to oppose: *to meet charges with countercharges.* **10.** to deal effectively with: *met the challenge.* **11.** to comply with: *to meet a deadline.* —*v.i.* **12.** to come together, face to face, or into company: *We met on the street.* **13.** to assemble for action or conference: *The directors will meet on Tuesday.* **14.** to become personally acquainted. **15.** to come into contact or form a junction: *The streets meet.* **16.** to concur; agree. **17.** to come together in opposition or conflict. **18. meet with,** to encounter; experience: *to meet with opposition.* —*n.* **19.** an assembly for athletic or sports competition, as for racing: *a track meet.* —**meet′er,** *n.*

meet[2] (mēt), *adj.* suitable; fitting; proper. —**meet′ly,** *adv.*

meet•ing (mē′ting), *n.* **1.** the act of coming together. **2.** an assembly or conference of persons. **3.** an assembly for religious worship, esp. by Quakers. **4.** a place or point of contact: *the meeting of two roads.* —***Idiom.*** **5. meeting of minds,** agreement; accord. **6. take a meeting,** to hold or participate in a meeting.

meet•ing•house (mē′ting hous′), *n.* a building for religious worship.

mega-, a combining form meaning "extremely large, huge," orig. a variant of MEGALO- (*megalith; megathere*), used also in the names of units of measure equal to one million of the units denoted by the base word (*megahertz; megaton*). By extension from the latter sense, **mega-** is now freely used to form words denoting very large quantities (*megabucks; megadose*), large things (*megastructure*) or, more generally, things that are extraordinary examples of their kind (*megahit; megatrend*). Abbr.: M Also, *esp. before a vowel,* **meg-.**

meg·a·bit (meg′ə bit′), *n.* **1.** 2^{20} (1,048,576) bits. **2.** (loosely) one million bits. *Abbr.:* Mb

meg·a·buck (meg′ə buk′), *n. Informal.* **1.** one million dollars. **2.** megabucks, very large sums of money.

meg·a·byte (meg′ə bīt′), *n.* **1.** 2^{20} (1,048,576) bytes. **2.** (loosely) one million bytes. *Abbr.:* MB

meg·a·cy·cle (meg′ə sī′kəl), *n.* MEGAHERTZ.

meg·a·deal (meg′ə dēl′), *n.* a large business transaction.

meg·a·death (meg′ə deth′), *n.* a unit of one million deaths used in predicting the fatalities in a nuclear war.

meg·a·dose (meg′ə dōs′), *n.* a very large dose, as of a vitamin.

meg·a·flops (meg′ə flops′), *n.* a measure of computer speed, equal to one million floating-point operations per second.

meg·a·hertz (meg′ə hûrts′), *n., pl.* **-hertz, -hertz·es.** a unit of frequency equal to one million cycles per second.

meg·a·hit (meg′ə hit′), *n.* an enterprise, as a movie, that is outstandingly successful.

meg·a·lith (meg′ə lith), *n.* a stone of great size, esp. in ancient constructions, as at Stonehenge. —**meg′a·lith′ic,** *adj.*

megalith

megalo-, a combining form meaning "very large" (*megalopolis*), "abnormally large" (*megaloblast*). Compare MEGA-.

meg·a·lo·ma·ni·a (meg′ə lō mā′nē ə), *n.* **1.** a highly exaggerated or delusional concept of one's own importance. **2.** an obsession with doing extravagant or grand things. —**meg′a·lo·ma′ni·ac,** *n.* —**meg′a·lo·ma·ni′a·cal** (-mə nī′kəl), **meg′a·lo·man′ic** (-man′ik), *adj.*

meg·a·lop·o·lis (meg′ə lop′ə lis) also **megapolis**, *n.* **1.** a very large city. **2.** an urban region, esp. of large adjoining cities and suburbs. —**meg′a·lo·pol′i·tan** (-lō pol′i tn), *adj., n.*

Meg′an's Law′ (mā′gənz), *n.* any of various laws aimed at people convicted of sex-related crimes that require community notification of the release of offenders, establishment of a registry of offenders, etc. [after *Megan* Kanka, young New Jersey girl killed by a previously convicted criminal]

meg·a·phone (meg′ə fōn′), *n., v.,* **-phoned, -phon·ing.** —*n.* **1.** a cone-shaped device for amplifying the voice. —*v.t.* **2.** to transmit through a megaphone.

meg·a·ton (meg′ə tun′), *n.* **1.** one million tons. **2.** an explosive force equal to that of one million tons of TNT. *Abbr.:* MT

meg·a·vi·ta·min (meg′ə vī′tə min; *Brit. also* -vit′ə-), *adj.* **1.** of, pertaining to, or using very large amounts of vitamins: *megavitamin therapy.* —*n.* **2.** megavitamins, doses of vitamins much larger than the recommended dietary allowances.

meg·a·watt (meg′ə wot′), *n.* a unit of power equal to one million watts. *Abbr.:* MW

Me·gid·do (mə gid′ō), *n.* an ancient city in N Israel, on the plain of Esdraelon: often identified with the Biblical Armageddon.

me·gil·lah or **me·gil·la** (mə gil′ə; *for 2 also Heb.* mə gē lä′), *n., pl.* **-gil·lahs** or **-gil·las,** *Heb.* **-gil·loth, -gil·lot** (-gē lôt′). **1.** *Slang.* **a.** a lengthy explanation or account. **b.** a lengthy and tediously complicated situation or matter. **2.** (*italics*) *Hebrew.* a scroll, esp. one containing the Book of Esther, that is read aloud in the synagogue on Purim.

me·grim (mē′grim), *n.* **1.** megrims, low spirits; blues. **2.** whim; caprice. **3.** MIGRAINE.

Mein Kampf (mīn kämpf′), the autobiography (1925–27) of Adolf Hitler, setting forth his political philosophy and his plan for German conquest.

mei·o·sis (mī ō′sis), *n.* **1.** part of the process of gamete formation in sexual reproduction consisting of chromosome conjugation and two cell divisions after which the chromosome number is reduced by half. Compare MITOSIS. **2.** expressive understatement, esp. litotes. —**mei·ot′ic** (mī ot′ik), *adj.*

Me·ir (mä ēr′, mī′ər), *n.* **Golda** (*Goldie Mabovitch, Goldie Myerson*), 1898–1978, prime minister of Israel 1969–74, born in Russia.

-meister, a combining form meaning "a person expert in or renowned for" something specified by the initial element (often used derisively): *schlockmeister; opinionmeister; dealmeister.* [< German *Meister* master]

mel·a·mine (mel′ə mēn′), *n.* **1.** a crystalline solid, $C_3H_6N_6$, used in organic synthesis and in manufacturing resins. **2.** any of the melamine resins.

mel·an·chol·y (mel′ən kol′ē), *n., pl.* **-chol·ies,** *adj.* —*n.* **1.** a gloomy state of mind; dejection. **2.** thoughtfulness; pensiveness. **3. a.** a condition of depression and irritability formerly attributed to an excess of black bile. **b.** BLACK BILE. —*adj.* **4.** affected with melancholy; depressed: *a melancholy mood.* **5.** causing melancholy: *a melancholy occasion.* **6.** pensive. —**mel′an·chol′ic,** *adj.* —**mel′an·chol′i·cal·ly,** *adv.*

Me·lanch·thon (mə langk′thən), *n.* **Philipp** (*Philipp Schwarzert*), 1497–1560, German Protestant reformer.

Mel·a·ne·sia (mel′ə nē′zhə, -shə), *n.* one of the three principal divisions of Oceania, comprising the island groups in the S Pacific NE of Australia. —**Mel′a·ne′sian,** *adj., n.*

mé·lange (mā länzh′, -länj′), *n., pl.* **-langes** (-länzh′, -län′jiz). mixture; medley.

mel·a·nin (mel′ə nin), *n.* any of a class of insoluble pigments that are found in all forms of animal life and account for the dark color of skin, hair, fur, scales, and feathers.

mel·a·no·ma (mel′ə nō′mə), *n., pl.* **-mas, -ma·ta** (-mə tə). any of several types of skin tumors characterized by the malignant growth of melanocytes.

mel·a·no·sis (mel′ə nō′sis), *n., pl.* **-ses** (-sēz). **1.** abnormal deposition or development of black or dark pigment in the tissues. **2.** a discoloration caused by this.

mel·a·to·nin (mel′ə tō′nin), *n.* a hormone secreted by the pineal gland in inverse proportion to the amount of light received by the retina, important in regulating biorhythms.

Mel·ba (mel′bə), *n.* **(Dame) Nellie** (*Helen Porter Mitchell Armstrong*), 1861–1931, Australian soprano.

Mel′ba toast′, *n.* narrow slices of thin crisp toast. [after N. MELBA]

Mel·bourne (mel′bərn), *n.* **1. 2nd Viscount,** LAMB, William. **2.** the capital of Victoria, in SE Australia. 2,942,000. **3.** a city on the E coast of Florida. 59,690.

Mel·chior (mel′kyôr, -kē ôr′), *n.* **1.** one of the three Magi. **2. Lauritz** (*Lebrecht Hommel*), 1890–1973, U.S. tenor, born in Denmark.

Mel·chite (mel′kīt), *n.* a Christian in Egypt or Syria who accepts the definition of faith adopted by the Council of Chalcedon in A.D. 451.

Mel·chiz·e·dek (mel kiz′i dek′), *n.* **1.** a priest and king of Salem. Gen. 14:18. **2.** the higher order of priests in the Mormon Church.

meld¹ (meld), *v.t.* **1.** to announce and display (a counting combination of playing cards) for a score. —*v.i.* **2.** to announce and display such a combination of cards. —*n.* **3.** the act of melding. **4.** any combination of cards to be melded.

meld² (meld), *v.t., v.i.* **1.** to merge; blend. —*n.* **2.** a blend.

me·lee or **mê·lée** (mā′lā, mā lā′, mel′ā), *n.* **1.** a confused hand-to-hand fight or struggle among several people. **2.** tumult; confusion.

me·lio·rate (mēl′yə rāt′, mē′lē ə-), *v.t., v.i.,* **-rat·ed, -rat·ing.** AMELIORATE. —**mel′io·ra·ble** (mēl′yər ə bəl, mē′lē ər ə-), *adj.* —**mel′io·ra′tive** (-yə rā′tiv, -yər ə tiv), *adj.* —**mel′io·ra′tor,** *n.*

mel·io·ra·tion (mēl′yə rā′shən, mē′lē ə-), *n.* **1.** semantic change in a word over the course of time to a more approved or respectable meaning. Compare PEJORATION (def. 2). **2.** amelioration.

mel·lif·er·ous (mə lif′ər əs), *adj.* yielding or producing honey.

mel·lif·lu·ent (mə lif′lōō ənt), *adj.* MELLIFLUOUS. —**mel·lif′lu·ence,** *n.* —**mel·lif′lu·ent·ly,** *adv.*

mel·lif·lu·ous (mə lif′lōō əs), *adj.* Also, **mellifluent,** *adj.* **1.** sweetly or smoothly flowing: *a mellifluous voice.* **2.** sweetened with or as if with honey. —**mel·lif′lu·ous·ly,** *adv.* —**mel·lif′lu·ous·ness,** *n.*

Mel·lon (mel′ən), *n.* **Andrew William,** 1855–1937, U.S. financier.

mel·low (mel′ō), *adj.,* **-low·er, -low·est,** *v.* —*adj.* **1.** sweet and full-flavored from ripeness, as fruit. **2.** soft and rich, as sound, lights, or colors. **3.** made gentle by age or maturity. **4.** friable or loamy, as soil. **5.** pleasantly intoxicated. **6.** free from tension or discord. —*v.t., v.i.* **7.** to make or become mellow. **8. mellow out,** *Slang.* to relax. —**mel′low·ly,** *adv.* —**mel′low·ness,** *n.*

me·lo·de·on (mə lō′dē ən), *n.* a small reed organ.

me·lo·di·ous (mə lō′dē əs), *adj.* **1.** of the nature of or characterized by melody; tuneful. **2.** producing melody; sweet-sounding; musical. —**me·lo′di·ous·ly,** *adv.* —**me·lo′di·ous·ness,** *n.*

mel·o·dra·ma (mel′ə dră′mə, -dram′ə), *n., pl.* **-mas.** **1.** a dramatic form that exaggerates emotion and emphasizes plot or action at the expense of characterization. **2.** melodramatic behavior or events. **3.** (in the 17th, 18th, and early 19th centuries) a romantic dramatic composition with music interspersed. —**mel′o·dra·mat′ic,** *adj.* —**mel′o·dra·mat′ics,** *n.* —**mel′o·dra·mat′i·cal·ly,** *adv.*

mel·o·dy (mel′ə dē), *n., pl.* **-dies.** **1.** musical sounds in agreeable succession or arrangement. **2.** a rhythmical succession of musical tones organized as a distinct phrase or sequence of phrases. —**me·lod·ic** (mə lod′ik), *adj.* —**me·lod′i·cal·ly,** *adv.*

mel·on (mel′ən), *n.* the fruit of any of various plants of the gourd family, as the muskmelon or watermelon.

melt (melt), *v.i.* **1.** to become liquefied by heat. **2.** to dissolve: *The lozenge will melt on your tongue.* **3.** to diminish to nothing: *His fortune slowly melted away.* **4.** to pass; blend: *Night melted into day.* **5.** to become softened in feeling. —*v.t.* **6.** to reduce to a liquid state by heat: *Fire melts ice.* **7.** to cause to dwindle or dissipate. **8.** to cause to change or blend gradually. **9.** to soften in feeling: *a story to melt your heart.* —*n.* **10.** the act or process of melting or the state of being melted. **11.** something that is melted. **12.** a sandwich or other dish topped with melted cheese. —**melt′a•ble,** *adj.* —**melt′a•bil′i•ty,** *n.* —**melt′ing•ly,** *adv.* —**melt′ing•ness,** *n.* —**melt′er,** *n.*

melt•down (melt′doun′), *n.* **1.** the melting of a significant portion of a nuclear-reactor core due to inadequate cooling of the fuel elements. **2.** any quickly developing breakdown, mishap, or accident.

melt′ing point′, *n.* the temperature at which a solid substance melts or fuses.

melt′ing pot′, *n.* **1.** a container in which metals or other substances are heated until they fuse. **2.** a country, locality, or situation in which a blending of races, peoples, or cultures takes place.

Mel•ville (mel′vil), *n.* **1. Andrew,** 1545–1622, Scottish theologian. **2. Herman,** 1819–91, U.S. novelist. **3. Lake,** a saltwater lake on the E coast of Labrador, Newfoundland, in E Canada. ab. 1133 sq. mi. (2935 sq. km). —**Mel•vil′le•an,** *adj., n.*

mem•ber (mem′bər), *n.* **1.** a person, animal, plant, or thing belonging to or forming part of an organization, taxon, or other group. **2.** a part or organ of an animal body; a limb, as a leg, arm, or wing. **3.** a structural entity of a plant body. **4.** a constituent part of any structural or composite whole, as a subordinate architectural feature of a building. **5.** a person belonging to a legislative body. **6.** *Math.* **a.** either side of an equation. **b.** an element of a set. **7.** a stratigraphic unit recognized within a geologic formation and mapped as such. —**mem′ber•less,** *adj.*

mem•ber•ship (mem′bər ship′), *n.* **1.** the state of being a member, as of a society. **2.** the status of a member. **3.** the total number of members belonging to an organization, society, etc.

mem•brane (mem′brān), *n.* **1.** a thin, pliable sheet or layer of animal or vegetable tissue, serving to line an organ, connect parts, etc. **2.** any thin, pliable material used as a filter, separator, resonator, etc. —**mem′bra•nous** (-brə nəs), *adj.*

me•men•to (mə men′tō), *n., pl.* **-tos, -toes. 1.** something that serves as a reminder of what is past or gone; keepsake; souvenir. **2.** anything serving as a reminder or warning. **3.** (*cap.*) either of two prayers in the canon of the Roman Catholic Mass, one for persons living and the other for persons dead.

mem•o (mem′ō), *n., pl.* **mem•os.** memorandum.

mem•oir (mem′wär, -wôr), *n.* **1.** a record of events based on the writer's personal observation. **2.** Usu., **memoirs. a.** an autobiography. **b.** the published proceedings of an organization, as of a learned society. **3.** a biography or biographical sketch.

mem•o•ra•bil•i•a (mem′ər ə bil′ē ə, -bil′yə), *n.pl.* **1.** mementos; souvenirs. **2.** matters or events worth remembering.

mem•o•ra•ble (mem′ər ə bəl), *adj.* **1.** worth remembering; notable: *a memorable speech.* **2.** easily remembered. —**mem′o•ra•bil′i•ty, mem′o•ra•ble•ness,** *n.* —**mem′o•ra•bly,** *adv.*

mem•o•ran•dum (mem′ə ran′dəm), *n., pl.* **-dums, -da** (-də). **1.** a short note designating something to be remembered. **2.** a record or written statement of something. **3.** a written message, esp. one sent between two or more employees of a company. **4.** *Law.* a writing, usu. informal, containing the terms of a transaction. **5.** (in diplomacy) a written summary of an issue, the reasons for a decision, etc. **6.** a document transferring title to goods but authorizing their return to the seller at the option of the buyer.

me•mo•ri•al (mə môr′ē əl, -mōr′-), *n.* **1.** something designed to preserve the memory of a person, event, etc., as a monument or a holiday. **2.** a written statement of facts presented to a governing body in the form of or along with a petition. —*adj.* **3.** serving to preserve the memory; commemorative: *memorial services.* **4.** of or pertaining to the memory. —**me•mo′ri•al•ize′,** *v.t.,* **-ized, -iz•ing.** —**me•mo′ri•al•ly,** *adv.*

Memo′rial Day′, *n.* **1.** Formerly, **Decoration Day.** the last Monday in May, a U.S. holiday in remembrance of members of the armed forces killed in war. **2.** Also called **Confederate Memorial Day.** any of several days similarly observed in various southern states.

mem•o•rize (mem′ə rīz′), *v.,* **-rized, -riz•ing.** —*v.t.* **1.** to commit to memory; learn by heart: *to memorize a poem.* —*v.i.* **2.** to learn something by heart. —**mem′o•riz′a•ble,** *adj.* —**mem′o•ri•za′tion,** *n.*

mem•o•ry (mem′ə rē), *n., pl.* **-ries. 1.** the mental capacity or faculty of retaining or recalling facts, events, impressions, or previous experiences. **2.** this faculty as possessed by a particular individual: *to have a good memory.* **3.** the act or fact of retaining and recalling impressions, facts, etc.; remembrance: *to draw from memory.* **4.** the length of time over which recollection extends: *within the memory of living persons.* **5.** a mental impression retained; a recollection: *an early memory.* **6.** the reputation of a person or thing, esp. after death. **7.** the state or fact of being remembered. **8.** a person or thing remembered. **9.** commemorative remembrance; commemoration. **10.** Also called **storage. a.** the capacity of a computer to store information subject to recall. **b.** the components of the computer in which such information is stored. **11.** the ability of certain materials to return to an original shape after deformation. **12.** the ability of a cell of the immune system to respond to an antigen it has previously encountered.

mem′ory cell′, *n.* a long-lived cell of the immune system that has previously encountered a specific antigen and that upon reexposure produces large amounts of antibody **(memory B cell)** or rapidly initiates cell-mediated immunity **(memory T cell).**

mem′ory lane′, *n.* the memory of one's past life likened to a road down which one may travel: *to walk down memory lane.*

Mem•phis (mem′fis), *n.* **1.** a port in SW Tennessee, on the Mississippi. 614,289. **2.** a ruined city in N Egypt, on the Nile, S of Cairo: ancient capital of Egypt. —**Mem•phi•an, Mem′phite,** *adj., n.*

men (men), *n.* pl. of MAN.

men-, var. of MENO- before a vowel: *menarche.*

men•ace (men′is), *n., v.,* **-aced, -ac•ing.** —*n.* **1.** something that threatens to cause evil, harm, etc.; threat. **2.** a person whose actions or ideas are considered dangerous or harmful. **3.** an extremely annoying person. —*v.t.* **4.** to utter or direct a threat against; threaten. **5.** to serve as a probable threat to; imperil. —*v.i.* **6.** to act as a threat; be threatening. —**men′ac•er,** *n.* —**men′ac•ing•ly,** *adv.*

men•a•di•one (men′ə dī′ōn), *n.* a synthetic yellow crystalline powder, $C_{11}H_8O_2$, insoluble in water, used as a vitamin K supplement. Also called **vitamin K$_3$.**

mé•nage or **me•nage** (mā näzh′), *n.* **1.** a domestic establishment; household. **2.** housekeeping.

me•nag•er•ie (mə naj′ə rē, -nazh′-), *n.* **1.** a collection of wild or unusual animals, esp. for exhibition. **2.** a place where they are kept or exhibited. **3.** an unusual and varied group of people.

men•ar•che (mə när′kē, men′är-), *n.* the first menstrual period; the establishment of menstruation. —**men•ar′che•al, men•ar′chi•al,** *adj.*

men′-chil′dren or **men′chil′dren,** *n.* pl. of MAN-CHILD.

Menck•en (meng′kən), *n.* **H(enry) L(ouis),** 1880–1956, U.S. writer, editor, and critic. —**Menc•ke•ni•an** (meng kē′nē ən), *adj., n.*

mend (mend), *v.t.* **1.** to make (something broken, torn, or otherwise damaged) whole, sound, or usable by repairing: *to mend clothes.* **2.** to correct defects or errors in. **3.** to set right; make better; improve: *to mend matters.* —*v.i.* **4.** to progress toward recovery, as a sick person. **5.** (of broken bones) to grow together; knit. **6.** to improve, as conditions or affairs. —*n.* **7.** the act of mending; repair or improvement. **8.** a mended place. —***Idiom.*** **9. mend one's fences,** to strengthen or reestablish one's position by conciliation or negotiation. **10. on the mend,** improving, esp. in health. —***Proverb.*** **11. It's never too late to mend,** moral improvement is always possible. —**mend′a•ble,** *adj.*

men•da•cious (men dā′shəs), *adj.* **1.** telling lies, esp. habitually; dishonest. **2.** false or untrue: *a mendacious report.* —**men•da′cious•ly,** *adv.* —**men•dac′i•ty** (-das′i tē), *n.*

Men•de (men′dē), *n., pl.* **-des,** (*esp. collectively*) **-de. 1.** a member of an African people of SE Sierra Leone and adjacent areas of Liberia. **2.** the Mande language of the Mende.

Men•del (men′dl), *n.* **Gregor Johann,** 1822–84, Austrian botanist.

Men•de•le•ev or **Men•de•ley•ev** (men′dl ā′əf, -ā′yef), *n.* **Dmitri Ivanovich,** 1834–1907, Russian chemist.

men•de•le•vi•um (men′dl ē′vē əm), *n.* a transuranic element. *Symbol:* Md, Mv; *at. no.:* 101.

Men′del's law′, *n.* **1.** Also called **law of segregation.** the principle stating that during the production of gametes the two copies of each hereditary factor segregate so that offspring acquire one factor from each parent. **2.** Also called **law of independent assortment.** the principle stating that the laws of chance govern which particular characteristics of the parental pairs will occur in each individual offspring. **3.** Also called **law of dominance.** the principle stating that one factor in a pair of traits dominates the other in inheritance unless both factors in the pair are recessive. [after G. J. MENDEL]

Men•dels•sohn (men′dl sən), *n.* **1. Felix** (*Jacob Ludwig Felix Mendelssohn-Bartholdy*), 1809–47, German composer. **2.** his grandfather, **Moses,** 1729–86, German philosopher.

men•di•cant (men′di kənt), *adj.* **1.** begging; living on alms. **2.** pertaining to or characteristic of a beggar. —*n.* **3.** a person who lives by begging; beggar. **4.** a mendicant friar. —**men′di•can•cy,** (-dis′i tē), *n.*

mend•ing (men′ding), *n.* articles, esp. clothes, to be mended.

men•folk (men′fōk′) also **men′folks′,** *n.pl.* men, esp. those of a family or community.

men•ha•den (men hād′n), *n., pl.* **-den.** a herringlike W Atlantic fish, *Brevoortia tyrannus:* important as a source of oil and fertilizer.

men•hir (men′hir), *n.* an upright monumental stone standing alone or in an alignment with others, found chiefly in Cornwall and Brittany.

me•ni•al (mē′nē əl, mēn′yəl), *adj.* **1.** servile; degrading: *menial work.* **2.** of or suitable for servants; humble. —*n.* **3.** a domestic servant. **4.** a servile person. —**me′ni•al•ly,** *adv.*

me•nin•ges (mi nin′jēz), *n.pl., sing.* **me•ninx** (mē′ningks). the three membranes covering the brain and spinal cord. Compare ARACHNOID (def. 4), DURA MATER, PIA MATER. —**me•nin′ge•al** (-jē əl), *adj.*

men•in•gi•tis (men′in jī′tis), *n.* inflammation of the meninges, esp. of the pia mater and arachnoid, caused by a bacterial or viral infection and characterized by high fever, severe headache, and stiff neck or back muscles. —**men′in•git′ic** (-jit′ik), *adj.*

me•nis•cus (mi nis′kəs), *n., pl.* **-nis•ci** (-nis′ī, -nis′kī, -kē), **-nis•cus•es. 1.** a crescent or a crescent-shaped body. **2.** the convex or concave upper surface of a column of liquid, the curvature of which is caused by surface tension. **3.** a lens with a crescent-shaped section. **4.** a wedge of cartilage between the articulating ends of the bones in certain joints. —**me•nis′coid,** *adj.*

Men·non·ite (men′ə nīt′), *n.* a member of a Protestant sect that refuses oaths and the bearing of arms and is noted for simplicity of living. [< German *Mennonit*, after *Menno* Simons (1492–1559), Frisian religious leader] —**Men′no·nit·ism,** *n.*

meno-, a combining form meaning "month," "menstrual cycle": *menopause.* Also, *esp. before a vowel,* **men-.**

men·o·pause (men′ə pôz′), *n.* the period of natural cessation of menstruation, usu. occurring between the ages of 45 and 55. —**men′o·pau′sal,** *adj.*

me·no·rah (mə nôr′ə, -nōr′ə), *n.* **1.** a candelabrum used in the Temple in Jerusalem and in modern synagogues. **2.** a nine-branched candelabrum used during the festival of Hanukah.

menorah
(def. 2)

Me·not·ti (mə not′ē), *n.* **Gian Carlo,** born 1911, U.S. composer, born in Italy.

men·sa (men′sə), *n., pl.* **-sas, -sae** (-sē) the top of a church altar.

men·sal[1] (men′səl), *adj.* MONTHLY.

men·sal[2] (men′səl), *adj.* of, pertaining to, or used at the table.

men·serv·ants (men′sûr′vənts), *n.* pl. of MANSERVANT.

men·ses (men′sēz), *n.* (*used with a sing. or pl. v.*) the periodic flow of blood and mucosal tissue from the uterus; menstrual flow.

men's′ room′, *n.* a public lavatory for men.

men·stru·a·tion (men′strōō ā′shən, -strā′-), *n.* **1.** the periodic discharge of blood and mucosal tissue from the uterus, occurring approximately monthly from puberty to menopause in nonpregnant women and females of other primate species. **2.** the period of menstruating. —**men′stru·al,** *adj.* —**men′stru·ate′,** *v.i.* **-at·ed, -at·ing.**

men·sur·a·ble (men′shər ə bəl, -sər ə-), *adj.* MEASURABLE. —**men′sur·a·bil′i·ty,** *n.*

men·su·ral (men′shər əl, -sər-), *adj.* pertaining to measure.

men·su·ra·tion (men′shə rā′shən, -sə-), *n.* the act or process of measuring. —**men′su·ra′tive,** *adj.*

mens·wear (menz′wâr′), *n.* Also, **men's′ wear′.** apparel and accessories for men.

-ment, a suffix of nouns that denote an action or resulting state (*abridgment; refreshment*), a product (*fragment*), or means (*ornament*).

men·tal (men′tl), *adj.* **1.** of or pertaining to the mind. **2.** of, pertaining to, or affected by a disorder of the mind: *a mental patient.* **3.** for persons with a psychiatric disorder: *a mental hospital.* **4.** performed by or existing in the mind: *mental arithmetic.* **5.** pertaining to intellectuals or intellectual activity. **6.** *Informal.* insane; crazy. —**men·tal·ly,** *adv.*

men′tal age′, *n.* the level of mental ability of an individual, usu. a child, expressed as the chronological age of the average individual at this level of ability, as determined by an intelligence test.

men′tal health′, *n.* psychological well-being and satisfactory adjustment to society and to the ordinary demands of life.

men′tal ill′ness, *n.* any of the various forms of psychosis or severe neurosis. Also called **men′tal disor′der, men′tal disease′.**

men·tal·i·ty (men tal′i tē), *n., pl.* **-ties. 1.** mental capacity or endowment. **2.** mental inclination; outlook: *a liberal mentality.*

men′tal retarda′tion, *n.* a developmental disorder characterized by varying degrees by a subnormal ability to learn, a substantially low IQ, and impaired social adjustment.

men·thol (men′thôl, -thol), *n.* a colorless, crystalline, slightly water-soluble alcohol, $C_{10}H_{20}O$, obtained from peppermint oil or synthesized: used chiefly in perfumes, confections, cigarettes, and liqueurs and in nasal medications.

men·tho·lat·ed (men′thə lā′tid), *adj.* containing, covered, or treated with menthol.

men·tion (men′shən), *v.t.* **1.** to refer briefly to; name, specify, or speak of. —*n.* **2.** a brief or incidental reference; a mentioning. —*Idiom.* **3. not to mention,** in addition to: *They own two houses, not to mention a boat.* —**men′tion·a·ble,** *adj.* —**men′tion·er,** *n.*

men·tor (men′tôr, -tər), *n.* **1.** a wise and trusted counselor or teacher. —*v.i.* **2.** to act as a mentor to. —*v.t.* **3.** to act as a mentor to.

men·u (men′yōō, mā′nyōō), *n., pl.* **men·us. 1.** a list of the dishes that can or will be served at a meal. **2.** the dishes served. **3.** any list or set of items from which to choose. **4.** a list of options available to a user, as displayed on a computer or TV screen.

me′nu-driv′en, *adj.* of or pertaining to computer software that makes extensive use of menus to enable users to choose program options.

Men·zies (men′zēz), *n.* **Sir Robert Gordon,** 1894–1978, prime minister of Australia 1939–41 and 1949–66.

me·ow (mē ou′, myou), *n.* **1.** the characteristic sound a cat makes. **2.** a spiteful or catty remark. —*v.i.* **3.** to make the sound of a cat. **4.** to make a spiteful or catty remark.

Me·phib·o·sheth (mə fib′ə sheth′), *n.* a son of Jonathan, and the grandson of Saul. II Sam. 4:4.

Meph·i·stoph·e·les (mef′ə stof′ə lēz′) also **Me·phis·to** (mə fis′tō), *n.* (in the Faust legend) the devil who tempts Faust. —**Meph′is·to·phe′li·an, Meph′is·to·phe′le·an** (-stə fē′lē ən), *adj.*

Me·rab (mēr′ab), *n.* the older daughter of King Saul, promised in marriage to anyone who killed Goliath. I Sam. 14:49; 17:25.

mer·can·tile (mûr′kən tēl′, -tīl′, -til), *adj.* **1.** of or pertaining to merchants or trade; commercial. **2.** of or pertaining to mercantilism.

mer·can·til·ism (mûr′kən ti liz′əm, -tē-, -tī-), *n.* **1.** an economic and political policy, evolving with the modern nation-state, in which a government regulated the national economy with a view to the accumulation of gold and silver, esp. by achieving a balance of exports over imports. **2.** mercantile practices or spirit; commercialism. —**mer′can·til·ist,** *n., adj.* —**mer′can·til·is′tic,** *adj.*

Mer·ca·tor (mər kā′tər), *n.* **Ger·har·dus** (jər här′dəs), (*Gerhard Kremer*), 1512–94, Flemish cartographer and geographer.

Merca′tor (or **Merca′tor's**) **projec′tion,** *n.* a conformal map projection on which any rhumb line is represented as a straight line, used chiefly in navigation, though the scale varies with latitude and areal size and the shapes of large areas are distorted.

mer·ce·nar·y (mûr′sə ner′ē), *adj., n., pl.* **-nar·ies.** —*adj.* **1.** working or acting merely for money or other reward; venal. **2.** hired to serve in a foreign army. —*n.* **3.** a professional soldier hired to serve in a foreign army. **4.** any hireling. —**mer′ce·nar′i·ly** (-när′ə lē), *adv.* —**mer′ce·nar′i·ness,** *n.*

mer·cer·ize (mûr′sə rīz′), *v.t.,* **-ized, -iz·ing.** to treat (cotton yarns or fabric) with caustic alkali under tension, in order to increase strength, luster, and affinity for dye. —**mer′cer·i·za′tion,** *n.* —**mer′cer·iz′er,** *n.*

mer·chan·dise (*n.* mûr′chən dīz′, -dīs′; *v.* -dīz′), *n., v.,* **-dised, -dis·ing.** —*n.* **1.** goods bought and sold; commodities. **2.** the stock of goods in a store. —*v.i.* **3.** to carry on trade. —*v.t.* **4.** to buy and sell; trade. **5.** to plan for and promote the sales of. —**mer′chan·dis′er,** *n.*

mer·chan·dis·ing (mûr′chən dī′zing), *n.* the marketing of a product, including sales promotion, advertising, and the like.

mer·chan·dize (mûr′chən dīz′), *v.i., v.t.,* **-dized, -diz·ing.** MERCHANDISE.

mer·chant (mûr′chənt), *n.* **1.** a person whose business is buying and selling goods for profit; dealer; trader. **2.** a storekeeper; retailer. **3.** a person who deals or indulges in something undesirable: *merchants of gloom and doom.* —*adj.* **4.** used for trade or commerce: *a merchant ship.* **5.** pertaining to the merchant marine.

mer′chant marine′, *n.* **1.** the ships of a nation that are engaged in commerce. **2.** the officers and crews of such ships.

mer′chant of death′, *n.* a company, nation, or person that sells military arms on the international market, usually to the highest bidder and without scruple or regard for political ramifications. [phrase popularized by the book *Merchants of Death* (1934) by U.S. writers Helmut C. Engelbrecht (1895–1939) and Frank C. Hanighen (1899–1964)]

Mer′chant of Ven′ice, The, a comedy (1596?) by William Shakespeare.

mer·cu·ri·al (mər kyŏŏr′ē əl), *adj.* **1.** changeable; fickle; erratic: *a mercurial nature.* **2.** animated; sprightly. **3.** (*cap.*) of or pertaining to the planet Mercury. —**mer·cu′ri·al·ly,** *adv.* —**mer·cu′ri·al·i·ty,** *n.*

mer·cu·ric (mər kyŏŏr′ik), *adj.* of or containing bivalent mercury.

mer·cu·ry (mûr′kyə rē), *n., pl.* **-ries. 1.** a heavy, silver-white, toxic metallic element, liquid at room temperature: used in barometers, thermometers, pesticides, pharmaceuticals, mirror surfaces, and as a laboratory catalyst; quicksilver. *Symbol:* Hg; *at. wt.:* 200.59; *at. no.:* 80; *sp. gr.:* 13.546 at 20°C; *freezing point:* –38.9°C; *boiling point:* 357°C. **2.** this metal as used in medicine, in the form of various organic and inorganic compounds, usu. for skin infections. **3.** *temperature: The mercury climbed to over a hundred today.* **4.** (*cap.*) the Roman god of commerce, thievery, eloquence, and science, and messenger to the other gods: identified with the Greek god Hermes. **5.** (*cap.*) the planet nearest the sun, having a diameter of 3031 mi. (4878 km), a mean distance from the sun of 36 million mi. (57.9 million km), and a period of revolution of 87.96 days, and having no satellites: the smallest planet in the solar system. **6.** any plant belonging to the genus *Mercurialis,* of the spurge family, esp. the poisonous, weedy *M. perennis* of Europe. **7.** any of several common weeds with spinachlike leaves, esp. weeds of the goosefoot family. **8.** a messenger.

mer′cury-va′por lamp′, *n.* a lamp producing a light with a high actinic and ultraviolet content by means of an electric arc in mercury vapor.

mer·cy (mûr′sē), *n., pl.* **-cies. 1.** compassionate or kindly forbearance shown toward an offender, an enemy, or other person in one's power; compassion, pity, or benevolence. **2.** the disposition or discretionary power to be compassionate or forbearing. **3.** an act of kindness, compassion, or favor. **4.** something of good fortune; blessing: *It was a mercy they weren't hurt.* —*Idiom.* **5. at the mercy of,** wholly in the power of; subject to. —**mer′ci·ful,** *adj.* —**mer′ci·ful·ly,** *adv.* —**mer′ci·less,** *adj.* —**mer′ci·less·ly,** *adv.*

mer′cy kill′ing, *n.* EUTHANASIA (def. 1).

mer′cy seat′, *n.* **1. a.** the gold covering on the ark of the covenant, regarded as the resting place of God. Ex. 25:17–22. **b.** the throne of God. **2.** *South Midland and Southern U.S.* MOURNER'S BENCH.

mere (mēr), *adj., superl.* **mer·est.** being nothing more nor better than what is specified: *a mere child.* —**mere′ly,** *adv.*

me·ren·gue (mə reng′gā), *n.* a ballroom dance of Dominican and Haitian origin, characterized by a stiff-legged, limping step.

mer·e·tri·cious (mer′i trish′əs), *adj.* **1.** alluring by a show of flashy or vulgar attractions; tawdry. **2.** based on pretense or insincerity. —**mer′e·tri′cious·ly**, *adv.* —**mer′e·tri′cious·ness**, *n.*

mer·gan·ser (mər gan′sər), *n., pl.* **-sers**, (*esp. collectively*) **-ser**. any of several fish-eating diving ducks of the genera *Mergus* and *Lophodytes*, having a narrow, serrated bill. Also called **fish duck, goosander.**

merge (mûrj), *v.*, **merged, merg·ing.** —*v.t.* **1.** to cause to combine or coalesce; unite. **2.** to combine, blend, or unite gradually so as to blur the differences of. —*v.i.* **3.** to become combined, united, or absorbed; lose identity by blending: *The stream merges into the river.* **4.** to combine or unite into a single organization, body, etc.: *The two firms merged.* —**mer′gence**, *n.*

merg·er (mûr′jər), *n.* **1.** a statutory combination of two or more corporations by the transfer of the properties to one surviving corporation. **2.** an act or instance of merging.

me·ringue (mə rang′), *n.* **1.** egg whites stiffly beaten with sugar and browned in the oven, often used as topping for pies. **2.** a dessert shell made by baking such a mixture, often filled with fruit or cream.

me·ri·no (mə rē′nō), *n., pl.* **-nos**. **1.** (*often cap.*) one of a breed of sheep, raised orig. in Spain, valued for their fine wool. **2.** wool from such sheep.

merino,
Ovis aries,
2 ft. (0.6 m)
high at shoulder

mer·it (mer′it), *n.* **1.** claim to respect and praise; excellence; worth. **2.** something that deserves praise or reward; commendable quality or act: *Its chief merit is sincerity.* **3. merits,** the inherent rights and wrongs of a matter unobscured by procedural details, personal feelings, etc.: *to decide a case on its merits.* **4.** Often, **merits.** the state or fact of deserving; desert: *to treat people according to their merits.* **5.** claim to spiritual reward, earned by the performance of righteous acts. —*v.t.* **6.** to be worthy of; deserve. —**mer′i·to′ri·ous**, *adj.* —**mer′i·to′ri·ous·ly**, *adv.* —**mer′i·to′ri·ous·ness**, *n.*

mer′it badge′, *n.* an insignia or device granted by the Boy Scouts, worn esp. on a uniform to indicate special achievement.

mer·i·toc·ra·cy (mer′i tok′rə sē), *n., pl.* **-cies.** **1.** a system in which able and talented persons are rewarded and advanced. **2.** an elite group of able and talented persons. **3.** leadership by such a group. —**mer′i·to·crat′ic** (-tə krat′ik), *adj.* —**mer′i·to·crat′**, *n.*

mer′it sys′tem, *n.* (esp. in the U.S. civil service) the system or practice in which persons are hired or promoted on the basis of ability rather than patronage.

merle or **merl** (mûrl), *n.* BLACKBIRD (def. 2).

mer·lin (mûr′lin), *n.* a small falcon, *Falco columbarius,* of the Northern Hemisphere, that feeds largely on birds taken in flight. Also called **pigeon hawk.**

Mer·lin (mûr′lin), *n.* a magician and seer in Arthurian legend.

mer·maid (mûr′mād′), *n.* (in folklore) a female marine creature, having the head, torso, and arms of a woman and the tail of a fish.

mer·man (mûr′man′), *n., pl.* **-men.** (in folklore) a male marine creature, having the head, torso, and arms of a man and the tail of a fish.

Mer·o·dach (mer′ə däk′), *n.* MARDUK.

-merous, a combining form meaning "having parts" of the kind or number specified by the initial element: *dimerous.*

Mer·o·vin·gi·an (mer′ə vin′jē ən, -jən), *adj.* **1.** of or pertaining to the Frankish dynasty established by Clovis I, which reigned in Gaul and Germany from A.D. 476 to 751. —*n.* **2.** a member or supporter of the Merovingian dynasty.

Mer·ri·mack (mer′ə mak′), *n.* **1.** a river in central New Hampshire and NE Massachusetts, flowing S and NE to the Atlantic. 110 mi. (175 km) long. **2.** (*italics*) Also, *Mer′ri·mac′.* a Union steamer that the Confederates converted into an ironclad warship, renamed the *Virginia,* and used against the *Monitor* in 1862 in the first battle between ironclads.

mer·ri·ment (mer′i mənt), *n.* cheerful gaiety; mirth; laughter.

mer·ry (mer′ē), *adj.*, **-ri·er, -ri·est.** **1.** full of cheerfulness or gaiety; joyous in disposition or spirit. **2.** characterized by rejoicing or festive conviviality. **3. Proverb. A merry heart makes a cheerful countenance,** how one looks is affected by how one feels. Prov. 15:13. —**mer′ri·ly**, *adv.* —**mer′ri·ness**, *n.*

mer′ry-an′drew (-an′drōo), *n.* a clown; buffoon.

mer′ry-go-round′, *n.* **1.** a revolving circular platform with wooden horses or other animals, benches, etc., on which people ride, usu. to the accompaniment of music, as at an amusement park or carnival; carousel. **2.** a whirl or busy round, of events or activities.

mer·ry·mak·ing (mer′ē mā′king), *n.* **1.** the act of taking part gaily or convivially in some festivity. **2.** a merry festivity; revel.

Mer·ton (mûr′tn), *n.* **Thomas,** 1915–68, U.S. poet and religious writer, born in France.

me·sa (mā′sə), *n., pl.* **-sas.** a land formation, less extensive than a plateau, having steep walls and a relatively flat top: common in arid and semiarid parts of the southwestern U.S. and Mexico.

Me·sa (mā′sə), *n.* a city in central Arizona, near Phoenix. 280,360.

mé·sal·li·ance (mā′zə lī′əns, -zal yäns′), *n., pl.* **-li·anc·es** (-lī′ən siz, -zal′yäns′). a marriage with someone who is considered socially inferior; misalliance. [< French]

Me·sa Ver·de (mā′sə vûrd′, vûr′dē), *n.* a national park in SW Colorado: ruins of prehistoric cliff dwellings. 80 sq. mi. (207 sq. km).

mes·cal (me skal′), *n.* **1.** an alcoholic beverage distilled from certain species of agave. **2.** any agave yielding this spirit. **3.** Also called **peyote.** a species of spineless, dome-shaped cactus, *Lophophora williamsii,* of Texas and N Mexico.

mes·dames (mā däm′, -dämz′, -dam′, -damz′), *n.* **1.** a pl. of MADAM. **2.** pl. of MADAME.

mes·de·moi·selles (mā′də mə zel′, -zelz′, mād′mwə-), *n.* a pl. of MADEMOISELLE.

mesh (mesh), *n.* **1.** an arrangement of interlocking metal links or wires with evenly spaced, uniform small openings between, as used in jewelry, sieves, etc. **2.** any knit, woven, or knotted fabric of open texture. **3.** an interwoven or intertwined structure; network. **4.** one of the open spaces between the cords, wires, etc., of a net or screen. **5. meshes, a.** the cords, wires, etc., that bind such spaces. **b.** a means of catching or holding fast: *the meshes of the law.* **6.** the engagement of gear teeth. —*v.t.* **7.** to catch or entangle in or as if in a net; enmesh. **8.** to form with meshes, as a net. **9.** to engage, as gear teeth. **10.** to cause to match, coordinate, or interlock. —*v.i.* **11.** to become enmeshed. **12.** to become or be engaged, as the teeth of gears. **13.** to match, coordinate, or interlock. —**mesh′y**, *adj.*, **-i·er, -i·est.**

Me·shach (mē′shak), *n.* a companion of Daniel. Compare SHADRACH. Dan. 3:12–30.

Me·shed (me shed′), *n.* MASHHAD.

Mes·mer (mez′mər, mes′-), *n.* **Franz** or **Friedrich Anton,** 1733–1815, Austrian physician.

mes·mer·ize (mez′mə rīz′, mes′-), *v.t.,* **-ized, -iz·ing. 1.** to hypnotize. **2.** to spellbind; fascinate. **3.** to compel by fascination. —**mes′mer·ism,** *n.* —**mes′mer·ist,** *n.* —**mes′mer·i·za′tion,** *n.* —**mes′mer·iz′er,** *n.*

meso-, a combining form meaning "middle": *mesoderm.* Also, *esp. before a vowel,* **mes-.**

Mes·o·a·mer·i·ca or **Mes·o·A·mer·i·ca** (mez′ō ə mer′i kə, mes′-, mē′zō-, -sō-), *n.* **1.** the area extending approximately from central Mexico to Honduras and Nicaragua where pre-Columbian civilizations flourished. **2.** Central America. —**Mes′o·a·mer′i·can,** *adj., n.*

mes·o·carp (mez′ə kärp′, mes′-, mē′zə-, -sə-), *n.* the middle layer of pericarp, as the fleshy part of certain fruits.

mes·o·derm (mez′ə dûrm′, mes′-, mē′zə-, -sə-), *n.* the embryonic germ layer between the ectoderm and endoderm, from which connective tissue, muscles, and blood vessels develop. —**mes′o·der′mal,** *adj.*

Mes·o·lith·ic (mez′ə lith′ik, mes′-, mē′zə-, -sə-), *adj.* (*sometimes l.c.*) of, designating, or characteristic of a transitional period of the Stone Age intermediate between the Paleolithic and Neolithic periods.

mes·o·mor·phic (mez′ə môr′fik, mes′-, mē′zə-, -sə-), *adj.* pertaining to or having a muscular or sturdy body build characterized by the relative prominence of structures among the embryonic mesoderm (contrasted with *ectomorphic, endomorphic*). —**mes′o·mor′phism,** *n.*

mes·o·pause (mez′ə pôz′, mes′-, mē′zə-, -sə-), *n.* the top of the mesosphere, determined by the appearance of a temperature minimum near an altitude of 50 mi. (80 km).

Mes·o·po·ta·mi·a (mez′ə pə tā′mē ə), *n.* an ancient region in W Asia between the Tigris and Euphrates rivers: now part of Iraq. —**Mes′o·po·ta′mi·an,** *adj., n.*

mes·o·some (mez′ə sōm′, mes′-, mē′zə-, -sə-), *n.* **1.** the anterior portion of the abdomen in arachnids. **2.** a whorled structure in bacteria, extending inward from the cell membrane and containing respiratory enzymes.

mes·o·sphere (mez′ə sfēr′, mes′-, mē′zə-, -sə-), *n.* the region between the stratosphere and the thermosphere, extending from about 20 to 50 mi. (32–80 km) above the surface of the earth. —**mes′o·spher′ic** (-sfer′ik), *adj.*

mes·o·zo·an (mez′ə zō′ən, mes′-, mē′zə-, -sə-), *n.* **1.** any of several parasitic wormlike organisms, of the phylum Mesozoa, that are multicellular but of an extremely simple organization. —*adj.* **2.** of or pertaining to the mesozoans.

Mes·o·zo·ic (mez′ə zō′ik, mes′-, mē′zə-, -sə-), *adj.* **1.** noting or pertaining to a geologic era occurring between 230 million and 65 million years ago, characterized by the appearance of flowering plants and by dinosaurs. —*n.* **2.** the Mesozoic Era or group of systems.

mes·quite or **mes·quit** (me skēt′, mes′kēt), *n.* **1.** any of several usu. spiny trees or shrubs belonging to the genus *Prosopis,* of the legume family, as *P. juliflora* or *P. glandulosa,* of W North America, having bipinnate leaves and beanlike pods and often forming dense thickets. **2.** the wood of such a tree or shrub, used esp. in grilling or barbecuing food. [1830–40, *Amer.*; < MexSp *mezquite* < Nahuatl *mizquitl*]

Mes•quite (me skēt′, mi-), *n.* a city in NE Texas, E of Dallas. 113,631.

mess (mes), *n.* **1.** a dirty or untidy condition. **2.** a person or thing that is dirty, untidy, or disordered. **3.** a state of embarrassing confusion. **4.** an unpleasant or difficult situation. **5.** a dirty or untidy mass; jumble: *a mess of papers.* **6.** a group regularly taking their meals together. **7.** the meal so taken. **8.** MESS HALL. **9.** a quantity of food sufficient for a dish or a single occasion. **10.** sloppy or unappetizing food. **11.** a dish or quantity of soft or liquid food. **12.** a person whose life, mental state, or affairs are in a state of confusion. —*v.t.* **13.** to make dirty or untidy (often fol. by *up*): *Don't mess up the room.* **14.** to make a mess or muddle of (affairs, responsibilities, etc.) (often fol. by *up*). —*v.i.* **15.** to make a mess. **16.** to eat in company, esp. as a member of a mess. **17. mess around** or **about, a.** to busy oneself aimlessly; waste time. **b.** to involve oneself, esp. for reprehensible purposes: *to mess around with gamblers.* **18. mess in** or **with,** to intervene officiously; meddle. **19. mess up, a.** to perform poorly; produce errors or confusion. **b.** to treat roughly; beat up.

mes•sage (mes′ij), *n.* **1.** a communication delivered in writing, speech, by means of signals, etc. **2.** an official communication, as from a chief executive to a legislative body. **3.** the main point, moral, or meaning of something, as of a speech, work of art, or book.

mes•sei•gneurs (*Fr.* mā se nyŒR′), *n.* (*sometimes cap.*) pl. of MONSEI-GNEUR.

mes•sen•ger (mes′ən jər), *n.* **1.** a person who conveys messages or parcels. **2.** a light line for pulling a heavier line to a ship, pier, etc.

messenger RNA, *n.* a molecule of RNA that is synthesized in the nucleus from a DNA template and then enters the cytoplasm, where its genetic code specifies the amino acid sequence for protein synthesis. *Abbr.:* mRNA

mess′ hall′, *n.* a dining hall, esp. at a military base.

Mes•si•ah (mi sī′ə), *n.* **1.** the promised and expected deliverer of the Jewish people. **2.** Jesus Christ, regarded by Christians as fulfilling this promise and expectation. John 4:25, 26. **3.** (*l.c.*) any expected deliverer or savior. **4.** (*italics*) an oratorio (1742) by George Frideric Handel. —**Mes•si•an•ic** (mes′ē an′ik), *adj.* —**Mes′si•an′i•cal•ly,** *adv.*

mes•sieurs (mes syœ′), *n.* pl. of MONSIEUR.

mess′ kit′, *n.* a portable set of usu. metal cooking and eating utensils, used esp. by soldiers and campers. Also called **mess′ gear′.**

Messrs. (mes′ərz), pl. of MR.

mess•y (mes′ē), *adj.,* **mess•i•er, mess•i•est. 1.** characterized by dirt, disorder, or confusion. **2.** causing a mess. **3.** embarrassing, difficult, or unpleasant. —**mess′i•ly,** *adv.* —**mess′i•ness,** *n.*

mes•ti•za (me stē′zə), *n., pl.* **-zas.** a woman who is a mestizo.

mes•ti•zo (me stē′zō), *n., pl.* **-zos, -zoes.** a person of racially mixed ancestry; in Latin America, of mixed American Indian and European ancestry, or, in the Philippines, of mixed native and foreign ancestry.

met•a (met′ə), *adj.* pertaining to or occupying positions (1, 3) in the benzene ring separated by one carbon atom. Compare ORTHO, PARA[1].

meta-, 1. a prefix appearing in loanwords from Greek, with the meanings "after," "along with," "beyond," "among," "behind," and productive in English on the Greek model: *metacarpus; metalinguistics.* **2. a.** a combining form used in the names of acids, salts, or their organic derivatives that are the least hydrated of a given series: *meta-antimonic* $HSbO_3$. Compare ORTHO- (def. 2a), PYRO- (def. 2a). **b.** a combining form used in the names of benzene derivatives in which the substituting group occupies the meta position in the benzene ring. *Abbr.:* m- Also, *esp. before a vowel,* **met-.**

me•tab•o•lism (mə tab′ə liz′əm), *n.* the sum of the physical and chemical processes in an organism by which its substance is produced, maintained, and destroyed, and by which energy is made available. Compare ANABOLISM, CATABOLISM. —**met•a•bol•ic** (met′ə bol′ik), *adj.* —**met′a•bol′i•cal•ly,** *adv.*

me•tab•o•lite (mə tab′ə līt′), *n.* a product of metabolism.

me•tab•o•lize (mə tab′ə līz′), *v.,* **-lized, -liz•ing.** —*v.t.* **1.** to subject to or change by metabolism. —*v.i.* **2.** to effect metabolism.

met•a•car•pal (met′ə kär′pəl), *adj.* **1.** of or pertaining to the metacarpus. —*n.* **2.** a metacarpal bone.

met•a•car•pus (met′ə kär′pəs), *n., pl.* **-pi** (-pī). the bones of a vertebrate forelimb between the wrist, or carpus, and the fingers, or phalanges.

met•a•cen•ter (met′ə sen′tər), *n. Naval Archit.* the intersection between two vertical lines, one through the center of buoyancy of a hull in equilibrium, the other through the center of buoyancy when the hull is inclined slightly to one side or toward one end.

met•a•eth•ics (met′ə eth′iks, met′ə eth′-), *n.* (*usu. with a sing. v.*) the branch of ethics dealing with the meaning of ethical terms, the nature of moral discourse, and the foundations of morality.

met•a•gal•ax•y (met′ə gal′ək sē), *n., pl.* **-ax•ies.** the complete system of galaxies; the Milky Way and all the surrounding galaxies. —**met′a•ga•lac′tic** (-gə lak′tik), *adj.*

met•al (met′l), *n.* **1.** any of a class of elementary substances, as gold, silver, or copper, all of which are crystalline when solid and many of which are characterized by opacity, ductility, conductivity, and a unique luster when freshly fractured. **2.** such a substance in its pure state, as distinguished from alloys. **3.** an alloy or mixture of such substances, as brass. **4.** an element yielding positively charged ions in aqueous solutions of its salts. **5.** formative material; stuff. **6.** METTLE. **7.** printing type

made of metallic alloy. **8.** molten glass in the pot or melting tank. **9.** HEAVY METAL. —*v.t.* **10.** to furnish or cover with metal.

met•a•lan•guage (met′ə lang′gwij), *n.* a language or symbolic system used to discuss, describe, or analyze another language or symbolic system.

met•al•head (met′l hed′), *n. Slang.* a fan of heavy-metal music.

met•a•lin•guis•tic (met′ə ling gwis′tik), *adj.* of or pertaining to metalinguistics or a metalanguage. —**met′a•lin•guis′ti•cal•ly,** *adv.*

met•a•lin•guis•tics (met′ə ling gwis′tiks), *n.* (*used with a sing. v.*) the study of the relation between languages and the other cultural systems they refer to.

me•tal•lic (mə tal′ik), *adj.* **1.** of, pertaining to, or consisting of metal. **2.** of the nature of or suggesting metal, as in luster, resonance, or hardness. **3. a.** (of a metal element) being in the free or uncombined state: *metallic iron.* **b.** containing or yielding metal. —*n.* **4. a.** a yarn or fiber made partly or entirely of metal and having a metallic appearance. **b.** a fabric made of such a yarn or fiber. —**me•tal′li•cal•ly,** *adv.*

met•al•lif•er•ous (met′l if′ər əs), *adj.* containing or yielding metal.

metallo-, a combining form representing METAL: *metallography.* Also, *metalli-; esp. before a vowel,* **metall-.**

met•al•log•ra•phy (met′l og′rə fē), *n.* the study of the structure of metals and alloys by means of microscopy. —**met′al•log′ra•pher,** *n.*

met•al•lur•gy (met′l ûr′jē; *esp. Brit.* mə tal′ər jē), *n.* **1.** the technique or science of working or heating metals. **2.** the technique or science of making and compounding alloys. **3.** the technique or science of separating metals from their ores. —**met′al•lur′gic, met′al•lur′gi•cal,** *adj.* —**met′al•lur′gi•cal•ly,** *adv.* —**met′al•lur′gist,** *n.*

met′al tape′, *n.* a high-performance recording tape with a magnetic metal-particle coating that is not an oxide.

met•al•work•ing (met′l wûr′king), *n.* the act or technique of making metal objects. —**met′al•work′er,** *n.*

met•a•mor•phic (met′ə môr′fik), *adj.* **1.** pertaining to or characterized by change of form, or metamorphosis. **2.** pertaining to or exhibiting structural change or metamorphism: *metamorphic rock.*

met•a•mor•phose (met′ə môr′fōz, -fōs), *v.,* **-phosed, -phos•ing.** —*v.t.* **1.** to change the form or nature of; transform. **2.** to subject to metamorphosis or metamorphism. —*v.i.* **3.** to undergo or be capable of undergoing a change in form or nature.

met•a•mor•pho•sis (met′ə môr′fə sis), *n., pl.* **-ses** (-sēz). **1.** a profound change in form from one stage to the next in the life history of an organism, as from the caterpillar to the pupa and from the pupa to the adult butterfly. **2.** a complete change of form, structure, or substance, as transformation by magic. **3.** any complete change in appearance, character, circumstances, etc. **4. a.** a type of alteration or degeneration in which tissues are changed. **b.** the resultant form. [< Latin < Greek: transformation]

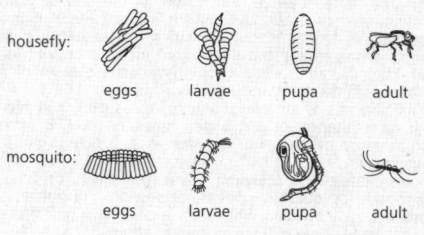

housefly: eggs larvae pupa adult

mosquito: eggs larvae pupa adult

metamorphosis

met•a•phase (met′ə fāz′), *n.* the stage in mitosis or meiosis in which the duplicated chromosomes line up along the equatorial plate of the spindle.

met•a•phor (met′ə fôr′, -fər), *n.* the application of a word or phrase to an object or concept it does not literally denote, suggesting comparison to that object or concept, as in "A mighty fortress is our God." —**met′a•phor′i•cal** (-fôr′i kəl, -for′-), *adj.* —**met′a•phor′i•cal•ly,** *adv.*

met•a•phys•i•cal (met′ə fiz′i kəl), *adj.* **1.** pertaining to or of the nature of metaphysics. **2.** highly abstract, subtle, or abstruse. **3.** of or pertaining to a 17th-century group of English poets who used extensive imaginative conceits and turns of wit. **4.** beyond the physical; incorporeal or supernatural. —**met′a•phys′i•cal•ly,** *adv.*

met•a•phys•ics (met′ə fiz′iks), *n.* (*used with a sing. v.*) **1.** the branch of philosophy that treats of first principles, includes ontology and cosmology, and is intimately connected with epistemology. **2.** philosophy, esp. in its more abstruse branches.

me•tas•ta•sis (mə tas′tə sis), *n., pl.* **-ses** (-sēz). **1.** the spread of disease-producing organisms or of malignant or cancerous cells to other parts of the body by way of the blood or lymphatic vessels or membranous surfaces. **2.** the condition produced by this. —**met•a•stat•ic** (met′-ə stat′ik), *adj.* —**met′a•stat′i•cal•ly,** *adv.*

me•tas•ta•size (mə tas′tə sīz′), *v.i.,* **-sized, -siz•ing.** to spread by metastasis.

met·a·tar·sal (met/ə tär/səl), *adj.* **1.** of or pertaining to the metatarsus. —*n.* **2.** a bone in the metatarsus. —**met/a·tar/sal·ly,** *adv.*

met·a·tar·sus (met/ə tär/səs), *n., pl.* **-si** (-sī). the bones of a vertebrate hind limb between the tarsus and the toes, or phalanges.

me·ta·te (mə tä/tē, -tā), *n.* a flat stone with a depression for holding maize or other grains to be ground.

me·tath·e·sis (mə tath/ə sis), *n., pl.* **-ses** (-sēz/). the transposition of letters, syllables, or sounds in a word, as in the pronunciation (kumf/tər bəl) for *comfortable* or (aks) for *ask.* —**met·a·thet·ic** (met/ə-thet/ik), **met/a·thet/i·cal,** *adj.*

mete¹ (mēt), *v.t.,* **met·ed, met·ing.** to distribute or apportion by measure; allot; dole (usu. fol. by *out*): *to mete out praise.*

mete² (mēt), *n.* **1.** a limiting mark. **2.** a limit or boundary: *metes and bounds.*

me·tem·psy·cho·sis (mə tem/sə kō/sis, -temp/-, met/əm sī-), *n., pl.* **-ses** (-sēz). the transmigration of the soul, esp. the passage of the soul after death into the body of another being. —**met·em·psy·chic** (met/-əm sī/kik, me·tem/psy·cho/sic, me·tem/psy·cho/si·cal,** *adj.*

met·en·ceph·a·lon (met/en sef/ə lon/), *n., pl.* **-lons, -la** (-lə). the anterior section of the hindbrain developing into the cerebellum and the pons. —**met·en·ce·phal/ic** (-sə fal/ik), *adj.*

me·te·or (mē/tē ər, -ôr/), *n.* **1. a.** a meteoroid that has entered the earth's atmosphere. **b.** a transient fiery streak in the sky produced by a meteoroid passing through the earth's atmosphere; a shooting star. **2.** any atmospheric phenomenon, as hail or a typhoon.

me·te·or·ic (mē/tē ôr/ik, -or/-), *adj.* **1.** of, pertaining to, or consisting of meteors. **2.** resembling a meteor in transient brilliance, suddenness of appearance, swiftness, etc.: *a meteoric rise in politics.* **3.** of or coming from the atmosphere; meteorological. —**me/te·or/i·cal·ly,** *adv.*

me·te·or·ite (mē/tē ə rīt/), *n.* **1.** the remains of a meteorid that has reached the earth from outer space. **2.** a meteoroid. —**me/te·or·it/ic** (-rit/ik), **me/te·or·it/i·cal, me·te·or·it/al** (-rīt/l), *adj.*

me·te·or·it·ics (mē/tē ə rit/iks), *n.* (*used with a sing. v.*) the science that deals with meteors. —**me/te·or·it/i·cist** (-ə sist), *n.*

me·te·or·oid (mē/tē ə roid/), *n.* any of the small bodies of rock or metal traveling through space that, upon entering the earth's atmosphere, are heated to glowing and become meteors.

me·te·or·ol·o·gy (mē/tē ə rol/ə jē), *n.* **1.** the science dealing with the atmosphere, weather, and climate. **2.** the atmospheric conditions and weather of an area. —**me/te·or·o·log/i·cal,** *adj.* —**me/te·or·o·log/i·cal·ly,** *adv.* —**me/te·or·ol/o·gist,** *n.*

me/teor show/er, *n.* the profusion of meteors observed when the earth passes through a swarm of meteors.

me·ter¹ (mē/tər), *n.* the base SI unit of length, equivalent to 39.37 U.S. inches; now defined as $^1/_{299,792,458}$ of the distance light travels in a vacuum in one second. *Abbr.:* m

me·ter² (mē/tər), *n.* **1. a.** the rhythmic element in music as measured by division into parts of equal time value. **b.** the unit of measurement, in terms of number of beats, adopted for a given piece of music. **2. a.** the arrangement of words in rhythmic lines; poetic measure. **b.** a particular rhythmic arrangement in a line, based on kind or kind and number of feet per line: *dactylic meter.* **c.** rhythmic arrangement of stanzas or strophes, based on the kind and number of lines.

me·ter³ (mē/tər), *n.* **1.** an instrument for measuring and recording the quantity of something, as of gas, water, miles, or time. **2.** PARKING METER. —*v.t.* **3.** to measure by means of a meter. **4.** to process (mail) by means of a postage meter.

-meter, a combining form meaning "measure," used in the names of instruments measuring quantity, extent, degree, etc.: *altimeter; barometer.*

me/ter maid/, *n.* a woman who is a member of a police or traffic department that issues tickets for parking violations.

meth·a·done (meth/ə dōn/) also **meth·a·don** (-don/), *n.* a synthetic narcotic, $C_{21}H_{28}ClNO$, similar to morphine but effective orally, used to relieve pain and as a heroin substitute to treat heroin addiction.

meth·am·phet·a·mine (meth/am fet/ə mēn/, -min), *n.* a central nervous system stimulant, $C_{10}H_{15}N$, used in treating narcolepsy, hyperkinesia, and for blood pressure maintenance in hypotensive states.

meth·ane (meth/ān; *Brit.* mē/thān), *n.* a colorless, odorless, flammable gas, CH_4, the main constituent of marsh gas and the firedamp of coal mines, obtained commercially from natural gas: the first member of the alkane series of hydrocarbons.

meth·a·nol (meth/ə nôl/, -nol/), *n.* METHYL ALCOHOL.

me·tha·qua·lone (mə thak/wə lōn/, meth/ə kwä/lōn, -kwol/ōn) *n.* a nonbarbiturate substance, $C_{16}H_{14}N_2O$, used to induce sleep.

me·thi·o·nine (me thī/ə nēn/, -nin), *n.* an essential amino acid, $C_5H_{11}NO_2S$, occurring in casein, yeast, and other proteins. *Abbr.:* Met; *Symbol:* M

meth·od (meth/əd), *n.* **1.** a procedure, technique, or planned way of doing something. **2.** order or system in doing anything: *to work with method.* **3.** orderly or systematic arrangement, sequence, or the like. **4.** **the Method.** Also called **Stanislavsky Method** (or **System**). a theory and technique of acting in which the actor attempts to experience the inner life of the character being portrayed. —*adj.* **5.** (*usu. cap.*) of, pertaining to, or employing the Method. —**meth/od·less,** *adj.*

me·thod·i·cal (mə thod/i kəl) also **me·thod/ic,** *adj.* **1.** performed, disposed, or acting in a systematic way. **2.** painstaking, esp. slow and careful; deliberate. —**me·thod/i·cal·ly,** *adv.*

Meth·od·ism (meth/ə diz/əm), *n.* the doctrines, polity, beliefs, and methods of worship of the Methodists.

Meth·od·ist (meth/ə dist), *n.* **1.** a member of a Protestant denomination that developed out of John Wesley's religious revival and has an Arminian doctrine and, in the U.S., a modified episcopal polity. —*adj.* **2.** Also, **Meth/od·is/tic, Meth/od·is/ti·cal.** of or pertaining to the Methodists or Methodism.

meth·od·ol·o·gy (meth/ə dol/ə jē), *n., pl.* **-gies. 1.** a set or system of methods, principles, and rules used in a given discipline, as in the arts or sciences. **2.** a branch of pedagogics dealing with analysis of subjects to be taught and of the methods of teaching them. —**meth/od·o·log/i·cal** (-dl oj/i kal), *adj.* —**meth/od·o·log/i·cal·ly,** *adv.*

Me·thu·se·lah (mə thōō/zə lə), *n.* **1.** a patriarch who lived 969 years. Gen. 5:27. **2.** (*often l.c.*) a wine bottle holding 6½ quarts (6 l).

meth/yl al/cohol, *n.* a colorless, volatile, poisonous liquid, CH_4O, used chiefly as a solvent, fuel, and antifreeze and in the synthesis of formaldehyde. Also called **methanol, wood alcohol.**

me·tic·u·lous (mə tik/yə ləs), *adj.* **1.** taking or showing extreme care about minute details; precise; thorough. **2.** finicky; fussy. —**me·tic/u·lous·ly,** *adv.* —**me·tic/u·lous·ness,** *n.*

mé·tier or **me·tier** (mā/tyā, mā tyā/), *n.* **1.** a field of work; occupation or profession. **2.** a field of activity in which one has special ability or training; forte.

mé·tis or **me·tis** (mā tēs/, -tē/), *n., pl.* **-tis** (-tēs/, -tēz/). **1.** any person of mixed ancestry. **2.** (*cap.*) (in Canada) the offspring of an American Indian and a white person, esp. one of French ancestry.

mé·tisse or **me·tisse** (mā tēs/), *n., pl.* **-tisses** (-tēs/, -tē/siz). **1.** a woman of mixed ancestry. **2.** (*cap.*) (in Canada) a woman of white, esp. French, and American Indian parentage.

met·o·nym (met/ə nim), *n.* a word used in metonymy.

me·ton·y·my (mi ton/ə mē), *n.* the use of the name of one object or concept for that of another to which it is related or of which it is a part, as "scepter" for "sovereignty." —**met·o·nym·ic** (met/ə nim/ik), **met/o·nym/i·cal,** *adj.* —**met/o·nym/i·cal·ly,** *adv.*

me·too·ism (mē/tōō/iz əm), *n.* **1.** the adopting of policies or practices similar or identical to those of a peer or competitor. **2.** the making of a product, offering of a service, etc., that duplicates one that has become successful. —**me/-too/er,** *n.*

me·tre (mē/tər), *n., v.,* **-tred, -tring.** *Chiefly Brit.* METER.

met·ric¹ (me/trik), *adj.* pertaining to the meter or to the metric system.

met·ric² (me/trik), *adj.* **1.** pertaining to distance: *metric geometry.* **2.** METRICAL. —*n.* **3.** a geometric function having properties analogous to those of the distance between points on a real line.

-metric, a combining form occurring in adjectives that correspond to nouns ending in -METER (*barometric*) or -METRY (*geometric*).

met·ri·cal (me/tri kal) also **metric,** *adj.* **1.** pertaining to or composed in meter. **2.** pertaining to measurement. —**met/ri·cal·ly,** *adv.*

met/rical psalm/, *n.* a Biblical psalm paraphrased and put into meter to be sung as a hymn.

met·ri·ca·tion (me/tri kā/shən), *n.* the process or result of establishing the metric system as the standard system of measurement.

met·ri·cize (me/trə sīz/), *v.t.,* **-cized, -ciz·ing.** to express in terms of the metric system. —**met/ri·cism,** *n.*

met·rics (me/triks), *n.* (*used with a sing. v.*) **1.** the study of prosodic meter. **2.** the art of metrical composition.

met/ric sys/tem, *n.* a decimal system of weights and measures, universally used in science, and the official system of measurement in many countries.

met/ric ton/, *n.* a unit of 1000 kilograms, equivalent to 2204.62 avoirdupois pounds. Also called **tonne.**

met·ro¹ (me/trō), *n., pl.* **-ros.** (*often cap.*) the underground electric railway of certain cities, as Washington, D.C., and Paris, France.

met·ro² (me/trō), *adj., n., pl.* **-ros.** *Informal.* —*adj.* **1.** METROPOLITAN (defs. 1, 2). —*n.* **2.** METROPOLIS (def. 1).

metro-¹, a combining form meaning "measure": *metronome.*

metro-², a combining form representing METROPOLIS or METROPOLITAN: *metroflight; metroland; Metroliner.*

me·trol·o·gy (mi trol/ə jē), *n.* the science of weights and measures. —**met·ro·log·i·cal** (me/trə loj/i kəl), *adj.* —**met/ro·log/i·cal·ly,** *adv.*

met·ro·nome (me/trə nōm/), *n.* an instrument that makes repeated clicks at an adjustable pace for marking rhythm, esp. in practicing music. —**met/ro·nom/ic** (-nom/ik), *adj.* —**met/ro·nom/i·cal·ly,** *adv.*

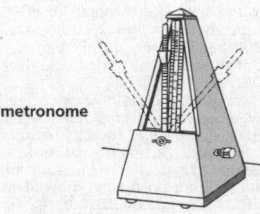

metronome

me·trop·o·lis (mi trop′ə lis), *n., pl.* **-lis·es. 1.** any large, busy city, esp. the chief city of a country or region. **2.** a central place of some activity: *a trading metropolis.* **3.** the mother city or parent state of a colony, esp. of an ancient Greek colony. [< Latin < Greek: a mother state or city]

met·ro·pol·i·tan (me′trə pol′i tn), *adj.* **1.** characteristic of a metropolis or its inhabitants, esp. in sophistication. **2.** of or pertaining to a large city and its surrounding communities: *the New York metropolitan area.* **3.** pertaining to or constituting a mother country. —*n.* **4.** an inhabitant of a metropolis. **5.** a person who has the manners associated with those who live in a metropolis. **6.** the head of an ecclesiastical province in an Eastern Church. **7.** an archbishop in the Church of England. **8.** a Roman Catholic archbishop who has authority over one or more suffragan sees. —**met′ro·pol′i·tan·ism,** *n.*

Metropol′itan Commu′nity Church′es, *n.pl.* a group of Christian churches in the United States that emphasizes ministry to homosexuals.

-metry, a combining form with the meaning "the process of measuring" that specified by the initial element: *anthropometry.*

Met·ter·nich (met′ər niкн, -nik), *n.* **Prince Klemens Wenzel Nepomuk Lothar von,** 1773–1859, Austrian statesman and diplomat.

met·tle (met′l), *n.* **1.** courage and fortitude: *a man of mettle.* **2.** disposition or temperament: *of fine mettle.*

met·tle·some (met′l səm), *adj.* spirited; courageous.

meu·nière (mən yâr′; *Fr.* mœ nyer′), *adj.* (esp. of fish) dipped in flour and sautéed in butter.

mew¹ (myōō), *n.* **1.** the high-pitched cry of a cat. **2.** the characteristic sound a gull makes. —*v.i.* **3.** to emit a mew or similar sound.

mew² (myōō), *n.* a small gull, *Larus canus,* of Eurasia and NW North America. Also called **mew′ gull′.**

mew³ (myōō), *n.* **1.** a cage for hawks. **2.** a place of retirement or concealment. **3. mews,** (*usu. with a sing. v.*) **a.** stables and usu. servants' quarters built around a courtyard. **b.** a street having apartments converted from such stables. **c.** a secluded street.

mewl (myōōl), *v.i.* to cry, as a baby, young child, or the like; whimper.

Mex·i·can (mek′si kən), *n.* **1.** a native or inhabitant of Mexico. —*adj.* **2.** of or pertaining to Mexico or its people.

Mex′ican bean′ beet′le, *n.* a ladybird beetle, *Epilachna varivestis,* introduced into the U.S. from Mexico, that feeds on the foliage of the bean plant.

Mex′ican hair′less, *n.* one of a breed of small dogs having no hair except for tufts on the top of the head and the lower part of the tail.

Mex′ican jump′ing bean′, *n.* JUMPING BEAN.

Mex′ican War′, *n.* the war between the U.S. and Mexico, 1846–48.

Mex·i·co (mek′si kō′), *n.* **1.** a republic in S North America. 97,563,374; 761,604 sq. mi. (1,972,545 sq. km). *Cap.:* Mexico City. **2.** a state in central Mexico. 11,571,000; 8268 sq. mi. (21,415 sq. km). *Cap.:* Toluca. **3.** **Gulf of,** an arm of the Atlantic surrounded by the U.S., Cuba, and Mexico. 700,000 sq. mi. (1,813,000 sq. km). Mexican, **Mé·xi·co** (me′нē kō′); Spanish, **Méjico** (for defs. 1, 2).

Mex′ico Cit′y, *n.* the capital of Mexico, in the Federal District, in the central part of Mexico. 18,748,000. Official name, **Mexico, D(istrito) F(ederal).**

Mey·er (mī′ər), *n.* **Frederick Brotherton,** 1847–1929, English clergyman and Biblical commentator.

me·zu·zah or **me·zu·za** (mə zŏŏz′ə, -zŏŏ′zə), *n., pl.* **-zu·zoth, -zu·zot** (-zŏŏ zôt′), **-zu·zahs** or **-zu·zas.** *Judaism.* a parchment scroll inscribed with Deut. 6:4–9 and 11:13–21 and with the word *Shaddai* (a name for God), inserted in a case and attached to the doorpost of the home.

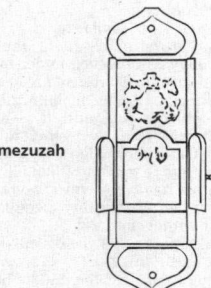

mezuzah

mez·za·nine (mez′ə nēn′, mez′ə nēn′), *n.* **1.** the lowest balcony or forward part of such a balcony in a theater. **2.** a low-ceilinged story between two other stories of greater height in a building, usu. built immediately above the ground floor, esp. when the low story and the one beneath it form part of one composition. [< French < Italian *mezzanino,* dim. of *mezzo* middle < Latin *mediānus* median]

mez·zo (met′sō, med′zō, mez′ō), *adj., n., pl.* **-zos.** —*adj.* **1.** middle; medium; half. —*n.* **2.** a mezzo-soprano.

mez′zo for′te (fôr′tā), *adj., adv. Music.* somewhat softer than forte but louder than piano; moderately loud.

mez′zo pia′no (pē ä′nō), *adj., adv. Music.* somewhat louder than piano but softer than forte; moderately soft.

mez′zo-sopran′o, *n., pl.* **-pran·os,** *adj.* —*n.* **1.** a voice or voice part intermediate in compass between soprano and contralto. **2.** a person having such a voice. —*adj.* **3.** of, pertaining to, characteristic of, or suitable to a mezzo-soprano.

MF, **1.** medium frequency. **2.** mezzo forte.

mf., microfarad.

m/f or **M/F,** male or female.

M.F.A., Master of Fine Arts.

mfg., manufacturing.

mfr., **1.** manufacture. **2.** *pl.* **mfrs.** manufacturer.

Mg, *Chem. Symbol.* magnesium.

mg, milligram.

mgr or **Mgr,** **1.** manager. **2.** Monseigneur. **3.** Monsignor.

mgt, management.

MHz, megahertz.

MI, **1.** Michigan. **2.** myocardial infarction.

mi (mē), *n. Music.* the syllable used for the third tone of a diatonic scale.

M.I., Military Intelligence.

MIA, **1.** Also, **M.I.A.** missing in action. **2.** *pl.* **MIAs, MIA′s.** a missing combatant whose whereabouts or death cannot be ascertained.

Mi·am·i (mī am′ē, -am′ə), *n.* **1.** a city in SE Florida. 373,024. **2.** a river in W Ohio, flowing S into the Ohio River. 160 mi. (260 km) long. —**Mi·am′i·an,** *n.*

mi·as·ma (mī az′mə, mē-), *n., pl.* **-mas, -ma·ta** (-mə tə). **1.** noxious exhalations from putrescent organic matter; poisonous effluvia or germs polluting the atmosphere. **2.** a dangerous, foreboding, or deathlike influence or atmosphere. —**mi·as′mal, mi·as·mat′ic** (-mat′ik), **mi·as′mic,** *adj.*

Mic., Micah.

mi·ca (mī′kə), *n.* any member of a group of minerals, hydrous silicates of aluminum usu. with potassium, sodium, or calcium, that separate readily into thin, tough, often transparent laminae. —**mi·ca′ceous** (-kā′shəs), *adj.*

Mi·cah (mī′kə), *n.* **1.** a Minor Prophet of the 8th century B.C. **2.** a book of the Bible bearing his name.

mice (mīs), *n.* pl. of MOUSE.

Mi·chael (mī′kəl), *n.* a militant archangel. Dan. 10:13; Rev. 12:7.

Mi·chal (mī′kəl), *n.* a daughter of Saul and David's wife. I Sam. 14:49; 18:27.

Mi·chel·an·ge·lo (mī′kəl an′jə lō′, mik′əl-), *n.* (Michelangelo Buonarroti), 1475–1564, Italian artist, architect, and poet.

Mich·i·gan (mish′i gən), *n.* **1.** a state in the N central United States. 9,328,784; 58,216 sq. mi. (150,780 sq. km). *Cap.:* Lansing. *Abbr.:* MI, Mich. **2. Lake,** a lake in the N central U.S., between Wisconsin and Michigan: one of the five Great Lakes. 22,400 sq. mi. (58,015 sq. km). —**Mich′i·gan′der** (-gan′dər), **Mich′i·gan·ite′,** *n.*

Mich′igan bank′roll, *n. Slang.* **1.** a large roll of paper money in small denominations. **2.** a roll of counterfeit paper money or a roll of money-sized paper surrounded by one or more genuine bills. Also called **Mich′igan roll.**

Mich·mash (mik′mash), *n.* a Benjamite city near Jerusalem where Jonathan defeated the Philistines. I Sam. 13:2–16.

mick′ey mouse′, *adj.* (*often caps.*) **1.** trite; corny: *mickey mouse music.* **2.** petty or trivial: *mickey mouse activities.*

mi·cra (mī′krə), *n.* a pl. of MICRON.

mi·cro (mī′krō), *adj., n., pl.* **-cros.** —*adj.* **1.** extremely small. **2.** minute in scope or capability. —*n.* **3.** MICROCOMPUTER.

micro-, a combining form with the meanings "small" (*microgamete*), "very small in comparison with others of its kind" (*microcapsule*), "too small to be seen by the unaided eye" (*microorganism*), "dealing with extremely minute organisms, organic structures, or quantities" (*microanalysis*), "localized, restricted in scope or area" (*microhabitat*), "(of a discipline) focusing on a restricted area" (*microeconomics*), "containing or dealing with texts that require enlargement to be read" (*microfilm*), "one millionth" (*microgram*). Also, *esp. before a vowel,* **micr-.**

mi·cro·am·pere (mī′krō am′pēr, -am pēr′), *n.* a unit of electric current, equal to one millionth of an ampere.

mi·cro·a·nal·y·sis (mī′krō ə nal′ə sis), *n., pl.* **-ses** (-sēz′). the chemical analysis of minute samples of substances. —**mi′cro·an′a·lyst** (-an′l-ist), *n.* —**mi′cro·an′a·lyt′i·cal** (-it′i kəl), **mi′cro·an′a·lyt′ic,** *adj.*

mi·cro·a·nat·o·my (mī′krō ə nat′ə mē), *n.* the branch of anatomy dealing with microscopic structures. —**mi′cro·an′a·tom′ic** (-an′ə-tom′ik), **mi′cro·an′a·tom′i·cal,** *adj.* —**mi′cro·an′a·tom′i·cal·ly,** *adv.* —**mi′cro·a·nat′o·mist,** *n.*

mi·crobe (mī′krōb), *n.* a microorganism, esp. a disease-causing bacterium. —**mi′crobe·less,** *adj.* —**mi·cro′bi·al, mi·cro′bic,** *adj.*

mi·cro·bi·ol·o·gy (mī′krō bī ol′ə jē), *n.* the branch of biology dealing with microscopic organisms. —**mi′cro·bi′o·log′i·cal** (-ə loj′i kəl), **mi′cro·bi′o·log′ic,** *adj.* —**mi′cro·bi·ol′o·gist,** *n.*

mi·cro·brew·er·y (mī′krō brōō′ə rē, -brōōr′ē), *n.* a brewery producing less than 15,000 barrels per year and usu. concentrating on exotic or high-quality beer.

mi·cro·cap·sule (mī′krō kap′səl, -sōol, -syōol), *n.* a tiny capsule, 20–150 microns in diameter, used for slow-release application of drugs, pesticides, flavors, etc.

mi·cro·chem·is·try (mī′krō kem′ə strē) *n.* the branch of chemistry dealing with minute quantities of substances. —**mi′cro·chem′i·cal** (-kem′i kəl), *adj.*

mi·cro·chip (mī′krō chip′), *n.* CHIP[1] (def. 5).

mi·cro·cir·cuit (mī′krō sûr′kit), *n.* INTEGRATED CIRCUIT. —**mi′cro·cir′cuit·ry,** *n.*

mi·cro·cli·mate (mī′krə klī′mit), *n.* the climate of a small area, as of confined spaces such as caves or houses, of plant communities, wooded areas, etc., or of urban communities, which may be different from that in the general region. Compare MACROCLIMATE. —**mi′cro·cli·mat′ic** (-mat′ik), *adj.* —**mi′cro·cli·mat′i·cal·ly,** *adv.*

mi·cro·cline (mī′krə klīn′), *n.* a mineral of the feldspar group, potassium aluminum silicate, KAlSi$_3$O$_8$, chemically identical with orthoclase but differing in internal structure: used in making porcelain.

mi·cro·com·put·er (mī′krō kəm pyōo′tər), *n.* a compact computer having less capability than a minicomputer and employing a microprocessor. Compare MAINFRAME, MINICOMPUTER.

mi·cro·cosm (mī′krə koz′əm) also **mi·cro·cos·mos** (mī′krə koz′məs, -mōs), *n.* **1.** a little world; a world in miniature (opposed to *macrocosm*). **2.** anything that is regarded as a world in miniature, as an individual or a town. —**mi′cro·cos′mic, mi′cro·cos′mi·cal,** *adj.*

mi·cro·cul·ture (mī′krō kul′chər), *n.* the culture of a group living within a limited geographical area.

mi·cro·cu·rie (mī′krə kyōor′ē, mī′krō kyōo rē′), *n.* a unit of radioactivity, equal to one millionth of a curie; 3.70 × 10⁴ disintegrations per second. *Symbol:* μCi, μc

mi·cro·ec·o·nom·ics (mī′krō ek′ə nom′iks, -ē′kə-), *n.* (*used with a sing. v.*) the branch of economics dealing with particular aspects of an economy, as the price-cost relationship of a firm. Compare MACROECONOMICS. —**mi′cro·ec′o·nom′ic,** *adj.* —**mi′cro·e·con′o·mist** (-i kon′ə mist), *n.*

mi·cro·e·lec·tron·ics (mī′krō i lek tron′iks, -ē′lek-), *n.* (*used with a sing. v.*) the technology dealing with electronic systems utilizing extremely small elements, esp. solid-state devices employing microminiaturization. —**mi′cro·e·lec·tron′ic,** *adj.*

mi·cro·en·vi·ron·ment (mī′krō en vī′ərn mənt, -vī′rən-), *n.* the environment of a small area or of an organism; microhabitat. —**mi′cro·en·vi′ron·men′tal** (-men′tl), *adj.*

mi·cro·ev·o·lu·tion (mī′krō ev′ə lōo′shən; *esp. Brit.* -ē′və-), *n.* evolutionary change involving the gradual accumulation of mutations leading to new varieties within a species. —**mi′cro·ev′o·lu′tion·ar′y,** *adj.*

mi·cro·far·ad (mī′krə far′əd, -ad), *n.* a unit of capacitance, equal to one millionth of a farad. *Abbr.:* mf.

mi·cro·fi·ber (mī′krō fī′bər), *n.* a very fine polyester fiber, weighing less than one denier per filament, used esp. for clothing.

mi·cro·fiche (mī′krə fēsh′), *n., pl.* **-fiche, -fich·es.** a flat sheet of microfilm, containing reproductions of printed or graphic matter. Also called **fiche.**

mi·cro·fil·a·ment (mī′krə fil′ə mənt), *n.* a tubelike protein structure that is involved in cell movement and changes in cell shape. —**mi′cro·fil·a·men′tous** (mī′krō fil′ə men′təs), *adj.*

mi·cro·film (mī′krə film′), *n.* **1.** a film bearing a miniature photographic copy of printed matter. —*v.t.* **2.** to make a microfilm of.

mi·cro·groove (mī′krə grōov′), *n.* a very narrow spiral needle groove on a long-playing record.

mi·cro·man·age (mī′krō man′ij), *v.t.,* **-aged, -ag·ing.** to manage or control with excessive attention to minor details: *micromanaging every facet of government.* —**mi′cro·man′age·ment,** *n.*

mi·crom·e·ter[1] (mī krom′i tər), *n.* any of various devices for measuring minute distances, angles, etc., as in connection with a telescope or microscope.

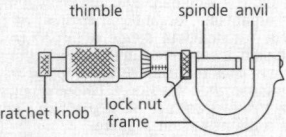

micrometer

mi·crom·e·ter[2] (mī′krō mē′tər), *n.* MICRON.

micromicro-, PICO-.

mi·cro·min·i (mī′krō min′ē), *adj., n., pl.* **-min·is.** —*adj.* **1.** MICROMINIATURE. —*n.* **2.** something of a microminiature size. **3.** a very short miniskirt.

mi·cro·min·i·a·ture (mī′krō min′ē ə chər, -chōor′, -min′ə chər), *adj.* built on an extremely small scale: used esp. of electronic equipment with small solid-state components.

mi·cron (mī′kron), *n., pl.* **-crons, -cra** (-krə). the millionth part of a meter. Also called **micrometer.** *Symbol:* μ, mu

Mi·cro·ne·sia (mī′krə nē′zhə, -shə), *n.* **1.** one of the three principal divisions of Oceania, comprising the small Pacific islands N of the equator and E of the Philippines, whose main groups are the Mariana Islands, the Caroline Islands, and the Marshall Islands. **2. Federated States of,** a group of islands in the W Pacific, in the Caroline Islands, comprising the islands of Pohnpei, Truk, Yap, and Kosrae: formerly a part of the Trust Territory of the Pacific Islands; now a self-governing area associated with the U.S. 127,616; 271 sq. mi. (701 sq. km).

mi·cro·nu·tri·ent (mī′krō nōo′trē ənt, -nyōo′-), *n.* an essential nutrient, as a trace mineral, that is required in minute amounts.

mi·cro·or·gan·ism (mī′krō ôr′gə niz′əm), *n.* any organism too small to be viewed by the unaided eye, as bacteria or some fungi and algae. —**mi′cro·or·gan′ic** (-ôr gan′ik), **mi′cro·or′gan·is′mal,** *adj.*

mi·cro·pa·le·on·tol·o·gy (mī′krō pā′lē ən tol′ə jē, -pal′ē-), *n.* the branch of paleontology dealing with the study of microscopic fossils. —**mi′cro·pa′le·on′to·log′i·cal** (-on′tl oj′i kəl, -pal′ē-), **mi′cro·pa′le·on′to·log′ic,** *adj.* —**mi′cro·pa′le·on·tol′o·gist,** *n.*

mi·cro·phage (mī′krə fāj′), *n.* a small phagocyte in blood and lymph that migrates to tissues in the inflammatory immune response.

mi·cro·phone (mī′krə fōn′), *n.* an instrument capable of transforming sound waves into changes in electric currents or voltage, used in recording or transmitting sound. —**mi′cro·phon′ic** (-fon′ik), *adj.*

mi·cro·pho·to·graph (mī′krə fō′tə graf′, -gräf′), *n.* **1.** MICROFILM. **2.** a small photograph requiring optical enlargement to render it visible in detail. **3.** PHOTOMICROGRAPH. —**mi′cro·pho′to·graph′ic** (-graf′ik), *adj.* —**mi′cro·pho·tog′ra·phy** (-krō fə tog′rə fē), *n.*

mi·cro·phys·ics (mī′krə fiz′iks), *n.* (*used with a sing. v.*) the branch of physics dealing with elementary particles, atoms, and molecules. —**mi′cro·phys′i·cal,** *adj.*

mi·cro·proc·es·sor (mī′krō pros′es ər, -ə sər; *esp. Brit.* -prō′ses ər, -sə sər), *n.* an integrated computer circuit that performs all the functions of a CPU. —**mi′cro·proc′es·sing,** *n.*

mi·cro·scope (mī′krə skōp′), *n.* **1.** an optical instrument having a magnifying lens or a combination of lenses for inspecting objects too small to be seen distinctly by the unaided eye. **2.** any of various high-powered electronic magnifying devices, as the electron microscope.

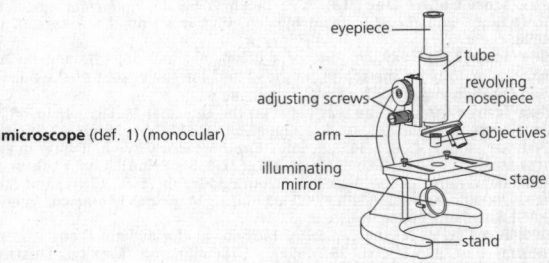

microscope (def. 1) (monocular)

mi·cro·scop·ic (mī′krə skop′ik) also **mi·cro·scop′i·cal,** *adj.* **1.** so small as to be invisible without the use of the microscope. Compare MACROSCOPIC (def. 1). **2.** very small; tiny. **3.** involving or requiring the use of a microscope: *microscopic investigation.* **4.** very detailed; meticulous: *a microscopic analysis.* —**mi′cro·scop′i·cal·ly,** *adv.*

mi·cros·co·py (mī kros′kə pē, mī′krə skō′pē), *n.* **1.** the use of the microscope. **2.** microscopic investigation.

mi·cro·sec·ond (mī′krə sek′ənd), *n.* a unit of time equal to one millionth of a second. *Symbol:* μsec

mi·cro·state (mī′krō stāt′), *n.* MINISTATE.

mi·cro·struc·ture (mī′krō struk′chər), *n.* the structure of an etched and polished metal or alloy as observed under magnification.

mi·cro·sur·ger·y (mī′krō sûr′jə rē, mī′krō sûr′-), *n.* any of various surgical procedures performed under magnification and with small specialized instruments. —**mi′cro·sur′geon,** *n.* —**mi′cro·sur′gi·cal,** *adj.*

mi·cro·wave (mī′krō wāv′), *n., v.,* **-waved, -wav·ing.** —*n.* **1.** an electromagnetic wave of extremely high frequency, 1 GHz or more, and having wavelengths of from 1 mm to 30 cm. **2.** MICROWAVE OVEN. —*v.t.* **3.** to cook or heat in a microwave. —**mi′cro·wav′a·ble,** *adj.*

mi′crowave ov′en, *n.* an electrically operated oven that uses microwaves to generate heat within the food.

mic·tu·rate (mik′chə rāt′), *v.i.,* **-rat·ed, -rat·ing.** to pass urine; urinate. —**mic′tu·ri′tion** (-rish′ən), *n.*

mid[1] (mid), *adj.* **1.** being at or near the middle point of: *in mid autumn.* **2.** (of a vowel) articulated with an opening above the tongue approximately intermediate between those for high and low, as the vowels of *bet, bait, but,* and *boat.* Compare HIGH (def. 20), LOW[1] (def. 27).

mid[2] or **'mid** (mid), *prep.* AMID.

mid-, a combining form representing MID[1]: *midday; mid-Victorian.*

mid·af·ter·noon (mid′af′tər nōon′, -äf′-), *n.* **1.** the part of the afternoon approximately halfway between noon and sunset. —*adj.* **2.** pertaining to or occurring in midafternoon: *a midafternoon nap.*

mid·air (mid âr′), *n.* **1.** any point in the air not contiguous with the earth or other solid surface. —*adj.* **2.** occurring in midair.

Mi·das (mī′dəs), *n.* a legendary Phrygian king endowed by Dionysus with the power to turn whatever he touched into gold.

mid·brain (mid′brān′), *n.* the middle of the three primary divisions of the brain in the embryo of a vertebrate or the part of the adult brain derived from this tissue; mesencephalon.

mid·day (*n.* mid′dā′, -dā′; *adj.* -dā′), *n.* **1.** the middle of the day; noon or the time shortly before or after noon. —*adj.* **2.** of or pertaining to the middle part of the day: *a midday news broadcast.*

mid·den (mid′n), *n.* a dunghill or refuse heap.

mid·dle (mid′l), *adj.* **1.** equally distant from the extremes or outer limits; central: *the middle part of a room.* **2.** intermediate or intervening: *the middle distance.* **3.** medium or average: *a man of middle size.* **4.** (*cap.*) (in the history of a language) intermediate between periods classified as Old and New or Modern: *Middle English.* **5.** of, pertaining to, or being a verb form or voice, as in Greek, in which the subject is represented as acting on or for itself, in contrast to the active voice in which the subject acts and the passive voice in which the subject is acted upon. **6.** (*often cap.*) noting the division intermediate between the upper and lower divisions of a geologic period, system, or the like: *the Middle Devonian.* —*n.* **7.** the point, part, position, etc., equidistant from extremes or limits: *in the middle of the pool.* **8.** the central part of the human body, esp. the waist: *He bent at the middle.*

mid′dle age′, *n.* the period of human life between youth and old age, usu. considered as the years between 45 and 65. —**mid′dle-aged′,** *adj.*

Mid′dle Ag′es, *n.* the time in European history between classical antiquity and the Renaissance, from the late 5th century to about 1350: sometimes restricted to the period after 1100 and sometimes extended to 1450 or 1500.

Mid′dle Amer′ica, *n.* **1.** average middle-class Americans as a group, as distinguished from the rich or poor or the politically extreme. **2.** the Midwest. **3.** continental North America S of the U.S., comprising Mexico, Central America, and usually the West Indies. 92,000,000; 1,060,118 sq. mi. (2,745,705 sq. km). —**Mid′dle-A·mer′i·can,** *adj.*

Mid′dle Atlan′tic States′, *n.pl.* New York, New Jersey, and Pennsylvania.

middle C, *n.* the musical note indicated by the first leger line above the bass staff and the first below the treble staff.

mid′dle class′, *n.* **1.** a class of people intermediate between those of higher and lower economic or social standing, generally characterized by average income and education, conventional values, and conservative attitudes. **2.** the class traditionally intermediate between the aristocracy and the working class. —**mid′dle-class′,** *adj.*

mid′dle ear′, *n.* the middle portion of the ear consisting of the eardrum and an air-filled chamber lined with mucous membrane that contains the malleus, incus, and stapes.

Mid′dle Eng′lish, *n.* the English language of the period c1150–c1475. *Abbr.:* ME

mid′dle fin′ger, *n.* the finger between the forefinger and the third finger.

mid′dle ground′, *n.* an intermediate position, area, or recourse between two opposites or extremes; a halfway or neutral standpoint.

Mid′dle King′dom, *n.* **1.** the period in the history of ancient Egypt, c2000–1785 B.C., comprising the 11th and 12th dynasties. Compare NEW KINGDOM, OLD KINGDOM. **2.** (formerly) the 18 inner provinces of China. **3.** the Chinese Empire.

mid·dle·man (mid′l man′), *n., pl.* **-men. 1.** a person who buys goods from the producer and resells them to the retailer or consumer. **2.** a person who acts as an intermediary.

mid′dle man′agement, *n.* the middle echelon of administration in business and industry.

Mid·dle·march (mid′l märch′), a novel (1871–72) by George Eliot.

mid′dle name′, *n.* a name occurring between a person's first and family names.

mid′dle-of-the-road′, *adj.* following or favoring an intermediate position between two extremes, esp. in politics; moderate. —**mid′dle-of-the-road′er,** *n.* —**mid′dle-of-the-road′ism,** *n.*

mid′dle pas′sage, *n.* (*sometimes caps.*) the part of the Atlantic Ocean between the W coast of Africa and the West Indies: the longest part of the journey formerly made by slave ships.

Mid′dle Path′, *Buddhism.* the conduct of life by a religious person in such a way as to avoid the extremes of luxury and asceticism.

mid′dle school′, *n.* a school encompassing grades five or six through eight.

mid′dle-sized′ or **mid′dle-size′,** *adj.* MEDIUM-SIZED.

mid′dle term′, *n.* the term of a syllogism that appears in both premises but not in the conclusion.

mid·dle·weight (mid′l wāt′), *n.* **1.** a boxer or weightlifter intermediate in weight between a welterweight and a light heavyweight, esp. a professional boxer weighing up to 160 pounds (72.5 kg). —*adj.* **2.** of or pertaining to middleweights: *the middleweight division.*

Mid′dle West′, *n.* MIDWEST (def. 1). —**Mid′dle West′erner,** *n.*

mid·dling (mid′ling), *adj.* **1.** medium, moderate, or average in size, quantity, or quality. **2.** mediocre; ordinary; commonplace; pedestrian. **3.** *Older Use.* in fairly good health. —*adv.* **4.** moderately; fairly. —*n.* **5.** **middlings, a.** any of various products or commodities of intermediate quality, grade, size, etc. **b.** coarser particles of ground wheat mingled with bran. —**mid′dling·ly,** *adv.*

mid·dy (mid′ē), *n., pl.* **-dies. 1.** *Informal.* a midshipman. **2.** MIDDY BLOUSE.

mid′dy blouse′, *n.* any of various loose, usu. hip-length pullover blouses with a sailor collar.

midge (mij), *n.* **1.** any of numerous minute dipterous insects, esp. of the family Chironomidae, resembling a mosquito. **2.** a tiny person.

midg·et (mij′it), *n.* **1.** (not in technical use) an extremely small person having normal physical proportions. **2.** any animal or thing that is very small for its kind. —*adj.* **3.** very small or of a class below the usual size; miniature.

mid·gut (mid′gut′), *n.* **1. a.** the middle portion of the vertebrate alimentary canal, posterior to the stomach or gizzard and extending to the cecum; small intestine. **b.** the anterior portion of the arthropod colon. **2.** the middle part of the embryonic alimentary canal, from which the intestines develop. Compare FOREGUT, HINDGUT.

mid·i (mid′ē), *n., pl.* **mid·is. 1.** MIDISKIRT. **2.** a garment with a midiskirt, as a coat.

MIDI (mid′ē), *n.* Musical Instrument Digital Interface: a standard means of sending digitally encoded information about music between electronic devices, as between synthesizers and computers.

Mid·i·an (mid′ē ən), *n.* a son of Abraham. Gen. 25:1–4.

Mid·i·an·ite (mid′ē ə nīt′), *n.* (in the Bible) a member of a pastoral people of NW Arabia, said to be descendants of Midian.

mid·i·skirt (mid′ē skûrt′), *n.* a skirt or skirt part, as of a dress or coat, ending at the middle of the calf.

mid·land (mid′lənd), *n.* **1.** the middle or interior part of a country. **2.** (*cap.*) the dialect or dialects of English spoken in the Midlands of England. **3.** (*cap.*) the dialect of English spoken in the S parts of Illinois, Indiana, Ohio, Pennsylvania, and New Jersey, in West Virginia, Kentucky, and E Tennessee, and throughout the S Appalachians. —*adj.* **4.** in or of the midland; inland. **5.** (*cap.*) of the Midlands.

Mid·lands (mid′ləndz), *n.pl.* the central part of England.

mid·life or **mid-life** (*n.* mid′līf′; *adj.* mid′līf′), *n.* **1.** MIDDLE AGE. —*adj.* **2.** MIDDLE-AGED.

mid′life cri′sis, *n.* a period of stress and self-doubt occurring in middle age.

mid·morn·ing (mid′môr′ning), *n.* **1.** the middle of the morning; the time between early morning and noon. —*adj.* **2.** of, pertaining to, or occurring in the middle of the morning: *a midmorning coffee break.*

mid·night (mid′nīt′), *n.* **1.** the middle of the night, esp. twelve o'clock at night. —*adj.* **2.** of or pertaining to midnight. **3.** resembling midnight, as in darkness. —**mid′night·ly,** *adj., adv.*

mid′night sun′, *n.* the sun visible at midnight in summer in arctic and antarctic regions.

mid·point (mid′point′), *n.* **1.** a point at or near the middle of something, as a line. **2.** a point in time halfway between the beginning and end, as of a period or process. **3.** *Geom.* the point on a line segment or an arc that is equidistant, when measured along the line or the arc, from both endpoints. **4.** *Statistics.* MEDIAN (def. 5).

mid·rash (mē dräsh′), *n., pl.* **mid·ra·shim** (mē′drä shēm′), **mid·ra·shoth, mid·ra·shot** (mē′drä shôt′). **1.** an early Jewish interpretation of or commentary on a Biblical text. **2.** (*cap.*) a collection of such commentaries, esp. those written in the first ten centuries A.D. [< Hebrew *midrāsh* lit., exposition] —**mid′rash·ic** (mid rash′ik), *adj.*

mid·riff (mid′rif), *n.* **1.** DIAPHRAGM (def. 1). **2.** the middle portion of the human body, between the chest and the waist. **3.** the part of a dress or bodice that covers this area. **4.** a garment that exposes this area.

mid·rise (mid′rīz′), *adj.* **1.** (of a building) moderately high, usu. of five to ten stories. —*n.* **2.** a mid-rise apartment or office building.

mid·sec·tion (mid′sek′shən), *n.* **1.** the middle section or part of anything. **2.** the solar plexus; midriff.

mid·ship (mid′ship′), *adj.* in or belonging to the middle part of a ship.

mid·ship·man (mid′ship′mən, mid ship′-) *n., pl.* **-men. 1.** a student, as at the U.S. Naval Academy, in training for commission as ensign in the Navy or second lieutenant in the Marine Corps. Compare CADET (def. 2). **2. a.** (*often cap.*) a recent graduate of a British government naval school having officer rank. **b.** (formerly) a candidate for officer rank in the British navy.

mid-size (mid′sīz′) also **mid′sized′,** *adj.* **1.** (of an automobile) being between a compact and a full-size car in size. **2.** intermediate in size.

midst¹ (midst), *n.* **1.** the position of anything surrounded by or among other things or parts (usu. prec. by *the*): *in the midst of the crowd.* **2.** the position of something occurring in the middle of or during a period of time, course of action, etc. (usu. prec. by *the*): *in the midst of the concert.* **3.** the state of being surrounded by or engaged in (usu. prec. by *the*): *in the midst of work.* **4.** the middle or central point or part.

midst² (midst), *prep.* AMIDST.

mid·stream (mid′strēm′), *n.* **1.** the middle of a stream. **2.** the middle period of a process, course, or the like.

mid·sum·mer (mid′sum′ər, -sum′-), *n.* **1.** the middle of summer. **2.** the summer solstice, around June 21. —*adj.* **3.** of, pertaining to, or occurring in the middle of the summer.

Mid′summer Day′, *n. Chiefly Brit.* the saint's day of St. John the Baptist, celebrated on June 24.

Mid′summer Night's′ Dream′, A, a comedy (1595?) by William Shakespeare.

mid-teen (mid′tēn′), *adj.* **1.** of or pertaining to a person 15–17 years

old. —*n.* **2.** a person 15–17 years old. **3. mid-teens,** numbers, amounts, etc., midway between 13 and 19: *a salary in the mid-teens.*
mid•term (mid′tûrm′), *n.* **1.** the halfway point of a term, as a school term or term of office. **2.** an examination given halfway through a school term. —*adj.* **3.** pertaining to, at, or near the middle of a term.
mid•town (mid′toun′, -toun′), *n.* **1.** the central part of a city or town between uptown and downtown. —*adj.* **2.** of, pertaining to, or situated in this part: *a midtown restaurant.*
Mid-Trib•u•la•tion•ist (mid′trib yə lā′shə nist), *n.* one who believes the Great Tribulation will be preceded by a period of peace and safety.
mid•way (*adv., adj.* mid′wā′; *n.* -wā′), *adv., adj.* **1.** in the middle of the way or distance; halfway. —*n.* **2.** (*often cap.*) a place or way, as at a fair or carnival, on or along which sideshows, games, concessions, etc., are located. **3.** a place or part situated midway.
Mid•way (mid′wā′), *n.* several U.S. islets in the N Pacific, about 1300 mi. (2095 km) NW of Hawaii. 2 sq. mi. (5 sq. km).
mid•week (*n.* mid′wēk′, -wēk′; *adj.* -wēk′), *n.* **1.** the middle of the week. —*adj.* **2.** pertaining to or occurring in the middle of the week.
Mid•west (mid′west′), *n.* **1.** Also called **Middle West.** a region in the N central United States, including Illinois, Indiana, Iowa, Kansas, Michigan, Minnesota, Missouri, Nebraska, North Dakota, Ohio, South Dakota, and Wisconsin. —*adj.* **2.** MIDWESTERN. —**Mid′west′ern•er,** *n.*
Mid•west•ern (mid wes′tərn), *adj.* (*sometimes l.c.*) of or pertaining to the Midwest. Often, **Middle Western.**
mid•wife (mid′wīf′), *n., pl.* **-wives** (-wīvz′), *v.,* **-wifed** or **-wived, -wif•ing** or **wiv•ing.** —*n.* **1.** a person who assists women in childbirth. **2.** a person or thing that assists in producing something new. —*v.t.* **3.** to assist in the birth of (a baby). **4.** to assist in producing or bringing about (something new).
mid•wife•ry (mid wif′ə rē, -wif′rē, mid′wī′fə rē, -wīf′rē), *n.* the technique or practice of a midwife.
mid•win•ter (*n.* mid′win′tər, -win′-; *adj.* -win′-), *n.* **1.** the middle of winter. **2.** the winter solstice, around December 22. —*adj.* **3.** of, pertaining to, or occurring in the middle of the winter.
mid•year (mid′yēr′, -yēr′ *for 1;* -yēr′ *for 2, 3*), *n.* **1.** the middle of the year. **2.** Often, **midyears.** an examination at the middle of a school year. —*adj.* **3.** of, pertaining to, or occurring in midyear.
mien (mēn), *n.* air, bearing, or demeanor, as showing character, feeling, etc.: *a person of noble mien.*
Mies van der Ro•he (mēz′ van dər rō′ə, fän, mēs′), *n.* **Ludwig,** 1886–1969, U.S. architect, born in Germany. —**Mies′i•an,** *adj., n.*
miff (mif), *v.t.* **1.** to put into an irritable mood, esp. by offending; annoy; vex. —*n.* **2.** petulant displeasure; ill humor.
MiG or **Mig** or **MIG** (mig), *n.* any of several Russian-built fighter aircraft.
might[1] (mīt), *auxiliary v., pres. sing. and pl.* **might;** *past* **might. 1.** pt. of MAY[1]: *I asked if we might borrow their car.* **2.** (used to express tentative possibility): *She might have called while you were out.* **3.** (used to express an unrealized possibility): *He might have been killed!* **4.** (used to express advisability or offer a suggestion): *They might at least have tried.* **5.** (used to express contingency, esp. in clauses indicating condition, concession, result, etc.): *difficult as it might be.* **6.** (used in polite requests for permission): *Might I speak to you for a moment?*
might[2] (mīt), *n.* **1.** physical strength: *He swung with all his might.* **2.** superior power or strength; force: *the theory that might makes right.* **3.** power or ability to be effective: *the might of the ballot box.*
might•y (mī′tē), *adj.,* **might•i•er, might•i•est,** *adv., n.* —*adj.* **1.** having, characterized by, or showing superior power or strength: *mighty rulers.* **2.** of great size; huge: *a mighty oak.* **3.** great in amount, extent, degree, or importance; exceptional: *a mighty accomplishment.* —*adv.* **4.** *Informal.* very; extremely: *I'm mighty pleased.* —*n.* **5. the mighty,** mighty persons collectively. —**might′i•ly,** *adv.* —**might′i•ness,** *n.*
Might′y For′tress Is′ Our′ God′, A, a Christian hymn (1529) with words and music by Martin Luther.
might′y men′, *n.pl.* brave soldiers loyal to David before and after he became king. II Sam. 23:8–39; I Chron. 11:10–47.
mi•graine (mī′grān *or, Brit.,* mē′-), *n.* a severe, recurrent headache characterized by pressure or throbbing on one side of the head and accompanied by nausea and other disturbances. —**mi•grain′ous,** *adj.*
mi•grant (mī′grənt), *adj.* **1.** migrating; migratory. —*n.* **2.** a person or animal that migrates. **3.** Also called **mi′grant work′er.** a person who moves from place to place to get work, esp. in seasonal harvesting.
mi•grate (mī′grāt), *v.i.,* **-grat•ed, -grat•ing. 1.** to move from one country, region, or place to another. **2.** to pass periodically from one region or climate to another, as certain birds, fishes, and animals. **3.** to shift, as from one system or enterprise to another. **4. a.** (of ions) to move toward an electrode during electrolysis. **b.** (of atoms within a molecule) to change position. **5.** (of a chemical or other substance) to spread, as by seepage, from an area or site of containment into a larger environment. —**mi′gra•tor,** *n.*
mi•gra•tion (mī grā′shən), *n.* **1.** the process or act of migrating. **2.** a migratory movement. **3.** a number or body of persons or animals migrating together. —**mi•gra′tion•al,** *adj.*
mi•gra•to•ry (mī′grə tôr′ē, -tōr′ē), *adj.* **1.** migrating. **2.** periodically migrating: *migratory birds.* **3.** pertaining to a migration: *migratory movements of birds.* **4.** roving; wandering; migrant.
mi•ka•do (mi kä′dō), *n., pl.* **-dos. 1.** (*sometimes cap.*) a title of the emperor of Japan. **2.** (*cap., italics*) ***The,*** an operetta (1885) by Sir William S. Gilbert and Sir Arthur Sullivan.
mike (mīk), *n.* a microphone.
mil (mil), *n. Slang.* a million.
mi•la•dy or **mi•la•di** (mi lā′dē), *n., pl.* **-dies** or **-dis. 1.** an English noblewoman (often used as a term of address). **2.** a woman regarded as having fashionable or expensive tastes.
mil•age (mī′lij), *n.* MILEAGE.
Mi•lan (mi lan′, -län′), *n.* an industrial city in central Lombardy, in N Italy. 1,478,505. Italian, **Mi•la•no** (mē lä′nô). —**Mil•an•ese** (mil′ə nēz′, -nēs′), *adj., n.*
milch (milch), *adj.* (of a domestic animal) yielding milk; kept or suitable for milk production.
mil•chig (mil′KHig, -KHik), *adj. Judaism.* (in the dietary laws) consisting of, made from, or used only for milk or dairy products. Compare FLEISHIG, PAREVE.
mild (mīld), *adj.,* **-er, -est. 1.** amiably gentle or temperate in feeling, behavior, manner, etc. **2.** not cold, severe, or extreme; temperate: *a mild winter.* **3.** not sharp, pungent, or strong: *a mild cheese.* **4.** moderate in intensity, degree, or character; not acute: *mild regret.* **5.** gentle or moderate in force or effect: *a mild drug.* —**mild′ly,** *adv.* —**mild′ness,** *n.*
mil•dew (mil′dōō′, -dyōō′), *n.* **1.** a disease of plants, characterized by a cottony, usu. whitish coating on the affected parts, caused by any of various fungi. **2.** any of these fungi, esp. downy mildew or powdery mildew. **3.** any similar coating or discoloration caused by fungi, as on fabrics, paper, leather, etc., when exposed to moisture. —*v.t., v.i.* **4.** to affect or become affected with mildew. —**mil′dew′y,** *adj.*
mile (mīl), *n.* **1.** Also called **statute mile.** a unit of distance on land in English-speaking countries equal to 5280 feet, or 1760 yards (1.609 kilometers). *Abbr.:* mi, mi. **2.** NAUTICAL MILE (def. 2). **3.** INTERNATIONAL NAUTICAL MILE. **4.** any of various other units of distance at different periods and in different countries. Compare ROMAN MILE. **5.** a notable distance or margin: *missed it by a mile.* —***Idiom.*** **6. go the extra mile,** to make an extra effort.
mile•age or **mil•age** (mī′lij), *n.* **1.** the aggregate number of miles traveled in a given time. **2.** length, extent, or distance in miles. **3.** the number of miles or average distance that a vehicle can travel on a specified quantity of fuel. **4.** wear, use, or profit: *to get good mileage out of an old coat.* **5.** an allowance for traveling expenses at a fixed rate per mile. **6.** a fixed charge per mile, as for haulage.
mile•post (mīl′pōst′), *n.* **1.** any of a series of posts set up to mark distance by miles, as along a highway, or an individual post showing the distance to or from a place. **2.** MILESTONE (def. 2).
mil•er (mī′lər), *n.* **1.** a participant in a one-mile race. **2.** an athlete who specializes in one-mile races. **3.** a racehorse that can compete well in a one-mile race.
Miles (mīlz), *n.* **Austin,** 1868–1946, U.S. hymn writer.
mile•stone (mīl′stōn′), *n.* **1.** a stone functioning as a milepost. **2.** a significant event or point in development.
Mi•le•tus (mī lē′təs), *n.* an ancient city in Asia Minor, on the Aegean.
mi•lieu (mil yōō′, mēl-; *Fr.* mē lyœ′), *n., pl.* **mi•lieus** (mil yōōz′, mēl-), **mi•lieux** (*Fr.* mē lyœ′). surroundings; environment.
mil•i•tant (mil′i tənt), *adj.* **1.** vigorously active, aggressive, and often combative, esp. in support of a cause: *militant reformers.* —*n.* **2.** a militant person. —**mil′i•tan•cy, mil′i•tant•ness,** *n.* —**mil′i•tant•ly,** *adv.*
mil•i•ta•rism (mil′i tə riz′əm), *n.* **1.** a strong military spirit or policy. **2.** the principle or policy of maintaining a large military establishment. **3.** the tendency to regard military efficiency as the supreme ideal of the state, with other interests subordinate.
mil•i•ta•rist (mil′i tər ist), *n.* **1.** a person imbued with militarism. **2.** a person skilled in the conduct of war and military affairs. —**mil′i•ta•ris′tic,** *adj.* —**mil′i•ta•ris′ti•cal•ly,** *adv.*
mil•i•ta•rize (mil′i tə rīz′), *v.t.,* **-rized, -riz•ing. 1.** to equip with armed forces, military supplies, etc. **2.** to make military. **3.** to imbue with militarism. —**mil′i•ta•ri•za′tion,** *n.*
mil•i•tar•y (mil′i ter′ē), *adj., n., pl.* **-tar•y,** sometimes **-tar•ies.** —*adj.* **1.** of, for, or pertaining to the army or armed forces, often as distinguished from the navy. **2.** of, for, or pertaining to war: *military preparedness.* **3.** of, pertaining to, or performed by soldiers: *military duty.* **4.** befitting or characteristic of a soldier: *a military bearing.* —*n.* **5. the military, a.** the armed forces of a nation; the military establishment. **b.** military personnel, esp. commissioned officers. —**mil′i•tar′i•ly,** *adv.*
mil′itary acad′emy, *n.* **1.** a private school following some of the procedures of military life. **2.** a school that trains people for military careers as officers. Also called **military school.**
mil′itary-indus′trial com′plex, *n.* a nation's armed forces together with the industries that supply them.
mil′itary police′, *n.* soldiers who perform police duties within the army. *Abbr.:* MP Compare SHORE PATROL.
mil′itary school′, *n.* MILITARY ACADEMY.
mil′itary sci′ence, *n.* a course of study dealing with the logistic, tactical, and other principles of warfare.
mil•i•tate (mil′i tāt′), *v.i.,* **-tat•ed, -tat•ing.** to have a substantial effect; weigh heavily: *His prison record militated against him.* —**mil′i•ta′tion,** *n.* —**Usage.** See MITIGATE.
mi•li•tia (mi lish′ə), *n.* **1.** a body of citizens enrolled for military service, and called out periodically for drill but serving full time only in

emergencies. **2.** a body of citizen soldiers as distinguished from professional soldiers. **3.** all able-bodied males considered by law eligible for military service. **4.** a body of citizens organized in a paramilitary group and typically regarding themselves as defenders of individual rights against the presumed interference of the federal government. [< Latin *mīlitia* soldiery, der. of *mīles* soldier]

mi·li·tia·man (mi lish′ə mən), *n., pl.* **-men.** a person serving in the militia.

mil·i·um (mil′ē əm), *n., pl.* **mil·i·a** (mil′ē ə). a small white or yellowish nodule resembling a millet seed, produced in the skin by the retention of sebaceous secretion.

milk (milk), *n.* **1.** an opaque white or bluish-white liquid secreted by the mammary glands of female mammals, serving for the nourishment of their young. **2.** this liquid as secreted by cows, goats, or certain other animals and used by humans for food or to make butter, cheese, yogurt, etc. **3.** any liquid resembling this, as the liquid within a coconut, the sap of certain plants, or a pharmaceutical preparation. —*v.t.* **4.** to press or draw milk from the udder or breast of. **5.** to extract something from as if by milking. **6.** to get something from; exploit: *The swindler milked her of all her savings.* **7.** to extract; draw out: *He's good at milking laughs from the audience.* —**milk′·ness,** *n.* —**milk′y,** *adj.,* **-i·er, -i·est.**

milk′ choc′olate, *n.* chocolate made with milk.

milk·fish (milk′fish′), *n., pl.* **-fish·es,** (*esp. collectively*) **-fish.** a tropical Pacific silvery food fish, *Chanos chanos.*

milk′ glass′, *n.* an opaque white glass.

milk·man (milk′man′), *n., pl.* **-men.** a person who sells or delivers milk.

milk′ of magne′sia, *n.* a milky white suspension in water of magnesium hydroxide, Mg (OH)$_2$, used as an antacid or laxative.

milk′ pow′der, *n.* DRY MILK.

milk′ run′, *n.* a routine trip or undertaking.

milk′ shake′ or **milk′shake′,** *n.* a beverage of cold milk, flavoring, and often ice cream, blended in a mixer.

milk′ snake′, *n.* any of numerous, usu. brightly marked king snakes of the subspecies *Lampropeltis triangulum* (*doliata*), of North America. Also called **milk adder.**

milk·sop (milk′sop′), *n.* a weak or ineffectual person.

milk′ sug′ar, *n.* LACTOSE.

milk′ toast′, *n.* buttered toast, served in hot milk.

milk′-toast′, *adj.* meek or ineffectual. —*n.* **2.** MILQUETOAST.

milk′ tooth′, *n.* DECIDUOUS TOOTH.

milk′ vetch′, *n.* any of various plants of the genus *Astragalus,* of the legume family, esp. a European plant, *A. glycyphyllos,* believed to increase the secretion of milk in goats.

milk·weed (milk′wēd′), *n.* **1.** any of several plants of the genus *Asclepias,* characterized by a milky juice, clusters of white-to-purple flowers, and pods filled with silky tufted seeds. **2.** any of various other plants having a milky juice, as certain spurges.

milk′weed bug′, *n.* any of several red and black bugs, as *Oncopeltus fasciatus,* that feed on the juice of the milkweed.

milk·wort (milk′wûrt′, -wôrt′), *n.* any of numerous plants or shrubs of the genus *Polygala,* having flowers with winged petals.

Milk′y Way′, *n.* the spiral galaxy containing our solar system, seen as a luminous band stretching across the night sky and composed of approximately a trillion stars.

mill (mil), *n.* **1.** a factory for certain kinds of manufacture, as paper, steel, or textiles. **2.** a building equipped with machinery for grinding grain into flour and other cereal products. **3.** a machine for grinding, crushing, or pulverizing any solid substance: *a coffee mill.* **4.** any of various machines that modify the shape or size of a workpiece by rotating tools or the work: *rolling mill.* **5.** any of various other apparatuses for shaping materials or performing other mechanical operations. **6.** a business or institution that dispenses products or services in an impersonal or mechanical manner: *a divorce mill; a diploma mill.* **7.** *Slang.* a boxing match or fistfight. —*v.t.* **8.** to grind, work, treat, or shape in or with a mill. **9. a.** to make a raised edge on (a coin or the like). **b.** to make radial grooves on the raised edge of (a coin or the like). **10.** to beat or stir, as to a froth: *to mill chocolate.* **11.** *Slang.* to beat or strike; fight. —*v.i.* **12.** to move around aimlessly, slowly, or confusedly (often fol. by *about* or *around*). **13.** *Slang.* to fight or box. —*Idiom.* **14. through the mill,** through a set of difficult or painful experiences. —**mill′a·ble,** *adj.*

Mill (mil), *n.* **1. James,** 1773–1836, English philosopher, historian, and economist, born in Scotland. **2.** his son **John Stuart,** 1806–73, English philosopher and economist.

milled (mild), *v.* **1.** pt. and pp. of MILL. —*adj.* **2.** ground or hulled in a mill: *milled wheat.* **3.** (of a coin) struck by a mill or press and usu. finished with transverse ribs or grooves. **4.** pressed flat by rolling: *milled board.*

mil·le·nar·i·an (mil′ə nâr′ē ən), *adj.* **1.** MILLENARY. —*n.* **2.** a believer in the millennium.

mil·le·nar·y (mil′ə ner′ē), *adj., n., pl.* **-nar·ies.** —*adj.* **1.** of or pertaining to 1000, esp. 1000 years. **2.** pertaining to the millennium or millenarians. —*n.* **3.** an aggregate of 1000. **4.** MILLENNIUM. **5.** MILLENARIAN.

mil·len·ni·al (mi len′ē əl), *adj.* **1.** of or pertaining to a millennium or the millennium. **2.** worthy or suggestive of the millennium. —**mil·len′ni·al·ly,** *adv.*

mil·len·ni·al·ism (mi len′ē ə liz′əm), *n.* a belief in the millennium. Also called **mil·le·nar·i·an·ism** (mil′ə nâr′ē ə niz′əm). —**mil·len′ni·al·ist,** *n.*

mil·len·ni·um (mi len′ē əm), *n., pl.* **-ni·ums, -ni·a** (-nē ə). **1.** a period of 1000 years. **2. the millennium,** the period of 1000 years during which Christ will reign on earth. Rev. 20:1–7. **3.** a period of general righteousness and happiness. **4.** a thousandth anniversary.

mill·er (mil′ər), *n.* **1.** a person who owns or operates a mill, esp. a mill that grinds grain into flour. **2.** any moth, esp. of the family Noctuídae, having wings that appear powdery.

Mil·ler (mil′ər), *n.* **1. Arthur,** born 1915, U.S. playwright. **2. Glenn,** 1904–44, U.S. bandleader. **3. Joaquin** (*Cincinnatus Heine Miller*), 1841–1913, U.S. poet. **4. William,** 1782–1849, U.S. religious leader: founder of the Adventist Church.

Mill·er·ite (mil′ə rīt′), *n.* a follower of William Miller, a U.S. preacher who taught that the Second Advent of Christ and the beginning of the millennium were to occur in 1843.

milli-, a combining form meaning "thousand" (*millipede*); in the metric system, used in the names of units equal to ^{1}/$_{1000}$ of the given base unit (*millimeter*).

mil·li·gram (mil′i gram′), *n.* a unit of mass or weight equal to ^{1}/$_{1000}$ of a gram, and equivalent to 0.0154 grain. *Abbr.:* mg Also, *esp. Brit.,* **mil′·li·gramme′.**

Mil·li·kan (mil′i kən), *n.* **Robert Andrews,** 1868–1953, U.S. physicist: Nobel prize 1923.

mil·li·li·ter (mil′ə lē′tər), *n.* a unit of capacity equal to ^{1}/$_{1000}$ of a liter, equivalent to 0.033815 fluid ounce, or 0.061025 cubic inch. *Abbr.:* ml

mil·li·me·ter (mil′ə mē′tər), *n.* a unit of length equal to ^{1}/$_{1000}$ of a meter, equivalent to 0.03937 inch. *Abbr.:* mm —**mil′li·met′ric** (-me′trik), *adj.*

mil·li·mi·cron (mil′ə mī′kron), *n., pl.* **-crons, -cra** (-krə). NANOMETER. *Symbol:* mμ

mil·li·mole (mil′ə mōl′), *n.* 1/1000 of a mole. *Abbr.:* mM

mil·line (mil′līn′, mil līn′), *n.* **1.** one agate line of advertising one column in width appearing in one million copies of a periodical. **2.** Also called **mil′line rate′.** the charge or cost per milline.

mil·li·ner (mil′ə nər), *n.* a person who creates or sells hats for women.

mil·li·ner·y (mil′ə ner′ē, -nə rē), *n.* **1.** women's hats and related articles. **2.** the business or trade of a milliner.

mil·lion (mil′yən), *n., pl.* **-lions,** (*as after a numeral*) **-lion,** *adj.* —*n.* **1.** a cardinal number, 1000 times 1000. **2.** a symbol for this number, as 1,000,000 or M̄. **3. millions,** a number between 1,000,000 and 999,999,999. **4.** the amount of a thousand thousand units of money: *The three paintings fetched a million.* **5.** a very great number: *Thanks a million.* **6. the million(s),** the mass of the common people: *poetry for the millions.* —*adj.* **7.** amounting to one million in number. —**mil′lionth,** *adj., n.*

mil·lion·aire or **mil·lion·naire** (mil′yə nâr′, mil′yə nâr′), *n.* a person whose wealth amounts to a million or more in some currency.

mil·li·pede or **mil·le·pede** (mil′ə pēd′), *n.* any terrestrial arthropod of the class Diplopoda, having a cylindrical body composed of 20 to more than 100 segments, each with two pairs of legs.

mil·li·sec·ond (mil′ə sek′ənd), *n.* 1/1000 of a second. *Abbr.:* msec

Mill′ on the Floss′, The, a novel (1860) by George Eliot.

mill·stone (mil′stōn′), *n.* **1.** either of a pair of circular stones between which grain or another substance is ground, as in a mill. **2.** anything that grinds or crushes. **3.** any heavy mental or emotional burden (often used in the phrase *a millstone around one's neck*).

mill·work (mil′wûrk′), *n.* **1.** ready-made carpentry work from a mill. **2.** work done in a mill. **3.** finished woodwork, as moldings.

mill·wright (mil′rīt′), *n.* **1.** a person who erects the machinery of a mill. **2.** a person who designs and erects mills and mill machinery. **3.** a person who maintains and repairs machinery in a mill.

Milne (miln), *n.* **A(lan) A(lexander),** 1882–1956, English writer.

milque·toast (milk′tōst′), *n.* (*often cap.*) a timid, spineless person.

milt (milt), *n.* **1.** the sperm-containing secretion of fish testes. **2.** fish testes and sperm ducts when filled with milt.

Mil·ton (mil′tən), *n.* **John,** 1608–74, English poet. —**Mil·ton′ic** (-ton′ik), **Mil·to′ni·an** (-tō′nē ən), *adj.*

Mil·wau·kee (mil wô′kē), *n.* a port in SE Wisconsin, on Lake Michigan. 617,044. —**Mil·wau·ke·an,** *n.*

mime (mīm, mēm), *n., v.,* **mimed, mim·ing.** —*n.* **1.** the art or technique of portraying a character, mood, idea, or narration by gestures and body movements; pantomime. **2.** an actor who specializes in this art. **3. a.** (in ancient Greece and Rome) a farcical, often licentious type of popular drama. **b.** a performer in such entertainment. **4.** MIMIC (def. 4). **5.** a jester, clown, or comedian. —*v.t.* **6.** to mimic. **7.** to act in mime. —*v.i.* **8.** to play a part by mime or mimicry. —**mim′er,** *n.*

mim·e·o (mim′ē ō′), *n., pl.* **mim·e·os.** mimeograph.

mim·e·o·graph (mim′ē ə graf′, -gräf′), *n.* **1.** a printing machine with an ink-fed drum, around which a cut waxed stencil is placed and which rotates as successive sheets of paper are fed into it. **2.** a copy made from a mimeograph. —*v.t.* **3.** to duplicate (something) by means of a mimeograph.

mi·me·sis (mi mē′sis, mī-), *n.* MIMICRY.

mi•met•ic (mi met′ik, mī-), *adj.* characterized by, exhibiting, or of the nature of mimicry: *mimetic gestures.* —**mi•met′i•cal•ly,** *adv.*

mim•ic (mim′ik), *v.,* **-icked, -ick•ing,** *n.* —*v.t.* **1.** to imitate or copy in action, speech, etc., often playfully or derisively. **2.** to imitate in a servile or unthinking way; ape. **3.** to be an imitation of; simulate; resemble closely. —*n.* **4.** a person or thing that mimics, esp. a performer skilled at mimicking others. **5.** a copy or imitation of something. **6.** a performer in a mime. —*adj.* **7.** imitating or copying something, often on a smaller scale: *a mimic battle.* **8.** apt at or given to imitating; imitative; simulative. —**mim′ick•er,** *n.*

mim•ic•ry (mim′ik rē), *n.,* *pl.* **-ries. 1.** the act, practice, or art of mimicking. **2.** the close external resemblance of an organism to a different organism, such that it benefits from the mistaken identity, as in seeming to be unpalatable or harmful. **3.** an instance or result of mimicking.

mi•mo•sa (mi mō′sə, -zə), *n.,* *pl.* **-sas. 1.** any of numerous plants, shrubs, or trees belonging to the genus *Mimosa,* of the legume family, native to tropical or warm regions, having small flowers in globular heads or cylindrical spikes. **2.** any of various similar or related plants, as the silk tree. **3.** a cocktail of orange juice and champagne.

mi•na (mī′nə), *n.,* *pl.* **-nae** (-nē), **-nas.** an ancient unit of weight and value equal to the sixtieth part of a talent.

min•a•ret (min′ə ret′, min′ə ret′), *n.* a lofty, often slender tower attached to a mosque, having one or more balconies from which the muezzin calls the people to prayer.

minaret

mince (mins), *v.,* **minced, minc•ing,** *n.* —*v.t.* **1.** to cut or chop into very small pieces. **2.** to moderate or soften, esp. for the sake of decorum or courtesy: *He was angry and didn't mince words.* **3.** to perform or utter with affected elegance. —*v.i.* **4.** to move with short, affectedly dainty steps. —*n.* **5.** something cut up very small; mincemeat.

mince•meat (mins′mēt′), *n.* **1.** a diced mixture, as of minced apples, suet, raisins, and sometimes meat, for filling a pie. —*Idiom.* **2. make mincemeat of,** to destroy utterly.

mince′ (or **minced′**) **pie′,** *n.* a pie filled with mincemeat.

minc•ing (min′sing), *adj.* affectedly dainty, or elegant: *mincing steps.* —**minc′ing•ly,** *adv.*

mind (mīnd), *n.* **1.** the element, part, or process in a human or other conscious being that reasons, thinks, feels, wills, perceives, judges, etc. **2.** *Psychol.* the totality of conscious and unconscious mental processes and activities. **3.** intellect or understanding, esp. as distinguished from the emotions and will; intelligence. **4.** a person considered with reference to intellectual power: *the great minds of the day.* **5.** intellectual power or ability. **6.** reason, sanity, or sound mental condition: *to lose one's mind.* **7.** a way of thinking and feeling; disposition; temper: *a liberal mind.* **8.** opinion, view, or sentiments: *to change one's mind.* **9.** inclination, intention, or desire: *to be of a mind to listen.* **10.** remembrance or recollection; memory: *to call to mind; The party put me in mind of my college days.* **11.** psychic or spiritual being, as opposed to matter. **12.** a conscious or intelligent agency or being: *an awareness of a mind ordering the universe.* **13.** attention; thoughts: *He can't keep his mind on his studies.* **14.** *Chiefly South Midland and Southern U.S.* notice; attention: *When he's like that, just pay him no mind.* **15.** *Rom. Cath. Ch.* a commemoration of a person's death, esp. by a Requiem Mass. **16.** (*cap.*) *Christian Science.* God; the incorporeal source of life, substance, and intelligence. —*v.t.* **17.** to pay attention to. **18.** to heed or obey (a person, advice, instructions, etc.). **19.** to apply oneself or attend to: *to mind one's own business.* **20.** to look after; take care of; tend: *to mind the baby.* **21.** to be careful, cautious, or wary about: *Mind what you say.* **22.** to feel concern at; care about. **23.** to feel disturbed or inconvenienced by; object to: *I hope you don't mind the interruption.* **24.** to regard as concerning oneself or as mattering: *Don't mind his bluntness.* **25.** *Dial.* **a.** to perceive or notice. **b.** to remember. **c.** to mind. —*v.i.* **26.** to pay attention. **27.** to obey. **28.** to take notice, observe, or understand (used chiefly in the imperative): *Mind now, I want you home by twelve.* **29.** to be careful or wary. **30.** to care, feel concern, or object (often used in negative or interrogative constructions): *Mind if I go?* **31.** to regard a thing as concerning oneself or as mattering: *You mustn't mind about their gossiping.* —*Idiom.* **32. be of one mind,** to share an intent or opinion. **33. be of two minds,** to be ambivalent. **34. bear** or **keep in mind,** to hold in one's memory; remember: *Bear in mind that your taxes are due next week.* **35. have half a mind to,** to be almost decided to; be inclined to. **36. on one's mind,** in one's thoughts;

of concern to one. **37. out of one's mind, a.** insane; mad. **b.** emotionally overwhelmed; frantic: *out of my mind with worry.* **38. A mind is a terrible thing to waste,** mental ability must be nurtured: slogan of the United Negro College Fund.

mind′-bend•ing, *adj.* MIND-BLOWING. —**mind′bend′er,** *n.* —**mind′-bend′ing•ly,** *adv.*

mind′-bog•gling, *adj.* overwhelming; stunning: *mind-boggling prices.* —**mind′-bog′gler,** *n.* —**mind′-bog′gling•ly,** *adv.*

mind′ con•trol′ cult′, *n.* a cult that enforces strict adherence to its leader and principles by means of psychological coercion.

mind•ed (mīn′did), *adj.* **1.** having a certain kind of mind (usu. used in combination): *strong-minded.* **2.** inclined or disposed.

mind•ful (mīnd′fəl), *adj.* attentive; aware: *Be mindful of the consequences.* —**mind′ful•ly,** *adv.* —**mind′ful•ness,** *n.*

mind′ games′, *n.pl.* psychological manipulation or strategy, used esp. to gain advantage or to intimidate.

mind•less (mīnd′lis), *adj.* **1.** showing, using, or requiring no intelligence or thought. **2.** unmindful; heedless: *mindless of all dangers.* —**mind′less•ly,** *adv.* —**mind′less•ness,** *n.*

mind′ read′ing, *n.* the supposed ability to discern the thoughts of others without the normal means of communication, esp. by means of a preternatural power. —**mind′ read′er,** *n.*

mind′-set′ or **mind′set′,** *n.* **1.** a fixed attitude or state of mind. **2.** intention; inclination.

mind's′ eye′, *n.* the hypothetical site of recollection or imagination.

mine¹ (mīn), *pron.* **1.** a form of the possessive case of I used as a predicate adjective: *The yellow sweater is mine.* **2.** that or those belonging to me: *Mine is on the left.*

mine² (mīn), *n.,* *v.,* **mined, min•ing.** —*n.* **1.** an excavation made in the earth for the purpose of extracting mineral substances, as ore, coal, or precious stones. **2.** a natural deposit of such substances. **3.** an abundant source; store: *a mine of information.* **4.** an explosive device floating on or moored just below the surface of the water, used for blowing up an enemy ship that strikes it or passes close by it. **5.** a similar device used on land against personnel or vehicles; land mine. **6.** an underground passage dug under an enemy's position so as to deposit explosives that will blow up the position. **7.** a passageway in the tissue of a leaf, made by certain insects. —*v.i.* **8.** to dig in the earth for the purpose of extracting a mineral substance; make a mine. **9.** to extract mineral substance from a mine. **10.** to make subterranean passages. **11.** to place or lay mines, as in military or naval operations. —*v.t.* **12.** to dig in (earth) in order to extract a mineral substance. **13.** to extract (a mineral substance) from a mine. **14.** to use for extracting useful or valuable material from: *to mine every reference book available.* **15.** to use, esp. a natural resource: *to mine the nation's forests.* **16.** to make subterranean passages in or under; burrow. **17.** to make, as a passage or tunnel, by digging or burrowing. **18.** to dig away or remove the foundations of. **19.** to place or lay military or naval mines under. **20.** to remove (a natural resource) from its source without attempting to replenish it.

mine•field (mīn′fēld′), *n.* **1.** an area of land or water where explosive mines have been laid. **2.** a situation fraught with potential problems or dangers: *a legislative minefield facing the city council.*

mine•lay•er (mīn′lā′ər), *n.* a naval ship equipped for laying mines in the water.

min•er (mī′nər), *n.* **1.** a person who works in a mine, esp. a commercial mine producing coal or metallic ores. **2.** a mechanical device for extracting ores.

min•er•al (min′ər əl, min′rəl), *n.* **1.** any of a class of substances occurring in nature, usu. comprising inorganic substances, as quartz or feldspar, of definite chemical composition and usu. of definite crystal structure, but sometimes also including rocks formed by these substances as well as certain natural products of organic origin, as asphalt or coal. **2.** a substance obtained by mining, as ore. **3.** any substance that is neither animal nor vegetable. **4.** any of the inorganic elements, as calcium, iron, magnesium, potassium, or sodium, essential to the functioning of the human body and obtained from foods. —*adj.* **5.** of, pertaining to, or of the nature of a mineral. **6.** containing or impregnated with minerals. **7.** neither animal nor vegetable; inorganic: *mineral matter.*

min′eral king′dom, *n.* minerals or inorganic substances collectively (contrasted with *animal kingdom, vegetable kingdom*).

min•er•al•o•gy (min′ə rol′ə jē, -ral′ə-), *n.* the science or study of minerals. —**min′er•al•og′i•cal** (-ər ə loj′i kəl), *adj.* —**min′er•al′o•gist,** *n.*

min′eral oil′, *n.* a colorless, oily, almost tasteless oil obtained from petroleum by distillation and used chiefly as a lubricant, in cosmetics, and as a laxative.

min′eral spring′, *n.* a spring of water that contains a significant amount of dissolved minerals.

min′eral wa′ter, *n.* water containing dissolved mineral salts or gases, esp. such water considered healthful to drink.

Mi•ner•va (mi nûr′və), *n.* the Roman goddess of wisdom and the arts, identified with the Greek goddess Athena.

min•e•stro•ne (min′ə strō′nē), *n.* a thick vegetable soup, often containing beans, herbs, and bits of pasta.

mine•sweep•er (mīn′swē′pər), *n.* a ship used for dragging a body of water to remove or destroy mines. —**mine′sweep′ing,** *n.*

mine′work′er or **mine′ work′er,** *n.* MINER (def. 1).

min·gle (ming′gəl), *v.,* **-gled, -gling,** *n.* —*v.i.* **1.** to become mixed, blended, or united. **2.** to mix in company. —*v.t.* **3.** to mix or combine; put together in a mixture; blend. **4.** to unite, join, or conjoin. **5.** to cause to mix in company. **6.** to form by mixing; compound; concoct. —*n.* **7. mingles,** two or more single, unrelated adults who live together. —**min′gler,** *n.*

ming′ tree′ (ming), *n.* **1.** any of various trees or shrubs used in bonsai arrangements, esp. when shaped to have flat-topped, asymmetrical branches. **2.** an artificial tree created to resemble a bonsai.

min·gy (min′jē), *adj.,* **-gi·er, -gi·est.** stingy; niggardly.

min·i (min′ē), *n., pl.* **min·is. 1. a.** MINISKIRT. **b.** a garment with a miniskirt, esp. a dress. **2.** MINICOMPUTER. **3.** anything small of its kind.

mini-, a combining form with the meanings "of a small or reduced size in comparison with others of its kind" (*minicar; minigun*); "limited in scope, intensity, or duration" (*miniboom; minicourse*); (of clothing) "short, not reaching the knee" (*minidress; miniskirt*).

min·i·a·ture (min′ē ə chər, -chŏŏr′, min′ə chər), *n.* **1.** a representation or image of something on a small or reduced scale. **2.** something small of its class or kind. **3.** a very small painting, esp. a portrait, on ivory, vellum, or the like. **4.** the art of executing such a painting. **5.** an illumination in an illuminated manuscript or book. —*adj.* **6.** on or represented on a small or reduced scale: *a miniature poodle.* —**Idiom. 7. in miniature,** of a reduced size; on a small scale: *a terrarium resembling a jungle in miniature.*

min′iature golf′, *n.* a game modeled on golf and played on a small obstacle course.

min·i·a·tur·ize (min′ē ə chə rīz′, min′ə-), *v.t.,* **-ized, -iz·ing.** to make in greatly reduced size: *to miniaturize electronic equipment.* —**min′i·a·tur·i·za′tion,** *n.*

min·i·bike (min′ē bīk′), *n.* a small, lightweight motorcycle with a low frame. —**min′i·bik′er,** *n.*

min·i·bus (min′ē bus′), *n.* a small bus typically used for transporting people short distances.

min·i·cam (min′ē kam′), *n.* a lightweight, hand-held television camera.

min·i·com·put·er (min′ē kəm pyŏŏ′tər), *n.* a computer with processing and storage capabilities smaller than those of a mainframe but larger than those of a microcomputer. Compare MAINFRAME, MICROCOMPUTER.

min·i·dress (min′ē dres′), *n.* a dress with a miniskirt.

min·im (min′əm), *n.* **1.** the smallest unit of liquid measure, ¹⁄₆₀ of a fluid dram, roughly equivalent to one drop. *Abbr.:* min, min.; *Symbol:* M, ♍ **2.** the least quantity of anything. **3.** something very small or insignificant. —*adj.* **4.** smallest or very small.

min·i·ma (min′ə mə), *n.* a pl. of MINIMUM.

min·i·mal (min′ə məl), *adj.* **1.** constituting a minimum: *a minimal weight loss of two pounds a week.* **2.** of or pertaining to minimalism or minimal art. —**min′i·mal·ly,** *adv.*

min′imal art′, *n.* modern abstract art marked by extreme simplicity of form and by impersonality. Also called **minimalism.**

min·i·mal·ism (min′ə mə liz′əm), *n.* **1.** MINIMAL ART. **2.** any style or method, as in literature, dance, or music, that is spare, simple, and often repetitious and impersonal in tone.

min·i·mal·ist (min′ə mə list), *n.* **1.** a person favoring a moderate approach to, or holding minimal expectations for, the achievement of specific goals or programs. **2.** a practitioner of minimalism. —*adj.* **3.** pertaining to or characteristic of minimalism. **4.** being or offering no more than what is required or essential: *a minimalist program for tax reform.*

min·i·mize (min′ə mīz′), *v.t.,* **-mized, -miz·ing. 1.** to reduce to the smallest possible amount or degree. **2.** to represent at the lowest possible value or importance, esp. in a disparaging way; belittle. —**min′i·mi·za′tion,** *n.* —**min′i·miz′er,** *n.*

min·i·mum (min′ə məm), *n., pl.* **-mums, -ma** (-mə), *adj.* —*n.* **1.** the least amount possible, allowable, or the like. **2.** the lowest amount, value, or degree attained or recorded. **3.** *Math.* **a.** the value of a function at a certain point in its domain, which is less than or equal to the values at all other points in the immediate vicinity of the point. **b.** the point in the domain at which a minimum occurs. —*adj.* **4.** of, pertaining to, or being a minimum.

min′imum wage′, *n.* the lowest hourly wage that may be paid to an employee, as fixed by law or by union contract.

min·ing (mī′ning), *n.* the act, process, or industry of extracting mineral substances from mines.

min·ion (min′yən), *n.* a servile follower or subordinate.

min·i·pill (min′ē pil′), *n.* a birth control pill that contains only a progestin and is to be taken daily without monthly cessation.

min·is·cule (min′ē skyŏŏl′), *adj.* MINUSCULE.

min·i·se·ries (min′ē sēr′ēz), *n., pl.* **-ries. 1.** a television film broadcast in consecutive parts over a span of several days or weeks. **2.** any short series of events or presentations.

min·i·skirt (min′ē skûrt′), *n.* a short skirt or skirt part ending several inches above the knee.

min·i·state (min′ē stāt′), *n.* a small, independent nation. Also called **microstate.**

min·is·ter (min′ə stər), *n.* **1.** a person authorized to conduct religious worship; member of the clergy; pastor. **2.** a person authorized to administer sacraments, as at mass. **3.** a person appointed to some high office of state, esp. to that of head of an administrative department. **4.** a diplomatic representative, usu. ranking below an ambassador. **5.** a person acting as the agent or instrument of another. —*v.i.* **6.** to perform the functions of a religious minister. **7.** to give service, care, or aid: *to minister to the needs of the hungry.*

min·is·te·ri·al (min′ə stēr′ē əl), *adj.* **1.** pertaining to a religious minister or ministry. **2.** pertaining to a ministry or minister of state. **3.** pertaining to or invested with delegated executive authority. **4.** serving as an instrument or means; instrumental.

min·is·trant (min′ə strənt), *adj.* **1.** ministering. —*n.* **2.** a person who ministers.

min·is·tra·tion (min′ə strā′shən), *n.* **1.** the administration of care, aid, or religious service. **2.** an instance of this. —**min′is·tra′tive,** *adj.*

min·is·try (min′ə strē), *n., pl.* **-tries. 1.** the service, functions, or profession of a minister of religion. **2.** the body or class of ministers of religion; clergy. **3.** the service, function, or office of a minister of state. **4.** the body of ministers of state. **5.** an administrative department headed by a minister of state. **6.** the building that houses such an administrative department. **7.** the term of office of a minister of state. **8.** an act or instance of ministering; ministration; service.

min·i·van (min′ē van′), *n.* a small passenger van, typically with side or rear windows and removable rear seats for hauling small loads.

mink (mingk), *n., pl.* **minks,** (*esp. collectively*) **mink. 1.** either of two semiaquatic weasels: *Mustela vison,* of North America, and *M. lutreola,* of Eurasia. **2.** the soft, lustrous fur of this animal, brownish in the natural state. **3.** a garment made of this fur.

min·ke (ming′kē), *n.* a finback whale, *Baleanoptera acutorostrata,* of temperate and polar seas. Also called **min′ke whale′.**

Min·ne·ap·o·lis (min′ē ap′ə lis), *n.* a city in SE Minnesota, on the Mississippi. 354,590. —**Min′ne·a·pol′i·tan** (-ə pol′i tn), *n.*

Min·ne·so·ta (min′ə sō′tə), *n.* **1.** a state in the N central United States. 4,657,758; 84,068 sq. mi. (217,735 sq. km). *Cap.:* St. Paul; *Abbr.:* MN, Minn. **2.** a river flowing SE from the W border of Minnesota into the Mississippi near St. Paul. 332 mi. (535 km) long. —**Min′ne·so′tan,** *adj., n.*

min·now (min′ō), *n., pl.* (*esp. for kinds or species*) **-nows,** (*esp. collectively, Rare*) **-now. 1.** a small European cyprinoid fish, *Phoxinus phoxinus.* **2.** any fish of the family Cyprinidae, characterized by jaws without teeth and smooth overlapping scales and including the carps, goldfishes, and daces.

Mi·no·an (mi nō′ən, mī-), *adj.* **1.** of or designating the Bronze Age civilization of Crete, c2400–1400 B.C. —*n.* **2.** a native or inhabitant of Crete during the Minoan period.

mi·nor (mī′nər), *adj.* **1.** lesser, as in size, extent, or amount, or being or noting the lesser of two: *a minor share.* **2.** lesser, as in seriousness, importance, or rank: *a minor wound; a minor role; a minor official.* **3.** under full legal age. **4.** of or pertaining to a student's academic minor. **5. a.** (of a musical interval) smaller by a chromatic half step than the corresponding major interval. **b.** (of a chord) containing a minor third. **c.** based on a minor scale: *a minor key.* **6.** of or pertaining to the minority. —*n.* **7.** a person under full legal age. **8.** a subject or course of study pursued secondarily to a major subject or course. **9.** a minor musical interval, chord, scale, etc. **10. the minors,** the minor leagues. —*v.i.* **11.** to choose or study as a secondary academic subject or course: *to minor in biology.*

mi·nor·i·ty (mi nôr′i tē, -nor′-, mī-), *n., pl.* **-ties,** *adj.* —*n.* **1.** the smaller part or number; a number, part, or amount forming less than half of the whole. **2.** a smaller group opposed to a majority. **3.** Also called **minor′ity group′.** a group differing, esp. in race, religion, or ethnic background, from the majority of a population. **4.** a member of such a group. **5.** the state or period of being under full legal age. —*adj.* **6.** of or pertaining to a minority.

minor′ity lead′er, *n.* the floor leader of the minority party in a legislature.

mi′nor league′, *n.* any association of professional sports teams other than the major leagues. —**mi′nor-league′,** *adj.* —**mi′nor-lea′guer,** *n.*

Mi′nor Proph′et, *n.* any of a group of Old Testament prophets including Hosea, Joel, Amos, Obadiah, Jonah, Micah, Nahum, Habakkuk, Zephaniah, Haggai, Zechariah, and Malachi. Compare MAJOR PROPHET.

mi′nor scale′, *n.* a musical scale having half steps between the second and third, fifth and sixth, and seventh and eighth degrees.

mi′nor suit′, *n.* (in bridge) diamonds or clubs. Compare MAJOR SUIT.

Mi·nos (mī′nəs, -nos), *n.* a legendary ruler of Crete who ordered Daedalus to build a labyrinth to house the Minotaur.

Min·o·taur (min′ə tôr′, mī′nə-), *n.* (in Greek myth) a monster with the head of a bull and the body of a man: housed in a labyrinth on Crete, it was fed on human flesh until Theseus killed it.

min·ox·i·dil (mi nok′si dil′), *n.* a vasodilating drug used for treating severe hypertension and also applied topically to promote hair growth in some types of baldness.

Minsk (minsk), *n.* the capital of Belarus, in the central part, on a tributary of the Berezina. 1,589,000.

min·ster (min′stər), *n.* any of certain large or important churches. [< Late Latin *monastērium* MONASTERY]

min·strel (min′strəl), *n.* **1.** a medieval poet, singer, and musician, who was either an itinerant or a member of a noble household. **2.** a musician, singer, or poet. **3.** a performer in a minstrel show.

M

min′strel show′, *n.* a highly conventionalized theatrical entertainment of the 19th and early 20th centuries, usu. performed by whites in blackface and featuring comic dialogue, songs, and dances based on stereotypes of blacks.

mint¹ (mint), *n.* **1.** any aromatic herb of the genus *Mentha,* having opposite leaves and small, whorled flowers, as the spearmint and peppermint. **2.** a mint-flavored candy. —*adj.* **3.** flavored with mint: *mint tea.*

mint² (mint), *n.* **1.** a place where coins, paper currency, special medals, etc., are produced under government authority. **2.** a place where something is manufactured. **3.** a vast amount, esp. of money. —*adj.* **4.** being in its original, unused condition, as if newly made: *a book in mint condition.* —*v.t.* **5.** to make (money) by stamping metal. **6.** to make or invent: *to mint words.* —**mint′er,** *n.*

mint•age (min′tij), *n.* **1.** the act or process of minting coins. **2.** the coins made by minting.

mint′ ju′lep, *n.* an alcoholic drink traditionally made with bourbon, sugar, finely cracked ice, and sprigs of mint.

min•u•end (min′yoo end′), *n.* a number from which another is subtracted. Compare SUBTRAHEND.

min•u•et (min′yoo et′), *n.* **1.** a slow, stately dance in triple meter, popular in the 17th and 18th centuries. **2.** a piece of music for such a dance or in its rhythm.

mi•nus (mī′nəs), *prep.* **1.** less by the subtraction of: *Ten minus six is four.* **2.** lacking or without: *a book minus a page.* —*adj.* **3.** involving or noting subtraction. **4.** algebraically negative: *a minus quantity.* **5.** less than; just below: *to get a C minus on a test.* —*n.* **6.** MINUS SIGN. **7.** a minus quantity. **8.** a deficiency or loss.

mi•nus•cule (min′ə skyool′, mi nus′kyool), *adj.* **1.** very small. **2.** (of letters or writing) small; not capital. **3.** written in such letters (opposed to *majuscule*). —*n.* **4.** a minuscule letter. **5.** a small cursive script developed in the 7th century A.D. from the uncial, which it afterward superseded. —**mi•nus′cu•lar,** *adj.*

mi′nus sign′, *n.* the symbol (−) denoting subtraction or a negative quantity.

min•ute¹ (min′it), *n.* **1.** the sixtieth part (¹⁄₆₀) of an hour; 60 seconds. **2.** an indefinitely short space of time: *Wait a minute!* **3.** an exact point in time; instant; moment: *Come here this minute!* **4. minutes,** the official record of the proceedings at a meeting of a society, committee, or other group. **5.** an informal written notation; note; memorandum. **6.** *Geom.* the sixtieth part of a degree of angular measure, often represented by the sign ′. —*v.t.* **7.** to time exactly, as movements or speed. **8.** to record in a memorandum; note down. **9.** to enter in the minutes of a meeting. —*adj.* **10.** prepared in a very short time: *minute pudding.* —*Idiom.* **11.** up to the minute, modern; up-to-date.

mi•nute² (mī noot′, -nyoot′, mi-), *adj.,* **-nut•er, -nut•est. 1.** extremely small, as in size, amount, extent, or degree: *minute differences.* **2.** of minor importance; insignificant; trifling. **3.** attentive to or concerned with even the smallest details: *a minute examination.*

min′ute hand′ (min′it), *n.* the hand that indicates the minutes on a clock or watch, usu. longer than the hour hand.

mi•nute•ly (mī noot′lē, -nyoot′-, mi-), *adv.* **1.** in a minute manner, form, or degree; in minute detail. **2.** into tiny or very small pieces.

Min•ute•man (min′it man′), *n., pl.* **-men.** (*sometimes l.c.*) a member of an American militia before and during the Revolutionary War who held themselves in readiness for instant military service.

mi•nu•ti•a (mi noo′shē ə, -shə, -nyoo′-), *n., pl.* **-ti•ae** (-shē ē′). Usu., **minutiae.** precise details; small or trifling matters. —**mi•nu′ti•al,** *adj.*

minx (mingks), *n.* a pert or flirtatious girl. —**minx′ish,** *adj.*

min•yan (min′yən, min yän′), *n., pl.* **min•yans, min•yan•im** (min′yä-nēm′) the quorum of ten adult Jewish males required by Jewish law to be present for public prayers.

Mi•o•cene (mī′ə sēn′), *adj.* **1.** pertaining to an epoch of the Tertiary Period, occurring from 25 million to 10 million years ago, when grazing mammals became widespread. —*n.* **2.** the Miocene Epoch or Series.

MIPS (mips), *n.* millions of instructions per second: a measure of computer speed.

mir•a•cle (mir′ə kəl), *n.* **1.** an extraordinary occurrence that surpasses all known human powers or natural causes and is ascribed to a divine or supernatural cause, esp. to God. **2.** a superb or surpassing example of something; wonder; marvel.

mir′acle drug′, *n.* WONDER DRUG.

mir′acle play′, *n.* a medieval drama based on a Bible story, a saint's life, or the like, usu. presented as part of a series or cycle. Compare MORALITY PLAY, MYSTERY PLAY.

mi•rac•u•lous (mi rak′yə ləs), *adj.* **1.** performed by or involving a supernatural power or agency: *a miraculous cure.* **2.** of the nature of a miracle; marvelous. **3.** having or seeming to have the power to work miracles: *miraculous herbs.* —**mi•rac′u•lous•ly,** *adv.*

mi•rage (mi räzh′), *n.* **1.** an optical phenomenon, esp. in the desert or at sea, by which the image of an object appears displaced above, below, or to one side of its true position as a result of spatial variations of the index of refraction of air. **2.** something illusory.

Mi•ran•da (mi ran′də), *n.* **1. Francisco de,** 1750–1816, Venezuelan revolutionist and patriot. **2.** a moon of the planet Uranus. —*adj.* **3.** *Law.* of, pertaining to, or being upheld by the Supreme Court ruling (Miranda v. Arizona, 1966) requiring law-enforcement officers to warn a

person who has been taken into custody of his or her rights to remain silent and to have legal counsel.

Miran′da rule′, *n.* a ruling, based upon a U.S. Supreme Court decision in a 1966 case, that law-enforcement officers must warn a person taken into custody that he or she has the right to remain silent and is entitled to legal counsel.

mire (mī°r), *n., v.,* **mired, mir•ing.** —*n.* **1.** an area of wet, swampy ground; bog; marsh. **2.** ground of this kind, as deep mud. —*v.t.* **3.** to cause to stick in mire. **4.** to involve; entangle. **5.** to soil with mire. —*v.i.* **6.** to sink or stick in mire. —**mir′y,** *adj.*

Mir•i•am (mir′ē əm), *n.* the sister of Moses and Aaron. Num. 26:59.

mir•ror (mir′ər), *n.* **1.** a reflecting surface, usu. of glass with a silvery, metallic, or amalgam backing. **2.** any reflecting surface, as of calm water under certain lighting conditions. **3.** something that gives a faithful representation, image, or idea of something else: *Gershwin's music was a mirror of its time.* **4.** a pattern for imitation; exemplar: *a man who was the mirror of fashion.* —*v.t.* **5.** to reflect in or as if in a mirror. **6.** to imitate. —**mir′ror•like′,** *adj.*

mir′ror im′age, *n.* **1.** an image of an object as it would appear if viewed in a mirror. **2.** an object having a spatial arrangement corresponding to another object except that the right-to-left sense on one object corresponds to the left-to-right sense on the other.

mirth (mûrth), *n.* gaiety or jollity, esp. when accompanied by laughter. —**mirth′ful,** *adj.* —**mirth′ful•ly,** *adv.* —**mirth′less,** *adj.*

MIRV (mûrv), *n., v.,* **MIRVed, MIRV•ing.** —*n.* **1.** a missile carrying several nuclear warheads, each of which can be directed to a different target. —*v.t.* **2.** to arm or attack with MIRVs. Also, **M.I.R.V.** [*m(ultiple) i(ndependently) t(argetable) r(eentry) v(ehicle)*]

MIS or **M.I.S.,** management information system.

mis-, a prefix applied to various parts of speech, meaning "ill," "mistaken," "wrong," "wrongly," "incorrectly," or simply negating: *mistrial; misprint; mistrust.*

mis•ad•ven•ture (mis′əd ven′chər), *n.* misfortune; mishap.

mis•al•li•ance (mis′ə lī′əns), *n.* **1.** an incompatible association, esp. in marriage. **2.** MÉSALLIANCE.

mis•al•ly (mis′ə lī′), *v.t.,* **-lied, -ly•ing.** to ally improperly or unsuitably.

mis•an•dry (mis′an drē), *n.* hatred of or hostility toward men. Compare MISOGYNY.

mis•an•thrope (mis′ən thrōp′, miz′-) also **mis•an•thro•pist** (mis-an′thrə pist, miz-), *n.* a hater of humankind.

mis•ap•pre•hend (mis′ap ri hend′), *v.t.* MISUNDERSTAND. —**mis′ap•pre•hend′ing•ly,** *adv.* —**mis′ap•pre•hen′sion** (-hen′shən), *n.* —**mis′ap•pre•hen′sive** (-hen′siv), *adj.* —**mis′ap•pre•hen′sive•ly,** *adv.*

mis•ap•pro•pri•ate (mis′ə prō′prē āt′), *v.t.,* **-at•ed, -at•ing. 1.** to put to a wrong use. **2.** to apply wrongfully or dishonestly, as funds entrusted to one's care. —**mis′ap•pro′pri•a′tion,** *n.*

mis•be•got•ten (mis′bi got′n) also **mis′be•got′,** *adj.* **1.** unlawfully or irregularly begotten; illegitimate: *his misbegotten son.* **2.** badly conceived, made, or carried out: *a misbegotten plan.*

mis•be•have (mis′bi hāv′), *v.,* **-haved, -hav•ing.** —*v.i.* **1.** to behave badly or improperly. —*v.t.* **2.** to conduct (oneself) badly or improperly.

mis•be•hav•ior (mis′bi hāv′yər), *n.* inappropriate or bad behavior.

mis•car•riage (mis kar′ij; *for 1 also* mis′kar′ij), *n.* **1.** the expulsion of a fetus before it is viable, esp. between the third and seventh months of pregnancy; spontaneous abortion. **2.** failure to attain the just, right, or desired result: *a miscarriage of justice.* **3.** failure of something sent, as a letter, to reach its destination. —**mis•car′ry,** *v.i.,* **-ried, -ry•ing.**

mis•cast (mis kast′, -käst′), *v.t.,* **-cast, -cast•ing. 1.** to cast (an actor) in an unsuitable role. **2.** to cast (a play, film, etc.) inappropriately.

mis•ceg•e•na•tion (mis sej′ə nā′shən, mis′i jə-), *n.* **1.** marriage or cohabitation between a man and woman of different races, esp., in the U.S., between a black and a white person. **2.** interbreeding between members of different races. —**mis′ce•ge•net′ic** (-net′ik), *adj.*

mis•cel•la•ne•a (mis′ə lā′nē ə), *n.pl.* miscellaneous collected writings, papers, or objects.

mis•cel•la•ne•ous (mis′ə lā′nē əs), *adj.* **1.** consisting of members or elements of different kinds; of mixed character. **2.** having various qualities, aspects, or subjects: *a miscellaneous discussion.* —**mis′cel•la′ne•ous•ly,** *adv.* —**mis′cel•la′ne•ous•ness,** *n.*

mis•cel•la•ny (mis′ə lā′nē; *Brit.* mi sel′ə nē), *n., pl.* **-nies. 1.** a collection of various items or parts. **2.** a book of literary works by several authors on various topics. **3. miscellanies,** miscellaneous articles or entries, as in a book.

mis•chief (mis′chif), *n.* **1.** conduct or activity that causes petty annoyance. **2.** a tendency to tease or annoy. **3.** harm or trouble: *to come to mischief.* **4.** an injury or evil caused by a person or thing. **5.** a cause or source of harm, evil, or annoyance.

mis•chie•vous (mis′chə vəs), *adj.* **1.** maliciously or playfully annoying. **2.** causing annoyance, harm, or trouble. **3.** roguishly or slyly teasing, as a glance. **4.** harmful; injurious. —**mis′chie•vous•ly,** *adv.* —**mis′chie•vous•ness,** *n.* —**Pronunciation.** The pronunciation of MISCHIEVOUS as (mis chē′vē əs), with stress on *-chie-* and an extra vowel before *-ous,* is usually considered nonstandard, although a spelling *mischievious,* which reflects this pronunciation, had some currency between the 16th and 19th centuries.

mis·ci·ble (mis′ə bəl), *adj.* capable of being mixed. —**mis′ci·bil′i·ty,** *n.*

mis·con·ceive (mis′kən sēv′), *v.t., v.i.,* **-ceived, -ceiv·ing.** to interpret wrongly; misunderstand. —**mis′con·ceiv′er,** *n.* —**mis′con·cep′tion** (-kən sep′shən), *n.*

mis·con·duct (*n.* mis kon′dukt; *v.*mis′kon dukt′), *n.* **1.** improper behavior. **2.** unlawful conduct by an official in regard to his or her office, or by a person in the administration of justice; malfeasance. —*v.t.* **3.** to mismanage. **4.** to misbehave (oneself).

mis·con·strue (mis′kən strōō′; *esp. Brit.* mis kon′strōō), *v.t.,* **-strued, -stru·ing.** to misunderstand the meaning of; misinterpret.

mis·count (*v.* mis kount′; *n.* mis′kount′), *v.i., v.t.* **1.** to count erroneously. —*n.* **2.** an erroneous counting; miscalculation.

mis·cre·ant (mis′krē ənt), *adj.* **1.** depraved; villainous. **2.** heretical. —*n.* **3.** a vicious or depraved person. **4.** infidel. —**mis′cre·an·cy,** *n.*

mis·cue[1] (mis kyōō′), *n., v.,* **-cued, -cu·ing.** —*n.* **1.** an error in sports. **2.** a mistake; blunder. —*v.i.* **3.** to make a mistake. **4.** to miss a stage cue. —*v.t.* **5.** to give the wrong cue to.

mis·cue[2] (mis kyōō′), *n., v.,* **-cued, -cu·ing.** —*n.* **1.** a stroke in billiards or pool in which the cue fails to make solid contact with the cue ball. —*v.i.* **2.** to make a miscue.

mis·deed (mis dēd′), *n.* an immoral deed.

mis·de·mean·or (mis′di mē′nər), *n.* **1.** a criminal offense less serious than a felony. **2.** an instance of misbehavior; misdeed. Also, *esp. Brit.,* **mis′de·mean′our.**

mis·di·rect (mis′di rekt′), *v.t.* to direct, instruct, or address wrongly: *to misdirect a person; to misdirect a letter.*

mis·di·rec·tion (mis′di rek′shən), *n.* **1.** a wrong direction or guidance. **2.** an erroneous charge to the jury by a judge.

mis·do (mis dōō′), *v.t.,* **-did, -done, -do·ing.** —*v.t.* to do badly or wrongly; botch. —**mis·do′er,** *n.* —**mis·do′ing,** *n.*

mis·doubt (mis dout′), *v.i., v.t.* to doubt; suspect.

mise-en-scène (mē zän sen′), *n., pl.* **-scènes** (-sens′, -sen′). **1.** the process of setting a stage, with regard to placement of actors, scenery, properties, etc. **2.** the stage setting or scenery of a play. **3.** surroundings; environment.

mi·ser (mī′zər), *n.* **1.** a person who lives poorly in order to save and hoard money. **2.** a stingy, avaricious person.

mis·er·a·ble (miz′ər ə bəl, miz′rə-), *adj.* **1.** wretchedly unhappy or uncomfortable: *a miserable beggar.* **2.** of wretched character or quality; contemptible: *a miserable villain.* **3.** attended with or causing misery: *a miserable existence.* **4.** manifesting misery. **5.** worthy of pity: *a miserable failure.* —**mis′er·a·ble·ness,** *n.* —**mis′er·a·bly,** *adv.*

Mis·e·re·re (miz′ə rȧr′ē, -rēr′ē), *n.* **1.** the 51st Psalm, or the 50th in the Douay Bible. **2.** (*l.c.*) a prayer or expression of appeal for mercy. [< Latin *miserēre* lit., have pity, first word of the psalm]

mis·er·i·cord or **mis·er·i·corde** (miz′ər i kôrd′, mi zer′i kôrd′), *n.* a small projection on the underside of a hinged seat of a church stall that when the seat is lifted gives support to a person. [< Latin *misericordia* pity]

mi·ser·ly (mī′zər lē), *adj.* of, like, or befitting a miser; penurious; stingy; niggardly. —**mi′ser·li·ness,** *n.*

mis·er·y (miz′ə rē), *n., pl.* **-er·ies. 1.** wretchedness of condition or circumstances. **2.** suffering caused by privation or poverty. **3.** great mental or emotional distress; extreme unhappiness.

mis·fea·sance (mis fē′zəns), *n.* the wrongful and injurious exercise of lawful authority. Compare MALFEASANCE. —**mis·fea′sor,** *n.*

mis·fire (*v.* mis fī^ər′; *n.* mis′fī^ər′), *v.,* **-fired, -fir·ing,** *n.* —*v.i.* **1.** (of a firearm; bullet; shell) to fail to fire or explode. **2.** (of an internal-combustion engine) to fail to ignite properly or when expected. **3.** to fail to achieve the desired result, effect, etc.: *His criticisms completely misfired.* —*n.* **4.** an act or instance of misfiring.

mis·fit (mis fit′ *for 1;* mis fit′, mis′fit′ *for 2), n.* **1.** something, as a garment, that fits badly. **2.** a person who is not suited or is unable to adjust to a situation: *a misfit in one's job.*

mis·for·tune (mis fôr′chən), *n.* **1.** adverse fortune; bad luck. **2.** an instance of this; mishap.

mis·give (mis giv′), *v.,* **-gave, -giv·en, -giv·ing.** —*v.t.* **1.** to cause doubt or fear in. —*v.i.* **2.** to be apprehensive.

mis·giv·ing (mis giv′ing), *n.* Often, **misgivings.** a feeling of doubt, distrust, or apprehension. —**mis·giv′ing·ly,** *adv.*

mis·guide (mis gīd′), *v.t.,* **-guid·ed, -guid·ing.** to guide wrongly; misdirect. —**mis·guid′ance,** *n.* —**mis·guid′er,** *n.*

mis·guid·ed (mis gī′did), *adj.* misled; mistaken: *a misguided attempt to save time.* —**mis·guid′ed·ness,** *n.*

mis·han·dle (mis han′dl), *v.t.,* **-dled, -dling. 1.** to handle roughly; maltreat. **2.** to manage badly: *to mishandle an estate.*

mis·hap (mis′hap, mis hap′), *n.* an unfortunate accident.

mish·mash (mish′mäsh′, -mash′) also **mish·mosh** (-mosh′), *n.* a confused mess; hodgepodge; jumble.

Mish·nah or **Mish·na** (mish′nä, mish nä′), *n., pl.* **Mish·na·yoth, Mish·na·yot** (mish′nä yōt′), **Mish·nahs.** *Judaism.* **1.** the collection of oral laws compiled about A.D. 200 and forming the basic part of the Talmud. **2.** an article or section of this collection.

mis·in·form (mis′in fôrm′), *v.t.* to give false or misleading information to. —**mis′in·for·ma′tion** (-fər mā′shən), *n.*

mis·in·ter·pret (mis′in tûr′prit), *v.t., v.i.* to interpret, explain, or understand incorrectly. —**mis′in·ter′pret·a·ble,** *adj.* —**mis′in·ter′pre·ta′tion,** *n.* —**mis′in·ter′pret·er,** *n.*

mis·judge (mis juj′), *v.t., v.i.,* **-judged, -judg·ing.** to judge or estimate wrongly or unjustly. —**mis·judg′er,** *n.* —**mis·judg′ment,** *n.*

mis·lay (mis lā′), *v.t.,* **-laid, -lay·ing. 1.** to lose temporarily; misplace: *I mislaid my keys.* **2.** to lay or place wrongly; arrange or situate improperly: *to mislay linoleum.* —**mis·lay′er,** *n.*

mis·lead (mis lēd′), *v.t.,* **-led, -lead·ing. 1.** to lead or guide in the wrong direction. **2.** to lead into error of conduct, thought, or judgment; lead astray. —**mis·lead′er,** *n.*

mis·lead·ing (mis lē′ding), *adj.* tending to mislead; deceptive. —**mis·lead′ing·ly,** *adv.* —**mis·lead′ing·ness,** *n.*

mis·man·age (mis man′ij), *v.t., v.i.,* **-aged, -ag·ing.** to manage incompetently or dishonestly. —**mis·man′age·ment,** *n.*

mis·match (mis mach′; *for 2 also* mis′mach′), *v.t.* **1.** to match badly or unsuitably. —*n.* **2.** a bad or unsuitable match.

mis·no·mer (mis nō′mər), *n.* **1.** a misapplied or inappropriate name or designation. **2.** an error in naming a person or thing.

mi·sog·a·my (mi sog′ə mē, mī-), *n.* hatred of marriage. —**mis·o·gam′ic** (mis′ə gam′ik, mī′sə-), *adj.* —**mi·sog′a·mist,** *n.*

mi·sog·y·ny (mi soj′ə nē, mī-), *n.* hatred of women. Compare MISANDRY. —**mi·sog′y·nous, mi·sog′y·nis′tic,** *adj.* —**mi·sog′y·nist,** *n.*

mis·place (mis plās′), *v.t.,* **-placed, -plac·ing. 1.** to put in a wrong place. **2.** to put in a place afterward forgotten; lose; mislay. **3.** to place or bestow improperly, unsuitably, or unwisely: *to misplace one's trust.* —**mis·place′ment,** *n.*

mis′placed mod′ifier, *n.* a word, phrase, or clause that seems to refer to or modify an unintended word because of its placement in a sentence, as *when young in When young, circuses appeal to all of us.* —**Usage.** Sometimes, as in the example above, a MISPLACED MODIFIER can cause a comic misreading. Rearrangement or modification of the sentence elements can clarify the thought: *Circuses appeal to all of us when young.* See also DANGLING PARTICIPLE.

mis·print (*n.* mis′print′, mis print′; *v.* mis print′), *n.* **1.** a mistake in printing. —*v.t.* **2.** to print incorrectly.

mis·pro·nounce (mis′prə nouns′), *v.t., v.i.,* **-nounced, -nounc·ing.** to pronounce incorrectly. —**mis′pro·nun′ci·a′tion** (-nun′sē ā′shən), *n.*

mis·quote (mis kwōt′), *v.,* **-quot·ed, -quot·ing,** *n.* —*v.t., v.i.* **1.** to quote incorrectly. —*n.* **2.** Also, **mis′quo·ta′tion.** an incorrect quotation.

mis·read (mis rēd′), *v.t., v.i.,* **-read** (red), **-read·ing. 1.** to read wrongly. **2.** to misunderstand or misinterpret.

mis·rep·re·sent (mis′rep ri zent′), *v.t.* **1.** to represent incorrectly, improperly, or falsely. **2.** to represent in an unsatisfactory manner. —**mis′rep·re·sen·ta′tion,** *n.*

mis·rule (mis rōōl′), *n., v.,* **-ruled, -rul·ing.** —*n.* **1.** bad or unwise rule; misgovernment. —*v.t.* **2.** to rule badly; misgovern.

miss[1] (mis), *v.t.* **1.** to fail to hit or strike. **2.** to fail to encounter, meet, catch, etc.: *to miss a train.* **3.** to fail to take advantage of: *to miss a chance.* **4.** to fail to be present at or for: *to miss a day of school.* **5.** to notice the absence or loss of: *When did you first miss your wallet?* **6.** to regret the absence or loss of: *I miss you all dreadfully.* **7.** to escape or avoid: *He just missed being caught.* **8.** to fail to perceive or understand: *to miss the point of a remark.* **9.** to omit; leave out. —*v.i.* **10.** to fail to hit something. **11.** to fail; be unsuccessful. **12.** to misfire. **13. miss out,** to fail to experience or take advantage of something. —*n.* **14.** a failure to hit something. **15.** a failure of any kind. **16.** MISFIRE. —*Idiom.* **17. miss the boat,** *Informal.* to fail to take advantage of an opportunity. —*Proverb.* **18. A miss is as good as a mile,** a loss, no matter how little, is still a loss.

miss[2] (mis), *n., pl.* **miss·es. 1.** (*cap.*) a title of respect prefixed to the name of an unmarried woman: *Miss Mary Jones.* **2.** (used by itself as a term of address to a young woman): *Miss, please bring me some ketchup.* **3.** (*cap.*) a title prefixed to the name of something that a young woman has been selected to represent: *Miss Sweden.* **4.** (*cap.*) a title

---

mis′ad·dress′, *v.t.*
mis′ad·vise′, *v.t.,* -vised, -vis·ing.
mis·aim′, *v. n.*
mis′a·lign′ment, *n.*
mis′al·lo·ca′tion, *n.*
mis′al·lot′ment, *n.*
mis′ap·pel·la′tion, *n.*
mis′ap·pli·ca′tion, *n.*

mis′ap·prais′al, *n.*
mis′ar·range′ment, *n.*
mis′as·sign′ment, *n.*
mis′cal·cu·la′tion, *n.*
mis′clas′si·fy′, *v.t.,* -fied, -fy·ing.
mis′code′, *v.t.,* -cod·ed, -cod·ing.
mis′com·mu′ni·cate′, *v.,* -cat·ed, -cat·ing.

mis′con·jec′ture, *v.,* -tured, -tur·ing, *n.*
mis′con·struc′tion, *n.*
mis′co·or′di·nate′, *v.,* -nat·ed, -nat·ing.
mis′cop·y, *v.,* -cop·ied, -cop·y·ing.
mis′cor·re·la′tion, *n.*
mis′de·clare′, *v.,* -clared, -clar·ing.

mis′de·fine′, *v.t.,* -fined, -fin·ing.
mis′di·ag·nose′, *v.,* -nosed, -nos·ing.
mis′di·ag·no′sis, *n., pl.* -ses.
mis·di′al, *n.*
mis′dis·tri·bu′tion, *n.*
mis′em·ploy′, *v.t.*
mis·es′ti·ma′tion, *n.*
mis′e·val′u·a′tion, *n.*

prefixed to a mock surname that is used to represent possession of a particular attribute, identity, etc.: *Miss Congeniality.* **5.** a young unmarried woman; girl. **6. misses, a.** a range of sizes, chiefly from 6 to 20, for garments that fit women of average height and build. **b.** a garment in this size range. [short for *mistress*]

mis·sal (mis′əl), *n.* **1.** (*sometimes cap.*) a book containing the prayers and rites used in celebrating the Roman Catholic mass over the course of the year. **2.** any book of prayers or devotions.

mis·shape (mis shāp′, mish-), *v.t.,* **-shaped, -shaped** or **-shap·en, -shap·ing.** to shape badly or wrongly; deform. —**mis·shap′er,** *n.*

mis·shap·en (mis shā′pən, mish-), *adj.* badly shaped; deformed. —**mis·shap′en·ly,** *adv.* —**mis·shap′en·ness,** *n.*

mis·sile (mis′əl; *esp. Brit.* -īl), *n.* **1.** an object or weapon that is thrown, shot, or otherwise propelled at a target, as a stone, bullet, arrow, or rocket. **2.** GUIDED MISSILE. —*adj.* **3.** capable of being used as a missile. **4.** used for discharging missiles.

miss·ing (mis′ing), *adj.* lacking, absent, or not found.

miss′ing link′, *n.* **1.** a hypothetical form of animal assumed to have been a connecting link between the anthropoid apes and humans. **2.** anything lacking for the completion of a series or sequence.

mis·sion (mish′ən), *n.* **1.** a group or committee of persons sent to a foreign country to conduct negotiations, establish relations, provide technical assistance, or the like. **2.** a specific task that a person or group of persons is sent to perform. **3.** a permanent diplomatic establishment abroad; embassy. **4.** a group of persons sent by a church to carry on religious work, esp. evangelization in foreign lands, and often to establish schools, hospitals, etc. **5.** the place of work of such persons, or the territory of their responsibility. **6.** a military operational task, usu. assigned by a higher headquarters: *a bombing mission.* **7.** an aerospace operation designed to carry out the goals of a specific program: *a space mission.* **8.** an allotted or self-imposed duty or task; calling: *one's mission in life.* **9.** a place for evangelical and philanthropic work, esp. in a poor urban area. **10.** a series of special religious services for increasing religious devotion and for conversion. **11.** a church or region with a nonresident minister or priest. —*adj.* **12.** of or pertaining to a mission. **13.** (*usu. cap.*) of or designating a style of U.S. furniture of the early 20th century, developed in supposed imitation of the furnishings of Spanish missions in California and characterized by simple, rectilinear shapes and the use of dark, stained oak.

mis·sion·ar·y (mish′ə ner′ē), *n., pl.* **-ar·ies,** *adj.* —*n.* Also, **mis′-sion·er. 1.** a person sent by a church into an area for religious or humanitarian work. **2.** a person who attempts to convert others. —*adj.* **3.** pertaining to religious missions. **4.** characteristic of a missionary.

Mis′sionary Ridge′, *n.* a ridge in NW Georgia and SE Tennessee: Civil War battle 1863.

mis′sion control′, *n.* a command center for the control, monitoring, and support of activities connected with manned space flight. Also called **mis′sion control′** (-trōl′).

mis′sion impos′sible, *n.* an extremely difficult task.

Mis·sis·sip·pi (mis′ə sip′ē), *n.* **1.** a state in the S United States. 2,716,115; 47,716 sq. mi. (123,585 sq. km). *Cap.:* Jackson. *Abbr.:* MS, Miss. **2.** a river flowing S from N Minnesota to the Gulf of Mexico: the principal river of the U.S. 2470 mi. (3975 km) long; from the headwaters of the Missouri to the Gulf of Mexico 3988 mi. (6418 km) long.

Mis·sis·sip·pi·an (mis′ə sip′ē ən), *adj.* **1.** of or pertaining to the state of Mississippi or the Mississippi River. **2.** noting or pertaining to a period of the Paleozoic Era, occurring from about 345 million to 310 million years ago and characterized as the age of amphibians: sometimes considered an epoch of the Carboniferous Period. —*n.* **3.** a native or inhabitant of Mississippi. **4.** the Mississippian Period or System.

mis·sive (mis′iv), *n.* a written message; letter.

Mis·sou·ri (mi zŏŏr′ē, -zŏŏr′ə), *n.* **1.** a state in the central United States. 5,358,692; 69,674 sq. mi. (180,455 sq. km). *Cap.:* Jefferson City. *Abbr.:* MO, Mo. **2.** a river flowing from SW Montana into the Mississippi N of St. Louis, Mo. 2723 mi. (4382 km) long. —**Mis·sou′ri·an,** *adj., n.*

Missour′i Com′promise, *n.* a group of U.S. laws (1820–21) that admitted Missouri as a slave state and Maine as a free state to the Union, and prohibited slavery in the Louisiana Purchase north of latitude 36°30′N, except in Missouri.

mis·spell (mis spel′), *v.t., v.i.* **-spelled** or **-spelt, -spell·ing.** to spell incorrectly. —**mis·spell′ing,** *n.*

mis·spend (mis spend′), *v.t., v.i.,* **-spent, -spend·ing.** to spend wrongly or unwisely; squander; waste.

mis·state (mis stāt′), *v.t.,* **-stat·ed, -stat·ing.** to state wrongly or misleadingly. —**mis·state′ment,** *n.*

mis·step (mis step′), *n.* **1.** a wrong step. **2.** an error or slip in conduct.

miss·y (mis′ē), *n., pl.* **miss·ies.** young girl; miss.

mist (mist), *n.* **1.** a mass of minute globules of water suspended in the atmosphere at or near the earth's surface, resembling fog but not as dense. **2.** a cloud of particles or a fine spray of liquid resembling this: *a mist of perfume.* **3.** something that dims, obscures, or blurs: *the mists of time.* **4.** a haze before the eyes that dims the vision: *a mist of tears.* **5.** a suspension of a liquid in a gas. —*v.i.* **6.** to become misty. **7.** to rain in very fine drops. —*v.t.* **8.** to make misty. **9.** to cover with mist.

mis·take (mi stāk′), *n., v.,* **-took, -tak·en, -tak·ing.** —*n.* **1.** an error in action, opinion, or judgment caused by poor reasoning, carelessness, insufficient knowledge, etc. **2.** a misunderstanding or misconception. —*v.t.* **3.** to regard or identify wrongly as something or someone else: *I mistook her for the mayor.* **4.** to understand, interpret, or evaluate wrongly. —**mis·tak′a·ble,** *adj.* —**mis·tak′a·bly,** *adv.*

mis·tak·en (mi stā′kən), *adj.* **1.** wrongly conceived, held, or done: *a mistaken notion.* **2.** erroneous; wrong. **3.** having made a mistake; being in error. —**mis·tak′en·ly,** *adv.*

mis·ter (mis′tər), *n.* **1.** (*cap.*) a title of respect prefixed to a man's name or position (usu. written *Mr.*). **2.** (used by itself as an informal term of address to a man): *Watch out, mister!*

mis·tle·toe (mis′əl tō′), *n.* **1.** a European plant, *Viscum album,* having yellowish flowers and white berries, growing parasitically on trees: used in Christmas decorations. **2.** any of several other similar and related plants, as *Phoradendron serotinum,* of the U.S.

mis·treat (mis trēt′), *v.t.* to treat badly or abusively. —**mis·treat′-ment,** *n.*

mis·tress (mis′tris), *n.* **1.** a woman who has authority, esp. the female head of a household or other establishment. **2.** a woman employing servants or attendants. **3.** a female owner of an animal, or formerly, a slave. **4.** a woman who has a continuing extramarital sexual relationship with a man, esp. a man who provides her with financial support. **5.** a woman who has possession or control of something: *mistress of a great fortune.* **6.** a woman who is skilled in an occupation or art. **7.** (*sometimes cap.*) something regarded as feminine that has control or supremacy: *Great Britain, mistress of the seas.* **8.** (*cap.*) a term of address in former use corresponding to Mrs., Miss, or Ms.

mis′tress of cer′emonies, *n.* a woman who directs events, as at a formal occasion or television broadcast, acting as hostess and introducing the speakers or performers.

mis·tri·al (mis trī′əl, -trīl′), *n.* **1.** a trial terminated without conclusion on the merits of the case because of some prejudicial error in the proceedings. **2.** an inconclusive trial, as where the jury cannot agree on a verdict.

mis·trust (mis trust′), *n.* **1.** lack of trust or confidence; distrust. —*v.t.* **2.** to regard with mistrust, suspicion, or doubt. **3.** to suspect or surmise. —*v.i.* **4.** to be distrustful. —**mis·trust′ful,** *adj.* —**mis·trust′ing·ly,** *adv.*

mist·y (mis′tē), *adj.,* **mist·i·er, mist·i·est. 1.** covered or obscured by mist. **2.** consisting of or resembling mist. **3.** indistinct or blurred. —**mist′i·ly,** *adv.* —**mist′i·ness,** *n.*

mist′y-eyed′, *adj.* **1.** having the eyes obscured by tears. **2.** sentimental or dreamy: *a misty-eyed romantic.*

mis·un·der·stand (mis′un dər stand′), *v.t.,* **-stood, -stand·ing.** to understand or interpret incorrectly; attach a wrong meaning to.

mis·un·der·stand·ing (mis′un dər stan′ding), *n.* **1.** a failure to understand or interpret correctly. **2.** a disagreement or quarrel.

mis·un·der·stood (mis′un dər stŏŏd′), *adj.* **1.** incorrectly understood or interpreted. **2.** unappreciated; misjudged.

mis·us·age (mis yŏŏ′sij, -zij), *n.* **1.** incorrect or improper usage, as of words. **2.** bad or abusive treatment.

mis·use (*n.* mis yŏŏs′; *v.* -yŏŏz′), *n., v.,* **-used, -us·ing.** —*n.* **1.** wrong or improper use; misapplication. —*v.t.* **2.** to use incorrectly or improperly: *to misuse a word.* **3.** to treat badly or abusively; mistreat: *to misuse a friend.* —**mis·us′er,** *n.*

mis·word (mis wûrd′), *v.t.* to word incorrectly.

Mitch·ell (mich′əl), *n.* **1. John,** 1870–1919, U.S. labor leader. **2. Maria,** 1818–89, U.S. astronomer. **3. William,** 1879–1936, U.S. general: pioneer in the field of aviation. **4. Mount,** a mountain in W North Carolina: highest peak in the eastern U.S., 6684 ft. (2037 m).

mite[1] (mīt), *n.* any of numerous small to microscopic arachnids of the subclass Acari, including species that are parasitic on animals and plants or that feed on decaying matter and stored foods.

mite[2] (mīt), *n.* **1.** a very small contribution or sum of money. **2.** a coin of very small value. **3.** a very small creature, person, or thing. —*Idiom.* **4. a mite,** somewhat; a bit: *a mite selfish.*

mi·ter (mī′tər), *n.* **1.** the official headdress of a bishop or abbot, a tall cap having an outline resembling a pointed arch in the front and back. **2.** the official headdress of the ancient Jewish high priest. **3.** a fillet

---

mis·file′, *v.t.,* -filed, -fil·ing.
mis·formed′, *adj.*
mis·func′tion, *n., v.i.*
mis·gauge′, *v.t.,* -gauged, -gaug·ing.
mis·gov′ern, *v.t.*
mis·hear′, *v.,* -heard, -hear·ing.
mis·i·den′ti·fi·ca′tion, *n.*
mis·i·den′ti·fy′, *v.t.,* -fied, -fy·ing.

mis·la′bel, *v.t.*
mis·lo′cate, *v.t.,* -cat·ed, -cat·ing.
mis·name′, *v.t.,* -named, -nam·ing.
mis·num′ber, *v.,* -bered, -ber·ing.
mis·per·ceive′, *v.t.,* -ceived, -ceiv·ing.
mis·per·cep′tion, *n.*
mis·pro·duce′, *v.,* -duced, -duc·ing.

mis·punc′tu·a′tion, *n.*
mis·reck′on, *v.*
mis·rec·ol·lect′, *v.*
mis·rec·ol·lec′tion, *n.*
mis·reg′u·late′, *v.t.,* -lat·ed, -lat·ing.
mis·route′, *v.t.,* -rout·ed, -rout·ing.
mis·say′, *v.,* -said, -say·ing.
mis·speak′, *v.,* -spoke, -spok·en,

-speak·ing.
mis·throw′, *v.,* -threw, -thrown, -throw·ing.
mis′trans·late′, *v.t.,* -lat·ed, -lat·ing.
mis′trans·la′tion, *n.*
mis·type′, *v.,* -typed, -typ·ing.
mis·write′, *v.t.,* -wrote, -writ·ten, -writ·ing.

worn by women of ancient Greece. **4.** MITER JOINT. **5.** an oblique surface formed on a piece of wood or the like so as to butt against an oblique surface on another piece to be joined with it. **6.** MITER SQUARE. —*v.t.* **7.** to bestow a miter upon, or raise to a rank entitled to it. **8. a.** to join with a miter joint. **b.** to cut to a miter. Also, *esp. Brit.*, **mitre.**

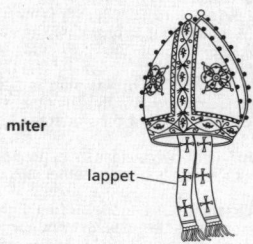

miter
lappet

mi′ter box′, *n.* any of various fixed or adjustable guides for a saw in making miters or cross cuts, esp. a troughlike box with slots in each side to guide the saw in making angular cuts.
mi′ter joint′, *n.* a joint between two pieces of wood or the like, meeting at an angle in which each of the butting surfaces is cut to an angle equal to half the angle of junction.

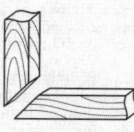

miter joint

mi′ter square′, *n.* an instrument for laying out miter joints, consisting of two straightedges joined at a 45° angle.
mi·ter·wort (mī′tər wûrt′, -wôrt′), *n.* any of several plants belonging to the genus *Mitella*, of the saxifrage family, having a capsule that resembles a bishop's miter.
Mith·ra·ism (mith′rə iz′əm), *n.* an ancient religion in which Mithras was worshipped: a rival of Christianity in the Roman Empire. —**Mith′ra′ic** (-rā′ik), **Mith′ra·is′tic,** *adj.* —**Mith′ra·ist,** *n.*
Mith·ras (mith′ras) also **Mith·ra** (-rə), *n.* the ancient Persian god of light and truth, later of the sun.
mith·ri·date (mith′ri dāt′), *n.* a sweetened medicinal preparation believed to contain an antidote to every poison.
mit·i·gate (mit′i gāt′), *v.,* **-gat·ed, -gat·ing.** —*v.t.* **1.** to lessen in force or intensity; make less severe: *to mitigate the harshness of a punishment.* **2.** to make milder or more gentle; mollify. —*v.i.* **3.** to become milder; lessen in severity. —**mit′i·gat′ed·ly,** *adv.* —**mit′i·ga′tion,** *n.* —**mit′i·ga·tive, mit′i·ga·to·ry** (-gə tôr′ē, -tōr′ē), *adj.* —**mit′i·ga′tor,** *n.* —**Usage.** MITIGATE AGAINST (to weigh against) is widely regarded as an error. The actual phrase is MILITATE AGAINST: *This criticism in no way militates against your continuing the research.*
mi·to·chon·dri·on (mī′tə kon′drē ən), *n., pl.* **-dri·a** (-drē ə). an organelle in the cell cytoplasm that has its own DNA, inherited solely from the maternal line, and that produces enzymes essential for energy metabolism. *Abbr.:* mt —**mi′to·chon′dri·al,** *adj.*
mi·to·sis (mī tō′sis), *n.* the usual method of cell division, characterized by the resolving of the chromatin of the nucleus into a threadlike form that condenses into chromosomes, each of which separates longitudinally into two parts, one part of each chromosome being retained in each of the two new daughter cells. Compare MEIOSIS (def. 1). —**mi·tot·ic** (mī tot′ik), *adj.* —**mi·tot′i·cal·ly,** *adv.*
mitt (mit), *n.* **1. a.** a rounded, thickly padded, mittenlike glove used by catchers in baseball. **b.** a similar glove used by first basemen. **2.** *Slang.* a hand. **3.** a padded or cloth mitten for a particular use: *oven mitt.* **4.** a glove that leaves the lower ends of the fingers bare.
mit·ten (mit′n), *n.* a hand covering enclosing the four fingers together and the thumb separately. —**mit′ten·like′,** *adj.*
mitz·vah or **mits·vah** (mēts vä′, mits-; *Eng.* mits′və), *n., pl.* **-voth, -vot, -vos** (-vôt′), *Eng.* **-vahs.** *Hebrew.* **1.** any of the collection of 613 commandments or precepts in the Bible and additional ones of rabbinic origin that relate chiefly to the religious and moral conduct of Jews. **2.** any good or praiseworthy deed. [< Hebrew *miṣwāh* commandment]
mix (miks), *v.t.* **1.** to combine into one mass or assemblage. **2.** to put together indiscriminately or confusedly (often fol. by *up*). **3.** to combine or unite: *to mix business and pleasure.* **4.** to add as an element or ingredient: *Mix some salt into the flour.* **5.** to form or make by combining ingredients: *to mix mortar.* **6.** to crossbreed. **7. a.** to combine, blend, or edit (the various components of a film soundtrack). **b.** to complete the mixing process on (a film or soundtrack). **8.** to combine (two or more recordings or microphone signals) to make a single recording or com-

posite signal. —*v.i.* **9.** to become mixed or capable of mixing: *a paint that mixes with water.* **10.** to associate or mingle, as in company: *to mix with the other guests.* **11.** to crossbreed. **12. mix up, a.** to confuse completely, esp. to mistake one person or thing for another. **b.** to involve or entangle. —*n.* **13.** an act or instance of mixing. **14.** the result of mixing; mixture. **15.** a commercial preparation to which usu. only a liquid must be added before cooking or baking: *a cake mix.* **16.** MIXER (def. 4). **17.** *Informal.* a mess or muddle; mix-up. **18.** an electronic blending of tracks or sounds made to produce a recording. —*Idiom.* **19. mix it (up),** *Slang.* **a.** to engage in a quarrel. **b.** to fight with the fists. —**mix′a·ble,** *adj.* —**mix′a·bil′i·ty, mix′a·ble·ness,** *n.*
mixed (mikst), *adj.* **1.** assembled or formed by mixing. **2.** incorporating different systems or elements: *a mixed economy.* **3.** of different kinds combined: *mixed nuts.* **4.** involving or comprised of persons of different sex: *a mixed doubles tennis match.* **5.** involving or comprised of persons of different class, character, belief, religion, or race: *a mixed neighborhood.* **6.** including contrasting, sometimes incompatible elements: *mixed emotions.* —**mix′ed·ly,** *adv.* —**mix′ed·ness,** *n.*
mixed′ bag′, *n.* a varied assortment.
mixed′ drink′, *n.* an alcoholic drink with two or more ingredients.
mixed′ grill′, *n.* various grilled meats, as a lamb chop, liver, sausage, and often vegetables served together.
mixed′ mar′riage, *n.* a marriage between persons of different religions or races.
mixed′ me′dia, *n.* **1.** MULTIMEDIA. **2.** artistic media used in combination in a single work. —**mixed′-me′di·a,** *adj.*
mixed′ met′aphor, *n.* an expression combining incongruous metaphors, as in *putting the ship of state on its feet.*
mixed′ mul′titude, *n.* in the Bible, a crowd of different races and nationalities. Ex. 12:38; Num. 11:4; Neh. 13:3; Jer. 25:20–24.
mixed′ num′ber, *n.* a number consisting of a whole number and a fraction or decimal, as 4½ or 4.5.
mixed′-up′, *adj.* confused or unstable: *a mixed-up kid.*
mix·er (mik′sər), *n.* **1.** a person or thing that mixes. **2.** a person with reference to sociability: *She's a good mixer at a party.* **3.** a kitchen device or appliance for mixing or beating foods. **4.** a nonalcoholic beverage, as soda water, used in a mixed drink. **5. a.** an electronic device for controlling and balancing sounds from various sources for broadcast or recording. **b.** a technician who operates such a device in a recording studio. **6.** a technician who combines various recorded elements and effects into a single soundtrack, as of a motion picture. **7.** a social event, as a dance, where people can meet informally.
mix·ture (miks′chər), *n.* **1.** a product of mixing. **2.** any combination or blend of different elements. **3.** an aggregate of substances not chemically united and existing in no fixed proportion to each other. **4.** a fabric woven of yarns combining various colors: *a heather mixture.* **5.** the act of mixing or the state of being mixed.
mix-up (miks′up′), *n.* **1.** a state of confusion. **2.** a fight.
Miz·pah (miz′pə), *n.* a mound of stones set up by Jacob in Gilead to mark a truce. Gen. 31:49.
miz·zen or **miz·en** (miz′ən), *n.* **1.** a fore-and-aft sail set on a mizzenmast. **2.** MIZZENMAST. —*adj.* **3.** of or pertaining to the mizzenmast.
miz·zen·mast or **miz·en·mast** (miz′ən mast′, -mäst′; *Naut.* -məst), *n.* **1.** the third mast from forward in a vessel having three or more masts. **2.** the after and shorter mast of a yawl or ketch; jiggermast.
mks or **MKS,** meter-kilogram-second.
mkt., market.
mktg., marketing.
Mlle., Mademoiselle.
Mlles., Mesdemoiselles.
M.L.S., Master of Library Science.
mm, millimeter.
MM., Messieurs.
Mme., Madame.
Mmes., Mesdames.
MN, Minnesota.
Mn, *Chem. Symbol.* manganese.
mne·mon·ic (ni mon′ik), *adj.* **1.** assisting or intended to assist the memory. **2.** pertaining to mnemonics or to memory. —*n.* **3.** something intended to assist the memory, as a verse or formula. **4.** a symbol, acronym, or other short form used as a computer code or function, as in programming. —**mne·mon′i·cal·ly,** *adv.*
mne·mon·ics (ni mon′iks), *n.* (*used with a sing. v.*) the process or technique of improving or developing the memory.
mo (mō), *n. Informal.* moment.
-mo, a suffix occurring in a series of words that describe book sizes according to the number of leaves formed by the folding of a single sheet of paper: *sixteenmo.*
MO, **1.** method or mode of operation. **2.** Missouri. **3.** modus operandi.
Mo, *Chem. Symbol.* molybdenum.
Mo., Missouri.
M.O., **1.** mail order. **2.** Medical Officer. **3.** method or mode of operation. **4.** modus operandi. **5.** money order.
m.o., **1.** mail order. **2.** modus operandi. **3.** money order.
mo·a (mō′ə), *n., pl.* **mo·as.** any of various flightless birds of the order Dinornithiformes, of New Zealand, some of which resembled the ostrich in size and appearance: extinct since c1800.

Mo·ab (mō′ab), *n.* an ancient kingdom E of the Dead Sea, in what is now Jordan.

Mo·ab·ite (mō′ə bīt′), *n.* **1.** a native or inhabitant of Moab. **2.** Also, **Mo·a·bit·ic** (-bit′ik). the extinct western Semitic language of the Moabites. —*adj.* **3.** of or pertaining to Moab, its people, or their language.

moan (mōn), *n.* **1.** a prolonged, low, inarticulate sound uttered from physical or mental suffering. **2.** any similar sound: *the moan of the wind.* **3.** a complaint or lamentation. —*v.i.* **4.** to utter moans, as of pain or grief. **5.** (of the wind, sea, trees, etc.) to make a sound suggestive of such moans. **6.** to complain; grumble. —*v.t.* **7.** to utter with a moan. **8.** to lament or bemoan: *to moan one's fate.* —**moan′er,** *n.*

moat (mōt), *n.* **1.** a deep, wide trench, usu. filled with water, surrounding the rampart of a fortified place, as a town or a castle. **2.** any similar trench, as one used for confining animals in a zoo.

mob (mob), *n., v.,* **mobbed, mob·bing.** —*n.* **1.** a disorderly or riotous crowd of people. **2.** a crowd bent on or engaged in lawless violence. **3.** any large group of persons or things. **4.** the common people; the masses. **5.** *Informal.* a criminal gang, esp. one involved in organized crime. —*v.t.* **6.** to crowd around noisily, as from curiosity or hostility: *Fans mobbed the actor.* **7.** to attack in a riotous mob: *The crowd mobbed the consulate.* **8.** to fill with people; crowd. —**mob′ber,** *n.* —**mob′bish,** *adj.* —**mob′bism,** *n.*

mobe′ pearl′ (mōb′, mō′bē), *n.* MABE PEARL.

mo·bile (mō′bal, -bēl; *esp. Brit.* -bīl *for 1–7;* mō′bēl *or, Brit,* -bīl *for 8),* *adj.* **1.** capable of moving or being moved readily. **2.** contained in or utilizing a motor vehicle for ready movement: *a mobile x-ray unit.* **3.** changing easily in expression, mood, purpose, etc.: *a mobile face.* **4.** quickly responding to impulses, emotions, etc., as the mind. **5. a.** characterized by or permitting the mixing of social groups. **b.** characterized by or permitting relatively free movement from one social class or level to another. **6.** flowing freely, as a liquid. **7.** of or pertaining to a mobile. —*n.* **8.** an abstract sculpture having delicately balanced units constructed of rods and sheets of metal or other material suspended in mid-air by wire or twine so that the individual parts can move independently, as when stirred by a breeze. [< Latin *mōbilis* movable]

Mo·bile (mō bēl′, mō′bēl), *n.* **1.** a seaport in SW Alabama at the mouth of the Mobile River. 204,490. **2.** a river in SW Alabama, formed by the confluence of the Alabama and Tombigbee rivers. 38 mi. (61 km) long.

-mobile, a combining form extracted from AUTOMOBILE, occurring in coinages denoting types of motorized conveyances, esp. vehicles equipped to procure or deliver objects, provide services, etc., to people without regular access to these: *bloodmobile; bookmobile; snowmobile.*

mo′bile home′, *n.* a large house trailer, designed for year-round living in one place.

mo′bile phone′, *n.* CELLULAR PHONE.

mo·bil·i·ty (mō bil′i tē), *n.* **1.** the quality of being mobile. **2.** the movement of individuals or groups from place to place, job to job, or one social or economic level to another.

mo·bi·lize (mō′bə līz′), *v.,* **-lized, -liz·ing.** —*v.t.* **1.** to assemble (armed forces) into readiness for active service: *to mobilize troops.* **2.** to organize or adapt for service in time of war or other emergency: *to mobilize industry.* **3.** to bring together or marshal for action or use: *to mobilize support.* **4.** to make mobile; put into movement or action. —*v.i.* **5.** to be or become assembled, organized, etc., as for war. —**mo′bi·liz′a·ble,** *adj.* —**mo′bi·li·za′tion,** *n.* —**mo′bi·liz′er,** *n.*

Mö·bi·us strip′ (mœ′bē əs, mā′-, mō′-), *n.* a continuous, one-sided surface formed by twisting one end of a rectangular strip through 180° about the longitudinal axis of the strip and attaching this end to the other. Also called **Mö′bius band′.** [after August Ferdinand *Möbius* (1790–1868), German mathematician]

Möbius strip
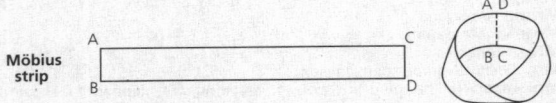

mob·ster (mob′stər), *n.* a member of a criminal mob.

Mo·by Dick (mō′bē dik′), a novel (1851) by Herman Melville.

moc·ca·sin (mok′ə sin, -zən), *n.* **1.** a heelless shoe made entirely of soft leather, as deerskin, with the sole brought up and attached to a piece of U-shaped leather on top of the foot, worn orig. by American Indians. **2.** a hard-soled shoe or slipper resembling this. **3.** COTTONMOUTH.

mo·cha (mō′kə), *n.* **1.** a choice variety of coffee, orig. grown in Arabia. **2.** a flavoring obtained by blending coffee with chocolate. **3.** a brownish chocolate color. **4.** a fine grade of soft leather with a suedelike finish, made of goatskin or sheepskin.

mock (mok), *v.t.* **1.** to treat with ridicule or contempt; deride. **2.** to mimic; imitate; counterfeit. **3.** to challenge; defy: *His actions mock convention.* **4.** to delude; disappoint. —*v.i.* **5.** to scoff; jeer (often fol. by *at*). —*n.* **6.** an act of mocking. **7.** something mocked. **8.** an imitation; counterfeit. —*adj.* **9.** feigned: *a mock battle.* —**mock′a·ble,** *adj.*

mock·er·y (mok′ə rē), *n., pl.* **-er·ies. 1.** ridicule; derision. **2.** a derisive, imitative action or speech. **3.** a subject or occasion of derision. **4.**

a mocking pretense or imitation; travesty: *a mockery of justice.* **5.** something absurdly or offensively inadequate or unfitting.

mock′-hero′ic, *adj.* **1.** imitating or burlesquing that which is heroic, as in manner, character, or action. **2.** satirizing the heroic style of literature: *a mock-heroic poem.* **3.** a literary work written in mock-heroic style. —**mock′-hero′ically,** *adv.*

mock·ing·bird (mok′ing bûrd′), *n.* any of several New World songbirds of the family Mimidae that appropriate the calls of other bird species, esp. *Mimus polyglottos,* of the U.S. and Mexico, having gray, white, and black plumage.

mock′ or′ange, *n.* **1.** any of various shrubs belonging to the genus *Philadelphus,* of the saxifrage family, having white, often fragrant flowers. **2.** any of various other shrubs or trees having flowers or fruit resembling those of the orange.

mock′ tur′tle soup′, *n.* a rich, clear soup prepared to resemble green turtle soup, made with a calf 's head or other meat, seasonings, and often with wine.

mock′-up′ or **mock′up′,** *n.* a model, often full-size, for study, testing, or teaching: *a mock-up of an experimental aircraft.*

mod (mod), *adj.* **1.** very modern in style, dress, etc. **2.** (*sometimes cap.*) of or pertaining to a style of dress of the 1960s, typified by miniskirts, bell-bottom trousers, and boots. —*n.* **3.** a person who is very modern in style, dress, etc. **4.** (*sometimes cap.*) a British teenager of the 1960s who affected Edwardian dress.

mod·al (mōd′l), *adj.* **1.** of or pertaining to mode, manner, or form. **2.** of or pertaining to a musical mode. **3.** of, pertaining to, or expressing the mood of a verb. **4.** exhibiting or expressing some phase of logical modality. —*n.* **5.** MODAL AUXILIARY. —**mod′al·ly,** *adv.*

mod′al auxil′iary, *n.* any of a group of auxiliary verbs, in English including *can, could, may, might, shall, should, will, would,* and *must,* used with the base form of another verb to express distinctions of mood.

mo·dal·i·ty (mō dal′i tē), *n., pl.* **-ties. 1.** the quality or state of being modal. **2.** an attribute or circumstance that denotes mode or manner. **3.** Also called **mode.** the classification of logical propositions according to whether they are contingently true or false, possible, impossible, or necessary. **4.** *Med.* a therapeutic method. **5.** one of the primary forms of sensation, as vision or touch.

mode¹ (mōd), *n.* **1.** a manner of acting or doing; method; way: *modern modes of transportation.* **2.** a particular type or form of something: *Heat is a mode of motion.* **3.** a designated condition or status, as for performing a task or responding to a problem: *a machine in the automatic mode.* **4.** *Philos.* appearance, form, or disposition taken by a thing, or by one of its essential properties or attributes. **5. a.** MODALITY (def. 3). **b.** any of the forms of categorical syllogisms according to the quantity and quality of their constituent propositions. **6.** any of various arrangements of the diatonic tones of an octave, differing from one another in the order of the whole steps and half steps; scale. **7.** MOOD². **8.** *Statistics.* the value of the variate at which a relative or absolute maximum occurs in the frequency distribution of the variate. **9.** the actual mineral composition of a rock, expressed in percentages by weight.

mode² (mōd), *n.* **1.** fashion or style in manners, dress, etc. **2.** a light gray or drab color.

mod·el (mod′l), *n., adj., v.,* **-eled, -el·ing** or (*esp. Brit.*) **-elled, -el·ling.** —*n.* **1.** a standard or example for imitation or comparison. **2.** a representation, generally in miniature, to show the construction or appearance of something. **3.** an image in clay, wax, or the like, to be reproduced in more durable material. **4.** a person or thing that serves as a subject for an artist, sculptor, writer, etc. **5.** a person whose profession is posing for artists or photographers. **6.** a person employed to wear clothing or pose with a product for purposes of display and advertising. **7.** a style or design of a particular product. —*adj.* **8.** serving as an example or model: *a model home.* **9.** worthy to serve as a model; exemplary: *a model student.* **10.** being a small or miniature version of something: *model ships.* —*v.t.* **11.** to form or plan according to a model. **12.** to give shape or form to; fashion. **13.** to make a miniature model of. **14.** to fashion in clay, wax, or the like. **15.** to display to other persons or to prospective customers, esp. by wearing: *to model dresses.* —*v.i.* **16.** to make models. **17.** to produce designs in some plastic material. **18.** to serve or be employed as a model.

Model T, *n.* an automobile with a 2.9-liter, 4-cylinder engine, produced by the Ford Motor Company from 1909 through 1927, considered to be the first motor vehicle successfully mass-produced on an assembly line.

mo·dem (mō′dəm, -dem), *n.* an electronic device that makes possible the transmission of data to or from a computer via telephone or other communication lines. [*mo(dulator)-dem(odulator)*]

mod·er·ate (*adj., n.* mod′ər it, mod′rit; *v.* -ə rāt′), *adj., n., v.,* **-at·ed, -at·ing.** —*adj.* **1.** kept or keeping within reasonable or proper limits; not extreme, excessive, or intense: *a moderate price.* **2.** of medium quantity, extent, or amount: *a moderate income.* **3.** mediocre or fair: *moderate talent.* **4.** calm or mild, as of the weather. **5.** of or pertaining to moderates, as in politics or religion. —*n.* **6.** a person who is moderate in opinion or opposed to extreme views and actions, as in politics. —*v.t.* **7.** to reduce the excessiveness of; make less violent, severe, intense, or rigorous: *to moderate one's criticism.* **8.** to preside over or at (a public forum, meeting, discussion, etc.). —*v.i.* **9.** to become less violent, severe, intense, or rigorous. **10.** to act as moderator; preside. —**mod′er·ate·ly,** *adv.* —**mod′er·ate·ness,** *n.*

mod′erate breeze′, *n.* a wind of 13–18 mph (5.8–8 m/sec).
mod′erate gale′, *n.* a wind of 32–38 mph (14–17 m/sec).
mod•er•a•tion (mod′ə rā′shən), *n.* **1.** the quality of being moderate; restraint; temperance. **2.** the act of moderating. —***Idiom.*** **3. in moderation,** without excess; temperately: *to drink in moderation.*
mod•er•a•tor (mod′ə rā′tər), *n.* **1.** a person or thing that moderates. **2.** a person who presides over any of various group events or meetings. **3.** a substance, as graphite or heavy water, used to slow neutrons to speeds at which they are more efficient in causing fission.
mod•ern (mod′ərn), *adj.* **1.** of or pertaining to present and recent time. **2.** characteristic of present and recent time; contemporary. **3.** of or pertaining to the historical period following the Middle Ages. **4.** of, pertaining to, or characteristic of contemporary styles of art, literature, music, etc., that reject traditionally accepted or sanctioned forms and emphasize individual experimentation and sensibility. **5.** (*cap.*) NEW (def. 12). —*n.* **6.** a person of modern times. **7.** a person whose views and tastes are modern. **8.** a type style differentiated from old style by heavy vertical strokes and straight serifs. —**mod′ern•ly,** *adv.* —**mod′ern•ness,** *n.*
mod′ern dance′, *n.* dance using specialized movement and techniques to convey a story, atmosphere, or design.
Mod′ern Eng′lish, *n.* the English language since c1475. *Abbr.:* ModE Also called **New English.**
Mod′ern Greek′, *n.* the Greek language since c1500. *Abbr.:* ModGk Also called **New Greek.**
mod•ern•ism (mod′ər niz′əm), *n.* **1.** modern character, tendencies, or values; adherence to or sympathy with what is modern. **2.** a modern usage or characteristic. **3.** (*cap.*) **a.** the movement in Roman Catholic thought that interpreted the teachings of the Church in the light of modern philosophic and scientific thought. **b.** the liberal theological tendency in 20th-century Protestantism. **4.** (*sometimes cap.*) estrangement or divergence from the past in the arts and literature, esp. in the 20th century and taking form in any of various innovative movements and styles. —**mod′ern•ist,** *n., adj.* —**mod′ern•is′tic,** *adj.*
mo•der•ni•ty (mo dûr′ni tē, mō-), *n., pl.* **-ties.** **1.** the quality of being modern. **2.** something modern.
mod•ern•ize (mod′ər nīz′), *v.,* **-ized, -iz•ing.** —*v.t.* **1.** to make modern; give a new or modern character or appearance to. —*v.i.* **2.** to become modern; adopt modern ways. —**mod′ern•i•za′tion,** *n.* —**mod′ern•iz′er,** *n.*
mod′ern lan′guages, *n.* current literary languages, esp. those in use in Europe, treated as a departmental course of study.
Mod′ern Per′sian, *n.* the Persian language since c900 A.D., written in Arabic script.
mod•est (mod′ist), *adj.* **1.** having or showing a moderate or humble estimate of one's merits, importance, etc. **2.** free from ostentation or showy extravagance: *a modest house.* **3.** having or showing regard for the decencies of behavior, speech, dress, etc.; decent. **4.** limited or moderate in amount, extent, etc. —**mod′est•ly,** *adv.*
Mo•des•to (mə des′tō), *n.* a city in central California. 176,357.
mod•es•ty (mod′ə stē), *n.* **1.** regard for decency of behavior, speech, dress, etc. **2.** lack of vanity.
mod•i•cum (mod′i kəm), *n.* a moderate or small amount.
mod•i•fi•ca•tion (mod′ə fi kā′shən), *n.* **1.** an act or instance of modifying or the state of being modified. **2.** a modified form; variety. **3.** a change in an organism acquired during its lifetime and not inheritable. **4.** limitation or qualification. **5. a.** the use of modifiers in a construction or language. **b.** the meaning a modifier has, esp. as it affects the meaning of the word or other form modified. **6.** a change in the phonological shape of a morpheme, word, or other form when it functions as an element in a construction, as the change of *not* to *n't* in *doesn't.*
mod•i•fi•er (mod′ə fī′ər), *n.* **1.** a person or thing that modifies. **2.** a word, phrase, or sentence element that limits or qualifies the sense of another word, phrase, or element in the same construction. —**Usage.** See DANGLING PARTICIPLE, MISPLACED MODIFIER.
mod•i•fy (mod′ə fī′), *v.,* **-fied, -fy•ing.** —*v.t.* **1.** to change somewhat the form or qualities of; alter partially; amend: *to modify a contract.* **2.** (of a word, phrase, or clause) to stand in a syntactically subordinate relation to (another word, phrase, or clause), usu. with descriptive, limiting, or particularizing meaning; act as a modifier: In *a good cook, good* modifies *cook.* **3.** to change (a vowel) by umlaut. **4.** to reduce in degree or extent: *to modify one's demands.* —*v.i.* **5.** to be or become modified. —**mod′i•fi′a•ble,** *adj.* —**mod′i•fi′a•bil′i•ty, mod′i•fi′a•ble•ness,** *n.*
mod•ish (mō′dish), *adj.* fashionable; stylish. —**mod′ish•ly,** *adv.* —**mod′ish•ness,** *n.*
mod•u•lar (moj′ə lər), *adj.* **1.** of or pertaining to a module. **2.** composed of standardized units or sections for easy construction or flexible arrangement. —*n.* **3.** something built or organized in self-contained units or sections. **4.** a self-contained unit or item that can be combined or interchanged with others like it to create different shapes or designs.
mod•u•late (moj′ə lāt′), *v.,* **-lat•ed, -lat•ing.** —*v.t.* **1.** to regulate by or adjust to a certain measure or proportion. **2.** to alter or adapt (the voice) according to the circumstances, one's listener, etc. **3.** to cause the amplitude, frequency, phase, or intensity of (a carrier wave) to vary in accordance with a sound wave or other signal. —*v.i.* **4.** to modulate a carrier wave. **5.** to move harmonically from one key to a related key. —**mod′u•la•to′ry** (-tôr′ē, -tōr′ē), *adj.* —**mod′u•la′tor,** *n.*
mod•u•la•tion (moj′ə lā′shən, mod′yə-), *n.* **1.** the act of modulating. **2.** the state of being modulated. **3.** harmonic movement from one key to a related key. **4.** the use of a particular distribution of stress or pitch in an utterance to show meaning, as the use of rising pitch on *here* in *John is here?*
mod•ule (moj′o͞ol), *n.* **1.** a separable component, frequently one that is interchangeable with others, for assembly into units of differing size, complexity, or function. **2.** any of the self-contained segments of a spacecraft, designed for a particular task. **3.** a standard or unit for measuring. **4.** a selected unit of measure used as a basis for the planning and standardization of building materials.
mo•dus op•e•ran•di (mō′dəs op′ə ran′dē, -dī), *n., pl.* **mo•di operandi** (mō′dē, -dī). mode of operating; method of working. [< Latin]
mo•dus vi•ven•di (mō′dəs vi ven′dē, -dī), *n., pl.* **mo•di vivendi** (mō′dē, -dī). **1.** manner of living; way of life; lifestyle. **2.** a temporary arrangement between persons or parties pending a settlement of matters in debate. [< Latin]
Mo•ga•di•shu (mō′gə dē′sho͞o), *n.* the capital of Somalia, in the S part. 444,882. Italian, **Mo•ga•di•scio** (mô′gä dē′shô).
Mo•gen Da•vid (mō′gən dā′vid, mô′gən dô′vid), *n.* STAR OF DAVID.
mo•gul (mō′gəl), *n.* a bump or mound of hard snow on a ski slope. —**mo′guled,** *adj.*
Mo•gul (mō′gəl, -gul, mō gul′), *n.* **1.** a member of the dynasty of Muslim rulers that dominated N India and parts of the Deccan from the 16th to the early 18th centuries. **2.** (*l.c.*) a powerful or influential person: *a mogul of the movie industry.* —*adj.* **3.** of or pertaining to the Moguls or their empire. Often, **Moghul, Mughal** (for defs. 1, 3).
mo•hair (mō′hâr′), *n.* **1.** the hair of an Angora goat. **2.** a fabric made wholly or partly of yarn from this hair, used in clothing and upholstery.
Mo•ham•med (mo͝o ham′id, -hä′mid, mō-), *n.* MUHAMMAD.
Mo•har•ram or **Mu•har•ram** (mo͝o har′əm), *n.* the first month of the Islamic calendar.
Mo•hawk (mō′hôk), *n., pl.* **-hawks,** (*esp. collectively*) **-hawk.** **1.** a member of an American Indian people, orig. residing in the middle Mohawk River valley in New York: the easternmost of the Iroquois Five Nations. **2.** the Iroquoian language of the Mohawks. **3.** a river flowing E from central New York to the Hudson. 148 mi. (240 km) long. **4.** (*often l.c.*) a hairstyle with the scalp shaved except for a center strip of stiff, bluntly cut hair running front to back.
Mo•he•gan (mō hē′gən), *n., pl.* **-gans,** (*esp. collectively*) **-gan.** **1.** a member of an American Indian people of E Connecticut. **2.** the extinct Eastern Algonquian language of the Mohegan.
Mohr (môr, mōr), *n.* **Joseph,** 1792–1848, German clergyman and hymn writer, author of *Silent Night.*
Mohs′ scale′ (mōz), *n.* a scale of hardness for minerals, consisting of the following degrees, in increasing hardness: talc 1; gypsum 2; calcite 3; fluorite 4; apatite 5; orthoclase 6; quartz 7; topaz 8; corundum 9; diamond 10. [after F. *Mohs* (1773–1839), German mineralogist]
moi•e•ty (moi′i tē), *n., pl.* **-ties.** **1.** a half. **2.** an indefinite portion, part, or share. **3.** (in certain unilateral societies or communities) one of the two descent groups into which the population falls.
moil (moil), *v.i.* **1.** to work hard; drudge. **2.** to whirl or eddy. —*n.* **3.** DRUDGERY. **4.** TURMOIL. —**moil′er,** *n.*
moi•ré (mwä rā′, mô-, mō-), *adj., n., pl.* **-rés.** —*adj.* **1.** (of silks and other fabrics) presenting a watery or wavelike appearance. —*n.* **2.** a design pressed on silk, rayon, etc., by engraved rollers. **3.** any silk, rayon, etc., fabric with a watery or wavelike appearance.
moist (moist), *adj.,* **-er, -est.** **1.** slightly wet; damp. **2.** (of the eyes) tearful. **3.** (of the air) having high humidity. —**moist′ly,** *adv.*
mois•ten (moi′sən), *v.t., v.i.* to make or become moist. —**moist′en•er,** *n.*
mois•ture (mois′chər), *n.* condensed or diffused liquid, esp. water. —**mois′ture•less,** *adj.*
mois•tur•ize (mois′chə rīz′), *v.,* **-ized, -iz•ing.** —*v.t.* **1.** to add or restore moisture to. —*v.i.* **2.** to make something moist.
mois•tur•iz•er (mois′chə rī′zər), *n.* a cream or lotion for the skin used to help restore or retain moisture.
Mo•ja′ve (or **Mo•ha′ve**) **Des′ert** (mō hä′vē), *n.* a desert in S California: part of the Great Basin. ab. 15,000 sq. mi. (38,850 sq. km).
mo•jo (mō′jō), *n., pl.* **-jos, -joes.** **1.** the art or practice of casting magic or voodoo spells. **2.** an amulet or charm believed to carry such a spell.
mo•lar[1] (mō′lər), *n.* **1.** Also called **mo′lar tooth′.** a tooth having a broad biting surface adapted for grinding, being one of 12 in humans, with 3 on each side of the upper and lower jaws. —*adj.* **2.** adapted for grinding, as teeth. **3.** pertaining to such teeth.
mo•lar[2] (mō′lər), *adj.* pertaining to a body of matter as a whole, as contrasted with molecular and atomic.
mo•lar[3] (mō′lər), *adj.* describing a solution containing one mole of solute per liter of solution.
mo•lar•i•ty (mō lar′i tē), *n.* the number of moles of solute per liter of solution.
mo•las•ses (mə las′iz), *n.* a thick syrup produced during the refining of sugar or from sorghum, usu. dark brown in color.
mold[1] (mōld), *n.* **1.** a hollow form or matrix for giving a particular shape to something in a molten or plastic state. **2.** the shape imparted to a thing by a mold. **3.** something formed in or on a mold: *a mold of jelly.* **4.** a frame on which something is formed or made. **5.** shape; form. **6.** prototype; precursor. **7.** a distinctive nature, character, or type: *a person of a simple mold.* **8.** *Archit.* a molding. —*v.t.* **9.** to work into a

required shape or form; shape. **10.** to shape or form in or on a mold. **11.** *Metall.* to make a mold of or from, in order to make a casting. **12.** to produce by or as if by shaping material; form. **13.** to have influence in determining or forming. **14.** to ornament with moldings. Also, *esp. Brit.,* **mould.** **—mold′a•ble,** *adj.* **—mold′er,** *n.*

mold² (mōld), *n.* **1.** a growth of minute fungi forming on vegetable or animal matter, commonly as a downy or furry coating, and associated with decay or dampness. **2.** any of the fungi that produce such a growth; mildew. *—v.t.* **3.** to cause to become overgrown with mold. *—v.i.* **4.** to become overgrown with mold. Also, *esp. Brit.,* **mould.**

Mol•da•vi•a (mol dā′vē ə, -vyə), *n.* **1.** a region in NE Romania: formerly a principality that united with Wallachia to form Romania. *Cap.:* Jassy. **2.** former name of **Moldova.** **—Mol•da′vi•an,** *adj., n.*

mold•board (mōld′bôrd′, -bōrd′), *n.* **1.** the curved metal plate in a plow that turns over the earth from the furrow. **2.** a large blade mounted on the front of a bulldozer to push loose earth. **3.** a board forming one side or surface of a mold for concrete.

mold•er (mōl′dər), *v.i.* to turn to dust by natural decay; crumble; disintegrate; waste away.

mold•ing (mōl′ding), *n.* **1.** the act or process of shaping into a mold. **2.** something molded. **3. a.** a long, narrow ornamental surface with a modeled profile that casts strong shadows: used on furniture, frames, and architectural members, as cornices, stringcourses, or bases. **b.** a strip of wood, stone, etc., having such a surface. **c.** a strip of contoured wood or other material placed on a wall, as just below the juncture with the ceiling.

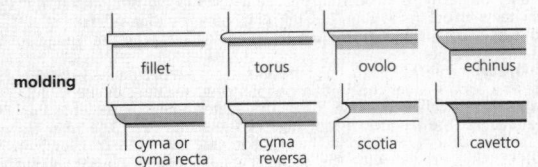

| molding | fillet | torus | ovolo | echinus |
| | cyma or cyma recta | cyma reversa | scotia | cavetto |

Mol•do•va (môl dō′və), *n.* a republic in S central Europe: a former constituent republic of the U.S.S.R. 4,475,232; 13,000 sq. mi. (33,700 sq. km). *Cap.:* Chişinău. Formerly, **Moldavia.** **—Mol•do′van,** *adj., n.*

mold•y (mōl′dē), *adj.,* **mold•i•er, mold•i•est.** **1.** overgrown or covered with mold. **2.** musty, as from decay or age. **3.** *Informal.* old-fashioned; outmoded. **—mold′i•ness,** *n.*

mole¹ (mōl), *n.* **1.** any of various small, insect-eating mammals, esp. of the family Talpidae, living chiefly underground and having velvety fur, very small eyes, and strong forefeet. **2.** a spy who becomes part of and works from within the ranks of an enemy governmental staff or intelligence agency.

mole² (mōl), *n.* a small, congenital spot or blemish on the human skin, usu. of a dark color, slightly elevated, and sometimes hairy; nevus.

mole³ (mōl), *n.* a massive structure, esp. of stone, set up in the water, as for a breakwater or a pier.

mole⁴ or **mol** (mōl), *n.* the quantity of a substance the weight of which equals the substance's molecular weight expressed in grams, and which contains 6.02×10^{23} molecules of the substance.

mo•le⁵ (mō′lā), *n.* a spicy Mexican sauce made with chocolate and chili peppers, usu. served with poultry.

mole′ crab′, *n.* a burrowing crustacean of the genus *Emerita,* found on sandy ocean beaches of North America, having a curved carapace.

mole′ crick′et, *n.* a burrowing cricket, of the subfamily Gryllotalpidae, having spadelike front legs and feeding on the roots of plants.

mo•lec•u•lar (mə lek′yə lər), *adj.* of or pertaining to or caused by molecules: *molecular structure.* **—mo•lec′u•lar•ly,** *adv.*

molec′ular biol′ogy, *n.* the branch of biology that deals with the nature of biological phenomena at the molecular level through the study of DNA and RNA, proteins, and other large molecules involved in genetic information and cell function.

molec′ular clock′, *n.* the changes over time that take place in the amino acid sequences of proteins, from which approximate ages and relationships of life forms can be deduced.

molec′ular for′mula, *n.* a chemical formula that indicates the kind and number of atoms in a molecule of a compound.

molec′ular genet′ics, *n.* a subdivision of genetics concerned with the structure and function of genes at the molecular level.

molec′ular sieve′, *n.* a compound with molecule-size pores, as some sodium aluminum silicates, that chemically locks molecules in them: used in purification and separation processes.

molec′ular weight′, *n.* the average weight of a molecule of an element or compound measured in units based on $1/12$ the weight of the carbon-12 atom; the sum of the atomic weights of all the atoms in a molecule. *Abbr.:* mol. wt.

mol•e•cule (mol′ə kyōōl′), *n.* **1.** the smallest physical unit of an element or compound, consisting of one or more like atoms in an element and two or more different atoms in a compound. **2.** a quantity of a substance, the weight of which is numerically equal to the molecular weight; gram molecule. **3.** any very small particle.

mole•hill (mōl′hil′), *n.* a small mound or ridge of earth raised up by a mole or moles burrowing under the ground.

mole•skin (mōl′skin′), *n.* **1.** the soft, deep gray, fragile fur of the mole. **2.** a strong, heavy cotton fabric with a suedelike finish, used for sportswear and work clothing. **3.** **moleskins,** a garment, esp. trousers, of this fabric. **4.** an adhesive-backed felt applied to parts of the feet subject to abrasion from footwear.

mo•lest (mə lest′), *v.t.* **1.** to bother, interfere with, or annoy. **2.** to make indecent sexual advances to. **—mo•les•ta•tion** (mō′le stā′shən, mol′e-), *n.* **—mo•lest′er,** *n.*

Mo•lière (mōl yâr′), *n.* (*Jean Baptiste Poquelin*) 1622–73, French playwright.

moll (mol), *n. Slang.* **1.** GUN MOLL. **2.** a casual female companion.

mol•li•fy (mol′ə fī′), *v.t.,* **-fied, -fy•ing.** **1.** to soften in feeling or temper; pacify; appease. **2.** to mitigate; reduce: *to mollify one's demands.* **—mol′li•fi•ca′tion,** *n.* **—mol′li•fi′er,** *n.*

mol•lusk or **mol•lusc** (mol′əsk), *n.* any invertebrate of the phylum Mollusca, typically having a calcareous shell of one, two, or more pieces that wholly or partly enclose the soft, unsegmented body: includes the chitons, snails, bivalves, squids, and octopuses. **—mol•lus•kan, mol•lus•can** (mə lus′kən), *adj., n.*

mol•ly (mol′ē), *n., pl.* **-lies.** any of certain livebearing freshwater fishes of the genus *Poecilia,* popular in home aquariums.

mol•ly•cod•dle (mol′ē kod′l), *v.,* **-dled, -dling,** *n.* *—v.t.* **1.** to coddle; pamper. *—n.* **2.** a man or boy who is used to being coddled; a milksop.

Mol′ly Ma•guire′ *n.* (mə gwīr′), **1.** *Irish Hist.* a member of a secret terrorist society organized in Ireland in 1843 to prevent evictions by the government: so called because the members disguised themselves as women. **2.** *U.S. Hist.* a member of a former secret association, organized about 1865, that terrorized the mine operators' agents in an effort to get relief from oppressive conditions in the anthracite coal-mining regions of Pennsylvania: ceased to function about 1877.

Mo•loch (mō′lok, mol′ək), *n.* **1.** a deity who was propitiated by the sacrificial burning of children. II Kings 23:10; Jer. 32:35. **2.** (*l.c.*) a spiny lizard, *Moloch horridus,* of Australian deserts.

molt (mōlt), *v.i.* **1.** to cast or shed the feathers, skin, or the like, in the process of renewal or growth. *—v.t.* **2.** to cast or shed (feathers, skin, etc.) in the process of renewal. *—n.* **3.** an act, process, or an instance of molting. **4.** something that is dropped in molting. Also, *esp. Brit.,* **moult.** **—molt′er,** *esp. Brit.,* **moult′er,** *n.*

mol•ten (mōl′tn), *v.* **1.** a pp. of MELT. *—adj.* **2.** liquefied by heat; in a state of fusion. **3.** produced by melting and casting: *a molten image.*

mo•lyb•de•nite (mə lib′də nīt′), *n.* a soft, graphitelike mineral, molybdenum sulfide, MoS_2, occurring in foliated masses or scales: the principal ore of molybdenum.

mo•lyb•de•num (mə lib′də nəm), *n.* a silver-white metallic element, used as an alloy with iron in making hard, high-speed cutting tools. *Symbol:* Mo; *at. wt.:* 95.94; *at. no.:* 42; *sp. gr.:* 10.2.

mom (mom), *n. Informal.* MOTHER¹ (defs. 1,2).

mom-and-pop (mom′ən pop′), *adj., n., pl.* **-pops.** *—adj.* **1.** of or pertaining to a small retail business, usually owned and operated by members of a family: *a mom-and-pop grocery.* **2.** of something, as an enterprise, investment, or project, that is independent, small in scope, and modestly financed. *—n.* **3.** a small-scale, owner-operated business.

mo•ment (mō′mənt), *n.* **1.** an indefinitely short period of time; instant. **2.** the present time or any other particular time (usu. prec. by *the*): *He is busy at the moment.* **3.** a definite period or stage, as in a course of events: *At that moment in history Rome was a republic.* **4.** importance or consequence: *a decision of great moment.* **5.** a time of success, excellence, satisfaction, etc.: *My job has its moments.* **6.** *Statistics.* the mean or expected value of the product formed by multiplying together a set of one or more variates or variables each to a specified power. **7.** *Mech.* **a.** a tendency to produce motion, esp. about an axis. **b.** the product of a physical quantity and its directed distance from an axis.

mo•men•tar•i•ly (mō′mən târ′ə lē, mō′mən ter′-), *adv.* **1.** for a moment; briefly. **2.** at any moment; imminently. **3.** instantly.

mo•men•tar•y (mō′mən ter′ē), *adj.* **1.** lasting but a moment; very brief. **2.** likely to occur at any moment: *to live in fear of momentary annihilation.* **3.** effective or recurring constantly.

mo•men•to (mə men′tō, mō-), *n., pl.* **-tos, -toes.** MEMENTO.

mo′ment of truth′, *n.* **1.** the moment in a bullfight at which the matador is about to make the kill. **2.** the moment at which one's character, courage, skill, etc., is put to an extreme test; critical moment.

mo•men•tous (mō men′təs), *adj.* of great importance or consequence. **—mo•men′tous•ly,** *adv.* **—mo•men′tous•ness,** *n.*

mo•men•tum (mō men′təm), *n., pl.* **-ta** (-tə), **-tums.** **1.** force or speed of movement; impetus, as of a physical object or course of events: *a career that lost momentum.* **2.** *Mech.* a quantity expressing the motion of a body or system, equal to the product of the mass of a body and its velocity.

mom•ism (mom′iz əm), *n.* (*sometimes cap.*) undue dependence on maternal protection, resulting in loss of maturity and independence.

mom•ma (mom′ə), *n., pl.* **-mas.** *Informal.* MOTHER¹ (defs. 1, 2).

mom•my or **mom•mie** (mom′ē), *n., pl.* **-mies.** *Informal.* MOTHER¹ (defs. 1, 2).

mom′my track′, *n.* a path of career advancement for women who are willing to forgo some promotions and pay increases so that they can spend more time with their children.

Mon·a·co (mon′ə kō′, mə nä′kō), *n.* **1.** a principality on the Mediterranean coast, bordering SE France. 31,892; ½ sq. mi. (1.3 sq. km). **2.** the capital of this principality. 1234.

mon·ad (mon′ad, mō′nad), *n.* **1.** a flagellated protozoan, esp. of the genus *Monas.* **2.** an element, atom, or group having a valence of one. **3.** an indivisible metaphysical entity, esp. one having an autonomous life. **4.** a single unit or entity. —**mo·nad·ic** (mə nad′ik), **mo·nad′i·cal, mo·nad′al,** *adj.*

Mo·na Li·sa (mō′nə lē′sə, lē′zə), (Italian, *La Gioconda*), a portrait (1503?–05?) by Leonardo da Vinci.

mo·nan·dry (mə nan′drē), *n.* **1.** the practice or condition of having one husband at a time. **2.** (of a female animal) the condition of having one mate at a time.

mon·arch (mon′ərk, -ärk), *n.* **1.** a hereditary sovereign, as a king, queen, or emperor. **2.** a sole and absolute ruler of a state or nation. **3.** a person or thing that holds a dominant position. **4.** MONARCH BUTTERFLY. [< Late Latin < Greek *monárchēs* sole ruler] —**mo·nar·chal** (mə när′kəl), **mo·nar′chi·al** (-kē əl), *adj.* —**mo·nar′chal·ly,** *adv.*

mon′arch but′terfly, *n.* a large, deep orange butterfly, *Danaus plexippus,* having black-and-white markings and larvae that feed on the leaves of milkweed. Also called **monarch.**

Mo·nar·chi·an·ism (mə när′kē ə niz′əm), *n.* any of several Christian doctrines in the 2nd and 3rd centuries A.D., emphasizing the unity of God. —**Mo·nar′chi·an,** *adj., n.* —**Mo·nar′chi·an·ist,** *n.*

mo·nar·chi·cal (mə när′ki kəl) also **mo·nar′chic,** *adj.* of, pertaining to, or favoring a monarch or monarchy. —**mo·nar′chi·cal·ly,** *adv.*

mon·ar·chism (mon′ər kiz′əm), *n.* **1.** the principles of monarchy. **2.** advocacy of monarchical rule. —**mon′ar·chist,** *n., adj.* —**mon′ar·chist′ic,** *adj.*

mon·ar·chy (mon′ər kē), *n., pl.* **-chies. 1.** a government or state in which the supreme power is actually or nominally lodged in a monarch. **2.** supreme power or sovereignty held by a single person. **3.** the fact or state of being a monarchy.

mo·nar·da (mə när′də), *n., pl.* **-das.** any aromatic, erect plant belonging to the genus *Monarda,* of the mint family, native to North America, including horsemint and Oswego tea.

mon·as·ter·y (mon′ə ster′ē), *n., pl.* **-ter·ies. 1.** a place of residence occupied by a community of persons, esp. monks, living in seclusion under religious vows. **2.** the community itself.

mo·nas·tic (mə nas′tik) *adj.* Also, **mo·nas′ti·cal. 1.** of or pertaining to monks, nuns, or monasteries: *monastic vows.* **2.** of or resembling the secluded, dedicated, or austere life characteristic of a monastery. —*n.* **3.** a member of a monastic community or order, esp. a monk. —**mo·nas′ti·cal·ly,** *adv.* —**mo·nas′ti·cism,** *n.*

Mon·dale (mon′dāl′), *n.* **Walter Frederick** (*"Fritz"*), born 1928, U.S. vice president 1977–81.

Mon·day (mun′dā, -dē), *n.* the second day of the week, following Sunday.

Mon′day morn′ing quar′terback, *n.* a person who offers hindsight solutions to problems already faced by others. —**Mon′day morn′ing quar′terbacking,** *n.*

mon·de·green (mon′di grēn′), *n.* a word or phrase resulting from a misinterpretation of a word or phrase that has been heard. [coined by British author S. Wright fr. the line *laid him on the green,* interpreted as *Lady Mondegreen,* in a Scottish ballad]

Mon·dri·an (môn′drē än′, mon′-), *n.* **Piet** (pēt) (*Pieter Cornelis Mondriaan*), 1872–1944, Dutch painter.

mo·ne·cious (mə nē′shəs, mō-), *adj.* MONOECIOUS.

Mo·ne·ra (mə nēr′ə), *n.* (*used with a pl. v.*) a taxonomic kingdom of prokaryotic organisms that typically reproduce by asexual budding or fission, comprising the bacteria, blue-green algae, and various primitive pathogens.

mo·ne·ran (mə nēr′ən), *n.* **1.** any organism of the taxonomic kingdom Monera, comprising prokaryotes and other primitive forms that do not have their genetic material organized into chromosomes or enclosed by membranes. —*adj.* **2.** of or pertaining to the kingdom Monera.

mon·e·ta·rism (mon′i tə riz′əm, mun′-), *n.* a doctrine holding that changes in the money supply determine the direction of a nation's economy. —**mon′e·ta·rist,** *n., adj.*

mon·e·tar·y (mon′i ter′ē, mun′-), *adj.* **1.** of or pertaining to the coinage or currency of a country. **2.** of or pertaining to money; pecuniary. —**mon′e·tar′i·ly** (-târ′ə lē), *adv.*

mon′etary u′nit, *n.* the standard unit of value of the currency of a country, as the dollar in the U.S.

mon·e·tize (mon′i tīz′, mun′-), *v.t.,* **-tized, -tiz·ing. 1.** to legalize as money. **2.** to coin into money: *to monetize gold.* —**mon′e·ti·za′tion,** *n.*

mon·ey (mun′ē), *n., pl.* **mon·eys, mon·ies,** *adj.* —*n.* **1.** any circulating medium of exchange, including coins, paper money, and demand deposits. **2.** PAPER MONEY. **3.** gold, silver, or other metal in pieces of convenient form stamped by public authority and issued as a medium of exchange and measure of value. **4.** any article or substance used as a medium of exchange, means of payment, or measure of wealth, as checks on demand deposit. **5.** a particular form or denomination of currency. **6.** capital to be borrowed, loaned, or invested: *mortgage money.*

7. an amount or sum of money. **8. moneys** or **monies,** *Chiefly Law.* pecuniary sums. —*adj.* **9.** of or pertaining to money. **10.** used for carrying, keeping, or handling money: *a money drawer.* **11.** of or pertaining to capital or finance: *the money business.* —**Idiom. 12. for my money,** according to my opinion: *For my money, she'd make a perfect president.* **13. in the money,** *Informal.* **a.** financially successful; affluent. **b.** finishing among the top winners, as of a race. **14. (right) on the money,** *Informal.* **a.** at just the exact spot or time; on target. **b.** exhibiting or done with great accuracy or expertise. —*Proverb.* **15. Money begets money,** those who have money are likely to accumulate more.

mon·ey·bag (mun′ē bag′), *n.* **1.** a bag for money. **2. moneybags,** (*used with a sing. v.*) a very wealthy person.

mon′ey belt′, *n.* a belt with a concealed section for holding money.

mon·ey-chang·er, *n.* **1.** a person whose business is the exchange of currency, esp. the exchange of one country's currency for that of another. **2.** a portable device, for dispensing coins in change.

mon·eyed (mun′ēd), *adj.* **1.** having much money; wealthy. **2.** of or pertaining to the wealthy: *moneyed interests.*

mon·ey-grub·ber (mun′ē grub′ər), *n.* a person who is preoccupied with making money. —**mon′ey·grub′bing,** *adj., n.*

mon·ey·lend·er (mun′ē len′dər), *n.* a person or organization whose business it is to lend money at interest.

mon·ey·mak·er (mun′ē mā′kər), *n.* **1.** a person who is successful at making large amounts of money. **2.** something that yields a large pecuniary profit. —**mon′ey·mak′ing,** *adj.,n.*

mon′ey mar′ket, *n.* the short-term trade in money, as in the sale and purchase of bonds and certificates.

mon′ey or′der, *n.* an order for the payment of money, as one issued by one bank or post office and payable at another.

mon·ey·wort (mun′ē wûrt′, -wôrt′), *n.* a creeping plant, *Lysimachia nummularia,* of the primrose family, having roundish leaves and solitary yellow flowers.

mon·ger (mung′gər, mong′-), *n.* **1.** a person who is involved with something in a petty or contemptible way (usu. used in combination): *a gossipmonger.* **2.** *Chiefly Brit.* a dealer in or trader of a commodity (usu. used in combination): *fishmonger.* —*v.t.* **3.** to sell; hawk.

Mon·gol (mong′gəl, -gōl, mon′-), *n.* **1. a.** a member of a pastoral people or group of peoples of Mongolia prominent in medieval Asian history under Genghis Khan and his successors. **b.** a member of any of the modern peoples descended from the historical Mongols, esp. the present inhabitants of Mongolia. **2.** MONGOLOID (def. 3).

Mon′gol Em′pire, *n.* an empire founded in the 12th century by Genghis Khan, which reached its greatest territorial extent in the 13th century, encompassing the larger part of Asia and extending westward to the Dnieper River in E Europe.

Mon·go·li·a (mong gō′lē ə, mon-), *n.* **1.** a region in Asia including Inner Mongolia in China and the Mongolian People's Republic. **2.** MONGOLIAN PEOPLE'S REPUBLIC. —**Mon·go′li·an,** *adj.*

Mongo′lian Peo′ple's Repub′lic, *n.* a republic in E central Asia, in N Mongolia. 2,538,211; ab. 604,250 sq. mi. (1,566,500 sq. km). *Cap.:* Ulan Bator. Formerly, **Outer Mongolia.** Also called **Mongolia.**

mon·gol·ism (mong′gə liz′əm, mon′-), *n.* (*sometimes cap.*) (no longer in technical use) DOWN SYNDROME.

Mon·gol·oid (mong′gə loid′, mon′-), *adj.* **1.** of, designating, or characteristic of one of the traditional racial divisions of humankind, marked by yellowish complexion, prominent cheekbones, epicanthic folds, and straight black hair and including the Mongols, Chinese, Japanese, Siamese, Eskimos, and, in some classifications, the American Indians. **2.** (*often l.c.*) (no longer in technical use) of or affected with Down syndrome. —*n.* **3.** a member of the Mongoloid race. **4.** (*usu. l.c.*) (no longer in technical use) a person affected with Down syndrome.

mon·goose (mong′gōōs′, mon′-), *n., pl.* **-goos·es.** any of several Old World genera of slender, ferretlike carnivores, esp. of the genus *Herpestes,* some species of which are noted for their ability to kill cobras.

mon·grel (mung′grəl, mong′-), *n.* **1.** a dog of mixed or indeterminate breed. **2.** an animal or plant resulting from an uncontrolled or accidental crossing of breeds or varieties. **3.** any cross between different types of persons or things. —*adj.* **4.** being a mongrel. —**mon′grel·ism,** *n.*

mon·ies (mun′ēz), *n.* a pl. of MONEY.

mon·i·ker or **mon·ick·er** (mon′i kər), *n. Slang.* name; nickname.

mon·ism (mon′iz əm, mō′niz əm), *n.* **1. a.** (in metaphysics) any of various theories holding that there is only one basic substance or principle as the ground of reality or that reality consists of a single element. Compare DUALISM (def. 2a), PLURALISM (def. 1a). **b.** (in epistemology) a theory that the object and datum of cognition are identical. **2.** the reduction of all processes, structures, etc., to a single governing principle. **3.** the notion that there is only one causal factor in history. —**mon′ist,** *n.* —**mo·nis·tic** (mə nis′tik, mō-), *adj.* —**mo·nis′ti·cal·ly,** *adv.*

mo·ni·tion (mə nish′ən), *n.* **1.** admonition; warning. **2.** an official or legal notice.

mon·i·tor (mon′i tər), *n.* **1.** a student appointed to assist in the conduct of a class or school, as to help keep order. **2.** a person who admonishes, esp. with reference to conduct. **3.** something that serves to remind or give warning. **4.** a device or arrangement for observing, detecting, or recording the operation of a machine or system, esp. an automatic control system. **5.** an instrument for detecting dangerous gases, radiation, etc. **6.** *Radio and Television.* a receiving apparatus used in a

Ⓜ

control room or studio for monitoring transmissions. **7.** a component with a display screen for viewing computer data, television programs, etc. **8. a.** a former U.S. steam-propelled, armored warship of very low freeboard. **b.** (*cap.*, *italics*) the first of such warships, used by Union forces against the *Merrimack* in 1862. **9.** a raised construction straddling the ridge of a roof and having windows or louvers for lighting or ventilating a building. **10.** any large lizard of the family Varanidae, of Africa, S Asia, the East Indies, and Australia, fabled to give warning of the presence of crocodiles. —*v.t.* **11.** *Radio and Television.* to listen to (transmitted signals) on a receiving set in order to check the quality of the transmission. **12.** to observe, record, or detect (an operation or condition) with instruments that have no effect upon the operation or condition. **13.** to oversee, supervise, or regulate. **14.** to watch closely for purposes of control, surveillance, etc.; keep track of. —*v.i.* **15.** to serve as a monitor, detector, supervisor, etc. —**mon/i·tor·ship/,** *n.*

mon·i·to·ry (mon′i tôr′ē, -tōr′ē), *adj.*, *n.*, *pl.* **-ries.** —*adj.* **1.** admonitory. —*n.* **2.** a letter containing a warning.

monk (mungk), *n.* a man who is a member of a religious order, usu. living in a monastery according to a particular rule and under vows of poverty, chastity, and obedience.

Monk (mungk), *n.* **1.** Thelonious (Sphere), 1917–82, U.S. jazz pianist and composer. **2.** William H(enry), 1823–89, English musician and hymn writer.

mon·key (mung′kē), *n.*, *pl.* **-keys,** *v.* **-ied, -eying.** —*n.* **1.** any nonhuman mammal of two major groupings of Primates, both characterized by flattened faces, binocular vision, and usu. long tails. **2.** the fur of certain long-haired monkeys. **3. a.** a mischievous, agile child. **b.** fool; dupe. —*v.i.* **4.** *Informal.* to trifle idly; fool (often fol. by *around* or *with*). —*v.t.* **5.** to imitate; mimic. —**Idiom. 6. make a monkey (out) of,** to cause to appear ridiculous; make a fool of. —**mon′key·ish,** *adj.*

mon′key bars′, *n.* JUNGLEGYM.

mon′key bread′, *n.* the gourdlike fruit of the baobab, eaten by monkeys.

mon′key busi′ness, *n.* **1.** frivolous or mischievous behavior. **2.** improper or underhanded conduct; trickery.

mon′key flow′er, *n.* any plant belonging to the genus *Mimulus*, of the figwort family, having flowers that resemble a face.

mon′key·pod, *n.* (mŭng′kē pod′), *n.* a tropical American tree, *Pithecolabrium saman*, of the legume family, having spreading branches and dense heads of small pink flowers. Also called **rain tree.**

mon′key·pot (mung′kē pot′), *n.* the covered seed vessel of certain large South American trees of the genus *Lecythis*, of the lecythis family.

mon′key puz′zle, *n.* a South American coniferous timber tree, *Araucaria araucana*, of the family Araucariaceae, with candelabralike branches, stiff sharp leaves, and edible nuts.

mon′key·shine (mung′kē shīn′), *n.* Usu., **monkeyshines.** MONKEY BUSINESS (def. 1).

mon′key suit′, *n.* *Slang.* **1.** a tuxedo or full-dress suit. **2.** any uniform.

Mon′key Tri′al, *n.* See under SCOPES.

mon′key wrench′, *n.* **1.** a wrench having a movable jaw that can be adjusted for grasping nuts of different sizes. **2.** something that interferes: *That throws a monkey wrench into our plans.*

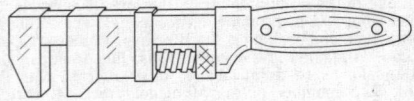

monkey wrench (def. 1)

mon′key-wrench′, *v.i.*, to prevent, delay, or sabotage industrialization or development of wilderness areas, esp. through vandalism. —**mon′key-wrench′er,** *n.*

monk·fish (mungk′fish′), *n.*, *pl.* (*esp. collectively*) **-fish,** (*esp. for kinds or species*) **-fish·es.** ANGLER (def. 3).

monk·hood (mungk′hŏŏd′), *n.* **1.** the condition or profession of a monk. **2.** monks collectively.

monk′ seal′, *n.* any of several small earless seals of the subtropical genus *Monachus.*

monks·hood (mungks′hŏŏd′), *n.* any plant of the genus *Aconitum*, of the buttercup family, esp. *A. napellus*, bearing flowers with a hood-shaped sepal and yielding a poisonous alkaloid used medicinally.

mon·o¹ (mon′ō), *n.* INFECTIOUS MONONUCLEOSIS.

mon·o² (mon′ō), *adj.* MONOPHONIC (def. 2).

mono-, a combining form meaning "one, single, lone" (*monochromatic; monogamy*), "having a thickness of one molecule" (*monolayer*), "containing one atom or group of a given kind" (*monoamine*). Also, *esp. before a vowel,* **mon-.**

mon·o·chro·mat·ic (mon′ə krō mat′ik, -ō krə-), *adj.* **1.** of or having one color. **2.** of, pertaining to, or having tones of one color in addition to the ground hue: *monochromatic pottery.* **3.** pertaining to light of one color or to radiation of a single wavelength or narrow range of wavelengths. —**mon′o·chro·mat′i·cal·ly,** *adv.*

mon·o·chrome (mon′ə krōm′), *n.* **1.** a painting, drawing, or photo-

graph in different shades of a single color. —*adj.* **2.** being in the shades of a single color. —**mon′o·chro/mic,** —**mon′o·chrom′ist,** *n.*

mon·o·cle (mon′ə kəl), *n.* an eyeglass for one eye. —**mon′o·cled,** *adj.*

mon·o·cot·y·le·don (mon′ə kot′l ēd′n), *n.* a plant of the class Monocotyledones characterized by an embryo containing a single seed leaf and floral parts in multiples of three and comprising grasses, orchids, and lilies. —**mon′o·cot′y·le′don·ous,** *adj.*

mo·noc·ra·cy (mō nok′rə sē, mə-), *n.*, *pl.* **-cies.** government by only one person; autocracy. —**mon·o·crat** (mon′ə krat′), *n.* —**mon′o·crat′ic,** *adj.*

mo·noe·cious or **mo·ne·cious** (mə nē′shəs), *adj.* **1.** having the stamens and the pistils in separate flowers on the same plant. **2.** having both male and female organs in the same individual; hermaphroditic. —**mo·noe′cious·ly,** *adv.* —**mo·noe′cism** (-siz əm), **mo·noe′cy,** *n.*

mo·nog·a·my (mə nog′ə mē), *n.* **1.** the practice or condition of having only one spouse at a time. Compare BIGAMY, POLYGAMY (def. 1). **2.** *Zool.* the condition of having only one mate at a time. **3.** the practice of marrying only once during life. Compare DIGAMY. —**mo·nog′a·mous,** *adj.* —**mo·nog′a·mous·ly,** *adv.*

mon·o·gram (mon′ə gram′), *n.*, *v.*, **-grammed, -gram·ming.** —*n.* **1.** a design consisting usu. of combined alphabetic letters, commonly one's initials. —*v.t.* **2.** to decorate with a monogram. —**mon′o·gram·mat′ic** (-grə mat′ik), *adj.*

mon·o·graph (mon′ə graf′, -gräf′), *n.* **1.** a learned treatise on a particular subject. **2.** a written account of a single thing. —**mo·nog·ra·pher** (mə nog′rə fər), *n.* —**mon′o·graph′ic** (-graf′ik), *adj.*

mon·o·lin·gual (mon′ə ling′gwəl), *adj.* **1.** knowing or able to use only one language. **2.** spoken or written in only one language. —*n.* **3.** a monolingual person. —**mon′o·lin′gual·ism,** *n.*

mon·o·lith (mon′ə lith′), *n.* **1.** an obelisk, column, large statue, etc., formed of a single block of stone. **2.** a single block or piece of stone of considerable size. **3.** something having a uniform, massive, redoubtable, or inflexible quality or character.

mon·o·logue or **mon·o·log** (mon′ə lôg′, -log′), *n.* **1. a.** a dramatic or comic piece spoken entirely by a single performer. **b.** SOLILOQUY (def. 1). **2.** a prolonged talk or discourse by a single speaker. **3.** any composition, as a poem, in which a single person speaks alone. —**mon·o·log·ist** (mon′ə lô′gist, -log′ist, mə nol′ə jist), **mon·o·logu·ist** (mon′ə lô′gist, -log′ist), *n.*

mon·o·ma·ni·a (mon′ə mā′nē ə, -mān′yə), *n.*, *pl.* **-ni·as. 1.** (no longer in technical use) a pathological obsession with one idea or group of ideas. **2.** an inordinate or obsessive zeal for or interest in a single thing. —**mon′o·ma′ni·ac,** —**mon′o·ma·ni′a·cal** (-mə nī′ə kəl), *adj.*

mon·o·mer (mon′ə mər), *n.* a molecule of low molecular weight capable of reacting with other molecules of low molecular weight to form a polymer. —**mon′o·mer′ic** (-mer′ik), *adj.*

mon·o·nu·cle·ar (mon′ə nōō′klē ər, -nyōō′- or, by metathesis, -kyə-lər) also **mon·o·nu·cle·ate** (-klē it, -āt′), *adj.* having only one nucleus.

mon·o·nu·cle·o·sis (mon′ə nōō′klē ō′sis, -nyōō′-), *n.* **1.** the presence of an abnormally large number of mononuclear leukocytes in the blood. **2.** INFECTIOUS MONONUCLEOSIS.

mon·o·pho·bi·a (mon′ə fō′bē ə), *n.*, *pl.* **-bi·as.** an abnormal fear of being alone.

mon·o·phon·ic (mon′ə fon′ik), *adj.* **1.** of or pertaining to monophony. **2.** of or noting a system of sound recording and reproduction using only a single channel. —**mon′o·phon′i·cal·ly,** *adv.*

mo·noph·o·ny (mə nof′ə nē), *n.*, *pl.* **-nies.** a musical style employing a single melodic line without accompaniment.

Mo·noph·y·site (mə nof′ə sīt′), *n.* a person who maintains that Christ has one nature, partly divine and partly human. —**Mo·noph′y·sit′ic** (-sit′ik), *adj.* —**Mo·noph′y·sit·ism,** *n.*

mon·o·plane (mon′ə plān′), *n.* an airplane with one set of wings.

mo·nop·o·lize (mə nop′ə līz′), *v.t.*, **-lized, -liz·ing. 1.** to acquire, have, or exercise a monopoly of. **2.** to obtain exclusive possession of; keep entirely to oneself. —**mo·nop′o·li·za′tion,** *n.*

mo·nop·o·ly (mə nop′ə lē), *n.*, *pl.* **-lies. 1.** exclusive control of a commodity or service that makes possible the manipulation of prices. **2.** the exclusive possession or control of something. **3.** something that is the subject of such control, as a commodity or service. **4.** a company or group that has such control. **5.** the market condition that exists when there is only one seller.

Mo·nop·o·ly (mə nop′ə lē), *n.* a board game involving the acquisition of real estate properties with play money.

mon·o·rail (mon′ə rāl′), *n.* **1.** a single rail functioning as a track for wheeled vehicles, as railroad cars, balanced upon or suspended from it. **2.** a transportation system using such a rail.

mon·o·so·di·um glu′tamate (mon′ə sō′dē əm), *n.* a white, crystalline, water-soluble powder, $C_5H_8NNaO_4 \cdot H_2O$, used to intensify the flavor of foods. Also called **MSG.**

mon·o·syl·lab·ic (mon′ə si lab′ik), *adj.* **1.** having only one syllable, as the word *no.* **2.** using, composed of, or uttering monosyllables or short, simple words. **3.** very brief; terse or blunt: *a monosyllabic reply.* —**mon′o·syl·lab′i·cal·ly,** *adv.*

mon·o·the·ism (mon′ə thē iz′əm), *n.* the doctrine or belief that there is only one God. —**mon′o•the•ist,** n., adj. —**mon′o•the•is′tic, mon′o•the•is′ti•cal,** adj. —**mon′o•the•is′ti•cal•ly,** adv.

mon•o•tone (mon′ə tōn′), n. **1.** a vocal utterance or series of speech sounds in one unvaried tone. **2.** a single musical tone without variation in pitch. **3.** recitation or singing of words in such a tone. **4.** a person who is unable to discriminate between or to reproduce differences in musical pitch, esp. in singing. **5.** any unrelieved sameness or boring repetition. —adj. **6.** MONOTONOUS. **7.** consisting of or characterized by a uniform tone of one color: *a monotone drape.*

mo•not•o•nous (mə not′n əs), adj. **1.** lacking in variety; tediously unvarying. **2.** sounded or uttered in one unvarying tone. —**mo•not′o•nous•ly,** adv.

mo•not•o•ny (mə not′n ē), n. **1.** wearisome uniformity or lack of variety, as in action or aspect. **2.** sameness of tone or pitch, as in speaking.

mon•o•treme (mon′ə trēm′), n. any egg-laying mammal of the order Monotremata, comprising only the duckbill and the echidnas of Australia and New Guinea.

mon•o•un•sat•u•rate (mon′ō un sach′ər it), n. a monounsaturated fat or fatty acid, as olive oil.

mon•o•va•lent (mon′ə vā′lənt), adj. **1.** UNIVALENT (def. 1). **2. a.** containing only one kind of antibody. **b.** pertaining to an antibody fragment with one antigen-binding site. —**mon′o•va′lence,** n.

mon•ox•ide (mon ok′sīd, mə nok′-), n. an oxide containing one oxygen atom in each molecule.

mon•o•zy•got•ic (mon′ə zī got′ik) also **mon•o•zy•gous** (-zī′gəs), adj. developed from a single fertilized ovum, as identical twins.

Mon•roe (mən rō′), n. **1. James,** 1758–1831, 5th president of the U.S. 1817–25. **2. Marilyn** (*Norma Jean Baker* or *Mortenson*), 1926–62, U.S. film actress. **3.** a city in N Louisiana. 54,520.

Monroe′ Doc′trine, n. the doctrine, essentially stated by President Monroe in 1823, that the U.S. opposed further European colonization of or intervention in the Western Hemisphere.

Mon•ro•vi•a (mən rō′vē ə), n. the capital of Liberia, in W Africa. 425,000.

mon•sei•gneur (môn se nyœr′), n., pl. **mes•sei•gneurs** (mā senyœr′). **1.** a French title of honor for princes, bishops, and other eminent persons. **2.** a person with this title.

mon•sieur (mə syœ′), n., pl. **mes•sieurs** (me syœ′). the conventional French title of respect and term of address for a man, corresponding to *Mr.* or *sir.*

mon•si•gnor (mon sē′nyər, mon′sē nyôr′), n., pl. **mon•si•gnors, mon•si•gno•ri** (môn′sē nyôr′ē). **1.** a title conferred upon certain Roman Catholic prelates. **2.** someone with this title. —**mon′si•gno′ri•al,** adj.

mon•soon (mon sōōn′), n. **1.** the seasonal wind of the Indian Ocean and S Asia, blowing from the SW in summer and from the NE in winter. **2.** (in India and nearby lands) the season during which the SW monsoon blows, commonly marked by heavy rains; rainy season. —**mon•soon′al,** adj.

mons pu•bis (monz′ pyōō′bis), n., pl. **mon•tes pubis** (mon′tēz). a rounded prominence of fatty tissue over the pubic symphysis, covered with hair after puberty. Also called **mons.** Compare MONS VENERIS.

mon•ster (mon′stər), n. **1.** any animal or human grotesquely deviating from the normal shape, behavior, or character. **2.** a person who excites horror by wickedness, cruelty, etc. **3.** any creature so ugly or monstrous as to frighten people. **4.** any animal or thing huge in size. **5.** a legendary creature having a body with both human and animal features, or the features of various animals in combination, as a centaur, griffin, or sphinx. **6.** a markedly malformed animal or plant. **7.** a grossly anomalous fetus or infant, esp. one that is not viable. —adj. **8.** huge; enormous; monstrous.

mon•ster•a (mon′stər ə), n., pl. **-ster•as.** any of various tropical American climbing plants belonging to the genus *Monstera,* of the arum family, esp. the ceriman, *M. deliciosa.*

mon•strance (mon′strəns), n. a receptacle used in the Roman Catholic Church for the display of the Host after its consecration by a priest.

mon•stros•i•ty (mon stros′i tē), n., pl. **-ties. 1.** a monster or something monstrous. **2.** the state or character of being monstrous.

mon•strous (mon′strəs), adj. **1.** frightful or hideous, esp. in appearance; extremely ugly. **2.** shocking or revolting; outrageous: *monstrous cruelty.* **3.** extraordinarily great; huge; immense: *a monstrous building.* —**mon′strous•ly,** adv. —**mon′strous•ness,** n.

mons ve•ne•ris (monz′ ven′ər is), n., pl. **mon•tes veneris** (mon′tēz). the mons pubis, esp. of the human female. Also called **mons.**

mon•tage (mon täzh′; Fr. môn täzh′), n., pl. **-tag•es** (-tä′zhiz; Fr. -täzh′). **1.** the combining of pictorial elements from different sources in a single composition. **2.** Motion Pictures, Television. **a.** juxtaposition or partial superimposition of several shots to form a single image. **b.** a technique of film editing in which this is used to present an idea or set of interconnected ideas. **3.** any combination of disparate elements that forms or is felt to form a unified whole, single image, etc. —v.t. **4.** to make or incorporate into a montage.

Mon•taigne (mon tān′; Fr. môn ten′yə), n. **Michel Eyquem, Seigneur de,** 1533–92, French essayist.

Mon•tan•a (mon tan′ə), n. a state in the NW United States. 879,372; 147,138 sq. mi. (381,085 sq. km). *Cap.:* Helena. *Abbr.:* MT, Mont. —**Mon•tan′an,** adj., n.

mon•tane (mon′tān), adj. pertaining to, growing in, or inhabiting mountainous regions.

Mont Blanc (môn blän′), n. a mountain in SE France, near the Italian border: highest peak of the Alps, 15,781 ft. (4810 m).

Mont•calm (mont käm′, Fr. môn-), n. **Louis Joseph,** 1712–59, French general in Canada.

mon•te (mon′tē), n. **1.** Also called **mon′te bank′.** a gambling game played with a 40-card pack. **2.** THREE-CARD MONTE.

Mon•te Al•bán (môn′te äl bän′), n. a major ceremonial center of the Zapotec culture, near the city of Oaxaca, Mexico, occupied 600 B.C.–A.D. 700.

Mon•te′go Bay′ (mon tē′gō), n. a city in NW Jamaica: seaside resort. 70,265.

Mon•te•ne•gro (mon′tə nē′grō, -neg′rō), n. a constituent republic of Yugoslavia, in the SW part. 615,267; 5333 sq. mi. (13,812 sq. km). *Cap.:* Podgorica. —**Mon•te•ne′grin** (-nē′grin, -neg′rin), adj., n.

Mon•te•rey (mon′tə rā′), n. a city in W California, on Monterey Bay: the capital of California until 1847. 27,558.

Mon′terey Jack′, n. a soft, mild cheddar, first made in Monterey County, California.

Mon•ter•rey (mon′tə rā′), n. the capital of Nuevo León, in NE Mexico. 1,916,472.

Mon•tes•quieu (mon′tə skyōō′; Fr. môn tes kyœ′), n. (*Charles Louis de Secondat, Baron de la Brède et de Montesquieu*) 1689–1755, French philosophical writer.

Mon•tes•so•ri (mon′tə sôr′ē, -sōr′ē), n. **Maria,** 1870–1952, Italian educator.

Montesso′ri meth′od, n. a system for teaching children to be self-motivated learners, with special emphasis on sensory training. Also called **Montesso′ri sys′tem.**

Mon•te•ver•di (mon′tə vâr′dē), n. **Claudio,** 1567–1643, Italian composer.

Mon•te•vi•de•o (mon′tə vi dā′ō, -vid′ē ō′), n. the capital of Uruguay. 1,309,100.

Mon•te•zu•ma II (mon′tə zōō′mə) also **Moctezuma,** n. c1470–1520, last Aztec emperor of Mexico 1502–20.

Montezu′ma′s revenge′, n. Slang. traveler's diarrhea, esp. as experienced by some visitors to Mexico.

Mont•gom•er•y (mont gum′ə rē, -gum′rē), n. **1. Bernard Law, 1st Viscount Montgomery of Alamein** (*"Monty"*), 1887–1976, British field marshal. **2. James,** 1771–1854, English hymn writer. **3. Richard,** 1736–75, American Revolutionary general. **4.** the capital of Alabama, in the central part, on the Alabama River. 195,471.

month (munth), n. **1.** Also called **calendar month.** any of the 12 parts, as January or February, into which the calendar year is divided. **2.** the time from any day of one calendar month to the corresponding day of the next. **3.** a period of four weeks or 30 days. **4. a.** Also called **solar month.** one-twelfth of a solar year. **b.** Also called **lunar month.** the period of a complete revolution of the moon around the earth, as between successive new moons or between successive conjunctions with a star. **5. months,** an indefinitely long period of time: *I haven't seen him for months.* —Idiom. **6. a month of Sundays,** an indeterminately great length of time.

month•ly (munth′lē), adj., n., pl. **-lies,** adv. —adj. **1.** pertaining to a month, or to each month. **2.** done, happening, etc., once a month: *a monthly magazine.* **3.** computed or determined by the month: *a monthly salary.* —n. **4.** a periodical published once a month. **5.** Sometimes, **monthlies.** Informal. a menstrual period. —adv. **6.** once a month.

Mon•ti•cel•lo (mon′ti chel′ō, -sel′ō), n. the estate and residence of Thomas Jefferson, in central Virginia, near Charlottesville.

Mont•par•nasse (môn PAR nAs′), n. a district in S Paris, France, on the left bank of the Seine: noted for its cafés and the artists and writers who have frequented and lived in the area.

Mont•pel•ier (mont pēl′yər), n. the capital of Vermont, in the central part. 8241.

Mont•re•al (mon′trē ôl′, mun′-), n. a port in S Quebec, in E Canada, on an island (**Mon′treal Is′land**) in the St. Lawrence. 1,015,420. French, **Mont•ré•al** (môn RĀ Al′). —**Mont′re•al′er,** n.

mon•u•ment (mon′yə mənt), n. **1.** something erected in memory of a person, event, etc., as a building, pillar, or statue. **2.** any building, megalith, etc., surviving from a past age, and regarded as of historical or archaeological importance. **3.** any enduring evidence or notable example of something: *a monument to human ingenuity; a monument of respectability.* **4.** something written, esp. a legal document or a tribute to a person. **5.** NATIONAL MONUMENT. **6.** an object, as a stone shaft, to mark a boundary or a survey station. **7.** a person considered as being of heroic proportions: *a monument in her lifetime.*

mon•u•men•tal (mon′yə men′tl), adj. **1.** of, pertaining to, or resembling a monument. **2.** exceptionally great, as in quality or degree: *a monumental book.* **3.** of historical or enduring significance: *a monumental victory.* —**mon′u•men′tal•ism,** n. —**mon′u•men•tal′i•ty,** n. —**mon′u•men′tal•ly,** adv.

moo (mōō), n., pl. **moos,** v., **mooed, moo•ing.** —n. **1.** the deep, low sound characteristic of a cow. —v.i. **2.** to utter such a sound; low.

mooch (mōōch), Slang. v.t. **1.** to borrow without intending to return or repay; scrounge. —v.i. **2.** to sponge; cadge; scrounge. **3.** to skulk or sneak. **4.** to loiter or wander about. —*n.* **5.** Also, **mooch'er.** a person who mooches.

mood[1] (mōōd), *n.* **1.** a person's emotional state or outlook at a particular time. **2.** a distinctive emotional quality or character: *a festive mood.* **3.** a prevailing emotional tone or general attitude: *the country's mood.* **4.** a frame of mind receptive, as to some activity: *in the mood to see a movie.* **5.** a state of sullenness, gloom, or bad temper.

mood[2] (mōōd), *n.* a category or set of categories of the verb serving typically to indicate the attitude of the speaker toward what is being said, as in expressing a fact, possibility, wish, or command, and indicated by inflection of the verb or by the use of syntactic devices, as modal auxiliaries: *the indicative, imperative, and subjunctive moods.*

mood•y (mōō'dē), *adj.,* **mood•i•er, mood•i•est. 1.** given to moods, esp. gloomy or sullen moods. **2.** expressing such a mood: *a moody silence.* —**mood'i•ly,** *adv.* —**mood'i•ness,** *n.*

moo•la or **moo•lah** (mōō'lə, -lä), *n. Slang.* money.

moon (mōōn), *n.* **1.** the earth's natural satellite, orbiting the earth at a mean distance of 238,857 miles (384,393 km) and having a diameter of 2160 miles (3476 km). **2.** this body during a particular lunar month, or during a certain period of time, or at a certain point of time, regarded as a distinct object or entity. **3.** a lunar month, or, in general, a month. **4.** any planetary satellite: *the moons of Jupiter.* **5.** something shaped like an orb or a crescent. **6.** MOONLIGHT. —*v.i.* **7.** to act or wander abstractedly, listlessly, or dreamily: *to moon about all day.* **8.** to sentimentalize or remember nostalgically. —*v.t.* **9.** to spend (time) idly: *to moon the afternoon away.* —**moon'less,** *adj.*

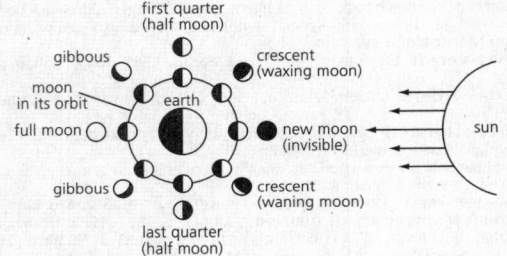

first quarter
(half moon)

gibbous

crescent
(waxing moon)

moon
in its orbit

earth

full moon

new moon
(invisible)

sun

gibbous

crescent
(waning moon)

last quarter
(half moon)

moon

Moon (mōōn), *n.* **Sun Myung** (sun myung), born 1920, Korean religious leader: founder of the Unification Church.

moon•beam (mōōn'bēm'), *n.* a ray of moonlight.

moon' blind'ness, *n.* a disease of horses in which the eyes suffer from recurring attacks of inflammation, eventually resulting in opacity and blindness.

moon•eye (mōōn'ī'), *n., pl.* **-eyes.** a large-eyed silvery freshwater fish, *Hiodon tergisus.*

moon•fish (mōōn'fish'), *n., pl.* (*esp. collectively*) **-fish,** (*esp. for kinds or species*) **-fish•es. 1.** any of several deep-bodied, compressed carangid fishes of the genus *Selene.* **2.** OPAH.

moon•flow•er (mōōn'flou'ər), *n.* any of several genera of vines of the morning glory family, having fragrant white flowers that bloom at night.

moon•light (mōōn'līt'), *n.* **1.** the light of the moon. —*adj.* **2.** pertaining to moonlight. **3.** occurring by moonlight, or at night. —*v.i.* **4.** to work at an additional job after one's regular, full-time employment, as at night. —**moon'light•er,** *n.*

moon•lit (mōōn'lit'), *adj.* lighted by the moon.

moon•rise (mōōn'rīz'), *n.* **1.** the rising of the moon above the horizon. **2.** the time at which this happens.

moon•set (mōōn'set'), *n.* **1.** the setting of the moon below the horizon. **2.** the time at which this happens.

moon•shine (mōōn'shīn'), *n.* **1.** *Informal.* smuggled or illicitly distilled liquor. **2.** empty or foolish talk, ideas, etc.; nonsense. **3.** MOONLIGHT.

moon•shin•er (mōōn'shī'nər), *n. Informal.* a person who distills or sells liquor, esp. corn liquor, illegally.

moon•shot' or **moon' shot',** *n.* the act or procedure of launching a rocket or spacecraft to the moon.

moon•stone (mōōn'stōn'), *n.* an opalescent, pearly blue variety of feldspar, used as a gem.

moon•struck (mōōn'struk') also **moon•strick•en** (-strik'ən), *adj.* **1.** mentally deranged, supposedly by the influence of the moon; crazed. **2.** dreamily romantic or bemused.

moon•walk (mōōn'wôk'), *n.* **1.** an exploratory walk by an astronaut on the surface of the moon. **2.** a dance step in which the dancer moves backwards while giving the illusion of walking forward.

moon•wort (mōōn'wûrt', -wôrt'), *n.* a small fern, *Botrychium lunaria,* of the adder's-tongue family, native to temperate regions, having a single frond with crescent-shaped leaflets. (See HONESTY (def. 4).

moon•y (mōō'nē), *adj.,* **moon•i•er, moon•i•est. 1.** dreamy, listless, or silly. **2.** pertaining to or characteristic of the moon. **3.** moonlit. —**moon'i•ly,** *adv.* —**moon'i•ness,** *n.*

moor[1] (mŏŏr), *n.* **1.** a tract of open, peaty wasteland, often overgrown with heath, common in high altitudes where drainage is poor; heath. **2.** a tract of land preserved for game. —**moor'y,** *adj.*

moor[2] (mŏŏr), *v.t.* **1.** to secure (a ship, boat, dirigible, etc.) in a particular place, as by cables and anchors or by lines. **2.** to fix firmly; secure. —*v.i.* **3.** to moor a ship, small boat, etc. **4.** to be made secure by cables or the like.

Moor (mŏŏr), *n.* a member of any of the groups of North African Arabs and Berbers who ruled parts of the Iberian Peninsula from the 8th century to 1492.

moor•age (mŏŏr'ij), *n.* **1.** a place for mooring. **2.** a charge or payment for the use of moorings. **3.** an act or instance of mooring or the state of being moored.

Moore (mŏŏr, môr, mōr), *n.* **1. Clement Clarke,** 1779–1863, U.S. scholar and writer. **2. George,** 1852–1933, Irish writer. **3. G(eorge) E(dward),** 1873–1958, English philosopher. **4. Henry,** 1898–1986, English sculptor. **5. Marianne (Craig),** 1887–1972, U.S. poet and critic. **6. Thomas,** 1779–1852, Irish poet.

moor•hen (mŏŏr'hen'), *n.* a common species of gallinule, *Gallinula chloropus,* of nearly worldwide distribution. Also called **water hen.**

moor•ing (mŏŏr'ing), *n.* **1.** the act of a person or thing that moors. **2.** Usu., **moorings.** the means by which a ship, boat, or aircraft is moored. **3. moorings,** a place where a ship, boat, or aircraft may be moored. **4.** Usu., **moorings.** a source of stability or security: *to lose one's moorings.*

Moor•ish (mŏŏr'ish), *adj.* of, pertaining to, or characteristic of the Moors or Moorish culture.

moose (mōōs), *n., pl.* **moose. 1.** a large, long-headed deer, *Alces alces,* of the Northern Hemisphere: the male has enormous palmate antlers. **2.** (*cap.*) a member of a fraternal and benevolent organization (**Loyal Order of Moose**).

moot (mōōt), *adj.* **1.** open to discussion or debate; debatable; doubtful. **2.** of little or no practical value or meaning; purely academic. **3.** *Chiefly Law.* not actual; theoretical; hypothetical. —*v.t.* **4.** to present or introduce for discussion. **5.** to reduce or remove the practical significance of; make theoretical or academic. —*n.* **6.** an assembly of the people in early England, exercising political, administrative, and judicial powers. **7.** an argument or discussion, esp. of a hypothetical legal case.

moot' court', *n.* a mock court for the conduct of hypothetical legal cases, as for students of law.

mop (mop), *n., v.,* **mopped, mop•ping.** —*n.* **1.** a bundle of coarse yarn, a sponge, or other absorbent material, fastened at the end of a stick or handle for washing floors, dishes, etc. **2.** a thick mass of hair. —*v.t.* **3.** to wipe, clean, or remove with a mop (often fol. by *up*). **4.** to wipe as if with a mop. —*v.i.* **5.** to clean or wipe with or as if with a mop (often fol. by *up*). **6. mop up, a.** to clear (an area, town, etc.) of remaining enemy combatants following a victory. **b.** to complete, as by finishing the remaining details of a task.

mop•board (mop'bôrd', -bōrd'), *n.* BASEBOARD.

mope (mōp), *v.,* **moped, mop•ing,** *n.* —*v.i.* **1.** to be sunk in dejection or apathy; sulk; brood. —*v.t.* **2.** to pass in a dejected or apathetic way (usu. fol. by *away*). —*n.* **3.** a person who mopes or is given to moping. **4. mopes,** depressed spirits; blues.

mo•ped (mō'ped'), *n.* a motorized bicycle with pedals that is designed for low-speed operation. [< Swedish (*trampcykel med*) *mo(tor och) ped(aler)* pedal cycle with engine and pedals]

mop•ey or **mop•y** (mō'pē), *adj.,* **mop•i•er, mop•i•est.** languishing, listless, droopy, or glum. —**mop'i•ness,** *n.*

mop•ish (mō'pish), *adj.* given to moping; listless, apathetic, or dejected. —**mop'ish•ly,** *adv.* —**mop'ish•ness,** *n.*

mop•pet (mop'it), *n.* a young child.

mop'-up', *n.* the act or process of mopping up; completion of an operation or action.

mo•raine (mə rān'), *n.* a ridge, mound, or irregular mass of unstratified glacial drift, chiefly boulders, gravel, sand, and clay.

mor•al (môr'əl, mor'-), *adj.* **1.** of, pertaining to, or concerned with the principles of right conduct or the distinction between right and wrong; ethical: *moral attitudes.* **2.** conforming to accepted or established principles of right conduct (opposed to *immoral*); virtuous; upright: *a moral man.* **3.** expressing or conveying truths or counsel as to right conduct: *a moral novel.* **4.** based on fundamental principles of right conduct rather than on law, custom, etc.: *moral obligations.* **5.** capable of recognizing and conforming to the rules of right conduct: *a moral being.* **6.** virtuous in sexual matters; chaste. **7.** of, pertaining to, or acting on the mind, feelings, will, or character: *moral support.* **8.** based on strong probability; virtual: *a moral certainty.* —*n.* **9.** the moral teaching or practical lesson contained in a fable, tale, experience, etc. **10. morals,** principles, standards, or habits with respect to right or wrong conduct. —**mor'al•ly,** *adv.*

mo•rale (mə ral'), *n.* emotional or mental condition with respect to confidence, zeal, etc., esp. in the face of opposition, hardship, etc.: *the morale of the troops.*

mor'al educa'tion, *n.* the teaching of good conduct and ethical behavior, esp. as part of a curriculum: *Parents, and the public in general, have indicated clearly that they want our schools to take a more direct role in children's moral education* (Edward Wynne and Kevin Ryan).

mor•al•ist (môr'ə list, mor'-), *n.* **1.** a person who practices, teaches, or inculcates morality. **2.** a philosopher concerned with the principles of

morality. 3. a person concerned with regulating morals, as by censorship. —**mor'al·is'tic,** *adj.* —**mor'al·is'ti·cal·ly,** *adv.*

mo·ral·i·ty (mə ral'i tē, mô-), *n., pl.* **-ties** for 4–6. **1.** conformity to the rules of right conduct; moral or virtuous conduct. **2.** moral quality or character. **3.** virtue in sexual matters; chastity. **4.** a doctrine or system of morals. **5.** moral instruction; a moral lesson, precept, discourse, or utterance. **6.** MORALITY PLAY.

moral'ity play', *n.* an allegorical drama of the 15th and 16th centuries in which personified virtues, vices, and other abstractions are characters. Compare MIRACLE PLAY, MYSTERY PLAY.

mor·al·ize (môr'ə līz', mor'-), *v.,* **-ized, -iz·ing.** —*v.i.* **1.** to reflect on or express opinions about matters of right and wrong, esp. in a self-righteous or tiresome way. —*v.t.* **2.** to explain in a moral sense, or draw a moral from. **3.** to improve the morals of. —**mor'al·i·za'tion,** *n.* —**mor'al·iz'er,** *n.* —**mor'al·iz'ing·ly,** *adv.*

Mor'al Major'ity, *n.* former name of the LIBERTY FOUNDATION.

mor'al philos'ophy, *n.* philosophy dealing with the principles of morality; ethics.

Mor'al Re-Ar'ma·ment (rē är'mə mənt), *n.* a worldwide movement initiated by Frank Buchman in 1938 as a successor to the Oxford Group, and maintaining that the practice of high morality in public and private life is the key to world betterment. *Abbr.:* MRA

mo·rass (mə ras'), *n.* **1.** a tract of low, soft, wet ground. **2.** a marsh or bog. **3.** something that is confusing or troublesome or from which it is difficult to free oneself.

mor·a·to·ri·um (môr'ə tôr'ē əm, -tōr'-, mor'-), *n., pl.* **-to·ri·a** (-tôr'ē ə, -tōr'-), **-to·ri·ums. 1.** a suspension of activity: *a moratorium on the testing of nuclear weapons.* **2.** a legally authorized period to delay payment of money due or the performance of some other legal obligation, as in an emergency. **3.** an authorized period of delay or waiting.

Mo·ra·tu·wa (mô rä'tōō wə), *n.* a city in W Sri Lanka. 134,826.

Mo·ra·vi·a (mô rä'vē ə, -rä'-, mō-), *n.* **1. Alberto** (*Alberto Pincherle*), 1907–90, Italian writer. **2.** Czech, **Morava.** a region in the E Czech Republic: former province of Austria.

Mo·ra·vi·an (mô rä'vē ən, mō-), *adj.* **1.** of or pertaining to Moravia or its inhabitants. **2.** of or pertaining to the religious denomination of Moravians. —*n.* **3.** a native or inhabitant of Moravia. **4.** a member of a Christian denomination descended from the Bohemian Brethren. —**Mo·ra'vi·an·ism,** *n.*

mo·ray (môr'ā, mōr'ā; mô rā', mō-), *n., pl.* **-rays.** any tropical eel of the family Muraenidae, lacking pectoral fins. Also called **mo'ray eel'.**

mor·bid (môr'bid), *adj.* **1.** suggesting an unhealthy mental state or attitude; unwholesomely gloomy. **2.** gruesome; grisly. **3.** affected by, caused by, causing, or characteristic of disease. —**mor'bid·ly,** *adv.*

mor·bid·i·ty (môr bid'i tē), *n.* **1.** a morbid state or quality. **2.** the proportion of a specific disease in a geographical locality.

mor·dant (môr'dnt), *adj.* **1.** sharply caustic or sarcastic; biting; cutting: *mordant wit.* **2.** burning; corrosive. **3.** having the property of fixing colors, as in dyeing. —*n.* **4.** a substance used in dyeing to fix the coloring matter. **5.** an acid or other corrosive substance used in etching. —*v.t.* **6.** to impregnate or treat with a mordant. —**mor'dan·cy,** *n.* —**mor'dant·ly,** *adv.*

Mor·de·cai (môr'di kī', -kī'), *n.* the cousin of Esther who delivered the Jews from the destruction planned by Haman. Esther 2–8.

more (môr, mōr), *adj., compar. of* **much** *or* **many** *with* **most** *as superl.* **1.** in greater quantity, amount, measure, degree, or number: *I need more money.* **2.** additional or further: *Do you need more time?* —*n.* **3.** an additional quantity, amount, or number: *Would you like more?* **4.** a greater quantity, amount, or degree: *The price is more than I thought.* **5.** something of greater importance, scope, etc.: *Their report is more than a survey.* —*pron.* **6.** (*used with a pl. v.*) a greater number of persons or of a class specified: *More will attend than ever before.* —*adv., compar. of* **much** *with* **most** *as superl.* **7.** in or to a greater extent or degree (often used before adjectives and adverbs, and regularly before those of more than two syllables, to form the comparative): *more interesting; more slowly.* **8.** in addition; further; again: *Let's talk more tomorrow.* **9.** MORE-OVER. —*Idiom.* **10.** more and more, to an increasing extent or degree: *I love you more and more every day.* **11.** more or less, to some extent; somewhat: *We came to more or less the same conclusion.*

More (môr, mōr), *n.* **1. Hannah,** 1745–1833, English writer on religious subjects. **2. Sir Thomas,** 1478–1535, English statesman and author: canonized in 1935.

mo·rel (mə rel'), *n.* any edible mushroom of the genus *Morchella,* characterized by a deeply furrowed, brownish cap.

mo·rel·lo (mə rel'ō), *n., pl.* **-los.** a variety of sour cherry having dark-colored skin and juice.

Mo·re·no Val'ley (mə rē'nō), *n.* a city in SW California, E of Riverside. 139,311.

more·o·ver (môr ō'vər, mōr-, môr'ō'vər, mōr'-), *adv.* in addition to what has been said; further; besides.

mo·res (môr'āz, -ēz, mōr'-), *n.pl.* folkways of central importance accepted without question and embodying the fundamental moral views of a social group.

Mor·gan[1] (môr'gən), *n.* any of a breed of light carriage and saddle horses descended from the stallion Justin Morgan. [after the original sire, owned by J. *Morgan* (1747–98)]

Mor·gan[2] (môr'gən), *n.* **1. Daniel,** 1736–1802, American Revolutionary

general. **2. Sir Henry,** 1635?–88, Welsh buccaneer in the Americas. **3. John Hunt,** 1826–64, Confederate general. **4. J(ohn) P(ierpont),** 1837–1913, U.S. financier and philanthropist. **5.** his son **John Pierpont,** 1867–1943, U.S. financier.

mor·ga·nat·ic (môr'gə nat'ik), *adj.* designating or pertaining to a marriage in which a person of high rank, as a member of the nobility, marries someone of lower station with the stipulation that neither the low-ranking spouse nor their children will have any claim to the titles or property of the high-ranking partner. —**mor'ga·nat'i·cal·ly,** *adv.*

mor·gan·ite (môr'gə nīt'), *n.* rose-colored beryl.

morgue (môrg), *n.* **1.** a place in which dead bodies are kept, esp. the bodies of victims of violence or accidents, pending identification or burial. **2.** a reference file of old clippings, photographs, etc., esp. in a newspaper office. **3.** the room containing such a reference file.

Mo·ri·ah (mô rī'ə, mō-), *n.* **1.** a mountainous region in S Palestine, where Abraham prepared to sacrifice Isaac. Gen. 22:3. **2.** a site usually identified with Zion, where Solomon built the Temple. II Chron. 3:1.

mor·i·bund (môr'ə bund', mor'-), *adj.* **1.** near death or termination. **2.** not progressing; stagnant; lifeless.

Mor·mon (môr'mən), *n.* **1.** a member of a church (**Mor'mon Church'**) founded in the U.S. in 1830 by Joseph Smith. **2.** See under BOOK OF MORMON. —*adj.* **3.** of or pertaining to the Mormons or their beliefs. —**Mor'mon·ism,** *n.*

morn·ing (môr'ning), *n.* **1.** the first period of the day, extending from dawn, or from midnight, to noon. **2.** the beginning of day; dawn. **3.** the early period of anything; beginning: *the morning of life.* —*adj.* **4.** of or in the morning.

morn'ing af'ter, *n., pl.* **mornings after. 1.** a morning when the aftereffects of overindulgence, esp. in alcohol, are felt. **2.** any time when the consequences of an earlier ill-advised act are felt.

morn'ing glo'ry or **morn'ing-glo'ry,** *n.* any of various plants, esp. of the genera *Ipomoea* and *Convolvulus,* as *I. purpurea,* a twining plant having cordate leaves and funnel-shaped flowers of various colors, often opening only in the morning.

Morn'ing Prayer', *n.* MATIN (def. 1b).

morn'ing sick'ness, *n.* nausea occurring in the early part of the day during the first months of pregnancy.

morn'ing star', *n.* a bright planet, esp. Venus, seen in the E immediately before sunrise.

Mo·roc·co (mə rok'ō), *n.* **1.** French, **Maroc.** a kingdom in NW Africa: formed from a sultanate that was divided into two protectorates (**French Morocco** and **Spanish Morocco**) and an international zone. 30,391,423; 172,104 sq. mi. (445,749 sq. km). *Cap.:* Rabat. **2.** (*l.c.*) a pebble-grained leather orig. made in Morocco from goatskin tanned with sumac. —**Mo·roc'can,** *adj., n.*

mo·ron (môr'on, mōr'-), *n.* **1.** a person who is notably stupid or lacking in good judgment. **2.** a person of borderline intelligence in a former classification of mental retardation, having an intelligence quotient of 50 to 69. —**mo·ron·ic** (mə ron'ik), *adj.* —**mo·ron'i·cal·ly,** *adv.* —**mo'ron·ism, mo·ron'i·ty** (-i tē), *n.*

Mo·ro·ni (mô rō'nē), *n.* the capital of the Comoros. 20,112.

mo·rose (mə rōs'), *adj.* **1.** gloomily or sullenly ill-humored, as a person or mood. **2.** characterized by or expressing gloom: *a morose silence.* —**mo·rose'ly,** *adv.* —**mo·rose'ness, mo·ros·i·ty** (mə ros'i tē), *n.*

morph (môrf), *n.* **1.** *Ling.* a sequence of phonemes constituting a minimal unit of grammar or syntax, and, as such, a representation, member, or contextual variant of a morpheme in a specific environment. **2.** *Biol.* an individual of one particular form, as a worker ant, in a species that occurs in two or more forms. —*v.t.* **3.** to transform (an image) by computer. —**mor'phic,** *adj.*

-morph, a combining form meaning "form, structure," of the kind specified by the initial element: *isomorph.*

mor·pheme (môr'fēm), *n.* any of the minimal grammatical units of a language, each constituting a word or meaningful part of a word that cannot be divided into smaller meaningful parts, as *the, write,* or the *-ed* of *waited.* Compare ALLOMORPH (def. 2). —**mor·phe·mic,** *adj.* —**mor·phe'mi·cal·ly,** *adv.*

mor·phe·mics (môr fē'miks), *n.* (*used with a sing. v.*) **1.** the study of the classification, description, and functions of morphemes; morphology. **2.** the manner by which morphemes combine to form words.

-morphic, var. of -MORPHOUS: *anthropomorphic.*

mor·phine (môr'fēn) also **mor·phi·a** (-fē ə), *n.* a white, bitter, crystalline alkaloid, $C_{17}H_{19}NO_3 \cdot H_2O$, the most important narcotic and addictive principle of opium, obtained by extraction and crystallization and used chiefly in medicine as a pain reliever and sedative. —**mor·phin'ic** (-fin'ik), *adj.*

-morphism, a combining form occurring in nouns that correspond to adjectives ending in -MORPHIC or -MORPHOUS: *monomorphism.*

morpho-, a combining form meaning "form, structure": *morphology.* Also, *esp. before a vowel,* **morph-.**

mor·phol·o·gy (môr fol'ə jē), *n.* **1.** the branch of biology that deals with the form and structure of organisms. **2.** the form and structure of an organism considered as a whole. **3. a.** the patterns of word formation in a particular language, including inflection, derivation, and the formation of compounds. **b.** the study and description of such patterns. **c.** the study of the behavior and combination of morphemes. **4.** GEOMORPHOLOGY. **5.** form or structure. **6.** the study of form or structure. —**mor'-**

pho·log·ic (-fə loj'ik), **mor'pho·log'i·cal,** *adj.* —**mor'pho·log'i·cal·ly,** *adv.* —**mor·phol'o·gist,** *n.*

mor·pho·pho·ne·mics (môr'fō fə nē'miks, -fə fō nē'-), *n.* (*used with a sing. v.*) **1.** the study of the relations between morphemes and their phonological realizations, components, or mappings. **2.** the body of data concerning these relations in a given language. —**mor'pho·pho·ne'mic,** *adj.*

-morphous or **-morphic,** a combining form with the meaning "having the shape, form, or structure" of the kind or number specified by the initial element: *polymorphous.*

Mor'rill Act' (môr'il, mor'-), **1.** an act of Congress (1862) granting each state 30,000 acres of land for each member it had in Congress, 90 percent of the gross proceeds of which were to be used for the endowment and maintenance of colleges and universities teaching agricultural and mechanical arts and other subjects. **2.** either of two supplementary acts (1890 and 1907) in which Congress made direct financial grants to assist the land-grant colleges and universities. [after Justin Smith *Morrill* (1810–98), congressman and senator from Vermont]

Mor·ris (môr'is, mor'-), *n.* **1. Gouv·er·neur** (guv'ər nēr'), 1752–1816, U.S. statesman. **2. Robert,** 1734–1806, U.S. financier and statesman, born in England. **3. William,** 1834–96, English artist, poet, and writer.

Mor'ris chair', *n.* a large armchair with an adjustable back and removable cushions.

mor'ris dance' (môr'is, mor'-), *n.* a rural folk dance of N English origin, performed by costumed dancers who orig. represented characters of the Robin Hood legend, esp. in May Day festivities. Also called **mor'ris.**

Mor·ri·son (môr'ə sən, mor'-), *n.* **1. Herbert Stanley,** 1888–1965, English labor leader and statesman. **2. Toni,** born 1931, U.S. novelist: Nobel prize 1993.

mor·row (môr'ō, mor'ō), *n. Literary.* the next day; tomorrow.

Morse (môrs), *n.* **1. Samuel F(inley) B(reese),** 1791–1872, U.S. artist and developer of the telegraph. **2.** MORSE CODE.

Morse' code', *n.* either of two systems of clicks and spaces, short and long sounds, or flashes of light, used to represent letters, numerals, etc.: now used primarily in radiotelegraphy by ham operators. Also called **Morse' al'phabet.** [after S. F. B. *Morse* (1791–1872), U.S. inventor]

mor·sel (môr'səl), *n.* **1.** a small portion of food; bite. **2.** a small piece or amount of anything; scrap; bit. **3.** an appetizing dish; treat.

mor·tal (môr'tl), *adj.* **1.** subject to death; having a transitory life: *mortal creatures.* **2.** of or pertaining to human beings as subject to death: *this mortal life.* **3.** belonging to this world. **4.** implacable; relentless: *a mortal enemy.* **5.** severe; dire; grievous: *in mortal fear.* **6.** causing or liable to cause death; fatal: *a mortal wound.* **7.** to the death: *mortal combat.* **8.** of or pertaining to death. **9.** long and wearisome. **10.** extreme; very great: *in a mortal hurry.* **11.** conceivable; possible: *of no mortal value to the owners.* **12.** involving spiritual death: *mortal transgressions.* —*n.* **13.** a human being. —**mor'tal·ly,** *adv.*

mor·tal·i·ty (môr tal'i tē), *n., pl.* **-ties. 1.** the state or condition of being subject to death. **2.** the relative frequency of deaths in a specific population; death rate. **3.** mortal beings collectively; humanity. **4.** death or destruction on a large scale, as from war, plague, or famine.

mortal'ity ta'ble, *n.* an actuarial table showing the percentage of persons who die at any given age, often based on former policyholders. Also called **life table.**

mor'tal sin', *n. Rom. Cath. Ch.* a willfully committed sin, as murder, serious enough to deprive the soul of divine grace. Compare VENIAL SIN.

mor·tar[1] (môr'tər), *n.* **1.** a bowl-shaped receptacle of hard material in which substances are pounded or ground to a powder or paste with a pestle. **2.** any of various mechanical appliances in which substances are pounded or ground. **3.** a cannon very short in proportion to its bore, for throwing shells at high angles.

mortar

pestle

mortar[1] (def. 1)

mor·tar[2] (môr'tər), *n.* **1.** a mixture of lime or cement or a combination of both with sand and water, used as a bonding agent between bricks, stones, etc. —*v.t.* **2.** to plaster or fix with mortar. —**mor'tar·y,** *adj.*

mor·tar·board (môr'tər bôrd', -bōrd'), *n.* **1.** a board, usu. square, used by masons to hold mortar. **2.** a close-fitting cap with a square, flat top and a tassel, worn at formal academic ceremonies.

mort·gage (môr'gij), *n., v.,* **-gaged, -gag·ing.** —*n.* **1.** a conveyance of an interest in property as security for the repayment of money borrowed. **2.** the deed by which such a transaction is effected. **3.** the rights conferred by it, or the state of the property conveyed. —*v.t.* **4.** to convey or place (property) under a mortgage. **5.** to place under advance obligation; pledge. —**mort'gage·a·ble,** *adj.*

mort·ga·gee (môr'gə jē'), *n.* a person to whom property is mortgaged.

mort·ga·gor or **mort·gag·er** (môr'gə jər), *n.* a person who mortgages property.

mor·ti·cian (môr tish'ən), *n.* FUNERAL DIRECTOR.

mor·ti·fi·ca·tion (môr'tə fi kā'shən), *n.* **1.** a feeling of humiliation or shame, as through some injury to one's pride or self-respect. **2.** a cause or source of such humiliation or shame. **3.** the practice of asceticism by penitential discipline to overcome desire for sin and to strengthen the will. **4.** the death of one part of a live body; gangrene; necrosis.

mor·ti·fy (môr'tə fī'), *v.,* **-fied, -fy·ing.** —*v.t.* **1.** to humiliate or shame, as by an injury to one's pride or self-respect. **2.** to subjugate (the body, passions, etc.) by abstinence, ascetic discipline, or self-inflicted suffering. **3.** to affect with gangrene. —*v.i.* **4.** to practice mortification or disciplinary austerities. **5.** to become gangrened. —**mor'ti·fi'er,** *n.*

mor·tise or **mor·tice** (môr'tis), *n., v.,* **-tised, -tis·ing.** —*n.* **1.** a notch, hole, or slot made in a piece of wood or the like to receive a tenon of the same dimensions. **2.** a deep recess cut into wood for other purposes, as for receiving a mortise lock. —*v.t.* **3.** to join securely, esp. with a mortise and tenon. **4.** to cut or form a mortise in.

mor'tise joint', *n.* any of various joints between two pieces of timber or the like in which a tenon is housed in or secured to a mortise. Also called **mor'tise and ten'on joint'.**

Mor·ton (môr'tn), *n.* **1. Jelly Roll** (*Ferdinand Morton*), 1885–1941, U.S. jazz pianist, composer, and band leader. **2. Levi Parsons,** 1824–1920, vice president of the U.S. 1889–93; governor of New York 1895–96. **3. William Thomas Green,** 1819–68, U.S. dentist: first to employ ether as an anesthetic.

mor·tu·ar·y (môr'chōo er'ē), *n., pl.* **-ar·ies,** *adj.* —*n.* **1.** FUNERAL HOME. —*adj.* **2.** of or pertaining to burial of the dead. **3.** pertaining to or connected with death.

mo·sa·ic (mō zā'ik), *n., adj., v.,* **-icked, -ick·ing.** —*n.* **1.** a picture or decoration made of small, usu. colored pieces of inlaid stone, glass, etc. **2.** the process of producing such a picture or decoration. **3.** something resembling a mosaic, esp. in being made up of diverse elements: *a cultural mosaic.* **4.** Also called **photomosaic.** an assembly of aerial photographs matched to show a continuous photographic representation of an area. **5.** Also called **mosa'ic disease'.** any of several diseases of plants, characterized by mottled green or green and yellow areas on the leaves, caused by certain viruses. **6.** an organism exhibiting mosaicism. —*adj.* **7.** pertaining to, resembling, or used for making a mosaic or mosaic work: *a mosaic tile.* **8.** composed of a combination of diverse elements. —*v.t.* **9.** to make a mosaic of or from. **10.** to decorate with mosaic. —**mo·sa'i·cal·ly,** *adv.* —**mo·sa'i·cist** (-ə sist), *n.*

Mo·sa·ic (mō zā'ik) also **Mo·sa'i·cal,** *adj.* of or pertaining to Moses or the writings, laws, and principles attributed to him.

Mosa'ic Law', *n.* the ancient law of the Hebrews; the Law of Moses.

mo·sa·saur (mō'sə sôr'), *n.* any of several extinct carnivorous marine lizards from the Cretaceous Period, having the limbs modified into broad, webbed paddles.

Mos·cow (mos'kō, -kou), *n.* the capital of the Russian Federation: capital of the former Soviet Union. 8,967,000. Russian, **Moskva.**

Mo·ses (mō'ziz, -zis), *n.* the Hebrew prophet who led the Israelites out of Egypt and delivered the Law during their years in the desert.

mo·sey (mō'zē), *v.i.,* **-seyed, -sey·ing.** *Informal.* **1.** to wander leisurely; stroll; saunter (often fol. by *along, about,* etc.). **2.** to leave quickly; decamp.

Mos·lem (moz'ləm, mos'-), *adj., n., pl.* **-lems, -lem.** MUSLIM. —**Usage.** See MUSLIM.

mosque (mosk, môsk), *n.* a Muslim temple or place of public worship.

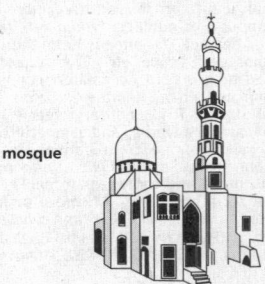

mosque

mos·qui·to (mə skē'tō), *n., pl.* **-toes, -tos.** any of numerous dipterous insects of the family Culicidae, the females of which suck the blood of animals and humans, some species transmitting certain diseases, as malaria and yellow fever. —**mos·qui'to·ey,** *adj.*

mos·qui·to·fish (mə skē'tō fish'), *n., pl.* (*esp. collectively*) **-fish** (*esp. for kinds or species*) **-fish·es.** any of several fishes used for mosquito control, esp. *Gambusia affinis,* native to the southeast U.S.

mosqui'to hawk', *n.* **1.** NIGHTHAWK. **2.** *Chiefly Southern U.S.* DRAGONFLY.

mosqui'to net', *n.* a screen, curtain, or canopy of net, gauze, or the like, for keeping out mosquitoes.

moss (môs, mos), *n.* **1.** any tiny, leafy-stemmed, filamentous bryophyte of the class Musci, growing in tufts, sods, or mats on moist ground, tree trunks, rocks, etc. **2.** a growth of such plants. **3.** any of various similar plants, as Iceland moss or club moss. —*v.t.* **4.** to cover with moss.

moss′ ag′ate, *n.* a kind of agate or chalcedony containing brown or black mosslike dendritic markings from various impurities.

moss·back (môs′bak′, mos′-), *n.* **1.** *Informal.* **a.** a person holding very antiquated notions; reactionary. **2.** an old turtle. **3.** a large and old fish, as a bass. —**moss′backed′,** *adj.*

most (mōst), *adj., superl. of* **much** *or* **many** *with* **more** *as compar.* **1.** in the greatest number, amount, or degree: *the most votes; the most talent.* **2.** in the majority of instances: *Most operations are successful.* —*n.* **3.** the greatest quantity, amount, or degree: *The most I can hope for is a passing grade.* **4.** the greatest number or greater part of what is specified: *Most of his writing is rubbish.* **5.** the greatest number: *The most this room will seat is 150.* **6.** the majority of persons: *to be happier than most.* **7. the most,** *Slang.* the ultimate in something. —*adv., superl. of* **much** *with* **more** *as compar.* **8.** in or to the greatest extent or degree (often used before adjectives and adverbs, and regularly before those of more than two syllables, to form superlative phrases having the same force and effect as the superlative degree formed by the termination *-est*): *most rapid; most wisely.* **9.** very: *a most puzzling case.* **10.** *Informal.* almost or nearly. —*Idiom.* **11. at (the) most,** to an extent not exceeding the amount specified; at the maximum: *Jog for one hour at most.* **12. for the most part,** on the whole; generally; usually. **13. make the most of,** to use to greatest advantage; utilize fully.

-most, a combining form of MOST occurring in a series of superlatives: *foremost; utmost.*

most·est (mōs′tist), *adj., n. Slang.* MOST.

most′-fa′vored-na′tion clause′ (mōst′fā′vərd nā′shən), *n.* a clause in a commercial treaty or contract by which each signatory agrees to give the other the same treatment that is or will be accorded any other nation.

Most′ High′, *n.* God. Ps. 21:7; 91:1.

most·ly (mōst′lē), *adv.* **1.** for the most part; in the main. **2.** chiefly; generally; customarily.

Most′ Rev′erend, *n.* the official form of address for cardinals, heads of religious orders, and certain prelates, as archbishops and bishops.

mot (mō), *n.* a pithy or witty remark; bon mot.

mote (mōt), *n.* a small particle or speck, esp. of dust.

mo·tel (mō tel′), *n.* a hotel designed for motorists, typically having rooms adjacent to an outside parking area.

moth (môth, moth), *n., pl.* **moths** (môthz, mothz, môths, moths). any of numerous insects of the order Lepidoptera, generally distinguished from the butterflies by having feathery antennae and by having nocturnal habits.

moth·ball (môth′bôl′, moth′-), *n.* **1.** a small ball of naphthalene or camphor for placing in closets or other storage areas to repel moths. **2. in mothballs,** **a.** in reserve or storage. **b.** in a state of disuse, rejection, or repudiation: *That idea belongs in mothballs.* —*v.t.* **3.** to put into storage; inactivate. **4.** inactive; stored away: *a mothball fleet.*

moth′-eat′en, *adj.* **1.** eaten or damaged by or as if by the larvae of moths. **2.** decayed or worn-out. **3.** out of fashion.

moth·er¹ (muth′ər), *n.* **1.** a female parent. **2.** (*often cap.*) one's own mother. **3.** a mother-in-law, stepmother, or adoptive mother. **4.** a woman looked upon as a mother, or exercising authority like that of a mother. **5.** a term of familiar address for an elderly woman. **6.** the qualities characteristic of a mother, as maternal affection. **7.** something that gives rise to or exercises protective care over something else **8.** MOTHER SUPERIOR. —*adj.* **9.** being a mother: *a mother bird.* **10.** pertaining to or characteristic of a mother: *mother love.* **11.** derived from or as if from one's mother; native: *his mother culture.* **12.** bearing a relation like that of a mother, as in being the origin, source, or protector: *a mother church.* —*v.t.* **13.** to be the mother of. **14.** to give origin or rise to. **15.** to care for or protect like a mother. —**moth′er·less,** *adj.*

moth·er² (muth′ər), *n.* a stringy, viscid film of yeast cells and various bacteria that forms on a fermenting liquid and is used to ferment other liquids, as in changing wine or cider to vinegar.

moth·er·board (muth′ər bôrd′, -bōrd′), *n.* a rigid slotted board upon which other boards that contain the basic circuitry of a computer or of a computer component can be mounted.

Moth′er Goose′, *n.* the fictitious author of a collection of nursery rhymes first published in London about 1760.

moth′er hen′, *n.* a person who attends to the welfare of others, esp. one who is fussily protective.

moth·er·hood (muth′ər hŏŏd′), *n.* **1.** the state of being a mother. **2.** the qualities or spirit of a mother. **3.** mothers collectively.

moth′er house′, *n.* **1.** a convent housing a mother superior. **2.** a self-governing convent having authority over other houses.

Moth′er Hub′bard (hub′ərd), *n.* a women's loose gown, usu. fitted at the shoulders. [after a nursery rhyme character]

moth′er-in-law′, *n., pl.* **mothers-in-law.** the mother of one's husband or wife.

moth·er·land (muth′ər land′), *n.* **1.** one's native land. **2.** the land of one's ancestors.

moth′er lan′guage, *n.* a language from which another language is descended; parent language. Also called **mother tongue.**

moth′er lode′, *n.* a rich or important lode.

moth·er·ly (muth′ər lē), *adj.* **1.** pertaining to, characteristic of, or befitting a mother. **2.** like a mother. —*adv.* **3.** in the manner of a mother.

Moth′er Na′ture, *n.* nature personified as a maternal figure.

Moth′er of God′, *n.* a title of the Virgin Mary.

moth′er-of-pearl′, *n.* **1.** a hard, iridescent substance that forms the inner layer of certain mollusk shells, used for making buttons, beads, etc.; nacre. —*adj.* **2.** made of or resembling mother-of-pearl.

Moth′er's Day′, *n.* a day, usu. the second Sunday in May, set aside in honor of mothers.

moth′er's help′er, *n.* a person who is hired to assist in household chores, esp. caring for children.

moth′er supe′rior, *n., pl.* **mother superiors, mothers superior.** the head of a Christian religious community for women.

moth·er tongue (muth′ər tung′ for 1; muth′ər tung′ for 2), *n.* **1.** the language first learned by a person; native language. **2.** MOTHER LANGUAGE.

moth·er·wort (muth′ər wûrt′, -wôrt′), *n.* a European plant, *Leonorus cardiaca,* of the mint family, an introduced weed in the U.S., having cut leaves with a whorl of lavender flowers in the axils.

moth·proof (môth′prŏŏf′, moth′-), *adj.* **1.** resistant to attack by moths. —*v.t.* **2.** to render (fabric, clothing, etc.) mothproof.

mo·tif (mō tēf′), *n.* **1.** a recurring subject, theme, idea, etc., esp. in a literary, artistic, or musical work. **2.** a distinctive and recurring form, shape, figure, etc., in a design.

mo·tile (mōt′l, mō′til), *adj.* moving or capable of moving spontaneously: *motile cells; motile spores.* —**mo·til′i·ty,** *n.*

mo·tion (mō′shən), *n.* **1.** the action or process of moving or of changing place or position; movement. **2.** power of movement, as of a living body. **3.** the manner of moving the body in walking; gait. **4.** a bodily movement or change of posture; gesture. **5.** a formal proposal, esp. one made to a deliberative assembly. **6.** an application made to a court or judge for an order, ruling, or the like. **7.** an inward prompting or impulse; inclination. **8.** melodic progression from one pitch to another. **9.** *Mach.* **a.** a piece of mechanism with a particular action or function. **b.** the action of such a mechanism. **10. in motion,** in active operation; moving. —*v.t.* **11.** to direct by a significant motion or gesture, as with the hand. —*v.i.* **12.** to make a meaningful motion, as with the hand. —**mo′tion·less,** *adj.* —**mo′tion·less·ly,** *adv.* —**mo′tion·less·ness,** *n.*

mo′tion pic′ture, *n.* **1.** a sequence of consecutive photographic images projected onto a screen in such rapid succession as to give the illusion of natural movement. **2.** a story, narrative, incident, or message presented in this form. **3.** motion pictures, MOVIE (def. 3).

mo′tion sick′ness, *n.* nausea and dizziness resulting from the effect of motion on the semicircular canals of the ear, as during car or plane travel.

mo·ti·vate (mō′tə vāt′), *v.t.,* **-vat·ed, -vat·ing.** to provide with a motive or motives; incite; impel. —**mo′ti·va′tor,** *n.*

mo·ti·va·tion (mō′tə vā′shən), *n.* **1.** an act or instance of motivating. **2.** the state of being motivated. **3.** something that motivates; inducement. —**mo′ti·va′tion·al,** *adj.* —**mo′ti·va′tive,** *adj.*

mo·tive (mō′tiv), *n.* **1.** something that causes a person to act in a certain way, do a certain thing, etc.; incentive. **2.** the goal or object of a person's actions: *Her motive was revenge.* —**mo′tive·less,** *adj.*

mo·to·cross (mō′tō krôs′, -kros′), *n.* a motorcycle race over a course of very rough terrain.

mo·tor (mō′tər), *n.* **1.** a comparatively small and powerful engine, esp. an internal-combustion engine in an automobile, motorboat, or the like. **2.** any self-powered vehicle. **3.** something that imparts motion, esp. a contrivance, as a steam engine, that receives and modifies energy from some natural source in order to utilize it in driving machinery. **4.** a machine that converts electrical energy into mechanical energy. —*adj.* **5.** designed for or operated by a motor. **6.** of, by, or for motor vehicles. **7.** designed for motorists: *a motor inn.* **8.** causing or producing motion. **9.** conveying an impulse that results or tends to result in motion: *a motor nerve cell.* **10.** of, pertaining to, or involving muscular movement: *a motor response.* —*v.i.* **11.** to ride in an automobile; drive. —*v.t.* **12.** to drive or transport by car.

mo·tor·bike (mō′tər bīk′), *n., v.,* **-biked, -bik·ing.** —*n.* **1.** a small, lightweight motorcycle. **2.** a bicycle propelled by an attached motor. —*v.i.* **3.** to drive or ride a motorbike. —**mo′tor·bik′er,** *n.*

mo·tor·boat (mō′tər bōt′), *n.* **1.** a boat propelled by an inboard or outboard motor. —*v.i.* **2.** to travel in or operate a motorboat.

mo·tor·bus (mō′tər bus′), *n., pl.* **-bus·es, -bus·ses.** a passenger bus powered by a motor. Also called **mo′tor coach′.**

mo·tor·cade (mō′tər kād′), *n.* a procession or parade of automobiles or other motor vehicles.

mo·tor·car (mō′tər kär′), *n.* AUTOMOBILE.

mo′tor court′, *n.* MOTEL.

mo·tor·cy·cle (mō′tər sī′kəl), *n., v.,* **-cled, -cling.** —*n.* **1.** a motor vehicle similar to a bicycle but usually larger and heavier, chiefly for one rider but sometimes having two saddles or an attached sidecar for passengers. —*v.i.* **2.** to ride on a motorcycle. —**mo′tor·cy′clist,** *n.*

mo′tor home′, *n.* a van or trucklike vehicle outfitted as living quarters for camping or extended motor trips.

mo·tor·ist (mō′tər ist), *n.* a person who drives or travels in a privately owned automobile.

mo·tor·ize (mō′tə rīz′), *v.t.,* **-ized, -iz·ing. 1.** to furnish with a motor. **2.** to supply with motor vehicles. —**mo′tor·i·za′tion,** *n.*

mo'tor lodge', *n.* MOTEL.

mo·tor·man (mō'tər mən), *n.*, *pl.* **-men.** a person who drives an electrically operated vehicle, as a streetcar or subway train.

mo'tor pool', *n.* a fleet of motor vehicles available for temporary use by personnel, as at a military installation.

mo'tor scoot'er, *n.* SCOOTER (def. 2).

mo'tor truck' or **mo'tor·truck'**, *n.* TRUCK[1] (def. 1).

mo'tor ve'hicle, *n.* an automobile, truck, bus, or similar motor-driven conveyance.

Mott (mot), *n.* **1. John Raleigh,** 1865–1955, U.S. religious leader: Nobel peace prize 1946. **2. Lucretia Coffin,** 1793–1880, U.S. advocate of women's rights and the abolition of slavery. **3. Sir Nevill Francis,** 1905–96, British physicist.

mot·tle (mot'l), *v.t.*, **-tled, -tling.** to mark with spots or blotches of different colors or shades.

mot·to (mot'ō), *n.*, *pl.* **-toes, -tos. 1.** a maxim adopted as an expression of one's guiding principle. **2.** a sentence, phrase, or word expressing the spirit or purpose of an organization or other group, often inscribed on a badge, banner, etc. [< Italian < Late Latin *muttum* sound, utterance]

mound (mound), *n.* **1.** a natural elevation of earth; hillock or knoll. **2.** an artificial elevation of earth, as for a defense work or a dam; embankment. **3.** a heap or raised mass: *a mound of papers.* **4.** the slightly raised ground from which a baseball pitcher delivers the ball. —*v.t.* **5.** to form into a mound; heap up. **6.** to furnish with a mound of earth, as for a defense.

Mound' Build'ers, *n.pl.* the various American Indian tribes who, in prehistoric and early historic times, erected the burial mounds and other earthworks of the Mississippi drainage basin and southeastern U.S.

mount¹ (mount), *v.t.* **1.** to go up; climb; ascend. **2.** to get up on (a platform, a horse, etc.). **3.** to set or place at an elevation: *to mount a house on stilts.* **4.** to furnish with a horse or other animal for riding. **5.** to set or place (a person) on horseback. **6.** to organize and launch (an attack, campaign, etc.). **7.** to raise or put (a gun) into position for use. **8.** (of a fortress or warship) to have (guns) in position for use. **9.** to put (a sentry or watch) on guard. **10.** to fix on or in a support, backing, setting, etc.: *to mount a photograph.* **11.** to provide (a play, opera, etc.) with scenery, costumes, and other equipment for production. **12.** to prepare (an animal body or skeleton) for exhibition as a specimen. **13.** (of an animal) to climb upon (another animal) for copulation. **14. a.** to prepare (a slide) for microscopic investigation. **b.** to prepare (a sample) for examination by a microscope, as by placing it on a slide. —*v.i.* **15.** to increase in amount or intensity (often fol. by *up*): *The costs mounted up.* **16.** to get up on the back of a horse or other animal for riding. **17.** to rise or go to a higher position, level, degree, etc.; ascend. **18.** to get up on something, as a platform. —*n.* **19.** the act or a manner of mounting. **20.** a horse, other animal, or sometimes a vehicle, as a bicycle, used, provided, or available for riding. **21.** an act or occasion of riding a horse, esp. in a race. **22.** a support, backing, setting, or the like, on or in which something is mounted. **23.** an ornamental or functional metal piece on furniture. **24.** a slide prepared for examination by a microscope. **25.** any means of holding a stamp on a page for display. —**mount'a·ble,** *adj.*

mount² (mount), *n.* a mountain: often used as part of a place name.

NOTABLE MOUNTAIN PEAKS OF THE WORLD

Name	Country or Region	Altitude ft.	Altitude m
Mt. Everest	Nepal-Tibet	29,028	8848
K2	Kashmir	28,250	8611
Kanchenjunga	Nepal-Sikkim	28,146	8579
Lhotse	Nepal-Tibet	27,890	8501
Makalu	Nepal-Tibet	27,790	8470
Dhaulagiri	Nepal	26,826	8180
Nanga Parbax	Kashmir	26,660	8125
Annapurna	Nepal	26,503	8078
Gasherbrum	Kashmir	26,470	8068
Gosainthan	Tibet	26,291	8013
Nanda Devi	India	25,661	7820
Tirich Mir	Pakistan	25,230	7690
Muztagh Ata	China	24,757	7546
Communism Peak	Tajikistan	24,590	7495
Pobeda Peak	Kyrgyzstan-China	24,406	7439
Lenin Peak	Kyrgyzstan-Tajikistan	23,382	7127
Aconcagua	Argentina	22,834	6960
Huascaran	Peru	22,205	6768
Illimani	Bolivia	21,188	6458
Chimborazo	Ecuador	20,702	6310
Mt. McKinley	United States (Alaska)	20,320	6194
Mt. Logan	Canada (Yukon)	19,850	6050
Cotopaxi	Ecuador	19,498	5943
Kilimanjaro	Tanzania	19,321	5889
El Misti	Peru	19,200	5880
Demavend	Iran	18,606	5671
Orizaba (Citlaltepetl)	Mexico	18,546	5653
Mt. Elbrus	Russian Federation	18,465	5628
Popocatepetl	Mexico	17,887	5450
Ixtaccihuatl	Mexico	17,342	5286
Mt. Kenya	Kenya	17,040	5194
Arafat	Turkey	16,945	5165
Mt. Ngaliema (Mt. Stanley)	Zaire-Uganda	16,790	5119
Mont-Blanc	France	15,781	4810
Mt. Wilhelm	Papua New Guinea	15,400	4694
Monte Rosa	Italy-Switzerland	15,217	4638
Mt. Kirkpatrick	Antarctica	14,855	4528
Weisshorn	Switzerland	14,804	4512
Matterhorn	Switzerland	14,780	4505
Mt. Whitney	United States (California)	14,495	4418
Mt. Elbert	United States (Colorado)	14,431	4399
Mt. Rainier	United States (Washington)	14,408	4392
Longs Peak	United States (Colorado)	14,255	4345
Mt. Shasta	United States (California)	14,161	4315
Pikes Peak	United States (Colorado)	14,108	4300
Mauna Kea	United States (Hawaii)	13,784	4201
Grand Teton	United States (Wyoming)	13,766	4196
Mauna Loa	United States (Hawaii)	13,680	4170
Jungfrau	Switzerland	13,668	4166
Mt. Victoria	Papua New Guinea	13,240	4036
Mt. Erebus	Antarctica	13,202	4024
Eiger	Switzerland	13,025	3970
Mt. Robson	Canada (B.C.)	12,972	3954
Mt.Fuji	Japan	12,395	3778
Mt. Cook	New Zealand	12,349	3764
Mt. Hood	United States (Oregon)	11,253	3430
Mt. Etna	Italy	10,758	3280
Lassen Peak	United States (California)	10,465	3190
Haleakala	United States (Hawaii)	10,032	3058
Mt. Olympus	Greece	9730	2966
Mt. Kosciusko	Australia	7316	2230

moun·tain (moun′tn), *n.* **1.** a natural elevation of land rising more or less abruptly to a summit, and attaining an altitude greater than that of a hill. **2.** a large mass or heap; pile. **3.** a huge amount: *a mountain of mail.* —*adj.* **4.** of or pertaining to mountains. **5.** living, growing, or located in the mountains. **6.** resembling or suggesting a mountain, as in size. —*Idiom.* **7. make a mountain out of a molehill,** to exaggerate a minor difficulty.

moun′tain ash′, *n.* any of several small trees of the genus *Sorbus,* of the rose family, having flat-topped clusters of small, white flowers and bright red to orange berries.

moun′tain cat′, *n.* **1.** COUGAR. **2.** BOBCAT.

moun′tain cran′berry, *n.* a low-growing shrub, *Vaccinium vitis-idaea,* of the heath family, growing in northern regions and having tart, red, edible berries. Also called **cowberry, lingonberry.**

moun·tain·eer (moun′tn ēr′), *n.* **1.** an inhabitant of a mountainous district. **2.** a climber of mountains, esp. for sport. —*v.i.* **3.** to climb mountains.

moun′tain goat′, *n.* ROCKY MOUNTAIN GOAT.

moun′tain goril′la, *n.* a subspecies of gorilla, *Gorilla gorilla beringei.*

moun′tain lau′rel, *n.* a shrub, *Kalmia latifolia,* of the heath family, having terminal clusters of rose to white flowers: the state flower of Connecticut and Pennsylvania.

moun′tain li′on, *n.* COUGAR.

moun′tain mahog′any, *n.* any of several W North American shrubs or small trees of the genus *Cercocarpus,* of the rose family, having simple, leathery leaves and small, whitish flowers.

moun·tain·ous (moun′tn əs), *adj.* **1.** abounding in mountains. **2.** resembling a mountain, as being very large and high. —**moun′tain·ous·ly,** *adv.* —**moun′tain·ous·ness,** *n.*

moun′tain range′, *n.* a series of more or less connected mountains ranged in a line or related in origin.

moun′tain sheep′, *n.* **1.** BIGHORN. **2.** any of various wild sheep inhabiting mountains.

moun′tain sick′ness, *n.* ALTITUDE SICKNESS.

moun·tain·side (moun′tn sīd′), *n.* the side of a mountain.

Moun′tain time′, *n.* See under STANDARD TIME. Also called **Moun′tain Stand′ard Time′.**

Mount·bat·ten (mount bat′n), *n.* **Louis, 1st Earl Mountbatten of Burma,** 1900–79, British admiral: viceroy of India 1947; governor general of India 1947–48.

moun·te·bank (moun′tə bangk′), *n.* **1.** a person who sells quack medicines, as from a platform, appealing to an audience by tricks, storytelling, etc. **2.** any charlatan or quack.

mount·ed (moun′tid), *adj.* **1.** seated or riding on a horse or other animal. **2.** serving on horseback: *mounted police.* **3.** having or set in a mounting: *mounted gems.*

Moun·tie or **Moun·ty** (moun′tē), *n., pl.* **-ties.** *Informal.* a member of the Royal Canadian Mounted Police.

mount·ing (moun′ting), *n.* **1.** the act of a person or thing that mounts. **2.** a mount, support, or setting: *a mounting for a jewel.*

Mount′ McKin′ley Na′tional Park′, *n.* former name of DENALI NATIONAL PARK.

Mount′ Rainier′ Na′tional Park′, *n.* a national park in W Washington, including Mount Rainier. 378 sq. mi. (980 sq. km).

Mount′ Rush′more Na′tional Memo′rial, *n.* See under RUSHMORE.

Mount′ Ver′non, *n.* the home and tomb of George Washington in NE Virginia, on the Potomac, 15 mi. (24 km) below Washington, D.C.

Mount′ Wil′son Observ′atory, *n.* an astronomical observatory on Mount Wilson, near Los Angeles, Ca., having a 100-in. (254-cm) reflecting telescope.

mourn (môrn, mōrn), *v.i.* **1.** to feel or express sorrow or grief. **2.** to grieve for the dead. **3.** to show the conventional signs of sorrow over a person's death. —*v.t.* **4.** to feel or express sorrow or grief over (misfortune, loss, etc.); deplore. **5.** to grieve or lament over (the dead).

mourn·er (môr′nər, mōr′-), *n.* **1.** a person who mourns. **2.** a person who attends a funeral to mourn for the deceased. **3.** (at religious revival meetings) a person who professes penitence.

mourn′ers′ bench′, *n.* (at religious revival meetings) a bench or seat at the front of the church or room, set apart for mourners or penitent sinners seeking salvation.

mourn·ful (môrn′fəl, mōrn′-), *adj.* **1.** feeling or expressing sorrow or grief. **2.** causing grief. **3.** gloomy, somber, or dreary, as in appearance or sound. —**mourn′ful·ly,** *adv.* —**mourn′ful·ness,** *n.*

mourn·ing (môr′ning, mōr′-), *n.* **1.** the act of a person who mourns; sorrowing or lamentation. **2.** the conventional manifestation of sorrow for a person's death, esp. by the wearing of black, the hanging of flags at half-mast, etc. **3.** the outward symbols of such sorrow, as black garments. **4.** the period during which a bereft person grieves.

mourn′ing band′, *n.* a piece of black cloth that is worn, esp. as a band on the arm, to indicate mourning.

mourn′ing cloak′, *n.* an anglewing butterfly, *Nymphalis antiopa,* widely distributed in Europe and North America, having velvety, dark brown wings with intense blue spots and pale yellow edges.

mourn′ing dove′, *n.* a dove, *Zenaida (Zenaidura) macroura,* of North America, noted for its plaintive cooing.

mouse (*n.* mous; *v.* mouz), *n., pl.* **mice** (mīs), *v.,* **moused, mous·ing.**
—*n.* **1.** any of numerous small rodents of various families, having small ears and a long, thin tail, esp. an Old World mouse, *Mus musculus,* introduced worldwide. **2.** a quiet, timid person. **3.** a palm-sized device equipped with one or more buttons, used to point at and select items on a computer display screen, with the displayed pointer controlled by means of analogous movement of the device on a nearby surface. **4.** *Informal.* a black eye. —*v.i.* **5.** to hunt for or catch mice.

mouse′ pad′, *n.* a small typically foam rubber sheet used to provide a stable surface on which a computer mouse can be moved.

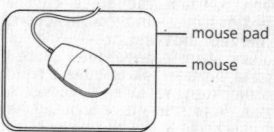

mouse pad

mous·er (mou′zər), *n.* an animal that catches mice.

mouse·trap (mous′trap′), *n.* **1.** a trap for mice, esp. a wooden one with a metal spring. **2.** a device or ruse for trapping someone.

mous·sa·ka (moo sä′kə, moo′sä kä′), *n., pl.* **-kas.** a Greek dish consisting of layers of eggplant and seasoned ground lamb, topped usu. with a custard or cheese sauce and baked.

mousse (moos), *n., v.,* **moussed, mouss·ing.** —*n.* **1. a.** a sweetened dessert, usu. made with whipped cream and gelatin or beaten egg whites and chilled in a mold. **b.** an unsweetened aspic containing fish, vegetables, meat, etc. **2.** a foamy preparation used to set or style the hair. —*v.t.* **3.** to set or style (the hair) with mousse.

mous·tache (mus′tash, mə stash′), *n.* MUSTACHE.

mous·y or **mous·ey** (mou′sē, -zē), *adj.,* **mous·i·er, mous·i·est. 1.** resembling or suggesting a mouse, as in being drab and colorless or meek and timid. **2.** infested with mice. —**mous′i·ness,** *n.*

mouth (*n.* mouth; *v.* mouth), *n., pl.* **mouths** (mouthz). **1.** the opening through which an animal takes in food. **2.** a person or animal dependent on someone for sustenance: *another mouth to feed.* **3.** the oral opening or cavity considered as the source of vocal utterance. **4.** utterance or expression: *to give mouth to one's thoughts.* **5.** talk, esp. loud, empty, or boastful talk. **6.** disrespectful talk or language. **7.** a grimace made with the lips. **8.** an opening leading out of or into any cavity or hollow place or thing. **9.** the outlet at the lower end of a river or stream, where flowing water is discharged, as into a larger body of water. **10.** the opening between the jaws of a vise or the like. **11.** the lateral hole of an organ pipe. **12.** the lateral blowhole of a flute. —*v.t.* **13.** to utter in a sonorous or pompous manner, or with excessive mouth movements. **14.** to form (a word, sound, etc.) silently or indistinctly in one's mouth. **15.** to put or take into the mouth, as food. **16.** to press, rub, or chew at with the mouth or lips. **17.** to accustom (a horse) to the use of the bit and bridle. —*v.i.* **18.** to speak sonorously and oratorically, or with excessive mouth movement. **19.** to grimace with the lips. **20. mouth off,** *Slang.* **a.** to talk back; sass. **b.** to express one's opinions in a forceful or uninhibited manner. —*Idiom.* **21. down in** or **at the mouth,** dejected; depressed; disheartened. —**mouth′er,** *n.*

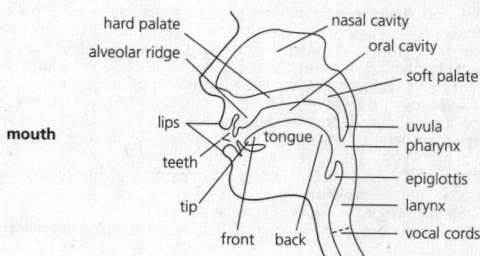

mouth

mouth·ful (mouth′fool′), *n., pl.* **-fuls. 1.** the amount a mouth can hold. **2.** the amount taken into the mouth at one time. **3.** a spoken remark of great truth, relevance, etc. **4.** a long word or phrase, esp. one that is hard to pronounce.

mouth′ or′gan, *n.* HARMONICA.

mouth·piece (mouth′pēs′), *n.* **1.** a piece placed at or forming the mouth, as of a receptacle or tube. **2.** a piece or part, as of a musical instrument, applied to or held in the mouth. **3.** *Slang.* a lawyer, esp. a criminal lawyer.

mouth′-to-mouth′ resuscita′tion, *n.* a method of artificial respiration in which a person rhythmically blows air into the victim's lungs.

mouth·wash (mouth′wôsh′, -wosh′), *n.* a solution, often containing an antiseptic or astringent, for cleaning the mouth.

mouth′-wa′tering, *adj.* very appetizing in appearance, aroma, or description.

mouth•y (mou′thē, -thē), *adj.,* **mouth•i•er, mouth•i•est.** garrulous, often in a bombastic manner. —**mouth′i•ly,** *adv.* —**mouth′i•ness,** *n.*

mou•ton (mōō′ton), *n.* sheepskin that has been processed to resemble another fur, esp. seal or beaver.

mov•a•ble or **move•a•ble** (mōō′və bəl), *adj.* **1.** capable of being moved; not fixed in one place or position. **2.** *Law.* (of property) personal, as distinguished from real. **3.** changing from one date to another in different years: *a movable holiday.* —*n.* **4.** an article of furniture that is not fixed in place. **5.** Often, **movables.** *Law.* an article of personal property not attached to land. —**mov′a•bil′i•ty,** *n.* —**mov′a•bly,** *adv.*

move (mōōv), *v.,* **moved, mov•ing,** *n.* —*v.i.* **1.** to pass from one place or position to another. **2.** to change one's place of residence or business. **3.** to advance or progress. **4.** to have a regular motion, as an implement or a machine; turn; revolve. **5.** to sell or be sold: *That new model is moving well.* **6.** to start off or leave. **7.** to transfer a piece in a game, as chess or checkers. **8.** (of the bowels) to discharge the feces; evacuate. **9.** to be active in a particular sphere: *to move in society.* **10.** to take action; proceed. **11.** to make a formal request, application, or proposal. —*v.t.* **12.** to change from one place or position to another. **13.** to set or keep in motion. **14.** to prompt, actuate, or impel to some action. **15.** to arouse or excite the feelings or passions of (usu. fol. by *to*): *to move someone to anger.* **16.** to affect with tender or compassionate emotion; touch. **17.** to dispose of (goods) by sale. **18.** to cause (the bowels) to evacuate. **19.** to propose formally, as to a court or judge, or for consideration by a deliberative assembly. **20.** to submit a formal request or proposal to (a court, a sovereign, etc.). **21. move in,** to begin to occupy a residence or workplace, esp. by installing one's possessions. **22. move in on,** to make aggressive advances toward, as to exploit, plunder, or possess. **23. move on,** to approach or attack as a military target. **24. move over,** to shift to a nearby place, as to make room for another. **25. move up,** to advance to a higher level. —*n.* **26.** an act or instance of moving; movement. **27.** a change of location or residence. **28.** an action toward an objective or goal; step. **29.** (in chess, checkers, etc.) a player's right or turn to make a play. **30.** a play or maneuver, as in a game or sport. —*Idiom.* **31. get a move on,** *Informal.* to hasten to act or proceed; hurry up. **32. move heaven and earth,** to do one's utmost to bring something about. **33. move the goalposts,** to change rules arbitrarily. **34. on the move, a.** busy; active. **b.** going from place to place. **c.** advancing; progressing.

move•ment (mōōv′mənt), *n.* **1.** the act, process, or result of moving. **2.** a particular manner or style of moving. **3.** Usu., **movements.** actions or activities, as of a person or a body of persons. **4.** a change of position or location of troops or ships. **5.** abundance of events or incidents. **6.** rapid progress of events. **7.** the progress of events, as in a narrative or drama. **8.** the stylistic representation of motion in a work of art. **9.** a series of actions or activities directed or tending toward a particular end. **10.** the course, tendency, or trend of affairs in a particular field. **11.** a diffusely organized or heterogeneous group of people or organizations tending toward or favoring a generalized common goal. **12.** the price change in the market of some commodity or security. **13.** BOWEL MOVEMENT. **14.** the working parts or a distinct portion of the working parts of a mechanism, as of a watch. **15.** *Music.* **a.** a principal division or section of a sonata, symphony, or the like. **b.** motion; rhythm; time; tempo. **16.** *Pros.* rhythmical structure or character.

mov•er (mōō′vər), *n.* **1.** one that moves. **2.** Often, **movers.** a person or company that moves household effects, office equipment, etc. **3. movers and shakers,** powerful and influential people, as in politics and business.

mov•ie (mōō′vē), *n.* **1.** MOTION PICTURE. **2.** a motion-picture theater (often prec. by *the*). **3. movies, a.** the business of making motion pictures; motion-picture industry. **b.** the showing of a motion picture.

mov•ie•go•er (mōō′vē gō′ər), *n.* a person who goes to see motion pictures frequently. —**mov′ie•go′ing,** *adj.*

mov•ie•mak•er (mōō′vē mā′kər), *n.* FILMMAKER. —**mov′ie•mak′ing,** *n.*

mov•ing (mōō′ving), *adj.* stirring or evoking strong feelings or emotions; touching. —**mov′ing•ly,** *adv.*

mov′ing pic′ture, *n.* MOTION PICTURE.

mov′ing stair′way, *n.* ESCALATOR (def. 1). Also called **mov′ing stair′case.**

mow[1] (mō), *v.,* **mowed, mowed** or **mown, mow•ing.** —*v.t.* **1.** to cut down (grass, grain, etc.) with a scythe or a machine. **2.** to cut grass, grain, etc., from. —*v.i.* **3.** to cut down grass, grain, etc. **4. mow down, a.** to destroy or kill in great numbers, as in a battle. **b.** to overwhelm. **c.** to knock down. —**mow′er,** *n.*

mow[2] (mou), *n.* **1.** the place in a barn where hay, grain, etc., are stored. **2.** a heap or pile of hay or grain in a barn.

mox•ie (mok′sē), *n. Slang.* **1.** vigor; verve; pep. **2.** courage and boldness; nerve.

Mo•zam•bique (mō′zam bēk′, -zəm-), *n.* Formerly, **Portuguese East Africa.** a republic in SE Africa: formerly an overseas province of Portugal; gained independence in 1975. 18,165,476; 308,642 sq. mi. (799,380 sq. km). *Cap.:* Maputo. Portuguese, **Moçambique.** —**Mo′zam•bi′can,** *adj., n.*

Moz•ar•ab (mō zar′əb), *n.* a Christian in Moorish Spain.

Mo•zart (mōt′särt), *n.* Wolfgang Amadeus, 1756–91, Austrian composer. —**Mo•zar′te•an, Mo•zar′ti•an,** *adj.*

moz•za•rel•la (mot′sə rel′ə, mōt′-), *n.* a mild, white, semisoft Italian cheese.

MP, 1. Member of Parliament. **2.** Military Police. **3.** Mounted Police.

mpg or **m.p.g.,** miles per gallon.

mph or **m.p.h.,** miles per hour.

Mr. (mis′tər), *pl.* **Messrs.** (mes′ərz). **1.** mister: a title of respect prefixed to a man's name or position: *Mr. Lawson; Mr. President.* **2.** a title prefixed to a mock surname that is used to represent possession of a particular attribute, identity, etc.: *Mr. Perfect.* [abbr. of *mister*]

Mr. Doo•ley (dōō′lē), *n.* a fictional character in humorous works by Finley Peter Dunne, known for skeptical remarks about politics.

MRI, magnetic resonance imaging.

Mrs. (mis′iz, miz′iz), *pl.* **Mmes.** (mā däm′, -dam′). **1.** a title of respect prefixed to the name of a married woman: *Mrs. Jones.* **2.** a title prefixed to a mock surname that is used to represent possession of a particular attribute, identity, etc.: *Mrs. Punctuality.*

MRV or **M.R.V.,** multiple reentry vehicle.

MS, 1. manuscript. **2.** Mississippi. **3.** multiple sclerosis.

Ms. (miz), *pl.* **Mses.** (miz′əz). **1.** a title of respect prefixed to a woman's name: unlike *Miss* or *Mrs.,* it does not depend upon or indicate her marital status. **2.** a title prefixed to a mock surname that is used to represent possession of a particular attribute, identity, etc.: *Ms. Cooperation.* [blend of *Miss* and *Mrs.*] —*Usage.* Ms. came into use in the 1950s. In the early 1970s the women's movement adopted and encouraged the use of Ms. on the grounds that since a man's marital status is not revealed by *Mr.,* a woman's status should not be revealed by her title. Since then Ms. has gained wide currency, esp. in business and professional spheres. —**Pronunciation.** The pronunciation of Ms. (miz) is identical with one standard South Midland and Southern U.S. pronunciation of *Mrs.*

M.S., 1. Master of Science. **2.** Master of Surgery.

M.Sc., Master of Science.

MS DOS or **MS-DOS** (em′es′ dôs′, -dos′), *Trademark.* a microcomputer operating system.

MSG, monosodium glutamate.

msg., message.

M.Sgt., master sergeant.

MST or **M.S.T.,** Mountain Standard Time.

MSW or **M.S.W., 1.** Master of Social Work or Master in Social Work. **2.** Master of Social Welfare.

MT, 1. megaton. **2.** metric ton. **3.** Montana. **4.** Mountain time.

Mt. or **mt., 1.** mount: *Mt. Rainier.* **2.** mountain.

mtg., **1.** meeting. **2.** Also, **mtge.** mortgage.

mtn. or **mtn,** mountain.

Mts. or **mts.,** mountains.

Mu•ba•rak (mōō bär′ək), *n.* **(Mohammed) Hosni,** born 1928, president of Egypt since 1981.

much (much), *adj.,* **more, most,** *n., pron., adv.,* **more, most.** —*adj.* **1.** great in quantity, measure, or degree: *too much cake.* —*n., pron.* **2.** a great quantity, measure, or degree: *There wasn't much to do.* **3.** a great, important, or notable thing or matter: *not much to look at.* —*adv.* **4.** to a great extent or degree: *to talk too much.* **5.** nearly, approximately, or about: *much like the others.* **6. much as, a.** almost to the same degree as: *Babies need love, much as they need food.* **b.** however much: *Much as I'd like to go, I can't.*

mu•ci•lage (myōō′sə lij), *n.* any of various, usu. liquid, preparations of gum, glue, or the like, used as an adhesive.

mu•ci•lag•i•nous (myōō′sə laj′ə nəs), *adj.* **1.** of, pertaining to, or secreting mucilage. **2.** of the nature of or resembling mucilage; moist, soft, and viscid.

muck (muk), *n.* **1.** moist farmyard dung; manure. **2.** a highly organic dark or black soil, often used as a manure. **3.** mire; mud. **4.** filth, dirt, or slime. **5.** defamatory or sullying remarks. **6.** *Informal.* a state of confusion; mess: *to make a muck of things.* **7.** *Chiefly Brit. Informal.* something of no value; trash. **8.** earth, rock, or other useless matter removed in excavation or mining. —*v.t.* **9.** to manure. **10.** *Informal.* to make dirty; soil (often fol. by *up*). **11.** to remove muck from (often fol. by *out*). **12.** *Informal.* to make a mess of; bungle (often fol. by *up*). **13. muck about** or **around,** *Informal.* to idle; waste time. —**muck′y,** *adj.,* **muck•i•er, muck•i•est.**

muck′-a-muck′, *n.* HIGH-MUCK-A-MUCK.

muck•rake (muk′rāk′), *v.i.,* **-raked, -rak•ing.** to search for and expose real or alleged corruption or scandal, esp. in politics. —**muck′rak′er,** *n.*

mu•cous (myōō′kəs), *adj.* **1.** of, consisting of, or resembling mucus. **2.** containing or secreting mucus. —**mu•cos′i•ty** (-kos′i tē), *n.*

mu′cous mem′brane, *n.* a mucus-secreting membrane lining all bodily passages that are open to the air, as parts of the digestive and respiratory tracts.

mu•cus (myōō′kəs), *n.* a viscous solution of mucins, water, electrolytes, and white blood cells that is secreted by mucous membranes and serves to protect and lubricate the internal surfaces of the body.

mud (mud), *n., v.,* **mud•ded, mud•ding.** —*n.* **1.** wet, soft earth or earthy matter; mire. **2.** scandalous or malicious assertions or information. —*v.t.* **3.** to cover or spatter with mud. **4.** to stir up the mud or sediment in.

mud′ daub′er, *n.* any of several wasps of the family Sphecidae that build a nest of mud cells and provision it with paralyzed spiders or insects for the larvae to feed on.

mud•dle (mud′l), *v.,* **-dled, -dling,** *n.* —*v.t.* **1.** to mix up in a confused or bungling manner. **2.** to cause to become mentally confused. **3.** to cause to become confused or stupid with or as if with liquor. **4.** to make muddy or turbid, as water. **5.** to mix or stir (a drink). —*v.i.* **6.** to think or act in a confused or bungling manner. **7. muddle through,** to make progress or reach a goal despite lack of knowledge, skill, or direction. —*n.* **8.** the state of being muddled, esp. a confused mental state. **9.** a confused or disordered state of affairs; mess.

mud•dle•head•ed (mud′l hed′id), *adj.* confused in one's thinking; blundering.

mud•dy (mud′ē), *adj.,* **-di•er, -di•est,** *v.,* **-died, -dy•ing.** —*adj.* **1.** abounding in or covered with mud. **2.** not clear or pure: *muddy colors.* **3.** vague, as thought or expression. —*v.t.* **4.** to make muddy. **5.** to make turbid. **6.** to cause to be confused or obscure. —**mud′di•ly,** *adv.*

mud′ eel′, *n.* a salamander, *Siren lacertina,* having external gills, tiny front legs, and no hind legs, inhabiting shallow waters in the southeastern U.S.

Mu•dé•jar (*Sp.* mōō тнe′här), *n., pl.* **-ja•res** (-hä ʀᴇs′), *adj.* —*n.* **1.** a Muslim allowed to remain in Spain after the Christian reconquest, esp. during the 8th–13th centuries. —*adj.* **2.** of, pertaining to, or characteristic of the Mudéjars.

mud′ flat′, *n.* a mud-covered, gently sloping tract of land alternately covered and exposed by tidal waters.

mud•guard (mud′gärd′), *n.* **1.** FENDER (def. 1). **2.** Also called **mud′ flap′.** SPLASH GUARD.

mud′ hen′ or **mud′hen′,** *n.* any of various marsh-inhabiting birds, esp. the North American coot.

mud•pack (mud′pak′), *n.* a pastelike preparation, as one containing fuller's earth, used on the face as a cosmetic restorative.

mud•pup•py (mud′pup′ē), *n., pl.* **-pies.** any of several often large, aquatic salamanders of the genus *Necturus,* of E North America, having bushy, red gills and well-developed limbs.

mud′ room′ or **mud′room′,** *n.* a vestibule or other area in a house, in which wet and muddy clothes or footwear are removed.

mud•skip•per (mud′skip′ər), *n.* any African or Asian goby of the genera *Periophthalmus* and *Boleophthalmus,* of tropical Pacific coasts, living around mud flats and able to maneuver out of water for limited periods.

mud•sling•ing (mud′sling′ing), *n.* efforts to discredit one's opponent by malicious or scandalous attacks. —**mud′sling′er,** *n.*

mud′ snake′, *n.* an iridescent black and red colubrine snake, *Farancia abacura,* of the SE and S central U.S., having a sharp, stiff tail tip used in manipulating prey into position for swallowing.

mud′ tur′tle, *n.* any of several small freshwater turtles of the family Kinosternidae, of North and South America, characterized by two transverse hinges on the lower shell.

muen•ster (mun′stər, mōōn′-), *n.* (*often cap.*) a semisoft cheese made from whole milk.

mu•ez•zin (myōō ez′in, mōō-), *n.* a crier who calls Muslims to prayer. Compare MINARET.

muff (muf), *n.* **1.** a thick tubular case for the hands that is covered with fur or other material. **2.** a bungled action or performance. —*v.t.* **3.** to handle clumsily. —*v.i.* **4.** to act clumsily.

muf•fin (muf′in), *n.* **1.** a small quick bread made with flour or cornmeal, eggs, milk, etc., and baked in a pan containing a series of cuplike molds. **2.** ENGLISH MUFFIN.

muf•fle (muf′əl), *n.,* **-fled, -fling,** *n.* —*v.t.* **1.** to wrap with something to deaden or prevent sound: *to muffle drums.* **2.** to deaden (sound) by wrappings or other means. **3.** to wrap or envelop in a shawl, coat, etc., esp. to keep warm or protect the face and neck (often fol. by *up*). **4.** to wrap (oneself) in a garment or other covering: *muffled in silk.* **5.** to suppress; stifle. —*n.* **6.** something that muffles.

muf•fler (muf′lər), *n.* **1.** a scarf worn around the neck for warmth. **2.** any of various devices for deadening sound, as that of an internal-combustion engine. **3.** anything used for muffling.

muf•ti (muf′tē), *n., pl.* **-tis. 1.** civilian clothes, as worn by a person who usu. wears a uniform. **2.** a Muslim legal adviser consulted in applying the religious law.

mug (mug), *n., v.,* **mugged, mug•ging.** —*n.* **1.** a cylindrical drinking cup with a handle. **2.** the quantity it holds. **3.** *Slang.* **a.** a person's face or mouth. **b.** GRIMACE. **c.** thug; ruffian. —*v.t.* **4.** to assault or menace, usu. with intent to rob. **5.** to photograph (a suspect or criminal). —*v.i.* **6.** to exaggerate facial expressions; grimace.

mug•ger¹ (mug′ər), *n.* one who mugs, esp. one who assaults a person with intent to rob.

mug•ger² (mug′ər), *n.* one who grimaces in an attention-getting way.

mug•gy (mug′ē), *adj.,* **-gi•er, -gi•est.** (of the atmosphere, weather, etc.) oppressively humid; damp and close. —**mug′gi•ness,** *n.*

mug′ shot′, *n.* a photograph of the face of a criminal suspect.

mug•wump (mug′wump′), *n.* **1.** a Republican who refused to support the party nominee, James G. Blaine, in the presidential campaign of 1884. **2.** a person who takes an independent position.

Mu•ham•mad (mōō ham′əd, -hä′məd), *n.* **1.** Also, **Mohammed.** A.D. 570–632, Arab prophet: founder of Islam. **2. Elijah** (*Elijah Poole*), 1897–1975, U.S. leader of the Black Muslims 1934–75.

Mu•ham•mad•an (mōō ham′ə dn), *adj.* **1.** of or pertaining to Muhammad or Islam. —*n.* **2.** a follower of Muhammad; an adherent of Islam. —**Usage.** See MUSLIM.

Mu•ham•mad•an•ism or **Mo•ham•med•an•ism** (mōō ham′ə dniz′əm, mō-), *n.* ISLAM. —**Usage.** See MUSLIM.

Muh•len•berg (myōō′lən bûrg′), *n.* **1. Frederick Augustus Conrad,** 1750–1801, U.S. clergyman and statesman: first Speaker of the House 1789–91, 1793–95. **2.** his father, **Henry Melchior,** 1711–87, American Lutheran clergyman, born in Germany.

Muir (myŏŏr), *n.* **John,** 1838–1914, U.S. naturalist, explorer, and writer; born in Scotland.

muk•luk or **muc•luc** or **muck•luck** (muk′luk), *n.* **1.** a soft boot worn by Eskimos, often lined with fur and usu. made of sealskin or reindeer skin. **2.** a slipper or lounging boot resembling this.

mu•lat•to (mə lat′ō, -lä′tō, myōō-), *n., pl.* **-toes. 1.** the offspring of one white parent and one black parent. **2.** a person whose ancestry is a mixture of Negro and Caucasian. —*adj.* **3.** of a light brown color.

mul•ber•ry (mul′ber′ē, -bə rē), *n., pl.* **-ries. 1.** the edible, berrylike collective fruit of any tree of the genus *Morus.* **2.** a tree of this genus, as the red mulberry.

mulch (mulch), *n.* **1.** a covering, as of straw, compost, or plastic sheeting, spread on the ground around plants to prevent excessive evaporation or erosion, enrich the soil, inhibit weed growth, etc. —*v.t.* **2.** to cover with mulch.

mulct (mulkt), *v.t.* **1.** to defraud of something; swindle. **2.** to obtain by fraud, extortion, etc. **3.** to punish by fine, esp. for a misdemeanor.

mule¹ (myōōl), *n.* **1.** the sterile offspring of a female horse and a male donkey. **2.** a stubborn person. **3.** a hybrid songbird, esp. of the canary and another finch. **4.** any sterile hybrid plant. **5.** *Slang,* a person paid to transport contraband, esp. drugs, for a smuggler. **6.** a machine for spinning cotton or other fibers into yarn and winding the yarn on spindles. **7.** a hybrid coin having the obverse of one issue and the reverse of the succeeding issue.

mule² (myōōl), *n.* a lounging slipper that covers the toes and instep or only the instep.

mule′ deer′, *n.* a deer, *Odocoileus hemionus,* of W North America, having large ears and a gray coat.

mu•le•ta (mōō lā′tə, -let′ə), *n., pl.* **-tas.** a matador's red cloth, smaller than the cape, used with a sword at the climax of a bullfight.

mu•li•eb•ri•ty (myōō′lē eb′ri tē), *n.* **1.** womanly nature or qualities. **2.** WOMANHOOD. —**mu′li•eb′ral,** *adj.*

mul•ish (myōō′lish), *adj.* unyieldingly stubborn; obdurate. —**mul′ish•ly,** *adv.* —**mul′ish•ness,** *n.*

mull¹ (mul), *v.t.* **1.** to think about carefully; consider (often fol. by *over*). —*v.i.* **2.** to ruminate; ponder.

mull² (mul), *v.t.* to heat, sweeten, and flavor (ale or wine) with spices.

mul•lah (mul′ə, mōōl′ə), *n.* **1.** (in Islamic countries) a title of respect for a person who is learned in, teaches, or expounds the sacred law. **2.** (in Turkey) a provincial judge.

mul•lein or **mul•len** (mul′ən), *n.* any of various plants belonging to the genus *Verbascum,* of the figwort family, native to the Old World, esp. *V. thapsus,* a tall plant with woolly leaves and a dense spike of yellow flowers.

Mul•ler (mul′ər), *n.* **George,** 1805–98, English evangelist.

mul•let (mul′it), *n., pl.* **-let,** (*esp. collectively*) **-let,** (*esp. for kinds or species*) **-lets.** any marine or freshwater spiny-finned fish of the family Mugilidae.

mul′li•gan stew′ (mul′i gən), *n.* a stew of any ingredients that are available. Also called **mulligan.**

mul•li•ga•taw•ny (mul′i gə tô′nē), *n.* a curry-flavored soup of East Indian origin, made with chicken or meat stock.

mul•lion *n.* **1.** a vertical member, as of stone or wood, between the lights of a window, the panels in wainscoting, or the like. —*v.t.* **2.** to furnish with, or to form into divisions by the use of, mullions.

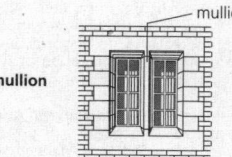

mullion

Mul•ro•ney (mul rō′nē), *n.* **(Martin) Brian,** born 1939, prime minister of Canada 1984–93.

multi-, a combining form meaning "many," "much," "multiple," "many times," "more than one," "more than two," "composed of many like parts," "in many respects": *multiply; multivitamin.*

mul•ti•cul•tur•al•ism (mul′tē kul′chər ə liz′əm, mul′tī-), *n.* the preservation of different cultures or cultural identities within a society, state, or nation. —**mul′ti•cul′tur•al,** *adj.*

mul•ti•dis•ci•pli•nar•y (mul′tē dis′ə plə ner′ē, mul′tī-), *adj.* combining several specialized branches of learning or fields of expertise.

M

mul·ti·eth·nic (mul′tē eth′nik, mul′tī-), *adj.* involving or pertaining to two or more distinct ethnic groups.

mul·ti·far·i·ous (mul′tə fâr′ē əs), *adj.* **1.** having many different parts, elements, forms, etc. **2.** numerous and varied; manifold: *multifarious activities.* —**mul′ti·far′i·ous·ly,** *adv.* —**mul′ti·far′i·ous·ness,** *n.*

mul·ti·lat·er·al (mul′ti lat′ər əl), *adj.* **1.** having several or many sides. **2.** participated in by more than two nations, parties, etc.: *multilateral agreements on disarmament.* —**mul′ti·lat′er·al·ly,** *adv.*

mul·ti·lin·gual (mul′tē ling′gwəl, mul′tī-), *adj.* **1.** using or able to speak several languages with some facility. **2.** of or expressed in several or many languages: *a multilingual broadcast.* —*n.* **3.** a multilingual person. —**mul′ti·lin′gual·ly,** *adv.* —**mul′ti·lin′gual·ism,** *n.*

mul·ti·me·di·a (mul′tē mē′dē ə, mul′tī-), *n. (used with a sing. v.)* **1.** the combined use of several media, as films, video, music, etc. —*adj.* **2.** of, pertaining to, or involving the use of several media simultaneously. **3.** having or offering the use of various communications or promotional media. —**mul′ti·me′di·al,** *adj.*

mul·ti·na·tion·al (mul′tē nash′ə nl, mul′tī-), *n.* **1.** a large corporation with operations and subsidiaries in several countries. —*adj.* **2.** of, pertaining to, or involving several nations or multinationals.

mul·ti·ple (mul′tə pəl), *adj.* **1.** consisting of, having, or involving several or many individuals, parts, elements, relations, etc.; manifold. **2.** *Elect.* **a.** (of circuits) arranged in parallel. **b.** (of a circuit or circuits) having a number of points at which connection can be made. —*n.* **3.** a number that contains another number an integral number of times without a remainder: *12 is a multiple of 3.*

mul′tiple-choice′, *adj.* **1.** consisting of several possible answers from which the correct one must be selected. **2.** made up of multiple-choice questions: *a multiple-choice exam.*

mul′tiple personal′ity, *n.* a mental disorder in which a person acquires several personalities that function independently.

mul′tiple sclero′sis, *n.* a chronic degenerative disease marked by patchy destruction of the myelin that surrounds and insulates nerve fibers and mild to severe neural and muscular impairments.

mul′tiple star′, *n.* a system of three or more stars appearing as one star to the naked eye.

mul·ti·plex (mul′tə pleks′), *adj.* **1.** having many parts or aspects. **2.** manifold; multiple. —*v.t.* **3. a.** to arrange (a circuit) for use by multiplex telegraphy. **b.** to transmit (two or more signals or messages) by a multiplex system, circuit, or the like. —*v.i.* **4.** to send several messages or signals simultaneously, as by multiplex telegraphy. —*n.* **5.** a multiplex electronics system. **6.** (in map making) a stereoscopic device that makes it possible to view pairs of aerial photographs in three dimensions. **7.** a building containing a number of motion-picture theaters or, sometimes, a cluster of adjoining theaters on the same site. —**mul′ti·plex′er, mul′ti·plex′or,** *n.*

mul·ti·pli·cand (mul′tə pli kand′), *n.* a number to be multiplied by another.

mul·ti·pli·ca·tion (mul′tə pli kā′shən), *n.* **1.** the act or process of multiplying or the state of being multiplied. **2.** a mathematical operation, symbolized by $a \times b$, $a \cdot b$, $a * b$, or ab, and signifying, when a and b are positive integers, that a is to be added to itself as many times as there are units in b; the addition of a number to itself as often as is indicated by another number, as in 2×3 or 5×10. **3.** any generalization of this operation applicable to numbers other than integers, as fractions or irrational numbers. —**mul′ti·pli·ca′tion·al,** *adj.*

multiplica′tion sign′, *n.* the symbol (·), (×), or (*) between two mathematical expressions, denoting multiplication of the second expression by the first. Also called **times sign.**

multiplica′tion ta′ble, *n.* a tabular listing of the products of any two numbers of a set, usu. of the integers 1 through 10 or 1 through 12.

mul·ti·plic·i·ty (mul′tə plis′i tē), *n., pl.* **-ties. 1.** a large number. **2.** the state of being multiplex or manifold; manifold variety.

mul·ti·pli·er (mul′tə plī′ər), *n.* **1.** a person or thing that multiplies. **2.** a number by which another is multiplied.

mul·ti·ply¹ (mul′tə plī′), *v.,* **-plied, -ply·ing.** —*v.t.* **1.** to make many or manifold; increase the number, quantity, etc., of. **2.** to find the product of by multiplication. **3.** to increase by procreation. —*v.i.* **4.** to grow in number, quantity, etc.; increase. **5.** to perform the process of multiplication. **6.** to increase in number by procreation or natural generation.

mul·ti·ply² (mul′tə plē), *adv.* in several or many ways; in a multiple manner; manifoldly.

mul·ti·task·ing (mul′tē tas′king, -tä′sking, mul′tī-), *n. Computers.* the concurrent execution of two or more jobs or programs by a single CPU.

mul·ti·tude (mul′ti tood′, -tyood′), *n.* **1.** a great number; host. **2.** a great number of people gathered together; crowd; throng. **3.** the state or character of being many; numerousness. **4.** populace; masses.

mul·ti·tu·di·nous (mul′ti tood′n əs, -tyood′-), *adj.* **1.** existing in great numbers; very numerous. **2.** comprising many parts or elements. —**mul′ti·tu′di·nous·ly,** *adv.* —**mul′ti·tu′di·nous·ness,** *n.*

mul·ti·us′er sys′tem (mul′tē yoo′zər, mul′tī-), *n.* a computer system in which multiple terminals connect to a host computer that handles processing tasks.

mul·ti·va·lent (mul′ti vā′lənt, mul tiv′ə lənt), *adj.* **1.** having a chemical valence of three or higher. **2. a.** containing several kinds of antibody. **b.** pertaining to an antibody that contains many antigen-binding sites. —**mul′ti·va′lence,** *n.*

mul·ti·var·i·ate (mul′ti vâr′ē it), *adj. Statistics.* (of a combined distribution) having more than one variate or variable.

mul·ti·ver·si·ty (mul′ti vûr′si tē), *n., pl.* **-ties.** a university with several campuses, each with many component schools, divisions, etc.

mul·ti·vi·ta·min (mul′ti vī′tə min, mul′ti vī′-), *adj.* **1.** containing or consisting of several vitamins. —*n.* **2.** a compound of several vitamins.

mum¹ (mum), *adj.* silent: *to keep mum.*

mum² (mum), *n.* CHRYSANTHEMUM.

mum·ble (mum′bəl), *v.,* **-bled, -bling,** *n.* —*v.i., v.t.* **1.** to utter in a soft, indistinct manner. —*n.* **2.** a soft, indistinct utterance or sound. —**mum′bler,** *n.* —**mum′bling·ly,** *adv.*

mum·bo jum·bo (mum′bō jum′bō), *n., pl.* **mumbo jum·bos. 1.** meaningless incantation or ritual. **2.** senseless or pretentious language, usu. designed to obscure or confuse. **3.** an object of superstitious awe or reverence.

mum·mer (mum′ər), *n.* **1.** a person who wears a mask or fantastic costume while merrymaking or taking part in a pantomime, as at Christmas. **2.** an actor, esp. a pantomimist.

mum·mi·fy (mum′ə fī′), *v.,* **-fied, -fy·ing.** —*v.t.* **1.** to make (a dead body) into a mummy. **2.** to make (something) resemble a mummy. —*v.i.* **3.** to dry or shrivel up. —**mum′mi·fi·ca′tion,** *n.*

mum·my (mum′ē), *n., pl.* **-mies. 1.** the dead body of a human being or animal preserved by the ancient Egyptian process or some similar method of embalming. **2.** a dead body dried and preserved by nature. **3.** a withered living being. —*v.t.* **4.** to mummify.

mum′my bag′, *n.* a snug-fitting sleeping bag tapered from the shoulders to the feet, enclosing both the body and head except for a small opening for the face. [so called because its shape resembles a wrapped Egyptian mummy]

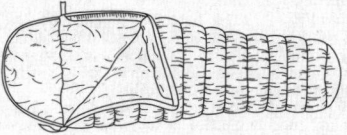

mummy bag

mumps (mumps), *n. (used with a sing. v.)* an infectious disease characterized by inflammatory swelling of the parotid and usu. other salivary glands, and sometimes by inflammation of the testes or ovaries, caused by a paramyxovirus.

munch (munch), *v.t., v.i.* to chew steadily or vigorously and often audibly. —**munch′a·ble,** *adj., n.* —**munch′er,** *n.*

munch·ies (mun′chēz), *n.pl. Informal.* **1.** food suitable for snacking. **2.** hunger pangs: *an attack of the munchies.*

munch·kin (munch′kin), *n. (often cap.)* a small person, esp. one who is dwarfish or elfin in appearance.

mun·dane (mun dān′, mun′dān), *adj.* **1.** of or pertaining to this world or earth as contrasted with heaven; earthly: *mundane affairs.* **2.** ordinary; banal. —**mun·dane′ly,** *adv.* —**mun·dan′i·ty** (-dan′i tē), *n.*

mung′ bean′ (mung), *n.* **1.** a plant, *Vigna radiata,* of the legume family, cultivated for its edible seeds, pods, and young sprouts. **2.** the seed or pod of this plant.

Mu·nich (myoo′nik), *n.* the capital of Bavaria, in SW Germany. 1,188,800. German, **München.**

Mu′nich Pact′, *n.* a pact signed by Great Britain, France, Italy, and Germany in 1938, by which the Sudetenland was ceded to Germany: cited as an instance of political appeasement. Also called **Mu′nich Agree′ment.**

mu·nic·i·pal (myoo nis′ə pəl), *adj.* **1.** of or pertaining to a city, town, etc., or its local government: *municipal elections.* —*n.* **2.** a municipal bond. —**mu·nic′i·pal·ly,** *adv.*

munic′ipal bond′, *n.* a bond issued by a state or local authority to finance projects.

munic′ipal court′, *n.* a court whose jurisdiction is confined to a city or municipality, with criminal jurisdiction usu. corresponding to that of a police court and civil jurisdiction over small cases.

mu·nic·i·pal·i·ty (myoo nis′ə pal′i tē), *n., pl.* **-ties.** a city, town, village, or borough possessing corporate existence and usu. its own local government.

mu·nif·i·cent (myoo nif′ə sənt), *adj.* characterized by or displaying great generosity. —**mu·nif′i·cence,** *n.* —**mu·nif′i·cent·ly,** *adv.*

mu·ni·tion (myoo nish′ən), *n.* **1.** Usu., **munitions.** materials used in war, esp. weapons and ammunition. —*v.t.* **2.** to provide with munitions.

mu·on (myoo′on), *n.* an unstable lepton of mass approximately 207 times greater than the electron's mass. —**mu·on′ic,** *adj.*

mu·ral (myoor′əl), *n.* **1.** a large picture painted directly on a wall or ceiling. **2.** a greatly enlarged photograph attached directly to a wall. —*adj.* **3.** of, pertaining to, or like a wall. **4.** painted on or attached to a wall. —**mu′ral·ist,** *n.*

mur·der (mûr′dər), *n.* **1.** the unlawful killing of a person, esp. when done with deliberation or premeditation or occurring during the commission of another serious crime **(first-degree murder)** or with intent but without deliberation or premeditation (**second-degree murder**). **2.** something injurious, immoral, or otherwise censurable: *to get away with murder.* **3.** something extremely difficult or unpleasant: *That exam was murder!* —*v.t.* **4.** to kill by an act constituting murder. **5.** to kill or slaughter barbarously. **6.** to spoil or mar through incompetence: *The singer murdered the aria.* **7.** *Informal.* to defeat thoroughly. —*v.i.* **8.** to commit murder. —*Proverb.* **9. Murder will out,** wrongdoing will be discovered eventually.

mur•der•er (mûr′dər ər), *n.* a person who commits murder.

mur•der•ess (mûr′dər is), *n.* a woman who commits murder.

mur′der one′, *n.* first-degree murder. See under MURDER (def. 1).

mur•der•ous (mûr′dər əs), *adj.* **1.** of the nature of or involving murder: *a murderous deed.* **2.** guilty of, bent on, or capable of murder. **3.** *Informal.* extremely difficult, dangerous, or unpleasant: *murderous heat.* —**mur′der•ous•ly,** *adv.* —**mur′der•ous•ness,** *n.*

mur′der two′, *n.* second-degree murder. See under MURDER (def. 1).

Mur•frees•bor•o (mûr′frēz bûr′ō, -bur′ō), *n.* a city in central Tennessee: Civil War battle 1862. 32,845.

mu′ri•at′ic ac′id (myŏŏr′ē at′ik, myōōr′-), *n.* HYDROCHLORIC ACID.

murk•y (mûr′kē), *adj.,* **murk•i•er, murk•i•est. 1.** dark, gloomy, and cheerless. **2.** obscure or thick, as with mist. **3.** vague; unclear: *a murky statement.* —**murk′i•ly,** *adv.* —**murk′i•ness,** *n.*

mur•mur (mûr′mər), *n.* **1.** a low and indistinct continuous sound, as of a brook or the wind, or of distant voices. **2.** a mumbled or private expression of discontent. **3.** an abnormal continuous or periodic sound heard within the body by auscultation, esp. one originating in the heart valves. —*v.i.* **4.** to make a low and indistinct continuous sound. **5.** to complain in a low tone or in private. —*v.t.* **6.** to express in murmurs.

Mur′phy bed′ (mûr′fē), *n.* a bed built so that it can be folded or swung into a closet.

Mur′phy's Law′, *n.* the facetious proposition that if something can go wrong, it will. Also called **Mur′phy's First′ Law′.** [after a fictitious *Murphy,* allegedly the name of a bungling mechanic in U.S. Navy educational cartoons of the 1950s]

Mur•ray (mûr′ē, mur′ē), *n.* **1. Andrew,** 1818–1917, South African clergyman. **2. Sir (George) Gilbert (Aimé),** 1866–1957, English classical scholar. **3. Sir James Augustus Henry,** 1837–1915, Scottish lexicographer and philologist. **4. Lindley,** 1745–1826, English grammarian, born in the U.S. **5.** a river in SE Australia, flowing W along the border between Victoria and New South Wales, through SE South Australia into the Indian Ocean. 1200 mi. (1930 km) long.

mus•ca•dine (mus′kə din, -dīn′), *n.* a grape, *Vitis rotundifolia,* of the southern U.S., having dull purple, thick-skinned musky fruit and being the origin of many grape varieties.

mus•cat (mus′kat, -kat), *n.* **1.** a variety of grape having a pronounced sweet aroma and flavor, used for making wine and raisins. **2.** the vine bearing this fruit.

Mus•cat or **Mas•qat** (mus kat′), *n.* the capital of Oman. 250,000.

mus•ca•tel (mus′kə tel′, mus′kə tel′), *n.* **1.** a sweet wine made from muscat grapes. **2.** a muscat grape or raisin.

mus•cle (mus′əl), *n., v.,* **-cled, -cling.** —*n.* **1.** a tissue composed of elongated cells, the contraction of which produces movement in the body. **2.** a specific bundle of such tissue. **3.** muscular strength; brawn. **4.** power or force, esp. of a coercive nature: *They put muscle into their policy and sent the marines.* —*v.i.* **5.** *Informal.* to make one's way by force or fraud (often fol. by *in* or *into*). —*v.t.* **6.** *Informal.* to push or move by force or muscular strength: *to muscle a bill through Congress.* —**mus′cly,** *adj.*

mus•cle-bound (mus′əl bound′), *adj.* **1.** having enlarged and inelastic muscles, as from excessive exercise. **2.** rigid; inflexible: *musclebound rules.*

mus′cle fi′ber, *n.* one of the structural cells of a muscle.

mus•cle•man (mus′əl man′), *n., pl.* **-men. 1.** a man with a muscular physique. **2.** *Slang.* BODYGUARD.

mus′cle spin′dle, *n.* a proprioceptor in skeletal muscle, composed of muscle fibers and sensory nerve endings, that conveys information on the state of muscle stretch.

Mus•co•vite (mus′kə vīt′), *n.* **1.** a native or inhabitant of Moscow. **2.** a native or inhabitant of the Grand Duchy of Muscovy. **3.** (*l.c.*) common light-colored mica, essentially $KAl_3Si_3O_{10}(OH)_2$, used as an electrical insulator. **4.** RUSSIAN (def. 1a). —*adj.* **5.** of or pertaining to Moscow, Muscovy, or the Muscovites.

Mus•co•vy (mus′kə vē), *n.* Also called **Grand Duchy of Muscovy.** a principality founded c1271 and centered on Moscow: gained control over the neighboring Great Russian principalities and established the Russian Empire under the czars.

Mus′covy duck′, *n.* a large, crested, widely domesticated wild duck, *Cairina moschata,* of tropical America. Also called **musk duck.**

mus•cu•lar (mus′kyə lər), *adj.* **1.** of or pertaining to muscle or the muscles. **2.** having well-developed muscles; brawny. —**mus′cu•lar′i•ty,** *n.* —**mus′cu•lar•ly,** *adv.*

mus′cular dys′trophy, *n.* a hereditary disease characterized by gradual wasting of the muscles.

mus•cu•la•ture (mus′kyə lə chər, -chŏŏr′), *n.* the muscular system of the body or of its parts.

muse (myŏŏz), *v.,* **mused, mus•ing.** —*v.i.* **1.** to think or meditate in silence. —*v.t.* **2.** to say or think meditatively. —**mus′er,** *n.*

Muse (myŏŏz), *n.* **1.** one of the nine Greek goddesses, daughters of Zeus and Mnemosyne, who presided over the arts: Calliope, Clio, Erato, Euterpe, Melpomene, Polyhymnia, Terpsichore, Thalia, and Urania. **2.** (*sometimes l.c.*) the inspiration that motivates a poet, artist, or thinker. **3.** (*l.c.*) a poet.

mu•se•um (myŏŏ zē′əm), *n.* a place where works of art, scientific specimens, or other objects of permanent value are kept and displayed.

muse′um piece′, *n.* **1.** something suitable for keeping and exhibiting in a museum. **2.** something very old-fashioned or decrepit.

mush¹ (mush *or,* esp. for 2–4, mŏŏsh), *n.* **1.** a thick mixture made by boiling meal, water, or milk. **2.** cornmeal, in water or milk. **3.** any thick, soft mass. **3.** mawkish sentimentality or amorousness. —*v.t.* **4.** to squeeze or crush; crunch.

mush² (mush), *v.i.* **1.** to go or travel, esp. over snow with a dog team and sled. —*interj.* **2.** (used as an order to start or speed up a dog team).

mush•room (mush′rŏŏm, -rŏŏm), *n.* **1.** any of various fleshy fungi, including the toadstools, puffballs, coral fungi, and morels. **2.** MEADOW MUSHROOM. **3.** anything of similar shape or correspondingly rapid growth. **4.** a large, mushroom-shaped cloud of smoke or rubble, formed in the atmosphere as a result of an explosion, esp. a nuclear explosion. —*adj.* **5.** of or containing mushrooms. **6.** resembling a mushroom in shape or rapid growth. —*v.i.* **7.** to spread, grow, or develop quickly. **8.** to gather mushrooms. **9.** to assume the shape of a mushroom.

mush′room cloud′, *n.* MUSHROOM (def. 4).

mush•y (mush′ē, mŏŏsh′ē), *adj.,* **mush•i•er, mush•i•est. 1.** resembling mush; pulpy. **2.** overly emotional or sentimental: *mushy love letters.* —**mush′i•ly,** *adv.* —**mush′i•ness,** *n.*

mu•sic (myŏŏ′zik), *n.* **1.** an art of sound in time that expresses ideas and emotions through the elements of rhythm, melody, harmony, and dynamics. **2.** sounds organized to have melody, rhythm, harmony, and dynamics. **3.** the written or printed score of a musical composition. —*Idiom.* **4. music to one's ears,** excellent news.

mu•si•cal (myŏŏ′zi kəl), *adj.* **1.** of, pertaining to, or producing music: *a musical instrument.* **2.** of the nature of or resembling music; melodious; harmonious. **3.** fond of or skilled in music. **4.** set to or accompanied by music: *a musical entertainment.* —*n.* **5.** Also called **musical comedy.** a play or motion picture in which the story line is interspersed with or developed by songs, dances, and the like. —**mu′si•cal•ly,** *adv.* —**mu′si•cal•i•ty, mu′si•cal•ness,** *n.*

mu′sical chairs′, *n.* **1.** a children's game in which players march to music around a set of chairs one less in number than the number of players, the object being to find a seat when the music stops abruptly. **2.** a situation or series of events in which jobs, decisions, prospects, etc., are changed with confusing rapidity.

mu′sical com′edy, *n.* **1.** MUSICAL (def. 5). **2.** the genre comprising musical comedy.

mu•si•cale (myŏŏ′zi kal′), *n.* a social occasion featuring music.

mu′sical saw′, *n.* a handsaw played as a musical instrument with a violin bow or a hammer while the saw is bent with varying tension to change the pitch.

mu′sic box′, *n.* a small container holding a device to produce music mechanically, esp. when the lid is lifted.

mu′sic hall′, *n.* **1.** an auditorium for musical performances. **2.** a vaudeville theater. **3.** Also called **variety.** a form of entertainment in Britain that resembled American vaudeville.

mu•si•cian (myŏŏ zish′ən), *n.* a person who performs music, esp. professionally. —**mu•si′cian•ly,** *adv.* —**mu•si′cian•ship′,** *n.*

mu•si•col•o•gy (myŏŏ′zi kol′ə jē), *n.* the scholarly or scientific study of music, as in historical research, musical theory, or the physical nature of sound. —**mu′si•co•log′i•cal** (-kə loj′i kəl), *adj.* —**mu′si•co•log′i•cal•ly,** *adv.* —**mu′si•col′o•gist,** *n.*

mu′sic vid′eo, *n.* a videotape featuring a dramatized rendition of a popular song.

musk (musk), *n.* **1.** a pungent glandular secretion of the male musk deer: used in perfumery. **2.** a similar secretion of other animals, as the muskrat. **3.** the odor of musk, or some similar odor. **4.** any of several plants, as the monkey flower, having a musky fragrance.

musk′ deer′, *n.* a small, antlerless deer, *Moschus moschiferus,* of central Asia: the male has tusks and secretes musk.

musk′ duck′, *n.* **1.** MUSCOVY DUCK. **2.** a drab-plumaged Australian duck, *Biziura lobata,* having a leathery flap under the bill.

musk•eg (mus′keg), *n.* a bog of N North America, commonly having sphagnum mosses, sedge, and stunted black spruce and tamarack trees.

mus•kel•lunge (mus′kə lunj′), *n., pl.* **-lung•es,** (*esp. collectively*) **-lunge.** a large pike, *Esox masquinongy,* of the Great Lakes and Mississippi drainage.

mus•ket (mus′kit), *n.* a heavy, large-caliber smoothbore gun for infantry soldiers: predecessor of the modern rifle.

mus•ket•eer (mus′ki tēr′), *n.* a soldier armed with a musket.

mus•ket•ry (mus′ki trē), *n.* **1.** the technique of bringing small arms fire to bear on specific targets. **2.** muskets collectively. **3.** musketeers collectively.

musk•mel•on (musk′mel′ən), *n.* **1.** a round or oblong melon, occurring in many varieties, having a juicy, often aromatic, sweet, yellow, white, or green, edible flesh. **2.** the plant, *Cucumis melo reticulatus,* of the gourd family, bearing this fruit. **3.** CANTALOUPE (def. 1).

Mus•ko•ge•an or **Mus•kho•ge•an** (mus kō′gē ən), *n.* a family of

American Indian languages spoken or formerly spoken in the southeastern U.S., and, since the Indian removals of the 1830s, in Oklahoma, including the languages of the Choctaw, Chickasaw, Creek, and Mikasuki.

Mus·ko·gee (mus kō′gē), *n., pl.* **-gees,** (*esp. collectively*) **-gee. 1. a.** a member of a group of American Indian tribes that formed the dominant element in the Creek confederacy. **b.** any member of the Creek confederacy. **2.** the language of the Muskogee; Creek.

musk′ox′ or **musk′ ox′,** *n., pl.* **-ox·en.** a large bovid, *Ovibos moschatus,* of arctic regions of North America and Greenland, with shaggy fur and horns that curve downward.

musk·rat (musk′rat′), *n., pl.* **-rats,** (*esp. collectively*) **-rat. 1.** either of two large, aquatic, North American cricetid rodents of the genus *Ondatra.* **2.** its glossy, dark brown fur, used for coats, hats, trimming, etc.

musk′ rose′, *n.* a rose, *Rosa moschata,* of the Mediterranean region, having white, musk-scented flowers.

musk′ tur′tle, *n.* any of several aquatic turtles of the genus *Sternotherus,* of North America, having a musky odor.

musk·y (mus′kē), *adj.,* **musk·i·er, musk·i·est.** of or like musk, as an odor: *a musky perfume.* **—musk′i·ness,** *n.*

Mus·lim (muz′lim, mŏŏz′-, mŏŏs′-) also **Moslem,** *adj., n., pl.* **-lims, -lim. —adj. 1.** pertaining to the religion, law, or civilization of Islam. **—n. 2.** an adherent of Islam. **3.** BLACK MUSLIM. **—Usage.** MOSLEM, once the more widely used form, still has currency but has declined in favor of MUSLIM. The use of MUHAMMADAN in reference to Islam or its adherents is rejected by Muslims themselves, as is MUHAMMADANISM for Islam.

mus·lin (muz′lin) *n.* a plain-weave cotton fabric made in various degrees of fineness, used esp. for sheets.

muss (mus), *v.t.* **1.** to put into disorder; make messy; rumple (often fol. by *up*). **—n. 2.** a state of disorder or untidiness.

mus·sel (mus′əl), *n.* any bivalve mollusk, an edible marine bivalve of the family Mytilidae and a freshwater clam of the family Unionidae.

Mus·so·li·ni (mŏŏs′ə lē′nē, mōō′sə-), *n.* **Benito** (*"Il Duce"*), 1883–1945, Italian Fascist leader: premier of Italy 1922–43.

muss·y (mus′ē), *adj.,* **muss·i·er, muss·i·est.** untidy, messy, or rumpled. **—muss′i·ly,** *adv.* **—muss′i·ness,** *n.*

must[1] (must), *auxiliary v. pres. sing.* and *pl. 1st, 2nd,* and *3rd pers.* **must,** *past* **must;** *adj., n.* **—auxiliary verb. 1.** (used to express obligation or imperative requirement): *I must keep my promise. We really must go now.* **2.** (used to express requirement or compulsion by law, social convention, or morality): *The rules must be obeyed. I must say, you look wonderful.* **3.** (used to express advisability or desirability): *You really must read this book.* **4.** (used to express inevitability, necessity, or compulsion by natural laws): *All good things must come to an end. One must eat to live.* **5.** (used to express logical necessity): *There must be some mistake.* **6.** (used to express strong probability or reasonable expectation): *You must be joking. He must be at least 70.* **7.** (used to express intention or determination, often persistence in something unwelcome): *if you must know; Must you repeat everything I say?* **—adj. 8.** necessary; vital: *A raincoat is must clothing in this area.* **—n. 9.** something necessary, vital, or required: *Getting enough sleep is a must.*

must[2] (must), *n.* (in winemaking) the juice of grapes or other fruit during fermentation.

must[3] (must), *n.* mold; moldiness; mustiness: *a castle harboring the must of centuries.*

mus·tache (mus′tash, mə stash′), *n.* **1.** the hair growing on the upper lip. **2.** such hair on men, often trimmed in various shapes. **3.** hairs or bristles near the mouth of an animal. **4.** a stripe of color, or elongated feathers, on the side of the head of a bird. **—mus′tached,** *adj.*

mus·tang (mus′tang), *n.* a small, hardy horse of the American plains, descended from Spanish stock. [< Spanish *mestengo* stray beast]

mus·tard (mus′tərd), *n.* **1.** a pungent powder or paste prepared from the seed of the mustard plant, used esp. as a food seasoning or condiment. **2.** any of various acrid or pungent plants, esp. of the genus *Brassica,* as *B. juncea,* the chief source of commercial mustard, and *Sinapis alba,* the white mustard.

mus′tard gas′, *n.* an oily liquid, $C_4H_8Cl_2S$, used, esp. in World War I, as a chemical-warfare gas for its irritating, blinding, and poisonous properties.

Mus′tard Seed′, The, a parable of Jesus. Matt. 13:31–32; Mark 4:30–32; Luke 13:18–19.

mus·ter (mus′tər), *v.t.* **1.** to assemble (troops, a ship's crew, etc.), as for battle or inspection. **2.** to gather or summon (often fol. by *up*): *He mustered all his courage.* **—v.i. 3.** to assemble for inspection, service, etc. **4.** to come together; collect; assemble; gather. **5. muster out,** to discharge from military service. **—n. 6.** an assembling of troops or persons for formal inspection or other purposes. **7.** an assemblage or collection. **8.** Also called **mus′ter roll′.** (formerly) a list of the persons in a military or naval unit. **—Idiom. 9. pass muster,** to be judged as acceptable in appearance or performance.

Mus′ter Day′, *n.* the annual day for enrollment in the militia of all able men aged 18 to 45, according to a law established in 1792 and in effect until after the Civil War.

musth or **must** (must), *n.* a state or condition of violent, destructive frenzy occurring with the rutting season in male elephants.

must·n't (mus′ənt), contraction of *must not.*

mus·ty (mus′tē), *adj.,* **-ti·er, -ti·est. 1.** having an odor or flavor sug-

gestive of mold, as old buildings or stale food. **2.** obsolete; outdated; antiquated: *musty laws.* **3.** dull; apathetic. **—mus′ti·ness,** *n.*

mu·ta·ble (myōō′tə bəl), *adj.* **1.** liable or subject to change or alteration. **2.** given to changing; constantly changing; fickle or inconstant: *the mutable ways of fortune.* **—mu′ta·bil′i·ty,** *n.* **—mu′ta·bly,** *adv.*

mu·ta·gen (myōō′tə jan, -jen′), *n.* a substance or preparation capable of inducing or accelerating mutation. **—mu′ta·gen′ic,** *adj.* **—mu′ta·gen′i·cal·ly,** *adv.* **—mu′ta·ge·nic′i·ty** (-jə nis′i tē), *n.*

mu·ta·gen·e·sis (myōō′tə jen′ə sis), *n.* the origin and development of a mutation. **—mu′ta·ge·net′ic** (-jə net′ik), *adj.*

mu·tant (myōōt′nt), *n.* **1.** a new type of organism produced as the result of mutation. **—adj. 2.** undergoing or resulting from mutation.

mu·tate (myōō′tāt), *v.,* **-tat·ed, -tat·ing. —v.i. 1.** to undergo mutation. **—v.t. 2.** to cause to undergo mutation. **—mu′ta·tive** (-tə tiv), *adj.*

mu·ta·tion (myōō tā′shən), *n.* **1.** *Biol.* **a.** a sudden departure from the parent type in one or more heritable characteristics, caused by a change in a gene or a chromosome. **b.** an individual, species, or the like resulting from such a departure. **2.** the act or process of changing. **3.** a change or alteration, as in form or nature. **4.** a change in a speech sound caused by assimilation to a nearby sound, esp. umlaut. **—mu·ta′tion·al,** *adj.* **—mu·ta′tion·al·ly,** *adv.*

mute (myōōt), *adj., mut·er, mut·est, n., v., mut·ed, mut·ing. —adj.* **1.** silent; refraining from speech or utterance. **2.** not emitting or having sound of any kind. **3.** incapable of speech; dumb. **4.** (of letters) silent; not pronounced. **5.** *Law.* (of a person who has been arraigned) making no plea or refusing to stand trial: *to stand mute.* **—n. 6.** a person incapable of speech. **7.** *Law.* a person who stands mute when arraigned. **8.** a mechanical device for muffling the tone of a musical instrument. **9.** STOP (def. 37). **—v.t. 10.** to deaden or muffle the sound of. **11.** to reduce the intensity of (a color) by the addition of another color. **—mute′ly,** *adv.* **—mute′ness,** *n.*

mute′ swan′, *n.* a soundless white Eurasian swan, *Cygnus olor,* widely introduced in other parts of the world.

mu·ti·late (myōōt′l āt′), *v.t.,* **-lat·ed, -lat·ing. 1.** to injure or disfigure by removing or irreparably damaging parts: *to mutilate a painting.* **2.** to deprive (a person or animal) of a limb or other essential part. **—mu′ti·la′tion,** *n.* **—mu′ti·la′tor,** *n.*

mu·ti·neer (myōōt′n ēr′), *n.* a person who mutinies.

mu·ti·nous (myōōt′n əs), *adj.* **1.** disposed to or engaged in revolt against authority. **2.** characterized by mutiny; rebellious. **3.** difficult to control: *mutinous feelings.* **—mu′ti·nous·ly,** *adv.*

mu·ti·ny (myōōt′n ē), *n., pl.* **-nies,** *v.,* **-nied, -ny·ing. —n. 1.** rebellion against constituted authority, esp. by sailors or soldiers against their officers. **—v.i. 2.** to commit mutiny.

mutt (mut), *n. Slang.* a mongrel dog.

Mutt′ and Jeff′, *n.* a very short and a very tall person who are paired as companions, teammates, or associates. [after the characters in a cartoon strip of the same name created by U.S. cartoonist Harry C. "Bud" Fisher (1885–1954)]

mut·ter (mut′ər), *v.i.* **1.** to utter words indistinctly or in a low tone; murmur. **2.** to complain murmuringly; grumble. **—v.t. 3.** to utter indistinctly or in a low tone. **—n. 4.** the act or utterance of a person who mutters. **—mut′ter·er,** *n.* **—mut′ter·ing·ly,** *adv.*

mut·ton (mut′n), *n.* the flesh of a mature sheep, used as food. **—mut′ton·y,** *adj.*

mut·ton·chops (mut′n chops′), *n.pl.* side whiskers that are narrow at the temples and broad and trimmed short at the jawline, the chin being shaved both in front and beneath. Also called **mut′tonchop whisk′ers.**

mu·tu·al (myōō′chōō əl), *adj.* **1.** possessed, experienced, performed, etc., by each of two or more with respect to the other; reciprocal: *mutual respect.* **2.** having the same relation each toward the other: *mutual enemies.* **3.** held in common; shared: *mutual interests.* **4.** pertaining to a form of corporate organization without stockholders, in which members proportionately share profits and losses, expenses, etc. **—mu′tu·al′i·ty** (-al′i tē), *n.* **—mu′tu·al·ly,** *adv.*

mu′tual fund′, *n.* an investment company that is capitalized by the constant sale of its stock, which it is obligated to repurchase from its shareholders on demand.

mu′tually exclu′sive, *adj.* pertaining to a situation involving two or more events, possibilities, etc., in which the occurrence of one precludes the occurrence of the other: *mutually exclusive plans of action.*

mu·tule (myōō′chōōl), *n.* a projecting flat block under the corona of the Doric cornice.

muu·muu (mōō′mōō′), *n., pl.* **-muus. 1.** a long, loose-hanging dress, usu. brightly colored or patterned, worn esp. by Hawaiian women. **2.** a similar dress worn as a housedress.

Mu·zak (myōō′zak), *Trademark.* recorded background music transmitted by radio, telephone, or satellite, as to offices or restaurants.

muz·zle (muz′əl), *n., v.,* **-zled, -zling. —n. 1.** the projecting part of the head of an animal, including jaws, mouth, and nose. **2.** the mouth, or end for discharge, of the barrel of a gun, pistol, etc. **3.** a device, usu. an arrangement of straps or wires, placed over an animal's mouth to prevent the animal from biting, eating, etc. **—v.t. 4.** to put a muzzle on (an animal or its mouth). **5.** to restrain from speech, the expression of opinion, etc. **—muz′zler,** *n.*

muz·zy (muz′ē), *adj.,* **-zi·er, -zi·est.** *Informal.* **1.** confused; muddled. **2.** dull; mentally hazy. **—muz′zi·ly,** *adv.* **—muz′zi·ness,** *n.*

Mv, *Chem. Symbol.* mendelevium.

MVP or **M.V.P.,** Most Valuable Player.

MX, missile, experimental: a ten-warhead U.S. intercontinental ballistic missile.

my (mī), *pron.* **1.** a form of the possessive case of **I** used as an attributive adjective: *My soup is cold.* **2.** (used in various forms of address): *my lord; my dear Mrs. Adams.* **3.** (used in various exclamations of surprise, dismay, disagreement, etc.): *My goodness! my foot!* —*interj.* **4.** (used as an exclamation of mild surprise or dismay): *My, what a big house this is!* —**Usage.** See **ME.**

My·an·mar (mī än′mär), *n.* Union of, official name of BURMA.

My′ An·to·ni′a (an′tə nē′ə), a novel (1918) by Willa Cather.

my·as·the·ni·a (mī′əs thē′nē ə), *n.* muscle weakness. —**my′as·then′ic** (-then′ik), *adj.*

my·ce·li·um (mī sē′lē əm), *n., pl.* **-li·a** (-lē ə). the mass of hyphae that form the vegetative part of a fungus. —**my·ce′li·al,** *adj.*

My·ce·nae (mī sē′nē), *n.* an ancient city in S Greece, in Argolis: important ruins. —**My·ce′nae·an, My·ce′ne·an,** *adj., n.*

-mycete, a combining form meaning "mushroom, fungus."

-mycin, a combining form used in the names of antibiotics, usu. fungal derivatives: *erythromycin.*

myco-, a combining form meaning "mushroom, fungus": *mycology.* Also, *esp. before a vowel,* **myc-.**

my·col·o·gy (mī kol′ə jē), *n.* **1.** the branch of biology dealing with fungi. **2.** fungi as a whole. —**my′co·log′i·cal** (-kə loj′i kəl), **my′co·log′ic,** *adj.* —**my·col′o·gist,** *n.*

my·co·sis (mī kō′sis), *n.* **1.** the presence of parasitic fungi in or on any part of the body. **2.** the condition caused by the presence of such fungi. —**my·cot′ic** (-kot′ik), *adj.*

My′ Coun′try, 'Tis′ of Thee′, AMERICA (def. 5).

my·e·lin (mī′ə lin), *n.* a soft, white, fatty material in the membrane of Schwann cells and certain neuroglial cells of the nervous system: the substance of the myelin sheath. —**my′e·lin′ic,** *adj.*

my′elin sheath′, *n.* a discontinuous wrapping of myelin around certain nerve axons, serving to speed nerve impulses to muscles and other effectors.

my·e·li·tis (mī′ə lī′tis), *n.* **1.** inflammation of the substance of the spinal cord. **2.** inflammation of the bone marrow; osteomyelitis.

My′ Fair′ La′dy, a musical (1956) with lyrics by Alan Jay Lerner and music by Frederick Loewe: based on George Bernard Shaw's play *Pygmalion.*

My Lai (mē′ lī′), *n.* a hamlet in S Vietnam: U.S. forces' massacre of South Vietnamese civilians 1968.

my·na or **myn·ah** or **mi·na** (mī′nə), *n., pl.* **-nas** or **-nahs.** any of various Asian birds of the starling family, esp. of the genera *Acridotheres* and *Gracula,* certain species of which have the ability to mimic speech when kept as pets.

myocar′dial infarc′tion (or **in′farct**), *n.* HEART ATTACK. *Abbr.:* MI

my·o·car·di·um (mī′ə kär′dē əm), *n., pl.* **-di·a** (-dē ə). the muscular substance of the heart. —**my′o·car′di·al,** *adj.*

my·o·glo·bin (mī′ə glō′bin, mī′ə glō′-) also **my·o·he·mo·glo·bin** (mī′ə hē′mə glō′bin), *n.* hemoglobin of muscle, weighing less and carrying more oxygen and less carbon monoxide than blood hemoglobin.

My′ Old′ Kentuck′y Home′, a song (1853) by Stephen Foster.

my·ol·o·gy (mī ol′ə jē), *n.* the science or branch of anatomy dealing with muscles. —**my·o·log′ic** (mī′ə loj′ik), *adj.* —**my·ol′o·gist,** *n.*

my·op·a·thy (mī op′ə thē), *n., pl.* **-thies.** any abnormality or disease of muscle tissue. —**my′o·path′ic** (mī′ə path′ik), *adj.*

my·o·pi·a (mī ō′pē ə), *n.* **1.** a condition of the eye in which parallel rays are focused in front of the retina, objects being seen distinctly only when near to the eye; nearsightedness. **2.** lack of foresight or discernment; obtuseness. **3.** narrow-mindedness; intolerance. —**my·op′ic** (-op′ik, -ō′pik), *adj.* —**my·op′i·cal·ly,** *adv.*

my·o·si·tis (mī′ə sī′tis), *n.* inflammation of muscle tissue. —**my′o·sit′ic** (-sit′ik), *adj.*

my·o·so·tis (mī′ə sō′tis) also **my′o·sote,** *n.* any plant belonging to the genus *Myosotis,* of the borage family, having basal leaves and pink or white flowers, as the forget-me-not.

myria-, a combining form meaning "10,000," used esp. in the names of metric units equal to 10,000 of the unit denoted by the base word: *myriagram; myriameter.*

myr·i·ad (mir′ē əd), *n.* **1.** an indefinitely great number of persons or things. **2.** ten thousand. —*adj.* **3.** of an indefinitely great number; innumerable. **4.** having innumerable phases, aspects, variations, etc.

myrrh (mûr), *n.* **1.** an aromatic, bitter gum resin from certain Arabian and E African woody plants, used chiefly in making incense and perfumes: one of three gifts, the other two being gold and frankincense, given by the Magi to the infant Jesus. Matt. 2:11. **2.** any of these plants, esp. a small thorny tree, *Commiphora myrrha,* of the bursera family.

myr·tle (mûr′tl), *n.* **1.** any plant of the genus *Myrtus,* esp. *M. communis* of S Europe, having evergreen leaves, fragrant white flowers, and aromatic berries. **2.** any of certain unrelated plants, as the periwinkle, *Vinca minor,* and California laurel, *Umbellularia californica.* **3.** Also called **myr′tle green′.** dark bluish green.

my·self (mī self′), *pron.* **1.** a reflexive form of **ME** (used as the direct or indirect object of a verb or as the object of a preposition): *I excused my-*

self from the table. **2.** (used as an intensive of I or ME): *I myself don't like it.* **3.** (used in place of I or ME in various compound and comparative constructions): *My wife and myself agree. He knows as much about the case as myself. No one is more to blame than myself.* **4.** my normal or customary self: *I wasn't myself when I said that.* —**Usage.** Questions are raised with certain uses of MYSELF and other -SELF forms in place of the personal pronouns (*I, me, you,* etc.). MYSELF as a single subject (*Myself shall be the messenger*) is mainly poetic or literary. As a simple nonreflexive object, the -SELF form is not uncommon in speech: *The letter was addressed to myself. Packages had come for everyone but themselves.* As part of a compound subject, object, or complement, MYSELF and to a lesser extent the other -SELF forms are common in informal speech and personal writing, somewhat less common in more formal speech and writing: *Many friends welcomed my husband and myself back home. His agent and himself spoke to the press.* Such forms are similarly used after *as* or *than* in all varieties of speech and writing: *No contributors have been more generous than yourselves.* Many usage guides advise that these uses of the -SELF forms are characteristic only of informal speech and should not occur in writing. See also ME.

My′ Song′ Is′ Love′ Unknown′, a Christian hymn with words by Samuel Crossman (1624–83).

mys·te·ri·ous (mi stēr′ē əs), *adj.* **1.** involving or full of mystery: *a mysterious phone call.* **2.** suggesting or implying a mystery: *a mysterious smile.* **3.** of obscure nature; puzzling; inexplicable: *a mysterious inscription on an ancient tomb.* —**mys·te′ri·ous·ly,** *adv.*

mys·ter·y (mis′tə rē, -trē), *n., pl.* **-ter·ies. 1.** anything that is kept secret or remains unexplained or unknown: *the mysteries of nature.* **2.** a person or thing having qualities that arouse curiosity or speculation: *The masked guest was a mystery to everyone.* **3.** a novel, film, or the like whose plot involves the solving of a puzzle, esp. a crime. **4.** the quality of being obscure or puzzling: *an air of mystery.* **5.** any truth unknowable except by divine revelation. **6.** (in the Christian religion) **a.** a sacramental rite. **b.** the Eucharist. **7.** an incident or scene in the life or passion of Christ, or in the life of the Virgin Mary. **8. mysteries, a.** ancient religions with secret rites and rituals known only to initiates. **b.** any rites or secrets known only to initiates. **c.** (in the Christian religion) the Eucharistic elements. **9.** MYSTERY PLAY.

mys′tery play′, *n.* a medieval drama based on a Bible story, usu. about Christ. Compare MIRACLE PLAY, MORALITY PLAY.

mys·tic (mis′tik), *adj.* **1.** characterized by esoteric, otherworldly, or symbolic practices or content, as certain religious ceremonies and art. **2.** involving mysteries known only to the initiated. **3.** of occult character or significance. **4.** involving mystics or mysticism. —*n.* **5.** a person who claims insight into mysteries transcending ordinary human knowledge, as by direct communication with the divine or immediate intuition in a state of spiritual ecstasy. **6.** a person initiated into religious mysteries.

mys·ti·cal (mis′ti kəl), *adj.* **1.** mystic; occult. **2.** of or pertaining to mystics or mysticism. **3.** spiritually symbolic. —**mys′ti·cal·ly,** *adv.*

mys·ti·cism (mis′tə siz′əm), *n.* **1.** the beliefs, ideas, or mode of thought of mystics. **2.** the doctrine of an immediate spiritual intuition of truths believed to transcend ordinary understanding, or of a direct, intimate union of the soul with God through contemplation or spiritual ecstasy. **3.** obscure thought or speculation.

mys·ti·fy (mis′tə fī′), *v.t.,* **-fied, -fy·ing. 1.** to perplex or bewilder. **2.** to make mysterious or difficult to understand. —**mys′ti·fi·ca′tion,** *n.* —**mys′ti·fi′er,** *n.* —**mys′ti·fy′ing·ly,** *adv.*

mys·tique (mi stēk′), *n.* **1.** a framework of doctrines, beliefs, etc., constructed around a person or object and lending enhanced value or meaning. **2.** an aura of mystery or mystical power surrounding a particular occupation or pursuit.

myth (mith), *n.* **1.** a traditional or legendary story, esp. one that involves gods and heroes and explains a cultural practice or natural phenomenon. **2.** such stories; mythology. **3.** an invented story, fictitious person, etc.: *His account of the event is pure myth.* **4.** a belief or set of beliefs, often unproven or false, that have accrued around a person, phenomenon, or institution: *myths of racial superiority.*

myth·i·cal (mith′i kəl) also **myth′ic,** *adj.* **1.** pertaining to, of the nature of, or involving a myth. **2.** dealt with in myth, as a prehistoric period. **3.** existing only in myth or legend. **4.** without foundation in fact; fictitious: *a mythical explanation.* —**myth′i·cal·ly,** *adv.*

mytho-, a combining form representing MYTH: *mythography.*

myth·o·log·i·cal (mith′ə loj′i kəl) also **myth′o·log′ic,** *adj.* **1.** of or pertaining to mythology. **2.** imaginary; fictitious. —**myth′o·log′i·cal·ly,** *adv.*

my·thol·o·gy (mi thol′ə jē), *n., pl.* **-gies. 1.** a body of myths, as that of a particular people. **2.** myths collectively. **3.** the science or study of myths. **4.** a set of stories, traditions, or beliefs that have accrued around a particular person, event, or institution. —**my·thol′o·gist,** *n.*

myth·os (mith′os, mī′thos), *n., pl.* **myth·oi** (mith′oi, mī′thoi). **1.** the underlying system of beliefs, esp. those dealing with supernatural forces, characteristic of a particular cultural group. **2.** MYTH (def. 1). **3.** MYTHOLOGY (def. 1).

myxo-, a combining form meaning "mucus" or "slime": *myxovirus.* Also, *esp. before a vowel,* **myx-.**

myx·o·ma (mik sō′mə), *n., pl.* **-mas, -ma·ta** (-mə tə). a soft tumor composed of connective and mucoid tissue. —**myx·om′a·tous** (-som′ə-təs), *adj.*

N

N, n (en), *n.*, *pl.* **Ns** or **N's, ns** or **n's.** **1.** the 14th letter of the English alphabet, a consonant. **2.** any spoken sound represented by this letter. **3.** something shaped like an N. **4.** a written or printed representation of the letter N or n.

N, *Chem. Symbol.* nitrogen.

n., **1.** name. **2.** born. [< Latin *nātus*] **3.** neuter. **4.** nominative. **5.** noun.

NA, **1.** not applicable. **2.** not available.

Na, *Chem. Symbol.* sodium. [< New Latin *natrium*]

N.A., **1.** North America. **2.** not applicable.

NAACP, National Association for the Advancement of Colored People.

Na·a·man (nā′ə mən), *n.* a leper who was healed by Elisha. II Kings 5:1–14.

nab (nab), *v.t.*, **nabbed, nab·bing.** *Informal.* **1.** to arrest or capture. **2.** to catch or seize, esp. suddenly. **3.** to snatch or steal. —**nab′ber,** *n.*

Na·bal (nā′bəl), *n.* a wealthy Calebite, husband of Abigail, who refused rightful tribute to King David for protecting Nabal's flocks. I Sam. 25. —**Na′bal·ism,** *n.* —**Na′bal·ite′,** *n.* —**Na·bal·it·ic** (nā′bə lit′ik), *adj.*

Nab·lus (nab′ləs, nä′bləs), *n.* a city in Samaria, formerly in W Jordan, occupied by Israel 1967–96; since 1996 under Palestinian self-rule. 50,000. Hebrew, **Shechem.**

na·bob (nā′bob), *n.* any very wealthy, influential, or powerful person.

Na·bo·kov (nə bô′kəf, nab′ə kôf′, -kof′), *n.* **Vladimir Vladimirovich,** 1899–1977, U.S. novelist, short-story writer, and poet, born in Russia.

Na·both (nā′both, -bŏth), *n.* the owner of a vineyard coveted by Ahab, slain by the scheming of Jezebel so that Ahab could secure the vineyard. I Kings 21.

na·cho (nä′chō), *n.*, *pl.* **-chos.** a snack or appetizer consisting of a small piece of tortilla topped with cheese, hot peppers, etc., and broiled.

na·cre (nā′kər), *n.* MOTHER-OF-PEARL. —**na′cre·ous** (-krē əs), *adj.*

Na·dab (nā′dab), *n.* a son of Aaron. Lev. 10. Compare ABIHU.

Na·der (nā′dər), *n.* **Ralph,** born 1934, U.S. lawyer, author, political reformer, and consumer advocate.

na·dir (nā′dər, -dēr), *n.* **1.** the point on the celestial sphere directly beneath a given position or observer and diametrically opposite the zenith. **2.** the lowest point; point of greatest adversity or despair.

nae (nā), *Scot. and North Eng.* —*adv.* **1.** no; not. —*adj.* **2.** no.

Nae·ge·li (neg′ə lē), *n.* **Hans,** 1773–1836, Swiss musician and hymn writer.

Na·fl (nä′fl) or **Na·fi·la, Na·fi·lah** (-fə lə), *n.* *Islam.* a prayer, charitable act, etc., that goes beyond the requirements of one's religion.

NAFTA, *n.* North American Free Trade Agreement.

nag¹ (nag), *v.*, **nagged, nag·ging,** *n.* —*v.t.* **1.** to annoy by persistent faultfinding, complaints, or demands: *Her doubts nagged her.* **2.** to be a constant source of unease or irritation to: —*v.i.* **3.** to find fault or complain, esp. in an irritating and persistent manner. **4.** to cause pain, distress, etc. —*n.* **5.** a person who nags. —**nag′ger,** *n.*

nag² (nag), *n.* **1.** an old or worthless horse. **2.** any horse, esp. a racehorse.

na·ga·na (nə gä′nə), *n.* a disease of livestock and other animals, widespread in parts of Africa, caused by several species of trypanosomes and transmitted by a variety of tsetse fly.

Na·ga·sa·ki (nä′gə sä′kē, nag′ə sak′ē), *n.* a seaport on W Kyushu, in SW Japan: second military use of the atomic bomb August 9, 1945. 447,000.

Nah., Nahum.

Na·hua·tl (nä′wät l), *n.* a Uto-Aztecan language spoken by American Indian peoples of Mexico and Central America, esp. the form of the language used in literature and legal documents of colonial Mexico, written in the Latin alphabet **(Classical Nahuatl).** Compare MEXICANO.

Na·hum (nā′həm), *n.* **1.** a Minor Prophet of the 7th century B.C. **2.** a book of the Bible bearing his name.

nai·ad (nā′ad, -ad, nī′-), *n.*, *pl.* **-ads, -a·des** (-ə dēz′). **1.** (in Greek myth) any of a group of nymphs presiding over rivers and springs. **2.** the aquatic nymph of certain insects, as the dragonfly or mayfly. **3.** any of several aquatic plants of the genus *Najas* and family Najadaceae, having narrow opposite leaves and solitary flowers.

na·if or **na·ïf** (nä ēf′), *n.* a naive or inexperienced person. —*adj.* naive.

nail (nāl), *n.* **1.** a slender, rod-shaped piece of metal, typically having a pointed tip and a flattened head, made to be hammered into wood or other material as a fastener or support. **2.** a thin, horny plate, consisting of modified epidermis, growing on the upper side of the end of a finger or toe. **3.** a former measure of length for cloth, equal to 2¼ in. (6.4 cm). —*v.t.* **4.** to fasten with a nail or nails. **5.** to enclose or shut by nailing (often fol. by *up*). **6.** to keep firmly in one place or position; make fast. **7.** *Informal.* to catch or seize. **8. nail down,** to make final; settle once and for all. —*Idiom.* **9. hit the nail on the head,** to say or do exactly the right thing. —*Proverb.* **10. For want of a nail the kingdom was lost,** no detail is so small as to be insignificant.

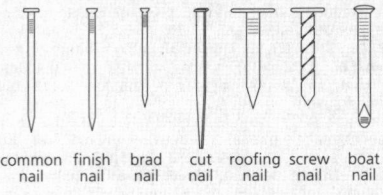

common finish brad cut roofing screw boat
nail nail nail nail nail nail nail

nails

nail′ file′, *n.* a small file of metal or cardboard, for trimming, smoothing, or shaping the fingernails.

nail·head (nāl′hed′), *n.* **1.** the flattened or rounded top of a nail. **2.** an ornament that resembles this.

nail′ pol′ish, *n.* a polish of quick-drying lacquer, often colored, used to paint the fingernails or toenails. Also called **nail′ enam′el.**

nail′ set′, *n.* a short rod of steel used to drive a nail below or flush with a surface.

Nai·paul (nī′pôl′), *n.* **V(idiadhar) S(urajprasad),** born 1932, English novelist and nonfiction writer, born in Trinidad.

Nai·ro·bi (nī rō′bē), *n.* the capital of Kenya, in the SW part. 827,775.

Nai·smith (nā′smith), *n.* **James,** 1861–1939, U.S. physical-education teacher and originator of basketball, born in Canada.

na·ive or **na·ïve** (nä ēv′), *adj.* **1.** having unaffected simplicity of nature; unsophisticated; ingenuous. **2.** having a lack of experience, judgment, or information; credulous. [< French, fem. of *naif*, Old French *naif* natural, instinctive < Latin *nātivus* native]

na·ive·té or **na·ïve·té** or **na·ive·te** (nä ēv tā′, -ē′və tā′, -ēv′tā, -ē′və-), *n.* **1.** the quality or state of being naive; unaffected simplicity. **2.** a naive action, remark, etc. [< French]

na·ked (nā′kid), *adj.* **1.** being without clothing or covering; nude. **2.** without adequate clothing. **3.** bare of vegetation, foliage, or the like. **4.** without the customary covering or protection: *a naked sword.* **5.** without furnishings, as rooms or walls. **6.** (of the eye, sight, etc.) unassisted by a microscope, telescope, or other instrument. **7.** defenseless; unprotected. **8.** plain; simple; unadorned: *the naked truth.* **9.** plainly revealed: *a naked threat.* **10.** *Law.* unsupported: *a naked promise.* **11. a.** (of seeds) not enclosed in an ovary. **b.** (of flowers) without a calyx or perianth. **c.** (of stalks, branches, etc.) without leaves. **d.** (of stalks, leaves, etc.) without hairs or pubescence. **12.** *Zool.* having no covering of hair, feathers, shell, etc. —**na′ked·ly,** *adv.* —**na′ked·ness,** *n.*

nam·by-pam·by (nam′bē pam′bē), *adj.*, *n.*, *pl.* **-bies.** —*adj.* **1.** lacking decisiveness; irresolute: *namby-pamby opinions.* **2.** wanting in character or moral strength. **3.** weakly sentimental; insipid: *namby-pamby poetry.* —*n.* **4.** a namby-pamby person or thing.

name (nām), *n.*, *v.*, **named, nam·ing,** *adj.* —*n.* **1.** a word or phrase by which a person or thing is designated. **2.** mere designation rather than fact: *a king in name only.* **3.** an often abusive descriptive epithet: *calling people names.* **4. a.** reputation: *a bad name.* **b.** a reputation of distinction: *making a name for oneself.* **5.** a celebrity: *one of music's great names.* **6.** a clan; family. **7.** a word or symbol in logic that respresents an entity. **8.** (*cap.*) a symbol or vehicle of divinity: *Holy Name.* —*v.t.* **9.** to give a name to; call: *to name a baby.* **10. a.** to accuse by name: *named the thief.* **b.** to identify by name. **11.** to designate or nominate for duty or office. **12.** to specify: *Name your price.* —*adj.* **13.** famous; well-known: *a name author.* **14.** designed for or bearing a name: *name tags.* **15.** being used as the title of a collection or production: *the name piece in the anthology.* —*Idiom.* **16. in the name of, a.** with appeal to: *Stop, in the name of mercy.* **b.** by the authority of: *Open, in the name of the law.* **c.** in behalf of. **17. name names,** to specify or accuse people by name. **18.** to one's **name,** within one's resources: *not a penny to his name.* —*Proverb.* **19. A good name is better than precious ointment,** reputation is one's most important possession. Eccl. 7:1. —**name′a·ble, nam′a·ble,** *adj.* —**nam′er,** *n.*

name′-brand′, *adj.* **1.** BRAND-NAME (def. 1). —*n.* **2.** BRAND NAME (def. 2).

name′ day′, *n.* **1.** the feast day of the saint after whom a person is named. **2.** the day on which a person is christened.

name′-drop′ping, *n.* the mention of famous or important people as friends or associates in order to impress others. —**name′-drop′,** *v.i.,* **-dropped, -drop·ping.** —**name′-drop′per,** *n.*

name·less (nām′lis), *adj.* **1.** having no name. **2.** not referred to by name. **3.** anonymous: *a nameless source of information.* **4.** incapable of being specified or described. **5.** too shocking or vile to be specified: *a nameless crime.* **6.** having no legitimate paternal name, as a child born out of wedlock. **7.** unknown to fame; obscure. —**name′less·ness,** *n.*

name·ly (nām′lē), *adv.* that is to say; specifically: *a new item of legislation, namely, the housing bill.*

name′ of the game′, *n.* *Informal.* the essential element or ultimate purpose; key: *Profit is the name of the game in business.*

name·plate (nām′plāt′), *n.* **1.** a rectangular piece of metal, wood, or plastic on which the name of a person, company, etc., is printed or engraved. **2.** Also called **masthead, flag.** the name of a newspaper printed on its front page or of a magazine printed on its cover.

name·sake (nām′sāk′), *n.* **1.** a person named after another. **2.** a person having the same name as another.

Na·mib·i·a (nə mib′ē ə), *n.* a republic in SW Africa: a former German protectorate; a mandate of South Africa (1919–66); gained independence 1990. 1,727,183; 318,261 sq. mi. (824,296 sq. km). *Cap.:* Windhoek. Formerly, **German Southwest Africa,** (1884–1919), **South-West Africa** (1920–68). —**Na·mib′i·an,** *adj., n.*

nan·a (nan′ə), *n., pl.* **nan·as.** grandmother; grandma.

nan·keen (nan′kēn′) also **nan·kin** (-kin′), *n.* **1.** a firm, durable, yellow or buff fabric, formerly made from a natural-colored Chinese cotton. **2.** nankeens, garments made of this material. **3.** Also called **Nan′keen por′celain, Nan′king chi′na, Nan′king′ ware′.** a type of Chinese porcelain having blue ornament on a white ground.

nan·no·fos·sil or **nan·o·fos·sil** (nan′ə fos′əl), *n.* any fossil so small that it is near the limit of resolution of a light microscope.

nan·ny (nan′ē), *n., pl.* **-nies.** a child's nursemaid.

nan′ny goat′, *n.* a female goat.

nano-, a combining form with the meaning "very small, minute" (*nanoplankton*); in the names of units of measure it has the specific sense "one billionth" (10^{-9}): *nanomole; nanosecond.* Also, **nanno-.**

nan·o·me·ter (nan′ə mē′tər, nä′nə-), *n.* a unit of measure equal to one billionth of a meter. *Abbr.:* nm

nan·o·sec·ond (nan′ə sek′ənd, nä′nə-), *n.* one billionth of a second. *Abbr.:* ns, nsec

Nan·sen (nan′sən, nän′-), *n.* **Fridtjof,** 1861–1930, Norwegian arctic explorer, zoologist, and statesman.

Nantes (nants; *Fr.* nänt), *n.* **1.** a seaport in W France, on the Loire River. 263,689. **2. Edict of,** a law, promulgated by Henry IV of France in 1598, granting religious and civil liberty to the Huguenots: revoked in 1685.

Na·o·mi (nā ō′mē), *n.* the mother-in-law of Ruth. Ruth 1.

nap¹ (nap), *v.,* **napped, nap·ping,** *n.* —*v.i.* **1.** to sleep for a short time; doze. **2.** to be off one's guard: *The question caught him napping.* —*v.t.* **3.** to sleep or doze through: *I napped the afternoon away.* —*n.* **4.** a brief period of sleep, esp. one taken during daytime.

nap² (nap), *n., v.,* **napped, nap·ping.** —*n.* **1.** the short fuzzy ends of fibers on the surface of cloth. —*v.t.* **2.** to raise a nap on. —**nap′less,** *adj.*

na·palm (nā′päm), *n.* **1.** a highly incendiary jellylike substance used in fire bombs, flamethrowers, etc. —*v.t.* **2.** to bomb or attack with napalm.

nape (nāp, nap), *n.* the back of the neck.

Na·per·ville (nā′pər vil′), *n.* a city in NE Illinois. 101,163.

na·per·y (nā′pə rē), *n.* **1.** table linen, as tablecloths or napkins. **2.** any linen for household use.

Naph·ta·li (naf′tə lī′), *n.* **1.** the sixth son of Jacob and Bilhah. Gen. 30:7, 8. **2.** one of the 12 tribes of Israel, descended from him.

naph·tha (naf′thə, nap′-), *n.* **1.** a colorless, volatile petroleum distillate, usu. an intermediate product between gasoline and benzine, used as a solvent and as a fuel. **2.** any of various similar liquids distilled from other products. —**naph′thous,** *adj.*

Na·pi·er (nā′pē ər, nə pēr′), *n.* **1. Sir Charles James,** 1782–1853, British general. **2. John,** 1550–1617, Scottish mathematician: inventor of logarithms.

nap·kin (nap′kin), *n.* **1.** a piece of cloth or paper, usu. square, wiping the lips and fingers and to protect the clothes while eating. **2. SANITARY NAPKIN.**

Na·ples (nā′pəlz), *n.* **1.** Italian, **Napoli.** a seaport in SW Italy, on the Bay of Naples. 1,200,958. **2. Bay of,** an inlet of the Tyrrhenian Sea. 22 mi. (35 km) long.

na·po·le·on (nə pō′lē ən, -pōl′yən), *n.* **1.** a pastry made of thin layers of puff paste and custard or cream filling. **2.** a former French gold coin equal to 20 francs. [< F *napoléon*]

Na·po·le·on (nə pō′lē ən, -pōl′yən), *n.* **1. Napoleon I,** (*Napoleon Bonaparte*) ("*the Little Corporal*") 1769–1821, French general born in Corsica: emperor of France 1804–15. **2. Napoleon II,** (*François Charles Joseph Bonaparte*) (*Duke of Reichstadt*) 1811–32, titular king of Rome (son of Napoleon I). **3. Napoleon III,** (*Louis Napoléon*) (*Charles Louis Napoléon Bonaparte*) 1808–73, president of France 1848–52, emperor of France 1852–70 (nephew of Napoleon I). —**Na·po·le·on·ic** (nə pō′lē on′ik), *adj.*

Napo′leon′ic Code′, *n.* **CODE NAPOLÉON.**

nap·py¹ or **nap·pie** (nap′ē), *n., pl.* **-pies.** a small shallow dish for serving food.

nap·py² (nap′ē), *adj.,* **-pi·er, -pi·est. 1.** covered with nap; downy. **2.** (of hair) kinky. —**nap′pi·ness,** *n.*

nap·py³ (nap′ē), *n., pl.* **-pies.** Chiefly Brit. **DIAPER** (def. 1).

narc or **nark** (närk), *n.* Slang. a government narcotics agent.

nar·cis·sism (när′sə siz′əm) also **nar·cism** (när′siz əm), *n.* inordinate fascination with oneself; excessive self-love; vanity. —**nar′cis·sist, nar′cist,** *n.* —**nar′cis·sis′tic, nar·cis′tic,** *adj.*

nar·cis·sus (när sis′əs), *n., pl.* **-cis·sus, -cis·sus·es, -cis·si** (-sis′ē, -sis′ī). **1.** any bulbous plant belonging to the genus *Narcissus*, of the amaryllis family, having showy yellow or white flowers with a cup-shaped corona. **2.** (*cap.*) (in Greek myth) a youth who fell in love with his own reflection in a pool: after his death he was transformed into the narcissus flower.

nar·co·lep·sy (när′kə lep′sē), *n.* a disorder characterized by frequent and uncontrollable attacks of deep sleep. —**nar′co·lep′tic,** *adj., n.*

nar·co·ma (när kō′mə), *n., pl.* **-mas, -ma·ta** (-mə tə). stupor produced by narcotics. —**nar·com′a·tous** (-kom′ə təs), *adj.*

nar·co·sis (när kō′sis), *n.* a state of drowsiness or stupor.

nar·co·ter·ror·ism (när′kō ter′ə riz′əm), *n.* terrorist tactics employed by dealers in illicit drugs, as against competitors or government agents. —**nar′co·ter′ror·ist,** *n., adj.*

nar·cot·ic (när kot′ik), *n.* **1.** any of a class of habituating or addictive substances that blunt the senses and in increasing doses cause confusion, stupor, coma, and death: some are used in medicine to relieve intractable pain or induce anesthesia. **2.** anything that exercises a soothing or numbing effect or influence. —*adj.* **3.** of or having the power to produce narcosis, as a drug. **4.** pertaining to or of the nature of narcosis. **5.** of or pertaining to narcotics or their use. **6.** used by, or in the treatment of, narcotic addicts. —**nar·cot′i·cal·ly,** *adv.*

nar·es (nâr′ēz), *n.pl., sing.* **nar·is** (nâr′is). the nostrils or the nasal passages.

nar·rate (nar′āt, na rāt′), *v.,* **-rat·ed, -rat·ing.** —*v.t.* **1.** to tell the story of (events, experiences, etc.). **2.** to add a spoken commentary to (a film, television program, etc.). —*v.i.* **3.** to relate or recount events, experiences, etc., in speech or writing. —**nar′ra·tor, nar′rat·er,** *n.*

nar·ra·tion (na rā′shən), *n.* **1.** something narrated; an account, story, or narrative. **2.** the act or process of narrating. **3.** a recital of events, esp. in chronological order. —**nar·ra′tion·al,** *adj.*

nar·ra·tive (nar′ə tiv), *n.* **1.** a story or account of events, experiences, or the like, whether true or fictitious. **2.** the art, technique, or process of narrating. —*adj.* **3.** consisting of or being a narrative: *narrative poetry.* **4.** of or pertaining to narration. **5.** representing stories or events pictorially or sculpturally: *narrative painting.* —**nar′ra·tive·ly,** *adv.*

nar·row (nar′ō), *adj.,* **-row·er, -row·est. 1.** of little breadth or width. **2.** affording little room: *narrow quarters.* **3.** limited in range or scope. **4.** lacking breadth of view or sympathy. **5.** barely adequate or successful; close: *a narrow escape.* **6.** careful or minute, as a scrutiny, search, or inquiry. **7.** limited in amount; meager: *narrow resources.* **8. a.** (of a speech sound) **TENSE¹** (def. 4). **b.** (of a phonetic transcription) using a symbol for each phoneme together with supplementary symbols or diacritics to indicate phonetic details. Compare **BROAD** (def. 13). —*v.i.* **9.** to decrease in width or breadth. —*v.t.* **10.** to make narrower. **11.** to limit or restrict (often fol. by *down*). **12.** to make narrow-minded. —*n.* **13. narrows,** (*used with a sing. or pl. v.*) a narrow part of a strait, river, ocean current, etc. —**nar′row·ly,** *adv.* —**nar′row·ness,** *n.*

nar·row·cast (nar′ō kast′, -käst′), *v.i.,* **-cast** or **-cast·ed, -cast·ing.** to aim a program or programming at a specific audience or sales market.

nar′row-mind′ed, *adj.* having a closed mind; biased. —**nar′row-mind′ed·ly,** *adv.* —**nar′row-mind′ed·ness,** *n.*

nar·whal or **nar·wal** (när′wəl), also **nar·whale** (-hwāl′, -wāl′), *n.* a small arctic whale, *Monodon monoceros*, the male of which has a long, spirally twisted tusk extending forward from the upper jaw. —**nar·whal′i·an** (-hwā′lē ən, -wā′-, -wol′ē-), *adj.*

nar·y (nâr′ē), *adj.* not any: *nary a sound.*

NAS or **N.A.S.,** National Academy of Sciences.

NASA (nas′ə), *n.* National Aeronautics and Space Administration.

na·sal (nā′zəl), *adj.* **1.** of or pertaining to the nose. **2.** (of a speech sound) pronounced with the soft palate lowered and the voice issuing through the nose, either partly, as in French nasal vowels, or entirely, as in the sounds (m), (n), or the (ng) of *song.* **3.** characterized by or resembling such sounds: *a nasal voice.* —*n.* **4.** a nasal speech sound. —**na·sal′i·ty, na′sal·ly,** *adv.*

na·sal·ize (nā′zə līz′), *v.,* **-ized, -iz·ing.** —*v.t.* **1.** to pronounce as a nasal sound. —*v.i.* **2.** to pronounce normally oral sounds as nasal sounds. —**na′sal·i·za′tion,** *n.*

NASCAR or **N.A.S.C.A.R.** (nas′kär), *n.* National Association for Stock Car Auto Racing.

nas·cent (nas′ənt, nā′sənt), *adj.* beginning to exist or develop. —**nas′cence, nas′cen·cy,** *n.*

NASDAQ (nas′dak, naz′-), *n.* National Association of Securities Dealers Automated Quotations: a system for quoting over-the-counter securities.

Nash·ville (nash′vil), *n.* the capital of Tennessee, in the central part. 481,380.

Nas·sau (nas′ô; *for 2, also* nä′sou), *n.* **1.** a seaport on New Providence Island: capital of the Bahamas. 132,000. **2.** a former duchy in central Germany: now a part of Hesse.

Nas·ser (nä′sər, nas′ər), *n.* **1. Gamal Abdel,** 1918–70, president of Egypt 1956–58; president of the United Arab Republic 1958–70. **2. Lake,** a reservoir in SE Egypt, formed in the Nile River S of the Aswan High Dam. ab. 300 mi. (500 km) long; 6 mi. (10 km) wide.

Nast (nast), *n.* **Thomas,** 1840–1902, U.S. illustrator and cartoonist.

nas·tur·tium (nə stûr′shəm, na-), *n., pl.* **-tiums.** any garden plant of the genus *Tropaeolum* and family Tropaeolaceae, having shield-shaped leaves and bright, irregular flowers.

nas•ty (nas′tē), *adj.,* **-ti•er, -ti•est,** *n., pl.* **-ties.** —*adj.* **1.** disgustingly unclean; filthy. **2.** offensive to taste or smell; nauseating. **3.** indecent or obscene: *a nasty word.* **4.** highly objectionable or unpleasant. **5.** vicious, spiteful, or ugly. **6.** bad to deal with or experience: *a nasty cut; a nasty accident.* **7.** *Slang.* formidable: *a nasty pitching arm.* —*n.* **8.** a nasty person or thing. —**nas′ti•ly,** *adv.* —**nas′ti•ness,** *n.*

na•tal (nāt′l), *adj.* **1.** of or pertaining to a person's birth. **2.** presiding over or affecting a person at birth.

na•tal•i•ty (nā tal′i tē, nə-), *n.* BIRTHRATE.

na•tant (nāt′nt), *adj.* swimming; floating.

na•ta•to•ri•um (nā′tə tôr′ē əm, -tōr′-, nat′ə-), *n., pl.* **-to•ri•ums, -to•ri•a** (-tôr′ē ə, -tōr′-). a swimming pool, esp. one that is indoors.

natch (nach), *adv. Slang.* of course; naturally.

Natch′ez Trace′, *n.* a road begun in 1806 between Natchez, Miss., and Nashville, Tenn.: about 500 mi. (800 km) long.

na•tes (nā′tēz), *n.pl.* the buttocks.

Na•than (nā′thən), *n.* **1.** a prophet during the reigns of David and Solomon. II Sam. 12; I Kings 1:34. **2. George Jean,** 1882–1958, U.S. drama critic.

Na•than•a•el (nə than′ē əl, -than′yəl), *n.* a disciple of Jesus, possibly Bartholomew. John 1:45–51.

na•tion (nā′shən), *n.* **1.** a body of people in a particular territory, that is sufficiently conscious of its unity to seek or have a government peculiarly its own. **2.** the territory or country itself. **3. a.** an American Indian people or tribe. **b.** a member tribe of an American Indian confederation. [< Latin *nātiō* birth, people, nation] —**na′tion•hood,** *n.*

Na•tion (nā′shən), *n.* **Carry** or **Carrie (Amelia Moore),** 1846–1911, U.S. temperance leader.

na•tion•al (nash′ə nl,), *adj.* **1.** of, pertaining to, or belonging to a nation: *our national anthem; national affairs.* **2.** peculiar or common to the people of a nation: *national customs.* **3.** devoted to one's own nation, its interests, etc.; patriotic: *national pride.* —*n.* **4.** a citizen or subject of a particular nation who is entitled to its protection. **5.** Often, **nationals.** a national competition, tournament, or the like. **6.** a national company or organization. —**na′tion•al•ly,** *adv.*

Na′tional Acad′emy of Sci′ences, *n.* a private organization, created by Congress (1863), that furthers science and advises the U.S. government on scientific and technical issues Abbr.: NAS, N.A.S.

Na′tional Aeronau′tics and Space′ Administra′tion, *n.* the federal agency that institutes and administers the civilian programs of the U.S. government that deal with aeronautical research and the development of launch vehicles and spacecraft. *Abbr.:* NASA

Na′tional Associa′tion for the Advance′ment of Col′ored Peo′ple, *n.* an interracial U.S. organization working for political and civil equality of black people: organized in 1910. *Abbr.:* NAACP

na′tional bank′, *n.* **1.** a bank chartered by the U.S. government and formerly authorized to issue notes that served as money. **2.** a bank owned and administered by the government, as in some European countries.

Na′tional Bap′tist Conven′tion of Amer′ica, *n.* a Christian denomination founded in 1895, now the third-largest Baptist group in the United States.

National Baptist Convention of the U.S.A., Inc., *n.* a Christian denomination, originally part of the National Baptist Convention of America, now the second-largest Baptist group in the United States.

Na′tional Bu′reau of Stand′ards, *n.* the federal agency that establishes the standards for units used in measuring the physical properties of substances. *Abbr.:* NBS, N.B.S.

na′tional cem′etery, *n.* a cemetery, maintained by the U.S. government, for persons who have served honorably in the armed forces.

na′tional church′, *n.* an independent church within a country, usually representing the prevalent religion. Compare ESTABLISHED CHURCH.

Na′tional Conven′tion, *n.* a convention held every four years by each major U.S. political party to nominate a presidential candidate.

Na′tional Cov′enant, *n.* an agreement (1638) among Scottish Presbyterians to uphold their faith in Scotland. Compare SOLEMN LEAGUE AND COVENANT.

na′tional debt′, *n.* the financial obligations of a national government. Also called **public debt.**

Na′tional Endow′ment for the Arts′, *n.* an independent agency that stimulates the growth and development of the arts in the U.S. by awarding grants to individuals and organizations. *Abbr.:* NEA

Na′tional Endow′ment for the Human′ities, *n.* an independent agency that stimulates the growth and development of the humanities in the U.S. by awarding grants to individuals and organizations. *Abbr.:* NEH

Na′tional Guard′, *n.* a state military force that is subject to call by the state or federal government in emergencies.

na′tional in′come, *n.* the total net earnings from the production of goods and services in a country over a period of time, usually one year, and consisting essentially of wages, salaries, rent, profits, and interest. Compare GROSS NATIONAL PRODUCT, NET NATIONAL PRODUCT.

na•tion•al•ism (nash′ə nl iz′əm, nash′nə liz′-), *n.* **1.** devotion and loyalty to one's own nation; patriotism. **2.** excessive patriotism; chauvinism. **3.** the desire for national advancement or independence. **4.** the doctrine or policy of asserting the interests of a particular nation over the interests of other nations. **5.** a movement, as in the arts, based upon the folk idioms, history, aspirations, etc., of a nation. —**na′tion•al•ist,** *adj., n.* —**na′tion•al•is′tic,** *adj.* —**na′tion•al•is′ti•cal•ly,** *adv.*

na•tion•al•i•ty (nash′ ə nal′i tē), *n., pl.* **-ties** for 1, 4, 5. **1.** the status of belonging to a particular nation, whether by birth or naturalization. **2.** NATIONALISM. **3.** existence as a distinct nation; national independence. **4.** a nation or people. **5.** national quality or character.

na•tion•al•ize (nash′ə nl īz′), *v.,* **-ized, -iz•ing.** —*v.t.* **1.** to bring under the ownership or control of a nation, as an industry or land. **2.** to make into a nation. **3.** to make national in extent or scope. —*v.i.* **4.** to become nationalized. —**na′tion•al•i•za′tion,** *n.*

Na′tional La′bor Rela′tions Act′, *n.* an act of Congress (1935)

MAJOR NATIONAL PARKS OF THE UNITED STATES

Park	Location	Highlights
Acadia	S Maine	Granite Mountains; coastal scenery
Badlands	SW South Dakota	Fossils; prairie grasslands; rugged, eroded slopes
Big Bend	SW Texas	Mountain and desert scenery
Bryce Canyon	SW Utah	Canyon with brilliantly colored pinnacles
Canyonlands	SE Utah	Red rock canyons, sandstone structures
Carlsbad Caverns	SE New Mexico	Huge natural caves
Crater Lake	SW Oregon	Clear blue lake in extinct volcano
Denali*	S central Alaska	Mount McKinley, highest peak in North America
Everglades	S Florida	Mangrove swamps; rare birds and plants
Glacier	NW Montana	Mountain scenery with lakes and glaciers
Glacier Bay	SE Alaska	Tidewater glaciers; wildlife
Grand Canyon	NW Arizona	Huge river gorge with varicolored cliffs
Grand Teton	NW Wyoming	Snow-capped peaks; evergreen forests
Great Smoky Mountains	E Tennessee/W North Carolina	Mountain scenery; primeval hardwood forests
Haleakala	Maui Isl., Hawaii	Large dormant volcano
Hawaii Volcanoes	Isl. of Hawaii	Active volcanoes
Hot Springs	W central Arkansas	Forty-seven mineral hot springs
Isle Royale	N Michigan	Forested islands
Kings Canyon	E central California	Imposing peaks and canyons; giant sequoias
Lassen Volcanic	N California	Recently active volcano; hot springs; geysers
Mammoth Cave	S central Kentucky	Limestone caverns; underground river and lakes
Mesa Verde	SW Colorado	Prehistoric cliff dwellings; pueblo houses
Mount Rainier	W central Washington	Glacier system; dense forests
North Cascades	NW Washington	Alpine region; glaciers; jagged peaks
Olympic	NW Washington	Temperate rainforest; mountain wilderness
Petrified Forest	N Arizona	Petrified wood in brilliant colors
Rocky Mountain	N central Colorado	Heart of Colorado Rockies; wildlife; alpine tundra
Sequoia	E central California	Stands of sequoias; lakes; high mountains
Shenandoah	N Virginia	Skyline drive along crest of Blue Ridges
Virgin Islands	E Caribbean	Tropical area; prehistoric and historic relics
Wind Cave	SW South Dakota	Limestone caverns; buffalo herd
Wrangell-St. Elias	E Alaska	Glaciers; high peaks
Yellowstone	NW Wyoming	Geysers; hot springs; lakes; waterfalls; wildlife
Yosemite	E central California	Lofty cliffs; domes; high waterfalls; giant sequoias
Zion	SW Utah	Colorful canyons; picturesque sandstone cliffs

*Formerly, Mount McKinley

that forbade any interference by employers with the formation and operation of labor unions. Also called **Wagner Act.** Compare TAFT-HARTLEY ACT.

Na′tional League′, *n.* the older of the two major professional U.S. baseball leagues, established in 1876. *Abbr.:* N.L.

na′tional li′brary, *n.* a library established and funded by a national government with the designation *national,* to serve the needs of this government, often to function as a library of record for the nation's publishing output, and in some cases to act as a central agency for library and bibliographic development in the nation.

Na′tional Mer′it Schol′arship, *n.* one of some 6000 college scholarships awarded annually since 1956, by the nonprofit, grant-supported National Merit Scholarship Corporation, to high-school students **(Na′tional Mer′it Schol′ars)** on the basis of scholastic record, personal character, and score on a test administered nationally.

na′tional mon′ument, *n.* a historic site or natural landmark maintained in the public interest by the federal government.

Na′tional Organiza′tion for Wom′en, *n.* a women's rights organization founded in 1966. *Abbr.:* NOW

na′tional park′, *n.* an area of scenic beauty, historical importance, or the like owned and maintained by a national government.

Na′tional Park′ Serv′ice, *n.* a division of the Department of the Interior, created in 1916, that administers national parks, monuments, historic sites, and recreational areas.

Na′tional Pub′lic Ra′dio, *n.* a nationwide network of nonprofit radio stations supported in part by U.S. government funds distributed by the Corporation for Public Broadcasting, often affiliated with a public television station or educational institution. *Abbr.:* NPR

Na′tional Ri′fle Associa′tion, *n.* a U.S. association of gun-owners, founded in 1871, that supports the right to bear arms. *Abbr.:* NRA

na′tional sea′shore, *n.* (*sometimes caps.*) an area of seacoast maintained by the U.S. government for public recreation or wildlife study.

Na′tional Secur′ity Coun′cil, *n.* the council, composed of the President, Vice President, Secretary of State, Secretary of Defense, director of the Central Intelligence Agency and the Chairman of the Joint Chiefs of Staff, that determines how domestic, foreign, and military policy can best be integrated for safeguarding the national security. *Abbr.:* NSC

Na′tional So′cialism, *n.* the principles and practices of the Nazis.

Na′tional Transporta′tion Safe′ty Board′, *n.* an independent agency, created in 1975, that promotes safe transportation in the U.S. through accident investigations, studies, and recommendations. *Abbr.:* NTSB

Na′tional Weath′er Serv′ice, *n.* a division of the U.S. Department of Commerce responsible for meteorological observations and weather forecasts.

Na′tion of Islam′, *n.* an organization composed chiefly of American blacks, advocating the teachings of Islam and originally favoring the separation of races: members are known as Black Muslims.

na′tion-state′, *n.* a sovereign state inhabited by a fairly homogeneous group of people who share a feeling of common nationality.

na•tion•wide (nā′shən wīd′), *adj.* extending throughout the nation.

na•tive (nā′tiv), *adj.* **1.** being the place or environment in which a person was born or a thing came into being: *one's native land.* **2.** belonging to a person by birth or to a thing by nature; inherent: *native ability.* **3.** belonging to or originating in a certain place; local; indigenous: *native dress.* **4.** born in a particular place: *a native Chicagoan.* **5.** of or pertaining to something first acquired by a person: *one's native language.* **6.** remaining or growing in a natural state: *the desert's native beauty.* **7.** originating naturally in a particular country or region, as animals or plants. **8.** (of metals) occurring in nature pure or uncombined. —*n.* **9.** one of the people indigenous to a place, esp. as distinguished from strangers, foreigners, colonizers, etc.: *the natives of Chile.* **10.** a person born in a particular place or country: *a native of Ohio.* **11.** an animal, plant, etc., that is indigenous to a particular region. —***Idiom.*** **12. go native,** to imitate the behavior of a surrounding culture, esp. behavior that seems simple, natural, or primitive. [< Middle French < Latin *nātīvus* inborn, natural] —**na′tive•ly,** *adv.* —**na′tive•ness,** *n.*

Na′tive Amer′ican, *n.* AMERICAN INDIAN. —**Usage.** See INDIAN, ESKIMO.

na′tive-born′, *adj.* born in the place indicated.

na′tive son′, *n.* a person born in a particular place: *The delegation from Iowa nominated a native son.*

Na′tive Son′, a novel (1940) by Richard Wright.

na•tiv•ism (nā′ti viz′əm), *n.* **1.** the policy of protecting the interests of native inhabitants against those of immigrants. **2.** the policy or practice of preserving or reviving an indigenous culture. **3.** the doctrine that certain knowledge, ideas, behavior, or capacities exist innately. —**na′tiv•ist,** *n., adj.* —**na′tiv•is′tic,** *adj.*

na•tiv•i•ty (nə tiv′i tē, nā-), *n., pl.* **-ties. 1.** birth, esp. with reference to place or attendant circumstances. **2.** (*cap.*) the birth of Christ. **3.** (*cap.*) Christmas. **4.** a horoscope of a person's birth.

natl., national.

NATO (nā′tō), *n.* a military alliance of Western nations for the purpose of collective defense.

nat•ter (nat′ər), *v.i.* to talk incessantly; chatter.

nat•ty (nat′ē), *adj.,* **-ti•er, -ti•est.** neatly or trimly smart; spruce: *a natty uniform.* —**nat′ti•ly,** *adv.* —**nat′ti•ness,** *n.*

nat•u•ral (nach′ər əl, nach′rəl), *adj.* **1.** existing in or formed by nature: *a natural bridge.* **2.** of or pertaining to nature: *the natural world.* **3.** in a state of nature; uncultivated, as land. **4.** having undergone little or no processing and containing no chemical additives: *natural food.* **5.** having a real or physical existence, as opposed to one that is spiritual, intellectual, fictitious, etc. **6.** belonging to the nature or essential constitution; inborn; innate: *natural ability.* **7.** being such because of one's inborn nature or abilities: *a natural mathematician.* **8.** free from affectation or constraint: *a natural manner.* **9.** in accordance with the nature of things; to be expected: *a natural result.* **10.** in accordance with human nature: *It's natural that they should miss their children.* **11.** based upon the innate moral feeling of humankind: *natural justice.* **12.** happening in the ordinary or usual course of things, without the intervention of accident, violence, etc.: *a natural death.* **13.** illegitimate: *a natural son.* **14.** related by blood rather than by adoption; biological: *one's natural parents.* **15.** based on what is learned from nature rather than on revelation: *natural religion.* **16.** true to or closely imitating nature: *a natural representation.* **17.** unenlightened or unregenerate: *natural man.* **18.** *Music.* **a.** neither sharp nor flat. **b.** changed in pitch by the sign

nat′ural child′birth, *n.* childbirth involving little or no use of drugs or anesthesia and usu. involving a program in which the mother is psychologically and physically prepared for the birth process.

nat′ural gas′, *n.* a combustible mixture of gaseous hydrocarbons that accumulates in porous sedimentary rocks: used as a fuel and to make acetylene.

nat′ural his′tory, *n.* the study of organisms and natural objects, esp. with reference to their history and native environment.

nat•u•ral•ism (nach′ər ə liz′əm, nach′rə-), *n.* **1.** a literary style combining a deterministic view of human nature and a nonidealistic, detailed observation of events. **2.** (in a work of art) treatment of forms, colors, etc., as they appear in nature. **3.** the theory of literary or artistic naturalism. **4.** *Philos.* the belief that all phenomena are covered by laws of science and that all teleological explanations are therefore without value. **5.** adherence or attachment to what is natural.

nat•u•ral•ist (nach′ər ə list, nach′rə-), *n.* **1.** a person who studies or is an expert in natural history, esp. a zoologist or botanist. **2.** an adherent of naturalism in literature or art.

nat•u•ral•is•tic (nach′ər ə lis′tik, nach′rə-), *adj.* **1.** imitating nature or the usual natural surroundings. **2.** pertaining to naturalists or natural history. **3.** pertaining to naturalism, esp. in literature and art. —**nat′u•ral•is′ti•cal•ly,** *adv.*

nat•u•ral•ize (nach′ər ə līz′, nach′rə-), *v.,* **-ized, -iz•ing.** —*v.t.* **1.** to confer upon (an alien) the rights and privileges of a citizen. **2.** to introduce (plants, birds, etc.) into a region and cause them to flourish as if native. **3.** to introduce or adopt (foreign practices, words, etc.) into a country or into general use. **4.** to bring into conformity with nature. **5.** to regard or explain as natural rather than supernatural. **6.** to adapt or accustom to a place or to new surroundings. —*v.i.* **7.** to become naturalized. **8.** to adapt as if native to a new environment, set of circumstances, etc. **9.** to study or carry on research in natural history. —**nat′u•ral•i•za′tion,** *n.* —**nat′u•ral•iz′er,** *n.*

nat′ural lan′guage, *n.* a language used as a native tongue by a group of speakers. Compare ARTIFICIAL LANGUAGE.

nat′ural law′, *n.* a principle or body of laws considered as derived from nature, right reason, or religion and as ethically binding in human society. Compare POSITIVE LAW.

nat•u•ral•ly (nach′ər ə lē, -əl lē, nach′rə lē, -rəl lē), *adv.* **1.** in a natural or normal manner. **2.** by nature; innately or inherently. **3.** of course; as would be expected; needless to say.

nat′ural num′ber, *n.* a positive integer or zero.

nat′ural reli′gion, *n.* religion based on principles derived solely from reason and the study of nature. Compare REVEALED RELIGION.

nat′ural re′sources, *n.pl.* the natural wealth of a country, consisting of land, forests, mineral deposits, water, etc.

nat′ural right′, *n.* any right that exists by virtue of natural law.

nat′ural sci′ence, *n.* a science or knowledge of objects or processes observable in nature, as biology, physics, chemistry, and geology.

nat′ural selec′tion, *n.* the process in nature by which forms of life having traits that better enable them to adapt to specific environmental pressures, as changes in climate or competition for food or mates, will tend to survive and reproduce in greater numbers than others of their kind, thus perpetuating those traits in succeeding generations.

nat′ural theol′ogy, *n.* theology based on knowledge of the natural world and on human reason, apart from revelation. Compare REVEALED THEOLOGY. —**nat′ural theolo′gian,** *n.*

nat′ural vir′tue, *n.* (esp. among the Scholastics) any moral virtue of which humankind is capable, esp. the cardinal virtues: justice, temperance, prudence, and fortitude. Compare THEOLOGICAL VIRTUE.

na•ture (nā′chər), *n.* **1.** the natural world as it exists without human beings or civilization. **2.** the elements of the natural world, as mountains, trees, animals, or rivers. **3.** natural scenery. **4.** the universe, with all its phenomena. **5.** the particular combination of qualities belonging to a person, animal, thing, or class by birth, origin, or constitution; native or inherent character. **6.** character, kind, or sort: *two books of the same nature.* **7.** characteristic disposition; temperament: *an evil nature.* **8.** the natural, primitive condition of humankind. **9.** biological functions or urges. **10.** the laws and principles that guide the universe or an individual. —***Idiom.*** **11. by nature,** as a result of inborn or inherent qualities; innately. —*Proverb.* **12. Nature abhors a vacuum,** something always fills a vacant space.

na′ture wor′ship, *n.* a religion based on the deification and worship of natural phenomena. —**na′ture wor′shiper,** *n.*

na·tur·op·a·thy (nā′chə rop′ə thē, nach′ə-), *n.* a method of treating disease that employs no surgery or synthetic drugs but uses fasting, special diets, massage, etc., to assist the natural healing processes. —**na′tur·o·path′** (-ə path′), *n.* —**na′tur·o·path′ic,** *adj.*

Nau·ga·hyde (nô′gə hīd′), *Trademark.* a brand of strong vinyl-coated fabric made to look like leather and used for upholstery, luggage, etc.

naught or **nought** (nôt), *n.* **1.** nothing. **2.** a cipher (0); zero. —*Idiom.* **3. come to naught,** to end in failure.

naugh·ty (nô′tē), *adj.,* **-ti·er, -ti·est. 1.** disobedient; mischievous. **2.** improper, indecorous, or indecent: *a naughty word.* —**naugh′ti·ly,** *adv.* —**naugh′ti·ness,** *n.*

Na·u·ru (nä ōō′rōō), *n.* **Republic of,** an island republic in the Pacific, near the equator, W of the Gilbert Islands: a UN trusteeship until 1968. 8042; 8 sq. mi. (21 sq. km). —**Na·u′ru·an,** *adj., n.*

nau·se·a (nô′zē ə, -zhə, -sē ə, -sha), *n.* **1.** sickness at the stomach, esp. when accompanied by a loathing for food and an involuntary impulse to vomit. **2.** extreme disgust; loathing; repugnance.

nau·se·ate (nô′zē āt′, -zhē-, -sē-, -shē-), *v.,* **-at·ed, -at·ing.** —*v.t.* **1.** to affect with nausea; sicken. **2.** to cause to feel extreme disgust. —*v.i.* **3.** to experience nausea. —**Usage.** See NAUSEOUS.

nau·se·at·ing (nô′zē ā′ting, -zhē-, -sē-, -shē-), *adj.* **1.** causing nausea; nauseous. **2.** such as to cause disgust, loathing, etc. —**nau′se·at′ing·ly,** *adv.* —**Usage.** See NAUSEOUS.

nau·seous (nô′shəs, -zē əs), *adj.* **1.** affected with nausea; nauseated. **2.** causing nausea; sickening; nauseating. **3.** disgusting; loathsome. —**nau′seous·ly,** *adv.* —**nau′seous·ness,** *n.* —**Usage.** The two literal senses of NAUSEOUS, "affected with nausea" (*to feel nauseous*) and "causing nausea" (*a nauseous smell*), appear in English at almost the same time in the early 17th century, and both are in standard use at present. NAUSEOUS is more common than NAUSEATED in the sense "affected with nausea," despite recent objections by those who imagine the sense to be new. In the sense "causing nausea," either literally or figuratively, NAUSEATING has become more common than NAUSEOUS: *a nauseating smell; nauseating eating habits.*

nau·ti·cal (nô′ti kəl, not′i-), *adj.* of or pertaining to sailors, ships, or navigation. —**nau′ti·cal·ly,** *adv.*

nau′tical mile′, *n.* **1.** INTERNATIONAL NAUTICAL MILE. **2.** a unit of distance, equal to 6080.20 feet (1853.25 m), formerly used in the U.S. for navigation.

nau·ti·lus (nôt′l əs, not′-), *n., pl.* **nau·ti·lus·es, nau·ti·li** (nôt′l ī′, not′--) **1.** Also called **chambered nautilus, pearly nautilus.** any cephalopod of the genus *Nautilus* having a spiral, chambered shell with a pearly interior. **2.** (*cap., italic*) the first nuclear-powered submarine launched by the U.S. Navy.

nautilus,
Nautilus macromphalus,
shell length 8 in. (20 cm)

Nav·a·jo or **Nav·a·ho** (nav′ə hō′, nä′və-), *n., pl.* **-jos, -joes** or **-hos, -hoes,** (*esp. collectively*) **-jo** or **-ho. 1.** a member of an American Indian people of the U.S. Southwest, now centered on a reservation in NE Arizona and adjacent areas of Utah and New Mexico. **2.** the Athabaskan language of the Navajo.

na·val (nā′vəl), *adj.* **1.** of or pertaining to warships. **2.** of or pertaining to ships of all kinds. **3.** belonging to, pertaining to, or connected with a navy: *naval affairs.* **4.** possessing a navy: *the great naval powers.*

nave (nāv), *n.* the principal longitudinal area of a church, extending from the main entrance or narthex to the chancel, usu. flanked by aisles of less height and breadth.

na·vel (nā′vəl), *n.* **1.** the depression in the surface of the abdomen where the umbilical cord was connected with the fetus; umbilicus. **2.** the central point or middle of any thing or place.

na′vel or′ange, *n.* a seedless variety of orange having at the apex a navellike formation containing a small secondary fruit.

nav·i·ga·ble (nav′i gə bəl), *adj.* **1.** deep and wide enough to provide passage to ships. **2.** capable of being steered or guided, as a ship, aircraft, or missile. —**nav′i·ga·bil′i·ty, nav′i·ga·ble·ness,** *n.*

nav·i·gate (nav′i gāt′), *v.,* **-gat·ed, -gat·ing.** —*v.t.* **1.** to move on, over, or through (water, air, or land), esp. in a ship or aircraft. **2.** to direct or manage (a ship, aircraft, spacecraft, etc.) on its course. **3.** to ascertain or plot and control the course or position of (a ship, aircraft, etc.). **4.** to walk or find one's way on, in, or across: *to navigate the stairs.* —*v.i.* **5.** to direct or manage a ship, aircraft, spacecraft, etc., on its course. **6.** to walk or find one's way.

nav·i·ga·tion (nav′i gā′shən), *n.* **1.** the act or process of navigating. **2.** the art or science of plotting, ascertaining, or directing the course of a ship, aircraft, spacecraft, etc. —**nav′i·ga′tion·al,** *adj.*

nav·i·ga·tor (nav′i gā′tər), *n.* **1.** a person skilled in navigation, as of ships or aircraft. **2.** a person who conducts explorations by sea.

na·vy (nā′vē), *n., pl.* **-vies. 1.** the warships and auxiliaries belonging to a country or ruler. **2.** (*often cap.*) the complete body of such warships, together with the personnel, equipment, etc., constituting the sea power of a nation. **3.** (*often cap.*) the department of government charged with its management. **4.** NAVY BLUE.

na′vy bean′, *n.* a small, white dried kidney bean.

na′vy blue′, *n.* a dark blue. —**na′vy-blue′,** *adj.*

na′vy yard′, *n.* a government dockyard where naval ships are built, repaired, etc.

na·wab (nə wob′, -wôb′), *n.* a provincial governor in Mogul India.

nay (nā), *adv.* **1.** not only so but; not only that but also; indeed: *many good, nay, noble qualities.* —*n.* **2.** a negative vote or voter.

nay·say·er (nā′sā′ər), *n.* a person who habitually expresses negative or pessimistic views. —**nay′say′,** *v.t.,* **-said, -say·ing.**

Naz·a·rene (naz′ə rēn′, naz′ə rēn′), *n.* **1.** a native or inhabitant of Nazareth. **2.** a member of a sect of early Jewish converts to Christianity who retained the Mosaic ritual. **3. the Nazarene,** JESUS (def. 1). —*adj.* **4.** of or pertaining to Nazareth or the Nazarenes. [< Late Latin *Nazarēnus* < Greek *Nazarēnós,* der. of *Nazar(ét)* NAZARETH]

Naz·a·reth (naz′ər əth), *n.* a town in N Israel: the childhood home of Jesus. 45,600.

Naz·a·rite or **Naz·i·rite** (naz′ə rīt′), *n.* **1.** (among the ancient Hebrews) a person who had taken certain strict religious vows. **2.** *Rare.* JESUS (def. 1). —**Naz′a·rit′ic** (-rit′ik), *adj.*

Na·zi (nät′sē, nat′-), *n., pl.* **-zis, 1.** a member of the National Socialist German Workers' Party, which controlled Germany from 1933 to 1945 under Adolf Hitler and advocated totalitarian government, territorial expansion, anti-Semitism, and Aryan supremacy, all these leading directly to World War II and the Holocaust. **2.** (*often l.c.*) a person elsewhere who holds similar views. **3.** *Sometimes Offensive.* (*often l.c.*) a person who is fanatically dedicated to or seeks to control a specified activity, practice, etc.: *a jazz nazi who disdains other forms of music; tobacco nazis trying to ban smoking.* [< German *Nazi,* short for *Nationalsozialist* National Socialist] —**Na′zism** (-siz əm), **Na′zi·ism,** *n.* —**Usage.** Definition 3 of NAZI has existed at least since 1980 and parallels other words such as POLICE (def. 5), as in *thought police,* and COP² (def. 2), as in *language cops.* Though this use is usually intended as jocular, it is sometime used intentionally to denigrate an opposing point of view. However, many people find these uses offensive, feeling that they trivialize the terrible crimes of the Nazis of Germany.

na·zir (nä′zir), *n.* **1.** (in Muslim countries) the title of any of various public officials. **2.** (formerly) a title of certain officials serving native rulers in India. —**na′zir·ship′,** *n.*

Nb, *Chem. Symbol.* niobium.

N.B., 1. New Brunswick. **2.** nota bene.

NBA, 1. National Basketball Association. **2.** National Boxing Association.

N-bomb (en′bom′), *n.* NEUTRON BOMB.

NBS or **N.B.S.,** National Bureau of Standards.

NC, 1. no charge. **2.** Also, **N.C.** North Carolina.

NCAA or **N.C.A.A.,** National Collegiate Athletic Association.

NCO, Noncommissioned Officer.

NC-17 (en′sē′sev′ən tēn′), *Trademark.* no children under 17: a motion-picture rating advising that persons under the age of 17 will not be admitted to the film. Compare G (def. 2), PG, PG-13, R (def. 4), X (def. 7).

ND or **N.D.,** North Dakota.

Nd, *Chem. Symbol.* neodymium.

n.d., no date.

N.Dak., North Dakota.

N′Dja·me·na (ən jä mä′nä), *n.* the capital of Chad, in the SW part. 511,700. Formerly, **Fort-Lamy.**

NE, 1. Nebraska. **2.** northeast. **3.** northeastern.

Ne, *Chem. Symbol.* neon.

N.E., 1. no error. **2.** New England. **3.** northeast. **4.** northeastern.

NEA or **N.E.A., 1.** National Education Association. **2.** National Endowment for the Arts.

Ne·an·der·thal (nē an′dər thôl′, nā än′dər täl′), *adj.* **1.** Also, **Ne·an′der·tal′** (-tôl′, -täl′). of or pertaining to Neanderthal man. **2.** (*often l.c.*) primitive, unenlightened, or reactionary. —*n.* **3.** NEANDERTHAL MAN. **4.** (*often l.c.*) an unenlightened, old-fashioned, or reactionary person. [after *Neanderthal,* valley in Germany where evidence of Neanderthal man was first found] —**Ne·an′der·thal′er,** *n.*

Nean′derthal man′, *n.* a member of an extinct subspecies of humans, *Homo sapiens neanderthalensis,* that inhabited Europe and W and central Asia c230,000–30,000 B.C.

neap (nēp), *adj.* designating those tides, midway between spring tides, that attain the least height.

near (nēr), *adv.* and *adj.,* **near·er, near·est,** *prep., v.* —*adv.* **1.** at, within, or to a short distance; close in space. **2.** close in time: *The new year draws near.* **3.** closely with respect to connection, similarity, etc. (often used in combination): *a near-standing position.* **4.** almost; nearly: *a period of near 30 years.* **5.** *Naut.* close to the wind. —*adj.* **6.** being close by; not distant: *the near fields.* **7.** being the lesser in distance: *the near side.* **8.** short or direct: *the near road.* **9.** close in time: *the near future.* **10.** closely related or connected: *our nearest relatives.* **11.** close to an original: *a near translation.* **12.** intimate or familiar: *a near and dear friend.* **13.** narrow or close: *a near escape.* **14.** thrifty or stingy. **15.** (of a vehicle, single animal, or pair of animals hitched side by side) desig-

nating the left as seen from the rider's or driver's viewpoint (opposed to *off*). —*prep.* **16.** at, to, or within a short distance, or no great distance, from: *regions near the equator.* **17.** close to in time: *near the beginning of the year.* **18.** close to a condition or state: *to be near death.* —*v.t., v.i.* **19.** to come or draw near; approach. —***Idiom.*** **20. near at hand, a.** in the immediate vicinity. **b.** in the near future. —**near′ness,** *n.*

near′ beer′, *n.* a malt beverage similar to beer but containing less than ½ percent alcohol.

near•by (nēr′bī′), *adj.* **1.** close at hand; adjacent; neighboring. —*adv.* **2.** in the vicinity; close by.

Near′er My′ God′ to Thee′, a hymn (1833) with words by Sarah F. Adams and music by Lowell Mason: often sung at funerals.

near•ly (nēr′lē), *adv.* **1.** all but; almost: *nearly dead with cold; a plan nearly like our own.* **2.** with close approximation: *a nearly perfect likeness.* **3.** with close kinship, interest, or connection; intimately.

near′ miss′ or **near′-miss′,** *n.* **1.** a strike by a missile that is not a direct hit. **2.** the narrow avoidance of a collision. **3.** something that falls narrowly short of its object.

near′ mon′ey, *n.* any asset easily made liquid, as government bonds or savings deposits.

near•sight•ed (nēr′sī′tid, -sī′-), *adj.* **1.** seeing distinctly at a short distance only; myopic. **2.** SHORTSIGHTED (def. 2). —**near′sight′ed•ly,** *adv.* —**near′sight′ed•ness,** *n.*

neat (nēt), *adj.,* **-er, -est,** *adv.* —*adj.* **1.** in a pleasingly orderly and clean condition: *a neat room.* **2.** habitually orderly and clean in personal appearance or habits. **3.** having a trim and graceful appearance, contour, style, etc.: *a neat figure.* **4.** cleverly effective; skillful; adroit: *a neat solution.* **5.** *Slang.* great; wonderful; fine: *What a neat car!* **6.** STRAIGHT (def. 15). **7.** NET[2] (def. 1). —*adv.* **8.** *Informal.* neatly. —**neat′ly,** *adv.* —**neat′ness,** *n.*

neat•en (nēt′n), *v.t.,* to make neat.

Ne•bo (nē′bō), *n.* **Mount.** See under PISGAH.

Ne•bras•ka (nə bras′kə), *n.* a state in the central United States. 1,652,093; 77,237 sq. mi. (200,044 sq. km). *Cap.:* Lincoln. *Abbr.:* NE, Nebr., Neb. —**Ne•bras′kan,** *adj., n.*

Neb•u•chad•nez•zar (neb′ə kəd nez′ər, neb′yŏŏ-), *n.* **1.** Also, **Neb′u•chad•rez′zar** (-rez′ər), died 562? B.C., king of Babylonia 605?–562? B.C.: conqueror of Jerusalem. II Kings 24, 25. **2.** (*sometimes l.c.*) a bottle for wine holding 20 quarts (18.9 liters).

neb•u•la (neb′yə lə), *n., pl.* **-lae** (-lē′, -lī′), **-las.** a cloud of interstellar gas and dust. —**neb′u•lar,** *adj.*

neb•u•lous (neb′yə ləs), *adj.* **1.** hazy, vague, indistinct, or confused. **2.** cloudy or cloudlike. **3.** of or resembling a nebula or nebulae; nebular. —**neb′u•lous•ly,** *adv.* —**neb′u•lous•ness,** *n.*

nec•es•sar•i•ly (nes′ə sâr′ə lē, -ser′-), *adv.* **1.** by or of necessity: *You don't necessarily have to attend.* **2.** as a necessary, logical, or inevitable result: *That conclusion doesn't necessarily follow.*

nec•es•sar•y (nes′ə ser′ē), *adj., n., pl.* **-sar•ies.** —*adj.* **1.** essential, indispensable, or requisite: *a necessary part of the motor.* **2.** happening or existing by necessity; unavoidable: *a necessary change in our plans.* **3.** acting or proceeding from compulsion or necessity; not free; involuntary. **4.** *Logic.* **a.** (of a proposition) such that a denial of it involves a self-contradiction. **b.** (of an inference or argument) such that its conclusion cannot be false if its supporting premises are true. **c.** (of a condition) such that it must exist if a given event is to occur or a given thing is to exist. Compare SUFFICIENT (def. 2). —*n.* **5.** something necessary or requisite; necessity. **6.** *Chiefly New Eng.* a privy or toilet.

ne•ces•si•tar•i•an (nə ses′i târ′ē ən), *n.* **1.** a person who advocates or supports necessitarianism (disting. from *libertarian*). —*adj.* **2.** pertaining to necessitarians or necessitarianism.

ne•ces•si•tar•i•an•ism (nə ses′i târ′ē ə niz′əm), *n.* the doctrine that all events, including acts of the will, are determined by antecedent causes; determinism.

ne•ces•si•tate (nə ses′i tāt′), *v.t.,* **-tat•ed, -tat•ing. 1.** to make necessary or unavoidable. **2.** to compel, oblige, or force.

ne•ces•si•ty (nə ses′i tē), *n., pl.* **-ties. 1.** something necessary or indispensable: *food, shelter, and other necessities of life.* **2.** the fact of being necessary or indispensable; indispensability: *the necessity of adequate housing.* **3.** an imperative requirement or need for something: *a necessity for a quick decision.* **4.** the state or fact of being necessary or inevitable: *to face the necessity of testifying in court.* **5.** an unavoidable need or compulsion to do something: *not by choice but by necessity.* **6.** a state of being in financial need; poverty: *a family in dire necessity.* **7.** *Philos.* the quality of following inevitably from logical, physical, or moral laws. —***Idiom.*** **8. of necessity,** inevitably; unavoidably; necessarily. —***Proverb.*** **9. Necessity is the mother of invention,** ingenuity will fill a need.

Ne•cho (nē′kō), *n.* **Prince of Sais** and **Prince of Memphis,** fl. 633? B.C., chief of the Egyptian delta lords (father of Psamtik I). Also called **Necho I.**

neck (nek), *n.* **1.** the part of the body connecting the head and the trunk. **2.** the part of a garment encircling or closest to the neck; neckline. **3.** the slender part near the top of a bottle, vase, or similar object. **4.** the longer and more slender part of a violin or similar stringed instrument, extending from the body to the head. **5.** any narrow, connecting, or projecting part suggesting a neck. **6.** a narrow strip of land, as an isthmus or a cape. **7.** a strait; channel. **8.** a narrowed part of a bone, organ, or the like. **9.** the slightly narrowed region of a tooth between the crown and the root. **10.** the approximate length of a horse's head and neck, as indicating a margin of victory in a race. **11.** BEARD (def. 5). —*v.i.* **12.** *Informal.* to embrace, kiss, and caress amorously. —*v.t.* **13.** *Informal.* to embrace, kiss, and caress (someone) amorously. **14.** to strangle or behead. —***Idiom.*** **15. break one's neck,** *Informal.* to make a great effort. **16. neck and neck,** just even or very close: *two horses crossing the finish line neck and neck.* **17. neck of the woods,** *Informal.* neighborhood, area, or vicinity. **18. stick one's neck out,** *Informal.* to put oneself in jeopardy, esp. by acting courageously.

necked (nekt), *adj.* having a neck of a kind specified (usu. used in combination): *a square-necked blouse.*

neck•er•chief (nek′ər chif, -chēf′), *n.* a cloth or scarf worn around the neck.

neck•lace (nek′lis), *n.,* a piece of jewelry worn around the neck, as a chain or a string of gemstones, pearls, etc.

neck•line (nek′līn′), *n.* the opening at the neck of a garment, often with reference to its shape or its position on the body: *a V-neckline; a high neckline.*

neck•tie (nek′tī′), *n.* **1.** a band of decorative fabric worn around the collar and tied in front with the ends hanging down or looped into a bow. **2.** any band or scarf fastened at the front of the neck.

necro-, a combining form meaning "the dead," "corpse," "dead tissue": *necrology.* Also, *esp. before a vowel,* **necr-.**

ne•crol•o•gy (nə krol′ə jē, ne-), *n., pl.* **-gies. 1.** a list of persons who have died within a certain time. **2.** a notice of death; obituary. —**ne•crol′o•gist,** *n.*

nec•ro•man•cy (nek′rə man′sē), *n.* **1.** a method of divination through invocation of the dead. **2.** magic in general, esp. that practiced by a witch or sorcerer; conjuration. —**nec′ro•man′cer,** *n.* —**nec′ro•man′tic,** *adj.*

nec•ro•phil•i•a (nek′rə fil′ē ə), *n.* an erotic attraction to corpses. —**nec′ro•phile′** (-fīl′), *n.* —**nec′ro•phil′i•ac, nec′ro•phil′ic,** *adj., n.*

nec•ro•pho•bi•a (nek′rə fō′bē ə), *n.* an abnormal fear of dead bodies. —**nec′ro•pho′bic,** *adj.*

ne•crop•o•lis (nə krop′ə lis), *n., pl.* **-lis•es.** an esp. large cemetery of an ancient city. —**nec•ro•pol•i•tan** (nek′rə pol′i tn), *adj.*

ne•cro•sis (nə krō′sis), *n.* death of a circumscribed portion of animal or plant tissue. —**ne•crot′ic** (-krot′ik), *adj.* —**nec•ro•tize** (nek′rə tīz′), *v.i., v.t.,* **-tized, -tiz•ing.**

nec•tar (nek′tər), *n.* **1.** the saccharine secretion of a plant, which attracts the insects or birds that pollinate the flower. **2.** the juice of a fruit, esp. when not diluted, or a blend of fruit juices. **3.** (in Greek myth) the life-giving drink of the gods. **4.** any delicious drink.

nec•tar•ine (nek′tə rēn′, nek′tə rēn′), *n.* a variety of peach having a smooth, downless skin.

nee or **née** (nā), *adj.* born (used to introduce the maiden name of a married woman): *Mrs. Jones, nee Berg.*

need (nēd), *n., v.,* **need•ed, need•ing,** *auxiliary v., pres. sing. 3rd pers.* **need.** —*n.* **1.** a requirement, necessary duty, or obligation: *There is no need to go there.* **2.** a lack of something wanted or deemed necessary: *the needs of the poor.* **3.** urgent want, as of something requisite: *They have need of your charity.* **4.** necessity arising from existing circumstances: *There is need for caution now.* **5.** a situation or time of difficulty; exigency: *to help a friend in need.* **6.** a condition marked by the lack of something requisite: *the need for leadership.* **7.** destitution; extreme poverty: *The family's need is acute.* —*v.t.* **8.** to have need of; require: *to need money.* —*v.i.* **9.** to be in need or want. —*auxiliary v.* **10.** (used to express obligation or necessity, esp. in interrogative or negative statements): *Need I say more?* —***Idiom.*** **11. if need be,** should the necessity arise. —**need′er,** *n.*

need•i•ness (nē′dē nis), *n.* a condition of need; poverty; indigence.

nee•dle (nēd′l), *n., v.,* **-dled, -dling.** —*n.* **1.** a small, slender, rodlike instrument, usu. of polished steel, with a sharp point at one end and an eye or hole for thread at the other, for passing thread through cloth to make stitches in sewing. **2.** any of various related, usu. considerably larger, implements for making stitches, as in knitting or crocheting. Compare CROCHET (def. 1). **3.** *Med.* **a.** a slender, pointed, steel instrument used in sewing or piercing tissues, as in suturing. **b.** a hypodermic needle. **4.** an injection of a drug or medicine; shot. **5.** any of various objects resembling or suggesting a needle. **6.** the tapered stylus at the end of a phonographic tonearm, used to transmit vibrations from a record groove to a transducer for conversion to audible signals. **7.** a pointed instrument, or stylus, used in engraving, etching, or the like. **8.** *Bot.* a needle-shaped leaf, as of a pine. **9.** *Zool.* a slender, sharp spicule. **10.** *Chem., Mineral.* a needlelike crystal. **11.** a sharp-pointed mass or pinnacle of rock. **12.** an obelisk or a tapering, four-sided shaft of stone. **13. the needle,** *Informal.* teasing or harassing remarks. —*v.t.* **14.** to sew or pierce with or as if with a needle. **15.** *Informal.* **a.** to prod or goad (someone) to a specified action: *We needled her into going with us.* **b.** to tease. —*v.i.* **16.** to form needles in crystallization. **17.** to work with a needle. —***Idiom.*** **18. needle in a haystack,** something very difficult to locate. —**nee′dler,** *n.*

nee′dle bi′opsy, *n.* the removal for diagnostic study of a small amount of tissue by means of a long, hollow needle.

nee•dle•craft (nēd′l kraft′, -kräft′), *n.* NEEDLEWORK.

nee•dle•point (nēd′l point′), *n.* **1.** embroidery upon canvas, usu. with uniform spacing of stitches in a pattern. —*adj.* **2.** done or executed in needlepoint: *a needlepoint cushion.* **3.** noting a lace **(nee′dlepoint**

lace′) in which a needle works out the design upon parchment or paper. —*v.t., v.i.* **4.** to execute in or create needlepoint.

need•less (nēd′lis), *adj.* unnecessary; not needed: *a needless waste of food.* —**need′less•ly,** *adv.* —**need′less•ness,** *n.*

nee•dle•work (nēd′l wûrk′), *n.* **1.** the art, process, or product of working with a needle, esp. in embroidery, needlepoint, tapestry, quilting, and appliqué. **2.** the occupation or employment of one skilled in embroidery, needlepoint, etc. Also called **needlecraft, stitchery.**

need•n't (nēd′nt), contraction of *need not.*

needs (nēdz), *adv.* of necessity; necessarily (usu. prec. or fol. by *must*): *It must needs be so. It needs must be.*

need•y (nē′dē), *adj.,* **need•i•er, need•i•est,** *n.* —*adj.* **1.** in a condition of need or want; extremely poor; destitute. —*n.* **2. the needy,** needy persons collectively: *to help the needy.* —**need′i•ly,** *adv.*

ne'er (nâr), *adv. Literary.* never.

ne'er′-do-well′, *n.* **1.** an idle, worthless person; good-for-nothing. —*adj.* **2.** worthless; ineffectual; good-for-nothing.

ne•far•i•ous (ni fâr′ē əs), *adj.* extremely wicked or villainous; iniquitous: *a nefarious plot.* —**ne•far′i•ous•ly,** *adv.* —**ne•far′i•ous•ness,** *n.*

Nef•er•ti•ti (nef′ər tē′tē) also **Nef•re•te•te** (nef′ri-), *n.* fl. early 14th century B.C., Egyptian queen: wife of Akhenaton.

ne•gate (ni gāt′, neg′āt), *v.,* **-gat•ed, -gat•ing.** —*v.t.* **1.** to deny the existence, evidence, or truth of (something). **2.** to cause to be ineffective; nullify or invalidate (something). —*v.i.* **3.** to be negative; bring or cause negative results: *a pessimism that always negates.* —**ne•ga′tor, ne•gat′er,** *n.*

ne•ga•tion (ni gā′shən), *n.* **1.** the act of denying: *He shook his head in negation of the charge.* **2.** a denial: *a negation of one's former beliefs.* **3.** something that is without existence; nonentity. **4.** the absence or opposite of something considered positive or affirmative: *Darkness is the negation of light.* **5.** a negative statement, idea, concept, doctrine, etc.; a contradiction, refutation, or rebuttal. —**ne•ga′tion•al,** *adj.*

neg•a•tive (neg′ə tiv), *adj., n., v.,* **-tived, -tiv•ing,** *interj.* —*adj.* **1.** expressing or containing negation or denial: *a negative response to the question.* **2.** refusing consent, as to a proposal: *a negative reply to my request.* **3.** expressing refusal or resistance: *a negative attitude about cooperating.* **4.** unfavorable: *negative criticism.* **5.** prohibitory, as a command or order. **6.** lacking positive attributes (opposed to *positive*): *a negative character.* **7.** lacking in helpfulness, optimism, or the like: *a negative approach to problem solving.* **8.** being without rewards, results, or effectiveness: *a search of the premises proved negative.* **9.** *Math.* **a.** involving or noting subtraction; minus. **b.** measured or proceeding in the direction opposite to that which is considered as positive. **10.** *Photog.* noting an image in which the brightness values of the subject are reproduced so that the lightest areas are shown as the darkest. **11. a.** of or pertaining to the electric charge of a body that has an excess of electrons. **b.** (of a point in a circuit) having lower potential, therefore drawing the flow of current. **12.** *Med.* failing to show a positive result in a diagnostic test. **13.** *Chem.* (of an element or group) tending to gain electrons and become negatively charged; acid. **14.** *Physiol.* responding in a direction away from the stimulus. **15.** of, pertaining to, or noting the S pole of a magnet. **16.** *Logic.* (of a proposition) denying the truth of the predicate with regard to the subject. —*n.* **17.** a negative statement, answer, word, gesture, etc.: *The ship signaled back a negative.* **18.** a refusal of assent: *to answer a request with a negative.* **19.** the negative form of statement. **20.** one or more persons arguing against a resolution, statement, etc., esp. a team in a formal debate. **21.** a negative quality or characteristic. **22.** disadvantage; drawback: *a brilliant plan with only one negative.* **23.** *Math.* **a.** a minus sign. **b.** a negative quantity or symbol. **24.** *Photog.* a negative image, as on a film, used chiefly for making positives. —*v.t.* **25.** to deny; contradict. **26.** to refute or disprove (something). **27.** to refuse assent or consent to; veto. **28.** to neutralize or counteract. —*interj.* **29.** (used to indicate disagreement, denial of permission, etc.) —*Idiom.* **30. in the negative,** in the form of a negative response: *to answer in the negative.* —**neg′a•tive•ly,** *adv.* —**neg′a•tive•ness, neg′a•tiv′i•ty,** *n.*

neg′ative in′come tax′, *n.* a system of income subsidy through which persons having less than a certain annual income receive money from the government rather than pay taxes to it.

neg′ative op′tion, *n.* a clause in a sales contract, as for books or records, that provides that merchandise will be sent periodically to the subscriber unless he or she notifies the company in writing that it is not wanted. —**neg′ative-op′tion,** *adj.*

neg•a•tiv•ism (neg′ə ti viz′əm), *n.* **1.** a negative or pessimistic attitude. **2.** *Psychol.* a tendency to resist external commands, suggestions, or expectations, or internal stimuli, as hunger, by doing nothing or something contrary or unrelated to the stimulus. —**neg′a•tiv•ist,** *n.* —**neg′a•tiv•is′tic,** *adj.*

neg•a•to•ry (neg′ə tôr′ē, -tōr′ē), *adj.* marked by negation; denying; negative.

Neg•ev (neg′ev) also **Neg•eb** (-eb), *n.* a partly desert region in S Israel, bordering on the Sinai Peninsula. 4700 sq. mi. (12,173 sq. km).

ne•glect (ni glekt′), *v.t.* **1.** to pay no attention or too little attention to; disregard or slight. **2.** to be remiss in the care or treatment of: *to neglect one's appearance.* **3.** to omit, as through indifference or carelessness: *to neglect to reply to an invitation.* **4.** to fail to carry out or perform: *to neglect the household chores.* —*n.* **5.** an act or instance of neglecting; negligence: *The neglect of the property was shameful.* **6.** the fact or state of being neglected: *a beauty marred by neglect.*

ne•glect•ful (ni glekt′fəl), *adj.* characterized by neglect; careless; negligent. —**ne•glect′ful•ly,** *adv.* —**ne•glect′ful•ness,** *n.*

neg•li•gee or **neg•li•gée** or **neg•li•gé** (neg′li zhā′, neg′li zhā′), *n., pl.* **-gees** or **-gées** or **-gés.** a woman's dressing gown or robe, usu. of sheer, soft fabric.

neg•li•gence (neg′li jəns), *n.* **1.** the quality, fact, or result of being negligent; neglect. **2.** an instance of being negligent. **3.** *Law.* the failure to exercise a reasonable degree of care, esp. for the protection of other persons.

neg•li•gent (neg′li jənt), *adj.* **1.** guilty of or characterized by neglect, as of duty: *negligent officials.* **2.** careless and indifferent; offhand: *a negligent shrug.* —**neg′li•gent•ly,** *adv.*

neg•li•gi•ble (neg′li jə bəl), *adj.* so small or unimportant as to be safely disregarded: *negligible expenses.* —**neg′li•gi•bil′i•ty, neg′li•gi•ble•ness,** *n.* —**neg′li•gi•bly,** *adv.*

ne•go•ti•a•ble (ni gō′shē ə bəl, -shə bəl), *adj.* **1.** capable of being negotiated. **2.** (esp. of securities) transferable by delivery, with or without endorsement, the title then passing to the transferee. —*n.* **3. negotiables,** negotiable bonds, stocks, etc. —**ne•go′ti•a•bil′i•ty,** *n.*

ne•go•ti•ate (ni gō′shē āt′), *v.,* **-at•ed, -at•ing.** —*v.i.* **1.** to deal or bargain with another or others, as in the preparation of a treaty or contract. —*v.t.* **2.** to arrange for or bring about by discussion and settlement of terms: *to negotiate a loan.* **3.** to move through, around, or over in a satisfactory manner: *to negotiate a sharp curve.* **4.** to transfer (a draft, promissory note, etc.) to a new owner by endorsement and delivery or by delivery. —**ne•go′ti•a′tor,** *n.*

ne•go•ti•a•tion (ni gō′shē ā′shən, -sē-), *n.* **1.** mutual discussion and arrangement of the terms of a transaction or agreement. **2.** the act or process of negotiating. **3.** an instance or the result of negotiating.

Ne•gro[1] (nē′grō), *adj., n., pl.* **-groes.** *Sometimes Offensive.* —*adj.* **1.** of, designating, or characteristic of one of the traditional racial divisions of humankind, marked by brown to black skin, dark eyes, and woolly or crisp hair and including esp. the indigenous peoples of sub-Saharan Africa and their descendents. —*n.* **2.** a member of the peoples traditionally classified as the Negro race. [< Spanish and Portuguese *negro* black < Latin *nigrum,* masc. acc. of *niger* black] —**Usage.** See BLACK.

Ne•gro[2] (nā′grō; *Sp.* ne′ɢʀô; *Port.* ne′ɢʀoo), *n.* **1.** a river in NW South America, flowing SE from Colombia into the Amazon. 1400 mi. (2255 km) long. **2.** a river in S Argentina, flowing E from the Andes to the Atlantic. 700 mi. (1125 km) long. **3.** a river in SE South America, flowing SW from Brazil into the Uruguay River. ab. 500 mi. (800 km) long. Portuguese, **Rio Negro.** Spanish, **Río Negro.**

NEH, National Endowment for the Humanities.

Neh., Nehemiah.

Ne•he•mi•ah (nē′ə mī′ə), *n.* **1.** a Hebrew leader of the 5th century B.C. **2.** a book of the Bible bearing his name.

Neh•ru (nā′rōō, nâr′ōō), *n.* **1. Jawaharlal,** 1889–1964, first prime minister of the republic of India 1947–64. **2.** his father **Motilal,** 1861–1931, Indian lawyer and statesman.

neigh (nā), *n.* **1.** the complex, high-pitched, snorting sound of a horse. —*v.i.* **2.** to utter such a sound.

neigh•bor (nā′bər), *n.* **1.** a person who lives near another. **2.** a person or thing that is near another. **3.** one's fellow human being. **4.** a person who shows helpfulness toward fellow humans. **5.** (used as a term of address, esp. in greeting a stranger). —*adj.* **6.** situated or living near another: *neighbor nations.* —*v.t.* **7.** to live or be situated near to; adjoin. —*v.i.* **8.** to live or be situated nearby. **9.** to associate with or as if with one's neighbors (often fol. by *with*). Also, *esp. Brit.,* **neigh′bour.**

neigh•bor•hood (nā′bər hŏŏd′), *n.* **1.** the area or region around or near some place or thing; vicinity. **2.** a district or locality, often with reference to its character or inhabitants: *a fashionable neighborhood.* **3.** a number of persons living in a particular locality. **4.** *Math.* an open set that contains a given point. —*Idiom.* **5. in the neighborhood of,** approximately; nearly; about.

neigh•bor•ing (nā′bər ing), *adj.* adjacent; adjoining.

neigh•bor•ly (nā′bər lē), *adj.* having or showing qualities befitting a neighbor; friendly. —**neigh′bor•li•ness,** *n.*

nei•ther (nē′thər, nī′-), *conj.* **1.** not either, as of persons or things specified (usu. fol. by *nor*): *Neither John nor Betty is here.* **2.** nor; nor yet: *Bob can't go; neither can I.* —*adj.* **3.** not either; not the one or the other: *neither path.* —*pron.* **4.** not either; not one person or the other; not one thing or the other: *Neither is correct.* —**Pronunciation.** See EITHER.

nel•son (nel′sən), *n.* a wrestling hold in which pressure is applied to the head, back of the neck, and one or both arms of the opponent. Compare FULL NELSON, HALF NELSON.

Nel•son (nel′sən), *n.* **1. Viscount Horatio,** 1758–1805, British admiral. **2.** a river in central Canada, flowing NE from Lake Winnipeg to Hudson Bay. 400 mi. (645 km) long. **3.** a seaport on N South Island, in New Zealand. 45,200.

nem•a•tode (nem′ə tōd′), *n.* any unsegmented worm of the phylum Nematoda, having an elongated, cylindrical body and often parasitic on animals and plants; a roundworm.

nem•e•sis (nem′ə sis), *n., pl.* **-ses** (-sēz′). **1.** a source or cause of harm or failure. **2.** an unconquerable opponent or rival. **3.** (*cap.*) the ancient Greek goddess of divine retribution. **4.** an agent or act of retribution.

ne·ne (nā′nā), *n., pl.* **-ne.** a barred, gray-brown wild goose, *Nesochen sandvicensis*, native to Hawaii. Also called **Hawaiian goose.**

neo-, 1. a combining form meaning "new," "recent," "revived," "modified": *Neolithic; neoorthodoxy; neophyte.* **2.** a combining form used in the names of isomers having a carbon atom attached to four carbon atoms: *neoarsphenamine.* Also, *esp. before a vowel,* **ne-.**

Ne·o·Ar·a·ma·ic (nē′ō ar′ə mā′ik), *n.* any of the modern Aramaic dialects or languages, spoken in a small number of Jewish and Christian communities in the Near East, and in émigré communities elsewhere.

ne·o·clas·sic (nē′ō klas′ik) also **ne·o·clas·si·cal,** *adj.* (*sometimes cap.*) of, pertaining to, or designating a revival or adaptation of classical styles, forms, principles, etc., as in art, literature, music, or architecture. —**ne′o·clas′si·cism** (-ə siz′əm), *n.* —**ne′o·clas′si·cist,** *n.*

ne·o·co·lo·ni·al·ism (nē′ō kə lō′nē ə liz′əm), *n.* the policy by which a nation exerts political and economic control over a less powerful independent nation or region. —**ne′o·co·lo′ni·al,** *adj., n.* —**ne′o·co·lo′ni·al·ist,** *n., adj.*

ne·o·con (nē′ō kon′), *n.* a neoconservative.

ne·o·con·serv·a·tism (nē′ō kən sûr′və tiz′əm), *n.* moderate political conservatism espoused or advocated by former liberals or socialists. —**ne′o·con·serv′a·tive,** *n., adj.*

ne·o·Dar·win·ism (nē′ō där′wi niz′əm), *n.* a modification of Darwin's theory of evolution holding that species evolve by natural selection acting on genetic variation. —**ne′o·Dar′win·ist,** *n.*

ne·o·dym·i·um (nē′ō dim′ē əm), *n.* a rare-earth metallic trivalent element; occurs with cerium and other rare-earth metals and has rose-colored salts. *Symbol:* Nd; *at. wt.:* 144.24; *at. no.:* 60; *sp. gr.:* 6.9 at 20°C.

ne·o·gen·e·sis (nē′ō jen′ə sis), *n.* the regeneration of tissue.

neo-im·pres·sion·ism (nē′ō im presh′ə niz′əm), *n.* a late 19th-century French artistic theory and practice, characterized chiefly by the use of pointillist techniques. —**ne′o·im·pres′sion·ist,** *n., adj.*

ne·o·lib·er·al·ism (nē′ō lib′ər ə liz′əm, -lib′rə-), *n.* an outgrowth of the U.S. liberal movement, beginning in the late 1960s, that modified somewhat its traditional endorsement of all trade unions and opposition to big business and military buildup. —**ne′o·lib′er·al,** *adj., n.*

ne·o·lith (nē′ə lith), *n.* a Neolithic stone implement.

Ne·o·lith·ic (nē′ə lith′ik), *adj.* **1.** (*sometimes l.c.*) of, designating, or characteristic of the last phase of the Stone Age, commonly thought to have begun c9000–8000 B.C. in the Middle East. Compare MESOLITHIC, PALEOLITHIC. **2.** (*usu. l.c.*) belonging to or remaining from an earlier era; outdated; passé.

ne·ol·o·gism (nē ol′ə jiz′əm), *n.* **1.** a new word or phrase or an existing word used in a new sense. **2.** the introduction or use of new words or new senses of existing words. **3.** a word invented and understood only by the speaker, occurring most often in the speech of schizophrenics. —**ne·ol′o·gist,** *n.* —**ne·ol′o·gis′tic,** *adj.* —**ne·ol′o·gize′,** *v.i.,* **-gized, -giz·ing.**

ne·on (nē′on), *n.* **1.** a chemically inert gaseous element occurring in small amounts in the earth's atmosphere, used chiefly in a type of electrical lamp. *Symbol:* Ne; *at. wt.:* 20.183; *at. no.:* 10; *density:* 0.9002 g/l at 0°C and 760 mm pressure. **2.** a sign formed from neon lamps.

ne·o·nate (nē′ə nāt′), *n.* a newborn child, or one in its first 28 days. —**ne′o·na′tal,** *adj.*

ne·o·Na·zi (nē′ō nät′sē, -nat′-), *n., pl.* **-zis.** a person, esp. a member of a group, who embraces Nazism. —**ne′o·Na′zism** (-siz əm), *n.*

ne′on tet′ra, a small, bright red and blue South American characin fish, *Pracheirodon innesi:* a popular aquarium fish.

ne·o·or·tho·dox·y or **ne·o·or·tho·dox·y** (nē′ō ôr′thə dok′sē), *n.* a 20th-century movement in Protestant theology reacting against liberal theology and reaffirming certain doctrines of the Reformation. —**ne′o·or′tho·dox,** *adj.*

ne·o·pa·gan·ism (nē′ō pā′gə niz′əm), *n.* any modern religion reconstructed from an ancient pagan religion. —**ne′o·pa′gan·ist,** *n.*

ne·o·phyte (nē′ə fīt′), *n.* **1.** a beginner or a novice. **2.** a new convert to a belief, religion, etc.; proselyte. **3.** a novice in a religious order. **4.** (in the early Christian Church) a person newly baptized. —**ne′o·phyt′ic** (-fit′ik), *adj.* —**ne′o·phyt·ism** (-fī tiz′əm), *n.*

ne·o·plasm (nē′ə plaz′əm), *n.* a new, often uncontrolled growth of abnormal tissue; tumor. —**ne′o·plas′tic** (-plas′tik), *adj.*

Ne·o·pla·to·nism (nē′ō plāt′n iz′əm), *n.* (*sometimes l.c.*) a philosophic system founded by Plotinus in the 3rd century A.D. on Platonic doctrine and Oriental mysticism to which Christian influences were later added and holding that all existence emanates from a single source to which souls can be reunited. —**Ne′o·pla′to·nist,** *n.*

ne·o·prene (nē′ə prēn′), *n.* an oil-resistant synthetic rubber: used in putty, paint, crepe soles for shoes, etc.

Ne·o·ri·can (nē′ō rē′kən) also **Nuyorican,** *n.* **1.** a Puerto Rican living in New York or one who has lived in New York and returned to Puerto Rico. —*adj.* **2.** of or pertaining to Neoricans.

ne·o·Scho·las·ti·cism (nē′ō skə las′tə siz′əm), *n.* a contemporary application of the doctrine of Scholasticism to problems of everyday life. —**ne′o·Scho·las′tic,** *adj., n.*

Ne·o·Sy·neph·rine (nē′ō si nef′rin, -rēn), *Trademark.* a brand of phenylephrine.

Ne·pal (nə pôl′, -päl′, -pal′, nā-), *n.* a constitutional monarchy in the Himalayas between N India and Tibet. 22,641,061; ab. 56,827 sq. mi. (147,181 sq. km). *Cap.:* Katmandu. —**Nep·a·lese** (nep′ə lēz′, -lēs′), *adj., n.*

ne·pen·the (ni pen′thē), *n., pl.* **-thes. 1.** a drug or drink, or the plant yielding it, mentioned by ancient writers as having the power to bring forgetfulness. **2.** anything inducing a pleasurable sensation of forgetfulness. —**ne·pen′the·an,** *adj.*

neph·ew (nef′yōō; *esp. Brit.* nev′yōō), *n.* **1.** a son of one's brother or sister. **2.** a son of one's spouse's brother or sister.

Neph·i·lim (nef′ə lim), *n.pl.* a race of giants. Gen. 6:4; Num. 13:33.

neph·rite (nef′rīt), *n.* a compact granular variety of actinolite, varying from whitish to dark green: a form of jade.

ne·phri·tis (nə frī′tis), *n.* inflammation of the kidneys, esp. in Bright's disease. —**ne·phrit′ic** (-frit′ik), *adj.*

ne·phrol·o·gy (nə frol′ə jē), *n.* the branch of medical science that deals with the kidney. —**ne·phrol′o·gist,** *n.*

ne plus ul·tra (nē′ plus′ ul′trə, nā′), *n.* **1.** the highest point or stage; acme. **2.** the most intense degree of a quality or state. [< Latin: not further beyond]

nep·o·tism (nep′ə tiz′əm), *n.* patronage or favoritism based on family relationship. —**ne·pot′ic** (nə pot′ik), **nep′o·tis′tic,** *adj.*

Nep·tune (nep′tōōn, -tyōōn), *n.* **1.** the Roman god of the sea, identified with the Greek god Poseidon. **2.** the sea or ocean: *Neptune's mighty roar.* **3.** the planet eighth in order from the sun, having an equatorial diameter of 30,200 mi. (48,600 km), a mean distance from the sun of 2794.4 million mi. (4497.1 million km), a period of revolution of 164.81 years, and at least six moons. —**Nep·tu′ni·an,** *adj.*

nep·tu·ni·um (nep tōō′nē əm, -tyōō′-), *n.* a short-lived radioactive transuranic element produced in nuclear reactors by the neutron bombardment of U-238. *Symbol:* Np; *at. no.:* 93; *at. wt.:* 237.

nerd (nûrd), *n. Slang.* **1.** a dull, ineffectual, or unattractive person. **2.** a person dedicated to a nonsocial pursuit: *a computer nerd.* —**nerd′y,** *adj.,* **nerd·i·er, nerd·i·est.**

Ne·ro (nēr′ō), *n.* (*Lucius Domitius Ahenobarbus*) ("*Nero Claudius Caesar Drusus Germanicus*") A.D. 37–68, emperor of Rome 54–68.

nerve (nûrv), *n., v.,* **nerved, nerv·ing.** —*n.* **1.** one or more bundles of fibers forming part of a system that conveys impulses of sensation, motion, etc., between the brain or spinal cord and other parts of the body. **2.** courage under trying circumstances. **3.** boldness; impudence; impertinence. **4.** nerves, nervousness: *an attack of nerves.* **5.** strength, vigor, or energy. **6.** a sinew or tendon: *to strain every nerve.* —*v.t.* **7.** to give strength, vigor, or courage to. —*Idiom.* **8. get on someone's nerves,** to irritate or annoy someone.

nerve′ cell′, *n.* NEURON.

nerve′ cen′ter, *n.* **1.** a group of nerves that act together to perform a function. **2.** a source of information or activity; control center.

nerve′ cord′, *n.* **1.** the hollow dorsal tract of nervous tissue that constitutes the central nervous system of all chordates and that developed as the spinal cord and brain of vertebrates. **2.** a double strand of nerve fibers in elongate invertebrates, as earthworms, that connects with a pair of nerve ganglia at each body segment.

nerve′ fi′ber, *n.* an axon or dendrite of a neuron.

nerve′ gas′, *n.* any of several poison gases, derived chiefly from phosphoric acid, that interfere with nerve conduction and respiration.

nerve′ growth′ fac′tor, *n.* a protein that promotes the growth, organization, and maintenance of sympathetic and some sensory nerve cells. *Abbr.:* NGF

nerve′ im′pulse, *n.* a progressive wave of electric and chemical activity along a nerve fiber, stimulating or inhibiting action.

nerve·less (nûrv′lis), *adj.* **1.** without nervousness; calm. **2.** lacking strength or vigor; weak. **3.** lacking firmness or courage. **4.** having no nerves. —**nerve′less·ly,** *adv.* —**nerve′less·ness,** *n.*

nerve′-rack′ing or **nerve′-wrack′ing,** *adj.* producing great anxiety, tension, or irritation.

nerv·ous (nûr′vəs), *adj.* **1.** acutely uneasy or apprehensive; fearful; timid. **2.** highly excitable or agitated. **3.** of, pertaining to, or affecting the nerves: *nervous tension.* **4.** suffering from, characterized by, or originating in disordered nerves. **5.** characterized by acute uneasiness or apprehension: *a nervous moment.* **6.** having or containing nerves. **7.** vigorous or spirited. —**nerv′ous·ly,** *adv.* —**nerv′ous·ness,** *n.*

nerv′ous break′down, *n.* (not in technical use) any disabling mental or emotional disorder requiring treatment.

nerv′ous Nel′lie (or **Nel′ly**) (nel′ē), *n., pl.* **-lies.** *Informal.* a timid or fearful person.

nerv′ous sys′tem, *n.* the system of neurons, neurochemicals, and allied structures involved in receiving sensory stimuli, generating and coordinating responses, and controlling bodily activities: in vertebrates it includes the brain, spinal cord, nerves, and ganglia.

nerv·y (nûr′vē), *adj.,* **nerv·i·er, nerv·i·est. 1.** brashly presumptuous or insolent; pushy. **2.** having or showing courage. **3.** nervous; excitable. **4.** strong; vigorous. —**nerv′i·ly,** *adv.* —**nerv′i·ness,** *n.*

n.e.s. or **N.E.S.,** not elsewhere specified.

nes·ci·ence (nesh′əns, nesh′ē əns, nes′ē-), *n.* **1.** lack of knowledge; ignorance. **2.** AGNOSTICISM. —**nes′cient,** *adj.*

ness (nes), *n.* a headland; promontory; cape.

-ness, a suffix attached to adjectives and participles, forming abstract nouns denoting quality and state (and often, by extension, something exemplifying a quality or state): *darkness; goodness; obligingness; preparedness.*

Ness (nes), *n.* **Loch,** a lake in SW Scotland, near Inverness. 23 mi. (37 km) long.

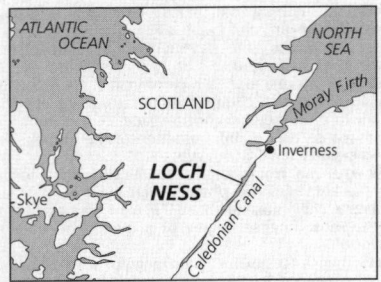

nest (nest), *n.* **1.** a bowl-shaped or pocketlike structure, often of twigs, grasses, and mud, prepared by a bird for incubating eggs and rearing young. **2.** any structure or shelter used for depositing eggs or raising young. **3.** a number of birds, insects, animals, etc., inhabiting one such place. **4.** a snug retreat or refuge; resting place; home. **5.** an assemblage of things lying or set close together. **6.** a set of items, often of graduated size, that fit close together or one within another: *a nest of tables.* **7.** a set of items or parts forming a hierarchical structure, with larger parts enclosing smaller ones. **8.** a place where something bad flourishes: *a nest of thieves.* **9.** the occupants or frequenters of such a place. —*v.i.* **10.** to build or have a nest: *to nest in trees.* **11.** to settle in or as if in a nest. **12.** to fit together, as one within another: *bowls that nest for storage.* **13.** to search for or collect nests. —*v.t.* **14.** to settle or place (something) in or as if in a nest. **15.** to fit or place one within another.

nest′ egg′, *n.* **1.** money saved and held as a reserve for emergencies, retirement, etc. **2.** a natural or artificial egg placed in a nest to induce a hen to continue laying eggs there.

nes·tle (nes′əl), *v.,* **-tled, -tling.** —*v.i.* **1.** to lie close and snug; snuggle; cuddle. **2.** to be located in a sheltered spot: *a cottage nestling in a grove.* **3.** to settle snugly. **4.** to put or press affectionately: *She nestled her head on his shoulder.* —**nes′tler,** *n.*

nest·ling (nest′ling, nes′ling), *n.* **1.** a bird too young to leave the nest. **2.** a young child or infant.

Nes·to·ri·an (ne stôr′ē ən, -stôr′-), *n.* **1.** any of the followers of Nestorius, who denied the hypostasis of Christ and maintained the existence of two distinct persons in Him. —*adj.* **2.** of or pertaining to the Nestorians. —**Nes′to′ri·an·ism,** *n.*

Nes·to·ri·us (ne stôr′ē əs, -stôr′-), *n.* died A.D. 451?, Syrian ecclesiastic: patriarch of Constantinople 428–431; condemned as a heretic.

net¹ (net), *n., v.,* **net·ted, net·ting.** —*n.* **1.** a fabric consisting of a uniform open mesh made by weaving, twisting, knotting, etc. **2.** a bag or other contrivance of such fabric, for catching fish or other animals: *a butterfly net.* **3.** a piece of meshed fabric designed for a specific purpose, as to divide a court in racket games or to protect against insects. **4.** anything serving to catch or ensnare. **5.** HAIR NET. **6.** (in racket games) a ball that hits the net. **7.** the goal in hockey or lacrosse. **8.** any network of filaments, lines, veins, or the like. **9.** a computer or telecommunications network. **10.** a broadcasting network. —*v.t.* **11.** to cover, screen, or enclose with a net or netting. **12.** to take with a net: *to net fish.* **13.** to set or use nets in (a river, stream, etc.). **14.** to catch or ensnare: *to net a criminal.* **15.** (in racket games) to hit (the ball) into the net.

net² (net), *adj., n., v.,* **net·ted, net·ting.** —*adj.* **1.** remaining after deductions, as for charges or expenses (opposed to *gross*): *net earnings.* **2.** sold at a stated price with all parts and charges included and with all deductions having been made. **3.** final; totally conclusive: *the net result.* **4.** (of weight) after deduction of tare, tret, or both. —*n.* **5.** net income, profit, etc. (opposed to *gross*). —*v.t.* **6.** to gain or produce as clear profit.

neth·er (neth′ər), *adj.* **1.** lying or believed to lie beneath the earth's surface; infernal: *the nether regions.* **2.** lower or under: *his nether lip.* —**neth′er·ward,** *adj.*

Neth·er·lands (neth′ər ləndz), *n.* **the,** (*used with a sing. or pl. v.*) a kingdom in W Europe, on the North Sea. 15,653,091; 16,065 sq. mi. (41,447 sq. km). *Capitals:* Amsterdam *and* The Hague. Also called **Holland.** Dutch, **Nederland.** —**Neth′er·land·er** (-lan′dər, -lən-), *n.* —**Neth′er·land/i·an,** *adj.*

Neth′erlands Antil′les, *n.pl.* a Netherlands overseas territory in the Caribbean Sea, N and NE of Venezuela: includes the islands of Bonaire, Curaçao, Saba, and St. Eustatius, and the S part of St. Martin. 188,501; 308 sq. mi. (800 sq. km). *Cap.:* Willemstad. Formerly, **Curaçao.** —**Neth′erlands Antil′lean,** *adj., n.*

Neth′erlands Gui·an′a, *n.* a former name of SURINAME.

neth·er·most (neth′ər mōst′, -məst), *adj.* lowest; farthest down.

neth′er world′ or **neth′er·world′,** *n.* **1.** the infernal regions; hell. **2.** the criminal underworld.

net′ in′come, *n.* the excess of revenues over expenses and losses.

net·i·quette (net′i kit, -ket′), *n.* the etiquette of computer networks.

net′ na′tional prod′uct, *n.* the gross national product less depreciation of capital goods.

net′ prof′it, *n.* the actual profit gained, usu. gross receipts less costs.

net·ting (net′ing), *n.* any of various kinds of net fabric.

net·tle (net′l), *n., v.,* **-tled, -tling.** —*n.* **1.** any plant of the genus *Urtica,* covered with stinging hairs. —*v.t.* **2.** to irritate, annoy, or provoke. **3.** to sting as a nettle does. —**net′tler,** *n.* —**net′tly,** *adj.*

net·work (net′wûrk′), *n.* **1.** any combination of intersecting or interconnecting filaments, lines, passages, etc.: *a network of caves.* **2. a.** a group of transmitting stations linked by wire or microwave relay so that the same radio or television program can be broadcast by all. **b.** a company or organization that provides the programs for these stations. **3.** any system or group of interrelated or interconnected elements esp. over a large area: *a network of supply depots.* **4.** a netting or net. **5.** a computer or telecommunications system linked to permit exchange of information. **6.** an association of individuals having a common interest and often providing mutual assistance, information, etc. —*v.i.* **7.** to engage in networking, so as to advance esp. one's career. —*v.t.* **8.** to place in or connect to a network. **9.** to organize into a network.

net·work·ing (net′wûr′king), *n.* **1.** the informal sharing of information and services among individuals or groups linked by a common interest. **2.** the design, establishment, or utilization of a computer network. —*adj.* **3.** of or pertaining to a network or networking.

Neuf·châ·tel (nœ′shə tel′, nyœ′-, nœ′-), *n.* a soft white cheese made in Neufchâtel, a town in N France.

neu·ral (nŏor′əl, nyŏor′-), *adj.* of or pertaining to a nerve or the nervous system. —**neu′ral·ly,** *adv.*

neu·ral·gia (nŏo ral′jə, nyŏo-), *n.* sharp and paroxysmal pain along the course of a nerve. —**neu·ral′gic,** *adj.*

neu′ral net′work, *n.* **1.** any group of neurons that conduct impulses in a coordinated manner, as the assemblages of brain cells that record a visual stimulus. **2.** Also called **neu′ral net′.** a computer model designed to simulate the behavior of biological neural networks, as in pattern recognition, language processing, and problem solving, with the goal of self-directed information processing.

neu′ral tube′, *n.* a tube formed in the early embryo by the closure of ectodermal tissue and later developing into the spinal cord and brain.

neur·as·the·ni·a (nŏor′əs thē′nē ə, nyŏor′-), *n.* **1.** a pattern of symptoms including chronic fatigue, sleep disturbances, and persistent aches, often linked with depression. **2.** prostration due to extreme emotional distress or dejection. —**neur′as·then′ic** (-then′ik), *adj., n.*

neu·ri·tis (nŏo rī′tis, nyŏo-), *n.* inflammation of a nerve, often marked by pain, numbness or tingling, or paralysis. —**neu·rit′ic** (-rit′ik), *adj.*

neuro-, a combining form meaning "nerve," "nerves," "nervous system": *neurology.* Also, *esp. before a vowel,* **neur-.**

neu·ro·a·nat·o·my (nŏor′ō ə nat′ə mē, nyŏor′-), *n., pl.* **-mies. 1.** the branch of anatomy that deals with the nervous system. **2.** the nerve structure of an organism. —**neu′ro·a·nat′o·mist,** *n.* —**neu′ro·an′a·tom′i·cal** (-an′ə tom′i kəl), **neu′ro·an′a·tom′ic,** *adj.*

neu·ro·bi·ol·o·gy (nŏor′ō bī ol′ə jē, nyŏor′-), *n.* the branch of biology that deals with the anatomy and physiology of the nervous system. —**neu′ro·bi′o·log′i·cal** (-ə loj′i kəl), *adj.* —**neu′ro·bi′o·log′i·cal·ly,** *adv.* —**neu′ro·bi·ol′o·gist,** *n.*

neu·ro·chem·i·cal (nŏor′ō kem′i kəl, nyŏor′-), *adj.* **1.** of or pertaining to neurochemistry. —*n.* **2.** a substance that affects the nervous system.

neu·ro·chem·is·try (nŏor′ō kem′ə strē, nyŏor′-), *n.* the study of the chemistry of the nervous system. —**neu′ro·chem′ist,** *n.*

neu·ro·en·do·cri·nol·o·gy (nŏor′ō en′dō krə nol′ə jē, nyŏor′-), *n.* the study of the anatomical and physiological interactions between the nervous and endocrine systems. —**neu′ro·en′do·crin′o·log′i·cal** (-krin′l oj′i kəl), *adj.* —**neu′ro·en′do·cri·nol′o·gist,** *n.*

neu·ro·im·mu·nol·o·gy (nŏor′ō im′yə nol′ə jē, nyŏor′-), *n.* a branch of immunology concerned with the interactions between immunological and nervous system functions, esp. as they apply to various autoimmune diseases.

neu·ro·lin·guis·tics (nŏor′ō ling gwis′tiks, nyŏor′-), *n.* (*used with a sing. v.*) the study of the neurological processes underlying the development and use of language. —**neu′ro·lin′guist,** *n.* —**neu′ro·lin·guis′tic,** *adj.*

neu·rol·o·gy (nŏo rol′ə jē, nyŏo-), *n.* the branch of medicine dealing with the nervous system. —**neu′ro·log′i·cal** (-ə loj′i kəl), **neu′ro·log′ic,** *adj.* —**neu′ro·log′i·cal·ly,** *adv.* —**neu·rol′o·gist,** *n.*

neu·ro·mo·tor (nŏor′ō mō′tər, nyŏor′-), *adj.* **1.** NEUROMUSCULAR. **2.** of or pertaining to the effects of nerve impulses on muscles.

neu·ro·mus·cu·lar (nŏor′ō mus′kyə lər, nyŏor′-), *adj.* pertaining to or affecting both nerves and muscles.

neu·ron (nŏor′on, nyŏor′-), *n.* a specialized, impulse-conducting cell that is the functional unit of the nervous system, consisting of the cell body and its processes, the axon and dendrites. Also called **nerve cell.** Also, *esp. Brit.,* **neu·rone** (-ōn). —**neu·ron·al** (nŏor′ə nl, nyŏor′-), *adj.*

neu·ro·pa·thol·o·gy (nŏor′ō pə thol′ə jē, nyŏor′-), *n.* the pathology of the nervous system. **—neu·ro·path'o·log'i·cal** (-path'ə loj'i kəl), *adj.* **—neu'ro·pa·thol'o·gist,** *n.*

neu·ro·phar·ma·col·o·gy (nŏŏr'ō fär'mə kol'ə jē, nyŏŏr'-), *n.* the branch of pharmacology dealing with the nervous system. **—neu'ro·phar'ma·co·log'ic** (-kə loj'ik), **neu'ro·phar'ma·co·log'i·cal,** *adj.* **—neu'ro·phar'ma·co·log'i·cal·ly,** *adv.* **—neu'ro·phar'ma·col'o·gist,** *n.*

neu·ro·phys·i·ol·o·gy (nŏŏr'ō fiz'ē ol'ə jē, nyŏŏr'-), *n.* the branch of physiology dealing with the nervous system. **—neu'ro·phys'i·o·log'i·cal** (-ə loj'i kəl), **neu'ro·phys'i·o·log'ic,** *adj.* **—neu'ro·phys'i·o·log'i·cal·ly,** *adv.* **—neu'ro·phys'i·ol'o·gist,** *n.*

neu·ro·psy·chi·a·try (nŏŏr'ō sī kī'ə trē, -sī-, nyŏŏr'-), *n.* the branch of medicine dealing with diseases of the mind and nervous system. **—neu'ro·psy·chi·at'ric** (-sī'kē a'trik), *adj.* **—neu'ro·psy·chi'a·trist,** *n.*

neu·ro·sis (nŏŏ rō'sis, nyŏŏ-), *n., pl.* **-ses** (-sēz). **1.** Also called **psy·cho·neu·ro·sis.** a functional disorder in which feelings of anxiety, obsessional thoughts, compulsive acts, and physical complaints without objective evidence of disease, occurring in various degrees and patterns, dominate the personality. **2.** a relatively mild personality disorder typified by excessive anxiety or indecision and some of social maladjustment.

neu·ro·sur·ger·y (nŏŏr'ō sûr'jə rē, nyŏŏr'-), *n.* surgery of the brain or other nerve tissue. **—neu'ro·sur'geon** (-jən), *n.* **—neu'ro·sur'gi·cal,** *adj.*

neu·rot·ic (nŏŏ rot'ik, nyŏŏ-), *adj.* **1.** of, pertaining to, or characteristic of neurosis. **—n. 2.** a neurotic person. **—neu·rot'i·cal·ly,** *adv.* **—neu·rot'i·cism** (-ə siz'əm), *n.*

neu·ro·trans·mit·ter (nŏŏr'ō trans'mit ər, -tranz'-, nyŏŏr'-), *n.* any of several chemical substances, as epinephrine or acetylcholine, that transmit nerve impulses across a synapse.

neu·ter (nŏŏ'tər, nyŏŏ'-), *adj.* **1. a.** of, pertaining to, or being a grammatical gender that refers to things classed as neither masculine nor feminine. **b.** (of a verb) intransitive. **2.** *Biol.* having no organs of reproduction; without sex; asexual. **3.** *Zool.* having imperfectly developed sexual organs, as worker bees. **4.** *Bot.* having neither stamens nor pistils; asexual. **5.** neutral; siding with no one. **—n. 6. a.** the neuter gender. **b.** a word or other linguistic form in or marking the neuter gender. **7.** an animal made sterile by castration or spaying. **8.** a neuter insect. **9.** an asexual plant. **10.** a person or thing that is neutral. **—v.t. 11.** to spay or castrate (a dog, cat, etc.).

neu·tral (nŏŏ'trəl, nyŏŏ'-), *adj.* **1.** not taking part or giving assistance in a dispute or war between others: *a neutral nation.* **2.** not aligned with or supporting any side or position in a controversy. **3.** of or belonging to a neutral state or party: *neutral territory.* **4.** of no particular kind, characteristics, etc.; indefinite: *a neutral personality.* **5.** (of a color or shade) **a.** without hue; achromatic. **b.** matching well with many or most other colors or shades, as white or beige. **6.** exhibiting neither acid nor alkaline qualities: *neutral salts.* **7. a.** (of a particle) having no electric charge. **b.** (of an atom, molecule, or collection of particles) having no net electric charge. **c.** not magnetized. **8.** (of a vowel) pronounced with the tongue relaxed in a central position, as the *a* in *alive.* **—n. 9.** a person or nation that is neutral. **10.** a citizen of a neutral nation during a war. **11.** the position or state of disengaged gears or other interconnecting parts. **12.** a neutral color. **—neu'tral·ly,** *adv.*

neu·tral·ism (nŏŏ'trə liz'əm, nyŏŏ'-), *n.* **1.** the policy of neutrality in foreign affairs. **2.** the theory that some changes in evolution are governed by chance mutations rather than natural selection.

neu·tral·ist (nŏŏ'trə list, nyŏŏ'-), *n.* **1.** a person who advocates or adheres to a policy of strict neutrality in foreign affairs. **2.** a person who advocates or adheres to a policy or theory of neutralism. **—adj. 3.** of, pertaining to, or advocating neutralism.

neu·tral·i·ty (nŏŏ tral'i tē, nyŏŏ-), *n.* **1.** the state of being neutral. **2.** the policy or status of a nation that does not participate in a war between other nations. **3.** neutral status, as of a seaport during a war.

neu·tral·ize (nŏŏ'trə līz', nyŏŏ'-), *v.,* **-ized, -iz·ing.** **—v.t. 1.** to make neutral. **2.** to make (something) ineffective; counteract; nullify. **3.** to declare neutral and exempt from involvement in war. **4.** to make (a solution) chemically neutral. **5.** to render electrically or magnetically neutral. **6.** *Ling.* to cause to lose the feature that normally differentiates a pair of phonemes. **—v.i. 7.** to become neutral or neutralized. **—neu'tral·iz'er,** *n.* **—neu'tral·i·za'tion,** *n.*

neu·tri·no (nŏŏ trē'nō, nyŏŏ-), *n., pl.* **-nos.** a massless or nearly massless electrically neutral lepton.

neu·tron (nŏŏ'tron, nyŏŏ'-), *n.* an elementary particle found in most atomic nuclei, having no charge, mass slightly greater than that of a proton, and spin of ½. *Symbol:* n

neu'tron bomb', *n.* a nuclear weapon designed to release an intense burst of neutrons and gamma rays, with a weaker blast wave and less residual radiation than other nuclear bombs.

neu'tron star', *n.* an extremely dense, compact star composed primarily of neutrons, esp. the collapsed core of a supernova.

Ne·vad·a (nə vad'ə, -vä'də), *n.* a state in the W United States. 1,603,163; 110,540 sq. mi. (286,300 sq. km). *Cap.:* Carson City. *Abbr.:* NV, Nev. **—Ne·vad'an, Ne·vad'i·an,** *adj., n.*

nev·er (nev'ər), *adv.* **1.** not ever; at no time: *It never happened.* **2.** not at all; absolutely not: *This will never do.* **3.** to no extent or degree: *He was never the wiser.* **—Idiom. 4. never mind,** don't bother; don't concern yourself. **—Proverb. 5. Never say never,** one never knows what the future holds.

nev·er·mind (nev'ər mīnd', nev'ər mīnd'), *n. Chiefly Dial.* concern (used chiefly in the phrase *pay no nevermind*).

nev·er·more (nev'ər môr'), *adv.* never again.

nev·er-nev·er (nev'ər nev'ər), *adj.* not real or true; imaginary; illusory: *the never-never world of films.*

nev·er-nev'er land', *n.* an unreal, imaginary, or ideal state, condition, place, etc.

nev·er·the·less (nev'ər *th*ə les'), *adv.* nonetheless; notwithstanding; however; in spite of that: *a small but nevertheless important change.*

ne·vus (nē'vəs), *n., pl.* **-vi** (-vī). any congenital anomaly of the skin, including moles and various types of birthmarks. **—ne'void,** *adj.*

new (nŏŏ, nyŏŏ), *adj.,* **-er, -est,** *adv., n.* **—adj. 1.** of recent origin, production, purchase, etc.; having but lately come or been brought into being: *a new book.* **2.** of a kind now appearing for the first time; novel: *a new concept of the universe.* **3.** having but lately or but now become known: *a new elementary particle.* **4.** unfamiliar or strange (often fol. by *to*): *ideas new to us; to explore new worlds.* **5.** having but lately come to a place, position, status, etc.: *a new minister.* **6.** unaccustomed (usu. fol. by *to*): *people new to such work.* **7.** further; additional: *new gains.* **8.** fresh or unused: *a new sheet of paper.* **9.** different and better in physical or moral quality: *It made a new man of him.* **10.** other than the former or the old: *a new era.* **11.** being the later or latest of two or more things of the same kind: *a new edition of Shakespeare.* **12.** (*cap.*) (of a language) in its latest known period, esp. as a living language at the present time: *New High German.* **—adv. 13.** recently or freshly (usu. used in combination): *new-mown hay.* **—n. 14.** something new: *Ring out the old, ring in the new.* **—Proverb. 15. There is nothing new under the sun,** everything has happened at least once before. Eccl. 1:9. **—new'ness,** *n.*

New' Age', *adj.* **1.** of or pertaining to a movement espousing a broad range of philosophies and practices traditionally viewed as occult, metaphysical, or paranormal. **2.** of or pertaining to an unintrusive style of music using both acoustic and electronic instruments and drawing on classical music, jazz, and rock. **—n. 3.** the New Age movement. **—New' Ag'er,** *n.*

New' Amer'ican Bi'ble, *n.* an English translation of the Bible based on the original languages, prepared by Catholic Biblical scholars, and first published in 1970.

New' Am'ster·dam (am'stər dam'), *n.* a former Dutch town on Manhattan Island; renamed New York by the British in 1664.

New·ark (nŏŏ'ərk, nyŏŏ'), *n.* a city in NE New Jersey. 258,751.

New·ber·ry (nŏŏ'ber'ē, -bə rē, nyŏŏ'-), *n.* **Thomas,** 1811–1901, English Bible editor.

New'bery Award', *n.* an annual award for the most distinguished book for juveniles.

new·bie (nŏŏ'bē, nyŏŏ'-), *n.* an inexperienced user of the Internet or of computers in general.

new·born (nŏŏ'bôrn', nyŏŏ'-), *adj., n., pl.* **-born, -borns.** **—adj. 1.** recently or only just born. **—n. 2.** a newborn infant; neonate.

New' Bruns'wick (brunz'wik), *n.* a province in SE Canada. 709,442; 27,985 sq. mi. (72,480 sq. km). *Cap.:* Fredericton.

New·cas·tle (nŏŏ'kas'əl, -kä'səl, nyŏŏ'-), *n.* **1.** Also called **New'cas·tle-up·on'-Tyne'.** a seaport in NE England, on the Tyne River; coal center. 282,700. **2.** a seaport in E New South Wales, in SE Australia. 429,300. **—Saying. 3. carry coals to Newcastle,** to provide something already present in abundance; to do something obviously superfluous.

New' Church', *n.* New Jerusalem Church.

new' class', *n.* the technical and managerial elite of a government.

New' Cloth' on Old' Gar'ments, a parable of Jesus. Matt. 9:16; Mark 2:21; Luke 5:36.

new'-col'lar, *adj.* pertaining to or designating middle-class wage earners holding jobs in a service industry. Compare BLUE-COLLAR.

New' Colos'sus, The, a poem (1883) by Emma Lazarus inscribed on the base of the Statue of Liberty in New York. The first stanza is: "Give me your tired, your poor,/ Your huddled masses yearning to breathe free;/ The wretched refuse of your teeming shore./ Send these, the homeless, tempest-tossed, to me:/ I lift my lamp beside the golden door."

New·comb (nŏŏ'kəm, nyŏŏ'-), *n.* **Simon,** 1835–1909, U.S. astronomer.

new·com·er (nŏŏ'kum'ər, nyŏŏ'-), *n.* a person or thing that has recently arrived; new arrival.

new' cov'enant, *n.* (*sometimes caps.*) (in Christian exegesis) the promises of salvation made by God to humans individually, based on divine grace rather than Mosaic Law.

new' crit'icism, *n.* (*often caps.*) a method of literary criticism that concentrates on textual explication and considers historical and biographical study as secondary. **—new' crit'ic,** *n.*

New' Deal', *n.* **1.** the economic and social policies and programs introduced by President Franklin D. Roosevelt and his administration. Compare FAIR DEAL, GREAT SOCIETY, NEW FRONTIER. **2.** the Roosevelt administration, esp. the period from 1933 to 1941. **—New' Deal'er,** *n.*

New' Del'hi (del'ē), *n.* the capital of India, in the N part, adjacent to Delhi. 271,990. Compare DELHI (def. 2).

New' Eng'land, *n.* an area in the NE United States, including the states of Connecticut, Maine, Massachusetts, New Hampshire, Rhode Island, and Vermont. —**New′ Eng′land·er,** *n.*

New′ Eng′land theol′ogy, *n.* Calvinism as modified and interpreted by the descendants of the Puritans in New England, esp. Jonathan Edwards, becoming the dominant theology there from about 1730 to 1880.

New′ Eng′lish Bi′ble, *n.* a British translation (1970) of the Bible into contemporary idiom, directed by Protestant churches.

new·fan·gled (nōō′fang′gəld, -fang′-, nyōō′-), *adj.* **1.** of a new kind or fashion. **2.** fond of or given to novelty. —**new′fan′gled·ness,** *n.*

new′ fed′eralism, *n.* (*sometimes caps.*) a plan, announced in 1969, to turn over the control of some federal programs to state and local governments and institute block grants, revenue sharing, etc.

new·found (nōō′found′, nyōō′-), *adj.* newly found or discovered: *newfound friends.*

New·found·land (nōō′fən lənd, -land′, -fänd-, nyōō′-; nōō found′lənd, nyōō-), *n.* **1.** a large island in E Canada. 42,734 sq. mi. (110,680 sq. km). **2.** a province in E Canada, composed of Newfoundland island and Labrador. 568,349; 155,364 sq. mi. (402,390 sq. km). *Cap.:* St. John's. **3.** one of a breed of large, powerful dogs having a dense, oily, usu. black coat, raised orig. in Newfoundland.

New′ France′, *n.* the French possessions in North America up to 1763.

New′ Frontier′, *n.* the principles and policies of the liberal wing of the Democratic party under the leadership of President John F. Kennedy. Compare FAIR DEAL, GREAT SOCIETY, NEW DEAL. [as a political catchphrase, appar. first used by Henry Wallace in a book of the same title (1934)]

New′ Guin′ea, *n.* **1.** a large island N of Australia, politically divided into the Indonesian province of Irian Jaya (West Irian) and the independent country of Papua New Guinea. 3,480,000; ab. 316,000 sq. mi. (818,000 sq. km). **2. Trust Territory of,** a former United Nations trust territory that included NE New Guinea, the Bismarck Archipelago, Bougainville, and other islands, administered by Australia jointly with the Territory of Papua until 1975: now part of Papua New Guinea. —**New′ Guin′ean,** *n.*

New′ Hamp′shire (hamp′shər, -shēr), *n.* **1.** a state in the NE United States. 1,162,481; 9304 sq. mi. (24,100 sq. km). *Cap.:* Concord. *Abbr.:* NH, N.H. **2.** one of an American breed of chestnut-red chickens.

New′ Ha′ven, *n.* a seaport in S Connecticut, on Long Island Sound. 119,604.

New′ Ha′ven Col′ony, *n.* a settlement founded in 1638 by John Davenport and Theophilus Eaton at Quinnipiac (now New Haven, Conn.).

New′ Interna′tional Bi′ble, *n.* a Bible in modern English: first published in 1978 under the direction of the New York Bible Society.

new·ish (nōō′ish, nyōō′-), *adj.* rather new.

New′ Jer′sey, *n.* a state in the E United States, on the Atlantic coast. 7,987,933; 7836 sq. mi. (20,295 sq. km). *Cap.:* Trenton. *Abbr.:* NJ, N.J. —**New′ Jer′sey·an, New′ Jer′sey·ite′,** *n.*

New′ Jer′sey plan′, *n.* a plan, unsuccessfully proposed at the Constitutional Convention, providing for a single legislative house with equal representation for each state. Compare CONNECTICUT COMPROMISE, VIRGINIA PLAN.

New′ Jer′sey tea′, *n.* a North American shrub, *Ceanothus americanus,* of the buckthorn family, the leaves of which were used as a substitute for tea during the American Revolution.

New′ Jeru′salem, *n.* the abode of God and His saints; heaven.

New′ Jeru′salem Church′, *n.* the church composed of the followers of Swedenborg; the Swedenborgian church. Also called **New Church.**

New′ Jour′nalism, *n.* journalism containing the writer's personal opinions and reactions and often fictional asides as added color.

New′ King′dom, *n.* the period in the history of ancient Egypt, c1580–1085 B.C., comprising the 18th to 20th dynasties. Compare MIDDLE KINGDOM (def. 1), OLD KINGDOM.

New′ King′ James′ Ver′sion, *n.* a revision of the KING JAMES VERSION, published in 1982, that eliminated many archaic expressions.

New′ Lat′in, *n.* the Latin of literature and learned writing from c1500 to the present, including the Greco-Latin taxonomic nomenclature of biology. *Abbr.:* NL

New′ Left′, *n.* a political movement of the 1960s and 1970s that sought radical changes in the political, social, and economic system. —**New′ Left′ist,** *n.*

new′ look′, *n.* **1.** a new or changed appearance, approach, etc., esp. one characterized by marked departure from the previous or traditional one. **2.** (*usually caps.*) a style of women's clothing introduced by the designer Christian Dior in 1947, characterized by a silhouette with broad shoulders, a narrow waist, a long, full skirt, and often emphasized hips. —**new′-look′,** *adj.*

new·ly (nōō′lē, nyōō′-), *adv.* **1.** recently; lately. **2.** anew or afresh. **3.** in a new manner or form.

new·ly·wed (nōō′lē wed′, nyōō′-), *n.* a person who has recently married.

New·man (nōō′mən, nyōō′-), *n.* **John Henry, Cardinal,** 1801–90, English Roman Catholic theologian and author.

new′ math′, *n.* a trend in mathematics teaching of the 1960s and 1970s that de-emphasized rote learning and introduced topics not in the traditional curriculum. Also called **new′ mathemat′ics.**

New′ Mex′ico, *n.* a state in the SW United States. 1,713,407; 121,666

sq. mi. (315,115 sq. km). *Cap.:* Santa Fe. *Abbr.:* NM, N. Mex., N.M. —**New′ Mex′i·can,** *n.*

new′ moon′, *n.* **1.** the moon either when in conjunction with the sun or soon after, being either invisible or visible only as a slender crescent. **2.** the phase of the moon at this time.

New′ Neth′erland, *n.* a Dutch colony in the Hudson River region, captured by England in 1664 and divided into New York and New Jersey.

new′ or′der, *n.* **1.** a new or revised system of operation, form of government, plan of attack, or the like. **2.** (*caps.*) the system of political and economic control and of social organization that prevailed in Germany and its subject countries during the Nazi era; National Socialism.

New′ Or′le·ans (ôr′lē ənz, -lənz, ôr lēnz′), *n.* a seaport in SE Louisiana, on the Mississippi: British defeated (1815) by Americans under Andrew Jackson. 484,149. —**New′ Or·lea′ni·an** (ôr lē′nē ən), *adj., n.*

New′ Pol′itics, *n.* (*sometimes l.c.*) politics concerned more with grassroots participation in the political process than with party loyalty or affiliation: identified esp. with the candidacies of Senators Eugene McCarthy and George McGovern.

New′port News′ (nōō′pôrt′, -pōrt′, -pərt, nyōō′-), *n.* a seaport in SE Virginia: shipbuilding and ship-repair center. 179,127.

New′ Revised′ Stand′ard Ver′sion, *n.* a revision of the 1952 REVISED STANDARD VERSION: published in 1989.

New′ Right′, *n.* (*sometimes l.c.*) a political movement advocating conservative social values and a nationalistic foreign policy. —**New′ Right′ist,** *n.*

news (nōōz, nyōōz), *n.* (*usu. with a sing. v.*) **1.** a report of a recent event; information: *to hear news of a relative.* **2.** a report on recent or new events in a newspaper or other periodical or on radio or television. **3.** such reports taken collectively; information reported: *to listen to the news.* **4.** a person, event, etc., regarded as newsworthy material. **5.** a newspaper. —*Proverb.* **6. No news is good news,** if nothing is heard about something, all must be well. —**news′less,** *adj.*

news′ a′gency, *n.* a business organization that gathers news for transmittal to newspapers, magazines, broadcasting stations, etc.

news′ an′alyst, *n.* COMMENTATOR (def. 1).

news·beat (nōōz′bēt′, nyōōz′-), *n.* BEAT (def. 38b).

news·break (nōōz′brāk′, nyōōz′-), *n.* **1.** a newsworthy event. **2.** a station break that consists typically of short news items.

news·cast (nōōz′kast′, -käst′, nyōōz′-), *n.* a broadcast of news on radio or television. —**news′cast′er,** *n.* —**news′cast′ing,** *n.*

news′ con′ference, *n.* a press conference, esp. one held by a government official.

news·deal·er (nōōz′dē′lər, nyōōz′-), *n.* a person who sells newspapers and periodicals.

news·desk (nōōz′desk′, nyōōz′-), *n.* the department of a newspaper, broadcasting station, etc., that receives late-breaking news.

news·let·ter (nōōz′let′ər, nyōōz′-), *n.* a written report, usu. issued periodically by an organization or agency to present information to employees, contributors, stockholders, or the public.

news·mag·a·zine (nōōz′mag′ə zēn′, nyōōz′-), *n.* **1.** a periodical, usu. issued weekly, that specializes in reports and commentaries on current events. **2.** MAGAZINE (def. 2).

news·man (nōōz′man′, -mən, nyōōz′-), *n., pl.* **-men** (-men′, -mən). a person employed to gather and report news; reporter or correspondent.

news·mon·ger (nōōz′mung′gər, -mong′-, nyōōz′-), *n.* a person who spreads gossip or idle talk; a gossip or gossipmonger.

New′ Spain′, *n.* a former Spanish viceroyalty (1535–1821) including Central America N of Panama, Mexico, the West Indies, the SW United States, and the Philippines.

news·pa·per (nōōz′pā′pər, nyōōz′-, nōōs′-, nyōōs′-), *n.* **1.** a publication, usu. issued daily or weekly and containing news, comment, features, and advertising. **2.** a business organization that prints and distributes such a publication. **3.** a single issue or copy of such a publication. **4.** NEWSPRINT.

news·pa·per·man (nōōz′pā′pər man′, nyōōz′-, nōōs′-, nyōōs′-), *n., pl.* **-men. 1.** a person employed by a newspaper or wire service as a reporter, writer, or editor. **2.** the owner or operator of a newspaper or news service.

news·pa·per·wom·an (nōōz′pā′pər wŏm′ən, nyōōz′pā′-, nōōs′pā′-, nyōōs′pā′-), *n., pl.* **-wom·en. 1.** a woman employed by a newspaper or wire service as a reporter, writer, or editor. **2.** a woman who owns or operates a newspaper or news service.

new·speak (nōō′spēk′, nyōō′-), *n.* (*sometimes cap.*) a propagandistic language marked by ambiguity, misstatement, and contradiction.

news·per·son (nōōz′pûr′sən, nyōōz′-), *n.* a person employed to gather, report, or broadcast news.

news·print (nōōz′print′, nyōōz′-), *n.* a low-grade paper made mainly from wood pulp, used chiefly for newspapers.

news·reel (nōōz′rēl′, nyōōz′-), *n.* a short motion picture presenting current or recent events.

news′ release′, *n.* PRESS RELEASE.

news′room′ or **news′ room′,** *n.* an office, as of a newspaper or broadcasting organization, in which the news is processed.

news′ serv′ice, *n.* NEWS AGENCY.

news·stand (nōōz′stand′, nyōōz′-), *n.* a stall or other place at which newspapers and often periodicals are sold.

New′ Stone′ Age′, *n.* the Neolithic period.

news•week•ly (nōōz′wēk′lē, nyōōz′-), *n., pl.* **-lies.** a newsmagazine or newspaper published weekly.

news•wire (nōōz′wīᵊr′, nyōōz′-), *n.* **1.** a service, esp. by teletypewriter, providing news or other up-to-the-minute information. **2.** a teletypewriter or other machine by which such information is transmitted.

news•wom•an (nōōz′wŏŏm′ən, nyōōz′-), *n., pl.* **-wom•en.** a woman employed to gather and report news.

news•wor•thy (nōōz′wûr′thē, nyōōz′-), *adj.* of sufficient interest to warrant press coverage. **—news′wor′thi•ness,** *n.*

news•writ•ing (nōōz′rī′ting, nyōōz′-), *n.* **1.** writing for publication in a newspaper; journalism. **2.** the reporting of current events. **—news′-writ′er,** *n.*

newt (nōōt, nyōōt), *n.* any of several brilliantly colored, semiaquatic salamanders of the worldwide family Salamandridae, esp. those of the genera *Triturus* and *Notophthalmus.*

New′ Tes′tament, *n.* **1.** the collection of the books of the Christian Bible, comprising the Gospels, Acts of the Apostles, the Epistles, and the Revelation of St. John the Divine. See table at BIBLE. **2.** the covenant in which God's dispensation of grace is revealed through Jesus Christ.

new′ theol′ogy, *n.* a movement away from orthodox or fundamentalist theological thought, originating in the late 19th century and aimed at reconciling modern concepts and discoveries in science and philosophy with theology.

new•ton (nōōt′n, nyōōt′n), *n.* the SI unit of force, equal to the force that produces an acceleration of one meter per second per second on a mass of one kilogram. [after I. NEWTON]

New•ton (nōōt′n, nyōōt′n), *n.* **1. Sir Isaac,** 1642–1727, English physicist and mathematician. **2. John,** 1725–1807, English clergyman and hymn writer. **3.** a city in E Massachusetts, near Boston. 82,230.

new′ wave′, *n.* **1.** a movement, esp. in art, literature, or politics, that breaks with traditional values, techniques, or the like. **2.** (*often caps.*) **a.** a movement in filmmaking that started in France in the 1950s, characterized by loosely structured plots and unconventional photographic techniques. **b.** the members of this movement. **—new′-wave′,** *adj.*

New′ Wine′ in Old′ Wine′skins, a parable of Jesus. Matt. 9:17; Mark 2:22; Luke 5:37–39.

New′ World′, *n.* WESTERN HEMISPHERE (def. 1).

New′ World′ mon′key, *n.* any primate of the superfamily Platyrrhini, inhabiting forests from Mexico to Argentina and characterized by widely separated nostrils, nonopposable thumbs, and usu. a long prehensile tail. Compare OLD WORLD MONKEY.

new′ world′ or′der, *n.* (*sometimes caps.*) the post-Cold War organization of power in which nations tend to cooperate.

new year (nōō′ yēr′, nyōō′ for 1; yēr′ for 2), *n.* **1.** the year approaching or newly begun. **2.** (*caps.*) **a. New Year's Day. b.** the first few days of a given year. **c.** the Jewish new year; Rosh Hashanah.

New′ Year's′ Day′, *n.* January 1, celebrated as a holiday in many countries.

New′ Year's′ Eve′, *n.* the night of December 31.

New′ York′, *n.* **1.** Also called **New′ York′ State′.** a state in the NE United States. 18,184,774; 49,576 sq. mi. (128,400 sq. km). *Cap.:* Albany. *Abbr.:* NY, N.Y. **2.** Also called **New′ York′ Cit′y.** a seaport in SE New York at the mouth of the Hudson: comprising the boroughs of Manhattan, Queens, Brooklyn, the Bronx, and Staten Island. 7,333,253. **3. Greater New York,** New York City, the counties of Nassau, Suffolk, Rockland, and Westchester in New York, and the counties of Bergen, Essex, Hudson, Middlesex, Morris, Passaic, Somerset, and Union in New Jersey: the metropolitan area as defined by the U.S. census. 17,412,652. **4.** the borough of Manhattan. **—New′ York′er,** *n.*

New′ York′ State′ Barge′ Canal′, *n.* **1.** a New York State waterway system. 575 mi. (925 km) long. **2.** the main canal of this system, between the Hudson River and Lake Erie: consists of the rebuilt Erie Canal. 352 mi. (565 km) long.

New′ York′ Stock′ Exchange′, *n.* the largest stock exchange in the U.S., located in New York City. *Abbr.:* NYSE, N.Y.S.E. Compare AMERICAN STOCK EXCHANGE.

New′ Zea′land (zē′lənd), *n.* a country in the S Pacific, SE of Australia, consisting of North Island, South Island, and adjacent small islands: a member of the Commonwealth of Nations. 3,587,275; 104,454 sq. mi. (270,534 sq. km). *Cap.:* Wellington. **—New′ Zea′land•er,** *n.*

next (nekst), *adj.* **1.** immediately following in time, order, importance, etc.: *the next day.* **2.** nearest or adjacent in place or position: *the next room.* **—adv. 3.** in the place, time, order, etc., nearest or immediately following: *We're going to London next. This is my next oldest daughter.* **4.** on the first occasion to follow: *when next we meet.* **—prep. 5.** adjacent to; nearest: *the closet next the blackboard.* **—Idiom. 6. next door to, a.** in a house, apartment, office, etc., adjacent to. **b.** next to; verging on. **7. next to, a.** adjacent to: *Sit next to me.* **b.** almost; nearly: *next to impossible.* **c.** aside from: *Next to me, you're the best.*

next-door (*adv.* neks′dôr′, -dōr′, nekst′-; *adj.* -dôr′, -dōr′), *adv.* **1.** Also, **next′ door′.** to, at, or in the next house, building, apartment, etc.: *go next-door.* **—adj. 2.** situated or living in the next house, building, apartment, etc.: *next-door neighbors.*

next′ of kin′, *n.* a person's nearest relative or relatives.

nex•us (nek′səs), *n., pl.* **nex•us. 1.** a means of connection; tie; link. **2.** a connected series or group. **3.** the core or center, as of a matter or situation. **4.** a specialized area of the cell membrane involved in intercellular communication and adhesion.

Nez Percé (nez′ pûrs′), *n., pl.* **Nez Per•cés,** (*esp. collectively*) **Nez Percé. 1.** a member of an American Indian people of the lower Snake and Salmon river regions in Idaho, SE Washington, and NE Oregon. **2.** the language of the Nez Percé, akin to Sahaptin.

NF, 1. Newfoundland, Canada. **2.** no funds.

NFL, National Football League.

NFS or **N.F.S.,** not for sale.

Nga•li•e•ma (əng gä′lē ā′mə), *n.* **Mount,** a mountain with two summits, in central Africa, between Uganda and Zaire: highest peak in the Ruwenzori group. 16,763 ft. (5109 m). Formerly, **Mount Stanley.**

NGO, Nongovernmental Organization.

NH or **N.H.,** New Hampshire.

NHL, National Hockey League.

Ni, *Chem. Symbol.* nickel.

ni•a•cin (nī′ə sin), *n.* NICOTINIC ACID.

Ni•ag•a•ra (nī ag′rə, -ag′ər ə), *n.* **1.** a river on the boundary between W New York and Ontario, Canada, flowing from Lake Erie into Lake Ontario. 34 mi. (55 km) long. **2.** NIAGARA FALLS. **3.** (*l.c.*) anything seen as resembling Niagara Falls in force and relentlessness; deluge: *a niagara of criticism.* **4.** a variety of white grape, grown for table use.

Niag′ara Falls′, *n.* **1.** the falls of the Niagara River: in Canada, the Horseshoe Falls, 158 ft. (48 m) high; 2600 ft. (792 m) wide; in the U.S., American Falls, 167 ft. (51 m) high; 1000 ft. (305 m) wide. **2.** a city in W New York, on the falls. 62,640. **3.** a city in SE Ontario, on the falls. 72,107.

Nia•mey (nyä mā′), *n.* the capital of Niger, in the SW part, on the Niger River. 399,100.

nib (nib), *n.* **1. a.** PENPOINT (def. 1). **b.** one of the two segments of a split penpoint. **2.** any pointed end. **3.** a bill or beak, as of a bird. **—nib′-like′,** *adj.*

nib•ble (nib′əl), *v.,* **-bled, -bling,** *n.* **—v.i. 1.** to bite off small bits: *to nibble on a cracker.* **2.** to eat or chew in small bites. **3.** to bite lightly or gently. **—v.t. 4.** to bite off or take small bits of (something). **5.** to eat (food) by biting off small pieces. **6.** to bite gently. **7. nibble (away) at,** to cause to decrease or diminish bit by bit. **—n. 8.** a small piece bitten off; morsel or bite. **9.** an act or instance of nibbling. **10.** a response by a fish to bait on a fishing line. **11.** a tentative but positive response or reaction. **—nib′bler,** *n.*

Ni•be•lung (nē′bə lŏŏng′), *n., pl.* **-lungs, -lung•en.** (in Germanic legend) any of a race of dwarfs who possess a treasure that confers unlimited power on its owner.

nibs (nibz), *n.* **his** or **her nibs,** *Informal.* a person in authority, esp. one who is exacting.

Ni•cae•a (nī sē′ə), *n.* an ancient city in NW Asia Minor: Nicene Creed formulated here A.D. 325.

Ni•cae•an (nī sē′ən), *adj.* NICENE.

Nic•a•ra•gua (nik′ə rä′gwä), *n.* **1.** a republic in Central America. 4,386,399; 50,193 sq. mi. (130,000 sq. km). *Cap.:* Managua. **2. Lake,** a lake in SW Nicaragua. 92 mi. (148 km) long; 34 mi. (55 km) wide; 3060 sq. mi. (7925 sq. km). **—Nic′a•ra′guan,** *n., adj.*

nice (nīs), *adj.,* **nic•er, nic•est. 1.** pleasing; agreeable; delightful: *a nice visit.* **2.** amiable; pleasant; kind: *to be nice to strangers.* **3.** requiring or displaying great skill, tact, or precision: *a nice handling of a crisis.* **4.** indicating very small differences; minutely accurate, as instruments or measurements. **5.** minute, fine, or subtle: *a nice distinction.* **6.** having or showing delicate perception: *a nice sense of color.* **7.** refined in manners, language, etc. **8.** virtuous; respectable; decorous. **9.** suitable or proper: *a nice wedding.* **10.** carefully neat in dress, habits, etc. **11.** having fastidious or fussy tastes. **—Idiom. 12. nice and,** (used as an intensifier to indicate sufficiency, pleasure, comfort, or the like): *It's nice and warm in here.* [< Old French: silly, simple < Latin *nescius* ignorant] **—nice′ly,** *adv.* **—nice′ness,** *n.*

Ni•cene (nī sēn′, nī′sēn) also **Nicaean,** *adj.* of or pertaining to Nicaea.

Ni′cene Coun′cil, *n.* either of two church councils that met at Nicaea, the first in A.D. 325 to deal with the Arian heresy, the second in A.D. 787 to consider the question of the veneration of images.

Ni′cene Creed′, *n.* **1.** a formal statement of the chief tenets of Christian belief, adopted by the first Nicene Council. **2.** a later creed of similar form accepted generally throughout Christendom.

ni•ce•ty (nī′si tē), *n., pl.* **-ties. 1.** a delicate or fine point; subtlety: *the niceties of protocol.* **2.** exactness or preciseness, as in workmanship; detail. **3.** Usu., **niceties.** refined or fine things or manners: *the niceties of life.* **4.** the quality of being nice; niceness. **5.** delicacy; care or tact: *a matter of considerable nicety.*

niche (nich), *n.* **1.** a recess in a wall or the like, as for a statue or other decorative object. **2.** a suitable place or position: *to find one's niche in the world.* **3.** the position and function of a particular species or population in an ecological community.

Nich•o•las¹ (nik′ə ləs, nik′ləs), *n.* **1. of Cusa,** 1401–64, German cardinal, mathematician, and philosopher. **2. Saint,** fl. 4th century A.D., bishop in Asia Minor: patron saint of Russia; protector of children and prototype of Santa Claus.

Nich•o•las² (nik′ə ləs, nik′ləs), *n.* **1. Nicholas I,** 1796–1855, czar of Russia 1825–55. **2. Nicholas II,** 1868–1918, czar of Russia 1894–1917: executed 1918.

N

nick (nik), *n.* **1.** a small notch, groove, chip, or the like. **2.** a small dent or wound. **3.** a small groove on one side of the shank of a printing type. **4.** a break in a strand of a DNA or RNA molecule. **5.** *Brit. Slang.* prison. —*v.t.* **6.** to cut into or through. **7.** to hit or injure slightly. **8.** to make a nick or nicks in (something); notch, groove, or chip. **9.** to incise certain tendons at the root of (a horse's tail) to give it a higher carrying position; make an incision under the tail of (a horse). **10.** to hit, guess, catch, etc., exactly. **11.** *Slang.* to trick, cheat, or defraud. **12.** *Brit. Slang.* **a.** to arrest (a criminal or suspect). **b.** to capture; nab. **c.** to steal. —*Idiom.* **13. in the nick of time,** at the right moment and no sooner; at the last possible moment.

nick•el (nik′əl), *n., v.,* **-eled, -el•ing** or (*esp. Brit.*) **-elled, -el•ling,** *adj.* —*n.* **1.** a hard, silvery white, ductile and malleable metallic element, not readily oxidized: used in alloys and in electroplating. Symbol: Ni; *at. wt.:* 58.71; *at. no.:* 28; *sp. gr.:* 8.9 at 20°C. **2.** a cupronickel coin of the U.S., equal to five cents. —*v.t.* **3.** to coat with nickel; nickel-plate. —*adj.* **4.** *Slang.* costing five dollars.

nick′el-and-dime′, *adj., v.,* **nick•el-and-dimed** or **nick•eled-and-dimed, nick•el-and-dim•ing** or **nick•el•ing-and-dim•ing.** *Informal.* —*adj.* **1.** insignificant; trivial; petty. —*v.t.* **2.** to expose to financial hardship by the accumulation of small expenses. **3.** to hinder, annoy, or harass with trivialities or nonessentials.

nick•el•o•de•on (nik′ə lō′dē ən), *n.* **1.** an early jukebox that was operated by inserting nickels. **2.** an early motion-picture theater, orig. with an admission price of one nickel.

Nick•laus (nik′ləs), *n.* **Jack (William),** born 1940, U.S. golfer.

nick•nack (nik′nak′), *n.* KNICKKNACK.

nick•name (nik′nām′), *n., v.,* **-named, -nam•ing.** —*n.* **1.** a name added to or substituted for the proper name of a person, place, etc., as in affection, ridicule, or familiarity. **2.** a familiar form of a proper name, as *Jim* for *James* and *Peg* for *Margaret.* —*v.t.* **3.** to give a nickname to.

Nic•o•de•mus (nik′ə dē′məs), *n.* a Pharisee and member of the Sanhedrin who became a secret follower of Jesus. John 3:1–21; 7:50–52; 19:39.

ni•çoise (nē swäz′; *Fr.* nē swAZ′), *adj.* made with tomatoes, black olives, capers, garlic, and often anchovies: *salad niçoise.*

Nic•o•si•a (nik′ə sē′ə), *n.* the capital of Cyprus, in the central part. 164,500.

nic•o•tine (nik′ə tēn′, -tin, nik′ə tēn′), *n.* a colorless, oily, water-soluble, highly toxic liquid alkaloid, $C_{10}H_{14}N_2$, found in tobacco and valued as an insecticide. —**nic′o•tined′,** *adj.* —**nic′o•tine•less,** *adj.*

nic•o•tin•ic (nik′ə tin′ik, -tē′nik), *adj.* **1.** of, pertaining to, or containing nicotine. **2.** related to or imitating the effects of nicotine.

nic′otin′ic ac′id, *n.* a crystalline acid, $C_6H_5NO_2$, that is a component of the vitamin B complex, occurring in animal products, yeast, etc. Also called **niacin, vitamin B₃.**

nic•ti•tate (nik′ti tāt′), *v.i.,* **-tat•ed, -tat•ing.** to wink.

nic′titating mem′brane, *n.* a thin membrane, present in many animals, that can be drawn across the eyeball for protection.

Nie•buhr (nē′bŏŏr), *n.* **Reinhold,** 1892–1971, U.S. theologian and philosopher.

niece (nēs), *n.* **1.** a daughter of one's brother or sister. **2.** a daughter of one's spouse's brother or sister.

ni•el•lo (nē el′ō), *n., pl.* **-el•li** (-el′ē) *v.,* **-el•loed, -el•lo•ing.** —*n.* **1.** a black metallic substance, consisting of silver, copper, lead, and sulfur, with which an incised design or ground is filled to create an ornamental effect on metal. **2.** ornamental work so created. —*v.t.* **3.** to decorate with niello. —**ni•el′list,** *n.*

Niel′sen rat′ing, *n.* an estimate of the total number of viewers for a television program, expressed as a percentage of the total number of viewers whose sets are on at the time and based on a monitoring of the sets of a preselected sample of viewers. [after the A.C. *Nielsen* Co., its originator]

Nie•tzsche (nē′chə, -chē), *n.* **Friedrich Wilhelm,** 1844–1900, German philosopher.

nif•ty (nif′tē), *adj.,* **-ti•er, -ti•est.** *Informal.* **1.** very good; fine; excellent: *a nifty idea.* **2.** attractively stylish or smart: *a nifty new suit.*

Ni•ger (nī′jər, nē zhâr′), *n.* **1.** a republic in NW Africa: formerly part of French West Africa. 9,388,859; 489,191 sq. mi. (1,267,000 sq. km). *Cap.:* Niamey. **2.** a river in W Africa, rising in S Guinea and flowing into the Gulf of Guinea. 2600 mi. (4185 km) long. —**Ni•ge•ri•en** (nī jēr′ē en′), *adj., n.*

Ni•ge•ri•a (nī jēr′ē ə), *n.* a republic in W Africa: member of the Commonwealth of Nations. 107,129,469; 356,669 sq. mi. (923,773 sq. km). *Cap.:* Abuja. —**Ni•ge′ri•an,** *adj., n.*

nig•gard (nig′ərd), *n.* **1.** an extremely stingy person. —*adj.* **2.** niggardly; stingy.

nig•gard•ly (nig′ərd lē) *adj.* **1.** reluctant to give or spend; stingy; miserly. **2.** meanly or ungenerously small or scanty: *a niggardly tip to a waiter.* —*adv.* **3.** in the manner of a niggard.

nig•gle (nig′əl), *v.i.,* **-gled, -gling. 1.** to spend too much time and effort on inconsequential details; trifle. **2.** to criticize in a peevish way; carp. —**nig′gler,** *n.* —**nig′gly,** *adj.*

nig•gling (nig′ling), *adj.* **1.** petty; trivial; inconsequential. **2.** demanding too much care, attention, time, etc. —**nig′gling•ly,** *adv.*

nigh (nī), *adv., adj.,* **nigh•er, nigh•est,** *prep.* —*adv.* **3.** near in space, time, or relation. **2.** nearly; almost (often fol. by *on* or *onto*). —*adj.* **3.**

near; approaching. **4.** short or direct. **5.** (of an animal or vehicle) being on the left side. —*prep.* **6.** NEAR.

night (nīt), *n.* **1.** the period of darkness between sunset and sunrise. **2.** the beginning of this period; nightfall. **3.** the darkness of night; the dark. **4.** a condition or time of obscurity, ignorance, sinfulness, misfortune, etc. **5.** (*sometimes cap.*) an evening used or set aside for a particular event or purpose. —*adj.* **6.** of or pertaining to night: *the night hours.* **7.** occurring or seen at night: *a night spectacle.* **8.** used or designed to be used at night. **9.** active or working at night: *night people.* —*Idiom.* **10. night and day,** unceasingly; continually.

night′ blind′ness, *n.* a condition in which vision is normal in daylight but abnormally poor in dim light. —**night′blind′,** *adj.*

night′-bloom′ing ce′reus, *n.* any of various cacti, as of the genera *Hylocereus, Peniocereus, Nyctocereus,* and *Selenicereus,* having large, usu. white flowers that open at night.

night•cap (nīt′kap′), *n.* **1.** an alcoholic drink taken at the end of the day. **2.** a cap for the head, intended primarily to be worn in bed. **3.** *Informal.* the last of a day's sports events, esp. the second game of a doubleheader in baseball.

night•clothes (nīt′klōz′, -klōthz′), *n.pl.* garments for wearing in bed, as pajamas or nightgowns.

night•club (nīt′klub′), *n., v.,* **-clubbed, -club•bing.** —*n.* **1.** Also, **night′ club′.** an establishment open at night, offering food, drink, floor shows, dancing, etc. —*v.i.* **2.** to visit nightclubs.

night′ crawl′er, *n. Chiefly Northern, North Midland,* and *Western U.S.* an earthworm.

night•fall (nīt′fôl′), *n.* the coming of night; dusk.

night•gown (nīt′goun′), *n.* a loose gown, worn in bed by women or children.

night•hawk (nīt′hôk′), *n.* any of several long-winged New World goatsuckers of the subfamily Chordeilinae, esp. *Chordeiles minor,* often nesting on flat rooftops in urban areas.

night′ her′on, *n.* any of several stocky herons that are most active at night, esp. *Nycticorax nycticorax,* of nearly cosmopolitan distribution.

night•ie or **night•y** (nī′tē), *n., pl.* **night•ies.** *Informal.* NIGHTGOWN.

night•in•gale (nīt′n gāl′, nī′ting-), *n.* any of several small Old World birds of the thrush subfamily, esp. *Luscinia megarhynchos,* noted for the melodious song of the male, often heard at night.

Night•in•gale (nīt′n gāl′, nī′ting-), *n.* **Florence,** 1820–1910, English nurse.

night•jar (nīt′jär′), *n.* **1.** any of numerous nocturnal goatsuckers of the subfamily Caprimulginae, having a short bill and a wide mouth for scooping up insects in flight. **2.** the common Eurasian nightjar *Caprimulgus europaeus,* known for its distinctive chirring song.

night′ jas′mine, *n.* **1.** a jasminelike Indian shrub or small tree, *Nyctanthes arbor-tristis,* of the verbena family, having fragrant, white and orange flowers that bloom at night. **2.** Also called **night′ jes′samine.** a West Indian shrub, *Cestrum nocturnum,* of the nightshade family, having fragrant, creamy white flowers that bloom at night.

night′ let′ter, *n.* a telegram sent at night for next-day delivery.

night′-light′, *n.* a light kept burning at night, as in a sickroom.

night•ly (nīt′lē), *adj.* **1.** occurring each night or at night. **2.** appearing or active at night. **3.** of, pertaining to, or characteristic of night. —*adv.* **4.** on every night: *performances given nightly.* **5.** at or by night.

night•mare (nīt′mâr′), *n.* **1.** a terrifying dream producing feelings of extreme fear and anxiety. **2.** a condition, thought, or experience suggestive of a nightmare. **3.** (formerly) a monster or evil spirit believed to oppress persons during sleep. —**night′mar′ish,** *adj.*

night′ owl′, *n.* a person who often stays up late at night.

night•rid•er (nīt′rī′dər), *n.* one of a band of mounted men who commit acts of violence and intimidation at night, esp. a member of such a band in the southern U.S. during Reconstruction.

night′ school′, *n.* a school held in the evening.

night•shade (nīt′shād′), *n.* **1.** any of various plants of the genus *Solanum,* as the black nightshade. **2.** BELLADONNA (def. 1).

night′ shift′, *n.* **1.** the work force, as of a factory, scheduled to work during the nighttime. **2.** the scheduled period of their labor.

night•shirt (nīt′shûrt′), *n.* a loose shirtlike garment reaching to the knees or lower, for wearing in bed.

night•side (nīt′sīd′), *n.* the dark side of a planet or moon.

night•spot (nīt′spot′), *n.* NIGHTCLUB.

night•stand (nīt′stand′), *n.* NIGHT TABLE.

night′ stick′, *n.* a billy carried by police officers.

night′ ta′ble, *n.* a small table set next to a bed.

night′ ter′ror, *n.* a sudden feeling of extreme fear that awakens a sleeping person and is not associated with a dream.

night•time (nīt′tīm′), *n.* the time between evening and morning.

night′ watch′, *n.* **1.** a watch or guard kept during the night. **2.** a person or the persons keeping such a watch. **3.** Usu., **night watches.** the periods into which the night was divided in ancient times.

ni•hil•ism (nī′ə liz′əm, nē′-), *n.* **1.** total rejection of established laws and institutions. **2.** anarchy, terrorism, or other revolutionary activity. **3. a.** the belief that all existence is senseless and that there is no possibility of an objective basis for truth. **b.** nothingness or nonexistence. —**ni′hil•ist,** *n.* —**ni′hil•is′tic,** *adj.*

Ni•jin•sky (ni zhin′skē, -jin′-), *n.* **Vaslav,** 1890–1950, Russian ballet dancer and choreographer.

nil (nil), *n.* **1.** nothing; naught; zero. —*adj.* **2.** having no value or existence.

Nile (nīl), *n.* a river in E Africa, the longest in the world, flowing N from Lake Victoria in Uganda to the Mediterranean. 3473 mi. (5592 km) long; from the headwaters of the Kagera River, 4000 mi. (6440 km) long.

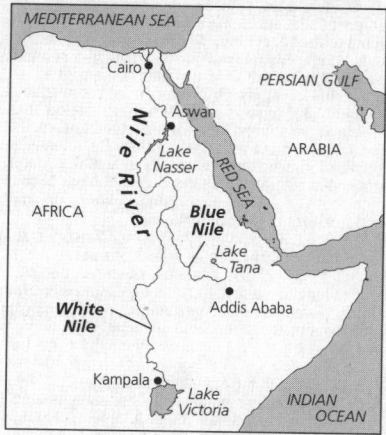

MEDITERRANEAN SEA
Cairo
PERSIAN GULF
Aswan
ARABIA
RED SEA
Lake Nasser
AFRICA
Blue Nile
Lake Tana
White Nile
Addis Ababa
Kampala
Lake Victoria
INDIAN OCEAN

nimbo-, a combining form representing NIMBUS: *nimbostratus.*

nim·bo·stra·tus (nim′bō strā′təs, -strat′əs), *n., pl.* **-stra·ti** (-strā′tī, -strat′ī). a cloud of a class characterized by a formless dark layer; a rain cloud of the layer type, of low altitude, usu. below 8000 ft. (2440 m).

nim·bus (nim′bəs), *n., pl.* **-bi** (-bī), **-bus·es. 1.** (in classical myth) a cloud that sometimes surrounds a deity appearing on earth. **2.** a cloud, aura, atmosphere, etc., surrounding a person or thing. **3.** HALO (def. 1). **4.** the type of dense cloud that yields rain or snow.

NIMBY or **Nim·by** (nim′bē), not in my backyard (used to refer to persons or groups that oppose the introduction into their neighborhood of an institution they consider objectionable, as a prison or psychiatric clinic). —**Nim′by·ism,** *n.*

Nim·itz (nim′its), *n.* **Chester William,** 1885–1966, U.S. admiral.

Nim·rod (nim′rod), *n.* **1.** the great-grandson of Noah: noted as a hunter. Gen. 10:8–10. **2.** (*sometimes l.c.*) a skilled hunter.

nin·com·poop (nin′kəm poop′, ning′-), *n.* a fool or simpleton. —**nin′·com·poop′er·y,** *n.*

nine (nīn), *n.* **1.** a cardinal number, eight plus one. **2.** a symbol for this number, as 9 or IX. **3.** a set of this many persons or things. **4.** a baseball team. **5. the Nine,** the Muses. —*adj.* **6.** amounting to nine in number. —*Idiom.* **7. dressed to the nines,** dressed splendidly, esp. in formal clothing. **8. nine days′ wonder,** a fad or transient trend.

nine′-band′ed armadil′lo, *n.* an armadillo, *Dasypus novemcinctus,* of the southern U.S. to Argentina, having nine hinged bands of bony plates.

nine·fold (*adj.* nīn′fōld′; *adv.* nīn′fōld′), *adj.* **1.** nine times as great or as much. **2.** having nine elements or parts. —*adv.* **3.** in a ninefold manner or measure; to or by nine times as much.

900 number, *n.* a telephone number preceded by the three-digit code "900," used to provide information or entertainment for a fee charged directly to the caller's telephone bill.

nine·pins (nīn′pinz′), *n.* **1.** (*used with a sing. v.*) tenpins played without the head pin. **2.** ninepin, a pin used in this game.

nine·teen (nīn′tēn′), *n.* **1.** a cardinal number, ten plus nine. **2.** a symbol for this number, as 19 or XIX. **3.** a set of this many persons or things. —*adj.* **4.** amounting to 19 in number.

1984, an antiutopian novel (1949) by George Orwell.

nine·teenth (nīn′tēnth′), *adj.* **1.** next after the eighteenth; being the ordinal number for 19. **2.** being one of 19 equal parts. —*n.* **3.** a nineteenth part, esp. of one (¹⁄₁₉). **4.** the nineteenth member of a series.

Nine′teenth Amend′ment, *n.* an amendment to the U.S. Constitution, ratified in 1920, guaranteeing women the right to vote.

nine′teenth hole′, *n. Informal.* a place where golfers gather after play to relax.

nine·ty (nīn′tē), *n., pl.* **-ties,** *adj.* —*n.* **1.** a cardinal number, ten times nine. **2.** a symbol for this number, as 90 or XC. **3.** a set of this many persons or things. **4. nineties,** the numbers from 90 through 99, as in referring to the years of a lifetime or of a century or to degrees of temperature. —*adj.* **5.** amounting to 90 in number. —**nine′ti·eth,** *adj., n.*

Nine′ty-Five′ The′ses, *n.pl.* the theses of Martin Luther against the sale of indulgences in the Roman Catholic Church, posted by him on the door of a church in Wittenberg, October 31, 1517.

Nin·e·veh (nin′ə və), *n.* the ancient capital of Assyria: ruins are opposite Mosul, on the Tigris River, in N Iraq. —**Nin′e·vite′** (-vīt′), *n.*

nin·ja (nin′jə), *n., pl.* **-ja, -jas.** (*often cap.*) a member of a feudal Japanese society of mercenaries highly trained in martial arts and stealth.

nin·ny (nin′ē), *n., pl.* **-nies.** a fool or simpleton.

Nin·ten·do (nin ten′dō), *Trademark.* **1.** a system for playing video games. **2.** any game designed for this system.

ninth (nīnth), *adj.* **1.** next after the eighth; being the ordinal number for nine. **2.** being one of nine equal parts. —*n.* **3.** a ninth part, esp. of one (¹⁄₉). **4.** the ninth member of a series. **5.** *Music.* **a.** a tone distant from another tone by an interval of an octave and a second. **b.** the interval between such tones. **c.** harmonic combination of such tones. —*adv.* **6.** in the ninth place. —**ninth′ly,** *adv.*

Ninth′ Amend′ment, *n.* an amendment to the U.S. Constitution, ratified in 1791 as part of the Bill of Rights, guaranteeing that the rights enumerated in the Constitution would not be construed as denying or jeopardizing other rights of the people.

Ninth′ Command′ment, *n.* "Thou shalt not bear false witness against thy neighbor": ninth of the Ten Commandments. Compare TEN COMMANDMENTS.

ni·o·bi·um (nī ō′bē əm), *n.* a steel-gray metallic element resembling tantalum in its chemical properties; becomes a superconductor below 9 K; used chiefly in alloy steels. *Symbol:* Nb; *at. no.:* 41; *at. wt.:* 92.906; *sp. gr.:* 8.4 at 20°C.

nip[1] (nip), *v.,* **nipped, nip·ping,** *n.* —*v.t.* **1.** to compress tightly between two surfaces or points; pinch; bite. **2.** to sever by pinching, biting, or snipping. **3.** to check in growth or development. **4.** to affect sharply and painfully or injuriously, as cold does. **5.** to snatch away suddenly. **6.** to steal or pilfer. —*v.i.* **7.** *Chiefly Brit.* to step or move nimbly. —*n.* **8.** an act of nipping. **9.** a biting quality, as of frosty air. **10.** sharp cold. **11.** a sharp or biting remark. **12.** a biting taste or tang. **13.** a small bit or quantity of anything; pinch; small bite. —*Idiom.* **14. nip and tuck,** closely contested, esp. with competitors alternately gaining advantage. **15. nip in the bud,** to stop (something) before it can develop or mature: *an ambitious project nipped in the bud.*

nip[2] (nip), *n.* a small drink of alcoholic liquor; sip.

nip·per (nip′ər), *n.* **1.** a person or thing that nips. **2.** Usu., **nippers.** a device for nipping, as pincers or forceps.

nip·ping (nip′ing), *adj.* **1.** sharp or biting, as cold. **2.** sarcastic; caustic.

nip·ple (nip′əl), *n.* **1.** a protuberance of the mamma or breast where, in the female, the milk ducts discharge; teat. **2.** something resembling it, as the mouthpiece of a nursing bottle or pacifier.

nip·py (nip′ē), *adj.,* **-pi·er, -pi·est. 1.** chilly; cold. **2.** sharp; pungent.

nir·va·na (nir vä′nə, -van′ə, nər-), *n.* **1.** (*often cap.*) (in Buddhism) the final release from the cycle of reincarnations as a result of the extinction of individual passion, hatred, and delusion. **2.** (*often cap.*) (in Hinduism) salvation through the union of Atman with Brahma. **3.** a place or state characterized by freedom from pain and worry. —**nir·va′nic,** *adj.*

Ni·san (nē′sän, nis′ən, nē sän′), *n.* the seventh month of the Jewish calendar.

Ni·sei (nē′sā, nē sā′), *n., pl.* **-sei.** (*sometimes l.c.*) a child of Japanese immigrants, born and educated in North America. Compare ISSEI, KIBEI, SANSEI.

nit (nit), *n.* **1.** the egg of a parasitic insect, esp. of a louse. **2.** the young of such an insect.

nite (nīt), *n.* an informal, simplified spelling of NIGHT.

nit′pick′ or **nit′-pick′,** *v.i.* **1.** to be critical of inconsequential details; niggle. —*v.t.* **2.** to criticize by focusing on minute details.

ni·trate (nī′trāt), *n.* **1.** a salt or ester of nitric acid, or any compound containing the univalent group ONO₂ or NO₃. **2.** fertilizer consisting of potassium nitrate or sodium nitrate. —**ni·tra′tion,** *n.*

ni′tric ac′id, *n.* a colorless or yellowish, fuming, suffocating, caustic, water-soluble liquid, HNO₃, used chiefly in the manufacture of explosives and fertilizers and in organic synthesis.

ni′tric ox′ide, *n.* a colorless, slightly water-soluble gas, NO, an intermediate in the manufacture of nitric acid.

ni·trite (nī′trīt), *n.* **1.** a salt or ester of nitrous acid. **2.** SODIUM NITRITE.

ni·tro (nī′trō), *n.* **1.** the univalent group NO₂. **2.** NITROGLYCERIN.

nitro-, a combining form used in the names of chemical compounds in which the nitro group is present: *nitroglycerin.*

ni·tro·cel·lu·lose (nī′trə sel′yə lōs′), *n.* any of a group of compounds produced by adding sulfuric and nitric acids to cellulose, used in the manufacture of lacquers and explosives.

ni·tro·gen (nī′trə jən), *n.* a colorless, odorless, gaseous element that constitutes about four-fifths of the volume of the atmosphere and is present in combined form in animal and vegetable tissues, esp. in proteins. *Symbol:* N; *at. wt.:* 14.0067; *at. no.:* 7; *density:* 1.2506 g/l at 0°C and 760 mm pressure.

ni′trogen cy′cle, *n.* the continuous sequence of natural processes by which nitrogen in the atmosphere and nitrogenous compounds in the soil are converted, as by nitrification and nitrogen fixation, into substances that can be utilized by green plants and then returned to the air and soil as a result of denitrification and plant decay.

ni·trog·e·nous (nī troj′ə nəs), *adj.* containing nitrogen.

ni·tro·glyc·er·in (nī′trə glis′ər in) also **ni·tro·glyc·er·ine** (-ər in, -ə rēn′), *n.* a highly explosive oily liquid, $C_3H_5N_3O_9$, used in explosives and as a vasodilator.

ni′trous ac′id, *n.* an acid, HNO₂, known only in solution.

ni′trous ox′ide, *n.* a colorless, sweet-smelling gas, N₂O, that may induce euphoria when inhaled: used for mild anesthesia.

nit′ty-grit′ty, *n., pl.* **-grit·ties.** the essential substance or details of a matter; crux: *Let's get down to the nitty-gritty of the issue.*

nit·wit (nit′wit′), *n.* a slow-witted, stupid, or foolish person.

nix (niks), *n. Slang.* **1.** nothing. —*adv.* **2.** no. —*v.t.* **3.** to veto.

Nix·on (nik′sən), *n.* **Richard M(ilhous),** 1913–94, president of the U.S. 1969–74 (resigned).

Nix′on Doc′trine, *n.* the policy declared by President Nixon in 1969 that the U.S. would supply arms but not military forces to its allies in Asia and elsewhere.

NJ or **N.J.,** New Jersey.

NL, night letter.

N.L., National League.

NLRB or **N.L.R.B.,** National Labor Relations Board.

NM or **N.M.,** New Mexico.

nm, **1.** nanometer. **2.** nautical mile.

N. Mex., New Mexico.

no¹ (nō), *adv., n., pl.* **noes, nos.** —*adv.* **1.** (a negative expressing dissent, denial, or refusal, as in response to a question.) **2.** (used to emphasize or introduce a negative statement): *No, not one of them came.* **3.** not in any degree or manner; not at all (used with a comparative): *He is no better.* **4.** not: *whether or no.* —*n.* **5.** an utterance of the word "no." **6.** a denial or refusal. **7.** a negative vote or voter.

no² (nō), *adj.* **1.** not any: *no money.* **2.** not at all; far from being: *He is no genius.*

No, *Chem. Symbol.* nobelium.

no. or **No.,** **1.** north. **2.** northern. **3.** number. [< Latin *numero*]

no′-account′, *Informal.* —*adj.* **1.** worthless; good-for-nothing; trifling. —*n.* **2.** a worthless person; good-for-nothing.

No·a·chi·an (nō ā′kē ən), *adj.* of or pertaining to the patriarch Noah or his time.

No·ah (nō′ə), *n.* the patriarch who built a ship (**No′ah's Ark′**) in which he, his family, and animals of every species survived the Flood. Gen. 5–9.

No′ah's Ark′, *n.* **1.** See under NOAH. **2.** an ark shell, *Arca noae.*

No·bel (nō bel′), *n.* **Alfred Bernhard,** 1833–96, Swedish engineer, manufacturer, and philanthropist.

no·bel·i·um (nō bel′ē əm, -bēl′ē-), *n.* a transuranic element in the actinium series. *Symbol:* No; *at. no.:* 102.

No′bel prize′, *n.* any of various awards made annually from funds orig. established by Alfred B. Nobel for achievements in physics, chemistry, medicine or physiology, literature, and the promotion of peace.

no·bil·i·ty (nō bil′i tē), *n., pl.* **-ties.** **1.** the noble class or the body of nobles in a country. **2.** the state or quality of being noble. **3.** nobleness of mind, character, or spirit; exalted moral excellence. **4.** grandeur or magnificence. **5.** noble birth or rank.

no·ble (nō′bəl), *adj.,* **-bler, -blest,** *n.* —*adj.* **1.** distinguished by rank or title. **2.** pertaining to persons so distinguished. **3.** of, belonging to, or constituting a hereditary class that has special social or political status in a country or state; aristocratic. **4.** of an exalted moral character or excellence. **5.** imposing in appearance; magnificent. **6.** of an admirably high quality. **7.** inert; chemically inactive. —*n.* **8.** a person of noble birth or rank; nobleman or noblewoman. **9.** a former gold coin of England, equal to 6s. 8d. —**no′ble·ness,** *n.* —**no′bly,** *adv.*

no·ble·man (nō′bəl mən), *n., pl.* **-men.** a man of noble birth or rank; noble; peer. —**no′ble·man·ly,** *adv.*

no·blesse o·blige (nō bles′ ō blēzh′), *n.* the moral obligation of the rich or highborn to display honorable and generous conduct.

no·ble·wom·an (nō′bəl wŏŏm′ən), *n., pl.* **-wom·en.** a woman of noble birth or rank.

no·bod·y (nō′bod′ē, -bud′ē, -bə dē), *pron., n., pl.* **-bod·ies.** —*pron.* **1.** no person; not anyone; no one. —*n.* **2.** a person of no importance, influence, or power.

No′body Knows′ the Trou′ble I've′ Seen′, a traditional American spiritual.

no-cal (nō′kal′), *adj.* containing no calories.

nock (nok), *n.* **1.** a metal or plastic piece at the end of an arrow, having a notch for the bowstring. **2.** a notch or groove at the end of an arrow into which the bowstring fits. **3.** a notch or groove at each end of a bow, to hold the bowstring in place. —*v.t.* **4.** to furnish with a nock. **5.** to adjust (the arrow) to the bowstring.

noc·tu·id (nok′chōō id), *n.* any of numerous dull-colored moths of the family Noctuidae; the larvae include armyworms and cutworms.

noc·tur·nal (nok tûr′nl), *adj.* **1.** of or pertaining to the night. **2.** done, occurring, or coming at night. **3.** active at night (opposed to *diurnal*): *nocturnal animals.* —**noc·tur′nal·i·ty,** *n.* —**noc·tur′nal·ly,** *adv.*

noc·u·ous (nok′yōō əs), *adj.* likely to cause damage or injury; harmful. —**noc′u·ous·ly,** *adv.* —**noc′u·ous·ness,** *n.*

nod (nod), *v.,* **nod·ded, nod·ding,** *n.* —*v.i.* **1.** to make a slight, quick inclination of the head, as in assent or greeting. **2.** to let the head fall slightly forward with a sudden, involuntary movement when sleepy. **3.** to become careless or listless; make an error through lack of attention. **4.** (of trees, flowers, plumes, etc.) to droop or incline with a swaying motion. —*v.t.* **5.** to bend (the head) in a short, quick downward movement, as of assent or greeting. **6.** to express or signify by such a movement: *to nod one's agreement.* **7.** to summon, bring, or send by a nod

of the head: *nodded us to follow him.* —*n.* **8.** a short, quick inclination of the head, as in assent, greeting, command, or drowsiness. —**Idiom.** **9. give the nod to,** to express approval of; agree to.

Nod (nod), *n.* **1.** the land east of Eden where Cain went to dwell. Gen. 4:16. **2.** LAND OF NOD.

nod·al (nōd′l), *adj.* pertaining to or of the nature of a node.

node (nōd), *n.* **1.** a knot, protuberance, or knob. **2.** a centering point of component parts. **3.** *Anat.* a knotlike mass of tissue: *lymph node.* **4.** *Pathol.* circumscribed swelling. **5.** *Bot.* a part of a stem that bears a leaf or branch. **6.** *Math.* Also called **joint, knot.** in interpolation, one of the points at which the values of a function are assigned. **7.** *Geom.* a point on a curve or surface at which there can be more than one tangent line or tangent plane. **8.** *Physics.* a point, line, or region in a standing wave at which there is relatively little or no vibration. **9.** either of the two points at which the orbit of a heavenly body intersects a given plane, esp. the plane of the ecliptic or of the celestial equator. **10.** a labeled point in a tree diagram at which subordinate lines branch off.

nod·ule (noj′ōōl), *n.* **1.** a small node, knot, or knob. **2.** a small, rounded mass or lump. —**nod′u·lar,** *adj.*

No·el (nō el′), *n.* **1.** CHRISTMAS. **2.** *(l.c.)* a Christmas song or carol. [< French: Christmas < Latin *nātālis (diēs)* birthday]

no′-fault′, *n.* **1.** a form of auto insurance entitling a policyholder in case of an accident to collect basic compensation without a determination of liability. —*adj.* **2.** of or pertaining to such insurance. **3.** holding neither party responsible: *a no-fault divorce.*

no′-fly′ zone′ (nō′flī′), *n.* an area over which no military flights are allowed.

no′-frills′, *adj.* lacking extras; basic; plain.

nog (nog), *n.* any beverage made with beaten eggs; eggnog.

nog·gin (nog′ən), *n.* **1.** a small mug. **2.** a small amount of liquor, usu. a gill. **3.** *Informal.* a person's head.

no′-go′, *adj.* **1.** not functioning properly; not ready to proceed. **2.** denying permission to proceed: *a go or no-go decision.*

no-good (*adj.* nō′gŏŏd′; *n.* nō′gŏŏd′), *adj.* **1.** lacking worth or merit; useless; bad. —*n.* **2.** a worthless or usseless person or thing.

no-good·nik (nō′gŏŏd′nik), *n. Slang.* a no-good person.

no′-hit′ter, *n.* a baseball game in which a pitcher allows no base hits to the opposing team. —**no′-hit′,** *adj.*

no·how (nō′hou′), *adv. Nonstandard.* in no case; in no way.

noise (noiz), *n., v.,* **noised, nois·ing.** —*n.* **1.** sound, esp. of a loud, harsh, or confused kind. **2.** a sound of any kind. **3.** loud shouting or clamor. **4.** an electric disturbance in a communications system that interferes with or prevents reception of a signal or of information. **5.** extraneous, excessive data or information. **6.** rumor or gossip, esp. slander. —*v.t.* **7.** to spread, as a report or rumor; disseminate (usu. fol. by *about* or *abroad*). —*v.i.* **8.** to talk much or publicly. **9.** to make a noise, outcry, or clamor. [< Old French < Latin *nausea* seasickness] —**noise′less,** *adj.* —**noise′less·ly,** *adv.* —**noise′less·ness,** *n.*

noise·mak·er (noiz′mā′kər), *n.* a person or thing that makes noise, esp. a rattle, horn, or other device used on festive occasions.

noi·sette (nwä zet′; *Fr.* nwA-), *n., pl.* **-settes** (-zets′; *Fr.* -zet′). a small piece of lean meat.

noi·some (noi′səm), *adj.* **1.** offensive or disgusting, as an odor. **2.** harmful or injurious to health; noxious. —**noi′some·ly,** *adv.*

nois·y (noi′zē), *adj.,* **-i·er, -i·est.** **1.** making much noise: *noisy children.* **2.** abounding in or full of noise: *a noisy party.* —**nois′i·ly,** *adv.*

no·li me tan·ge·re (nō′lī mē tan′jə rē, nō′lē; *Lat.* nō′lē me täng′ge·Rĕ′), *n.* a person or thing that must not be touched or interfered with.

no·lo con·ten·de·re (nō′lō kən ten′də rē), *n. Law.* a plea that does not admit guilt but subjects the defendant to punishment as if guilty.

no·mad (nō′mad), *n.* **1.** a member of a people that has no permanent abode but moves from place to place along a traditional circuit in search of pasturage or food. **2.** any wanderer; itinerant. —*adj.* **3.** nomadic.

no·mad·ic (nō mad′ik), *adj.* of, pertaining to, or characteristic of nomads: *a nomadic people.* —**no·mad′i·cal·ly,** *adv.*

no′ man's land′, *n.* **1.** an area between warring armies that no one controls. **2.** an area where guidelines and authority are not clear.

nom de guerre (nom′ də gâr′), *n., pl.* **noms de guerre.** an assumed name, as one under which a person fights or writes, etc.; pseudonym.

nom de plume (nom′ də plōōm′), *n., pl.* **noms de plume.** PEN NAME.

no·men·cla·ture (nō′mən klā′chər), *n.* **1.** a set or system of names or terms, as those of a particular science or art. **2.** the names or terms comprising a set or system. —**no′men·cla′tur·al,** *adj.*

-nomics a combining form abstracted from *economics* to indicate someone's economic policies or practices: *Reaganomics.*

nom·i·nal (nom′ə nl), *adj.* **1.** being such in name only; so-called; putative: *the nominal head of the country.* **2.** (of a price, fee, etc.) named as a matter of form, being trifling in comparison with the actual value: *a nominal price.* **3.** of, pertaining to, or constituting a name or names. **4.** of, pertaining to, functioning as, or producing a noun: *a nominal suffix.* **5.** containing, bearing, or giving a name or names. **6.** *Aerospace.* performing or achieved within expected limits; normal and satisfactory. —*n.* **7.** a word or group of words functioning as a noun.

nom·i·nal·ism (nom′ə nl iz′əm), *n.* the philosophical doctrine that general or abstract words do not stand for objectively existing entities and that universals are no more than names assigned to them. Compare

CONCEPTUALISM (def. 1), REALISM (def. 5a). —**nom′i·nal·ist,** *n.* —**nom′i·nal·is′tic,** *adj.* —**nom′i·nal·is′ti·cal·ly,** *adv.*

nom·i·nal·ize (nom′ə nl īz′), *v.t.,* **-ized, -iz·ing.** to convert into or use as a noun or nominal, as in changing the verb *legalize* into *legalization.* —**nom′i·nal·i·za′tion,** *n.*

nom′i·nal·ly (nom′ə nl ē), *adv.* in name or in name only.

nom′inal val′ue, *n.* FACE VALUE (def. 1).

nom·i·nate (*v.* nom′ə nāt′; *adj.* -nit), *v.,* **-nat·ed, -nat·ing,** *adj.* —*v.t.* **1.** to propose (someone) for appointment or election to an office. **2.** to appoint to a duty or office. **3.** to propose for an honor, award, or the like. **4.** to name; designate. —*adj.* **5.** having a particular name.

nom·i·na·tion (nom′ə nā′shən), *n.* **1.** an act or instance of nominating, esp. to office. **2.** the state of being nominated.

nom·i·na·tive (nom′ə nə tiv, nom′nə- *or, for 2,* nom′ə nā′tiv), *adj.* **1.** of, pertaining to, or being a grammatical case typically indicating the subject of a finite verb. **2.** nominated; appointed by nomination. —*n.* **3.** the nominative case. —**nom′i·na·tive·ly,** *adv.*

nom·i·nee (nom′ə nē′), *n.* a person nominated, as to run for elective office.

non-, a prefix meaning "not," usu. having a simple negative force, as implying mere negation or absence of something (rather than the opposite or reverse of it, as often expressed by UN-[1]): *nonadherence; nonpayment; nonprofessional.*

non·age (non′ij, nō′nij), *n.* **1.** the period of legal minority. **2.** any period of immaturity.

non·a·ge·nar·i·an (non′ə jə nâr′ē ən, nō′nə-), *adj.* **1.** of the age of 90 years, or between 90 and 100 years old. —*n.* **2.** a nonagenarian person.

non·a·ligned (non′ə līnd′), *adj.* not politically aligned, esp. with either one of two opposing powers or ideologies. —**non′a·lign′ment,** *n.*

no′-name′, *adj.* packaged and sold without a brand name or with a brand name that is not nationally recognized.

non·as·sess·a·ble (non′ə ses′ə bəl), *adj.* (of stock) exempting the investor from any expense or liability beyond the amount of his or her investment. —**non′as·ses′sa·bil′i·ty,** *n.*

non·be·liev·er (non′bi lē′vər), *n.* a person who lacks belief or faith, as in a religion, idea, or undertaking. —**non′be·liev′ing,** *adj.*

nonce (nons), *n.* the immediate occasion or purpose: *We'll stay, for the nonce.*

nonce′ word′, *n.* a word coined and used only for a particular occasion.

non·cha·lance (non′shə läns′, non′shə läns′, -ləns), *n.* cool indifference or lack of concern; casualness.

non·cha·lant (non′shə länt′, non′shə länt′, -lənt), *adj.* coolly unconcerned; indifferent or unexcited. —**non′cha·lant′ly,** *adv.*

non·com (non′kom′), *n. Informal.* NONCOMMISSIONED OFFICER.

non·com·bat·ant (non′kəm bat′nt, non kom′bə tnt), *n.* **1.** a member of a military force who is not a fighter, as a surgeon or chaplain. **2.** a person who is not a combatant; a civilian in wartime.

non′com·mis′sioned of′ficer (non′kə mish′ənd, non′-), *n.* an enlisted person, as a sergeant or corporal, holding a rank below commissioned or warrant officer in a branch of the armed forces.

non·com·mit·tal (non′kə mit′l), *adj.* having or giving no clear or particular view, feeling, character, or the like.

non·com·mu·ni·ca·ble (non′kə myoo̅′ni kə bəl), *adj.* not communicable; not contagious: *noncommunicable diseases.*

non·com·pli·ance (non′kəm plī′əns), *n.* failure or refusal to comply, as with the terms of an agreement or a prescribed medical regimen. —**non′com·pli′ant,** *adj.* —**non′com·ply′ing,** *adj.*

non com·pos men·tis (non′ kom′pəs men′tis), *adj.* not of sound mind; mentally incompetent. [< Latin]

non·con·duc·tor (non′kən duk′tər), *n.* a substance that does not readily conduct heat, sound, or electricity. —**non′con·duct′ing,** *adj.*

non·con·form·ist (non′kən fôr′mist), *n.* **1.** a person who refuses to conform, as to established customs or ideas. **2.** (*often cap.*) a Protestant in England who is not a member of the Church of England; dissenter.

non·con·form·i·ty (non′kən fôr′mi tē), *n.* **1.** failure or refusal to conform, as to established customs, attitudes, or ideas. **2.** lack of conformity or agreement. **3.** (*often cap.*) refusal to conform to the Church of England. **4.** an unconformity that separates crystalline rocks, either igneous or metamorphic, from sedimentary rocks.

---

non′a·bra′sive, *adj.*
non′ab·sorb′ent, *adj., n.*
non′ac·cept′ance, *n.*
non′ac·ces′si·ble, *adj.*
non′a·chiev′er, *n.*
non′ac′tive, *adj.*
non′a·dap′tive, *adj.*
non′ad·dic′tive, *adj.*
non′ad·he′sive, *adj.*
non′ad·join′ing, *adj.*
non′ad·just′a·ble, *adj.;* **-bly,** *adv.*
non′ag·gres′sion, *n.*
non′ag·gres′sive, *adj.*
non′a·gree′ment, *n.*
non′al·co·hol′ic, *adj.*
non′al·ler·gen′ic, *adj.*
non′ap·pli·ca·ble, *adj.;* **-ness,** *n.*
non′a·quat′ic, *adj.*
non′as·ser′tive, *adj.;* **-ly,** *adv.;* **-ness,** *n.*
non′ath·lete, *n.*
non′ath·let′ic, *adj.*
non′at·tend′ance, *n.*
non′au·to·mat′ed, *adj.*
non′au·to·mo′tive, *adj.*
non′bind′ing, *adj.*
non′break′a·ble, *adj.*
non′can′cer·ous, *adj.*
non′can′di·date′, *n.*
non′car′bo·nat′ed, *adj.*
non′cer′ti·fied′, *adj.*
non′chal·leng·ing, *adj.*
non′chem′i·cal, *adj.*
non′cir′cu·lar, *adj.;* **-ly,** *adv.*
non′civ′i·lized′, *adj.*
non′clas′si·fied′, *adj.*
non′cler′i·cal, *adj.;* **-ly,** *adv.*
non′clin′i·cal, *adj.;* **-ly,** *adv.*
non′co·her′ent, *adj.;* **-ly,** *adv.*
non′col·laps′i·ble, *adj.*
non′com·mer′cial, *adj., n.;* **-ly,** *adv.*
non′com·mu′ni·cat′ing, *adj.*
non′com·mu′ni·ca′tion, *n.*
non′com·pet′ing, *adj.*
non′com·pet′i·tive, *adj.;* **-ly,** *adv.;* **-ness,** *n.*
non′com·pul′so·ry, *adj.*
non′con·clu′sive, *adj.;* **-ly,** *adv.;* **-ness,** *n.*
non′con·di′tion·al, *adj.*
non′con·flict′ing, *adj.*

non′con·form′ing, *adj.*
non′con·sec′u·tive, *adj.;* **-ly,** *adv.*
non′con·sen′su·al, *adj.;* **-ly,** *adv.*
non′con·sent′ing, *adj.*
non′con·struc′tive, *adj.;* **-ly,** *adv.;* **-ness,** *n.*
non′con·sum′er, *adj.;* *n.*
non′con′tact, *n.;* *adj.*
non′con·ta′gious, *adj.;* **-ly,** *adv.;* **-ness,** *n.*
non′con·tend′ing, *adj.*
non′con·tin′u·ous, *adj.;* **-ly,** *adv.;* **-ness,** *n.*
non′con·trib′ut·ing, *adj.*
non′con·trib′u·tor, *n.*
non′con·trol′la·ble, *adj.;* **-ly,** *adv.*
non′con·trol′ling, *adj.*
non′con·tro·ver′sial, *adj.;* **-ly,** *adv.*
non′con·ven′tion·al, *adj.;* **-ly,** *adv.*
non′cor·rob′o·ra′tion, *n.*
non′de·bat′a·ble, *adj.*
non′de·duct′i·ble, *adj.*
non′de·fer′ra·ble, *adj.*
non′de·lib′er·ate, *adj.;* **-ly,** *adv.*
non′de·liv′er·y, *n.;* *pl.* **-er·ies.**
non′de·nom′i·na′tion·al, *adj.;* **-ly,** *adv.*
non′de·part·men′tal, *adj.;* **-ly,** *adv.*
non′de·pend′ence, *n.*
non′de·pre′ci·at′ing, *adj.*
non′de·riv′a·ble, *adj.*
non′de·riv′a·tive, *adj., n.;* **-ly,** *adv.*
non′de·ter′mi·na·ble, *adj.*
non′de·ter′mi·nant, *n.*
non′de·ter′mi·nate, *adj.*
non′di·chot′o·mous, *adj.;* **-ly,** *adv.*
non′di·dac′tic, *adj.*
non′di·e·tet′ic, *adj.*
non′dif·fer·en′ti·a·ble, *adj.*
non′dif·fer·en′ti·a′tion, *n.*
non′dif·fus′i·ble, *adj.;* **-bly,** *adv.*
non′di·gest′i·ble, *adj.*
non′dip·lo·mat′ic, *adj.*
non′dip·lo·mat′i·cal·ly, *adv.*
non′dis·burs′a·ble, *adj.*
non′dis·burse′ment, *n.*
non′dis·ci·pli·nar′y, *adj.*
non′dis·clo′sure, *n.*
non′dis·cre′tion·ar′y, *adj.*
non′dis·crim′i·nat′ing, *adj.;* **-ly,** *adv.*
non′dis·crim′i·na·to′ry, *adj.*
non′dis·in′te·grat′ing, *adj.*

non′dis·in′te·gra′tion, *n.*
non′dis·junc′tive, *adj.;* **-ly,** *adv.*
non′dis·par′i·ty, *n.;* *pl.* **-ties.**
non′dis·per′sal, *n.*
non′dis·pos′a·ble, *adj.*
non′dis·solv′ing, *adj.*
non′dis·tin′guish·a·ble, *adj.;* **-bly,** *adv.*
non′dis·tin′guish·ing, *adj.*
non′dis·tort′ed, *adj.;* **-ly,** *adv.*
non′dis·tor′tive, *adj.*
non′dis·trib′u·tive, *adj.;* **-ly,** *adv.*
non′di·ver′gence, *n.*
non′di·ver′si·fied′, *adj.*
non′di·vis′i·bil′i·ty, *n.*
non′di·vis′i·ble, *adj.*
non′doc·tri·naire′, *adj.*
non′dog·mat′ic, *adj.*
non′drip′, *adj.*
non′earn′ing, *adj., n.*
non′e·co·nom′ic, *adj.*
non′ec·u·men′i·cal, *adj.*
non′ed′u·ca·ble, *adj.*
non′ef·fec′tive, *adj.*
non′e·las′tic, *adj.*
non′el·i·gi·bil′i·ty, *n.*
non′el·i·gi·ble, *adj.;* **-bly,** *adv.*
non′e·mer′gence, *n.*
non′e·mer′gent, *adj.*
non′em·pir′i·cal, *adj.;* **-ly,** *adv.*
non′en·force′a·ble, *adj.*
non′en′trant, *n.*
non′en·tre·pre·neur′i·al, *adj.*
non′eq′ua·ble, *adj.*
non′e′qual, *adj., n.*
non′e·qui·lib′ri·um, *n.*
non′eq′ui·ta·ble, *adj.;* **-bly,** *adv.*
non′e·quiv′a·lence, *n.*
non′e·quiv′a·lent, *adj., n.;* **-ly,** *adv.*
non′e·quiv′o·cal, *adj.;* **-ly,** *adv.*
non′e·ras′a·ble, *adj.*
non′ex·empt′, *adj., n.*
non′ex·ist′ing, *adj.*
non′ex·pect′ant, *adj.;* **-ly,** *adv.*
non′ex·per′i·men′tal, *adj.;* **-ly,** *adv.*
non′ex·po′sure, *n.*
non′ex·pres′sive, *adj.;* **-ly,** *adv.*
non′ex·tin′guish·a·ble, *adj.*
non′ex·tract′a·ble, *adj.*
non′ex·tract′i·ble, *adj.*
non′ex·tra·dit′a·ble, *adj.*

non′fac′tu·al, *adj.;* **-ly,** *adv.*
non′fa′tal, *adj.;* **-ly,** *adv.*
non′fa′vor·ite, *n.*
non′fea′si·ble, *adj.*
non′fed′er·al, *adj.*
non′fi·du′ci·ar′y, *adj., n.,* *pl.* **-ar·ies.**
non′fight′ing, *adj.*
non′fil′ter·a·ble, *adj.*
non′fi·nan′cial, *adj.;* **-ly,** *adv.*
non′fi′nite, *adj.*
non′fis′sion·a·ble, *adj.*
non′flex′i·ble, *adj.;* **-bly,** *adv.*
non′flow′er·ing, *adj.*
non′fluc′tu·at′ing, *adj.*
non′fluo·res′cent, *adj.*
non′for·feit·a·ble, *adj.*
non′form′a·tive, *adj.;* **-ly,** *adv.*
non′fright′en·ing, *adj.;* **-ly,** *adv.*
non′func′tion·al, *adj.;* **-ly,** *adv.*
non′func′tion·ing, *adj.*
non′fund′ed, *adj.*
non′ge·ner′ic, *adj.*
non′glazed′, *adj.*
non′gloss′y, *adj.*
non′gov·ern·men′tal, *adj.*
non′grad′ed, *adj.*
non′grad′u·ate, *n.*
non′grad′u·at′ed, *adj.*
non′gram·mat′i·cal, *adj.*
non′gran′u·lar, *adj.*
non′gran′u·lat′ed, *adj.*
non′graph′ic, *adj.*
non′ha·bit′u·al, *adj.;* **-ly,** *adv.*
non′har·mon′ic, *adj.*
non′he·red′i·tar′y, *adj.*
non′her′it·a·ble, *adj.;* **-bly,** *adv.*
non′he·ro′ic, *adj.*
non′heu·ris′tic, *adj.*
non′hi·er·ar′chi·cal, *adj.;* **-ly,** *adv.*
non′his·tor′ic, *adj.*
non′his·tor′i·cal, *adj.;* **-ly,** *adv.*
non′hos′tile, *adj.*
non′hu·man·is′tic, *adj.*
non′hu′mor·ous, *adj.;* **-ly,** *adv.*
non′hy·drau′lic, *adj.*
non′hy·gi·en′ic, *adj.*
non′hyp·not′ic, *adj., n.*
non′i·de·al·is′tic, *adj.*
non′i·de·o·log′i·cal, *adj.;* **-ly,** *adv.*
non′id·i·o·mat′ic, *adj.*
non′i·dyl′lic, *adj.*
non′il·lu′mi·nat′ing, *adj.;* **-ly,** *adv.*

non·co·op·er·a·tion or **non·co-op·er·a·tion** (non′kō op′ə rā′shən), n. 1. failure or refusal to cooperate. 2. a method of showing opposition to a government by refusing to participate in civic and political life or to obey governmental regulations. Compare CIVIL DISOBEDIENCE, PASSIVE RESISTANCE. —**non′co·op′er·a′tive** (-op′ər ə tiv, -ə rā′tiv), adj.

non·dair·y (non dâr′ē), adj. being a substitute for milk or milk products; containing no dairy ingredients: a nondairy creamer.

non·de·script (non′di skript′), adj. 1. undistinguished or dull; without interest or character: nondescript clothes. 2. of no recognized or specific type or kind. —n. 3. a nondescript person or thing.

non·di·rec·tion·al (non′di rek′shə nl, -dī-), adj. functioning equally well in all directions; omnidirectional.

non·dis·tinc·tive (non′di stingk′tiv), adj. Ling. not serving to distinguish meanings: a nondistinctive difference in sound.

non·drink·er (non dring′kər), n. a person who abstains from alcohol. —**non·drink′ing**, adj., n.

none (nun), pron. 1. no one; not one: None of the members is going. 2. not any: None of the pie is left. That is none of your business. 3. no part; nothing: I'll have none of that. 4. (used with a pl. v.) no or not any persons or things: There were two coats on the rack and now there are none. —adv. 5. to no extent; in no way; not at all: We saw the ceremony none too well.

non·en·ti·ty (non en′ti tē), n., pl. -ties. 1. a person or thing of no importance. 2. something that does not exist or exists only in imagination.

none·such (nun′such′), n. a person or thing without equal.

none·the·less (nun′thə les′), adv. nevertheless.

non-Eu·clid·e·an (non′yōō klid′ē ən), adj. differing from the postulates of Euclid or based upon postulates other than those of Euclid: non-Euclidean geometry.

non·e·vent (non′i vent′), n. 1. a usu. well publicized event that is anticipated but does not occur or occurs with little impact; anticlimax. 2. an occasion that creates little or no interest.

non·ex·ist·ence (non′ig zis′təns), n. 1. absence of existence. 2. something that has no existence. —**non′ex·ist′ent**, adj.

non·fat (non′fat′), adj. having the fat solids removed.

non·fea·sance (non fē′zəns), n. failure to perform an act that is part of one's responsibility.

non·fer·rous (non fer′əs), adj. 1. (of a metal) containing little or no iron. 2. pertaining to metals other than iron or steel.

non·fic·tion (non fik′shən), n. literature comprising works that are not fictional. —**non·fic′tion·al**, adj.

non·flam·ma·ble (non flam′ə bəl), adj. not flammable; not combustible or easily set on fire.

non·hu·man (non hyōō′mən; often -yōō′-), adj. 1. not human or for humans. 2. not worthy of human beings.

non·in·ter·ven·tion (non′in tər ven′shən), n. 1. abstention by a nation from interference in the affairs of other nations. 2. failure or refusal to intervene. —**non′in·ter·ven′tion·ist**, n., adj.

non·in·va·sive (non′in vā′siv), adj. 1. not invading adjacent cells, vessels, or tissues; localized: a noninvasive tumor. 2. not entering or penetrating the body. —**non′in·va′sive·ly**, adv.

non·judg·men·tal (non′juj men′tl), adj. not judging on the basis of one's personal standards or opinions. —**non′judg·men′tal·ly**, adv.

non·lit·er·ate (non lit′ər it), adj. preliterate.

non·mem·ber (non mem′bər), n. a person who is not a member of an organization.

non·mil·len·ni·al·ism (non′mi len′ē ə liz′əm), n. AMILLENNIALISM.

non·mor·al (non môr′əl, -mor′-), adj. neither moral nor immoral. —**non′mo·ral′i·ty**, n. —**non·mor′al·ly**, adv.

non·ne·go·ti·a·ble (non′ni gō′shē ə bəl, -shə bəl), adj. not subject to negotiation, discussion, or change: nonnegotiable demands.

no′-no′, n., pl. -nos, -no's. Informal. anything that is forbidden or not advisable, as because of being improper or unsafe.

no′-non′sense, adj. serious; businesslike.

non·pa·reil (non′pə rel′), adj. 1. having no equal; peerless. —n. 2. a person or thing having no equal. 3. a pellet of colored sugar for decorating candy, cakes, or cookies. 4. a bite-sized disk of chocolate covered with these pellets. 5. PAINTED BUNTING. 6. Print. a. a 6-point type. b. a slug occupying 6 points between lines.

non·par·ti·san or **non·par·ti·zan** (non pär′tə zən), adj. 1. not par-

non′il·lus′tra·tive, adj.; -ly, adv.	non·lay′ered, adj.	non·mo′tor·ized′, adj.	non′pa·ter′nal, adj.; -ly, adv.
non′im·mer′sion, n.	non·le·git′i·mate, adj.	non·mov′a·ble, adj.; -ble·ness, n.;	non′path·o·gen′ic, adj.
non′im·mune′, adj.	non·le′thal, adj.; -ly, adv.	-bly, adv.	non′path·o·log′i·cal, adj.; -ly, adv.
non′im·mu′ni·ty, n., pl. -ties.	non·li′a·ble, adj.	non′mu·nic′i·pal, adj.; -ly, adv.	non′pa·tri·ot′ic, adj.
non′im·pe′ri·al, adj.; -ly, adv.	non′li·bel′ous, adj.; -ly, adv.	non·mus′cu·lar, adj.; -ly, adv.	non·pay′ing, adj.
non′im·pe′ri·al·is′tic, adj.	non·lim′it·ing, adj.	non·mu′si·cal, adj.; -ly, adv.	non·pay′ment, n.
non′im·pres′sion·is′tic, adj.	non·lin′e·ar, adj.	non′mu·ta′tion·al, adj.; -ly, adv.	non′pe·des′tri·an, n., adj.
non′in·can·des′cent, adj.; -ly, adv.	non·lit′er·ar′y, adj.	non·nar·cot′ic, adj., n.	non·ped′i·greed′, adj.
non′in·cum′bent, n., adj.	non′li·ti′gious, adj.	non′na·tion·al·is′tic, adj.	non′per·ceiv′a·ble, adj.; -bly, adv.
non′in′dexed, adj.	non′li·tur′gi·cal, adj.; -ly, adv.	non·na′tive, adj., n.; -ly, adv.	non′per·cep′tive, adj.; -ly, adv.;
non′in·dict′a·ble, adj.	non·liv′ing, adj., n.	non·nat′u·ral, adj.; -ly, adv.	-ness, n.
non′in·dig′e·nous, adj.	non·lov′ing, adj.	non·neu′tral, adj., n.; -ly, adv.	non′per·fect′i·bil′i·ty, n.
non′in·di·vid′u·al, adj.	non·loy′al, adj.; -ly, adv.	non·nour′ish·ing, adj.	non′per·fect′i·ble, adj.
non-In′do-Eu′ro·pe′an, adj., n.	non·lu′bri·cat′ing, adj.	non·nu′cle·ar, adj.	non′per·fo′rat·ed, adj.
non′in·duc′tive, adj.	non·lyr′ic, adj.	non·nur′tur·ant, adj.	non′per·form′ance, n.
non′in·duced′, adj.	non·mag·net′ic, adj.	non′nu·tri′tious, adj.; -ly, adv.;	non′per·form′er, n.
non′in·dul′gent, adj.; -ly, adv.	non·mag′net·ized′, adj.	-ness, n.	non′pe·ri·od′ic, adj.
non′in·dus′tri·al, adj.; -ly, adv.	non·ma·li′cious, adj.; -ly, adv.	non′o·be′di·ence, n.	non′per·ish·a·ble, adj., n.
non′in·dus′tri·al·ized′, adj.	non·ma·lig′nant, adj.; -ly, adv.	non′o·be′di·ent, adj.	non′per·me·a·bil′i·ty, n.
non′in·fec′tious, adj.; -ness, n.	non·mam·ma′li·an, n., adj.	non′ob·jec′tive, adj.	non′per′me·a·ble, adj.
non′in·flam′ma·ble, adj.	non′man·da·to′ry, adj., n., pl. -ries.	non·ob′lig·a·to′ry, adj.	non′per·mis′si·ble, adj.; -bly, adv.
non′in·her′it·a·ble, adj.; -ness, n.	non·ma·nip′u·la·tive, adj.	non′ob·serv′a·ble, adj.; -bly, adv.	non′per·mis′sive, adj.; -ly, adv.;
non′in·sist′ent, adj.	non·man′u·al, adj.	non′ob·serv′ance, n.	-ness, n.
non′in·stall′ment, n.	non·mar′i·tal, adj.; -ly, adv.	non′ob·serv′ing, adj.; -ly, adv.	non′per·sist′ent, adj.; -ly, adv.
non′in·stru·men′tal, adj.; -ly, adv.	non·mar′ket, n., adj.	non′ob·ses′sive, adj.; -ly, adv.	non′per·son·al, adj.; -ly, adv.
non·in′su·lat′ing, adj.	non·mar′riage·a·ble, adj.	non′oc·cur′rence, n.	non′per·sua′sive, adj.; -ly, adv.;
non·in′te·grat′ed, adj.	non·mar′tial, adj.; -ly, adv.	non′o′dor·ous, adj.; -ly, adv.	-ness, n.
non·in′te·ger, n.	non·match′ing, adj.	non′of·fen′sive, adj.; -ly, adv.	non·per′ti·nent, adj.; -ly, adv.
non′in·tel·lec′tu·al, adj., n.; -ly, adv.	non·ma·te′ri·al, adj.	non′of·fi′cial, adj.; -ly, adv.	non′phil·o·soph′i·cal, adj.; -ly, adv.
non′in·ter·ac′tive, adj.	non·ma·te′ri·al·is′tic, adj.	non·oil′y, adj.	non′pho·to·graph′ic, adj.
non′in·ter·change′a·ble, adj.	non·ma·ter′nal, adj.; -ly, adv.	non·op′er·a·ble, adj.	non·phys′i·cal, adj.; -ly, adv.
non′in·ter·fer′ence, n.	non′math·e·mat′i·cal, adj.; -ly, adv.	non·op′er·at′ing, adj.	non·phys′i·o·log′i·cal, adj.; -ly, adv.
non′in·ter·fer′ing, adj.; -ly, adv.	non′mat·ri·mo′ni·al, adj.; -ly, adv.	non′op·er·a′tion·al, adj.	non′pic·to′ri·al, adj.; -ly, adv.
non′in·ter·pret·a·ble, adj.	non·ma·ture′, adj.; -ly, adv.	non·op′er·a·tive, adj.	non·plau′si·ble, adj.; -ble·ness, n.;
non′in·ter′pre·tive, adj.; -ly, adv.	non′me·chan′i·cal, adj.; -ly, adv.	non·or′bit·ing, adj.	-bly, adv.
non′in·ter·sect′ing, adj.	non′med′i·cal, adj.; -ly, adv.	non·or·gan′ic, adj.	non·play′er, n.
non′in·tox′i·cant, adj.	non′me·dic′i·nal, adj.; -ly, adv.	non′o·rig′i·nal, adj., n.; -ly, adv.	non·play′ing, adj.
non′in·tox′i·cat′ing, adj.; -ly, adv.	non·me·lod′ic, adj.	non′or·na·men′tal, adj.; -ly, adv.	non·pli′a·ble, adj.; -ble·ness, n.;
non′in·tru′sive, adj.; -ly, adv.	non′me·lod′i·cal·ly, adv.	non·ox′i·diz′ing, adj.	-bly, adv.
non′in·ves′tor, n.	non·melt′ing, adj.	non·pac′i·fist, n.	non·po′lar·ized′, adj.
non′in·volve′ment, n.	non′met·a·phor′i·cal, adj.; -ly, adv.	non·pa′gan, n., adj.	non′po·lit′i·cal, adj.; -ly, adv.
non·i′o·dized′, adj.	non′me·thod′ic, adj.	non·paid′, n.	non·pol′lut′ing, adj.
non·i′on·ized′, adj.	non·met′ric, adj.	non·pal′a·tal, adj., n.	non′por·no·graph′ic, adj.
non′i·on·iz′ing, adj.	non·mi′grant, adj., n.	non·par′al·lel′, adj.	non·po′rous, adj.; -ness, n.
non′ir·ra′di·at′ed, adj.	non·mi′gra·to′ry, adj.	non′par·a·sit′ic, adj.	non′port′a·ble, adj.
non′ir′ri·tat′ing, adj.	non·mil′i·tar′y, adj.	non·par′i·ty, n.	non′pos·ses′sive, adj.; -ly, adv.;
non·is′sue, n.	non·min′er·al, n., adj.	non′par·lia·men′ta·ry, adj.	-ness, n.
non′i·tem·ized′, adj.	non·mo′bile, adj.	non′pa·ro′chi·al, adj.; -ly, adv.	non·po′ta·ble, adj., n.
non′ju·di′cial, adj.; -ly, adv.	non·mod′ern, adj., n.; -ly, adv.	non·par′tic′i·pant, n.	non·pred′a·to′ry, adj.
non·ju′ry, adj., n., pl. -ries.	non·mo·lec′u·lar, adj.	non′par·tic′i·pa′tion, n.	non′pref·er·en′tial, adj.; -ly, adv.
non·ko′sher, adj., n.	non′mo·nog′a·mous, adj.; -ly, adv.	non·pat′ent·a·ble, adj.	non′prej·u·di′cial, adj.; -ly, adv.
	non·mor′tal, adj., n.; -ly, adv.	non·pat′ent·ed, adj.	non′pre·scrip′tive, adj.

tisan; objective. **2.** not supporting, controlled by, or affiliated with any of the established political parties. —*n.* **3.** a person who is nonpartisan. —**non·par′ti·san·ship′**, *n.*

non·per·son (non pûr′sən), *n.* a person whose existence is not recognized.

non·plus (non plus′, non′plus), *v.t.*, **-plussed** or **-plused**, **-plus·sing** or **-plus·ing.** to render utterly perplexed; puzzle completely.

non·pre·scrip·tion (non′pri skrip′shən), *adj.* (of drugs) legally purchasable without a doctor's prescription; over-the-counter.

non·pro·duc·tive (non′prə duk′tiv), *adj.* **1.** not productive. **2.** not producing goods directly, as supervisors or inspectors. —**non′pro·duc′·tive·ness, non′pro·duc·tiv′i·ty** (-prō duk tiv′i tē, -prod ək-), *n.*

non·prof·it (non prof′it), *adj.* **1.** not established for the purpose of making a profit. —*n.* **2.** a nonprofit organization.

non·pro·lif·er·a·tion (non′prə lif′ə rā′shən), *n.* **1.** the action or practice of curbing proliferation, esp. of nuclear weapons. —*adj.* **2.** of or pertaining to nonproliferation.

non·res·i·dent (non rez′i dənt), *adj.* **1.** not resident in a particular place. —*n.* **2.** a person who is nonresident. —**non·res′i·dence, non·res′i·den·cy**, *n.*

non·re·sis·tant (non′ri zis′tənt), *adj.* **1.** not able to resist something, as a disease; susceptible. **2.** not resistant; passively obedient. —*n.* **3.** a person who maintains that established authority, even when tyrannical, should not be resisted by force. **4.** a person who does not use force to resist violence. —**non′re·sis′tance**, *n.*

non·re·stric·tive (non′ri strik′tiv), *adj.* **1.** not restrictive or limiting. **2.** of or pertaining to a word, phrase, or clause that describes or supplements a modified element but is not essential in establishing its identity, as the relative clause *which has been dry* in the sentence *This year, which has been dry, was bad for crops.* In English a nonrestrictive clause is usu. set off by commas. Compare RESTRICTIVE (def. 3).

non·re·turn·a·ble (non′ri tûr′nə bəl), *adj.* **1.** not returnable, esp. to a vendor for refund of a deposit. —*n.* **2.** something not returnable.

non·sched·uled (non skej′ōōld, -ōōld, -ōō əld; *Brit.* -shed′yōōld, -shej′-ōōld), *adj.* (of an airline or plane) authorized to carry passengers or freight between specified points as demand warrants, rather than on a regular schedule.

non·sec·tar·i·an (non′sek târ′ē ən), *adj.* not affiliated with or limited to a specific religious denomination.

non·sense (non′sens, -səns), *n.* **1.** words without sense or conveying absurd ideas. **2.** conduct or action that is senseless or absurd. **3.** something that makes no sense. **4.** impudent, insubordinate, or otherwise objectionable behavior: *Don't take any nonsense from him.* —**non·sen′si·cal**, *adj.* —**non·sen′si·cal·ly**, *adv.*

non se·qui·tur (non sek′wi tər, -tōōr′), *n.* **1.** an inference or a conclusion that does not follow from the premises. **2.** a comment that is unrelated to a preceding one.

non·sex·ist (non sek′sist), *adj.* not showing, advocating, or involving sexism: *nonsexist language; nonsexist toys.*

non·sked (non′sked′), *n. Informal.* a nonscheduled airline or plane.

non·skid (non′skid′), *adj.* resistant to skidding.

non·stand·ard (non′stan′dərd), *adj.* **1.** not standard. **2.** not conforming in pronunciation, grammar, vocabulary, etc., to the usage characteristic of and considered acceptable by most educated native speakers. Compare STANDARD (def. 25).

non·start·er (non stär′tər), *n.* **1.** someone or something that does not start. **2.** an inoperative idea or proposal.

non·stick (non′stik′), *adj.* having a finish designed to prevent food from sticking during cooking or baking.

non·stop (non′stop′), *adj.* **1.** being without a single stop en route: *a nonstop flight from New York to Dallas.* **2.** happening, done, or held without a pause: *nonstop meetings.* —*adv.* **3.** without a single stop en route. **4.** without interruption; continually.

non·sup·port (non′sə pôrt′, -pōrt′), *n.* failure to provide financial support for a spouse, child, or other dependent.

non-U (non yōō′), *adj.* not characteristic of the upper classes.

non·un·ion (non yōōn′yən), *adj.* **1.** not belonging to a labor union. **2.** not recognizing or accepting labor unions: *a nonunion factory.* **3.** not produced by union workers. —**non·un′ion·ism**, *n.*

non·us·er (non yōō′zər), *n.* a person who does not use or partake of something, as harmful drugs.

---

non·prin′ci·pled, *adj.*
non·priv′i·leged, *adj.*
non·pro·fes′sion·al, *adj., n.*
non·pro·fi′cien·cy, *n.*
non·pro·fi′cient, *adj.*
non·prof′it·a·ble, *adj.;* -ly, *adv.*
non·pro·gram′ma·ble, *adj.*
non·pro·por′tion·al, *adj.;* -ly, *adv.*
non·psy·chi·at′ric, *adj.*
non·psy·cho·log′i·cal, *adj.;* -ly, *adv.*
non·pun′ish·a·ble, *adj.*
non·qual′i·fied, *adj.*
non·quan′ti·fi′a·ble, *adj.*
non·quan′ti·ta·tive, *adj.;* -ly, *adv.;* -ness, *n.*
non·ra′di·at′ing, *adj.*
non·ra·di·o·ac′tive, *adj.*
non·ran′dom, *adj.;* -ly, *adv.*
non·ra′tion·al, *adj.;* -ly, *adv.*
non·re·ac′tive, *adj.*
non·read′er, *n.*
non·re·al·is′tic, *adj.*
non·re·al·is′ti·cal·ly, *adv.*
non·re·al·iz′a·ble, *adj.*
non·re·cep·tiv′i·ty, *n.*
non·re·charge′a·ble, *adj.*
non·re·cip′ro·cal, *adj., n.;* -ly, *adv.*
non·rec·og·ni′tion, *n.*
non·rec′on·cil′a·ble, *adj.;* -bly, *adv.*
non·re·cov′er·a·ble, *adj.*
non·re·cur′rent, *adj.*
non·re·cur′ring, *adj.*
non·re·cy′cla·ble, *adj.*
non·re·deem′a·ble, *adj.*
non·re·fill′a·ble, *adj.*
non·re·flect′ing, *adj.*
non·re·fund′a·ble, *adj.*
non·reg′is·tered, *adj.*
non·reg′u·lat′ed, *adj.*
non·re·me′di·al, *adj.;* -ly, *adv.*
non·re·mov′a·ble, *adj.*
non·re·new′a·ble, *adj.*
non·rep′a·ra·ble, *adj.*
non·rep·re·sent′a·ble, *adj.*
non·rep·re·sen·ta′tion, *n.*
non·rep·re·sen′ta·tive, *n., adj.*
non·req′ui·site, *adj., n.;* -ly, *adv.*
non·res·i·den′tial, *adj.*
non·re·spon′sive, *adj.*
non·re·straint′, *n.*
non·re·strict′ed, *adj.;* -ly, *adv.*
non·re·strict′ing, *adj.*

non·re·ten′tion, *n.*
non·re·triev′a·ble, *adj.*
non·ret·ro·ac′tive, *adj.;* -ly, *adv.*
non·re·us′a·ble, *adj.*
non·re·view′a·ble, *adj.*
non·re·vers′i·bil′i·ty, *n.*
non·re·vers′i·ble, *adj.;* -bly, *adv.*
non·rev′o·ca·ble, *adj.;* -bly, *adv.*
non·re·vok′a·ble, *adj.*
non·rhym′ing, *adj.*
non·rig′id, *adj.*
non·sal′a·ble, *adj.;* -bly, *adv.*
non·sal′a·ried, *adj.*
non·sa′line, *adj.*
non·sal′vage·a·ble, *adj.*
non·sat·is·fac′tion, *n.*
non·sat′u·rat′ed, *adj.*
non·sci′ence, *n.*
non·scrip′tur·al, *adj.*
non·sea′son·a·ble, *adj.;* -ble·ness, *n.;* -bly, *adv.*
non·sea′son·al, *adj.;* -ly, *adv.*
non·sec·re·tar′i·al, *adj.*
non·sec′tion·al, *adj.;* -ly, *adv.*
non·sec′u·lar, *adj.*
non·seg′re·gat′ed, *adj.*
non·se·lec′tive, *adj.*
non·sen′tient, *adj.;* -ly, *adv.*
non·se·quen′tial, *adj.;* -ly, *adv.*
non·se′ri·al, *n., adj.;* -ly, *adv.*
non·sev′er·a·ble, *adj.*
non·shrink′a·ble, *adj.*
non·sim·i·lar′i·ty, *n., pl.* -ties.
non·skilled′, *adj.*
non·slip′, *adj.*
non·smok′er, *n.*
non·smok′ing, *adj.*
non·sol′id, *adj., n.;* -ly, *adv.*
non·sol′u·ble, *adj.;* -ble·ness, *n.*
non·spe′cial·ized′, *adj.*
non·spe·cif′ic, *adj.*
non·spher′i·cal, *adj.;* -ly, *adv.*
non·spill′a·ble, *adj.*
non·spir′it·u·al, *adj., n.;* -ly, *adv.*
non·spir·it·u·al′i·ty, *n.*
non·stain′ing, *adj.*
non·stand′ard·ized′, *adj.*
non·sta′ple, *n.*
non·stat′u·to·ry, *adj.*
non·stel′lar, *adj.*
non·ster·e·o·typ′i·cal, *adj.*
non·ster′ile, *adj.;* -ly, *adv.*
non·stick′y, *adj.*

non·stim′u·lant, *n., adj.*
non·stra·te′gic, *adj.*
non·strat′i·fied′, *adj.*
non·stretch′a·ble, *adj.*
non·strin′gent, *adj.*
non·struc′tur·al, *adj.;* -ly, *adv.*
non·struc′tured, *adj.*
non·stu′dent, *n.*
non·styl′ized, *adj.*
non·sub·lim′i·nal, *adj.;* -ly, *adv.*
non·sub·mers′i·ble, *adj.*
non·sub·mis′sive, *adj.;* -ly, *adv.;* -ness, *n.*
non·sub·scrib′er, *n.*
non·sub·sid′i·ar′y, *adj., n., pl.* -ar·ies.
non·sub′si·dized′, *adj.*
non·sub·sist′ence, *n.*
non·sub·stan′tial, *adj.;* -ly, *adv.*
non·sub·ur′ban, *adj., n.*
non·sub·ver′sive, *adj.;* -ly, *adv.*
non·sup·port′er, *n.*
non·sup·port′ing, *adj.*
non·sup·port′ive, *adj.*
non·sur′gi·cal, *adj.;* -ly, *adv.*
non·sur·viv′a·ble, *adj.*
non·sus·cep′ti·ble, *adj.*
non·sus·tain′a·ble, *adj.*
non·sweet′ened, *adj.*
non·swim′mer, *n.*
non·syl·lab′ic, *adj.*
non·sym·bi·ot′ic, *adj.*
non·sym·bol′ic, *adj.*
non·sym·met′ri·cal, *adj.*
non·sym·pa·thet′ic, *adj.*
non·symp·to·mat′ic, *adj.*
non·syn·on′y·mous, *adj.;* -ly, *adv.*
non·syn′the·sized′, *adj.*
non·sys·tem·at′ic, *adj.*
non·sys·tem′ic, *adj.*
non·tac′ti·cal, *adj.;* -ly, *adv.*
non·tac′tile, *adj.*
non·talk′er, *n.*
non·tar′nish·a·ble, *adj.*
non·tax′a·ble, *adj.*
non·teach′ing, *adj.*
non·tech′ni·cal, *adj.;* -ly, *adv.*
non·tem′po·ral, *adj., n.;* -ly, *adv.*
non·ten′ured, *adj.*
non·ter′mi·nal, *adj.;* -ly, *adv.*
non·ter·res′tri·al, *adj.*
non·ter·ri·to′ri·al, *adj.;* -ly, *adv.*

non·tex′tu·al, *adj.;* -ly, *adv.*
non·the·at′ri·cal, *adj.;* -ly, *adv.*
non·the·mat′ic, *adj.*
non·the·o·ret′i·cal, *adj.;* -ly, *adv.*
non·ther·a·peu′tic, *adj.*
non·ther′mal, *adj.;* -ly, *adv.*
non·think′ing, *adj.*
non·threat′en·ing, *adj.;* -ly, *adv.*
non·till′a·ble, *adj.*
non·top·o·graph′i·cal, *adj.*
non·to·tal′i·tar′i·an, *adj.*
non·tour′ist, *n.*
non·tox′ic, *adj.*
non·tra·di′tion·al, *adj.;* -ly, *adv.*
non·trans·fer′a·ble, *adj.*
non·trans·form′ing, *adj.*
non·tran′sient, *adj.;* -ly, *adv.*
non·trans·mit′ta·ble, *adj.*
non·trans·par′ent, *adj.;* -ly, *adv.*
non·trans·port′a·ble, *adj.*
non·treat′a·ble, *adj.*
non·trop′i·cal, *adj.;* -ly, *adv.*
non·ty·po·graph′ic, *adj.*
non·u·nan′i·mous, *adj.;* -ly, *adv.*
non·u′ni·fied′, *adj.*
non·u′ni·form′, *adj.*
non·u·ni·ver′sal, *adj., n.;* -ly, *adv.*
non·ur′ban, *adj.*
non·use′, *n.*
non·u′ter·ine, *adj.*
non·u·til′i·tar′i·an, *adj., n.*
non·u·til′i·ty, *n., pl.* -ties.
non·va′cant, *adj.*
non·val′id, *adj.;* -ly, *adv.*
non·var′i·ant, *adj., n.*
non·ven′om·ous, *adj.*
non·ver′bal, *adj.;* -ly, *adv.*
non·ver′i·fi′a·ble, *adj.*
non·vest′ed, *adj.*
non·vet′er·an, *n.*
non·vi′brat·ing, *adj.*
non·vir′ile, *adj.*
non·vir′u·lent, *adj.;* -ly, *adv.*
non·vis′cer·al, *adj.*
non·vis′u·al, *adj.*
non·vo′cal, *adj., n.;* -ly, *adv.*
non·vo·ca′tion·al, *adj.;* -ly, *adv.*
non·waiv′a·ble, *adj.*
non·wash′a·ble, *adj.*
non·west′ern, *adj., n.*
non·wool′, *adj.*
non·zeal′ous, *adj.;* -ly, *adv.*

non·vi·a·ble (non vī′ə bəl), *adj.* **1.** not capable of living, growing, and developing, as an embryo or seed. **2.** not practicable or workable. —**non′vi·a·bil′i·ty,** *n.*

non·vi·o·lence (non vī′ə ləns), *n.* **1.** absence or lack of violence. **2.** the policy or practice of refraining from the use of violence, as in protesting oppressive authority or injustice. —**non·vi′o·lent,** *adj.*

non·vol·a·tile (non vol′ə tl, -til; *esp. Brit.* -tīl′), *adj.* **1.** not volatile. **2.** (of computer memory) having the property of retaining data when electrical power fails or is turned off.

non·white (non hwīt′, -wīt′), *n.* **1.** a person who is not Caucasian. —*adj.* **2.** not Caucasian. **3.** of or pertaining to nonwhite persons or peoples.

non·word (non wûrd′), *n.* a meaningless word or one that is not recognized or accepted as legitimate.

noo·dle¹ (nood′l), *n.* a dried strip of egg dough that is boiled and served as a side dish or in soups, casseroles, etc.

noo·dle² (nood′l), *n. Slang.* the head.

nook (nook), *n.* **1.** a corner, as in a room. **2.** any secluded or obscure corner. **3.** any small recess: *a breakfast nook.* **4.** any remote or sheltered spot.

noon (noon), *n.* **1.** midday. **2.** twelve o'clock in the daytime.

noon·day (noon′dā′), *adj.* of or at noon or midday: *the noonday meal.*

no′ one′, *pron.* no person; not anyone: *No one is home.*

noon·time (noon′tīm′), *n.* noon; midday.

noose (noos), *n., v.,* **noosed, noos·ing.** —*n.* **1.** a loop with a slipknot, as in a snare, lasso, or hangman's halter, that tightens as the rope is pulled. **2.** a tie; snare. —*v.t.* **3.** to secure by or as if by a noose. **4.** to make a noose with or in (a rope or the like).

no·o·sphere (no′ə sfēr′), *n.* the part of the biosphere that is affected by human structures and activities.

no·pal (nō′pəl, nō pāl′, -pal′), *n.* **1.** any of several cacti of the genus *Nopalea,* resembling the prickly pear. **2.** the fruit of such a cactus.

nope (nōp), *adv. Informal.* no.

no·place (nō′plās′), *adv.* nowhere. —**Usage.** See ANYPLACE.

nor (nôr; *unstressed* nər), *conj.* **1.** (used in negative phrases, esp. after *neither,* to introduce the second member in a series, or any subsequent member): *Neither he nor I will be there. They won't wait for you, nor for me, nor for anybody.* **2.** (used to continue the force of a negative, as *not, no, never,* etc., occurring in a preceding clause): *I never saw him again, nor did I regret it.* —**Usage.** See NEITHER.

NOR (nôr), *n.* a Boolean operator that returns a positive result when both operands are negative.

Nor·dau (nôr′dou), *n.* **Max Simon,** 1849–1923, Hungarian author, physician, and Zionist leader.

Nor·dic (nôr′dik), *adj.* having or suggesting the physical features associated with the peoples of northern Europe, typically tall stature, blond hair, blue eyes, and elongated head.

nor′east·er (nôr′ē′stər), *n.* NORTHEASTER.

nor·ep·i·neph·rine (nôr′ep ə nef′rin, -rēn), *n.* a neurotransmitter similar to epinephrine, that constricts blood vessels and dilates bronchi and is used esp. in medical emergencies to raise blood pressure.

Nor·folk (nôr′fək; *for 2 also* nôr′fôk), *n.* **1.** a county in E England. 736,200; 2068 sq. mi. (5355 sq. km). **2.** a seaport in SE Virginia: naval base. 241,426.

Nor′folk Is′land pine′, *n.* a pine tree, *Araucaria heterophylla,* of the monkey puzzle family, having whorled branches and needlelike foliage: cultivated as a houseplant. Also called **Nor′folk pine′.**

Nor′folk ter′rier, *n.* one of an English breed of terriers resembling the Norwich terrier but with ears folded forward.

norm (nôrm), *n.* **1.** a standard, model, or pattern. **2.** a rule or standard of behavior expected to be followed by each member of a social group. **3.** a behavior pattern or trait considered to be typical of a particular social group. **4.** the general level or average. **5.** *Educ.* **a.** a designated standard of average performance of people of a given age, background, etc. **b.** a standard based on the past average performance of a given individual. **6.** *Math.* **a.** a real-valued, nonnegative function whose domain is a vector space. **b.** the greatest difference between two successive points of a given partition.

nor·mal (nôr′məl), *adj.* **1.** conforming to the standard or the common type; usual; regular; natural. **2.** serving to fix a standard. **3.** of natural occurrence. **4.** approximately average in any psychological trait, as intelligence or personality. **5.** free from any mental disorder; sane. **6.** free from disease or malformation. **7. a.** being at right angles, as a line; perpendicular. **b.** of the nature of or pertaining to a mathematical normal. —*n.* **8.** the normal form or state; the average or mean. **9.** the standard or common type. **10. a.** a perpendicular line or plane, esp. one perpendicular to a tangent line of a curve, or a tangent plane of a surface, at the point of contact. **b.** the portion of this line included between its point of contact with the curve and the x-axis. —**nor·mal′i·ty,** *n.*

nor·mal·cy (nôr′məl sē), *n.* the state of being normal.

nor·mal·ize (nôr′mə līz′), *v.,* **-ized, -iz·ing.** —*v.t.* **1.** to make normal. **2.** to establish or resume (relations) in a normal manner, as between countries. —*v.i.* **3.** to become normal; resume a normal state. —**nor′mal·i·za′tion,** *n.* —**nor′mal·iz′er,** *n.*

nor·mal·ly (nôr′mə lē), *adv.* **1.** in a normal or regular way. **2.** according to rule, custom, etc.; ordinarily; usually.

Nor·man (nôr′mən), *n.* **1. a.** any of the Scandinavian raiders who in the 10th century settled in N France and established the duchy of Normandy. **b.** any of their Gallicized and Christianized descendants who established feudal regimes in the British Isles, Sicily, and S Italy who in the 11th and 12th centuries. **2.** a native or inhabitant of modern Normandy. **3. a.** NORMAN FRENCH (def. 1). **b.** the French dialect of modern Normandy. **4.** a city in central Oklahoma. 78,280. —*adj.* **5.** of or pertaining to Normandy, the Normans, or their speech. **6.** of or pertaining to Romanesque architecture built by the Normans, esp. in England after 1066.

Nor′man Con′quest, *n.* the conquest of England by the Normans in 1066.

Nor·man·dy (nôr′mən dē), *n.* a historic region in NW France along the English Channel: Allied invasion in World War II began here June 6, 1944.

Nor′man French′, *n.* **1.** the form of French spoken by the Normans in the 11th and 12th centuries. **2.** NORMAN (def. 3b). —**Nor′man-French′,** *adj.*

nor·ma·tive (nôr′mə tiv), *adj.* **1.** of or pertaining to a norm or standard. **2.** tending or attempting to establish such a norm, esp. by the prescription of rules: *normative grammar.* —**nor′ma·tive·ly,** *adv.*

Nor·plant (nôr′plant′, -plänt′), *Trademark.* a long-term contraceptive for women, usu. effective for five years, consisting of several small slow-release capsules of progestin implanted under the skin.

Norse·man (nôrs′mən), *n., pl.* **-men.** a native or inhabitant of medieval Scandinavia during the Viking period.

north (nôrth), *n.* **1.** a cardinal point of the compass, lying to the left of a person facing the rising sun. *Abbr.:* N **2.** the direction in which this point lies. **3.** (*usu. cap.*) a region situated in this direction. **4. the North,** the northern area of the United States, esp. the states that fought to preserve the Union in the Civil War. —*adj.* **5.** in, toward, or facing the north: *the north gate.* **6.** directed or proceeding toward the north: *a north course.* **7.** coming from the north: *a north wind.* **8.** (*usu. cap.*) designating the northern part of a region, nation, country, etc.: *North Atlantic.* —*adv.* **9.** to, toward, or in the north.

North (nôrth), *n.* **Frederick, 2nd Earl of Guilford** (*"Lord North"*), 1732–92, English statesman: prime minister 1770–82.

North′ Af′rica, *n.* the northern part of Africa, esp. between the Mediterranean Sea and the Sahara Desert. —**North′ Af′rican,** *adj., n.*

North′ Amer′ica, *n.* the northern continent of the Western Hemisphere, extending from Central America to the Arctic Ocean. Highest point, Mount McKinley, 20,300 ft. (6187 m); lowest, Death Valley, 276 ft. (84 m) below sea level; ab. 9,360,000 sq. mi. (24,242,400 sq. km). —**North′ Amer′ican,** *adj., n.*

North′ Atlan′tic Cur′rent, *n.* an ocean current flowing NE toward the British Isles, formed by the convergence of the Gulf Stream and the Labrador Current SE of Newfoundland. Also called **North′ Atlan′tic Drift′.**

north·bound (nôrth′bound′), *adj.* proceeding or headed north.

north′ by east′, *n.* a point on the compass 11°15′ east of north. *Abbr.:* NbE

north′ by west′, *n.* a point on the compass 11°15′ west of north. *Abbr.:* NbW

North′ Caroli′na, *n.* a state in the SE United States. 7,332,870; 52,586 sq. mi. (136,198 sq. km). *Cap.:* Raleigh. *Abbr.:* NC, N.C. —**North′ Carolin′ian,** *n., adj.*

North′ Cascades′, *n.* a national park in NW Washington: site of glaciers and mountain lakes. 789 sq. mi. (2043 sq. km).

North′ Dako′ta, *n.* a state in the N central United States. 643,539; 70,665 sq. mi. (183,020 sq. km). *Cap.:* Bismarck. *Abbr.:* ND, N. Dak. —**North′ Dako′tan,** *adj., n.*

north·east (nôrth′ēst′; *Naut.* nôr′-), *n.* **1.** a point on the compass midway between north and east. *Abbr.:* NE **2.** a region in this direction. **3. the Northeast,** the northeastern part of the U.S.. —*adj.* **4.** in, toward, or facing the northeast: *a northeast course.* **5.** coming from the northeast: *a northeast wind.* —*adv.* **6.** toward the northeast: *sailing northeast.* **7.** from the northeast. —**north′east′ern,** *adj.*

northeast′ by east′, *n.* a point on the compass 11°15′ east of northeast. *Abbr.:* NEbE

northeast′ by north′, *n.* a point on the compass 11°15′ north of northeast. *Abbr.:* NEbN

north·east·er (nôrth′ē′stər; *Naut.* nôr′-), *n.* a storm or gale from the northeast.

north·east·er·ly (nôrth′ē′stər lē; *Naut.* nôr′-), *adj., adv.* toward or from the northeast.

north·east·ern·er (nôrth′ē′stər nər), *n.* (*often cap.*) a native or inhabitant of the northeast, esp. the northeastern U.S.

North′east Pas′sage, *n.* a ship route between the Atlantic and the Pacific along the N coast of Europe and Asia.

north·east·ward (nôrth′ēst′wərd; *Naut.* nôr′-), *adv., adj.* **1.** Also, **north′east′ward·ly.** toward the northeast. —*n.* **2.** the northeast.

north·er (nôr′thər), *n.* a storm or gale from the north.

north·er·ly (nôr′thər lē), *adj., adv., n., pl.* **-lies.** —*adj.* **1.** moving, directed, or situated toward the north. **2.** (esp. of a wind) coming from the north. —*adv.* **3.** toward the north. **4.** from the north. —*n.* **5.** a wind that blows from the north. —**north′er·li·ness,** *n.*

north·ern (nôr′thərn), *adj.* **1.** lying toward or situated in the north. **2.**

directed or proceeding northward. **3.** coming from the north, as a wind. **4.** (*often cap.*) of or pertaining to the North, esp. the northern U.S.

North′ern Cross′, *n.* six stars in the constellation Cygnus, arranged in the form of a cross.

north•ern•er (nôr′thər nər), *n.* (*often cap.*) a native or inhabitant of the north, esp. the northern U.S.

North′ern Hem′isphere, *n.* the half of the earth between the North Pole and the equator.

North′ern Ire′land, *n.* a political division of the United Kingdom, in the NE part of Ireland. 1,575,200; 5452 sq. mi. (14,121 sq. km). *Cap.*: Belfast.

north′ern king′dom, *n.* Israel under King Jeroboam.

north′ern lights′, *n.pl.* AURORA BOREALIS.

North′ern Marian′a Is′lands, *n.pl.* a group of islands in the W Pacific, N of Guam: formerly a part of the Trust Territory of the Pacific Islands; since 1986 a commonwealth associated with the U.S. 18,400; 184 sq. mi. (477 sq. km). *Cap.*: Saipan.

north′ern o′riole, *n.* a North American oriole, *Icterus galbula,* with distinctive eastern and western subspecies that interbreed in the Great Plains region. Compare BALTIMORE ORIOLE, BULLOCK'S ORIOLE.

North′ern pike′, *n.* a pike, *Esox lucius,* of North American and Eurasian waters, valued as a game fish.

North′ern Rhode′sia, *n.* former name of ZAMBIA.

North′ern Spy′, *n.* an American variety of red-striped apple that ripens in autumn or early winter.

north′ern white′ ce′dar, *n.* an evergreen tree, *Thuja occidentalis,* of the cypress family, native to NE North America, having short, spreading branches. Also called **white cedar.**

North′ Kore′a, *n.* a country in E Asia: formed 1948 after the division of the former country of Korea at 38° N. 24,317,004; 50,000 sq. mi. (129,500 sq. km). *Cap.*: Pyongyang. Compare KOREA. Official name, **Democratic People's Republic of Korea. —North′ Kore′an,** *adj., n.*

north′-northeast′, *n.* **1.** the point on the compass midway between north and northeast. *Abbr.:* NNE **—adj. 2.** coming from this point, as a wind. **3.** in the direction of or toward this point. **—adv. 4.** toward this point.

north′-northwest′, *n.* **1.** the point on the compass midway between north and northwest. *Abbr.:* NNW **—adj. 2.** coming from this point, as a wind. **3.** in the direction of or toward this point. **—adv. 4.** toward this point.

North′ Pacif′ic Cur′rent, *n.* a warm current flowing eastward across the Pacific Ocean.

North′ Pole′, *n.* **1.** the end of the earth's axis of rotation, marking the northernmost point on earth. **2.** the point at which the extended axis of the earth cuts the northern half of the celestial sphere, about 1° from the North Star; the north celestial pole. **3.** (*l.c.*) See under MAGNETIC POLE (def. 1).

North′ Sea′, *n.* an arm of the Atlantic between Great Britain and the European mainland. ab. 201,000 sq. mi. (520,600 sq. km); greatest depth, 1998 ft. (610 m).

North′ Slope′, *n.* the northern coastal area of Alaska, rich in oil and natural gas: so called because it is N of the Brooks Range sloping down to the Arctic Ocean.

North′-South′ divide′, *n.* the difference in living standards between the economically developed nations, chiefly in the northern hemisphere, and the undeveloped nations of the southern hemisphere.

North′ Star′, *n.* POLARIS.

North′ Tem′perate Zone′, *n.* the part of the earth's surface between the tropic of Cancer and the Arctic Circle.

North′ Vietnam′, *n.* the part of Vietnam north of the 17th parallel; a separate state 1954–75; now part of reunified Vietnam. Compare SOUTH VIETNAM, VIETNAM.

north•ward (nôrth′wərd; *Naut.* nôr′thərd), *adv.* **1.** Also, **north′wards.** toward the north. **—adj. 2.** moving, bearing, facing, or situated toward the north. **—n. 3.** the northward part, direction, or point. Also, **north′ward•ly** (for defs. 1, 2).

north•west (nôrth′west′; *Naut.* nôr′-), *n.* **1.** a point on the compass midway between north and west. *Abbr.:* NW **2.** a region in this direction. **3. the Northwest, a.** the northwestern part of the United States, esp. Washington, Oregon, and Idaho. **b.** the northwestern part of the United States when its western boundary was the Mississippi River. **c.** the northwestern part of Canada. **—adj. 4.** in, toward, or facing the northwest: *the northwest corner.* **5.** coming from the northwest, as a wind. **—adv. 6.** toward the northwest: *heading northwest.* **7.** from the northwest. **—north′west′ern,** *adj.*

northwest′ by north′, *n.* a point on the compass 11°15′ north of northwest. *Abbr.:* NWbN

northwest′ by west′, *n.* a point on the compass 11°15′ west of northwest. *Abbr.:* NWbW

north•west•er (nôrth′wes′tər; *Naut.* nôr′-), *n.* a storm or gale from the northwest.

north•west•er•ly (nôrth′wes′tər lē; *Naut.* nôr′-), *adj., adv.* toward or from the northwest.

north•west•ern•er (nôrth′wes′tər nər), *n.* (*often cap.*) a native or inhabitant of the northwest, esp. the northwestern U.S.

North′west Or′dinance, *n.* the act of Congress in 1787 providing for

the government of the Northwest Territory and setting forth the steps by which its subdivisions might become states.

North′west Pas′sage, *n.* a ship route along the Arctic coast of Canada and Alaska, joining the Atlantic and Pacific oceans.

North′west Ter′ritories, *n.* a territory of Canada lying N of the provinces and extending E from Yukon territory to Davis Strait. 52,238; 1,304,903 sq. mi. (3,379,700 sq. km). *Cap.*: Yellowknife.

North′west Ter′ritory, *n.* the region north of the Ohio River, organized by Congress in 1787, comprising present-day Ohio, Indiana, Illinois, Michigan, Wisconsin, and the eastern part of Minnesota.

Nor•walk (nôr′wôk), *n.* **1.** a city in SW California. 100,744. **2.** a city in SW Connecticut. 76,130.

Nor•way (nôr′wā), *n.* a kingdom in N Europe, in the W part of the Scandinavian Peninsula. 4,404,456; 125,000 sq. mi. (323,752 sq. km). *Cap.*: Oslo. Norwegian, **Norge.**

Nor′way ma′ple, *n.* a European maple, *Acer platanoides,* having bright green leaves, grown as a shade tree in the U.S.

Nor′way pine′, *n.* RED PINE.

Nor′way rat′, *n.* an Old World rat, *Rattus norvegicus,* having a grayish brown body and a long, scaly tail: introduced worldwide. Also called **brown rat.**

Nor′way spruce′, *n.* a European spruce, *Picea abies,* having shiny, dark green needles, grown as an ornamental.

Nor•we•gian (nôr wē′jən), *n.* **1.** a native or inhabitant of Norway. **2.** the North Germanic language of Norway. **—adj. 3.** of or pertaining to Norway, its inhabitants, or their language.

Norwe′gian elk′hound, *n.* one of a Norwegian breed of hunting dogs having a short body, a thick, gray coat, and a tail curled over the back.

Nor•wich (nôr′ich, -ij, nor′-, nôr′wich), *n.* a city in E Norfolk, in E England: cathedral. 118,600.

Nor′wich ter′rier, *n.* one of an English breed of small, short-legged terriers with a straight, wiry coat and erect ears that distinguish it from the Norfolk terrier.

nos. or **Nos.,** numbers.

nose (nōz), *n., v.,* **nosed, nos•ing. —n. 1.** the part of the face that contains the nostrils and organs of smell and that functions as a passageway for air in respiration. **2.** this part as the organ of smell. **3.** the sense of smell. **4.** the snout, muzzle, or proboscis of an animal. **5.** the forward end of something, as of an aircraft or ship. **6.** a projecting part of something: *the nose of a pair of pliers.* **7.** anything regarded as resembling a nose, as a spout or nozzle. **8.** a faculty of perceiving or detecting: *a nose for news.* **9.** the human nose as a symbol of meddling or prying: *Keep your nose out of my business!* **10.** the length of a nose: *to win by a nose.* **11.** distinctive aroma, esp. of a wine; bouquet. **—v.t. 12.** to perceive by or as if by the sense of smell. **13.** to approach the nose to, as in examining; sniff. **14.** to move or push forward with or as if with the nose: *The boat nosed its way toward shore.* **15.** to touch or rub with the nose; nuzzle. **—v.i. 16.** to smell or sniff. **17.** to seek as if by smelling or scent. **18.** to move or push forward. **19.** to meddle or pry: *to nose about in other people's business.* **20. nose out, a.** to defeat, esp. by a narrow margin. **b.** to learn or discover, esp. by snooping or prying. **—Idiom. 21. follow one's nose, a.** to go forward in a straight course. **b.** to guide oneself by instinct. **22. keep one's nose clean,** to behave properly; avoid trouble. **23. lead (around) by the nose,** to exercise complete control over; dominate. **24. look down one's nose at,** to regard with disdain or condescension. **25. on the nose, a.** precisely; exactly: *3 o'clock on the nose.* **b.** (of a bet) for win only. **26. put** or **keep one's nose to the grindstone,** to work intensely and persistently. **27. put someone's nose out of joint, a.** to annoy or irritate. **b.** to supersede someone, as by superseding or supplanting the person. **28. turn up one's nose at,** to dismiss or reject disdainfully. **29. under someone's nose,** plainly visible; in full view. **—nose′less,** *adj.* **—nose′like′,** *adj.*

nose•bleed (nōz′blēd′), *n.* bleeding from the nostril.

nose′ cone′, *n.* the cone-shaped forward section of a rocket or guided missile, including a heat shield and containing the payload.

nose•count (nōz′kount′), *n. Informal.* the counting of individual persons, as for a census.

nose•dive (nōz′dīv′), *n., v.,* **-dived** or **-dove, -dived, -div•ing. —n.** Also, **nose′ dive′. 1.** a plunge of an aircraft with the forward part pointing downward. **2.** a sudden sharp drop or rapid decline: *Stock prices took a nosedive.* **—v.i.** Also, **nose′-dive′. 3.** to go into a nosedive.

no-see-um (nō sē′əm), *n. Northern and Western U.S.* PUNKIE.

nose′ job′, *n. Informal.* RHINOPLASTY.

nose•piece (nōz′pēs′), *n.* **1.** the part of a frame for eyeglasses that passes over the bridge of the nose. **2.** the part of a microscope to which the objectives are attached.

nose′ ring′, *n.* **1.** a ring inserted in the nose of an animal for leading it about. **2.** a decorative ornament worn in the nose.

nos•ey (nō′zē), *adj.,* **nos•i•er, nos•i•est.** NOSY.

nosh (nosh), *Informal. —v.i.* **1.** to snack or eat between meals. **—v.t. 2.** to snack on: *to nosh potato chips.* **—n. 3.** a snack. [< Yiddish *nashn*] **—nosh′er,** *n.*

no′-show′, *n.* **1.** a person who fails to use or cancel a reservation or ticket. **2.** a person who fails to show up, as for an appointment.

nos•ing (nō′zing), *n.* a projecting edge, as the part of the tread of a step extending beyond the riser.

no·sol·o·gy (nō sol′ə jē), *n.* **1.** the branch of medicine dealing with the systematic classification of diseases. **2.** a list or classification of diseases. —**nos·o·log·i·cal** (nos′ə loj′i kəl), *adj.* —**nos′o·log′i·cal·ly,** *adv.* —**no·sol′o·gist,** *n.*

nos·tal·gia (no stal′jə, -jē ə, nə-), *n.* **1.** a wistful or sentimental longing for places, things, acquaintances, or conditions belonging to the past. **2.** a longing for home; homesickness. **3.** something that elicits nostalgia. —**nos·tal′gic,** *adj.* —**nos·tal′gi·cal·ly,** *adv.*

Nos·tra·da·mus (nos′trə dä′məs, -dä′-, nō′strə-), *n.* (Michel de Nostredame), 1503–66, French astrologer.

nos·tril (nos′trəl), *n.* either of the two external openings of the nose.

nos·trum (nos′trəm), *n.* **1.** a medicine sold with false or exaggerated claims; quack medicine. **2.** a pet scheme or remedy, esp. for social or political ills; panacea. **3.** a medicine made by the person who recommends it; proprietary medicine.

nos·y or **nos·ey** (nō′zē), *adj.,* **nos·i·er, nos·i·est.** unduly curious about the affairs of others; prying. —**nos′i·ly,** *adv.* —**nos′i·ness,** *n.*

not (not), *adv.* (used to express negation, denial, refusal, prohibition, etc.): *It's not far from here. Are they coming or not? You will not go.*

NOT (not), *n.* a Boolean operator that returns a positive result if its operand is negative and a negative result if its operand is positive.

NOTA, none of the above.

no·ta·bil·i·a (nō′tə bil′ē ə), *n.pl.* matters, events, or items worthy of note.

no·ta·bil·i·ty (nō′tə bil′i tē), *n., pl.* **-ties. 1.** the state or quality of being notable. **2.** a notable or prominent person.

no·ta·ble (nō′tə bəl), *adj.* **1.** worthy of note or notice; remarkable; outstanding: *a notable success.* **2.** prominent, important, or distinguished; eminent: *notable artists.* —*n.* **3.** a prominent, distinguished, or important person. —**no′ta·ble·ness,** *n.* —**no′ta·bly,** *adv.*

no·ta·rize (nō′tə rīz′), *v.t.,* **-rized, -riz·ing.** to certify (a document) through a notary public. —**no′ta·ri·za′tion,** *n.*

no·ta·ry (nō′tə rē), *n., pl.* **-ries.** NOTARY PUBLIC.

no′ta·ry pub′lic, *n., pl.* **notaries public.** a person authorized to take affidavits, authenticate contracts, etc.

no·tate (nō′tāt), *v.t.,* **-tat·ed, -tat·ing.** to write in notation.

no·ta·tion (nō tā′shən), *n.* **1.** a system of graphic symbols or signs for a specialized use: *musical notation.* **2.** the process or method of writing down by means of such a system. **3.** the act of noting or marking down in writing. **4.** a short note; jotting; annotation. —**no·ta′tion·al,** *adj.*

notch (noch), *n.* **1.** an angular or V-shaped cut or indentation. **2.** a nick made in an object for keeping a record. **3.** a narrow pass between mountains; gap. **4.** a step; degree: *a notch above the average.* —*v.t.* **5.** to make a notch in. **6.** to record by notches. **7.** to score: *He notched up another win.*

notched′ col′lar, *n.* a collar forming a notch with the lapels of a garment at the seam where collar and lapels join. Also called **notched′ lapel′.**

note (nōt), *n., v.,* **not·ed, not·ing.** —*n.* **1.** a brief written record of something to assist the memory or for future reference. **2.** a short, informal letter: *a thank-you note.* **3. notes,** a written record or outline of something heard, read, experienced, etc., or of one's impressions. **4.** an explanatory or critical comment appended to a passage of text. **5.** a brief written or printed statement giving particulars or information. **6.** a formal diplomatic or official communication in writing. **7.** eminence, distinction, or importance: *a person of note.* **8.** notice, observation, or heed: *to take note of a sign.* **9.** an underlying expression of a quality, emotion, etc.; hint: *a note of whimsy in an essay.* **10.** a distinctive quality, mood, etc.: *The speech began on a serious note.* **11.** a quality or tone, as of voice, signaling or intimating some emotion, attitude, etc.: *a note of warning.* **12.** *Music.* **a.** a sign or character used to represent a tone, its position and form indicating the pitch and duration of the tone. **b.** a key, as of a piano. **13.** a sound of musical quality, as one uttered by a bird. **14.** PROMISSORY NOTE. **15.** a certificate, as of a government or a bank, accepted as money. —*v.t.* **16.** to write or mark down briefly; make a memorandum, record, or note of. **17.** to make particular mention of: *She noted their efforts in her report.* **18.** to annotate. **19.** to observe carefully; give attention or heed to. **20.** to take notice of; perceive. **21.** to indicate or designate; signify; denote. —**not′er,** *n.*

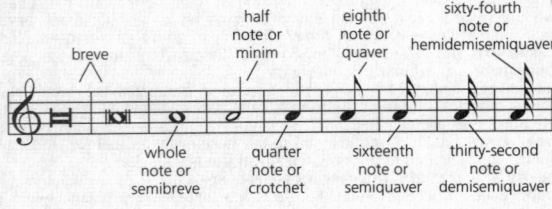

breve
half note or minim
eighth note or quaver
sixty-fourth note or hemidemisemiquaver
whole note or semibreve
quarter note or crotchet
sixteenth note or semiquaver
thirty-second note or demisemiquaver

note

note·book (nōt′bŏŏk′), *n.* **1.** a book or binder of blank, often ruled pages for recording notes. **2.** a small, lightweight laptop computer measuring approximately 8½ × 11 in. (22 × 28 cm).

not·ed (nō′tid), *adj.* well-known; celebrated; famous; renowned: *a noted scholar.* —**not′ed·ly,** *adv.* —**not′ed·ness,** *n.*

note·pad (nōt′pad′), *n.* a pad of blank paper for writing notes.

note·pa·per (nōt′pā′pər), *n.* writing paper, esp. for writing letters.

note·wor·thy (nōt′wûr′t͟hē), *adj.* worthy of notice or attention; notable; remarkable: *a noteworthy addition to the library.* —**note′wor′thi·ly,** *adv.* —**note′wor′thi·ness,** *n.*

not′-for-prof′it, *adj.* NONPROFIT.

noth·ing (nuth′ing), *pron.* **1.** no thing; not anything: *to say nothing.* **2.** no part, share, or trace: *The house showed nothing of its former splendor.* **3.** something of no importance, significance, or value: *Money is nothing to him.* **4.** something that is nonexistent. **5.** something that is without quantity or magnitude. **6.** no great effort, trouble, etc.: *Nothing to it.* —*n.* **7.** a trivial action, matter, circumstance, or remark: *to exchange nothings.* **8.** a person of little or no importance; a nobody. **9.** nonexistence; nothingness. **10.** a cipher or naught; zero. —*adv.* **11.** in no respect or degree; not at all: *It was nothing like that.* —*adj.* **12.** amounting to nothing: *a nothing job.* —**Idiom. 13. for nothing, a.** free of charge. **b.** for no apparent reason or motive. **c.** futilely; to no avail: *We went to all that trouble for nothing.* **14. in nothing flat,** in very little time. **15. make nothing of, a.** to fail to comprehend. **b.** to treat lightly; regard as easy. **16. nothing doing,** *Informal.* certainly not. **17. nothing to write home about,** ordinary, mediocre, or inconsequential. **18. think nothing of,** to regard as routine. —*Proverb.* **19. Nothing ventured, nothing gained,** rewards require taking risks.

noth·ing·ness (nuth′ing nis), *n.* **1.** the state or quality of being nothing. **2.** lack of being. **3.** unconsciousness or death. **4.** absence of meaning or worth; emptiness. **5.** something insignificant or without value.

no·tice (nō′tis), *n., v.,* **-ticed, -tic·ing.** —*n.* **1.** information, warning, or announcement of something impending; notification: *to give notice of one's intentions.* **2.** a written or printed statement conveying such information or warning: *to post a notice.* **3.** a notification by one of the parties to an agreement, as for renting or employment, that the agreement will terminate on a specified date: *She gave her employer two-weeks' notice.* **4.** observation, attention, or heed; note: *to take notice of one's surroundings.* **5.** interested or favorable attention: *singled out for notice.* **6.** a brief written review or critique of a book, play, etc. —*v.t.* **7.** to become aware of or pay attention to; take notice of; observe; note. **8.** to mention or refer to; point out. **9.** to acknowledge acquaintance with. **10.** to give notice to; serve with a notice. —**no′tic·er,** *n.*

no·tice·a·ble (nō′ti sə bəl), *adj.* **1.** attracting notice or attention; capable of being noticed. **2.** worthy or deserving of notice or attention; noteworthy. —**no′tice·a·bil′i·ty,** *n.* —**no′tice·a·bly,** *adv.*

no·ti·fi·ca·tion (nō′tə fi kā′shən), *n.* **1.** a formal notifying or informing. **2.** an act or instance of notifying, making known, or giving notice. **3.** a written or printed notice, announcement, or warning.

no·ti·fy (nō′tə fī′), *v.t.,* **-fied, -fy·ing.** to inform; give notice to: *to notify the police of a crime.* —**no′ti·fi′a·ble,** *adj.* —**no′ti·fi′er,** *n.*

no·tion (nō′shən), *n.* **1.** a general, vague, or imperfect conception or idea. **2.** an opinion, view, or belief. **3.** a conception or idea: *his notion of democracy.* **4.** a fanciful or foolish idea; whim. **5. notions,** small articles, as buttons, thread, or ribbon, displayed together for sale.

no·tion·al (nō′shə nl), *adj.* **1.** pertaining to, expressing, or like a notion. **2.** abstract, theoretical, or speculative. **3.** not real or actual; imaginary. **4.** given to or full of fanciful ideas or moods. **5. a.** pertaining to or based on the meaning expressed by a linguistic item: *the notional definition of a noun as "a person, place, or thing."* **b.** (of a word) having full lexical rather than just grammatical meaning (contrasted with *relational*). —**no′tion·al′i·ty,** *n.* —**no′tion·al·ly,** *adv.*

no·to·ri·e·ty (nō′tə rī′i tē), *n., pl.* **-ties. 1.** the state or quality of being notorious. **2.** *Chiefly Brit.* a notorious person.

no·to·ri·ous (nō tôr′ē əs, -tōr′-, nə-), *adj.* **1.** widely and unfavorably known: *a notorious thief.* **2.** publicly or generally known: *a notorious scandal.* —**no·to′ri·ous·ly,** *adv.* —**no·to′ri·ous·ness,** *n.*

no′-trump′, *adj.* **1.** (of a hand, bid, or contract in bridge) without a trump suit; noting a bid or contract to be played without naming a trump suit. —*n.* **2.** the bid to play a no-trump contract.

not·with·stand·ing (not′with stan′ding, -with-), *prep.* **1.** in spite of: *Notwithstanding a brilliant defense, he was found guilty. The doctor's orders notwithstanding, she returned to work.* —*adv.* **2.** nevertheless; anyway; yet. —*conj.* **3.** in spite of the fact that; although.

Nouak·chott (nwäk shot′), *n.* the capital of Mauritania, on the W coast. 500,000.

nou·gat (nōō′gət; esp. Brit. -gä), *n.* a candy containing nuts and sometimes fruit in a sugar or honey paste.

nought (nôt), *n., adj., adv.* NAUGHT.

nou·me·non (nōō′mə non′), *n., pl.* **-na** (-nə). (in the philosophy of Kant) something that can be the object only of a purely intellectual, nonsensuous intuition. Compare PHENOMENON (def. 4b). —**nou′me·nal,** *adj.*

noun (noun), *n.* a member of a class of words that can function as the subject or object in a construction, are often formally distinguished, as by taking the plural and possessive endings, and typically refer to persons, places, animals, things, states, or qualities, as *cat, desk, Ohio, darkness. Abbr.:* n.

noun′ ad′junct, *n.* a noun that occurs before and modifies another noun, as *toy* in *toy store* or *tour* in *tour group.*

noun′ phrase′, *n.* a grammatical construction that functions syntactically as a noun, consisting of a noun and any modifiers, as *all the people in the room*, or of a noun substitute, as a pronoun. *Abbr.:* NP

nour·ish (nûr′ish, nur′-), *v.t.* **1.** to sustain with food or nutriment; supply with what is necessary for life, health, and growth. **2.** to cherish; keep alive: *to nourish a hope.* **3.** to strengthen or promote; foster: *to nourish the arts.* —**nour′ish·a·ble,** *adj.* —**nour′ish·er,** *n.*

nour·ish·ing (nûr′i shing, nur′-), *adj.* promoting or sustaining life, growth, or strength: *a nourishing diet.* —**nour′ish·ing·ly,** *adv.*

nour·ish·ment (nûr′ish mənt, nur′-), *n.* **1.** something that nourishes; food. **2.** the act of nourishing. **3.** the state of being nourished.

nou·veau (nōō′vō, nōō vō′), *adj.* newly or recently created, developed, or come to prominence.

nou·veau riche (nōō′vō rēsh′), *n., pl.* **nou·veaux riches** (nōō′vō rēsh′). a person who is newly rich, esp. one regarded as ostentatious or uncultivated. [< French]

nou·velle′ cuisine′ (nōō vel′), *n.* a style of cooking that emphasizes the use of fresh ingredients, unusual combinations of foods, light sauces, and the artful presentation of each. [< French]

no·va (nō′və), *n., pl.* **-vas, -vae** (-vē). a star that suddenly becomes thousands of times brighter and then gradually fades to its original intensity.

No·va Sco·tia (nō′və skō′shə), *n.* a peninsula and province in SE Canada: once a part of the French province of Acadia. 873,176; 21,068 sq. mi. (54,565 sq. km) *Cap.:* Halifax. —**No′va Sco′tian,** *adj., n.*

nov·el¹ (nov′əl), *n.* a fictitious prose narrative of considerable length and complexity, portraying characters and usu. presenting a sequential organization of action and scenes. —**nov′el·is′tic,** *adj.*

nov·el² (nov′əl), *adj.* of a new kind; different from anything seen or known before: *a novel idea.*

nov·el·ette (nov′ə let′), *n.* a brief novel or long short story.

nov·el·ist (nov′ə list), *n.* a person who writes novels.

no·vel·la (nō vel′ə), *n., pl.* **-vel·las** for 1, **-vel·le** (-vel′ē, -vel′ā) for 2. **1.** a fictional prose narrative that is longer and more complex than a short story; a short novel. **2.** a tale or short story of the type contained in the *Decameron* of Boccaccio.

nov·el·ty (nov′əl tē), *n., pl.* **-ties,** *adj.* —*n.* **1.** the state or quality of being novel, new, or unique; newness. **2.** a novel occurrence, experience, etc. **3.** a small decorative or amusing article, usu. mass-produced. —*adj.* **4. a.** (of a weave) consisting of a combination of basic weaves. **b.** (of a fabric or garment) having a pattern or design produced by a novelty weave. **c.** (of yarn) made of fibers with an unusual surface, texture, or color. **5.** of or pertaining to novelties as articles of trade.

No·vem·ber (nō vem′bər), *n.* the 11th month of the year, containing 30 days. *Abbr.:* Nov.

no·ve·na (nō vē′nə, nə-), *n., pl.* **-nae** (-nē) **-nas.** a Roman Catholic devotion occurring on nine consecutive days.

nov·ice (nov′is), *n.* **1.** a person who is new to the circumstances, work, etc., in which he or she is placed; beginner. **2.** a person admitted into a religious order or congregation for a period of probation before taking vows. —**nov′ice·hood′,** *n.*

no·vi·ti·ate (nō vish′ē it, -āt′), *n.* **1.** the state or period of being a novice, as of a religious order. **2.** the quarters occupied by religious novices. **3.** NOVICE.

now (nou), *adv.* **1.** at the present time or moment. **2.** without further delay; immediately: *Do it now or not at all.* **3.** at the time being referred to: *The case was now ready for the jury.* **4.** in the very recent past: *I saw them just now.* **5.** in these times; nowadays. **6.** under the present circumstances: *I see now what you meant.* **7.** (used to introduce a statement or question): *Now, may I ask you something?* **8.** (used to strengthen a command, entreaty, or the like): *Now stop that!* —*conj.* **9.** inasmuch as; since (often fol. by *that*): *Now that you're here, stay for dinner.* —*n.* **10.** the present time or moment. —*adj.* **11.** current; very fashionable: *the now look.* —**Idiom. 12. now and again,** occasionally. Also, **now and then. 13. now you see it, now you don't,** (said of a quick disappearance.) —**now′ness,** *n.*

NOW (nou), National Organization for Women.

now·a·days (nou′ə dāz′), *adv.* **1.** at the present time; these days. —*n.* **2.** the present.

no′ way′, *adv. Informal.* absolutely not; no.

no·way (nō′wā′) a. also **no′ways′,** *adv.* in no way; not at all.

no·where (nō′hwâr′, -wâr′), *adv.* **1.** in or at no place; not anywhere. **2.** to no place: *We went nowhere last weekend.* —*n.* **3.** the state of nonexistence or seeming nonexistence: *Thieves appeared from nowhere.* **4.** anonymity or obscurity. **5.** an unknown, remote, or nonexistent place or region. —**Idiom. 6. miles from nowhere,** in a remote or inaccessible area. **7. nowhere near,** not nearly: *nowhere near enough food.* —**Usage.** See ANYPLACE.

no-win (nō′win′), *adj. Informal.* denoting a condition in which one cannot benefit, succeed, or win: *a no-win situation; a no-win war.*

Now′ the Day′ Is′ O′ver, a Christian hymn (1860s) with words by Sabine Baring-Gould.

nox·ious (nok′shəs), *adj.* **1.** harmful to health or physical well-being: *noxious fumes.* **2.** morally harmful; corrupting. —**nox′ious·ly,** *adv.*

noz·zle (noz′əl), *n.* **1.** a spout, terminal discharging pipe, or the like, as of a hose or bellows. **2.** a duct in a rocket engine in which the velocity of fluid is increased. **3.** *Slang.* NOSE.

NP, 1. noun phrase. **2.** nurse-practitioner.

Np, *Chem. Symbol.* neptunium.

N.P., notary public.

NPR, National Public Radio.

NRA, National Rifle Association.

NRC, Nuclear Regulatory Commission.

NS, 1. not sufficient (funds). **2.** Nova Scotia, Canada.

ns, nanosecond; nanoseconds. Also, **nsec**

N.S., Nova Scotia.

n.s., not specified.

NSA or **N.S.A.,** National Security Agency.

NSC, 1. National Safety Council. **2.** National Security Council.

NSF, 1. National Science Foundation. **2.** not sufficient funds. Also, **N.S.F.**

N/S/F, not sufficient funds.

N.S.P.C.A., National Society for the Prevention of Cruelty to Animals.

-n't, a contraction of **not:** *didn't; hadn't; couldn't; shouldn't; won't; mustn't.*

NT, 1. New Testament. **2.** Northwest Territories, Canada.

N.T., 1. New Testament. **2.** Northern Territory.

nth (enth), *adj.* **1.** being the last in a series of infinitely decreasing or increasing values, amounts, etc. **2.** being the latest in a lengthy series: *This is the nth time I've told you.* **3.** utmost; extreme: *to the nth degree.*

NTSB, National Transportation Safety Board.

nt. wt., net weight.

nu·ance (nōō′äns, nyōō′-), *n.* **1.** a subtle difference or distinction, as in expression or meaning. **2.** a slight difference or variation in color or tone.

nub (nub), *n.* **1.** the point, gist, or heart of something. **2.** a knob or protuberance. **3.** a lump or small piece.

nubbed (nubd), *adj.* NUBBY.

nub·bin (nub′in), *n.* **1.** a small lump or stunted piece; stub. **2.** a small or imperfect ear of corn.

nub·ble (nub′əl), *n.* a small lump or knob. —**nub′bly,** *adj.,* **-bli·er, -bli·est.**

nub·by (nub′ē), *adj.* **-bi·er, -bi·est.** having nubs; knobby or lumpy.

Nu·bi·a (nōō′bē ə, nyōō′-), *n.* **1.** a region in S Egypt and N Sudan, extending from the Nile to the Red Sea. **2.** an ancient kingdom in this region. —**Nu′bi·an,** *adj., n.*

nu·bile (nōō′bil, -bīl, nyōō′-), *adj.* **1.** (of a young woman) suitable for marriage, esp. in age or physical development; marriageable. **2.** (of a young woman) sexually developed and attractive. —**nu·bil′i·ty,** *n.*

nu·cle·ar (nōō′klē ər, nyōō′-; *by metathesis* -kyə lər), *adj.* **1.** pertaining to or involving atomic weapons: *nuclear war.* **2.** operated or powered by atomic energy: *a nuclear power plant.* **3.** having atomic weapons: *a nuclear submarine.* **4.** of, pertaining to, or forming a nucleus: *nuclear particles.* —**Pronunciation.** The second and third syllables of NU·CLE·AR are commonly pronounced as (-klē ər), transcribed more broadly as (-klə yər). The somewhat controversial pronunciation of these two syllables as (-kyə lər), prominent in recent years, results from a process of metathesis in which the sounds (l) and (y) change places. This pronunciation, reinforced by analogy with words like *molecular,* is disapproved of by many, although it occurs among such highly educated speakers as scientists, professors, and government officials.

nu′clear en′ergy, *n.* energy released by reactions within atomic nuclei, as in nuclear fission or fusion; atomic energy.

nu′clear fam′ily, *n.* a social unit composed of father, mother, and children. Compare EXTENDED FAMILY.

nu·cle·ar·ize (nōō′klē ə rīz′, nyōō′-; *by metathesis* -kyə lə-), *v.t.,* **-ized, -iz·ing.** to equip with nuclear weapons. —**nu′cle·ar·i·za′tion,** *n.*

nu′clear magnet′ic res′onance, *n.* the selective absorption of electromagnetic radiation by an atomic nucleus in the presence of a strong, static, magnetic field: used in research and in medicine to monitor tissue metabolism and to distinguish between normal and abnormal cells. *Abbr.:* NMR

nu′clear mem′brane, *n.* the double membrane surrounding the nucleus within a cell. Also called **nu′clear en′velope.**

nu′clear phys′ics, *n.* the branch of physics that deals with atomic nuclei. —**nu′clear phys′icist,** *n.*

nu′clear reac′tion, *n.* REACTION (def. 5b).

nu′clear reac′tor, *n.* REACTOR (def. 3). Also called **nu′clear pile′.**

Nu′clear Reg′ulatory Commis′sion, *n.* an independent agency, created in 1975, that licenses and regulates the nonmilitary use of nuclear energy. *Abbr.:* NRC

Nu′clear Test′-Ban′ Trea′ty, *n.* an agreement signed by Britain, the Soviet Union, and the U.S. in 1963, committing nations to halt atmospheric tests of nuclear weapons: by the end of 1963, 96 additional nations had signed the treaty.

nu′clear weap′on, *n.* an explosive device whose destructive potential derives from the release of energy that accompanies the splitting or combining of atomic nuclei.

nu′clear win′ter, *n.* the worldwide devastation, darkness, and cold that conceivably could result from a nuclear war.

nu·cle·ase (nōō′klē ās′, -āz′, nyōō′-), *n.* any enzyme that catalyzes the hydrolysis of nucleic acids.

nu·cle·ate (*adj.* nōō′klē it, -āt′, nyōō′-; *v.* -āt′), *adj., v.,* **-at·ed, -at·ing.** —*adj.* **1.** having a nucleus. —*v.t.* **2.** to form (something) into a nucleus. —*v.i.* **3.** to form a nucleus. —**nu′cle·a′tion,** *n.* —**nu′cle·a′tor,** *n.*

nu·cle·i (nōō′klē ī′, nyōō′-), *n.* a pl. of NUCLEUS.

nu·cle·ic ac·id (noō klē′ik, -klā′-, nyoō-), *n.* any of a group of long, linear molecules, either DNA or various types of RNA, that carry genetic information directing all cellular functions: composed of linked nucleotides.

nucleo-, a combining form representing NUCLEUS, NUCLEAR, or NUCLEIC ACID: *nucleoprotein.*

nu·cle·o·lus (noō klē′ə ləs, nyoō-), *n., pl.* **-li** (-lī′). a small, rounded body within the cell nucleus, functioning in ribosome manufacture. —**nu·cle′o·lar,** *adj.*

nu·cle·on (noō′klē on′, nyoō′-), *n.* a proton or neutron, esp. when considered as a component of a nucleus. —**nu′cle·on′ic,** *adj.*

nu·cle·on·ics (noō′klē ō′niks, nyoō′-), *n.* (*used with a sing. v.*) the branch of science that deals with nuclear phenomena, as radioactivity, fission, or fusion, esp. practical applications.

nu·cle·o·syn·the·sis (noō′klē ō sin′thə sis, nyoō′-), *n.* the formation of new atomic nuclei by nuclear reactions, as in stellar evolution. —**nu′cle·o·syn·thet′ic** (-thet′ik), *adj.*

nu·cle·o·tide (noō′klē ə tīd′, nyoō′-), *n.* any of a group of molecules that, when linked together, form the building blocks of DNA or RNA.

nu·cle·us (noō′klē əs, nyoō′-), *n., pl.* **-cle·i** (-klē ī′), **-cle·us·es.** **1.** a central part about which other parts are grouped or gathered; core. **2.** a specialized, usu. spherical mass of protoplasm encased in a double membrane and found in eukaryotic cells, directing their growth, metabolism, and reproduction, and containing most of the genetic material. **3.** the positively charged mass within an atom, composed of neutrons and protons and possessing most of the mass but occupying only a small fraction of the volume of the atom. **4.** a mass of nerve cells in the brain or spinal cord in which nerve fibers form connections. **5.** a fundamental arrangement of atoms, as the benzene ring, that may occur in many compounds by substitution of atoms without a change in structure. **6.** the condensed portion of the head of a comet. **7. a.** the central, most prominent segment in a syllable, consisting of a vowel or vowellike consonant, as the *a*-sound in *cat* or the *l*-sound in *bottle*. **b.** the most prominent syllable in an utterance or stress group; tonic syllable.

nu·clide (noō′klīd, nyoō′-), *n.* **1.** an atomic species in which the atoms all have the same atomic number and mass number. **2.** an individual atom in such a species.

nude (noōd, nyoōd), *adj.,* **nud·er, nud·est,** *n.* —*adj.* **1.** naked or unclothed, as a person or the body. **2.** without the usual coverings, furnishings, etc.; bare. **3.** (of a photograph, painting, statue, etc.) representing the nude human figure. **4.** lacking some legal essential: *a nude contract.* **5.** of the color nude. —*n.* **6.** a sculpture, painting, etc., of a nude human figure. **7.** an unclothed human figure. **8.** the condition of being unclothed: *to sleep in the nude.* **9.** a light grayish yellow brown to brownish pink color. —**nude′ly,** *adv.* —**nu′di·ty, nude′ness,** *n.*

nudge (nuj), *v.,* **nudged, nudg·ing,** *n.* —*v.t.* **1.** to push slightly or gently with the elbow, esp. to get someone's attention. —*v.i.* **2.** to give a nudge. —*n.* **3.** a slight or gentle push with the elbow. —**nudg′er,** *n.*

nu·di·branch (noō′də brangk′, nyoō′-), *n.* any shell-less marine gastropod mollusk of the suborder Nudibranchia, having external, often branched respiratory appendages.

nud·ism (noō′diz əm, nyoō′-), *n.* the practice of going nude, esp. in places that allow sexually mixed groups. —**nud′ist,** *n., adj.*

nud·nik (noōd′nik), *n. Slang.* a bore; pest.

nu·ga·to·ry (noō′gə tôr′ē, -tōr′ē, nyoō′-), *adj.* **1.** trifling or worthless. **2.** ineffective or futile.

nug·get (nug′it), *n.* **1.** a lump, esp. of native gold or other precious metal. **2.** anything small but of great value or significance: *nuggets of wisdom.* **3.** a small batter-fried piece of chicken or fish.

nui·sance (noō′səns, nyoō′-), *n.* **1.** an obnoxious or annoying person, thing, practice, etc. **2.** *Law.* harm, injury, or disturbance, as to use of property, health, safety, or decency.

nui′sance tax′, *n.* a small excise tax collected from consumers on a wide variety of inexpensive items.

nuke (noōk, nyoōk), *n., v.,* **nuked, nuk·ing.** *Informal.* —*n.* **1.** a nuclear or thermonuclear weapon. **2.** a nuclear power plant or nuclear reactor. —*v.t.* **3.** to attack with nuclear weapons. **4.** *Slang.* to heat or cook in a microwave oven.

null (nul), *adj.* **1.** without value or significance. **2.** being or amounting to nothing; nil. **3.** *Math.* (of a set) **a.** empty. **b.** of measure zero. **4.** being or amounting to zero. —*n.* **5.** a point of minimum signal reception, as on a radio direction finder. —*v.t.* **6.** to cancel; make null. —*Idiom.* **7. null and void,** without force or effect; not valid.

nul·li·fi·ca·tion (nul′ə fi kā′shən), *n.* **1.** an act or instance of nullifying. **2.** the state of being nullified. **3.** the failure or refusal of a U.S. state to aid in the enforcement of federal laws within its territory. —**nul′li·fi·ca′tion·ist,** *n.*

nul·li·fy (nul′ə fī′), *v.t.,* **-fied, -fy·ing.** **1.** to render or declare legally void: *to nullify a contract.* **2.** to deprive (something) of value or effectiveness; invalidate. [< Late Latin *nūllificāre* to despise] —**nul′li·fi′er,** *n.*

nul·lip·a·ra (nu lip′ər ə), *n., pl.* **-a·rae** (-ə rē′). a woman who has never borne a child. —**nul·li·par·i·ty** (nul′ə par′i tē), *n.* —**nul·lip′a·rous,** *adj.*

nul·li·ty (nul′i tē), *n., pl.* **-ties.** **1.** the state or quality of being null; nothingness; invalidity. **2.** something null. **3.** something of no legal force or validity.

Num., Numbers.

num., **1.** number. **2.** numeral.

numb (num), *adj.,* **numb·er, numb·est.** **1.** deprived of sensation, as by anesthesia: *fingers numb with cold.* **2.** incapable of feeling emotion. —*v.t.* **3.** to make numb. —**numb′ly,** *adv.* —**numb′ness,** *n.*

num·ber (num′bər), *n.* **1.** a mathematical unit used to express an amount, quantity, etc., usu. having precise relations with other such units: *Six is an even number.* **2.** a numeral or group of numerals. **3.** the sum, total, or aggregate of a collection of units: *the number of people with reserved seats.* **4.** the particular numeral assigned to an object so as to designate its place in a series: *a house number; a license number.* **5.** one of a series of things distinguished by or marked with numerals. **6.** a certain collection or quantity not precisely reckoned, but considerable: *a number of times.* **7.** a collection or company. **8. numbers, a.** a considerable amount or quantity; many: *Numbers came to the parade.* **b.** numerical strength or superiority. **c.** metrical feet; verse. **d.** NUMBERS POOL (def. 1). **e.** *Informal.* the figures representing the actual cost, expense, profit, etc. **f.** arithmetic. **9.** a tune or arrangement for singing or dancing. **10.** a distinct performance within a show, as a song or dance. **11.** a single issue of a periodical. **12.** a code of numerals, letters, or a combination of these, as that assigned to a particular telephone. **13.** *Gram.* a category of inflection or other variation in the form of a word serving to indicate whether the word has one or more than one referent, as in the distinction between singular and plural and, in some languages, dual or trial. **14.** *Informal.* person; individual: *a cute number.* **15.** *Informal.* an article of merchandise, esp. of wearing apparel, offered for sale. —*v.t.* **16.** to mark with or distinguish by numbers. **17.** to amount to or comprise in number; total. **18.** to consider or include in a number: *I number myself among his friends.* **19.** to count over one by one; enumerate; tell. **20.** to fix the number of. **21.** to ascertain the amount or quantity of; count. **22.** to apportion or divide. —*v.i.* **23.** to make a total; reach an amount. **24.** to count. —*Idiom.* **25. by the numbers, a.** according to standard procedures; by the book. **b.** together or in unison to a called-out count. **26. do a number on,** *Slang.* to undermine or humiliate. **27. get** or **have someone's number,** *Informal.* to discern someone's character, intentions, or underlying motives. **28. one's number is up,** *Slang.* it is time for fate to strike in the form of retribution, death, etc. **29. without number,** of unknown or countless number; vast. —**num′ber·a·ble,** *adj.* —*Usage.* See AMOUNT, COLLECTIVE NOUN.

num′ber-crunch′er, *n. Informal.* a person, computer, or computer program that performs a great many numerical calculations. —**num′ber-crunch′ing,** *adj.*

num·ber·less (num′bər lis), *adj.* **1.** innumerable; countless; myriad. **2.** without a number.

num′ber of the beast′, *n.* the number 666, considered to represent the Antichrist. Rev. 13:18.

num′ber one′, *n.* **1.** oneself, esp. one's own well-being or interests. —*adj.* **2.** of the highest in quality; first-rate: *a number one performance.*

Num·bers (num′bərz), *n.* the fourth book of the Old Testament, containing the census of the Israelites after the Exodus.

num′bers game′, *n.* a misleading or deceptive use of statistics.

num′ber sign′, *n.* a symbol (#) for "number" or "numbered": *item #8 on the list.*

num′bers pool′, *n.* **1.** Also called **numbers, num′bers game′, num′bers rack′et.** a lottery in which bets are made on numbers that appear in a regularly published listing or tabulation. **2.** POLICY[2] (def. 2).

num′ber the′ory, *n.* the study of integers and their relation to one another.

numb·ing (num′ing), *adj.* causing numbness or insensibility; stupefying. —**numb′ing·ly,** *adv.*

numb·skull (num′skul′), *n.* NUMSKULL.

nu·men (noō′min, nyoō′-), *n., pl.* **-mi·na** (-mə nə). divine or supernatural power or presence, esp. as associated with a particular place or object.

nu·mer·a·ble (noō′mər ə bəl, nyoō′-), *adj.* capable of being counted, totaled, or numbered. —**nu′mer·a·bly,** *adv.*

nu·mer·al (noō′mər əl, nyoō′-; noōm′rəl, nyoōm′-), *n.* **1.** a word, letter, symbol, or figure representing a number: *the Roman numerals.* —*adj.* **2.** of, pertaining to, or consisting of numbers or numerals. **3.** expressing or noting a number or numbers.

nu·mer·ate (*v.* noō′mə rāt′, nyoō′-; *adj.* -mər it), *v.,* **-at·ed, -at·ing,** *adj.* —*v.t.* **1.** to represent numbers by symbols. **2.** ENUMERATE (def. 2). —**nu′mer·a·cy,** *n.*

nu·mer·a·tion (noō′mə rā′shən, nyoō′-), *n.* **1.** an act or instance of or the process or result of numbering or counting. **2.** the process or a method of calculating. **3.** the act or method of reading off numerals, esp. those written decimally. —**nu′mer·a′tive,** *adj.*

nu·mer·a·tor (noō′mə rā′tər, nyoō′-), *n.* **1.** the term of a fraction, usu. written above or before the line, that indicates the number of equal parts that are to be added together; the dividend placed over a divisor. Compare DENOMINATOR (def. 1). **2.** a person or thing that numbers.

nu·mer·i·cal (noō mer′i kəl, nyoō-) also **nu·mer′ic,** *adj.* **1.** of or pertaining to numbers; of the nature of a number. **2.** indicating a number, as a symbol. **3.** bearing or designated by a number. **4.** expressed in numbers: *numerical equations.* —**nu·mer′i·cal·ly,** *adv.*

numer′ic key′pad, *n.* KEYPAD. Also called **numer′ic pad′.**

nu·mer·ol·o·gy (noō′mə rol′ə jē, nyoō′-), *n.* the study of numbers, as the figures designating the year of one's birth, to determine their supernatural meaning or influence. **—nu′mer•o•log′i•cal** (-mər ə loj′i kəl), *adj.* **—nu′mer•ol′o•gist,** *n.*

nu•me•ro u•no (nōō′mə rō′ ōō′nō, nyōō′-), *n., adj.* NUMBER ONE.

nu•mer•ous (nōō′mər əs, nyōō′-), *adj.* **1.** very many; being or existing in great quantity. **2.** comprising a great number of units or individuals: *Recent audiences have been more numerous.* **—nu′mer•ous•ly,** *adv.* **—nu′mer•ous•ness, nu/me•ros′i•ty** (-mə ros′i tē), *n.*

nu•mi•nous (nōō′mə nəs, nyōō′-), *adj.* **1.** of, pertaining to, or like a numen; spiritual or supernatural. **2.** surpassing comprehension or understanding; mysterious. **3.** arousing one's elevated feelings of duty, honor, loyalty, etc.

nu•mis•mat•ic (nōō′miz mat′ik, -mis-, nyōō′-) also **nu/mis•mat′i•cal,** *adj.* **1.** of or pertaining to coins or paper money. **2.** of or pertaining to numismatics. **—nu/mis•mat′i•cal•ly,** *adv.*

nu•mis•mat•ics (nōō′miz mat′iks, -mis-, nyōō′-), *n.* (*used with a sing. v.*) the study or collecting of coins, medals, paper money, etc. **—nu•mis′ma•tist** (-mə tist), *n.*

num•skull or **numb•skull** (num′skul′), *n.* a dull-witted or stupid person; dolt.

nun (nun), *n.* a woman who is a member of a religious order, esp. one bound by vows of poverty, chastity, and obedience. **—nun′like,** *adj.*

nun•cha•ku (nun chä′kōō), *n., pl.* **-kus.** Sometimes, **nunchakus.** an Oriental hand weapon consisting of two sticks joined by a chain or cord. Also called **nun•chucks** (nun′chuks′).

nun•ci•o (nun′shē ō′, -sē ō′, nōōn′-), *n., pl.* **-ci•os.** a permanent diplomatic representative of the pope at a foreign court or capital.

nun•ner•y (nun′ə rē), *n., pl.* **-ner•ies.** a convent for nuns.

nup•tial (nup′shəl, -chəl), *adj.* **1.** of or pertaining to marriage or the marriage ceremony. **2.** of or pertaining to mating or the mating season of animals. **—n. 3.** Usu., **nuptials.** a wedding or marriage. **—nup′tial•ly,** *adv.* **—Pronunciation.** The pronunciations (nup′choo əl) and (nup′shoo əl), reinforced by analogy with words like *mutual* and *actual,* are not considered standard.

Nu•rem•berg (nōōr′əm bûrg′, nyōōr′-), *n.* a city in central Bavaria, in SE Germany: site of international trials (1945–46) of Nazis accused of war crimes. 471,800. German, **Nürn•berg** (nʏRN′bɛrk′).

nurse (nûrs), *n., v.,* **nursed, nurs•ing.** **—n. 1.** a person formally educated and trained in the care of the sick or infirm, esp. a registered nurse. **2.** a woman who has the general care of a child or children; dry nurse. **3.** WET NURSE. **4.** a worker that attends the young in a colony of social insects. **—v.t. 5.** to tend or minister to in sickness, infirmity, etc. **6.** to try to cure (an ailment) by taking care of oneself: *to nurse a cold.* **7.** to suckle (an infant). **8.** to handle carefully or fondly. **9.** to use, consume, or dispense slowly or carefully: *to nurse a cup of tea.* **10.** to keep steadily in mind or memory: *He nursed a grudge.* **11.** to feed and tend in infancy. **12.** to bring up, train, or nurture. **—v.i. 13.** to suckle a child, esp. one's own. **14.** (of a child) to suckle. **15.** to act as nurse; tend the sick or infirm. **—nurs′er,** *n.*

nurse•ling (nûrs′ling), *n.* NURSLING.

nurse•maid (nûrs′mād′), *n.* a woman or girl employed to care for children, esp. in a household. Also called **nurs′er•y•maid′.**

nurse′-practi•ti•tioner, *n.* a registered nurse qualified to diagnose and treat common or minor ailments. *Abbr.:* NP

nurs•er•y (nûr′sə rē), *n., pl.* **-er•ies. 1.** a room or place set apart for infants or very young children. **2.** a nursery school or day nursery. **3.** a place where young trees or other plants are raised.

nurs•er•y•man (nûr′sə rē mən), *n., pl.* **-men.** a person who owns or conducts a plant nursery.

nurs′er•y rhyme′, *n.* a short, simple poem or song for very young children.

nurs′er•y school′, *n.* a prekindergarten school for children.

nurse′′s aide′, *n.* a person who assists professional nurses, as in a hospital, by making beds and serving meals.

nurse′ shark′, *n.* any scavenging shark of the family Orectolobidae, having a barbel and deep groove at either side of the mouth, esp. *Ginglymostoma cirratum.*

nurs′ing home′, *n.* a residential institution caring for the aged or infirm.

nurs•ling or **nurse•ling** (nûrs′ling), *n.* **1.** a nursing infant or young animal. **2.** any person or thing under fostering care.

nur•ture (nûr′chər), *v.,* **-tured, -tur•ing,** *n.* **—v.t. 1.** to feed and protect or support and encourage. **2.** to bring up; train; educate. **—n. 3.** upbringing; training; education. **4.** development: *the nurture of young artists.* **5.** something that nourishes; nourishment; food. **—nur′tur•er,** *n.*

nut (nut), *n.* **1.** a dry fruit consisting of an edible kernel or meat enclosed in a woody or leathery shell. **2.** the kernel itself. **3.** a hard, indehiscent, one-seeded fruit, as the chestnut or the acorn. **4.** a block, usu. of metal, perforated with a threaded hole so that it can be screwed down on a bolt to hold together objects through which the bolt passes. **5.** *Slang.* a devotee or zealot. **6.** *Slang.* **a.** a foolish, silly, or eccentric person. **b.** an insane person. **7. a.** the operating expenses of a commercial enterprise, usu. figured weekly; break-even point. **b.** the total cost of opening a new business or financing a venture. **8.** (in an instrument

of the violin family) a ledge at the upper end of the fingerboard over which the strings pass. **—v.i. 9.** to seek for or gather nuts. **—Idiom. 10. a hard** or **tough nut to crack, a.** a difficult problem. **b.** a person difficult to understand or convince.

nut•crack•er (nut′krak′ər), *n.* **1.** an instrument for cracking the shells of nuts. **2.** either of two corvine birds of the genus *Nucifraga* that feed on pine nuts, *N. caryocatactes,* of N Eurasia, and *N. columbiana,* of W North America.

Nut′cracker Suite′, a ballet and concert suite (1892) arranged by Peter Ilyich Tchaikovsky from his orchestral work for a ballet, *The Nutcracker.*

nut•gall (nut′gôl′), *n.* a small nutlike gall, esp. one formed on an oak.

nut•hatch (nut′hach′), *n.* any of various small, sharp-beaked songbirds of the family Sittidae, mainly of the Northern Hemisphere, that seek food along tree trunks and branches.

nut•let (nut′lit), *n.* **1.** a small nut or nutlike fruit. **2.** the stone of a drupe.

nut•meat (nut′mēt′), *n.* the kernel of a nut, usu. edible.

nut•meg (nut′meg), *n.* **1.** the hard, aromatic seed of an East Indian tree, *Myristica fragrans,* of the nutmeg family, used in grated form as a spice. **2.** a similar seed of certain related trees. **3.** a tree bearing the nutmeg seed.

nu•tri•ent (nōō′trē ənt, nyōō′-), *adj.* **1.** nourishing; providing nourishment or nutriment. **2.** containing or conveying nutriment, as solutions or vessels of the body. **—n. 3.** a nutrient substance.

nu•tri•ment (nōō′trə mənt, nyōō′-), *n.* **1.** any substance that, taken into a living organism, serves to sustain it, promoting growth, replacing loss, and providing energy. **2.** anything that nourishes; nourishment; food. **—nu/tri•men′tal** (-men′tl), *adj.*

nu•tri•tion (nōō trish′ən, nyōō′-), *n.* **1.** the act or process of nourishing or of being nourished. **2.** the study or science of the dietary requirements of humans and animals for proper health and development. **3.** the process by which organisms take in and utilize food material. **4.** food; nutriment. **—nu•tri′tion•al,** *adj.* **—nu•tri′tion•al•ly,** *adv.*

nu•tri•tion•ist (nōō trish′ə nist, nyōō-), *n.* a person who is trained or expert in the science of nutrition.

nu•tri•tious (nōō trish′əs, nyōō-), *adj.* providing nourishment, esp. to a high degree; nourishing; healthful. **—nu•tri′tious•ly,** *adv.* **—nu•tri′tious•ness,** *n.*

nu•tri•tive (nōō′tri tiv, nyōō′-), *adj.* **1.** serving to nourish; nutritious. **2.** of, pertaining to, or concerned with nutrition. **—n. 3.** an item of nourishing food. **—nu′tri•tive•ly,** *adv.* **—nu′tri•tive•ness,** *n.*

nuts (nuts), *Slang.* **—interj. 1.** (used to express disgust, defiance, disapproval, despair.) **—adj. 2.** insane; crazy. **—Idiom. 3. be nuts about,** to admire fervently; love deeply.

nuts′ and bolts′, *n.pl.* the essential or basic aspects.

nut•shell (nut′shel′), *n.* **1.** the shell of a nut. **—Idiom. 2. in a nutshell,** briefly; succinctly.

nut•ty (nut′ē), *adj.,* **-ti•er, -ti•est. 1.** abounding in or producing nuts. **2.** nutlike, esp. in flavor. **3.** *Slang.* **a.** silly or ridiculous. **b.** eccentric; queer. **c.** insane. **—nut′ti•ly,** *adv.* **—nut′ti•ness,** *n.*

Nu•yo•ri•can (nōō′yô rē′kən, nyōō′-), *n., adj.* NEORICAN. [by alteration (influence of Sp *Nu(eva) Yor(k)* New York)]

nuz•zle (nuz′əl), *v.,* **-zled, -zling,** *n.* **—v.i. 1.** to burrow or root with the nose, snout, etc., as an animal does. **2.** to thrust the nose, muzzle, etc.: *The dog nuzzled up to its master.* **3.** to lie very close; cuddle or snuggle up. **—v.t. 4.** to root up with the nose or snout. **5.** to touch or rub with the nose, snout, muzzle, etc. **6.** to thrust the nose, muzzle, snout, etc., against or into. **7.** to thrust (the nose or head), as into something. **8.** to lie very close to; cuddle or snuggle up to. **—n. 9.** an affectionate embrace or cuddle.

NV, Nevada.

NW or **N.W.** or **n.w., 1.** northwest. **2.** northwestern.

NWS, National Weather Service.

NY or **N.Y.,** New York.

NYC or **N.Y.C.,** New York City.

nyet (nyet), *adv., n. Russian.* no.

ny•lon (nī′lon), *n.* **1.** any of a class of thermoplastic polyamides capable of extruding when molten into fibers, sheets, etc., of extreme toughness, strength, and elasticity: used esp. for yarn, fabrics, and bristles. **2. nylons,** stockings made of nylon, esp. sheer ones. [coined by the du Pont Chemical Co.]

nymph (nimf), *n.* **1.** any of a class of lesser deities in classical mythology, conceived of as beautiful young women inhabiting the sea, rivers, trees, or mountains. **2.** a beautiful or graceful young woman. **3.** the young of an insect that undergoes incomplete metamorphosis. **—nymph′al, nym/phe•an** (-fē ən), *adj.*

nym•pho•ma•ni•a (nim′fə mā′nē ə, -mān′yə), *n.* abnormal, uncontrollable sexual desire in a female. Compare SATYRIASIS. **—nym′pho•ma′ni•ac′** (-mā′nē ak′), *n., adj.* **—nym′pho•ma•ni′a•cal** (-mə nī′ə kəl), *adj.*

NYSE or **N.Y.S.E.,** New York Stock Exchange.

O

O, o (ō), *n., pl.* **O's** or **Os, o's** or **os** or **oes. 1.** the 15th letter of the English alphabet, a vowel. **2.** any spoken sound represented by this letter. **3.** something shaped like an O. **4.** a written or printed representation of the letter *O* or *o.*

O (ō), *interj.* **1.** (used before a name in direct address, esp. in solemn or poetic language, to lend earnestness to an appeal): *Hear, O Israel!* **2.** (used as an expression of surprise, pain, annoyance, longing, gladness, etc.)

O, *Symbol.* **1.** the 15th in order or in a series. **2.** a major blood group. Compare ABO SYSTEM. **3.** oxygen.

o' (ə, ō), *prep.* **1.** of: *o'clock; will-o'-the-wisp.* **2.** *Chiefly Dial.* on.

-o, 1. a suffix occurring as the final element in informal shortenings of nouns (*combo; promo*); **-o** also forms nouns, usu. derogatory, for persons or things exemplifying or associated with that specified by the base noun or adjective (*weirdo*). **2.** a suffix occurring in informal noun or adjective derivatives: *kiddo; neato; righto.*

oaf (ōf), *n.* **1.** a crudely clumsy person; lout. **2.** a stupid person; idiot. —**oaf′ish,** *adj.* —**oaf′ish•ly,** *adv.* —**oaf′ish•ness,** *n.*

oak (ōk), *n.* **1.** any tree or shrub belonging to the genus *Quercus,* of the beech family, bearing the acorn as fruit. **2.** the hard, durable wood of such a tree, used in making furniture and in construction. **3.** the leaves of this tree, esp. as worn in a chaplet. **4.** something made of oak wood. —*Proverb.* **5. Great oaks from little acorns grow,** mighty people or projects may develop from small beginnings. —**oak′en,** *adj.*

oak′ ap′ple, *n.* any of various rounded galls produced on oaks. Also called **oak′ gall′.**

Oak•land (ōk′lənd), *n.* a seaport in W California, on San Francisco Bay. 366,926.

oak•moss (ōk′môs′, -mos′), *n.* a lichen, *Evernia pranastri,* growing on oak and other trees, yielding a resin used in the manufacture of perfumes.

oa•kum (ō′kəm), *n.* loose fiber obtained by untwisting and picking apart old ropes, used as a material for caulking.

oar (ōr, ôr), *n.* **1.** a long shaft with a broad blade at one end, used as a lever for rowing or otherwise propelling or steering a boat. **2.** OARSMAN. —*v.t.* **3.** to propel with or as if with oars; row. —*v.i.* **4.** to row. —*Idiom.* **5. put in one's oar,** to meddle; interfere. Also, **put one's oar in. 6. rest on one's oars,** to cease to make further effort; relax.

oar•fish (ōr′fish′, ôr′-), *n., pl.* (*esp. collectively*) **-fish,** (*esp. for kinds or species*) **-fish•es.** any long, ribbon-shaped, deep-sea fish of the genus *Regalecus,* having a fin along the back that rises to a crest: up to 30 ft. (9 m) long.

oar•lock (ōr′lok′, ôr′-), *n.* a usu. U-shaped device providing a pivot for an oar in rowing.

oars•man (ōrz′mən, ôrz′-), *n., pl.* **-men.** a person who rows a boat, esp. a racing boat. —**oars′man•ship′,** *n.*

o•a•sis (ō ā′sis), *n., pl.* **-ses** (-sēz). **1.** a fertile area in a desert region, usu. having a spring or well. **2.** a refuge, as from work or stress; haven.

oat (ōt), *n.* **1.** a cereal grass, *Avena sativa,* cultivated for its edible grain. **2.** Usu., **oats.** the grain of this plant. **3.** any of several other plants of the genus *Avena,* as the wild oat. —*Idiom.* **4. feel one's oats,** to have a strong sense of one's own power.

oath (ōth), *n., pl.* **oaths** (ōthz, ōths). **1.** a solemn appeal to a deity or to some reverend person or thing to witness one's determination to speak the truth or keep a promise. **2.** any statement, promise, or affirmation accepted as the equivalent of such an appeal. **3.** the form of words in which an oath is made. **4.** an irreverent or blasphemous use of the name of God or anything sacred. **5.** any profane expression; curse. —*Idiom.* **6. take an oath,** to swear solemnly; vow. **7. under oath,** solemnly bound by the obligations of an oath.

Oat•man (ōt′mən), *n.* **Johnson,** 1856–1922, U.S. businessman and hymn writer.

oat•meal (ōt′mēl′, -mēl′), *n.* **1.** meal made from ground or rolled oats. **2.** a cooked breakfast food made from this.

Oa•xa•ca (wä hä′kä, wä-), *n.* **1.** a state in S Mexico. 2,650,232; 36,375 sq. mi. (94,210 sq. km). **2.** the capital of this state, in the central part. 157,284.

Ob (ôb, ob), *n.* **1.** a river in the W Russian Federation in Asia, flowing NW to the Gulf of Ob. 2500 mi. (4025 km) long. **2. Gulf of,** an inlet of the Arctic Ocean. ab. 500 mi. (800 km) long.

OB, Also, ob *Med.* **1.** obstetrical. **2.** obstetrician. **3.** obstetrics.

ob-, a prefix meaning "toward," "to," "on," "over," "against," occurring in loanwords from Latin; used also, with the senses "reversely," "inversely," to form New Latin and English scientific terms: *object; obligate; oblanceolate.* Also, **o-, oc-, of-, op-.**

ob., **1.** he died; she died. [< Latin *obiit*] **2.** incidentally. [< Latin *obiter*]

O•ba•di•ah (ō′bə dī′ə), *n.* **1.** a Minor Prophet. **2.** a book of the Bible bearing his name.

ob•bli•ga•to or **ob•li•ga•to** (ob′li gä′tō), *adj., n., pl.* **-tos, -ti** (-tē) **—***adj.* **1.** (used as a musical direction) obligatory; not to be omitted. —*n.* **2.** a musical line performed by a single instrument in accompaniment to a solo part.

ob•du•ra•cy (ob′dŏŏ rə sē, -dyŏŏ-), *n.* the state or quality of being obdurate.

ob•du•rate (ob′dŏŏ rit, -dyŏŏ-), *adj.* **1.** unmoved by persuasion or pity; unyielding. **2.** stubbornly resistant to moral influence; impenitent: *an obdurate sinner.* —**ob′du•rate•ly,** *adv.* —**ob′du•rate•ness,** *n.*

o•be•di•ence (ō bē′dē əns), *n.* **1.** the state or quality of being obedient. **2.** the act or practice of obeying. **3.** a sphere of ecclesiastical or secular authority or jurisdiction.

o•be•di•ent (ō bē′dē ənt), *adj.* complying with or submissive to authority. —**o•be′di•ent•ly,** *adv.*

o•bei•sance (ō bā′səns, ō bē′-), *n.* **1.** a movement of the body, as a bow or curtsy, expressing deep respect or deferential courtesy. **2.** deference; homage. —**o•bei′sant,** *adj.* —**o•bei′sant•ly,** *adv.*

ob•e•lisk (ob′ə lisk), *n.* **1.** a tapering, four-sided shaft of stone, usu. monolithic and having a pyramidal apex. **2.** OBELUS. **3.** DAGGER (def. 2).

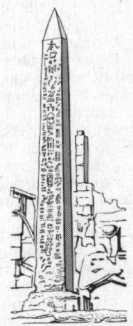

obelisk

ob•e•lus (ob′ə ləs), *n., pl.* **-li** (-lī′). a mark (− or ÷) used in ancient manuscripts to point out questionable words or passages.

o•bese (ō bēs′), *adj.* very fat or overweight; corpulent. —**o•bese′ly,** *adv.* —**o•be′si•ty,** *n.*

o•bey (ō bā′), *v.t.* **1.** to comply with the wishes, instructions, or commands of. **2.** to comply with or follow: *to obey orders.* **3.** to respond readily to: *The car obeys my slightest touch on the steering wheel.* **4.** to submit or conform to: *to obey the law of gravity.* —*v.i.* **5.** to be obedient. —**o•bey′a•ble,** *adj.* —**o•bey′er,** *n.*

ob•fus•cate (ob′fə skāt′, ob fus′kāt), *v.t.,* **-cat•ed, -cat•ing. 1.** to confuse. **2.** to make unclear. —**ob′fus•ca′tion,** *n.* —**ob•fus′ca•to•ry** (-kə tôr′ē, -tōr′ē), *adj.*

ob-gyn or **ob/gyn** (ō′bē′jē′wī′en′; *sometimes* ob′gīn′), **1.** obstetrics and gynecology. **2.** obstetrician-gynecologist. **3.** obstetrical-gynecological.

o•bit (ō bit′; *esp. Brit.* ob′it), *n.* an obituary.

ob•i•ter dic•tum (ob′i tər dik′təm), *n., pl.* **obiter dic•ta** (dik′tə). **1.** an incidental remark or opinion. **2.** a judicial opinion in a matter related but not essential to a case. [< Latin: (a) saying by the way]

o•bit•u•ar•y (ō bich′ŏŏ er′ē), *n., pl.* **-ar•ies,** *adj.* —*n.* **1.** a notice of the death of a person, often with a biographical sketch, as in a newspaper. —*adj.* **2.** of, pertaining to, or recording obituaries. —**o•bit′u•ar•ist,** *n.*

ob•ject (*n.* ob′jikt, -jekt; *v.* əb jekt′), *n.* **1.** anything that is visible or tangible and is relatively stable in form. **2.** a thing, person, or matter to which thought or action is directed: *an object of investigation.* **3.** the end toward which effort or action is directed; goal; objective. **4.** anything that may be apprehended intellectually: *objects of thought.* **5.** a noun, noun phrase, or pronoun representing either the goal or recipient of the action of a verb or the goal of a preposition, as *ball* in *I hit the ball, her* and *question* in *He asked her a question,* or *table* in *under the table.* Compare DIRECT OBJECT, INDIRECT OBJECT. —*v.i.* **6.** to offer a reason or argument in opposition. **7.** to express or feel disapproval, dislike, or distaste. —*v.t.* **8.** to state or cite in opposition: *They objected that the rules were unfair.* —**ob•jec′tor,** *n.*

ob′ject com′plement, *n.* a noun, noun phrase, pronoun, or adjective used in the predicate following a factitive verb and referring to or identified with its direct object, as *treasurer* in *We appointed him treasurer* or *white* in *They painted the house white.* Also called **objective complement.**

ob′ject glass′, *n.* OBJECTIVE (def. 3).

ob•jec•tion (əb jek′shən), *n.* **1.** a reason or argument offered in opposition. **2.** the act of objecting. **3.** a feeling of disapproval, dislike, or disagreement.

ob•jec•tion•a•ble (əb jek′shə nə bəl), *adj.* causing or tending to cause objection; offensive. —**ob•jec′tion•a•bly,** *adv.*

ob•jec•tive (əb jek′tiv), *n.* **1.** something that one's efforts or actions are intended to attain or accomplish; purpose; goal. **2. a.** the objective case in grammar. **b.** a word or other form in the objective case. **3.** Also called **object glass, object lens, object′ive lens′.** (in an optical system) the lens or combination of lenses that first receives the rays from an observed object, forming its image in an optical device, as a microscope or camera. —*adj.* **4.** not influenced by personal feelings or prejudice; unbiased: *an objective opinion.* **5. a.** being the object of perception or thought. **b.** belonging to the object of thought rather than to the thinking subject (opposed to *subjective*). **6. a.** of, pertaining to, or being a grammatical case that typically indicates the object of a transitive verb or a preposition (contrasted with *subjective*). **b.** of or pertaining to the object of a sentence. **7.** *Med.* (of a symptom) discernible to others as well as the patient. —**ob•jec′tive•ly,** *adv.* —**ob•jec′tive•ness,** *n.*

ob•jec•tiv•ism (əb jek′tə viz′əm), *n.* **1.** a tendency to lay stress on the objective or external elements of cognition. **2.** the tendency, as of a writer, to deal with things external to the mind rather than with thoughts or feelings. **3.** a doctrine or philosophy emphasizing individualism and self-interest. —**ob•jec′tiv•ist,** *n., adj.* —**ob•jec′ti•vis′tic,** *adj.*

ob•jec•tiv•i•ty (ob′jik tiv′i tē, -jek-), *n.* **1.** the state or quality of being objective. **2.** external reality.

ob′ject lan′guage, *n.* the language to which a metalanguage refers.

ob′ject les′son, *n.* a practical or concrete illustration of a principle.

ob•jet d'art (ob′zhā där′), *n., pl.* **ob•jets d'art** (ob′zhā där′). an object of artistic worth or interest. Also called **ob•jet′.**

ob•late¹ (ob′lāt, o blāt′), *adj.* flattened at the poles, as a spheroid generated by the revolution of an ellipse about its shorter axis.

ob•late² (ob′lāt, o blāt′), *n.* **1.** a person serving and living in a monastery but not under monastic rule or full monastic vows. **2.** a lay member of a Roman Catholic society devoted to special religious work.

ob•la•tion (o blā′shən), *n.* **1.** an offering made to a deity, esp. the offering of bread and wine in the celebration of the Eucharist. **2.** the act of making such an offering. **3.** any offering for religious or charitable uses. —**ob•la•to•ry** (ob′lə tôr′ē, -tōr′ē), **ob•la′tion•al,** *adj.*

ob•li•gate (*v.* ob′li gāt′; *adj.* ob′li git, -gāt′), *v.* **-gat•ed, -gat•ing,** *adj.* —*v.t.* **1.** to bind or oblige morally or legally. **2.** to commit (funds, property, etc.) to meet an obligation. —*adj.* **3.** restricted to a particular condition of life, as certain organisms that can survive only in the absence of oxygen (opposed to *facultative*).

ob•li•ga•tion (ob′li gā′shən), *n.* **1.** something by which a person is bound to do certain things, and which arises out of a sense of duty or results from custom, law, etc. **2.** something done or to be done for such reasons: *to fulfill one's obligations.* **3.** a binding promise, contract, sense of duty, etc. **4. a.** an agreement enforceable by law. **b.** a document setting forth such an agreement. **5.** any bond, certificate, or the like, as of a government or a corporation, serving as evidence of indebtedness. **6.** an indebtedness or amount of indebtedness. **7.** a debt of gratitude. **8.** the state of being under a debt.

ob•li•ga•to (ob′li gä′tō), *adj., n., pl.* **-tos, -ti** (tē). OBBLIGATO.

o•blig•a•to•ry (ə blig′ə tôr′ē, -tōr′ē, ob′li gə-), *adj.* **1.** required as a matter of obligation; mandatory. **2.** incumbent or compulsory: *duties obligatory on all.* **3.** imposing or stipulating an obligation. —**o•blig′a•to′ri•ly,** *adv.*

o•blige (ə blīj′), *v.,* **o•bliged, o•blig•ing.** —*v.t.* **1.** to require or constrain, as by law, conscience, or force. **2.** to bind morally or legally, as by a promise or contract. **3.** to place under a debt of gratitude for a favor or service: *We are much obliged for the ride.* **4.** to do a favor or service for; accommodate: *He obliged us with a song.* —*v.i.* **5.** to do a favor or service. —**o•blig′er,** *n.*

o•blique (ə blēk′, ō blēk′; *Mil.* ə blīk′, ō blīk′), *adj.* **1.** neither perpendicular nor parallel to a given line or surface; slanting; sloping. **2.** (of a solid) not having the axis perpendicular to the plane of the base. **3.** diverging from a given straight line or course. **4.** not straight or direct, as a course. **5.** indirectly stated or expressed. **6.** indirectly or deviously aimed at or reached. **7.** pertaining to or denoting muscles running obliquely in the body as opposed to those running transversely or longitudinally. **8.** *Bot.* having unequal sides, as a leaf. **9.** *Gram.* of or pertaining to any case of inflection except the nominative or vocative. —*adv.* **10.** *Mil.* at an angle of 45°. —*n.* **11.** something that is oblique. **12.** *Gram.* an oblique case. **13.** any of several oblique muscles, esp. in the walls of the abdomen. —**o•blique′ly,** *adv.* —**o•blique′ness,** *n.*

oblique′ tri′angle, *n.* any triangle that does not have a right angle (contrasted with *right triangle*).

o•bliq•ui•ty (ə blik′wi tē, ō blik′-), *n., pl.* **-ties.** **1.** the state of being oblique. **2.** an inclination or a degree of inclination. **3.** intellectual deviousness. **4.** deliberate evasiveness in speech or writing. **5.** a confusing or obscure statement or passage of writing. **6.** the angle between the plane of the earth's orbit and that of the earth's equator, equal to 23°27′; the inclination of the earth's equator.

ob•lit•er•ate (ə blit′ə rāt′), *v.t.,* **-at•ed, -at•ing.** **1.** to remove or destroy all traces of. **2.** to blot out or render indecipherable; efface. —**ob•lit′er•a•ble** (-ər ə bəl), *adj.* —**ob•lit′er•a′tion,** *n.* —**ob•lit′er•a′tor,** *n.*

ob•liv•i•on (ə bliv′ē ən), *n.* **1.** the state of being completely forgotten. **2.** the state of forgetting or of being oblivious: *the oblivion of sleep.*

ob•liv•i•ous (ə bliv′ē əs), *adj.* **1.** unmindful or unaware (usu. fol. by *to* or *of*): *oblivious to someone's stare.* **2.** forgetful; without remembrance or memory. —**ob•liv′i•ous•ly,** *adv.* —**ob•liv′i•ous•ness,** *n.*

ob•long (ob′lông′, -long′), *adj.* **1.** elongated, usu. from the square or circular form. **2.** in the form of a rectangle one of whose dimensions is greater than the other. —*n.* **3.** an oblong figure.

ob•lo•quy (ob′lə kwē), *n., pl.* **-quies.** **1.** censure, blame, or abusive language. **2.** discredit, disgrace, or bad repute. —**ob•lo•qui•al** (o blō′kwē əl), *adj.*

ob•nox•ious (əb nok′shəs), *adj.* highly objectionable or offensive. —**ob•nox′ious•ly,** *adv.* —**ob•nox′ious•ness,** *n.*

o•boe (ō′bō), *n.* a woodwind instrument having a slender conical, tubular body and a double-reed mouthpiece. [< Italian < French *hautbois* = *haut* high + *bois* wood] —**o′bo•ist,** *n.*

ob•scene (əb sēn′), *adj.* **1.** offensive to morality or decency; indecent: *obscene language.* **2.** intended to stimulate sexual appetite or lust; lewd: *obscene movies.* **3.** abominable; disgusting; repulsive. —**ob•scene′ly,** *adv.* —**ob•scene′ness,** *n.*

ob•scen•i•ty (əb sen′i tē, -sē′ni-), *n., pl.* **-ties.** **1.** the state or quality of being obscene. **2.** something obscene, as a word or story.

ob•scu•rant•ism (əb skyŏŏr′ən tiz′əm, ob′skyŏŏ ran′tiz əm), *n.* **1.** opposition to the increase and spread of knowledge. **2.** deliberate obscurity or evasion of clarity. —**ob•scu′rant•ist,** *n., adj.*

ob•scure (əb skyŏŏr′), *adj.,* **-scur•er, -scur•est,** *v.,* **-scured, -scur•ing,** *n.* —*adj.* **1.** (of meaning) not clear or plain; ambiguous, vague, or uncertain. **2.** not clear to the understanding; hard to perceive: *obscure motives.* **3.** (of language, style, a speaker, etc.) not expressing the meaning clearly or plainly. **4.** not readily seen, heard, etc.; indistinct; faint. **5.** inconspicuous: *the obscure beginnings of a movement.* **6.** of little or no prominence or distinction; unknown: *an obscure artist; an obscure little town.* **7.** lacking in light or illumination; dark; dim; murky. **8.** (of a vowel) having the reduced or neutral sound usu. represented by the schwa (ə). —*v.t.* **9.** to conceal or confuse (meaning, intention, or the like); cover; mask. **10.** to make dark, dim, indistinct, etc. **11.** to reduce or neutralize (a vowel) to the sound usu. represented by a schwa (ə). —*n.* **12.** OBSCURITY. —**ob•scu•ra•tion** (ob′skyŏŏ rā′shən), *n.* —**ob•scure′ly,** *adv.* —**ob•scure′ness,** *n.*

ob•scu•ri•ty (əb skyŏŏr′i tē), *n., pl.* **-ties.** **1.** the state or quality of being obscure. **2.** a person or thing that is obscure.

ob•se•qui•ous (əb sē′kwē əs), *adj.* characterized by or showing servile complaisance or deference; fawning: *an obsequious bow; obsequious servants.* —**ob•se′qui•ous•ly,** *adv.* —**ob•se′qui•ous•ness,** *n.*

ob•se•quy (ob′si kwē), *n., pl.* **-quies.** Usu., **obsequies.** a funeral rite or ceremony.

ob•serv•a•ble (əb zûr′və bəl), *adj.* **1.** capable of being or liable to be observed; discernible. **2.** worthy of being celebrated or observed: *an observable holiday.* **3.** deserving of attention; noteworthy. —**ob•serv′a•bil′i•ty, ob•serv′a•ble•ness,** *n.* —**ob•serv′a•bly,** *adv.*

ob•serv•ance (əb zûr′vəns), *n.* **1.** an act or instance of following, obeying, or conforming to a law, custom, etc. **2.** a celebration by appropriate procedure, ceremonies, etc.: *the observance of the Sabbath.* **3.** a procedure, ceremony, or rite, as for a particular occasion. **4.** a rule governing a Roman Catholic religious house or order.

ob•serv•ant (əb zûr′vənt), *adj.* **1.** quick to notice or perceive; alert. **2.** looking at, watching, or regarding attentively. **3.** careful in the observing of a law, religious ritual, custom, etc. —**ob•serv′ant•ly,** *adv.*

ob•ser•va•tion (ob′zûr vā′shən), *n.* **1.** an act or instance of noticing or perceiving. **2.** an act or instance of regarding attentively or watching. **3.** the faculty or habit of observing or noticing. **4.** notice: *to escape observation.* **5.** an act or instance of watching or noting something for a scientific or other special purpose. **6.** the information or record secured by such an act. **7.** something learned in the course of observing things. **8.** a remark or statement based on what one has observed; pronouncement. **9.** the condition of being observed. **10.** the measurement of the altitude or azimuth of a heavenly body for navigational purposes. —**ob′ser•va′tion•al,** *adj.* —**ob′ser•va′tion•al•ly,** *adv.*

ob•serv•a•to•ry (əb zûr′və tôr′ē, -tōr′ē), *n., pl.* **-ries.** **1.** a place or building used for making observations of astronomical or other natural phenomena, esp. a place equipped with a powerful telescope for observing the planets and stars. **2.** an institution that controls or carries on the work of such a place. **3.** a place or structure that provides an extensive view; lookout.

ob•serve (əb zûrv′), *v.,* **-served, -serv•ing.** —*v.t.* **1.** to see, watch, or notice. **2.** to regard with attention, esp. so as to see or learn something. **3.** to watch, view, or note for a scientific, official, or other special purpose: *to observe an eclipse.* **4.** to state by way of comment; remark. **5.** to keep or maintain in one's action, conduct, etc.: *to observe quiet.* **6.** to obey, comply with, or conform to: *to observe laws.* **7.** to celebrate, as a holiday, in an appropriate way. **8.** to perform duly or solemnize (ceremonies, rites, etc.). **9.** to note or inspect closely, as for an omen. —*v.i.* **10.** to notice. **11.** to act as an observer. **12.** to remark or comment (usu. fol. by *on* or *upon*). —**ob•serv′ing•ly,** *adv.*

ob•serv•er (əb zûr′vər), *n.* **1.** someone or something that observes. **2.** a delegate to an assembly or gathering, who is sent to observe and report but not to take part officially in its activities.

ob•sess (əb ses′), *v.* **1.** to dominate or excessively preoccupy the thoughts, feelings, or desires of; haunt. —*v.i.* **2.** to think about something unceasingly. —**ob•sess′ing•ly,** *adv.* —**ob•ses′sor,** *n.*

ob·ses·sion (əb sesh′ən), n. **1.** the domination of one's thoughts or feelings by a persistent idea, image, desire, etc. **2.** the idea, image, desire, etc., itself. **3.** the state of being obsessed. —**ob·ses′sion·al**, adj.

ob·ses·sive (əb ses′iv), adj. **1.** being, pertaining to, or resembling an obsession: an obsessive fear of illness. **2.** causing an obsession. **3.** excessive, esp. extremely so. —n. **4.** a person who has an obsession or obsessions. —**ob·ses′sive·ly**, adv. —**ob·ses′sive·ness**, n.

obses′sive-compul′sive, adj. **1.** of, pertaining to, or characterized by the persistent intrusion of unwanted thoughts accompanied by ritualistic actions, regarded as a form of neurosis. —n. **2.** a person with obsessive-compulsive characteristics.

ob·sid·i·an (əb sid′ē ən), n. a volcanic glass similar in composition to granite, usu. dark but transparent in thin pieces.

ob·so·les·cent (ob′sə les′ənt), adj. becoming obsolete; passing out of use, as a word. —**ob′so·les′cence,** n. —**ob′so·les′cent·ly,** adv.

ob·so·lete (ob′sə lēt′, ob′sə lēt′), adj., v., **-let·ed, -let·ing.** —adj. **1.** no longer in general use; fallen into disuse: obsolete customs. **2.** of a discarded or outmoded type; out-of-date: an obsolete battleship. **3.** (of a linguistic form) no longer in use, esp., out of use for at least the past century. **4.** Biol. rudimentary in comparison with the corresponding part or trait in related species or in individuals of the opposite sex. —v.t. **5.** to make obsolete; antiquate. —**ob′so·lete′ly,** adv.

ob·sta·cle (ob′stə kəl), n. something that obstructs or hinders progress.

ob′stacle course′, n. **1.** a military training area having obstacles, as hurdles and ditches that must be surmounted or crossed in succession. **2.** an event, situation, or the like with many challenges or difficulties.

ob·stet·ri·cal (əb ste′tri kəl) also **ob·stet′ric,** adj. **1.** of or pertaining to the care and treatment of women in childbirth and during the period before and after delivery. **2.** of or pertaining to childbirth or obstetrics. —**ob·stet′ri·cal·ly,** adv.

ob·ste·tri·cian (ob′sti trish′ən), n. a physician who specializes in obstetrics.

ob·stet·rics (əb ste′triks), n. (used with a sing. v.) the branch of medical science concerned with childbirth and caring for and treating women in or in connection with childbirth.

ob·sti·na·cy (ob′stə nə sē), n., pl. **-cies. 1.** the quality or state of being obstinate; stubbornness. **2.** an instance of being obstinate; an obstinate act, viewpoint, etc.

ob·sti·nate (ob′stə nit), adj. **1.** firmly or stubbornly adhering to a purpose, opinion, or course of action. **2.** not easily or readily treated, controlled, or overcome, as a disease. —**ob·sti·nate·ly,** adv.

ob·strep·er·ous (əb strep′ər əs), adj. **1.** resisting control or restraint in a difficult manner; unruly. **2.** noisy, clamorous, or boisterous: obstreperous children. —**ob·strep′er·ous·ly,** adv. —**ob·strep′er·ous·ness,** n.

ob·struct (əb strukt′), v.t. **1.** to block or close up with an obstacle: Debris obstructed the road. **2.** to hinder, interrupt, or delay the passage, progress, course, etc., of. **3.** to block from sight; be in the way of (a view, passage, etc.). —**ob·struct′er, ob·struc′tor,** n. —**ob·struc′tive,** adj. —**ob·struc′tive·ness,** n.

ob·struc·tion (əb struk′shən), n. **1.** something that obstructs; an obstacle or hindrance: obstructions to navigation. **2.** an act or instance of obstructing. **3.** the state of being obstructed. **4.** the delaying of business before a deliberative body.

ob·struc·tion·ist (əb struk′shə nist), n. a person who deliberately delays or obstructs progress, esp. of business before a deliberative body. —**ob·struc′tion·ism,** n.

ob·tain (əb tān′), v.t. **1.** to come into possession of; get, acquire, or procure, as through effort or request. —v.i. **2.** to be prevalent, customary, or in vogue: the morals that obtained in Rome. —**ob·tain′a·ble,** adj. —**ob·tain′a·bil′i·ty,** n. —**ob·tain′er,** n. —**ob·tain′ment,** n.

ob·trude (əb trōōd′), v., **-trud·ed, -trud·ing.** —v.t. **1.** to thrust (something) forward or upon a person, esp. without warrant or invitation. **2.** to thrust forth; push out. —v.i. **3.** to thrust forward, esp. unduly; intrude. —**ob·trud′er,** n. —**ob·tru′sion** (-trōō′zhən), n.

ob·tru·sive (əb trōō′siv), adj. **1.** having a disposition to impose oneself or one's opinions on others. **2.** (of a thing) obtruding itself; blatant: an obtrusive error. **3.** protruding; projecting. —**ob·tru′sive·ly,** adv. —**ob·tru′sive·ness,** n.

ob·tund (ob tund′), v.t. to blunt; dull; deaden. —**ob·tund′ent,** adj., n.

ob·tuse (əb tōōs′, -tyōōs′), adj. **1.** not quick or alert in perception, feeling, or intellect; insensitive; dull. **2.** not sharp, acute, or pointed; blunt. **3.** Bot. (of a leaf, petal, etc.) rounded at the extremity. **4.** indistinctly perceived, as pain or sound. —**ob·tuse′ly,** adv. —**ob·tuse′ness,** n.

obtuse′ an′gle, n. an angle greater than 90° but less than 180°. —**ob·tuse′-an′gled,** adj.

ob·verse (ob′vûrs; adj. ob vûrs′, ob′vûrs), n. **1.** the side of a coin, medal, flag, etc., that bears the principal design (opposed to reverse). **2.** the front or principal surface of anything. **3.** a counterpart. **4.** a proposition obtained from another by obversion. **5.** facing the observer. **6.** corresponding to something else as a counterpart. **7.** Bot. having the base narrower than the top, as a leaf.

ob·vert (ob vûrt′), v.t. to turn (something) so as to show a different surface.

ob·vi·ate (ob′vē āt′), v.t., **-at·ed, -at·ing.** to anticipate and prevent or render unnecessary by effective measures. —**ob′vi·a·ble** (-ə bəl), adj. —**ob′vi·a′tion,** n. —**ob′vi·a′tor,** n.

ob·vi·ous (ob′vē əs), adj. **1.** easily seen, recognized, or understood; open to view or knowledge; evident. **2.** lacking in subtlety. —**ob′vi·ous·ly,** adv. —**ob′vi·ous·ness,** n.

ob·vo·lute (ob′və lōōt′), adj. **1.** rolled or turned in. **2.** Bot. having alternately overlapping margins, as leaves or petals in bud. —**ob′vo·lu′tion,** n. —**ob′vo·lu′tive,** adj.

oc-, var. of OB- (by assimilation) before c: occident.

o.c., in the work cited.

o·ca or **o·ka** (ō′kə), n., pl. **o·cas** or **o·kas. 1.** a wood sorrel, Oxalis tuberosa, of the Andes, cultivated in South America for its edible tubers. **2.** a tuber of this plant.

O′ Can′ada, the national anthem of Canada.

O′ Cap′tain! My′ Cap′tain!, a poem (1865) by Walt Whitman in memory of Abraham Lincoln: published in Leaves of Grass.

oc·a·ri·na (ok′ə rē′nə), n., pl. **-nas.** a simple musical wind instrument shaped somewhat like an elongated egg with a mouthpiece and finger holes. Also called **sweet potato.**

O′Ca·sey (ō kā′sē), n. **Sean** (shôn), 1880–1964, Irish playwright.

Oc·cam or **Ock·ham** (ok′əm), n. **William of,** died 1349?, English Scholastic philosopher. —**Oc′cam·is′tic,** adj.

Oc′cam's ra′zor, n. the principle in philosophy and science that assumptions introduced to explain a thing must not be multiplied beyond necessity, and hence the simplest of several hypotheses is always the best in accounting for unexplained facts.

oc·ca·sion (ə kā′zhən), n. **1.** a particular time, esp. as marked by certain circumstances or occurrences. **2.** a special or important time, event, ceremony, etc.: The party was quite an occasion. **3.** a convenient or favorable time; opportunity: a good occasion to take inventory. **4.** the immediate or incidental cause or reason for some action or result: What is the occasion for this uproar? —v.t. **5.** to give occasion or cause for; bring about. —**Idiom. 6. on occasion,** once in a while; occasionally.

oc·ca·sion·al (ə kā′zhə nl), adj. **1.** occurring or appearing at irregular or infrequent intervals: an occasional headache. **2.** intended for supplementary use when needed: an occasional chair. **3.** pertaining to, arising out of, or intended for the occasion: occasional verses. **4.** acting or serving for the occasion or only on particular occasions. **5.** serving as the occasion or incidental cause.

oc·ca·sion·al·ly (ə kā′zhə nl ē), adv. at times; from time to time; now and then.

Oc·ci·dent (ok′si dənt), n. **1. the Occident, a.** the West; the countries of Europe and America. **b.** WESTERN HEMISPHERE. **2.** (l.c.) the west; the western regions. [< Latin occidere to fall, (of the sun) to set]

oc·ci·den·tal (ok′si den′tl), adj. **1.** (usu. cap.) of or pertaining to the Occident or its inhabitants. **2.** western. —n. **3.** (usu. cap.) a native or inhabitant of the Occident. —**oc′ci·den′tal·ly,** adv.

oc·cip·i·tal (ok sip′i tl), adj. **1.** of, pertaining to, or situated near the occiput or the occipital bone. —n. **2.** any of several parts of the occiput, esp. the occipital bone. —**oc·cip′i·tal·ly,** adv.

occip′ital bone′, n. a curved, compound bone forming the back and part of the base of the skull.

occip′ital lobe′, n. the most posterior lobe of each cerebral hemisphere, behind the parietal and temporal lobes.

oc·ci·put (ok′sə put′, -pət), n., pl. **oc·ci·puts, oc·cip·i·ta** (ok sip′i tə). the back part of the head or skull.

Oc·ci·tan (ok′si tan′), n. the Romance speech of S France.

oc·clude (ə klōōd′), v., **-clud·ed, -clud·ing.** —v.t. **1.** to close, shut, or stop up (a passage, opening, etc.); block. **2.** to shut in, out, or off. **3.** (of certain metals and other solids) to incorporate (gases and other foreign substances), as by absorption or adsorption. —v.i. **4.** to become occluded. **5.** (of a tooth) to make contact with the surface of an opposing tooth when the jaws are closed. **6.** to form an occluded front. —**oc·clud′ent,** adj.

occlud′ed front′, n. a composite front formed when a cold front overtakes a warm front and forces it aloft; occlusion.

oc·clu·sion (ə klōō′zhən), n. **1.** the act of occluding or the state of being occluded. **2.** the fitting together of the teeth of the upper and lower jaws when the jaws are closed. **3.** Phonet. momentary complete closure at some area in the vocal tract, causing stoppage of the flow of air and accumulation of pressure. **4. a.** OCCLUDED FRONT. **b.** the formation of an occluded front. —**oc·clu′sive** (-siv), adj.

oc·cult (ə kult′, ok′ult), adj. **1.** of or pertaining to any system claiming use or knowledge of secret or supernatural powers or agencies. **2.** beyond ordinary knowledge or understanding. **3.** secret; disclosed or communicated only to the initiated. **4.** hidden from view. **5.** Med. not readily detectable, esp. at the place of origin: occult bleeding. —n. **6. the occult,** the supernatural, or supernatural agencies and affairs considered as a whole. —v.t. **7.** to block or shut off (an object) from view; hide. **8.** to hide (a celestial body) by occultation. —v.i. **9.** to become hidden or shut off from view. —**oc·cult′ly,** adv. —**oc·cult′ness,** n.

oc·cul·ta·tion (ok′ul tā′shən), n. **1.** the passage of one celestial body in front of another, thus hiding the other from view: applied esp. to the moon's coming between an observer and a star or planet. **2.** the act of blocking or hiding from view. **3.** the resulting hidden or concealed state.

oc·cult·ism (ə kul′tiz əm), n. **1.** belief in the existence of secret, mysterious, or supernatural agencies. **2.** the study or practice of occult arts. —**oc·cult′ist,** *n., adj.*

oc·cu·pan·cy (ok′yə pən sē), *n., pl.* **-cies. 1.** the act, state, or condition of being or becoming a tenant or of living in or taking up quarters or space in or on something. **2.** the possession or tenancy of a property. **3.** the act of taking possession, as of a property. **4.** the term during which one is an occupant. **5.** the condition of being occupied. **6.** the use to which property is put.

oc·cu·pant (ok′yə pənt), *n.* **1.** a person or group that occupies or has quarters or space in or on something: *the occupants of a taxicab.* **2.** a tenant of a house, estate, office, etc.; resident. **3.** an owner through occupancy.

oc·cu·pa·tion (ok′yə pā′shən), *n.* **1.** a person's usual or principal work, esp. in earning a living; vocation. **2.** any activity in which a person is engaged. **3.** possession, settlement, or use of land or property. **4.** the act of occupying. **5.** the state of being occupied. **6.** the seizure and control of an area by military forces, esp. foreign territory. **7.** the term of control of a territory by foreign military forces.

oc·cu·pa·tion·al (ok′yə pā′shə nl), *adj.* of, pertaining to, or caused by the conditions of a particular occupation: *an occupational disease.* —**oc′cu·pa′tion·al·ly,** *adv.*

occupa′tional ther′apy, therapy that utilizes useful and creative activities to facilitate psychological or physical rehabilitation. —**occupa′tional ther′apist,** *n.*

oc·cu·py (ok′yə pī′), *v.,* **-pied, -py·ing.** —*v.t.* **1.** to have, hold, or take as a separate space; possess, reside in or on, or claim: *The orchard occupies half the farm.* **2.** to be a resident or tenant of; dwell in. **3.** to fill up, employ, or engage: *to occupy time reading.* **4.** to engage or employ the mind, energy, or attention of: *We occupied the children with a game.* **5.** to take possession and control of (a place), as by military invasion. —*v.i.* **6.** to take or hold possession. —**oc′cu·pi·er,** *n.*

oc·cur (ə kûr′), *v.i.,* **-curred, -cur·ring. 1.** to happen; take place; come to pass. **2.** to be met with or found; present itself; appear: *Irregularities occur throughout the fabric.* **3.** to suggest itself in thought; come to mind (usu. fol. by *to*).

oc·cur·rence (ə kûr′əns, ə kur′-), *n.* **1.** the action, fact, or instance of occurring. **2.** something that happens; event; incident: *several unexpected occurrences.* —**oc·cur′rent,** *adj.*

o·cean (ō′shən), *n.* **1.** the vast body of salt water that covers almost three-fourths of the earth's surface. **2.** any of the geographical divisions of this body, commonly given as the Atlantic, Pacific, Indian, Arctic, and Antarctic oceans. **3.** a vast expanse or quantity: *an ocean of grass.* —**o′cean·like′,** *adj.*

o·cea·nar·i·um (ō′shə nâr′ē əm), *n., pl.* **-nar·i·ums, -nar·i·a** (-nâr′ē ə). a large saltwater aquarium for marine life.

o·cean·front (ō′shən frunt′), *n.* the land along the shore of an ocean.

o′cean·go′ing or **o′cean-go′ing,** *adj.* **1.** (of a ship) designed and equipped to travel on the open sea. **2.** noting or pertaining to sea transportation: *oceangoing traffic.*

O·ce·an·i·a (ō′shē an′ē ə, -ā′nē ə) also **O·ce·an·i·ca** (-an′i kə), *n.* the islands of the central and S Pacific, including Micronesia, Melanesia, Polynesia, and usu. Australasia. —**O′ce·an′i·an,** *adj.*

o·ce·an·ic (ō′shē an′ik), *adj.* **1.** of, living in, or produced by the ocean: *oceanic currents.* **2.** of or pertaining to the region of water lying above the bathyal, abyssal, and hadal zones of the sea bottom. —*n.* **3.** (*cap.*) (in most classifications) a branch of the Austronesian language family that includes all Austronesian languages spoken from New Guinea and the Caroline Islands E through Polynesia.

o·cea·nog·ra·phy (ō′shə nog′rə fē, ō′shē ə-), *n.* the branch of physical geography dealing with the ocean. —**o′cea·nog′ra·pher,** *n.* —**o′**

cea·no·graph′ic (-graf′ik), **o′cea·no·graph′i·cal,** *adj.* —**o′cea·no·graph′i·cal·ly,** *adv.*

o·cea·nol·o·gy (ō′shə nol′ə jē, ō′shē ə-), *n.* the science concerned with the practical application of oceanography. —**o′cea·no·log′ic, o′cea·no·log′i·cal,** *adj.* —**o′cea·nol′o·gist,** *n.*

o′cean perch′, *n.* REDFISH (def. 1).

O·cean·side (ō′shən sīd′), *n.* a city in SW California. 146,229.

o′cean sun′fish, *n.* a large sluggish mola, *Mola mola.*

O·ce·a·nus (ō sē′ə nəs), *n.* (in Greek myth) a Titan who rules over a great stream of water that encircles the earth.

oc·e·lot (os′ə lot′, ō′sə-), *n.* a spotted wildcat, *Felis pardalis,* ranging from Texas through South America.

o·cher or **o·chre** (ō′kər), *n.* **1.** any of a class of natural earths, mixtures of hydrated oxide of iron with various earthy materials, ranging in color from pale yellow to orange and red, and used as pigments. **2.** the color of this; pale to orangish or reddish yellow. —**o′cher·ous, o′cher·y,** *adj.*

Ochs (oks), *n.* **Adolph Simon,** 1858–1935, U.S. newspaper publisher.

o′clock (ə klok′), *adv.* of, by, or according to the clock (used in specifying the hour of the day): *11 o'clock.*

O′ Come′, All′ Ye′ Faith′ful, a Christmas hymn dating from the 18th century.

O′Con·nor (ō kon′ər), *n.* **1. Frank** (*Michael Donovan*), 1903–66, Irish writer. **2.** (**Mary**) **Flannery,** 1925–64, U.S. author. **3. Sandra Day,** born 1930, associate justice of the U.S. Supreme Court since 1981. **4. Thomas Power,** 1848–1929, Irish journalist and political leader.

oc·ta·gon (ok′tə gon′, -gən), *n.* a polygon having eight angles and eight sides. —**oc·tag′o·nal** (-tag′ə nl), *adj.* —**oc·tag′o·nal·ly,** *adv.*

oc·ta·he·dron (ok′tə hē′drən), *n., pl.* **-drons, -dra** (-drə). a solid figure having eight faces. —**oc′ta·he′dral,** *adj.*

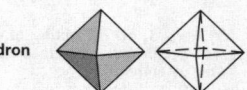

octahedron

oc·tane (ok′tān), *n.* any of 18 isomeric saturated hydrocarbons having the formula C_8H_{18}, some of which are obtained in the distillation of petroleum.

oc′tane num′ber, *n.* a designation of antiknock quality of gasoline, numerically equal to the percentage of isooctane by volume in a mixture of isooctane and normal heptane that matches the given gasoline in antiknock characteristics. Also called **oc′tane rat′ing.**

oc·tave (ok′tiv, -tāv), *n.* **1. a.** a tone on the eighth degree from a given musical tone. **b.** the interval encompassed by such tones. **c.** the harmonic combination of such tones. **d.** a series of tones, or of keys of an instrument, extending through this interval. **2.** a series or group of eight. **3. a.** a group of eight lines of verse, esp. the first eight lines of a sonnet in the Italian form. **b.** a stanza of eight lines. **4. a.** the eighth day from a religious festival, counting the festival as the first. **b.** the period of eight days beginning with such a day. —**oc·ta·val** (ok tā′vəl, ok′tə-), *adj.*

oc·ta·vo (ok tā′vō, -tä′-), *n., pl.* **-vos,** *adj.* —*n.* **1.** a book size of about 6 × 9 in. (16 × 23 cm), determined by printing on sheets folded to form 8 leaves or 16 pages. *Symbol:* 8vo, 8° **2.** a book of this size. —*adj.* **3.** in octavo.

oc·tet or **oc·tette** (ok tet′), *n.* **1.** a company of eight singers or musicians. **2.** a musical composition for eight voices or instruments. **3.** a group or stanza of eight lines, esp. the first eight lines in an Italian sonnet. **4.** any group of eight.

GREAT OCEANS AND SEAS OF THE WORLD

Ocean or Sea	Area		Location
	sq. mi.	sq. k	
Pacific Ocean	70,000,000	181,300,000	Bounded by N and S America, Asia, and Australia
Atlantic Ocean	31,530,000	81,663,000	Bounded by N and S America, Europe and Africa
Indian Ocean	28,357,000	73,444,630	S of Asia, E of Africa, and W of Australia
Arctic Ocean	5,540,000	14,350,000	N of North America, Asia, and the Arctic Circle
Mediterranean Sea	1,145,000	2,965,550	Between Europe, Africa, and Asia
Caribbean Sea	1,049,500	2,718,200	Between Central America, West Indies, and S America
South China Sea	895,000	2,318,050	Part of N Pacific, off coast of SE Asia
Bering Sea	878,000	2,274,000	Part of N Pacific, between N America and N Asia
Gulf of Mexico	700,000	1,813,000	Arm of N Atlantic, off SE coast of North America
Sea of Okhotsk	582,000	1,507,380	Arm of N Pacific, off E coast of Asia
East China Sea	480,000	1,243,200	Part of N Pacific, off E coast of Asia
Yellow Sea	480,000	1,243,200	Part of N Pacific, off E coast of Asia
Hudson Bay	400,000	1,036,000	N North America
Sea of Japan	389,000	1,008,000	Arm of N Pacific, between Asia and mainland and Japanese Isles
Andaman Sea	300,000	777,000	Part of Bay of Bengal (Indian Ocean), off S coast of Asia
North Sea	201,000	520,600	Arm of N Atlantic, off coast of NW Europe
Red Sea	170,000	440,300	Arm of Indian Ocean, between N Africa and Arabian Peninsula
Black Sea	164,000	424,760	SE Europe-SW Asia
Baltic Sea	160,000	414,000	N Europe
Persian Gulf	92,200	238,800	Between Iran and Arabian Peninsula
Gulf of St. Lawrence	92,000	238,280	Arm of N Atlantic, between mainland of SE Canada and Newfoundland
Gulf of California	62,600	162,100	Arm of N Pacific, between W coast of Mexico and peninsula of Lower California

oc·til·lion (ok til′yən), *n., pl.* **-lions,** (*as after a numeral*) **-lion,** *adj.* **—n. 1.** a cardinal number represented in the U.S. by 1 followed by 27 zeros, and in Great Britain by 1 followed by 48 zeros. **—adj. 2.** amounting to one octillion in number. **—oc·til′lionth,** *adj., n.*

Oc·to·ber (ok tō′bər), *n.* the tenth month of the year, containing 31 days. *Abbr.:* Oct.

Oc·to·ber·fest (ok tō′bər fest′), *n.* OKTOBERFEST.

Octo′ber surprise′, *n.* a surprising, last-minute announcement or development that may affect esp. a presidential election in November.

oc·to·de·cil·lion (ok′tō di sil′yən), *n., pl.* **-lions,** (*as after a numeral*) **-lion,** *adj.* **—n. 1.** a cardinal number represented in the U.S. by 1 followed by 57 zeros, and in Great Britain by 1 followed by 108 zeros. **—adj. 2.** amounting to one octodecillion in number. **—oc′to·de·cil′lionth,** *adj., n.*

oc·to·ge·nar·i·an (ok′tə jə när′ē ən), *n.* **1.** a person who is between 80 and 90 years old. **—adj. 2.** between 80 and 90 years old. **—oc′to·ge·nar′i·an·ism,** *n.*

oc·to·pus (ok′tə pəs), *n., pl.* **-pus·es, -pi** (-pī′). **1.** any octopod of the genus *Octopus,* having a soft, oval body and eight sucker-bearing arms, living mostly at the bottom of the sea. **2.** something likened to an octopus, as an organization that exercises far-reaching control. [< New Latin < Greek *oktṓpous* eight-footed]

octopus, *Octopus vulgaris,*
radial span about 10 ft. (3 m)

oc·u·lar (ok′yə lər), *adj.* **1.** of, pertaining to, or for the eyes. **2.** of the nature of an eye. **3.** performed or perceived by the eye or eyesight. **—n. 4.** EYEPIECE. **—oc′u·lar·ly,** *adv.*

odd (od), *adj.,* **-er, -est. 1.** differing in nature from what is usual or expected: *an odd creature; an odd choice.* **2.** peculiar or eccentric: *an odd person.* **3.** fantastic; bizarre: *an odd taste in clothing.* **4.** leaving a remainder of 1 when divided by 2, as a number (opposed to *even*): *3, 15, and 181 are odd numbers.* **5.** more or less, esp. a little more (used in combination with a round number): *I owe three hundred-odd dollars.* **6.** being part of a pair, set, or series of which the rest is lacking: *an odd glove.* **7.** remaining after all others are paired, grouped, or divided into equal numbers or parts: *Who gets the odd burger?* **8.** not forming part of any particular group, set, or class: *to pick up odd bits of information.* **9.** not regular or full-time; occasional: *odd jobs.* **10.** *Math.* (of a function) having a sign that changes when the sign of each independent variable is changed at the same time. **—odd′ly,** *adv.* **—odd′ness,** *n.*

odd·ball (od′bôl′), *Informal.* **—n. 1.** an eccentric or peculiar person or thing. **—adj. 2.** eccentric; atypical.

Odd′ Fel′low or **Odd′fel′low,** *n.* a member of a social and benevolent society that originated in England in the 18th century. **—Odd′fel′low·ship′,** *n.*

odd·i·ty (od′i tē), *n., pl.* **-ties. 1.** an odd or remarkably unusual person, thing, or event. **2.** an odd characteristic or trait; peculiarity. **3.** the quality of being odd; strangeness or eccentricity.

odd′ lot′, *n.* **1.** a quantity or amount less than the conventional unit of trading. **2.** (in a stock transaction) a quantity of stock less than 100 shares. **—odd′-lot′,** *adj* **—odd′-lot′ter,** *n.*

odd′ man′ out′, *n.* **1.** a way of selecting or eliminating a person from a group, esp. in a game, as by tossing coins. **2.** the person so selected or eliminated. **3.** OUTSIDER (def. 1).

odds (odz), *n.* (*usu. with a pl. v.*) **1.** the probability that something is so or is more likely to occur than something else: *The odds are that it will rain today.* **2.** this probability, expressed as a ratio: *The odds are two-to-one that it will rain today.* **3.** an equalizing allowance, as that given the weaker player in a contest; handicap. **4.** an advantage or degree of superiority favoring one of two contestants. **5.** an amount or degree by which one thing is better or worse than another. **—Idiom. 6. at odds,** at variance; in disagreement: *at odds over politics.* **7. by all odds,** in every respect; undoubtedly.

odds′ and ends′, *n.pl.* **1.** miscellaneous items, matters, etc. **2.** fragments; remnants; scraps; bits.

odds·mak·er (odz′mā′kər), *n.* a person who calculates or predicts the outcome of a contest, as in sports, and sets betting odds.

odds′-on′, *adj.* being the one more or most likely to attain or achieve something: *the odds-on favorite.*

ode (ōd), *n.* a lyric poem, typically with an irregular metrical form and expressing exalted or enthusiastic emotion. **—od′ic,** *adj.*

O·des·sa (ō des′ə), *n.* **1.** a seaport in S Ukraine, on the Black Sea. 1,115,000. **2.** a city in W Texas. 95,010.

O·din (ō′din), *n.* the principal god of pagan Scandinavia.

o·di·ous (ō′dē əs), *adj.* **1.** deserving or causing hatred; hateful; detestable. **2.** highly offensive; repugnant; disgusting. **—o′di·ous·ly,** *adv.* **—o′di·ous·ness,** *n.*

o·di·um (ō′dē əm), *n.* **1.** intense hatred or dislike. **2.** the reproach, dis-

credit, etc., attaching to some discreditable action. **3.** the state or quality of being hated.

o·dom·e·ter (ō dom′i tər), *n.* an instrument for measuring distance traveled, as by an automobile. **—o·do·met·ri·cal** (ō′də me′tri kəl), *adj.* **—o·dom′e·try,** *n.*

o·dor (ō′dər), *n.* **1.** the property of a substance that activates the sense of smell: *a beautiful flower with an unpleasant odor.* **2.** a sensation perceived by the sense of smell; scent. **3.** a quality or property characteristic or suggestive of something: *an odor of suspicion.* **4.** repute: *in bad odor with one's creditors.* Also, *esp. Brit.,* **odour.** **—o′dor·less,** *adj.*

o·dor·if·er·ous (ō′də rif′ər əs), *adj.* yielding an odor, esp. one that is pungent or unpleasant; odorous. **—o′dor·if·er·ous·ly,** *adv.* **—o′dor·if′er·ous·ness,** *n.*

o·dor·ous (ō′dər əs), *adj.* ODORIFEROUS. **—o′dor·ous·ly,** *adv.* **—o′dor·ous·ness,** *n.*

O·dys·se·us (ō dis′ē əs, ō dis′yōōs), *n.* a legendary king of Ithaca, one of the heroes of the *Iliad* and protagonist of the *Odyssey.* Latin, **Ulysses.**

Od·ys·sey (od′ə sē), *n., pl.* **-seys. 1.** (*italics*) an epic poem attributed to Homer, describing Odysseus's adventures in his ten-year attempt to return home to Ithaca after the Trojan War. **2.** (*often l.c.*) any long journey, esp. when filled with adventure, hardships, etc. **—Od′ys·se′an,** *adj.*

OE or **O.E.,** Old English.

Oed·i·pus (ed′ə pəs, ē′də-), *n.* a legendary king of Thebes, the son of Laius and Jocasta, who fulfilled a prophecy made at his birth by unwittingly killing his father and marrying his mother.

Oed′ipus com′plex, *n. Psychoanal.* libidinous feelings toward the parent of the opposite sex, often also involving rivalry with the parent of the same sex: esp. applied to males and considered normal in young children. Compare ELECTRA COMPLEX.

oe·nol·o·gy or **e·nol·o·gy** (ē nol′ə jē), *n.* the science of winemaking. Compare VINICULTURE. **—oe·no·log·i·cal** (ēn′l oj′i kəl), *adj.* **—oe·nol′o·gist,** *n.*

oe·no·phile (ē′nə fīl′), *n.* one who loves or is a connoisseur of wine.

o′er (ôr, ōr), *prep., adv. Literary.* OVER.

oeu·vre (Fr. œ′vʀᵊ), *n., pl.* **oeu·vres** (Fr. œ′vʀᵊ). **1.** the works of a writer, painter, or the like, taken as a whole. **2.** any one of such works.

of¹ (uv, ov; *unstressed* əv *or, esp. before consonants,* ə), *prep.* **1.** (used to indicate distance or direction from, separation, deprivation, etc.): *within a mile of the house; robbed of one's money.* **2.** (used to indicate derivation or origin): *the songs of Gershwin.* **3.** (used to indicate cause or reason): *dead of hunger.* **4.** (used to indicate material, substance, or contents): *a dress of silk; a book of poems.* **5.** (used to indicate apposition or identity): *a genius of a pilot.* **6.** (used to indicate possession or association): *property of the church.* **7.** (used to indicate inclusion in a number, class, or whole): *one of us.* **8.** (used to indicate the object of the action noted by the preceding noun, verb, or adjective): *the ringing of bells; to write of home; tired of working.* **9.** (used to indicate qualities or attributes): *a woman of courage.* **10.** before the hour of; until: *ten minutes of one.* **11.** on the part of: *It was nice of you to come.* **12.** set aside for or devoted to: *a minute of prayer.* **—Usage.** OF with an adjective after the adverb *how* or *too* is largely characteristic of informal speech: *How long of a drive will it be? It's too hot of a day for tennis.*

of² (əv), *auxiliary v. Nonstandard.* have: *He should of asked me.* Compare A⁴.

off (ôf, of), *adv.* **1.** so as to be no longer supported or attached: *This button is about to come off.* **2.** so as to be no longer covering or enclosing: *Pull the wrapping off.* **3.** away from a place: *to run off; to loaf off toward the west.* **4.** away from a path, course, etc.: *The road branches off to Grove City.* **5.** so as to be away or on one's way: *to start off early.* **6.** away from what is considered normal, standard, or the like: *to go off on a tangent.* **7.** from a charge or price: *Take 10 percent off for cash.* **8.** at a distance in space or future time: *Summer is only a week off.* **9.** out of operation: *Turn the lights off.* **10.** into operation or action: *The alarm goes off at noon.* **11.** in absence from work, service, etc.: *to get two days off at Christmas.* **12.** completely; utterly: *to cut off communications.* **13.** to fulfillment, or into execution or effect: *The contest went off as planned.* **14.** so as to be delineated, divided, or apportioned: *Mark it off into equal parts.* **15.** *Naut.* away from the land, a ship, the wind, etc. **—prep. 16.** so as no longer to be supported by, resting on, etc.: *Wipe the dirt off your shoes.* **17.** deviating from: *to be off course.* **18.** below the usual level or standard: *20 percent off the marked price.* **19.** away, disengaged, or resting from: *to be off duty on Tuesdays.* **20.** refraining or abstaining from: *He's off gambling.* **21.** located apart from: *a village off the main road.* **22.** leading away from: *an alley off 12th Street.* **23.** *Informal.* from (a specified source): *I bought it off a street vendor.* **24.** from or of, indicating material or component parts: *to lunch off fruit.* **25.** by means of: *living off his parents.* **26.** *Naut.* at some distance to seaward of: *off Cape Hatteras.* **—adj. 27.** in error; wrong: *You are off on that point.* **28.** less than normal or sane: *a little off, but harmless.* **29.** not up to the usual or expected standard; comparatively weak or inferior: *a play with off moments.* **30.** affected by spoilage; bad: *The cream is a bit off.* **31.** no longer in effect, in operation, or in process: *The agreement is off.* **32.** in a specified state, circumstance, etc.: *to be badly off for money.* **33.** free from work or duty: *a pastime for one's off hours.* **34.** of less than the ordinary activity; slack: *an off season in the tourist trade.* **35.** unlikely; remote: *on the off chance that we'd find her at home.* **36.** more distant; farther: *the off side of a wall.*

37. (of a vehicle, single animal, or pair of animals hitched side by side) designating the right as seen from the rider's or driver's viewpoint (opposed to *near*): *the off side; the off horse.* **38.** starting on one's way; leaving: *I'm off to Europe on Monday.* **39.** lower in price or value; down: *Stock prices were off this morning.* **40.** *Naut.* noting one of two like things that is the farther from the shore; seaward: *the off side of the ship.* —*n.* **41.** the state or fact of being off. —***Idiom.*** **42. off and on,** with intervals between; intermittently: *to work off and on.* Also, **on and off. 43. off of,** off: *Take your feet off of the table!* **44. off with, a.** take away; remove: *Off with those muddy boots!* **b.** cut off: *Off with his head!*

of•fal (ô′fəl, of′əl), *n.* **1.** waste parts, esp. the viscera or inedible remains of a butchered animal. **2.** refuse or rubbish; garbage.

off•beat (*adj.* ôf′bēt′, of′-; *n.* -bēt′), *adj.* **1.** differing from the usual or expected; unconventional: *an offbeat comedian.* —*n.* **2.** an unaccented beat of a measure in music.

off′ (or **Off′**) **Broad′way,** *n.* professional drama produced in New York City in small theaters usu. outside the Broadway area. —**off′-Broad′way,** *adj., adv.*

off′-cam′era, *adj.* **1.** OFFSCREEN. **2.** not intended to be filmed or recorded by a camera, esp. a TV camera: *off-camera remarks.* —*adv.* **3.** out of the range of the camera. **4.** OFFSCREEN (def. 3).

off′-cen′ter or **off′-cen′tered,** *adj.* **1.** not centered; diverging from the exact center. **2.** out of balance or alignment.

off′-col′or, *adj.* **1.** not having the usual or standard color. **2.** of doubtful propriety or taste; risqué. **3.** not in one's usual health. Also, **off′-col′ored** (for defs. 1, 2).

off′-du′ty, *adj.* **1.** not engaged in the performance of one's usual work: *an off-duty police officer.* **2.** pertaining to or during a period when a person is not at work.

of•fend (ə fend′), *v.t.* **1.** to irritate, annoy, or anger; cause resentful displeasure in; insult. **2.** to affect (the sense, taste, etc.) disagreeably. —*v.i.* **3.** to cause resentful displeasure; irritate. —**of•fend′er,** *n.*

of•fense or **of•fence** (ə fens′ *or, for 8,* ô′fens, of′ens), *n.* **1.** a violation or breaking of a social or moral rule; transgression; sin. **2.** a transgression of the law; misdemeanor. **3.** something that offends or displeases. **4.** the act of offending or displeasing. **5.** the feeling of resentment caused: *to give offense.* **6.** aggression or assault: *weapons of offense.* **7.** a person, army, etc., that is attacking. **8. a.** the team unit responsible for scoring in a game. **b.** a pattern or style of scoring attack. **c.** offensive effectiveness; ability to score.

of•fen•sive (ə fen′siv *or, for 4, 5,* ô′fen-, of′en-), *adj.* **1.** causing resentful displeasure; highly irritating or annoying. **2.** unpleasant or disagreeable to the sense; disgusting. **3.** repugnant to the moral sense, good taste, or the like; repulsive. **4.** pertaining to offense or attack. **5.** characterized by attack; aggressive: *offensive warfare.* —*n.* **6.** the position or attitude of aggression or attack: *to take the offensive.* **7.** an aggressive movement or attack. —**of•fen′sive•ly,** *adv.* —**of•fen′sive•ness,** *n.*

of•fer (ô′fər, of′ər), *v.t.* **1.** to present for acceptance or rejection: *to offer a drink.* **2.** to propose or put forward for consideration: *to offer a suggestion.* **3.** to show willingness (to do something): *I offered to go first.* **4.** to give, make, or promise: *She offered no response.* **5.** to present solemnly as an act of worship. **6.** to present for sale. **7.** to tender or bid as a price. **8.** to put forth; exert: *to offer resistance.* **9.** to present or volunteer (oneself) as a spouse. —*v.i.* **10.** to present itself; occur. **11.** to make a proposal or suggestion. —*n.* **12.** an act or instance of offering. **13.** a proposal or bid to give or pay something. **14.** a proposal of marriage. —**of′fer•er, of′fer•or,** *n.*

of•fer•ing (ô′fər ing, of′ər-), *n.* **1.** something offered in worship or devotion. **2.** a contribution given to or through the church. **3.** anything offered as a gift. **4.** something presented for inspection or sale.

of•fer•to•ry (ô′fər tôr′ē, -tōr′ē, of′ər-), *n., pl.* **-ries. 1.** (*sometimes cap.*) the offering to God of the unconsecrated elements in a Eucharistic service. **2. a.** the verses, anthem, or music accompanying the offerings made at a religious service. **b.** that part of a service at which offerings are made. **c.** the offerings themselves. —**of′fer•to′ri•al,** *adj.*

off•hand (ôf′hand′, of′-), *adv.* **1.** cavalierly, curtly, or brusquely. **2.** without previous thought or preparation; extempore. —*adj.* **3.** informal, casual, curt, or brusque. **4.** Also, **off′hand′ed.** done or made offhand. —**off′hand′ed•ly,** *adv.* —**off′hand′ed•ness,** *n.*

off′-hour′, *n.* **1.** an hour or other period when a person is not at a job. **2.** a period outside of rush hours or greatest activity. —*adj.* **3.** of, pertaining to, or during an off-hour.

of•fice (ô′fis, of′is), *n.* **1.** a place where business is conducted. **2.** a room assigned to a specific person or a group of persons in such a place. **3.** a business or professional organization: *working in an architect's office.* **4.** the staff that works in a place of business. **5.** a position of duty, trust, or authority: *the office of president.* **6.** employment or position as an official: *to seek office.* **7.** the duty, function, or part of a particular person or agency; responsibility; charge. **8.** (*usu. cap.*) a government agency, or a division of a government department: *Office of Community Services.* **9.** (*usu. cap.*) a department of the national government in Great Britain: *the Foreign Office.* **10.** Often, **offices.** something, whether good or bad, done or said for or to another: *the good offices of a friend.* **11. a.** the prescribed order or form for a service of the church or for devotional use. **b.** the services so prescribed. **c.** Also called **divine office.** the prayers, readings from Scripture, and psalms that must be recited every day by all who are in major orders. **d.** a ceremony or rite, esp. for the dead. **12. offices,** *Chiefly Brit.* the parts of a house, as the kitchen, pantry, or laundry, devoted mainly to household work.

of′fice-block′ bal′lot, *n.* a ballot on which the candidates are listed alphabetically, with or without their party designations, in columns under the office for which they were nominated. Compare INDIANA BALLOT, MASSACHUSETTS BALLOT.

of′fice boy′, *n.* a person, traditionally a boy, employed in an office to run errands, do odd jobs, etc.

of•fice•hold•er (ô′fis hōl′dər, of′is-), *n.* a person filling a governmental position; public official.

of′fice park′, *n.* a commercial complex consisting of an office building set in parklike surroundings.

of•fi•cer (ô′fə sər, of′ə-), *n.* **1.** a person who holds a position of rank or authority in the armed services, esp. one holding a commission. **2.** a member of a police department or a constable. **3.** a person appointed or elected to some position of responsibility or authority in some organization. **4.** a person licensed to take full or partial responsibility for the operation of a ship. **5.** (in some honorary orders) a member of any rank except the lowest. —*v.t.* **6.** to furnish with officers. **7.** to direct, conduct, or manage. —**of′fi•ce′ri•al** (-sēr′ē əl), *adj.*

of•fi•cial (ə fish′əl), *n.* **1.** a person appointed or elected to an office or charged with certain duties. —*adj.* **2.** of or pertaining to an office or position of duty, trust, or authority: *official powers.* **3.** appointed, authorized, or approved by a government or organization. —**of•fi′cial•ly,** *adv.*

of•fi•cial•dom (ə fish′əl dəm), *n.* the domain or class of officials.

of•fi•cial•ese (ə fish′ə lēz′, -lēs′), *n.* a style of language used in some official statements, often criticized for its use of polysyllabic jargon and obscure, pretentiously wordy phrasing.

offi′cial fam′ily, *n.* the executives or officials chiefly responsible for the operation of an organization or government.

of•fi•ci•ate (ə fish′ē āt′), *v.i.,* **-at•ed, -at•ing. 1.** to perform the duties or function of some office or position. **2.** to perform the office of a cleric, as at a divine service. **3.** to serve as referee, umpire, etc., in a contest or game. —**of•fi′ci•a′tion,** *n.* —**of•fi′ci•a′tor,** *n.*

of•fi•cious (ə fish′əs), *adj.* **1.** objectionably aggressive in offering unrequested and unwanted help or advice; meddlesome. **2.** marked by or proceeding from such forwardness. —**of•fi′cious•ly,** *adv.* —**of•fi′cious•ness,** *n.*

off•ing (ô′fing, of′ing), *n.* **1.** the more distant part of the sea seen from the shore. —***Idiom.*** **2. in the offing, a.** at a distance but within sight. **b.** in the projected future; likely to happen.

off′-key′, *adj.* **1.** deviating from the correct tone or pitch; out of tune. **2.** somewhat irregular, abnormal, or incongruous.

off′-lim′its, *adj.* forbidden to be patronized, frequented, used, etc., by certain persons, as soldiers.

off′-line′ or **off′line′,** *adj.* operating independently of, or disconnected from, an associated computer. Compare ON-LINE.

off′-load′ or **off′load′,** *v.t., v.i.* UNLOAD. —**off′-load′er,** *n.*

off′ off′ (or **Off′ Off′**) **Broad′way,** *n.* experimental or avant-garde drama produced in New York City, in small theaters, halls, churches, etc. —**off′-off′-Broad′way,** *adj., adv.*

off′-peak′, *adj.* **1.** of, pertaining to, or during a period of less than maximum frequency, demand, intensity, or use. **2.** lower than the maximum.

off•print (ôf′print′, of′-), *n.* a reprint of an article that orig. appeared as part of a larger publication.

off′-put′ting, *adj.* provoking uneasiness, dislike, annoyance, or repugnance: *off-putting remarks.*

off′-road′, *adj.* designed, built, or used for traveling off public roads, esp. on unpaved roads or rough terrain.

off•screen (ôf′skrēn′, of′-), *adj.* **1.** occurring as part of a motion picture or a television program but not seen or embodied by the camera; off-camera. **2.** in private life apart from one's professional image or work as a film or TV performer. —*adv.* **3.** in private life. **4.** OFF-CAMERA (def. 3).

off′-sea′son, *n.* **1.** a time of year other than the regular or busiest one for a specific activity. —*adj.* **2.** of, pertaining to, or during the off-season. —*adv.* **3.** in or during the off-season.

off•set (*n., adj.* ôf′set′, of′-; *v.* ôf′set′, of′-), *n., adj., v.,* **-set, -set•ting.** —*n.* **1.** something that compensates for something else. **2.** the start, beginning, or outset. **3.** a short lateral shoot by which certain plants are propagated. **4.** an offshoot or branch. **5. a.** a process in which a lithographic stone or metal or paper plate is used to make an inked impression on a rubber blanket that transfers it to the paper being printed. **b.** the impression itself. **6.** *Geol.* (in faults) the magnitude of displacement between two previously aligned bodies. **7.** a flat or sloping projecting ledge on a wall, buttress, or the like, produced by a reduction in thickness above; setoff. **8. a.** a short distance measured perpendicularly from a main survey line. **b.** Also called **off′set line′.** a line a short distance from and parallel to a main survey line. —*adj.* **9.** of, noting, or pertaining to an offset. **10.** pertaining to, printed by, or suitable for printing by offset. **11.** placed away from a center line; off-center. **12.** placed at an angle to something. —*v.t.* **13.** to compensate for: *The gains offset the losses.* **14.** to juxtapose with something else, as for comparison. **15.** *Print.* **a.** to make an offset of. **b.** to print by the process of offset lithography. **16.** to build (a wall) with an offset. —*v.i.* **17.** to project as an offset or branch. **18.** *Print.* to make an offset.

off•shoot (ôf′shoōt′, of′-), *n.* **1.** a branch or lateral shoot from a main stem, as of a plant. **2.** anything conceived of as springing or proceeding from a main stock.

off•shore (ôf′shôr′, -shōr′, of′-), *adv.* **1.** off or away from the shore. **2.** at a distance from the shore, on or in a body of water. **3.** in a foreign country. —*adj.* **4.** moving or tending away from the shore toward or into a body of water: *an offshore wind.* **5.** located or operating on or in a body of water, at some distance from the shore. **6.** registered, located, conducted, or operated in a foreign country.

off•side (ôf′sīd′, of′-), *adj.*, *adv. Sports.* illegally beyond a prescribed line or area or in advance of the ball or puck at the beginning of or during play.

off•spring (ôf′spring′, of′-), *n.*, *pl.* **-spring, -springs. 1.** children or young of a particular parent or progenitor; descendants; progeny. **2.** a child or animal in relation to its parent or parents. **3.** the product or result of something.

off•stage (ôf′stāj′, of′-), *adv.* **1.** off the stage or in the wings; away from the view of the audience (opposed to *onstage*). **2.** in private life. —*adj.* **3.** not in view of the audience; backstage, in the wings, etc. **4.** withheld from public view or attention; private.

off′-the-books′, *adj.* not recorded in account books or not reported as taxable income: *off-the-books payments.*

off′-the-cuff′, *adj.* with little or no preparation; impromptu.

off′-the-rack′, *adj.* ready-made: *off-the-rack clothes.*

off′-the-rec′ord, *adj.* **1.** not for publication; not to be quoted. **2.** confidential: *off-the-record information.*

off′-the-shelf′, *adj.* **1.** readily available from merchandise in stock. **2.** made according to a standardized format; ready-made.

off′-the-wall′, *adj. Informal.* markedly unconventional; bizarre; odd-ball.

off•track (ôf′trak′, of′-), *adj.* occurring or carried on away from a race-track: *offtrack betting.*

off′-white′, *adj.* **1.** white mixed with a small amount of gray, yellow, or other light color. —*n.* **2.** an off-white color.

off′ year′, *n.* **1.** a year without a major, esp. presidential, election. **2.** a year marked by reduced or inferior production or activity in a particular field, as a business. —**off′-year′,** *adj.*

O′ for a Clos′er Walk′ with God′, a Christian hymn (1772) with words by William Cowper.

oft (ôft, oft), *adv. Literary.* OFTEN.

of•ten (ô′fən, of′ən; ôf′tən, of′-), *adv.* **1.** many times; frequently. **2.** in many cases.

Of′ Thee′ I′ Sing′, a musical (1931) with music by George and Ira Gershwin.

Og (og), *n.* the king of Bashan, defeated by the Israelites before they crossed the Jordan. Deut. 3:1-4.

og•ham or **og•am** (og′əm, ô′gəm), *n.* **1.** an alphabetical script used for inscriptions in an archaic form of Irish from about the 5th to the 10th century. **2.** any of the 20 characters of this script, each consisting of one or more strokes for consonants and of notches for vowels cut across or upon a central line on a stone or piece of wood.

o•gle (ō′gəl), *v.*, **o•gled, o•gling.** —*v.t.* **1.** to look at amorously, flirtatiously, or impertinently. **2.** to look or stare at. —*v.i.* **3.** to look amorously, flirtatiously, or impertinently. **4.** to look or stare. —*n.* **5.** an amorous, flirtatious, or impertinent look. —**o′gler,** *n.*

O•gle•thorpe (ō′gəl thôrp′), *n.* **James Edward,** 1696–1785, British general: founder of the colony of Georgia.

O′ God′ Our′ Help′ in A′ges Past′, a Christian hymn (1719) with words by Isaac Watts: based on Psalm 90.

o•gre (ō′gər), *n.* **1.** a monster in fairy tales, usu. represented as a hideous giant who feeds on human flesh. **2.** a monstrously ugly, cruel, or barbarous person. —**o′gre•ish, o•grish** (ō′grish), *adj.* —**o′gre•ish•ly, o′grish•ly,** *adv.*

o•gress (ō′gris), *n.* **1.** a female ogre. **2.** a monstrously ugly, cruel, or barbarous woman.

oh (ō), *interj.*, *n.*, *pl.* **oh's, ohs,** *v.*, **ohed, oh•ing.** —*interj.* **1.** (used as an exclamation of surprise, pain, disapprobation, sympathy, agreement, etc.) **2.** (used in direct address to attract the attention of the person spoken to.) —*n.* **3.** the exclamation "oh." —*v.i.* **4.** to utter or exclaim "oh."

OH, Ohio.

O′ Hap′py Day′, a Christian hymn (1755) with words by Philip Doddridge and music by Edward F. Rimbault: often sung at baptisms.

O′Har•a (ō hâr′ə, ō har′ə), *n.* **John (Henry),** 1905–70, U.S. journalist, novelist, short-story writer, and scenarist.

O. Hen•ry (ō hen′rē), *n.* pen name of William S. PORTER.

Oh′ Free′dom, a traditional American spiritual.

O•hi•o (ō hī′ō), *n.* **1.** a state in the NE central United States. 11,172,782; 41,222 sq. mi. (106,765 sq. km). *Cap.:* Columbus. *Abbr.:* OH **2.** a river formed by the confluence of the Allegheny and Monongahela rivers, flowing SW from Pittsburgh, Pa., to the Mississippi in S Illinois. 981 mi. (1580 km) long. —**O•hi′o•an,** *adj., n.*

Ohi′o buck′eye, *n.* a horse chestnut tree, *Aesculus glabra,* native to the U.S., having palmate leaves and bell-shaped greenish-yellow flowers in upright clusters: the state tree of Ohio.

ohm (ōm), *n.* the SI unit of electrical resistance, equal to the resistance between two points when a constant potential difference applied be-

tween the points produces a current of 1 ampere. —**ohm′ic,** *adj.* —**ohm′i•cal•ly,** *adv.*

ohm•age (ō′mij), *n.* electric resistance expressed in ohms.

Oh′, Mar′y, Don′t′ You′ Weep′, a traditional American spiritual.

-oholic, var. of -AHOLIC: *cokeoholic.*

Oh!′ Susan′nah, a song (1848) by Stephen Foster.

oi (oi), *interj.* OY.

-oid, a suffix meaning "resembling," "like," used in the formation of adjectives and nouns, and often implying an incomplete or imperfect resemblance to what is indicated by the preceding element: *alkaloid; humanoid; planetoid.*

oil (oil), *n.* **1.** any of a large class of substances typically unctuous, viscous, combustible, liquid at ordinary temperatures, and soluble in ether or alcohol but not in water. **2.** a substance of this or similar consistency. **3.** refined or crude petroleum. **4. a.** OIL COLOR. **b.** OIL PAINTING. **5.** unctuous hypocrisy; flattery. —*v.t.* **6.** to smear, lubricate, or supply with oil. **7.** to bribe. **8.** pertaining to or resembling oil. **9.** using oil, esp. as a fuel. **10.** concerned with the production or use of oil. **11.** made with oil. **12.** obtained from oil. —*Idiom.* **13.** pour oil on troubled waters, to attempt to calm a difficult or tense situation. **14.** strike oil, a. to discover petroleum by drilling an oil well. b. to have good luck, esp. financially. —*Proverb.* **15.** Oil and water don't mix, very different qualities or things are incompatible.

oil′ bee′tle, *n.* any of several beetles of the genus *Meloe* that exude oily fluid from their leg joints when disturbed.

oil•bird (oil′bûrd′), *n.* a nocturnal cave-nesting bird of tropical South America, *Steatornis caripensis,* akin to the goatsuckers: the rendered fat of its young has been used as a cooking and lighting oil.

oil•cloth (oil′klôth′, -kloth′), *n.* a cotton fabric made waterproof by treatment with oil and pigment, for use as tablecloths, shelf coverings, and the like.

oil′ col′or, *n.* a paint made by grinding a pigment in oil, usu. linseed oil.

oil′ field′, *n.* an area having large deposits of petroleum.

oil•man (oil′man′, -mən), *n.*, *pl.* **-men** (-men′, -mən). **1.** a person in the petroleum industry. **2.** a person who retails or delivers fuel oil.

oil′ of vit′riol, *n.* SULFURIC ACID. [1570–80]

oil′ paint′, *n.* **1.** OIL COLOR. **2.** a commercial paint in which a drying oil is the vehicle.

oil′ paint′ing, *n.* **1.** the art or technique of painting with oil colors. **2.** a painting executed in oil colors. —**oil′ paint′er,** *n.*

oil′ pan′, *n.* the bottom part of the crankcase of an internal-combustion engine, in which the oil used to lubricate the engine accumulates.

oil•skin (oil′skin′), *n.* **1.** a cotton fabric made waterproof by treatment with oil and used for rain gear and fishermen's clothing. **2.** Often, **oilskins,** a garment made of this, as a long, full raincoat.

oil′ slick′, *n.* a smooth area on the surface of water caused by the presence of oil.

oil•stone (oil′stōn′), *n.* a block of fine-grained stone, usu. oiled, for putting the final edge on certain cutting tools by abrasion.

oil′ well′, *n.* a well drilled to obtain petroleum.

oil•y (oi′lē), *adj.*, **oil•i•er, oil•i•est. 1.** smeared or covered with oil; greasy. **2.** of the nature of, consisting of, or resembling oil. **3.** of or pertaining to oil. **4.** full of or containing oil. **5.** smooth or unctuous, as in manner or speech. —**oil′i•ly,** *adv.* —**oil′i•ness,** *n.*

oink (oingk), *n.* **1.** the grunting sound made by a hog. —*v.i.* **2.** to utter such a sound.

oint•ment (oint′mənt), *n.* a soft, unctuous preparation, often medicated, for application to the skin; unguent; salve.

OK, Oklahoma.

OK or **O.K.** or **o•kay** (ō′kā′, ō′kā′, ō′kā′), *adj.*, *adv.*, *n.*, *pl.* **OKs** or **OK's** or **O.K.'s** or **o•kays,** *v.*, **OK'd** or **O.K.'ed** or **o•kayed, OK′•ing** or **O.K.′•ing** or **o•kay•ing.** —*adj.* **1.** all right; satisfactory: *Is everything OK?* **2.** correct, permissible, or acceptable. **3.** feeling well. **4.** safe; sound. **5.** estimable, likable, or dependable. —*adv.* **7.** all right; well enough; successfully; fine: *He sings OK.* **8.** (used to request or express agreement, acknowledgment, approval, etc.) —*n.* **9.** an approval, agreement, or endorsement. —*v.t.* **10.** to endorse or indicate approval of; authorize. [initials of *oll korrect,* facetious spelling of *all correct*]

o•ka•pi (ō kä′pē), *n.*, *pl.* **-pis,** (*esp. collectively*) **-pi.** a central African ruminant, *Okapia johnstoni,* of the same family as the giraffe, but smaller and with a much shorter neck.

o•kay (ō′kā′, ō′kā′, ō′kā′), *adj.*, *adv.*, *n.*, *pl.* **o•kays,** *v.t.*, **o•kayed, o•kay•ing.** See OK.

O′Keefe (ō kēf′), *n.* **Georgia,** 1887–1986, U.S. painter.

o•key-doke (ō′kē dōk′) also **o•key-do•key** (-dō′kē), *adj., adv. Informal.* OK.

O•ki•na•wa (ō′kə nou′wə, -nä′wə), *n.* the largest of the Ryukyu Islands: occupied by U.S. 1945–72. 544 sq. mi. (1409 sq. km). *Cap.:* Naha. —**O•ki•na′wan,** *adj., n.*

O•kla•ho•ma (ō′klə hō′mə), *n.* a state in the S central United States. 3,300,902; 69,919 sq. mi. (181,090 sq. km). *Cap.:* Oklahoma City. *Abbr.:* OK, Okla. —**O•kla•ho′man,** *adj., n.*

O•kla•ho•ma! (ō′klə hō′mə), a Broadway musical (1943) with words and music by Richard Rodgers and Oscar Hammerstein.

O·klaho'ma Cit'y, *n.* the capital of Oklahoma, in the central part. 463,201.

o·kra (ō'krə), *n., pl.* **o·kras. 1.** a shrub, *Abelmoschus esculentus,* of the mallow family, bearing beaked pods. **2.** the pods, used in soups, stews, etc., or eaten as a vegetable. Also called **gumbo.**

Ok·to·ber·fest or **Oc·to·ber·fest** (ok tō'bər fest'), *n.* **1.** a traditional beer festival held each October in Munich, Germany. **2.** any similar festival held in the autumn.

-ola, 1. a formative of no precise significance found in a variety of commercial coinages (*Crayola; granola; Victrola*) and jocular variations of words (*crapola*). **2.** a suffix extracted from PAYOLA, used in coinages that have the general sense "covert payments, esp. to an entertainment figure in return for promoting a product, making an appearance, etc." (*playola; plugola*).

O·laf or **O·lav** (ō'läf, ō'ləf), *n.* **1.** Olaf (or Olav) I (*Olaf Tryggvason*), A.D. 969–1000, king of Norway 995–1000. **2.** Olaf (or Olav) II, Saint (*Olaf Haraldsson*), A.D. 995–1030, king of Norway 1016–29: patron saint of Norway. **3.** Olaf (or Olav) V, born 1903, king of Norway since 1957.

old (ōld), *adj.,* **old·er, old·est** or **eld·er, eld·est,** *n.* —*adj.* **1.** having lived or existed for a comparatively long time; far advanced in years or life: *an old man; an old building.* **2.** of or pertaining to the latter part of life or existence: *old age.* **3.** having lived or existed for a specified time: *a six-month-old company.* **4.** having lived or existed as specified with relation to younger or newer ones: *our oldest child.* **5.** deteriorated through age or long use; worn or dilapidated: *old clothes.* **6.** of long standing; having been such for a comparatively long time: *an old friend.* **7.** no longer in general use: *This typewriter is an old model.* **8.** having been replaced or supplanted by something newer or more recent: *We sold our old house.* **9.** long known or in use: *the same old excuse.* **10.** belonging to the past: *the good old days.* **11.** of or originating at an earlier period or date: *old maps.* **12.** having been in existence since the distant past: *an old family.* **13.** prehistoric; ancient: *old civilizations.* **14.** (*cap.*) (of a language) in its oldest known period, as attested by the earliest written records: *Old Czech.* **15.** experienced: *an old sailor.* **16.** sedate, sensible, mature, or wise: *a child old beyond her years.* **17.** as if or appearing to be far advanced in years: *Worry had made him old.* **18.** (of colors) dull, faded, or subdued. **19.** (of land forms) far advanced in reduction by erosion or the like. **20.** (used to indicate affection, familiarity, disparagement, or a personalization): *good old Bob; that dirty old thing.* **21.** (used as an intensive): *a high old time.* —*n.* **22.** the old, the persons collectively. **23.** a person or animal of a specified age or age group (used in combination): *a program for six-year-olds.* **24.** old or former time, often time long past: *days of old.* —**old'ness,** *n.*

old'-boy' net'work (ōld'boi'), *n.* a network through which men of the same profession, social class, school, affiliation, or the like assist one another in business, politics, etc.

Old' Cath'olic, 1. a member of any of several European churches professing to be truly Catholic but rejecting certain modern Roman Catholic doctrines, dogmas, and practices, esp. the dogma of papal infallibility. **2.** a member of any of several minor churches, esp. in the U.S., differing from the Roman Catholic Church chiefly in their rejection of the ecclesiastical authority of the Roman Catholic hierarchy.

old' coun'try, *n.* the original home country of an immigrant or a person's ancestors, usu. a European country.

old·en (ōl'dən), *adj.* of or pertaining to the distant past or bygone times; ancient; old.

Old' Eng'lish, *n.* **1.** the English language before c1150. *Abbr.*: OE, O.E. **2.** *Print.* a style of black letter.

Old' Eng'lish sheep'dog, *n.* one of an English breed of large, stocky sheepdogs having a bobbed tail and a long, shaggy gray or blue-gray and white coat that hangs over the eyes.

Old' Faith'ful, *n.* one of the best known geysers of Yellowstone National Park. [so named because of the longevity and regularity of its activity]

old'-fash'ioned, *adj.* **1.** of a kind that is no longer in style: *an old-fashioned bathing suit.* **2.** favored or prevalent in former times: *old-fashioned ideas.* **3.** having the conservative behavior, ways, ideas, or tastes of earlier times. —**old'-fash'ioned·ness,** *n.*

old' fo'gy (or **fo'gey**), *n.* a person excessively old-fashioned in attitude, ideas, manners, etc. —**old'-fo'gy·ish,** *adj.*

old'-girl' net'work, *n.* an association among women that is comparable to or modeled on an old-boy network.

Old' Glo'ry, *n.* STARS AND STRIPES.

Old' Guard', *n.* **1.** the imperial guard created in 1804 by Napoleon: it made the last French charge at Waterloo. **2.** (in the U.S.) the conservative element of any political party, esp. the Republican party. **3.** (*usually l.c.*) the influential, established, more conservative members of any body, group, movement, etc.: *the old guard of New York society.* [trans. of French *Vieille Garde*]

old' hand', *n.* a person with long experience in a subject, area, procedure, etc.; veteran.

Old' Har'ry, *n. Older Use.* the devil; Satan.

old' hat', *adj.* **1.** old-fashioned; dated. **2.** trite; hackneyed.

Old' Hick'ory, *n.* epithet of Andrew Jackson.

old·ie (ōl'dē), *n. Informal.* a popular song, joke, movie, etc., that was in vogue at a time in the past.

Old' King'dom, *n.* the period in the history of ancient Egypt, c2780–

c2280 B.C., comprising the 3rd to 6th dynasties. Compare MIDDLE KINGDOM (def. 1), NEW KINGDOM.

old' la'dy, *n. Slang.* **1.** one's mother. **2.** one's wife. **3.** one's girlfriend or female lover, esp. a lover with whom one cohabits.

Old' Lat'in, *n.* the Latin language as used in inscriptions and literature prior to c100 B.C. *Abbr.*: OL

old'-line', *adj.* **1.** following or supporting conservative or traditional ideas, customs, etc. **2.** traditional; established.

old' maid', *n.* **1.** an elderly or confirmed spinster. **2.** a fussy, timid, prudish person. **3.** a simple card game, played with a deck having one card removed, in which players match pairs, the loser being the holder of the odd card, usu. a queen. —**old'-maid'ish,** *adj.*

Old' Man' of the Sea', *n.* **1.** (in *The Arabian Nights' Entertainments*) an old man who clung to the shoulders of Sindbad the Sailor for many days and nights. **2.** a burden, annoyance, care, or the like, from which it is extremely difficult to free oneself.

Old' Man' Riv'er, a song (1927) by Jerome Kern, from the musical *Show Boat.*

old' mon'ey, *n.* inherited wealth.

Old' Nick', *n. Informal.* the devil; Satan.

Old' Rug'ged Cross', The, a Christian hymn (1913) with words and music by George Bennard.

old' school', *n.* advocates or supporters of established custom or of conservatism.

Old' South', *n.* the U.S. South before the Civil War.

Old' Span'ish Trail', *n.* an overland route from Santa Fe, N. Mex., to Los Angeles, Calif., first marked out in 1776 by Spanish explorers and missionaries.

Old' Tes'tament, *n.* **1.** the collection of the books of the Hebrew Bible, comprising the Law of Moses or Pentateuch, the Prophets, and the Hagiographa, being the first of the two main divisions of the Christian Bible. See table at BIBLE. **2.** the covenant between God and Israel on Mount Sinai, constituting the basis of the Jewish religion.

old'-time', *adj.* **1.** belonging to or characteristic of old or former times, methods, ideas, etc. **2.** being long established: *old-time residents.*

old'-tim'er, *n.* **1.** a person whose residence, membership, or experience dates from long ago. **2.** an elderly person; oldster.

old' wives'' tale', *n.* a traditional, often superstitious, belief or story.

Old' World', *n.* **1. a.** Europe, Asia, and Africa. **b.** Europe. **2.** EASTERN HEMISPHERE (def. 1).

o·lé (ō lā'), *interj., n., pl.* **o·les.** —*interj.* **1.** (used as a shout of approval, triumph, or encouragement.) —*n.* **2.** a cry of "olé."

o·le·ag·i·nous (ō'lē aj'ə nəs), *adj.* **1.** having the nature or qualities of oil. **2.** containing oil. **3.** producing oil. **4.** unctuous; fawning; smarmy.

o·le·an·der (ō'lē an'dər, ō'lē an'-), *n.* an ornamental, poisonous evergreen shrub, *Nerium oleander,* of the dogbane family, native to S Eurasia, having showy clusters of pink, red, or white flowers.

o·le·o (ō'lē ō'), *n. Older Use.* MARGARINE.

o·le·o·mar·ga·rine (ō'lē ō mär'jə rin, -rēn', -märj'rin, -rēn) also **o·le·o·mar·ga·rin** (-rin), *n. Older Use.* MARGARINE.

o·le·o·res·in (ō'lē ō rez'ən), *n.* **1.** a natural mixture of an essential oil and a resin, as found in certain plants. **2.** a prepared mixture of an oil and a resin in solution.

ol·fac·to·ry (ol fak'tə rē, -trē, ōl-), *adj., n., pl.* **-ries.** —*adj.* **1.** of or pertaining to the sense of smell. —*n.* **2.** Usu. **olfactories.** an olfactory organ.

ol·i·gar·chy (ol'i gär'kē), *n., pl.* **-chies. 1.** a form of government in which power is vested in a few persons or in a dominant class or clique. **2.** a state or organization so ruled. **3.** the persons or class so ruling. —**ol'i·gar'chic, ol'i·gar'chi·cal,** *adj.*

Ol·i·go·cene (ol'i gō sēn'), *adj.* **1.** noting or pertaining to an epoch of the Tertiary Period, occurring from 40 million to 25 million years ago. See table at GEOLOGIC TIME. —*n.* **2.** the Oligocene Epoch or Series.

ol·i·gop·o·ly (ol'i gop'ə lē), *n., pl.* **-lies.** a market situation in which prices and other factors are controlled by a few sellers. —**ol'i·gop'o·lis'tic,** *adj.*

o·li·o (ō'lē ō'), *n., pl.* **o·li·os. 1.** a mixture of heterogeneous elements; potpourri; miscellany. **2.** OLLA PODRIDA (def. 1).

O' Lit'tle Town' of Beth'lehem, a Christmas hymn (1867) with words by Phillips Brooks.

ol·ive (ol'iv), *n.* **1.** an evergreen tree, *Olea europaea,* of Mediterranean and other warm regions, cultivated chiefly for its fruit. **2.** the fruit of this tree, a small oval drupe, eaten as a relish and used as a source of oil. **3.** the wood of this tree. **4.** a wreath of its foliage. **5.** OLIVE BRANCH. **6.** the ocher green or dull yellow green of the unripe olive fruit. —*adj.* **7.** of, pertaining to, or made of olive or olives. **8.** of the color olive.

ol·ive branch', *n.* **1.** a branch of the olive tree as an emblem of peace. **2.** any token of peace.

ol·ive drab', *n.* **1.** a deep olive color. **2.** woolen cloth of this color, used esp. for military uniforms. **3.** Usu. **olive drabs.** a military uniform made from this cloth.

ol·ive green', *n.* green with a yellowish or brownish tinge. —**ol'ive-green',** *adj.*

ol·ive oil', *n.* an oil expressed from the olive fruit, used in cooking, in salad dressings, in medicine, etc.

Ol'iver Twist', a novel (1838) by Charles Dickens.

Ol•ives (ol′ivz) also **Ol•i•vet** (ol′ə vet′, -vit), *n.* **Mount of,** a small ridge E of Jerusalem. Highest point, 2737 ft. (834 m).

O•liv•i•er (ō liv′ē ā′), *n.* **Laurence (Kerr)** (*Baron Olivier of Brighton*), 1907–89, English actor and director.

ol•i•vine (ol′ə vēn′, ol′ə vēn′), *n.* any of a group of magnesium iron silicates, $(Mg,Fe)_2SiO_4$, occurring in olive-green to gray-green masses as an important constituent of basic igneous rocks.

ol•la (ol′ə, ol′yə, oi′ə), *n., pl.* **-las.** an earthen pot used esp. for holding water or cooking.

ol′la po•dri′da (pə drē′də), *n., pl.* **olla po•dri•das, ollas po•dri•das.** **1.** a spicy Spanish stew usu. containing sausage and other meat, chick-peas, and often tomatoes and other vegetables. **2.** a hodgepodge; olio.

Ol′ney Hym′nal (ol′nē), *n.* a collection of hymns (1799) written by John Newton and William Cowper. [after *Olney,* town in Buckinghamshire, England]

O•lym•pi•a (ə lim′pē ə, ō lim′-), *n.* **1.** a plain in Elis, Greece, where the ancient Olympic Games were held. **2.** the capital of Washington, in the W part, on Puget Sound. 27,447.

O•lym•pi•ad (ə lim′pē ad′, ō lim′-), *n.* (*often l.c.*) **1.** a period of four years reckoned from one celebration of the Olympic Games to the next, by which the Greeks computed time from 776 B.C. **2. a.** a celebration of the modern Olympic Games. **b.** OLYMPIC GAMES (def. 2).

O•lym•pi•an (ə lim′pē ən, ō lim′-), *adj.* **1.** pertaining to Mount Olympus or dwelling thereon, as the gods of classical Greece. **2.** pertaining to Olympia in Elis. **3.** characteristic of or resembling the gods of Olympus; majestic or aloof: *an Olympian disdain.* —*n.* **4.** an Olympian deity. **5.** a contender in the Olympic Games. **6.** a native or inhabitant of Olympia.

Olym′pic Games′, *n.pl.* **1.** Also, **Olym′pian Games′.** the greatest of the national festivals of ancient Greece, held every four years on the plain of Olympia in Elis. **2.** a modern international sports competition traditionally held every four years but, after 1992, with Summer Games and Winter Games alternating every two years.

Olym′pic Na′tional Park′, *n.* a national park in NW Washington. 1323 sq. mi. (3425 sq. km).

O•lym•pus (ə lim′pəs, ō lim′-), *n.* **Mount, 1.** a mountain in NE Greece, on the boundary between Thessaly and Macedonia: mythical abode of the Greek gods. 9730 ft. (2966 m). **2.** a mountain in NW Washington: highest peak of the Olympic Mountains. 7954 ft. (2424 m).

O•ma•ha (ō′mə hô′, -hä′), *n.* **1.** a city in E Nebraska, on the Missouri River. 345,033. **2.** *Mil.* the World War II Allied code name for one of the five D-Day invasion beaches on France's Normandy coast, attacked by American troops.

O•man (ō män′), *n.* **1. Sultanate of.** Formerly, **Muscat and Oman.** an independent sultanate in SE Arabia. 2,264,590; ab. 119,969 sq. mi. (309,500 sq. km). *Cap.:* Muscat. **2. Gulf of,** a NW arm of the Arabian Sea, at the entrance to the Persian Gulf. —**O•ma•ni** (ō mä′nē), *n., pl.*

om•buds•man (om′bədz mən, -man′, -bo͝odz-, ôm′-, om bo͝odz′-, ôm-), *n., pl.* **-men. 1.** a public official, esp. in Scandinavian countries, who investigates complaints by private citizens against government agencies or officials. **2.** a person who investigates and resolves complaints, as from employees or students. [< Swedish: legal representative] —**Usage.** See -MAN.

o•me•ga (ō mē′gə, ō mā′-, ō meg′ə), *n., pl.* **-gas. 1.** the 24th and last letter of the Greek alphabet (Ω, ω). **2.** the last of any series; the end.

om•e•let or **om•e•lette** (om′lit, om′ə-), *n.* a dish of beaten eggs cooked until set and often served folded around a filling, as of cheese, ham, or mushrooms.

o•men (ō′mən), *n.* **1.** any event believed to portend something good or evil; augury; portent. **2.** prophetic significance; presage: *a bird of ill omen.* —*v.t.* **3.** to be an omen of; portend. **4.** to divine, as if from omens.

o•men•tum (ō men′təm), *n., pl.* **-ta** (-tə). a fold of the peritoneum connecting the stomach and other abdominal viscera and forming a protective and supportive covering. —**o•men′tal,** *adj.*

o•mer (ō′mər; *Heb.* ô meʀ′), *n.* **1.** an ancient Hebrew unit of dry measure, the tenth part of an ephah. **2.** (*usu. cap.*) the period of 49 days from the second day of Passover to the first day of Shavuoth, a period of semimourning.

om•i•nous (om′ə nəs), *adj.* **1.** portending evil or harm; foreboding; threatening; inauspicious. **2.** having the significance of an omen. —**om′i•nous•ly,** *adv.* —**om′i•nous•ness,** *n.*

o•mis•sion (ō mish′ən), *n.* **1.** the act of omitting. **2.** the state of being omitted. **3.** something left out, not done, or neglected.

o•mit (ō mit′), *v.t.,* **o•mit•ted, o•mit•ting. 1.** to leave out; fail to include. **2.** to forbear or fail (to do, make, use, send, etc.).

omni-, a combining form meaning "all": *omnidirectional.*

om•ni•bus (om′nə bus′, -bəs), *n., pl.* **-bus•es** or, for 1, **bus•ses,** *adj.* —*n.* **1.** BUS[1] (def. 1). **2.** a volume of reprints by a single author or on a single subject. —*adj.* **3.** pertaining to, including, or dealing with numerous objects or items at once: *an omnibus bill submitted to a legislature.*

om•ni•far•i•ous (om′nə fâr′ē əs), *adj.* of all forms, varieties, or kinds. —**om′ni•far′i•ous•ly,** *adv.* —**om′ni•far′i•ous•ness,** *n.*

om•nip•o•tence (om nip′ə təns), *n.* **1.** the quality or state of being omnipotent. **2.** (*cap.*) GOD.

om•nip•o•tent (om nip′ə tənt), *adj.* **1.** infinite in power, as God. **2.** having very great or unlimited authority or power. —*n.* **3.** an omnipotent being. **4. the Omnipotent,** GOD. —**om•nip′o•tent•ly,** *adv.*

om•ni•pres•ent (om′nə prez′ənt), *adj.* present everywhere at the same time. —**om′ni•pres′ence,** *n.*

om•nis•cience (om nish′əns), *n.* **1.** the quality or state of being omniscient. **2.** infinite knowledge.

om•nis•cient (om nish′ənt), *adj.* **1.** having complete or unlimited knowledge, awareness, or understanding. —*n.* **2.** an omniscient being. **3. the Omniscient,** GOD. —**om•nis′cient•ly,** *adv.*

om•ni•vore (om′nə vôr′, -vōr′), *n.* **1.** someone or something that is omnivorous. **2.** an omnivorous animal.

om•niv•o•rous (om niv′ər əs), *adj.* **1.** feeding on both animals and plants. **2.** eating all kinds of foods indiscriminately. **3.** taking in everything, as with the mind: *an omnivorous reader.* —**om•niv′o•rous•ly,** *adv.* —**om•niv′o•rous•ness,** *n.*

Om•ri (om′rī), *n.* a king of Israel and the father of Ahab. I Kings 16:16–28.

on (on, ôn), *prep.* **1.** so as to be or remain supported by or suspended from: *Put the package on the table. Hang your coat on the hook.* **2.** so as to be attached to or unified with: *a label on a jar.* **3.** so as to be a covering or wrapping for: *Put the blanket on the baby.* **4.** in connection, association, or cooperation with: *to serve on a jury.* **5.** so as to be a supporting part or base of: *legs on a chair.* **6.** having as a place, location, situation, etc.: *a scar on the face; a store on 19th Street.* **7.** in immediate proximity to: *a house on the lake.* **8.** in the direction of: *to sail on a southerly course.* **9.** using as a means of conveyance or of supporting or supplying movement: *arriving on the noon plane; a car that runs on electricity.* **10.** by the agency or means of: *drunk on wine; talking on the phone.* **11.** directed against or toward: *played a joke on him.* **12.** having as a subject; about: *a book on birds.* **13.** in a state, condition, or process of: *on strike.* **14.** engaged in or involved with: *I'm on the second chapter now.* **15.** subject to: *a doctor on call.* **16.** having as a source or agent: *to depend on friends for support.* **17.** having as a basis or ground: *on my word of honor.* **18.** assigned to or working at: *Who's on the switchboard today?* **19.** at the time or occasion of: *on Sunday; cash on delivery.* **20.** within the required limits of: *on time.* **21.** having as the object or end of motion: *to march on the capital; to creep up on someone.* **22.** having as the object or end of action, thought, desire, etc.: *to gaze on a scene.* **23.** having as the subject or reference; with respect to: *views on public matters.* **24.** paid for by, esp. as a treat or gift: *Dinner is on me.* **25.** taking or using as a prescribed measure, cure, etc.: *on a low-salt diet.* **26.** regularly taking or addicted to: *on drugs.* **27.** with; carried by: *I have no money on me.* **28.** so as to disturb or affect adversely: *My hair dryer broke on me.* **29.** having as a risk or liability: *on pain of death.* **30.** in addition to: *millions on millions of stars.* —*adv.* **31.** in, into, or onto a position of being supported or attached: *Sew the buttons on.* **32.** in, into, or onto a position of covering or wrapping: *Put your raincoat on.* **33.** fast to a thing, as for support: *Hold on!* **34.** toward a place, point, activity, or object: *to look on while others work.* **35.** forward, onward, or along, as in any course or process: *further on.* **36.** with continuous activity: *to work on.* **37.** into or in active operation or performance: *Turn the gas on.* —*adj.* **38.** operating or in use: *Is the radio on?* **39.** taking place; occurring: *Don't you know there's a war on?* **40.** performing or broadcasting: *The radio announcer told us we were on.* **41. a.** behaving in a very animated or theatrical manner. **b.** functioning or performing at one's best. **42.** scheduled or planned: *Anything on tonight?* —***Idiom.*** **43. on and off,** OFF (def. 46). **44. on and on,** at great length, so as to become tiresome: *to chatter on and on.*

On (on), *n.* Biblical name of HELIOPOLIS.

ON, Ontario, Canada.

on′-again′, off′-again′ or **on′-again′-off′-again′,** *adj.* being in force or inoperative by turns, esp. spasmodically and unpredictably: *an on-again, off-again romance.*

o•nan•ism (ō′nə niz′əm), *n.* **1.** withdrawal of the penis in sexual intercourse so that ejaculation takes place outside the vagina; coitus interruptus. **2.** MASTURBATION. —**o′nan•ist,** *n.* —**o′nan•is′tic,** *adj.*

O•nas•sis (ō nas′is, ō nä′sis), *n.* **1. Aristotle Socrates,** 1906–75, Greek businessman, born in Turkey. **2. Jacqueline (Lee Bouvier Kennedy)** ("*Jackie*"), 1929–94, wife of John F. Kennedy (1953–63) and Aristotle Onassis (1968–75).

once (wuns), *adv.* **1.** at one time in the past; formerly: *a once powerful nation.* **2.** a single time: *We eat out once a week.* **3.** even a single time; at any time; ever: *if the facts once become known.* **4.** by a single step, degree, or grade: *a cousin once removed.* —*n.* **5.** a single occasion; one time only: *Once is enough.* —*conj.* **6.** if or when at any time; if ever. **7.** whenever; as soon as: *Once you're finished, you can leave.* —*adj.* **8.** former; one-time: *the once and future king.* —***Idiom.*** **9. all at once,** suddenly: *All at once it started to rain.* **10. at once, a.** at the same time; simultaneously. **b.** immediately; promptly. **11. once (and) for all,** decisively; finally: *Let's settle this once and for all.* **12. once in a while,** at intervals; occasionally. **13. once or twice,** a very few times; infrequently. **14. once upon a time,** (used as a conventional opening phrase to set a fairy tale or the like in the distant, imaginary past.)

Once′ in Roy′al Da′vid's Cit′y, a Christmas hymn (1848) with words by Cecil Alexander.

once′-o′ver, *n.* **1.** a quick look, examination, or appraisal. **2.** a quick, superficial job.

Once′ to Eve′ry Man′ and Na′tion, a Christian hymn (1845) with words by James Russell Lowell.

on•col•o•gy (ong kol′ə jē), *n.* the branch of medical science dealing with tumors, including the origin, development, diagnosis, and treatment of cancer. —**on′co•log′ic** (-kə loj′ik), **on′co•log′i•cal,** *adj.* —**on•col′o•gist,** *n.*

on•com•ing (on′kum′ing, ôn′-), *adj.* **1.** approaching; nearing: *an oncoming train.* **2.** emerging: *the oncoming generation.* —*n.* **3.** approach; onset: *the oncoming of winter.*

one (wun), *adj.* **1.** being or amounting to a single unit or individual or entire thing: *one child; one piece of cake.* **2.** being an individual instance or member of a number, kind, or group indicated: *one member of the party.* **3.** existing, acting, or considered as a single unit or entity. **4.** of the same or having a single kind, nature, or condition: *of one mind.* **5.** denoting an unspecified day or time: *one evening last week.* **6.** denoting some indefinite day or time in the future: *You'll see him one day.* **7.** a certain (used in naming a person otherwise unknown or undescribed): *One John Smith was chosen.* **8.** being a particular, unique, or only individual, item, or unit: *the one person I can trust.* **9.** of no consequence as to the character, outcome, etc.; the same: *It's all one to me.* **10.** a or an (used with intensifying force): *That is one smart dog.* —*n.* **11.** the first and lowest whole number; the lowest cardinal number; unity. **12.** a symbol of this number, as 1 or I. **13.** a single person or thing: *one at a time.* **14.** a one-dollar bill. —*pron.* **15.** a person or thing of a number or kind indicated or understood: *one of the Elizabethan poets.* **16.** a person or a personified being: *the evil one.* **17.** any person or thing indefinitely; anyone or anything: *as good as one could desire.* **18.** something or someone of the kind just mentioned: *The portraits are good ones.* —*Idiom.* **19. as one (man), a.** with complete accord; unanimously: *They voted as one.* **b.** in unison: *We rose to our feet as one man.* **20. at one,** united in thought or feeling; attuned: *to feel at one with the world.* **21. one and all,** everyone. **22. one by one,** singly and successively. —**Usage.** ONE meaning "any person indefinitely" is more formal than *you,* in the same sense: *One* (or *you*) *should never give up hope.* When the pronoun must be repeated, either ONE or a personal pronoun is used; the latter is more common in the U.S.: *Wherever one looks, he* or *she finds industrial pollution.* In speech or informal writing, a form of *they* sometimes occurs: *Can one read this without thinking of their own childhood?* In the construction *one of those who* (or *that* or *which*), the antecedent of *who* is considered to be the plural form, correctly followed by a plural verb: *one of those people who find fault.* Yet so strong is the feeling for ONE as antecedent that a singular verb is commonly found in all types of writing: *one of those people who finds fault.* When ONE is preceded by *only* in such a construction, the singular verb is called for: *the only one of her sons who visits her.* See also HE[1], THEY.

one′ anoth′er, *pron.* EACH OTHER.

one′-dimen′sional, *adj.* **1.** having one dimension only. **2.** having no depth or scope: *a novel with one-dimensional characters.* —**one′-dimensional′ity,** *n.*

one′-hand′ed, *adj.* **1.** having or using only one hand. **2.** involving or requiring the use of only one hand. —*adv.* **3.** with one hand: *to drive one-handed.*

one′-horse′, *adj.* **1.** using or having only a single horse. **2.** small and unimportant; limited: *a one-horse town.*

one′-house′ bill′, *n.* a piece of legislation not expected to pass both houses of the legislature, intended only to create a good impression.

one′-house′ ve′to, *n.* a provision in a law that enables either the House of Representatives or the Senate to cancel presidential actions.

O•nei•da (ō nī′də), *n., pl.* **-das,** (*esp. collectively*) **-da. 1.** a member of an American Indian people, orig. residing near Oneida Lake and the upper Mohawk River valley in New York: one of the Iroquois Five Nations. **2.** the Iroquoian language of the Oneidas.

O'Neill (ō nēl′), *n.* **Eugene (Gladstone),** 1888–1953, U.S. playwright.

one′-lin′er, *n.* a brief joke or witty remark.

one′-man′ band′, *n.* **1.** an entertainer who plays several musical instruments simultaneously. **2.** a person who works alone on all aspects of a task or project.

one′ man′, one′ vote′, *adj.* of or pertaining to a system of legislative representation in which each member represents about the same number of people.

one′-on′-one′, *adj.* **1.** consisting of or involving direct individual communication, confrontation, or competition; person-to-person. —*adv.* **2.** in direct encounter. —*n.* **3.** a meeting or confrontation between two persons. —*Idiom.* **4. go one-on-one with,** *Sports.* to play directly against (an opposing player).

one′-par′ty press′, *n.* favoritism considered to be shown by the media toward one political party.

one′-par′ty rule′, *n.* prolonged political domination by one party.

one′-piece′, *adj.* complete in one piece, as a garment: *a one-piece snowsuit.*

on•er•ous (on′ər əs, ō′nər-), *adj.* **1.** burdensome, oppressive, or troublesome: *onerous duties.* **2.** having or involving obligations or responsibilities, esp. legal ones, that outweigh the advantages: *an onerous agreement.* —**on′er•ous•ly,** *adv.* —**on′er•ous•ness,** *n.*

one•self or **one's self** (wun self′, wunz-), *pron.* **1.** a person's self (used as a reflexive or emphatic form of ONE): *One should be able to laugh at oneself.* —*Idiom.* **2. be oneself, a.** to be in one's normal state of mind or physical condition. **b.** to be unpretentious and sincere. **3. by oneself, a.** without a companion; alone. **b.** through one's own efforts; unaided.

one′-shot′, *adj.* **1.** occurring, appearing, done, etc., only once. **2.**

achieved or accomplished with a single try: *a one-shot solution.* —*n.* Also, **one′ shot′. 3.** a magazine, brochure, etc., published only one time and usu. devoted to one subject. **4.** a single appearance by a performer, as in a television program. **5.** a close-up camera shot of one person. **6.** something occurring, done, used, etc., only once.

one′-sid′ed, *adj.* **1.** considering but one side of a matter or question; partial or unfair: *a one-sided judgment.* **2.** one side far superior or having all the advantage; unequal: *a one-sided fight.* **3.** *Biol.* existing, occurring, or developing more fully on one side, as certain flower clusters or crabs. —**one′-sid′ed•ly,** *adv.* —**one′-sid′ed•ness,** *n.*

O•nes•i•mus (ō nes′ə məs), *n.* a slave of Philemon who was converted to Christianity by the Apostle Paul. Col. 4:9; Philem. 10.

one′-step′, *n., v.,* **-stepped, -step•ping.** —*n.* **1.** a dance for couples with quick walking steps to a ragtime rhythm. —*v.i.* **2.** to dance the one-step.

one′-time′ or **one′time′,** *adj.* **1.** having been as specified at one time; former: *my one-time partners.* **2.** occurring, done, etc., only once.

one′-to-one′, *adj.* **1.** (of the relationship between two or more groups of things) corresponding element by element. **2.** ONE-ON-ONE.

one′-track′, *adj.* **1.** unable or unwilling to cope with more than one idea, subject, etc., at a time: *a one-track mind.* **2.** having only one track.

one′-two′, *n.* **1.** a left-hand boxing jab immediately followed by a right cross. **2.** any combination of two people, things, or actions producing a rapid and powerful effect. Also called **one′-two′ punch′.**

one′ up′, *adj.* having gained an advantage, esp. over a rival.

one′-up′, *v.t.,* **-upped, -up•ping.** to gain an advantage over; be a move, step, etc., ahead of: *to one-up the competition.*

one′-up′manship or **one′-ups′manship,** *n.* the art or practice of maneuvering for or gaining the advantage in a competitive relationship, as through status symbols or displays of superiority.

one′-way′, *adj.* **1.** moving or allowing movement in one direction only: *one-way traffic; a one-way street.* **2.** valid for travel in one direction only: *a one-way ticket.* **3.** operating, developing, etc., in one direction only: *a one-way window.* **4.** without reciprocal feeling, responsibility, etc.: *a one-way friendship.*

on•go•ing (on′gō′ing, ôn′-), *adj.* continuing without termination or interruption: *ongoing research projects.*

on•ion (un′yən), *n.* **1.** a plant, *Allium cepa,* of the amaryllis family, having an edible, succulent, pungent bulb. **2.** this bulb. **3.** any of certain similar plants. —**on′ion•y,** *adj.*

on•ion•skin (un′yən skin′), *n.* a thin, lightweight, translucent glazed paper, used esp. for making carbon copies.

On′ Lib′erty, a treatise (1859) by John Stuart Mill on the rights of the individual within the state.

on′-line′ or **on′line′,** *adj.* operating under the direct control of, or connected to, a main computer. Compare OFF-LINE.

on•look•er (on′lŏŏk′ər, ôn′-), *n.* a spectator; observer; witness. —**on′look′ing,** *adj.*

on•ly (ōn′lē), *adv.* **1.** without others or anything further; alone; solely; exclusively: *This information is for your eyes only.* **2.** no more than; merely; just: *only on weekends; If it were only true!* **3.** as recently as: *I read that article only yesterday.* **4.** in the final outcome or decision: *That will only make matters worse.* —*adj.* **5.** being the single one or the relatively few of the kind; lone; sole: *the only seat left.* **6.** having no sibling: *an only child.* —*conj.* **7.** but (introducing a single restriction, restraining circumstance, or the like): *I would have gone, only you objected.* —*Idiom.* **8. only too,** very; extremely.

on•o•mas•tic (on′ə mas′tik), *adj.* **1.** of or pertaining to proper names. **2.** of or pertaining to onomastics. **3.** (of a signature) not in the same hand as the document to which it is appended.

on•o•mas•tics (on′ə mas′tiks), *n.* (*used with a sing. v.*) the study of the origin, history, and use of proper names.

on•o•mat•o•poe•ia (on′ə mat′ə pē′ə, -mä′tə-), *n.* **1.** the formation of a word, as *cuckoo* or *boom,* by imitation of a sound made by or associated with its referent. **2.** the use of such imitative words. —**on′o•mat′o•poe′ic,** **on′o•mat′o•po•et′ic** (-pō et′ik), *adj.* —**on′o•mat′o•poe′i•cal•ly,** **on′o•mat′o•po•et′i•cal•ly,** *adv.*

on•rush (on′rush′, ôn′-), *n.* a strong forward rush, flow, etc. —**on′rush′ing,** *adj.*

on′-screen′, *adj.* **1.** seen or displayed on a motion-picture, television, or computer screen. —*adv.* **2.** on a motion-picture, television, or computer screen: *The wrong weather map appeared on-screen.*

on•set (on′set′, ôn′-), *n.* **1.** a beginning or start: *the onset of winter.* **2.** an assault or attack: *the onset of the enemy.*

on•shore (on′shôr′, -shōr′, ôn′-), *adv.* **1.** onto or in the direction of the shore from a body of water. **2.** on land, esp. within the area adjoining a port; ashore. —*adj.* **3.** moving or proceeding toward shore or onto land from a body of water: *an onshore breeze.* **4.** located on or close to the shore. **5.** done or taking place on land.

on•side (on′sīd′, ôn′-), *adj., adv. Sports.* within the prescribed line or area at the beginning of or during play or a play.

on′side kick′, *n. Football.* a short-distance kickoff resorted to in hopes of immediately recovering possession of the ball.

on′-site′, *adj.* accomplished or located at the site of a particular activity or concern: *on-site medical treatment for accident victims.*

on•slaught (on′slôt′, ôn′-), *n.* an onset or assault, esp. a vigorous one.

on•stage (on′stāj′, ôn′-), *adv.* **1.** on or onto the stage (opposed to *offstage*). **—***adj.* **2.** of, pertaining to, or used in that part of the stage seen by the audience.

On•tar•i•o (on târ′ē ō′), *n.* **1.** a province in S Canada, bordering on the Great Lakes. 9,101,694; 412,582 sq. mi. (1,068,585 sq. km). *Cap.:* Toronto. **2. Lake,** a lake between the northeastern U.S. and S Canada, between New York and Ontario: the smallest of the Great Lakes. 7540 sq. mi. (19,530 sq. km). **3.** a city in SW California, E of Los Angeles. 134,825. —**On•tar′i•an,** *adj., n.*

on′-the-job′, *adj.* done, received, or happening while in actual performance of one's work: *on-the-job training.*

on′-the-spot′, *adj.* **1.** done or occurring at the time or place in question: *an on-the-spot recording.* **2.** done without delay; immediate; instant: *on-the-spot decisions.*

on•to (on′to͞o, ôn′-; *unstressed* on′tə, ôn′-), *prep.* **1.** to a place or position on; upon; on. **2.** *Informal.* aware of the true nature, motive, or meaning of: *I'm onto your tricks.* **—***adj.* **3.** *Math.* pertaining to a function or map from one set to another set, the range of which is the entire second set.

on•tog•e•ny (on toj′ə nē) also **on•to•gen•e•sis** (on′tə jen′ə sis), *n.* the development or developmental history of an individual organism. Compare PHYLOGENY. —**on′to•ge•net′ic** (-jə net′ik), **on′to•gen′ic,** *adj.* —**on′to•ge•net′i•cal•ly, on′to•gen′i•cal•ly,** *adv.* —**on•tog′e•nist,** *n.*

ontolog′ical ar′gument, *n.* an a priori argument for the existence of God, asserting that as existence is a perfection, and as God is conceived of as the most perfect being, it follows that God must exist.

on•tol•o•gy (on tol′ə jē), *n.* **1.** the branch of metaphysics that studies the nature of existence or being as such. **2.** (loosely) metaphysics. —**on•to•log•i•cal** (on′tl oj′i kəl), **on′to•log′ic,** *adj.* —**on•tol′o•gist,** *n.*

o•nus (ō′nəs), *n., pl.* **o•nus•es. 1.** a difficult or disagreeable obligation or task. **2.** BURDEN OF PROOF. **3.** blame; responsibility.

on•ward (on′wərd, ôn′-), *adv.* Also, **on′wards. 1.** toward a point ahead or in front; forward, as in space or time. **2.** at a position or point in advance. **—***adj.* **3.** directed or moving onward; forward.

On′ward, Chris′tian Sol′diers, a Christian hymn (1864) with words by Sabine Baring-Gould and music by Arthur S. Sullivan.

-onym, a combining form meaning "word," "name": *pseudonym.*

on•yx (on′iks, ō′niks), *n.* **1.** a variety of chalcedony having straight parallel bands of alternating colors. **2.** (not in technical use) an unbanded chalcedony dyed for ornamental purposes. **3.** black, esp. a pure or jet black. **—***adj.* **4.** black, esp. jet black.

oo-, a combining form meaning "egg": *oogamete.*

o•o•cyte (ō′ə sīt′), *n.* an immature egg cell of the animal ovary: in humans, one oocyte matures during the menstrual cycle while several others partially mature and disintegrate.

oo•dles (o͞od′lz), *n.* (*sometimes used with a sing. v.*) *Informal.* a large quantity: *oodles of money.*

ooh (o͞o), *interj.* **1.** (used as an exclamation of amazement, satisfaction, excitement, etc.) **—***n.* **2.** the exclamation "ooh."

oo•long (o͞o′lông′, -long′), *n.* a brown or amber tea grown in China and Taiwan and partially fermented before being dried.

oom•pah (o͞om′pä, o͞om′-) also **oom′pah-pah′,** *n.* **1.** a repetitive, rhythmic bass accompaniment in music typically provided by brasses. **—***adj.* **2.** marked by an oompah: *an oompah band.*

oops (o͝ops, o͞ops), *interj.* (used as an exclamation of mild dismay or chagrin, as at one's own mistake or blunder.)

o•o•the•ca (ō′ə thē′kə), *n., pl.* **-cae** (-sē). a case or capsule containing eggs, as that of certain insects and mollusks. —**o′o•the′cal,** *adj.*

ooze[1] (o͞oz), *v.,* **oozed, ooz•ing,** *n.* **—***v.i.* **1.** (of moisture, liquid, etc.) to flow, percolate, or exude slowly, as through holes or small openings. **2.** to move or pass slowly or gradually, as if through a small opening or passage. **3.** (of a substance) to exude moisture. **4.** (of something abstract, as courage) to appear or disappear slowly or imperceptibly (often fol. by *out* or *away*). **5.** to display some characteristic or quality. **—***v.t.* **6.** to make by oozing. **7.** to exude (moisture, air, etc.) slowly. **8.** to display or dispense freely and conspicuously: *to ooze charm.* **—***n.* **9.** the act of oozing. **10.** something that oozes. **11.** an infusion of oak bark, sumac, etc., used in tanning.

ooze[2] (o͞oz), *n.* **1.** a calcareous or siliceous mud composed chiefly of the shells of one-celled organisms, found on the ocean bottom. **2.** soft mud or slime. **3.** a marsh or bog.

O.P., or, **o.p.,** out of print.

OPA, Office of Price Administration: the federal agency (1941–46) charged with regulating rents and the distribution and prices of goods during World War II.

o•pac•i•ty (ō pas′i tē), *n., pl.* **-ties. 1.** the state or quality of being opaque. **2.** something opaque. **3.** the degree to which a substance is or may be opaque. **4.** the proportion of light absorbed by the emulsion on an area of a photographic film or plate. **5.** obscurity of meaning. **6.** mental dullness.

o•pal (ō′pəl), *n.* **1.** a mineral, an amorphous form of silica, SiO_2, with some water of hydration, found in many varieties and colors, including milky white. **2.** a gemstone made of this, esp. of an iridescent variety.

o•pal•es•cent (ō′pə les′ənt), *adj.* **1.** exhibiting a play of colors like that of the opal. **2.** having a milky iridescence. —**o′pal•es′cence,** *n.*

o•paque (ō pāk′), *adj., n., v.,* **o•paqued, o•paqu•ing. —***adj.* **1.** not allowing light to pass through. **2.** not shining or bright; dark; dull. **3.** hard to understand; not clear or lucid. —**o•paque′ly,** *adv.*

opaque′ projec′tor, *n.* a machine for projecting opaque objects, as books, on a screen, by means of reflected light.

op′ art′ (op), *n.* a style of art in which lines, forms, and space are distributed so as to produce optical effects, as illusory movement. —**op′-art′,** *adj.* —**op′ art′ist,** *n.*

op. cit. (op′ sit′), in the work cited. [< Latin *opere citātō*]

OPEC (ō′pek), *n.* Organization of Petroleum Exporting Countries.

Op′-Ed′, *n.* a newspaper page or section devoted to signed articles by commentators, essayists, etc., and sometimes to letters from readers. [*op(posite) ed(itorial page)*]

o•pen (ō′pən), *adj.* **1.** not closed or barred at the time, as a doorway or passageway, by a door. **2.** (of a door, window sash, or the like) set so as to permit passage through the opening it can be used to close. **3.** having the interior immediately accessible, as a box with the lid raised. **4.** relatively free of obstructions. **5.** constructed so as not to be fully enclosed: *an open boat.* **6.** having relatively large or numerous spaces, voids, or intervals: *open ranks of soldiers.* **7.** relatively unoccupied by buildings, trees, etc.: *open country.* **8.** not covered or closed; with certain parts apart: *open eyes.* **9.** without a covering, esp. a protective covering; exposed: *an open wound.* **10.** extended or unfolded: *an open newspaper.* **11.** without restrictions as to who may participate: *an open session.* **12.** accessible or available: *Which job is open?* **13.** ready for or carrying on normal trade or business: *The new store is now open.* **14.** not engaged or committed: *open time.* **15.** exposed to general view or knowledge: *open disregard of the rules.* **16.** unreserved, candid, or frank, as a person or speech. **17.** generous, liberal, or bounteous: *to give with an open hand.* **18.** liable or subject: *open to question.* **19.** undecided; unsettled: *several open questions.* **20.** without effective or enforced legal, commercial, or moral regulations: *an open town.* **21.** unguarded by an opponent: *An open receiver caught the pass.* **22.** noting the part of the sea beyond headlands or enclosing areas of land. **23.** free of navigational hazards: *an open coast.* **24.** not yet balanced or adjusted, as an account. **25. a.** (of a vowel) articulated with a relatively large opening above the tongue or with a relatively large oral aperture, as the vowel sound of *cot;* low. Compare CLOSE (def. 50). **b.** (of a syllable) ending with a vowel. Compare CLOSED (def. 6). **26.** (of a compound word) written with the constituent words separated by a space, as *police officer.* **27.** *Music.* (of a string) not stopped by a finger. **28.** *Math.* (of a set) consisting of points having neighborhoods wholly contained in the set, as the set of points within a circle. **29.** (of a fabric or weave) so loosely constructed that spaces are visible between warp and filling yarns. **—***v.t.* **30.** to move (a door, window sash, etc.) from a shut or closed position. **31.** to render the interior of (a box, drawer, etc.) readily accessible. **32.** to make accessible or available: *to open a port for trade.* **33.** to establish for business purposes or for public use: *to open an office.* **34.** to set in action, begin, start, or commence (sometimes fol. by *up*): *to open the bidding.* **35.** to uncover, lay bare, or expose to view. **36.** to expand, unfold, or spread out: *to open a map.* **37.** to make less compact or less closely spaced: *to open ranks.* **38.** to disclose, reveal, or divulge. **39.** to render (the mind) accessible to knowledge, sympathy, etc. **40.** to make or produce (an opening): *to open a way through a crowd.* **41.** to make an opening in. **42.** *Law.* to revoke (a decree, judgment, etc.) esp. so as to hear further arguments. **—***v.i.* **43.** to become open. **44.** to afford access or have an opening to a place: *a door that opens into a garden.* **45.** (of a building) to open its doors to the public. **46.** to begin, start, or commence: *The game opened with the national anthem.* **47.** to part or seem to part: *The clouds opened.* **48.** to become disclosed or revealed. **49.** to come into view; become more visible or plain. **50.** (of the mind) to become receptive to knowledge, sympathy, etc. **51.** to spread out or expand, as the hand or a fan. **52.** to turn the pages of a book, newspaper, etc.: *Open to page 22.* **53.** to spread or come apart; burst: *The wound opened.* **54.** to become less compact or less closely spaced: *The ranks began to open.* **55. open up, a.** to make or become open. **b.** to begin firing a gun, or the like. **c.** to share one's feelings, confidences, etc. **—***n.* **56.** an open or clear space. **57.** the open air or the outdoors, esp. the countryside. **58.** the open water, as of the sea. **59.** an opening or aperture. **60.** an opening or opportunity. **61.** a contest or tournament in which both amateurs and professionals may compete. **—*Idiom.* 62. open someone's eyes,** to make someone alert to a situation. **63. out in** or **in the open,** unconcealed or publicly known. —**o′pen•ly,** *adv.* —**o′pen•ness,** *n.*

o′pen admis′sions, *n.* a policy of admitting applicants to a college, university, etc., regardless of previous academic grades.

o′pen-and-shut′, *adj.* immediately obvious upon consideration; easily decided: *an open-and-shut case of larceny.*

o′pen conven′tion, *n.* a party convention at which delegates are free to vote for the candidate of their choice. Compare BROKERED CONVENTION.

o′pen door′, *n.* **1.** the policy or practice of trading with all nations on an equal basis. **2.** admission or access; unrestricted opportunity. —**o′pen-door′,** *adj.*

o′pen-end′, *adj.* **1.** continuously issuing shares of stock or repurchasing them from shareholders. **2.** OPEN-ENDED.

o′pen-end′ed, *adj.* **1.** not having fixed limits; unrestricted; broad. **2.** allowing for future changes, revisions, or additions: *an open-ended mortgage.* **3.** having no fixed answer: *an open-ended question.* —**o′pen-end′ed•ness,** *n.*

o•pen•er (ō′pə nər), *n.* **1.** a person or thing that opens. **2.** a device for opening sealed containers. **3.** the first of several theatrical numbers, sports events, etc. **4. openers,** cards in poker whose value enables the holder to make the first bet of the deal, as a pair of jacks or better. —*Idiom.* **5. for openers,** as an initially stated reason or argument; to begin with.

o•pen-hand•ed (ō′pən han′did), *adj.* generous; liberal. —**o′pen•hand′ed•ly,** *adv.* —**o′pen•hand′ed•ness,** *n.*

o′pen-heart′ed, *adj.* **1.** candid or frank. **2.** kindly; benevolent. —**o′pen-heart′ed•ly,** *adv.* —**o′pen-heart′ed•ness,** *n.*

o′pen-heart′ sur′gery, *n.* surgery performed on the exposed heart with the aid of a heart-lung machine.

o′pen house′, *n.* **1.** a party or reception during which a person's home is open to visitors. **2.** a time during which a school, institution, etc., is open to the public, as for exhibition. **3.** a house or apartment for sale or rent that is available for inspection by prospective clients.

o•pen•ing (ō′pə ning), *n.* **1.** an act or instance of making or becoming open. **2.** an unobstructed or unoccupied space or place. **3.** a hole or void in solid matter. **4.** the act of beginning; start. **5.** the first part or initial stage of anything. **6.** an employment vacancy. **7.** an opportunity; chance. **8. a.** the formal or official beginning of an activity, event, presentation, etc. **b.** a celebration marking this. **9.** the statement of the case made by legal counsel to the court or jury before presenting evidence. **10.** a mode of beginning a game: *chess openings.*

o′pen let′ter, *n.* a letter, often of protest, addressed to a specific person, but intended to be brought to public attention.

o′pen mar′ket, *n.* an unrestricted competitive market in which any buyer and seller is free to participate.

o′pen-mind′ed, *adj.* **1.** having or showing a mind receptive to new ideas or arguments. **2.** unprejudiced; unbigoted; impartial. —**o′pen-mind′ed•ness,** *n.*

o′pen-mouthed′, *adj.* **1.** having the mouth open. **2.** gaping, as with surprise or astonishment. **3.** having a wide mouth, as a pitcher or jar.

o′pen pri′mary, *n.* a direct primary in which voters need not meet a test of party membership.

o′pen sand′wich, *n.* a sandwich served on only one slice of bread, without a covering slice.

o′pen sea′son, *n.* a specific season or time of year when it is legal to catch or hunt for fish or game protected at all other times by the law.

o′pen se′cret, *n.* something supposedly secret but actually known quite generally.

o′pen ses′ame, *n.* any marvelously effective means for bringing about a desired result.

o′pen shop′, *n.* a business establishment in which a union acts as representative of all the employees but in which union membership is not a condition of employment.

o′pen-skies′, *n.* relatively unrestricted aircraft traffic across international boundaries: *an open-skies treaty.*

o•pen•work (ō′pən wûrk′), *n.* any kind of ornamental work, as in lace, stone, or metal, having open spaces in the material.

op•er•a[1] (op′ər ə, op′rə), *n., pl.* **-er•as. 1.** an extended dramatic work in which the parts are sung to orchestral accompaniment. Compare ARIA, COMIC OPERA, GRAND OPERA, RECITATIVE[2]. **2.** the score of such a work. **3.** an opera house or resident company.

o•pe•ra[2] (ō′pər ə, op′ər ə), *n.* a pl. of OPUS.

op•er•a•ble (op′ər ə bəl, op′rə-), *adj.* **1.** treatable by a surgical operation. Compare INOPERABLE (def. 2). **2.** capable of being put into use, operation, or practice. —**op′er•a•bil′i•ty,** *n.* —**op′er•a•bly,** *adv.*

op′era glass′es (or **glass′**), *n.* a small, low-power pair of binoculars without prisms.

op′era house′, *n.* a theater devoted chiefly to operas.

op•er•and (op′ə rand′), *n.* a quantity upon which a mathematical operation is performed.

op•er•ate (op′ə rāt′), *v.*, **-at•ed, -at•ing.** —*v.i.* **1.** to work, perform, or function, as a machine does. **2.** to exert force or influence (often fol. by *on* or *upon*). **3.** to perform some process of work or treatment. **4.** to perform a surgical procedure. **5.** to carry on military operations in war. **6.** to carry on transactions in securities, or some commodity, esp. speculatively or on a large scale. **7.** *Informal.* to insinuate oneself; finagle. —*v.t.* **8.** to manage or use (a machine, device, etc.). **9.** to put or keep (a factory, industrial system, ranch, etc.) in operation. **10.** to bring about, effect, or produce, as by action or the exertion of force or influence. —**op′er•at′a•ble,** *adj.*

op•er•at•ic (op′ə rat′ik), *adj.* **1.** of, resembling, or suitable for opera. —*n.* Usu. **operatics.** (*used with a sing. or pl. v.*) **2.** the production or staging of operas. **3.** exaggerated or melodramatic behavior. —**op′er•at′i•cal•ly,** *adv.*

op′erating sys′tem, *n.* the software that directs a computer's operations, as by controlling and scheduling the execution of other programs and managing storage and input/output.

op•er•a•tion (op′ə rā′shən), *n.* **1.** an act or instance, process, or manner of functioning or operating. **2.** the state of being operative (usu. prec. by *in* or *into*): *a rule no longer in operation.* **3.** the power to act; efficacy, influence, or force. **4.** the exertion of force, power, or influence; agency. **5.** a process of a practical or mechanical nature. **6.** a business transaction, esp. one of a speculative nature; deal. **7.** a business, esp. one run on a large scale. **8.** a procedure aimed at restoring or

improving the health of a patient, as by correcting a malformation, removing diseased parts, implanting new parts, etc. **9. a.** a mathematical process, as addition, multiplication, or differentiation. **b.** the action of applying a mathematical process to a quantity or quantities. **10. a.** a military campaign, mission, maneuver, or action. **b.** Usu., **operations.** the conduct of such a campaign, mission, etc. **c. operations,** a headquarters, office, etc., from which such activity is conducted. **d. operations,** the staff at such a headquarters.

op•er•a•tion•al (op′ə rā′shə nl), *adj.* **1.** able to function or be used; functional. **2. a.** of, pertaining to, or involved in military operations. **b.** on active service or combat duty. **3.** of or pertaining to operations or an operation. —**op′er•a′tion•al•ly,** *adv.*

opera′tions research′, *n.* the analysis, usu. involving mathematical treatment, of a process, problem, or operation to determine its purpose and effectiveness and to gain maximum efficiency.

op•er•a•tive (op′ər ə tiv, op′rə tiv, op′ə rā′tiv), *n.* **1.** a person engaged or skilled in some branch of work, esp. productive or industrial work; worker. **2.** DETECTIVE. **3.** a secret agent; spy. **4.** a clever manipulator; operator. —*adj.* **5.** operating, or exerting force or influence. **6.** being in effect or operation. **7.** effective or efficacious. **8.** significant; key: *The operative word in that sentence is "sometimes."* **9.** concerned with, involving, or pertaining to surgical operations. —**op′er•a•tive•ly,** *adv.*

op•er•a•tor (op′ə rā′tər), *n.* **1.** a person who operates a machine, apparatus, or the like. **2.** a person who operates a telephone switchboard. **3.** a person who manages an industrial establishment. **4.** a person who trades in securities, esp. speculatively or on a large scale. **5. a.** a symbol for expressing a mathematical or logical operation. **b.** a function, esp. one transforming a function, set, etc., into another. **6.** a person who accomplishes his or her purposes by cleverness or devious means. **7.** a segment of DNA that interacts with a regulatory molecule, preventing transcription of the adjacent region.

op•er•et•ta (op′ə ret′ə), *n., pl.* **-tas.** a short opera usu. of a light and amusing character.

O′ Per′fect Love′, a Christian hymn (1882) with words by Dorothy B. Gurney and music by Joseph Barnby: often sung at weddings.

o•phid•i•an (ō fid′ē ən), *adj.* **1.** belonging or pertaining to the suborder Serpentes (formerly Ophidia), comprising the snakes. —*n.* **2.** a snake.

oph•i•ol•o•gy (of′ē ol′ə jē, ō′fē-), *n.* the study of snakes, a branch of herpetology. —**oph′i•o•log′i•cal** (-ə loj′i kəl), **oph′i•o•log′ic,** *adj.* —**oph′i•ol′o•gist,** *n.*

O•phir (ō′fər), *n.* a country of uncertain location from which gold and precious stones and trees were brought for Solomon. I Kings 10:11.

oph•thal•mic (of thal′mik, op-), *adj.* of or pertaining to the eye.

ophthalmo-, a combining form meaning "eye": *ophthalmology.*

oph•thal•mol•o•gist (of′thal mol′ə jist, -thə-, -thal-, op′-), *n.* a physician specializing in ophthalmology.

oph•thal•mol•o•gy (of′thal mol′ə jē, -thə-, -thal-, op′-), *n.* the branch of medicine dealing with the anatomy, functions, and diseases of the eye. —**oph•thal′mo•log′i•cal** (-mə loj′i kəl), *adj.*

o•pi•ate (*n., adj.* ō′pē it, -āt′; *v.* ō′pē āt′), *n., v.,* **-ated, -ating.** —*n.* **1.** a drug containing opium or its derivatives. **2.** any sedative, soporific, or narcotic. **3.** anything that induces lethargy or that soothes the feelings. —*adj.* **4.** mixed or prepared with opium. **5.** inducing sleep; narcotic. **6.** causing lethargy or inaction. —*v.t.* **7.** to subject to an opiate; sedate or stupefy.

o•pine (ō pīn′), *v.,* **o•pined, o•pin•ing.** —*v.t.* **1.** to express as an opinion. —*v.i.* **2.** to express opinions.

o•pin•ion (ə pin′yən), *n.* **1.** a belief or judgment based on grounds insufficient to produce complete certainty. **2.** a personal view, attitude, or appraisal. **3.** the formal expression of a professional judgment: *a second medical opinion.* **4.** the formal statement by a judge or court of the principles used in reaching a decision on a case. **5.** a judgment or estimate of a person or thing with respect to character, merit, etc. **6.** a favorable estimate; esteem. —**o•pin′ioned,** *adj.*

o•pin•ion•at•ed (ə pin′yə nā′tid), *adj.* obstinate or conceited regarding the merit of one's own opinions; dogmatic. —**o•pin′ion•at′ed•ly,** *adv.* —**o•pin′ion•at′ed•ness,** *n.*

O′ Pioneers′, a novel (1913) by Willa Cather.

o•pi•um (ō′pē əm), *n.* **1.** the dried, condensed juice of the seed capsules of a poppy, *Papaver somniferum,* that has a narcotic effect and contains morphine, codeine, and other alkaloids. **2.** OPIATE (def. 3).

o′pium pop′py, *n.* a Eurasian poppy, *Papaver somniferum,* having white, pink, red, or purple flowers, cultivated as the source of opium and as an ornamental.

o•pos•sum (ə pos′əm, pos′əm), *n., pl.* **-sums,** (*esp. collectively*) **-sum. 1.** a prehensile-tailed marsupial, *Didelphis virginiana,* of the eastern U.S.: noted for feigning death when in danger. **2.** any marsupial of the New World family Didelphidae. **3.** POSSUM (def. 2).

opossum, *Didelphis virginiana,* head and body 18 in. (0.5 m); tail 13 in. (33 cm)

op·po·nent (ə pō′nənt), *n.* **1.** a person who is on an opposing side in a game, controversy, or the like; adversary. —*adj.* **2.** being opposite, as in position. **3.** opposing; adverse; antagonistic. **4.** *Anat.* bringing parts together or into opposition, as a muscle.

op·por·tune (op′ər tōōn′, -tyōōn′), *adj.* **1.** suitable; apt: *an opportune comment.* **2.** occurring at an appropriate time; well-timed: *an opportune appearance.* —**op′por·tune′ly,** *adv.* —**op′por·tune′ness,** *n.*

op·por·tun·ism (op′ər tōō′niz əm, -tyōō′-), *n.* the policy or practice, as in politics or business, of adapting actions, decisions, etc., to expediency or effectiveness without regard to principles or consequences. —**op′por·tun′ist,** *n.*

op·por·tun·is·tic (op′ər tōō nis′tik, -tyōō-), *adj.* **1.** adhering to a policy of opportunism; practicing opportunism. **2. a.** (of a microorganism) causing disease only under certain conditions, as when a person's immune system is impaired. **b.** (of a disease or infection) caused by such an organism, as pneumocystis pneumonia in a person with AIDS. —**op′por·tun·is′ti·cal·ly,** *adv.*

op·por·tu·ni·ty (op′ər tōō′ni tē, -tyōō′-), *n., pl.* **-ties. 1.** an appropriate or favorable time or occasion. **2.** a situation or condition favorable for attainment of a goal. **3.** a good position, chance, or prospect, as for success. —*Proverb.* **4. Opportunity knocks but once,** seize a chance when it occurs or you may not get another.

op·pos·a·ble (ə pō′zə bəl), *adj.* **1.** capable of being opposed or resisted. **2.** able to be placed against something else: *the opposable thumb of primates.* —**op·pos′a·bil′i·ty,** *n.*

op·pose (ə pōz′), *v.,* **-posed, -pos·ing.** —*v.t.* **1.** to act against or furnish resistance to; combat. **2.** to hinder or obstruct. **3.** to set as an opponent or adversary. **4.** to be hostile or adverse to, as in opinion: *to oppose new tax legislation.* **5.** to set against, esp. for comparison or contrast: *to oppose advantages to disadvantages.* **6.** to set (something) opposite something else, or to set (two things) so as to be opposite one another. —*v.i.* **7.** to be in opposition.

op·po·site (op′ə zit, -sit), *adj.* **1.** situated or lying face to face with something else or each other, or placed in corresponding positions across an intervening line, space, etc.: *at opposite ends of a room.* **2.** contrary or radically different, as in nature, qualities, or significance; opposed: *opposite sides in a controversy.* **3.** *Bot.* situated on diametrically opposite sides of a stem, as leaves occurring in pairs at a node. **4.** adverse or inimical. —*n.* **5.** a person or thing that is opposite or contrary. **6.** ANTONYM. —*prep.* **7.** across from; facing: *to sit opposite the fireplace.* **8.** in a role parallel or complementary to: *He has played opposite many leading ladies.* —*adv.* **9.** on or to the opposite side: *I was at one end and she sat opposite.* —**op′po·site·ly,** *adv.* —**op′po·site·ness,** *n.*

op′po·site num′ber, *n.* counterpart; equivalent: *New members with an interest in folk art will find their opposite numbers in the association's directory.*

op·po·si·tion (op′ə zish′ən), *n.* **1.** the action of opposing, resisting, or combating. **2.** antagonism or hostility. **3.** a person or group of people opposing, criticizing, or protesting something, someone, or another group. **4.** (*sometimes cap.*) the major political party opposed to the party in power and seeking to replace it. **5.** the act of placing opposite, or the state or position of being placed opposite. **6.** the act of opposing, or the state of being opposed by way of comparison or contrast. **7.** the relation between two propositions in logic that have the same subject and predicate, but which differ in quantity or quality, or in both. **8.** the situation of two heavenly bodies when their longitudes or right ascensions differ by 180°: *The moon is in opposition to the sun when the earth is directly between them.* **9.** the relationship between two alternative units within a linguistic system, esp. between minimally distinct phonemes. —**op′po·si′tion·al,** *adj.* —**op′po·si′tion·ist,** *n., adj.*

op·press (ə pres′), *v.t.* **1.** to govern or manage with cruel or unjust impositions or restraints; exercise harsh authority or power over. **2.** to lie heavily upon (the mind, a person, etc.); weigh down. —**op·press′i·ble,** *adj.* —**op·press′or,** *n.*

op·pres·sion (ə presh′ən), *n.* **1.** the exercise of authority or power in a cruel or unjust manner. **2.** something that oppresses. **3.** the feeling of being oppressed.

op·pres·sive (ə pres′iv), *adj.* **1.** burdensome, unjustly harsh, or tyrannical. **2.** causing discomfort. **3.** distressing or grievous. —**op·pres′sive·ly,** *adv.* —**op·pres′sive·ness,** *n.*

op·pro·bri·ous (ə prō′brē əs), *adj.* conveying or expressing opprobrium, as language or a speaker. **2.** disgraceful or shameful. —**op·pro′bri·ous·ly,** *adv.* —**op·pro′bri·ous·ness,** *n.*

op·pro·bri·um (ə prō′brē əm), *n.* **1.** the disgrace or reproach incurred by shameful conduct. **2.** the cause of such disgrace or reproach. **3.** reproach; scorn.

Ops (ops), *n.* the Roman goddess of plenty and the wife of Saturn.

-opsy, a combining form occurring in words denoting a medical examination or inspection: *biopsy.*

opt (opt), *v.i.* **1.** to make a choice; choose: *Voters opted for conservative candidates.* **2. opt out,** to decide to leave or withdraw: *to opt out of the urban congestion.*

op·tic (op′tik), *adj.* **1.** of or pertaining to the eye or sight. —*n.* **2.** Usu. **optics.** *Slang.* the eye. **3.** a lens of an optical instrument.

op·ti·cal (op′ti kəl), *adj.* **1.** of, pertaining to, or applying optics. **2.** of or pertaining to the eye or sight. **3.** constructed to assist sight. **4.** dealing with or skilled in optics. —**op′ti·cal·ly,** *adv.*

op′tical art′, *n.* OP ART.

op′tical char′acter recogni′tion, *n.* the process or technology of reading printed or typed text by electronic means and converting it to digital data. *Abbr.:* OCR

op′tical disc′, *n.* **1.** Also called **laser disc.** a grooveless disk on which digital data, as text, music, or pictures, are stored as tiny pits in the surface and read or replayed by a laser beam scanning the surface. **2.** VIDEODISC. Compare COMPACT DISC.

op′tical illu′sion, *n.* See under ILLUSION (def. 4).

op′tical scan′ning, *n.* the process of interpreting data in printed, handwritten, bar-code, or other visual form by a device (**op′tical scan′ner**) that scans and identifies the data.

op·ti·cian (op tish′ən), *n.* a person who makes or sells eyeglasses and contact lenses in accordance with the prescriptions of ophthalmologists and optometrists.

op′tic nerve′, *n.* either of a pair of cranial nerves consisting of sensory fibers that conduct impulses from the retina to the brain.

op·tics (op′tiks), *n.* (*used with a sing. v.*) the branch of physical science that deals with the properties and phenomena of both visible and invisible light and with vision.

op·ti·mal (op′tə məl), *adj.* OPTIMUM. —**op′ti·mal·ly,** *adv.*

op·ti·mism (op′tə miz′əm), *n.* **1.** a tendency to look on the more favorable side or to expect the most favorable outcome of events or conditions. **2.** the belief that good will ultimately triumph over evil and that virtue will be rewarded. **3.** the doctrine that the existing world is the best of all possible worlds. —**op′ti·mist,** *n.* —**op′ti·mis′tic,** *adj.* —**op′ti·mis′ti·cal·ly,** *adv.*

op·ti·mize (op′tə mīz′), *v.,* **-mized, -miz·ing.** —*v.t.* **1.** to make as effective, perfect, or useful as possible. **2.** to make the best of. **3.** to write or rewrite (the instructions in a computer program) for maximum efficiency and speed in retrieval, storage, or execution. **4.** *Math.* to determine the maximum or minimum values of (a specified function that is subject to a set of constraints). —*v.i.* **5.** to be optimistic. —**op′ti·mi·za′tion,** *n.* —**op′ti·miz′er,** *n.*

op·ti·mum (op′tə məm), *n., pl.* **-ma** (-mə), **-mums,** *adj.* —*n.* **1.** the most favorable point, degree, or amount of something for obtaining a given result. **2.** the most favorable conditions for the growth or reproduction of an organism. **3.** the best result obtainable under specific conditions. —*adj.* **4.** most favorable or desirable; best: *optimum conditions.*

op·tion (op′shən), *n.* **1.** the power or right of choosing. **2.** something that may be chosen; choice. **3.** the act of choosing. **4.** an item of equipment or an extra feature that may be chosen. **5.** part of a legal agreement giving one the right to buy property, use services, etc., after a specified time or for an additional period under the terms of the agreement. —*v.t.* **6.** to acquire or grant an option on. —**op′tion·a·ble,** *adj.*

op·tion·al (op′shə nl), *adj.* left to one's choice; not required or mandatory: *Formal dress is optional.* —**op′tion·al·ly,** *adv.*

opto-, a combining form meaning "optic" or "vision": *optometry.*

op·to·e·lec·tron·ics (op′tō i lek tron′iks, -ē′lek-), *n.* (*used with a sing. v.*) the branch of electronics dealing with devices that generate, transform, transmit, or sense optical, infrared, or ultraviolet radiation, as solar cells and lasers. —**op′to·e·lec·tron′ic,** *adj.*

op·tom·e·trist (op tom′i trist), *n.* a licensed professional who practices optometry.

op·tom·e·try (op tom′i trē), *n.* the practice or profession of examining the eyes for defects of vision and eye disorders in order to prescribe corrective lenses or other appropriate treatment. —**op·to·met′ri·cal** (op′tə me′tri kəl), *adj.*

op·u·lence (op′yə ləns) also **op′u·len·cy,** *n.* **1.** wealth, riches, or affluence. **2.** abundance, as of resources or goods. **3.** the state of being opulent.

op·u·lent (op′yə lənt), *adj.* **1.** characterized by opulence: *an opulent lifestyle.* **2.** wealthy, rich, or affluent. **3.** richly supplied; plentiful: *opulent sunshine.* —**op′u·lent·ly,** *adv.*

o·pus (ō′pəs), *n., pl.* **o·pus·es** or, esp. for 1, **o·pe·ra** (ō′pər ə, op′ər ə). **1.** one of the compositions of a composer, usu. numbered according to the order of publication. **2.** a literary work or composition.

O′pus De′i (dā′ē), *n.* an international Roman Catholic order with lay and clerical members: founded in Spain in 1928.

or¹ (ôr; *unstressed* ər), *conj.* **1.** (used to connect words, phrases, or clauses representing alternatives): *to be or not to be.* **2.** (used to connect alternative terms for the same thing): *the Hawaiian, or Sandwich, Islands.* **3.** (used in correlation): *Either we go now or wait till tomorrow.* **4.** (used to correct or rephrase what was previously said): *His autobiography, or rather memoirs, will be published soon.* **5.** otherwise; or else: *Be here on time, or we'll leave without you.* **6.** *Logic.* the connective used in disjunction. —**Usage.** See EITHER.

or² (ôr), *n.* the heraldic color yellow or gold. [Latin *aurum* gold]

OR, *n.* a Boolean operator that returns a positive result when either or both operands are positive.

OR, 1. operating room. **2.** operations research. **3.** Oregon.

-or¹, a suffix occurring in loanwords from Latin, directly or through Anglo-French, usu. denoting a condition or property of things or persons, sometimes corresponding to qualitative adjectives ending in -ID⁴ (*honor; horror; liquor; pallor*); a few other words that orig. ended in different suffixes have been assimilated to this group (*behavior; demeanor; glamour*). —**Usage.** The *-or* spelling of the suffix -OR¹ is characteristic of

American English, with occasional exceptions. In British English *-our* is still the most common spelling, *-or* often being retained when certain suffixes are added, as in *color*ation, *honor*ary, and *labor*ious. The English of Australia, New Zealand, and South Africa tends to mirror British practice, whereas Canadian English is about equally divided between U.S. and British forms.

The suffix -OR[2] is now spelled *-or* in all forms of English, except for the word *savior,* once often spelled *saviour* in the U.S. as in Britain, esp. with reference to Jesus. But the official spelling of Catholics, Episcopalians, Presbyterians, and Methodists is now SAVIOR; SAVIOUR is now only British.

-or[2], a suffix forming animate or inanimate agent nouns, occurring orig. in loanwords from Anglo-French (*debtor; tailor; traitor*); it now functions in English as an orthographic variant of -ER[1], usu. joined to bases of Latin origin, in imitation of borrowed Latin words containing the suffix -TOR (and alternant *-sor*). Resultant formations often denote machines or less tangible entities that behave in an agentlike way: *projector; repressor; sensor; tractor.*

or•a•cle (ôr′ə kəl, or′-), *n.* **1.** (esp. in the ancient world) **a.** a shrine at which inquiries are made of a particular deity through a means of divination. **b.** the agency by which the inquiry is answered, as a priest or priestess. **c.** the typically terse, ambiguous response of the deity. **2.** a person who delivers authoritative and usu. influential pronouncements. **3.** any utterance regarded as authoritative, unquestionably wise, or infallible. **4.** the holy of holies of the Temple built by Solomon in Jerusalem. I Kings 6:16, 19–23.

o•rac•u•lar (ô rak′yə lər, ō rak′-), *adj.* **1.** of the nature of an oracle. **2.** making pronouncements as if by special inspiration or authority. **3.** uttered or delivered as if divinely inspired or infallible. **4.** ambiguous; obscure. —**o•rac′u•lar•ly,** *adv.* —**o•rac′u•lar′i•ty** (-lar′i tē), *n.*

o•ral (ôr′əl, ōr′-), *adj.* **1.** uttered by the mouth; spoken: *oral testimony.* **2.** of, using, or transmitted by speech: *oral traditions.* **3.** of or involving the mouth: *oral hygiene.* **4.** done or administered through the mouth. **5.** (of a speech sound) pronounced with all the air issuing through the mouth and none through the nose, as the normal English vowels or the consonants (b) and (v). **6.** *Psychoanal.* **a.** of, pertaining to, or characteristic of the earliest phase of psychosexual development, during which pleasure is derived from activities involving the mouth, as sucking, eating, and babbling. **b.** of or pertaining to a group of adult behaviors and personality traits including eating, talking, feeding, and being friendly and generous. **7.** LINGUAL (def. 4). —*n.* **8.** an oral examination in a school, college, or university, given esp. to a candidate for an advanced degree. —**o′ral•ly,** *adv.* —**Usage.** See VERBAL.

o′ral contracep′tive, *n.* BIRTH-CONTROL PILL.

o′ral her′pes, *n.* a disease caused by a herpes simplex virus, characterized chiefly by a cluster of small, transient blisters **(cold sore)** at the edge of the lip or nostril.

o′ral his′tory, *n.* **1.** historical information obtained by interviews with persons whose experiences have been representative or of special significance. **2.** a book, article, recording, or transcription of such information. —**o′ral histo′rian,** *n.*

-orama or **-ama** or **-arama** or **-rama,** a combining form extracted from PANORAMA, DIORAMA, or CYCLORAMA, occurring as the final element in coinages that denote a display or spectacle, or the space, as a store or hall, containing it: *audiorama; scoutorama; smellorama.*

o•rang (ô rang′, ō rang′), *n.* ORANGUTAN.

or•ange (ôr′inj, or′-), *n.* **1.** any of various globose, reddish yellow, bitter or sweet, edible citrus fruits. **2.** any of various white-flowered evergreen trees of the genus *Citrus,* bearing such fruit, and cultivated in warm countries. **3.** a color between yellow and red in the spectrum, an effect of light with a wavelength between 590 and 610 nm. —*adj.* **4.** of or pertaining to the orange. **5.** prepared with oranges or orangelike flavoring: *orange sherbet.* **6.** of the color orange; reddish yellow.

or•ange•ade (ôr′inj ād′, -in jād′, or′-), *n.* a beverage of orange juice, sugar, and plain or carbonated water.

Or•ange•man (ôr′inj mən, or′-), *n., pl.* **-men. 1.** a member of a secret Protestant society formed in the north of Ireland in 1795. **2.** a Protestant of Northern Ireland.

or′ange milk′weed, *n.* BUTTERFLY WEED.

or′ange pe′koe, *n.* a black tea composed of the smallest top leaves and grown in India and Ceylon.

or•ange•ry (ôr′inj rē, or′-), *n., pl.* **-ries.** a warm place in which orange trees are cultivated in cool climates.

or•ange•wood (ôr′inj wo͝od′, or′-), *n.* the hard, fine-grained, yellowish wood of the orange tree, used in inlaid work and fine turnery.

o•rang•u•tan (ô rang′o͞o tan′, ō rang′-, ə rang′-) also **o•rang′u•tang′, o•rang′ou•tang′** (-tang′), *n.* a large, mostly arboreal, long-armed anthropoid ape, *Pongo pygmaeus,* of Borneo and Sumatra.

or•ang•y or **or•ang•ey** (ôr′in jē, or′-), also **or′ang•ish,** *adj.* resembling an orange, as in taste, appearance, or color.

o•rate (ô rāt′, ō rāt′, ôr′āt, ōr′āt), *v.i., v.t.,* **-rat•ed, -rat•ing.** to deliver an oration, esp. to speak pompously.

o•ra•tion (ô rā′shən, ō rā′-), *n.* a formal public speech, esp. for a special occasion.

or•a•tor (ôr′ə tər, or′-), *n.* a person who delivers an oration; a public speaker, esp. one of great eloquence.

or•a•tor•i•cal (ôr′ə tôr′i kəl, or′ə tor′-), *adj.* **1.** of, pertaining to, or characteristic of an orator or oratory. **2.** given to oratory. —**or′a•tor′i•cal•ly,** *adv.*

or•a•to•ri•o (ôr′ə tôr′ē ō′, -tōr′-, or′-), *n., pl.* **-ri•os.** an extended musical work usu. based upon a religious theme, for solo voices, chorus, and orchestra, and performed without action, costume, or scenery.

or•a•to•ry[1] (ôr′ə tôr′ē, -tōr′ē, or′-), *n.* **1.** skill or eloquence in public speaking. **2.** the art of public speaking, esp. in a formal and eloquent manner.

or•a•to•ry[2] (ôr′ə tôr′ē, -tōr′ē, or′-), *n., pl.* **-ries. 1.** a place of prayer, as a small chapel or a room for private devotions. **2.** (*cap.*) any of the Roman Catholic religious societies of secular priests who live in religious communities but do not take vows.

orb (ôrb), *n.* **1.** a sphere or globe. **2.** the eyeball or eye. **3.** any of the heavenly bodies, as the sun or moon. **4.** a sphere bearing a cross as emblem of sovereignty and justice. **5.** any of the hollow concentric spheres that in pre-Copernican astronomy were thought to surround the earth and carry the planets and stars. —*v.t.* **6.** to form into a circle or sphere. —*v.i.* **7.** to move in an orbit. —**orb′less,** *adj.*

or•bic•u•lar (ôr bik′yə lər), *adj.* circular; spherical. —**or•bic′u•lar′i•ty,** *n.* —**or•bic′u•lar•ly,** *adv.*

or•bit (ôr′bit), *n.* **1.** the curved path, usu. elliptical, described by a planet, satellite, spaceship, etc., around a celestial body. **2.** the usual course of one's life. **3.** the sphere of influence, as of a nation or person. **4.** (in Bohr theory) the path traced by an electron revolving around the nucleus of an atom. **5.** the bony cavity of the skull that contains the eye; eye socket. **6.** the part surrounding the eye of a bird or insect. —*v.t.* **7.** to move or travel around in an orbital or elliptical path. **8.** to send into orbit, as a satellite. —*v.i.* **9.** to travel in an orbit.

or•bit•al (ôr′bi tl), *adj.* **1.** of or pertaining to an orbit. —*n.* **2. a.** a wave function describing the state of a single electron in an atom or in a molecule. **b.** the electron in that state.

or•bit•er (ôr′bi tər), *n.* **1.** a space probe designed to orbit a planetary body or moon. **2.** the crew- and payload-carrying component of a space shuttle.

orb′ weav′er, *n.* any spider of the family Araneidae that weaves spiraling webs with crossing support lines.

or•ca (ôr′kə), *n., pl.* **-cas.** KILLER WHALE.

or•chard (ôr′chərd), *n.* **1.** an area of land devoted to the cultivation of fruit or nut trees. **2.** a group or collection of such trees.

or•ches•tra (ôr′kə strə, -kes trə), *n., pl.* **-tras. 1.** a group of performers on various musical instruments, including esp. strings, winds, and percussion, who play music together. **2.** (in a modern theater) **a.** the space reserved for the musicians, usu. the front part of the main floor **(or′chestra pit′). b.** the entire main-floor space for the audience. **c.** the front section of seats on the main floor; parquet.

or•ches•tral (ôr kes′trəl), *adj.* **1.** of, pertaining to, or resembling an orchestra. **2.** composed for or performed by an orchestra: *orchestral works.* —**or•ches′tral•ly,** *adv.*

or•ches•trate (ôr′kə strāt′), *v.t.,* **-trat•ed, -trat•ing. 1.** to compose or arrange (music) for orchestra. **2.** to arrange, coordinate, or manipulate the elements of to achieve a goal or effect: *to orchestrate negotiations.* —**or′ches•tra′tion,** *n.* —**or′ches•tra′tor, or′ches•trat′er,** *n.*

or•chid (ôr′kid), *n.* **1.** any terrestrial or epiphytic plant of the family Orchidaceae, of temperate and tropical regions, having showy flowers. **2.** the flower of any of these plants. **3.** a bluish to reddish purple.

or•dain (ôr dān′), *v.t.* **1.** to invest with ministerial or sacerdotal functions; confer holy orders upon. **2.** to enact or establish by law, edict, etc. **3.** to decree; give orders for. **4.** (of God, fate, etc.) to destine or predestine. —*v.i.* **5.** to order or command. —**or•dain′er,** *n.*

or•deal (ôr dēl′, -dē′əl, ôr′dēl), *n.* **1.** any extremely severe or trying test, experience, or trial. **2.** a former method of trial used to determine guilt or innocence by subjecting the accused person to serious physical danger, the result being regarded as a divine judgment.

or•der (ôr′dər), *n.* **1.** an authoritative direction or instruction; command. **2.** the disposition of things following one after another; succession or sequence: *alphabetical order.* **3.** a condition in which each thing is properly disposed with reference to other things and to its purpose; methodical or harmonious arrangement. **4.** formal disposition or array. **5.** proper, satisfactory, or working condition. **6.** state or condition generally: *in good working order.* **7.** conformity or obedience to law or established authority: *to maintain law and order.* **8.** customary mode of procedure; established practice or usage. **9.** the customary or prescribed mode of proceeding in debates, legislative bodies, meetings, etc.: *parliamentary rules of order.* **10.** prevailing course or arrangement of things; established system or regime: *The old order is changing.* **11.** a direction or commission to make, provide, or furnish something. **12.** a quantity of goods or items purchased or sold. **13.** a portion of food requested or served in a restaurant. **14.** *Math.* **a.** degree, as in algebra. **b.** the number of rows or columns of a square matrix or determinant. **c.** the number of times a function has been differentiated to produce a given derivative: *a second-order derivative.* **d.** the highest derivative appearing in a given differential equation. **e.** the number of elements of a given group. **15.** a class, kind, or sort distinguished from others by character or rank: *talents of a high order.* **16.** *Biol.* the usual major subdivision of a class or subclass in the classification of organisms, consisting of one or more families. **17.** a rank or class of persons in a community. **18.** a group or body of persons of the same profession, occupation, or pursuits. **19.** a body or society of persons living by common consent under the same religious, moral, or social regulations. **20.** any of the degrees or grades of clerical office. **21.** a monastic society or fraternity: *the Franciscan order.* **22.** any of the nine grades of angels in medieval angelology. Compare ANGEL (def. 1). **23.** a written direction to pay money or deliver goods, given by a person legally entitled to dispose of it. **24.** *Archit.* **a.** an arrangement of columns with an entablature. **b.** any of five styles of column and entablature typical of classical architecture, including the Doric, Ionic, Corinthian, Tuscan, and Composite styles. **25. orders,** the rank or status of an ordained Christian minister. **26.** Usu., **orders.** the rite or sacrament of ordination. **27.** a prescribed form of religious service or of administration of a rite. **28.** a society or fraternity of knights, of combined military and monastic character, as the medieval Knights Templars. **29.** an organization or fraternal society in some way resembling the knightly orders. **30.** (*cap.*) **a.** a special honor or rank conferred by a sovereign upon a person for distinguished achievement. **b.** the insignia worn by such persons. —*v.t.* **31.** to give an order or command to. **32.** to direct or command to go or come as specified: *She ordered them out of her house.* **33.** to direct to be made or supplied: *to order a copy of a book.* **34.** to prescribe. **35.** to regulate, conduct, or manage. **36.** to arrange methodically or suitably. **37.** *Math.* to arrange (the elements of a set) so that if one element precedes another, it cannot be preceded by the other or by elements that the other precedes. **38.** to ordain. —*v.i.* **39.** to give an order or issue orders. —*Idiom.* **40. a tall** or **large order,** a difficult or formidable task. **41. call to order,** to begin (a meeting). **42. in order, a.** rightful and proper; appropriate: *An apology is certainly in order.* **b.** properly arranged or prepared; ready. **c.** correct according to the rules of parliamentary procedure. **43. in order that,** so that; to the end that. **44. in order to,** as a means to; with the purpose of. **45. in short order,** with promptness or speed; rapidly. **46. on order,** ordered but not yet received. **47. on the order of, a.** resembling to some extent; like. **b.** approximately; about. **48. out of order, a.** not in correct sequence or arrangement. **b.** inappropriate; unsuitable. **c.** not operating properly; in disrepair. **d.** incorrect according to the rules of parliamentary procedure. **49. to order,** according to the purchaser's requirements or stipulations. —**or′der•a•ble,** *adj.*

Doric   Ionic   Corinthian   Tuscan   Composite

orders (def. 24b)

or•der•ly (ôr′dər lē), *adj., n., pl.* **-lies,** *adv.* —*adj.* **1.** arranged or disposed in a neat, tidy manner or in a regular sequence: *an orderly desk.* **2.** observant of or governed by system or method. **3.** characterized by or observant of law, rule, or discipline; well-behaved; law-abiding. **4.** pertaining to or charged with the communication or execution of orders. —*n.* **5.** a hospital attendant having general, nonmedical duties. **6.** an enlisted soldier assigned to perform various chores for a commanding officer or group of officers. —*adv.* **7.** methodically; regularly. **8.** according to established order or rule. —**or′der•li•ness,** *n.*

or′der of busi′ness, *n.* a task assigned or to be dealt with: *Our first order of business is to reduce expenses.*

or′der of the day′, *n.* **1.** the agenda for a meeting, group, or organization. **2.** an activity of primary importance.

or•di•nal¹ (ôr′dn əl), *adj.* **1.** of or pertaining to an order, as of animals or plants. **2.** of or pertaining to order, rank, or position in a series. —*n.* **3.** an ordinal number or numeral. —**or′di•nal•ly,** *adv.*

or•di•nal² (ôr′dn əl), *n.* **1.** a directory of ecclesiastical services. **2.** a book containing the forms for the ordination of priests, consecration of bishops, etc.

or′dinal num′ber, *n.* any of the numbers that express degree, quality, or position in a series, as *first, second,* and *third* (disting. from *cardinal number*).

or•di•nance (ôr′dn əns), *n.* **1.** an authoritative rule or law; a decree or command. **2.** a public injunction or regulation: *a city ordinance against excessive horn blowing.* **3.** something believed to have been ordained, as by a deity or destiny. **4.** an established rite or ceremony.

or•di•nand (ôr′dn and′), *n.* a candidate for ordination.

or•di•nar•i•ly (ôr′dn âr′ə lē, ôr′dn er′ə lē), *adv.* **1.** most of the time; generally; usually. **2.** in an unexceptional manner or fashion; modestly. **3.** to the usual extent; reasonably.

or•di•nar•y (ôr′dn er′ē), *adj., n., pl.* **-nar•ies.** —*adj.* **1.** of no special quality or interest; commonplace; unexceptional. **2.** plain or undistinguished. **3.** somewhat inferior or below average; mediocre. **4.** customary; usual; normal. **5.** (of jurisdiction) immediate, as contrasted with

that which is delegated. **6.** (of officials) belonging to the regular staff or the fully recognized class. —*n.* **7.** the commonplace or average condition, degree, etc.: *ability far above the ordinary.* **8.** something regular, customary, or usual. **9.** the service of the Mass exclusive of the proper. **10.** a bishop, archbishop, or other ecclesiastic or his deputy, in his capacity as an ex officio ecclesiastical authority. **11.** (in some U.S. states) a judge of a court of probate. **12.** *Brit.* a complete meal at a restaurant or inn with all courses included at one fixed price. **13.** a restaurant, public house, or dining room serving all customers the same standard meal or fare. **14.** a high bicycle of an early type, with one large wheel in front and one small wheel behind. **15.** a simple, common heraldic charge, as the chevron. —*Idiom.* **16. in ordinary,** in regular service: *a physician in ordinary to the king.* **17. out of the ordinary, a.** unusual. **b.** unusually good. —**or′di•nar′i•ness,** *n.*

or•di•nate (ôr′dn it′, -āt′), *n.* (in plane Cartesian coordinates) the y-coordinate of a point: its distance from the x-axis measured parallel to the y-axis.

or•di•na•tion (ôr′dn ā′shən), *n.* **1.** the act or ceremony of ordaining as a priest, minister, etc. **2.** the fact or state of being ordained. **3.** a decreeing. **4.** the act of arranging. **5.** the resulting state; disposition; arrangement.

ord•nance (ôrd′nəns), *n.* **1.** cannon or artillery. **2.** military weapons with their equipment, ammunition, etc. **3.** the army branch that deals with ordnance.

Or•do•vi•cian (ôr′də vish′ən), *adj.* **1.** noting or pertaining to a geologic period of the Paleozoic Era, from 500 million to 425 million years ago, notable for the advent of fish. —*n.* **2.** the Ordovician Period or System.

ore (ôr, ōr), *n.* **1.** a metal-bearing mineral or rock, or a native metal, that can be mined at a profit. **2.** a mineral or natural product serving as a source of some nonmetallic substance, as sulfur.

o•reg•a•no (ə reg′ə nō′, ô reg′-), *n.* an aromatic herb, *Origanum vulgare,* of the mint family, having leaves used as seasoning in cooking.

Or•e•gon (ôr′i gən, -gon′, or′-), *n.* a state in the NW United States, on the Pacific coast. 3,203,735; 96,981 sq. mi. (251,180 sq. km). *Cap.:* Salem. *Abbr.:* OR, Ore. —**Or•e•go•ni•an** (ôr′i gō′nē ən, or′-), *adj., n.*

Or′egon Trail′, *n.* a route used during the U.S. westward migrations, esp. in the period from 1840 to 1860, starting in Missouri and ending in Oregon. ab. 2000 mi. (3200 km) long.

O•res•te•ia (ôr′e stē′ə, ōr′-), a trilogy of tragic dramas (458 B.C.) by Aeschylus, consisting of the *Agamemnon,* the *Choëphori,* and the *Eumenides.*

O•res•tes (ô res′tēz, ō res′-), *n.* **1.** the legendary son of Agamemnon and Clytemnestra, who, together with his sister Electra, avenged the murder of his father by killing his mother and her lover. **2.** (*italics*) a tragedy (408 B.C.) by Euripides.

or•gan (ôr′gən), *n.* **1. a.** Also called **pipe organ.** a musical instrument having one or more sets of pipes actuated by keyboard and sounded by compressed air. **b.** a similar musical instrument having the tones produced electronically: *an electronic organ.* **c.** REED ORGAN. **d.** HAND ORGAN. **2.** a grouping of tissues into a distinct structure, as a heart or kidney in animals or a leaf or stamen in plants, that performs a specialized task. **3.** a newspaper, magazine, or other means of communicating information, thoughts, or opinions, esp. in behalf of some organization or political group. **4.** an instrument or means, as of action. **5.** PENIS.

or•gan•dy or **or•gan•die** (ôr′gən dē), *n., pl.* **-dies.** a fine, thin cotton fabric usu. having a crisp finish, used for dresses, curtains, etc.

or•gan•elle (ôr′gə nel′, ôr′gə nel′), *n.* a specialized cell structure that has a specific function; a cell organ.

or′gan grind′er, *n.* an itinerant street musician who earns a living by playing a hand organ or hurdy-gurdy.

or•gan•ic (ôr gan′ik), *adj.* **1.** noting or pertaining to a class of chemical compounds that formerly comprised only those existing in or derived from plants or animals, but that now includes all other compounds of carbon. Compare INORGANIC (def. 3). **2.** pertaining to, characteristic of, or derived from living organisms. **3.** of, pertaining to, or involving animals, produce, etc., raised or grown without synthetic fertilizers, pesticides, or drugs: *organic farming; organic chicken.* **4.** of or pertaining to an organ or the organs of an animal, plant, or fungus. **5.** of, pertaining to, or affecting living tissue. **6.** caused by physical change or impairment: *organic disorder.* Compare FUNCTIONAL (def. 5). **7.** characterized by the systematic arrangement of parts; organized; systematic. **8.** of or pertaining to the basic constitution or structure of a thing; constitutional; inherent; fundamental. **9.** developing in the manner of living organisms: *a view of history as organic.* **10.** *Law.* pertaining to the laws organizing the government of a state. —*n.* **11.** a substance, as a fertilizer or pesticide, of animal or vegetable origin. —**or·gan′i·cal·ly,** *adv.* —**or·ga·nic·i·ty** (ôr′gə nis′i tē), *n.*

or·gan′ic chem′istry, *n.* the branch of chemistry dealing with the compounds of carbon.

or·gan·ism (ôr′gə niz′əm), *n.* **1.** any individual life form considered as an entity; an animal, plant, fungus, protistan, or moneran. **2.** any complex, organized body or system analogous to a living being, esp. one composed of mutually interdependent parts functioning together. —**or′gan·is′mic, or′gan·is′mal,** *adj.* —**or′gan·is′mi·cal·ly,** *adv.*

or·gan·ist (ôr′gə nist), *n.* a person who plays the organ.

or·gan·i·za·tion (ôr′gə nə zā′shən), *n.* **1.** the act or process of organizing. **2.** the state or manner of being organized. **3.** something that is organized. **4.** organic structure; composition. **5.** a group of persons organized for some end or work; association. **6.** the administrative personnel or apparatus of a business. **7.** the functionaries of a political party along with the offices, committees, etc., that they fill. —*adj.* **8.** of or pertaining to an organization. **9.** conforming completely to the standards, rules, or demands of an organization, esp. that of one's employer: *an organization man.* —**or′gan·i·za′tion·al,** *adj.* —**or′gan·i·za′tion·al·ly,** *adv.*

organiza′tion man′, *n.* a person who conforms and is loyal to the standards and values of an organization. [from a 1972 novel of that name by William H. Whyte, Jr.]

Organiza′tion of Amer′ican States′, *n.* an organization composed of the U.S. and other republics in the Western Hemisphere, formed in 1948 to promote regional peace and cooperation. *Abbr.:* OAS

or·gan·ize (ôr′gə nīz′), *v.,* **-ized, -iz·ing.** —*v.t.* **1.** to form as or into a whole consisting of interdependent or coordinated parts, esp. for united action: *to organize a committee.* **2.** to systematize; order. **3.** to give organic structure or character to. **4.** to enlist or attempt to enlist into a labor union: *to organize workers.* **5.** to enlist the employees of (a business) into a labor union: *to organize a factory.* **6.** to put (oneself) in a state of mental competence to perform a task. —*v.i.* **7.** to combine in an organized company, party, or the like. **8.** to form a labor union.

or·gan·iz·er (ôr′gə nī′zər), *n.* **1.** a person who organizes. **2.** a person who enlists employees into membership in a union. **3.** a file folder or other container with multiple compartments for sorting the contents. **4.** any part of an embryo that stimulates the development and differentiation of another part.

organo-, a combining form with the meanings "organ of the body," "organic": *organogenesis; organophosphate.*

or·ga·non (ôr′gə non′), *n.,* *pl.* **-na** (-nə), **-nons. 1.** an instrument of thought or knowledge. **2.** a system of rules or principles of demonstration or investigation.

or′gan-pipe′ cac′tus, *n.* any of several treelike cacti of the southwest U.S. and Mexico, esp. the saguaro and a species, *Lemaireocereus marginatus,* having tall, columnlike stems.

or·gan·za (ôr gan′zə), *n.,* *pl.* **-zas.** a sheer, plain-weave fabric with a crisp finish, used for evening dresses, trimmings, etc.

or·gasm (ôr′gaz əm), *n.* **1.** the intense physical and emotional sensation experienced at the peak of sexual excitation, usually accompanied in the male by ejaculation; climax. **2.** intense or unrestrained excitement. —*v.i.* **3.** to have an orgasm. —**or·gas′mic, or·gas′tic** (-gas′-), *adj.*

or·gi·as·tic (ôr′jē as′tik), *adj.* **1.** of, pertaining to, or having the nature of an orgy. **2.** tending to arouse or excite unrestrained emotion: *orgiastic rhythms.*

or·gy (ôr′jē), *n.,* *pl.* **-gies. 1.** drunken or licentious revelry. **2.** any actions or proceedings marked by unbridled indulgence of passions: *an orgy of killing.*

o·ri·ent (*n., adj.* ôr′ē ənt, -ē ent′, ōr′-; *v.* ôr′ē ent′, ōr′-), *n.* **1. the Orient, a.** the countries of Asia, esp. East Asia. **b.** (formerly) the countries to the E of the Mediterranean. **2. a.** an orient pearl. **b.** the iridescent luster of a pearl or of mother-of-pearl. **3.** the east; the eastern region of the heavens or the world. —*v.t.* **4.** to adjust or bring into due relation to surroundings, circumstances, facts, etc. **5.** to familiarize with new surroundings or circumstances: *lectures to orient visitors.* **6.** to place in a position with reference to the points of the compass or other locations: *to orient a building north and south.* **7.** to direct or position toward a particular object. **8.** to determine the position of in relation to the points of the compass; get the bearings of. **9.** to place so as to face the east, esp. to build (a church) with the chief altar to the east and the chief entrance to the west. **10.** to set (the horizontal circle of a surveying instrument) so that readings give correct azimuths. —*adj.* **11.** (of a gem or pearl) exceptionally fine and lustrous. —**o′ri·ent′er,** *n.*

o·ri·en·tal (ôr′ē en′tl, ōr′-), *adj.* **1.** (*usu. cap.*) of, pertaining to, or characteristic of the Orient, or East; Eastern. **2.** eastern. **3.** (*cap.*) belonging to a zoogeographical division comprising S Asia and the Malay Archipelago as far as and including the Philippines, Borneo, and Java. **4. a.** (*usu. cap.*) (not in technical use) designating a variety of corundum resembling the color of the specified gemstone, crystal, or mineral: *Oriental amethyst.* **b.** of very fine quality: *oriental garnet.* **c.** (*often cap.*)

designating a natural saltwater pearl, esp. one found from the Red Sea eastward. —**o′ri·en·tal·ly,** *adv.*

O′rien′tal pop′py, *n.* an ornamental poppy, *Papaver orientale,* of Asia, having bristly stems and leaves and showy scarlet, pink, or white flowers.

O′rien′tal rug′, *n.* a rug or carpet woven usu. in Asia and characterized by hand-knotted pile. Also called **O′rien′tal car′pet.**

o·ri·en·tate (ôr′ē ən tāt′, -en-, ōr′-), *v.,* **-tat·ed, -tat·ing.** —*v.t.* **1.** to orient. —*v.i.* **2.** to turn toward the east.

o·ri·en·ta·tion (ôr′ē ən tā′shən, -en-, ōr′-), *n.* **1.** the act or process of orienting. **2.** the state of being oriented. **3.** an introductory program to guide a person in adjusting to new surroundings, employment, or the like. **4.** the ability to locate oneself in one's environment with reference to time, place, and people. **5.** position in relation to true north, to points on the compass, or to a specific place or object. **6.** the ascertainment of one's true position, as in a novel situation. **7.** the general direction or tendency of one's approach, thoughts, etc. **8.** the relative positions of certain atoms or groups, esp. in aromatic compounds.

o·ri·en·teer·ing (ôr′ē en tēr′ing, ōr′-), *n.* a sport in which competitors navigate unfamiliar terrain and locate checkpoints with the aid of a map and compass, the winner being the person who finishes with the lowest elapsed time.

or·i·fice (ôr′ə fis, or′-), *n.* an opening or aperture, as of a tube or pipe; a mouthlike opening or hole; mouth; vent. —**or′i·fi′cial** (-fish′əl), *adj.*

or·i·flamme (ôr′ə flam′, or′-), *n.* **1.** the red banner of St. Denis, near Paris. **2.** any ensign, banner, or standard that serves as a rallying point or symbol.

o·ri·ga·mi (ôr′i gä′mē), *n.* the Japanese art of folding paper into decorative or representational forms, as of animals or flowers. [< Japanese: folding paper]

Or·i·gen (ôr′i jen′, -jən, or′-), *n.* (*Origenes Admantius*) A.D. 185?–254?, Alexandrian writer and Christian theologian.

or·i·gin (ôr′i jin, or′-), *n.* **1.** something from which anything arises or is derived; source. **2.** rise or derivation from a particular source: *the origin of a word.* **3.** the first stage of existence; beginning. **4.** ancestry; parentage: *of Scottish origin.* **5.** *Anat.* **a.** the point of derivation. **b.** the more fixed portion of a muscle. **6.** *Math.* **a.** the point in a Cartesian coordinate system where the axes intersect. **b.** Also called **pole.** the point from which rays designating specific angles originate in a polar coordinate system with no axes.

o·rig·i·nal (ə rij′ə nl), *adj.* **1.** belonging or pertaining to the origin or beginning of something. **2.** arising or proceeding independently; inventive; novel: *an original idea.* **3.** capable of or given to thinking or acting in an independent, creative, or individual manner: *an original thinker.* **4.** created, undertaken, or presented for the first time: *the original performance of a play.* **5.** being that from which a copy, translation, or the like is made. —*n.* **6.** a primary form or type from which varieties are derived. **7.** an original work, document, or the like, as opposed to a copy or imitation. **8.** a person whose ways of thinking or acting are original.

o·rig·i·nal·i·ty (ə rij′ə nal′i tē), *n.* **1.** the quality or state of being original. **2.** the ability to think or express oneself in an independent and individual manner; creative ability. **3.** freshness or novelty, as of an idea, method, or performance.

o·rig·i·nal·ly (ə rij′ə nl ē), *adv.* **1.** at the origin; at first; initially. **2.** with respect to origin. **3.** in an original or individual manner.

orig′inal sin′, *n.* a depravity, or tendency to evil, held to be innate in humankind and transmitted from Adam to the race in consequence of his sin.

o·rig·i·nate (ə rij′ə nāt′), *v.,* **-nat·ed, -nat·ing.** —*v.i.* **1.** to take or have origin; arise. **2.** (of a public conveyance) to begin a scheduled run at a specified place. —*v.t.* **3.** to give origin or rise to; initiate. —**o·rig′i·na′tion,** *n.* —**o·rig′i·na′tor,** *n.*

Or′igin of Spe′cies, The, (*On the Origin of Species by Means of Natural Selection, or the Preservation of Favoured Races in the Struggle for Life*) a treatise (1859) by Charles Darwin setting forth his theory of evolution.

o·ri·ole (ôr′ē ōl′, ōr′-), *n.* **1.** any of various New World songbirds of the subfamily Icterinae (family Emberizidae), the males of which are usu. black and orange or black and yellow. Compare NORTHERN ORIOLE. **2.** any of various Old World songbirds of the family Oriolidae, as the golden oriole, *Oriolus oriolus,* having a bright yellow body and black wings and tail.

O·ri·on (ə rī′ən), *n., gen.* **Or·i·o·nis** (ôr′ē ō′nis, or′-, ə rī′ə nis) for 2. **1.** (in Greek myth) a hunter who was killed by Artemis and placed in the sky as a constellation. **2.** the Hunter, a constellation lying on the celestial equator between Canis Major and Taurus, containing the stars Betelgeuse and Rigel.

or·is·mol·o·gy (ôr′iz mol′ə jē, or′-), *n.* the science of defining the technical terms of a field of study.

or·i·son (ôr′ə zən, or′-), *n.* PRAYER.

Or·lan·do (ôr lan′dō), *n.* **1.** Vittorio Emanuele, 1860–1952, Italian statesman. **2.** a city in central Florida. 176,948.

Or·lon (ôr′lon), *Trademark.* a brand of acrylic textile fiber.

or·na·ment (*n.* ôr′nə mənt; *v.* -ment′, -mənt), *n.* **1.** an object or feature intended to beautify the appearance of that to which it is added or of which it is a part; embellishment; decoration. **2.** a group or style of such objects or features; ornamentation. **3.** any adornment or means of adornment. **4.** a person or thing that adds to the credit or glory of a society, era, etc. **5.** the act of adorning. **6.** a tone or group of tones applied as decoration to a principal melodic tone. **7.** any religious accessory, adjunct, or equipment. —*v.t.* **8.** to furnish with ornaments; embellish; decorate. **9.** to serve as an ornament to.

or·na·men·tal (ôr′nə men′tl), *adj.* **1.** used or grown for ornament: *ornamental plants.* **2.** providing ornament; decorative. **3.** of or pertaining to ornament. —*n.* **4.** something ornamental, esp. a plant cultivated for decorative purposes. —**or′na·men·tal′i·ty,** *n.* —**or′na·men′tal·ly,** *adv.*

or·na·men·ta·tion (ôr′nə men tā′shən, -mən-), *n.* **1.** the act of ornamenting. **2.** the state of being ornamented. **3.** something with which a thing is ornamented; embellishment. **4.** ornaments collectively.

or·nate (ôr nāt′), *adj.* **1.** elaborately adorned, often excessively or showily so. **2.** rhetorically florid: *ornate writing.* —**or·nate′ly,** *adv.* —**or·nate′ness,** *n.*

or·ner·y (ôr′nə rē), *adj.,* **-ner·i·er, -ner·i·est. 1.** disagreeable in disposition; mean; crotchety. **2.** stubborn. —**or′ner·i·ness,** *n.*

or·ni·thol·o·gy (ôr′nə thol′ə jē), *n.* the branch of zoology that deals with birds. —**or′ni·tho·log′i·cal** (-thə loj′i kal), **or′ni·tho·log′ic,** *adj.* —**or′ni·tho·log′i·cal·ly,** *adv.* —**or′ni·thol′o·gist,** *n.*

o·rog·e·ny (ô roj′ə nē, ō roj′-), *n.* the process of mountain formation or upheaval. —**or·o·gen·ic** (ôr′ə jen′ik, or′ə-), *adj.*

o·rog·ra·phy (ô rog′rə fē, ō rog′-), *n.* the branch of physical geography dealing with mountains. Also called **o·rol·o·gy** (ô rol′ə jē, ō rol′-). —**or·o·graph·ic** (ôr′ə graf′ik, or′ə-), **or′o·graph′i·cal,** *adj.* —**or′o·graph′i·cal·ly,** *adv.*

o·ro·tund (ôr′ə tund′, or′-), *adj.* **1.** (of the voice or speech) characterized by strength, fullness, and clearness. **2.** (of speech or writing) pompous or bombastic. —**o′ro·tun′di·ty,** *n.*

O·roz·co (ô rôs′kō), *n.* **José Clemente,** 1883–1949, Mexican painter.

or·phan (ôr′fən), *n.* **1.** a child who has lost both parents or, less commonly, one parent through death. **2.** a young animal that is without its mother. **3.** a person or thing that is without protective affiliation, sponsorship, etc. **4.** (esp. in word processing) the first line of a paragraph when it appears alone at the bottom of a printed page. Compare WIDOW (def. 3b). —*adj.* **5.** bereft of parents. **6.** of or for orphans. **7.** lacking sponsorship or funding: *an orphan disease.* —*v.t.* **8.** to cause to become an orphan. —**or′phan·hood′,** *n.*

or·phan·age (ôr′fə nij), *n.* an institution for the housing and care of orphans.

Or·phe·us (ôr′fē əs, -fyōōs), *n.* a poet and lyre-player of Greek legend who tried to free his dead wife Eurydice from the underworld by charming the god Hades with his music. —**Or·phe·an** (ôr fē′ən, ôr′fē ən), *adj.*

Or·phism (ôr′fiz əm), *n.* a Greek religious movement of the 6th to 5th centuries B.C. whose mystic beliefs were expounded in poems allegedly written by Orpheus.

or·ris (ôr′is, or′-), *n.* an iris, *Iris germanica florentina,* having a fragrant rootstock.

or·tho (ôr′thō), *adj.* pertaining to or occupying two adjacent positions in the benzene ring. Compare META, PARA¹.

ortho-, 1. a combining form meaning "straight," "upright," "right," "correct": *orthodontics; orthopedic.* **2. a.** a combining form used in the name of the most hydrated acid in a given series: *orthoboric acid.* Compare META- (def. 2a), PYRO- (def. 2a). **b.** a combining form used in the names of benzene derivatives in which the substituting group occupies the ortho position in the benzene ring. Also, *esp. before a vowel,* **orth-.**

or·tho·clase (ôr′thə klās′, -klāz′), *n.* a common white or pink potassium feldspar mineral, KAlSi₃O₈, having two good cleavages at right angles, and found in silica-rich igneous rocks.

or·tho·don·tia (ôr′thə don′shə, -shē ə), *n.* **1.** ORTHODONTICS. **2.** treatment for the correction of irregular teeth.

or·tho·don·tics (ôr′thə don′tiks), *n.* (*used with a sing. v.*) the branch of dentistry dealing with the prevention and correction of irregular teeth, as by means of braces. —**or′tho·don′tic, or′tho·don′tal,** *adj.* —**or′tho·don′tist,** *n.*

or·tho·dox (ôr′thə doks′), *adj.* **1.** conforming to the approved form of any doctrine, philosophy, ideology, etc. **2.** conforming to generally approved beliefs, attitudes, or modes of conduct. **3.** customary or conventional; established. **4.** sound or correct in matters of theological doctrine or opinion. **5.** conforming to the Christian faith as represented in the creeds of the early church. **6.** (*cap.*) of, pertaining to, or designating the Eastern Church, esp. the Greek Orthodox Church. **7.** (*cap.*) conforming to or characteristic of Orthodox Judaism. [< Late Latin *orthodoxus* < Greek *orthódoxos* = *ortho-* straight, right + *-doxos,* belief, opinion]

Or′thodox Church′, *n.* **1.** the Christian church comprising the local and national Eastern churches that are in communion with the ecumenical patriarch of Constantinople; Byzantine Church. **2.** (originally) the Christian church of those countries formerly comprising the Eastern Roman Empire and of countries evangelized from it; Greek Orthodox Church.

Or′thodox Ju′daism, *n.* a branch of Judaism that faithfully adheres to traditional beliefs and practices as evidenced by Torah study, daily synagogue attendance, and strict observance of the Sabbath, festivals, and dietary laws. Compare CONSERVATIVE JUDAISM, REFORM JUDAISM.

or·tho·dox·y (ôr′thə dok′sē), *n., pl.* **-dox·ies. 1.** orthodox belief or practice. **2.** the state or quality of being orthodox.

or·tho·e·py (ôr thō′ə pē, ôr′thō ep′ē), *n.* the study of correct pronunciation. —**or′tho·ep′ic, or′tho·ep′i·cal,** *adj.* —**or·tho′e·pist,** *n.*

or·tho·gen·e·sis (ôr′thō jen′ə sis), *n.* **1. a.** evolution of a species proceeding by continuous structural changes without presenting a branching pattern of descent. **b.** a theory that such evolution of a species is due to a predetermined series of alterations and not subject to natural selection. **2.** a hypothetical parallelism between the stages through which every culture necessarily passes in spite of secondary conditioning factors. —**or′tho·ge·net′ic** (-jə net′ik), *adj.*

or·tho·gen·ic (ôr′thə jen′ik), *adj.* concerned with or providing corrective treatment for mentally retarded or seriously disturbed children.

or·thog·o·nal (ôr thog′ə nl), *adj.* **1.** Also, **orthographic.** *Math.* pertaining to or involving right angles or perpendiculars. **2.** *Crystall.* referable to a rectangular set of axes. —**or·thog′o·nal·ly,** *adv.* —**or·thog′o·nal′i·ty,** *n.*

or·thog·ra·phy (ôr thog′rə fē), *n., pl.* **-phies. 1.** the art of writing words with the proper letters according to accepted usage; correct spelling. **2.** language study concerned with letters and spelling. **3.** a method of spelling, as by the use of an alphabet or other system of symbols. **4.** a system of such symbols. —**or·thog′ra·pher, or·thog′ra·phist,** *n.*

or·tho·pe·dics or **or·tho·pae·dics** (ôr′thə pē′diks), *n.* (*used with a sing. v.*) the medical specialty concerned with correction of deformities or functional impairments of the skeletal system, esp. the extremities and the spine, and associated structures, as muscles and ligaments. —**or′tho·pe′dic, or′tho·pae′dic,** *adj.* —**or′tho·pe′dist, or′tho·pae′dist,** *n.*

or·thop·ter·an (ôr thop′tər ən), *n.* an insect of the order Orthoptera, characterized by leathery forewings, membranous hind wings, and chewing mouthparts: includes the cockroaches, crickets, grasshoppers, and katydids. —**or·thop′ter·ous,** *adj.*

or·thot·ic (ôr thot′ik), *n.* **1.** a device or support used to relieve or correct an orthopedic problem, esp. of the foot. —*adj.* **2.** of or pertaining to orthotics.

or·thot·ics (ôr thot′iks), *n.* (*used with a sing. v.*) a branch of medicine dealing with the making and fitting of orthotic devices. —**or·thot′ist** (ôr thot′ist, ôr′thə tist), *n.*

Or·well (ôr′wel, -wəl), *n.* **George** (*Eric Arthur Blair*), 1903–50, English novelist and essayist. —**Or·well′i·an,** *adj.*

-ory¹, an adjective-forming suffix, joined to bases of Latin origin in imitation of borrowed Latin words containing the suffix -TORY¹ (and its alternant -*sory*): *excretory; sensory; statutory.*

-ory², a suffix forming nouns denoting places or receptacles, joined to bases of Latin origin in imitation of borrowed Latin words containing the suffix -TORY² (and its alternant -*sory*): *crematory.*

o·ryx (ôr′iks, or′-), *n., pl.* **o·ryx·es,** (*esp. collectively*) **o·ryx. 1.** any of several large African antelopes of the genus *Oryx,* with black markings and long, nearly straight horns. **2.** GEMSBOK.

or·zo (ôr′zō), *n.* pasta in the form of small ricelike grains.

Os, *Chem. Symbol.* osmium.

O′sage o·range′, *n.* **1.** a tree, *Maclura pomifera,* of the mulberry family, native to the south-central U.S., that has hard, yellowish wood and is often cultivated for hedges. **2.** the round, rough-skinned, inedible fruit of this tree.

O·sa·ka (ō sä′kə, ō′sä kä′), *n.* a city on S Honshu, in S Japan. 2,546,000.

Os·car (os′kər), *Trademark.* ACADEMY AWARD.

os·cil·late (os′ə lāt′), *v.,* **-lat·ed, -lat·ing.** —*v.i.* **1.** to swing or move to and fro, as a pendulum does. **2.** to vary or vacillate between differing beliefs, conditions, etc.

os·cil·la·tion (os′ə lā′shən), *n.* **1.** an act or instance of oscillating. **2. a.** a single swing in one direction of an oscillating body. **b.** a single fluctuation between the maximum and minimum values of an oscillatory cycle. —**os′cil·la·to′ry** (-lə tôr′ē, -tōr′ē), *adj.*

os·cine (os′in, -īn), *adj.* **1.** of or pertaining to birds of the suborder Oscines, of the order Passeriformes, comprising members of the order that have highly developed vocal organs. —*n.* **2.** an oscine bird; songbird.

os·cu·late (os′kyə lāt′), *v.t.,* **-lat·ed, -lat·ing.** to kiss.

-ose¹, a suffix occurring in adjectives borrowed from Latin, meaning "full of," "abounding in," "given to," "like": *jocose; otiose; verbose.*

-ose², a suffix used in the names of sugars and other carbohydrates (*fructose; lactose*), and of protein derivatives (*proteose*).

OSHA (ō′shə), *n.* Occupational Safety and Health Administration.

o·sier (ō′zhər), *n.* **1.** any of various willows having tough, flexible twigs or branches that are used for wickerwork. **2.** a twig from such a willow. —**o′siered,** *adj.*

O′ Sing′ a New′ Song′ to′ the Lord′, a Christian hymn based on Psalm 98.

O·si·ris (ō sī′ris), *n.* the Egyptian god and judge of the dead, husband and brother of Isis. —**O·si′ri·an** (-rē ən), *adj.*

-osis, a suffix occurring in nouns that denote actions, conditions, or states (*hypnosis; osmosis*), esp. disorders or abnormal states (*neurofibromatosis; tuberculosis*). Compare -OTIC.

Os·lo (oz′lō, os′-), *n.* the capital of Norway, in the SE part, at the head of Oslo Fjord. 453,700. Formerly, **Christiania.**

Os·man (oz′mən, os′-, os män′), *n.* 1259–1326, Turkish emir 1299–1326: founder of the Ottoman dynasty.

os·mi·um (oz′mē əm), *n.* a hard, heavy, metallic element, densest of the known elements, able to form octavalent compounds: used chiefly as a catalyst, in alloys, and in the manufacture of electric-light filaments. *Symbol:* Os; *at. wt.:* 190.2; *at. no.:* 76; *sp. gr.:* 22.57.

os•mose (oz′mōs, os′-), *v.,* **-mosed, -mos•ing.** *n.* —*v.i.* **1.** to undergo osmosis. —*v.t.* **2.** to subject to osmosis. —*n.* **3.** OSMOSIS.

os•mo•sis (oz mō′sis, os-), *n.* **1. a.** the tendency of a fluid, usu. water, to pass through a semipermeable membrane into a solution where the solvent concentration is higher, thus equalizing the concentrations of materials on either side of the membrane. **b.** the diffusion of fluids through membranes or porous partitions. **2.** a subtle or gradual absorption: *to learn by osmosis.* —**os•mot′ic** (-mot′ik), *adj.* —**os•mot′i•cal•ly,** *adv.*

osmot′ic pres′sure, *n.* the force that a dissolved substance exerts on a semipermeable membrane, through which it cannot penetrate, when separated by it from pure solvent.

os•mun•da (oz mun′də), *n., pl.* **-das.** any of several large, coarse ferns of the genus *Osmunda* and family Osmundaceae, that have dense clusters of globular spore cases, as the royal fern.

os•prey (os′prē, -prā), *n., pl.* **-preys.** a large, nearly cosmopolitan bird of prey, *Pandion haliaetus,* that feeds on fish.

Os•sa (os′ə), *n.* a mountain in E Greece, in Thessaly. 6490 ft. (1978 m).

os•se•ous (os′ē əs), *adj.* composed of, containing, or resembling bone; bony.

os•si•cle (os′i kəl), *n.* a small bone. —**os•sic′u•lar** (o sik′yə lər), *adj.*

os•sif•er•ous (o sif′ər əs), *adj.* containing bones, esp. fossil bones.

os•si•fy (os′ə fī′), *v.,* **-fied, -fy•ing.** —*v.t.* **1.** to convert into or cause to harden like bone. —*v.i.* **2.** to become bone or harden like bone. **3.** to become rigid or inflexible in habits, opinions, etc. —**os′si•fi•ca′tion,** *n.* —**os′si•fi′er,** *n.*

os•so bu•co (os′ō boo̅′kō), *n.* an Italian dish of veal shanks cooked with olive oil, tomatoes, white wine, and seasonings.

os•su•ar•y (osh′oo̅ er′ē, os′yoo̅-), *n., pl.* **-ar•ies.** a place or receptacle for the bones of the dead.

os•ten•si•ble (o sten′sə bəl), *adj.* outwardly appearing as such; professed; pretended. —**os•ten′si•bly,** *adv.*

os•ten•sive (o sten′siv), *adj.* **1.** clearly or manifestly demonstrative. **2.** OSTENSIBLE. —**os•ten′sive•ly,** *adv.*

os•ten•ta•tion (os′ten tā′shən, -tən-), *n.* pretentious or conspicuous display intended to impress others.

os•ten•ta•tious (os′ten tā′shəs, -tən-), *adj.* **1.** characterized by pretentious show in an attempt to impress others. **2.** intended to attract notice: *ostentatious charity.* —**os′ten•ta′tious•ly,** *adv.*

osteo-, a combining form meaning "bone": *osteoarthritis.*

os•te•o•ar•thri•tis (os′tē ō är thrī′tis), *n.* arthritis marked by chronic breakdown of cartilage in the joints leading to pain, stiffness, and swelling. Also called **degenerative joint disease.**

os•te•ol•o•gy (os′tē ol′ə jē), *n.* the branch of anatomy dealing with the skeleton. —**os′te•o•log′i•cal** (-ə loj′i kəl), **os′te•o•log′ic,** *adj.* —**os′te•ol′o•gist,** *n.*

os•te•o•my•e•li•tis (os′tē ō mī′ə lī′tis), *n.* an inflammation of bone and bone marrow, usu. caused by bacterial infection.

os•te•o•path (os′tē ə path′) also **os•te•op•a•thist** (os′tē op′ə thist), *n.* a practitioner of osteopathy.

os•te•op•a•thy (os′tē op′ə thē), *n.* a system of medical practice emphasizing the manipulation of muscles and bones to promote structural integrity and the relief of certain disorders. —**os′te•o•path′ic** (-ə path′ik), *adj.* —**os′te•o•path′i•cal•ly,** *adv.*

os•te•o•po•ro•sis (os′tē ō pə rō′sis), *n.* a disorder in which the bones become increasingly porous, brittle, and subject to fracture, owing to loss of calcium and other mineral components. —**os′te•o•po•rot′ic** (-rot′ik), *adj.*

os•tra•cism (os′trə siz′əm), *n.* **1.** exclusion, by general consent, from social acceptance, privileges, friendship, etc. **2.** (in ancient Greece) temporary banishment of a citizen, decided upon by popular vote.

os•tra•cize (os′trə sīz′), *v.t.,* **-cized, -ciz•ing.** **1.** to exclude, by general consent, from society, privileges, etc. **2.** to banish (a person) from his or her native country; expatriate. **3.** (in ancient Greece) to banish (a citizen) temporarily by popular vote. —**os′tra•ciz′a•ble,** *adj.* —**os′tra•ci•za′tion,** *n.* —**os′tra•ciz′er,** *n.*

os•trich (ô′strich, os′trich), *n.* **1.** a two-toed, swift-footed, flightless bird, *Struthio camelus,* orig. of Africa and SW Asia: the largest of living birds. **2.** a person who attempts to ignore unpleasant facts or situations.

ostrich (def.1), *Struthio camelus,*
height 8 ft. (2.4 m);
length 6 ft. (1.8 m)

Os•tro•goth (os′trə goth′), *n.* a member of the eastern division of the Goths, who entered Italy in A.D. 488, maintaining a kingdom there until 555. —**Os′tro•goth′ic,** *adj.*

Os•wald (oz′wôld), *n.* **Lee Harvey,** 1939–63, determined by a presidential commission to be the lone assassin of John F. Kennedy.

Os•we′go tea′, *n.* (os wē′gō), *n.* a North American plant, *Monarda didyma,* of the mint family, having a cluster of showy, bright red tubular flowers.

OT, 1. Also, **O.T.** Old Testament. **2.** Also, **o.t.** overtime.

o•tal•gi•a (ō tal′jē ə, -jə), *n.* EARACHE. —**o•tal′gic,** *adj.*

OTB, offtrack betting.

OTC, 1. Also, **O.T.C.** Officers' Training Corps. **2.** over-the-counter.

O•thel•lo (ō thel′ō, ə thel′ō), a tragedy (1604) by William Shakespeare.

oth•er (uth′ər), *adj.* **1.** additional or further: *she and one other person.* **2.** different from the one mentioned: *in some other city.* **3.** different in nature or kind: *I would not have him other than he is.* **4.** being the remaining one of two or more: *the other hand.* **5.** being the remaining ones of a number (usu. fol. by a pl. n.): *the other men.* **6.** former; earlier: *sailing ships of other days.* **7.** not long past: *the other night.* —*n.* **8.** the other one: *Each praises the other.* —*pron.* **9.** Usu., **others.** other persons or things: *others in the medical profession.* **10.** some person or thing else: *Surely some friend or other will help me.* —*adv.* **11.** otherwise; differently (usu. fol. by *than*): *We can't collect the rent other than by suing the tenant.* —*Idiom.* **12. the other side of the coin,** the alternative consideration or point of view. —**oth′er•ness,** *n.*

oth′er-di•rect′ed, *adj.* guided by a set of values derived from other people or external influences rather than from within oneself. Compare INNER-DIRECTED.

oth•er•wise (uth′ər wīz′), *adv.* **1.** under other circumstances. **2.** in another manner; differently: *I refuse to believe otherwise.* **3.** in other respects: *an otherwise happy life.* —*conj.* **4.** or else: *Button up your coat, otherwise you'll catch cold.* —*adj.* **5.** of a different kind: *We hoped his behavior would be otherwise.* **6.** in different circumstances: *An otherwise pleasure had become a chore.*

oth′er world′, *n.* the world after death; the next world.

Oth•ni•el (oth′nē əl), *n.* a judge of Israel. Judg. 3:9.

o•tic (ō′tik, ot′ik), *adj.* of or pertaining to the ear; auricular.

-otic, a suffix of adjectives corresponding to nouns ending in -OSIS: *hypnotic; neurotic.*

o•ti•ose (ō′shē ōs′, ō′tē-), *adj.* **1.** being at leisure; idle. **2.** ineffective or futile. **3.** superfluous or useless. —**o′ti•ose′ly,** *adv.* —**o′ti•os′i•ty** (-os′i tē), **o′ti•ose′ness,** *n.*

O•tis (ō′tis), *n.* **James,** 1725–83, American Revolutionary lawyer and public official.

o•ti•tis (ō tī′tis), *n.* inflammation of the ear.

oti′tis me′di•a (mē′dē ə), *n.* inflammation of the middle ear, characterized by pain, dizziness, and impaired hearing.

oto-, a combining form meaning "ear": *otology.*

o•tol•o•gy (ō tol′ə jē), *n.* the study and treatment of diseases of the ear. —**o′to•log′i•cal** (ōt′l oj′i kəl), *adj.* —**o•tol′o•gist,** *n.*

Ot•ta•wa (ot′ə wə), *n., pl.* **-was,** (*esp. collectively*) **-wa. 1.** the capital of Canada, in SE Ontario. 300,763. **2.** a river in SE Canada, flowing SE into the St. Lawrence at Montreal. 685 mi. (1105 km) long. **3. a.** a member of an American Indian people living on Manitoulin Island and adjacent shores of Lake Huron and Georgian Bay at time of first contact: later dispersed in large part, and now living also on reserves in lower Michigan and in Oklahoma. **b.** the dialect of Ojibwa spoken by the Ottawas.

ot•ter (ot′ər), *n., pl.* **-ters,** (*esp. collectively*) **-ter. 1.** any of several aquatic, furbearing, weasellike mammals of the genus *Lutra* and related genera, having webbed feet and a long, slightly flattened tail. **2.** the fur of an otter.

Ot•to•man (ot′ə mən), *adj., n., pl.* **-mans.** —*adj.* **1.** of or pertaining to the Ottoman Empire or its rulers. —*n.* **2. a.** a member of the dynasty descended from Osman that ruled the Ottoman Empire. **b.** a Turkish citizen of the Ottoman state. **3.** (*l.c.*) **a.** a cushioned footstool. **b.** a low cushioned seat without back or arms. **c.** a kind of divan or sofa, with or without a back. **4.** (*l.c.*) a heavy, lustrous fabric of wool, silk, or other fibers woven with broad, horizontal ribs. —**Ot′to•man•like′,** *adj.*

Ot′toman Em′pire, *n.* a Turkish state that was founded about 1300 by Osman and reached its greatest territorial extent under Suleiman in the 16th century; collapsed after World War I. *Cap.:* Constantinople.

Oua•ga•dou•gou (wä′gə doo̅′goo̅), *n.* the capital of Burkina Faso, in the central part. 442,223.

ouch (ouch), *interj.* (used to express sudden pain or dismay.)

ought•n't (ôt′nt), contraction of *ought not.*

ounce¹ (ouns), *n.* **1.** a unit of weight equal to 437.5 grains or $\frac{1}{16}$ of a pound (28.349 grams) avoirdupois. **2.** a unit of weight equal to 480 grains or $\frac{1}{12}$ of a pound (31.103 grams) troy or apothecaries' weight. **3.** a fluid ounce. **4.** a small quantity or portion. —*Proverb.* **5. An ounce of prevention is worth a pound of cure,** taking the right measures beforehand is easier than correcting a problem later.

ounce² (ouns), *n.* SNOW LEOPARD.

our (ou∂r, ou′ər; *unstressed* är), *pron.* a form of the possessive case of WE used as an attributive adjective: *Our team won.* Compare OURS. —*Usage.* See ME.

Our′ Fa′ther, *n.* the Lord's Prayer.

Our′ La′dy, *n.* a title of the Virgin Mary.

ours (ouᵊrz, ou′ərz *or, often,* ärz), *pron.* **1.** a form of the possessive case of WE used as a predicate adjective: *Which house is ours?* **2.** that or those belonging to us: *Ours are the pink ones.*

our•self (är self′, ouᵊr-, ou′ər-), *pron.* **1.** one's own person, individuality, etc., considered apart from others: *It is for ourself that we must work harder.* **2.** (a form corresponding to *ourselves,* used by a single person, esp. in the formal or regal style, as *we* for *I*): *We have taken unto ourself such powers as may be necessary.*

our•selves (är selvz′, ouᵊr-, ou′ər-), *pron.pl.* **1.** a reflexive form of WE (used as the direct or indirect object of a verb or the direct object of a preposition): *We may be deceiving ourselves.* **2.** (used as an intensive with *we*): *We ourselves would never say such a thing.* **3.** (used in place of WE or US in various compound and comparative constructions): *The children and ourselves want to thank you. No one is more fortunate than ourselves.* **4.** (used in absolute constructions): *Ourselves too poor to help, we were forced to turn them away.* **5.** our customary, normal, or healthy selves: *We were ourselves again after a nap.* **—Usage.** See MYSELF.

Our′ Town′, a play (1938) by Thornton Wilder.

-ous, 1. a suffix forming adjectives that have the general sense "possessing, full of" a given quality (*covetous; glorious; nervous; wondrous*); *-ous* and its variant *-ious* have often been used to Anglicize Latin adjectives with terminations that cannot be directly adapted into English (*atrocious; contiguous; garrulous; obvious; stupendous*). As an adjective-forming suffix of neutral value, it regularly Anglicizes Greek and Latin adjectives derived without suffix from nouns and verbs; many such formations are productive combining forms in English, sometimes with a corresponding nominal combining form that has no suffix; compare -FER, -FEROUS; -PHORE, -PHOROUS. **2.** a suffix forming adjectival correspondents to the names of chemical elements; specialized, in opposition to like adjectives ending in -IC, to mean the lower of two possible valences (*stannous chloride,* $SnCl_2$, and *stannic chloride,* $SnCl_4$).

oust (oust), *v.t.* to expel or remove from a place or position occupied.

oust•er (ou′stər), *n.* expulsion or removal from a place or position occupied.

out (out), *adv.* **1.** not in the usual place, position, state, etc.: *out of alphabetical order.* **2.** away from one's home, country, work, etc., as specified: *to go out of town.* **3.** in or into the outdoors: *to go out for a walk.* **4.** to a state of exhaustion or depletion: *to pump a well out.* **5.** to the end or conclusion, a final decision, etc.: *to say it all out.* **6.** to a point or state of extinction: *a practice on the way out.* **7.** in or into a state of neglect, disuse, etc.: *That style has gone out.* **8.** so as not to be in the normal or proper position or state; out of joint: *Her back went out after her fall.* **9.** in or into public notice or knowledge: *The truth is out at last.* **10.** on strike: *The miners go out at midnight.* **11.** so as to project or extend: *to stretch out.* **12.** from a specified source or material: *made out of scraps.* **13.** so as to deprive or be deprived: *to be cheated out of one's money.* **14.** aloud or loudly: *to cry out.* **15.** thoroughly; completely; entirely: *The children tired me out.* **16.** so as to obliterate or make undecipherable: *to cross out a misspelling; to ink out.* **—*adj.* 17.** not at one's home or place of employment; absent: *I stopped by to visit you, but you were out.* **18.** not open to consideration; out of the question: *She gets airsick, so flying is out.* **19.** wanting; lacking; without: *We had some but now we're out.* **20.** removed from or not in effective operation, play, etc., as in a game: *He's out for the season with a leg injury.* **21.** no longer holding a job, public office, etc.; unemployed (usu. fol. by *of*): *to be out of work.* **22.** inoperative; extinguished: *The elevator is out. Are the lights out?* **23.** finished; ended: *before the week is out.* **24.** not currently fashionable or in vogue: *Fitted waistlines are out this season.* **25.** unconscious; senseless. **26.** not in power, authority, or the like: *a member of the out party.* **27.** *Baseball.* **a.** (of a batter) not succeeding in getting on base. **b.** (of a base runner) not successful in an attempt to advance a base or bases. **28.** out of bounds. **29.** having a financial loss to an indicated extent: *out millions when the market crashed.* **30.** incorrect or inaccurate: *calculations out by $247.* **31.** not in practice: *Your bow hand is out.* **32.** beyond the usual range, size, weight, etc. (often used in combination): *an outsize bed.* **33.** threadbare or having holes: *out at the knees.* **34.** not available: *Mums are out till next fall.* **35.** external; outer. **36.** located at a distance; outlying: *the out islands.* **37.** indicating the first nine holes of an 18-hole golf course (opposed to *in*): *an out score of 33.* **—*prep.* 38.** (used to indicate movement or direction from the inside to the outside of something): *She ran out the door.* **39.** (used to indicate location): *The car is out back.* **40.** (used to indicate movement away from a central point): *Let's drive out the old parkway.* **—*interj.* 41.** begone! away! **42.** (used in radio communications to signify that the sender has finished the message and is not expecting a reply.) Compare OVER (def. 46). **—*n.* 43.** a means of escape from responsibility, embarrassment, etc.: *I had no out.* **44.** Usu., **outs.** those persons or groups not in office or lacking status, power, or authority. **45.** *Baseball.* **a.** PUT-OUT. **b.** a turn at bat that results in a put-out. **46.** (in tennis, squash, handball, etc.) an out-of-bounds return or service. **47.** something that is out, as a projecting corner. **48.** *Print.* an omission or deletion. **—*v.i.* 49.** to go or come out. **50.** to become public, evident, known, etc.: *The truth will out.* **51.** to make known; tell (fol. by *with*): *Out with the truth!* **—*v.t.* 52.** to eject or expel. **—*Idiom.* 53. all out,** with maximum effort; thoroughly or wholeheartedly: *They went all out to finish by Friday.* **54. on the outs,** in a state of disagreement; quarreling; at odds. **55. out and away,** to a surpassing extent; far and away; by far. **56. out for,** aggressively determined to acquire, achieve, etc. **57. out from under,** rid of burdensome responsibilities, esp. free of debt. **58. out of, a.** not within: *out of the house.* **b.** beyond the reach of: *out of hearing.* **c.** not in a condition of: *out of danger.* **d.** so as to deprive or be deprived of. **e.** from within or among: *Take the jokers out of the pack.* **f.** because of; owing to: *out of loyalty.* **g.** foaled by: *Grey Dancer out of Lady Grey.* **59. out of it,** *Informal.* **a.** not participating. **b.** not conscious. **c.** confused; muddled. **60. out of place, a.** not in the correct position or order. **b.** unsuitable to the circumstances or surroundings.

out-, a prefixal use of OUT, occurring in various senses in compounds (*outcast; outcome; outside*), and serving also to form transitive verbs denoting a going beyond, surpassing, or outdoing of the particular action indicated (*outbid; outdo; outlast; outrate*).

out•age (ou′tij), *n.* **1. a.** an interruption or failure in the supply of power, esp. electricity. **b.** the period during which power is lost. **2.** a stoppage in the functioning of a machine due to a power failure.

out′-and-out′, *adj.* complete; absolute: *an out-and-out lie.*

out•back (out′bak′), *n.* (*sometimes cap.*) *Chiefly Australian.* the back country or remote settlements; the bush (usu. prec. by *the*).

out•bal•ance (out′bal′əns), *v.t.*, **-anced, -anc•ing.** to outweigh.

out•board (out′bôrd′, -bōrd′), *adj.* **1.** located on the exterior of a hull or aircraft. **2.** located farther from the center, as of an aircraft: *the outboard engine.* **3.** (of a motorboat) having an outboard motor. **—*adv.* 4.** away from the center of a hull, aircraft, etc. **—*n.* 5.** OUTBOARD MOTOR. **6.** a boat equipped with an outboard motor.

out′board mo′tor, *n.* a portable gasoline engine with propeller and tiller, clamped on the stern of a boat.

out•bound (out′bound′), *adj.* outward bound: *an outbound freighter.*

out•break (out′brāk′), *n.* **1.** a sudden occurrence; eruption: *the outbreak of war.* **2.** a sudden manifestation: *an outbreak of hives.* **3.** an outburst.

out•build•ing (out′bil′ding), *n.* a detached building subordinate to a main building.

out•burst (out′bûrst′), *n.* **1.** a sudden and violent release or outpouring: *an outburst of tears.* **2.** a sudden spell of activity. **3.** a public disturbance; riot. **4.** a bursting forth; eruption.

out•cast (out′kast′, -käst′), *n.* **1.** a person who is rejected or cast out, as from home or society. **2.** a homeless wanderer; vagabond. **—*adj.* 3.** cast out, as from one's home or society: *an outcast son.*

out•class (out′klas′, -kläs′), *v.t.* to surpass in excellence; be superior to: *She outclassed her teammates.*

out•come (out′kum′), *n.* **1.** a final product or end result. **2.** a conclusion reached through a process of logical thinking.

out•crop (*n.* out′krop′; *v.* out′krop′), *n., v.,* **-cropped, -crop•ping.** **—*n.* 1. a.** a cropping out, as of a stratum or vein at the surface of the earth. **b.** the exposed portion of such a stratum or vein. **2.** something that emerges suddenly or violently in the manner of an outcrop; outbreak: *an outcrop of wildcat strikes.* **—*v.i.* 3.** to crop out, as strata.

out•cry (out′krī′), *n., pl.* **-cries. 1.** a strong and usu. public expression of protest or indignation. **2.** a crying out. **3.** a loud cry or shout; clamor. **4.** an auction.

out•date (out′dāt′), *v.t.*, **-dat•ed, -dat•ing.** to put out of date; make obsolete.

out•dat•ed (out′dā′tid), *adj.* out-of-date; outmoded.

out•dis•tance (out′dis′təns), *v.t.*, **-tanced, -tanc•ing.** to leave behind, as in running.

out•do (out′do͞o′), *v.t.*, **-did, -done, -do•ing.** to surpass in execution or performance: *The cook outdid himself last night.*

out•door (out′dôr′, -dōr′), *adj.* **1.** Also, **outdoors.** located, occurring, or belonging outdoors: *outdoor sports.* **2.** OUTDOORSY.

out•doors (out′dôrz′, -dōrz′), *adv.* **1.** out of doors; in the open air. **—*n.* 2.** (*used with a sing. v.*) the world outside of or away from houses; open air. **—*adj.* 3.** OUTDOOR.

out•doors•man (out′dôrz′mən, -dōr′-), *n., pl.* **-men.** a person devoted to outdoor sports and recreational activities. **—out′doors′man•ship,** *n.*

out•doors•wom•an (out′dôrz′wo͝om′ən, -dōrz′-), *n., pl.* **-wom•en. 1.** a woman devoted to outdoor sports and recreational activities. **2.** a woman who spends much time in the outdoors.

out•doors•y (out′dôr′zē, -dōr′-), *adj.* **1.** characteristic of or suitable to the outdoors. **2.** unusually fond of outdoor life.

out•draw (out′drô′), *v.t.*, **-drew, -drawn, -draw•ing. 1.** to draw a gun, revolver, etc., from a holster, faster than (an opponent or competitor). **2.** to prove a greater attraction than.

out•er (ou′tər), *adj.* **1.** situated on or toward the outside: *an outer wall.* **2.** situated farther out or farther from the center. **3.** of or pertaining to the external world. **—out′er•ness,** *n.*

Out′er Banks′, *n.pl.* a chain of sandy barrier islands along the coast of North Carolina.

out•er•most (ou′tər mōst′), *adj.* farthest out; remotest from the interior or center: *the outermost limits.*

out′er plan′et, *n.* any of the five planets with orbits outside the orbit of Mars: Jupiter, Saturn, Uranus, Neptune, and Pluto.

out′er space′, *n.* **1.** space beyond the atmosphere of the earth. **2.** DEEP SPACE.

out•er•wear (ou′tər wâr′), *n.* **1.** garments, as overcoats, worn over other clothing for warmth or protection outdoors; overclothes. **2.** clothing, as dresses, sweaters, or suits, worn over undergarments.

out·field (out′fēld′), n. **1. a.** the part of a baseball field beyond the diamond. **b.** the positions played by the right, center, and left fielders. **c.** the outfielders considered as a group (contrasted with *infield*). **2.** the part of a cricket field farthest from the batsman.

out·field·er (out′fēl′dər), n. one of the players, esp. in baseball, stationed in the outfield.

out·fit (out′fit′), n., v., **-fit·ted, -fit·ting.** —n. **1.** an assemblage of gear for a particular task or role: *a cowboy's outfit.* **2.** a set of usu. harmonious garments and accessories worn together: *a new spring outfit.* **3.** a set of articles for any purpose: *a barbecue outfit.* **4.** a military unit. **5.** a business firm engaged in a particular commercial enterprise: *a construction outfit.* **6.** any company, party, or set. **7.** the act of equipping for any purpose. —v.t. **8.** to furnish with an outfit. —v.i. **9.** to furnish oneself with an outfit. —**out′fit′ter,** n.

out·flank (out′flangk′), v.t. **1.** to go or extend beyond the flank of (an enemy force). **2.** to outmaneuver.

out·flow (out′flō′), n. **1.** the act of flowing out. **2.** something, as an amount or measure, that flows out.

out·fox (out′foks′), v.t. to outsmart.

out′-front′, adj. candid; frank; honest.

out·go (n. out′gō′; v. out′gō′), n., pl. *goes,* v., **-went, -gone, -go·ing** —n. **1.** the act or process of going out. **2.** money paid out. **3.** something that goes out; outflow. —v.t. **4.** to go beyond; outdistance or exceed. **5.** to surpass or excel.

out·go·ing (out′gō′ing or, for 5, -gō′-), adj. **1.** going out; departing: *outgoing trains.* **2.** leaving or retiring from a position or office: *the outgoing mayor.* **3.** addressed and ready for posting: *outgoing mail.* **4.** of or pertaining to food prepared for delivery or consumption off the premises. **5.** interested in and responsive to others; friendly; sociable. —n. **6.** the act of going out. **7.** something that goes out; effluence.

out·group′, n. a group outside one's own with which one feels no sense of identity. Compare IN-GROUP.

out·grow (out′grō′), v.t., **-grew, -grown, -grow·ing. 1.** to grow too large for. **2.** to discard or lose in the course of one's development: *to outgrow a fear of the dark.* **3.** to surpass in growing.

out·growth (out′grōth′), n. **1.** a natural development or result. **2.** an additional, supplementary result.

out·guess (out′ges′), v.t. to anticipate the actions or intentions of; outwit.

out·gun (out′gun′), v.t., **-gunned, -gun·ning. 1.** to exceed in firepower. **2.** to outdo or overwhelm, as by superior forces.

out·house (out′hous′), n., pl. **-hous·es** (-hou′ziz). **1.** an outbuilding serving as a toilet; privy. **2.** any outbuilding.

out·ing (ou′ting), n. **1.** a pleasure trip, picnic, or the like. **2.** a public appearance, as by a participant in an athletic contest.

out·land·ish (out lan′dish), adj. **1.** freakishly or grotesquely strange or odd. **2.** having a foreign appearance. **3.** remote; out-of-the-way. —**out·land′ish·ly,** adv. —**out·land′ish·ness,** n.

out·last (out′last′, -läst′), v.t. to endure or last longer than. **2.** to live longer than; outlive.

out·law (out′lô′), n. **1.** a lawless person or habitual criminal, esp. one who is a fugitive from the law. **2.** a person, group, etc., excluded from the benefits or protection of the law. **3.** a person or group that has been banned or restricted. **4.** a person who rebels against established rules or practices; nonconformist. **5.** *Western U.S.* **a.** a horse that cannot be broken. **b.** any rogue animal. —v.t. **6.** to make unlawful or illegal. **7.** to deprive of the benefits and protection of the law. **8.** to prohibit: *to outlaw smoking.* **9.** to remove from legal jurisdiction. —adj. **10.** of, pertaining to, or characteristic of an outlaw. —**out·law′ry,** n., pl. **-ries.**

out·lay (n. out′lā′; v. out′lā′), n., v., **-laid, -lay·ing.** —n. **1.** an expending or spending, as of money. **2.** an amount expended; expenditure. —v.t. **3.** to expend, as money.

out·let (out′let, -lit), n. **1.** an opening or passage by which anything is let out; vent. **2. a.** a point on a wiring system at which current may be taken to supply electric devices. **b.** Also called **out′let box′.** the metal box or receptacle designed to facilitate connections to a wiring system. **3.** a means of expression: *an outlet for one's artistic impulses.* **4. a.** a market for goods. **b.** a store selling the goods of a particular manufacturer or wholesaler. **5. a.** a river or stream flowing from a body of water, as a lake or pond. **b.** the channel such a river or stream follows. **c.** the lower end or mouth of a river where it meets a large body of water.

out·line (out′līn′), n., v., **-lined, -lin·ing.** —n. **1.** the line by which a figure or object is defined or bounded; contour. **2.** a drawing restricted to line without shading or modeling of form. **3.** a general account or re-

port, indicating only the main features of a subject. **4.** outlines, the essential features or main aspects of something under discussion. —v.t. **5.** to draw the outline of, or draw in outline. **6.** to indicate the main features of.

out·live (out′liv′), v.t., **-lived, -liv·ing. 1.** to live longer than; survive. **2.** to outlast; live through.

out·look (out′lŏŏk′), n. **1.** the view or prospect from a particular place. **2.** mental attitude or view; point of view. **3.** prospect for the future: *the political outlook.* **4.** the place from which an observer looks out. **5.** the act or state of looking out.

out·ly·ing (out′lī′ing), adj. **1.** lying at a distance from the center or the main body; remote. **2.** lying outside the boundary or limit.

out·ma·neu·ver (out′mə nōō′vər), v.t. **1.** to outwit or defeat by maneuvering. **2.** to outdo or surpass in maneuvering or maneuverability.

out·match (out′mach′), v.t. to be superior to; surpass; outdo.

out·mod·ed (out′mō′did), adj. **1.** no longer fashionable or stylish. **2.** no longer acceptable or usable; obsolete: *outmoded teaching methods.*

out·most (out′mōst′; esp. Brit -məst), adj. farthest out; outermost.

out·num·ber (out′num′bər), v.t. to exceed in number.

out′-of-bod′y, adj. of, pertaining to, or characterized by the dissociative sensation of perceiving oneself from an external vantage point, as though the mind or soul has left the body and is acting on its own: *an out-of-body experience.*

out′-of-bounds′, adv., adj. outside or beyond designated or established limits.

out′-of-date′, adj. gone out of style or fashion; outmoded; obsolete.

out′-of-doors′, adj. **1.** Also, **out′-of-door′.** OUTDOOR. —n. **2.** (used with a sing. v.) OUTDOORS.

out′-of-pock′et, adj. paid out or owed in cash: *out-of-pocket expenses.*

out′-of-sight′, adj. **1.** Slang. marvelous; great. **2.** exceedingly high: *an out-of-sight hospital bill.*

out′-of-state′, adj. in or from another state of the U.S. —**out′-of-stat′er,** n.

out′-of-the-way′, adj. **1.** remote from much-traveled or populous regions; isolated. **2.** seldom encountered; unusual. **3.** giving offense; improper or uncalled-for: *an out-of-the-way remark.*

out′-of-town′, adj. **1.** coming from another city or town: *out-of-town visitors.* **2.** taking place in another city or town: *an out-of-town ballgame.* —**out′-of-town′er,** n.

out·pace (out′pās′), v.t., **-paced, -pac·ing. 1.** to go faster than. **2.** to outdo.

out′pa′tient or **out′-pa′tient,** n. a person who receives treatment at a hospital but is not hospitalized.

out·per·form (out′pər fôrm′), v.t. to surpass in excellence of performance.

out·place·ment (out′plās′mənt), n. assistance in finding a new job, provided by a company for an employee who is being let go. —**out′place′,** v.t., **-placed, -plac·ing.**

out·post (out′pōst′), n. **1.** a station established at a distance from an army to protect it from surprise attack. **2.** the body of troops stationed there. **3.** a post or settlement in a foreign environment.

out·pour (n. out′pôr′, -pōr′; v. out′pôr′, -pōr′), **1.** OUTPOURING. —v.t. **2.** to pour out.

out·pour·ing (out′pôr′ing, -pōr′-), n. something that pours out; outflow; overflow: *an outpouring of sympathy.*

out·put (out′pŏŏt′), n., v., **-put·ted** or **-put, -put·ting.** —n. **1.** the quantity of something produced, esp. in a specified period. **2.** the material produced; product; yield. **3.** the current, voltage, power, or signal produced by an electrical or electronic circuit or device. Compare INPUT (def. 4). **4. a.** any information made available by computer, as on a printout, display screen, or disk. **b.** the process of transferring such information from computer memory to or by means of an output device. **5.** the power or force produced by a machine. —v.t. **6.** to transfer (computer output). **7.** to produce; yield; turn out.

out·race (out′rās′), v.t., **-raced, -rac·ing.** to outpace.

out·rage (out′rāj′), n., v., **-raged, -rag·ing.** —n. **1.** an act of wanton cruelty or violence. **2.** anything that strongly offends or affronts the feelings. **3.** a powerful feeling of resentment or anger aroused by an injury, insult, or injustice. —v.t. **4.** to subject to grievous violence or indignity. **5.** to anger or offend; shock. **6.** to offend against (right, decency, feelings, etc.) grossly or shamelessly.

out·ra·geous (out rā′jəs), adj. **1.** of or involving gross injury or wrong. **2.** grossly offensive to the sense of right or decency: *outrageous behavior.* **3.** passing reasonable bounds: *an outrageous price.* **4.** violent

---

out′ar′gue, v.t., -gued, -gu·ing.
out′bar′gain, v.t.
out′bid′, v.t., -bid, -bid·ding.
out·bluff′, v.t
out′boast′, v.t.
out′brag′, v.t.
out′climb′, v.t.
out′dance′, v.t., -danced, -danc·ing.
out′dare′, v.t., -dared, -dar·ing.

out′daz′zle, v.t., -zled, -zling.
out′earn′, v.t.
out′fight′, v.t., -fought, -fight·ing.
out′flat′ter, v.t.
out′glit′ter, v.t.
out′hit′, v.t., -hit, -hit·ting.
out′jump′, v.t.
out′kick′, v.t.
out′mas′ter, v.t.

out′mus′cle, v.t., -cled, -cling.
out′play′, v.t., -played, -play·ing.
out′pro·duce′, v.t., -duced, -duc·ing.
out′ri′val, v.t.
out′score′, v.t., -scored, -scor·ing.
out′shout′, v.t.
out′sing′, v.t., -sang, -sung, -sing·ing.
out′speed′, v.t., -sped or -speed·ed,

-speed·ing.
out′spell′, v.t., -spelled or -spelt, spel·ling.
out′sprint′, v.t.
out′stride′, v.t., -strode, -strid·den, -strid·ing.
out′swim′, v., -swam, -swum, -swim·ming.
out′trav′el, v.t.

in action or temper. **5.** extravagant; remarkable: *outrageous cleverness.* —**out·ra'geous·ly,** *adv.* —**out·ra'geous·ness,** *n.*

out·rank (out'rangk'), *v.t.,* to have a higher rank than.

ou·tré (ōō trā'), *adj.* passing the bounds of what is usual or considered proper; unconventional; bizarre.

out·reach (*v.* out'rēch'; *n., adj.* out'rēch'), *v.t.* **1.** to exceed: *Demand has outreached supply.* —*n.* **2.** an act or instance of reaching out. **3.** length or extent of reach. **4.** the act of extending community services to a wider section of the population. —*adj.* **5.** concerned with extending community services: *outreach programs in education.*

out·rid·er (out'rī'dər), *n.* **1.** a mounted attendant riding before or beside a carriage. **2.** a person who goes in advance.

out·rig·ger (out'rig'ər), *n.* **1.** a framework supporting a float extended outboard from the side of a boat for increasing stability. **2.** a bracket extending outward from the side of a racing shell to support an oarlock. **3.** the shell itself. **4.** a projecting beam, as for supporting a hoisting tackle. **5.** a structure extending outward from an aircraft or the like to increase stability or provide support.

outrigger (def. 1)

out·right (*adj.* out'rīt'; *adv.* out'rīt', -rīt'), *adj.* **1.** complete; total. **2.** downright; unqualified: *an outright refusal.* **3.** involving no further payments due or other restrictions: *an outright sale.* —*adv.* **4.** completely; entirely. **5.** without restraint, reserve, or concealment; openly. **6.** at once; instantly: *to be killed outright.* **7.** without further payments due or other restrictions: *to own the house outright.* —**out'right·ness,** *n.*

out·run (out'run'), *v.t.,* **-ran, -run, -run·ning. 1.** to run faster or farther than. **2.** to exceed; surpass. —**out'run'ner,** *n.*

out·sell (out'sel'), *v.t.,* **-sold, -sell·ing. 1.** to surpass in salesmanship or selling. **2.** to exceed in number of sales: *The soap outsells all other brands.*

out·set (out'set'), *n.* beginning; start.

out·shine (out'shīn'), *v.,* **-shone** or **shined, -shin·ing.** —*v.t.* **1.** to shine more brightly than. **2.** to surpass in excellence, achievement, etc.

out·shoot (*v.* out'shōōt'; *n.* out'shōōt'), *v.,* **-shot, -shoot·ing,** *n.* —*v.t.* **1.** to surpass in shooting, esp. in accuracy. **2.** to shoot beyond. —*v.i.* **3.** to shoot forth; project. —*n.* **4.** an act or instance of shooting out. **5.** something that shoots out.

out·side (*n.* out'sīd', -sīd'; *adj.* out'sīd', out'-; *adv.* out'sīd'; *prep.* out'sīd', out'sīd'), *n.* **1.** the outer side, surface, or part; exterior. **2.** the external aspect or appearance. **3.** the space beyond an enclosure, boundary, etc. **4.** a position away or away from the inside or center: *the horse on the outside.* **5.** *Basketball.* a position away or further away from the basket, usu. fifteen feet or more. —*adj.* **6.** originating beyond an enclosure, boundary, etc.: *news from the outside world.* **7.** situated on or pertaining to the outside; exterior. **8.** situated away from the inside or center: *the outside lane.* **9.** not belonging to a specified group: *outside influences.* **10.** extremely unlikely or remote: *an outside chance for recovery.* **11.** extreme or maximum: *an outside estimate.* **12.** being in addition to one's regular work or duties: *an outside job.* **13.** working on the outside, as of a place: *an outside man to care for the grounds.* **14.** *Baseball.* (of a pitched ball) passing, but not going over, home plate on the side opposite the batter. —*adv.* **15.** on or to the outside: *Take the dog outside.* —*prep.* **16.** on the outside of: *a noise outside the door.* **17.** beyond the confines or borders of: *visitors from outside the country.* **18.** aside from: *She has no interests outside her work.* —*Idiom.* **19. at the outside,** at the utmost limit; at the maximum. **20. outside of,** other than; excepting.

out·sid·er (out'sī'dər), *n.* a person not part of a particular group.

out·size (out'sīz'), *n.* **1.** an uncommon or irregular size, esp. one larger than average. **2.** a garment of such a size. —*adj.* **3.** Also, **out'sized'.** being unusually or abnormally large, heavy, extensive, etc.

out·skirt (out'skûrt'), *n.* **1.** Often, **outskirts.** the outlying district or region, as of a city. **2.** Usu., **outskirts.** border; fringes: *the outskirts of respectability.*

out·smart (out'smärt'), *v.t.* **1.** to get the better of (someone); outwit. —*Idiom.* **2. outsmart oneself,** to defeat oneself through the very schemes one has perpetrated to promote one's own welfare or profit.

out·sole (out'sōl'), *n.* the outer sole of a shoe or boot.

out·source (out'sôrs'), *v.t.,* **-sourced, -sourc·ing.** to buy from a foreign or nonunion supplier.

out·spend (out'spend'), *v.t.,* **-spent, -spend·ing. 1.** to outdo in spending. **2.** to exceed (one's resources) in spending.

out·spo·ken (out'spō'kən), *adj.* **1.** uttered or expressed with frankness or without reserve: *outspoken criticism.* **2.** unreserved in speech. —**out'spo'ken·ly,** *adv.* —**out'spo'ken·ness,** *n.*

out·spread (*v.* out'spred'; *n.* out'spred'), *v.,* **-spread, -spread·ing,** *n.* —*v.t., v.i.* **1.** to spread or stretch out; extend. —*n.* **2.** something that is spread out; an expanse.

out·stand·ing (out'stan'ding), *adj.* **1.** prominent; conspicuous; striking: *outstanding courage.* **2.** marked by superiority or distinction; excellent; distinguished: *an outstanding student.* **3.** continuing in existence; remaining unpaid, unresolved, etc.: *outstanding debts; outstanding questions on procedure.* —**out'stand'ing·ly,** *adv.* —**out'stand'ing·ness,** *n.*

out·stare (out'stâr'), *v.t.,* **-stared, -star·ing.** to outdo in staring; stare down.

out·sta·tion (out'stā'shən), *n.* a post, station, or settlement in a remote or outlying area.

out·stay (out'stā'), *v.t.* **1.** to stay longer than. **2.** to stay beyond the time or duration of; overstay.

out·stretch (out'strech'), *v.t.* **1.** to stretch forth; extend: *to outstretch one's hand.* **2.** to stretch out; expand: *The rising population has outstretched the city.* **3.** to stretch beyond: *His behavior outstretches my patience.* —**out'stretch'er,** *n.*

out·strip (out'strip'), *v.t.,* **-stripped, -strip·ping. 1.** to outdo; surpass; excel. **2.** to pass in running or swift travel. **3.** to get ahead of in or as if in a race. **4.** to exceed: *a demand that outstrips the supply.*

out·take (out'tāk'), *n.* **1.** a segment of film or videotape or a part of a recording edited out of the final version. **2.** an outlet for the outflow of something, as water.

out·talk (out'tôk'), *v.t.* to outdo or overcome in talking.

out·think (out'thingk'), *v.t.,* **-thought, -think·ing. 1.** to think faster, more accurately, or more perceptively than. **2.** to get the advantage of (someone) by quick or clever thinking; outwit.

out·ward (out'wərd), *adj.* **1.** proceeding or directed toward the outside or away from a center. **2.** pertaining to or being what is seen or apparent; pertaining to surface qualities only; superficial: *outward appearances.* **3.** lying toward or on the outside; exterior: *an outward court.* **4.** of or pertaining to the outside or outer surface: *the outward walls of a house.* **5.** pertaining to the outside of the body; external. **6.** pertaining to the body, as opposed to the mind or spirit. **7.** belonging or pertaining to what is external to oneself: *outward influences.* —*n.* **8.** that which is external or material; external appearance or reality. —*adv.* Also, **out'wards. 9.** toward the outside; out. **10.** away from port: *a ship bound outward.* —**out'ward·ness,** *n.*

out'ward-bound', *adj.* headed in an outward direction.

out·ward·ly (out'wərd lē), *adv.* **1.** as regards appearance or outward manifestation: *outwardly charming.* **2.** on the outside: *Outwardly, the fruit was rough to the touch.* **3.** toward the outside.

out·wash (out'wosh', -wôsh'), *n.* material, chiefly sand or gravel, deposited by meltwater streams in front of a glacier.

out·wear (out'wâr'), *v.t.,* **-wore, -worn, -wear·ing. 1.** to wear or last longer than; outlast. **2.** to exhaust in strength or endurance. **3.** to wear out; destroy by wearing.

out·weigh (out'wā'), *v.t.* **1.** to exceed in value or importance. **2.** to exceed in weight.

out·wit (out'wit'), *v.t.,* **-wit·ted, -wit·ting.** to get the better of by superior cleverness.

out·work (*v.* out'wûrk'; *n.* out'wûrk'), *v.t.* **1.** to work harder, better, or faster than. **2.** to work out or carry on to a conclusion; finish. —*n.* **3.** an earthwork or other defensive structure established outside the limits of a larger fortification.

out·worn (out'wôrn', -wōrn'), *adj.* **1.** out-of-date, outmoded, or obsolete. **2.** worn-out, as clothes.

ou·zo (ōō'zō), *n.* a colorless, anise-flavored liqueur of Greece.

o·va (ō'və), *n.* pl. of OVUM.

o·val (ō'vəl), *adj.* **1.** having the general form or outline of an egg; egg-shaped. **2.** ellipsoidal or elliptical. —*n.* **3.** something that is oval in shape or outline. **4.** an elliptical field or a field on which an elliptical track is laid out, as for athletic contests. —**o'val·ly,** *adv.*

O'val Of'fice, *n.* **1.** the office of the president of the United States, located in the White House. **2.** this office regarded as the seat of executive power in the United States federal government.

o·var·i·an (ō vâr'ē ən) also **o·var'i·al,** *adj.* of or pertaining to an ovary.

o·va·ry (ō'və rē), *n., pl.* **-ries. 1.** the female gonad or reproductive gland, in which the ova and the female sex hormones develop. **2.** the enlarged lower part of the pistil in flowering plants enclosing the ovules or new seeds.

o·vate (ō'vāt), *adj.* **1.** egg-shaped. **2.** *Bot.* egg-shaped in longitudinal section with the broader end at the base, as a leaf. —**o'vate·ly,** *adv.*

o·va·tion (ō vā'shən), *n.* **1.** an enthusiastic public acclamation, marked esp. by loud, prolonged applause. **2.** (in ancient Rome) the ceremonial entrance of a commander whose victories did not warrant a triumph. —**o·va'tion·al,** *adj.*

ov·en (uv'ən), *n.* a chamber, as in a stove, for baking, roasting, heating, or drying. —**ov'en·like',** *adj.*

ov·en·bird (uv'ən bûrd'), *n.* **1.** a North American wood warbler, *Seiurus aurocapillus,* that builds an oven-shaped nest on the forest floor. **2.** any of numerous suboscine songbirds of the family Furnariidae, ranging from S Mexico through South America, some species of which build an oven-shaped nest.

ov•en•proof (uv′ən pro͞of′), *adj.* capable of withstanding the heat of an oven; safe for use in an oven: *an ovenproof dish.*

o•ver (ō′vər), *prep.* **1.** above in place or position: *the roof over one's head.* **2.** above and to the other side of: *to leap over a wall.* **3.** above in authority, rank, power, etc.: *no one over her in the department.* **4.** so as to rest on or cover; on or upon: *Throw a sheet over the bed.* **5.** on top of: *to hit someone over the head.* **6.** here and there on or in; about: *at various places over the country.* **7.** through all parts of; all through: *to show someone over the house.* **8.** to and fro on or in; across; throughout: *to travel over Europe.* **9.** from one side to the other of; to the other side of; across: *to go over a bridge.* **10.** on the other side of; across: *lands over the sea.* **11.** reaching higher than, so as to submerge: *The water is over his shoulders.* **12.** in excess of; more than: *not over five dollars.* **13.** above in degree, quantity, etc.: *a big improvement over last year's turnout.* **14.** in preference to: *chosen over another applicant.* **15.** throughout the length or duration of: *The message was sent over a great distance; over a long period of years.* **16.** until after the end of: *to adjourn over the holidays.* **17.** in reference to, concerning, or about: *to quarrel over a matter.* **18.** while doing or attending to: *to fall asleep over one's work.* **19.** via; by means of: *I heard it over the radio.* —*adv.* **20.** beyond the top or upper part of something: *a roof that hangs over.* **21.** so as to cover or affect the whole surface: *The furniture was covered over with dust.* **22.** through a region, area, etc.: *known the world over.* **23.** at some distance, as in a direction indicated: *They live over by the hill.* **24.** from one side or place to another or across an intervening space: *to sail over; Toss the ball over, will you? Let's walk over to the coffee shop.* **25.** across or beyond an edge or rim: *The soup boiled over.* **26.** from beginning to end; throughout: *Think it over.* **27.** from one person, party, etc., to another: *He made the property over to his brother.* **28.** on the other side, as of a sea, a river, or any space: *over in Japan.* **29.** so as to displace from an upright position: *to knock over a glass.* **30.** so as to put or be in the reversed position: *The dog rolled over.* **31.** once more; again: *Do the work over.* **32.** in repetition or succession: *20 times over.* **33.** in excess or addition: *to pay the full sum and something over.* **34.** in excess of or beyond a certain amount: *Five goes into seven once, with two over.* **35.** throughout or beyond a period of time: *to stay over till Monday.* —*adj.* **36.** upper; higher up. **37.** higher in authority, station, etc. **38.** serving or intended as an outer covering; outer (often used in combination): *a gown with an overskirt.* **39.** remaining or additional, surplus; extra. **40.** too great; excessive (usu. used in combination): *overaggressive behavior.* **41.** ended; done; past: *when the war was over.* —*n.* **42.** an amount in excess or addition; extra. **43.** a shot that strikes or bursts beyond the target. **44.** *Cricket.* the part of the game played between such changes. —*v.t.* **45.** to go or get over; leap over. —*interj.* **46.** (used in radio communications to signify that the sender is awaiting a reply to or acknowledgment of a transmission.) —***Idiom.*** **47. all over, a.** throughout; everywhere. **b.** ended; finished; over with. **48. over again,** once more; again. **49. over and above,** in addition to; besides. **50. over and over,** many times; repeatedly. **51. over the hill,** past one's prime. **52. over there,** (in the U.S. during and after World War I) in or to Europe. **53. over with,** finished; ended; done.

over-, a prefixal use of OVER, occurring in various senses in compounds (*overboard; overcoat; overhang; overthrow*), and esp. employed, with the senses "over the limit," "to excess," "too much," "too," to form verbs, adjectives, adverbs, and nouns (*overact; overcrowd; overweight*).

o•ver•a•chieve (ō′vər ə chēv′), *v.i.*, **-chieved, -chiev•ing.** to perform better or achieve more than is usual or expected. —**o′ver•a•chieve′ment,** *n.* —**o′ver•a•chiev′er,** *n.*

o•ver•act (ō′vər akt′), *v.t.* **1.** to perform (a role) in an exaggerated manner. —*v.i.* **2.** to overact a role.

o•ver•ac•tive (ō′vər ak′tiv), *adj.* exceptionally or excessively active; too active. —**o′ver•ac•tiv′i•ty, o′ver•ac′tive•ness,** *n.*

o•ver•age[1] (ō′vər āj′), *adj.* **1.** beyond the acceptable, desired, or usual age. **2.** too old to be serviceable; antiquated.

o•ver•age[2] (ō′vər ij), *n.* an excess supply of merchandise.

o•ver•all (*adv.* ō′vər ôl′; *adj., n.* ō′vər ôl′), *adv., adj.* **1.** from one end or limit to the other. **2.** covering or including everything. —*n.* **3. overalls,** (*used with a pl. v.*) loose, sturdy trousers, usu. having a bib with attached shoulder straps, orig. worn over other trousers to protect them while working.

o•ver•arch (ō′vər ärch′), *v.t.* **1.** to span with or like an arch. —*v.i.* **2.** to form an arch over something.

o•ver•arch•ing (ō′vər är′ching), *adj.* encompassing or overshadowing everything.

o•ver•arm (ō′vər ärm′), *adj.* thrown or performed by raising the arm above the shoulder.

o•ver•bal•ance (*v.* ō′vər bal′əns; *n.* ō′vər bal′əns), *v.*, **-anced, -anc•ing,** *n.* —*v.t.* **1.** to outweigh. **2.** to cause to lose balance or to fall or turn over. —*n.* **3.** an excessive weight or amount. **4.** something that more than balances or more than equals.

o•ver•bear (ō′vər bâr′), *v.*, **-bore, -borne, -bear•ing.** —*v.t.* **1.** to overwhelm by weight or force. **2.** to dominate. —*v.i.* **3.** to produce fruit or progeny so abundantly as to impair the health. —**o′ver•bear′er,** *n.*

o•ver•bear•ing (ō′vər bâr′ing), *adj.* **1.** domineering; dictatorial; haughtily or rudely arrogant. **2.** of overwhelming or critical importance. —**o′ver•bear′ing•ly,** *adv.* —**o′ver•bear′ing•ness,** *n.*

o•ver•bid (*v.* ō′vər bid′; *n.* ō′vər bid′), *v.*, **-bid, -bid•ding,** *n.* —*v.t.* **1.** to bid more than the value of. —*v.i.* **2.** to bid more than the actual value or worth. —*n.* **3.** a higher bid.

o•ver•bite (ō′vər bīt′), *n.* occlusion in which the upper incisor teeth overlap the lower ones.

o•ver•blow (ō′vər blō′), *v.t.*, **-blew, -blown, -blow•ing. 1.** to give excessive importance or value to. **2.** to overinflate. **3.** to blow over the surface of, as the wind or something carried by it.

o•ver•blown[1] (ō′vər blōn′), *adj.* **1.** overdone or excessive: *overblown praise.* **2.** of unusually large size or proportions. **3.** overinflated; turgid; bombastic; pretentious.

o•ver•blown[2] (ō′vər blōn′), *adj.* past the stage of full bloom: *an overblown rose.*

O

o•ver•board (ō′vər bôrd′, -bōrd′), *adv.* **1.** over the side of a ship or boat, esp. into or in the water: *to fall overboard.* —***Idiom.*** **2. go overboard,** to go to extremes, as in speech, behavior, or dress.

o•ver•book (ō′vər bo͝ok′), *v.t.* **1.** to accept reservations for in excess of the available space: *to overbook a flight.* —*v.i.* **2.** to accept reservations in excess of the available space: *The hotel has overbooked this weekend.*

o•ver•build (ō′vər bild′), *v.*, **-built, -build•ing.** —*v.t.* **1.** to erect too many buildings in (an area). —*v.i.* **2.** to build too many dwellings or commercial buildings in an area.

o•ver•bur•den (*v.* ō′vər bûr′dn; *n.* ō′vər bûr′dn), *v.t.* **1.** to load with too great a burden. —*n.* **2.** an excessive burden. **3.** waste earth and rock covering a mineral deposit.

o•ver•buy (ō′vər bī′), *v.*, **-bought, -buy•ing.** —*v.t.* **1.** to purchase in excessive quantities. —*v.i.* **2.** to buy regardless of one's needs or financial means.

o•ver•call (*n.* ō′vər kôl′; *v.* ō′vər kôl′, ō′vər kôl′), *n.* **1.** a bid in cards higher than the previous bid. **2.** a bid in bridge higher than an opponent's bid that was not followed by a bid or double by one's partner. —*v.i.* **3.** to make an overcall.

o•ver•ca•pac•i•ty (ō′vər kə pas′i tē), *n.*, *pl.* **-ties.** capacity beyond what is normal, necessary, or desirable.

o•ver•cap•i•tal•ize (ō′vər kap′i tl īz′), *v.t.*, **-ized, -iz•ing. 1.** to capitalize (a corporation) in excess of legal limits or sound financial policy. **2.** to overestimate the capital value of (a property or enterprise). —**o′ver•cap′i•tal•i•za′tion,** *n.*

o•ver•cast (*adj.* ō′vər kast′, -käst′, -kast′, -käst′; *v.* ō′vər kast′, -käst′, ō′vər kast′, -käst′; *n.* ō′vər kast′, -käst′), *adj.* **1. a.** overspread with clouds; cloudy. **b.** (of the sky) more than 95 percent covered by clouds. **2.** dark; gloomy. —*v.t.* **3.** to overcloud; darken. **4.** to sew (fabric) with long, spaced stitches passing successively over an edge to prevent raveling. —*n.* **5.** the condition of the sky when more than 95 percent covered by clouds.

o′vercast stitch′, *n.* **1.** a sewing stitch done by overcasting. **2.** a fine embroidery stitch used to create decorative patterns on the thread bundles in openwork or drawn work.

o•ver•charge (*v.* ō′vər chärj′; *n.* ō′vər chärj′), *v.*, **-charged, -charg•ing,** *n.* —*v.t.* **1.** to charge (a purchaser) too high a price. **2.** to overload. **3.** to express too elaborately or dramatically. —*v.i.* **4.** to charge too high a price. —*n.* **5.** a charge in excess of a stated or just price. **6.** an act of overcharging. **7.** an excessive load. —**o′ver•charg′er,** *n.*

o•ver•clothes (ō′vər klōz′, -klōthz′), *n.* (*used with a pl. v.*) clothing worn outside other garments.

o•ver•cloud (ō′vər kloud′), *v.t.* **1.** to overspread with or as if with clouds. **2.** to make gloomy; darken.

o•ver•coat (ō′vər kōt′), *n.* **1.** a coat worn over the ordinary indoor clothing, as in cold weather. **2.** Also called **o′ver•coat′ing.** an added coating, as of paint, applied for protection.

o•ver•come (ō′vər kum′), *v.*, **-came, -come, -com•ing.** —*v.t.* **1.** to get the better of in a struggle or conflict. **2.** to prevail over (opposition, a debility, temptations, etc.). **3.** to overpower or overwhelm in body or mind: *overcome by smoke; overcome with grief.* —*v.i.* **4.** to gain the victory; win; conquer. —**o′ver•com′er,** *n.*

o•ver•com•mit (ō′vər kə mit′), *v.t.*, **-mit•ted, -mit•ting.** to commit more than is feasible or desirable. —**o′ver•com•mit′ment,** *n.*

o•ver•com•pen•sate (ō′vər kom′pən sāt′), *v.*, **-sat•ed, -sat•ing.** —*v.t.* **1.** to compensate excessively. —*v.i.* **2.** to perform more strenuously than required to overcome a physical or psychological defect. —**o′ver•com•pen′sa•to′ry** (-kəm pen′sə tôr′ē, -tōr′ē), *adj.*

o•ver•com•pen•sa•tion (ō′vər kom′pən sā′shən), *n.* **1.** compensation to an unnecessary or unreasonable degree. **2.** *Psychoanal.* a pronounced striving to overcome a trait perceived as unacceptable by substituting an opposite trait.

o•ver•crop (ō′vər krop′), *v.t.*, **-cropped, -crop•ping.** to crop (land) to excess; exhaust the fertility of by continuous cultivation.

o•ver•crowd (ō′vər kroud′), *v.t., v.i.* to crowd to an uncomfortable or undesirable excess.

o•ver•de•vel•op (ō′vər di vel′əp), *v.t.* **1.** to develop to excess: *to overdevelop a waterfront area.* **2.** to develop a (photograph) for too long or in too strong a solution. —**o′ver•de•vel′op•ment,** *n.*

o•ver•do (ō′vər do͞o′), *v.*, **-did, -done, -do•ing.** —*v.t.* **1.** to do to excess; overindulge in. **2.** to carry to excess or beyond the proper limit: *to overdo the charm with the boss.* **3.** to overact (a part); exaggerate. **4.** to overtax the strength of; exhaust. **5.** to cook too much; overcook. —*v.i.* **6.** to do too much; go to extremes. —**o′ver•do′er,** *n.*

o•ver•dose (*n.* ō′vər dōs′; *v.* ō′vər dōs′, ō′vər dōs′), *n., v.*, **-dosed,**

-dos•ing. —*n.* **1.** an excessive dose of a drug. —*v.i.* **2.** to take an excessive dose, esp. of a narcotic. —*v.t.* **3.** to give an excessive dose to.

o•ver•draft (ō′vər draft′, -dräft′), *n.* **1.** an act of overdrawing a checking account. **2.** a check overdrawn on an account. **3.** the amount overdrawn. **4.** an excessive drawing on or drawing off of something. **5.** a draft made to pass over a fire, as in a furnace.

o•ver•draw (ō′vər drô′), *v.*, **-drew, -drawn, -draw•ing.** —*v.t.* **1.** to draw upon (an account, allowance, etc.) in excess of the balance standing to one's credit or at one's disposal. **2.** to strain, as a bow, by drawing too far. **3.** to exaggerate in drawing, depicting, or describing. —*v.i.* **4.** to overdraw an account or the like. —**o′ver•draw′er,** *n.*

o•ver•dress (*v.* ō′vər dres′; *n.* ō′vər dres′), *v.t., v.i.* **1.** to dress with too much finery or formality. **2.** to dress with too much clothing. —*n.* **3.** a dress worn over another.

o•ver•drive (*n.* ō′vər drīv′; *v.* ō′vər drīv′), *n., v.,* **-drove, -driven, -driving.** —*n.* **1.** a device in a motor vehicle containing a gear that provides a drive shaft speed greater than the engine crankshaft speed. **2.** *Informal.* a state of intense activity or productivity. —*v.t.* **3.** to push or carry to excess; overwork. **4.** to drive too hard.

o•ver•dub (*v.* ō′vər dub′; *n.* ō′vər dub′), *v.,* **-dubbed, -dub•bing,** *n.* —*v.i.* **1.** to add additional sound or music to an existing recording. —*v.t.* **2.** to add (a track or tracks) to a recording. —*n.* **3.** an act of overdubbing. **4.** a recorded segment or layer of sound integrated into a recording.

o•ver•due (ō′vər dōō′, -dyōō′), *adj.* **1.** past due, as a delayed train or a bill not paid by the assigned date; late. **2.** too long awaited: *an overdue improvement in attitude.* **3.** more than sufficiently advanced or ready: *a country overdue for industrial development.*

o′ver eas′y, *adj., adv.* (of an egg) fried on one side until nearly done and then fried briefly on the reverse side so that the yolk remains somewhat liquid but hard on top.

o•ver•eat (ō′vər ēt′), *v.i.,* **-ate, -eat•en, -eat•ing.** to eat too much. —**o′ver•eat′er,** *n.*

o•ver•es•ti•mate (*v.* ō′vər es′tə māt′; *n.* ō′vər es′tə mit), *v.,* **-mat•ed, -mat•ing,** *n.* —*v.t.* **1.** to estimate at too high a value, amount, or rate. **2.** to hold in too great esteem; overrate. —*n.* **3.** an estimate that is too high. —**o′ver•es′ti•ma′tion,** *n.*

o•ver•ex•pose (ō′vər ik spōz′), *v.t.,* **-posed, -pos•ing. 1.** to expose too much, as to the sun, cold, or public view. **2.** to expose (a photographic film, plate, etc.) to too much light. —**o′ver•ex•po′sure** (-spō′zhər), *n.*

o•ver•ex•tend (ō′vər ik stend′), *v.t.* **1.** to extend or expand beyond a proper, safe, or reasonable point. **2.** to obligate (oneself) to more activities, commitments, etc., than one has time or resources for. —**o′ver•ex•ten′sion** (-sten′shən), *n.*

o•ver•fill (ō′vər fil′), *v.t.* **1.** to fill too full, so as to cause overflowing. —*v.i.* **2.** to become too full.

o•ver•fish (ō′vər fish′), *v.t.* to fish (an area) excessively; exhaust the supply of usable fish in (a body of water).

o•ver•flight (ō′vər flīt′), *n.* an air flight that passes over a specific area, country, or territory.

o•ver•flow (*v.* ō′vər flō′; *n.* ō′vər flō′), *v.i.* **1.** to flow or run over, as rivers or water. **2.** to have the contents flowing over or spilling. **3.** to pass from one part to another as if flowing from an overfull space: *The population overflowed into the adjoining territory.* **4.** to be supplied with in great measure: *a heart overflowing with gratitude.* —*v.t.* **5.** to flow over; flood; inundate. **6.** to flow over or beyond (the brim, banks, borders, etc.). **7.** to flow over the edge or brim of. **8.** to cause to overflow. —*n.* **9.** an overflowing. **10.** something that flows or runs over: *the overflow from a fountain.* **11.** a portion crowded out of an overfilled place. **12.** an excess or superabundance: *an overflow of applicants for the job.* **13.** an outlet or receptacle for excess liquid.

o•ver•fly (ō′vər flī′), *v.t.,* **-flew, -flown, -fly•ing. 1.** to fly over (a specified area, country, etc.). **2.** to fly farther than or beyond; overshoot. **3.** to fly over or past instead of making a scheduled stop.

o•ver•gar•ment (ō′vər gär′mənt), *n.* an outer garment.

o•ver•graze (ō′vər grāz′, ō′vər grāz′), *v.t.,* **-grazed, -graz•ing.** to graze (land) to excess.

o•ver•grow (ō′vər grō′, ō′vər grō′), *v.,* **-grew, -grown, -grow•ing.** —*v.t.* **1.** to grow over; cover with a growth of something. **2.** to grow beyond, grow too large for, or outgrow. —*v.i.* **3.** to grow to excess; grow too large. **4.** to become grown over, as with weeds.

o•ver•growth (ō′vər grōth′), *n.* **1.** a growth overspreading or covering something. **2.** excessive growth.

o•ver•hang (*v.* ō′vər hang′; *n.* ō′vər hang′), *v.,* **-hung, -hang•ing,** *n.* —*v.t.* **1.** to hang or be suspended over. **2.** to extend, project, or jut over. **3.** to impend over or threaten; loom over. —*v.i.* **4.** to hang over; project or jut out over something below. —*n.* **5.** something that extends or juts out over; projection. **6.** the extent of a projection. **7.** an excess or surplus, as of securities, currency, or inventory. **8.** a projecting upper part of a building, as a roof or balcony.

o•ver•haul (*v.* ō′vər hôl′, ō′vər hôl′; *n.* ō′vər hôl′), *v.t.* **1.** to make necessary repairs on; restore to working condition. **2.** to examine thoroughly and revise or refurbish: *to overhaul the curriculum.* **3.** to gain upon, catch up with, or overtake. **4.** *Naut.* **a.** to slacken (a rope) by hauling in the opposite direction to that in which the rope was drawn taut. **b.** to release the blocks of (a tackle). —*n.* **5.** Also, **o′ver•haul′ing.** a general examination and repair. —**o′ver•haul′er,** *n.*

o•ver•head (*adv.* ō′vər hed′; *adj., n.* ō′vər hed′), *adv.* **1.** above one's head; aloft; up in the air or sky, esp. near the zenith. **2.** so as to be completely submerged or engulfed: *to plunge overhead in water.* —*adj.* **3.** situated, operating, or passing above, aloft, or over the head. **4.** of or pertaining to the general costs of running a business. —*n.* **5.** the general, fixed costs of running a business, as rent, lighting, and heating expenses, that cannot be charged to a specific product or part of the work operation. **6.** a stroke in tennis or badminton in which the ball or shuttlecock is hit with a downward motion from above the head; smash. **7.** an overhead compartment, shelf, etc. **8.** a ceiling light. **9.** Also called **o′verhead projec′tor.** an apparatus that projects images above and behind the operator when transparencies are placed horizontally on its surface and lighted from below. **10.** Also called **o′verhead projec′tion.** a picture or image thus projected.

o•ver•hear (ō′vər hēr′), *v.t.,* **-heard, -hear•ing.** to hear (speech or a speaker) without the speaker's intention or knowledge.

o•ver•heat (ō′vər hēt′), *v.t.* **1.** to heat to excess. **2.** to excite or agitate (the economy) to excess. —*v.i.* **3.** to become overheated.

o•ver•in•dulge (ō′vər in dulj′), *v.t., v.i.,* **-dulged, -dulg•ing.** to indulge to excess. —**o′ver•in•dul′gence,** *n.* —**o′ver•in•dul′gent,** *adj.* —**o′ver•in•dul′gent•ly,** *adv.*

o•ver•joy (ō′vər joi′), *v.t.* to cause to feel great joy or delight; elate. —**o′ver•joyed′,** *adj.*

o•ver•kill (ō′vər kil′), *n.* **1.** the capacity of a nation to destroy by nuclear weapons more of an enemy than would be necessary for a victory. **2.** an excess of what is required or suitable.

o•ver•land (ō′vər land′, -lənd), *adv.* **1.** by, over, or across land. —*adj.* **2.** proceeding, performed, or carried on overland.

O′ver•land Park′ (ō′vər lənd), *n.* a town in E Kansas, near Kansas City. 125,225.

o•ver•lap (*v.* ō′vər lap′; *n.* ō′vər lap′), *v.,* **-lapped, -lap•ping,** *n.* —*v.t.* **1.** to extend over and cover a part of. **2.** to coincide in part with; have in common with. **3.** to cover and extend beyond. —*v.i.* **4.** to lap over. **5.** to coincide partly. —*n.* **6.** an act or instance of overlapping. **7.** the extent, amount, or place of overlapping. **8.** an overlapping part.

o•ver•lay (*v.* ō′vər lā′; *n.* ō′vər lā′), *v.,* **-laid, -lay•ing,** *n.* —*v.t.* **1.** to lay or place (one thing) over or upon another. **2.** to cover, overspread, or surmount with something. **3.** to finish with an overlay: *wood overlaid with gold.* —*n.* **4.** something laid over something else; covering. **5.** a superimposed decorative layer. **6.** a sheet laid on the tympan of a printing press to increase or distribute the impression. **7.** a transparent sheet placed over artwork, a map, or the like for noting corrections, instructions, additional information, etc.

o•ver•leaf (ō′vər lēf′), *adv.* on the other side of the page or sheet.

o•ver•lie (ō′vər lī′), *v.t.,* **-lay, -lain, -ly•ing. 1.** to lie over or on, as a

---

o′ver•ab•sorp′tion, *n.*
o′ver•a•bun′dance, *n.*
o′ver•a•bun′dant, *adj.;* -ly, *adv.*
o′ver•ac•cel′er•a′tion, *n.*
o′ver•ac•cen′tu•ate′, *v.t.,* -at•ed, -at•ing.
o′ver•ac•cu′mu•la′tion, *n.*
o′ver•a•cid′i•ty, *n.*
o′ver•a•dorned′, *adj.*
o′ver•af•fect′, *v.t.*
o′ver•ag•gres′sive, *adj.;* -ly, *adv.;* -ness, *n.*
o′ver•am•bi′tious, *adj.;* -ly, *adv.*
o′ver•am•pli•fy′, *v.,* -fied, -fy•ing.
o′ver•an′a•lyt′i•cal, *adj.;* -ly, *adv.*
o′ver•an′i•mat′ed, *adj.;* -ly, *adv.*
o′ver•anx′ious, *adj.*

o′ver•ap•pre′ci•a′tion, *n.*
o′ver•ap•pre′cia•tive, *adj.;* -ness, *n.*
o′ver•ap•pre•hen′sive, *adj.;* -ness, *n.*
o′ver•ar′gu•men′ta•tive, *adj.*
o′ver•ar•tic′u•late, *adj.*
o′ver•as•ser′tive, *adj.;* -ly, *adv.;* -ness, *n.*
o′ver•at•ten′tive, *adj.;* -ly, *adv.;* -ness, *n.*
o′ver•a•ware′ness, *n.*
o′ver•bake′, *v.,* -baked, -bak•ing.
o′ver•bleach′, *v.*
o′ver•boil′, *v.,* -boiled, -boil•ing.
o′ver•bold′, *adj.;* -ly, *adv.;* -ness, *n.*
o′ver•boun′te•ous, *adj.*
o′ver•brake′, *v.,* -braked, -brak•ing.
o′ver•bus′y, *adj.*
o′ver•care′ful, *adj.;* -ly, *adv.*

o′ver•cau′tious, *adj.;* -ly, *adv.*
o′ver•com•mer′cial•i•za′tion, *n.*
o′ver•com•pet′i•tive, *adj.;* -ness, *n.*
o′ver•com•plex′, *adj.*
o′ver•com•pli′ance, *n.*
o′ver•com′pli•cate′, *v.t.,* -cat•ed, -cat•ing.
o′ver•con′cen•tra′tion, *n.*
o′ver•con′fi•dent, *adj.;* -ly, *adv.*
o′ver•con•sci•en′tious, *adj.;* -ly, *adv.;* -ness, *n.*
o′ver•con•sump′tion, *n.*
o′ver•cook′, *v.t.,* -cooked, -cook•ing.
o′ver•cor•rect′, *adj.; v.*
o′ver•crit′i•cal, *adj.;* -ly, *adv.*
o′ver•crowd′ed, *adj.;* -ly, *adv.;* -ness, *n.*
o′ver•cul′ti•va′tion, *n.*

o′ver•cu′ri•ous, *adj.;* -ness, *n.*
o′ver•dec′o•rate′, *v.,* -rat•ed, -rat•ing.
o′ver•ded′i•cate′, *v.t.,* -cat•ed, -cat•ing.
o′ver•de•fen′sive, *adj.;* -ly, *adv.;* -ness, *n.*
o′ver•de•mand′ing, *adj.*
o′ver•de•pend′ent, *adj.*
o′ver•de•ter′mined, *adj.*
o′ver•dif•fuse′, *adj.*
o′ver•dil′i•gent, *adj.;* -lat•ed, -lat•ing.
o′ver•di•rect′ed, *adj.*
o′ver•dis•ci•pline, *v.,* -plined, -plin•ing.
o′ver•dis•crim′i•nat′ing, *adj.*
o′ver•di•ver′si•ty, *n.*

covering or stratum. **2.** to smother (an infant) by lying upon it, as in sleep.

o·ver·load (*v.* ō′vər lōd′; *n.* ō′vər lōd′), *v.t.* **1.** to load to excess; overburden. —*n.* **2.** an excessive load.

o·ver·look (*v.* ō′vər lŏok′; *n.* ō′vər lŏok′), *v.t.* **1.** to fail to notice or consider. **2.** to disregard indulgently: *to overlook misbehavior.* **3.** to excuse; pardon. **4.** to look over, as from a higher position. **5.** to rise above, esp. so as to afford a view over. **6.** to inspect or peruse. **7.** to look after; supervise. —*n.* **8.** terrain that affords a good view of things below.

o·ver·lord (ō′vər lôrd′), *n.* **1.** a person who is lord over other lords. **2.** a person of great influence or power. —*v.t.* **3.** to rule or govern arbitrarily or tyrannically. —**o′ver·lord′ship,** *n.*

o·ver·ly (ō′vər lē), *adv.* excessively; too.

o·ver·much (ō′vər much′), *adj., n., adv.* too much.

o·ver·night (*adv.* ō′vər nīt′; *adj., n.* ō′vər nīt′), *adv.* **1.** for or during the night. **2.** very quickly; suddenly: *New suburbs sprang up overnight.* **3.** on the previous evening. —*adj.* **4.** done, made, occurring, or continuing during the night: *an overnight stop.* **5.** staying for one night: *overnight guests.* **6.** intended for delivery on the next day. **7.** valid for one night: *an overnight pass.* **8.** occurring suddenly or within a very short time: *an overnight sensation.* —*n.* **9.** an overnight stay or trip.

overnight′ bag′, *n.* a travel bag large enough to hold personal articles and clothing for use on an overnight trip.

o·ver·night·er (ō′vər nī′tər), *n.* **1.** OVERNIGHT (def. 9). **2.** a person making an overnight stay. **3.** something serving overnight travel, as a special train or an overnight bag.

o·ver·pass (*n.* ō′vər pas′, -päs′; *v.* ō′vər pas′, -päs′), *n., v.,* **-passed** or **-past, -pass·ing.** —*n.* **1.** a road, walkway, or bridge providing access over another route. —*v.t.* **2.** to pass over; traverse. **3.** to exceed; overstep; transgress. **4.** to surpass. **5.** to ignore; disregard. —*v.i.* **6.** to pass over or by.

o·ver·pay (ō′vər pā′), *v.t.,* **-paid, -pay·ing. 1.** to pay more than (an amount due). **2.** to pay (a person) in excess. —**o′ver·pay′ment** (-pā′mənt), *n.*

o·ver·play (ō′vər plā′), *v.t.* **1.** to exaggerate or overemphasize (an emotion, an effect, etc.). **2.** to put too much stress on the value or importance of. **3.** to hit (a golf ball) past the putting green. —*Idiom.* **4. overplay one's hand,** to overestimate the strength of one's position.

o·ver·pop·u·late (ō′vər pop′yə lāt′), *v.t.,* **-lat·ed, -lat·ing.** to fill with too many people, straining available resources and facilities. —**o′ver·pop′u·la′tion,** *n.*

o·ver·pow·er (ō′vər pou′ər), *v.t.* **1.** to overcome by superior force; vanquish. **2.** to affect or impress excessively; overwhelm. **3.** to furnish with excessive power: *an overpowered car.*

o·ver·price (ō′vər prīs′), *v.t.,* **-priced, -pric·ing.** to set too high a price on.

o·ver·print (*v.* ō′vər print′; *n.* ō′vər print′), *v.t.* **1.** to print (additional material) over something already printed. —*n.* **2.** something overprinted, esp. something printed on the face of a stamp that signifies a new or altered function for the stamp or a change in the authority issuing it. **3.** a stamp with an overprint.

o·ver·qual·i·fied (ō′vər kwol′ə fīd′), *adj.* having more education, training, or experience than is required for a job.

o·ver·rate (ō′vər rāt′), *v.t.,* **-rat·ed, -rat·ing.** to rate or appraise too highly.

o·ver·reach (ō′vər rēch′), *v.t.* **1.** to reach or extend over or beyond. **2.** to exceed (a goal) by excessive effort. **3.** to defeat (oneself) by excessive eagerness. **4.** to strain (oneself) to the point of exceeding a purpose. **5.** to get the better of, esp. by deceit or trickery; outwit. —*v.i.* **6.** to reach or extend over something. **7.** to reach too far. **8.** to cheat others. **9.** (of a horse) to strike the forefoot with the hind foot. —**o′ver·reach′er,** *n.*

o·ver·re·act (ō′vər rē akt′), *v.i.* to react more strongly than is appropriate. —**o′ver·re·ac′tion,** *n.*

o·ver·ride (*v.* ō′vər rīd′; *n.* ō′vər rīd′), *v.,* **-rode, -rid·den, -rid·ing,** *n.* —*v.t.* **1.** to prevail over; overrule. **2.** to set aside or nullify; counter-

mand. **3.** to take precedence over; preempt. **4.** to extend beyond or spread over; overlap. **5.** to modify or suspend the ordinary functioning of. **6.** to ride over or across. **7.** to ride past or beyond. **8.** to trample or crush. **9.** to ride (a horse) too much. —*n.* **10.** an act or instance of overriding. **11.** a commission on sales or profits paid esp. at the executive or managerial level. **12.** budgetary or expense increase; exceeding of an estimate: *cost overrides.* **13.** a system or device for overriding an otherwise automatic operation.

o·ver·ripe (ō′vər rīp′), *adj.* **1.** ripe beyond succulence: *overripe fruit.* **2.** effete; decadent. —**o′ver·ripe′ness,** *n.*

o·ver·rule (ō′vər rōol′), *v.t.,* **-ruled, -rul·ing. 1.** to rule against or disallow the arguments of (a person). **2.** to rule against (a plea, argument, etc.); reject. **3.** to prevail over so as to change the purpose or action. **4.** to exercise control or influence over.

o·ver·run (*v.* ō′vər run′; *n.* ō′vər run′), *v.,* **-ran, -run, -run·ning,** *n.* —*v.t.* **1.** to swarm or spread over in great numbers. **2.** to attack and defeat decisively and occupy the position of; overwhelm. **3.** to run or go beyond: *to overrun the finish line.* **4.** to exceed, as a budget or estimate. **5.** to run over; overflow. **6.** to print extra copies of. —*v.i.* **7.** to overflow. **8.** to exceed the proper or desired limits. —*n.* **9.** an amount in excess of that needed or ordered. **10.** the exceeding of estimated costs of production.

o·ver·seas (*adv.* ō′vər sēz′; *adj.* ō′vər sēz′) also **o·ver·sea** (*adv.* ō′vər sē′; *adj.* ō′vər sē′), *adv.* **1.** over, across, or beyond the sea; abroad. —*adj.* **2.** of or pertaining to passage over the sea. **3.** of, from, or located in places across the sea; foreign.

o·ver·see (ō′vər sē′), *v.t.,* **-saw, -seen, -see·ing. 1.** to supervise; manage. **2.** to observe secretly or unintentionally. **3.** to survey or watch, as from a higher postition. **4.** to examine; inspect.

o·ver·se·er (ō′vər sē′ər, -sēr′), *n.* a supervisor; manager.

o·ver·sell (ō′vər sel′), *v.t.,* **-sold, -sell·ing. 1.** to sell more of than can be delivered. **2.** to sell too aggressively to. **3.** to emphasize the good points of excessively; praise too highly.

o·ver·shad·ow (ō′vər shad′ō), *v.t.* **1.** to exceed in importance or significance. **2.** to cast a shadow over; darken.

o·ver·shoe (ō′vər shōō′), *n.* a shoe or boot worn over another, esp. for protection in wet or cold weather.

o·ver·shoot (ō′vər shōōt′), *v.,* **-shot, -shoot·ing.** —*v.t.* **1.** to shoot or go over, beyond, or above so as to miss. **2.** to pass or go by or beyond. **3.** to fly beyond the end of (a landing strip) when landing. —*v.i.* **4.** to fly or go beyond. **5.** to shoot over or above a mark.

o·ver·shot (ō′vər shot′), *adj.* **1.** driven by water passing over the top from above: *an overshot water wheel.* **2.** having the upper jaw projecting beyond the lower, as a dog. **3.** (in weaving) a pattern formed when filling threads are passed over several warp threads at a time.

o·ver·sight (ō′vər sīt′), *n.* **1.** unintentional failure to notice or consider. **2.** a careless omission. **3.** the act of overseeing; supervision.

o·ver·sim·pli·fy (ō′vər sim′plə fī′), *v.t., v.i.,* **-fied, -fy·ing.** to simplify to the point of error, distortion, or misrepresentation. —**o′ver·sim′pli·fi·ca′tion,** *n.*

o·ver·size (ō′vər sīz′) also **o′ver·sized′,** *adj.* of a size larger than is usual or necessary.

o·ver·sleep (ō′vər slēp′), *v.i.,* **-slept, -sleep·ing.** to sleep beyond the proper or intended time of waking.

o·ver·spend (ō′vər spend′), *v.,* **-spent, -spend·ing.** —*v.i.* **1.** to spend more than one can afford. —*v.t.* **2.** to spend in excess of: *to overspend one's salary.* **3.** to wear out; exhaust.

o·ver·spread (ō′vər spred′), *v.t.,* **-spread, -spread·ing.** to spread or diffuse over: *A smile overspread her face.*

o·ver·state (ō′vər stāt′), *v.t.,* **-stat·ed, -stat·ing.** to state too strongly; exaggerate. —**o·ver·state·ment** (ō′vər stāt′mənt, ō′vər stāt′-), *n.*

o·ver·stay (ō′vər stā′), *v.t.* to stay beyond the time, limit, or duration of: *to overstay one's welcome.*

o·ver·step (ō′vər step′), *v.t.,* **-stepped, -step·ping.** to go beyond; exceed: *to overstep one's authority.*

o·ver·strung (ō′vər strung′), *adj.* too highly strung; overly tense or sensitive.

O

---

o′ver·dra·mat′ic, *adj.*
o′ver·dram′a·tize′, *v.,* -tized, -tiz·ing.
o′ver·dry′, *adj.;* -ness, *n.*
o′ver·ea′ger, *adj.;* -ly, *adv.;* -ness, *n.*
o′ver·ear′nest, *adj.*
o′ver·ed′u·cate′, *v.t.,* -cat·ed, -cat·ing.
o′ver·e·mo′tion·al, *adj.*
o′ver·em′pha·size′, *v.,* -sized, -siz·ing.
o′ver·en·dowed′, *adj.*
o′ver·en·rolled′, *adj.*
o′ver·en·thu′si·as′tic, *adj.*
o′ver·e·quipped′, *adj.*
o′ver·ex·act′ing, *adj.*
o′ver·ex·ag′ger·ate′, *v.,* -at·ed, -at·ing.

o′ver·ex·cit′a·ble, *adj.;* -bly, *adv.*
o′ver·ex·er′tion, *n.*
o′ver·ex·pan′sion, *n.*
o′ver·ex·pend′i·ture, *n.*
o′ver·ex·trav′a·gant, *adj.;* -ly, *adv.*
o′ver·ex·u′ber·ant, *adj.;* -ly, *adv.*
o′ver·fa·mil′i·ar′i·ty, *n.*
o′ver·fan′ci·ful, *adj.*
o′ver·fas·tid′i·ous, *adj.;* -ly, *adv.;* -ness, *n.*
o′ver·feed′, *v.,* -fed, -feed·ing.
o′ver·frag′ment·ed, *adj.*
o′ver·fund′, *v.t.*
o′ver·fur′nish, *v.t.*
o′ver·fuss′y, *adj.*
o′ver·gen′er·al·i·za′tion, *n.*
o′ver·gen′er·ous, *adj.;* -ly, *adv.*
o′ver·hast′y, *adj.*

o′ver·i·de′al·ize′, *v.,* -ized, -iz·ing.
o′ver·im·ag′i·na·tive, *adj.*
o′ver·im′i·ta·tive, *adj.*
o′ver·in·dus′tri·al·i·za′tion, *n.*
o′ver·in·flate′, *v.t.,* -flat·ed, -flat·ing.
o′ver·in·hib′it·ed, *adj.*
o′ver·in·sist′ence, *n.*
o′ver·in·tel·lec′tu·al, *adj.;* -ly, *adv.*
o′ver·in·ter·fer′ence, *n.*
o′ver·in·vest′, *v.*
o′ver·in·volve′, *v.t.,* -volved, -volv·ing.
o′ver·lad′en, *adj.*
o′ver·loud′, *adj.;* -ness, *n.*
o′ver·mag′ni·fy′, *v.t.,* -fied, -fy·ing.
o′ver·med′i·cate′, *v.t.,* -cat·ed, -cat·ing.

o′ver·mod′est, *adj.;* -ly, *adv.*
o′ver·o·pin′ion·at′ed, *adj.*
o′ver·op′ti·mis′tic, *adj.*
o′ver·or′ches·trate′, *v.t.,* -trat·ed, -trat·ing.
o′ver·or′gan·ize′, *v.,* -ized, -iz·ing.
o′ver·pes′si·mis′tic, *adj.*
o′ver·plan′, *v.,* -planned, -plan·ning.
o′ver·plant′, *v.t.*
o′ver·plen′ti·ful, *adj.*
o′ver·prac′tice, *v.t.,* -ticed, -tic·ing.
o′ver·praise′, *v.t.,* -praised, -prais·ing, *n.*
o′ver·pre·cise′, *adj.;* -ly, *adv.;*
o′ver·pre·scribe′, *v.,* -scribed, -scrib·ing.
o′ver·pres′sure, *n., v.t.,* -sured, -sur·ing.

o·ver·stuff (ō′vər stuf′), *v.t.* **1.** to stuff too much into. **2.** to cover (a sofa, chair, etc.) completely with thick upholstery.

o·ver·sub·scribe (ō′vər səb skrīb′), *v.t.*, **-scribed, -scrib·ing.** to subscribe for more of than is available, expected, or required. —**o′ver·sub·scrip′tion** (-skrip′shən), *n.*

o·vert (ō vûrt′, ō′vûrt), *adj.* open to view or knowledge; not concealed or secret: *overt hostility.* —**overt′ly,** *adv.*

o·ver·take (ō′vər tāk′), *v.t.*, **-took, -tak·en, -tak·ing. 1.** to catch up with. **2.** to catch up with and pass. **3.** to befall suddenly: *Bad luck overtook them.*

o·ver·tax (ō′vər taks′), *v.t.* **1.** to tax too heavily. **2.** to make too great demands on. —**o′ver·tax·a′tion,** *n.*

o′ver-the-count′er, *adj.* **1.** not listed on or transacted through an organized securities exchange: *over-the-counter stocks.* **2.** sold legally without a prescription: *over-the-counter drugs.*

o·ver·throw (*v.* ō′vər thrō′; *n.* ō′vər thrō′), *v.*, **-threw, -thrown, -throw·ing,** *n.* —*v.t.* **1.** to depose, as from a position of power. **2.** to put an end to by force: *to overthrow tyranny.* **3.** to overturn; topple. **4.** to throw past or over: *to overthrow first base.* —*n.* **5.** an act or instance of overthrowing or being overthrown. —**o′ver·throw′er,** *n.*

o·ver·time (ō′vər tīm′), *n.* **1.** working time before or after one's regularly scheduled working hours. **2.** pay for such time. **3.** time in excess of a set period. **4.** an additional period in a game, played when the score is tied at the end of the regular playing period. —*adv.* **5.** during overtime: *to work overtime.* —*adj.* **6.** of or for overtime.

o·ver·tone (ō′vər tōn′), *n.* **1.** an acoustical frequency that is higher than and simultaneous with the fundamental in a complex musical tone. **2.** an additional, usu. implicit meaning or quality.

o·ver·top (ō′vər top′), *v.t.*, **-topped, -top·ping. 1.** to rise above the top of. **2.** to rise above in authority. **3.** to surpass or excel.

o·ver·trick (ō′vər trik′), *n.* a trick in bridge in excess of the number bid.

o·ver·ture (ō′vər chər, -chŏŏr′), *n.*, *v.*, **-tured, -tur·ing.** —*n.* **1.** an initiating move in negotiating an agreement or action; proposal; offer. **2. a.** an orchestral composition introducing a musical work, as an opera. **b.** an independent piece of similar character. **3.** an introductory part; prelude; prologue. —*v.t.* **4.** to submit as an overture or proposal. **5.** to make an overture or proposal to.

o·ver·turn (*v.* ō′vər tûrn′; *n.* ō′vər tûrn′), *v.t.* **1.** to cause to turn over on the side, face, or back. **2.** to destroy the power of; overthrow. —*v.i.* **3.** to turn over; capsize. —*n.* **4.** the act of overturning. **5.** the state of being overturned. **6.** the thorough circulation of water and nutrients brought about in a lake by the action of wind in the spring and fall.

o·ver·use (*v.* ō′vər yōōz′; *n.* ō′vər yōōs′), *v.*, **-used, -us·ing,** *n.* —*v.t.* **1.** to use too much or too often. —*n.* **2.** excessive use.

o·ver·view (ō′vər vyōō′), *n.* a general outline of a subject or situation; survey or summary.

o·ver·ween·ing (ō′vər wē′ning), *adj.* **1.** presumptuously conceited, overconfident, or proud. **2.** exaggerated; excessive: *overweening pride.* —**o′ver·ween′ing·ly,** *adv.*

o·ver·weight (*adj.* ō′vər wāt′; *n.* ō′vər wāt′; *v.* ō′vər wāt′), *adj.* **1.** weighing more than is allowed or considered normal, proper, or healthful. —*n.* **2.** weight above what law or regulation allows: *baggage overweight.* **3.** weight in excess of what is considered normal, proper, or healthful. —*v.t.* **4.** to weight excessively. **5.** to give too much consideration or emphasis to.

o·ver·whelm (ō′vər hwelm′, -welm′), *v.t.* **1.** to overpower in mind or feeling: *overwhelmed by remorse.* **2.** to overpower with superior force or numbers. **3.** to cover or bury beneath a mass of something. **4.** to burden excessively.

o·ver·whelm·ing (ō′vər hwel′ming, -wel′-), *adj.* so great as to render resistance or opposition useless; overpowering. —**o′ver·whelm′ing·ly,** *adv.*

o·ver·wind (ō′vər wīnd′), *v.t.*, **-wound, -wind·ing.** to wind too far or too much: *to overwind a watch.*

o·ver·win·ter (ō′vər win′tər), *v.i.* to pass or survive the winter.

o·ver·work (*v.* ō′vər wûrk′; *n.* ō′vər wûrk′), *v.t.* **1.** to cause to work

too hard, too much, or too long. **2.** to excite excessively. **3.** to use or elaborate to excess. **4.** to decorate the surface of. —*v.i.* **5.** to work too hard, too much, or too long.

o·ver·write (ō′vər rīt′), *v.*, **-wrote, -writ·ten, -writ·ing.** —*v.t.* **1.** to write in too elaborate or prolix a style. **2.** to write on or over. —*v.i.* **3.** to write too elaborately or lengthily.

o·ver·wrought (ō′vər rôt′, ō′vər-), *adj.* **1.** extremely excited or agitated. **2.** excessively complex or ornate.

ovi-, a combining form meaning "egg": *oviform.*

Ov·id (ov′id), *n.* (*Publius Ovidius Naso*) 43 B.C.–A.D. 17?, Roman poet. —**O·vid·i·an** (ō vid′ē ən), *adj.*

o·vi·duct (ō′vi dukt′), *n.* a tube through which ova are transported from the ovary to the outside or into the uterus. —**o′vi·duc′tal,** *adj.*

o·vi·form (ō′və fôrm′), *adj.* egg-shaped; ovoid.

o·vine (ō′vīn, ō′vin), *adj.* of, pertaining to, or resembling a sheep.

o·vip·a·rous (ō vip′ər əs), *adj.* producing eggs that hatch outside the body. —**o·vi·par·i·ty** (ō′və par′i tē), *n.* —**o·vip′a·rous·ly,** *adv.*

o·vi·pos·it (ō′və poz′it, ō′və poz′-), *v.i.* to deposit or lay eggs, esp. by means of an ovipositor. —**o′vi·po·si′tion** (-pə zish′ən), *n.*

o·vi·pos·i·tor (ō′və poz′i tər), *n.* **1.** an organ at the end of the abdomen in certain female insects, through which eggs are deposited. **2.** a similar organ in certain fishes and other creatures.

o·void (ō′void), *adj.* **1.** egg-shaped; having the solid form of an egg. **2.** OVATE (def. 2). —*n.* **3.** an ovoid body.

o·vo·vi·vip·a·rous (ō′vō vī vip′ər əs), *adj.* producing eggs that are hatched within the body, so that the young are born alive but without placental attachment, as certain reptiles or fishes. —**o′vo·vi·vi·par′i·ty** (-vī′və par′i tē), *n.* —**o′vo·vi·vip′a·rous·ly,** *adv.*

ov·u·lar (ov′yə lər, ō′vyə-), *adj.* pertaining to or of the nature of an ovule.

ov·u·late (ov′yə lāt′, ō′vyə-), *v.i.*, **-lat·ed, -lat·ing.** to produce and discharge eggs from an ovary or ovarian follicle. —**ov′u·la′tion,** *n.* —**ov′u·la·to·ry** (-lə tôr′ē, -tōr′ē), *adj.*

ov·ule (ov′yōōl, ō′vyōōl), *n.* **1.** the structure in seed plants that contains the embryo sac and that develops into a seed after fertilization. **2.** a small egg.

o·vum (ō′vəm), *n.*, *pl.* **o·va** (ō′və). the female reproductive cell, developed in the ovary; female gamete; egg cell.

ow (ou), *interj.* (used esp. as an expression of intense or sudden pain.)

owe (ō), *v.*, **owed, ow·ing.** —*v.t.* **1.** to be under obligation to pay or repay, or to render: *I owe him a dollar. She owes me an apology.* **2.** to be in debt to. **3.** to be indebted or beholden for: *to owe one's fame to good fortune.* **4.** to have or bear (a feeling or attitude) toward someone or something. —*v.i.* **5.** to be in debt.

Ow·en (ō′ən), *n.* **1. John,** 1616–83, English theologian. **2. Robert,** 1771–1858, Welsh social reformer in Great Britain and the U.S.

Ow·ens (ō′ənz), *n.* **Jesse** (*John Cleveland*), 1913–80, U.S. athlete.

ow·ing (ō′ing), *adj.* owed, unpaid, or due for payment: *to pay what is owing.* —**Idiom. 2. owing to,** because of; as a result of.

owl (oul), *n.* **1.** any of numerous chiefly nocturnal birds of prey comprising the order Strigiformes, having a broad head with large, forward-directed eyes that are usu. surrounded by disks of modified feathers. **2.** a person of owllike solemnity or appearance. —**owl′like′,** *adj.*

owl·et (ou′lit), *n.* a young owl.

owl·ish (ou′lish), *adj.* resembling or characteristic of an owl. —**owl′ish·ly,** *adv.* —**owl′ish·ness,** *n.*

own (ōn), *adj.* **1.** of, pertaining to, or belonging to oneself or itself (usu. used after a possessive to emphasize the idea of ownership, interest, or relation conveyed by the possessive): *He spent only his own money.* **2.** (used as an intensifier to indicate oneself as the sole agent of some activity or action, prec. by a possessive): *She insists on being her own doctor.* —*pron.* **3.** something that belongs to oneself. —*v.t.* **4.** to have or hold as one's own; possess. **5.** to acknowledge or admit: *to own a fault.* **6.** to acknowledge as one's own. —*v.i.* **7.** to confess (often fol. by *to,* *up,* or *up to*). —**Idiom. 8. come into one's own,** to achieve the recognition, professional stature, or self-respect that one deserves. **9. get one's own back,** to gain revenge. **10. hold one's own, a.** to maintain

o′ver·proc′ess, *v.t.*
o′ver·pro·duce′, *v.*, -duced, -duc·ing.
o′ver·pro·duc′tion, *n.*
o′ver·prompt′, *adj.*; -ly, *adv.*
o′ver·proud′, *adj.*; -ly, *adv.*
o′ver·re·fine′, *v.t.*, -fined, -fin·ing.
o′ver·re·fine′ment, *n.*
o′ver·reg′i·ment′, *v.t.*
o′ver·reg′u·late′, *v.*, -lat·ed, -lat·ing.
o′ver·re·li′ance, *n.*
o′ver·rep′re·sen·ta′tion, *n.*
o′ver·re·stric′tion, *n.*
o′ver·rich′, *adj.*; -ly, *adv.*; -ness, *n.*

o′ver·rig′id, *adj.*; -ly, *adv.*; -ness, *n.*
o′ver·roast′, *v.*
o′ver·ro·man′ti·cize′, *v.*, -cized, -ciz·ing.
o′ver·salt′, *v.t.*
o′ver·sat′u·ra′tion, *n.*
o′ver·scru′pu·lous, *adj.*; -ly, *adv.*; -ness, *n.*
o′ver·sea′son, *v.t.*
o′ver·sen′si·tive, *adj.*; -ly, *adv.*; -ness, *n.*
o′ver·sen′ti·men′tal, *adj.*; -ly, *adv.*
o′ver·sen′ti·men′tal·ize′, *v.*, -ized, -iz·ing.
o′ver·sharp′, *adj.*
o′ver·skep′ti·cal, *adj.*; -ly, *adv.*
o′ver·skilled′, *adj.*
o′ver·so·lic′i·tous, *adj.*

o′ver·so·phis′ti·cat′ed, *adj.*
o′ver·spe′cial·i·za′tion, *n.*
o′ver·staff′, *v.t.*
o′ver·stim′u·late′, *v.*, -lat·ed, -lat·ing.
o′ver·stim′u·la′tion, *n.*
o′ver·stock′, *v.*
o′ver·strain′, *v.*
o′ver·stress′, *v.t.*
o′ver·stretch′, *v.t.*, *v.i.*
o′ver·strict′, *adj.*
o′ver·stri′dent, *adj.*; -ly, *adv.*
o′ver·struc′tured, *adj.*
o′ver·stud′y, *v.*, -stud·ied, -stud·y·ing.
o′ver·sub′tle, *adj.*
o′ver·sup·ply′, *n.*, *pl.* -plies.
o′ver·sure′, *adj.*

o′ver·sus·cep′ti·ble, *adj.*
o′ver·sus·pi′cious, *adj.*; -ly, *adv.*
o′ver·sweet′en, *v.t.*
o′ver·tech′ni·cal, *adj.*; -ly, *adv.*
o′ver·the·at′ri·cal, *adj.*; -ly, *adv.*
o′ver·tim′id, *adj.*
o′ver·tire′, *v.*, -tired, -tir·ing.
o′ver·train′, *v.*
o′ver·treat′, *v.t.*
o′ver·u′ti·li·za′tion, *n.*
o′ver·val′ue, *v.t.*, -ued, -u·ing.
o′ver·vi′o·lent, *adj.*
o′ver·weak′, *adj.*; -ness, *n.*
o′ver·wea′ry, *v.t.*, -ried, -ry·ing.
o′ver·will′ing, *adj.*; -ly, *adv.*; -ness, *n.*
o′ver·zeal′ous, *adj.*; -ly, *adv.*; -ness, *n.*

one's position or condition. **b.** to be equal to the opposition. **11. of one's own,** belonging to oneself. **12. on one's own, a.** through one's own efforts or resources. **b.** living or functioning independently: *She was on her own at 17.* —**own′er,** *n.*

own•er•ship (ō′nər ship′), *n.* **1.** the state or fact of being an owner. **2.** legal right of possession; proprietorship.

ox (oks), *n., pl.* **ox•en** for 1, **ox•es** for 2. **1.** any of various large, bulky bovids, as domestic cattle, water buffaloes, and yaks, esp. a castrated adult male used as a draft animal. **2.** *Informal.* a clumsy, stupid fellow. —**ox′like′,** *adj.*

ox•blood (oks′blud′), *n.* a deep, dull red color.

ox•bow (oks′bō′), *n.* **1.** a U-shaped piece of wood placed under and around the neck of an ox with its upper ends in the bar of the yoke. **2. a.** a bow-shaped bend in a river, or the land embraced by it. **b.** Also called **ox′bow lake′.** a bow-shaped lake formed in a former channel of a river. —*adj.* **3.** (esp. of a furniture front) having a compound curve with a concave section between two convex ones.

ox•en (ok′sən), *n.* a pl. of ox.

ox•eye (oks′ī′), *n., pl.* **-eyes.** any of several composite plants, esp. of the genera *Heliopsis* and *Buphthalum,* having ray flowers surrounding a conspicuous disk.

ox′eye dai′sy, *n.* a composite plant, *Chrysanthemum leucanthemum,* having flowers with white rays and a yellow disk.

ox•ford (oks′fərd), *n.* **1.** a low shoe laced over the instep. **2.** Also called **ox′ford cloth′.** a cotton or synthetic fabric constructed in plain or basket weave and having a lustrous finish and soft hand, used for shirts, blouses, and sportswear.

Ox•ford (oks′fərd), *n.* **1.** a city in S Oxfordshire, in S England, NW of London: university, founded in 12th century. 115,800. **2.** Also called **Ox′ford Down′.** one of an English breed of large sheep.

Ox′ford Group′, *n.* an organization founded at Oxford University in 1921 by Frank Buchman, advocating absolute morality in public and private life. Compare MORAL RE-ARMAMENT.

Ox′ford move′ment, *n.* the movement toward High Church principles within the Church of England, originating at Oxford University in 1833. Compare TRACTARIANISM.

ox•i•dant (ok′si dənt), *n.* a chemical agent that oxidizes.

ox•i•da•tion (ok′si dā′shən) also **ox•i•di•za•tion** (-də zā′shən), *n.* **1.** the process or result of oxidizing. **2.** the deposit that forms on the surface of a metal as it oxidizes. —**ox′i•da′tion•al, ox′i•da′tive,** *adj.*

oxida′tion-reduc′tion, *n.* a chemical reaction between two substances in which one substance is oxidized and the other reduced. Also called **redox.**

oxida′tion state′, *n.* the state of an element or ion in a compound with regard to the loss or gain of electrons, expressed as a positive or negative number. Also called **oxida′tion num′ber.**

ox•ide (ok′sīd, -sid) also **ox•id** (ok′sid), *n.* a compound in which oxygen is bonded to one or more electropositive atoms. —**ox•id′ic** (-sid′ik), *adj.*

ox•i•dize (ok′si dīz′), *v.,* **-dized, -diz•ing.** —*v.t.* **1.** to combine chemically with oxygen; convert into an oxide. **2.** to cover with a coating of oxide or rust. **3.** to increase the valence of (an atom or molecule) by removing electrons. Compare REDUCE (def. 9c). —*v.i.* **4.** to become oxidized. —**ox′i•diz′a•ble,** *adj.* —**ox′i•diz′er,** *n.*

Ox•nard (oks′närd), *n.* a city in SW California, NW of Los Angeles. 145,863.

ox•tail (oks′tāl′), *n.* the skinned tail of an ox or steer, used as an ingredient in soup, stew, etc.

oxy-[1], a combining form meaning "sharp," "acute," "keen," "pointed," "acid": *oxycephaly; oxygen; oxymoron.*

oxy-[2], a combining form representing OXYGEN in compound words, sometimes as an equivalent of *hydroxy-: oxyhemoglobin.*

ox•y•gen (ok′si jən), *n.* a colorless, odorless, gaseous element constituting about one-fifth of the volume of the atmosphere and present in a combined state in nature. *Symbol:* O; *at. wt.:* 15.9994; *at. no.:* 8; *density:* 1.4290 g/l at 0°C and 760 mm pressure. —**ox′y•gen′ic** (-jen′ik), **ox•yg′e•nous** (-sij′ə nəs), *adj.*

ox•y•gen•ate (ok′si jə nāt′), *v.t.,* **-at•ed, -at•ing.** to treat, combine, or enrich with oxygen: *to oxygenate the blood.* —**ox′y•gen•a′tion,** *n.* —**ox′y•gen•a′tor,** *n.*

ox′ygen debt′, *n.* the body's oxygen deficiency resulting from strenuous physical activity.

ox′ygen mask′, *n.* a masklike device placed or worn over the nose and mouth when inhaling supplementary oxygen from an attached tank.

ox′ygen tent′, *n.* a small transparent canopy placed over a patient for delivering an increased concentration of oxygen.

ox•y•mo•ron (ok′si môr′on, -mōr′-), *n., pl.* **-mo•ra** (-môr′ə, -mōr′ə). a figure of speech that uses seeming contradictions, as "cruel kindness" or "to make haste slowly." —**ox•y•mo•ron•ic** (ok′sē mə ron′ik), *adj.*

oy or **oi** (oi), *interj.* (used to express dismay, pain, annoyance, grief, etc.)

o•yez or **o•yes** (ō′yes, ō′yez), *interj.* hear! attend! (uttered by court officers, and formerly by public criers, to command silence before a proclamation.)

oys•ter (oi′stər), *n.* **1.** any of several edible, marine, bivalve mollusks of the family Ostreidae, having an irregularly shaped shell. **2.** the oyster-shaped bit of dark meat in the front hollow of the pelvic bone of a fowl. **3.** *Informal.* a closemouthed or uncommunicative person. **4.** something from which one may extract or derive advantage: *The world is my oyster.* —*v.i.* **5.** to dredge for or otherwise take oysters.

oys′ter bed′, *n.* a place where oysters breed or are cultivated.

oys′ter cap′, *n.* an edible, brownish gray to white mushroom, *Pleurotus ostreatus,* that grows in clusters on fallen trees and their stumps.

oys′ter•catch′er or **oys′ter catch′er,** *n.* any of several heavy-billed shorebirds comprising the family Haematopodidae, that have chiefly black-and-white plumage and feed largely on bivalve mollusks.

oys′ter crab′, *n.* any small, thin-shelled crab of the family Pinnotheridae: the female lives as a commensal in the gill cavity of bivalves.

oys′ter crack′er, *n.* a small, round, usu. salted cracker.

oz., ounce.

O′zark Moun′tains, *n.pl.* a group of low mountains in S Missouri, N Arkansas, and NE Oklahoma. Also called **Ozarks.**

o•zone (ō′zōn, ō zōn′), *n.* **1.** a form of oxygen, O_3, produced when an electric spark or ultraviolet light passes through air or oxygen, that in the upper atmosphere absorbs ultraviolet rays, thereby preventing them from reaching the earth's surface, but that near the earth's surface is a harmful irritant and pollutant: used commercially for bleaching, oxidizing, sterilizing, etc. **2.** OZONE LAYER. **3.** clear, fresh, invigorating air.

o′zone hole′, *n.* any part of the ozone layer that has become depleted by atmospheric pollution, resulting in excess ultraviolet radiation passing through the atmosphere.

o′zone lay′er, *n.* the layer of the upper atmosphere where most atmospheric ozone is concentrated, from about 8 to 30 mi. (12 to 48 km) above the earth.

o•zon•o•sphere (ō zō′nə sfēr′), *n.* OZONE LAYER.

O

P

P, p (pē), *n., pl.* **Ps** or **P's, ps** or **p's.** **1.** the 16th letter of the English alphabet, a consonant. **2.** any spoken sound represented by this letter. **3.** something shaped like a P. **4.** a written or printed representation of the letter *P* or *p*.

P, *Symbol.* **1.** the 16th in order or in a series. **2.** phosphorus. **3.** *Physics.* **a.** power. **b.** pressure. **c.** proton. **4.** proline.

p, **1.** penny; pence. **2.** *Music.* softly.

p-, *Chem.* PARA-[1] (def. 2).

pa (pä, pô), *n. Informal.* father.

PA, **1.** Pennsylvania. **2.** public-address system.

Pa, *Chem. Symbol.* protactinium.

Pa., Pennsylvania.

PABA (pä′bə), *n.* para-aminobenzoic acid.

Pab·lum (pab′ləm), **1.** *Trademark.* a brand of soft cereal for infants. **—n.** **2.** (*l.c.*) trite, naive, or simplistic ideas or writings; intellectual pap.

pab·u·lum (pab′yə ləm), *n.* **1.** something that nourishes; food. **2.** intellectual nourishment. **3.** a soft, bland cereal for infants.

PAC (pak), *n., pl.* **PAC's, PACs.** political action committee.

pa·ca (pä′kə, pak′ə), *n., pl.* **-cas.** either of two large, white-spotted, almost tailless tropical American rodents of the genus *Cuniculus.*

pace¹ (pās), *n., v.,* **paced, pac·ing.** **—n.** **1.** a rate of movement, esp. in stepping, walking, etc.: *to hike at a rapid pace.* **2.** a rate of activity, progress, growth, etc.; tempo. **3.** any of various standard linear measures representing the space measured by a single step in walking. **4.** a single step. **5.** the distance covered in a step. **6.** a manner of stepping; gait. **7.** a gait of a horse or other animal in which the feet on the same side are lifted and put down together. **—v.t.** **8.** to set or regulate the pace for, as in racing. **9.** to traverse with slow, regular steps: *to pace the floor nervously.* **10.** to measure by paces. **11.** to train to a certain pace: *to pace a horse.* **12.** (of a horse) to run (a distance) at a pace. **—v.i.** **13.** to take slow, regular steps. **14.** to walk up and down. **15.** (of a horse) to go at a pace. **—Idiom.** **16.** **put through one's paces,** to cause to demonstrate a set of skills or practiced routines. **17.** **set the pace,** to act as an example for others to rival; be first or first-rate.

pa·ce² (pä′sē, pä′chā; *Lat.* pä′ke), *prep.* with all due respect to: *I do not, pace my rivals, agree with their ideas.* [< Latin *pace* in peace, by favor]

pace′ car′ (pās), *n.* a car that leads the competing cars through a pace lap and leaves the course before the race begins.

pace·mak·er (pās′mā′kər), *n.* **1.** PACESETTER. **2.** an electronic device surgically implanted beneath the skin to provide a normal heartbeat by electrical stimulation of the heart muscle. **3.** any specialized body tissue governing a rhythmic physiological activity, esp. the sinoatrial node of the heart that regulates heartbeat. **—pace′mak′ing,** *n.*

pac·er (pā′sər), *n.* **1.** a person or thing that paces. **2.** a standardbred horse used for pacing in harness racing. **3.** PACESETTER.

pace·set·ter (pās′set′ər), *n.* **1.** a person or group that serves as a model to be imitated or followed; leader. **2.** a person, animal, or thing that sets the pace, as in racing. Also called **pacemaker.**

pa·chi·si (pə chē′zē, pä-), *n.* a game, orig. from ancient India, similar to backgammon but played on a cross-shaped board.

pach·y·derm (pak′i dûrm′), *n.* any large, thick-skinned, hoofed mammal, as the elephant, hippopotamus, and rhinoceros. **—pach′y·der′mal, pach′y·der′mic,** *adj.*

pach·y·san·dra (pak′ə san′drə), *n., pl.* **-dras.** any of several low-growing plants of the genus *Pachysandra,* of the box family, widely grown as a ground cover.

pa·cif·ic (pə sif′ik), *adj.* **1.** tending to make or preserve peace; conciliatory. **2.** not warlike; peaceable; mild. **3.** at peace; peaceful. **4.** calm; tranquil. **—pa·cif′i·cal·ly,** *adv.*

pac·i·fi·ca·tion (pas′ə fi kā′shən), *n.* **1.** the act of pacifying or the state of being pacified; appeasement. **2.** the process of attempting to rid an area of terrorists or other enemies by military force or psychological persuasion. **—pa·cif′i·ca·tor** (pə sif′i kā′tər), *n.* **—pa·cif′i·ca·to·ry** (-kə tôr′ē, -tōr′ē), *adj.*

Pacif′ic Is′lands, Trust′ Ter′ritory of the, *n.* a group of islands in the W Pacific, established in 1947 by the United Nations as a U.S. trusteeship: orig. composed of the Caroline, Marshall, and Mariana Islands (except Guam); the Republic of Palau is the only remaining trust territory.

Pacif′ic O′cean, *n.* an ocean bordered by the American continents, Asia, and Australia: largest ocean in the world; divided by the equator into the North Pacific and the South Pacific. 70,000,000 sq. mi. (181,300,000 sq. km); greatest known depth, 35,433 ft. (10,800 m).

Pacif′ic Rim′, *n.* the group of countries bordering on the Pacific Ocean, esp. the industrialized nations of Asia.

Pacif′ic time′, *n.* See under STANDARD TIME. Also called **Pacif′ic Stand′ard Time′.**

pac·i·fi·er (pas′ə fī′ər), *n.* **1.** a person or thing that pacifies. **2.** a device, often shaped like a nipple, for a baby to suck or bite on.

pac·i·fism (pas′ə fiz′əm), *n.* **1.** opposition to war or violence as a resort in the settlement of disputes. **2.** refusal to engage in military activity because of one's principles or beliefs. **—pac′i·fist,** *n., adj.* **—pac′i·fis′tic,** *adj.* **—pac′i·fis′ti·cal·ly,** *adv.*

pac·i·fy (pas′ə fī′), *v.t.,* **-fied, -fy·ing.** **1.** to bring or restore to a state of peace or tranquillity; quiet; calm. **2.** to appease: *to pacify one's appetite.* **3.** to reduce to a submissive state; subdue. **—pac′i·fi·a·ble,** *adj.*

pack¹ (pak), *n.* **1.** a group of things wrapped or tied together for easy handling or carrying; a bundle, esp. one carried on the back of an animal or person. **2.** a definite quantity or standard measure of merchandise together with its wrapping or package: *a pack of cigarettes.* **3.** the quantity of something that is packaged at one time or in one season: *last year's salmon pack.* **4.** a group of people or things: *a pack of lies.* **5.** a group of animals of the same kind, esp. predatory ones: *a pack of wolves.* **6.** a number of hounds used together in a hunt. **7.** a set of playing cards; deck. **8.** BACKPACK. **9.** PACK ICE. **10. a.** a wrapping of the body in wet or dry cloths for therapeutic purposes. **b.** the cloths so used. **11.** a pastelike substance used as a cosmetic restorative, esp. on the face. **—v.t.** **12.** to make into a pack or bundle. **13.** to form into a compact mass. **14.** to fill with anything compactly arranged: *to pack a trunk.* **15.** to put into a case, trunk, etc., as for traveling: *to pack clothes for a trip.* **16.** to press or crowd together within; cram: *The crowd packed the gallery.* **17.** to prepare for marketing by putting into packages. **18.** to make airtight, vaportight, or watertight by stuffing: *to pack the engine.* **19.** to load, as with packs. **20.** to carry or wear as part of one's usual equipment: *to pack a gun.* *Informal.* to be able to deliver: *to pack a mean punch.* **—v.i.** **22.** to pack goods in compact form, as for shipping. **23.** to place clothes and personal items in a suitcase, trunk, etc., preparatory to traveling. **24.** to adapt to compact storage or packing: *dresses that pack well.* **25.** to crowd together. **26.** to become compacted: *Wet snow packs readily.* **27. pack in** or **up,** to relinquish, abandon, or renounce: *to pack in one's career at 35.* **28. pack off** or **away,** to send away with dispatch: *to pack the kids off to camp.* **—adj.** **29.** used in transporting a pack or load. **30.** compressed into a pack; packed. **31.** used in or adapted for packing. **—pack′a·ble,** *adj.*

pack² (pak), *v.t.* to choose, collect, arrange, or manipulate (cards, persons, facts, etc.) so as to serve one's own purposes: *to pack a jury.*

pack·age (pak′ij), *n., v.,* **-aged, -ag·ing.** **—n.** **1.** a bundle of something that is packed and wrapped or boxed; parcel. **2.** a container, as a box or case, in which something is packed. **3.** a person or thing conceived of as a compact unit having particular characteristics: *a package of mischief.* **4.** a finished product contained in a unit suitable for immediate installation and operation, as a heating unit. **5.** a group or combination of related parts or elements offered as a single unit: *a contract package; a tax package.* **6.** a complete program or series of programs produced for the theater, television, etc., and sold as a unit. **—v.t.** **7.** to make or put into a package. **8.** to design and manufacture a package for (a product). **9.** to combine or offer as a single unit. **—pack′ag·er,** *n.*

pack′age deal′, *n.* **1.** an agreement in which the buyer pays a stipulated price for a group of related products or services. **2.** the products or services included in such an agreement. **3.** an agreement or plan in which the approval of one element is contingent upon the approval of all the others.

pack′age store′, *n.* a store selling sealed bottles or cans of alcoholic beverages for consumption off the premises.

pack′ an′imal, *n.* an animal, as a mule or horse, used for carrying loads.

packed (pakt), *adj.* **1.** filled to capacity. **2.** pressed together; compressed: *packed snow.* **3.** abundantly supplied with a specified element (used in combination): *an action-packed movie.*

pack·er (pak′ər), *n.* **1.** a person or thing that packs, esp. a person or company that packs food for market: *a meat packer.*

pack·et (pak′it), *n.* **1.** a small package or parcel: *a packet of letters.* **2.** a small vessel that carries mail, passengers, and goods regularly on a fixed route. **3.** *Informal.* a large amount of money. **—v.t.** **4.** to bind up in a package or parcel.

pack·horse (pak′hôrs′), *n.* a horse used for carrying loads.

pack′ ice′, *n.* a large area of floating marine ice whose pieces are driven together by wind, current, etc. Also called **ice pack.**

pack·ing (pak′ing), *n.* **1.** the act or work of a person or thing that packs. **2.** the preparation and packaging of foodstuffs, esp. to be sold at wholesale. **3.** the way in which something is packed. **4.** material used to cushion or protect goods packed in a container.

pack′ rat′, *n.* **1.** any North and Central American rat of the genus *Neotoma,* noted for carrying off shiny articles to its nest. **2.** *Informal.* a person who collects, saves, or hoards useless small items.

pack·sad·dle (pak′sad′l), *n.* a saddle designed for supporting the load on a pack animal.

pact (pakt), *n.* **1.** an agreement or compact. **2.** an agreement or treaty between two or more nations.

pad¹ (pad), *n., v.,* **pad·ded, pad·ding.** —*n.* **1.** a cushionlike mass of soft material used for comfort, protection, or stuffing. **2.** a soft, stuffed cushion used as a saddle. **3.** a number of sheets of paper glued together at one edge to form a tablet. **4.** a soft, ink-soaked block of absorbent material for inking a rubber stamp. **5. a.** the fleshy mass of tissue on the underside of each finger and toe. **b.** any of the cushionlike parts on the feet of vertebrates. **c.** the enlarged structure at the tip of the legs in certain insects; pulvillus. **6.** LILY PAD. **7.** *Slang.* **a.** one's living quarters. **b.** one's bed. —*v.t.* **8.** to furnish or stuff with a pad or padding. **9.** to expand or add to unnecessarily or dishonestly: *to pad an expense account.*

pad² (pad), *n., v.,* **pad·ded, pad·ding.** —*n.* **1.** a dull, muffled sound, as of footsteps on the ground. **2.** a slow-paced road horse. **3.** *Brit. Dial.* a path. —*v.i.* **4.** to travel on foot; walk. **5.** to walk so that one's footsteps make a dull, muffled sound. —*v.t.* **6.** to travel along on foot. **7.** to beat down by treading.

pad·ding (pad′ing), *n.* **1.** material, as cotton or straw, used to pad something. **2.** something added unnecessarily or dishonestly.

pad·dle¹ (pad′l), *n., v.,* **-dled, -dling.** —*n.* **1.** a short, flat-bladed oar for propelling and steering a canoe or small boat, usu. held by both hands and moved through a vertical arc. **2.** any of various similar implements used for mixing, stirring, or beating. **3.** a similarly shaped implement used to spank or beat someone. **4.** a racket with a short handle and a wide, rounded blade, used in table tennis, paddle tennis, etc. **5.** an implement used for beating garments while washing them in running water, as in a stream. **6.** a blade of a paddle wheel. **7.** PADDLE WHEEL. **8.** a flipper or limb of a penguin, turtle, whale, etc. **9.** an act of paddling. —*v.i.* **10.** to propel or travel in a canoe or the like by using a paddle. —*v.t.* **11.** to propel with a paddle. **12.** to spank with or as if with a paddle. **13.** to stir, mix, or beat with or as if with a paddle. **14.** to hit (a ball) with a paddle. —**pad′dler,** *n.*

pad·dle² (pad′l), *v.i.,* **-dled, -dling.** **1.** to move the feet or hands playfully in shallow water; dabble. **2.** TODDLE (def. 1). **3.** to toy with the fingers. —**pad′dler,** *n.*

pad·dle·ball (pad′l bôl′), *n.* a game in which players use short-handled, perforated paddles to hit a ball against a wall.

pad·dle·board (pad′l bôrd′, -bōrd′), *n.* a long, round-tipped board used for surfing or in rescuing swimmers.

pad·dle·fish (pad′l fish′), *n., pl.* **-fish·es,** (*esp. collectively*) **-fish.** a large fish, *Polyodon spathula,* of the Mississippi River and its larger tributaries, having a long, flat, paddlelike snout.

pad′dle ten′nis, *n.* a game combining elements of tennis and handball, played with paddles and a rubber ball on a court about half the size of a tennis court.

pad′dle wheel′, *n.* a wheel for propelling a ship, having a number of paddles entering the water more or less perpendicularly.

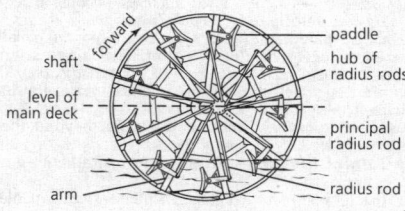

paddle wheel

pad·dock (pad′ək), *n.* **1.** a small, usu. enclosed field near a stable or barn for pasturing or exercising animals. **2.** the enclosure in which horses are saddled and mounted before a race. —*v.t.* **3.** to confine in a paddock.

pad·dy (pad′ē), *n., pl.* **-dies. 1.** a rice field. **2.** rice, esp. in the husk, either uncut or gathered.

pad′dy wag′on, *n.* an enclosed truck or van used by the police to transport prisoners.

pad·dy·whack (pad′ē hwak′, -wak′) also **pad·dy·wack** (-wak′). *Informal.* —*n.* **1.** a spanking. —*v.t.* **2.** to spank.

pad·lock (pad′lok′), *n.* **1.** a portable or detachable lock with a pivoted or sliding shackle that can be passed through a link, ring, staple, or the like. —*v.t.* **2.** to fasten with or as if with a padlock.

pa·dre (pä′drā, -drē), *n., pl.* **-dres. 1.** a priest or clergyman. **2.** a military chaplain. [< Spanish, Portuguese, Italian: father < Latin *pater*]

pa·dro·ne (pə drō′nē, -nā), *n., pl.* **-nes, -ni** (-nē). **1.** a master; boss. **2.** an employer, esp. of immigrant laborers. **3.** an innkeeper.

pae·an (pē′ən), *n.* a song of praise, joy, thanksgiving, or triumph.

pa·el·la (pä äl′lə, -ā′lə, pä ā′ə), *n., pl.* **-las.** a Spanish dish of rice cooked with chicken, seafood, vegetables, etc., and flavored with saffron.

pa·gan (pā′gən), *n.* **1.** one of a people or community observing a polytheistic religion, as the ancient Romans and Greeks. **2.** a person who is not a Christian, Jew, or Muslim; heathen. **3.** an irreligious or hedonistic person. —*adj.* **4.** of or pertaining to pagans or their religion. **5.** irreligious or hedonistic. —**pa′gan·ish,** *adj.* —**pa′gan·ism,** *n.*

pa·gan·ize (pā′gə nīz′), *v.t., v.i.,* **-ized, -iz·ing.** to make or become pagan. —**pa′gan·i·za′tion,** *n.*

page¹ (pāj), *n., v.,* **paged, pag·ing.** —*n.* **1.** one side of a leaf of something printed or written, as a book, manuscript, or letter. **2.** the entire leaf. **3.** a noteworthy event or period: *a bright page in English history.* **4. a.** a block of computer memory up to 4,096 bytes long. **b.** a portion of a program that can be moved to a computer's internal memory from external storage. **5.** WEB PAGE. —*v.t.* **6.** PAGINATE. **7.** to turn pages (usu. fol. by *through*).

page² (pāj), *n., v.,* **paged, pag·ing.** —*n.* **1.** a boy servant or attendant. **2.** (in medieval times) a youth in attendance on a person of rank. **b.** a youth being trained for knighthood. **3.** an employee who carries messages, runs errands, etc., as in a hotel or a legislative body. —*v.t.* **4.** to summon (a person) by calling out his or her name, as over a public-address system. **5.** to summon or alert by electronic pager. **6.** to attend as a page.

pag·eant (paj′ənt), *n.* **1.** an elaborate costumed procession or parade, often with floats, forming part of public or social festivities. **2.** an elaborate public spectacle illustrative of the history of a place, institution, or the like. **3.** something comparable to such a spectacle or procession in its variety or grandeur: *the pageant of Renaissance history.* **4.** a show or exhibition: *a beauty pageant.* **5.** a pretentious display.

pag·eant·ry (paj′ən trē), *n., pl.* **-ries. 1.** spectacular display; pomp. **2.** mere show; empty display. **3.** pageants collectively.

page′boy′ or **page′ boy′,** *n.* **1.** a hairstyle in which the hair is rolled under, usu. at shoulder-length. **2.** a youth serving as a page.

page′ descrip′tion lan′guage, *n.* a high-level programming language for determining the output of a page printer designed to work with it, independent of the printer's internal codes. *Abbr.:* PDL

page′ print′er, *n.* a high-speed, high-resolution computer printer that uses a light source, as a laser beam or electrically charged ions, to print a full page of text or graphics at a time.

pag·er (pā′jər), *n.* BEEPER (def. 1).

page′-turn′er, *n.* a book so exciting or gripping that one is compelled to read it very rapidly.

pag·i·nate (paj′ə nāt′), *v.t.,* **-nat·ed, -nat·ing. 1.** to indicate the sequence of pages in (a book, manuscript, etc.) by placing numbers or other characters on each leaf. **2.** to divide an electronic document into pages, as for printing.

pag·i·na·tion (paj′ə nā′shən), *n.* **1.** the act of paginating. **2. a.** the figures by which the leaves of a book, manuscript, etc., are marked to indicate their sequence. **b.** the total number of leaves so marked and their order, as part of a bibliographic description.

pa·go·da (pə gō′də), *n., pl.* **-das.** a temple or sacred building of the Far East, usu. a tower having an upward-curving roof over each story.

Pa·go Pa·go (päng′ō päng′ō, pä′gō pä′gō), *n.* the chief harbor and town of American Samoa, on Tutuila Island. 2451.

Pah·la·vi¹ (pä′lə vē′), *n., pl.* **-vis. 1.** Muhammad Re·za (rez′ä), 1919–80, shah of Iran 1941–79. **2.** his father, **Reza Shah,** 1877–1944, shah of Iran 1925–41.

Pah·la·vi² (pä′lə vē′), *n.* **1.** a form of Middle Persian used in Zoroastrian literature of the 3rd to 10th centuries. **2.** the script used in writing Middle Persian.

paid (pād), *v.* a pt. and pp. of PAY.

pail (pāl), *n.* **1.** a container, usu. cylindrical, with a handle; bucket. **2.** the amount filling a pail.

pail·lette (pī yet′, pā-, pə let′), *n.* a spangle for ornamenting a costume. —**pail·let′ted,** *adj.*

pain (pān), *n.* **1.** physical suffering typically from injury or illness. **2.** an instance of such suffering; a distressing sensation in a part of the body: *a back pain.* **3.** severe mental or emotional distress: *the pain of loneliness.* **4. pains, a.** assiduous care: *Take pains with your work.* **b.** the uterine contractions of childbirth. **5.** Also called **pain in the neck.** an annoying or troublesome person or thing. —*v.t.* **6.** to cause physical or emotional pain to. —*v.i.* **7.** to have or give pain. —*Idiom.* **8. on** or **under pain of,** subject to the penalty of; risking: *on pain of death.*

Paine (pān), *n.* **Thomas,** 1737–1809, U.S. patriot and political writer, born in England.

pained (pānd), *adj.* **1.** hurt; injured. **2.** showing or expressing distress, resentment, or hurt feelings: *a pained look.*

pain·ful (pān′fəl), *adj.* **1.** affected with, causing, or characterized by pain. **2.** laborious; exacting; difficult. —**pain′ful·ly,** *adv.*

pain·kill·er (pān′kil′ər), *n.* something, as a drug or treatment, that relieves pain, esp. an analgesic. —**pain′kill′ing,** *adj.*

pain·less (pān′lis), *adj.* **1.** without pain; causing little or no pain. **2.** not difficult; requiring little exertion. —**pain′less·ly,** *adv.*

pains·tak·ing (pānz′tā′king, pān′stā′-), *adj.* taking or characterized by taking pains; expending or showing diligent care and effort; careful: *a painstaking craftsman; painstaking research.* —**pains′tak′ing·ly,** *adv.* —**pains′tak′ing·ness,** *n.*

paint (pānt), *n.* **1.** a substance composed of solid coloring matter suspended in a liquid medium and applied as a protective or decorative coating to various surfaces, or to canvas or other materials in producing a work of art. **2.** an application of this. **3.** the dried surface pigment: *Don't scuff the paint.* **4.** the solid coloring matter alone; pigment. **5.** facial cosmetics, esp. lipstick or rouge, designed to heighten natural color. **6.** *Chiefly Western U.S.* a pied, calico, or spotted horse or pony; pinto.

—*v.t.* **7.** to coat, cover, or decorate with paint. **8.** to produce (a picture, design, etc.) in paint. **9.** to represent in paint: *to paint a sunset.* **10.** to describe vividly in words: *The ads painted the resort as a paradise.* **11.** to color by or as if by painting. **12.** to coat or brush, as with a liquid medicine or a cosmetic. —*v.i.* **13.** to coat or cover anything with paint. **14.** to engage in painting as an art. **15.** to use facial cosmetics. —***Idiom.*** **16. paint the town (red),** to go out and celebrate, esp. uninhibitedly. —**paint′a•ble,** *adj.*

paint•brush (pānt′brush′), *n.* **1.** a brush for applying paint, as one used in painting houses or pictures. **2.** INDIAN PAINTBRUSH.

paint′ed bunt′ing, *n.* a brilliantly colored bunting, *Passerina ciris,* of the southern U.S. and northern Mexico.

paint′ed cup′, *n.* INDIAN PAINTBRUSH.

Paint′ed Des′ert, *n.* a region in N central Arizona, E of the Colorado River.

paint′ed la′dy, *n.* a butterfly, *Vanessa cardui,* having brownish black and orange wings and hind wings each with four eyelike spots.

paint′ed tril′lium, *n.* a North American trillium, *Trillium undulatum,* having white flowers streaked with pink or purple.

paint′ed tur′tle, *n.* a freshwater turtle, *Chrysemys picta,* common in the U.S., having bright yellow markings on the head and neck and red markings on the margin of the carapace.

paint•ing (pān′ting), *n.* **1.** a picture or design executed in paints. **2.** the act, art, or work of a person who paints.

pair (pâr), *n., pl.* **pairs, pair.** **1.** two identical, similar, or corresponding things that are matched for use together: *a pair of gloves.* **2.** something consisting of or regarded as having two parts or pieces joined together: *a pair of scissors.* **3.** two individuals who are similar or in some way associated: *a pair of liars; a pair of seal pups.* **4.** a married, engaged, or dating couple. **5.** two mated animals. **6.** a span or team: *a pair of horses.* **7. a.** two members on opposite sides in a legislature who arrange to forgo voting on a given occasion. **b.** the arrangement thus made. **8.** two playing cards of the same denomination without regard to suit or color. **9.** *Mech.* two parts or pieces so connected that they mutually constrain relative motion. **10.** a set or combination of more than two objects forming a collective whole: *a pair of beads.* —*v.t.* **11.** to arrange or designate in pairs or groups of two. **12.** to form into a pair, as by matching or joining: *to pair socks.* **13.** (of animals) to cause to mate. —*v.i.* **14.** to separate into pairs or groups of two (usu. fol. by *off*): *to pair off for a dance.* **15.** to form a pair or pairs. **16.** to be a member of a pair. **17.** to match with or resemble another. **18.** to unite in close association with another, as in a business partnership, friendship, or marriage. **19.** (of animals) to mate. —**Usage.** When modified by a number, the plural of PAIR is more commonly PAIRS, esp. of persons: *six pairs of masked dancers in the procession.* The unmarked plural PAIR is used mainly in reference to inanimate objects or nonhumans: *four pair* (or *pairs*) *of loafers; two pair* (or *pairs*) *of boots.* See also COLLECTIVE NOUN.

pair′ bond′, *n.* **1.** a partnership between a pair of mating animals that lasts through at least one breeding season, usu. involving joint rearing of the young. **2.** any monogamous bond. —**pair′-bond′,** *v.i.,* **-bond•ed, -bond•ing.**

pair•ing (pâr′ing), *n.* **1.** a coupling. **2.** the lining up of the two homologous chromosomes or chromatids of each chromosome pair in meiosis or mitosis.

pair′ (or **pairs′**) **skat′ing,** *n.* a form of competitive skating in which a couple skate together in performing a choreographed series of jumps, lifts, and other acrobatic moves to a selection of music.

pai•sa•no (pī sä′nō, -zä′-), *n., pl.* **-nos.** **1.** compatriot; countryman. **2.** *Slang.* pal; buddy.

pais•ley (pāz′lē), *n., pl.* **-leys,** *adj.* —*n.* **1.** a pattern of colorful, minutely detailed, usu. curving figures. **2.** a fabric woven or printed in this pattern. **3.** a shawl or other article made of this fabric. —*adj.* **4.** made of paisley fabric. **5.** having the pattern of paisley.

Pai•ute (pī o͞ot′, pī′o͞ot), *n., pl.* **-utes,** (*esp. collectively*) **-ute.** **1.** a member of an American Indian people of the U.S. Great Basin region. **2.** either of two Uto-Aztecan languages spoken by the Paiutes.

pa•ja•mas (pə jä′məz, -jam′əz), *n.* (*used with a pl. v.*) **1.** nightclothes consisting of loose-fitting trousers and a jacket. **2.** loose trousers of silk, cotton, etc., orig. worn in India and parts of the Middle East. Also, *esp. Brit.,* **pyjamas.** —**pa•ja′maed,** *adj.*

Pak•i•stan (pak′ə stan′, pä′kə stän′), *n.* **Islamic Republic of,** a republic in S Asia, between India and Afghanistan: formerly part of British India; known as West Pakistan from 1947–71 to distinguish it from East Pakistan (now Bangladesh). 132,185,299; 307,293 sq. mi. (796,095 sq. km). *Cap.:* Islamabad.

Pak•i•stan•i (pak′ə stan′ē, pä′kə stä′nē), *n., pl.* **-stan•is, -stan•i,** *adj.* —*n.* **1.** a native or inhabitant of Pakistan. —*adj.* **2.** of or pertaining to Pakistan or its inhabitants.

pal (pal), *n., v.,* **palled, pal•ling.** *Informal.* —*n.* **1.** a close friend; comrade; chum. —*v.i.* **2.** to associate as pals: *they always pal around.*

pal•ace (pal′is), *n.* **1.** the official residence of a sovereign, bishop, or other exalted personage. **2.** a large and stately mansion or building. **3.** a large and often ornate place for entertainment, exhibitions, etc. —**pal′aced,** *adj.*

pal′ace guard′, *n.* **1.** the security force protecting a palace. **2.** a group of trusted advisers who often control access to a sovereign, president, or other chief executive.

pal•a•din (pal′ə din), *n.* **1.** any of the 12 legendary peers or knightly champions in attendance on Charlemagne. **2.** any knightly or heroic champion. **3.** a determined advocate or defender of a cause.

pal•at•a•ble (pal′ə tə bəl), *adj.* **1.** acceptable or agreeable to the palate or taste. **2.** acceptable or agreeable to the mind or feelings: *palatable ideas.* —**pal′at•a•bil′i•ty, pal′at•a•ble•ness,** *n.* —**pal′at•a•bly,** *adv.*

pal•a•tal (pal′ə tl), *adj.* **1.** *Anat.* of or pertaining to the palate. **2.** (of a speech sound, esp. a consonant) articulated with the blade of the tongue held close to or touching the hard palate. —*n.* **3.** a palatal consonant, as the sound (y) in *yes* or (KH) in German *ich.* —**pal′a•tal•ly,** *adv.*

pal•a•tal•ize (pal′ə tl īz′), *v.t.,* **-ized, -iz•ing.** to articulate (a consonant other than a palatal) with the blade of the tongue raised toward the hard palate; change into a palatal sound. —**pal′a•tal•i•za′tion,** *n.*

pal•ate (pal′it), *n.* **1.** the roof of the mouth in mammals, consisting of an anterior bony portion **(hard palate)** and a posterior fleshy portion **(soft palate)** that separate the oral cavity from the nasal cavity. **2.** the sense of taste: *a dinner to delight the palate.* **3.** intellectual or aesthetic taste.

pa•la•tial (pə lā′shəl), *adj.* **1.** of, pertaining to, or resembling a palace: *a palatial house.* **2.** suitable for a palace; magnificent. —**pa•la′tial•ly,** *adv.* —**pa•la′tial•ness,** *n.*

Pa•lat•i•nate (pə lat′n āt′, -it), *n.* **1. the.** German, **Pfalz.** either of two historic regions of Germany that constituted an electorate of the Holy Roman Empire: one **(Lower Palatinate** or **Rhine Palatinate)** is now part of Rhineland-Palatinate, and the other **(Upper Palatinate)** is now part of Bavaria. **2.** a native or inhabitant of the Palatinate. **3.** (*l.c.*) the territory under a palatine.

pal•a•tine (pal′ə tīn′, -tin), *adj.* **1.** having royal privileges: *a count palatine.* **2.** of or pertaining to a palace; palatial. —*n.* **3.** a vassal exercising royal privileges in a province; a count or earl palatine. **4.** a high official of an imperial court.

Pa•lau (pə lou′), *n.* **Republic of,** a group of islands in the W Pacific part of the Caroline group: since 1947 part of the Trust Territory of the Pacific Islands. 11,210; 192 sq. mi. (497 sq. km). Formerly, **Palau′ Is′lands.**

pa•lav•er (pə lav′ər, -lä′vər), *n.* **1.** profuse and idle talk. **2.** persuasive talk; flattery; cajolery. **3.** a conference or discussion, orig. one between European explorers, etc., and people indigenous to a region. —*v.i.* **4.** to talk profusely and idly. **5.** to confer. [< Portuguese *palavra* word, speech]

pa•laz•zo (pə lät′sō), *n., pl.* **-laz•zi** (-lät′sē). an impressive public building or private residence, esp. in Italy; palace.

pale[1] (pāl), *adj.,* **pal•er, pal•est,** *v.,* **paled, pal•ing.** —*adj.* **1.** lacking intensity of color; colorless or whitish: *a pale complexion.* **2.** of a low degree of chroma, saturation, or purity; approaching white or gray: *pale yellow.* **3.** not bright or brilliant; dim: *the pale moon.* **4.** faint or feeble; weak: *a pale protest.* —*v.i., v.t.* **5.** to make or become pale: *to pale at the sight of blood.* —**pale′ly,** *adv.* —**pale′ness,** *n.*

pale[2] (pāl), *n., v.,* **paled, pal•ing.** —*n.* **1.** a stake or picket, as of a fence. **2.** an enclosing or confining barrier; enclosure. **3.** an enclosed area. **4.** limits; bounds: *outside the pale of my jurisdiction.* **5.** a district or region within designated bounds. **6.** a central vertical stripe in a heraldic escutcheon. —*v.t.* **7.** to enclose with pales; fence. **8.** to encircle or encompass. —***Idiom.*** **9. beyond the pale,** beyond the limits of propriety, courtesy, etc.

Pale′ Horse′, Pale′ Rid′er, a novel (1939) by Katherine Anne Porter. Rev. 6:8.

Pa•len•que (pä leng′ke), *n.* a village in SE Mexico, in Chiapas state: ruins of an ancient Mayan city.

paleo-, a combining form meaning "old" or "ancient," used esp. in reference to former geologic time periods: *paleobotany.* Also, **pale–;** *esp. Brit.,* **palae-, palaeo-.**

pa•le•o•an•thro•pol•o•gy (pā′lē ō an′thrə pol′ə jē; *esp. Brit.* pal′ē-), *n.* the study of the origins and predecessors of the present human species. —**pa′le•o•an′thro•pol′o•gist,** *n.* —**pa′le•o•an′thro•po•log′i•cal** (-pə loj′i kəl), *adj.*

pa•le•o•bi•o•ge•og•ra•phy (pā′lē ō bī′ō jē og′rə fē; *esp. Brit.* pal′ē-), *n.* the study of the distribution of ancient plants and animals. —**pa′le•o•bi′o•ge′o•graph′ic** (-ə graf′ik), **pa′le•o•bi′o•ge′o•graph′i•cal,** *adj.* —**pa′le•o•bi′o•ge•og′ra•pher,** *n.*

pa•le•o•bi•ol•o•gy (pā′lē ō bī ol′ə jē; *esp. Brit.* pal′ē-), *n.* the branch of paleontology that deals with fossil animals, plants, and other organisms. —**pa′le•o•bi′o•log′i•cal** (-bī′ə loj′i kəl), **pa′le•o•bi′o•log′ic,** *adj.* —**pa′le•o•bi•ol′o•gist,** *n.*

pa•le•o•bot•a•ny (pā′lē ō bot′n ē; *esp. Brit.* pal′ē-), *n.* the branch of paleontology that deals with fossil plants. —**pa′le•o•bo•tan′i•cal** (-bə tan′i kəl), **pa′le•o•bo•tan′ic,** *adj.* —**pa′le•o•bot′a•nist,** *n.*

Pa•le•o•cene (pā′lē ə sēn′; *esp. Brit.* pal′ē-), *adj.* **1.** noting or pertaining to an epoch of the Tertiary Period, from 65 million to 55 million years ago, a time of mammalian proliferation. —*n.* **2.** the Paleocene Epoch or Series.

pa•le•o•cli•mate (pā′lē ō klī′mit; *esp. Brit.* pal′ē-), *n.* the climate of some former period of geologic time.

pa•le•o•cli•ma•tol•o•gy (pā′lē ō klī′mə tol′ə jē; *esp. Brit.* pal′ē-), *n.* the study of paleoclimates. —**pa′le•o•cli′ma•tol′o•gist,** *n.*

pa•le•o•ge•og•ra•phy (pā′lē ō jē og′rə fē; *esp. Brit.* pal′ē-), *n.* the science of representing the earth's geographic features belonging to any part of the geologic past. —**pa/le·o·ge·og/ra·pher,** *n.* —**pa/le·o·ge/o·graph/ic** (-jē/ə graf/ik), **pa/le·o·ge/o·graph/i·cal,** *adj.*

pa·le·og·ra·phy (pā/lē og/rə fē; *esp. Brit.* pal/ē-), *n.* **1.** ancient writing or forms of writing, as in documents and inscriptions. **2.** the study of ancient writings. —**pa/le·og/ra·pher,** *n.* —**pa/le·o·graph/ic** (-ə graf/ik), **pa/le·o·graph/i·cal,** *adj.* —**pa/le·o·graph/i·cal·ly,** *adv.*

Pa·le·o·In·di·an (pā/lē ō in/dē ən; *esp. Brit.* pal/ē-), *adj.* **1.** of, pertaining to, or characteristic of a New World cultural stage, c22,000–6000 B.C., distinguished by fluted-point tools and cooperative hunting methods. —*n.* **2.** a member of the American Indian people of this cultural stage, believed to have migrated orig. from Asia.

pa·le·o·lith (pā/lē ə lith; *esp. Brit.* pal/ē-), *n.* a Paleolithic stone implement.

Pa·le·o·lith·ic (pā/lē ə lith/ik; *esp. Brit.* pal/ē-), *adj.* (*sometimes l.c.*) of, designating, or characteristic of the early phase of the Stone Age: usu. divided into three periods (**Lower Paleolithic,** c2,000,000–c200,000 B.C., **Middle Paleolithic,** c150,000–c40,000 B.C., **Upper Paleolithic,** c40,000–c10,000 B.C.). Compare MESOLITHIC, NEOLITHIC.

pa·le·ol·o·gy (pā/lē ol/ə jē; *esp. Brit.* pal/ē-), *n.* the study of antiquities. —**pa/le·o·log/i·cal** (-ə loj/i kəl), *adj.* —**pa/le·ol/o·gist,** *n.*

pa·le·o·mag·net·ism (pā/lē ō mag/ni tiz/əm; *esp. Brit.* pal/ē-), *n.* magnetic polarization acquired by the minerals in a rock at the time the rock was deposited or solidified. —**pa/le·o·mag·net/ic** (-net/ik), *adj.*

pa·le·on·tol·o·gy (pā/lē ən tol/ə jē; *esp. Brit.* pal/ē-), *n.* the science of the forms of life existing in former geologic periods, as represented by their fossils. —**pa/le·on/to·log/ic** (-on/tl oj/ik), **pa/le·on/to·log/i·cal,** *adj.* —**pa/le·on/tol/o·gist,** *n.*

Pa·le·o·zo·ic (pā/lē ə zō/ik; *esp. Brit.* pal/ē-), *adj.* **1.** noting or pertaining to a geologic era occurring between 570 million and 230 million years ago, when fish, insects, and reptiles first appeared. —*n.* **2.** the Paleozoic Era or group of systems.

pa·le·o·zo·ol·o·gy (pā/lē ō zō ol/ə jē; *esp. Brit.* pal/ē-), *n.* the branch of paleontology dealing with fossil animals. —**pa/le·o·zo/o·log/i·cal** (-zō/ə loj/i kəl), *adj.* —**pa/le·o·zo·ol/o·gist,** *n.*

Pal·es·tine (pal/ə stīn/), *n.* **1.** Biblical name, **Canaan.** an ancient country in SW Asia, on the E coast of the Mediterranean. **2.** a former British mandate (1923–48) comprising part of this country, divided between Israel, Jordan, and Egypt in 1948: the Jordanian and Egyptian parts were occupied by Israel in 1967.

Pal/estine Libera/tion Organiza/tion, *n.* an umbrella organization for several Arab groups dedicated to the recovery of Palestine from the state of Israel and the return of refugees from the area to their homeland through diplomatic, military, and terrorist means. *Abbr.:* PLO

Pa·le·stri·na (pal/ə strē/nə), *n.* **Giovanni Pierluigi da,** 1526?–94, Italian composer.

pal·ette (pal/it), *n.* **1.** a thin, usu. oval or oblong board or tablet used by painters for holding and mixing colors. **2.** the set of colors on such a board. **3.** the range of colors used by a particular artist. **4.** the variety of techniques or range of any art: *a composer's musical palette.* **5.** the complete range of colors made available by a computer graphics card, from which a user or program may choose those to be displayed.

pal/ette knife/, *n.* a thin blade of varying flexibility set in a handle and used for mixing colors or applying them to a canvas.

Pa·ley (pā/lē), *n.* **William,** 1743–1805, English philosopher.

pal·imp·sest (pal/imp sest/), *n.* a parchment or the like from which writing has been partially or completely erased to make room for another text. —**pal/imp·ses/tic,** *adj.*

pal·in·drome (pal/in drōm/), *n.* a word, line, verse, number, etc., reading the same backward as forward, as *Madam, I'm Adam.* —**pal/in·drom/ic** (-drom/ik, -drō/mik), *adj.*

pal·ing (pā/ling), *n.* **1.** Also called **pal/ing fence/.** PICKET FENCE. **2.** a pale or picket for a fence. **3.** pales collectively. **4.** the act of building a fence with pales.

pal·in·gen·e·sis (pal/in jen/ə sis), *n.* **1.** rebirth; regeneration. **2. a.** embryonic development that reproduces the ancestral features of the species. **b.** a former theory that organisms are generated from other organisms preformed in the germ cells. **3.** the doctrine of transmigration of souls. —**pal/in·ge·net/ic** (-jə net/ik), *adj.*

pal·i·sade (pal/ə sād/), *n., v.,* **-sad·ed, -sad·ing.** —*n.* **1.** a fence of pales or stakes set firmly in the ground, as for enclosure or defense. **2.** a pale or stake pointed at the top and set firmly in the ground in a close row with others to form a defense. **3.** palisades, a line of cliffs. —*v.t.* **4.** to furnish or fortify with a palisade.

palisades
(def. 3)

pall¹ (pôl), *n.* **1.** something that covers, shrouds, or overspreads, esp. with darkness or gloom. **2.** a cloth for spreading over a coffin, bier, or tomb. **3.** a coffin. **4. a.** PALLIUM (def. 2). **b.** a linen cloth or a square cloth-covered piece of cardboard used to cover a chalice. —*v.t.* **5.** to cover with or as if with a pall. —**pall/-like/,** *adj.*

pall² (pôl), *v.i.* **1.** to have a wearying or tiresome effect. **2.** to become distasteful or unpleasant. **3.** to become satiated or cloyed with something. —*v.t.* **4.** to satiate or cloy. **5.** to make dull, distasteful, or unpleasant.

pal·la·di·um (pə lā/dē əm), *n.* a rare silver-white ductile metallic element of the platinum group, used chiefly as a catalyst and in dental and other alloys. *Symbol:* Pd; *at. wt.:* 106.4; *at. no.:* 46; *sp. gr.:* 12 at 20°C. —**pal·lad/ic** (-lad/ik), **pal·la/dous** (pə lā/dəs, pal/ə dəs), *adj.*

pall·bear·er (pôl/bâr/ər), *n.* one of several persons who carry or attend the coffin at a funeral.

pal·let¹ (pal/it), *n.* **1.** a bed or mattress of straw. **2.** a small or makeshift bed.

pal·let² (pal/it), *n.* **1.** a small, low, portable platform on which goods are placed for storage or moving. **2.** a flat board or metal plate used to support ceramic articles during drying. **3.** a painter's palette. **4.** (on a pawl) a lip or projection that engages with the teeth of a ratchet wheel. **5.** a shaping tool used by potters and consisting of a flat blade or plate with a handle at one end.

pal·li·ate (pal/ē āt/), *v.t.,* **-at·ed, -at·ing. 1.** to relieve without curing; mitigate; alleviate: *to palliate a chronic disease.* **2.** to try to mitigate or conceal the gravity of (an offense) by excuses, apologies, etc.; extenuate. —**pal/li·a/tion,** *n.* —**pal/li·a/tor,** *n.*

pal·li·a·tive (pal/ē ā/tiv, -ē ə tiv), *adj.* **1.** serving to palliate: *a palliative medicine.* —*n.* **2.** something that palliates. —**pal/li·a/tive·ly,** *adv.*

pal·lid (pal/id), *adj.* **1.** pale; faint or deficient in color; wan: *a pallid face.* **2.** lacking in vitality or interest: *a pallid performance.* —**pal/lid·ly,** *adv.* —**pal/lid·ness,** *n.*

pal·li·um (pal/ē əm), *n., pl.* **pal·li·a** (pal/ē ə), **pal·li·ums. 1.** a piece of cloth wrapped about the body as an outer garment in ancient Greece and Rome. **2.** a woolen vestment worn by the pope and by archbishops. **3.** CEREBRAL CORTEX. **4.** the mantle of a mollusk or bird.

pal·lor (pal/ər), *n.* unusual or extreme paleness, as from fear, ill health, or death.

pal·ly (pal/ē), *adj.,* **-li·er, -li·est.** *Informal.* friendly; chummy.

palm¹ (päm), *n.* **1.** the part of the inner surface of the hand that extends from the wrist to the bases of the fingers. **2.** the corresponding part of the forefoot of an animal. **3.** the part of a glove covering this part of the hand. **4. a.** a unit of measure ranging from 3 to 4 inches (7.5 to 10 cm), based on the breadth of the hand. **b.** a unit of measure ranging from 7 to 10 inches (17.5 to 25 cm), based on the length of the hand. **5.** the flat, expanded part of the antler of a deer. **6. a.** the blade of an oar. **b.** the inner face of an anchor fluke. —*v.t.* **7.** to conceal in the palm, as in sleight of hand. **8.** to pick up stealthily. **9.** to hold in the hand. **10.** to impose (something) fraudulently: *to palm stolen jewels on tourists.* **11.** to touch or stroke with the palm or hand. **12.** to shake hands with. **13.** to grip (a basketball) momentarily with the hand while dribbling: a rule violation. **14. palm off,** to foist upon someone, as by deception or fraud: *to palm off a forgery on a museum.* —**palm/er,** *n.*

royal palm, *Roystonea regia*

palm² (päm), *n.* **1.** any of numerous plants of the palm family, most species being tall, unbranched trees surmounted by a crown of large pinnate or palmately cleft leaves. **2.** a leaf or branch of such a tree, esp. as formerly carried to signify victory. **3.** a representation of such a leaf or branch, as on a military decoration, indicating a second award of the decoration. **4.** victory; triumph; success. —**palm/like/,** *adj.*

pal·mate (pal/māt, -mit, päl/-, pä/māt) also **pal/mat·ed,** *adj.* **1.** shaped like an open palm or like a hand with the fingers extended, as a leaf or an antler. **2.** web-footed. **3.** having four or more lobes or leaflets radiating from a single point. —**pal/mate·ly,** *adv.* —**pal·ma/tion,** *n.*

Palm·dale (päm/dāl/), *n.* a city in SW California, NE of Los Angeles. 103,423.

Palm·er (pä/mər), *n.* **1. Alice Elvira,** 1855–1902, U.S. educator. **2. Daniel David,** 1845–1913, Canadian originator of chiropractic medicine. **3. George Herbert,** 1842–1933, U.S. educator, philosopher, and author.

pal·met·to (pal met/ō, päl-, pä met/ō), *n., pl.* **-tos, -toes.** any of various palms having fan-shaped leaves, as of the genera *Sabal* and *Serenoa.*

palm·is·try (pä/mə strē), *n.* the art or practice of telling fortunes and interpreting character from the lines and configurations on the palm of a person's hand. —**palm′ist**, *n.*

Palm′ Sun′day, *n.* the Sunday before Easter, celebrated in commemoration of Christ's triumphal entry into Jerusalem.

palm·top (päm′top′), *n.* a battery-powered microcomputer small enough to fit in the palm.

Pal·my·ra (pal mī′rə), *n.* an ancient city in central Syria, NE of Damascus: reputedly built by Solomon. Biblical name, **Tadmor.**

pal·o·mi·no (pal′ə mē′nō), *n., pl.* **-nos.** a horse with a golden coat, a white mane and tail, and often white markings on the face and legs, developed chiefly in the southwestern U.S.

pal·pa·ble (pal′pə bəl), *adj.* **1.** readily or plainly seen or perceived; obvious. **2.** capable of being touched or felt; tangible. —**pal′pa·bil′i·ty, pal′pa·ble·ness,** *n.* —**pal′pa·bly,** *adv.*

pal·pate (pal′pāt), *v.t.,* **-pat·ed, -pat·ing.** to examine by touch, esp. for the purpose of diagnosing disease or illness. —**pal·pa′tion,** *n.* —**pal′pa·to′ry** (-pə tôr′ē, -tōr′ē), *adj.*

pal·pi·tate (pal′pi tāt′), *v.,* **-tat·ed, -tat·ing.** —*v.i.* **1.** to pulsate, as the heart, with unusual rapidity; flutter. **2.** to quiver; throb; tremble. —*v.t.* **3.** to cause to pulsate or tremble. —**pal′pi·tant** (-tənt), *adj.* —**pal′pi·tat′ing·ly,** *adv.* —**pal′pi·ta′tion,** *n.*

pal·sy (pôl′zē), *n., pl.* **-sies. 1.** any of several conditions characterized by paralysis, as Bell's palsy. **2.** any of a variety of atonal muscular conditions characterized by tremors of the body parts or of the entire body. —**pal′sy·like′,** *adj.*

pal·sy-wal·sy (pal′zē wal′zē), *adj. Slang.* friendly in a very intimate or hearty way.

pal·try (pôl′trē), *adj.,* **-tri·er, -tri·est. 1.** ridiculously or insultingly small: *a paltry sum.* **2.** utterly worthless: *paltry clothes.* **3.** mean or contemptible: *a paltry coward.* —**pal′tri·ness,** *n.*

pam·pas (pam′pəz; *attributively* pam′pəs), *n.pl., sing.* **-pa.** the vast grassy plains of S South America, esp. in Argentina. —**pam·pe·an** (pam pē′ən, pam′pē ən), *adj.*

pam′pas grass′, *n.* a tall, ornamental grass, *Cortaderia selloana,* native to South America, having large, thick, feathery, silvery white panicles.

pam·per (pam′pər), *v.t.* to treat with extreme or excessive indulgence, kindness, or care: *to pamper a child.* —**pam′per·er,** *n.*

pam·phlet (pam′flit), *n.* **1.** a short unbound publication held together by staples or stitching, typically containing factual information. **2.** a short treatise or essay, generally on a contemporary or controversial subject. —**pam′phlet·ar′y,** *adj.*

pam·phlet·eer (pam′fli tēr′), *n.* **1.** a person who writes or publishes pamphlets. —*v.i.* **2.** to write or publish pamphlets.

Pam·phyl·i·a (pam fil′ē ə), *n.* an ancient country in S Asia Minor: later a Roman province.

pan¹ (pan), *n., v.,* **panned, pan·ning.** —*n.* **1.** a broad, usu. shallow, metal container, used in various forms for frying, baking, washing, etc. **2.** any similar receptacle or part, as the scales of a balance. **3.** the amount a pan holds or can hold; panful. **4.** a container in which gold or other valuable metals are separated from gravel or other substances by agitation with water. **5.** a drifting piece of flat, thin ice, as formed on a shore or bay. **6.** a natural depression in the ground, as one containing water, mud, or mineral salts. **7.** (in old guns) the hollow part of the lock, holding the priming. **8.** *Informal.* an unfavorable review or critique. **9.** *Slang.* the face. —*v.t.* **10.** *Informal.* to criticize harshly, as in a review. **11.** to wash (gravel, sand, etc.) in a pan to separate gold or other valuable metal. **12.** to cook in a pan. —*v.i.* **13.** to wash gravel, sand, etc., in a pan in seeking gold or the like. **14.** to yield gold or the like, as gravel washed in a pan. **15. pan out,** *Informal.* to have an outcome, esp. a successful one. —**pan′ner,** *n.*

pan² (pan), *v.,* **panned, pan·ning,** *n.* —*v.i.* **1.** to swivel a television or motion-picture camera horizontally in order to keep a moving subject in view or record a panorama. **2.** (of a camera) to be moved in such a manner. —*v.t.* **3.** to move (a camera) in such a manner. —*n.* **4.** the act of panning a camera. **5.** the filmed shot resulting from this.

Pan (pan), *n.* an ancient Greek god of shepherds and hunters, usu. represented as a man with the legs, horns, and ears of a goat.

pan-, a combining form meaning "all": *panorama; pantheism;* used esp. in terms implying the union of all branches of a group: *Pan-American; Panhellenic; Pan-Slavism.*

pan·a·ce·a (pan′ə sē′ə), *n., pl.* **-ce·as. 1.** a remedy for all ills; cure-all. **2.** a solution for all difficulties. —**pan′a·ce′an,** *adj.*

pa·nache (pə nash′, -näsh′), *n.* **1.** a grand or flamboyant manner; flair; verve; style. **2.** an ornamental plume of feathers, tassels, or the like, esp. one worn on a helmet or cap.

Pan·a·ma (pan′ə mä′, -mô′), *n., pl.* **-mas** for 5. **1.** a republic in S Central America. 2,693,417; 29,762 sq. mi. (77,082 sq. km). **2.** Also called **Panama City.** the capital of Panama, at the Pacific end of the Panama Canal. 386,393. **3. Isthmus of,** an isthmus between North and South America. **4. Gulf of,** the portion of the Pacific in the bend of the Isthmus of Panama. **5.** (*sometimes l.c.*) **panama hat.** Also, **Pa·na·má** (Sp. pä′nä mä′) (for defs. 1, 2). —**Pan·a·ma′ni·an** (-mā′nē ən), *adj., n.*

Pan′ama Canal′, *n.* a canal extending SE from the Atlantic to the Pacific across the Isthmus of Panama. 40 mi. (64 km) long.

Pan′ama hat′, *n.* a hat made of finely plaited young leaves of the jipijapa plant.

Pan-A·mer·i·can (pan′ə mer′i kən), *adj.* of or representing the countries or people of North, Central, and South America.

Pan′-Amer′ican Games′, *n.pl.* an amateur athletic competition, held every four years in a different host city for all the nations of the Western Hemisphere.

pan′-broil′ or **pan/broil′,** *v.t., v.i.* to cook in an uncovered frying pan over direct heat using little or no fat.

pan·cake (pan′kāk′), *n., v.,* **-caked, -cak·ing.** —*n.* **1.** a thin, flat cake of batter fried on both sides on a griddle or in a frying pan; griddlecake or flapjack. **2.** Also called **pan′cake land′ing.** an airplane landing made by pancaking. —*v.i.* **3.** (of an airplane) to drop flat to the ground after leveling off a few feet above it. —*v.t.* **4.** *Informal.* to flatten, esp. as the result of a mishap. **5.** to cause (an airplane) to pancake.

pan·cre·as (pan′krē əs, pang′-), *n.* a large compound gland, situated near the stomach, that secretes digestive enzymes into the intestine and insulin into the bloodstream. —**pan′cre·at′ic** (-at′ik), *adj.*

pan·da (pan′də), *n., pl.* **-das. 1.** a white-and-black bearlike mammal, *Ailuropoda melanoleuca,* now restricted to Central China, where it feeds mainly on bamboo: classified either as a bear or as a raccoon, or more generally the sole member of its own family, the Ailuropodidae. **2.** Also called **lesser panda, red panda.** a reddish brown, raccoonlike mammal, *Ailurus fulgens,* of the Himalayas and adjacent regions, feeding mainly on bamboo and other vegetation: usu. classified as the only Old World member of the raccoon family.

giant panda, *Ailuropoda melanoleuca,*
2 ft. (0.6 m) high at shoulder;
length 5 ft. (1.5 m)

lesser panda, *Ailurus fulgens,*
head and body 2 ft. (0.6 m);
tail 1 ½ ft. (0.5 m)

pan·dem·ic (pan dem′ik), *adj.* **1.** (of a disease) prevalent throughout an entire country, continent, or the whole world; epidemic over a large area. —*n.* **2.** a pandemic disease.

pan·de·mo·ni·um (pan′də mō′nē əm), *n., pl.* **-ums. 1.** wild uproar or disorder; tumult or chaos. **2.** a place or scene of turmoil or utter chaos.

pan·der (pan′dər), *n.* **1.** a person who caters to or profits from the weaknesses or vices of others. —*v.i.* **2.** to act as a pander; cater basely: *to pander to vulgar tastes.*

pan·dit (pun′dit; *spelling pron.* pan′dit) also **pundit,** *n.* (in India) a man esteemed for his wisdom and learning: used as a title of respect.

P. and L. or **p. and l.,** profit and loss.

Pan·do·ra (pan dôr′ə, -dōr′ə), *n.* (in Greek myth) the first woman, created by Hephaestus and endowed with every grace: out of curiosity, she opened a box and released all the evils that might plague humankind. [< Greek *Pandóra* = *pan-* all + *dôr(on)* gift]

pane (pān), *n.* **1.** one of the divisions of a window or the like, consisting of a single plate of glass in a frame. **2.** a plate of glass for such a division. **3.** a panel, as of a wainscot, ceiling, or door. **4.** a section of a full sheet of stamps, as sold at a post office window.

pan·e·gyr·ic (pan′i jir′ik, -jī′rik), *n.* **1.** a lofty oration or writing in praise of a person or thing; eulogy. **2.** formal or elaborate praise. —**pan′e·gyr′i·cal,** *adj.* —**pan′e·gyr′i·cal·ly,** *adv.* —**pan′e·gyr′ist,** *n.* —**pan′e·gyr·ize′** (-jə rīz′), *v.t., v.i.,* **-rized, -riz·ing.**

pan·el (pan′l), *n., v.,* **-eled, -el·ing** or (*esp. Brit.*) **-elled, -el·ling.** —*n.* **1.** a distinct section of a wall, wainscot, door, etc., esp. one sunk below or raised above the surface or enclosed by a frame or border. **2.** a comparatively thin, flat piece of wood or the like, as a large piece of plywood. **3. a.** a group of persons gathered to conduct a public discussion, judge a contest, or the like: *a panel of experts.* **b.** PANEL DISCUSSION. **4. a.** a list of persons summoned for service as jurors. **b.** the body of persons composing a jury. **c.** (in Scotland) the person or persons arraigned for trial. **5.** a surface on a machine on which controls and dials are mounted. **6.** a switchboard or control board containing a set of related electrical cords, jacks, relays, etc. **7.** a broad strip of material set vertically in or on a dress, skirt, etc. **8. a.** a flat piece of wood of varying kinds on which a picture is painted. **b.** a picture painted on such a piece of wood. **9.** a lateral subdivision of an airfoil with internal girder construction. **10.** *Engin.* an area or section of a truss bounded by principal web members and chords. **11.** a pad placed under a saddle. —*v.t.* **12.** to arrange in or furnish with a panel or panels. **13.** to ornament with a panel or panels. **14.** to set in a frame as a panel. **15.** IMPANEL (def. 2). —**Usage.** See COLLECTIVE NOUN.

pan′el discus′sion, *n.* a formal discussion before an audience for which the topic and speakers have been arranged in advance.

pan·el·ing (pan′l ing), *n.* **1.** wood or other material made into panels. **2.** a surface of panels, esp. of decorative wood or woodlike panels. **3.** panels collectively. Also, *esp. Brit.,* **pan′el·ling.**

pan·el·ist (pan′l ist), *n.* a member of a panel convened for public discussion, judging, playing a radio or television game, etc.

pan·el truck′, *n.* a small truck having a fully enclosed body.

pan·e·tel·la or **pan·e·tel·a** or **pan·a·tel·la** or **pan·a·tel·a** (pan′ə tel′ə), *n.*, *pl.* **-tel·las** or **-tel·as**. a long, slender cigar, usu. with straight sides and tapering to a point at the closed end.

pan·fish (pan′fish′), *n.*, *pl.* **-fish·es**, (*esp. collectively*) **-fish**. any small, freshwater food fish, as a perch or sunfish, that is usu. cooked by pan-frying.

pan′-fry′, *v.t.*, **-fried, -fry·ing**. to sauté in a frying pan.

pang (pang), *n.* **1.** a sudden feeling of mental or emotional distress: *a pang of guilt.* **2.** a sudden, brief, and sharp pain: *the pangs of childbirth.*

pan′ gra′vy, *n.* meat juices, as from a roast, seasoned but not usu. thickened.

pan·han·dle[1] (pan′han′dl), *n.* **1.** the handle of a pan. **2.** a long, narrow, projecting strip of a larger territory, as of a state: *the Texas panhandle.*

pan·han·dle[2] (pan′han′dl), *v.*, **-dled, -dling.** —*v.i.* **1.** to accost passers-by on the street and beg from them. —*v.t.* **2.** to accost and beg from. **3.** to obtain by accosting and begging. —**pan′han′dler,** *n.*

pan·ic (pan′ik), *n.*, *adj.*, *v.*, **-icked, -ick·ing.** —*n.* **1.** a sudden overwhelming fear that produces hysterical behavior and that can spread quickly through a crowd. **2.** an instance, outbreak, or period of such fear. **3.** an anxiety disorder characterized by feelings of impending doom and physical symptoms such as trembling and hyperventilation. **4.** a sudden widespread fear that the economy is faltering, causing stock values to fall and some banks to fail, as investments and savings are hastily withdrawn. **5.** *Informal.* someone or something that is considered hilariously funny. —*adj.* **6.** of the nature of, caused by, or indicating panic: *panic selling of stocks.* **7.** (*cap.*) of or pertaining to the god Pan. —*v.t.* **8.** to affect with panic. **9.** *Informal.* to keep (an audience or the like) highly amused. —*v.i.* **10.** to be stricken with panic; become frantic with fear.

pan′ic-strick′en or **pan′ic-struck′,** *adj.* overcome with, characterized by, or resulting from fear or panic.

pan·jan·drum (pan jan′drəm), *n.* a self-important or pretentious official.

Pank·hurst (pangk′hûrst′), *n.* **Emmeline (Goulden),** 1858–1928, English suffragist leader.

Pan·mun·jom (pän′mŏŏn′jom′), *n.* a village on the border of North Korea and South Korea: site of truce talks ending the Korean War.

pan·nier or **pan·ier** (pan′yər, -ē ər), *n.* **1.** a basket, esp. a large one, for carrying goods, provisions, etc. **2.** one of a pair of baskets to be slung across the back of a pack animal. **3.** Also called **pan′nier drape′.** (on a dress, skirt, etc.) a puffed arrangement of drapery at the hips. **4.** Often, **panniers.** an oval framework or a pair of hoops formerly used for distending the skirt of a dress at the hips. —**pan′niered,** *adj.*

pan·o·ply (pan′ə plē), *n.*, *pl.* **-plies. 1.** a wide-ranging and impressive array or display. **2.** a complete suit of armor. —**pan′o·plied,** *adj.*

pan·o·ram·a (pan′ə ram′ə, -rä′mə), *n.*, *pl.* **-ram·as. 1.** an unobstructed and wide view of an extensive area. **2.** an extended pictorial representation of a landscape or other scene, often exhibited a part at a time before spectators. **3.** a continuously passing or changing scene or an unfolding of events: *the panorama of Chinese history.* **4.** a comprehensive survey, as of a subject. —**pan′o·ram′ic,** *adj.* —**pan′o·ram′i·cal·ly,** *adv.*

pan·pipe (pan′pīp′), *n.* a primitive wind instrument consisting of a series of hollow pipes of graduated length, the tones being produced by blowing across the upper ends. Often, **pan′pipes′.**

panpipe

pan·sy (pan′zē), *n.*, *pl.* **-sies.** a violet, *Viola tricolor hortensis,* cultivated in many varieties, having richly and variously colored flowers.

pant (pant), *v.i.* **1.** to breathe hard and quickly, as after exertion. **2.** to long with breathless or intense eagerness; yearn: *to pant for revenge.* **3.** to emit steam or the like in loud puffs. —*v.t.* **4.** to breathe or utter rapidly or gaspingly. —*n.* **5.** the act of panting. **6.** a short, quick, labored effort at breathing; gasp. —**pant′ing·ly,** *adv.*

pan·ta·loon (pan′tl ōōn′), *n.* **1.** pantaloons, a man's close-fitting garment for the hips and legs, worn esp. in the 19th century, but varying in form from period to period. **2.** (in the modern pantomime) a foolish, vicious old man, the butt and accomplice of the clown. **3.** (*usu. cap.*) Also, **Pan·ta·lo·ne** (pan′tl ō′nä, pän′-). (in commedia dell'arte) a foolish old Venetian merchant, generally lascivious and frequently deceived in the course of lovers' intrigues.

pan·the·ism (pan′thē iz′əm), *n.* **1.** the doctrine that God is the transcendent reality of which the material world and humanity are only manifestations. **2.** any religious belief or philosophical doctrine that identifies God with the universe. —**pan′the·ist,** *n.* —**pan′the·is′tic, pan′the·is′ti·cal,** *adj.* —**pan′the·is′ti·cal·ly,** *adv.*

pan·the·on (pan′thē on′, -ən *or, esp. Brit.,* pan thē′ən), *n.* **1.** a public building containing tombs or memorials of the illustrious dead of a nation. **2.** the realm of the heroes or idols of any group, movement, etc.: *a place in the pantheon of American literature.* **3.** a temple dedicated to all the gods. **4.** the gods of a particular mythology considered collectively. **5.** (*cap.*) a domed circular temple in Rome, completed A.D. 120–124 by Hadrian, used as a church since A.D. 609. —**pan′the·on′ic,** *adj.*

pan·ther (pan′thər), *n.*, *pl.* **-thers,** (*esp. collectively*) **-ther. 1.** the cougar, *Felis concolor.* **2.** the leopard, *Panthera pardus.* **3.** any leopard in the black color phase.

pant·ies (pan′tēz), *n.* (*used with a pl. v.*) short underpants for women and children. Often, **pant′ie, panty.**

pan·to·mime (pan′tə mīm′), *n.*, *v.*, **-mimed, -mim·ing.** —*n.* **1.** the art of conveying emotions, actions, and thoughts by gestures without speech. **2.** a play or entertainment in which the performers express themselves by gesture alone, often to the accompaniment of music. **3.** significant gesture without speech. **4.** (in the Roman Empire) **a.** a masked dancer, who was accompanied by a chorus. **b.** a dramatic performance by such a dancer and chorus. **5.** a theatrical spectacle common in England at Christmastime, with stock characters who sing, dance, and tell jokes. **6.** a pantomimist. —*v.t.* **7.** to represent or express in pantomime. —*v.i.* **8.** to express oneself in pantomime. —**pan′to·mim′ic** (-mim′ik), *adj.*

pan·try (pan′trē), *n.*, *pl.* **-tries.** a room or closet, usu. near a kitchen, in which food, silverware, dishes, etc., are kept.

pants (pants), *n.* (*used with a pl. v.*) **1.** TROUSERS. **2.** underpants, esp. for women and children; panties. —*Idiom.* **3. wear the pants,** to have the dominant role, as in a household.

pant·suit (pant′sŏŏt′) also **pants′ suit′,** *n.* a woman's suit consisting of trousers and a matching jacket.

pant·y·hose or **pant·i·hose** (pan′tē hōz′), *n.* (*used with a pl. v.*) a one-piece, skintight garment worn by women, combining panties and stockings.

pant·y·waist (pan′tē wāst′), *n.* **1.** *Informal.* an effeminate man; sissy. **2.** (formerly) a child's undergarment consisting of short pants and a shirt that buttoned together at the waist.

pan·zer (pan′zər), *adj.* **1.** (esp. in the German army) armored. **2.** of or designating an armored unit in the German army, esp. in World War II. —*n.* **3.** a vehicle, esp. a tank, forming part of an armored unit.

pap[1] (pap), *n.* **1.** soft food for infants or invalids, as bread soaked in milk. **2.** ideas, writings, or the like, lacking substance or real value.

pap[2] (pap), *n. Chiefly Dial.* a teat or nipple or something resembling one.

pa·pa (pä′pə, pə pä′), *n.*, *pl.* **-pas.** FATHER.

pa·pa·cy (pä′pə sē), *n.*, *pl.* **-cies. 1.** the office, dignity, or jurisdiction of the pope. **2.** the system of Roman Catholic ecclesiastical government. **3.** the period during which a certain pope is in office. **4.** the succession or line of the popes.

pa·pal (pä′pəl), *adj.* **1.** of or pertaining to the pope or the papacy. **2.** of or pertaining to the Roman Catholic Church. —**pa′pal·ly,** *adv.*

Pa·pa·ni·co·laou′ test′ (pä′pə nē′kə lou′, pap′ə nik′əlou′), *n.* PAP TEST.

pa·pa·raz·zo (pä′pə rät′sō), *n.*, *pl.* **-raz·zi** (-rät′sē). a freelance photographer, esp. one who takes candid pictures of celebrities for publication.

pa·pa·ya (pə pä′yə), *n.*, *pl.* **-yas. 1.** a small tropical American tree, *Carica papaya,* resembling a palm with broad leaves at the top, bearing a yellow melonlike fruit. **2.** the fruit itself. —**pa·pa′yan,** *adj.*

Pa·pe·e·te (pä′pē ā′tā, pə pē′tē), *n.* a seaport on NW Tahiti, in the Society Islands: capital of the Society Islands and of French Polynesia. 22,967.

pa·per (pä′pər), *n.* **1.** a substance made from wood pulp, rags, straw, or other fibrous material, usu. in thin sheets, used to write or print on, for wrapping, for decorating walls, etc. **2.** a piece, sheet, or leaf of this. **3.** something resembling this substance, as papyrus. **4.** a written or printed document or the like. **5.** a newspaper or journal. **6.** a scholarly essay, article, or dissertation, usu. intended for publication. **7.** a written piece of schoolwork, as a composition or report. **8.** Often, **papers.** a document establishing or verifying identity, status, or the like: *citizenship papers.* **9.** negotiable notes, bills, etc., as commercial paper or paper money. **10.** a promissory note. **11.** WALLPAPER. **12.** a sheet of paper with pins or needles stuck through it in rows. **13.** *Slang.* a free pass to an entertainment. —*v.t.* **14.** to cover with wallpaper. **15.** to line or cover with paper. **16.** to distribute handbills, posters, etc., throughout (an area). **17.** to fold or wrap in paper. **18.** to supply with paper. **19.** *Informal.* to deluge with documents, esp. those requiring response or compliance. **20.** *Slang.* to fill (a theater or the like) by giving away free tickets. —*v.i.* **21.** to apply wallpaper to walls. **22. paper over,** to conceal or cover up (dissension, controversy, etc.), esp. to preserve an impression of accord. —*adj.* **23.** made of paper: *a paper bag.* **24.** paperlike, as in being thin or flimsy. **25.** of or pertaining to routine clerical duties. **26.** conducted by means of letters, articles, books, etc.: *a paper war.* **27.** existing on paper only; not realized: *paper profits.* —*Idiom.* **28. on paper, a.** in written or printed form. **b.** in theory only. —*Saying.* **29. not worth the paper it's written on,** worthless. —**pa′per·er,** *n.* —**pa′per·less,** *adj.*

pa·per·back (pā′pər bak′), *n.* **1.** a book bound in a flexible paper cover. —*adj.* **2.** (of a book) bound in a flexible paper cover. **3.** of or pertaining to paperbacks. Compare HARDCOVER.

pa′per birch′, *n.* a North American birch, *Betula papyrifera,* having a tough bark and yielding a valuable wood.

pa·per·board (pā′pər bôrd′, -bōrd′), *n.* **1.** a thick, stiff cardboard composed of layers of paper or paper pulp compressed together; pasteboard. —*adj.* **2.** of, pertaining to, or made of paperboard.

pa·per·boy (pā′pər boi′), *n.* a youth or man who sells newspapers on the street or delivers them to homes.

pa′per chase′, *n.* the paperwork necessary to obtain a college degree or a professional license, apply for financial aid, etc.

pa′per clip′, *n.* **1.** a flat clip that holds sheets of paper between two loops. **2.** a spring clamp for holding papers.

pa′per cut′ter, *n.* any device for cutting or trimming sheets of paper to a required size. —**pa′per-cut′ting,** *adj.*

pa′per doll′, *n.* **1.** a paper or cardboard doll, usu. two-dimensional. **2.** Usu., **paper dolls.** a connected series of doll-like figures cut from folded paper.

pa·per·hang·er (pā′pər hang′ər), *n.* **1.** a person whose job is covering walls with wallpaper. **2.** *Slang.* a person who passes worthless checks. —**pa′per·hang′ing,** *n.*

pa′per knife′, *n.* a small, often decorative, knifelike instrument for slitting open envelopes, folded papers, etc.

pa′per mon′ey, *n.* currency in paper form, such as government and bank notes, as distinguished from metal currency.

pa′per mul′berry, *n.* a mulberry tree, *Broussonetia papyrifera,* of E Asia, having alternate leaves that vary in size, and orange-red fruit: grown as a shade tree.

pa′per nau′tilus, *n.* any swimming octopod mollusk of the genus *Argonauta:* the female produces a delicate shell into which she lays her eggs.

pa′per-push′er, *n. Informal.* **1.** a person who has a routine desk job. **2.** BUREAUCRAT.

pa′per-thin′, *adj.* **1.** extremely thin: *paper-thin pastry.* **2.** inadequate or unconvincing; flimsy: *a paper-thin excuse.*

pa′per ti′ger, *n.* a person, nation, etc., that has the appearance of power but is actually weak and ineffectual.

pa′per trail′, *n.* a written or printed record, as of transactions or judicial opinions, esp. when used to incriminate someone.

pa′per-train′, *v.t.* to train (a pet) to defecate or urinate on sheets of disposable paper.

pa′per wasp′, *n.* any of several social wasps, as the yellow jacket or hornet, that construct a nest of a paperlike substance.

pa·per·weight (pā′pər wāt′), *n.* a small, heavy object placed on papers to keep them from scattering.

pa·per·work (pā′pər wûrk′), *n.* written or clerical work, forming an incidental but necessary part of some work or job.

Pa·phos (pā′fos), *n.* an ancient city in SW Cyprus.

pa·pier-mâ·ché (pā′pər mə shā′, pä pyä′-), *n.* **1.** moistened paper pulp mixed with glue and other materials or layers of paper glued and pressed together, molded when moist to form various articles and becoming hard and strong when dry. —*adj.* **2.** made of papier-mâché. **3.** easily destroyed or discredited; false or illusory: *a papier-mâché economy.* [< French: lit., chewed paper]

pa·pil·la (pə pil′ə), *n., pl.* **-pil·lae** (-pil′ē). any small, nipplelike projection, as on the surface of the tongue or at the root of a developing hair. —**pap·il·lar·y** (pap′ə ler′ē, pə pil′ə rē), *adj.*

pap·il·lo·ma (pap′ə lō′mə), *n., pl.* **-ma·ta** (-mə tə), **-mas.** a benign tumor of the skin or mucous membrane consisting of hypertrophied epithelial tissue, as a wart or corn. —**pap·il·lo′ma·to′sis,** *n.* —**pap·il·lo′ma·tous** (-lō′mə təs, -lom′ə-), *adj.*

pap·il·lon (pap′ə lon′; *Fr.* PA pē yôn′), *n., pl.* **-lons** (-lon′; *Fr.* -yôn′). one of a breed of toy spaniels having a long, silky coat and large, erect ears held so that they resemble the wings of a butterfly.

pa·poose or **pap·poose** (pa pōōs′, pə-), *n.* a North American Indian baby or young child.

Pap′ (or **pap′**) **test′** (pap), *n.* **1.** a test for cancer of the cervix, consisting of the staining of cells taken in a cervical or vaginal smear **(Pap** (or **pap′**) **smear′)** for examination of exfoliated cells. **2.** a vaginal Pap smear used to evaluate estrogen levels. **3.** an examination of exfoliated cells in any body fluid, as sputum or urine, for cancer cells. Also called **Papanicolaou test.** [after *George Papanicolaou* (1883–1962), U.S. cytologist]

Pap·u·a (pap′yōō ə, pä′pōō ä′), *n.* **1. Territory of,** a former Australian territory that included SE New Guinea and adjacent islands: now part of Papua New Guinea. **2. Gulf of,** an inlet of the Coral Sea on the SE coast of New Guinea.

Pap·u·an (pap′yōō ən), *adj.* **1.** of or pertaining to Papua or Papua New Guinea, or the inhabitants of either. **2.** of or pertaining to the island of New Guinea or its indigenous inhabitants. **3.** of, pertaining to, or denoting the group of more than 700 languages, belonging to an as yet undetermined number of language families, spoken on New Guinea, several islands of E Indonesia, and parts of the Bismarck Archipelago, Bougainville, and the W Solomon Islands. —*n.* **4.** a native or inhabitant of Papua or Papua New Guinea. **5. a.** a member of any of the indigenous peoples of New Guinea. **b.** a speaker of a Papuan language. **6.** the Papuan languages collectively.

Pap′ua New′ Guin′ea, *n.* an independent country comprising the E part of the island of New Guinea and nearby islands: a former Australian Trusteeship Territory; independent since 1975; member of the Commonwealth of Nations. 4,496,221; 178,704 sq. mi. (462,840 sq. km). *Cap.:* Port Moresby. —**Pap′ua New′ Guin′ean,** *adj., n.*

pa·py·rus (pə pī′rəs), *n., pl.* **-py·ri** (-pī′rī, -rē), **-py·rus·es. 1.** a tall, aquatic plant, *Cyperus papyrus,* of the sedge family, native to the Nile valley. **2.** a material on which to write, prepared from thin strips of the pith of this plant laid and pressed together, used by the ancient Egyptians, Greeks, and Romans. **3.** a document written on this material. —**pa·py′ral, pa·py′rine** (-rin), *adj.*

par (pär), *n., adj., v.,* **parred, parring.** —*n.* **1.** an equality in value or standing; a level of equality: *gains on a par with losses.* **2.** an average or normal amount, degree, condition, etc.: *to feel below par.* **3.** the number of golf strokes set as a standard for a specific hole or a complete course. **4. a.** the value of the monetary unit of one country in terms of that of another, based on the same metal. **b.** the face value, original price, or principal of a note, stock, or bond. —*adj.* **5.** average or normal. —*v.t.* **6.** *Golf.* to equal par on (a hole or course). —*Idiom.* **7. par for the course,** exactly what one might expect; typical.

par·a¹ (par′ə), *adj.* pertaining to or occupying two positions (1, 4) in the benzene ring that are separated by two carbon atoms. *Abbr.:* p- Compare ORTHO, META.

par·a² (par′ə), *n., pl.* **par·as.** *Informal.* **1.** paraprofessional. **2.** paratrooper.

par·a³ (par′ə), *n., pl.* **par·as, par·ae** (par′ē). **1.** Also called **parity.** a woman's status regarding the bearing of offspring: usu. followed by a numeral designating the number of times the woman has given birth. **2.** the woman herself. Compare GRAVIDA.

para-¹, **1.** a prefix appearing in loanwords from Greek, with the meanings "at or to one side of, beside, side by side" (*parabola; paragraph*), "beyond, past, by" (*paradox; paragoge*); by extension designating objects or activities auxiliary to or derivative of that denoted by the base word (*parody; paronomasia*), and hence abnormal or defective (*paranoia*). As an English prefix, **para-¹** is also productive in the naming of occupational roles considered ancillary or subsidiary to roles requiring more training, or of a higher status: *paralegal; paraprofessional.* **2.** a combining form used in the names of benzene derivatives in which the substituting group occupies the para position in the benzene ring. *Abbr.:* p- Also, *esp. before a vowel,* **par-.**

para-², a combining form meaning "guard against": *parachute; parasol.*

para-³, a combining form extracted from PARACHUTE, forming compounds denoting persons or things utilizing parachutes: *paratrooper.*

par·a·ble (par′ə bəl), *n.* **1.** a short allegorical story designed to illustrate or teach some truth, religious principle, or moral lesson. **2.** a statement or comment that conveys a meaning indirectly by the use of comparison, analogy, or the like. [< Late Latin *parabola* comparison, parable, word < Greek *parabolē* comparison]

pa·rab·o·la (pə rab′ə lə), *n., pl.* **-las.** a plane curve formed by the intersection of a right circular cone with a plane parallel to a generator of the cone; the set of points in a plane that are equidistant from a fixed line and a fixed point in the same plane or in a parallel plane.

par·a·bol·ic (par′ə bol′ik), *adj.* **1.** having the form or outline of a parabola. **2.** of, pertaining to, or resembling a parabola.

par·a·chute (par′ə shōōt′), *n., v.,* **-chut·ed, -chut·ing.** —*n.* **1.** a folding, umbrellalike, fabric device with cords supporting a harness or straps for allowing a person, object, etc., to descend slowly from a height, esp. from an aircraft. —*v.t.* **2.** to drop or land (troops, supplies, etc.) by parachute. —*v.i.* **3.** to descend by parachute. —**par′a·chut′ist, par′a·chut′er,** *n.*

par·a·clete (par′ə klēt′), *n.* **1.** an advocate or intercessor. **2.** (*cap.*) the Holy Spirit.

pa·rade (pə rād′), *n., v.,* **-rad·ed, -rad·ing.** —*n.* **1.** a public procession, often including a marching band, held in honor of an event, person, etc. **2. a.** a military ceremony involving the formation and marching of troops. **b.** the assembly of troops for inspection or display. **c.** Also called **parade′ ground′.** a place where such assembly regularly occurs. **3.** a continual passing by, as of people, objects, or events: *the parade of the seasons.* **4.** an ostentatious display: *to make a parade of one's beliefs.* **5.** *Chiefly Brit.* **a.** a group of promenaders. **b.** a promenade. —*v.t.* **6.** to walk up and down on. **7.** to display ostentatiously. **8.** to cause to march. —*v.i.* **9.** to march in a procession. **10.** to promenade in a public place. **11.** to assemble in military order for display. **12.** to assume a false or misleading appearance. —**pa·rad′er,** *n.*

par·a·digm (par′ə dīm′, -dim), *n.* **1.** a set of all the inflected forms of a word based on a single stem or root, as *boy, boy's, boys, boys'.* **2.** an example serving as a model; pattern: *a paradigm of virtue.*

par·a·dig·mat·ic (par′ə dig mat′ik), *adj.* **1.** of or pertaining to a paradigm. **2.** pertaining to or being a relationship among linguistic elements that can substitute for each other in a given context, as the relationship of *sun* in *The sun is shining* to other nouns that could substitute for it, as *star* or *light.*. —**par′a·dig·mat′i·cal·ly,** *adv.*

par′adigm shift′, *n.* a great change in overall thinking and assumptions, creating a large number of smaller changes.

par·a·dise (par′ə dīs′, -dīz′), *n.* **1.** heaven, as the final abode of the righteous. **2.** (*often cap.*) EDEN (def. 1). **3.** a place of great beauty or happiness. **4.** a state of supreme happiness.

Par′a·dise Lost′, an epic poem (1667) by John Milton about Adam and Eve's explusion from the Garden of Eden and the misery that ensues.

par·a·di·si·a·cal (par′ə di sī′ə kəl, -zī′-) also **par·a·dis·i·ac** (-dis′ē ak′, -diz′-), *adj.* of, like, or befitting paradise.

pa·ra·dor (par′ə dôr′), *n.* a government-sponsored inn, esp. in Spain.

par·a·dox (par′ə doks′), *n.* **1.** a seemingly contradictory or absurd statement that expresses a possible truth. **2.** a self-contradictory and false proposition. **3.** a person, thing, or situation, exhibiting an apparently contradictory nature. —**par′a·dox′i·cal,** *adj.* —**par′a·dox′i·cal·ly,** *adv.*

par·af·fin (par′ə fin), *n.* **1.** a white or colorless, tasteless, odorless, waxy, solid mixture of alkanes, used esp. in candles and sealing materials. **2.** Also called **par′affin oil′.** *Brit.* KEROSENE. —*v.t.* **3.** to cover or impregnate with paraffin.

par·a·gon (par′ə gon′, -gən), *n.* a model or pattern of excellence.

par·a·graph (par′ə graf′, -gräf′), *n.* **1.** a distinct portion of written or printed matter dealing with a particular idea, beginning on a new line that is usu. indented. **2.** a brief article or notice, as in a newspaper. —*v.t.* **3.** to divide into paragraphs.

par′agraph mark′, *n.* a character, usu. ¶, used to indicate the beginning of a new paragraph, as in copy for typesetting. Also called **par′agraph sign′.**

Par·a·guay (par′ə gwī′, -gwā′), *n.* **1.** a republic in central South America between Bolivia, Brazil, and Argentina. 5,651,634; 157,047 sq. mi. (406,750 sq. km). *Cap.*: Asunción. **2.** a river in central South America, flowing S from W Brazil through Paraguay to the Paraná. 1500 mi. (2400 km) long. —**Par′a·guay′an,** *adj., n.*

par·a·keet (par′ə kēt′), *n.* any of various small to medium-sized parrots having a long, graduated tail, as the budgerigar and New World parrots of the genus *Aratinga* and allied genera.

par·a·lan·guage (par′ə lang′gwij), *n.* features that accompany speech and contribute to communication but are not considered part of the language system, esp. vocal features, as voice quality, loudness, and tempo.

par·a·le·gal (par′ə lē′gəl), *n.* **1.** an attorney's assistant trained to perform certain legal tasks but not licensed to practice law. —*adj.* **2.** of or pertaining to paralegals.

par·a·lin·guis·tics (par′ə ling gwis′tiks), *n.* (*used with a sing. v.*) the study of paralanguage. —**par′a·lin·guis′tic,** *adj.*

par·al·lax (par′ə laks′), *n.* **1.** the apparent displacement of an observed object due to a change in the position of the observer. **2.** the apparent angular displacement of a celestial body due to its being observed from the surface instead of from the center of the earth or due to its being observed from the earth instead of from the sun. **3.** the difference between the view of an object as seen through the picture-taking lens of a camera and the view as seen through a separate viewfinder. —**par′al·lac′tic** (-lak′tik), *adj.* —**par′al·lac′ti·cal·ly,** *adv.*

par·al·lel (par′ə lel′, -ləl), *adj., n., v.,* **-leled, -lel·ing** or (*esp. Brit.*) **-lelled, -lel·ling,** *adv.* —*adj.* **1.** extending in the same direction, equidistant at all points, and never converging or diverging: *parallel rows of chairs.* **2.** having the same direction, nature, tendency, or course; corresponding; similar: *parallel interests.* **3. a.** (of straight lines) lying in the same plane but never meeting no matter how far extended. **b.** (of planes) having common perpendiculars. **c.** (of a single line, plane, etc.) equidistant from another or others (usu. fol. by *to* or *with*). **4.** having parts that are parallel. **5.** having electrical components connected in parallel: *a parallel circuit.* **6. a.** progressing at the same intervalic distance: *parallel lines in music.* **b.** sharing the same tonic: *A major and A minor are parallel keys.* **7. a.** of or pertaining to operations within a computer that are performed simultaneously: *parallel processing.* **b.** pertaining to or supporting the transfer of electronic data several bits at a time (disting. from *serial*). —*n.* **8.** a parallel line or plane. **9.** anything parallel or comparable in direction, course, nature, or tendency, to something else. **10.** any of the imaginary lines bearing E and W on the earth's surface, parallel to the equator, that mark the latitude. **11.** something identical in essential respects: *a case without a parallel.* **12.** correspondence or analogy. **13.** a comparison of things as if regarded side by side. **14.** an arrangement of an electrical circuit whereby all positive terminals are connected to one point and all negative ones to another. **15.** a pair of vertical parallel lines (‖) used in printing as a reference mark. —*v.t.* **16.** to provide a parallel for; match. **17.** to be in a parallel course to: *The road parallels the river.* **18.** to form a parallel to; equal. **19.** to compare. **20.** to make parallel. —*adv.* **21.** in a parallel course or manner. [< Latin *parallēlus* < Greek *parállēlos* side by side]

par′allel bars′, *n.pl.* a gymnasium apparatus consisting of two horizontal bars on uprights, used for various exercises.

par·al·lel·e·pi·ped (par′ə lel′ə pī′pid, -pip′id), *n.* a prism with six faces, all parallelograms.

par·al·lel·ism (par′ə lel′iz′əm, -lə liz′-), *n.* **1.** the fact or condition of being parallel; agreement in character, direction, etc. **2.** the position or relation of parallels. **3.** a parallel or comparison. **4.** the philosophical theory that mental and physical processes are concomitant but not causally related. **5.** the repetition of a syntactic structure for rhetorical effect. —**par′al·lel·ist,** *n.*

par·al·lel·o·gram (par′ə lel′ə gram′), *n.* a quadrilateral having both pairs of opposite sides parallel to each other.

parallelogram

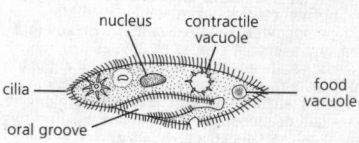

pa·ral·y·sis (pə ral′ə sis), *n., pl.* **-ses** (-sēz′). **1. a.** a loss or impairment of movement or sensation in a body part, caused by injury or disease of the nerves, brain, or spinal cord. **b.** a disease characterized by this, esp. palsy. **2.** a state of helpless stoppage or inability to act.

par·a·lyt·ic (par′ə lit′ik), *n.* **1.** a person affected with paralysis. —*adj.* **2.** affected with or subject to paralysis. **3.** pertaining to or of the nature of paralysis. —**par′a·lyt′i·cal·ly,** *adv.*

par·a·lyze (par′ə līz′), *v.t.,* **-lyzed, -lyz·ing. 1.** to affect with paralysis. **2.** to bring to a condition of helpless stoppage or inability to act. Also, *esp. Brit.,* **par′a·lyse′.** —**par′a·ly·za′tion,** *n.* —**par′a·lyz′er,** *n.* —**par′a·lyz′ing·ly,** *adv.*

Par·a·mar·i·bo (par′ə mar′ə bō′), *n.* a seaport in and the capital of Suriname. 110,867.

par·a·me·ci·um (par′ə mē′shē əm, -shəm, -sē əm), *n., pl.* **-ci·a** (-shē ə, -sē ə). a freshwater protozoan of the genus *Paramecium*, having an oval body with a long, deep oral groove and a fringe of cilia.

nucleus   contractile vacuole

cilia   food vacuole

oral groove

paramecium

par·a·med·ic (par′ə med′ik), *n.* a person who is trained to assist a physician or to give first aid or other health care in the absence of a physician.

par·a·med·i·cal (par′ə med′i kəl), *adj.* related to the medical profession in a secondary or supplementary capacity.

pa·ram·e·ter (pə ram′i tər), *n.* **1. a.** a constant or variable term in a mathematical function that determines the specific form of the function but not its general nature, as a in $f(x) = ax$, where a determines only the slope of the line described by $f(x)$. **b.** one of the independent variables in a set of parametric equations. **2.** a variable entering into the mathematical form of any statistical distribution such that the possible values of the variable correspond to different distributions. **3.** a variable that must be given a specific value during the execution of either a computer program or a procedure within a program. **4.** Usu., **parameters.** limits or boundaries; guidelines: *to keep within the parameters of the discussion.* **5.** a determining characteristic; factor: *a useful parameter for judging long-term success.* —**par·a·met′ric** (par′ə me′trik), **par′a·met′ri·cal,** *adj.* —**Usage.** Some object strongly to the use of PARAMETER in the newer senses, "limits" or "characteristic." Nevertheless, the criticized uses are now well established both in educated speech and in edited writing.

par·a·mil·i·tar·y (par′ə mil′i ter′ē), *adj., n., pl.* **-tar·ies.** —*adj.* **1.** of or designating an organization operating in place of, as a supplement to, or in a manner resembling a regular military force. —*n.* **2.** Also, **par′a·mil′i·ta·rist** (-tər ist). a person employed in such a force.

par·a·mount (par′ə mount′), *adj.* **1.** chief in importance or impact; supreme; preeminent. **2.** above others in rank or authority; superior. —**par′a·mount·ly,** *adv.*

par·a·mour (par′ə mŏŏr′), *n.* **1.** an illicit lover. **2.** any lover.

par·a·myx·o·vi·rus (par′ə mik′sə vī′rəs, -mik′sə vī′-), *n., pl.* **-rus·es.** any of various RNA-containing viruses of the family Paramyxoviridae: includes viruses causing measles and mumps.

Pa·ran (pā′ran), *n.* a desert in Palestine. Gen. 14:6; 21:21; Num. 10:12; 12:16; I Sam. 25:1; I Kings 11:18.

par·a·noi·a (par′ə noi′ə), *n.* **1.** a mental disorder characterized by systematized delusions ascribing hostile intentions to other persons, often linked with a sense of mission. **2.** baseless or excessive distrust of others.

par·a·noid (par′ə noid′), *adj.* **1.** Also, **par′a·noi′dal.** of, like, or suffering from paranoia. —*n.* **2.** a person suffering from paranoia.

par·a·nor·mal (par′ə nôr′məl), *adj.* of or pertaining to events or perceptions occurring without scientific explanation, as clairvoyance or extrasensory perception. —**par′a·nor′mal·ly,** *adv.*

par·a·pet (par′ə pit, -pet′), *n.* **1.** a wall or elevation in a fortification, esp. one at the outer edge of a rampart. **2.** any low protective wall or barrier at the edge of a balcony, roof, bridge, or the like. —**par′a·pet·ed,** *adj.*

par·a·pher·na·lia (par′ə fər nāl′yə, -fə nāl′-), *n.* **1.** (*often used with a pl. v.*) equipment, apparatus, or furnishings used in or necessary for a particular activity. **2.** (*used with a pl. v.*) personal belongings. **3.** (*used with a sing. v.*) *Law.* the personal property of a married woman, which she may bequeath.

par·a·phrase (par′ə frāz′), *n., v.,* **-phrased, -phras·ing.** —*n.* **1.** a restatement of a text or passage giving the meaning in another form, as

P

for clearness; rewording. **2.** the act or process of restating or rewording. —*v.t.* **3.** to render the meaning of in a paraphrase. —*v.i.* **4.** to make a paraphrase. —**par′a•phras′a•ble,** *adj.* —**par′a•phras′er,** *n.*

par•a•phras•tic (par′ə fras′tik), *adj.* having the nature of a paraphrase. —**par′a•phras′ti•cal•ly,** *adv.*

par•a•ple•gi•a (par′ə plē′jē ə, -jə), *n.* paralysis of both lower limbs due to spinal disease or injury. —**par′a•ple′gic** (-plē′jik), *adj., n.*

par•a•pro•fes•sion•al (par′ə prə fesh′ə nl), *n.* **1.** a person trained to assist a doctor, lawyer, teacher, or other professional. —*adj.* **2.** of or pertaining to paraprofessionals.

par•a•psy•chol•o•gy (par′ə sī kol′ə jē), *n.* the branch of psychology that studies psychic phenomena, as clairvoyance and telepathy. —**par′a•psy′cho•log′i•cal,** *adj.* —**par′a•psy•chol′o•gist,** *n.*

par•a•sail (par′ə sāl′), *n.* **1.** a parachutelike device that enables the user to soar when towed behind a car or motorboat. —*v.i.* **2.** to engage in parasailing.

par•a•sail•ing (par′ə sā′ling), *n.* the sport of soaring while harnessed to a parasail.

pa•ra•shah (pär′ə shä′), *n., pl.* **pa•ra•shoth, pa•ra•shot** (pär′ə shōt′). **1.** a portion of the Torah read in the synagogue on the Sabbath and holy days. **2.** a selection from such a portion.

par•a•site (par′ə sīt′), *n.* **1.** an organism that lives on or within a plant or animal of another species, from which it obtains nutrients (opposed to *host*). **2.** a person who receives support or advantage from another without giving any useful or proper return, as one who lives on the hospitality of others. **3.** (esp. in ancient Greece) a person receiving free meals in return for amusing conversation or flattery.

par•a•sit•ic (par′ə sit′ik) also **par′a•sit′i•cal,** *adj.* **1.** of, pertaining to, or characteristic of parasites. **2.** (of diseases) due to parasites. **3.** EXCRESCENT (def. 2). —**par′a•sit′i•cal•ly,** *adv.*

par•a•si•tol•o•gy (par′ə sī tol′ə jē, -si-), *n.* the branch of biology dealing with parasites and parasitism. —**par′a•si•to•log′i•cal** (-sīt′ə loj′i kəl), *adj.* —**par′a•si•tol′o•gist,** *n.*

par•a•sol (par′ə sôl′, -sol′), *n.* a lightweight umbrella used by women as a sunshade.

par′asol mush′room, *n.* a common edible field mushroom, *Macrolepiota (Lepiota) procera,* with a light brown, scaly cap.

par•a•sym•pa•thet•ic (par′ə sim′pə thet′ik), *adj.* pertaining to that part of the autonomic nervous system consisting of nerves and ganglia that arise from the cranial and sacral regions and generally function in regulatory opposition to the sympathetic system, as in slowing heartbeat or contracting the pupil of the eye.

par•a•thy•roid (par′ə thī′roid), *adj.* **1.** situated near the thyroid gland. —*n.* **2.** PARATHYROID GLAND.

parathy′roid gland′, *n.* any of several small paired glands in vertebrates, lying near or embedded in the thyroid gland, that secrete parathyroid hormone.

parathy′roid hor′mone, *n.* a polypeptide hormone, produced in the parathyroid glands, that helps regulate the blood levels of calcium and phosphate. *Abbr.:* PTH

par•a•troop•er (par′ə trōō′pər), *n.* a member of an infantry unit trained to land in combat areas by parachuting from airplanes.

par•boil (pär′boil′), *v.t.* to boil partially or for a short time, as to facilitate further cooking.

par•cel (pär′səl), *n., v.,* **-celed, -cel•ing** or (*esp. Brit.*) **-celled, -cel•ling,** —*n.* **1.** an object or objects wrapped or packed up to form a small bundle; package. **2.** a quantity or unit of something, as of a commodity for sale; lot. **3.** a group or assemblage of persons or things. **4.** a distinct, continuous tract of land. **5.** a part, portion, or fragment. —*v.t.* **6.** to divide into or distribute in portions (usu. fol. by *out*). **7.** to make into or wrap as a parcel. **8.** to cover or wrap (a rope) with strips of canvas.

par′cel post′, *n.* **1.** (in the U.S. Postal Service) parcels weighing one pound or more sent at fourth-class rates. **2.** the branch of a postal service that delivers parcels.

parch (pärch), *v.t.* **1.** to make extremely, excessively, or completely dry, as heat, sun, and wind do. **2.** to make thirsty. **3.** to dry (peas, beans, grain, etc.) by exposure to heat without burning. **4.** to dry or shrivel with cold. —*v.i.* **5.** to suffer from heat, thirst, or need of water. **6.** to become parched; undergo drying by heat.

parch•ment (pärch′mənt), *n.* **1.** the skin of sheep, goats, etc., prepared for writing on. **2.** a manuscript or document on such material. **3.** a stiff off-white paper treated to resemble this material. **4.** a diploma.

pard•ner (pärd′nər), *n. Informal.* partner; friend (often used in direct address).

par•don (pär′dn), *n.* **1.** kind indulgence, as in forgiveness for an offense or in tolerance of an inconvenience: *I beg your pardon.* **2. a.** a legal release from the penalty of an offense, as by a government official. **b.** a document declaring such release. **3.** forgiveness of a serious offense or offender. —*v.t.* **4.** to excuse or make courteous allowance for: *Pardon me for interfering.* **5.** to release (a person) from liability for an offense. **6.** to remit the penalty of (an offense). —*interj.* **7.** (used with rising inflection when asking a speaker to repeat something.) —**par′don•a•ble,** *adj.* —**par′don•a•bly,** *adv.*

par•don•er (pär′dn ər), *n.* **1.** a person who pardons. **2.** (during the Middle Ages) an ecclesiastic authorized to sell indulgences.

pare (pâr), *v.t.,* **pared, par•ing. 1.** to cut off or trim the outer coating, layer, edge, or part of: *to pare an apple; to pare one's nails.* **2.** to reduce

or remove by or as if by cutting; diminish or decrease gradually (often fol. by *down*): *to pare down expenses.*

par•e•gor•ic (par′i gôr′ik, -gor′-), *n.* an opium derivative used as a mild sedative and to treat diarrhea.

pa•ren•chy•ma (pə reng′kə mə), *n.* **1.** the fundamental tissue of plants, composed of thin-walled cells able to divide. **2.** the functional tissue of an animal organ as distinguished from its connective or supporting tissue. **3.** a soft, spongy connective tissue of certain invertebrates, as the flatworms. —**pa•ren′chy•mal, par•en•chym•a•tous** (par′əng kim′ə təs), *adj.*

par•ent (pâr′ənt, par′-), *n.* **1.** a father or a mother. **2.** a source, origin, or cause. **3.** any organism that produces another. **4.** a precursor; progenitor. —*adj.* **5.** being the original source. **6.** pertaining to an organism, cell, or structure that produces another. **7.** of or designating an enterprise that owns controlling interests in one or more subsidiaries. —*v.t.* **8.** to be or act as parent of. —**par′ent•hood,** *n.*

par•ent•age (pâr′ən tij, par′-), *n.* **1.** derivation or descent from parents or ancestors; birth, origin, or lineage. **2.** the state or relation of a parent; parenthood.

pa•ren•tal (pə ren′tl), *adj.* **1.** of or pertaining to a parent. **2.** proper to or characteristic of a parent. **3.** *Genetics.* pertaining to the sequence of generations preceding the filial generation, each generation being designated by a P followed by a subscript number indicating its place in the sequence. —**pa•ren′tal•ly,** *adv.*

paren′tal leave′, *n.* a leave of absence for a parent to care for a new baby.

pa•ren•the•sis (pə ren′thə sis), *n., pl.* **-ses** (-sēz′). **1.** either or both of a pair of signs ( ) used in writing to mark off an interjected explanatory or qualifying remark, to indicate separate groupings of symbols in mathematics or symbolic logic, etc. **2.** Usu., **parentheses.** the material contained within these marks. **3.** a qualifying, explanatory, or appositive word, phrase, or clause that interrupts a syntactic construction without otherwise affecting it, set off in speech by intonation and in writing by commas, parentheses, or dashes, as *Bill Smith—you've met him—is coming tonight.* **4.** an interval.

par•en•thet•ic (par′ən thet′ik) also **par′en•thet′i•cal,** *adj.* **1.** of, pertaining to, or of the nature of a parenthesis: *parenthetic remarks.* **2.** using or placed within parentheses. —**par′en•thet′i•cal•ly,** *adv.*

par•ent•ing (pâr′ən ting, par′-), *n.* the rearing of children by parents.

par′ent-in-law′, *n., pl.* **par•ents-in-law.** the father or mother of one's wife or husband.

par•es•the•sia or **par•aes•the•sia** (par′əs thē′zhə, -zhē ə, -zē ə), *n.* an abnormal tingling or prickling sensation; pins and needles. —**par′es•thet′ic** (-thet′ik), *adj.*

pa•re•ve (pär′ə və, pär′və) also **parve,** *adj. Judaism.* containing neither meat nor milk nor their derivatives and thus permissible for use with either meat or dairy meals in accordance with the dietary laws: *pareve margarine.*

par ex•cel•lence (pär ek′sə läns′, ek′sə lans′), *adj.* being an example of excellence; superior: *an orator par excellence.* [< French]

par•fait (pär fā′), *n.* **1.** a dessert of layered ice cream, fruit, or syrup, and whipped cream. **2.** a frozen dessert of flavored whipped cream or custard.

par•he•li•on (pär hē′lē ən, -hēl′yən), *n., pl.* **-he•li•a** (-hē′lē ə, -hēl′yə). a bright spot on the solar halo similar in origin to the parhelic circle. —**par•he′lic, par/he•li•a•cal** (-hi lī′ə kəl), *adj.*

pa•ri•ah (pə rī′ə), *n.* **1.** OUTCAST. **2.** any person or animal that is generally despised or avoided.

pa•ri•es (pâr′ē ēz′), *n., pl.* **pa•ri•e•tes** (pə rī′i tēz′). Often, **parietes.** the wall of an internal organ or cavity.

pa•ri•e•tal (pə rī′i tl), *adj.* **1.** of or pertaining to the wall of an organ or cavity. **2.** of, pertaining to, or situated near the parietal bones of the skull. **3.** proceeding or arising from a wall, as ovules from an ovary in certain plants. **4.** pertaining to or having authority over residence within the walls of a college. —*n.* **5.** any of several parts in the parietal region of the skull, esp. the parietal bone.

pari′etal bone′, *n.* either of a pair of bones forming, by their union at the sagittal suture, part of the sides and top of the skull.

pari′etal lobe′, *n.* the middle part of each cerebral hemisphere behind the central sulcus.

par•i•mu•tu•el or **par•i•mu•tu•el** (par′i myōō′chōō əl), *n.* **1.** a form of betting on horse races, in which those holding winning tickets divide the total amount bet in proportion to their wagers. **2.** Also called **pari-mu′tuel machine′.** an electronic machine that registers bets in pari-mutuel betting as they are made and calculates and posts the changing odds and final payoffs.

par•ing (pâr′ing), *n.* **1.** the act of a person or thing that pares. **2.** a piece or part pared off: *apple parings.*

par′ing knife′, *n.* a short-bladed kitchen knife for paring fruits and vegetables.

Par•is[1] (par′is; *Fr.* pA rē′), *n.* **1.** the capital of France, in the N part, on the Seine. 2,188,918. **2. Treaty of, a.** a treaty signed in 1763 by France, Spain, and Great Britain that ended the Seven Years' War and the French and Indian War. **b.** a treaty signed in 1783 by the United States and Great Britain that ended the American Revolution. **c.** a treaty signed in 1898 by the United States and Spain that ended the Spanish-American War. —**Pa•ri•sian** (pə rē′zhən, -rizh′ən), *adj., n.*

Par·is[2] (par′is), *n.* a Trojan prince, son of Priam and Hecuba, whose abduction of Helen led to the Trojan War.

Par′is Com·mune′, *n.* COMMUNE[3] (def. 6).

par·ish (par′ish), *n.* **1.** an ecclesiastical district having its own church and cleric. **2.** a local church with its field of activity. **3.** (in Louisiana) a county. **4.** the people of a parish. **5.** HOUSE (def. 13).

pa·rish·ion·er (pə rish′ə nər), *n.* one of the members or inhabitants of a parish. —**pa·rish′ion·er·ship′,** *n.*

par·i·ty[1] (par′i tē), *n., pl.* **-ties. 1.** equality, as in amount, status, or character. **2.** equivalence or correspondence; similarity. **3. a.** equivalent value in the currency of another country. **b.** equivalent value at a fixed ratio between moneys of different metals. **4.** the property of symmetry between a subatomic particle and its mirror image, indicated by +1 if the two are indistinguishable and by −1 if they are different. **5.** a system of regulating prices of farm commodities, usu. by government price supports, to provide farmers with the same purchasing power they had in a selected base period. **6.** the status, as even or odd, of the total number of bits per byte or word: used to detect errors in a computer system or in data communications.

par·i·ty[2] (par′i tē), *n.* **1.** the condition of having borne offspring. **2.** PARA[3] (def. 1).

par′ity check′, *n.* a method for detecting errors in data communications or within a computer system by counting the number of ones or zeros per byte or per word, including a special check bit (**par′ity bit′,**) to see if the value is even or odd.

park (pärk), *n.* **1.** a public area of land, usu. in a natural state, having facilities for recreation. **2.** an enclosed area or a stadium used for sports. **3.** the grounds of a country house. **4.** *Western U.S.* a broad valley in a mountainous region. **5.** a space where vehicles, esp. automobiles, may be assembled or stationed. **6.** AMUSEMENT PARK. **7.** THEME PARK. **8.** INDUSTRIAL PARK. **9.** a setting in an automatic transmission in which the transmission is in neutral and the brake is engaged. —*v.t.* **10.** to leave (a vehicle) in a certain place for a period of time. **11.** *Informal.* to put, leave, or settle. **12.** to place (a satellite) in orbit. —*v.i.* **13.** to park a vehicle. —**park′like′,** *adj.*

Park (pärk), *n.* **Mungo,** 1771–1806?, Scottish explorer in Africa.

par·ka (pär′kə), *n., pl.* **-kas.** a hooded, usu. straight-cut coat or jacket made of materials that protect against very cold temperatures.

Par·ker (pär′kər), *n.* **1. Charles Christopher, Jr.** (*Charlie, "Bird"*), 1920–55, U.S. jazz saxophonist and composer. **2. Dorothy (Rothschild),** 1893–1967, U.S. author. **3. Sir Gilbert,** 1862–1932, Canadian novelist and politician in England. **4. Matthew,** 1504–75, English theologian. **5. Theodore,** 1810–60, U.S. preacher, theologian, and reformer.

Par′ker House′ roll′, *n.* a soft dinner roll made by folding a flat disk of dough in half. [after the *Parker House* hotel in Boston, which originally served the rolls]

park′ing brake′, *n.* EMERGENCY BRAKE.

park′ing lot′, *n.* an area intended for parking motor vehicles.

park′ing me′ter, *n.* a mechanical device for receiving and registering payment for the length of time that a vehicle occupies a parking space.

Par′kin·son's disease′ (pär′kin sənz), *n.* a neurologic disease believed to be caused by deterioration of the brain cells that produce dopamine, occurring primarily after the age of 60, and characterized by tremors, esp. of the fingers and hands, muscle rigidity, and a shuffling gait. Also called **par′kin·son·ism** (-sə niz′əm), **paralysis agitans.** [after James *Parkinson* (1755–1824), English physician who first described it]

Par′kinson's law′ (or **Law′**), *n.* any of various statements about business and office management expressed facetiously as if a law of physics, as the statement that work expands to fill the time allotted for its completion. [after C. Northcote *Parkinson* (born 1909), English historian, who proposed them]

park·way (pärk′wā′), *n.* a broad thoroughfare with a dividing strip or side strips planted with grass, trees, etc.

par·lance (pär′ləns), *n.* a way or manner of speaking; vernacular; jargon: *legal parlance.*

par·lay (pär′lā, -lē), *v.t.* **1.** to bet or gamble (an original amount and its winnings) on a subsequent contest. **2.** to use (assets) to achieve a relatively great gain: *to parlay a modest inheritance into a fortune.* —*n.* **3.** a bet of an original sum and the subsequent winnings.

par·ley (pär′lē), *n., pl.* **-leys. 1.** discussion; conference. **2.** a conference between enemies under a truce. —*v.i.* **3.** to hold a parley.

par·lia·ment (pär′lə mənt; *sometimes* pärl′yə-), *n.* **1.** (*cap.*) the national legislature of Great Britain, consisting of the House of Commons and the House of Lords. **2.** (*cap.*) the national legislature of certain former British colonies and possessions. **3.** (*cap.*) the national legislature in various other countries. **4.** any of several high courts of justice in France before 1789. **5.** an assembly on public or national affairs.

par·lia·men·tar·i·an (pär′lə men târ′ē ən, -mən-; *sometimes* pärl′yə-), *n.* **1.** an expert in parliamentary rules and procedures. **2.** (*cap.*) a partisan of the British Parliament in opposition to Charles I.

par·lia·men·ta·ry (pär′lə men′tə rē, -trē; *sometimes* pärl′yə-), *adj.* **1.** of, characteristic of, dealt with, or enacted by a Parliament. **2.** having a Parliament. **3.** in accordance with parliamentary law: *parliamentary procedure.* —**par′lia·men·ta·ri·ly,** *adv.*

par′liamen′tary gov′ernment, *n.* government by a body of cabinet ministers who are chosen from and responsible to the legislature and act as advisers to a nominal chief of state.

par′liamen′tary law′, *n.* the body of rules, usages, and precedents governing the proceedings of legislative and deliberative assemblies.

par·lor (pär′lər), *n.* **1.** a room in a home for receiving visitors; living room. **2.** a shop or business establishment: *ice-cream parlor; beauty parlor.* **3.** a somewhat private room in a hotel, club, or the like for relaxation, conversation, etc.; lounge. —*adj.* **4.** advocating a political view or doctrine at a safe remove from actual involvement or commitment to action: *parlor socialist.* Also, *esp. Brit.,* **parlour.**

par′lor car′, *n.* a railroad passenger car that has individual reserved seats and is more comfortable than a day coach.

par′lor game′, *n.* any game usu. played indoors, as a word game.

par′lor grand′, *n.* a grand piano smaller than a concert grand but larger than a baby grand.

par·lous (pär′ləs), *adj.* perilous; dangerous. —**par′lous·ly,** *adv.* —**par′lous·ness,** *n.*

Par·me·san (pär′mə zän′, -zan′, -zən; pär′mə zän′, -zan′), *adj.* **1.** of or from Parma, in N Italy. —*n.* **2.** (*sometimes l.c.*) Also called **Par′mesan cheese′.** a hard, dry Italian cheese made from skim milk and usu. grated.

par·mi·gia·na (pär′mə zhä′nə, -zhän′, -jä′nə, -jän′) also **par·mi·gia·no** (-zhä′nō, -jä′-), *adj.* cooked with Parmesan cheese: *veal parmigiana.*

Par·nas·sus (pär nas′əs), *n.* **Mount,** a mountain in central Greece, N of the Gulf of Corinth and near Delphi. ab. 8000 ft. (2440 m).

Par·nell (pär nel′, pär′nl), *n.* **Charles Stewart,** 1846–91, Irish political leader. —**Par·nell′ite,** *n.*

pa·ro·chi·al (pə rō′kē əl), *adj.* **1.** of or pertaining to a parish or parishes. **2.** of or pertaining to parochial schools. **3.** very limited or narrow in scope or outlook; provincial. —**pa·ro′chi·al·ly,** *adv.*

pa·ro·chi·al·ism (pə rō′kē ə liz′əm), *n.* a parochial attitude or outlook; narrowness or provincialism. —**pa·ro′chi·al·ist,** *n.*

paro′chial school′, *n.* a primary or secondary school maintained by a religious organization.

par·o·dy (par′ə dē), *n., pl.* **-dies,** *v.,* **-died, -dy·ing.** —*n.* **1.** a humorous or satirical imitation of a serious piece of literature or writing. **2.** any humorous, satirical, or burlesque imitation, as of a person, event, etc. **3.** a burlesque imitation of a musical composition. **4.** a poor or feeble imitation; travesty. —*v.t.* **5.** to imitate (a composition, author, etc.) for purposes of ridicule or satire. **6.** to imitate feebly; travesty. —**par′o·di·a·ble,** *adj.*

pa·role (pə rōl′), *n., v.,* **-roled, -rol·ing.** —*n.* **1.** the conditional release of a person from prison prior to the end of the sentence imposed. **2. a.** the promise of a prisoner of war not to take up arms again if released or to abide by other conditions. **b.** a password given by authorized personnel in passing by a guard. **3.** word of honor given or pledged. —*v.t.* **4.** to place or release on parole. —*adj.* **5.** of or pertaining to parole or parolees: *a parole violation.* [< Middle French, short for *parole d'honneur* word of honor] —**pa·rol′a·ble,** *adj.*

pa·rol·ee (pə rō lē′, -rō′lē), *n.* a person receiving a parole.

par·o·nym (par′ə nim), *n.* a paronymous word.

pa·ron·y·mous (pə ron′ə məs), *adj.* containing the same root or stem, as the words *wise* and *wisdom.*

Par·ou·si·a (pə rōō′zē ə, -sē ə, pär′ōō sē′ə), *n.* SECOND COMING. [< Greek *parousía* a being present, presence]

par·ox·ysm (par′ək siz′əm), *n.* **1.** any sudden, violent outburst, as of action or emotion: *paroxysms of rage.* **2.** a severe attack or a sudden increase in intensity of a disease, usu. recurring periodically. —**par′ox·ys′mal, par′ox·ys′mic,** *adj.* —**par′ox·ys′mal·ly,** *adv.*

par·quet (pär kā′), *n.* (-kād′), *v.,* **-quet·ing** (-kā′ing), *v.,* **-queted. 1.** a floor composed of short strips or blocks of wood forming a pattern, sometimes with inlays of other woods or other materials. **2.** the front part of the main floor of a theater, opera house, etc., between the musicians' area and the parterre or, esp. in the U.S., the entire main-floor space for spectators. —*v.t.* **3.** to construct (a floor) of parquetry.

par·que·try (pär′ki trē), *n.* mosaic work of wood used for floors, wainscoting, etc.; marquetry.

par·ri·cide (par′ə sīd′), *n.* **1.** the killing of one's father, mother, or other close relative. **2.** a person who commits such an act. —**par′ri·cid′al,** *adj.*

par·rot (par′ət), *n.* **1.** any of numerous gregarious, noisy, often brilliantly colored birds of the order Psittaciformes, principally of the tropics and warmer regions of the Southern Hemisphere: some species have the ability to mimic speech when in captivity. **2.** a person who, without thought or understanding, repeats the words of another. —*v.t.* **3.** to repeat without thought or understanding.

par′rot fe′ver, *n.* PSITTACOSIS.

par·rot·fish (par′ət fish′), *n., pl.* (*esp. collectively*) **-fish,** (*esp. for kinds or species*) **-fish·es.** any tropical marine fish of the family Scaridae, having brilliant coloring and parrotlike jaws.

parse (pärs, pärz), *v.,* **parsed, pars·ing.** —*v.t.* **1.** to analyze (a sentence) in terms of grammatical constituents, identifying the parts of speech, syntactic relations, etc. **2.** to describe (a word in a sentence) grammatically, identifying the part of speech, inflectional form, syntactic function, etc. —*v.i.* **3.** to admit of being parsed. —**pars′a·ble,** *adj.*

par·sec (pär′sek′), *n.* a unit of distance equal to 206,265 times the distance from the earth to the sun, or 3.26 light years.

Par·see or **Par·si** (pär′sē, pär sē′), *n., pl.* **-sees** or **-sis.** an Indian Zoroastrian whose ancestors fled Muslim persecution in Persia in the 7th and 8th centuries. —**Par′see•ism,** *n.*

par•si•mo•ni•ous (pär′sə mō′nē əs), *adj.* given to parsimony; frugal or stingy. —**par′si•mo′ni•ous•ly,** *adv.* —**par′si•mo′ni•ous•ness,** *n.*

par•si•mo•ny (pär′sə mō′nē), *n.* extreme or excessive economy or frugality; stinginess.

pars•ley (pärs′lē), *n.* **1.** an herb, *Petroselinum crispum,* native to the Mediterranean, having either curled leaf clusters (French parsley) or flat compound leaves (Italian parsley). —*adj.* **2.** Also, **pars′lied, pars′leyed.** cooked or garnished with parsley: *parsley potatoes.*

pars•nip (pär′snip), *n.* **1.** a plant, *Pastinaca sativa,* of the parsley family, cultivated varieties of which have a large white edible root. **2.** the root of this plant.

par•son (pär′sən), *n.* a member of the clergy, esp. a Protestant minister; pastor; rector. —**par′son•ish, par′son•like′,** *adj.*

par•son•age (pär′sə nij), *n.* the residence provided by a parish for its pastor.

part (pärt), *n.* **1.** a portion or division of a whole that is separate or distinct; piece, fraction, or section; constituent: *the rear part of the house.* **2.** an essential or integral quality. **3.** a section or division of a literary work. **4.** a portion, member, or organ of an animal body. **5.** any of a number of quantities that compose a whole: *two parts sugar to one part cocoa.* **6.** an allotted portion; share. **7.** Usu., **parts. a.** a region, quarter, or district: *a journey to foreign parts.* **b.** an attribute establishing the possessor as a person of superior worth. **8.** either of the opposing sides in a contest, contractual agreement, etc. **9.** the dividing line formed in separating the hair of the head when combing it. **10.** a constituent piece of a machine or tool, esp. a replacement for the original piece. **11. a.** the written or printed matter extracted from the score that a single performer or section uses in the performance of concerted music: *a horn part.* **b.** a section or division of a composition. **12.** participation or concern in something; role. **13.** a person's contribution to some effort or action; duty. **14.** a role acted in a play or sustained in real life. —*v.t.* **15.** to divide (a thing) into parts. **16.** to comb (the hair) away from a dividing line. **17.** to divide into shares; apportion. **18.** to put or keep apart; separate: *to part the calves from the herd.* —*v.i.* **19.** to be or become divided into parts; break or cleave. **20.** to go apart from or leave one another, as persons. **21.** to break or become torn apart, as a cable. **22.** to depart. **23.** to die. **24. part with,** to relinquish. —*adj.* **25.** partial; of a part: *part owner.* —*adv.* **26.** in part; partly: *part wool.* —***Idiom.*** **27. for one's part,** as far as concerns one: *For my part, you can do whatever you please.* **28. in good part,** to a great extent; largely. **29. in part,** in some measure or degree. **30. on the part of, a.** on behalf of; concerning. **b.** as done or manifested by: *too much noise on the part of the class.* **31. part and parcel,** an essential, integral part. **32. take part,** to participate; share or partake. **33. take someone's part,** to support or defend someone.

par•take (pär tāk′), *v.,* **-took, -tak•en, -tak•ing.** —*v.i.* **1.** to take part in along with others (usu. fol. by *in*): *to partake in a celebration.* **2.** to receive, take, or have a portion (usu. fol. by *of*): *to partake of a meal.* **3.** to have the nature or character (usu. fol. by *of*): *feelings partaking of both joy and regret.* —*v.t.* **4.** to take or have a part in; share. —**par•tak′er,** *n.*

part•ed (pär′tid), *adj.* **1.** divided into parts; cleft. **2.** divided by a part: *parted hair.* **3.** set or kept apart; separated. **4.** *Bot.* separated into rather distinct portions by incisions that extend nearly to the midrib or the base. —**part′ed•ness,** *n.*

par•terre (pär târ′), *n.* **1.** Also called **parquet circle.** the rear section of seats on the main floor of a theater, opera house, etc., under the balcony. **2.** an arrangement of ornamental flower beds separated by walks. —**par•terred′,** *adj.*

partheno-, a combining form meaning "without fertilization": *parthenogenesis.*

Par•the•non (pär′thə non′, -nən), *n.* a Doric temple of Athena on the Acropolis in Athens, completed c438 B.C.

Par′thian shot′, *n.* a sharp, telling remark made in departing.

par•tial (pär′shəl), *adj.* **1.** being such in part only; incomplete: *partial payment.* **2.** biased or prejudiced in favor of one person, group, side, etc., over another: *The judge was partial.* **3.** pertaining to or affecting a part. **4.** being a part; component; constituent. —***Idiom.*** **5. partial to,** favoring; especially fond of. —**par′tial•ly,** *adv.*

par•ti•al•i•ty (pär′shē al′i tē, pär shal′-), *n., pl.* **-ties. 1.** a favorable bias. **2.** a special fondness or liking.

par•ti•ble (pär′tə bəl), *adj.* capable of being divided or separated; divisible. —**par′ti•bil′i•ty,** *n.*

par•tic•i•pant (pär tis′ə pənt), *n.* **1.** a person or group that participates. —*adj.* **2.** participating; sharing.

par•tic•i•pate (pär tis′ə pāt′), *v.i.,* **-pat•ed, -pat•ing.** to take part or have a share, as with others (usu. fol. by *in*): *to participate in profits; to participate in a conversation.* —**par•tic′i•pa′tive,** *adj.* —**par•tic′i•pa′tor,** *n.* —**par•tic′i•pa•to′ry** (-pə tôr′ē, -tōr′ē), *adj.*

par•tic•i•pa•tion (pär tis′ə pā′shən), *n.* **1.** an act or instance of participating. **2.** a sharing, as in benefits.

par•ti•cip•i•al (pär′tə sip′ē əl), *adj.* of, pertaining to, formed from, or containing a participle. —**par′ti•cip′i•al•ly,** *adv.*

par•ti•ci•ple (pär′tə sip′əl, -sə pəl), *n.* a nonfinite verbal form that can function as an adjective or be used with certain auxiliaries to make compound verb forms, as *burning* in *a burning candle* or *devoted* in *your devoted friend. Abbr.:* part. Compare PAST PARTICIPLE, PRESENT PARTICIPLE. —**Usage.** See DANGLING PARTICIPLE, MISPLACED MODIFIER.

par•ti•cle (pär′ti kəl), *n.* **1.** a minute portion, piece, or amount; a very small bit: *a particle of dust.* **2.** one of the extremely small constituents of matter, as an atom, proton, or quark. **3.** a clause or article, as of a document. **4.** *Gram.* any of various small, usu. uninflected words or affixes having functional or relational rather than lexical use and in some languages constituting a form class: in English often applied to words like *to* used in forming the infinitive or the word following the verb in a phrasal verb, as *up* in *get up.* **5.** a small piece of the Host given to each lay communicant in a Eucharistic service.

par′ticle accel′erator, *n.* an electrostatic or electromagnetic device, as a cyclotron, that produces high-energy particles and focuses them on a target.

par′ticle beam′, *n.* a concentrated stream of subatomic particles generated for studying nuclear structure, crystal structure, etc., or as a military weapon.

par′ticle board′, *n.* any of various composition boards formed from small particles of wood, as flakes, bonded with a resin.

par′ticle phys′ics, *n.* the branch of physics that deals with the properties and behavior of elementary particles.

par•ti-col•ored or **par•ty-col•ored** (pär′tē kul′ərd), *adj.* having different colors in different areas or patches; variegated.

par•tic•u•lar (pər tik′yə lər, pə tik′-), *adj.* **1.** pertaining to a single or specific person, thing, group, etc.; not general: *one's particular interests.* **2.** considered separately from others; specific: *a particular item on a list.* **3.** exceptional or special; unusual: *Take particular pains with this job.* **4.** being such in an exceptional degree: *a particular friend.* **5.** exceptionally selective; fussy: *to be particular about one's food.* **6.** dealing with or giving details; minute. **7.** *Logic.* referring to an indefinite part of a whole class. —*n.* **8.** an individual or distinct part, as an item of a list. **9.** Usu., **particulars.** specific points, details, or circumstances: *the particulars of a case.* **10.** *Logic.* an individual or a specific group within a general class. —***Idiom.*** **11. in particular,** particularly; especially.

par•tic•u•lar•ism (pər tik′yə lə riz′əm, pə tik′-), *n.* **1.** exclusive attention or devotion to one's own particular interests, party, etc. **2.** the principle of leaving each member of a federation or other political group free to promote its interests.

par•tic•u•lar•i•ty (pər tik′yə lar′i tē, pə tik′-), *n., pl.* **-ties. 1.** the quality or state of being particular. **2.** detailed character, as of description or statement. **3.** attention to details; fastidiousness. **4.** an individual or characteristic feature or trait; peculiarity.

par•tic•u•lar•ize (pər tik′yə lə rīz′, pə tik′-), *v.,* **-ized, -iz•ing.** —*v.t.* **1.** to state or treat in detail. —*v.i.* **2.** to give details; be specific. —**par•tic′u•lar•i•za′tion,** *n.*

par•tic•u•lar•ly (pər tik′yə lər lē, pə tik′-), *adv.* **1.** to an exceptional degree; especially. **2.** specifically; individually. **3.** in detail.

par•tic•u•late (pər tik′yə lit, -lāt′, pə tik′-, pär-), *adj.* **1.** of, pertaining to, or composed of distinct particles. —*n.* **2.** a separate and distinct particle. **3.** a material composed of such particles. **4. particulates, a.** the aggregate of such particles: *diesel particulates.* **b.** particles suspended in the atmosphere, esp. pollutants.

part•ing (pär′ting), *n.* **1.** a division; separation. **2.** a place of division or separation. **3.** departure; leave-taking. —*adj.* **4.** given, taken, or done at parting: *a parting glance.* **5.** departing: *the parting day.*

par•ti•san¹ (pär′tə zən, -sən; *Brit.* pär′tə zan′), *n.* **1.** an adherent or supporter of a person, party, or cause, esp. one who shows a biased, unthinking allegiance. **2.** a member of a guerrilla band engaged in fighting an occupying army. —*adj.* **3.** of, pertaining to, or characteristic of partisans. —**par′ti•san•ship′,** *n.*

par•ti•san² (pär′tə zən, -sən), *n.* a shafted weapon of the 16th and 17th centuries, having as a head a long spear blade with a pair of curved lobes at the base.

par•tite (pär′tīt), *adj.* **1.** divided into parts (usu. used in combination): *a tripartite agreement.* **2.** *Bot.* parted.

par•ti•tion (pär tish′ən, pər-), *n.* **1.** a division into or distribution in portions or shares. **2.** a separation, as of two or more things. **3.** something that separates or divides. **4.** a part, division, or section. **5.** an interior wall or barrier dividing space into separate areas. **6.** *Logic.* the separation of a whole into its integral parts. **7.** *Math.* a mode of separating a positive whole number into a sum of positive whole numbers. —*v.t.* **8.** to divide into parts or portions. **9.** to divide or separate by a partition (often fol. by *off*): *to partition off a dining area.* **10.** to divide (a country or territory) into separate political entities. —**par•ti′tion•er,** *n.*

par•ti•tive (pär′ti tiv), *adj.* **1.** serving to divide into parts. **2.** (of a word, construction, or grammatical case) indicating a part or quantity of a whole. —*n.* **3.** a partitive word, case, or construction, as *a slice of cake* or the word *some.* —**par′ti•tive•ly,** *adv.*

part•ly (pärt′lē), *adv.* in some degree; partially.

part•ner (pärt′nər), *n.* **1.** a person who shares or is associated with another in some action or endeavor; associate. **2.** one of two or more persons who contribute capital to establish or maintain a commercial venture and who usu. share in the risks and profits. **3.** SILENT PARTNER. **4.** a husband, wife, or lover. **5.** either of two people who dance together. **6.** a player on the same side or team as another. **7. partners,** a framework of timber around a hole in a ship's deck, to support a mast, capstan, etc. —*v.t.* **8.** to associate as a partner or partners with. **9.** to serve as the partner of.

part•ner•ship (pärt′nər ship′), *n.* **1.** the state or condition of being a partner; participation; association; joint interest. **2.** *Law.* **a.** the relation subsisting between partners. **b.** the contract creating this relation. **c.** the persons joined together as partners in business.

part′ of speech′, *n.* any of the classes into which words in a language have traditionally been divided on the basis of their meaning, form, or syntactic function, as, in English, noun, pronoun, verb, adverb, adjective, preposition, conjunction, and interjection.

par•took (pär tŏŏk′), *v.* pt. of PARTAKE.

par•tridge (pär′trij), *n., pl.* **-tridg•es**, (*esp. collectively*) **-tridge. 1.** any of various rotund, orig. Old World gallinaceous birds of the pheasant family, esp. *Perdix perdix*, widely introduced in North America. **2.** any game bird resembling the partridge, as the ruffed grouse or bobwhite.

partridge, *Perdix perdix,*
length 1 to 1 ½ ft. (0.3 to 0.5 m)

par•tridge•ber•ry (pär′trij ber′ē), *n., pl.* **-ries.** a North American trailing plant, *Mitchella repens,* of the madder family, having roundish evergreen leaves, fragrant white flowers, and scarlet berries.

part′-song′, *n.* a song with parts for several voices, esp. one meant to be sung without accompaniment.

part-time (*adj.* pärt′tīm′; *adv.* pärt′tīm′), *adj.* **1.** working or attending school less than the usual or full time. **2.** pertaining to or noting such work or study: *part-time employment.* —*adv.* **3.** on a part-time basis: *to work part-time.* —**part′-tim′er,** *n.*

par•tu•ri•ent (pär tŏŏr′ē ənt, -tyŏŏr′-), *adj.* **1.** bearing or about to bear young. **2.** pertaining to parturition. **3.** bringing forth or about to produce something, as an idea. —**par•tu′ri•en•cy,** *n.*

par•tu•ri•tion (pär′tŏŏ rish′ən, -tyŏō-, -chŏō-), *n.* the act or process of bringing forth young; childbirth.

part•way (pärt′wā′, -wā′), *adv.* **1.** at or to a part of the way: *I'm already partway home.* **2.** in some degree; partly.

par•ty (pär′tē), *n., pl.* **-ties,** *adj., v.,* **-tied, -ty•ing.** —*n.* **1.** a social gathering for conversation, refreshments, entertainment, etc. **2.** a group gathered for some special purpose or task: *a search party.* **3.** a group of persons who support one side of a dispute, question, etc. **4.** a political group organized for gaining political influence and governmental control and for directing government policy. **5.** a person or group that participates in some action, affair, or plan: *He was a party to the merger deal.* **6.** *Law.* **a.** one of the litigants in a legal proceeding; a plaintiff or defendant. **b.** a signatory to a legal instrument. **7.** a detail of troops. **8.** a specific individual. —*adj.* **9.** of or pertaining to a party or faction; partisan: *party leaders.* **10.** of or for a social gathering: *a party dress.* —*v.i.* **11.** to go to or give parties. **12.** to revel; carouse.

par′ty-col′umn bal′lot, *n.* INDIANA BALLOT.

par′ty eld′ers, *n.pl.* veteran, respected members of a political party.

par′ty faith′ful, *n.* (*used with a pl. v.*) loyal supporters of a political party.

par′ty line (pär′tē līn′ *for 1, 2;* pär′tē līn′ *for 3, 4*), *n.* **1.** the authoritatively announced policies and practices of a group, esp. of the Communist Party. **2.** the guiding policy, tenets, or practices of a political party: *The delegates voted along party lines.* **3.** a telephone line connecting the telephones of a number of subscribers by one circuit to a central office. **4.** the boundary line separating adjoining properties. —**par′ty-line′,** *adj.* —**par′ty lin′er,** *n.*

par′ty pol′itics, *n.* politics based on adherence to the policies and principles of a political party regardless of the public interest.

par′ty poop′er (pŏō′pər), *n. Slang.* a person who spoils the enjoyment of others; spoilsport.

par•u•la (par′yə lə, -ə lə), *n., pl.* **-las.** any of several New World wood warblers of the genus *Parula,* esp. *P. americana,* having bluish plumage with a yellow throat and breast. Also called **par′ula war′bler.**

par′ val′ue, *n.* FACE VALUE (def. 1).

par•ve (pär′və), *adj.* PAREVE.

par•ve•nu (pär′və nŏō′, -nyŏō′, pär′və nŏō′, -nyŏō′), *n., pl.* **-nus,** *adj.* —*n.* **1.** a person who has newly acquired wealth or influence, but has not yet acquired the acceptance or social qualifications associated with it. —*adj.* **2.** characteristic of a parvenu.

pas (pä), *n., pl.* **pas** (pä, päz). **1.** a step or series of steps in ballet. **2.** right of precedence.

Pas•a•de•na (pas′ə dē′nə), *n.* **1.** a city in SW California, near Los Angeles. 134,170. **2.** a city in SE Texas, near Houston. 116,880.

pas•cal (pa skal′, pä skäl′), *n.* the SI unit of pressure or stress, equal to one newton per square meter. *Abbr.:* Pa [after Blaise PASCAL]

Pas•cal (pa skal′), *n.* **1.** Blaise, 1623–62, French philosopher and mathematician. **2.** Also, **PASCAL** a high-level computer language, a descendant of ALGOL, designed to facilitate structured programming.

Pasch (pask), *n.* **1.** PASSOVER. **2.** EASTER. —**pas′chal,** *adj.*

pas′chal lamb′, *n.* **1.** a lamb slaughtered and eaten by the ancient Hebrews at Passover. **2.** (*caps.*) JESUS. **3.** (*caps.*) any of several symbolic representations of Christ, as the Agnus Dei.

pas de deux (pä′ də dœ′), *n., pl.* **pas de deux** (dœ′, dœz′). **1.** a dance for two persons. **2.** a set dance for a ballerina and a danseur noble, consisting typically of an entrée, an adagio, a variation for each dancer, and a coda.

pas•quin•ade (pas′kwə nād′), *n., v.,* **-ad•ed, -ad•ing.** —*n.* **1.** a satire or lampoon, esp. one posted in a public place. —*v.t.* **2.** to satirize in a pasquinade. —**pas′quin•ad′er,** *n.*

pass (pas, päs), *v.t.* **1.** to move past; go by: *to pass a car on the road.* **2.** to let go without notice, action, etc.; disregard. **3.** to cause or allow to go through a barrier, obstacle, etc.: *The guard passed the visitor.* **4.** to go across or over (a stream, threshold, etc.); cross. **5.** to endure or undergo. **6.** to undergo or complete successfully: *to pass an examination.* **7.** to cause or permit (a person) to complete an examination, course of study, etc., successfully. **8.** to go beyond (a point, degree, stage, etc.); surpass. **9.** to cause to go or move onward: *to pass a rope through a hole.* **10.** to cause to go or march by: *to pass troops in review.* **11.** to allow to elapse or slip by; spend: *How did you pass the time?* **12.** to cause to circulate or spread: *to pass rumors.* **13.** to cause to be accepted or received: *to pass bad checks.* **14.** to convey from one person to another. **15.** to discharge or void from the body. **16.** to sanction or approve, esp. by vote: *Congress passed the bill.* **17.** to obtain the approval or sanction of: *The bill passed the Senate.* **18.** to express; pronounce: *to pass judgment.* **19.** to omit the usual or regular payment of (a dividend). **20.** to transfer (a ball or puck) to a teammate. **21.** to pledge. —*v.i.* **22.** to go or move onward; proceed. **23.** to come to or toward, then go beyond: *to pass through town.* **24.** to go away; depart: *The feeling will pass.* **25.** to elapse: *The day passed quickly.* **26.** to come to an end: *The crisis soon passed.* **27.** to die (often fol. by *away* or *on*). **28.** to take place; happen; occur. **29.** to go by or move past. **30.** to go about or circulate. **31.** to serve as a marginally acceptable substitute: *The copy isn't very good but it will pass.* **32.** to live or be known as a member of a racial or ethnic group other than one's own, esp. to live and be known as a white person though having some black ancestry. **33.** to be transferred: *The crown passed to the king's nephew.* **34.** to be interchanged: *Sharp words passed between them.* **35.** to undergo transition or conversion: *to pass from a solid to a liquid state.* **36.** to go or get through a barrier, test, etc., successfully. **37.** to go unheeded or unchallenged: *I let the insult pass.* **38.** to express or pronounce an opinion or judgment: *Will you pass on the authenticity of this drawing?* **39.** to be voided, as excrement or a kidney stone. **40.** to obtain the approval or sanction of a legislative body, committee, or the like. **41.** to make a pass, as in football or ice hockey. **42.** *Cards.* **a.** to forgo one's opportunity to bid. **b.** to throw in one's hand. **43.** (in fencing) to thrust. **44. pass off, a.** to present, offer, or sell by fraud or deceit. **b.** to cause to be accepted under a false identity: *He passed himself off as a doctor.* **c.** to continue to completion; occur: *The meeting passed off without incident.* **45. pass out,** to faint. **46. pass over,** to disregard; ignore. **47. pass up,** to refuse or neglect to take advantage of, as an opportunity. —*n.* **48.** an act of passing. **49.** a narrow route across a low notch or depression in a mountain barrier. **50.** a road, channel, or other means of passage, as through an obstructed region. **51.** a permission or license to pass, go, come, or enter. **52.** written permission given a soldier to be absent briefly from a station. **53.** a free ticket or permit. **54.** a particular stage or state of affairs: *The situation came to a dreadful pass.* **55.** a single movement, effort, etc.: *We made a pass at the enemy airfield.* **56.** a jab with the arm, esp. one that misses its mark. **57.** the transfer of a ball or puck from one teammate to another. **58.** WALK (def. 31). **59.** *Cards.* the act or statement of not bidding or raising another bid. **60.** a thrust or lunge made in fencing. —*Idiom.* **61. bring to pass,** to cause to happen; bring about. **62. come to pass,** to happen; occur. **63. pass the buck,** to shift responsibility to another person. **64. pass the time of day,** to chat.

pass•a•ble (pas′ə bəl, pä′sə-), *adj.* **1.** capable of being passed, penetrated, or crossed. **2.** marginally acceptable; adequate: *a passable knowledge of French.* **3.** capable of being circulated legally, as a coin. **4.** capable of being ratified or enacted: *passable legislation.* —**pass′a•ble•ness,** *n.* —**pass′a•bly,** *adv.*

pas•sage (pas′ij), *n., v.,* **-saged, -sag•ing.** —*n.* **1.** a portion or section of a written work; a paragraph, verse, etc.: *a passage of Scripture.* **2.** a phrase or other division of a musical work. **3.** an act or instance of passing from one place, condition, etc., to another. **4.** the permission, right, or freedom to pass. **5.** the route or course by which a person or thing passes or travels. **6.** a hall or corridor; passageway. **7.** an opening or entrance into, through, or out of something: *the nasal passages.* **8.** a voyage by water. **9.** the accommodation on a ship. **10.** the price charged for such accommodation. **11.** a lapse or passing, as of time. **12.** a progress or course, as of events. **13.** the enactment into law of a legislative measure. **14.** an interchange of communications, confidences, etc., between persons. **15.** an exchange of blows; altercation or dispute: *a passage at arms.* **16.** the act of causing something to pass; transference; transmission. **17.** an occurrence, incident, or event. —*v.i.* **18.** to make a passage; cross; pass.

pas′sage grave′, *n.* a chamber tomb with a narrow entrance passage leading to the burial chamber.

pas·sage·way (pas′ij wā′), *n.* a way affording passage, as a corridor, alley, or the like.

pas·sage·work (pas′ij wûrk′), *n.* **1.** musical writing of a virtuosic or decorative character. **2.** the performance of such writing.

pas·sé (pa sā′), *adj.* **1.** old-fashioned; out-of-date; outmoded. **2.** past one's prime.

passed′ ball′, *n.* a pitched baseball that the catcher can reasonably be expected to catch but misses. Compare WILD PITCH.

pas·sel (pas′əl), *n.* a group or lot of indeterminate number: *a passel of kids.*

pas·sen·ger (pas′ən jər), *n.* **1.** a person traveling in an automobile, train, airplane, or other conveyance, esp. one who is not the operator. **2.** a wayfarer.

pas′senger pi′geon, *n.* a North American pigeon, *Ectopistes migratorius,* that once nested in great numbers in hardwood forests: extinct since 1914.

passe-par·tout (pas′pär tōō′), *n.* **1.** something that passes or provides passage everywhere, as a master key. **2.** an ornamental mat for a picture. **3.** a method of framing in which a piece of glass is placed over a picture and is affixed to a backing by means of adhesive strips of paper pasted over the edges. **4.** paper prepared for this purpose.

pass·er·by or **pass·er-by** (pas′ər bī′, -bī′, pä′sər-), *n., pl.* **pass·ers·by** or **pass·ers-by** (pas′ərz bī′, -bī′, pä′sərz-). a person passing by.

pas·ser·ine (pas′ər in, -ə rīn′, -ə rēn′), *adj.* **1.** of, belonging, or pertaining to the order Passeriformes, comprising more than half of all birds and typically having the feet adapted for perching. —*n.* **2.** any bird of the order Passeriformes.

pas·si·ble (pas′ə bəl), *adj.* capable of feeling; susceptible of sensation or emotion. —**pas′si·bil′i·ty,** *n.*

pas·sim (pas′im), *adv.* here and there (used in bibliographic references).

pass·ing (pas′ing, pä′sing), *adj.* **1.** going past; elapsing: *each passing day.* **2.** brief; fleeting: *a passing fancy.* **3.** superficial; cursory: *a passing mention.* **4.** indicating satisfactory performance, as in a test: *a passing grade.* —*adv.* **5.** surpassingly; very: *passing strange.* —*n.* **6.** the act of a person or thing that passes or causes to pass. **7.** DEATH. —*Idiom.* **8. in passing,** by the way; incidentally. —**pass′ing·ly,** *adv.*

pas·sion (pash′ən), *n.* **1.** compelling emotion. **2.** strong amorous feeling; love. **3.** strong sexual desire; lust. **4.** a strong fondness, enthusiasm, or desire for something: *a passion for music.* **5.** the object of one's passion. **6.** an outburst of emotion. **7.** violent anger; wrath; rage. **8.** (*often cap.*) **a.** the sufferings of Christ on the cross or subsequent to the Last Supper. **b.** the Gospel narrative of Christ's sufferings or a musical setting of this. —**pas′sion·ful,** *adj.*

pas·sion·ate (pash′ə nit), *adj.* **1.** having, compelled by, or ruled by intense emotion or strong feeling; fervid; zealous. **2.** easily aroused to or influenced by sexual desire; ardently sensual. **3.** expressing, showing, or marked by intense or strong feeling; emotional: *passionate language.* **4.** intense or vehement, as emotions or feelings: *passionate grief.* **5.** easily moved to anger; hotheaded. —**pas′sion·ate·ly,** *adv.*

pas·sion·flow·er (pash′ən flou′ər), *n.* any of numerous American climbing vines or shrubs of the genus *Passiflora,* having showy flowers and a pulpy berry or fruit that is edible in some species.

pas·sion·fruit (pash′ən frōōt′), *n.* any edible fruit of a passionflower, as the maypop.

pas·sion·less (pash′ən lis), *adj.* not feeling or moved by passion; cold; detached. —**pas′sion·less·ly,** *adv.* —**pas′sion·less·ness,** *n.*

pas′sion play′, *n.* (*sometimes caps.*) a dramatization of Christ's Passion, typically performed by amateur actors, usu. during Lent.

Pas′sion Sun′day, *n.* the fifth Sunday in Lent, being the second week before Easter.

Pas·sion·tide (pash′ən tīd′), *n.* the two-week period from Passion Sunday to Holy Saturday.

Pas′sion Week′, *n.* **1.** the week preceding Easter; Holy Week. **2.** the week before Holy Week, beginning with Passion Sunday.

pas·sive (pas′iv), *adj.* **1.** not reacting visibly to something that might be expected to produce manifestations of an emotion or feeling. **2.** not participating readily or actively; inactive: *a passive member of a committee.* **3.** inert or quiescent. **4.** influenced, acted upon, or affected by some external force, cause, or agency (opposed to *active*). **5.** receiving or characterized by the reception of impressions or influences from external sources. **6.** produced or caused by an external agency. **7.** receiving, enduring, or submitting without resistance; submissive. **8.** of, pertaining to, or being a voice, verb form, or construction having a subject represented as undergoing the action expressed by the verb, as the sentence *The letter was written last week* (opposed to *active*). **9.** chemically inactive, esp. under conditions in which chemical activity is to be expected. **10.** (of a metal) treated so as to render corrosion-resistant. **11.** (of a solar heating system) functioning without the aid of machinery, as pumps. —*n.* **12.** the passive voice. **13.** a passive verb form or construction. —**pas′sive·ly,** *adv.*

pas′sive euthana′sia, *n.* See under EUTHANASIA.

pas′sive immu′nity, *n.* immunity that results from an external source, as injected antibody, or in infants from maternal antibody that has passed through the placenta or been received from breast milk.

pas′sive resist′ance, *n.* opposition to a government or to specific laws by the use of noncooperation or other nonviolent methods. —**pas′sive resist′er,** *n.*

pas′sive smok′ing, *n.* the inhaling of the cigarette, cigar, or pipe smoke of others, esp. by a nonsmoker in an enclosed area.

pas·siv·ism (pas′ə viz′əm), *n.* **1.** the quality of being passive. **2.** the principle or practice of passive resistance. —**pas′siv·ist,** *n.*

pas·siv·i·ty (pa siv′i tē), *n.* **1.** Also, **pas·sive·ness** (pas′iv nis). the state or condition of being passive. **2.** chemical inactivity, esp. the resistance to corrosion of certain metals when covered with a coherent oxide layer.

pass·key (pas′kē′, päs′-), *n., pl.* **-keys. 1.** MASTER KEY. **2.** SKELETON KEY.

Pass·o·ver (pas′ō′vər, päs′-), *n.* **1.** Also called **Pesach.** a Jewish festival, beginning on the 14th of Nisan and celebrated for either seven or eight days, that commemorates the Exodus of the Israelites from Egypt. **2.** (*l.c.*) PASCHAL LAMB (def. 1). [trans. of Hebrew *pesaḥ*]

pass·port (pas′pôrt, -pōrt, päs′-), *n.* **1.** an official document issued by a government to one of its citizens, authenticating the bearer's identity and right to travel to and return from other countries. **2.** anything that ensures admission or acceptance: *Education is a passport to success.* —**pass′port·less,** *adj.*

pass·word (pas′wûrd′, päs′-), *n.* **1.** a secret word or expression used by authorized persons to gain access, information, etc. **2.** a string of characters typed into a computer to identify and obtain access for an authorized user.

past (past, päst), *adj.* **1.** gone by or elapsed in time: *The bad times are all past now.* **2.** of, having existed in, or having occurred during a previous time; bygone: *past glories.* **3.** gone by just before the present time; just passed: *during the past year.* **4.** ago: *six days past.* **5.** having formerly been or served as; previous; earlier: *three past presidents.* **6.** of, pertaining to, or being a verb tense or form referring to events or states in times gone by. —*n.* **7.** the time gone by: *far back in the past.* **8.** the history of a person, nation, etc.: *our country's glorious past.* **9.** what has existed or happened at some earlier time: *Try to learn from the past.* **10.** an earlier period of a person's life, career, etc., that is characterized by imprudent or immoral conduct. **11. a.** the past tense. **b.** a form in the past tense, as *looked* or *ate.* —*adv.* **12.** so as to pass by or beyond; by: *The troops marched past.* —*prep.* **13.** beyond in time; later than; after: *past noon.* **14.** beyond in space or position; farther on than: *the house just past the church.* **15.** in a direction so as to pass by or go beyond: *We went past the house by mistake.* **16.** beyond in amount, number, etc.; over: *past the maximum age.* **17.** beyond the reach, scope, influence, or power of: *past hope of recovery.* —*Proverb.* **18.** Those who cannot remember the past are condemned to repeat it, the study of history can teach how to avoid mistakes. George Santayana, *Life of Reason* (1905–06).

pas·ta (pä′stə; *esp. Brit.* pas′tə), *n., pl.* **-tas.** thin, unleavened dough, processed into a variety of forms, as spaghetti or ravioli.

paste (pāst), *n., v.,* **past·ed, past·ing.** —*n.* **1.** a mixture of flour and water, often with starch or the like, used for causing paper or other material to adhere to something. **2.** any soft, smooth, plastic material or preparation. **3.** dough, esp. when prepared with shortening. **4.** a semisoft confection of pulverized or puréed fruit or the like: *almond paste.* **5.** a preparation of puréed fish, tomatoes, or other food. **6.** PASTA. **7.** a mixture of clay, water, etc., for making pottery or porcelain. **8.** a brilliant, heavy glass used for making artificial gems. **9.** *Slang.* a hard slap or blow. —*v.t.* **10.** to fasten or stick with paste or the like (sometimes fol. by *up*). **11.** to cover with something applied by paste.

paste·board (pāst′bôrd′, -bōrd′), *n.* **1.** a stiff board made of sheets of paper pasted or layers of paper pulp pressed together. —*adj.* **2.** made of pasteboard. **3.** unsubstantial or sham. —**paste′board′y,** *adj.*

pas·tel (pa stel′; *esp. Brit.* pas′tl), *n.* **1.** a color having a soft, subdued shade. **2.** a dried paste made of ground pigment and compounded with gum water. **3.** a crayon made from such paste. **4.** the art of drawing with such crayons. **5.** a drawing so made. **6.** a light sketch in prose. —*adj.* **7.** having a soft, subdued shade. **8.** drawn with pastels.

pas·tel·ist (pa stel′ist; *esp. Brit.* pas′tl ist), *n.* an artist who draws with pastels. Also, *esp. Brit.,* **pas′tel·list.**

pas·tern (pas′tərn), *n.* the part of the foot of a horse, cow, etc., between the fetlock and the hoof.

Pas·ter·nak (pas′tər nak′), *n.* **Boris (Leonidovich),** 1890–1960, Russian poet, novelist, and translator.

paste′-up′, *n.* MECHANICAL (def. 8).

Pas·teur (pa stûr′), *n.* **Louis,** 1822–95, French chemist and bacteriologist. —**Pas·teur′i·an,** *adj.*

pas·teur·ize (pas′chə rīz′, pas′tə-), *v.t.,* **-ized, -iz·ing.** to expose (a food, as milk, cheese, yogurt, beer, or wine) to an elevated temperature for a period of time sufficient to destroy harmful or undesirable microorganisms without radically altering taste or quality. —**pas′teur·i·za′tion,** *n.* —**pas′teur·iz′er,** *n.*

pas·tiche (pa stēsh′, pä-), *n.* **1.** a literary, musical, or artistic piece consisting wholly or chiefly of motifs or techniques from borrowed sources. **2.** HODGEPODGE.

pas·time (pas′tīm′, päs′-), *n.* something, as a game, sport, or hobby, that serves to make time pass agreeably.

past′ mas′ter, *n.* **1.** a person who is thoroughly skilled in a profession or art; expert. **2.** a person who has held the office of master in a guild, lodge, etc.

pas·tor (pas′tər, pä′stər), *n.* **1.** a minister or priest in charge of a church. **2.** a person having spiritual care of a number of persons. —**pas′tor•like′, pas′tor•ly,** *adj.* —**pas′tor•ship′,** *n.*

pas•to•ral (pas′tər əl, pä′stər-), *adj.* **1.** having the simplicity, serenity, etc., generally attributed to rural areas. **2.** pertaining to the country or to life in the country; rural; rustic. **3.** portraying idyllically the life of shepherds or of the country. **4.** of, pertaining to, or consisting of shepherds. **5.** of or pertaining to a pastor or the duties of a pastor: *pastoral visits to a hospital.* **6.** pertaining to or designating the herding of domesticated animals as the chief means of subsistence. —*n.* **7.** a literary work dealing with the life of shepherds, commonly in a conventional manner; bucolic. **8.** a treatise on the duties of a pastor. **9.** a letter from an ecclesiastic, esp. a bishop. —**pas′to•ral•ly,** *adv.*

pas•to•rale (pas′tə räl′, -ral′, -rä′lē, -lā), *n., pl.* **-rales, -ra•li** (-rä′lē). **1.** an opera or cantata with a pastoral subject. **2.** a piece of music suggestive of pastoral life.

Pas′toral Epis′tles, *n.pl.* the Epistles I and II Timothy and Titus.

pas•to•ral•ism (pas′tər ə liz′əm, pä′stər-), *n.* the herding of domesticated animals as the primary economic activity of a society.

pas•tor•ate (pas′tər it, pä′stər-), *n.* **1.** the office or term of office of a pastor. **2.** a body of pastors. **3.** PARSONAGE.

past′ par′ticiple, *n.* a participle with past, perfect, or passive meaning, as *fallen, sung,* or *defeated,* used in English and other languages in forming the present perfect, past perfect, and passive and as an adjective.

past′ per′fect, *adj.* **1.** pertaining to or being a verb tense or form indicating that the action or state expressed by the verb was completed prior to a point of reference in the past or that it extended up to or had results continuing up to that point, and consisting in English of *had* followed by a past participle, as *had seen* in *I had never seen anything like it.* —*n.* **2.** the past perfect tense. **3.** a form in this tense.

pas•tra•mi (pə strä′mē), *n.* a brisket of beef cured in a mixture of seasonings and smoked before cooking. [< Yiddish < Romanian *pastramă* pressed, cured meat]

pas•try (pā′strē), *n., pl.* **-tries. 1.** a sweet baked food made of dough. **2.** a piece of such food.

pas•tur•age (pas′chər ij, päs′-), *n.* **1.** PASTURE (defs. 1, 2). **2.** the activity or business of pasturing livestock.

pas•ture (pas′chər, päs′-), *n., v.,* **-tured, -tur•ing.** —*n.* **1.** Also called **pas′ture•land′** (-land′). an area of ground covered with plants suitable for the grazing of livestock; grassland. **2.** grass or other plants for feeding livestock. —*v.t.* **3.** to feed (livestock) by putting out to graze on pasture. **4.** (of livestock) to graze upon. —*v.i.* **5.** (of livestock) to graze in a pasture. —***Idiom.*** **6. put out to pasture, a.** to put in a pasture to graze. **b.** to dismiss or retire as being past one's prime. —**pas′tur•al,** *adj.* —**pas′ture•less,** *adj.* —**pas′tur•er,** *n.*

past•y (pā′stē), *adj.,* **-i•er, -i•est.** of or like paste, as in texture or color: *a pasty complexion.* —**past′i•ness,** *n.*

PA system, *n.* PUBLIC-ADDRESS SYSTEM.

pat[1] (pat), *v.,* **pat•ted, pat•ting,** *n.* —*v.t.* **1.** to strike lightly, as with the hand or a small object, usu. to flatten, smooth, or shape. **2.** to stroke or tap gently with the palm or fingers as an expression of affection, approbation, etc. —*v.i.* **3.** to strike lightly or gently. **4.** to walk or run with light footsteps. —*n.* **5.** a light stroke, tap, or blow, as with the hand or a small object. **6.** the sound of a light stroke or of light footsteps. **7.** a small piece, usu. flat and square, formed by patting, cutting, etc.: *a pat of butter.* —***Idiom.*** **8. pat on the back, a.** praise, congratulations, or encouragement. **b.** to praise, congratulate, or encourage.

pat[2] (pat), *adj.* **1.** exactly to the point or purpose; apt; opportune. **2.** excessively glib; unconvincingly facile: *pat answers.* **3.** learned, known, or mastered perfectly or exactly: *to have something pat.* —*adv.* **4.** exactly or perfectly. **5.** aptly; opportunely. —***Idiom.*** **6. stand pat, a.** to cling firmly to one's decision, policy, or beliefs. **b.** (in draw poker) to play a hand as dealt, without replacing any cards. —**pat′ness,** *n.*

Pat•a•go•ni•a (pat′ə gō′nē ə, -gōn′yə), *n.* a region in S South America, in S Argentina and S Chile, extending from the Andes to the Atlantic. —**Pat′a•go′ni•an,** *adj., n.*

patch (pach), *n.* **1.** a small piece of material used to mend a tear or break, cover a hole, or strengthen a weak place. **2.** a piece of material used to cover or protect a wound, an injured part, etc. **3.** an adhesive patch that applies to the skin and gradually delivers medication to the user. **4.** any of the pieces of cloth sewn together to form patchwork. **5.** a small piece or area of anything: *a patch of ice on the road.* **6.** a small plot, esp. one in which a specific type of plant grows or is cultivated: *a cabbage patch.* **7.** a cloth emblem worn on the sleeve of a military uniform to identify the wearer's unit. **8.** an organizational or affiliational emblem of cloth sewn to one's jacket, shirt, cap, etc. **9.** a tiny, usu. black piece of material applied to the face or neck, as to set off a feature or to cover a flaw. **10.** a connection or hookup, as between radio circuits or telephone lines. **11.** *Computers.* a temporary fix inserted into program code to fix a bug. —*v.t.* **12.** to mend, cover, or strengthen with or as if with a patch. **13.** to repair or restore, esp. in a hasty or makeshift way (usu. fol. by *up*). **14.** to make by joining patches or pieces together: *to patch a quilt.* **15.** to settle or smooth over (a quarrel or difference) (often fol. by *up*). **16.** (esp. in radio and telephone communications) to connect or hook up (circuits, programs, conversations, etc.) (often fol. by *through, into,* etc.). —*v.i.* **17.** to make a connection between radio circuits, telephone lines, etc. (often fol. by *in* or *into*).

patch•ou•li or **patch•ou•ly** (pach′o͝o lē, pə cho͞o′lē), *n., pl.* **-lis** or **-lies. 1.** a tropical Asian plant, *Pogostemon cablin,* of the mint family, yielding a fragrant oil. **2.** a perfume made from this oil.

patch′ pock′et, *n.* a pocket formed by sewing a piece of shaped material to the outside of a garment.

patch′ test′, *n.* a test for suspected allergy in which a patch impregnated with an allergen is applied to the skin.

patch′-up′, *n.* **1.** an act or instance of patching or repair. —*adj.* **2.** done by patching: *a quick patch-up job.*

patch•work (pach′wûrk′), *n.* **1.** something made up of incongruous pieces or parts; mélange. **2.** sewn work made of pieces of material in various colors or shapes. —*adj.* **3.** resembling a patchwork; makeshift.

patch•y (pach′ē), *adj.,* **-i•er, -i•est. 1.** occurring in, forming, or made up of patches. **2.** irregular in quality, texture, or distribution: *patchy fog.* —**patch′i•ly,** *adv.* —**patch′i•ness,** *n.*

pate (pāt), *n.* **1.** the crown of the head. **2.** the head. **3.** the brain.

pâte (pät), *n.* PASTE (def. 7).

pâ•té (pä tā′, pa-), *n., pl.* **-tés.** a paste of puréed or chopped meat, liver, game, etc., usu. served as an appetizer.

pâ•té de foie gras (pä tā′ də fwä′ grä′, pa tā′), *n., pl.* **pâ•tés de foie gras.** See under FOIE GRAS.

pa•tel•la (pə tel′ə), *n., pl.* **-tel•las, -tel•lae** (-tel′ē). **1.** the flat, movable bone at the front of the knee; kneecap. **2.** any other disklike or pan-shaped anatomical structure. —**pa•tel′lar,** *adj.*

pat•en (pat′n), *n.* a metal plate for holding the bread of the Eucharist.

pat•ent (pat′nt; *for 8, 10, 11* pāt′-; *esp. Brit.* pāt′-), *n.* **1.** the exclusive right granted to an inventor to manufacture or sell an invention for a specified number of years. **2.** an invention or process protected by this right. **3.** LETTERS PATENT. **4.** the instrument by which the U.S. government grants title to public land. **5.** PATENT LEATHER. —*adj.* **6.** protected by a patent. **7.** dealing with patents: *patent law.* **8.** readily open to notice; evident; obvious. **9.** made of patent leather: *patent shoes.* **10.** *Chiefly Bot.* expanded or spreading. **11.** open; unobstructed, as a bodily passage. —*v.t.* **12.** to obtain a patent on. **13.** to grant (public land) by a patent. —**pat′ent•a•ble,** *adj.* —**pat′ent•a•bil′i•ty,** *n.* —**pat′ent•a•bly,** *adv.* —**pat′ent•ly,** *adv.*

pat•ent•ee (pat′n tē′; *esp. Brit.* pāt′-), *n.* a person, group, or company granted a patent.

pat′ent leath′er (pat′nt, pat′n; *esp. Brit.* pāt′nt), *n.* a hard, glossy, smooth leather used esp. for shoes and accessories.

pat′ent med′icine, *n.* **1.** a nonprescription drug that is protected by the trademark of a company that owns the patent on its manufacture or is licensed to distribute it. **2.** any proprietary drug.

pa•ter (pā′tər; *for 2 also* pat′ər), *n.* **1.** *Brit. Informal.* FATHER. **2.** (*often cap.*) PATERNOSTER.

pa•ter•fa•mil•i•as (pā′tər fə mil′ē əs, pä′-, pat′ər-), *n.* the male head of a household or family, usu. the father.

pa•ter•nal (pə tûr′nl), *adj.* **1.** characteristic of or befitting a father; fatherly. **2.** of or pertaining to a father: *paternal rights.* **3.** related on the father's side: *one's paternal grandfather.* **4.** derived or inherited from a father. —**pa•ter′nal•ly,** *adv.*

pa•ter•ni•ty (pə tûr′ni tē), *n.* **1.** the state of being a father; fatherhood. **2.** derivation or descent from a father. **3.** origin or authorship. —*adj.* **4.** of or pertaining to a legal dispute in which a woman accuses a man of having fathered her child: *a paternity suit.*

pater′nity leave′, *n.* a leave of absence for a father to care for a new baby.

pa•ter•nos•ter (pā′tər nos′tər, pä′-, pat′ər-), *n.* **1.** (*often cap.*) Also, **Pa′ter Nos′ter.** the Lord's Prayer, esp. in the Latin form. **2.** a recitation of this prayer as an act of worship. **3.** one of certain large beads in a rosary, indicating that the Lord's Prayer is to be said. **4.** any fixed recital of words used as a prayer or magical charm. [Lord's prayer < Latin *pater noster* our father, its first two words in the Vulgate]

Pat•er•son (pat′ər sən), *n.* a city in NE New Jersey. 138,290.

path (path, päth), *n., pl.* **paths** (pat͟hz, pät͟hz, paths, päths). **1.** a way beaten, formed, or trodden by the feet of persons or animals. **2.** a narrow walk or way: *a bicycle path.* **3.** a route, course, or track along which something moves: *the path of a hurricane.* **4.** a course of action, conduct, or procedure: *the path of righteousness.* **5.** (in some computer operating systems) **a.** a listing of the route through directories and subdirectories that locates and thereby names a specific file or program on a disk drive. **b.** the currently active list of all such routes that tells the operating system where to find programs, enabling a user to run them from other directories.

-path, a combining form occurring in personal nouns corresponding to abstract nouns ending in -PATHY, with the general sense "one practicing such a treatment" (*osteopath*) or "one suffering from such an ailment" (*psychopath*).

pa•thet•ic (pə thet′ik) also **pa•thet′i•cal,** *adj.* **1.** causing or evoking pity, either sympathetically or contemptibly; pitiful; pitiable: *a pathetic sight; a pathetic return on our investment.* **2.** sad; sorrowful; mournful: *a pathetic tone of voice.* —**pa•thet′i•cal•ly,** *adv.*

path•find•er (path′fīn′dər, päth′-), *n.* a person who finds a path or way, esp. through an unexplored wilderness. —**path′find′ing,** *n., adj.*

-pathic, a combining form occurring in adjectives that correspond to nouns ending in -PATHY: *psychopathic.*

patho-, a combining form meaning "suffering," "disease": *pathology.*

path•o•gen (path′ə jən, -jen′), *n.* any disease-producing agent, esp. a virus, bacterium, or other microorganism.

path•o•gen•e•sis (path′ə jen′ə sis) also **pa•thog•e•ny** (pə thoj′ə nē), *n.* the production and development of disease. —**path′o•ge•net′ic** (-ō jə net′ik), *adj.*

path•o•gen•ic (path′ə jen′ik), *adj.* capable of producing disease. —**path′o•ge•nic′i•ty** (-ō jə nis′i tē), *n.*

path•o•log•i•cal (path′ə loj′i kəl) also **path′o•log′ic,** *adj.* **1.** of or pertaining to pathology. **2.** caused or affected by disease. **3.** characterized by an unhealthy compulsion: *a pathological liar.* —**path′o•log′i•cal•ly,** *adv.*

pa•thol•o•gy (pə thol′ə jē), *n., pl.* **-gies.** **1.** the science or the study of the origin, nature, and course of diseases. **2.** the conditions and processes of a disease. **3.** any deviation from a healthy, normal, or efficient condition. —**pa•thol′o•gist,** *n.*

pa•thos (pā′thos, -thōs, -thôs), *n.* **1.** the quality or power in life or art of evoking a feeling of pity or compassion. **2.** pity.

path•way (path′wā′, päth′-), *n.* **1.** a path, course, route, or way. **2.** a sequence of reactions, usu. controlled and catalyzed by enzymes, by which one organic substance is converted to another.

-pathy, a combining form meaning "feeling" (*antipathy; sympathy*), "suffering," "disease" (*cardiopathy; psychopathy*), "system or method of treating a disease" (*homeopathy; osteopathy*).

pa•tience (pā′shəns), *n.* **1.** the bearing of provocation, annoyance, misfortune, or pain without complaint, loss of temper, or anger. **2.** an ability or willingness to suppress restlessness or annoyance when confronted with delay. **3.** quiet, steady perseverance; even-tempered care; diligence. **4.** *Chiefly Brit.* SOLITAIRE (def. 1).

pa•tient (pā′shənt), *n.* **1.** a person who is under medical care or treatment. **2.** a person or thing that undergoes some action. —*adj.* **3.** bearing provocation, annoyance, pain, etc., without complaint or anger. **4.** characterized by or expressing such a quality. **5.** persevering or diligent; steady. **6.** undergoing the action of another (opposed to *agent*). —***Idiom.*** **7. patient of, a.** able and willing to endure: *patient of others' mistakes.* **b.** susceptible of. —**pa′tient•ly,** *adv.*

pat•i•na (pat′n ə, pə tē′nə) also **pa•tine** (pə tēn′), *n., pl.* **-ti•nas** also **-tines.** **1.** a film or incrustation, usu. green, produced by oxidation on the surface of old bronze and often esteemed as being of ornamental value. **2.** a similar film or coloring appearing gradually on some other surface, esp. as a result of age or long use. **3.** a surface calcification of implements, usu. indicating great age. —**pat′i•nate′** (-āt′), *v.t.,* **-nat•ed, -nat•ing.**

pat•i•o (pat′ē ō′, pä′tē ō′), *n., pl.* **-i•os.** **1.** an area, usu. paved, adjoining a house and used for outdoor lounging, dining, etc. **2.** a courtyard, esp. of a house, enclosed by low buildings or walls.

pa•tis•se•rie (pə tis′ə rē), *n.* a shop where pastry, esp. French pastry, is made and sold.

Pat•mos (pat′mos, -mōs, -məs; *Gk.* pät′môs), *n.* one of the Dodecanese Islands, off the SW coast of Asia Minor: St. John is supposed to have been exiled here (Rev. 1:9). 2432; 13 sq. mi. (34 sq. km). Italian, **Pat•mo** (pät′mô). —**Pat′mi•an,** *adj.*

pat•ois (pat′wä, pä′twä, pa twä′), *n., pl.* **pat•ois** (pat′wäz, pä′twäz, pa twäz′). **1.** a regional form of a language, esp. of French, differing from the standard, literary form of the language. **2.** a rural or provincial form of speech. **3.** jargon; cant; argot.

pat. pend., patent pending.

patri-, a combining form meaning "father": *patrilineal.*

pa•tri•arch (pā′trē ärk′), *n.* **1.** the male head of a family or tribal line. **2.** a person regarded as the father or founder of an order, class, etc. **3.** any of the Biblical personages regarded as the fathers of the human race or any of the three great progenitors of the Israelites: Abraham, Isaac, and Jacob. **4.** any of the 12 sons of Jacob from whom the tribes of Israel were descended. **5.** (in the early Christian church) any of the bishops of the sees of Alexandria, Antioch, Constantinople, Jerusalem, or Rome having authority over other bishops. **6.** *Gk. Orth. Ch.* the head of any of the ancient sees of Alexandria, Antioch, Constantinople, or Jerusalem. **7.** the head of certain other churches. **8.** *Rom. Cath. Ch.* **a.** the pope as patriarch of the West. **b.** any of certain bishops of the Eastern rites. **9.** any of the high Mormon dignitaries who pronounce the blessing of the church. **10.** one of the elders or leading older members of a community. **11.** a venerable old man. —**pa′tri•ar′chal,** *adj.*

pa•tri•arch•y (pā′trē är′kē), *n., pl.* **-chies.** **1. a.** a form of social organization in which the father is the head of the family, clan, or tribe and descent is reckoned in the male line. **b.** a society based on this social organization. **2. a.** an institution or organization in which power is held by and transferred through males. **b.** the principles or philosophy upon which control by male authority is based.

pa•tri•cian (pə trish′ən), *n.* **1.** a person of noble or high rank; aristocrat. **2.** a person of breeding, education, and refinement. **3.** a member of the original hereditary aristocracy of ancient Rome, having such privileges as the exclusive right to hold certain offices. Compare PLEBS (def. 1). **4.** (in the later Roman and Byzantine empires) a nonhereditary honorary title or dignity conferred by the emperor. **5.** a member of a hereditary ruling class in certain medieval German, Swiss, and Italian free cities. —*adj.* **6.** of high social rank or noble family; aristocratic. **7.** befitting of, or characteristic of, patricians.

pat•ri•cide (pa′trə sīd′, pā′-), *n.* **1.** the act of killing one's own father. **2.** a person who commits such an act. —**pat′ri•cid′al,** *adj.*

Pat•rick (pa′trik), *n.* **Saint,** A.D. 389?–461?, British missionary and bishop in Ireland: patron saint of Ireland.

pat•ri•lin•e•age (pa′trə lin′ē ij, pā′-), *n.* lineal descent traced through the male line.

pat•ri•lin•e•al (pa′trə lin′ē əl, pā′-) also **pat′ri•lin′e•ar,** *adj.* tracing, signifying, or based upon descent through the male line. Compare MATRILINEAL. —**pat′ri•lin′e•al•ly,** *adv.* —**pat′ri•li′ny** (-lī′nē), *n.*

pat•ri•mo•ny (pa′trə mō′nē), *n., pl.* **-nies.** **1.** an estate inherited from one's father or ancestors. **2.** any quality, characteristic, etc., that is inherited; heritage. **3.** the estate or endowment of a religious institution. —**pat′ri•mo′ni•al,** *adj.*

pa•tri•ot (pā′trē ət, -ot′; *esp. Brit.* pa′trē ət), *n.* **1.** a person who loves, supports, and defends his or her country and its interests. **2.** a person who regards himself or herself as a defender, esp. of individual rights, against presumed interference by the federal government. **3.** (*cap.*) a U.S. Army antiaircraft missile launched from a tracked vehicle with radar and computer guidance. [< Middle French < Late Latin < Greek *patriṓtēs* fellow-countrymen]

pa•tri•ot•ic (pā′trē ot′ik; *esp. Brit.* pa′-), *adj.* **1.** of, like, or characteristic of a patriot. **2.** expressing or inspired by patriotism. —**pa′tri•ot′i•cal•ly,** *adv.*

pa•tri•ot•ism (pā′trē ə tiz′əm; *esp. Brit.* pa′-), *n.* devoted love, support, and defense of one's country; national loyalty.

Pa′triots' Day′, *n.* the anniversary of the battles of Lexington and Concord (1775), celebrated the third Monday in April: a legal holiday in Massachusetts and Maine.

pa•tris•tic (pə tris′tik) also **pa•tris′ti•cal,** *adj.* of or pertaining to the fathers of the Christian church or their writings.

pa•trol (pə trōl′), *v.,* **-trolled, -trol•ling,** *n.* —*v.t.* **1.** (of a police officer, soldier, etc.) to pass regularly along (a specified route) or through (a specified area) in order to maintain order and security. —*v.i.* **2.** to pass along or through such a route or area for this purpose. —*n.* **3.** a person or group of persons that patrols. **4.** an automobile, ship, plane, squadron, fleet, etc., assigned to patrol an area. **5.** a military detachment detailed for reconnaissance, combat, or other special assignment. **6.** the act of patrolling. **7.** (in the Boy Scouts and Girl Scouts) a subdivision of a troop, usu. consisting of about eight members. —**pa•trol′ler,** *n.*

patrol′ car′, *n.* SQUAD CAR.

pa•trol•man (pə trōl′mən), *n., pl.* **-men.** a police officer who is assigned to patrol a specific route or area.

pa•trol•wom•an (pə trōl′wŏŏm′ən), *n., pl.* **-wom•en.** a policewoman who is assigned to patrol a specific route or area.

pa•tron (pā′trən), *n.* **1.** a person who is a customer, client, or paying guest, esp. a regular one, of a store, hotel, or the like. **2.** a person who supports with money, efforts, or endorsement an artist, charity, etc. **3.** PATRON SAINT. **4.** (in ancient Rome) **a.** the protector of a dependent or client. **b.** the former master of a freed slave still retaining some rights over him. **5.** a person who has the right of presenting a member of the clergy to a benefice. —**pa′tron•ly,** *adj.*

pa•tron•age (pā′trə nij, pa′-), *n.* **1.** the financial support or business provided to a store, hotel, or the like, by customers, clients, or paying guests. **2.** patrons collectively; clientele. **3. a.** the power of public officials to make appointments to government jobs or grant other favors to their supporters. **b.** the distribution of such jobs or favors. **c.** the jobs or favors so distributed. **4.** a condescending manner or attitude in granting favors, in dealing with people, etc.; condescension. **5.** the encouragement or support of a patron, as toward an artist or institution. **6.** ADVOWSON.

pa•tron•ess (pā′trə nis), *n.* a woman who protects, supports, or sponsors someone or something.

pa•tron•ize (pā′trə nīz′, pa′-), *v.t.,* **-ized, -iz•ing.** **1.** to give (a store, restaurant, hotel, etc.) one's regular patronage. **2.** to behave in an offensively condescending manner toward. **3.** to act as a patron toward (an artist, institution, etc.); support. —**pa′tron•i•za′tion,** *n.* —**pa′tron•iz′er,** *n.* —**pa′tron•iz′ing•ly,** *adv.*

pa′tron saint′, *n.* a saint regarded as the special guardian of a person, group, trade, country, etc.

pat•ro•nym•ic (pa′trə nim′ik), *n.* **1.** a name derived from the name of a father or ancestor, esp. by the addition of a suffix or prefix indicating descent, as *Williamson* (son of *William*) or *Macdonald* (son of Donald). —*adj.* **2.** (of a family name) derived from the name of a father or ancestor. **3.** (of a suffix or prefix) indicating descent from a father or ancestor. —**pat′ro•nym′i•cal•ly,** *adv.*

pa•troon (pə trōōn′), *n.* a person who held an estate in land with certain manorial privileges granted under the old Dutch governments of New York and New Jersey.

pat•sy (pat′sē), *n., pl.* **-sies.** *Slang.* **1.** a person who is easily swindled or manipulated. **2.** a person upon whom the blame for something falls; scapegoat; fall guy.

pat•ter[1] (pat′ər), *v.i.* **1.** to make a rapid succession of light taps. **2.** to move or walk lightly or quickly. —*v.t.* **3.** to cause to patter. **4.** to spatter with something. —*n.* **5.** a rapid succession of light tapping sounds. **6.** the act of pattering.

pat•ter[2] (pat′ər), *n.* **1.** glib and rapid talk used to attract attention, entertain, etc. **2.** meaningless, rapid talk; chatter. **3.** amusing lines delivered rapidly by an entertainer or performer. **4.** the jargon or cant of any class, group, etc. —*v.i.* **5.** to talk glibly or rapidly, esp. with little regard to meaning; chatter. —*v.t.* **6.** to repeat or say rapidly or glibly.

pat•ter[3] (pat′ər), *n.* a person or thing that pats.

pat•tern (pat′ərn; *Brit.* pat′n), *n.* **1.** a decorative design, as for wallpaper, china, or textile fabrics, composed of elements in a regular arrangement. **2.** a natural or chance marking, configuration, or design. **3.** a distinctive style, model, or form: *a new pattern of army helmet.* **4.** a combination of qualities, acts, tendencies, etc., forming a consistent or characteristic arrangement: *the behavior patterns of teenagers.* **5.** an original or model considered for or deserving of imitation. **6.** anything designed to serve as a model or guide for something to be made. **7.** an example, instance, sample, or specimen. **8.** the path of flight established for an aircraft approaching an airport at which it is to land. **9.** the distribution of strikes around a target at which artillery rounds have been fired or on which bombs have been dropped.

pat′tern•mak′er or **pat′tern mak′er,** *n.* a person who makes patterns, as for clothing. —**pat′tern•mak′ing,** *n.*

Pat•ton (pat′n), *n.* **George S(mith),** 1885–1945, U.S. general.

pat•ty (pat′ē), *n., pl.* **-ties. 1.** a thin, round piece of ground or minced food, as of meat or the like: *a hamburger patty.* **2.** a thin, round piece, as of candy. **3.** a little pie.

pat′ty•pan squash′ (pat′ē pan′), *n.* a flat, whitish variety of squash, *Cucurbita pepo melopepo,* having a scalloped edge.

pau•ci•ty (pô′si tē), *n.* **1.** smallness of quantity; scarcity; scantiness. **2.** smallness or insufficiency of number; fewness.

Paul[1] (pôl), *n.* **Saint,** died A.D. c67, a missionary and apostle to the gentiles: author of several of the Epistles. Compare SAUL (def. 2).

Paul[2] (pôl), *n.* **1. Paul I, a.** (*Pavel Petrovich*), 1754–1801, emperor of Russia 1796–1801 (son of Peter III). **b.** 1901–64, king of Greece 1947–64. **2. Paul II** (*Pietro Barbo*), 1417–71, Italian pope 1464–71. **3. Paul III** (*Alessandro Farnese*), 1468–1549, Italian pope 1534–49. **4. Paul V** (*Camillo Borghese*), 1552–1621, Italian pope 1605–21. **5. Paul VI** (*Giovanni Battista Montini*), 1897–1978, Italian pope 1963–78.

Paul′ Bun′yan, *n.* a legendary giant lumberjack of the North American forests.

Paul•ine (pô′līn, -lēn), *adj.* of or pertaining to the apostle Paul or to his doctrines or writings.

Paul•ing (pô′ling), *n.* **Linus Carl,** 1901–94, U.S. chemist.

paunch (pônch, pänch), *n.* **1.** a large and protruding belly; potbelly. **2.** the belly or abdomen. **3.** RUMEN (def. 1). —**paunched,** *adj.*

paunch•y (pôn′chē, pän′-), *adj.,* **-i•er, -i•est.** having a large and protruding belly; potbellied. —**paunch′i•ness,** *n.*

pau•per (pô′pər), *n.* **1.** a person without any personal means of support. **2.** a very poor person.

pau•per•ize (pô′pə rīz′), *v.t.,* **-ized, -iz•ing.** to make a pauper of.

pause (pôz), *n., v.,* **paused, paus•ing.** —*n.* **1.** a temporary stop or rest, esp. in speech or action. **2.** a break in speaking or reading to emphasize or clarify meaning, indicated in writing with punctuation. **3.** a break or suspension, as a caesura, in a line of verse. **4.** FERMATA. —*v.i.* **5.** to make a brief stop or delay; wait; hesitate. **6.** to dwell or linger (usu. fol. by *on* or *upon*). —***Idiom.* 7. give pause,** to cause to hesitate or reconsider, as from surprise or doubt.

pave (pāv), *v.t.,* **paved, pav•ing. 1.** to cover or lay (a road, walk, etc.) with concrete, stones, bricks, or the like, so as to make a firm, level surface. —***Idiom.* 2. pave the way for,** to prepare the way for; make possible; lead up to. —**pav′er,** *n.*

pa•vé (pə vā′, pav′ā), *adj.* pertaining to or designating a setting of gemstones, esp. diamonds, placed so close together as to show no metal between them.

pave•ment (pāv′mənt), *n.* **1.** a paved road, highway, etc. **2.** a paved surface, ground covering, or floor. **3.** a material used for paving. **4.** *Atlantic States and Brit.* SIDEWALK.

pa•vil•ion (pə vil′yən), *n.* **1.** a light, usu. open building, used for concerts, exhibits, etc. **2.** any of a number of separate or attached buildings forming a hospital or the like. **3.** a projecting element of a building facade, esp. at the center or ends, usu. suggesting a tower. **4.** a tent, esp. a large and elaborate one. **5.** Also called **base.** the part of a cut gem below the girdle.

pav•ing (pā′ving), *n.* **1.** a pavement. **2.** material for paving. **3.** the laying of a pavement.

Pav•lov (pav′lof, -lôf), *n.* **Ivan Petrovich,** 1849–1936, Russian physiologist. —**Pav•lov′i•an** (-lō′vē ən, -lô′-), *adj.*

paw[1] (pô), *n.* **1.** the foot of an animal that has claws; broadly, the foot of a quadruped. **2.** *Informal.* the human hand, esp. one that is large, rough, or clumsy. —*v.t.* **3.** to strike or scrape with the paws or feet. **4.** to handle or caress clumsily, rudely, or with unwelcome familiarity. —*v.i.* **5.** to beat or scrape the floor, ground, etc., with the paws or feet. **6.** to use one's hands in an awkward manner. —**paw′er,** *n.*

paw[2] (pô), *n. Informal.* father; pa.

pawl (pôl), *n.* a pivoted bar adapted to engage with the teeth of a wheel so as to prevent movement or to impart motion.

pawn[1] (pôn), *v.t.* **1.** to deposit as security, as for money borrowed, esp. with a pawnbroker. **2.** to pledge; stake; risk: *to pawn one's life.* —*n.* **3.** the state of being pawned: *jewels in pawn.* **4.** something that is pawned. **5.** a person serving as security; hostage. **6.** the act of pawning. —**pawn′a•ble,** *adj.* —**pawn•er** (pô′nər), **paw′nor** (-nər, -nôr), *n.*

pawn[2] (pôn), *n.* **1.** one of eight chess pieces of one color and of the lowest value, usu. moved one square at a time vertically and capturing diagonally. **2.** someone who is used or manipulated to further another person's purposes.

pawn•bro•ker (pôn′brō′kər), *n.* a person whose business is lending money at interest on personal, movable property deposited with the lender until redeemed. —**pawn′bro′king, pawn′bro′ker•age, pawn′bro′ker•y,** *n.*

Paw•nee (pô nē′), *n., pl.* **-nees,** (*esp. collectively*) **-nee. 1.** a member of an American Indian people living along the Platte River and its tributaries in Nebraska during the first half of the 19th century: confined to a reservation in the Indian Territory in 1874–75. **2.** the Caddoan language of the Pawnees, closely related to Arikara.

pawn•shop (pôn′shop′), *n.* the shop of a pawnbroker.

pawn′ tick′et, *n.* a receipt given for goods left with a pawnbroker.

paw•paw or **pa•paw** (pô′pô′, pə pô′), *n.* **1.** a tree, *Asimina triloba,* of the annona family, native to the eastern U.S., having large, oblong leaves and purplish flowers. **2.** the fleshy, edible fruit of this tree. **3.** PAPAYA.

pax (paks, päks), *n.* **1.** KISS OF PEACE. **2.** (*often cap.*) a period in history marked by general peace, usu. imposed by a predominant nation.

pax′ America′na *n.* a peace imposed by the United States upon hostile nations, esp. in the 20th century.

Pax Ro•ma•na (paks′ rō mā′nə, -mä′-, päks′), *n.* **1.** the peace imposed by ancient Rome on its dominions. **2.** any state of peace imposed by a strong nation on weaker or defeated nations. [< Latin: Roman peace]

pay (pā), *v.,* **paid** or **payed, pay•ing,** *n., adj.* —*v.t.* **1.** to discharge or settle (a debt, obligation, etc.), as by transferring money or goods, or by doing something. **2.** to give over (money) in exchange for something. **3.** to transfer money to (a person or organization) as compensation for work done or services rendered. **4.** to defray (cost or expense). **5.** to be profitable to: *Your training will pay you well in the future.* **6.** to yield as a return: *The stock paid six percent last year.* **7.** to reward or retaliate against, as for good, harm, or an offense. **8.** to give or render (attention, respects, a compliment, etc.), as if due or fitting. **9.** to make (a call, visit, etc.). **10.** to suffer in retribution; undergo: *to pay the penalty for a crime.* —*v.i.* **11.** to transfer money, goods, etc., as in making a purchase or settling a debt. **12.** to discharge a debt or obligation. **13.** to yield a return, profit, or advantage; be worthwhile: *It pays to be courteous.* **14.** to give compensation, as for damage or loss sustained. **15.** to suffer or be punished for something: *to pay with one's life.* **16. pay back, a.** to repay or return. **b.** to retaliate against; punish. **17. pay off, a.** to pay (someone) everything that is due that person, esp. final wages. **b.** to pay (a debt) in full. **c.** *Informal.* to bribe. **d.** to retaliate against; punish. **e.** to result in success or failure. **18. pay out, a.** to distribute (money, wages, etc.); disburse. **b.** to let out (a rope) by slackening. **19. pay up, a.** to pay fully. **b.** to pay on demand. —*n.* **20.** the act of paying or being paid; payment. **21.** wages, salary, or a stipend. **22.** paid employment. —*adj.* **23.** operable or accessible on deposit of coins: *a pay toilet.* **24.** pertaining to or requiring payment. —***Idiom.* 25. pay as you go, a.** to pay for goods or services at the time of purchase, as opposed to buying on credit. **b.** to spend no more than income permits; keep out of debt. **c.** to pay income tax by regular deductions from one's salary or wages. **26. pay through the nose,** to pay an exorbitant price. —***Saying.* 27. You get what you pay for,** value tends to reflect cost.

pay•a•ble (pā′ə bəl), *adj.* **1.** to be paid; due: *a loan payable in 30 days.* **2.** capable of being or liable to be paid. **3.** profitable. —*n.* **4.** a bill that is to be paid. **5. payables,** accounts payable.

pay•back (pā′bak′), *n.* **1.** the period of time required to recoup a capital investment. **2.** the return on an investment.

pay•check (pā′chek′), *n.* **1.** a bank check given as salary or wages. **2.** salary or wages.

pay•day (pā′dā′), *n.* the day on which wages are paid.

pay′ dirt′, *n.* **1.** soil, gravel, or ore that can be mined profitably. **2.** *Informal.* any source of success or wealth.

pay•ee (pā ē′), *n.* a person to whom a check, money, etc., is payable.

pay•load (pā′lōd′), *n.* **1.** the part of a cargo producing revenue or income, usu. expressed in weight. **2.** the number of paying passengers, as on an airplane. **3. a.** the bomb load, warhead, cargo, or passengers of an aircraft, rocket, missile, etc. **b.** the equipment carried by a spacecraft to perform a specified mission. **c.** the explosive energy of a warhead or of the bomb load of an aircraft.

pay•ment (pā′mənt), *n.* **1.** something that is paid. **2.** the act of paying. **3.** reward or punishment; requital.

Payne (pān), *n.* **John Howard,** 1791–1852, U.S. actor and dramatist.

pay•off (pā′ôf′, -of′), *n.* **1.** the payment of a salary, debt, wager, etc. **2.** the time at which such payment is made. **3.** *Informal.* the outcome of a series of events or circumstances; climax. **4.** a settlement or reckoning, as in retribution or reward. **5.** *Informal.* BRIBE.

pay•o•la (pā ō′lə), *n.* secret payment in return for the promotion of a product, service, etc., through the abuse of one's position or influence, as a bribe paid to a disc jockey to promote a record.

pay•out (pā′out′), *n.* **1.** an act or instance of paying or disbursing. **2.** money paid or disbursed, as a dividend or winning.

pay′-per-view′, *n.* **1.** a pay television service in which a subscriber pays for each program viewed. —*adj.* **2.** noting or pertaining to such a system. *Abbr.:* ppv

pay′ phone′, *n.* a public telephone requiring that the caller deposit coins or use a credit card to pay for a call. Also called **pay′ sta′tion.**

P

pay·roll (pā'rōl'), *n.* **1.** a list of employees to be paid, with the amount due to each. **2.** the sum total of these amounts. **3.** the actual money on hand for distribution.

pay' tel'evision, *n.* **1.** a commercial service that broadcasts television programs to viewers who pay a monthly charge or a per-program fee. **2.** the programming provided. Also called **pay-TV, subscription television.**

Pb, *Chem. Symbol.* lead. [< Latin *plumbum*]

PBS, Public Broadcasting Service.

PBX, a telephone facility that handles communications within an office, building, or organization and is connected to the public telephone network. [*P(rivate) B(ranch) Ex(change)*]

PC or **P.C., 1.** Peace Corps. **2.** *pl.* **PCs** or **PC's** or **P.C.'s.** personal computer. **3.** political correctness. **4.** politically correct.

pc., 1. *pl.* **pcs.** piece. **2.** prices.

P/C or **p/c, 1.** petty cash. **2.** price current.

p.c., 1. percent. **2.** postcard. **3.** (in prescriptions) after meals. [< Latin *post cibos*]

PCB, *pl.* **PCB's, PCBs.** any of a family of highly toxic, possibly carcinogenic compounds consisting of two benzene rings in which chlorine replaces hydrogen, formerly used in industry: banned in the U.S. because of concern over contamination of water supplies. [*p(oly)c(hlorinated) b(iphenyl)*]

PC card, *n.* a small, removable, externally accessible circuit board housing a device, as a modem or disk drive, and conforming to the PCMCIA standard: used esp. for laptop computers.

pct., percent.

Pd, *Chem. Symbol.* palladium.

PD or **P.D., 1.** Also, **p.d.** per diem. **2.** Police Department. **3.** postal district.

pd., paid.

PDA, personal digital assistant.

PDQ or **P.D.Q.,** *Informal.* immediately; at once.

p/e, price-earnings ratio.

PE, 1. physical education. **2.** printer's error. **3.** *Statistics.* probable error. **4.** Prince Edward Island, Canada.

pea (pē), *n.*, *pl.* **peas,** *adj.* —*n.* **1.** the round edible seed of a widely cultivated plant, *Pisum sativum,* of the legume family. **2.** the plant itself. **3.** the green, somewhat inflated pod of this plant. **4.** any of various related or similar plants or their seed, as the chickpea. **5.** something resembling a pea, esp. in being small and round. —*adj.* **6.** pertaining to, containing, or cooked with peas. **7.** small or small and round (usu. used in combination).

pea' a'phid, *n.* a large green aphid, *Acyrthosiphon pisum,* that is a pest of peas, clovers, alfalfa, and similar plants and occurs throughout North America.

pea' bean', *n.* a variety of kidney bean with a small white seed.

peace (pēs), *n.* **1.** freedom from war; cessation or absence of hostilities between nations. **2.** a state of harmony between people or groups; freedom from dissension. **3.** freedom from civil commotion; public order and security. **4.** freedom from anxiety, annoyance, or other mental disturbance: *peace of mind.* **5.** a state of tranquillity or serenity. **6.** silence; stillness. **7.** (*often cap.*) an agreement or treaty that ends a war or hostilities. —*interj.* **8.** (used to express greeting or farewell or to request silence.) —*Idiom.* **9. at peace, a.** in a state of nonbelligerence; not at war. **b.** untroubled; tranquil. **c.** deceased. **10. hold** or **keep one's peace,** to refrain from or cease speaking; keep silent. **11. keep the peace, a.** to maintain public order. **b.** to prevent discord. **12. make one's peace with,** to become reconciled with or to. **13. make peace,** to arrange a cessation of hostilities or antagonism. —*Proverb.* **14. If you want peace, prepare for war,** a strong defense is the best safeguard against the outbreak of hostilities.

peace·a·ble (pē'sə bəl), *adj.* **1.** inclined or disposed to avoid strife or dissension. **2.** peaceful; tranquil. —**peace'a·bly,** *adv.*

Peace' Corps', *n.* a civilian organization, sponsored by the U.S. government, that sends volunteers to instruct citizens of underdeveloped countries in the execution of industrial, agricultural, educational, and health programs.

peace' div'idend, *n.* money cut by a government from its defense budget as a result of the cessation of hostilities with other countries.

peace' feel'er, *n.* a subtle diplomatic enquiry about the possibility of ending hostilities between nations.

peace·ful (pēs'fəl), *adj.* **1.** characterized by peace; free from war, strife, commotion, violence, or disorder. **2.** of, pertaining to, or characteristic of a state or time of peace. **3.** peaceable; not argumentative or quarrelsome. —**peace'ful·ly,** *adv.* —**peace'ful·ness,** *n.*

peace'ful coexist'ence, *n.* competition without war, or a policy of peace between nations of widely differing political systems and ideologies, esp. between Communist and non-Communist nations: *peaceful coexistence between the U.S. and the Soviet Union.*

peace·keep·ing (pēs'kē'ping), *n.* **1.** the maintenance of international peace and security, as by the enforcement of a truce. —*adj.* **2.** for or pertaining to peacekeeping. —**peace'keep'er,** *n.*

peace·mak·er (pēs'mā'kər), *n.* a person, group, or nation that tries to make peace. —**peace'mak'ing,** *n.*, *adj.*

peace' offen'sive, *n.* an active program, policy, propaganda campaign, etc., by a national government for the purpose of terminating a

war or period of hostility, lessening international tensions, or promoting peaceful cooperation with other nations.

peace' of'fering, *n.* **1.** any offering made to procure peace. **2.** a sacrificial offering made in order to assure communion with God. Ex. 20:24; Lev. 7:11–18.

peace' of'ficer, *n.* a civil officer appointed to preserve the public peace, as a sheriff or constable.

peace' pipe', *n.* CALUMET.

peace' proc'ess, *n.* a series of negotiations aimed at ending hostilities between nations.

peace·time (pēs'tīm'), *n.* a period of freedom from war.

peach (pēch), *n.* **1.** the round, pink-to-yellow, fuzzy-skinned fruit of a tree, *Prunus persica,* of the rose family. **2.** the tree itself, cultivated in temperate climates. **3.** a light pinkish yellow color. **4.** *Informal.* a person or thing that is especially attractive, liked, or enjoyed.

peach' Mel'ba, *n.* a dessert of peach halves topped with vanilla ice cream and raspberry sauce.

peach·y (pē'chē), *adj.,* **-i·er, -i·est. 1.** resembling a peach, as in color or appearance. **2.** *Informal.* excellent; wonderful; fine. —**peach'i·ness,** *n.*

pea'coat' or **pea' coat',** *n.* PEA JACKET.

pea·cock (pē'kok'), *n.,* *pl.* **-cocks,** (*esp. collectively*) **-cock,** *v.,* **-cocked, -cock·ing.** —*n.* **1.** the male of the peafowl, distinguished by its long, erectile, iridescent tail feathers that are marked with eyelike spots and can be spread in a fan. **2.** any peafowl. **3.** a vain, self-conscious person. —*v.i.* **4.** to display oneself vainly; strut like a peacock. —**pea'cock'ish,** **pea'cock'y,** *adj.* —**pea'cock'ish·ly,** *adv.*

peacock (peafowl), *Pavo cristatus,* head and body 2 ½ ft. (0.8 m); train 5 ft. (1.5 m)

pea'cock blue', *n.* a lustrous greenish blue.

pea'cock chair', *n.* a wicker armchair with a high circular back.

pea·fowl (pē'foul'), *n.,* *pl.* **-fowls,** (*esp. collectively*) **-fowl.** any of several large gallinaceous birds of the genera *Pavo,* of S and SE Asia, and *Afropavo,* of central Africa. Compare PEACOCK, PEAHEN.

pea' green', *n.* a medium or yellowish green.

pea·hen (pē'hen'), *n.* the female peafowl.

pea' jack'et, *n.* **1.** a short, double-breasted coat of navy-blue wool, worn by seamen. **2.** any jacket or short coat resembling this. Also called **peacoat.**

peak[1] (pēk), *n.* **1.** the pointed top of a mountain or ridge. **2.** a mountain with a pointed summit. **3.** the pointed top of anything. **4.** the highest or most important point or level. **5.** the maximum point, degree, or volume of anything. **6.** the time of the day or year when traffic, use, or demand is greatest and charges, fares, etc., are highest. **7.** a projecting point. **8.** WIDOW's PEAK. **9.** the projecting front piece of a cap or hat. **10.** NUCLEUS (def. 7a). **11. a.** the contracted part of a ship's hull at the bow or the stern. **b.** the upper after corner of a sail that is extended by a gaff. —*v.i.* **12.** to project in a peak. **13.** to attain a peak of activity, development, popularity, etc. —*v.t.* **14.** to raise the after end of (a yard, gaff, etc.) to or toward an angle above the horizontal. —*adj.* **15.** attaining or being at the highest or maximum level, point, use, etc: *peak performance; the peak travel season.*

peak[2] (pēk), *v.i.* to become weak, thin, and sickly. —**peak'ish,** *adj.* —**peak'ish·ness,** *n.*

peaked[1] (pēkt, pē'kid), *adj.* having a peak: *a peaked cap.*

peak·ed[2] (pē'kid), *adj.* pale and drawn; wan. —**peak'ed·ness,** *n.*

peal (pēl), *n.* **1.** a loud, prolonged ringing of bells. **2.** a set of bells tuned to one another. **3.** a series of changes rung on a set of bells. **4.** any loud, sustained sound or series of sounds, as of thunder or laughter. —*v.t.* **5.** to sound loudly and sonorously. —*v.i.* **6.** to sound forth in a peal; resound.

Peale (pēl), *n.* **1. Charles Willson,** 1741–1827, and his brother **James,** 1749–1831, U.S. painters. **2. Norman Vincent,** born 1898, U.S. Protestant clergyman and author. **3. Rembrandt,** 1778–1860, U.S. painter (son of Charles Willson Peale).

pea·nut (pē'nut', -nət), *n.* **1.** the pod or the enclosed edible seed of a plant, *Arachis hypogaea,* of the legume family: the pod is forced underground in growing, where it ripens. **2.** the plant itself. **3.** any small or insignificant person or thing. **4. peanuts,** *Informal.* a very small amount of money.

pea'nut but'ter, *n.* a paste made from ground roasted peanuts, used as a spread or in cooking.

pea'nut gal'lery, *n.* *Slang.* the rearmost and cheapest section of seats in the balcony of a theater.

pea'nut oil', *n.* the yellowish oil expressed from peanuts, used in cooking and in margarine, soap, and medicines.

Pea·nuts (pē'nuts, -nəts), a syndicated comic strip by Charles M. Schulz: begun in 1950.

pear (pâr), *n.* **1.** the edible fruit, typically rounded but elongated and growing smaller toward the stem, of a tree, *Pyrus communis,* of the rose family. **2.** the tree itself. **3.** a type of cut for a gemstone, esp. a diamond, yielding a faceted oval with one end tapered to a point.

pearl (pûrl), *n.* **1.** a smooth, rounded bead, composed chiefly of aragonite, formed around an irritating foreign body within the shells of oysters and other mollusks: valued as a gem when lustrous and finely colored. Compare CULTURED PEARL. **2.** something resembling this, as various synthetic substances used in costume jewelry. **3.** something similar in form or luster. **4.** something precious or choice: *pearls of wisdom.* **5.** a very pale gray, often with a bluish tinge. **6.** MOTHER-OF-PEARL. **7.** a 5-point type. —*v.t.* **8.** to adorn with or as if with pearls. **9.** to make like a pearl, as in form or color. —*v.i.* **10.** to dive or search for pearls. **11.** to assume a pearllike form or appearance. —*adj.* **12.** of or resembling a pearl. **13.** set or adorned with or consisting of pearls or mother-of-pearl. **14.** having or reduced to small, round grains. —*Saying.* **15. Do not cast your pearls before swine,** do not offer good things to people who can't appreciate their value. Matt. 7:6.

pearl′ bar′ley, *n.* barley milled into small, round grains, used esp. in soups.

pearl′ div′er, *n.* a person who dives for pearl oysters or other pearl-bearing mollusks.

pearl•es•cent (pər les′ənt), *adj.* having an iridescent luster resembling that of pearl or mother-of-pearl; nacreous.

pearl′ gray′, *n.* a very pale bluish gray.

Pearl′ Har′bor, *n.* a harbor near Honolulu, on S Oahu, in Hawaii: surprise attack by Japan on U.S. naval base Dec. 7, 1941.

pearl•ite (pûr′līt), *n.* **1.** a microscopic lamellar structure found in iron or steel, composed of alternating layers of ferrite and cementite. **2.** PERLITE. —**pearl•it′ic** (-lit′ik), *adj.*

pearl•ized (pûr′līzd), *adj.* resembling or made to resemble mother-of-pearl; iridescent.

pearl′ mil′let, *n.* a tall grass, *Pennisetum glaucum,* cultivated for its edible seeds and as a forage plant.

Pearl′ of Great′ Price′, a parable of Jesus. Matt. 13:45–46.

pearl′ on′ion, *n.* a very small white onion, often pickled and used as a garnish.

pearl′ oys′ter, *n.* any of several marine bivalve mollusks of the family Pteriidae, inhabiting tropical waters, some of which form pearls of great value.

pearl′ tapio′ca, *n.* See under TAPIOCA.

pearl•y (pûr′lē), *adj.,* **-i•er, -i•est. 1.** like a pearl, esp. in being white or lustrous: *pearly teeth.* **2.** adorned with or abounding in pearls or mother-of-pearl. —**pearl′i•ness,** *n.*

Pearl′y Gates′, *n.pl.* the entrance to heaven.

pearl′y nau′tilus, *n.* NAUTILUS (def. 1).

pear′-shaped′, *adj.* **1.** having the shape of a pear; tapering near the top and bulging toward the base or bottom. **2.** (of a vocal tone) clear, resonant, and without harshness; full-bodied.

Pea•ry (pēr′ē), *n.* **Robert Edwin,** 1856–1920, U.S. admiral and arctic explorer.

peas•ant (pez′ənt), *n.* **1.** a member of a class of small farmers or farm laborers of low social rank, as in Europe, Asia, or Latin America. **2.** a coarse, boorish, uneducated person of little financial means. —*adj.* **3.** of or characteristic of peasants or their traditions, way of life, etc. **4.** modeled on the folk costumes of Western cultures: *peasant blouses.*

peas•ant•ry (pez′ən trē), *n.* **1.** peasants collectively. **2.** the status or character of a peasant.

pea•shoot•er (pē′shōō′tər), *n.* a tube through which dried peas, beans, or pellets are blown, used as a toy. Also called **beanshooter.**

pea′ soup′, *n.* **1.** a thick soup made from split peas. **2.** a dense fog.

peat (pēt), *n.* **1.** a highly organic material found in marshy or damp regions, composed of partially decayed vegetable matter: it is cut and dried for use as fuel. **2.** such vegetable matter used as fertilizer. —**peat′y,** *adj.,* **-i•er, -i•est.**

peat′ moss′, *n.* **1.** any moss, esp. of the genus *Sphagnum,* from which peat may form. **2.** such moss when dried, used chiefly as a mulch or seedbed.

peb•ble (peb′əl), *n., v.,* **-bled, -bling.** —*n.* **1.** a small, rounded stone, esp. one worn by the action of water. **2.** Also called **peb′ble leath′er.** leather that has been given a granulated surface. **3.** any granulated or crinkled surface, as of a textile. **4.** a transparent colorless rock crystal used for the lenses of eyeglasses. **5.** a lens made from this. —*v.t.* **6.** to prepare (leather) so as to have a granulated surface. —**peb′bly,** *adj.*

pe•can (pi kän′, -kan′, pē′kan), *n.* a tall hickory tree, *Carya illinoinensis,* of the southern U.S. and Mexico, cultivated for its oval, smooth-shelled, edible nuts. **2.** a nut of this tree.

pec•ca•dil•lo (pek′ə dil′ō), *n., pl.* **-loes, -los.** a minor or slight sin or offense; trifling fault.

pec•cant (pek′ənt), *adj.* **1.** sinning; guilty of a moral offense. **2.** violating a rule or principle; faulty; wrong. —**pec′can•cy,** *n.*

pec•ca•ry (pek′ə rē), *n., pl.* **-ries,** *(esp. collectively)* **-ry.** either of two piglike mammals constituting the New World family Tayassuidae, esp. *Tayassu tajacu,* **(collared peccary** or **javelina),** having a dark gray coat with a white collar.

peck¹ (pek), *n.* **1.** a dry measure of 8 quarts; the fourth part of a bushel, equal to 537.6 cubic inches (8.81 liters). *Abbr.:* pk **2.** a container for measuring this quantity. **3.** a considerable quantity: *a peck of trouble.*

peck² (pek), *v.t.* **1.** to strike or pierce with the beak, as a bird does, or with some pointed instrument. **2.** to make (a hole, puncture, etc.) by doing this. **3.** to take (food) bit by bit, with or as if with the beak. —*v.i.* **4.** to make strokes with the beak or a pointed instrument. **5. peck at, a.** to nibble indifferently at (food). **b.** to nag or carp at. —*n.* **6.** a quick stroke, as in pecking. **7.** a hole or mark made by or as if by pecking. **8.** a quick, almost impersonal kiss.

peck′ing or′der, *n.* **1.** Also, **peck′ or′der.** a dominance hierarchy of domestic poultry in which each bird's status is maintained by pecking a bird of lower status. **2.** a hierarchy of status in a social group.

Peck′s′ Bad′ Boy′, *n.* **1.** the mischievous boy in a series of newspaper stories and collected volumes by the American newspaperman and humorist George Wilbur Peck (1840–1916). **2.** Usually, **Peck's bad boy. a.** any mischievous boy. **b.** a recalcitrant person or organization.

Pe′cos Bill′, *n.* a legendary cowboy of the American frontier who performed such fabulous feats as digging the Rio Grande.

pecs (peks), *n.pl. Informal.* pectoral muscles.

pec•tase (pek′tās, -tāz), *n.* an enzyme occurring in various fruits, involved in the formation of pectic acid from pectin.

pec•ten (pek′tən), *n., pl.* **-tens, -ti•nes** (-tə nēz′). **1.** a comblike part or process. **2.** a pigmented vascular membrane with parallel folds suggesting the teeth of a comb, projecting into the vitreous humor of the eye in birds and reptiles. **3.** SCALLOP (def. 1).

pec′tic ac′id, *n.* any of several products of the hydrolysis of pectin esters.

pec•tin (pek′tin), *n.* a white colloidal carbohydrate of high molecular weight, present in ripe fruits: used in fruit jellies for its thickening and emulsifying properties. —**pec′tic, pec′tin•ous,** *adj.*

pec•to•ral (pek′tər əl), *adj.* **1.** of, in, on, or pertaining to the chest or breast; thoracic. **2.** worn on the breast or chest. —*n.* **3.** a pectoral body part or organ. **4.** something worn on the breast for ornament, protection, etc., as a breastplate. —**pec′to•ral•ly,** *adv.*

pec′toral cross′, *n.* a cross worn on the breast by various prelates, as a designation of office. [1720–30]

pec′toral fin′, *n.* (in fishes) either of a pair of fins usu. situated behind the head, one on each side, and corresponding to the forelimbs of higher vertebrates.

pec′toral gir′dle, *n.* the compound bony or cartilaginous arch supporting the forelimbs or analogous parts in vertebrates.

pec′toral mus′cle, *n.* any of four muscles, two on each side, originating in the chest wall and extending to the shoulders and upper arms.

pec•u•late (pek′yə lāt′), *v.t., v.i.,* **-lat•ed, -lat•ing.** to steal or take dishonestly (money, esp. public funds, or property entrusted to one's care); embezzle. —**pec′u•la′tion,** *n.* —**pec′u•la′tor,** *n.*

pe•cu•liar (pi kyōōl′yər), *adj.* **1.** strange; queer; odd. **2.** uncommon; unusual. **3.** distinctive in nature or character from others. **4.** belonging characteristically or exclusively to some person, group, or thing (often fol. by *to*): *an expression peculiar to Canadians; the peculiar properties of a drug.* —*n.* **5.** a property or privilege belonging exclusively to a person. **6.** a church or parish of the Church of England under jurisdiction outside of the diocese in which it lies. —**pe•cu′liar•ly,** *adv.*

pe•cu•li•ar•i•ty (pi kyōō′lē ar′i tē, -kyōōl yar′-), *n., pl.* **-ties. 1.** a trait, manner, characteristic, or habit that is odd or unusual. **2.** oddity; singularity; eccentricity. **3.** a distinguishing quality or characteristic. **4.** the quality or condition of being peculiar.

pe•cu•ni•ar•y (pi kyōō′nē er′ē), *adj.* **1.** of, pertaining to, or consisting of money. **2.** (of a legal offense) involving a money penalty or fine. —**pe•cu′ni•ar′i•ly** (-âr′i lē), *adv.*

ped- or **paed-,** var. of PEDO- before a vowel: *pedagogue.*

-ped, a combining form with the meaning "having a foot" of the kind specified by the initial element: *pinniped.* Compare -POD.

ped•a•gog•ic (ped′ə goj′ik) also **ped′a•gog′i•cal,** *adj.* of or pertaining to a pedagogue or pedagogy. —**ped′a•gog′i•cal•ly,** *adv.*

ped•a•gog•ics (ped′ə goj′iks, -gō′jiks), *n. (used with a sing. v.)* the science or art of teaching; pedagogy.

ped•a•gogue or **ped•a•gog** (ped′ə gog′, -gôg′), *n.* **1.** a teacher; schoolteacher. **2.** a person who is pedantic, dogmatic, and formal. —**ped′a•gogu′ism,** *n.*

ped•a•go•gy (ped′ə gō′jē, -goj′ē), *n., pl.* **-gies. 1.** the function or work of a teacher; teaching. **2.** the art or science of teaching; education; instructional methods.

ped•al (ped′l; *for 5 also* pēd′l), *n., v.,* **-aled, -al•ing** or *(esp. Brit.)* **-alled, -al•ling,** *adj.* —*n.* **1.** a foot-operated lever or part used to control, activate, or supply power to various mechanisms. **2. a.** a foot-operated lever on a keyboard musical instrument, esp. one of a set serving as a secondary keyboard on a pipe organ. **b.** PEDAL POINT. —*v.i.* **3.** to work or use pedals, as in riding a bicycle. —*v.t.* **4.** to work the pedals of. —*adj.* **5.** of or pertaining to a foot or the feet. **6.** of, pertaining to, or using pedals.

ped′al point′, *n.* a musical tone, as the dominant or tonic, held by the bass while the other parts move independently above it. Also called **ped′al note′.**

ped′al push′ers, *n. (used with a pl. v.)* girls' and women's casual slacks reaching to mid-calf.

ped′al steel′ guitar′, *n.* an oblong, floor-mounted electrified guitar fretted with a steel bar and producing a wailing sound that is modulated by use of a foot pedal. Also called **ped′al steel′.**

P

ped·ant (ped′nt), *n.* **1.** a person who makes an excessive or inappropriate display of learning. **2.** a person who overemphasizes rules or minor details, esp. in teaching. **3.** a person who adheres rigidly to book knowledge without regard to common sense. —**pe·dan·tic** (pə dan′tik), *adj.* —**pe·dan′ti·cal·ly,** *adv.*

ped·ant·ry (ped′n trē), *n., pl.* **ped·ant·ries. 1.** the character or practices of a pedant, esp. undue display of learning. **2.** slavish attention to formal rules or minute details. **3.** an instance of being pedantic.

ped·ate (ped′āt), *adj.* **1.** having a foot or feet. **2.** resembling a foot. **3.** having divisions like toes. **4.** (of a leaf) palmately parted or divided with the lateral lobes or divisions cleft or divided.

ped·dle (ped′l), *v.,* **-dled, -dling.** —*v.t.* **1.** to carry (goods, esp. small articles) from place to place for sale; hawk. **2.** to deal out or attempt to spread: *to peddle radical ideas.* —*v.i.* **3.** to go from place to place with goods for sale. **4.** to occupy oneself with trifles.

ped·dler (ped′lər), *n.* **1.** a person who sells from door to door or in the street. **2.** a person who tries to promote some cause, candidate, viewpoint, etc. Sometimes, **pedlar, pedler.**

-pede, var. of **-PED:** *centipede.*

ped·es·tal (ped′ə stl), *n., v.,* **-taled, -tal·ing** or (*esp. Brit.*) **-talled, -tal·ling.** —*n.* **1.** an architectural support for a column, statue, vase, or the like. **2.** a supporting structure or piece; base. **3.** a columnar support, often flaring outward at the bottom, for a tabletop or chair seat. —*v.t.* **4.** to put on or supply with a pedestal. —*Idiom.* **5.** set or put on a pedestal, to glorify; idealize.

pe·des·tri·an (pə des′trē ən), *n.* **1.** a person who goes or travels on foot. —*adj.* **2.** going or performed on foot. **3.** of or intended for walking. **4.** lacking in vitality, imagination, or distinction; commonplace; prosaic.

pe·des·tri·an·ism (pə des′trē ə niz′əm), *n.* **1.** the exercise or practice of walking. **2.** commonplace or prosaic manner or quality.

pedi-, a combining form meaning "foot": *pedicab.*

pe·di·a·tri·cian (pē′dē ə trish′ən), *n.* a physician who specializes in pediatrics. Sometimes, **pe′di·at′rist** (-ə′trist).

pe·di·at·rics (pē′dē ə′triks), *n.* (*used with a sing. v.*) the branch of medicine concerned with the development, care, and diseases of babies and children. —**pe′di·at′ric,** *adj.*

ped·i·cab (ped′i kab′), *n.* (esp. in Southeast Asia) a three-wheeled public conveyance operated by pedals, typically one having a hooded cab for two passengers mounted behind the driver.

ped·i·cel (ped′ə səl, -sel′), *n.* **1.** the stalk of a single flower in a branched inflorescence. **2.** PEDUNCLE (def. 3).

ped·i·cle (ped′i kal), *n.* **1.** PEDUNCLE (def. 3).

pe·dic·u·lar (pə dik′yə lər), *adj.* of or pertaining to lice.

pe·dic·u·late (pə dik′yə lit, -lāt′), *adj.* **1.** of or pertaining to the Lophiiformes (Pediculati), an order of marine fishes characterized by armlike pectoral fins and a dorsal spine modified into a lure. —*n.* **2.** a pediculate fish.

pe·dic·u·lo·sis (pə dik′yə lō′sis), *n.* infestation with lice of the genus *Pediculus* or *Pthirus.* —**pe·dic′u·lous** (-ləs), *adj.*

ped·i·cure (ped′i kyŏŏr′), *n.* **1.** professional care of the feet, as removal of corns and trimming of toenails. **2.** a single treatment of the feet. **3.** a podiatrist. —**ped′i·cur′ist,** *n.*

ped·i·gree (ped′i grē′), *n.* **1.** an ancestral line; lineage; ancestry. **2.** a genealogical record, esp. of a purebred animal. **3.** distinguished or pure ancestry. **4.** derivation; history. —*adj.* Also, **ped′i·greed′. 5.** having established purebred ancestry: *a pedigree collie.*

ped·i·ment (ped′ə mənt), *n.* **1.** (in classical architecture) a low triangular gable outlined by a horizontal cornice below and sloping cornices above, surmounting a colonnade, an end wall, or a major division of a facade. **2.** a feature resembling this, used to crown an opening, monument, etc., or as decoration. **3.** a gently sloping rock surface at the foot of a steep slope, usu. thinly covered with alluvium. —**ped′i·men′tal** (-men′tl), *adj.* —**ped′i·ment′ed,** *adj.*

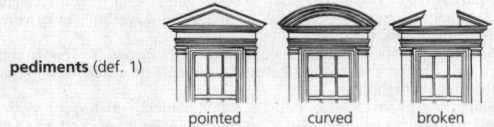

pediments (def. 1)

pointed   curved   broken

ped·lar or **ped·ler** (ped′lər), *n.* PEDDLER.

pedo-, a combining form meaning "child," "boy": *pedophilia.* Also, **paedo-;** *esp. before a vowel,* **ped-.**

pe·dol·o·gy[1] (pi dol′ə jē), *n.* the scientific study of soils. —**ped·o·log·i·cal** (ped′l oj′i kəl), —**ped·o·log′ic,** or **pe·dol′o·gist,** *n.*

pe·dol·o·gy[2] (pi dol′ə jē), *n.* **1.** the scientific study of the nature and development of children. **2.** PEDIATRICS. —**pe·do·log·i·cal** (pēd′l oj′i kəl), **pe′do·log′ic,** *adj.* —**pe·dol′o·gist,** *n.*

pe·dom·e·ter (pə dom′i tər), *n.* an instrument that measures the distance walked or run by recording the number of steps taken.

pe·do·mor·phism or **pae·do·mor·phism** (pē′də môr′fiz əm), *n.* the retention by an adult organism of a juvenile or larval form. —**pe′do·mor′phic,** *adj.*

pe·do·phil·i·a (pē′də fil′ē ə), *n.* sexual desire in an adult for a child. —**pe′do·phile′** (-fīl′), —**pe′do·phil′i·ac,** *adj., n.*

pe·dun·cle (pi dung′kəl, pē′dung-), *n.* **1.** the stalk that supports a flower or flower cluster. **2.** the stem bearing a mushroom cap. **3.** any stalklike process serving as a support. **4.** a band of nervous tissue connecting different parts of the brain. —**pe·dun′cled, pe·dun′cu·lar** (-kyə lər), *adj.*

pee (pē), *n., pl.* **pees** for 1; **pee** for 2. **1.** the letter *p.* **2.** *Brit.* PENNY (def. 2).

peek (pēk), *v.* **1.** to look or glance quickly or furtively, esp. through a small opening or from a concealed location; peep. —*n.* **2.** a quick or furtive look or glance; peep.

peek·a·boo (pēk′ə bōō′), *n.* **1.** a game in which one amuses a baby by suddenly revealing one's face from hiding, as from behind one's hands, and calling "Peekaboo!" —*adj.* **2.** (of clothing) decorated with openwork. **3.** made of a sheer and revealing material.

peek·a·poo or **pe·ke·poo** (pē′kə pōō′), *n., pl.* **-poos.** one of a variety of dogs crossbred from a Pekingese and a miniature poodle.

peel (pēl), *v.t.* **1.** to strip (something) of its skin, rind, bark, etc. **2.** to strip away from something: *to peel paint from a car.* —*v.i.* **3.** (of skin, bark, paint, etc.) to come off in pieces. **4.** to lose the skin, rind, bark, paint, etc. **5.** *Informal.* to undress. **6.** peel off, a. (of an aircraft) to leave a flight formation with a banking turn. b. to veer away from a path or group. —*n.* **7.** the skin or rind of a fruit or vegetable. —*Idiom.* **8.** keep one's eyes peeled, to watch closely or carefully; be alert.

Peel (pēl), *n.* **Sir Robert,** 1788–1850, British statesman: founder of the London constabulary; prime minister 1834–35, 1841–46.

peel·er (pē′lər), *n.* **1.** a kitchen implement for removing the peel from a vegetable or fruit. **2.** one that peels.

peel·ing (pē′ling), *n.* a piece, as of skin or rind, peeled off: *potato peelings.*

peen (pēn), *n.* **1.** the usu. wedgelike or spherical end of a hammer head opposite the face. —*v.t.* **2.** to enlarge, straighten, or smooth with a peen.

peep[1] (pēp), *v.i.* **1.** to look through a small opening or from a concealed location. **2.** to look slyly, pryingly, or furtively. **3.** to look curiously or playfully. **4.** to come partially into view; begin to appear. —*v.t.* **5.** to show or protrude slightly. —*n.* **6.** a quick or furtive look. **7.** the first appearance, as of dawn. **8.** an aperture for looking through.

peep[2] (pēp), *n.* **1.** a short, shrill little cry or sound, as of a young bird. **2.** any of various small sandpipers, esp. of the genus *Calidris.* **3.** a slight sound or remark, as of complaint: *I don't want to hear a peep out of you!* —*v.i.* **4.** to utter a short, shrill little cry. **5.** to speak in a weak voice.

peep·er[1] (pē′pər), *n.* **1.** a person who peeps in a prying manner; voyeur. **2.** **peepers,** *Slang.* the eyes.

peep·er[2] (pē′pər), *n.* **1.** one that makes a peeping sound. **2.** any of several frogs having a peeping call, esp. the spring peeper.

peep·hole (pēp′hōl′), *n.* a small hole, as in a door, through which to look.

pee·pul (pē′pəl), *n.* PIPAL.

peer[1] (pēr), *n.* **1.** a person who is the equal of another in abilities, qualifications, age, background, or social status. **2.** a person of the same legal status as another. **3.** something of equal worth or quality. **4.** a noble. **5.** a member of any of the five degrees of the nobility in Great Britain and Ireland (duke, marquis, earl, viscount, and baron).

peer[2] (pēr), *v.i.* **1.** to look narrowly or searchingly, as in the effort to discern clearly. **2.** to appear slightly; peep out. **3.** to come into view. —**peer′ing·ly,** *adv.*

peer·age (pēr′ij), *n.* **1.** the body of peers of a country. **2.** the rank or dignity of a peer. **3.** a book listing the peers and giving their genealogies.

peer·ess (pēr′is), *n.* **1.** the wife or widow of a peer. **2.** a woman having in her own right the rank of a peer.

peer′ group′, *n.* a group of friends or associates, usu. of similar background, social status, and esp. age, who are likely to influence a person's beliefs and behavior.

peer·less (pēr′lis), *adj.* having no equal; matchless; unrivaled. —**peer′less·ly,** *adv.* —**peer′less·ness,** *n.*

peeve (pēv), *v.,* **peeved, peev·ing,** *n.* —*v.t.* **1.** to render peevish; annoy. —*n.* **2.** a source of annoyance or irritation. **3.** an annoyed or irritated mood.

peeved (pēvd), *adj.* annoyed; irritated; vexed.

pee·vish (pē′vish), *adj.* cross, querulous, or fretful. —**pee′vish·ly,** *adv.* —**pee′vish·ness,** *n.*

pee·wee (pē′wē′), *n. Informal.* a person or thing that is unusually small.

peg (peg), *n., v.,* **pegged, peg·ging,** *adj.* —*n.* **1.** a cylindrical or tapered pin of wood, metal, etc., driven or fitted into something as a fastening, support, stopper, or marker. **2.** a notch or degree: *to come down a peg.* **3.** an occasion, basis, or reason: *a peg to hang a grievance on.* **4.** one of the wooden or metal pins in the neck of a musical stringed instrument that are turned to adjust the tension and pitch of the strings. **5.** *Informal.* a leg. **6.** *Informal.* a hard, accurate throw, esp. in baseball. **7.** *Brit.* CLOTHESPIN. **8.** *Brit.* an alcoholic drink, esp. a whiskey or brandy and soda. —*v.t.* **9.** to fasten with or as if with pegs. **10.** to mark with pegs. **11.** to strike or pierce with or as if with a peg. **12.**

to keep (a price, exchange rate, etc.) at a set level. **13.** *Informal.* to throw (a ball) forcefully. **14.** *Informal.* to identify: *to peg someone as a good prospect.* **15.** to base upon: *The feature story was pegged on the riots.* —*v.i.* **16.** to work persistently: *pegging away at homework.* —*adj.* **17.** Also, **pegged.** PEG-TOP.

Peg·a·sus (peg′ə səs), *n., gen.* **-si** (-sī′) for 2. **1.** a winged horse of Greek myth. **2.** the Winged Horse, a northern constellation between Cygnus and Aquarius. —**Pe·ga·si·an** (pə gā′sē ən), *adj.*

peg′ leg′, *n.* **1.** an artificial leg, esp. a wooden one. **2.** a person with an artificial leg. —**peg′legged′,** *adj.*

peg′-top′, *adj.* wide or full at the top and tapered narrowly at the bottom: *peg-top trousers; peg-top sleeves.*

peign·oir (pān wär′, pen-, pān′wär, pen′-), *n.* a woman's loose dressing gown.

Pei·ping (pā′ping′, bā′-), *n.* former name of BEIJING.

pej·o·ra·tion (pej′ə rā′shən, pē′jə-), *n.* **1.** a lessening in worth or quality; depreciation. **2.** semantic change in a word over the course of time to a less favorable or less respectable meaning. Compare MELIORATION (def. 1).

pe·jo·ra·tive (pi jôr′ə tiv, -jor′-, pej′ə rā′-, pē′jə-), *adj.* **1.** having a disparaging, derogatory, or belittling effect or force, as a word. —*n.* **2.** a pejorative form or word, as *poetaster.* —**pe·jo′ra·tive·ly,** *adv.*

Pe·kah (pē′kä, -kə), *n.* an idolatrous king of Israel. II Kings 15:25–31; II Chron. 28:5–31.

Pek·a·hi·ah (pek′ə hī′ə), *n.* an idolatrous king of Israel who was assassinated by Pekah. II Kings 15:22–26.

Pe·king (pē′king′, pā′-), *n.* BEIJING.

Pe′king duck′, *n.* a Chinese dish of the crisp skin and meat of a roasted duck combined with scallions and hoisin sauce and folded in thin pancakes.

Pe·king·ese (pē′kə nēz′, -nēs′; *esp. for 2–4 also* pē′king ēz′, -ēs′) *also* **Pe·kin·ese** (pē′kə nēz′, -nēs′), *n., pl.* **-ese** for 1, 3, *adj.* —*n.* **1.** one of a Chinese breed of small dogs having a long, silky coat and a flat, wrinkled muzzle. **2. a.** the Mandarin dialect of Beijing. **b.** PUTONGHUA. **3.** a native or inhabitant of Beijing. —*adj.* **4.** of or pertaining to Beijing or its inhabitants.

Pe′king′ man′, *n.* the skeletal remains of *Homo erectus* found at Zhoukoudian, near Peking (Beijing), China, in the late 1920s to mid-1930s and subsequently lost during World War II.

pe·koe (pē′kō), *n.* a black tea from Sri Lanka, India, and Java, made from leaves coarser than those used for orange pekoe.

pel·age (pel′ij), *n.* the hair, fur, wool, or other soft covering of a mammal. —**pe·la·gi·al** (pə lā′jē əl), *adj.*

Pe·la·gi·an (pə lā′jē ən, -jən), *n.* **1.** a follower of Pelagius, who denied original sin and believed in freedom of the will. —*adj.* **2.** of or pertaining to Pelagius or his beliefs.

pe·lag·ic (pə laj′ik), *adj.* **1.** of or pertaining to the open seas or oceans. **2.** living at or near the surface of the open seas.

Pe·la·gi·us (pə lā′jē əs), *n.* A.D. 360?–420?, British monk and theologian who lived in Rome: teachings opposed by St. Augustine.

pel·ar·go·ni·um (pel′är gō′nē əm, -ər-), *n., pl.* **-ums.** any plant of the genus *Pelargonium,* the cultivated species of which are usu. called geranium.

Pe·lée (pə lā′), *n.* **Mount,** a volcano in the West Indies, on the island of Martinique: eruption 1902. 4428 ft. (1350 m).

pel·i·can (pel′i kən), *n.* any of several large web-footed birds of the family Pelecanidae, of warmer regions of the world, having an expandable throat pouch.

pel·la·gra (pə lag′rə, -lā′grə, -lä′-), *n.* a disease caused by a deficiency of niacin in the diet, characterized by skin changes, severe nerve dysfunction, mental symptoms, and diarrhea. —**pel·la′grose, pel·la′grous,** *adj.*

pel·let (pel′it), *n.* **1.** a small, rounded body, as of food or medicine. **2.** a small wad or ball of wax, paper, etc., for throwing, shooting, or the like. **3.** one of a charge of small shot, as for a shotgun. **4.** a bullet. **5.** a ball, usu. of stone, formerly used as a missile. **6.** a small, roundish mass of matter regurgitated by certain predatory birds, consisting of the indigestible remains of the prey. —*v.t.* **7.** to hit with pellets. **8.** to form into pellets; pelletize. —**pel′let·like′,** *adj.*

pell-mell or **pell·mell** (pel′mel′), *adv.* **1.** in a recklessly hurried manner. **2.** in a disordered mass. —*adj.* **3.** disorderly or confused. **4.** overhasty or precipitate; rash. —*n.* **5.** a jumbled mass, crowd, etc. **6.** disorderly, headlong haste.

pel·lu·cid (pə lōō′sid), *adj.* **1.** allowing the maximum passage of light, as glass; translucent. **2.** clear or limpid: *pellucid waters.* **3.** clear in meaning or expression. —**pel·lu·cid·i·ty** (pel′ōō sid′i tē), **pel·lu′cid·ness,** *n.* —**pel·lu′cid·ly,** *adv.*

Pel′oponne′sian War′, *n.* a war between Athens and Sparta, 431–404 B.C., that resulted in the transfer of hegemony in Greece from Athens to Sparta.

pe·lo·rus (pə lôr′əs, -lōr′-), *n., pl.* **-rus·es.** *Navigation.* a device for measuring in degrees the relative bearings of observed objects.

pe·lo·ta (pə lō′tə), *n., pl.* **-tas.** **1.** a game from which jai alai was developed. **2.** the game of jai alai. **3.** the ball used in pelota and jai alai.

pelt¹ (pelt), *v.t.* **1.** to attack with repeated blows or with missiles. **2.** to throw (missiles). **3.** to assail vigorously with words, questions, etc. **4.** to beat or rush against with repeated forceful blows. —*v.i.* **5.** to beat or pound unrelentingly. **6.** to throw missiles. **7.** to hurry. —*n.* **8.** the act of pelting. **9.** a blow, esp. with something thrown. —**pelt′er,** *n.*

pelt² (pelt), *n.* the untanned hide or skin of an animal. —**pelt′less,** *adj.*

pel′vic fin′, *n.* (in fishes) either of a pair of fins behind and below the pectoral fins, corresponding to the hind limbs of a land vertebrate.

pel′vic gir′dle, *n.* the compound bony or cartilaginous arch supporting the hind limbs or analogous parts in vertebrates.

pel·vis (pel′vis), *n., pl.* **-vis·es, -ves** (-vēz). **1. a.** the basinlike cavity in the lower trunk of the body, formed by the sacrum, ilium, ischium, and pubis. **b.** the bones forming this cavity. **2.** the cavity of the kidney that receives the urine before it is passed into the ureter. [< Latin: basin] —**pel′vic,** *adj.*

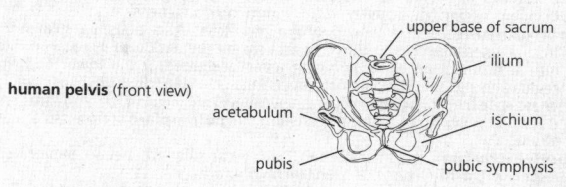

human pelvis (front view)

upper base of sacrum
ilium
acetabulum
ischium
pubis
pubic symphysis

pen¹ (pen), *n., v.,* **penned, pen·ning.** —*n.* **1.** any of various instruments for writing or drawing with ink or a similar substance. Compare BALLPOINT, FOUNTAIN PEN, QUILL (def. 3). **2.** a detachable metal penpoint; nib. **3.** such a penpoint with its penholder. **4.** the pen as a symbol of authorship. **5.** a writer. **6.** QUILL (def. 1). —*v.t.* **7.** to write or draw with or as if with a pen: *to pen an essay; to pen a likeness.* —*Proverb.* **8. The pen is mightier than the sword,** words have more lasting influence than violence. —**pen′like′,** *adj.* —**pen′ner,** *n.*

pen² (pen), *n., v.,* **penned, pen·ning.** —*n.* **1.** a small enclosure for domestic animals. **2.** the animals so enclosed. **3.** PLAYPEN. **4.** BULL PEN (defs. 1, 2). **5.** a dock used in the repair of submarines. —*v.t.* **6.** to confine in or as if in a pen.

pen³ (pen), *n.* *Slang.* PENITENTIARY (def. 1).

pen⁴ (pen), *n.* a female swan.

pe·nal (pēn′l), *adj.* **1.** of or pertaining to punishment, as for crimes or offenses. **2.** prescribing punishment: *penal laws.* **3.** used as a place of confinement and punishment: *a penal colony.* **4.** subject to or incurring punishment: *a penal offense.*

pe′nal code′, *n.* the body of statutes dealing with crimes and their punishment.

pe·nal·ize (pēn′l īz′, pen′-), *v.t.,* **-ized, -iz·ing.** **1.** to subject to a penalty. **2.** to declare (an action) punishable by law or rule. **3.** to put under a disadvantage or handicap. —**pe′nal·i·za′tion,** *n.*

pen·al·ty (pen′l tē), *n., pl.* **-ties.** **1.** a punishment imposed or incurred for a violation of law or rule. **2.** a loss, forfeiture, etc., incurred by nonfulfillment of some obligation. **3.** something forfeited, as a sum of money. **4.** a disadvantage imposed upon one side for infraction of the rules of a game or sport.

pen′alty box′, *n.* an enclosed space at the side of an ice hockey rink for penalized players and certain officials.

pen′alty kick′, *n.* (in soccer) a free kick awarded for an infraction committed by a defensive player in the penalty area.

pen′alty shot′, *n.* (in ice hockey) a free shot at the goal defended only by the goalkeeper, awarded to an offensive player for certain defensive violations.

pen·ance (pen′əns), *n.* **1.** a punishment undergone as penitence for sin. **2.** a penitential discipline imposed by church authority. **3.** a sacrament, as in the Roman Catholic Church, consisting of confession, repentance, and forgiveness for one's sins.

pen′-based′, *adj.* (of a computer) having an electronic stylus rather than a keyboard as the primary input device.

pence (pens), *n.* *Brit.* a pl. of PENNY; used in referring to a sum of money rather than to the coins themselves (often used in combination): *sixpence.*

pen·chant (pen′chənt; (*esp. Brit.*) Fr. pän shän′), *n.* a strong inclination, taste, or liking for something.

pen·cil (pen′səl), *n., v.,* **-ciled, -cil·ing** or (*esp. Brit.*) **-cilled, -cil·ling.** —*n.* **1.** a slender tube of wood, metal, etc., containing a core of graphite, a solid coloring material, or the like, used for writing or drawing. **2.** a stick of cosmetic coloring material for use on the eyebrows, eyelids, etc. **3.** a stick of medicated material. **4.** a narrow set of lines, light rays, or the like, diverging from or converging to a point: *a pencil of sunlight.* **5.** a slender, pointed piece of a substance used for marking. **6.** skill in drawing. —*v.t.* **7.** to write, draw, or mark with or as if with a pencil. **8. pencil in,** to schedule or list tentatively, by or as if by writing down in pencil rather than in ink. —**pen′cil·er;** *esp. Brit.* **pen′cil·ler,** *n.*

pen′cil push′er, *n.* *Often Disparaging.* a person, as a bookkeeper or clerk, whose job involves much paperwork.

pend (pend), *v.i.* **1.** to remain undecided or unsettled. **2.** to hang.

pend·ant (pen′dənt), *n.* Also, **pendent. 1.** a hanging ornament, as a jewel suspended from a necklace. **2.** an ornament suspended from a vault or ceiling, used esp. in Gothic architecture. **3.** a hanging electrical lighting fixture; chandelier. **4.** that by which something is suspended, as the ringed stem of a pocket watch. **5.** a parallel or counterpart. **6.** *Naut.* a hanging length of rope with a block or thimble attached to its free end. —*adj.* **7.** PENDENT.

pen·den·cy (pen′dən sē), *n., pl.* **-cies.** the state or time of being pending, as of a lawsuit awaiting settlement.

pend·ent (pen′dənt), *adj.* Also, **pendant. 1.** hanging or suspended. **2.** overhanging; jutting. **3.** (esp. of a lawsuit) undecided; pending. —*n.* **4.** PENDANT. —**pend′ent·ly,** *adv.*

pend·ing (pen′ding), *prep.* **1.** while awaiting; until: *pending his return.* **2.** during: *pending the trial.* —*adj.* **3.** awaiting decision or settlement. **4.** about to happen; impending.

pen·du·lous (pen′jə ləs, pen′dyə-, -də-), *adj.* **1.** hanging down loosely: *pendulous blossoms.* **2.** swinging freely; oscillating. **3.** vacillating or undecided. —**pen′du·lous·ly,** *adv.* —**pen′du·lous·ness,** *n.*

pen·du·lum (pen′jə ləm, pen′dyə-, -də-), *n.* **1.** a body so suspended from a fixed point as to move to and fro by the action of gravity and acquired momentum. **2.** a swinging lever, weighted at the lower end, for regulating the speed of a clock mechanism. —**pen′du·lum·like′,** *adj.*

pe·ne·plain or **pe·ne·plane** (pē′nə plān′, pen′ə-), *n.* an area reduced almost to a plain by erosion. —**pe′ne·pla·na′tion** (-plə nā′shən), *n.*

pen·e·tra·ble (pen′i trə bəl), *adj.* capable of being penetrated. —**pen′e·tra·bil′i·ty,** *n.* —**pen′e·tra·bly,** *adv.*

pen·e·trant (pen′i trənt), *n.* **1.** a person or thing that penetrates. **2.** a lotion, cream, etc., that penetrates the skin. —*adj.* **3.** PENETRATING.

pen·e·trate (pen′i trāt′), *v.,* **-trat·ed, -trat·ing.** —*v.t.* **1.** to pierce or pass into or through. **2.** to enter the interior of. **3.** to permeate. **4.** to arrive at the meaning of; comprehend. **5.** to obtain a share of (a market). **6.** to affect (the mind or feelings) deeply. **7.** to influence the affairs of (another country). —*v.i.* **8.** to enter or pass through something, as by piercing. **9.** to be diffused through something. **10.** to see or reach by intense searching or study (often fol. by *to* or *into*). **11.** to have a deep effect on someone. —**pen′e·tra′tor,** *n.*

pen·e·trat·ing (pen′i trā′ting), *adj.* **1.** able or tending to penetrate; piercing; sharp. **2.** acute; discerning: *a penetrating remark.* —**pen′e·trat′ing·ly,** *adv.* —**pen′e·trat′ing·ness,** *n.*

pen·e·tra·tion (pen′i trā′shən), *n.* **1.** the act or power of penetrating. **2.** mental acuteness; discernment or insight. **3.** the obtaining of a share of a market for some commodity or service. **4.** the extension of influence into the affairs of another nation. **5.** a military attack that penetrates into enemy territory. **6.** the depth to which a projectile goes into the target.

pen·guin (peng′gwin, pen′-), *n.* any of various flightless aquatic birds of the order Sphenisciformes, of the Southern Hemisphere, having webbed feet and wings reduced to flippers.

emperor penguin, *Aptenodytes forsteri,* length 4 ft. (1.2 m)

pen·i·cil·lin (pen′ə sil′in), *n.* any of several antibiotics produced naturally or semisynthetically from molds of the genus *Penicillium,* widely used to prevent and treat bacterial infection and other diseases.

pen·i·cil·li·um (pen′ə sil′ē əm), *n., pl.* **-cil·li·ums, -cil·li·a** (-sil′ē ə). any fungus of the genus *Penicillium,* certain species of which are used in making cheese and as the source of penicillin.

pen·in·su·la (pə nin′sə lə, -nins′yə lə), *n., pl.* **-las.** an area of land almost completely surrounded by water except for an isthmus connecting it with the mainland. [< Latin *paenīnsula* = *paene* almost + *īnsula* island] —**pen·in′su·lar,** *adj.*

pe·nis (pē′nis), *n., pl.* **-nis·es, -nes** (-nēz). the male organ of copulation and, in mammals, of urinary excretion. —**pe·nile** (pēn′l, pē′nīl), *adj.*

pen·i·tence (pen′i təns), *n.* the state of being penitent; regret for one's wrongdoing or sinning; contrition; repentance.

pen·i·tent (pen′i tənt), *adj.* **1.** feeling or expressing sorrow for sin or wrongdoing and disposed to atonement; repentant; contrite. —*n.* **2.** a penitent person. **3.** *Rom. Cath. Ch.* a person who confesses sin and submits to a penance. —**pen′i·tent·ly,** *adv.*

pen·i·ten·tial (pen′i ten′shəl), *adj.* of, pertaining to, proceeding from, or expressive of penitence or repentance. —**pen′i·ten′tial·ly,** *adv.*

pen·i·ten·tia·ry (pen′i ten′shə rē), *n., pl.* **-ries,** *adj.* —*n.* **1.** a place for imprisonment, reformatory discipline, or punishment, esp., in the U.S., a state or federal institution for serious offenders. **2.** a tribunal in the Curia Romana, presided over by a cardinal having jurisdiction over certain matters, as penance, confession, or dispensation. —*adj.* **3.** (of an offense) punishable by imprisonment in a penitentiary. **4.** of, pertaining

to, or intended for imprisonment, reformatory discipline, or punishment. **5.** PENITENTIAL.

pen·knife (pen′nīf′), *n., pl.* **-knives.** a small pocketknife, formerly one used for making and sharpening quill pens.

pen·light or **pen·lite** (pen′līt′), *n.* a flashlight similar in size and shape to a fountain pen.

pen·man (pen′mən), *n., pl.* **-men. 1.** a person who writes or copies; scribe; copyist. **2.** an expert in penmanship. **3.** a writer or author.

pen·man·ship (pen′mən ship′), *n.* **1.** the art of handwriting; use of the pen in writing. **2.** a person's style or manner of handwriting.

pen·na (pen′ə), *n., pl.* **pen·nae** (pen′ē). a contour feather, as distinguished from a down feather.

pen′ name′, a writer's pseudonym; nom de plume.

pen·nant (pen′ənt), *n.* **1.** a long, tapering flag. **2.** a flag serving as an emblem of victory or championship. **3.** PENDANT (def. 6).

pen·nate (pen′āt) also **pen·nat·ed,** *adj.* winged; feathered.

pen·ni·less (pen′i lis), *adj.* totally without money; destitute. —**pen′ni·less·ly,** *adv.* —**pen′ni·less·ness,** *n.*

Penn·syl·va·nia (pen′səl vān′yə, -vā′nē ə), *n.* a state in the E United States. 12,056,112; 45,333 sq. mi. (117,410 sq. km). *Cap.:* Harrisburg. *Abbr.:* PA, Pa., Penn., Penna.

Penn·syl·va·nian (pen′səl vān′yən, -vā′nē ən), *adj.* **1.** of or pertaining to the state of Pennsylvania. **2.** of or pertaining to a period of the Paleozoic Era, occurring from about 310 to 280 million years ago and characterized by warm climates, swampy land areas, and the development of insects and reptiles: sometimes considered as an epoch of the Carboniferous Period. —*n.* **3.** a native or inhabitant of Pennsylvania. **4.** the Pennsylvanian Period or System.

Penn′sylva′nia ri′fle, *n.* KENTUCKY RIFLE.

pen·ny (pen′ē), *n., pl.* **pen·nies,** (*esp. collectively for 2-4*) **pence. 1.** a monetary unit of various nations, as Australia, Canada, New Zealand, and the U.S., equal to ¹/₁₀₀ of a dollar; one cent. **2.** a monetary unit of the United Kingdom, equal to ¹/₁₀₀ of a pound. **3.** a monetary unit equal to ¹/₂₄₀ of the former British pound or to ¹/₁₂ of the former British shilling. **4.** a monetary unit of Ireland, equal to ¹/₁₀₀ of the Irish pound. **5.** a sum of money: *to spend every penny.* **6.** the unit of measurement describing the size of a nail in standard designations from twopenny to sixtypenny. *Abbr.:* d —*Idiom.* **7. a bad penny,** someone or something undesirable. **8. a pretty penny,** a considerable sum of money. **9. turn an honest penny,** to earn one's living honestly.

-penny, a combining form for adjectives denoting nail sizes: *sixpenny; eightpenny. Abbr.:* d

pen′ny an′te, *n.* **1.** a game of poker in which the ante or limit is one cent. **2.** any arrangement or transaction involving a trifling or paltry sum of money.

pen′ny arcade′, *n.* a gallery or area that contains coin-operated entertainment devices, orig. costing a penny a play.

pen·ny·cress′ or **pen′ny-cress′,** *n.* any of several plants belonging to the genus *Thlaspi,* of the mustard family, esp. *T. arvense,* of Europe, bearing somewhat round, flat pods.

pen′ny pinch′er, *n.* a stingy person. —**pen′ny-pinch′ing,** *n., adj.*

pen·ny·roy·al (pen′ē roi′əl), *n.* **1.** an aromatic Old World plant, *Mentha pulegium,* of the mint family, having clusters of small purple flowers. **2.** a similar related plant, *Hedeoma pulegioides,* of E North America, having bluish flowers growing from the leaf axils.

pen·ny·weight (pen′ē wāt′), *n.* (in troy weight) a unit of 24 grains or ¹/₂₀ of an ounce (1.555 grams). *Abbr.:* dwt, pwt

pen·ny·wort (pen′ē wûrt′, -wôrt′), *n.* any of several plants having round or roundish leaves, as *Obolaria virginica,* of North America.

pe·nol·o·gy (pē nol′ə jē), *n.* **1.** the study of the punishment of crime. **2.** the study of the management of prisons. —**pe·no·log·i·cal** (pēn′l oj′i kəl), *adj.* —**pe·nol′o·gist,** *n.*

pen′ pal′, *n.* a person with whom one keeps up an exchange of letters, usu. someone far away.

pen·point (pen′point′), *n.* **1.** the writing end of a pen, esp. a small, tapering, metallic device with a split tip for drawing up ink and for writing; nib. **2.** the tip or point of a ballpoint or other pen.

pen·sile (pen′sīl, -sil), *adj.* **1.** hanging, as a bird's nest. **2.** building a hanging nest.

pen·sion (pen′shən; *Fr.* päN syôN′ *for* 3), *n., pl.* **-sions. 1.** a fixed amount, other than wages, paid at regular intervals to a person or to the person's surviving dependents for past services, injury or loss sustained, etc. **2.** an allowance, annuity, or subsidy. **3.** (in Europe) **a.** a boardinghouse or small hotel. **b.** room and board. —*v.t.* **4.** to grant or pay a pension to. **5.** to cause to retire on a pension (usu. fol. by *off*).

pen·sion·er (pen′shə nər), *n.* **1.** a person who receives or lives on a pension. **2.** a hireling.

pen′sion plan′, *n.* a plan maintained by a company or organization, either with or without contributions by employees, for making regular payments of benefits to retired or disabled employees.

pen·sive (pen′siv), *adj.* **1.** dreamily or wistfully thoughtful. **2.** expressing thoughtfulness or sadness. —**pen′sive·ly,** *adv.* —**pen′sive·ness,** *n.*

pen·ste·mon (pen stē′mən, pen′stə mən), *n.* any of numerous chiefly North American plants belonging to the genus *Penstemon,* of the figwort family, some species of which are cultivated for their showy, variously colored flowers. Also called **beardtongue.**

pent (pent), *adj.* shut in; confined: *pent cattle; pent emotions.*

penta-, a combining form meaning "five": *pentavalent*. Also, *esp. before a vowel*, **pent-**.

pen·ta·cle (pen′tə kəl), *n.* **1.** PENTAGRAM. **2.** a similar figure, as a hexagram.

pen·tad (pen′tad), *n.* **1.** a period of five years. **2.** a group of five. **3.** the number five. **4.** a pentavalent element or group.

pen·ta·dac·tyl (pen′tə dak′tl, -til), *adj.* having five digits on each hand or foot.

pen·ta·gon (pen′tə gon′), *n.* **1.** a polygon having five angles and five sides. **2. the Pentagon, a.** a building in Arlington, Va., built in the form of a pentagon and containing most of the offices of the U.S. Department of Defense. **b.** the U.S. Department of Defense; the U.S. military establishment. —**pen·tag′o·nal** (-tag′ə nl), *adj.*

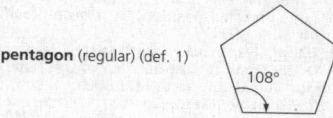

pentagon (regular) (def. 1)

108°

pen·ta·gram (pen′tə gram′), *n.* a regular five-pointed, star-shaped figure, used as an occult symbol. Also called **pentacle, pentangle.**

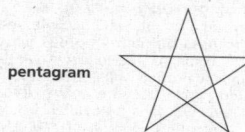

pentagram

pen·tam·e·ter (pen tam′i tər), *n.* **1.** a line of verse consisting of five metrical feet. **2.** unrhymed verse of five iambic feet; English heroic verse. —*adj.* **3.** consisting of five metrical feet. —**pen·tam′e·trist,** *n.*

pen·tane (pen′tān), *n.* a hydrocarbon of the methane series having three liquid isomers, the most important of which, C_5H_{12}, is a highly volatile petroleum distillate used as a solvent and an anesthetic.

pen·tan·gle (pen′tang gəl), *n.* PENTAGRAM.

Pen·ta·teuch (pen′tə tōōk′, -tyōōk′), *n.* the first five books of the Old Testament: Genesis, Exodus, Leviticus, Numbers, and Deuteronomy. Compare HAGIOGRAPHA, PROPHETS. —**Pen′ta·teuch′al,** *adj.*

pen·tath·lete (pen tath′lēt), *n.* an athlete participating or specializing in the pentathlon.

pen·tath·lon (pen tath′lən, -lon), *n.* an athletic contest comprising five different track and field events and won by the contestant amassing the highest total score.

Pen·te·cost (pen′ti kôst′, -kost′), *n.* **1.** a Christian festival celebrated on the seventh Sunday after Easter, commemorating the descent of the Holy Ghost upon the apostles; Whitsunday. **2.** SHAVUOTH. [Middle English *pentecoste,* Old English *pentecosten* < Late Latin *pentēcostē* < Greek *pentēkostē* (*hēméra*) fiftieth (day)]

Pen·te·cos·tal (pen′ti kô′stl, -kos′tl), *adj.* **1.** of or pertaining to Pentecost. **2.** noting or pertaining to any of various Christian groups, usu. fundamentalist, that emphasize the activity of the Holy Spirit, stress holiness of living, and express their religious feelings uninhibitedly, as by speaking in tongues.

pent·house (pent′hous′), *n., pl.* **-hous·es** (-hou′ziz). **1.** an apartment or dwelling on the roof of a building, usu. set back from the outer walls. **2.** any specially designed apartment on an upper floor, esp. the top floor, of a building. **3.** a structure on a roof for housing elevator machinery, a water tank, etc. **4.** a sloping roof or a shed with a sloping roof projecting from a wall or the side of a building, as to shelter a door.

pen·ti·men·to (pen′tə men′tō), *n., pl.* **-ti** (-tē). the reemergence in a painting of an image that has been painted over.

pent·land·ite (pent′lən dīt′), *n.* a mineral, iron-nickel sulfide, (FeNi),S₈, occurring in the form of bronze-colored granular aggregates: the principal source of nickel.

pent′-up′, *adj.* confined; restrained; not vented or expressed; curbed: *pent-up rage.*

pen·tyl (pen′tl), *n.* AMYL.

pe·nu·che (pə nōō′chē), *n.* a fudge made of brown sugar, butter, milk, and usu. nuts.

pe·nuch·le or **pe·nuck·le** (pē′nuk əl), *n.* PINOCHLE.

Pe·nu·el (pi nōō′el, -nyōō′-) also **Pe·ni·el** (pi nī′el), *n.* a place where Jacob wrestled with God, later a city. Gen. 32:30; Judg. 8:17.

pe·nult (pē′nult, pi nult′), *n.* the next to the last syllable in a word.

pe·nul·ti·mate (pi nul′tə mit), *adj.* **1.** next to the last. **2.** of or pertaining to a penult. —*n.* **3.** PENULT.

pe·num·bra (pi num′brə), *n., pl.* **-brae** (-brē), **-bras. 1. a.** the partial or imperfect shadow outside the complete shadow of an opaque body, as a planet, where the light from the source of illumination is only partly cut off. **b.** the grayish marginal portion of a sunspot. **2.** a shadowy, indefinite, or marginal area. —**pe·num′bral, pe·num′brous,** *adj.*

pe·nu·ri·ous (pə nŏŏr′ē əs, -nyŏŏr′-), *adj.* **1.** extremely stingy. **2.** extremely poor; indigent. **3.** poorly or inadequately supplied. —**pe·nu′ri·ous·ness,** *n.*

pen·u·ry (pen′yə rē), *n.* **1.** extreme poverty; destitution. **2.** scarcity or lack; insufficiency.

pe·on (pē′ən, pē′on), *n.* **1.** (in Spanish America) a farm worker or unskilled laborer. **2.** (formerly, esp. in Mexico) a person held in servitude to work off debts or other obligations. **3.** any person of low social status, esp. one who does menial or unskilled work; drudge.

pe·on·age (pē′ə nij), *n.* **1.** the condition or service of a peon. **2.** the practice of holding persons in servitude or partial slavery, as to work off a debt or to serve a penal sentence.

pe·o·ny (pē′ə nē), *n., pl.* **-nies.** any of various plants of the genus *Paeonia,* having large showy flowers, as *P. lactiflora.*

peo·ple (pē′pəl), *n., pl.* **-ples** for 4, *v.,* **-pled, -pling.** —*n.* **1.** persons indefinitely or collectively; persons in general. **2.** persons considered as numerable individuals forming a group. **3.** human beings, as distinguished from animals or other beings. **4.** the entire body of persons who constitute a community or other group by virtue of a common culture, religion, or the like. **5.** the persons of any particular group, company, or number (sometimes used in combination): *salespeople.* **6.** the ordinary persons, as distinguished from those who have wealth, rank, influence, etc. **7.** the subjects, followers, or subordinates of a ruler, leader, employer, etc. **8.** the body of enfranchised citizens of a state. **9.** a person's family or relatives. —*v.t.* **10.** to furnish with people; populate. **11.** to supply or stock as if with people. —**Usage.** PEOPLE is usu. followed by a plural verb and referred to by a plural pronoun: *The people have made their choice.* When PEOPLE means "the entire body of persons who constitute a community by virtue of a common culture, religion, etc.," it is singular, with the plural PEOPLES: *This people shares characteristics with certain inhabitants of central Asia. The aboriginal peoples of the Western Hemisphere speak many different languages.* At one time, some usage guides maintained that PEOPLE could not be preceded by a number, as in *Fewer than 30 people showed up.* This use is now standard.

peo′ple me′ter, *n.* an electronic device used in registering the television viewing habits of selected viewers.

peo′ple mov′er, *n.* any of various forms of mass transit for fixed routes, as moving sidewalks or automated driverless vehicles.

Peo′ple's Libera′tion Ar′my, *n.* **1.** the name of the armed forces of the People's Republic of China. **2.** a rebel army or army of liberation in any of various other countries.

Peo′ple's Par′ty, *n.* a political party (1891–1904), advocating expansion of currency, state control of railroads, the placing of restrictions upon ownership of land, etc.; Populist party.

Pe·o·ri·a (pē ôr′ē ə, -ōr′-), *n.* a city in central Illinois, on the Illinois River. 112,878.

pep (pep), *n., v.,* **pepped, pep·ping.** —*n.* **1.** lively spirits or energy; vigor. —*v.* **2. pep up,** to make or become spirited or vigorous.

pep·er·o·mi·a (pep′ə rō′mē ə), *n., pl.* **-mi·as.** any of various plants of the genus *Peperomia,* of the pepper family, cultivated as houseplants.

pep·er·o·ni (pep′ə rō′nē), *n., pl.* **-nis.** PEPPERONI.

pep·lum (pep′ləm), *n., pl.* **-lums, -la** (-lə). a piece of fabric, as a full flounce, attached to or extending from the waistline of a jacket, dress, or the like.

pe·po (pē′pō), *n., pl.* **-pos.** the characteristic fruit of plants of the gourd family, having a fleshy, many-seeded interior and a hard or firm rind, as the gourd, melon, and cucumber.

pep·per (pep′ər), *n.* **1. a.** the pungent dried berries of the tropical climbing shrub *Piper nigrum,* used whole, crushed, or ground as a condiment. **b.** any plant of the genus *Piper,* of the pepper family, several of which yield similar pungent berries. **2. a.** any of several plants belonging to the genus *Capsicum,* of the nightshade family, esp. *C. annuum* and *C. frutescens.* **b.** the usu. green or red fruit of any of these plants, ranging from mild to very pungent in flavor. **c.** the pungent seeds of several varieties of *C. annuum* or *C. frutescens,* used ground or whole as a condiment. —*v.t.* **3.** to season with or as if with pepper. **4.** to sprinkle or cover, as if with pepper; dot. **5.** to pelt with or as if with shot or missiles. —**pep′per·ish,** *adj.*

pep′per-and-salt′, *adj.* composed of a fine mixture of black and white or sometimes (in fabric) of two colors.

pep·per·corn (pep′ər kôrn′), *n.* **1.** the dried berry of the pepper plant, *Piper nigrum.* **2.** anything very small or insignificant. —*adj.* **3.** (of hair) growing in tight spirals.

pep·per·grass (pep′ər gras′, -gräs′), *n.* any of various pungent plants belonging to the genus *Lepidium,* of the mustard family: used as a potherb or salad vegetable. Compare GARDEN CRESS.

pep′per mill′, *n.* a small hand-held device for storing and grinding peppercorns.

pep·per·mint (pep′ər mint′, -mənt), *n.* **1.** an aromatic herb, *Mentha piperita,* of the mint family, having lance-shaped leaves and spikes of purplish flowers. **2.** the pungent oil of this plant, used as a flavoring. **3.** a lozenge or confection flavored with peppermint.

pep·per·o·ni or **pep·er·o·ni** (pep′ə rō′nē), *n., pl.* **-nis.** a highly seasoned hard sausage of beef and pork.

pep′per pot′, *n.* **1.** a highly seasoned soup of tripe, vegetables, and often dumplings. **2.** a highly seasoned West Indian stew of meat or fish and vegetables.

pep′per shak′er, *n.* a small container with a perforated top, for sprinkling pepper.

pep′per tree′, *n.* a South American evergreen tree, *Schinus molle,* of the cashew family, cultivated as an ornamental.

pep·per·y (pep′ə rē), *adj.* **1.** full of or tasting like pepper; hot. **2.** of, pertaining to, or resembling pepper. **3.** sharp or stinging: *a peppery speech.* **4.** easily angered; irascible. —**pep′per·i·ness,** *n.*

pep·py (pep′ē), *adj.,* **-pi·er, -pi·est.** energetic; vigorous; lively. —**pep′pi·ly,** *adv.* —**pep′pi·ness,** *n.*

pep′ ral′ly, *n.* a meeting, as of students before an athletic contest, to stimulate group enthusiasm by rousing talks, cheers, etc.

pep·sin (pep′sin), *n.* **1.** an enzyme, produced in the stomach, that in the presence of hydrochloric acid splits proteins into proteoses and peptones. **2.** a commercial preparation containing pepsin, obtained from hog stomachs, used as a digestive and as a ferment in making cheese.

pep′ talk′, *n.* a vigorous, emotional talk intended to inspire enthusiasm, increase determination to succeed, etc. —**pep′talk′,** *v.t., v.i.*

pep·tic (pep′tik), *adj.* **1.** pertaining to or associated with digestion; digestive. **2.** promoting digestion. **3.** of or pertaining to pepsin. —*n.* **4.** a substance promoting digestion.

pep′tic ul′cer, *n.* an erosion of the mucous membrane of the lower esophagus, stomach, or duodenum, caused in part by the corrosive action of the gastric juice.

pep·ti·dase (pep′ti dās′, -dāz′), *n.* any of the class of enzymes that catalyze the hydrolysis of peptides or peptones to amino acids.

pep·tide (pep′tīd), *n.* a compound containing two or more amino acids in which the carboxyl group of one acid is linked to the amino group of the other.

pep·tone (pep′tōn), *n.* any of a class of diffusible, soluble substances into which proteins are converted by partial hydrolysis. —**pep·ton′ic** (-ton′ik), *adj.*

Pe′quot War′, *n.* a war in 1637 between Connecticut colonists, aided by British soldiers and friendly Indian tribes, and the Pequot Indians under their chief, Sassacus, that resulted in the defeat and dispersion of the Pequot tribe.

per (pûr; *unstressed* pər), *prep.* **1.** for or in each or every; a or an: *Membership costs $10 per year.* **2.** according to; in accordance with: *I delivered the box per your instructions.* **3.** by means of; by; through: *Send it per messenger.* —*adv.* **4.** *Informal.* each; for each one: *The charge was five dollars per.*

per-, 1. a prefix meaning "through," "thoroughly," "utterly," "very": *pervert; pervade; perfect.* **2.** a prefix used in the names of inorganic acids and their salts that possess the maximum amount of the element specified in the base word: *percarbonic* ($H_2C_2O_5$) *acid; potassium permanganate* ($KMnO_4$).

per·ad·ven·ture (pûr′əd ven′chər, per′-), *n.* **1.** chance, doubt, or uncertainty. **2.** surmise.

per·am·bu·late (pər am′byə lāt′), *v.,* **-lat·ed, -lat·ing.** —*v.t.* **1.** to walk through, about, or over; traverse. **2.** to examine or inspect the boundaries of by walking through. —*v.i.* **3.** to walk or travel about; stroll. —**per·am′bu·la′tion,** *n.* —**per·am′bu·la·to′ry** (-lə tôr′ē, -tōr′ē), *adj.*

per·am·bu·la·tor (pər am′byə lā′tər), *n.* **1.** baby carriage. **2.** an odometer pushed by a person walking. **3.** a person who makes a tour of inspection on foot.

per an·num (pər an′əm), *adv.* by the year; yearly.

per·cale (pər kāl′), *n.* a smooth, plain-weave cotton cloth, used esp. for bedsheets and clothing.

per cap·i·ta (pər kap′i tə), *adj., adv.* by or for each individual person: *income per capita.*

per·ceive (pər sēv′), *v.t.,* **-ceived, -ceiv·ing. 1.** to become aware of, know, or identify by means of the senses. **2.** to recognize or understand: *to perceive difficulties.* —**per·ceiv′a·ble,** *adj.* —**per·ceiv′a·bly,** *adv.*

per·cent or **per cent** (pər sent′), *n.* **1.** one one-hundredth part; $1/100$. **2.** PERCENTAGE (defs. 1, 3). **3.** *Brit.* stocks, bonds, etc., that bear an indicated rate of interest. —*adj.* **4.** figured or expressed on the basis of a rate or proportion per hundred (used in combination with a number in expressing rates of interest, proportions, etc.). *Symbol:* % [short for Medieval Latin *per centum* by the hundred] —**per·cent′al,** *adj.*

per·cent·age (pər sen′tij), *n.* **1.** a rate or proportion per hundred. **2.** an allowance, commission, or rate of interest calculated by percent. **3.** a proportion in general; part: *a small percentage of the class.* **4.** gain; benefit; profit; advantage. —**per·cent′aged,** *adj.*

per·cen·tile (pər sen′tīl, -til), *n.* one of the values of a statistical variable that divides the distribution of the variable into 100 groups having equal frequencies: *Ninety percent of the values lie at or below the ninetieth percentile, ten percent above it.*

per·cept (pûr′sept), *n.* **1.** the mental result or product of perceiving; an impression or sensation of something perceived. **2.** a thing perceived; the object of perception.

per·cep·ti·ble (pər sep′tə bəl), *adj.* capable of being perceived; recognizable; discernible: *a perceptible change in behavior.* —**per·cep′ti·bil′i·ty,** *n.* —**per·cep′ti·bly,** *adv.*

per·cep·tion (pər sep′shən), *n.* **1.** the act or faculty of apprehending by means of the senses or the mind; cognition; awareness. **2.** a single unified awareness derived from sensory processes while a stimulus is present. **3.** immediate or intuitive recognition or appreciation, as of moral, psychological, or aesthetic qualities; insight; discernment. **4.** the result or product of perceiving; percept. —**per·cep′tion·al,** *adj.*

per·cep·tive (pər sep′tiv), *adj.* **1.** having or showing keenness of insight, understanding, or intuition. **2.** having the power or faculty of perceiving. **3.** of, pertaining to, or showing perception. —**per·cep′tive·ly,** *adv.* —**per′cep·tiv′i·ty, per·cep′tive·ness,** *n.*

per·cep·tu·al (pər sep′chōō əl), *adj.* of, pertaining to, or involving perception. —**per·cep′tu·al·ly,** *adv.*

perch¹ (pûrch), *n.* **1.** a pole or rod, usu. horizontal, serving as a roost for birds. **2.** any place or object for a bird, animal, or person to alight or rest upon. **3.** a high or elevated position, resting place, or the like. **4.** a small, elevated seat for the driver of any of certain vehicles. **5.** *Brit.* **a.** a linear or square rod. **b.** a measure of volume for stone, about 24 cubic feet (0.7 cubic meters). —*v.i.* **6.** to alight or rest upon a perch. **7.** to settle or rest in some elevated position, as if on a perch. —*v.t.* **8.** to set or place on or as if on a perch.

perch² (pûrch), *n., pl.* (*esp. collectively*) **perch,** (*esp. for kinds or species*) **perch·es. 1.** any small freshwater fish of the family Percidae, having a spiny anterior dorsal fin, as the European perch, *Perca fluviatilis,* and the North American yellow perch, *P. flavescens.* **2.** any of various related or similar spiny-finned fishes.

per·chance (pər chans′, -chäns′), *adv.* perhaps; maybe; possibly.

per·cip·i·ent (pər sip′ē ənt), *adj.* **1.** perceiving or capable of perceiving. **2.** having or showing perception; discerning. —*n.* **3.** one that perceives. —**per·cip′i·ence, per·cip′i·en·cy,** *n.*

per·co·late (*v.* pûr′kə lāt′, *n.* -lit, -lāt′), *v.,* **-lat·ed, -lat·ing,** *n.* —*v.t.* **1.** to cause (a liquid) to pass through a porous body; filter. **2.** (of a liquid) to filter through; permeate. **3.** to brew (coffee) in a percolator. —*v.i.* **4.** to pass through a porous substance; filter; ooze; seep; trickle. **5.** to become percolated. **6.** to become active, lively, or spirited. **7.** to spread or grow gradually. —*n.* **8.** a percolated liquid. —**per′co·la′tion,** *n.* —**Pronunciation.** The pronunciation of PERCOLATE with an intrusive *y*-glide results from analogy with words like *circulate* and *matriculate,* where the *y*-glide is mandatory. In words like *percolate* and *escalate,* where (k) is followed by *-o-* or *-a-* rather than *-u-,* the (y), as in the pronunciations (pûr′kyə lāt′) and (es′kyə lāt′), represents a hypercorrection. See COUPON.

per·co·la·tor (pûr′kə lā′tər), *n.* **1.** a type of coffeepot in which boiling water is continuously forced up a hollow stem and filters down through ground coffee, collecting in the bottom of the pot. **2.** something that percolates.

per·cuss (pər kus′), *v.t.* **1.** to use percussion for diagnosis or therapy. **2.** to strike (something) so as to shake or shock.

per·cus·sion (pər kush′ən), *n.* **1.** the striking of one body against another with some sharpness; impact; blow. **2.** the striking of a musical instrument to produce tones. **3.** the percussion instruments of an orchestra or band. **4.** the striking or tapping of the surface of a part of the body for diagnostic or therapeutic purposes. **5.** a sharp blow for detonating a percussion cap or the fuze of an artillery shell. **6.** the striking of sound on the ear. **7.** the act of percussing. —**per·cus′sion·al,** *adj.*

percus′sion cap′, *n.* a small metallic cap containing an explosive powder, formerly detonated by percussion to fire the charge of small arms.

percus′sion in′strument, *n.* a musical instrument, as the drum, cymbal, triangle, xylophone, or piano, that is struck to produce a sound, as distinguished from a string or wind instrument.

per·cus·sion·ist (pər kush′ə nist), *n.* a musician who plays percussion instruments.

per di·em (pər dē′əm, dī′əm), *adv.* **1.** by the day; for each day. —*n.* **2.** a daily allowance for living expenses, as while traveling in connection with one's job. —*adj.* **3.** paid by the day. [< Latin]

per·di·tion (pər dish′ən), *n.* **1.** a state of final spiritual ruin; loss of the soul; damnation. **2.** hell.

per·du or **per·due** (pər dōō′, -dyōō′, per-), *adj.* hidden; concealed; obscured. [< French: lost]

per·dur·a·ble (pər dōōr′ə bəl, -dyōōr′-), *adj.* very durable; permanent; imperishable. —**per·dur′a·bil′i·ty,** *n.* —**per·dur′a·bly,** *adv.*

per·dure (pər dōōr′, -dyōōr′), *v.i.,* **-dured, -dur·ing.** to continue or last permanently; endure.

per·e·gri·nate (per′i grə nāt′), *v.,* **-nat·ed, -nat·ing.** —*v.i.* **1.** to travel or journey, esp. on foot. —*v.t.* **2.** to travel or walk over; traverse. —**per′e·gri·na′tion,** *n.* —**per′e·gri·na′tor,** *n.*

per·e·grine (per′i grin, -grēn′, -grīn′), *adj.* **1.** wandering or migrating. **2.** foreign; alien; coming from abroad. —*n.* **3.** PEREGRINE FALCON.

per′egrine fal′con, *n.* a cosmopolitan falcon, *Falco peregrinus,* that feeds on birds taken in flight.

per·emp·to·ry (pə remp′tə rē), *adj.* **1.** leaving no opportunity for denial or refusal; imperative: *a peremptory command.* **2.** imperious or dictatorial. **3.** positive or assertive in speech, tone, manner, etc. **4.** *Law.* **a.** precluding or not admitting of debate or question: *a peremptory edict.* **b.** decisive or final. —**per·emp′to·ri·ly,** *adv.* —**per·emp′to·ri·ness,** *n.*

per·en·ni·al (pə ren′ē əl), *adj.* **1.** lasting for an indefinitely long time; enduring. **2.** (of plants) having a life cycle lasting more than two years. **3.** lasting or continuing throughout the entire year, as a stream. **4.** perpetual; continuing; recurrent. —*n.* **5.** a perennial plant. **6.** something that is continuing or recurrent. —**per·en′ni·al′i·ty,** *n.* —**per·en′ni·al·ly,** *adv.*

peren′nial can′didate, *n.* one who repeatedly runs and fails in elections.

pe•re•stroi•ka (per′ə stroi′kə; *Russ.* pyi ryi stroi′kə), *n. Russian.* the program of economic and political reform in the Soviet Union initiated by Mikhail Gorbachev in 1986. [< Russian *perestróĭka* lit., rebuilding, reorganization]

per•fect (*adj., n.* pûr′fikt; *v.* pər fekt′), *adj.* **1.** conforming absolutely to the description or definition of an ideal type: *a perfect gentleman.* **2.** excellent or complete beyond practical or theoretical improvement. **3.** exactly fitting the need in a certain situation or for a certain purpose: *the perfect actor for the part.* **4.** entirely without any flaws, defects, or shortcomings: *a perfect apple.* **5.** accurate, exact, or correct in every detail: *a perfect copy.* **6.** thorough; complete; utter: *perfect strangers.* **7.** unqualified; absolute: *perfect control.* **8.** expert; accomplished; proficient. **9.** unmitigated: *a perfect fool.* **10. a.** of or designating a verb tense, aspect, or form typically indicating an action or state extending up to, or having results continuing up to, the present or some other temporal point of reference. **b.** of or designating a verb tense, as in Greek, indicating an action or state brought to a close prior to some temporal point of reference, in contrast to imperfect or incomplete action. **11.** pertaining to or being the consonant musical intervals of an octave, fifth, or fourth. —*v.t.* **12.** to bring to perfection; make flawless or faultless. **13.** to bring nearer to perfection; improve. **14.** to bring to completion; finish. —*n.* **15.** the perfect tense or aspect. **16.** a verb form or construction in the perfect tense or aspect. —**per•fect′er,** *n.* —**per′fect•ness,** *n.*

per•fec•ta (pər fek′tə), *n., pl.* **-tas.** EXACTA.

per′fect bind′ing, *n.* a method of binding books in which the backs of the sections are cut off and the leaves glued to a cloth or paper backing. —**per′fect-bound′,** *adj.*

per′fect game′, *n.* a baseball no-hitter in which no members of the opposing team reach base.

per•fec•tion (pər fek′shən), *n.* **1.** the state or quality of being or becoming perfect. **2.** the highest degree of proficiency, skill, or excellence, as in an art. **3.** a perfect embodiment or example of something. **4.** a quality, trait, or feature of the highest degree of excellence. **5.** the highest or most nearly perfect degree of a quality or trait. **6.** the act or fact of perfecting.

per•fec•tion•ism (pər fek′shə niz′əm), *n.* **1.** any of various doctrines holding that religious, moral, social, or political perfection is attainable. **2.** a personal standard, attitude, or philosophy that demands perfection and rejects anything less. —**per•fec′tion•ist,** *n., adj.* —**per•fec′tion•is′tic,** *adj.*

per•fec•tive (pər fek′tiv), *adj.* **1.** tending to make perfect; conducive to perfection. **2.** of or designating an aspect of verbal inflection, as in Russian, that indicates completion of the action or state denoted by the verb. —*n.* **3.** the perfective aspect. **4.** a form in this aspect. —**per•fec′tive•ly,** *adv.* —**per•fec′tive•ness, per′fec•tiv′i•ty,** *n.*

per•fect•ly (pûr′fikt lē), *adv.* **1.** in a perfect manner or to a perfect degree. **2.** completely; fully; adequately.

per′fect num′ber, *n.* a positive number that is equal to the sum of all positive integers that are submultiples of it, as 6, which is equal to the sum of 1, 2, and 3.

per•fec•to (pər fek′tō), *n., pl.* **-tos.** a rather thick, medium-sized cigar tapered at each end.

per′fect par′ticiple, *n.* PAST PARTICIPLE.

per′fect pitch′, *n.* ABSOLUTE PITCH (def. 2).

per•fer•vid (pər fûr′vid), *adj.* very fervent; extremely ardent; impassioned. —**per•fer′vid•ly,** *adv.* —**per•fer′vid•ness,** *n.*

per•fid•i•ous (pər fid′ē əs), *adj.* deliberately faithless; treacherous; deceitful. —**per•fid′i•ous•ly,** *adv.* —**per•fid′i•ous•ness,** *n.*

per•fi•dy (pûr′fi dē), *n., pl.* **-dies.** **1.** deliberate breach of faith or trust; treachery. **2.** an act or instance of treachery.

per•fo•rate (*v.* pûr′fə rāt′; *adj.* -fər it, -fə rāt′), *v.,* **-rat•ed, -rat•ing.** —*v.t.* **1.** to make a hole or holes through by boring, punching, piercing, or the like. **2.** to pierce through or to the interior of; penetrate. —*v.i.* **3.** to make a way through or into something; penetrate. —**per′for•a•ble,** *adj.* —**per′fo•ra′tive,** *adj.* —**per′fo•ra′tor,** *n.*

per•fo•rat•ed (pûr′fə rā′tid) also **perforate,** *adj.* **1.** pierced with a hole or holes. **2.** (of a stamp) having closely spaced perforations along its edges. **3.** marked by or having perforation: *a perforated ulcer.*

per•fo•ra•tion (pûr′fə rā′shən), *n.* **1.** a hole made by or as if by boring, punching, or piercing through something. **2.** one of a series of holes between individual postage stamps on a sheet. **3.** the act of perforating. **4.** the condition or state of being perforated.

per•force (pər fôrs′, -fōrs′), *adv.* of necessity; necessarily; by force of circumstance.

per•form (pər fôrm′), *v.t.* **1.** to carry out; execute; do: *to perform surgery.* **2.** to execute in the proper, customary, or established manner: *to perform a marriage ceremony.* **3.** to carry into effect; fulfill: *to perform a contract.* **4.** to act (a play, part, etc.), as on the stage. **5.** to render (music), as by playing or singing. **6.** to accomplish (an action involving skill or ability), as before an audience: *to perform a juggling act.* —*v.i.* **7.** to execute or do something; function. **8.** to carry out or fulfill a command, promise, or contract. **9.** to give a performance, esp. before an audience. **10.** to engage in the performing arts, esp. professionally.

per•for•mance (pər fôr′məns), *n.* **1.** an entertainment presented before an audience. **2.** the act of performing a ceremony, play, piece of music, etc. **3.** the execution or accomplishment of work, acts, feats, etc. **4.** a particular action, deed, or proceeding. **5.** an action or proceeding of an unusual or spectacular kind. **6.** the act of performing. **7.** the manner in which or the efficiency with which something reacts or fulfills its intended purpose. **8.** *Ling.* a person's actual use of language in real situations. Compare COMPETENCE (def. 4).

perfor′mance art′, *n.* an often collaborative art form involving a fusion of several artistic media, as painting, film, video, music, drama, and dance. —**perfor′mance art′ist,** *n.*

per•form•er (pər fôr′mər), *n.* **1.** a person who performs in plays, motion pictures, operas, etc. **2.** one who performs or does something.

perform′ing arts′, *n.pl.* arts or skills that require public performance, as acting, singing, and dancing.

per•fume (*n.* pûr′fyo͞om, pər fyo͞om′; *v.* pər fyo͞om′, pûr′fyo͞om), *n., v.,* **-fumed, -fum•ing.** —*n.* **1.** a substance that diffuses or imparts an agreeable or attractive smell, esp. a fluid containing fragrant natural oils extracted from flowers, woods, etc., or similar synthetic oils. **2.** the scent, odor, or volatile particles emitted by substances that smell agreeable. —*v.t.* **3.** (of substances, flowers, etc.) to impart a pleasant fragrance to. **4.** to permeate with a sweet odor; scent. —**per′fume•less,** *adj.* —**per′fum•y,** *adj.*

P

per•fum•er•y (pər fyo͞o′mə rē), *n., pl.* **-er•ies.** **1.** perfumes collectively. **2.** the art or business of a perfumer. **3.** the place of business of a perfumer. **4.** the preparation of perfumes.

per•func•to•ry (pər fungk′tə rē), *adj.* **1.** performed merely as a routine duty; hasty and superficial: *perfunctory courtesy.* **2.** lacking interest or enthusiasm; apathetic: *a perfunctory speaker.* —**per•func′to•ri•ly,** *adv.* —**per•func′to•ri•ness,** *n.*

per•fuse (pər fyo͞oz′), *v.t.,* **-fused, -fus•ing.** **1.** to overspread with moisture, color, etc.; suffuse. **2.** to diffuse (a liquid, color, etc.) through or over something. **3.** to pass (fluid) through blood vessels or the lymphatic system to an organ or tissue. —**per•fu′sion** (-fyo͞o′zhən), *n.* —**per•fu′sive** (-siv), *adj.*

Per•ga (pûr′gə), *n.* the capital of Pamphylia, twice visited by the Apostle Paul. Acts 13:13–14; 14:25.

Per•ga•mum (pûr′gə məm), *n.* **1.** an ancient Greek kingdom on the coast of Asia Minor: later a Roman province. **2.** the ancient capital of this kingdom, the site of the one of the seven churches of Asia (Rev. 1:11): now the site of Bergama, in W Turkey.

per•haps (pər haps′), *adv.* maybe; possibly: *Perhaps I misunderstood.*

peri-, a prefix meaning "about," "around" (*perimeter; periscope*), "enclosing," "surrounding" (*pericardium*), "near" (*perigee; perihelion*).

per•i•anth (per′ē anth′), *n.* the envelope of a flower, whether calyx or corolla or both. —**per′i•an′thi•al,** *adj.*

per•i•car•di•tis (per′i kär dī′tis), *n.* inflammation of the pericardium. —**per′i•car•dit′ic** (-dit′ik), *adj.*

per•i•car•di•um (per′i kär′dē əm), *n., pl.* **-di•a** (-dē ə). the membranous sac enclosing the heart.

per•i•carp (per′i kärp′), *n.* the walls of a ripened ovary or fruit, sometimes consisting of three layers, the epicarp, mesocarp, and endocarp. —**per′i•car′pi•al,** *adj.*

per•i•chon•dri•um (per′i kon′drē əm), *n., pl.* **-dri•a** (-drē ə). the membrane of fibrous connective tissue covering the surface of cartilages except at the joints. —**per′i•chon′dral, per′i•chon′dri•al,** *adj.*

Per•i•cles (per′i klēz′), *n.* c495–429 B.C., Athenian statesman.

pe•ric•o•pe (pə rik′ə pē′), *n., pl.* **-pes, -pae** (-pē′). a selection or extract from a book. —**pe•ric′o•pal, per•i•cop•ic** (per′i kop′ik), *adj.*

per•i•cy•cle (per′ə sī′kəl), *n.* the cell layer of the stele in a plant, bounded by the endodermis and the phloem.

per•i•derm (per′i dûrm′), *n.* **1.** the cork-producing tissue of plant stems together with the cork layers and other tissues derived from it. **2.** the outermost layer of epidermal skin in most mammalian fetuses, usu. disappearing before birth. —**per′i•der′mal, per′i•der′mic,** *adj.*

pe•rid•i•um (pə rid′ē əm), *n., pl.* **-rid•e•a** (-rid′ē ə). the outer enveloping coat of the fruiting body in many fungi. —**pe•rid′i•al,** *adj.* —**pe•rid′i•i•form′** (-ə fôrm′), *adj.*

per•i•dot (per′i dō′, -dot′), *n.* a green transparent variety of olivine, used as a gem. —**per′i•dot′ic** (-dot′ik, -dō′tik), *adj.*

per•i•do•tite (per′i dō′tīt, pə rid′ə tīt′), *n.* a coarsely granular igneous rock composed chiefly of olivine admixed with various other minerals. —**per′i•do•tit′ic** (-tit′ik), *adj.*

per•i•gee (per′i jē′), *n.* the point in the orbit of a heavenly body, esp. the moon, or of an artificial satellite at which it is nearest to the earth. —**per′i•ge′al, per′i•ge′an,** *adj.*

pe•rig•y•nous (pə rij′ə nəs), *adj.* **1.** situated around the pistil on the edge of a cuplike receptacle, as stamens or petals. **2.** having stamens, petals, etc., so arranged. —**pe•rig′y•ny,** *n.*

per•i•he•li•on (per′ə hē′lē ən, -hēl′yən), *n., pl.* **-he•li•a** (-hē′lē ə, -hēl′yə). the point in the orbit of a planet or comet at which it is nearest to the sun. —**per′i•he′li•al, per′i•he′li•an,** *adj.*

per•il (per′əl), *n., v.,* **-iled, -il•ing** or (*esp. Brit.*) **-illed, -il•ling.** —*n.* **1.** exposure to injury, loss, or destruction; grave risk; jeopardy. **2.** something that causes or may cause injury, loss, or destruction. —*v.t.* **3.** to imperil. —**per′il•less,** *adj.*

pe•ril•la (pə ril′ə), *n., pl.* **-las.** any of several aromatic Asian plants belonging to the genus *Perilla,* of the mint family, esp. *P. frutescens,* from which perilla oil is obtained.

peril′la oil′, *n.* a light yellow oil, obtained from the seeds of mints of the genus *Perilla*, used in Asia as a cooking oil and elsewhere in the manufacture of varnish, printing ink, and artificial leather.

per·il·ous (per′ə ləs), *adj.* involving grave risk or peril; hazardous; dangerous: *a perilous sea voyage.* —**per′il·ous·ly,** *adv.* —**per′il·ous·ness,** *n.*

per·i·lymph (per′i limf′), *n.* the fluid between the bony and membranous labyrinths of the ear. —**per′i·lym·phat′ic,** *adj.*

pe·rim·e·ter (pə rim′i tər), *n.* **1.** the border or outer boundary of a two-dimensional figure. **2.** the length of such a boundary. **3.** a line marking a boundary. **4.** the outermost limits. **5.** an instrument for determining the peripheral field of vision. —**pe·rim′e·ter·less,** *adj.* —**pe·rim′e·tral, per·i·met′ric** (per′ə me′trik), **per′i·met′ri·cal,** *adj.* —**per′i·met′ri·cal·ly,** *adv.* —**pe·rim′e·try,** *n.*

per·i·na·tal (per′ə nāt′l), *adj.* occurring during or pertaining to the phase surrounding the time of birth, from the 20th week of gestation to the 28th day of newborn life. —**per′i·na′tal·ly,** *adv.*

per·i·ne·um (per′ə nē′əm), *n., pl.* **-ne·a** (-nē′ə). the area in front of the anus extending from the fourchette of the vulva in the female and to the scrotum in the male. —**per′i·ne′al,** *adj.*

pe·ri·od (pēr′ē əd), *n.* **1.** an extent of time that is meaningful in the life of a person, in history, etc.: *a period of illness; a period of social unrest.* **2.** a specific division or portion of time: *the postwar period.* **3.** a round of time, esp. as marked by the recurrence of some phenomenon: *the rainy period.* **4.** any of the parts of equal length into which a particular thing, as a sports contest, is divided. **5.** the time during which something is completed or runs its course: *the gestation period.* **6.** the point or character (.) used to mark the end of a declarative sentence or to indicate an abbreviation; full stop. **7.** a full pause, as is made at the end of a complete sentence; full stop. **8.** a sentence, esp. a well-balanced, impressive sentence: *the stately periods of Churchill.* **9. a.** an occurrence of menstruation. **b.** a time of the month during which menstruation occurs. **10.** the basic unit of geologic time, during which a standard rock system is formed: comprising two or more epochs and included with other periods in an era. **11.** *Physics.* the duration of one complete cycle of a wave or oscillation; the reciprocal of the frequency. **12.** a division of a musical composition commonly consisting of two or more contrasted or complementary phrases ending with a cadence. **13.** *Astron.* **a.** the time in which a body rotates once on its axis. **b.** the time in which a planet or satellite revolves once about its primary. **14.** (in classical prosody) a group of two or more cola. —*adj.* **15.** noting or pertaining to a historical period: *a period play.* —*interj.* **16.** (used to indicate that a decision is final): *I forbid you to go, period.*

pe·ri·od·ic (pēr′ē od′ik), *adj.* **1.** recurring at intervals of time: *periodic revivals of interest in handicrafts.* **2.** occurring at regular intervals: *periodic visits of a mailboat to the island.* **3.** recurring irregularly; intermittent: *periodic outbreaks of smallpox.* **4.** *Physics.* recurring at equal intervals of time. **5.** *Math.* (of a function) having a graph that repeats after a fixed interval of the independent variable. **6.** *Astron.* **a.** characterized by a series of successive circuits or revolutions, as the motion of a planet or satellite. **b.** of or pertaining to a period, as of the revolution of a heavenly body. **7.** pertaining to or characterized by periodic sentences. —**pe′ri·od′i·cal·ly,** *adv.*

pe·ri·od·i·cal (pēr′ē od′i kəl), *n.* **1.** a publication, as a magazine, that is issued under the same title at regular intervals. —*adj.* **2.** of or per-

taining to such publications. **3.** published at regular intervals. **4.** PERIODIC (defs. 1–3).

pe·ri·o·dic·i·ty (pēr′ē ə dis′i tē), *n.* the character of being periodic; the tendency to recur at regular intervals.

pe′ri·od′ic law′ (pēr′ē od′ik, pēr′-), *n.* **1.** the law that the properties of the chemical elements are periodic functions of their atomic numbers. **2.** (formerly) the statement that the chemical and physical properties of the elements recur periodically when the elements are arranged in the order of their atomic weights.

pe′ri·od′ic ta′ble (pēr′ē od′ik, pēr′-), *n.* a table in which the chemical elements, arranged according to their atomic numbers, are shown in related groups.

per·i·o·don·tal (per′ē ə don′tl), *adj.* **1.** of or pertaining to the periodontium or the periodontal membrane. **2.** of or pertaining to periodontics. **3.** surrounding or associated with a tooth.

per·i·o·don·tics (per′ē ə don′tiks) also **per·i·o·don·tia** (-don′shə, -shē ə), *n.* (*used with a sing. v.*) the branch of dentistry dealing with the study and treatment of diseases of the periodontium. —**per′i·o·don′tic,** *adj.* —**per′i·o·don′tist,** *n.*

per·i·o·don·tium (per′ē ə don′shəm, -shē əm), *n., pl.* **-tia** (-shə, -shē ə). the bone, connective tissue, and gum surrounding and supporting a tooth.

per·i·o·don·tol·o·gy (per′ē ō don tol′ə jē), *n.* PERIODONTICS.

pe′ri·od piece′, *n.* something, as a novel, painting, or building, of interest or value primarily because it evokes or epitomizes a particular period of history.

per·i·o·nych·i·um (per′ē ō nik′ē əm), *n., pl.* **-nych·i·a** (-nik′ē ə). the epidermis surrounding the base and sides of a fingernail or toenail.

per·i·os·te·um (per′ē os′tē əm), *n., pl.* **-te·a** (-tē ə). the dense, fibrous connective tissue covering all bones except where ligaments attach and on the surfaces of joints. —**per′i·os′te·al, per′i·os′te·ous,** *adj.* —**per′i·os′te·al·ly,** *adv.*

per·i·pa·tet·ic (per′ə pə tet′ik), *adj.* **1.** walking or traveling about; itinerant. **2.** (*cap.*) of or pertaining to Aristotle, who taught philosophy while walking in the Lyceum. **3.** (*cap.*) of or pertaining to the Aristotelian school of philosophy. —*n.* **4.** an itinerant person. **5.** (*cap.*) a member of the Aristotelian school. —**per′i·pa·tet′i·cal·ly,** *adv.* —**per′i·pa·tet′i·cism** (-ə siz′əm), *n.*

pe·riph·er·al (pə rif′ər əl), *adj.* **1.** pertaining to or constituting the periphery. **2.** concerned with the minor or superficial aspects of a question. **3.** *Anat.* near the surface or outside of; external. **4.** of or pertaining to a computer peripheral. —*n.* **5.** an external hardware device, as a keyboard, printer, or tape drive, connected to a computer's CPU. —**pe·riph′er·al·ly,** *adv.*

periph′eral nerv′ous sys′tem, *n.* the portion of the nervous system lying outside the brain and spinal cord.

periph′eral vi′sion, *n.* all that is visible to the eye outside the central area of focus; side vision.

pe·riph·er·y (pə rif′ə rē), *n., pl.* **-er·ies. 1.** the boundary or perimeter of any surface or area. **2.** the external surface of a body. **3.** the outskirts of a city or urban area. **4.** the minor or superficial aspects of a question.

pe·riph·ra·sis (pə rif′rə sis), *n., pl.* **-ses** (-sēz′). **1.** the use of a verbose or roundabout form of expression; circumlocution. **2.** an expression phrased in this way. **3. a.** the use of two or more words instead of

PERIODIC TABLES OF THE ELEMENTS

1A																	8A
1 H 1.00797	2 A		— Group									3A	4A	5A	6A	7A	2 He 4.0026
3 Li 6.939	4 Be 9.0122		1 H 1.00797	— Atomic number — Symbol — Atomic mass (Approx. values in parentheses)								5 B 10.811	6 C 12.011	7 N 14.0067	8 O 15.9994	9 F 18.9984	10 Ne 20.183
11 Na 22.9898	12 Mg 24.312	3B	4B	5B	6B	7B		8B		1B	2B	13 Al 26.9815	14 Si 28.086	15 P 30.9738	16 S 32.064	17 Cl 35.453	18 Ar 39.948
19 K 39.102	20 Ca 40.08	21 Sc 44.956	22 Ti 47.90	23 V 50.942	24 Cr 51.996	25 Mn 54.938	26 Fe 55.847	27 Co 58.933	28 Ni 58.71	29 Cu 63.54	30 Zn 65.37	31 Ga 69.72	32 Ge 72.59	33 As 74.922	34 Se 78.96	35 Br 79.909	36 Kr 83.80
37 Rb 85.47	38 Sr 87.62	39 Y 88.905	40 Zr 91.22	41 Nb 92.906	42 Mo 95.94	43 Tc (98)	44 Ru 101.07	45 Rh 102.905	46 Pd 106.4	47 Ag 107.870	48 Cd 112.40	49 In 114.82	50 Sn 118.69	51 Sb 121.75	52 Te 127.60	53 I 126.904	54 Xe 131.30
55 Cs 132.905	56 Ba 137.34	57 La 138.91	72 Hf 178.49	73 Ta 180.948	74 W 183.85	75 Re 186.2	76 Os 190.2	77 Ir 192.2	78 Pt 195.09	79 Au 196.967	80 Hg 200.59	81 Tl 204.37	82 Pb 207.19	83 Bi 208.980	84 Po (210)	85 At (210)	86 Rn (222)
87 Fr (223)	88 Ra (226)	89 Ac (227)	104 Unq (257)	105 Unp (260)	106 Unh (263)	107 Uns (262)											

			58 Ce 140.12	59 Pr 140.907	60 Nd 144.24	61 Pm (147)	62 Sm 150.35	63 Eu 151.96	64 Gd 157.25	65 Tb 158.924	66 Dy 162.50	67 Ho 164.930	68 Er 167.26	69 Tm 168.934	70 Yb 173.04	71 Lu 174.97
			90 Th 232.038	91 Pa (231)	92 U 238.03	93 Np (237)	94 Pu (242)	95 Am (243)	96 Cm (247)	97 Bk (247)	98 Cf (249)	99 Es (254)	100 Fm (253)	101 Md (256)	102 No (254)	103 Lw (257)

an inflected word to express the same grammatical function. **b.** an example of this. Sometimes, **per·i·phrase** (per′ə frāz′).

per·i·phras·tic (per′ə fras′tik), *adj.* **1.** circumlocutory; roundabout. **2.** expressed by or using grammatical periphrasis, as the construction *more friendly* rather than *friendlier.* —**per/i·phras/ti·cal·ly,** *adv.*

per·i·scope (per′ə skōp′), *n.* an optical instrument for viewing objects in an obstructed field of vision, consisting of a tube with an arrangement of prisms or mirrors and, usu., lenses: used esp. in submarines.

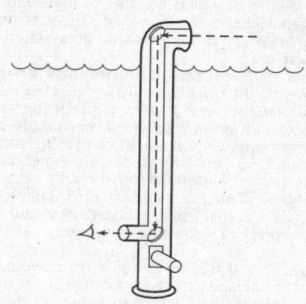

periscope

per·ish (per′ish), *v.i.* **1.** to die as a result of violence, privation, etc. **2.** to pass away or disappear. **3.** to suffer destruction or ruin. —*Idiom.* **4. perish the thought,** may it never happen: used facetiously or as an afterthought of foreboding.

per·ish·a·ble (per′i shə bəl), *adj.* **1.** subject to decay, ruin, or destruction. —*n.* **2.** Usu., **perishables.** something perishable, esp. food. —**per/ish·a·bil/i·ty, per/ish·a·ble·ness,** *n.* —**per/ish·a·bly,** *adv.*

pe·ris·so·dac·tyl (pə ris′ō dak′til), *adj.* **1.** having an uneven number of toes or digits on each foot. —*n.* **2.** any mammal of the order Perissodactyla, comprising the odd-toed hoofed quadrupeds and including the tapirs, rhinoceroses, and horses. Compare ARTIODACTYL. —**pe·ris/so·dac/ty·lous,** *adj.*

per·i·stal·sis (per′ə stôl′sis, -stal′-), *n., pl.* **-ses** (-sēz). progressive waves of involuntary muscle contractions and relaxations that move matter along certain tubelike structures of the body, as ingested food along the alimentary canal. —**per/i·stal/tic,** *adj.*

per·i·style (per′ə stīl′), *n.* **1.** a colonnade surrounding a building or an open space. **2.** an open space, as a courtyard, surrounded by a colonnade. —**per/i·sty/lar,** *adj.*

per·i·to·ne·um (per′i tn ē′əm), *n., pl.* **-to·ne·ums, -to·ne·a** (-tn ē′ə). the serous membrane lining the abdominal cavity and investing its viscera. —**per/i·to·ne/al,** *adj.* —**per/i·to·ne/al·ly,** *adv.*

per·i·to·ni·tis (per′i tn ī′tis), *n.* inflammation of the peritoneum. —**per/i·to·nit/ic,** **per/i·to·nit/ic,** *adj.*

per·i·win·kle¹ (per′i wing′kəl), *n.* any of various small gastropod mollusks of the family Littorinidae, of intertidal waters.

per·i·win·kle² (per′i wing′kəl), *n.* any plant of the genus *Vinca,* of the dogbane family, esp. *V. minor,* having glossy evergreen foliage and usu. blue-violet flowers. Also called **myrtle.** —**per/i·win/kled,** *adj.*

per·jure (pûr′jər), *v.t.,* **-jured, -jur·ing.** to make (oneself) guilty of swearing falsely, esp. in a court of law. —**per/jur·er,** *n.*

per·ju·ry (pûr′jə rē), *n., pl.* **-ries.** the willful giving of false testimony under oath, esp. in a legal inquiry. —**per·ju/ri·ous** (pər jŏŏr′ē əs), *adj.* —**per·ju/ri·ous·ly,** *adv.*

perk¹ (pûrk), *v.i.* **1.** to become lively, cheerful, vigorous, etc., again, as after decline or neglect (usu. fol. by *up*). —*v.t.* **2.** to enhance or enliven (often fol. by *up*): *to perk up a suit with a new blouse.* **3.** to raise smartly or briskly (often fol. by *up*): *to perk one's head up.*

perk² (pûrk), *v.i., v.t.* to percolate.

perk³ (pûrk), *n.* perquisite.

perk·y (pûr′kē), *adj.,* **-i·er, -i·est.** jaunty; cheerful; pert. —**perk/i·ly,** *adv.* —**perk/i·ness,** *n.*

perm (pûrm), *n.* **1.** PERMANENT (def. 4). —*v.t.* **2.** to give (the hair) a permanent. —*v.i.* **3.** to apply a permanent to the hair.

per·ma·frost (pûr′mə frôst′, -frost′), *n.* (in arctic or subarctic regions) permanently frozen subsoil.

per·ma·nence (pûr′mə nəns), *n.* the condition or quality of being permanent.

per·ma·nen·cy (pûr′mə nən sē), *n., pl.* **-cies. 1.** PERMANENCE. **2.** something that is permanent.

per·ma·nent (pûr′mə nənt), *adj.* **1.** existing perpetually; everlasting. **2.** intended to serve, function, etc., for a long, indefinite period: *permanent headquarters.* **3.** long-lasting or nonfading: *permanent pleats; permanent ink.* —*n.* **4.** Also called **per/manent wave/.** a wave or curl set into the hair by the application of chemical preparations or heat and lasting for a number of months. —**per/ma·nent·ly,** *adv.*

Per/manent Court/ of Interna/tional Jus/tice, *n.* an international tribunal established under the Covenant of the League of Nations

and replaced in 1945 by the International Court of Justice. Also called **World Court.**

per/manent press/, *n.* **1.** a process in which a fabric is chemically treated to make it wrinkle-resistant so as to require little or no ironing after washing. **2.** the condition of a fabric so treated.

per/manent tooth/, *n.* one of the teeth of a mammal, in humans amounting to 32, that erupt with or after the loss of the deciduous teeth and remain for most of adult life.

per·me·a·bil·i·ty (pûr′mē ə bil′i tē), *n.* **1.** the quality or state of being permeable. **2.** *Physics.* **a.** the rate at which a pressurized gas or liquid passes through a porous medium. **b.** the ability of a medium to permit such flow. **3.** a measure of the ability of a material to alter the magnetic field in the area that it occupies. **4.** the capability of a porous rock or sediment to permit the flow of fluids through its pore spaces.

per·me·a·ble (pûr′mē ə bəl), *adj.* capable of being permeated. —**per/me·a·ble·ness,** *n.* —**per/me·a·bly,** *adv.*

per·me·ate (pûr′mē āt′), *v.,* **-at·ed, -at·ing.** —*v.t.* **1.** to pass into or through every part of: *sunshine permeating the room.* **2.** to penetrate through the pores, interstices, etc., of. **3.** to be diffused through; pervade: *Bias permeated the report.* —*v.i.* **4.** to become diffused; spread. —**per/me·a/tion,** *n.* —**per/me·a/tive,** *adj.* —**per/me·a/tor,** *n.*

Per·mi·an (pûr′mē ən), *adj.* **1.** noting or pertaining to a period of the Paleozoic Era occurring from about 280 million to 230 million years ago, a time of mass extinctions and a profusion of amphibian species. —*n.* **2.** the Permian Period or System.

per mill or **per mil** (pûr′ mil′, pər), *adv.* per thousand.

per·mis·si·ble (pər mis′ə bəl), *adj.* capable of being permitted; allowable. —**per·mis/si·bly,** *adv.*

per·mis·sion (pər mish′ən), *n.* **1.** authorization granted to do something; formal consent: *to ask permission to leave the room.* **2.** the act of permitting. —**per·mis/sioned,** *adj.* —**per·mis/so·ry** (-is′ə rē), *adj.*

per·mis·sive (pər mis′iv), *adj.* **1.** tolerant of something, as social behavior or linguistic usage, that others might disapprove or forbid. **2.** granting or expressing permission: *a permissive nod.* **3.** optional. **4.** *Genetics.* (of a cell) permitting replication of a strand of DNA that could be lethal, as a viral segment or mutant gene. —**per·mis/sive·ly,** *adv.* —**per·mis/sive·ness,** *n.*

per·mis·siv·ism (pər mis′ə viz′əm), *n.* lenience toward a wide variety of social behavior. —**per·mis/siv·ist,** *n.*

per·mit (*v.* pər mit′; *n.* pûr′mit, pər mit′), *v.,* **-mit·ted, -mit·ting,** *n.* —*v.t.* **1.** to allow to do something: *Permit me to explain.* **2.** to allow to be done or occur: *laws permitting the sale of drugs.* **3.** to tolerate; consent to: *a decree permitting religious worship.* **4.** to afford opportunity for, or admit of: *vents to permit the escape of gases.* —*v.i.* **5.** to grant permission; allow a person to do something. **6.** to afford opportunity: *when time permits.* —*n.* **7.** an authoritative or official certificate of permission; license: *a fishing permit.* **8.** a decree granting permission to do something. **9.** PERMISSION.

per·mu·ta·tion (pûr′myŏŏ tā′shən), *n.* **1.** the act of permuting or permutating; alteration; transformation. **2.** *Math.* **a.** the act of changing the order of set elements arranged in a particular way, as *abc* into *acb* or *bac.* **b.** any of the resulting arrangements. Compare COMBINATION (def. 8). —**per/mu·ta/tion·al,** *adj.* —**per/mu·ta/tion·ist,** *n.*

per·mute (pər myŏŏt′), *v.t.,* **-mut·ed, -mut·ing. 1.** to alter; change. **2.** *Math.* to subject to permutation. —**per·mut/a·ble,** *adj.* —**per·mut/a·bil/i·ty, per·mut/a·ble·ness,** *n.* —**per·mut/a·bly,** *adv.*

per·ni·cious (pər nish′əs), *adj.* causing insidious harm or ruin; ruinous: *a pernicious lie.* —**per·ni/cious·ly,** *adv.* —**per·ni/cious·ness,** *n.*

perni/cious ane/mia, *n.* a severe anemia associated with inadequate intake or absorption of vitamin B₁₂, characterized by defective production of red blood cells.

per·nick·et·y (pər nik′i tē), *adj.* PERSNICKETY. —**per·nick/et·i·ness,** *n.*

Pe·rón (pə rōn′, pā-), *n.* **1. Eva Duarte de,** 1919–52, Argentine political figure (wife of Juan Perón). **2. Juan (Domingo),** 1895–1974, president of Argentina 1946–55, 1973–74.

per·o·ral (pə rôr′əl, -rōr′-), *adj.* administered or performed through the mouth, as surgery or administration of a drug. —**per·o/ral·ly,** *adv.*

per·o·rate (per′ə rāt′), *v.i.,* **-rat·ed, -rat·ing. 1.** to speak at length or elaborately. **2.** to end a speech with a peroration. —**per/o·ra/tor,** *n.*

per·o·ra·tion (per′ə rā′shən), *n.* **1.** the concluding part of a speech or discourse, which recapitulates the principal points. **2.** a long speech, often highly rhetorical. —**per/o·ra/tion·al,** *adj.*

per·ox·ide (pə rok′sīd), *n., v.,* **-id·ed, -id·ing.** —*n.* **1. a.** hydrogen peroxide, H_2O_2 or H–O–O–H. **b.** a compound containing the bivalent group –O₂–, derived from hydrogen peroxide. —*v.t.* **2.** to use peroxide as a bleaching agent on (esp. the hair).

perp (pûrp), *n. Slang.* a person who perpetrates a crime.

per·pend¹ (pûr′pənd), *n.* a large stone passing through the entire thickness of a wall.

per·pend² (pər pend′), *v.t.* **1.** to consider. —*v.i.* **2.** to ponder; deliberate.

per·pen·dic·u·lar (pûr′pən dik′yə lər), *adj.* **1.** vertical; straight up and down; upright. **2.** meeting a given line or surface at right angles. **3.** maintaining a standing or upright position; standing up. **4.** having a sharp pitch or slope; steep. **5.** (*cap.*) of or pertaining to the last phase of English Gothic architecture, prevailing from the late 14th to early 16th century, characterized by predominantly vertical tracery. —*n.* **6.** a perpendicular line, plane, or position. **7.** an instrument for indicating the vertical line from any point. **—per′pen•dic′u•lar′i•ty,** *n.* **—per′pen•dic′u•lar•ly,** *adv.*

per•pe•trate (pûr′pi trāt′), *v.t.,* **-trat•ed, -trat•ing.** to carry out; enact; commit: *to perpetrate a hoax.* **—per′pe•tra′tor,** *n.*

per•pet•u•al (pər pech′o͞o əl), *adj.* **1.** continuing or enduring forever; everlasting. **2.** lasting an indefinitely long time. **3.** continuing without interruption: *a perpetual stream of visitors.* **4.** blooming throughout the growing season. **—*n.* 5.** a perpetual plant. **6.** a variety of continuously blooming hybrid rose. **—per•pet′u•al•ly,** *adv.*

perpet′ual cal′endar, *n.* a calendar devised to be used for many years, as one for determining the day of the week on which a given date falls.

perpet′ual mo′tion, *n.* the motion of a theoretical mechanism that, without any losses due to friction or other forms of dissipation of energy, would continue to operate indefinitely at the same rate without any external energy being applied to it.

per•pet•u•ate (pər pech′o͞o āt′), *v.t.,* **-at•ed, -at•ing.** to make perpetual; preserve from extinction or oblivion. **—per•pet′u•a′tion,** *n.* **—per•pet′u•a′tor,** *n.*

per•pe•tu•i•ty (pûr′pi to͞o′i tē, -tyo͞o′-), *n., pl.* **-ties. 1.** the state or character of being perpetual. **2.** endless or indefinitely long duration or existence. **3.** an annuity paid for life.

per•plex (pər pleks′), *v.t.* **1.** to cause to be puzzled or bewildered over what is not understood or certain. **2.** to make complicated; confuse. **3.** to hamper with complications, confusion, or uncertainty. **—per•plex′er,** *n.* **—per•plex′ing•ly,** *adv.*

per•plexed (pər plekst′), *adj.* **1.** bewildered; puzzled. **2.** complicated; involved; entangled. **—per•plex′ed•ly,** *adv.*

per•plex•i•ty (pər plek′si tē), *n., pl.* **-ties. 1.** the state of being perplexed; bewilderment. **2.** something that perplexes. **3.** an entangled or confused condition or situation.

per•qui•site (pûr′kwə zit), *n.* **1.** an incidental payment, benefit, or privilege over and above regular income or salary: *One of the perquisites is use of a company car.* **2.** a gratuity; tip. **3.** something due as a particular privilege: *homage that was once the perquisite of royalty.*

Per•rault (pə rō′, pe-), *n.* **Charles,** 1628–1703, French poet, critic, and author of fairy tales.

Per•ry (per′ē), *n.* **1. Matthew Calbraith,** 1794–1858, U.S. commodore. **2.** his brother, **Oliver Hazard,** 1785–1819, U.S. naval officer.

per se (pûr sā′, sē′, pər), *adv.* by, of, for, or in itself; intrinsically.

per•se•cute (pûr′si kyo͞ot′), *v.t.,* **-cut•ed, -cut•ing. 1.** to subject to harassing or cruel treatment, as because of religion, race, or beliefs; oppress. **2.** to annoy or trouble persistently. **—per′se•cu′tive,** *adj.* **—per′se•cu′tor,** *n.* **—per′se•cu′to•ry** (-kyo͞o′tə rē, -kyə tôr′ē, -tōr′ē), *adj.*

per•se•cu•tion (pûr′si kyo͞o′shən), *n.* **1.** the act of persecuting. **2.** the state of being persecuted. **—per′se•cu′tion•al,** *adj.*

Per•seph•o•ne (pər sef′ə nē), *n.* in Greek mythology, the daughter of Zeus and Demeter, abducted by Hades to be queen of the underworld.

Per•se•us (pûr′sē əs, -syo͞os), *n., gen.* **-se•i** (-sē ī′) for 2. **1.** a hero, the son of Zeus and Danaë, who slew the Gorgon Medusa and afterward saved Andromeda from a sea monster. **2.** a northern constellation between Cassiopeia and Taurus containing the variable star Algol.

per•se•ver•ance (pûr′sə vēr′əns), *n.* **1.** steady persistence in a course of action, a purpose, a state, etc., esp. in spite of difficulties, obstacles, or discouragement. **2.** *Theol.* continuance in a state of grace to the end, leading to eternal salvation. **—per′se•ver′ant,** *adj.*

per•se•vere (pûr′sə vēr′), *v.i.,* **-vered, -ver•ing.** to persist in pursuing something in spite of obstacles or opposition. **—per′se•ver′ing•ly,** *adv.*

Per•shing (pûr′shing, -zhing), *n.* **John Joseph** (*"Blackjack"*), 1860–1948, U.S. general in World War I.

Per•sia (pûr′zhə, -shə), *n.* **1.** Also called **Persian Empire.** an ancient empire located in W and SW Asia: at its height it extended from Egypt and the Aegean to India; conquered by Alexander the Great 334–331 B.C. **2.** former official name (until 1935) of IRAN.

Per•sian (pûr′zhən, -shən), *adj.* **1.** of or pertaining to ancient, medieval, or modern Persia, its people, or their language. **—*n.* 2.** a native, inhabitant, or citizen of Persia. **3.** an Iranian language, the principal language of Iran and much of Afghanistan. **4.** PERSIAN CAT.

Per′sian blinds′, *n.pl.* outside window shutters made of thin, movable horizontal slats.

Per′sian car′pet, *n.* a handwoven carpet or rug produced in Iran and characteristically having a tight, velvety pile and intricate designs of flowers, leaves, animals, etc., in rich, harmonious colors. Also called **Per′sian rug′.**

Per′sian cat′, *n.* one of a breed of longhaired domestic cats with a short, stocky body and a broad, round head.

Per′sian Em′pire, *n.* PERSIA (def. 1).

Per′sian Gulf′, *n.* an arm of the Arabian Sea, between SW Iran and Arabia. 600 mi. (965 km) long.

Per′sian Gulf′ States′, *n.pl.* GULF STATES (def. 2).

Per′sian lamb′, *n.* **1.** the lamb of the Karakul sheep. **2.** its lustrous, tightly curled fur, used by furriers.

Per′sian mel′on, *n.* **1.** a round variety of muskmelon having a green, reticulate, unribbed rind and orange flesh. **2.** the plant bearing this fruit.

Per′sian vi′olet, *n.* any of several plants belonging to the genus *Exacum,* native to the Old World, as *E. affine,* having glossy ovate leaves and fragrant bluish flowers: cultivated as a houseplant.

per•si•flage (pûr′sə fläzh′, pâr′-), *n.* light, bantering talk.

per•sim•mon (pər sim′ən), *n.* **1.** any of several trees of the genus *Diospyros,* of the ebony family, bearing showy white flowers and a large, plumlike orange fruit that is edible and sweet when very ripe and soft. **2.** the fruit itself.

per•sist (pər sist′, -zist′), *v.i.* **1.** to continue steadily or firmly in some state, purpose, or course of action, in spite of opposition or criticism. **2.** to last or endure tenaciously: *The legend of King Arthur has persisted for nearly fifteen centuries.* **3.** to be insistent in a statement, request, or question. **—per•sist′er,** *n.*

per•sist•ence (pər sis′təns, -zis′-) also **per•sist′en•cy,** *n.* **1.** the act or fact of persisting. **2.** the quality of being persistent.

per•sist•ent (pər sis′tənt, -zis′-), *adj.* **1.** persisting stubbornly; insistent. **2.** lasting or enduring tenaciously. **3.** constantly repeated; continued. **4.** *Biol.* **a.** continuing or permanent. **b.** having continuity of phylogenetic characteristics. **5.** *Bot.* remaining attached beyond the usual time, as flowers or leaves. **—per•sist′ent•ly,** *adv.*

Persist′ent Wid′ow, The, a parable of Jesus. Luke 18:1–8.

per•snick•et•y (pər snik′i tē) also **pernickety,** *adj. Informal.* **1.** excessively particular; fussy. **2.** requiring painstaking care. **—per•snick′et•i•ness,** *n.*

per•son (pûr′sən), *n.* **1.** a human being; a man, woman, or child. **2.** a human being as distinguished from an animal or a thing. **3.** the actual self or individual personality of a human being. **4.** the body of a living human being, sometimes including the clothes being worn: *He had no money on his person.* **5.** the body in its external aspect. **6.** a human being or other entity, as a partnership or corporation, recognized by law as having rights and duties. **7.** a grammatical category applied esp. to pronouns and verbs, used to distinguish between the speaker of an utterance, the person addressed, and other people or things spoken about. Compare FIRST PERSON, SECOND PERSON, THIRD PERSON. **8.** any of the three modes of being in the Trinity: the Father, the Son, and the Holy Ghost. **—*Idiom.* 9. in person,** in one's own bodily presence; personally: *Applicants are requested to apply in person.* **—per′son•hood′,** *n.*

-person, a combining form of PERSON, replacing in existing compound words such paired, sex-specific forms as -MAN and -WOMAN or -ER[1] and -ESS: *salesperson.* **—Usage.** The -PERSON compounds are used, esp. by the media and in government and business communications, to avoid the -MAN compounds (*anchorman; businessman*) for individuals of either sex or the -WOMAN compounds (*anchorwoman; businesswoman*) to specify the individual's sex. Some find the new -PERSON compounds unnecessary, regarding the long-used compounds in *-man* as generic, not sex-marked. Alternatives to some of the -PERSON forms have won acceptance, as *anchor* and *chair;* other coinages, as *congressmember,* have had only marginal use. See also -ESS, LADY, -MAN, -WOMAN.

per•so•na (pər sō′nə), *n., pl.* **-nae** (-nē), **-nas. 1.** a character in a fictional literary work. **2.** (in the psychology of C. G. Jung) the public role or personality a person assumes or is perceived to assume (contrasted with *anima*).

per•son•a•ble (pûr′sə nə bəl), *adj.* having an agreeable or pleasing personality. **—per′son•a•ble•ness,** *n.* **—per′son•a•bly,** *adv.*

per•son•age (pûr′sə nij), *n.* **1.** a person of distinction or importance. **2.** any person. **3.** a character in a play, story, etc.

per•so•na gra•ta (pər sō′nə grä′tə, grā′tə, grat′ə), *adj.* being personally acceptable or welcome.

per•son•al (pûr′sə nl), *adj.* **1.** of, pertaining to, or concerning a particular person; individual; private: *a personal opinion.* **2.** directed to or intended for a particular person: *a personal favor.* **3.** referring or directed to a particular person in an offensive sense or manner: *personal remarks.* **4.** done, carried out, held, etc., in person: *a personal interview.* **5.** pertaining to the body, clothing, or appearance: *personal cleanliness.* **6.** of, pertaining to, or indicating grammatical person: *the personal ending -o in Spanish* hablo *"I speak."* **7.** pertaining to or characteristic of a person or self-conscious being. **8.** of the nature of an individual rational being. **9.** *Law.* of or pertaining to personal property: *personal interests.* **—*n.* 10. a.** a short news item concerning a socially prominent person. **b.** a brief, private message to a particular person, as one who is missing, either unsigned or using initials, first names, etc. **c.** a notice placed by a person seeking companionship, marriage, etc. **d. personals,** the section of a newspaper or magazine reserved for such notices.

per′sonal comput′er, *n.* a microcomputer designed for individual use, as for word processing, financial analysis, desktop publishing, or playing computer games. *Abbr.:* PC

per′sonal dig′ital assis′tant, *n.* a hand-held computer, often pen-based, that provides esp. organizational software, as an appointment calendar, and communications hardware, as a fax modem. *Abbr.:* PDA

per′sonal effects′, *n.pl.* privately owned articles consisting chiefly of clothing, toilet items, etc., for intimate use by an individual.

per′sonal foul′, *n.* a foul called in a game, as basketball or football, for illegal body contact or rough, unsportsmanlike play.

per′sonal identifica′tion num′ber, *n.* See PIN.

per•son•al•i•ty (pûr′sə nal′i tē), *n., pl.* **-ties. 1.** the visible aspect of one's character as it impresses others. **2.** a person as an embodiment of a collection of qualities. **3. a.** the sum total of the physical, mental, emotional, and social characteristics of an individual. **b.** the organized pattern of behavioral characteristics of the individual. **4.** the quality of being a person; personal existence or identity. **5.** something apprehended as analogous to a distinctive human personality, as the atmosphere of a place or thing. **6.** a famous or prominent person; celebrity. **7.** Usu. **personalities.** a disparaging or offensive personal remark.

per·son·al·ize (pûr′sə nl īz′), *v.t.,* **-ized, -iz·ing. 1.** to have marked with one's initials or name: *to personalize stationery.* **2.** to make personal, as by applying a general statement to oneself. **3.** to personify. **—per′son·al·i·za′tion,** *n.*

per·son·al·ly (pûr′sə nl ē), *adv.* **1.** in person; directly: *I thanked them personally.* **2.** as if intended for or directed at oneself: *Don't take his comments personally.* **3.** as regards oneself: *Personally, I don't care to go.* **4.** as the person: *I like her personally, but not as a boss.*

per′sonal pro′noun, *n.* a pronoun indicating grammatical person, as *I, me, we, us, you, he, she, it, they, him, her, them.*

per′sonal prop′erty, *n.* an estate or property consisting of movable articles both corporeal, as furniture or jewelry, and incorporeal, as stocks or bonds (disting. from *real property*).

per·so·na non gra·ta (pər sō′nə non grä′tə, grā′tə, grat′ə), *adj.* not being personally acceptable or welcome.

per·son·ate[1] (pûr′sə nāt′), *v.t.,* **-at·ed, -at·ing. 1.** to portray (as a character in a play). **2.** to impersonate, esp. with fraudulent intent. **3.** to personify. **—per′son·a′tion,** *n.* **—per′son·a′tor,** *n.*

per·son·ate[2] (pûr′sə nit, -nāt′), *adj. Zool.* having a disguised or masklike form or markings. **—per′son·ate·ly,** *adv.*

per·son·i·fi·ca·tion (pər son′ə fi kā′shən), *n.* **1.** the attribution of a human nature or character to inanimate objects or abstract notions, esp. as a rhetorical figure. **2.** the representation of a thing or abstraction in the form of a person, as in art. **3.** an embodiment, as of a quality: *He is the personification of evil.* **—per·son′i·fi·ca′tor,** *n.*

per·son·i·fy (pər son′ə fī′), *v.t.,* **-fied, -fy·ing. 1.** to attribute a human nature or character to (an inanimate object or an abstraction). **2.** to represent (a thing or abstraction) in the form of a person, as in art. **3.** to be an embodiment; typify: *He personifies the ruthless ambition of some executives.* **—per·son′i·fi′a·ble,** *adj.* **—per·son′i·fi′er,** *n.*

per·son·nel (pûr′sə nel′), *n.* **1.** the body of persons employed in an organization. Compare MATERIEL. **2.** (*used with a pl. v.*) persons. **3.** a department of an organization supervising matters of personnel.

per′son-to-per′son, *adj.* **1.** (of a long-distance telephone call) chargeable only upon speaking with a specified person at the number called. **2.** involving personal contact between persons. **—adv. 3.** (in making a long-distance telephone call) to a specified person. **4.** in person.

per·spec·tive (pər spek′tiv), *n.* **1.** a technique of depicting volumes and spatial relationships on a flat surface. Compare LINEAR PERSPECTIVE. **2.** a picture employing this technique, esp. one in which it is prominent. **3.** a visible scene, esp. one extending to a distance; vista. **4.** the manner in which objects appear to the eye in respect to their relative positions and distance. **5.** one's mental view of facts, ideas, etc., and their interrelationships. **6.** the ability to see all the relevant data in a meaningful relationship. **7.** a mental view or prospect. **—adj. 8.** of or pertaining to the art of perspective, or represented according to its laws. **—per·spec′·tiv·al,** *adj.* **—per·spec′tive·ly,** *adv.*

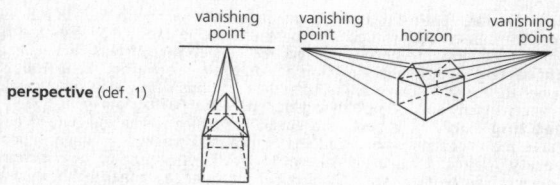

vanishing point   vanishing point   horizon   vanishing point

perspective (def. 1)

per·spi·ca·cious (pûr′spi kā′shəs), *adj.* having keen mental perception and understanding; discerning. **—per′spi·ca′cious·ly,** *adv.* **—per′·spi·cac′i·ty** (-kas′i tē), per′spi·ca′cious·ness, *n.*

per·spi·cu·i·ty (pûr′spi kyōō′i tē), *n.* clearness or lucidity, as of a statement.

per·spic·u·ous (pər spik′yōō əs), *adj.* clearly expressed or presented; lucid. **—per·spic′u·ous·ly,** *adv.* **—per·spic′u·ous·ness,** *n.*

per·spi·ra·tion (pûr′spə rā′shən), *n.* **1.** a salty, watery fluid secreted by the sweat glands of the skin; sweat. **2.** the act or process of perspiring.

per·spire (pər spīr′), *v.,* **-spired, -spir·ing. —v.i. 1.** to secrete a salty, watery fluid from the sweat glands of the skin; sweat. **—v.t. 2.** to emit through pores; exude.

per·suade (pər swād′), *v.t.,* **-suad·ed, -suad·ing. 1.** to prevail on (a person) to do something, as by advising or urging. **2.** to induce to believe; convince. **—per·suad′a·ble,** *adj.* **—per·suad′a·bil′i·ty,** *n.*

per·sua·sion (pər swā′zhən), *n.* **1.** the act of persuading or seeking to persuade. **2.** power to persuade; persuasive force. **3.** the state or fact of being persuaded or convinced. **4.** a deep conviction or belief. **5.** a form or system of belief, esp. religious belief: *the Quaker persuasion.* **6.** a sect, group, or faction. **7.** kind; sort.

per·sua·sive (pər swā′siv, -ziv), *adj.* able, fitted, or intended to persuade: *a persuasive argument.* **—per·sua′sive·ly,** *adv.* **—per·sua′sive·ness,** *n.*

pert (pûrt), *adj.,* **-er, -est. 1.** boldly forward in speech or behavior; impertinent; saucy. **2.** jaunty and stylish; chic. **3.** lively; sprightly; in good health. **—pert′ly,** *adv.* **—pert′ness,** *n.*

per·tain (pər tān′), *v.i.* **1.** to have reference or relation; relate: *documents pertaining to the lawsuit.* **2.** to belong or be connected as a part, adjunct, possession, or attribute. **3.** to belong properly or fittingly; be appropriate.

per·ti·na·cious (pûr′tn ā′shəs), *adj.* **1.** holding tenaciously to a purpose, course of action, or opinion; resolute. **2.** extremely or stubbornly persistent: *a pertinacious investigator.* **—per′ti·na′cious·ly,** *adv.* **—per′ti·nac′i·ty** (-as′i tē), per′ti·na′cious·ness, *n.*

per·ti·nent (pûr′tn ənt), *adj.* pertaining directly and significantly to the matter at hand; relevant: *pertinent details.* **—per′ti·nence, per′ti·nen·cy,** *n.* **—per′ti·nent·ly,** *adv.*

per·turb (pər tûrb′), *v.t.* **1.** to disturb or disquiet greatly in mind; agitate. **2.** to throw into great disorder; derange. **3.** to cause perturbation in the orbit of (a celestial body). **—per·turb′a·ble,** *adj.*

per·tur·ba·tion (pûr′tər bā′shən), *n.* **1.** the act of perturbing. **2.** the state of being perturbed. **3.** deviation of a celestial body from a regular orbit about its primary, caused by the presence of one or more other bodies that act upon it. **—per′tur·ba′tion·al,** *adj.*

per·tus·sis (pər tus′is), *n.* WHOOPING COUGH. **—per·tus′sal,** *adj.*

Pe·ru (pə rōō′), *n.* a republic in W South America. 24,949,512. 496,222 sq. mi. (1,285,215 sq. km.) *Cap.:* Lima. Spanish, **Pe·rú** (pe RŌŌ′).

pe·rus·al (pə rōō′zəl), *n.* the act of perusing.

pe·ruse (pə rōōz′), *v.t.,* **-rused, -rus·ing. 1.** to read through with thoroughness or care: *to peruse a report.* **2.** to read in an often desultory way. **3.** to survey or examine in detail. **—pe·rus′a·ble,** *adj.*

Pe·ru·vi·an (pə rōō′vē ən), *adj.* **1.** of or pertaining to Peru or its inhabitants. **—n. 2.** a native or inhabitant of Peru.

per·vade (pər vād′), *v.t.,* **-vad·ed, -vad·ing.** to become spread throughout all parts of: *Spring pervaded the air.* **—per·vad′er,** *n.* **—per·va′sion** (-vā′zhən), *n.* **—per·va′sive** (-siv), *adj.* **—per·va′sive·ly,** *adv.* **—per·va′sive·ness,** *n.*

per·verse (pər vûrs′), *adj.* **1.** willfully determined not to do what is expected or desired; contrary. **2.** characterized by or proceeding from such a determination: *a perverse mood.* **3.** wayward or cantankerous. **4.** turned away from what is right, good, or proper; wicked or corrupt. **—per·verse′ly,** *adv.* **—per·verse′ness,** *n.* **—per·ver′si·ty,** *n., pl.* **-ties.**

per·ver·sion (pər vûr′zhən, -shən), *n.* **1.** the act of perverting. **2.** the state of being perverted. **3.** a perverted form of something.

per·vert (*v.* pər vûrt′; *n.* pûr′vərt), *v.t.* **1.** to lead astray morally. **2.** to turn away from the right course. **3.** to lead into mental error or false judgment. **4.** to turn to an improper use; misapply. **5.** to misconstrue or misinterpret, esp. deliberately; distort. **6.** to bring to a less excellent state; debase. **—per·vert′er,** *n.* **—per·vert′i·ble,** *adj.*

per·vert·ed (pər vûr′tid), *adj.* **1.** of an unnatural or abnormal nature: *a perverted interest in death.* **2.** misguided; distorted; misinterpreted. **3.** turned from what is considered right or true. **—per·vert′ed·ly,** *adv.* **—per·vert′ed·ness,** *n.*

per·vi·ous (pûr′vē əs), *adj.* **1.** permeable. **2.** accessible to reason. **—per′vi·ous·ness,** *n.*

pes (pēs, pās), *n., pl.* **pe·des** (pē′dēz, ped′ēz). *Anat., Zool.* a foot or footlike part.

Pe·sach (pä′säKH), *n. Judaism.* PASSOVER (def. 1).

pe·se·ta (pə sā′tə), *n., pl.* **-tas** (-təz). the basic monetary unit of Spain.

pes·ky (pes′kē), *adj.,* **-ki·er, -ki·est.** annoying; troublesome: *a pesky fly.* **—pesk′i·ly,** *adv.* **—pesk′i·ness,** *n.*

pe·so (pā′sō), *n., pl.* **-sos. 1.** the basic monetary unit of Argentina, Chile, Colombia, Cuba, the Dominican Republic, Guinea-Bissau, Mexico, the Philippines, and Uruguay. **2.** a former monetary unit of Peru, equal to 100 centavos. **3.** a former silver coin of Spain and Spanish America, equal to eight reals.

pes·si·mism (pes′ə miz′əm), *n.* **1.** the tendency to see only what is disadvantageous or gloomy or to anticipate the worst outcome. **2.** the doctrine that the existing world is the worst of all possible worlds or that all things naturally tend toward evil. **3.** the belief that the evil and pain in the world outweigh any goodness or happiness. **—pes′si·mist,** *n.* **—pes′si·mis′tic,** *adj.* **—pes′si·mis′ti·cal·ly,** *adv.*

pest (pest), *n.* **1.** an annoying or troublesome person, animal, or thing; nuisance. **2.** an insect or other small animal that harms or destroys garden plants, trees, etc.

pes·ter (pes′tər), *v.t.* to bother persistently with petty annoyances; trouble. **—pes′ter·ing·ly,** *adv.* **—pes′ter·some,** *adj.*

pes·ti·cide (pes′tə sīd′), *n.* a chemical preparation for destroying plant, fungal, or animal pests. **—pes′ti·cid′al,** *adj.*

pes·tif·er·ous (pe stif′ər əs), *adj.* **1.** bringing or bearing disease. **2.** pernicious; dangerous. **3.** troublesome; annoying. **—pes·tif′er·ous·ly,** *adv.* **—pes·tif′er·ous·ness,** *n.*

pes·ti·lence (pes′tl əns), *n.* **1.** a deadly or virulent epidemic disease. **2.** BUBONIC PLAGUE. **3.** something regarded as harmful or destructive.

pes·ti·lent (pes′tl ənt), *adj.* **1.** producing or tending to produce infectious or contagious, often epidemic, disease; pestilential. **2.** destructive to life; deadly. **3.** injurious to peace, morals, etc.; pernicious. **4.** troublesome or annoying. **—pes′ti·lent·ly,** *adv.*

pes·tle (pes′əl, pes′tl), *n., v.,* **-tled, -tling. —n. 1.** a tool for pounding or grinding substances in a mortar. **2.** any of various appliances for pounding or stamping. —*v.t.* **3.** to pound or grind with a pestle.

pes·to (pes/tō), *n.* an uncooked sauce usu. of fresh bašil ground together with pine nuts, garlic, olive oil, and cheese.

pet¹ (pet), *n., adj., v.,* **pet·ted, pet·ting.** —*n.* **1.** any domesticated animal kept as a companion. **2.** a person especially cherished or indulged: *teacher's pet.* **3.** a thing particularly cherished. —*adj.* **4.** kept or treated as a pet. **5.** cherished or indulged, as a child. **6.** favorite; preferred: *a pet theory.* **7.** showing fondness or affection: *pet names.* —*v.t.* **8.** to treat as a pet; indulge. **9.** to fondle or caress: *I like to pet the cat and listen to her purr.* —*v.i.* **10.** to engage in amorous fondling and caressing. —**pet/ta·ble,** *adj.*

pet² (pet), *n., v.,* **pet·ted, pet·ting.** —*n.* **1.** a fit of peevishness or sulking. —*v.i.* **2.** to be peevish; sulk.

PET (pet), *n.* positron emission tomography: a technique for revealing active areas of the brain while information is being processed by detecting radiolabeled glucose in the cerebral blood flow. Compare PET SCANNER.

Pé·tain (pā taN/), *n.* **Henri Philippe Omer,** 1856–1951, marshal of France: premier of the Vichy government 1940–44.

pet·al (pet/l), *n.* one of the often colored segments of the corolla of a flower. —**pet/al·age,** *n.* —**pet/aled, pet/alled,** *adj.* —**pet/al·less,** *adj.* —**pet/al·like/,** *adj.*

pe·ter (pē/tər), *v.i.* to tire; become exhausted (usu. fol. by *out*).

Pe·ter¹ (pē/tər), *n.* **1.** Also called **Simon Peter.** died A.D. 67?, one of the 12 apostles and the reputed author of two of the Epistles. **2.** either of these two Epistles in the New Testament, I Peter or II Peter.

Pe·ter² (pē/tər), *n.* **1.** Peter I (*"the Great"*), 1672–1725, czar of Russia 1682–1725. **2.** Peter II, 1923–70, king of Yugoslavia 1934–45. **3.** Peter III, 1728–62, czar of Russia 1762 (husband of Catherine II).

Pe/ter Pan/, *n.* **1.** the hero of Sir James M. Barrie's play about a boy who never grew up. **2.** (*italics*) the play itself (1904).

Pe/ter Pan/ col/lar, *n.* a close-fitting flat or rolled collar with rounded ends that meet in front of a high, round neckline.

Pe/ter Prin/ciple, *n.* a satirical observation that in any organizational structure people tend to be promoted until they reach their level of incompetence. [from the title of a book by Laurence J. *Peter* (b. 1919), Canadian educator]

Pe/ter's pence/ or **Pe/ter pence/,** *n.* **1.** an annual tax of a penny from each household, formerly paid to the papal see. **2.** a voluntary contribution to the pope, made by Roman Catholics.

Pe/ter the Her/mit, *n.* c1050–1115, French monk: preacher of the first Crusade 1095–99. Also called **Pe/ter of Amiens/.**

pet·i·ole (pet/ē ōl/), *n.* **1.** the slender stalk by which a leaf is attached to the stem; leafstalk. **2.** a stalk or peduncle, as that connecting the abdomen and thorax in wasps.

pet·it (pet/ē, pə tē/), *adj. Law.* small; petty; minor.

pet·it bour·geois (pə tē/ bŏŏr zhwä/; pet/ē bŏŏr/zhwä), *n., pl.* **pe·tits bour·geois** (pə tē/ bŏŏr zhwäz/; pet/ē bŏŏr/zhwäz). a person who belongs to the petite bourgeoisie. —**petit/-bourgeois/,** *adj.*

pe·tite (pə tēt/), *adj.* **1.** (of a woman) short and having a small, trim figure; diminutive. —*n.* **2.** a size of garments for women of less than average height and with average or diminutive figures. **3.** a garment in this size. —**pe·tite/ness,** *n.*

pe·tite bour·geoise (pə tēt/ bŏŏr zhwäz/), *n., pl.* **pe·tites bour·geoises** (pə tēt/ bŏŏr zhwäz/). a woman who belongs to the petite bourgeoisie.

pe·tite bour·geoi·sie (pə tēt/ bŏŏr/zhwä zē/), *n.* the part of the bourgeoisie having the least wealth and lowest social status; the lower middle class.

pet·it four (pet/ē fôr/, fōr/), *n., pl.* **pet·its fours** (pet/ē fôrz/, fōrz/). a small frosted teacake.

pe·ti·tion (pə tish/ən), *n.* **1.** a formally drawn request, often signed by those endorsing it, that is addressed to a person or group of persons in authority, soliciting some favor, right, mercy, or other benefit. **2.** a respectful or humble request, as to a superior; a supplication or prayer. **3.** something that is sought by request or entreaty. —*v.t.* **4.** to address a formal petition to (a sovereign, a legislative body, etc.). **5.** to ask by petition for (something). **6.** to beg for or request. —*v.i.* **7.** to present a petition. **8.** to make a request or entreaty. —**pe·ti/tion·a·ble,** *adj.* —**pe·ti/tion·ar/y,** *adj.* —**pe·ti/tion·er,** *n.*

pe·tit mal (pet/ē mäl/, mal/; pə tē/), *n.* See under EPILEPSY.

pet/it point/ (pet/ē), *n.* **1.** a small stitch used in embroidery. **2.** embroidery done on a canvas backing and resembling woven tapestry.

pet·nap·ping or **pet·nap·ing** (pet/nap/ing), *n.* the stealing of a pet. —**pet/nap/per, pet/nap/er,** *n.*

pet/ peeve/, *n.* a continual source of personal annoyance or complaint.

Pe·tra (pē/trə, pe/-), *n.* an ancient city in what is now SW Jordan: capital of the Nabataeans.

Pe·trarch (pē/trärk, pe/-), *n.* (*Francesco Petrarca*), 1304–74, Italian poet and scholar. —**Pe·trar·chan** (pi trär/kən), *adj.*

pet·rel (pe/trəl), *n.* any of various oceanic tube-nosed seabirds of the families Procellariidae, Hydrobatidae, and Pelecanoididae.

petri-, var. of PETRO-¹ before elements of Latin origin: *petrifaction.*

pe/tri dish/ (pē/trē), *n.* a shallow, circular, glass or plastic dish with a

loose-fitting cover over the top and sides, used for culturing microorganisms.

Pet/rified For/est Na/tional Park/, *n.* a national park in E Arizona: buried tree trunks turned to stone by the action of mineral-laden water. 147 sq. mi. (381 sq. km).

pet·ri·fy (pe/trə fī/), *v., -fied, -fy·ing.* —*v.t.* **1.** to convert into stone or a stony substance. **2.** to numb with strong emotion, as fear. **3.** to harden; deaden: *The tragedy petrified his emotions.* —*v.i.* **4.** to become petrified. —**pet/ri·fi/a·ble,** *adj.* —**pe·trif·i·cant** (pi trif/i kənt), *adj.* —**pet/ri·fi/er,** *n.*

Pe·trine (pē/trīn, -trin), *adj.* of or pertaining to the apostle Peter or the Epistles bearing his name.

pet·ro (pe/trō), *adj.* of or pertaining to petroleum or the petroleum industry.

petro-¹, a combining form meaning "rock," "stone": *petrology.*

petro-², a combining form meaning "petroleum," "the extraction and export of petroleum": *petrochemistry; petropower.*

pet·ro·chem·i·cal (pe/trō kem/i kəl), *n.* **1.** a chemical substance obtained from petroleum or natural gas, as gasoline, kerosene, or petrolatum. —*adj.* **2.** of or pertaining to petrochemistry or a petrochemical.

pet·ro·chem·is·try (pe/trō kem/ə strē), *n.* **1.** the branch of chemistry dealing with petroleum or its products. **2.** the chemistry of rocks.

pet·ro·dol·lars (pe/trō dol/ərz), *n.pl.* revenues in dollars accumulated by petroleum-exporting countries, esp. of the Middle East.

pet·ro·gen·e·sis (pe/trō jen/ə sis) also **pe·trog·e·ny** (pi troj/ə nē), *n.* the origin and formation of rocks. —**pet/ro·ge·net/ic** (-jə net/ik), *adj.*

pet·ro·glyph (pe/trə glif/), *n.* a prehistoric drawing or carving on rock. Also called **pet·ro·graph** (-graf/, -gräf/). —**pet/ro·glyph/ic,** *adj.* —**pe·trog·ly·phy** (pi trog/lə fē), *n.*

pe·trog·ra·phy (pi trog/rə fē), *n.* the branch of petrology dealing with the description and classification of rocks, esp. by microscopic examination. —**pe·trog/ra·pher,** *n.* —**pet·ro·graph·ic** (pe/trə graf/ik), **pet/ro·graph/i·cal,** *adj.* —**pet/ro·graph/i·cal·ly,** *adv.*

pet·rol (pe/trəl), *n. Brit.* GASOLINE.

pet·ro·la·tum (pe/trə lā/təm, -lä/-), *n.* a gelatinous mass obtained from petroleum, used as a lubricant, rust preventive, protective dressing, and ointment base.

pe·tro·le·um (pə trō/lē əm), *n.* an oily, thick, flammable, usu. dark-colored liquid that is a form of bitumen or a mixture of various hydrocarbons, occurring naturally and commonly obtained by drilling: used as fuel, or separated by distillation into gasoline, naphtha, benzene, kerosene, paraffin, etc. —**pe·tro/le·ous,** *adj.*

petro/leum jel/ly, *n.* PETROLATUM.

pe·trol·o·gy (pi trol/ə jē), *n.* the scientific study of rocks, including petrography and petrogenesis. —**pet·ro·log·ic** (pe/trə loj/ik), **pet/ro·log/i·cal,** *adj.* —**pe·trol/o·gist,** *n.*

PET/ scan/ner, *n.* a tomographic device that produces computerized cross-sectional images of biochemical activity in the brain or other organ through the use of radioactive tracers. [*p(ositron) e(mission) t(omography)*]

pet·ti·coat (pet/ē kōt/), *n.* **1.** an underskirt, esp. one that is full and often trimmed and ruffled and of a decorative fabric. **2.** any skirtlike part or covering. —**pet/ti·coat/ed,** *adj.* —**pet/ti·coat/less,** *adj.*

pet·ti·fog (pet/ē fog/, -fôg/), *v.i., -fogged, -fog·ging.* **1.** to quibble over trifles. **2.** to carry on an unethical law business. **3.** to practice chicanery of any sort. —**pet/ti·fog/ger,** *n.* —**pet/ti·fog/ger·y,** *n.*

pet/ting zoo/, *n.* a zoo, or a special part of a larger zoo, where children may hold and stroke and sometimes feed small or young animals.

pet·ty (pet/ē), *adj., -ti·er, -ti·est.* **1.** of little or no importance; inconsequential: *petty grievances.* **2.** of lesser importance or merit; minor: *petty considerations.* **3.** having or showing narrow ideas, interests, etc.: *petty minds.* **4.** ungenerous in trifling matters: *a petty person.* **5.** showing meanness of spirit: *a petty revenge.* —**pet/ti·ly,** *adv.* —**pet/ti·ness,** *n.*

pet/ty cash/, *n.* a cash fund for paying small charges, as for minor office supplies or deliveries.

pet/ty (or **pet/it**) **ju/ry,** *n.* a jury, usu. of 12 persons, impaneled to render a verdict in a civil or criminal proceeding (disting. from *grand jury*). —**pet/ty ju/ror,** *n.*

pet/ty (or **pet/it**) **lar/ceny,** *n. Law.* larceny in which the value of the goods taken is below a certain legally specified amount.

pet/ty of/ficer, *n.* **1.** a noncommissioned officer in the navy or coast guard. **2.** one of the minor officers on a merchant ship, as a boatswain.

pet·u·lant (pech/ə lənt), *adj.* showing sudden irritation, esp. over some trifling annoyance; peevish. —**pet/u·lance, pet/u·lan·cy,** *n.* —**pet/u·lant·ly,** *adv.*

pe·tu·nia (pi tōō/nyə, -nē ə, -tyōō/-), *n., pl.* **-nias.** any garden plant belonging to the genus *Petunia,* of the nightshade family, native to tropical America, having funnel-shaped flowers of various colors.

pew (pyōō), *n.* **1.** (in a church) one of a number of fixed benches with backs, accessible by aisles, for the use of the congregation. **2.** an enclosure with seats in a church, assigned to the use of a family or other group of worshipers.

pew·ter (pyōō/tər), *n.* **1.** any of various alloys in which tin is the chief constituent, orig. one of tin and lead. **2.** utensils and vessels made of pewter. —*adj.* **3.** consisting or made of pewter.

pe·yo·te (pā ō′tē) *n., pl.* **-tes. 1.** MESCAL (def. 3). **2.** (in Mexico) any of several cacti related to or resembling mescal.

Pfc. or **PFC,** *Mil.* private first class.

PG, parental guidance: a motion-picture rating advising parents that some material in the film may be unsuitable for children. Compare G (def. 2), NC-17, PG-13, R (def. 4), X (def. 7).

PG-13 (pē′jē′thûr′tēn′), a motion-picture rating advising parents that some material in the film may be unsuitable for children under the age of 13. Compare G (def. 2), NC-17, PG, R (def. 4), X (def. 7).

pg., page.

PGA or **P.G.A.,** Professional Golfers' Association.

pH, the symbol for the logarithm of the reciprocal of hydrogen ion concentration in gram atoms per liter, used to describe the acidity or alkalinity of a chemical solution on a scale of 0 (more acidic) to 14 (more alkaline).

phage (fāj) *n.* BACTERIOPHAGE.

-phage, a combining form meaning "a thing that devours," used esp. in the names of viruses and phagocytes: *bacteriophage; macrophage.*

-phagia, var. of -PHAGY.

phago-, a combining form meaning "eating," "devouring": *phagocyte.*

phag·o·cyte (fag′ə sīt′), *n.* any cell, as a macrophage, that ingests foreign particles, bacteria, or cell debris. —**phag′o·cyt′ic** (-sit′ik), *adj.*

-phagy or **-phagia,** a combining form meaning "eating," "feeding on," esp. as a practice or means of gaining sustenance: *anthropophagy; monophagy.*

phal·ange (fal′ənj, fə lanj′, fā′lanj) *n., pl.* **pha·lan·ges** (fə lan′jēz) PHALANX (def. 6).

pha·lan·ger (fə lan′jər), *n.* any tree-dwelling Australian marsupial of the family Phalangeridae, including mouselike, squirrellike, and lemurlike forms.

pha·lan·ges (fə lan′jēz), *n.* **1.** a pl. of PHALANX. **2.** pl. of PHALANGE.

pha·lanx (fā′langks, fal′angks), *n., pl.* **pha·lanx·es** for 1–5, **pha·lan·ges** (fə lan′jēz) for 6. **1.** (in ancient Greece) a group of heavily armed infantry formed in ranks and files close and deep, with shields joined and long spears overlapping. **2.** any body of troops in close array. **3.** a number of persons united for a common purpose. **4.** a compact or closely massed body of persons, animals, or things. **5.** (in Fourierism) a group of about 1800 persons, living together and holding their property in common. **6.** any of the bones of the fingers or toes.

phal·a·rope (fal′ə rōp′), *n.* any of three small aquatic birds, akin to or part of the sandpiper family, having lobed toes adapted for swimming: the males are the sole or primary tenders of the eggs and young.

phal·lic (fal′ik), *adj.* **1.** of, pertaining to, or resembling a phallus. **2.** of or pertaining to phallicism. **3.** GENITAL (def. 3b).

phal·lus (fal′əs), *n., pl.* **phal·li** (fal′ī), **phal·lus·es. 1.** a representation of the penis, employed in the art and religious practices of various cultures, usu. as a symbol of male generative powers. **2.** PENIS. **3.** the undifferentiated embryonic organ out of which either the penis or the clitoris develops.

phan·tasm (fan′taz əm), *n.* **1.** an apparition or specter. **2.** a creation of the imagination or fancy; fantasy. **3.** a mental image or representation of a real object. **4.** an illusory likeness of something. —**phan·tas′mal, phan·tas′mic, phan·tas′mi·cal,** *adj.*

phan·tas·ma·go·ri·a (fan taz′mə gôr′ē ə, -gōr′-), *n., pl.* **-ri·as. 1.** a shifting series of phantasms, illusions, or deceptive appearances, as in a dream. **2.** a changing scene made up of many elements. **3.** an optical illusion produced by a magic lantern or the like in which figures increase or diminish in size, pass into each other, dissolve, etc. —**phan·tas′ma·gor′ic** (-gôr′ik, -gor′-), **phan·tas′ma·gor′i·cal,** *adj.* —**phan·tas′ma·gor′i·cal·ly,** *adv.* —**phan·tas′ma·gor′ist,** *n.*

phan·tom (fan′təm), *n.* **1.** an apparition or specter. **2.** an appearance or illusion without material substance, as a dream image, mirage, or optical illusion. **3.** a person or thing of merely illusory power, status, efficacy, etc.: *the phantom of fear.* —*adj.* **4.** of, pertaining to, or of the nature of a phantom; illusory: *a phantom ship; an amputee with a phantom limb.* **5.** nonexistent; fictitious: *phantom employees on the payroll.* —**phan′tom·like′,** *adj.*

Phar·aoh (fâr′ō, far′ō, fā′rō), *n.* **1.** a title of an ancient Egyptian king. **2.** (*l.c.*) TYRANT. —**phar·a·on·ic** (fâr′ā on′ik, far′-), *adj.*

Phar′aoh ant′ or **Phar′aoh's ant′,** *n.* a red or yellow ant, *Monomorium pharaonis,* introduced from Europe into North America: a common household pest.

Phar·i·sa·ic (far′ə sā′ik) also **Phar′i·sa′i·cal,** *adj.* **1.** of or pertaining to the Pharisees. **2.** (*l.c.*) practicing or advocating strict observance of external forms and ceremonies of religion or conduct without regard to the spirit; self-righteous; sanctimonious; hypocritical. —**phar′i·sa′i·cal·ly,** *adv.*

Phar·i·sa·ism (far′ə sā iz′əm) also **Phar·i·see·ism** (-sē iz′əm), *n.* **1.** the principles and practices of the Pharisees. **2.** (*l.c.*) pharisaic character, behavior, or practice; sanctimoniousness. —**Phar′i·sa·ist,** *adj.*

Phar·i·see (far′ə sē′), *n.* **1.** a member of an ancient Jewish sect that differed from the Sadducees chiefly in its strict observance of religious practices, liberal interpretation of the Bible, and adherence to oral laws and traditions. **2.** (*l.c.*) a sanctimonious, self-righteous, or hypocritical person.

Phar′isee and the Tax′ Collec′tor, The, a parable of Jesus. Luke 18:9–14.

phar·ma·ceu·ti·cal (fär′mə sōō′ti kəl) also **phar′ma·ceu′tic,** *adj.* **1.** pertaining to pharmacy or pharmacists. —*n.* **2.** a pharmaceutical preparation or product. —**phar′ma·ceu′ti·cal·ly,** *adv.*

phar·ma·ceu·tics (fär′mə sōō′tiks), *n.* (*used with a sing. v.*) PHARMACY (def. 2).

phar·ma·cist (fär′mə sist), *n.* a person licensed to prepare and dispense drugs and medicines; druggist.

pharmaco-, a combining form meaning "drug": *pharmacology.*

phar·ma·co·ki·net·ics (fär′mə kō ki net′iks, -kī-), *n.* **1.** (*used with a pl. v.*) the actions of drugs within the body, as their absorption, distribution, metabolism, and elimination. **2.** (*used with a sing. v.*) the study of such actions.

phar·ma·col·o·gy (fär′mə kol′ə jē), *n.* the science dealing with the preparation, uses, and esp. the effects of drugs. —**phar′ma·co·log′i·cal** (-kə loj′i kəl), **phar′ma·co·log′ic,** *adj.* —**phar′ma·co·log′i·cal·ly,** *adv.* —**phar′ma·col′o·gist,** *n.*

phar·ma·co·poe·ia or **phar·ma·co·pe·ia** (fär′mə kə pē′ə), *n., pl.* **-ias. 1.** a book published usu. under the jurisdiction of the government and containing a list of drugs, their formulas, methods for making medicinal preparations, and other related information. **2.** a stock of drugs. —**phar′ma·co·poe′ial,** *adj.* —**phar′ma·co·poe′ist,** *n.*

phar·ma·cy (fär′mə sē), *n., pl.* **-cies. 1.** DRUGSTORE. **2.** Also called **pharmaceutics.** the art and science of preparing and dispensing drugs and medicines.

pha·ryn·ge·al (fə rin′jē əl, -jəl, far′in jē′əl) also **pha·ryn·gal** (fə ring′gəl), *adj.* **1.** of, pertaining to, or situated near the pharynx. **2.** (of a speech sound) articulated with retraction of the root of the tongue and constriction of the pharynx. —*n.* **3.** a pharyngeal speech sound.

phar·yn·gi·tis (far′in jī′tis), *n.* inflammation of the mucous membrane of the pharynx; sore throat.

phar·ynx (far′ingks), *n., pl.* **pha·ryn·ges** (fə rin′jēz), **phar·ynx·es.** the portion of the alimentary canal, with its membranes and muscles, that connects the mouth and nasal passages with the larynx.

phase (fāz), *n., v.,* **phased, phas·ing.** —*n.* **1.** any of the major appearances or aspects in which a thing of varying modes or conditions manifests itself; facet. **2.** a stage in a process of change or development. **3.** a side, aspect, or point of view. **4.** a state of synchronous operation. **5. a.** the particular appearance presented by the moon or a planet at a given time. **b.** one of the recurring appearances or states of the moon or a planet in respect to the form, or the absence, of its illuminated disk. **6.** a mechanically separate, homogeneous part of a heterogeneous system, as a solution: *liquid, solid, and gaseous phases.* **7.** *Physics.* **a.** a particular stage or point of advancement in a cycle of motion or change. **b.** the fractional part of the cycle that has elapsed, measured from a fixed datum. —*v.t.* **8.** to schedule or order so as to be available when or as needed. **9.** to put in phase; synchronize. **10. phase down,** to reduce or diminish by gradual stages. **11. phase in,** to put or come into use gradually. **12. phase out,** to bring or come to an end gradually; ease out of service. —**pha′sic,** *adj.*

phase′ modu·la′tion, *n.* radio transmission in which the carrier wave is modulated by changing its phase to transmit the amplitude and pitch of the signal.

phase′out′ or **phase′-out′,** *n.* an act or instance of phasing out; planned discontinuation or expiration.

phas·mid (faz′mid), *n.* any insect of the order Phasmida, characterized by long slender legs and antennae and a wingless, twiglike body: includes walking sticks and leaf insects.

Ph.D., Doctor of Philosophy. [< New Latin *Philosophiae Doctor*]

pheas·ant (fez′ənt), *n.* **1.** any of numerous large, typically long-tailed gallinaceous birds of the family Phasianidae, principally of Asia, though introduced in other parts of the world. **2.** *Southern U.S.* the ruffed grouse.

pheno-, **1.** a combining form meaning "shining," "appearing, seeming": *phenotype.* **2.** a combining form used in the names of chemical compounds that contain phenol or the phenyl group, are related to aromatic compounds, or derive from benzene: *phenobarbital.* Also, *esp. before a vowel,* **phen-.**

phe·no·bar·bi·tal (fē′nō bär′bi tôl′, -tal′, -nə-), *n.* a white, crystalline powder, $C_{12}H_{12}N_2O_3$, used as a sedative, a hypnotic, and as an antispasmodic in epilepsy.

phe·no·cop·y (fē′nə kop′ē), *n., pl.* **-cop·ies.** a trait or condition that resembles a known genetic defect but is externally caused and not inheritable.

phe·nol (fē′nôl, -nol), *n.* **1.** a white, crystalline, water-soluble, poisonous substance, C_6H_5OH, used chiefly as a disinfectant, as an antiseptic, and in organic synthesis. **2.** any analogous hydroxyl derivative of benzene. —**phe·no·lic** (fi nō′lik, -nol′ik), *adj.*

phe·nol·o·gy (fi nol′ə jē), *n.* the science dealing with the influence of climate on the recurrence of such annual phenomena of animal and plant life as budding and bird migrations. —**phe′no·log′i·cal** (fēn′l oj′i kəl), *adj.* —**phe′no·log′i·cal·ly,** *adv.* —**phe·nol′o·gist,** *n.*

phe·nom (fē′nom, fi nom′), *n. Slang.* a person of remarkable talent or ability; phenomenon: *a tennis phenom.*

phe·nom·e·na (fi nom′ə nə), *n.* a pl. of PHENOMENON.

phe·nom·e·nal (fi nom′ə nl), *adj.* **1.** highly extraordinary or prodigious; exceptional: *phenomenal speed.* **2.** of or pertaining to phenomena. **3.** of the nature of a phenomenon; cognizable by the senses. —**phe·nom′e·nal/i·ty,** *n.* —**phe·nom′e·nal·ly,** *adv.*

phe·nom·e·nol·o·gy (fi nom′ə nol/ə jē), *n.* **1.** the study of phenomena as distinct from ontology. **2.** the branch of a field of study that classifies phenomena relevant to itself. **3.** the system of Husserl and his followers stressing the description of phenomena. —**phe·nom′e·no·log′i·cal** (-nl oj′i kəl), *adj.* —**phe·nom′e·no·log′i·cal·ly,** *adv.* —**phe·nom′e·nol/o·gist,** *n.*

phe·nom·e·non (fi nom′ə non′, -nən), *n., pl.* **-na** (-nə) or, esp. for 3, **-nons. 1.** a fact, occurrence, or circumstance observed or observable: *the phenomena of nature.* **2.** something that is remarkable or extraordinary. **3.** a remarkable or exceptional person; prodigy. **4.** *Philos.* **a.** an appearance or immediate object of awareness in experience. **b.** (in Kantian philosophy) a thing as it appears to and is constructed by the mind, as distinguished from a noumenon, or thing-in-itself. —**Usage.** As with other plurals of Latin or Greek origin, there is a tendency to use the plural PHENOMENA as a singular (*This phenomena will not be seen again*), but such use occurs infrequently in edited writing. See also CRITERION, MEDIA[1].

phe·no·type (fē/nə tīp′), *n.* **1.** the observable constitution of an organism. **2.** the appearance of an organism resulting from the interaction of the genotype and the environment. Compare GENOTYPE. —**phe/no·typ′ic** (-tip′ik), **phe/no·typ′i·cal,** *adj.* —**phe/no·typ′i·cal·ly,** *adv.*

phen·yl (fen/l, fēn/l), *n.* the univalent group C_6H_5, derived from benzene.

phen·yl·al·a·nine (fen/l al/ə nēn′, -nin, fēn′-), *n.* a crystalline, water-soluble, essential amino acid, $C_6H_5CH_2CH(NH_2)COOH$, necessary to the nutrition of humans and most animals, occurring in egg white and skim milk. *Abbr.*: Phe; *Symbol:* F

pher·o·mone (fer/ə mōn′), *n.* any chemical substance released by an animal that serves to influence the physiology or behavior of other members of the same species. —**pher/o·mo′nal,** *adj.*

phew (hwyōō, fyōō), *interj.* an exclamation to express relief, disgust, exhaustion, surprise, etc.): *Phew, it's hot!*

Phi Be·ta Kap·pa (fī/ bā/tə kap/ə, bē/tə), *n.* **1.** a national honor society, founded in 1776, whose members are chosen, for lifetime membership, usually from among college undergraduates of high academic distinction. **2.** a member of Phi Beta Kappa.

phil-, var. of PHILO- before a vowel: *philanthropy.*

-phil, var. of -PHILE: *eosinophil.*

Phil., 1. Philemon. **2.** Philippians. **3.** Philippine.

phil., 1. philosophical. **2.** philosophy.

Phil·a·del·phi·a (fil/ə del/fē ə), *n.* **1.** a city in SE Pennsylvania, on the Delaware River. 1,524,249 **2.** a city of Lydia, the site of one of the seven churches of Asia. Rev. 1:11.

phi·lan·der (fi lan/dər), *v.i.* (of a man) to make love with a woman one cannot or will not marry; carry on flirtations. —**phi·lan/der·er,** *n.*

phil·an·throp·ic (fil/ən throp/ik) also **phil/an·throp/i·cal,** *adj.* of, pertaining to, or characterized by philanthropy; benevolent. —**phil/an·throp/i·cal·ly,** *adv.*

phi·lan·thro·pist (fi lan/thrə pist), *n.* a person who practices philanthropy.

phi·lan·thro·py (fi lan/thrə pē), *n., pl.* **-pies. 1.** altruistic concern for human beings, esp. as manifested by donations of money, property, or work to needy persons or to institutions advancing human welfare. **2.** a philanthropic act or donation. **3.** a philanthropic institution.

phi·lat·e·ly (fi lat/l·ē), *n.* the collection and study of postage and revenue stamps and other material relating to postal or fiscal history. —**phil·a·tel·ic** (fil/ə tel/ik), *adj.* —**phi·lat/e·list,** *n.*

-phile or **-phil,** a combining form meaning "lover of, enthusiast for (a given object)" (*bibliophile; Francophile*), "person sexually attracted to or obsessively interested in (a given object)" (*pedophile*), "organism having an affinity for (a given thing)" (*siderophile*); used also as a synonym of -PHILIC (*lyophile*).

Phi·le·mon (fi lē/mən, fī-), *n.* **1.** an Epistle written by Paul. **2.** a person who was probably a convert of Paul and to whom this Epistle is addressed. **3.** (in Greek myth) the husband of Baucis.

Phi·le·tus (fi lē/təs), *n.* a false teacher of the early Christian church. II Tim. 2:17–18.

phil·har·mon·ic (fil/här mon/ik, fil/ər-), *n.* (*often cap.*) SYMPHONY ORCHESTRA.

-philia or **-phily,** a combining form occurring in abstract nouns that correspond to adjectives ending in -PHILIC or -PHILOUS or nouns ending in -PHILE.

-philiac, a combining form occurring in personal nouns that correspond to nouns ending in -PHILIA: *hemophiliac; necrophiliac.*

-philic or **-philous,** a combining form occurring in adjectives that characterize classes of organisms having an affinity for or thriving in a given substance or environment (*acidophilic; thermophilic*); used also to form adjectives corresponding to nouns ending in -PHILE (*Anglophilic*).

Phil·ip[1] (fil/ip), *n.* **1.** one of the 12 apostles. Mark 3:18; John 1:43–48; 6:5–7. **2. King** (*Metacomet*), died 1676, sachem of the Wampanoag Indians 1662–76. **3. Prince, Duke of Edinburgh,** born 1921, consort of Elizabeth II.

Phil·ip[2] (fil/ip), *n.* **1. Philip I,** 1052–1108, king of France 1060–1108 (son of Henry I of France). **2. Philip II, a.** (*"Philip of Macedon"*) 382–336 B.C., king of Macedonia 359–336 (father of Alexander the Great). **b.**

(*"Philip Augustus"*) 1165–1223, king of France 1180–1223. **c.** 1527–98, king of Spain 1556–98 (husband of Mary I). **3. Philip IV** (*"Philip the Fair"*), 1268–1314, king of France 1285–1314. **4. Philip V,** 1683–1746, king of Spain 1700–46. **5. Philip VI,** 1293–1350, king of France 1328–50: first ruler of the house of Valois.

Philip., Philippians.

Phi·lip·pi (fi lip/ī, fil/ə pī/), *n.* a ruined city in NE Greece, in Macedonia: Octavian and Mark Antony defeated Brutus and Cassius here, 42 B.C. —**Phi·lip/pi·an** (-ē ən), *adj., n.*

Phi·lip·pi·ans (fi lip/ē ənz), *n.* (*used with a sing. v.*) an Epistle written by Paul to the Christians in Philippi.

Phi·lip·pic (fi lip/ik), *n.* **1.** any of the orations delivered by Demosthenes, the Athenian orator, in the 4th century B.C., against Philip, king of Macedon. **2.** (*l.c.*) any speech or discourse of bitter denunciation.

Phil/ippine mahog/any, *n.* **1.** any of several Philippine trees of the genus *Shorea* and related genera, having brown or reddish wood used as lumber and in cabinetry. **2.** the wood of any of these trees. Also called **lauan.**

Phil·ip·pines (fil/ə pēnz′, fil/ə pēnz′), *n.pl.* an archipelago of 7083 islands in the Pacific, SE of China: formerly (1898–1946) under the guardianship of the U.S.; now an independent republic. 76,103,564; 115,831 sq. mi. (300,000 sq. km). *Cap.:* Manila. Also called **Phil/ippine Is/lands.** Official name, **Republic of the Philippines.**

Phi·lis·ti·a (fi lis/tē ə), *n.* an ancient country in SW Palestine on the Mediterranean coast: the land of the Philistines.

phil·is·tine (fil/ə stēn′, -stīn′, fi lis/tin, -tēn), *n.* **1.** (*sometimes cap.*) a person who is lacking in or smugly indifferent to culture, aesthetic refinement, etc., or is contentedly commonplace in ideas and tastes. **2.** (*cap.*) a member of a maritime people of Anatolian or Aegean origin who controlled SW Palestine from c1200 to 604 B.C. —*adj.* **3.** (*sometimes cap.*) lacking in or indifferent to cultural values; uncultivated or smugly conventional. **4.** (*cap.*) of or pertaining to the ancient Philistines. —**phil/is·tin·ism,** *n.*

Phil/lips head/, *n.* a screw head having two partial slots crossed at right angles, driven by a special screwdriver (**Phil/lips screw/driver**).

philo-, a combining form with the meanings "loving," "having an affinity for": *philology.* Also, *esp. before a vowel,* **phil-.**

phil·o·den·dron (fil/ə den/drən), *n., pl.* **-drons, -dra.** any tropical American climbing plant belonging to the genus *Philodendron,* of the arum family, usu. having smooth, shiny, evergreen leaves: grown as a houseplant.

phi·log·y·ny (fi loj/ə nē), *n.* love of or liking for women. —**phi·log/y·nist,** *n.* —**phi·log/y·nous,** *adj.*

Phi·lo Ju·dae·us (fī/lō jōō dē/əs), *n.* c20 B.C.–A.D. c50, Alexandrian Jewish theologian and philosopher.

phi·lol·o·gy (fi lol/ə jē), *n.* **1.** the study of literary texts and of written records, the establishment of their authenticity and their original form, and the determination of their meaning. **2.** (esp. in older use) linguistics, esp. historical and comparative linguistics. —**phil·o·log·i·cal** (fil/ə loj′i kəl), **phil/o·log/ic,** *adj.* —**phil/o·log/i·cal·ly,** *adv.* —**phi·lol/o·gist, phi·lol/o·ger,** *n.*

phil·o·mel (fil/ə mel′) also **philomela,** *n. Literary.* NIGHTINGALE.

phi·los·o·pher (fi los/ə fər), *n.* **1.** a person who offers views or theories on profound questions in ethics, metaphysics, logic, and other related fields. **2.** a person who is deeply versed in philosophy. **3.** a person who establishes the central ideas of some movement, cult, etc. **4.** a person who regulates his or her life by the light of philosophy or reason. **5.** a person who is sensibly calm or rational, esp. under trying circumstances.

philos/opher king/, *n.* the Platonic ideal of a ruler, philosophically trained and enlightened.

phil·o·soph·i·cal (fil/ə sof/i kəl) also **phil/o·soph/ic,** *adj.* **1.** of or pertaining to philosophy. **2.** versed in or occupied with philosophy. **3.** proper to or befitting a philosopher. **4.** sensibly calm or rational. —**phil/o·soph/i·cal·ly,** *adv.*

phi·los·o·phize (fi los/ə fīz′), *v.i.,* **-phized, -phiz·ing. 1.** to speculate or theorize, usu. in a superficial or imprecise manner. **2.** to think or reason as a philosopher. —**phi·los/o·phiz/er,** *n.*

phi·los·o·phy (fi los/ə fē), *n., pl.* **-phies. 1.** the rational investigation of the truths and principles of being, knowledge, or conduct. **2.** a system of philosophical doctrine: *the philosophy of Spinoza.* **3.** the critical study of the basic principles and concepts of a particular branch of knowledge: *the philosophy of science.* **4.** a system of principles for guidance in practical affairs: *a philosophy of life.* **5.** a calm or philosophical attitude.

-philous, var. of -PHILIC: *zoophilous.*

phil·ter (fil/tər), *n.* **1.** a potion, charm, or drug supposed to cause a person to fall in love. **2.** a magic potion for any purpose. —*v.t.* **3.** to enchant or bewitch with a philter. Also, *esp. Brit.,* **phil/tre.**

-phily, var. of -PHILIA.

Phin·e·as (fin/ē əs), *n.* **1.** a son of Eleazar and third high priest of Israel. Ex. 6:25; Num. 25:13. **2.** a son of Eli who was in battle with the Philistines. I Sam. 1:3; 2:12–17, 22–25.

phle·bi·tis (flə bī/tis), *n.* inflammation of a vein, often occurring in the legs and involving the formation of a thrombus, characterized by swelling, pain, and change of skin color. —**phle·bit/ic** (-bit/ik), *adj.*

phlebo-, a combining form meaning "vein": *phlebotomy.*

phle·bol·o·gy (flə bol′ə jē), *n.* the study of the anatomy, physiology, and diseases of veins. Also called **venology.** —**phle·bol′o·gist,** *n.*

phle·bot·o·my (flə bot′ə mē), *n., pl.* **-mies.** the act or practice of opening a vein to let or draw blood as a therapeutic or diagnostic measure. Also called **venesection.** —**phleb·o·tom·ic** (fleb′ə tom′ik), *adj.* —**phle′bot′o·mize,** *v.t.,* **-mized, -miz·ing.**

phlegm (flem), *n.* **1.** the thick mucus secreted in the respiratory passages and discharged through the mouth, esp. that occurring in the lungs and throat passages, as during a cold. **2.** one of the four elemental bodily humors of medieval physiology, regarded as causing sluggishness or apathy. **3.** sluggishness or apathy. **4.** calmness; composure. —**phlegm′y,** *adj.,* **phlegm·i·er, phlegm·i·est.**

phlo·em (flō′em), *n.* the part of a vascular bundle consisting of sieve tubes, companion cells, parenchyma, and fibers and forming the food-conducting tissue of a plant.

phlox (floks), *n., pl.* **phlox, phlox·es.** any plant of the genus *Phlox,* of North America, certain species of which are cultivated for their showy flowers.

Phnom (or **Pnom**) **Penh** (nom′ pen′, pə nôm′), *n.* the capital of Cambodia, in the S part. 500,000.

-phobe or **-phobiac,** a combining form used to form personal nouns corresponding to nouns ending in -PHOBIA: *Anglophobe.*

pho·bi·a (fō′bē ə), *n., pl.* **-bi·as.** a persistent, irrational fear of a specific object, activity, or situation that leads to a compelling desire to avoid it. —**pho′bic,** *adj.,* *n.*

-phobia, a combining form meaning "dread of," "phobic aversion toward," "unreasonable antipathy toward" a given object: *agoraphobia; xenophobia.*

-phobic, a combining form used to form adjectives corresponding to nouns ending in -PHOBE: *acrophobic; xenophobic.*

phoe·be (fē′bē), *n., pl.* **-bes.** any of several New World flycatchers of the genus *Sayornis,* esp. *S. phoebe,* of E North America.

Phoe·be (fē′bē), *n.* **1.** a Titan, later identified with Artemis and the Roman goddess Diana. **2.** the moon personified.

Phoe·ni·cia (fi nish′ə, -nē′shə), *n.* an ancient kingdom on the Mediterranean, in the region of modern Lebanon and Syria.

Phoe·ni·cian (fi nish′ən, -nē′shən), *n.* **1.** a member of a Semitic people of Phoenicia, prominent in Mediterranean history from c1100 to c625 B.C. as merchants and colonizers. **2.** the extinct western Semitic language of the Phoenicians. —*adj.* **3.** of or pertaining to Phoenicia, its people, or their language.

phoe·nix (fē′niks), *n.* **1.** (*sometimes cap.*) a fabulous bird that after a life of five or six centuries immolates itself on a pyre and rises from the ashes to begin a new cycle of years: often an emblem of immortality or of reborn idealism or hope. **2.** a person or thing that has been restored after suffering calamity or apparent annihilation.

Phoe·nix (fē′niks), *n.* the capital of Arizona, in the central part. 1,048,949.

pho·nate (fō′nāt), *v.i.,* **-nat·ed, -nat·ing.** to produce a sound, esp. a speech sound, by vibration of the vocal cords. —**pho·na′tion,** *n.*

phone[1] (fōn), *n., v.t., v.i.,* **phoned, phon·ing.** TELEPHONE.

phone[2] (fōn), *n.* a single speech sound. Compare ALLOPHONE, PHONEME.

-phone, a combining form meaning "speech sound" (*homophone*), "speaker" (of the language specified) (*Francophone*), "an instrument of sound transmission or reproduction" (*telephone*), "a musical instrument" (*saxophone; xylophone*).

phone′ book′, *n.* TELEPHONE BOOK.

pho·neme (fō′nēm), *n.* any of the minimal units of speech sound in a language that can serve to distinguish one word from another: The (p) of *pit* and the (b) of *bit* are considered two different phonemes, while the unaspirated (p) of *spin* and the aspirated (p) of *pin* are not. Compare ALLOPHONE.

pho·ne·mic (fə nē′mik, fō-), *adj.* **1.** of or pertaining to phonemes: *a phonemic system.* **2.** of or pertaining to phonemics. **3.** concerning or involving the discrimination of distinctive speech elements of a language: *a phonemic contrast.* —**pho·ne′mi·cal·ly,** *adv.*

pho·ne·mics (fə nē′miks, fō-), *n.* (*used with a sing. v.*) **1.** the study of phonemes and phonemic systems. **2.** the phonemic system of a language, or an analysis of this. —**pho·ne′mi·cist** (-mə sist), *n.*

pho·net·ic (fə net′ik, fō-), *adj.* **1.** pertaining to speech sounds, their production, or their transcription in written symbols. **2.** representing speech sounds: *phonetic transcription.* **3.** agreeing with pronunciation: *a phonetic spelling.* **4.** pertaining to or involving the discrimination of nondistinctive speech elements of a language: *In English, the features of length and aspiration are phonetic rather than phonemic.* —*n.* **5.** (in Chinese writing) a written element that represents a sound and is used in combination with a radical to form a character. —**pho·net′i·cal·ly,** *adv.*

phonet′ic al′phabet, *n.* an alphabet containing a separate character for each distinguishable speech sound.

pho·ne·ti·cian (fō′ni tish′ən), *n.* a specialist in phonetics or in some aspect of phonetics.

pho·net·ics (fə net′iks, fō-), *n.* **1.** (*used with a sing. v.*) the study of speech sounds and their production, transmission, reception, analysis, classification, and transcription. **2.** (*used with a sing. or pl. v.*) the phonetic system or the body of phonetic facts of a particular language.

phon·ic (fon′ik, fō′nik), *adj.* **1.** of or pertaining to speech sounds. **2.** of or pertaining to phonics. —**phon′i·cal·ly,** *adv.*

phon·ics (fon′iks), *n.* (*used with a sing. v.*) a method of teaching reading and spelling based upon the phonetic interpretation of ordinary spelling.

phono-, a combining form meaning "sound," "voice": *phonology.*

pho·no·graph (fō′nə graf′, -gräf′), *n.* any sound-reproducing machine using records in the form of cylinders or grooved disks.

pho·no·graph·ic (fō′nə graf′ik), *adj.* **1.** of, pertaining to, or characteristic of a phonograph. **2.** of or pertaining to phonography. —**pho′no·graph′i·cal·ly,** *adv.*

pho·nol·o·gy (fə nol′ə jē, fō-), *n., pl.* **-gies. 1.** the study of the distribution and patterning of speech sounds in a language and of the tacit rules governing pronunciation. **2.** the phonological system or the body of phonological facts of a language. —**pho·no·log·i·cal** (fōn′l oj′i kəl), *adj.* —**pho·no·log′i·cal·ly,** *adv.* —**pho·nol′o·gist** (-jist), *n.*

pho·ny or **pho·ney** (fō′nē), *adj.,* **-ni·er, -ni·est,** *n., pl.* **-nies** or **-neys,** *v.,* **-nied** or **-neyed, -ny·ing** or **-ney·ing.** —*adj.* **1.** not real or genuine; fake: *phony diamonds.* **2.** false or deceiving: *a phony excuse.* **3.** affected or pretentious. —*n.* **4.** something that is phony; a counterfeit or fake. **5.** an insincere or affected person. —*v.t.* **6.** to falsify (often fol. by *up*): *to phony up a document.* —**pho′ni·ly,** *adv.* —**pho′ni·ness,** *n.*

-phony, a combining form used in the formation of abstract nouns corresponding to nouns ending in -PHONE: *telephony.*

Pho′ny War′, *n.* the period of World War II between the fall of Poland in 1939 and the German attack on Norway and Denmark in the spring of 1940, during which there was relatively little fighting.

phoo·ey (fōō′ē), *interj. Informal.* (used as an exclamation of contempt or disgust.)

-phore, a combining form meaning "bearer of," "thing or part bearing" that specified by the initial element: *gonophore.*

-phorous, a combining form occurring in adjectives that correspond to nouns ending in -PHORE: *gonophorous.*

phos·phate (fos′fāt), *n.* **1. a.** (loosely) a salt or ester of phosphoric acid. **b.** a tertiary salt of orthophosphoric acid, as sodium phosphate. **2.** a fertilizing material containing compounds of phosphorus. **3.** *Older Use.* a carbonated drink of water and fruit syrup orig. with a little phosphoric acid. —**phos·phat′ic** (-fat′ik, -fā′tik), *adj.*

phos·phene (fos′fēn), *n.* a luminous visual image produced by mechanical stimulation of the retina, as when pressing on closed eyelids.

phospho-, a combining form representing PHOSPHORUS: *phospholipid.*

phos·pho·lip·id (fos′fō lip′id), *n.* any of a group of fatty compounds, composed of phosphoric esters, present in living cells.

phos·phor (fos′fər, -fôr), *n.* any of a number of substances that exhibit luminescence when struck by light of certain wavelengths, as by ultraviolet.

phos·pho·res·cence (fos′fə res′əns), *n.* **1.** the property of being luminous at temperatures below incandescence, as from slow oxidation or after exposure to light or other radiation. **2.** a luminous appearance resulting from this. **3.** any luminous radiation emitted from a substance after the removal of the exciting agent. —**phos′pho·res′cent,** *adj.*

phos·phor·ic (fos fôr′ik, -for′-), *adj.* of or containing phosphorus, esp. in the pentavalent state.

phosphor′ic ac′id, *n.* any of three acids, orthophosphoric acid, H_3PO_4, metaphosphoric acid, HPO_3, or pyrophosphoric acid, $H_4P_2O_7$, derived from phosphorus pentoxide, P_2O_5, and various amounts of water.

phos·pho·rous (fos′fər əs, fos fôr′əs, -fôr′-), *adj.* containing trivalent phosphorus.

phos·pho·rus (fos′fər əs), *n., pl.* **-pho·ri** (-fə rī′). **1.** a nonmetallic element existing in yellow, red, and black allotropic forms and an essential constituent of plant and animal tissue: used, in combined form, in matches and fertilizers. Symbol: P; *at. wt.:* 30.974; *at. no.:* 15; *sp. gr.:* (yellow) 1.82 at 20°C, (red) 2.20 at 20°C, (black) 2.25–2.69 at 20°C. **2.** any phosphorescent substance. **3.** PHOSPHOR.

phot (fot, fōt), *n.* a unit of illumination, equal to one lumen per square centimeter. Abbr.: **ph**

pho·tic (fō′tik), *adj.* **1.** of or pertaining to light. **2.** pertaining to the generation of light by organisms, or their excitation by means of light. **3.** pertaining to the upper zone of a body of water, delineated by the depth to which sufficient sunlight penetrates to support photosynthesis.

pho·tics (fō′tiks), *n.* (*used with a sing. v.*) the science of light.

pho·to (fō′tō), *n., pl.* **-tos.** a photograph.

photo-, a combining form meaning "light" (*photobiology*); also used to represent PHOTOGRAPHIC or PHOTOGRAPH: *photocopy.*

pho·to·ac·ti·va·tion (fō′tō ak′tə vā′shən), *n.* the activation or control of a chemical, chemical reaction, or organism by light, as the activation of chlorophyll by sunlight during photosynthesis. —**pho′to·ac′tive,** *adj.* —**pho′to·ac·tiv′i·ty,** *n.*

pho·to·ag·ing (fō′tō ā′jing), *n.* damage to the skin, as wrinkles or discoloration, caused by prolonged exposure to sunlight.

pho·to·au·to·troph (fō′tō ô′tə trof′, -trōf′), *n.* any organism that derives its energy for food synthesis from light and is capable of using carbon dioxide as its principal source of carbon. —**pho′to·au′to·troph′ic,** *adj.*

pho·to·bi·ol·o·gy (fō′tō bī ol′ə jē), *n.* the study of the effects of light on biological systems. —**pho′to·bi′o·log′i·cal** (-bī′ə loj′i kəl), **pho′to·bi′o·log′ic,** *adj.* —**pho′to·bi·ol′o·gist,** *n.*

P

pho·to·bi·ot·ic (fō′tō bī ot′ik, -bē-), *adj.* living or thriving only in the presence of light.

pho·to·cell (fō′tō sel′), *n.* a solid-state electronic device that converts light into electrical energy by producing a voltage or that uses light to regulate the flow of current: used in automatic control systems for doors, burglar alarms, lighting, etc.

pho·to·chem·is·try (fō′tō kem′ə strē), *n.* the branch of chemistry that deals with the chemical action of light. —**pho′to·chem′i·cal** (-i kəl), *adj.* —**pho′to·chem′i·cal·ly,** *adv.* —**pho′to·chem′ist,** *n.*

pho·to·com·po·si·tion (fō′tō kom′pə zish′ən), *n.* a method of composition in which type is set photographically.

pho·to·cop·i·er (fō′tə kop′ē ər), *n.* any electrically operated machine using a photographic method, as the electrostatic process, for making instant copies of written, drawn, or printed material. Also called **pho′tocopying machine′.**

pho·to·cop·y (fō′tə kop′ē), *n., pl.* **-cop·ies,** *v.,* **-cop·ied, -cop·y·ing.** —*n.* **1.** a photographic reproduction of a document, print, or the like. —*v.t.* **2.** to make a photocopy of.

pho·to·dy·nam·ics (fō′tō dī nam′iks), *n.* (*used with a sing. v.*) the branch of biology dealing with light and its effects on living organisms. —**pho′to·dy·nam′ic,** *adj.* —**pho′to·dy·nam′i·cal·ly,** *adv.*

pho·to·e·lec·tric (fō′tō i lek′trik) also **pho′to·e·lec′tri·cal,** *adj.* of or pertaining to electronic effects produced by light, esp. the phenomenon whereby a surface emits electrons when exposed to light. —**pho′to·e·lec′tri·cal·ly,** *adv.* —**pho′to·e·lec·tric′i·ty** (-i lek tris′i tē, -ē′lek-), *n.*

pho′toelec′tric cell′, *n.* PHOTOCELL.

pho·to·en·grave (fō′tō en grāv′), *v.t.,* **-graved, -grav·ing.** to make a photoengraving of. —**pho′to·en·grav′er,** *n.*

pho·to·en·grav·ing (fō′tō en grā′ving), *n.* **1.** a photographic process of preparing printing plates for letterpress printing. **2.** a plate so produced. **3.** a print made from it.

pho′to es′say, *n.* a series of photographs, accompanied by a brief text, that conveys a unified story and is published as a book or a feature in a magazine or newspaper. —**pho′to es′sayist,** *n.*

pho·to fin′ish, *n.* a finish of a race so close as to require scrutiny of a photograph to determine the winner.

pho·to·fin·ish·ing (fō′tō fin′i shing), *n.* the act or occupation of developing films, printing photographs, etc. —**pho·to·fin′ish·er,** *n.*

pho·tog (fə tog′), *n. Informal.* photographer.

pho·to·gen·ic (fō′tō jen′ik), *adj.* **1.** forming an appealing subject for photography or having features that look attractive in a photograph. **2.** producing or emitting light. **3.** produced or caused by light. —**pho′to·gen′i·cal·ly,** *adv.*

pho·to·gram·me·try (fō′tə gram′i trē), *n.* the process of making surveys and maps through the use of photographs, esp. aerial photographs. —**pho′to·gram·met′ric** (-grə me′trik), *adj.* —**pho′to·gram·met′ri·cal·ly,** *adv.* —**pho′to·gram′me·trist,** *n.*

pho·to·graph (fō′tə graf′, -gräf′), *n.* **1.** a picture produced by photography. —*v.t.* **2.** to take a photograph of. —*v.i.* **3.** to practice photography. **4.** to be photographed; be the subject of a photograph, esp. in some specified way: *The children photographed well.* —**pho′to·graph′a·ble,** *adj.*

pho·tog·ra·pher (fə tog′rə fər), *n.* a person who takes photographs, esp. one who practices photography professionally.

pho·to·graph·ic (fō′tə graf′ik), *adj.* **1.** of, pertaining to, used in, or produced by photography. **2.** suggestive of a photograph; extremely realistic and detailed: *photographic accuracy.* **3.** remembering, reproducing, or functioning with the precision of a photograph: *a photographic memory.* —**pho′to·graph′i·cal·ly,** *adv.*

pho·tog·ra·phy (fə tog′rə fē), *n.* **1.** the process or art of producing images of objects on sensitized surfaces by the chemical action of light or of other forms of radiant energy. **2.** CINEMATOGRAPHY.

pho·to·gra·vure (fō′tə grə vyŏŏr′, -grā′vyər), *n.* **1.** a process, based on photography, by which an intaglio engraving is formed on a metal plate, from which ink reproductions are made. **2.** the plate itself. **3.** a print made from it.

pho·to·jour·nal·ism (fō′tō jûr′nl iz′əm), *n.* journalism in which the story is told largely in captioned photographs. —**pho′to·jour′nal·ist,** *n.*

pho·to·lu·mi·nes·cence (fō′tə lōō′mə nes′əns), *n.* luminescence induced by the absorption of infrared radiation, visible light, or ultraviolet radiation. —**pho′to·lu′mi·nes′cent,** *adj.*

pho·tom·e·try (fō tom′i trē), *n.* the measurement of the intensity of light or of relative illuminating power. —**pho′to·met′ric** (-tə me′trik), **pho′to·met′ri·cal,** *adj.* —**pho·tom′e·trist, pho′to·me·tri′cian** (-trish′ən), *n.*

pho·to·mi·cro·graph (fō′tə mī′krə graf′, -gräf′), *n.* a photograph taken through a microscope. —**pho′to·mi·crog′ra·phy** (-krog′rə fē), *n.*

pho·to·mon·tage (fō′tə mon täzh′), *n.* a combination of several photographs joined together for artistic effect or to show more of the subject than can be shown in a single photograph.

pho·ton (fō′ton), *n.* a quantum of electromagnetic radiation, usu. considered as an elementary particle that is its own antiparticle and that has zero rest mass and charge and a spin of one. —**pho·ton′ic,** *adj.*

pho′to opportu′nity, *n.* a brief period set aside, esp. for the media, to take photographs of public figures or noteworthy events. *Informal.* **pho′to op′** (op).

pho·to·play (fō′tə plā′), *n.* **1.** a motion picture. **2.** the scenario for it; screenplay. —**pho′to·play′er,** *n.*

pho·to·scan (fō′tə skan′), *v.t.,* **-scanned, -scan·ning.** to study the distribution of a radioactive isotope or radiopaque dye in (a body organ or part) through the use of x-rays.

pho·to·sen·si·tive (fō′tə sen′si tiv), *adj.* sensitive to light or similar radiation.

Pho·to·stat (fō′tə stat′), *n., v.,* **-stat·ed** or **-stat·ted, -stat·ing** or **-stat·ting. 1.** *Trademark.* a camera for making facsimile copies of documents, drawings, etc., in the form of paper negatives. —*n.* **2.** (*often l.c.*) a copy made with this camera. —*v.t., v.i.* **3.** (*l.c.*) to copy with this camera. —**pho′to·stat′er, pho′to·stat′ter,** *n.* —**pho′to·stat′ic,** *adj.*

pho·to·syn·the·sis (fō′tə sin′thə sis), *n.* the production of complex organic materials, esp. carbohydrates, from carbon dioxide, water, and inorganic salts, using sunlight as the source of energy and with the aid of chlorophyll and associated pigments. —**pho′to·syn·thet′ic** (-thet′ik), *adj.* —**pho′to·syn·thet′i·cal·ly,** *adv.*

pho·to·ty·pog·ra·phy (fō′tō tī pog′rə fē), *n.* **1.** the art or technique of making printing surfaces by light or photography, by any of a number of processes. **2.** PHOTOCOMPOSITION. —**pho′to·ty′po·graph′ic** (-pə graf′ik), *adj.*

pho·to·vol·ta·ics (fō′tō vol tā′iks, -vōl-), *n.* (*used with a sing. v.*) a field of semiconductor technology involving the direct conversion of electromagnetic radiation, as sunlight, into electricity. **2.** (*used with a pl. v.*) devices designed to perform such conversion.

phrag·mi·tes (frag mī′tēz), *n.* any of several tall grasses of the genus *Phragmites,* having plumed heads, growing in marshy areas, esp. the common reed *P. australis* (or *P. communis*).

phrag·mo·plast (frag′mə plast′), *n.* the cytoplasmic structure that forms at the equator of the spindle after the chromosomes have divided during the anaphase of plant mitosis, and that initiates cell division.

phras·al (frā′zəl), *adj.* of, pertaining to, or consisting of a phrase or phrases. —**phras′al·ly,** *adv.*

phras′al verb′, *n.* a combination of verb and one or more adverbs or prepositions, as *catch on, take off,* or *put up with,* functioning as a single semantic unit and often having an idiomatic meaning not predictable from the meanings of the individual parts.

phrase (frāz), *n., v.,* **phrased, phras·ing.** —*n.* **1.** a sequence of two or more words arranged in a grammatical unit and lacking a finite verb or such elements of clause structure as subject and verb, as a preposition and a noun or pronoun, an adjective and noun, or an adverb and verb, esp. such a construction acting as a unit in a sentence. **2.** a characteristic, current, or proverbial expression. **3.** a way of speaking, mode of expression, or phraseology. **4.** a brief utterance or remark. **5.** a division of a musical composition, commonly a passage of four or eight measures, forming part of a period. **6.** a sequence of dance motions making up part of a choreographic pattern. —*v.t.* **7.** to express or word in a particular way. **8.** to express in words. **9. a.** to mark off or bring out the phrases of (a piece of music), esp. in execution. **b.** to group (notes) into a phrase. —*v.i.* **10.** to perform a musical passage or piece with proper phrasing.

phrase′ book′, *n.* a small book containing everyday phrases and sentences and their equivalents in a foreign language, written esp. for travelers.

phrase·mak·er (frāz′mā′kər), *n.* **1.** a person who is skilled in coining well-turned phrases. **2.** a person who makes catchy but often meaningless or empty statements. —**phrase′mak′ing,** *n.*

phra·se·ol·o·gy (frā′zē ol′ə jē), *n.* **1.** manner or style of verbal expression; characteristic language: *legal phraseology.* **2.** expressions; phrases: *obscure phraseology.* —**phra′se·o·log′i·cal** (-ə loj′i kəl), **phra′se·o·log′ic,** *adj.* —**phra′se·o·log′i·cal·ly,** *adv.*

phrase′ struc′ture, *n.* the hierarchical arrangement of the constituent words and phrases of a sentence.

phras·ing (frā′zing), *n.* **1.** the act of forming phrases. **2.** a manner or method of forming phrases; phraseology. **3.** the grouping of the notes of a musical line into distinct phrases.

phre·net·ic (fri net′ik) also **phre·net′i·cal,** *adj.* FRENETIC.

-phrenia, a combining form used in the names of mental conditions or states, as specified by the preceding element: *schizophrenia.*

phre·nol·o·gy (fri nol′ə jē, fre-), *n.* a system of character analysis based upon the belief that certain faculties and personality traits are indicated by the configurations of the skull. —**phren·o·log·ic** (fren′l oj′ik), **phren′o·log′i·cal,** *adj.* —**phren′o·log′i·cal·ly,** *adv.* —**phre·nol′o·gist,** *n.*

Phryg·i·a (frij′ē ə), *n.* an ancient country in central and NW Asia Minor.

phy·col·o·gy (fī kol′ə jē), *n.* the branch of botany dealing with algae. —**phy′co·log′i·cal** (-kə loj′i kəl), *adj.* —**phy·col′o·gist,** *n.*

phy·lac·ter·y (fi lak′tə rē), *n., pl.* **-ter·ies. 1.** *Judaism.* either of two small black leather cubes containing pieces of parchment inscribed with specific Biblical verses: worn by Orthodox or Conservative Jewish men during weekday morning prayers, one usu. strapped to the left arm, the other to the head above the hairline. **2.** (in the early Christian church) a receptacle containing a holy relic. **3.** an amulet or charm. [< Greek *phylaktērion* safeguard, amulet, der. of *phylássein* to protect, guard]

phyl·lo (fē′lō), *n.* flaky, tissue-thin layers of pastry used in baked desserts and appetizers.

phyllo-, a combining form meaning "leaf": *phyllotaxy.*

-phyllous, a combining form meaning "having leaves" of the kind or number specified by the initial element: *diphyllous; heterophyllous.*

phylo-, a combining form meaning "group having common ancestry": *phylogeny.*

phylogenet′ic classifica′tion, *n.* classification of organisms based on their assumed evolutionary histories and relationships.

phy·log·e·ny (fī loj′ə nē), *n.* **1.** the development or evolution of a particular group of organisms. **2.** the evolutionary history of a group of organisms, esp. as depicted in a family tree. Compare ONTOGENY. **—phy·log′e·nist,** *n.*

phy·lum (fī′ləm), *n., pl.* **-la** (-lə). **1.** the primary subdivision of a taxonomic kingdom, grouping together all classes of organisms that have the same body plan. **2.** a category consisting of language stocks that, because of cognates in vocabulary, are considered likely to be related by common origin. **—phy′lar,** *adj.*

phys ed or **phys. ed.** (fiz′ ed′), *n.* physical education.

phys·i·cal (fiz′i kəl), *adj.* **1.** of or pertaining to the body. **2.** of or pertaining to that which is material: *the physical universe.* **3.** noting or pertaining to the properties of matter and energy other than those peculiar to living matter. **4.** carnal; sexual: *a physical attraction.* **5.** physically demonstrative. **6.** requiring, characterized by, or liking rough physical contact or strenuous physical activity. **7.** contained in or being computer hardware: *a physical disk drive; physical memory contained on a chip.* **—n. 8.** PHYSICAL EXAMINATION. **—phys′i·cal·ly,** *adv.*

phys′ical anthropol′ogy, *n.* the branch of anthropology dealing with the evolutionary changes in human body structure and the classification of modern races, using mensurational and descriptive techniques. Compare CULTURAL ANTHROPOLOGY. **—phys′ical anthropol′ogist,** *n.*

phys′ical chem′istry, *n.* the branch of chemistry dealing with the relations between the physical properties of substances and their chemical composition and transformations.

phys′ical educa′tion, *n.* instruction in sports, exercise, and hygiene, esp. as part of a school or college program.

phys′ical examina′tion, *n.* an examination, usu. by a physician, of a person's body in order to determine his or her state of health or physical fitness.

phys′ical geog′raphy, *n.* the branch of geography concerned with natural features and phenomena of the earth's surface, as landforms, drainage features, climates, soils, and vegetation.

phys·i·cal·i·ty (fiz′i kal′i tē), *n., pl.* **-ties. 1.** the quality of being physical, esp. when emphasized or overemphasized. **2.** preoccupation with one's body, physical needs, or appetites.

phys′ical sci′ence, *n.* any of the natural sciences dealing with inanimate matter or with energy, as physics, chemistry, and astronomy. **—phys′ical sci′entist,** *n.*

phys′ical ther′apy, *n.* the treatment or management of physical disability, malfunction, or pain by physical techniques, as exercise, massage, hydrotherapy, etc. **—phys′ical ther′apist,** *n.*

phy·si·cian (fi zish′ən), *n.* **1.** a person who is legally qualified to practice medicine; doctor of medicine. **2.** a person engaged in general medical practice, as distinguished from a surgeon. **—*Proverb.* 3.** Physician, heal thyself, one should look after one's own problems first. Luke 4:23.

physi′cian assis′tant or **physi′cian's assis′tant,** *n.* a person trained and certified to perform many clinical procedures under the supervision of a physician. *Abbr.:* PA

phys·i·cist (fiz′ə sist), *n.* a scientist who specializes in physics.

phys·ics (fiz′iks), *n.* (*used with a sing. v.*) the science that deals with matter, energy, motion, and force.

physio-, a combining form representing PHYSICAL OR PHYSIOLOGICAL: *physiotherapy.*

phys·i·og·no·my (fiz′ē og′nə mē, -on′ə mē), *n., pl.* **-mies. 1.** the face or countenance, esp. when considered as an index to the character. **2.** the art of determining character or personal characteristics from the form or features of the body, esp. of the face. **—phys′i·og·nom′ic** (-og-nom′ik, ə nom′-), **phys′i·og·nom′i·cal,** *adj.* **—phys′i·og·nom′i·cal·ly,** *adv.* **—phys′i·og′no·mist,** *n.*

phys·i·og·ra·phy (fiz′ē og′rə fē), *n.* **1.** PHYSICAL GEOGRAPHY. **2.** (formerly) GEOMORPHOLOGY. **—phys′i·og′ra·pher,** *n.* **—phys′i·o·graph′ic** (-ə graf′ik), **phys′i·o·graph′i·cal,** *adj.*

phys·i·o·log·i·cal (fiz′ē ə loj′i kəl) also **phys′i·o·log′ic,** *adj.* **1.** of or pertaining to physiology. **2.** consistent with the normal functioning of an organism. **—phys′i·o·log′i·cal·ly,** *adv.*

physiolog′ical psychol′ogy, *n.* the branch of psychology concerned with the relationship between the physical functioning of an organism and its behavior.

phys·i·ol·o·gy (fiz′ē ol′ə jē), *n.* **1.** the branch of biology dealing with the functions and activities of living organisms and their parts. **2.** the organic processes or functions in an organism or in any of its parts.

phys·i·o·ther·a·py (fiz′ē ō ther′ə pē), *n.* PHYSICAL THERAPY. **—phys′i·o·ther′a·pist,** *n.*

phy·sique (fi zēk′), *n.* bodily structure, proportions, appearance, and development: *the physique of an athlete.*

-phyte, var. of PHYTO- as final element of compound words: *lithophyte.*

phyto-, a combining form meaning "plant": *phytogenesis.*

phy·to·chem·is·try (fī′tə kem′ə strē), *n.* the branch of biochemistry dealing with plants and plant processes.

phy·to·ge·og·ra·phy (fī′tō jē og′rə fē), *n.* the science dealing with the geographical relationships of plants.

phy·tol·o·gy (fī tol′ə jē), *n.* BOTANY. **—phy·to·log′ic** (fīt′l oj′ik), **phy′to·log′i·cal,** *adj.*

phy·ton (fī′ton), *n.* the smallest part of a stem, root, or leaf, that, when removed from a plant, may grow into a new plant. **—phy·ton′ic,** *adj.*

phy·to·pa·thol·o·gy (fī′tō pə thol′ə jē), *n.* PLANT PATHOLOGY. **—phy′to·path′o·log′i·cal** (-path′ə loj′i kəl), **phy′to·path′o·log′ic,** *adj.*

pi¹ (pī), *n., pl.* **pis. 1.** the 16th letter of the Greek alphabet (Π, π). **2. a.** the letter π, used as the symbol for the ratio of the circumference of a circle to its diameter. **b.** the ratio itself: 3.14159 + .

pi² or **pie** (pī), *n., pl.* **pies,** *v.,* **pied, pi·ing. —n. 1.** printing type mixed together indiscriminately. **2.** any confused mixture; jumble. **—v.t. 3.** to jumble (printing type). **4.** to mix up; jumble.

Pia·get (pē·ä zhā′, pyä-), *n.* **Jean** (zhän), 1896–1980, Swiss cognitive psychologist. **—Pi·a·get′ian,** *adj.*

pi·al (pī′əl, pē′-), *adj.* of or pertaining to the pia mater.

pi·a ma·ter (pī′ə mā′tər, pē′ə), *n.* the delicate, fibrous, and highly vascular membrane forming the innermost of the three coverings of the brain and spinal cord. Compare ARACHNOID (def. 4), DURA MATER.

pi·a·nis·si·mo (pē′ə nis′ə mō′, pyä-), *adj., adv., adj., n.* **-mos.** *Music.* **—adj. 1.** very soft. **—adv. 2.** very softly. **—n. 3.** a passage or movement played in this way.

pi·an·ist (pē an′ist, pyan′-, pē′ə nist), *n.* a person who plays the piano, esp. one who performs expertly or professionally.

pi·an·o¹ (pē an′ō, pyan′ō), *n., pl.* **-an·os.** a musical instrument in which felt-covered hammers, operated from a keyboard, strike upon metal strings.

pi·a·no² (pē ä′nō, pyä′-), *Music.* **—adj. 1.** soft; subdued. **—adv. 2.** softly. *Abbr.:* p

pian′o bar′, *n.* a cocktail lounge featuring live piano music.

pi·an·o·forte (pē an′ə fôrt′, -fōrt′; pē an′ə fôr′tē, -tä, -fōr′-), *n.* PIANO¹.

pian′o roll′, *n.* a roll of paper containing perforations such that air passing through them actuates the keys of a player piano.

pi·az·za (pē az′ə, -ä′zə or, for 1, 3, pē at′sə, -ät′-), *n., pl.* **pi·az·zas,** *It. piaz·ze* (pyät′tse). **1.** an open public square in a city or town, esp. in Italy. **2.** *Chiefly New Eng. and Southern U.S.* a large porch; veranda. **3.** *Chiefly Brit.* an arcade or covered walk or gallery.

pic (pik), *n., pl.* **pix** (piks), **pics.** *Slang.* **1.** motion picture. **2.** photograph.

pi·ca¹ (pī′kə), *n., pl.* **-cas. 1.** a 12-point type of a size between small pica and English. **2.** the depth of this type size as a unit of linear measurement for type, pages containing type, etc.; one sixth of an inch. **3.** a 12-point type, widely used for typewriters, having 10 characters to the inch. Compare ELITE (def. 4).

pi·ca² (pī′kə), *n.* an abnormal appetite or craving for substances that are not fit to eat, as chalk or clay.

pi·ca·dor (pik′ə dôr′, pik′ə dôr′), *n., pl.* **-dors, -do·res** (-dôr′ēz). one of the mounted assistants to a matador, who opens a bullfight by jabbing the bull's shoulder muscles with a lance.

pi·can·te (pi kän′tā), *adj.* (of food) spicy; hot.

pic·a·ra (pik′ər ə, pē′kär ə), *n., pl.* **-ras.** a woman who is a rogue or vagabond.

pic·a·resque (pik′ə resk′), *adj.* **1.** of or pertaining to a form of prose fiction, orig. developed in Spain, in which the adventures of a roguish hero are described in a series of usu. humorous or satiric episodes. **2.** of, pertaining to, or resembling rogues.

pic·a·ro (pik′ə rō′, pē′kə-), *n., pl.* **-ros.** a rogue or vagabond. [< Spanish *pícaro* rogue]

pic·a·roon (pik′ə rōōn′), *n.* **1.** a rogue, vagabond, thief, or brigand. **2.** a pirate or corsair.

Pi·cas·so (pi kä′sō, -kas′ō), *n.* **Pablo,** 1881–1973, Spanish painter and sculptor in France.

pic·a·yune (pik′ē yōōn′, pik′ə-), *adj.* Also, **pic′a·yun′ish. 1.** of little value or account; small; trifling. **2.** petty, carping, or prejudiced. **—n. 3.** (formerly, in Louisiana, Florida, etc.) a coin equal to half a Spanish real. **4.** any small coin, as a five-cent piece. **5.** an insignificant person or thing.

pic·co·lo (pik′ə lō′), *n., pl.* **-los.** a small flute sounding an octave higher than the ordinary flute. [< Italian: lit., small] **—pic′co·lo·ist,** *n.*

pick¹ (pik), *v.t.* **1.** to choose or select, esp. with care. **2.** to seek and find occasion for; provoke: *to pick a fight.* **3.** to attempt to find; seek out: *to pick flaws in an argument.* **4.** to steal the contents of: *to pick a pocket.* **5.** to open (a lock) with a device other than the key, esp. for the purpose of burglary. **6.** to pierce, dig into, or break up (something) with a pointed instrument: *to pick ore.* **7.** to form (a hole) by such action. **8.** to use a pointed instrument or the fingers on (a thing), to remove particles or adhering matter: *to pick one's teeth.* **9.** to prepare for use by removing a covering, as feathers: *to pick a fowl.* **10.** to detach or remove piece by piece with the fingers: *to pick meat from the bones.* **11.** to pluck or gather one by one: *to pick flowers.* **12.** (of birds or other animals) to take up (small bits of food) with the bill or teeth. **13.** to eat daintily or in small morsels. **14.** to separate, pull apart, or pull to pieces: *to pick fibers.* **15. a.** to pluck (the strings of a musical instrument). **b.** to play (a stringed instrument) by plucking with the fingers.

—*v.i.* **16.** to use a pick or other pointed instrument on something. **17.** to select carefully or fastidiously. **18.** to pilfer; steal. **19.** to pluck or gather fruit, flowers, etc. **20. pick apart,** to criticize severely or in great detail. **21. pick at, a.** to find fault with; nag. **b.** to eat sparingly or daintily. **c.** to grasp at; touch; handle. **22. pick off, a.** to remove by pulling or plucking off. **b.** to single out and shoot: *The hunter picked off a duck rising from the marsh.* **c.** *Baseball.* to put out (a base runner) in a pick-off play. **23. pick on, a.** to criticize or blame; tease; harass. **b.** to single out; choose. **24. pick out, a.** to choose; select. **b.** to distinguish from that which surrounds or accompanies: *to pick out a well-known face in a crowd.* **c.** to discern (sense or meaning). **d.** to work out (a melody) note by note; play by ear. **e.** to extract by picking. **25. pick over,** to examine (an assortment of items) in order to make a selection. **26. pick up, a.** to lift or take up: *to pick up a stone.* **b.** to cause (one's courage, health, etc.) to recover. **c.** to gain, obtain, or learn casually or by occasional opportunity: *I've picked up a few Japanese phrases.* **d.** to take on as a passenger. **e.** to bring into range of reception, observation, etc.: *to pick up Rome on one's radio.* **f.** to accelerate; gain (speed). **g.** to put in good order; tidy. **h.** to make progress; improve: *Business is picking up.* **i.** to become acquainted with informally or casually, often in hope of a sexual relationship. **j.** to resume or continue after being left off: *Let's pick up the discussion in our next meeting.* **k.** to take into custody; arrest. **l.** to accept, as in order to pay: *to pick up the check.* **27. pick up on,** *Informal.* become aware of; notice: *I picked up on his hostility.* —*n.* **28.** the act of choosing or selecting; choice; selection: *Take your pick.* **29.** a person or thing selected. **30.** the choicest or most desirable part, example, or examples: *This horse is the pick of the stable.* **31.** the right of selection. **32.** the quantity of a crop picked at a particular time. **33.** a stroke with something pointed. **34.** a basketball maneuver or positioning to prevent a defender from interfering with a teammate's shot. —***Idiom.*** **35. pick and choose,** to be very careful or particular in choosing. **36. pick someone's brains,** to obtain information or ideas by questioning someone closely.

pick² (pik), *n.* **1.** a heavy tool consisting of a metal head, usu. curved, tapering to a point at one or both ends, mounted on a wooden handle, and used for breaking up soil, rock, etc. **2.** any of various other pointed tools or instruments for picking: *an ice pick.* **3.** PLECTRUM. **4.** a comb with long, widely spaced teeth.

pick•ax or **pick•axe** (pik′aks′), *n., pl.* **-ax•es,** *v.,* **-axed, -ax•ing.** —*n.* **1.** PICK² (def. 1). —*v.t.* **2.** to cut or clear away with a pickax.

picked (pikt), *adj.* **1.** specially selected: *a crew of picked men.* **2.** cleared or cleaned by or as if by picking: *picked fruit.*

pick•er (pik′ər), *n.* **1.** someone or something that picks. **2.** a tool or machine for picking fruit, vegetables, or fibers.

pick•er•el (pik′ər əl, pik′rəl), *n., pl.* (*esp. collectively*) **-el,** (*esp. for kinds or species*) **-els. 1.** any of several small pikes of the genus *Esox.* **2.** the walleye, blue pike, or pikeperch. **3.** *Brit.* a young pike.

pick•er•el•weed (pik′ər əl wēd′, pik′rəl-), *n.* any of several North American aquatic plants of the genus *Pontederia,* esp. *P. cordata,* with spikes of blue flowers, common in shallow fresh waters.

Pick•er•ing (pik′ər ing, pik′ring), *n.* **Edward Charles,** 1846–1919, and his brother, **William Henry,** 1858–1938, U.S. astronomers.

pick′er-up′per, *n.* PICK-ME-UP.

pick•et (pik′it), *n.* **1.** a post, stake, or peg that is driven into the ground for use in a fence, to fasten down a tent, etc. **2.** a person stationed, as by a union, outside a factory, store, etc., to dissuade workers or customers from entering it during a strike. **3.** a person engaged in any similar demonstration, as against a government's policies. **4.** an aircraft or ship performing similar sentinel duty. —*v.t.* **5.** to enclose within a picket fence or stockade, as for protection or imprisonment. **6.** to fasten or tether to a picket. **7.** to place pickets in front of or around (a factory, embassy, etc.), as during a strike or demonstration. **8. a.** to guard, as with pickets. **b.** to station as a picket. —*v.i.* **9.** to stand or march as a picket. —**pick′et•er,** *n.*

pick′et fence′, *n.* a fence consisting of pickets nailed to horizontal stringers between upright posts.

pick′et line′, *n.* a line of strikers or other pickets.

Pick•ford (pik′fərd), *n.* **Mary** (*Gladys Marie Smith*), 1893–1979, U.S. motion-picture actress, born in Canada.

pick•ings (pik′ingz), *n.pl.* **1.** scraps or gleanings: *the pickings of a feast.* **2.** profits or gains; spoils.

pick•le (pik′əl), *n., v.,* **-led, -ling.** —*n.* **1.** a cucumber that has been preserved and flavored in brine, vinegar, or the like. **2.** any other vegetable, as cauliflower, preserved in vinegar and eaten as a relish. **3.** any food preserved in a brine or marinade. **4.** a liquid usu. prepared with salt or vinegar for preserving or flavoring meat, vegetables, etc.; brine or marinade. **5.** an acid or other chemical solution in which metal objects are dipped to remove oxide scale or other adhering substances. **6.** a troublesome situation; predicament. —*v.t.* **7.** to preserve or steep in brine or other liquid. **8.** to treat with a chemical solution, as for the purpose of cleaning. **9.** to antique (woodwork), as by bleaching.

pick•led (pik′əld), *adj.* **1.** preserved or steeped in brine or vinegar. **2.** (of woodwork) given an antique appearance, as by bleaching.

pick′-me-up′, *n.* **1.** something, as a drink or snack, taken to restore one's energy or good spirits. **2.** any restorative.

pick′-off′, *n.* a baseball play in which a base runner, caught off base, is tagged out by an infielder on a quick throw.

pick•pock•et (pik′pok′it), *n.* **1.** a person who steals from the pockets of people, as in a crowded public place. —*v.t.* **2.** to steal from the pocket of.

pick•up (pik′up′), *n.* **1.** an improvement, as in health, business conditions, production, etc. **2.** an instance of taking aboard passengers or freight. **3.** the passengers or freight taken aboard. **4.** acceleration, or the capacity for acceleration. **5.** Also called **pick′up truck′.** a small truck with a low-sided open body, used for deliveries and light hauling. **6.** a device at the end of the tone arm of a phonograph that translates the movement of the stylus into a changing electrical voltage; cartridge. **7. a.** the reception of sound waves in a radio transmitter for conversion into electrical waves. **b.** a receiving or recording device. —*adj.* **8.** composed of or using whatever persons, ingredients, etc., are available: *a pickup dance band; a pickup supper.*

Pick′wick Pa′pers, The, (*The Posthumous Papers of the Pickwick Club*) a novel (1837) by Charles Dickens.

pick•y (pik′ē), *adj.,* **-i•er, -i•est.** extremely fussy or finicky, usu. over trifles. —**pick′i•ness,** *n.*

pic•nic (pik′nik), *n., v.,* **-nicked, -nick•ing.** —*n.* **1.** an excursion in which the participants carry food with them and share a meal in the open air. **2.** the food eaten on such an excursion. **3.** Also called **pic′nic ham′.** a section of pork shoulder, usu. boned and smoked. **4.** *Informal.* an enjoyable experience, task, etc.: *That job was no picnic.* —*v.i.* **5.** to go on or take part in a picnic. —**pic′nick•er,** *n.*

pico-, a combining form meaning "one trillionth" (10^{-12}): *picosecond.*

pi•cor•na•vi•rus (pi kôr′nə vī′rəs, -kôr′nə vī′-), *n., pl.* **-rus•es.** any of several small, RNA-containing viruses of the family Picornaviridae, including poliovirus and the rhinoviruses that cause the common cold.

pi•co•sec•ond (pē′kə sek′ənd, pī′-), *n.* one trillionth of a second. *Abbr.:* ps, psec

pi•cot (pē′kō), *n.* **1.** one of a number of small decorative loops worked or attached along the edge of fabric, lace, ribbon, etc. —*v.i.* **2.** to make picots; do picot work.

pic•to•graph (pik′tə graf′, -gräf′), *n.* **1.** a single pictorial sign or symbol, as in a system of picture writing. **2.** a record consisting of pictorial symbols, as a graph or chart with figures representing a certain number of people, objects, etc. **3.** a painting or drawing on a rock wall or the like by ancient or prehistoric peoples. —**pic′to•graph′ic** (-graf′ik), *adj.* —**pic′to•graph′i•cal•ly,** *adv.*

pic•to•ri•al (pik tôr′ē əl, -tōr′ē əl), *adj.* **1.** pertaining to, expressed in, or of the nature of a picture. **2.** illustrated by or containing pictures: *a pictorial history.* **3.** of or pertaining to the art of painting and drawing pictures, the pictures themselves, or their makers. **4.** having or suggesting the visual appeal or imagery of a picture: *a pictorial metaphor.* —*n.* **5.** a periodical in which pictures constitute an important feature. **6.** a magazine feature that is primarily photographic. —**pic•to′ri•al•i•za′tion,** *n.* —**pic•to′ri•al•ize′,** *v.t.,* **-ized, -iz•ing.** —**pic•to′ri•al•ly,** *adv.*

pic•ture (pik′chər), *n., v.,* **-tured, -tur•ing.** —*n.* **1.** a visual representation of a person, object, or scene, as a painting, drawing, or photograph. **2.** any visible image, however produced. **3.** a mental image. **4.** a graphic or vivid account or description. **5.** a tableau, as in theatrical representation. **6. a.** MOTION PICTURE (def. 2). **b. pictures,** *Older Use.* MOVIE (defs. 2, 3). **7.** a person, thing, group, or scene regarded as resembling a work of pictorial art in beauty, fineness of appearance, etc. **8.** the image or perfect likeness of someone else: *She is the picture of her father.* **9.** a visible or concrete embodiment of some quality or condition: *the picture of health.* **10.** a situation or set of circumstances: *the economic picture.* **11.** the image on a television screen, motion-picture screen, or computer monitor. —*v.t.* **12.** to represent in a picture or pictorially, as by painting or drawing. **13.** to form a mental picture of; imagine. **14.** to depict in words; describe graphically.

pic′ture hat′, *n.* a woman's hat with a broad brim.

pic•tur•esque (pik′chə resk′), *adj.* **1.** visually charming or quaint, as if resembling or suitable for a painting: *a picturesque village.* **2.** (of writing, speech, etc.) strikingly graphic or vivid. **3.** having pleasing or interesting qualities; strikingly effective in appearance. —**pic′tur•esque′ly,** *adv.* —**pic′tur•esque′ness,** *n.*

pic′ture tube′, *n.* a cathode-ray tube with a screen at one end on which televised images are reproduced.

pic′ture win′dow, *n.* a large, usu. single-paned window.

pid•dle (pid′l), *v.i.,* **-dled, -dling. 1.** to waste time; dawdle. **2.** *Informal.* to urinate. —**pid′dler,** *n.*

pid•dling (pid′ling), *adj.* trifling; negligible.

pidg•in (pij′ən), *n.* **1.** an auxiliary language that has developed from the need of speakers of two different languages to communicate and is primarily a simplified form of one of the languages, with a reduced vocabulary and grammatical structure. **2.** (loosely) any simplified form of a language, esp. when used for communication between speakers of different languages.

pidg′in (or **Pidg′in**) **Eng′lish,** *n.* any of various other pidgins with lexicons taken primarily from English, as Bislama and New Guinea Pidgin.

pie (pī), *n.* **1.** a pastry crust filled with fruit, meat, pudding, etc., and baked, often with a top crust. **2.** a layer cake with a cream or custard filling: *Boston cream pie.* **3.** a total or whole that can be divided: *They want a bigger part of the profit pie.* **4.** an activity or affair: *I'm sure he had a finger in the pie.* —***Idiom.*** **5. easy as pie,** extremely easy or simple. **6. pie in the sky,** the illusory prospect of future benefits.

pie·bald (pī′bôld′), *adj.* **1.** having patches of two colors, esp. black and white. —*n.* **2.** a piebald animal.

piece (pēs), *n., v.,* **pieced, piec·ing.** —*n.* **1.** a limited portion or quantity of something: *a piece of land.* **2.** a quantity of some substance or material forming a single mass or body: *a piece of lumber.* **3.** a portion or quantity of a whole: *a piece of pie.* **4.** a particular length, as of certain goods prepared for the market: *cloth sold by the piece.* **5.** an amount of work forming a single job: *to be paid by the piece.* **6.** an example of artistic creativity or workmanship, as a painting or a musical or literary composition. **7. a.** one of the figures, disks, or the like, used in playing a board game. **b.** (in chess) a superior man, as distinguished from a pawn. **8.** an individual thing of a particular class or set: *a piece of furniture.* **9.** an example, specimen, or instance of something: *a fine piece of work.* **10.** a part, fragment, or shred: *to tear a letter into pieces.* **11.** one's opinion or thoughts on a subject. **12.** a cannon or other unit of ordnance: *field piece.* **13.** a coin: *a five-cent piece.* **14.** *Midland and Southern U.S.* a distance: *down the road a piece.* —*v.t.* **15.** to mend by adding a piece or pieces; patch. **16.** to complete or extend by an added piece or something additional (often fol. by *out*): *to piece out a library with new books.* **17.** to make by or as if by joining pieces (often fol. by *together*): *to piece together a musical program.* **18.** to join together, as pieces or parts. **19.** to join as a piece or addition to something: *to piece new wire into the cable.* **20.** to assemble into a meaningful whole by combining available facts, information, etc. —*Idiom.* **21. go to pieces, a.** to break into fragments. **b.** to lose control of oneself; become emotionally or physically upset. **22. of a piece,** of the same kind; harmonious; consistent. Also, **of one piece. 23. piece of cake,** *Informal.* something easily done. **24. piece of one's mind,** a sharp rebuke or scolding. **25. piece of the action,** *Informal.* a share of the profits. —**piec′er,** *n.*

piece′ goods′, *n.pl.* goods, esp. fabrics, sold at retail by linear measure. Also called **yard goods.**

piece·meal (pēs′mēl′), *adv.* **1.** one piece at a time; gradually: *to work piecemeal.* **2.** into pieces. —*adj.* **3.** done piecemeal.

piece′ of eight′, *n.* PESO (def. 3).

piece·work (pēs′wûrk′), *n.* work done and paid for by the piece. —**piece′work′er,** *n.*

pie′ chart′, *n.* a graphic data display in which sectors of a circle correspond in area to the relative size of the quantities represented.

pie·crust (pī′krust′), *n.* the crust or shell of a pie.

pied (pīd), *adj.* having two or more colors in a pattern of patches or spots; piebald.

pied-à-terre (pē ā′də târ′, -dä-, pyā′-), *n., pl.* **pieds-à-terre** (pē ā′də târ′, -dä-, pyā′-). a residence, as an apartment, for part-time or temporary use. [< French: lit., foot on ground]

Pied′ Pip′er, *n.* **1.** the hero of a German folk legend, popularized in *The Pied Piper of Hamelin* (1842) by Robert Browning, who charms the city's rats into a river with his magical pipe-playing. **2.** (*sometimes l.c.*) a person who induces others to follow or imitate him or her.

pie′ in the sky′, *n.* PIE¹ (def. 6).

pie·plant (pī′plant′, -plänt′), *n.* the edible rhubarb, *Rheum rhaponticum.*

pier (pēr), *n.* **1.** a structure built on posts extending from land out over water, used as a landing place for ships, an entertainment area, etc. **2.** (in a bridge or the like) a support for the ends of adjacent spans. **3.** a square pillar. **4.** a portion of wall between doors, windows, etc. **5.** a pillar or post on which a gate or door is hung. **6.** a support of masonry, steel, or the like for sustaining vertical pressure.

pierce (pērs), *v.,* **pierced, pierc·ing.** —*v.t.* **1.** to penetrate (something), as a pointed object does. **2.** to make a hole or opening in; perforate. **3.** to make (a hole or opening) by or as if by boring or perforating. **4.** to force or make a way into or through: *a road that pierces the jungle.* **5.** to penetrate with the eye or mind. **6.** to affect sharply with some sensation or emotion, as pain. **7.** to sound sharply through (the air, stillness, etc.), as a cry. —*v.i.* **8.** to force or make a way into or through something. —**pierce′a·ble,** *adj.* —**pierc′er,** *n.*

Pierce (pērs), *n.* **Franklin,** 1804–69, 14th president of the U.S. 1853–57.

pierced (pērst), *adj.* **1.** punctured or perforated, as to form a decorative design. **2.** (of the ear) having the lobe punctured, as for earrings. **3.** (of an earring) made to be worn in a pierced ear.

pierc·ing (pēr′sing), *adj.* **1.** loud; shrill. **2.** extremely cold or bitter. **3.** appearing to gaze deeply into something. **4.** perceptive or aware. **5.** sarcastic; cutting. —**pierc′ing·ly,** *adv.*

Pierre (pēr), *n.* the capital of South Dakota, in the central part, on the Missouri River. 11,973.

Pier·son (pēr′sən), *n.* **Arthur Tappan,** 1837–1911, U.S. clergyman.

Pie·tà (pē′ā tä′, pyā tä′), *n., pl.* **-tàs.** (*sometimes l.c.*) a representation of the Virgin Mary mourning over the body of the dead Christ, usu. shown held on her lap.

Pi·e·tism (pī′i tiz′əm), *n.* **1.** a movement in the Lutheran Church in Germany in the 17th century that stressed personal piety over religious formality and orthodoxy. **2.** (*l.c.*) intensity of religious devotion or feeling. **3.** (*l.c.*) exaggeration or affectation of piety. —**Pi′e·tist,** *n.* —**pi·e·tis′tic, pi′e·tis′ti·cal,** *adj.* —**pi′e·tis′ti·cal·ly,** *adv.*

pi·e·ty (pī′i tē), *n., pl.* **-ties. 1.** reverence for God or devout fulfillment of religious obligations. **2.** the quality or state of being pious. **3.** dutiful respect or regard for parents, homeland, etc.: *filial piety.* **4.** a pious act, remark, belief, or the like.

pi·e·zo·e·lec·tric·i·ty (pī ē′zō i lek tris′i tē, -ē′lek-, pē ā′zō-), *n.*

electricity or electric polarity produced in certain nonconducting crystals, as quartz, when subjected to pressure or strain. —**pi·e′zo·e·lec′tric** (-i lek′trik), *adj.* —**pi·e′zo·e·lec′tri·cal·ly,** *adv.*

pif·fle (pif′əl), *n., v.,* **-fled, -fling.** *Informal.* —*n.* **1.** nonsense, as idle talk or trivial writing. —*v.i.* **2.** to talk or behave in a nonsensical way.

pig (pig), *n., v.,* **pigged, pig·ging.** —*n.* **1.** a young swine of either sex, esp. a domestic hog, *Sus scrofa,* weighing less than 120 lb. (220 kg). **2.** any wild or domestic swine. **3.** the flesh of swine; pork. **4.** a person who is gluttonous, greedy, or slovenly. **5. a.** an oblong mass of metal that has been run while still molten into a mold of sand or the like. **b.** one of the molds for such masses of metal. **c.** metal in the form of such masses. **d.** PIG IRON. —*v.i.* **6.** to bring forth pigs; farrow. **7. pig out,** *Slang.* to overindulge in eating: *We pigged out on pizza last night.* —*Saying.* **8. pig in a poke,** something not adequately appraised or of undetermined value, as an offering or purchase.

pi·geon (pij′ən), *n.* **1.** any bird of the family Columbidae, having a plump body and small head, esp. the larger species with square or rounded tails. Compare DOVE¹ (def. 1). **2.** *Slang.* a person who is easily fooled or cheated.

pi·geon·hole (pij′ən hōl′), *n., v.,* **-holed, -hol·ing.** —*n.* **1.** one of a series of small, open compartments in a desk, cabinet, or the like, used for filing papers, letters, etc. **2.** a hole or recess, or one of a series of recesses, for pigeons to nest in. —*v.t.* **3.** to assign to a definite place in an orderly system. **4.** to put aside for the present; defer. **5.** to place in or as if in a pigeonhole.

pi′geon pea′, *n.* **1.** a tropical shrub, *Cajanus cajan,* of the legume family, with yellow flowers. **2.** the brown, edible seed of this plant.

pi′geon-toed′, *adj.* having the toes or feet turned inward.

pi·geon-wing (pij′ən wing′), *n.* **1.** a fancy figure in skating. **2.** a fancy step in dancing.

pig·fish (pig′fish′), *n., pl.* **-fish·es,** (*esp. collectively*) **-fish.** a grunt, *Orthopristis chrysoptera,* living in waters off the Atlantic coast of the southern U.S.

pig·gy or **pig·gie** (pig′ē), *n., pl.* **-gies,** *adj.,* **-gi·er, -gi·est.** —*n.* **1.** a small or young pig. —*adj.* **2.** PIGGISH. —**pig′gi·ness,** *n.*

pig·gy·back (pig′ē bak′), *adv.* **1.** on the back or shoulders: *The child rode piggyback on her father.* —*adj.* **2.** astride the back or shoulders: *a piggyback ride.* **3.** attached to, carried on, or allied with something else: *a piggyback clause.* **4.** noting or pertaining to the carrying of one vehicle on another, as the carrying of truck trailers on flatcars. —*v.t.* **5.** to attach to, carry on, or ally with something else. **6.** to carry on the back or shoulders. **7.** to carry (one vehicle) on another. —*v.i.* **8.** to be attached to or carried on something else. —*n.* **9.** a piggyback ride. **10.** a vehicle on which another is carried. **11.** anything attached to or carried on something else.

pig′gy bank′, *n.* a small bank, usu. having the shape of a pig, provided with a slot to receive coins.

pig·head·ed (pig′hed′id), *adj.* stupidly obstinate; stubborn. —**pig′head′ed·ly,** *adv.* —**pig′head′ed·ness,** *n.*

pig′ in a poke′, *n.* something purchased, accepted, or acquired without a preliminary examination.

pig′ i′ron, *n.* **1.** iron tapped from a blast furnace and cast into pigs in preparation for conversion into steel, cast iron, or wrought iron. **2.** iron in the chemical state in which it exists when tapped from the blast furnace, without alloying or refinement.

pig′ Lat′in, *n.* a form of language, used esp. by children, derived from ordinary English by moving the first consonant or consonant cluster of each word to the end of the word and adding the sound (ā), as in *Eakspay igpay atinlay* for "Speak Pig Latin."

pig·let (pig′lit), *n.* a little pig.

pig·ment (pig′mənt), *n.* **1.** a dry insoluble substance, usu. pulverized, that when suspended in a liquid vehicle becomes a paint, ink, etc. **2.** a coloring matter or substance. **3.** any of various biological substances, as chlorophyll and melanin, that produce color in the tissues of organisms. —*v.t.* **4.** to color; add pigment to. —*v.i.* **5.** to acquire color. —**pig′men·tar′y,** *adj.*

pig·men·ta·tion (pig′mən tā′shən), *n.* **1.** coloration, esp. of the skin. **2.** *Biol.* coloration with or deposition of pigment.

pi·gno·li·a (pēn yō′lē ə) also **pi·gno′li,** *n., pl.* **-li·as** also **-lis.** PINE NUT.

pig′-out′, *n. Slang.* an instance of overindulging in eating; food binge.

pig·pen (pig′pen′), *n.* **1.** a pen for keeping pigs. **2.** a filthy or flagrantly untidy place.

pig·skin (pig′skin′), *n.* **1.** the skin of a pig. **2.** leather made from it. **3.** FOOTBALL (def. 2).

pig·sty (pig′stī′), *n., pl.* **-sties.** PIGPEN.

pig·tail (pig′tāl′), *n.* **1.** a braid of hair hanging down the back of the head. **2.** tobacco in a thin, twisted roll.

pig·weed (pig′wēd′), *n.* **1.** any goosefoot of the genus *Chenopodium.* **2.** any of various amaranths, as *Amaranthus retroflexus.*

pi·ka (pī′kə), *n., pl.* **-kas.** any short-eared, short-legged, tailless lagomorph of the genus *Ochotona,* of western mountains of North America and parts of E Europe and Asia.

pike¹ (pīk), *n., pl.* (*esp. collectively*) **pike,** (*esp. for kinds or species*) **pikes. 1.** any of several large, slender, voracious freshwater fishes of the genus *Esox,* having a long, flat snout. **2.** any of various superficially similar fishes, as the walleye or pikeperch.

pike² (pīk), *n., v.,* **piked, pik·ing.** —*n.* **1.** a shafted weapon having a pointed head, formerly used by infantry. —*v.t.* **2.** to pierce, wound, or kill with a pike.

pike³ (pīk), *n.* **1.** a toll road or highway; turnpike. **2.** a tollgate. **3.** the toll paid at a tollgate.

pike⁴ (pīk), *n.* **1.** a sharply pointed projection or spike. **2.** the pointed end of anything, as of an arrow or a spear.

pike⁵ (pīk), *n.* a midair position assumed by divers and gymnasts in which the torso and head are bent forward and the legs held together with knees straight.

Pike (pīk), *n.* **Zebulon Montgomery,** 1779–1813, U.S. general and explorer.

Pikes′ Peak′, *n.* a mountain in central Colorado: a peak of the Rocky Mountains. 14,108 ft. (4300 m).

pi·laf or **pi·laff** (pē′läf, pi läf′), also **pilau,** *n.* a Middle Eastern dish of rice cooked in bouillon, sometimes with meat or shellfish.

pi·lar (pī′lər), *adj.* of, pertaining to, or covered with hair.

pi·las·ter (pi las′tər), *n.* a shallow rectangular feature projecting from a wall, usu. having a capital and base and imitating the form of a column. —**pi·las′tered,** *adj.*

pilasters

Pi·late (pī′lət), *n.* **Pon·tius** (pon′shəs, -tē əs), fl. early 1st century A.D., Roman procurator of Judea A.D. 26–36?.

pi·lau or **pi·law** (pē′lô, -lou, pi lô′, -lou′), *n.* PILAF.

pile¹ (pīl), *n.* **1.** an assemblage of things laid or lying one upon the other: *a pile of papers.* **2.** a large number, quantity, or amount of anything: *a pile of work.* **3.** a heap of wood on which a dead body, a living person, or a sacrifice is burned; pyre. **4.** a lofty or large building or group of buildings: *the noble pile of Windsor Castle.* **5.** *Informal.* a large accumulation of money. **6.** REACTOR (def. 3). **7.** VOLTAIC PILE. —*v.t.* **8.** to lay or dispose in a pile: *to pile up leaves.* **9.** to accumulate or store (often fol. by *up*): *to pile up money.* **10.** to cover or load with a pile. —*v.i.* **11.** to accumulate, as money, debts, evidence, etc. (usu. fol. by *up*). **12.** to move as a group in a more or less confused, disorderly cluster: *to pile off a train.* **13.** to gather or rise in a pile or piles (often fol. by *up*).

pile² (pīl), *n., v.,* **piled, pil·ing.** —*n.* a cylindrical or flat member of wood, steel, concrete, etc., hammered vertically into soil to form part of a foundation or retaining wall.

pile³ (pīl), *n.* **1.** a surface or thickness of soft hair, down, wool, or other pelage. **2.** a soft or brushy surface on cloth, rugs, etc., formed by upright yarns that have been cut straight across, as in velvet, or left standing in loops, as in terry.

pile⁴ (pīl), *n.* Usu. **piles. 1.** HEMORRHOID. **2.** the condition of having hemorrhoids.

pi·le·at·ed (pī′lē ā′tid, pil′ē-), *adj. Ornith.* crested.

pi′leated wood′pecker, *n.* a large, black-and-white North American woodpecker, *Dryocopus pileatus,* having a prominent red crest.

pile′ driv′er, *n.* a machine for driving piles, usu. composed of a tall framework in which either a weight is raised and dropped on a pile head or in which a steam hammer drives the pile.

pi·le·um (pī′lē əm, pil′ē-), *n., pl.* **pi·le·a** (pī′lē ə, pil′ē ə). the top of the head of a bird, from the base of the bill to the nape.

pile·up (pīl′up′), *n.* **1.** a collision of several or many moving vehicles. **2.** an accumulation, as of chores or bills. **3.** a rough or disorderly falling of people upon one another, as in a football game.

pil·fer (pil′fər), *v.i., v.t.,* to steal, esp. in small quantities. —**pil′fer·age** (-ij), *n.* —**pil′fer·er,** *n.*

pil·grim (pil′grim, -grəm), *n.* **1.** a person who journeys, esp. a long distance, to some sacred place as an act of religious devotion. **2.** a traveler or wanderer, esp. in a foreign place. **3.** (*cap.*) one of the band of Puritans who founded the colony of Plymouth, Mass., in 1620.

pil·grim·age (pil′grə mij), *n.* **1.** a journey, esp. a long one, made to some sacred place as an act of religious devotion. **2.** *Islam.* **a.** the Pilgrimage, hajj. **b.** ‘umrah. **3.** any long journey, esp. one undertaken as a quest or act of devotion.

Pil′grim's Prog′ress, The, a religious allegory by John Bunyan, published between 1678 and 1684, whose main character, Christian, flees the City of Destruction, wanders through the Slough of Despond, and finally arrives at the Celestial City.

pil·ing (pī′ling), *n.* a mass of building piles considered collectively.

pill (pil), *n.* **1.** a small tablet or capsule of medicine, usu. designed to be swallowed whole or dissolved in the mouth. **2.** something unpleasant that has to be accepted or endured. **3.** *Slang.* a tiresomely disagreeable person. **4.** *Slang.* a ball, esp. a baseball or golf ball. **5. the pill,** (*sometimes cap.*) BIRTH-CONTROL PILL. —*v.t.* **6.** to form or make into pills. **7.** *Slang.* to blackball. —*v.i.* **8.** to develop small, pill-like balls of fuzz on the surface, as a wool sweater.

pil·lage (pil′ij), *v.,* **-laged, -lag·ing,** *n.* —*v.t.* **1.** to strip ruthlessly of money or goods by open violence, as in war; plunder. **2.** to take as booty. —*v.i.* **3.** to rob with open violence; take booty. —*n.* **4.** the act of plundering, esp. in war. **5.** booty or spoil. —**pil′lag·er,** *n.*

pil·lar (pil′ər), *n.* **1.** an upright shaft or structure, of stone, brick, or other material, relatively slender in proportion to its height, and of any shape in section, used as a building support, or standing alone, as for a monument. **2.** a natural formation resembling such a construction: *a pillar of smoke.* **3.** any upright, supporting part; post. **4.** a person who is a chief supporter of a state, institution, etc. **5.** (in a mine) an isolated mass of rock or ore, usu. serving as a roof support. —*v.t.* **6.** to provide or support with pillars. —*Idiom.* **7. from pillar to post, a.** from place to place, esp. aimlessly. **b.** from one bad situation or predicament to another. —**pil′lared,** *adj.*

pil′lar of salt′, *n.* the object into which Lot's wife was turned after she disobeyed God and looked back at the cities of Sodom and Gomorrah. Gen. 19:26.

Pil′lars of Is′lam, *n.* the five bases of the Islamic faith: shahada (confession of faith), salat (prayer), zakat (almsgiving), sawm (fasting, esp. during the month of Ramadan), and hajj (the pilgrimage to Mecca). Also called **Pil′lars of the Faith′.**

pill·box (pil′boks′), *n.* **1.** a small box for holding pills. **2.** a small, box-like fortification for machine guns or antitank weapons. **3.** a small, round, brimless hat with straight sides and a flat top.

pill′ bug′, *n.* any of various small terrestrial isopods, esp. of the genera *Armadillidium* and *Oniscus,* that can roll themselves up into a spherical shape.

pil·lo·ry (pil′ə rē), *n., pl.* **-ries,** *v.,* **-ried, -ry·ing.** —*n.* **1.** a wooden framework erected on a post, with holes for securing the head and hands, formerly used to expose an offender to public derision. —*v.t.* **2.** to set in the pillory. **3.** to expose to public derision or abuse.

pil·low (pil′ō), *n.* **1.** a cloth bag or case filled with feathers, foam rubber, or other soft material, used to cushion the head during sleep or rest. **2.** a similar cushion, esp. a small one used for decoration, as on a sofa. **3.** anything used to cushion the head: *a pillow of moss.* **4.** Also called **lace pillow.** a hard cushion or pad that supports the pattern and threads in the making of bobbin lace. **5.** a supporting piece or part, as the block on which the inner end of a bowsprit rests. —*v.t.* **6.** to rest on or as if on a pillow. **7.** to support with pillows. **8.** to serve as a pillow for. —*v.i.* **9.** to rest on or as if on a pillow.

pil·low·case (pil′ō kās′), *n.* a removable sacklike covering, usu. of cotton, drawn over a pillow. Also called **pil′low·slip′** (-slip′).

pil′low sham′, *n.* an ornamental cover for a bed pillow.

pi·lot (pī′lət), *n.* **1.** a person qualified to operate an airplane, balloon, or other aircraft. **2.** a person qualified to steer ships into or out of a harbor or through certain difficult waters. **3.** a person who steers a ship. **4.** a guide or leader. **5.** PILOT LIGHT. **6.** a guide for positioning two adjacent machine parts, often consisting of a projection on one part fitting into a recess in the other. **7.** a filmed or taped television program serving to introduce a possible new series. **8.** a preliminary or experimental trial or test. —*v.t.* **9.** to act as pilot on, in, or over. **10.** to lead or guide, as through unknown places or intricate affairs. **11.** to steer. —*adj.* **12.** serving as a guide. **13.** serving as an experimental or trial undertaking prior to full-scale operation or use: *a pilot project.* —**pi′lot·less,** *adj.*

pi′lot burn′er, *n.* PILOT LIGHT.

pi·lot·fish (pī′lət fish′), *n., pl.* (*esp. collectively*) **-fish,** (*esp. for kinds or species*) **-fish·es.** a small, marine fish, *Naucrates ductor,* often swimming with sharks or alongside boats.

pi′lot light′, *n.* a small flame burning continuously, as in a gas stove, to relight the main gas burners.

pi′lot whale′, *n.* either of two large, black, bulbous-headed species of dolphin of the genus *Globicephala.*

PIM, *pl.* **PIMs, PIM's.** personal information manager.

Pi′ma cot′ton, (*often l.c.*) a variety of smooth, strong-fibered cotton developed from Egyptian cotton and grown in the southwestern U.S.

pi·men·to (pi men′tō), *n., pl.* **-tos. 1.** the red, mild-flavored fruit of the sweet pepper, *Capsicum annuum,* used esp. as a stuffing for olives. **2.** the plant itself. **3.** ALLSPICE.

pimen′to (or **pimien′to**) **cheese′,** *n.* a cheese spread flavored with chopped pimentos.

pim·per·nel (pim′pər nel′, -nl), *n.* any plant belonging to the genus *Anagallis,* of the primrose family, esp. *A. arvensis* (**scarlet pimpernel**), having scarlet or white flowers that close at the approach of bad weather.

pimp·ing (pim′ping), *adj.* petty; insignificant; trivial.

pim·ple (pim′pal), *n.* a small, usu. inflammatory swelling or elevation of the skin; papule or pustule.

pim·ply (pim′plē), *adj.* **-pli·er, -pli·est.** having many pimples. Often, **pim·pled** (pim′pald).

pin (pin), *n., v.,* **pinned, pin·ning.** —*n.* **1.** a small, slender, often pointed piece of metal, wood, etc., used as a fastener or support. **2.** a short, slender piece of wire with a point at one end and a head at the other, for fastening things together. **3.** any of various forms of fasteners, badges, or ornaments consisting essentially or partly of a penetrating wire or shaft (often used in combination): *a fraternity pin; a tiepin.* **4. a.** a short metal rod, as a linchpin, driven through holes in adjacent parts, as a hub and an axle, to keep the parts together. **b.** a short cylindrical rod or tube, as a crankpin, joining two parts so as to permit them to move in one plane relative to each other. **5.** the part of a cylindrical key stem entering a lock. **6.** CLOTHESPIN. **7.** HAIRPIN. **8.** a peg, nail, or stud marking the center of a target. **9.** any one of the rounded wooden clubs set up as the target in tenpins, ninepins, duckpins, etc. **10.** *Golf.* the pole, with flag, which identifies a hole. **11.** *Informal.* a human leg. **12.** PEG (def. 4). **13.** *Naut.* **14.** a very small amount; a trifle. **15.** a pin-shaped connection, as the terminals on the base of an electron tube or the connections on an integrated circuit. —*v.t.* **16.** to fasten or attach with or as with a pin or pins. **17.** to hold fast in a spot or position (sometimes fol. by *down*). **18.** to give one's fraternity pin to (a young woman) as a pledge of one's attachment. **19. pin down,** to force (someone) to deal with a situation or to come to a decision. —*Idiom.* **20. pin something on someone,** *Informal.* to ascribe the blame or guilt for something to a person.

PIN (pin), *n.* an identification number assigned to an individual to gain access to a computer system via an automated-teller machine, a point-of-sale terminal, or other device.

pi•ña co•la•da (kə lä′də), *n., pl.* **piña co•la•das.** a frappéed drink of rum, coconut cream, and pineapple juice.

pin•a•fore (pin′ə fôr′, -fōr′), *n.* a sleeveless, apronlike garment usu. having buttons or a sash at the back, worn by girls and women over a dress or with a blouse. —**pin′a•fored′,** *adj.*

pi•ña•ta (pēn yä′tə, pin yä′-), *n., pl.* **-tas.** (in Mexico and Central America) a gaily decorated crock or papier-mâché figure filled with toys, candy, etc., and suspended from above, esp. for birthday parties and Christmas festivities, so that blindfolded children may break it with sticks and release the contents.

pin•ball (pin′bôl′), *n.* any of various games played on a sloping table, the object usu. being to shoot a ball, driven by a spring-operated plunger, up a side passage and cause it to roll back down against pins and bumpers and through channels that flash or ring and electronically record the score.

pin′ball machine′, *n.* the sloping, usu. coin-operated tablelike device on which pinball is played.

pince-nez (pans′nā′, pins′-; *Fr.* pans nā′), *n., pl.* **pince-nez** (pans′nāz′, pins′-; *Fr.* pans nā′) a pair of glasses held on the face by a spring that grips the nose.

pin•cers (pin′sərz), *n.* (*usu. with a pl. v.*) **1.** a gripping tool consisting of two pivoted limbs forming a pair of jaws and a pair of handles (usu. used with *pair of*). **2.** a grasping organ or pair of organs resembling this, as the claw of a lobster.

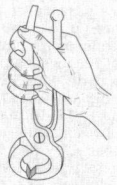

pincers

pinch (pinch), *v.t.* **1.** to squeeze or compress between the finger and thumb, the jaws of an instrument, or the like. **2.** to constrict or squeeze painfully, as a tight shoe does. **3.** to render unnaturally constricted or drawn: *a face pinched with fear.* **4.** to remove or shorten (buds or shoots) in order to produce a certain plant shape or to encourage growth. **5.** to affect with sharp discomfort or distress, as cold, hunger, or need does. **6.** to straiten in means or circumstances: *a family pinched by the recession.* **7.** to hamper or inconvenience by the lack of something specified. **8.** to stint the supply or amount of (a thing). **9.** *Slang.* **a.** to steal. **b.** to arrest. **10.** to sail (a ship) so close to the wind that the sails shake and the speed is reduced. —*v.i.* **11.** to exert a sharp or painful constricting force: *shoes that pinch.* **12.** to cause sharp discomfort or distress. **13.** to economize unduly; stint oneself: *pinched and saved to buy a new car.* **14.** (of a vein of ore or the like) to diminish. —*n.* **15.** the act of pinching; nip; squeeze. **16.** as much of something as can be taken up between the finger and thumb. **17.** a very small quantity of anything. **18.** sharp or painful stress, as of hunger, need, or any trying circumstances. **19.** a situation or time of special stress, esp. an emergency. **20.** *Slang.* **a.** a raid or an arrest. **b.** a theft. —*Idiom.* **21. pinch pennies,** to stint on or be frugal with expenditures. —**pinch′a•ble,** *adj.*

pinch′-hit′, *v.,* **-hit, -hit•ting.** —*v.i.* **1.** to substitute at bat for a teammate in baseball, often at a critical moment of a game. **2.** to substitute for someone, esp. in an emergency. —*v.t.* **3.** to make (a hit) in pinch-hitting. —**pinch′ hit′ter,** *n.*

pinch•pen•ny (pinch′pen′ē), *n., pl.* **-nies,** *adj.* —*n.* **1.** a miser or niggard; penny pincher. —*adj.* **2.** stingy; miserly.

pin′ curl′, *n.* a small coil of dampened hair held flat to the head by a clip or bobby pin so as to form a curl when the hair dries.

pin•cush•ion (pin′kŏosh′ən), *n.* a small cushion into which pins are stuck until needed.

pine¹ (pīn), *n.* **1.** any evergreen tree of the genus *Pinus,* having needlelike leaves borne in bundles and woody cones enclosing winged seeds;

many are valued for their wood and their resinous products, as turpentine and tar. **2.** the wood of a pine tree.

pine² (pīn), *v.i.,* **pined, pin•ing. 1.** to yearn deeply; long painfully: *to pine for one's family.* **2.** to fail gradually in health or vitality from grief, regret, or longing (often fol. by *away*).

pin•e•al (pin′ē əl, pī′nē-, pī nē′-), *adj.* **1.** resembling a pine cone in shape. **2.** of or pertaining to the pineal gland.

pin′eal gland′, *n.* a small, cone-shaped endocrine organ in the posterior forebrain, secreting melatonin and involved in biorhythms and gonadal development.

pine•ap•ple (pī′nap′əl), *n.* **1.** the edible, juicy, collective fruit of a tropical bromeliad, *Ananas comosus,* that develops from a spike or head of flowers and is surmounted by a crown of leaves. **2.** the plant itself, having a short stem and rigid, spiny-margined, recurved leaves. **3.** a small hand grenade shaped like a pineapple.

pine′ cone′, *n.* the cone of a pine tree.

pine′ mar′ten, *n.* **1.** a Eurasian marten, *Martes martes.* **2.** a North American marten, *Martes americana.*

pine′ nee′dle, *n.* the needlelike leaf of a pine tree.

pine′ nut′, *n.* the edible seed of any of several pine trees, as the piñon. Also called **pignolia, pignoli.**

pine•sap (pīn′sap′), *n.* any of several parasitic or saprophytic plants of the genus *Monotropa,* as the reddish *M. hypopithys,* and *M. uniflora,* the Indian pipe.

pine′ sis′kin, *n.* a small North American finch, *Carduelis pinus,* of coniferous forests, having yellow markings on the wings and tail.

pine′ snake′, *n.* any of several subspecies of bullsnake of the eastern and southeastern U.S., chiefly inhabiting pine woods.

pine′ tar′, *n.* a viscid, blackish brown liquid with an odor resembling that of turpentine, obtained by the destructive distillation of pine wood, used in paints, roofing, soaps, and as an antiseptic.

pine′ war′bler, *n.* a North American wood warbler, *Dendroica pinus,* inhabiting pine forests of the eastern U.S.

pin•ey (pī′nē), *adj.,* **pin•i•er, pin•i•est.** PINY.

pin•fish (pin′fish′), *n., pl.* **-fish•es,** (*esp. collectively*) **-fish.** a small, spiny-finned porgy, *Lagodon rhomboides,* inhabiting bays of the S Atlantic and Gulf coasts of the U.S.

ping (ping), *v.i.* **1.** to produce a sharp sound like that of a bullet striking a sheet of metal. —*n.* **2.** a pinging sound.

ping-pong (ping′pong′, -pông′), *v.t.* **1.** to move or transfer back and forth: *The patient was ping-ponged from one specialist to another.* —*v.i.* **2.** to move or shift back and forth.

Ping-Pong (ping′pong′, -pông′), *Trademark.* TABLE TENNIS.

pin•head (pin′hed′), *n.* **1.** the head of a pin. **2.** a stupid person; nitwit. **3.** something very small or insignificant.

pin•hole (pin′hōl′), *n.* **1.** a small hole made by or as if by a pin. **2.** a hole for a pin to go through; tiny aperture.

pin•ion¹ (pin′yən), *n.* **1.** a gear with a small number of teeth, esp. one engaging a rack or larger gear. **2.** a shaft or spindle cut with teeth engaging a gear.

pin•ion² (pin′yən), *n.* **1.** the distal or terminal segment of the wing of a bird consisting of the carpus, metacarpus, and phalanges. **2.** the wing of a bird. **3.** a feather. —*v.t.* **4.** to cut off the pinion of (a wing) or bind (the wings), as in order to prevent a bird from flying. **5.** to bind (a person's arms or hands) so they cannot be used. **6.** to disable (someone) in such a manner; shackle. **7.** to bind or hold fast, as to a thing.

pink¹ (pingk), *n., adj.,* **-er, -est.** —*n.* **1.** a color varying from light crimson to pale reddish purple. **2.** any of several plants of the genus *Dianthus,* as the clove pink or carnation. **3.** the flower of such a plant; carnation. **4.** the highest form or degree; prime: *in the pink of condition.* **5.** *Slang (disparaging).* **a.** a person with left-wing, but not extreme, political opinions. **b.** a person who leans toward Communist ideology. **6. pinks,** the usu. scarlet coat worn by fox hunters. **7.** the scarlet color of this coat. —*adj.* **8.** of the color pink. —**pink′ness,** *n.*

pink² (pingk), *v.t.* **1.** to pierce with a rapier or the like; stab. **2.** to cut (fabric) at the edge with a notched pattern, as to prevent fraying or for ornament. **3.** to pierce (fabric, leather, etc.) with small holes or slits for ornament.

pink′-col′lar, *adj.* of or pertaining to employment traditionally held by women, as nursing and secretarial work. Compare BLUE-COLLAR.

pink′ el′ephants, *n.pl.* any of various visual hallucinations sometimes experienced after sustained alcoholic drinking.

Pink•er•ton (ping′kər tən), *n.* Allan, 1819–84, U.S. detective, born in Scotland.

pink•eye (pingk′ī′), *n.* a contagious, epidemic form of acute conjunctivitis occurring in humans and certain animals: so called from the color of the inflamed eye.

pink•ie (ping′kē), *n.* pl. **pink•ies.** *Informal.* the little finger.

pink′ing shears′, *n.* (*used with a sing. or pl. v.*) shears with notched blades, for simultaneously cutting and pinking fabric (often used with *pair of*).

pink′ la′dy, *n.* a cocktail made with gin, grenadine, and egg white, shaken and strained before serving.

pink′ salm′on, *n.* a small Pacific salmon, *Oncorhynchus gorbuscha,* distinguished by its small scales and long anal fin and by the bright red spawning coloration of males.

pink′ slip′, *n.* a notice of dismissal from one's job.

pin′ mon′ey, *n.* **1.** any small sum set aside for nonessential minor expenditures. **2.** (formerly) an allowance of money given by a husband to his wife for her personal expenditures.

pin•na•cle (pin′ə kəl), *n., v.,* **-cled, -cling.** —*n.* **1.** a lofty peak. **2.** the highest or culminating point, as of success, power, fame, etc. **3.** any pointed, towering part or formation, as of rock. **4.** a relatively small upright structure, commonly terminating in a pyramid or cone, rising above a roof or coping or capping a tower or buttress. —*v.t.* **5.** to place on or as if on a pinnacle. **6.** to form a pinnacle on; crown.

pin•nate (pin′āt, -it) also **pin′nat•ed,** *adj.* **1.** resembling a feather, as in construction or arrangement; having parts arranged on each side of a common axis: *a pinnate branch.* **2.** (of a leaf) having leaflets or primary divisions arranged on each side of a common stalk. —**pin′nate•ly,** *adv.*

pin•ni•ped (pin′ə ped′), *adj.* **1.** belonging to the Pinnipedia, a group-ing of carnivorous aquatic mammals that have their limbs broadened and flattened into flippers, as seals and walruses. —*n.* **2.** a pinniped animal.

pin′ oak′, *n.* an oak, *Quercus palustris,* having branches that grow in a pyramidal manner and deeply lobed leaves.

Pi•no•cchi•o (pi nō′kē ō′), *n.* the hero of Carlo Collodi's children's story, *The Adventures of Pinocchio* (1883), a wooden puppet who comes to life as a boy and whose nose grows longer whenever he tells a lie.

pi•noch•le or **pi•noc•le** (pē′nuk əl, -nok-), *n.* **1.** a card game played by two, three, or four persons, with a 48-card deck. **2.** a meld of the queen of spades and the jack of diamonds in this game.

pi•ñon or **pin•yon** (pin′yən, pēn′yōn, pēn yōn′), *n., pl.* **pi•ñons, pi•ño•nes** (pē nyô′nes), or **pin•yons. 1.** any of several pines of SW North America, as *Pinus monophylla* or *P. edulis,* bearing edible nutlike seeds. **2.** Also called **pi′ñon nut′.** the seed. Compare PINE NUT, PIGNOLIA.

pi•not (pē nō′), *n.* (*often cap.*) **1.** any of several varieties of purple or white vinifera grapes yielding a red or white wine, used esp. in making burgundies and champagnes. **2.** a red or white wine made from such a grape.

pin•point (pin′point′), *n.* **1.** the point of a pin. **2.** a trifle; pinhead. **3.** a tiny spot or sharp point. —*v.t.* **4.** to locate or describe exactly or precisely. —*adj.* **5.** exact; precise.

pin•prick (pin′prik′), *n.* **1.** any minute puncture made by a pin or the like. **2.** a negligible irritation or annoyance.

pins′ and nee′dles, *n.pl.* **1.** a tingly, prickly sensation in a limb that is recovering from numbness. —***Idiom.*** **2. on pins and needles,** in a state of nervous anticipation.

pin•scher (pin′shər), *n.* any of a group of related dogs including the Doberman pinscher, miniature pinscher, and affenpinscher.

pin•set•ter (pin′set′ər), *n.* a person or mechanical apparatus in a bowling alley that places the pins in position.

pin•stripe (pin′strīp′), *n.* **1.** a very thin stripe, esp. (in fabrics) a thin white stripe on a dark background. **2.** a fabric or garment having such stripes. —**pin′striped′,** *adj.* —**pin′strip′ing,** *n.*

pint (pīnt), *n.* a liquid and dry measure of capacity, equal to one half of a quart, approximately 35 cubic inches (0.6 liter). *Abbr.:* pt.

pin•tail (pin′tāl′), *n., pl.* **-tails,** (*esp. collectively*) **-tail.** any of several slim dabbling ducks with a long, pointed tail, esp. *Anas acuta,* of the Northern Hemisphere.

Pin•ter (pin′tər), *n.* **Harold,** born 1930, English playwright.

pin•to (pin′tō, pēn′-), *adj., n., pl.* **-tos.** —*adj.* **1.** marked with spots of white and other colors; mottled; spotted. —*n.* **2.** a pinto horse.

pin′to bean′, *n.* a variety of the common bean, *Phaseolus vulgaris,* having pinkish mottled seeds, grown chiefly in the southern U.S.

pint′-size′ or **pint′-sized′,** *adj.* small in size.

pin•up (pin′up′), *n.* **1.** a large photograph, as of a sexually attractive person, suitable for pinning on a wall. **2.** a person in such a photograph. —*adj.* **3.** of, suitable for, or appearing in a pinup. **4.** designed or suitable for hanging or fastening on a wall: *a pinup lamp.*

pin•wale (pin′wāl′), *adj.* (of a fabric) having very thin wales.

pin•wheel (pin′hwēl′, -wēl′), *n.* **1.** a toy consisting of a small wheel with paper or plastic vanes attached by a pin to a stick, designed to revolve when blown. **2.** a firework that revolves rapidly on a pin when ignited, making a wheel of fire or sparks; Catherine wheel. —*v.i.* **3.** to revolve rapidly like a pinwheel.

pin•worm (pin′wûrm′), *n.* a small nematode worm, *Enterobius vermicularis,* infesting the intestine and migrating to the anus, esp. in children.

pinx′ter (or **pink′ster**) **flow′er,** *n.* a wild azalea, *Rhododendron nudiflorum,* of the U.S., having pink or purplish flowers.

pin•y or **pin•ey** (pī′nē), *adj.,* **-i•er, -i•est. 1.** abounding in or covered with pine trees. **2.** pertaining to or suggestive of pine trees: *a piny fragrance.*

pin•yon (pin′yən, pēn′yōn, pēn yōn′), *n.* PIÑON.

pi•o•let (pē′ə lā′), *n.* an ice ax used in mountaineering.

pi•o•neer (pī′ə nēr′), *n.* **1.** a person who is among those who first enter or settle a region, thus opening it for occupation and development by others. **2.** one who is first or among the earliest in any field of inquiry, enterprise, or progress. **3.** one of a group of foot soldiers detailed to make roads, dig entrenchments, etc., in advance of the main body. **4.** an organism that successfully establishes itself in a barren area, thus starting an ecological cycle of life. —*v.i.* **5.** to act as a pioneer. —*v.t.* **6.** to be the first to open or prepare (a way, settlement, etc.). **7.** to take part in the beginnings of; initiate. **8.** to lead the way for (a group); guide. —*adj.* **9.** being the earliest or original. **10.** of, pertaining to, or characteristic of pioneers. **11.** being a pioneer. [< Middle French < Old French *peonier* foot soldier]

Pioneer′ Day′, *n.* a legal holiday in Utah on July 24 to commemorate Brigham Young's founding of Salt Lake City in 1847.

pi•ous (pī′əs), *adj.* **1.** having or showing a dutiful spirit of reverence for God or an earnest wish to fulfill religious obligations. **2.** characterized by a hypocritical concern with virtue or religious devotion; sanctimonious. **3.** practiced or used in the name of real or pretended religious motives or for an ostensibly good object: *a pious deception.* **4.** sacred rather than secular. **5.** showing due respect or regard, as for parents. —**pi′ous•ly,** *adv.* —**pi′ous•ness,** *n.*

pip[1] (pip), *n.* **1.** one of the spots on dice, playing cards, or dominoes. **2.** each of the small segments into which the surface of a pineapple is divided. **3.** a metal insignia of rank worn on the shoulders of junior officers in the British army. **4.** an individual rootstock of a plant, esp. of the lily of the valley.

pip[2] (pip), *n.* **1.** a contagious disease of birds, esp. poultry, characterized by the secretion of a thick mucus in the mouth and throat. **2.** *Slang.* any minor or unspecified ailment in a person.

pip[3] (pip), *n.* **1.** a small seed, esp. of a fleshy fruit, as an apple or orange. **2.** *Informal.* someone or something wonderful or amazing.

pip[4] (pip), *v.,* **pipped, pip•ping.** —*v.i.* **1.** to peep or chirp. **2.** (of a hatching bird) to break out from the shell. —*v.t.* **3.** to crack or chip a hole through (the shell), as a hatching bird.

pip[5] (pip), *n.* BLIP (def. 1).

pi•pal (pī′pəl, pē′-) also **peepul,** *n.* a fig tree, *Ficus religiosa,* of India, somewhat resembling the banyan.

pipe[1] (pīp), *n., v.,* **piped, pip•ing.** —*n.* **1.** a hollow cylinder of metal, wood, or other material, used for the conveyance of water, gas, steam, etc. **2.** a tube of wood, clay, or other material, with a small bowl at one end, used for smoking tobacco, opium, etc. **3.** a quantity, as of tobacco, filling the bowl of such a smoking utensil. **4. a.** a musical wind instrument, as a flute or oboe, constructed of a single tube. **b.** a small flute held with one hand while the other beats a drum. **c.** one of the tubes from which the tones of an organ are produced; flue pipe or reed pipe. **d. pipes,** BAGPIPE. **e. pipes,** PANPIPE. **5.** a high-pitched whistle used by a boatswain for giving signals. **6.** the call or utterance of a bird, frog, etc. **7. pipes,** the human vocal cords or the voice, esp. as used in singing. **8. a.** a tubular organ or passage. **b.** Usu., **pipes.** the human respiratory passage. **9.** any of various tubular or cylindrical objects or natural formations, as an eruptive passage of a volcano or geyser. **10. a.** a cylindrical vein or body of ore. **b.** (in South Africa) a vertical, cylindrical matrix, of intrusive igneous origin, in which diamonds are found. —*v.i.* **11.** to play on a pipe. **12.** to speak in a high-pitched or piercing tone. **13.** to make or utter a shrill sound like that of a pipe. **14.** to signal, as with a boatswain's pipe. —*v.t.* **15.** to convey by or as if by pipes. **16.** to supply with pipes. **17.** to play (music) on a pipe or pipes. **18.** to summon, order, etc., by sounding a boatswain's pipe or whistle. **19.** to bring, lead, etc., by or as if by playing on a pipe: *to pipe dancers.* **20.** to utter in a shrill tone: *to pipe a command.* **21.** to trim or finish with piping, as an article of clothing. **22.** to force (dough, frosting, etc.) through a pastry tube onto a baking sheet, cake or pie, etc. **23.** to convey by an electrical wire or cable: *to pipe in music.* **24. pipe down,** *Slang.* to stop talking; be quiet. **25. pipe up,** to make oneself heard, esp. as to assert oneself; speak up. —**pipe′less,** *adj.* —**pipe′like′,** *adj.*

pipe[2] (pīp), *n.* **1.** a large cask, of varying capacity, esp. for wine or oil. **2.** such a cask as a measure of liquid capacity, equal to 4 barrels, 2 hogsheads, or 126 gallons.

pipe′ bomb′, *n.* a small homemade bomb typically contained in a metal pipe.

pipe′ clean′er, *n.* a short length of twisted flexible wires covered with tufted fabric, used to clean the stem of a smoker's pipe and for various handicrafts.

pipe′ dream′, *n.* a fanciful or unrealistic notion, hope, or plan.

pipe•fish (pīp′fish′), *n., pl.* (*esp. collectively*) **-fish,** (*esp. for kinds or species*) **-fish•es.** any small, elongated fish of the family Syngnathidae, having a tubular snout and a covering of bony plates.

pipe′ fit′ter, *n.* a person who installs and repairs pipe systems.

pipe′ fit′ting, *n.* **1.** a joint or connector, as an elbow, union, or tee, used in a pipe system. **2.** the work performed by a pipe fitter.

pipe•line (pīp′līn′), *n., v.,* **-lined, -lin•ing.** —*n.* **1.** a linked series of pipes with pumps and valves for flow control, used to transport crude oil, water, etc., esp. over great distances. **2.** a route or channel along which supplies pass. **3.** a channel of information, esp. one that is direct, privileged, or confidential. —*v.t.* **4.** to convey by or as if by pipeline. —*v.i.* **5.** to install a pipeline. —***Idiom.*** **6. in the pipeline,** in the process of being developed, provided, or completed. —**pipe′lin′er,** *n.*

pipe′ or′gan, *n.* ORGAN (def. 1a).

pip•er (pī′pər), *n.* **1.** a person who plays on a pipe. **2.** a bagpiper. —***Idiom.*** **3. pay the piper, a.** to pay the cost of something. **b.** to bear the unfavorable consequences of one's actions or indulgences. —***Proverb.*** **4. He who pays the piper calls the tune,** financial control dictates what decisions are made.

pi•pette (pī pet′, pi-), *n., v.,* **-pet•ted, -pet•ting.** —*n.* **1.** a slender graduated tube for measuring liquids or transferring them from one container to another. —*v.t.* **2.** to measure or transfer with a pipette.

pipe′ wrench′, *n.* a tool having two toothed jaws, one fixed and the other free, that can be adjusted to grip pipes and other tubular objects when the tool is turned in one direction only.

pip•ing (pī′ping), *n.* **1.** pipes collectively; a system of pipes. **2.** material formed into pipes. **3.** the act of a person or thing that pipes. **4.** the sound of pipes. **5.** a shrill sound. **6.** the music of pipes. **7.** a usu. narrow band of ornamental material used for trimming the edges and seams of clothing, upholstery, etc. —*adj.* **8.** making a shrill sound. **9.** characterized by the peaceful music of the pipe. —*Idiom.* **10. piping hot,** (of food or drink) very hot. —**pip′ing•ly,** *adv.*

pip′ing plo′ver, *n.* a small, pale, brown and white plover of E North America, *Charadrius melodus,* nesting on sandy or pebbly beaches.

pip•it (pip′it), *n.* any of various slim, brown-streaked songbirds of the genus *Anthus,* of the family Motacillidae, found in treeless country over much of the world.

pip•pin (pip′in), *n.* any of numerous roundish or oblate varieties of apple.

pip•squeak (pip′skwēk′), *n. Informal.* a contemptibly small or unimportant person.

pi•quant (pē′kənt, -känt, pē känt′), *adj.* **1.** agreeably pungent or sharp in taste. **2.** of an interestingly provocative or lively character: *a piquant wit.* —**pi′quan•cy, pi′quant•ness,** *n.* —**pi′quant•ly,** *adv.*

pique (pēk), *v.,* **piqued, piqu•ing,** *n.* —*v.t.* **1.** to affect with sharp irritation and resentment, esp. by some wound to pride. **2.** to wound (the pride, vanity, etc.). **3.** to excite, arouse, or provoke: *The remark piqued my curiosity.* —*v.i.* **4.** to arouse pique in someone. —*n.* **5.** a feeling of irritation or resentment, as from a wound to pride.

pir (pēr), *n. Islam.* **1.** a term of respect for the head of a religious group, esp. in Pakistan and various areas of the Middle and Near East. **2.** a religious instructor, esp. in mystical sects.

pi•ra•cy (pī′rə sē), *n., pl.* **-cies. 1.** practice of a pirate; robbery or illegal violence at sea. **2.** the unauthorized reproduction or use of copyrighted material, a patented invention, a trademarked product, etc.

pi•ra•nha (pi rän′yə, -ran′-, -rä′nə, -ran′ə), *n., pl.* **-nhas,** (*esp. collectively*) **-nha.** any of several small South American freshwater fishes of the genus *Serrasalmus,* family Serrasalmidae, with sharp interlocking teeth: predatory on fishes and mammals and dangerous when swimming in schools.

pi•rate (pī′rət), *n., v.,* **-rat•ed, -rat•ing.** —*n.* **1.** a person who robs or commits illegal violence at sea or on the shores of the sea. **2.** a ship used by such persons. **3.** a person who uses or reproduces the work or invention of another without authorization. **4.** a person who transmits radio or television signals illicitly. —*v.t.* **5.** to commit piracy upon; plunder; rob. **6.** to take by piracy. **7.** to use or reproduce (a book, an invention, etc.) without authorization or legal right. —*v.i.* **8.** to commit or practice piracy. —**pi•rat•i•cal** (pī rat′i kəl, pi-), **pi•rat′ic,** *adj.* —**pi•rat′i•cal•ly,** *adv.*

pi•ro•gen (pi rō′gən), *n.pl.* dumplings with a filling, as of meat or potatoes.

pi•rosh•ki (pi rôsh′kē, -rosh′-), *n.pl.* small turnovers with a filling, as of meat or vegetables.

pir•ou•ette (pir′ o̅o̅ et′), *n., v.,* **-et•ted, -et•ting.** —*n.* **1.** a whirling about on one foot or on the points of the toes, as in ballet dancing. —*v.i.* **2.** to perform a pirouette.

Pi•sa (pē′zə, -zä), *n.* a city in NW Italy, on the Arno River: leaning tower. 103,527. —**Pi′san,** *adj., n.*

Pis•ces (pī′sēz, pis′ēz), *n.* **1.** the Fishes, a zodiacal constellation between Aquarius and Aries. **2.** the 12th sign of the zodiac. [< Latin: fish]

pisci-, a combining form meaning "fish": *piscine.*

pis•cine (pī′sēn, pis′īn, -ēn, -in), *adj.* pertaining to fish.

Pis•gah (piz′gə), *n.* **Mount,** a mountain ridge of ancient Moab, now in Jordan, NE of the Dead Sea: from its summit **(Mount Nebo)** Moses viewed the Promised Land. Deut. 34:1.

pish (psh; *spelling pron.* pish), *interj.* **1.** (used as an exclamation of mild contempt or impatience.) —*v.i.* **2.** to say "pish."

Pish•pek (pish pek′), *n.* former name (until 1926) of **BISHKEK.**

Pi•sid•i•a (pi sid′ē ə, pī-), *n.* an ancient country in S Asia Minor: later a Roman province.

pis′mo clam′ (piz′mō), *n.* a large edible clam, *Tivela stultorum,* of sandy shores of California and Mexico.

pis•tach•i•o (pi stash′ē ō′, -stä′shē ō′), *n., pl.* **-chi•os. 1.** the nut of a Eurasian tree, *Pistacia vera,* of the cashew family, containing an edible, greenish kernel. **2.** the tree itself. **3.** a light or medium shade of yellow-green. Also, **pis•tache** (pi stash′), **pistach′io nut′** (for def. 1).

pis•til (pis′tl), *n.* the seed-bearing organ of a flower, consisting when complete of ovary, style, and stigma.

pis•til•late (pis′tl it, -āt′), *adj.* **1.** having a pistil or pistils. **2.** having a pistil or pistils but no stamens.

pis•tol (pis′tl), *n., v.,* **-toled, -tol•ing** or (*esp. Brit.*) **-tolled, -tol•ling.** —*n.* **1.** a short firearm intended to be held and fired with one hand. —*v.t.* **2.** to shoot with a pistol.

pis′tol-whip′, *v.t.* to beat with a pistol.

pis•ton (pis′tən), *n.* **1.** a disk or solid cylinder moving within a longer cylinder and exerting pressure on, or receiving pressure from, a fluid or gas. **2.** a pumplike valve used to change the pitch in a cornet, etc.

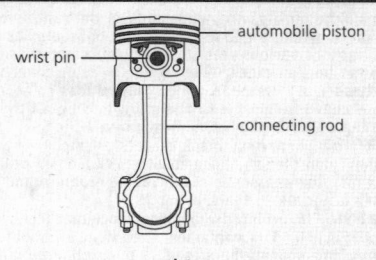

piston

P

pit¹ (pit), *n., v.,* **pit•ted, pit•ting.** —*n.* **1.** a hole or cavity in the ground. **2.** a covered or concealed excavation in the ground, serving as a trap. **3. a.** an excavation made in exploring for or removing a mineral deposit, as by open-cut methods. **b.** the shaft of a coal mine. **c.** the mine itself. **4.** the abode of evil spirits and lost souls; hell. **5. the pits,** *Slang.* an extremely unpleasant or depressing place, condition, etc. **6.** a hollow or indentation in a surface. **7.** a natural hollow or depression in the body: *the pit of the back.* **8.** POCKMARK. **9.** an enclosure for staging fights, esp. between dogs or cocks. **10.** a place where slam dances are performed. **11.** a part of the floor of a commodity exchange where trading in a particular commodity takes place. **12. a.** all that part of the main floor of a theater behind the musicians. **b.** ORCHESTRA (def. 2a). **13.** an area at the side of a racing track, for servicing and refueling the cars. —*v.t.* **14.** to mark or indent with pits or depressions. **15.** to scar with pockmarks. **16.** to place or bury in a pit, as for storage. **17.** to set in opposition or combat, as one against another. **18.** to put (animals) in a pit for fighting. —*v.i.* **19.** to become marked with pits or depressions. **20.** (of body tissue) to retain temporarily a mark of pressure, as by a finger or instrument.

pit² (pit), *n., v.,* **pit•ted, pit•ting.** —*n.* **1.** the stone of a fruit, as of a cherry, peach, or plum. —*v.t.* **2.** to remove the pit from (a fruit).

pi•ta¹ (pē′tə), *n., pl.* **-tas. 1.** a fiber obtained from plants of the genera *Agave, Aechmea,* etc., used for cordage, mats, etc. **2.** any of these plants.

pi•ta² (pē′tä, -tə), *n.* a round, flat Middle Eastern bread having a pocket that can be filled to make a sandwich. Also called **pi′ta bread′.**

pit-a-pat (pit′ə pat′), *adv., n., v.,* **-pat•ted, -pat•ting.** —*adv.* **1.** with a quick succession of beats or taps. —*n.* **2.** the movement or the sound of something going pitapat. —*v.i.* **3.** to go pitapat.

pit′ bull′ ter′rier, *n.* **1.** AMERICAN STAFFORDSHIRE TERRIER. **2.** a dog developed by crossbreeding the American Staffordshire terrier and another breed, as the bull terrier. Also called **pit′ bull′.**

pitch¹ (pich), *v.t.* **1.** to erect or set up (a tent, camp, or the like). **2.** to put, set, or plant in a fixed or definite place or position. **3.** to throw, fling, hurl, or toss. **4.** *Baseball.* **a.** to deliver or serve (the ball) to the batter. **b.** to serve as pitcher of (a game). **5.** to set at a certain point, degree, level, etc.: *He pitched his hopes too high.* **6.** to establish the musical key of. **7.** to set or build with a downward slope: *a pitched roof.* **8.** to pave with small stones. —*v.i.* **9.** to plunge or fall forward or headlong. **10.** to lurch. **11.** to throw or toss. **12.** *Baseball.* **a.** to deliver or serve the ball to the batter. **b.** to fill the position of pitcher. **13.** to slope downward; dip. **14.** to plunge with alternate fall and rise of bow and stern, as a ship. **15.** (of a rocket or guided missile) to deviate from a stable flight attitude by oscillations of the longitudinal axis in a vertical plane about the center of gravity. **16.** to fix a tent or temporary habitation; encamp. **17.** *Golf.* to play a pitch shot. **18. pitch in,** *Informal.* to contribute to a common cause. **19. pitch into,** *Informal.* to attack verbally or physically. —*n.* **20.** relative point, position, or degree: *a high pitch of excitement.* **21.** the degree of inclination or slope; angle. **22.** (in music, speech, etc.) the degree of height or depth of a tone or of sound, depending upon the relative rapidity of the vibrations by which it is produced. **23.** *Music.* the particular tonal standard with which given tones may be compared in respect to their relative level. **24.** the apparent predominant frequency sounded by an acoustical source. **25.** the act or manner of pitching. **26.** a throw or toss. **27.** *Baseball.* the serving of the ball to the batter by the pitcher. **28.** a pitching movement, as of a ship. **29.** a sloping part or place: *the pitch of a hill.* **30.** a quantity of something pitched or placed somewhere. **31.** *Cricket.* the central part of the field; the area between the wickets. **32.** *Informal.* a sales talk, often high-pressured. **33.** *Aeron.* **a.** the nosing of an airplane or spacecraft up or down about a transverse axis. **b.** the distance that a given propeller would advance in one revolution. **34.** (of a rocket or guided missile) **a.** the motion due to pitching. **b.** the extent of the rotation of the longitudinal axis involved in pitching. **35.** *Geol.* the inclination of a linear feature, as the axis of a fold or an oreshoot, from the horizontal. **36. a.** the distance between the corresponding surfaces of two adjacent gear teeth, measured between perpendiculars to the root surfaces. **b.** the distance between any two adjacent things in a series, as screw threads or rivets. **37.** *Cards.* ALL FOURS (def. 2). **38.** a unit of typographic measurement indicating the number of characters to a horizontal inch.

pitch² (pich), *n.* **1.** any of various dark, tenacious, and viscous substances for caulking and paving, consisting of the residue of the distillation of coal tar or wood tar. **2.** any of certain bitumens, as asphalt: *mineral pitch.* **3.** any of various resins. **4.** the sap or crude turpentine that exudes from the bark of pines. —*v.t.* **5.** to smear or cover with pitch.

pitch′-and-toss′, *n.* a game in which players toss coins at a mark, the person whose coin hits closest to the mark tossing all the coins in the air and winning all those that come down heads up.

pitch′-black′, *adj.* extremely black or dark as pitch.

pitch•blende (pich′blend′), *n.* a massive variety of uraninite, occurring in black pitchlike masses: a major ore of uranium and radium.

pitch′-dark′, *adj.* dark or black as pitch.

pitched′ bat′tle, *n.* an intense battle at close quarters.

pitch•er[1] (pich′ər), *n.* **1.** a container, usu. with a handle and spout or lip, for holding and pouring liquids. **2.** a pitcherlike modification of the leaf of certain plants; ascidium. —***Proverb.*** **3. Little pitchers have big ears,** adults should be careful what they say when children are around.

pitch•er[2] (pich′ər), *n.* **1.** a person who pitches. **2.** *Baseball.* the player who throws the ball to the opposing batter.

pitch′er plant′, *n.* any of various insectivorous bog plants of the family Sarraceniaceae, with hooded, pitcher-shaped leaves containing a liquid in which insects are trapped.

pitch•fork (pich′fôrk′), *n.* **1.** a large, long-handled fork for manually lifting and pitching hay, stalks of grain, etc. —*v.t.* **2.** to pitch or throw with or as if with a pitchfork.

pitch•man (pich′mən), *n., pl.* **-men. 1.** a person who makes a sales pitch, as on a radio or TV commercial. **2.** an itinerant vendor or hawker of small wares.

pitch•out (pich′out′), *n.* **1.** *Baseball.* a ball purposely thrown by a pitcher too far outside of the plate for the batter to hit, esp. in anticipation of an attempted steal by a base runner. **2.** *Football.* a lateral pass thrown behind the line of scrimmage by one back, esp. a T-formation quarterback, to another.

pit•e•ous (pit′ē əs), *adj.* evoking or deserving pity; pathetic. —**pit′e•ous•ly,** *adv.* —**pit′e•ous•ness,** *n.*

pit•fall (pit′fôl′), *n.* **1.** a lightly covered and unnoticeable pit prepared as a trap for people or animals. **2.** any trap or danger for the unwary.

pith (pith), *n.* **1.** the soft, spongy central cylinder of parenchymatous tissue in the stems of dicotyledonous plants. **2.** the soft inner part of a feather, a hair, etc. **3.** the important or essential part; core: *the pith of the matter.* **4.** substance; solidity: *an argument without pith.* —*v.t.* **5.** to remove the pith from (plants). **6.** to destroy the spinal cord or brain of. **7.** to slaughter, as cattle, by severing the spinal cord.

Pith•e•can•thro•pus (pith′i kan′thrə pəs, -kən thrō′pəs), *n.* a former genus of extinct hominids whose members have now been assigned to the proposed species *Homo erectus.*

Pi•thom (pī′thəm), *n.* one of the two cities built by Israelite slaves in Egypt. Ex. 1:11. Compare RAAMSES.

pith•y (pith′ē), *adj.,* **-i•er, -i•est. 1.** brief, forceful, and meaningful in expression; terse; forcible: *a pithy observation.* **2.** of, like, or abounding in pith. —**pith′i•ly,** *adv.* —**pith′i•ness,** *n.*

pit•i•a•ble (pit′ē ə bəl), *adj.* **1.** evoking or deserving pity; lamentable. **2.** evoking or deserving contemptuous pity; miserable; contemptible.

pit•i•ful (pit′i fəl), *adj.* **1.** evoking or deserving pity: *a pitiful fate.* **2.** arousing contempt by smallness, poor quality, etc.: *pitiful attempts.* —**pit′i•ful•ly,** *adv.*

pit•i•less (pit′i lis, pit′ē-), *adj.* feeling or showing no pity; merciless. —**pit′i•less•ly,** *adv.* —**pit′i•less•ness,** *n.*

pi•ton (pē′ton), *n.* a metal spike with an eye through which a rope may be passed: used in mountain climbing.

Pi′tot tube′, *n.* (*often l.c.*) an instrument for measuring fluid velocity, consisting of a narrow tube, one end of which is open and faces upstream, the other end being connected to a manometer. [after Henri *Pitot* (1695–1771), French physicist, who invented it]

pit′ stop′, *n.* **1.** a stop in a pit during an auto race. **2.** *Informal.* any brief stop, as during an automobile ride, to eat, rest, etc. **3.** a place where one makes such stops.

Pitt (pit), *n.* **1. William, 1st Earl of Chatham** (*"the Elder"*), 1708–78, British statesman. **2.** his son **William** (*"the Younger"*), 1759–1806, British prime minister 1783–1801, 1804–06.

pit•tance (pit′ns), *n.* **1.** a small amount or share. **2.** a small allowance of money. **3.** a scanty wage or remuneration.

pit•ter-pat•ter (pit′ər pat′ər), *n.* **1.** the sound of a rapid succession of light beats or taps, as of rain or footsteps. —*v.i.* **2.** to produce or move with this sound. —*adv.* **3.** with such a sound.

Pitts•burgh (pits′bûrg), *n.* a port in SW Pennsylvania, at the confluence of the Allegheny and Monongahela rivers that forms the Ohio River. 375,230.

Pitts•burgh (pits′bûrg), *n.* a port in SW Pennsylvania, at the confluence of the Allegheny and Monongahela rivers that forms the Ohio River. 358,883.

pi•tu•i•tar•y (pi tōō′i ter′ē, -tyōō′-), *n., pl.* **-tar•ies,** *adj.* —*n.* **1.** PITUITARY GLAND. **2.** a hormonal extract obtained from pituitary glands for use as a medicine. —*adj.* **3.** of, pertaining to, or involving the pituitary gland. **4.** noting an abnormal physical type resulting from excessive pituitary secretion.

pitu′itary gland′, *n.* a small, somewhat cherry-shaped double-lobed structure attached to the base of the brain, constituting the master endocrine gland affecting all hormonal functions of the body.

pit′ vi′per, *n.* any of various vipers, as the rattlesnake and copperhead, that have a heat-sensitive pit above each nostril.

pit•y (pit′ē), *n., pl.* **pit•ies,** *v.,* **pit•ied, pit•y•ing.** —*n.* **1.** sympathetic or kindly sorrow evoked by the suffering, distress, or misfortune of another, often leading one to give relief or aid or to show mercy. **2.** a cause or reason for pity, sorrow, or regret: *What a pity you couldn't go!* —*v.t.* **3.** to feel pity or compassion for; be sorry for; commiserate with. —*v.i.* **4.** to have compassion; feel pity. —***Idiom.*** **5. have** or **take pity,** to have compassion or show mercy. —**pit′y•ing•ly,** *adv.*

Pi•us (pī′əs), *n.* **1. Pius II,** (*Enea Silvio de Piccolomini*) 1405–64, Italian pope 1458–64. **2. Pius V, Saint** (*Michele Ghislieri*) 1504–72, Italian pope 1566–72. **3. Pius VII,** (*Luigi Barnaba Chiaramonti*) 1740–1823, Italian pope 1800–23. **4. Pius IX,** (*Giovanni Maria Mastai-Ferretti*) 1792–1878, Italian pope 1846–78. **5. Pius X, Saint** (*Giuseppe Sarto*) 1835–1914, Italian pope 1903–14. **6. Pius XI,** (*Achille Ratti*) 1857–1939, Italian pope 1922–39. **7. Pius XII,** (*Eugenio Pacelli*) 1876–1958, Italian pope 1939–58.

piv•ot (piv′ət), *n.* **1.** a pin, point, or short shaft on the end of which something rests and turns, or upon and around which something rotates or oscillates. **2.** the end of a shaft or arbor, resting and turning in a bearing. **3.** a person or thing on which something turns, hinges, or depends: *She was the pivot of the campaign's success.* **4.** the person in a line, as of troops on parade, whom the others use as a point around which to wheel or maneuver. **5.** a whirling around on one foot. **6.** *Basketball.* **a.** an offensive position in the front court, usu. played by the center, in which the player stands facing away from the offensive basket. **b.** the player who plays in the pivot position. —*v.i.* **7.** to turn on or as if on a pivot. —*v.t.* **8.** to mount on, attach by, or provide with a pivot or pivots.

piv•ot•al (piv′ə tl), *adj.* **1.** of, pertaining to, or serving as a pivot. **2.** of vital or critical importance. —**piv′ot•al•ly,** *adv.*

pix (piks), *n.* a pl. of PIC.

pix•el (pik′səl, -sel), *n.* the smallest element of an image that can be individually processed in a video display system.

pix•ie or **pix•y** (pik′sē), *n., pl.* **pix•ies,** *adj.* —*n.* **1.** a fairy or sprite, esp. a mischievous one. **2.** a playfully mischievous person. —*adj.* **3.** Also, **pix′ie•ish, pix′y•ish.** playfully impish or mischievous; prankish.

pix•i•lat•ed (pik′sə lā′tid), *adj.* **1.** slightly eccentric or mentally disordered. **2.** whimsical or prankish. —**pix′i•la′tion,** *n.*

pi•zazz or **piz•zazz** (pə zaz′), *n. Informal.* **1.** energy; vitality; vigor. **2.** attractive style; dash; flair. —**pi•zazz′y,** *adj.*

piz•za (pēt′sə), *n., pl.* **-zas.** a baked, open-faced pie consisting of a thin layer of dough topped with tomato sauce and cheese, and often peppers, sausage, mushrooms, etc. Also called **piz′za pie′.**

piz•ze•ri•a (pēt′sə rē′ə), *n., pl.* **-ri•as.** a restaurant or bakery where pizzas are made and sold.

piz•zi•ca•to (pit′si kä′tō), *adj., n., pl.* **-ti** (-tē). *Music.* —*adj.* **1.** played by plucking the strings with the finger instead of using the bow, as on a violin. —*n.* **2.** a note or passage so played.

piz•zle (piz′əl), *n.* **1.** the penis of an animal, esp. a bull. **2.** a whip made from a bull's pizzle.

pj's or **p.j.'s** or **P.J.'s** (pē′jāz′), *n.* (*used with a pl. v.*) *Informal.* PAJAMAS.

pk., *pl.* **pks. 1.** pack. **2.** park. **3.** peak.

pkg., *pl.* **pkgs.** package.

pkwy., parkway.

PL, Public Law: *PL #480.*

P/L, profit and loss.

plac•ard (plak′ärd, -ərd), *n.* **1.** a sign or notice, as one posted in a public place or carried by a demonstrator or picketer. —*v.t.* **2.** to display placards on or in. **3.** to publicize by means of placards. **4.** to post as a placard. —**plac′ard•er,** *n.*

pla•cate (plā′kāt, plak′āt), *v.t.,* **-cat•ed, -cat•ing.** to appease or pacify, esp. by concessions. —**pla′cat•er,** *n.* —**pla•ca′tion,** *n.* —**pla′ca•tive, pla′ca•to′ry** (-tôr′ē, -tōr′ē), *adj.*

place (plās), *n., v.,* **placed, plac•ing.** —*n.* **1.** a particular portion of space, whether of definite or indefinite extent. **2.** space in general: *time and place.* **3.** the portion of space normally occupied by a person or thing. **4.** any part of a body or surface; spot: *a decayed place in a tree.* **5.** a particular passage in a book or writing. **6.** a space or seat for a person, as in a theater or train. **7.** position, situation, or circumstances: *I would complain if I were in your place.* **8.** a proper or appropriate location, position, or time: *A restaurant is no place for an argument.* **9.** a job, post, or office: *persons in high places.* **10.** a function or duty: *It is not your place to offer criticism.* **11.** proper sequence or relationship, as of ideas or details. **12.** high position or rank. **13.** a region or area: *to travel to distant places.* **14.** an open space or square in a city or town. **15.** a short street or court. **16.** an area of habitation, as a city, town, or village. **17.** a building, location, etc., set aside for a specific purpose: *a place of worship.* **18.** a part of a building: *The kitchen is the sunniest place in the house.* **19.** a residence, dwelling, or house. **20.** lieu; substitution (usu. fol. by *of*): *Use yogurt in place of sour cream.* **21.** a step or point in order of proceeding: *in the first place.* **22.** *Arith.* **a.** the position of a figure in a series, as in decimal notation. **b.** Usu., **places.** the figures of the series. **23.** one of the three dramatic unities. Compare UNITY (def. 8). **24.** *Sports.* **a.** a position among the leading competitors, usu. the first, second, or third at the finish line. **b.** the position of the competitor who comes in second in a horse race. Compare SHOW (def. 26), WIN (def. 15). **25.** space for entry or passage: *to make place for the crowds.* —*v.t.* **26.** to put in the proper position or order; arrange; dispose: *Place the silverware on the table.* **27.** to put or set in a particular place. **28.** to put in a suitable place for some purpose: *to place an advertisement in the newspaper.* **29.** to put into particular or proper hands. **30.** to give (an order or the like) to a supplier. **31.** to appoint (a person) to a post or office. **32.** to find a place, situation, etc., for (a person). **33.** to determine or indicate the place of: *We place health high among our aims.* **34.** to assign a certain position or rank to. **35.** to identify by connecting with the proper place, circumstances, etc: *to place a face.* **36.** to employ (the voice) to sing or speak with resonant tones. —*v.i.* **37. a.** to finish among the first three competitors in a race. **b.** to finish second in a horse race. **38.** to earn a specified standing, as in an examination or competition: *He placed fifth in the class.* —**Idiom. 39. give place to, a.** to give precedence to. **b.** to be succeeded or replaced by. **40. go places,** to advance in one's career; succeed. **41. in place, a.** in the correct or usual position or order. **b.** in the same spot, without advancing or retreating: *to jog in place.* **42. know** or **keep one's place,** to behave according to one's position or rank, esp. if inferior. **43. out of place, a.** not in the correct or usual position or order. **b.** unsuitable; inappropriate. **44. place in the sun,** a favorable position; prominence. **45. put someone in his** or **her place,** to rebuke or belittle someone. —*Proverb.* **46. A place for everything and everything in its place,** everything should be neat and in proper order. —**place′a•ble,** *adj.*

pla•ce•bo (plə sē′bō for 1; plä chā′bō for 2), *n., pl.* **-bos, -boes. 1.** a substance having no pharmacological effect but given to placate a patient who supposes it to be a medicine. **2.** a pharmacologically inactive substance or a sham procedure administered as a control in testing the efficacy of a drug or course of action.

place•hold•er (plās′hōl′dər), *n.* a symbol in a mathematical or logical expression that may be replaced by the name of any element of the set.

place′ kick′, *n.* a kick in which a football is held nearly upright on the ground either by means of a tee or by a teammate, as in a kickoff. —**place′-kick′,** *v.t., v.i.* —**place′-kick′er,** *n.*

place′ mat′, *n.* a mat set on a dining table beneath a place setting.

place•ment (plās′mənt), *n.* **1.** the act of placing, as in a suitable job, grade, or school. **2.** the state of being placed. **3.** location; arrangement: *the placement of furniture.* **4.** (in sports) the placing or directing of a ball, regarded in terms of tactics or skill.

place′ name′ or **place′-name′,** *n.* the name of a geographical location, as a town, city, or village.

pla•cen•ta (plə sen′tə), *n., pl.* **-tas, -tae** (-tē). **1.** the organ in most mammals, formed in the lining of the uterus by the union of the uterine mucous membrane with the membranes of the fetus, that provides for the nourishment of the fetus and the elimination of its waste products. **2. a.** the part of the ovary of flowering plants that bears the ovules. **b.** (in ferns and related plants) the tissue giving rise to sporangia. —**pla•cen′tal, plac•en•tar•y** (plas′ən ter′ē, plə sen′tə rē), *adj.*

place′ set′ting, *n.* the group of dishes, silverware, glasses, etc., for one person at a meal.

plac•id (plas′id), *adj.* pleasantly calm or peaceful; tranquil. —**pla•cid•i•ty** (plə sid′i tē), **plac′id•ness,** *n.* —**plac′id•ly,** *adv.*

plack•et (plak′it), *n.* **1.** a slit, usu. with fastenings, at the neck, waist, or wrist of a garment for ease in putting it on or taking it off. **2.** a pocket, esp. one in a woman's skirt.

pla•gia•rism (plā′jə riz′əm, -jē ə riz′-), *n.* **1.** the unauthorized use of the language and thoughts of another author and the representation of them as one's own. **2.** something used and represented in this manner. —**pla′gia•rist,** *n.* —**pla′gia•ris′tic,** *adj.*

pla•gia•rize (plā′jə rīz′, -jē ə rīz′), *v.,* **-rized, -riz•ing.** —*v.t.* **1.** to take and use by plagiarism. **2.** to take and use ideas, passages, etc., from (another's work) by plagiarism. —*v.i.* **3.** to commit plagiarism.

plague (plāg), *n., v.,* **plagued, pla•guing.** —*n.* **1.** an epidemic disease that causes high mortality; pestilence. **2.** an infectious, epidemic disease caused by a bacterium, *Yersinia pestis,* characterized by fever, chills, and prostration, transmitted to humans from rats by means of the bites of fleas. Compare BUBONIC PLAGUE. **3.** any widespread affliction, calamity, or evil. **4.** any cause of trouble, annoyance, or vexation. —*v.t.* **5.** to trouble, annoy, or torment in any manner. **6.** to smite with a plague or pestilence. **7.** to cause an epidemic in or among. **8.** to afflict with any evil. —*Saying.* **9. A plague on both your houses,** may both of you be cursed. William Shakespeare, *Romeo and Juliet.* —**pla′guer,** *n.*

plaice (plās), *n., pl.* **plaice. 1.** a European flatfish, *Pleuronectes platessa,* used for food. **2.** any of various American flatfishes or flounders.

plaid (plad), *n.* **1.** any fabric woven of differently colored yarns in a cross-barred pattern. **2.** a long, rectangular piece of cloth, usu. with such a pattern and worn across the left shoulder by Scottish Highlanders. —*adj.* **3.** having the pattern of a plaid. Compare TARTAN.

plain (plān), *adj.,* **-er, -est,** *adv., n.* —*adj.* **1.** clear or distinct to the eye or ear: *in plain view.* **2.** clear to the mind; evident: *to make one's meaning plain.* **3.** easily understood: *plain talk.* **4.** downright; sheer; utter: *plain stupidity.* **5.** free from ambiguity or evasion; candid: *the plain truth.* **6.** without special pretensions; ordinary: *plain people.* **7.** not beautiful; unattractive: *a plain face.* **8.** without intricacies or difficulties. **9.** with little or no embellishment or decoration: *a plain blue suit.* **10.** without a pattern, figure, or device: *a plain fabric.* **11.** not rich, highly seasoned, or elaborately prepared, as food. **12.** flat or level: *plain coun-*

try. —*adv.* **13.** clearly and simply: *They're just plain stupid.* —*n.* **14.** an area of land not significantly higher than adjacent areas and with relatively minor differences in elevation, commonly less than 500 ft. (150 m), within the area. —**plain′ly,** *adv.* —**plain′ness,** *n.*

plain•clothes•man (plān′klōz′mən, -man′, -klōthz′-) also **plain′-clothes′ man′,** *n., pl.* **-men** (-mən, -men′). a police officer, esp. a detective, who wears civilian clothes while on duty.

plain′-Jane′ or **plain′-jane′,** *adj.* simple; ordinary.

Plain′ Peo′ple, *n.pl.* members of the Amish, the Mennonites, or the Dunkers: so named because they stress simple living.

plain′ sail′ing, *n.* an easy and unobstructed way, course, or plan.

Plains′ In′dian, *n.* a member of any of the American Indian peoples of the Great Plains who shared certain cultural features, including mounted hunting of bison and shifting residence in tepees.

plain•song (plān′sông′, -song′), *n.* the ancient traditional unisonal music of the Christian Church, having its form set and its use prescribed by ecclesiastical tradition.

plaint (plānt), *n.* **1.** a complaint. **2.** a lament; lamentation.

plain•tiff (plān′tif), *n.* one who brings a legal action or suit in a court (opposed to *defendant*). —**plain′tiff•ship′,** *n.*

plain•tive (plān′tiv), *adj.* expressing sorrow or melancholy; mournful: *a plaintive melody.* —**plain′tive•ly,** *adv.* —**plain′tive•ness,** *n.*

plain′-vanil′la, *adj.* having no embellishments; simple; basic.

plain′ weave′, *n.* the most common and important of the three basic weave structures, with each filling thread passing alternately over and under or under and over successive warp threads, producing a checkered surface. Compare SATIN WEAVE, TWILL WEAVE.

plain′-wo′ven, *adj.* constructed of plain weave: *plain-woven silk.*

plait (plāt, plat), *n.* **1.** a braid, esp. of hair or straw. **2.** a pleat or fold, as of cloth. —*v.t.* **3.** to braid, as hair or straw. **4.** to make, as a mat, by braiding. **5.** to pleat.

plait•ing (plā′ting, plat′ing), *n.* **1.** anything that is braided or pleated. **2.** plaits collectively.

plan (plan), *n., v.,* **planned, plan•ning.** —*n.* **1.** a scheme or method of acting, proceeding, etc., developed in advance: *a battle plan.* **2.** a design or arrangement: *a seating plan.* **3.** a specific project or definite goal: *plans for the future.* **4.** a drawing made to scale to represent the top view or a horizontal section of a structure or a machine, as a floor layout of a building. **5.** an outline, diagram, or sketch. **6.** (in perspective drawing) one of several planes in front of a represented object. **7.** a program for specified benefits, needs, etc.: *a pension plan.* —*v.t.* **8.** to formulate a plan or scheme for: *to plan a new park.* **9.** to make plans for: *to plan a vacation.* **10.** to draw or make a plan of, as a building. **11.** to have in mind as an intention. —*v.i.* **12.** to make plans: *to plan for retirement.* —**plan′ner,** *n.*

pla•nar (plā′nər), *adj.* **1.** of or pertaining to a geometric plane. **2.** flat or level. —**pla•nar•i•ty** (plə nâr′i tē), *n.*

pla•nar•i•an (plə nâr′ē ən), *n.* any of various free-swimming, mostly freshwater flatworms, having an undulating or sluglike motion.

planch•et (plan′chit), *n.* a blank metal disk for stamping as a coin.

plan•chette (plan shet′, -chet′), *n.* a small, heart-shaped board supported by two casters and a pencil or stylus that, when moved by the fingertips across a surface, supposedly writes clairvoyant messages or subconscious thoughts.

Planck's′ (or **Planck′**) **con′stant,** *n.* a unit used in quantum mechanics that equals the ratio of the energy of a quantum of radiation to the frequency of the radiation, approximately 6.626 × 10⁻³⁴ joule second. *Symbol:* h [after M.K.E. *Planck,* 1858–1947, German physicist]

plane¹ (plān), *n., adj., v.,* **planed, plan•ing.** —*n.* **1.** a flat or level surface. **2.** *Geom.* a surface generated by a straight line moving at a constant velocity with respect to a fixed point. **3.** an area of a two-dimensional surface having determinate extension and spatial direction or position: *horizontal plane.* **4.** a level of dignity, character, or the like: *a high moral plane.* **5. a.** an airplane or a hydroplane. **b.** a thin, flat or curved, extended section of an airplane or a hydroplane, affording a supporting surface. —*adj.* **6.** flat or level, as a surface. **7.** of or pertaining to planes or plane figures. —*v.i.* **8.** to glide or soar. **9.** (of a boat) to rise partly out of the water when moving at high speed. **10.** *Informal.* to fly or travel in an airplane.

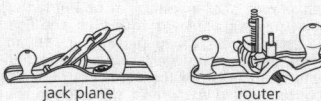

jack plane   router

plane¹

plane² (plān), *n., v.,* **planed, plan•ing.** —*n.* **1.** any of various woodworking instruments for paring, truing, or smoothing, or for forming moldings, chamfers, etc., by means of an inclined, adjustable blade moved along and against the piece being worked. —*v.t.* **2.** to smooth or dress with or as if with a plane or a planer. **3.** to remove by or as if by means of a plane (usu. fol. by *away* or *off*). —*v.i.* **4.** to work with a plane. **5.** to function as a plane.

plane′ geom′etry, *n.* the geometry of figures whose parts all lie in one plane.

plan•er (plā′nər), *n.* **1.** a machine for removing the rough or excess surface from a board. **2.** a machine for cutting flat surfaces, having a cutting tool supported by an overhead frame beneath which the work slides back and forth.

pla′ner tree′, *n.* a small swamp elm, *Planera aquatica,* of the southern U.S., bearing a small, ovoid, nutlike fruit.

plan•et (plan′it), *n.* **1. a.** any of the nine large heavenly bodies revolving about the sun and shining by reflected light: Mercury, Venus, Earth, Mars, Jupiter, Saturn, Uranus, Neptune, or Pluto in the order of their proximity to the sun. **b.** a similar body revolving about a star other than the sun. **c.** (formerly) a moving celestial body, as distinguished from a fixed star, applied also to the sun and moon. **2.** *Astrol.* any celestial body regarded as exerting an influence on human affairs. **3.** (*often cap.*) the planet Earth considered as a single ecosystem.

plan•e•tar•i•um (plan′i târ′ē əm), *n., pl.* **-tar•i•ums, -tar•i•a** (-târ′ē ə). **1.** an apparatus or model representing the planetary system. **2.** a device that produces a representation of the heavens by the use of a number of moving projectors. **3.** the building or room in which such a device is housed.

plan•e•tar•y (plan′i ter′ē), *adj.* **1.** of, pertaining to, or resembling a planet or the planets. **2.** wandering; erratic. **3.** terrestrial; global.

plan•e•tol•o•gy (plan′i tol′ə jē), *n.* the scientific study of the planets. —**plan′e•to•log′i•cal** (-tl oj′i kəl), *adj.* —**plan′e′tol′o•gist,** *n.*

plane′ tree′, *n.* any of several trees of the genus *Platanus,* esp. *P. occidentalis,* the North American sycamore.

planet X (eks), *n.* a hypothetical tenth planet beyond the orbit of Pluto.

plan•gent (plan′jənt), *adj.* resounding loudly, esp. with a plaintive sound, as a bell. —**plan′gen•cy,** *n.* —**plan′gent•ly,** *adv.*

plan•i•sphere (plan′ə sfēr′, plā′nə-), *n.* **1.** a map of half or more of the celestial sphere with a device for indicating the part of a given location visible at a given time. **2.** a projection or representation of the whole or a part of a sphere on a plane. —**plan′i•spher′i•cal** (-sfer′i-kəl), **plan′i•spher′ic, plan′i•spher′al,** *adj.*

plank (plangk), *n.* **1.** a long, flat piece of timber, thicker than a board. **2.** something to stand on or to cling to for support. **3.** any one of the principles or objectives that make up the platform of a political party. —*v.t.* **4.** to lay, cover, or furnish with planks. **5.** to bake or broil and serve (steak, fish, etc.) on a wooden board. **6.** PLUNK (def. 2).

plank•ton (plangk′tən), *n.* the aggregate of passively floating, drifting, or somewhat motile organisms occurring in a body of water, primarily comprising microscopic algae and protozoa. —**plank•ton′ic** (-ton′ik), *adj.*

planned′ obsoles′cence, *n.* the designing of products so that they will wear out or become outmoded in a few years.

Pla•no (plā′nō), *n.* a town in N Texas. 157,394.

plano- or **plani-,** a combining form meaning "flat," "plane": *planography.*

pla•no-con•cave (plā′nō kon kāv′, -kon′kāv), *adj.* pertaining to or noting a lens that is plane on one side and concave on the other.

pla•no-con•vex (plā′nō kon veks′, -kən-), *adj.* pertaining to or noting a lens that is plane on one side and convex on the other.

pla•nog•ra•phy (plə nog′rə fē), *n.* the art or technique of printing from a flat surface directly or by offset. —**pla•no•graph•ic** (plā′nə-graf′ik, plan′ə-), *adj.* —**pla′no•graph′i•cal•ly,** *adv.*

plant (plant, plänt), *n.* **1.** any member of the kingdom Plantae, comprising multicellular organisms that produce food from sunlight and inorganic matter by the process of photosynthesis and that have rigid cell walls containing cellulose, including the vascular plants, mosses, liverworts, and hornworts. **2.** an herb or other small vegetable growth, in contrast with a tree or a shrub. **3.** a seedling or a growing slip, esp. one ready for transplanting. **4.** a factory, workshop, etc., where a product is manufactured: *a steel plant.* **5.** the equipment, machinery, tools, etc., necessary to carry on any industrial business. **6.** the complete equipment or apparatus for a particular mechanical operation: *a heating plant.* **7.** the buildings, equipment, etc., of an institution: *the university plant.* **8.** a scheme to trap, trick, swindle, or defraud. **9.** a person or thing placed secretly or strategically, as to gather information, provoke responses, or advance a plot or scheme. —*v.t.* **10.** to put or set in the ground for growth, as seeds, shrubs, or young trees. **11.** to furnish or stock (land) with plants. **12.** to establish or implant (ideas, principles, etc.). **13.** to bed (oysters). **14.** to insert or set firmly in or on the ground: *to plant fence posts.* **15.** to place; put. **16.** to place or station with great force or determination: *He planted himself in the doorway.* **17.** to place (something) in order to advance a plot, obtain a desired result, etc.: *The police planted a story in the newspaper to trap the thief.* **18.** to place (a person) secretly in a situation, as to gather information or stir up reactions: *to plant a spy.* **19.** to hide or conceal, as stolen goods. **20.** to settle or found (a colony, city, etc.). —*v.i.* **21.** to plant crops, seeds, etc., esp. as an annual task. —**plant′a•ble,** *adj.*

Plan•tae (plan′tē), *n.* (*used with a pl. v.*) the taxonomic kingdom comprising all plants.

Plan•tag•e•net (plan taj′ə nit), *n.* a member of the royal house that ruled England from the accession of Henry II in 1154 to the death of Richard III in 1485.

plan•tain¹ (plan′tin, -tn), *n.* **1.** a tropical plant, *Musa paradisiaca,* of the banana family, resembling the banana. **2.** its fruit, cooked and eaten as a staple food in tropical regions.

plan•tain² (plan′tin, -tn), *n.* any of numerous plants of the genus *Plantago,* of the family Plantaginaceae, esp. *P. major,* a weed with large, spreading basal leaves and long spikes of small flowers.

plan′tain lil′y, *n.* any Japanese or Chinese plant of the genus *Hosta,* of the lily family, having large leaves and spikes or one-sided clusters of white, lilac, or blue flowers.

plan•tar (plan′tər), *adj.* of or pertaining to the sole of the foot.

plan•ta•tion (plan tā′shən), *n.* **1.** a usu. large farm or estate, esp. in a tropical or semitropical country, usu. worked by resident laborers: *a coffee plantation..* **2.** a group of planted trees or plants. **3.** a colony or new settlement.

plant′er's punch′, *n.* a punch made with rum, lime juice, sugar, and water or soda.

plan•ti•grade (plan′ti grād′), *adj.* **1.** walking on the entire sole of the foot, as humans and bears. —*n.* **2.** a plantigrade animal.

plant′ king′dom, *n.* **1.** PLANTAE. **2.** VEGETABLE KINGDOM.

plant•let (plant′lit, plänt′-), *n.* a little plant.

plant′ louse′, *n.* APHID.

plant′ pathol′ogy, *n.* the branch of botany dealing with diseases of plants. Also called **phytopathology.**

plaque (plak), *n.* **1.** a thin, flat plate or tablet of metal, porcelain, etc., intended for ornament, as on a wall, or set in a piece of furniture. **2.** an inscribed commemorative tablet, usu. of metal, placed on a building or monument. **3.** a platelike brooch or ornament, esp. one worn as a badge. **4. a.** a flat, often raised patch on any external or internal body surface. **b.** an abnormal hardened deposit on the inner wall of an artery. **5.** a soft, sticky, whitish film formed on tooth surfaces, composed of bacteria, mucin, and other matter. **6.** a clear area in a laboratory dish of a bacterial culture, indicating dead bacteria.

plasm-, var. of PLASMO- before a vowel: *plasmapheresis.*

-plasm, a combining form with the meanings "living substance," "tissue," "substance of a cell": *cytoplasm; neoplasm.*

plas•ma (plaz′mə), *n.* **1.** the fluid part of blood or lymph, as distinguished from the cellular components. **2.** PROTOPLASM. **3.** a green, faintly translucent chalcedony. **4.** a highly ionized gas containing an approximately equal number of positive ions and electrons. Also, **plasm** (plaz′əm) (for defs. 1, 2). —**plas•mat′ic** (-mat′ik), **plas′mic,** *adj.*

plas•ma•sphere (plaz′mə sfēr′), *n.* a region of cool plasma surrounding the earth, extending 8000–25,000 mi. (13,000–40,000 km) into space.

plasmo-, a combining form representing PLASMA or CYTOPLASM: *plasmolysis.* Also, *esp. before a vowel,* **plasm-.**

-plast, a combining form meaning "living substance," "organelle," "cell": *chloroplast; protoplast; spheroplast.*

plas•ter (plas′tər, plä′stər), *n.* **1.** a composition, as of lime or gypsum, sand, and water, applied in a pasty form to walls, ceilings, etc., and allowed to harden and dry. **2.** powdered gypsum. **3.** PLASTER OF PARIS. **4.** a solid or semisolid preparation spread upon cloth or other material and applied to the body, esp. for some healing purpose. —*v.t.* **5.** to cover, fill, or daub with plaster. **6.** to treat with gypsum or plaster of Paris. **7.** to lay flat (often fol. by *down*): *to plaster one's hair down.* **8.** to apply a plaster to (the body, a wound, etc.). **9.** to overspread with something, esp. thickly or excessively: *to plaster a wall with posters.* **10.** *Informal.* **a.** to defeat decisively. **b.** to knock down or injure. **c.** to inflict serious damage on, as by bombing. —**plas′ter•er,** *n.* —**plas′ter•y,** *adj.*

plas•ter•board (plas′tər bôrd′, -bōrd′, plä′stər-), *n.* a material used for insulating or covering walls, or as a lath, consisting of paper-covered sheets of gypsum and felt.

plas′ter cast′, *n.* any piece of sculpture reproduced in plaster of Paris.

plas′ter of Par′is (or **par′is**), *n.* calcined gypsum in white, powdery form, used as a base for gypsum plasters, as an additive of lime plasters, and as a material for making fine and ornamental casts.

plas•tic (plas′tik), *n.* **1.** any of a group of synthetic or natural organic materials that may be shaped when soft and then hardened, including many types of resins, polymers, cellulose derivatives, casein materials, and proteins. **2.** a credit card or cards. **3.** credit represented by the use of credit cards. **4.** an object or objects made of plastic. —*adj.* **5.** made of plastic. **6.** capable of being molded. **7.** produced by molding. **8.** having the power to mold or shape material: *the plastic forces of nature.* **9.** concerned with or pertaining to molding or modeling; sculptural. **10.** pliable; impressionable: *the plastic mind of youth.* **11.** artificial or synthetic. **12.** insincere; phony: *a plastic smile.* **13.** pertaining to the use of credit cards: *plastic credit.* **14.** *Mech.* able to deform continuously and permanently without rupturing. **15.** *Biol.* FORMATIVE (def. 3). **16.** of or pertaining to plastic surgery. [< Latin *plasticus* that may be molded < Greek *plastikós*] —**plas′ti•cal•ly, plas′tic•ly,** *adv.*

plas′tic art′, *n.* **1.** an art, as sculpture, in which forms are carved or modeled. **2.** an art, as painting or sculpture, in which forms are rendered in or as if in three dimensions.

plas′tic explo′sive, *n.* a mixture of TNT or RDX and a plasticizer that can be shaped by hand into an explosive charge.

plas•tic•i•ty (pla stis′i tē), *n.* **1.** the quality or state of being plastic. **2.** the capability of being molded: *the plasticity of clay.*

plas•ti•cize (plas′tə sīz′), *v.* **-cized, -ciz•ing.** —*v.t.* **1.** to make plastic. —*v.i.* **2.** to become plastic. —**plas′ti•ci•za′tion,** *n.*

plas•ti•ciz•er (plas′tə sī′zər), *n.* **1.** any of a group of substances that are used in plastics or other materials to impart viscosity, flexibility, softness, or other properties to the finished product. **2.** an admixture for making mortar or concrete workable with little water.

plas′tic sur′gery, *n.* the branch of surgery dealing with the repair, replacement, or reshaping of malformed, injured, or lost parts of the body. —**plas′tic sur′geon,** *n.*

plas′tic wrap′, *n.* a very thin, transparent sheet of plastic packaged in rolls and used to wrap and store food.

plas•tid (plas′tid), *n.* a small, double-membraned organelle of plant cells and certain protists, occurring in several varieties, as the chloroplast, and containing ribosomes, prokaryotic DNA, and, often, pigment.

plat (plat), *n., v.,* **plat•ted, plat•ting.** —*n.* **1.** a plot of ground. **2.** a plan or map, as of land. —*v.t.* **3.** to make a plat of.

plat du jour (plä′ də zho͝or′; *Fr.* plᴀ dʏ zho͞oʀ′), *n., pl.* **plats du jour** (pläz′ də zho͝or′; *Fr.* plᴀ dʏ zho͞oʀ′). a special dish offered by a restaurant on a particular day.

plate (plāt), *n., v.,* **plat•ed, plat•ing.** —*n.* **1.** a shallow, usu. circular dish from which food is eaten. **2.** the contents of such a dish; plateful. **3.** an entire course of a meal served on such a dish: *a vegetable plate.* **4.** the food and service for one person, as at a catered meal: *a benefit dinner at $100 a plate.* **5. a.** household dishes, utensils, etc., of metal plated with gold or silver. **b.** household dishes, utensils, etc., made of gold or silver. **6.** a dish used for collecting offerings, as in a church. **7.** a thin, flat sheet or piece of metal or other material, esp. of uniform thickness. **8.** metal in such sheets. **9.** a flat, polished piece of metal on which something may be or is engraved. **10.** LICENSE PLATE. **11.** a flat or curved sheet, usu. of metal, plastic, or glass, on which a picture or text has been engraved, etched, molded, photographically developed, or drawn, to be inked, as in a press, for printing impressions on other surfaces. **12.** a printed impression from such a piece or from some similar piece, as a woodcut. **13.** a full-page illustration in a book, esp. on paper different from the text pages. **14.** any of the flat metal pieces used in armor. **15. a.** the part of a denture that conforms to the mouth and contains the teeth. **b.** the entire denture. **16. the plate,** HOME PLATE. **17.** a sheet, usu. of glass or metal, coated with a sensitized emulsion, used for taking a photograph. **18.** *Anat., Zool.* a platelike part, structure, or organ. **19.** a cut of beef from the lower end of the ribs. **20.** any of a number of rigid sections of the earth's crust, movement of which gives rise to continental drift. **21.** one of the interior elements of a vacuum tube, toward which electrons are attracted by virtue of its positive charge; anode. **22.** a horizontal timber or board laid flat to support joists, rafters, or studs at or near their ends. **23.** a gold or silver cup or the like awarded as the prize in a horse race or some other contest. **24.** a horse race or some other contest for such a prize. —*v.t.* **25.** to coat (metal) with a thin film of gold, silver, nickel, etc., by mechanical or chemical means. **26.** to cover or overlay with metal plates for protection. **27.** to make a stereotype from (type). **28.** to give a high gloss to (paper), as on supercalendered paper. —***Idiom.*** **29. have on one's plate,** *Informal.* to have as an immediate obligation.

pla•teau (pla tō′; *esp. Brit.* plat′ō), *n., pl.* **-teaus, -teaux** (-tōz′, -tōz). **1.** a land area having a relatively level surface considerably raised above adjoining land on at least one side. **2.** a period or state of little or no growth or decline, esp. one in which increase or progress ceases: *to reach a plateau in one's career.* —*v.i.* **3.** to reach a state or level of little or no growth or decline; stabilize.

plate′ glass′, *n.* a soda-lime-silica glass formed by rolling the hot glass into a plate that is subsequently ground and polished and used in large windows, mirrors, etc.

plate•let (plāt′lit), *n.* a small platelike body, esp. a blood platelet.

plat•en (plat′n), *n.* **1.** a cylinder or flat plate in a printing press for pressing the paper against an inked surface to produce an impression. **2.** the roller of a typewriter or impact printer used for guiding paper through the device.

plate′ tecton′ics, *n.* a geologic theory that describes the earth's crust as divided into a number of rigid plates, movement of which accounts for such phenomena as continental drift and the distribution of earthquakes. —**plate′-tecton′ic,** *adj.*

plat•form (plat′fôrm), *n.* **1.** a horizontal surface, or a structure with a horizontal surface, usu. raised above the level of the surrounding area. **2.** a raised flooring or other horizontal surface for use as a stage. **3.** the raised area between or alongside the tracks of a railroad station, from which the cars of the train are entered. **4.** the open entrance area, or vestibule, at the end of a railroad passenger car. **5.** a public statement of the principles on which a person or group, esp. a political party, takes a stand in appealing to the public. **6.** a set of principles; plan. **7.** a place for public discussion; forum. **8.** a decklike construction on which the drill rig of an offshore oil or gas well is erected. **9.** a flat, elevated piece of ground. **10. a.** a thick insert of leather, cork, or other sturdy material between the uppers and the sole of a shoe. **b.** a shoe with this feature. **11. a.** HARDWARE PLATFORM. **b.** SOFTWARE PLATFORM.

plat′form ten′nis, *n.* a variation of tennis played on a wooden platform fenced with wire in which the players hit a rubber ball with wooden paddles.

plat•ing (plā′ting), *n.* **1.** a thin coating of gold, silver, etc. **2.** an external layer of metal plates. **3.** the act or process of a person or thing that plates.

plat•i•num (plat′n əm, plat′nəm), *n.* **1.** a heavy, grayish white, highly malleable and ductile metallic chemical element, resistant to most chemicals, practically unoxidizable except in the presence of bases, and fusible only at extremely high temperatures: used for making chemical and scientific apparatus, as a catalyst in the oxidation of ammonia to nitric acid, and in jewelry. *Symbol:* Pt; *at. wt.:* 195.09; *at. no.:* 78; *sp. gr.:* 21.5 at 20°C. **2.** a light, metallic gray with very slight bluish tinge when compared with silver. —*adj.* **3.** (of a recording, compact disc, or cassette) having sold a minimum of one million copies.

plat′inum blonde′ (or **blond′**), *n.* **1.** a person whose hair is a pale, silvery, often artificially colored blond. **2.** a pale blond or silver color.

plat•i•tude (plat′i to͞od′, -tyo͞od′), *n.* **1.** a dull or trite remark, esp. one uttered as if it were fresh or profound. **2.** the quality or state of being dull or trite.

plat•i•tu•di•nous (plat′i to͞od′n əs, -tyo͞od′-), *adj.* **1.** characterized by or given to platitudes. **2.** of the nature of or resembling a platitude. —**plat′i•tu′di•nous•ly,** *adv.* —**plat′i•tu′di•nous•ness,** *n.*

Pla•to (plā′tō), *n.* 427–347 B.C., Greek philosopher.

Pla•ton•ic (plə ton′ik, plā-), *adj.* **1.** of, pertaining to, or characteristic of Plato or Platonism. **2.** (*usu. l.c.*) of or pertaining to an intimate relationship between two persons that is characterized by the absence of sexual involvement: *platonic love.* **3.** (*usu. l.c.*) free from sensual desire; purely spiritual: *a platonic relationship.* —**Pla•ton′i•cal•ly,** *adv.*

Pla•to•nism (plāt′n iz′əm), *n.* **1.** the philosophy or doctrines of Plato or his followers. **2.** the belief that physical objects are impermanent representations of unchanging Ideas, and that the Ideas alone give true knowledge as they are known by the mind. **3.** (*sometimes l.c.*) the doctrine or practice of platonic love. —**Pla′to•nist,** *n., adj.*

pla•toon (plə to͞on′), *n.* **1.** a military unit consisting of two or more squads or sections and a headquarters. **2.** a small unit of a police force. **3.** a company or group: *a platoon of visitors.* **4.** *Football.* a group of players specially trained in one aspect of the game, as offense or defense. —*v.t.* **5.** *Sports.* **a.** to use (a player) at a position in a game alternately with another player. **b.** to alternate (two different teams or units). —*v.i.* **6.** *Sports.* **a.** to alternate at a position with another player. **b.** to use players alternately at the same position. **c.** to alternate different teams.

plat•ter (plat′ər), *n.* **1.** a large, shallow dish for holding and serving food. **2.** a course of a meal, usu. consisting of a variety of foods served on the same plate. **3.** a phonograph record.

plat•y[1] (plā′tē), *adj.,* **-i•er, -i•est.** (of an igneous rock) split into thin, flat sheets, often resembling strata, as a result of uneven cooling.

plat•y[2] (plat′ē), *n., pl.* (*esp. collectively*) **plat•y,** (*esp. for kinds or species*) **plat•ys, plat•ies.** PLATYFISH.

platy-, a combining form meaning "flat," "broad": *platyhelminth.*

plat•y•fish (plat′ē fish′), *n., pl.* (*esp. collectively*) **-fish,** (*esp. for kinds or species*) **-fish•es.** any of several small, yellow-gray freshwater fishes of the genus *Xiphophorus,* esp. the Mexican *X. variatus* of which home aquarium varieties occur in a range of colors.

plat•y•hel•minth (plat′i hel′minth), *n.* any of various unsegmented worms of the phylum Platyhelminthes, with a soft, flattened body, including the tapeworm, planarian, and trematode. Also called **flatworm.** —**plat′y•hel•min′thic,** *adj.*

plat•y•pus (plat′i pəs, -po͝os′), *n., pl.* **-pus•es, -pi** (-pī′). an aquatic, egg-laying monotreme, *Ornithorhynchus anatinus,* of Australia and Tasmania, having webbed feet, a broad, flat tail, and a ducklike bill. Also called **duckbill.**

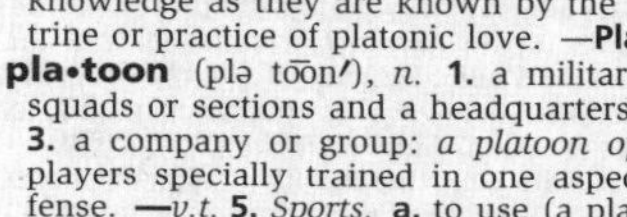

platypus, *Ornithorhynchus anatinus,* head and body 1 1/2 ft. (0.5 m); tail 6 in. (15 cm)

plau•dit (plô′dit), *n.* Usu., **plaudits. 1.** an enthusiastic expression of approval: *Her performance won the plaudits of the critics.* **2.** a demonstration or round of applause.

plau•si•ble (plô′zə bəl), *adj.* **1.** having an appearance of truth or reason; credible; believable: *a plausible excuse.* **2.** well-spoken and apparently worthy of confidence: *a plausible commentator.* —**plau′si•bil′i•ty, plau′si•ble•ness,** *n.* —**plau′si•bly,** *adv.*

play (plā), *n.* **1.** a dramatic composition; drama. **2.** a dramatic performance, as on the stage. **3.** activity, often spontaneous, engaged in for recreation, as by children. **4.** fun or jest, as opposed to earnest: *I said it merely in play.* **5.** a pun. **6.** the action or conduct of a game: *the fourth inning of play.* **7.** an act or instance of playing: *a play that cost us the match.* **8.** manner or style of playing. **9.** one's turn to play. **10.** a playing for stakes; gambling. **11.** an often crafty maneuver: *a takeover play.* **12.** an enterprise; venture. **13.** action of a specified kind: *fair play; foul play.* **14.** action, activity, or operation: *the play of fancy.* **15.** brisk, light, or changing movement or action: *the play of a water fountain.* **16.** elusive change: *the play of a searchlight against the night sky.* **17.** a space in which something, as a part of a mechanism, can move. **18.** freedom of movement within a space. **19.** freedom or scope for activity: *full play of the mind.* **20.** attention; coverage: *The scandal got a big play in the papers.* **21.** an act or instance of being broadcast. —*v.t.* **22.** to portray; enact: *to play Lady Macbeth.* **23.** to perform (a drama, pantomime, etc.). **24.** to act the part or character of in real life: *to play the*

P

fool; to play God. **25.** to act or sustain (a part): *Economics played an important part in the decision.* **26.** to give performances in: *to play the big cities.* **27.** to engage in (a game, pastime, etc.). **28.** to contend against in a game. **29.** to perform in (a specified position or role) in a game or competition: *to play center field.* **30.** to employ in a game: *I played my highest card.* **31.** to use as if in playing a game, esp. for one's own advantage: *He played his brothers against each other.* **32.** to stake or wager, as in a game. **33.** to lay a wager or wagers on (something). **34.** to represent or imitate, as for recreation: *to play cowboys and Indians.* **35.** to perform or be able to perform on (a musical instrument). **36.** to perform (music) on an instrument. **37.** to perform the music of (a composer). **38.** to cause to produce sound or pictures: *played the VCR.* **39.** to perform or carry out, esp. as a sly or deceitful action: *to play tricks.* **40.** to put into operation; act upon: *to play a hunch.* **41.** to cause to move or change lightly or quickly: *to play colored lights on a fountain.* **42.** to operate or cause to operate, esp. continuously or with repeated action: *to play a hose on a fire.* **43.** to allow (a hooked fish) to exhaust itself by pulling on the line. **44.** to display or feature (a news story, photograph, etc.), esp. prominently: *Play the flood photos on page one.* **45.** to exploit or trade in: *to play the stock market.* —*v.i.* **46.** to occupy oneself in diversion, amusement, or recreation. **47.** to do something that is not to be taken seriously; sport. **48.** to amuse oneself; toy; trifle (often fol. by *with*). **49.** to take part in a game. **50.** to take part in a game for stakes; gamble. **51.** to conduct oneself or act in a specified way: *to play fair.* **52.** to act on or as if on the stage; perform. **53.** to perform on a musical instrument. **54.** (of an instrument or music) to sound in performance. **55.** to give forth sound: *The radio played all night.* **56.** to be performed or shown: *What's playing at the theater?* **57.** to be capable of or suitable for performance, as a dramatic script. **58.** to be received; go over: *How will the proposal play with the public?* **59.** to move freely within a space, as a part of a mechanism. **60.** to move about lightly, quickly, or irregularly: *A smile played about her lips.* **61.** to operate continuously or with repeated action. **62.** to comply; cooperate. **63. play along, a.** to cooperate or concur. **b.** to pretend to cooperate or concur. **64. play around,** to behave in a playful or frivolous manner. **65. play at, a.** to pretend to do or be. **b.** to do without seriousness. **66. play back,** to play (a recording, esp. one newly made). **67. play down,** to treat as of little importance; minimize; belittle. **68. play off, a.** to play an extra game or round in order to settle a tie. **b.** to set (one person or thing) against another, usu. for one's own gain or advantage. **69. play on** or **upon,** to exploit the weaknesses of; take advantage of: *to play on someone's generosity.* **70. play out, a.** to bring to an end; finish. **b.** to use up; exhaust. **c.** to reel or pay out, as a rope or line. **71. play up,** to emphasize the importance of; highlight or publicize. **72. play up to,** to attempt to please or impress in order to gain the favor of. —***Idiom.*** **73. bring into play,** to cause to be introduced, considered, or used. **74. make a play for,** to employ stratagems to attract or gain. **75. play both ends against the middle,** to maneuver opposing groups in order to benefit oneself. **76. play cat and mouse with,** to toy with, as while waiting to strike. **77. play fast and loose with,** to behave cavalierly toward; deal irresponsibly with. **78. play for time,** to forestall an event or decision. **79. play into the hands of,** to act in such a way as to give an advantage to (someone, esp. an opponent). Also, **play into someone's hands. 80. play one's cards right** or **well,** to maneuver skillfully. **81. play the field,** to date a number of persons during the same period of time. **82. play with a full deck,** *Slang.* to be sane (used esp. in the negative). **83. play with fire,** to take risks by trifling with serious or dangerous matters. —***Saying.*** **84. But will it play in Peoria?** will it appeal to people in Middle America?

play•act (plā′akt′), *v.i.* **1.** to engage in make-believe. **2.** to be insincere or affected in speech, manner, etc. **3.** to perform in a play. —*v.t.* **4.** to dramatize; act out. —**play′act′ing,** *n.* —**play′ac′tor,** *n.*

play′-ac′tion pass′, *n. Football.* a pass play in which the quarterback fakes a hand-off to a back before throwing a forward pass.

play•back (plā′bak′), *n.* **1.** the act of reproducing a sound or video recording, esp. in order to check a recording that is newly made. **2.** the apparatus used in producing playbacks. **3.** response; feedback.

play•bill (plā′bil′), *n.* a program or announcement of a play.

play•book (plā′bo͝ok′), *n.* **1.** a book containing the scripts of one or more plays. **2.** a notebook containing descriptions and diagrams of the plays used by a football team.

play•boy (plā′boi′), *n.* a man who pursues a life of pleasure without responsibility or attachments.

play′-by-play′, *adj.* **1.** pertaining to or being a sequential account of each incident or act of an event, as in sports. —*n.* **2.** a detailed and sequential description of a sports contest or other event, usu. as it is taking place.

play′ date′ or **play′date′,** *n.* an appointment made by parents from separate families to have their young children play together.

play•er (plā′ər), *n.* **1.** a person or thing that plays. **2.** a person who takes part or is skilled in some game or sport. **3.** a person who plays parts on the stage; actor. **4.** a performer on a musical instrument. **5.** a sound- or image-reproducing machine: *a cassette tape player; a laserdisc player.* **6.** a participant, as in a business deal. **7.** a gambler. **8.** a mechanical or electrical device that actuates the playing mechanism of a musical instrument.

play′er pian′o, *n.* a piano using a mechanical player.

play•fel•low (plā′fel′ō), *n.* a playmate.

play•ful (plā′fəl), *adj.* **1.** full of play or fun; sportive; frolicsome. **2.** pleasantly humorous or jesting: *a playful remark.* —**play′ful•ly,** *adv.* —**play′ful•ness,** *n.*

play•girl (plā′gûrl′), *n.* a girl or woman who pursues a life of pleasure without responsibility or attachments.

play•go•er (plā′gō′ər), *n.* a person who attends the theater often or habitually.

play•ground (plā′ground′), *n.* **1.** an area used by children for outdoor recreation, usu. containing play equipment such as slides and swings. **2.** any popular recreation area, as a resort. **3.** the area or sphere of a particular activity.

play•group (plā′gro͞op′), *n.* a group of children, esp. preschoolers, organized for play.

play•house (plā′hous′), *n., pl.* **-hous•es** (-hou′ziz). **1.** THEATER (def. 1). **2.** a small house for children to play in.

play′ing card′, *n.* one of a set of cards used in playing various games, esp. one of a set of 52 numbered or ranked cards of four suits (diamonds, clubs, hearts, and spades).

play′ing field′, *n.* an expanse of level ground, as in a park or stadium, where athletic events are held.

play•list (plā′list′), *n.* a list or schedule of the recordings to be played on the radio during a particular program or time period.

play•mak•er (plā′mā′kər), *n.* an offensive player, as in basketball or ice hockey, who executes plays designed to put one or more teammates in a position to score. —**play′mak′ing,** *n.*

play•mate (plā′māt′), *n.* **1.** a companion, esp. of a child, in play or recreation. **2.** a social companion or lover.

play′-off′, *n. Sports.* **1.** an extra game, round, inning, etc., played in order to settle a tie. **2.** a series of games or matches, as between the leading teams of two leagues, played in order to decide a championship.

play′ on words′, *n.* a pun or the act of punning.

play•pen (plā′pen′), *n.* a small enclosure, usu. portable, in which a baby or young child can play.

play•room (plā′ro͞om′, -ro͝om′), *n.* a room set aside for recreation.

play•suit (plā′so͞ot′), *n.* an outfit consisting of shorts and a top, sometimes in one piece, worn by children as sportswear.

play•thing (plā′thing′), *n.* **1.** a thing to play with; toy. **2.** a person who is used capriciously and selfishly by another.

play•wright (plā′rīt′), *n.* a writer of plays; dramatist.

pla•za (plä′zə, plaz′ə), *n., pl.* **-zas. 1.** a public square or open space in a city or town. **2.** a complex of stores, banks, movie theaters, etc.; shopping center. **3.** an area along an expressway where public facilities, as service stations and rest rooms, are available.

plea (plē), *n., pl.* **pleas. 1.** an appeal or entreaty: *a plea for mercy.* **2.** something that is alleged, urged, or pleaded in defense or justification. **3.** an excuse; pretext: *He begged off on the plea that his car wasn't working.* **4. a.** an allegation made by, or on behalf of, a party to a legal suit, in support of his or her claim or defense. **b.** a defendant's answer to a legal declaration or charge. **c.** a plea of guilty.

plea′ bar′gaining, *n.* a practice in which a defendant in a criminal case is allowed to plead guilty to a lesser charge rather than risk conviction for a graver crime.

plead (plēd), *v.,* **plead•ed** or **pled, plead•ing.** —*v.i.* **1.** to appeal or entreat earnestly; beg: *to plead for time.* **2.** to use arguments or persuasions. **3.** to afford an argument or appeal: *His youth pleads for him.* **4. a.** to make any allegation or plea in an action at law. **b.** (of a defendant) to answer a charge. **c.** to address a court as an advocate. **d.** to prosecute a suit or action at law. —*v.t.* **5.** to allege or urge in defense, justification, or excuse: *to plead ignorance.* **6. a.** to argue (a cause) before a court. **b.** to allege formally in a court action. **c.** to allege or cite as a defense. —**plead′a•ble,** *adj.* —**plead′er,** *n.*

pleas•ant (plez′ənt), *adj.* **1.** pleasing, agreeable, or enjoyable; giving pleasure: *pleasant news.* **2.** (of persons, manners, disposition, etc.) socially acceptable or adept; amiable; agreeable; polite. **3.** fair, as weather: *a pleasant day.* —**pleas′ant•ly,** *adv.* —**pleas′ant•ness,** *n.*

pleas•ant•ry (plez′ən trē), *n., pl.* **-ries. 1.** good-humored teasing; banter. **2.** a humorous action or remark. **3.** a courteous remark used to facilitate a conversation.

please (plēz), *adv., v.,* **pleased, pleas•ing.** —*adv.* **1.** (used as a polite addition to requests, commands, etc.) if you would be so obliging; kindly: *Please come here.* —*v.t.* **2.** to give pleasure or gratification to: *to please the public.* **3.** to be the pleasure or will of: *May it please your Majesty.* —*v.i.* **4.** to like, wish, or feel inclined: *Go where you please.* **5.** to give pleasure or satisfaction; be agreeable: *manners that please.* —***Idiom.*** **6. if you please, a.** if it be your pleasure; if you like or wish. **b.** (used as an exclamation expressing astonishment, indignation, etc.)

pleas•ing (plē′zing), *adj.* giving pleasure; agreeable; gratifying. —**pleas′ing•ly,** *adv.* —**pleas′ing•ness,** *n.*

pleas•ur•a•ble (plezh′ər ə bəl), *adj.* such as to give pleasure; enjoyable; agreeable; pleasant: *a pleasurable experience.* —**pleas′ur•a•ble•ness,** *n.* —**pleas′ur•a•bly,** *adv.*

pleas•ure (plezh′ər), *n., v.,* **-ured, -ur•ing.** —*n.* **1.** enjoyment or satisfaction derived from something that is to one's liking; gratification; delight. **2.** a cause or source of enjoyment or delight: *It was a pleasure to see you.* **3.** worldly or frivolous enjoyment: *the pursuit of pleasure.* **4.** recreation or amusement: *to travel for pleasure.* **5.** sensual gratification. **6.** pleasurable quality. **7.** one's will or desire; preference: *to make* *known one's pleasure.* —*v.t.* **8.** to give pleasure to; gratify; please. —*v.i.* **9.** to take pleasure; delight (often fol. by *in*). **10.** to seek pleasure, as by taking a holiday. —**pleas′ure·ful,** *adj.* —**pleas′ure·less,** *adj.* —**pleas′ure·less·ly,** *adv.*

pleas′ure prin′ciple, *n. Psychoanal.* an automatic mental drive or instinct seeking to avoid pain and to obtain pleasure.

pleat (plēt), *n.* **1.** a fold of definite, even width made by doubling cloth or the like upon itself. **2.** something resembling this, as a crease or mark. —*v.t.* **3.** to arrange in pleats. —**pleat′er,** *n.* —**pleat′less,** *adj.*

pleb (pleb), *n.* a plebeian.

plebe (plēb), *n.* (at the U.S. Military and Naval academies) a member of the freshman class.

ple·be·ian (pli bē′ən), *adj.* **1.** of or pertaining to the common people. **2.** of or pertaining to the ancient Roman plebs. **3.** common, commonplace, or vulgar. —*n.* **4.** a member of the common people. **5.** a member of the ancient Roman plebs. —**ple·be′ian·ism,** *n.*

pleb·i·scite (pleb′ə sīt′, -sit), *n.* **1.** a direct vote of the qualified voters of a state in regard to some important public question. **2.** the vote by which the people of a political unit determine autonomy or affiliation with another country.

plebs (plebz), *n.pl.* **1.** the general body of citizens in ancient Rome; the common people. Compare PATRICIAN (def. 3). **2.** the common people; the general populace.

plec·trum (plek′trəm), *n., pl.* **-tra** (-trə), **-trums.** a small piece of rigid material, as plastic, ivory, or metal, used to pluck the strings of a musical instrument.

pled (pled), *v.* a pt. and pp. of PLEAD.

pledge (plej), *n., v.,* **pledged, pledg·ing.** —*n.* **1.** a solemn promise or agreement to do or refrain from doing something: *a pledge of aid.* **2.** something delivered as security for the payment of a debt or fulfillment of a promise. **3.** the state of being given or held as security. **4.** *Law.* **a.** the act of delivering goods, property, etc., to another for security. **b.** the resulting legal relationship. **5.** something given or regarded as an earnest or token, as of friendship or love. **6.** a person accepted for membership in a club, fraternity, or sorority, but not yet formally approved or initiated. **7.** an assurance of support or goodwill conveyed by drinking a person's health; toast. —*v.t.* **8.** to bind by or as if by a pledge: *to pledge hearers to secrecy.* **9.** to promise solemnly: *to pledge support.* **10.** to give or deposit as a pledge; pawn. **11.** to stake, as one's honor. **12.** to secure by a pledge; give a pledge for. **13.** to accept as a pledge for club, fraternity, or sorority membership. **14.** to drink a toast to. —*v.i.* **15.** to make or give a pledge. —*Idiom.* **16. take the pledge,** to make a vow to abstain from intoxicating drink. —**pledge′a·ble,** *adj.*

pledg·ee (plej ē′), *n.* a person to whom something is pledged.

Pledge′ of Alle′giance, *n.* a solemn oath of allegiance or fidelity to the U.S., beginning, "I pledge allegiance to the flag," and forming part of many flag-saluting ceremonies in the U.S.

-plegia, a combining form meaning "paralysis, cessation of motion" in the limbs or region of the body specified by the initial element: *quadriplegia.*

pleio-, var. of PLEO-.

Pleis·to·cene (plī′stə sēn′), *adj.* **1.** of or pertaining to the geologic epoch forming the earlier half of the Quaternary Period, beginning about two million years ago and ending ten thousand years ago, the time of the last Ice Age and the advent of modern humans. —*n.* **2.** the Pleistocene Epoch or Series.

ple·na·ry (plē′nə rē, plen′ə-), *adj., n., pl.* **-ries.** —*adj.* **1.** full; complete; entire; absolute; unqualified: *plenary powers.* **2.** attended by all qualified members; fully constituted: *a plenary session of Congress.* —*n.* **3.** a plenary session, meeting, or the like. —**ple′na·ri·ly,** *adv.*

ple′nary indul′gence, *n.* (in Roman Catholicism) a remission of all temporal punishment that is still due to sin after absolution.

ple·nip·o·tent (plə nip′ə tənt), *adj.* invested with or possessing full power.

plen·i·po·ten·ti·ar·y (plen′ə pə ten′shē er′ē, -shə rē), *n., pl.* **-ar·ies,** *adj.* —*n.* **1.** a person, esp. a diplomatic agent, invested with full power or authority to transact business on behalf of another. —*adj.* **2.** invested with full power or authority, as a diplomatic agent. **3.** conferring full power, as a commission.

plen·i·tude (plen′i tōōd′, -tyōōd′), *n.* **1.** fullness or adequacy; abundance: *a plenitude of food.* **2.** the state of being full or complete.

plen·te·ous (plen′tē əs), *adj.* **1.** plentiful; abundant. **2.** yielding abundantly; fruitful: *a plenteous harvest.* —**plen′te·ous·ly,** *adv.* —**plen′te·ous·ness,** *n.*

plen·ti·ful (plen′ti fəl), *adj.* existing or yielding in abundance. —**plen′ti·ful·ly,** *adv.* —**plen′ti·ful·ness,** *n.*

plen·ty (plen′tē), *n., pl.* **-ties,** *adj., adv.* —*n.* **1.** a full or abundant supply or amount: *There is plenty of time.* **2.** the state or quality of being plentiful; abundance: *resources in plenty.* **3.** an abundance, as of goods or luxuries, or a time of such abundance: *the years of plenty.* —*adj.* **4.** plentiful; abundant. **5.** more than sufficient; ample: *This helping is plenty for me.* —*adv.* **6.** *Informal.* fully; quite: *plenty good enough.*

ple·num (plē′nəm, plen′əm), *n., pl.* **ple·nums, ple·na** (plē′nə, plen′ə). **1. a.** the space in which a gas, usu. air, is contained at a pressure greater than atmospheric pressure. **b.** the gas in such a state. **2.** a full assembly, as a joint legislative assembly. **3.** a space serving as a receiving chamber for heated or cooled air.

pleo- or **pleio-,** or **plio-,** a combining form meaning "more": *pleomorphism.*

ple·on (plē′on), *n.* the abdomen of a crustacean. —**ple′on·al** (-ə nl), **ple·on′ic,** *adj.*

ple·o·nasm (plē′ə naz′əm), *n.* **1.** the use of more words than are necessary to express an idea; redundancy. **2.** an instance of this, as *free gift* or *true fact.* —**ple′o·nas′tic,** *adj.* —**ple′o·nas′ti·cal·ly,** *adv.*

ple·si·o·saur (plē′sē ə sôr′), *n.* any extinct marine reptile of the Jurassic and Cretaceous suborder Plesiosauroidea, having a thick body and paddlelike limbs. —**ple′si·o·sau′ri·an,** *adj.*

Plessy v. Ferguson (ples′ē; fûr′gə sən), *n.* a U.S. Supreme Court decision of 1896 that upheld segregation by declaring that the 13th Amendment of the Constituion only provided for a guarantee of political, not social, rights for blacks, thereby establishing the "separate but equal" doctrine.

pleth·o·ra (pleth′ər ə), *n.* **1.** overabundance; excess. **2.** a morbid condition due to excess of red corpuscles in the blood or increase in the quantity of blood.

ple·thor·ic (ple thôr′ik, -thor′-, pleth′ə rik), *adj.* **1.** turgid; overinflated: *a plethoric, pompous speech.* **2.** characterized by plethora. —**ple·thor′i·cal·ly,** *adv.*

pleu·ra (plŏŏr′ə), *n., pl.* **pleu·rae** (plŏŏr′ē). one of a pair of serous membranes each of which covers a lung and folds back to line the corresponding side of the chest wall.

pleu·ral (plŏŏr′əl), *adj.* of or pertaining to the pleura.

pleu·ri·sy (plŏŏr′ə sē), *n.* inflammation of the pleura, characterized by a dry cough and pain in the affected side. —**pleu·rit·ic** (plŏŏ rit′ik), *adj.*

pleuro-, a combining form meaning "side," "rib," "lateral," "pleura": *pleuropneumonia.* Also, *esp. before a vowel,* **pleur-.**

-plex, a combining form meaning "having parts or units" of the number specified by the initial element, occurring orig. in loanwords from Latin (*duplex; quadruplex*); recent English coinages ending in *-plex* are probably in part new formations with this suffix and in part based on the noun COMPLEX: *eightplex; Cineplex; Metroplex.*

Plex·i·glas (plek′si glas′, -gläs′), *Trademark.* a lightweight, transparent plastic material made from methyl methacrylate, used for signs, windows, and furniture.

plex·or (plek′sər) also **plessor,** *n.* a small hammer with a soft head, used in medicine for diagnostic percussion.

plex·us (plek′səs), *n., pl.* **-us·es, -us.** **1.** a network, as of nerves or blood vessels. **2.** any complex structure containing an intricate network of parts: *the plexus of international relations.* —**plex′al,** *adj.*

pli·a·ble (plī′ə bəl), *adj.* **1.** easily bent; flexible; supple. **2.** easily influenced or persuaded; yielding. **3.** adjusting readily; adaptable. —**pli′a·bil′i·ty, pli′a·ble·ness,** *n.* —**pli′a·bly,** *adv.*

pli·ant (plī′ənt), *adj.* **1.** pliable. **2.** having a variety of uses; adaptable. —**pli′an·cy, pli′ant·ness,** *n.* —**pli′ant·ly,** *adv.*

pli·cate (plī′kāt, -kit) also **pli′cat·ed,** *adj.* folded like a fan; pleated. —**pli′cate·ly,** *adv.* —**pli′cate·ness,** *n.*

pli·é (plē ā′), *n., pl.* **pli·és** (plē āz′; *Fr.* plē ā′). a ballet movement in which the knees are bent and the back is held straight.

pli·ers (plī′ərz), *n.* (*used with a sing. or pl. n.*) small pincers with long jaws, for bending wire, holding small objects, etc. (often used with *pair of*).

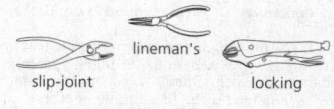

slip-joint   lineman's   locking

pliers

plight¹ (plīt), *n.* a distressing condition or situation: *in a sorry plight.*

plight² (plīt), *v.t.* **1.** to pledge (one's troth) in engagement to marry. **2.** to give in pledge, as one's word, or to pledge, as one's honor.

plink (plingk), *v.i.* **1.** to shoot, as with a rifle, at random targets. **2.** to make a series of short, light, ringing sounds. —*v.t.* **3.** to shoot at randomly, as with a rifle. **4.** to cause to make a series of short, light, ringing sounds. —*n.* **5.** a plinking sound. —**plink′er,** *n.*

plinth (plinth), *n.* **1.** a slablike member beneath the base of a column or pier. **2.** a square base or lower block, as of a pedestal. **3.** Also called **plinth′ course′.** a projecting course of stones at the base of a wall; earth table. **4.** a flat member at the bottom of an architrave, dado, baseboard, or the like. —**plinth′less,** *adj.*

Plin·y (plin′ē), *n.* **1.** ("the Elder," Gaius Plinius Secundus) A.D. 23–79, Roman naturalist and writer. **2.** his nephew ("the Younger," Gaius Plinius Caecilius Secundus) A.D. 62?–c113, Roman writer and orator.

Pli·o·cene (plī′ə sēn′), *adj.* **1.** noting or pertaining to an epoch of the Tertiary Period, occurring from ten million to two million years ago when mammalian life was proliferating and climatic cooling had begun. —*n.* **2.** the Pliocene Epoch or Series.

PLO, Palestine Liberation Organization.

plod (plod), *v.,* **plod·ded, plod·ding,** *n.* —*v.i.* **1.** to walk heavily or move laboriously; trudge. **2.** to proceed in a tediously slow manner. **3.** to work with steady and monotonous perseverance; drudge. —*v.t.* **4.** to walk heavily over or along. —*n.* **5.** the act or a course of plodding. **6.** a sound of a heavy tread. —**plod′der,** *n.* —**plod′ding•ly,** *adv.*

plop (plop), *v.*, **plopped, plop•ping,** *n.*, *adv.* —*v.i.* **1.** to make a sound like that of something falling or dropping into water. **2.** to fall with such a sound. **3.** to drop or fall with full force or direct impact: *to plop into a chair.* —*v.t.* **4.** to drop or set down heavily. —*n.* **5.** a plopping sound or fall. **6.** the act of plopping. —*adv.* **7.** with a plop.

plo•sion (plō′zhən), *n.* the release of the occlusive phase of a stop consonant, with the forced outward release of compressed air. Compare IMPLOSION (def. 2).

plo•sive (plō′siv), *adj.* **1.** of or pertaining to a consonant characterized by momentary complete closure at some part of the vocal tract causing stoppage of the flow of air, followed by sudden release of the compressed air. —*n.* **2.** a plosive consonant, as (p) or (d); stop.

plot (plot), *n.*, *v.*, **plot•ted, plot•ting.** —*n.* **1.** a secret plan or scheme to accomplish some purpose: *a plot to overthrow the government.* **2.** the main story of a literary or dramatic work. **3.** a small piece of ground: *a garden plot.* **4.** a measured parcel of land: *a two-acre plot.* **5.** GROUND PLAN (def. 1). —*v.t.* **6.** to plan secretly or conspiratorially: *to plot mutiny.* **7.** to mark on a plan, map, or chart, as the course of a ship or aircraft. **8.** to draw a plan or map of, as a tract of land or a building. **9.** to divide (land) into plots. **10. a.** to determine and mark (points), as on graph paper, by means of measurements or coordinates. **b.** to draw (a curve) by means of points so marked. **c.** to represent by means of such a curve. **d.** to make (a calculation) by graph. **11.** to devise or construct the plot of (a play, novel, etc.). —*v.i.* **12.** to plan or scheme secretly; conspire. **13.** to devise the plot of a literary work. —**plot′less,** *adj.*

plot•ter (plot′ər), *n.* **1.** a person or thing that plots. **2.** an instrument, as a protractor, for plotting lines and measuring angles on a chart. **3.** a type of computer printer that draws a graphical representation on paper with one or more attached pens.

plough (plou), *n.*, *v.t.*, *v.i.* *Chiefly Brit.* PLOW.

plov•er (pluv′ər, plō′vər), *n.* **1.** any of various shorebirds of the family Charadriidae, of worldwide distribution, having a thick neck, compact body, and a pigeonlike beak. **2.** any of various similar shorebirds.

plow (plou), *n.* **1.** an agricultural implement used for cutting, lifting, turning over, and partly pulverizing soil. **2.** any of various implements resembling or suggesting this, as a contrivance for clearing away snow from a road or track. **3.** (*cap.*) *Astron.* the Big Dipper. —*v.t.* **4.** to turn up (soil) with a plow. **5.** to make (a furrow) with a plow. **6.** to tear up, cut into, or make furrows or grooves in (a surface) with or as if with a plow (often fol. by *up*): *The tornado plowed up an acre of trees.* **7.** to clear by the use of a plow, esp. a snowplow. **8.** to reinvest or reutilize (usu. fol. by *back*): *to plow profits back into new equipment.* **9.** (of a ship, boat, animal, etc.) **a.** to cleave the surface of (the water). **b.** to make (a way) or follow (a course) in this manner: *plowing an easterly course.* —*v.i.* **10.** to till the soil or work with a plow. **11.** to take plowing in a specified way: *land that plows easily.* **12.** to move forcefully through something in the manner of a plow (often fol. by *through, along,* etc.): *to plow through a crowd; The car plowed into a tree.* **13.** to proceed laboriously (often fol. by *through*): *to plow through a pile of reports.* **14. plow under, a.** to bury under soil by plowing. **b.** to force out of existence; overwhelm. Also, *esp. Brit.*, **plough.** —**plow′a•ble,** *adj.* —**plow′a•bil′i•ty,** *n.* —**plow′er,** *n.*

plow•share (plou′shâr′), *n.* the cutting part of the moldboard of a plow; share.

ploy (ploi), *n.* a maneuver or stratagem to gain the advantage; ruse; subterfuge; gambit.

pluck (pluk), *v.t.* **1.** to pull off or out from the place of growth, as fruit, flowers, or feathers. **2.** to grasp or grab: *to pluck someone's sleeve.* **3.** to pull with sudden force or with a jerk. **4.** to pull or detach by force (often fol. by *away, off,* or *out*). **5.** to remove feathers or hair from by pulling: *to pluck a chicken.* **6.** *Slang.* to rob; cheat. **7.** to sound (the strings of a musical instrument) by pulling at them with the fingers or a plectrum. —*v.i.* **8.** to pull or tug sharply (often fol. by *at*). **9.** to snatch (often fol. by *at*). —*n.* **10.** the act of plucking; a tug. **11.** courage; resolution. —**pluck′er,** *n.*

pluck•y (pluk′ē), *adj.*, **-i•er, -i•est.** having or showing pluck; brave. —**pluck′i•ly,** *adv.* —**pluck′i•ness,** *n.*

plug (plug), *n.*, *v.*, **plugged, plug•ging.** —*n.* **1.** a piece of wood or other material used to stop up a hole or aperture. **2.** a core or interior segment taken from a larger matrix. **3.** an attachment at the end of an electrical cord that allows its insertion into an outlet or jack. **4.** SPARK PLUG (def. 1). **5.** fireplug; hydrant. **6.** a cake of pressed tobacco. **7.** the favorable mention of a product, performer, etc., as in a radio or television interview; advertisement. **8.** an artificial fishing lure made of wood, plastic, or metal and fitted with one or more gang hooks. **9.** *Geol.* NECK (def. 12). **10.** Also called **plug hat.** a man's tall, cylindrical hat, esp. a top hat. —*v.t.* **11.** to stop or fill with or as if with a plug (often fol. by *up*): *to plug up a leak.* **12.** to insert or drive a plug into. **13.** to secure with or as if with a plug. **14.** to remove a core or a small plug-shaped piece from, as for a sample: *to plug a watermelon.* **15.** to mention (a product or the like) favorably, as in a radio or television interview. **16.** *Slang.* to punch with the fist. **17.** *Slang.* to shoot or kill with a bullet. —*v.i.* **18.** to work with stubborn persistence (often fol. by *along* or *away*): *to plug away at a novel for years.* **19. plug in, a.** to connect to an electrical power source. **b.** to include; incorporate: *to plug in more data.* **20. plug into,** to connect (something) by means of a plug. **21. plug up,** to become plugged. —***Idiom.*** **22. pull the plug on,** *Informal.* **a.** to discontinue or terminate. **b.** to disconnect life-sustaining equipment from (a moribund patient).

Plug′ and Play′, *n.* (*sometimes l.c.*) a standard for the production of compatible computers, peripherals, and software that facilitates device installation and enables automatic configuration of the system.

plug′-compat′ible, *adj.* designating computers or peripherals that are compatible with another vendor's models and could replace them.

plug′-in′, *adj.* **1.** designed to be plugged into an electrical power source: *a plug-in hair dryer.* —*n.* **2.** PLUG (def. 3). **3.** JACK (def. 3). **4.** a plug-in appliance.

plum (plum), *n.*, *adj.*, **plum•mer, plum•mest.** —*n.* **1.** the drupaceous fruit of any of several trees belonging to the genus *Prunus,* of the rose family, having an oblong stone. **2.** the tree itself. **3.** any of various other trees bearing a plumlike fruit. **4.** the fruit itself. **5.** a sugarplum. **6.** a raisin, as in a cake or pudding. **7.** a deep purple varying from bluish to reddish. **8.** an excellent or desirable thing, as a rewarding job. —*adj.* **9.** extremely desirable or rewarding. —**plum′like′,** *adj.*

plum•age (plōō′mij), *n.* the entire feathery covering of a bird.

plumb (plum), *n.* **1.** a small mass of lead or other heavy material, as that suspended by a line and used to measure the depth of water or to ascertain a vertical line. Compare PLUMB LINE. —*adj.* **2.** true according to a plumb line; perpendicular. **3.** downright or absolute. —*adv.* **4.** in a perpendicular or vertical direction. **5.** exactly, precisely, or directly. **6.** completely or absolutely: *You're plumb right.* —*v.t.* **7.** to test or adjust by a plumb line. **8.** to make vertical. **9.** to sound with or as if with a plumb line. **10.** to measure (depth) by sounding. **11.** to examine closely: *to plumb the poem's meaning.* **12.** to seal with lead. **13.** to install plumbing in (a house, building, etc.). —*v.i.* **14.** to work as a plumber. —***Idiom.*** **15. out of** or **off plumb,** not corresponding to the perpendicular; out of true. Also, **plum** (for defs. 2–6). [< Latin *plumbum* lead] —**plumb′a•ble,** *adj.* —**plumb′less,** *adj.*

plum•ba•go (plum bā′gō), *n.*, *pl.* **-gos. 1.** GRAPHITE. **2.** a drawing made by an instrument with a lead point.

plumb′ bob′, *n.* PLUMMET (def. 1).

plumb•er (plum′ər), *n.* **1.** a person who installs and repairs piping, fixtures, and the like, in connection with the water supply, drainage systems, etc., of a house or other building. **2.** an undercover operative hired to detect or stop leaks of confidential information, often using questionable or illegal methods.

plumb′er's help′er, *n.* PLUNGER (def. 2). Also called **plumb′er's friend′.**

plumb•ing (plum′ing), *n.* **1.** the system of pipes and other apparatus for conveying water, liquid wastes, etc., as in a building. **2.** the work or trade of a plumber. **3.** the action of using a plumb.

plumb′ line′, *n.* a cord with a lead bob attached to one end, used to determine perpendicularity, the depth of water, etc. Compare PLUMB (def. 1).

plume (plōōm), *n.*, *v.*, **plumed, plum•ing.** —*n.* **1.** a large, long, or conspicuous feather. **2.** any feathery or plumelike part or formation. **3.** a feather or tuft of feathers worn as an ornament, token of honor or distinction, etc. **4.** PLUMAGE. **5.** a rising or expanding fluid body, as of smoke or water, with a plumelike shape. —*v.t.* **6.** to adorn with plumes. **7.** (of a bird) to preen (itself or its feathers). **8.** to feel complacent satisfaction with (oneself); pride (oneself) (often fol. by *on* or *upon*). —**plume′less,** *adj.* —**plume′like′,** *adj.*

plumed (plōōmd), *adj.* adorned with a plume or plumes.

plum•met (plum′it), *n.* **1.** the piece of lead or other weight attached to a plumb line; bob of a plumb line. —*v.i.* **2.** to fall straight or sharply down; plunge.

plum•my (plum′ē), *adj.*, **-mi•er, -mi•est. 1.** containing or resembling plums. **2.** highly desirable. **3.** richly resonant: *a plummy voice.*

plump[1] (plump), *adj.* **plump•er, plump•est. 1.** well filled out or rounded in form; fleshy or fat. —*v.i.* **2.** to become plump (often fol. by *up* or *out*). —*v.t.* **3.** to make plump (often fol. by *up* or *out*): *to plump up the sofa pillows.* —**plump′ly,** *adv.* —**plump′ness,** *n.*

plump[2] (plump), *v.i.* **1.** to drop or fall heavily or suddenly (often fol. by *down*): *to plump down on the sofa.* —*v.t.* **2.** to drop or throw heavily or suddenly (often fol. by *down*). **3. plump for,** to support enthusiastically: *to plump for the home team.* —*n.* **4.** a heavy or sudden fall. **5.** the sound of such a fall. —*adv.* **6.** with a heavy or sudden fall or drop. **7.** directly or bluntly. **8.** straight down. **9.** with direct impact. —*adj.* **10.** direct; downright; blunt.

plump•ish (plum′pish), *adj.* rather plump; tending to plumpness.

plum′ pud′ding, *n.* a rich pudding made with suet, raisins, citron, spices, etc., and steamed or boiled.

plum′ toma′to, *n.* an egg-shaped or oblong variety of tomato.

plum•y (plōō′mē), *adj.*, **plum•i•er, plum•i•est. 1.** having plumes or feathers. **2.** adorned with a plume or plumes: *a plumy helmet.* **3.** resembling a plume; feathery.

plun•der (plun′dər), *v.t.* **1.** to rob of goods or valuables by open force, as in war: *to plunder a town.* **2.** to rob or fleece: *to plunder the public treasury.* **3.** to take by pillage, robbery, or fraud. —*v.i.* **4.** to take plunder; pillage. —*n.* **5.** plundering or pillage. **6.** that which is taken in plundering; loot. **7.** anything taken by robbery, theft, or fraud. —**plun′der•a•ble,** *adj.* —**plun′der•er,** *n.* —**plun′der•ous,** *adj.*

plunge (plunj), *v.*, **plunged, plung•ing,** *n.* —*v.t.* **1.** to cast or thrust forcibly or suddenly into something: *to plunge a dagger into one's heart.* **2.** to bring suddenly or forcibly into some condition, situation, etc.: *to plunge a house into darkness.* —*v.i.* **3.** to cast oneself, or fall as if cast, into water, from a great height, etc.; plummet. **4.** to rush or dash with headlong haste: *to plunge through a crowd.* **5.** to bet or speculate recklessly. **6.** to throw oneself impetuously or abruptly into some condition or situation: *to plunge into debt.* **7.** to descend abruptly or precipitously, as a cliff or road. **8.** to pitch violently forward, as a ship. —*n.* **9.** the act of plunging. **10.** a leap or dive, as into water. **11.** a headlong or impetuous rush or dash. **12.** a sudden, violent pitching movement. —*Idiom.* **13. take the plunge,** to enter upon a course of action, esp. after hesitation.

plung•er (plun′jər), *n.* **1.** a pistonlike reciprocating part moving within the cylinder of a pump or hydraulic device. **2.** a device consisting of a handle with a rubber suction cup at one end, used as a force pump to free clogged drains and toilet traps. **3.** a person or thing that plunges. **4.** a reckless bettor or speculator.

plunk (plungk), *v.t.* **1.** PLUCK (def. 7). **2.** to throw, put, drop, etc., heavily or suddenly; plump (often fol. by *down*). **3.** to push, shove, toss, etc. (sometimes fol. by *in, over,* etc.): *to plunk the ball over the net.* —*v.i.* **4.** to give forth a twanging sound. **5.** to drop heavily or suddenly; plump (often fol. by *down*): *to plunk down somewhere and take a nap.* —*n.* **6.** the act or sound of plunking. **7.** a direct, forcible blow. —*adv.* **8.** with a plunking sound. **9.** squarely; exactly: *The ball landed plunk in the middle of the net.* —**plunk′er,** *n.*

plu•per•fect (ploo pûr′fikt), *adj.* **1.** PAST PERFECT (def. 1). **2.** more than perfect: *with pluperfect precision.* —*n.* **3.** PAST PERFECT (defs. 2, 3).

plu•ral (ploor′əl), *adj.* **1.** pertaining to or involving more than one. **2.** pertaining to or involving a plurality of persons or things. **3.** of or belonging to the grammatical category of number used to indicate that a word has more than one referent, as plural *children* or, in some languages more than two referents, as Old English *ge* "you." —*n.* **4.** the plural number. **5.** a word or other form in the plural. *Abbr.:* pl.

plu•ral•ism (ploor′ə liz′əm), *n.* **1.** (in philosophy) **a.** a theory that there is more than one basic substance or principle. **b.** a theory that reality consists of two or more independent elements. **2. a.** a condition in which minority groups participate fully in the dominant society, yet maintain their cultural differences. **b.** a doctrine that society benefits from such a condition. **3.** the holding by one person of two or more ecclesiastical offices at the same time. **4.** the state or quality of being plural. —**plu′ral•ist,** *n., adj.* —**plu′ral•is′tic,** *adj.*

plu•ral•i•ty (ploo ral′i tē), *n., pl.* **-ties. 1.** (in an election involving three or more candidates) the excess of votes received by the leading candidate over those received by the next candidate (disting. from *majority*). **2.** more than half of the whole; the majority. **3.** a number greater than one. **4.** the fact of being numerous. **5.** a large number; multitude. **6.** the state or fact of being plural.

plus (plus), *prep., adj., n., pl.* **plus•es** or **plus•ses,** *conj., adv.* —*prep.* **1.** increased by: *Ten plus two is twelve.* **2.** in addition to: *to have wealth plus fame.* —*adj.* **3.** involving or noting addition. **4.** positive: *on the plus side.* **5.** more or greater, as in relation to a certain amount or level: *A plus for effort.* **6.** pertaining to or characterized by positive electricity: *the plus terminal.* **7.** of a remarkable degree: *She has personality plus.* —*n.* **8.** a plus quantity. **9.** PLUS SIGN. **10.** something additional. **11.** a surplus or gain. —*conj.* **12.** also; furthermore: *It's safe plus it's economical.* —*adv.* **13.** in addition; besides.

plus′ fours′, *n.* (*used with a pl. v.*) long, baggy knickers for men, worn for golfing and other sports, esp. during the 1920s.

plush (plush), *n., adj.,* **-er, -est.** —*n.* **1.** a pile fabric whose pile is generally no less than ⅛ inch (0.3 cm) high. —*adj.* **2.** expensively or showily luxurious. **3.** abundantly rich; luxuriant: *plush lawns.* —**plush′like′,** *adj.* —**plush′ly,** *adv.* —**plush′ness,** *n.*

plush•y (plush′ē), *adj.,* **-i•er, -i•est. 1.** of, pertaining to, or resembling plush. **2.** characterized by luxury, wealth, or ease: *a plushy resort.* —**plush′i•ness,** *n.*

plus′ sign′, *n.* the symbol (+) indicating summation or a positive quality.

Plu•tarch (ploo′tärk), *n.* A.D. c46–c120, Greek biographer. —**Plu•tarch′i•an,** *adj.*

Plu•to (ploo′tō), *n.* **1.** HADES (def. 2). **2.** the planet ninth in order from the sun, having an equatorial diameter of about 1400 mi. (2250 km), a mean distance from the sun of 3.674 billion mi. (5.914 billion km), a period of revolution of 248.53 years, and one known moon.

plu•toc•ra•cy (ploo tok′rə sē), *n., pl.* **-cies. 1.** the rule or power of wealth or of the wealthy. **2.** a government or state in which the wealthy class rules. **3.** a class or group ruling, or exercising power or influence, by virtue of its wealth.

plu•to•ni•um (ploo tō′nē əm), *n.* a radioactive metallic transuranic element with a fissile isotope of mass number 239 that can be produced from nonfissile uranium 238. *Symbol:* Pu; *at. no.:* 94.

plu•vi•al (ploo′vē əl), *adj.* **1.** of or pertaining to rain, esp. much rain; rainy. **2.** occurring through or formed by the action of rain.

ply¹ (plī), *v.,* **plied, ply•ing.** —*v.t.* **1.** to work with diligently; employ busily; wield: *to ply the needle.* **2.** to carry on, practice, or pursue busily or steadily: *to ply a trade.* **3.** to assail repeatedly or persistently: *to ply horses with a whip.* **4.** to supply or offer something pressingly to: *to ply a person with drink.* **5.** to address persistently, as with questions; importune. **6.** to pass over or along (a river, stream, etc.) steadily or regu-

larly: *boats plying the Mississippi.* —*v.i.* **7.** to run or travel regularly over a fixed course or between certain places, as a boat or bus. **8.** to perform one's work or office busily or steadily: *to ply with the oars.*

ply² (plī), *n., pl.* **plies. 1.** a thickness or layer. **2.** a layer of reinforcing fabric for an automobile tire. **3.** a unit of yarn: *single ply.* **4.** one of the sheets of veneer glued together to make plywood. **5.** bent, bias, or inclination.

Plym•outh (plim′əth), *n.* **1.** a seaport in SW Devonshire, in SW England, on the English Channel: the departing point of the *Mayflower* 1620. 257,900. **2.** a city in SE Massachusetts: the oldest town in New England, founded by the Pilgrims 1620. 35,913.

Plym′outh Breth′ren, *n.* a loosely organized body of Christians founded in Plymouth, England, about 1830, having no ordained ministry, no formal creed or ritual, and accepting the Bible as the only guide.

Plym′outh Col′ony, *n.* the colony established in SE Massachusetts by the Pilgrims in 1620.

Plym′outh Rock′, *n.* **1.** a rock at Plymouth, Mass., on which the Pilgrims who sailed on the *Mayflower* are said to have stepped ashore when they landed in America in 1620. **2.** one of an American breed of medium-sized chickens, raised for meat and eggs.

ply•wood (plī′wŏŏd′), *n.* a building material consisting usu. of an odd number of wood veneers glued over each other, usu. at right angles.

Pm, *Chem. Symbol.* promethium.

P.M., 1. Past Master. **2.** Paymaster. **3.** Police Magistrate. **4.** Postmaster. **5.** postmortem. **6.** Prime Minister. **7.** Provost Marshal.

p.m. or **P.M., 1.** after noon. **2.** the period between noon and midnight. [< Latin *post merīdiem*] —**Usage.** See A.M.

P.M.G., Postmaster General.

PMS, premenstrual syndrome.

pmt., payment.

PN or **pn, 1.** please note. **2.** promissory note.

-pnea or **-pnoea,** a combining form meaning "breath, respiration," used esp. to form nouns denoting a kind of breathing or condition of the respiratory system, as specified by the initial element: *dyspnea; hyperpnea.*

pneu•mat•ic (nŏŏ mat′ik, nyŏŏ-), *adj.* **1.** of or pertaining to air, gases, or wind. **2.** of or pertaining to pneumatics. **3.** operated by air or by the pressure or exhaustion of air: *a pneumatic drill.* **4.** filled with or containing compressed air, as a tire. **5.** of or pertaining to the spirit; spiritual. **6.** having lungs or air cavities. —*n.* **7.** a pneumatic tire. —**pneu•mat′i•cal•ly,** *adv.* —**pneu•ma•tic′i•ty** (nŏŏ′mə tis′i tē, nyŏŏ′-), *n.*

pneu•mat•ics (nŏŏ mat′iks, nyŏŏ-), *n.* (*used with a sing. v.*) the branch of physics that deals with the mechanical properties of air and other gases.

pneumato-, a combining form meaning "air," "breath," "spirit": *pneumatology; pneumatophore.*

pneu•ma•tol•o•gy (nŏŏ′mə tol′ə jē, nyŏŏ′-), *n.* **1.** doctrine concerning the Holy Spirit. **2.** the doctrine or study of spiritual beings. —**pneu′mat•o•log′ic** (-mə tl oj′ik), **pneu′ma•to•log′i•cal,** *adj.*

pneumo-, a combining form meaning "lung," "thorax": *pneumograph.* Also, **pneumono-;** *esp. before a vowel,* **pneum-, pneumon-.**

pneu•mo•ba•cil•lus (nŏŏ′mō bə sil′əs, nyŏŏ′-), *n., pl.* **-cil•li** (-sil′ī). an enterobacterium, *Klebsiella pneumoniae,* that is a cause of pneumonia and urinary tract infection.

pneu•mo•coc•cus (nŏŏ′mə kok′əs, nyŏŏ′-), *n., pl.* **-coc•ci** (-kok′sī, -sē). a bacterium, *Streptococcus (Diplococcus) pneumoniae,* that invades the respiratory tract and is a major cause of pneumonia. —**pneu′mo•coc′cal** (-kok′əl), *adj.*

pneu•mo•cys′tis pneumo′nia (nŏŏ′mə sis′tis, nyŏŏ′-), *n.* a rare form of pulmonary infection caused by the protozoan *Pneumocystis carinii,* occurring as an opportunistic disease in persons with impaired immune systems, as persons with AIDS. *Abbr.:* PCP

pneumon-, var. of PNEUMO- before a vowel: *pneumonectomy.*

pneu•mo•nia (nŏŏ mōn′yə, -mō′nē ə, nyŏŏ-), *n.* **1.** inflammation of the lungs with congestion. **2.** an acute infection of the lungs caused by the bacterium *Streptococcus pneumoniae.*

pneu•mon•ic (nŏŏ mon′ik, nyŏŏ-), *adj.* **1.** of, pertaining to, or affecting the lungs; pulmonary. **2.** pertaining to or affected with pneumonia.

Po, *Chem. Symbol.* polonium.

P.O., 1. parole officer. **2.** petty officer. **3.** post office.

poach¹ (pōch), *v.i.* **1.** to trespass, as on another's game preserve, in order to steal or hunt animals. **2.** to take game or fish illegally. **3.** to encroach; trespass. **4.** (of land) to become broken up or slushy through trampling. **5.** to sink into wet ground. —*v.t.* **6.** to trespass on (private property), esp. in order to hunt or fish. **7.** to steal (game or fish) from another's property. **8.** to take without permission and use as one's own. **9.** to trample (wet ground).

poach² (pōch), *v.t.* to cook (eggs, fruit, etc.) in a hot liquid just below the boiling point.

poach•er¹ (pō′chər), *n.* a person who trespasses on private property, esp. to catch fish or game illegally.

poach•er² (pō′chər), *n.* **1.** a covered pan in which eggs are broken into metal cups and cooked over steam. **2.** a pan for simmering food.

POB, post-office box.

POC, port of call.

po•chard (pō′chərd, -kərd), *n., pl.* **-chards,** (*esp. collectively*) **-chard.**

any of various Old World diving ducks of the genus *Aythya*, esp. *A. ferina*, having a chestnut-red head.

pock (pok), *n.* **1.** a pustule on the body in an eruptive disease, as small-pox. **2.** a pockmark. **3.** a pit, hole, or the like.

pocked (pokt), *adj.* having pustules, pockmarks, or pits.

pock·et (pok′it), *n.* **1.** a shaped piece of fabric attached inside or out-side a garment and forming a pouch used esp. for carrying small arti-cles. **2.** means; financial resources: *gifts to suit every pocket.* **3.** a bag or pouch. **4.** any pouchlike receptacle, compartment, envelope, hollow, or cavity. **5.** an isolated group, area, or element contrasted with a sur-rounding element or group: *pockets of resistance.* **6.** a small orebody or mass of ore, frequently isolated. **7.** any of the pouches at the corners and sides of a pool table. **8.** a position in which a competitor in a race is so hemmed in by others that his or her progress is impeded. **9.** a re-cess, as in a wall, for receiving a sliding door, sash weights, etc. **10.** AIR POCKET. —*adj.* **11.** small enough for carrying in the pocket: *a pocket calculator.* **12.** relatively small; small-scale: *a pocket war.* —*v.t.* **13.** to put into one's pocket: *to pocket one's keys.* **14.** to take as one's own, often dishonestly; appropriate: *to pocket public funds.* **15.** to endure without protest: *to pocket an insult.* **16.** to conceal or suppress: *to pocket one's pride.* **17.** to enclose; confine; hem in or as if in a pocket: *The town was pocketed in a small valley.* **18.** to drive (a ball) into the pocket of a pool table. **19.** to retain (a legislative bill) without action and thus prevent from becoming a law. —*Idiom.* **20. in someone's pocket,** completely under someone's influence. **21. line one's pockets,** to profit, esp. at the expense of others. **22. out of pocket,** having suffered a financial loss.

pock′et bil′liards, *n.* POOL² (def. 1).

poc·ket·book (pok′it bŏŏk′), *n.* **1.** a woman's purse or handbag. **2.** a person's financial resources or means: *out of reach of my pocketbook.* **3.** Also, **pock′et book′.** a book, usu. paperback, that is small enough to carry in a coat pocket. **4.** *Chiefly Brit.* **a.** a notebook for carrying in one's pocket. **b.** a wallet or billfold.

pock′etbook is′sue, *n.* BREAD-AND-BUTTER ISSUE.

pock′et edi′tion, *n.* **1.** POCKETBOOK (def. 3). **2.** a small or smaller than usual form of something; miniature version.

pock′et go′pher, *n.* GOPHER¹.

pock′et-hand′kerchief, *n.* a handkerchief.

pock·et·knife (pok′it nīf′), *n., pl.* **-knives.** a knife with one or more blades that fold into the handle, suitable for carrying in the pocket.

pock′et mon′ey, *n.* money for small current expenses.

pock′et mouse′, *n.* any burrowing rodent of the family Heteromyi-dae, esp. of the genus *Perognathus*, of arid regions of W North America, having fur-lined cheek pouches and a long tail.

pock′et sec′retary, *n.* a long, narrow, walletlike case with compart-ments for credit and business cards, money, notepad, etc.

pock′et-size′ or **pock′et-sized′,** *adj.* small enough to fit in one's pocket.

pock′et ve′to, *n.* **1.** an automatic veto of a bill, occurring when Con-gress adjourns within the ten-day period allowed for presidential action on the bill and the president has retained it unsigned. **2.** a similar ac-tion on the part of any legislative executive. —**pock′et-ve′to,** *v.t.,* **-ve-toed, -ve·to·ing.**

pock·mark (pok′märk′), *n.* **1.** a scar or pit on the skin left by a pus-tule of smallpox, chickenpox, acne, etc. **2.** a small pit or scar resem-bling this. —*v.t.* **3.** to mark or scar with or as if with pockmarks.

pock·y (pok′ē), *adj.,* **-i·er, -i·est.** of, pertaining to, characterized by, or covered with pocks.

po·co (pō′kō), *adv. Music.* somewhat; rather: *poco presto.*

po·co a po·co (pō′kō ä pō′kō), *adv. Music.* gradually; little by little: *poco a poco accelerando.*

pod¹ (pod), *n., v.,* **pod·ded, pod·ding.** —*n.* **1.** an elongated seed vessel that splits easily along the sides at maturity, as that of the pea or bean. **2.** an insect egg case. **3.** a streamlined enclosure, housing, or detacha-ble container, esp. on an aircraft or other vehicle. —*v.i.* **4.** to produce pods. **5.** to swell out like a pod. —**pod/like′,** *adj.*

pod² (pod), *n.* a small herd or school, esp. of seals or whales.

pod³ (pod), *n.* the straight groove or channel in the body of certain au-gers or bits.

pod-, a combining form meaning "foot": *podiatry.* Also, *esp. before a consonant,* **podo-.**

-pod, a combining form meaning "one having a foot" of the kind or number specified by the initial element; often corresponding to New Latin class names ending in -PODA, with **-pod** used in English to name a member of such a class: *cephalopod.* Compare -PED.

P.O.D., **1.** pay on delivery. **2.** Post Office Department.

-poda, a combining form meaning "those having feet" of the kind or number specified by the initial element, used in the names of classes in zoology: *Cephalopoda.* Compare -POD.

-pode, var. of -POD or -PODIUM: *megapode.*

po·di·a·trist (pə dī′ə trist, pō-), *n.* a person qualified to diagnose and treat foot disorders. Also called **chiropodist.**

po·di·a·try (pə dī′ə trē, pō-), *n.* the care of the human foot, esp. the diagnosis and treatment of foot disorders. Also called **chiropody.**

po·di·um (pō′dē əm), *n., pl.* **-di·ums, -di·a** (-dē ə). **1.** a small plat-form for an orchestra conductor, speaker, etc. **2.** LECTERN (def. 2). **3. a.** a low wall or platform forming a base for a structure, as the masonry supporting the colonnade of a classical temple. **b.** a raised platform sur-

rounding the arena of a Roman amphitheater, forming the base of the seating area. **4.** *Anat.* a foot.

-podium, a combining form meaning "footlike appendage," "support," "stem": *monopodium.*

-podous, a combining form meaning "footed, having a foot" of the kind or number specified by the initial element; often occurring in adjectives corresponding to nouns ending in -POD: *gastropodous.*

pod·sol (pod′sol, -sôl) also **pod·zol** (-zol, -zôl), *n.* SPODOSOL. —**pod·sol′ic,** *adj.*

Poe (pō), *n.* Edgar Allan, 1809–49, U.S. short-story writer and poet.

POE, **1.** port of embarkation. **2.** port of entry.

po·em (pō′əm), *n.* **1.** a composition in verse, esp. one characterized by a highly developed form and the use of heightened language and rhythm to express an imaginative interpretation of the subject. **2.** some-thing having qualities that are suggestive of those of poetry.

po·e·sy (pō′ə sē, -zē), *n., pl.* **-sies.** *Literary.* poetry.

po·et (pō′it), *n.* **1.** one who writes poetry. **2.** one who displays imagi-nation and sensitivity along with eloquent expression.

po·et·as·ter (pō′it as′tər), *n.* an inferior poet; a writer of indifferent verse. —**po′et·as′ter·ing, po′et·as′ter·y,** *n.*

po·et·ic (pō et′ik), *adj.* Also, **po·et′i·cal.** **1.** of the nature of or resem-bling poetry; possessing the qualities of poems. **2.** pertaining to, charac-teristic of, or befitting a poet or poetry. **3.** having or showing the sensi-bility of a poet. **4.** of or pertaining to literature in verse form. —*n.* **5.** POETICS. —**po·et′i·cal·ly,** *adv.*

poet′ic jus′tice, *n.* an ideal or particularly fitting distribution of re-wards and punishments.

poet′ic li′cense, *n.* license or liberty, esp. as taken by a poet or other writer, in deviating from conventional form, logic, fact, etc., to produce a desired effect.

po·et·ics (pō et′iks), *n. (used with a sing. v.)* **1.** literary criticism treat-ing of the nature and laws of poetry. **2.** the study of prosody. **3.** a trea-tise on poetry.

po′et lau′reate, *n., pl.* **poets laureate. 1.** (in Great Britain) a poet appointed for life as an officer of the royal household. **2.** (in the U.S.) a poet appointed for a term as the national laureate poet.

po·et·ry (pō′i trē), *n.* **1.** literary work in metrical form; poetic works; poems; verse. **2.** the art of writing poems. **3.** prose with poetic quali-ties. **4.** poetic qualities however manifested. **5.** poetic spirit or feeling. **6.** something suggestive of poetry.

po′go stick′ or **po′go-stick′** (pō′gō), *n.* a long stick with footrests and a spring, used as a toy for leaping.

po·grom (pə grum′, -grom′, pō′grəm), *n.* an organized massacre, esp. of Jews. [< Russian *pogróm* lit., destruction]

poi (poi, pō′ē), *n.* a Hawaiian food made of taro root pounded into a paste.

poign·ant (poin′yənt, poi′nənt), *adj.* **1.** keenly distressing to the feelings. **2.** affecting or moving the emotions: *a poignant scene.* **3.** keen or strong in appeal; sharp; pointed: *a subject of poignant interest.* **4.** pungent to the smell. —**poign′an·cy,** *n.* —**poign′ant·ly,** *adv.*

poin·ci·an·a (poin′sē an′ə), *n., pl.* **-an·as.** any of several tropical leg-ume trees of the genus *Caesalpinia*, having showy red, orange, or yel-low flowers.

poin·set·ti·a (poin set′ē ə, -set′ə), *n., pl.* **-ti·as.** a plant, *Euphorbia pulcherrima*, of the spurge family, native to Mexico and Central Amer-ica, having variously lobed leaves and brilliant scarlet, pink, or white petallike bracts.

point (point), *n.* **1.** a sharp or tapering end, as of a dagger. **2.** a project-ing part of anything: *A point of land juts into the bay.* **3.** something having a sharp or tapering end (often used in combination): *a penpoint.* **4.** something that has position but not extension, as the intersection of two lines. **5.** See under DECIMAL FRACTION. **6.** a pointed tool or instru-ment, as an etching needle. **7.** any of 32 separate horizontal directions on a compass, 11° 15′ apart. **8.** a degree or stage: *frankness to the point of insult.* **9.** a particular instant of time. **10.** a critical position in a course of affairs. **11.** the important or essential thing: *the point of the matter.* **12.** an individual part or element of something: *noble points in her character.* **13.** a distinguishing mark or quality, esp. one of an ani-mal, used as a standard in stockbreeding, judging, etc. **14.** a stone im-plement with a tapering end found in some Middle and Upper Paleo-lithic and Mesolithic industries, used primarily for hunting. **15. points,** *Brit.* a railroad switch. **16.** a unit of count in the score of a game. **17. a.** the action of a hunting dog in locating game by direction of its head to-ward the game. **b.** such a position taken by a hunting dog. **18.** a branch of an antler of a deer: *an eight-point buck.* **19.** *Educ.* a credit hour. **20.** Also called **breaker point.** either of a pair of electrical con-tacts that make or break current flow in a distributor, as in an automo-bile. **21. a.** a unit of price quotation, as, in the U.S., one dollar in stock transactions. **b.** one percent of gross profits or of the face value of a loan, paid to an investor as compensation or by a borrower as a fee. **22.** *Jewelry.* a unit of weight equal to ¹/₁₀₀ of a carat. **23.** *Mil.* **a.** a patrol that goes ahead of the advance party, or, sometimes, follows the rear party. **b.** POINT MAN. **24.** *Print.* a unit of type measurement equal to 0. 013835 inch (¹/₇₂ inch), or ¹/₁₂ pica. **25.** one of the divisions of a heral-dic shield by which the position of a charge is determined. **26.** the act of pointing. —*v.t.* **27.** to direct (the finger, a weapon, the attention, etc.) at, to, or upon something. **28.** to indicate the presence or position of (usu. fol. by *out*): *to point out an object in the sky.* **29.** to direct attention to (usu. fol. by *out*): *to point out advantages.* **30.** to furnish with a point; sharpen. **31.** to mark with points, dots, or the like. **32.** to separate (figures) by dots or points (usu. fol. by *off*). **33.** to give greater or added force to (often fol. by *up*): *to point up the need for caution.* **34.** (of a hunting dog) to indicate the presence and location of (game) by standing rigid and facing toward the game. **35.** *Masonry.* to fill the joints of (brickwork, stonework, etc.) with new mortar or cement. —*v.i.* **36.** to indicate position or direction, as with the finger. **37.** to direct the mind or thought in some direction; call attention to: *Everything points to their guilt.* **38.** to aim. **39.** to have or signify a tendency toward something: *Conditions point to inflation.* **40.** (of a hunting dog) to point game. —*Idiom.* **41. beside the point,** irrelevant. **42. in point,** pertinent; applicable: *a case in point.* **43. in point of,** as regards; in reference to: *in point of fact.* **44. make a point of,** to regard as important; insist upon. **45. strain** or **stretch a point,** to make a concession or exception. **46. to the point,** relevant.

point′-blank′, *adj.* **1.** aimed or fired straight at the mark esp. from close range; direct. **2.** straightforward, plain, or explicit. —*adv.* **3.** with a direct aim; directly; straight. **4.** bluntly; frankly.

point′ count′, *n.* **1.** a method of evaluating a bridge hand by assigning values to high cards and certain distributions. **2.** the total of such points in a hand.

pointe (pwant), *n.* a ballet position with the body balanced on the extreme tip of the toe.

point•ed (poin′tid), *adj.* **1.** having a point or points. **2.** sharp or piercing: *pointed wit.* **3.** having direct significance; relevant. **4.** directed or aimed, as at a particular person: *a pointed remark.* **5.** marked; emphasized. —**point′ed•ly,** *adv.* —**point′ed•ness,** *n.*

point•er (poin′tər), *n.* **1.** a person or thing that points. **2.** a long, tapering stick used in pointing things out on a map, blackboard, or the like. **3.** the hand on a watch dial, clock face, scale, etc. **4.** one of a breed of large shorthaired hunting dogs that point game. **5.** a piece of advice, esp. on how to succeed in a specific area.

poin•til•lism (pwan′tl iz′əm, -tē iz′-, poin′tl iz′-), *n.* (*sometimes cap.*) a theory and technique developed by the neo-impressionists, based on the principle that juxtaposed dots of pure color, as blue and yellow, are optically mixed into the resulting hue, as green, by the viewer. —**poin′-til•list,** *n., adj.* —**poin′til•list′ic,** *adj.*

point•ing (poin′ting), *n.* (in masonry) mortar used as a finishing touch to brickwork.

point′ lace′, *n.* lace made with a needle rather than with bobbins; needlepoint lace. —**point′-laced′,** *adj.*

point•less (point′lis), *adj.* **1.** without relevance or force; meaningless; useless. **2.** without a point scored, as in a game. **3.** blunt, as an instrument. —**point′less•ly,** *adv.* —**point′less•ness,** *n.*

point′ man′, *n.* **1.** the lead soldier of an infantry patrol on combat operations. **2.** a person in the forefront of an economic or political issue.

point′ of hon′or, *n.* an issue that affects one's honor, reputation, etc.

point′ of no′ return′, *n.* **1.** the point in a flight at which an aircraft will lack sufficient fuel to return to its starting point. **2.** the critical point in an undertaking where one has committed oneself irrevocably to a course of action.

point′ of or′der, *n.* a question raised as to whether proceedings are in order, or in conformity with parliamentary law.

point′ of pur′chase, *n.* a retail outlet, mail-order house, or other place where an item can be purchased. *Abbr.:* POP, P.O.P. Also called **point′-of-pur′chase,** *adj.*

point′ of view′, *n.* **1.** a specified or stated manner of consideration or appraisal; standpoint. **2.** an opinion, attitude, or judgment. **3.** (in a literary work) the position of the narrator in relation to the story.

point′ source′, *n.* a source of radiation sufficiently distant compared to its length and width that it can be considered as a point.

point′ spread′, *n.* a betting device used to attract bettors for uneven competitions, indicating the estimated number of points by which a stronger team can be expected to defeat a weaker team.

point′ sys′tem, *n.* **1.** a system of promoting students on the basis of points representing their letter grades and credit hours. **2.** any of certain systems of writing and printing for the blind that employ embossed symbols for letters. **3.** *Print.* a system for grading the sizes of type bodies, leads, etc., that employs the point as a unit of measurement.

point•y (poin′tē), *adj.,* **-i•er, -i•est. 1.** having a comparatively sharp point. **2.** having numerous pointed parts.

poise (poiz), *v.,* **poised, pois•ing.** —*n.* **1.** a state of balance or equilibrium, as from equality or equal distribution of weight. **2.** a dignified, self-confident manner or bearing; composure; self-possession: *showed great poise in company.* **3.** steadiness; stability: *intellectual poise.* **4.** the way of being poised, held, or carried. **5.** the state or position of hovering. —*v.t.* **6.** to adjust, hold, or carry in equilibrium; balance evenly. **7.** to hold supported or raised, as in position for casting, using, etc. —*v.i.* **8.** to rest in equilibrium; be balanced. **9.** to hover, as a bird in the air.

poised (poizd), *adj.* **1.** composed, dignified, and self-assured. **2.** being in balance or equilibrium. **3.** hovering or suspended in or as if in midair: *a bird poised in flight.*

poi•son (poi′zən), *n.* **1.** a substance that has an inherent tendency to destroy life or impair health. **2.** something harmful, as to happiness or well-being. —*v.t.* **3.** to administer poison to (a person or animal). **4.** to kill or injure with or as if with poison. **5.** to put poison into or upon;

saturate with poison. **6.** to ruin, vitiate, or corrupt: *Hatred had poisoned their minds.* —*adj.* **7.** poisonous: *a poison shrub.* —**poi′son•er,** *n.*

poi′son gas′, *n.* any of various toxic gases, esp. those used in chemical warfare to kill or incapacitate on inhalation or contact.

poi′son hem′lock, *n.* HEMLOCK (defs. 1, 3).

poi′son i′vy, *n.* **1.** a vine or shrub, *Rhus radicans,* of the cashew family, with trifoliate leaves and whitish berries: may cause allergic dermatitis when touched. **2.** POISON OAK. **3.** the rash caused by touching poison ivy.

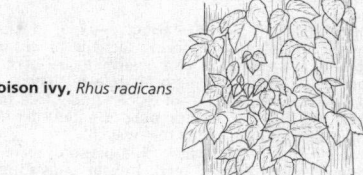

poison ivy, *Rhus radicans*

poi′son oak′, *n.* either of two North American shrubs of the cashew family, *Rhus toxicodendron,* of the eastern U.S., or *R. diversiloba,* of the Pacific coastal area, with leaves resembling those of poison ivy: may cause allergic dermatitis when touched.

poi•son•ous (poi′zə nəs), *adj.* **1.** full of or containing poison. **2.** deeply malicious; malevolent. —**poi′son•ous•ly,** *adv.* —**poi′son•ous•ness,** *n.*

poi′son-pen′, *adj.* composed or sent maliciously and usu. anonymously, as an anonymous letter.

poi′son pill′, *n.* a means of preventing a hostile takeover of a corporation, as by issuing a new class of stock or guaranteeing generous benefits to employees, which would be a burden to a buyer.

poi′son su′mac, *n.* a swamp shrub or small tree, *Rhus vernix,* of the cashew family, common in the eastern U.S., having pinnate leaves and pale green flower clusters: may cause allergic dermatitis when touched.

poke¹ (pōk), *v.,* **poked, pok•ing,** *n.* —*v.t.* **1.** to prod or push, esp. with something narrow or pointed. **2.** to make (a hole, one's way, etc.) by or as if by prodding or pushing. **3.** to thrust or push: *She poked her head out of the window.* **4.** to force, drive, or stir by or as if by pushing or thrusting: *to poke the fire up.* —*v.i.* **5.** to make a pushing or thrusting movement with the finger, a stick, etc. **6.** to extend or project (often fol. by *out*). **7.** to thrust oneself obtrusively. **8.** to search curiously; pry (often fol. by *around* or *about*). **9.** to go or proceed in a slow or aimless way (often fol. by *along*). —*n.* **10.** a thrust or push. **11.** SLOWPOKE. —*Idiom.* **12. poke fun at,** to ridicule or mock. **13. poke one's nose into,** to meddle in; pry into. —**pok′a•ble,** *adj.*

poke² (pōk), *n. Chiefly Midland U.S.* a bag or sack, esp. a small one.

poke³ (pōk), *n.* **1.** a projecting brim at the front of a bonnet, framing the face. **2.** Also called **poke′ bon′net.** a bonnet with such a brim.

poke•ber•ry (pōk′ber′ē, -bə rē), *n., pl.* **-ries. 1.** the berry of the pokeweed. **2.** the plant.

pok•er¹ (pō′kər), *n.* **1.** a person or thing that pokes. **2.** a metal rod for poking or stirring a fire.

pok•er² (pō′kər), *n.* a card game played by two or more persons, in which the players bet on the value of their hands, the winner taking the pool.

pok′er face′, *n.* a face that shows no emotion or intention. —**pok′er-faced′,** *adj.*

poke•weed (pōk′wēd′), *n.* a North American treelike plant, *Phytolacca americana,* of the pokeweed family, with edible shoots and juicy deep-purple berries in depressed round clusters. Also called **poke′root′** (-root′, -root′).

pok•ey (pō′kē), *adj.,* **-i•er, -i•est.** POKY¹.

pok•y¹ (pō′kē), *adj.,* **-i•er, -i•est. 1.** slow; dawdling. **2.** (of a place) small and cramped. —**pok′i•ness,** *n.*

pok•y² (pō′kē), *n., pl.* **pok•ies.** *Slang.* a jail.

pol (pol), *n. Informal.* a politician, esp. one experienced in making political deals.

Po•land (pō′lənd), *n.* a republic in E central Europe, on the Baltic Sea. 38,700,291; ab. 120,628 sq. mi. (312,683 sq. km). *Cap.:* Warsaw. Polish, Polska.

po•lar (pō′lər), *adj.* **1.** of or pertaining to the North or South Pole. **2.** of or pertaining to any pole, as of a sphere, a magnet, or an electric cell. **3.** opposite in character or action. **4.** capable of ionizing, as NaCl, HCl, or NaOH; electrolytic. **5.** central; pivotal. **6.** analogous to the polestar as a guide; guiding: *a polar precept.*

po′lar bear′, *n.* a large white bear, *Ursus (Thalarctos) maritimus,* of arctic regions.

po′lar front′, *n.* the variable frontal zone of middle latitudes separating air masses of polar and tropical origin.

Po•lar•is (pō lâr′is, -lar′-, pə-), *n.* the polestar or North Star, a star of the second magnitude situated close to the north pole of the heavens, in the constellation Ursa Minor: the outermost star in the handle of the Little Dipper.

po•lar•i•ty (pō lar′i tē, pə-), *n., pl.* **-ties. 1.** *Physics.* **a.** the property or characteristic that produces unequal physical effects at different points in a body or system, as a magnet or storage battery. **b.** the positive or negative state in which a body reacts to a magnetic, electric, or other field. **2.** the presence or manifestation of two opposite or contrasting principles or tendencies. **3.** *Ling.* the positive or negative character of a word or other item in a language.

po·lar·i·za·tion (pō′lər ə zā′shən), *n.* **1.** a sharp division, as of a population or group, into opposing factions. **2.** a state, or the production of a state, in which rays of light or similar radiation exhibit different properties in different directions. **3.** the induction of polarity in a ferromagnetic substance; magnetization. **4.** the production or acquisition of polarity.

po·lar·ize (pō′lə rīz′), *v.*, **-ized, -iz·ing.** —*v.t.* **1.** to cause polarization in. **2.** to divide into sharply opposing factions or groups: *The controversy has polarized voters.* **3.** to give polarity to. —*v.i.* **4.** to become polarized. —**po′lar·iz′a·ble,** *adj.* —**po·lar·iz·a·bil′i·ty,** *n.*

po·lar·ized (pō′lə rīzd′), *adj.* **1.** of or pertaining to a medium that exhibits polarization. **2.** (of an electric plug or outlet) designed so that the plug and outlet fit together in only one way.

Po·lar·oid (pō′lə roid′), *Trademark.* **1.** a brand of glare-reducing material that produces polarized light by dichroism, consisting typically of an iodine-treated sheet of clear plastic. **2.** the first brand of instant camera, developed by Edwin H. Land and marketed since 1948. **3.** a print made by such a camera.

Po′lar Re′gions, *n.pl.* the regions within the Arctic and Antarctic circles.

pole[1] (pōl), *n.*, *v.*, **poled, pol·ing.** —*n.* **1.** a long, cylindrical, often slender piece of wood, metal, etc. **2.** a long, tapering piece of wood or other material that extends from the front axle of a vehicle between the animals drawing it. **3.** the inside position on the front row of the starting line of a race. **4. a.** ROD (def. 4b). **b.** ROD (def. 4c). —*v.t.* **5.** to furnish with poles. **6.** to push, strike, or propel with a pole: *to pole a raft.* —*v.i.* **7.** to use a pole or poles, as to propel a boat or raft or push oneself on skis.

pole[2] (pōl), *n.* **1.** each of the extremities of the earth's axis or of any spherical body. **2.** one of two opposite or contrasted principles or tendencies. **3.** a point of concentration of interest, attention, etc. **4.** either of the two regions or parts of an electric battery, magnet, or the like, that exhibits electrical or magnetic polarity. **5.** *Cell Biol.* **a.** either end of an ideal axis in a nucleus, cell, or ovum, about which parts are more or less symmetrically arranged. **b.** either end of a spindle-shaped figure formed in a cell during mitosis. **c.** the place at which a cell extension or process begins, as a nerve cell axon or a flagellum. **6.** *Math.* ORIGIN (def. 6b). —*Idiom.* **7. poles apart,** having widely divergent or opposing attitudes, interests, etc.: *On political issues they are poles apart.*

Pole[1] (pōl), *n.* a native or inhabitant of Poland.

Pole[2] (pōl), *n.* **Reginald,** 1500–58, English cardinal and last Roman Catholic archbishop of Canterbury.

pole·ax (pōl′aks′), *n.*, *pl.* **-ax·es,** *v.* **1.** a medieval shafted weapon with blade combining ax, hammer, and apical spike, used for fighting on foot. —*v.t.* **2.** to strike down or kill with or as if with a poleax.

pole′ bean′, *n.* any vinelike variety of bean that is trained to grow upright on a pole, trellis, fence, etc.

pole·cat (pōl′kat′), *n.*, *pl.* **-cats,** (*esp. collectively*) **-cat. 1.** a European weasel, *Mustela putorius,* having blackish fur and ejecting a fetid fluid when attacked or disturbed. Compare FERRET[1] (def. 1). **2.** any of various North American skunks.

po·lem·ic (pə lem′ik, pō-), *n.* **1.** a controversial argument, as one against some opinion, doctrine, etc. **2.** a person who argues in opposition to another; controversialist. —*adj.* **3.** Also, **po·lem′i·cal.** of or pertaining to a controversy; controversial. —**po·lem′i·cal·ly,** *adv.*

po·lem·i·cize (pə lem′ə sīz′, pō-), *v.i.,* **-cized, -ciz·ing.** to practice the art of disputation; engage in polemics or controversy.

po·lem·ics (pə lem′iks, pō-), *n.* (*used with a sing. v.*) **1.** the art or practice of disputation or controversy. **2.** the branch of theology dealing with ecclesiastical disputation and controversy.

pol·e·mist (pol′ə mist, pə lem′ist, pō-), *n.* a person who is engaged or versed in polemics. Also, **po·lem·i·cist** (pə lem′ə sist, pō-).

po·len·ta (pō len′tə), *n.* a thick mush of cornmeal.

pole·star (pōl′stär′), *n.* **1.** POLARIS. **2.** something that serves as a guiding principle.

pole′ vault′, *n.* **1.** a field event in which a vault over a crossbar is performed with the aid of a long pole. **2.** a vault so performed. —**pole′vault′,** *v.i.* —**pole′-vault′er,** *n.*

po·lice (pə lēs′), *n.*, *v.*, **-liced, -lic·ing.** —*n.* **1.** an organized civil force for maintaining order, preventing and detecting crime, and enforcing the laws. **2.** (*used with a pl. v.*) members of such a force. **3.** the regulation and control of a community, esp. for the maintenance of public order, safety, health, etc. **4.** the department of a government concerned with this, esp. with the maintenance of order. **5.** any body of people employed to keep order, enforce regulations, etc. **6.** the cleaning and keeping clean of a military camp, post, etc. —*v.t.* **7.** to regulate, control, or keep in order by or as if by means of police. **8.** to clean and keep clean (a military camp, post, etc.).

police′ ac′tion, *n.* a localized military action undertaken by regular armed forces, without a formal declaration of war, against those who violate international peace and order.

police′ car′, *n.* SQUAD CAR.

police′ court′, *n.* an inferior court empowered to try persons accused of minor offenses and to hold those charged with more serious crimes for trial in superior court.

police′ dog′, *n.* **1.** a dog trained to assist the police. **2.** GERMAN SHEPHERD.

police′ force′, *n.* POLICE (def. 1).

po·lice·man (pə lēs′mən), *n., pl.* **-men.** a member of a police force.

police′ of′ficer, *n.* a policeman or policewoman.

po·lice·per·son (pə lēs′pûr′sən), *n.* a member of a police force.

police′ pow′er, *n.* the power of a nation to regulate the conduct of its citizens in the interest of the common good.

police′ proce′dural, *n.* a mystery novel, film, or television drama that deals realistically with police work. Also called **procedural.**

police′ report′er, *n.* a reporter assigned to gather news at a police department, precinct, etc.

police′ state′, *n.* a totalitarian state or country in which a national police force, esp. a secret police, suppresses any act that conflicts with government policy.

police′ sta′tion, *n.* the police headquarters for a particular district. Also called **station house.**

police′ wag′on, *n.* PADDY WAGON.

po·lice·wom·an (pə lēs′wŏŏm′ən), *n., pl.* **-wom·en.** a woman who is a member of a police force.

pol·i·cy[1] (pol′ə sē), *n., pl.* **-cies. 1.** a definite course of action adopted for the sake of expediency, facility, etc.: *a new company policy.* **2.** a course of action adopted and pursued by a government, ruler, political party, etc.: *U.S. trade policy.* **3.** action or procedure conforming to or considered with reference to prudence or expediency. **4.** prudence, practical wisdom, or expediency. **5.** government; polity.

pol·i·cy[2] (pol′ə sē), *n., pl.* **-cies. 1.** a document embodying a contract of insurance. **2.** a method of gambling in which bets are made on numbers to be drawn by lottery. **3.** NUMBERS POOL (def. 1).

pol·i·cy·hold·er (pol′ə sē hōl′dər), *n.* the individual or firm in whose name an insurance policy is written; an insured.

pol′icy wonk′, *n. Slang.* an obsessive student of public policy.

po·li·o (pō′lē ō′), *n.* poliomyelitis.

po·li·o·my·e·li·tis (pō′lē ō mī′ə lī′tis), *n.* an acute infectious disease of motor nerves of the spinal cord and brain stem, caused by a poliovirus and sometimes resulting in muscular atrophy and skeletal deformity: formerly epidemic in children and young adults, now controlled by vaccination.

po·li·o·vi·rus (pō′lē ō vī′rəs, pō′lē ō vī′-), *n., pl.* **-rus·es.** any of three picornaviruses of the genus *Enterovirus,* that cause poliomyelitis.

-polis, a combining form meaning "city" (*metropolis*), often used in the formation of place names (*Annapolis*).

pole vault (def.1)

pol·ish (pol′ish), *v.t.* **1.** to make smooth and glossy, esp. by rubbing or friction. **2.** to render finished, refined, or elegant: *to polish a speech.* —*v.i.* **3.** to become smooth and glossy through polishing. **4. polish off, a.** to finish or dispose of quickly: *to polish off a gallon of ice cream.* **b.** to subdue or get rid of (an enemy or opponent). **5. polish up,** to improve; refine. —*n.* **6.** a substance used to give smoothness or gloss: *shoe polish.* **7.** the act of polishing. **8.** the state of being polished. **9.** smoothness and gloss of surface. **10.** superiority of manner or execution; refinement; elegance. —**pol′ish·er,** *n.*

Po·lish (pō′lish), *n.* **1.** the West Slavic language of Poland. *Abbr.:* Pol —*adj.* **2.** of or pertaining to Poland, its inhabitants, or the language Polish.

pol·ished (pol′isht), *adj.* **1.** made smooth and glossy. **2.** naturally smooth and glossy. **3.** refined or elegant. **4.** flawless; expert: *a polished conversationalist.*

po·lite (pə līt′), *adj.,* **-lit·er, -lit·est. 1.** showing good manners toward others, as in behavior or speech; courteous: *a polite reply.* **2.** refined or cultured: *polite society.* **3.** of a refined or elegant kind: *polite learning.* —**po·lite′ly,** *adv.* —**po·lite′ness,** *n.*

pol·i·tesse (pol′i tes′, pô′lē-), *n.* formal politeness; courtesy. [< French]

pol·i·tic (pol′i tik), *adj.* **1.** shrewd or prudent in practical matters; tactful; diplomatic. **2.** contrived in a shrewd and practical way; expedient: *a politic reply.* **3.** political: *the body politic.* —**pol′i·tic·ly,** *adv.*

po·lit·i·cal (pə lit′i kəl), *adj.* **1.** of, pertaining to, or concerned with politics. **2.** exercising or seeking power in the governmental or public affairs of a state, municipality, etc.: *a political party.* **3.** of, pertaining to, or involving the state or its government. **4.** having a definite policy or system of government. **5.** of or pertaining to citizens: *political rights.* —**po·lit′i·cal·ly,** *adv.*

polit′ical an′imal, *n.* a human being, considered as a member of society.

polit′ical econ′omy, *n.* the science of economics.

polit′ically correct′, *adj.* marked by or adhering to a typically progressive orthodoxy on issues involving esp. race, gender, sexual affinity, or ecology. *Abbr.:* PC, P.C. —**polit′ical correct′ness,** *n.*

polit′ical pris′oner, *n.* a person who is imprisoned because of political beliefs or offenses.

polit′ical sci′ence, *n.* a social science dealing with political institutions and with the principles and conduct of government. —**polit′ical sci′entist,** *n.*

pol·i·ti·cian (pol′i tish′ən), *n.* **1.** a person who is active in politics, esp. as a career. **2.** a seeker or holder of public office. **3.** a person who uses public office to advance personal or partisan interests. **4.** a person who is skilled in politics.

po·lit·i·cize (pə lit′ə sīz′), *v.,* **-cized, -ciz·ing.** —*v.t.* **1.** to give a political character or bias to: *to politicize a religious debate.* —*v.i.* **2.** to engage in or discuss politics. —**po·lit′i·ci·za′tion,** *n.*

pol·i·tick·ing (pol′i tik′ing), *n.* activity undertaken for political reasons or ends, esp. campaigning for votes.

po·lit·i·co (pə lit′i kō′), *n., pl.* **-cos.** POLITICIAN.

pol·i·tics (pol′i tiks), *n.* (*used with a sing. or pl. v.*) **1.** the science or art of political government. **2.** the practice or profession of conducting political affairs. **3.** political affairs. **4.** political methods or maneuvers. **5.** political principles or opinions. **6.** the use of strategy or intrigue in obtaining power, control, or status. —*Idiom.* **7. above politics,** more concerned with the public interest than with partisan gain. **8. play politics, a.** to engage in political intrigue. **b.** to deal with people in an opportunistic or manipulative way, as for job advancement.

pol·i·ty (pol′i tē), *n., pl.* **-ties. 1.** a particular form or system of government: *civil polity; ecclesiastical polity.* **2.** a state or other organized community. **3.** the condition of being constituted as a state or other organized community. **4.** government or administrative regulation.

Polk (pōk), *n.* **James Knox,** 1795–1849, the 11th president of the U.S. 1845–49.

pol·ka (pōl′kə, pō′kə), *n., pl.* **-kas,** *v.,* **-kaed, -ka·ing.** —*n.* **1.** a lively couple dance of Bohemian origin, with music in duple meter. **2.** a piece of music for such a dance or in its rhythm. —*v.i.* **3.** to dance the polka. [< Czech: lit., Polish woman]

pol′ka dot′ (pō′kə), *n.* **1.** a dot or round spot repeated to form a pattern, esp. on a textile fabric. **2.** a pattern of such dots or something having such a pattern, as a fabric. —**pol′ka-dot′,** *adj.*

poll (pōl), *n.* **1.** a sampling or collection of opinions on a subject, taken from a selected or random group of persons, as for the purpose of analysis. **2.** the act of voting in an election. **3.** the registration of such votes. **4.** Usu. **polls.** the place where votes are cast. **5.** a list or enumeration of individuals, as for purposes of taxing or voting. **6.** the head, esp. the part of it on which the hair grows. **7.** the rear portion of the head of a horse; the nape. **8.** the part of the head between the ears of certain animals, as the horse and cow. —*v.t.* **9.** to take a sampling of the attitudes or opinions of. **10.** to receive at the polls, as votes. **11.** to enroll (someone) in a list or register, as for purposes of taxing or voting. **12.** to take or register the votes of (persons). **13.** to deposit or cast at the polls, as a vote. **14.** to bring to the polls, as voters. **15.** to cut short or cut off the hair, wool, etc., of (an animal) or the horns of (cattle). —*v.i.* **16.** to vote at the polls; cast one's vote. —**poll′er,** *n.*

pol·lack (pol′ək), *n., pl.* **-lacks,** (*esp. collectively*) **-lack.** POLLOCK (def. 2).

pol·lard (pol′ərd), *n.* **1.** a tree cut back nearly to the trunk, so as to produce a dense mass of branches. **2.** a hornless stag, ox, sheep, etc. —*v.t.* **3.** to make a pollard of.

pol·len (pol′ən), *n.* **1.** the fertilizing element of flowering plants, consisting of fine, powdery, yellowish grains or spores. —*v.t.* **2.** to pollinate. —**pol·lin·ic** (pə lin′ik), **pol·lin′i·cal,** *adj.*

pol′len count′, *n.* a count of the pollen in the air, based on the average number of pollen grains collected from the air in a given time.

pol·lex (pol′eks), *n., pl.* **pol·li·ces** (pol′ə sēz′). the innermost digit of the forelimb; thumb.

pol·li·nate (pol′ə nāt′), *v.t.,* **-nated, -nat·ing.** to convey pollen to the stigma of (a flower). —**pol′li·na′tion,** *n.* —**pol′li·na′tor,** *n.*

pol·li·wog or **pol·ly·wog** (pol′ē wog′), *n.* TADPOLE.

pol·lock (pol′ək), *n., pl.* **-locks,** (*esp. collectively*) **-lock. 1.** a greenish North Atlantic food fish, *Pollachius virens,* of the cod family, with a white lateral stripe and a jutting lower jaw. **2.** Also, **pollack.** a related, brownish food fish, *P. pollachius.*

Pol·lock (pol′ək), *n.* **Jackson,** 1912–56, U.S. painter.

poll·ster (pōl′stər), *n.* a person whose occupation is the taking of public-opinion polls.

poll′ tax′, *n.* a capitation tax, sometimes levied as a prerequisite for voting.

pol·lu·tant (pə loot′nt), *n.* **1.** something that pollutes. **2.** any substance, as a chemical or waste product, that renders the air, water, or other natural resource harmful or generally unusable.

pol·lute (pə loot′), *v.t.,* **-luted, -lut·ing. 1.** to make foul or unclean, esp. with harmful chemical or waste products; contaminate: *to pollute the air with smoke.* **2.** to make impure or morally unclean; defile; debase: *to pollute the mind.* —**pol·lut′er,** *n.*

pol·lut·ed (pə loo′tid), *adj.* made unclean or impure; contaminated; tainted. —**pol·lut′ed·ness,** *n.*

pol·lu·tion (pə loo′shən), *n.* **1.** the act of polluting or the state of being polluted. **2.** the introduction of harmful substances or products into the environment: *air pollution.*

Pol·lux (pol′əks), *n.* **1.** the brother of Castor. Compare CASTOR AND POLLUX. **2.** a first-magnitude star in the constellation Gemini.

Pol·ly·an·na (pol′ē an′ə), *n.* **1.** an excessively or blindly optimistic person. —*adj.* **2.** (*often l.c.*) Also, **Pol′ly·an′na·ish.** unreasonably or illogically optimistic: *some pollyanna notions about world peace.* [from the name of the child heroine created by Eleanor Porter (1868–1920), American writer] —**Pol′ly·an′na·ism,** *n.*

pol·ly·wog or **pol·li·wog** (pol′ē wog′), *n.* TADPOLE.

po·lo (pō′lō), *n., pl.* **-los. 1.** a game played on horseback between two teams of four players each, who score points by driving a wooden ball into the opponents' goal with a long-handled mallet. **2.** any game broadly resembling this, esp. water polo. **3.** POLO SHIRT. —**po′lo·ist,** *n.*

pol·o·naise (pol′ə nāz′, pō′lə-), *n.* **1.** a slow dance of Polish origin, in triple meter, consisting chiefly of a march or promenade in couples. **2.** a piece of music for, or in the rhythm of, such a dance. **3.** a fitted, low-necked, often elaborate outer dress with a cutaway overskirt draped at the hips, worn by women in the 18th century.

po·lo·ni·um (pə lō′nē əm), *n.* a radioactive chemical element discovered by Pierre and Marie Curie in 1898. *Symbol:* Po; *at. no.:* 84; *at. wt.:* about 210.

po′lo po′ny, *n.* a small, swift horse used in polo.

po′lo shirt′, *n.* a pullover sport shirt, usu. of cotton or cottonlike knit, with a round neckband or a turnover collar. Also called **polo.**

pol·ter·geist (pōl′tər gīst′), *n.* a ghost or spirit supposed to manifest its presence by noises, knockings, etc.

poly-, a combining form with the meanings "much, many" and, in the names of chemical compounds, "polymeric": *polyandry; polyethylene.*

pol·y·an·drous (pol′ē an′drəs), *adj.* **1.** of, pertaining to, characterized by, or practicing polyandry. **2.** having an indefinite number of stamens.

pol·y·an·dry (pol′ē an′drē, pol′ē an′-), *n.* **1.** the practice or condition of having more than one husband at one time. **2.** (among female animals) the habit of having two or more mates. **3.** *Bot.* the state of being polyandrous.

pol·y·an·thus (pol′ē an′thəs), *n., pl.* **-thus·es. 1.** any of various many-flowered primroses. **2.** a narcissus, *Narcissus tazetta,* having small white or yellow flowers.

Pol·y·carp (pol′ē kärp′), *n.* **Saint,** A.D. 69?–155, bishop of Smyrna and a Christian martyr.

pol·y·cen·trism (pol′ē sen′triz əm), *n.* the existence or advocacy of several independent centers of leadership, power, or ideology within a single political system, esp. in Communism. —**pol′y·cen′tric,** *adj.*

pol·y·chrome (pol′ē krōm′), *adj., v.,* **-chromed, -chrom·ing,** *n.* —*adj.* **1.** being of many or various colors. **2.** decorated or executed in many colors, as a statue, vase, or mural. —*v.t.* **3.** to paint in many or various colors. —*n.* **4.** a polychrome object or work.

pol·y·clin·ic (pol′ē klin′ik), *n.* a clinic or a hospital dealing with various diseases.

pol·y·es·ter (pol′ē es′tər, pol′ē es′tər), *n.* **1.** a polymer in which the monomer units are linked by the group –COO–, used in the manufacture of resins, plastics, and textile fibers. **2.** a fabric made of such textile fibers. —**pol′y·es′ter·i·fi·ca′tion** (-ə fi kā′shən), *n.*

pol·y·eth·yl·ene (pol′ē eth′ə lēn′), *n.* a plastic polymer of ethylene used chiefly for containers, electrical insulation, and packaging. Also, *Brit.,* **polythene.**

polyeth′ylene gly′col, *n.* any of a series of polymers of ethylene glycol, having a molecular weight from about 200 to 6000, used as an emulsifying agent and lubricant.

po·lyg·a·mous (pə lig′ə məs) also **pol·y·gam·ic** (pol′ē gam′ik), *adj.* **1.** practicing polygamy. **2.** *Bot.* bearing both unisexual and hermaphrodite flowers on the same plant or on different plants of the same species. —**po·lyg′a·mous·ly,** *adv.*

po·lyg·a·my (pə lig′ə mē), *n.* **1.** the practice or condition of having more than one spouse, esp. a wife, at one time. Compare BIGAMY, MONOGAMY (def. 1). **2.** *Zool.* the habit or system of mating with more than one individual, either simultaneously or successively. —**po·lyg′a·mist,** *n.* —**po·lyg′a·mis′tic,** *adj.*

pol·y·glot (pol′ē glot′), *adj.* **1.** able to speak or write several languages; multilingual. **2.** containing, composed of, or written in several languages. —*n.* **3.** a mixture or confusion of languages. **4.** a person who speaks, writes, or reads several languages. **5.** (*often cap.*) a book, esp. a Bible, containing the same text in several languages. —**pol′y‧glot′ism,** *n.*

pol‧y‧gon (pol′ē gon′), *n.* a figure, esp. a closed plane figure, having three or more, usu. straight, sides. —**po‧lyg‧o‧nal** (pə lig′ə nl), *adj.*

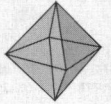 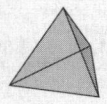 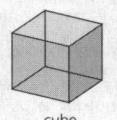 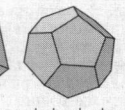

octahedron   tetrahedron   cube   icosahedron   dodecahedron

polygon

pol‧y‧graph (pol′i graf′, -gräf′), *n.* **1.** an instrument for receiving and recording simultaneously tracings of variations in certain body activities. **2.** LIE DETECTOR. **3.** a test using a lie detector to determine the subject's veracity. —*v.t.* **4.** to test (a person) with a polygraph. —**pol′y‧graph′ic** (-graf′ik), *adj.* —**po‧lyg‧ra‧phist** (pə lig′rə fist), **po‧lyg′ra‧pher,** *n.*

pol‧y‧he‧dron (pol′ē hē′drən), *n., pl.* **-drons, -dra** (-drə). a solid figure having many faces. —**pol′y‧he′dral,** *adj.*

pol‧y‧math (pol′ē math′), *n.* a person of great learning in several fields of study. —**pol′y‧math′ic,** *adj.* —**po‧lym‧a‧thy** (pə lim′ə thē), *n.*

pol‧y‧mer (pol′ə mər), *n.* a compound of high molecular weight derived either by the addition of many smaller molecules, as polyethylene, or by the condensation of many smaller molecules with the elimination of water, alcohol, or the like, as nylon. —**pol‧y‧mer‧ic** (pol′ə mer′ik), *adj.*

pol‧y‧morph (pol′ē môrf′), *n.* **1. a.** an organism that exists in different forms. **b.** one of the forms. **2.** any of the crystal forms assumed by a substance that exhibits polymorphism. —**pol′y‧mor′phic,** *adj.* —**pol′y‧mor′phi‧cal‧ly,** *adv.*

pol‧y‧mor‧phous (pol′ē môr′fəs), *adj.* having, assuming, or passing through many or various forms, stages, or the like; polymorphic.

Pol‧y‧ne‧sia (pol′ə nē′zhə, -shə), *n.* one of the three principal divisions of Oceania, comprising those island groups in the Pacific lying E of Melanesia and Micronesia and extending from the Hawaiian Islands S to New Zealand.

Pol‧y‧ne‧sian (pol′ə nē′zhən, -shən) *adj.* **1.** of or pertaining to Polynesia, its inhabitants, or their languages. —*n.* **2.** a member of any of the indigenous peoples of Polynesia. **3.** the languages of the Polynesians, constituting a relatively homogeneous subgroup within the Oceanic branch of the Austronesian family.

pol‧y‧no‧mi‧al (pol′ə nō′mē əl), *adj.* **1.** characterized by two or more names or terms. —*n.* **2.** an algebraic expression consisting of the sum of two or more terms. **3.** a polynomial name or term.

pol‧yp (pol′ip), *n.* **1.** the cylindrical body form in the life cycle of a jellyfish, sea anemone, or other cnidarian, having stinging tentacles around the mouth and usu. having the opposite end attached to a surface. Compare MEDUSA. **2.** the individual zooid of a colonial organism, as the bryozoan. **3.** a projecting growth from a mucous surface, as of the nose, being either a tumor or a hypertrophy of the mucous membrane. —**pol′yp‧ous,** *adj.*

pol‧y‧pep‧tide (pol′ē pep′tīd, -tid), *n.* a chain of amino acids linked together by peptide bonds and having a molecular weight of up to about 10,000.

Pol‧y‧phe‧mus (pol′ə fē′məs), *n.* a Cyclops who was blinded by Odysseus.

polyphe′mus moth′ (pol′ə fē′məs), a large, yellowish brown American moth, *Antheraea polyphemus,* having a prominent eyelike spot on each hind wing.

po‧lyph‧o‧ny (pə lif′ə nē), *n.* **1.** a musical technique or style in which two or more melodic lines are in equitable juxtaposition. **2.** representation of different sounds by the same letter or symbol. —**po‧lyph′o‧nous,** *adj.* —**po‧lyph′o‧nous‧ly,** *adv.*

pol‧yp‧ne‧a (pol′ip nē′ə), *n.* rapid breathing; panting.

pol‧y‧po‧dy (pol′ē pō′dē), *n., pl.* **-dies.** any of various evergreen ferns of the genus *Polypodium,* with branching rhizomes and deeply cleft fronds.

pol‧y‧pro‧pyl‧ene (pol′ē prō′pə lēn′), *n.* a plastic polymer of propylene, $(C_3H_6)_n$, used chiefly for molded parts, electrical insulation, packaging, and fibers for wearing apparel.

pol‧y‧sac‧cha‧ride (pol′ē sak′ə rīd′, -rid), *n.* a complex carbohydrate, as starch, inulin, or cellulose, formed by the combination of nine or more monosaccharides and capable of hydrolyzing to these simpler sugars. Also, **pol′y‧sac′cha‧rose′** (-rōs′).

pol‧y‧sty‧rene (pol′ē stī′rēn, -stēr′ēn), *n.* a polymer of styrene in the form of a clear plastic or stiff foam, used in molded objects and as an insulator in refrigerators and air conditioners.

pol‧y‧syl‧lab‧ic (pol′ē si lab′ik) also **pol′y‧syl‧lab′i‧cal,** *adj.* **1.** consisting of several, esp. four or more, syllables. **2.** characterized by polysyllabic words, as a language or piece of writing. —**pol′y‧syl‧lab′i‧cal‧ly,** *adv.*

pol‧y‧syn‧thet‧ic (pol′ē sin thet′ik) also **pol′y‧syn‧thet′i‧cal,** *adj.* (of a language) characterized by the use of long words containing a large number of affixes to express syntactic relationships and meanings,

as many American Indian languages. Compare ANALYTIC (def. 3), SYNTHETIC (def. 4).

pol‧y‧tech‧nic (pol′ē tek′nik), *adj.* **1.** of, pertaining to, or offering instruction in a variety of industrial arts, applied sciences, or technical subjects. —*n.* **2.** a school or other institution providing instruction in such subjects.

pol‧y‧the‧ism (pol′ē thē iz′əm, pol′ē thē′iz əm), *n.* the doctrine of or belief in more than one god or in many gods. —**pol′y‧the′ist,** *n., adj.* —**pol′y‧the‧is′tic,** *adj.* —**pol′y‧the‧is′ti‧cal‧ly,** *adv.*

pol‧y‧un‧sat‧u‧rate (pol′ē un sach′ər it, -ə rāt′), *n.* a polyunsaturated fat or fatty acid.

pol‧y‧un‧sat‧u‧rat‧ed (pol′ē un sach′ə rā′tid), *adj.* (of an organic compound) having many unsaturated double bonds: in vegetable oils associated with a low cholesterol content of the blood.

pol‧y‧u‧re‧thane (pol′ē yŏŏr′ə thān′) also **pol‧y‧u‧re‧than** (-than′), *n.* a thermoplastic polymer containing the group NHCOO, used for padding and insulation in furniture, clothing, and packaging, in spandex fibers, and in the manufacture of resins.

pom‧ace (pum′is, pom′-), *n.* the pulpy residue from fruit, seeds, or the like after crushing, as from apples in cider making.

po‧made (po mād′, -mäd′, pō-), *n., v.,* **-mad‧ed, -mad‧ing.** —*n.* **1.** a scented ointment, esp. for dressing the hair. —*v.t.* **2.** to dress with pomade; apply pomade to.

po‧man‧der (pō′man dər, pō man′dər), *n.* **1.** a mixture of aromatic substances, often in the form of a ball, formerly carried on the person as a supposed guard against infection but now placed for fragrance in closets, dressers, etc. **2.** an orange or apple stuck with cloves, used to impart fragrance to closets, dressers, etc.

pome (pōm), *n.* the characteristic fruit of the apple subfamily, as an apple, pear, or quince, in which the edible flesh arises from the greatly swollen receptacle and not from the carpels. —**pome′like′,** *adj.*

pome‧gran‧ate (pom′gran′it, pom′i-, pum′i′-), *n.* **1.** a round fruit with a leathery red rind, containing membranous chambers filled with a juicy, tart red pulp and white seeds. **2.** the small tree, *Punica granatum,* of the family Punicaceae, that bears this fruit.

pom‧e‧lo (pom′ə lō′), *n., pl.* **-los. 1.** the very large, yellow or orange citrus fruit of a tree, *Citrus maxima,* of SE Asia, closely related to the grapefruit. **2.** the tree itself. Also called **shaddock.**

pom‧mel (pum′əl, pom′-), *n., v.,* **-meled, -mel‧ing** or (*esp. Brit.*) **-melled, -mel‧ling.** —*n.* **1.** a knob, as on the hilt of a sword. **2.** the protuberant part at the front and top of a saddle. **3.** either of the two curved handles on the top surface of a pommel horse. —*v.t.* **4.** to beat or strike with or as if with the fists or a pommel.

pom′mel horse′, *n.* **1.** a padded, somewhat cylindrical, floor-supported gymnastic apparatus with two graspable pommels on top, used for hand-supported balancing and swinging maneuvers. **2.** the gymnastic competition involving this apparatus.

po‧mol‧o‧gy (pō mol′ə jē), *n.* the science that deals with fruits and fruit growing. —**po′mo‧log′i‧cal** (-mə loj′i kəl), *adj.* —**po‧mol′o‧gi‧cal‧ly,** *adv.* —**po‧mol′o‧gist,** *n.*

Po‧mo‧na (pə mō′nə), *n.* **1.** the Roman goddess of fruit. **2.** a city in SW California, E of Los Angeles. 143,870. **3.** Also called **Mainland.** the largest of the Orkney Islands, N of Scotland. 6502; 190 sq. mi. (490 sq. km).

pomp (pomp), *n.* **1.** stately or splendid display; splendor; magnificence. **2.** ostentatious or vain display, esp. of dignity or importance. **3. pomps,** pompous displays, actions, or things.

pom‧pa‧dour (pom′pə dôr′, -dōr′, -dŏŏr′), *n.* **1.** an arrangement of a man's hair in which it is brushed up high from the forehead. **2.** an arrangement of a woman's hair in which it is raised over the forehead and often the temples in a roll, sometimes over a pad. **3.** any fabric, as cotton or silk, having a design of small pink, blue, and sometimes gold flowers or bouquets on a white background. —**pom′pa‧doured′,** *adj.*

pom‧pa‧no (pom′pə nō′), *n., pl.* (*esp. collectively*) **-no,** (*esp. for kinds or species*) **-nos. 1.** a deep-bodied food fish, *Trachinotus carolinus,* inhabiting waters off the S Atlantic and Gulf states. **2.** a food fish, *Peprilus simillimus,* of California. **3.** COQUINA (def. 1).

Pom‧pei‧i (pom pā′, -pā′ē), *n.* an ancient city in SW Italy, on the Bay of Naples: buried along with Herculaneum by an eruption of nearby Mount Vesuvius in A.D. 79; much of the city has been excavated. —**Pom‧pe′ian, Pom‧pei′ian,** *adj., n.*

Pom‧pey (pom′pē), *n.* (*Gnaeus Pompeius Magnus*) ("*the Great*") 106–48 B.C., Roman general and statesman.

pom‧pom¹ or **pom-pom** (pom′pom′), *n.* an automatic, 40-millimeter antiaircraft gun, usu. mounted, esp. on ships, in groups of four.

pom‧pom² or **pom-pom** (pom′pom′), *n.* **1.** Also, **pompon.** an ornamental tuft or ball of feathers, wool, or the like, used esp. on clothing or waved at sporting events. **2.** POMPON (def. 2).

pom‧pon (pom′pon), *n.* **1.** POMPOM² (def. 1). **2.** a form of small, globe-shaped flower head that characterizes a type of flowering plant, esp. chrysanthemums and dahlias.

pom‧pos‧i‧ty (pom pos′i tē), *n., pl.* **-ties. 1.** the quality of being pompous. **2.** pompous flaunting of importance. **3.** an instance of being pompous, as by ostentatious loftiness of language or behavior. Also, **pomp′ous‧ness** (-pəs nis) (for defs. 1, 2).

pomp‧ous (pom′pəs), *adj.* **1.** characterized by an ostentatious display of dignity or importance. **2.** ostentatiously lofty or high-flown: *a pomp-*

ous speech. **3.** characterized by pomp or stately splendor. —**pomp′-ous•ly,** *adv.*

Ponce de Le•ón (pons′ də lē′ən, pon′sä dä lē ôn′), *n.* **Juan,** c1460–1521, Spanish explorer.

pon•cho (pon′chō), *n., pl.* **-chos. 1.** a blanketlike cloak with an opening in the center to admit the head, orig. worn in South America. **2.** a waterproof garment styled like this, worn as a raincoat. —**pon′choed,** *adj.*

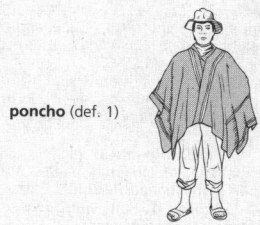

poncho (def. 1)

pond (pond), *n.* **1.** a body of water smaller than a lake, sometimes artificially formed, as by damming a stream. —*v.i.* **2.** (esp. of water) to collect into a pond or large puddle.

pon•der (pon′dər), *v.i.* **1.** to consider something deeply and thoroughly; meditate. —*v.t.* **2.** to weigh carefully in the mind; consider thoughtfully: *to ponder one's next move.* —**pon′der•er,** *n.*

pon•der•a•ble (pon′dər ə bəl), *adj.* **1.** worth serious consideration. **2.** having appreciable weight. —**pon′der•a•bil′i•ty,** *n.*

pon•der•o′sa pine′ (pon′də rō′sə, pon′-), *n.* **1.** a large pine, *Pinus ponderosa,* of W North America, having yellowish brown bark. **2.** the light, soft wood of this tree, used for making furniture and in the construction of houses, ships, etc.

pon•der•ous (pon′dər əs), *adj.* **1.** of great weight; heavy; massive: *a ponderous creature.* **2.** awkward or unwieldy. **3.** dull and labored: *a ponderous dissertation.* —**pon′der•ous•ly,** *adv.* —**pon′der•ous•ness,** **pon•der•os′i•ty** (-də ros′i tē), *n.*

pond′ lil′y, *n.* any of several water lilies, as the common water lily, *Nymphaea odorata.*

pond′ scum′, *n.* a mass of free-floating freshwater algae that forms a green scum on water.

pone (pōn), *n. South Midland and Southern U.S.* a loaf or oval-shaped cake of any type of bread, esp. corn bread.

pon•gid (pon′jid), *n.* any anthropoid ape of the family Pongidae, usu. comprising the gorilla, chimpanzee, and orangutan.

pons (ponz), *n., pl.* **pon•tes** (pon′tēz). **1.** a band of nerve fibers forming the part of the brainstem that lies between the medulla oblongata and the midbrain. **2.** any tissue connecting two parts of a body organ or structure.

pon•tiff (pon′tif), *n.* **1. a.** the Roman Catholic pope; the Bishop of Rome. **b.** a bishop. **2.** any high or chief priest.

pon•tif•i•cal (pon tif′i kəl), *adj.* **1.** of, pertaining to, or characteristic of a pontiff; papal. **2.** pompous, dogmatic, or pretentious. —*n.* **3. pontificals,** the vestments and other insignia of a pontiff, esp. a bishop. —**pon•tif′i•cal•ly,** *adv.*

pon•tif•i•cate (*v.* pon tif′i kāt′; *n.* -kit, -kāt′), *v.,* **-cat•ed, -cat•ing,** *n.* —*v.i.* **1.** to speak in a pompous or dogmatic manner. **2.** to discharge the duties of a pontiff. —*n.* **3.** the office or term of office of a pontiff.

Pon′tius Pi′late (pon′shəs, -tē əs), *n.* PILATE, Pontius.

pon•toon (pon tōōn′) also **pon•ton** (pon′tn), *n.* **1.** a boat or some other floating structure used as one of the supports for a temporary bridge over a river. **2.** a float for a derrick, landing stage, etc. **3.** a seaplane float.

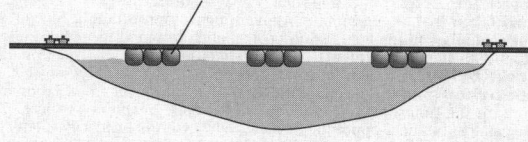

pontoon bridge

Pon•tus (pon′təs), *n.* an ancient country in NE Asia Minor, bordering on the Black Sea: later a Roman province. —**Pon′tic,** *adj.*

po•ny (pō′nē), *n., pl.* **-nies,** *v.,* **-nied, -ny•ing.** —*n.* **1.** a small horse of any of several breeds, usu. not higher at the shoulder than 14½ hands (58 in./146 cm). **2.** *Slang.* a racehorse. **3.** *Informal.* a literal translation or summary of a text, used illicitly as an aid in schoolwork; crib. **4.** something small of its kind. **5.** a small glass holding about one ounce (30 ml) of liqueur. **6.** a small beverage bottle, often holding seven ounces (196 g). —*v.* **7. pony up,** *Informal.* to pay (money), as in settling an account.

po′ny express′, *n.* a system of carrying mail by relays of riders on

ponies, esp. the system in use between Missouri and California in 1860–61.

po•ny•tail (pō′nē tāl′), *n.* a hairstyle in which the hair is gathered at the back of the head and fastened so as to hang freely there.

pooch (pōōch), *n. Informal.* a dog.

poo•dle (pōōd′l), *n.* one of a breed of dogs with long, thick, frizzy or curly hair usu. trimmed in standard patterns, occurring in three varieties (standard, miniature, and toy) that differ only in size: orig. used as a water retriever.

pooh (pōō, pŏŏ), *interj.* **1.** (used as an exclamation of disdain or contempt.) —*n.* **2.** an exclamation of "pooh."

Pooh Bah (pōō′ bä′), *(often l.c.)* **1.** a person who holds several positions, esp. ones that give him or her bureaucratic importance. **2.** a leader, authority, or other important person: *one of the pooh bahs of the record industry.* **3.** a pompous, self-important person. Also, **Pooh′-Bah′, poobah.** [after a character in Gilbert and Sullivan's *The Mikado,* who holds all of the high offices of state simultaneously and uses them for personal gain]

pooh-pooh (pōō′pōō′), *v.t.* **1.** to express disdain or contempt for; dismiss lightly. —*v.i.* **2.** to express disdain or contempt. —**pooh′-pooh′-er,** *n.*

pool¹ (pōōl), *n.* **1.** a small body of standing water; a small pond. **2.** a still, deep place in a stream. **3.** any small collection of liquid on a surface; puddle: *a pool of blood.* **4.** SWIMMING POOL. **5.** a subterranean accumulation of oil or gas. **6.** (of water) to accumulate in a pool. **7.** (of blood) to accumulate in a body part or organ. —*v.t.* **8.** to cause pools to form in.

pool² (pōōl), *n.* **1.** Also called **pocket billiards.** any of various games played on a pool table with a cue ball and 15 other balls that are driven into pockets. **2. a.** the total amount staked by a combination of bettors, as on a race. **b.** the combination of such bettors. **3.** an association of competitors who conspire to control the production, market, and price of a commodity for their mutual benefit. **4. a.** a combination of resources, funds, etc., for common advantage. **b.** the combined resources or funds. **5. a.** a facility or service shared by a group of people: *a car pool; a typing pool.* **b.** the persons involved. **6.** the stakes in certain games. —*v.t.* **7.** to put (resources, money, etc.) into a pool, or common fund, as for a financial venture. **8.** to form a pool of. —*v.i.* **9.** to enter into or form a pool. —**pool′er,** *n.*

pool′ hall′ or **pool′hall′,** *n.* POOLROOM (def. 1).

pool•room (pōōl′rōōm′, -rŏŏm′), *n.* **1.** an establishment or room for the playing of pool or billiards. **2.** a bookmaker's establishment.

pool•side (pōōl′sīd′), *n.* the lounging area around a swimming pool.

pool′ ta′ble, *n.* a billiard table with six pockets, on which pool is played.

poon (pōōn), *n.* **1.** any of several East Indian trees of the genus *Calophyllum,* family Guttiferae, that yield a light, hard wood used for masts, spars, etc. **2.** the wood of these trees.

poop¹ (pōōp), *n.* **1.** a superstructure at the stern of a vessel. **2.** POOP DECK. —*v.t.* **3.** (of a wave) to break over the stern of (a ship). **4.** to take (seas) over the stern.

poop² (pōōp), *v.t., Informal.* **1.** to cause to become out of breath or exhausted: **2. poop out, a.** to become exhausted. **b.** to give up or cease to participate. **c.** to break down; stop functioning.

poop³ (pōōp), *n. Slang.* a candid or pertinent factual report; low-down.

poop′ deck′, *n.* a weather deck on top of a poop.

poor (pŏŏr), *adj.,* **-er, -est,** *n.* —*adj.* **1.** having little or no money, goods, or other means of support. **2.** *Law.* dependent upon charity or public support. **3.** (of a country, institution, etc.) meagerly supplied or endowed with resources or funds. **4.** lacking in something specified: *a region poor in mineral deposits.* **5.** faulty or inferior: *poor workmanship.* **6.** deficient in desirable ingredients or qualities: *poor soil.* **7.** lacking in ability or training: *a poor cook.* **8.** wretched; unfortunate: *The poor thing has no friends.* **9.** scanty or meager: *poor attendance.* **10.** humble; modest. —*n.* **11. the poor,** poor persons collectively: *aid for the poor.*

poor′ boy′, *n. Chiefly New Orleans.* a hero sandwich.

poor•house (pŏŏr′hous′), *n., pl.* **-hous•es** (-hou′ziz). (formerly) an institution in which paupers were maintained at public expense.

poor•ly (pŏŏr′lē), *adv.* **1.** in a poor manner or way: *to write poorly.* —*adj.* **2.** in poor health; somewhat ill.

poor′ mouth′, *n. Informal.* **1.** a person who continually complains about a lack of money. **2.** a plea or complaint of poverty, often as an excuse for not contributing to charities, paying bills, etc.

poor′-mouth′ (-mouth′), *v.,* **-mouthed** (-moutht, -mouthd), **-mouth•ing.** *Informal.* —*v.i.* **1.** to plead or complain poverty. —*v.t.* **2.** to disparage; bad-mouth.

Poor′ Rich′ard's Al′manac, an almanac (1732–58) written and published by Benjamin Franklin.

pop¹ (pop), *v.,* **popped, pop•ping,** *n., adv., adj.* —*v.i.* **1.** to make a short, quick, explosive sound. **2.** to burst open with such a sound, as chestnuts or corn in roasting. **3.** to come or go quickly, suddenly, or unexpectedly. **4.** (of eyes) to protrude from the sockets. —*v.t.* **5.** to cause to make a sudden, explosive sound. **6.** to cause to burst open with such a sound. **7.** to put or thrust quickly: *Pop the muffins into the oven.* **8.** to shoot; fire at. **9. pop for,** *Slang.* to pay for, esp. as a treat. **10. pop in,** *Informal.* to visit briefly; drop by. **11. pop off,** *Informal.* **a.** to die suddenly. **b.** to depart abruptly. **c.** to express oneself volubly or indiscreetly. **12. pop up,** *Baseball.* to hit a pop fly. —*n.* **13.** a short, quick, explosive sound. **14.** a popping. **15.** a shot with a firearm. **16.** SODA POP. —*adv.* **17.** with an explosive sound. —*adj.* **18.** *Informal.* unexpected; without warning: *a pop quiz.* —*Idiom.* **19. a pop,** *Slang.* each; apiece. **20. pop the question,** *Informal.* to propose marriage.

pop² (pop), *adj.* **1.** of or pertaining to popular songs: *pop singers.* **2.** of or pertaining to pop art. **3.** reflecting or aimed at the tastes of the general masses of people: *pop culture.* —*n.* **4.** popular music. **5.** POP ART.

pop³ (pop), *n. Informal.* father.

pop⁴ (pop), *n.* a frozen ice or ice-cream confection on a stick.

POP or **P.O.P.** or **p.o.p.,** **1.** point of purchase. **2.** proof of purchase.

pop′ art′ or **Pop′ Art′,** *n.* art in which everyday objects and subjects are depicted with the flat naturalism of advertising or comic strips. —**pop′ ar′tist,** *n.*

pop·corn (pop′kôrn′), *n.* **1.** any of several varieties of corn whose kernels burst open and puff out when subjected to dry heat. **2.** such corn when popped.

pope (pōp), *n.* **1.** (*often cap.*) the bishop of Rome as head of the Roman Catholic Church. **2.** a person regarded as comparable in authority or position. **3.** *Eastern Ch.* **a.** the Orthodox patriarch of Alexandria. **b.** (in certain churches) a parish priest. [Old English *pāpa* < Late Latin: bishop, pope < Late Greek *pápas* bishop, priest, var. of *páppas* father]

Pope (pōp), *n.* **1. Alexander,** 1688–1744, English poet. **2. John,** 1822–92, Union general in the U.S. Civil War.

pop′ fly′, *n.* (in baseball) a high fly ball hit to the infield or immediately beyond it that can easily be caught before reaching the ground. Also called **pop-up.**

pop·gun (pop′gun′), *n.* a toy gun from which a pellet is shot by compressed air.

pop·in·jay (pop′in jā′), *n.* a vain, pretentious, shallow person.

pop·lar (pop′lər), *n.* **1.** any of several rapidly growing softwood trees of the genus *Populus,* of the willow family, usu. with a columnar or spirelike shape. **2.** any of various similar trees, as the tulip tree. **3.** the wood of any of these trees, used esp. for pulp. —**pop′lared,** *adj.*

pop·lin (pop′lin), *n.* a finely corded fabric of cotton, rayon, silk, or wool, for dresses, draperies, etc.

Po·po·ca·té·petl (pō′pō kä te′pet′l, pō′pə kat′ə pet′l), *n.* a volcano in S central Mexico, SE of Mexico City. 17,887 ft. (5450 m).

pop·off (pop′ôf′, -of′), *n. Slang.* a person given to loud and often indiscreet arguing or complaining.

pop·o·ver (pop′ō′vər), *n.* a hollow muffin made with a batter of milk, egg, and flour.

pop·pa (pop′ə), *n., pl.* **-pas.** *Informal.* father.

pop·pet (pop′it), *n.* **1.** a rising and falling valve consisting of a disk at the end of a vertically set stem, used in internal-combustion and steam engines. **2.** *Brit. Dial.* a term of endearment for a girl or child.

pop·ple (pop′əl), *v.,* **-pled, -pling,** *n.* —*v.i.* **1.** to move in a tumbling, irregular manner, as boiling water. —*n.* **2.** a popping motion.

pop·py (pop′ē), *n., pl.* **-pies** for 1, 2. **1.** any plant of the genus *Papaver,* having showy, usu. red flowers. **2.** any of several related or similar plants, as the California poppy or the prickly poppy. **3.** an extract from the juice of the poppy, as opium. **4.** Also called **pop′py red′.** an orangish red resembling scarlet. —**pop′py·like′,** *adj.*

pop·py·cock (pop′ē kok′), *n.* nonsense; foolishness.

pop·py·head (pop′ē hed′), *n.* a finial or other ornament, often richly carved, as the top of the upright end of a bench or pew.

pop′py seed′, *n.* seed of the poppy plant, used as an ingredient or topping for breads, rolls, etc.

pops (pops), *n.* (*used with a sing. or pl. v.*) a symphony orchestra specializing in popular and light classical music.

pop′-top′, *adj.* (of a can) able to be opened by pulling the tab or ring on its top.

pop·u·lace (pop′yə ləs), *n.* **1.** (in a community or nation) the common people as distinguished from the higher classes. **2.** the inhabitants of a place; population.

pop·u·lar (pop′yə lər), *adj.* **1.** regarded with approval or affection by people in general: *a popular preacher.* **2.** of, pertaining to, or representing the common people or the people as a whole: *popular government; popular suffrage.* **3.** prevailing among the people generally: *a popular superstition.* **4.** appealing to or intended for the public at large: *popular music.* **5.** adapted to the tastes, means, etc., of ordinary persons: *popular lectures; popular prices.* —**pop′u·lar·ly,** *adv.*

pop′ular front′, *n.* a coalition, usu. temporary, of leftist and sometimes centrist political parties, formed against a common opponent, as fascism.

pop·u·lar·i·ty (pop′yə lar′i tē), *n.* the quality or fact of being popular.

pop·u·lar·ize (pop′yə lə rīz′), *v.t.,* **-ized, -iz·ing.** to make popular. —**pop′u·lar·i·za′tion,** *n.* —**pop′u·lar·iz′er,** *n.*

pop′ular sov′ereignty, *n.* **1.** the doctrine that sovereign power is vested in the people and that those chosen to govern, as trustees of such power, must exercise it in conformity with the general will. **2.** (before the Civil War) a doctrine, held chiefly by the opponents of the abolitionists, that the people living in a territory should be free of federal interference in determining domestic policy, esp. with respect to slavery.

pop·u·late (pop′yə lāt′), *v.t.,* **-lat·ed, -lat·ing.** **1.** to inhabit; live in. **2.** to furnish with inhabitants; people.

pop·u·la·tion (pop′yə lā′shən), *n.* **1.** the total number of persons inhabiting a country, city, or any district or area. **2.** the number or body

of inhabitants of a particular race, class, or group in a place: *the working-class population.* **3.** any aggregation of things or individuals subject to statistical study. **4.** the assemblage of organisms living in a given area. **5.** the act or process of populating. —**pop′u·la′tion·al,** *adj.*

popula′tion explo′sion, *n.* the rapid increase in numbers of a particular species, esp. in the world's human population since the end of World War II, attributed to an accelerating birthrate, a decrease in infant mortality, and an increase in life expectancy.

Pop·u·lism (pop′yə liz′əm), *n.* **1.** the political philosophy of the Populist or People's Party. **2.** (*l.c.*) an egalitarian political philosophy or movement that promotes the interests of the common people. **3.** (*l.c.*) representation or celebration of the views, interests, etc., of the common people.

Pop·u·list (pop′yə list), *n.* **1.** a member of the Populist or People's Party. **2.** (*l.c.*) a supporter of populism. —*adj.* **3.** of or pertaining to the Populist Party. **4.** (*l.c.*) of, pertaining to, or characteristic of populism or its supporters.

Pop′ulist Par′ty, *n.* a U.S. political party (1891–1904) advocating agrarian interests, expansion of currency, state control of railroads, and a graduated income tax. Also called **People's Party.**

pop·u·lous (pop′yə ləs), *adj.* **1.** containing many residents or inhabitants; heavily populated: *a populous area.* **2.** jammed or crowded with people. **3.** forming or comprising a large number or quantity; numerous. —**pop′u·lous·ly,** *adv.* —**pop′u·lous·ness,** *n.*

pop′-up′, *adj.* **1.** (of a book, greeting card, etc.) having artwork fastened to a page in such a way that when the page is opened, a three-dimensional cutout or object unfolds or springs up. **2.** of, pertaining to, or equipped with a device that springs up or that causes something to spring up or out: *a pop-up toaster.* —*n.* **3.** a pop-up book. **4.** something, as an illustration, that pops up. **5.** *Baseball.* POP FLY.

por·ce·lain (pôr′sə lin, pōr′-; pôrs′lin, pōrs′-), *n.* **1.** a strong, vitreous, translucent ceramic material, made of kaolin and feldspar, with a transparent glaze fired at a high temperature. **2.** ware made from this. —**por′ce·la′ne·ous, por′cel·la′ne·ous** (-lā′nē əs), *adj.*

porch (pôrch, pōrch), *n.* **1.** an exterior appendage to a building, forming a covered approach or vestibule to a doorway. **2.** a veranda.

por·cine (pôr′sīn, -sin), *adj.* **1.** of or pertaining to swine. **2.** resembling swine; hoggish; piggish.

por·cu·pine (pôr′kyə pīn′), *n.* any large rodent of the New World family Erethizontidae or the Old World family Hystricidae, having stiff, sharp, erectile spines or quills.

por·cu·pine·fish (pôr′kyə pīn′fish′), *n., pl.* (*esp. collectively*) **-fish,** (*esp. for kinds or species*) **-fish·es.** a spiny fish, *Diodon hystrix,* of tropical seas, capable of inflating itself when disturbed.

pore¹ (pôr, pōr), *v.i.,* **pored, por·ing.** **1.** to read or study with steady attention or application (usu. fol. by *over*): *to pore over old manuscripts.* **2.** to meditate or ponder intently (usu. fol. by *over, on,* or *upon*). **3.** to gaze earnestly or steadily.

pore² (pôr, pōr), *n.* **1.** a minute opening or orifice, as in the skin or a leaf, for perspiration, absorption, etc. **2.** a minute interstice, as in a rock. —**pore′like′,** *adj.*

pore′ fun′gus, *n.* any of a group of fleshy to woody porous mushrooms and fungi, having the spores in tiny tubules.

por·gy (pôr′gē), *n., pl.* (*esp. collectively*) **-gy,** (*esp. for kinds or species*) **-gies.** any of various marine food fishes of the family Sparidae, having a deep body and large scales.

Por·gy and Bess (pôr′gē ən bes′), an opera (1935) with music by George Gershwin and lyrics by Ira Gershwin.

po·rif·er·an (pô rif′ər ən, pō-, pə-), *n.* **1.** any animal of the phylum Porifera, comprising the sponges. —*adj.* **2.** belonging or pertaining to the phylum Porifera.

po·rif·er·ous (pô rif′ər əs, pō-, pə-), *adj.* bearing or having pores.

pork (pôrk, pōrk), *n.* **1.** the flesh of a hog or pig used as food. **2.** *Informal.* appropriations, appointments, etc., made by the government for political reasons. [< Old French < Latin *porcus* hog]

pork′ bar′rel, *n. Informal.* a government appropriation, bill, or policy that supplies funds for local improvements designed to ingratiate legislators with their constituents. —**pork′-bar′rel,** *adj.*

pork′ bel′ly, *n.* a side of fresh pork.

pork·chop·per (pôrk′chop′ər, pōrk′-), *n. Informal.* **1.** a labor official put on the union payroll as a reward for past loyalty or services. **2.** any legislator, political appointee, official, etc., who is primarily interested in personal gain or the perquisites of power.

pork·er (pôr′kər, pōr′-), *n.* a pig, esp. one being fattened for its meat.

pork·y (pôr′kē, pōr′-), *adj.,* **-i·er, -i·est.** **1.** of, pertaining to, or resembling pork. **2.** fat; obese. —**pork′i·ness,** *n.*

por·nog·ra·pher (pôr nog′rə fər), *n.* a person who writes or sells pornography.

por·nog·ra·phy (pôr nog′rə fē), *n.* **1.** writings, photographs, movies, etc., intended to arouse sexual excitement, esp. such materials considered as having little or no artistic merit. **2.** the production of such materials. —**por′no·graph′ic** (-nə graf′ik), *adj.*

po·ros·i·ty (pô ros′i tē, pō-, pə-), *n., pl.* **-ties. 1.** the state or quality of being porous. **2.** (in rock or other natural material) the ratio of aggregated pore space to the volume of the entire mass: used as a measure of the amount of fluid, as oil or gas, that a geologic stratum might hold.

po·rous (pôr′əs, pōr′-), *adj.* **1.** permeable by water, air, etc. **2.** full of pores. —**po′rous·ly,** *adv.* —**po′rous·ness,** *n.*

por·phy·ry (pôr′fə rē), *n., pl.* **-ries. 1.** a very hard rock, anciently quarried in Egypt, having a dark, purplish red groundmass containing small crystals of feldspar. **2.** any igneous rock containing coarse crystals, as phenocrysts, in a finer-grained groundmass. —**por′phy·rit′ic** (-rit′ik), *adj.*

por·poise (pôr′pəs), *n., pl.* (*esp. collectively*) **-poise,** (*esp. for kinds or species*) **-pois·es,** *v.,* **-poised, -pois·ing.** —*n.* **1.** any of certain toothed cetaceans of the family Delphinidae having a blunt, rounded snout, as the common porpoise. Compare DOLPHIN. —*v.i.* **2.** (of a speeding motorboat) to leap clear of the water after striking a wave. **3.** (of a vehicle) to move forward with an alternately rising and falling motion. —**por′poise·like′,** *adj.*

por·ridge (pôr′ij, por′-), *n.* a thick cereal made esp. of oatmeal boiled in water or milk.

port[1] (pôrt, pōrt), *n.* **1.** a city, town, or other place where ships load or unload. **2.** a place along a coast in which ships may take refuge from storms; harbor. **3.** Also called **port of entry. a.** any place where imported goods may be received into a country subject to inspection by customs officials. **b.** any place where travelers or immigrants may enter a country. **4.** a geographical area that forms a harbor. —*Proverb.* **5. Any port in a storm** any place of safety will do in an emergency.

port[2] (pôrt, pōrt), *n.* **1.** the left-hand side of a vessel or aircraft, facing forward. —*adj.* **2.** located on the left side of a vessel or aircraft. —*v.t., v.i.* **3.** to turn or shift to the port, or left, side.

port[3] (pôrt, pōrt), *n.* a very sweet, usu. dark red, fortified wine, orig. from Portugal.

port[4] (pôrt, pōrt), *n.* **1.** an opening in the side or other exterior part of a ship for admitting air and light or for taking on cargo. Compare PORTHOLE (def. 1). **2.** an aperture in the surface of a cylinder, as in machinery, for the passage of steam, air, water, etc. **3.** a small aperture in an armored vehicle, aircraft, or fortification through which a gun can be fired or a camera directed. **4.** a data connection in a computer to which a peripheral device or a transmission line from a remote terminal can be attached. —*v.t.* **5.** to create a new version of (an application program) to run on a different hardware platform.

port[5] (pôrt, pōrt), *v.t.* **1.** to carry (a rifle or other weapon) in the port arms position. —*n.* **2.** PORT ARMS.

port·a·bil·i·ty (pôr′tə bil′i tē, pōr′-), *n., pl.* **-ties. 1.** the state or quality of being portable. **2.** a system under which employees may transfer pension or retirement benefits from one employer's plan to that of another, as when they change jobs.

port·a·ble (pôr′tə bəl, pōr′-), *adj.* **1.** capable of being transported or conveyed: *a portable stage.* **2.** easily carried or conveyed by hand: *a portable typewriter.* **3.** (of data, software, etc.) able to be used on different computer systems. **4.** capable of being transferred, as pension benefits, from one employer's plan to that of another. —*n.* **5.** something that is portable, esp. as distinguished from a nonportable counterpart.

por·tage (pôr′tij, por-, for 2, 3, 5, 6, pôr täzh′), *n., v.,* **-taged, -tag·ing.** —*n.* **1.** the act of carrying; carriage. **2.** the carrying of boats, supplies, etc., overland from one navigable water to another. **3.** the route over which this is done. **4.** the cost of carriage. —*v.i.* **5.** to make a portage. —*v.t.* **6.** to carry over a portage: *to portage a canoe.*

por·tal[1] (pôr′tl, pōr′-), *n.* **1.** a door, gate, or entrance, esp. one of imposing size and appearance. **2.** an iron or steel bent for bracing a framed structure, having curved braces between the vertical members and a horizontal member at the top. **3.** an entrance to a tunnel or mine.

por·tal[2] (pôr′tl, pōr′-), *adj.* **1.** noting or pertaining to the transverse fissure of the liver. —*n.* **2.** PORTAL VEIN.

por′tal vein′, *n.* a large vein conveying blood to the liver from the veins of the stomach, intestine, spleen, and pancreas.

port′ arms′, *n.* a position in military drill in which one's rifle is held diagonally in front of the body, with the muzzle pointing upward to the left.

Port-au-Prince (pôrt′ō prins′, pōrt′-; *Fr.* pôr tō prans′), *n.* the capital of Haiti, in the S part. 763,188.

port′ author′ity, *n.* a government commission that manages bridges, tunnels, airports, and other such facilities of a port or city.

port·cul·lis (pôrt kul′is, pōrt-), *n.* a strong grating, as of iron, made to slide along vertical grooves at the sides of the gateway of a castle or fortified place and let down to prevent passage.

portcullis

por·tend (pôr tend′, pōr-), *v.t.* **1.** to indicate in advance, as an omen does; foreshadow or presage. **2.** to signify; mean.

por·tent (pôr′tent, pōr′-), *n.* **1.** an indication or omen of something about to happen, esp. something momentous. **2.** threatening or disquieting significance: *an occurrence of dire portent.* **3.** a prodigy or marvel.

por·ten·tous (pôr ten′təs, pōr-), *adj.* **1.** of the nature of a portent; momentous. **2.** ominously significant or indicative: *a portentous defeat.* **3.** solemnly self-important; pompous; overinflated. **4.** marvelous; amazing; prodigious. —**por·ten′tous·ly,** *adv.* —**por·ten′tous·ness,** *n.*

por·ter[1] (pôr′tər, pōr′-), *n.* **1.** a person hired to carry packages or baggage, as at a railroad station or a hotel. **2.** a person who does cleaning and maintenance work in a building, factory, store, etc. **3.** an attendant in a railroad parlor car or sleeping car.

por·ter[2] (pôr′tər, pōr′-), *n.* a person who has charge of a door or gate; doorkeeper.

Por·ter (pôr′tər, pōr′-), *n.* **1. Cole,** 1893–1964, U.S. composer. **2. Katherine Anne,** 1890–1980, U.S. writer. **3. William Sydney** ("*O. Henry*"), 1862–1910, U.S. short-story writer.

por·ter·house (pôr′tər hous′, pōr′-), *n., pl.* **-hous·es** (-hou′ziz). Also called **por′terhouse steak′.** a choice cut of beef from between the prime ribs and the sirloin.

port·fo·li·o (pôrt fō′lē ō′, pōrt-), *n., pl.* **-li·os. 1.** a flat, portable case for carrying loose papers, drawings, etc. **2.** the contents of such a case, esp. a collection of drawings, photographs, etc., representative of a person's work. **3.** the securities, commercial paper, etc., held by a private investor, financial institution, etc. **4.** the office or post of a minister of state or member of a cabinet.

port·hole (pôrt′hōl′, pōrt′-), *n.* **1.** a round, windowlike opening with a hinged, watertight glass cover in the side of a vessel for admitting air and light. Compare PORT[4] (def. 1). **2.** an opening in a wall, door, etc., as one through which to shoot.

por·ti·co (pôr′ti kō′, pōr′-), *n., pl.* **-coes, -cos.** a structure consisting of a roof supported by columns or piers, usu. attached to a building as a porch. —**por′ti·coed′,** *adj.*

portico

por·tion (pôr′shən, pōr′-), *n.* **1.** a part of a whole, either separated from or integrated with it; segment. **2.** an amount of food served to one person; serving; helping. **3.** the part of a whole allotted to or belonging to a person or group; share. **4.** the part of an estate that goes to an heir or a next of kin. **5.** that which is allotted to a person by God or fate; lot. **6.** a woman's dowry. —*v.t.* **7.** to divide into or distribute in portions or shares (often fol. by *out*). **8.** to furnish with a portion, as with an inheritance or dowry. —**por′tion·a·ble,** *adj.*

Port·land (pôrt′lənd, pōrt′-), *n.* **1.** a seaport in NW Oregon, at the confluence of the Willamette and Columbia rivers. 450,777. **2.** a seaport in SW Maine, on Casco Bay. 61,280.

Port′land cement′, *n.* a type of hydraulic cement usu. made by burning a mixture of limestone and clay in a kiln.

Port′ Lou′is (lōō′is, lōō′ē), *n.* a seaport in and the capital of Mauritius, on the NW coast. 139,038.

port·ly (pôrt′lē, pōrt′-), *adj.,* **-li·er, -li·est.** rather heavy or fat; stout; corpulent. —**port′li·ness,** *n.*

port·man·teau (pôrt man′tō, pōrt-; pôrt′man tō′, pōrt′-), *n., pl.* **-teaus, -teaux** (-tōz, -tō; -tōz′, -tō′), *adj.* —*n.* **1.** *Chiefly Brit.* a case or bag to carry clothing in while traveling, esp. a leather trunk or suitcase that opens into two halves. —*adj.* **2.** combining or blending several items, features, or qualities: *a portmanteau show.*

Port′ Mores′by (môrz′bē, mōrz′-), *n.* a seaport in SE New Guinea: capital of Papua New Guinea. 152,100.

port′ of call′, *n.* a port visited briefly by a ship, as to take on or discharge passengers and cargo or to undergo repairs.

port′ of en′try, *n.* PORT[1] (def. 3).

Port′-of-Spain′, *n.* a seaport on NW Trinidad, in the SE West Indies: national capital of Trinidad and Tobago. 58,400.

por·trait (pôr′trit, -trāt, pōr′-), *n.* **1.** a likeness of a person, esp. of the face, as a painting, drawing, sculpture, or photograph. **2.** a verbal picture or description, usu. of a person. —*adj.* **3.** pertaining to, designating, or producing standard vertical orientation of computer output, with lines of data parallel to the two shorter sides of a page (contrasted with *landscape*). —**por′trait·like′,** *adj.*

Por′trait of a La′dy, The, a novel (1881) by Henry James.

por·trai·ture (pôr′tri chər, pōr′-), *n.* **1.** the art or practice of making portraits. **2.** a pictorial representation; portrait. **3.** a verbal picture.

por·tray (pôr trā′, pōr-), *v.t.* **1.** to make a likeness of by drawing, painting, carving, etc.; depict. **2.** to depict in words; describe graphically. **3.** to represent dramatically, as on the stage: *the actor who portrayed Napoleon.* —**por·tray′a·ble,** *adj.* —**por·tray′er,** *n.*

por•tray•al (pôr trā′əl, pōr-), *n.* **1.** the act of portraying. **2.** a portrait.

Ports•mouth (pôrts′məth, pōrts′-), *n.* **1.** a seaport in S Hampshire, in S England, on the English Channel. 186,800. **2.** a seaport in SE Virginia. 103,464. **3.** a seaport in SE New Hampshire: Russian-Japanese peace treaty 1905. 26,254.

Por•tu•gal (pôr′chə gəl, pōr′-), *n.* a republic in SW Europe, on the Iberian Peninsula, W of Spain. (including the Azores and the Madeira Islands). 9,867,654; 35,414 sq. mi. (91,720 sq. km). *Cap.:* Lisbon.

Por•tu•guese (pôr′chə gēz′, -gēs′, pōr′-), *n., pl.* **-guese,** *adj.* **—***n.* **1.** a native or inhabitant of Portugal. **2.** a Romance language spoken in Portugal, Brazil, the Azores, and Madeira, and used as an auxiliary language in former colonies of Portugal, as Angola and Mozambique. *Abbr.:* Pg, Pg. **—***adj.* **3.** of or pertaining to Portugal, its people, or the language Portuguese.

Por′tuguese man′-of-war′, *n.* any of several large, colonial marine hydrozoans of the genus *Physalia,* having a buoyant saillike sac from which dangle poisonous stinging tentacles.

por•tu•lac•a (pôr′chə lak′ə, pōr′-), *n., pl.* **-lac•as.** any of various plants belonging to the genus *Portulaca,* of the purslane family, esp. *P. grandiflora,* cultivated for its showy, variously colored flowers.

POS, point-of-sale.

pose¹ (pōz), *v.,* **posed, pos•ing,** *n.* **—***v.i.* **1.** to assume or hold a physical position or attitude, as for an artistic purpose: *to pose for a painter.* **2.** to pretend to be what one is not, esp. in order to impress or deceive: *to pose as a police officer.* **3.** to behave in an affected manner. **—***v.t.* **4.** to place in a suitable position or attitude for a picture, tableau, etc: *to pose a group for a photograph.* **5.** to assert, state, or put forward; present: *That poses a problem.* **6.** to put or place. **—***n.* **7.** a bodily attitude or posture, esp. one assumed deliberately, as for an artistic purpose. **8.** a mental attitude or posture, esp. one that is studied or assumed for effect; affectation: *His liberalism is merely a pose.*

pose² (pōz), *v.t.,* **posed, pos•ing.** to embarrass or baffle, as by a difficult question or problem.

Po•sei•don (pō sīd′n, pə-), *n.* the ancient Greek god of the sea and of horses: identified by the Romans with Neptune.

po•seur (pō zûr′), *n.* a person who assumes or affects a character, manner, sentiment, etc., in order to impress others.

posh (posh), *adj.* stylishly elegant; luxurious: *a posh new restaurant.*

pos•it (poz′it), *v.t.* **1.** to lay down or assume as a fact or principle; postulate. **2.** to place, put, or set. **—***n.* **3.** something that is posited; assumption; postulate.

po•si•tion (pə zish′ən), *n.* **1.** condition with reference to place, often relative to the location of others; location; situation. **2.** a place occupied or to be occupied; site: *a fortified position.* **3.** the proper or usual place: *out of position.* **4.** situation or condition, esp. with relation to favorable or unfavorable circumstances: *The question put me in an awkward position.* **5.** status or standing; rank. **6.** a post of employment; job. **7.** the manner of being placed or arranged; arrangement. **8.** bodily posture or attitude: *sitting in an uncomfortable position.* **9.** attitude or opinion; stand: *his position on capital punishment.* **10.** the part of a sports field or playing area covered by a particular player. **11.** a commitment to buy or sell securities, as stocks. **—***v.t.* **12.** to put in a particular or appropriate position; place; situate. **13.** to determine the position of; locate. **—po•si′tion•al,** *adj.*

posi′tion pa′per, *n.* a formal, usu. detailed written statement, esp. on a single issue, articulating a position, viewpoint, or proposed policy.

pos•i•tive (poz′i tiv), *adj.* **1.** confident in opinion or assertion; sure: *He is positive that he'll win.* **2.** showing or expressing approval or agreement; favorable: *a positive reaction to the speech.* **3.** expressing or containing an assertion or affirmation; affirmative: *a positive answer.* **4.** emphasizing what is laudable, hopeful, or to the good; constructive: *a positive attitude.* **5.** admitting of no question; incontrovertible: *positive proof.* **6.** without relation to or comparison with other things; not relative or comparative; absolute. **7.** downright; out-and-out: *a positive genius.* **8.** not speculative or theoretical; practical: *a positive approach to the problem.* **9.** possessing an actual force, being, existence, etc. **10.** *Philos.* **a.** constructive and sure, rather than skeptical. **b.** concerned with or based on matters of experience: *positive philosophy.* **11.** consisting in or characterized by the presence or possession of distinguishing or marked qualities or features (opposed to *negative*). **12.** noting the presence of such qualities, as a term. **13.** determined by enactment or convention; arbitrarily laid down: *positive laws.* **14. a.** noting or pertaining to the electricity in a body or substance that is deficient in electrons. **b.** indicating a point in a circuit that has a higher potential than that of another point, the current flowing from the point of higher potential to the point of lower potential. **15.** of, pertaining to, or noting the north pole of a magnet. **16. a.** (of blood, affected tissue, etc.) showing the presence of disease. **b.** (of a diagnostic test) indicating the presence of the disease, condition, etc., tested for. **17.** noting a numerical quantity greater than zero. **18.** of or designating the initial degree of grammatical comparison, used with reference to the simple, base form of an adjective or adverb, as *good* or *smoothly.* Compare COMPARATIVE (def. 4), SUPERLATIVE (def. 2). **19.** (of government) assuming control or regulation of activities beyond those involved merely with the maintenance of law and order. **20.** of or designating a photographic print or transparency showing the brightness values as they are in the subject. **—***n.* **21.** something positive. **22.** a positive quality or characteristic. **23.** a positive quantity or symbol. **24. a.** the positive degree in grammatical comparison. **b.** the positive form of an adjective or adverb. **25.** a positive photographic image, as on a print or transparency.

pos′itive law′, *n.* customary law or law enacted by governmental authority (as distinguished from *natural law*).

pos•i•tive•ly (poz′i tiv lē *or, esp. for* , poz′i tiv′lē), *adv.* **1.** with certainty; absolutely. **2.** decidedly; unquestionably; definitely.

pos•i•tron (poz′i tron′), *n.* an elementary particle with the same mass as an electron but a positive charge; the antiparticle of the electron.

pos′itron emis′sion tomog′raphy, *n.* the process of producing a PET scan. Compare PET SCANNER.

po•sol•o•gy (pə sol′ə jē, pō-), *n.* the branch of pharmacology dealing with the determination of dosage. **—pos•o•log•ic** (pos′ə loj′ik), **pos′o•log′i•cal,** *adj.* **—po•sol′o•gist,** *n.*

pos•se (pos′ē), *n.* **1.** a body of persons given legal authority to assist a peace officer esp. in an emergency. **2.** a body of persons summoned for the purpose of making a search.

pos•sess (pə zes′), *v.t.* **1.** to have as belonging to one; have as property; own. **2.** to have as a faculty, quality, or the like: *possess intelligence.* **3.** (of a spirit, esp. an evil one) to occupy or control (a person) from within: *be possessed by demons.* **4.** (of a feeling, idea, etc.) to dominate or actuate in the manner of such a spirit. **5.** to keep or maintain in a certain state, as of peace or patience. **6.** to seize or take; gain. **—pos•ses′sor,** *n.*

pos•sessed (pə zest′), *adj.* **1.** spurred or moved by a strong feeling, madness, or a supernatural power (often fol. by *by, of,* or *with*). **2.** self-possessed; poised. **—*Idiom.*** **3. possessed of,** having; possessing: *He is possessed of intelligence and ambition.*

pos•ses•sion (pə zesh′ən), *n.* **1.** the act or fact of possessing. **2.** the state of being possessed. **3.** ownership. **4.** *Law.* actual holding or occupancy, either with or without rights of ownership. **5.** a thing possessed or owned. **6. possessions,** property or wealth. **7.** a territorial dominion of a state. **8.** physical control of the ball or puck by a player or team. **9.** control over oneself, one's mind, etc. **10.** domination or obsession by a feeling or idea.

pos•ses•sive (pə zes′iv), *adj.* **1.** desiring to dominate or be the only influence on someone. **2.** of or pertaining to possession or ownership. **3.** (of a word, construction, or grammatical case) indicating possession, ownership, origin, etc., as *Jane's* in *Jane's coat. His* in *his book* is a possessive adjective. *His* in *The book is his* is a possessive pronoun. Compare GENITIVE (def. 1). **—***n.* **4.** the possessive case. **5.** a possessive form or construction. **—pos•ses′sive•ly,** *adv.* **—pos•ses′sive•ness,** *n.*

pos•si•bil•i•ty (pos′ə bil′i tē), *n., pl.* **-ties.** **1.** the state or fact of being possible. **2.** something that is possible.

pos•si•ble (pos′ə bəl), *adj.* **1.** that may or can exist, happen, be done, be used, etc.: *a possible cure.* **2.** that may be true or may be the case: *It is possible that she has already gone.*

pos•si•bly (pos′ə blē), *adv.* **1.** perhaps; maybe. **2.** by any possibility; conceivably: *Could you possibly help me?*

POSSLQ (pos′əl kyo͞o′), *n., pl.* **POSSLQs, POSSLQ's.** either of two persons, one of each sex, who share living quarters but are not related by blood, marriage, or adoption. [*p(erson of the) o(pposite) s(ex) s(haring) l(iving) q(uarters)*]

pos•sum (pos′əm), *n., pl.* **-sums,** (*esp. collectively*) **-sum.** **1.** OPOSSUM. **2.** any of many marsupials of the families Phalangeridae, Petauridae, and Burramidae, of Australia and neighboring islands. **—*Idiom.*** **3. play possum,** to feign sleep or death.

post¹ (pōst), *n.* **1.** a piece of timber, metal, or the like, set upright as a support, a point of attachment, etc. **2.** one of the principal uprights of a piece of furniture, as one supporting a chair back. **3.** a pole on a racetrack indicating the point where a race begins or ends: *the starting post.* **—***v.t.* **4.** to affix (a public notice or bulletin) to a post, wall, or the like. **5.** to bring to public notice by means of a poster or bill: *to post a reward.* **6.** to enter the name of in a published list. **7.** to placard (a wall, fence, etc.) with public notices or bills.

post² (pōst), *n.* **1.** a position of duty, employment, or trust to which one is assigned or appointed: *a diplomatic post.* **2.** the station or rounds of a person on duty, as a soldier or sentry. **3.** a military station with permanent buildings. **4.** the body of troops occupying a military station. **5.** a local unit of a veterans' organization. **6.** TRADING POST. **7.** a place in the stock exchange where a particular stock is traded. **8.** *Brit. Mil.* either of two bugle calls signaling tattoo. **—***v.t.* **9.** to place or station at a post. **10.** to provide or put up, as bail. **11.** to appoint to a military or naval command.

post³ (pōst), *n.* **1.** *Chiefly Brit.* **a.** a single dispatch or delivery of mail. **b.** the mail itself. **c.** an established mail system or service. **2.** one of a series of stations along a route, for furnishing relays of men and horses. **—***v.t.* **3.** to supply with up-to-date information; inform: *Keep me posted on your activities.* **4.** *Chiefly Brit.* to send by mail. **5.** *Bookkeeping.* to transfer (an entry or item), from a journal to a ledger. **—***v.i.* **6.** to rise from and descend to the saddle in accordance with the rhythm of a horse at a trot. **7.** to travel with post horses. **8.** to travel with speed; hasten. **—***adv.* **9.** with speed or haste; posthaste. **10.** by post or courier. **11.** with post horses.

post- a prefix meaning "after, subsequent to," "behind:" *postmeridian; postscript.*

post•age (pō′stij), *n.* the charge for the conveyance of a letter or other matter sent by mail.

post′age me′ter, *n.* an office machine used in bulk mailing that imprints prepaid postage and a dated postmark.

post′age stamp′, *n.* a small gummed label issued by postal authorities that can be affixed to an envelope, postcard, or package as evidence that postal charges have been paid. Also called **stamp.**

post·al (pōs′tl), *adj.* of or pertaining to the post office or mail service: *postal delivery; postal employees.*

post′al serv′ice, *n.* POST OFFICE (def. 2).

post′card′ or **post′ card′,** *n.* a small, commercially printed card usu. having a picture on one side and space for a postage stamp, address, and message on the other.

post′ chaise′, *n.* a four-wheeled coach for rapid transportation of passengers and mail, used in the 18th and early 19th centuries.

post·date (pōst dāt′, pōst′-), *v.t.,* **-dat·ed, -dat·ing. 1.** to date (a check, invoice, document, etc.) with a date later than the current date. **2.** to give a date later than the true date: *to postdate the termination of one's employment.* **3.** to follow in time.

post·doc·tor·al (pōst dok′tər əl), *adj.* of or pertaining to study or professional work undertaken after the receipt of a doctorate.

post·er (pō′stər), *n.* a placard or bill posted or intended for posting in a public place, as for advertising.

pos·te·ri·or (po stēr′ē ər, pō-), *adj.* **1.** situated behind or at the rear of; hinder (opposed to *anterior*). **2.** coming after in order, as in a series. **3.** coming after in time; later. **4.** pertaining to or toward the back plane of the body, equivalent to the dorsal surface of quadrupeds. **5.** *Bot.* toward the back and near the main axis, as the upper lip of a flower. **—n. 6.** the hinder parts or rump of the body. **—pos·te′ri·or·ly,** *adv.*

pos·ter·i·ty (po ster′i tē), *n.* **1.** succeeding or future generations collectively. **2.** all descendants of one person.

pos·tern (pō′stərn, pos′tərn), *n.* **1.** a back door or gate. **2.** a private entrance or any entrance other than the main one. **—adj. 3.** of, pertaining to, or resembling a postern.

post·fem·i·nist (pōst fem′ə nist), *adj.* **1.** pertaining to or occurring in the period after the feminist movement of the 1970s. **2.** reflecting any of the ideologies emerging from this movement. **—n. 3.** a supporter of a postfeminist ideology. **—post·fem′i·nism,** *n.*

post·grad·u·ate (pōst graj′ōō it, -āt′), *adj.* **1.** of, pertaining to, characteristic of, or consisting of postgraduates: *a postgraduate seminar.* **—n. 2.** a student who is taking advanced work after graduation, as from a high school or college.

post·haste (pōst′hāst′), *adv.* with the greatest possible speed or promptness.

post·hu·mous (pos′chə məs, -chōō-), *adj.* **1.** arising, occurring, or continuing after one's death. **2.** published after the death of the author. **—post′hu·mous·ly,** *adv.* **—post′hu·mous·ness,** *n.*

post·hyp·not·ic (pōst′hip not′ik), *adj.* of or pertaining to the period after hypnosis. **—post′hyp·not′i·cal·ly,** *adv.*

post·ing (pō′sting), *n.* **1.** the act or process of entering data in an accounts ledger. **2.** the record in a ledger after such entry.

post·lude (pōst′lōōd), *n.* a concluding piece of music, esp. an organ voluntary at the end of a church service.

post·man (pōst′mən), *n., pl.* **-men.** MAIL CARRIER.

post·mark (pōst′märk′), *n.* **1.** an official mark stamped on mail passed through a postal system, showing the place and date of sending or receipt. **—v.t. 2.** to stamp with a postmark.

post·mas·ter (pōst′mas′tər, -mä′stər), *n.* **1.** the official in charge of a post office. **2.** (formerly) the master of a station that furnished post horses to travelers. **—post′mas′ter·ship′,** *n.*

post′master gen′eral, *n., pl.* **postmasters general.** the executive head of the postal system of a country.

post·me·rid·i·an (pōst′mə rid′ē ən), *adj.* **1.** of or pertaining to the afternoon. **2.** occurring after noon.

post me·rid·i·em (pōst′ mə rid′ē əm, -em′), *adj.* See P.M.

post·mil·len·ni·al·ism (pōst′mi len′ē ə liz′əm), *n.* the doctrine or belief that the second coming of Christ will follow the millennium. **—post′mil·len′ni·al·ist,** *n.*

post·mod·ern (pōst mod′ərn), *adj.* (*sometimes cap.*) of or pertaining to any of various movements in architecture, the arts, and literature developing in the late 20th century in reaction to the precepts and austere forms of modernism and characterized by the use of historical and vernacular style elements and often fantasy, decoration, and complexity. **—post·mod′ern·ism,** *n.* **—post·mod′ern·ist,** *adj., n.*

post·mor·tem (pōst môr′təm), *adj.* **1.** of, pertaining to, or occurring in the time following death. **2.** of or pertaining to examination of the body after death. **3.** occurring after the end of something; after the event. **—n. 4.** a postmortem examination; autopsy. **5.** a discussion or evaluation after the end or fact of something, esp. a card game.

post′nasal drip′, *n.* a trickling of mucus onto the pharyngeal surface from the posterior portion of the nasal cavity.

post′ of′fice, *n.* **1.** an office or station of a government postal system at which mail is received and sorted, from which it is dispatched and distributed, and at which stamps are sold or other services rendered. **2.** (*often caps.*) the department of a government charged with the transportation of mail. **—post′-of′fice,** *adj.*

post·op·er·a·tive (pōst op′ər ə tiv, -ə rā′tiv, -op′rə tiv), *adj.* occurring after a surgical operation. **—post·op′er·a·tive·ly,** *adv.*

post·paid (pōst′pād′), *adj., adv.* with the postage prepaid.

post·par·tum (pōst pär′təm), *adj.* following childbirth.

post·pone (pōst pōn′, pōs-), *v.t.,* **-poned, -pon·ing. 1.** to put off to a later time; defer: *We have postponed our departure until tomorrow.* **2.** to place after in order of importance or estimation; subordinate. **—post·pon′a·ble,** *adj.* **—post·pone′ment,** *n.*

post·pro·duc·tion (pōst′prə duk′shən), *n.* the final phase of technical work, as editing or synchronizing of sound elements, that must be done before a film, tape, recording, or the like can be released.

post·script (pōst′skript′, pōs′-), *n.* **1.** a paragraph, phrase, etc., added to a letter that has already been concluded and signed by the writer. **2.** any addition or supplement, as one appended by a writer to a book to supply further information. [< Latin *postscrībere* to write after]

Post·Script (pōst′skript′, pōs′-), *Trademark.* a page description computer language using scalable fonts that can be printed on a variety of appropriately equipped devices, including laser printers and professional-quality imagesetters.

pos·tu·lant (pos′chə lənt), *n.* a candidate, esp. for admission into a religious order.

pos·tu·late (*v.* pos′chə lāt′; *n.* -lit, -lāt′), *v.,* **-lat·ed, -lat·ing,** *n.* **—v.t. 1.** to claim or assume the existence or truth of, esp. as a basis for reasoning or arguing. **2.** to assume without proof, or as self-evident; take for granted. **3.** *Math., Logic.* to assume as a postulate. **—n. 4.** something taken as self-evident or assumed without proof as a basis for reasoning. **5.** *Math., Logic.* a proposition that requires no proof, being self-evident, or that is for a specific purpose assumed true, and that is used in the proof of other propositions; axiom. **6.** a fundamental principle. **7.** a necessary condition; prerequisite. **—pos′tu·la′tion,** *n.*

pos·ture (pos′chər), *n., v.,* **-tured, -tur·ing. —n. 1.** the position of the limbs or the carriage of the body as a whole. **2.** an affected or unnatural attitude. **3.** the relative disposition of the parts of something. **4.** a mental or spiritual attitude. **5.** a policy or stance, as that adopted by a company or government. **6.** position, condition, or state, as of affairs. **—v.t. 7.** to place in a particular posture or attitude. **—v.i. 8.** to assume a particular posture. **9.** to assume affected or unnatural postures, as by bending or contorting the body. **10.** to act in an affected or artificial manner, as to create a certain impression. **—pos′tur·al,** *adj.*

po·sy (pō′zē), *n., pl.* **-sies.** a flower, nosegay, or bouquet.

pot¹ (pot), *n., v.,* **pot·ted, pot·ting. —n. 1.** a container of earthenware, metal, etc., usu. round and deep and having a handle or handles and often a lid, used for cooking, serving, and other purposes. **2.** such a container with its contents: *a pot of stew.* **3.** the amount that can be held by a pot. **4.** FLOWERPOT. **5.** a container of liquor or other drink: *a pot of ale.* **6.** a cagelike vessel for trapping fish, lobsters, etc. **7.** CHAMBER POT. **8.** a large sum of money. **9.** all the money bet at a single time; pool. **10.** POTSHOT. **11.** POTBELLY. **—v.t. 12.** to put or transplant into a pot. **13.** to preserve (food) in a pot. **14.** to shoot (game birds) on the ground or water, or (game animals) at rest, instead of in flight or running. **—v.i. 15.** *Informal.* to take a potshot; shoot. **—Idiom. 16. go to pot,** to become ruined; deteriorate. **17. sweeten the pot.** See SWEETEN (def. 8). **—Saying. 18. pot calling the kettle black,** hypocrisy.

pot² (pot), *n. Slang.* MARIJUANA.

po·ta·ble (pō′tə bəl), *adj.* **1.** fit for drinking. **—n. 2.** Usu., **potables.** drinkable liquids; beverages. **—po′ta·bil′i·ty, po′ta·ble·ness,** *n.*

po·tage (pō täzh′), *n.* a thick soup.

pot·ash (pot′ash′), *n.* **1.** potassium carbonate, esp. the crude impure form obtained from wood ashes. **2.** potassium hydroxide. **3.** any of several potassium compounds, as the oxide of potassium, K_2O.

po·tas·si·um (pə tas′ē əm), *n.* a silvery white metallic element that oxidizes rapidly in the air and whose compounds are used as fertilizer and in special hard glasses. Symbol: K; *at. wt.:* 39.102; *at. no.:* 19; *sp. gr.:* 0.86 at 20°C.

potas′sium-ar′gon dat′ing, *n.* a method for estimating the age of a mineral or rock, based on measurement of the rate of decay of radioactive potassium into argon.

po·ta·tion (pō tā′shən), *n.* **1.** the act of drinking. **2.** a drink or draft, esp. of an alcoholic beverage.

po·ta·to (pə tā′tō, -tə), *n., pl.* **-toes. 1.** Also called **Irish potato, white potato.** the edible tuber of a cultivated plant, *Solanum tuberosum,* of the nightshade family. **2.** the plant itself. **3.** SWEET POTATO (defs. 1, 2).

po·ta′to·bug′ or **pota′to bug′,** *n.* COLORADO BEETLE. Also called **pota′to beet′le.**

pota′to chip′, *n.* a thin slice of potato fried until crisp and usu. salted.

pot-au-feu (Fr. pô tō fœ′), *n., pl.* **pot-au-feu.** a dish of boiled meat and vegetables.

pot·bel·ly (pot′bel′ē), *n., pl.* **-lies.** a distended or protuberant belly. **—pot·bel′lied,** *adj.*

pot′ cheese′, *n.* a usu. dry-textured form of cottage cheese.

Po·tem·kin vil′lage, *n.* a pretentiously showy or imposing façade intended to mask or divert attention from an embarrassing or shabby fact or condition. [after Prince *Potemkin* (1739–91), who allegedly had villages of cardboard constructed for Catherine II's visit to the Ukraine and the Crimea in 1787]

po·tence (pōt′ns), *n.* POTENCY.

po·ten·cy (pōt′n sē), *n., pl.* **-cies. 1.** the state or quality of being potent; strength. **2.** power; authority. **3.** capacity to be, become, or develop; potentiality. **4.** a person or thing exerting power or influence.

P

po•tent[1] (pōt′nt), *adj.* **1.** powerful; mighty. **2.** cogent; persuasive. **3.** producing powerful physical or chemical effects: *a potent drug.* **4.** having or exercising great power or influence. **5.** (of a male) capable of sexual intercourse. —**po′tent•ly,** *adv.*

po•tent[2] (pōt′nt), *adj.* (of a heraldic cross) having a crosspiece at the extremity of each arm.

po•ten•tate (pōt′n tāt′), *n.* a person who possesses great power, as a sovereign, monarch, or ruler.

po•ten•tial (pə ten′shəl), *adj.* **1.** possible, as opposed to actual: *the potential uses of nuclear energy.* **2.** capable of being or becoming: *a potential danger.* **3.** (esp. of a verb form, or mood) expressing possibility, as by using the auxiliaries *can* or *may.* —*n.* **4.** possibility; potentiality: *an investment that has little growth potential.* **5.** a latent ability that may or may not be developed. **6.** *Physics.* **a.** a scalar quantity equal to the work done in moving a body from a standard reference point to a given point in a field of force. **b.** a scalar quantity equal, at a given point in an electric field, to the work done in moving a unit charge from an infinite distance from the field's origin. —**po•ten′tial•ly,** *adv.*

poten′tial en′ergy, *n.* the energy of a body or a system with respect to the position of the body or the arrangement of the particles of the system. Compare KINETIC ENERGY.

po•ten•ti•al•i•ty (pə ten′shē al′i tē), *n., pl.* **-ties. 1.** the state or quality of being potential. **2.** something potential; a possibility.

po•ten•ti•ate (pə ten′shē āt′), *v.t.,* **-at•ed, -at•ing. 1.** to cause to be potent; make powerful. **2.** to increase the effectiveness of; intensify.

poth•er (poth′ər), *n.* **1.** commotion; uproar. **2.** a heated discussion, debate, or argument; fuss; to-do. **3.** a choking or suffocating cloud, as of smoke or dust. —*v.t., v.i.* **4.** to worry; bother.

pot•herb (pot′ûrb′, -hûrb′), *n.* any herb boiled for use as a vegetable or added to food as a seasoning.

pot•hold•er (pot′hōl′dər), *n.* a thick piece of material, as a quilted or woven pad, used in handling hot pots and dishes.

pot•hole (pot′hōl′), *n.* **1.** a hole formed in pavement, as by excessive use or by extremes of weather. **2.** a hole cut in submerged bedrock by the eroding action of sand and gravel whirled about by eddying water.

pot•hook (pot′hŏŏk′), *n.* **1.** a hook for suspending a pot or kettle over an open fire. **2.** an iron rod with a hook at the end used to lift hot pots, stove lids, etc. **3.** an S-shaped stroke in writing.

po•tion (pō′shən), *n.* a drink or draft, esp. one having or reputed to have medicinal, poisonous, or magical powers.

Pot•i•phar (pot′ə fər), *n.* the Egyptian officer whose wife tried to seduce Joseph. Gen. 39:1–20.

pot•latch (pot′lach), *n.* **1.** (among American Indians of the N Pacific coast, esp. the Kwakiutl) a ceremonial festival at which the sponsor bestows gifts lavishly upon the guests. **2.** *Pacific Northwest.* a party or celebration.

pot′ liq′uor or **pot′-liq′uor,** *n. Midland and Southern U.S.* the broth in which meat or vegetables, as salt pork or greens, have been cooked.

pot•luck (pot′luk′, -luk′), *n.* **1.** a meal that happens to be available without special preparation or purchase. **2.** Also called **pot′luck sup′per.** a meal, esp. for a large group, to which participants bring food to be shared. **3.** whatever is available or comes one's way.

pot′ mar′igold, *n.* CALENDULA (def. 1).

Po•to•mac (pə tō′mək), *n.* a river flowing SE from the Allegheny Mountains in West Virginia, along the boundary between Maryland and Virginia to the Chesapeake Bay. 287 mi. (460 km) long.

Poto′mac fe′ver, *n.* the determination or fervor to share in the power and prestige of the U.S. government in Washington, D.C., esp. by being appointed or elected to a government position. [after the POTOMAC River, on which Washington, D.C., is located]

pot•pie (pot′pī′, -pī′), *n.* a pie of meat or chicken and vegetables cooked in a deep dish and topped with a crust.

pot•pour•ri (pō′pŏŏ rē′, pō′pŏŏ rē′), *n., pl.* **-ris. 1.** a fragrant mixture of dried flower petals and spices, usu. kept in a jar. **2.** any miscellaneous grouping; medley.

pot′ roast′, *n.* a cut of beef stewed in one piece in a covered pot and served in its own gravy.

Pots•dam (pots′dam; *for 1 also Ger.* pôts′däm), *n.* a city in and the capital of Brandenburg, in NE Germany, SW of Berlin: formerly the residence of German emperors; wartime conference July–August 1945 of Truman, Stalin, Churchill, and later, Attlee. 142,860.

pot•sherd (pot′shûrd′), *n.* a broken pottery fragment, esp. one of archaeological value.

pot•shot (pot′shot′), *n.* **1.** a shot fired at game merely for food, with little regard to skill or the rules of sport. **2.** a shot at an animal or person within easy range, as from ambush. **3.** a casual or aimless shot. **4.** a random or incidental criticism.

pot•tage (pot′ij), *n.* a thick soup made of vegetables, with or without meat.

pot•ted (pot′id), *adj.* **1.** transplanted into or grown in a pot. **2.** *Brit.* concise and superficial: *potted biographies.*

pot•ter (pot′ər), *n.* a person who makes pottery.

Pot•ter (pot′ər), *n.* **1. Beatrix,** 1866–1943, English writer and illustrator of children's books. **2. Paul,** 1625–54, Dutch painter.

pot′ter's field′, *n.* (*sometimes caps.*) a burial place for unidentified persons and the poor. Matt. 27:7.

pot′ter's wheel′, *n.* a device with a rotating horizontal disk upon which clay is molded by a potter.

pot•ter•y (pot′ə rē), *n., pl.* **-ter•ies. 1.** ceramic ware, esp. earthenware and stoneware. **2.** the art or business of a potter; ceramics. **3.** a place where earthen pots or vessels are made.

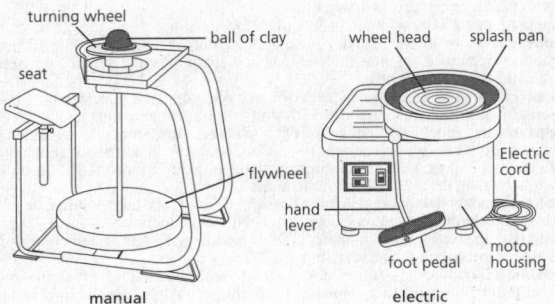

turning wheel   ball of clay   wheel head   splash pan
seat   flywheel   hand lever   foot pedal   Electric cord   motor housing
manual   electric

potter's wheel

pot′ting soil′, *n.* enriched topsoil for potting plants.

pot•ty (pot′ē), *n., pl.* **-ties. 1.** a seat of reduced size fitting over a toilet seat, for use by a small child. **2.** the pot of a potty-chair.

pot′ty-chair′, *n.* a small chair with an open seat over a removable pot, for use by a child during toilet training.

pouch (pouch), *n.* **1.** a bag, sack, or similar receptacle, esp. one for small articles or quantities: *a tobacco pouch.* **2.** a small moneybag. **3.** a bag for carrying mail. **4.** a bag or case of leather, used by soldiers to carry ammunition. **5.** something shaped like or resembling a bag or pocket. **6.** a baggy fold of flesh under the eye. **7.** a baglike anatomical structure, as the dilated cheeks of certain rodents or the receptacle for the young of marsupials. —*v.t.* **8.** to put into or enclose in a pouch, bag, or pocket; pocket. **9.** (of a fish or bird) to swallow. —*v.i.* **10.** to form a pouch or a cavity resembling a pouch.

pouf (pŏŏf), *n.* **1.** a high headdress with the hair rolled in puffs, worn by women in the late 18th century. **2.** PUFF (def. 8). **3.** Also, **pouffe.** a backless, usu. round, cushionlike seat, often large enough for several people. —**poufed, pouffed,** *adj.*

poult (pōlt), *n.* a young fowl, as of the turkey, the pheasant, or a similar bird.

poul•tice (pōl′tis), *n., v.,* **-ticed, -tic•ing. —n. 1.** a soft, moist mass of cloth, bread, meal, herbs, etc., applied hot as a medicament to the body. —*v.t.* **2.** to apply a poultice to.

poul•try (pōl′trē), *n.* domesticated fowl, esp. those valued for their meat and eggs, as chickens, turkeys, ducks, geese, and guinea fowl.

pounce[1] (pouns), *v.,* **pounced, pounc•ing,** *n.* —*v.i.* **1.** to swoop down or spring suddenly, as an animal in seizing its prey. **2.** to seize eagerly. **3.** to make a sudden attack: *to pounce on every mistake.* —*n.* **4.** a sudden swoop, as or as if on an object of prey. **5.** the claw or talon of a bird of prey. —**pounc′ing•ly,** *adv.*

pounce[2] (pouns), *n., v.,* **pounced, pounc•ing. —n. 1.** a fine powder, as of cuttlefish bone, formerly used to prevent ink from spreading in writing, or to prepare parchment for writing. **2.** a fine powder, often of charcoal, used in transferring a design through a perforated pattern. —*v.t.* **3.** to sprinkle, smooth, or prepare with pounce. **4.** to trace (a design) with pounce.

pound[1] (pound), *v.t.* **1.** to strike repeatedly with great force, as with an instrument, the fist, heavy missiles, etc. **2.** to produce or effect by or as if by striking or thumping (often fol. by *out*). **3.** to force (a way) by battering; batter (often fol. by *down*). **4.** to crush into a powder or paste by beating repeatedly. —*v.i.* **5.** to strike heavy blows repeatedly. **6.** to beat or throb violently, as the heart. **7.** to give forth a thumping sound. **8.** to walk or go with heavy steps. **9.** to work with force or vigor (often fol. by *away*). —*n.* **10.** the act of pounding. **11.** a heavy or forcible blow. **12.** a thump. —*Idiom.* **13. pound the pavement,** *Informal.* to walk the streets unremittingly, as to find work.

pound[2] (pound), *n., pl.* **pounds,** (*collectively*) **pound. 1.** a unit of weight and of mass, varying in different periods and countries. **2.** a. (in English-speaking countries) an avoirdupois unit of weight equal to 7000 grains, divided into 16 ounces (0.453 kg), used for ordinary commerce. *Abbr.:* lb., lb. av. **b.** a troy unit of weight, in the U.S. and formerly in Britain, equal to 5760 grains, divided into 12 ounces (0.373 kg), used for precious metals. *Abbr.:* lb. t. **c.** (in the U.S.) a unit of apothecaries' weight equal to 5760 grains, divided into 12 ounces (0.373 kg). **3.** Also called **pound sterling.** the basic monetary unit of the United Kingdom, equal to 100 pence. *Abbr.:* L; *Symbol:* £ **4.** the basic monetary unit of Cyprus, Egypt, Ireland, Lebanon, Sudan, and Syria. See table at CURRENCY. —*Idiom.* **5. pound of flesh,** something justly owed but ruinous to the payer.

pound[3] (pound), *n.,* **1.** an enclosure maintained by public authorities for confining stray or homeless animals. **2.** an enclosure for sheltering, keeping, confining, or trapping animals. **3.** an enclosure or trap for fish. **4.** a place of confinement or imprisonment. **5.** a place where illegally parked vehicles are impounded.

Pound (pound), *n.* **Ezra Loomis,** 1885–1972, U.S. poet.

pound•age[1] (poun'dij), *n.* **1.** a charge of so much per pound sterling or per pound weight. **2.** weight in pounds.

pound•age[2] (poun'dij), *n.* **1.** confinement within an enclosure or within certain limits. **2.** the fee demanded to free animals from a pound.

pound′ cake′, *n.* a rich cake made with flour, butter, sugar, and eggs, orig. in proportions of a pound each.

pound•er (poun'dər), *n.* a person or thing having or associated with a weight or value of a pound or a specified number of pounds (often used in combination): *The lobster is a two-pounder.*

pound′ sign′, *n.* **1.** a symbol (#) for "pound" or "pounds" as a monetary unit of the United Kingdom. **2.** a symbol (#) for "pound" or "pounds" as a unit of weight or mass. Compare NUMBER SIGN, SPACE MARK.

pound′ ster′ling, *n.* POUND[1] (def. 3).

pour (pôr, pōr), *v.t.* **1.** to send (a liquid, fluid, or anything in loose particles) flowing or falling, as from one container to another, or into, over, or on something. **2.** to emit or propel, esp. continuously or rapidly. **3.** to produce or utter in or as if in a stream (often fol. by *out*). —*v.i.* **4.** to issue, move, or proceed in great quantity or number: *Crowds poured from the stadium after the game.* **5.** to flow forth or along; stream. **6.** to rain heavily (often used impersonally with *it* as subject). —*n.* **7.** the act of pouring. **8.** an abundant or continuous flow: *a pour of invective.* **9.** DOWNPOUR. —**pour′a•ble,** *adj.* —**pour′a•bil′i•ty,** *n.* —**pour′er,** *n.*

pout[1] (pout), *v.i.* **1.** to thrust out the lips, esp. in displeasure or sullenness. **2.** to look or be sullen. **3.** to swell out or protrude, as lips. —*v.t.* **4.** to protrude (the lips). **5.** to utter with a pout. —*n.* **6.** the act of pouting; a protrusion of the lips. **7.** a fit of sullenness: *to be in a pout.* —**pout′ing•ly,** *adv.*

pout[2] (pout), *n., pl.* (*esp. collectively*) **pout,** (*esp. for kinds or species*) **pouts.** a northern marine food fish, *Trisopterus luscus.*

pout•y (pou'tē), *adj.,* **-i•er, -i•est.** inclined to pout; sulky.

POV, point of view.

pov•er•ty (pov'ər tē), *n.* **1.** condition of being poor; indigence. **2.** deficiency of necessary or desirable ingredients, qualities, etc. **3.** scantiness; insufficiency.

pov′erty-strick′en, *adj.* extremely poor.

pow (pou), *interj.* **1.** (used to suggest a heavy blow or an explosive noise.) —*n.* **2.** a heavy blow or explosive noise.

POW, *pl.* **POW's, POWs.** prisoner of war.

pow•der (pou'dər), *n.* **1.** matter reduced to a state of fine, loose particles by crushing, grinding, disintegration, etc. **2.** a preparation in this form, as gunpowder or face powder. **3.** loose, usu. fresh snow that is not granular, wet, or packed. —*v.t.* **4.** to reduce to powder; pulverize. **5.** to sprinkle or cover with or as if with powder. *A light snowfall powdered the ground.* **6.** to apply powder to (the face, skin, etc.) as a cosmetic. —*v.i.* **7.** to become pulverized. **8.** to use powder as a cosmetic.

pow′der blue′, *n.* a pale blue diluted with gray. —**pow′der-blue′,** *adj.*

pow′der burn′, *n.* a skin burn caused by exploding gunpowder.

pow′dered sug′ar, *n.* a sugar produced by pulverizing granulated sugar. *Symbol:* XX Compare CONFECTIONERS′ SUGAR.

pow′der keg′, *n.* **1.** a small, metal, barrellike container for gunpowder or blasting powder. **2.** a potentially dangerous situation, esp. one involving violent repercussions.

pow′der puff′, *n.* a soft ball or pad, as of cotton or down, for applying powder to the skin.

pow′der room′, *n.* **1.** lavatory; half bath. **2.** LADIES′ ROOM.

pow•der•y (pou'də rē), *adj.* **1.** consisting of or resembling powder. **2.** easily reduced to powder: *powdery plaster.* **3.** sprinkled or covered with or as if with powder.

pow′dery mil′dew, *n.* **1.** any of various fungi that produce a powderlike film of mycelium on the surface of host plants. **2.** the plant disease caused by powdery mildew.

Pow•ell (pou'əl), *n.* **1. Adam Clayton, Jr.,** 1908–72, U.S. clergyman, politician, and civil-rights leader: congressman 1945–67, 1969–71. **2. Colin** (kō'lin, kol'in), born 1937, U.S. general. **3. Lewis Franklin, Jr.,** born 1907, U.S. jurist: associate justice of the U.S. Supreme Court 1972–87.

pow•er (pou'ər), *n.* **1.** ability to do or act; capability of doing or accomplishing something. **2.** political or national strength. **3.** great or marked ability to do or act; strength; might; force. **4.** the possession of control or command over others; authority; ascendancy: *power over people's minds.* **5.** political ascendancy or control in the government of a country, state, etc. **6.** legal ability, capacity, or authority. **7.** delegated authority; authority granted to a person or persons in a particular office or capacity: *the powers of the president.* **8.** a document or written statement conferring legal authority. **9.** a person or thing that possesses or exercises authority or influence. **10.** a state or nation having international authority or influence. **11.** a military or naval force. **12.** Often, **powers.** a deity; divinity: *the heavenly powers.* **13. powers,** an order of angels. Compare ANGEL (def. 1). **14.** *Physics.* work done or energy transferred per unit of time. *Symbol:* P **15.** mechanical energy as distinguished from hand labor: *a loom driven by power.* **16.** a particular form of mechanical or physical energy: *hydroelectric power.* **17.** energy, force,

or momentum. **18.** *Math.* **a.** the product obtained by multiplying a quantity by itself one or more times: *The third power of 2 is 8.* **b.** the exponent of an expression, as a in x^a. **19. a.** the magnifying capacity of a microscope, telescope, etc., expressed as the ratio of the diameter of the image to the diameter of the object. Compare MAGNIFICATION (def. 2). **b.** the reciprocal of the focal length of a lens. —*v.t.* **20.** to supply with electricity or other means of power. **21.** to give power to; make powerful. **22.** to inspire; spur; sustain. **23.** (of a fuel, engine, or any source able to do work) to supply force to operate (a machine). —*adj.* **24.** operated or driven by a motor or electricity: *a power mower; power tools.* **25.** operated by a procedure in which manual effort is supplemented or replaced by hydraulic, mechanical, or electric means: *power brakes.* **26.** conducting electricity: *a power cable.* **27.** *Informal.* expressing power; involving or characteristic of those having authority or influence: *a power breakfast.* —*Idiom.* **28. the powers that be,** those in supreme command; the authorities.

pow′er base′, *n.* a source of political power founded esp. on support by an organized body of voters or ethnic minority.

pow•er•boat (pou'ər bōt′), *n.* MOTORBOAT. —**pow′er•boat′ing,** *n.*

pow•er•bro•ker or **pow′er bro′ker,** *n.* a person who wields power and influence, esp. a politician who controls votes.

pow′er curve′, *n. Informal.* the capacity to sustain leadership or influence.

pow′er elite′, *n.* a closely knit alliance of military, government, and corporate officials perceived as the center of wealth and political power in the U.S.

pow•er•ful (pou'ər fəl), *adj.* **1.** having or exerting great power or force. **2.** physically strong, as a person. **3.** potent; efficacious: *a powerful drug.* **4.** having great power, authority, or influence; mighty. **5.** *Chiefly South Midland and Southern U.S.* great in number or amount: *a powerful lot of money.* —**pow′er•ful•ly,** *adv.* —**pow′er•ful•ness,** *n.*

pow•er•house (pou'ər hous′), *n., pl.* **-hous•es** (-hou'ziz). **1.** POWER STATION. **2.** a person or group with great energy, strength, or potential for success.

pow•er•less (pou'ər lis), *adj.* **1.** unable to produce an effect; ineffective. **2.** lacking power to act; helpless. —**pow′er•less•ly,** *adv.* —**pow′er•less•ness,** *n.*

pow′er line′, *n.* a line for conducting electric power.

pow′er lunch′, *n.* a meal at which business or political matters are discussed.

pow′er mow′er, *n.* a lawn mower that is powered and propelled by an electric motor or gasoline engine.

pow′er of attor′ney, *n.* written legal authorization for another person to act in one's place.

Pow′er of Pos′itive Think′ing, The, a self-help book (1952) by Norman Vincent Peale.

pow′er of the purse′, *n.* the influence of money.

pow′er plant′ *n.* **1.** a plant, including engines, dynamos, etc., and the building or buildings necessary for the generation of power, as electric or nuclear power. **2.** the machinery for supplying power for a particular mechanical process or operation.

pow′er play′, *n.* **1.** *Football.* an aggressive running play in which numerous offensive players clear a path for the ballcarrier. **2.** a maneuver, as in business, in which advantage is sought through the use of power or influence.

pow′er pol′itics, *n.* (*used with a sing. or pl. v.*) international politics characterized by the use or threatened use of military or economic power as a means of coercion.

pow′er shov′el, *n.* any self-propelled shovel for excavating earth, ore, or coal with a dipper that is powered by a diesel engine or electric motor. Compare SHOVEL (def. 2).

pow′er sta′tion, *n.* a power plant that generates and distributes electricity.

pow′er steer′ing, *n.* an automotive steering system in which the engine's power is used to supplement the driver's effort in turning the steering wheel.

pow′er struc′ture, *n.* **1.** the system of authority or influence in government, politics, education, etc. **2.** the people who participate in such a system.

pow′er train′, *n.* a train of gears and shafting transmitting power from an engine, motor, etc., to a mechanism being driven.

pow•wow (pou'wou′), *n.* **1.** (among North American Indians) a ceremony performed for the cure of disease, success in a hunt, etc. **2.** a council or conference of or with Indians. **3.** (among North American Indians) a priest or shaman. **4.** *Informal.* any conference or meeting. —*v.i.* **5.** to hold a powwow. **6.** *Informal.* to confer.

pox (poks), *n.* **1.** a disease characterized by multiple skin pustules, as smallpox. **2.** syphilis. **3.** curse; plague: *A pox on you and your bright ideas!*

pp, pianissimo.

pp., **1.** pages. **2.** past participle. **3.** privately printed.

p.p., **1.** parcel post. **2.** past participle. **3.** per person. **4.** postpaid.

ppb or **p.p.b.,** parts per billion.

ppd., **1.** postpaid. **2.** prepaid.

ppm, **1.** Also, **p.p.m.** parts per million. **2.** pulse per minute.

PPO, preferred-provider organization.

ppp, pianississimo; double pianissimo.

P

ppr. or **p.pr.,** present participle.
P.P.S. or **p.p.s.,** an additional postscript.
ppv or **PPV,** pay-per-view.
Pr, *Chem. Symbol.* praseodymium.
PR, 1. public relations. **2.** Puerto Rico.
pr., 1. pair. **2.** present. **3.** price. **4.** pronoun.
Pr., 1. (of stock) preferred. **2.** Priest. **3.** Prince. **4.** Provençal.
P.R., 1. proportional representation. **2.** public relations.
prac·ti·ca·ble (prak′ti kə bəl), *adj.* **1.** capable of being done or put into practice with the available means; feasible. **2.** capable of being used. —**prac′ti·ca·bil′i·ty, prac′ti·ca·ble·ness,** *n.*
prac·ti·cal (prak′ti kəl), *adj.* **1.** pertaining to or concerned with practice or action: *practical mathematics.* **2.** consisting of, involving, or resulting from practice or action: *a practical application of a rule.* **3.** adapted or suited for actual use; useful or utilitarian: *practical instructions; a practical vinyl floor.* **4.** inclined toward or fitted for action or useful activities. **5.** mindful of the results, usefulness, etc., of action or procedure; sensible. **6.** of or concerned with ordinary activities or work: *practical affairs.* **7.** engaged or experienced in actual practice or work: *a practical politician.* **8.** matter-of-fact; prosaic. **9.** being such in practice or effect; virtual: *a practical certainty.* —**prac′ti·cal·i·ty,** *n.*
prac′tical joke′, *n.* a playful trick, often involving some physical agent or means, in which the victim is placed in an embarrassing or disadvantageous position. —**prac′tical jok′er,** *n.*
prac·ti·cal·ly (prak′tik lē), *adv.* **1.** in a practical manner: *to think practically.* **2.** from a practical point of view. **3.** almost; nearly.
prac′tical nurse′, *n.* a person with less training than a registered nurse whose occupation is caring for the sick.
prac·tice (prak′tis), *n., v.,* **-ticed, -tic·ing.** —*n.* **1.** habitual or customary course of action or way of doing something: *office practice.* **2.** a habit; custom: *to make a practice of borrowing money.* **3.** repeated performance or systematic exercise for the purpose of acquiring proficiency. **4.** condition arrived at by experience or exercise: *out of practice.* **5.** the action or process of doing something or carrying something out: *to put a scheme into practice.* **6.** the exercise or pursuit of a profession, esp. law or medicine. **7.** the business of a professional person. **8.** the established method of conducting legal proceedings. —*v.t.* **9.** to perform or do habitually or usually: *to practice a strict regimen.* **10.** to follow or observe habitually or customarily: *to practice one's religion.* **11.** to exercise or pursue as a profession, art, or occupation. **12.** to perform on or do repeatedly in order to acquire skill or proficiency: *to practice the violin.* —*v.i.* **13.** to do something habitually or as a practice. **14.** to pursue a profession, esp. law or medicine. **15.** to do something repeatedly in order to acquire skill. Also, *Brit.,* **practise** (for defs. 9–15). —*Proverb.* **16. Practice makes perfect,** practice improves skill. **17. Practice what you preach,** do what you tell others to do. —**prac′tic·er,** *n.*
prac·ticed (prak′tist), *adj.* **1.** skilled or expert; proficient through practice or experience. **2.** acquired or perfected through practice: *a practiced English accent.*
prac′tice teach′er, *n.* STUDENT TEACHER. —**prac′tice-teach′,** *v.i.*
prac·tic·ing (prak′ti sing), *adj.* **1.** actively working at a profession. **2.** actively following a religion, philosophy, or way of life.
prac·tise (prak′tis), *v.t., v.i.,* **-tised, -tis·ing.** *Brit.* PRACTICE.
prac·ti·tion·er (prak tish′ə nər), *n.* **1.** a person engaged in the practice of a profession or occupation. **2.** a person who practices something specified. **3.** a person authorized to practice Christian Science healing.
prag·mat·ic (prag mat′ik), *adj.* **1.** concerned with practical considerations or consequences; having a practical point of view. **2.** of or pertaining to philosophical pragmatism. **3.** treating historical phenomena with special reference to their causes, antecedent conditions, and results. Also, **prag·mat′i·cal** (for defs. 1, 2). —**prag·mat′i·cal·ly,** *adv.*
prag·mat·ics (prag mat′iks), *n.* **1.** (*used with a pl. v.*) practical considerations. **2.** (*used with a sing. v.*) a branch of semiotics dealing with the causal and other relations between words, expressions, or symbols and their users. **3.** (*used with a sing. v.*) a branch of linguistics dealing with language in its situational context, including the knowledge and beliefs of the speaker and the relationship and interaction between speaker and listener.
prag·ma·tism (prag′mə tiz′əm), *n.* **1.** character or conduct that emphasizes practical results or concerns rather than theory or principle. **2.** a philosophical movement or system having various forms, but generally stressing practical consequences as constituting the essential criterion in determining meaning, truth, or value. —**prag′ma·tist,** *n., adj.*
Prague (präg), *n.* the capital of the Czech Republic, in the W central part, on the Vltava: formerly the capital of Czechoslovakia. 1,215,000. Czech, **Pra·ha** (prä′hä).
Prai·a (prī′ə), *n.* the capital of Cape Verde, in the S Atlantic Ocean, on S São Tiago Island. 39,000.
prai·rie (prâr′ē), *n.* **1.** an extensive, level or undulating, mostly treeless tract of land esp. in the Mississippi valley, orig. covered with coarse grasses. **2.** a tract of grassland; meadow.
prai′rie chick′en, *n.* either of two gallinaceous birds of central North American grasslands, *Tympanuchus cupido* or *T. pallidicinctus,* of the grouse subfamily, noted for the booming sounds made by males during courtship displays.
prai′rie dog′, *n.* any burrowing squirrel of the genus *Cynomys,* of W

prairie dog, *Cynomys ludovicianus,*
head and body 1 ½ ft. (0.5 m);
tail 3 ½ in (8.9 cm)

North American and N Mexican plains and prairies, having a barklike cry.
Prai′rie School′, *n.* a group of early 20th-century architects of the Chicago area who designed houses and other buildings with strong horizontal lines reflecting the flatness of the Midwestern prairie; the best-known member was Frank Lloyd Wright.
prai′rie schoon′er, *n.* a covered wagon similar to the Conestoga wagon, used by pioneers in crossing the prairies and plains of North America.
prai′rie wolf′, *n.* COYOTE.
praise (prāz), *n., v.,* **praised, prais·ing.** —*n.* **1.** the act of expressing approval or admiration; commendation. **2.** the offering of grateful homage in words or song as an act of worship. **3.** the state of being approved or admired. —*v.t.* **4.** to express approval or admiration of; commend. **5.** to offer grateful homage to (God or a deity), as in words or song. —*Proverb.* **6. Praise the Lord and pass the ammunition,** rely on your own efforts as well as on God: title of a popular song in World War II. —**praise′ful,** *adj.* —**praise′less,** *adj.* —**prais′er,** *n.*
Praise′ God′ from′ Whom′ All′ Bless′ings Flow′, a doxology (1709) by Thomas Ken.
praise·wor·thy (prāz′wûr′thē), *adj.* deserving of praise: *a praiseworthy motive.* —**praise′wor′thi·ness,** *n.*
praj·na (pruj′nyä, -nə), *n. Buddhism, Hinduism.* pure and unqualified knowledge; Enlightenment.
pra·line (prā′lēn, prä′-), *n.* **1.** a confection made of nuts, esp. almonds, and sugar cooked until caramelized, often ground into a powder and used as a flavoring. **2.** a cookie-size confection, originating in New Orleans, made chiefly of brown sugar, pecans, and butter. **3.** a sugarcoated almond.
pram (pram), *n. Chiefly Brit.* a perambulator.
prance (prans, präns), *v.,* **pranced, pranc·ing,** *n.* —*v.i.* **1.** to dance or move in a lively or spirited manner; caper. **2.** to move or walk in a proud or insolent manner. **3.** (esp. of a horse) to spring from the hind legs, or move by springing. **4.** to ride on a horse doing this. —*v.t.* **5.** to cause to prance. —*n.* **6.** the act of prancing; a prancing movement. —**pranc′er,** *n.* —**pranc′ing·ly,** *adv.*
pran·di·al (pran′dē əl), *adj.* of or pertaining to a meal, esp. dinner. —**pran′di·al·ly,** *adv.*
prank¹ (prangk), *n.* a trick of an amusing, playful, or sometimes malicious nature.
prank² (prangk), *v.t.* **1.** to dress or adorn in an ostentatious manner. —*v.i.* **2.** to make an ostentatious show or display.
prank·ish (prang′kish), *adj.* **1.** of the nature of a prank: *a prankish plan.* **2.** full of pranks; playful: *a prankish child.* —**prank′ish·ly,** *adv.* —**prank′ish·ness,** *n.*
prank·ster (prangk′stər), *n.* a person who is given to pranks.
pra·se·o·dym·i·um (prā′zē ō dim′ē əm, prā′sē-), *n.* a rare-earth metallic trivalent element. *Symbol:* Pr; *at. wt.:* 140.91; *at. no.:* 59; *sp. gr.:* 6.77 at 20°C.
prate (prāt), *v.,* **prat·ed, prat·ing,** *n.* —*v.i.* **1.** to talk excessively and pointlessly; babble. —*v.t.* **2.** to utter in empty or foolish talk. —*n.* **3.** the act of prating. **4.** empty or foolish talk. —**prat′er,** *n.* —**prat′ing·ly,** *adv.*
prat·fall (prat′fôl′), *n.* **1.** a fall on the buttocks, esp. when often regarded as comical or humiliating. **2.** a humiliating blunder.
prat·tle (prat′l), *v.,* **-tled, -tling,** *n.* —*v.i.* **1.** to talk in a childish or simple-minded way; chatter or babble; prate. —*v.t.* **2.** to utter by chattering or babbling. —*n.* **3.** the act of prattling. **4.** chatter; babble. —**prat′tler,** *n.* —**prat′tling·ly,** *adv.*
prawn (prôn), *n.* **1.** any of various shrimplike crustaceans of the genera *Palaemonetes, Penaeus,* etc., some of which are used as food. **2.** any shrimp. —*v.i.* **3.** to catch prawns, as for food. —**prawn′er,** *n.*
Prax·it·e·les (prak sit′l ēz′), *n.* fl. c350 B.C., Greek sculptor.
pray (prā), *v.t.* **1.** to offer devout petition, praise, thanks, etc., to (God or an object of worship). **2.** to offer (a prayer). **3.** to make earnest petition to (a person). **4.** to make entreaty for; crave: *I pray your forgiveness.* **5.** to bring, put, etc., by praying: *to pray a soul into heaven.* —*v.i.* **6.** to offer devout petition, praise, thanks, etc., to God or to an object of worship; engage in prayer. **7.** to make entreaty to a person or for a thing. —**pray′ing·ly,** *adv.*
prayer¹ (prâr), *n.* **1.** a devout petition to God or an object of worship. **2.** a spiritual communion with God or an object of worship, as in supplication, thanksgiving, or adoration. **3.** the act or practice of praying to God or an object of worship. **4.** a formula or sequence of words used in praying: *the Lord's Prayer.* **5. prayers,** a religious observance consisting

mainly of prayer. **6.** something prayed for. **7.** a petition; entreaty. **8.** a negligible hope or chance: *We don't have a prayer of winning.* —**prayer/less,** *adj.*

pray•er² (prā/ər), *n.* a person who prays.

prayer/ beads/ (prâr), *n.* a rosary.

prayer/ book/ (prâr), *n.* a book containing formal prayers for religious devotions.

prayer/ flag/ (prâr), *n.* a flag stamped with printed prayers, used by Himalayan Buddhists, who believe that its fluttering sends out the prayers inscribed on it.

prayer/ meet/ing (prâr), *n.* **1.** a meeting chiefly for prayer. **2.** (in certain Protestant churches) a meeting in midweek, chiefly for individual prayer and the offering of testimonies of faith. Also called **prayer service.**

Prayer/ of Manas/seh, *n.* a book of the Apocrypha.

prayer/ plant/ (prâr), *n.* a Brazilian plant cultivated for its variegated leaves, which close up at night.

prayer/ rug/ (prâr), *n.* a small rug upon which a Muslim kneels and prostrates himself during his devotions.

prayer/ wheel/ (prâr), *n.* a wheel or cylinder inscribed with or containing prayers, used chiefly by Buddhists of Tibet.

pray/ing man/tis, *n.* MANTIS.

PRC, Postal Rate Commission.

pre-, a prefix, occurring orig. in loanwords from Latin, meaning "before, in front of," "prior to, in advance of," "surpassing" (*predict; preeminent; preface; premaxilla*); in English, esp. productive in forming verbs that specify an activity taking place before or instead of the usual occurrence of the same activity (*preboard; precook; prepay*), or in forming adjectives that specify a period of time prior to the event, period, person, etc., denoted by the headword (*pre-Columbian; preschool; prewar*).

preach (prēch), *v.t.* **1.** to proclaim or make known in a sermon. **2.** to deliver (a sermon). **3.** to advocate (moral principles, conduct, etc.) as right or advisable. —*v.i.* **4.** to deliver a sermon. **5.** to give earnest advice, esp. in an insistent, tedious, or moralizing way.

preach•er (prē/chər), *n.* **1.** a person whose occupation or function it is to preach the gospel. **2.** a person who preaches.

preach•y (prē/chē), *adj.*, **-i•er, -i•est.** tediously or obtrusively didactic. —**preach/i•ly,** *adv.* —**preach/i•ness,** *n.*

pre-Ad•am•ite (prē ad/ə mīt/), *n.* **1.** a person supposed to have existed before Adam. **2.** a person who believes that there were people in existence before Adam. —*adj.* **3.** Also, **pre-A•dam•ic** (prē/ə dam/ik). **4.** existing before Adam. **5.** of or pertaining to the pre-Adamites.

pre•ad•o•les•cence (prē/ad l es/əns), *n.* the period preceding adolescence, usu. designated as the years from 10 to 13. —**pre/ad•o•les/cent,** *adj., n.*

pre•am•ble (prē/am/bəl, prē am/-), *n.* **1.** an introductory statement; preface. **2.** the introductory part of a statute, deed or other document, stating the intent of what follows. **3.** a preliminary fact or circumstance. —**pre/am/bled,** *adj.*

pre/ar•range (prē/ə rānj/), *v.t.,* **-ranged, -rang•ing.** to arrange in advance. —**pre/ar•range/ment,** *n.*

pre•ax•i•al (prē ak/sē əl), *adj. Anat.* situated in front of an axis of the body. —**pre•ax/i•al•ly,** *adv.*

Pre•cam•bri•an or **Pre-Cam•bri•an** (prē kam/brē ən, -kām/-), *adj.* **1.** noting or pertaining to the earliest era of earth history, ending 570 million years ago, during which the earth's crust formed and life first appeared in the seas. —*n.* **2.** the Precambrian Era.

pre•can•cer•ous (prē kan/sər əs), *adj.* showing pathological changes that may be preliminary to malignancy.

pre•car•i•ous (pri kâr/ē əs), *adj.* **1.** dependent on circumstances beyond one's control; uncertain: *a precarious livelihood.* **2.** dangerous because insecure or unsteady. **3.** based upon insufficient evidence. **4.** dependent on the will of another. —**pre•car/i•ous•ly,** *adv.* —**pre•car/i•ous•ness,** *n.*

pre•cast (prē kast/, -käst/), *v.,* **-cast, -cast•ing,** *adj.* —*v.t.* **1.** to cast (a concrete block or slab, etc.) in a place other than where it is to be installed in a structure. —*adj.* **2.** (of a building material or member) cast before being transported to the site of installation.

pre•cau•tion (pri kô/shən), *n.* **1.** a measure taken in advance to avert possible harm or misfortune. **2.** caution employed beforehand; prudent foresight. —*v.t.* **3.** to forewarn; put on guard. —**pre•cau/tion•ar/y,** *adj.*

pre•cede (pri sēd/), *v.,* **-ced•ed, -ced•ing.** —*v.t.* **1.** to go before, as in place, rank, importance, or time. **2.** to introduce by something preliminary; preface. —*v.i.* **3.** to go or come before. —**pre•ced/a•ble,** *adj.*

prec•e•dence (pres/i dəns, pri sēd/ns), *n.* **1.** the act or fact of preceding. **2.** the right to be dealt with or placed before others; priority in order, rank, or importance. **3.** the order of rank to be observed in ceremonies, as by diplomatic protocol.

prec•e•dent (*n.* pres/i dənt; *adj.* pri sēd/nt, pres/i dənt), *n.* **1.** an act or instance that may serve as an example or justification for subsequent situations. **2.** a legal decision serving as an authoritative rule or pattern in similar cases that follow. **3.** established practice; custom: *to break with precedent.* —*adj.* **4.** preceding; prior. —**prec/e•den/tial** (-den/shəl), *adj.* —**prec/e•dent•less,** *adj.*

pre•ced•ing (pri sē/ding), *adj.* that precedes; coming before; previous: *the preceding page.*

pre•cen•tor (pri sen/tər), *n.* a person who leads a church choir or congregation in singing.

pre•cept (prē/sept), *n.* **1.** a commandment or direction given as a rule of action or conduct. **2.** an injunction as to moral conduct; maxim. **3.** a direction for performing a technical operation. **4.** a written order issued pursuant to law.

pre•cep•tor (pri sep/tər, prē/sep-), *n.* **1.** an instructor; teacher; tutor. **2.** the head of a school. —**pre•cep/to/ri•al** (-tôr/ē əl, -tōr/-), *adj.* —**pre/cep•to/ri•al•ly,** *adv.* —**pre•cep/tor•ship/,** *n.*

pre•ces•sion (prē sesh/ən), *n.* **1.** the act or fact of preceding; precedence. **2.** the movement of the axis of rotation of a spinning body around another axis, an effect exhibited by a spinning top or gyroscope. **3.** the slow, conical motion of the earth's axis of rotation caused by forces exerted on the earth by the sun and moon. —**pre•ces/sion•al,** *adj.*

pre•cinct (prē/singkt), *n.* **1.** a district, as of a city, marked out for administrative purposes or for police protection. **2.** Also called **pre/cinct house/.** the police station in such a district. **3.** one of a fixed number of districts, each containing one polling place, into which a city, town, etc., is divided for voting purposes. **4.** Often, **precincts.** an enclosing boundary or limit. **5. precincts,** the parts or regions immediately surrounding a place; environs. **6.** a walled or bounded space within which a building or place is situated.

pre•cious (presh/əs), *adj.* **1.** of high price or great value: *precious metals.* **2.** highly esteemed for some nonmaterial quality: *precious memories.* **3.** dear; beloved: *a precious child.* **4.** designating a stone or crystal, esp. a diamond, ruby, sapphire, or emerald, valued as rare and beautiful, used in jewelry. **5.** affectedly or excessively refined. **6.** flagrant; gross: *a precious fool.* —*n.* **7.** a dearly beloved person; darling. —*adv.* **8.** extremely; very: *We have precious little time.* —**pre/cious•ly,** *adv.* —**pre/cious•ness,** *n.*

pre/cious met/al, *n.* a metal of the gold, silver, or platinum group.

prec•i•pice (pres/ə pis), *n.* **1.** a cliff with a vertical or overhanging face. **2.** a situation of great peril. —**prec/i•piced,** *adj.*

pre•cip•i•tant (pri sip/i tənt), *adj.* **1.** hasty, sudden, or headlong; precipitate. —*n.* **2.** *Chem.* something that causes precipitation. —**pre•cip/i•tan•cy** (-tən sē), **pre•cip/i•tance,** *n.* —**pre•cip/i•tant•ly,** *adv.*

pre•cip•i•tate (*v.* pri sip/i tāt/; *adj., n.* -tit, -tāt/), *v.,* **-tat•ed, -tat•ing,** *adj., n.* —*v.t.* **1.** to hasten the occurrence of; bring about prematurely or suddenly: *to precipitate a crisis.* **2.** to fling or hurl down. **3.** to cast violently or abruptly: *to precipitate oneself into a struggle.* **4.** to separate (a substance) in solid form from a solution. —*v.i.* **5.** to fall to the earth's surface as a condensed form of water; to rain, snow, hail, drizzle, etc. **6.** to separate from a solution as a precipitate. **7.** to be cast down headlong. —*adj.* **8.** done or made without sufficient deliberation; overhasty. **9.** rushing or falling headlong. **10.** proceeding rapidly or with great haste. **11.** exceedingly sudden or abrupt. —*n.* **12.** a substance precipitated from a solution. **13.** moisture condensed in the form of rain, snow, etc. —**pre•cip/i•tate•ly,** *adv.* —**pre•cip/i•ta•tor,** *n.*

pre•cip•i•ta•tion (pri sip/i tā/shən), *n.* **1. a.** falling products of condensation in the atmosphere, as rain, snow, or hail. **b.** the amount of rain, snow, hail, or the like that has fallen at a given place within a given period, usu. expressed in inches or centimeters of water. **2.** the act of precipitating; state of being precipitated. **3.** the precipitating of a substance from a solution. **4.** sudden or rash haste.

pre•cip•i•tous (pri sip/i təs), *adj.* **1.** of the nature of a precipice: *a precipitous wall of rock.* **2.** extremely steep: *precipitous mountain trails.* **3.** PRECIPITATE. —**pre•cip/i•tous•ly,** *adv.* —**pre•cip/i•tous•ness,** *n.*

pré•cis (prā sē/, prā/sē), *n., pl.* **-cis** (-sēz/, -sēz), *v.* —*n.* **1.** a concise summary. —*v.t.* **2.** to make a précis of.

pre•cise (pri sīs/), *adj.* **1.** definitely or strictly stated, defined, or fixed: *precise directions.* **2.** being that one and no other: *the precise dress I wanted.* **3.** exact in expressing oneself. **4.** carefully distinct: *precise articulation.* **5.** exact in measuring, recording, etc.: *a precise instrument.* —**pre•cise/ly,** *adv.* —**pre•cise/ness,** *n.*

pre•ci•sion (pri sizh/ən), *n.* **1.** the state or quality of being precise. **2.** mechanical or scientific exactness: *a lens ground with precision.* **3.** strict observance; punctiliousness. **4.** *Math.* the degree to which the correctness of a quantity is expressed. Compare ACCURACY (def. 3). —*adj.* **5.** of, pertaining to, or characterized by precision: *precision instruments.* —**pre•ci/sion•al,** *adj.*

preci/sion bomb/ing, *n.* aerial bombing in which bombs are dropped, as accurately as possible, on a specific, usually small, target.

pre•clin•i•cal (prē klin/i kəl), *adj.* of or pertaining to the period prior to the appearance of symptoms.

pre•clude (pri klōōd/), *v.t.,* **-clud•ed, -clud•ing. 1.** to prevent the presence or occurrence of; make impossible: *evidence that precludes a conviction.* **2.** to exclude or debar. —**pre•clud/a•ble,** *adj.* —**pre•clu/sion** (-klōō/zhən), *n.* —**pre•clu/sive** (-siv), *adj.* —**pre•clu/sive•ly,** *adv.*

pre•co•cious (pri kō/shəs), *adj.* **1.** unusually advanced or mature in mental development or talent: *a precocious child.* **2.** prematurely developed. —**pre•co/cious•ly,** *adv.* —**pre•co/cious•ness, pre•coc/i•ty** (-kos/i tē), *n.*

pre•cog•ni•tion (prē/kog nish/ən), *n.* knowledge of a future event or situation, esp. through extrasensory means. —**pre•cog/ni•tive** (-kog/ni•tiv), *adj.*

pre•co•lo•ni•al (prē/kə lō/nē əl), *adj.* of or pertaining to the time before a region or country became a colony.

P

pre·Co·lum·bi·an (prē′kə lum′bē ən), *adj.* of or pertaining to the Americas before the arrival of Columbus.

pre·con·ceive (prē′kən sēv′), *v.t.,* **-ceived, -ceiv·ing.** to form (as an opinion) beforehand, esp. from previously held prejudice.

pre·con·cep·tion (prē′kən sep′shən), *n.* **1.** a conception or opinion formed beforehand. **2.** a prejudice or bias. **—pre′con·cep′tion·al,** *adj.*

pre·con·di·tion (prē′kən dish′ən), *n.* **1.** something that is necessary to a subsequent result: *a precondition for a promotion.* **—v.t. 2.** to subject to a special preparation that will permit or facilitate a subsequent experience, process, etc.: *to precondition a surface to receive paint.*

pre·cook (prē kŏŏk′), *v.t.* to cook (food) partly or completely beforehand, esp. to facilitate preparation before serving.

pre·cur·sor (pri kûr′sər, prē′kûr-), *n.* **1.** a person or thing that precedes, as in a job or a method; predecessor. **2.** a person, animal, or thing regarded as a harbinger: *The first robin is a precursor of spring.* **3.** a chemical that is transformed into another compound, as in the course of a chemical reaction: *Cholesterol is a precursor of testosterone.* **4.** a cell or tissue that gives rise to a variant or more mature form. **—pre·cur′so·ry,** *adj.*

pre·date (prē′dāt′), *v.t.,* **-dat·ed, -dat·ing. 1.** to date before the actual time: *to predate a check.* **2.** to precede in time.

pre·da·tion (pri dā′shən), *n.* **1.** the act of plundering or robbing; depredation. **2.** predatory behavior. **3.** *Ecol.* the capture and consumption of prey.

pred·a·tor (pred′ə tər, -tôr′), *n.* **1.** an animal that hunts and seizes other animals for food. **2.** a predatory person.

pred·a·to·ry (pred′ə tôr′ē, -tōr′ē), *adj.* **1.** preying upon other organisms for food. **2.** characterized by plunder, robbery, or exploitation. **3.** engaging in or living by these activities: *predatory brigands.* **4.** acting with or indicative of rapacious, greedy, or selfish motives. **—pred′a·to′ri·ly,** *adv.* **—pred′a·to′ri·ness,** *n.*

pre·dawn (prē dôn′, prē′-), *n.* **1.** the period immediately preceding dawn. **—adj. 2.** occurring just before dawn.

pre·de·cease (prē′di sēs′), *v.t.,* **-ceased, -ceas·ing.** to die before (another person).

pred·e·ces·sor (pred′ə ses′ər; *esp. Brit.* prē′də-), *n.* **1.** a person who precedes another in an office, position, etc. **2.** something succeeded or replaced by something else.

pre·des·ti·nate (*v.* pri des′tə nāt′; *adj.* -nit, -nāt′), *v.,* **-nat·ed, -nat·ing,** *adj.* **—v.t. 1.** to foreordain by divine decree or purpose. **—adj. 2.** foreordained. **—pre·des′ti·nate·ly,** *adv.*

pre·des·ti·na·tion (pri des′tə nā′shən, prē′des-), *n.* **1.** an act of predestinating or predestining. **2.** the state of being predestinated or predestined. **3.** fate; destiny. **4.** the foreordination by God of whatever comes to pass, esp. the salvation and damnation of souls.

pre·des·tine (prē des′tin), *v.t.,* **-tined, -tin·ing.** to destine in advance; foreordain; predetermine. **—pre·des′ti·na·ble,** *adj.*

pre·de·ter·mine (prē′di tûr′min), *v.t.,* **-mined, -min·ing. 1.** to settle or decide in advance. **2.** to ordain in advance; predestine. **3.** to direct or impel; influence strongly. **—pre′de·ter′mi·nate,** *adj.* **—pre′de·ter′mi·nate·ly,** *adv.* **—pre′de·ter′mi·na′tion,** *n.* **—pre′de·ter′mi·na′tive** (-nā′tiv, -nə tiv), *adj.*

pred·i·ca·ble (pred′i kə bəl), *adj.* **1.** able to be predicated or affirmed; assertable. **—n. 2.** that which may be predicated; an attribute. **—pred′i·ca·bil′i·ty,** *n.* **—pred′i·ca·bly,** *adv.*

pre·dic·a·ment (pri dik′ə mənt *for 1;* pred′i kə- *for 2*), *n.* **1.** an unpleasantly difficult, perplexing, or dangerous situation. **2.** a class or category of logical or philosophical predication.

pred·i·cate (*v.* pred′i kāt′; *adj., n.* -kit), *v.,* **-cat·ed, -cat·ing,** *adj., n.* **—v.t. 1.** to proclaim; declare; affirm; assert. **2.** *Logic.* to affirm or assert (something) of the subject of a proposition. **3.** to connote; imply. **4.** to found or derive (a statement, action, etc.); base (usu. fol. by *on*): *to predicate one's behavior on faith in humanity.* **—v.i. 5.** to make an affirmation or assertion. **—adj. 6.** predicated. **7.** belonging to or used in the predicate of a sentence. **—n. 8.** a syntactic unit that functions as one of the two main constituents of a sentence, the other being the subject, as *is here* in *The package is here.* **9.** *Logic.* that which is affirmed or denied concerning the subject of a proposition. **—pred′i·ca′tion,** *n.* **—pred′i·ca′tion·al,** **pred′i·ca′tive** (-kā′tiv, -kə-), *adj.* **—pred′i·ca′tive·ly,** *adv.*

pred′icate ad′jective, *n.* an adjective that is used in the predicate

and has the same referent as the subject of the copulative verb or the direct object, as *sick* in *He is sick* or *It made him sick.*

pred′icate noun′, *n.* a noun that is used in the predicate with a copulative or factitive verb and has the same referent as the subject of the copulative verb or the direct object of the factitive verb, as *mayor* in *She is the mayor* or *They elected her mayor.*

pred·i·ca·to·ry (pred′i kə tôr′ē, -tōr′ē), *adj.* of or pertaining to preaching.

pre·dict (pri dikt′), *v.t.* **1.** to declare or tell in advance; foretell. **—v.i. 2.** to foretell the future; make a prediction. **—pre·dict′a·ble,** *adj.* **—pre·dict′a·bil′i·ty,** *n.* **—pre·dict′a·bly,** *adv.* **—pre·dic′tive,** *adj.* **—pre·dic′tive·ly,** *adv.* **—pre·dic′tive·ness,** *n.* **—pre·dic′tor,** *n.*

pre·dic·tion (pri dik′shən), *n.* **1.** the act of predicting. **2.** an instance of this; something predicted; prophecy.

pre·di·lec·tion (pred′l ek′shən, prēd′-), *n.* a tendency to think favorably of something in particular; partiality; preference; liking.

pre·dis·pose (prē′di spōz′), *v.,* **-posed, -pos·ing. —v.t. 1.** to make susceptible or liable: *genetic factors predisposing us to disease.* **2.** to dispose beforehand; incline; bias. **—v.i. 3.** to give or furnish a tendency or inclination. **—pre′dis·pos′al,** *n.* **—pre′dis·pos′ed·ly** (-spō′zid lē, -spōzd′-), *adv.* **—pre·dis′po·si′tion** (-dis′pə zish′ən), *n.*

pre·dom·i·nant (pri dom′ə nənt), *adj.* **1.** having ascendancy, power, authority, or influence over others; preeminent. **2.** preponderant; prominent: *the predominant color of a painting.* **—pre·dom′i·nant·ly,** *adv.*

pre·dom·i·nate (pri dom′ə nāt′), *v.,* **-nat·ed, -nat·ing. —v.i. 1.** to be the stronger or leading element or force. **2.** to have numerical superiority or advantage. **3.** to surpass others; be preeminent. **4.** to have or exert controlling power (often fol. by *over*): *Good sense predominated over anger.* **—v.t. 5.** to dominate or prevail over. **—pre·dom′i·nate·ly** (-nit-lē), *adv.* **—pre·dom′i·nat′ing·ly,** *adv.* **—pre·dom′i·na′tion,** *n.*

pree·mie (prē′mē), *n.* an infant born prematurely; a preterm.

pre·em·i·nence or **pre-em·i·nence** (prē em′ə nəns), *n.* the state or character of being preeminent.

pre·em·i·nent or **pre-em·i·nent** (prē em′ə nənt), *adj.* eminent above or before others; superior; outstanding. **—pre·em′i·nent·ly,** *adv.*

pre·empt or **pre-empt** (prē empt′), *v.t.* **1.** to occupy (land) in order to establish a prior right to buy; claim. **2.** to acquire or appropriate before someone else; arrogate. **3.** to take the place of because of priorities, rescheduling, etc.; supplant: *A special news report preempted the game show.* **4.** to forestall or prevent (something anticipated) by acting first; head off. **—v.i. 5.** *Bridge.* to make a preemptive bid. **—n. 6.** *Bridge.* a preemptive bid. **—pre·emp′ti·ble,** *adj.* **—pre·emp′tor** (-tôr, -tər), *n.* **—pre·emp′to·ry** (-tə rē), *adj.*

pre·emp·tion or **pre-emp·tion** (prē emp′shən), *n.* **1.** the act or right of claiming or purchasing before or in preference to others. **2.** the act of preempting.

pre·emp·tive or **pre-emp·tive** (prē emp′tiv), *adj.* **1.** of or pertaining to preemption. **2.** taken as a measure against something possible, anticipated, or feared; preventive; deterrent: *a preemptive strike against the enemy.* **3.** pertaining to an opening bid in bridge that is unnecessarily high, designed to prevent further bidding. **—pre·emp′tive·ly,** *adv.*

preemp′tive strike′, *n.* PREVENTIVE WAR.

preen (prēn), *v.t.* **1.** to trim or dress (feathers, fur, etc.) with the beak or tongue. **2.** to dress (oneself) carefully or smartly; primp. **3.** to pride (oneself) on an achievement, personal quality, etc. **—v.i. 4.** to make oneself appear striking or smart in dress or appearance. **5.** to be exultant or proud. **—preen′er,** *n.*

pre·ex·ist or **pre-ex·ist** (prē′ig zist′), *v.i.* **1.** to exist beforehand. **—v.t. 2.** to antedate; precede. **—pre′ex·ist′ence,** *n.* **—pre′ex·ist′ent,** *adj.*

pre·fab (*adj., n.* prē′fab′; *v.* prē fab′), *adj., n., v.,* **-fabbed, -fab·bing.** *Informal.* **—adj. 1.** prefabricated. **—n. 2.** something that is prefabricated, as a building or fixture. **—v.t. 3.** to prefabricate.

pre·fab·ri·cate (prē fab′ri kāt′), *v.t.,* **-cat·ed, -cat·ing. 1.** to fabricate or construct beforehand. **2.** to manufacture in standardized parts or sections ready for quick assembly and erection, as buildings. **—pre′fab·ri·ca′tion,** *n.* **—pre·fab′ri·ca′tor,** *n.*

pref·ace (pref′is), *n., v.,* **-aced, -ac·ing. —n. 1.** a preliminary statement in a book by the author or editor, setting forth the book's purpose, acknowledging the assistance of others, etc. **2.** an introductory part, as

---

of a speech. **3.** a preliminary or introductory event, circumstance, etc. —*v.t.* **4.** to provide with or introduce by a preface. **5.** to serve as a preface to. —**pref′ac•er,** *n.*

pref•a•to•ry (pref′ə tôr′ē, -tōr′ē) also **pref′a•to′ri•al,** *adj.* of, pertaining to, or of the nature of a preface: *prefatory explanations.* —**pref′a•to′ri•ly,** *adv.*

pre•fect (prē′fekt) *n.* **1.** a person appointed to any of various positions of command, authority, or superintendence, as a chief magistrate in ancient Rome or the chief administrative official of a department of France or Italy. **2.** the dean of a Jesuit school or college. —**pre•fec′to•ri•al,** *adj.*

pre•fec•ture (prē′fek chər), *n.* the office, jurisdiction, territory, or official residence of a prefect. —**pre•fec′tur•al** (pri-), *adj.*

pre•fer (pri fûr′), *v.t.,* **-ferred, -fer•ring. 1.** to set or hold before or above other persons or things in estimation; like better: *I prefer school to work.* **2.** to give priority to, as to one creditor over another. **3.** to put forward or present for consideration or sanction. **4.** to put forward or advance, as in rank or office; promote. —*Idiom.* **5. prefer charges,** to make or place an accusation of misconduct, wrongdoing, etc., against another. —**pre•fer′red•ly** (-fûr′id lē, -fûrd′lē), *adv.* —**pre•fer′red•ness,** *n.* —**pre•fer′rer,** *n.*

pref•er•a•ble (pref′ər ə bəl, pref′rə- *or, often,* pri fûr′-), *adj.* **1.** more desirable. **2.** worthy to be preferred. —**pref′er•a•bil′i•ty, pref′er•a•ble•ness,** *n.* —**pref′er•a•bly,** *adv.*

pref•er•ence (pref′ər əns, pref′rəns), *n.* **1.** the act of preferring. **2.** the state of being preferred. **3.** something preferred; choice; selection: *Her preference is vanilla.* **4.** a practical advantage given to one over others. **5.** a prior right or claim, as to payment.

pref•er•en•tial (pref′ə ren′shəl), *adj.* **1.** of, pertaining to, or of the nature of preference. **2.** showing or giving preference. **3.** receiving preference, as a country in trade relations. —**pref′er•en′tial•ism,** *n.* —**pref′er•en′tial•ist,** *n.* —**pref′er•en′tial•ly,** *adv.*

pre•fer•ment (pri fûr′mənt), *n.* **1.** the act of preferring. **2.** the state of being preferred. **3.** advancement or promotion, esp. in the church. **4.** a position or office affording social or pecuniary advancement.

pre•ferred′-pro•vid′er organiza′tion (pri fûrd′prə vī′dər), *n.* a comprehensive health-care plan that allows corporate employees to choose their own physicians and hospitals within certain limits. *Abbr.:* PPO

preferred′ stock′, *n.* stock that has a superior claim to that of common stock with respect to dividends and often to assets in the event of liquidation.

pre•fig•ure (prē fig′yər), *v.t.,* **-ured, -ur•ing. 1.** to show or represent beforehand by a figure or type; foreshadow. **2.** to picture or represent to oneself beforehand; imagine. —**pre•fig′ur•a•tive, pre•fig′ur•a•tive•ly,** *adv.* —**pre•fig′ur•a•tive•ness,** *n.* —**pre•fig′ure•ment,** *n.*

pre•fix (*n.* prē′fiks; *v. also* prē fiks′), *n.* **1.** an affix placed before a base or another prefix, as *un-* in *unkind, un-* and *re-* in *unrewarding.* **2.** something prefixed, as a title before a person's name. —*v.t.* **3.** to fix or put before or in front. **4.** to add as a prefix. **5.** to fix, settle, or appoint beforehand. —**pre•fix′al** (prē′fik səl, prē fik′-), *adj.* —**pre′fix•al•ly,** *adv.* —**pre′fix•a′tion, pre•fix′ion** (-fik′shən), *n.*

pre•flight (prē flīt′), *adj.* occurring or done before a flight.

pre•form (*v.* prē′fôrm′; *n.* prē′fôrm′), *v.t.* **1.** to form beforehand. **2.** to shape beforehand: *to preform a mold.* —*n.* **3.** something preformed.

pre•for•ma•tion (prē′fôr mā′shən), *n.* **1.** previous formation. **2.** a former biological theory that the individual preexists fully formed in the germ cell and grows from microscopic to normal proportions during the embryo phase.

pre′frontal lobe′, *n.* the anterior region of the frontal lobe of the brain.

preg•na•ble (preg′nə bəl), *adj.* **1.** capable of being taken by force: *a pregnable fortress.* **2.** open to rebuttal: *a pregnable argument.* —**preg′na•bil′i•ty,** *n.*

preg•nan•cy (preg′nən sē), *n., pl.* **-cies.** the state, condition, or quality of being pregnant.

preg•nant (preg′nənt), *adj.* **1.** having a child or other offspring developing in the body. **2.** abounding (usu. fol. by *with*): *a silence pregnant with suspense.* **3.** fertile; rich (often fol. by *in*): *a mind pregnant in ideas.* **4.** full of meaning: *a pregnant utterance.* **5.** of great importance or

potential; momentous: *a pregnant epoch in history.* **6.** teeming with ideas or imagination.

pre•heat (prē hēt′), *v.t.* to heat before using or before subjecting to a further process. —**pre•heat′er,** *n.*

pre•hen•sile (pri hen′sil, -sīl) *adj.* **1.** adapted for seizing, grasping, or taking hold of something: *a prehensile tail.* **2.** able to perceive quickly; having keen mental grasp. **3.** greedy; grasping; avaricious. —**pre•hen•sil•i•ty** (prē′hen sil′i tē), *n.*

pre•hen•sion (pri hen′shən), *n.* **1.** the act of seizing or grasping. **2.** mental apprehension.

pre•his•tor•ic (prē′hi stôr′ik, -stor′-, prē′i-) also **pre′his•tor′i•cal,** *adj.* of or pertaining to the time prior to recorded history. —**pre′his•tor′i•cal•ly,** *adv.*

pre•his•to•ry (prē his′tə rē, -his′trē), *n., pl.* **-ries. 1.** human history in the period before recorded events. **2.** a history of the events or circumstances leading to something.

pre•judge (prē juj′), *v.t.,* **-judged, -judg•ing.** to pass judgment on prematurely or without sufficient reflection or investigation. —**pre•judg′er,** *n.* —**pre•judg′ment;** *esp. Brit.,* **pre•judge′ment,** *n.*

prej•u•dice (prej′ə dis), *n., v.,* **-diced, -dic•ing.** —*n.* **1.** an unfavorable opinion or feeling formed beforehand or without knowledge or reason. **2.** any preconceived opinion or feeling, either favorable or unfavorable. **3.** unreasonable feelings or attitudes, esp. of a hostile nature, regarding a racial, religious, or national group. **4.** damage or injury; detriment: *a law that operated to the prejudice of the majority.* —*v.t.* **5.** to affect with a prejudice. —*Idiom.* **6. without prejudice,** without waiving or losing any rights or privileges of the party concerned. —**prej′u•diced•ly,** *adv.*

prej•u•di•cial (prej′ə dish′əl), *adj.* causing prejudice or disadvantage; detrimental. —**prej′u•di′cial•ly,** *adv.* —**prej′u•di′cial•ness,** *n.*

pre-K (prē kā′), prekindergarten.

prel•a•cy (prel′ə sē), *n., pl.* **-cies. 1.** the office or dignity of a prelate. **2.** the order of prelates. **3.** the body of prelates collectively. **4.** *Sometimes Disparaging.* the system of church government by prelates.

prel•ate (prel′it), *n.* an ecclesiastic of a high order, as an archbishop or a bishop; a church dignitary. —**prel′ate•ship;** *n.* —**pre•lat•ic** (pri lat′ik), *adj.*

pre•launch (prē lônch′, -länch′), *adj.* preparatory to launch, as of a spacecraft.

pre•lim•i•nar•y (pri lim′ə ner′ē), *adj., n., pl.* **-nar•ies.** —*adj.* **1.** preceding and leading up to the main part, matter, or business; introductory; preparatory. —*n.* **2.** something preliminary, as an introductory or preparatory step, measure, or stage. **3.** a sports or athletic contest, esp. a boxing match, that takes place before the main event on the program. **4.** a preliminary examination, as of a candidate for an academic degree. —**pre•lim′i•nar′i•ly,** *adv.*

Prelim′inary Scholas′tic Assess′ment Test′, a standardized multiple-choice assessment test administered by the College Entrance Examination Board, and usually taken by eleventh graders, to help secondary-school students prepare for the Scholastic Assessment Test. *Abbr.:* PSAT

pre•lit•er•ate (prē lit′ər it), *adj.* **1.** lacking a written language; nonliterate: *a preliterate culture.* **2.** occurring before the development or use of writing.

prel•ude (prel′yōōd, prāl′-, prā′lōōd, prē′-), *n., v.,* **-ud•ed, -ud•ing.** —*n.* **1.** any action, event, comment, etc., that precedes something else. **2.** *Music.* **a.** a relatively short, independent instrumental composition, free in form and resembling an improvisation. **b.** a piece that is introductory to another piece, as a fugue. **c.** the overture to an opera. **d.** music opening a church service. —*v.t.* **3.** to serve as a prelude or introduction to. **4.** to introduce by a prelude. —*v.i.* **5.** to serve as a prelude. —**pre•lu•di•al** (pri lōō′dē əl), *adj.* —**pre•lu′di•ous•ly,** *adv.*

prem., premium.

pre•mar•i•tal (prē mar′i tl), *adj.* preceding marriage. —**pre•mar′i•tal•ly,** *adv.*

pre•ma•ture (prē′mə chŏŏr′, -tŏŏr′, -tyŏŏr′; *esp. Brit.* prem′ə-), *adj.* **1.** occurring, coming, or done too soon: *a premature announcement.* **2.** mature or ripe before the proper time. **3.** born before gestation is complete; preterm. —**pre′ma•ture′ly,** *adv.* —**pre′ma•tu′ri•ty, pre′ma•ture′ness,** *n.*

P

pre·med (prē med′), *adj.* **1.** premedical. —*n.* **2.** a program of premedical study. **3.** a student enrolled in such a program.

pre·med·i·cal (prē med′i kəl), *adj.* of, pertaining to, or engaged in studies in preparation for the formal study of medicine.

pre·med·i·tate (pri med′i tāt′), *v.t., v.i.* **-tat·ed, -tat·ing.** to meditate, consider, or plan beforehand. —**pre·med′i·ta·tive,** *adj.* —**pre·med′i·ta·tor,** *n.*

pre·med·i·tat·ed (pri med′i tā′tid), *adj.* done with willful deliberation; planned in advance: *a premeditated murder.* —**pre·med′i·tat′-ed·ly,** *adv.*

pre·med·i·ta·tion (pri med′i tā′shən), *n.* **1.** an act or instance of premeditating. **2.** *Law.* sufficient forethought to impute deliberation and intent to commit an act.

pre·men′stru·al syn′drome, *n.* a complex of physical and emotional changes that may be experienced in the several days before the onset of menstrual flow. *Abbr.:* PMS

pre·mier (pri mēr′, -myēr′, prē′mēr), *n.* **1.** the head of the cabinet in France and certain other countries; prime minister. —*adj.* Also, **pre·miere. 2.** first in rank; chief; leading. **3.** first in time; earliest. —*v.t., v.i.* **4.** PREMIERE. —**pre·mier′ship,** *n.*

pre·miere (pri mēr′, -myâr′), *n.* **1.** a first public performance or showing of a play, opera, film, etc. **2.** the leading woman, as in a drama. —*v.t.* **3.** to present publicly for the first time: *to premiere a new film.* —*v.i.* **4.** to perform publicly for the first time. —*adj.* **5.** PREMIER. [< French: lit., first]

pre·mil·len·ni·al·ism (prē′mi len′ē ə liz′əm), *n.* the doctrine or belief that the Second Coming of Christ will precede the millennium. —**pre′mil·len′ni·al·ist,** *n.*

prem·ise (prem′is), *n., v.,* **-ised, -is·ing.** —*n.* **1.** Also, **prem′iss.** *Logic.* a proposition supporting or helping to support a conclusion. **2. premises, a.** a tract of land including its buildings. **b.** a building together with its grounds or other appurtenances. **c.** the property forming the subject of a conveyance or bequest. **3.** *Law.* **a.** a basis, stated or assumed, on which reasoning proceeds. **b.** an earlier statement in a document. —*v.t.* **4.** to set forth beforehand, as by way of introduction or explanation. **5.** to state or assume (a proposition) as a premise for a conclusion. —*v.i.* **6.** to state or assume a premise.

pre·mi·um (prē′mē əm), *n.* **1.** a prize or bonus given as an inducement, as to purchase products. **2.** a bonus, gift, or sum additional to price, wages, interest, or the like. **3.** the amount usu. paid in installments by a policyholder for coverage under a contract. **4.** a sum above the nominal or par value of a thing. **5.** great value or esteem: *She puts a premium on loyalty.* —*adj.* **6.** of exceptional quality or greater value than others of its kind; superior. **7.** of higher price or cost. —**Idiom. 8. at a premium, a.** at an unusually high price. **b.** in short supply; in demand.

pre·mo·lar (prē mō′lər), *adj.* **1.** situated in front of the molar teeth. —*n.* **2.** a premolar tooth. **3.** Also called **bicuspid.** (in humans) any of eight teeth located in pairs on each side of the upper and lower jaws between the cuspids and the molar teeth.

pre·mo·ni·tion (prē′mə nish′ən, prem′ə-), *n.* a feeling of anticipation of or anxiety over a future event: *a premonition of danger.*

pre·na·tal (prē nāt′l), *adj.* previous to birth or to giving birth; antenatal: *prenatal care for mothers.* —**pre·na′tal·ly,** *adv.*

pren·tice (pren′tis), *n., v.,* **-ticed, -tic·ing.** APPRENTICE.

pre·nup·tial (prē nup′shəl, -chəl), *adj.* before marriage: *a prenuptial agreement.* —**Pronunciation.** See NUPTIAL.

pre·oc·cu·pa·tion (prē ok′yə pā′shən, prē′ok-), *n.* **1.** the state of being preoccupied. **2.** an act of preoccupying.

pre·oc·cu·pied (prē ok′yə pīd′), *adj.* **1.** completely engrossed in thought; absorbed. **2.** previously occupied; taken; filled. **3.** already used as a name, as for a species or genus, and not available as a designation for any other. —**pre·oc′cu·pied′ly** (-pīd′lē, -pī′id-), *adv.* —**pre·oc′cu·pied′ness,** *n.*

pre·oc·cu·py (prē ok′yə pī′), *v.t.,* **-pied, -py·ing. 1.** to absorb or engross to the exclusion of other things. **2.** to occupy beforehand or before others. —**pre·oc′cu·pi′er,** *n.*

pre·op·er·a·tive (prē op′ər ə tiv, -ə rā′tiv, -op′rə tiv), *adj.* occurring or related to the period or preparations before a surgical operation. —**pre·op′er·a·tive·ly,** *adv.*

pre·or·dain (prē′ôr dān′), *v.t.* to ordain beforehand; foreordain. —**pre′or·di·na′tion** (-dn ā′shən), *n.*

pre-owned (prē ōnd′), *adj.* secondhand.

prep (prep), *n., adj., v.,* **prepped, prep·ping.** —*n.* **1.** a preparatory school. **2.** a preliminary or warm-up activity or event; trial run. **3.** preparation. —*adj.* **4.** preparatory. **5.** involving or used for preparation. —*v.t.* **6.** to prepare (a person) for a test, debate, etc. **7.** to prepare (a patient) for a medical or surgical procedure. —*v.i.* **8.** to prepare; get ready. **9.** to attend a preparatory school.

pre·pack (*n.* prē′pak′; *v.* prē pak′), *n.* **1.** a package assembled by a manufacturer, distributor, or retailer and containing a specific number of items or a specific assortment of a product. —*v.t.* **2.** to prepackage.

pre·pack·age (prē pak′ij), *v.t.,* **-aged, -ag·ing.** to package (foodstuffs or manufactured goods) before retail sale.

prep·a·ra·tion (prep′ə rā′shən), *n.* **1.** a proceeding, measure, or provision by which one prepares for something: *preparations for a journey.* **2.** any proceeding, experience, or the like considered as a mode of preparing for the future. **3.** an act of preparing. **4.** something prepared, manufactured, or compounded: *a preparation for burns.*

pre·par·a·tive (pri par′ə tiv, -pâr′-), *adj.* **1.** preparatory. —*n.* **2.** something that prepares; preparation. —**pre·par′a·tive·ly,** *adv.*

pre·par·a·to·ry (pri par′ə tôr′ē, -tōr′ē, -pâr′-, prep′ər ə-), *adj.* **1.** serving or designed to prepare. **2.** preliminary; introductory: *preparatory remarks.* **3.** of or pertaining to training that prepares for more advanced education. —**pre·par′a·to′ri·ly,** *adv.*

prepar′atory school′, *n.* **1.** a private secondary school providing a college-preparatory education. **2.** *Brit.* a private elementary school.

pre·pare (pri pâr′), *v.,* **-pared, -par·ing.** —*v.t.* **1.** to put in proper condition or readiness. **2.** to get (a meal) ready for eating, as by proper assembling, cooking, etc. **3.** to manufacture, compound, or compose: *to prepare a cough syrup.* —*v.i.* **4.** to put things or oneself in readiness; get ready: *to prepare for exams.* —**pre·par′er,** *n.*

pre·par·ed·ness (pri pâr′id nis, -pârd′nis), *n.* the state of being prepared; readiness, esp. for war.

pre·pay (prē pā′), *v.t.,* **-paid, -pay·ing.** to pay beforehand or before due. —**pre·pay′a·ble,** *adj.* —**pre·pay′ment,** *n.*

pre·pon·der·ance (pri pon′dər əns) also **pre·pon′der·an·cy,** *n.* the fact or quality of being preponderant; superiority in weight, power, numbers, etc.

pre·pon·der·ant (pri pon′dər ənt), *adj.* superior in weight, force, influence, numbers, etc.; predominant: *a preponderant misconception.* —**pre·pon′der·ant·ly,** *adv.*

prep·o·si·tion¹ (prep′ə zish′ən), *n.* a member of a class of words that are typically used before nouns, pronouns, or other substantives to form phrases with adverbial, nominal, or adjectival function, and that typically express a spatial, temporal, or other relationship, as *on, by, to, with,* or *since.* —**prep′o·si′tion·al,** *adj.* —**prep′o·si′tion·al·ly,** *adv.* —**Usage.** The often heard "rule" that a sentence should not end with a preposition is transferred from Latin, where it is an accurate description of practice. But the Latin rule does not fit English grammar. In speech, the final preposition is normal and idiomatic, esp. in questions: *What are we waiting for? Where did he come from? You didn't tell me which floor you worked on.* In writing, the problem of placing the preposition arises most often when a sentence ends with a relative clause in which the relative pronoun (*that; whom; which; etc.*) is the object of a preposition. In edited writing, esp. formal writing, when a pronoun other than *that* introduces a final relative clause, the preposition usu. precedes its object: *He abandoned the project to which he had devoted his whole life. I finally telephoned the representative with whom I had been corresponding.* If the pronoun is *that,* or if the pronoun is omitted, then the preposition must occur at the end: *The librarian found the books that the child had scribbled in. There is the woman he spoke of.*

prep·o·si·tion² or **pre·po·si·tion** (prē′pə zish′ən), *v.t.* to position in advance or beforehand.

preposi′tional phrase′, *n.* a phrase consisting of a preposition, its object, and any modifiers, as *in the gray desk I use.*

pre·pos·sess (prē′pə zes′), *v.t.* **1.** to possess or dominate mentally beforehand. **2.** to prejudice, esp. favorably. **3.** to impress favorably beforehand or at the outset.

pre·pos·ter·ous (pri pos′tər əs, -trəs), *adj.* completely contrary to na-

---

pre′oc·cur′rence, *n.*

pre·o′ral, *adj.*

pre·or′bit·al, *adj.*

pre·or′der, *v.*

pre·plan′, *v.,* -planned, -plan·ning.

pre·pro′gram, *v.t.,* -grammed or -gramed, -gram·ming or -gram·ing.

pre′reg·is·tra′tion, *n.*

pre·Ren′ais·sance′, *adj.*

pre′re·quest′, *n., v.t.*

pre′re·quire′, *v.t.,* -quired, -quir·ing.

pre′res·o·lu′tion, *n.*

pre′re·tire′ment, *adj., n.*

pre′rev·o·lu′tion·ar′y, *adj.*

pre·rinse′, *v.t.,* -rinsed, -rins·ing.

pre·ro·man′tic, *adj.*

pre·sched′ule, *v.t.,* -uled, -ul·ing.

pre·score′, *v.t.,* -scored, -scor·ing.

pre·screen′, *v.t.*

pre·sea′son, *n.*

pre·se·lect′, *v.t.*

pre·set′tle, *v.t.,* -tled, -tling.

pre-Shake′spear′i·an, *adj.*

pre·shape′, *n., v.t.,* -shaped, -shap·ing.

pre·sharp′en, *v.t.*

pre·slice′, *v.t.,* -sliced, -slic·ing.

pre·ster′i·lize′, *v.t.,* -lized, -liz·ing.

pre·stim′u·late′, *v.t.,* -lat·ed, -lat·ing.

pre·sur′gi·cal, *adj.*

pre′sur·vey′, *v.t.,* -veyed, -vey·ing.

pre·sweet′en, *v.t.*

pre′symp·to·mat′ic, *adj.*

pre·tel′e·vi′sion, *adj.*

pre·tell′, *v.,* -told, -tell·ing.

pre·tes′ti·fy′, *v.t.,* -fied, -fy·ing.

pre·tes′ti·mo′ny, *n., pl.* -nies.

pre·tick′et·ed, *adj.*

pre·train′, *v.t.*

pre′u·ni·ver′si·ty, *adj.*

pre′vac′ci·nate′, *v.t.,* -nat·ed, -nat·ing.

pre′vac·ci·na′tion, *n.*

pre′val·u·a′tion, *n.*

pre·val′ue, *n., v.t.,* -ued, -u·ing.

pre·ver′bal, *adj.*

pre′-Vic·to′ri·an, *adj.*

pre·war′, *adj.*

pre·warm′, *v.t.*

pre·warn′, *v.t.*

pre·wash′, *n., v.t.*

pre·worn′, *adj.*

pre·weigh′, *v.t.*

pre·wrap′, *v.t.,* -wrapped, -wrap·ping.

pre·writ′ten, *adj.*

ture, reason, or common sense; senseless; foolish. **—pre•pos′ter•ous•ly,** *adv.* **—pre•pos′ter•ous•ness,** *n.*

prep•py or **prep•pie** (prep′ē), *n., pl.* **-pies,** *adj.,* **-pi•er, -pi•est.** *—n.* **1.** a student at or a graduate of a preparatory school. **2.** a person whose clothing or behavior is associated with traditional preparatory schools. *—adj.* **3.** of, pertaining to, or characteristic of a preppy: *preppy clothes.*

pre•pran•di•al (prē pran′dē əl), *adj.* appropriate to the period just before dinner.

pre•pro•duc•tion (prē′prə duk′shən), *n.* the work necessary to prepare a film for production, as casting, designing sets, etc.

prep′ school′, *n.* PREPARATORY SCHOOL.

pre•pu•ber•ty (prē pyo͞o′bər tē), *n.* the period of life just before sexual maturation. **—pre•pu′ber•tal,** *adj.*

pre•pu•bes•cence (prē′pyo͞o bes′əns), *n.* PREPUBERTY. **—pre′pu•bes′cent,** *adj., n.*

pre•puce (prē′pyo͞os), *n.* **1.** the fold of skin that covers the head of the penis; foreskin. **2.** a similar covering of the clitoris. **—pre•pu•tial** (pri pyo͞o′shəl), *adj.*

pre•quel (prē′kwəl), *n.* a sequel to a film, play, or piece of fiction that prefigures the original. [PRE- + (SE)QUEL]

Pre-Raph•a•el•ite (prē raf′ē ə līt′, -rā′fē-), *n.* **1.** any of a group of English artists **(Pre-Raph′aelite Broth′erhood)** formed in 1848, and including Holman Hunt, John Everett Millais, and Dante Gabriel Rossetti, who aimed to revive the style and spirit of the Italian artists before the time of Raphael. *—adj.* **2.** of, pertaining to, or characteristic of the Pre-Raphaelites. **—Pre-Raph′a•el•it′ism,** *n.*

pre•re•cord (prē′ri kôrd′), *v.t.* to record beforehand or in advance, as a television program before broadcast.

pre•re•cord•ed (prē′ri kôr′did), *adj.* (of a video or audio tape) containing previously recorded information.

pre•req•ui•site (pri rek′wə zit, prē-), *adj.* **1.** required beforehand. *—n.* **2.** something prerequisite; precondition.

pre•rog•a•tive (pri rog′ə tiv, pə rog′-), *n.* **1.** an exclusive right, privilege, etc., exercised by virtue of rank, office, or the like. **2.** a right, privilege, etc., limited to persons of a particular category. **3.** a power, immunity, or the like restricted to a sovereign government or its representative. *—adj.* **4.** having or exercising a prerogative.

pres•age (pres′ij; *v. also* pri sāj′), *v.,* **-aged, -ag•ing,** *n. —v.t.* **1.** to portend; foreshadow. **2.** to forecast; predict. *—v.i.* **3.** to make a prediction. *—n.* **4.** presentiment; foreboding. **5.** something that portends or foreshadows a future event; an omen. **6.** prophetic significance; augury.

pres•by•o•pi•a (prez′bē ō′pē ə, pres′-), *n.* farsightedness due to ciliary muscle weakness and loss of elasticity in the crystalline lens, usu. associated with aging. **—pres′by•op′ic** (-op′ik), *adj.*

pres•by•ter (prez′bi tər, pres′-), *n.* **1.** (in the early Christian church) an office bearer who exercised teaching, priestly, and administrative functions. **2.** (in hierarchical churches) a priest. **3.** an elder in a Presbyterian church. **—pres•byt′er•al** (-bit′ər əl), *adj.*

pres•by•te•ri•an (prez′bi tēr′ē ən, pres′-), *adj.* **1.** pertaining to or based on the principle of ecclesiastical government by presbyters or presbyteries. **2.** (*cap.*) designating or pertaining to various churches having this form of government and professing more or less modified forms of Calvinism. *—n.* **3.** (*cap.*) a member of a Presbyterian church; a person who supports Presbyterianism.

Pres•by•te•ri•an•ism (prez′bi tēr′ē ə niz′əm, pres′-), *n.* **1.** church government by presbyters or elders, equal in rank and organized into graded administrative courts. **2.** the doctrines of Presbyterian churches.

pres•by•ter•y (prez′bi ter′ē, pres′-), *n., pl.* **-ter•ies. 1.** a body of presbyters or elders. **2.** (in Presbyterian churches) an ecclesiastical assembly consisting of all the ministers and one or two presbyters from each congregation in a district. **3.** the churches under the jurisdiction of a presbytery. **4.** the part of a church appropriated to the clergy. **5.** *Rom. Cath. Ch.* RECTORY. [Late Middle English *presbetory* priests' bench < Late Latin *presbyterium* group of elders < Greek *presbytérion,* der. of *presbyteros* elder, priest]

pre•school (*adj.* prē′sko͞ol′; *n.* prē′sko͞ol′), *adj.* **1.** of, for, or concerning a child between infancy and kindergarten age. *—n.* **2.** a school or nursery for preschool children. **—pre′school′er,** *n.*

pre•science (presh′əns, -ē əns, prē′shəns, -shē əns), *n.* knowledge of things before they exist or happen; foreknowledge; foresight. **—pre′scient,** *adj.* **—pre′scient•ly,** *adv.*

Pres•cott (pres′kət, -kot), *n.* **William Hickling,** 1796–1859, U.S. historian.

pre•scribe (pri skrīb′), *v.,* **-scribed, -scrib•ing.** *—v.t.* **1.** to lay down, in writing or otherwise, as a rule or a course of action to be followed; appoint, ordain, or enjoin. **2.** to designate or order the use of (a medicine, remedy, treatment, etc.). *—v.i.* **3.** to lay down rules; direct; dictate. **4.** to order a treatment or medicine. **—pre•scrib′a•ble,** *adj.* **—pre•scrib′er,** *n.*

pre•script (*adj.* pri skript′, prē′skript; *n.* prē′skript), *adj.* **1.** prescribed. *—n.* **2.** something prescribed, as a rule, precept, or order.

pre•scrip•tion (pri skrip′shən), *n.* **1. a.** a written direction by a physician for the preparation and use of a medicine or remedy. **b.** the medicine prescribed. **2.** an act of prescribing. **3.** something prescribed. **4.** the long, unchallenged use of some legal right, which sanctions such a right. *—adj.* **5.** (of drugs) sold only upon medical prescription.

pre•scrip•tive (pri skrip′tiv), *adj.* **1.** that prescribes; giving directions or injunctions. **2.** based on or arising from long-standing usage or custom. **3.** concerned with or involving the establishment of norms of correct and incorrect language usage or rules based on these norms; normative: *prescriptive grammar.* **4.** depending on or arising from effective legal prescription, as a right or title established by a long unchallenged tenure. **—pre•scrip′tive•ly,** *adv.* **—pre•scrip′tive•ness,** *n.* **—pre•scrip′tiv•ism,** *n.* **—pre•scrip′tiv•ist,** *n., adj.*

pres•ence (prez′əns), *n.* **1.** the state or fact of being present. **2.** immediate vicinity; proximity. **3.** the military or economic power of a country as reflected abroad by the stationing of its troops, sale of its goods, etc. **4.** *Chiefly Brit.* the immediate personal vicinity of a great personage giving audience. **5.** personal appearance or bearing, esp. of a dignified or imposing kind. **6.** a person, esp. of noteworthy appearance or compelling personality. **7.** a divine or supernatural spirit felt to be present.

pres′ence of mind′, *n.* the ability to think clearly and act appropriately, as during a crisis.

pres•ent[1] (prez′ənt), *adj.* **1.** being, existing, or occurring at this time or now; current: *the present economic situation.* **2.** at this time; at hand; immediate: *articles for present use.* **3.** of, pertaining to, or being a verb tense or form used to refer to an action or state occurring or existing at the moment of speaking (*They're eating. I know the answer*) or to a habitual event (*He drives to work*), and also sometimes used to express the future (*The plane leaves at six tomorrow*) or past. **4.** being with one or others or in the specified or understood place: *to be present at the wedding.* **5.** existing or occurring. **6.** being actually here or under consideration. **7.** being before the mind. *—n.* **8.** the present time. **9. a.** the present tense. **b.** a verb form in the present tense, as *knows.* **10. presents,** (in a deed of conveyance) the present document or writings: *Know all men by these presents.* **—*Idiom.*** **11. at present,** at the present time or moment; now. **12. for the present,** for now; temporarily.

pre•sent[2] (*v.* pri zent′; *n.* prez′ənt), *v.t.* **1.** to furnish or endow with a gift or the like, esp. by formal act. **2.** to bring, offer, or give, often in a formal or ceremonious way: *to present one's credentials.* **3.** to afford or furnish (an opportunity, possibility, etc.). **4.** to hand over or submit (a bill or check). **5.** to introduce (a person) to another, esp. in a formal manner. **6.** to bring before or introduce to the public: *to present a new play.* **7.** to come to show (oneself) before a person, in or at a place, etc. **8.** to bring forth or render for or before another or others; offer for consideration: *to present an alternative plan.* **9.** to set forth in words; frame or articulate: *to present arguments.* **10.** to represent, impersonate, or act, as on the stage. **11.** to direct, point, or turn (something) to something or someone: *He presented his back to the audience.* **12.** to level or aim (a weapon, esp. a firearm). **13.** *Law.* **a.** to bring (a formal charge) against a person. **b.** to bring (an offense) to the notice of the proper authority. *—n.* **14.** a thing presented as a gift; gift: *Christmas presents.*

pre•sent•a•ble (pri zen′tə bəl), *adj.* **1.** capable of being presented. **2.** of sufficiently good appearance; fit to be seen. **—pre•sent′a•bil′i•ty, pre•sent′a•ble•ness,** *n.* **—pre•sent′a•bly,** *adv.*

present′ arms′, *n.* **1.** a position of salute in the manual of arms in which the rifle is held in both hands vertically in front of the body, with the muzzle upward. **2.** a command to take this position or, for troops not under arms, to give a hand salute.

pres•en•ta•tion (prez′ən tā′shən, prē′zen-), *n.* **1.** an act of presenting. **2.** the state of being presented. **3.** a social introduction, as of a person at court. **4.** an exhibition or performance, as of a play or film. **5.** an offering, as of a gift. **6.** GIFT. **7.** a demonstration, lecture, or welcoming speech. **8.** a manner or style of speaking, instructing, or putting oneself forward. **9.** the presentment of a bill, note, or the like. **10.** the position of the fetus in the uterus during labor, esp. in relation to its appearance at the cervix: *a breech presentation.* **11.** the act or the right of presenting a cleric to the bishop for institution to a benefice. **—pres′en•ta′tion•al,** *adj.*

pres′ent-day′, *adj.* current; modern: *present-day English.*

pre•sen•tient (prē sen′shənt), *adj.* having a presentiment.

pre•sen•ti•ment (pri zen′tə mənt), *n.* a feeling or impression that something is about to happen, esp. something evil; foreboding. **—pre•sen′ti•ment′al,** *adj.*

pres•ent•ly (prez′ənt lē), *adv.* **1.** in a little while; soon. **2.** at the present time; now.

pre•sent•ment (pri zent′mənt), *n.* **1.** an act of presenting, esp. to the mind, as an idea, view, etc. **2.** the state of being presented. **3.** a presentation. **4.** the presenting of a bill, note, or the like, as for payment. **5.** the written statement of an offense by a grand jury when no indictment has been laid before them.

pres′ent par′ticiple, *n.* a participle form, in English having the suffix *-ing,* denoting repetition or duration of an activity or event: used as an adjective, as in *the growing weeds,* and in forming progressive verb forms, as in *The weeds are growing.*

pres′ent per′fect, *adj.* **1.** of, pertaining to, or being a verb tense or form indicating that the action or state expressed by the verb was completed prior to the present or that it extends up to or has results continuing up to the present, and consisting in English of *have* followed by a past participle, as *have lived* in *We have lived here for two years.* *—n.* **2.** the present perfect tense.

pres•er•va•tion (prez′ər vā′shən), *n.* **1.** the act or process of preserving. **2.** the state of being preserved.

pres•er•va•tion•ist (prez′ər vā′shə nist), *n.* a person who advocates or promotes preservation, esp. of wildlife, natural areas, or historical places. —**pres′er•va′tion•ism,** *n.*

pre•serv•a•tive (pri zûr′və tiv), *n.* **1.** something that preserves or tends to preserve. **2.** a chemical substance used to preserve foods or other organic materials from decomposition or fermentation. —*adj.* **3.** tending to preserve.

pre•serve (pri zûrv′), *v.*, **-served, -serv•ing,** *n.* —*v.t.* **1.** to keep alive or in existence: *to preserve our liberties.* **2.** to keep safe from harm or injury; protect or spare. **3.** to keep up; maintain. **4.** to prepare (food or any perishable substance) so as to resist decomposition or fermentation. **5.** to prepare (fruit, vegetables, etc.) by cooking with sugar, pickling, canning, or the like. **6.** to maintain and reserve (game, fish, etc.) for

continued survival or for private use, as in hunting or fishing. —*v.i.* **7.** to preserve fruit, vegetables, etc.; make preserves. —*n.* **8.** something that preserves. **9.** that which is preserved. **10.** Usu., **preserves.** fruit, vegetables, etc., prepared by cooking with sugar. **11.** a place set apart for protection and propagation of game or fish. —**pre•serv′a•ble,** *adj.* —**pre•serv′a•bil′i•ty,** *n.* —**pre•serv′er,** *n.*

pre•set (prē set′), *v.t.* **-set, -set•ting.** to set beforehand. —**pre•set′ta•ble,** *adj.*

pre•shrink (prē shringk′), *v.t.* **-shrank** or, often, **-shrunk; -shrunk** or **-shrunk•en; -shrink•ing.** to cause (a fabric) to contract during finishing in order to prevent or minimize shrinkage later.

pre•side (pri zīd′), *v.i.*, **-sid•ed, -sid•ing. 1.** to occupy the place of au-

PRESIDENTS AND VICE PRESIDENTS OF THE UNITED STATES

President	Born	Died	Birthplace	Residence	Religious Affiliation	Party	Dates in Office	Vice President	Dates in Office
1. GEORGE WASHINGTON	Feb. 22, 1732	Dec. 14, 1799	Westmoreland Co., Va.	Va.	Episcopalian	Fed.	1789-1797	JOHN ADAMS	1789-1797
2. JOHN ADAMS	Oct. 30, 1735	July 4, 1826	Quincy, Mass	Mass.	Unitarian	Fed.	1797-1801	THOMAS JEFFERSON	1797-1801
3. THOMAS JEFFERSON	Apr. 13, 1743	July 4, 1826	Shadwell, Va.	Va.	Deist	Rep.*	1801-1809	AARON BURR	1801-1805
								GEORGE CLINTON	1805-1809
4. JAMES MADISON	Mar. 16, 1751	June 28, 1836	Port Conway, Va.	Va.	Episcopalian	Rep.*	1809-1817	GEORGE CLINTON**	1809-1812
								ELBRIDGE GERRY	1813-1814
5. JAMES MONROE	Apr. 28, 1758	July 4, 1831	Westmoreland Co., Va.	Va.	Episcopalian	Rep.*	1817-1825	DANIEL D. TOMPKINS	1817-1825
6. JOHN QUINCY ADAMS	July 11, 1767	Feb. 23, 1848	Quincy, Mass.		Unitarian	Rep.*	1825-1829	JOHN C. CALHOUN	1825-1829
7. ANDREW JACKSON	Mar. 15, 1767	June 8, 1845	New Lancaster Co., S.C.	Tenn.	Presbyterian	Dem.	1829-1837	JOHN C. CALHOUN	1829-1832
								MARTIN VAN BUREN (4*)	1833-1837
8. MARTIN VAN BUREN	Dec. 5, 1782	July 24, 1862	Kinderhook, N.Y.	N.Y.	Reformed Church	Dem.	1837-1841	RICHARD M. JOHNSON	1837-1841
9. WILLIAM HENRY HARRISON**	Feb. 9, 1773	Apr. 4, 1841	Berkeley, Va.	Ohio	Episcopalian	Whig	1841	JOHN TYLER (4*)	1841
10. JOHN TYLER	Mar. 29, 1790	Jan. 18, 1862	Greenway, Va.	Va.	Episcopalian	Whig	1841-1845		
11. JAMES KNOX POLK	Nov. 2, 1795	June 15, 1849	Mecklenburg Co., N.C.	Tenn.	Methodist	Dem.	1845-1849	GEORGE M. DALLAS	1845-1849
12. ZACHARY TAYLOR**	Nov. 24, 1784	July 9, 1850	Orange Co., Va.	La.	Episcopalian	Whig	1849-1850	MILLARD FILLMORE (4*)	1849-1850
13. MILLARD FILLMORE	Jan. 7, 1800	Mar. 8, 1874	Cayuga Co., N.Y.	N.Y.	Unitarian	Whig	1850-1853		
14. FRANKLIN PIERCE	Nov. 23, 1804	Oct. 8, 1869	Hillsboro, N.H.	N.H.	Episcopalian	Dem.	1853-1857	WILLIAM R. KING**	1853
15. JAMES BUCHANAN	Apr. 23, 1791	June 1, 1868	Mercersburg, Pa.	Pa.	Presbyterian	Dem.	1857-1861	JOHN C. BRECKINRIDGE	1857-1861
16. ABRAHAM LINCOLN**	Feb. 12, 1809	Apr. 15 1865	Hardin Co., Ky.	Ill.	Nonaffiliated	Rep.***	1861-1865	HANNIBAL HAMLIN	1861-1865
								ANDREW JOHNSON (4*)	1865
17. ANDREW JOHNSON	Dec. 29, 1808	July 31, 1875	Raleigh, N.C.	Tenn.	Nonaffiliated	Dem.***	1865-1869		
18. ULYSSES SIMPSON GRANT	Apr. 27, 1822	July 23, 1885	Point Pleasant, Ohio	Ill.	Methodist	Rep.	1869-1877	SCHUYLER COLFAX	1869-1873
								HENRY WILSON**	1873-1875
19. RUTHERFORD BIRCHARD HAYES	Oct. 4, 1822	Jan. 17, 1893	Delaware, Ohio	Ohio	Methodist	Rep.	1877-1881	WILLIAM A. WHEELER	1877-1881
20. JAMES ABRAM GARFIELD**	Nov. 19, 1831	Sept. 19, 1881	Orange, Ohio	Ohio	Disciples of Christ	Rep.	1881	CHESTER A. ARTHUR (4*)	1881
21. CHESTER ALAN ARTHUR	Oct. 5, 1830	Nov. 18, 1886	Fairfield, Vt.	N.Y.	Episcopalian	Rep.	1881-1885		
22. GROVER CLEVELAND	Mar. 18, 1837	June 24, 1908	Caldwell, N.J.	N.Y.	Presbyterian	Dem.	1885-1889	THOMAS A. HENDRICKS**	1885
23. BENJAMIN HARRISON	Aug. 20, 1833	Mar. 13, 1901	North Bend, Ohio	Ind.	Presbyterian	Rep.	1889-1893	LEVI P. MORTON	1889-1893
24. GROVER CLEVELAND	See number 22						1893-1897	ADLAI E. STEVENSON	1893-1897
25. WILLIAM MCKINLEY**	Jan. 29, 1843	Sept. 14, 1901	Niles, Ohio	Ohio	Methodist	Rep.	1897-1901	GARRET A. HOBART**	1897-1899
								THEODORE ROOSEVELT (4*)	1901
26. THEODORE ROOSEVELT	Oct. 27, 1858	Jan. 6, 1919	New York, N.Y.	N.Y.	Reformed Dutch	Rep.	1901-1909	CHARLES W. FAIRBANKS	1905-1909
27. WILLIAM HOWARD TAFT	Sept. 15, 1857	Mar. 8, 1930	Cincinnati, Ohio	Ohio	Unitarian	Rep.	1909-1913	JAMES S. SHERMAN	1909-1912
28. WOODROW WILSON	Dec. 28, 1856	Feb. 3, 1924	Staunton, Va.	N.J.	Presbyterian	Dem.	1913-1921	THOMAS R. MARSHALL	1913-1921
29. WARREN GAMALIEL HARDING**	Nov. 2, 1865	Aug. 2, 1923	Bloomington Grove, Ohio	Ohio	Baptist	Rep.	1921-1923	CALVIN COOLIDGE (4*)	1921-1923
30. CALVIN COOLIDGE	July 4, 1872	Jan. 5, 1933	Plymouth, Vt.	Mass.	Congregational	Rep.	1923-1929	CHARLES G. DAWES	1925-1929
31. HERBERT CLARK HOOVER	Aug. 10, 1874	Oct. 20, 1964	West Branch, Iowa	Calif.	Society of Friends	Rep.	1929-1933	CHARLES CURTIS	1929-1933
32. FRANKLIN DELANO ROOSEVELT**	Jan. 30, 1882	Apr. 12, 1945	Hyde Park, N.Y.	N.Y.	Episcopalian	Dem.	1933-1945	JOHN NANCE GARNER	1933-1941
								HENRY AGARD WALLACE	1941-1945
								HARRY S TRUMAN (4*)	1945
33. HARRY S TRUMAN	May 8, 1884	Dec. 26, 1972	Lamar, Mo.	Mo.	Baptist	Dem.	1945-1953	ALBEN W. BARKLEY	1949-1953
34. DWIGHT DAVID EISENHOWER	Oct. 14, 1890	Mar. 28, 1969	Denison, Tex.	N.Y.	Presbyterian	Rep.	1953-1961	RICHARD M. NIXON	1953-1961
35. JOHN FITZGERALD KENNEDY**	May 29, 1917	Nov. 22, 1963	Brookline, Mass.	Mass.	Roman Catholic	Dem.	1961-1963	LYNDON B. JOHNSON (4*)	1961-1963
36. LYDON BAINES JOHNSON	Aug. 27, 1908	Jan. 22, 1973	Johnson City, Tex.	Tex.	Disciples of Christ	Dem.	1963-1969	HUBERT H. HUMPHREY	1965-1969
37. RICHARD MILHOUS NIXON (5*)	Jan. 9, 1913	Apr. 22, 1994	Yorba Linda, Calif.	Calif.	Society of Friends	Rep.	1969-1974	SPIRO T. AGNEW	1969-1973
								GERALD R. FORD (4*)	1973-1974
38. GERALD RUDOLPH FORD	July 14, 1913		Omaha, Nebr.	Mich.	Episcopalian	Rep.	1974-1977	NELSON A. ROCKEFELLER	1974-1977
39. JAMES EARL CARTER, JR.	Oct. 1, 1924		Plains, Ga.	Ga.	Southern Baptist	Dem.	1977-1981	WALTER F. MONDALE	1977-1981
40. RONALD WILSON REAGAN	Feb. 6, 1911		Tampico, Ill.	Calif.	Disciples of Christ	Rep.	1981-1989	GEORGE H.W. BUSH	1981-1989
41. GEORGE HERBERT WALKER BUSH	June 12, 1924		Milton, Mass.	Tex.	Episcopalian	Rep.	1989-1993	JAMES DANFORTH QUAYLE	1989-1993
42. WILLIAM JEFFERSON CLINTON	Aug. 19, 1946		Hope, Ark.	Ark.	Baptist	Dem.	1993-	ALBERT A. GORE, JR.	1993-

*Now the Democratic Party   **Died in office   ***Elected on the Union party ticket   (4*)Succeeded to Presidency   (5*)Resigned

thority or control, as in an assembly or meeting; act as president or chairperson. **2.** to exercise management or control (usu. fol. by *over*): *The lawyer presided over the estate.* —**pre•sid′er,** *n.*

pres•i•den•cy (prez′i dən sē), *n., pl.* **-cies. 1.** the office, function, or term of office of a president. **2.** (*often cap.*) the office of President of the United States. **3.** (in the Mormon Church) **a.** a local governing body consisting of a council of three. **b.** (*often cap.*) the highest administrative body, composed of the prophet and his two councilors. **4.** (*often cap.*) the former designation of any of the three original provinces of British India: Bengal, Bombay, and Madras.

pres•i•dent (prez′i dənt), *n.* **1.** (*often cap.*) the chief of state and often the chief executive officer of a republic, as the United States. **2.** an officer appointed or elected to preside over an organized body of persons.

pres′ident-elect′, *n.* a president after election but before induction into office.

pres•i•den•tial (prez′i den′shəl), *adj.* **1.** of or pertaining to a president or presidency. **2.** of the nature of a president: *a presidential bearing.* —**pres′i•den′tial•ly,** *adv.*

pres′iden′tial pri′mary, *n.* a direct primary for the selection of state delegates to a national party convention and the expression of preference for a U.S. presidential nominee.

pres′iden′tial tim′ber, *n.* one with the abilities and appeal to become president.

pres′ident pro tem′pore, *n.* a senator, usu. a senior member of the majority party, who is chosen to preside over the Senate in the absence of the vice president. Also called **pres′ident pro tem′.**

Pres′idents′ Day′, *n.* the third Monday in February, a legal holiday in the U.S., commemorating the birthdays of George Washington and Abraham Lincoln.

pre•sid•i•o (pri sid′ē ō′), *n., pl.* **-sid•i•os. 1.** a garrisoned fort; military post. **2.** a Spanish penal settlement. —**pre•sid′i•al, pre•sid′i•ar′y,** *adj.*

pre•sid•i•um (pri sid′ē əm), *n., pl.* **-sid•i•ums, -sid•i•a** (-sid′ē ə). **1.** (*often cap.*) (esp. in Communist countries) an administrative committee, usu. permanent and governmental, acting when its parent body is in recess but exercising full powers. **2.** an executive board or committee.

Pres•ley (pres′lē, prez′-), *n.* **Elvis (Aron),** 1935–77, U.S. rock-and-roll singer.

pre•sort (prē sôrt′), *v.t.* to sort (letters, packages, etc.) by ZIP code or class before collection or delivery to a post office.

pres. part., present participle.

press[1] (pres), *v.t.* **1.** to act upon with steadily applied weight or force. **2.** to move by weight or force in a certain direction or into a certain position. **3.** to compress or squeeze, as to alter in shape or size. **4.** to subject to pressure. **5.** to hold closely, as in an embrace; clasp. **6.** to flatten or make smooth, esp. by ironing. **7.** to extract juice or contents from by pressure. **8.** to squeeze out (juice). **9.** to beset; harass. **10.** to trouble or oppress, as by lack of something. **11.** to urge or entreat insistently: *to press someone for an explanation.* **12.** to emphasize or propound forcefully: *He pressed his own ideas on us.* **13.** to urge onward; hasten. **14.** to push forward. **15.** to manufacture by stamping from a mold. —*v.i.* **16.** to exert weight, force, or pressure. **17.** to raise or lift, esp. a specified amount of weight, in a press. **18.** to iron clothing, curtains, etc. **19.** to bear heavily, as upon the mind. **20.** (of athletes and competitors) to strain because of frustration. **21.** to compel haste or attention. **22.** to use urgent entreaty: *to press for an answer.* **23.** to push forward or advance with force or haste: *The army pressed on.* **24.** to crowd; throng. **25.** *Basketball.* to employ a press. —*n.* **26.** an act of pressing. **27.** the state of being pressed. **28.** PRINTING PRESS. **29.** printed publications collectively, esp. newspapers and periodicals. **30. a.** all the media and agencies that print, broadcast, or gather and transmit news. **b.** their editorial employees. **31.** (*often used with a pl. v.*) a group from the news media, as reporters and photographers. **32.** the consensus of critical commentary or amount of coverage in the news: *The play received a good press.* **33.** an establishment for printing books, magazines, etc. **34.** the process or art of printing. **35.** any of various devices or machines for exerting pressure, stamping, or crushing. **36.** a crowding, thronging, or pressing together: *the press of the crowd.* **37.** a crowd; throng. **38.** the desired smooth or creased effect caused by ironing or pressing. **39.** urgency, as of affairs or business. **40.** a large upright case or cupboard for holding clothes, linens, books, etc. **41.** *Basketball.* an aggressive form of defense in which players guard opponents very closely. **42.** a lift in which a barbell is pushed overhead from chest level with the arms extended straight up, without moving the legs or feet. —***Idiom.*** **43. go to press,** to begin being printed. —**press′a•ble,** *adj.*

press[2] (pres), *v.t.* **1.** to force into service, esp. naval or military service; impress. **2.** to make use of in a manner different from that intended or desired: *A bus was pressed into service as an ambulance.* —*n.* **3.** impressment into service, esp. naval or military service.

press′ a′gent, *n.* a person employed to promote an individual or organization by obtaining favorable publicity. —**press′-a′gent•ry,** *n.*

press•board (pres′bôrd′, -bōrd′), *n.* a kind of millboard or pasteboard.

press′ box′, *n.* a press section, esp. at a sports event.

press′ con′ference, *n.* a usu. prearranged interview with reporters held by a government official or prominent person.

press′ corps′, *n.* journalists from various publications who regularly cover the same beat.

pressed′ glass′, *n.* molded glass shaped or given its pattern while molten by the action of a plunger thrust into the mold.

press•ing (pres′ing), *adj.* demanding immediate attention: *a pressing need.* —**press′ing•ly,** *adv.*

press•man (pres′mən), *n., pl.* **-men. 1.** a person who operates or has charge of a printing press. **2.** *Brit.* a writer or reporter for the press.

press′ release′, *n.* a statement or news story prepared and distributed to the press by a public relations firm, governmental agency, etc. Also called **news release, release.**

press•room (pres′ro͞om′, -ro͝om′), *n.* **1.** the room in a printing or newspaper publishing establishment where the printing presses are installed. **2.** a room set aside for members of the press, as at a government or military center.

press•run (pres′run′), *n.* **1.** the running of a printing press for a specific job. **2.** the quantity that is run. Also called **run.**

press′ sec′retary, *n.* a person officially responsible for press and public relations for a prominent figure or organization and who often holds press conferences to answer journalists' questions.

pres•sure (presh′ər), *n., v.,* **-sured, -sur•ing.** —*n.* **1.** the exertion of force upon a surface by an object, fluid, etc., in contact with it. **2.** *Physics.* force per unit area. *Symbol:* P **3.** the state of being pressed or compressed. **4.** harassment; oppression; stress: *the pressures of daily life.* **5.** ATMOSPHERIC PRESSURE. **6.** BLOOD PRESSURE. —*v.t.* **7.** to force toward a particular end by exerting a constraining or compelling influence; coerce: *They pressured him into accepting.* **8.** to pressurize.

pres′sure cook′er, *n.* **1.** a reinforced metal cooking pot with an airtight lid, in which food may be cooked quickly in heat above boiling point by steam maintained under pressure. **2.** a situation that subjects one to urgent demands, a hectic pace, or other stressful conditions. **3.** a volatile situation. —**pres′sure-cook′,** *v.t.*

pres′sure gauge′, *n.* **1.** an instrument for measuring the pressure of a gas or liquid. **2.** an instrument used to determine the pressure in the bore or chamber of a gun when the charge explodes.

pres′sure group′, *n.* an interest group that attempts to influence legislation through the use of lobbying and propaganda.

pres′sure point′, *n.* **1.** a point on the skin that is extremely sensitive to pressure. **2.** a point on the body where pressure serves to press an artery against underlying bony tissue, so as to arrest the flow of blood distally. **3.** a sensitive or vulnerable area or item, esp. one subject to the application of pressure to produce a desired result.

pres•sur•ize (presh′ə rīz′), *v.t.,* **-ized, -iz•ing. 1.** to produce or maintain normal air pressure in (an airplane cabin, a spacesuit, etc.), esp. at high altitudes or in space. **2.** to exert pressure on; pressure. **3.** to pressure-cook. —**pres′sur•i•za′tion,** *n.* —**pres′sur•iz′er,** *n.*

pres′surized suit′, *n.* an airtight suit that can be inflated to maintain approximately normal atmospheric pressure on a person in space or at high altitudes. Also called **pressure suit.**

pres•tige (pre stēzh′, -stēj′), *n.* **1.** reputation or influence arising from success, achievement, etc. **2.** distinction or reputation attaching to a person or thing. —*adj.* **3.** having or showing success, rank, wealth, etc.: *a prestige car.*

pres•tig•ious (pre stij′əs, -stij′ē əs, -stē′jəs, -stē′jē əs), *adj.* **1.** indicative of or conferring prestige: *a prestigious address.* **2.** having a high reputation; honored; esteemed: *a prestigious university.* —**pres•tig′ious•ly,** *adv.* —**pres•tig′ious•ness,** *n.*

pres•to (pres′tō), *adv., adj., n., pl.* **-tos.** —*adv.* **1.** quickly, rapidly, or immediately. **2.** at a rapid tempo. —*adj.* **3.** quick or rapid. **4.** executed at a rapid tempo (used as a musical direction). —*n.* **5.** a presto musical piece or movement. [< Italian: quick, quickly < Latin *praestō* ready, at hand]

pres′to chan′go (chān′jō), *v.i.* **1.** change at once (used imperatively, as in a magician's command). —*n.* **2.** a change occurring suddenly and as if by magic.

pre•stress (prē stres′), *v.t.* **1.** (in concrete construction) to apply stress to (reinforcing strands) before subjecting to a load. **2.** to make (a concrete member) with prestressed reinforcing strands.

pre•sum•a•ble (pri zo͞o′mə bəl), *adj.* capable of being presumed or taken for granted; probable. —**pre•sum′a•bly,** *adv.*

pre•sume (pri zo͞om′), *v.,* **-sumed, -sum•ing.** —*v.t.* **1.** to take for granted, assume, or suppose. **2.** *Law.* to assume as true in the absence of proof to the contrary. **3.** to undertake with unwarrantable boldness. —*v.i.* **4.** to take something for granted; suppose. **5.** to act or proceed with unwarrantable or impertinent boldness. —**pre•sum′ed•ly,** *adv.*

pre•sump•tion (pri zump′shən), *n.* **1.** the act of presuming. **2.** belief on reasonable grounds or probable evidence. **3.** something that is presumed; an assumption. **4.** a ground or reason for presuming or believing. **5.** *Law.* an inference permitted as to the existence of one fact from proof of the existence of other facts. **6.** unwarrantable or impertinent boldness; audacity; effrontery.

pre•sump•tive (pri zump′tiv), *adj.* **1.** affording ground for presumption: *presumptive evidence.* **2.** based on likelihood or presumption: *the presumptive heir.* **3.** pertaining to the part of an embryo that, in the course of normal development, will predictably become a particular structure or region. —**pre•sump′tive•ly,** *adv.*

pre•sump•tu•ous (pri zump′cho͞o əs), *adj.* characterized by presumption or readiness to presume; unwarrantedly or impertinently bold; forward. —**pre•sump′tu•ous•ly,** *adv.* —**pre•sump′tu•ous•ness,** *n.*

pre•sup•pose (prē′sə pōz′), *v.t.,* **-posed, -pos•ing. 1.** to suppose or assume beforehand; take for granted in advance. **2.** to require or imply as an antecedent condition: *An effect presupposes a cause.* —**pre′sup•po•si′tion** (-sup ə zish′ən), *n.*

pre•tax (prē taks′), *adj., adv.* prior to the payment of taxes: *pretax income; bonds earning 12 percent pretax.*

pre•teen (prē tēn′), *n.* **1.** a boy or girl under the age of 13, esp. one between the ages of 10 and 13; preadolescent. —*adj.* **2.** of, pertaining to, characteristic of, or designed for preteens.

pre•tend (pri tend′), *v.t.* **1.** to cause or attempt to cause (what is not so) to seem so; claim: *pretending that nothing is wrong.* **2.** to deceive; feign: *to pretend illness.* **3.** to make believe: *The children pretended they were cowboys.* **4.** to presume; venture: *I can't pretend to say what went wrong.* **5.** to allege or profess, esp. insincerely or falsely. —*v.i.* **6.** to make believe. **7.** to lay claim (usu. fol. by *to*): *to pretend to the throne.* **8.** to make pretensions (usu. fol. by *to*): *to pretend to great knowledge.* —*adj.* **9.** simulated; imaginary: *pretend diamonds.*

pre•tense (pri tens′, prē′tens), *n.* **1.** a false show of something; semblance: *a pretense of friendship.* **2.** a pretending or feigning; make-believe: *My sleepiness was all pretense.* **3.** the act of pretending or alleging falsely. **4.** an ostensible claim or justification; pretext: *to obtain money under false pretenses.* **5.** an unwarranted or false claim. **6.** pretension (usu. fol. by *to*): *no pretense to wit.*

pre•ten•sion (pri ten′shən), *n.* **1.** the laying of a claim to something. **2.** a claim or title to something. **3.** Often, **pretensions.** a claim made, often indirectly or by implication, to some quality, merit, dignity, or importance. **4.** the act of pretending or alleging. **5.** an allegation of doubtful veracity.

pre•ten•tious (pri ten′shəs), *adj.* **1.** full of pretension; characterized by the assumption of dignity, importance, artistic distinction, etc. **2.** making an exaggerated outward show; ostentatious; showy. —**pre•ten′tious•ly,** *adv.* —**pre•ten′tious•ness,** *n.*

preter-, a prefix meaning "beyond," "by," "past": *preterit.*

pret•er•it or **pret•er•ite** (pret′ər it), *n.* **1.** a verb tense referring to a past, esp. completed, action or state, and expressed in English by using a verb inflected for the past tense with no auxiliaries; simple past. **2.** a verb form in this tense, as *took* or *lived.* —*adj.* **3.** (of a verb tense or form) expressing a past action or state.

pre•term (prē tûrm′), *adj.* **1.** occurring earlier in pregnancy than expected. —*n.* **2.** a baby born before the 37th week of pregnancy, esp. when undersized.

pre•ter•mit (prē′tər mit′), *v.t.,* **-mit•ted, -mit•ting. 1.** to let pass without notice; disregard. **2.** to leave undone; neglect; omit. **3.** to suspend or interrupt. —**pre′ter•mis′sion** (-mish′ən), *n.*

pre•ter•nat•u•ral (prē′tər nach′ər əl, -nach′rəl), *adj.* **1.** existing or occurring out of the ordinary course of nature; exceptional or abnormal; extraordinary: *preternatural powers.* **2.** being outside of nature; supernatural. —**pre′ter•nat′u•ral•ism, pre′ter•nat′u•ral•ness,** *n.* —**pre′ter•nat′u•ral•ly,** *adv.*

pre•test (*n.* prē′test′; *v.* prē test′), *n.* **1.** an advance or preliminary testing or trial, as of a new product. **2.** a test given to determine if students are sufficiently prepared to begin a new course of study. —*v.t.* **3.** to give a pretest to. —*v.i.* **4.** to conduct a pretest.

pre•text (prē′tekst), *n.* **1.** something put forward to conceal a true purpose or object; ostensible reason; excuse. **2.** the misleading appearance or behavior assumed with this intention; subterfuge.

Pre•to•ri•a (pri tôr′ē ə, -tōr′-), *n.* the administrative capital of the Republic of South Africa, in the NE part: also the capital of Transvaal. 822,925.

pre•tri•al (prē trī′əl, -trīl′), *n.* **1.** a proceeding held by a judge, arbitrator, etc., before a trial to clarify issues of law and fact and stipulate certain matters between the parties. —*adj.* **2.** of or pertaining to such a proceeding.

pret•ti•fy (prit′ə fī′), *v.t.,* **-fied, -fy•ing. 1.** to make pretty, esp. in a small, petty way. **2.** to minimize or gloss over (something unpleasant). —**pret′ti•fi•ca′tion,** *n.* —**pret′ti•fi′er,** *n.*

pret•ty (prit′ē), *adj.,* **-ti•er, -ti•est,** *n., pl.* **-ties,** *adv., v.,* **-tied, -ty•ing.** —*adj.* **1.** pleasing or attractive, esp. in a delicate or graceful way: *a pretty face.* **2.** pleasing or charming but lacking in grandeur, importance, or force. **3.** fine; grand (often used ironically): *This is a pretty mess!* **4.** *Informal.* considerable; fairly great. —*n.* **5.** Usu., **pretties.** pretty ornaments or clothes. —*adv.* **6.** fairly or moderately: *a pretty good time.* **7.** quite; very: *The wind blew pretty hard.* —*v.t.* **8.** to make pretty in appearance. —**pret′ti•ly,** *adv.* —**pret′ti•ness,** *n.*

pret•zel (pret′səl), *n.* a usu. crisp, dry biscuit, typically in the form of a knot or stick, usu. salted on the outside.

pre•vail (pri vāl′), *v.i.* **1.** to be widespread or current; exist generally. **2.** to appear or occur as the most important or frequent feature or element; predominate. **3.** to be or prove superior in strength, power, or influence (usu. fol. by *over*): *to prevail over one's enemies.* **4.** to succeed; become dominant; win out. **5.** to use persuasion or inducement successfully (usu. fol. by *on* or *upon*): *Can you prevail on him to go?*

pre•vail•ing (pri vā′ling), *adj.* **1.** most frequent; predominant: *prevailing winds.* **2.** generally current: *the prevailing opinion.* **3.** having superior power or influence. —**pre•vail′ing•ly,** *adv.* —**pre•vail′ing•ness,** *n.*

prev•a•lent (prev′ə lənt), *adj.* **1.** widespread; in general use or acceptance. **2.** having the superiority or ascendancy; dominant. —**prev′a•lence,** *n.* —**prev′a•lent•ly,** *adv.*

pre•var•i•cate (pri var′i kāt′), *v.i.,* **-cat•ed, -cat•ing.** to speak falsely; deliberately misstate; lie. —**pre•var′i•ca′tion,** *n.* —**pre•var′i•ca′tor,** *n.*

pre•ven•ient (pri vēn′yənt), *adj.* **1.** coming before; antecedent. **2.** anticipatory. —**pre•ven′ience,** *n.* —**pre•ven′ient•ly,** *adv.*

pre•vent (pri vent′), *v.t.* **1.** to keep from occurring; stop: *to prevent illness.* **2.** to stop from doing something. —*v.i.* **3.** to interpose a hindrance. —**pre•vent′a•ble, pre•vent′i•ble,** *adj.* —**pre•vent′a•bil′ty,** *n.* —**pre•vent′er,** *n.*

pre•ven•tion (pri ven′shən), *n.* **1.** the act of preventing; effectual hindrance. **2.** something that prevents; preventive.

pre•ven•tive (pri ven′tiv) also **pre•vent•a•tive** (-tə tiv), *adj.* **1.** serving to prevent or hinder: *preventive measures.* **2.** concerned with prevention, as of disease: *preventive medicine.* —*n.* **3.** a drug or other substance for preventing disease. **4.** a preventive agent or measure. —**pre•ven′tive•ly,** *adv.* —**pre•ven′tive•ness,** *n.*

preven′tive war′, *n.* an attack against a possible enemy to prevent an attack by that enemy at a later time. Also called **preemptive strike.**

pre•view (prē′vyo͞o′), *n.* **1.** an earlier or advance view. **2.** an advance showing of a motion picture, play, etc., before its public opening. **3.** anything that gives an advance idea or impression of something to come. —*v.t.* **4.** to view or show beforehand or in advance.

pre•vi•ous (prē′vē əs), *adj.* **1.** coming or occurring before something else; prior: *the previous owner.* **2.** *Informal.* done, occurring, etc., before the proper time; premature. —***Idiom.*** **3. previous to,** before; prior to. —**pre′vi•ous•ly,** *adv.* —**pre′vi•ous•ness,** *n.*

pre•vue (prē′vyo͞o′), *n., v.t.,* **-vued, -vu•ing.** PREVIEW.

pre•washed (prē′wosht′, -wôsht′), *adj.* washed before sale, esp. to produce a soft texture or a worn look: *prewashed jeans.*

prex•y (prek′sē) also **prex,** *n., pl.* **prex•ies** also **prex•es.** *Slang.* a president, esp. of a college or university.

prey (prā), *n.* **1.** an animal hunted or seized for food, esp. by a carnivorous animal. **2.** a person or thing that is the victim of an enemy, disease, swindler, injurious agency, etc. **3.** the action or habit of preying: *a beast of prey.* —*v.i.* (usu. fol. by *on* or *upon*) **4.** to seize and devour prey. **5.** to make raids or attacks for booty or plunder. **6.** to exert a harmful or destructive and often influence: *The problem preyed upon his mind.* **7.** to victimize another or others. —**prey′er,** *n.*

PRF, Puerto Rican female.

price (prīs), *n., v.,* **priced, pric•ing.** —*n.* **1.** the sum or amount of money or its equivalent for which anything is bought, sold, or offered for sale. **2.** a sum offered for the capture of a person: *to put a price on someone's head.* **3.** an amount of money for which a person will forsake principles or obligations. **4.** that which must be given, done, or undergone in order to obtain a thing: *We won, but at a heavy price.* —*v.t.* **5.** to fix the price of. **6.** to ask or find out the price of. —***Idiom.*** **7. at any price,** at any cost, no matter how great. —**pric′er,** *n.*

price′ control′, *n.* government regulation of prices by establishing maximum levels for goods or services, as during a period of inflation.

price′-earn′ings ra′tio, *n.* the current price of a share of common stock divided by earnings per share over a 12-month period, often used in stock evaluation. *Abbr.:* p/e

price′ fix′ing or **price′-fix′ing,** *n.* the establishing of prices at a determined level, either by a government or by mutual consent among producers or sellers of a commodity.

price′ in′dex, *n.* an index of the changes in the prices of goods and services, based on the prices of a previous period, with the base level usu. expressed as 100.

price•less (prīs′lis), *adj.* **1.** having a value beyond all price; invaluable. **2.** delightfully amusing or absurd. —**price′less•ness,** *n.*

price′ support′, *n.* the maintenance of the price of a commodity, product, etc., esp. by means of public subsidy or government purchase of surpluses.

price′ tag′, *n.* **1.** a label or tag that shows the price of the item to which it is attached. **2.** cost; price.

price′ war′, *n.* intensive competition, esp. among retailers, in which prices are repeatedly cut in order to undersell competitors or force competitors out of business.

pric•ey or **pric•y** (prī′sē), *adj.,* **-i•er, -i•est.** expensive or unduly expensive: *a pricey wine.* —**pric′ey•ness,** *n.*

prick (prik), *n.* **1.** a puncture made by a needle, thorn, or the like. **2.** the act of pricking: *the prick of a needle.* **3.** the state or sensation of being pricked. **4.** a sharp pain caused by or as if by being pricked; twinge. **5.** a sharp point or part; prickle. —*v.t.* **6.** to pierce with a sharp point; puncture. **7.** to affect with sharp pain, as from piercing. **8.** to cause sharp mental pain to; sting, as with remorse. **9.** to urge on with or as if with a goad or spur. **10.** to cause to stand erect or point upward (usu. fol. by *up*): *The dog pricked up its ears.* **11.** —*v.i.* **12.** to perform the action of piercing or puncturing something. **13.** to have a sensation of being pricked. **14.** to rise erect or point upward, as the ears of an animal (usu. fol. by *up*). **15.** to spur or urge a horse on. —***Idiom.*** **16. prick up one's ears,** to listen attentively. —**prick′er,** *n.*

prick•le (prik′əl), *n., v.,* **-led, -ling.** —*n.* **1.** a sharp point. **2.** a small, sharp thorn or projection, as on a plant. **3.** a pricking sensation. —*v.t.* **4.** to prick lightly. **5.** to cause a pricking or tingling sensation in. —*v.i.* **6.** to tingle as if pricked.

prick•ly (prik′lē), *adj.,* **-li•er, -li•est. 1.** full of or armed with prickles. **2.** full of troublesome points: *a prickly problem.* **3.** prickling; smarting. **4.** irritable; touchy. —**prick′li•ness,** *n.*

prick′ly heat′, *n.* a cutaneous eruption accompanied by a prickling and itching sensation, due to an inflammation of the sweat glands. Also called **heat rash.**

prick′ly pear′, *n.* **1.** any of numerous cacti of the genus *Opuntia,* having flattened, usu. spiny stem joints, yellow, orange, or reddish flowers, and ovoid, often edible fruit. **2.** the usu. prickly fruit of such a cactus.

pric•y (prī′sē), *adj.,* **-i•er, -i•est.** PRICEY. **—pric′i•ness,** *n.*

pride (prīd), *n., v.,* **prid•ed, prid•ing.** **—***n.* **1.** the state or quality of being proud; self-respect; self-esteem: one of the seven deadly sins. **2.** a feeling of gratification arising from association with something good or laudable: *civic pride.* **3.** a high or inordinate opinion of one's own importance or superiority; conceit. **4.** something that causes one to be proud: *Her paintings were the pride of the family.* **5.** the best of a group, class, etc. **6.** a group of lions. **7.** the most flourishing state or period; prime. **8.** splendor, magnificence, or pomp. **—***v.t.* **9.** to indulge (oneself) in a feeling of pride (usu. fol. by *on* or *upon*): *He prides himself on his good memory.* **—*Proverb.*** **10. Pride goes before a fall,** excessive pride leads to humiliation. Prov. 16:18. **—pride′ful,** *adj.* **—pride′ful•ly,** *adv.* **—pride′ful•ness,** *n.*

Pride′ and Prej′udice, a novel (1813) by Jane Austen (written 1796–97).

prie-dieu (prē′dyōō′; *Fr.* PRē dyœ′), *n., pl.* **-dieus, -dieux** (-dyōōz′), *Fr.* ***-dieu.*** a piece of furniture for kneeling on during prayer, having a rest above, as for a book. [< French: lit., pray God]

priest (prēst), *n.* **1.** (in Christian use) **a.** a person ordained to the sacerdotal or pastoral office; a member of the clergy; minister. **b.** (in hierarchical churches) a member of the clergy of the order next below that of bishop, authorized to carry out the Christian ministry. **2.** a minister of any religion. **3.** a person whose office it is to perform religious rites, and esp. to make sacrificial offerings. **—***v.t.* **4.** to ordain as a priest. **—priest′like′,** *adj.*

priest•ess (prē′stis), *n.* a woman who officiates in sacred rites.

priest•hood (prēst′ho͝od), *n.* **1.** the condition or office of a priest. **2.** priests collectively.

priest•ly (prēst′lē), *adj.,* **-li•er, -li•est.** **1.** of or pertaining to a priest; sacerdotal. **2.** characteristic of or befitting a priest.

prig (prig), *n.* a person self-righteously concerned with the punctilious observance of proprieties. **—prig′gish,** *adj.* **—prig′gish•ly,** *adv.* **—prig′gish•ness,** *n.*

prim (prim), *adj.,* **prim•mer, prim•mest,** *v.,* **primmed, prim•ming.** **—***adj.* **1.** formally proper; prissy; prudish. **2.** stiffly neat. **—***v.i.* **3.** to draw up the mouth in an affectedly nice or precise way. **—***v.t.* **4.** to make prim, as in appearance. **5.** to draw (one's features) into a prim expression. **—prim′ly,** *adv.* **—prim′ness,** *n.*

pri′ma balleri′na (prē′mə), *n., pl.* **prima ballerinas.** the principal ballerina in a ballet company.

pri•ma•cy (prī′mə sē), *n., pl.* **-cies.** **1.** the state of being first in order, rank, importance, etc. **2.** the office, rank, or dignity of an ecclesiastical primate. **3.** the supreme jurisdiction of the pope as supreme bishop.

pri•ma don•na (prē′mə don′ə, prim′ə), *n., pl.* **prima don•nas.** **1.** a first or principal female singer of an opera company. **2.** a vain, temperamental person who expects privileged treatment.

pri•ma fa•ci•e (prī′mə fā′shē ē′, fā′shē, fā′shə, prē′-), *adv.* **1.** at first view; before investigation. **—***adj.* **2.** obvious; self-evident. **3.** sufficient to establish a fact or to raise a presumption of fact unless rebutted: *prima facie evidence.*

pri•mal (prī′məl), *adj.* **1.** first; original; primeval. **2.** of first importance; fundamental.

pri•ma•ri•ly (prī mâr′ə lē, -mer′-, prī′mer ə lē, -mər ə-), *adv.* **1.** essentially; chiefly: *Their income is primarily from farming.* **2.** at first; originally: *Primarily a doctor, he later turned to teaching.*

pri•ma•ry (prī′mer ē, -mə rē), *adj., n., pl.* **-ries.** **—***adj.* **1.** first in rank or importance; chief: *one's primary goal in life.* **2.** first in time; earliest. **3.** of or pertaining to primary school: *the primary grades.* **4.** being of the simplest or most basic order of its or their kind: *a primary constituent.* **5.** immediate or direct; not involving intermediate agency: *primary perceptions.* **6.** noting or pertaining to the circuit, coil, winding, or current that induces electric current in secondary windings in an induction coil, transformer, or the like. **7.** *Chem.* **a.** involving or obtained by replacement of one atom or group. **b.** noting or containing a carbon atom united to no other or to only one other carbon atom in a molecule. **—***n.* **8.** something that is first in order or importance. **9. a.** a preliminary election in which voters of each political party nominate candidates for office, party officers, etc. **b.** a local meeting of party members to select candidates or delegates; caucus. **10.** PRIMARY COLOR. **11. a.** a body in relation to a smaller body or smaller bodies revolving around it, as a planet in relation to its satellites. **b.** the brighter of the two stars comprising a double star. **—pri′ma•ri•ness,** *n.*

pri′mary cell′, *n.* an electric battery that produces current by means of an irreversible chemical reaction and is therefore not rechargeable.

pri′mary col′or, *n.* a color, as red, yellow, or blue, that in mixture yields other colors.

pri′mary school′, *n.* an elementary school, esp. one covering the first three or four grades and sometimes kindergarten.

pri′mary stress′, *n.* the principal or strongest degree of stress in a word or phrase: indicated in this dictionary by the mark (′). Compare SECONDARY STRESS.

pri•mate (prī′māt *or, esp. for 1,* -mit), *n.* **1.** an archbishop or bishop ranking first among the bishops of a province or country. **2.** any mammal of the order Primates, comprising the three suborders Anthropoidea (humans, apes, Old World monkeys, and New World monkeys), Prosimii (lemurs, lorises, and bush babies), and Tarsioidea (tarsiers). **—pri•ma′tial** (-mā′shəl), *adj.* **—pri′mate•ship′** (-mit ship′, -māt-), *n.*

prime (prīm), *adj., n., v.,* **primed, prim•ing.** **—***adj.* **1.** of the first importance: *a prime requisite.* **2.** of the greatest relevance or significance: *a prime example.* **3.** of the highest eminence or rank. **4.** of the greatest commercial value. **5.** first-rate. **6.** (of meat) of the highest grade or best quality. **7.** first in order of time, existence, or development. **8.** basic; fundamental. **9.** (of any two or more numbers) having no common divisor except unity: *The number 2 is prime to 9.* **—***n.* **10.** the most flourishing stage or state. **11.** the period of greatest vigor of human life: *a man in his prime.* **12.** the choicest or best part of anything. **13.** PRIME RATE. **14.** *Math.* **a.** PRIME NUMBER. **b.** one of the equal parts into which a unit is primarily divided. **c.** the mark (′) indicating such a division: *a, a′.* **15.** *Music.* (in a scale) the tonic or keynote. **—***v.t.* **16.** to prepare for a particular purpose or operation. **17.** to supply (a firearm) with powder for igniting a charge. **18.** to pour or admit liquid into (a pump) to expel air and prepare for action. **19.** to put fuel into (a carburetor) before starting an engine, in order to insure a sufficiently rich mixture at the start. **20.** to cover (a surface) with an undercoat of paint or the like. **21.** to supply with needed information, facts, etc. **—***v.i.* **22.** to harvest the bottom leaves from a tobacco plant. **—*Idiom.*** **23. prime the pump, a.** to increase government expenditure in an effort to stimulate the economy. **b.** to support or promote the operation or improvement of something. **—prime′ly,** *adv.* **—prime′ness,** *n.*

prime′ merid′ian, *n.* the meridian running through Greenwich, England, from which longitude east and west is reckoned.

prime′ min′ister, *n.* the head of government and the head of the cabinet in parliamentary systems. **—prime′ min′is•ter•ship′,** *n.*

prime′ mov′er, *n.* **1. a.** the initial agent, as wind or electricity, that puts a machine in motion. **b.** a machine, as a waterwheel or steam engine, that receives and modifies energy as supplied by some natural source. **2.** a person or thing that initiates or gives power and cohesion to an idea, endeavor, etc.

prime′ num′ber, *n.* a positive integer that is not divisible without remainder by any integer except itself and 1.

prim•er[1] (prim′ər; *esp. Brit.* prī′mər), *n.* **1.** an elementary book for teaching children to read. **2.** any book of elementary principles.

prim•er[2] (prī′mər), *n.* **1.** a person or thing that primes. **2.** a cap, cylinder, etc., that supplies a compound for igniting a charge of powder. **3.** a first coat of paint, size, etc., given to any surface as a base, sealer, or the like. **4.** a short piece of DNA added to one end of a strand of DNA in order to define the portion to be copied.

prime′ rate′, *n.* the minimum interest rate charged by a commercial bank on short-term business loans to large, best-rated customers or corporations. Also called **prime, prime′ in′terest rate′, prime′ lend′ing rate′.**

prime′ ribs′ (or **rib′**), *n.* a serving of the roasted ribs and meat from a prime cut of beef.

prime′ time′, *n.* the hours, generally between 7 and 11 P.M., considered to have the largest television audience of the day.

pri•me•val or **pri•mae•val** (prī mē′vəl), *adj.* of or pertaining to the first age or ages, esp. of the world; primordial: *primeval forms of life.* **—pri•me′val•ly,** *adv.*

prim•ing (prī′ming), *n.* **1.** the powder or other material used to ignite a charge. **2.** the act of a person or thing that primes. **3.** a first coat or layer of paint, size, etc.

prim•i•tive (prim′i tiv), *adj.* **1.** being the first or earliest of the kind or in existence, esp. in an early age of the world: *primitive forms of life.* **2.** early in the history of the world or of humankind. **3.** characteristic of early ages or of an early state of human development: *primitive toolmaking.* **4.** *Anthropol.* **a.** of or indicating a people or society organized in bands or tribes and having a simple economy and technology. **b.** (no longer in technical use) of or indicating a preliterate people having cultural or physical similarities with their early ancestors. **5.** unaffected or little affected by civilizing influences; uncivilized; savage: *primitive passions.* **6.** of an early or the earliest period. **7.** old-fashioned: *primitive notions of style.* **8.** simple or crude: *primitive housing.* **9. a.** of or pertaining to a form from which a word or other linguistic form is derived; not derivative. **b.** of or pertaining to a protolanguage. **10.** primary, as distinguished from secondary. **11.** *Biol.* **a.** rudimentary; primordial. **b.** noting species, etc., only slightly evolved from early antecedent types. **c.** of early formation and temporary, as a part that subsequently disappears. **—***n.* **12.** someone or something primitive. **13. a.** an artist of a preliterate culture. **b.** a naive or unschooled artist. **c.** an artist belonging to the early stage in the development of a style. **d.** a work of art by a primitive artist. **14.** a geometric or algebraic form or expression from which another is derived. **15.** a form from which a given linguistic form has been derived by morphological or historical processes, as *take* in *undertake.* **—prim′i•tive•ly,** *adv.* **—prim′i•tive•ness,** *n.*

prim•i•tiv•ism (prim′i ti viz′əm), *n.* **1.** a recurrent theory or belief, as in philosophy or art, that the qualities of primitive or chronologically early cultures are superior to those of contemporary civilization. **2.** the state of being primitive: *the primitivism of Stone Age culture.* **3.** the qualities or style characterizing primitive art. **—prim′i•tiv•ist,** *n.* **—prim′i•tiv•is′tic,** *adj.*

pri•mo•gen•i•tor (prī′mə jen′i tər), *n.* forefather; ancestor.

pri•mo•gen•i•ture (prī′mə jen′i chər, -cho͝or′), *n.* **1.** the state or fact of being the firstborn of children of the same parents. **2.** inheritance by the firstborn, specifically the eldest son. —**pri′mo•gen′i•tar′y, pri′mo•gen′i•tal,** *adj.*

pri•mor•di•al (prī môr′dē əl), *adj.* **1.** constituting the earliest stages; original: *primordial forms of life.* **2.** existing at or from the very beginning: *primordial matter.* —**pri•mor′di•al′i•ty** (-al′i tē), *n.* —**pri•mor′di•al•ly,** *adv.*

primp (primp), *v.t.* **1.** to dress or adorn with care. —*v.i.* **2.** to groom oneself carefully.

prim•rose (prim′rōz′), *n.* **1.** any plant of the genus *Primula,* with showy five-lobed flowers in a variety of colors. **2.** EVENING PRIMROSE. **3.** pale yellow. —*adj.* **4.** of a pale yellow.

prince (prins), *n.* **1.** a nonreigning male member of a royal family. **2.** (in Great Britain) a son of the sovereign or of a son of the sovereign. **3.** any of various titles of nobility in other countries. **4.** a holder of such a title. **5.** the ruler of a small or subordinate state. **6.** a person who is preeminent in any class or group. **7.** an admirable person.

Prince (prins), *n.* **Harold S.,** born 1928, U.S. stage director and producer.

Prince, The (prins), (Italian, *Il Principe*), a treatise on statecraft (1513) by Niccolò Machiavelli.

Prince′ Charm′ing, *n.* a man who embodies a woman's romantic ideal. [after *Prince Charming,* hero of *Cinderella*]

prince′ con′sort, *n.* a prince who is the husband of a reigning female sovereign.

Prince′ Ed′ward Is′land, *n.* an island in the Gulf of St. Lawrence, forming a province of Canada. 126,646; 2184 sq. mi. (5657 sq. km). *Cap.:* Charlottetown.

Prince′ of Dark′ness, *n.* Satan.

Prince′ of Peace′, *n.* the Messiah. Is. 9:6.

Prince′ of Wales′, *n.* **1.** a title conferred by the British sovereign on the male heir apparent, usu. the eldest son. **2. Cape,** a cape in W Alaska, on Bering Strait: the westernmost point of North America.

prince′'s-feath′er, *n.* a tall, showy plant, *Amaranthus hybridus erythrostachys,* of the amaranth family, having reddish foliage and thick spikes of small, red flowers.

prin•cess (prin′sis, -ses, prin ses′), *n.* **1.** a nonreigning female member of a royal family. **2.** the wife and consort of a prince. **3.** (in Great Britain) a daughter of the sovereign or of a son of the sovereign. **4.** a woman or girl regarded or treated as a princess. —*adj.* **5.** Also, **prin′cesse.** (of a woman's dress, coat, or the like) styled with a close-fitting bodice and flared skirt.

Prin′cess and the Pea′, The, a fairy tale by Hans Christian Andersen.

prin•ci•pal (prin′sə pəl), *adj.* **1.** first or highest in rank, importance, value, etc. **2.** of or constituting principal or capital: *a principal investment.* —*n.* **3.** a chief or head. **4.** the head or director of a school. **5.** a chief actor or performer. **6.** a matter of the greatest importance. **7.** *Law.* **a.** a person who authorizes another to act for him or her. **b.** a person who commits a crime or is present and acts as an abettor. **8.** a capital sum, as distinguished from interest or profit. **9.** the main body of an estate, or the like, as distinguished from income. **10.** each of the combatants in a duel. —**prin′ci•pal•ly,** *adv.* —**prin′ci•pal•ship′,** *n.* —**Usage.** Although pronounced alike, PRINCIPLE and PRINCIPAL are not interchangeable in writing. A PRINCIPLE is broadly "a rule of action or conduct" or "a fundamental doctrine or tenet." The adjective PRINCIPAL has the general sense "chief, first, foremost." The noun PRINCIPAL has among other meanings "the head or director of a school" and "a capital sum, as distinguished from interest or profit."

prin•ci•pal•i•ty (prin′sə pal′i tē), *n., pl.* **-ties. 1.** a state ruled by a prince. **2.** the position or authority of a prince. **3.** the rule of a prince. **4. principalities,** an order of angels.

prin′cipal parts′, *n.* a set of inflected forms of a verb from which all the other inflected forms can be derived, as *sing, sang, sung* or *smoke, smoked.*

prin•ci•ple (prin′sə pəl), *n.* **1.** an accepted or professed rule of action or conduct. **2.** a fundamental law, axiom, or doctrine: *the principles of modern physics.* **3. principles,** a personal or specific basis of conduct or management: *to adhere to one's principles.* **4.** a guiding sense of the requirements and obligations of right conduct. **5.** a rule or law exemplified in natural phenomena, the construction or operation of a machine, or the like. **6.** the method of formation, operation, or procedure exhibited in a given instance. **7.** a determining characteristic of something; essential quality. **8.** *Chem.* a constituent of a substance, esp. one giving to it some distinctive quality or effect. —*Idiom.* **9. in principle,** in essence; fundamentally. **10. on principle, a.** according to rules for right and moral conduct. **b.** according to habit or self-imposed regulations. —**Usage.** See **principal.**

prin•ci•pled (prin′sə pəld), *adj.* imbued with moral principles (often used in combination): *high-principled.*

print (print), *v.t.* **1.** to produce (a text, picture, etc.) by applying inked types, plates, blocks, or the like, to paper or other material. **2.** to reproduce (a design or pattern) by engraving on a plate or block. **3.** to publish in printed form. **4.** to write in letters like those commonly used in print. **5.** to produce (an indentation, mark, etc.), as by pressure. **6.** to impress on the mind, memory, etc. **7.** *Photog.* to produce a positive picture from (a negative) by the transmission of light. —*v.i.* **8.** to produce printed material: *to print in color.* **9.** to produce something in printed form. **10.** to write in characters such as are used in print. **11. print out,** to produce (data) in printed form; make a printout of. —*n.* **12.** the state of being printed. **13.** printed material. **14.** NEWSPRINT. **15.** a picture, design, or the like, printed from an engraved or otherwise prepared block, plate, etc. **16.** an indentation, mark, etc., made by the pressure of one body or thing on another. **17.** something with which an impression is made; a stamp or die. **18.** FINGERPRINT. **19. a.** a design or pattern on cloth made by dyeing, weaving, or printing with engraved rollers, blocks of wood, stencils, etc. **b.** a cloth so treated. **c.** an article of apparel made of this cloth. **20.** a photograph, esp. a positive made from a negative. **21.** any reproduced image, as a blueprint. **22.** a positive copy of a completed motion picture ready for showing. —*adj.* **23.** of or pertaining to newspapers and magazines: *the print media.* —*Idiom.* **24. in print, a.** in printed form; published. **b.** (of a book or the like) still available for purchase from the publisher. **25. out of print,** (of a book or the like) no longer available for purchase from the publisher.

print′ed cir′cuit, *n.* a circuit in which the interconnecting conductors and some of the circuit components have been printed, etched, etc., onto a sheet or board of dielectric material.

print′ed mat′ter, *n.* **1.** any of various kinds of printed material that qualify for a special postal rate. **2.** a classification of international mail consisting of such items.

print•er (prin′tər), *n.* **1.** a person or firm engaged in the business of printing. **2.** a machine used for printing. **3.** a computer output device that produces a paper copy of data or graphics.

print•ing (prin′ting), *n.* **1.** the skill, process, or business of producing books, newspapers, etc., by impression from movable types, plates, etc. **2.** the act of a person or thing that prints. **3.** printed material. **4.** the total number of copies of a book or other publication printed at one time.

print′ing press′, *n.* a machine, as a cylinder press or rotary press, for printing on paper or the like from type, plates, etc.

print•out (print′out′), *n.* computer output produced by a printer.

print′ shop′, *n.* **1.** a shop where prints or graphics are sold. **2.** a shop where printing is done.

pri•or[1] (prī′ər), *adj.* **1.** preceding in time or order; earlier: *a prior commitment.* —*Idiom.* **2. prior to,** preceding; before. —**pri′or•ly,** *adv.*

pri•or[2] (prī′ər), *n.* an officer in a monastic order or religious house, sometimes next in rank below an abbot. —**pri′or•ship′,** *n.*

pri•or•ess (prī′ər is), *n.* a woman holding a position corresponding to that of a prior.

pri•or•i•tize (prī ôr′i tīz′, -or′-), *v.,* **-tized, -tiz•ing.** —*v.t.* **1.** to arrange or do in order of priority. **2.** to give a high priority to. —*v.i.* **3.** to organize material according to its priority. —**pri•or′i•ti•za′tion,** *n.*

pri•or•i•ty (prī ôr′i tē, -or′-), *n., pl.* **-ties. 1.** the state or quality of being earlier in time or occurrence. **2.** the right to take precedence in a given situation. **3.** something given special or prior attention.

prior′ity mail′, *n.* (in the U.S. Postal Service) mail consisting of merchandise weighing more than 12 ounces sent at first-class rates.

pri•o•ry (prī′ə rē), *n., pl.* **-ries.** a religious house governed by a prior or prioress, often dependent upon an abbey.

Pris•cil•la (pri sil′ə), *n.* a Christian of Corinth who was married to Aquila and was a leader in the early church. Acts 18:2.

prism (priz′əm), *n.* **1.** *Optics.* a transparent solid body, often having triangular bases, used for dispersing light into a spectrum or for reflecting rays of light. **2.** *Geom.* a solid having bases or ends that are parallel, congruent polygons and sides that are parallelograms.

pris•mat•ic (priz mat′ik), *adj.* **1.** of, pertaining to, or like a prism. **2.** formed by or as if by a transparent prism. **3.** spectral in color; brilliant. **4.** highly varied or faceted. —**pris•mat′i•cal•ly,** *adv.*

pris•on (priz′ən), *n.* **1.** a building for the confinement of accused persons awaiting trial or persons sentenced after conviction. **2.** any place of confinement or involuntary restraint. **3.** imprisonment.

pris′on camp′, *n.* **1.** a camp for the confinement of prisoners of war or political prisoners. **2.** a camp for less dangerous prisoners assigned to outdoor work, usu. for the government.

pris•on•er (priz′ə nər, priz′nər), *n.* **1.** a person who is confined in prison or kept in custody, esp. as the result of legal process. **2.** a person or thing deprived of liberty or kept in restraint.

pris′oner of war′, *n.* a person who is captured and held by an enemy during war, esp. a member of the armed forces. *Abbr.:* POW

pris•sy (pris′ē), *adj.,* **-si•er, -si•est.** excessively proper; affectedly correct; prim. —**pris′si•ly,** *adv.* —**pris′si•ness,** *n.*

pris•tine (pris′tēn, pri stēn′; *esp. Brit.* pris′tīn), *adj.* **1.** having its original purity; uncorrupted or unsullied. **2.** of or pertaining to the earliest period or state.

pri•va•cy (prī′və sē; *Brit. also* priv′ə sē), *n., pl.* **-cies. 1.** the state of being private; retirement or seclusion. **2.** freedom from the intrusion of others in one's private life or affairs: *the right to privacy.*

pri•vate (prī′vit), *adj.* **1.** belonging to some particular person or persons: *private property.* **2.** pertaining to or affecting a particular person or a small group of persons. **3.** confined to or intended only for the person or persons immediately concerned. **4.** not holding public office or employment: *private citizens.* **5.** not of an official or public character: *to return to private life.* **6.** removed from or out of public view or knowledge; personal; secret: *private papers.* **7.** not open or accessible to the general public: *a private beach.* **8.** undertaken or operated independently: *private research.* **9.** working as an independent individual: *a private detective.* **10.** solitary; secluded. **11.** preferring privacy; retiring. —*n.* **12.** a soldier of one of the three lowest enlisted ranks. —***Idiom.*** **13. in private,** not publicly; secretly. —**pri′vate•ly,** *adv.*

pri•va•teer (prī′və tēr′), *n.* a privately owned ship commissioned to fight or harass enemy ships.

pri′vate eye′, *n. Informal.* a private detective.

pri′vate first′ class′, *n.* a soldier ranking above a private and below a corporal or specialist fourth class in the U.S. Army, and above a private and below a lance corporal in the U.S. Marine Corps.

pri′vate law′, *n.* a branch of law dealing with the legal relationships of private individuals. Compare PUBLIC LAW (def. 2).

pri′vate place′ment, *n.* a sale of an issue of securities by the issuing company directly to a limited number of investors, often only one or two large institutional investors, such as a bank or an insurance company (opposed to *public offering*): required to be cleared but not registered with the Securities and Exchange Commission.

pri′vate sec′retary, *n.* a person employed to attend to the individual or confidential correspondence, files, etc., of a business executive, official, or the like.

pri•va•tion (prī vā′shən), *n.* **1.** lack of the usual comforts or necessaries of life. **2.** an instance of this. **3.** the act of depriving. **4.** the state of being deprived.

pri•va•tism (prī′və tiz′əm), *n.* concern with or pursuit of one's personal interests, welfare, or ideals to the exclusion of broader social issues or relationships. —**pri′va•tist, pri′va•tis′tic,** *adj.*

priv•a•tive (priv′ə tiv), *adj.* **1.** causing, or tending to cause, deprivation. **2.** consisting in or characterized by the taking away, loss, or lack of something. —**priv′a•tive•ly,** *adv.*

pri•va•tize (prī′və tīz′), *v.t.*, **-tized, -tiz•ing. 1.** to transfer from public or government control or ownership to private enterprise. **2.** to make private. —**pri′va•ti•za′tion,** *n.*

priv•et (priv′it), *n.* any deciduous or evergreen shrubs of the genus *Ligustrum,* of the olive family, esp. *L. vulgare,* having clusters of small white flowers and commonly grown as a hedge.

priv•i•lege (priv′ə lij, priv′lij), *n., v.,* **-leged, -leg•ing.** —*n.* **1.** a right or benefit enjoyed by a particular person or group of persons. **2.** a special right, immunity, or exemption granted to persons in authority or office to free them from certain obligations. **3.** a grant of a special right or immunity, under certain conditions. **4.** the principle or condition of enjoying special rights or immunities. **5.** any of the rights common to all citizens under a modern constitutional government. **6.** an advantage or source of pleasure granted to a person: *It's my privilege to be here.* —*v.t.* **7.** to grant a privilege to. **8.** to exempt (usu. fol. by *from*).

priv•i•leged (priv′ə lijd, priv′lijd), *adj.* **1.** belonging to a class that enjoys special privileges. **2.** entitled to or exercising a privilege. **3.** restricted to a select group or individual: *privileged information.* **4.** *Law.* (of statements or communications) **a.** confidential; not making the participants liable to prosecution for libel or slander. **b.** protected against being used as evidence in court. **5.** (of a vessel) having the right of way. Compare BURDENED.

priv′ileged sanc′tuary, *n. Mil.* a base from which attacks can be made without risk of retaliation.

priv•i•ty (priv′i tē), *n., pl.* **-ties. 1.** private or secret knowledge. **2.** participation in the knowledge of something private or secret, esp. as implying concurrence or consent. **3.** *Law.* the relation between privies.

priv•y (priv′ē), *adj.,* **priv•i•er, priv•i•est,** *n., pl.* **priv•ies.** —*adj.* **1.** participating in the knowledge of something private or secret (usu. fol. by *to*): *Many people were privy to the plot.* **2.** private; assigned to private uses. **3.** belonging or pertaining to some particular person, esp. a sovereign. **4.** secret, concealed, hidden, or secluded. **5.** acting or done in secret. —*n.* **6.** OUTHOUSE (def. 1). **7.** *Law.* a person who participates directly in or has an interest in a legal transaction.

priv′y cham′ber, *n.* a private apartment in a royal residence.

priv′y coun′cil, *n.* **1.** a board or select body of personal advisers, as of a sovereign. **2.** (*caps.*) (in Great Britain) a body of persons who advise the sovereign in matters of state, the majority of members being selected by the prime minister. —**priv′y coun′cilor,** *n.*

prix fixe (prē′ fiks′; *Fr.* prē fēks′), *n., pl.* **prix fixes** (prē′ fiks′; *Fr.* prē fēks′). a fixed price charged for a complete meal chosen usu. from a limited menu.

prize[1] (prīz), *n.* **1.** a reward for victory or superiority, as in a contest or competition. **2.** something won in a lottery or the like. **3.** anything striven for, worth striving for, or much valued. **4.** something seized or captured, esp. an enemy's ship and cargo captured at sea in wartime. **5.** the act of taking or capturing, esp. a ship at sea. —*adj.* **6.** having won a prize: *a prize play.* **7.** worthy of a prize. **8.** given or awarded as a prize.

prize[2] (prīz), *v.t.,* **prized, priz•ing. 1.** to value or esteem highly. **2.** to estimate the worth or value of.

prize[3] or **prise** (prīz), *v.,* **prized, priz•ing** or **prised, pris•ing,** *n.* —*v.t.* **1.** PRY[2]. —*n.* **2.** LEVERAGE. **3.** LEVER (def. 1).

prize′fight′ or **prize′ fight′,** *n.* a professional boxing match. —**prize′fight′er,** *n.* —**prize′fight′ing,** *n.*

prize′ mon′ey, *n.* **1.** money offered, won, or received in prizes. **2.** a portion of the money realized from the sale of a prize, esp. an enemy's vessel, divided among the captors.

PRM, Puerto Rican male.

pro[1] (prō), *adv., n., pl.* **pros.** —*adv.* **1.** in favor of a proposition, opinion, etc. —*n.* **2.** the argument, position, arguer, or voter for something. Compare CON[1].

pro[2] (prō), *adj., n., pl.* **pros.** professional.

pro-[1], **1.** a prefix, having ANTI- as its opposite, used to form adjectives that have the general sense "favoring" the group, interests, course of action, etc., denoted by the headword: *pro-American; prowar.* **2.** a prefix occurring in loanwords from Latin, with the meanings "forward," forming esp. verbs denoting forward movement or location (*proceed; progress*), advancement (*promote; propose*), or bringing into existence (*produce*); "before, outside of" (*profane*); "in place of" (*pronoun*).

pro-[2], a prefix, occurring orig. in loanwords from Greek, with the meanings "before, beforehand, in front of" (*prognosis; prophylactic; prothesis*), "front part, extremity" (*proboscis; proglottis*), "primitive or embryonic form," "precursor" (*prodrug; pronephros; prosimian*).

pro•a (prō′ə), *n., pl.* **pro•as.** any of various Indonesian vessels, esp. a swift sailboat with a single outrigger.

pro•ac•tive (prō ak′tiv), *adj.* serving to prepare for, intervene in, or control an expected occurrence or situation: *proactive measures against crime.* —**pro•ac′tive•ly,** *adv.*

prob•a•bil•i•ty (prob′ə bil′i tē), *n., pl.* **-ties. 1.** the quality or fact of being probable. **2.** a probable event, circumstance, etc. **3.** *Statistics.* the relative possibility that an event will occur, as expressed by the ratio of the number of actual occurrences to the total number of possible occurrences. —***Idiom.*** **4. in all probability,** very probably; quite likely.

probabil′ity the′ory, *n.* the theory of analyzing and making mathematical statements concerning the probability of the occurrence of uncertain events.

prob•a•ble (prob′ə bəl), *adj.* **1.** likely to occur or prove true. **2.** having more evidence for than against, or evidence that inclines the mind to belief but leaves some room for doubt. **3.** affording ground for belief.

prob′able cause′, *n. Law.* **1.** (in a criminal case) reasonable ground for a belief that the accused was guilty of the crime. **2.** (in a civil case) the probability that grounds for the action existed.

prob•a•bly (prob′ə blē), *adv.* in all likelihood; very likely.

pro•bate (prō′bāt), *n., adj., v.,* **-bat•ed, -bat•ing.** —*n.* **1.** the official proving of a will as authentic or valid in a probate court. —*adj.* **2.** of or pertaining to probate or a probate court. —*v.t.* **3.** to establish the authenticity or validity of (a will).

pro′bate court′, *n.* a special court with power over administration of estates of deceased persons, the probate of wills, etc.

pro•ba•tion (prō bā′shən), *n.* **1.** the testing or trial of a person's conduct, character, qualifications, or the like. **2.** the state or period of such testing or trial. **3.** the conditional release of an offender under the supervision of a probation officer. **4.** the trial period or condition of a student who is being permitted to redeem failures, misconduct, etc. **5.** the act of testing. —**pro•ba′tion•al, pro•ba′tion•ar′y,** *adj.*

proba′tion of′ficer, *n.* an officer who investigates and reports on the conduct of offenders who are free on probation.

pro•ba•tive (prō′bə tiv) also **pro•ba•to•ry** (-tôr′ē, -tōr′ē), *adj.* **1.** serving or designed for testing or trial. **2.** affording proof or evidence. —**pro′ba•tive•ly,** *adv.*

probe (prōb), *v.,* **probed, prob•ing,** *n.* —*v.t.* **1.** to search into or examine thoroughly: *to probe one's conscience.* **2.** to examine or explore with a probe. —*v.i.* **3.** to examine or explore with or as if with a probe. —*n.* **4.** a slender surgical instrument for exploring the depth or direction of a wound, sinus, or the like. **5.** any slender device inserted into something in order to explore, test, or examine. **6.** the act of probing. **7.** an investigation, esp. by a legislative committee, of suspected illegal activity. **8.** SPACE PROBE. —**probe′a•ble,** *adj.* —**prob′er,** *n.*

pro•bi•ty (prō′bi tē, prob′i-), *n.* integrity and uprightness; honesty. [< Latin *probitās,* der. of *probus* upright]

prob•lem (prob′ləm), *n.* **1.** any question or matter involving doubt, uncertainty, or difficulty. **2.** a question proposed for solution or discussion. **3.** *Math.* a statement requiring a solution, usu. by means of a mathematical operation or geometric construction. —*adj.* **4.** difficult to train or guide; unruly: *a problem child.* **5.** *Literature.* dealing with difficult choices: *a problem play.* —***Proverb.*** **6. If you're not part of the solution, you're part of the problem,** direct action is necessary to solve a problem.

prob•lem•at•ic (prob′lə mat′ik) also **prob′lem•at′i•cal,** *adj.* of the nature of a problem; doubtful; questionable. —**prob′lem•at′i•cal•ly,** *adv.*

pro bo•no or **pro-bo•no** (prō′ bō′nō), *adj.* done or donated without charge; free: *pro bono legal services.*

pro•bos•cid•e•an or **pro•bos•cid•i•an** (prō′bə sid′ē ən, -bo-, prō-bos′i dē′ən), *adj.* **1.** belonging or pertaining to the Proboscidea, an order of massive tusked mammals with a flexible trunk and columnar legs, comprising the elephant and the now extinct mammoth and mastodon. —*n.* **2.** a proboscidean animal.

pro•bos•cis (prō bos′is, -kis), *n., pl.* **-bos•cis•es, -bos•ci•des** (-bos′i-dēz′). **1.** the trunk of an elephant. **2.** any long flexible snout, as of the tapir. **3.** the elongate, protruding process on the head of certain insects or worms, used for feeding.

pro•ce•dur•al (prə sē′jər əl), *adj.* **1.** of or pertaining to a procedure. —*n.* **2.** POLICE PROCEDURAL. —**pro•ce′dur•al•ly,** *adv.*

pro•ce•dure (prə sē′jər), *n.* **1.** the act or manner of proceeding in any

P

action or process; conduct. **2.** a particular course or mode of action. **3.** any given mode of conducting legal, parliamentary, or similar business.

pro•ceed (*v.* prə sēd′; *n.* prō′sēd), *v.i.* **1.** to move or go forward or onward, esp. after stopping. **2.** to carry on or continue any action or process. **3.** to continue one's discourse. **4.** to initiate a legal action (often fol. by *against*). **5.** to go or come forth; issue (often fol. by *from*). **6.** to arise, originate, or result (usu. fol. by *from*). —*n.* **proceeds**, **7.** something that results or accrues. **8.** the total amount or profit derived from a sale or other transaction. —**pro•ceed′er**, *n.*

pro•ceed•ing (prə sē′ding), *n.* **1.** a particular action, or course or manner of action. **2. proceedings**, a series of activities or events; happenings. **3. proceedings**, a record of the business discussed at a meeting of an academic society or other formal group. **4. proceedings**, legal action, esp. as carried on in a court of law. **5.** the act of a person or thing that proceeds.

proc•ess (pros′es; *esp. Brit.* prō′ses), *n., pl.* **proc•ess•es** (pros′es iz, -ə siz, -ə sēz′; *esp. Brit.* prō′ses-, prō′sə-), *v. adj.* —*n.* **1.** a systematic series of actions directed to some end: *a process for homogenizing milk.* **2.** a continuous action, operation, or series of changes taking place in a definite manner: *the process of decay.* **3.** *Law.* **a.** the summons, mandate, or writ by which a defendant is brought before court for litigation. **b.** the whole course of the proceedings in an action at law. **4.** photomechanical or photoengraving methods collectively. **5.** *Anat.* a natural outgrowth or appendage: *a process of a bone.* **6.** the action of going forward or on. **7.** the condition of being carried on. **8.** course or lapse, as of time. **9.** CONK⁴ (defs. 1, 2). —*v.t.* **10.** to treat by some particular process, as in manufacturing. **11.** to handle (persons, papers, etc.) according to a routine procedure. **12.** to institute a legal process against. **13.** to serve a process or summons on. **14.** CONK⁴ (def. 3). —*adj.* **15.** prepared or modified by a special process. **16.** noting, pertaining to, or involving photomechanical or photoengraving methods: *a process print.*

proc′essed cheese′ or **proc′ess cheese′**, *n.* a mass-produced product made of one or more types of cheese that have been heated and blended with flavorings and emulsifiers.

pro•ces•sion (prə sesh′ən), *n.* **1.** the act of moving along or proceeding in orderly succession or in a formal and ceremonious manner. **2.** a line or body of persons, vehicles, etc., moving along in such a manner. **3.** the act of coming forth from a source. —*v.i.* **4.** to go in procession.

pro•ces•sion•al (prə sesh′ə nl), *adj.* **1.** of or pertaining to a procession. **2.** of the nature of a procession. **3.** used in processions. **4.** sung or played during a procession, as a hymn. —*n.* **5.** a piece of music, as a hymn or slow march, suitable for accompanying a procession. —**pro•ces′sion•al•ly**, *adv.*

proc•es•sor or **proc•ess•er** (pros′es ər; *esp. Brit.* prō′ses-), *n.* **1.** a person or thing that processes. **2.** a computer.

proc′ess print′ing, *n.* a method of printing almost any color by using a limited number of separate color plates, as yellow, magenta, cyan, and black, in combination.

proc′ess serv′er, *n.* a person who serves subpoenas or other legal documents, esp. those requiring appearance in court.

pro•choice or **pro•choice** (prō chois′), *adj.* supporting or advocating the right to legalized abortion. Compare PRO-LIFE. —**pro•choic′er**, *n.*

pro•claim (prō klām′, prə-), *v.t.* **1.** to announce or declare in an official or formal manner. **2.** to announce or declare in an open or ostentatious way. **3.** to indicate or make known publicly or openly. **4.** to extol or praise publicly. **5.** to denounce or prohibit publicly. —*v.i.* **6.** to make a proclamation. —**pro•claim′er**, *n.*

proc•la•ma•tion (prok′lə mā′shən), *n.* **1.** something that is proclaimed; a public and official announcement. **2.** the act of proclaiming.

pro•cliv•i•ty (prō kliv′i tē), *n., pl.* **-ties.** natural or habitual inclination or tendency; propensity; predisposition.

pro•cras•ti•nate (prō kras′tə nāt′, prə-), *v.,* **-nat•ed, -nat•ing.** —*v.i.* **1.** to defer action; delay: *to procrastinate until an opportunity is lost.* —*v.t.* **2.** to put off till another day or time; defer; delay. —**pro•cras′ti•na′tion**, *n.* —**pro•cras′ti•na′tor**, *n.*

pro•cre•ate (prō′krē āt′), *v.,* **-at•ed, -at•ing.** —*v.t.* **1.** to beget or generate (offspring). **2.** to produce; bring into being. —*v.i.* **3.** to beget offspring. —**pro′cre•a′tion**, *n.* —**pro′cre•a′tive**, *adj.* —**pro′cre•a′tor**, *n.*

Pro•crus•te•an (prō krus′tē ən), *adj.* **1.** pertaining to or suggestive of Procrustes. **2.** (*often l.c.*) tending to produce conformity by violent or arbitrary means.

Pro•crus•tes (prō krus′tēz), *n.* (in Greek myth) a robber who stretched or amputated the limbs of travelers to make them conform to the length of his bed.

procto-, a combining form meaning "anus," "rectum": *proctoscope.*

proc•tol•o•gy (prok tol′ə jē), *n.* the branch of medicine dealing with the rectum and anus. —**proc′to•log′ic** (-tl oj′ik), **proc′to•log′i•cal**, *adj.* —**proc•tol′o•gist**, *n.*

proc•tor (prok′tər), *n.* **1.** a person appointed to keep watch over students at examinations. **2.** a school official charged with any of various supervisory or disciplinary duties. —*v.t., v.i.* **3.** to supervise or monitor. —**proc•to′ri•al** (-tôr′ē əl, -tōr′-), *adj.* —**proc′tor•ship′**, *n.*

pro•cum•bent (prō kum′bənt), *adj.* **1.** lying on the face; prone; prostrate. **2.** (of a plant or stem) lying along the ground, but not putting forth roots.

pro•cu•ra•tor (prok′yə rā′tər), *n.* **1.** (in ancient Rome) any of various imperial agents with fiscal or administrative powers, esp. in a province. **2.** an agent, attorney, etc., employed to manage one's affairs. —**proc′u•ra′tor•ship′**, *n.* —**proc′u•ra•to′ri•al** (-yər ə tôr′ē əl, -tōr′-), *adj.*

pro•cure (prō kyŏŏr′, prə-), *v.,* **-cured, -cur•ing.** —*v.t.* **1.** to obtain by care, effort, or the use of special means. **2.** to bring about, esp. by complicated or indirect means. —**pro•cur′a•ble**, *adj.* —**pro•cure′ment**, *n.*

Pro•cy•on (prō′sē on′), *n.* a first-magnitude star in the constellation Canis Minor.

prod (prod), *v.,* **prod•ded, prod•ding**, *n.* —*v.t.* **1.** to poke or jab with or as if with something pointed. **2.** to rouse or incite as if by poking; nag; goad. —*n.* **3.** the act of prodding; a poke or jab. **4.** any of various pointed instruments, as an electrified rod, used as a goad: *a cattle prod.* —**prod′der**, *n.*

prod•i•gal (prod′i gəl), *adj.* **1.** wastefully or recklessly extravagant. **2.** giving or yielding profusely; lavish (usu. fol. by *of* or *with*): *to be prodigal with money.* **3.** lavishly abundant; profuse. —*n.* **4.** a person who spends money or uses resources with wasteful extravagance; wastrel or profligate. —**prod′i•gal•ly**, *adv.*

prod′igal son′, *n.* a wayward son who squanders his inheritance but returns home to find that his father forgives him. Luke 15:11–32.

pro•di•gious (prə dij′əs), *adj.* **1.** extraordinary in size, amount, extent, etc. **2.** arousing admiration or amazement: *a prodigious feat.* —**pro•di′gious•ly**, *adv.* —**pro•di′gious•ness**, *n.*

prod•i•gy (prod′i jē), *n., pl.* **-gies. 1.** a person, esp. a child or young person, having extraordinary talent or ability: *a musical prodigy.* **2.** something that excites wonder or amazement.

pro•duce (*v.* prə dōōs′, -dyōōs′; *n.* prod′ōōs, -yōōs, prō′dōōs, -dyōōs), *v.,* **-duced, -duc•ing**, *n.* —*v.t.* **1.** to cause to exist; give rise to: *to produce steam.* **2.** to bring into existence by intellectual or creative ability: *to produce a great painting.* **3.** to make or manufacture. **4.** to give birth to; bear. **5.** to furnish or supply; yield. **6.** to present; exhibit. **7.** to bring (a play, movie, opera, etc.) before the public. **8.** to extend or prolong, as a line. —*v.i.* **9.** to yield products, offspring, etc. —*n.* **prod•uce 10.** something that is produced; yield; product. **11.** agricultural products collectively, esp. vegetables and fruits. —**pro•duc′i•ble, pro•duct′i•ble** (-duk′tə bəl), *adj.* —**pro•duc′i•bil′i•ty, pro•duct′i•bil′i•ty**, *n.*

pro•duc•er (prə dōō′sər, -dyōō′-), *n.* **1.** a person who produces. **3.** a person who produces goods and services or creates economic value. **3.** the person responsible for raising money, hiring personnel, and generally supervising business matters for a stage, film, television, or radio production. **4.** an organism, as a plant, that is able to produce its own food from inorganic substances.

produc′er goods′, *n.pl.* goods, as machinery or raw materials, that are used in the process of creating consumer goods.

prod•uct (prod′əkt, -ukt), *n.* **1.** a thing produced by labor: *farm products.* **2.** the totality of goods or services that a company produces. **3.** material created or produced and viewed in terms of potential sales: *an artist who provided dealers with reliable product.* **4.** a person or thing seen as resulting from a process, as a social or historical one: *He is a product of his time.* **5.** *Math.* the result obtained by multiplying two or more quantities together.

pro•duc•tion (prə duk′shən), *n.* **1.** the act of producing; creation or manufacture. **2.** something that is produced; a product. **3.** the total amount produced. **4.** a work of literature or art. **5.** the act of presenting for display; presentation; exhibition: *the production of evidence.* **6.** an unnecessarily or exaggeratedly complicated situation or activity: *That child makes a production out of going to bed.* **7. a.** the organization and presentation of a play, motion picture, or other entertainment. **b.** the entertainment itself. —*adj.* **8.** regularly manufactured; not custom-made or specially produced: *a production model.* —**pro•duc′tion•al**, *adj.*

produc′tion line′, *n.* ASSEMBLY LINE.

pro•duc•tive (prə duk′tiv), *adj.* **1.** able to produce; generative; creative. **2.** producing abundantly; fertile: *productive land.* **3.** causing; bringing about (usu. fol. by *of*): *conditions productive of crime.* **4.** *Econ.*

---

pro′-A•mer′i•can, *adj., n.*
pro′an•nex•a′tion, *adj.*
pro′ar•bi•tra′tion, *adj.*
pro′au•to•ma′tion, *adj.*
pro•busi′ness, *adj.*
pro•cap′i•tal•ist, *n., adj.*
pro-Cath′o•lic, *adj., n.*
pro•church′, *adj.*
pro′-Con•fed′er•ate, *adj.*
pro′con•ser•va′tion, *adj.*

pro′-Dar•win′i•an, *adj., n.*
pro′dem•o•crat′ic, *adj.*
pro′dis•ar′ma•ment, *adj.*
pro′en•vi′ron•men′tal, *adj.*
pro•fas′cist, *adj., n.*
pro•fem′i•nist, *n., adj.*
pro•gov′ern•ment, *adj.*
pro•gun′, *adj.*
pro′im•mi•gra′tion, *adj.*
pro′in•dus′try, *adj.*

pro′in•te•gra′tion, *adj.*
pro′in•ter•ven′tion, *adj.*
pro•la′bor, *adj.*
pro•mar′riage, *adj.*
pro•mil′i•tar′y, *adj.*
pro′mi•nor′i•ty, *adj.*
pro•mod′ern, *adj.*
pro•mon′ar•chist, *n., adj.*
pro•na′tion•al•ist, *adj., n.*
pro•or′tho•dox′, *adj.*

pro-Prot′es•tant, *adj., n.*
pro′re•form′, *adj.*
pro′re•pub′li•can, *adj., n.*
pro′rev•o•lu′tion•ar′y, *adj.*
pro•syn′di•cal•ism, *n.*
pro•trade′, *adj.*
pro•un′ion, *adj.*
pro•war′, *adj.*
pro-West′, *adj.*
pro-Zi′on•ist, *n., adj.*

producing goods and services that have exchange value. **5.** (of a derivational affix or pattern) readily used in forming new words, as the suffix *-ness.* —**pro•duc′tive•ly,** *adv.* —**pro•duc′tive•ness,** *n.*

pro•em (prō′em), *n.* an introductory discourse; introduction; preface. —**pro•e′mi•al** (-ē′mē əl, -em′ē-), *adj.*

prof•a•na•tion (prof′ə nā′shən), *n.* the act of profaning; desecration. —**pro•fan•a•to•ry** (prə fan′ə tôr′ē, -tōr′ē, prō-), *adj.*

pro•fane (prə fān′, prō-), *adj., v.,* **-faned, -fan•ing.** —*adj.* **1.** showing irreverence toward God or sacred things; blasphemous. **2.** not devoted to holy purposes; secular (opposed to *sacred*). **3.** unholy; heathen; pagan: *profane rites.* **4.** not initiated into religious rites or mysteries. **5.** coarse or vulgar. —*v.t.* **6.** to misuse (anything sacred); defile; debase. —**pro•fane′ly,** *adv.* —**pro•fane′ness,** *n.* —**pro•fan′er,** *n.*

pro•fan•i•ty (prə fan′i tē, prō-), *n., pl.* **-ties. 1.** the quality of being profane; irreverence. **2.** irreverent or blasphemous speech. **3.** a blasphemous act or utterance.

pro•fess (prə fes′), *v.t.* **1.** to lay claim to, often insincerely; pretend to: *He professed extreme regret.* **2.** to declare openly; announce or affirm: *to profess one's satisfaction.* **3.** to affirm one's faith in (a religion, God, etc.). **4.** to declare oneself skilled or expert in; claim to have good knowledge of. **5.** to receive into a religious order. —*v.i.* **6.** to make a profession, avowal, or declaration. **7.** to take the vows of a religious order.

pro•fessed (prə fest′), *adj.* **1.** avowed; acknowledged. **2.** professing to be qualified. **3.** having been received into a religious order. **4.** alleged; pretended. —**pro•fess′ed•ly** (-fes′id-), *adv.*

pro•fes•sion (prə fesh′ən), *n.* **1.** a vocation requiring extensive education in science or the liberal arts and often specialized training. **2.** any vocation or business. **3.** the body of persons engaged in an occupation: *the medical profession.* **4.** the act of professing; avowal. **5.** the declaration of belief in religion or a faith. **6.** the declaration made on entering into membership of a church or religious order.

pro•fes•sion•al (prə fesh′ə nl), *adj.* **1.** following an occupation as a means of livelihood. **2.** pertaining to a profession. **3.** appropriate to a profession: *professional objectivity.* **4.** engaged in one of the learned professions, as law or medicine. **5.** following as a business something usu. regarded as a pastime: *a professional golfer.* **6.** making a constant practice of something: *A salesman has to be a professional optimist.* **7.** engaged in for competitive gain: *professional baseball.* **8.** of or for a professional person or such a person's place of business: *a professional apartment.* **9.** done by a professional; expert: *professional car repairs.* —*n.* **10.** a member of a profession, esp. one of the learned professions. **11.** a person who earns a living in a sport or other occupation frequently engaged in by amateurs. **12.** a person who is expert at his or her work. —**pro•fes′sion•al•ly,** *adv.*

pro•fes•sion•al•ism (prə fesh′ə nl iz′əm), *n.* **1.** professional character, spirit, or methods. **2.** the standing, practice, or methods of a professional, as distinguished from those of an amateur.

pro•fes•sor (prə fes′ər), *n.* **1.** a college or university teacher of the highest academic rank in a particular branch of learning. **2.** any teacher who has the rank of professor, associate professor, or assistant professor. **3.** a teacher. **4.** an instructor in some art or skilled sport. **5.** a person who professes his or her sentiments, beliefs, etc. —**pro•fes′sor•ate, pro•fes•so•ri•ate** (prō′fə sôr′ē it, -sōr′-, prof′ə-), *n.* —**pro′fes•so′ri•al,** *adj.* —**pro′fes•so′ri•al•ly,** *adv.* —**pro•fes′sor•ship′,** *n.*

prof•fer (prof′ər), *v.t.* **1.** to put before a person for acceptance; offer. —*n.* **2.** the act of proffering. **3.** an offer or proposal. —**prof′fer•er,** *n.*

pro•fi•cient (prə fish′ənt), *adj.* **1.** fully competent in any art, science, or subject; skilled: *a proficient swimmer.* —*n.* **2.** an expert. —**pro•fi′cien•cy** (-sē), *n.* —**pro•fi′cient•ly,** *adv.*

pro•file (prō′fīl), *n., v.,* **-filed, -fil•ing.** —*n.* **1.** a picture or representation of the side view of a head. **2.** an outlined view, as of a city or mountain. **3.** an outline of an object, as a molding. **4.** a graphic representation of this. **5.** a verbal, arithmetical, or graphic summary of a process, activity, or set of characteristics. **6.** an informal biographical sketch. **7.** a set of characteristics or qualities that identify a type or category of person or thing. **8.** the look or general contour of something. **9.** degree of noticeability; visibility. —*v.t.* **10.** to draw, write, or produce a profile of. —**pro′fil•er,** *n.*

Pro′files in Cour′age, a biographical work (1955) by John F. Kennedy.

prof•it (prof′it), *n.* **1.** Often, **profits. a.** pecuniary gain resulting from the employment of capital in any transaction. **b.** the ratio of such gain to the amount of capital invested. **c.** proceeds or revenue from property, investments, etc. **2.** the monetary surplus left to a producer or employer after deducting wages, rent, cost of materials, etc. **3.** advantage; benefit; gain. —*v.i.* **4.** to gain an advantage or benefit: *to profit from one's schooling.* **5.** to make a profit. **6.** to take advantage: *to profit from the weaknesses of others.* **7.** to be of service or benefit. —*v.t.* **8.** to be of advantage or profit to. —**prof′it•er,** *n.* —**prof′it•less,** *adj.*

prof•it•a•ble (prof′i tə bəl), *adj.* **1.** yielding profit. **2.** beneficial or useful. —**prof′it•a•bil′i•ty,** *n.* —**prof′it•a•bly,** *adv.*

prof′it and loss′, *n.* the gain and loss arising from commercial transactions, esp. as shown on a balance sheet. *Abbrev.: P. and L., p. and l.*

prof•it•eer (prof′i tēr′), *n.* **1.** a person who makes profits on the sale of scarce or rationed goods. —*v.i.* **2.** to act as a profiteer.

pro•fit•er•ole (prə fit′ə rōl′), *n.* a small cream puff, usu. filled with cream and topped with chocolate sauce.

prof′it shar′ing, *n.* the sharing of a portion of the profits from a business with employees, who receive it in addition to wages. —**prof′it-shar′ing,** *adj.*

prof•li•ga•cy (prof′li gə sē), *n.* **1.** shameless dissoluteness. **2.** reckless extravagance. **3.** great abundance.

prof•li•gate (prof′li git, -gāt′), *adj.* **1.** utterly and shamelessly immoral or dissipated; thoroughly dissolute. **2.** recklessly prodigal or extravagant. —*n.* **3.** a profligate person. —**prof′li•gate•ly,** *adv.* —**prof′li•gate•ness,** *n.*

pro for•ma (prō fôr′mə), *adj.* **1.** done as a matter of form or for the sake of form: *a pro forma apology.* **2.** Also, **pro•for′ma.** provided in advance of shipment and merely showing the description and quantity of goods shipped without terms of payment: *a pro forma invoice.*

P

pro•found (prə found′), *adj.* **1.** showing deep insight or understanding: *a profound thinker.* **2.** originating in the depths of one's being: *profound grief.* **3.** going beyond what is superficial or obvious: *profound insight.* **4.** of deep significance: *a profound book.* **5.** complete and pervasive: *a profound silence.* **6.** extending or situated far beneath the surface: *the profound depths of the ocean.* **7.** low: *a profound bow.* —**pro•found′ly,** *adv.* —**pro•found′ness,** *n.*

pro•fun•di•ty (prə fun′di tē), *n., pl.* **-ties. 1.** the quality or state of being profound; depth. **2.** Usu., **profundities.** profound or deep matters. **3.** a profoundly deep place; abyss.

pro•fuse (prə fyōōs′), *adj.* **1.** spending or giving freely, often to excess; extravagant (often fol. by *in*): *profuse in their praise.* **2.** made or done freely and abundantly: *profuse apologies.* **3.** abundant; in great amount. —**pro•fuse′ly,** *adv.* —**pro•fuse′ness,** *n.*

pro•fu•sion (prə fyōō′zhən), *n.* **1.** abundance; abundant quantity. **2.** a great quantity or amount (often fol. by *of*). **3.** lavish spending; extravagance.

Prog., Progressive.

pro•gen•i•tive (prō jen′i tiv), *adj.* capable of having offspring; reproductive. —**pro•gen′i•tive•ness,** *n.*

pro•gen•i•tor (prō jen′i tər), *n.* **1.** a biologically related ancestor. **2.** a person or thing that originates something or serves as a model; precursor. —**pro•gen′i•tor•ship′,** *n.*

prog•e•ny (proj′ə nē), *n., pl.* **-ny** or, for plants or animals, **-nies. 1. a.** offspring collectively; children. **b.** (broadly) descendants. **2.** something that originates or results from something else; outcome; issue.

pro•ges•ter•one (prō jes′tə rōn′), *n.* a female hormone that functions in the menstrual cycle to prepare the lining of the uterus for a fertilized ovum.

pro•ges•tin (prō jes′tin) also **pro•ges•to•gen** (-jes′tə jən), *n.* any substance having progesteronelike activity.

prog•na•thous (prog′nə thəs, prog nā′-) also **prog•nath•ic** (prog-nath′ik), *adj.* having protruding jaws. —**prog′na•thism,** *n.*

prog•no•sis (prog nō′sis), *n., pl.* **-ses** (-sēz). **1.** a forecasting of the probable course and outcome of a disease, esp. of the chances of recovery. **2.** a forecast or prognostication.

prog•nos•ti•cate (prog nos′ti kāt′), *v.,* **-cat•ed, -cat•ing.** —*v.t.* **1.** to forecast from present signs or indications; prophesy. **2.** to foretoken; presage. —*v.i.* **3.** to make a forecast; prophesy. —**prog•nos′ti•ca′tor,** *n.*

pro•gram (prō′gram, -grəm), *n., v.,* **-grammed** or **-gramed, -gram•ming** or **-gram•ing.** —*n.* **1.** a plan of action to accomplish a specified end. **2.** a schedule of activities, procedures, etc., to be followed. **3.** a radio or television performance or production. **4.** a list of items, pieces, performers, etc., in a musical, theatrical, or other entertainment. **5.** an entertainment with reference to its pieces or numbers: *a program of French songs.* **6.** a planned, coordinated group of activities, procedures, etc., often for a specific purpose: *a drug rehabilitation program.* **7.** a prospectus or syllabus: *a program of courses.* **8.** a sequence of instructions enabling a computer to perform a task; piece of software. —*v.t.* **9.** to schedule or establish as part of a program. **10.** to provide a program for (a computer). **11. a.** to insert or encode specific operating instructions into (a machine or apparatus). **b.** to insert (instructions) into a machine or apparatus. **12.** to inculcate with attitudes, behavior patterns, or the like; condition: *to program children to respect their elders.* **13.** to regulate or modify: *Program your eating habits to eliminate sweets.* —*v.i.* **14.** to plan or write a program. Also, *esp. Brit.,* **pro′gramme.** —**pro′gram•ma•ble,** *adj.* —**pro′gram•ma•bil′i•ty,** *n.*

pro•gram•mat•ic (prō′grə mat′ik), *adj.* **1.** having or following a plan or program. **2.** of or pertaining to program music. —**pro′gram•mat′i•cal•ly,** *adv.*

pro•gram•mer or **pro•gram•er** (prō′gram ər), *n.* **1.** a person who programs or who is in charge of programming. **2.** a person who programs a device, esp. one who writes computer programs.

pro•gram•ming or **pro•gram•ing** (prō′gram ing, -grə ming), *n.* **1.** the act or process of planning or writing a computer program. **2. a.** the selection and scheduling of television or radio programs. **b.** the programs so scheduled.

pro′gram trad′ing, *n.* the use of computer programs that automatically buy and sell large quantities of stock. —**pro′gram trad′er,** *n.*

prog•ress (*n.* prog′res, -rəs; *esp. Brit.* prō′gres; *v.* prə gres′), *n.* **1.** advancement toward a goal or to a further or higher stage. **2.** the development of an individual or society in a direction considered superior to the previous level. **3.** growth or development; continuous improvement. **4.** forward or onward movement. **5.** an official tour or procession, as by a sovereign or dignitary. —*v.i.* **pro•gress 6.** to go forward or onward in space or time. **7.** to grow or develop; advance: *a disease progressing slowly.* —*Idiom.* **8. in progress,** going on; under way.

pro•gres•sion (prə gresh′ən), *n.* **1.** the act of progressing; forward or onward movement. **2.** a passing successively from one member of a series to the next; succession. **3.** a succession of quantities in which there is a constant relation between each member and the one succeeding it: *an arithmetic progression.* **4.** *Music.* the manner in which chords or melodic tones follow each other; a succession of chords or tones. —**pro•gres′sion•al,** *adj.* —**pro•gres′sion•al•ly,** *adv.*

pro•gres•sive (prə gres′iv), *adj.* **1.** advocating progress or reform, esp. in political and social matters. **2.** employing or advocating more liberal ideas, new methods, etc.: *a progressive community.* **3.** noting or characterized by progress, progression, reform, innovation, etc. **4.** (*cap.*) of or pertaining to a Progressive Party. **5.** going forward or onward; passing successively from one stage to the next. **6.** continuously increasing in extent or severity, as a disease. **7.** pertaining to a form of taxation in which the rate increases as taxable income increases. **8.** pertaining to or practicing progressive education: *progressive schools.* **9.** of or designating a verb tense, aspect, or form typically used to indicate that an action or event is, was, or will be going on at some temporal point of reference. —*n.* **10.** a person who favors progress or reform, as in politics. **11.** (*cap.*) a member of a Progressive Party. **12. a.** the progressive tense or aspect. **b.** a verb form or construction in the progressive tense or aspect, as *am listening* or *was sleeping.* —**pro•gres′sive•ly,** *adv.* —**pro•gres′sive•ness, pro•gres•siv•i•ty** (prō′gre siv′i tē), *n.*

Progres′sive Conserv′ative Par′ty, *n.* a political party in Canada characterized by conservatism.

progres′sive lens′, *n.* a multifocal eyeglass lens that provides a continuous range of focal power between near and far distances.

Progres′sive Par′ty, *n.* **1.** a political party formed in 1912 under the leadership of Theodore Roosevelt, advocating social and political reforms. **2.** a similar party formed in 1924 under the leadership of Robert M. La Follette. **3.** a political party formed in 1948 under the leadership of Henry A. Wallace.

pro•gres•siv•ism (prə gres′ə viz′əm), *n.* **1.** the principles and practices of progressives. **2.** (*cap.*) the doctrines and beliefs of a Progressive Party. —**pro•gres′siv•ist,** *n., adj.*

pro•hib•it (prō hib′it), *v.t.* **1.** to forbid (an action, activity, etc.) by authority or law. **2.** to forbid the action of (a person). **3.** to prevent; hinder. —**pro•hib′it•er, pro•hib′i•tor,** *n.*

pro•hi•bi•tion (prō′ə bish′ən), *n.* **1.** the act of prohibiting. **2. a.** the legal prohibiting of the manufacture, sale, and transportation of alcoholic beverages. **b.** (*usu. cap.*) the period (1920–33) during which such prohibition was in effect in the U.S. **3.** a law or decree that forbids. —**pro′hi•bi′tion•ar′y,** *adj.*

Prohibi′tion Par′ty, *n.* a U.S. political party organized in 1869, advocating the prohibition of alcoholic beverages.

pro•hib•i•tive (prō hib′i tiv), *adj.* **1.** serving to prohibit or forbid something. **2.** sufficing to prevent the use, purchase, etc., of something: *prohibitive prices.* —**pro•hib′i•tive•ly,** *adv.* —**pro•hib′i•tive•ness,** *n.*

proj•ect (*n.* proj′ekt, -ikt *or, esp. Brit.,* prō′jekt; *v.* prə jekt′), *n.* **1.** something that is planned or devised; a plan or scheme. **2.** a large or important undertaking. **3.** a specific task of investigation. **4.** a supplementary long-term assignment given by a teacher to students. **5.** Often, **projects.** HOUSING PROJECT. —*v.t.* **pro•ject 6.** to devise, propose, or plan. **7.** to throw or impel forward, onward, or outward. **8.** to calculate (some future cost, schedule, etc.). **9.** to throw or cause to fall upon a surface or into space, as a ray of light. **10.** to ascribe (one's own feelings, prejudices, etc.) to another or others. **11.** to cause to jut out or protrude. **12.** *Geom.* to transform the points of (one figure) into those of another. **13.** to present (an idea, program, etc.) for consideration or action. **14.** to use (one's voice, gestures, etc.) forcefully enough to be heard or understood by all members of an audience. **15.** to communicate clearly and forcefully (one's thoughts, feelings, etc.) to an audience. —*v.i.* **pro•ject 16.** to extend or protrude beyond something else. **17.** to use one's voice forcefully enough to be heard at a distance, as in a theater. **18.** to communicate clearly and forcefully one's thoughts, feelings, etc., to an audience. **19.** to ascribe one's own feelings, thoughts, or attitudes to another or others. —**pro•ject′a•ble,** *adj.* —**pro•ject′ing•ly,** *adv.*

pro•jec•tile (prə jek′til, -tīl), *n.* **1.** an object fired from a gun with an explosive propelling charge, as a bullet, shell, or grenade. **2.** a body projected or impelled forward, as through the air. —*adj.* **3.** impelling or driving forward, as a force. **4.** caused by impulse, as motion. **5.** capable of being thrust or flung forward, as a missile or the tongue of a frog.

pro•jec•tion (prə jek′shən), *n.* **1.** the act, process, or result of projecting. **2.** a projecting or protruding part. **3.** the state or fact of jutting out or protruding. **4.** a systematic construction of lines drawn on a plane surface representative of and corresponding to the meridians and parallels of the curved surface of the earth or celestial sphere. **5. a.** the act of reproducing on a surface, by optical means, a remote image on a film, slide, etc. **b.** the image reproduced. **6. a.** the act of visualizing an idea as an objective reality. **b.** something that is so visualized. **7.** calculation of some future cost, revenue, etc.: *a projection for the rate of growth.* **8.** the act of communicating distinctly and forcefully to an audience. **9.** *Psychoanal.* the attribution to another person or object the

feelings, thoughts, or attitudes present in oneself. **10.** the act of planning or scheming. —**pro•jec′tion•al,** *adj.*

projec′tion booth′, *n.* **1.** a compartment in a theater from which a motion picture is projected onto the screen. **2.** a compartment at the rear of or above an auditorium, in which spotlights and other lighting units are operated.

projec′tion room′, *n.* **1.** PROJECTION BOOTH. **2.** a room with a projector and screen for the private viewing of motion pictures.

pro•jec•tor (prə jek′tər), *n.* **1.** an apparatus for throwing an image onto a screen, as a motion-picture projector or magic lantern. **2.** a device for projecting a beam of light. **3.** a person who forms projects; planner or promoter.

pro•kar•y•ote or **pro•car•y•ote** (prō kar′ē ōt′, -ē ət), *n.* any one-celled organism that lacks a distinct membrane-bound nucleus and has its genetic material in a continuous strand forming loops or coils: characteristic of monerans. Compare EUKARYOTE. —**pro•kar′y•ot′ic** (-ot′ik), *adj.*

pro•lac•tin (prō lak′tin), *n.* a pituitary hormone that in mammals stimulates milk production at parturition and in birds activates the crop for feeding the young.

pro•lapse (*n.* prō laps′, prō′laps; *v.* prō laps′), *n., v.,* **-lapsed, -laps•ing.** —*n.* **1.** a falling down of an organ or part, as the uterus, from its normal position. —*v.i.* **2.** to fall or slip down or out of place.

pro•le•gom•e•non (prō′li gom′ə non′, -nən), *n., pl.* **-na** (-nə). a preliminary or introductory commentary, esp. a scholarly preface or introduction to a book. —**pro′le•gom′e•nous** (-nəs), *adj.*

pro•lep•sis (prō lep′sis), *n., pl.* **-ses** (-sēz). **1.** *Rhet.* the anticipation of possible objections in order to answer them in advance. **2.** the representation of something in the future as if it already existed or had occurred. —**pro•lep′tic** (-tik), **pro•lep′ti•cal,** *adj.* —**pro•lep′ti•cal•ly,** *adv.*

pro•le•tar•i•an (prō′li târ′ē ən), *adj.* **1.** pertaining or belonging to the proletariat. —*n.* **2.** a member of the proletariat. —**pro′le•tar′i•an•ism,** *n.*

pro•le•tar•i•at (prō′li târ′ē ət), *n.* **1.** the class of wage earners, esp. those who earn their living by manual labor or who are dependent for support on daily or casual employment; the working class. **2.** (in Marxist theory) the class of workers, esp. industrial wage earners, who do not possess capital or property and must sell their labor to survive. **3.** the lowest or poorest class of people, possessing no property, esp. in ancient Rome.

pro-life′, *adj.* opposed to legalized abortion; right-to-life. Compare PRO-CHOICE. —**pro-lif′er,** *n.*

pro•lif•er•ate (prə lif′ə rāt′), *v.i., v.t.,* **-at•ed, -at•ing.** to increase in number or spread rapidly. —**pro•lif′er•a′tion,** *n.* —**pro•lif′er•a′tive,** *adj.*

pro•lif•er•ous (prə lif′ər əs), *adj.* **1.** tending to proliferate; proliferative. **2.** *Biol.* producing new individuals by budding or the like.

pro•lif•ic (prə lif′ik), *adj.* **1.** producing offspring, young, fruit, etc., abundantly; highly fruitful. **2.** highly productive: *a prolific writer.* —**pro•lif′i•ca•cy** (-kə sē), **pro•lif′ic•ness,** *n.* —**pro•lif′i•cal•ly,** *adv.*

pro•lix (prō liks′, prō′liks), *adj.* **1.** extended to unnecessary or tedious length; long and wordy. **2.** (of a person) given to speaking or writing at great or tedious length. —**pro•lix′i•ty,** *n.* —**pro•lix′ly,** *adv.*

pro•logue or **pro•log** (prō′lôg, -log), *n., v.,* **-logued, -logu•ing.** —*n.* **1.** a preface or introductory part of a discourse, poem, or novel. **2. a.** an introductory speech or scene in a play or opera. **b.** the person or persons who perform this. **3.** anything that serves as a preamble or introduction. —*v.t.* **4.** to introduce with or as if with a prologue. —**pro′logu•ist, pro′log•ist,** *n.* —**pro′logue•like′, pro′log•like′,** *adj.*

pro•long (prə lông′, -long′), *v.t.* **1.** to extend the duration of; cause to continue longer. **2.** to make longer in spatial extent: *to prolong a line.* —**pro•long′a•ble,** *adj.* —**pro•long′er,** *n.* —**pro•long′ment,** *n.*

pro•lon•ga•tion (prō′lông gā′shən, -long-), *n.* **1.** the act of prolonging. **2.** the state of being prolonged. **3.** a prolonged or extended form. **4.** an added part.

prom (prom), *n.* a formal dance held by a high school or college class. [short for *promenade*]

prom•e•nade (prom′ə nād′, -näd′), *n., v.,* **-nad•ed, -nad•ing.** —*n.* **1.** a stroll or walk, esp. in a public place. **2.** an area used for such walking. **3.** a march of guests into a ballroom opening a formal ball. **4.** a march of dancers in square dancing. **5.** a prom. —*v.i.* **6.** to go for or take part in a promenade. **7.** to execute a promenade in square dancing. —*v.t.* **8.** to take a promenade through or about. **9.** to display as in a promenade; parade. —**prom′e•nad′er,** *n.*

promenade′ deck′, *n.* an upper deck or part of a deck on a passenger ship where passengers can stroll.

pro•me•thi•um (prə mē′thē əm), *n.* a rare-earth, metallic, trivalent element. *Symbol:* Pm; *at. no.:* 61.

prom•i•nence (prom′ə nəns), *n.* **1.** Also, **prom′i•nen•cy.** the state of being prominent; conspicuousness. **2.** something that is prominent; a projection or protuberance: *a prominence high over a ravine.* **3.** an eruption of a flamelike tongue of relatively cool, high-density gas from the solar chromosphere into the corona.

prom•i•nent (prom′ə nənt), *adj.* **1.** standing out so as to be seen easily; conspicuous. **2.** standing out beyond the adjacent surface or line; projecting. **3.** leading, important, or well-known; eminent. —**prom′i•nent•ly,** *adv.*

prom•is•cu•i•ty (prom′i skyo͞o′i tē, prō′mi-), *n., pl.* **-ties. 1.** promiscuous sexual behavior. **2.** an indiscriminate mixture.

pro•mis•cu•ous (prə mis′kyo͞o əs), *adj.* **1.** characterized by or having numerous sexual partners on a casual basis. **2.** consisting of a disordered mixture of various elements. **3.** indiscriminate. —**pro•mis′cu•ous•ly,** *adv.* —**pro•mis′cu•ous•ness,** *n.*

prom•ise (prom′is), *n., v.,* **-ised, -is•ing.** —*n.* **1.** a declaration that something will or will not be done, given, etc: *He kept his promise to write regularly.* **2.** indication of future excellence or achievement: *a writer who shows promise.* **3.** something that is promised. —*v.t.* **4.** to pledge or undertake by promise (usu. with an infinitive or a clause as object): *She promised to visit us.* **5.** to make a promise of. **6.** to afford ground for expecting: *The sky promises a storm.* **7.** to engage to join in marriage. **8.** to assure (used in emphatic declarations): *I won't go there again, I promise you!* —*v.i.* **9.** to make a promise. **10.** to afford ground for expectation (often fol. by *well* or *fair*). —***Saying.* 11. A promise is a promise,** a promise must be kept. —**prom′is•er,** *n.*

Prom′ised Land′, *n.* Canaan, the land promised by God to Abraham and his descendants. Gen. 12:7.

prom•is•ing (prom′ə sing), *adj.* giving favorable promise; likely to turn out well. —**prom′is•ing•ly,** *adv.*

prom•is•so•ry (prom′ə sôr′ē, -sōr′ē), *adj.* **1.** containing or implying a promise. **2.** of the nature of a promise.

prom′issory note′, *n.* a written promise to pay a specified sum of money at a fixed time or on demand.

pro•mo (prō′mō), *n., pl.* **-mos,** *adj.* —*n.* **1.** PROMOTION (def. 5). —*adj.* **2.** of, pertaining to, or involving the promotion of a product, event, etc.; promotional.

prom•on•to•ry (prom′ən tôr′ē, -tōr′ē), *n., pl.* **-ries. 1.** a high point of land or rock projecting into water beyond the line of coast; headland. **2.** a bluff, or part of a plateau, overlooking a lowland. **3.** *Anat.* a prominent or protuberant part.

pro•mote (prə mōt′), *v.t.,* **-mot•ed, -mot•ing. 1.** to help or encourage to exist or flourish; further. **2.** to advance in rank, dignity, position, etc. **3.** to advance to the next higher grade in a school. **4.** to aid in organizing (business undertakings). **5.** to encourage the sales, acceptance, or recognition of, esp. through advertising or publicity. **6.** to obtain (something) by trickery. —**pro•mot′able,** *adj.* —**pro•mot′a•bil′i•ty,** *n.*

pro•mot•er (prə mō′tər), *n.* **1.** a person or thing that promotes, furthers, or encourages. **2.** a person who initiates or takes part in the organizing of a company, development of a project, etc. **3.** a person who organizes and finances a sporting event or entertainment.

pro•mo•tion (prə mō′shən), *n.* **1.** advancement in rank or position. **2.** furtherance or encouragement. **3.** the act of promoting. **4.** the state of being promoted. **5. a.** the publicizing or advertising of a product, cause, institution, etc. **b.** materials, events, etc., generated for this purpose. —**pro•mo′tion•al,** *adj.* —**pro•mo′tive,** *adj.*

prompt (prompt), *adj.* **1.** done, performed, delivered, etc., at once or without delay: *a prompt reply.* **2.** quick to act or respond. **3.** punctual. —*v.t.* **4.** to induce (someone) to action. **5.** to occasion or inspire (an act). **6.** to assist (a speaker or performer) by suggesting something to be said, offering a missed cue, etc. —*n.* **7. a.** a limit of time given for payment for merchandise purchased. **b.** the contract setting the time limit. **8.** the act of prompting. **9.** something serving to suggest or remind. **10.** a symbol or message on a computer screen requesting more information or indicating readiness to accept instructions. —**prompt′ly,** *adv.* —**prompt′ness,** *n.*

prom•ul•gate (prom′əl gāt′, prō mul′gāt), *v.t.,* **-gat•ed, -gat•ing. 1.** to put into operation (a law, decree of a court, etc.) by formal proclamation. **2.** to set forth or teach publicly (a creed, doctrine, etc.). —**prom′ul•ga′tion,** *n.* —**prom′ul•ga′tor,** *n.*

pro•na•tion (prō nā′shən), *n.* **1.** rotation of the hand or forearm so as to bring the palm downward or rearward. **2.** an everting motion of the foot so as to turn the sole outward. —**pro′nate,** *v.t., v.i.,* **-nat•ed, -nat•ing.**

prone (prōn), *adj.* **1.** having a natural tendency toward something; disposed; liable: *prone to anger.* **2.** with the front or ventral part downward; lying facedown. **3.** lying flat; prostrate. **4.** having a downward direction or slope. —**prone′ly,** *adv.* —**prone′ness,** *n.*

prong (prông, prong), *n.* **1.** one of the pointed tines of a fork. **2.** any pointed, projecting part, as of an antler. **3.** a subdivision; fork. —*v.t.* **4.** to pierce or stab with or as if with a prong. **5.** to supply with prongs.

pronged (prôngd, prongd), *adj.* having prongs (often used in combination): *a four-pronged fork; a three-pronged attack.*

prong•horn (prông′hôrn′, prong′-), *n., pl.* **-horns,** (*esp. collectively*) **-horn.** a fleet, antelopelike ruminant, *Antilocapra americana,* of the plains of W North America. Also called **prong′horn an′telope.**

pro•nom•i•nal (prō nom′ə nl), *adj.* **1.** pertaining to, derived from, functioning as, or resembling a pronoun: *My* in *my book* is a pronominal adjective. —*n.* **2.** a pronominal word or expression. —**pro•nom′i•nal•ly,** *adv.*

pro•noun (prō′noun′), *n.* any of a small class of words used as replacements or substitutes for nouns and noun phrases, as *I, you, he, them, this, who, what. Abbr.:* pron.

pro•nounce (prə nouns′), *v.,* **-nounced, -nounc•ing.** —*v.t.* **1.** to enunciate or articulate (sounds, words, sentences, etc.). **2.** to utter or articulate in the accepted or correct manner: *I can't pronounce this word.* **3.** to declare (a person or thing) to be as specified: *She pronounced it the best book she had ever read.* **4.** to utter formally or solemnly: *to pronounce sentence.* **5.** to announce authoritatively or officially: *The judge pronounced the defendant guilty.* **6.** to indicate the pronunciation of (words) by providing a phonetic transcription. —*v.i.* **7.** to pronounce words, phrases, etc. **8.** to make an authoritative statement (often fol. by *on*). —**pro•nounce′a•ble,** *adj.* —**pro•nounc′er,** *n.*

pro•nounced (prə nounst′), *adj.* **1.** strongly or clearly apparent. **2.** decided; unequivocal: *pronounced views.* —**pro•nounc′ed•ly** (-noun′sid lē, -nounst′lē), *adv.* —**pro•nounc′ed•ness,** *n.*

pro•nounce•ment (prə nouns′mənt), *n.* **1.** a formal or authoritative statement. **2.** an opinion or decision. **3.** act of pronouncing.

pron•to (pron′tō), *adv.* promptly; quickly.

pro•nun•ci•a•tion (prə nun′sē ā′shən), *n.* **1.** the act, manner, or result of producing the sounds of speech, including articulation, stress, and intonation. **2.** a way of pronouncing a word, syllable, etc., that is accepted or considered correct. **3.** the conventional patterns of treatment of the sounds of a language: *the pronunciation of French.* **4.** a phonetic transcription of a given word, sound, etc. —**pro•nun′ci•a′tion•al,** *adj.*

proof (pro͞of), *n.* **1.** evidence sufficient to establish a thing as true or believable. **2.** anything serving as such evidence. **3.** the act of testing or trying anything; test; trial: *to put a thing to the proof.* **4.** the establishment of the truth of anything; demonstration. **5.** (in judicial proceedings) evidence that seems to substantiate or corroborate an allegation. **6.** a test to determine the quality, durability, etc., of materials used in manufacture. **7.** the strength of an alcoholic liquor, esp. with reference to the standard whereby 100 proof signifies an alcoholic content of 50 percent. **8.** *Photog.* a trial print from a negative. **9.** *Print.* a trial impression, as of composed type, taken to correct errors and make alterations. **10.** one of a limited number of coins of a new issue struck from polished dies on a blank having a polished or matte surface. **11.** the state of having been tested. —*adj.* **12.** able to withstand; impenetrable, impervious, or invulnerable: *proof against attack; proof against leakage.* **13.** used for testing or proving; serving as proof. **14.** of standard strength, as an alcoholic liquor. **15.** of tested or proven strength or quality: *proof armor.* —*v.t.* **16.** to examine for flaws, errors, etc. **17.** *Print.* PROVE (def. 7). **18.** PROOFREAD. **19.** to treat or coat for the purpose of rendering resistant to deterioration, damage, etc. (often used in combination). **20.** to cause (bread dough, etc.) to rise by adding baker's yeast. —*v.i.* **21.** (of yeast) to bubble when mixed with warm water, milk, etc. —***Proverb.* 22. The proof of the pudding is in the eating,** the worth of something is proved by experience and results.

-proof, a combining form of PROOF, with the meaning "resistant, impervious to" that specified by the initial element: *childproof; waterproof.*

proof•read (pro͞of′rēd′), *v.,* **-read** (-red′), **-read•ing.** —*v.t.* **1.** to read (printers' proofs, copy, etc.) in order to detect and mark errors to be corrected. —*v.i.* **2.** to read printers' proofs, copy, etc., to detect errors, esp. as an employee of a newspaper or publishing house. —**proof′read′er,** *n.*

prop[1] (prop), *v.,* **propped, prop•ping,** *n.* —*v.t.* **1.** to support, or prevent from falling, with or as if with a prop (often fol. by *up*). **2.** to rest (a thing) against a support: *He propped the ladder against the wall.* **3.** to support or sustain (often fol. by *up*). —*n.* **4.** a stick, rod, pole, beam, or other rigid support. **5.** a person or thing serving as a support or stay.

prop[2] (prop), *n.* PROPERTY (def. 7).

prop[3] (prop), *n.* a propeller.

prop•a•gan•da (prop′ə gan′də), *n.* **1.** information or ideas methodically spread to promote or injure a cause, movement, nation, etc. **2.** the deliberate spreading of such information or ideas. **3.** the particular doctrines or principles propagated by an organization or movement.

prop•a•gan•dize (prop′ə gan′dīz), *v.,* **-dized, -diz•ing.** —*v.t.* **1.** to propagate or publicize (principles, dogma, etc.) by means of propaganda. **2.** to subject to propaganda. —*v.i.* **3.** to carry on or disseminate propaganda. —**prop′a•gan′dism,** *n.* —**prop′a•gan′dist,** *n., adj.* —**prop′a•gan•dis′tic,** *adj.*

prop•a•gate (prop′ə gāt′), *v.,* **-gat•ed, -gat•ing.** —*v.t.* **1.** to cause (an organism) to multiply by any process of natural reproduction from the parent stock. **2.** to reproduce (itself, its kind, etc.), as an organism does. **3.** to transmit (hereditary features or elements) to or through offspring. **4.** to spread (a report, doctrine, practice, etc.) from person to person; disseminate. **5.** to cause to increase in number or amount. —*v.i.* **6.** to multiply by any process of natural reproduction, as organisms; breed. **7.** (of electromagnetic waves, compression waves, etc.) to travel through space or a physical medium. —**prop′a•ga′tion,** *n.* —**prop′a•ga′tion•al,** *adj.* —**prop′a•ga′tive,** *adj.* —**prop′a•ga′tor,** *n.*

pro•pane (prō′pān), *n.* a colorless, flammable gas, C_3H_8, of the alkane series, occurring in petroleum and natural gas: used chiefly as a fuel and in organic synthesis.

pro pa•tri•a (PRŌ pä′TRI ä′; *Eng.* prō pā′trē ə, pa′-), *adv. Latin.* for one's country.

pro•pel (prə pel′), *v.t.,* **-pelled, -pel•ling.** to drive, or cause to move, forward or onward: *to propel a boat.*

pro•pel•lant (prə pel′ənt), *n.* **1.** a propelling agent. **2.** the charge of explosive used to propel the projectile from a gun. **3.** a substance, usu. a mixture of fuel and oxidizer, for propelling a rocket. **4.** a compressed inert gas that serves to dispense the contents of an aerosol container when the pressure is released.

PROOFREADER'S MARKS

The marks shown below are used in (1) preparing a manuscript to be typeset or (2) proofreading or revising printed material. The mark should be written in the margin, directly in line with the sentence or part of the text in which the change is being made, and the line of text should also be marked to indicate the exact place of the change.

When more than one change is being made in the same line, diagonal or vertical slashes are used in the margin to separate the respective marks. Marks that are actual words, such as "OK?," "run over," and "set?," as well as editorial comments or queries noted in the margin, are often circled to distinguish them from textual corrections (words to be inserted) themselves.

In practice, these marks often differ slightly from person to person. For example, some proofreaders use slash marks even when making only one correction in a line. In all cases, however, the marks must be legible and carefully placed to avoid creating uncertainty or introducing new errors.

Mark in margin	Indication in text	Instruction or comment
LETTERS, WORDS, SPACING, AND QUERIES		
a	Peter left town in hurry.	Insert at caret (∧)
a/r	Peter left town in hurry.	Insert at carets
℘ or ℽ	Joan sent me the the book.	Delete
⌒	ma ke	Close up; no space
⌒͢	I haven't seen the m in years.	Delete and close up
stet	They phoned both Betty and Jack.	Let it stand; disregard indicated deletion or change
¶	up the river. Two years	Start new paragraph
no ¶ or, run in	many unnecessary additives. The most dangerous one	No new paragraph
tr	Put the book on the table. Put the book table on the Put the table on the book.	Transpose
tr up or tr↑	to Betty Steinberg, who was traveling abroad. Mrs. Steinberg, an actress,	Transpose to place indicated above
tr down or tr↓	in the clutch. The final score was 6–5. He pitched the last three innings but didn't have it.	Transpose to place indicated below
sp.	Lunch cost me 6 dollars.	Spell out; use letters
fig	There were eighteen members present.	Set in figures; use numbers
#	It was a small village.	Insert one letter space
##	too late After the dance	Insert two letter spaces
hr #	jeroboam	Insert hair space (very thin space, as between letters)
line #	Oscar Picks # This year's Academy Awards nomination.	Insert line space
eq #	Ronnie got rid of the dog.	Equalize spacing between words or between lines
=	thre e d a ys later	Align horizontally
‖	from one hand to another without spilling it	Align vertically
run over	enhance production. 2. It will	Start new line
□	□ Rose asked the price.	Indent or insert one em (space)
□□	□□ The Use of the Comma	Indent or insert two ems
⌐	⌐ What's Ellen's last name?	Move left
¬	April 2, 1945¬	Move right
⊓	Please go now.	Move up
⊔	Well, that's that!	Move down
⊐⊏	⊐ "The Birth of Atomic Energy" ⊏	Center (heading, title, etc.)
fl	2. Three (3) skirts	Flush left; no indention
fr	Total: $89.50 ⌐	Flush right; no indention
sent/? [the specific word that appears to be missing]	He the copy.	Insert this word here?
OK? or ?	by Francis G. Kellsey. She wrote	Query or verify; is this correct?
out: see copy	the discovery of but near the hull	Something left out in typesetting
set?	arrived in 1922 wrong date and	Is this part of the copy, to be set (or a marginal note)?

Mark in margin	Indication in text	Instruction or comment
PUNCTUATION		
⊙	Christine teaches fifth grade	Insert period (.)
∧͵	We expect Eileen, Tom, and Ken.	Insert comma (,)
∧͵	I came; I saw, conquered.	Insert semicolon (;)
⊙͵	Jenny worked until 6:30 P.M.	Insert colon (:)
=	Douglas got a two thirds majority.	Insert hyphen (-)
=	Douglas got a two= thirds majority.	End-of-line hyphen is part of word
1/M	Mike then left, very reluctantly.	Insert one-em dash or long dash (—)
1/N	See pages 96, 124.	Insert one-en dash or short dash (–)
∨	Don't mark the authors copy. Don't mark the authors copy.	Insert apostrophe (')
!	Watch out	Insert exclamation point (!)
?	Did Seth write to you	Insert question mark (?)
∨/∨	I always liked Stopping by Woods on a Snowy Evening.	Insert quotation marks (" ")
∨/∨	She said, "Read The Raven tonight."	Insert single quotation marks (' ')
(/) or {/}	Dorothy paid 8 pesos 800 centavos for it.	Insert parentheses (())
[/] or {/}	The "portly and profane author, Dickson, presumably, in his cups" was noticed by nobody else.	Insert brackets ([ ])
TYPOGRAPHIC CASE, STYLE, AND ADJUSTMENT		
ital	I've read Paradise Lost twice.	Set in italic (not roman) type
bf	See the definition at peace.	Set in boldface (heavier) type
lf	She repaired the motor easily.	Set in lightface (standard) type
rom	Gregory drove to Winnipeg.	Set in roman (not italic) type
cap or caps or uc or u/c	the italian role in Nato	Set as CAPITAL letter(s)
sc	He lived about 350 B.C.	Set in SMALL CAPITAL letter(s)
lc or l/c	Arlene enjoys Reading. I do NOT.	Set in lowercase; not capitalized
u+lc or c+lc or uc+lc	STOP STOP!	Set in uppercase and lowercase
⌄2	H2O	Set as subscript; inferior figure
∨2	A² + B²	Set as superscript; superior figure
X	They drove to Miami.	Broken (damaged) letter of type
wf	Turn Right	Wrong font; not the proper typeface style or size
⊙	Bert proofread the book	Turn inverted (upside-down) letter

pro·pel·lent (prə pel′ənt), *adj.* **1.** serving or tending to propel or drive forward. —*n.* **2.** PROPELLANT.
pro·pel·ler (prə pel′ər), *n.* **1.** a device having a revolving hub with radiating blades, for propelling an airplane, ship, etc. **2.** a person or thing that propels. **3.** a wind-driven, usu. three-bladed device that provides mechanical energy.

 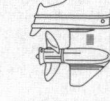 

aircraft propeller   outboard-engine   marine propeller
propeller

propellers (def. 1)

pro·pen·si·ty (prə pen′si tē), *n.*, *pl.* **-ties.** a natural inclination or tendency.
prop·er (prop′ər), *adj.* **1.** adapted or appropriate to the purpose or circumstances; suitable. **2.** conforming to established standards of behavior or manners; correct or decorous. **3.** fitting; right. **4.** belonging or pertaining exclusively to a person, thing, or group. **5.** strict; accurate. **6.** in the strict sense (usu. used postpositively): *Shellfish do not belong to the fishes proper.* **7.** normal or regular. **8.** belonging to oneself or itself; own. **9.** *Chiefly Brit.* complete; thorough: *a proper thrashing.* **10.** *Eccles.* used only on a particular day or festival. **11.** *Math.* (of a subset of a set) not equal to the whole set. —**prop′er·ly,** *adv.* —**prop′er·ness,** *n.*
prop′er ad′jective, *n.* an adjective formed from a proper noun, as *American* from *America.*
prop′er frac′tion, *n.* a fraction having the numerator less, or lower in degree, than the denominator.
prop′er noun′, *n.* a noun that designates a particular person, place, or thing, is not normally preceded by an article or other limiting modifier, and is usu. capitalized in English, as *Lincoln, Beth, Pittsburgh.* Also called **prop′er name′.** Compare COMMON NOUN.
prop·er·tied (prop′ər tēd), *adj.* owning property.
prop·er·ty (prop′ər tē), *n.*, *pl.* **-ties.** **1.** that which a person owns; the possession or possessions of a particular owner. **2.** goods, land, etc., considered as possessions. **3.** a piece of land or real estate. **4.** ownership; right of possession, enjoyment, or disposal, esp. of something tangible. **5.** something at the disposal of a person, a group of persons, or the community or public. **6.** an essential or distinctive attribute of a thing: *the chemical properties of alcohol.* **7.** Also called **prop.** a usu. movable item used onstage or in a film. **8.** a written work, play, movie, etc., bought or optioned for commercial production or distribution.
pro·phase (prō′fāz′), *n.* the first stage of mitosis or meiosis in cell division, during which the nuclear envelope breaks down and strands of chromatin form into chromosomes.
proph·e·cy (prof′ə sē), *n.*, *pl.* **-cies.** **1.** the foretelling or prediction of what is to come. **2.** something that is declared by a prophet, esp. a divinely inspired prediction, instruction, or exhortation. **3.** any prediction or forecast. **4.** the action, function, or faculty of a prophet.
proph·e·sy (prof′ə sī′), *v.*, **-sied, -sy·ing.** —*v.t.* **1.** to foretell or predict. **2.** to indicate beforehand. **3.** to utter in prophecy or as a prophet, esp. by divine inspiration. —*v.i.* **4.** to make predictions, esp. by divine inspiration. **5.** to speak as a mediator between God and humankind or in God's stead. —**proph′e·si′er,** *n.*
proph·et (prof′it), *n.* **1.** a person who speaks for God or a deity, or by divine inspiration. **2.** (in the Old Testament) **a.** a person chosen to speak for God and to guide the people of Israel. **b.** (*often cap.*) one of the Major or Minor Prophets. **c.** one of a band of ecstatic visionaries claiming divine inspiration and, according to popular belief, possessing magical powers. **3.** one of a class of persons in the early Christian church recognized as inspired to utter special revelations and predictions. 1 Cor. 12:28. **4. the Prophet,** Muhammad, the founder of Islam. **5.** a person regarded as, or claiming to be, an inspired teacher or leader. **6.** a person who foretells the future. —*Proverb.* **7. A prophet is not without honor, save in his own country,** one is often valued less by those close to one than by the world at large. Matt. 13:57. —**proph′et·hood,** *n.*
pro·phet·ic (prə fet′ik) also **pro·phet′i·cal,** *adj.* **1.** of or pertaining to a prophet. **2.** of the nature of or containing prophecy: *prophetic writings.* **3.** having the function or powers of a prophet, as a person. **4.** predictive; presageful or portentous; ominous: *prophetic signs.* —**pro·phet′i·cal·ly,** *adv.*
Proph·ets (prof′its), *n.* (*used with a sing. v.*) the canonical group of prophetic books that forms the second of the three Jewish divisions of the Old Testament. Compare PENTATEUCH, HAGIOGRAPHA.
pro·phy·lac·tic (prō′fə lak′tik, prof′ə-), *adj.* **1.** preventive or protective, esp. from disease or infection. —*n.* **2.** a prophylactic medicine or measure. **3.** a preventive. **4.** a device used to prevent conception or venereal infection, esp. a condom. —**pro′phy·lac′ti·cal·ly,** *adv.*
pro·phy·lax·is (prō′fə lak′sis, prof′ə-), *n.*, *pl.* **-lax·es.** **1.** the prevention of disease, as by protective measures. **2.** prophylactic treatment.

pro·pin·qui·ty (prō ping′kwi tē), *n.* **1.** nearness in time or place; proximity. **2.** nearness of relation; kinship.
pro·pi·ti·ate (prə pish′ē āt′), *v.t.* **-at·ed, -at·ing.** to make favorably inclined; appease; conciliate: *tried to propitiate the angry gods.* —**pro·pi′ti·a·ble,** *adj.* —**pro·pi′ti·at′ing·ly,** *adv.* —**pro·pi′ti·a′tive, pro·pi′ti·a·to′ry** (-ə tôr′ē, -tōr′ē), *adj.* —**pro·pi′ti·a′tor,** *n.*
pro·pi·tious (prə pish′əs), *adj.* **1.** presenting favorable conditions; favorable: *propitious weather.* **2.** indicative of favor; auspicious: *propitious omens.* **3.** favorably disposed: *a propitious ruler.* —**pro·pi′tious·ly,** *adv.* —**pro·pi′tious·ness,** *n.*
prop′jet en′gine, *n.* TURBO-PROPELLER ENGINE.
prop·man (prop′man′), *n.*, *pl.* **-men.** a person in charge of the properties used esp. in a theatrical production.
pro·po·nent (prə pō′nənt), *n.* **1.** a person who puts forward a proposition or proposal. **2.** an advocate for or adherent of a cause or doctrine. **3.** a person who propounds a legal instrument, as a will for probate.
pro·por·tion (prə pôr′shən, -pōr′-), *n.* **1.** comparative relation between things or magnitudes as to size, quantity, number, etc.; ratio. **2.** proper relation between things or parts. **3.** relative size or extent. **4. proportions,** dimensions or size. **5.** a portion or part in its relation to the whole. **6.** symmetry, harmony, or balance. —*v.t.* **7.** to adjust in proper proportion or relation, as to size or quantity. **8.** to balance or harmonize the proportions of. —**pro·por′tion·er,** *n.*
pro·por·tion·al (prə pôr′shə nl, -pōr′-), *adj.* **1.** having due proportion; corresponding. **2.** being in or characterized by proportion. **3.** of, pertaining to, or based on proportion; relative. **4.** (of two quantities) having the same or a constant ratio or relation. —**pro·por′tion·al·i·ty,** *n.* —**pro·por′tion·al·ly,** *adv.*
propor′tional representa′tion, *n.* a method of voting by which political parties are given legislative representation in proportion to their popular vote.
pro·por·tion·ate (*adj.* prə pôr′shə nit, -pōr′-; *v.* -nāt′), *adj.*, *v.*, **-at·ed, -at·ing.** —*adj.* **1.** proportioned; being in due proportion; proportional. —*v.t.* **2.** to make proportionate. —**pro·por′tion·ate·ly,** *adv.*
pro·pos·al (prə pō′zəl), *n.* **1.** the act of offering or suggesting something for acceptance, adoption, or performance. **2.** a plan or scheme proposed. **3.** an offer of marriage.
pro·pose (prə pōz′), *v.*, **-posed, -pos·ing.** —*v.t.* **1.** to offer for consideration, acceptance, or action: *proposed a new method.* **2.** to offer (a toast). **3.** to suggest. **4.** to nominate (a person) for office, membership, etc. **5.** to plan; intend. —*v.i.* **6.** to make an offer, esp. of marriage. **7.** to form or consider a purpose or design. —*Proverb.* **8. Man proposes, God disposes,** things do not always work out according to plan. —**pro·pos′er,** *n.*
prop·o·si·tion (prop′ə zish′ən), *n.* **1.** the act of proposing. **2.** a plan or scheme proposed. **3.** an offer of terms for a transaction, as in business. **4.** a thing, matter, or person considered as something to be dealt with: *a tough proposition.* **5.** anything stated for discussion or illustration. **6.** *Logic.* a statement in which something is affirmed or denied, so that it can therefore be significantly characterized as either true or false. **7.** *Math.* a formal statement of either a truth to be demonstrated or an operation to be performed; a theorem or a problem. —*v.t.* **8.** to propose a plan, etc., to. —**prop′o·si′tion·al,** *adj.* —**prop′o·si′tion·al·ly,** *adv.*
pro·pound (prə pound′), *v.t.* to put forward or offer for consideration, acceptance, or adoption; set forth; propose: *to propound a theory.* —**pro·pound′er,** *n.*
pro·pri·e·tar·y (prə prī′i ter′ē), *adj.*, *n.*, *pl.* **-tar·ies.** —*adj.* **1.** pertaining to, belonging to, or being a proprietor. **2.** pertaining to property or ownership. **3.** manufactured and sold only by the owner of the patent, trademark, etc.: *proprietary medicine.* —*n.* **4.** an owner or proprietor. **5.** a body of proprietors. **6.** ownership. **7.** something owned, esp. real estate. **8.** a proprietary medicine. —**pro·pri′e·tar′i·ly** (-tär′i lē), *adv.*
propri′etary col′ony, *n.* any of certain colonies, as Maryland and Pennsylvania, that were granted to an individual or group by the British crown and that were granted full rights of self-government. Compare CHARTER COLONY, ROYAL COLONY.
pro·pri·e·tor (prə prī′i tər), *n.* **1.** the owner of a business establishment. **2.** a person who has the exclusive right or title to something; an owner, as of real property. **3.** a proprietary of a colony in America. —**pro·pri′e·tor·ship′,** *n.*
pro·pri·e·ty (prə prī′i tē), *n.*, *pl.* **-ties.** **1.** conformity to established standards of good or proper behavior or manners. **2.** appropriateness to the purpose or circumstances; suitability. **3.** rightness or justness. **4. the proprieties,** the conventional standards of proper behavior; manners.
pro·pul·sion (prə pul′shən), *n.* **1.** the act of propelling. **2.** the state of being propelled. **3.** a propelling force, impulse, etc. —**pro·pul′sive** (-siv), **pro·pul′so·ry,** *adj.*
pro·pyl (prō′pil), *n.* either of two univalent isomeric groups with the formula C_3H_7.
pro′pyl al′cohol, *n.* a colorless, water-soluble liquid, C_3H_8O, used chiefly in organic synthesis and as a solvent.
pro·pyl·ene (prō′pə lēn′), *n.* a colorless, flammable gas, C_3H_6, of the olefin series: used chiefly in organic synthesis.
pro ra·ta (prō rā′tə, rä′-), *adv.* in proportion; according to a certain rate. —**pro-ra′ta,** *adj.*
pro·rate (prō rāt′, prō′rāt′), *v.*, **-rat·ed, -rat·ing.** —*v.t.* **1.** to divide, distribute, or calculate proportionately. —*v.i.* **2.** to make an arrange-

ment on a basis of proportional distribution. —**pro•rat′a•ble,** *adj.* —**pro•ra′tion,** *n.*

pro•rogue (prō rōg′), *v.t.,* **-rogued, -ro•guing. 1.** to discontinue a session of (the British Parliament or a similar body). **2.** to defer; postpone. —**pro′ro•ga′tion** (-rə gā′shən), *n.*

pro•sa•ic (prō zā′ik) also **pro•sa′i•cal,** *adj.* **1.** commonplace or dull; unimaginative: *a prosaic mind.* **2.** of or like prose rather than poetry. —**pro•sa′i•cal•ly,** *adv.* —**pro•sa′ic•ness,** *n.*

pro•sa•ism (prō zā′iz əm) also **pro•sa•i•cism** (-ə siz′əm), *n.* **1.** prosaic character or style. **2.** a prosaic expression.

pro•sciut•to (prō shōō′tō), *n.* salted ham that has been cured by drying, sliced paper-thin for serving.

pro•scribe (prō skrīb′), *v.t.,* **-scribed, -scrib•ing. 1.** to condemn (a thing) as harmful or odious; prohibit. **2.** to put outside legal protection; outlaw. **3.** to banish or exile. **4.** (in ancient Rome) to announce the name of (a person) as condemned to death and subject to confiscation of property. —**pro•scrib′er,** *n.*

pro•scrip•tion (prō skrip′shən), *n.* **1.** the act of proscribing. **2.** the state of being proscribed. **3.** outlawry, interdiction, or prohibition. —**pro•scrip′tive** (-tiv), *adj.* —**pro•scrip′tive•ly,** *adv.*

prose (prōz), *n., adj., v.,* **prosed, pros•ing.** —*n.* **1.** the ordinary form of spoken or written language, without metrical structure, as distinguished from poetry or verse. **2.** commonplace or dull expression, quality, etc. —*adj.* **3.** of, in, or pertaining to prose. **4.** commonplace; prosaic. —*v.t.* **5.** to turn into or express in prose. —*v.i.* **6.** to write or talk in a dull, matter-of-fact manner.

pros•e•cute (pros′i kyōōt′), *v.,* **-cut•ed, -cut•ing.** —*v.t.* **1. a.** to institute or conduct legal proceedings against (a person). **b.** to seek to conduct, obtain, or enforce by legal process. **2.** to follow up or carry forward (an undertaking), usu. to completion: *to prosecute a war.* **3.** to carry on or practice. —*v.i.* **4.** to institute and carry on a legal prosecution. **5.** to act as prosecutor. —**pros′e•cut′a•ble,** *adj.* —**pros′e•cut′a•bil′i•ty,** *n.*

pros′ecuting attor′ney, *n.* (*sometimes caps.*) the public officer in a county or other jurisdiction charged with prosecuting criminal cases.

pros•e•cu•tion (pros′i kyōō′shən), *n.* **1. a.** the institution and carrying on of legal proceedings against a person. **b.** the officials who institute and conduct such proceedings. **2.** the following up of something undertaken or begun, usu. to its completion.

pros•e•cu•tor (pros′i kyōō′tər), *n.* **1.** PROSECUTING ATTORNEY. **2.** a complainant, chief witness, or the like who instigates prosecution in a criminal proceeding. **3.** a person who prosecutes.

pros•e•lyte (pros′ə līt′), *n., v.,* **-lyt•ed, -lyt•ing.** —*n.* **1.** a person who has changed from one opinion, religious belief, sect, or the like to another; convert. —*v.i., v.t.* **2.** PROSELYTIZE. —**pros′e•lyt′er,** *n.*

pros•e•lyt•ize (pros′ə li tīz′), *v.t., v.i.,* **-ized, -iz•ing.** to convert or attempt to convert as a proselyte; recruit. —**pros′e•lyt•i•za′tion,** *n.* —**pros′e•lyt•iz′er,** *n.*

pros•en•ceph•a•lon (pros′en sef′ə lon′, -lən), *n., pl.* **-lons, -la** (-lə). the forebrain. —**pros′en•ce•phal′ic** (-sə fal′ik), *adj.*

pro•sim•i•an (prō sim′ē ən), *adj.* **1.** of or pertaining to primates of the suborder Prosimii, characterized by nocturnal habits and large eyes and ears: includes lemurs. —*n.* **2.** a prosimian animal.

pros•o•dy (pros′ə dē), *n., pl.* **-dies. 1.** the science or study of poetic meters and versification. **2.** a particular or distinctive system of metrics and versification: *Milton's prosody.* **3.** the stress and intonation patterns of an utterance. —**pro•sod•ic** (prə sod′ik), **pro•sod′i•cal,** *adj.*

pros•pect (pros′pekt), *n.* **1.** Usu., **prospects. a.** an apparent probability of advancement, success, profit, etc. **b.** the outlook for the future: *good business prospects.* **2.** anticipation; expectation; a looking forward. **3.** something in view as a source of profit. **4.** a potential or likely customer, client, candidate, etc. **5.** a view, esp. of scenery; scene. **6.** outlook or view over a region or in a particular direction. **7.** a mental view or survey, as of a subject. **8. a.** a place giving indication of a mineral deposit. **b.** the mineral yielded by such a test. **c.** a mine working or excavation undertaken in a search for ore. —*v.t.* **9.** to search or explore (a region), as for gold. **10.** to work (a mine or claim) experimentally in order to test its value. —*v.i.* **11.** to search or explore a region for gold or the like. —***Idiom.*** **12. in prospect,** expected; in view: *no other alternative in prospect.* —**pros•pec•tor** (pros′pek tər, prə spek′-), *n.*

pro•spec•tive (prə spek′tiv), *adj.* **1.** of or in the future. **2.** potential, likely, or expected. —**pro•spec′tive•ly,** *adv.*

pro•spec•tus (prə spek′təs), *n., pl.* **-tus•es. 1.** a document describing the major features of a proposed business venture, literary work, etc., in enough detail so that prospective investors, participants, or buyers may evaluate it. **2.** a brochure describing the facilities, services, or attractions of a place or institution, as a university.

pros•per (pros′pər), *v.i.* to be successful or fortunate, esp. in financial respects; thrive; flourish.

pros•per•i•ty (pro sper′i tē), *n.* a successful, flourishing, or thriving condition, esp. in financial respects; good fortune.

pros•per•ous (pros′pər əs), *adj.* **1.** having or characterized by good fortune, success, or wealth. **2.** favorable or propitious. —**pros′per•ous•ly,** *adv.* —**pros′per•ous•ness,** *n.*

pros•ta•glan•din (pros′tə glan′din), *n.* any of a class of unsaturated fatty acids that are involved in the contraction of smooth muscle, the control of inflammation and body temperature, etc.

pros•tate (pros′tāt), *adj.* **1.** Also, **pros•tat•ic** (pro stat′ik). of or pertaining to the prostate gland. —*n.* **2.** PROSTATE GLAND.

pros′tate gland′, *n.* a partly muscular gland that surrounds the urethra of males at the base of the bladder and secretes an alkaline fluid that makes up part of the semen.

pros•the•sis (pros thē′sis *for 1;* pros′thə sis *for 2*), *n., pl.* **-ses** (-sēz *for 1;* -sēz′ *for 2*). **1.** a device, either external or implanted, that substitutes for or supplements a missing or defective part of the body. **2.** PROTHESIS (def. 1). —**pros•thet′ic** (-thet′ik), *adj.* —**pros•thet′i•cal•ly,** *adv.*

pros•thet•ics (pros thet′iks), *n.* (*used with a sing. v.*) **1.** the branch of surgery or of dentistry that deals with the replacement of missing parts with artificial structures. **2.** the fabrication and fitting of prosthetic devices. —**pros′the•tist** (-thə tist), *n.*

pros•tho•don•tics (pros′thə don′tiks) also **pros•tho•don•tia** (-don′shə, -shē ə), *n.* (*used with a sing. v.*) the branch of dentistry that deals with the replacement of missing teeth and related oral structures by artificial devices.

pros•ti•tute (pros′ti tōōt′, -tyōōt′), *n., v.,* **-tut•ed, -tut•ing.** —*n.* **1.** a woman who engages in sexual intercourse for money. **2.** a man who engages in sexual acts for money. **3.** a person who willingly uses his or her talent or ability in a base and unworthy way, usu. for money. —*v.t.* **4.** to sell or offer (oneself) as a prostitute. **5.** to put (one's talent or ability) to unworthy use.

pros•ti•tu•tion (pros′ti tōō′shən, -tyōō′-), *n.* **1.** the act or practice of engaging in sexual intercourse for money. **2.** base or unworthy use, as of talent or ability.

pros•trate (pros′trāt), *v.,* **-trat•ed, -trat•ing,** *adj.* —*v.t.* **1.** to cast (oneself) facedown on the ground in humility, submission, or adoration. **2.** to lay flat, as on the ground. **3.** to throw down level with the ground. **4.** to overthrow, overcome, or reduce to helplessness. **5.** to reduce to physical weakness or exhaustion. —*adj.* **6.** lying flat or at full length, as on the ground. **7.** lying facedown on the ground, as in humility. **8.** overthrown, overcome, or helpless: *a country left prostrate by natural disasters.* **9.** physically weak or exhausted. **10.** submissive. **11.** utterly dejected; disconsolate. **12.** (of a plant or stem) lying flat on the ground. —**pros•tra′tion,** *n.*

pro•style (prō′stīl), *adj.* (of a classical temple or other building) having a portico with columns on the front only.

pros•y (prō′zē), *adj.,* **-i•er, -i•est. 1.** resembling prose. **2.** prosaic; dull or commonplace. —**pros′i•ly,** *adv.* —**pros′i•ness,** *n.*

prot•ac•tin•i•um (prō′tak tin′ē əm) also **protoactinium,** *n.* a radioactive, metallic chemical element. *Symbol:* Pa; *at. no.:* 91.

pro•tag•o•nist (prō tag′ə nist), *n.* **1.** the leading character of a drama or other literary work. **2.** a chief proponent or leader of a movement, cause, etc. —**pro•tag′o•nism,** *n.*

pro•te•an (prō′tē ən, prō tē′-), *adj.* **1.** readily assuming different forms or characters. **2.** changeable in shape or form, as an ameba. **3.** (of an actor) versatile. —**pro′te•an•ism,** *n.*

pro•tect (prə tekt′), *v.t.* **1.** to defend or guard from attack, invasion, loss, insult, etc.; cover; shield. **2.** to guard (an industry) from foreign competition by imposing import duties. —*v.i.* **3.** to provide, or be capable of providing, protection. —**pro•tect′i•ble, pro•tect′a•ble,** *adj.*

pro•tec•tion (prə tek′shən), *n.* **1.** the act of protecting or the state of being protected. **2.** a thing, person, or group that protects. **3.** *Insurance.* COVERAGE (def. 1). **4.** money paid to racketeers for a guarantee against threatened violence. **5.** a document that assures safety for the person, persons, or property specified in it.

pro•tec•tive (prə tek′tiv), *adj.* **1.** having the quality or function of protecting. **2.** tending to protect. **3.** pertaining to or favoring protectionism. —**pro•tec′tive•ly,** *adv.* —**pro•tec′tive•ness,** *n.*

pro•tec•tor (prə tek′tər), *n.* **1.** a person or thing that protects; defender; guardian. **2.** (*cap.*) Also called **Lord Protector.** the title of the head of the government during the British Protectorate, held by Oliver Cromwell (1653–58) and by Richard Cromwell (1658–59). —**pro•tec′tor•al,** *adj.* —**pro•tec′tor•ship′,** *n.*

pro•tec•tor•ate (prə tek′tər it), *n.* **1.** the relation of a strong state toward a weaker state or territory that it protects and partly controls. **2.** a state or territory so protected. **3.** the office or position, or the term of office, of a protector. **4.** the government of a protector. **5.** (*cap.*) the period (1653–59) when the Cromwells governed England.

pro•té•gé (prō′tə zhā′, prō′tə zhā′), *n., pl.* **-gés.** a person under the patronage or protection of someone interested in his or her welfare.

pro•tein (prō′tēn, -tē in), *n.* **1.** any of numerous organic molecules constituting a large portion of the mass of every life form, composed of 20 or more amino acids linked in chains. **2.** plant or animal tissue rich in such molecules, considered as a food source. —**pro′tein•a′ceous** (-tē nā′shəs, -tē i nā′-), **pro•tein′ic, pro•tei′nous,** *adj.*

pro′tein syn′thesis, *n.* the process by which amino acids are linearly arranged into proteins through the involvement of ribosomal RNA, transfer RNA, messenger RNA, and various enzymes.

pro tem (prō′ tem′), *adv.* PRO TEMPORE.

pro tem•po•re (prō′ tem′pə rē′, -rā′), *adv.* **1.** temporarily; for the time being. —*adj.* **2.** temporary.

Prot•er•o•zo•ic (prot′ər ə zō′ik, prō′tər-), *adj.* **1.** noting or pertaining to the latter half of the Precambrian Era, from about 2.5 billion to 570 million years ago, when bacteria and marine algae were the principal forms of life. —*n.* **2.** the Proterozoic division of geologic time or the rock systems formed then.

pro•test (n. prō′test; v. prə test′, prō′test), n. **1.** an expression or declaration of objection, disapproval, or dissent, often in opposition to something a person is powerless to prevent or avoid. **2.** Law. a formal statement of protest, disputing the legality of a tax or other exaction. —v.i. **3.** to give expression to objection or disapproval; remonstrate. **4.** to make a solemn or earnest declaration. —v.t. **5.** to make a protest or remonstrance against; object to. **6.** to say in protest or remonstrance. **7.** to declare solemnly or earnestly. —**pro•test′er, pro•tes′tor,** n.

Prot•es•tant (prot′ə stənt), n. **1.** (loosely) any Christian not an adherent of a Catholic, Anglican, or Eastern church. **2.** an adherent of one of the Christian churches arising from the Reformation. —adj. **3.** belonging or pertaining to Protestants or their religion. —**Prot′es•tant•ism,** n.

Prot′estant Epis′copal Church′, n. EPISCOPAL CHURCH.

Prot′estant eth′ic, n. WORK ETHIC.

Prot•es•tant•ism (prot′ə stən tiz′əm), n. **1.** the religion of Protestants. **2.** the Protestant churches collectively. **3.** adherence to Protestant principles.

Prot′estant Reforma′tion, n. REFORMATION (def. 2).

prot•es•ta•tion (prot′ə stā′shən, prō′tə-, -te-), n. **1.** the act of protesting or affirming. **2.** a solemn or earnest declaration or affirmation. **3.** formal expression or declaration of objection, dissent, or disapproval.

proth•e•sis (proth′ə sis), n. **1.** the addition of a sound or syllable at the beginning of a word, as in Spanish *escala* "ladder" from Latin *scala*. **2.** *Eastern Ch.* the preparation and preliminary oblation of the Eucharistic elements. [< Late Latin < Greek *próthesis* placing in public, offering] —**pro•thet•ic** (prə thet′ik), adj. —**Prot•het′i•cal•ly,** adv.

pro•tist (prō′tist), n. any of various complex one-celled organisms, of the kingdom Protista, that have nuclei and organelles and that are either free-living or aggregated into simple colonies: includes the protozoans, slime molds, and eukaryotic algae. —**pro•tis′tan,** adj., n. —**pro•tis′tic,** adj.

proto-, a combining form meaning "first," "foremost," "earliest form of" (*protolithic; protoplasm*); used also in the names of chemical compounds that are the first in a given series.

pro•to•col (prō′tə kôl′, -kol′, -kōl′), n. **1.** the customs and regulations dealing with diplomatic formality, precedence, and etiquette. **2.** an original draft, minute, or record from which a document, esp. a treaty, is prepared. **3.** a supplementary international agreement. **4.** an agreement between states. **5.** an annex to a treaty giving data relating to it. **6.** a plan for carrying out a scientific study or a patient's treatment regimen. **7.** a set of rules governing the format of messages that are exchanged between computers. —v.i. **8.** to draft or issue a protocol. —**pro′to•col′ar** (-kol′ər), **pro′to•col′a•ry, pro′to•col′ic,** adj.

Pro•to-In•do-Eu•ro•pe•an (prō′tō in′dō yoŏr′ə pē′ən), n. the unattested prehistoric parent language of the Indo-European languages.

pro•ton (prō′ton), n. a positively charged elementary particle found in all atomic nuclei, the lightest and most stable of the baryons, and having a positive charge of 1.602×10^{19} coulombs: the number of protons in an atom equals that element's atomic number. —**pro•ton′ic,** adj.

pro•to•plasm (prō′tə plaz′əm), n. **1.** the colloidal and liquid substance of which cells are formed, excluding horny, chitinous, and other structural material; the cytoplasm and nucleus. **2.** (formerly) CYTOPLASM. —**pro′to•plas′mic,** adj.

pro•to•plast (prō′tə plast′), n. **1. a.** the contents of a cell within the cell membrane, considered as a fundamental entity. **b.** the primordial living unit or cell. **2.** a person or thing that is formed first; original; prototype. **3.** the hypothetical first individual or one of the supposed first pair of a species or the like. —**pro′to•plas′tic,** adj.

pro•to•type (prō′tə tīp′), n., v. **-typed, -typ•ing.** —n. **1.** the original or model on which something is based or formed; pattern. **2.** someone or something that serves as a typical example of a class; model; exemplar. **3.** something analogous to a thing of a later period: *a Renaissance prototype of modern public housing.* **4.** a first or experimental working model of something to be manufactured, usu. on a large scale. —v.t. **5.** to create a prototype of. —v.i. **6.** to create prototypes. —**pro′to•typ′i•cal** (-tip′i kal), **pro′to•typ′ic, pro′to•typ′al** (-tī′pəl), adj. —**pro′to•typ′i•cal•ly,** adv.

pro•to•zo•an (prō′tə zō′ən), n., pl. **-zo•ans,** (esp. collectively) **-zo•a** (-zō′ə), adj. —n. **1.** any of various one-celled protist organisms that usu. obtain nourishment by ingesting food particles rather than by photosynthesis: classified as the superphylum Protozoa encompassing separate phyla according to means of movement, as by pseudopod, flagella, or cilia. —adj. **2.** of, pertaining to, or characteristic of a protozoan.

pro•to•zo•on (prō′tə zō′on, -ən), n., pl. **-zo•a** (-zō′ə). PROTOZOAN.

pro•tract (prō trakt′, prə-), v.t. **1.** to draw out or lengthen, esp. in time; prolong. **2.** Anat. to extend or protrude. **3.** (in surveying, mathematics, etc.) to plot and draw (lines) with a scale and a protractor. —**pro•tract′ed•ly,** adv. —**pro•tract′ed•ness,** n. —**pro•tract′i•ble,** adj. —**pro•trac′tive,** adj.

pro•trac•tion (prō trak′shən, prə-), n. **1.** the act of protracting; prolongation; extension. **2.** protrusion. **3.** something that is protracted. **4.** a drawing or rendering to scale.

pro•trac•tor (prō trak′tər, prə-), n. **1.** (in surveying, mathematics, etc.) an instrument having a graduated arc for plotting or measuring angles. **2.** one that protracts. **3.** any muscle that serves to extend a part of the body; extensor.

protractor (def. 1)

pro•trude (prō trōōd′, prə-), v., **-trud•ed, -trud•ing.** —v.i. **1.** to project; jut or stick out. —v.t. **2.** to thrust forward; cause to project. —**pro•trud′ent,** adj. —**pro•tru′si•ble** (-sə bəl, -zə-), **pro•trud′a•ble,** adj.

pro•tru•sion (prō trōō′zhən, prə-), n. **1.** the act of protruding or the state of being protruded. **2.** something that protrudes; projection.

pro•tu•ber•ant (prō tōō′bər ənt, -tyōō′-, prə-), adj. bulging out beyond the surrounding surface; protruding; projecting: *protuberant eyes.* —**pro•tu′ber•ant•ly,** adv.

proud (proud), adj. **1.** feeling pleasure or satisfaction over something regarded as honorable or creditable to oneself. **2.** having or showing self-respect or self-esteem. **3.** giving a sense of pride: *a proud moment.* **4.** highly honorable or creditable. **5.** having or showing an inordinate opinion of one's own dignity, superiority, etc.; arrogant; haughty. **6.** stately or magnificent: *proud cities.* **7.** Southern U.S. pleased: *I'm proud to meet you.* **8.** full of vigor and spirit: *a proud stallion.* —**Idiom. 9. do one proud, a.** to be a source of pride or credit to a person. **b.** to treat someone or oneself generously or lavishly. —**proud′ly,** adv.

Prov., 1. Proverbs. **2.** Province. **3.** Provost.

prove (prōōv), v., **proved, proved** or **prov•en, prov•ing.** —v.t. **1.** to establish the truth or validity of, as by evidence or argument. **2.** to give demonstration of; cause to be shown as specified: *Events have proved me right.* **3.** to subject to a test, experiment, or analysis to determine quality, characteristics, etc.: *to prove ore.* **4.** to show (oneself) to have the character or ability expected, esp. through one's actions. **5.** to verify the correctness or validity of by mathematical demonstration or arithmetical proof. **6.** Law. to probate (a will). **7.** Also, **proof.** Print. to take a trial impression of (type, a cut, etc.). **8.** to cause (dough) to rise to the necessary lightness. —v.i. **9.** to turn out: *The experiment proved to be successful.* **10.** to be found by trial or experience to be: *His story proved false.* **11.** (of dough) to rise to a specified lightness. —**prov′a•ble,** adj. —**prov′a•bil′i•ty,** n. —**prov′a•bly,** adv. —**Usage.** Either PROVED or PROVEN is standard as the past participle of PROVE. As a modifier, PROVEN is by far the more common: *a proven fact.*

prov•e•nance (prov′ə nəns, -näns′), n. place or source of origin: *a manuscript of unknown provenance.*

prov•en•der (prov′ən dər), n. **1.** dry food for livestock; fodder. **2.** food; provisions.

pro•ve•ni•ence (prō vē′nē əns, -vēn′yəns), n. provenance; origin; source.

pro′-verb′, n. a word that can substitute for a verb or verb phrase, as *do* in *They never attend meetings, but I do.*

prov•erb (prov′ərb), n. **1.** a short popular saying, usu. of unknown and ancient origin, that expresses effectively some commonplace truth or useful thought; adage; saw. **2.** a person or thing commonly regarded as an embodiment or representation of some quality; byword. **3.** a profound Biblical saying, maxim, or oracular utterance requiring interpretation. —v.t. **4.** to make the subject of a proverb. **5.** to make a byword of.

pro•ver•bi•al (prə vûr′bē əl), adj. **1.** of, characteristic of, or resembling a proverb. **2.** expressed in or as if in a proverb. **3.** having been the subject of a proverb: *the proverbial stitch in time.* **4.** having become an object of common mention or reference: *his proverbial wit.* —**pro•ver′bi•al•ly,** adv.

Prov•erbs (prov′ərbz), n. (used with a sing. v.) a book of the Bible, containing the sayings of sages.

pro•vide (prə vīd′), v., **-vid•ed, -vid•ing.** —v.t. **1.** to make available; furnish: *to provide employees with benefits.* **2.** to supply or equip: *to provide the army with tanks.* **3.** to afford or yield. **4.** to stipulate beforehand, as by a provision. —v.i. **5.** to take measures with due foresight (usu. fol. by *for* or *against*). **6.** to make a stipulation or provision. **7.** to supply means of support (usu. fol. by *for*): *to provide for one's children.*

pro•vid•ed (prə vī′did), conj. on the condition or understanding (that); providing. —**Usage.** The conjunctions PROVIDED and PROVIDING are interchangeable. Both mean "on the condition or understanding that," with *that* sometimes expressed: *Provided (or Providing) (that) sales remain steady all summer, the business will show a profit by September.*

prov•i•dence (prov′i dəns), n. **1.** (often cap.) the foreseeing care and guidance of God or nature over the creatures of the earth. **2.** (cap.) God, esp. when conceived as exercising such care and guidance in directing human affairs. **3.** a manifestation of divine care or direction. **4.** provident or prudent management of resources. **5.** foresight; provident care. [< Latin *prōvidentia* foresight, forethought]

Prov•i•dence (prov′i dəns), n. the capital of Rhode Island, in the NE part, at the head of Narragansett Bay. 150,639.

prov•i•dent (prov′i dənt), adj. **1.** having or showing foresight; providing carefully for the future. **2.** mindful in making provision (usu. fol. by *of*). **3.** economical; frugal; thrifty. —**prov′i•dent•ly,** adv.

prov•i•den•tial (prov′i den′shəl), adj. **1.** of, pertaining to, or resulting

P

from divine providence. **2.** opportune, fortunate, or lucky: *a providential event.* —**prov′i•den′tial•ly,** *adv.*

pro•vid•er (prə vī′dər), *n.* **1.** a person or thing that provides. **2.** a person who supports a family or another person.

pro•vid•ing (prə vī′ding), *conj.* on the condition or understanding (that); provided: *You can stay providing you do some work.*

prov•ince (prov′ins), *n.* **1.** an administrative division or unit of a country. **2. the provinces,** the parts of a country outside of the capital or the largest cities. **3.** a country, district, or region. **4.** a major region of the earth or biosphere. **5.** a department or branch of learning or activity. **6.** a sphere or field of activity or authority, as of a person. **7.** an ecclesiastical territorial division. **8.** a country or territory of the Roman Empire outside of Italy administered by a governor sent from Rome.

pro•vin•cial (prə vin′shəl), *adj.* **1.** belonging or peculiar to a particular province or provinces; local. **2.** of or pertaining to the provinces. **3.** rustic, narrow, or illiberal; unsophisticated; parochial. **4.** (*often cap.*) of or pertaining to styles of furniture, architecture, etc., developed in the provinces, esp. when based on styles originating in or around the capital: *Italian provincial.* —*n.* **5.** a person who lives in or comes from the provinces. **6.** a person lacking in urban sophistication or broad-mindedness. —**pro•vin′cial•ly,** *adv.*

pro•vin•cial•ism (prə vin′shə liz′əm), *n.* **1.** narrowness of views or interests; lack of sophistication. **2.** a trait, habit of thought, etc., characteristic of a provincial, a province, or the provinces. **3.** a word, expression, or pronunciation peculiar to a region. **4.** devotion to one's own province before the nation as a whole.

prov′ing ground′, *n.* any place, context, or area for testing something, as scientific equipment or a theory.

pro•vi•sion (prə vizh′ən), *n.* **1.** the act of providing or supplying. **2.** something provided or supplied. **3.** an arrangement or preparation made beforehand. **4.** a clause in a law, legal instrument, etc., providing for something; stipulation; proviso. **5.** provisions, supplies of food. **6.** to supply with provisions. —**pro•vi′sion•er,** *n.*

pro•vi•sion•al (prə vizh′ə nl), *adj.* **1.** serving for the time being only; temporary: *a provisional government.* **2.** accepted or adopted tentatively; conditional. **3.** (*usu. cap.*) of or being the wing of the Irish Republican Army that follows a policy of terrorism and violence. —*n.* **4.** a postage stamp issued for temporary use, as by a local post office prior to regular government issues. **5.** a provisional member of a group. **6.** (*usu. cap.*) a member of the Provisional wing of the Irish Republican Army. Also, **pro•vi′sion•ar′y** (-vizh′ə ner′ē) (for defs. 1, 2). —**pro•vi′sion•al′i•ty, pro•vi′sion•al•ness,** *n.* —**pro•vi′sion•al•ly,** *adv.*

pro•vi•so (prə vī′zō), *n., pl.* **-sos, -soes. 1.** a clause, as in a statute or contract, by which a condition is introduced. **2.** a stipulation or condition.

pro•vo•ca•teur (prə vok′ə tûr′, -tŏŏr′), *n.* a person who provokes trouble or incites dissension; agitator; agent provocateur.

prov•o•ca•tion (prov′ə kā′shən), *n.* **1.** the act of provoking. **2.** something that provokes, esp. by inciting, instigating, angering, or irritating. —**prov′o•ca′tion•al,** *adj.*

pro•voc•a•tive (prə vok′ə tiv), *adj.* **1.** tending or serving to provoke; stimulating, exciting, or vexing. —*n.* **2.** something provocative. —**pro•voc′a•tive•ly,** *adv.* —**pro•voc′a•tive•ness,** *n.*

pro•voke (prə vōk′), *v.t.,* **-voked, -vok•ing. 1.** to anger, exasperate, or vex. **2.** to stir up, arouse, or call forth (feelings, desires, or activity). **3.** to incite or stimulate to action. **4.** to give rise to, induce, or bring about. —**pro•vok′er,** *n.*

pro•vo•lo•ne (prō′və lō′nē), *n.* a mellow, light-colored Italian cheese.

pro•vost (prō′vōst, prov′əst *or, esp. in military usage,* prō′vō), *n.* **1.** a person appointed to superintend or preside. **2.** a high-ranking administrative officer of some colleges and universities, concerned with the curriculum, faculty appointments, etc. **3.** the chief dignitary of a cathedral or collegiate church. **4.** the mayor of a municipality in Scotland. [< Old English < Medieval Latin *prōpositus* abbot, lit., (one) placed before] —**pro′vost•ship′,** *n.*

prow (prou), *n.* **1.** the forepart of a ship or boat; bow. **2.** a similar projecting forepart, as the nose of an airplane.

prow•ess (prou′is), *n.* **1.** exceptional ability, skill, or strength. **2.** exceptional valor or bravery, esp. in combat or battle.

prowl (proul), *v.i.* **1.** to rove or go about stealthily, as in search of prey or something to steal. **2.** to rove over or through in search of what may be found: *to prowl the streets.* —*n.* **3.** the act of prowling. —*Idiom.* **4. on the prowl,** in the act of prowling; searching stealthily. —**prowl′ing•ly,** *adv.*

prowl•er (prou′lər), *n.* **1.** one that prowls. **2.** a person who goes stealthily about with an unlawful intention, as to commit theft.

prox•i•mal (prok′sə məl), *adj.* **1.** situated toward the point of origin or attachment, as of a limb or bone. Compare DISTAL (def. 1). **2.** of or designating the surface of a tooth nearest to a specified adjacent tooth. **3.** nearest; proximate. —**prox′i•mal•ly,** *adv.*

prox•i•mate (prok′sə mit), *adj.* **1.** next; nearest; immediately before or after in order, place, occurrence, etc. **2.** close; very near. **3.** forthcoming; imminent. **4.** approximate; fairly accurate. —**prox′i•mate•ly,** *adv.* —**prox′i•mate•ness,** *n.*

prox•im•i•ty (prok sim′i tē), *n.* nearness in place, time, relation, etc.

prox•y (prok′sē), *n., pl.* **prox•ies. 1.** the agency, function, or power of a person authorized to act as the deputy or substitute for another. **2.** the person so authorized; substitute; agent. **3.** a written authorization

empowering another person to vote or act for the signer, as at a meeting of stockholders.

prox′y mar′riage, *n.* a marriage performed between one of the two contracting parties and a proxy representing the other.

Pro•zac (prō′zak), *Trademark.* a drug that inhibits the release of serotonin and is used chiefly as an antidepressant.

prp., present participle.

prs., pairs.

prude (prŏŏd), *n.* a person who is excessively proper or modest and is or affects to be easily shocked, esp. in matters involving sex.

pru•dence (prŏŏd′ns), *n.* **1.** the quality or fact of being prudent. **2.** wisdom with regard to practical matters. **3.** cautiousness; circumspection. **4.** provident care in the management of resources; economy.

pru•dent (prŏŏd′nt), *adj.* **1.** wise or judicious in practical affairs. **2.** discreet or circumspect; cautious. **3.** careful in providing for the future; provident. —**pru′dent•ly,** *adv.*

pru•den•tial (prŏŏ den′shəl), *adj.* **1.** of, characterized by, or resulting from prudence. **2.** exercising prudence. **3.** having discretionary or advisory authority, as in business matters. —**pru•den′tial•ly,** *adv.*

prud•ish (prŏŏ′dish), *adj.* of or characteristic of a prude; excessively proper or modest. —**prud′ish•ly,** *adv.* —**prud′ish•ness,** *n.*

prune¹ (prŏŏn), *n.* **1.** a variety of plum that dries without spoiling. **2.** any plum when dried.

prune² (prŏŏn), *v.,* **pruned, prun•ing.** —*v.t.* **1.** to cut or lop superfluous or undesired twigs, branches, or roots from; trim. **2.** to cut or lop off (twigs, branches, or roots). **3.** to rid or clear of (anything superfluous or undesirable). —*v.i.* **4.** to remove or cut away superfluous or undesired parts. —**prun′er,** *n.*

pru•ri•ent (prŏŏr′ē ənt), *adj.* **1.** having or characterized by lascivious or lustful thoughts, desires, etc. **2.** causing lasciviousness or lust. —**pru′ri•ence, pru′ri•en•cy,** *n.* —**pru′ri•ent•ly,** *adv.*

Prus•sia (prush′ə), *n.* a former state in N Europe: became a military power in the 18th century and in 1871 led the formation of the German empire; formally abolished as an administrative unit in 1947. German, **Preussen.** —**Prus′sian,** *adj., n.*

Prus′sian blue′, *n.* **1.** a moderate to deep greenish blue. **2.** a dark blue, crystalline, water-insoluble ferrocyanide pigment, $C_{18}Fe_7N_{18}$, used in painting, fabric printing, and laundry bluing.

prus′sic ac′id (prus′ik), *n.* HYDROCYANIC ACID.

pry¹ (prī), *v.i.,* **pried, pry•ing. 1.** to inquire impertinently or unnecessarily into something: *to pry into the personal affairs of others.* **2.** to look closely or curiously; peer.

pry² (prī), *v.,* **pried, pry•ing,** *n., pl.* **pries.** —*v.t.* **1.** to move, raise, or open by leverage. **2.** to obtain, extract, or separate with difficulty: *to pry a secret out of someone.* —*n.* **3.** a tool, as a crowbar, for raising, moving, or opening something by leverage. **4.** the leverage exerted.

pry•ing (prī′ing), *adj.* impertinently or unnecessarily curious or inquisitive. —**pry′ing•ly,** *adv.*

PS, phrase structure.

P.S., 1. Also, **p.s.** postscript. **2.** Privy Seal. **3.** Public School.

ps, picosecond.

Ps. or **Psa.,** Psalm.

ps., 1. pieces. **2.** pseudonym.

PSA, prostate specific antigen: a protein, produced by the prostate, elevated levels of which may indicate the presence of cancer.

psalm (säm), *n.* **1.** a sacred song or hymn. **2.** (*cap.*) any of the songs, hymns, or prayers contained in the Book of Psalms. —**psalm′ic,** *adj.*

Psalms (sämz), *n.* (*used with a sing. v.*) a book of the Bible composed of 150 songs, hymns, and prayers.

psal•ter•y (sôl′tə rē), *n., pl.* **-ter•ies.** an ancient musical instrument similar to a zither.

psaltery

p's and q's, *n.pl., Idiom.* **mind** or **watch one's p's and q's,** to pay careful attention to one's own behavior or affairs; be discreet.

PSAT, *Trademark.* Preliminary Scholastic Assessment Test.

psec, picosecond.

pse•phol•o•gy (sē fol′ə jē), *n.* the study of elections. [< Greek *psêphos* pebble; so called from the Athenian custom of casting votes by means of pebbles] —**pse′pho•log′i•cal** (-fə loj′i kəl), *adj.* —**pse•phol′o•gist,** *n.*

pseud•e•pig•ra•pha (sŏŏ′də pig′rə fə), *n.pl.* certain writings other than the canonical books and the Apocrypha professing to be Biblical in character. —**pseud′ep•i•graph′ic** (-dep i graf′ik), *adj.*

pseu•do (sŏŏ′dō), *adj., n., pl.* **-dos.** —*adj.* **1.** false or spurious; pretended. —*n.* **2.** a false or pretentious person, esp. a pseudointellectual.

pseudo-, a combining form meaning "false," "pretended," "unreal" (*pseudoclassic; pseudointellectual*), "closely or deceptively resembling" (*pseudocarp*). Also, *esp. before a vowel,* **pseud-**.

pseu·do·e·vent (sōō′dō i vent′), *n.* an event that is staged primarily so that it can be reported in the media.

pseu·do·in·tel·lec·tu·al (sōō′dō in′tl ek′chōō əl), *n.* a person who pretends an interest in intellectual matters.

pseu·do·morph (sōō′də môrf′), *n.* **1.** an irregular or unclassifiable form. **2.** a mineral having the outward appearance of another mineral that it has replaced. **—pseu′do·mor′phic, pseu′do·mor′phous,** *adj.* **—pseu′do·mor′phism,** *n.*

pseu·do·nym (sōōd′n im), *n.* a fictitious name used by an author to conceal his or her identity; pen name. Compare ALLONYM (def. 1). **—pseu′do·nym′i·ty,** *n.*

pseu·don·y·mous (sōō don′ə məs), *adj.* **1.** bearing a false or fictitious name. **2.** writing or written under a fictitious name. **—pseu·don′y·mous·ly,** *adv.*

psf or **p.s.f.,** pounds per square foot.

pshaw (shô), *interj.* (used to express impatience, contempt, or disbelief.)

psi or **p.s.i.,** pounds per square inch.

psit·ta·co·sis (sit′ə kō′sis), *n.* a rickettsial disease affecting birds of the parrot family, pigeons, and domestic fowl, caused by the chlamydia *Chlamydia psittaci* and transmissible to humans. Also called **parrot fever.**

pso·ri·a·sis (sə rī′ə sis), *n.* a common chronic, inflammatory skin disease characterized by scaly patches. **—pso·ri·at·ic** (sôr′ē at′ik), *adj.*

P.SS. or **p.ss.,** postscripts.

psst or **pst** (pst), *interj.* (used to attract someone's attention in an unobtrusive manner.)

PST or **P.S.T.** or **p.s.t.,** Pacific Standard Time.

psych (sīk), *v.t., Informal.* **1.** to intimidate or frighten psychologically (often fol. by *out*). **2.** to prepare psychologically to be in the right frame of mind or to give one's best (often fol. by *up*). **3.** to figure out; decipher (often fol. by *out*).

psych-, var. of PSYCHO- before vowels: *psychiatry.*

psy·che (sī′kē), *n.* **1.** the human soul, spirit, or mind. **2.** the mental or psychological structure of a person, esp. as a motive force. **3.** (*cap.*) a personification of the soul in the form of a beautiful girl visited at night by Cupid.

psych·e·del·ic (sī′ki del′ik), *adj.* **1.** of or noting a mental state of intensified sensory perception. **2.** of or pertaining to any of various drugs that produce this state. **3.** resembling, characteristic of, or reproducing images, sounds, or the like, experienced while in such a state: *psychedelic painting.* **—n. 4.** a psychedelic drug. **5.** a person who uses such a substance. **—psych′e·del′i·cal·ly,** *adv.*

psy·chi·a·try (si kī′ə trē, sī-), *n.* the branch of medicine concerned with the study, diagnosis, and treatment of mental disorders. **—psy·chi·at·ric** (sī′kē a′trik), *adj.* **—psy′chi·at′ri·cal·ly,** *adv.* **—psy·chi′a·trist,** *n.*

psy·chic (sī′kik), *adj.* Also, **psy′chi·cal. 1.** of or pertaining to the human soul or mind; mental (opposed to *physical*). **2.** *Psychol.* pertaining to or noting mental phenomena. **3.** outside of natural or scientific knowledge; spiritual. **4.** of or pertaining to some apparently nonphysical force or agency. **5.** sensitive to influences or forces of a nonphysical or supernatural nature. **—n. 6.** a person who is sensitive to psychic influences or forces; medium. **—psy′chi·cal·ly,** *adv.*

psy·cho (sī′kō), *n., pl.* **-chos,** *adj. Slang.* **—n. 1.** a psychopathic person; psychopath. **—adj. 2.** psychopathic.

psycho-, a combining form representing PSYCHE (*psychological*) or PSYCHOLOGICAL (*psychoanalysis*). Also, *esp. before a vowel,* **psych-.**

psy·cho·a·nal·y·sis (sī′kō ə nal′ə sis), *n.* **1.** a systematic structure of theories concerning the relation of conscious and unconscious psychological processes. **2.** a technical procedure for investigating unconscious mental processes and for treating mental illness. **—psy′cho·an′a·lyst** (-an′l ist), *n.* **—psy′cho·an′a·lyt′ic, psy′cho·an′a·lyt′i·cal,** *adj.* **—psy′cho·an′a·lyt′i·cal·ly,** *adv.*

psy·cho·an·a·lyze (sī′kō an′l īz′), *v.t.,* **-lyzed, -lyz·ing.** to investigate or treat by psychoanalysis.

psy·cho·bab·ble (sī′kō bab′əl), *n.* writing or talk using jargon from psychiatry or psychotherapy without particular accuracy or relevance.

psy·cho·bi·ol·o·gy (sī′kō bī ol′ə jē), *n.* **1.** the use of biological methods to study normal and abnormal emotional and cognitive processes. **2.** the branch of biology dealing with the relations or interactions between body and behavior, esp. as exhibited in the nervous system, receptors, effectors, or the like. **—psy′cho·bi′o·log′i·cal** (-ə loj′i kəl), **psy′cho·bi′o·log′ic,** *adj.* **—psy′cho·bi·ol′o·gist,** *n.*

psy·cho·dra·ma (sī′kō drä′mə, -dram′ə, sī′kō drä′mə, -dram′ə), *n.* a method of group psychotherapy in which participants take roles in improvisational dramatizations of emotionally charged situations. **—psy′cho·dra·mat′ic** (-drə mat′ik), *adj.*

psy·cho·ki·ne·sis (sī′kō ki nē′sis, -kī-), *n.* TELEKINESIS. **—psy′cho·ki·net′ic** (-net′ik), *adj.*

psy·cho·lin·guis·tics (sī′kō ling gwis′tiks), *n.* (*used with a sing. v.*) the study of the relationship between language and the cognitive or behavioral characteristics of those who use it. **—psy′cho·lin′guist,** *n.* **—psy′cho·lin·guis′tic,** *adj.*

psy·cho·log·i·cal (sī′kə loj′i kəl) also **psy′cho·log′ic,** *adj.* **1.** of or pertaining to psychology. **2.** pertaining to the mind or to mental phenomena as the subject matter of psychology. **3.** of, pertaining to, dealing with, or affecting the mind, esp. as a function of awareness, feeling, or motivation. **—psy′cho·log′i·cal·ly,** *adv.*

psycholog′ical war′fare, *n.* the use of propaganda and other psychological techniques, esp. in wartime, to demoralize or intimidate an enemy nation and bolster national morale.

psy·chol·o·gist (sī kol′ə jist), *n.* a specialist in psychology.

psy·chol·o·gy (sī kol′ə jē), *n., pl.* **-gies. 1.** the science of the mind or of mental states and processes. **2.** the science of human and animal behavior. **3.** the sum of the mental states and processes characteristic of a person or class of persons. **4.** mental ploys or strategy: *He used psychology to get a promotion.*

psy·cho·neu·ro·im·mu·nol·o·gy (sī′kō nŏŏr′ō im′yə nol′ə jē, -nyŏŏr′-), *n.* the study of molecular interconnections among the central nervous system, endocrine system, and immune system. **—psy′cho·neu′ro·im′mu·no·log′i·cal** (-nl oj′i kəl), *adj.* **—psy′cho·neu′ro·im′mu·nol′o·gist,** *n.*

psy·cho·path (sī′kə path′), *n.* a person having a character disorder distinguished by amoral or antisocial behavior without feelings of remorse; psychopathic person.

psy·cho·path·ic (sī′kə path′ik), *adj.* of, pertaining to, or affected with psychopathy; engaging in amoral or antisocial acts without feeling remorse. **—psy′cho·path′i·cal·ly,** *adv.*

psy·cho·pa·thol·o·gy (sī′kō pə thol′ə jē), *n., pl.* **-gies. 1.** the study of the causes, conditions, and processes of mental disorders. **2.** the systematic description of a mental disorder. **3.** PSYCHOSIS. **—psy′cho·path′o·log′i·cal** (-path′ə loj′i kəl), **psy′cho·path′o·log′ic,** *adj.* **—psy′cho·pa·thol′o·gist,** *n.*

psy·cho·phar·ma·col·o·gy (sī′kō fär′mə kol′ə jē), *n.* the branch of pharmacology dealing with the psychological effects of drugs. **—psy′cho·phar′ma·co·log′ic** (-kə loj′ik), **psy′cho·phar′ma·co·log′i·cal,** *adj.*

psy·cho·phys·ics (sī′kō fiz′iks), *n.* (*used with a sing. v.*) the branch of psychology that deals with the relationships between physical stimuli and resulting sensations and mental states. **—psy′cho·phys′i·cal** (-i kəl), **psy′cho·phys′i·cist** (-ə sist), *n.*

psy·cho·phys·i·ol·o·gy (sī′kō fiz′ē ol′ə jē), *n.* the branch of physiology that deals with the interrelation of mental and physical phenomena. **—psy′cho·phys′i·o·log′i·cal** (-ə loj′i kəl), **psy′cho·phys′i·o·log′ic,** *adj.* **—psy′cho·phys′i·ol′o·gist,** *n.*

psy·cho·sex·u·al (sī′kō sek′shōō əl), *adj.* of or pertaining to the relationship of psychological and sexual phenomena. **—psy′cho·sex′u·al′i·ty,** *n.* **—psy′cho·sex′u·al·ly,** *adv.*

psy·cho·sis (sī kō′sis), *n., pl.* **-ses** (-sēz). **1.** a mental disorder characterized by symptoms, as delusions or hallucinations, that indicate impaired contact with reality. **2.** any severe form of mental disorder, as schizophrenia or paranoia.

psy·cho·so·mat·ic (sī′kō sə mat′ik, -sō-), *adj.* **1.** of or pertaining to a physical disorder that is caused or notably influenced by emotional factors. **2.** pertaining to or involving both the mind and the body. **—psy′cho·so·mat′i·cal·ly,** *adv.*

psy·cho·ther·a·py (sī′kō ther′ə pē), *n., pl.* **-pies.** the treatment of psychological disorders or maladjustments by a professional technique, as psychoanalysis, group therapy, or behavioral therapy. **—psy′cho·ther′a·pist,** *n.*

psy·chot·ic (sī kot′ik), *adj.* **1.** characterized by or afflicted with psychosis. **—n. 2.** a person afflicted with psychosis. **—psy·chot′i·cal·ly,** *adv.*

psyl·li·um (sil′ē əm), *n.* **1.** FLEAWORT. **2.** the seeds of the fleawort, used as a mild laxative esp. in breakfast cereals.

Pt, *Chem. Symbol.* platinum.

Pt., 1. point. **2.** port.

pt., 1. part. **2.** payment. **3.** pint. **4.** point. **5.** port. **6.** preterit.

P.T., 1. Also, **PT** Pacific time. **2.** physical therapy. **3.** physical training.

p.t., 1. past tense. **2.** pro tempore.

PTA or **P.T.A.,** Parent-Teacher Association.

ptar·mi·gan (tär′mi gən), *n., pl.* **-gans,** (*esp. collectively*) **-gan.** any of several grouses of mountainous and cold northern regions, having white or nearly white plumage in the winter.

PT boat, *n.* a small, fast, highly maneuverable, lightly armed boat used esp. in World War II for torpedoing enemy shipping.

PTC, phenylthiocarbamide.

ptero-, a combining form meaning "wing," "feather": *pterodactyl.*

pter·o·dac·tyl (ter′ə dak′til), *n.* any pterosaur, esp. of the sparrow-sized genus *Pterodactylus,* having a stubby tail and toothed jaws. **—pter′o·dac·tyl′ic, pter′o·dac′tyl·ous,** *adj.* **—pter′o·dac′tyl·id,** *adj.,* *n.* **—pter′o·dac′tyl·oid′,** *adj.*

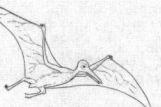

pterodactyl, *genus Pterodactylus,*
wingspread to 20 ft. (0.3 to 6 m)

P

pter·o·pod (terʹə pod′), *adj.* **1.** belonging or pertaining to the Pteropoda, a group of gastropod mollusks having a foot with winglike lobes used in swimming. —*n.* **2.** a pteropod mollusk.

pter·o·saur (terʹə sôr′), *n.* any extinct flying reptile of the Jurassic and Cretaceous order Pterosauria characterized by membranous wings supported by one elongated finger on each hand.

-pterous, a combining form meaning "having wings" of the kind or number specified: *dipterous.*

PTO, 1. Patent and Trademark Office. **2.** *Mach.* power takeoff.

P.T.O. or **p.t.o.,** please turn over (a page or leaf).

Ptol·e·ma·ic (tol′ə māʹik), *adj.* **1.** of or pertaining to Ptolemy or his system of astronomy. **2.** of or pertaining to the dynastic house of the Ptolemies or the period of their rule in Egypt.

Ptol·e·my[1] (tol′ə mē), *n., pl.* **-mies. 1.** (*Claudius Ptolemaeus*) fl. A.D. 127–151, Alexandrian mathematician, astronomer, and geographer. **2.** any of the kings of the Macedonian dynasty in Egypt 323–30 B.C.

Ptol·e·my[2] (tol′ə mē), *n.* **1.** **Ptolemy I,** (surnamed *Soter*) 367?–280 B.C., ruler of Egypt 323–285: founder of Macedonian dynasty in Egypt. **2.** **Ptolemy II,** (surnamed *Philadelphus*) 309?–247? B.C., king of Egypt 285–247? (son of Ptolemy I).

pto·maine (tōʹmān, tō mānʹ), *n.* any of a class of foul-smelling nitrogenous substances produced by bacteria during putrefaction of animal or plant protein: formerly thought to cause food poisoning (**ptomaine/ poiʹsoning**). —**pto·mainʹic,** *adj.*

pto·sis (tōʹsis), *n., pl.* **-ses** (-sēz). prolapse or drooping of an organ or part, esp. a drooping of the upper eyelid. —**pto·tic** (tōʹtik), *adj.*

ptp., past participle.

Pu, *Chem. Symbol.* plutonium.

pub (pub), *n.* a bar or tavern.

pu·ber·ty (pyōōʹbər tē), *n.* the period of life during which the genital organs mature, secondary sex characteristics develop, and the individual becomes capable of sexual reproduction. —**puʹber·tal, puʹber·al,** *adj.*

pu·bes (pyōōʹbēz), *n., pl.* **-bes. 1.** the lower part of the abdomen, esp. the area between the right and left iliac regions. **2.** the hair appearing on the lower part of the abdomen at puberty.

pu·bes·cent (pyōō besʹənt), *adj.* **1.** arriving or arrived at puberty. **2.** *Bot., Zool.* covered with down or fine short hairs. —**pu·besʹcence,** *n.*

pu·bic (pyōōʹbik), *adj.* of, pertaining to, or situated near the pubes or the pubis.

pu·bis (pyōōʹbis), *n., pl.* **-bes** (-bēz). one of the paired anterior bones of the vertebrate pelvic girdle, forming the front of each innominate bone in humans.

pub·lic (pubʹlik), *adj.* **1.** of, pertaining to, or affecting a population or a community as a whole: *a public nuisance.* **2.** done, made, acting, etc., for the community as a whole: *public prosecution.* **3.** open to all persons: *a public meeting.* **4.** of, pertaining to, or being in the service of a community or nation: *a public official.* **5.** maintained at the public expense and under public control: *a public library.* **6.** generally known: *The fact became public.* **7.** familiar to the public; prominent: *public figures.* **8.** open to the view of all; existing or conducted in public: *a public dispute.* **9.** pertaining or devoted to the welfare or well-being of the community: *public spirit.* **10.** of or pertaining to all humankind; universal. —*n.* **11.** the people constituting a community, state, or nation. **12.** a particular group of people with a common interest, aim, etc.: *the book-buying public.* —*Idiom.* **13. go public, a.** to issue stock for sale to the general public. **b.** to present previously concealed information to the public. **14. in public,** in a situation open to public notice, view, or access; publicly: *to quarrel in public.* **15. make public,** to cause to become known generally, as through the news media. —**pubʹlic·ness,** *n.*

pub·lic-ac·cess tel·evision, *n.* **1.** a noncommercial system of broadcasting on television channels made available to independent or community groups. **2.** one or more channels on cable television that by law are reserved for noncommercial broadcasting.

pubʹlic-addressʹ sysʹtem, *n.* a combination of electronic devices that makes sound audible via loudspeakers to many people, as in an auditorium or out of doors.

pubʹlic affairsʹ, *n.* matters of general interest or concern, esp. those dealing with current social or political issues.

pub·li·can (pubʹli kən), *n.* **1.** a tax collector in the Roman Empire, frequently despised because the job offered considerable opportunity for theft. Matt. 9:10, 11; 11:19; Mark 2:15, 16; Luke 18:10–14; 19:2–8. **2.** any collector of taxes, tolls, or the like.

pubʹlic assisʹtance, *n.* government aid to the poor, disabled, blind, or aged, or to dependent children.

pub·li·ca·tion (pubʹli kāʹshən), *n.* **1.** the act of publishing a book, periodical, map, piece of music, engraving, or the like. **2.** the act of bringing before the public; announcement. **3.** the state or fact of being published. **4.** something that is published, esp. a periodical.

Pubʹlic Broadʹcasting Servʹice, *n.* a network of independent, noncommercial television stations devoted to educational and other quality programming and funded by members' contributions, government allocations, and grants from private industry instead of revenues from advertising. *Abbr.:* PBS

pubʹlic corporaʹtion, *n.* a corporation, owned and operated by a government, established for the administration of certain public programs.

pubʹlic debtʹ, *n.* NATIONAL DEBT.

pubʹlic defendʹer, *n.* a full-time lawyer appointed to represent indigents in criminal cases at public expense.

pubʹlic domainʹ, *n.* **1.** the legal status of a literary work or invention whose copyright or patent has expired, or for which there never was such protection. **2.** PUBLIC LAND.

pubʹlic enʹemy, *n.* a person or thing considered a danger or menace to the public.

Pubʹlic Enʹemy Numʹber Oneʹ, *n.* **1.** (not in official use) a criminal at the top of the FBI's list of the ten most wanted criminals. **2.** a major menace to public safety, health, etc.

pubʹlic healthʹ, *n.* health services to improve and protect community health, esp. preventive medicine, immunization, and sanitation.

pubʹlic houseʹ, *n.* **1.** *Brit.* TAVERN. **2.** an inn or hostelry.

pubʹlic housʹing, *n.* housing owned or operated by a government and usually offered at low rent to the needy.

pubʹlic inʹterest, *n.* **1.** the welfare or well-being of the general public; commonwealth: *health programs that directly affect the public interest.* **2.** appeal or relevance to the general populace: *a news story of public interest.* —**pubʹlic-in·ʹterest,** *adj.*

pub·li·cist (pubʹlə sist), *n.* a person who publicizes, esp. a press agent or public-relations consultant.

pub·lic·i·ty (pu blisʹi tē), *n.* **1.** extensive mention in the news media or by word of mouth or other means of communication. **2.** public notice so gained. **3.** the technique, process, or business of securing public notice. **4.** information, articles, or advertisements issued to secure public notice or attention. **5.** the state of being public, or open to general observation or knowledge.

pub·li·cize (pubʹlə sīz′), *v.t.,* **-cized, -ciz·ing.** to give publicity to; bring to public notice; announce or advertise.

pubʹlic landʹ, *n.* Often, **public lands.** land owned by the government.

pubʹlic lawʹ, *n.* **1.** a law or statute that applies to all the people of a state or nation. **2.** the laws dealing with individuals and the state or with relations among government agencies. Compare PRIVATE LAW.

pubʹlic liʹbrary, *n.* a nonprofit library established for the use of the general public and maintained chiefly by public funds.

pub·lic·ly (pubʹlik lē), *adv.* **1.** in a public or open manner or place. **2.** by the public. **3.** in the name of the community. **4.** by public action or consent.

pubʹlic ofʹfering, *n.* a sale of a new issue of securities to the general public through a managing underwriter (opposed to *private placement*): required to be registered with the Securities and Exchange Commission.

pubʹlic opinʹion, *n.* the collective opinion of many people on some issue.

pubʹlic polʹicy, *n.* **1.** the fundamental policy on which laws rest, esp. policy not yet enunciated in specific rules. **2.** *Law.* the principle that injury to the public good or public order constitutes a basis for setting aside, or denying effect to, acts or transactions.

pubʹlic prosʹecutor, *n.* an officer charged with the conduct of criminal prosecution in the interest of the public.

pubʹlic relaʹtions, *n.* (*used with a pl. v.*) the actions of a corporation, individual, government, etc., in promoting goodwill with the public.

pubʹlic schoolʹ, *n.* **1.** (in the U.S.) a school, usu. for primary or secondary grades, that is maintained at public expense. **2.** (in England) any of a number of endowed secondary boarding schools that prepare students chiefly for the universities or for public service.

pubʹlic servʹant, *n.* a person holding a government office or job by election or appointment.

pubʹlic servʹice, *n.* **1.** the business of supplying an essential commodity, as electricity, or a service, as transportation, to the general public. **2.** government employment; civil service. **3.** a service to the public rendered without charge by a profit-making organization.

pubʹlic troughʹ, *n. Informal.* the greedy or self-interested use of public funds.

pubʹlic utilʹity, *n.* a business enterprise, as a gas company, performing an essential public service and regulated by the federal, state, or local government.

pubʹlic worksʹ, *n.pl.* structures, as roads, dams, or post offices, paid for by government funds for public use.

Pubʹlic Worksʹ Administraʹtion, *n.* the U.S. federal agency (1933–44) that instituted and administered projects for the construction of public works. *Abbr.:* PWA, P.W.A.

pub·lish (pubʹlish), *v.t.* **1.** to issue (printed or otherwise reproduced textual or graphic material, computer software, etc.) for sale or distribution to the public. **2.** to issue publicly the work of. **3.** to announce formally or officially; proclaim; promulgate. **4.** to make publicly or generally known. —*v.i.* **5.** to issue newspapers, books, computer software, etc.; engage in publishing. **6.** to have one's work published: *She publishes with another house now.* —**pubʹlish·a·ble,** *adj.*

pub·lish·er (pubʹli shər), *n.* a person or company whose business is the publishing of books, periodicals, computer software, etc.

pub·lish·ing (pubʹli shing), *n.* the business of a publisher.

Puc·ci·ni (pōō chēʹnē), *n.* **Giacomo,** 1858–1924, Italian composer.

puck (puk), *n.* a black disk of vulcanized rubber that is hit into the goal in a game of ice hockey.

puck·er (pukʹər), *v.t., v.i.* **1.** to draw or gather into wrinkles or irregular folds; constrict. —*n.* **2.** an irregular fold; wrinkle. **3.** a puckered part, as of cloth tightly or crookedly sewn. —**puck′er·er,** n. —**puck′-er·y,** adj.

pud·ding (pŏŏd′ing), n. **1.** a soft, thickened dessert, typically made with milk, sugar, flour, and flavoring. **2.** a similar dish unsweetened and served as or with the main dish: corn pudding. **3.** Brit. the dessert course of a meal. —**pud′ding·like′,** adj.

pud·dle (pud′l), n., v., **-dled, -dling.** —n. **1.** a small pool of water, as of rainwater on the ground. **2.** a small pool of any liquid. **3.** clay or the like mixed with water and tempered, used as a waterproof lining for the walls of canals, ditches, etc. —v.t. **4.** to mark or scatter with puddles. **5.** to make (water) muddy or dirty. **6.** to muddle or confuse. —v.i. **7.** to wade in a puddle. **8.** to be or become puddled. —**pud′dly,** adj.

pud′dle-jump′er or **pud′dle-jump′er,** n. Slang. LIGHTPLANE.

pu·den·dum (pyŏŏ den′dəm), n., pl. **-da** (-də). Usu. **pudenda.** the external genital organs, esp. those of the female; vulva.

pudg·y (puj′ē), adj., **-i·er, -i·est.** short and fat or thick: an infant's pudgy fingers. —**pudg′i·ly,** adv. —**pudg′i·ness,** n.

pueb·lo (pweb′lō), n., pl. **-los,** adj. —n. **1.** a communal dwelling of certain agricultural Indians of the southwestern U.S., consisting of a number of adjoining houses of stone or adobe, typically flat-roofed, multistoried, and terraced, with access provided by ladder. **2.** (cap.) PUEBLO INDIAN. **3.** any Indian village in the southwestern U.S. **4.** (in Spanish America) a town or village. —adj. **5.** of or pertaining to the Pueblo Indians. [< Spanish: town, people < Latin populus people]

Pueb·lo (pweb′lō), n. a city in central Colorado. 100,471.

Pueb′lo In′dian, a member of any of a number of American Indian peoples of the U.S. Southwest whose traditional way of life includes residence in pueblos, agriculture, and an annual cycle of community rituals.

pu·er·ile (pyŏŏ′ər il, -ə rīl′, pyŏŏr′il, -īl), adj. **1.** youthful; juvenile. **2.** childishly foolish; immature; silly. —**pu′er·ile·ly,** adv.

pu·er·per·al (pyŏŏ ûr′pər əl), adj. **1.** of or pertaining to a woman in childbirth. **2.** pertaining to or connected with childbirth.

Puer·to Ri·co (pwer′tə rē′kō, pwer′tō, pôr′tə, pōr′-), n. an island in the central West Indies: a commonwealth associated with the U.S. 3,196,520; 3435 sq. mi. (8895 sq. km). Cap.: San Juan. Abbr.: PR, P.R. Formerly (until 1932), Porto Rico. —**Puer′to Ri′can,** adj., n.

puff (puf), n. **1.** a short, quick blast or emission of air, smoke, etc. **2.** a small emission of vapor, smoke, etc. **3.** the sound of an emission of vapor, smoke, etc. **4.** an act of inhaling and exhaling, as on a cigarette or pipe. **5.** an inflated or distended part. **6.** a ball of light pastry baked and filled with whipped cream, jam, etc. **7.** a portion of material gathered but left full in the middle, as on a sleeve. **8.** a cylindrical roll of hair. **9.** a quilted bed covering, usu. filled with down. **10.** an exaggerated commendation. **11.** POWDER PUFF. **12.** a ball or pad of soft material. —v.i. **13.** to blow with short, quick blasts, as the wind. **14.** to be emitted in a puff. **15.** to emit a puff or puffs of air. **16.** to emit puffs of vapor or smoke. **17.** to go or move with puffing or puffs. **18.** to take puffs at a cigar, cigarette, etc. **19.** to become inflated or distended (usu. fol. by up). —v.t. **20.** to send forth (air, vapor, etc.) in short, quick blasts. **21.** to drive or impel by puffing, or with a short, quick blast. **22.** to smoke (a cigarette, etc.). **23.** to inflate or distend, esp. with air. **24.** to make fluffy; fluff (often fol. by up): to puff up a pillow. **25.** to inflate with pride, vanity, etc. (often fol. by up). **26.** to praise unduly. **27.** to arrange in puffs, as the hair. —**puff′y,** adj. —**puff′i·ness,** n.

puff′ ad′der, n. **1.** a large, thick-bodied, African viper, Bitis arietans, that inflates its body and hisses when disturbed. **2.** HOGNOSE SNAKE.

puff·ball (puf′bôl′), n. any of various globular stalkless fungi, of the genus Lycoperdon and allied genera, that emit a cloud of spores when pressed or broken.

puff·er (puf′ər), n. **1.** a person or thing that puffs. **2.** Also called **blow-fish, globefish.** any of various spiny fishes, capable of inflating the body: several species contain a potent nerve poison.

puff·er·y (puf′ə rē), n., pl. **-er·ies.** publicity, acclaim, or praise that is unduly exaggerated.

puf·fin (puf′in), n. any of several sea birds of the genus Fratercula, of the auk family, with a short neck and a colorful, triangular bill.

Atlantic puffin, Fratercula arctica, length 1 ft. (0.3m)

pug (pug), n. **1.** one of a breed of small, squarely built dogs with a deeply wrinkled face, tightly curled tail, and a short, smooth, usu. silver or fawn coat with a black mask. **2.** a pug nose. —**pug′gish, pug′gy,** adj.

pu·gi·lism (pyŏŏ′jə liz′əm), n. the art or practice of fighting with the fists; boxing.

pu·gi·list (pyŏŏ′jə list), n. a person who fights with the fists; a boxer, usu. a professional. —**pu′gi·lis′tic,** adj. —**pu′gi·lis′ti·cal·ly,** adv.

pug·na·cious (pug nā′shəs), adj. inclined to quarrel or fight readily;

quarrelsome; belligerent; combative. —**pug·na′cious·ly,** adv. —**pug·nac′i·ty** (-nas′i tē), **pug·na′cious·ness,** n.

pug′ nose′, n. a short, broad, somewhat turned-up nose. —**pug′-nosed′,** adj.

pu·is·sance (pyŏŏ′ə səns, pyŏŏ is′əns, pwis′əns), n. power; might. —**pu′is·sant,** adj. —**pu′is·sant·ly,** adv.

Pul (pul, pŏŏl), n. TIGLATH-PILESER.

Pu·las·ki (pə las′kē), n. **1. Count Casimir,** 1748–79, Polish patriot; general in the American Revolutionary army. **2. Fort.** FORT PULASKI.

pul·chri·tude (pul′kri tŏŏd′, -tyŏŏd′), n. physical beauty; comeliness. —**pul′chri·tu′di·nous,** adj.

pule (pyŏŏl), v.i., **puled, pul·ing.** to cry in a thin voice; whine; whimper. —**pul′er,** n.

pu·li (pŏŏl′ē, pyŏŏ′lē), n., pl. **pu·lik** (pŏŏl′ēk, pyŏŏ′lēk), **pu·lis.** one of a Hungarian breed of medium-sized sheepdogs having long, fine hair that often mats, giving the coat a corded appearance.

Pu·litz·er (pŏŏl′it sər, pyŏŏ′lit-), n. **Joseph,** 1847–1911, U.S. journalist and publisher, born in Hungary.

Pu′litzer Prize′, n. any of the annual prizes, as in journalism, literature, or music, established by Joseph Pulitzer.

pull (pŏŏl), v.t. **1.** to draw or haul toward oneself or itself, in a particular direction, or into a particular position. **2.** to draw or tug at with force. **3.** to rend; tear: to pull a cloth to pieces. **4.** to draw or pluck away from a place of growth, attachment, etc.: to pull a tooth. **5.** to draw out (a weapon) for ready use. **6.** to perform; carry out: They pulled a spectacular coup. **7.** to put on; affect: He pulled a long face when I reprimanded him. **8.** to withdraw; remove: to pull an ineffective pitcher. **9.** to attract; win: to pull votes. **10.** to take (an impression or proof) from type, a cut or plate, etc. **11.** to propel by rowing, as a boat. **12.** to strain (a muscle, ligament, or tendon). **13.** to be assigned (a specific duty). **14.** to hold in (a racehorse), esp. so as to prevent from winning. **15.** to hit (a baseball) so that it follows the direction in which the bat is being swung. —v.i. **16.** to exert a drawing, tugging, or hauling force (often fol. by at). **17.** to inhale through a pipe, cigarette, etc. **18.** to move or go: The train pulled away from the station. **19.** to row. **20. pull apart,** to analyze critically esp. for errors. **21. pull down, a.** to draw downward. **b.** to demolish; wreck. **c.** to lower; reduce. **d.** Informal. to receive as a salary; earn: He is pulling down more than fifty thousand a year. **22. pull for,** to support actively; encourage: They were pulling for the Republican candidate. **23. pull in, a.** to arrive. **b.** to tighten; curb: to pull in the reins. **c.** Informal. to arrest (someone). **24. pull off,** Informal. to perform successfully, esp. something difficult. **25. pull out, a.** to depart. **b.** to abandon abruptly: to pull out of an agreement. **26. pull over,** to direct one's automobile or other vehicle to the curb. **27. pull through,** to come safely through (a crisis, illness, etc.). **28. pull up, a.** to bring or come to a halt. **b.** to bring or draw closer. **c.** to root up. —n. **29.** the act of pulling or drawing. **30.** force used in pulling; pulling power. **31.** a drawing in of smoke or a liquid through the mouth. **32.** influence, as with persons able to grant favors. **33.** a part or thing to be pulled, as a handle on a drawer. **34.** a spell, or turn, at rowing. **35.** a stroke of an oar. **36.** a pulled muscle. **37.** a pulling of the ball, as in baseball or golf. **38.** the ability to attract; drawing power. —Idiom. **39. pull oneself together,** to regain command of one's emotions. **40. pull strings** or **wires,** to use influence, as with powerful associates, to gain one's objectives. —**pull′er,** n.

pull·back (pŏŏl′bak′), n. **1.** the act of pulling back, esp. a retreat or a strategic withdrawal of troops. **2.** a device for pulling a moving part to its original position.

pul·let (pŏŏl′it), n. a hen less than one year old.

pul·ley (pŏŏl′ē), n., pl. **-leys. 1.** a wheel for supporting, guiding, or transmitting force to or from a moving rope or cable that rides in a groove in its edge. **2.** a combination of such wheels in a block, or of such wheels or blocks in a tackle, to increase the force applied.

Pull·man (pŏŏl′mən), pl. **-mans. 1.** Trademark. a railroad sleeping car or parlor car. —n. **2.** (often l.c.) Also called **Pull′man case′.** a large suitcase. [after G. M. Pullman (1831–97), U.S. inventor]

pull′man (or Pull′man) kitch′en, n. a small, compact kitchen or kitchen unit, often recessed into a wall.

pull′-on′, n. **1.** an item of apparel that is pulled on, as a sweater or glove. —adj. **2.** designed to be put on by being pulled on.

pull·out (pŏŏl′out′), n. **1.** an act or instance of pulling out; removal. **2.** a withdrawal, as of troops or funds. **3.** a maneuver by which an airplane levels into horizontal flight after a dive. **4.** a section of a newspaper or magazine that can be pulled out.

pull·o·ver (pŏŏl′ō′vər), n. **1.** Also called **slipover.** a garment, esp. a sweater, that must be drawn over the head to be put on. —adj. **2.** designed to be put on by being drawn over the head.

pul·lu·late (pul′yə lāt′), v.i., **-lat·ed, -lat·ing. 1.** to germinate; sprout. **2.** to breed or increase rapidly. **3.** to swarm; teem. —**pul′lu·la′tion,** n.

pull′-up′ or **pull′up′,** n. CHIN-UP.

pul·mo·nar·y (pul′mə ner′ē, pŏŏl′-), adj. **1.** of or affecting the lungs. **2.** having lungs or lunglike organs.

pul′monary ar′tery, n. one of a pair of arteries conveying venous blood from the right ventricle of the heart to the lungs.

pulp (pulp), n. **1.** the soft, juicy, edible part of a fruit. **2.** the pith of the stem of a plant. **3.** Also called **dental pulp.** the inner substance of the tooth, containing arteries, veins, and lymphatic and nerve tissue. **4.** any soft, moist, slightly cohering mass, as that into which linen, wood, etc., are converted in making paper. **5.** a magazine, etc., printed on low-quality paper, usu. containing lurid material. **6.** ore pulverized and mixed with water. *—v.t.* **7.** to reduce to pulp. **8.** to remove pulp from. *—v.i.* **9.** to become reduced to pulp. —**pulp′i•ness,** *n.* —**pulp′y,** *adj.,* -**i•er, -i•est.**

pul•pit (po͝ol′pit, pul′-), *n.* **1.** a platform or raised structure in a church, from which the sermon is delivered or the service is conducted. **2. the pulpit,** the clerical profession; ministry. **3.** (esp. in Protestantism and Judaism) the position of pastor or rabbi: *He heard of a pulpit in Chicago that was about to be vacated.* **4.** (in small craft) **a.** a safety rail rising from the deck near the bow and extending around it. **b.** a similar rail at the stern. **5.** an elevated control booth in a factory.

pulp•wood (pulp′wo͝od′), *n.* spruce or other soft wood suitable for making paper.

pul•sar (pul′sär), *n.* any of several hundred known celestial objects, generally believed to be rapidly rotating neutron stars, that emit pulses of radiation, esp. radio waves, with a high degree of regularity.

pul•sate (pul′sāt), *v.i.,* **-sat•ed, -sat•ing. 1.** to expand and contract rhythmically, as the heart; beat; throb. **2.** to vibrate; quiver. —**pul′sa•tive,** *adj.*

pulse[1] (puls), *n., v.,* **pulsed, puls•ing.** *—n.* **1.** the regular throbbing of the arteries, caused by the successive contractions of the heart, esp. as may be felt at an artery, as at the wrist. **2.** a single pulsation of the arteries or heart. **3.** a stroke, vibration, or undulation, or a rhythmic series of these. **4.** the prevailing attitudes, as of the public. **5.** a momentary, sudden fluctuation in an electrical quantity, as in voltage or current. **6.** a single, abrupt emission of particles or radiation. *—v.i.* **7.** to beat or throb; pulsate. **8.** to vibrate or undulate. **9.** to emit particles or radiation periodically in short bursts. *—v.t.* **10.** to cause to pulse.

pulse[2] (puls), *n.* **1.** the edible seeds of certain leguminous plants, as peas or beans. **2.** a plant producing such seeds.

pulse•jet (puls′jet′), *n.* a jet engine in which combustion occurs intermittently, owing to the opening and shutting of flap valves at the air intake.

pul•ver•ize (pul′və rīz′), *v.,* **-ized, -iz•ing.** *—v.t.* **1.** to reduce to dust or powder, as by pounding or grinding. **2.** to demolish or crush completely. *—v.i.* **3.** to become reduced to dust. —**pul′ver•iz′a•ble,** *adj.* —**pul′ver•i•za′tion,** *n.* —**pul′ver•iz′er,** *n.*

pu•ma (pyo͞o′mə, po͞o′-), *n., pl.* **-mas.** COUGAR.

pum•ice (pum′is), *n., v.,* **-iced, -ic•ing.** *—n.* **1.** a porous or spongy form of volcanic glass, used as an abrasive. *—v.t.* **2.** to rub, smooth, clean, etc., with pumice. —**pu•mi•ceous** (pyo͞o mish′əs), *adj.*

pum•mel (pum′əl), *v.t.,* **-meled, -mel•ing** or (*esp. Brit.*) **-melled, -mel•ling.** to beat or thrash with or as if with the fists.

pump[1] (pump), *n.* **1.** an apparatus or machine for raising, driving, exhausting, or compressing fluids or gases by means of a piston, plunger, or set of rotating vanes. **2.** *Informal.* the heart. **3.** a biological system that supplies energy for the transport of molecular substances against a chemical gradient, as sodium and potassium ions across the cell membrane. *—v.t.* **4.** to raise or drive with a pump. **5.** to force or inject like a pump or as if by using a pump: *The gangster pumped ten bullets into him.* **6.** to free from water or other liquid by means of a pump. **7.** to operate or move by an up-and-down or back-and-forth action. **8.** to question (someone) artfully or persistently so as to elicit information. **9.** to elicit (information) by questioning. *—v.i.* **10.** to work a pump. **11.** to operate as a pump does. **12.** to move up and down like a pump handle. **13.** to come out in spurts. **14. pump up, a.** to inflate by pumping: *to pump up a tire.* **b.** to infuse with enthusiasm, competitive spirit, etc. *—Idiom.* **15. pump iron,** to lift weights as an exercise or in competition. —**pump′er,** *n.*

pump[2] (pump), *n.* **1.** a lightweight, low-cut shoe without fastenings for women. **2.** a slip-on black patent leather man's shoe for wear with formal dress.

pum•per•nick•el (pum′pər nik′əl), *n.* a coarse, dark, slightly sour bread made of unbolted rye.

pump•kin (pump′kin *or, commonly,* pung′kin), *n.* **1.** a large, edible, orange-yellow fruit borne by a coarse vine of the gourd family. **2.** the similar fruit of related species. **3.** a plant bearing such fruit.

pun (pun), *n., v.,* **punned, pun•ning.** *—n.* **1.** the humorous use of a word or phrase so as to emphasize or suggest its different meanings or applications, or the use of words that are alike or nearly alike in sound but different in meaning; a play on words. **2.** a word or phrase used in this way. *—v.i.* **3.** to make puns.

pu•na (po͞o′nä), *n., pl.* **-nas. 1.** a high, cold, arid plateau, as in the Peruvian Andes. **2.** ALTITUDE SICKNESS.

punch[1] (punch), *n.* **1.** a thrusting blow, esp. with the fist. **2.** forcefulness or effectiveness; power. *—v.t.* **3.** to give a sharp thrust or blow to, esp. with the fist. **4.** *Western U.S. and Canada.* to drive (cattle). **5.** to poke or prod, as with a stick. **6.** to strike or hit in operating: *to punch an elevator button.* **7.** to put into operation with or as if with a blow: *to punch a time clock.* **8.** to produce or extract, as from a computer, by striking keys: *to punch out data on sales.* **9.** to hit (a baseball) with a short, chopping motion rather than with a full swing. *—v.i.* **10.** to give sharp blows, as with the fist. **11. punch in, a.** to record one's time of arrival at work by punching a time clock. **b.** to enter (data), as into a computer, by striking keys. **12. punch out, a.** to record one's time of departure from work by punching a time clock. **b.** *Slang.* to beat up or knock out with the fists. **13. punch up,** to add zest or vigor to; enliven. *—Idiom.* **14. pull punches, a.** to lessen the force of one's punches deliberately. **b.** *Informal.* to restrain oneself from full action; hold back.

punch[2] (punch), *n.* **1.** a tool or machine for perforating or stamping materials, driving nails, etc. **2.** a device for making holes, as in paper. *—v.t.* **3.** to perforate, stamp, drive, etc., with a punch. **4.** to make (a hole) with a punch.

punch[3] (punch), *n.* **1.** a drink consisting of wine or spirits mixed with fruit juice, soda, etc., and often sweetened and spiced. **2.** a beverage of two or more fruit juices, sugar, and water.

Punch′-and-Ju′dy show′ (punch′ən jo͞o′dē), *n.* a puppet show having a conventional plot consisting chiefly of slapstick humor and the tragicomic misadventures of the grotesque, hook-nosed, humpback buffoon Punch and his wife Judy.

punch′ card′, *n.* a rectangular card on which data is stored in the form of a pattern of small holes.

punch′-drunk′, *adj.* **1.** (of a boxer) showing symptoms of cerebral injury, as unsteadiness, slow muscular movement, and dulled thinking capacity, caused by repeated blows to the head. **2.** befuddled; dazed.

punch′ing bag′, *n.* an inflated or stuffed bag, usu. suspended, punched with the fists as an exercise.

punch′ line′, *n.* the climactic phrase or sentence in a joke, speech, or humorous story that produces the desired effect.

punch•y (pun′chē), *adj.,* **-i•er, -i•est. 1.** punch-drunk. **2.** vigorously effective; forceful. —**punch′i•ness,** *n.*

punc•tate (pungk′tāt) also **punc′tat•ed,** *adj.* marked with points or dots; having minute spots or depressions. —**punc•ta′tion,** *n.*

punc•til•i•o (pungk til′ē ō′), *n., pl.* **-til•i•os. 1.** a fine point, particular, or detail, as of conduct, ceremony, or procedure. **2.** strictness or exactness in the observance of formalities or amenities.

punc•til•i•ous (pungk til′ē əs), *adj.* strict or exact in the observance of the formalities or amenities of conduct or actions. —**punc•til′i•ous•ly,** *adv.* —**punc•til′i•ous•ness,** *n.*

punc•tu•al (pungk′cho͞o əl), *adj.* **1.** arriving, acting, or happening at the time or times appointed; prompt. **2.** pertaining to or of the nature of a point. —**punc′tu•al′i•ty,** *n.* —**punc′tu•al•ly,** *adv.*

punc•tu•ate (pungk′cho͞o āt′), *v.,* **-at•ed, -at•ing.** *—v.t.* **1.** to mark or divide (something written) with punctuation marks in order to make the meaning clear. **2.** to interrupt at intervals: *Cheers punctuated the mayor's speech.* **3.** to give emphasis or force to. *—v.i.* **4.** to insert or use marks of punctuation. —**punc′tu•a′tor,** *n.*

punc′tuated equilib′rium, *n.* a theory that the evolution of species proceeds with long periods of relative stability interspersed with rapid change. Compare GRADUALISM (def. 2).

punc•tu•a•tion (pungk′cho͞o ā′shən), *n.* **1.** the practice or system of using certain conventional marks or characters in writing or printing in order to separate elements and make the meaning clear, as in ending a sentence or separating clauses. **2.** punctuation marks. **3.** the act of punctuating. —**punc′tu•a′tive,** *adj.*

punctua′tion mark′, *n.* any of a group of marks or characters used in punctuation, as the period, comma, or question mark.

punc•ture (pungk′chər), *n., v.,* **-tured, -tur•ing.** *—n.* **1.** the act of piercing or perforating, as with a pointed instrument or object. **2.** a hole or mark so made. *—v.t.* **3.** to pierce or perforate, as with a pointed instrument. **4.** to make (a hole, perforation, etc.) by piercing or perforating. **5.** to reduce or diminish as if by piercing: *to puncture a person's pride.* **6.** to cause to collapse or disintegrate: *to puncture one's dream of success.* *—v.i.* **7.** to become punctured. —**punc′tur•a•ble,** *adj.*

pun•dit (pun′dit), *n.* **1.** a learned person; an expert or authority. **2.** a person who makes comments or judgments in an authoritative manner. **3.** PANDIT. —**pun′dit•ry,** *n.*

pun•gent (pun′jənt), *adj.* **1.** sharply affecting the organs of taste or smell, as if by a penetrating power; biting; acrid. **2.** caustic or sharply expressive: *pungent remarks.* **3.** incisive; mordant: *pungent wit.* **4.** acutely distressing; poignant. **5.** *Bot.* sharp-pointed: *a pungent leaf.* —**pun′gen•cy,** *n.* —**pun′gent•ly,** *adv.*

Pu′nic Wars′, *n.pl.* the three wars waged by Rome against Carthage, 264–241, 218–201, and 149–146 B.C., resulting in the destruction of Carthage and the annexation of its territory by Rome.

pun•ish (pun′ish), *v.t.* **1.** to subject to pain, loss, confinement, or death as a penalty for some offense or fault. **2.** to inflict such a penalty for (an offense or fault): *to punish theft.* **3.** to handle or treat harshly or roughly; hurt. **4.** *Informal.* to consume; deplete. *—v.i.* **5.** to inflict punishment. —**pun′ish•er,** *n.* —**pun′ish•ing•ly,** *adv.*

pun•ish•a•ble (pun′i shə bəl), *adj.* liable to or deserving punishment. —**pun′ish•a•bil′i•ty,** *n.*

pun•ish•ment (pun′ish mənt), *n.* **1.** the act of punishing. **2.** the fact of being punished. **3.** a penalty inflicted for an offense or fault. **4.** severe handling or treatment.

pu•ni•tive (pyo͞o′ni tiv) also **pu•ni•to•ry** (-tôr′ē, -tōr′ē), *adj.* serving for, concerned with, or inflicting punishment. —**pu′ni•tive•ly,** *adv.* —**pu′ni•tive•ness,** *n.*

pu′nitive dam′ages, *n.pl.* damages awarded a plaintiff in addition to compensatory damages in order to punish the defendant for a reckless or willful act.

punk[1] (pungk), *n.* **1.** any prepared substance, usu. in stick form, that will smolder and can be used to light fireworks, fuses, etc. **2.** dry, decayed wood that can be used as tinder; touchwood. **3.** a spongy substance derived from fungi.

punk² (pungk), *n.* **1.** *Slang.* **a.** something or someone worthless or unimportant. **b.** a young ruffian; hoodlum. **c.** an inexperienced youth. **2.** PUNK ROCK. **3.** a style or movement characterized by the adoption of aggressively unconventional and often bizarre or shocking clothing, hairstyles, etc., and the defiance of social norms, usu. associated with punk rock musicians and fans. —*adj.* **4.** *Informal.* poor in quality or condition. **5.** ill; sick: *feeling punk.* **6.** of or pertaining to punk rock or the punk style. —**punk′y,** *adj.*

punk′ rock′, *n.* rock music marked by loud, insistent music and aggressive, often abusive or violent lyrics. —**punk′ rock′er,** *n.*

punt¹ (punt), *n.* **1.** a kick, as in football or rugby, executed by dropping the ball and kicking it before it touches the ground. —*v.t.* **2.** to kick (a dropped ball) before it touches the ground. —*v.i.* **3.** to punt a ball. **4.** *Informal.* to equivocate or delay: *If they ask you for exact sales figures, you'll have to punt.* —**punt′er,** *n.*

punt² (punt), *n.* **1.** a small, shallow, flat-bottomed boat with square ends, propelled by poling. —*v.t.* **2.** to pole (a small boat) along. **3.** to convey in a punt. —*v.i.* **4.** to pole a boat along. **5.** to travel or have an outing in a punt. —**punt′er,** *n.*

punt³ (po͝ont, punt), *n., pl.* **punt.** the basic monetary unit of the Republic of Ireland.

pu•ny (pyo͞o′nē), *adj.,* **-ni•er, -ni•est. 1.** of less than normal size and strength; weak. **2.** unimportant; insignificant: *a puny excuse.* —**pu′ni•ness,** *n.*

pup (pup), *n., v.,* **pupped, pup•ping.** —*n.* **1.** a young dog; puppy. **2.** the young of certain other animals, as the rat or fur seal. —*v.i.* **3.** to give birth to pups.

pu•pa (pyo͞o′pə), *n., pl.* **-pae** (-pē), **-pas.** an insect in the nonfeeding, usu. immobile, transformation stage between the larva and the adult. —**pu′pal,** *adj.*

pup•fish (pup′fish′), *n., pl.* (*esp. collectively*) **-fish,** (*esp. for kinds or species*) **-fish•es.** any of several tiny, stout killifishes inhabiting marshy waters in W North America.

pu•pil¹ (pyo͞o′pəl), *n.* a person, usu. young, who is learning under the supervision of a teacher at school or a private tutor; student.

pu•pil² (pyo͞o′pəl), *n.* the expanding and contracting opening in the iris of the eye, through which light passes to the retina.

pup•pet (pup′it), *n.* **1.** a usu. small, doll-like figure representing a human being or an animal, manipulated by the hand or by rods, wires, etc. Compare HAND PUPPET, MARIONETTE. **2.** a person, group, or government whose actions are prompted and controlled by another or others. **3.** a small doll. —**pup′pet•like′,** *adj.*

pup•pet•eer (pup′i tēr′), *n.* **1.** a person who manipulates puppets, as in a puppet show. —*v.i.* **2.** to work as a puppeteer.

pup•pet•ry (pup′i trē), *n., pl.* **-ries. 1.** the art of making puppets or presenting puppet shows. **2.** puppets collectively.

pup′pet show′, *n.* an entertainment in which the performers are puppets. Also called **pup′pet play′.**

pup•py (pup′ē), *n., pl.* **-pies.** a young dog, esp. one less than a year old. —**pup′py•ish,** *adj.* —**pup′py•like′,** *adj.*

pup′py love′, *n.* temporary infatuation between a boy and girl.

pur•blind (pûr′blīnd′), *adj.* **1.** nearly or partially blind; dim-sighted. **2.** deficient in understanding, imagination, or vision. —**pur′blind′ly,** *adv.* —**pur′blind′ness,** *n.*

Pur•cell (pûr sel′ *for 1;* pûr′səl *for 2*), *n.* **1. Edward Mills,** born 1912, U.S. physicist. **2. Henry,** 1659–95, English composer.

pur•chase (pûr′chəs), *v.,* **-chased, -chas•ing,** *n.* —*v.t.* **1.** to acquire by the payment of money or its equivalent; buy. **2.** to acquire by effort, sacrifice, flattery, etc. **3.** to influence by a bribe. **4.** to be sufficient to buy. **5.** to move, haul, or raise, esp. by applying mechanical power. **6.** to apply a lever, pulley, or other aid to. —*v.i.* **7.** to buy something. —*n.* **8.** acquisition by the payment of money or its equivalent. **9.** something that is bought. **10.** acquisition by means of effort, labor, etc. **11.** *Law.* the acquisition of land or other property by means other than inheritance. **12.** a lever, pulley, or other device that provides mechanical advantage or power for moving a heavy object. **13.** an effective hold or position for applying power in moving a heavy object; leverage. **14.** any means of applying or increasing power, influence, etc. **15.** a firm grip or footing on something. —**pur′chas•a•ble,** *adj.* —**pur′chas•er,** *n.*

pur•dah or **pur•da** or **par•dah** (pûr′də), *n.* (in India, Pakistan, etc.) the seclusion of women from the sight of men or strangers, practiced by some Muslims and Hindus.

pure (pyo͝or), *adj.,* **pur•er, pur•est. 1.** free from adulterating or extraneous matter: *pure gold.* **2.** free from contamination, pollution, or dirt; clean: *pure water.* **3.** unmodified by an admixture; simple or homogeneous: *pure white.* **4.** absolute; utter; sheer: *pure joy.* **5.** being that and nothing else. **6.** of unmixed descent or ancestry. **7.** free from blemishes; clear; spotless: *pure skin.* **8.** (of literary style) straightforward; unaffected. **9.** abstract or theoretical (opposed to *applied*): *pure science.* **10.** without any discordant quality; clear and true: *a pure tone in music.* **11.** untainted with evil or guilt; innocent. **12.** physically chaste; virgin. **13.** ceremonially or ritually clean. **14.** independent of sense or experience: *pure knowledge.* **15.** (of a vowel sound) maintaining the same quality throughout its duration. —**pure′ness,** *n.*

pure•blood (pyo͝or′blud′), *n.* **1.** an individual whose ancestry consists of a single strain or type unmixed with any other. —*adj.* Also, **pure′-blood′ed. 2.** of or pertaining to a pureblood. **3.** PUREBRED (def. 1).

pure•bred (*adj.* pyo͝or′bred′; *n.* pyo͝or′bred′), *adj.* **1.** of or pertaining to an individual whose ancestors derive over many generations from a recognized breed. —*n.* **2.** a purebred animal, esp. one of registered pedigree.

pu•rée or **pu•ree** (pyo͝o rā′, -rē′), *n., v.* **-réed, -rée•ing.** —*n.* **1.** a thick liquid or pulp prepared from cooked vegetables, fruit, etc., passed through a sieve or broken down in a blender or similar device. **2.** a soup made of puréed ingredients. —*v.t.* **3.** to make a purée of.

Pure′ Food′ and Drug′ Act′, *n.* a law passed in 1906 to remove harmful and misrepresented foods and drugs from the market and regulate the manufacture and sale of drugs and food involved in interstate trade.

pure•ly (pyo͝or′lē), *adv.* **1.** in a pure manner; without admixture. **2.** merely; only; solely: *purely accidental.* **3.** entirely; completely. **4.** innocently or chastely.

pur•ga•tion (pûr gā′shən), *n.* **1.** the act of purging. **2.** the result of purging, as a cleansing or purification.

pur•ga•tive (pûr′gə tiv), *adj.* **1.** purging or cleansing, esp. by causing evacuation of the bowels. —*n.* **2.** a purgative medicine or agent; cathartic. —**pur′ga•tive•ly,** *adv.*

pur•ga•to•ry (pûr′gə tôr′ē, -tōr′ē), *n., pl.* **-ries,** *adj.* —*n.* **1.** (esp. in Roman Catholic belief) a place or state following death in which penitent souls are made ready for heaven. **2.** any condition or place of temporary suffering or expiation. —*adj.* **3.** serving to cleanse or expiate.

purge (pûrj), *v.,* **purged, purg•ing,** *n.* —*v.t.* **1.** to rid of impurities; cleanse; purify. **2.** to rid, clear, or free: *to purge a political party of disloyal members.* **3.** to clear of imputed guilt. **4.** to remove by cleansing or purifying. **5.** to clear or empty (the stomach or intestines) by inducing vomiting or evacuation. **6.** to eliminate (undesirable members) from a government, political organization, etc. —*v.i.* **7.** to become cleansed or purified. **8.** to undergo or cause emptying of the stomach or intestines. —*n.* **9.** the act or process of purging. **10.** the removal or elimination of members of a political organization, government, etc., considered disloyal or otherwise undesirable, often in a summary or violent manner. **11.** something that purges, as a purgative medicine. —**purge′a•ble,** *adj.* —**purg′er,** *n.*

pu•ri•fi•ca•tor (pyo͝or′ə fi kā′tər), *n.* a linen cloth used during the celebration of communion to wipe the chalice or the celebrant's hands.

pu•ri•fy (pyo͝or′ə fī′), *v.,* **-fied, -fy•ing.** —*v.t.* **1.** to make pure; free from pollutants or contaminants. **2.** to free from extraneous or objectionable elements. **3.** to free from guilt or evil. **4.** to make clean for ceremonial or ritual use. —*v.i.* **5.** to become pure. —**pu′ri•fi•ca′tion,** *n.* —**pu•rif′i•ca•to′ry** (-rif′i kə tôr′ē, -tōr′ē), *adj.* —**pu′ri•fi′er,** *n.*

Pu•rim (po͝or′im; *Heb.* po͞o RĒM′), *n.* a Jewish festival celebrated on the 14th day of Adar in commemoration of the deliverance of the Jews in Persia from destruction by Haman.

pu•rine (pyo͝or′ēn, -in), *n.* a white, crystalline compound, $C_5H_4N_4$, from which is derived a group of compounds including uric acid, xanthine, and caffeine.

pur•ism (pyo͝or′iz əm), *n.* **1.** strict observance of or insistence on purity or correctness in language, style, etc. **2.** an instance of this. —**pur′ist,** *n.* —**pu•ris′tic,** *adj.* —**pu•ris′ti•cal•ly,** *adv.*

Pu•ri•tan (pyo͝or′i tn), *n.* **1.** a member of a group of Protestants that arose in the 16th century within the Church of England, demanding the simplification of doctrine and worship and greater strictness in religious discipline. **2.** (*l.c.*) a person who is strict in moral or religious matters, often to an excessive degree. —*adj.* **3.** of or pertaining to the Puritans. **4.** (*l.c.*) pertaining to or characteristic of a moral puritan.

pu•ri•tan•i•cal (pyo͝or′i tan′i kəl) also **pu′ri•tan′ic,** *adj.* **1.** very strict in moral or religious matters, often excessively so; rigidly austere. **2.** (*sometimes cap.*) of or pertaining to Puritans or Puritanism. —**pu′ri•tan′i•cal•ly,** *adv.* —**pu′ri•tan′i•cal•ness,** *n.*

Pu•ri•tan•ism (pyo͝or′i tn iz′əm), *n.* **1.** the principles and practices of the Puritans. **2.** (*usu. l.c.*) extreme, often excessive strictness in moral or religious matters, esp. rigid austerity.

pu•ri•ty (pyo͝or′i tē), *n.* **1.** the condition or quality of being pure; freedom from anything that contaminates, pollutes, etc. **2.** freedom from any admixture or modifying addition. **3.** cleanness. **4.** freedom from guilt or evil; innocence. **5.** freedom from foreign or inappropriate elements; careful correctness: *purity of expression.*

purl¹ (pûrl), *n.* **1.** a basic stitch in knitting, the reverse of the knit, formed by pulling a loop of the working yarn back through an existing stitch and then slipping that stitch off the needle. **2.** one of a series of small loops along the edge of lace braid. **3.** a twisted gold or silver embroidery thread. —*v.i.* **4.** to knit with a purl stitch. —*v.t.* **5.** to make with this stitch. **6.** to finish with loops or a looped edging.

purl² (pûrl), *v.i.* **1.** to flow with curling or rippling motion, as a shallow stream over stones. **2.** to flow with a murmuring sound. —*n.* **3.** the action or sound of purling. **4.** a ripple or eddy.

pur•lieu (pûr′lo͞o, pûrl′yo͞o), *n., pl.* **-lieus. 1. purlieus, a.** environs or neighborhood. **b.** confines or bounds. **2.** a place frequented by a person; haunt. **3.** an outlying district of a town or city. **4.** a piece of land on the edge of a forest, orig. land once part of a royal forest restored to private ownership.

pur•loin (pər loin′, pûr′loin), *v.t.* **1.** to take dishonestly; steal; filch. —*v.i.* **2.** to commit theft; steal. —**pur•loin′er,** *n.*

pur•ple (pûr′pəl), *n., adj.*, **-pler, -plest,** *v.*, **-pled, -pling.** —*n.* **1.** any color having components of both red and blue, esp. one deep in tone. **2.** cloth of this hue, esp. as formerly worn distinctively by persons of royal or other high rank. **3.** the office of a cardinal or bishop. **4.** imperial, regal, or princely rank or position. —*adj.* **5.** of the color purple. **6.** imperial, regal, or princely. **7.** brilliant or showy. **8.** full of exaggerated literary devices and effects: *purple prose.* **9.** profane or shocking, as language. —*v.t., v.i.* **10.** to make or become purple. —***Idiom.*** **11. born to the purple,** of royal or exalted birth. —**pur′ple•ness,** *n.*

Pur′ple Heart′, *n.* a medal awarded U.S. service personnel for wounds received in action against an enemy.

pur′ple loose′strife, *n.* an Old World wetland plant, of the loosestrife family, having spikes of reddish purple flowers: widely naturalized in North America.

pur′ple mar′tin, *n.* a large American swallow, the male of which is blue-black.

pur•port (*v.* pər pôrt′, -pōrt′; *n.* pûr′pôrt, -pōrt), *v.t.* **1.** to present the appearance of being; profess or claim: *a man purporting to be the manager.* **2.** to convey; express or imply. —*n.* **3.** the meaning, import, or sense. **4.** a purpose or intention.

pur•port•ed (pər pôr′tid, -pōr′-), *adj.* reputed or claimed; alleged: *no evidence of their purported wealth.* —**pur•port′ed•ly,** *adv.*

pur•pose (pûr′pəs), *n., v.*, **-posed, -pos•ing.** —*n.* **1.** the reason for which something exists or is done, made, etc. **2.** an intended or desired result; aim; goal. **3.** determination; resoluteness. **4.** the subject in hand; point at issue. **5.** practical result or effect: *to act to good purpose.* —*v.t.* **6.** to intend; design; resolve. —*v.i.* **7.** to have a purpose. —***Idiom.*** **8. on purpose,** intentionally. **9. to the purpose,** to the point; relevant.

pur•pose•ful (pûr′pəs fəl), *adj.* **1.** having a purpose. **2.** determined; resolute. **3.** full of meaning; significant. —**pur′pose•ful•ly,** *adv.* —**pur′pose•ful•ness,** *n.*

pur•pose•less (pûr′pəs lis), *adj.* **1.** having no purpose or apparent meaning. **2.** having no aim or goal; aimless: *a purposeless existence.* —**pur′pose•less•ly,** *adv.* —**pur′pose•less•ness,** *n.*

pur•pose•ly (pûr′pəs lē), *adv.* **1.** intentionally; deliberately. **2.** with the particular purpose specified; expressly: *I wore that suit purposely to make a good impression.*

purr (pûr), *n.* **1.** the low, continuous, vibrating sound a cat makes, as when contented. **2.** any similar sound, esp. one expressive of ease or contentment: *the purr of the new motor.* —*v.i.* **3.** to utter such a sound. **4.** to speak in a murmuring tone, esp. one indicative of smugness or malice. —*v.t.* **5.** to express in or as if in a purr. —**purr′ing•ly,** *adv.*

purse (pûrs), *n.* **1.** a woman's handbag or pocketbook. **2.** a small bag, pouch, or case for carrying money: *a change purse.* **3.** anything resembling a purse in appearance, use, etc. **4.** a sum of money offered as a prize or collected as a gift. **5.** financial resources; wealth. —*v.t.* **6.** to contract into folds; pucker: *to purse one's lips.* **7.** to put into a purse. —***Proverb.*** **8. You can't make a silk purse out of a sow's ear,** one cannot make something good out of inferior material.

purs•er (pûr′sər), *n.* an officer who is in charge of the accounts and documents of a ship and who keeps valuables for passengers.

purse′ strings′, *n.pl.* the disposition of financial resources: *to control the family purse strings.*

purs•lane (pûrs′lān, -lin), *n.* any low, trailing plant of the purslane family having yellow flowers, used as a salad plant.

pur•su•ance (pər sōō′əns), *n.* the carrying out of some plan, course, or the like.

pur•su•ant (pər sōō′ənt), *adj.* **1.** pursuing. —***Idiom.*** **2. pursuant to,** in accordance with: *Pursuant to instructions, I enclose the documents.* —**pur•su′ant•ly,** *adv.*

pur•sue (pər sōō′), *v.*, **-sued, -su•ing.** —*v.t.* **1.** to follow in order to overtake, capture, etc.; chase. **2.** to follow close upon; attend: *Bad luck pursued us.* **3.** to strive to attain or accomplish (a goal, purpose, etc.). **4.** to proceed in accordance with (a method, plan, etc.). **5.** to carry on or continue (a course of action, etc.): *to pursue one's studies.* **6.** to continue to trouble. **7.** to practice (an occupation or pastime). **8.** to continue to discuss (a subject). **9.** to follow. —*v.i.* **10.** to follow in pursuit. **11.** to continue. —**pur•su′a•ble,** *adj.* —**pur•su′er,** *n.*

pur•suit (pər sōōt′), *n.* **1.** the act of pursuing. **2.** an effort to secure or attain; quest. **3.** an occupation or pastime one regularly engages in: *literary pursuits.*

pursuit′ plane′, *n.* (formerly) FIGHTER (def. 2).

pu•ru•lent (pyŏŏr′ə lənt, pyŏŏr′yə-), *adj.* **1.** full of, forming, or discharging pus; suppurating. **2.** attended with suppuration: *purulent appendicitis.* **3.** of the nature of or like pus. —**pu′ru•lent•ly,** *adv.*

pur•vey (pər vā′), *v.t.* to supply (esp. food or provisions), usu. as a business. —**pur•vey′or,** *n.*

pur•view (pûr′vyōō), *n.* **1.** the range of operation, authority, concern, etc. **2.** the range of vision, insight, or understanding. **3. a.** the body, as distinguished from the preamble, of a statute. **b.** the purpose or scope of a statute. **4.** the full scope or compass of any document, statement, subject, etc.

pus (pus), *n.* a more or less viscid substance produced by suppuration and found in abscesses, sores, etc. —**pus′like′,** *adj.*

push (pŏŏsh), *v.t.* **1.** to press against (a thing) with force in order to move it away. **2.** to move (something) in a specified way by exerting force: *to push the door open.* **3.** to accomplish by pushing: *to push one's way through a crowd.* **4.** to cause to extend or project; thrust. **5.** to urge to some action or course. **6.** to press (an action, proposal, etc.) with energy and insistence. **7.** to carry (an action) toward a conclusion or completion. **8.** to press the adoption, use, sale, etc., of: *to push inferior merchandise.* **9.** to press or bear hard upon: *to push a witness for an answer.* **10.** to cause difficulties because of a specified lack (usu. fol. by *for*): *I'm pushed for time.* **11.** *Slang.* to peddle (illicit drugs). **12.** *Informal.* to be approaching a specified age, speed, etc. —*v.i.* **13.** to exert a thrusting force upon something. **14.** to proceed by shoving. **15.** to make one's way with effort or persistence. **16.** to extend or project. **17.** to put forth vigorous or persistent efforts. **18.** to move on being pushed. **19. push around,** to intimidate or bully. **20. push off,** *Informal.* to go away; depart. **21. push on,** to proceed; press forward. —*n.* **22.** the act of pushing; a shove or thrust. **23.** a vigorous effort or campaign. **24.** a vigorous and determined advance or military attack. **25.** the pressure of circumstances, activities, etc. **26.** *Informal.* persevering energy; enterprise. —***Idiom.*** **27. push the envelope,** to reach the forefront and stretch the limits of technological advance. **28. when** or **if push comes to shove,** when or if a problem must finally be faced; in a crucial situation.

push′ but′ton, *n.* a button or knob that opens or closes an electric circuit when depressed or released.

push′-but′ton, *adj.* **1.** operated by or as if by push buttons: *push-button tuning.* **2.** utilizing devices that can be easily activated from a distant location: *push-button warfare.*

push•er (pŏŏsh′ər), *n.* **1.** a person or thing that pushes. **2.** *Slang.* a peddler of illegal drugs. **3.** an aircraft driven by propellers located on the trailing rather than the leading edge of the wings.

Push•kin (pŏŏsh′kin), *n.* **Alexander Sergeevich,** 1799–1837, Russian poet and dramatist.

push•o•ver (pŏŏsh′ō′vər), *n.* **1.** anything done easily. **2.** an easily defeated person or team. **3.** a person who is easily persuaded, influenced, or seduced.

push•pin (pŏŏsh′pin′), *n.* a short pin with a spool-shaped head of plastic, glass, or metal, used for affixing material to a bulletin board, wall, or the like.

push′-up′, *n.* **1.** an exercise in which a person lies in a prone position with the hands palms down under the shoulders and raises and lowers the body using only the arms. —*adj.* **2.** (of a sleeve) made to be pushed up the arm so as to create a puffed or creased fullness.

push•y (pŏŏsh′ē), *adj.*, **-i•er, -i•est.** obnoxiously forward or self-assertive. —**push′i•ly,** *adv.* —**push′i•ness,** *n.*

pu•sil•lan•i•mous (pyōō′sə lan′ə məs), *adj.* **1.** lacking courage or resolution; cowardly; faint-hearted. **2.** indicating a cowardly spirit. —**pu′sil•la•nim′i•ty** (-lə nim′i tē), *n.* —**pu′sil•lan′i•mous•ly,** *adv.*

puss (pŏŏs), *n.* a cat. —**puss′like′,** *adj.*

puss•y[1] (pŏŏs′ē), *n., pl.* **-ies.** a cat, esp. a kitten.

pus•sy[2] (pus′ē), *adj.*, **-si•er, -si•est.** puslike.

puss•y•cat (pŏŏs′ē kat′), *n.* **1.** a cat; pussy. **2.** *Informal.* an agreeable, nonthreatening person.

puss•y•foot (pŏŏs′ē fŏŏt′), *v.i.* **1.** to go or move in a stealthy or cautious manner. **2.** to act timidly or irresolutely, as if afraid to commit oneself. —**puss′y•foot′er,** *n.*

puss′y wil′low (pŏŏs′ē), *n.* **1.** a small willow, *Salix discolor,* of E North America, having silky catkins. **2.** any of various similar willows.

pus•tu•lant (pus′chə lənt), *adj.* causing the formation of pustules.

pus•tu•lar (pus′chə lər), *adj.* **1.** of, pertaining to, or of the nature of pustules. **2.** characterized by or covered with pustules.

pus•tule (pus′chōōl), *n.* **1.** a small elevation of the skin containing pus. **2.** any pimplelike or blisterlike swelling or elevation. —**pus′tuled,** *adj.*

put (pŏŏt), *v.*, **put, put•ting,** *n.* —*v.t.* **1.** to move (anything) into a specific location or position; place. **2.** to bring into some condition, relation, etc.: *to put affairs in order.* **3.** to force to undergo something. **4.** to set to a duty, task, action, etc. **5.** to render or translate, as into another language. **6.** to provide musical accompaniment for (words); set. **7.** to assign or attribute: *to put the blame on others.* **8.** to estimate (distance, time, etc.). **9.** to bet or wager. **10.** to express or state: *To put it honestly, I don't care.* **11.** to apply (knowledge, skill, etc.) to a use or purpose. **12.** to submit for answer, consideration, etc. **13.** to impose (a tax, charge, etc.). **14.** to invest (money, resources, etc.). **15.** to throw: *to put the shot.* —*v.i.* **16.** to go or proceed: *to put to sea.* **17.** to shoot out or grow, or send forth shoots or sprouts. **18. put about, a.** *Naut.* to change direction, as on a course. **b.** to turn in a different direction. **19. put across, a.** to cause to be understood or received favorably. **b.** to do successfully; accomplish. **20. put aside** or **by, a.** to store up; save. **b.** to put out of the way **21. put away, a.** to put in the designated place for storage. **b.** to save, esp. for later use. **c.** to discard. **d.** to drink or eat, esp. in a large quantity. **e.** to confine in a jail or a mental institution. **f.** to kill (an animal, esp. a pet) by humane means. **22. put down, a.** to write down; record. **b.** to enter in a list, as of subscribers or contributors. **c.** to suppress. **d.** to attribute; ascribe. **e.** to regard or categorize: *He was put down as a chronic complainer.* **f.** to disparage, humiliate, or embarrass. **g.** to pay as a deposit. **h.** to land an aircraft. **23. put forth, a.** to bear or grow: *trees putting forth green shoots.* **b.** to propose; present. **c.** to exert. **d.** to set out; depart. **24. put forward, a.** to propose; advance. **b.** to nominate or support. **25. put in, a.** Also, **put into.** *Naut.* to enter (a port or harbor). **b.** to spend (time) as indicated. **26. put in for,** to apply for or request: *to put in for a transfer.*

27. put off, a. to postpone; defer. **b.** to get rid of by evasion or delay. **c.** to disconcert or perturb: *We were put off by the book's abusive tone.* **28. put on, a.** to clothe oneself in. **b.** to assume or pretend. **c.** to produce or stage, as a show. **d.** *Informal.* to deceive (someone) as a joke; tease: *You're putting me on, aren't you?* **29. put out, a.** to extinguish, as a fire. **b.** to be vexed or annoyed. **c.** to subject to inconvenience. **d.** *Baseball, Softball.* to cause to be denied an opportunity to reach base or score; retire. **e.** to publish. **f.** to go out to sea. **g.** to manufacture; produce. **30. put over,** to accomplish successfully. **31. put through, a.** to complete successfully. **b.** to bring about. **c.** to make a telephone connection for: *Put me through to Los Angeles.* **d.** to make (a telephone connection): *to put a call through to Hong Kong.* **e.** to cause to suffer or endure. **32. put up, a.** to construct; erect. **b.** to can (vegetables, fruits, etc.); preserve (jam, jelly, etc.). **c.** to set or arrange (the hair). **d.** to provide or stake (money). **e.** to accommodate; lodge. **f.** to propose as a candidate; nominate. **g.** to offer, esp. for public sale. **h.** to sheathe (one's sword). **33. put upon,** to take unfair advantage of; impose upon. **34. put up to,** to provoke or incite. **35. put up with,** to endure; tolerate. **—n. 36.** a throw or cast, esp. with a forward motion of the hand. **37.** Also called **put option.** an option to sell stock at a specified price and by a specified date. Compare CALL (def. 55). **—Idiom. 38. put one's best foot forward,** to try to make as good an impression as possible. **39. put oneself out,** to take pains; go to trouble or expense. **40. put one's shoulder to the wheel,** to exert extra effort and work hard. **41. put on the dog** or **the ritz,** to assume an attitude of wealth or importance; put on airs. **42. put something over on,** to deceive. **43. put to it,** to be confronted with a serious problem. **44. stay put,** to remain in the same position; refuse to move. **—Proverb. 45. Never put off until tomorrow what you can do today,** it is best not to procrastinate.

pu•ta•tive (pyōō′tə tiv), *adj.* commonly regarded as such; reputed. **—pu′ta•tive•ly,** *adv.*

put′-call′ ra′tio, *n.* (in stock trading) the ratio of put options to call options, by which an increase in puts signals a falling market and an increase in calls a rising market.

put′-down′ or **put′down′,** *n.* **1.** a landing of an aircraft. **2.** *Informal.* a disparaging or snubbing remark.

Put•nam (put′nəm), *n.* **1. Israel,** 1718–90, American Revolutionary general. **2. Rufus,** 1738–1824, American Revolutionary officer: engineer and colonizer in Ohio.

put-on (*n.* pŏŏt′on′, -ôn′; *adj.* -on′, -ôn′), *n. Informal.* **1.** an act or instance of putting someone on. **2.** a hoax or spoof. **—adj. 3.** feigned or assumed.

pu•tong•hua or **p′u•t′ung hua** (pōō′tung′hwä′), *n.* the form of spoken Chinese, based on the dialect of Beijing, adopted as the official national language of China. [< Chinese *pŭtōnghuà* lit., common (spoken) language]

put′-out′, *n.* an instance of putting out a batter or base runner in a baseball game.

pu•tre•fac•tion (pyōō′trə fak′shən), *n.* **1.** bacterial or fungal decomposition of organic matter with resulting obnoxious odors; rotting. **2.** the state of being putrefied; decay. **—pu′tre•fac′tive, pu′tre•fa′cient** (-fā′shənt), *adj.*

pu•tre•fy (pyōō′trə fī′), *v.*, **-fied, -fy•ing. —v.i. 1.** to become putrid; rot. **2.** to become gangrenous. **—v.t. 3.** to render putrid; cause to rot or decay with an offensive odor. **—pu′tre•fi′a•ble,** *adj.* **—pu′tre•fi′er,** *n.*

pu•tres•cent (pyōō tres′ənt), *adj.* **1.** becoming putrid; undergoing putrefaction. **2.** of or pertaining to putrefaction. **—pu•tres′cence, pu•tres′cen•cy,** *n.*

pu•trid (pyōō′trid), *adj.* **1.** (of organic material) in a state of foul decay or decomposition. **2.** of, pertaining to, or attended by putrefaction. **3.** having the odor of decaying flesh. **4.** of very low quality; rotten. **—pu•trid′i•ty, pu′trid•ness,** *n.* **—pu′trid•ly,** *adv.*

putsch (pŏŏch), *n.* a sudden political revolt or uprising. [< German *Putsch,* orig. Swiss German: lit., violent blow, clash, shock; introduced into standard German through reports of Swiss popular uprisings of the 1830s, esp. the Zurich revolt of Sept., 1839]

putt (put), *v.t.* **1.** to strike (a golf ball) gently so as to make it roll along the green into the hole. **—v.i. 2.** to putt a golf ball. **—n. 3.** an act of putting. **4.** a stroke made in putting.

put•ter¹ (put′ər), *v.i.* to busy or occupy oneself in a leisurely, casual, or ineffective manner. **—put′ter•er,** *n.* **—put′ter•ing•ly,** *adv.*

putt•er² (put′ər), *n.* **1.** a golf club used in putting. **2.** a person who putts a golf ball.

put•ter³ (pŏŏt′ər), *n.* a person or thing that puts.

putt′ing green′, *n.* GREEN (def. 24).

put•ty (put′ē), *n., pl.* **-ties,** *v.,* **-tied, -ty•ing. —n. 1.** a compound, usu. of whiting and linseed oil, used to secure windowpanes, patch woodwork defects, etc. **2.** any of various substances for sealing the joints of tubes or pipes. **3.** a mixture of lime and water with sand and plaster of Paris, used as a finish plaster coat. **4.** a person or thing easily molded, influenced, etc. **—v.t. 5.** to secure, cover, etc., with putty.

put′ty knife′, *n.* a tool for puttying, having a broad flexible blade.

put′-upon′, *adj.* imposed upon; ill-used.

Pu•zo (pōō′zō), *n.* **Mario,** born 1920, U.S. novelist.

puz•zle (puz′əl), *n., v.,* **-zled, -zling. —n. 1.** a toy, problem, or other contrivance designed to amuse by presenting difficulties to be solved by ingenuity or patience. **2.** a puzzling question, matter, or person. **3.** a puzzled or perplexed condition. **—v.t. 4.** to mystify; confuse; baffle. **5.**

to exercise (one's brain, etc.) over some problem. **—v.i. 6.** to ponder over some perplexing problem or matter. **7. puzzle out,** to solve by careful study or effort. **—puz′zled•ly,** *adv.* **—puz′zle•ment,** *n.* **—puz′zler,** *n.*

Pvt., Private.

PW, 1. prisoner of war. **2.** public works.

PWA or **P.W.A.,** Public Works Administration.

pwr, power.

pwt or **pwt.,** pennyweight.

PX, *pl.* **PXs.** post exchange.

Pyg•ma•li•on (pig mā′lē ən, -māl′yən), *n.* **1.** (in classical myth) a sculptor who fell in love with the ivory statue of a woman that he had carved. Compare GALATEA. **2.** (*italics*) a comedy (1912) by George Bernard Shaw.

Pyg•my or **Pigmy** (pig′mē), *n., pl.* **-mies,** *adj.* **—n. 1. a.** a member of any of several small-statured peoples of Africa, esp. the forested regions of central Africa. **b.** a Negrito of SE Asia, or of the Andaman or Philippine islands. **2.** (*l.c.*) a small or dwarfish person. **3.** (*l.c.*) anything very small of its kind. **4.** (*l.c.*) a person of small importance or lacking in some important quality, attribute, etc. **—adj. 5.** (*sometimes l.c.*) of or pertaining to the Pygmies. **6.** (*l.c.*) of very small size, capacity, power, etc. **—pyg′moid,** *adj.* **—pyg′my•ism,** *n.*

py•lon (pī′lon), *n.* **1.** a marking post or tower for guiding aviators. **2.** a relatively tall structure at the side of a gate, bridge, or avenue. **3. a.** a monumental gateway to an ancient Egyptian temple, usu. consisting of two towers with sloping sides flanking a doorway. **b.** either of these towers. **4.** a steel tower used as a support. **5.** a finlike device used to attach auxiliary equipment to an aircraft. [< Greek: gateway]

Pyong•yang (pyung′yäng′, -yang′, pyong′-), *n.* the capital of North Korea, in the SW part. 2,639,448.

pyr•a•lid (pir′ə lid), *n.* **1.** any of numerous slender-bodied moths of the family Pyralidae, with elongated triangular forewings. **—adj. 2.** belonging or pertaining to the family Pyralidae.

pyr•a•mid (pir′ə mid), *n.* **1.** a massive quadrilateral masonry structure having smooth, steeply sloping sides meeting at an apex, as a tomb built in ancient Egypt. **2.** any object or arrangement of objects shaped like a pyramid. **3.** a system or structure resembling a pyramid, as in hierarchical form. **4.** a solid having a polygonal base, and triangular sides that meet in a point. **5.** any crystalline form the planes of which intersect all three of the axes. **6.** the series of transactions involved in pyramiding. **—v.i. 7.** to take the form of a pyramid. **8.** to speculate in securities trading by using paper profits as margin for additional buying and selling. **9.** to increase gradually, as with the completion of each phase. **—v.t. 10.** to arrange in the form of a pyramid. **11.** to cause to increase at a steady and progressive rate. **12.** to employ in speculative pyramiding. **—py•ram′i•dal** (-ram′i dl), *adj.* **—py•ram′i•dal•ly,** *adv.*

pyramids (def. 4)

Pyr′a•mus and This′be (pir′ə məs), *n.pl.* two young lovers of classical legend: mistakenly believing that Thisbe is dead, Pyramus kills himself, and Thisbe, in turn, kills herself upon finding his body.

pyre (pīr), *n.* **1.** a pile or heap of wood or other combustible material. **2.** such a pile for burning a dead body, esp. as part of a funeral rite, as in India.

Pyr•e•nees (pir′ə nēz′), *n.pl.* a mountain range between Spain and France. Highest peak, Pico de Aneto, 11,165 ft. (3400 m). **—Pyr′e•ne′an,** *adj.*

py•re•thrum (pī rē′thrəm, -reth′rəm), *n., pl.* **-thrums, -thrum.** any of several chrysanthemums, having finely divided leaves and showy red, pink, lilac, or white flowers.

py•ret•ic (pī ret′ik), *adj.* of, pertaining to, affected by, or producing fever.

Py•rex (pī′reks), *Trademark.* a brand name for any of a class of heat- and chemical-resistant glass products.

pyr•i•dine (pir′i dēn′, -din), *n.* a colorless, flammable, liquid organic base, used chiefly as a solvent and in organic synthesis. **—py•rid′ic** (pī-rid′ik), *adj.*

pyr•i•dox•ine (pir′i dok′sēn, -sin) also **pyr•i•dox•in** (-sin), *n.* a derivative of pyridine, required for the formation of hemoglobin and the prevention of pellagra; vitamin B_6.

pyr•i•form (pir′ə fôrm′), *adj.* pear-shaped.

py•rim•i•dine (pī rim′i dēn′, pi-), *n.* a heterocyclic compound, $C_4H_4N_2$, that is the basis of several important biochemical substances.

py•rite (pī′rīt) also **pyrites,** *n.* a brass-yellow mineral, iron sulfide, FeS_2. Also called **iron pyrites, iron pyrite.** **—py•rit′ic** (pī rit′ik, pə-), **py•rit′i•cal,** *adj.*

py•ri•tes (pī rī′tēz, pə-, pī′rīts), *n., pl.* **-tes. 1.** any of various metallic sulfides, as of copper or tin. **2.** PYRITE.

pyro-, 1. a combining form meaning "fire," "heat," "high temperature," used in the formation of compound words: *pyrogen; pyromancy.* **2. a.** a combining form used in the names of inorganic acids, the water content of which is intermediate between the ortho and meta forms of an acid: *pyrophosphoric acid.* **b.** a combining form used in the names of the salts of these acids. Also, *esp. before h or a vowel,* **pyr-**.

py·ro·chem·i·cal (pī′rə kem′i kəl), *adj.* pertaining to or producing chemical change at high temperatures. **—py′ro·chem′i·cal·ly,** *adv.*

py·ro·e·lec·tric·i·ty (pī′rō i lek tris′i tē, -ē′lek-), *n.* electrification or electrical polarity produced in certain crystals by temperature changes. **—py′ro·e·lec′tric,** *adj.*

py·ro·ma·ni·a (pī′rə mā′nē ə, -mān′yə), *n.* a compulsion to set things on fire. **—py′ro·ma′ni·ac,** *n.* **—py′ro·ma·ni′a·cal** (-mə nī′ə kəl), *adj.*

py·ro·met·al·lur·gy (pī′rə met′l ûr′jē), *n.* the process or technique of refining ores with heat, as in roasting or smelting. **—py′ro·met′al·lur′gi·cal,** *adj.*

py·ro·sis (pī rō′sis), *n.* HEARTBURN (def. 1).

py·ro·tech·nics (pī′rə tek′niks), *n.* (*used with a sing. or pl. v.*) **1.** the art of making fireworks. **2.** a display of fireworks. **3.** a brilliant or sensational display, as of rhetoric or musicianship. **—py′ro·tech′nic,** *adj.*

py·rox·ene (pī rok′sēn, pə-, pī′rok sēn′), *n.* any of a group of silicate minerals whose silica tetrahedra are arranged in single chains, usu. with ions of magnesium, iron, and calcium in between, and that constitute many igneous rocks. **—py′rox·en′ic** (-sen′ik), *adj.*

pyr·rhic (pir′ik), *adj.* **1.** consisting of two short or unaccented syllables. **2.** composed of or pertaining to pyrrhics. **—n. 3.** a pyrrhic foot.

Pyr′rhic vic′tory, *n.* a victory or goal achieved at too great a cost. [< Greek *Pyrrhikós;* after a remark attributed by Plutarch to PYRRHUS, who declared, after a costly victory over the Romans, that another similar victory would ruin him.]

pyr·rhu·lox·i·a (pir′ə lok′sē·ə), *n.,* *pl.* **-lox·i·as.** a songbird, *Cardinalis (Pyrrhuloxia) sinuatus,* of the southwestern U.S. and Mexico, resembling the cardinal but with a red breast and gray back.

Pyr·rhus (pir′əs), *n.* c318–272 B.C., king of Epirus c300–272.

Py·thag·o·ras (pi thag′ər əs), *n.* c582–c500 B.C., Greek philosopher and mathematician. **—Py·thag·o·re·an** (pi thag′ə rē′ən), *adj., n.*

Pythag′ore′an the′orem, *n.* the theorem that the square of the hypotenuse of a right triangle is equal to the sum of the squares of the other two sides.

py·thon (pī′thon, -thən), *n.* any of several Old World constrictors of the subfamily Pythoninae (family Boidae), often growing to a length of more than 20 ft. (6 m).

pyx·ie (pik′sē), *n.* either of two trailing, shrubby, evergreen plants of the family Diapensiaceae, of E North America, having numerous small, starlike blossoms.

Q

Q, q (kyōō), *n., pl.* **Qs** or **Q's, qs** or **q's. 1.** the 17th letter of the English alphabet, a consonant. **2.** any spoken sound represented by this letter. **3.** something shaped like a Q. **4.** a written or printed representation of the letter *Q* or *q*.

Q, quarterly.

Q, *Symbol.* **1.** the 17th in order or in a series. **2.** *Biochem.* glutamine. **3.** *Physics.* heat.

Qad·da·fi or **Qa·dha·fi** (kə dä′fē), *n.* **Mu·am·mar (Muhammad)** al- or el- (mōō ä′mär), born 1942, Libyan chief of state since 1969.

Q and A or **Q&A** (kyōō′ ən ā′, ənd), *n. Informal.* an exchange of questions and answers.

Qa·tar (kä′tär, kə tär′), *n.* an independent emirate on the Persian Gulf; under British protection until 1971. 665,485; 4416 sq. mi. (11,437 sq. km). *Cap.:* Doha. —**Qa·tar′i,** *adj., n.*

q.b., *Football.* quarterback.

QC or **Q.C., 1.** quality control. **2.** Quartermaster Corps. **3.** Queen's Counsel.

QED, quantum electrodynamics.

Q.E.D., which was to be shown or demonstrated (used esp. in mathematical proofs). [< Latin *quod erat dēmōnstrandum*]

ql., quintal.

QM or **Q.M.,** Quartermaster.

Qq., quartos.

qq., questions.

qq. v., (in formal writing) which (words, things, etc.) see. Compare Q.V.

qr., *pl.* **qrs. 1.** quarter. **2.** quire.

q.s., quarter section.

qt., 1. quantity. **2.** *pl.* **qt., qts.** quart.

q.t. or **Q.T.,** *Informal.* **1.** quiet. —*Idiom.* **2. on the q.t.,** stealthily; secretly: *to meet someone on the q.t.*

Q-Tip (kyōō′tip′), *Trademark.* a brand of cotton-tipped swab used esp. for applying medications or cosmetics.

qto., quarto.

qtr., 1. quarter. **2.** quarterly.

qty., quantity.

qua (kwā, kwä), *adv.* as; as being; in the character or capacity of: *The work of art qua art can be judged by aesthetic criteria only.*

quack¹ (kwak), *n.* **1.** the harsh, throaty cry of a duck or any similar sound. —*v.i.* **2.** to utter a quack.

quack² (kwak), *n.* **1.** a fraudulent pretender to medical skill. **2.** a person who pretends, professionally or publicly, to skill, knowledge, or qualifications he or she does not possess; a charlatan. —*adj.* **3.** being a quack: *a quack psychologist.* **4.** of, pertaining to, or befitting a quack or quackery: *quack methods; quack medicine.* —**quack′ish,** *adj.* —**quack′ish·ness,** *n.*

quack·er·y (kwak′ə rē), *n., pl.* **-er·ies. 1.** the practice or methods of a quack. **2.** an instance of this.

quack′ grass′, *n. Inland North and North Midland U.S.* a couch grass, *Agropyron repens,* a pernicious weed in cultivated fields.

quad¹ (kwod), *n.* a quadrangle, as on a college campus.

quad² (kwod), *n.* a quadruplet.

quad³ (kwod), *adj.* **1.** quadraphonic. —*n.* **2.** quadraphonic sound, or an electronic system for reproducing it.

quadr-, var. of QUADRI- before a vowel: *quadrennial.*

Quad·ra·ges·i·ma (kwod′rə jes′ə mə), *n.* the first Sunday in Lent.

quad·ran·gle (kwod′rang′gəl), *n.* **1.** a plane figure having four angles and four sides, as a square. **2.** a square or quadrangular space or court that is surrounded by a building or buildings, as on a college campus. **3.** the building or buildings around such a space or court. **4.** the area shown on a topographic map sheet of a standard size. —**quad·ran′gu·lar** (-gyə lər), *adj.*

quad·rant (kwod′rənt), *n.* **1.** a quarter of a circle; an arc of 90°. **2.** the area included between such an arc and two radii drawn one to each extremity. **3.** something shaped like a quarter of a circle, as a part of a machine. **4.** one of the four parts into which a plane, as the face of a heavenly body, is divided by two perpendicular lines: *the first quadrant of the moon.* **5.** an instrument, usu. containing a graduated arc of 90°, used in astronomy, navigation, etc., for measuring altitudes. —**quad·ran′tal** (-dran′tl), *adj.*

quad·ra·phon·ic or **quad·ri·phon·ic** (kwod′rə fon′ik), *adj.* of or pertaining to the recording, reproduction, or transmission of sound by means of four channels instead of two; four-channel. —**quad′ra·phon′ics, qua·draph·o·ny** (kwo draf′ə nē), *n.*

quad·rat (kwod′rət), *n.* **1.** a piece of type metal of less height than the lettered types, serving to cause a blank in printed matter, used for spacing. **2.** a square or rectangular plot of land marked off for the study of plants and animals.

quad·rate (*adj., n.* kwod′rit, -rāt; *v.* -rāt), *adj., n., v.,* **-rat·ed, -rat·ing.** —*adj.* **1.** square or rectangular. —*n.* **2.** a square. **3.** something square

or rectangular. —*v.t.* **4.** to cause to conform or harmonize; adapt. —*v.i.* **5.** to agree; conform.

quad·rat·ic (kwo drat′ik), *adj.* **1.** *Algebra.* involving the square and no higher power of the unknown quantity; of the second degree. —*n.* **2.** a quadratic polynomial or equation. —**quad·rat′i·cal·ly,** *adv.*

quadrat′ic equa′tion, *n.* an equation containing a single variable of degree 2. Its general form is $ax^2 + bx + c = 0$, where x is the variable and a, b, and c are constants ($a \neq 0$).

quad·rat·ics (kwo drat′iks), *n.* (*used with a sing. v.*) the branch of algebra that deals with quadratic equations.

quad·ren·ni·al (kwo dren′ē əl), *adj.* **1.** occurring every four years: *a quadrennial festival.* **2.** of or lasting for four years: *a quadrennial period.* —*n.* **3.** an event occurring every four years. **4.** QUADRENNIUM. —**quad·ren′ni·al·ly,** *adv.*

quad·ren·ni·um (kwo dren′ē əm), *n., pl.* **quad·ren·ni·ums, quad·ren·ni·a** (kwo dren′ē ə). a period of four years.

quadri-, a combining form meaning "four": *quadrilateral.* Also, **qua·dru-;** *esp. before a vowel,* **quadr-.**

quad·ri·ceps (kwod′rə seps′), *n., pl.* **-ceps·es** (-sep′siz), **-ceps.** a large, four-part muscle at the front of the thigh that extends the leg or bends it at the hip joint. —**quad′ri·cip′i·tal** (-sip′i tl), *adj.*

quad·ri·lat·er·al (kwod′rə lat′ər əl), *adj.* **1.** having four sides. —*n.* **2. a.** a polygon with four sides. **b.** a figure formed by four straight lines that have six points of intersection. —**quad′ri·lat′er·al·ly,** *adv.*

quad·rille¹ (kwo dril′, kwə-, kə-), *n.* a square dance for four couples, consisting of five parts or movements, each complete in itself.

quad·rille² (kwo dril′, kwə-, kə-), *adj.* ruled in squares, as graph paper.

quad·ril·lion (kwo dril′yən), *n., pl.* **-lions,** (*as after a numeral*) **-lion,** *adj.* —*n.* **1.** a cardinal number represented in the U.S. by 1 followed by 15 zeros, and in Great Britain by 1 followed by 24 zeros. —*adj.* **2.** amounting to one quadrillion in number. —**quad·ril′lionth,** *n., adj.*

quad·ri·ple·gi·a (kwod′rə plē′jē ə, -jə), *n.* paralysis of all four limbs or of the entire body below the neck. —**quad′ri·ple′gic,** *n., adj.*

quad·riv·i·um (kwo driv′ē əm), *n., pl.* **quad·riv·i·a** (kwo driv′ē ə). (during the Middle Ages) the more advanced division of the seven liberal arts, comprising arithmetic, geometry, astronomy, and music. Compare TRIVIUM.

quadru-, var. of QUADRI-.

quad·ru·ped (kwod′rŏŏ ped′), *adj.* **1.** four-footed. —*n.* **2.** an animal, esp. a mammal, that has four feet. —**quad·ru·pe·dal** (kwo drŏŏ′pi dl, kwod′rŏŏ ped′l), *adj.* —**quad′ru·ped′ism,** *n.*

quad·ru·ple (kwo drŏŏ′pəl, -drup′əl, kwod′rŏŏ pəl), *adj., n., v.,* **-pled, -pling.** —*adj.* **1.** fourfold; consisting of four parts: *a quadruple alliance.* **2.** four times as great. **3.** *Music.* having four beats to a measure. —*n.* **4.** a number, amount, etc., four times as great as another. —*v.t., v.i.* **5.** to make or become four times as great. —**quad·ru′ple·ness,** *n.* —**quad·ru′ply,** *adv.*

quad·ru·plet (kwo drup′lit, -drŏŏ′plit, kwod′rŏŏ plit), *n.* **1.** any group or combination of four. **2. quadruplets,** four children or offspring born of one pregnancy. **3.** one of four such children or offspring. **4.** *Music.* a group of four notes of equal value performed in the time normally taken for three.

quads (kwodz), *n.pl. Informal.* quadriceps muscles.

quaff (kwof, kwaf, kwôf), *v.i., v.t.* **1.** to drink copiously and with hearty enjoyment. —*n.* **2.** an act or instance of quaffing. **3.** a beverage quaffed. —**quaff′er,** *n.*

quag·mire (kwag′mīʳ′, kwog′-), *n.* **1.** an area of miry or boggy ground whose surface yields under the tread; a bog. **2.** a situation from which extrication is very difficult.

qua·hog or **qua·haug** (kwô′hôg, -hog, kwō′-, kō′-), *n.* a thick-shelled, edible clam of Atlantic North American coasts.

quail¹ (kwāl), *n., pl.* **quails,** (*esp. collectively*) **quail. 1.** any of various small, plump New World gallinaceous birds of the subfamily Odontophorinae, of the pheasant family, as the bobwhite. **2.** any of various similar Old World gallinaceous birds of the genus *Coturnix,* esp. *C. coturnix,* of Eurasia.

quail² (kwāl), *v.i.* to lose heart or courage in difficulty or danger; shrink with fear.

quaint (kwānt), *adj.,* **-er, -est. 1.** having an old-fashioned charm; oddly picturesque: *a quaint old house.* **2.** peculiar or unusual in an interesting or amusing way: *a quaint sense of humor.* **3.** skillfully or cleverly made. —**quaint′ly,** *adv.* —**quaint′ness,** *n.*

quake (kwāk), *v.,* **quaked, quak·ing,** *n.* —*v.i.* **1.** to shudder or quiver, as from cold or fear. **2.** to shake or tremble, as from shock or instability: *The earth quaked.* —*n.* **3.** an earthquake. **4.** an act or instance of quaking. —**quak′ing·ly,** *adv.*

quake·proof (kwāk′prŏŏf′), *adj.* **1.** designed or built to withstand an earthquake. —*v.t.* **2.** to make quakeproof.

Quak·er (kwā′kər), *n.* a member of the Society of Friends, a Christian denomination founded by George Fox in 1650; Friend. —**Quak′er•ish**, *adj.* —**Quak′er•ism**, *n.* —**Quak′er•ly**, *adj., adv.*

quak•y (kwā′kē), *adj.*, **-i•er, -i•est.** tending to quake; shaky or tremulous. —**quak′i•ly**, *adv.* —**quak′i•ness**, *n.*

qual•i•fi•ca•tion (kwol′ə fi kā′shən), *n.* **1.** a quality, accomplishment, etc., that fits a person for some function, office, or the like. **2.** a circumstance or condition required by law or custom for exercising a right, holding an office, etc. **3.** the act of qualifying or the state of being qualified. **4.** modification, limitation, or restriction: *to agree without qualification.*

qual•i•fied (kwol′ə fīd′), *adj.* **1.** having the qualities, accomplishments, etc., that fit one for some function, office, etc.; competent. **2.** having met the conditions required by law or custom for exercising a right, holding an office, etc. **3.** modified, limited, or restricted in some way: *qualified approval.* —**qual′i•fied′ly**, *adv.* —**qual′i•fied′ness**, *n.*

qual•i•fi•er (kwol′ə fī′ər), *n.* **1.** a person or thing that qualifies. **2.** a word, as an adverb or adjective, that qualifies or limits the meaning of another; modifier.

qual•i•fy (kwol′ə fī′), *v.*, **-fied, -fy•ing.** —*v.t.* **1.** to provide with proper or necessary skills, knowledge, credentials, etc.: *The training program qualified her for the job.* **2.** to make less strong, general, or positive; modify or limit: *to qualify an endorsement.* **3.** to make less violent, severe, or unpleasant; moderate; mitigate. **4.** to attribute some quality to; characterize, call, or name: *I can't qualify his approach as either good or bad.* **5.** *Gram.* MODIFY (def. 2). **6.** to modify or alter the flavor or strength of. **7.** to certify as legally competent or entitled. —*v.i.* **8.** to be fitted or competent for something. **9.** to get authority, license, power, etc., as by fulfilling required conditions. **10.** to demonstrate the required ability in an initial or preliminary contest. **11.** to perform the actions necessary to acquire legal authority: *to qualify as executor.* —**qual′i•fi•a•ble**, *adj.* —**qual′i•fi•ca•to•ry** (-fi kə tôr′ē, -tōr′ē), *adj.* —**qual′i•fy′ing•ly**, *adv.*

qual•i•ta•tive (kwol′i tā′tiv), *adj.* pertaining to or concerned with quality or qualities. —**qual′i•ta•tive•ly**, *adv.*

qual′itative anal′ysis, *n.* the analysis of a substance in order to ascertain the identity of its chemical constituents.

qual•i•ty (kwol′i tē), *n.*, *pl.* **-ties**, *adj.* —*n.* **1.** an essential characteristic, property, or attribute: *the qualities found in great writing.* **2.** character or nature, as belonging to or distinguishing a thing: *the quality of a color.* **3.** character with respect to grade of excellence or fineness: *materials of poor quality.* **4.** superiority; excellence: *a reputation for quality.* **5.** a personality or character trait: *Generosity is one of her many good qualities.* **6.** an accomplishment or attainment. **7.** high social position: *a man of quality.* **8.** TIMBRE (def. 1). **9.** the tonal color, or timbre, that characterizes a particular vowel sound. **10.** *Logic.* the character of a proposition as affirmative or negative. **11.** social status or position. **12.** a person or persons of high social position. —*adj.* **13.** of or having superior quality: *quality paper.* **14.** producing or providing products or services of high quality: *a quality publisher.*

qual′ity control′, *n.* a system for verifying and maintaining a desired level of quality in a product or process, as by planning, continued inspection, and corrective action as required.

qual•i•ty-of-life (kwol′i tē əv līf′), *adj.* affecting the quality of urban life: *such quality-of-life crimes as fare-beating and graffiti writing.*

qual′ity time′, *n.* time devoted exclusively to nurturing a cherished person or activity.

qualm (kwäm, kwôm), *n.* **1.** an uneasy feeling or pang of conscience as to conduct; compunction: *He has no qualms about lying.* **2.** a sudden feeling of apprehensive uneasiness; misgiving. **3.** a sudden sensation or onset of faintness or illness, esp. of nausea.

quan•da•ry (kwon′də rē, -drē), *n.*, *pl.* **-ries.** a state of perplexity or uncertainty, esp. as to what to do; dilemma.

quan•ta (kwon′tə), *n.* *pl.* of QUANTUM.

quan•ti•fi•er (kwon′tə fī′ər), *n.* **1.** *Logic.* an expression, as "all" or "some," that indicates the quantity of a proposition. **2.** a word or phrase, usu. modifying a noun, that indicates quantity, as *much, few,* or *a lot of.*

quan•ti•fy (kwon′tə fī′), *v.t.*, **-fied, -fy•ing. 1.** to determine, indicate, or express the quantity of. **2.** *Logic.* to make explicit the quantity of (a proposition). **3.** to give quantity to (something regarded as having only quality). —**quan′ti•fi•a•ble**, *adj.* —**quan′ti•fi•a•bly**, *adv.* —**quan′ti•fi•ca′tion**, *n.*

quan•ti•ta•tive (kwon′ti tā′tiv), *adj.* **1.** being or capable of being measured by quantity. **2.** pertaining to or based on the relative duration of syllables: *Classical prosody was quantitative.* —**quan′ti•ta′tive•ly**, *adv.* —**quan′ti•ta′tive•ness**, *n.*

quan′titative anal′ysis, *n.* **1.** the analysis of a substance to determine the amounts and proportions of its chemical constituents. **2.** *Business.* the use of esp. computerized mathematical analysis to support decision making, make business forecasts or investment recommendations, etc.

quan′titative inher′itance, *n.* the process in which the additive action of a group of genes results in a trait, as height or shape, showing continuous variability.

quan•ti•ty (kwon′ti tē), *n.*, *pl.* **-ties. 1.** an indefinite or aggregate amount: *a quantity of sugar.* **2.** an exact or specified amount or measure: *in the quantities called for.* **3.** a considerable or great amount: *to*

buy food in quantity. **4. a.** the property of magnitude involving comparability with other magnitudes. **b.** something having magnitude, or size, extent, amount, or the like. **c.** magnitude, size, volume, area, or length. **5.** the amount, degree, etc., in terms of which another can be greater or lesser. **6.** the character of a proposition as singular, universal, or particular. **7.** the relative duration of a speech sound, esp. a vowel, or a syllable; length. **8.** any person, thing, or factor taken into consideration: *The nominee was an unknown quantity.*

quan•tize (kwon′tīz), *v.t.*, **-tized, -tiz•ing. 1.** to restrict (a variable quantity) to discrete values rather than to a continuous set of values. **2.** to use quantum mechanics to calculate or express (the behavior of a physical system). —**quan′ti•za′tion**, *n.*

quan•tum (kwon′təm), *n.*, *pl.* **-ta** (-tə), *adj.* —*n.* **1.** quantity or amount: *the least quantum of evidence.* **2.** share; portion. **3.** a large quantity; bulk. **4. a.** the smallest excitation of a quantized wave or field, as a photon. **b.** the fundamental unit of a quantized physical property, and the smallest amount by which its magnitude can change. —*adj.* **5.** sudden and significant: *a quantum increase in productivity.*

quan′tum mechan′ics, *n.* (*used with a sing. v.*) a quantum theory of the mechanics of atoms, molecules, and other physical systems that are subject to the uncertainty principle. —**quan′tum-me•chan′i•cal**, *adj.*

quan′tum the′ory, *n.* **1.** a theory for predicting the discrete energy states of atoms and of radiation. **2.** any theory that describes a force or field using the methods of quantum mechanics: *a quantum theory of gravitation.*

quar•an•tine (kwôr′ən tēn′, kwor′-, kwôr′ən tēn′, kwor′-), *n.*, *v.*, **-tined, -tin•ing.** —*n.* **1.** a strict isolation imposed to prevent the spread of disease. **2.** a period, orig. 40 days, of detention or isolation imposed upon ships, people, animals, or plants on arrival at a port or place, when suspected of carrying a contagious disease. **3.** a system of measures maintained at ports, frontiers, etc., for preventing the spread of disease. **4.** a place or station at which such measures are carried out, as a place where ships are detained. **5.** the detention or isolation enforced. **6.** the place, as a hospital, where people are detained. **7.** social, political, or economic isolation imposed as a punishment. **8.** a period of 40 days. —*v.t.* **9.** to put in or subject to quarantine. **10.** to exclude, detain, or isolate for political or social reasons. —**quar′an•tin′a•ble**, *adj.* —**quar′an•tin′er**, *n.*

quark (kwôrk, kwärk), *n.* any of a group of subatomic particles having a fractional electric charge and thought to constitute, together with their antiparticles, all baryons and mesons. [coined in 1963 by U.S. physicist Murray Gell-Mann who associated it with a word in James Joyce's *Finnegans Wake*]

quar•rel¹ (kwôr′əl, kwor′-), *n.* **1.** an angry dispute or altercation, often marked by a temporary or permanent break in friendly relations. **2.** a cause of dispute, complaint, or hostile feeling: *She has no quarrel with her present salary.* —*v.i.* **3.** to disagree angrily; squabble; wrangle. **4.** to end a friendship as a result of a disagreement; fall out. **5.** to make a complaint; find fault. —**quar′rel•er**, *n.* —**quar′rel•ing•ly**, *adv.*

quar•rel² (kwôr′əl, kwor′-), *n.* **1.** a square-headed bolt or arrow, formerly used with a crossbow. **2.** a small square or diamond-shaped pane of glass, as used in latticed windows.

quar•rel•some (kwôr′əl səm, kwor′-), *adj.* inclined to quarrel; argumentative; contentious. —**quar′rel•some•ly**, *adv.* —**quar′rel•some•ness**, *n.*

quar•ry¹ (kwôr′ē, kwor′ē), *n.*, *pl.* **-ries**, *v.*, **-ried, -ry•ing.** —*n.* **1.** an excavation or pit, usu. open to the air, from which building stone, slate, or the like, is obtained by cutting, blasting, etc. **2.** an abundant source or supply. —*v.t.* **3.** to obtain from or as if from a quarry. **4.** to make a quarry in.

quar•ry² (kwôr′ē, kwor′ē), *n.*, *pl.* **-ries. 1.** an animal or bird hunted or pursued. **2.** game, esp. game hunted with hounds or hawks. **3.** any object of search, pursuit, or attack.

quar•ry³ (kwôr′ē, kwor′ē), *n.*, *pl.* **-ries.** a square stone or tile.

quart (kwôrt), *n.* **1.** a unit of liquid measure of capacity, equal to one fourth of a gallon, or 57.749 cubic inches (0.946 liter) in the U.S. and 69.355 cubic inches (1.136 liters) in Great Britain. **2.** a unit of dry measure of capacity, equal to one eighth of a peck, or 67.201 cubic inches (1.101 liters). **3.** a container holding or capable of holding a quart. *Abbr.:* qt.

quar•ter (kwôr′tər), *n.* **1.** one of the four equal or equivalent parts into which anything is or may be divided. **2.** a fourth part, esp. of one (¼). **3.** one fourth of a U.S. or Canadian dollar, equivalent to 25 cents. **4.** a coin of this value. **5.** one fourth of an hour; 15 minutes. **6.** one fourth of a calendar or fiscal year. **7.** a term of instruction at a school or college lasting about 10 to 12 weeks. **8.** any of the four equal periods of play in certain games, as football and basketball. Compare HALF (def. 3). **9.** one fourth of a pound. **10.** one fourth of a mile; 2 furlongs. **11.** one fourth of a yard; 9 inches. **12.** one fourth of a hundredweight: in the U.S. equaling 25 lbs. and in Britain 28 lbs. **13. a.** the region of any of the four principal points of the compass or divisions of the horizon. **b.** such a point or division. **c.** any point or direction of the compass. **d.** the fourth part of the distance between any two adjacent points of the 32 marked on a compass. **14.** a region, district, or place. **15.** a district of a city or town, esp. one largely occupied by a particular group: *the Turkish quarter.* **16.** Usu., **quarters. a.** housing accommodations, as a place of residence; lodgings. **b.** the buildings, rooms, etc., occupied by military personnel or their families. **17.** Often, **quarters.** an unspecified person or group serving as a source: *secret information from a high quarter.* **18.** mercy or indulgence, esp. as shown in sparing the life of a vanquished enemy: *to give quarter.* **19.** the part of a boot or shoe on each side of the foot, from the middle of the back to the vamp. **20. a.** the after part of a ship's side, usu. from about the aftermost mast to the stern. **b.** the general horizontal direction 45° from the stern of a ship on either side. **c.** one of the stations to which crew members are called for battle, emergencies, or drills. **d.** the part of a yard between the slings and the yardarm. **21.** any of the four equal areas into which an escutcheon can be divided. —*v.t.* **22.** to divide into four equal or equivalent parts. **23.** to divide into parts fewer or more than four. **24.** to cut the body of (a person) into quarters, esp. after executing for treason. **25.** to furnish with lodging. **26.** to traverse (the ground) from left to right and right to left while advancing, as dogs in search of game. **27. a.** to divide (an escutcheon) into four or more parts. **b.** to display (a coat of arms) with one's own on an escutcheon. —*v.i.* **28.** to take up or be in quarters; lodge. **29.** to range to and fro, as dogs in search of game. **30.** to sail so as to have the wind or sea on the quarter. —*adj.* **31.** being one of four equal or approximately equal parts. **32.** being equal to only about one fourth of the full measure. —**quar′ter·er,** *n.*

quar·ter·back (kwôr′tər bak′), *n.* **1.** a back in football who usu. lines up immediately behind the center and directs the offense of the team. **2.** the position played by this back. —*v.t.* **3.** to direct the offense of (a team). **4.** to lead; direct. —*v.i.* **5.** to play the position of quarterback.

quar·ter·deck (kwôr′tər dek′), *n.* the part of the weather deck of a vessel that runs from the midship area to the poop or stern.

quar·ter·fi·nal (kwôr′tər fīn′l), *adj.* **1.** of or pertaining to the contest or round preceding the semifinal one in a tournament. —*n.* **2.** a quarterfinal contest or round. —**quar′ter·fi′nal·ist,** *n.*

quar′ter horse′, *n.* one of an American breed of strong, agile horses capable of great speed over short distances, often used in herding livestock.

quar·ter-hour (kwôr′tər ou′r′, -ou′ər), *n.* **1.** a period of 15 minutes. **2.** a point 15 minutes after or before the hour.

quar·ter·ing (kwôr′tər ing), *n.* **1.** the act of a person or thing that quarters. **2.** the assignment of quarters or lodgings. —*adj.* **3.** lying at right angles.

quar·ter·ly (kwôr′tər lē), *adj., n., pl.* **-lies,** *adv.* —*adj.* **1.** occurring, done, paid, issued, etc., at the end of every quarter of a year: *a quarterly report.* **2.** pertaining to or consisting of a quarter. —*n.* **3.** a periodical issued every three months. —*adv.* **4.** once each quarter of a year: *to pay interest quarterly.* **5.** with division into four quarters.

quar·ter·mas·ter (kwôr′tər mas′tər, -mä′stər), *n.* **1.** a military officer charged with providing quarters, clothing, food, etc., for a body of troops. **2.** a petty officer having charge of a ship's helm and its navigating apparatus.

quar′ter note′, *n.* a musical note equal in time value to one quarter of a whole note.

quar′ter rest′, *n.* a musical rest equal in time value to a quarter note.

quar′ter sec′tion, *n.* (in surveying) a square tract of land, half a mile on each side, containing ¼ sq. mi. or 160 acres.

quar′ter tone′, *n.* a musical interval equal to half a semitone.

quar·tet (kwôr tet′), *n.* **1.** an organized group of four singers or players. **2.** a musical composition for four voices or instruments. **3.** any group of four persons or things. Also, *esp. Brit.,* **quar·tette′.**

quar·to (kwôr′tō), *n., pl.* **-tos,** *adj.* —*n.* **1.** a book size of about 9½ × 12 in. (24 × 30 cm), determined by folding printed sheets twice to form four leaves or eight pages. *Symbol:* 4to, 4°. **2.** a book of this size. —*adj.* **3.** bound in quarto.

quartz (kwôrts), *n.* the commonest mineral, silicon dioxide, SiO_2, occurring in crystals and grains: the chief component of sand. —**quartz·ose** (kwôrt′sōs), *adj.*

quartz′ heat′er, *n.* a small infrared radiant heater having heating elements contained within quartz-glass rods.

quartz·ite (kwôrt′sīt), *n.* a granular metamorphic rock consisting essentially of quartz in interlocking grains. —**quartz·it′ic** (-sit′ik), *adj.*

quartz′ move′ment, *n.* an extremely accurate electronic movement utilizing the natural frequency of vibrations of a quartz crystal to regulate the operation of a timepiece (**quartz′ clock′** or **quartz′ watch′**).

qua·sar (kwā′zär, -zər, -sär, -sər), *n.* any of numerous starlike celestial objects that may be the most distant and brightest objects in the universe. Also called **quasi-stellar object.**

quash (kwosh), *v.t.* **1.** to put down or suppress completely; quell; subdue: *to quash a rebellion.* **2.** to make void, annul, or set aside (a law, indictment, decision, etc.).

qua·si (kwā′zī, -sī, kwä′sē, -zē), *adj.* resembling; seeming; virtual: *a quasi member.*

quasi-, a combining form meaning "resembling," "having some, but not all of the features of": *quasi-definition; quasi-scientific.*

quat·er·cen·ten·ar·y (kwot′ər sen ten′ə rē, -sen′tn er′ē; *esp. Brit.* kwot′ər sen tē′nə rē), *n., pl.* **-ar·ies.** **1.** a 400th anniversary or its celebration. —*adj.* **2.** pertaining to or marking a period of 400 years.

quat·er·cen·ten·ni·al (kwot′ər sen ten′ē əl), *adj., n.* QUATERCENTENARY.

quat·er·nar·y (kwot′ər ner′ē, kwə tûr′nə rē), *adj., n., pl.* **-nar·ies.** —*adj.* **1.** consisting of four. **2.** arranged in fours. **3.** (*cap.*) of or pertaining to the present period of earth history forming the latter part of the Cenozoic Era, originating about two million years ago, and including the

Recent and Pleistocene Epochs. —*n.* **4.** a group of four. **5.** the number four. **6.** (*cap.*) the Quaternary Period or System.

quat·rain (kwo′trān), *n.* a stanza or poem of four lines, usu. with alternate rhymes.

quat·re·foil (kat′ər foil′, ka′trə-), *n.* **1.** a leaf composed of four leaflets. **2.** an architectural ornament composed of four lobes, separated by cusps, radiating from a common center.

quatrefoils (def. 2)

qua·ver (kwā′vər), *v.i.* **1.** to shake tremulously; quiver or tremble. **2.** to sound, speak, or sing tremulously. **3.** to perform trills in music. —*v.t.* **4.** to utter, say, or sing with a quavering voice. —*n.* **5.** a quavering or trembling, esp. in the voice. **6.** a quavering tone or utterance. **7.** EIGHTH NOTE. —**qua′ver·er,** *n.* —**qua′ver·ing·ly,** *adv.* —**qua′ver·y,** *adj.*

quay (kē, kā, kwā), *n.* a landing place, esp. one of solid masonry, constructed along the edge of a body of water; wharf.

Quayle (kwāl), *n.* James Danforth (*Dan*), born 1947, vice president of the U.S. 1989–93.

quea·sy (kwē′zē), *adj.,* **-si·er, -si·est. 1.** inclined to or feeling nausea. **2.** causing nausea; nauseating. **3.** uneasy; uncomfortable. **4.** squeamish; fastidious. —**quea′si·ly,** *adv.* —**quea′si·ness,** *n.*

Que·bec (kwi bek′, ki-), *n.* **1.** a province in E Canada. 6,532,461; 594,860 sq. mi. (1,540,685 sq. km). **2.** the capital of this province, on the St. Lawrence. 164,580. French, **Qué·bec′** (kā-). —**Que·bec′er, Que·beck′er,** *n.*

que·bra·cho (kā brä′chō), *n., pl.* **-chos. 1.** any of several tropical American trees, the wood and bark of which are used in tanning and dyeing. **2.** a tree of the dogbane family, yielding a medicinal bark. **3.** the wood or bark of any of these trees.

Quech·ua (kech′wä, -wə), *n., pl.* **-uas,** (*esp. collectively*) **-ua** for 3. **1.** a group of closely related American Indian languages spoken in Andean South America, from S Colombia and Ecuador to NE Argentina. **2.** the form of Quechua spoken in Cuzco and its environs that served as the administrative language of the Inca state. **3.** an American Indian speaker of Quechua. —**Quech′uan,** *adj., n.*

queen (kwēn), *n.* **1.** a female sovereign or monarch. **2.** the wife or consort of a king. **3.** a woman, or something personified as a woman, preeminent in some respect: *a beauty queen; Athens, the queen of the Aegean.* **4.** a playing card bearing a picture of a queen. **5.** the most powerful chess piece of either color, able to be moved across any number of empty squares in any direction. **6.** a fertile female ant, bee, termite, or wasp. —*v.i.* **7.** to reign as queen. **8.** to behave in an imperious or pretentious manner (usu. fol. by *it*). **9.** (of a pawn in chess) to become promoted to a queen. —*v.t.* **10.** to make a queen of; crown. —**queen′dom,** *n.* —**queen′hood,** *n.* —**queen′like′,** *adj.*

Queen′ Anne′s′ lace′, *n.* a plant, *Daucus carota,* the wild form of the carrot, having broad umbels of white flowers. Also called **wild carrot.**

Queen′ Anne′s′ War′, *n.* the war (1702–13) in which England and its American colonies opposed France and its Indian allies. It constituted the American phase of the War of the Spanish Succession.

queen′ bee′, *n.* **1.** a fertile female bee. **2.** a woman who is in a favored or preeminent position.

queen′-cup′, *n.* a North American plant, *Clintonia uniflora,* of the lily family, having solitary white flowers and blue berries.

queen′ moth′er, *n.* a queen dowager who is mother of a reigning sovereign.

Queen′ of Heav′en, *n.* **1.** a designation of the Virgin Mary. **2.** (*l.c.*) an ancient Semitic goddess, variously identified with other ancient goddesses, as Isis and Ashtoreth. **3.** an epithet of Ishtar.

Queen′ of She′ba, *n.* SHEBA (def. 1).

queen′ of the prai′rie or **queen′-of-the-prai′rie,** *n.* a tall meadow plant, *Filipendula rubra,* of the rose family.

queen′ post′, *n.* either of a pair of timbers or posts extending vertically upward from the tie beam of a roof truss or the like, one on each side of the center.

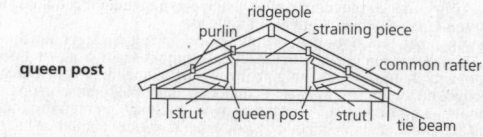

queen post

ridgepole
purlin — straining piece
common rafter
strut   queen post   strut
tie beam

queen's′ Eng′lish, *n.* See KING'S ENGLISH.
queen′-size′ or **queen′-sized′,** *adj.* **1.** (of a bed) larger than a double bed, but smaller than king-size, usu. 60 in. (152 cm) wide and 80 in. (203 cm) long. **2.** of or for a queen-size bed. **3.** of a size larger than average: *queen-size clothing.*
queer (kwēr), *adj.* **1.** strange or odd from a conventional viewpoint; unusually different; singular; eccentric. **2.** of a questionable nature or character; suspicious; shady: *something queer in the wording of the document.* **3.** not physically right or well; giddy or faint. **4.** mentally unbalanced or deranged. **5.** *Slang.* bad, worthless, or counterfeit. —*v.t.* **6.** to spoil; ruin. **7.** to put (a person) in a hopeless or disadvantageous situation as to success, favor, etc. —**queer′ly,** *adv.* —**queer′ness,** *n.*
quell (kwel), *v.t.* **1.** to suppress; subdue; crush: *to quell an uprising.* **2.** to quiet; allay: *to quell a child's fear of thunder.* —**quell′a•ble,** *adj.* —**quell′er,** *n.*
quench (kwench), *v.t.* **1.** to satisfy; allay (thirst, desires, etc.). **2.** to put out; extinguish (fire, flames, etc.). **3.** to cool suddenly by plunging into a liquid, as in tempering steel by immersion in water. **4.** to overcome; quell. —**quench′a•ble,** *adj.* —**quench′a•ble•ness,** *n.* —**quench′er,** *n.* —**quench′less,** *adj.*
que•nelle (kə nel′), *n.* a poached dumpling of finely chopped fish or meat, usu. served with a sauce.
quer•u•lous (kwer′ə ləs, kwer′yə-), *adj.* **1.** full of complaints; complaining; carping. **2.** characterized by or uttered in complaint; peevish: *querulous demands.* —**quer′u•lous•ly,** *adv.* —**quer′u•lous•ness,** *n.*
que•ry (kwēr′ē, kwer′ē), *n., pl.* **-ries,** *v.,* **-ried, -ry•ing.** —*n.* **1.** a question; an inquiry. **2.** mental reservation; doubt. **3.** QUESTION MARK (def. 1). —*v.t.* **4.** to put as a question. **5.** to question as doubtful or obscure: *to query a statement.* **6.** to mark with a question mark. **7.** to ask questions of. —**que′ri•er,** *n.* —**que′ry•ing•ly,** *adv.*
quest (kwest), *n.* **1.** a search or pursuit made in order to find or obtain something. **2.** an adventurous expedition, as by knights in medieval romances. **3.** those engaged in such an expedition. —*v.i.* **4.** to search; seek: *to quest after hidden treasure.* **5.** to go on a quest. —*v.t.* **6.** to search or seek for; pursue. —**quest′er,** *n.* —**quest′ing•ly,** *adv.*
ques•tion (kwes′chən), *n.* **1.** a sentence in an interrogative form addressed to someone in order to get information in reply. **2.** a problem for discussion or under discussion. **3.** a matter of some uncertainty or difficulty; problem: *It was mainly a question of time.* **4.** a subject of dispute or controversy. **5.** a proposal to be debated or voted on, as in a meeting or a deliberative assembly. **6.** the procedure of putting a proposal to vote. **7.** *Law.* a controversy that is submitted to a judicial tribunal for decision. **8.** the act of asking or inquiring; interrogation; query. **9.** inquiry into or discussion of some problem. —*v.t.* **10.** to ask questions of; interrogate. **11.** to ask; inquire. **12.** to make a question of; doubt: *They questioned our sincerity.* —*v.i.* **13.** to ask a question or questions. —***Idiom.*** **14. beyond (all) question,** beyond dispute; without doubt. **15. call in** or **into question, a.** to dispute; challenge. **b.** to cast doubt upon; question. **16. in question, a.** under consideration. **b.** in dispute. **17. out of the question,** not to be considered; unthinkable; impossible. **18. the $64,000 question,** the most important and difficult question. [so called from a 1950s television quiz show in which the top prize was $64,000] —**ques′tion•er,** *n.*
ques•tion•a•ble (kwes′chə nə bəl), *adj.* **1.** of doubtful propriety, honesty, morality, or propriety: *questionable activities.* **2.** open to question; uncertain: *questionable accuracy.* **3.** open to question as to being of the nature or value suggested: *a questionable privilege.* —**ques′tion•a•ble•ness, ques′tion•a•bil′i•ty,** *n.* —**ques′tion•a•bly,** *adv.*
ques′tion mark′, *n.* **1.** Also called **interrogation point.** a mark indicating a question: usu., as in English, the mark (?) placed after a question. **2.** something unanswered or unknown.
ques•tion•naire (kwes′chə nâr′), *n.* a list of questions, usu. printed, submitted for replies that can be analyzed for usable information.
quet•zal (ket säl′) also **que•zal** (ke-), *n., pl.* **-zals, -za•les** (-sä′lās). **1.** any of several large New World trogons of the genus *Pharomachrus,* esp. *P. mocinno,* of S Mexico and Central America, with golden-green and scarlet plumage and, in the male, greatly elongated tail coverts. **2.** the basic monetary unit of Guatemala.
Quet•zal•co•a•tl (ket säl′kō ät′l), *n.* an Aztec god, associated esp. with the arts of civilization and worshiped in a number of guises.
queue (kyōō), *n., v.,* **queued, queu•ing.** —*n.* **1.** a braid of hair worn hanging down behind. **2.** a file or line, esp. of people waiting their turn. **3.** a sequence of items waiting in order for electronic action in a computer system. —*v.i.* **4.** to form in a line while waiting (often fol. by *up*). —*v.t.* **5.** to arrange or organize into a queue. —**queu′er,** *n.*
quib•ble (kwib′əl), *n., v.,* **-bled, -bling.** —*n.* **1.** a petty or carping criticism. **2.** an instance of the use of ambiguous, deceptive, or irrelevant language or arguments to evade a point at issue. —*v.i.* **3.** to argue or complain about trivial matters; bicker, carp, or cavil. **4.** to use evasive or ambiguous language; equivocate. —**quib′bler,** *n.*
quiche (kēsh), *n.* a pie containing unsweetened custard baked with other ingredients, as cheese, meat, or onions.
quick (kwik), *adj.* **1.** done, proceeding, or occurring with promptness or rapidity: *a quick response.* **2.** finished or completed in a short time: *a quick shower.* **3.** moving or able to move with speed: *a quick fox.* **4.** easily provoked or excited; hasty: *a quick temper.* **5.** keenly responsive; lively; acute: *a quick wit.* **6.** prompt or swift in doing, perceiving, or understanding: *quick to respond; a quick eye; a quick student.* **7.** (of a bend or curve) sharp: *a quick bend in the road.* **8.** brisk, as fire, flames, or heat. —*n.* **9.** living persons. **10.** the tender, sensitive flesh of the living body, esp. that under the nails. **11.** the vital or most important part. —*adv.* **12.** quickly. —**quick′ness,** *n.* —**Usage.** The difference between the adverbial forms QUICK and QUICKLY is frequently stylistic. QUICK is more often used in short spoken sentences, esp. imperative ones: *Come quick! The roof is leaking.* QUICKLY is the usual form in writing, both in the preverb position (*We quickly realized that attempts to negotiate would be futile*) and following verbs other than imperatives (*She turned quickly and sat down*). See also SLOW, SURE.
quick′-and-dirt′y, *adj. Informal.* slipshod.
quick′ and the dead′, *n.* the living and the dead: a phrase from the Apostles' Creed.
quick′ bread′, *n.* bread made with a leavening agent, as baking powder or soda, that permits immediate baking.
quick•en (kwik′ən), *v.t.* **1.** to make more rapid; accelerate; hasten: *She quickened her pace.* **2.** to give or restore vigor or activity to; stimulate: *to quicken the imagination.* **3.** to restore life to; revive: *The spring rains quickened the earth.* —*v.i.* **4.** to become more rapid: *This drug causes the pulse to quicken.* **5.** to become alive; receive life. **6.** to enter that stage of pregnancy in which the fetus gives indications of life. **7.** (of a fetus in the womb) to begin to manifest signs of life. —**quick′en•er,** *n.*
quick′ fix′, *n.* an expedient temporary solution, esp. one that merely postpones coping with an overall problem.
quick′-freeze′, *v.t.,* **-froze, -fro•zen, -freez•ing.** to freeze (food) rapidly so that it can be stored at freezing temperatures.
quick•ie (kwik′ē), *n.* **1.** something produced, done, or enjoyed in only a short time. —*adj.* **2.** accomplished quickly with minimal formality: *a quickie meal.*
quick•ly (kwik′lē), *adv.* with speed; rapidly; very soon. —**Usage.** See QUICK.
quick•sand (kwik′sand′), *n.* a bed of soft or loose sand saturated with water and having considerable depth, yielding under weight and therefore tending to cause an object resting on its surface to sink. —**quick′sand′y,** *adj.*
quick•sil•ver (kwik′sil′vər), *n.* **1.** MERCURY (def. 1). —*v.t.* **2.** to amalgamate (metal). —*adj.* **3.** unpredictably changeable; mercurial. —**quick′sil′ver•y,** *adj.*
quick•step (kwik′step′), *n.* **1.** QUICK TIME. **2.** martial music for a march in quick time.
quick′ stud′y, *n.* a person who is able to learn or adapt to something in a short time or on short notice.
quick′-tem′pered, *adj.* easily angered; touchy.
quick′ time′, *n.* a rate of marching in which 120 paces, each of 30 in. (76.2 cm), are taken in a minute.
quick′-wit′ted, *adj.* having a nimble, alert mind; keen; clever. —**quick′-wit′ted•ly,** *adv.* —**quick′-wit′ted•ness,** *n.*
quid[1] (kwid), *n.* a portion of something, esp. tobacco, that is to be chewed but not swallowed.
quid[2] (kwid), *n., pl.* **quid.** *Brit. Informal.* one pound sterling.
quid•di•ty (kwid′i tē), *n., pl.* **-ties. 1.** the quality that makes a thing what it is; essential nature. **2.** a trifling nicety of subtle distinction, as in argument.
quid pro quo (kwid′ prō kwō′), *n., pl.* **quid pro quos, quids pro quo.** something that is given or taken in return for something else; substitute.
qui•es•cent (kwē es′ənt, kwī-), *adj.* being at rest; quiet; still; inactive or motionless: *a quiescent mind.* —**qui•es′cent•ly,** *adv.* —**qui•es′cence, qui•es′cen•cy,** *n.*
qui•et[1] (kwī′it), *adj.* **1.** making little or no noise or sound: *quiet neighbors.* **2.** free or comparatively free from noise: *a quiet street.* **3.** silent: *Be quiet!* **4.** restrained in speech or manner: *a quiet person.* **5.** free from disturbance or tumult; tranquil; peaceful: *a quiet life.* **6.** being at rest. **7.** free from activity, esp. busy or vigorous activity: *a quiet Sunday afternoon.* **8.** quiescent; peaceable: *The factions have been quiet for years.* **9.** motionless or moving very gently: *quiet waters.* **10.** free from disturbing thoughts, emotions, etc.; mentally peaceful: *a quiet conscience.* **11.** said, expressed, done, etc., in a restrained or unobtrusive way: *a quiet reproach.* **12.** not showy or obtrusive; subdued: *quiet colors.* **13.** not busy or active: *The stock market was quiet last week.* —*v.t.* **14.** to make quiet. **15.** to make tranquil or peaceful; pacify. **16.** to calm mentally, as a person. **17.** to allay (tumult, doubt, fear, etc.). **18.** to silence. —*v.i.* **19.** to become quiet (often fol. by *down*). —***Idiom.*** **20. All quiet on the Potomac,** everything is calm; there is no fighting: phrase popularized during the Civil War. —**qui′et•er,** *n.* —**qui′et•ly,** *adv.* —**qui′et•ness,** *n.*
qui•et[2] (kwī′it), *n.* **1.** freedom from noise, unwanted sound, etc. **2.** freedom from disturbance or tumult; tranquillity; rest; repose. **3.** peace; peaceful condition of affairs.
qui′et diplo′macy, *n.* diplomacy conducted without publicity.
qui•et•ism (kwī′i tiz′əm), *n.* **1.** a form of Christian mysticism first promulgated in the late 17th century, requiring extinction of the will and worldly interests, and passive meditation on the divine. **2.** mental or bodily repose or passivity. —**qui′et•ist,** *n., adj.* —**qui′et•is′tic,** *adj.*
qui•e•tude (kwī′i tōōd′, -tyōōd′), *n.* the state of being quiet; tranquillity.
qui•e•tus (kwī ē′təs), *n., pl.* **-tus•es. 1.** a finishing stroke; anything

that effectually ends or settles. **2.** discharge or release from life. **3.** a period of retirement or inactivity.

quill (kwil), *n.* **1.** one of the large feathers of the wing or tail of a bird. **2.** the hard, hollow, basal part of a feather. **3.** a feather, as of a goose, formed into a pen for writing. **4.** one of the hollow spines on a porcupine or hedgehog. **5.** a plectrum of a harpsichord. **6.** a roll of bark, as of cinnamon, formed in drying. **7.** a reed, spindle, or tube upon which filling yarn is wound for weaving. **8.** *Mach.* a hollow shaft or sleeve through which another independently rotating shaft may pass. —*v.t.* **9.** to arrange (fabric) in flutes or cylindrical ridges, as along the edge of a garment. **10.** to wind on a quill, as yarn. **11.** to penetrate with, or as if with, a quill or quills. **12.** to extract a quill or quills from. —**quill/-like/**, *adj.*

quilt (kwilt), *n.* **1.** a coverlet for a bed, made of two layers of fabric with some soft substance between them and stitched in patterns through all thicknesses to prevent the filling from shifting. **2.** anything quilted or resembling a quilt. —*v.t.* **3.** to stitch together (two pieces of cloth and a soft interlining), usu. in an ornamental pattern. **4.** to sew or stitch with patterns like those of quilts. **5.** to pad or line with material. —*v.i.* **6.** to make quilts or quilted work. —**quilt/er**, *n.*

quilt·ing (kwil/ting), *n.* **1.** the act or process of making quilts or quilted work. **2.** material for making quilts. **3.** material or work that has been quilted.

quilt/ing bee/, *n.* a social gathering at which the participants make quilts.

quince (kwins), *n.* **1.** a small tree, *Cydonia oblonga*, of the rose family, bearing hard, fragrant, yellowish fruit used chiefly for making jelly or preserves. **2.** the fruit of such a tree.

quin·cen·ten·ni·al (kwin/sen ten/ē əl), *adj.* **1.** pertaining to or marking a period of 500 years. —*n.* **2.** a 500th anniversary or its celebration.

Quin·cy (kwin/zē, -sē), *n.* **1.** Josiah, 1744–75, American patriot and writer. **2.** a city in E Massachusetts, near Boston. 82,640.

qui·nel·la (kē nel/ə, kwi-) also **qui·nie·la** (kēn yel/ə), *n., pl.* **-las.** a type of bet, esp. on horse races, in which the bettor, in order to win, must select the first- and second-place finishers without specifying their order of finishing.

quin·i·dine (kwin/i dēn′, -din), *n.* a colorless, crystalline alkaloid, isomeric with quinine, obtained from cinchona bark and used for treating malaria and arrhythmia.

qui·nine (kwī/nīn, kwin/īn; *esp. Brit.* kwi nēn′), *n.* **1.** a white crystalline alkaloid, $C_{20}H_{24}N_2O_2$, obtained from cinchona bark, used chiefly for treating resistant forms of malaria. **2.** a salt of this alkaloid, esp. the sulfate.

qui/nine wa/ter, *n.* TONIC WATER.

qui·none (kwi nōn′, kwin/ōn), *n.* **1.** a yellow, crystalline, cyclic compound, $C_6H_4O_2$, used chiefly in photography and in tanning leather. **2.** any of a class of compounds of this type.

quin·qua·ge·nar·i·an (kwing/kwə jə när/ē ən, kwin/-), *n.* a person who is 50 years old or between 50 and 60.

Quin·qua·ges·i·ma (kwing/kwə jes/ə mə, kwin/-), *n.* the Sunday before Lent; Shrove Sunday.

quinque-, a combining form meaning "five": *quinquevalent.*

quin·quen·ni·al (kwin kwen/ē əl, kwing-), *adj.* **1.** of or lasting for five years. **2.** occurring every five years. —*n.* **3.** a quinquennium. **4.** something that occurs every five years. —**quin·quen/ni·al·ly**, *adv.*

quin·quen·ni·um (kwin kwen/ē əm, kwing-) also **quin·quen·ni·ad** (-ad′), *n., pl.* **-quen·ni·ums, -quen·ni·a** (-kwen/ē ə) also **-quen·ni·ads.** a period of five years.

quint (kwint), *n.* a quintuplet.

quin·tal (kwin/tl), *n.* **1.** a unit of weight equal to 100 kilograms (220.5 avoirdupois pounds). **2.** HUNDREDWEIGHT.

quin·tes·sence (kwin tes/əns), *n.* **1.** the pure and concentrated essence of a substance. **2.** the most perfect embodiment of something. **3.** (in ancient and medieval philosophy) the fifth essence or element, ether, supposed to be with air, fire, earth, and water the constituent matter of the heavenly bodies. —**quin/tes·sen/tial** (-tə sen/shəl), *adj.* —**quin/tes·sen/tial·ly**, *adv.*

quin·tet or **quin·tette** (kwin tet′), *n.* **1.** any set or group of five persons or things. **2.** a group of five singers or players. **3.** a musical composition scored for five voices or instruments.

quin·tu·ple (kwin tōō/pəl, -tyōō′-, -tup/əl, kwin/tōō pəl, -tyōō-), *adj., n., v.,* **-pled, -pling.** —*adj.* **1.** fivefold; consisting of five parts. **2.** five times as great or as much. **3.** having five beats to a musical measure. —*n.* **4.** a number, amount, etc., five times as great as another. —*v.t., v.i.* **5.** to make or become five times as great.

quin·tu·plet (kwin tup/lit, -tōō/plit, -tyōō′-, kwin/tōō plit, -tyōō-), *n.* **1.** any group or combination of five, esp. of the same kind. **2.** quintuplets, five children or offspring born of one pregnancy. **3.** one of five such children or offspring. **4.** a group of five musical notes of equal value performed in the time normally taken for four.

quip (kwip), *n., v.,* **quipped, quip·ping.** —*n.* **1.** a clever or witty remark or comment. **2.** a sharp, sarcastic remark. **3.** quibble; cavil. **4.** an odd or fantastic action or thing. —*v.i.* **5.** to utter quips. —**quip/ster**, *n.*

quire (kwī°r), *n.* **1.** a set of 24 uniform sheets of paper. **2.** *Bookbinding.* a section of printed leaves in proper sequence after folding; gathering.

Qui·ri·i·us (kwī rin/ē əs), *n.* CYRENIUS.

quirk (kwûrk), *n.* **1.** a peculiarity of action, behavior, or personality; mannerism. **2.** caprice; vagary; accident: *a quirk of fate.* **3.** a showy stroke, as in writing. **4.** an acute angle or channel, as one dividing two parts of a molding. —*adj.* **5.** formed with a quirk or channel, as a molding. —**quirk/i·ly**, *adv.* —**quirk/i·ness**, *n.* —**quirk/y**, *adj.*

quirt (kwûrt), *n.* **1.** a riding whip consisting of a short, stout stock and a lash of braided leather. —*v.t.* **2.** to strike with a quirt.

quis·ling (kwiz/ling), *n.* a person who betrays his or her own country by aiding an invading enemy, often serving later in a puppet government; fifth columnist. [after Vidkun *Quisling* (1887–1945), pro-Nazi Norwegian leader]

quit (kwit), *v.,* **quit** or **quit·ted, quit·ting,** *adj.* —*v.t.* **1.** to stop, cease, or discontinue. **2.** to depart from; leave (a place or person). **3.** to give up or resign; let go; relinquish: *He quit his claim to the throne.* **4.** to release one's hold of (something grasped). **5.** to free or rid (oneself). **6.** to clear (a debt); repay. **7.** to acquit or conduct (oneself). —*v.i.* **8.** to cease from doing something; stop. **9.** to give up or resign one's job or position. **10.** to depart or leave. **11.** to stop trying, struggling, or the like; accept or acknowledge defeat. —*adj.* **12.** released from obligation, penalty, etc.; rid (usu. fol. by *of*): *quit of all further responsibilities.*

quit·claim (kwit/klām′), *n.* **1.** a transfer of one's interest in a property, esp. without a warranty of title. —*v.t.* **2.** to give up claim to (property) by means of a quitclaim deed.

quit/claim deed/, *n.* a deed that conveys to the grantee only such interests in property as the grantor may have, the grantee assuming responsibility for any claims brought against the property. Compare WARRANTY DEED.

quite (kwīt), *adv.* **1.** completely, wholly, or entirely: *not quite finished.* **2.** actually, really, or truly: *quite a sudden change.* **3.** to a considerable extent or degree: *quite small.*

Qui·to (kē/tō), *n.* the capital of Ecuador, in the N part. 1,110,248; 9348 ft. (2849 m) above sea level.

quits (kwits), *adj.* **1.** on equal terms by repayment or retaliation. —*Idiom.* **2. call it quits,** to end an activity, relationship, etc.

quit·tance (kwit/ns), *n.* **1.** recompense or requital. **2.** discharge from a debt or obligation. **3.** a document certifying discharge from debt or obligation, as a receipt.

quit·ter (kwit/ər), *n.* a person who quits or gives up easily, esp. in the face of difficulty.

quiv·er (kwiv/ər), *v.t., v.i.* **1.** to shake with a slight but rapid motion; tremble. —*n.* **2.** the act or state of quivering. —**quiv/er·er**, *n.* —**quiv/er·ing·ly**, *adv.* —**quiv/er·y**, *adj.*

Quix·o·te (kē hō/tē, kwik/sət; *Sp.* kē hô/te), *n.* Don, DON QUIXOTE.

quix·ot·ic (kwik sot/ik) also **quix·ot/i·cal**, *adj.* **1.** (*sometimes cap.*) resembling or befitting Don Quixote. **2.** extravagantly chivalrous or romantic; visionary; impractical. [after Don *Quixote*, hero of Cervantes' novel of the same name] —**quix·ot/i·cal·ly**, *adv.*

quiz (kwiz), *n., pl.* **quiz·zes,** *v.,* **quizzed, quiz·zing.** —*n.* **1.** an informal test or examination. **2.** a questioning. **3.** a practical joke; hoax. **4.** an eccentric person. —*v.t.* **5.** to examine or test (a student or class) informally by questions. **6.** to question closely. **7.** *Chiefly Brit.* to make fun of. —**quiz/zer**, *n.*

quiz·mas·ter (kwiz/mas′tər, -mä′stər), *n.* a person who asks questions of contestants in a quiz show.

quiz/ show/, *n.* a radio or television program in which contestants compete, often for prizes, by answering questions. Also called **quiz/ pro/gram.** Compare GAME SHOW.

quiz·zi·cal (kwiz/i kəl), *adj.* **1.** odd or comical. **2.** questioning or puzzled: *a quizzical expression on her face.* **3.** derisively questioning or ridiculing. —**quiz/zi·cal/i·ty**, *n.* —**quiz/zi·cal·ly**, *adv.*

Qum·ran (kōōm/rän′), *n.* KHIRBET QUMRAN.

quoin (koin, kwoin), *n.* **1.** an external solid angle of a wall or the like. **2.** one of the stones forming it; cornerstone. **3.** a wedge-shaped piece of wood, stone, or other material, used for any of various purposes. **4.** a wedge of wood or metal for securing type in a chase. —*v.t.* **5.** to provide with quoins, as a corner of a wall. **6.** to secure or raise with a quoin or wedge.

quoit (kwoit, koit), *n.* **1. quoits,** (*used with a sing. v.*) a game in which rings of rope or flattened metal are thrown at an upright peg, the object being to encircle it. **2.** a ring used in the game of quoits. —*v.t.* **3.** to throw like a quoit.

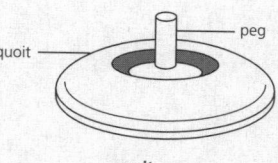

quoit

quon·dam (kwon/dəm, -dam), *adj.* former; onetime: *his quondam partner.* [< Latin]

Quon/set hut/ (kwon/sit), *Trademark.* a semicylindrical metal shelter having end walls, usually serving as a barracks, storage shed, or the like, developed for the U.S. military forces from the British Nissen hut at Quonset Naval Base in Rhode Island.

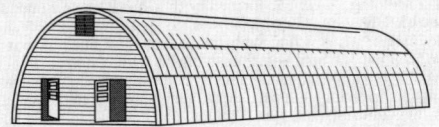

Quonset hut

quo•rum (kwôr′əm, kwōr′-), *n.* **1.** the number of members of a group required to be present to transact business or carry out an activity legally, usu. a majority. **2.** a particularly chosen group.

quo•ta (kwō′tə), *n.* **1.** the share or proportional part of a total that is required from, or is due or belongs to, a particular district, state, person, group, etc. **2.** a proportional part or share of a fixed total amount or quantity. **3.** the number or percentage of persons of a specified kind permitted to enroll in a college, join a club, immigrate to a country, etc.

quot•a•ble (kwō′tə bəl), *adj.* **1.** able to be quoted or easily quoted, as by reason of effectiveness, succinctness, or the like. **2.** suitable or appropriate for quotation. —**quot′a•bil′i•ty,** *n.* —**quot′a•bly,** *adv.*

quo•ta•tion (kwō tā′shən), *n.* **1.** something quoted; a passage quoted from a book, speech, etc. **2.** the act or practice of quoting. **3.** the statement of the current or market price of a commodity or security.

quota′tion mark′, *n.* one of the marks used to indicate the beginning and end of a quotation, in English usu. shown as (") at the beginning and (") at the end, or, for a quotation within a quotation, as single marks of this kind, as *"He said, 'I will go.'"*

quote (kwōt), *v.,* **quot•ed, quot•ing,** *n.* —*v.t.* **1.** to repeat (a passage, phrase, etc.) from a book, speech, or the like, as by way of authority or illustration. **2.** to repeat words from (a book, author, etc.). **3.** to cite, offer, or bring forward as evidence or support. **4.** to enclose (words) within quotation marks. **5.** to state the current or market price of (a stock, bond, etc.). —*v.i.* **6.** to make a quotation or quotations, as from a book or author. **7.** (used by a speaker to indicate the beginning of a quotation.) —*n.* **8.** QUOTATION. **9.** QUOTATION MARK. —**quot′er,** *n.*

quo•tid•i•an (kwō tid′ē ən), *adj.* **1.** daily: *a quotidian report.* **2.** ordinary; everyday. **3.** recurring daily: *quotidian fever.* —*n.* **4.** something recurring daily. **5.** a quotidian fever or ague.

quo•tient (kwō′shənt), *n.* the result of division; the number of times one quantity is contained in another.

q.v., *pl.* **qq.v.** (used in formal writing after a cross reference) which see. [< Latin *quod vidē*]

QWERTY (kwûr′tē, kwer′-), *adj.* of or noting the standard typewriter or computer keyboard with *q, w, e, r, t,* and *y* being the first six of the top row of letters, starting from the left.

Qy. or **qy.,** query.

R

R, r (är), *n., pl.* **Rs** or **R's, rs** or **r's. 1.** the 18th letter of the English alphabet, a consonant. **2.** any spoken sound represented by this letter. **3.** something shaped like an R. **4.** a written or printed representation of the letter *R* or *r*.

R, 1. *Chem.* radical. **2.** *Math.* ratio. **3.** regular: a man's suit or coat size. **4.** restricted: a motion-picture rating advising that children under the age of 17 will not be admitted unless accompanied by an adult. **5.** right. **6.** roentgen.

R, *Symbol.* **1.** the 18th in order or in a series. **2.** arginine. **3.** registered trademark: written as superscript ® following a name registered with the U.S. Patent and Trademark Office. **4.** *Elect.* resistance.

r, 1. radius. **2.** *Elect.* resistance. **3.** roentgen.

r, *Ecol.* the intrinsic rate of increase of a population, equivalent to the difference between the birth and death rates divided by the number of individuals in the population. Also called **Malthusian paramenter.**

Ra (rä) also **Re,** *n.* a sun god of Heliopolis, worshipped throughout ancient Egypt and typically represented as a hawk-headed man crowned with a solar disk and uraeus.

RA, regular army.

Ra, *Chem. Symbol.* radium.

R.A., 1. right ascension. **2.** royal academician. **3.** Royal Academy.

Ra•am•ses (rä am′sēz), *n.* a city that was built for the Pharaoh by the Israelites and from which the Exodus began. Ex. 1:11. Compare PITHOM.

ra•bat (rab′ē, rə bat′), *n. Eccles.* a sleeveless, backless, vestlike garment extending to the waist, worn by a cleric beneath the clerical collar, esp. in the Roman Catholic and Anglican churches.

Ra•bat (rä bät′, rə-), *n.* the capital of Morocco, in the NW part on the Atlantic. 518,616.

Rab•bah (rab′ə), *n.* **1.** the ancient Biblical capital of the Ammonite kingdom east of the Jordan River. **2.** a city in Judah, near Jerusalem.

rab•bet (rab′it), *n.* **1.** a deep notch formed in or near one edge of a board, framing timber, etc., so that something else can be fitted into it or so that a door or the like can be closed against it. —*v.t.* **2.** to cut a rabbet in (a board). **3.** to join (boards) by means of a rabbet or rabbets. —*v.i.* **4.** to join by a rabbet (usu. fol. by *on* or *over*).

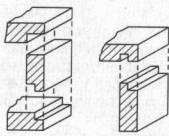

boards joined by means of **rabbets**

rab•bi (rab′ī), *n., pl.* **-bis. 1.** the chief religious official of a synagogue who performs ritualistic, educational, and other functions as spiritual leader of the congregation. **2.** a title of respect for a Jewish scholar or teacher. **3.** a Jewish scholar qualified to rule on questions of Jewish law. **4.** any of the Jewish scholars of the 1st to 6th centuries A.D. who contributed to the Talmud. [< Hebrew: my master]

rab•bin•ate (rab′ə nit, -nāt′), *n.* **1.** the office or term of office of a rabbi. **2.** a group of rabbis: *the Orthodox rabbinate.*

rab•bin•i•cal (rə bin′i kəl) also **rab•bin′ic,** *adj.* **1.** pertaining to rabbis or their writings. **2.** for the rabbinate: *a rabbinical school.*

rab•bit (rab′it), *n., pl.* **-bits,** (*esp. collectively*) **-bit. 1.** any of several large-eared, hopping lagomorphs of the family Leporidae, usu. smaller than the hares and characterized by bearing blind and furless young in nests. **2.** the fur of a rabbit or hare.

rab′bit-eared′ ban′dicoot, *n.* any bandicoot of the Australian genus *Thylacomis,* esp. *T. lagotis,* with rabbitlike ears and a long, pointed snout. Also called **bilby, rab′bit ban′dicoot.**

rab′bit punch′, *n.* a short, sharp blow to the nape of the neck or the lower part of the skull.

rab•bit•ry (rab′i trē), *n., pl.* **-ries. 1.** a collection of rabbits. **2.** a place where rabbits are kept.

rab•ble[1] (rab′əl), *n., v.,* **-bled, -bling.** —*n.* **1.** a disorderly crowd; mob. **2.** the rabble, the lower classes; the common people. —*v.t.* **3.** to beset as a rabble does; mob.

rab•ble[2] (rab′əl), *n., v.,* **-bled, -bling.** *Metall.* —*n.* **1.** a tool or mechanically operated device used for stirring or mixing a charge in a roasting furnace. —*v.t.* **2.** to stir (a charge) in a roasting furnace. —**rab′bler,** *n.*

rab′ble-rous′er, *n.* a person who stirs up the passions or prejudices of the public, usu. for his or her own interests; demagogue. —**rab′ble-rous′ing,** *n., adj.*

Rab•e•lais (rab′ə lā′, rab′ə lā′), *n.* **François,** c1490–1553, French satirist and humorist.

Rab•e•lai•si•an (rab′ə lā′zē ən, -zhən), *adj.* of, pertaining to, or suggesting Rabelais or his broad, coarse humor.

Ra•bi[1] (rä′bē), *n.* **Isidor Isaac,** 1898–1988, U.S. physicist.

Ra•bi[2] (rub′ē), *n.* **1.** Rabi I, the third month of the Islamic calendar. **2.** Rabi II, the fourth month of the Islamic calendar.

rab•id (rab′id), *adj.* **1.** irrationally extreme in opinion or practice. **2.** furious, raging; violently intense. **3.** affected with or pertaining to rabies: *a rabid dog.* —**rab•id•i•ty** (rə bid′i tē, ra-), *n.* —**rab′id•ly,** *adv.*

ra•bies (rā′bēz), *n.* an infectious, usu. fatal disease of dogs, cats, and other warm-blooded animals, and transmitted to humans by the bite of a rabid animal.

Ra•bin (rä bēn′), *n.* **Yitz•hak** (yits кнäk′), 1922–95, Israeli military and political leader: prime minister 1974–77 and 1992–95: Nobel peace prize 1994.

Rab•sha•keh (rab′shə ke′), *n.* an Assyrian military officer at the time of Hezekiah. II Kings 18:17–37; Is. 36:2–22.

rac•coon (ra kōōn′), *n., pl.* **-coons,** (*esp. collectively*) **-coon.** any small, nocturnal carnivore of the genus *Procyon,* esp. *P. lotor,* having a mask-like black stripe across the eyes and a bushy, ringed tail, native to North and Central America.

race[1] (rās), *n., v.,* **raced, rac•ing.** —*n.* **1.** a contest of speed, as in running, riding, driving, or sailing. **2.** races, a series of races, run at a set time over a regular course. **3.** any contest or competition, esp. to achieve superiority: *an arms race.* **4.** an urgent effort, as when a solution is imperative: *a race to find a vaccine.* **5.** onward movement; an onward or regular course. **6.** the course of time or life. **7. a.** a strong or rapid current of water, as in the sea or a river. **b.** the channel or bed of such a current or of any stream. **8.** an artificial channel leading water to or from a place where its energy is utilized. **9.** a channel, groove, or the like, for sliding or rolling a part or parts, as the balls of a ball bearing. —*v.i.* **10.** to engage in a contest of speed; run a race. **11.** to run horses or dogs in races. **12.** to run, move, or go swiftly. **13.** (of an engine, wheel, etc.) to run with undue or uncontrolled speed when the load is diminished without corresponding diminution of fuel, force, etc. —*v.t.* **14.** to run a race against. **15.** to enter (a horse, car, etc.) in a race. **16.** to cause to run, move, or go at high speed: *to race a motor.* —*Proverb.* **17. The race is not to the swift,** the expected winner may not be the one who succeeds. Eccl. 9:11.

race[2] (rās), *n.* **1.** a group of persons related by common descent or heredity. **2. a.** a classification of modern humans, sometimes, esp. formerly, based on an arbitrary selection of physical characteristics, now frequently based on such genetic markers as blood groups. **b.** a human population partially isolated reproductively from other populations, whose members share a greater degree of physical and genetic similarity with one another than with other humans. **3.** any people united by common history, language, cultural traits, etc.: *the Dutch race.* **4.** the human race or family; humankind. **5.** *Zool.* a variety; subspecies. **6.** any group, class, or kind, esp. of persons.

race•course (rās′kôrs′, -kōrs′), *n.* **1.** RACETRACK. **2.** a current of water.

race•horse (rās′hôrs′), *n.* a horse bred or kept for racing, esp. in flat races or steeplechases.

ra•ceme (rā sēm′, rə-), *n.* a simple indeterminate inflorescence in which the flowers are borne on short stalks lying along an elongated main stem, as in the lily of the valley. —**ra•cemed′,** *adj.*

race′ norm′ing, *n.* the process of statistically adjusting the scores of minority job applicants on job-qualification tests by rating each test-taker's score against those of others in his or her racial or ethnic group.

rac•er (rā′sər), *n.* **1.** a person, animal, or thing that races or takes part in a race. **2.** anything having great speed. **3.** any of several slender, active snakes of the genera *Coluber* and *Masticophis.*

race•track (rās′trak′), *n.* **1.** a plot of ground, usu. oval, laid out for horse racing. **2.** the course for any race.

race′ walk′ing, *n.* the sport of rapid walking, in which one foot must be in contact with the ground at all times. —**race′ walk′,** *v.i.,*

race•way (rās′wā′), *n.* **1.** a racetrack on which harness races are held. **2.** a channel for protecting and holding electrical wires.

Ra•chel (rā′chəl), *n.* Jacob's favorite wife, the mother of Joseph and Benjamin. Gen. 29–35.

ra•cial (rā′shəl), *adj.* **1.** of, pertaining to, or characteristic of one race or the races of humankind. **2.** between races: *racial harmony; racial relations.* —**ra′cial•ly,** *adv.*

Ra•cine (rā sēn′, ra- for 1; rə sēn′, rā- for 2), *n.* **1. Jean Baptiste,** 1639–99, French dramatist. **2.** a city in SE Wisconsin. 82,510.

rac′ing form′, *n.* a sheet that provides detailed information about horse races, including data on the horses, jockeys, etc.

rac•ism (rā′siz əm), *n.* **1.** a belief or doctrine that inherent differences among the various human races determine cultural or individual achievement, usu. involving the idea that one's own race is superior. **2.** a policy, system of government, etc., based on such a doctrine. **3.** hatred or intolerance of another race or other races. —**rac′ist,** *n., adj.*

rack¹ (rak), *n.* **1.** a framework of bars, pegs, etc., on which articles are arranged or deposited: *a clothes rack.* **2.** a fixture containing tiered shelves, often affixed to a wall: *a spice rack.* **3.** a framework set up on a vehicle to carry loads. **4. a.** a triangular wooden frame in which balls are arranged before a game of pool. **b.** the balls so arranged. **5. a.** a bar, with teeth on one of its sides, adapted to engage with the teeth of a pinion **(rack and pinion)** or the like, as for converting circular into rectilinear motion or vice versa. **b.** a bar having a series of notches engaging with a pawl or the like. **6.** a former instrument of torture on which a victim was slowly stretched. **7.** a cause or state of intense suffering of body or mind. **8.** violent strain. **9.** a pair of antlers. —*v.t.* **10.** to torture; distress acutely; torment. **11.** to strain in mental effort: *to rack one's brains.* **12.** to strain by physical force or violence. **13.** to stretch the body of (a person) on a rack. **14. rack up, a.** *Pool.* to put (the balls) in a rack. **b.** to gain, achieve, or score: *The new store is racking up profits.* —**rack′ing•ly,** *adv.*

rack² (rak), *n.* wreckage or destruction; wrack: *to go to rack and ruin.*

rack³ (rak), *n.* **1.** the fast pace of a horse in which the legs move in lateral pairs but not simultaneously. —*v.i.* **2.** (of horses) to move in a rack.

rack⁴ (rak), *n.* **1.** a group of drifting clouds. —*v.i.* **2.** to drive or move, esp. before the wind.

rack⁵ (rak), *v.t.* to draw off (wine, cider, etc.) from the lees.

rack⁶ (rak), *n.* **1.** the neck portion of mutton, pork, or veal. **2.** the rib section of a foresaddle of lamb, veal, etc.

rack′ and pin′ion, *n.* See under RACK¹ (def. 5a).

rack•et¹ (rak′it), *n.* **1.** a loud noise or clamor, esp. of a disturbing or confusing kind; din; uproar. **2.** social excitement, gaiety, or dissipation. **3.** an organized illegal activity, such as the extortion of money by threat or violence. **4.** a dishonest scheme, business, activity, etc. **5.** *Slang.* **a.** an occupation, livelihood, or business. **b.** an easy or profitable source of livelihood. —*v.i.* **6.** to make a racket or noise. **7.** to take part in social gaiety or dissipation.

tennis court tennis squash squash tennis badminton paddle tennis table tennis

racket² (defs. 1, 2)

rack•et² (rak′it), *n.* **1.** a light bat having a netting of catgut or nylon stretched in a more or less oval frame and used in tennis, badminton, etc. **2.** the short-handled paddle used to strike the ball in table tennis and paddle tennis. **3. rackets,** (*used with a sing. v.*) RACQUET (def. 1). **4.** a snowshoe made in the form of a tennis racket. Also, **racquet** (for defs. 1, 2, 4).

rack•et•eer (rak′i tēr′), *n.* **1.** a person engaged in an organized illegal activity, as extortion. —*v.i.* **2.** to engage in a racket.

ra•clette (rä klet′, ra-), *n.* a Swiss dish of melted cheese served with boiled potatoes.

rac•on•teur (rak′on tûr′, -tŏor′, -ən-), *n.* a person who is skilled in relating stories and anecdotes interestingly.

ra•coon (ra kōon′), *n., pl.* **-coons,** (*esp. collectively*) **-coon.** RACCOON.

rac•quet (rak′it), *n.* **1. racquets,** (*used with a sing. v.*) a game played with rackets and a ball by two or four persons on a four-walled court. **2.** RACKET² (defs. 1, 2, 4).

rac•quet•ball (rak′it bôl′), *n.* a game similar to handball, played with rackets on a four-walled court.

rac•y (rā′sē), *adj.,* **-i•er, -i•est. 1.** slightly improper or indelicate; suggestive; risqué. **2.** vigorous; lively; spirited. **3.** sprightly; piquant; pungent: *a racy literary style.* **4.** having an agreeably peculiar taste or flavor, as wine or fruit. —**rac′i•ly,** *adv.* —**rac′i•ness,** *n.*

rad, *Math.* radian.

ra•dar (rā′där), *n.* a device or system for determining the presence and location of an object by measuring the direction and timing of radio waves. [*ra(dio) d(etecting) a(nd) r(anging)*]

ra′dar astron′omy, *n.* the branch of astronomy that uses radar to map the surfaces of planetary bodies, as the moon and Venus, and to determine periods of rotation.

ra′dar bea′con, *n.* a radar device at a fixed location, used as a navigational aid.

ra•di•al (rā′dē əl), *adj.* **1.** arranged or having parts arranged like radii or rays. **2.** made in the direction of a radius; going from the center outward or from the circumference inward along a radius: *a radial cut.* **3.** of, like, or pertaining to a radius or a ray. **4.** of, pertaining to, or situated near the radius of the forearm. **5.** acting along or in the direction of the radius of a circle: *radial motion.* —*n.* **6.** a radial section, part, or structure. **7.** RADIAL TIRE. —**ra′di•al•ly,** *adv.*

ra′dial sym′metry, *n.* a basic body plan in which the organism can be divided into similar halves by passing a plane at any angle along a central axis. Compare BILATERAL SYMMETRY.

ra′dial tire′, *n.* a motor-vehicle tire in which the plies or cords run from one bead to the other at right angles to both beads.

ra•di•an (rā′dē ən), *n.* the measure of a central angle subtending an arc equal in length to the radius: equal to 57.2958°. *Abbr.:* rad

ra•di•ance (rā′dē əns) also **ra′di•an•cy,** *n.* **1.** radiant brightness or light. **2.** warm, cheerful brightness.

ra•di•ant (rā′dē ənt), *adj.* **1.** emitting rays of light; shining. **2.** bright with joy, hope, etc. **3.** *Physics.* emitted or propagated by radiation. —*n.* **4.** a point or object from which rays proceed. —**ra′di•ant•ly,** *adv.*

ra′diant en′ergy, *n.* **1.** energy transmitted in wave motion, esp. electromagnetic wave motion. **2.** LIGHT¹ (def. 2a).

ra′diant heat′, *n.* heat energy transmitted by electromagnetic waves in contrast to heat transmitted by conduction or convection.

ra′diant heat′ing, *n.* **1.** the means of heating objects or persons by radiation in which the intervening air is not heated. **2.** a system for heating by radiation from a surface, esp. from a surface heated by means of electric resistance, hot water, etc.

ra•di•ate (*v.* rā′dē āt′; *adj.* -it, -āt′), *v.,* **-at•ed, -at•ing,** *adj.* —*v.i.* **1.** to extend, spread, or move like rays or radii from a center. **2.** to emit rays, as of light or heat; irradiate. **3.** to issue or proceed in rays. **4.** (of persons) to project or glow with cheerfulness, joy, etc. —*v.t.* **5.** to emit in rays; disseminate, as from a center. **6.** (of persons) to project (joy, goodwill, etc.). —*adj.* **7.** radiating from a center. **8.** having rays extending from a central point or part. **9.** radiating symmetrically.

ra•di•a•tion (rā′dē ā′shən), *n.* **1. a.** the process in which energy is emitted as particles or waves. **b.** the complete process in which energy is emitted by one body, transmitted through an intervening medium or space, and absorbed by another body. **c.** the energy transferred by these processes. **2.** the act or process of radiating. **3.** something that is radiated. **4.** radial arrangement of parts. —**ra′di•a′tion•al,** *adj.*

radia′tion sick′ness, *n.* sickness caused by irradiation with x-rays or radioactive materials, characterized by nausea and vomiting, headache, diarrhea, loss of hair and teeth, destruction of white blood cells, and hemorrhage.

ra•di•a•tor (rā′dē ā′tər), *n.* **1.** heating device, as a series of pipes through which steam or hot water passes. **2.** a person or thing that radiates. **3.** a device constructed from thin-walled tubes and metal fins, used for cooling circulating water, as in an automobile engine.

rad•i•cal (rad′i kəl), *adj.* **1.** of or going to the root or origin; fundamental. **2.** thoroughgoing or extreme: *a radical change in company policy.* **3.** favoring drastic political, economic, or social reforms. **4.** existing inherently in a thing or person: *radical defects of character.* **5.** *Math.* **a.** pertaining to or forming a root. **b.** denoting or pertaining to the radical sign. **c.** IRRATIONAL (def. 4b). **6.** of or pertaining to the root of a word. **7.** *Bot.* of or arising from the root or the base of the stem. **8.** *Slang.* great; marvelous; wonderful. —*n.* **9.** a person who holds or follows strong convictions or extreme principles; extremist. **10.** a person who advocates fundamental political, economic, and social reforms by direct and often uncompromising methods. **11.** *Math.* **a.** a quantity expressed as a root of another quantity. **b.** RADICAL SIGN. **12.** *Chem.* **a.** GROUP (def. 3). **b.** FREE RADICAL. **13.** ROOT¹ (def. 10).

rad′ical chic′, *n.* the espousal of radical political and social causes because they are fashionable.

rad•i•cal•ly (rad′ik lē), *adv.* **1.** with regard to origin or root. **2.** in a complete or basic manner; thoroughly; fundamentally.

rad′ical sign′, *n. Math.* the symbol $\sqrt{}$ or $\sqrt[n]{}$ indicating extraction of a root of the quantity that follows it, as $\sqrt{25} = 5$.

rad•i•cand (rad′i kand′, rad′i kand′), *n. Math.* the quantity under a radical sign.

ra•dic•chi•o (rə dē′kē ō′), *n.* a variety of chicory having a compact head of reddish, white-streaked leaves.

rad•i•ces (rad′ə sēz′, rā′də-), *n.* a pl. of RADIX.

rad•i•cle (rad′i kəl), *n.* **1.** *Bot.* an embryonic root. **2.** *Anat.* a small rootlike part or structure, as the beginning of a nerve or vein. —**ra•dic•u•lar** (rə dik′yə lər), *adj.*

ra•di•i (rā′dē ī′), *n.* a pl. of RADIUS.

ra•di•o (rā′dē ō′), *n.* **1.** a system of telecommunication employing electromagnetic waves of a particular frequency range to transmit speech or other sound over long distances without the use of wires. **2.** an apparatus for receiving or transmitting radio broadcasts. —*adj.* **3.** pertaining to, used in, or sent by radio. **4.** pertaining to electromagnetic radiation having frequencies in the range of 10 kHz to 300,000 MHz: *radio waves.* —*v.t.* **5.** to transmit (a message, music, etc.) by radio.

radio-, a combining form with the meanings "radiant energy" (*radiometer*), "radio waves" (*radiolocation; radiotelephone*), "emission of rays as a result of the breakup of atomic nuclei" (*radioactivity; radiocarbon*), "x-rays" (*radiograph; radiotherapy*).

ra•di•o•ac•tive (rā′dē ō ak′tiv), *adj.* of, pertaining to, exhibiting, or caused by radioactivity. —**ra′di•o•ac′tive•ly,** *adv.*

ra′dioac′tive dat′ing, *n.* RADIOMETRIC DATING.

ra•di•o•ac•tiv•i•ty (rā′dē ō ak tiv′i tē), *n.* the phenomenon, exhibited by and being a property of certain elements, of spontaneously emitting radiation resulting from changes in the nuclei of atoms of the element.

ra′dio astron′omy, *n.* the branch of astronomy that utilizes extraterrestrial radiation in radio wavelengths rather than visible light for the study of the universe.

ra•di•o•bi•ol•o•gy (rā′dē ō bī ol′ə jē), *n.* the branch of biology dealing with the effects of radiation on living matter. —ra/di•o•bi•o•log/i•cal (-ə loj/i kəl), *adj.* —ra/di•o•bi•ol/o•gist, *n.*

ra•di•o•car•bon (rā/dē ō kär/bən), *n.* **1.** Also called **carbon 14.** a radioactive isotope of carbon with mass number 14 and a half-life of about 5730 years: widely used in the dating of organic materials. **2.** any radioactive isotope of carbon.

radiocar/bon dat/ing, *n.* determination of the age of objects of organic origin by measurement of their radiocarbon content.

ra•di•o•fre/quen•cy or **ra/dio fre/quency,** *n., pl.* **-cies. 1.** the frequency of the transmitting waves of a given radio message or broadcast. **2.** a frequency within the range of radio transmission, from about 15,000 to 10¹¹ hertz. *Abbr.:* RF, rf

ra•di•o•graph (rā/dē ō graf/, -gräf/), *n.* **1.** a photographic image produced by the action of x-rays or nuclear radiation. —*v.t.* **2.** to make a radiograph of. —ra/di•og/ra•phy (-og/rə fē), *n.* —ra/di•o•graph/ic (-graf/ik), *adj.* —n. **1.** LABEL (def. 8). —*v.t.* **2.** LABEL (def. 14).

ra•di•o•i•so•tope (rā/dē ō ī/sə tōp/), *n.* a radioactive isotope, usu. artificially produced: used in physical and biological research and therapeutics. —ra/di•o•i/so•top/ic (-top/ik), *adj.*

ra•di•o•la•bel (rā/dē ō lā/bəl), *n., v.t.,* **-beled, -bel•ing** or (*esp. Brit.*) **-belled, -bel•ling.** —*n.* **1.** LABEL (def. 8). —*v.t.* **2.** LABEL (def. 14).

ra•di•o•log•i•cal (rā/dē ō loj/i kəl) also **ra/di•o•log/ic,** *adj.* **1.** of or pertaining to radiology. **2.** involving radioactive materials: *radiological warfare.* —ra/di•o•log/i•cal•ly, *adv.*

ra•di•ol•o•gy (rā dē ol/ə jē), *n.* the branch of medicine dealing with x-rays, other radiation, and various imaging techniques for diagnosis and treatment. —ra/di•ol/o•gist, *n.*

ra/diomet/ric dat/ing, *n.* any method of determining the age of earth materials or objects of organic origin based on measurement of either short-lived radioactive elements or the amount of a long-lived radioactive element plus its decay product.

ra•di•o•paque (rā/dē ō pāk/), *adj.* opaque to radiation; visible in x-ray photographs and under fluoroscopy. —ra/di•o•pac/i•ty (-pas/i tē), *n.*

ra•di•o•sonde (rā/dē ō sond/), *n.* an instrument carried aloft by balloon to transmit meteorological data by radio.

ra•di•o•tel•e•graph (rā/dē ō tel/ə graf/, -gräf/), *n.* **1.** a telegraph in which messages or signals are sent by means of radio waves rather than through wires or cables. —*v.t.* **2.** to send (a message) by radiotelegraph. —ra/di•o•te•leg/ra•phy (-ə leg/rə fē), *n.*

ra•di•o•tel•e•phone (rā/dē ō tel/ə fōn/), *n., v.,* **-phoned, -phon•ing.** —*n.* **1.** a telephone in which sound or speech is transmitted by means of radio waves instead of through wires or cables. —*v.t., v.i.* **2.** to communicate by radiotelephone.

ra/dio tel/escope, *n.* a parabolic or dipolar antenna used to detect radio waves emitted by stars, galaxies, and other sources in space.

radio telescope

ra•di•o•ther•a•py (rā/dē ō ther/ə pē), *n.* the treatment of disease by means of x-rays or radioactive substances.

ra/dio wave/, *n.* an electromagnetic wave having a wavelength between 1 mm and 30,000 m, or a frequency between 10 kHz and 300,000 MHz.

rad•ish (rad/ish), *n.* **1.** the crisp, pungent, edible root of the plant, *Raphanus sativus,* of the mustard family. **2.** the plant itself.

ra•di•um (rā/dē əm), *n.* a highly radioactive metallic element whose decay yields radon gas and alpha rays. *Symbol:* Ra; *at. wt.:* 226; *at. no.:* 88.

ra•di•us (rā/dē əs), *n., pl.* **-di•i** (-dē ī/), **-di•us•es. 1.** a straight line extending from the center of a circle or sphere to the circumference or surface: *The radius of a circle is half the diameter.* **2.** the length of such a line. **3.** any radial or radiating part. **4.** a circular area having an extent determined by the length of the radius from a given or specified central point: *every house within a radius of 50 miles.* **5.** a field or range of operation or influence. **6.** extent of possible operation, travel, etc., as under a single supply of fuel. **7.** the bone of the forearm on the thumb side. **8.** a corresponding bone in the forelimb of other vertebrates. [< Latin: staff, spoke]

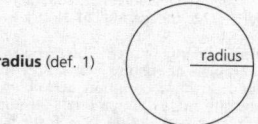

radius (def. 1)

ra•dix (rā/diks), *n., pl.* **rad•i•ces** (rad/ə sēz/, rā/də-), **ra•dix•es. 1.** *Math.* a number taken as the base of a system of numbers, logarithms, or the like. **2.** *Anat., Bot.* a root; radicle.

ra•don (rā/don), *n.* a chemically inert, radioactive gaseous element produced by the decay of radium: emissions from outgassing of rock, brick, etc., are a health hazard. *Symbol:* Rn; *at. no.:* 86; *at. wt.:* 222.

RAF or **R.A.F.,** Royal Air Force.

raf•fi•a (raf/ē ə), *n.* a fiber from the leaves of the raffia palm, used to tie plants and other objects and to make mats, baskets, hats, etc.

raf•fi•nose (raf/ə nōs/), *n.* a colorless, crystalline sugar, $C_{18}H_{32}O_{16} \cdot 5H_2O$, with little or no sweetness, obtained from cottonseed and sugar beets and breaking down to fructose, glucose, and galactose on hydrolysis.

raff•ish (raf/ish), *adj.* **1.** disreputable or nonconformist; rakish. **2.** gaudily vulgar or cheap; tawdry.

raf•fle (raf/əl), *n., v.,* **-fled, -fling.** —*n.* **1.** a form of lottery in which a number of persons buy one or more chances to win a prize. —*v.t.* **2.** to dispose of by a raffle (often fol. by *off*). —*v.i.* **3.** to take part in a raffle.

raf•fle•sia (rə flē/zhə, -zhē ə, ra-), *n., pl.* **-sias.** a stemless, leafless Malaysian plant of the genus *Rafflesia,* of the family Rafflesiaceae, bearing a flower that grows to 3 ft. (90 cm) in diameter, the world's largest.

raft¹ (raft, räft), *n.* **1.** a more or less rigid floating platform made of buoyant materials: *an inflatable rubber raft.* **2.** a collection of logs, planks, casks, etc., fastened together for floating on water. **3.** LIFE RAFT. **4.** a slab of reinforced concrete providing a footing on yielding soil, usu. for a whole building. —*v.t.* **5.** to transport on a raft. **6.** to form (logs or the like) into a raft. **7.** to travel or cross by raft. **8.** (of an ice floe) to transport (embedded organic or rock debris) from the shore out to sea. —*v.i.* **9.** to use a raft; go or travel on a raft.

raft² (raft, räft), *n. Informal.* a great quantity; a lot.

raf•ter (raf/tər, räf/-), *n.* any of a series of timbers etc. having a pronounced slope, for supporting the sheathing and covering of a roof.

rag¹ (rag), *n.* **1.** a worthless piece of cloth, esp. one that is torn or worn. **2. rags,** ragged or tattered clothing. **3.** any article of apparel regarded deprecatingly. **4.** a cloth-based pulp used in making high-quality paper, as bond. **5.** a shred, scrap, or fragmentary bit of anything. **6.** something of very low value or in very poor condition. **7.** *Informal.* a newspaper or magazine regarded with contempt or distaste.

rag² (rag), *v.,* **ragged, rag•ging,** *n. Informal.* —*v.t.* **1.** to scold. **2.** to subject to a teasing. **3.** *Brit.* to torment; tease. —*n.* **4.** *Brit.* an act of ragging.

rag³ (rag), *n.* a musical composition in ragtime.

rag•a•muf•fin (rag/ə muf/in), *n.* **1.** a child in ragged, ill-fitting, dirty clothes. **2.** a ragged, disreputable person.

rag•bag (rag/bag/), *n.* **1.** a bag in which rags are kept. **2.** a mixture or conglomeration.

rag/ doll/, *n.* a stuffed doll, esp. of cloth.

rage (rāj), *n., v.,* **raged, rag•ing.** —*n.* **1.** angry fury; violent anger. **2.** a fit of violent anger. **3.** fury or violence of wind, waves, fire, disease, etc. **4.** violence of feeling, desire, or appetite. **5.** a violent desire or passion. **6.** ardor; fervor; enthusiasm. **7.** an object of current popularity; fad: *I remember when long hair was all the rage.* —*v.i.* **8.** to act or speak with fury; show or feel violent anger. **9.** to move, rush, dash, or surge furiously. **10.** to proceed, continue, or prevail with great violence. —**rag/ing•ly,** *adv.*

ragg (rag), *n.* **1.** a sturdy wool fiber treated so as to retain the natural oils. **2.** a flecked, grayish yarn made from this, usu. blended with nylon. **3.** a garment made from this yarn.

rag•ged (rag/id), *adj.* **1.** clothed in tattered garments. **2.** torn or worn to rags; tattered. **3.** shaggy, as an animal or its coat. **4.** having loose or hanging shreds or fragmentary bits. **5.** full of rough or sharp projections; jagged. **6.** in a wild or neglected state. **7.** rough, imperfect, or faulty. **8.** harsh, as the voice.

rag/ged edge/, *n.* **1.** the brink, as of a cliff. **2.** any extreme or precarious edge: *on the ragged edge of despair.*

rag•ged•y (rag/i dē), *adj.* somewhat ragged, tattered, or shaggy.

rag•i or **rag•gee** (rag/ē, rä/gē), *n.* a cereal grass, *Eleusine coracana,* cultivated in the Old World for its grain.

rag/lan (rag/lən), *n.* a loose overcoat with raglan sleeves.

rag/lan sleeve/, *n.* a set-in sleeve that starts at the neck of the garment and has a long, slanting seam from neckline to armhole.

ra•gout (ra gōō/), *n.* a highly seasoned stew of meat or fish, with or without vegetables.

rag•tag (rag/tag/), *adj.* **1.** ragged or shabby; disheveled. **2.** made up of mixed, often diverse, elements; motley.

rag•time (rag/tīm/), *n.* **1.** rhythm in which the accompaniment is strict two-four time and the melody, with ragtime embellishments, is in steady syncopation. **2.** music in ragtime rhythm.

rag•weed (rag/wēd/), *n.* any of the composite plants of the genus *Ambrosia,* the airborne pollen of which is the most prevalent cause of autumnal hay fever.

rag•wort (rag/wûrt/, -wôrt/), *n.* any of various composite plants of the genus *Senecio,* usu. bearing yellow, slender-rayed flower heads.

rah (rä), *interj.* (an exclamation of encouragement to a player or team.)

Ra•hab (rā/hab), *n.* a harlot of Jericho who gave shelter to the two agents sent by Joshua to spy on the city. Josh. 2.

R

rah-rah (rä′rä′), *adj. Informal.* marked by or expressive of ardently enthusiastic spirit: *a group of rah-rah undergraduates.*

raid (rād), *n.* **1.** a sudden assault or attack, as upon something to be seized or suppressed: *a police raid on a narcotics ring.* **2.** a sudden attack on an enemy, as by air or by a small land force. **3.** an effort to lure away a competitor's employees, members, etc. **4.** a concerted attempt of speculators to force stock prices down. —*v.t.* **5.** to make a raid on. —*v.i.* **6.** to engage in a raid.

raid•er (rā′dər), *n.* **1.** a person or thing that raids. **2. a.** a commando, ranger, etc., trained to participate in military raids. **b.** a light, fast warship, aircraft, etc., used in raids. **3.** CORPORATE RAIDER.

Raikes (rāks), *n.* **Robert,** 1735–1811, English publisher and philanthropist who organized the first Sunday school.

rail[1] (rāl), *n.* **1.** a bar of wood, metal, etc., fixed horizontally, as for a support, barrier, fence, or railing. **2.** a fence; railing. **3.** one of a pair of steel bars that provide the running surfaces for the wheels of locomotives and railroad cars. **4.** the railroad as a means of transportation: *to travel by rail.* **5. rails,** stocks or bonds of railroad companies. **6.** one of two fences marking the inside and outside boundaries of a racetrack. **7.** a horizontal member capping a ship's bulwark. **8.** any of the horizontal members framing paneling, as in a paneled door or a window sash. Compare STILE[2]. —*v.t.* **9.** to furnish or enclose with a rail or railing.

rail[2] (rāl), *v.i.* to utter bitter complaints or vehement denunciation (often fol. by *at* or *against*): *to rail at fate.*

rail[3] (rāl), *n.* any of numerous usu. secretive birds of the family Rallidae, having short wings, a narrow body, and long toes, and inhabiting forests, grasslands, and esp. marshes in most parts of the world.

rail•ing (rā′ling), *n.* **1.** a fencelike barrier composed of one or more horizontal rails supported by widely spaced uprights; balustrade. **2.** a banister. **3.** rails collectively.

rail•ler•y (rā′lə rē), *n., pl.* **-ler•ies. 1.** good-humored ridicule; banter. **2.** a bantering remark.

rail•road (rāl′rōd′), *n.* **1.** a permanent road laid with rails, commonly in one or more pairs of continuous lines forming a track or tracks, on which locomotives and cars are run for the transportation of passengers, freight, and mail. **2.** an entire system of such roads together with its rolling stock, buildings, etc. —*v.t.* **3.** to transport by means of a railroad. **4.** to supply with railroads. **5.** to push (a law or bill) hastily through a legislature so that there is not time enough for objections to be considered. **6.** to pressure or coerce into a hasty action or decision. **7.** to convict in a hasty manner by means of false charges or insufficient evidence. —*v.i.* **8.** to work on a railroad.

rail•way (rāl′wā′), *n.* **1.** a railroad using lightweight equipment or operating over short distances. **2.** a line of rails forming a road for flanged-wheel equipment.

rai•ment (rā′mənt), *n.* clothing; apparel; attire.

rain (rān), *n.* **1.** water that is condensed from the aqueous vapor in the atmosphere and falls to earth in drops. **2.** a rainfall, rainstorm, or shower. **3. rains,** the rainy season; seasonal rainfall. **4.** weather marked by steady or frequent rainfall. **5.** a heavy, continuous descent or inflicting of anything: *a rain of blows.* —*v.i.* **6.** (of rain) to fall (usu. used impersonally with *it* as subject): *It rained all night.* **7.** to fall like rain. **8.** to send down rain. —*v.t.* **9.** to send down like rain. **10.** to offer or bestow in great quantity; shower: *to rain favors upon a person.* **11. rain out,** to cancel or postpone because of rain. —***Idiom.*** **12. rain cats and dogs,** to rain very heavily or steadily. —***Proverb.*** **13. It never rains but it pours,** instances of good or bad fortune come in groups.

rain•bow (rān′bō′), *n.* **1.** a bow or arc of prismatic colors appearing in the heavens opposite the sun and caused by the refraction and reflection of the sun's rays in drops of rain. **2.** a similar bow of colors, esp. one appearing in the spray of a waterfall or fountain. **3.** any brightly multicolored arrangement or display. **4.** a wide variety or range; gamut. —*adj.* **5.** of many colors; multicolored. **6.** made up of diverse races, groups, etc.: *a rainbow coalition.*

rain′bow fish′, *n.* GUPPY.

rain′bow trout′, *n.* a plump trout, *Salmo gairdneri,* native to W North American streams, having vertical reddish stripes on a black-speckled, green-to-turquoise body.

rain′ check′ or **rain′check′,** *n.* **1.** an offered or requested postponement of an invitation until a more convenient, usu. unspecified time. **2.** a voucher entitling a customer to purchase at a later date and for the same price a sale item that is temporarily out of stock. **3.** a ticket for future use given to spectators at an outdoor event that has been postponed or interrupted by rain.

rain•coat (rān′kōt′), *n.* a waterproof or water-repellent coat worn as protection against rain.

rain•drop (rān′drop′), *n.* a drop of rain.

rain•fall (rān′fôl′), *n.* **1.** a fall of rain. **2.** the amount of water falling in rain, snow, etc., within a given time and area, usu. expressed as a hypothetical depth of coverage: *a rainfall of 70 inches a year.*

rain′ for′est or **rain′for′est,** *n.* a tropical forest, usu. of tall, densely growing, broad-leaved evergreen trees in an area of high annual rainfall.

Rai•nier (rə nēr′, rā-, rā′nēr), *n.* **Mount,** a volcanic peak in W Washington, in the Cascade Range. 14,408 ft. (4392 m).

rain•mak•er (rān′mā′kər), *n.* **1.** (among American Indians) a medicine man who by various rituals and incantations seeks to cause rain. **2.** a person who induces or tries to induce rainfall by artificial techniques. **3.** *Informal.* an executive able to secure clients, generate income, etc., esp. by using political or other connections.

rain•out (rān′out′), *n.* **1.** the cancellation or postponement of a sports event, etc., because of rain. **2.** the removal of radioactive particles or other foreign substances from the atmosphere by precipitation.

rain•proof (rān′pro͞of′), *adj.* **1.** impervious to rain; keeping out or unaffected by rain. —*v.t.* **2.** to make rainproof.

rain•spout (rān′spout′), *n.* DOWNSPOUT.

rain′ tree′, *n.* MONKEYPOD.

rain•y (rā′nē), *adj.,* **-i•er, -i•est. 1.** characterized by rain: *rainy weather.* **2.** wet with rain: *rainy streets.* **3.** bringing rain: *rainy clouds.* —**rain′i•ly,** *adv.* —**rain′i•ness,** *n.*

rain′y day′, *n.* a future time of need.

raise (rāz), *v.,* **raised, rais•ing,** *n.* —*v.t.* **1.** to move to a higher position; elevate: *to raise one's hand.* **2.** to set upright. **3.** to cause to rise or stand up; rouse. **4.** to increase the height or vertical measurement of. **5.** to increase in amount: *to raise rents.* **6.** to increase in degree, intensity, pitch, or force: *to raise one's voice.* **7.** to promote the growth or development of; grow or breed: *to raise corn.* **8.** to bring up; rear: *to raise children.* **9.** to present for consideration; put forward: *to raise a question.* **10.** to give rise to; bring about: *to raise a ripple of applause.* **11.** to build; erect: *to raise a house.* **12.** to restore to life: *to raise the dead.* **13.** to stir up: *to raise a rebellion.* **14.** to give vigor to; animate: *to raise one's spirits.* **15.** to advance in rank or position; elevate: *to raise someone to the peerage.* **16.** to assemble or collect: *to raise an army; to raise money.* **17.** to utter (a cry, shout, etc.). **18.** to cause to be heard: *to raise an alarm.* **19.** to make (an issue at law). **20.** to cause (dough or bread) to rise by expansion and become light, as by the use of yeast. **21.** to increase (the value or price) of a commodity, stock, bond, etc. **22. a.** to increase (another player's bet) in poker. **b.** to bet at a higher level than (a preceding bettor). **23.** to increase (the bid for a bridge contract) by repeating one's partner's bid at a higher level. **24.** to increase the amount specified in (a check, money order, etc.) by fraudulent alteration. **25.** to end (a siege) by withdrawing forces or compelling them to withdraw. **26.** to establish communication with by radio: *to raise headquarters.* —*v.i.* **27.** to lift up: *The window raises easily.* —*n.* **28.** an increase in amount, as of wages. **29.** the amount of such an increase. **30.** an act or instance of raising. **31.** a raised or ascending place; rise. —**Usage.** Although similar in form and meaning, RISE and RAISE differ in grammatical use. RAISE is almost always used transitively. Its forms are regular: *Raise the window. The flag had been raised before we arrived.* RAISE in the intransitive sense "to rise up, arise" is nonstandard: *Dough rises* (not *raises*) *better in warm temperature.* RISE is almost exclusively intransitive in its standard uses. Its forms are irregular: *My husband usually rises before seven. The latest he has ever risen is eight. The sun rose in a cloudless sky.* In American English a person receives a RAISE in salary; in British English, a RISE. Both RAISE and REAR are used in the U.S. to refer to the upbringing of children. Although RAISE was formerly condemned in this sense, it is now standard.

raised (rāzd), *adj.* **1.** fashioned or made as a surface design in relief. **2.** made light by the use of yeast or other ferment and not with baking powder, soda, or the like.

rai•sin (rā′zin), *n.* a grape of any of various sweet varieties dried in the sun or by artificial means.

rai•son d'ê•tre (rā′zōn de′trə, rez′ôɴ), *n., pl.* **rai•sons d'ê•tre** (rā′zōnz de′trə, rez′ôɴ). reason or justification for existence. [< French]

Ra•jab (rə jab′), *n.* the seventh month of the Islamic calendar.

ra•jah or **ra•ja** (rä′jə), *n.* **1.** a king or prince in India. **2.** a minor chief or dignitary. **3.** an honorary title conferred on Hindus in India. **4.** a title of rulers, princes, or chiefs in Java, Borneo, etc.

rake[1] (rāk), *n., v.,* **raked, rak•ing.** —*n.* **1.** an agricultural implement with teeth or tines for gathering cut grass, hay, etc., or for smoothing the surface of the ground. **2.** any of various implements of similar form and use. —*v.t.* **3.** to gather, draw, or remove with a rake. **4.** to clear, smooth, or prepare with a rake. **5.** to clear (a fire, embers, etc.) by stirring with a poker or the like. **6.** to collect in abundance (usu. fol. by *in*): *to rake in money.* **7.** to bring to light, usu. for discreditable reasons (usu. fol. by *up*): *to rake up a scandal.* **8.** to search thoroughly through. **9.** to scrape; scratch. **10.** to fire guns along the length of (a position, body of troops, ship, etc.). **11.** to sweep with the eyes. —*v.i.* **12.** to use a rake. **13.** to search, as if with a rake. **14.** to scrape or scratch.

rake[2] (rāk), *n.* a dissolute and profligate and usu. licentious man; roué; libertine.

rake[3] (rāk), *v.,* **raked, rak•ing,** *n.* —*v.i.* **1.** to incline from the vertical, as a mast, or from the horizontal. —*v.t.* **2.** to cause (something) to incline from the vertical or the horizontal. —*n.* **3.** inclination or slope away from the perpendicular or the horizontal.

rak•ish[1] (rā′kish), *adj.* like a rake; dissolute. —**rak′ish•ly,** *adv.*

rak•ish[2] (rā′kish), *adj.* **1.** smart; jaunty; dashing: *a rakish hat.* **2.** (of a vessel) having an appearance suggesting speed.

Ra•leigh (rô′lē, rä′-), *n.* **1. Sir Walter.** Also, **Ra′legh.** 1552?–1618, English explorer and writer. **2.** the capital of North Carolina, in the central part. 236,707.

ral•ly (ral′ē), *v.,* **-lied, -ly•ing,** *n., pl.* **-lies.** —*v.t.* **1.** to bring into order again; gather and organize or inspire anew: *to rally scattered troops.* **2.** to draw or call together for a common action or effort: *to rally one's friends.* **3.** to concentrate or revive, as one's strength or spirits. —*v.i.* **4.** to come together for common action or effort. **5.** to come together or into order again, as troops. **6.** to come to the assistance of a person, party, or cause: *to rally around the president.* **7.** to recover partially from illness. **8.** to find renewed strength or vigor. **9. a.** (of securities) to rise sharply in price after a drop. **b.** (of a market) to show increased activity after a slow period. **10.** (in tennis, badminton, etc.) to engage in a rally. **11.** to participate in a long-distance automobile race. **12.** (of a baseball team) to score one or more runs in one inning. **—***n.* **13.** a recovery from dispersion or disorder, as of troops. **14.** a renewal or recovery of strength, activity, etc. **15.** a partial recovery of strength during illness. **16.** a mass meeting of people gathered for a common cause: *a political rally.* **17.** a sharp rise in price or active trading after a declining market. **18.** (in tennis, badminton, etc.) **a.** an exchange of strokes between players before a point is scored. **b.** the hitting of the ball back and forth prior to the start of a match. **19.** the scoring of one or more runs in one inning in baseball. **20.** Also, **ral′lye.** a long-distance automobile race, esp. for sports cars, held over public roads unfamiliar to the drivers, with numerous checkpoints along the route. **—ral′li•er,** *n.*

ram (ram), *n., v.,* **rammed, ram•ming. —***n.* **1.** a male sheep. **2.** any of various devices for battering, crushing, driving, or forcing something, as a battering ram. **3.** (formerly) a heavy beak or spur projecting from the bow of a warship for penetrating the hull of an enemy's ship. **4.** a warship so equipped. **—***v.t.* **5.** to drive or force by heavy blows. **6.** to strike with great force; dash violently against. **7.** to cram; stuff. **8.** to push firmly; force: *to ram a bill through the Senate.* **9.** to force (a charge) into a firearm, as with a ramrod. **—ram′mer,** *n.*

RAM (ram), *n.* random-access memory: volatile computer memory, used for creating, loading, and running programs and for manipulating and temporarily storing data; main memory. Compare ROM.

ra•ma•da (rə mä′də), *n., pl.* **-das.** an open shelter, often with a thatched roof.

Ram•a•dan (ram′ə dän′), *n.* **1.** the ninth month of the Islamic calendar. **2.** the daily fast enjoined from dawn until sunset during this month.

ram•ble (ram′bəl), *v.,* **-bled, -bling,** *n.* **—***v.i.* **1.** to wander around in a leisurely, aimless manner; stroll. **2.** to take a course with many turns or windings, as a stream or path. **3.** to grow or spread in a random, unsystematic fashion, as a vine. **4.** to talk or write in a discursive, aimless manner: *The speaker rambled on endlessly.* **—***v.t.* **5.** to walk aimlessly or idly over or through. **—***n.* **6.** a leisurely walk without a definite route, taken merely for pleasure.

ram•bler (ram′blər), *n.* **1.** one that rambles. **2.** RANCH HOUSE (def. 2). **3.** any of several climbing roses with clusters of small flowers.

ram•bunc•tious (ram bungk′shəs), *adj.* **1.** difficult to control or handle; wildly boisterous. **2.** turbulently active and noisy. **—ram•bunc′tious•ly,** *adv.* **—ram•bunc′tious•ness,** *n.*

ram•bu•tan (ram bo͞ot′n), *n.* **1.** the bright red, oval, edible fruit of a Malayan tree of the soapberry family, covered with soft spines or hairs and having a mildly acid taste. **2.** the tree itself.

ram•e•kin or **ram•e•quin** (ram′i kin), *n.* **1.** a portion of food, esp. a cheese preparation, baked and served in an open dish. **2.** the dish itself.

ram•ie (ram′ē, rā′mē), *n.* **1.** an Asian shrub of the nettle family, yielding a fiber used esp. in making textiles. **2.** the fiber itself.

ram•i•fi•ca•tion (ram′ə fi kā′shən), *n.* **1.** the act or process of ramifying. **2.** a related or derived development; consequence; implication. **3.** a branch: *ramifications of a nerve.* **4.** a structure formed of branches.

ram•i•fy (ram′ə fī′), *v.t., v.i.,* **-fied, -fy•ing.** to spread out into branches or branchlike parts; extend into subdivisions.

ram•jet (ram′jet′), *n.* a jet engine operated by fuel injected into a stream of air compressed by the aircraft's forward speed.

ra•mose (rā′mōs, rə mōs′), *adj.* having many branches; branching. **—ra•mos•i•ty** (rə mos′i tē), *n.*

Ra′moth-Gil′ead (rā′moth), *n.* a city in Gad near the border of Israel and Syria, one of the cities of refuge. Deut. 4:43; Josh. 20:8.

ramp (ramp), *n.* **1.** a sloping surface connecting two levels; incline. **2.** any extensive sloping walk or passageway. **3.** a concave slope or bend, as one connecting the higher and lower parts of a staircase railing at a landing. **4.** the act of ramping. **5. a.** BOARDING RAMP. **b.** APRON (def. 3). **—***v.i.* **6.** to rise or rear with arms or forelegs raised as if to spring. **7.** (of a lion or other large quadruped represented on a coat of arms) to rise or stand on the hind legs. **8.** to leap or dash with fury. **9.** to act violently; rage; storm: *to ramp and rage.* **—***v.t.* **10.** to provide with a ramp.

ram•page (ram′pāj; *v. also* ram pāj′), *n., v.,* **-paged, -pag•ing. —***n.* **1.** an eruption of violently uncontrolled, reckless, or destructive behavior. **—***v.i.* **2.** to rush or behave furiously or violently.

ramp•ant (ram′pənt), *adj.* **1.** prevailing or unchecked; widespread; rife: *a rampant rumor.* **2.** growing luxuriantly, as weeds. **3.** violent in action or spirit; raging. **4.** (of an animal) standing on the hind legs; ramping. **5.** (of a heraldic animal) **a.** having the body upraised on the left hind leg, the head in profile, and one foreleg above the other. **b.** rearing in profile upon the hind legs with the forelegs extended. **6.** (of an arch or vault) springing at one side from one level of support and resting at the other on a higher level. **—ramp′an•cy,** *n.* **—ramp′ant•ly,** *adv.*

ram•part (ram′pärt, -pərt), *n.* **1. a.** a mound of earth, rubble, or similar material raised around a place as a fortification. **b.** such a fortification together with a stone or earth parapet capping it. **2.** anything serving as a bulwark or defense. **—***v.t.* **3.** to furnish with a rampart.

ram•pi•on (ram′pē ən), *n.* a European bellflower, *Campanula rapunculus,* having an edible white tuberous root used in salad.

ram•rod (ram′rod′), *n., v.,* **-rod•ded, -rod•ding. —***n.* **1.** a rod for ramming down the charge of a muzzleloading firearm. **2.** a cleaning rod for the barrel of a firearm. **3.** a rigid, strict disciplinarian. **4.** a boss. **—***v.t.* **5.** to exert discipline and authority on. **6.** to direct or oversee. **7.** to accomplish by force. **8.** to strike with or as if with a ramrod.

Ram•ses (ram′sēz) also **Rameses,** *n.* **1.** the name of several kings of ancient Egypt. **2. Ramses II,** king of ancient Egypt 1292–1225 B.C. **3. Ramses III,** king of ancient Egypt 1198–1167 B.C.

Ram•sey (ram′zē), *n.* **Arthur Michael,** (*Baron Ramsey of Canterbury*), born 1904, English clergyman and scholar: archbishop of Canterbury 1961–74.

ram•shack•le (ram′shak′əl), *adj.* loosely made or held together; rickety; shaky: *a ramshackle house.*

ran (ran), *v.* pt. of RUN.

ranch (ranch), *n.* **1.** an establishment maintained for raising livestock under range conditions. **2.** a farm or ranchlike enterprise that raises a single crop or animal: *a fruit ranch; a mink ranch.* **3.** the persons working or living on a ranch. **—***v.i.* **4.** to own, manage, or work on a ranch.

ranch•er (ran′chər), *n.* a person who owns or works on a ranch.

ran•che•ro (ran châr′ō, rän-), *n., pl.* **-che•ros.** (in Spanish America and the southwestern U.S.) a rancher.

ranch•ette (ran chet′), *n.* a house on a parcel of land large enough for the maintenance of a horse or small farm animals, as goats or sheep.

ranch′ house′, *n.* **1.** the house of the owner of a ranch, usu. of one story and with a low-pitched roof. **2.** any one-story house of the same general form, esp. one built in the suburbs.

ranch′ mink′, *n.* a semiaquatic mink, *Mustela vision,* raised commercially for its fur.

Ran′cho Cu•ca•mon′ga (ko͞o′kə mung′gə, -mong′-), *n.* a city in SE California. 114,799.

ran•cid (ran′sid), *adj.* **1.** having a rank, unpleasant smell or taste: *rancid oil.* **2.** (of an odor or taste) rank, unpleasant, and stale. **3.** offensive or nasty. **—ran•cid′i•ty,** *n.*

ran•cor (rang′kər), *n.* bitter resentment or ill will; malice. Also, *esp. Brit.,* **ran′cour. —ran′cored;** *esp. Brit.,* **ran′coured,** *adj.*

ran•cor•ous (rang′kər əs), *adj.* full of or showing rancor.

rand (rand), *n.* a coin and monetary unit of the Republic of South Africa, equal to 100 cents. *Abbr.:* R.

Rand (rand), *n.* **Ayn** (īn), 1905–82, U.S. novelist and essayist, born in Russia.

Rand, The (rand), Witwatersrand.

Ran•dolph (ran′dolf, -dəlf), *n.* **1. A(sa) Philip,** 1889–1979, U.S. labor leader: president of the Brotherhood of Sleeping Car Porters 1925–68. **2. Edmund Jennings** (jen′ings), 1753–1813, U.S. statesman: first U.S. Attorney General 1789–94; Secretary of State 1794–95. **3. John,** 1773–1833, U.S. statesman and author.

ran•dom (ran′dəm), *adj.* **1.** occurring or done without definite aim, reason, or pattern: *random examples.* **2.** *Statistics.* of or characterizing a process of selection in which each item of a set has an equal probability of being chosen. **3.** *Building Trades.* **a.** (of building materials) lacking uniformity of dimensions: *random shingles.* **b.** constructed or applied without regularity: *random bond.* **—***adv.* **4.** *Building Trades.* without uniformity: *random-sized slates.* **—*Idiom.*** **5. at random,** without regard to rules, schedules, etc.; haphazardly. **—ran′dom•ly,** *adv.*

ran′dom ac′cess, *n.* a feature of a videodisc or compact disc player that allows the user to select and replay any portion without starting at the beginning.

ran′dom-ac′cess, *adj.* designating an electronic storage medium that allows information to be stored and retrieved in arbitrary sequence.

ran′dom-ac′cess mem′ory, *n.* See RAM.

ran•dom•ize (ran′də mīz′), *v.t.,* **-ized, -iz•ing.** to arrange, select, or distribute in a random manner. **—ran′dom•i•za′tion,** *n.*

ran′dom sam′pling, *n.* a method of selecting a sample **(ran′dom sam′ple)** from a statistical population in such a way that every sample that could be selected has a predetermined probability of being selected.

ran′dom var′iable, *n.* a statistical quantity that can take any of the values of a specified set in accordance with an associated probability distribution. Also called **variate.**

R and R or **R&R,** **1.** rest and recreation. **2.** rest and recuperation. **3.** rest and relaxation. **4.** rock and roll.

ra•nee or **ra•ni** (rä′nē, rä nē′), *n.* (in India) **1.** the wife of a rajah. **2.** a reigning queen or princess.

rang (rang), *v.* pt. of RING².

range (rānj), *n., adj., v.,* **ranged, rang•ing. —***n.* **1.** the extent to which or the limits between which variation is possible: *the range of steel prices.* **2.** the extent or scope of something: *one's range of vision.* **3.** the distance to which a projectile may be sent by a weapon. **4.** the distance of the target from the weapon. **5.** an area equipped with targets for practice in shooting: *a rifle range.* **6.** an area used for flight-testing missiles. **7.** the distance of something from the point of operation, as in sound ranging. **8.** the distance that can be covered by an aircraft, ship, etc., carrying a normal load without refueling. **9.** (in navigation) a line established by markers or lights on shore for the location of soundings. **10.** a rank, class, or order. **11.** a row, line, or series, as of persons or things. **12.** the act of moving around, as over an area or region. **13.** an area or tract that is or may be ranged over, esp. an open region for the grazing of livestock. **14.** the region over which a population or species is distributed: *the range of the Baltimore oriole.* **15.** *Math.* the set of all values attained by a given function throughout its domain. **16.** a chain of mountains forming a single system: *the Cascade Range.* **17.** a large cooking stove having burners on the top surface and containing one or more ovens. **—*adj.*** **18.** working or grazing on a range. **—*v.t.*** **19.** to draw up or arrange (persons or things) in rows or lines or in a specific position. **20.** to place in a particular class; classify. **21.** to make straight, level, or even, as lines of type. **22.** to pass over or through (an area or region), as in exploring or searching. **23.** to pasture (cattle) on a range. **24.** to direct or train, as a telescope. **25.** to ascertain the distance of. **26.** to lay out (an anchor cable) so that the anchor may descend smoothly. **—*v.i.*** **27.** to vary within certain limits: *Prices range from $20 to $50.* **28.** to extend within extreme points of a scale: *emotions ranging from smugness to despair.* **29.** to move around or through a region, as people or animals. **30.** to roam or wander: *talks ranging over a variety of subjects.* **31.** to extend in a certain direction: *a boundary ranging from east and west.* **32.** to lie or extend in the same line or plane as another or others. **33.** to extend or occur over an area or throughout a period, as an animal or plant. **—*Idiom.*** **34. in range,** *Naut.* (of two or more objects observed from a vessel) located one directly behind the other.

range′ find′er or **range′find′er,** *n.* any of various instruments for determining the distance from the observer to a particular object, as for sighting a gun or adjusting the focus of a camera.

rang•er (rān′jər), *n.* **1.** FOREST RANGER. **2.** one of a body of armed guards who patrol a region. **3.** (*often cap.*) a U.S. soldier trained for making surprise raids and attacks in small groups. **4.** a person who ranges or roves. **5.** (esp. in Texas) a member of the state police. **6.** *Brit.* a keeper of a royal forest or park.

Ran•goon (rang go͞on′), *n.* former name of YANGON.

rang•y (rān′jē), *adj.*, **-i•er, -i•est.** **1.** (of animals or people) slender and long-limbed. **2.** able to range over large areas, as animals. **3.** (of terrain) mountainous. —**rang′i•ness,** *n.*

ra•ni (rä′nē, rä nē′), *n., pl.* **-nis.** RANEE.

rank[1] (rangk), *n.* **1.** a social or official position or standing, as in the armed forces: *the rank of captain.* **2.** high position or station: *a person of rank.* **3.** relative position or standing: *a writer of the first rank.* **4.** a row or series of things or persons: *orchestra players arranged in ranks.* **5.** a number of persons forming a separate class, as in a social hierarchy. **6. ranks, a.** the members of an armed service apart from its officers; enlisted personnel. **b.** military enlisted personnel as a group. **7.** Usu., **ranks.** the general body of any organization apart from the officers or leaders. **8.** orderly arrangement; array. **9.** a line of persons, esp. soldiers, standing abreast in close-order formation (disting. from *file*). **10.** one of the horizontal lines of squares on a chessboard. **11.** a set of organ pipes of the same kind and tonal color. **12.** the classification of coal according to hardness, from lignite to anthracite. **—*v.t.*** **13.** to arrange in ranks or in regular formation. **14.** to assign to a particular position, class, etc.: *to be ranked among the experts.* **15.** to outrank. **—*v.i.*** **16.** to form a rank or ranks. **17.** to take up or occupy a place in a particular rank, class, etc.: *to rank well ahead of the other students.* **18.** to have rank or standing. **19.** to be the senior in rank. **—*Idiom.*** **20. break ranks, a.** to leave an assigned position in a military formation. **b.** to withdraw support from one's colleagues, political party, or the like.

rank[2] (rangk), *adj.*, **-er, -est.** **1.** growing with excessive luxuriance; vigorous and tall of growth. **2.** having an offensive smell or taste: *a rank cigar.* **3.** utter; absolute: *a rank amateur.* **4.** highly offensive to one's moral sense; disgusting. **5.** grossly coarse or vulgar: *rank language.*

rank′ and file′, *n.* **1.** the members of any organization, esp. a union, apart from its leaders or officers. **2.** RANK[1] (def. 6a).

Ran•kin (rang′kən), *n.* **Jeremiah,** 1828–1904, U.S. clergyman and hymn writer.

rank•ing (rang′king), *adj.* **1.** senior or superior in rank, position, etc.: *a ranking diplomat.* **2.** highly regarded; renowned: *a ranking authority.* **3.** of a specific rank (often used in combination): *a low-ranking executive.* **—*n.*** **4.** an act or instance of indicating relative standing. **5.** a list showing such standing.

ran•kle (rang′kəl), *v.*, **-kled, -kling.** **—*v.i.*** **1.** (of feelings, experiences, etc.) to continue to irritate or cause bitter resentment. **—*v.t.*** **2.** to cause (a person) keen irritation or bitter resentment.

ran•sack (ran′sak), *v.t.* **1.** to search thoroughly or vigorously through (a house, receptacle, etc.). **2.** to search through for plunder; pillage.

ran•som (ran′səm), *n.* **1.** the redemption of a prisoner, kidnapped person, etc., for a price. **2.** the price paid or demanded for such redemption. **3.** deliverance or rescue from punishment for sin or the means for this, esp. the payment of a redemptive fine. **—*v.t.*** **4.** to redeem from detention, bondage, etc., by paying a demanded price.

rant (rant), *v.i.* **1.** to speak or declaim extravagantly or violently; talk in a wild or vehement way; rave. **—*v.t.*** **2.** to utter or declaim in a ranting manner. **—*n.*** **3.** extravagant or vehement declamation. **4.** a ranting speech or other utterance. —**rant′ing•ly,** *adv.*

rap[1] (rap), *v.*, **rapped, rap•ping,** *n.* **—*v.t.*** **1.** to strike, esp. with a quick, smart blow. **2.** to utter sharply or vigorously: *to rap out orders.* **3.** (of a spirit summoned by a medium) to communicate (a message) by raps (often fol. by *out*). **4.** *Slang.* to criticize severely. **5.** *Slang.* to arrest, detain, or sentence for a crime. **—*v.i.*** **6.** to knock smartly or vigorously: *to rap on a door.* **7.** *Slang.* to talk or discuss, esp. freely and volubly; chat. **8.** to talk rhythmically to the beat of rap music. **—*n.*** **9.** a quick, smart blow: *a rap on the knuckles.* **10.** the sound produced by such a blow. **11.** *Slang.* blame or punishment. **12.** *Slang.* a criminal charge: *a murder rap.* **13.** *Slang.* response or reception. **14.** *Slang.* a talk or conversation; chat. **15.** RAP MUSIC. **—*Idiom.*** **16. beat the rap,** *Slang.* to avoid retribution or punishment, as for a crime. **17. take the rap,** *Slang.* to be blamed and punished for another's crime.

rap[2] (rap), *n.* the least bit: *I don't care a rap.*

ra•pa•cious (rə pā′shəs), *adj.* **1.** given to plundering. **2.** inordinately greedy; predatory. **3.** (of animals) subsisting by the capture of living prey; predatory. —**ra•pa′cious•ly,** *adv.* —**ra•pac′i•ty** (-pas′i tē), **ra•pa′cious•ness,** *n.*

rape[1] (rāp), *n., v.*, **raped, rap•ing.** **—*n.*** **1.** the unlawful act of forcing a female to have sexual intercourse, as by physical attack or threats. **2.** any act of sexual intercourse that is forced upon a person. **3.** STATUTORY RAPE. **4.** an act of plunder: *the rape of the countryside.* **—*v.t.*** **5.** to force to have sexual intercourse. **6.** to plunder (a place); despoil. **7.** to seize and carry off by force. **—*v.i.*** **8.** to commit rape. —**rap′ist,** *n.*

rape[2] (rāp), *n.* a plant, *Brassica napus,* of the mustard family, whose leaves are used as fodder, and whose seeds yield rape oil.

rape[3] (rāp), *n.* the residue of grapes, after the juice has been extracted, used as a filter in making vinegar.

rape•seed (rāp′sēd′), *n.* the seed of the rape plant.

Raph•a•el (raf′ē əl, rā′fē-, rä′fī el′), *n.* **1.** (*Raffaello Santi* or *Sanzio*) 1483–1520, Italian painter. **2.** one of the archangels.

rap•id (rap′id), *adj.*, **-er, -est,** *n.* **—*adj.*** **1.** occurring within a short time: *rapid growth.* **2.** moving or acting with great speed; swift: *a rapid worker.* **3.** characterized by speed: *rapid motion.* **—*n.*** **4.** Usu., **rapids.** a part of a river where the current runs very swiftly. —**rap′id•ly,** *adv.*

rap′id eye′ move′ment, *n.* rapidly shifting movements of the eyes under closed lids, associated with the dreaming phase of the sleep cycle. Compare REM SLEEP.

rap′id-fire′, *adj.* **1.** done or occurring in rapid succession: *rapid-fire questions.* **2.** discharging, operating, etc., at a faster rate than normal.

ra•pid•i•ty (rə pid′i tē) also **rap•id•ness** (rap′id nis), *n.* a rapid state or quality; swiftness.

rap′id tran′sit, *n.* a system of public transportation in a metropolitan area, usu. a subway or elevated train system.

ra•pi•er (rā′pē ər), *n.* **1.** a small sword, esp. of the 18th century, having a narrow blade. **2.** a longer, heavier sword, esp. of the 16th and 17th centuries, having a double-edged blade. —**ra′pi•ered,** *adj.*

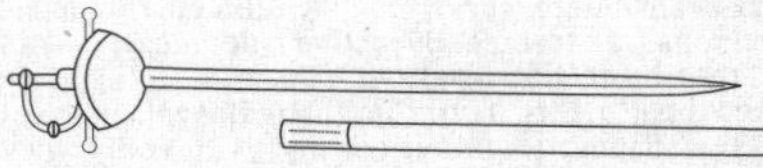

rapier (def. 2) and scabbard (17th century)

rap•ine (rap′in, -īn), *n.* the violent seizure and carrying off of another's property; plunder.

rap′ mu′sic, *n.* a popular music idiom marked by the rhythmical intoning of rhymed couplets to an insistent beat.

rap•pel (ra pel′, rə-), *n., v.*, **-pelled, -pel•ling.** **—*n.*** **1.** (in mountaineering) the act or method of moving down a vertical face by means of a double rope secured above and placed around the body and paid out gradually in the descent. **—*v.i.*** **2.** to descend by means of a rappel.

rap•per (rap′ər), *n.* **1.** a person or thing that raps or knocks. **2.** *Slang.* a person who chats or talks, esp. freely. **3.** a person who performs rap music, esp. professionally.

rap•port (ra pôr′, -pōr′, rə-), *n.* relation, esp. one that is harmonious or sympathetic: *a close rapport between teacher and students.*

rap•proche•ment (rap′rōsh mäN′), *n.* an establishment or renewal of harmonious relations.

rap•scal•lion (rap skal′yən), *n.* a rascal; rogue.

rap′ sheet′, *n. Slang.* a record kept by law-enforcement authorities of a person's arrests and convictions.

rapt (rapt), *adj.* **1.** deeply engrossed or absorbed: *a rapt listener.* **2.** transported with emotion; enraptured. **3.** indicative of or expressing rapture: *a rapt smile.* —**rapt′ly,** *adv.* —**rapt′ness,** *n.*

rap•tor (rap′tər, -tôr), *n.* a raptorial bird; bird of prey.

rap•to•ri•al (rap tôr′ē əl, -tōr′-), *adj.* **1.** preying upon other animals; predatory. **2.** adapted for seizing prey, as an eagle's claws. **3.** of or pertaining to a bird of prey.

rap•ture (rap′chər), *n., v.*, **-tured, -tur•ing.** **—*n.*** **1.** ecstatic joy or delight. **2.** Often, **raptures.** an utterance or expression of ecstatic delight. **3.** the feeling of being transported to another place or sphere of existence. **4. the Rapture,** *Theol.* the experience, anticipated by some fundamentalist Christians, of meeting Christ midway in the air upon his return to earth. **—*v.t.*** **5.** to enrapture.

rap•tur•ous (rap′chər əs), *adj.* **1.** feeling or manifesting ecstatic joy or delight. **2.** characterized by or expressive of such rapture: *rapturous praise.* —**rap′tur•ous•ly,** *adv.* —**rap′tur•ous•ness,** *n.*

ra•ra a•vis (râr′ə ā′vis; *Lat.* RÄ′RÄ ä′wis), *n., pl.* **ra•rae a•ves** (râr′ē ā′vēz; *Lat.* RÄ′RĪ ä′wes). a rare person or thing; rarity. [< Latin: rare bird]

rare[1] (râr), *adj.,* **rar•er, rar•est. 1.** occurring or found infrequently; markedly uncommon: *a rare disease; the rare gas station on that stretch of the road.* **2.** having the component parts loosely compacted; thin: *rare gases.* **3.** unusually great: *a rare display of courage.* **4.** admirable; exemplary: *rare tact.* —**rare′ness,** *n.*

rare[2] (râr), *adj.,* **rar•er, rar•est.** (of meat) cooked just slightly: *rare steak.* —**rare′ness,** *n.*

rare•bit (râr′bit), *n.* WELSH RABBIT.

rare′ earth′, *n.* the oxide of any of the rare-earth elements contained in various minerals.

rare′-earth′ el′ement, *n.* any of a group of closely related metallic elements, comprising the lanthanides, scandium, and yttrium, that are chemically similar in having the same number of valence electrons. Also called **rare′-earth′ met′al.**

rar•e•fac•tion (râr′ə fak′shən), *n.* **1.** the act or process of rarefying. **2.** the state of being rarefied. —**rar′e•fac′tion•al,** *adj.* —**rar′e•fac′tive** (-fak′tiv), *adj.*

rar•e•fied (râr′ə fīd′), *adj.* **1.** lofty or elevated; exalted: *the rarefied atmosphere of a scholarly symposium.* **2.** appealing to or exemplifying an exclusive group; select; esoteric: *rarefied tastes.*

rar•e•fy (râr′ə fī′), *v.,* **-fied, -fy•ing.** —*v.t.* **1.** to make rare or rarer; make less dense: *to rarefy a gas.* **2.** to make more refined or spiritual. —*v.i.* **3.** to become less dense; become thinned.

rare•ly (râr′lē), *adv.* **1.** on rare occasions; seldom. **2.** exceptionally; in or to an unusual degree. **3.** unusually or remarkably well.

rar•ing (râr′ing), *adj.* very eager or anxious; enthusiastic: *raring to go.*

rar•i•ty (râr′i tē), *n., pl.* **-ties. 1.** the state or quality of being rare. **2.** something rare or extremely uncommon. **3.** rare occurrence; infrequency. **4.** thinness, as of air or a gas.

Ras Ad•dar (räs′ a där′). See **Bon, Cape.**

ras•cal (ras′kəl), *n.* **1.** a dishonest or unscrupulous person. **2.** a mischievous person or animal.

rash[1] (rash), *adj.* **-er, -est. 1.** acting too hastily or without due consideration. **2.** made or done with reckless or ill-considered haste: *rash promises.* —**rash′ly,** *adv.* —**rash′ness,** *n.*

rash[2] (rash), *n.* **1.** an eruption of spots on the skin. **2.** multiple occurrences of something at about the same time: *a rash of robberies last month.* —**rash′like′,** *adj.*

rash•er (rash′ər), *n.* **1.** a thin slice of bacon or ham for frying or broiling. **2.** a serving of three or four slices, esp. of bacon.

rasp (rasp, räsp), *v.t.* **1.** to scrape or abrade with or as if with a rough instrument. **2.** to grate upon or irritate: *The sound rasped his nerves.* **3.** to utter with a grating sound: *to rasp out an order.* —*v.i.* **4.** to scrape or grate. **5.** to make a grating sound. —*n.* **6.** an act of rasping. **7.** a rasping sound. **8.** a coarse file, used mainly on wood, having separate conical teeth. **9.** (in an insect) a roughened surface used in stridulation.

rasp•ber•ry (raz′ber′ē, -bə rē, räz′-), *n., pl.* **-ries. 1.** the fruit of any of several shrubs belonging to the genus *Rubus,* of the rose family, consisting of small and juicy red, black, or pale yellow drupelets. **2.** any shrub bearing this fruit. **3.** a dark reddish purple color. **4. a.** a loud, abrasive, vibrating or spluttering noise made with the lips and tongue to express contempt. **b.** any sign or expression of displeasure or derision.

rasp•ing (ras′ping, rä′sping), *adj.* **1.** harsh; grating: *a rasping voice.* —*n.* **2.** a minute piece of wood, etc., removed with a rasp. **3. raspings,** dry breadcrumbs. —**rasp′ing•ly,** *adv.*

Ra•spu•tin (ra spyōō′tin, -spyōōt′n), *n.* **Grigori Efimovich,** 1871–1916, Russian mystic.

rasp•y (ras′pē, rä′spē), *adj.,* **-i•er, -i•est. 1.** harsh or grating; rasping. **2.** easily annoyed; irritable. —**rasp′i•ness,** *n.*

Ras•ta•far•i•an (ras′tə fâr′ē ən, -fär′-, rä′stə-), *n.* **1.** a follower of Rastafarianism. —*adj.* **2.** of, pertaining to, or characteristic of Rastafarianism or Rastafarians.

Ras•ta•far•i•an•ism (ras′tə fâr′ē ə niz′əm, -fär′-, rä′stə-), *n.* a religious sect, orig. of Jamaica, that regards the late Haile Selassie I of Ethiopia as the messiah and Africa as the Promised Land.

ras•ter (ras′tər), *n.* **1.** a pattern of scanning lines covering the area upon which the image is projected on the cathode-ray tube of a television set. **2.** a set of horizontal lines composed of individual pixels, used to form an image on a CRT or other screen.

rat (rat), *n., interj., v.,* **rat•ted, rat•ting.** —*n.* **1.** any of several long-tailed rodents of the Old World family Muridae, esp. of the genus *Rattus,* resembling but larger than mice. **2.** any of various similar rodents of other families. **3.** *Slang.* a scoundrel. **4.** *Slang.* **a.** a person who abandons or betrays associates. **b.** an informer. **c.** a scab laborer. **5.** a roll of padding used to give shape or fullness to a woman's hairstyle. —*interj.* **6. rats,** (used as an exclamation of disgust or disappointment.) —*v.i.* **7.** *Slang.* **a.** to inform on one's associates; squeal. **b.** to work as a scab. **8.** to hunt or catch rats. —*v.t.* **9.** to dress (hair) with a rat or by teasing. —***Proverb.*** **10. Rats desert a sinking ship,** the cowardly flee during a crisis. —**rat′like′,** *adj.*

rat•a•ble or **rate•a•ble** (rā′tə bəl), *adj.* **1.** capable of being rated or appraised. **2.** proportional: *a ratable distribution of wealth.*

rat•a•tat (rat′ə tat′) also **rat′-a-tat′-tat′,** *n.* a sound of knocking or rapping.

ra•ta•touille (rat′ə tōō′ē, rä′tə-), *n.* a vegetable stew of Provence containing eggplant, tomatoes, onions, and green peppers.

ratch•et (rach′it), *n.* **1. a.** a toothed bar or wheel with which a pawl engages. **b.** a pawl or the like used with a ratchet. **c.** a mechanism consisting of such a bar or wheel with the pawl. —*v.t., v.i.* **2.** to move by degrees (often fol. by *up* or *down*).

rate[1] (rāt), *n., v.,* **rat•ed, rat•ing.** —*n.* **1.** the amount of a charge or payment with reference to some basis of calculation: *a high rate of interest on loans.* **2.** a certain amount of one thing considered in relation to a unit of another: *at the rate of 60 miles an hour.* **3.** a fixed charge per unit of quantity: *a rate of 10 cents a pound.* **4.** degree of speed or progress: *to work at a rapid rate.* **5.** assigned position in any of a series of graded classes; rating. **6.** the premium charge per unit of insurance. **7.** a charge by a common carrier for transportation. **8.** a wage paid on a specified time basis: *an hourly rate.* —*v.t.* **9.** to estimate the value or worth of; appraise. **10.** to esteem, consider, or account: *He is rated one of the best writers around.* **11.** to fix at a certain rate, as of charge or payment. **12.** to value for purposes of taxation or the like. **13.** to make subject to the payment of a certain rate or tax. **14.** to place in a certain rank or class, as a ship or a sailor. —*v.i.* **15.** to have value or standing. —***Idiom.*** **16. at any rate, a.** in any event; in any case. **b.** at least.

rate[2] (rāt), *v.t., v.i.,* **rat•ed, rat•ing.** to chide vehemently.

rate•a•ble (rā′tə bəl), *adj.* RATABLE.

ra•tel (rāt′l, rät′l), *n.* a badgerlike carnivore, *Mellivora capensis,* of Africa and India. Also called **honey badger.**

rate′ of exchange′, *n.* EXCHANGE RATE.

rath•er (rath′ər, rä′thər), *adv.* **1.** to some extent: *rather good.* **2.** in some degree: *I rather expect you'll regret it.* **3.** more properly or justly: *The contrary is rather to be supposed.* **4.** sooner: *to die rather than yield.* **5.** more truly: *He is a painter or, rather, a watercolorist.* **6.** on the contrary: *It's not generosity, rather self-interest.* —***Idiom.*** **7. had** or **would rather,** to prefer that or to: *I had much rather we not stay.*

raths•kel•ler (rät′skel′ər, rat′-, rath′-), *n.* a restaurant or bar located below street level.

rat•i•fy (rat′ə fī′), *v.t.,* **-fied, -fy•ing.** to confirm by expressing consent, approval, or formal sanction: *to ratify a constitutional amendment.* —**rat′i•fi•ca′tion,** *n.* —**rat′i•fi′er,** *n.*

rat•ing (rā′ting), *n.* **1.** classification according to grade or rank, as in the armed forces. **2.** the estimated credit standing of a person or firm. **3.** a percentage indicating the number of listeners to or viewers of a radio or television broadcast. **4.** a designated operating limit for a machine, based on specified conditions.

ra•tio (rā′shō, -shē ō′), *n., pl.* **-tios. 1.** the relation between two similar magnitudes with respect to the number of times the first contains the second: *the ratio of 5 to 2, written 5:2 or 5/2.* **2.** proportional relation; rate: *the ratio between acceptances and rejections.* **3.** the relative value of gold and silver when both are used as a country's monetary standard. [< Latin *ratiō* reckoning, proportion]

ra•ti•oc•i•nate (rash′ē os′ə nāt′, -ō′sə-, rat′ē-), *v.i.,* **-nat•ed, -nat•ing.** to reason logically. —**ra′ti•oc′i•na′tion,** *n.*

ra•tion (rash′ən, rā′shən), *n.* **1.** a fixed allowance of food, esp. for one day. **2.** an allotted amount. —*v.t.* **3.** to distribute as rations (often fol. by *out*): *to ration out food to an army.* **4.** to provide with or put on rations. **5.** to restrict consumption of: *to ration meat.*

ra•tion•al (rash′ə nl, rash′nl), *adj.* **1.** based on or agreeable to reason: *a rational decision.* **2.** exercising reason: *a rational negotiator.* **3.** sane; lucid: *The patient seems perfectly rational.* **4.** *Math.* **a.** capable of being expressed exactly by a ratio of two integers. **b.** (of a function) capable of being expressed exactly by a ratio of two polynomials. —*n.* **5.** RATIONAL NUMBER. —**ra′tion•al•ly,** *adv.*

ra•tion•ale (rash′ə nal′), *n.* **1.** the fundamental reason or reasons serving to account for something. **2.** a statement of reasons or principles.

ra•tion•al•ism (rash′ə nl iz′əm), *n.* **1.** the principle or habit of accepting reason as the supreme authority in matters of opinion, belief, or conduct. **2.** a philosophic doctrine that reason alone is a source of knowledge and is independent of experience. **3.** a doctrine that human reason, unaided by divine revelation, is an adequate or the sole guide to all attainable religious truth. —**ra′tion•al•ist,** *n.*

ra•tion•al•ize (rash′ə nl īz′, rash′nl-), *v.,* **-ized, -iz•ing.** —*v.t.* **1.** to ascribe (one's actions) to causes that seem reasonable but do not reflect true, unconscious, or less creditable causes. **2.** to make conformable to reason. **3.** *Math.* to eliminate radicals from (an equation or expression): *to rationalize the denominator of a fraction.* —*v.i.* **4.** to invent plausible explanations for actions that are actually based on less acceptable causes. **5.** to employ reason. —**ra′tion•al•i•za′tion,** *n.*

ra′tional num′ber, *n.* a number that can be expressed exactly by a ratio of two integers.

rat′-kangaroo′, *n., pl.* **-roos.** any of several rabbit-sized, ratlike Australian kangaroos of the subfamily Potoroinae.

rat′ race′, *n.* an exhausting and usu. competitive routine activity.

rat′ snake′, *n.* any of several harmless New and Old World snakes, of the genus *Elaphe,* that feed chiefly on small mammals and birds. Also called **chicken snake.**

rat's′ nest′, *n.* MARE'S NEST (def. 2).

rat′-tail′ cac′tus, *n.* a cactus, *Aporocactus flagelliformis,* of Mexico, having slim cylindrical stems that are easily trained into strange designs, and crimson flowers.

rat•tan (ra tan′, rə-), *n.* **1.** Also called **rattan′ palm′.** any of various climbing palms of the genus *Calamus* or allied genera. **2.** the tough stems of such palms, used for wickerwork, canes, etc. **3.** a stick or switch of rattan.

rat·tle (rat′l), v., **-tled, -tling,** n. —v.i. **1.** to make a rapid succession of short, sharp sounds: *The doors rattled in the storm.* **2.** to move noisily: *The car rattled along the back roads.* **3.** to chatter: *rattling on about his ailments.* —v.t. **4.** to cause to make a rattling noise: *to rattle a doorknob.* **5.** to impel with a rattling noise: *The wind rattled the metal can across the roadway.* **6.** to utter or perform in a rapid or lively manner (usu. with *off*). **7.** to disconcert; confuse. **8.** *Hunting.* to stir up (a cover). —n. **9.** a rapid succession of short, sharp sounds. **10.** a contrivance that makes a rattling sound, esp. a baby's toy filled with small pellets that rattle when shaken. **11.** the series of horny, interlocking hollow rings at the end of a rattlesnake's tail, with which it produces a rattling sound. **12.** a rattling sound in the throat, as a death rattle.

rat·tler (rat′lər), n. **1.** a rattlesnake. **2.** one that rattles.

rat·tle·snake (rat′l snāk′), n. any of several New World pit vipers of the genera *Crotalus* and *Sistrurus*, having a rattle at the end of the tail.

rat·tle·trap (rat′l trap′), n. a rattling object, as a rickety vehicle.

rat·tling (rat′ling), adj. **1.** brisk: *a rattling pace.* **2.** splendid; fine. —adv. **3.** very: *a rattling good time.* —**rat′tling·ly,** adv.

rat·trap (rat′trap′), n. **1.** a device for catching rats. **2.** a run-down, filthy, or dilapidated place. **3.** a daunting situation.

rat·ty (rat′ē), adj., **-ti·er, -ti·est. 1.** full of rats. **2.** of or characteristic of a rat. **3.** wretched; shabby. **4.** irritable; angry.

rau·cous (rô′kəs), adj. **1.** harsh; strident: *raucous laughter.* **2.** rowdy; disorderly: *a raucous party.* —**rau′cous·ly,** adv. —**rau′cous·ness,** n.

raunch (rônch, ränch), n. **1.** smuttiness; vulgarity. —adj. **2.** using or characterized by raunch; vulgar: *raunch radio.*

raun·chy (rôn′chē, rän′-), adj., **-chi·er, -chi·est. 1.** vulgar; smutty. **2.** lecherous. **3.** dirty; slovenly. —**raun′chi·ly,** adv.

Rau·schen·busch (rou′shan bŏŏsh′), n. **Walter,** 1861–1918, U.S. clergyman and social reformer.

rav·age (rav′ij), v., **-aged, -ag·ing,** n. —v.t. **1.** to damage or mar severely: *a face ravaged by grief.* —v.i. **2.** to do ruinous damage. —n. **3.** ruinous damage: *the ravages of war.* **4.** devastating or destructive action. —**rav′age·ment,** n. —**rav′ag·er,** n.

rave (rāv), v., **raved, rav·ing,** n. —v.i. **1.** to talk irrationally, as in delirium. **2.** to talk or write with extravagant enthusiasm: *They raved about the performance.* **3.** to make a wild or furious sound, as the wind; rage. —v.t. **4.** to utter as if in delirium. —n. **5.** an act of raving. **6.** an extravagantly approving appraisal or review. —**rav′er,** n.

rav·el (rav′əl), v., **-eled, -el·ing** or (esp. *Brit.*) **-elled, -el·ling.** —v.t. **1.** to disentangle the threads or fibers of; unravel. **2.** to make clear; unravel. **3.** to entangle; enmesh; confuse. —v.i. **4.** to become unwound; fray. —n. **5.** a tangle or complication. —**rav′el·ment,** n.

Ra·vel (rə vel′), n. **Maurice Joseph,** 1875–1937, French composer.

rav·el·ing (rav′ə ling), n. something raveled out, as a loose thread.

ra·ven¹ (rā′vən), n. **1.** any of several very large corvine birds having lustrous black plumage and a loud, harsh call, esp. *Corvus corax,* of North America and Eurasia. —adj. **2.** lustrous black: *raven hair.*

rav·en² (rav′ən), v., **-ened, -en·ing.** —v.i. **1.** to pillage; plunder. **2.** to prowl for food. **3.** to eat or feed greedily. —v.t. **4.** to pillage: *armies ravening the land.* **5.** to devour greedily.

Ra·ven, The, (rā′vən), a lyric poem (1845) by Edgar Allan Poe.

rav·en·ous (rav′ə nəs), adj. **1.** extremely hungry; famished. **2.** predatory: *a ravenous jungle beast.* **3.** intensely eager: *ravenous for affection.* —**rav′en·ous·ly,** adv. —**rav′en·ous·ness,** n.

rav·in (rav′in), n. **1.** something taken as prey. **2.** plunder; despoliation.

ra·vine (rə vēn′), n. a narrow, steep-sided valley typically eroded by running water. —**ra·vined′,** adj.

rav·ing (rā′ving), adj. **1.** talking wildly; delirious: *a raving maniac.* **2.** extraordinary in degree: *a raving beauty.* —adv. **3.** furiously; wildly: *raving mad.* —n. **4.** Usu., **ravings.** incoherent or extravagant talk. —**rav′ing·ly,** adv.

ra·vi·o·li (rav′ē ō′lē), n. (used with a sing. or pl. v.) small, square pockets of pasta, filled with cheese, meat, etc., and served in a sauce.

rav·ish (rav′ish), v.t. **1.** to transport with strong emotion, esp. joy. **2.** to rape; violate. **3.** to seize and carry off by force. **4.** to rob; plunder. —**rav′ish·er,** n. —**rav′ish·ment,** n.

rav·ish·ing (rav′i shing), adj. extremely beautiful or attractive. —**rav′ish·ing·ly,** adv.

raw (rô), adj., **-er, -est,** n. —adj. **1.** uncooked: *a raw carrot.* **2.** not processed, finished, or refined: *raw cotton.* **3.** not pasteurized: *raw milk.* **4.** unnaturally or painfully exposed: *raw flesh.* **5.** indelicate; crude: *raw jokes.* **6.** inexperienced; untrained: *a raw recruit.* **7.** frank; unvarnished: *a raw portrayal of human passions.* **8.** brutally harsh or unfair: *a raw deal.* **9.** damp and chilly: *a raw day.* **10.** (of whiskey, rum, etc.) unaged or of undiluted strength. **11.** unprocessed; unevaluated: *raw data.* —n. **12.** a raw condition or substance. —*Idiom.* **13. in the raw, a.** in the natural, uncultivated, or unrefined state: *nature in the raw.* **b.** nude; naked. —**raw′ly,** adv. —**raw′ness,** n.

raw·boned (rô′bōnd′), adj. having the flesh seemingly stretched over a large-boned frame.

raw·hide (rô′hīd′), n., v., **-hid·ed, -hid·ing.** —n. **1.** untanned skin of cattle or other animals. **2.** a rope or whip made of rawhide. —v.t. **3.** to whip with or as if with a rawhide.

raw′ mate′rial, n. material before being processed or manufactured into a final form.

raw′ silk′, n. reeled silk with its sericin intact.

ray¹ (rā), n. **1.** a narrow beam of light. **2.** a slight manifestation: *a ray of hope.* **3.** radiance. **4. a.** any of the lines or streams in which light appears to radiate from a luminous body. **b.** the straight line normal to the wave front in the propagation of radiant energy. **c.** a stream of particles all moving in the same straight line. Compare GAMMA RAY, ALPHA RAY. **5. a.** one of a system of straight lines emanating from a point. **b.** the part of a straight line considered as originating at a point on the line and as extending in one direction from that point. **6.** any of a system of parts radially arranged. **7. a.** one of the branches or arms of a starfish or other radiate animal. **b.** one of the bony or cartilaginous rods in the fin of a fish. **8.** *Bot.* one of the branches of an umbel. **9.** one of many long, bright streaks radiating from some large lunar craters. —v.i. **10.** to emit rays. **11.** to issue in rays. —v.t. **12.** to send forth in rays. **13.** to throw rays upon; irradiate. **14.** to subject to the action of rays, as in radiotherapy. —*Idiom.* **15. get** or **grab some rays,** *Slang.* to sunbathe.

ray² (rā), n. any of numerous elasmobranch fishes having a flattened body and greatly enlarged pectoral fins with the gills on the undersides.

ray·on (rā′on), n. **1.** a regenerated, semisynthetic textile filament made from cellulose, cotton linters, or wood chips treated with caustic soda and carbon disulfide and passed through spinnerets. **2.** a fabric or yarn of rayon.

raze or **rase** (rāz), v.t., **razed** or **rased, raz·ing** or **ras·ing. 1.** to level to the ground; tear down. **2.** to shave; scrape off.

ra·zor (rā′zər), n. a sharp-edged instrument used esp. for shaving the face or trimming hair.

ra·zor·back (rā′zər bak′), n. **1.** a feral hog with a ridgelike back, common in the southern U.S. **2.** a finback or rorqual whale. **3.** a sharp, narrow ridge or range of hills. —adj. **4.** Also, **ra′zor·backed′, ra′zor-backed′.** having a sharp ridge along the back.

ra′zor-billed′ auk′, n. a black-and-white auk, *Alca torda,* of the N Atlantic, having a compressed black bill encircled by a white band. Also called **ra′zor·bill′.**

ra′zor clam′, n. any narrow, elongated bivalve mollusk of the family Solenidae, having a shell with razor-sharp edges.

ra·zor·fish (rā′zər fish′), n., pl. (esp. collectively) **-fish,** (esp. for kinds or species) **-fish·es.** any of several wrasses having a vertically compressed, sharp-edged head.

razz (raz), v.t. **1.** to make fun of; mock. —n. **2.** RASPBERRY (def. 4).

raz·zle-daz·zle (raz′əl daz′əl), n. **1.** showy technique or effect. **2.** confusion, commotion, or riotous gaiety. —adj. **3.** marked by razzle-dazzle.

razz·ma·tazz (raz′mə taz′), n. RAZZLE-DAZZLE.

Rb, *Chem. Symbol.* rubidium.

RBC, red blood cell.

RBI, run batted in: a run scored in baseball as a result of the batter advancing a runner to home.

RC, 1. Red Cross. **2.** Roman Catholic.

RCAF or **R.C.A.F.,** Royal Canadian Air Force.

RCMP or **R.C.M.P.,** Royal Canadian Mounted Police.

RCN, Royal Canadian Navy.

rd., road.

RD, Rural Delivery.

RDA or **R.D.A., 1.** recommended daily allowance. **2.** recommended dietary allowance.

re¹ (rā), n. the musical syllable used for the second tone in the ascending diatonic scale.

re² (rē, rā), prep. with reference to; regarding.

Re (rā), n. RA.

Re, *Chem. Symbol.* rhenium.

re-, a prefix, occurring orig. in loanwords from Latin, used to form verbs denoting action in a backward direction (*recede; return; revert*), action in answer to or intended to undo a situation (*rebel; remove; respond; restore; revoke*), or action done over, often with the implication that the outcome of the original action was in some way impermanent or inadequate, or that the performance of the new action brings back an earlier state of affairs (*recapture; reoccur; repossess; resole; retype*). Also, **red-.**

reach (rēch), v.t. **1.** to get to or as far as; arrive at: *The boat reached the shore.* **2.** to succeed in touching or seizing, as with an outstretched hand or a pole: *to reach a book on a high shelf.* **3.** to take and convey or pass along: *Will you reach me that pencil?* **4.** to stretch or hold out; extend: *reaching out a hand in greeting.* **5.** to stretch or extend so as to touch or meet: *The bookcase reaches the ceiling.* **6.** to establish communication with: *I called but couldn't reach you.* **7.** to amount to: *The cost will reach millions.* **8.** to carry to; penetrate to: *The loud bang reached our ears.* **9.** to succeed in influencing, impressing, rousing, etc. —v.i. **10.** to make a stretch, as with the hand or arm. **11.** to become outstretched, as the hand or arm. **12.** to make a movement or effort as if to touch or seize something: *to reach for a weapon.* **13.** to extend, as in operation, effect, direction, length, or distance. **14.** to carry or penetrate: *as far as the eye could reach.* **15. a.** to sail on a reach. **b.** to sail with the wind forward of the beam but so as not to require sailing close-hauled. —n. **16.** an act or instance of reaching. **17.** the extent or distance of reaching. **18.** range of effective action, power, or capacity. **19.** Usu., **reaches.** level, rank, or stratum. **20.** a continuous stretch or extent of something, as of land or a river. **21.** a straight portion of a river between two bends. **22. One's reach should exceed one's grasp,** one should strive for as much as possible in one's endeavors. —**reach′a·ble,** adj.

re•act (rē akt′), *v.i.* **1.** to act in response to an agent, influence, stimulus, etc.: *to react to a drug; reacted to the noise by jumping.* **2.** to act reciprocally upon each other. **3.** to act in a reverse direction or manner, esp. so as to return to a prior condition. **4.** to act in opposition, as against some force. **5.** to undergo a chemical reaction.

re•ac•tance (rē ak′təns), *n.* the opposition of inductance and capacitance to alternating electrical current, expressed in ohms. *Symbol:* X

re•ac•tant (rē ak′tənt), *n.* **1.** a person or thing that reacts. **2.** any substance that undergoes a chemical change in a given reaction.

re•ac•tion (rē ak′shən), *n.* **1.** a reverse movement or tendency; an action in a reverse direction or manner. **2.** a movement toward extreme political conservatism; a desire to return to an earlier system or order. **3.** action in response to some influence, event, etc.: *the nation's reaction to the president's speech.* **4. a.** a physiological response to an action or condition. **b.** a physiological change indicating sensitivity to foreign matter: *an allergic reaction.* **5.** the reciprocal action of chemical agents upon each other; chemical change. **6.** *Mech.* the instantaneous response of a system to an applied force, manifested as the exertion of a force equal in magnitude, but opposite in direction, to the applied force.

re•ac•tion•ar•y (rē ak′shə ner′ē), *adj., n., pl.* **-ar•ies.** *—adj.* **1.** pertaining to, marked by, or favoring reaction, esp. in politics; extremely conservative. *—n.* **2.** a reactionary person.

reac′tion en′gine, *n.* an engine that produces power as a reaction to the momentum given to gases ejected from it, as a rocket or jet engine.

reac′tion time′, *n. Psychol.* the interval between stimulation and response.

re•ac•ti•vate (rē ak′tə vāt′), *v.,* **-vat•ed, -vat•ing.** *—v.t.* **1.** to render active again; revive. *—v.i.* **2.** to be active again. **—re•ac′ti•va′tion,** *n.*

re•ac•tive (rē ak′tiv), *adj.* **1.** tending to react. **2.** pertaining to or characterized by reaction. **3.** pertaining to or characterized by reactance. **—re•ac′tive•ly,** *adv.* **—re•ac′tive•ness,** *n.*

re•ac•tiv•i•ty (rē′ak tiv′i tē), *n.* **1.** the quality or condition of being reactive. **2.** the relative capacity of an atom, molecule, or radical to undergo a chemical reaction with another atom, molecule, or compound. **3.** the ability of an antigen to combine with an antibody.

re•ac•tor (rē ak′tər), *n.* **1.** one that reacts or undergoes reaction. **2.** *Elect.* a device whose primary purpose is to introduce reactance into a circuit. **3.** Also called **nuclear reactor.** an apparatus in which a nuclear-fission chain reaction is sustained and controlled, for generating heat or producing useful radiation. **4.** (esp. in industry) a large container, as a vat, for substances undergoing chemical reactions.

read¹ (rēd), *v.,* **read** (red), **read•ing** (rē′ding). *—v.t.* **1.** to look at so as to understand the meaning of (something written, printed, etc.). **2.** to utter aloud or render in speech (something written, printed, etc.): *to read a story to a child.* **3.** to have such knowledge of (a language) as to be able to understand things written in it. **4.** to apprehend the meaning of (signs, characters, etc.) otherwise than with the eyes: *to read Braille.* **5.** to recognize and understand the meaning of (gestures, symbols, signals, or the like): *to read a semaphore.* **6.** to study the speech movements of (lips) so as to understand what is being said by a speaker who cannot be heard. **7.** to make out the significance of by scrutiny or observation: *to read the dark sky as the threat of a storm.* **8.** to foretell or predict. **9.** to make out the character, motivations, etc., of (a person), as by the interpretation of outward signs. **10.** to interpret or attribute a meaning to (a written text, a musical composition, etc.). **11.** to infer (something not expressed) from what is read, considered, or observed: *He read sarcasm into her letter.* **12.** to adopt or give as a reading in a particular passage: *For "one thousand" another version reads "ten thousand."* **13.** to register or indicate, as a thermometer. **14.** to learn by or as if by reading: *to read a person's thoughts.* **15.** to hear and understand (a transmitted message or the person transmitting it): *I read you loud and clear.* **16.** to bring, put, etc., by reading: *to read oneself to sleep.* **17.** to discover or explain the meaning of (a riddle, dream, etc.). **18.** *Brit.* to study (a subject), as at a university. *—v.i.* **19.** to read written or printed matter. **20.** to render aloud a text that one is reading. **21.** (of an actor) to audition by reading aloud from a given script or other text. **22.** to give a public reading or recital. **23.** to inspect and apprehend the meaning of written or other signs or characters. **24.** to occupy oneself with reading or study. **25.** to obtain knowledge or learn of something by reading. **26.** to admit of being read as specified: *The essay reads well.* **27.** to have a certain wording. **28.** to admit of being interpreted: *a rule that reads two different ways.* **29. read out of,** to oust from membership in, esp. publicly. **30. read up on,** to learn about by reading. *—n.* **31.** an act or instance of reading. **32.** something that is read: *Her new novel is a good read.* *—Idiom.* **33. read between the lines,** to understand from implications only. **34. read someone's lips,** to accept the truth of someone's statements, esp. after protracted argument: *Read my lips—I don't want the job.*

read² (red), *adj.* having knowledge gained by reading (usu. used in combination): *a well-read person.*

read•a•ble (rē′də bəl), *adj.* **1.** easy or interesting to read. **2.** capable of being read; legible. **—read′a•bil′i•ty,** *n.*

read•er (rē′dər), *n.* **1.** a person who reads. **2.** a schoolbook for instruction and practice in reading. **3.** a book of collected writings; anthology. **4. a.** a person employed to read and evaluate manuscripts for publication, theatrical production, etc. **b.** a proofreader. **5.** a person authorized to read the lessons, Bible, etc., in a church service. **6.** a lecturer or instructor, esp. in some British universities. **7.** an assistant to a professor, who grades examinations, papers, etc. **8.** a person who interprets tea leaves, dreams, etc., in order to predict future events.

read•er•ship (rē′dər ship′), *n.* **1.** the people who read or are thought to read a publication. **2.** the duty, status, or profession of a reader.

read•i•ly (red′l ē), *adv.* **1.** promptly; quickly; easily. **2.** in a ready manner; willingly.

read•i•ness (red′ē nis), *n.* **1.** the condition of being ready. **2.** ready action or movement; promptness; quickness; facility. **3.** willingness; inclination; cheerful consent.

read•ing (rē′ding), *n.* **1.** the action or practice of a person who reads. **2.** the oral interpretation of written language. **3.** the interpretation given in the performance of a dramatic part, musical composition, etc. **4.** the extent to which a person has read; literary knowledge. **5.** matter read or for reading: *light reading.* **6.** the form or version of a given passage in a particular text: *the various readings of a line in Shakespeare.* **7.** an instance or occasion in which a text or literary work is read or recited in public. **8.** an interpretation given to anything: *What is your reading of the situation?* **9.** the indication of a graduated instrument: *The thermometer reading is 101.2°F.* *—adj.* **10.** pertaining to or used for reading: *reading glasses.* **11.** given to reading: *the reading public.*

read′ing desk′, *n.* **1.** a desk for use in reading, esp. by a person standing. **2.** a lectern in a church.

re•ad•just (rē′ə just′), *v.t., v.i.* to adjust again or anew; rearrange or readapt. **—re′ad•just′a•ble,** *adj.* **—re′ad•just′ment,** *n.*

read′-on′ly mem′ory, *n.* See ROM.

read′out′ or **read′-out′,** *n.* **1.** the output of information from a computer in readable form. **2.** the information displayed on a graduated instrument.

read•y (red′ē), *adj.,* **-i•er, -i•est,** *v.,* **read•ied, read•y•ing.** *—adj.* **1.** completely prepared or in fit condition for action or use: *ready for battle.* **2.** not hesitant; willing: *ready to forgive.* **3.** prompt or quick in perceiving, comprehending, speaking, etc. **4.** proceeding from or showing such quickness: *a ready reply.* **5.** prompt or quick in action, performance, manifestation, etc.: *a ready wit.* **6.** inclined; disposed; apt: *too ready to criticize.* **7.** in such a condition as to be imminent; likely at any moment: *a tree ready to fall.* **8.** immediately available for use: *ready money.* *—v.t.* **9.** to make ready; prepare. *—n.* **10.** *Slang.* ready money; cash. *—Idiom.* **11. at the ready,** in a condition or position of being ready for use: *soldiers with weapons at the ready.* **12. make ready,** to bring to a state of readiness; prepare. *—Usage.* See ALREADY.

read′y-made′, *adj.* **1.** made in advance for sale to any purchaser: *a ready-made coat.* **2.** made for immediate use. **3.** unoriginal; conventional. *—n.* **4.** something that is ready-made, as a garment or a piece of furniture. **5.** READYMADE.

read′y-made′ or **read′y-made′,** *n.* an everyday, manufactured object that comes to be regarded as a work of art.

read′y-to-wear′, *n.* **1.** ready-made clothing. *—adj.* **2.** being, pertaining to, or dealing in such clothing.

Rea•gan (rā′gən), *n.* **Ronald (Wilson),** born 1911, 40th president of the U.S. 1981–89.

Rea•gan•om•ics (rā′gə nom′iks), *n.* (*used with a sing. v.*) the conservative economic policies of the administration of President Ronald Reagan, esp. those based on supply-side theory.

---

re′ab•sorb′, *v.t.*
re′ab•sorp′tion, *n.*
re′ac•claim′, *v.t.*
re′ac•cus′tom, *v.t.*
re′a•dapt′, *v.*
re′ad•dress′, *v.t.*
re′ad•mis′sion, *n.*
re′ad•mit′, *v.,* -mit•ted, -mit•ting.
re′a•dopt′, *v.t.*
re′af•firm′, *v.t.*
re′a•lign′, *v.t.*
re•al′lot′ment, *n.*
re′an•nex′, *v.t.*

re′ap•pear′, *v.i.*
re′ap•ply′, *v.,* -plied, -ply•ing.
re′ap•point′, *v.t.*
re′ap•prais′al, *n.*
re′ap•pro•pri•a′tion, *n.*
re′ap•prov′al, *n.*
re′ar•range′, *v.,* -ranged, -rang•ing.
re′ar•range′ment, *n.*
re′ar•rest′, *n., v.t.*
re′as•sem′ble, *v.,* -bled, -bling.
re′as•ser′tion, *n.*
re′as•sess′ment, *n.*
re′as•sign′ment, *n.*
re′at•tack′, *v.*

re′au•thor•ize′, *v.t.,* -ized, -iz•ing.
re′a•wak′en, *v.*
re•build′, *v.,* -built, -build•ing.
re•cal′cu•late′, *v.t.,* -lat•ed, -lat•ing.
re•cap′i•tal•ize′, *v.t.,* -ized, -iz•ing.
re•cau′tion, *v.t.*
re•cer′ti•fy′, *v.t.,* -fied, -fy•ing.
re•check′, *v.*
re•cir′cu•late′, *v.,* -lat•ed, -lat•ing.
re•clothe′, *v.t.,* -clothed or -clad, -cloth•ing.
re•code′, *v.t.,* -cod•ed, -cod•ing.
re•coin′, *v.t.*
re′com•bine′, *v.,* -bined, -bin•ing.

re′com•mit′ment, *n.*
re′com•pose′, *v.t.,* -posed, -pos•ing.
re′com•pu•ta′tion, *n.*
re•con•fig′ure, *v.t.,* -ured, -ur•ing.
re′con•firm′, *v.t.*
re′con•nect′, *v.t.*
re•con′quer, *v.t.*
re•con′se•crate′, *v.t.,* -crat•ed, -crat•ing.
re′con•sol′i•date′, *v.,* -dat•ed, -dat•ing.
re′con•vene′, *v.,* -vened, -ven•ing.
re′con•vert′, *v.t.*
re′con•vert′er, *n.*

re·a·gent (rē ā′jənt), *n. Chem.* a substance that, because of the reactions it causes, is used in analysis and synthesis.

re·al (rē′əl, rēl), *adj.* **1.** true; not merely ostensible, nominal, or apparent: *the real reason for an act.* **2.** actual rather than imaginary, ideal, or fictitious: *real events; a story taken from real life.* **3.** being actually such; not merely so-called: *a real victory.* **4.** genuine; authentic: *real pearls.* **5.** unfeigned or sincere: *real sympathy.* **6.** *Informal.* absolute; complete; utter: *She's a real brain.* **7.** *Philos.* **a.** existent as opposed to nonexistent. **b.** actual as opposed to possible or potential. **8.** (of wages, income, or money) measured in purchasing power rather than in nominal value. **9.** noting an optical image formed by the actual convergence of rays, as the image produced in a camera (opposed to *virtual*). **10.** *Law.* of or pertaining to immovable or permanent things, as lands or buildings. **11.** *Math.* of, pertaining to, or having the value of a real number. —*adv.* **12.** *Informal.* very or extremely: *You did a real nice job.* —*n.* **13. the real, a.** something that actually exists. **b.** reality in general. —*Idiom.* **14. for real, a.** in reality; actually. **b.** genuine; sincere.

re′al estate′, *n.* **1.** property, esp. in land. **2.** REAL PROPERTY.

re·a·li·a (rē ā′lē ə, -al′ē ə, rä ä′lē ə), *n.pl.* objects, as coins or tools, used by a teacher to illustrate everyday living.

re·al·ism (rē′ə liz′əm), *n.* **1.** interest in or concern for the actual or real, as distinguished from the abstract, speculative, etc. **2.** the tendency to view or represent things as they really are. **3.** (*usu. cap.*) a style of painting and sculpture developed about the mid-19th century in which figures and scenes are depicted as they are or might be experienced in everyday life. **4.** a style or theory of literature in which familiar aspects of life are represented in a straightforward or plain manner. **5.** *Philos.* the doctrine that universals have a real objective existence.

re·al·ist (rē′ə list), *n.* **1.** a person who tends to view or represent things as they really are. **2.** a writer or artist whose work is characterized by realism. **3.** an adherent of philosophic realism.

re·al·is·tic (rē′ə lis′tik), *adj.* **1.** concerned with or based on what is real or practical: *a realistic estimate of costs; a realistic planner.* **2.** characterized by or given to the representation in literature or art of things as they really are: *a realistic novel.* **3.** resembling or simulating real life: *a realistic decoy.* **4.** of or pertaining to philosophic realists or realism. —**re′al·is′ti·cal·ly,** *adv.*

re·al·i·ty (rē al′i tē), *n., pl.* **-ties. 1.** the state or quality of being real. **2.** resemblance to what is real. **3.** a real thing or fact. **4.** real things, facts, or events taken as a whole: *reading fantasy books to escape from reality.* **5.** *Philos.* **a.** something that exists independently of ideas concerning it. **b.** something that exists independently of all other things and from which all other things derive. —*Idiom.* **6. in reality,** in fact or truth; actually.

re·al·i·za·tion (rē′ə lə zā′shən), *n.* **1.** the act of realizing or the state of being realized. **2.** an instance or result of realizing.

re·al·ize (rē′ə līz′), *v.*, **-ized, -iz·ing.** —*v.t.* **1.** to grasp or understand clearly. **2.** to make real; give reality to (a hope, fear, plan, etc.). **3.** to bring vividly to the mind. **4.** to convert into cash or money: *to realize securities.* **5.** to obtain for oneself by trade, labor, or investment, as a profit or income. **6.** to bring as proceeds, as from a sale. **7.** to write out or sight-read on a keyboard instrument the full musical harmonization of (a figured bass). **8.** *Ling.* to serve as an actual instance in speech or writing of (an abstract linguistic element or category). —*v.i.* **9.** to convert property or goods into cash or money. —**re′al·iz′a·ble,** *adj.*

re′al-life′ (rē′əl, rēl′), *adj.* existing or happening in reality: *real-life drama.*

re·al·ly (rē′ə lē, rē′lē), *adv.* **1.** actually: *things as they really are.* **2.** genuinely; truly: *a really hot day.* **3.** indeed: *Really, this is too much.* —*interj.* **4.** (used to express surprise, reproof, etc.)

realm (relm), *n.* **1.** a royal domain; kingdom: *the realm of England.* **2.** any sphere, domain, or province: *the realm of dreams.*

re·al·po·li·tik (rā äl′pō′li tēk′, rē-), *n.* (*often cap.*) political realism or practical politics, esp. policy based on power rather than ideals.

re′al prop′erty, *n.* property consisting of lands, buildings, mineral rights, and the like (disting. from *personal property*).

Re·al·tor (rē′əl tər, -tôr′, rēl′-), *Trademark.* a person in the real-estate business who is a member of the National Association of Real Estate Boards.

re·al·ty (rē′əl tē, rēl′-), *n.* real property or real estate.

ream¹ (rēm), *n.* **1.** a standard quantity of paper, consisting of 20 quires

or 500 sheets (formerly 480 sheets), or 516 sheets. **2.** Usu., **reams.** a large quantity, as of writing.

ream² (rēm), *v.t.* **1.** to enlarge to desired size (a previously bored hole) by means of a reamer. **2.** to remove or press out with a reamer. **3.** to extract the juice from: *to ream an orange.* **4.** *Slang.* to cheat; defraud.

ream·er (rē′mər), *n.* **1.** any of various rotary tools, with helical or straight flutes, for finishing or enlarging holes drilled in metal. **2.** any bladelike pick or rod used for scraping, shaping, or enlarging a hole: *a pipe reamer.* **3.** a deep, saucerlike dish with a grooved cone in the center for extracting the juice from a fruit. **4.** a dental drill with a spiral shaft, for enlarging root canals.

re·an·i·mate (rē an′ə māt′), *v.t.,* **-mat·ed, -mat·ing. 1.** to restore to life; resuscitate. **2.** to give fresh vigor, spirit, or courage to.

reap (rēp), *v.* **1.** to cut (wheat, rye, etc.) with a sickle or other implement or a machine, as in harvest. **2.** to gather or take (a crop, harvest, etc.). **3.** to get as a return, recompense, or result: *to reap large profits.* —*v.i.* **4.** to reap a crop, harvest, etc.

reap·er (rē′pər), *n.* **1.** a machine for cutting standing grain; reaping machine. **2.** a person who reaps. **3.** (*cap.*) GRIM REAPER.

re·ap·por·tion (rē′ə pôr′shən, -pōr′-), *v.t.* to apportion or distribute anew.

re·ap·por·tion·ment (rē′ə pôr′shən mənt, -pōr′-), *n.* **1.** the act of redistributing or changing the apportionment of something. **2.** the redistribution of representation in a legislative body.

rear¹ (rēr), *n.* **1.** the back of something, as distinguished from the front. **2.** the space or position at the back of something: *Move to the rear of the bus.* **3.** the buttocks; rump. **4.** the hindmost portion of an army, fleet, etc. —*adj.* **5.** pertaining to or situated at the rear: *the rear door.* —*Idiom.* **6. bring up the rear,** to be at the end; follow behind.

rear² (rēr), *v.t.* **1.** to take care of and support up to maturity: *to rear a child.* **2.** to breed and raise (livestock). **3.** to raise by building; erect. **4.** to raise to an upright position: *to rear a ladder.* **5.** to lift or hold up; elevate. —*v.i.* **6.** to rise on the hind legs, as a horse. **7.** to start up in angry excitement or the like (usu. fol. by *up*). **8.** to rise high, as a building or tower. —**Usage.** See RAISE.

rear′ ad′miral, *n.* a commissioned officer in the U.S. Navy or Coast Guard ranking above a captain.

rear′ end′, *n.* **1.** the hindmost part. **2.** the buttocks; behind.

rear′-end′, *v.t.* to drive or crash a vehicle into the back end of (another vehicle).

rear′ guard′, *n.* a part of a military force assigned to guard the rear from attack, esp. in a retreat. —**rear′guard′,** *adj.*

re·arm (rē ärm′), *v.t.* **1.** to arm again. **2.** to furnish with new or better weapons. —*v.i.* **3.** to become armed again. —**re·ar′ma·ment** (-mə-mənt), *n.*

rear′view mir′ror (rēr′vyōō′), *n.* an automobile mirror mounted so as to provide the driver with a view of the road to the rear.

rear·ward (rēr′wərd), *adv.* **1.** Also, **rear′wards.** toward or in the rear. —*adj.* **2.** located in, near, or toward the rear. **3.** directed toward the rear. —*n.* **4.** a position at the rear.

rea·son (rē′zən), *n.* **1.** a basis or cause, as for some belief, action, fact, or event. **2.** a statement presented in justification or explanation of a belief or action. **3.** the mental powers concerned with forming conclusions, judgments, or inferences. **4.** sound judgment; good sense. **5.** normal or sound powers of mind; sanity. **6.** *Logic.* a premise of an argument. **7.** *Philos.* the faculty or power of acquiring intellectual knowledge, either by direct understanding of first principles or by argument. —*v.i.* **8.** to think or argue in a logical manner. **9.** to form conclusions, judgments, or inferences from facts or premises. —*v.t.* **10.** to think through logically, as a problem (often fol. by *out*). **11.** to conclude or infer. **12.** to convince, persuade, etc., by reasoning. **13.** to support with reasons. —*Idiom.* **14. by reason of,** on account of; because of. **15. in** or **within reason,** in accord with reason; justifiable. **16. with reason,** with ample justification; fittingly. —**Usage.** The construction REASON IS BECAUSE is criticized in a number of usage guides: *The reason for the long delays was because the costs far exceeded the original estimates.* One objection is based on redundancy: the word BECAUSE (literally, *by cause*) contains within it the meaning "reason," so that saying the REASON IS BECAUSE is like saying "The cause is by cause," which would never be said. A second objection is based on the claim that BECAUSE can introduce only adverbial clauses and that REASON IS requires

---

completion by a noun clause. Critics would substitute *that* for BECAUSE in the offending construction: *The reason for the long delays was that the costs.* ... Nevertheless, REASON IS BECAUSE is still common in almost all levels of speech and occurs often in edited writing as well. A similar charge of redundancy is made against THE REASON WHY, which is also a well-established idiom: *The reason why the bill failed to pass was the defection of three key senators.*

rea•son•a•ble (rē′zə nə bəl, rēz′nə-), *adj.* **1.** agreeable to or in accord with reason; logical. **2.** not exceeding the limit prescribed by reason; not excessive: *reasonable terms.* **3.** moderate, esp. in price; not expensive. **4.** endowed with reason. **5.** capable of rational behavior, decision, etc. —**rea′son•a•ble•ness,** *n.* —**rea′son•a•bly,** *adv.*

rea•son•ing (rē′zə ning, rēz′ning), *n.* **1.** the act or process of a person who reasons. **2.** the process of forming conclusions, judgments, or inferences from facts or premises. **3.** the reasons, arguments, proofs, etc., resulting from this process.

re•as•sure (rē′ə shŏŏr′, -shûr′), *v.t.,* **-sured, -sur•ing. 1.** to restore to assurance or confidence. **2.** to assure again. **3.** *Chiefly Brit.* to reinsure. —**re′as•sur′ance,** *n.* —**re′as•sur′ing•ly,** *adv.*

Ré•au•mur (rā′ə myŏŏr′), *n.* **1. René Antoine Ferchault de,** 1683–1757, French physicist and inventor. —*adj.* **2.** Also, **Re′au•mur′.** noting or pertaining to a temperature scale **(Ré′aumur scale′)** in which 0° represents the ice point and 80° represents the steam point.

Reb or **reb** (reb), *n.* REBEL (def. 3).

Reb (reb), *n. Yiddish.* Mister (used with the given name as a title of respect). [short for *rebi* my master]

re•bate (rē′bāt; *v. also* ri bāt′), *n., v.,* **-bat•ed, -bat•ing.** —*n.* **1.** a return of part of the original payment for some service or merchandise. —*v.t.* **2.** to allow as a discount. **3.** to deduct (a certain amount), as from a total. **4.** to return (part of an original payment). **5.** to provide a rebate for (merchandise) after purchase. —**re′bat•a•ble, re′bate•a•ble,** *adj.*

reb•be (REB′ə), *n. Yiddish.* **1.** a teacher in a Jewish school. **2.** (*often cap.*) a title of respect for the leader of a Hasidic group. [lit., rabbi]

Re•bek•ah (ri bek′ə), *n.* the wife of Isaac, and mother of Esau and Jacob. Gen. 24–27.

reb•el (*n., adj.* reb′əl; *v.* ri bel′), *n., adj., v.,* **-belled, -bel•ling.** —*n.* **1.** a person who refuses allegiance to, resists, or rises in arms against a government or ruler. **2.** a person who resists any authority, control, or tradition. **3.** (*usu. cap.*) a Confederate soldier: used chiefly by Northerners. —*adj.* **4.** rebellious; defiant. **5.** of or pertaining to rebels. —*v.i.* **re•bel 6.** to act as a rebel. **7.** to show or feel utter repugnance.

re•bel•lion (ri bel′yən), *n.* **1.** open, organized, and armed resistance to a government or ruler. **2.** resistance to or defiance of any authority, control, or tradition.

re•bel•lious (ri bel′yəs), *adj.* **1.** defying or resisting some established authority, government, or tradition. **2.** pertaining to or characteristic of rebels or rebellion. **3.** (of things or animals) resisting management or treatment; refractory. —**re•bel′lious•ly,** *adv.* —**re•bel′lious•ness,** *n.*

re•birth (rē bûrth′, rē′bûrth′), *n.* **1.** a new or second birth. **2.** a renewed existence, activity, or growth; renaissance; revival.

re•born (rē bôrn′), *adj.* having undergone rebirth.

re•bound (*v.* ri bound′, rē′bound′; *n.* rē′bound′, ri bound′), *v.* **1.** to bound or spring back from force of impact. **2.** to recover, as from ill health or discouragement. **3.** *Basketball.* to gain hold of rebounds. —*v.t.* **4.** to cause to bound back; cast back. **5.** *Basketball.* to gain hold of (a rebound). —*n.* **6.** the act of rebounding; recoil. **7.** *Basketball.* an instance of seizing the ball off the backboard or rim. —***Idiom.* 8. on the rebound, a.** (of a bounced ball) while still in the air. **b.** in an attempt to replace a recently lost relationship, esp. a romance: *to marry on the rebound.*

re•buff (*n.* ri buf′, rē′buf; *v.* ri buf′), *n.* **1.** a blunt rejection, as of a person making advances. **2.** a peremptory refusal of a request or offer. **3.** a check to action or progress. —*v.t.* **4.** to give a rebuff to; check; repel.

re•buke (ri byōōk′), *v.,* **-buked, -buk•ing,** *n.* —*v.t.* **1.** to express sharp, stern disapproval of; reprove; reprimand. —*n.* **2.** a sharp reproof; reprimand. —**re•buk′er,** *n.*

re•bus (rē′bəs), *n., pl.* **-bus•es.** a representation of a word or phrase by pictures, symbols, etc., that suggest that word or phrase or its syllables: *Two gates and a head is a rebus for Gateshead.*

re•but (ri but′), *v.,* **-but•ted, -but•ting.** —*v.t.* **1.** to refute by evidence or argument. **2.** to oppose by contrary proof. —*v.i.* **3.** to provide some evidence or argument that refutes or opposes. —**re•but′ta•ble,** *adj.*

re•but•tal (ri but′l), *n.* an act of rebutting, as in a debate.

re•cal•ci•trant (ri kal′si trənt), *adj.* **1.** resisting authority or control: *a recalcitrant prisoner.* **2.** hard to deal with, manage, or operate. —*n.* **3.** a recalcitrant person. —**re•cal′ci•trance,** *n.*

re•call (*v.* ri kôl′; *n.* ri kôl′, rē′kôl *for 6–8;* rē′kôl *for 9, 10*), *v.t,* **1.** to bring back from memory; recollect; remember. **2.** to call or order back: *to recall an ambassador.* **3.** to bring (one's thoughts, attention, etc.) back to matters previously considered. **4.** to revoke or withdraw. **5.** to revive. —*n.* **6.** an act of recalling. **7.** recollection; remembrance. **8.** the act or possibility of revoking something. **9.** the removal or the right of removal of a public official from office by a vote of the people. **10.** a summons by a manufacturer for the return of a product, as from a consumer, because of a known defect in it. —**re•call′a•ble,** *adj.*

re•cant (ri kant′), *v.t.* **1.** to withdraw or disavow (a statement, opinion, etc.), esp. formally; retract. —*v.i.* **2.** to withdraw or disavow a statement, opinion, etc., esp. formally. —**re•can•ta•tion** (rē′kan tā′shən), *n.*

re•cap[1] (*v.* rē′kap′, rē kap′; *n.* rē′kap′), *v.,* **-capped, -cap•ping,** *n.* —*v.t.* **1.** to recondition (a worn automobile tire) by cementing on a strip of prepared rubber and vulcanizing by subjecting to heat and pressure in a mold. —*n.* **2.** a recapped tire. —**re•cap′pa•ble,** *adj.*

re•cap[2] (rē′kap′), *n., v.,* **-capped, -cap•ping.** —*n.* **1.** a recapitulation. —*v.t., v.i.* **2.** to recapitulate.

re•cap•i•tal•i•za•tion (rē kap′i tl ə zā′shən), *n.* a revision of a corporation's capital structure by an exchange of securities.

re•ca•pit•u•late (rē′kə pich′ə lāt′), *v.,* **-lated, -lat•ing.** —*v.t.* **1.** to review by a brief summary, as at the end of a speech or discussion. **2.** to repeat (ancestral evolutionary stages) during embryonic development or during a life cycle. —*v.i.* **3.** to sum up statements or matters.

re•ca•pit•u•la•tion (rē′kə pich′ə lā′shən), *n.* **1.** the act of recapitulating or the state of being recapitulated. **2.** a brief review or summary, as of a speech. **3.** the theory that the evolutionary history of a species is made evident in the developmental stages of each of its representative organisms. **4.** the last section of a musical sonata form, restating the exposition. —**re′ca•pit′u•la′tive, re′ca•pit′u•la•to′ry** (-lə tôr′ē, -tōr′ē), *adj.*

re•cap•ture (rē kap′chər), *v.,* **-tured, -tur•ing,** *n.* —*v.t.* **1.** to capture again; retake. **2.** (of a government) to take by recapture. **3.** to recollect or reexperience (something past). —*n.* **4.** recovery or retaking by capture. **5.** the taking by the government of a fixed part of all earnings in excess of a certain percentage of property value. **6.** *Internat. Law.* the lawful reacquisition of a former possession. **7.** the state or fact of being recaptured. —**re•cap′tur•a•ble,** *adj.*

re•cast (*v.* rē kast′, -käst′; *n.* rē′kast′, -käst′), *v.,* **-cast, -cast•ing,** *n.* —*v.t.* **1.** to cast again or anew. **2.** to form, fashion, or arrange again. **3.** to remodel or reconstruct (a literary work, sentence, etc.). **4.** to provide (a play, role, etc.) with a different cast or performer. —*n.* **5.** a recasting. **6.** a new form produced by recasting. —**re•cast′er,** *n.*

recd. or **rec'd.,** received.

re•cede[1] (ri sēd′), *v.i.,* **-ced•ed, -ced•ing. 1.** to go back to a more distant point; retreat; withdraw. **2.** to become or seem to become more distant. **3.** to slope backward: *a chin that recedes.*

re•cede[2] (rē sēd′), *v.t.* to cede back; give to a former possessor.

re•ceipt (ri sēt′), *n.* **1.** a written acknowledgment of having received money or goods as specified. **2. receipts,** the amount or quantity received. **3.** the act of receiving or the state of being received. **4.** something that is received. **5.** a recipe. —*v.t.* **6.** to acknowledge in writing the payment of (a bill). **7.** to give a receipt for (money, goods, etc.). —*v.i.* **8.** to give a receipt, as for money or goods. —**re•ceipt′or,** *n.*

re•ceiv•a•ble (ri sē′və bəl), *adj.* **1.** fit for acceptance; acceptable. **2.** awaiting receipt of payment. **3.** capable of being received. —*n.* **4. receivables,** business assets in the form of money owed by customers, clients, etc. —**re•ceiv′a•bil′i•ty,** *n.*

re•ceive (ri sēv′), *v.,* **-ceived, -ceiv•ing.** —*v.t.* **1.** to take into one's possession (something offered or delivered): *to receive gifts.* **2.** to have (something) bestowed, conferred, etc.: *received an honorary degree.* **3.** to have delivered or brought to one: *to receive a letter.* **4.** to get or be informed of: *received news of the baby's birth.* **5.** to be burdened with; sustain. **6.** to hold, bear, or contain: *The socket receives the plug.* **7.** to take into the mind; apprehend mentally. **8.** to accept from another by

re′in•ter′ro•gate′, *v.,* **-gat•ed, -gat•ing.**
re′in•tro•duce′, *v.t.,* **-duced, -duc•ing.**
re′in•tro•duc′tion, *n.*
re′in•vade′, *v.t.,* **-vad•ed, -vad•ing.**
re′in•vest′, *v.t.*
re′in•ves′ti•gate′, *v.,* **-gat•ed, -gat•ing.**
re′in•ves′ti•ga′tion, *n.*
re′in•vest′ment, *n.*
re′in•vig′or•ate′, *v.t.,* **-at•ed, -at•ing.**
re′in•vite′, *v.,* **-vit•ed, -vit•ing.**
re′in•voke′, *v.t.,* **-voked, -vok•ing.**
re′in•volve′, *v.t.,* **-volved, -volv•ing.**
re′in•volve′ment, *n.*
rejigger, *v.t.,* **-gered, -gering.**
re•la′bel, *v.t.,* **-beled, -bel•ing.**
re•launch′, *v.t.*
re•learn′, *v.*
re•load′, *n., v.*
re•mar′riage, *n.*
re•mar′ry, *v.,* **-ried, -ry•ing.**
re•mas′ter, *v.t.*
re′ma•te′ri•al•ize′, *v.,* **-ized, -iz•ing.**
re′ma•tric′u•late′, *v.,* **-lat•ed, -lat•ing.**
re•meas′ure, *v.t.,* **-ured, -ur•ing.**
re•mend′, *v.*
re•mod′i•fy′, *v.,* **-fied, -fy•ing.**
re•mod′u•late′, *v.t.,* **-lat•ed, -lat•ing.**
re•mold′, *v.*
re•mort′gage, *v.t.,* **-gaged, -gag•ing.**
re•name′, *v.t.,* **-named, -nam•ing.**
re•nom′i•nate′, *v.t.,* **-nat•ed, -nat•ing.**
re•num′ber, *v.t.*
re•oc′cu•py′, *v.t.,* **-pied, -py•ing.**
re′oc•cur′, *v.i.,* **-curred, -cur•ring.**
re′oc•cur′rence, *n.*
re•o′ri•ent′, *v.*
re•pag′i•nate′, *v.t.,* **-nat•ed, -nat•ing.**
re•paint′, *v.t.*
re•pave′, *v.t.,* **-paved, -pav•ing.**
re•pol′ish, *v.,* **-ished, -ish•ing,** *n.*
re•pop′u•lar•ize′, *v.t.,* **-ized, -iz•ing.**
re•pop′u•late′, *v.t.,* **-lat•ed, -lat•ing.**
re•pro′gram, *v.t.,* **-grammed** or **-gramed, -gram•ming** or **-gram•ing.**
re•qual′i•fy′, *v.,* **-fied, -fy•ing.**
re•read′, *v.,* **-read, -read•ing.**
re•reg′is•ter, *v.*

hearing or listening: *A priest received his confession.* **9.** to meet with; experience. **10.** to suffer the injury of: *receiving a sharp blow on the forehead.* **11.** to be at home to (visitors). **12.** to greet or welcome (guests, visitors, etc.) upon arriving. **13.** to admit (a person) to a place: *The butler received him into the hall.* **14.** to admit into an organization, membership, etc. **15.** to accept as true, valid, or approved. **16.** to react to in the manner specified: *to receive a proposal with joy.* —*v.i.* **17.** to take, get, accept, or meet with something. **18.** to meet with or greet visitors or guests. **19.** *Radio.* to convert incoming electromagnetic waves into the original signal.

re·ceived (ri sēvd′), *adj.* generally or traditionally accepted; conventional; standard: *received ideas.*

re·ceiv·er (ri sē′vər), *n.* **1.** a person or thing that receives. **2.** a device or apparatus, as an earphone, radio, or television, that receives electrical signals, waves, or the like and renders them intelligible and perceptible to the senses. **3.** a person appointed by a court to manage the affairs of a bankrupt business or person or to care for property in litigation. **4.** a person who knowingly receives stolen goods for an illegal purpose. **5.** a receptacle; container. **6.** a vessel for collecting and containing a distillate. **7.** *Football.* a player on the offensive team who catches or is eligible to catch a forward pass.

re·ceiv·er·ship (ri sē′vər ship′), *n.* **1.** the condition of being in the hands of a receiver. **2.** the position or function of being a receiver in charge of administering the property of others.

receiv′ing line′, *n.* a row formed by the hosts, guests of honor, or the like, to greet guests formally, as at a reception.

re·cen·sion (ri sen′shən), *n.* a critical revision of a text, esp. one based on examination of its sources. —**re·cen′sion·ist,** *n.*

re·cent (rē′sənt), *adj.* **1.** of late occurrence, appearance, or origin; lately happening, done, made, etc.: *recent events.* **2.** of or belonging to a time not long past. **3.** (*cap.*) *Geol.* noting or pertaining to the present epoch, originating at the end of the glacial period, about 10,000 years ago, and forming the latter part of the Quaternary Period. —*n.* **4.** (*cap.*) *Geol.* the Recent Epoch. —**re′cent·ly,** *adv.*

re·cep·ta·cle (ri sep′tə kəl), *n.* **1.** a container, device, etc., that receives or holds something. **2.** the modified or expanded portion of a plant stem or axis that bears the organs of a single flower or the florets of a flower head. **3.** a contact device installed at an electrical outlet, equipped with one or more sockets.

re·cep·tion (ri sep′shən), *n.* **1.** the act of receiving or the state of being received. **2.** a manner of being received: *The book met with a favorable reception.* **3.** a function or occasion when persons are formally received. **4.** the quality or fidelity attained in receiving radio or television broadcasts under given circumstances.

re·cep·tion·ist (ri sep′shə nist), *n.* a person employed to receive and assist callers, clients, etc., as in an office.

re·cep·tive (ri sep′tiv), *adj.* **1.** having the quality of receiving, taking in, or admitting. **2.** able or quick to receive knowledge, ideas, etc. **3.** willing or inclined to receive suggestions, offers, etc. **4.** of or pertaining to reception or receptors. **5.** of or pertaining to the language skills of listening and reading. —**re·cep′tive·ly,** *adv.* —**re·cep·tiv·i·ty** (rē′sep tiv′i tē), **re·cep′tive·ness,** *n.*

re·cep·tor (ri sep′tər), *n.* **1.** a protein molecule, usu. on the surface of a cell, that is capable of binding to a complementary molecule, as a hormone, antibody, or antigen. **2.** a sensory nerve ending or sense organ that is sensitive to stimuli.

re·cess (ri ses′, rē′ses), *n.* **1.** a temporary withdrawal or cessation from the usual work or activity; break. **2.** a period of such withdrawal: *a five-minute recess.* **3.** a receding part or space, as an alcove in a room. **4.** an indentation, as in a coastline or a hill. **5.** **recesses,** a secluded or inner area or part: *in the recesses of the palace.* —*v.t.* **6.** to place or set in a recess. **7.** to set or form as or like a recess: *to recess a wall.* **8.** to suspend or defer for a recess: *to recess the Senate.* —*v.i.* **9.** to take a recess.

re·ces·sion (ri sesh′ən), *n.* **1.** a period of economic decline when production, employment, and earnings fall below normal levels. **2.** the act of receding or withdrawing. **3.** a receding part of a wall, building, etc. **4.** a withdrawing procession, as at the end of a religious service. —**re·ces′sion·ar′y,** *adj.*

re·ces·sion·al (ri sesh′ə nl), *adj.* **1.** of or pertaining to a recession of the clergy and choir after a service. **2.** of or pertaining to a recess, as of

a legislative body. —*n.* **3.** a piece of music played at the end of a church service or other gathering.

re·ces·sive (ri ses′iv), *adj.* **1.** tending to recede; receding. **2.** *Genetics.* **a.** of or pertaining to that allele of a gene pair whose effect is masked by the second allele when both are present in the same cell or organism. **b.** of or pertaining to the hereditary trait determined by such an allele. —*n.* **3.** *Genetics.* **a.** the recessive allele of a gene pair. **b.** a recessive trait. —**re·ces′sive·ly,** *adv.* —**re·ces′sive·ness,** *n.*

Rech·a·bite (rek′ə bīt′), *n.* one of a nomadic clan that aided Jehu in his struggle against Ahab. Jer. 35:2.

re·charge (rē chärj′; *n. also* rē′chärj′), *v.,* **-charged, -charg·ing,** *n.* —*v.t.* **1.** to charge again with electricity: *recharged the battery.* **2.** to refresh or restore; revitalize. —*v.i.* **3.** to make a new charge, esp. to attack again. **4.** to revive or restore energy, stamina, enthusiasm, etc. —*n.* **5.** an act or instance of recharging. —**re·charge′a·ble,** *adj.* —**re·charge′a·bil′i·ty,** *n.* —**re·charg′er,** *n.*

ré·chauf·fé (rā′shō fā′), *n., pl.* **-fés.** **1.** a warmed-up dish of food. **2.** anything old or stale brought into service again.

re·cher·ché (rə shâr′shā, rə shâr shā′), *adj.* **1.** carefully selected. **2.** very rare or choice; exotic. **3.** of studied refinement or elegance; affected; pretentious.

re·cid·i·vism (ri sid′ə viz′əm), *n.* repeated or habitual relapse, as into crime. —**re·cid′i·vist,** *n., adj.*

rec·i·pe (res′ə pē), *n., pl.* **-pes.** **1.** a set of instructions for making or preparing something, esp. a food dish. **2.** a method to attain a desired end: *a recipe for a happy marriage.*

re·cip·i·ent (ri sip′ē ənt), *n.* **1.** one that receives; receiver. —*adj.* **2.** receiving or able to receive.

re·cip·ro·cal (ri sip′rə kəl), *adj.* **1.** given or felt by each toward the other; mutual. **2.** given, performed, felt, etc., in return: *reciprocal aid.* **3.** corresponding; matching; equivalent. **4.** (of a pronoun or verb) expressing mutual relationship or action, as the pronouns *each other* and *one another.* **5.** inversely related or proportional; opposite. **6.** *Math.* noting expressions, relations, etc., involving reciprocals. **7.** bearing in a direction 180° to a given direction; back. —*n.* **8.** one that is reciprocal to another; equivalent; counterpart; complement. **9.** *Math.* the ratio of unity to a given quantity or expression; that by which the given quantity or expression is multiplied to produce unity: *The reciprocal of x is 1/x.* —**re·cip′ro·cal·ly,** *adv.*

re·cip·ro·cate (ri sip′rə kāt′), *v.,* **-cat·ed, -cat·ing.** —*v.t.* **1.** to give, feel, etc., in return. **2.** to give and receive reciprocally; interchange: *to reciprocate favors.* **3.** to cause to move alternately backward and forward. —*v.i.* **4.** to make a return, as for something given. **5.** to make interchange. **6.** to be correspondent. **7.** to move alternately backward and forward. —**re·cip′ro·ca′tion,** *n.* —**re·cip′ro·ca′tive,** *adj.*

rec·i·proc·i·ty (res′ə pros′i tē), *n.* **1.** a reciprocal state or relation. **2.** reciprocation; mutual exchange. **3.** the policy between countries by which corresponding advantages or privileges are granted by each country to the citizens of the other.

re·ci·sion (ri sizh′ən), *n.* an act of canceling or voiding.

re·cit·al (ri sīt′l), *n.* **1.** a musical or dance entertainment given by one or more performers. **2.** a presentation by dance or music students to demonstrate their progress. **3.** an act or instance of reciting, esp. from memory. **4.** a detailed statement: *a recital of grievances.* **5.** an account, narrative, or description. —**re·cit′al·ist,** *n.*

rec·i·ta·tion (res′i tā′shən), *n.* **1.** an act of reciting. **2.** a reciting or repeating of something from memory, esp. formally or publicly. **3.** oral response by a pupil or pupils to a teacher on a prepared lesson. **4.** a period of classroom instruction.

rec·i·ta·tive¹ (res′i tā′tiv, ri sīt′ə-), *adj.* pertaining to or of the nature of recital.

rec·i·ta·tive² (res′i tə tēv′), *n.* **1.** a style of vocal music intermediate between speaking and singing. **2.** a passage, part, or piece in this style.

re·cite (ri sīt′), *v.,* **-cit·ed, -cit·ing.** —*v.t.* **1.** to repeat the words of, as from memory, esp. in a formal manner: *to recite a lesson.* **2.** to repeat (a piece of poetry or prose) before an audience, as for entertainment. **3.** to narrate; describe. **4.** to enumerate; detail. —*v.i.* **5.** to recite a lesson for a teacher. **6.** to repeat something from memory. —**re·cit′a·ble,** *adj.*

reck·less (rek′lis), *adj.* **1.** utterly unconcerned about consequences; rash; careless (sometimes fol. by *of*): *reckless drivers; to be reckless of*

---

re·seal′a·ble, *adj.*
re′se·lect′, *v.t.*
re·sell′, *v.*
re·send′, *v.t.,* **-sent, -send·ing.**
re·set′tle·ment, *n.*
re·shape′, *v.t.,* **-shaped, -shap·ing.**
re·sit′u·ate′, *v.t.,* **-at·ed, -at·ing.**
re·size′, *v.t.,* **-sized, -siz·ing.**
re·sod′, *v.t.,* **-sod·ded, -sod·ding.**
re·sof′ten, *v.*
re·soil, *v.,* **-soiled, -soiling.**
re′so·lid′i·fy′, *v.,* **-fied, fy·ing.**
re·sta′bi·lize′, *v.t.,* **-lized, -liz·ing.**
re·stack′, *v.t.,* **-stacked, -stack·ing.**

re·stage′, *v.t.,* **-staged, -stag·ing.**
re·start′, *v., n.*
re·state′, *v.t.,* **-stat·ed, -stat·ing.**
re·sta′tion, *v.t.*
re′ster·i·li·za′tion, *n.*
re·ster′i·lize′, *v.t.,* **-lized, -liz·ing.**
re·stock′, *v.*
re·string′, *v.,* **-strung, -string·ing.**
re·style′, *v.t.,* **-styled, -styl·ing.**
re′sub·scribe′, *v.,* **-scribed, -scrib·ing.**
re·tal′ly, *n., pl.* **-lies,** *v.,* **-lied, -ly·ing.**

re·tell′, *v.,* **-told, -tell·ing.**
re·test′, *v.t.*
re·thread′, *v.*
re·tie′, *v.t.,* **-tied, -ty·ing.**
re·tight′en, *v.*
re·ti′tle, *v.t.,* **-tled, -tling.**
re·train′, *v.*
re′trans·late′, *v.t.,* **-lat·ed, -lat·ing.**
re′trans·mit′, *v.t.,* **-mit·ted, -mit·ting.**
re·tri′al, *n.*
re·try′, *v.,* **-tried, -try·ing.**
re·type′, *v.t.,* **-typed, -typ·ing.**
re·u′ni·fy′, *v.t.,* **-fied, -fy·ing.**

re′up·hol′ster, *v.t.*
re·use′, *v.,* **-used, -us·ing,** *n.*
re′val·i·da′tion, *n.*
re·var′nish, *v.*
re·ver′i·fy′, *v.t.,* **-fied, -fy·ing.**
re·vi′o·late′, *v.t.,* **-lat·ed, -lat·ing.**
re·vis′it, *v.,* **-it·ed, -it·ing.**
re·wak′en, *v.*
re·warm′, *v.*
re·wash′, *v.*
re·weave′, *v.,* **-wove, -wo·ven** or **-wove, -weav·ing.**
re·weigh′, *v.*
re·wrap′, *v.,* **-wrapped, -wrap·ping.**

danger. **2.** characterized by or proceeding from such carelessness. —**reck′less•ly,** *adv.* —**reck′less•ness,** *n.*

reck•on (rek′ən), *v.t.* **1.** to count, compute, or calculate, as in number or amount. **2.** to esteem or consider; regard as; deem: *to be reckoned an authority.* **3.** *Chiefly Midland and Southern U.S.* to think or suppose. —*v.i.* **4.** to count; make a computation or calculation. **5.** to settle accounts, as with a person (often fol. by *up*). **6.** to count, depend, or rely (usu. fol. by *on* or *upon*). **7.** *Southern U.S.* to think or suppose. **8. reckon with,** to consider, deal with, or anticipate. **9. reckon without,** to fail to consider, deal with, or anticipate. —**reck′on•a•ble,** *adj.*

reck•on•ing (rek′ə ning), *n.* **1.** count; computation; calculation. **2.** the settlement of accounts, as between two companies. **3.** a statement of an amount due; bill. **4.** an accounting, as for things received or done: *a day of reckoning.* **5.** an appraisal or judgment.

re-claim or **re•claim** (rē klām′), *v.t.* to claim the return or restoration of, as a right or possession.

re•claim (ri klām′), *v.t,* **1.** to bring (wasteland) into a condition for cultivation or other use. **2.** to recover (substances) in a pure or usable form from refuse, discarded articles, etc. **3.** to bring back to a more positive or wholesome way of life; rescue or reform. **4.** to tame. **5.** RECLAIM. —*n.* **6.** reclamation: *beyond reclaim.* —**re•claim′a•ble,** *adj.*

rec•la•ma•tion (rek′lə mā′shən), *n.* **1.** the act or process of reclaiming. **2.** the state of being reclaimed. **3.** the reclaiming of uncultivated areas or wastelands for productive use.

ré•clame (*Fr.* rā kläm′), *n.* publicity; notoriety.

re•clas•si•fy (rē klas′ə fī′), *v.t.,* **-fied, -fy•ing. 1.** to classify anew. **2.** to alter the security classification of. —**re•clas′si•fi•ca′tion,** *n.*

re•cline (ri klīn′), *v.,* **-clined, -clin•ing.** —*v.i.* **1.** to lean back or lie; rest in a recumbent position. —*v.t.* **2.** to cause to lean back or lie; place in a recumbent position. —**re•clin′a•ble,** *adj.*

re•clin•er (ri klī′nər), *n.* **1.** a person or thing that reclines. **2.** Also called **reclin′ing chair′.** an easy chair with a back and footrest adjustable up or down.

re•clos•a•ble or **re•close•a•ble** (rē klō′zə bəl), *adj.* capable of being closed again easily or tightly after opening.

rec•luse (*n.* rek′lo͞os, ri klo͞os′; *adj.* ri klo͞os′, rek′lo͞os), *n.* **1.** a person living in seclusion, apart from society. —*adj.* **re•cluse 2.** RECLUSIVE.

re•clu•sive (ri klo͞o′siv, -ziv), *adj.* **1.** shut off or apart from the world; living in seclusion. **2.** characterized by seclusion; solitary.

rec•og•ni•tion (rek′əg nish′ən), *n.* **1.** an act of recognizing or the state of being recognized. **2.** identification of a person or thing as having previously been seen, heard, known, etc. **3.** perception of something as existing, true, or valid; realization or acceptance. **4.** the acknowledgment of achievement, service, merit, etc. **5.** formal acknowledgment conveying approval, sanction, or validity. **6.** an official act by which one state acknowledges the existence of another state or of a new government. **7.** the automated conversion of words or images into a form that can be processed by a computer. Compare OPTICAL CHARACTER RECOGNITION. **8.** *Biochem.* the responsiveness of one substance to another based on the reciprocal fit of a portion of their molecular shapes. —**rec′og•ni′tion•al,** *adj.* —**re•cog•ni•tive** (ri kog′ni tiv), *adj.*

re•cog•ni•zance (ri kog′nə zəns, -kon′ə-), *n. Law.* **1.** a bond or obligation of record entered into before a court of record or a magistrate, usu. binding a person to appear for trial or forfeit a specified amount of money. **2.** the sum pledged as surety.

re-coil (rē koil′), *v.t., v.i.* to coil again.

re•coil (*v.* ri koil′; *n.* rē′koil′, ri koil′), *v.i.* **1.** to start or shrink back, as in alarm, horror, or disgust. **2.** to spring or fly back, as in consequence of force of impact or of a discharge of ammunition: *The rifle recoiled with a powerful slam.* **3.** to spring or come back; rebound (usu. fol. by *on* or *upon*): *plots recoiling upon the plotters.* **4.** to undergo a change in momentum as a result either of a collision with an atom, a nucleus, or a particle or of the emission of a particle. —*n.* **5.** the act or an instance of recoiling. **6.** the distance through which a weapon moves backward after discharging.

re-col•lect (rē′kə lekt′), *v.t.* **1.** to collect, gather, or assemble again (something scattered). **2.** to rally (one's faculties, powers, etc.); recover or compose (oneself).

rec•ol•lect (rek′ə lekt′), *v.t., v.i.* to remember; recall.

rec•ol•lect•ed (rek′ə lek′tid), *adj.* **1.** calm; composed. **2.** remembered; recalled. —**rec′ol•lect′ed•ly,** *adv.*

rec•ol•lec•tion (rek′ə lek′shən), *n.* **1.** the act or power of recalling to mind; remembrance. **2.** something recollected.

re•com•bi•nant (rē kom′bə nənt), *adj.* **1.** of or resulting from new combinations of genetic material: *recombinant cells.* —*n.* **2.** a cell or organism whose genetic material results from recombination.

recombinant DNA, *n.* DNA in which one or more segments or genes have been inserted, either naturally or by laboratory manipulation, from a different molecule or from another part of the same molecule, resulting in a new genetic combination.

re•com•bi•na•tion (rē′kom bə nā′shən), *n.* the formation of new combinations of genes, either naturally or in the laboratory.

rec•om•mend (rek′ə mend′), *v.t.* **1.** to present as worthy of confidence, acceptance, or use; commend. **2.** to urge or suggest as appropriate, satisfying, or beneficial: *to recommend a special diet.* **3.** to make desirable or attractive: *The plan has little to recommend it.* —*v.i.* **4.** to make a recommendation. —**rec′om•mend′a•ble,** *adj.*

rec•om•men•da•tion (rek′ə men dā′shən, -mən-), *n.* **1.** the act of recommending. **2.** the person or thing recommended. **3.** something, as a letter, expressing commendation.

recommend′ed di′etary allow′ance, *n.* the amount of an essential nutrient, as a vitamin or mineral, that has been established by the Food and Nutrition Board of the National Academy of Sciences as adequate to meet the average daily nutritional needs of most healthy persons according to age group and sex. *Abbr.:* RDA Compare U.S. RDA

rec•om•pense (rek′əm pens′), *v.,* **-pensed, -pens•ing,** *n.* —*v.t.* **1.** to make payment or return to, as for work done, injury sustained, or favors received. **2.** to pay or give compensation for; make restitution for. —*v.i.* **3.** to make compensation or return for something; repay or requite someone. —*n.* **4.** a repayment, requital, or reward, as for services, gifts, or favors. **5.** compensation, as for an injury; reparation. —**rec′om•pen′sa•ble,** *adj.*

rec•on•cile (rek′ən sīl′), *v.,* **-ciled, -cil•ing.** —*v.t.* **1.** to cause (a person) to accept or be resigned to something not desired. **2.** to cause to become friendly or peaceable again: *to reconcile hostile persons.* **3.** to compose or settle (a quarrel, dispute, etc.). **4.** to bring into agreement or harmony; make compatible or consistent: *to reconcile accounts.* **5.** to restore (an excommunicate or penitent) to communion in a church. —*v.i.* **6.** to become reconciled. —**rec′on•cil′a•ble,** *adj.* —**rec′on•cil′a•bil′i•ty,** *n.* —**rec′on•cil′a•bly,** *adv.* —**rec′on•cile′ment,** *n.*

rec•on•cil•i•a•tion (rek′ən sil′ē ā′shən), *n.* **1.** the act of reconciling or the state of being reconciled. **2.** the process of making consistent or compatible. —**rec′on•cil′i•ate′,** *v.t., v.i.,* **-at•ed, -at•ing.**

rec•on•dite (rek′ən dīt′, ri kon′dīt), *adj.* **1.** pertaining to or dealing with very profound, difficult, or abstruse subject matter: *a recondite treatise.* **2.** known or understood by relatively few; esoteric; arcane. **3.** obscure. —**rec′on•dite′ly,** *adv.* —**rec′on•dite′ness,** *n.*

re•con•di•tion (rē′kən dish′ən), *v.t.* to restore to a satisfactory condition; repair; make over.

re•con•nais•sance (ri kon′ə səns, -zəns), *n.* **1.** the act of reconnoitering. **2.** a general examination or survey of a region, usu. followed by a detailed survey.

re•con•noi•ter (rē′kə noi′tər, rek′ə-), *v.t.* **1.** to inspect, observe, or survey (an enemy position, strength, etc.) in order to gain information for military purposes. **2.** to examine or survey (a region, area, etc.) for engineering, geological, or other purposes. —*v.i.* **3.** to make a reconnaissance. —**re′con•noi′ter•er,** *n.*

re•con•sid•er (rē′kən sid′ər), *v.t.* **1.** to consider again, esp. with a view to a change of decision: *to reconsider a refusal.* —*v.i.* **2.** to consider something again. —**re′con•sid′er•a′tion,** *n.*

re•con•sti•tute (rē kon′sti to͞ot′, -tyo͞ot′), *v.t.,* **-tut•ed, -tut•ing. 1.** to constitute again; reconstruct. **2.** to return (a dehydrated or concentrated food) to the liquid state by adding water. —**re′con•sti•tu′tion,** *n.*

re•con•struct (rē′kən strukt′), *v.t.* **1.** to construct again; rebuild; make over. **2.** to re-create in the mind from available information. —**re′con•struct′i•ble,** *adj.*

re•con•struc•tion (rē′kən struk′shən), *n.* **1.** the act of reconstructing. **2.** (*cap.*) **a.** the process by which the states that had seceded were reorganized as part of the Union after the Civil War. **b.** the period during which this took place, 1865–77.

Re•con•struc•tion•ism (rē′kən struk′shə niz′əm), *n.* a 20th-century Jewish movement originated in the U.S. that views Judaism as an evolving religious civilization requiring constant adaptation to contemporary conditions. —**Re′con•struc′tion•ist,** *n., adj.*

re•cord (*v.* ri kôrd′; *n., adj.* rek′ərd), *v.t.* **1.** to set down in writing or the like, as for the purpose of preserving evidence. **2.** to cause to be set down or registered: *to record one's vote.* **3.** to state or indicate, so as to be noted. **4.** to serve to tell of. **5.** to set down, register, or fix by characteristic marks, incisions, magnetism, etc., for the purpose of reproduction by a phonograph or magnetic reproducer. **6.** to make a recording of. —*v.i.* **7.** to record something; make a record. —*n.* **rec•ord 8.** an account in writing or the like preserving the memory or knowledge of facts or events. **9.** information or knowledge preserved in writing or the like. **10.** a report, list, or aggregate of actions or achievements: *a fine sailing record.* **11.** a legally documented history of criminal activity: *All the suspects had records.* **12.** something or someone serving as a remembrance; memorial. **13.** something on which sound or images have been recorded for subsequent reproduction, as a grooved disk that is played on a phonograph. **14.** the standing of a team or individual with respect to contests won, lost, and tied. **15.** a group of related fields treated as a unit in a database. **16.** an official written report of proceedings of a court of justice. —*adj.* **rec•ord 17.** making or affording a record. **18.** surpassing or superior to all others. —***Idiom.* 19. for the record,** meant for publication or dissemination. **20. off the record,** not for publication; unofficial; confidential. **21. on record, a.** existing as a matter of public knowledge; known. **b.** existing in a publication, document, file, etc. **c.** having stated one's opinion or position publicly. —**re•cord′a•ble,** *adj.*

re•cord•er (ri kôr′dər), *n.* **1.** a person who records, esp. as an official duty. **2.** a recording or registering apparatus or device. **3.** a device for recording sound, images, or data by electrical, magnetic, or optical means. **4.** an end-blown flute having a mouthpiece like a whistle, eight finger holes, and a soft, mellow tone.

rec′ord•hold′er or **rec′ord-hold′er,** *n.* a person or thing recog-

R

nized for the accomplishment of a feat to a better or greater degree than any other.

re·cord·ing (ri kôr′ding), *n.* **1.** the act or practice of a person or thing that records. **2.** sound recorded on a disk or tape. **3.** a disk or tape on which something is recorded.

re·count (*v.* rē kount′; *n.* rē′kount′, rē kount′), *v.t.* **1.** to count again. —*n.* **2.** a second or additional count.

re·count (ri kount′), *v.t.* to relate or narrate; tell in detail. —**re·count′al,** *n.*

re·coup (ri kōōp′), *v.t.* **1.** to get back the equivalent of: *to recoup one's losses.* **2.** to regain; recover. **3.** to reimburse; recompense. —*v.i.* **4.** to get back an equivalent, as of something lost. —**re·coup′a·ble,** *adj.*

re·course (rē′kôrs, -kōrs, ri kôrs′, -kōrs′), *n.* **1.** access or resort to a person or thing for help or protection. **2.** a person or thing resorted to for help or protection. **3.** the right to collect from a maker or endorser of a negotiable instrument.

re·cov·er (rē kuv′ər), *v.t.* to cover again or anew: *re-covered the couch with new upholstery.*

re·cov·er (ri kuv′ər), *v.t.* **1.** to get back or regain (something lost or taken away). **2.** to make up for or make good (loss, damage, etc.) to oneself. **3.** to regain the strength, composure, balance, or the like, of (oneself). **4. a.** to obtain by judgment in a court of law. **b.** to acquire title to through judicial process. **5.** to reclaim from a bad state, practice, etc. **6.** to regain (a substance) in usable form; reclaim. —*v.i.* **7.** to regain one's health, strength, composure, balance, etc., after illness, trouble, disturbance, or the like (sometimes fol. by *from*): *to recover from the flu.* **8.** to regain a former and better state or condition. **9.** to obtain a favorable judgment in a suit for something. **10.** to make a recovery, as in a sport or game. —**re·cov′er·a·ble,** *adj.*

re·cov·er·y (ri kuv′ə rē), *n., pl.* **-er·ies. 1.** the act or process of recovering. **2.** the regaining of something lost or taken away. **3.** restoration or return to any former and better condition, esp. to health from sickness, injury, addiction, etc. **4.** something that is gained in recovering. **5.** an improvement in the economy marking the end of a recession. **6.** a movement or return to a particular position, esp. in preparation for the next movement.

rec·re·ant (rek′rē ənt), *adj.* **1.** cowardly. **2.** unfaithful; disloyal. —*n.* **3.** COWARD. **4.** APOSTATE. —**rec′re·ance, rec′re·an·cy,** *n.*

re·cre·ate (rē′krē āt′), *v.t.,* **-at·ed, -at·ing.** to create anew. —**re′-cre·a′tion,** *n.* —**re′-cre·a′tor,** *n.*

rec·re·ate (rek′rē āt′), *v.,* **-at·ed, -at·ing.** —*v.t.* **1.** to refresh through recreation. —*v.i.* **2.** to take recreation.

rec·re·a·tion (rek′rē ā′shən), *n.* **1.** refreshment by means of a pastime, agreeable exercise, or the like. **2.** a means of enjoyable relaxation. —**rec′re·a′tion·al,** *adj.*

recrea′tional ve′hicle, *n.* a van or utility vehicle used for recreational purposes, as camping. *Abbr.:* RV

recrea′tion room′, *n.* (in a home or public building) a room for informal entertaining, as with dancing or games.

re·cruit (ri krōōt′), *n.* **1.** a newly enlisted or drafted member of the armed forces. **2.** a new member of a group, organization, or the like. **3.** a fresh supply of something. —*v.t.* **4.** to enlist (a person) for service in one of the armed forces. **5.** to raise (a force) by enlistment. **6.** to strengthen or supply (an armed force) with new members. **7.** to furnish with a fresh supply; replenish; renew. **8.** to renew or restore (health, strength, etc.). **9.** to seek to hire, enroll, or enlist: *to recruit executives.* —*v.i.* **10.** to enlist persons for service in one of the armed forces. **11.** to engage in finding and attracting new members. —**re·cruit′er,** *n.* —**re·cruit′ment,** *n.*

rec·ta (rek′tə), *n.* a pl. of RECTUM.

rec·tal (rek′tl), *adj.* of or for the rectum. —**rec′tal·ly,** *adv.*

rec·tan·gle (rek′tang′gəl), *n.* a parallelogram having four right angles.

rectangle

rec·tan·gu·lar (rek tang′gyə lər), *adj.* **1.** shaped like a rectangle. **2.** having the base or section in the form of a rectangle: *a rectangular pyramid.* **3.** having one or more right angles. **4.** forming a right angle.

rec·ti·fi·a·ble (rek′tə fī′ə bəl), *adj.* able to be rectified.

rec·ti·fy (rek′tə fī′), *v.t.,* **-fied, -fy·ing. 1.** to make, put, or set right; remedy; correct: *to rectify an error.* **2.** to put right by adjustment or calculation, as an instrument or a course at sea. **3.** to purify (esp. a spirit or liquor) by repeated distillation. **4.** to change (an alternating current) into a direct current. **5.** to determine the length of (a curve). —**rec′ti·fi·ca′tion,** *n.*

rec·ti·lin·e·ar (rek′tl in′ē ər) also **rec′ti·lin′e·al,** *adj.* **1.** forming a straight line. **2.** formed or characterized by straight lines. **3.** moving in a straight line. —**rec′ti·lin′e·ar·ly,** *adv.*

rec·ti·tude (rek′ti tōōd′, -tyōōd′), *n.* **1.** rightness of principle or conduct; moral virtue; righteousness. **2.** correctness. **3.** straightness.

rec·to (rek′tō), *n., pl.* **-tos.** a right-hand page of an open book or manuscript; the front of a leaf (opposed to *verso*).

rec·tor (rek′tər), *n.* **1.** a member of the clergy in charge of a parish in the Episcopal Church. **2.** a Roman Catholic ecclesiastic in charge of a

college, religious house, or congregation. **3.** a member of the Anglican clergy who has the charge of a parish with full possession of all its rights, tithes, etc. **4.** the head of certain universities, colleges, or schools. —**rec′tor·ate, rec′tor·ship′,** *n.*

rec·to·ry (rek′tə rē), *n., pl.* **-ries. 1.** a rector's house; parsonage. **2.** a benefice held by an Anglican rector.

rec·tum (rek′təm), *n., pl.* **-tums, -ta** (-tə). the terminal section of the large intestine, ending in the anus.

re·cum·bent (ri kum′bənt), *adj.* **1.** lying down; reclining; leaning. **2.** inactive; idle. **3.** *Zool., Bot.* noting a part that leans or reposes upon its surface of origin. —**re·cum′ben·cy,** *n.* —**re·cum′bent·ly,** *adv.*

re·cu·per·ate (ri kōō′pə rāt′, -kyōō′-), *v.i.,* **-at·ed, -at·ing. 1.** to recover from sickness or exhaustion; regain health or strength. **2.** to recover from financial loss. —**re·cu′per·a′tion,** *n.*

re·cu·per·a·tive (ri kōō′pər ə tiv, -pə rā′tiv, -kyōō′-) also **re·cu·per·a·to·ry** (-tôr′ē, -tōr′ē), *adj.* **1.** having the power of recuperating. **2.** pertaining to recuperation: *recuperative powers.*

re·cur (ri kûr′), *v.i.,* **-curred, -cur·ring. 1.** to occur again, as an event, experience, etc. **2.** to return to the mind: *The idea kept recurring.* **3.** to come up again for consideration, as a question. **4.** to have recourse. —**re·cur′rence,** *n.*

re·cur·rent (ri kûr′ənt, -kur′-), *adj.* **1.** occurring or appearing repeatedly. **2.** turned back so as to run in a reverse direction, as a nerve, artery, branch, etc. —**re·cur′rent·ly,** *adv.*

recur′ring dec′imal, *n.* REPEATING DECIMAL.

re·cur·sive (ri kûr′siv), *adj.* pertaining to or using a rule or procedure that can be applied repeatedly. —**re·cur′sive·ly,** *adv.*

re·curve (ri kûrv′), *v.t., v.i.,* **-curved, -curv·ing.** to curve or bend backward or upward.

re·cu·sant (rek′yə zənt, ri kyōō′zənt), *n.* **1.** (in 16th to 18th century England) a person, esp. a Roman Catholic, who refused to attend the services of the Church of England. **2.** a person who refuses to submit or comply. —*adj.* **3.** of or characteristic of a recusant. —**rec′u·san·cy,** *n.*

re·cuse (ri kyōōz′), *v.t.,* **-cused, -cus·ing.** to reject or challenge (a judge or juror) as disqualified to act, esp. because of interest or bias. —**rec·u·sa·tion** (rek′yōō zā′shən), *n.*

re·cy·cle (rē sī′kəl), *v.t.,* **-cled, -cling. 1.** to treat or process (used or waste materials) so as to make suitable for reuse. **2.** to alter or adapt for new use. **3.** to use again in the original form or with minimal alteration: *to recycle a speech.* **4.** to cause to pass through a cycle again. —**re·cy′cla·ble,** *adj.*

red (red), *n., adj.,* **red·der, red·dest.** —*n.* **1.** any of various colors resembling the color of blood; the primary color at one extreme end of the visible spectrum, an effect of light with a wavelength between 610 and 780 nm. **2.** something red. **3.** (*often cap.*) a radical leftist in politics, esp. a communist. **4.** *Informal.* RED LIGHT (def. 1). **5.** *Informal.* red wine. —*adj.* **6.** of the color red. **7.** having distinctive areas or markings of red: *a red robin.* **8.** of or indicating a state of financial loss or indebtedness: *the red column in the ledger.* **9.** politically radical or leftist. **10.** (*often cap.*) communist. —**Idiom. 11. in the red,** operating at a loss or being in debt (opposed to *in the black*). —**red′ness,** *n.*

re·dact (ri dakt′), *v.t.* **1.** to put into suitable literary form; edit. **2.** to frame (a statement). —**re·dac′tion,** *n.* —**re·dac′tor,** *n.*

red′ alert′, *n.* a signal or warning that a critical situation is developing or has occurred.

red′ al′gae, *n.pl.* marine algae of the phylum Rhodophyta in which the chlorophyll is masked by a red or purplish pigment.

red′ ant′, *n.* any of various reddish ants, as a Pharaoh ant.

Red′ Badge′ of Cour′age, The, a novel (1895) by Stephen Crane.

red′ blood′ cell′, *n.* any of the blood cells that in mammals are enucleate disks concave on both sides, contain hemoglobin, and carry oxygen to the cells and tissues and carbon dioxide to the respiratory organs. Also called **erythrocyte, red′ blood′ cor′puscle.** *Abbr.:* RBC

red′-blood′ed, *adj.* vigorous; virile. —**red′-blood′ed·ness,** *n.*

red·bone (red′bōn′), *n.* an American hound with a red coat, used in hunting raccoons and larger game.

red·breast (red′brest′), *n.* **1.** any of various birds that have a red breast, as the robin. **2.** a freshwater sunfish, *Lepomis auritus,* of the eastern U.S.

red·bud (red′bud′), *n.* any American tree of the genus *Cercis,* of the legume family, having small, budlike, pink flowers.

red′ car′pet, *n.* **1.** a red strip of carpet for high-ranking dignitaries to walk on when entering or leaving a building, vehicle, or the like. **2.** a display of courtesy or deference, as that shown to persons of high station. —**red′-car′pet,** *adj.*

red′ ce′dar, *n.* an E North American juniper, *Juniperus virginiana,* yielding a fragrant, moth-repellent red wood used for making lead pencils and for lining drawers and chests. Also called **savin.**

red′ cent′, *n.* a cent as representative of triviality.

Red′ Chi′na, *n.* CHINA, People's Republic of.

red′ clo′ver, *n.* a clover, *Trifolium pratense,* that has red flowers and is grown for forage.

red·coat (red′kōt′), *n.* (esp. during the American Revolution) a British soldier.

Red′ Cres′cent, *n.* an organization functioning as the Red Cross in Muslim countries.

Red′ Cross′, *n.* **1.** an international philanthropic organization (**Red′**

Cross′ Soci′ety), formed in consequence of the Geneva Convention of 1864 chiefly to care for the sick and wounded in war. **2.** a branch of this organization. **3.** Also, **red′ cross′.** GENEVA CROSS.

red•den (red′n), *v.t.* **1.** to make or cause to become red. —*v.i.* **2.** to become red. **3.** to blush; flush.

red•dish (red′ish), *adj.* tending to red; tinged with red.

red′ dwarf′, *n.* any of the faint reddish stars having diameters about half that of the sun and low surface temperatures, about 2000–3000 K.

re•dec•o•rate (rē dek′ə rāt′), *v.,* **-rat•ed, -rat•ing.** —*v.t.* **1.** to decorate (a room, house, etc.) anew, as by repainting or refurnishing. —*v.i.* **2.** to change the décor. —**re•dec′o•ra′tion,** *n.*

re•deem (ri dēm′), *v.t.* **1.** to buy or pay off; clear by payment: *to redeem a mortgage.* **2.** to buy back, as after a tax sale or a mortgage foreclosure. **3.** to recover (something pledged or mortgaged) by payment or other satisfaction: *to redeem a pawned watch.* **4.** to exchange (bonds, trading stamps, etc.) for money or goods. **5.** to convert (paper money) into specie. **6.** to discharge or fulfill (a pledge, promise, etc.). **7.** to make up for; make amends for; offset (some fault, shortcoming, etc.). **8.** to deliver from sin and its consequences by means of a sacrifice offered for the sinner. —**re•deem′a•ble,** *adj.* —**re•deem′a•bil′i•ty,** *n.*

re•deem•er (ri dē′mər), *n.* **1.** a person who redeems. **2.** (*cap.*) Jesus Christ.

re•demp•tion (ri demp′shən), *n.* **1.** an act of redeeming or the state of being redeemed. **2.** deliverance; rescue. **3.** deliverance from sin. **4.** atonement for guilt. **5.** repurchase, as of something sold. **6.** paying off, as of a mortgage, bond, or note. **7.** recovery by payment, as of something pledged: **8.** conversion of paper money into specie.

re•demp•tion•er (ri demp′shə nər), *n.* an emigrant from Europe who obtained passage to America by becoming an indentured servant.

re•demp•tive (ri demp′tiv), *adj.* **1.** serving to redeem. **2.** pertaining to or centering on redemption or salvation. —**re•demp′tive•ly,** *adv.*

Re•demp•tor•ist (ri demp′tər ist), *n.* a member of the Roman Catholic Congregation of the Most Holy Redeemer, an order of priests and lay brothers founded by St. Alphonsus Liguori in 1732.

red′-eye′ or **red′eye′,** *adj. Informal.* of or indicating a long-distance flight that leaves late at night: *the red-eye special from New York to Los Angeles.*

red•eye (red′ī′), *n., pl.* **-eyes,** (*esp. collectively*) **-eye.** any of several fishes having red eyes, as the rock bass.

red′-eye′ gra′vy, *n.* pan gravy from fried ham.

red′ fes′cue, *n.* a grass, *Festuca rubra,* of the meadows of the North Temperate Zone, having green, reddish, or bluish green flower clusters.

red′ fir′, *n.* **1.** any of several firs, as *Abies magnifica,* of the western U.S., having a reddish bark. **2.** the light, soft wood of these trees.

red•fish (red′fish′), *n., pl.* (*esp. collectively*) **-fish,** (*esp. for kinds or species*) **-fish•es. 1.** Also called **ocean perch.** a North Atlantic rockfish. **2.** SHEEPHEAD.

red′ fox′, *n.* fox of the genus *Vulpes,* usu. having reddish fur.

red′ gi′ant, *n.* a star in an intermediate stage of evolution, characterized by a large volume, low surface temperature, and reddish hue.

Red′ Guard′, *n.* a member of a Chinese Communist youth movement in the late 1960s, committed to the militant support of Mao Zedong.

red′-hand′ed, *adj., adv.* in the very act of a crime, wrongdoing, etc., or in possession of self-incriminating evidence.

red•head (red′hed′), *n.* **1.** a person with red hair. **2.** a North American diving duck, *Aythya americana,* the male of which has a chestnut-red head. —**red′-headed,** *adj.*

red′ her′ring, *n.* **1.** a smoked herring. **2.** something intended to divert attention from the real problem or matter at hand; a misleading clue. **3.** a tentative financial prospectus describing a proposed offering, as of stocks, that has not yet been officially registered or approved.

red•horse (red′hôrs′), *n.* any North American sucker of the genus *Moxostoma,* often having reddish fins.

red′-hot′, *adj.* **1.** red with heat; very hot. **2.** violent; furious: *red-hot anger.* **3.** characterized by or creating intense excitement or passion. **4.** very fresh or new: *a red-hot tip on the stock market.*

red•in•te•grate (red in′ti grāt′), *v.t.,* **-grat•ed, -grat•ing.** to make whole again; restore to a perfect state; renew; reestablish.

re•di•rect (rē′di rekt′, -dī-), *v.t.* **1.** to direct again. **2.** to change the direction or focus of. —**re′di•rec′tion,** *n.*

re•dis•trib•ute (rē′di strib′yōōt), *v.t.,* **-ut•ed, -ut•ing. 1.** to distribute again or anew. **2.** to alter the distribution of; apportion differently.

re•dis•tri•bu•tion (rē′dis trə byōō′shən), *n.* **1.** a distribution performed again or anew. **2.** the economic theory that inequalities in income can be reduced by such measures as a progressive income tax and antipoverty programs.

re•dis•trict (rē dis′trikt), *v.t.* to divide anew into districts, as for administrative or electoral purposes.

red′leg•ged grass′hopper (red′leg′id, -legd′), *n.* a migratory grasshopper, *Melanoplus femur-rubrum,* of the southwestern and midwestern U.S., with reddish hind legs: an agricultural pest.

red′-let′ter, *adj.* **1.** marked by red letters, as festival days in the church calendar. **2.** memorable; especially important or happy: *a red-letter day in my life.*

red′ light′, *n.* **1.** a red-colored traffic light used as a signal to stop. **2.** an order or directive to halt an action, project, etc. **3.** a signal of danger; warning.

red′lin′ing or **red′-lin′ing,** *n.* a discriminatory practice by which some financial institutions refuse to grant mortgages or insurance in urban areas that they consider to be deteriorating. [as if such areas had been outlined in red on a map]

red′ ma′ple, *n.* a maple tree, *Acer rubrum,* of E North America, growing in moist soil and usu. having red flowers and leaves that turn bright red in autumn.

red′ mul′berry, *n.* a mulberry tree, *Morus rubra,* of North America, bearing long clusters of dark purple fruit.

re•do (*v.* rē dōō′; *n.* rē′dōō′), *v.,* **-did, -done, -do•ing,** *n., pl.* **-dos, -do's.** —*v.t.* **1.** to do again; repeat. **2.** to revise or reconstruct. **3.** to redecorate or remodel. —*n.* **4.** an act or instance of redoing.

red′ oak′, *n.* **1.** any of several oak trees, as *Quercus rubra,* or *Q. falcata,* of North America, characterized by leaves with pointed lobes and acorns that usu. mature every two years. **2.** the hard, reddish wood of these trees.

red′ o′cher, *n.* any of the red natural earths, mixtures of hematite, that are used as pigments.

red•o•lent (red′l ənt), *adj.* **1.** having a pleasant odor; fragrant. **2.** odorous or smelling (usu. fol. by *of*): *redolent of garlic.* **3.** suggestive; reminiscent (usu. fol. by *of*). —**red′o•lence,** *n.* —**red′o•lent•ly,** *adv.*

red′ o′sier, *n.* a North American dogwood, *Cornus sericea* (or *C. stolonifera*), having red twigs and branches and white fruits. Also called **red′-o′sier dog′wood.**

re•dou•ble (rē dub′əl), *v.,* **-bled, -bling,** *n.* —*v.t.* **1.** to double; make twice as great: *to redouble one's efforts.* **2.** to echo or reecho. **3.** *Bridge.* to double the double of (an opponent). —*v.i.* **4.** to become twice as great. **5.** *Bridge.* to double the double of an opponent.

re•doubt (ri dout′), *n.* an independent earthwork built inside or outside a larger fortification.

re•doubt•a•ble (ri dou′tə bəl), *adj.* **1.** evoking fear; fearsome; formidable. **2.** commanding respect or reverence. —**re•doubt′a•bly,** *adv.*

re•dound (ri dound′), *v.i.* **1.** to have a good or bad effect; work to one's advantage or disadvantage. **2.** to result or accrue. **3.** to reflect upon a person as honor or disgrace (usu. followed by *on* or *upon*).

red•out (red′out′), *n.* a condition experienced by pilots and astronauts in which rapid deceleration or a negative gravity force drives blood to the head, reddening the field of vision.

re•dox (rē′doks), *n.* OXIDATION-REDUCTION.

red′ pep′per, *n.* **1.** CAYENNE. **2.** a pepper, *Capsicum annuum longum,* cultivated in many varieties, the pods of which are used for flavoring, sauces, etc. **3.** the mild, ripe fruit of the sweet pepper, *Capsicum annuum grossum,* used as a vegetable.

red′ pine′, *n.* **1.** a pine, *Pinus resinosa,* of NE North America, having needles in groups of two and reddish bark. **2.** the wood of this tree, valued as timber. Also called **Norway pine.**

re•dress (*n.* rē′dres, ri dres′; *v.* ri dres′), *n.* **1.** the setting right of what is morally wrong. **2.** relief from wrong or injury. **3.** compensation for such wrong or injury. —*v.t.* **4.** to remedy (wrongs, injuries, etc.). **5.** to correct (abuses, evils, etc.). **6.** to relieve (suffering, want, etc.). **7.** to adjust evenly again, as a balance.

Red′ Riv′er, *n.* **1.** a river flowing E from NW Texas along the S boundary of Oklahoma into the Mississippi River in Louisiana. ab. 1300 mi. (2095 km) long. **2.** Also called **Red′ Riv′er of the North′.** a river flowing N along the boundary between Minnesota and North Dakota to Lake Winnipeg in S Canada. 533 mi. (860 km) long. **3.** Vietnamese, **Song Hong.** Chinese, **Yuan Jiang.** a river in SE Asia, flowing SE from Yunnan, China, through N Vietnam to the Gulf of Tonkin. 500 mi. (800 km) long.

Red′ Riv′er War′, *n.* a punitive campaign (1874–75) led by General Sheridan against hostile Indians in the region of the Red River and the Llano Estacado.

red•root (red′rōōt′, -root′), *n.* an E North American swamp plant, *Lachnanthes tintoria,* of the bloodwort family, having sword-shaped leaves, woolly yellowish flowers, and a red root.

red′ salm′on, *n.* SOCKEYE SALMON.

Red′ Sea′, *n.* an arm of the Indian Ocean, extending NW between Africa and Arabia; connected to the Mediterranean by the Suez Canal. 1450 mi. (2335 km) long; 170,000 sq. mi. (440,300 sq. km).

red′ snap′per, *n.* any of several snappers of the genus *Lutjanus,* esp. *L. campechanus,* a large food fish of the Gulf of Mexico.

red′ spi′der, *n.* SPIDER MITE.

red′-spot′ted newt′, *n.* a common central and E North American newt, *Notophthalmus viridescens viridescens,* orange with red spots in its immature terrestrial phase (**red eft**), darkening to a dull green as an aquatic adult.

red′ spruce′, *n.* a spruce, *Picea rubens,* of NE North America, having reddish brown inner bark and yielding a light, soft wood.

red′ squir′rel, *n.* a reddish squirrel, *Tamiasciurus hudsonicus,* of North America. Also called **chickaree.**

red•start (red′stärt′), *n.* any of several New World wood warblers that habitually fan their tails, esp. *Setophaga ruticilla,* the male of which is mostly black with orange wing and tail patches.

red′-tailed′ hawk′, *n.* a common North American hawk, *Buteo jamaicensis,* with whitish underparts, a dark back, head, and wings, and a reddish brown tail.

R

red′ tape′, *n.* bureaucratic routine required before official action can be taken.

red•top (red′top′), *n.* a grass of the genus *Agrostis* having reddish panicles, as *A. gigantea,* widely cultivated for lawns and pasturage.

Red′ To′ry, *n. Canadian.* a Progressive Conservative who suports fiscal conservatism but liberal social and cultural policies.

re•duce (ri do͞os′, -dyo͞os′), *v.,* **-duced, -duc•ing.** —*v.t.* **1.** to bring down to a smaller size, amount, price, etc. **2.** to lower in degree, intensity, etc. **3.** to demote to a lower rank or authority. **4.** to treat analytically, as a complex idea. **5.** to act destructively upon (a substance or object): *a house reduced to ashes.* **6.** to bring to a certain state: *to reduce someone to tears.* **7.** to evaporate water from (a sauce, soup, etc.) by boiling. **8.** to change the denomination or form, but not the value, of (a fraction, polynomial, etc.). **9. a.** to deoxidize. **b.** to add hydrogen to. **c.** to decrease the positive charge on (an ion) by adding electrons. **10.** to convert (ore minerals) to a metallic state by driving off nonmetallic elements; smelt. **11.** to thin or dilute: *to reduce paint with turpentine.* **12.** to restore to the normal place, relation, or condition, as a fractured bone. —*v.i.* **13.** to become reduced. **14.** to lose weight, as by dieting. **15.** to be equal to or turned into something. **16.** to undergo meiosis. —**re•duc′er,** *n.* —**re•duc•i•ble,** *adj.* —**re•duc′i•bil′i•ty,** *n.*

reduc′ing a′gent, *n.* a substance that causes another substance to undergo reduction and that is oxidized in the process.

re•duc•tion (ri duk′shən), *n.* **1.** the act or process of reducing, or the state of being reduced. **2.** the amount by which something is reduced. **3.** a form produced by reducing; a copy on a smaller scale. **4.** *Biol.* meiosis, esp. the first meiotic cell division in which the chromosome number is reduced by half. **5.** the process or result of reducing a chemical substance. —**re•duc′tion•al,** *adj.*

re•duc•tion•ism (ri duk′shə niz′əm), *n.* **1.** the theory that every complex phenomenon, esp. in biology or psychology, can be explained by analyzing the simplest, most basic physical mechanisms that are in operation during the phenomenon. **2.** the practice of oversimplifying a complex idea or issue to the point of minimizing or distorting it. —**re•duc′tion•ist,** *n., adj.*

re•duc•tive (ri duk′tiv), *adj.* **1.** of or pertaining to reduction or abridgment. **2.** of or pertaining to change from one form to another. **3.** of, pertaining to, or employing reductionism; reductionistic. —**re•duc′tive•ly,** *adv.* —**re•duc′tive•ness,** *n.*

re•dun•dan•cy (ri dun′dən sē) also **re•dun′dance,** *n., pl.* **-dan•cies** also **-danc•es. 1.** the state of being redundant. **2.** a redundant thing; superfluity. **3.** the provision of a duplicate system or equipment as a backup.

re•dun•dant (ri dun′dənt), *adj.* **1.** characterized by verbosity or unnecessary repetition in expressing ideas. **2.** exceeding what is usual or necessary: *a redundant part.* **3.** superabundant or superfluous: *lush, redundant vegetation.* **4.** (of a system, equipment, etc.) supplied as a backup, as in a spacecraft. **5.** (of language or a linguistic feature) characterized by redundancy; predictable. —**re•dun′dant•ly,** *adv.*

re•du•pli•cate (*v.* ri do͞o′pli kāt′, -dyo͞o′-; *adj.* -kit, -kāt′), *v.,* **-cat•ed, -cat•ing,** *adj.* —*v.t.* **1.** to double; repeat. **2.** to form (a derivative or inflected form) by doubling a syllable or other part of a word, sometimes with modifications. —*v.i.* **3.** to become doubled. **4.** to become reduplicated. —*adj.* **5.** doubled.

re•du•pli•ca•tion (ri do͞o′pli kā′shən, -dyo͞o′-), *n.* **1.** an act or instance of reduplicating; the state of being reduplicated. **2. a.** reduplicating as a grammatical pattern. **b.** the added element in a reduplicated form. **c.** a word formed by reduplication, as *hush-hush* or *helter-skelter.*

re•dux (ri duks′), *adj.* (used postpositively) brought back; resurgent: *the Victorian morality redux.*

red•ware (red′wâr′), *n.* a large brown seaweed, *Laminaria digitata,* common off N Atlantic coasts.

red′ wine′, *n.* wine having a predominantly red color derived from the skin pigment in the dark-colored grapes used in making it.

red•wing (red′wing′), *n.* **1.** a Eurasian thrush, *Turdus iliacus,* having chestnut-red feathers under the wings. **2.** RED-WINGED BLACKBIRD.

red′-winged′ black′bird, *n.* a North American blackbird, *Agelaius phoeniceus,* the male of which is black with scarlet patches, usu. bordered with yellow, on the bend of the wing.

red′ wolf′, *n.* a small, red gray North American canid, *Canis rufus.*

red•wood (red′wo͝od′), *n.* **1.** a coniferous tree, *Sequoia sempervirens,* of the bald cypress family, native to California, noted for its great height. **2.** its valuable brownish red timber.

Red′wood Na′tional Park′, *n.* a national park in N California: redwood forest with some of the world's tallest trees. 172 sq. mi. (445 sq. km).

red′ worm′, *n.* a freshwater bloodworm of the genus *Tubifex.*

re•ech•o or **re-ech•o** (rē ek′ō), *v., n., pl.* **-ech•oes.** —*v.i.* **1.** to echo back, as a sound. **2.** to give back an echo; resound. —*v.t.* **3.** to echo back. **4.** to repeat like an echo. —*n.* **5.** a repeated echo.

reed (rēd), *n.* **1.** the straight stalk of any of various tall grasses, esp. of the genus *Phragmites,* growing in marshy places. **2.** any of the plants themselves. **3.** such stalks or plants collectively, esp. as material for thatching. **4.** anything made from such a stalk, as an arrow. **5. a.** a small, flexible piece of cane or metal that, attached to the mouth of any of various wind instruments, is set into vibration by a stream of air and, in turn, sets into vibration the air column enclosed in the tube of the instrument. **b.** REED INSTRUMENT. **6.** the comblike device in a loom that separates the warp threads during weaving and is used to beat the filling yarns. **7.** a small convex molding, usu. one of a series set in parallel rows as decoration. **8.** an ancient unit of length, equal to 6 cubits. Ezek. 40:5. —*v.t.* **9.** to decorate with reed. **10.** to thatch with or as if with reed. **11.** to make vertical grooves on (the edge of a coin, medal, etc.).

Reed (rēd), *n.* **1. John,** 1887–1920, U.S. journalist and poet. **2. Walter C.,** 1851–1902, U.S. army surgeon.

reed•buck (rēd′buk′), *n., pl.* **-bucks,** (*esp. collectively*) **-buck.** any of several yellowish African antelopes of the genus *Redunca,* living near lakes and rivers, the male of which has short, forward-curving horns.

reed•ing (rē′ding), *n.* **1.** a set of moldings, as on a column, resembling small, convex fluting. **2.** ornamentation consisting of such moldings. **3.** a number of narrow, vertical grooves on the edge of a coin, medal, etc.

reed′ in′strument, *n.* a wind instrument with a single or double reed, as a saxophone or an oboe.

reed′ or′gan, *n.* a musical keyboard instrument, as the harmonium, with small metal reeds through which air is forced to produce sound.

reed′ pipe′, *n.* an organ pipe having a reed that is vibrated by air to produce the sound.

re•ed•u•cate or **re-ed•u•cate** (rē ej′o͝o kāt′), *v.t.,* **-cat•ed, -cat•ing. 1.** to educate again, as for new purposes. **2.** to educate or train for resumption of normal activities, as a disabled person. —**re•ed′u•ca′tion,** *n.* —**re•ed′u•ca′tive,** *adj.*

reef[1] (rēf), *n.* **1.** a ridge of rocks or sand, often of coral debris, at or near the surface of the water. **2.** *Mining.* a lode or vein.

reef[2] (rēf), *n.* **1.** a part of a sail that is rolled and tied down to reduce the area exposed to the wind. —*v.t.* **2.** to shorten (a sail) by tying in one or more reefs. **3.** to reduce the length of (a topmast, a bowsprit, etc.), as by lowering or sliding inboard.

reef•er (rē′fər), *n.* **1.** a fitted, usu. double-breasted coat or jacket made of heavy cloth and having wide lapels. **2.** a person who reefs.

reek (rēk), *v.i.* **1.** to smell strongly and unpleasantly. **2.** to be strongly pervaded with something unpleasant. **3.** to give off steam, smoke, etc. **4.** to be wet with sweat, blood, etc. —*v.t.* **5.** to give off; emit; exude. **6.** to expose to or treat with smoke. —*n.* **7.** a strong, unpleasant smell. **8.** vapor or steam.

reel[1] (rēl), *n.* **1.** a cylinder or other device that turns on an axis and is used to wind up or let out wire, rope, film, etc. **2.** a rotatory device attached to a fishing rod at the butt, for winding up or letting out the line. **3.** a quantity of something wound on a reel. —*v.t.* **4.** to wind on a reel. **5.** to unwind (silk filaments) from a cocoon. **6.** to pull by winding a line on a reel: *to reel a fish in.* **7. reel off,** to say or write fluently and quickly, as a sequence of items.

reel[2] (rēl), *v.i.* **1.** to sway or rock under a blow, shock, etc. **2.** to waver or retreat. **3.** to sway about in standing or walking, as from dizziness or intoxication; stagger. **4.** to turn round and round; whirl. **5.** to have a sensation of whirling: *His brain reeled.* —*v.t.* **6.** to cause to reel. —*n.* **7.** a reeling or staggering movement.

reel[3] (rēl), *n.* **1.** a lively Scottish dance. **2.** VIRGINIA REEL. **3.** music for a reel.

re•en•force or **re-en•force** (rē′ən fôrs′, -fōrs′), *v.t.,* **-forced, -forc•ing.** REINFORCE.

re•en•ter or **re-en•ter** (rē en′tər), *v.t.* **1.** to enter again. **2.** to participate in once more: *to reenter politics.* **3.** to record again, as in a list or account. —*v.i.* **4.** to enter again.

re•en•try (rē en′trē), *n., pl.* **-tries. 1.** the act of reentering. **2.** the return from outer space into the earth's atmosphere of an earth-orbiting satellite, spacecraft, rocket, or the like. **3.** *Law.* the retaking of possession under a right reserved in a prior conveyance. **4.** Also called **reen′try card′.** (in bridge) a card that will win a trick enabling one to regain the lead in a hand.

reeve[1] (rēv), *v.t.,* **rove** or **reeved, reev•ing. 1.** to pass (a rope or the like) through a hole, ring, or the like. **2.** to fasten by placing through or around something.

reeve[2] (rēv), *n.* the female of the ruff, *Philomachus pugnax.*

re•ex•am•ine or **re-ex•am•ine** (rē′ig zam′in), *v.t.,* **-ined, -in•ing. 1.** to examine again. **2.** *Law.* to examine (a witness) again after cross-examination. —**re′ex•am′i•na′tion,** *n.* —**re′ex•am′in•er,** *n.*

re•ex•port or **re-ex•port** (*v.* rē′ik spôrt′, -spōrt′, rē ek′spôrt, -spōrt; *n.* rē ek′spôrt, -spōrt), *v.t.* **1.** to export again, as imported goods. —*n.* **2.** the act of reexporting. **3.** a commodity that is reexported. —**re′ex•por•ta′tion,** *n.*

ref (ref), *n., v.t., v.i.,* **reffed, ref•fing.** REFEREE.

re•face (rē fās′), *v.t.,* **-faced, -fac•ing. 1.** to renew, restore, or repair the face or surface of (buildings, stone, etc.). **2.** to provide with a new facing, as a garment.

re•fec•to•ry (ri fek′tə rē), *n., pl.* **-ries.** a dining hall, esp. in a religious house.

re•fer (ri fûr′), *v.,* **-ferred, -fer•ring.** —*v.t.* **1.** to direct to a person, place, etc., for information or anything required. **2.** to direct the attention of: *The asterisk refers the reader to a footnote.* **3.** to submit for decision, information, etc.: *to refer a dispute to arbitration.* **4.** to assign to a class, period, etc.; classify. **5.** relate; apply. —*v.i.* **6.** to direct attention. **7.** to have recourse, as for aid or information. **8.** to make reference or allusion. —**ref•er•a•ble, re•fer•ra•ble** (ref′ər ə bəl, ri fûr′-), *adj.*

ref•er•ee (ref′ə rē′), *n., v.,* **-eed, -ee•ing.** —*n.* **1.** a person to whom something is referred for decision or settlement; arbitrator. **2.** (in certain games and sports) a judge having functions fixed by the rules of the game or sport; umpire. **3.** *Law.* a person selected by a court to take testimony and recommend a decision. —*v.t.* **4.** to preside over as referee. —*v.i.* **5.** to act as referee.

ref•er•ence (ref′ər əns, ref′rəns), *n., v.,* **-enced, -enc•ing.** —*n.* **1.** an act or instance of referring. **2.** a mention; allusion. **3.** something for which a name or designation stands; denotation. **4. a.** a direction of the attention, as in a book, to some other book, passage, etc. **b.** the book, passage, etc., to which one is directed. **5.** REFERENCE MARK. **6.** use or recourse for purposes of information: *a library for public reference.* **7.** a book or other source of useful facts or information. **8. a.** a person to whom one refers for testimony as to another's character, abilities, etc. **b.** a statement regarding a person's character, abilities, etc. **9.** regard or connection; relation: *without reference to age.* —*v.t.* **10.** to furnish with references. **11.** to mention in or as a reference. **12.** to arrange for easy reference.

ref′erence mark′, *n.* any of various symbols, as an asterisk (*), dagger (†), or superscript number, used to direct a reader to further information in a footnote, bibliography, or other text.

ref•er•en•dum (ref′ə ren′dəm), *n., pl.* **-dums, -da** (-də). **1.** the principle or practice of referring measures proposed or passed by a legislative body to the vote of the electorate for approval or rejection. Compare INITIATIVE (def. 4a). **2.** a vote on a measure thus referred.

ref•er•ent (ref′ər ənt, ref′rənt), *n.* the object or event to which a term or symbol refers.

ref•er•en•tial (ref′ə ren′shəl), *adj.* **1.** being a reference. **2.** containing one or more references. **3.** used for reference. —**ref′er•en′tial•ly,** *adv.*

re•fer•ral (ri fûr′əl), *n.* **1.** an act or instance of referring. **2.** the state of being referred. **3.** a person referred or recommended to someone or for something.

re•fill (*v.* rē fil′; *n.* rē′fil′), *v.t., v.i.* **1.** to fill again. —*n.* **2.** a material, supply, or the like, to replace something that has been used up. —**re•fill′a•ble,** *adj., n.*

re•fi•nance (rē′fi nans′, rē fī′nans), *v.,* **-nanced, -nanc•ing.** —*v.t.* **1.** to finance again. **2.** to satisfy (a debt) by making another loan on new terms. —*v.i.* **3.** to arrange new financing for something.

re•fine (ri fīn′), *v.,* **-fined, -fin•ing.** —*v.t.* **1.** to bring to a pure state; free or separate from impurities or other extraneous substances. **2.** to purify from what is coarse or debasing; make elegant or cultured. **3.** to bring to a finer state or form by purifying or polishing. **4.** to make more fine, subtle, or precise. —*v.i.* **5.** to become pure. **6.** to become more elegant or polished. **7.** to make fine distinctions in thought or language. **8.** refine on or upon, to improve by inserting finer distinctions, superior elements, etc. —**re•fin′a•ble,** *adj.* —**re•fin′er,** *n.*

re•fined (ri fīnd′), *adj.* **1.** having or showing well-bred feeling, taste, etc. **2.** freed or free from coarseness, vulgarity, etc. **3.** freed from impurities. **4.** very subtle or exact.

re•fine•ment (ri fīn′mənt), *n.* **1.** fineness or elegance of feeling, taste, manners, language, etc. **2.** an instance of this. **3.** the act or process of refining. **4.** the quality or state of being refined. **5.** a subtle point or distinction. **6.** an improved form of something. **7.** a detail or device added to improve something.

re•fin•er•y (ri fī′nə rē), *n., pl.* **-er•ies.** an establishment for refining something, as metal, sugar, or petroleum.

re•fin•ish (rē fin′ish), *v.t.* to give a new surface to (wood, furniture, etc.). —**re•fin′ish•er,** *n.*

re•fit (rē fit′), *v.,* **-fit•ted** or **-fit, -fit•ting,** *n.* —*v.t.* **1.** to fit, prepare, or equip again. —*v.i.* **2.** to renew supplies or equipment. **3.** to get refitted. —*n.* **4.** an act of refitting.

re•fla•tion (ri flā′shən), *n.* the attempt to restore economic activity by putting more money in circulation, esp. through tax cuts, lower interest rates, and increased government spending. —**re•fla′tion•ar′y** (-shə ner′ē), *adj.*

re•flect (ri flekt′), *v.t.* **1.** to cast back (light, heat, sound, etc.) from a surface. **2.** to give back or show an image of; mirror. **3.** to serve to cast or bring (credit, discredit, etc.). **4.** to express; show: *followers reflecting the views of the leader.* —*v.i.* **5.** to be turned or cast back, as light. **6.** to cast back light, heat, etc. **7.** to be reflected or mirrored. **8.** to give back or show an image. **9.** to think, ponder, or meditate: *to reflect on one's faults.* **10.** to serve or tend to bring reproach or discredit: *His crimes reflected on the whole community.* **11.** to serve to give a particular aspect or impression: *The test reflects well on your abilities.*

reflect′ing tel′escope, *n.* See under TELESCOPE (def. 1). Also called **reflector.**

re•flec•tion (ri flek′shən), *n.* **1.** the act of reflecting or the state of being reflected. **2.** the return of light, heat, or sound after striking a surface. **3.** something reflected, as an image. **4.** a fixing of the thoughts on something; careful consideration. **5.** a thought occurring in consideration or meditation. **6.** an unfavorable remark or observation. **7.** the casting of some imputation or reproach. Also, *esp. Brit.,* **reflexion.** —**re•flec′tion•al,** *adj.*

re•flec•tive (ri flek′tiv), *adj.* **1.** capable of reflecting. **2.** of or pertaining to reflection. **3.** cast by reflection. **4.** given to or marked by meditation. —**re•flec′tive•ly,** *adv.* —**re•flec•tiv•i•ty** (rē′flek tiv′i tē), *n.*

re•flec•tor (ri flek′tər), *n.* **1.** a person or thing that reflects. **2.** a body, surface, or device that reflects light, heat, sound, or the like. **3.** REFLECTING TELESCOPE.

re•flex (*adj., n.* rē′fleks; *v.* ri fleks′), *adj.* **1.** noting or pertaining to an involuntary response to a stimulus. **2.** occurring in reaction; responsive. **3.** cast back; reflected, as light or color. **4.** bent or turned back. —*n.* **5. a.** Also called **re′flex act′.** movement caused by a reflex response. **b.** Also called **re′flex ac′tion.** the entire physiological process activating such movement. **6.** any automatic, unthinking, often habitual behavior or response. **7.** the reflected image of an object. **8.** a reproduction, as if in a mirror. **9.** a copy; adaptation. **10.** reflected light, color, etc. —*v.t.* **11.** to subject to a reflex process. **12.** to bend, turn, or fold back.

re′flex an′gle, *n.* an angle greater than 180° and less than 360°.

re•flex•ive (ri flek′siv), *adj.* **1. a.** (of a verb) taking a subject and object with identical referents, as *cut* in *I cut myself.* **b.** (of a pronoun) used as an object with the same referent as the subject of a verb, as *myself* in *I cut myself.* **2.** reflex; responsive. **3.** able to reflect; reflective. —*n.* **4.** a reflexive verb or pronoun. —**re•flex′ive•ly,** *adv.* —**re•flex′ive•ness, re•flex•iv•i•ty** (rē′flek siv′i tē), *n.*

re•flex•ol•o•gy (rē′flek sol′ə jē), *n.* **1.** a system of massaging specific areas of the foot or sometimes the hand in order to promote healing, relieve stress, etc., in other parts of the body. **2.** the study of reflex movements and processes. —**re•flex′ol•o•gist,** *n.*

re•flux (rē′fluks′), *n.* a flowing back; ebb.

re•for•est (rē fôr′ist, -for′-), *v.t.* to replant trees on (land denuded by cutting or fire). —**re′for•est•a′tion,** *n.*

re-form (rē fôrm′), *v.t., v.i.* to form again.

re•form (ri fôrm′), *n.* **1.** the improvement or amendment of what is wrong, corrupt, unsatisfactory, etc.: *social reform.* **2.** an instance of this. **3.** the amendment of conduct, belief, etc. —*v.t.* **4.** to change to a better state, form, etc. **5.** to cause (a person) to abandon wrong or evil ways of life or conduct. **6.** to put an end to (abuses, evils, etc.). **7.** to subject (petroleum fractions) to a chemical process that increases the octane content. —*v.i.* **8.** to abandon evil conduct or error. —*adj.* **9.** (*cap.*) conforming to or characteristic of Reform Judaism. —**re•form′a•ble,** *adj.* —**re•form′a•tive,** *adj.*

ref•or•ma•tion (ref′ər mā′shən), *n.* **1.** the act of reforming or the state of being reformed. **2.** (*cap.*) the 16th-century movement for reforming the Roman Catholic Church, which resulted in the establishment of the Protestant churches. —**ref′or•ma′tion•al,** *adj.*

re•form•a•to•ry (ri fôr′mə tôr′ē, -tōr′ē), *adj., n., pl.* **-ries.** —*adj.* **1.** serving or designed to reform. —*n.* **2.** Also called **reform school.** a penal institution for reforming young offenders.

re•formed (ri fôrmd′), *adj.* **1.** amended by removal of faults, abuses, etc. **2.** improved in conduct, morals, etc. **3.** (*cap.*) noting or pertaining to Protestant churches, esp. Calvinist as distinguished from Lutheran. —**re•form′ed•ly,** *adv.*

Reformed′ Church′ in Amer′ica, *n.* a Protestant denomination having a Calvinist theology: originally, Dutch Reformed Church.

re•form•er (ri fôr′mər), *n.* **1.** a person devoted to bringing about reform, as in politics or society. **2.** (*cap.*) any of the leaders of the Reformation.

Reform′ Ju′daism, *n.* a branch of Judaism that stresses ethical teachings and frequently simplifies or rejects traditional beliefs and practices to meet the conditions of contemporary life. Compare ORTHODOX JUDAISM, CONSERVATIVE JUDAISM.

reform′ school′, *n.* REFORMATORY (def. 2).

re•for•mu•late (rē fôr′myə lāt′), *v.t.,* **-lat•ed, -lat•ing. 1.** to formulate in a different way; alter or revise. **2.** to formulate again. —**re′for•mu•la′tion,** *n.*

re•fract (ri frakt′), *v.t.* **1.** to subject to refraction. **2.** to determine the refractive condition of (an eye).

refract′ing tel′escope, *n.* See under TELESCOPE (def. 1). Also called **refractor.**

re•frac•tion (ri frak′shən), *n.* **1.** the change of direction of a ray of light, sound, heat, or the like, in passing obliquely from one medium into another in which its wave velocity is different. **2.** the ability of the eye to refract light that enters it so as to form an image on the retina. **3.** the amount, in angular measure, by which the altitude of a celestial body is increased by the refraction of its light in the earth's atmosphere. —**re•frac′tion•al,** *adj.*

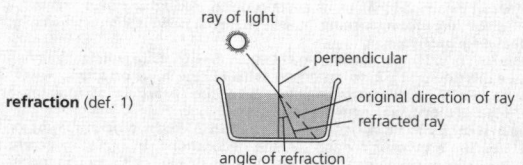

refraction (def. 1)

re•frac•tive (ri frak′tiv), *adj.* **1.** of or pertaining to refraction. **2.** having power to refract. —**re•frac′tive•ly,** *adv.*

re•frac•tor (ri frak′tər), *n.* **1.** a person or thing that refracts. **2.** REFRACTING TELESCOPE.

re•frac•to•ry (ri frak′tə rē), *adj., n., pl.* **-ries.** —*adj.* **1.** hard or impossible to manage; stubbornly disobedient: *a refractory child.* **2.** resisting ordinary methods of treatment. **3.** difficult to fuse, reduce, or work, as an ore or metal. —*n.* **4.** a material that retains its shape and composition even when heated to extreme temperatures.

re•frain[1] (ri frān′), *v.i.* to keep oneself from doing or saying something (often fol. by *from*).

re•frain[2] (ri frān′), *n.* **1.** a phrase or verse recurring in a song or poem, esp. at the end of each stanza; chorus. **2. a.** a musical setting for a poetic refrain. **b.** melody; tune. **c.** the recurrent section of a rondo.

re•fresh (ri fresh′), *v.t.* **1.** to provide new vigor and energy by rest, food, etc. (often used reflexively). **2.** to stimulate (the memory). **3.** to reinvigorate or cheer (the mind or spirits). **4.** to freshen in appearance, color, etc. **—***v.i.* **5.** to take refreshment, esp. food or drink. **6.** to become fresh or vigorous again; revive. **—re•fresh′er,** *n.*

re•fresh•ing (ri fresh′ing), *adj.* **1.** having the power to restore freshness, vitality, energy, etc. **2.** pleasingly fresh or different. **—re•fresh′ing•ly,** *adv.*

re•fresh•ment (ri fresh′mənt), *n.* **1.** something that refreshes, esp. food or drink. **2. refreshments,** articles or portions of food or drink, esp. for a light meal. **3.** the act of refreshing or the state of being refreshed.

re′fried beans′, *n.pl.* dried beans, cooked and mashed and then fried in lard, sometimes with onions and other seasonings.

re•frig•er•ant (ri frij′ər ənt), *adj.* **1.** refrigerating; cooling. **2.** reducing bodily heat or fever. **—***n.* **3.** a refrigerant agent, as a drug. **4.** a liquid capable of vaporizing at a low temperature, as ammonia, used in mechanical refrigeration.

re•frig•er•ate (ri frij′ə rāt′), *v.t.,* **-at•ed, -at•ing.** to make or keep cold or cool, as for preservation. **—re•frig′er•a′tion,** *n.* **—re•frig′er•a′tive, re•frig′er•a•to′ry** (-ər ə tôr′ē, -tōr′ē), *adj.*

re•frig•er•a•tor (ri frij′ə rā′tər), *n.* **1.** a box, room, or cabinet in which food, drink, etc., are kept cool by means of ice or mechanical refrigeration. **2.** the part of a distilling apparatus that cools the volatile material, causing it to condense; condenser.

re•fu•el (rē fyōō′əl), *v.,* **-eled, -el•ing** or (*esp. Brit.*) **-elled, -el•ling.** **—***v.t.* **1.** to supply again with fuel. **—***v.i.* **2.** to take on a fresh supply of fuel.

ref•uge (ref′yōōj), *n.* **1.** shelter or protection from danger, trouble, etc. **2.** a place of shelter, protection, or safety. **3.** anything to which one has recourse for aid, relief, or escape.

ref•u•gee (ref′yŏŏ jē′, ref′yŏŏ jē′), *n.* a person who flees for refuge or safety, esp. to a foreign country, as in time of political upheaval, war, etc.

re•ful•gent (ri ful′jənt), *adj.* shining brightly; radiant; gleaming. **—re•ful′gence, re•ful′gen•cy,** *n.* **—re•ful′gent•ly,** *adv.*

re•fund[1] (*v.* ri fund′, rē′fund; *n.* rē′fund), *v.t.* **1.** to give back or restore (esp. money); repay. **2.** to make repayment to; reimburse. **—***v.i.* **3.** to make repayment. **—***n.* **4.** an act or instance of refunding. **5.** an amount refunded. **—re•fund′a•ble,** *adj.*

re•fund[2] (rē fund′), *v.t.* to fund anew.

re•fur•bish (rē fûr′bish), *v.t.* to furbish again; renovate; brighten. **—re•fur′bish•ment,** *n.*

re•fus•al (ri fyōō′zəl), *n.* **1.** an act or instance of refusing. **2.** priority in refusing or taking something; option.

re•fuse[1] (ri fyōōz′), *v.,* **-fused, -fus•ing.** **—***v.t.* **1.** to decline to accept (something offered). **2.** to decline to give; deny (a request, demand, etc.). **3.** to express a determination not to (do something): *to refuse to discuss an issue.* **4.** to decline to submit to. **5.** to decline to accept (a suitor) in marriage. **6.** (of a horse) to decline to leap over (a barrier). **—***v.i.* **7.** to decline acceptance or compliance. **—re•fus′a•ble,** *adj.*

ref•use[2] (ref′yōōs), *n.* **1.** something that is discarded as worthless or useless; trash; garbage. **—***adj.* **2.** rejected as worthless; discarded.

re•fuse•nik (ri fyōōz′nik), *n.* (formerly) a Soviet citizen, usu. Jewish, who was denied permission to emigrate from the Soviet Union.

ref•u•ta•tion (ref′yŏŏ tā′shən) also **re•fut•al** (ri fyōōt′l), *n.* an act of refuting a statement, charge, etc.; disproof.

re•fute (ri fyōōt′), *v.t.,* **-fut•ed, -fut•ing.** **1.** to prove to be false or erroneous, as an opinion or charge. **2.** to prove (a person) to be in error. **—re•fut•a•ble** (ri fyōō′tə bəl, ref′yə tə-), *adj.*

re•gain (rē gān′), *v.t.* **1.** to get again; recover. **2.** to succeed in reaching again; get back to: *to regain the shore.* **—re•gain′a•ble,** *adj.*

re•gal (rē′gəl), *adj.* **1.** of or pertaining to a king or queen; royal. **2.** befitting or resembling a king or queen. **3.** stately; splendid. **—re′gal•ly,** *adv.* **—re′gal•ness,** *n.*

re•gale (ri gāl′), *v.,* **-galed, -gal•ing,** *n.* **—***v.t.* **1.** to entertain lavishly or agreeably; delight. **2.** to entertain with choice food or drink. **—***v.i.* **3.** to feast. **—***n.* **4.** a sumptuous feast. **5.** a choice article of food or drink. **—re•gale′ment,** *n.* **—re•gal′er,** *n.*

re•ga•li•a (ri gā′lē ə, -gāl′yə), *n.pl.* **1.** the ensigns or emblems of royalty, as the crown or scepter. **2.** the decorations, insignia, or ceremonial clothes of any office or order. **3.** fancy or dressy clothing; finery.

re•gard (ri gärd′), *v.t.* **1.** to look upon or think of with a particular feeling: *to regard a person with favor.* **2.** to have or show respect or concern for. **3.** to think highly of; esteem. **4.** to take into account; consider. **5.** to look at; observe. **6.** to relate to; concern. **7.** to see, look at, or conceive of in a particular way; judge. **—***v.i.* **8.** to pay attention. **9.** to look or gaze. **—***n.* **10.** reference; relation: *to err with regard to facts.* **11.** an aspect, point, or particular: *quite satisfactory in this regard.* **12.** thought; attention; concern. **13.** a look; gaze. **14.** respect, esteem, or deference. **15.** kindly feeling; liking. **16. regards,** sentiments of esteem or affection. **—*Idiom.* 17. as regards,** concerning; about. **18. with** or **in regard to,** with reference to; as regards; concerning. **—Usage.** Although sometimes considered poor substitutes for *about* or *concerning,* the phrases AS REGARDS, IN REGARD TO, and WITH REGARD TO are standard and occur in all varieties of spoken and written English, esp. in business writing: *As regards your letter of January 19. ...* The phrases IN REGARDS TO and WITH REGARDS TO are widely rejected as errors.

re•gard•ing (ri gär′ding), *prep.* with regard to; respecting; concerning.

re•gard•less (ri gärd′lis), *adj.* **1.** having or showing no regard; heedless; unmindful (often fol. by *of*). **—***adv.* **2.** without concern as to advice, warning, hardship, etc.; anyway. **—*Idiom.* 3. regardless of,** in spite of; without regard for. **—re•gard′less•ly,** *adv.*

re•gat•ta (ri gat′ə, -gä′tə), *n., pl.* **-tas.** a boat race, as of rowboats, yachts, or other vessels.

re•gen•cy (rē′jən sē), *n., pl.* **-cies,** *adj.* **—***n.* **1.** the office, jurisdiction, or control of a regent or regents. **2.** a body of regents. **3.** a government consisting of regents. **4.** a territory under the control of a regent or regents. **5.** the term of office of a regent. **6.** (*cap.*) the period (1811–20) during which the Prince of Wales, later George IV, was regent of England. **7.** (*cap.*) the period (1715–23) during which Philip, Duke of Orleans, was regent of France. **—***adj.* **8.** of or pertaining to a regency. **9.** (*cap.*) of or pertaining to the Regencies in England or France. **10.** (*often cap.*) of or designating the style of architecture, furniture, and decoration in England around the time of the Regency.

re•gen•er•ate (*v.* ri jen′ə rāt′; *adj.* -ər it), *v.,* **-at•ed, -at•ing,** *adj.* **—***v.t.* **1.** to effect a complete moral reform in. **2.** to re-create, reconstitute, or make over, esp. in a better form or condition. **3.** to revive or produce anew; bring into existence again. **4.** to restore or revive (a lost or injured body part) by the growth of new tissue. **5.** to make (a substance) usable again, as by restoring it to its original chemical composition. **6.** to magnify the amplification of, by relaying part of the output circuit power into the input circuit. **7.** to cause to be born again spiritually. **—***v.i.* **8.** to come into existence or be formed again. **9.** to reform; become regenerate. **10.** to produce a regenerative effect. **11.** to undergo regeneration. **—***adj.* **12.** reconstituted or made over in a better form. **13.** reformed. **—re•gen′er•a′tor,** *n.*

re•gen•er•a•tion (ri jen′ə rā′shən), *n.* **1.** the act of regenerating or the state of being regenerated. **2.** the regrowth of a lost or injured part of the body. **3.** spiritual rebirth; religious revival.

re•gen•er•a•tive (ri jen′ər ə tiv, -ə rā′tiv), *adj.* **1.** of or characterized by regeneration. **2.** tending to regenerate. **—re•gen′er•a•tive•ly,** *adv.*

re•gent (rē′jənt), *n.* **1.** a person who exercises the ruling power in a kingdom during the minority, absence, or disability of the sovereign. **2.** a ruler or governor. **3.** a member of the governing board of a state university or a state educational system. **4.** any of various officers of academic institutions. **—***adj.* **5.** acting as regent of a kingdom (usu. used postpositively): *a prince regent.* **—re′gent•ship′,** *n.*

reg•gae (reg′ā), *n.* a style of Jamaican music blending blues, calypso, and rock and characterized by a strongly syncopated rhythm.

reg•i•cide (rej′ə sīd′), *n.* **1.** the killing of a king. **2.** a person who kills a king or is responsible for his death. **—reg′i•cid′al,** *adj.*

re•gime or **ré•gime** (rə zhēm′, rā-; *sometimes* -jēm′), *n.* **1.** a mode or system of rule or government. **2.** a ruling or prevailing system. **3.** a government in power. **4.** the period during which a particular government or ruling system is in power. **5.** REGIMEN (def. 1).

reg•i•men (rej′ə mən, -men′, rezh′-), *n.* **1.** a regulated course, as of diet, exercise, or manner of living, to preserve or restore health or to attain some result. **2.** government or rule. [< Latin: rule]

reg•i•ment (*n.* rej′ə mənt; *v.* -ment′), *n.* **1.** a military unit of ground forces, consisting of two or more battalions, a headquarters unit, and supporting units. **—***v.t.* **2.** to manage or treat in a rigid, uniform manner; subject to strict discipline. **3.** to form into a regiment or regiments. **4.** to form into an organized group. **—reg′i•men•ta′tion,** *n.*

reg•i•men•tal (rej′ə men′tl), *adj.* **1.** pertaining to a regiment. **—***n.* **2. regimentals,** the uniform of a regiment. **—reg′i•men′tal•ly,** *adv.*

re•gion (rē′jən), *n.* **1.** an extensive, continuous part of a surface, space, or body: *a region of the earth.* **2.** Usu., **regions.** the vast or indefinite entirety of a space or area, or something compared to one: *the regions of the mind.* **3.** a part of the earth's surface of considerable and usu. indefinite extent: *a tropical region.* **4.** a district without respect to boundaries or extent: *an industrial region.* **5.** a large, indefinite area or range of something specified: *a region of authority.* **6.** an area of interest, activity, etc.; field. **7.** an administrative division of a country, territory, or city. **8.** a division or part of the body: *the abdominal region.*

re•gion•al (rē′jə nl), *adj.* **1.** of or pertaining to a region of considerable extent; not merely local. **2.** of or pertaining to a particular region, area, or part, as of a country or the body. **—re′gion•al•ly,** *adv.*

re•gion•al•ism (rē′jə nl iz′əm), *n.* **1.** a speech form, expression, custom, or other feature peculiar to or characteristic of a particular area. **2.** devotion to the interests of one's own region. **3.** (*sometimes cap.*) the theory or practice of emphasizing regional characteristics in a work of literature or a painting. **—re′gion•al•ist,** *n., adj.*

reg•is•ter (rej′ə stər), *n.* **1.** a book in which records of events, names, etc., are kept. **2.** a list or record of such events, names, etc. **3.** an entry in such a record or list. **4.** an official document issued to a merchant ship as evidence of its nationality. **5.** registration or registry. **6.** a mechanical device by which certain data are automatically recorded. **7.** CASH REGISTER. **8. a.** the compass or range of a voice or an instrument. **b.** a part of this range produced in the same way and having the same quality. **c.** STOP (def. 35c). **9.** a device for controlling the flow of warmed air or the like through an opening. **10.** proper relationship between two plane surfaces in photography. **11.** a precise adjustment or correspondence, as of lines or columns, esp. on the two sides of a printed leaf. —*v.t.* **12.** to enter or cause to be entered in a register. **13.** to cause (mail) to be recorded upon delivery to a post office for safeguarding against loss, damage, etc. **14.** to enroll (a student, voter, etc.). **15.** to indicate by a record or scale, as instruments do. **16.** to adjust (fire) on a known point. **17.** to show (surprise, joy, anger, etc.), as by facial expression or by actions. **18.** to document (a merchant ship engaged in foreign trade). —*v.i.* **19.** to enter one's name or cause it to be entered in a register; enroll. **20.** to show: *A smile registered on her face.* **21.** to have some effect; make some impression.

reg•is•tered (rej′ə stərd), *adj.* **1.** recorded, as in a register or book; enrolled. **2.** (of a bond) listed with the issuing corporation and inscribed with the owner's name. **3.** officially or legally certified by a government board: *a registered patent.* **4.** denoting cattle, horses, dogs, etc., having pedigrees verified and filed by authorized associations of breeders.

reg′istered nurse′, *n.* a graduate nurse who has passed a state board examination and been registered and licensed to practice nursing. *Abbr.:* RN, R.N.

reg′ister ton′, *n.* See under TON[1] (def. 6).

reg•is•trant (rej′ə strənt), *n.* a person who registers or is registered.

reg•is•trar (rej′ə strär′), *n.* **1.** a person who keeps a record; an official recorder. **2.** an official at a school or college who maintains students' records, issues reports of grades, mails out official publications, etc.

reg•is•tra•tion (rej′ə strā′shən), *n.* **1.** the act of registering. **2.** an instance of this. **3.** an entry in a register. **4.** the group or number registered. **5.** a certificate attesting to the fact that someone or something has been registered. **6.** the selection of stops made by an organist for a particular piece.

reg•is•try (rej′ə strē), *n., pl.* **-tries. 1.** the act of registering; registration. **2.** a place where a register is kept; an office of registration. **3.** an official record; register. **4.** the state of being registered. **5.** the nationality of a merchant ship as shown on its register.

reg•nant (reg′nənt), *adj.* reigning; ruling (usu. used postpositively): *a queen regnant.* —**reg′nan•cy,** *n.*

re•gress (*v.* ri gres′; *n.* rē′gres), *v.i.* **1.** to move backward; go back. **2.** to revert to an earlier or less advanced state or form. —*n.* **3.** the act of going back; return. **4.** the right to go back. **5.** backward movement or course; retrogression.

re•gres•sion (ri gresh′ən), *n.* **1.** the act of going back to a previous place or state; return or reversion. **2.** retrogradation; retrogression. **3.** *Biol.* reversion to an earlier or less advanced state or to a general type. **4.** *Psychoanal.* reversion to an earlier, less adaptive emotional state or behavior pattern. **5.** the subsidence of a disease or its symptoms.

re•gres•sive (ri gres′iv), *adj.* **1.** regressing or tending to regress; retrogressive. **2.** (of tax) decreasing proportionately with an increase in the tax base. —**re•gres′sive•ly,** *adv.*

re•gret (ri gret′), *v.,* **-gret•ted, -gret•ting,** *n.* —*v.t.* **1.** to feel sorrow or remorse for (an act, fault, disappointment, etc.). **2.** to think of with a sense of loss. —*n.* **3.** a sense of loss, disappointment, etc. **4.** a feeling of sorrow or remorse for a fault, act, loss, etc. **5. regrets,** a polite, usu. formal refusal of an invitation.

re•gret•ful (ri gret′fəl), *adj.* full of regret; sorrowful because of what is lost, gone, or done. —**re•gret′ful•ly,** *adv.* —**re•gret′ful•ness,** *n.*

re•gret•ta•ble (ri gret′ə bəl), *adj.* causing or deserving regret; unfortunate; deplorable. —**re•gret′ta•bly,** *adv.*

re•group (rē gro͞op′), *v.t.* **1.** to form into a new or restructured group or grouping. —*v.i.* **2.** to become reorganized in order to make a fresh start. **3.** *Mil.* to become organized in a new tactical formation.

reg•u•lar (reg′yə lər), *adj.* **1.** usual; normal; customary. **2.** evenly or uniformly arranged; symmetrical. **3.** characterized by fixed principle, uniform procedure, etc. **4.** recurring at fixed or uniform intervals. **5.** having regular menses or bowel movements. **6.** adhering to a rule or procedure; methodical. **7.** habitual or long-standing: *a regular user.* **8.** conforming to some accepted rule, discipline, etc. **9.** legitimate or proper: *a regular doctor.* **10.** *Informal.* **a.** decent; straightforward; nice: *a regular guy.* **b.** absolute; thoroughgoing: *a regular rascal.* **11.** conforming to the most prevalent pattern of formation, inflection, etc., in a language: *a regular verb.* **12.** *Math.* **a.** governed by one law throughout. **b.** (of a polygon) having all sides and angles equal. **c.** (of a polyhedron) having all faces congruent regular polygons, and all solid angles congruent. **d.** ANALYTIC (def. 5a). **13.** noting or belonging to the permanently organized, or standing, army of a state. **14.** subject to a religious rule, or belonging to a religious or monastic order (opposed to *secular*). **15.** of, pertaining to, or selected by the recognized agents of a political party: *the regular ticket.* **16.** (of coffee) containing an average amount of milk or cream. —*n.* **17.** a long-standing or habitual customer or client. **18.** a member of a duly constituted religious order under a rule. **19.** a professional soldier. **20.** a party member who faithfully stands by his or her party. **21.** a size of garments for persons of average proportions. **22.** an athlete who plays in most of the games. —**reg′u•lar′i•ty,** *n.*

reg•u•lar•ly (reg′yə lər lē), *adv.* **1.** at regular times or intervals. **2.** according to plan, custom, etc. **3.** usually; ordinarily.

reg•u•late (reg′yə lāt′), *v.t.,* **-lat•ed, -lat•ing. 1.** to control or direct by a rule, principle, or method. **2.** to adjust in accordance with some standard or requirement, as of amount or degree: *to regulate the temperature.* **3.** to adjust so as to ensure accuracy of operation: *to regulate a watch.* **4.** to put in good order: *to regulate the digestion.* —**reg′u•la′tive** (-yə lā′tiv, -yə lə tiv), **reg′u•la•to′ry** (-lə tôr′ē, -tōr′ē), *adj.*

reg•u•la•tion (reg′yə lā′shən), *n.* **1.** a law, rule, or other order prescribed by authority, esp. to regulate conduct. **2.** the act of regulating or the state of being regulated. —*adj.* **3.** prescribed by or conforming to regulation: *regulation army equipment.* **4.** usual; normal; customary.

reg•u•la•tor (reg′yə lā′tər), *n.* **1.** a person or thing that regulates. **2. a.** an adjustable device in a clock or a watch for making it go faster or slower. **b.** a master clock, usu. of great accuracy, against which other clocks are checked. **3.** any of various devices designed to control the flow of liquids, gases, or electrical current. **4.** (*cap.*) **a.** a member of any of several bands or committees in North Carolina (1767–71), formed to resist certain abuses, as extortion by officials. **b.** (in newly settled areas) a member of any band or committee organized to preserve order before the establishment of regular legal authority.

Reg•u•lus (reg′yə ləs), *n., pl.* **-lus•es, -li** (-lī′). a first-magnitude star in the constellation Leo.

re•gur•gi•tate (ri gûr′ji tāt′), *v.,* **-tat•ed, -tat•ing.** —*v.i.* **1.** to surge or rush back, as liquids, gases, or undigested food. —*v.t.* **2.** to cause to surge or rush back; vomit. **3.** to give back or repeat, esp. something not fully understood or assimilated.

re•gur•gi•ta•tion (ri gûr′ji tā′shən), *n.* **1.** the act of regurgitating. **2.** voluntary or involuntary return of partly digested food from the stomach to the mouth. **3.** the reflux of blood through defective heart valves.

re•hab (rē′hab′), *n., v.,* **-habbed, -hab•bing.** —*n.* **1.** rehabilitation. **2.** a rehabilitated building. —*v.t.* **3.** to rehabilitate.

re•ha•bil•i•tate (rē′hə bil′i tāt′, rē′ə-), *v.,* **-tat•ed, -tat•ing.** —*v.t.* **1.** to restore or bring to a condition of good health, ability to work, or productive activity. **2.** to restore to good condition, operation, or management. **3.** to reestablish the good reputation of. **4.** to restore formally to former capacity, standing, rank, rights, or privileges. —*v.i.* **5.** to undergo rehabilitation. —**re′ha•bil′i•ta′tion,** *n.* —**re′ha•bil′i•ta′tive,** *adj.*

re•hash (*v.* rē hash′; *n.* rē′hash′), *v.t.* **1.** to rework or reuse (old material) in a new form without significant change. —*n.* **2.** the act of rehashing. **3.** something rehashed.

re•hear (rē hēr′), *v.t.,* **-heard** (-hûrd′), **-hear•ing. 1.** to hear again. **2.** to reconsider officially, as a judge.

re•hears•al (ri hûr′səl), *n.* **1.** private session of exercise, drill, or practice in preparation for a public performance or ceremony. **2.** the act of rehearsing. **3.** a repeating or relating: *a rehearsal of grievances.*

re•hearse (ri hûrs′), *v.,* **-hearsed, -hears•ing.** —*v.t.* **1.** to practice (a play, speech, musical piece, etc.) in private prior to a public presentation. **2.** to drill or train (an actor, musician, etc.) by rehearsal. **3.** to relate the facts or particulars of; recount. —*v.i.* **4.** to rehearse a play, part, etc.; participate in a rehearsal.

Rehn•quist (ren′kwist), *n.* **William H(ubbs),** born 1924, Chief Justice of the U.S. Supreme Court since 1986.

Re•ho•bo•am (rē′ə bō′əm), *n.* the successor of Solomon and the first king of Judah, reigned 922?–915? B.C. I Kings 11:43.

Re•ho•both (ri hō′both), *n.* a well dug by Isaac. Gen. 26:22.

re•hy•drate (rē hī′drāt), *v.t.,* **-drat•ed, -drat•ing.** to restore moisture or fluid to (something dehydrated). —**re′hy•dra′tion,** *n.*

Reich (rīk, rīKH), *n.* the German state during the period 1871–1945. Compare THIRD REICH. [< German: kingdom]

re•i•fy (rē′ə fī′, rā′-), *v.t.,* **-fied, -fy•ing.** to convert into or regard as a concrete thing: *to reify a concept.* —**re′i•fi•ca′tion,** *n.*

reign (rān), *n.* **1.** the period during which a sovereign occupies the throne. **2.** royal rule or authority; sovereignty. **3.** dominating power or influence: *the reign of law.* —*v.i.* **4.** to possess or exercise sovereign power or authority; rule. **5.** to have control or influence. **6.** to predominate or be prevalent; prevail.

Reign′ of Ter′ror, *n.* **1.** a period of the French Revolution (1793–94) during which many persons were ruthlessly executed by the ruling faction. **2.** (*l.c.*) any period or situation of ruthless oppression or violence.

re•im•burse (rē′im bûrs′), *v.t.,* **-bursed, -burs•ing. 1.** to make repayment to for expense or loss incurred. **2.** to pay back; refund; repay. —**re′im•burs′a•ble,** *adj.* —**re′im•burse′ment,** *n.*

re•im•port (rē′im pôrt′, -pōrt′), *v.t.* to import back into the country of exportation. —**re′im•por•ta′tion,** *n.*

Reims or **Rheims** (rēmz; *Fr.* RANS), *n.* a city in NE France: cathedral; unconditional surrender of Germany May 7, 1945. 181,985.

rein (rān), *n.* **1.** Often, **reins.** a leather strap fastened to each end of the bit of a bridle, by which the rider or driver controls a horse or other animal. **2.** any of certain other straps or thongs forming part of a harness. **3.** a means of curbing, controlling, or directing; check; restraint. **4. reins,** the controlling or directing power: *the reins of government.* —*v.t.* **5.** to check or guide (a horse or other animal) by exerting pressure on a bridle bit by means of the reins. **6.** to curb; restrain; control. —*v.i.* **7.** to rein a horse or other animal. **8.** to obey the reins. —***Idiom.*** **9. draw rein,** to curtail one's speed or progress; halt. **10. give (free) rein to,** to give complete freedom to; indulge freely.

re•in•car•nate (*v.* rē′in kär′nāt; *adj.* -nit, -nāt), *v.,* **-nat•ed, -nat•ing,** *adj.* —*v.i., v.t.* **1.** to undergo or cause to undergo reincarnation. —*adj.* **2.** incarnate anew.

re•in•car•na•tion (rē′in kär nā′shən), *n.* **1.** the belief that the soul, upon death of the body, comes back to earth in another body or form.

2. rebirth of the soul in a new body. **3.** a new incarnation or embodiment, as of a person.
rein·deer (rān′dēr′), *n., pl.* **-deer,** (*occasionally*) **-deers.** a large deer, *Rangifer tarandus,* of N and arctic regions of the world: both male and female have antlers. Compare CARIBOU.

reindeer, *Rangifer tarandus,*
4 1/2 ft. (1.4 m) high at shoulder;
length 5 1/2 ft. (1.7 m)

re·in·force or **re·en·force** (rē′in fôrs′, -fōrs′), *v.t.,* **-forced, -forc·ing. 1.** to strengthen with some added piece, support, or material: *to reinforce a wall.* **2.** to make more forcible or effective; strengthen; support: *to reinforce efforts; to reinforce prejudices.* **3.** to augment; increase. **4.** to strengthen (a military force) with additional personnel, ships, or aircraft. **5.** to strengthen the probability of (a desired behavior) by giving or withholding a reward.
re′inforced con′crete, *n.* concrete containing steel bars, strands, mesh, etc., to absorb tensile and shearing stresses.
re·in·force·ment (rē′in fôrs′mənt, -fōrs′-), *n.* **1.** the act of reinforcing; the state of being reinforced. **2.** something that reinforces or strengthens. **3.** Often, **reinforcements.** an additional supply of personnel, ships, aircraft, etc., for a military force. **4.** a procedure, as a reward or punishment, that alters a behavioral response.
re·in·state (rē′in stāt′), *v.t.,* **-stat·ed, -stat·ing.** to put back or establish again, as in a former position or state: *to reinstate the ousted president.* —**re′in·state′ment,** *n.* —**re′in·sta′tor,** *n.*
re·in·sure (rē′in shŏŏr′, -shûr′), *v.t.,* **-sured, -sur·ing. 1.** to insure again. **2.** to insure under a contract by which a first insurer is relieved of all or part of the risk, which devolves upon another insurer. —**re′in·sur′ance,** *n.* —**re′in·sur′er,** *n.*
re·in·te·grate (rē in′tə grāt′), *v.t.,* **-grat·ed, -grat·ing.** to restore to a unified state. —**re′in·te·gra′tion,** *n.*
re·in·vent (rē′in vent′), *v.t.* to invent again or anew, esp. without knowing that the invention already exists. —**re′in·ven′tion,** *n.*
re·is·sue (rē ish′ōō; *esp. Brit.* -is′yōō), *n., v.,* **-sued, -su·ing.** —*n.* **1.** something that is issued again, as a book or movie. —*v.t.* **2.** to issue again. —**re·is′su·a·ble,** *adj.*
re·it·er·ate (rē it′ə rāt′), *v.t.,* **-at·ed, -at·ing.** to say or do again or repeatedly; repeat, often excessively. —**re·it′er·a′tion,** *n.*
re·ject (*v.* ri jekt′; *n.* rē′jekt), *v.t.* **1.** to refuse to have, take, use, recognize, etc.: *to reject a job offer.* **2.** to refuse to grant (a request, demand, etc.); deny. **3.** to refuse to accept or admit; rebuff. **4.** to discard as useless or unsatisfactory. **5.** to eject; vomit. **6.** to cast out or off. **7.** to have an immunological reaction against (a transplanted organ or grafted tissue). —*n.* **8.** something or someone that is rejected, as an imperfect or unwanted article. —**re·jec′tion,** *n.*
re·joice (ri jois′), *v.,* **-joiced, -joic·ing.** —*v.i.* **1.** to feel joy or gladness; take delight (often fol. by *in* or *at*). —*v.t.* **2.** to make joyful; gladden.
re·join[1] (rē join′), *v.t.* **1.** to come again into the company of: *to rejoin a party after a brief absence.* **2.** to join together again; reunite. —*v.i.* **3.** to become joined together again.
re·join[2] (ri join′), *v.t.* **1.** to say in answer; reply. —*v.i.* **2.** to reply, esp. in response to a reply or comment; retort. **3.** *Law.* to answer a plaintiff's replication.
re·join·der (ri join′dər), *n.* **1.** an answer to a reply; response. **2.** *Law.* a defendant's answer to a plaintiff's replication.
re·ju·ve·nate (ri jōō′və nāt′), *v.,* **-nat·ed, -nat·ing.** —*v.t.* **1.** to restore to youthful vigor, appearance, etc.; make young again. **2.** to restore to a former state; make fresh or new again. —*v.i.* **3.** to undergo rejuvenation. —**re·ju′ve·na′tion,** *n.* —**re·ju′ve·na′tive,** *adj.*
re·laid (rē lād′), *v.* pt. and pp. of RE-LAY.
re·lapse (*v.* ri laps′; *n. also* rē′laps), *v.,* **-lapsed, -laps·ing,** *n.* —*v.i.* **1.** to fall or slip back into a former state or practice: *to relapse into silence.* **2.** to fall back into illness after apparent recovery. **3.** to fall back into wrongdoing or error; backslide. —*n.* **4.** a return of a disease after partial recovery from it.
re·late (ri lāt′), *v.,* **-lat·ed, -lat·ing.** —*v.t.* **1.** to give an account of; tell; narrate. **2.** to bring into or establish association or connection: *to relate events to probable causes.* —*v.i.* **3.** to have reference or relation (often fol. by *to*). **4.** to have or establish a sympathetic relationship or understanding. —**re·lat′a·ble,** *adj.*
re·lat·ed (ri lā′tid), *adj.* **1.** associated; connected. **2.** allied by kinship, marriage, or common origin. **3.** harmonically interconnected: *related musical keys.*
re·la·tion (ri lā′shən), *n.* **1.** a significant association between or

among things; connection; relationship: *the relation between cause and effect.* **2. relations,** *n.* **a.** the various connections or dealings between peoples, countries, etc. **b.** the various connections in which persons are brought together: *business relations.* **c.** sexual intercourse. **3.** the mode or kind of connection between one person or thing and another. **4.** connection between persons by blood or marriage; relationship. **5.** a person who is related by blood or marriage; relative. **6.** the act of relating or narrating. **7.** *Law.* a principle whereby an act done at one time is presumed to have taken effect at a previous time. —*Idiom.* **8. in** or **with relation to,** with reference to; concerning.
re·la·tion·al (ri lā′shə nl), *adj.* **1.** of or pertaining to relations. **2.** indicating or specifying some relation.
rela′tional da′tabase, *n.* an electronic database comprising multiple files of related information, usu. stored in tables of rows (records) and columns (fields), and allowing a link to be established between separate files that have a matching field, as a column of invoice numbers, so that the two files can be queried simultaneously by the user.
re·la·tion·ship (ri lā′shən ship′), *n.* **1.** a connection, association, or involvement. **2.** connection between persons by blood or marriage; kinship. **3.** an emotional or other connection between people.
rel·a·tive (rel′ə tiv), *n.* **1.** a person who is connected with another by blood or marriage. **2.** something having, or standing in, some relation to something else. **3.** something dependent upon external conditions for its specific nature, size, etc. (opposed to *absolute*). **4.** a relative pronoun, adjective, or adverb. —*adj.* **5.** considered in relation to something else: *the relative merits of gas and electric heating.* **6.** existing or having its specific nature only by relation to something else; not absolute or independent: *Happiness is relative.* **7.** having relation or connection. **8.** having reference; relevant; pertinent (usu. fol. by *to*): *the facts relative to the case.* **9.** correspondent; proportionate. **10.** depending for significance upon something else: *"Better"* is a relative term. **11.** designating a word that introduces a subordinate clause and refers to an expressed or implied element of the principal clause: *the relative pronoun who in "That was the woman who called."* **12.** (of a musical key) having the same key signature as another key: *a relative minor.* —**rel′a·tive·ly,** *adv.*
rel′ative clause′, *n.* a subordinate clause that is introduced by a relative pronoun, adjective, or adverb and modifies an antecedent, as *"who saw you"* in *"That's the woman who saw you."*
rel′ative humid′ity, *n.* the amount of water vapor in the air, expressed as a percentage of the maximum amount that the air could hold at the given temperature.
rel·a·tiv·i·ty (rel′ə tiv′i tē), *n.* **1.** the state or fact of being relative. **2. a.** Also called **special relativity.** the first part of Albert Einstein's two-part theory, based on the axioms that physical laws have the same form throughout the universe and that the velocity of light in a vacuum is a universal constant, from which is derived the mass-energy equation, $E = mc^2$. **b.** Also called **general relativity.** the second part, a theory of gravitation based on the axiom that the local effects of a gravitational field and of the acceleration of an inertial system are identical.
re·lax (ri laks′), *v.t.* **1.** to make less tense, rigid, or firm: *to relax the muscles.* **2.** to diminish the force or intensity of, as effort or concentration; slacken or abate. **3.** to make less strict, as rules or discipline. **4.** to release or bring relief from the effects of tension, anxiety, etc. —*v.i.* **5.** to become less tense, or rigid. **6.** to become less strict or severe. **7.** to reduce or stop work or effort for the sake of rest or recreation.
re·lax·ant (ri lak′sənt), *adj.* **1.** of, pertaining to, or causing relaxation. —*n.* **2.** a drug that relaxes, esp. one that lessens strain in muscle.
re·lax·a·tion (rē′lak sā′shən), *n.* **1.** abatement or relief from work, effort, etc. **2.** an activity or recreation that provides such relief; diversion; entertainment. **3.** a loosening or slackening. **4.** diminution or remission of strictness or severity.
re·laxed (ri lakst′), *adj.* **1.** being free of or relieved from tension or anxiety. **2.** not strict; easy; informal.
re·lay or **re·lay** (rē lā′), *v.t.,* **-laid, -lay·ing.** to lay again.
re·lay[1] (rē′lā), *n., v.,* **-layed, -lay·ing.** —*n.* **1.** a series of persons relieving one another or taking turns; shift. **2.** a fresh set of dogs or horses posted in readiness for use in a hunt, on a journey, etc. **3. a.** RELAY RACE. **b.** a length or leg in a relay race. **4. a.** an electrical device that responds to a change of current or voltage in one circuit by making or breaking a connection in another. **b.** SERVOMECHANISM. **5.** an act or instance of conveying or transmitting by relay. —*v.t.* **6.** to carry or convey by or as if by relays: *to relay a message.* **7.** to provide with or replace by fresh relays. **8.** to retransmit (a signal, message, etc.) by or as if by means of an electrical relay.
re·lay[2] (rē lā′), *v.t.,* **-laid, -lay·ing.** RE-LAY.
re′lay race′, *n.* a race between teams of contestants, each contestant being relieved by a teammate after running part of the distance.
re·lease (rē lēs′), *v.t.,* **-leased, -leas·ing. 1.** to lease again. **2.** to make over (land, property, etc.), as to another.
re·lease (ri lēs′), *v.,* **-leased, -leas·ing,** *n.* —*v.t.* **1.** to free from confinement, bondage, obligation, pain, etc.; let go. **2.** to free from anything that restrains or fastens; loose. **3.** to allow to be known, issued, done, or exhibited: *to release an article for publication.* —*n.* **4.** a freeing or releasing from confinement, obligation, pain, emotional strain, etc. **5.** liberation from anything that restrains or fastens. **6.** a device or agency that effects such liberation. **7.** a grant of permission, as to publish, use, or sell something. **8.** the releasing of something for publication, performance, use, exhibition, or sale. **9.** a film, book, record, etc., that is re-

leased. **10.** PRESS RELEASE. **11.** the surrender of a legal right or the like to another. **12.** a control mechanism for starting or stopping a machine, esp. by removing some restrictive apparatus.

rel•e•gate (rel′i gāt′), *v.t.*, **-gat•ed, -gat•ing. 1.** to send or consign to an inferior position or condition. **2.** to consign or commit (a matter, task, etc.), as to a person. **3.** to assign or refer (something) to a particular class or kind. **4.** to send into exile; banish.

re•lent (ri lent′), *v.i.* **1.** to soften in feeling, temper, or determination; become more mild, compassionate, or forgiving. **2.** to become less severe; slacken. —**re•lent′ing•ly,** *adv.*

re•lent•less (ri lent′lis), *adj.* unyieldingly severe, strict, or harsh; unrelenting. —**re•lent′less•ly,** *adv.*

rel•e•vant (rel′ə vənt), *adj.* **1.** bearing upon or connected with the matter at hand; pertinent. **2.** having practical value or applicability. —**rel′e•vance,** *n.* —**Pronunciation.** See IRRELEVANT.

re•li•a•ble (ri lī′ə bəl), *adj.* capable of being relied on; consistently dependable in character, judgment, performance, or result. —**re•li•a•bil′i•ty,** *n.* —**re•li′a•bly,** *adv.*

re•li•ance (ri lī′əns), *n.* **1.** confident or trustful dependence. **2.** confidence. **3.** something or someone relied on.

re•li•ant (ri lī′ənt), *adj.* **1.** having or showing dependence. **2.** confident; trustful.

rel•ic (rel′ik), *n.* **1.** a surviving memorial of something past. **2.** an object having interest by reason of its age or its association with the past. **3.** a surviving trace of something: *a custom that is a relic of paganism.* **4. relics, a.** remaining parts or fragments. **b.** the remains of a deceased person. **5.** something kept in remembrance; souvenir; memento. **6.** a body, body part, or personal object associated with a saint or martyr and preserved as worthy of veneration.

re•lief¹ (ri lēf′), *n.* **1.** alleviation of or deliverance from pain, distress, etc. **2.** a feeling of comfort or ease caused by such alleviation or deliverance. **3.** money, food, or other help given to those in poverty or need. **4.** something affording a pleasing change. **5.** release from a post of duty, as by the arrival of a replacement. **6.** the person or persons acting as replacement. **7.** the rescue of a besieged town, fort, etc., from an attacking force. **8.** the freeing of a closed space, as a tank or boiler, from more than a desirable amount of pressure or vacuum. —*Idiom.* **9. on relief,** receiving financial assistance from a government agency.

bas-relief   high relief

relief² (def. 2)

re•lief² (ri lēf′), *n.* **1.** prominence, distinctness, or vividness due to contrast. **2.** the projection of a figure or part from the ground or plane on which it is formed, as in sculpture or similar work. **3.** a piece or work in such projection. **4.** an apparent projection of parts in a painting, drawing, etc., giving the appearance of the third dimension. **5.** the differences in elevation and slope between the higher and lower parts of the land surface of a given area. **6.** a printing process, as letterpress, in which ink is transferred to paper from raised printing surfaces.

relief′ map′, *n.* a map showing the relief of an area, usu. by generalized contour lines.

relief′ pitch′er, *n.* a baseball pitcher brought into a game to replace another pitcher, usu. in a critical situation.

re•lieve (ri lēv′), *v.,* **-lieved, -liev•ing.** —*v.t.* **1.** to ease or alleviate (pain, anxiety, need, etc.); mitigate; allay. **2.** to free from anxiety, fear, pain, etc. **3.** to free from need or poverty. **4.** to bring effective aid to (a besieged town, military position, etc.). **5.** to ease (a person) of a burden, wrong, or oppression. **6.** to reduce (a pressure, load, weight, etc., on a device or object under stress). **7.** to make less tedious, unpleasant, or monotonous. **8.** to bring into relief or prominence; heighten the effect of. **9.** to release (a person on duty) by coming as or providing a substitute or replacement. **10.** to replace (a baseball pitcher). **11.** to release from an obligation or position. **12.** *Informal.* to take something from; rob (usu. fol. by *of*): *The thief relieved me of my wallet.* —*v.i.* **13.** to act as a relief pitcher. —*Idiom.* **14. relieve oneself,** to urinate or defecate.

re•li•gion (ri lij′ən), *n.* **1.** a set of beliefs concerning the cause, nature, and purpose of the universe, esp. when considered as the creation of a superhuman agency or agencies, usu. involving devotional and ritual observances, and often containing a moral code for the conduct of human affairs. **2.** a specific fundamental set of beliefs and practices generally agreed upon by a number of persons or sects: *the Christian religion.*

3. the body of persons adhering to a particular set of beliefs and practices: *a world council of religions.* **4.** the life or state of a monk, nun, etc.: *to enter religion.* **5.** the practice of religious beliefs; ritual observance of faith. **6.** something a person believes in and follows devotedly. —*Idiom.* **7. get religion, a.** to become religious; acquire religious convictions. **b.** to resolve to mend one's errant ways.

re•li•gious (ri lij′əs), *adj., n., pl.* **-gious.** —*adj.* **1.** of, pertaining to, or concerned with religion: *a religious holiday.* **2.** imbued with or exhibiting religion; pious; devout. **3.** scrupulously faithful; conscientious: *with religious care.* **4.** pertaining to or connected with a monastic or religious order. **5.** appropriate to religion or to sacred rites or observances. —*n.* **6.** a member of a religious order; a monk, friar, or nun. —**re•li′gious•ly,** *adv.* —**re•li′gious•ness,** *n.*

reli′gious house′, *n.* a convent or monastery.

relig′ious right′, *n.* conservatives who support and promote fundamentalist Christian values in society, including prayer in the schools and opposition to abortion.

re•lin•quish (ri ling′kwish), *v.t.* **1.** to renounce or surrender (a possession, right, claim, etc.). **2.** to give up; put aside or desist from: *to relinquish a plan.* **3.** to let go; release: *to relinquish one's hold.*

rel•i•quar•y (rel′i kwer′ē), *n., pl.* **-quar•ies.** a repository or receptacle for relics.

rel•ish (rel′ish), *n.* **1.** enjoyment of the taste of something: *to eat with relish.* **2.** pleasurable appreciation of anything; liking. **3.** something savory or appetizing added to a meal, as olives or pickles. **b.** a sweet or pungent pickle made of various usu. chopped vegetables. **4.** a pleasing or appetizing flavor. **5.** a pleasing or enjoyable quality. **6.** a taste or flavor. **7.** a trace or touch of something. —*v.t.* **8.** to take pleasure in; enjoy. **9.** to make pleasing to the taste. **10.** to like the taste of. —*v.i.* **11.** to have taste or flavor. —**rel′ish•a•ble,** *adj.*

re•live (rē liv′), *v.t.,* **-lived, -liv•ing. 1.** to experience again, as an emotion. **2.** to live (one's life) again. —**re•liv′a•ble,** *adj.*

re•lo•cate (rē lō′kāt, rē′lō kāt′), *v.,* **-cat•ed, -cat•ing.** —*v.t.* **1.** to move to a different location. —*v.i.* **2.** to change one's residence or place of business; move. —**re′lo•ca′tion,** *n.*

re•luct (ri lukt′), *v.i.* to object; show reluctance.

re•luc•tance (ri luk′təns) also **re•luc′tan•cy,** *n.* **1.** the state or quality of being reluctant; unwillingness; disinclination. **2.** the resistance to magnetic flux offered by a magnetic circuit.

re•luc•tant (ri luk′tənt), *adj.* **1.** unwilling; disinclined: *a reluctant candidate.* **2.** marked by hesitation or slowness because of unwillingness: *a reluctant promise.* —**re•luc′tant•ly,** *adv.*

re•ly (ri lī′), *v.i.,* **-lied, -ly•ing.** to depend confidently; put trust in (usu. fol. by *on* or *upon*): *Can I rely on your support?* —**re•li′er,** *n.*

REM (rem), *n.* RAPID EYE MOVEMENT.

re•main (ri mān′), *v.i.* **1.** to continue to be as specified; continue in the same state. **2.** to stay behind or in the same place. **3.** to be left after the removal, loss, or destruction of all else. **4.** to be left to be done, told, shown, etc. **5.** to be reserved or in store. —*n.* **6.** Usu., **remains.** something that remains or is left. **7. remains, a.** traces of some quality, condition, etc. **b.** a dead body; corpse. **c.** parts or substances remaining from animal or plant life.

re•main•der (ri mān′dər), *n.* **1.** something that remains or is left; remaining part: *the remainder of the day.* **2.** *Math.* **a.** the quantity that remains after subtraction. **b.** the portion of the dividend that is not evenly divisible by the divisor. **3.** a copy of a book remaining in the publisher's stock when its sale has practically ceased, usu. sold at a reduced price. **4.** *Law.* a future interest so created as to take effect at the end of another estate, as when property is conveyed to one person for life and then to another. —*adj.* **5.** remaining; leftover. —*v.t.* **6.** to dispose of or sell as a remainder.

re•make (*v.* rē māk′; *n.* rē′māk′), *v.,* **-made, -mak•ing,** *n.* —*v.t.* **1.** to make again or anew. **2.** to film a new version of (an earlier motion picture, screenplay, or the like). **3.** a more recent version of an existing film, screenplay, or story. **4.** anything that has been remade, renovated, or rebuilt. —**re•mak′er,** *n.*

re•mand (ri mand′, -mänd′), *v.t.* **1.** to send back again. **2.** (of a court) to return (a prisoner or accused person) to custody, as to await further proceedings. **3.** to send back (a case) to a lower court for further proceedings. —*n.* **4.** the act of remanding or the state of being remanded.

re•mark (ri märk′), *v.t.* **1.** to say casually, as in making a comment. **2.** to note; perceive; observe. —*v.i.* **3.** to make a remark or observation (usu. fol. by *on* or *upon*). —*n.* **4.** notice, comment, or mention: *an act worthy of remark.* **5.** a casual or brief expression of thought or opinion.

re•mark•a•ble (ri mär′kə bəl), *adj.* notably or conspicuously unusual; noteworthy. —**re•mark′a•bly,** *adv.*

re•match (*n.* rē′mach′; *v.* rē mach′, rē′mach′), *n.* **1.** a second match between teams, challengers, etc.; return match. —*v.t.* **2.** to match again; duplicate. **3.** to schedule a second match for or between.

Rem•brandt (rem′brant, -bränt), *n.* (*Rembrandt Harmenszoon van Rijn* or *van Ryn*) 1606–69, Dutch painter.

re•me•di•al (ri mē′dē əl), *adj.* **1.** affording remedy. **2.** intended to improve poor skills in a specified field. —**re•me′di•al•ly,** *adv.*

rem•e•dy (rem′i dē), *n., pl.* **-dies,** *v.,* **-died, -dy•ing.** —*n.* **1.** something, as a medicine, that cures or relieves a disease or bodily disorder. **2.** something that corrects or removes an evil, error, or undesirable condition. **3.** legal redress; the legal means of enforcing a right or redressing a wrong. —*v.t.* **4.** to cure or relieve. **5.** to restore to the proper condition; put right: *to remedy a matter.* **6.** to counteract or remove: *to remedy an evil.* —**rem′e•di•less,** *adj.*

re•mem•ber (ri mem′bər), *v.t.* **1.** to recall to the mind; think of again. **2.** to retain in the mind; remain aware of. **3.** to have (something) come into the mind again: *I just remembered our date.* **4.** to bear (a person) in mind as deserving a gift, reward, or fee. **5.** to give a tip, donation, or gift to. **6.** to mention (a person) to another as sending kindly greetings: *Remember me to your family.* —*v.i.* **7.** to possess or exercise the faculty of memory. —**re•mem′ber•a•ble,** *adj.* —**re•mem′ber•er,** *n.*

Remem′ber the Al′amo!, —***Saying.*** a battle cry uttered by Col. Sidney Sherman (1805–73) at the Battle of San Jacinto during the Texan war for independence, recalling the earlier fall of the Alamo.

re•mem•brance (ri mem′brəns), *n.* **1.** a retained mental impression; memory. **2.** the act or fact of remembering. **3.** the ability to remember. **4.** the length of time over which memory extends. **5.** the state of being remembered; commemoration. **6.** something that serves to bring to or keep in mind some place, person, event, etc.; memento. **7.** a gift given as a token of love or friendship. **8. remembrances,** greetings; respects.

Remem′brance Day′, *n.* (in Canada) November 11, observed as a legal holiday in memory of those who died in World Wars I and II.

re•mind (ri mīnd′), *v.t.* to cause (a person) to remember; cause (a person) to think (of someone or something): *Remind me to call him. She reminds me of my mother.* —**re•mind′er,** *n.*

Rem•ing•ton (rem′ing tən), *n.* **Frederic,** 1861–1909, U.S. artist.

rem•i•nisce (rem′ə nis′), *v.i.,* **-nisced, -nisc•ing.** to recall or talk about past experiences, events, etc.

rem•i•nis•cence (rem′ə nis′əns), *n.* **1.** the act or process of recalling past experiences, events, etc. **2.** a mental impression retained and revived. **3.** Often, **reminiscences.** a recollection narrated or told.

rem•i•nis•cent (rem′ə nis′ənt), *adj.* **1.** awakening memories of something similar; suggestive (usu. fol. by *of*): *a style reminiscent of Hemingway's.* **2.** characterized by or of the nature of reminiscence. **3.** given to reminiscing. —**rem′i•nis′cent•ly,** *adv.*

re•mise (ri mīz′), *v.t.,* **-mised, -mis•ing.** *Law.* to give up a claim to; surrender by deed.

re•miss (ri mis′), *adj.* **1.** negligent or careless in performing one's duty, business, etc. **2.** characterized by negligence or carelessness.

re•mis•sion (ri mish′ən), *n.* **1.** the act of remitting. **2.** pardon; forgiveness, as of sins or offenses. **3.** abatement or diminution, as of diligence, labor, or intensity. **4.** the relinquishment of a payment, obligation, etc. **5.** a temporary or permanent decrease or subsidence of manifestations of a disease.

re•mit (ri mit′), *v.,* **-mit•ted, -mit•ting,** *n.* —*v.t.* **1.** to transmit or send (money, a check, etc.), usu. in payment. **2.** to refrain from inflicting or enforcing, as a punishment or sentence. **3.** to refrain from exacting, as a payment or service. **4.** to pardon or forgive (a sin, offense, etc.). **5.** to slacken; abate. **6.** to send back (a case) to an inferior court for further action; remand. **7.** to restore to a previous position or condition. **8.** to put off; postpone; defer. —*v.i.* **9.** to transmit money, as in payment. **10.** to slacken; abate. —*n.* **11.** a transfer of the record of an action from one tribunal to another, esp. from an appellate court to the court of original jurisdiction. —**re•mit′ta•ble,** *adj.* —**re•mit′ter, re•mit′tor,** *n.*

re•mit•tal (ri mit′l), *n.* a remission.

re•mit•tance (ri mit′ns), *n.* **1.** the sending of money, checks, etc., to a recipient at a distance. **2.** the money sent.

re•mit•tent (ri mit′nt), *adj.* abating and relapsing in cycles: *remittent fever.* —**re•mit′tence, re•mit′ten•cy,** *n.* —**re•mit′tent•ly,** *adv.*

re•mix (*v.* rē miks′; *n.* rē′miks′), *v.t.* **1.** to mix again. **2.** to mix and rerecord the elements of (a musical recording) in a different way. —*n.* **3.** a remixed recording.

rem•nant (rem′nənt), *n.* **1.** a remaining, usu. small part or number. **2.** a fragment or scrap. **3.** a small unsold or unused piece of fabric, as at the end of a bolt. **4.** a trace; vestige: *remnants of former greatness.* —*adj.* **5.** remaining; leftover. —**rem′nant•al,** *adj.*

re•mod•el (rē mod′l), *v.t.,* **-eled, -el•ing** or (*esp. Brit.*) **-elled, -el•ling.** **1.** to model again. **2.** to alter in structure or form; reconstruct; make over. —**re•mod′el•er;** *esp. Brit.,* **re•mod′el•ler,** *n.*

re•mon•strance (ri mon′strəns), *n.* **1.** an act or instance of remonstrating. **2.** a protest: *deaf to remonstrances.*

re•mon•strate (ri mon′strāt), *v.t., v.i.,* **-strat•ed, -strat•ing.** to reason or plead in protest, objection, or complaint. —**re•mon•stra•tion** (rē′mon strā′shən, rem′ən-), *n.* —**re•mon′stra•tive** (-strə tiv), *adj.*

rem•o•ra (rem′ər ə), *n., pl.* **-ras.** any of several fishes of the family Echeneidae, having on the top of the head a large sucking disk by which they attach themselves to moving objects above.

re•morse (ri môrs′), *n.* deep and painful regret for wrongdoing.

re•morse•ful (ri môrs′fəl), *adj.* full of, characterized by, or due to remorse. —**re•morse′ful•ly,** *adv.* —**re•morse′ful•ness,** *n.*

re•morse•less (ri môrs′lis), *adj.* without remorse; merciless; pitiless; cruel. —**re•morse′less•ly,** *adv.* —**re•morse′less•ness,** *n.*

re•mote (ri mōt′), *adj.,* **-mot•er, -mot•est,** *n.* —*adj.* **1.** far apart; far distant in space. **2.** out-of-the-way; secluded: *a remote village.* **3.** distant in time, relationship, connection, etc.: *remote antiquity; a remote ancestor.* **4.** far off; abstracted; removed: *principles remote from actions.* **5.** not direct or primary; not directly involved or influential. **6.** slight or faint; unlikely: *a remote chance.* **7.** reserved and distant in manner. **8.** operating or controlled from a distance, as by remote control. —*n.* **9.** a broadcast, usu. live, from outside a radio or television station. **10.** REMOTE CONTROL (def. 2). —**re•mote′ly,** *adv.* —**re•mote′ness,** *n.*

remote′ control′, *n.* **1.** control of an apparatus from a distance, as the control of a guided missile by radio signals. **2.** a device used to control the operation of an apparatus or machine, as a television set, from a distance. —**remote′-control′,** *adj.*

ré•mou•lade (rā′mə läd′, -mo͞o-), *n.* a cold sauce of mayonnaise with mustard, capers, chopped pickles, herbs, etc.

re•mount (*v.* rē mount′; *n.* rē′mount′, rē mount′), *v.t., v.i.* **1.** to mount again. —*n.* **2.** a fresh horse or supply of fresh horses.

re•mov•al (ri mo͞o′vəl), *n.* **1.** the act of removing. **2.** change of residence, position, etc. **3.** dismissal, as from an office.

re•move (ri mo͞ov′), *v.,* **-moved, -mov•ing,** *n.* —*v.t.* **1.** to move or shift from a place or position. **2.** to take off or shed (an article of clothing): *to remove one's jacket.* **3.** to put out; send away: *to remove a tenant.* **4.** to dismiss from a position; discharge. **5.** to eliminate; do away with or put an end to: *to remove a stain; to remove the threat of danger.* **6.** to kill; assassinate. —*v.i.* **7.** to move from one place to another, esp. to another locality or residence. **8.** to go away; disappear. —*n.* **9.** the act of removing. **10.** a removal from one place, as of residence, to another. **11.** a distance by which one person or thing is separated from another: *to see something at a remove.* **12.** a degree of difference: *a folk survival, at many removes, of a druidic rite.* —**re•mov′a•ble,** *adj.* —**re•mov′a•bly,** *adv.* —**re•mov′er,** *n.*

re•moved (ri mo͞ovd′), *adj.* **1.** remote; separate; not connected with. **2.** distant by a given number of degrees of descent or kinship.

REM′ sleep′, *n.* rapid eye movement sleep: a recurrent sleep pattern during which dreaming occurs while the eyes shift rapidly.

re•mu•ner•ate (ri myo͞o′nə rāt′), *v.t.,* **-at•ed, -at•ing.** **1.** to pay, recompense, or reward for work, trouble, etc. **2.** to yield a recompense for. —**re•mu′ner•a•ble,** *adj.* —**re•mu′ner•a′tor,** *n.*

re•mu•ner•a•tion (ri myo͞o′nə rā′shən), *n.* **1.** the act of remunerating. **2.** reward; pay.

re•mu•ner•a•tive (ri myo͞o′nər ə tiv, -nə rā′tiv) also **re•mu′ner•a•to′ry,** *adj.* **1.** affording remuneration; profitable. **2.** remunerating. —**re•mu′ner•a′tive•ly** (-nə rā′tiv lē, -nər ə tiv-), *adv.*

Re•mus (rē′məs), *n.* See under ROMULUS.

Ren•ais•sance (ren′ə säns′, -zäns′, -SÄNS′, ren′ə säns′, -zäns′, -SÄNS′; *esp. Brit.* ri nā′səns), *n.* **1.** the activity, spirit, or time of the great revival of art, literature, and learning in Europe beginning in the 14th century and extending to the 17th century, marking the transition from the medieval to the modern world. **2.** the forms and treatments in art used during this period. **3.** (*sometimes l.c.*) any similar revival in the world of art and learning. **4.** (*l.c.*) renewal; rebirth: *a moral renaissance.* —*adj.* **5.** of, pertaining to, or suggestive of the European Renaissance: *Renaissance attitudes.* **6.** of or pertaining to the style of architecture and decoration originating in Italy in the 15th century, characterized by the revival and adaptation of ancient Roman motifs and forms, including the classical orders, and by an emphasis on symmetry. [< French, Middle French: rebirth]

re•nal (rēn′l), *adj.* of or pertaining to the kidneys or the surrounding regions.

re•nas•cent (ri nas′ənt, -nā′sənt), *adj.* being reborn; springing again into being or vigor: *a renascent interest in Henry James.*

ren•coun•ter (ren koun′tər), *n.* Also, **rencontre.** **1.** a hostile meeting. **2.** a casual meeting. —*v.t., v.i.* **3.** to meet casually.

rend (rend), *v.,* **rent, rend•ing.** —*v.t.* **1.** to separate into parts with force or violence; tear apart. **2.** to tear (one's garments or hair) in grief or rage. **3.** to disturb (the air) sharply with noise. **4.** to distress (the heart) with painful feelings. —*v.i.* **5.** to split or tear something. **6.** to become torn or split.

ren•der[1] (ren′dər), *v.t.* **1.** to cause to be or become; make. **2.** to do; perform. **3.** to furnish; provide. **4.** to exhibit or show (obedience, attention, etc.). **5.** to present for approval, payment, etc. **6.** to pay as due (a tax, tribute, etc.). **7.** to officially hand down: *to render a verdict.* **8.** to translate into another language. **9.** to depict, as in painting: *to render a landscape.* **10.** to represent (a perspective view of a projected building) in drawing or painting. **11.** to interpret (a part in a drama or a piece of music). **12.** to give in return: *to render good for evil.* **13.** to give back; restore (often fol. by *back*). **14.** to give up; surrender. **15.** to melt down; extract the impurities from by melting: *to render fat.* **16.** to process, as for industrial use: *to render livestock carcasses.* —*v.i.* **17.** to provide due reward. **18.** to extract oil from fat, blubber, etc., by melting. —***Proverb.*** **19. Render unto Caesar the things that are Caesar's and unto God the things that are God's,** one should distinguish between one's duty to God and one's duty to the state. Matt. 22:19–21.

rend•er[2] (ren′dər), *n.* a person or thing that rends.

ren•der•ing (ren′dər ing), *n.* **1.** an interpretation of a dramatic part or a musical composition. **2.** a translation. **3.** a representation of a building, interior, etc., executed in perspective.

ren•dez•vous (rän′də vo͞o′, -dā-), *n., pl.* **-vous** (-vo͞oz′), *v.,* **-voused** (vo͞od′), **-vous•ing** (-vo͞o′ing). —*n.* **1.** an agreement to meet at a certain time and place. **2.** the meeting itself. **3.** a place designated for a meeting or assembling, esp. of troops or ships. **4.** a meeting of two or more spacecraft in outer space. **5.** a popular gathering place. —*v.t., v.i.* **6.** to assemble at an agreed time and place.

ren•di•tion (ren dish′ən), *n.* **1.** the act of rendering. **2.** a translation. **3.** an interpretation, as of a role or a piece of music.

ren•e•gade (ren′i gād′), *n.* **1.** a person who deserts a party or cause for another. **2.** an apostate from a religious faith. *—adj.* **3.** of or like a renegade; traitorous.

re•nege (ri nig′, -neg′, -nēg′), *v.i.*, **-neged, -neg•ing. 1.** to go back on one's word: *He has reneged on his promise.* **2.** to play a card that is not of the suit led when one can follow suit. **—re•neg′er,** *n.*

re•ne•go•ti•ate (rē′ni gō′shē āt′), *v.t.*, **-at•ed, -at•ing. 1.** to negotiate again, as a loan or treaty. **2.** to reexamine (a contract) with a view to eliminating or modifying those provisions found to represent excessive profits to the contractor. **—re′ne•go′ti•a•ble** (-shē ə bəl, -shə bəl), *adj.* **—re′ne•go′ti•a′tion,** *n.*

re•new (ri no͞o′, -nyo͞o′), *v.t.* **1.** to begin or take up again; resume: *to renew a friendship.* **2.** to make effective for an additional period. **3.** to restore or replenish. **4.** to make, say, or do again. **5.** to revive; reestablish. **6.** to recover (youth, strength, etc.). **7.** to restore to a former state. *—v.i.* **8.** to begin again; recommence. **9.** to renew a lease, note, etc. **10.** to be restored to a former state. **—re•new′a•ble,** *adj.*

re•new•al (ri no͞o′əl, -nyo͞o′-), *n.* **1.** the act of renewing. **2.** the state of being renewed. **3.** something renewed.

ren•net (ren′it), *n.* **1.** the lining membrane of the fourth stomach of a calf or of the stomach of certain other young animals. **2.** the rennin-containing substance from the stomach of an unweaned animal, esp. a calf. **3.** a preparation of the rennet membrane used esp. in making cheese.

ren•nin (ren′in), *n.* a coagulating enzyme in the gastric juice of the calf, forming the active principle of rennet and able to curdle milk.

Re•no (rē′nō), *n.* a city in W Nevada. 145,029.

Re•noir (ren′wär, ren wär′), *n.* **1. Jean** (zhän), 1894–1979, French film director. **2.** his father, **Pierre Auguste,** 1841–1919, French painter.

re•nounce (ri nouns′), *v.*, **-nounced, -nounc•ing,** *n.* *—v.t.* **1.** to give up or put aside. **2.** to repudiate; disown. *—v.i.* **3.** to fail to follow the suit led in cards. *—n.* **4.** failure to follow in the suit led in cards. **—re•nounce′ment,** *n.* **—re•nounc′er,** *n.*

ren•o•vate (ren′ə vāt′), *v.t.*, **-vat•ed, -vat•ing. 1.** to restore to good condition, as by repairing or remodeling. **2.** to reinvigorate; refresh. **—ren′o•va′tion,** *n.* **—ren′o•va′tor,** *n.*

re•nown (ri noun′), *n.* widespread and high repute; fame.

re•nowned (ri nound′), *adj.* celebrated; famous. **—re•nown′ed•ly,** *adv.* **—re•nown′ed•ness,** *n.*

rent¹ (rent), *n.* **1.** a payment made periodically by a tenant to a landlord in return for the use of land or property. **2.** a payment made by a lessee to an owner in return for the use of machinery, equipment, etc. **3.** the yield on a piece of land, as the profit on produce over the cost of production. **4.** profit or return derived from any differential advantage in production. *—v.t.* **5.** to grant the possession and use of (property, machinery, etc.) in return for payment of rent (often fol. by *out*). **6.** to take and hold (property, machinery, etc.) in return for payment of rent to the landlord or owner. *—v.i.* **7.** to be leased or let for rent. **8.** to lease or let property. **9.** to take possession of and use property by paying rent. *—**Idiom.*** **10. for rent,** available to be rented: *an apartment for rent.* **—rent′a•ble,** *adj.* **—rent′er,** *n.*

rent² (rent), *n.* **1.** an opening made by rending or tearing; fissure. **2.** a breach of relations; schism.

rent³ (rent), *v.* pt. and pp. of REND.

rent′-a-car′, *n.* **1.** a company that rents cars. **2.** a car rented.

rent•al (ren′tl), *n.* **1.** an amount received or paid as rent. **2.** the act of renting. **3.** something offered or given for rent. **4.** an income arising from rents received. *—adj.* **5.** of or pertaining to rent. **6.** available for rent. **7.** engaged in the business of providing rentals: *a rental agency.*

rent′-free′, *adv.* **1.** without payment of rent. *—adj.* **2.** not subject to rent.

rent′ strike′, *n.* an organized refusal by tenants to pay rent, as in protest over inadequate services.

re•nun•ci•a•tion (ri nun′sē ā′shən, -shē-), *n.* an act or instance of renouncing something, as a right, title, person, or ambition. **—re•nun′ci•a′tive, re•nun′ci•a•to′ry** (-ə tôr′ē, -tōr′ē), *adj.*

re•o•pen (rē ō′pən), *v.t., v.i.* **1.** to open again. **2.** to resume.

re•or•der (rē ôr′dər), *v.t.* **1.** to put in order again. **2.** to give a repeated order for. *—v.i.* **3.** to order goods again. *—n.* **4.** a second or repeated order for the same goods.

re•or•gan•i•za•tion (rē′ôr gə nə zā′shən), *n.* **1.** the act or process of reorganizing; state of being reorganized. **2.** a restructuring of the financial management of a company, esp. following bankruptcy. **—re•or′gan•ize′,** *v.t., v.i.*, **-ized, -iz•ing. —re•or′gan•iz′er,** *n.*

rep¹ or **repp** (rep), *n.* a horizontally ribbed fabric of wool, silk, rayon, or cotton. **—repped,** *adj.*

rep² (rep), *n. Informal.* **1.** a repertory theater or company. **2.** a representative, esp. a sales representative. **3.** reputation.

re•pack•age (rē pak′ij), *v.t.*, **-aged, -ag•ing. 1.** to package again or afresh. **2.** to remake or alter so as to be more appealing or desirable.

re•pair¹ (ri pâr′), *v.t.* **1.** to restore to a good or sound condition after decay or damage; mend. **2.** to restore or renew. **3.** to remedy; make up for; compensate for. *—n.* **4.** an act, process, or work of repairing. **5.** Usu., **repairs. a.** an instance or operation of repairing. **b.** a repaired part or an addition made in repairing. **6.** the good condition resulting from continued maintenance and repairing: *to keep in repair.* **7.** condition with respect to soundness and usability: *a house in good repair.* **—re•pair′a•ble,** *adj.* **—re•pair′er,** *n.*

re•pair² (ri pâr′), *v.i.* **1.** to betake oneself; go, as to a place. **2.** to go frequently or customarily. *—n.* **3.** a resort or haunt. **4.** the act of going or going customarily.

re•pair•man (ri pâr′man′, -mən), *n., pl.* **-men** (-men′, -mən). a person whose occupation is the making of repairs, readjustments, etc.

rep•a•ra•ble (rep′ər ə bəl *or, often,* ri pâr′-), *adj.* capable of being repaired or remedied. **—rep′a•ra•bly,** *adv.*

rep•a•ra•tion (rep′ə rā′shən), *n.* **1.** the making of amends for wrong or injury done. **2.** Usu., **reparations.** compensation payable by a defeated nation to the victor for damages or loss suffered during war. **3.** restoration to good condition.

rep•ar•tee (rep′ər tē′, -tā′, -är-), *n.* **1.** a quick, witty reply. **2.** conversation full of such replies. **3.** skill in repartee.

re•past (ri past′, -päst′), *n.* **1.** food and drink for a meal. **2.** the meal itself. **3.** MEALTIME. *—v.i.* **4.** to eat or feast (often fol. by *on* or *upon*).

re•pa•tri•ate (*v.* rē pā′trē āt′; *n.* -it; *esp. Brit.* -pa′-), *v.*, **-at•ed, -at•ing,** *n.* *—v.t.* **1.** to send back (a prisoner of war, a refugee, etc.) to his or her country. **2.** to send back (profits or other assets) to one's own country. *—v.i.* **3.** to return to one's own country, esp. after living abroad. *—n.* **4.** a person who has been repatriated. **—re•pa′tri•a•ble** (-ə bəl), *adj.* **—re•pa′tri•a′tion,** *n.*

re•pay (ri pā′), *v.*, **-paid, -pay•ing.** *—v.t.* **1.** to pay back or refund, as money. **2.** to make return for: *to repay a compliment with a smile.* **3.** to make return to in any way: *We can never repay you for your help.* **4.** to return: *to repay a visit.* *—v.i.* **5.** to make repayment or return. **—re•pay′ment,** *n.*

re•peal (ri pēl′), *v.t.* **1.** to revoke or withdraw formally or officially. **2.** to revoke or annul (a law, tax, etc.) by express legislative enactment. *—n.* **3.** the act of repealing; revocation. **—re•peal′a•ble,** *adj.*

re•peat (ri pēt′), *v.t.* **1.** to say or do again. **2.** to say or utter in reproducing the words, inflections, etc., of another: *Now repeat it after me.* **3.** to reproduce (sounds) in the manner of an echo. **4.** to tell (something heard) to another. **5.** to undergo again. *—v.i.* **6.** to say or do something again. **7.** to taste food after eating, esp. as a result of belching: *Onions always seem to repeat on me.* **8.** to vote illegally by casting more than one vote in the same election. *—n.* **9.** the act of repeating. **10.** something repeated; repetition. **11.** a duplication or reproduction. **12. a.** a musical passage to be performed anew. **b.** a sign placed in the score before and after such a passage. **13.** a radio or television program that has been broadcast at least once before. **—re•peat′a•ble,** *adj.*

re•peat•ed (ri pē′tid), *adj.* done or said again and again: *repeated attempts.* **—re•peat′ed•ly,** *adv.*

re•peat•er (ri pē′tər), *n.* **1.** a person or thing that repeats. **2.** a firearm that can discharge a number of shots without reloading. **3.** a timepiece, esp. a watch, that may be made to strike the hour or part of the hour. **4.** a pupil who repeats a course he or she has failed. **5.** a person who casts illegally more than one vote in the same election. **6.** a person who has been convicted and sentenced for more than one crime; recidivist.

repeat′ing dec′imal, *n.* a decimal that, after a certain point, includes a group of one or more digits repeated ad infinitum, as 2.33333 .... or 23.02181818 .... Also called **recurring decimal.**

re•pel (ri pel′), *v.*, **-pelled, -pel•ling.** *—v.t.* **1.** to drive or force back (an assailant, invader, etc.). **2.** to thrust back or away. **3.** to fail to mix with: *Water and oil repel each other.* **4.** to resist the absorption of: *This coat repels rain.* **5.** to cause distaste or aversion in. **6.** to push away by a force (opposed to *attract*): *The north pole of one magnet will repel the north pole of another.* *—v.i.* **7.** to act with a force that drives or keeps away something. **8.** to cause distaste or aversion. **—re•pel′len•cy,** *n.*

re•pel•lent or **re•pel•lant** (ri pel′ənt), *adj.* **1.** causing distaste or aversion; repulsive. **2.** serving or tending to ward off or drive away. **3.** impervious or resistant to something (often used in combination): *moth-repellent.* *—n.* **4.** something that repels, as a substance that keeps away insects. **5.** any solution applied to a fabric to increase its resistance to water, moths, etc.

re•pent (ri pent′), *v.i.* **1.** to feel regretful or contrite for past conduct: *to repent of an act.* **2.** to be penitent for one's sins and seek to change one's life for the better. *—v.t.* **3.** to remember with self-reproach or contrition: *to repent one's angry words.* **4.** to feel sorry for; regret: *to repent a hasty marriage.* **—re•pent′er,** *n.* **—re•pent′ing•ly,** *adv.*

re•pent•ance (ri pen′tns, -pen′təns), *n.* deep sorrow, compunction, or contrition for a past sin, wrongdoing, or error.

re•pent•ant (ri pen′tnt, -pen′tənt), *adj.* **1.** experiencing repentance; penitent. **2.** characterized by repentance. **—re•pent′ant•ly,** *adv.*

re•per•cus•sion (rē′pər kush′ən, rep′ər-), *n.* **1.** an effect or result of some previous action or event. **2.** a rebounding or recoil after impact. **3.** reverberation; echo. **—re′per•cus′sive** (-kus′iv), *adj.*

rep•er•toire (rep′ər twär′, -twôr′, rep′ə-), *n.* **1.** all the works that a performing company or artist is prepared to present. **2.** the entire stock of works existing in a particular artistic field: *the theatrical repertoire.* **3.** the skills, techniques, etc., used in a particular field or occupation.

rep•er•to•ry (rep′ər tôr′ē, -tōr′ē), *n., pl.* **-ries. 1.** a type of theatrical presentation in which a company performs several works regularly or in alternate sequence in one season. **2.** Also called **rep′ertory com′pany** (or **the′ater**). a theatrical company that presents productions in this manner. **3.** REPERTOIRE. **4.** a store or stock of things available. **5.** a storehouse or repository.

rep•e•ti•tion (rep′i tish′ən), *n.* **1.** the act of repeating; a repeated action, performance, etc. **2.** repeated utterance; reiteration. **3.** a reproduction or copy.

rep•e•ti•tious (rep′i tish′əs), *adj.* full of repetition; tending to repeat unnecessarily and tediously. —**rep′e•ti′tious•ly,** *adv.*

re•pet•i•tive (ri pet′i tiv), *adj.* pertaining to or characterized by repetition. —**re•pet′i•tive•ly,** *adv.* —**re•pet′i•tive•ness,** *n.*

repet′itive strain′ in′jury, *n.* any of a group of debilitating disorders, as of the hand and arm, characterized typically by pain, numbness, tingling, or loss of muscle control and caused by the stress of repeated movements. *Abbr.:* RSI

Reph•i•dim (ref′i dim), *n.* the last encampment of the Israelites during the Exodus from Egypt before they reached Mount Sinai: attacked by the Amalekites. Ex. 17:1–8.

re•phrase (rē frāz′), *v.t.,* **-phrased, -phras•ing.** to phrase again, esp. in a different manner.

re•pine (ri pīn′), *v.i.,* **-pined, -pin•ing. 1.** to fret or complain. **2.** to yearn for something. —**re•pin′er,** *n.*

re•place (ri plās′), *v.t.,* **-placed, -plac•ing. 1.** to assume the function of; substitute for: *to replace gas lights with electric lights.* **2.** to provide a substitute or equivalent for: *to replace a broken dish.* **3.** to return; make good: *to replace borrowed money.* **4.** to restore to the proper place. —**re•place′a•ble,** *adj.*

re•place•ment (ri plās′mənt), *n.* **1.** the act of replacing. **2.** a person or thing that replaces another. **3.** a person in the military assigned to fill a vacancy in a unit.

re•plant (rē plant′, -plänt′), *v.t.* **1.** to plant again. **2.** to provide again with plants. **3.** to reattach, as a severed finger, esp. with the use of microsurgery. —**re′plan•ta′tion,** *n.*

re•play (*v.* rē plā′; *n.* rē′plā′), *v.t.* **1.** to play again, as a tape. —*n.* **2.** an act or instance of replaying. **3.** a repetition of all or part of a broadcast or of the playing of a videocassette, etc. **4.** INSTANT REPLAY. **5.** a repetition or recurrence.

re•plen•ish (ri plen′ish), *v.t.* **1.** to make full or complete again. **2.** to supply with fresh fuel. **3.** to fill again or anew. —*v.i.* **4.** to become full or complete again. —**re•plen′ish•ment,** *n.*

re•plete (ri plēt′), *adj.* **1.** abundantly supplied: *a speech replete with humor.* **2.** stuffed with food and drink. —**re•plete′ly,** *adv.*

re•ple•tion (ri plē′shən), *n.* **1.** the condition of being filled or abundantly supplied; fullness. **2.** overfullness resulting from excessive eating or drinking; surfeit.

rep•li•ca (rep′li kə), *n., pl.* **-cas. 1.** a copy or reproduction of a work of art produced or supervised by the maker of the original. **2.** any close copy or reproduction.

rep•li•cate (*adj., n.* rep′li kit; *v.* -kāt′), *adj., v.,* **-cat•ed, -cat•ing,** *n.* —*adj.* **1.** Also, **rep′li•cat′ed.** folded; bent back on itself: *a replicate leaf.* —*v.t.* **2.** to repeat, duplicate, or reproduce. —*v.i.* **3.** to undergo replication. —*n.* **4.** something, as a scientific experiment, that can be replicated. —**rep′li•ca•ble,** *adj.*

rep•li•ca•tion (rep′li kā′shən), *n.* **1.** a reply; answer. **2.** the reply of a plaintiff or complainant to a defendant's plea or answer. **3.** reverberation; echo. **4.** copy; replica. **5.** the act or process of replicating, esp. in a scientific experiment. **6.** the process by which double-stranded DNA makes copies of itself, each strand, as it separates, synthesizing a complementary strand.

re•ply (ri plī′), *v.,* **-plied, -ply•ing,** *n., pl.* **-plies.** —*v.i.* **1.** to answer in words or writing; respond: *to reply to a question.* **2.** to respond by some action: *to reply to the enemy's fire.* **3.** to echo or resound. —*v.t.* **4.** to return as an answer: *He replied that no one would go.* —*n.* **5.** a response in words or writing. **6.** a response in the form of some action.

re•port (ri pôrt′, -pōrt′), *n.* **1.** a detailed account of an event, situation, etc., usu. based on observation or inquiry. **2.** a statement or announcement. **3.** a widely circulated item of news; rumor; gossip. **4.** an account of a speech, meeting, etc., esp. as taken down for publication. **5.** a loud noise, as from an explosion. **6.** a statement of a student's grades or academic standing. **7.** repute; reputation. —*v.t.* **8.** to carry and repeat, as an answer or message. **9.** to relate, as the results of one's observation or investigation. **10.** to give a formal account or statement of: *to report a deficit.* **11.** (of a committee) to return (a bill) to a legislative body with findings and recommendations. **12.** to make a charge against (a person), as to a superior. **13.** to make known the presence, absence, condition, etc., of: *to report an aircraft missing.* **14.** to write an account of, as for publication in a newspaper. **15.** to relate; tell. —*v.i.* **16.** to make a report of something observed. **17.** to work as a reporter, as for a newspaper. **18.** to make one's condition or whereabouts known, as to a person in authority: *to report sick.* **19.** to present oneself as ordered: *to report for duty.* —**re•port′a•ble,** *adj.*

re•port•age (ri pôr′tij, -pōr′-, rep′ôr täzh′, -ər-), *n.* **1.** the act or technique of reporting news. **2.** reported news collectively: *reportage on the war.*

report′ card′, *n.* **1.** a periodic written report of a pupil's grades and behavior, sent to the parents or guardian. **2.** an estimation of accomplishment as viewed by others.

re•port•ed•ly (ri pôr′tid lē, -pōr′-), *adv.* according to report or rumor: *Reportedly, he is a billionaire.*

re•port•er (ri pôr′tər, -pōr′-), *n.* **1.** a person who reports. **2.** a person employed to gather and report news, as for a newspaper or television station. **3.** a person who prepares official reports, as of legal or legislative proceedings.

re•pose[1] (ri pōz′), *n., v.,* **-posed, -pos•ing.** —*n.* **1.** the state of being at rest; sleep. **2.** peace or tranquillity; calm. **3.** dignified calmness; composure. **4.** absence of movement or animation. —*v.i.* **5.** to lie or be at rest, as from work or activity. **6.** to be peacefully calm and quiet. **7.** to lie dead. —*v.t.* **8.** to lay to rest; refresh by rest (often used reflexively).

re•pose[2] (ri pōz′), *v.t.,* **-posed, -pos•ing. 1.** to put (confidence, trust, etc.) in a person or thing. **2.** to put under the authority of a person.

re•pos•it (ri poz′it), *v.t.* **1.** to put back; replace. **2.** to store; deposit.

re•po•si•tion[1] (rē′pə zish′ən, rep′ə-), *n.* **1.** the act of depositing or storing. **2.** replacement, as of a bone.

re•po•si•tion[2] (rē′pə zish′ən), *v.t.* **1.** to put in a new position. **2.** to change the marketing strategy of (a product) so as to appeal to a different market.

re•pos•i•tor•y (ri poz′i tôr′ē, -tōr′ē), *n., pl.* **-tor•ies. 1.** a receptacle or place where things are deposited, stored, or offered for sale. **2.** an abundant source or supply. **3.** a burial place; sepulcher.

re•pos•sess (rē′pə zes′), *v.t.* **1.** to take possession of again, esp. for nonpayment of money due. **2.** to put again in possession of something: *to repossess the Bourbons of their throne.* —**re′pos•sess′a•ble,** *adj.* —**re′pos•ses′sion** (-zesh′ən), *n.*

re•pous•sé (rə pōō sā′), *adj.* **1.** (of a design) raised in relief by hammering on the reverse side. **2.** ornamented or made in this kind of raised work. —*n.* **3.** the art or process of producing repoussé designs.

rep•re•hend (rep′ri hend′), *v.t.* to find fault with; reprove; rebuke. —**rep′re•hend′a•ble,** *adj.*

rep•re•hen•si•ble (rep′ri hen′sə bəl), *adj.* deserving censure; blameworthy. —**rep′re•hen′si•bly,** *adv.* —**rep′re•hen′si•bil′i•ty,** *n.*

rep•re•hen•sion (rep′ri hen′shən), *n.* the act of reprehending; reproof. —**rep′re•hen′sive** (-siv), *adj.* —**rep′re•hen′sive•ly,** *adv.*

re-pre•sent (rē′pri zent′), *v.t.* to present again or anew.

rep•re•sent (rep′ri zent′), *v.t.* **1.** to serve to stand for or denote, as a word or symbol does; symbolize. **2.** to express or designate by some symbol, character, or the like: *to represent musical sounds by notes.* **3.** to stand or act in place of, as an agent or substitute. **4.** to speak and act for by delegated authority. **5.** to portray; depict. **6.** to describe as having a particular character. **7.** to set forth clearly or earnestly with a view to influencing opinion. **8.** to impersonate, as in acting. **9.** to serve as an example of. **10.** to be the equivalent of; correspond to. —*v.i.* **11.** to protest. —**rep′re•sent′a•ble,** *adj.*

rep•re•sen•ta•tion (rep′ri zen tā′shən, -zən-), *n.* **1.** the act of representing, or the state of being represented. **2.** the expression or designation by some term, character, symbol, or the like. **3.** action on behalf of a person or group by an agent or deputy. **4.** the state of being so represented. **5.** a body of representatives, as of a constituency. **6.** presentation to the mind, as of an idea. **7.** a mental image or idea so presented; concept. **8.** the act of rendering something in visible form. **9.** a picture, figure, statue, etc. **10.** the production or a performance of a play. **11.** Often, **representations.** a statement of things true or alleged. **12.** a protest or remonstrance. **13.** a statement of fact made to induce a party to enter into a contract.

rep•re•sen•ta•tion•al (rep′ri zen tā′shə nl, -zən-), *adj.* **1.** of or pertaining to representation. **2.** representing or depicting an object in a recognizable manner: *representational art.*

rep•re•sent•a•tive (rep′ri zen′tə tiv), *n.* **1.** a person or thing that represents another or others. **2.** an agent or deputy: *a legal representative.* **3.** a person who represents a constituency or community in a legislative body, esp. a member of the U.S. House of Representatives or a lower house in certain state legislatures. **4.** a typical example or specimen. —*adj.* **5.** serving to represent; representing. **6.** made up of representatives. **7.** of, characterized by, or founded on representation of the people in government: *a representative democracy.* **8.** exemplifying a group or kind; typical. —**rep′re•sent′a•tive•ly,** *adv.*

re-press (rē′pres′), *v.t., v.i.* to press again or anew.

re•press (ri pres′), *v.t.* **1.** to check or inhibit (actions or desires). **2.** to keep down or suppress (anything objectionable). **3.** to quell (disorder, sedition, etc.). **4.** to reduce (persons) to subjection. **5.** to suppress (memories, emotions, or impulses) unconsciously. —*v.i.* **6.** to initiate or undergo repression. —**re•press′i•ble,** *adj.*

re•pressed (ri prest′), *adj.* subjected to, affected by, or characteristic of psychological repression.

re•pres•sion (ri presh′ən), *n.* **1.** the act of repressing; state of being repressed. **2.** the suppression from consciousness of distressing or disagreeable ideas, memories, feelings, or impulses.

re•pres•sive (ri pres′iv), *adj.* tending or serving to repress: *repressive laws.* —**re•pres′sive•ly,** *adv.* —**re•pres′sive•ness,** *n.*

re•priev•al (ri prē′vəl), *n.* reprieve; respite.

re•prieve (ri prēv′), *v.,* **-prieved, -priev•ing,** *n.* —*v.t.* **1.** to delay the impending punishment or sentence of (a condemned person). **2.** to relieve temporarily from any evil. —*n.* **3.** a respite from impending punishment, esp. from execution. **4.** a warrant authorizing this. **5.** any respite or temporary relief. —**re•priev′er,** *n.*

rep•ri•mand (rep′rə mand′, -mänd′; *v. also* rep′rə mand′, -mänd′), *n.* **1.** a severe rebuke, esp. a formal or official one. —*v.t.* **2.** to reprove or rebuke severely.

re•print (*v.* rē print′; *n.* rē′print′), *v.t.* **1.** to print again; print a new impression of. —*n.* **2.** a reproduction of matter already printed. **3.** a new impression, without alteration, of printed work.

re•pris•al (ri prī′zəl), *n.* **1.** retaliation against an enemy by the infliction of equal or greater injuries. **2.** an act or instance of retaliation. **3.** the action or practice of using countermeasures against another nation to secure redress of a grievance.

re•prise (ri prīz′; *for 2, 3 usu.* rə prēz′), *n., v.,* **-prised, -pris•ing.** —*n.* **1.** Usu., **reprises.** *Law.* an annual deduction, duty, or payment out of an estate or manor, as an annuity. **2. a.** REPEAT (def. 12). **b.** RECAPITULATION (def. 4). —*v.t.* **3.** to repeat.

re•pro (rē′prō), *n., pl.* **-pros. 1.** REPRODUCTION (def. 2). **2.** reproduction proof: a printer's proof from which a usable plate can be made by photographic reproduction.

re•proach (ri prōch′), *v.t.* **1.** to find fault with (a person, group, etc.); blame; censure. **2.** to criticize severely; upbraid. **3.** to be a cause of blame or discredit to. —*n.* **4.** blame or censure conveyed in disapproval: *a term of reproach.* **5.** an expression of reproof or censure. **6.** disgrace or discredit. **7.** an object of scorn or contempt. —**re•proach′a•ble,** *adj.* —**re•proach′ing•ly,** *adv.*

rep•ro•bate (rep′rə bāt′), *n., adj., v.,* **-bat•ed, -bat•ing.** —*n.* **1.** a depraved or wicked person. **2.** a person who is beyond hope of salvation. —*adj.* **3.** morally depraved; wicked. **4.** being beyond hope of salvation. —*v.t.* **5.** to disapprove, condemn, or censure. **6.** to exclude from salvation, as for sin.

rep•ro•ba•tion (rep′rə bā′shən), *n.* **1.** disapproval, condemnation, or censure. **2.** rejection or exclusion. **3.** rejection by God. —**rep′ro•ba′tion•ar′y,** *adj.*

re•proc•essed (rē pros′est; *esp. Brit.* -prō′sest), *adj.* (of wool fiber) derived from previously woven, knitted, or felted wool that was never used or worn.

re•pro•duce (rē′prə do͞os′, -dyo͞os′), *v.,* **-duced, -duc•ing.** —*v.t.* **1.** to make a copy or close imitation of; duplicate. **2.** to produce again or anew by natural process. **3.** to produce one or more other individuals of (a given kind of organism) by some process of generation or propagation, sexual or asexual. **4.** to cause or foster the reproduction of (organisms). **5.** to produce, form, or bring about again or anew in any manner. **6.** to recall to the mind (a past incident). **7.** to produce again (a play produced previously). —*v.i.* **8.** to reproduce one's kind, as an organism; propagate; bear offspring. **9.** to turn out in a given manner when copied. —**re′pro•duc′er,** *n.* —**re′pro•duc′i•ble,** *adj.*

re•pro•duc•tion (rē′prə duk′shən), *n.* **1.** the act or process of reproducing. **2.** a copy or duplicate of an original. **3.** the process among organisms by which new individuals of the same kind are generated.

re•pro•duc•tive (rē′prə duk′tiv), *adj.* **1.** serving to reproduce. **2.** concerned with or pertaining to reproduction: *reproductive organs; the reproductive process.* —**re′pro•duc′tive•ly,** *adv.*

re•proof (ri pro͞of′), *n.* **1.** the act of reproving or censuring. **2.** an expression of censure or rebuke. —**re•proof′less,** *adj.*

re•prove (ri pro͞ov′), *v.,* **-proved, -prov•ing.** —*v.t.* **1.** to criticize or correct, esp. gently. **2.** to express strong disapproval of; censure. —*v.i.* **3.** to speak in reproof. —**re•prov′er,** *n.* —**re•prov′ing•ly,** *adv.*

rep•tile (rep′til, -tīl), *n.* **1.** any air-breathing vertebrate of the class Reptilia, characterized by a three-chambered heart, a completely bony skeleton, and a covering of dry scales or horny plates: includes the snakes, lizards, turtles, crocodilians, and various extinct forms. **2.** (loosely) any of various animals that crawl or creep. **3.** a groveling, mean, or despicable person. —*adj.* **4.** groveling, mean, or despicable.

rep•til•i•an (rep til′ē ən, -til′yən), *adj.* **1.** of or pertaining to the reptiles. **2.** characteristic of or resembling a reptile. **3.** groveling and contemptible. **4.** mean; treacherous. —*n.* **5.** a reptile.

re•pub•lic (ri pub′lik), *n.* **1.** a state in which the supreme power rests in the body of citizens entitled to vote and is exercised by representatives chosen by them. **2.** a state in which the head of government is not a monarch and is usu. an elected or nominated president. **3.** the form of government of such a state. **4.** any body of persons viewed as a commonwealth. **5.** (*cap., italics.*) a philosophical dialogue (4th century B.C.) by Plato dealing with the composition and structure of the ideal state. [< French < Latin *rēs pūblica* public affairs, the state]

re•pub•li•can (ri pub′li kən), *adj.* **1.** of, pertaining to, or of the nature of a republic. **2.** favoring a republic. **3.** fitting or appropriate for a citizen of a republic. **4.** (*cap.*) of or pertaining to the Republican Party. —*n.* **5.** a person who favors a republican form of government. **6.** (*cap.*) a member of the Republican Party.

Repub′lican Par′ty, *n.* one of the two major political parties in the U.S., originated (1854–56) to combat slavery.

re•pu•di•ate (ri pyo͞o′dē āt′), *v.t.,* **-at•ed, -at•ing. 1.** to reject as having no authority or binding force. **2.** to disown: *to repudiate a son.* **3.** to reject with disapproval or condemnation. **4.** to reject with denial: *to repudiate an accusation.* **5.** to refuse to acknowledge and pay (a debt). —**re•pu′di•a•ble,** *adj.* —**re•pu′di•a′tive,** *adj.* —**re•pu′di•a′tor,** *n.*

re•pu•di•a•tion (ri pyo͞o′dē ā′shən), *n.* **1.** the act of repudiating, or the state of being repudiated. **2.** refusal, as by a state or municipality, to pay a debt. —**re•pu′di•a•to′ry** (-ə tôr′ē, -tōr′ē), *adj.*

re•pugn (ri pyo͞on′), *v.t.* to oppose or refute.

re•pug•nance (ri pug′nəns) also **re•pug′nan•cy,** *n.* **1.** the state of being repugnant. **2.** strong distaste or aversion. **3.** contradictoriness or inconsistency.

re•pug•nant (ri pug′nənt), *adj.* **1.** objectionable or offensive; repellent. **2.** not consistent or compatible. **3.** opposed or antagonistic. —**re•pug′nant•ly,** *adv.*

re•pulse (ri puls′), *v.,* **-pulsed, -puls•ing,** *n.* —*v.t.* **1.** to drive back; repel. **2.** to repel with denial; refuse or reject. **3.** to cause feelings of repulsion in; disgust. —*n.* **4.** the act of repelling. **5.** a refusal or rejection. **6.** the fact of being repelled, as in hostile encounter.

re•pul•sion (ri pul′shən), *n.* **1.** the act of repulsing, or the state of being repulsed. **2.** being repelled; distaste or aversion. **3.** the force that tends to separate bodies of like electric charge or magnetic polarity.

re•pul•sive (ri pul′siv), *adj.* **1.** causing repugnance or aversion. **2.** serving to repulse. **3.** tending to drive away or keep at a distance; forbidding. —**re•pul′sive•ly,** *adv.* —**re•pul′sive•ness,** *n.*

repur′chase agree′ment, *n.* a deal to purchase securities between an investor and a bank, stipulating that the investor will sell back the bonds on a specified date, keeping the interest.

rep•u•ta•ble (rep′yə tə bəl), *adj.* **1.** held in good repute; honorable; respectable. **2.** considered to be good or acceptable usage; standard: *reputable speech.* —**rep′u•ta•bil′i•ty, rep′u•ta•ble•ness,** *n.* —**rep′u•ta•bly,** *adv.*

rep•u•ta•tion (rep′yə tā′shən), *n.* **1.** the estimation in which a person or thing is generally held; repute. **2.** favorable repute. **3.** a favorable and publicly recognized name or standing.

re•pute (ri pyo͞ot′), *n., v.,* **-put•ed, -put•ing.** —*n.* **1.** estimation in the view of others; reputation. **2.** favorable reputation. —*v.t.* **3.** to consider or believe (a person or thing) to be as specified (usu. used in the passive): *He was reputed to be a millionaire.*

re•put•ed (ri pyo͞o′tid), *adj.* reported or supposed to be such: *the reputed author of a book.* —**re•put′ed•ly,** *adv.*

re•quest (ri kwest′), *n.* **1.** the act of asking for something to be given or done; solicitation or petition. **2.** an instance of this: *a request for silence.* **3.** a written statement of petition. —*v.t.* **4.** to ask for, esp. formally or politely: *I request permission to speak.* **5.** to ask or beg (usu. fol. by a clause or an infinitive): *I request to be excused.* **6.** to ask or beg (someone) to do something: *He requested me to leave.* —***Idiom.* 7. by request,** in response to a request. —**re•quest′er,** *n.*

req•ui•em (rek′wē əm, rē′kwē-, rā′-), *n.* **1.** (*often cap.*) Also called **req′uiem mass′.** the mass celebrated for the repose of the souls of the dead. **2.** any musical service, hymn, or dirge for the repose of the dead.

req′uiem shark′, *n.* any of numerous, chiefly tropical sharks, including the tiger shark and soupfin shark.

re•qui•es•cat in pa•ce (re′kwē es′kät in pä′che), *Latin.* may he (or she) rest in peace.

re•quire (ri kwīər′), *v.,* **-quired, -quir•ing.** —*v.t.* **1.** to have need of; need: *He requires medical care.* **2.** to order or enjoin to do something: *to require a witness to testify.* **3.** to ask for authoritatively or imperatively; demand. **4.** to make necessary or indispensable: *The work required infinite patience.* **5.** to place under an obligation: *The situation requires me to take immediate action.* —*v.i.* **6.** to impose an obligation; demand: *to do as the law requires.*

re•quire•ment (ri kwīər′mənt), *n.* **1.** something required. **2.** an act or instance of requiring. **3.** a need or necessity.

req•ui•site (rek′wə zit), *adj.* **1.** required; necessary: *requisite skills.* —*n.* **2.** something required. —**req′ui•site•ly,** *adv.*

req•ui•si•tion (rek′wə zish′ən), *n.* **1.** the act of requiring or demanding something. **2.** a demand made. **3.** a formal or official demand. **4.** a written request for something, as supplies. **5.** the form on which such an order is drawn up. **6.** the state of being in use or required for use: *supplies in requisition.* —*v.t.* **7.** to require, order, or take for use. **8.** to demand or take, as for military purposes. —**req′ui•si′tion•er,** *n.*

re•quit•al (ri kwīt′l), *n.* **1.** the act of requiting. **2.** an action in return for service, kindness, etc. **3.** retaliation for a wrong, injury, etc.

re•quite (ri kwīt′), *v.t.,* **-quit•ed, -quit•ing. 1.** to make repayment for (service, benefits, etc.). **2.** to retaliate for (a wrong, injury, etc.); avenge. **3.** to repay in kind, either for a kindness or an injury. **4.** to give or do in return. —**re•quit′a•ble,** *adj.* —**re•quite′ment,** *n.*

re•re•cord (rē′ri kôrd′), *v.t.* **1.** to record (something) another time. **2.** to transfer (a recording) from one process to another, as from analog recording to digital recording.

rere•dos (rēr′dos, rēr′i-, râr′i-), *n.* a screen or a decorated part of the wall behind an altar in a church.

re•re•lease (rē′ri lēs′), *v.,* **-leased, -leas•ing,** *n.* —*v.t.* **1.** to release again. —*n.* **2.** something, as a film, that has been rereleased.

re•run (*v.* rē run′; *n.* rē′run′), *v.,* **-ran, -run, -running,** *n.* —*v.t.* **1.** to run or run off again. —*n.* **2.** the act of rerunning. **3. a.** the showing of a motion picture or television program after its initial run or showing. **b.** the motion picture or television program being shown again. **4.** a restatement or imitation of something familiar.

re•sale (rē′sāl′, rē sāl′), *n.* **1.** the act of selling a second time. **2.** the act of selling something secondhand. —*adj.* **3.** used; secondhand: *a rack of resale clothing.*

re•sched•ule (rē skej′o͞ol, -o͞ol, -o͞o əl; *Brit.* rē shed′yo͞ol, -shej′o͞ol), *v.t.,* **-uled, -ul•ing. 1.** to schedule for another or later time. **2.** to extend the time for repaying (a loan).

re•scind (ri sind′), *v.t.* **1.** to revoke, annul, or repeal. **2.** to invalidate (an act, measure, etc.) by a later action or a higher authority. —**re•scind′a•ble,** *adj.* —**re•scind′er,** *n.*

R

re•scis•sion (ri sizh′ən), *n.* the act of rescinding.

res•cue (res′kyo͞o), *v.*, **-cued, -cu•ing,** *n.* —*v.t.* **1.** to free from confinement or danger. **2.** to take by forcible means from lawful custody. —*n.* **3.** the act of rescuing. —**res′cu•er,** *n.*

re•search (ri sûrch′, rē′sûrch), *n.* **1.** diligent and systematic inquiry into a subject in order to discover or revise facts, theories, etc. **2.** a particular instance or piece of research. —*v.i.* **3.** to investigate carefully. —*v.t.* **4.** to make an extensive investigation into. —**re•search′er,** *n.*

re•sem•blance (ri zem′bləns), *n.* **1.** the state or fact of resembling; similarity. **2.** a degree, kind, or point of likeness. **3.** a likeness, appearance, or semblance of something.

re•sem•ble (ri zem′bəl), *v.t.*, **-bled, -bling.** to be like or similar to.

re•sent (ri zent′), *v.t.* to feel or show displeasure or indignation at from a sense of injury or insult. —**re•sent′ing•ly,** *adv.*

re•sent•ful (ri zent′fəl), *adj.* full of or marked by resentment. —**re•sent′ful•ly,** *adv.* —**re•sent′ful•ness,** *n.*

re•sent•ment (ri zent′mənt), *n.* a feeling of displeasure or indignation at someone or something regarded as the cause of injury or insult; pique; irritation.

res•er•pine (res′ər pin, -pēn′, rə sûr′-), *n.* an alkaloid obtained from the root of the rauwolfia, used in treating hypertension.

res•er•va•tion (rez′ər vā′shən), *n.* **1.** the act of keeping back, withholding, or setting apart. **2.** the act of making an exception or qualification. **3.** an exception or qualification: *to accept something with inner reservations.* **4.** a tract of public land set apart for a special purpose, as for the use of an American Indian people. **5.** an arrangement to secure accommodations, as at a restaurant or on a plane. **6.** the record kept or assurance given of such an arrangement.

re•serve (ri zûrv′), *v.*, **-served, -serv•ing,** *n., adj.* —*v.t.* **1.** to keep back or save for future use, consideration, handling, etc. **2.** to retain or secure by prior arrangement. **3.** to set apart for a particular use, purpose, service, etc. **4.** to delay; postpone: *to reserve judgment.* **5.** to retain (the original color) of a surface, as on a painted ceramic piece. —*n.* **6. a.** cash, or assets readily convertible into cash, held aside to meet unexpected demands. **b.** uninvested cash held to comply with legal requirements. **7.** something stored for use or need; stock. **8.** a resource not normally called upon but available if needed. **9.** a tract of public land set apart for a special purpose. **10.** an act of reserving; reservation, exception, or qualification. **11. a.** part of a military force held in readiness to augment the main force. **b.** the part of a country's fighting force not in active service. **c. reserves,** the enrolled but not regular components of the U.S. Army. **12.** formality and self-restraint; avoidance of familiarity or intimacy with others. **13.** reticence or silence; forebearance. —*adj.* **14.** kept in reserve; forming a reserve. —***Idiom.*** **15. in reserve,** put aside or withheld for a future need; reserved: *money in reserve.* **16. without reserve,** without restraint; frankly; freely.

reserve′ bank′, *n.* **1.** one of the 12 principal banks of the U.S. Federal Reserve System. **2.** a bank authorized by a government to hold the reserves of other banks.

re•served (ri zûrvd′), *adj.* **1.** kept, held, or set apart for someone or some particular use or purpose. **2.** avoiding familiarity or intimacy with others; formal or self-restrained. **3.** characterized by reserve: *reserved comments.* —**re•serv′ed•ly,** *adv.*

Reserve′ Of′ficers Train′ing Corps′, *n.* a body of students at some colleges and universities who are given training toward becoming officers in the armed forces. *Abbr.:* ROTC, R.O.T.C.

re•serv•ist (ri zûr′vist), *n.* a person who belongs to a reserve military force of a country.

res•er•voir (rez′ər vwär′, -vwôr′, -vôr′, rez′ə-), *n.* **1.** a natural or artificial place where water is collected and stored for use. **2.** a receptacle or chamber for holding a liquid or fluid. **3.** a body of porous, permeable rock in which a pool of oil or gas has accumulated. **4.** *Anat.* a cavity or part that holds some fluid or secretion. **5.** a place where anything is collected or accumulated in great amount. **6.** a large or extra supply or stock; reserve.

re•set (rē set′), *v.*, **-set, -set•ting.** —*v.t.* **1.** to set again. **2.** to set back the odometer on (an auto or other vehicle) to a lower reading. —*v.i.* **3.** to become set again.

re•side (ri zīd′), *v.i.*, **-sid•ed, -sid•ing. 1.** to dwell permanently or for a considerable time; live. **2.** (of things, qualities, etc.) to be present habitually; be inherent (usu. fol. by *in*). **3.** to rest or be vested, as powers or rights (usu. fol. by *in*).

res•i•dence (rez′i dəns), *n.* **1.** the place, esp. the house, in which a person lives or resides; dwelling place; home. **2.** the act or fact of residing. **3.** the act of living or staying in a specified place, as while performing official duties. **4.** the time during which a person resides in a place. **5.** the principal center of a business activity as registered under law. **6.** the period of time during which a substance, as a chemical, remains adsorbed, suspended, or dissolved.

res•i•den•cy (rez′i dən sē), *n., pl.* **-cies. 1.** RESIDENCE (def. 2). **2.** the position or tenure of a medical resident.

res•i•dent (rez′i dənt), *n.* **1.** a person who resides in a place. **2.** a physician employed by a hospital while receiving specialized training there. —*adj.* **3.** residing; dwelling in a place. **4.** living or staying at a place in discharge of duty. **5.** (of qualities) existing; intrinsic. **6.** (of birds) not migratory. **7.** encoded and permanently available to a computer user, as a font in a printer's ROM or software on a CD-ROM.

res•i•den•tial (rez′i den′shəl), *adj.* **1.** pertaining to residence or to residences: *a residential requirement for a doctorate.* **2.** characterized by private residences: *a residential neighborhood.*

re•sid•u•al (ri zij′o͞o əl), *adj.* **1.** pertaining to or constituting a residue or remainder; remaining; leftover. **2.** of or pertaining to the payment of residuals. **3.** *Geol.* remaining after the soluble elements have been dissolved: *residual soil.* —*n.* **4.** a residual quantity; remainder. **5.** Often, **residuals.** something that remains to discomfort or disable a person following an illness, injury, operation, or the like; disability. **6.** Usu., **residuals.** a fee paid, as to an actor or composer, for repeated broadcasts of a film, program, commercial, etc., after its original presentation or period of use. —**re•sid′u•al•ly,** *adv.*

res•i•due (rez′i do͞o′, -dyo͞o′), *n.* **1.** something that remains after a part is removed, disposed of, or used; remainder; rest; remnant. **2. a.** RESIDUUM (def. 2). **b.** an atom or group of atoms considered as a group or part of a molecule. **3.** the part of a testator's estate that remains after the payment of all debts, bequests, etc.

re•sid•u•um (ri zij′o͞o əm), *n., pl.* **-sid•u•a** (-zij′o͞o ə). **1.** a remainder or residue. **2.** the matter remaining after operation of any of a number of chemical processes, as filtration, evaporation, or combustion. **3.** any residual product.

re•sign (ri zīn′), *v.i.* **1.** to give up an office or position (often fol. by *from*). **2.** to submit; yield. —*v.t.* **3.** to give up (an office, position, etc.), often formally. **4.** to relinquish (a right, claim, etc.). **5.** to submit (oneself, one's mind, etc.) without resistance.

res•ig•na•tion (rez′ig nā′shən), *n.* **1.** the act of resigning. **2.** a formal statement, document, etc., stating that one gives up an office or position. **3.** an accepting, unresisting attitude, state, etc.

re•signed (ri zīnd′), *adj.* **1.** submissive or acquiescent. **2.** characterized by or indicative of resignation. —**re•sign′ed•ly,** *adv.*

re•sil•ience (ri zil′yəns, -zil′ē əns) also **re•sil′ien•cy,** *n.* **1.** the power or ability to return to the original form, position, etc., after being bent, compressed, or stretched; elasticity. **2.** ability to recover readily from illness, depression, adversity, or the like; buoyancy.

re•sil•ient (ri zil′yənt, -zil′ē ənt), *adj.* **1.** having resilience; able to spring back to an original form or position after compression, stretching, etc.; flexible. **2.** recovering readily from illness, adversity, or the like; buoyant. —**re•sil′ient•ly,** *adv.*

res•in (rez′in), *n.* **1.** any of a class of nonvolatile, solid or semisolid organic substances, as copal or mastic, that consist of amorphous mixtures of carboxylic acids: used in medicine and in the making of varnishes and plastics. **2.** a substance of this type obtained from certain pines; rosin. —*v.t.* **3.** to treat or rub with resin. —**res′in•like′,** *adj.*

res•in•ous (rez′ə nəs) also **res•in•y** (-ə nē), *adj.* **1.** full of or containing resin. **2.** pertaining to or resembling resin. —**res′in•ous•ly,** *adv.*

re•sist (ri zist′), *v.t.* **1.** to withstand, strive against, or oppose. **2.** to withstand the action or effect of. **3.** to refrain or abstain from, esp. with difficulty: *They couldn't resist the chocolates.* —*v.i.* **4.** to act or make efforts in opposition. —*n.* **5.** a coating on a surface of a metallic printing plate that prevents or inhibits corrosion of the metal by acid. **6.** a dye-resistant substance applied to specific areas of a fabric before its immersion in a dye bath and afterward removed, creating a pattern on a colored ground. —**re•sist′er,** *n.* —**re•sist′ing•ly,** *adv.*

re•sist•ance (ri zis′təns), *n.* **1.** the act or power of resisting, opposing, or withstanding. **2.** the opposition offered by one thing, force, etc., to another. **3. a.** the tendency of a conductor to oppose the flow of current, causing electrical energy to be changed into heat. *Symbol:* R **b.** a conductor or coil offering such opposition; resistor. **4.** (*often cap.*) an underground organization working to liberate a country occupied by a foreign power, as in France during World War II.

re•sist•ant (ri zis′tənt), *adj.* resisting (sometimes used in combination): *stain-resistant fabric.* —**re•sist′ant•ly,** *adv.*

re•sist•i•ble (ri zis′tə bəl), *adj.* able to be resisted. —**re•sist′i•bil′i•ty, re•sist′i•ble•ness,** *n.* —**re•sist′i•bly,** *adv.*

re•sis•tiv•i•ty (rē′zis tiv′i tē), *n.* **1.** the power or property of resistance. **2.** electrical resistance as a function of a given volume or area.

re•sis•tor (ri zis′tər), *n.* a device designed to introduce resistance into an electric circuit.

re•sole (rē sōl′), *v.t.*, **-soled, -sol•ing.** to put a new sole on (a shoe, boot, etc.).

re•sol•u•ble[1] (ri zol′yə bəl, rez′əl-), *adj.* capable of being resolved.

re•sol•u•ble[2] (rē sol′yə bəl), *adj.* able to be redissolved.

res•o•lute (rez′ə lo͞ot′), *adj.* **1.** firmly set in purpose or opinion; determined; resolved. **2.** characterized by firmness and determination. —**res′o•lute′ly,** *adv.* —**res′o•lute′ness,** *n.*

res•o•lu•tion (rez′ə lo͞o′shən), *n.* **1.** a formal expression of opinion or intention made, usu. after voting, by a formal organization, a legislature, a club, or other group. **2.** a resolve or determination. **3.** the act of resolving or determining upon a course of action, method, procedure, etc. **4.** the mental state or quality of being resolved or resolute; firmness of purpose. **5.** the act or process of resolving or separating into constituent or elementary parts. **6.** the resulting state. **7.** the act, process, or capability of distinguishing between two separate but adjacent parts, objects, or sources of light or between two nearly equal wavelengths. **8.** a solution or settlement of a problem, controversy, etc. **9.** the completion or conclusion of the actions, conflicts, issues, etc., in the plot of a play, novel, or other literary work. **10.** *Music.* the progression of a voice part or of the harmony as a whole from a dissonance to a consonance. **11.** reduction to a simpler form; conversion. **12.** the degree of sharpness of a computer-generated image as measured by the number of dots per linear inch in a hard-copy printout or the number of pixels across and down on a display screen.

re•solve (ri zolv′), *v.*, **-solved, -solv•ing,** *n.* **—***v.t.* **1.** to come to a definite or earnest decision about; determine. **2.** to separate into constituent or elementary parts; break up (usu. fol. by *into*). **3.** to reduce or convert by, or as if by, breaking up (usu. fol. by *to* or *into*). **4.** to convert or transform by any process (often used reflexively). **5.** to reduce by mental analysis (often fol. by *into*). **6.** to settle, determine, or state formally in a vote or resolution, as of a deliberative assembly. **7.** to deal with (a question, controversy, etc.) conclusively; settle. **8.** to clear away or dispel (doubts, fears, etc.); answer. **9.** to bring about the resolution of (the plot elements of a play, novel, or other literary work). **10.** to cause (a voice part or the harmony as a whole) to progress from a dissonance to a consonance. **11.** to separate (a racemic mixture) into optically active components. **12.** to separate and make visible the individual parts of (an image); distinguish between. **13.** to cause (swellings, inflammation, etc.) to disappear without suppuration. **—***v.i.* **14.** to come to a determination; make up one's mind (often fol. by *on* or *upon*). **15.** to break up or disintegrate. **16.** to be reduced or changed by breaking up, analysis, or the like (usu. fol. by *to* or *into*). **17.** to progress from a dissonance to a consonance. **—***n.* **18.** a resolution or determination made, as to follow some course of action. **19.** firmness of purpose or intent; determination. **—re•solv′a•ble,** *adj.*

re•solved (ri zolvd′), *adj.* firm in purpose or intent; determined.

res•o•nance (rez′ə nəns), *n.* **1.** the quality of being resonant. **2.** the prolongation of sound by reflection; reverberation. **3.** amplification of a source of speech sounds, esp. of phonation, by sympathetic vibration of the air, esp. in the cavities of the mouth, nose, and pharynx. **4.** a larger than normal vibration produced in response to a stimulus whose frequency is close to the natural frequency of the vibrating system. **5.** a quality of enriched significance, profundity, or allusiveness. **6.** the chemical phenomenon in which the arrangement of the valence electrons of a molecule changes back and forth between two or more states.

res•o•nant (rez′ə nənt), *adj.* **1.** resounding or echoing, as sounds. **2.** deep and full of resonance: *a resonant voice.* **3.** pertaining to resonance. **4.** producing resonance; causing amplification or sustention of sound. **5.** made intensely significant, profound, or allusive: *a land resonant with history.* **6.** pertaining to a system in a state of resonance. **—***n.* **7.** a speech sound produced without occlusion or audible friction. **—res′o•nant•ly,** *adv.*

res•o•nate (rez′ə nāt′), *v.*, **-nat•ed, -nat•ing.** **—***v.i.* **1.** to resound. **2.** to act as a resonator; exhibit resonance. **3.** to amplify vocal sound by the sympathetic vibration of air in certain cavities and bony structures. **—***v.t.* **4.** to cause to resound. **—res′o•na′tion,** *n.*

res•o•na•tor (rez′ə nā′tər), *n.* **1.** something that resonates. **2.** an appliance for increasing sound by resonance. **3.** an instrument for detecting the presence of a particular frequency by means of resonance. **4.** a hollow enclosure designed to cause energy of a certain frequency, as sound waves or microwaves, to resonate. **5.** an electrical circuit that exhibits resonance at a certain frequency.

re•sorb (ri sôrb′, -zôrb′), *v.t.* to absorb again, as an exudation. **—re•sorb′ence,** *n.* **—re•sorb′ent,** *adj.*

res•or•cin•ol (ri zôr′sə nôl′, -nol′, rez ôr′-) also **res•or′cin,** *n.* a white, needlelike, water-soluble solid, $C_6H_6O_2$, used chiefly in making dyes, as a reagent, in tanning, in the synthesis of certain resins, and as a skin medication.

re•sort (ri zôrt′), *v.i.* **1.** to have recourse for use, help, or accomplishing something, often as a final option: *to resort to war.* **2.** to go, esp. frequently or customarily: *a beach to which many people resort.* **—***n.* **3.** a place with facilities for vacationers. **4.** habitual or general going, as to a place or person. **5.** recourse; resource: *a court of last resort.* **6.** a person or thing resorted to for aid, satisfaction, service, etc.

re•sound (ri zound′), *v.i.* **1.** to echo or ring with sound. **2.** to make an echoing sound, or sound loudly. **3.** to ring or be echoed. **4.** to be celebrated or notably important. **—***v.t.* **5.** to reecho (a sound). **6.** to give forth or utter loudly or resonantly. **7.** to proclaim loudly or broadly.

re•sound•ing (ri zoun′ding), *adj.* **1.** making an echoing sound. **2.** uttered loudly. **3.** impressively thorough or complete: *a resounding popular success.* **—re•sound′ing•ly,** *adv.*

re•source (rē′sôrs, -sōrs, -zôrs, -zōrs; ri sôrs′, -sōrs′, -zôrs′, -zōrs′), *n.* **1.** a source of supply, support, or aid, esp. one held in reserve. **2. resources,** the collective wealth of a country or its means of producing wealth. **3.** Usu., **resources.** money, or any property that can be converted into money; assets. **4.** Often, **resources.** an available means afforded by the mind or one's personal capabilities: *to have resource against loneliness.* **5.** an action or measure to which one may have recourse in an emergency; expedient. **6.** capability in dealing with a situation or in meeting difficulties. **—re•source′less,** *adj.*

re•source•ful (ri sôrs′fəl, -sōrs′-, -zôrs′-, -zōrs′-), *adj.* able to deal skillfully and promptly with new situations, difficulties, etc. **—re•source′ful•ly,** *adv.* **—re•source′ful•ness,** *n.*

re•spect (ri spekt′), *n.* **1.** particular; detail; point: *to differ in some respect.* **2.** relation; reference: *inquiries with respect to a route.* **3.** esteem; admiration: *I have great respect for her judgment.* **4.** proper acceptance or courtesy. **5.** the condition of being esteemed or honored: *to be held in respect.* **6. respects,** a formal expression or gesture of greeting, esteem, friendship, or sympathy: *Give my respects to your parents.* **—***v.t.* **7.** to hold in esteem or honor. **8.** to refrain from intruding upon or interfering with: *to respect a person's privacy.* **9.** to relate or have reference to. **—*Idiom.*** **10. in respect of,** in reference to; concerning.

re•spect•a•ble (ri spek′tə bəl), *adj.* **1.** worthy of respect or esteem: *a respectable citizen.* **2.** of good social standing or reputation: *a respectable neighborhood.* **3.** good enough to be seen or used: *respectable shoes.* **4.** of moderate excellence: *a respectable performance.* **5.** appreciable in size, number, or amount: *a respectable turnout.* **—re•spect′a•bil′i•ty, re•spect′a•ble•ness,** *n.* **—re•spect′a•bly,** *adv.*

re•spect•ful (ri spekt′fəl), *adj.* characterized by or showing politeness or deference. **—re•spect′ful•ly,** *adv.*

re•spec•tive (ri spek′tiv), *adj.* pertaining individually to each of a number of persons; particular: *the respective merits of the candidates.*

re•spec•tive•ly (ri spek′tiv lē), *adv.* **1.** in precisely the order given; sequentially. **2.** (of two or more subjects, with reference to two or more subjects previously mentioned) in a parallel or sequential way: *Joe and Bob escorted Betty and Alice, respectively.*

res•pi•ra•tion (res′pə rā′shən), *n.* **1.** the act of respiring; inhalation and exhalation of air; breathing. **2.** the sum total of the physical and chemical processes by which oxygen is conveyed to tissues and cells and the oxidation products, carbon dioxide and water, are given off.

res•pi•ra•tor (res′pə rā′tər), *n.* **1.** an apparatus to produce artificial respiration. **2.** a filtering device worn over the nose and mouth to prevent inhalation of noxious substances.

res•pi•ra•to•ry (res′pər ə tôr′ē, -tōr′ē, ri spīᵊr′ə-), *adj.* pertaining to or serving for respiration.

res′piratory distress′ syn′drome, *n.* an acute lung disease of newborn, esp. premature, infants, caused by a deficiency of the surface-active substance that keeps the alveoli of the lungs expanded.

res′piratory sys′tem, *n.* the system of organs and tissues that draw oxygen into the body and remove carbon dioxide: in mammals, the nasal cavity, pharynx, trachea, bronchi, lungs, and the diaphragm.

re•spire (ri spīᵊr′), *v.*, **-spired, -spir•ing.** **—***v.i.* **1.** to inhale and exhale air for the purpose of maintaining life; breathe. **2.** (of a living system) to exchange oxygen for carbon dioxide and other products. **—***v.t.* **3.** to breathe; inhale and exhale.

res•pite (res′pit), *n.*, *v.*, **-pit•ed, -pit•ing.** **—***n.* **1.** a delay or cessation for a time, esp. of anything distressing or trying; an interval of relief. **2.** temporary suspension of a death sentence; reprieve; stay. **—***v.t.* **3.** to relieve temporarily, esp. from anything distressing or trying. **4.** to grant delay in the carrying out of (a punishment, obligation, etc.); postpone.

re•splend•ent (ri splen′dənt), *adj.* shining brilliantly; gleaming; radiant; splendid. **—re•splend′ence,** *n.* **—re•splend′ent•ly,** *adv.*

re•spond (ri spond′), *v.i.* **1.** to answer in words: *to respond to a question.* **2.** to make a return by some action: *to respond generously to a charity drive.* **3.** to react favorably. **4.** *Physiol.* to exhibit some action or effect; react: *Nerves respond to a stimulus.* **—***v.t.* **5.** to say in answer; reply. **—***n.* **6.** a half pier, pilaster, or the like projecting from a wall as a support for a lintel or an arch. **7.** a short anthem chanted at intervals during the reading of a lection.

re•spond•ent (ri spon′dənt), *n.* **1.** a person who responds or makes reply. **2.** a defendant, esp. in appellate and divorce proceedings. **—***adj.* **3.** giving a response; answering; responsive. **4.** being a respondent.

re•sponse (ri spons′), *n.* **1.** an answer; reply; rejoinder. **2.** any behavior of a living organism that results from an external or internal stimulus. **3.** a verse, sentence, phrase, or word said or sung by the choir or congregation in reply to the officiant in a religious service.

re•spon•si•bil•i•ty (ri spon′sə bil′i tē), *n.*, *pl.* **-ties.** **1.** the state or fact of being responsible. **2.** an instance of being responsible: *The responsibility for this mess is yours!* **3.** a particular burden of obligation upon one who is responsible: *the responsibilities of authority.* **4.** a person or thing for which one is responsible. **5.** reliability or dependability, esp. in meeting debts or payments.

re•spon•si•ble (ri spon′sə bəl), *adj.* **1.** accountable, as for something within one's power. **2.** involving responsibility: *a responsible position.* **3.** chargeable with being the source or occasion of something (usu. fol. by *for*). **4.** having a capacity for moral decisions and therefore accountable: *The defendant is not responsible for his actions.* **5.** able to discharge obligations or pay debts. **6.** reliable or dependable, as in conducting one's affairs; trustworthy. **—re•spon′si•bly,** *adv.*

re•spon•sive (ri spon′siv), *adj.* **1.** responding readily and sympathetically; receptive. **2.** characterized by the use of responses. **—re•spon′sive•ly,** *adv.* **—re•spon′sive•ness,** *n.*

re•spon•so•ry (ri spon′sə rē), *n.*, *pl.* **-ries.** an anthem sung after a lection by a soloist and choir alternately.

re•spon•sum (ri spon′səm), *n.*, *pl.* **-sa** (-sə). the written reply of a noted rabbi or Jewish scholar to a question concerning Jewish law.

rest[1] (rest), *n.* **1.** the refreshing quiet or repose of sleep. **2.** refreshing ease or inactivity after exertion or labor. **3.** relief, esp. from trouble, anxiety, etc. **4.** a period or interval of inactivity, repose, solitude, or tranquillity. **5.** mental or spiritual calm; tranquillity. **6.** the repose of death: *eternal rest.* **7.** cessation or absence of motion. **8.** *Music.* **a.** an interval of silence between tones. **b.** a mark or sign indicating it. **9.** any stopping or resting place. **10.** a piece or device by which something is supported or upon which it can rest. **—***v.i.* **11.** to refresh oneself, as by sleeping, lying down, or relaxing. **12.** to be at ease; have tranquillity or peace. **13.** to repose in death. **14.** to cease from motion or activity; stop. **15.** to remain without further action or notice. **16.** to lie, sit, lean, or be set: *His arm rested on the table.* **17.** (of land) to lie fallow or unworked. **18.** to be imposed as a burden or responsibility (usu. fol. by *on* or *upon*). **19.** to rely (usu. fol. by *on* or *upon*). **20.** to be based or founded (usu. fol. by *on* or *upon*). **21.** to belong; reside (often fol. by *with*): *The blame rests with them.* **22.** to be fixed or directed on something, as a gaze. **23.** *Law.* to conclude the introduction of evidence in a case. **—***v.t.* **24.** to give rest to; refresh with rest. **25.** to lay or place for rest, ease, or support. **26.** to direct or cast: *to rest one's eyes on someone.* **27.** to base, or let depend, as on some ground of reliance. **28.** to bring to rest; halt; stop. **29.** *Law.* to conclude the introduction of evidence on: *to rest one's case.* **—*Idiom.* 30. at rest, a.** in a state of repose, as in sleep. **b.** dead. **c.** quiescent; inactive; not in motion. **d.** free from worry; tranquil. **31. lay to rest, a.** to inter (a dead body); bury. **b.** to allay, suppress, or appease.

rest[1] (def. 8b)

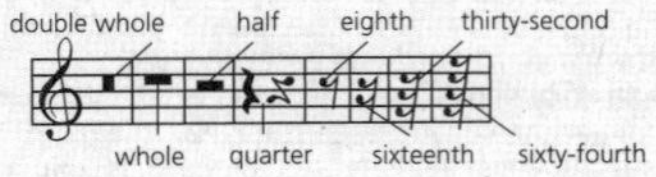
double whole
half
eighth
thirty-second
whole
quarter
sixteenth
sixty-fourth

rest[2] (rest), *n.* **1.** the part that is left or remains; remainder. **2.** the others: *All the rest are going.* **—***v.i.* **3.** to continue to be; remain as specified: *Rest assured that all is well.*

res•tau•rant (res′tər ənt, -tə ränt′, -tränt′), *n.* an establishment where meals are served to customers.

res•tau•ra•teur (res′tər ə tûr′; *Fr.* res tô ʀᴀ tœʀ′), *n., pl.* **-teurs** (-tûrz′; *Fr.* -tœʀ′). the owner or manager of a restaurant.

rest•ful (rest′fəl), *adj.* **1.** giving or conducive to rest. **2.** being at rest; tranquil; peaceful. **—rest′ful•ly,** *adv.* **—rest′ful•ness,** *n.*

rest′ home′, *n.* a residential establishment that provides special care for convalescents and aged or infirm persons.

res•ti•tu•tion (res′ti to͞o′shən, -tyo͞o′-), *n.* **1.** reparation made by giving an equivalent or compensation for loss, damage, or injury caused; indemnification. **2.** the restoration of property or rights previously taken away, conveyed, or surrendered. **3.** restoration to the former or original state or position. **—res′ti•tute′,** *v.t., v.i.,* **-tut•ed, -tut•ing.**

res•tive (res′tiv), *adj.* **1.** impatient of control, restraint, or delay, as persons; restless; uneasy. **2.** obstinately uncooperative; stubborn; balky. **—res′tive•ly,** *adv.* **—res′tive•ness,** *n.*

rest•less (rest′lis), *adj.* **1.** characterized by or showing inability to remain at rest: *a restless mood.* **2.** unquiet; uneasy. **3.** perpetually in motion: *the restless sea.* **4.** without rest: *a restless night.* **5.** unceasingly active: *a restless crowd.* **—rest′less•ly,** *adv.* **—rest′less•ness,** *n.*

rest′ mass′, *n.* the mass of a body as measured when the body is at rest relative to an observer, an inherent property of the body in the theory of relativity.

res•to•ra•tion (res′tə rā′shən), *n.* **1.** the act of restoring. **2.** the state of being restored. **3.** a return of something to an original or unimpaired condition. **4.** restitution of something taken away or lost. **5.** something that is restored, as by renovating. **6.** a reconstruction or reproduction, as of an extinct form, showing it in the original state. **7. a.** the work or process of replacing or restoring teeth or parts of teeth. **b.** something that restores or replaces teeth or parts of teeth, as a denture or filling. **8. the Restoration, a.** the reestablishment of the monarchy in England with the return of Charles II in 1660. **b.** the period of the reign of Charles II (1660–85).

re•stor•a•tive (ri stôr′ə tiv, -stōr′-), *adj.* **1.** of or pertaining to restoration. **2.** capable of renewing health or strength. **—***n.* **3.** a restorative agent, means, or the like.

re•store (ri stôr′, -stōr′), *v.t.,* **-stored, -stor•ing. 1.** to bring back into existence, use, or the like; reestablish: *to restore order.* **2.** to bring back to a former, more desirable condition: *to restore a painting.* **3.** to bring back to a state of health, soundness, or vigor. **4.** to put back; return, as to a former place, position, or rank. **5.** to give back; make return or restitution of (anything taken away or lost). **6.** to reproduce or reconstruct (an ancient building, extinct animal, etc.) in the original state. **—re•stor′a•ble,** *adj.* **—re•stor′er,** *n.*

re•strain (ri strān′), *v.t.* **1.** to hold back from action; check or control; repress. **2.** to deprive of liberty, as by arrest; confine. **3.** to limit or hamper the activity, growth, or effect of: *to restrain trade with Cuba.*

restrain′ing or′der, *n.* a judicial order to forbid a particular act until a decision is reached on an application for an injunction.

re•straint (ri strānt′), *n.* **1.** a restraining action or influence. **2.** a means of restraining. **3.** a device that restrains, as a harness. **4.** the act of restraining. **5.** the state or fact of being restrained; confinement. **6.** constraint or reserve in feelings, behavior, etc.

re•strict (ri strikt′), *v.t.* to confine or keep within limits, as of space, action, choice, or quantity.

re•strict•ed (ri strik′tid), *adj.* **1.** confined; limited. **2.** available only to authorized persons. **3.** excluding members of a particular group or class: *a restricted neighborhood.* **—re•strict′ed•ly,** *adv.*

re•stric•tion (ri strik′shən), *n.* **1.** something that restricts. **2.** the act of restricting. **3.** the state of being restricted.

re•stric•tive (ri strik′tiv), *adj.* **1.** tending or serving to restrict. **2.** of the nature of a restriction. **3.** of or pertaining to a word, phrase, or clause that identifies or limits the meaning of a modified element, as the relative clause *that just ended* in *The year that just ended was bad for crops:* in English a restrictive clause is usu. not set off by commas. Compare ɴᴏɴʀᴇsᴛʀɪᴄᴛɪᴠᴇ (def. 2). **—re•stric′tive•ly,** *adv.*

rest′ room′, *n.* a room or rooms, esp. in a public building, having washbowls, toilets, and other facilities.

re•struc•ture (rē struk′chər), *v.,* **-tured, -tur•ing. —***v.t.* **1.** to alter or restore the structure of. **2.** to effect a fundamental change in, as an organization. **—***v.i.* **3.** to restructure something.

re•sult (ri zult′), *v.i.* **1.** to arise or proceed as a consequence from actions, circumstances, premises, etc.; be the outcome. **2.** to end in a specified manner or thing: *to result in failure.* **—***n.* **3.** something that results; outcome. **4.** Often, **results.** a desirable consequence or outcome. **5.** *Math.* a quantity, expression, etc., obtained by calculation.

re•sult•ant (ri zul′tnt), *adj.* **1.** following as a result or consequence. **2.** resulting from the combination of two or more agents. **—***n.* **3.** something that results.

re•sume (ri zo͞om′), *v.,* **-sumed, -sum•ing. —***v.t.* **1.** to take up or go on with again after interruption; continue. **2.** to take or occupy again: *to resume one's seat.* **3.** to take on or assume again: *She resumed her maiden name.* **4.** to take back. **—***v.i.* **5.** to go on or continue after interruption. **6.** to begin again. **—re•sum′a•ble,** *adj.*

ré•su•mé or **re•su•me** or **re•su•mé** (rez′o͝o mā′, rez′o͝o mā′), *n.* **1.** sᴜᴍᴍᴀʀʏ. **2.** a brief written account of personal, educational, and professional qualifications and experience.

re•sump•tion (ri zump′shən), *n.* the act of resuming.

re•sur•face (rē sûr′fis), *v.,* **-faced, -fac•ing. —***v.t.* **1.** to give a new surface to. **—***v.i.* **2.** to come to the surface again.

re•sur•gent (ri sûr′jənt), *adj.* rising or tending to come back to life, activity, or prominence. **—re•sur′gence,** *n.*

res•ur•rect (rez′ə rekt′), *v.t.* **1.** to raise from the dead; bring to life again. **2.** to bring back into use, practice, etc.

res•ur•rec•tion (rez′ə rek′shən), *n.* **1.** the act of rising from the dead. **2.** (*cap.*) the rising of Christ after His death and burial. **3.** (*cap.*) the rising of the dead on Judgment Day. **4.** a rising again, as from decay or disuse; revival.

resurrec′tion plant′, *n.* **1.** any American desert plant of the genus *Selaginella,* of the family Selaginellaceae, having stems that curl inward until moistened. **2.** Rᴏsᴇ ᴏғ Jᴇʀɪᴄʜᴏ.

re•sus•ci•tate (ri sus′i tāt′), *v.t.,* **-tat•ed, -tat•ing.** to revive, esp. from apparent death or from unconsciousness. **—re•sus′ci•ta•ble** (-tə bəl), *adj.* **—re•sus′ci•ta′tion,** *n.* **—re•sus′ci•ta′tive,** *adj.*

re•tail (rē′tāl *for 1–4, 6;* ri tāl′ *for 5*), *n.* **1.** the sale of goods to ultimate consumers, usu. in small quantities (opposed to *wholesale*). **—***adj.* **2.** pertaining to or engaged in sale at retail. **—***adv.* **3.** in a retail quantity or at a retail price. **—***v.t.* **4.** to sell at retail; sell directly to the consumer. **5.** to relate or repeat in detail to others: *to retail scandal.* **—***v.i.* **6.** to be sold at retail. **—re′tail•er,** *n.*

re•tain (ri tān′), *v.t.* **1.** to keep possession of. **2.** to continue to use, practice, etc. **3.** to continue to hold or have: *a cloth that retains its color.* **4.** to keep in mind; remember. **5.** to hold in place or position. **6.** to engage, esp. by payment of a preliminary fee: *to retain a lawyer.* **—re•tain′a•ble,** *adj.* **—re•tain′ment,** *n.*

re•tain•er[1] (ri tā′nər), *n.* **1.** one that retains. **2.** a servant or attendant who has been with a family for many years. **3.** (esp. in feudal times) a person attached to a noble household and owing it occasional service. **4.** any of various devices for maintaining the position of the natural teeth, attaching or stabilizing a denture, etc.

re•tain•er[2] (ri tā′nər), *n.* **1.** the act of retaining in one's service. **2.** the fact of being so retained. **3.** a fee paid to secure services.

retain′ing wall′, *n.* a wall for holding in place a mass of earth or the like, as at the edge of a terrace or excavation.

re•take (*v.* rē tāk′; *n.* rē′tāk′), *v.,* **-took, -tak•en, -tak•ing,** *n.* **—***v.t.* **1.** to take again; take back. **2.** to recapture. **3.** to photograph or film again. **—***n.* **4.** the act of photographing or filming again. **5.** a picture, scene, etc., that is to be or has been photographed or filmed again.

re•tal•i•ate (ri tal′ē āt′), *v.,* **-at•ed, -at•ing. —***v.i.* **1.** to return like for like, esp. evil for evil: *to retaliate for an injury.* **—***v.t.* **2.** to requite or make return for (a wrong or injury) with the like. **—re•tal′i•a′tion,** *n.* **—re•tal′i•a′tive, re•tal′i•a•to′ry** (-ə tôr′ē, -tōr′ē), *adj.*

re•tard (ri tärd′), *v.t.* **1.** to make slow; delay the development or progress of; hinder. **—***v.i.* **2.** to be delayed. **—***n.* **3.** retardation; delay. **4.** an adjustment to the distributor of an internal-combustion engine that causes the spark for ignition to be generated later in the cycle. Compare ᴀᴅᴠᴀɴᴄᴇ (def. 22).

re•tard•ant (ri tär′dnt), *n.* **1.** any substance capable of reducing the speed of a chemical reaction. **—***adj.* **2.** retarding or tending to retard (usu. used in combination): *fire-retardant material.*

re•tar•da•tion (rē′tär dā′shən), *n.* **1.** the act of retarding or the state of being retarded. **2.** something that retards; hindrance. **3.** slowness or limitation in intellectual understanding and awareness, emotional development, academic progress, etc.

re•tard•ed (ri tär′did), *adj.* characterized by retardation: *a retarded child.*

retch (rech), *v.i.* to make efforts to vomit.

re•ten•tion (ri ten′shən), *n.* **1.** the act of retaining or the state of being retained. **2.** the power to retain; capacity for retaining. **3.** the act or power of remembering things; memory.

re·ten·tive (ri ten′tiv), *adj.* **1.** tending or serving to retain something. **2.** having power or capacity to retain. **3.** having power or ability to remember; having a good memory. **—re·ten′tive·ness,** *n.*

re·think (rē thingk′), *v.t., v.i.,* **-thought, -think·ing.** to reconsider, esp. profoundly.

ret·i·cent (ret′ə sənt), *adj.* **1.** disposed to be silent or not to speak freely; reserved. **2.** restrained, as in style or appearance. **—ret′i·cence, ret′i·cen·cy,** *n.* **—ret′i·cent·ly,** *adv.*

ret·i·cle (ret′i kal) also **reticule,** *n.* a network of fine lines, wires, or the like placed in the focus of the eyepiece of an optical instrument.

re·tic·u·lar (ri tik′yə lar), *adj.* **1.** having the form of a net; netlike. **2.** intricate or entangled. **3.** of or pertaining to a reticulum.

re·tic·u·late (*adj.* ri tik′yə lit, -lāt′; *v.* -lāt′), *adj., v.,* **-lat·ed, -lat·ing.** *—adj.* **1.** covered with a network. **2.** netlike. **3.** *Bot.* having the veins or nerves disposed like the threads of a net. *—v.t.* **4.** to form into a network. **5.** to cover or mark with a network. *—v.i.* **6.** to form a network. **—re·tic′u·late·ly,** *adv.*

ret·i·cule (ret′i kyōōl′), *n.* **1.** a small purse or bag, orig. of network but later of fabric. **2.** RETICLE.

re·tic·u·lum (ri tik′yə ləm), *n., pl.* **-la** (-lə). **1.** a network; any reticulated system or structure. **2. a.** a network of intercellular fibers in certain tissues. **b.** a network of structures in the endoplasm or nucleus of certain cells. **3.** the second stomach of cows and other ruminants, into which the coarse food regurgitated from the rumen is reswallowed.

ret·i·na (ret′n ə, ret′nə), *n., pl.* **ret·i·nas, ret·i·nae** (ret′n ē′). the innermost coat of the posterior part of the eyeball that receives the image produced by the lens, is continuous with the optic nerve, and consists of several layers, one of which contains the rods and cones that are sensitive to light.

ret·i·nol (ret′n ôl′, -ol′), *n.* VITAMIN A.

ret·i·nue (ret′n ōō′, -yōō′), *n.* a body of retainers in attendance upon an important personage; suite. **—ret′i·nued′,** *adj.*

re·tire (ri tīr′), *v.,* **-tired, -tir·ing.** *—v.i.* **1.** to withdraw or go away to a place of privacy, shelter, or seclusion. **2.** to go to bed. **3.** to give up or withdraw from an office, occupation, or career, usu. because of age. **4.** to fall back or retreat, as from battle or danger. **5.** to withdraw from view. *—v.t.* **6.** to withdraw from circulation by taking up and paying, as bonds or bills. **7.** to withdraw (troops, ships, etc.), as from battle or danger. **8.** to remove from an office or active service, as an army officer. **9.** to withdraw (a machine, ship, etc.) permanently from its normal service. **10.** *Sports.* to put out (a batter, side, etc.).

re·tired (ri tīrd′), *adj.* **1.** withdrawn from an office, occupation, or career: *a retired banker.* **2.** due or given a retired person: *retired pay.* **3.** secluded or sequestered.

re·tir·ee (ri tī rē′, -tīr′ē), *n.* a person who has retired from an office.

re·tire·ment (ri tīr′mənt), *n.* **1.** the act of retiring or the state of being retired. **2.** removal or withdrawal from an office or active service. **3.** privacy or seclusion. **4.** a private or secluded place.

re·tir·ing (ri tīr′ing), *adj.* **1.** that retires. **2.** withdrawing from contact with others; reserved; shy. **—re·tir′ing·ly,** *adv.*

re·took (rē tōōk′), *v.* pt. of RETAKE.

re·tool (rē tōōl′), *v.t.* **1.** to replace or rearrange the tools and machinery of (a factory). **2.** to reorganize, usu. for the purpose of updating. *—v.i.* **3.** to replace or rearrange the tools or machinery of a factory.

re·tort[1] (ri tôrt′), *v.t.* **1.** to reply to, usu. in a sharp or retaliatory way. **2.** to return (an accusation, epithet, etc.) upon the person uttering it. **3.** to answer (an argument or the like) by another to the contrary. *—v.i.* **4.** to reply, esp. sharply. *—n.* **5.** a severe, incisive, or witty reply, esp. one that counters a first speaker's statement, argument, etc. **6.** the act of retorting. **—re·tort′er,** *n.*

retort[2] (def. 1a)

re·tort[2] (ri tôrt′), *n.* **1. a.** a vessel, commonly a glass bulb with a long neck bent downward, used for distilling or decomposing substances by heat. **b.** a refractory chamber in which a substance, as ore or coal, is heated in smelting or manufacturing. **2.** a sterilizer for food cans. *—v.t.* **3.** to sterilize (food) after it is sealed in a container, by steam or other heating methods. **4.** to subject (shale, ore, etc.) to heat and possibly reduced pressure, as to produce fuel oil or a metal.

re·touch (*v.* rē tuch′; *n.* rē′tuch′, rē tuch′), *v.t.* **1.** to improve with new touches, details, or the like; touch up, as a painting or makeup. **2.** to alter (a photograph) after development by adding or removing lines, lightening areas, etc. **3.** to tint or bleach (a new growth of hair) to match previously dyed hair. *—n.* **4.** an added touch to a picture, painting, etc., by way of improvement or alteration. **5.** an act or instance of retouching.

re·trace (rē trās′), *v.t.,* **-traced, -trac·ing.** to trace again, as lines in writing or drawing.

re·trace (ri trās′), *v.t.,* **-traced, -trac·ing.** **1.** to trace backward; go back over: *to retrace one's steps.* **2.** to go back over with the memory. **—re·trace′a·ble,** *adj.*

re·tract[1] (ri trakt′), *v.t.* **1.** to draw back or in: *to retract fangs.* *—v.i.* **2.** to be capable of being drawn back or in.

re·tract[2] (ri trakt′), *v.t.* **1.** to withdraw (a statement, opinion, etc.) as inaccurate or unjustified, esp. formally. **2.** to withdraw or revoke (a decree, promise, etc.). *—v.i.* **3.** to withdraw a promise, vow, etc. **4.** to make a disavowal of a statement, opinion, etc.; recant. **—re·tract′a·ble, re·tract′i·ble,** *adj.* **—re·tract′a·bil′i·ty, re·tract′i·bil′i·ty,** *n.*

re·trac·tile (ri trak′til), *adj.* capable of being drawn back or in, as the head of a tortoise. **—re·trac·til′i·ty** (rē′trak til′i tē), *n.*

re·trac·tion (ri trak′shən), *n.* **1.** the act of retracting or the state of being retracted. **2.** withdrawal of a promise, statement, etc. **3.** retractile power.

re·tread (rē tred′), *v.t., v.i.,* **-trod, -trod·den** or **-trod, -tread·ing.** to tread again.

re·tread (*v.* rē tred′; *n.* rē′tred′), *v.t.* **1.** to put a new tread on (a worn pneumatic tire casing) either by recapping or by cutting fresh treads. **2.** to revive or rework, esp. without the inventiveness of the original. *—n.* **3.** a tire that has been retreaded. **4.** a reviving or reworking of an old or familiar idea, story, etc.

re·treat (rē trēt′), *v.t., v.i.* to treat again.

re·treat (ri trēt′), *n.* **1.** the forced or strategic withdrawal of a military force before an enemy. **2.** the act of withdrawing, as into safety or privacy; retirement. **3.** a place of refuge, seclusion, or privacy. **4.** an asylum, as for the insane. **5.** a retirement or a period of retirement for religious exercises and meditation. **6.** a flag-lowering ceremony held at sunset on a military post. *—v.i.* **7.** to withdraw, retire, or draw back, esp. for shelter or seclusion. **8.** to make a retreat. **9.** to slope backward; recede. **10.** to draw or lead back. **—Idiom. 11. beat a retreat,** to withdraw or retreat, esp. in disgrace.

re·trench (ri trench′), *v.t.* **1.** to cut down, reduce, or diminish; curtail (expenses). **2.** to cut off or remove. *—v.i.* **3.** to economize.

re·trench·ment (ri trench′mənt), *n.* **1.** the act of retrenching; a cutting down or off, as by the reduction of expenses. **2.** an interior work within a fortification, to which a garrison may retreat.

ret·ri·bu·tion (re′trə byōō′shən), *n.* **1.** requital according to merits or deserts, esp. for evil. **2.** something given or inflicted in such requital. **3.** *Theol.* the distribution of rewards and punishments in a future life.

re·triev·al (ri trē′vəl), *n.* **1.** the act of retrieving. **2.** the chance of recovery or restoration: *lost beyond retrieval.*

re·trieve (ri trēv′), *v.,* **-trieved, -triev·ing,** *n.* *—v.t.* **1.** to recover or regain. **2.** to bring back to a former and better state; restore. **3.** to make amends for; repair: *to retrieve an error.* **4.** to recall to mind. **5.** (of hunting dogs) to fetch (killed or wounded game). **6.** to rescue; save. **7.** (in tennis, handball, etc.) to make an in-bounds return of (a difficult shot). **8.** to locate and read (data) from computer storage, as for display on a monitor. *—v.i.* **9.** to retrieve game. *—n.* **10.** an act of retrieving; recovery. **11.** the possibility of recovery. **—re·triev′a·ble,** *adj.*

re·triev·er (ri trē′vər), *n.* **1.** a person or thing that retrieves. **2.** any of several medium- to large-sized breeds of dogs with a thick, oily, water-resistant coat, used esp. to retrieve game.

ret·ro (re′trō), *adj.* **1.** retroactive. **2.** of or designating the style of an earlier time: *retro clothes.*

retro-, a prefix meaning "back, backward": *retrogress; retrorocket.*

ret·ro·ac·tion (re′trō ak′shən), *n.* action that is opposed or contrary to the preceding action.

ret·ro·ac·tive (re′trō ak′tiv), *adj.* **1.** operative with respect to past occurrences, as a statute. **2.** (of a pay raise) effective as of a past date. **—ret′ro·ac′tive·ly,** *adv.* **—ret′ro·ac·tiv′i·ty,** *n.*

ret·ro·fit (*v.* re′trō fit′, re′trō fit′; *n.* re′trō fit′), *v.,* **-fit·ted** or **-fit, -fit·ting,** *n.* *—v.t.* **1.** to furnish (an automobile, airplane, etc.) with parts or equipment made available after the time of original manufacture. *—n.* **2.** something that has been retrofitted. **3.** the process of retrofitting.

ret·ro·flex (re′trə fleks′) also **ret·ro·flexed** (-flekst′), *adj.* **1.** bent backward. **2.** (of a speech sound) articulated with the tip of the tongue curled upward and back toward or against the hard palate.

ret·ro·grade (re′trə grād′), *adj., v.,* **-grad·ed, -grad·ing.** *—adj.* **1.** moving backward; having a backward motion or direction; retiring or retreating. **2.** inverse or reversed, as order. **3.** *Chiefly Biol.* exhibiting degeneration or deterioration. **4.** moving in an orbit in the direction opposite to that of the earth in its revolution around the sun. Compare DIRECT (def. 25). *—v.i.* **5.** to move or go backward; retire or retreat. **6.** *Chiefly Biol.* to decline to a worse condition; degenerate.

ret·ro·gress (re′trə gres′, re′trə gres′), *v.i.* **1.** to go backward into an earlier and usu. worse condition. **2.** to move backward. **—ret′ro·gress′ive,** *adj.* **—ret′ro·gress′ion,** *n.*

ret·ro·rock·et (re′trō rok′it), *n.* a small auxiliary rocket engine with its exhaust nozzle aimed in the direction of flight, used for decelerating a larger rocket, separating one stage from another, etc.

ret·ro·spect (re′trə spekt′), *n.* **1.** contemplation of the past; a survey of past events, etc. *—v.i.* **2.** to look back in thought; refer back (often fol. by *to*). *—v.t.* **3.** to look back upon; contemplate retrospectively. **—Idiom. 4. in retrospect,** on evaluating the past; upon reflection.

R

ret•ro•spec•tive (re′trə spek′tiv), *adj.* **1.** directed to the past; contemplative of past situations, events, etc. **2.** looking or directed backward. **3.** retroactive, as a statute. —*n.* **4.** an exhibit showing an entire phase or representative examples of an artist's lifework. **5.** an exhibit or series of performances representing the lifework of a composer, performer, etc. —**ret′ro•spec′tive•ly,** *adv.*

ret•ro•vi•rus (re′trə vī′rəs, re′trə vī′-), *n., pl.* **-rus•es.** any of various single-stranded RNA-containing viruses of the family Retroviridae. —**ret′ro•vi′ral,** *adj.*

re•turn (ri tûrn′), *v.i.* **1.** to go or come back, as to a former place, position, or state: *to return from abroad.* **2.** to revert to a former owner. **3.** to revert or recur, as in thought or discourse. **4.** to make a reply or retort. —*v.t.* **5.** to put, bring, take, give, or send back to the original or proper place, position, etc. **6.** to send or give back in reciprocation, recompense, or requital: *to return evil for good.* **7.** to reciprocate, repay, or react to (something sent, done, etc.) with something similar. **8.** to render (a verdict, decision, etc.). **9.** to give (a statement or a writ of actions done) to a judge or official. **10.** to reflect (light, sound, etc.). **11.** to yield (a profit, revenue, etc.). **12.** to report or announce officially. **13.** to elect or reelect, as to a legislative body. **14.** to send or hit back, as a served ball in tennis. **15.** *Chiefly Archit.* to cause to turn or proceed in a different direction: *to return a molding.* —*n.* **16.** the act or fact of returning, as by going or coming back or bringing, sending, or giving back. **17.** a recurrence. **18.** reciprocation, repayment, or requital: *profits in return for outlay.* **19.** response or reply. **20.** the gain realized on an exchange of goods. **21.** Often, **returns.** a yield or profit, as from labor or investment. **22.** Also called **tax return.** a statement on an official form showing income, deductions, exemptions, and taxes due. **23.** Usu., **returns.** an official or unofficial report on a count of votes, candidates elected, etc. **24.** *Archit.* **a.** the continuation of a molding, projection, etc., in a different direction. **b.** a side or part that falls away from the front of any straight or flat member or area. **25.** *Sports.* **a.** the act of returning a ball. **b.** the ball that is returned. **c.** (in football) a runback. **26.** *Law.* **a.** the sending back of a writ, summons, etc., with a brief report endorsed on it, by a sheriff to the court that issued it. **b.** a certified document by an assessor, election official, etc. **27. returns, a.** merchandise shipped back to a supplier from a retailer or distributor as unsold. **b.** merchandise returned to a retailer by a consumer. —*adj.* **28.** of or pertaining to a return or returning. **29.** sent, given, or done in return. **30.** done or occurring again. **31.** noting a person or thing that is returned or returning to a place: *return cargo.* **32.** changing in direction; doubling or returning on itself. **33.** used for returning, recirculating, etc.: *the return road.* **34.** played in order to provide the loser of an earlier game with the opportunity to win from the same opponent. **35.** provided to enable the return of mail to its sender: *a return envelope.*

re•turn•a•ble (ri tûr′nə bəl), *adj.* **1.** that may be returned. **2.** requiring a return, as a writ to the court from which it is issued. —*n.* **3.** a beverage bottle or can that can be returned for refund of a deposit.

Reu•ben (ro͞o′bən), *n.* **1.** the eldest son of Jacob and Leah. Gen. 29, 30. **2.** one of the 12 tribes of Israel, traditionally descended from him.

Reu•el (ro͞o′el), *n.* Jethro.

re•un•ion (rē yo͞on′yən), *n.* **1.** the act of uniting again. **2.** the state of being united again. **3.** a gathering of relatives, friends, or associates at regular intervals or after separation.

Ré•u•nion (rē yo͞on′yən, rā-), *n.* an island in the Indian Ocean, E of Madagascar: an overseas department of France. 692,204; 970 sq. mi. (2512 sq. km). *Cap.:* St. Denis.

re•u•nite (rē′yo͞o nīt′), *v.t., v.i.,* **-nit•ed, -nit•ing.** to unite again, as after separation. —**re′u•nit′a•ble,** *adj.*

re•used (rē yo͞ozd′), *adj.* designating wool fiber derived from used materials, as old wool clothing and rags.

Reu•ther (ro͞o′thər), *n.* **Walter Philip,** 1907–70, U.S. labor leader.

rev (rev), *n., v.,* **revved, rev•ving.** —*n.* **1.** a revolution of the crankshaft or other rotating part within an engine. —*v.t.* **2.** to accelerate sharply the speed of (an internal-combustion engine), esp. while the clutch is disengaged (often fol. by *up*). —*v.i.* **3.** (of an engine) to accelerate; become revved (often fol. by *up*). **4. rev up, a.** to increase in activity or speed; accelerate sharply: *The economy began to rev up.* **b.** to stimulate or stir up; excite. [short for *revolution*]

Rev., **1.** Revelation; Revelations. **2.** Reverend.

rev., **1.** revenue. **2.** reverse. **3.** review; reviewed. **4.** revise; revised. **5.** revision. **6.** revolution. **7.** revolving.

re•val•ue (rē val′yo͞o), *v.t.,* **-ued, -u•ing.** **1.** to revise or reestimate the value of: *to revalue the dollar.* **2.** to value again.

re•vamp (*v.* rē vamp′; *n.* rē′vamp′), *v.t.* **1.** to renovate or revise. —*n.* **2.** an act or instance of revamping. **3.** something revamped.

re•vanche (rə vanch′, -väɴsh′) also **re•vanch•ism** (-van′chiz əm, -väɴ′shiz-), *n.* the policy of a state intent on regaining areas of its original territory that have been lost to other states.

re•vanch•ist (rə van′chist, -väɴ′shist), *n.* **1.** an advocate or supporter of a political policy of revanche, esp. in order to seek vengeance for a previous military defeat. —*adj.* **2.** of or pertaining to a political policy of revanche. **3.** of or pertaining to revanchists or revanchism.

re•veal¹ (ri vēl′), *v.t.* **1.** to make known; disclose; divulge: *to reveal a secret.* **2.** to lay open to view; display; exhibit. —*n.* **3.** an act or instance of revealing; revelation; disclosure. —**re•veal′er,** *n.*

re•veal² (ri vēl′), *n.* **1.** the part of the jamb of a window or door opening between the outer wall surface and the frame. **2.** the whole jamb of an opening between the outer and inner surfaces of a wall.

revealed′ reli′gion, *n.* religion based on the revelations of God to humans, esp. as described in Scripture. Compare natural religion.

revealed′ theol′ogy, *n.* theology based on the doctrine that all religious truth is derived exclusively from the revelations of God to humans. Compare natural theology.

re•veal•ing (ri vē′ling), *adj.* **1.** giving information or insight, esp. of a striking or significant nature, about something previously concealed or private. **2.** exposing parts of the body that are usu. covered: *a revealing dress.* —**re•veal′ing•ly,** *adv.*

rev•eil•le (rev′ə lē; *Brit.* ri val′ē), *n., pl.* **-les.** **1.** a bugle call in the early morning to awaken military personnel and alert them for assembly. **2.** a signal to arise.

rev•el (rev′əl), *v.,* **-eled, -el•ing** or (*esp. Brit.*) **-elled, -el•ling,** *n.* —*v.i.* **1.** to take great pleasure or delight (usu. fol. by *in*): *to revel in luxury.* **2.** to make merry; indulge in boisterous festivities. —*n.* **3.** boisterous merrymaking or festivity; revelry. **4.** Often, **revels.** an occasion of merrymaking or noisy festivity. —**rev′el•er;** *esp. Brit.* **rev′el•ler,** *n.*

rev•e•la•tion (rev′ə lā′shən), *n.* **1.** the act of revealing or disclosing; disclosure. **2.** something revealed or disclosed, esp. a striking disclosure, as of something not before realized. **3.** *Theol.* **a.** God's disclosure of Himself and His will to His creatures. **b.** an instance of such communication or disclosure. **c.** something thus communicated or disclosed. **d.** something that contains such disclosure, as the Bible. **4.** (*cap.*) Usu., **Revelations.** Also called **The Revelation of St. John the Divine.** the last book in the New Testament; the Apocalypse.

rev•el•ry (rev′əl rē), *n., pl.* **-ries.** boisterous festivity or merrymaking.

re•venge (ri venj′), *v.,* **-venged, -veng•ing,** *n.* —*v.t.* **1.** to exact punishment or expiation for a wrong on behalf of, esp. in a vindictive spirit: *to revenge a murdered brother.* **2.** to inflict pain or harm for; take vengeance for; avenge. —*n.* **3.** the act of revenging; retaliation for injuries or wrongs; vengeance. **4.** something done in vengeance. **5.** the desire to revenge; vindictiveness. **6.** an opportunity to retaliate or gain satisfaction. —**re•veng′er,** *n.*

rev•e•nue (rev′ən yo͞o′, -ə no͞o′), *n.* **1.** the income of a government from taxation and other sources, appropriated for public expenses. **2.** the government department charged with the collection of such income. **3. revenues,** the collective items or amounts of income of a person, a state, etc. **4.** the return or yield from any kind of property, patent, service, etc.; income. **5.** an amount of money regularly coming in. **6.** a particular item or source of income.

rev′enue bond′, *n.* a bond issued, as by a municipal utility, to finance a specific project, the income from which will be used for repaying the bond.

rev′enue shar′ing, *n.* the system of disbursing part of federal tax revenues to state and local governments for their use. —**rev′e•nue-shar′ing,** *adj.*

rev′enue stamp′, *n.* a stamp showing that a governmental tax has been paid.

re•ver•ber•ant (ri vûr′bər ənt), *adj.* reverberating; reechoing. —**re•ver′ber•ant•ly,** *adv.*

re•ver•ber•ate (*v.* ri vûr′bə rāt′; *adj.* -bər it), *v.,* **-at•ed, -at•ing,** *adj.* —*v.i.* **1.** to reecho or resound. **2.** to be reflected many times, as sound waves from the walls of a confined space. **3.** to rebound or recoil. **4.** to have a lingering effect or impact. —*v.t.* **5.** to echo back or reecho (sound). **6.** to cast back or reflect (light, heat, etc.). —*adj.* **7.** reverberant. —**re•ver′ber•a′tive** (-bə rā′tiv), *adj.*

re•ver•ber•a•tion (ri vûr′bə rā′shən), *n.* **1.** a reechoed sound. **2.** the fact of being reverberated or reflected. **3.** something that is reverberated. **4.** an act or instance of reverberating.

re•vere (ri vēr′), *v.t.,* **-vered, -ver•ing.** to regard with respect tinged with awe; venerate. [< Latin *reverērī* = *re-* re- + *verērī* to stand in awe of, fear, feel reverence] —**re•ver′a•ble,** *adj.*

Re•vere (ri vēr′), *n.* **1. Paul,** 1735–1818, American silversmith and patriot. **2.** a city in E Massachusetts, on Massachusetts Bay, near Boston: seaside resort. 42,423.

rev•er•ence (rev′ər əns, rev′rəns), *n., v.,* **-enced, -enc•ing.** —*n.* **1.** a feeling or attitude of deep respect tinged with awe; veneration. **2.** the outward manifestation of this feeling: *to pay reverence.* **3.** a gesture indicative of deep respect; an obeisance, bow, or curtsy. **4.** the state of being revered. **5.** (*cap.*) a title used in addressing or mentioning a member of the clergy (usu. prec. by *Your, His,* or *Her*). —*v.t.* **6.** to regard or treat with reverence; venerate; revere. —**rev′er•enc•er,** *n.*

rev•er•end (rev′ər ənd, rev′rənd), *adj.* **1.** (*cap.*) (used as a title of respect applied or prefixed to the name of a member of the clergy or a religious order): *the Reverend Timothy Cranshaw; Reverend Mother.* **2.** worthy of being revered; entitled to reverence. **3.** pertaining to the clergy. —*n.* **4.** a member of the clergy.

rev•er•ent (rev′ər ənt, rev′rənt), *adj.* feeling, exhibiting, or characterized by reverence; deeply respectful. —**rev′er•ent•ly,** *adv.*

rev•er•en•tial (rev′ə ren′shəl), *adj.* of the nature of or characterized by reverence; reverent. —**rev′er•en′tial•ly,** *adv.*

rev•er•ie (rev′ə rē), *n.* **1.** a state of dreamy meditation or fanciful musing: *lost in reverie.* **2.** a daydream. **3.** a fantastic, or impractical idea.

re•ver•sal (ri vûr′səl), *n.* **1.** an act or instance of reversing. **2.** the state of being reversed. **3.** an adverse change of fortune; reverse. **4.** the setting aside of a decision of a lower court by a higher court.

re•verse (ri vûrs′), *adj., n., v.,* **-versed, -vers•ing.** —*adj.* **1.** opposite or contrary in position, direction, order, or character. **2.** with the back or rear part toward the observer: *the reverse side of a fabric.* **3.** pertaining to or producing movement in a mechanism opposite to that made under ordinary running conditions: *reverse gear.* **4.** acting in a manner opposite or contrary to that which is usual. **5.** of or pertaining to an image like that seen in a mirror; backward; reversed. —*n.* **6.** the opposite or contrary of something. **7.** the back or rear of anything. **8.** the side of a coin, medal, etc., that does not bear the principal design (opposed to *obverse*). **9.** an adverse change of fortune; a misfortune, check, or defeat. **10. a.** the condition of being reversed: *to put an engine into reverse.* **b.** a reversing mechanism. **11.** printed matter in which areas that normally appear as white are black, and vice versa. —*v.t.* **12.** to turn in an opposite position; transpose. **13.** to turn in the opposite direction; send on the opposite course. **14.** to turn in the opposite order. **15.** to turn inside out or upside down. **16.** to change the direction of running of (a mechanism). **17.** to revoke or annul (a decree, judgment, etc.): *to reverse a verdict.* **18.** to alter to the opposite in character or tendency; change completely. **19.** to have (the charges for a telephone call) billed to the recipient. —*v.i.* **20.** to shift into reverse gear. **21.** (of a mechanism) to be reversed. **22.** to turn or move in the opposite or contrary direction. —**re•verse′ly,** *adv.*

reverse′ annu′ity mort′gage, *n.* a type of home mortgage under which an elderly homeowner is allowed a long-term loan in the form of monthly payments against his or her paid-off equity as collateral, repayable when the home is eventually sold. *Abbr.:* RAM Also called **equity conversion, reverse mortgage.**

reverse′ discrimina′tion, *n.* discrimination against white persons or males resulting from preferential policies intended to remedy past discrimination against minorities or females.

reverse′-engineer′, *v.t.* to study or analyze (a device) to learn details of design, construction, and operation, as to produce a copy or an improved version.

reverse′ mort′gage, *n.* REVERSE ANNUITY MORTGAGE.

reverse′ osmo′sis, *n.* a process in which pure water is produced by forcing waste or saline water through a semipermeable membrane.

reverse′ psychol′ogy, *n.* a method of getting another person to do what one wants by pretending not to want it or to want something else.

re•vers•i•ble (ri vûr′sə bəl), *adj.* **1.** capable of reversing or of being reversed. **2.** capable of reestablishing the original condition after a change by a reversing the change. **3.** constructed so that both sides can be exposed: *a reversible jacket.* **4.** (of a chemical reaction) capable of proceeding in either of two directions. —*n.* **5.** a garment that can be worn with either side exposed. —**re•vers′i•bil′i•ty,** *n.*

re•ver•sion (ri vûr′zhən, -shən), *n.* **1.** return to a former practice, belief, condition, etc. **2.** the act of reversing or the state of being reversed; reversal. **3. a.** reappearance of ancestral characteristics that have been absent in intervening generations. **b.** return to an earlier or primitive type; atavism. **4.** the returning of an estate, property, etc., to the grantor at the expiration of a grant.

re•vert (ri vûrt′), *v.i.* **1.** to return to a former habit, practice, belief, condition, etc. **2.** to return to the former owner or that person's heirs. **3.** to return to an ancestral type or characteristic. **4.** to go back in thought or discussion. —*n.* **5.** a person or thing that reverts.

re•view (ri vyōō′), *n.* **1.** a critical article or report, as in a periodical, on a book, play, performance, etc.; critique. **2.** the process of going over a subject again in study or recitation in order to fix it in the memory or summarize the facts. **3.** an exercise designed for study of this kind. **4.** a general survey, esp. in words; report or account. **5.** an inspection or examination, esp. a formal inspection of a military or naval force, parade, etc. **6.** a periodical containing articles on current affairs, books, art, etc. **7.** a judicial reexamination, as by a higher court, of the decision or proceedings in a case. **8.** a second or repeated view of something. **9.** a viewing of the past; consideration of past events, circumstances, or facts. **10.** REVUE. —*v.t.* **11.** to go over (lessons, studies, work, etc.) in review. **12.** to view or look over again. **13.** to inspect, esp. formally or officially: *to review the troops.* **14.** to survey mentally; examine: *to review the situation.* **15.** to discuss (a book, play, etc.) in a critical review. **16.** to look back upon; view retrospectively. **17.** to present a survey of in speech or writing. **18.** to reexamine judicially: *to review a case.* —*v.i.* **19.** to go over or restudy material, as in preparation for a test. **20.** to review books, movies, etc., as for a newspaper or magazine. —**re•view′a•ble,** *adj.*

re•view•er (ri vyōō′ər), *n.* a person who reviews, esp. one who reviews books, plays, etc.

re•vile (ri vīl′), *v.,* **-viled, -vil•ing.** —*v.t.* **1.** to address or speak of with contemptuous, abusive, or opprobrious language. —*v.i.* **2.** to speak abusively. —**re•vil′ing•ly,** *adv.*

re•vise (ri vīz′), *v.,* **-vised, -vis•ing,** *n.* —*v.t.* **1.** to amend or alter: *to revise an opinion.* **2.** to alter something written or printed, in order to make corrections, improve, or update: *to revise a manuscript.* —*n.* **3.** an act of revising. **4.** a revised form of something. **5.** a printing proof taken after alterations have been made, for further examination or correction. —**re•vis′a•ble, re•vis′i•ble,** *adj.* —**re•vis′er, re•vi′sor,** *n.*

Revised′ Stand′ard Ver′sion, *n.* a revision of the Bible, based on the AMERICAN REVISED VERSION and the KING JAMES VERSION, prepared by American scholars and published in its completed form in 1952.

Revised′ Ver′sion, *n.* a recension of the KING JAMES VERSION, prepared by British and American scholars. The New Testament was published in 1881, and the Old Testament in 1885.

Revised′ Ver′sion of the Bi′ble, *n.* a recension of the Authorized Version, prepared by British and American scholars, the Old Testament being published in 1885, and the New Testament in 1881. Also called **Revised′ Ver′sion.**

re•vi•sion (ri vizh′ən), *n.* **1.** the act or work of revising. **2.** a process of revising. **3.** a revised form or version, as of a book. —**re•vi′sion•al, re•vi′sion•ar′y,** *adj.*

re•vi•sion•ism (ri vizh′ə niz′əm), *n.* **1.** advocacy or approval of revision. **2.** any departure from Marxist doctrine, theory, or practice, esp. favoring reform above revolutionary change. **3.** a departure from any authoritative or generally accepted doctrine, theory, practice, etc.

re•vi•tal•ize (rē vīt′l īz′), *v.t.,* **-ized, -iz•ing.** to give new life, vitality, or vigor to. —**re•vi′tal•i•za′tion,** *n.*

re•viv•al (ri vī′vəl), *n.* **1.** restoration to life, consciousness, vigor, or strength. **2.** restoration to use, acceptance, or currency: *the revival of old customs.* **3.** a new production of an old play. **4.** a showing of an old motion picture. **5.** a reawakening of interest in and care for religion. **6.** an evangelistic service or a series of services for the purpose of effecting a religious awakening. **7.** the act of reviving. **8.** the state of being revived. **9.** the reestablishment of legal force and effect.

re•viv•al•ist (ri vī′və list), *n.* **1.** a person, esp. a member of the clergy, who promotes or holds religious revivals. **2.** a person who revives former customs, methods, etc. —**re•viv′al•is′tic,** *adj.*

re•vive (ri vīv′), *v.,* **-vived, -viv•ing.** —*v.t.* **1.** to activate, set in motion, or take up again; renew. **2.** to restore to life or consciousness. **3.** to put on or show (an old play or motion picture) again. **4.** to make operative or valid again. **5.** to bring back into notice, use, or currency: *to revive an old word.* **6.** to renew in the mind; recall. **7.** to reanimate or cheer. —*v.i.* **8.** to return to life, consciousness, vigor, strength, or a flourishing condition. **9.** to be quickened, restored, or renewed. **10.** to become operative or valid again. —**re•viv′a•ble,** *adj.*

rev•o•ca•ble (rev′ə kə bəl *or, often,* ri vō′-) also **re•vok•a•ble** (ri vō′kə bəl, rev′ə-), *adj.* capable of being revoked. —**rev′o•ca•bil′i•ty, rev′o•ca•ble•ness,** *n.* —**rev′o•ca•bly,** *adv.*

rev•o•ca•tion (rev′ə kā′shən), *n.* the act of revoking; annulment. —**rev•o•ca•tive** (rev′ə kā′tiv, ri vok′ə-), *adj.*

re•voke (ri vōk′), *v.,* **-voked, -vok•ing,** *n.* —*v.t.* **1.** to take back or withdraw; annul or cancel: *to revoke a license.* **2.** to bring or summon back. —*v.i.* **3.** to fail to follow suit in a card game when possible and required; renege. —*n.* **4.** an act or instance of revoking.

re•volt (ri vōlt′), *v.i.* **1.** to break away from or rise against constituted authority, as by open rebellion; rebel: *to revolt against the government.* **2.** to refuse to accept or be subjected to some authority, condition, etc. **3.** to turn away in mental rebellion, disgust, or abhorrence: *to revolt from eating meat.* **4.** to feel horror or aversion. —*v.t.* **5.** to affect with disgust or abhorrence. —*n.* **6.** an act of revolting; insurrection or rebellion. **7.** an expression or movement of spirited protest or dissent.

re•volt•ing (ri vōl′ting), *adj.* **1.** disgusting; repulsive. **2.** rebellious.

rev•o•lu•tion (rev′ə lōō′shən), *n.* **1.** a complete and forcible overthrow and replacement of an established government or political system by the people governed. **2.** a sudden, complete, or radical change in something: *a revolution in church architecture; a social revolution caused by automation.* **3. a.** a procedure or course, as if in a circuit, back to a starting point. **b.** a single turn of this kind. **4. a.** a turning round or rotating, as on an axis. **b.** a moving in a circular or curving course, as about a central point. **c.** a single cycle in such a course. **5. a.** the orbiting of one heavenly body around another. **b.** (not in technical use) the rotation of a heavenly body on its axis. **c.** a single course of such movement. **6.** a cycle of events in time or in a recurring period of time.

rev•o•lu•tion•ar•y (rev′ə lōō′shə ner′ē), *adj., n., pl.* **-ar•ies.** —*adj.* **1.** pertaining to or of the nature of a revolution. **2.** productive of or characterized by radical change, **3.** (*cap.*) of or pertaining to the American Revolution or to the period contemporaneous with it. —*n.* **4.** Also, **rev′o•lu′tion•ist.** a person who advocates or takes part in a revolution.

revolu′tionary prax′is *n.* the practical actions required to overthrow an existing political system.

Revolu′tionary War′, *n.* AMERICAN REVOLUTION.

rev•o•lu•tion•ize (rev′ə lōō′shə nīz′), *v.t.,* **-ized, -iz•ing. 1.** to bring about a revolution in; effect a radical change in. **2.** to subject to a political revolution. —**rev′o•lu′tion•iz′er,** *n.*

revolu′tion of ris′ing expecta′tions, *n.* expectations of a higher standard of living based on optimism about a society's resources or perception of its affluence.

re•volve (ri volv′), *v.,* **-volved, -volv•ing.** —*v.i.* **1.** to move in a circular or curving course or orbit: *The earth revolves around the sun.* **2.** to turn or rotate, as on an axis: *The wheel revolved slowly.* **3.** to focus or center on. **4.** to proceed or occur in a round or cycle; recur. **5.** to be turned over in the mind. —*v.t.* **6.** to cause to turn around, as on an axis. **7.** to cause to move in a circular or curving course, as about a central point. **8.** to turn over in the mind; consider.

re•volv•er (ri vol′vər), *n.* **1.** a handgun having a revolving chambered cylinder for holding a number of cartridges, which may be discharged in succession without reloading. **2.** a person or thing that revolves.

revolv′ing cred′it, *n.* credit automatically available up to a predetermined limit while payments are periodically made.

revolv′ing door′, *n.* an entrance door to a building consisting of four rigid leaves in the form of a cross rotating about a central vertical pivot in the doorway, designed to keep out drafts.

re·volv'ing-door', *adj.* **1.** (of a company, institution, or organization) having a high turnover of employees, members, patients, etc. **2.** of or pertaining to a practice in which government officials return to positions in private companies that do business with the government.

re·vue or **re·view** (ri vyōō'), *n.* **1.** a form of theatrical entertainment in which recent events, popular fads, etc., are parodied. **2.** any entertainment featuring skits, dances, and songs.

re·vul·sion (ri vul'shən), *n.* **1.** a strong feeling of repugnance, distaste, or dislike; disgust; loathing. **2.** a sudden and violent change of feeling or response in sentiment, taste, etc. **3.** the act of drawing something back or away.

re·ward (ri wôrd'), *n.* **1.** a sum of money offered for the detection or capture of a criminal, the recovery of lost property, etc. **2.** something given or received in return or recompense for services rendered, merit, hardship, etc. —*v.t.* **3.** to recompense or requite (a person or animal) for service, merit, achievement, etc. **4.** to make return for or requite (service, merit, etc.); recompense.

re·ward·ing (ri wôr'ding), *adj.* **1.** affording satisfaction or valuable experience; gratifying; worthwhile. **2.** affording material gain; profitable. —**re·ward'ing·ly**, *adv.*

re·wind (*v.* rē wīnd'; *n.* rē'wīnd'), *v.*, **-wound, -wind·ing,** *n.* —*v.t., v.i.* **1.** to wind again. **2.** to wind back to or toward the beginning; reverse. —*n.* **3.** an act or instance of rewinding. **4.** a function or mechanism of a tape recorder, camera, etc., that causes tape or film to wind backward. —**re·wind'er**, *n.*

re·wire (rē wīr'), *v.*, **-wired, -wir·ing.** —*v.t.* **1.** to provide with new wiring: *to rewire a house.* —*v.i.* **2.** to install new wiring. —**re·wir'a·ble**, *adj.*

re·word (rē wûrd'), *v.t.* **1.** to put into other words: *to reword a contract.* **2.** to express in the same words; repeat.

re·work (*v.* rē wûrk'; *n.* rē'wûrk'), *v.*, **-worked** or **-wrought, -work·ing,** *n.* —*v.t.* **1.** to work or form again: *to rework gold.* **2.** to revise or rewrite: *to rework an essay.* **3.** to process again or anew for reuse: *to rework wool.* —*n.* **4.** an act or instance of reworking: *merely a rework of an earlier novel.*

re·write (*v.* rē rīt'; *n.* rē'rīt'), *v.*, **-wrote, -writ·ten, -writ·ing,** *n.* —*v.t.* **1.** to write in a different form or manner; revise. **2.** to write again. **3.** to write (news submitted by a reporter) for inclusion in a newspaper. —*n.* **4.** the news story rewritten. **5.** something written in a different form or manner; revision. —**re·writ'er**, *n.*

rex (reks; *Eng.* reks), *n., pl.* **re·ges** (rē'gēs; *Eng.* rē'jēz). *Latin.* king.

Reye's' syn'drome (rīz, rāz), *n.* a rare disorder occurring primarily in children after a viral illness and associated with aspirin usage, characterized by vomiting, swelling of the brain, and liver dysfunction.

Rey·kja·vik (rā'kyə vik, -vēk'), *n.* the capital of Iceland, on the SW coast. 93,245.

Reyn·olds (ren'ldz), *n.* **Sir Joshua,** 1723–92, English painter.

Re·zin (rē'zin), *n.* the last king of Syria, an ally of Pekah. II Kings 15:37; 16:5–9; Is. 7:4.

re·zone (*v.* rē zōn'; *n. also* rē'zōn'), *v.*, **-zoned, -zon·ing,** *n.* —*v.t.* **1.** to reclassify (a property, neighborhood, etc.) as belonging to a different zone or being subject to different zoning restrictions. —*n.* **2.** an act or instance of rezoning.

R factor, *n.* a genetic component of some bacteria that provides resistance to antibiotics and can be transferred from one bacterium to another by conjugation. [r(*esistance) factor*]

RFD or **R.F.D.,** rural free delivery.

Rh, RH FACTOR.

Rh, *Chem. Symbol.* rhodium.

rhab·do·vi·rus (rab'dō vī'rəs), *n., pl.* **-rus·es.** any of numerous bullet-shaped or oblong RNA-containing viruses, of the family Rhabdoviridae, that have spikes protruding from their envelope: includes the virus that causes rabies.

rhap·sod·ic (rap sod'ik) also **rhap·sod'i·cal,** *adj.* **1.** extravagantly enthusiastic; ecstatic. **2.** pertaining to, characteristic of, or of the nature or form of rhapsody. —**rhap·sod'i·cal·ly**, *adv.*

rhap·so·dize (rap'sə dīz'), *v.*, **-dized, -diz·ing.** —*v.i.* **1.** to talk with extravagant enthusiasm. **2.** to speak or write rhapsodies. —*v.t.* **3.** to recite as a rhapsody.

rhap·so·dy (rap'sə dē), *n., pl.* **-dies. 1.** a musical composition irregular in form and suggestive of improvisation. **2.** an ecstatic expression of feeling or enthusiasm. **3.** an epic poem, or a part of such a poem. **4.** an unusually intense, emotional literary work or discourse.

rhe·a (rē'ə), *n., pl.* **rhe·as.** either of two ostrichlike birds, *Rhea americana* or *Pterocnemia pennata,* of South America.

rhe·bok (rē'bok), *n., pl.* **-boks,** (*esp. collectively*) **-bok.** a large deerlike South African antelope, *Pelea capreolus,* with pale gray, curly fur and straight horns.

Rheims (rēmz; *Fr.* RANS), *n.* REIMS.

Rhein (*Ger.* rīn), *n.* RHINE.

rhe·ni·um (rē'nē əm), *n.* a rare metallic element of the manganese subgroup: used, because of its high melting point, in platinum-rhenium thermocouples. *Symbol:* Re; *at. no.:* 75; *at. wt.:* 186.2.

Rhe'sus fac'tor (rē'səs), *n.* RH FACTOR.

rhe'sus mon'key (rē'səs), *n.* a macaque, *Macaca mulatta,* of India, used in biological and medical research. Also called **rhe'sus.**

rhet·o·ric (ret'ər ik), *n.* **1. a.** the art of effectively using language in speech or writing, including the use of figures of speech. **b.** language skillfully used. **2.** the undue use of exaggerated language. **3.** the art of prose writing. **4.** the art of persuasive speaking; oratory.

rhe·tor·i·cal (ri tôr'i kəl, -tor'-), *adj.* **1.** used for mere style or effect. **2.** marked by or tending to use bombast. **3.** of, concerned with, or having the nature of rhetoric. —**rhe·tor'i·cal·ly**, *adv.*

rhetor'ical ques'tion, *n.* a question asked solely for effect and not to elicit a reply, as "What is so rare as a day in June?"

rheum (rōōm), *n.* **1.** a thin discharge of the mucous membranes, esp. during a cold. **2.** catarrh; cold. —**rheum'ic**, *adj.*

rheu·mat·ic (rōō mat'ik), *adj.* **1.** pertaining to or of the nature of rheumatism. **2.** affected with or subject to rheumatism. —*n.* **3.** a person affected with rheumatism. —**rheu·mat'i·cal·ly**, *adv.*

rheumat'ic fe'ver, *n.* an acute complication of certain streptococcal infections, usu. affecting children, characterized by fever, arthritis, chorea, and heart disturbances.

rheu·ma·tism (rōō'mə tiz'əm), *n.* **1.** disorder characterized by pain and stiffness in the joints or muscles. **2.** RHEUMATIC FEVER.

rheu'matoid arthri'tis, *n.* a chronic autoimmune disease characterized by inflammation and progressive deformity of the joints.

Rh factor (är'āch'), *n.* any of a group of antigens present on the surface of red blood cells, those having inherited such antigens being designated Rh + (**Rh positive**) and those lacking them, a much smaller group, being designated Rh − (**Rh negative**): transfused or fetal Rh + blood may induce a severe reaction in an Rh − individual. [so called because first found in the blood of rhesus monkeys]

Rhine (rīn), *n.* a river flowing from SE Switzerland through Germany and the Netherlands into the North Sea. 820 mi. (1320 km) long. German, **Rhein.** French, **Rhin** (RAN). Dutch, **Rijn.**

rhine·stone (rīn'stōn'), *n.* an artificial gemstone cut from rock crystal or various kinds of brilliant glass or paste, esp. in imitation of a diamond. —**rhine'stoned'**, *adj.*

Rhine' wine', *n.* **1.** a dry white wine of the Rhine valley. **2.** a similar wine produced elsewhere.

rhi·ni·tis (rī nī'tis), *n.* inflammation of the nose or its mucous membrane.

rhi·no (rī'nō), *n., pl.* **-nos,** (*esp. collectively*) **-no.** a rhinoceros.

rhino-, a combining form meaning "nose": *rhinology.* Also, *esp. before a vowel,* **rhin-.**

rhi·noc·er·os (rī nos'ər əs), *n., pl.* **-os·es,** (*esp. collectively*) **-os.** any of several large, thick-skinned, plant-eating mammals of the family Rhinocerotidae, of Africa and S and SE parts of Asia, with one or two upright horns on the snout.

Indian rhinoceros,
Rhinoceros unicornis,
5 1/2 ft. (1.7 m) high at shoulder;
horn to 2 ft. (0.6 m);
head and body 10 ft. (3 m);
tail 2 ft. (0.6 m)

rhinoc'eros bee'tle, *n.* any of several scarabaeid beetles, esp. of the genus *Dynastes,* which comprises the largest beetles, characterized by one or more horns on the head and prothorax.

rhi·no·plas·ty (rī'nə plas'tē), *n., pl.* **-ties.** plastic surgery of the nose. —**rhi/no·plas'tic,** *adj.*

rhi·no·vi·rus (rī'nō vī'rəs, rī'nō vī'-), *n., pl.* **-rus·es.** any of a varied and widespread group of picornaviruses responsible for many respiratory diseases, including the common cold.

rhizo-, a combining form meaning "root": *rhizogenic.*

rhi·zome (rī'zōm), *n.* a rootlike underground stem, commonly horizontal in position, that usu. produces roots below and sends up shoots progressively from the upper surface. —**rhi·zom'a·tous** (-zom'ə təs, -zō'mə-), *adj.*

rhi·zo·pod (rī'zə pod'), *n.* any of numerous protozoans of the subphylum (or superclass) Rhizopoda, characterized by locomotion with a pseudopod: comprises most members of the phylum Sarcodina, including the amebas and foraminifers. —**rhi·zop'o·dan** (-zop'ə dn), *adj., n.*

Rh negative (är'āch'), *adj.* See under RH FACTOR.

Rho·da (rō'də), *n.* a girl in the household of Mary, mother of Mark. Acts 12:13.

Rhode' Is'land (rōd), *n.* a state of the NE United States, on the Atlantic coast: a part of New England. 990,225; 1214 sq. mi. (3145 sq. km). *Cap.:* Providence. *Abbr.:* RI, R.I. —**Rhode' Is'lander,** *n.*

Rhodes (rōdz), *n.* **1. Cecil John,** 1853–1902, English capitalist and administrator in S Africa. **2.** Greek, **Rhodos. a.** a Greek island in the SE Aegean, off the SW coast of Turkey: largest Dodecanese Island. 66,606; 542 sq. mi. (1404 sq. km). **b.** a seaport on Rhodes. 32,019.

Rho·de·sia (rō dē'zhə), *n.* **1.** a historical region in S Africa that comprised the British territories of Northern Rhodesia (now Zambia) and

Southern Rhodesia (now Zimbabwe). **2.** a former name (1964–80) of Zimbabwe (def. 1). —**Rho·de′sian,** *adj.*, *n.*

Rhodes′ schol′arship, *n.* one of a number of scholarships at Oxford University, established by the will of Cecil Rhodes, for selected students (**Rhodes′ schol′ars**) from the British Commonwealth and the U.S.

rho·di·um (rō′dē əm), *n.* a silvery white metallic element of the platinum family, forming salts that give rose-colored solutions: used to electroplate metals to prevent corrosion. *Symbol:* Rh; *at. wt.:* 102.905; *at. no.:* 45; *sp. gr.:* 12.5 at 20°C.

rhodo-, a combining form meaning "rose": *rhodolite.* Also, *esp. before a vowel*, **rhod-.**

rho·do·den·dron (rō′də den′drən), *n.* any evergreen or deciduous shrub or tree belonging to the genus *Rhododendron*, of the heath family, having rounded clusters of showy pink, purple, or white flowers and oval or oblong leaves.

rho·do·ra (rō dôr′ə, -dōr′ə, rə-), *n.*, *pl.* **-ras.** a low North American shrub, *Rhododendron canadense*, of the heath family, having rose-colored flowers that appear before the leaves.

rhom·bic (rom′bik) also **rhom′bi·cal,** *adj.* **1.** having the form of a rhombus. **2.** having a rhombus as base or cross section. **3.** bounded by rhombuses, as a solid.

rhom·boid (rom′boid), *n.* **1.** an oblique-angled parallelogram with only the opposite sides equal. —*adj.* **2.** Also, **rhom·boi′dal.** having a form like or similar to that of a rhombus; shaped like a rhomboid.

rhom·bus (rom′bəs), *n.*, *pl.* **-bus·es, -bi** (-bī). an equilateral parallelogram having oblique angles.

Rh positive (är′āch′), *adj.* See under Rh FACTOR.

rhu·barb (rōō′bärb), *n.* **1.** any of several plants belonging to the genus *Rheum*, of the buckwheat family, as *R. officinale*, having a medicinal rhizome, and *R. rhabarbarum*, having edible leafstalks. **2.** the edible fleshy leafstalks of *R. rhabarbarum*, used in making pies, preserves, etc. **3.** *Slang.* a quarrel or squabble.

rhumb (rum, rumb), *n.* **1.** RHUMB LINE. **2.** a point of the compass.

rhumb′ line′, *n.* the path of a ship that maintains a constant compass direction.

rhyme (rīm), *n.*, *v.*, **rhymed, rhym·ing.** —*n.* **1.** identity in sound of some part, esp. the end, of words or lines of verse. **2.** a word agreeing with another in terminal sound: Find *is a rhyme for* mind *and* kind. **3.** verse or poetry having correspondence in the terminal sounds of the lines. **4.** a poem or piece of verse having such correspondence. —*v.t.* **5.** to treat in rhyme, as a subject; turn into rhyme, as something in prose. **6.** to compose (verse or the like) in metrical form with rhymes. **7.** to use (a word) as a rhyme to another word; use (words) as rhymes. —*v.i.* **8.** to make rhyme or verse. **9.** to use rhyme in writing verse. **10.** to form a rhyme, as one word or line with another. **11.** to be composed in metrical form with rhymes, as verse. —*Idiom.* **12. rhyme or reason,** logic, sense, or method (usu. used negatively): They ran off without rhyme or reason.

rhyn·cho·ce·pha·lian (ring′kō sə fāl′yən, -fā′lē ən), *adj.* **1.** belonging or pertaining to the Rhynchocephalia, an order of lizardlike reptiles. —*n.* **2.** a rhynchocephalian reptile.

rhythm (rith′əm), *n.* **1.** movement or procedure with uniform or patterned recurrence of a beat, accent, or the like. **2. a.** the pattern of regular and weak melodic and harmonic beats. **b.** a particular form of this: *triple rhythm.* **c.** RHYTHM SECTION. **3.** measured movement, as in dancing. **4.** the pattern of recurrent strong and weak accents, long and short syllables, and vocalization and silence in speech. *Pros.* **a.** metrical or rhythmical form; meter. **b.** metrical movement. **6.** a patterned repetition of a motif, formal element, etc., at regular or irregular intervals in the same or a modified form. **7.** *Physiol.* the regular recurrence of an action or function, as of the beat of the heart or the menstrual cycle. **8.** the regular recurrence of particular phases, elements, etc. **9.** the regular recurrence of related elements in a progression or other system of motion: *the importance of rhythm in film editing.* —**rhyth′mic** (-mik), **rhyth′mi·cal,** *adj.* —**rhyth′mi·cal·ly,** *adv.*

rhythm′ and blues′, *n.* a folk-based form of black popular music forerunning rock.

rhythm′ meth′od, *n.* a method of birth control by abstaining from sexual intercourse when ovulation is most likely to occur.

rhythm′ sec′tion, *n.* the group of band instruments, as drums and bass, that supplies musical rhythm.

RI or **R.I.,** Rhode Island.

ri·al¹ (rē ôl′, -äl′), *n.* the basic monetary unit of Iran, Oman, and the Republic of Yemen.

ri·al² (rē ôl′, -äl′), *n.* RIYAL.

ri·al·to (rē al′tō), *n.*, *pl.* **-tos.** an exchange or mart.

rib¹ (rib), *n.*, *v.*, **ribbed, rib·bing.** —*n.* **1.** one of a series of curved bones that are articulated with the vertebrae and occur in pairs, 12 in humans, on each side of the vertebrate body, certain pairs being connected with the sternum and forming the thoracic wall. **2.** a cut of meat containing a rib. **3.** ribs, SPARERIBS. **4. a.** one of several archlike members of a vault supporting it at the groins and defining its distinct surfaces. **b.** one of several ornamental projecting bands or moldings on the surface of a vault or ceiling dividing the surface into panels. **5.** something resembling a rib in form, position, or use, as a supporting part: *the ribs of an umbrella.* **6.** any of the curved framing members in a ship's hull that rise upward and outward from the keel; frame. **7.** a pri-

mary vein of a leaf. **8.** a vertical ridge in cloth, esp. in knitted fabrics. **9.** a wife (in allusion to the creation of Eve. Gen. 2:21–22). —*v.t.* **10.** to furnish or strengthen with ribs. **11.** to enclose as with ribs. **12.** to mark with riblike ridges.

rib² (rib), *v.t.*, **ribbed, rib·bing.** to tease; make fun of.

rib·ald (rib′əld; *spelling pron.* rī′bəld), *adj.* **1.** vulgar or indecent in speech, language, etc.; coarsely mocking or irreverent. —*n.* **2.** a ribald person. —**rib′ald·ly,** *adv.*

rib·bing (rib′ing), *n.* **1.** ribs collectively. **2.** an assemblage or arrangement of ribs, as in cloth or a ship.

rib·bon (rib′ən), *n.* **1.** a woven strip or band of fine material, used for ornament, tying, etc. **2.** material in such strips. **3.** anything resembling a ribbon. **4. ribbons,** torn or ragged strips; shreds: *torn to ribbons.* **5.** a band of inked material, as used in a typewriter. **6.** a strip of material, as satin or rayon, being or representing a medal or similar decoration, esp. a military one. **7.** a long, thin, flexible band of metal, as for a spring, a band saw, or a tapeline. **8.** *Carpentry.* a thin horizontal piece let into studding to support the ends of joists. —*v.t.* **9.** to adorn with ribbon. **10.** to mark with something suggesting ribbons. **11.** to separate into ribbonlike strips. —*v.i.* **12.** to form in ribbonlike strips.

rib′bon snake′, *n.* either of two long-tailed garter snakes, *Thamnophis proximus* or *T. sauritus*, of E and central North America, having a brownish body and yellow or orange stripes.

rib′ cage′, *n.* the enclosure formed by the ribs and connecting bones.

rib′-knit′, *adj.* **1.** (of a knitted garment or fabric) having a pattern of ribs. —*n.* **2.** Also, **ribbed-knit.** a garment with such a pattern.

ri·bo·fla·vin (rī′bō flā′vin, rī′bō flā′-, -bə-), *n.* a vitamin B complex factor essential for growth, occurring as a yellow crystalline compound, $C_{17}H_{20}N_4O_6$, abundant in milk, meat, eggs, and leafy vegetables and produced synthetically. Also called **vitamin B₂.**

ri·bo·nu·cle′ic ac′id (rī′bō nōō klē′ik, -klā′-, -nyōō-, rī′-), *n.* See RNA.

ri·bose (rī′bōs), *n.* a white, crystalline, water-soluble, slightly sweet solid, $C_5H_{10}O_5$, a pentose sugar obtained by the hydrolysis of RNA.

ribosomal RNA, *n.* a type of RNA, distinguished by its length and abundance, that functions in protein synthesis as a component of ribosomes. *Abbr.:* rRNA

Ri·car·do (ri kär′dō), *n.* **David,** 1772–1823, English economist.

rice (rīs), *n.*, *v.*, **riced, ric·ing.** —*n.* **1.** the starchy seeds or grain of an annual marsh grass, *Oryza sativa*, cultivated in warm climates and used for food. **2.** the grass itself. —*v.t.* **3.** to reduce to a form resembling rice: *to rice potatoes.*

rice′ pa′per, *n.* **1.** a thin paper made from the straw of rice, as in China. **2.** a Chinese paper consisting of the pith of certain plants cut and pressed into thin sheets.

ric·er (rī′sər), *n.* an implement for ricing cooked potatoes, squash, etc., by pressing them through small holes.

rich (rich), *adj.*, **-er, -est,** *n.* —*adj.* **1.** having wealth or great possessions; abundantly supplied with resources, means, or funds. **2.** abounding in natural resources: *a rich territory.* **3.** abounding (usu. fol. by *in* or *with*): *rich in beauty.* **4.** of great value or worth: *a rich harvest.* **5.** delectably and perhaps unhealthfully spicy, or sweet and abounding in butter or cream: *a rich gravy; a rich pastry.* **6.** costly, expensively elegant, or fine, as dress or jewels. **7.** made of valuable materials or with elaborate workmanship, as buildings or furniture. **8.** (of color) deep, strong, or vivid. **9.** full and mellow in tone: *a rich voice.* **10.** strongly fragrant; pungent: *a rich odor.* **11.** producing or yielding abundantly: *a rich soil.* **12.** abundant, plentiful, or ample: *a rich supply.* **13.** (of a mixture in a fuel system) having a relatively high ratio of fuel to air (contrasted with *lean*). **14.** *Informal.* **a.** highly amusing. **b.** ridiculous; absurd. —*n.* **15. the rich,** rich persons collectively. —**rich′ly,** *adv.*

Rich·ard (rich′ərd), *n.* **1. Richard I** ("Richard the Lion-Hearted," "Richard Coeur de Lion"), 1157–99, king of England 1189–99. **2. Richard II,** 1367–1400, king of England 1377–99 (son of Edward, Prince of Wales). **3. Richard III** (*Duke of Gloucester*), 1452–85, king of England 1483–85.

Rich′ard Roe′ (rō), *n.* a fictitious name for the second male of unknown identity in legal proceedings, the first being John Doe.

Rich·ard·son (rich′ərd sən), *n.* **1. Henry Hobson,** 1838–86, U.S. architect. **2. Samuel,** 1689–1761, English novelist.

Rich·e·lieu (rish′ə lōō′; *Fr.* Rēsh• lyœ′), *n.* **1. Armand Jean du Plessis** (zhäɴ), **Duc de,** 1585–1642, French cardinal and statesman. **2.** a river in SE Canada, in Quebec, flowing N from Lake Champlain to the St. Lawrence. 210 mi. (340 km) long.

rich·es (rich′iz), *n.pl.* abundant and valuable possessions; wealth.

Rich′ Fool′, The, a parable of Jesus. Luke 12:13–21.

Rich·mond (rich′mənd), *n.* **1.** former name of STATEN ISLAND (def. 2). **2.** the capital of Virginia, in the E part on the James River: capital of the Confederacy 1861–65. 201,108. **3.** Also called **Rich′mond-upon′-Thames′.** a borough of Greater London, England, on the Thames River. 163,000. **4.** a seaport in W California, on San Francisco Bay. 81,220.

Rich′ter scale′, *n.* a logarithmic scale, ranging from 1 to 10, for indicating the intensity of an earthquake. [after C. F. *Richter* (1900–85), U.S. seismologist]

Rick·en·back·er (rik′ən bak′ər), *n.* **Edward Vernon** (*"Eddie"*), 1890–1973, U.S. aviator and aviation executive.

rick·ets (rik′its), *n.* (*used with a sing. v.*) a childhood disease in which the bones soften from an inadequate intake of vitamin D and insufficient exposure to sunlight.

rick•ett•si•a (ri ket′sē ə), *n., pl.* **-si•as, -si•ae** (-sē ē′). any of various rod-shaped infectious microorganisms of the heterogeneous group Rickettsieae: parasitic in fleas, ticks, mites, or lice and transmitted by bite. —**rick•ett′si•al,** *adj.*

rick•et•y (rik′i tē), *adj.,* **-et•i•er, -et•i•est. 1.** likely to fall or collapse; shaky: *a rickety chair.* **2.** feeble in the joints; tottering: *a rickety old man.* **3.** old, dilapidated, or in disrepair. **4.** irregular, as motion or action. **5.** affected with rickets. **6.** pertaining to or of the nature of rickets.

Rick•o•ver (rik′ō vər), *n.* **Hyman George,** 1900–86, U.S. naval officer, born in Poland: helped to develop the nuclear submarine.

rick•sha or **rick•shaw** (rik′shô, -shä), *n., pl.* **-shas** or **-shaws.** JINRIKISHA.

RICO (rē′kō), *n.* Racketeer Influenced and Corrupt Organizations Act: a U.S. law, enacted in 1970, allowing victims of organized crime to sue those responsible for punitive damages.

ric•o•chet (rik′ə shā′, rik′ə shā′; *esp. Brit.* rik′ə shet′), *n., v.,* **-cheted** (-shād′, -shād′), **-chet•ing** (-shā′ing, -shā′ing) or (*esp. Brit.*) **-chet•ted** (-shet′id), **-chet•ting** (-shet′ing). —*n.* **1.** the rebound or skip of an object or projectile after it hits a glancing blow against a surface. —*v.i.* **2.** to move in this way, as a projectile.

ri•cot•ta (ri kot′ə, -kô′tə), *n.* a soft Italian cheese that resembles cottage cheese, made from the whey of milk.

rid (rid), *v.t.,* **rid** or **rid•ded, rid•ding. 1.** to free, disencumber, or relieve of something objectionable: *to rid the house of mice; to rid the mind of doubt.* —***Idiom.*** **2. be** or **get rid of,** to be or become free of.

rid•a•ble or **ride•a•ble** (rī′də bəl), *adj.* **1.** capable of being ridden, as a horse. **2.** capable of being ridden over, through, etc., as a road or a stream. —**rid′a•bil′i•ty,** *n.*

rid•dance (rid′ns), *n.* **1.** the act or fact of clearing away or out, as anything undesirable. **2.** relief or deliverance from something. —***Idiom.*** **3. good riddance,** (used to express relief at deliverance from something): *They're gone, and good riddance!*

rid•den (rid′n), *v.* a pp. of RIDE.

-ridden, a combining form meaning "obsessed with," "overwhelmed by" (*torment-ridden*) or "full of," "burdened with" (*debt-ridden*).

rid•dle¹ (rid′l), *n., v.,* **-dled, -dling.** —*n.* **1.** a question framed so as to exercise one's ingenuity in answering it or discovering its meaning; conundrum. **2.** a puzzling question, problem, or matter. **3.** a puzzling thing or person. —*v.i.* **4.** to propound riddles; speak enigmatically.

rid•dle² (rid′l), *v.,* **-dled, -dling,** *n.* —*v.t.* **1.** to pierce with many holes, suggesting a sieve. **2.** to fill or affect with (something undesirable): *a government riddled with graft.* **3.** to sift through a riddle, as gravel; screen. —*n.* **4.** a coarse sieve, as one for sifting sand in a foundry.

ride (rīd), *v.,* **rode, rid•den, rid•ing,** *n.* —*v.i.* **1.** to sit on and manage a horse or other animal in motion; be carried on the back of an animal. **2.** to be borne along on or in a vehicle or other conveyance. **3.** to move along in any way; be carried or supported: *riding on his friend's success.* **4.** to have a specified character for riding purposes: *The car rides smoothly.* **5.** to depend: *Her hopes are riding on a promotion.* **6.** to continue without interruption or interference: *to let the matter ride.* **7.** to turn or rest on something. **8.** to appear to float in space, as a heavenly body. **9.** to lie at anchor, as a ship. —*v.t.* **10.** to sit on and manage (a horse, bicycle, etc.) so as to be carried along. **11.** to sit or move along on; be carried or borne along on: *The ship rode the waves.* **12.** to ride over, along, or through (a road, region, etc.). **13.** to ridicule or harass persistently. **14.** to control, dominate, or tyrannize over: *a man ridden by fear.* **15.** to cause to ride. **16.** to carry (a person) on something as if on a horse: *He rode the child about on his back.* **17.** to execute by riding: *to ride a race.* **18.** to rest on, esp. by overlapping. **19.** to keep (a vessel) at anchor or moored. **20. ride out, a.** to sustain (a gale, storm, etc.) without damage, as while riding at anchor. **b.** to sustain or endure successfully. **21. ride up,** to move up from the proper place or position: *This skirt always rides up.* —*n.* **22.** a journey or excursion on a horse, camel, etc., or on or in a vehicle. **23.** a means of or arrangement for transportation by motor vehicle: *My ride's here.* **24.** a vehicle or device, as a roller coaster, on which people ride for amusement. **25.** a way, road, etc., made esp. for riding. —***Idiom.*** **26. ride a hobby** or **hobbyhorse,** to concern oneself excessively with a favorite notion or activity. **27. ride for a fall,** to conduct oneself so as to invite misfortune or injury. **28. ride herd on,** to have charge or control of: *teachers riding herd on their students.* **29. ride shotgun, a.** (formerly) to ride in a stagecoach as a shotgun-bearing guard. **b.** to ride in a motor vehicle or airplane as an armed escort. **c.** to ride as a passenger in the front seat of a car or truck. **30. take for a ride, a.** *Slang.* to abduct in order to murder. **b.** to deceive; trick.

ride•a•ble (rī′də bəl), *adj.* RIDABLE.

rid•er (rī′dər), *n.* **1.** a person who rides a horse, a bicycle, etc. **2.** something that rides. **3.** an additional, usu. unrelated clause attached to a legislative bill. **4.** an addition or amendment to a document. **5.** any object or device that straddles or moves along on something else.

rid•er•ship (rī′dər ship′), *n.* the number of passengers who use a given public transportation system.

ridge (rij), *n., v.,* **ridged, ridg•ing.** —*n.* **1.** a long, narrow elevation of land; a chain of hills or mountains. **2.** the long and narrow upper edge, angle, or crest of something, as a hill, wave, or vault. **3.** the back of an animal. **4.** any raised, narrow strip, as on cloth. **5.** (on a weather chart) a narrow, elongated area of high pressure. —*v.t.* **6.** to provide with or form into ridges. **7.** to mark with ridges. —*v.i.* **8.** to form ridges.

Ridg•way (rij′wā′), *n.* **Matthew Bunker,** born 1895, U.S. Army general: chief of staff 1953–55.

rid•i•cule (rid′i kyo͞ol′), *n., v.,* **-culed, -cul•ing.** —*n.* **1.** speech or action intended to cause contemptuous laughter; derision. —*v.t.* **2.** make fun of. —**rid′i•cul′er,** *n.*

ri•dic•u•lous (ri dik′yə ləs), *adj.* causing or worthy of ridicule or derision; laughable: *a ridiculous plan.* —**ri•dic′u•lous•ly,** *adv.* —**ri•dic′u•lous•ness,** *n.*

rid•ing¹ (rī′ding), *n.* **1.** the act of a person or thing that rides. —*adj.* **2.** used in or for traveling or riding: *riding boots.*

ri•ding² (rī′ding), *n.* **1.** (*cap.*) any of the three former administrative divisions of Yorkshire, England. **2.** any similar administrative division elsewhere.

rid′ing crop′, *n.* CROP (def. 6).

rid•ley (rid′lē), *n., pl.* **-leys. 1.** a gray sea turtle, *Lepidochelys kempi,* of the Atlantic and Gulf coasts of North America. **2.** an olive-colored sea turtle, *L. olivacea,* of the Indian, Pacific, and S Atlantic oceans.

Rid•ley (rid′lē), *n.* **Nicholas,** c1500–55, English bishop, reformer, and martyr.

Ries•ling (rēz′ling, rēs′-), *n.* **1.** a variety of white grape used in winemaking. **2.** a fragrant white wine made from this grape.

RIF (rif), *n.* **1.** a reduction in the personnel of an armed service or unit. **2.** a reduction in the number employed by a business, government department, etc., esp. for budgetary reasons. [*R(eduction) I(n) F(orce)*]

rife (rīf), *adj.* **1.** of common or frequent occurrence; prevalent; widespread: *Crime is rife in the city.* **2.** abundant, plentiful, or numerous. **3.** abounding (usu. fol. by *with*).

riff (rif), *n.* **1.** a constantly repeated melodic phrase accompanying a soloist in jazz or rock music. **2.** any variation or improvisation, as on an idea or topic. —*v.i.* **3.** to perform a riff.

rif•fle (rif′əl), *v.,* **-fled, -fling,** *n.* —*v.t.* **1.** to flip hastily with the fingers; flutter: *to riffle papers.* **2.** to shuffle (cards) by dividing a deck in two, raising the corners of the cards slightly, and allowing them to fall alternately together. **3.** to cause a ripple in or upon. —*v.i.* **4.** to become riffled; flutter or ripple; move in ripples. —*n.* **5.** a rapid, as in a stream. **6.** the act or method of riffling cards.

riff•raff (rif′raf′), *n.* **1.** disreputable people. **2.** the lowest classes; rabble. **3.** trash; rubbish.

ri•fle¹ (rī′fəl), *n., v.,* **-fled, -fling.** —*n.* **1.** a shoulder firearm with a rifled bore. **2.** a rifled cannon. **3. rifles,** a military unit equipped with rifles. —*v.t.* **4.** to cut spiral grooves within (a gun barrel, pipe, etc.). **5.** to propel (a ball) at high speed.

ri•fle² (rī′fəl), *v.t.,* **-fled, -fling. 1.** to ransack and rob. **2.** to steal and take away. —**ri′fler,** *n.*

rift (rift), *n.* **1.** a fissure; cleft. **2.** an open space or clear interval. **3.** a break in friendly relations. **4.** a cause of a break in friendly relations: *Economic rivalry was a rift between the two nations.* **5.** *Geol.* a fault. —*v.t., v.i.* **6.** to burst open; split.

rig (rig), *v.,* **rigged, rig•ging,** *n.* —*v.t.* **1.** to fit (a ship, mast, etc.) with rigging. **2.** to furnish with equipment or clothing (usu. fol. by *out* or *up*). **3.** to assemble, install, or prepare (often fol. by *up*). **4.** to manipulate fraudulently: *to rig prices.* —*n.* **5.** the arrangement of the masts, spars, sails, etc., on a boat or ship. **6.** apparatus designed for some purpose: *a hi-fi rig; oil-drilling rig.* **7.** a tractor-trailer. **8.** a carriage or wagon together with its horse. **9.** costume; clothing.

Ri•ga (rē′gə), *n.* **1.** the capital of Latvia, on the Gulf of Riga. 915,000. **2. Gulf of,** an arm of the Baltic between Latvia and Estonia. 90 mi. (145 km) long.

rig•a•ma•role (rig′ə mə rōl′), *n.* RIGMAROLE.

rig•a•to•ni (rig′ə tō′nē), *n.* (*used with a sing. or pl. v.*) a tubular pasta in short, ribbed pieces.

Ri•gel (rī′jəl, -gəl), *n.* a first-magnitude star in the constellation Orion.

rig•ging (rig′ing), *n.* **1.** the ropes, chains, etc., used to support and work the masts, yards, sails, etc., on a ship. **2.** lifting or hauling tackle. **3.** clothing; costume.

right (rīt), *adj.* **1.** in accordance with what is good, proper, or just: *right conduct.* **2.** in conformity with fact or reason: *the right answer.* **3.** correct in judgment, opinion, or action. **4.** appropriate; suitable: *to say the right thing.* **5.** most desirable. **6.** of, pertaining to, or located on or near the side of a person or thing that is turned toward the east when the subject is facing north (opposed to *left*). **7.** sound; sane: *in one's right mind.* **8.** in good health or spirits. **9.** principal, front, or upper: *right side up.* **10.** (*often cap.*) of or belonging to the political Right; having conservative or reactionary views in politics. **11.** socially desirable or influential. **12.** straight: *a right line.* **13.** having an axis perpendicular to the base: *a right cone.* **14.** *Math.* pertaining to an element of a set that has a given property when placed on the right of an element or set of elements of the given set: *a right identity.* **15.** genuine; authentic: *the right owner.* —*n.* **16.** something that is due to anyone by just claim, legal guarantees, moral principles, etc. **17.** that which is morally, legally, or ethically proper. **18.** a moral, ethical, or legal principle considered as an underlying cause of truth, justice, morality, or ethics. **19.** Sometimes, **rights.** the interest or ownership a person, group, or business has in property. **20.** the property itself or its value. **21.** Often, **rights.** the privilege of subscribing to a specified amount of a stock or bond issue, or the document certifying this privilege. **22.** that which is in accord with fact, reason, or propriety. **23.** the state or quality or an instance of being correct. **24.** the side that is normally opposite to that where the heart is: *to turn to the right.* **25.** a right-hand turn. **26.** the one of a pair, as of shoes or gloves, that is shaped for, used by, or situated on the right side. **27. the Right, a.** individuals or groups advocating maintenance of the established political, social, or economic order. **b.** the conservative position held by these people. **28.** (*usu. cap.*) **a.** the part of a legislative assembly, esp. in continental Europe, that is situated to the right of the presiding officer. **b.** the more conservative members of such an assembly, who customarily sit in this part. —*adv.* **29.** in a straight or direct line: *right to the bottom; to come right home.* **30.** quite; completely: *My hat was knocked right off.* **31.** immediately; promptly: *right after dinner.* **32.** exactly; precisely: *right here.* **33.** correctly or accurately: *to guess right.* **34.** righteously; properly: *to live right.* **35.** advantageously or well: *to turn out right.* **36.** on or to the right: *to turn right.* **37.** *Informal.* very; extremely: *a right fine day.* **38.** (*often cap.*) very (used in certain titles): *The Right Reverend John C. Stewart.* —*v.t.* **39.** to put in or restore to an upright position: *to right a fallen lamp.* **40.** to bring into conformity with fact; correct: *to right one's point of view.* **41.** to do justice to; avenge: *to be righted in court.* **42.** to redress: *to right a wrong.* —*v.i.* **43.** to resume an upright or proper position. —***Idiom.*** **44. by rights,** in fairness; justly. **45. in one's own right,** by reason of one's own ability, ownership, or qualifications. **46. in the right,** having the support of reason or law. **47. right away** or **off,** without hesitation; immediately. **48. right on,** *Slang.* exactly right; precisely. **49. to rights,** into proper condition or order: *to set a room to rights.* —**right′er,** *n.* —**right′ness,** *n.* —**Usage.** RIGHT in the sense of "very, extremely" is neither old-fashioned nor dialectal. It is most common in informal speech and writing: *You know right well what I mean.*

right′ an′gle, *n.* the angle formed by two intersecting perpendicular lines; an angle of 90°. —**right′-an′gled,** *adj.*

right′ ascen′sion, *n.* the arc of the celestial equator measured eastward from the vernal equinox to the foot of the great circle passing through the celestial poles and a given point on the celestial sphere, expressed in degrees or hours.

right′ brain′, *n.* the right cerebral hemisphere, controlling activity on the left side of the body: in humans, usu. showing specialization for spatial and nonverbal concepts. Compare LEFT BRAIN.

right•eous (rī′chəs), *adj.* **1.** characterized by uprightness or morality. **2.** morally right or justifiable: *righteous indignation.* **3.** acting in an upright, moral way; virtuous: *a righteous person.* **4.** *Slang.* genuinely good. —**right′eous•ly,** *adv.* —**right′eous•ness,** *n.*

right′ field′, *n.* **1.** the area of the baseball outfield to the right of center field, as viewed from home plate. **2.** the position of the player covering this area. —**right′ field′er,** *n.*

right•ful (rīt′fəl), *adj.* **1.** having a valid or just claim; legitimate: *the rightful heir.* **2.** belonging or held by a valid or just claim: *rightful access.* **3.** equitable or just, as actions or a cause. **4.** proper; appropriate. —**right′ful•ly,** *adv.* —**right′ful•ness,** *n.*

right′ hand′, *n.* **1.** the hand on a person's right side. **2.** the right side. **3.** a position of honor or trust. **4.** an indispensably valuable person.

right′-hand′, *adj.* **1.** located on the right. **2.** RIGHT-HANDED. **3.** being of great assistance: *my right-hand man.*

right′-hand′ed, *adj.* **1.** having the right hand or arm more serviceable than the left; using the right hand by preference. **2.** adapted to or performed by the right hand. **3. a.** rotating clockwise. **b.** (of a gear tooth or screw thread) twisting clockwise when receding from an observer. —*adv.* Also, **right′-hand′ed•ly. 4.** in a right-handed manner. **5.** with the right hand. **6.** toward the right hand; clockwise. —**right′-hand′edness,** *n.*

right•ist (rī′tist), *adj.* (*sometimes cap.*) **1.** of, pertaining to, characteristic of, or advocated by the political Right. —*n.* **2.** a member of the political Right; conservative or reactionary. —**right′ism,** *n.*

right•ly (rīt′lē), *adv.* **1.** in accordance with truth or fact; correctly: *if I understand rightly.* **2.** in accordance with morality or equity. **3.** properly; suitably: *rightly dressed.* **4.** *Informal.* with certainty; positively: *I don't rightly know.*

right′-mind′ed, *adj.* having proper principles or opinions.

right′ of way′ or **right′-of-way′,** *n., pl.* **rights of way, right of ways** or **rights-of-way, right-of-ways. 1.** a common law or statutory right granted to a vehicle, as an airplane or boat, to proceed ahead of another. **2.** a path or route that may lawfully be used. **3.** a right of passage, as over another's land. **4.** the strip of land acquired for use by a railroad for tracks. **5.** land covered by a public road. **6.** land over which a power line passes.

right′ stuff′, *n. Informal.* the necessary or ideal qualities or capabilities, as courage, confidence, dependability, toughness, or daring (usually prec. by *the*).

right′-to-die′, *adj.* asserting or advocating the right to refuse extraordinary medical measures to prolong one's life when one is terminally ill or irreversibly comatose.

right-to-know (rīt′tə nō′), *adj.* of or pertaining to laws or policies that make certain government or company data and records available to any individual who has a right or need to know their contents.

right′-to-life′, *adj.* pertaining to or advocating laws making abortion, esp. abortion-on-demand, illegal. —**right′-to-lif′er,** *n.*

right′-to-work′, *adj.* of or pertaining to the right of workers to be employed whether or not they belong to a labor union.

right′ tri′angle, *n.* a triangle having a right angle (contrasted with *oblique triangle*).

right•ward (rīt′wərd), *adv.* **1.** Also, **right′wards.** toward or on the right. —*adj.* **2.** situated on the right. **3.** directed toward the right.

right′ wing′, *n.* **1.** members of a conservative or reactionary political party, or those opposing extensive political reform. **2.** such a political party or a group of such parties. **3.** that part of a political or social organization advocating a conservative or reactionary position. —**right′-wing′,** *adj.* —**right′-wing′er,** *n.*

rig•id (rij′id), *adj.* **1.** stiff; unyielding; not pliant: *a rigid strip of metal.* **2.** firmly fixed or set. **3.** strict; severe: *rigid rules.* **4.** exacting; rigorous: *a rigid examination.* **5.** *Mech.* of or pertaining to a body in which the distance between any pair of points remains fixed under all forces. **6.** (of an airship or dirigible) having a form maintained by a stiff, unyielding structure contained within the envelope. —**ri•gid′i•ty,** *n.* —**rig′id•ly,** *adv.*

rig•ma•role (rig′mə rōl′) also **rigamarole,** *n.* **1.** an elaborate or complicated procedure. **2.** confused or meaningless talk.

rig•or (rig′ər), *n.* **1.** the quality of being strict; strictness; inflexibility. **2.** harshness of judgment or attitude; sternness. **3.** hardship of living conditions; austerity. **4.** a severe or harsh act or circumstance. **5.** scrupulous accuracy; precision. **6.** severity of weather or climate: *the rigors of winter.* **7.** a sudden coldness, as that preceding certain fevers; chill. **8.** muscular rigidity. Also, *esp. Brit.*, **rig′our.**

rig•or mor•tis (rig′ər môr′tis; *esp. Brit.* rī′gôr), *n.* the stiffening of the body after death.

rig•or•ous (rig′ər əs), *adj.* **1.** characterized by rigid severity: *rigorous laws.* **2.** severely exact; precise: *rigorous research.* **3.** extremely inclement; harsh: *rigorous weather.* **4.** logically valid. —**rig′or•ous•ly,** *adv.* —**rig′or•ous•ness,** *n.*

Riis (rēs), *n.* **Jacob August,** 1849–1914, U.S. journalist and social reformer, born in Denmark.

rile (rīl), *v.t.*, **riled, ril•ing. 1.** to irritate; vex. **2.** to make turbulent.

Ril•ke (ril′kə), *n.* **Rainer Maria,** 1875–1926, Austrian poet, born in Prague.

rill[1] (ril), *n.* a small rivulet or brook.

rill[2] or **rille** (ril), *n.* any of certain long, narrow trenches or valleys observed on the surface of the moon.

rim (rim), *n., v.,* **rimmed, rim•ming.** —*n.* **1.** the outer, often circular or curved edge or border of something. **2.** the outer circle of a wheel, attached to the hub by spokes. **3.** a circular strip of metal forming the connection between an automobile wheel and tire. **4.** a drive wheel or flywheel, as on a spinning mule. —*v.t.* **5.** to furnish with a rim. **6.** to roll around the edge of but not go in: *a basketball rimming the basket.*

Rim•bault (rim′bōlt), *n.* **Edward F(rancis),** 1816–76, English musician.

rime[1] (rīm), *n., v.,* **rimed, rim•ing.** —*n.* **1.** FROST (def. 2). —*v.t.* **2.** to cover with rime or hoarfrost. —**rim′y,** *adj.,* **rim•i•er, rim•i•est.**

rime[2] (rīm), *n., v.t., v.i.,* **rimed, rim•ing.** RHYME.

ri•mose (rī′mōs, rī mōs′) also **ri•mous** (-məs), *adj.* full of crevices, chinks, or cracks.

rind (rīnd), *n.* a thick and firm outer coat or covering: *watermelon rind; orange rind; bacon rind.*

ring[1] (ring), *n.* **1.** a typically circular band of durable material, as gold, worn on the finger as an ornament, a token of betrothal or marriage, etc. **2.** anything having the form of such a band: *a smoke ring.* **3.** a circular line or mark: *dark rings around the eyes.* **4.** a circular course: *to dance in a ring.* **5.** a number of persons or things situated in a circle: *a ring of hills.* **6.** an enclosed area, often circular, for a sports contest or exhibition: *a circus ring.* **7.** a bullring. **8.** a square enclosure in which boxing and wrestling matches take place. **9.** the sport of boxing. **10. rings, a.** a pair of suspended rings that can be grasped by a gymnast for performing feats of balance and strength. **b.** a competitive event in men's gymnastics using such an apparatus. **11.** a group of persons cooperating for unethical or illegal purposes: *a ring of dope smugglers.* **12.** a single turn in a spiral or helix or in a spiral course. **13.** ANNUAL RING. **14.** a number of atoms so united that they may be graphically represented in cyclic form. Compare CHAIN (def. 6). **15.** a bowlike or circular piece at the top of an anchor, to which the chain or cable is secured. —*v.t.* **16.** to surround with a ring; encircle. **17.** to form into a ring. **18.** GIRDLE (def. 10). **19.** to throw a ring or horseshoe over (a stake or peg). —*v.i.* **20.** to form a ring or rings. **21.** to move in a ring or a constantly curving course. —***Idiom.*** **22. run rings around,** to surpass; outdo.

ring[2] (ring), *v.,* **rang, rung, ring•ing,** *n.* —*v.i.* **1.** to give forth a clear resonant sound: *The doorbell rang twice.* **2.** to cause a bell, telephone, or the like to sound: *Just ring for service.* **3.** to resound; reecho: *The room rang with shouts.* **4.** (of the ears) to have the sensation of a continued ringing sound. **5.** to make a given impression on the mind; appear: *a story that rings true.* **6.** to telephone (usu. fol. by *up*). —*v.t.* **7.** to cause to ring; sound by striking: *to ring a bell.* **8.** to produce (sound) by or as if by ringing. **9.** to announce by or as if by the sound of a bell: *The bell rang the hour.* **10.** to telephone (usu. fol. by *up*). **11. ring off,** to terminate a telephone conversation. **12. ring up, a.** to register (the amount of a sale) on a cash register. **b.** to accomplish: *to ring up a series of successes.* —*n.* **13.** a ringing sound: *the ring of sleigh bells.* **14.** a sound like that of a ringing bell: *the ring of laughter.* **15.** reverberation: *the ring of iron upon stone.* **16.** a set of bells. **17.** a telephone call. **18.**

an act or instance of ringing a bell. **19.** a characteristic sound or quality: *the ring of truth.* **—Idiom. 20. ring a bell,** to evoke a memory; remind one of someone or something. **21. ring down the curtain, a.** to bring a performance or action to a close. **b.** to lower or close the curtain in front of a stage. **22. ring the bell,** to be outstandingly satisfactory; be just right. **23. ring the changes, a.** to ring variations on a set of bells. **b.** to range through the possible variations of something. **24. ring up the curtain, a.** to start a performance or action. **b.** to raise or open the curtain in front of a stage. **—ring′ing·ly,** *adv.*

ring′ bind′er, *n.* a loose-leaf binder in which the sheets are held in by two or more rings that can be made to snap open.

ringed (ringd), *adj.* **1.** wearing or marked or surrounded with rings. **2.** formed of or with rings; annular: *a ringed growth.*

ring·er[1] (ring′ər), *n.* **1.** a person or thing that encircles. **2.** a quoit or horseshoe thrown so as to encircle the peg.

ring·er[2] (ring′ər), *n.* **1.** one that rings or makes a ringing noise. **2.** DEAD RINGER. **3. a.** a racehorse, athlete, or the like entered in a competition under false representation. **b.** any person or thing that is fraudulent; impostor. **c.** a substitute; replacement.

ring′ fin′ger, *n.* the finger next to the little finger.

ring·hals (ring′hals), *n.* a highly venomous snake, *Hemachatus hemachatus,* of S Africa, related to the cobras, characterized by its ability to spit its venom up to 7 ft. (2.1 m).

ring·lead·er (ring′lē′dər), *n.* a person who leads others, esp. in unlawful or rebellious activities.

ring·let (ring′lit), *n.* **1.** a curled lock of hair. **2.** a small ring or circle.

ring·mas·ter (ring′mas′tər, -mä′stər), *n.* a person in charge of the performances in a circus ring.

ring′-necked′ pheas′ant, *n.* an Asian pheasant, *Phasianus colchicus,* the male of which has a white band around the neck: widely introduced as a game bird in North America.

ring·side (ring′sīd′), *n.* **1.** the area occupied by the first row of seats on all sides of a boxing or wrestling ring. **2.** a place providing a close view. **—adj. 3.** pertaining to or situated at the ringside.

ring′ spot′, *n.* plant disease caused by a virus or fungus and characterized by concentric rings of discoloration or necrosis on the leaves.

ring·tail (ring′tāl′), *n.* **1.** any phalanger of the genus *Pseudocheirus,* having the prehensile tail curled into a ring. **2.** CACOMISTLE.

ring·toss (ring′tôs′, -tos′), *n.* a game in which rings, often of rope, are tossed onto an upright peg.

ring·worm (ring′wûrm′), *n.* any of a number of contagious skin diseases caused by certain parasitic fungi and characterized by the formation of ring-shaped eruptive patches.

rink (ringk), *n.* **1.** a smooth expanse of ice for ice-skating, often artificially prepared. **2.** a smooth floor, usu. of wood, for roller-skating. **3.** a building or enclosure for ice-skating or roller-skating; skating arena. **4.** an area of ice marked off for the game of curling. **5.** a section of a bowling green where a match can be played.

rink·y-dink (ring′kē dingk′), *Slang.* **—adj. 1.** of generally inferior quality; small-time. **2.** outmoded or shabby; backward; antiquated.

rinse (rins), *v.,* **rinsed, rins·ing,** *n.* **—v.t. 1.** to wash lightly, as by pouring water over or by dipping in water. **2.** to douse or drench in clean water as a final stage in washing. **3.** to remove (soap, dirt, etc.) by such a process (often fol. by *off* or *out*). **4.** to use a rinse on (the hair). **—n. 5.** an act or instance of rinsing. **6.** the water used for rinsing. **7.** any preparation that may be used on the hair after washing, esp. to tint or condition the hair. **8.** an act or instance of using such a preparation.

Ri·o de Ja·nei·ro (rē′ō dā zhə nâr′ō, jə-, dē, də), *n.* **1.** a state in SE Brazil. 11,489,797; 17,091 sq. mi. (44,268 sq. km). **2.** the capital of this state, on Guanabara Bay: former capital of Brazil. 5,184,292.

Ri·o Grande (rē′ō grand′, gran′dē, grän′dā), *n.* **1.** Mexican, **Río Bravo.** a river flowing S from Colorado through central New Mexico and along the boundary between Texas and Mexico into the Gulf of Mexico. 1800 mi. (2900 km) long. **2.** a river flowing W from SE Brazil into the

Paraná River. 650 mi. (1050 km) long. **3.** a seaport in SE Rio Grande do Sul state, in Brazil. 124,706.

Ri·o Gran·de (rē′ō grän′dā, -dē), *n.* a river in central Nicaragua, flowing NE to the Caribbean Sea. ab. 200 mi. (320 km) long.

ri·ot (rī′ət), *n.* **1.** a noisy, violent public disorder caused by a group or crowd of persons. **2.** *Law.* a disturbance of the public peace by three or more persons acting together in a violent or tumultuous manner. **3.** violent or wild disorder or confusion. **4.** a profuse or unrestrained outpouring, display, etc., as of emotions or phenomena. **5.** something or someone hilariously funny: *You were a riot at the party.* **6.** unrestrained revelry. **7.** loose, wanton living; profligacy. **—v.i. 8.** to take part in a violent public disorder or disturbance. **9.** to live in a loose or wanton manner; indulge in unrestrained revelry. **—v.t. 10.** to spend (money, time, etc.) in riotous living (usu. fol. by *away* or *out*). **—Idiom. 11. run riot,** to behave with abandon. **—ri′ot·er,** *n.*

Ri′ot Act′, *n.* **1.** an English statute of 1715 providing that if 12 or more persons assemble unlawfully and riotously, to the disturbance of the public peace, and refuse to disperse upon proclamation they shall be considered guilty of felony. **2. read (someone) the riot act, a.** to reprimand; censure: *The principal read them the riot act for their behavior at the assembly.* **b.** to give (someone) a sharp warning.

ri·ot·ous (rī′ə təs), *adj.* **1.** (of an act) of or characterized by rioting or a disturbance of the peace. **2.** (of a person) inciting or taking part in a riot. **3.** given to or marked by unrestrained revelry. **4.** boisterous or uproarious: *riotous laughter.* **5.** hilariously funny. **—ri′ot·ous·ly,** *adv.*

rip (rip), *v.,* **ripped, rip·ping,** *n.* **—v.t. 1.** to cut or tear apart roughly or vigorously. **2.** to cut or tear away roughly or vigorously. **3.** to saw (wood) in the direction of the grain. **—v.i. 4.** to become torn apart or split open. **5.** to move with violence or great speed. **6. rip into,** to attack physically or verbally; assail. **7. rip off,** *Slang.* **a.** to steal. **b.** to steal from, cheat, or exploit. **—n. 8.** a rent made by ripping; tear. **—Idiom. 9. let her** or **it rip,** to allow something to go on or be done without restraint.

RIP or **R.I.P., 1.** may he or she rest in peace. **2.** may they rest in peace. [< Latin *requiēsca(n)t in pāce*]

ri·par·i·an (ri pâr′ē ən, rī-), *adj.* of, situated, or dwelling on the bank of a river or other body of water.

rip′ cord′, *n.* **1.** a cord on a parachute that, when pulled, opens the parachute for descent. **2.** a cord in the bag of a passenger balloon or dirigible that, when pulled, will open the bag and let the gas escape.

ripe (rīp), *adj.,* **rip·er, rip·est. 1.** completely matured or developed, as grain or fruit that is ready for harvesting or eating. **2.** resembling fruit, as in ruddiness and fullness: *ripe red lips.* **3.** advanced to the point of being in the best condition for use, as cheese or beer. **4.** characterized by full development of body or mind; mature: *of ripe years.* **5.** of mature judgment or knowledge: *a ripe mind.* **6.** (of time) advanced: *a ripe old age.* **7.** (of ideas, plans, etc.) ready for action, execution, etc. **8.** (of people) completely ready to do or undergo something: *ripe for a change in jobs.* **9.** ready enough; auspicious. **10.** ready for some operation or process: *a ripe abscess.* **—ripe′ly,** *adv.* **—ripe′ness,** *n.*

rip·en (rī′pən), *v.t., v.i.* **1.** to make or become ripe. **2.** to bring or come to maturity, the proper condition, etc.; mature. **3.** to bring or come by aging to the desired flavor, texture, etc. **—rip′en·er,** *n.*

rip′off′ or **rip′-off′,** *n. Slang.* **1.** a theft, cheat, or swindle. **2.** a copy or imitation. **3.** a person who rips off another.

ri·poste or **ri·post** (ri pōst′), *n., v.,* **-post·ed, -post·ing. —n. 1.** a quick, sharp return in speech or action; counterstroke: *a clever riposte.* **2.** *Fencing.* a quick thrust given after parrying a lunge. **—v.i. 3.** to make a riposte. **4.** to reply or retaliate.

rip·ple (rip′əl), *v.,* **-pled, -pling,** *n.* **—v.i. 1.** (of a liquid surface) to form small waves or undulations, as water agitated by a breeze. **2.** to flow with a light rise and fall or ruffling of the surface. **3.** to have or fall in small undulations, ruffles, or folds. **4.** (of sound) to move with a rising and falling tone, inflection, or magnitude. **—v.t. 5.** to form small waves or undulations on; agitate lightly. **6.** to mark as if with ripples; give a wavy form to. **—n. 7.** a small wave or undulation, as on water. **8.** any movement or form similar to this. **9.** a small rapid. **10.** a sound as of water rippling: *a ripple of laughter.* **—rip′pling·ly,** *adv.*

rip′ple effect′, *n.* a spreading effect or series of consequences caused by a single action or event.

rip′-roar′ing, *adj.* boisterously wild and exciting; riotous: *a rip-roaring good time.*

rip·snort·er (rip′snôr′tər), *n.* something exceedingly strong, exciting, etc.: *a ripsnorter of a storm.* **—rip′snort′ing,** *adj.*

rip·tide (rip′tīd′), *n.* a tide that opposes another or other tides, causing a violent disturbance in the sea.

Rip Van Win·kle (rip′ van wing′kəl), *n.* **1.** (in a story by Washington Irving) a ne'er-do-well who sleeps 20 years and upon waking is startled to find how much the world has changed. **2.** (*italics*) the story itself, published in *The Sketch Book* (1819).

RISC (risk), *n.* reduced instruction set computer: a computer whose central processing unit recognizes a relatively small number of instructions, which it can execute very rapidly. Compare CISC.

rise (rīz), *v.,* **rose, ris·en** (riz′ən), **ris·ing,** *n.* **—v.i. 1.** to get up from a lying, sitting, or kneeling posture; assume an upright position. **2.** to get up from bed, esp. to begin the day after a night's sleep. **3.** to become erect and stiff, as the hair in fright. **4.** to become active in opposition or resistance; revolt or rebel. **5.** to come into existence; appear. **6.** to occur. **7.** to originate, issue, or be derived. **8.** to move from a lower to a higher position; ascend. **9.** to ascend above the horizon, as a heavenly body. **10.** to extend directly upward; project vertically. **11.** to have an upward slant or curve. **12.** to attain a higher level, as of importance or financial security: *to rise in the world.* **13.** to prove oneself equal to a demand, emergency, etc. (usu. fol. by *to*): *to rise to the occasion.* **14.** to become animated, cheerful, or heartened, as the spirits. **15.** to become roused or stirred: *to feel one's temper rising.* **16.** to increase, as in height, amount, value, or intensity. **17.** to swell or puff up, as dough from the action of yeast. **18.** to become louder or of higher pitch, as the voice. **19.** to adjourn or close a session, as a deliberative body or court. **20.** (of fish) to come up toward the surface of the water in pursuit of food or bait. **21.** to return from the dead. —*v.t.* **22.** *Nonstandard.* to cause to rise. **23.** RAISE (def. 27). **24. rise above,** to ignore and overcome, as adversity. —*n.* **25.** an act or instance of rising. **26.** appearance above the horizon, as of the sun or moon. **27.** elevation or increase in rank, fortune, influence, etc. **28.** an increase, as in height, amount, or value. **29.** the amount of such increase. **30.** an increase in loudness or in pitch, as of the voice. **31.** the measured height of any of various things, as of a roof, a flight of steps, or a stair step. **32.** the vertical distance through which the floor of an elevator or the like passes. **33.** origin, source, or beginning. **34.** a coming into existence or notice: *the rise of a new talent.* **35.** extension upward. **36.** the amount of such extension. **37.** upward slope, as of ground. **38.** a piece of rising or high ground. **39.** the distance between the crotch and the waist of a pair of trousers. **40.** the coming up of a fish toward the surface in pursuit of food or bait. —**Usage.** See RAISE.

ris•er (rī′zər), *n.* **1.** a person who rises, esp. from bed. **2.** the vertical face of a stair step. **3. a.** a long low platform on which persons can stand for greater visibility, as on a stage. **b. risers,** a group of such platforms connected in stepwise fashion, often used for sitting. **4.** a vertical pipe, duct, or conduit.

ris•i•bil•i•ty (riz′ə bil′i tē), *n., pl.* **-ties. 1.** Often, **risibilities.** the ability or disposition to laugh; humorous awareness. **2.** laughter.

ris•i•ble (riz′ə bəl), *adj.* **1.** causing or capable of causing laughter; laughable; ludicrous. **2.** having the ability, disposition, or readiness to laugh. **3.** pertaining to or connected with laughing.

ris•ing (rī′zing), *adj.* **1.** advancing, ascending, or mounting. **2.** growing or advancing to adult years. —*adv.* **3.** somewhat more than: *The crop came to rising 6000 bushels.* **4.** in approach of; almost: *a lad rising sixteen.* —*n.* **5.** the act of a person or thing that rises. **6.** a rebellion; uprising. **7.** a projection or prominence. **8.** a stringer supporting the thwarts of an open boat.

risk (risk), *n.* **1.** exposure to the chance of injury or loss; a hazard or dangerous chance. **2.** *Insurance.* **a.** the hazard or chance of loss. **b.** the degree of probability of such loss. **c.** the amount that the insurance company may lose. **d.** a person or thing with reference to the hazard involved to the insurer. **e.** the type of loss against which a policy is drawn. —*v.t.* **3.** to expose to the chance of injury or loss; hazard: *to risk one's life.* **4.** to venture upon; take the chance of: *to risk a fall.*

risk•y (ris′kē), *adj.,* **-i•er, -i•est.** attended with or involving risk; hazardous. —**risk′i•ly,** *adv.* —**risk′i•ness,** *n.*

ri•sot•to (ri sô′tō, -sot′ō, -zô′tō, -zot′ō), *n.* rice cooked in broth and flavored with grated cheese and other ingredients.

ris•qué (ri skā′), *adj.* daringly close to indelicacy or impropriety; off-color: *a risqué story.*

rite (rīt), *n.* **1.** a formal ceremony or procedure prescribed or customary in religious or other solemn use. **2.** a particular form or system of religious or ceremonial practice. **3.** (*sometimes cap.*) a liturgy or liturgical system: *the Byzantine rite.* **4.** (*sometimes cap.*) a division of a Christian church based on differences in liturgical practice. **5.** any customary observance or practice.

rite′ of pas′sage, *n.* **1.** a ceremony to facilitate or mark a person's change of status on a significant occasion, as at the onset of puberty or upon entry into a select group. **2.** any act or event marking a passage from one stage of life to another.

Ritsch•li•an (rich′lē ən), *adj.* **1.** of or pertaining to the theology of Albrecht Ritschl (1822–89), who developed a liberal Christian theology and maintained that religious faith is based on value judgments. —*n.* **2.** a supporter of Ritschlian theology. —**Ritsch′li•an•ism,** *n.*

rit•u•al (rich′o͞o əl), *n.* **1. a.** an established procedure for a religious or other rite. **b.** a system of such rites. **2.** observance of set forms in public worship. **3.** a book of rites or ceremonies. **4.** prescribed, established, or ceremonial acts or features collectively. **5.** any practice or pattern of behavior regularly performed in a set manner. **6.** *Psychiatry.* a specific act, as hand-washing, performed repetitively to a pathological degree. —*adj.* **7.** being or practiced as a rite or ritual: *a ritual dance.* **8.** of or pertaining to rites or ritual: *ritual laws.* —**rit′u•al•ly,** *adv.*

rit•u•al•ism (rich′o͞o ə liz′əm), *n.* **1.** adherence to ritual. **2.** excessive fondness for ritual. —**rit′u•al•ist,** *n.* —**rit′u•al•is′tic,** *adj.* —**rit′u•al•is′ti•cal•ly,** *adv.*

rit•u•al•ize (rich′o͞o ə līz′), *v.,* **-ized, -iz•ing.** —*v.i.* **1.** to practice ritualism. —*v.t.* **2.** to make into a ritual. **3.** to convert (someone) to ritualism; impose ritualism upon. —**rit′u•al•i•za′tion,** *n.*

ritz•y (rit′sē), *adj.,* **-i•er, -i•est.** swanky; elegant; posh. [after the *Ritz* hotels founded by Swiss-born hotelier César Ritz (1850–1918)] —**ritz′i•ly,** *adv.* —**ritz′i•ness,** *n.*

ri•val (rī′vəl), *n., adj., v.,* **-valed, -val•ing** or (*esp. Brit.*) **-valled, -val•ling.** —*n.* **1.** a person who seeks to achieve the same object or goal as another or who tries to equal or outdo another in some endeavor; competitor. **2.** a person or thing that can dispute another's preeminence or superiority; equal; peer. —*adj.* **3.** competing or standing in rivalry. —*v.t.* **4.** to prove to be a worthy rival of. **5.** to equal (something) as if engaged in a rivalry; match; emulate. **6.** to compete with in rivalry. —*v.i.* **7.** to engage in rivalry; compete.

ri•val•ry (rī′vəl rē), *n., pl.* **-ries. 1.** the condition of being a rival or rivals; competition; antagonism. **2.** an instance of this.

rive (rīv), *v.,* **rived, rived** or **riv•en, riv•ing.** —*v.t.* **1.** to tear or rend apart. **2.** to split by striking; cleave. **3.** to harrow or distress (the feelings, heart, etc.). **4.** to split (wood) radially from a log. —*v.i.* **5.** to become rent or split apart.

riv•er (riv′ər), *n.* **1.** a natural stream of water of fairly large size flowing in a definite course or series of diverging and converging channels. **2.** a similar stream of something else: *a river of lava.* **3.** any abundant stream or copious flow; outpouring: *rivers of tears.* —***Idiom.*** **4. sell down the river,** to betray. **5. up the river,** *Slang.* to or in prison.

riv•er•bank (riv′ər bangk′), *n.* the slopes bordering a river.

riv•er•bed (riv′ər bed′), *n.* the channel in which a river flows or formerly flowed.

riv•er•boat (riv′ər bōt′), *n.* any shallow-draft boat used on rivers.

riv•er•ine (riv′ə rīn′, -rēn′, -ər in), *adj.* **1.** of or pertaining to a river. **2.** situated or dwelling beside a river.

riv•er•side (riv′ər sīd′), *n.* **1.** a bank of a river. —*adj.* **2.** on or near a bank of a river. [1325–75]

Riv•er•side (riv′ər sīd′), *n.* a city in SW California. 241,644.

riv•er•weed (riv′ər wēd′), *n.* any of several submerged aquatic plants of the genus *Podostemum,* family Podostemaceae, growing in rapid streams by clinging to stones with the roots.

riv•et (riv′it), *n., v.,* **-et•ed, -et•ing** or (*esp. Brit.*) **-et•ted, -et•ting.** —*n.* **1.** a metal pin for passing through holes in two or more plates or pieces to hold them together, usu. with a head at one end, the other end being hammered into a head after insertion. —*v.t.* **2.** to fasten with a rivet or rivets. **3.** to hammer or spread out the end of (a pin, bolt, etc.) in order to form a head and secure something; clinch. **4.** to fasten firmly. **5.** to hold (the eye, attention, etc.) firmly. —**riv′et•er,** *n.*

riv•u•let (riv′yə lit), *n.* a small stream; brook.

Ri•yadh (rē yäd′), *n.* the capital of Saudi Arabia, in the E central part. 1,500,000.

ri•yal (rē yôl′, -yäl′) also **rial,** *n.* the basic monetary unit of Qatar and Saudi Arabia.

Riz•pah (riz′pə), *n.* a concubine of King Saul. II Sam. 3:7; 21:8–11.

Rn, *Chem. Symbol.* radon.

RN or **R.N., 1.** registered nurse. **2.** *Brit.* Royal Navy.

RNA, ribonucleic acid: any of a class of single-stranded nucleic acid molecules composed of ribose and uracil, found chiefly in the cytoplasm of cells and in certain viruses, and important in protein synthesis.

RNA virus, *n.* any virus containing RNA; retrovirus.

roach[1] (rōch), *n.* a cockroach.

roach[2] (rōch), *n., pl.* **roach•es,** (*esp. collectively*) **roach. 1.** a European freshwater fish of the carp family. **2.** a freshwater sunfish found in E North America.

roach[3] (rōch), *n.* **1.** hair combed up from the forehead in a roll or curve. —*v.t.* **2.** to clip or cut off (the mane of a horse); hog. **3.** to comb (hair) into a roach.

road (rōd), *n.* **1.** a long, narrow stretch with a leveled or paved surface, made for traveling by motor vehicle, carriage, etc.; street or highway. **2.** a way or course: *the road to peace.* **3.** Often, **roads. 4.** RAILROAD. **5.** any tunnel in a mine used for hauling. —***Idiom.*** **6. down the road,** at some future time. **7. hit the road,** *Informal.* to begin or resume traveling. **8. on the road, a.** traveling or touring. **b.** moving or evolving, as from one condition to another: *on the road to recovery.* **9. take (to) the road,** to start to travel, tour, or wander.

road•block (rōd′blok′), *n.* **1.** an obstruction placed across a road for halting or hindering traffic, as by the police to facilitate a search or capture, or by the military to delay the enemy. **2.** an obstruction on a road, as a fallen tree. **3.** any obstruction to progress. —*v.t.* **4.** to halt or obstruct with a roadblock.

road′ com′pany, *n.* a theatrical group that tours cities and towns, usu. performing a single play.

road•house (rōd′hous′), *n., pl.* **-hous•es** (-hou′ziz). a tavern, nightclub, etc., located on a highway, usu. beyond city limits.

road•ie (rō′dē), *n.* a crew member for a traveling group of musicians who usu. sets up the equipment.

road′ kill′, *n.* the body of an animal killed by a motor vehicle.

road′ map′, *n.* **1.** a folding map designed for motorists. **2.** any plan or guide: *your road map to financial independence.*

road•run•ner (rōd′run′ər), *n.* either of two large terrestrial cuckoos of the genus *Geococcyx* of arid regions of the western U.S., Mexico, and Central America, esp. *G. californianus.*

road′ show′ or **road′show′,** *n.* **1.** a show, as a play or musical comedy, performed by a touring group of actors. **2.** an important motion picture presented at selected theaters, often with reserved seating and for higher prices. —**road′-show′,** *v.t.,* **-showed, -show•ing,** *adj.*

road•side (rōd′sīd′), *n.* **1.** the side or border of the road; wayside. —*adj.* **2.** on or near the side of a road.

road•ster (rōd′stər), *n.* **1.** an automobile with an open body, a single seat for two or three persons, and a large trunk or a rumble seat. **2.** a horse for riding or driving on the road.

road′ test′, *n.* **1.** a check of an automobile's performance in actual operation on the road. **2.** an examination of driving skill, conducted in normal traffic, esp. as a requirement for a driver's license.

road•way (rōd′wā′), *n.* **1.** the land over which a road is built; a road together with the land at its edge. **2.** the part of a road over which vehicles travel; road.

road•work (rōd′wûrk′), *n.* a conditioning exercise for an athlete, esp. a boxer, consisting of running considerable distances on roads.

roam (rōm), *v.i.* **1.** to walk or travel without purpose or direction; ramble; wander. —*v.t.* **2.** to wander over or through. —*n.* **3.** an act or instance of roaming; a ramble. —**roam′er,** *n.*

roan[1] (rōn), *adj.* **1.** (chiefly of horses) of the color sorrel, chestnut, or bay, sprinkled with gray or white. —*n.* **2.** a horse or other animal with a roan coat.

roan[2] (rōn), *n.* a soft, flexible sheepskin leather, used in bookbinding, often made to imitate morocco.

roar (rôr, rōr), *v.i.* **1.** to utter a loud, deep, extended sound, as in anger or excitement. **2.** to laugh loudly or boisterously. **3.** to make a loud din, as thunder, cannon, waves, or wind. **4.** to function or move with a loud, deep sound, as a vehicle: *The bus roared away.* **5.** to make a loud, inhaled snort, as a horse affected with roaring. —*v.t.* **6.** to utter or express in a roar. **7.** to affect (oneself) as indicated by roaring: *to roar oneself hoarse.* —*n.* **8.** a loud, deep, extended sound: *the roar of a lion.* **9.** a loud outburst: *a roar of laughter.*

roar•ing (rôr′ing, rōr′-), *n.* **1.** the act of a person, animal, or thing that roars. **2.** a loud, deep cry or sound or a series of such sounds. **3.** a disease of horses caused by respiratory obstruction or vocal cord paralysis and characterized by loud breathing. —*adj.* **4.** making or causing a roar, as an animal or thunder. **5.** brisk; active: *a roaring business.* **6.** complete; utter: *a roaring idiot.* —*adv.*

Roar′ing Twen′ties, *n.pl.* the 1920s regarded as a boisterous era of prosperity, fast cars, jazz, speakeasies, and wild youth.

roast (rōst), *v.t.* **1.** to cook (meat or other food) by direct exposure to dry heat, as in an oven or over live coals. **2.** to parch by exposure to heat, as coffee beans. **3.** to cook or heat by embedding in hot coals, embers, etc.: *to roast chestnuts.* **4.** to heat excessively. **5.** to heat (ore or the like) in air in order to oxidize. **6.** to warm (one's hands, etc.) at a hot fire. **7.** to ridicule or criticize severely or mercilessly. **8.** to honor with or subject to a roast. —*v.i.* **9.** to roast meat or other food. **10.** to undergo the process of becoming roasted. —*n.* **11.** a piece of meat that has been roasted or is suitable for roasting. **12.** something that is roasted. **13.** the act or process of roasting. **14.** severe criticism. **15.** a facetious ceremonial tribute in which the guest of honor is both praised and good-naturedly insulted. **16.** an outdoor get-together at which food is roasted: *a weenie roast.* —*adj.* **17.** roasted: *roast beef.*

roast•er (rō′stər), *n.* **1.** a person or thing that roasts. **2.** a pan, oven, or device for roasting. **3.** an animal suitable for roasting.

rob (rob), *v.,* **robbed, rob•bing.** —*v.t.* **1.** to take something by unlawful force or threat of violence; steal from. **2.** to deprive of some right or something legally due: *They robbed her of her inheritance.* **3.** to plunder or rifle (a house, shop, etc.). **4.** to deprive of something unjustly or injuriously: *The shock robbed him of speech.* —*v.i.* **5.** to commit or practice robbery. —*Idiom.* **6. rob the cradle,** to become romantically involved with someone much younger than oneself.

rob•ber (rob′ər), *n.* a person who robs.

LONGEST RIVERS OF THE WORLD

River	Countries of Transit	Outflow	Approx. Length Miles	Km
Nile	Uganda-Sudan-Egypt	Mediterranean Sea	4160	6695
Missouri-Mississippi	United States	Gulf of Mexico	3990	6420
Amazon	Peru-Brazil	Atlantic Ocean	3900	6280
Chang Jiang (Yangtze)	China	East China Sea	3200	5150
Congo (Zaire)	Zaire-Congo-Angola	Atlantic Ocean	3000	4800
Lena	Russian Federation	Arctic Ocean	2800	4510
Yenisei	Russian Federation	Arctic Ocean	2800	4510
Huang He (Yellow River)	China	Gulf of Bohai	2800	4510
Missouri	United States	Mississippi River	2720	4380
Amur	China-Russian Federation	Sea of Okhotsk	2700	4350
Mekong	China-Burma-Thailand-Laos-Cambodia-Vietnam	South China Sea	2600	4185
Niger	Guinea-Mali-Niger-Nigeria	Gulf of Guinea	2600	4185
Mackenzie	Canada	Beaufort Sea	2525	4065
Ob	Russian Federation	Gulf of Ob	2500	4025
Mississippi	United States	Gulf of Mexico	2470	3975
Volga	Russian Federation	Caspian Sea	2325	3745
Madeira	Brazil	Amazon River	2100	3380
Parana	Brazil-Paraguay-Argentina	Rio de la Plata	2050	3300
Purus	Peru-Brazil	Amazon River	2000	3220
Yukon	Canada-United States	Bering Sea	2000	3220
Indus	Tibet-India-Pakistan	Arabian Sea	1900	3060
Irtysh	China-Kazakhstan-Russian Federation	Ob River	1840	2960
Rio Grande	United States-Mexico	Gulf of Mexico	1800	2900
Sao Francisco	Brazil	Atlantic Ocean	1800	2900
Japura	Colombia-Brazil	Amazon River	1750	2815
Salween	China-Burma	Bay of Bengal	1750	2815
Danube	Germany-Austria-Slovakia-Hungary-Croatia-Yugoslavia-Rumania-Bulgaria-Ukraine	Black Sea	1725	2775
Euphrates	Turkey-Syria-Iraq	Perisan Gulf	1700	2735
Brahmaputra	Tibet-India-Bangladesh	Ganges River	1700	2735
Tocantins	Brazil	Para River	1700	2735
Zambezi	Angola-Zambia-Zimbabwe-Mozambique	Mozambique Channel	1650	2657
Orinoco	Venezuela-Colombia	Atlantic Ocean	1600	2575
Ganges	India	Bay of Bengal	1550	2495
Aldan	Russian Federation	Lena River	1500	2415
Paraguay	Brazil-Paraguay-Argentina	Parana River	1500	2415
Arkansas	United States	Mississippi River	1450	2335
Colorado	United States-Mexico	Gulf of California	1450	2335
Amu	Darya Afghanistan-Tadzhikistan-Turkmenistan-Uzbekistan	Aral Sea	1400	2250
Dnieper	Russian Federation-Belarus-Ukraine	Black Sea	1400	2250
Negro	Colombia-Brazil	Amazon River	1400	2250
Ural	Russian Federation	Caspian Sea	1400	2250
Orange	Lesotho-South Africa	Atlantic Ocean	1300	2095
Syr	Darya Kirghizia-Uzbekistan-Kazakhstan	Aral Sea	1300	2095
Red	United States	Mississippi River	1300	2095
Xingu	Brazil	Amazon River	1300	2095
Irrawaddy	Burma	Bay of Bengal	1250	2015
Xi Jiang	China	South China Sea	1250	2015
Columbia	Canada-United States	Pacific Ocean	1214	1955
Saskatchewan	Canada	Lake Winnipeg	1205	1940
Kama	Russian Federation	Volga	1200	1930
Don	Russian Federation	Sea of Azov	1200	1930
Jurua	Peru-Brazil	Amazon River	1200	1930
Murray	Australia	Indian Ocean	1200	1930
Salado	Argentina	Parana River	1200	1930
Ucayali	Peru	Amazon River	1200	1930
Darling	Australia	Murray River	1160	1870
Angara	Russian Federation	Yenisei River	1150	1855
Tigris	Turkey-Syria-Iraq	Euphrates River	1150	1850

rob′ber bar′on, *n.* **1.** a U.S. capitalist of the late 19th century who became wealthy by ruthless and unethical means. **2.** a feudal noble who robbed travelers passing through his lands.

rob•ber•y (rob′ə rē), *n., pl.* **-ber•ies. 1.** the act, the practice, or an instance of robbing. **2.** the felonious taking of property from another's person by violence or intimidation.

robe (rōb), *n., v.,* **robed, rob•ing. —n. 1.** a long, loose or flowing gown or outer garment worn as ceremonial dress or garb of office. **2.** any loose informal garment, as a bathrobe or dressing gown. **3.** a woman's gown or dress, esp. of a more elaborate kind. **4. robes,** apparel in general; dress; costume. **5.** a piece of fur, knitted work, etc., used as a blanket or wrap. —*v.t.* **6.** to clothe or invest with a robe or robes; dress; array. —*v.i.* **7.** to put on a robe or robes. —**rob′er,** *n.*

Rob•ert (rob′ərt), *n.* **Henry Martyn,** 1837–1923, U.S. engineer and authority on parliamentary procedure: author of *Robert's Rules of Order* (1876, revised 1915).

Robert I, *n.* **1.** (*"Robert the Devil"*) died 1035, duke of Normandy 1028–35 (father of William I of England). **2.** Also called **Rob′ert the Bruce′, Rob′ert Bruce′.** 1274–1329, king of Scotland 1306–29.

Rob•erts (rob′ərts), *n.* **1. Daniel,** 1841–1907, U.S. clergyman and hymn writer. **2. Kenneth (Lewis),** 1885–1957, U.S. novelist and essayist. **3. Oral,** born 1918, U.S. evangelist.

Rob•ert•son (rob′ərt sən), *n.* **1. Archibald Thomas,** 1863–1934, U.S. theologian. **2. Pat** (*Marion Gordon*), born 1930, U.S. evangelist.

Robe•son (rōb′sən), *n.* **Paul,** 1898–1976, U.S. singer and actor.

Robes•pierre (rōbz′pēr, -pē âr′, rō′bəs pē âr′), *n.* **Maximilien Fran-çois Marie Isidore de,** 1758–94, French revolutionary leader.

rob•in (rob′in), *n.* **1.** a large North American thrush, *Turdus migratorius,* having a chestnut-red breast and abdomen. **2.** any of several small Old World birds having a red or reddish breast, esp. *Erithacus rubecula,* of Eurasia. Also called **rob′in red′breast.**

Rob′in Hood′, *n.* a legendary English outlaw of the 12th century, celebrated in ballads, who robbed the rich to give to the poor.

rob′in's-egg′ blue′, *n.* a pale green to light greenish blue color.

Rob•in•son (rob′in sən), *n.* **1. Edward G.** (*Emanuel Goldenberg*), 1893–1973, U.S. actor, born in Romania. **2. Jack Roosevelt** (*Jackie*), 1919–72, U.S. baseball player. **3. Ray** (*Walker Smith*) (*"Sugar Ray"*), 1921–89, U.S. boxer.

Rob′inson Cru′soe (krōō′sō), *n.* **1.** in a novel by Daniel Defoe, a mariner who is shipwrecked and lives adventurously for years on a small island. **2.** (*italics*) the novel itself (1719).

ro•bot (rō′bət, -bot), *n.* **1.** a machine that resembles a human and does mechanical, routine tasks on command. **2.** a person who acts in a mechanical, routine manner; automaton. **3.** any machine or mechanical device that operates automatically with humanlike skill. [< Czech, coined by Karel Čapek in the play *R.U.R.* from *robota* labor] —**ro•bot′ic,** *adj.*

ro•bot•ics (rō bot′iks), *n.* (*used with a sing. v.*) the technology connected with using computer-controlled robots to perform manipulative tasks. —**ro•bot′i•cist,** *n.*

ro•bust (rō bust′, rō′bust), *adj.* **1.** strong and healthy; hardy; vigorous. **2.** strongly or stoutly built. **3.** suited to or requiring bodily strength or endurance. **4.** hearty; boisterous: *robust eaters.* **5.** rich and full-bodied: *robust flavor.* —**ro•bust′ly,** *adv.* —**ro•bust′ness,** *n.*

Roch•es•ter (roch′es tər, -ə stər), *n.* **1.** a city in W New York, on the Genesee River. 231,170. **2.** a town in SE Minnesota. 60,300. **3.** a city in N Kent, in SE England. 55,460.

roch•et (roch′it), *n.* a vestment of linen or lawn, resembling a surplice, worn esp. by bishops and abbots.

rock¹ (rok), *n.* **1.** a large mass of stone forming a hill, cliff, promontory, or the like. **2. a.** mineral matter of variable composition, consolidated or unconsolidated, assembled in masses or considerable quantities in nature, as by the action of heat or water. **b.** a particular kind of such matter: *igneous rock.* **3.** stone in the mass: *built on rock.* **4.** a stone of any size. **5.** something resembling a rock. **6.** a firm foundation or support: *The Lord is my rock.* **7.** ROCK CANDY. **8.** *Slang.* **a.** a diamond. **b.** any gem. —**Idiom. 9. between a rock and a hard place,** between undesirable alternatives.

rock² (rok), *v.i.* **1.** to move or sway to and fro or from side to side. **2.** to be moved or swayed powerfully with excitement, emotion, etc. **3.** (of ore) to be washed in a cradle. **4.** to dance to or play rock music. —*v.t.* **5.** to move or sway to and fro or from side to side, esp. gently and soothingly. **6.** to lull in security, hope, etc. **7.** to affect deeply; stun. **8.** to shake or disturb violently: *An earthquake rocked the dock.* —*n.* **9.** a rocking movement. **10.** a musical style derived in part from blues and folk music and marked by an accented beat and repetitive phrase structure. —*adj.* **11.** pertaining to or characteristic of musical rock. —**rock′a•ble,** *adj.* —**rock′ing•ly,** *adv.*

rock•a•bil•ly (rok′ə bil′ē), *n.* a style of popular music combining features of rock and hillbilly music.

rock′ and roll′ or **rock′ & roll′,** *n., v.,* **rolled, roll•ing. —n. 1.** ROCK² (def. 10). —*v.i.* **2.** ROCK² (def. 4).

rock′ bot′tom, *n.* the very lowest level.

rock′-bot′tom, *adj.* extremely low: *rock-bottom prices.*

rock′-bound′ or **rock′bound′,** *adj.* hemmed in or covered by rocks: *a rock-bound coast.*

rock′ can′dy, *n.* sugar in large, hard, cohering crystals.

Rock′ Cor′nish, *n.* a small hybrid chicken produced by mating Cor-

nish and white Plymouth Rock chickens. Also called **Rock′ Cor′nish game′ hen′.**

rock′ crys′tal, *n.* transparent quartz, esp. when colorless.

Rock•e•fel•ler (rok′ə fel′ər), *n.* **Nelson A(ldrich),** 1908–79, vice president of the U.S. 1974–77 (son of John D. Rockefeller, Jr.).

rock•er (rok′ər), *n.* **1.** Also called **runner.** one of the curved pieces on which a cradle or a rocking chair rocks. **2.** ROCKING CHAIR. **3.** any of various devices that operate with a rocking motion. **4.** *Mining.* CRADLE (def. 9). **5.** a performer, fan, or piece of rock music. —**Idiom. 6. off one's rocker,** *Slang.* insane; crazy.

rock′er arm′, *n.* a rocking or oscillating arm or lever rotating with a moving shaft or pivoted on a stationary shaft.

rock•et¹ (rok′it), *n.* **1.** any of various tubelike devices containing combustibles that on being ignited propel the tube through the air: used for pyrotechnic effect, signaling, hurling explosives, launching a space vehicle, etc. **2.** a space capsule or vehicle put into orbit by such devices. **3.** ROCKET ENGINE. —*v.t.* **4.** to move or transport by means of a rocket. —*v.i.* **5.** to move like a rocket. **6.** (of game birds) to fly straight up rapidly when flushed.

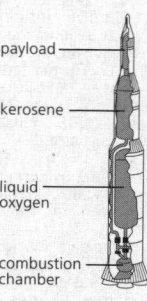

payload

kerosene

liquid oxygen

combustion chamber

rocket

rock•et² (rok′it), *n.* **1.** any of various plants belonging to the genus *Hesperis,* of the mustard family, and related genera. Compare DAME'S ROCKET. **2.** Also called **roquette.** ARUGULA.

rock′et en′gine, *n.* a reaction engine, supplied with its own fuel and oxidizer, used to power an aircraft or spacecraft. Also called **rocket, rock′et mo′tor.**

rock•et•ry (rok′i trē), *n.* the science of rocket design, development, and flight.

rock′et sci′entist, *n.* **1.** a specialist in rocketry. **2.** an exemplar of keen intelligence, esp. mathematical ability.

rock′et ship′, *n.* a rocket-propelled aircraft or spacecraft.

rock•fish (rok′fish′), *n., pl.* **(*esp. collectively*) -fish, (*esp. for kinds or species*) -fish•es. 1.** a fish found about rocks. **2.** STRIPED BASS.

Rock•ford (rok′fərd), *n.* a city in N Illinois. 143,263.

rock′ gar′den, *n.* a garden on rocky ground or among rocks, for the growing of alpine or other plants.

rock′ hound′ or **rock′hound′,** *n.* an amateur collector of rocks and minerals. —**rock′ hound′ing,** *n.*

Rock•ies (rok′ēz), *n.pl.* ROCKY MOUNTAINS.

rock′ing chair′, *n.* a chair mounted on rockers or springs so as to rock a sitter back and forth. Also called **rocker.**

rock′ing horse′, *n.* a toy horse, mounted on rockers or springs, on which children may ride; hobbyhorse.

rock′ lob′ster, *n.* SPINY LOBSTER.

Rock•ne (rok′nē), *n.* **Knute (Kenneth)** (nōōt), 1888–1931, U.S. football coach, born in Norway.

rock′n′roll′ (rok′ən rōl′), *n., v.i.,* **rock′n′rolled, rock′n′roll•ing.** ROCK AND ROLL. —**rock′′n′roll′er, rock′-′n′-roll′er,** *n.*

Rock′ of A′ges, a Christian hymn (1776) with words by August M. Toplady.

rock′-ribbed′, *adj.* **1.** having ribs or ridges of rock. **2.** unyielding; confirmed and uncompromising.

rock′ salt′, *n.* common salt, sodium chloride, occurring in rocklike masses.

Rock•well (rok′wel′, -wəl), *n.* **Norman,** 1894–1978, U.S. illustrator.

rock•y¹ (rok′ē), *adj.,* **-i•er, -i•est. 1.** full of or abounding in rocks. **2.** consisting of rock. **3.** rocklike. **4.** firm; steadfast: *rocky endurance.* **5.** unfeeling; without sympathy or emotion.

rock•y² (rok′ē), *adj.,* **-i•er, -i•est. 1.** wobbly; unsteady. **2.** full of hazards; uncertain: *a business with a rocky future.* **3.** physically unsteady or weak, as from sickness.

Rock′y Moun′tain goat′, *n.* a long-haired, white wild goat of W North America, having short black horns.

Rock′y Moun′tain Na′tional Park′, *n.* a national park in N Colorado. 405 sq. mi. (1050 sq. km).

Rock′y Moun′tains, *n.pl.* a mountain system in W North America, extending NW from central New Mexico through W Canada to N

Alaska. Highest peak in U.S., Mount Elbert, 14,431 ft. (4399 m); highest peak in Canada, Mount Robson, 12,972 ft. (3954 m). Also called **Rockies.**

Rock′y Moun′tain sheep′, *n.* BIGHORN.

Rock′y Moun′tain spot′ted fe′ver, *n.* an acute infectious disease caused by a rickettsia and transmitted by the bite of a wood tick, characterized by high fever, joint and muscle pain, and a rash.

ro•co•co (rə kō′kō, rō′kə kō′), *n.* **1.** an artistic style, chiefly of 18th-century France, marked by studied elegance and delicate ornamentation. **2.** an 18th-century musical style marked by a witty fluency. —*adj.* **3.** of, pertaining to, or characteristic of rococo. **4.** ornate or florid in speech, literary style, etc.

rod (rod), *n.* **1.** a stick, wand, staff, or the like, of wood, metal, or other material. **2.** a straight, slender shoot or stem of any woody plant, whether still growing or cut from the plant. **3.** a slender bar or tube for draping towels over, suspending curtains, etc. **4. a.** a stick used for measuring. **b.** a unit of linear measure, 5½ yards or 16½ feet (5.03 m); pole. **c.** a unit of square measure, 30¼ square yards (25.3 sq m); rood. **5.** a stick, or a bundle of sticks or switches bound together, used as an instrument of punishment. **6.** punishment or discipline. **7.** a staff or scepter carried as a symbol of office, authority, etc. **8.** authority, sway, or rule, esp. when tyrannical. **9.** FISHING ROD. **10.** LIGHTNING ROD. **11.** one of the rodlike cells in the retina of the eye, sensitive to low intensities of light. Compare CONE (def. 5). **12.** (in plastering or mortaring) a straightedge moved along screeds to even the plaster between them. **13.** *Bible.* a branch of a family; tribe. Ps. 74:2; Jer. 10:16. **14.** *Slang.* a pistol or revolver. **15.** a collapsible pole, conspicuously marked with graduations, held upright so that it can be read at a distance by a surveyor.

rode (rōd), *v.* a pt. of RIDE.

ro•dent (rōd′nt), *adj.* **1.** belonging or pertaining to the gnawing or nibbling mammals of the order Rodentia, characterized by four continually growing incisors: includes mice, squirrels, beavers, chipmunks, and rats. —*n.* **2.** a rodent mammal.

ro•den•ti•cide (rō den′tə sīd′), *n.* a substance for killing rodents.

ro•de•o (rō′dē ō′, rō dā′ō), *n., pl.* **-de•os. 1.** a public exhibition of cowboy skills, as bronco riding and calf roping. **2.** a roundup of cattle.

Rodg•ers (roj′ərz), *n.* **1. James Charles** (*Jimmie*), 1897–1933, U.S. country-and-western singer, guitarist, and composer. **2. Richard,** 1902–79, U.S. composer of popular music.

Ro•din (rō dan′, -daɴ′), *n.* **(François) Auguste (René),** 1840–1917, French sculptor.

rod•o•mon•tade (rod′ə mən tād′, -täd′, rō′də-), *n.* **1.** vainglorious boasting; blustering talk. —*adj.* **2.** boastful.

roe[1] (rō), *n.* **1.** the mass of eggs, or spawn, within the ovarian membrane of the female fish. **2.** the eggs of certain crustaceans, as lobsters.

roe[2] (rō), *n., pl.* **roes,** (*esp. collectively*) **roe.** ROE DEER.

roe•buck (rō′buk′), *n., pl.* **-bucks,** (*esp. collectively*) **-buck.** a male roe deer.

roe′ deer′, *n.* a small, agile Old World deer, *Capreolus capreolus,* the male of which has three-pointed antlers. Also called **roe.**

Roent•gen or **Rönt•gen** (rent′gən, -jən, runt′-), *n.* (*l.c.*) a unit of radiation dosage equal to the amount of ionizing radiation required to produce one electrostatic unit of charge per cubic centimeter of air. *Abbr.:* r, R

roent•gen•ol•o•gy (rent′gə nol′ə jē, -jə-, runt′-), *n.* the branch of medicine dealing with diagnosis and therapy through x-rays.

Roe v. Wade (rō; wād), *n.* a U.S. Supreme Court case in 1973 that legalized abortions in the U.S.

ro•ga•tion (rō gā′shən), *n.* **1.** Usu., **rogations.** solemn supplication, esp. as chanted during procession on the three days **(Roga′tion Days′)** before Ascension Day. **2.** (in ancient Rome) **a.** the proposing by the consuls or tribunes of a law to be passed by the people. **b.** a law so proposed. [< Latin *rogāre* to ask]

rog•er (roj′ər), *interj.* **1.** *Informal.* all right; OK. **2.** message received and understood (a response to radio communications).

Rog•ers (roj′ərz), *n.* **1. Ginger** (*Virginia Katherine McMath*), 1911–95, U.S. dancer and actress. **2. Will(iam Penn Adair),** 1879–1935, U.S. actor and humorist.

Ro•get (rō zhā′, rō′zhā), *n.* **Peter Mark,** 1779–1869, English physician and author of a thesaurus.

rogue (rōg), *n., v.,* **rogued, ro•guing.** —*n.* **1.** a dishonest person; scoundrel. **2.** a playfully mischievous person; scamp. **3.** a tramp or vagabond. **4.** a rogue elephant or other animal of similar disposition. **5.** a usu. inferior organism, esp. a plant, varying markedly from the normal. —*v.i.* **6.** to live or act as a rogue. —*v.t.* **7.** to uproot or destroy (plants, etc., that do not conform to a desired standard). **8.** to perform this operation upon: *to rogue a field.*

rogue′ el′ephant, *n.* a vicious elephant exiled from the herd.

ro•guish (rō′gish), *adj.* **1.** dishonest, knavish, or rascally. **2.** playfully mischievous: *a roguish smile.* —**ro′guish•ly,** *adv.* —**ro′guish•ness,** *n.*

roil (roil), *v.t.* **1.** to render (a fluid) turbid by stirring up sediment. **2.** to disturb or disquiet; irritate. —*v.i.* **3.** to move or proceed turbulently.

Ro•land (rō′lənd), *n.* the greatest of the paladins in the Charlemagne cycle of chansons de geste, renowned for his prowess and the manner of his death in the battle of Roncesvalles (A.D. 778).

role or **rôle** (rōl), *n.* **1.** a part or character played by an actor, singer, or other performer. **2.** the proper or customary function of a person or thing. **3.** the rights, obligations, and expected behavior patterns associated with a particular social status.

role′ mod′el, *n.* a person whose behavior in a particular social setting is imitated by others, esp. by younger persons.

role′-play′ing, *n.* **1.** modification of one's behavior to accord with a desired personal image, as to impress others or conform to a particular environment. **2.** a method of psychotherapy aimed at changing attitudes and behavior, in which participants act out designated roles relevant to real-life situations. —**role′-play′,** *v.t., v.i.*

roll (rōl), *v.i.* **1.** to move along a surface by turning over and over. **2.** to move or be moved on wheels. **3.** to flow or advance with an undulating motion, as waves. **4.** to extend in undulations, as land. **5.** to elapse, as time. **6.** to move as in a cycle, as seasons (usu. fol. by *round* or *around*). **7.** to emit or have a deep, prolonged sound, as thunder. **8.** to trill, as a bird. **9.** to turn over, as a person lying down. **10.** (of the eyes) to turn around in different directions. **11.** (of a vessel) **a.** to rock from side to side in open water. **b.** to sail with a side-to-side rocking motion. **12.** to walk with a swinging or swaying gait. **13.** *Informal.* **a.** to begin to move or operate: *Let's roll at sunrise.* **b.** to make progress; advance. **14.** to curl up so as to form a ball or cylinder. **15.** to become spread out or flattened. **16.** (of an aircraft or rocket) to deviate from a stable flight attitude by rotation about the longitudinal axis. —*v.t.* **17.** to cause to move along a surface by turning over and over. **18.** to move along on wheels or rollers. **19.** to drive or cause to flow onward with an undulating motion. **20.** to utter or give forth with a full, flowing, continuous sound. **21.** to trill: *to roll one's* r*'s.* **22.** to cause to turn over. **23.** to turn around in different directions: *to roll one's eyes.* **24.** to cause to sway or rock from side to side, as a ship. **25.** to wrap around an axis or around itself: *to roll string.* **26.** to make by forming into a cylinder: *to roll a cigarette.* **27.** to spread out flat (something curled up) (often fol. by *out*). **28.** to wrap or envelop, as in a covering. **29.** to spread out or level as with a rolling pin. **30.** to beat (a drum) with rapid, continuous strokes. **31.** (in certain games, as craps) to throw (dice). **32.** to apply (ink) with a roller or series of rollers. **33.** *Slang.* to rob, esp. by going through the pockets of a victim who is asleep or drunk. **34. roll back,** to reduce (prices, wages, etc.) to a former level. **35. roll in,** *Informal.* to arrive, esp. in large numbers or quantity: *When does the money start rolling in?* **36. roll out, a.** to spread out or flatten. **b.** *Informal.* to arise, as from bed. **c.** *Football.* to execute a rollout. **37. roll over,** to reinvest (funds), as from one stock or bond into another. **38. roll up, a.** to amass in increasing quantities or amounts. **b.** to arrive in a car, carriage, or other vehicle. —*n.* **39.** a piece of paper, parchment, or the like, that is rolled up. **40.** a register, catalog, or list, as of membership. **41.** anything rolled up in a ringlike or cylindrical form. **42.** a length of cloth, wallpaper, or the like, rolled up in cylindrical form, often forming a definite measure. **43.** a cylindrical or rounded mass of something. **44.** a roller. **45. a.** thin cake spread with jelly or the like and rolled up. **b.** a small cake of bread sometimes folded over before baking. **c.** meat rolled up and cooked. **46.** an act or instance of rolling. **47.** undulation, as of a surface. **48.** a sonorous or rhythmical flow of words. **49.** a deep, prolonged sound, as of thunder or drums. **50.** the trill of certain birds. **51.** a rolling motion or gait. **52.** (in various dice games) a single cast of or turn at casting the dice. —***Idiom.* 53. on a roll,** experiencing an interval of success and good fortune. **54. roll with the punches,** to cope by accommodating to adversity and remaining flexible. **55. strike off** or **from the rolls,** to remove from membership or practice.

roll•a•way (rōl′ə wā′), *adj.* **1.** designed to be rolled out of the way or out of sight when not in use: *a rollaway bed.* —*n.* **2.** a rollaway piece of furniture, esp. a bed.

roll•back (rōl′bak′), *n.* **1.** an act or instance of rolling back. **2.** a return to a lower level of prices, wages, etc.

roll′ bar′, *n.* a steel bar arching over an automobile from side to side, designed for passenger protection in the event of a rollover.

roll′ call′, *n.* the calling of a list of names, as of soldiers or students, for checking attendance.

rolled′ gold′, *n.* a thin layer of gold fused to a base metal, rolled out into sheets from which articles can be cut, esp. jewelry.

rolled′ oats′, *n.* oats flattened by rollers after hulling and steaming.

roll•er[1] (rō′lər), *n.* **1.** a person or thing that rolls. **2.** a cylinder, wheel, caster, or the like, upon which something is rolled along. **3.** a cylindrical object revolving on a fixed axis, esp. one that facilitates the movement of something passed over or around it. **4.** a cylindrical object upon which something is rolled up. **5.** a hollow, cylindrical object upon which hair is rolled up for setting. **6.** a cylindrical object for spreading or flattening something. **7.** a long, swelling wave advancing steadily.

roll•er[2] (rō′lər), *n.* any of various medium-sized, often brightly colored Old World birds of the family Coraciidae, that tumble or roll over during display flights.

Roll•er•blade (rō′lər blād′), *v.,* **-blad•ed, -blad•ing. 1.** *Trademark.* a brand of in-line skates. —*v.i.* **2.** (*often l.c.*) to skate on in-line skates. —**Roll′er•blad′er, roll′er•blad′er,** *n.*

roll′er coast′er, *n.* **1.** a small railroad, esp. in an amusement park, having a train with open cars that moves along a high, sharply winding trestle built with steep inclines. **2.** any phenomenon, period, or experience characterized by violent fluctuations.

roll′er rink′, *n.* a rink for roller-skating.

roll′er skate′, *n.* a form of skate with four wheels or rollers, for use on a sidewalk or other surface offering traction. —**roll′er-skate′**, *v.i.*, **-skat•ed, -skat•ing.** —**roll′er skat′er,** *n.*

roll′ film′, *n.* a strip of film with space for several exposures, rolled on a spool to permit ease of handling. —**roll′-film′,** *adj.*

rol•lick (rol′ik), *v.i.* to move or act in a carefree or boisterous manner.

roll•ing (rō′ling), *adj.* **1.** moving by turning over and over. **2.** rising and falling in gentle slopes, as land. **3.** moving in undulating billows, as clouds. **4.** rocking from side to side. **5.** turning or folding over, as a collar. **6.** producing a deep, continuous sound.

roll′ing mill′, *n.* **1.** a mill where metal is passed between rolls to give it a certain thickness or cross-sectional form. **2.** a machine or set of rollers for rolling out or shaping metal.

roll′ing pin′, *n.* a cylinder of wood or other material, usu. with a handle at each end, for rolling out dough.

roll′ing stock′, *n.* the wheeled vehicles of a railroad, including locomotives, freight cars, and passenger cars.

roll′-on′, *adj.* **1.** packaged in a container equipped with a rotating ball that dispenses the liquid content directly: *a roll-on deodorant.* —*n.* **2.** a roll-on preparation.

roll′out′ or **roll′-out′,** *n.* **1.** the first public showing of an aircraft. **2.** the introduction of a new product or service. **3.** a football maneuver in which the quarterback moves laterally with the ball.

roll•o•ver (rōl′ō′vər), *n.* the reinvestment of funds, as from one stock or bond into another.

roll′-top′ (or **roll′top′**) **desk′,** *n.* a desk with a flexible sliding cover, often of closely set wood strips, that can be pulled down over the working surface or rolled up beneath the top.

roll•way (rōl′wā′), *n.* **1.** a place on which things are rolled or moved on rollers. **2.** an incline for rolling or sliding logs into a stream to begin them on their journey from lumber camp to mill.

Ro•lo•dex (rō′lə deks′), *Trademark.* a small desktop file containing cards for names, addresses, and phone numbers.

ro•ly-po•ly (rō′lē pō′lē, -pō′lē), *adj., n., pl.* **-lies.** —*adj.* **1.** short and plumply round. —*n.* **2.** a roly-poly person or thing.

ROM (rom), *n.* read-only memory: nonvolatile, nonmodifiable computer memory, used to hold programmed instructions to the system. Compare RAM.

rom., roman (type).

ro•maine (rō mān′, rə-), *n.* a variety of lettuce, *Lactuca sativa longifolia,* having a cylindrical head of long, loose leaves. Also called **romaine′ let′tuce, cos, cos lettuce.**

ro•man (rô mäⁿ′), *n., pl.* **-mans** (-mäⁿ′). *French.* **1.** a metrical narrative, esp. in medieval French literature. **2.** a novel.

Ro•man (rō′mən), *adj.* **1.** of or pertaining to the ancient or modern city of Rome, or to its inhabitants. **2.** of or pertaining to the ancient kingdom, republic, and empire whose capital was the city of Rome. **3.** of a kind or character regarded as typical of the ancient Romans: *Roman virtues.* **4.** (*usu. l.c.*) designating or pertaining to the upright style of printing types most commonly used in modern books, periodicals, etc. **5.** of or pertaining to the Roman Catholic Church. **6.** of or pertaining to the architecture of ancient Rome, characterized by semicircular arches, domes, groin and barrel vaults, and the use of elaborated forms of the Greek orders. **7.** written in or pertaining to Roman numerals. —*n.* **8.** a native, inhabitant, or citizen of ancient or modern Rome. **9.** (*usu. l.c.*) roman type or lettering.

ro•man à clef (*Fr.* rô mä nA kle′), *n., pl.* **ro•mans à clef** (*Fr.* rô mäⁿ zA kle′). a novel that represents historical events and characters under the guise of fiction.

Ro′man al′phabet, *n.* LATIN ALPHABET.

Ro′man cal′endar, *n.* the calendar in use in ancient Rome until 46 B.C., when it was replaced with the Julian calendar.

Ro′man can′dle, *n.* a firework consisting of a tube that sends out a shower of sparks and a succession of balls of fire.

Ro′man Cath′olic, *adj.* **1.** of or pertaining to the Roman Catholic Church. —*n.* **2.** a member of the Roman Catholic Church.

Ro′man Cath′olic Church′, *n.* the Christian church of which the pope, or bishop of Rome, is the supreme head.

Ro′man Cathol′icism, *n.* the faith, practice, and system of government of the Roman Catholic Church.

ro•mance (*n., adj.* rō mans′, rō′mans; *v.* rō mans′), *n., v.,* **-manced, -manc•ing,** *adj.* —*n.* **1.** a novel or other prose narrative depicting heroic or marvelous deeds, pageantry, romantic exploits, etc., usu. in a historical or imaginary setting. **2.** a medieval narrative, orig. one in verse and in a Romance language, treating of heroic, fantastic, or supernatural events, often in the form of allegory. **3.** a made-up story, usu. full of exaggeration or fanciful invention. **4.** romantic aura, setting, character, or quality. **5.** a love affair. **6.** (*cap.*) the Romance languages. *Abbr.:* Rom —*v.i.* **7.** to indulge in fanciful stories or daydreams. **8.** to think or talk romantically. —*v.t.* **9.** to court or woo romantically. **10.** to court the favor of; play up to. —*adj.* **11.** (*cap.*) of, pertaining to, or denoting the group of languages descended from the spoken Latin of the Roman Empire, including French, Spanish, Portuguese, Italian, and Romanian.

Ro′man col′lar, *n.* CLERICAL COLLAR.

Ro′man Em′pire, *n.* **1.** the lands and peoples subject to the authority of ancient Rome. **2.** the imperial form of government established in Rome in 27 B.C., comprising the Principate or Early Empire (27 B.C.–A.D. 284) and the Autocracy or Later Empire (A.D. 284–476).

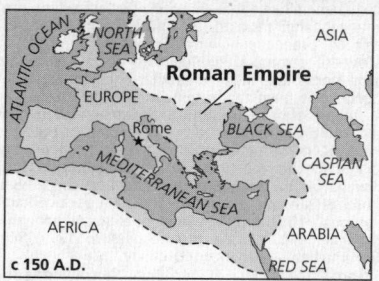

c 150 A.D.

Ro•man•esque (rō′mə nesk′), *adj.* of or pertaining to the style of architecture prevailing in W and S Europe from the 9th through the 12th centuries, characterized by heavy masonry construction with narrow openings and the use of the round arch.

Ro′man hol′iday, *n.* **1.** a riotous public disturbance, often marked by wanton destruction and licentiousness. **2.** pleasure or entertainment obtained from the discomfort or suffering of others.

Ro•ma•ni•a (rō mā′nē ə, -mān′yə), *n.* a republic in SE Europe, bordering on the Black Sea. 21,399,114; 91,699 sq. mi. (237,500 sq. km). *Cap.:* Bucharest. Romanian, **Ro•mâ•nia** (rō mä′nyä)

Ro•ma•ni•an (rō mā′nē ən, -mān′yən) also **Rumanian, Roumanian,** *n.* **1.** a native or inhabitant of Romania. **2.** the Romance language of Romania, spoken also in Moldavia. —*adj.* **3.** of or pertaining to Romania, its inhabitants, or the language Romanian.

Ro′man law′, *n.* the system of jurisprudence elaborated by the Romans, a strong varied influence on the legal systems of many countries.

Ro′man mile′, *n.* a unit of length used by the ancient Romans, equivalent to about 1620 yards (1480 m).

Ro′man nu′merals, *n.pl.* the numerals in the ancient Roman system of notation, still used occasionally, as in pagination and dates on buildings. The basic symbols are $I(=1)$, $V(=5)$, $X(=10)$, $L(=50)$, $C(=100)$, $D(=500)$, and $M(=1000)$. If a letter is immediately followed by one of equal or lesser value, the two values are added; if followed by one of greater value, the first is subtracted from the second; thus, XX equals 20 and IV equals 4. The year 1997 would usu. appear as MCMXCVII. Roman numerals are usu. written in capital letters.

ROMAN NUMERALS

Arabic Numeral	Roman Numeral	Arabic Numeral	Roman Numeral
1	I	29	XXIX
2	II	30	XXX
3	III	31	XXXI
4	IV	32	XXXII
5	V	40	XL
6	VI	41	XLI
7	VII	50	L
8	VIII	60	LX
9	IX	70	LXX
10	X	80	LXXX
11	XI	90	XC
12	XII	100	C
13	XIII	101	CI
14	XIV	102	CII
15	XV	200	CC
16	XVI	300	CCC
17	XVII	400	CD
18	XVIII	500	D
19	XIX	600	DC
20	XX	700	DCC
21	XXI	800	DCCC
22	XXII	900	CM
23	XXIII	1000	M
24	XXIV	2000	MM
25	XXV	5000	$\bar{V}$
26	XXVI	10,000	$\bar{X}$
27	XXVII	100,000	$\bar{C}$
28	XXVIII	1,000,000	$\bar{M}$

Ro•ma•no (rō mä′nō), *n.* (*sometimes l.c.*) a sharp Italian cheese made of ewe's milk and usu. grated before serving.

Ro•ma•nov or **Ro•ma•noff** (rō′mə nôf′, -nof′, rō mä′nəf), *n.* **1.** a member of the imperial dynasty of Russia that ruled from 1613 to 1917. **2. Mikhail Feodorovich,** 1596–1645, emperor of Russia 1613–45: first ruler of the house of Romanov.

Ro•mans (rō′mənz), *n.* (*used with a sing. v.*) an Epistle of the New Testament, written by Paul to the Christian community in Rome.

ro•man•tic (rō man′tik), *adj.* **1.** of or pertaining to romance. **2.** impractical or unrealistic; fanciful. **3.** imbued with idealism, a desire for adventure, etc. **4.** preoccupied with love or by the idealizing of love. **5.** expressing love or strong affection. **6.** ardent; passionate; fervent. **7.** (*often cap.*) of, pertaining to, or characteristic of a style of literature and art that subordinates form to content, encourages freedom of treatment, emphasizes imagination, emotion, and introspection, and often celebrates nature, the ordinary person, and freedom of the spirit (contrasted with *classical*). **8.** of or pertaining to a musical style, esp. of the 19th century, marked by the free expression of imagination and emotion, virtuosic display, experimentation with form, and the adventurous development of orchestral and piano music and opera. **9.** imaginary, fictitious, or fabulous. **10.** noting the role of a suitor in a play about love: *the romantic lead.* —*n.* **11.** a romantic person. **12.** (*often cap.*) an adherent of Romanticism. —**ro•man′ti•cal•ly,** *adv.*

ro•man•ti•cism (rō man′tə siz′əm), *n.* **1.** romantic spirit. **2.** (*often cap.*) the Romantic style or movement in literature and art, or adherence to its principles (contrasted with *classicism*). —**ro•man′ti•cist,** *n.*

ro•man•ti•cize (rō man′tə sīz′), *v.,* **-cized, -ciz•ing.** —*v.t.* **1.** to invest with a romantic character. —*v.i.* **2.** to hold romantic notions, ideas, etc.

Roman′tic Move′ment, *n.* a movement that led to the establishment of Romantic principles in art and literature around 1800.

Rom•a•ny or **Rom•a•ni** (rom′ə nē, rō′mə-), *n.* **1.** the Indo-Aryan language traditionally spoken by the Gypsies, comprising a broad range of dialects. **2.** the Gypsies collectively. —*adj.* **3.** of or pertaining to the Gypsies or Romany.

Rome (rōm), *n.* **1.** Italian, **Roma.** the capital of Italy, in the central part, on the Tiber: site of Vatican City. 2,817,227. **2.** the ancient Italian kingdom, republic, and empire whose capital was the city of Rome. **3.** the Roman Catholic Church. **4.** ROMAN CATHOLICISM. —*Proverb.* **5. Rome was not built in a day,** worthwhile projects take time to complete. **6. When in Rome, do as the Romans do,** one should follow the customs of one's hosts.

Ro′meo and Ju′liet, a tragedy (produced between 1591 and 1596) by William Shakespeare.

Rom•mel (rom′əl, rum′-), *n.* **Erwin** (*"the Desert Fox"*), 1891–1944, German field marshal.

romp (romp), *v.i.* **1.** to play or frolic in a lively or boisterous manner. **2.** to move rapidly and without effort, as in racing. **3.** to win easily. —*n.* **4.** a lively or boisterous frolic. **5.** a person who romps. **6.** a quick or effortless pace: *He did the work in a romp.* **7.** an easy victory.

romp•er (rom′pər), *n.* **1.** a person or thing that romps. **2.** Usu., **rompers.** (*used with a pl. v.*) **a.** a one-piece garment combining a shirt and short, bloomerlike pants, worn by young children. **b.** a similar garment worn by women and girls for leisure activity.

Rom•u•lus (rom′yə ləs), *n.* the legendary founder of Rome and its first king: a son of Mars, he and his twin brother (**Remus**) were abandoned as infants and suckled by a wolf.

ron•deau (ron′dō, ron dō′), *n., pl.* **-deaux** (-dōz, -dōz′). a short poem of 13 or 10 lines on two rhymes with the opening words or phrase used in two places as an unrhymed refrain.

ron•del (ron′dl, ron del′), *n.* a 14 line poem on two rhymes, with the initial couplet repeated in the middle and at the end.

ron•de•let (ron′dl et′, ron′dl et′), *n.* a short poem consisting of five lines on two rhymes, and having the opening words or word used after the second and fifth lines as an unrhymed refrain.

ron•do (ron′dō, ron dō′), *n., pl.* **-dos. 1.** a musical form in which a refrain recurs typically four times in the tonic with intervening couplets in contrasting keys. **2.** a movement in the form of a rondo.

Ron•sard (RÔN SAR′), *n.* **Pierre de,** 1524–85, French poet.

rood (rōōd), *n.* **1.** a crucifix, esp. a large one at the entrance to the choir or chancel of a church. **2. a.** a unit of length varying locally from 5½ to 8 yards (5 to 7 m). **b.** a unit of land measure equal to 40 square rods or ¼ acre (0.1 ha). **c.** a unit of square measure equal to one square rod (25.3 sq. m).

roof (rōōf, rŏŏf), *n.* **1.** the external upper covering of a house or other building. **2.** a frame for supporting this: *an open-timbered roof.* **3.** the highest part or summit of anything. **4.** something that covers in the manner of a roof, as the top of a car or the upper part of the mouth. **5.** a house. —*v.t.* **6.** to provide or cover with a roof. —*Idiom.* **7. go through the roof, a.** (esp. of costs) to increase dramatically. **b.** Also, **hit the roof.** to lose one's temper; become enraged.

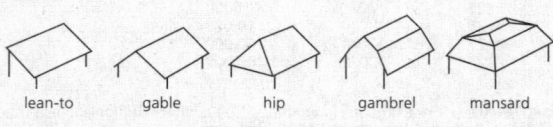

lean-to   gable   hip   gambrel   mansard

roofs (def. 1)

roof•er (rōō′fər, rŏŏf′ər), *n.* a person who makes or repairs roofs.

roof′ gar′den, *n.* **1.** a garden on the flat roof of a house or other building. **2.** the top or top story of a building, having a garden, restaurant, or the like.

roof•ing (rōō′fing, rŏŏf′ing), *n.* **1.** the act of covering with a roof. **2.** material for roofs. **3.** a roof.

rook[1] (rŏŏk), *n.* **1.** a black, bare-faced Eurasian crow, *Corvus frugilegus,* that nests and roosts colonially. **2.** a sharper at cards or dice; swindler. —*v.t.* **3.** to cheat or swindle.

rook[2] (rŏŏk), *n.* one of two chess pieces of the same color that may be moved any unobstructed distance horizontally or vertically; castle.

rook•er•y (rŏŏk′ə rē), *n., pl.* **-er•ies. 1.** a colony or breeding place of rooks or other gregarious creatures, as penguins or seals. **2.** any teeming, overcrowded place.

rook•ie (rŏŏk′ē), *n.* **1.** an athlete in the first season as a member of a professional team. **2.** an inexperienced military or police recruit. **3.** a novice; beginner.

room (rōōm, rŏŏm), *n.* **1.** a portion of space within a building that is enclosed or partitioned off from other parts. **2. rooms,** lodgings or quarters, as in a house. **3.** the persons present in a room: *The whole room laughed.* **4.** space or extent of space occupied by or available for something: *The desk will take up more room.* **5.** opportunity or scope for something: *room for improvement.* —*v.i.* **6.** to occupy a room or rooms; lodge.

room′ and board′, *n.* lodging and meals.

room•er (rōō′mər, rŏŏm′ər), *n.* a person who rents room; lodger.

room•ette (rōō met′, rŏŏ-), *n.* a small private compartment in the sleeping car of a train. **2.** a private room adjoining a box at a sports stadium or arena and used for entertaining guests.

room′ing house′, *n.* a house with furnished rooms to rent.

room•mate (rōōm′māt′, rŏŏm′-), *n.* a person who shares a room or apartment with another or others.

room′ serv′ice, *n.* **1.** the serving of food, drinks, etc., to a guest in a hotel room. **2.** the department offering this service.

room•y (rōō′mē, rŏŏm′ē), *adj.,* **-i•er, -i•est.** affording ample room; spacious. —**room′i•ly,** *adv.* —**room′i•ness,** *n.*

roor•back or **roor•bach** (rŏŏr′bak′), *n.* a false and more or less damaging report circulated for political effect, usually about a candidate seeking an office. [after a fictitious Baron von Roorback, in whose travelogue occurred an account of an incident damaging to the character of James K. Polk]

Roo•se•velt (rō′zə velt′, -vəlt, rōz′-; spelling pron. rōō′-), *n.* **1. (Anna) Eleanor,** 1884–1962, U.S. diplomat and author (wife of Franklin Delano Roosevelt). **2. Franklin Delano** (*"FDR"*), 1882–1945, 32nd president of the U.S. 1933–45. **3. Theodore** (*Teddy,* "*T.R.*"), 1858–1919, 26th president of the U.S. 1901–09. **4. Rio,** a river flowing N from W Brazil to the Madeira River. ab. 400 mi. (645 km) long.

Roo′sevelt Cor′ollary, *n.* a corollary (1904) to the Monroe Doctrine, asserting that the U.S. might intervene in the affairs of an American republic threatened with seizure or intervention by a European country. [after Theodore ROOSEVELT]

roost (rōōst), *n.* **1.** a perch upon which birds or fowls rest at night. **2.** a large cage, house, or other place for fowls or birds to roost in. **3.** a place for resting or lodging. —*v.i.* **4.** to sit or rest on a perch, branch, etc. **5.** to settle or stay, esp. for the night. —*Idiom.* **6. come home to roost,** (of an action) to react unfavorably on the doer; boomerang. **7. rule the roost,** to be in charge or control; dominate.

roost•er (rōō′stər), *n.* **1.** the male of domestic fowl and certain game birds; cock. **2.** *Informal.* a cocky person.

root[1] (rōōt, rŏŏt), *n.* **1.** a part of the body of a plant that develops, typically, from the radicle and grows downward into the soil, anchoring the plant and absorbing nutriment and moisture. **2.** any underground part of a plant, as a rhizome. **3.** something resembling or suggesting the root of a plant in position or function. **4.** the embedded or basal portion of a hair, tooth, nail, nerve, etc. **5.** the fundamental or essential part. **6.** the source or origin of a thing. **7.** a person or family as the source of offspring or descendants. **8. roots, a.** a person's original or ancestral home, environment, and culture. **b.** the personal relations, affinity for a place, habits, etc., that make a locale one's true home. **9. a.** *Math.* a quantity that, when multiplied by itself a certain number of times, produces a given quantity. **b.** *r*th root, the quantity raised to the power $1/r$: *2 is the ⅓ root of 8.* **c.** a value of the argument of a function for which the function takes the value zero. **10. a.** a morpheme that underlies an inflectional or derivational paradigm, as *dance,* the root in *danced, dancer* or *tend-,* the root of Latin *tendere* "to stretch." **b.** such a form reconstructed for a parent language, as **sed-,* the hypothetical proto-Indo-European root meaning "sit." **11. a.** the fundamental tone of a compound musical tone of a series of harmonies. **b.** the lowest tone of a chord when arranged as a series of thirds; fundamental. **12. a.** (in a

tap (ragweed),   fibrous (plantain),   fleshy (carrot),   tuberous (rue anemone),
Ambrosia trifida   *Plantago major*   *Daucus carota*   *Anemonella thalictroides*

roots (def. 1)

screw or other threaded object) the narrow inner surface between threads. **b.** (in a gear) the narrow inner surface between teeth. —*v.i.* **13.** to become fixed or established. —*v.t.* **14.** to fix by or as if by roots: *We were rooted to the spot in amazement.* **15.** to implant or establish deeply. **16.** to pull, tear, or dig up by the roots (often fol. by *up* or *out*). **17.** to extirpate; remove completely (often fol. by *up* or *out*): *to root out crime.* —*Idiom.* **18. root and branch,** utterly; entirely. **19. take root, a.** to send out roots; begin to grow. **b.** to become established.

root² (rōōt, rōōt), *v.i.* **1.** to turn up the soil with the snout, as swine. **2.** to poke, pry, or search, as if to find something: *to root around in a drawer for a cuff link.* —*v.t.* **3.** to turn over with the snout (often fol. by *up*). **4.** to unearth; bring to light (often fol. by *up*). —**root′er,** *n.*

root³ (rōōt *or, sometimes,* rŏŏt), *v.i.* **1.** to encourage a team or contestant by cheering enthusiastically. **2.** to lend moral support. —**root′er,** *n.*

Root (rōōt), *n.* **1. Elihu,** 1845–1937, U.S. statesman. **2. George F(rederick),** 1820–95, U.S. musician and hymn writer.

root′ beer′, *n.* a carbonated beverage flavored with syrup made from the extracted juices of roots, barks, and herbs.

root′ canal′, *n.* **1.** the root portion of the pulp cavity of a tooth. **2.** ROOT CANAL THERAPY (def. 2).

root′ canal′ ther′apy, *n.* **1.** the branch of endodontics that treats disease of the dental pulp. **2.** a treatment for such disease in which the pulp is removed from the pulp cavity and replaced by filling material.

root′ cel′lar, *n.* a cellar, often underground and usu. covered with dirt, where root crops and other vegetables are stored.

root•ed (rōō′tid, rŏŏt′id), *adj.* firmly implanted: *a deeply rooted dislike.*

root′er skunk′, *n.* HOG-NOSED SKUNK.

root′ hair′, *n.* an elongated tubular extension of an epidermal cell of a root, serving to absorb water and minerals from the soil.

root•less (rōōt′lis, rŏŏt′-), *adj.* **1.** having no roots. **2.** having no basis of stability; unsteady: *a rootless feeling.* **3.** having no place or position in society: *a rootless wanderer.* —**root′less•ness,** *n.*

root•let (rōōt′lit, rŏŏt′-), *n.* a little root or branch of a root.

Roots (rōōts, rŏŏts), a nonfiction work (1976) by Alex Haley, tracing the history of black Americans.

root•stock (rōōt′stok′, rŏŏt′-), *n.* **1.** a root and its associated growth buds, used as a stock in plant propagation. **2.** a rhizome.

rope (rōp), *n., v.,* **roped, rop•ing.** —*n.* **1.** a strong, thick line or cord, usu. made of twisted or braided strands of hemp, flax, wire, or the like. **2.** a lasso. **3. ropes, a.** the cords used to enclose a prize ring or other space. **b.** the operations of a business or the details of any undertaking: *to learn the ropes.* **4.** a hangman's noose. **5.** the sentence or punishment of death by hanging. **6.** material or objects twisted or strung together in the form of a cord. **7.** a stringy, viscid formation in a liquid. **8.** *Slang.* a thick, heavy gold chain worn as jewelry. —*v.t.* **9.** to tie, bind, or fasten with a rope. **10.** to enclose or mark off with a rope (often fol. by *off*): *to rope off the reserved seats.* **11.** to catch with a lasso; lasso. —*v.i.* **12.** to become ropy or stringy. **13. rope in,** to lure, esp. by trickery. —*Idiom.* **14. on the ropes,** close to defeat, failure, or utter collapse. —**rop′a•ble, rope′a•ble,** *adj.* —**rop′er,** *n.*

rope•mak•ing (rōp′mā′king), *n.* the act, process, or skill of making rope. —**rope′mak′er,** *n.*

rope′ tow′, *n.* SKI TOW.

rop•y (rō′pē), *adj.,* **-i•er, -i•est. 1.** resembling a rope or ropes: *ropy muscles.* **2.** forming viscid or glutinous threads, as a liquid. —**rop′i•ly,** *adv.* —**rop′i•ness,** *n.*

Roque•fort (rōk′fərt), *n.* a strong-flavored cheese veined with blue mold, made from sheep's milk.

ro•quette (rō ket′), *n.* ARUGULA.

ror•qual (rôr′kwəl), *n.* any of several whales of the genus *Balaenoptera;* finback.

Ror′schach test′ (rôr′shäk, rôr′-), *n.* a diagnostic test of personality and intellect based on the viewer's interpretations of a standard series of inkblot designs. Compare INKBLOT TEST. [after Hermann *Rorschach* (1884–1922), Swiss psychiatrist]

ro•sa•ce•a (rō zā′shē ə), *n.* a chronic form of acne affecting the nose, forehead, and cheeks, characterized by red pustular lesions.

ro•sa•ceous (rō zā′shəs), *adj.* **1.** belonging to the plant family Rosaceae. **2.** having a corolla of five broad petals, like that of a rose. **3.** like a rose; roselike. **4.** rose-colored; rosy.

ro•sa•ry (rō′zə rē), *n., pl.* **-ries. 1.** a series of prayers recited by Roman Catholics as a private devotion, usu. consisting of groups of ten *aves* preceded by a paternoster and followed by a Gloria Patri, each group being accompanied by meditation on a mystery in the lives of Jesus or Mary. **2.** a string of beads used in counting these prayers during their recitation. **3.** a similar string used in praying by other religious groups. [< Medieval Latin *rosārium* rose garden]

rose¹ (rōz), *n.* **1.** any of the wild or cultivated, usu. prickly-stemmed, pinnate-leaved, showy-flowered shrubs of the genus *Rosa.* **2.** any of various related or similar plants. **3.** the flower of any such shrub, of a red, pink, white, or yellow color. **4.** a pinkish red, purplish pink, or light crimson color. **5.** an ornament shaped like or suggesting a rose. **6.** any of various diagrams showing directions radiating from a common center, as a compass card or wind rose. **7. a.** an old style of gem cut having a flat base and a dome-shaped crown, typically with 24 triangular facets. **b.** a gem with this cut. **8.** a perforated cap or plate, as at the end of a pipe or the spout of a watering pot, to break a flow of water

into a spray. —*adj.* **9.** of the color rose. **10.** for, containing, or growing roses. **11.** scented like a rose. —*Idiom.* **12. come up roses,** to become or prove to be fine; turn out well. —**rose′like′,** *adj.*

rose² (rōz), *v.* pt. of RISE.

ro•sé (rō zā′), *n.* a pink wine made from red grapes by removing the grape skins from the must before fermentation is completed.

ro•se•ate (rō′zē it, -āt′), *adj.* **1.** tinged with rose; rosy. **2.** bright or promising. **3.** incautiously optimistic. —**ro′se•ate•ly,** *adv.*

ro′seate spoon′bill, *n.* a spoonbill, *Ajaia ajaja,* of warmer parts of the New World, having rose-colored plumage and a bare head.

Ro•seau (rō zō′), *n.* the capital of Dominica. 20,000.

rose′-breast′ed gros′beak, *n.* a North American grosbeak, *Pheucticus ludovicianus,* the male of which has a rose-pink breast patch.

rose•bush (rōz′bŏŏsh′), *n.* a shrub that bears roses.

rose′ chaf′er, *n.* a tan beetle, *Macrodactylus subspinosus,* that feeds on the flowers and foliage of roses, grapes, peach trees, etc. Also called **rose′ bee′tle.**

rose′-col′ored, *adj.* **1.** of the color rose; rosy. **2.** bright; cheerful. **3.** optimistic; sanguine.

rose′-col′ored glass′es, (*used with a pl. v.*) a cheerful or optimistic, esp. overly optimistic view of things.

rose′ gera′nium, *n.* any of several plants of the genus *Pelargonium,* cultivated for their fragrant leaves.

rose′ hip′, *n.* HIP².

rose•mar•y (rōz′mâr′ē, -mə rē), *n., pl.* **-mar•ies.** an aromatic evergreen shrub, *Rosmarinus officinalis,* of the mint family, native to the Mediterranean region, with narrow, leathery leaves used as a seasoning and in perfumes.

rose′ moss′, *n.* a portulaca, *Portulaca grandiflora,* widely cultivated for its showy flowers.

Ro•sen•berg (rō′zən bûrg′), *n.* **Julius,** 1918–53, and his wife, **Ethel Greenglass,** 1915–53, U.S. citizens executed for espionage.

rose′ of Jer′icho, *n.* an Asian plant, *Anastatica hierochuntica,* of the mustard family, that curls up when dry and expands when moistened. Also called **resurrection plant.**

rose′ of Shar′on, *n.* **1.** Also called **althea.** a widely cultivated shrub or small tree, *Hibiscus syriacus,* of the mallow family, having showy white, reddish, or purplish flowers. **2.** a St.-John's-wort, *Hypericum calycinum,* having evergreen foliage and showy yellow flowers. **3.** a plant mentioned in the Bible. Song of Solomon 2:1.

ro•se•o•la (rō zē′ə lə, rō′zē ō′lə), *n.* **1.** a rose-colored rash occurring in various febrile diseases. **2.** RUBELLA. —**ro•se′o•lar,** *adj.*

Roset′ta stone′, *n.* a stone slab, found in 1799 near Rosetta, with parallel inscriptions in Greek, Egyptian hieroglyphic, and demotic characters, enabling the decipherment of ancient Egyptian hieroglyphics.

ro•sette (rō zet′), *n.* **1.** any arrangement, part, or object more or less resembling a rose. **2.** a rose-shaped arrangement of ribbon or other material, used as an ornament or badge. **3.** an architectural ornament resembling a rose or having a generally circular combination of parts. **4.** a circular cluster of leaves or other plant organs. **5.** one of the compound spots on a leopard.

rose′ wa′ter, *n.* water containing oil distilled from roses, used in perfume and as a flavoring.

rose•wood (rōz′wŏŏd′), *n.* **1.** any of various reddish cabinet woods, sometimes with a roselike odor, yielded by certain tropical trees, esp. of the genus *Dalbergia.* **2.** a tree yielding such wood.

Rosh Ha•sha•nah (or **Ha•sha•na**) (rōsh′ hä shō′nə, -shä′-, hə-, rōsh′; *Heb.* rôsh′ hä shä nä′), *n.* the Jewish New Year, celebrated on the first or first and second days of Tishri.

Ro•si•cru•cian (rō′zi krōō′shən, roz′i-), *n.* **1.** a member of an international society professing esoteric religious principles and emphasizing occult knowledge and powers. —*adj.* **2.** characteristic of the Rosicrucians. —**Ro′si•cru′cian•ism,** *n.*

ros•in (roz′in), *n.* **1.** the yellowish to amber, translucent, brittle resin left after distilling the oil of turpentine from the crude oleoresin of the pine: used esp. in making varnishes and for rubbing on the bows of stringed instruments. **2.** RESIN. —*v.t.* **3.** to cover or rub with rosin.

Ross (rôs, ros), *n.* **1. Betsy Griscom,** 1752–1836, maker of the first U.S. flag. **2. Harold Wallace,** 1892–1951, U.S. publisher and editor. **3. Sir James Clark,** 1800–62, English explorer of the Arctic and the Antarctic. **4.** his uncle, **Sir John,** 1777–1856, Scottish Arctic explorer. **5. John** (*Coowescoowe* or *Kooweskoowe*), 1790–1866, Cherokee leader.

Ros•set•ti (rō set′ē, -zet′ē, rə-), *n.* **1. Christina Georgina,** 1830–94, English poet. **2.** her brother, **Dante Gabriel** (*Gabriel Charles Dante Rossetti*), 1828–82, English poet and painter.

Ros•si•ni (rō sē′nē, rô-), *n.* **Gio•ac•chi•no Antonio** 1792–1868, Italian composer.

ros•ter (ros′tər), *n.* **1.** a list of persons or groups, as of military personnel or units with their turns of duty. **2.** any list, roll, or register.

ros•trum (ros′trəm), *n., pl.* **-trums, -tra** (-trə). **1.** platform or stage for public speaking. **2.** a pulpit. **3.** a beaklike anatomical process or extension of a part. **4.** a beaklike projection from the prow of a ship, esp. one on an ancient warship for ramming an enemy ship; ram.

ros•y (rō′zē), *adj.,* **-i•er, -i•est. 1.** pink or pinkish red; roseate. **2.** having a fresh, healthy redness; flushed: *rosy cheeks.* **3.** bright or promising: *a rosy future.* **4.** cheerful or optimistic. **5.** made or consisting of roses: *a rosy bower.* —**ros′i•ness,** *n.*

R

rot (rot), v., **rot·ted, rot·ting,** n., interj. —v.i. **1.** to undergo decomposition; decay. **2.** to deteriorate, disintegrate, fall, or become weak due to decay (often fol. by *away, off,* etc.). **3.** to languish, as in confinement. **4.** to become morally corrupt or offensive. —v.t. **5.** to cause to rot. **6.** to cause to become morally corrupt. **7.** to ret (flax, hemp, etc.). —n. **8.** the process of rotting. **9.** the state of being rotten; decay; putrefaction. **10.** rotting or rotten matter. **11.** moral or social decay or corruption. **12.** any of various animal or plant diseases caused by a fungal or bacterial infection and characterized by decay. **13.** nonsense. —interj. **14.** (used to express disagreement or disgust.)

Ro·tar·i·an (rō târ′ē ən), n. **1.** a member of a Rotary Club. —adj. **2.** of or pertaining to Rotarians or Rotary Clubs.

ro·ta·ry (rō′tə rē), adj., n., pl. **-ries. 1.** turning or capable of turning around on an axis, as a wheel. **2.** taking place around an axis, as motion. **3.** having a part or parts that turn on an axis: *a rotary beater.* —n. **4.** TRAFFIC CIRCLE.

Ro′tary Club′, n. a local club of business and professional people belonging to a worldwide organization of similar clubs **(Ro′tary Interna′tional)** devoted to serving the community and promoting world peace.

ro′tary di′al, n. a disk with finger holes that is affixed to a telephone and rotated to match up the fingerholes with the letters and digits of a telephone number. —**ro′tary-di′al,** adj.

ro′tary en′gine, n. an engine, as a turbine, in which the impelling fluid produces torque directly rather than by acting upon reciprocating parts.

ro′tary press′, n. a printing press in which the type or plates to be printed are fastened upon a rotating cylinder and impressed on a continuous roll of moving paper. Compare CYLINDER PRESS.

ro·tate (rō′tāt; *esp. Brit.* rō tāt′), v., **-tat·ed, -tat·ing.** —v.i. **1.** to turn around on or as if on an axis; revolve. **2.** to proceed in a fixed routine of succession. —v.t. **3.** to cause to turn around an axis or center point. **4.** to cause to go through a cycle of changes or follow in a fixed routine of succession: *to rotate crops.* **5.** to replace (a person, troops, etc.) by another or others, usu. according to a schedule. —**ro′tat·a·ble,** adj.

ro·ta·tion (rō tā′shən), n. **1.** the act of rotating; a turning around as on an axis. **2. a.** the movement or path of the earth or a heavenly body turning on its axis. **b.** one complete turn of such a body. **3.** regularly recurring succession, as of people performing a job. **4.** CROP ROTATION. —**ro·ta′tion·al,** adj.

ro·ta·tor (rō′tā tər; *esp. Brit.* rō tā′-), n., pl. **ro·ta·tors** for 1, **ro·ta·tor·es** (rō′tə tôr′ēz, -tôr′-) for 2. **1.** a person or thing that rotates. **2.** a muscle serving to rotate a part of the body.

ro·ta·to·ry (rō′tə tôr′ē, -tōr′ē), adj. **1.** pertaining to, of the nature of, or causing rotation: *rotatory motion.* **2.** rotating, as an object. **3.** passing or following in rotation or succession.

ROTC or **R.O.T.C.** (är′ō tē sē′, rot′sē), Reserve Officers Training Corps.

rote (rōt), n. **1.** routine; a fixed, habitual, or mechanical course of procedure. —**Idiom. 2. by rote,** from memory, without thought of the meaning; in a mechanical way: *to learn a language by rote.*

Roth·schild (rōth′chīld, rōths′-, roth-, roths′-), n. **1. Mayer Amschel,** 1743–1812, German banker: founder of the Rothschild family and international banking firm. **2.** his son, **Nathan Mayer, Baron de,** 1777–1836, English banker, born in Germany.

ro·ti·fer (rō′tə fər), n. any microscopic animal of the phylum Rotifera, found in fresh and salt waters, having one or more rings of cilia on the anterior end. Also called **wheel animalcule.** —**ro·tif′er·ous,** adj.

ro·tis·ser·ie (rō tis′ə rē), n., v., **-ied, -i·ing.** —n. **1.** a cooking unit equipped with a motor-driven spit, for barbecuing poultry, beef, etc. —v.t. **2.** to broil on a rotisserie.

Rotis′serie League′ Base′ball, *Trademark.* a game in which participants compete by running imaginary baseball teams whose results are based on the actual performances of major-league players.

ro·to·gra·vure (rō′tə grə vyŏor′, -grā′vyər), n. **1.** a photomechanical process by which pictures, typeset matter, etc., are printed from an intaglio copper cylinder. **2.** a print made by this process. **3.** a section of a newspaper consisting of pages printed by the rotogravure process; magazine section.

ro·tor (rō′tər), n. **1.** a rotating member of a mechanical or electrical device, as in an electric motor. **2.** a system of rotating airfoils, as the horizontal ones of a helicopter or of the compressor of a jet engine.

ro·tor·craft (rō′tər kraft′, -kräft′), n. a rotary-wing aircraft. Also called **ro′tor plane′.**

ro·to·till·er (rō′tə til′ər), n. a motorized device with spoke-like spinning blades perpendicular to the ground, used for tilling soil.

rot·ten (rot′n), adj., **-er, -est. 1.** having rotted; decomposing or decaying. **2.** tainted or foul-smelling; putrid. **3.** corrupt or morally offensive. **4.** wretchedly bad or unsatisfactory; miserable: *a rotten day.* **5.** contemptible; despicable: *a rotten trick.* —**Proverb. 6. A rotten apple spoils the barrel,** one bad person or thing may corrupt or damage those nearby. —**Saying. 7. Something is rotten in Denmark,** something underhanded or suspicious is going on. William Shakespeare, *Hamlet.* —**rot′ten·ly,** adv. —**rot′ten·ness,** n.

rot′ten bor′ough, n. **1.** (before the Reform Bill of 1832) any English borough that had very few voters yet was represented in Parliament. **2.** an election district that has more representatives in a legislative body than the number of its constituents would normally call for.

Rott·wei·ler (rot′wī lər), n. one of a German breed of large, powerful dogs having a short, coarse black coat with tan markings.

ro·tund (rō tund′), adj. **1.** round in shape; rounded. **2.** plump; fat. **3.** full-toned or sonorous: *rotund phrases.* —**ro·tun′di·ty, ro·tund′ness,** n. —**ro·tund′ly,** adv.

ro·tun·da (rō tun′də), n., pl. **-das. 1.** a round building, esp. one with a dome. **2.** a large and high circular hall or room, esp. one surmounted by a dome.

rotunda (def. 1)

rou·ble (rōō′bəl), n. RUBLE.

rou·é (rōō ā′, rōō′ā), n., pl. **rou·és.** a dissolute and licentious man; rake.

rouge (rōōzh), n., v., **rouged, roug·ing.** —n. **1.** any of various red cosmetics for coloring the cheeks or lips. **2.** a reddish powder, chiefly ferric oxide, used for polishing metal, glass, etc. —v.t. **3.** to color with rouge. **4.** to cause to blush. —v.i. **5.** to use rouge.

rough (ruf), adj. **1.** having a coarse or uneven surface, as from projections, irregularities, or breaks. **2.** shaggy or coarse: *a dog with a rough coat.* **3.** steep or uneven and covered with high grass, brush, stones, etc.; wild: *rough country.* **4.** acting with or characterized by violence: *a rough sport.* **5.** characterized by turbulence: *rough seas; a rough flight.* **6.** stormy or tempestuous, as wind or weather. **7.** lacking in gentleness, care, or consideration: *rough handling.* **8.** sharp or harsh: *rough words.* **9.** unmannerly or rude. **10.** disorderly or riotous: *a rough mob.* **11.** difficult or unpleasant: *to have a rough time of it.* **12.** harsh to the ear. **13.** harsh to the taste. **14.** coarse, as food. **15.** lacking culture or refinement. **16.** without comforts or conveniences: *rough camping.* **17.** not elaborated, perfected, or corrected; unpolished: *a rough draft.* **18.** approximate or tentative: *a rough guess.* **19.** crude, unwrought, nonprocessed, or unprepared: *rough rice.* **20.** requiring exertion or strength: *rough manual labor.* —n. **21.** something that is rough, esp. rough ground. **22.** any part of a golf course bordering the fairway on which the grass, weeds, etc., are not trimmed. **23.** the unpleasant or difficult part of anything. **24.** anything in its crude or preliminary form, as a drawing. —adv. **25.** in a rough manner; roughly. —v.t. **26.** to make rough; roughen. **27.** to subject to physical violence: *The muggers roughed up their victim.* **28.** to subject to some rough, preliminary process of working or preparation. **29.** to sketch roughly or in outline (often fol. by *in* or *out*). **30.** to subject (a player on an opposing team) to unnecessary physical abuse, as in blocking or tackling. —v.i. **31.** to become rough, as a surface. **32.** to behave roughly. —**Idiom. 33. rough it,** to live without customary comforts or conveniences. —**Saying. 34. take the rough with the smooth,** one must accept and bad times as well as good. —**rough′ly,** adv. —**rough′ness,** n.

rough·age (ruf′ij), n. **1.** FIBER (def. 9). **2.** rough or coarse material. **3.** any coarse, rough food for livestock.

rough′-and-read′y, adj. **1.** rough, rude, or crude, but good enough for the purpose. **2.** exhibiting rough vigor rather than refinement or delicacy. —**rough′-and-read′i·ness,** n.

rough′-and-tum′ble, adj. **1.** characterized by violent, random, disorderly action and struggles. **2.** given to such action. —n. **3.** rough and unrestrained competition, fighting, struggling, etc.

rough·cast (ruf′kast′, -käst′), n., v., **-cast, -cast·ing.** —n. **1.** an exterior wall finish composed of mortar and fine pebbles mixed together and dashed against the wall. **2.** a crudely formed pattern or model. —v.t. **3.** to cover or coat with roughcast. **4.** to make, shape, or prepare in a rough form. —**rough′cast′er,** n.

rough′ cut′, n. the first assembly of a motion picture film following preliminary cutting and editing. Compare FINAL CUT.

rough·en (ruf′ən), v.t., v.i. to make or become rough or rougher.

rough′-hew′ or **rough′hew′,** v.t., **-hewed, -hewed** or **-hewn, -hew·ing. 1.** to hew (timber, stone, etc.) roughly or without smoothing or finishing. **2.** to shape roughly; give crude form to.

rough·house (n. ruf′hous′; v. also -houz′), n., pl. **-hous·es** (-hou′ziz), v., **-housed** (-houst′, -houzd′), **-hous·ing** (-hou′sing, -zing). —n. **1.** rough, disorderly horseplay, esp. indoors. —v.i. **2.** to engage in rough, disorderly play. —v.t. **3.** to handle roughly but with playful intent: *to roughhouse the cat.*

rough·neck (ruf′nek′), n. **1.** a rough, coarse person; tough. **2.** a laborer working on an oil-drilling rig. —v.i. **3.** to work as a roughneck.

rough·rid·er (ruf′rī′dər), n. **1.** a person who breaks horses to the saddle. **2.** a person accustomed to rough or hard riding.

Rough′ Rid′er, *n.* a member of a volunteer cavalry organized by Theodore Roosevelt and Leonard Wood in the Spanish-American War.
rough•shod (ruf′shod′), *adj.* **1.** shod with horseshoes having projecting nails or points. —***Idiom.*** **2. ride roughshod over,** to treat harshly, esp. in order to advance oneself.
rou•lade (ro͞o läd′), *n.* **1.** a slice of meat rolled around a filling, as of minced meat, and cooked. **2.** a musical embellishment consisting of a rapid succession of tones sung to a single syllable.
rou•lette (ro͞o let′), *n., v.,* **-let•ted, -let•ting.** —*n.* **1.** a game of chance in which a small ball is spun on a dishlike device **(roulette′ wheel′),** with players betting on which of the black or red numbered compartments the ball will come to rest in. **2.** a small wheel, esp. one with sharp teeth and a handle, for making lines of marks or perforations. **3.** a row of short cuts, in which no paper is removed, made between individual stamps to permit their ready separation. —*v.t.* **4.** to mark, impress, or perforate with a roulette.
round (round), *adj.* **1.** having a flat, circular form, as a disk or hoop. **2.** curved like part of a circle, as an outline. **3.** having a circular cross section, as a cylinder; cylindrical. **4.** spherical or globular, as a ball. **5.** shaped like part of a sphere; hemispherical. **6.** consisting of full, curved lines or shapes, as handwriting or parts of the body. **7.** executed with or involving circular motion. **8.** full or complete: *a round dozen.* **9.** noting, formed, or expressed by an integer or whole number with no fraction. **10.** expressed, given, or exact to the nearest multiple or power of ten: *in round numbers.* **11.** considerable in amount; ample: *a round sum of money.* **12.** brought to completeness or perfection. **13.** fully delineated or developed, as a character in fiction. **14.** full and sonorous, as sound. **15.** straightforward, plain, or candid; outspoken. —*n.* **16.** any round shape or object. **17.** something circular in cross section, as a rung of a ladder. **18.** Sometimes, **rounds.** a completed course of time, series of events or operations, etc., ending at a point corresponding to that at the beginning. **19.** any complete course, series, or succession: *a round of talks.* **20.** Often, **rounds.** a going around from place to place, as in a habitual or definite circuit: *a doctor's rounds.* **21.** a completed course or spell of activity, commonly one of a series, in some play or sport: *a round of bridge.* **22.** a single outburst, as of applause or cheers. **23.** a single discharge of shot by each of a number of guns, rifles, etc. **24.** a single discharge by one firearm. **25.** a charge of ammunition for a single shot. **26.** a single serving, esp. of drink, to everyone present. **27.** ROUND DANCE (def. 1). **28.** movement in a circle or around an axis. **29.** a cut of beef from the thigh, below the rump and above the leg. **30.** a short musical canon at the unison, in which the voices enter at equally spaced intervals of time. **31.** a specified number of arrows shot from a specified distance from the target in archery. **32.** one of a series of three-minute periods making up a boxing match. —*adv.* **33.** throughout or from the beginning to the end of a recurring period of time: *all year round.* **34.** Also, **'round.** around. —*prep.* **35.** throughout (a period of time): *a resort visited round the year.* **36.** around: *It happened round noon.* —*v.t.* **37.** to make round. **38.** to free from angularity; fill out symmetrically. **39.** to bring to completeness or perfection; finish (often fol. by *off* or *out*). **40.** to make a turn or partial circuit around or to the other side of: *to round a corner.* **41.** to make a complete circuit of; pass completely around. **42. a.** to make the opening at (the lips) relatively round or pursed. **b.** to pronounce (a speech sound, esp. a vowel) with rounded lips. **43.** to express as a round number, esp. to replace by the nearest multiple of 10, with 5 being increased to the next highest multiple (often fol. by *off*). —*v.i.* **44.** to become round, plump, or free from angularity (often fol. by *out*). **45.** to develop to completeness or perfection. **46.** to make a turn or a partial or complete circuit around something. **47.** to turn around as on an axis: *to round on one's heels.* **48.** to reduce the number of digits to the right of a decimal point by dropping the final digit and adding 1 to the next preceding digit if the digit dropped was 5 or more. **49. round to,** to turn a sailing vessel in the direction from which the wind is blowing. **50. round up, a.** to drive or bring (cattle, sheep, etc.) together. **b.** to assemble; gather. —***Idiom.*** **51. in the round, a.** (of a theater) having a stage completely surrounded by seats for the audience. **b.** in the style of theater-in-the-round. **c.** in complete detail; from all aspects. **d.** (of sculpture) not attached to a supporting background; freestanding. **52. make the rounds, a.** to go from one place to another, as in seeking employment. **b.** Also, **go the rounds.** (of a rumor, story, or the like) to spread from one person to another. —**round′ness,** *n.*
round•a•bout (*adj.* round′ə bout′, round′ə bout′; *n.* round′ə bout′), *adj.* **1.** circuitous or indirect, as a road, journey, method, statement, or person. —*n.* **2.** a circuitous or indirect road, method, etc.
round′ arch′, *n.* an arch formed in a continuous curve, esp. in a semicircle.
round′ dance′, *n.* **1.** a dance in which the dancers are arranged in or move about in a circle or ring. **2.** a dance performed by couples and characterized by circular or revolving movement.
round•ed (roun′did), *adj.* **1.** reduced to simple curves; made round. **2.** (of a speech sound) pronounced with rounded lips, as the vowel in *boot.* **3.** fully developed, perfected, or complete: *a rounded character.* **4.** ROUND (def. 10).
roun•de•lay (roun′dl ā′), *n.* a song in which a phrase, line, or the like, is continually repeated.
round•er (roun′dər), *n.* **1.** a person or thing that rounds something. **2.** a person who makes a round. **3.** a boxing match of a specified number of rounds (used in combination): *a 15-rounder.*
Round•head (round′hed′), *n.* a Puritan supporter of Parliament during the English Civil War: so called in derision by the Cavaliers because they wore their hair cut short.
round•house (round′hous′), *n., pl.* **-hous•es** (-hou′ziz). **1.** a building for the servicing and repair of locomotives, built around a turntable in the form of some part of a circle. **2.** a cabin on the after part of a quarterdeck. **3.** a punch delivered with an exaggerated circular motion. **4.** a meld in pinochle of one king and queen of each suit.
round•ish (roun′dish), *adj.* somewhat round.
round′ lot′, *n.* the conventional unit in which commodities or securities are bought and sold, esp. a quantity of 100 shares of a stock in a transaction. Compare ODD LOT.
round•ly (round′lē), *adv.* **1.** in a round manner. **2.** vigorously or briskly. **3.** outspokenly, severely, or unsparingly. **4.** completely or fully. **5.** in round numbers or in a vague or general way.
round′ rob′in, *n.* **1.** a sequence or series. **2.** a tournament in which all of the entrants play each other at least once, failure to win a contest not resulting in elimination. **3.** a letter, notice, or the like, circulated from person to person in a group.
round′ steak′, *n.* a steak cut from a round of beef.
round′ ta′ble, *n.* **1.** a number of persons gathered together for a conference or a discussion of some subject on equal terms. **2.** the discussion, topic of discussion, or the conference itself. **3.** (*cap.*) a table, made round to avoid quarrels as to precedence, at which King Arthur and his knights sat. Also, **round′ta′ble** (for defs. 1, 2). —**round′-ta′ble,** *adj.*
round′-the-clock′, *adj.* AROUND-THE-CLOCK.
round′ trip′, *n.* a trip to a given place and back again. —**round′-trip′,** *adj.*
round•up (round′up′), *n.* **1. a.** the driving together of cattle, horses, etc., for branding, shipping to market, or the like. **b.** the people and horses who do this. **c.** the herd so collected. **2.** the gathering together of scattered items or people: *a police roundup of suspects.* **3.** a summary or brief listing of facts, figures, or information: *a sports roundup.*
round•worm (round′wûrm′), *n.* any nematode that infests the intestine of humans and other mammals.
rouse (rouz), *v.,* **roused, rous•ing,** *n.* —*v.t.* **1.** to bring out of a state of sleep, unconsciousness, inactivity, fancied security, apathy, etc. **2.** to stir or incite to strong indignation or anger. **3.** to cause (game) to start from a covert or lair. —*v.i.* **4.** to come out of a state of sleep, unconsciousness, inactivity, apathy, etc. —*n.* **5.** a rousing. **6.** a signal for rousing; reveille. —**rous′er,** *n.*
rous•ing (rou′zing), *adj.* **1.** exciting; stirring: *a rousing speech.* **2.** active or vigorous. **3.** brisk; lively: *a rousing business.* **4.** exceptional; extraordinary. —**rous′ing•ly,** *adv.*
Rous•seau (ro͞o sō′), *n.* **1. Henri** (*"Le Douanier"*), 1844–1910, French painter. **2. Jean Jacques** (zhäɴ), 1712–78, French philosopher and social reformer, born in Switzerland. **3. (Pierre Étienne) Théodore,** 1812–67, French painter.
roust (roust), *v.t.* to rout, as from a place.
roust•a•bout (roust′ə bout′), *n.* **1.** a wharf laborer or deck hand. **2.** a circus laborer who helps in setting up tents, caring for the animals, etc. **3.** any unskilled laborer, esp. one working in an oil field.
rout[1] (rout), *n.* **1.** a defeat attended with disorderly flight: *to put an army to rout.* **2.** any overwhelming defeat. **3.** a tumultuous or disorderly crowd. **4.** *Law.* a disturbance of the public peace by three or more persons acting together in a manner that suggests an intention to riot. **5.** a large, formal evening party or social gathering. —*v.t.* **6.** to disperse in defeat and disorderly flight. **7.** to defeat decisively.
rout[2] (rout), *v.i.* **1.** to root, as swine. **2.** to poke, search, or rummage. —*v.t.* **3.** to turn over or dig up (something) with the snout. **4.** to find or get by searching, rummaging, etc. (usu. fol. by *out*). **5.** to cause to rise from bed. **6.** to force or drive out. **7.** to hollow out or furrow, as with a scoop, gouge, or machine.
route (ro͞ot, rout), *n., v.,* **rout•ed, rout•ing.** —*n.* **1.** a course or road for passage or travel. **2.** a customary or regular line of passage or travel. **3.** a specific itinerary or round of stops regularly visited by a person in the performance of a job: *a newspaper route.* —*v.t.* **4.** to fix the route of: *to route a tour.* **5.** to send, direct, or forward by a particular route. [< Old French < Latin *rupta (via)* broken (i.e., freshly made) (way)]
rout•er (rou′tər), *n.* any of various tools or machines for routing, hollowing out, or furrowing.
rou•tine (ro͞o tēn′), *n.* **1.** a customary or regular course of procedure: *office routine.* **2.** habitual, unvarying, unimaginative, or rote procedure. **3.** a set of instructions directing a computer to perform a specific task. **4.** a rehearsed act, performance, or part of a performance: *a comic routine; a dance routine.* **5.** an unvarying and often repeated piece of behavior or formula of speech: *He'd give me that brotherly love routine.* —*adj.* **6.** of the nature of, proceeding by, or adhering to routine. **7.** dull or uninteresting; commonplace. —**rou•tine′ly,** *adv.*
roux (ro͞o), *n., pl.* **roux.** a cooked mixture of butter or other fat and flour used to thicken soups, sauces, etc.
rove[1] (rōv), *v.,* **roved, rov•ing,** *n.* —*v.i.* **1.** to wander about without definite destination; move at random, esp. over a wide area. —*v.t.* **2.** to wander over or through; traverse. —*n.* **3.** an act of roving.
rove[2] (rōv), *v.* a pt. and pp. of REEVE[1].

rove[3] (rōv), v.t., **roved, rov•ing. 1.** to form (slivers of wool, cotton, etc.) into slightly twisted strands in a preparatory process of spinning. **2.** to draw fibers through an eye or other small opening. **3.** to attenuate, compress, and twist slightly in carding.

rov•er[1] (rō′vər), n. **1.** a person who roves; wanderer. **2. a.** a mark selected at random in archery. **b.** one of a group of fixed marks at a long distance. **c.** an archer who shoots at such a mark. **3.** a croquet ball that has been driven through all the arches and needs only to strike the last peg to be out of the game.

rov•er[2] (rō′vər), n. **1.** a pirate. **2.** a pirate ship.

rov•ing[1] (rō′ving), adj. **1.** roaming or wandering. **2.** not assigned or restricted to any particular location, area, topic, etc.: *a roving reporter.* **3.** inclined to wander or stray. —**rov′ing•ly,** adv.

rov•ing[2] (rō′ving), n. **1.** a soft strand of fiber that has been twisted, attenuated, and freed of foreign matter preparatory to its conversion into yarn. **2.** the final phase of carding, in which this is done.

row[1] (rō), n. **1.** a number of persons or things arranged in a line, esp. a straight line. **2.** a line of persons or things so arranged. **3.** a line of adjacent seats facing the same way, as in a theater. **4.** a street formed by two continuous lines of buildings. **5.** one of the horizontal lines of squares on a checkerboard; rank. —v.t. **6.** to put in a row (often fol. by *up*). —*Idiom.* **7. a hard, long,** or **tough row to hoe,** an extremely difficult set of circumstances to contend with.

row[2] (rō), v.i. **1.** to propel a vessel by the leverage of oars or the like. —v.t. **2.** to propel (a vessel) with oars or the like. **3.** to convey in a boat that is rowed. **4.** to convey or propel (something) in a manner suggestive of rowing. **5.** to require, use, or be equipped with (a number of oars). **6.** to use (oarsmen) for rowing. **7.** to row against in a race. —n. **8.** an act of rowing. **9.** an excursion in a rowboat. —**row′er,** n.

row[3] (rou), n. **1.** a noisy dispute or quarrel; commotion. **2.** noise or clamor. —v.i. **3.** to quarrel noisily.

row•an (rō′ən, rou′-), n. **1.** the European mountain ash, having pinnate leaves and clusters of bright red berries. **2.** the American mountain ash. **3.** the berry of either of these trees.

row•boat (rō′bōt′), n. a small boat designed for rowing.

row•dy (rou′dē), adj., **-di•er, -di•est,** n., pl. **-dies.** —adj. **1.** rough and disorderly: *rowdy behavior.* —n. **2.** a rough, disorderly person. —**row′di•ly,** adv. —**row′di•ness,** n. —**row′dy•ish,** adj.

row′ house′ (rō), n. one of a row of uniformly constructed houses, each of which has at least one sidewall in common.

Row•ley (rō′lē, rou′-), n. **Francis,** 1854–1952, U.S. clergyman and hymn writer.

roy•al (roi′əl), adj. **1.** of or pertaining to a king, queen, or other sovereign: *a royal palace.* **2.** descended from or related to a king or line of kings: *a royal prince.* **3.** noting or having the rank of a king or queen. **4.** established or chartered by or existing under the patronage of a sovereign: *a royal society.* **5.** proceeding from or performed by a sovereign: *a royal warrant.* **6.** appropriate to or befitting a sovereign; magnificent; stately. **7.** serving or subject to a sovereign. **8.** (*usu. cap.*) in the service of the British monarch or the Commonwealth: *Royal Air Force.* **9.** fine; excellent: *in royal spirits.* **10.** *Informal.* extreme or persistent; unmitigated: *a royal pain.* —n. **11.** a sail set on a royal mast. **12.** *Informal.* a royal person; member of the royalty. **13.** a size of printing paper, 20 × 25 in. (51 × 64 cm). **14.** a size of writing paper, 19 × 24 in. (48 × 61 cm). —**roy′al•ly,** adv.

roy′al blue′, n. a deep blue, often with a purplish tinge.

roy′al col′ony, n. **1.** a colony administered by officials appointed by and responsible to the sovereign of the parent state. **2.** (in colonial America) a colony, as New York, administered by a governor and council appointed by the British crown.

roy′al flush′, n. a hand in poker consisting of the five highest cards in a suit.

roy•al•ist (roi′ə list), n. **1.** a supporter of a monarch or royal government, esp. in times of rebellion or civil war. **2.** (*cap.*) a supporter of Charles I of England; Cavalier. **3.** (*often cap.*) a loyalist in the American Revolution; Tory. **4.** (*cap.*) a supporter of the Bourbons in France. —adj. **5.** of or pertaining to royalists.

roy′al mast′, n. a mast situated immediately above, and generally formed as a single spar with, a topgallant mast.

roy′al palm′, n. any of several tall, showy feather palms of the genus *Roystonea,* as *R. regia.*

roy•al•ty (roi′əl tē), n., pl. **-ties. 1.** royal persons collectively. **2.** royal status or power; sovereignty. **3.** a person of royal lineage; member of a royal family. **4.** Usu. **royalties.** prerogatives or rights of a sovereign. **5.** a royal domain; kingdom; realm. **6.** character or quality proper to or befitting a sovereign; nobility. **7.** a compensation or portion of the proceeds paid to the owner of a right, as a patent or oil or mineral right, for the use of it. **8.** an agreed portion of the income from a work paid to its author, composer, etc., usu. a percentage of the retail price of each copy sold. **9.** a royal right, as over minerals, granted by a sovereign to a person or corporation. **10.** the payment made for such a right.

rpm or **r.p.m.,** revolutions per minute.

rps or **r.p.s.,** revolutions per second.

RQ, respiratory quotient.

RR or **R.R., 1.** railroad. **2.** Right Reverend. **3.** rural route.

R-rat•ed (är′rā′tid), adj. (of a motion picture) suitable for those under 17 years of age only when accompanied by an adult.

rRNA, ribosomal RNA.

RSV, Revised Standard Version.

RSVP, (used on an invitation to indicate that the favor of a reply is requested.) [< French r(épondez) s(′il) v(ous) p(laît) please reply]

rt., right.

rte., route.

Rt. Hon., Right Honorable.

Rt. Rev., Right Reverend.

Rts., *Finance.* rights.

Ru, *Chem. Symbol.* ruthenium.

Ru•an•da (rōō än′də), n., pl. **-das,** (*esp. collectively*) **-da.** a member of an African people or group of peoples inhabiting Rwanda and parts of the Democratic Republic of the Congo and Uganda.

rub (rub), v., **rubbed, rub•bing,** n. —v.t. **1.** to subject (something) to pressure and friction, as in cleaning, polishing, or massaging; move one thing back and forth or with a rotary motion along the surface of (something else). **2.** to move, spread, or apply with pressure and friction over something: *to rub lotion on chapped hands.* **3.** to move (two things) with pressure and friction over each other: *He rubbed his hands together.* **4.** to force (something) by pressure and friction (fol. by *in* or *into*). **5.** to make sore from friction. **6.** to remove or erase by pressure and friction (often fol. by *off* or *out*). —v.i. **7.** to exert pressure and friction on something. **8.** to move with pressure against something. **9.** to admit of being rubbed in a specified manner: *Chalk rubs off easily.* **10. rub down, a.** to smooth, polish, or clean by rubbing. **b.** to massage. **11. rub off on,** to pass along to, as or as if by touching: *I wish your good luck would rub off on me.* **12. rub out, a.** to obliterate; erase. **b.** *Slang.* to murder. —n. **13.** an act or instance of rubbing: *an alcohol rub.* **14.** something that annoys or irritates one's feelings. **15.** an annoying experience or circumstance. **16.** an obstacle or difficulty. **17.** a rough or abraded area caused by rubbing. —*Idiom.* **18. rub elbows** or **shoulders with,** to associate or mingle with. **19. rub it in,** to emphasize or reiterate something unpleasant in order to tease or annoy. **20. rub someone's nose in,** to remind someone persistently of (a past mistake) in order to punish. **21. rub the wrong way,** to irritate; offend; annoy.

rub•ber[1] (rub′ər), n. **1.** a highly elastic solid substance, light cream or dark amber in color, polymerized by the drying and coagulation of the latex or milky juice of rubber trees and plants. **2.** a material made by chemically treating and toughening this substance, used in the manufacture of electrical insulation, elastic bands, tires, and other products. **3.** any of various similar substances and materials made synthetically. Compare SYNTHETIC RUBBER. **4.** an eraser of this material. **5.** a low overshoe of this material. **6.** RUBBER BAND. **7.** an instrument or tool used for rubbing, polishing, scraping, etc. **8.** a person who rubs something. —adj. **9.** made of, containing, or coated with rubber. **10.** pertaining to or producing rubber. —**rub′ber•like′,** adj.

rub•ber[2] (rub′ər), n. **1.** (in bridge) a series or round played until one side has won two out of three games. **2.** Also called **rub′ber match′.** a deciding contest when a competition is tied.

rub′ber band′, n. a narrow circular or oblong band of rubber, used for holding papers or other things together.

rub′ber cement′, n. a viscous, flammable liquid consisting of unvulcanized rubber dispersed in benzene, gasoline, or the like, used chiefly as an adhesive.

rub′ber check′, n. *Informal.* a check drawn on an account lacking the funds to pay it; a check that bounces.

rub′ber-chick′en cir′cuit, n. *Informal.* a monotonous round of dinners, often featuring chicken, that a lecturer or political candidate is obliged to attend.

rub•ber•ize (rub′ə rīz′), v.t., **-ized, -iz•ing.** to coat or impregnate with rubber or some preparation of it.

rub•ber•neck (rub′ər nek′), v.i. *Informal.* **1.** to look about or stare with curiosity, as by craning the neck or turning the head. —n. Also, **rub′ber•neck′er. 2.** a curious onlooker. **3.** a sightseer or tourist.

rub′ber plant′, n. an Asian tree, *Ficus elastica,* of the mulberry family, having oblong, shiny, leathery leaves, used as a source of rubber and cultivated as a houseplant.

rub′ber room′, n. *Informal.* a room padded with foam rubber for the confinement of a violent mentally ill person.

rub′ber stamp′, n. **1.** a device with a rubber printing surface that is coated with ink by pressing it on an ink-saturated pad, used for imprinting names, standard messages, etc. **2.** a person, government agency, etc., that gives approval automatically or routinely. **3.** such approval. —**rub′ber-stamp′,** v.t., adj.

rub′ber tree′, n. any tree that yields latex from which rubber is produced, esp. *Hevea brasiliensis,* of the spurge family, native to South America, the chief commercial source of rubber.

rub•ber•y (rub′ə rē), adj. like rubber; elastic; tough.

rub•bing (rub′ing), n. an impression of an incised or sculptured surface made by laying paper over it and rubbing with graphite or a similar substance until the image appears.

rub′bing al′cohol, n. a poisonous solution of about 70 percent isopropyl or denatured ethyl alcohol, used in massaging.

rub•bish (rub′ish), n. **1.** worthless material that is rejected or thrown out; litter; trash. **2.** nonsense, as in writing or art: *sentimenal rubbish.*

rub•ble (rub′əl *or, for 2,* rōō′bəl), n. **1.** broken bits and pieces of anything, as that which is demolished: *Bombing reduced the town to rubble.* **2.** rough fragments of broken stone, formed by geological processes, in quarrying, etc., and sometimes used in masonry.

rub•down (rub′doun′), *n.* a massage.

rube (rōōb), *n. Informal.* an unsophisticated country person; hick.

ru•be•fa•cient (rōō′bə fā′shənt), *adj.* **1.** causing redness of the skin, as a medicinal application. —*n.* **2.** a rubefacient application, as a mustard plaster.

Rube Gold•berg (rōōb′ gōld′bûrg), *adj.* **1.** having a fantastically complicated, improvised appearance: *a Rube Goldberg arrangement of flasks and test tubes.* **2.** deviously complex and impractical. [after *Rube (Reuben) Goldberg* (1883–1970), U.S. cartoonist]

ru•bel•la (rōō bel′ə), *n.* a usu. mild infection caused by a virus of the genus *Rubivirus,* characterized by fever, cough, and a fine red rash: may cause fetal damage if contracted during pregnancy. Also called **German measles.**

Ru•bens (rōō′bənz), *n.* Peter Paul, 1577–1640, Flemish painter.

ru•be•o•la (rōō bē′ə lə, rōō′bē ō′lə), *n.* MEASLES (def. 1a). —**ru•be′o•lar,** *adj.*

ru•bid•i•um (rōō bid′ē əm), *n.* a silver-white, metallic, active element resembling potassium, used in photoelectric cells and radio vacuum tubes. *Symbol:* Rb; *at. wt.:* 85.47; *at. no.:* 37; *sp. gr.:* 1.53 at 20°C. —**ru•bid′ic,** *adj.*

Ru′bik's Cube′ (rōō′biks), *Trademark.* a puzzle consisting of a cube with colored faces made of 26 smaller colored blocks attached to a spindle in the center, the object being to rotate the blocks until each face of the cube is a single color.

ru•ble or **rou•ble** (rōō′bəl), *n.* the basic monetary unit of Russia, the Soviet Union, and its successor states.

rub•out (rub′out′), *n. Slang.* a murder.

ru•bric (rōō′brik), *n.* **1.** a title, heading, or the like, in a manuscript, book, statute, etc., written or printed in red or otherwise distinguished from the rest of the text. **2.** a direction for the conduct of divine service or the administration of the sacraments, inserted in liturgical books. **3.** any established rule of conduct or procedure. **4.** a class or category. **5.** an explanatory comment; gloss. —*adj.* **6.** written or marked in red.

ru•by (rōō′bē), *n., pl.* **-bies,** *adj.* —*n.* **1.** a red variety of corundum, used as a gem. **2.** something made of this stone or an imitation, as a bearing in a watch. **3.** a deep red; carmine. —*adj.* **4.** ruby-colored. **5.** containing or set with a ruby or rubies.

ru′by-throat′ed hum′mingbird, *n.* a hummingbird, *Archilochus colubris,* of E North America, having metallic-green upper plumage and, in the male, a bright red throat.

ruck[1] (ruk), *n.* **1.** a large number or quantity; mass. **2.** the great mass of undistinguished or inferior persons or things.

ruck[2] (ruk), *n.* a fold or wrinkle; crease. —*v.t., v.i.* **2.** to make or become creased or wrinkled.

ruck•sack (ruk′sak′, rōōk′-), *n.* a type of knapsack carried by hikers, bicyclists, etc.

ruck•us (ruk′əs), *n.* **1.** a noisy commotion; uproar; rumpus. **2.** a heated controversy.

ruc•tion (ruk′shən), *n.* a disturbance, quarrel, or row.

rudd (rud), *n.* a European cyprinid fish, *Scardinius erythrophthalmus,* of the carp family.

rud•der (rud′ər), *n.* **1.** a vertical blade at the stern of a vessel that can be turned to change the vessel's direction when in motion. **2.** a movable control surface attached to a vertical stabilizer, located at the rear of an airplane and used, along with the ailerons, to turn the airplane. **3.** any means of directing or guiding a course. —**rud′der•less,** *adj.*

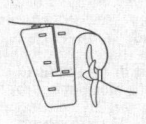 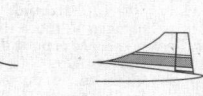 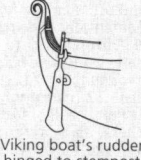

ship's rudder   supersonic–transport rudder   Viking boat's rudder hinged to stempost

rudder (defs. 1, 2)

rud•der•post (rud′ər pōst′), *n.* the vertical member on which a ship's rudder is hung.

rud•dy (rud′ē), *adj.,* **-di•er, -di•est. 1.** having a fresh, healthy red color. **2.** red or reddish. **3.** *Brit. Slang.* damned: *a ruddy fool.* —**rud′di•ly,** *adv.* —**rud′di•ness,** *n.*

rud′dy duck′, *n.* a stiff-tailed New World duck, the male of which has a brownish red body, black crown, and white cheeks.

rude (rōōd), *adj.,* **rud•er, rud•est. 1.** discourteous or impolite, esp. deliberately so: *a rude reply.* **2.** without culture, learning, or refinement. **3.** rough in manners or behavior; uncouth. **4.** rough, harsh, or ungentle: *a rude shock.* **5.** roughly built or made; crude: *a rude cottage.* **6.** harsh to the ear: *rude sounds.* **7.** lacking elegance; of a primitive simplicity: *a rude design.* **8.** robust, sturdy, or vigorous. —**rude′ly,** *adv.* —**rude′ness,** *n.*

ru•di•ment (rōō′də mənt), *n.* **1.** Usu., **rudiments. a.** the elements or first principles of a subject: *the rudiments of grammar.* **b.** a mere beginning, first appearance, or undeveloped or imperfect form of something: *the rudiments of a plan.* **2.** an incompletely developed organ or part.

ru•di•men•ta•ry (rōō′də men′tə rē, -trē) also **ru′di•men′tal,** *adj.* **1.** of or pertaining to rudiments or first principles; elementary. **2.** undeveloped or vestigial. **3.** primitive; crude.

rue[1] (rōō), *v.,* **rued, ru•ing,** *n.* —*v.t.* **1.** to feel sorrow over; repent for; regret bitterly: *to rue the loss of opportunities.* **2.** to wish that (something) had never been done or taken place: *rued the day he was born.* —*v.i.* **3.** to feel sorrow, repentance, or regret. —*n.* **4.** sorrow, repentance, or regret.

rue[2] (rōō), *n.* any strongly scented plant of the genus *Ruta,* esp. *R. graveolens,* having yellow flowers and leaves formerly used in medicine.

ruff[1] (ruf), *n.* **1.** a neckpiece or collar of lace, lawn, or the like, gathered into deep, full, regular folds, worn in the 16th and 17th centuries. **2.** a collar, or set of lengthened or specially marked hairs or feathers, on the neck of an animal. **3.** a Eurasian sandpiper, *Philomachus pugnax,* the male of which has a large erectile ruff of feathers during the breeding season. Compare REEVE[2].

ruff

ruff[2] (ruf), *n.* **1.** an act or instance of trumping in cards when one cannot follow suit. **2.** an old game of cards resembling whist. —*v.t., v.i.* **3.** to trump when unable to follow suit.

ruffed′ grouse′, *n.* a North American grouse of dense forests, *Bonasa umbellus,* having a tuft of black feathers on each side of the neck.

ruf•fi•an (ruf′ē ən, ruf′yən), *n.* **1.** a tough, lawless person; brutal bully. —*adj.* **2.** Also, **ruf′fi•an•ly.** tough; lawless; brutal.

ruf•fle[1] (ruf′əl), *v.,* **-fled, -fling,** *n.* —*v.t.* **1.** to destroy the smoothness or evenness of. **2.** to erect (the feathers), as a bird in anger. **3.** to disturb, vex, or irritate. **4.** to turn (pages) rapidly. **5.** to pass (cards) through the fingers rapidly in shuffling. **6.** to draw up (cloth, lace, etc.) into a ruffle by gathering along one edge. —*v.i.* **7.** to be or become ruffled. —*n.* **8.** a break in the smoothness or evenness of a surface; undulation. **9.** a strip of cloth, lace, etc., gathered along one edge and used as a trimming on a dress, curtains, etc. **10.** something resembling this, as the ruff of a bird. **11.** disturbance or vexation; irritation. —*Idiom.* **12. ruffle someone's feathers,** to upset or annoy someone somewhat. —**ruf′fly,** *adj.*

ruf•fle[2] (ruf′əl), *n., v.,* **-fled, -fling.** —*n.* **1.** a low, continuous beating of a drum. —*v.t.* **2.** to beat (a drum) in this manner.

ru•fous (rōō′fəs), *adj.* tinged with red; brownish red.

rug (rug), *n.* **1.** a piece of thick fabric for covering part of a floor, often having a design. Compare CARPET. **2.** the treated skin of an animal, used as a floor covering: *a bear rug.* **3.** *Chiefly Brit.* a piece of thick, warm cloth, used as a coverlet, lap robe, etc. **4.** *Slang.* a toupee; hairpiece.

Rug•by (rug′bē), *n. (sometimes l.c.)* Also called **Rug′by foot′ball.** a form of football, played between two teams of 15 members each, that differs from soccer in freedom to carry the ball, block with the hands and arms, and tackle, and is characterized by continuous action and prohibition against the use of substitute players.

Rug′by (or **rug′by**) **shirt′,** *n.* a knitted pullover sport shirt usu. in bold horizontal stripes, styled after the shirts traditionally worn by Rugby players. Also called **Rug′by jer′sey.**

rug•ged (rug′id), *adj.* **1.** having a roughly broken, rocky, hilly, or jagged surface. **2.** roughly irregular, heavy, or hard in outline or form: *Lincoln's rugged features.* **3.** (of a face) wrinkled or furrowed. **4.** rough, harsh, or severe: *a rugged life.* **5.** capable of enduring hardship, wear, etc.: *a rugged floor covering.* **6.** requiring great endurance, determination, etc.: *a rugged test.* **7.** tempestuous; stormy. **8.** rude, uncultivated, or unrefined. —**rug′ged•ly,** *adv.* —**rug′ged•ness,** *n.*

rug′ged individ′ualism, *n.* a way of living defined by economic freedom and private initiative.

rug•ger (rug′ər), *n.* RUGBY.

ru•go′sa rose′ (rōō gō′sə), *n.* a rose, *Rosa rugosa,* with densely bristled stems, wrinkled leaves, and fragrant red or white flowers.

ru•in (rōō′in), *n.* **1. ruins,** the remains of a building, city, etc., that has been destroyed or is decaying. **2.** a destroyed or decayed building, town, etc. **3.** a fallen, wrecked, or decayed condition: *The house fell into ruin.* **4.** the downfall, decay, or destruction of anything. **5.** the complete loss of health, means, position, hope, or the like. **6.** something that causes a downfall or destruction; blight: *Alcohol was my ruin.* **7.** the downfall of a person; undoing. **8.** a person as the wreck of his or her former self. **9.** the act of causing destruction or a downfall. —*v.t.* **10.** to reduce to ruin; devastate. **11.** to bring to financial ruin; bankrupt. **12.** to injure (a thing) irretrievably. **13.** to deflower (a woman) by seduction. —*v.i.* **14.** to fall into ruins. **15.** to come to ruin.

R

ru•in•a•tion (ro͞o′ə nā′shən), *n.* **1.** the act of ruining or the state of being ruined. **2.** something that ruins.

ru•in•ous (ro͞o′ə nəs), *adj.* **1.** bringing or tending to bring ruin; destructive; disastrous: *a ruinous war.* **2.** fallen into ruin; dilapidated. **3.** extremely expensive. —**ru′in•ous•ly,** *adv.* —**ru′in•ous•ness,** *n.*

rule (ro͞ol), *n., v.,* **ruled, rul•ing.** —*n.* **1.** a principle or regulation governing conduct, procedure, arrangement, etc. **2.** the customary or normal circumstance, occurrence, practice, quality, etc.: *the rule rather than the exception.* **3.** control, government, or dominion. **4.** tenure or conduct of reign or office. **5.** the code of regulations observed by a religious order or congregation. **6.** a prescribed mathematical method for performing a calculation or solving a problem. **7.** RULER (def. 2). **8.** a solid or decorative line, as used for separating newspaper columns. **9. a.** a formal order made by a law court, esp. for governing the procedure of the court. **b.** a legal principle. **c.** a court order in a particular case. —*v.t.* **10.** to exercise dominating power, authority, or influence over; govern: *to rule a kingdom.* **11.** to decide or declare judicially or authoritatively; decree. **12.** to mark with lines, esp. parallel straight lines, with the aid of a ruler or the like: *to rule paper.* **13.** to mark out or form (a line) by this method. **14.** to be superior or preeminent in (a field or group); hold sway over. —*v.i.* **15.** to exercise dominating power or influence; predominate. **16.** to exercise authority, dominion, or sovereignty. **17.** to make a formal decision or ruling, as on a point at law. **18.** to be prevalent or current. **19. rule out,** to eliminate from consideration. —***Idiom.*** **20. as a rule,** generally; usually.

rule′ of law′, *n.* conformity by the country's leaders to common or constitutional law.

rule′ of thumb′, *n.* **1.** a general principle or rule based on experience or practice, as opposed to a scientific calculation. **2.** a rough, practical method of procedure.

rul•er (ro͞o′lər), *n.* **1.** a person who rules or governs; sovereign. **2.** Also, **rule.** a strip of wood, metal, or other material having a straight edge marked off in inches or centimeters, used for drawing lines and measuring. **3.** a person or thing that rules lines on paper, wood, etc.

rules′ commit′tee, *n.* a special committee of a legislature, as of the U.S. House of Representatives, having the authority to establish rules or methods for expediting legislative action, and usually determining the date a bill is presented for consideration.

rules′ of or′der, *n.pl.* the rules by which a legislative or deliberative assembly governs its proceedings; parliamentary law.

rul•ing (ro͞o′ling), *n.* **1.** an authoritative decision, as one by a judge on a debated point of law. **2.** the act of drawing straight lines with a ruler. **3.** ruled lines. —*adj.* **4.** governing or dominating. **5.** controlling; predominating: *the ruling factor.* **6.** widespread; prevalent.

rum (rum), *n.* **1.** an alcoholic liquor or spirit distilled from molasses or some other fermented sugarcane product. **2.** any intoxicating liquor.

Ru•ma•ni•a (ro͞o mā′nē ə, -mān′yə), *n.* ROMANIA.

rum•ba (rum′bə, ro͝om′-, ro͞om′-), *n., pl.* **-bas** (-bəz), *v.,* **-baed** (-bəd), **-ba•ing** (-bə ing). —*n.* **1.** a dance, Cuban in origin and complex in rhythm. —*v.i.* **2.** to dance the rumba. [< American Spanish]

rum•ble (rum′bəl), *v.,* **-bled, -bling,** *n.* —*v.i.* **1.** to make a deep, somewhat muffled, continuous sound, as thunder. **2.** to move or travel with such a sound. —*v.t.* **3.** to give forth or utter with a rumbling sound. **4.** to cause to make or move with a rumbling sound. **5.** to subject to the action of a tumbling box, as for the purpose of polishing. —*n.* **6.** a deep, somewhat muffled, continuous sound. —**rum′bly,** *adj.*

rum′ble seat′, *n.* a seat recessed into the back of a coupe or roadster, covered by a hinged lid that opens to form the back of the seat when in use.

rum•bling (rum′bling), *n.* **1.** Often, **rumblings.** the first signs of dissatisfaction or grievance. **2.** RUMBLE (def. 7). —**rum′bling•ly,** *adv.*

ru•men (ro͞o′min), *n., pl.* **-mi•na** (-mə nə). **1.** the first stomach of a cow or other ruminant, in which food is softened and then regurgitated for cud-chewing. **2.** the cud of a ruminant.

ru•mi•nant (ro͞o′mə nənt), *n.* **1.** any even-toed ungulate of the suborder Ruminantia, characterized by cud-chewing and a three- or four-chambered stomach: includes cows, sheep, goats, deer, giraffes, and camels. —*adj.* **2.** ruminating; chewing the cud. **3.** contemplative; meditative. —**ru′mi•nant•ly,** *adv.*

ru•mi•nate (ro͞o′mə nāt′), *v.,* **-nat•ed, -nat•ing.** —*v.i.* **1.** to chew the cud, as a ruminant. **2.** to meditate or muse; ponder. —*v.t.* **3.** to chew again or over and over. **4.** to meditate on; ponder. —**ru′mi•nat′ing•ly,** *adv.* —**ru′mi•na′tion,** *n.* —**ru′mi•na′tive,** *adj.* —**ru′mi•na′tor,** *n.*

rum•mage (rum′ij), *v.,* **-maged, -mag•ing,** *n.* —*v.t.* **1.** to search thoroughly or actively through (a place, receptacle, etc.), esp. by moving around, turning over, or looking through contents. **2.** to find, bring, or fetch by searching (often fol. by *out* or *up*). —*v.i.* **3.** to search actively, as in a place or receptacle or within oneself. —*n.* **4.** miscellaneous articles; odds and ends. **5.** a rummaging search. —**rum′mag•er,** *n.*

rum′mage sale′, *n.* a sale of miscellaneous articles, esp. items contributed to raise money for charity.

rum•my (rum′ē), *n.* any of various card games for two, three, or four players, each dealt seven, nine, or ten cards, in which the object is to match cards into sets and sequences.

ru•mor (ro͞o′mər), *n.* **1.** a story or statement in general circulation without confirmation or certainty as to facts: *rumors of war.* **2.** gossip; hearsay. —*v.t.* **3.** to report or circulate by a rumor. Also, *esp. Brit.,* **ru′mour.**

rump (rump), *n.* **1.** the hind part of the body of an animal, as the hindquarters of a quadruped. **2.** a cut of beef from this part of the animal, behind the loin and above the round. **3.** the buttocks. **4.** the remnant of a legislature, council, etc., after a majority of the members have resigned or been expelled.

rum•ple (rum′pəl), *v.,* **-pled, -pling,** *n.* —*v.t.* **1.** to crumple or wrinkle. **2.** to ruffle; tousle: *The wind rumpled her hair.* —*v.i.* **3.** to become wrinkled or crumpled. —*n.* **4.** a wrinkle or crease. —**rum′ply,** *adj.,*

rum•pus (rum′pəs), *n.* **1.** a noisy or violent disturbance; commotion. **2.** a heated controversy.

run (run), *v.,* **ran, run, run•ning,** *n., adj.* —*v.i.* **1.** to go quickly by moving the legs more rapidly than at a walk and in such a manner that for an instant in each step all or both feet are off the ground. **2.** to move or pass quickly. **3.** to depart quickly; flee. **4.** to have recourse for aid, comfort, etc. **5.** to make a quick trip or visit: *to run up to New York.* **6.** to move freely and without restraint: *to run about in the park.* **7.** to move or roll forward. **8. a.** to take part in a race or contest. **b.** to finish a race in a specified sequence: *The horse ran second.* **c.** to advance a football by carrying it, as opposed to throwing or passing it. **9.** to be a candidate for election. **10.** (of fish) to migrate, as upstream or inshore for spawning. **11.** (of a ship) to be sailed or driven from a proper or given route: *to run aground.* **12.** to ply between places: *The bus runs between New Haven and Hartford.* **13.** to creep or climb, as growing vines. **14.** to unravel, as stitches or a fabric. **15.** to flow in or as if in a stream. **16.** to include a specific range of variations: *Your work runs from fair to bad.* **17.** to spread on being applied to a surface, as a liquid. **18.** to undergo a spreading of colors. **19.** to operate or function: *the noise of a dishwasher running.* **20.** to encounter a certain condition: *to run into trouble.* **21.** to amount; total: *The bill ran to $100.* **22.** to be stated or worded: *The text runs as follows.* **23.** to continue, extend, or stretch: *The story runs for eight pages.* **24.** to appear in print: *The story ran in all the papers.* **25.** to be performed: *The play ran for two years.* **26.** to last: *The movie runs for three hours.* **27.** to spread rapidly: *The news ran all over town.* **28.** to recur persistently: *Musical ability runs in my family.* **29.** to tend to have a specified quality, form, etc. **30.** to be of a certain size, number, etc.: *Potatoes are running large this year.* **31.** to sail before the wind. —*v.t.* **32.** to move along (a surface, path, etc.). **33.** to traverse (a distance) in running. **34.** to perform or accomplish by or as if by running: *to run an errand; to run a race.* **35.** to ride or cause to gallop. **36.** to enter in a race. **37.** to pursue or hunt, as game: *to run deer on foot.* **38.** to drive (an animal): *to run a fox to cover.* **39.** to cause to ply: *to run a ferry between New York and New Jersey.* **40.** to convey or transport. **41.** to cause to pass quickly: *He ran a comb through his hair.* **42.** to get past or through: *to run a blockade.* **43.** to disregard (a red traffic light) and continue ahead without stopping. **44.** to smuggle (contraband goods). **45.** to operate or drive: *Can you run a tractor?* **46.** to print or publish. **47.** to allow (a ship, automobile, etc.) to depart from a proper or given route: *ran the car up on the curb.* **48.** to sponsor as a candidate for election. **49.** to manage or conduct. **50.** to process (the instructions in a program) by computer. **51.** (in some games, as billiards) to continue or complete (a series of successful shots, strokes, or the like). **52.** to expose oneself to (danger, a risk, etc.). **53.** to cause (a liquid) to flow. **54.** to fill (a tub or bath) with water. **55.** to pour forth or discharge (a liquid). **56.** to cause to move freely: *to run a rope in a pulley.* **57.** to cause (a golf ball) to roll forward after landing from a stroke. **58.** to sew in a running stitch. **59.** to cause stitches in (a knitted fabric) to unravel: *to run a stocking.* **60.** to bring or lead into a certain condition: *They ran themselves into debt.* **61.** to drive or thrust. **62.** to graze; pasture. **63.** to extend in a particular direction or to a given place. **64.** to cause to fuse and flow, as metal. **65.** to cost (an amount): *This watch runs $30.* **66.** to cost (a person) an amount: *The car repair will run you $90.* **67. run across,** to meet or find accidentally. **68. run after, a.** to chase or pursue. **b.** to seek to acquire. **69. run along,** to leave; go away. **70. run around, a.** to engage in many and varied activities. **b.** to be engaged in more than one romantic involvement. **71. run away,** to flee or escape, esp. with no intent to return. **72. run away with, a.** to go away with, esp. to elope with. **b.** to abscond with; steal. **c.** to surpass others in. **d.** to get by surpassing others, as a prize. **e.** to overwhelm; get the better of. **73. run down, a.** to strike and overturn, esp. with a vehicle. **b.** to chase after and seize: *to run down criminals.* **c.** to read through quickly. **d.** to cease operation; stop. **e.** to speak disparagingly of. **f.** to search out; find: *to run down information.* **g.** *Baseball.* to tag out (a base runner) between bases. **74. run in, a.** to pay a casual visit. **b.** to arrest. **c.** Also, **run on.** to add (matter) to text without indenting. **75. run into, a.** to collide with. **b.** to meet accidentally. **c.** to amount to; total. **d.** to become contiguous or virtually intermingled: *one year running into the next.* **76. run in with,** to sail close to (a coast, vessel, etc.). **77. run off, a.** to leave quickly; run away. **b.** to create quickly and easily: *to run off a term paper in an hour.* **c.** to drive away; expel. **d.** to print or duplicate. **78. run off with, a.** to steal; abscond with. **b.** to elope with. **79. run on, a.** to continue without relief or interruption. **b.** to add at the end of a text. **80. run out, a.** to terminate; expire. **b.** to become used up. **c.** to drive out; expel. **81. run out of,** to use up a supply of. **82. run out on,** to withdraw one's support from; abandon. **83. run over, a.** to hit and drive over with a vehicle, esp. so as to injure severely. **b.** to go beyond; exceed. **c.** to repeat; review. **d.** to overflow, as a container. **84. run through, a.** to pierce or stab, as with a sword. **b.** to consume or squander. **c.** to practice or rehearse. **85. run up, a.** to sew rapidly. **b.** to amass; incur: *running up huge debts.* **c.** to cause to increase; raise: *to run up costs.* **d.** to build, esp. hurriedly. **86. run with, a.** to proceed with. **b.** to carry out with enthusiasm or speed. **—***n.* **87.** an act or instance of running: *a five-minute run.* **88.** a fleeing; flight. **89.** a running pace. **90.** an act or instance of moving rapidly, as in a boat or automobile. **91.** the distance covered, as by running or racing. **92.** a quick trip. **93.** a routine or regular trip. **94.** any portion of a military flight during which the aircraft flies directly toward the target in order to begin its attack. **95.** the rapid movement, under its own power, of an aircraft on a runway, water, or another surface. **96.** a period of continuous operation of a machine. **97.** the amount of anything produced in such a period. **98.** PRESSRUN. **99.** a place in knitted work where a series of stitches have come undone. **100.** the direction of something or of its elements. **101.** trend or tendency: *the normal run of events.* **102.** freedom to move around in or use something: *to have the run of the house.* **103.** a continuous series of performances or presentations. **104.** an uninterrupted course or spell: *a run of good luck.* **105.** a continuous extent of something, as a vein of ore. **106.** an uninterrupted series or sequence: *a run of 10 winning games.* **107.** a sequence of cards in a given suit: *run of hearts.* **108.** any extensive and continued demand. **109.** a series of sudden and urgent demands for payment, as on a bank. **110.** a period of being in demand or favor. **111.** a small stream or brook. **112.** a flow or rush, as of oil or water. **113.** a kind or class, as of goods. **114.** the typical or ordinary kind. **115.** an inclined course, as on a slope: *a bobsled run.* **116.** a trough or pipe for water or the like. **117.** a large enclosure for domestic animals: *a sheep run.* **118.** the usual trail of a group of animals: *a deer run.* **119.** the movement of fish upstream or inshore, as for spawning. **120.** *Music.* a rapid succession of notes; scale. **121.** *Baseball.* the score unit made by safely running around all the bases and reaching home plate. **122.** a series of successful shots, strokes, or the like in a game. **123. the runs,** (*used with a sing. or pl. v.*) *Informal.* DIARRHEA. **—***adj.* **124.** melted or liquefied: *run butter.* **125.** poured in a melted state, as into a mold: *run bronze.* **—*Idiom.* 126. in the long run,** in the course of long experience. **127. in the short run,** in the near or immediate future. **128. on the run, a.** scurrying about to perform one's activities. **b.** while rushing to get somewhere. **c.** moving from place to place so as to hide from the police. **129. run afoul of, a.** *Naut.* to collide with so as to cause damage and entanglement. **b.** to encounter or engender the animosity of; anger. **130. run for it,** to flee hurriedly, esp. to escape danger. **131. run off at the mouth,** *Informal.* to talk incessantly or indiscreetly. **132. run scared,** to be apprehensive about one's personal or professional survival. **133. run short,** to be in insufficient supply. **134. run wild, a.** to grow unchecked. **b.** to behave with lack of restraint or control. —**run′na•ble,** *adj.*

run•a•bout (run′ə bout′), *n.* **1.** a small, light automobile with an open top; roadster. **2.** a small pleasure motorboat. **3.** a person who roves around from place to place.

run′ against′ Wash′ington, to campaign as an outsider who does not belong to the centers of power, esp. in Congress.

run•a•round (run′ə round′), *n.* **1.** an indecisive or evasive response. **2.** *Print.* an arrangement of type in which several lines are set in narrower measure than the others in a column to accommodate an illustration, initial, or the like.

run•a•way (run′ə wā′), *n.* **1.** a person who runs away; fugitive; deserter. **2.** a horse or team that has broken away. **3.** the act of running away. **4.** an easy victory. **5.** a young person who has run away from home. **—***adj.* **6.** escaped; fugitive. **7.** (esp. of a horse) having escaped control. **8.** achieved by running away, esp. by eloping: *a runaway marriage.* **9.** (of a contest) easily won. **10.** unchecked; rampant: *runaway prices.*

run•back (run′bak′), *n. Football.* a run made by a player toward the opponent's goal line after receiving a kick, intercepting a pass, or recovering a fumble.

run′ci•ble spoon′ (run′sə bəl), *n.* a forklike utensil with two broad prongs a sharp, curved prong, for serving hors d'oeuvres.

Run•cie (run′sē), *n.* **Robert Alexander Kennedy,** born 1921, English clergyman: archbishop of Canterbury 1980–91.

run′-down′, *adj.* **1.** fatigued; exhausted. **2.** in poor health. **3.** in neglected or dilapidated condition. **4.** (of a clock, watch, etc.) not running because it is unwound.

run•down (run′doun′), *n.* **1.** a short summary. **2.** *Baseball.* pursuit of a runner caught between bases by two or more opposing players.

rune¹ (ro͞on), *n.* **1.** any of the characters of certain ancient alphabets, as of a script used for writing Germanic languages, esp. of Scandinavia and Britain, from about the 3rd to 13th centuries. **2.** something written or inscribed in such characters. **3.** something secret or mysterious, as an aphorism with mystical meaning. —**rune′like′,** *adj.*

rune² (ro͞on), *n. Literary.* a poem, song, or verse.

run′ for the ex′ercise, to campaign for election when there is no hope of winning, done as a means of practice for future races.

rung¹ (rung), *v.* pt. and pp. of RING².

rung² (rung), *n.* **1.** one of the crosspieces, usu. rounded, forming the steps of a ladder. **2.** a rounded or shaped piece fixed horizontally, for strengthening purposes, as between the legs of a chair. **3.** a spoke of a wheel. **4.** a level or degree, as in a hierarchy.

ru•nic (ro͞o′nik), *adj.* **1.** consisting of or set down in runes: *runic inscriptions.* **2.** having some secret or mysterious meaning.

run′-in′, *n.* **1.** a quarrel; argument. **2.** *Print.* matter added to a text without indenting for a new paragraph.

run•ner (run′ər), *n.* **1.** a person, animal, or thing that runs, esp. as a racer. **2.** a messenger, esp. of a bank or brokerage house. **3.** *Baseball.* BASE RUNNER. **4.** *Football.* the ball-carrier. **5.** a smuggler. **6.** a vessel engaged in smuggling. **7.** a person who takes and often pays off bets for a bookmaker. **8.** either of the long, bladelike strips of metal or wood on which a sled or sleigh slides. **9.** the blade of an ice skate. **10.** a long, narrow rug. **11.** a long, narrow strip of fabric used to adorn the top of a table, bureau, etc. **12. a.** a guiding or supporting strip for something that slides, as a drawer or sliding door. **b.** ROCKER (def. 1). **13.** *Bot.* a slender, trailing stem that runs along the surface of the ground and sends out roots. **14.** *Metall.* **a.** any of the channels in which molten metal flows from the furnace. **b.** GATE (def. 14a). **15.** any of several carangid fishes, as *Caranx crysos* or *Elagatis bipinnulata,* of deep waters from Cape Cod to Brazil. **16.** the rotating member of a pair of millstones. Compare BED STONE. **17.** a tackle consisting of a line rove through a single block and fixed at one end.

run′ner-up′, *n., pl.* **run•ners-up. 1.** the competitor, player, or team finishing in second place. **2. runners-up,** the competitors who place second, third, and fourth, or in the top ten.

run•ning (run′ing), *n.* **1.** the act of a person, animal, or thing that runs. **2.** management; direction: *the running of a business.* **3.** an act or instance of racing: *the 113th running of the Kentucky Derby.* **4.** the condition of a track or surface to be run or raced on. **5.** the amount, quality, or type of a liquid flow. **—***adj.* **6.** (of a horse) **a.** going or proceeding at a gallop. **b.** trained to proceed at a gallop. **7.** creeping or climbing, as plants. **8.** moving or proceeding smoothly. **9.** slipping or sliding easily, as a knot. **10.** operating or functioning, as a machine. **11.** (of measurement) linear; straight-line. **12.** flowing or fluid. **13.** carried on continuously: *a running commentary.* **14.** performed with or during a run: *a running leap.* **15.** discharging pus or other matter: *a running sore.* **16.** *Naut.* noting any of various objects or assemblages of objects that may be moved in ordinary use: *running bowsprit; running gaff.* **—***adv.* **17.** in succession; consecutively: *three nights running.* **—*Idiom.* 18. in the running, a.** participating as a competitor. **b.** under consideration as a candidate. **19. out of the running, a.** not competing. **b.** not among the winners or runners-up.

run′ning head′, *n.* a descriptive word, phrase, title, or the like, usu. repeated at the top of each page of a book, periodical, etc.

run′ning mate′, *n.* a candidate for an office linked with another and more important office, as for the vice-presidency.

run′ning stitch′, *n.* a sewing stitch made by passing the needle in and out repeatedly with short, even stitches.

run•ny (run′ē), *adj.,* **-ni•er, -ni•est. 1.** tending to run or drip: *a runny paste.* **2.** (of the nose) discharging mucus.

run•off (run′ôf′, -of′), *n.* **1.** something that drains or flows off, as rain water. **2.** a final contest held to break a tie or eliminate semifinalists.

run′off pri′mary, *n.* (esp. in the southern U.S.) a second primary between the two leading candidates of the first primary to provide nomination by majority rather than by plurality.

run′-of-the-mill′, *adj.* merely average; commonplace; mediocre.

run′-on′, *adj.* **1.** of or designating something that is added or run on: *a run-on entry in a dictionary.* **2.** (of a line of verse) having a thought that carries over to the next line. **—***n.* **3.** run-on matter.

run′-on′ sen′tence, *n.* a written sequence of two or more main clauses that are not separated by a period or semicolon or joined by a conjunction.

run•o•ver (run′ō′vər), *n.* the amount of type matter for a given article, story, etc., carried over to another page, column, or line.

runt (runt), *n.* **1.** an animal that is small or stunted as compared with others of its kind. **2.** the smallest or weakest of a litter, esp. of pigs or puppies. **3.** a person who is small and contemptible. —**runt′ish,** *adj.* —**runt′ish•ly,** *adv.* —**runt′ish•ness,** *n.* —**runt′y,** *adj.,*

run′-through′, *n.* **1.** a trial or practice performance, esp. an uninterrupted rehearsal of a play. **2.** a quick outline or review.

run•way (run′wā′), *n.* **1.** a way along which something runs. **2.** a paved or cleared strip on which planes land and take off. **3.** the beaten track or habitual path of deer or other wild animals. **4.** a fairly large enclosure in which domestic animals may range about: *a runway for dogs.* **5.** the bed of a stream. **6.** a narrow platform or ramp extending from a stage into the orchestra pit or into an aisle, as in a theater.

Run•yon (run′yən), *n.* **(Alfred) Da•mon** (dā′mən), 1884–1946, U.S. journalist and short-story writer. —**Run′yon•esque′,** *adj.*

ru•pee (ro͞o pē′, ro͞o′pē), *n.* the basic monetary unit of India, Mauritius, Nepal, and Pakistan.

rup•ture (rup′chər), *n., v.,* **-tured, -tur•ing. —***n.* **1.** the act of breaking or bursting. **2.** the state of being broken or burst. **3.** a breach of harmonious, friendly, or peaceful relations. **4.** hernia, esp. abdominal hernia. **—***v.t.* **5.** to break or burst. **6.** to cause a breach of. **—***v.i.* **7.** to suffer a break or rupture. —**rup′tur•a•ble,** *adj.*

rup′tured disk′, *n.* HERNIATED DISK.

ru•ral (ro͝or′əl), *adj.* **1.** characteristic of country life or people; rustic. **2.** living in the country. **3.** pertaining to agriculture. —**ru′ral•ism,** *n.*

ru′ral deliv′ery, *n.* delivery of mail in rural communities. Formerly, **ru′ral free′ deliv′ery.**

ruse (ro͞oz), *n.* a trick, stratagem, or artifice: *He used a ruse to get past the sentry.*

R

rush¹ (rush), *v.i.* **1.** to move, act, or progress with speed, impetuosity, or violence. **2.** to dash, esp. to dash forward for an attack or onslaught. **3.** to appear, go, pass, etc., rapidly or suddenly. **4.** to carry the football on a running play. —*v.t.* **5.** to perform, accomplish, or finish with speed, impetuosity, or violence. **6.** to carry or convey with haste. **7.** to cause to move, act, or progress quickly; hurry. **8.** to send, push, force, impel, etc., with unusual speed or haste. **9.** to attack suddenly and violently; charge. **10.** to overcome or capture (a person, place, etc.). **11.** to entertain (a prospective fraternity or sorority member) before making bids for membership. **12. a.** to carry (the football) forward across the line of scrimmage. **b.** to carry the football (a distance) forward from the line of scrimmage. **c.** (of a defensive team member) to attempt to force a way quickly into the backfield in pursuit of (the back in possession of the football). —*n.* **13.** the act of rushing; a rapid, impetuous, or violent onward movement. **14.** a hostile attack. **15.** a sudden appearance or access. **16.** hurried activity; busy haste. **17.** a hurried state, as from pressure of affairs. **18.** press of work, business, traffic, etc., requiring extraordinary effort or haste. **19.** an eager rushing of numbers of persons to some region: *the California gold rush.* **20.** a scrimmage held as a form of sport between classes or bodies of students in colleges. **21.** rushes, DAILY (def. 4). **22.** the rushing by a fraternity or sorority. —*adj.* **23.** requiring or done in haste. **24.** characterized by excessive business, a press of work or traffic, etc. —**rush′er,** *n.*

rush² (rush), *n.* **1.** any grasslike plant of the genus *Juncus,* having pithy or hollow stems, found in wet or marshy places. **2.** any of various similar plants. **3.** a stem of such a plant, used for making chair bottoms, baskets, etc. **4.** something of little or no value; trifle.

rush′ hour′, *n.* a time of day in which large numbers of people are in transit, as going to or returning from work.

Rush•more (rush′môr, -mōr), *n.* **Mount,** a peak in the Black Hills of South Dakota that is a memorial **(Mount Rushmore National Memorial)** having busts of Washington, Jefferson, Lincoln, and Theodore Roosevelt carved into its face. 5600 ft. (1707 m).

rusk (rusk), *n.* a sweet raised bread dried and baked again; zwieback.

Rus•kin (rus′kin), *n.* **John,** 1819–1900, English author, art critic, and social reformer.

Rus•sell (rus′əl), *n.* **1. Bertrand (Arthur William), 3rd Earl,** 1872–1970, English philosopher and mathematician. **2. John Russell, 1st Earl** (*Lord John Russell*), 1792–1878, British prime minister 1846–52, 1865–66. **3. Leon** (*Hank Wilson*), born 1941, U.S. rock singer and pianist. **4. Lillian** (*Helen Louise Leonard*), 1861–1922, U.S. singer and actress.

rus•set (rus′it), *n.* **1.** light brown, yellowish, or reddish brown. **2.** a coarse reddish brown or brownish homespun cloth formerly used for clothing. **3.** any of various apples that have a rough brownish skin and ripen in the autumn. —*adj.* **4.** light brown, yellowish, or reddish brown.

Rus•sia (rush′ə), *n.* **1.** Also called **Russian Empire.** Russian, **Rossiya.** a former empire in E Europe and N and W Asia: overthrown by the Russian Revolution 1917. *Cap.:* St. Petersburg (1703–1917). **2.** UNION OF SOVIET SOCIALIST REPUBLICS. **3.** RUSSIAN SOVIET FEDERATED SOCIALIST REPUBLIC. **4.** RUSSIAN FEDERATION.

Rus•sian (rush′ən), *n.* **1. a.** a member of a Slavic people, the dominant ethnic group in the Russian Federation, whose historical homeland lies along the upper Volga and Oka rivers and adjacent areas. **b.** the East Slavic language of this people: the official language of Russia or the Russian Federation. *Abbr.:* Russ **2.** any native or citizen of Russia or the Russian Federation. —*adj.* **3.** of or pertaining to Russia, its inhabitants, or their language.

Rus′sian Blue′, *n.* one of a breed of shorthaired domestic cats with large ears, green eyes, and a thick, plush bluish gray coat.

Rus′sian dress′ing, *n.* a mayonnaise dressing containing chili sauce, chopped pickles, pimientos, and other ingredients.

Rus′sian Federa′tion, *n.* a republic extending from E Europe to N and W Asia. 147,987,101; 6,592,849 sq. mi. (17,075,400 sq. km.). *Cap:* Moscow. Also called **Rus′sian Repub′lic.** Formerly (1918–91), **Russian Soviet Federated Socialist Republic.**

Rus′sian Or′thodox Church′, *n.* the autocephalous Eastern Church in Russia: the branch of the Orthodox Church that constituted the established church in Russia until 1917. Also called **Rus′sian Church′.**

Rus′sian Revolu′tion, *n.* **1.** Also called **February Revolution.** the uprising in Russia in March 1917 (February Old Style), in which the Czarist government collapsed and a provisional government was established. **2.** Also called **October Revolution.** the overthrow of this provisional government by a coup d'état on Nov. 7, 1917 (Oct. 25 Old Style), establishing the Soviet government.

Rus′sian roulette′, *n.* **1.** a lethal game of chance in which a person, using a revolver with one bullet, spins its cylinder, points the muzzle at his or her head, and pulls the trigger. **2.** any reckless act or activity.

Rus′sian wolf′hound, *n.* BORZOI.

rust (rust), *n.* **1.** the red or orange coating that forms on the surface of iron when exposed to air and moisture, consisting chiefly of ferric hydroxide and ferric oxide formed by oxidation. **2.** any film or coating on metal caused by oxidation. **3.** a stain resembling this coating. **4.** any

growth, habit, or agency tending to injure or impair the mind, abilities, etc. **5. a.** any of several diseases of plants, characterized by reddish, brownish, or black pustules on the leaves, stems, etc., caused by fungi of the order Uredinales. **b.** Also called **rust′ fun′gus.** a fungus causing this disease. **6.** reddish yellow or reddish brown. —*v.i.* **7.** to become or grow rusty, as iron. **8.** to contract rust. **9.** to deteriorate or become impaired, as through inaction or disuse. **10.** to become rust-colored. —*v.t.* **11.** to affect with rust. **12.** to make rust-colored.

rus•tic (rus′tik), *adj.* **1.** of or living in the country, as distinguished from towns or cities; rural. **2.** simple or unsophisticated. **3.** uncouth, rude, or boorish. **4.** (of stonework) having the surfaces rough or irregular and the joints sunken or beveled. —*n.* **5.** a country person. **6.** an unsophisticated country person. —**rus•tic•i•ty** (ru stis′i tē), *n.*

rus•ti•cate (rus′ti kāt′), *v.,* **-cat•ed, -cat•ing.** —*v.i.* **1.** to go to the country. **2.** to stay or sojourn in the country. —*v.t.* **3.** to send to or domicile in the country. **4.** to make rustic, as persons or manners. **5.** to finish (masonry) with deeply sunken or beveled joints between raised block faces. —**rus′ti•ca′tion,** *n.*

Rus•tin (rus′tin), *n.* **Bayard,** born 1910, U.S. civil rights leader.

rus•tle (rus′əl), *v.i.* **1.** to make the slight, soft sounds of gentle rubbing, of as leaves, silk, or paper. **2.** to cause such sounds by moving or stirring something. **3.** to move, proceed, or work energetically. —*v.t.* **4.** to move so as to cause a rustling sound. **5.** to move, bring, or get by energetic action. **6.** to steal (livestock, esp. cattle). **7. rustle up,** *Informal.* to find, gather, or assemble by effort or search. —*n.* **8.** the sound made by anything that rustles. —**rus′tler,** *n.*

rust•proof (rust′prōōf′), *adj.* **1.** not subject to rusting. —*v.t.* **2.** to coat with a substance that prevents rusting.

rust•y (rus′tē), *adj.,* **rust•i•er, rust•i•est. 1.** covered with or affected by rust. **2.** consisting of or produced by rust. **3.** of or tending toward the color rust. **4.** impaired through disuse or neglect. **5.** having lost agility or alertness; out of practice. **6.** faded or shabby. —**rust′i•ly,** *adv.*

rut¹ (rut), *n., v.,* **rut•ted, rut•ting.** —*n.* **1.** a furrow or track in the ground, esp. one made by the passage of vehicles. **2.** any furrow, groove, etc. **3.** a fixed mode of procedure or course of life, usu. dull or unpromising: *to fall into a rut.* —*v.t.* **4.** to make a rut or in; furrow.

rut² (rut), *n., v.,* **rut•ted, rut•ting.** —*n.* **1.** the periodically recurring sexual excitement of the deer, goat, sheep, etc. —*v.i.* **2.** to be in the condition of rut.

ru•ta•ba•ga (rōō′tə bā′gə, rōō′tə bā′-), *n., pl.* **-gas. 1.** a plant, *Brassica napobrassica,* of the mustard family, with a yellow- or white-fleshed, edible tuber. **2.** the edible tuber, a variety of turnip.

ruth (rōōth), *n.* **1.** pity or compassion. **2.** sorrow or grief. **3.** self-reproach; remorse.

Ruth¹ (rōōth), *n.* **1.** a Moabite who married Boaz and became an ancestor of David: the daughter-in-law of Naomi. **2.** a book of the Bible bearing her name.

Ruth² (rōōth), *n.* **George Herman** ("*Babe*"), 1895–1948, U.S. baseball player.

ru•the•ni•um (rōō thē′nē əm, -thēn′yəm), *n.* a steel-gray, rare metallic element, belonging to the platinum group of metals. *Symbol:* Ru; *at. wt.:* 101.07; *at. no.:* 44; *sp. gr.:* 12.2 at 20°C.

ruth•er•for•di•um (ruth′ər fôr′dē əm, -fôr′-), *n.* UNNILQUADIUM.

ruth•less (rōōth′lis), *adj.* without pity or compassion; cruel; merciless. —**ruth′less•ly,** *adv.* —**ruth′less•ness,** *n.*

ru•tile (rōō′tēl, -tīl), *n.* a dark red, brilliant mineral, titanium dioxide, TiO₂, occurring in needlelike crystals and granular masses: used to coat welding rods.

RV, 1. recreational vehicle. **2.** Revised Version (of the Bible).

R-val•ue (är′val′yōō), *n.* a measure of the resistance of an insulating or building material to heat flow, expressed as R-11, R-20, etc.; higher number signifies greater resistance to heat flow. Compare U-VALUE.

R/W, right of way.

Rwan•da (rōō än′də), *n.* a republic in central Africa, E of the Democratic Republic of the Congo: formerly comprising the N part of the Belgian trust territory of Ruanda-Urundi; became independent 1962. 7,737,537; 10,169 sq. mi. (26,338 sq. km). *Cap.:* Kigali. —**Rwan′dan,** *adj., n.*

Rx, 1. prescription. **2.** (in prescriptions) take.

rye¹ (rī), *n.* **1.** a widely cultivated cereal grass, *Secale cereale.* **2.** the seeds or grain of this plant, used for making flour and whiskey, and as a livestock feed. **3.** RYE BREAD. **4.** Also called **rye′ whis′key. a.** a straight whiskey distilled from a mash containing 51 percent or more rye grain. **b.** *Northeastern U.S. and Canada.* a blended whiskey.

rye² (rī), *n.* a Gypsy man.

rye′ bread′, *n.* bread that is made either entirely or partly from rye flour, often with caraway seeds.

rye•grass (rī′gras′, -gräs′), *n.* any of several European grasses of the genus *Lolium,* as *L. perenne,* grown for forage in the U.S.

Ryu′kyu Is′lands (rē ōō′kyōō), *n.pl.* a chain of Japanese islands in the W Pacific between Japan and Taiwan. 1,235,000; 1205 sq. mi. (3120 sq. km). —**Ryu′kyu•an,** *n., adj.*

S

S, s (es), *n., pl.* **Ss** or **S's, ss** or **s's. 1.** the 19th letter of the English alphabet, a consonant. **2.** any spoken sound represented by this letter. **3.** something shaped like an S. **4.** a written or printed representation of the letter *S* or *s.*

S, 1. satisfactory. **2.** sentence. **3.** siemens. **4.** signature. **5.** single. **6.** small. **7.** soft. **8.** soprano. **9.** Also, **s** south. **10.** southern. **11.** state (highway). **12.** *Gram.* subject.

S, *Symbol.* **1.** the 19th in order or in a series. **2.** entropy. **3.** sulfur.

s, *Symbol.* second.

's[1], an ending used to form the possessive of most singular nouns, plural nouns not ending in *s,* noun phrases, and noun substitutes: *man's; women's; James's; witness's* (or *witness'*); *king of England's; anyone's.*

's[2], **1.** contraction of *is: She's here.* **2.** contraction of *has: He's been there.* **3.** contraction of *does: What's he do for a living?*

-s or **-es,** an ending marking nouns as plural (*weeks; days; minutes*), occurring also on nouns that have no singular (*dregs; pants; scissors*), or on nouns that have a singular with a different meaning (*glasses; manners; thanks*); **-s** occurs with a number of nouns that now often take singular agreement, as the names of games (*billiards; checkers*), of diseases (*measles; pox; rickets*), or of various involuntary physical or mental conditions (*d.t.'s; giggles; hots; willies*). A parallel set of formations, where **-s** has no plural value, are adjectives denoting mental states (*bananas; crackers; nuts*); compare **-ERS.**

s.a., 1. semiannual. **2.** without year or date. **3.** subject to approval.

Saa·ri·nen (sär′ə nən, sar′-), *n.* **1. Eero,** 1910–61, U.S. architect, born in Finland. **2. (Gottlieb) Eliel,** 1873–1950, U.S. architect, born in Finland (father of Eero Saarinen).

Sa·ba (sä′bə), *n.* an ancient kingdom in SW Arabia. Biblical name, Sheba.

Sab·a·oth (sab′ē oth′, -ôth′, sab′ā-, sə bā′ôth), *n.* (*used with a pl. v.*) armies; hosts. Rom. 9:29; James 5:4. [< Hebrew *ṣ̌ebhā'ōth,* pl. of *ṣābhā* army]

Sab·ba·tar·i·an (sab′ə târ′ē ən), *n.* **1.** a person, esp. a Christian, who observes Saturday as the Sabbath. **2.** a person who adheres to or advocates a strict observance of Sunday as a day of rest. —*adj.* **3.** of or pertaining to the Sabbath and its observance. —**Sab′ba·tar′i·an·ism,** *n.*

Sab·bath (sab′əth), *n.* **1.** the seventh day of the week, Saturday, as the day of rest and religious observance among Jews and some Christians. Ex. 20:8–11. **2.** the first day of the week, Sunday, observed by most Christians in commemoration of the Resurrection of Christ. **3.** (*often l.c.*) a day of rest or prayer. [Old English < Latin *sabbatum* < Greek *sábbaton* < Hebrew *shabbāth* rest]

Sab′bath school′, 1. SUNDAY SCHOOL. **2.** (among Seventh-Day Adventists) such a school held on Saturday, their holy day.

sab·bat·i·cal (sə bat′i kal) also **sab·bat′ic,** *adj.* **1.** (*cap.*) of or appropriate to the Sabbath. **2.** pertaining to a sabbatical year. **3.** bringing a period of rest. —*n.* **4.** SABBATICAL YEAR. **5.** any extended period of leave from one's customary work, esp. for rest or study.

sabbat′ical year′, 1. Also called **sabbat′ical leave′.** a year, usu. every seventh, of release from normal teaching duties granted to a college professor for research, travel, etc. **2.** a yearlong period observed by Jews in ancient times and in modern Israel once every seven years, during which all agricultural labors are suspended. Lev. 25. Compare JUBILEE (def. 6).

Sa·be·an (sə bē′ən), *adj.* **1.** of or pertaining to ancient Saba. —*n.* **2.** a native or inhabitant of ancient Saba.

sa·ber (sā′bər), *n.* **1.** a one-edged sword, usu. slightly curved, used esp. by cavalry. **2.** a soldier armed with such a sword. **3. a.** a fencing sword having two cutting edges and a blunt point. **b.** the art or sport of fencing with the saber. —*v.t.* **4.** to strike, wound, or kill with a saber. —**sa′ber·like′,** *adj.*

sa′ber-rat′tling, *n.* a show or threat of military power.

sa′ber saw′, *n.* a portable electric jigsaw.

sa·ber·tooth (sā′bər tooth′), *n.* any of several extinct members of the cat family Felidae, from the Oligocene to Pleistocene epochs, having greatly elongated, saberlike upper canine teeth. Also called **sa′ber-toothed′ ti′ger.**

sa′ber-toothed′, *adj.* having long, saberlike upper canine teeth, sometimes extending below the margin of the lower jaw.

sa·bin (sā′bin), *n.* a unit of sound absorption, equal to the absorption of one square foot (929 square centimeters) of a perfectly absorptive surface. [after W.C. *Sabine* (1868–1919), U.S. physicist]

Sa·bin (sā′bin), *n.* **Albert Bruce,** 1906–93, U.S. physician, born in Russia: developed the Sabin vaccine.

Sa′bin vaccine′, *n.* an orally administered vaccine of live viruses for immunization against poliomyelitis. [after A. B. *Sabin*]

sa·ble[1] (sā′bəl), *n., pl.* **-bles,** (*esp. collectively*) **-ble,** *adj.* —*n.* **1.** a dark-colored Eurasian marten, *Martes zibellina,* valued for its fur. **2.** a North American marten, *Martes americana.* **3.** the fur of the sable. **4.** the color black. **5. sables,** black mourning garments. —*adj.* **6.** of the color black. **7.** made of sable fur.

sa·ble[2] (sā′bəl), *n., pl.* **-ble, -bles.** SABLEFISH.

sa′ble an′telope, *n.* a large African antelope, *Hippotragus niger,* with long, saberlike horns and, in the male, a black coat.

sa·ble·fish (sā′bəl fish′), *n., pl.* (*esp. collectively*) **-fish,** (*esp. for kinds or species*) **-fish·es.** a large, blackish food fish of the N Pacific.

sab·o·tage (sab′ə täzh′), *n., v.,* **-taged, -tag·ing.** —*n.* **1.** deliberate damage of equipment or underhand interference with production or work, as by employees during a trade dispute. **2.** destruction of property or obstruction of public services, as to undermine a government or military effort. **3.** any undermining of a cause, plan, or effort. —*v.t.* **4.** to injure or attack by sabotage.

sab·o·teur (sab′ə tûr′), *n.* a person who commits sabotage.

sac (sak), *n.* a baglike structure in an animal, plant, or fungus, esp. one containing fluid. —**sac′like′,** *adj.*

sacchar-, a word-forming base meaning "sugar," to which suffixes beginning in a vowel are added: *saccharide.*

sac·cha·ride (sak′ə rīd′, -ər id), *n.* **1.** an organic compound containing a sugar or sugars. **2.** a simple sugar; monosaccharide. **3.** an ester of sucrose.

sac·cha·rin (sak′ər in), *n.* a synthetic powder, $C_7H_5NO_3S$, which in dilute solution is 500 times as sweet as sugar: used as a noncaloric sugar substitute.

sac·cha·rine (sak′ər in, -ə rēn′, -ə rīn′), *adj.* **1.** of, resembling, or containing sugar. **2.** very sweet to the taste; sugary. **3.** cloyingly agreeable or ingratiating. **4.** exaggeratedly sweet or sentimental.

Sac·co (sak′ō, sä′kō), *n.* **Nicola,** 1891–1927, Italian anarchist, in the U.S. after 1908: together with Bartolomeo Vanzetti, found guilty of robbery and murder 1921; executed 1927.

sac·er·do·tal (sas′ər dōt′l), *adj.* of priests; priestly. —**sac′er·do′tal·ly,** *adv.*

sa·chem (sā′chəm), *n.* **1.** (among some North American Indians) the chief of a tribe or confederation. **2.** one of the high officials in the Tammany Society. —**sa·chem′ic** (-chem′ik), *adj.*

Sa·cher torte (sä′kər tôrt′, zä′-), *n.* a chocolate cake filled or spread with apricot jam and covered with a chocolate glaze. [after the *Sacher Hotel,* in Vienna, Austria]

sa·chet (sa shā′; *esp. Brit.* sash′ā), *n.* **1.** a small bag, case, or pad containing aromatic powder, flower parts, or the like. **2.** scented powder used in such a case. —**sa·cheted′** (-shād′), *adj.*

sack[1] (sak), *n.* **1.** a large bag of strong, coarsely woven material, as for grain, potatoes, or coal. **2.** the amount a sack holds. **3.** a bag. **4.** *Slang.* dismissal, as from a job: *to get the sack.* **5.** *Slang.* bed. **6. a.** a loose-fitting dress, esp. one fashionable in the late 17th–18th century. **b.** a loose-fitting coat, jacket, or cape. **7.** *Baseball.* a base. —*v.t.* **8.** to put into a sack or sacks. **9.** *Football.* to tackle (the quarterback) behind the line of scrimmage before the quarterback is able to throw a pass. **10.** *Slang.* to dismiss or discharge, as from a job. **11. sack out,** *Slang.* to go to bed; fall asleep. —**sack′er,** *n.* —**sack′like′,** *adj.*

sack[2] (sak), *v.t.* **1.** to pillage or loot (a place) after capture; plunder. —*n.* **2.** the plundering of a captured place: *the sack of Troy.* —**sack′er,** *n.*

sack[3] (sak), *n.* a strong white wine formerly imported by England from Spain and the Canary Islands.

sack·cloth (sak′klôth′, -kloth′), *n.* **1.** SACKING. **2. a.** a coarse cloth of various fibers, as goat hair, cotton, or linen. **b.** this cloth or a garment made from it worn to show repentance or grief. —*Idiom.* **3. in sackcloth and ashes,** in a state of repentance or sorrow; contrite.

sack·ing (sak′ing), *n.* stout, coarse woven material of hemp, jute, or the like, chiefly for sacks. Also called **sackcloth.**

sack′ race′, *n.* a race in which each contestant has the legs enclosed in a sack and moves forward by jumping.

sa·cral[1] (sā′krəl, sak′rəl), *adj.* of or pertaining to sacred rites or observances.

sa·cral[2] (sā′krəl, sak′rəl), *adj.* of or pertaining to the sacrum.

sac·ra·ment (sak′rə mənt), *n.* **1.** a rite considered to have been established by Christ as a channel for grace: the Roman Catholic and Greek Orthodox sacraments are baptism, the Eucharist, the anointing of the sick, confirmation, holy orders, penance, and matrimony; the Protestant sacraments are baptism and the Lord's Supper. **2.** (*often cap.*) the Eucharist. **3.** the consecrated elements of the Eucharist, esp. the bread. **4.** something regarded as possessing a sacred character or mysterious significance. [< Medieval Latin *sacrāmentum* obligation, oath < Latin *sacrāre* to consecrate]

sac·ra·men·tal (sak′rə men′tl), *adj.* **1.** of, pertaining to, or of the nature of a sacrament, esp. the sacrament of the Eucharist. **2.** powerfully binding: *a sacramental obligation.* —*n.* **3.** a sacred act, ceremony, or object instituted by the Church, as prayer, a blessing, or holy water. —**sac′ra·men′tal·ly,** *adv.*

sac·ra·men·tal·ism (sak′rə men′tl iz′əm), *n.* a belief in or emphasis on the importance and efficacy of the sacraments for achieving salvation and conferring grace. —**sac′ra·men′tal·ist,** *n.*

Sac·ra·men·tar·i·an (sak′rə men târ′ē ən), *n.* **1.** a person who maintains that the Eucharistic elements have only symbolic significance. **2.** (*l.c.*) a sacramentalist. —*adj.* **3.** of or pertaining to the Sacramentarians. —**Sac′ra·men·tar′i·an·ism,** *n.*

Sac·ra·men·to (sak′rə men′tō), *n.* **1.** the capital of California, in the central part, on the Sacramento River. 373,924. **2.** a river flowing S from N California to San Francisco Bay. 382 mi. (615 km) long.

sa·cred (sā′krid), *adj.* **1.** devoted or dedicated to a deity or to some religious purpose; consecrated. **2.** entitled to veneration or religious respect by association with divine things; holy. **3.** pertaining to or connected with religion (opposed to *secular* or *profane*). **4.** reverently dedicated to some person, purpose, or object; consecrated: *a morning hour sacred to study.* **5.** regarded with reverence: *the sacred memory of a dead hero.* **6.** secured against violation, infringement, etc., as by reverence or sense of right: *sacred oaths.* **7.** properly immune from violence, interference, etc.; inviolable. —**sa′cred·ly,** *adv.* —**sa′cred·ness,** *n.*

sa′cred cow′, *n.* someone or something considered to be exempt from criticism or questioning.

sa′cred i′bis, *n.* an African ibis, *Threskiornis aethiopica,* having a black, naked head: venerated by the ancient Egyptians.

sac′red mon′ster, *n.* a celebrity whose eccentricities or indiscretions are easily forgiven by admirers.

sac·ri·fice (sak′rə fīs′), *n., v.,* **-ficed, -fic·ing.** —*n.* **1.** the offering of animal, plant, or human life or of some object to a deity, as in propitiation or homage. **2.** the person, animal, or thing so offered. **3.** the surrender or destruction of something valued for the sake of something having a higher claim. **4.** something so surrendered or lost. **5.** a loss incurred in selling something below its value. **6.** Also called **sac′rifice bunt′, sac′rifice hit′.** a hit or bunted ball in baseball that results in an out for the batter, but allows a runner on base to advance or score. —*v.t.* **7.** to make a sacrifice or offering of. **8.** to surrender, give up, permit injury to, or destroy for the sake of something else. **9.** to dispose of (goods, property, etc.) regardless of profit. **10.** to cause the advance of (a base runner) in baseball by a sacrifice. —*v.i.* **11.** to offer or make a sacrifice. **12.** to make a sacrifice in baseball. —**sac′ri·fic′er,** *n.*

sac′rifice fly′, *n.* a fly ball in baseball that enables a base runner, usu. at third base, to score after the ball is caught.

sac·ri·fi·cial (sak′rə fish′əl), *adj.* pertaining to, concerned with, or used in sacrifice: *a sacrificial lamb.* —**sac′ri·fi′cial·ly,** *adv.*

sac·ri·lege (sak′rə lij), *n.* **1.** the violation or profanation of anything sacred or held sacred. **2.** an instance of this.

sac·ri·le·gious (sak′rə lij′əs, -lē′jəs), *adj.* **1.** involving sacrilege. **2.** guilty of sacrilege. —**sac′ri·le′gious·ly,** *adv.*

sac·ris·tan (sak′ri stən), *n.* an official in charge of a sacristy. Also called **sac′rist** (sak′rist, sā′krist).

sac·ris·ty (sak′ri stē), *n., pl.* **-ties.** a room in a church in which sacred vessels, vestments, etc., are kept.

sac·ro·il·i·ac (sak′rō il′ē ak′, sā′krō-), *n.* **1.** the joint where the sacrum and ilium meet. —*adj.* **2.** of, pertaining to, or affecting this joint or its associated ligaments.

sac·ro·sanct (sak′rō sangkt′), *adj.* **1.** extremely sacred or inviolable. **2.** regarded or treated as being above or beyond interference, criticism, etc. —**sac′ro·sanc′ti·ty, sac′ro·sanct′ness,** *n.*

sac·rum (sak′rəm, sā′krəm), *n., pl.* **sac·ra** (sak′rə, sā′krə). a bone between the lumbar vertebrae and tail vertebrae, in humans composed usu. of five fused vertebrae and forming the posterior wall of the pelvis.

sad (sad), *adj.,* **sad·der, sad·dest.** **1.** affected by unhappiness or grief; sorrowful or mournful: *to feel sad.* **2.** expressive of or characterized by sorrow: *a sad song.* **3.** causing sorrow: *sad news.* **4.** (of color) somber or dull; drab. **5.** deplorably bad; sorry: *a sad attempt.* —**sad′ly,** *adv.* —**sad′ness,** *n.*

SAD, seasonal affective disorder.

sad·den (sad′n), *v.t., v.i.* to make or become sad.

sad·dle (sad′l), *n., v.,* **-dled, -dling.** —*n.* **1.** a seat for a rider on the back of a horse or other animal. **2.** a similar seat on a bicycle, tractor, etc. **3.** the padded part of a harness laid across the back of an animal and girded under the belly. **4.** something resembling a saddle in shape, position, or function. **5.** the part of the back of an animal where a saddle is placed. **6.** a cut of lamb, venison, etc., comprising both loins. **7.**

the posterior part of the back of poultry. **8.** a ridge connecting two higher elevations. **9.** a strip of leather, often of a contrasting color, sewn across the instep of a shoe. **10.** SADDLE SHOE. —*v.t.* **11.** to put a saddle on. **12.** to load or charge, as with a burden or responsibility: *saddled with unwanted guests.* —*v.i.* **13.** to put a saddle on a horse (often fol. by *up*). **14.** to mount into the saddle (often fol. by *up*). —*Idiom.* **15.** in the saddle, **a.** in a position to direct or control; in command. **b.** at work; on the job.

sad′dle-backed′, *adj.* **1.** having the back or upper surface curved like a saddle. **2.** having a saddlelike marking on the back.

sad′dle·bag′, *n.* **1.** a large bag or pouch, usu. one of a pair, hung from a saddle, laid over the back of a horse behind the saddle, or mounted over the rear wheel of a motorcycle.

sad′dle horse′, *n.* **1.** a horse bred, trained, or used for riding. **2.** AMERICAN SADDLE HORSE.

sad′dle leath′er, *n.* **1.** hide, as from a cow or bull, that undergoes vegetable tanning and is used for saddlery. **2.** any leather that simulates this, used for clothing, accessories, etc.

sad′dle shoe′, *n.* an oxford-type shoe with a saddle of contrasting leather or color.

sad′dle soap′, *n.* a soft, mild soap, used for cleaning and preserving saddles and other leather articles.

sad′dle stitch′, *n.* **1.** an overcasting stitch, esp. one made with a strip of leather or a thick cord. **2.** a spaced running stitch in contrasting or heavy thread, usu. along an edge. —**sad′dle-stitch′,** *v.t.*

Sad·du·cee (saj′ə sē′, sad′yə-), *n.* a member of an ancient Jewish sect, consisting mainly of priests and aristocrats, that differed from the Pharisees esp. in its literal interpretation of the Bible and its rejection of oral laws and traditions. [Old English *saddūcēas* < Late Latin *saddūcaeī* < Greek *saddoukaîoi* < Hebrew *ṣəḏ·ūqī* adherent of Zadok] —**Sad′du·ce′an,** *adj.* —**Sad′du·cee′ism,** *n.*

Sa′die Haw′kins, *n.* **1.** Also called **Sadie, Sa′dies.** a party, dance, or other social event, esp. one held annually among high school or college students, to which each girl escorts the boy of her choice, or invites him to escort her. **2.** a day **(Sa′die Haw′kins Day′)** or night, often in November, when such an event or events are held. [after the race held on Sadie Hawkins Day (in the cartoon strip *Li'l Abner* by Al Capp), in which single women pursued bachelors]

sa·dism (sā′diz əm, sad′iz-), *n.* **1.** pleasure in being cruel. **2.** extreme cruelty. [after D. A. F. de *Sade* (1740–1814), French novelist] —**sa′dist,** *n., adj.* —**sa·dis′tic** (sə dis′tik), *adj.* —**sa·dis′ti·cal·ly,** *adv.*

sa·do·mas·o·chism (sā′dō mas′ə kiz′əm, -maz′-, sad′ō-), *n.* gratification, esp. sexual, gained through inflicting or receiving pain. —**sa′do·mas′o·chist,** *n., adj.* —**sa′do·mas·o·chis′tic,** *adj.*

sad′ sack′, *n.* a pathetically inept person.

S.A.E., **1.** self-addressed envelope. **2.** stamped addressed envelope.

Sa·far (sə fär′), *n.* the second month of the Islamic calendar.

sa·fa·ri (sə fär′ē), *n., pl.* **-ris,** *v.* **-ried, ri·ing.** —*n.* **1.** an expedition for hunting or exploration, esp. in East Africa. **2.** any long adventurous expedition. —*v.i.* **3.** to go on safari.

safa′ri jack′et, *n.* BUSH JACKET.

safe (sāf), *adj.,* **saf·er, saf·est,** *n.* —*adj.* **1.** offering security from harm or danger: *a safe haven.* **2.** free from injury or risk: *arrived safe and sound.* **3.** reasonably accurate: *a safe estimate.* **4.** dependable; trustworthy: *a safe guide.* **5.** careful to avoid danger or controversy: *a safe player.* **6.** securely confined: *a criminal safe in jail.* **7.** Baseball. reaching base without being put out. —*n.* **8.** a steel or iron box or repository for valuable items. —**safe′ly,** *adv.* —**safe′ness,** *n.*

safe′-con′duct, *n.* **1.** a document authorizing safe passage through a region, esp. in time of war. **2.** the authorization itself.

safe·crack·er (sāf′krak′ər), *n.* a person who breaks open safes to rob them. —**safe′crack′ing,** *n.*

safe′-depos′it box′, *n.* a lockable metal box, esp. in a bank vault, for storing valuable items. Also called **safe′ty-depos′it box′.**

safe·guard (sāf′gärd′), *n.* **1.** something that serves as a protection or defense. **2.** a permit for safe passage. **3.** a guard or convoy. **4.** a mechanical device for ensuring safety. —*v.t.* **5.** to guard; protect; secure.

safe′ house′, *n.* an inconspicuous place for refuge or clandestine activities.

safe·keep·ing (sāf′kē′ping), *n.* the act of keeping safe or the state of being kept safe; protection; care; custody.

safe·light (sāf′līt′), *n.* a darkroom light with a filter that transmits only those rays of the spectrum to which films, printing paper, etc., are not sensitive.

safe·ty (sāf′tē), *n., pl.* **-ties.** **1.** the state of being safe from the risk of experiencing or causing injury, danger, or loss. **2.** a device to prevent injury or avert danger. **3. a.** a football play in which a player on the offensive team is tackled in his own end zone or downs the ball there. **b.** a player on defense who lines up farthest behind the line of scrimmage. **4.** a base hit in baseball.

safe′ty belt′, *n.* **1.** SEAT BELT. **2.** a strap securing a person working at a height.

safe′ty glass′, *n.* glass made by joining two sheets of glass with a layer of usu. transparent plastic or artificial resin between them that retains the fragments on impact.

safe′ty match′, *n.* a match designed to ignite only when rubbed on a specially prepared surface.

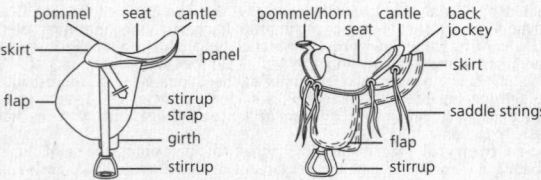

English saddle   **Western saddle**

safe′ty net′, *n.* **1.** a protective net suspended under a person working at a height. **2.** something that provides a margin of security.

safe′ty pin′, *n.* a pin bent back on itself to form a spring, with a guard to cover the point. **—safe′ty-pin′,** *v.t.,* **-pinned, -pin·ning.**

safe′ty ra′zor, *n.* a razor with a guard to prevent the blade from cutting the skin.

safe′ty valve′, *n.* **1.** a device that opens to release a fluid before pressure reaches dangerous levels. **2.** a harmless outlet for pent-up feelings.

saf·flow·er (saf′lou′ər), *n.* **1.** a thistlelike composite plant, *Carthamus tinctorius,* native to the Old World, having finely toothed leaves and large orange-red flower heads. **2.** its dried florets used medicinally or as a red dyestuff.

saf′flower oil′, *n.* an oil from safflower seeds used in cooking and in medicines, paints, and varnishes.

saf·fron (saf′rən), *n.* **1.** a crocus, *Crocus sativus,* having showy purple flowers. **2.** an orange-colored condiment consisting of its dried stigmas, used to color and flavor foods. **3.** Also called **saf′fron yel′low.** yellowish-orange.

sag (sag), *v.,* **sagged, sag·ging,** *n.* —*v.i.* **1.** to sink or bend downward by or as if by weight or pressure. **2.** to wane in vigor or intensity: *Our spirits began to sag.* **3.** to decline in value: *The stock market sagged today.* —*v.t.* **4.** to cause to sag. —*n.* **5.** an act or instance of sagging. **6.** the degree of sagging. **7.** a place where anything sags; depression. **8.** a moderate decline in prices.

sa·ga (sä′gə), *n., pl.* **-gas. 1.** a medieval Scandinavian prose narrative of events in the lives of historical or legendary individuals or families. **2.** any narrative of heroic exploits. **3.** Also called **sa′ga nov′el.** a form of novel that chronicles the members or generations of a family or social group.

sa·ga·cious (sə gā′shəs), *adj.* having or showing acute mental discernment and keen practical sense; shrewd: *a sagacious lawyer.* **—sa·ga′cious·ly,** *adv.* **—sa·ga′ci·ty,** *n.*

sage[1] (sāj), *n., adj.,* **sag·er, sag·est.** —*n.* **1.** a profoundly wise person, esp. one famed for wisdom. **2.** an experienced person respected for sound judgment. —*adj.* **3.** wise, judicious, or prudent: *sage advice.* **—sage′ly,** *adv.* **—sage′ness,** *n.*

sage[2] (sāj), *n.* any plant or shrub belonging to the genus *Salvia,* of the mint family, esp. the herb *S. officinalis,* whose grayish green leaves are used in medicine and in cooking.

sage·brush (sāj′brush′), *n.* any of several sagelike, bushy composite plants having silvery wedge-shaped leaves with three teeth at the tip: common on the dry plains of the western U.S.

sag·gy (sag′ē), *adj.,* **-gi·er, -gi·est.** sagging or tending to sag: *a saggy roof.* **—sag′gi·ness,** *n.*

sag·it·tal (saj′i tl), *adj.* **1.** of or pertaining to the suture between the parietal bones at the roof of the skull. **2.** from front to back in the body's median plane. **—sag′it·tal·ly,** *adv.*

Sag·it·tar·i·us (saj′i târ′ē əs), *n.* **1.** the Archer, a zodiacal constellation between Scorpius and Capricorn. **2.** the ninth sign of the zodiac. [< Latin: archer]

sa·go (sā′gō), *n.* a starch derived from the pith of sago palms and used in making puddings.

sa′go palm′, *n.* **1.** any of several tropical Old World palms, as of the genus *Metroxylon,* that yield sago. **2.** a cycad, *Cycas revoluta,* of Japan, having a crown of glossy fernlike leaves.

sa·gua·ro (sə gwär′ō, -wär′ō), *n., pl.* **-ros.** a tall, horizontally branched cactus of Arizona and neighboring regions yielding a useful wood and bearing an edible fruit.

Sa·har·a (sə har′ə, -hâr′ə, -hâr′ə), *n.* a desert in N Africa, extending from the Atlantic to the Nile valley. ab. 3,500,000 sq. mi. (9,065,000 sq. km). **—Sa·har′an, Sa·har′i·an,** *adj.*

sa·hib (sä′ib, -ēb), *n.* (in colonial India) sir; master: a term of respect used in addressing or referring to a European.

said (sed), *v.* **1.** pt. and pp. of SAY. —*adj.* **2.** aforesaid; aforementioned: *the said witness.*

Sa·i·da (sä′ē dä′), *n.* a seaport in SW Lebanon: the site of ancient Sidon. 24,740.

sai·ga (sī′gə), *n., pl.* **-gas.** a goatlike antelope, *Saiga tatarica,* of W Asia and E Russia, having a greatly enlarged muzzle.

Sai·gon (sī gon′), *n.* former name of HO CHI MINH CITY: capital of South Vietnam 1954–76.

sail (sāl), *n.* **1.** an area of canvas or other fabric extended on a ship or other vessel to catch the wind for propulsion. **2.** a similar apparatus, as on a windmill. **3.** a voyage, esp. in a vessel with sails. **4.** sailing vessels collectively. **5.** the sails of a ship or boat. —*v.i.* **6.** to travel on water in a ship or boat. **7.** to manage a sailboat, esp. for sport. **8.** to begin a journey by water. **9.** to move along in a manner suggestive of a sailing vessel: *caravans sailing along.* **10.** to move along in a stately, effortless way: *to sail into a room.* —*v.t.* **11.** to sail upon or over: *to sail the seven seas.* **12.** to navigate (a vessel). **13. sail into,** to attack vigorously; assail. **—Idiom. 14.** set or make sail, to start a voyage. **15. under sail,** with sails set; sailing. **—sail′a·ble,** *adj.* **—sail′less,** *adj.*

sail·boat (sāl′bōt′), *n.* a boat having sails as its principal means of propulsion. **—sail′boat′er,** *n.* **—sail′boat′ing,** *n.*

sail·cloth (sāl′klôth′, -kloth′), *n.* **1.** any of various fabrics, as of cotton, nylon, or Dacron, for boat sails or tents. **2.** a lightweight canvas or canvaslike fabric used esp. for clothing and curtains.

sail·er (sā′lər), *n.* a vessel with reference to its powers or manner of sailing.

sail·fish (sāl′fish′), *n., pl.* (*esp. collectively*) **-fish,** (*esp. for kinds or species*) **-fish·es.** either of two large marlinlike fish of the genus *Istiophorus,* distinguished by a long, high dorsal fin, long pelvic fins, and a swordlike snout.

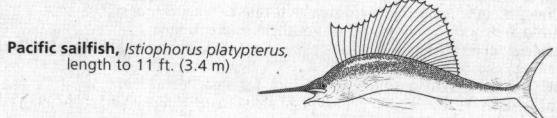
Pacific sailfish, *Istiophorus platypterus,* length to 11 ft. (3.4 m)

sail·ing (sā′ling), *n.* **1.** the activity of a person or thing that sails. **2.** any of various methods for determining courses and distances by means of charts or with reference to longitudes and latitudes, rhumb lines, great circles, etc.

sail·or (sā′lər), *n.* **1.** a person whose occupation is sailing or navigation; mariner. **2.** a seaman below the rank of officer. **3.** a naval enlistee. **4.** a flat-brimmed straw hat with a low flat crown.

sail′or col′lar, *n.* a collar, as on a middy blouse, that is broad and square in the back and tapers to a V in the front.

sail′or's-choice′, *n., pl.* **-choice.** any of several fishes living in waters along the Atlantic coast of the U.S., esp. a pinfish, *Lagodon rhomboides,* ranging from Massachusetts to Texas, and a grunt, *Haemulon parrai,* ranging from Florida to Brazil.

sail·plane (sāl′plān′), *n., v.,* **-planed, -plan·ing.** —*n.* **1.** a very light glider that can be lifted by an upward current of air. —*v.i.* **2.** to soar in a sailplane. **—sail′plan′er,** *n.*

saint (sānt), *n.* **1.** a person of exceptional holiness, formally recognized by the Christian Church esp. by canonization. **2.** a person of great virtue or benevolence. **3.** a founder or patron, as of a movement. **4.** a member of any of various Christian groups. —*v.t.* **5.** to acknowledge as a saint; canonize. [< Latin *sanctus* holy, sacred]

Saint′ Ag′nes's Eve′ (ag′ni siz), *n.* the night of January 20, regarded as a time when a woman dreams of her future husband.

Saint′ An′drew's Cross′, *n.* an X-shaped cross.

Saint′ Bernard′, *n.* one of a breed of very large, heavy dogs with a massive head and a dense red-and-white or brindle-and-white coat, bred in the Swiss Alps and used to rescue lost, snowbound travelers.

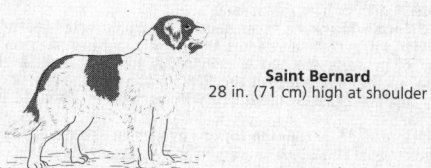
Saint Bernard
28 in. (71 cm) high at shoulder

saint·ed (sān′tid), *adj.* **1.** enrolled among the saints. **2.** sacred; hallowed. **3.** pious; saintly.

Saint-Ex·u·pé·ry (saN teg zУ pā Rē′), *n.* **Antoine de,** 1900–45, French author and aviator.

Saint-Gau·dens (sānt gôd′nz), *n.* **Augustus,** 1848–1907, U.S. sculptor, born in Ireland.

saint·hood (sānt′hŏŏd), *n.* **1.** the character or status of a saint. **2.** saints collectively.

saint·ly (sānt′lē), *adj.,* **-li·er, -li·est.** like or befitting a saint; holy. **—saint′li·ness,** *n.*

Saint′ Pat′rick's Day′, *n.* March 17, observed in honor of St. Patrick, the patron saint of Ireland.

saint's′ day′, *n.* a day in a church calendar commemorating a particular saint.

Sai·pan (sī pan′), *n.* an island in and the capital of the Northern Mariana Islands in the W Pacific. 15,000; 71 sq. mi. (184 sq. km).

sake[1] (sāk), *n.* **1.** benefit or well-being; interest; advantage: *for the sake of all students.* **2.** purpose; end: *art for art's sake.*

sa·ke[2] or **sa·ké** or **sa·ki** (sä′kē), *n.* a mildly alcoholic Japanese beverage made from fermented rice.

sa·ki[1] (sak′ē, sä′kē), *n., pl.* **-kis.** any of several monkeys of the genus *Pithecia,* of tropical South America, having a shaggy golden brown to black coat and a long nonprehensile tail.

sa·ki[2] (sä′kē), *n.* SAKE[2].

sa·laam (sə läm′), *n.* **1.** a salutation meaning "peace," used esp. in Islamic countries. **2.** a very low bow or obeisance, esp. with the palm of the right hand placed on the forehead. —*v.i., v.t.* **3.** to salute with a salaam. **—sa·laam′like′,** *adj.*

sal·a·ble or **sale·a·ble** (sā′lə bəl), *adj.* subject to or suitable for sale; readily sold. **—sal·a·bil′i·ty,** *n.* **—sal′a·bly,** *adv.*

sa·la·cious (sə lā′shəs), *adj.* **1.** lustful or lecherous. **2.** (of writings, pictures, etc.) grossly indecent; obscene. —**sa·la'cious·ly,** *adv.* —**sa·la'cious·ness, sa·lac'i·ty** (-las'i tē), *n.*

sal·ad (sal'əd), *n.* **1.** a cold dish of raw vegetables, as lettuce, and tomatoes, served with a dressing, sometimes with meat, cheese, etc., added. **2.** a dish of any of various raw or cold cooked foods, usu. sliced or chopped and mixed with a dressing. **3.** any leavy vegetable, as lettuce, eaten raw, as in salads. **4.** a mixture or assortment.

sal'ad bar', *n.* an assortment of salads, salad ingredients, and dressings, as in a restaurant, from which one can serve oneself.

sal'ad days', *n.* a period of youthful inexperience.

sal'ad dress'ing, *n.* a sauce for a salad, usu. with a base of oil and vinegar or of mayonnaise.

sal'ad fork', *n.* a small, broad fork for salad or dessert.

Sal·a·din (sal'ə din), *n.* (*Salāh-ed-Dīn Yūsuf ibn Ayyūb*) 1137–93, sultan of Egypt and Syria 1175–93.

sa·lal (sə lal', sa-), *n.* an evergreen shrub native to the W coast of North America, with leathery, oblong leaves, clusters of pink or white flowers, and edible purplish black fruit.

sal·a·man·der (sal'ə man'dər), *n.* **1.** any tailed amphibian of the order Caudata, having a soft, moist, scaleless skin, usu. aquatic as a larva and semiterrestrial as an adult. **2.** a mythical being, esp. a lizard or other reptile, thought to be able to live in fire. **3.** a portable stove or burner. —**sal'a·man'drine** (-drin), *adj.* —**sal'a·man'droid,** *adj.*

sa·la·mi (sə lä'mē), *n., pl.* **-mis.** a spicy, garlic-flavored sausage.

Sal·a·mis (sal'ə mis, sä'lä mēs'), *n.* **1.** an island off the SE coast of Greece, W of Athens, in the Gulf of Aegina; 39 sq. mi. (101 sq. km). **2.** an ancient city on Cyprus, in the E Mediterranean: the apostle Paul made his first missionary journey to Salamis. Acts 13:5.

sal·a·ried (sal'ə rēd), *adj.* **1.** receiving a salary: *a salaried employee.* **2.** providing a salary: *a salaried job.*

sal·a·ry (sal'ə rē), *n., pl.* **-ries.** a fixed compensation paid periodically to a person for regular work or services. —**sal'a·ry·less,** *adj.*

Sa·la·zar (sal'ə zär', sä'lə-), *n.* **Antonio de Oliveira,** 1889–1970, premier of Portugal 1933–68.

Sal·chow (sal'kou), *n.* a figure-skating jump in which the skater leaps from the back inside edge of one skate to make one full rotation in the air and lands on the back outside edge of the other skate.

sale (sāl), *n.* **1.** the act of selling. **2.** a special offering of goods, esp. at reduced prices. **3.** transfer of property for money or credit. **4. a.** an amount or quantity sold. **b. sales,** total receipts from selling. **5.** opportunity to sell; demand. **6.** an auction. **7. sales,** a department or division, as in a business, concerned with selling and promoting goods, services, etc. —*Idiom.* **8. for sale,** available for purchase. **9. on sale,** able to be bought at reduced prices.

sale·a·ble (sā'lə bəl), *adj.* SALABLE.

sale' and lease'back, *n.* LEASEBACK. Also called **sale'-lease'back.**

Sa·lem (sā'ləm), *n.* **1.** a seaport in NE Massachusetts: founded 1626; execution of persons accused of witchcraft 1692. 38,220. **2.** the capital of Oregon, in the NW part, on the Willamette River. 115,912. **3.** an ancient city of Canaan, later identified with Jerusalem. Gen. 14:18; Psalms 76:2.

sales (sālz), *adj.* of, pertaining to, or engaged in selling.

sales·clerk (sālz'klûrk'), *n.* a person who sells goods in a store.

sales·man (sālz'mən), *n., pl.* **-men.** a man who sells goods, services, etc.

sales·man·ship (sālz'mən ship'), *n.* the technique of or skill in selling a product, idea, etc.

sales·peo·ple (sālz'pē'pəl), *n.pl.* people engaged in selling; salespersons.

sales·per·son (sālz'pûr'sən), *n.* a person who sells goods, services, etc.

sales' pitch', *n.* SALES TALK.

sales' represent'ative, *n.* **1.** a person or organization authorized to solicit business for a company. **2.** TRAVELING SALESMAN.

sales' slip', *n.* a receipt issued by a store or other vendor showing the amount paid.

sales' talk', *n.* **1.** an argument intended to persuade someone to buy a product or service. **2.** any persuasive argument.

sales' tax', *n.* a tax on a purchase, added to the total sale.

sales·wom·an (sālz'wŏŏm'ən), *n., pl.* **-wom·en.** a woman who sells goods, services, etc. —*Usage.* See -WOMAN.

sal·i·cyl'ic ac'id (sal'ə sil'ik), *n.* a white crystalline substance, C₇H₆O₃: used as a food preservative and in the manufacture of aspirin.

sa·li·ence (sā'lē əns, sāl'yəns), *n.* **1.** the quality of being salient. **2.** a salient or projecting feature.

sa·li·ent (sā'lē ənt, sāl'yənt), *adj.* **1.** prominent or conspicuous: *salient features.* **2.** projecting or pointing outward. **3.** leaping or jumping: *a salient animal.* —*n.* **4.** a salient angle or part; an outward projection. —**sa'li·ent·ly,** *adv.*

Sa·li·nas (sə lē'nəs), *n.* a city in W California. 119,814.

sa·line (sā'lēn, -līn), *adj.* **1.** of, containing, or tasting of common salt; salty: *saline soil; a saline solution.* **2.** of or pertaining to a chemical salt, esp. of sodium, potassium, or magnesium, used as a cathartic. —*n.* **3.** a saline solution. —**sa·lin·i·ty** (sə lin'i tē), *n.*

Salis·bur·y (sôlz'ber'ē, -bə rē, -brē), *n.* **1. Robert Arthur Talbot Gascoyne Cecil, 3rd Marquis of,** 1830–1903, British prime minister 1885–

86, 1886–92, 1895–1902. **2.** former name of HARARE. **3.** a city in Wiltshire, in S England: cathedral. 104,700.

Salis'bury steak', *n.* ground beef, often mixed with breadcrumbs, onions, seasonings, etc., shaped into a large patty and broiled or fried.

Sa·lish (sā'lish), *n., pl.* **-lish·es,** (*esp. collectively*) **-lish. 1.** a member of any of a number of Salishan-speaking peoples of the Columbia and Fraser river drainage basins. **2.** the languages of these peoples.

Sa·lish·an (sā'lish ən, sal'ish-), *n.* a family of American Indian languages spoken or formerly spoken by peoples of S British Columbia and the northwest U.S.

sa·li·va (sə lī'və), *n.* a viscid, watery fluid, secreted into the mouth by the salivary glands, that functions in the tasting, chewing, and swallowing of food, moistens the mouth, and starts the digestion of starches. —**sal·i·var·y** (sal'ə ver'ē), *adj.*

sal'ivary gland', *n.* any of several glands of the mouth and jaw that secrete saliva.

sal·i·vate (sal'ə vāt'), *v.i.,* **-vat·ed, -vat·ing.** to produce saliva.

sal·i·va·tion (sal'ə vā'shən), *n.* **1.** the act or process of salivating. **2.** an abnormally profuse flow of saliva; ptyalism.

Salk (sôk, sôlk), *n.* **Jonas E(dward),** 1914–95, U.S. bacteriologist.

Salk' vaccine', *n.* a vaccine that contains three types of inactivated poliomyelitis viruses. [after J. E. *Salk*]

sal·low¹ (sal'ō), *adj.,* **-low·er, -low·est,** *v.* —*adj.* **1.** of a sickly, yellowish color: *a sallow complexion.* —*v.t.* **2.** to make sallow. —**sal'low·ish,** *adj.* —**sal'low·ness,** *n.*

sal·low² (sal'ō), *n. Brit.* any of several shrubby Old World willows, esp. the pussy willow, *Salix caprea.*

sal·ly (sal'ē), *n., pl.* **-lies,** *v.,* **-lied, -ly·ing.** —*n.* **1.** a sortie of troops from a besieged place against an enemy. **2.** a sudden rushing forth. **3.** an excursion or side trip. **4.** an outburst of passion, flight of fancy, etc. **5.** a witty remark; quip. —*v.i.* **6.** to make a sally, as a body of troops from a besieged place. **7.** to set out, as on an excursion; venture (often fol. by *forth*). **8.** to rush or burst out. —**sal'li·er,** *n.*

sal·ma·gun·di (sal'mə gun'dē), *n., pl.* **-dis. 1.** a salad dish of chopped meats, cubed poultry or fish, eggs, onions, anchovies, and other ingredients. **2.** any mixture or miscellany.

salm·on (sam'ən), *n., pl.* **-ons,** (*esp. collectively*) **-on** for 1, 2, *adj.* —*n.* **1.** a marine and freshwater food fish, *Salmo salar,* of the family Salmonidae, having pink flesh, inhabiting waters off the North Atlantic coasts of Europe and North America near the mouths of large rivers, which it enters to spawn. **2.** any of several similar food fishes of the genus *Oncorhynchus,* inhabiting the N Pacific. **3.** a light yellowish pink. —*adj.* **4.** of the color salmon. —**salm'on·like',** *adj.*

salm·on·ber·ry (sam'ən ber'ē), *n., pl.* **-ries. 1.** the salmon-colored, edible fruit of a raspberry, *Rubus spectabilis,* of the Pacific coast of North America. **2.** the plant itself.

sal·mo·nel·la (sal'mə nel'ə), *n., pl.* **-nel·lae** (-nel'ē), **-nel·las. 1.** any of several rod-shaped bacteria of the genus *Salmonella* that enter the digestive tract in contaminated food, causing food poisoning. **2.** SALMONELLOSIS.

sal·mo·nel·lo·sis (sal'mə nl ō'sis), *n.* food poisoning, esp. violent diarrhea and cramps, caused by consumption of food contaminated with salmonella bacteria.

Sa·lo·me or **Sa·lo·mé** (sə lō'mē), *n.* **1.** one of the women who was present at the Crucifixion and on Easter morning, assumed to be the wife of Zebedee and the mother of the apostles James and John. Matt. 27:56; Mark 15:40; 16:1. **2.** assumed to be the daughter of Herodias who danced for Herod Antipas and was granted the head of John the Baptist. Mark 6:22–25.

Sal·o·mon (sal'ə mən), *n.* **Haym** (hīm), 1740?–85, American financier and patriot, born in Poland.

sa·lon (sə lon'; *Fr.* SA lôn'), *n., pl.* **-lons** (-lonz'; *Fr.* -lôn'). **1.** a reception room in a large house. **2.** an assembly of fashionable guests in such a room, as leaders in society, politics, and the arts, esp. as a regular event. **3.** a hall used for the exhibition of works of art. **4.** a specialized shop, department of a store, etc., catering to fashionable clients.

sa·loon (sə lōōn'), *n.* **1.** a place where alcoholic drinks are sold and consumed. **2.** a room or place for general use for a specific purpose: *the dining saloon on a ship.* **3.** a large cabin for the common use of passengers on a passenger vessel. **4.** SALON (def. 1).

sal·sa (säl'sə, -sä), *n., pl.* **-sas. 1.** Latin American music blending Cuban rhythm with elements of jazz, rock, and soul. **2.** a dance of Puerto Rican origin performed to this music. **3.** a sauce, esp. a hot sauce containing chilies. [< American Spanish: sauce]

sal·si·fy (sal'sə fē), *n., pl.* **-fies.** a purple-flowered composite plant, *Tragopogon porrifolius,* whose root has an oysterlike flavor and is eaten as a vegetable. Also called **oyster plant.**

salt (sôlt), *n.* **1.** a crystalline compound, sodium chloride, NaCl, occurring chiefly as a mineral or a constituent of seawater, and used for seasoning and as a preservative. **2.** any of a class of chemical compounds formed by neutralization of an acid by a base, a reaction in which hydrogen atoms of the acid are replaced by cations supplied by the base. **3.** an element that gives liveliness or pungency. **4.** sharp, biting wit. **5.** a sailor, esp. an old or experienced one. —*v.t.* **6.** to season with salt. **7.** to cure or preserve with salt. **8.** to provide with salt: *to salt cattle.* **9.** to treat with any chemical salt. **10.** to spread salt on so as to melt ice. **11.** to introduce rich ore fraudulently into (a mine, a mineral sample, etc.)

to create a false impression of value. **12. salt away, a.** Also, **salt down.** to preserve by adding salt to. **b.** to save (money) for future use. —*adj.* **13.** containing salt, or tasting of salt. **14.** cured or preserved with salt: *salt cod.* **15.** inundated by salt water. **16.** SALTY (def. 1). —*Idiom.* **17. take with a grain of salt,** to be somewhat skeptical about. **18. worth one's salt,** deserving of one's wages or salary. —**salt/like/,** *adj.*
SALT (sôlt), *n.* Strategic Arms Limitation Talks (or Treaty).
salt/-and-pep/per, *adj.* PEPPER-AND-SALT.
salt•box (sôlt/boks/), *n.* **1.** a box in which salt is kept. **2.** a type of house found esp. in New England, generally two full stories high in front and one in back, the roof having about the same pitch in both directions so that the ridge is well toward the front of the house.
salt•ed (sôl/tid), *adj.* seasoned, preserved, or otherwise treated with salt: *salted nuts.*
salt/ flat/, *n.* an extensive level tract coated with salt deposits left by evaporation of rising ground water or a temporary body of surface water.
sal•tine (sôl tēn/), *n.* a crisp, salted cracker.
salt/ lake/, *n.* a body of water having no outlet to the sea and containing in solution a high concentration of salts, esp. sodium chloride.
Salt/ Lake/ Cit/y, *n.* the capital of Utah, in the N part, near the Great Salt Lake. 171,849.
salt/ lick/, *n.* **1.** a place to which animals go to lick naturally occurring salt deposits. **2.** a block of salt or salt preparation provided, as in a pasture, for cattle, horses, etc.
salt/ marsh/, *n.* a marshy tract that is wet with salt water or flooded by the sea.
salt/ of the earth/, *n.* an individual or group considered to embody the noblest human qualities. Matt. 5:13.
Sal/ton Sea/ (sôl/tn), *n.* a shallow saline lake in S California, in the Imperial Valley, formed by the diversion of water from the Colorado River into a salt-covered depression **(Sal/ton Sink/).** 236 ft. (72 m) below sea level.
salt•pe•ter or **salt•pe•tre** (sôlt/pē/tər), *n.* naturally occurring potassium nitrate, used in making fireworks, gunpowder, etc.; niter.
salt/ pork/, *n.* the fat pork from the back, sides, and belly, cured with salt.
salt/ wa/ter, *n.* **1.** water containing a large amount of salt. **2.** seawater.
salt•wa•ter (sôlt/wô/tər, -wot/ər), *adj.* **1.** of or pertaining to salt water. **2.** inhabiting salt water: *a saltwater fish.*
salt/water taf/fy, *n.* a taffy made with salted fresh water or, sometimes, with seawater.
salt•wort (sôlt/wûrt/, -wôrt/), *n.* any of various plants growing in saline soil, esp. those belonging to the genus *Salsola,* of the goosefoot family, as *S. kali,* a bushy plant with prickly leaves.
salt•y (sôl/tē), *adj.,* **-i•er, -i•est.** **1.** tasting of or containing salt; saline. **2.** piquant; sharp; witty. **3.** racy or coarse: *salty humor.* **4.** of the sea, sailing, or life at sea. —**salt/i•ness,** *n.*
sa•lu•bri•ous (sə lōō/brē əs), *adj.* favorable to or promoting health; healthful. —**sa•lu/bri•ous•ly,** *adv.* —**sa•lu/bri•ous•ness,** *n.*
sa•lu•ki (sə lōō/kē), *n., pl.* **-kis.** one of a breed of tall, slender, swift hounds raised orig. in Egypt and SW Asia, having a long, narrow head, drooping ears, and a short, silky coat with longer fringes on the ears, legs, and tail.
sal•u•tar•y (sal/yə ter/ē), *adj.* **1.** favorable to or promoting health; healthful. **2.** promoting or conducive to some beneficial purpose; wholesome. —**sal/u•tar/i•ly** (-ə lē), *adv.* —**sal/u•tar/i•ness,** *n.*
sal•u•ta•tion (sal/yə tā/shən), *n.* **1.** a. something uttered, written, or done by way of greeting, welcome, recognition, etc. **b. salutations,** greetings or regards. **2.** a word or phrase serving as the prefatory greeting in a letter or speech, as *Dear Sir* in a letter or *Ladies and Gentlemen* in a speech. **3.** the act of saluting. —**sal/u•ta/tion•al,** *adj.*
sa•lu•ta•to•ri•an (sə lōō/tə tôr/ē ən, -tōr/-), *n.* a student, usu. ranking second highest academically in a graduating class, who delivers the salutatory.
sa•lu•ta•to•ry (sə lōō/tə tôr/ē, -tōr/ē), *adj., n., pl.* **-ries.** —*adj.* **1.** pertaining to or of the nature of a salutation. —*n.* **2.** a welcoming address, esp. one given at the beginning of commencement exercises in some U.S. high schools and colleges by the salutatorian.
sa•lute (sə lōōt/), *n., v.* **-lut•ed, -lut•ing.** —*n.* **1.** a formal gesture of respect given to a person of superior military rank, as raising the right hand to the side of the head. **b.** a ceremonial gesture of respect, as the discharge of firearms, performed by a military or naval force to honor a dignitary or commemorate an occasion. **2.** any instance or occasion of formal greeting or welcome. —*v.t.* **3.** to give a salute to. **4.** to address with expressions of goodwill, respect, etc.; greet. **5.** to make a bow or other gesture to, as in greeting, farewell, or respect. **6.** to express respect or praise for; honor; commend. —*v.i.* **7.** to give a salute.
salv•a•ble (sal/və bəl), *adj.* fit for or capable of being saved or salvaged. —**sal/va•bly,** *adv.*
Sal•va•dor (sal/və dôr/), *n.* **1.** EL SALVADOR. **2.** Formerly, **Bahia, São Salvador.** the capital of Bahia in E Brazil. 1,525,831. —**Sal/va•do/ran, Sal/va•do/ri•an,** *adj., n.*
sal•vage (sal/vij), *n., v.,* **-vaged, -vag•ing.** —*n.* **1.** the act of saving a ship or its cargo from perils of the seas. **2.** the act of saving anything from destruction or danger. **3.** the property, goods, etc., so saved. **4.**

compensation given to those who voluntarily save a ship or its cargo. **5.** the value or proceeds upon sale of goods recovered from a fire. —*v.t.* **6.** to save from shipwreck, fire, or other peril; rescue; recover. —**sal/vage•a•ble,** *adj.* —**sal/vag•er,** *n.*
sal•va•tion (sal vā/shən), *n.* **1.** the act of saving or protecting from harm, risk, loss, etc. **2.** the state of being so saved or protected: *the company's salvation from bankruptcy.* **3.** a source, cause, or means of being saved or protected from harm, risk, etc. **4.** *Theol.* deliverance from the power and penalty of sin; redemption. —**sal•va/tion•al,** *adj.*
Salva/tion Ar/my, *n.* an international charitable and evangelistic Christian organization founded in England in 1895 by William Booth along quasi-military lines. *Abbr.:* SA or S.A.
Sal•va•tion•ist (sal vā/shə nist), *n.* **1.** a member of the Salvation Army. **2.** (*l.c.*) a person who preaches salvation.
salve[1] (sav, säv), *n., v.,* **salved, salv•ing.** —*n.* **1.** a medicinal ointment for treating wounds and sores. **2.** anything that soothes, mollifies, or relieves. —*v.t.* **3.** to soothe with or as if with salve; assuage; ease: *to salve one's conscience.*
salve[2] (salv), *v.t.,* **salved, salv•ing.** to salvage. —**sal/vor,** *n.*
sal•ver (sal/vər), *n.* a tray, esp. one used for serving food or drinks.
sal•vi•a (sal/vē ə), *n., pl.* **-vi•as.** any of various plants of the genus *Salvia,* of the mint family, that have opposite leaves and whorled flowers, esp. the red-flowered *S. splendens.*
sal•vo (sal/vō), *n., pl.* **-vos, -voes. 1.** a simultaneous or successive discharge of artillery, etc. **2.** a round of gunfire given as a salute. **3.** a round of cheers or applause. **4.** a verbal attack, as upon an opponent.
SAM (sam), *n.* surface-to-air missile.
Sam., Samuel.
sam•a•ra (sam/ər ə, sə mâr/ə), *n., pl.* **-ras.** a usu. one-seeded, winged fruit that does not split open, as of the elm or maple.
Sa•mar•i•a (sə mâr/ē ə), *n.* **1.** a district in ancient Palestine N of Judea: later part of the Roman province of Syria; taken by Jordan 1948; occupied by Israel 1967. **2.** the northern kingdom of the ancient Hebrews. **3.** the ancient capital of this kingdom.
Sa•mar•i•tan (sə mar/i tn), *n.* **1.** a native or inhabitant of ancient or modern Samaria. **2.** a member of a religious sect of Samaria that split from Judaism in the 4th century B.C. **3.** (*often l.c.*) GOOD SAMARITAN. —*adj.* **4.** of or pertaining to Samaria or to Samaritans.
sa•mar•i•um (sə mâr/ē əm), *n.* a rare-earth metallic element discovered in samarskite. *Symbol:* Sm; *at. wt.:* 150.35; *at. no.:* 62; *sp. gr.:* 7.49.
Sam•ar•kand (sam/ər kand/), *n.* a city in SE Uzbekistan: taken by Alexander the Great 329 B.C.; Tamerlane's capital in the 14th century. 388,000.
sam•ba (sam/bə, säm/-), *n., pl.* **-bas,** *v.,* **-baed, -ba•ing.** —*n.* **1.** a rhythmic Brazilian ballroom dance of African origin. —*v.i.* **2.** to dance the samba.
same (sām), *adj.* **1.** identical with what is about to be or has just been mentioned: *This street is the same one we were on yesterday.* **2.** being one or identical though having different names, aspects, etc.: *the same play with a different title.* **3.** agreeing in kind, amount, etc.; corresponding: *two boxes of the same dimensions.* **4.** unchanged in character, condition, etc.: *It's the same town after all these years.* —*pron.* **5.** the same person, thing, or kind of thing. **6.** the very person, thing, or set just mentioned: *Sighted sub sank same.* **7. the same,** in the same manner; in an identical or similar way: *I see the same through your glasses as through mine.* —*Idiom.* **8. all the same, a.** notwithstanding; nevertheless: *I know you're tired, but all the same, I wish you'd stay.* **b.** of no difference; immaterial: *It's all the same to me whether you go or not.* **9. just the same, a.** in the same way. **b.** nevertheless; all the same.
same•ness (sām/nis), *n.* **1.** the state or quality of being the same; identity; uniformity. **2.** lack of variety; monotony.
Sam•hi•ta (sum/hi tə/), *n., pl.* **-tas.** VEDA (def. 2).
Sam•mis (sam/is), *n.* **John,** 1836–1919, U.S. clergyman and hymn writer.
Sa•mo•a (sə mō/ə), *n.* a group of islands in the S Pacific, N of Tonga: divided into American Samoa and Western Samoa. —**Samoan,** *adj., n.*
sam•o•var (sam/ə vär/, sam/ə vär/), *n.* a metal urn, used esp. by Russians for heating water to make tea.
Sam•o•yed (sam/ə yed/, sə moi/id), *n.* **1.** a member of any of a group of Uralic peoples living in W Siberia and the far NE parts of European Russia. **2.** (*sometimes l.c.*) one of a Siberian breed of dogs with long, straight, dense white hair that forms a ruff around the neck.
samp (samp), *n.* **1.** coarsely ground corn. **2.** a porridge made of it.
sam•pan (sam/pan), *n.* any of various small boats of the Far East, as one propelled by a single scull over the stern and having a mat roof.

sampan

sam·ple (sam/pəl, säm/-), *n., adj., v.,* **-pled, -pling.** —*n.* **1.** a small part of or a selection from something, intended to show the quality, style, or nature of the whole; specimen. **2.** *Statistics.* a subset of a population. **3.** a sound of short duration, as a musical tone, digitally stored in a synthesizer for playback. —*adj.* **4.** serving as a specimen: *a sample piece of cloth.* —*v.t.* **5.** to take a sample of; judge by a sample.

sam·pler (sam/plər, säm/-), *n.* **1.** a person who samples. **2.** a piece of cloth embroidered with various stitches, showing a beginner's skill in needlework. **3.** a collection of representative pieces. **4.** an electronic device that digitally encodes and stores samples of sound.

sam·pling (sam/pling, säm/-), *n.* **1.** the act or process of selecting a sample for testing, analyzing, etc. **2.** the sample so selected.

sam·sa·ra (səm sär/ə), *n.* **1.** (in Buddhism) the process of coming into existence as a differentiated, mortal creature. **2.** (in Hinduism) the endless series of births, deaths, and rebirths to which all beings are subject.

Sam·son (sam/sən), *n.* **1.** a judge of Israel famous for his great strength. Judges 13–16. **2.** any man of extraordinary physical strength. —**Sam·so′ni·an** (-sō′nē ən), *adj.*

Sam·u·el (sam/yōō əl), *n.* **1.** a judge and prophet of Israel. I Sam. 1–3; 8–15. **2.** either of two books of the Bible bearing his name.

sam·u·rai (sam/ōō rī′), *n., pl.* **-rai.** (in feudal Japan) **1.** a member of the hereditary warrior class. **2.** a retainer of a daimyo.

Sa·n′a or **Sa·naa** (sä nä′), *n.* the political capital of the Republic of Yemen, in SW Arabia. 150,000.

San′ An·dre·as fault′ (san′ an drā′əs), *n.* an active geological fault in the western U.S., extending from San Francisco to S California. [after *San Andreas* Lake, located in the rift, in San Mateo County]

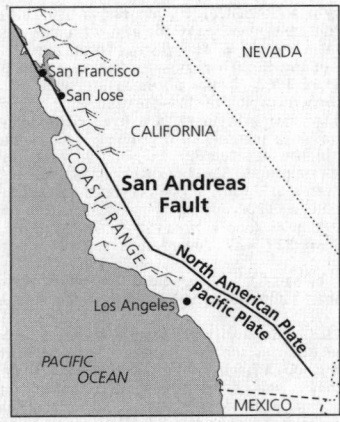

San An·to·ni·o (san′ an tō′nē ō′), *n.* a city in S Texas: site of the Alamo. 998,905. —**San′ An·to′ni·an,** *n., adj.*

san·a·tive (san/ə tiv), *adj.* having the power to heal.

san·a·to·ri·um (san/ə tōr/ē əm, -tōr/-), *n., pl.* **-to·ri·ums, -to·ri·a** (-tōr/ē ə, -tōr/ə). **1.** a hospital for the treatment of chronic diseases, as tuberculosis or various nervous or mental disorders. **2.** SANITARIUM.

San·bal·lat (san bal/ət), *n.* an opponent of the Israelites after their return from Babylonian captivity. Neh. 2:10, 19; 4:1–23; 6:1–19; 13:28.

sanc·ti·fy (sangk/tə fī/), *v.t.,* **-fied, -fy·ing. 1.** to make holy; consecrate. **2.** to free from sin. **3.** to impart religious sanction to. **4.** to entitle to reverence or respect. **5.** to make conducive to spiritual blessing. —**sanc′ti·fi·a·ble,** *adj.* —**sanc′ti·fi·ca′tion,** *n.* —**sanc′ti·fi′er,** *n.*

sanc·ti·mo·ni·ous (sangk/tə mō/nē əs), *adj.* showing or marked by false piety or righteousness; hypocritically religious or virtuous. —**sanc′ti·mo′ni·ous·ly,** *adv.* —**sanc′ti·mo′ni·ous·ness,** *n.*

sanc·ti·mo·ny (sangk/tə mō/nē), *n.* pretended, affected, or hypocritical religious devotion, righteousness, etc.

sanc·tion (sangk/shən), *n.* **1.** authoritative permission or approval, as for an action. **2.** something that serves to support an action, condition, etc. **3.** something that gives binding force, as to an oath or rule of conduct. **4. a.** a provision of a law enacting a penalty for disobedience. **b.** the penalty imposed. **5.** action by a state or states calculated to force another state to comply with its obligations: *to invoke sanctions against an aggressor.* —*v.t.* **6.** to authorize, approve, or allow. **7.** to ratify or confirm. **8.** to impose a sanction on; penalize, esp. by way of discipline. —**sanc′tion·a·ble,** *adj.* —**sanc′tion·er,** *n.*

sanc·ti·ty (sangk/ti tē), *n., pl.* **-ties. 1.** holiness, saintliness, or godliness. **2.** sacred or hallowed character. **3.** a sacred thing.

sanc·tu·ar·y (sangk/chōō er/ē), *n., pl.* **-ar·ies. 1.** a sacred or holy place. **2.** *Judaism.* **a.** the Biblical tabernacle or the Temple in Jerusalem. **b.** the holy of holies of these places of worship. **3.** an esp. holy place in a temple or church, as the chancel. **4.** a church or other sacred place formerly providing refuge, esp. immunity from arrest. **5.** the protection provided by such a place. **6.** any place of refuge; asylum. **7.** a

tract of land where wildlife can live and breed in safety from hunters; preserve. —**sanc′tu·ar′ied,** *adj.*

sanc·tum (sangk/təm), *n., pl.* **-tums, -ta** (-tə). **1.** a holy place. **2.** an inviolably private place or retreat. **3.** a sanctified custom, rite, etc.

sanc′tum sanc·to′rum (sangk tôr/əm, -tōr/-), *n.* **1.** the holy of holies of the Biblical tabernacle and the Temple in Jerusalem. **2.** SANCTUM (def. 2).

Sanc·tus (sangk/təs), *n.* the hymn with which the Eucharistic preface culminates. Is. 6:3. [< Latin *sānctus* inviolate, holy]

sand (sand), *n.* **1.** the more or less fine debris of rocks, consisting of small, loose grains, often of quartz. **2.** Usu., **sands.** a tract or region composed principally of sand. **3. sands,** moments of time or of one's life. **4.** a light reddish yellow or brownish yellow color. **5.** courage; pluck. —*v.t.* **6.** to smooth or polish with sandpaper or other abrasive. **7.** to sprinkle with or as if with sand. **8.** to fill up with sand, as a harbor. **9.** to add sand to. —**sand′a·ble,** *adj.* —**sand′less,** *adj.*

san·dal (san/dl), *n.* **1.** a shoe consisting of a sole of leather or other material fastened to the foot by thongs or straps. **2.** any of various low shoes or slippers. **3.** a band or strap that fastens a low shoe or slipper.

san·dal·wood (san/dl wŏŏd/), *n.* **1.** the fragrant reddish yellow heartwood of an Indian tree, *Santalum album,* or of related trees in the sandalwood family: used for incense and ornamental carving. **2.** any of various similar trees or their wood.

san′dalwood fam′ily, *n.* a S Asian family, Santalaceae, of semiparasitic evergreen trees and shrubs with small flowers borne in the leaf axils: most bear fragrant woods and some yield valued oils and dyes.

sand·bag (sand/bag/), *n., v.,* **-bagged, -bag·ging.** —*n.* **1.** a bag filled with sand, used in fortification, as ballast, etc. **2.** such a bag used as a weapon. —*v.t.* **3.** to furnish with sandbags. **4.** to hit or stun with a sandbag. **5.** to coerce or intimidate, as by threats. **6.** to trap (an opponent in poker) into greater loss by pretending one has a weak hand. —*v.i.* **7.** to sandbag an opponent in poker. —**sand′bag′ger,** *n.*

sand·bank (sand/bangk/), *n.* a large mass of sand, as on a shoal or hillside.

sand′ bar′, *n.* a bar of sand formed in a river or sea by the action of tides or currents.

sand·blast (sand/blast/, -bläst/), *n.* **1.** a blast of air or steam laden with sand, used to clean, grind, cut, or decorate hard surfaces, as of glass or stone. **2.** the apparatus used to apply such a blast. —*v.t.* **3.** to clean, smooth, etc., with a sandblast. —**sand′blast′er,** *n.*

sand·box (sand/boks/), *n.* a box or receptacle for holding sand, esp. one for children to play in.

sand·bur or **sand·burr** (sand/bûr/), *n.* **1.** any of various grasses of the genus *Cenchrus,* having grains enclosed in prickly burs. **2.** any of several bur-bearing weeds growing in sandy places.

Sand·burg (sand/bûrg, san/-), *n.* **Carl,** 1878–1967, U.S. author.

sand′cast′, *v.t.,* **-cast, -cast·ing.** to produce (a casting) by pouring molten metal into sand molds.

sand′ dab′, *n.* any of several flatfishes, esp. of the genus *Citharichthys,* inhabiting waters along the Pacific coast of North America.

sand′ dol′lar, *n.* any flat, disklike echinoderm of the order Clypeasteroidea, of the same class as sea urchins, living on sandy bottoms.

sand dollar, *Mellita testudinata,* width 3 in. (8 cm)

sand·er·ling (san/dər ling), *n.* a small sandpiper, *Calidris alba,* that breeds in the Arctic and frequents sandy beaches in the winter over much of the world.

San·der·son (san/dər sən), *n.* **James,** 1769–1841, U.S. musician, composer of HAIL TO THE CHIEF.

sand′ flea′, *n.* **1.** BEACH FLEA. **2.** CHIGOE.

sand·fly (sand/flī/), *n., pl.* **-flies. 1.** any of several small, bloodsucking insects of the family Psychodidae that are vectors of several diseases of humans. **2.** any of several other small, bloodsucking insects, as one of the family Heleidae or Simuliidae.

sand·glass (sand/glas/, -gläs/), *n.* an hourglass.

sand′hill crane′ (sand/hil/), *n.* a North American crane, *Grus canadensis,* having bluish gray plumage and a red forehead.

San Di·e·go (san′ dē ā/gō), *n.* a seaport in SW California. 1,151,977.

San·di·nis·ta (san/də nē′stə), *n., pl.* **-tas.** a member of the Nicaraguan revolutionary organization that controlled Nicaragua from 1979 to 1989.

S&L, savings and loan (association).

sand′ lil′y, *n.* a small, stemless lily, *Leucocrinum montanum,* of the western U.S., having white, fragrant flowers.

sand′ liz′ard, *n.* **1.** a common lizard, *Lacerta agilis,* of Europe and central Asia. **2.** any of several lizards that live in sandy areas.

sand·lot (sand/lot/), *n.* **1.** a vacant lot used by youngsters for games or sports. —*adj.* **2.** Also, **sand′-lot′.** of, pertaining to, or played in such a lot: *sandlot baseball.* —**sand′lot′ter,** *n.*

sand·man (sand′man′), *n., pl.* **-men.** a being of fairy tales and folklore who puts sand in the eyes of children to make them sleepy.

sand′ myr′tle, *n.* an evergreen shrub, *Leiophyllum buxifolium,* of the heath family, native to the eastern U.S., having simple, leathery leaves and clusters of white or pink flowers.

San Do·min·go (san′ də ming′gō), *n.* Santo Domingo (defs. 2, 3).

sand′ paint′ing, *n.* **1.** the ceremonial practice among Navajo and Pueblo Indians of creating symbolic designs on a flat surface with vari-colored sand. **2.** the designs so made.

sand·pa·per (sand′pā′pər), *n.* **1.** strong paper coated with a layer of sand or other abrasive, used for smoothing or polishing. —*v.t.* **2.** to smooth or polish with sandpaper.

sand·pi·per (sand′pī′pər), *n.* any of various plump, thin-billed shore-birds of the family Scolopacidae, of cosmopolitan distribution, typically with brown, gray, or white plumage.

spotted sandpiper, *Actitis macularia,*
length 7 in. (18 cm)

sand·stone (sand′stōn′), *n.* a common sedimentary rock consisting of sand, usu. quartz, cemented together by various substances, as silica, calcium carbonate, iron oxide, or clay.

sand·storm (sand′stôrm′), *n.* a windstorm, esp. in a desert, that blows along great clouds of sand.

sand′ trap′, *n.* (on a golf course) a shallow pit partly filled with sand and designed to serve as a hazard.

sand·wich (sand′wich, san′-), *n.* **1.** two or more slices of bread or the like with a layer of meat, fish, cheese, etc., between them. **2.** something that resembles or suggests a sandwich: *a plywood sandwich.* —*v.t.* **3.** to put into a sandwich. **4.** to insert between two other things. [after John Montagu, fourth Earl of *Sandwich* (1718–92)]

Sand·wich (sand′wich, san′-), *n.* a town in E Kent, in SE England: one of the Cinque Ports. 4467.

sand′wich board′, *n.* two connected signboards hanging in front of and behind a person (**sand′wich man′**) and bearing some advertisement, notice, or the like.

Sand′wich Is′lands, *n.pl.* former name of Hawaiian Islands.

sand·worm (sand′wûrm′), *n.* **1.** any of various marine worms that live in sand. **2.** clamworm.

sand·wort (sand′wûrt′, -wôrt′), *n.* any of various plants of the genus *Arenaria,* pink family, that have clusters of usu. white flowers and often grow in sandy soil.

sand·y (san′dē), *adj.,* **-i·er, -i·est. 1.** of the nature of or consisting of sand. **2.** containing or covered with sand. **3.** of a yellowish red color: *sandy hair.*

sane (sān), *adj.,* **san·er, san·est. 1.** free from mental derangement; having a sound, healthy mind. **2.** having or showing reason, sound judgment, or good sense. **3.** sound; healthy. —**sane′ly,** *adv.*

San·for·ized (san′fə rīzd′), *Trademark.* (of a fabric) specially processed to resist shrinking.

San Fran·cis·co (san′ frən sis′kō, fran-), *n.* a seaport in W central California. 734,676. —**San′ Fran·cis′can,** *n., adj.*

sang (sang), *v.* pt. of sing.

Sang·er (sang′ər), *n.* **1. Frederick,** born 1918, English biochemist: Nobel prize for chemistry 1958. **2. Margaret (Higgins),** 1883–1966, U.S. nurse and author: leader of birth-control movement.

sang-froid (Fr. sän frwA′), *n.* coolness of mind; calmness; composure. [< French: lit., cold blood]

san·gri·a or **san·gri·a** (sang grē′ə, san-), *n., pl.* **-grias.** an iced drink typically of red wine, sugar, sliced fruit and fruit juice, soda water, and spices.

san·guine (sang′gwin), *adj.* **1.** cheerfully optimistic, hopeful, or confident: *sanguine about the future.* **2.** reddish; ruddy: *a sanguine complexion.* **3.** (in old physiology) having blood as the predominating humor and consequently being ruddy-faced, cheerful, etc. **4.** bloody. **5.** of the color of blood; red. —**san′guine·ly,** *adv.* —**san′guine·ness,** *n.*

san·guin·e·ous (sang gwin′ē əs), *adj.* **1.** of, pertaining to, or containing blood. **2.** of the color of blood. **3.** involving much bloodshed. **4.** sanguine; confident. —**san·guin′e·ous·ness,** *n.*

San·hed·rin (san hed′rin, -hē′drin, sän-, san′i drin) also **San·he·drim** (san′hi drim, san′i-), *n.* the supreme legislative council and ecclesiastical and secular tribunal of the ancient Jews, exercising authority until A.D. 70.

san·i·cle (san′i kəl), *n.* any plant belonging to the genus *Sanicula,* of the parsley family, as *S. marilandica,* of North America, used in medicine.

san·i·tar·i·um (san′i târ′ē əm) also **sanatorium,** *n., pl.* **-tar·i·ums,** **-tar·i·a** (-târ′ē ə). an institution for the preservation of health; health resort.

san·i·tar·y (san′i ter′ē), *adj.* **1.** of or pertaining to health or the conditions affecting health, esp. with reference to cleanliness, precautions against disease, etc. **2.** favorable to health; free from dirt, bacteria,

etc. **3.** providing healthy cleanliness: *a sanitary wrapper on all sandwiches.* —**san′i·tar′i·ly,** *adv.* —**san′i·tar′i·ness,** *n.*

san′itary engineer′ing, *n.* a branch of civil engineering dealing with matters affecting public health, as water supply or sewage disposal. —**san′itary engineer′,** *n.*

san′itary land′fill, *n.* landfill (def. 1).

san′itary nap′kin, *n.* a disposable pad of absorbent material, as cotton, worn by women during menstruation to absorb the uterine flow.

san·i·ta·tion (san′i tā′shən), *n.* **1.** the development and application of sanitary measures for the sake of cleanliness, protecting health, etc. **2.** the disposal of sewage and solid waste.

san·i·tize (san′i tīz′), *v.t.,* **-tized, -tiz·ing. 1.** to free from dirt, germs, etc., as by cleaning or sterilizing. **2.** to make less offensive by eliminating anything unwholesome, objectionable, etc. —**san′i·ti·za′tion,** *n.*

san·i·ty (san′i tē), *n.* **1.** the state of being sane. **2.** soundness of judgment.

San Jo·se (san′ hō zā′), *n.* a city in W California. 816,884.

San Jo·sé (san′ hō zā′), *n.* the capital of Costa Rica, in the central part. 241,464.

San Juan (san′ wän′, hwän′), *n.* **1.** the capital of Puerto Rico, on the NE coast. 431,227. **2.** a city in W Argentina. 290,479.

San′ Juan′ Hill′, *n.* a hill in SE Cuba, near Santiago de Cuba: captured by U.S. forces during the Spanish-American War in 1898.

sank (sangk), *v.* a pt. of sink.

San Ma·ri·no (san′ mə rē′nō), *n.* **1.** a small republic in E Italy. 24,714; 24 sq. mi. (61 sq. km). **2.** the capital of this republic. 4363. —**San′ Mar·i·nese′** (mar′ə nēz′, -nēs′), *adj., n.*

San Mar·tín (san′ mär tēn′), *n.* **José de,** 1778–1850, South American general and statesman.

sans (sanz), *prep.* without: *a bird sans feathers.*

San Sal·va·dor (san sal′və dôr′), *n.* **1.** an island in the E central Bahamas. 825; 60 sq. mi. (155 sq. km). **2.** the capital of El Salvador. 452,614.

sans-cu·lotte (sanz′kyoō lot′, -koō-), *n.* **1.** a radical in the French Revolution. **2.** an extreme republican or revolutionary. [< French: lit., without knee breeches] —**sans′-cu·lot′tic,** *adj.* —**sans′-cu·lot′tism,** *n.*

San·sei (sän′sā, sän sā′), *n., pl.* **-sei.** (*sometimes l.c.*) a grandchild of Japanese immigrants to North America. Compare Issei, Kibei, Nisei.

San·skrit (san′skrit), *n.* the oldest extant Indo-Aryan language, retained in India in a codified, classical form as a language of literature, traditional learning, and Hinduism. *Abbr.:* Skt —**San·skrit′ic,** *adj.* —**San′skrit·ist,** *n.*

sans′ ser′if (sanz), *n.* a style of type without serifs. —**sans′-ser′if,** *adj.*

San·ta (san′tə), *n.* Santa Claus.

San′ta An′a (an′ə), *n.* **1.** a city in SW California. 290,827. **2.** a city in NW El Salvador. 174,546. **3.** (in S California) a weather condition in which strong, hot, dust-bearing winds descend to the Pacific coast around Los Angeles from inland desert regions.

San′ta Cla·ri′ta (kla rē′tə), *n.* a city in SW California, N of Los Angeles. 123,676.

San′ta Claus′ (or **Klaus**) (klôz), *n.* a white-bearded, plump, red-suited, grandfatherly man of folklore who brings gifts to well-behaved children at Christmas.

San′ta Cruz′ (krōōz), *n.* **1.** a city in central Bolivia. 441,717. **2.** an island in NW Santa Barbara Islands. **3.** St. Croix (def. 1).

San′ta Fe′ (fā), *n.* the capital of New Mexico, in the N part: founded c1605. 59,300. —**San′ta Fe′an,** *adj.*

San′ta Fé′ (fā), *n.* a city in E Argentina. 287,240.

San′ta Fe′ Trail′, *n.* a trade route between Independence, Missouri, and Santa Fe, New Mexico, used from about 1821 to 1880.

San′ta Ger·tru′dis (gər trōō′dis), *n.* any of an American breed of beef cattle, developed from Shorthorn and Brahman stock for endurance in hot climates.

San′ta Ro′sa (rō′zə), *n.* a city in W California, N of San Francisco. 116,962.

San·ta·ya·na (san′tē an′ə, -ä′nə), *n.* **George,** 1863–1952, U.S. philosopher and writer, born in Spain.

San·te·rí·a or **San·te·ri·a** (sän′tə rē′ə), *n.* (*sometimes l.c.*) a religion merging the worship of Yoruba deities with veneration of Roman Catholic saints: practiced in Cuba and spread to other parts of the Caribbean and to the U.S. by Cuban emigrés.

San·ti·a·go (san′tē ä′gō), *n.* **1.** the capital of Chile, in the central part. 4,858,342. **2.** Also called **Santia′go de Com·pos·te′la** (də kom′pə stel′ə). a city in NW Spain. 104,045.

San·to Do·min·go (san′tō də ming′gō), *n.* **1.** the capital of the Dominican Republic, on the S coast: first European settlement in the New World 1496. 1,313,172. **2.** a former name of Dominican Republic. **3.** a former name of Hispaniola. Also, **San Domingo** (for defs. 2, 3).

san·ton·i·ca (san ton′i kə), *n., pl.* **-cas. 1.** any of several European wormwoods, as *Artemisia cina.* **2.** dried wormwood flower heads, used as a vermifuge.

São Pau·lo (soun′ pou′lō, -lōō), *n.* **1.** a state in S. Brazil. 30,942,600; 95,714 sq. mi. (247,898 sq. km). **2.** the capital of this state. 7,032,547.

São To·mé (soun′ tōō mā′), *n.* **1.** an island in W Africa, off the W coast of Gabon: the larger component of the republic of São Tomé and

S

Príncipe. 106,900; 326 sq. mi. (847 sq. km). **2.** a city on this island: capital of the republic. 35,000. —**Sãoʹ To•meʹan,** *n.*, *adj.*

Sãoʹ Toméʹ and Prínʹcipe or **Saoʹ Toméʹ and Prinʹcipe,** *n.* a republic in W Africa, comprising the islands of São Tomé and Príncipe, in the Gulf of Guinea, N of the equator: a former overseas province of Portugal; gained independence in 1975. 147,865; 387 sq. mi. (1001 sq. km). *Cap.:* São Tomé.

sap¹ (sap), *n.*, *v.*, **sapped, sap•ping.** —*n.* **1.** a watery juice, containing mineral salts and sugar, that circulates through the tissues of a plant. **2.** any vital body fluid. **3.** energy; vitality. **4.** a fool; dupe. —*v.t.* **5.** to drain the sap from.

sap² (sap), *n.*, *v.*, **sapped, sap•ping.** —*n.* **1.** a trench constructed so as to form an approach to a besieged place. —*v.t.* **2.** to approach (a wall, glacis, or other part of a fortification) with saps, in order to move troops or artillery into a more forward position, or to dig below and undermine the fortification. **3.** to undermine; weaken or destroy insidiously.

sa•pheʹnous veinʹ (sə fēʹnəs), *n.* either of two large veins near the surface of the leg from thigh to foot, one along the inner side and the other outer and posterior.

sap•id (sapʹid), *adj.* **1.** having flavor. **2.** agreeable to the taste; palatable. **3.** agreeable to the mind. —**sa•pidʹi•ty, sapʹid•ness,** *n.*

sa•pi•ens (sapʹē ənz), *adj.* of, pertaining to, or resembling modern humans (*Homo sapiens*).

sa•pi•ent (sāʹpē ənt), *adj.* **1.** having or showing great wisdom or sound judgment. **2.** SAPIENS. —**saʹpi•ence, saʹpi•en•cy,** *n.* —**saʹpi•ent•ly,** *adv.*

sap•ling (sapʹling), *n.* **1.** a young tree. **2.** a young person.

sap•o•dil•la (sapʹə dilʹə), *n.*, *pl.* **-las. 1.** a large evergreen tree, *Achras zapota,* of tropical America, bearing an edible fruit: yields chicle. **2.** Also called **sapʹodilʹla plumʹ.** the fruit itself.

sap•o•na•ceous (sapʹə nāʹshəs), *adj.* resembling soap; soapy. —**sapʹo•naʹceous•ness,** *n.*

sa•pon•i•fy (sə ponʹə fīʹ), *v.*, **-fied, -fy•ing.** —*v.t.* **1.** to convert (a fat) into soap by treating with an alkali. **2.** to decompose (any ester), forming the corresponding alcohol and acid or salt. —*v.i.* **3.** to become converted into soap. —**sa•ponʹi•fiʹa•ble,** *adj.* —**sa•ponʹi•fi•caʹtion,** *n.* —**sa•ponʹi•fiʹer,** *n.*

sap•pan•wood (sə panʹwo͝od´), *n.* **1.** a dyewood yielding a red color, produced by a small, East Indian tree, *Caesalpinia sappan,* of the legume family. **2.** the tree itself.

Sap•phi•ra (sə fīʹrə), *n.* a woman who, with her husband, Ananias, was struck dead for lying. Acts 5.

sap•phire (safʹīr), *n.* **1.** any gem variety of corundum other than the ruby, esp. one of the blue varieties. **2.** a gem of this kind. **3.** the deep blue color of this gem. —*adj.* **4.** deep blue.

Sap•pho (safʹō), *n.* c620–c565 B.C., Greek poet of Lesbos.

sap•py (sapʹē), *adj.*, **-pi•er, -pi•est. 1.** abounding in sap. **2.** sentimental; mawkish. **3.** foolish: *a sappy grin.* —**sapʹpi•ness,** *n.*

sap•suck•er (sapʹsukʹər), *n.* any of several North American woodpeckers of the genus *Sphyrapicus* that drill holes in trees for sap and to catch insects attracted by sap.

sap•wood (sapʹwo͝od´), *n.* the living, softer part of the wood between the inner bark and the heartwood. Also called **alburnum.**

Sar•a•cen (sarʹə sən), *n.* any of the Muslim opponents of the Crusaders in the Middle Ages. —**Sarʹa•cenʹic** (-senʹik), *adj.*

Sar•ah (sârʹə), *n.* the wife of Abraham and mother of Isaac. Gen. 17:15–22.

Sa•ra•je•vo (sarʹə yāʹvō), *n.* the capital of Bosnia and Herzegovina, in the central part. 448,519.

sa•ran (sə ranʹ), *n.* a tough thermoplastic resin used as a fiber, in thin sheets for packaging, and for making acid-resistant pipe.

sa•ra•pe (sə räʹpē), *n.* SERAPE.

Sar•a•to•ga (sarʹə tōʹgə), *n.* former name of **Schuylerville.**

sarc-, var. of SARCO-, esp. before a vowel: *sarcoptic.*

sar•casm (särʹkaz əm), *n.* **1.** harsh or bitter derision or irony. **2.** a sharply ironical taunt; sneering or cutting remark.

sar•cas•tic (sär kasʹtik), *adj.* **1.** of, pertaining to, or characterized by sarcasm: *a sarcastic reply.* **2.** using or given to the use of sarcasm. —**sar•casʹti•cal•ly,** *adv.*

sar•ci•na (särʹsə nə), *n.*, *pl.* **-nas, -nae** (-nēʹ). any of several spherical saprophytic bacteria, of the genus *Sarcina,* that after division remain attached in cubelike groups of eight.

sarco-, a combining form meaning "flesh": *sarcolemma.* Also, *esp. before a vowel,* **sarc-.**

sar•co•carp (särʹkō kärpʹ), *n. Bot.* **1.** the fleshy mesocarp of certain fruits, as the peach. **2.** any fruit of fleshy consistency.

sar•co•lem•ma (särʹkə lemʹə), *n.*, *pl.* **-mas.** the membranous sheath of a muscle fiber. —**sarʹco•lemʹmic, sarʹco•lemʹmous,** *adj.*

sar•co•ma (sär kōʹmə), *n.*, *pl.* **-mas, -ma•ta** (-mə tə). any of various malignant tumors composed of neoplastic cells resembling embryonic connective tissue. —**sar•coʹma•toidʹ, sar•coʹma•tous** (-kōʹmə təs, -komʹə-), *adj.*

sar•coph•a•gous (sär kofʹə gəs) also **sar•co•phag•ic** (särʹkə fajʹik, -fāʹjik), *adj.* carnivorous.

sar•coph•a•gus (sär kofʹə gəs), *n.*, *pl.* **-gi** (-jīʹ, -gīʹ), **-gus•es.** a stone coffin, esp. one bearing sculpture, inscriptions, etc., often displayed as a monument.

sar•dine (sär dēnʹ), *n.*, *pl.* (*esp. collectively*) **-dine,** (*esp. for kinds or species*) **-dines. 1.** the pilchard, *Sardinops sagax,* often preserved in oil and used for food. **2.** any of various similar, closely related fishes of the herring family Clupeidae.

Sar•din•i•a (sär dinʹē ə, -dinʹyə), *n.* a large island in the Mediterranean, W of Italy: with small nearby islands it comprises a department of Italy. 1,594,175; 9301 sq. mi. (24,090 sq. km). *Cap.:* Cagliari. Italian, **Sar•deʹgna** (sär deʹnyä).

Sar•dis (särʹdis) also **Sar•des** (-dēz), *n.* an ancient city in W Asia Minor: the capital of Lydia and site of one of the seven churches of Asia (Rev. 1:11). —**Sarʹdi•an** (-dē ən), *adj.*, *n.*

sar•don•ic (sär donʹik), *adj.* characterized by scornful derision or bitter irony; mocking; cynical: *a sardonic grin.* —**sar•donʹi•cal•ly,** *adv.*

Sar•gasʹso Seaʹ (sär gasʹō), *n.* a relatively calm area of water in the N Atlantic, NE of the West Indies: central part covered with sargassum.

sar•gas•sum (sär gasʹəm), *n.* **1.** any seaweed of the genus *Sargassum,* widely distributed in the warmer waters of the globe. **2.** GULFWEED (def. 1). Also called **sargasso.**

serge (särj), *n. Informal.* sergeant.

Sar•gent (särʹjənt), *n.* **John Singer,** 1856–1925, U.S. painter.

Sar•gon (särʹgon), *n.* fl. c2300 B.C., Mesopotamian ruler: founder of Akkadian kingdom.

Sargon II, *n.* died 705 B.C., king of Assyria 722–705.

sa•ri or **sa•ree** (särʹē), *n.*, *pl.* **-ris** or **-rees.** a garment consisting of a long cloth wrapped around the body with one end draped over one shoulder or the head, worn by women chiefly in India.

sa•rong (sə rôngʹ, -rongʹ), *n.* **1.** a loose-fitting skirtlike garment formed by wrapping a strip of cloth around the lower part of the body, worn by both sexes in the Malay Archipelago and some Pacific islands. **2.** a cloth for such garments.

sar•sa•pa•ril•la (sasʹpə rilʹə, särʹsə pə-, särʹspə-), *n.*, *pl.* **-las. 1.** any of various tropical American vines of the genus *Smilax,* of the lily family, having serrated heart-shaped leaves. **2.** the root of any of these vines, used medicinally and as a flavoring. **3.** an extract or other preparation made of this root. **4.** a soft drink, as root beer, flavored with this extract. **5.** Also called **wild sarsaparilla.** a North American plant, *Aralia nudicaulis,* of the ginseng family, having a root with a similar flavor.

sar•to•ri•al (sär tôrʹē əl, -tōrʹ-), *adj.* **1.** pertaining to tailors or their trade. **2.** pertaining to clothing or style or manner of dress: *sartorial splendor.* **3.** pertaining to the sartorius. —**sar•toʹri•al•ly,** *adv.*

sar•to•ri•us (sär tôrʹē əs, -tōrʹ-), *n.*, *pl.* **-to•ri•i** (-tôrʹē īʹ, -tōrʹ-). a long, flat, narrow muscle extending obliquely from the front of the hip to the inner side of the tibia.

Sar•tre (SARʹtRə), *n.* **Jean-Paul** (zhäN), 1905–80, French philosopher, novelist, and dramatist.

SASE, self-addressed stamped envelope.

sash¹ (sash), *n.* **1.** a long band or scarf worn over one shoulder or around the waist, as a part of one's ensemble or a uniform. —*v.t.* **2.** to furnish or adorn with a sash: *a dress sashed at the waist.*

sash² (sash), *n.* **1.** a fixed or movable framework, as in a window or door, in which panes of glass are set. **2.** such frameworks collectively. —*v.t.* **3.** to furnish with sashes or with windows having sashes.

sa•shay (sa shāʹ), *v.i.* **1.** to walk, move, or proceed easily or nonchalantly. **2.** to strut. **3.** to chassé in dancing. —*n.* **4.** a chassé. **5.** a trip or excursion. **6.** a venture or foray.

Sas•katch•e•wan (sa skachʹə wonʹ, -wən), *n.* **1.** a province in W Canada. 1,009,613; 251,700 sq. mi. (651,900 sq. km). *Cap.:* Regina. **2.** a river in SW Canada, flowing E from the Rocky Mountains. 1205 mi. (1940 km) long.

Sas•quatch (sasʹkwoch, -kwach), *n.* BIG FOOT.

sas•sa•fras (sasʹə frasʹ), *n.* **1.** an E North American tree, *Sassafras albidum,* of the laurel family, having both oval and two- or three-lobed leaves. **2.** the aromatic bark of its root, used esp. as a flavoring agent.

sas•sy (sasʹē), *adj.*, **-si•er, -si•est. 1.** impudent; fresh: *a sassy child.* **2.** boldly smart; jaunty: *a sassy outfit.*

sat (sat), *v.* a pt. and pp. of SIT.

SAT, *Trademark.* Scholastic Assessment Test.

Sa•tan (sātʹn), *n.* **1.** the chief evil spirit, the great adversary of God and humanity; the devil. —*Proverb.* **2. Get thee behind me, Satan,** temptation must be resisted. Matt. 16:23.

sa•tan•ic (sə tanʹik, sā-) also **sa•tanʹi•cal,** *adj.* **1.** of Satan or Satanism. **2.** characteristic of or befitting Satan; extremely evil or wicked; fiendish; diabolical. —**sa•tanʹi•cal•ly,** *adv.* —**sa•tanʹi•cal•ness,** *n.*

Sa•tan•ism (sātʹn izʹəm), *n.* **1.** the worship of Satan or the powers of evil. **2.** a travesty of Christian rites in which Satan is worshiped. **3.** *sometimes* (*l.c.*) diabolical or satanic disposition, behavior, or activity. —**Saʹtan•ist,** *n.*

satch•el (sachʹəl), *n.* a small bag, sometimes with a shoulder strap. —**satchʹeled,** *adj.*

Sat•com (satʹkomʹ), *n.* one of a series of privately financed geosynchronous communications satellites that provide television, voice, and data transmissions to the U.S.

sate (sāt), *v.t.*, **sat•ed, sat•ing. 1.** to satisfy (an appetite or desire) fully. **2.** to fill to excess; surfeit; glut.

sa•teen (sa tēnʹ), *n.* a cotton fabric constructed in satin weave and. having a lustrous face.

sat•el•lite (satʹl ītʹ), *n.* **1.** a natural body that revolves around a planet; moon. **2.** a device designed to be launched into orbit around the earth, another planet, the sun, etc. **3.** a country under the domination or influence of another. **4.** something that depends on, accompanies, or is subordinate to something else. **5.** a place or facility physically separated from but associated with or dependent on another place or facility. **6.** an attendant or follower of another person, often subservient or obsequious in manner. **—***adj.* **7.** of or constituting a satellite. **8.** subordinate to another authority, outside power, or the like.

sat′ellite dish′, *n.* DISH (def. 8).

sa•tia•ble (sā′shə bəl, -shē ə-), *adj.* capable of being satiated. **—sa′tia•bil′i•ty,** *n.* **—sa′tia•bly,** *adv.*

sa•ti•ate (*v.* sā′shē āt′; *adj.* -it, -āt′), *v.,* **-at•ed, -at•ing,** *adj.* **—***v.t.* **1.** to supply with something to excess, as to disgust or weary; surfeit. **2.** to satisfy to the full; sate. **—***adj.* **3.** satisfied fully, as in appetite or desire. **—sa′ti•a′tion,** *n.*

sa•ti•e•ty (sə tī′i tē), *n.* the state of being satiated; surfeit.

sat•in (sat′n), *n.* **1.** a fabric, as acetate, rayon, nylon, or silk, constructed in a satin weave and often having a glossy face and a soft, slippery texture. **2.** a garment of satin. **—***adj.* **3.** of or like satin; smooth; glossy. **4.** made of or covered or decorated with satin.

sat′in stitch′, *n.* a long, straight embroidery stitch worked closely together to form a smooth surface resembling satin.

sat′in weave′, *n.* one of the three basic weave structures, in which the filling threads are interlaced with the warp at widely separated intervals, producing the effect of an unbroken surface. Compare PLAIN WEAVE, TWILL WEAVE.

sat•in•wood (sat′n wo͝od′), *n.* **1.** the satiny wood of any of several trees of the rue family, used to make furniture, esp. *Chloroxylon swietenia,* of the East Indies. **2.** any of these trees.

sat•in•y (sat′n ē), *adj.* like satin; smooth; glossy.

sat•ire (sat′īər), *n.* **1.** the use of irony, sarcasm, or ridicule in exposing, denouncing, or deriding vice, folly, etc. **2.** a literary composition or genre in which human folly and vice are held up to scorn, derision, or ridicule.

sa•tir•i•cal (sə tir′i kəl) also **sa•tir′ic,** *adj.* **1.** of or characterized by satire. **2.** indulging in or given to satire. **—sa•tir′i•cal•ly,** *adv.*

sat•i•rist (sat′ər ist), *n.* **1.** a writer of satires. **2.** a person who indulges in satire.

sat•i•rize (sat′ə rīz′), *v.,* **-rized, -riz•ing.** **—***v.t.* **1.** to attack or ridicule with satire. **—***v.i.* **2.** to write satires; attack with satire. **—sat′i•riz′a•ble,** *adj.* **—sat′i•ri•za′tion,** *n.* **—sat′i•riz′er,** *n.*

sat•is•fac•tion (sat′is fak′shən), *n.* **1.** the state or feeling of being satisfied; contentment; pleasure. **2.** a cause or means of fulfillment or contentment. **3.** the act of satisfying; fulfillment; gratification. **4.** confident acceptance of something as satisfactory, dependable, true, etc. **5.** reparation or compensation, as for a wrong or injury. **6.** the opportunity to redress or right a wrong, as by a duel. **7.** payment or discharge, as of a debt or obligation. **8. a.** an act of doing penance or making reparation for venial sin. **b.** the penance or reparation made.

sat•is•fac•to•ry (sat′is fak′tə rē, -fak′trē), *adj.* **1.** satisfying demands, expectations, or requirements; adequate. **2.** atoning or expiating. **—sat′is•fac′to•ri•ly,** *adv.* **—sat′is•fac′to•ri•ness,** *n.*

sat•is•fy (sat′is fī′), *v.,* **-fied, -fy•ing.** **—***v.t.* **1.** to fulfill the desires, expectations, needs, or demands of; make content. **2.** to put an end to (a desire, want, need, etc.) by sufficient or ample provision: *to satisfy one's hunger.* **3.** to give assurance to; convince: *to satisfy oneself by investigation.* **4.** to answer sufficiently, as an objection. **5.** to solve or dispel, as a doubt. **6.** to discharge fully (a debt, obligation, etc.). **7.** to make reparation to or for. **8.** to pay (a creditor). **9.** *Math.* **a.** to fulfill the requirements or conditions of: *to satisfy a theorem.* **b.** (of a value of an unknown) to change (an equation) into an identity when substituted for the unknown: $x = 2$ *satisfies* $3x = 6$. **—***v.i.* **10.** to give satisfaction. **—sat′is•fi′a•ble,** *adj.* **—sat′is•fi′er,** *n.* **—sat′is•fy′ing•ly,** *adv.*

sa•trap (sā′trap, sa′-), *n.* **1.** a governor of a province under the ancient Persian monarchy. **2.** a subordinate ruler, often a despotic one.

sat•u•ra•ble (sach′ər ə bəl), *adj.* capable of being saturated. **—sat′u•ra•bil′i•ty,** *n.*

sat•u•rate (*v.* sach′ə rāt′; *adj., n.* -ər it, -ə rāt′), *v.,* **-rat•ed, -rat•ing,** *adj., n.* **—***v.t.* **1.** to cause (a substance) to unite with the greatest possible amount of another substance, through solution, chemical combination, or the like. **2.** to load, fill, or charge to the utmost. **3.** to soak, impregnate, or imbue thoroughly or completely. **4.** to furnish (a market) with goods to the full purchasing capacity. **5.** to destroy (a target) completely with bombs and missiles. **—***v.i.* **6.** to become saturated. **—***adj.* **7.** saturated. **—***n.* **8.** a saturated fat or fatty acid.

sat•u•rat•ed (sach′ə rā′tid), *adj.* **1.** thoroughly or completely imbued, filled, or charged. **2.** thoroughly soaked with moisture; wet. **3.** (of colors) of maximum chroma or purity; free from admixture of white. **4. a.** (of a chemical solution) containing the maximum amount of solute capable of being dissolved under given conditions. **b.** (of an organic compound) containing no double or triple bonds.

sat′urated fat′, *n.* a single-bonded animal or vegetable fat, abundant in fatty meats, dairy products, coconut oil, and palm oil, tending to raise cholesterol levels in the blood.

sat•u•ra•tion (sach′ə rā′shən), *n.* **1.** the act or process of saturating. **2.** the state of being saturated. **3.** a condition in the atmosphere corresponding to 100 percent relative humidity. **4.** the degree of chroma or purity of a color; the degree of freedom from admixture with white. **5.** the state of maximum magnetization of a ferromagnetic material.

satura′tion point′, *n.* **1.** a point at which some capacity is at its fullest limit. **2.** the point at which a substance will receive no more of another substance in solution, chemical combination, etc.

Sat•ur•day (sat′ər dā′, -dē), *n.* the seventh day of the week, following Friday.

Sat′urday-night′ spe′cial, *n. Informal.* a cheap, small-caliber handgun that is easily obtainable and concealable.

Sat•urn (sat′ərn), *n.* **1.** a Roman god of agriculture, the consort of Ops, believed to have ruled the earth during an age of happiness and virtue: identified with the Greek god Cronus. **2.** the planet sixth in order from the sun, having an equatorial diameter of 74,600 mi. (120,000 km), a mean distance from the sun of 886.7 million mi. (1427 million km), a period of revolution of 29.46 years, and 23 known moons. It is the second largest planet in the solar system, encompassed by a series of thin, flat rings composed of small particles of ice.

Sat•ur•na•li•a (sat′ər nā′lē ə, -nāl′yə), *n., pl.* **-li•a, -li•as.** **1.** (*sometimes used with a pl. v.*) the festival of Saturn, celebrated in December in ancient Rome as a time of unrestrained merrymaking. **2.** (*l.c.*) any unrestrained revelry; orgy. **—Sat′ur•na′li•an,** *adj.*

sat•ur•nine (sat′ər nīn′), *adj.* **1.** sluggish or gloomy in temperament or appearance; somber; taciturn. **2.** suffering from lead poisoning. **3.** due to absorption of lead, as bodily disorders. **—sat′ur•nine′ly,** *adv.* **—sat′ur•nine′ness, sat′ur•nin′i•ty** (-nin′i tē), *n.*

sa•tyr (sā′tər, sat′ər), *n.* **1.** ancient Greek woodland deity, represented as part human and part horse or goat, and noted for riotousness and lasciviousness. **2.** a lecher. **3.** a man who has satyriasis. **4.** Also, **sa•tyr•id** (sā′tər id, sat′ər-, sə tī′rid). any of several butterflies of the family Satyridae, having gray or brown wings marked with eyelike spots. **—sa•tyr•ic** (sə tir′ik), **sa•tyr′i•cal,** *adj.* **—sa′tyr•like′,** *adj.*

sa•ty•ri•a•sis (sā′tə rī′ə sis, sat′ə-), *n.* abnormal, uncontrollable sexual desire in a male. Compare NYMPHOMANIA.

sauce (sôs), *n., v.,* **sauced, sauc•ing.** **—***n.* **1.** any liquid or semiliquid preparation, as gravy or a condiment, eaten as an accompaniment to food. **2.** stewed fruit, usu. puréed: *cranberry sauce.* **3.** something that adds piquance or zest. **4.** *Informal.* impertinence; sauciness. **—***v.t.* **5.** to dress or prepare with a sauce. **6.** *Informal.* to speak impertinently or saucily to; sass. **—*Proverb.*** **7. What's sauce for the goose is sauce for the gander,** people should be treated equally.

sauce•pan (sôs′pan′), *n.* a cooking pan of moderate depth, usu. with a long handle and sometimes a cover.

sau•cer (sô′sər), *n.* **1.** a small, round, shallow dish for holding a cup. **2.** something resembling a saucer, as in shape.

sau•cy (sô′sē), *adj.,* **-ci•er, -ci•est.** **1.** impertinent; insolent. **2.** pert; jaunty: *a saucy little hat.* **—sau′ci•ly,** *adv.* **—sau′ci•ness,** *n.*

Sau•di (sou′dē, sô′-, sä o͞o′-), *n., pl.* **-dis,** *adj.* **—***n.* **1.** SAUDI ARABIAN. **2.** a member of the Saud family of Arabia, rulers of most of the Arabian Peninsula since 1932. **—***adj.* **3.** SAUDI ARABIAN. **4.** of or pertaining to the Saud family.

Sau′di Ara′bia, *n.* a kingdom occupying most of Arabia. 20,087,965; ab. 849,425 sq. mi. (2,200,000 sq. km). *Cap.:* Riyadh. **—Sau′di Ara′bian,** *adj., n.*

sau•er•bra•ten (souər′brät′n, sou′ər-), *n.* a pot roast of beef, marinated before cooking in vinegar and seasonings.

sau•er•kraut (souər′krout′, sou′ər-), *n.* cabbage cut fine, salted, and allowed to ferment until sour. [< German: sour greens]

Saul (sôl), *n.* **1.** the first king of Israel. I Sam. 9. **2.** Also called **Saul′ of Tar′sus.** the original name of the apostle Paul. Acts 9:1–30; 22:3.

sault (so͞o), *n.* a waterfall or rapid.

Sault Ste. (or **Sainte**) **Marie** (so͞o′ sānt′ mə rē′), *n.* **1.** the rapids of the St. Marys River, between NE Michigan and Ontario, Canada. **2.** a city in S Ontario, in S Canada, near these rapids. 80,905.

sau•na (sô′nə, sou′-), *n., pl.* **-nas,** *v.,* **-naed, -na•ing.** **—***n.* **1.** a bath that uses dry heat to induce perspiration, and in which steam is produced by pouring water on heated stones. **2.** a bathhouse or room equipped for such a bath. **—***v.i.* **3.** to take a sauna. [< Finnish]

saun•ter (sôn′tər, sän′-), *v.i.* **1.** to walk with a leisurely gait; stroll. **—***n.* **2.** a leisurely walk or ramble; stroll. **3.** a leisurely gait.

sau•ri•an (sôr′ē ən), *adj.* **1.** belonging or pertaining to the Sauria, a group of reptiles orig. including the lizards, crocodiles, dinosaurs, and other reptilian types but now restricted to the lizards. **—***n.* **2.** a lizard or lizardlike creature.

saur•is•chi•an (sô ris′kē ən), *n.* **1.** any carnivorous or herbivorous dinosaur of the order Saurischia, in which the pelvic structure resembles that of lizards. **—***adj.* **2.** belonging or pertaining to the Saurischia.

sau•ro•pod (sôr′ə pod′), *n.* **1.** any of various huge, plant-eating saurischian dinosaurs, of the suborder Sauropoda, including the brontosaur, brachiosaur, and supersaur, that had small heads, very long necks and tails, and columnar limbs. **—***adj.* **2.** of or belonging to the sauropods.

sau•sage (sô′sij; *esp. Brit.* sos′ij), *n.* finely chopped, seasoned meat, usu. stuffed into a prepared intestine or other casing and often made into links. **—sau′sage•like′,** *adj.*

sau•té (sō tā′, sô-), *v.,* **-téed** (-tād′), **-té•ing** (-tā′ing), *n.* **—***v.t.* **1.** to cook in a small amount of butter, oil, etc. **—***n.* **2.** a dish of sautéed food.

Sau·terne (sō tûrn′, sô-), *n.* (*sometimes l.c.*) a semisweet white wine of California.

Sau·ternes (sō tûrn′, sô-), *n.* **1.** a rich, sweet white table wine of Bordeaux, in SW France. **2.** the district producing this wine.

Sau·vi·gnon (sō′vin yōN′), *n.* a small blue-black wine grape grown orig. in SW France.

Sau′vignon Blanc′ (bläNk′, blän′), *n.* a white table wine made esp. in France and California.

sav·age (sav′ij), *adj., n., v.,* **-aged, -ag·ing.** —*adj.* **1.** fierce or ferocious; wild; untamed. **2.** uncivilized; barbarous. **3.** enraged or furiously angry. **4.** rugged or uncultivated, as country or scenery. —*n.* **5.** an uncivilized human being. **6.** a fierce, brutal, or cruel person. **7.** a rude, boorish person. —*v.t.* **8.** to assault and maul brutally. **9.** to criticize remorselessly. —**sav′age·ly,** *adv.* —**sav′age·ness,** *n.*

sav·age·ry (sav′ij rē), *n., pl.* **-ries. 1.** an uncivilized or barbaric state; savage condition. **2.** savage action, nature, disposition, or behavior.

sa·van·na or **sa·van·nah** (sə van′ə), *n., pl.* **-nas** or **-nahs.** a plain characterized by coarse grasses and scattered tree growth, esp. on the margins of the tropics where the rainfall is seasonal, as in E Africa.

Sa·van·nah (sə van′ə), *n.* **1.** a seaport in E Georgia, near the mouth of the Savannah River. 140,597. **2.** a river flowing SE from E Georgia along most of the boundary between Georgia and South Carolina and into the Atlantic. 314 mi. (505 km) long. **3.** (*italics*) a U.S. vessel that was the first to cross the Atlantic Ocean under steam (1818), making the voyage in 26 days.

sa·vant (sa vänt′, sav′ənt; *Fr.* SA vän′), *n., pl.* **sa·vants** (sa vänts′, sav′ənts; *Fr.* SA vän′). a person of profound or extensive learning; scholar.

save¹ (sāv), *v.,* **saved, sav·ing,** *n.* —*v.t.* **1.** to rescue from danger or possible harm or loss. **2.** to keep safe, intact, or unhurt; safeguard: *God save the United States.* **3.** to keep from being lost: *tried to save the game.* **4.** to avoid the spending, consumption, or waste of: *to save fuel.* **5.** to set aside, reserve, or lay by: *to save money.* **6.** to treat carefully in order to reduce wear, fatigue, etc.: *to save one's strength.* **7.** to prevent the occurrence, use, or necessity of; obviate. **8.** to deliver from the power and consequences of sin. **9.** to copy (computer data) onto a hard or floppy disk, a tape, etc. **10.** to stop (a ball or puck) from entering one's goal. —*v.i.* **11.** to lay up money as the result of economy or thrift. **12.** to be economical in expenditure. **13.** to preserve something from harm, loss, etc. —*n.* **14.** a goalkeeper's act of preventing a goal. **15.** *Baseball.* a statistical credit given a relief pitcher for preserving a team's victory by holding its lead. —*Idiom.* **16. save one's neck** or **skin,** to rescue oneself or another from harm or danger. —**sav′a·ble, save′a·ble,** *adj.* —**sav′er,** *n.*

save² (sāv), *prep.* **1.** except; but: *They all left save one.* —*conj.* **2.** except; but: *He would have gone, save that he had no money for travel.*

sav·ing (sā′ving), *adj.* **1.** tending or serving to save; rescuing; preserving. **2.** compensating; redeeming. **3.** thrifty; economical. **4.** making a reservation: *a saving clause.* —*n.* **5.** a reduction or lessening of expenditure or outlay. **6.** something that is saved. **7. savings,** sums of money saved by economy and laid away. —*prep.* **8.** except. **9.** with all due respect to or for. —*conj.* **10.** except; save.

sav′ing grace′, *n.* a quality that makes up for other generally negative characteristics; redeeming feature.

sav′ings account′, *n.* a bank account on which interest is compounded and paid on a regular basis.

sav′ings and loan′ associa′tion, *n.* a government-regulated savings institution in which deposits are exchanged for shares of ownership and funds are invested chiefly in home mortgages. *Abbr.:* S&L Also called **building and loan association.**

sav′ings bank′, *n.* a bank that provides savings accounts primarily and pays interest to its depositors.

sav′ings bond′, *n.* a U.S. government bond with principal amounts issued in denominations up to $10,000.

sav·ior or **sav·iour** (sāv′yər), *n.* **1.** a person who saves, rescues, or delivers: *the savior of the country.* **2.** (*cap.*) a title of God, esp. of Jesus.

sa·voir-faire (sav′wär fâr′; *Fr.* SA vwar feR′), *n.* knowledge of just what to do in any situation; tact.

Sav·o·na·ro·la (sav′ə nə rō′lə), *n.* **Girolamo,** 1452–98, Italian monk, reformer, and martyr.

sa·vor (sā′vər), *n.* **1.** the quality in a substance that affects the sense of taste or smell. **2.** a particular taste or smell. **3.** distinctive quality or property. **4.** power to excite or interest. —*v.i.* **5.** to have savor, taste, or odor. **6.** to hint or smack (often fol. by *of*): *practices savoring of greed.* —*v.t.* **7.** to season; flavor. **8.** to perceive by taste or smell, esp. with relish. **9.** to give oneself to the enjoyment of: *to savor the best in life.* Also, *esp. Brit.,* **sa′vour.** —**sa′vor·er,** *n.* —**sa′vor·ing·ly,** *adv.*

sa·vor·y¹ (sā′və rē), *adj.,* **-vor·i·er, -vor·i·est,** *n., pl.* **-vor·ies.** —*adj.* **1.** pleasant or agreeable in taste or smell. **2.** piquant: *a savory jelly.* **3.** pleasing, attractive, or agreeable. —*n.* **4.** *Chiefly Brit.* a spicy or aromatic dish served as an appetizer or dessert, as pickled fish or brandied fruit. Also, *esp. Brit.,* **savoury.** —**sa′vor·i·ness,** *n.*

sa·vor·y² (sā′və rē), *n., pl.* **-vor·ies.** any aromatic herb of the genus *Satureja,* of the mint family, esp. *S. hortensis* (**summer savory**) or *S. montana* (**winter savory**), having leaves used in cooking.

Savoy′ cab′bage, *n.* a variety of cabbage having a compact head of crinkled, blistered leaves.

sav·vy (sav′ē), *n., adj.,* **-vi·er, -vi·est,** *v.,* **-vied, -vy·ing.** —*n.* **1.** Also, **sav′vi·ness.** practical understanding; shrewdness or intelligence: *politi-*

cal savvy. —*adj.* **2.** shrewdly informed; experienced and well-informed; canny. —*v.t., v.i.* **3.** to know; understand. —**sav′vi·ly,** *adv.*

saw¹ (sô), *n., v.,* **sawed, sawed** or **sawn, saw·ing.** —*n.* **1.** a tool or device for cutting, typically a thin blade of metal with a series of sharp teeth. **2.** any similar tool or device, as a rotating disk, in which a sharp continuous edge replaces the teeth. —*v.t.* **3.** to cut or divide with a saw. **4.** to form by cutting with a saw. **5.** to make cutting motions as if using a saw: *to saw the air with one's hands.* **6.** to work (something) from side to side like a saw. —*v.i.* **7.** to use a saw. **8.** to cut with or as if with a saw. —*Idiom.* **9. saw wood,** to snore loudly while sleeping.

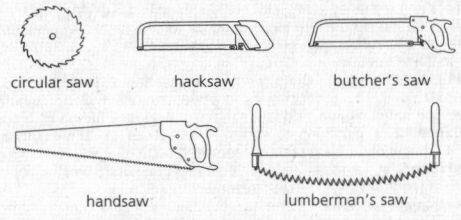

circular saw   hacksaw   butcher's saw

handsaw   lumberman's saw

saws (def. 1)

saw² (sô), *v.* pt. of SEE¹.

saw³ (sô), *n.* a maxim; proverb; saying: *an old saw.*

saw·buck (sô′buk′), *n.* **1.** a sawhorse. **2.** *Slang.* a ten-dollar bill.

saw·dust (sô′dust′), *n.* fine particles of wood produced in sawing.

saw·horse (sô′hôrs′), *n.* a movable frame or trestle for supporting wood while it is being sawed.

saw·mill (sô′mil′), *n.* a place or building in which timber is sawed into planks, boards, etc., by machinery.

sawn (sôn), *v.* a pp. of SAW¹.

saw′ palmet′to, *n.* a shrublike palmetto, *Serenoa repens,* native to the southern U.S., having green or blue leafstalks set with spiny teeth.

saw·tooth (sô′tōōth′), *n., pl.* **-teeth** (-tēth′), *adj.* —*n.* **1.** one of the cutting teeth of a saw. —*adj.* **2.** having a zigzag profile, like that of the cutting edge of a saw; serrate.

saw′-toothed′, *adj.* having sawlike teeth; serrate.

sax (saks), *n.* a saxophone.

sax·horn (saks′hôrn′), *n.* any of a family of brass instruments close to the cornets and tubas.

sax·i·frage (sak′sə frij), *n.* any of numerous plants of the genus *Saxifraga,* certain species of which grow wild in the clefts of rocks, other species of which are cultivated for their flowers.

sax·o·phone (sak′sə fōn′), *n.* a musical wind instrument consisting of a conical, usu. brass tube with keys or valves and a mouthpiece with one reed. —**sax′o·phon′ic** (-fon′ik), *adj.* —**sax′o·phon′ist,** *n.*

saxophone

say (sā), *v.,* **said, say·ing,** *adv., n., interj.* —*v.t.* **1.** to utter or pronounce; speak: *to say a word.* **2.** to express in words; state; declare: *Say what you think.* **3.** to state as an opinion or judgment: *I say we should wait here.* **4.** to recite or repeat. **5.** to report or allege; maintain. **6.** to express (a message, viewpoint, etc.), as through a literary or other artistic medium. **7.** to indicate or show: *What does your watch say?* —*v.i.* **8.** to speak; declare; express an opinion, idea, etc. —*adv.* **9.** approximately; about: *It's, say, 14 feet long.* **10.** for example. —*n.* **11.** what a person says or has to say. **12.** the right or opportunity to state an opinion or exercise influence: *to have one's say in a decision.* **13.** a turn to say something. —*interj.* **14.** (used to express surprise, get attention, etc.) —*Idiom.* **15. go without saying,** to be completely self-evident. **16. that is to say,** in other words; meaning that. —**say′er,** *n.*

say·a·ble (sā′ə bəl), *adj.* **1.** of the sort that can be said or spoken. **2.** capable of being said or stated clearly, effectively, etc.

Say·ers (sā′ərz, sârz), *n.* **Dorothy L(eigh),** 1893–1957, English detective-story writer, essayist, translator, and Christian apologist.

say·ing (sā′ing), *n.* something said, esp. a proverb or maxim.

sa·yo·na·ra (sī′ə när′ə; *Japn.* sä′yō nä′Rä), *interj., n.* farewell; goodbye.

says (sez), *v.* 3rd pers. sing. pres. indic. of SAY.

say'-so', *n., pl.* **say-sos. 1.** one's personal statement or assertion. **2.** right of final authority. **3.** an authoritative statement.

Sb, *Chem. Symbol.* antimony. [< Latin *stibium*]

SBA, Small Business Administration.

Sc, *Chem. Symbol.* scandium.

S.C. 1. Security Council (of the U.N.). **2.** South Carolina. **3.** Supreme Court.

scab (skab), *n., v.,* **scabbed, scab·bing.** —*n.* **1.** the incrustation that forms over a sore or wound during healing. **2.** any mangy skin disease in animals, esp. sheep. **3. a.** a fungal or bacterial disease of plants characterized by crustlike lesions on the affected parts. **b.** one such lesion. **4.** a worker who refuses to join a labor union or to participate in a union strike, who takes a striking worker's place on the job, or the like. **5.** *Slang.* a rascal or scoundrel. —*v.i.* **6.** to become covered with a scab. **7.** to act or work as a scab. —**scab'like'**, *adj.*

scab·bard (skab'ərd), *n.* **1.** a sheath for a sword or the like. —*v.t.* **2.** to put into a scabbard; sheathe.

scab·by (skab'ē), *adj.,* **-bi·er, -bi·est. 1.** covered with scabs; having many scabs. **2.** consisting of scabs. **3.** (of an animal or plant) having scab. **4.** *Informal.* mean or contemptible. —**scab'bi·ly**, *adv.*

sca·bies (skā'bēz, -bē ēz'), *n.* (*used with a sing. v.*) a form of mange caused by the itch mite, *Sarcoptes scabiei*, which burrows into the skin. —**sca'bi·et'ic** (-bē et'ik), *adj.*

scab·rous (skab'rəs), *adj.* **1.** having a rough surface because of minute points or projections. **2.** indecent; obscene: *scabrous books.* **3.** full of difficulties. —**scab'rous·ly**, *adv.*

scad (skad), *n.* Usu., **scads.** a great number or quantity.

scaf·fold (skaf'əld, -ōld), *n.* **1.** a platform or framework for raising workers and materials during the erection, repair, or maintenance of a building or the like. **2.** an elevated platform on which a criminal is executed, usu. by hanging. **3.** any raised platform or stage. **4.** any supporting framework. —*v.t.* **5.** to furnish with a scaffold or scaffolding. **6.** to support by or place on a scaffold.

scaf·fold·ing (skaf'əl ding, -ōl-), *n.* **1.** a scaffold or system of scaffolds. **2.** materials for scaffolds.

scal·a·ble (skā'lə bəl), *adj.* capable of being scaled.

sca·lar (skā'lər), *adj.* **1.** representable by position on a scale or line; having only magnitude: *a scalar variable.* **2.** of, pertaining to, or utilizing a scalar. **3.** ladderlike in arrangement or organization; graduated. —*n.* **4.** a quantity possessing only magnitude. Compare VECTOR (def. 1).

scal·a·wag (skal'ə wag'), *n.* **1.** a scamp; rascal. **2.** a white Southerner who supported Republican policy during Reconstruction, often for personal gain.

scald (skôld), *v.t.* **1.** to burn with or as if with hot liquid or steam. **2.** to subject to the action of boiling liquid or steam. **3.** to heat to a temperature just short of the boiling point: *to scald milk.* **4.** to parboil: *to scald vegetables.* —*v.i.* **5.** to become scalded. —*n.* **6.** a burn caused by the action of hot liquid or steam. **7. a.** a browning of fruit or plant tissue caused by extreme heat or overexposure to the sun. **b.** a browning of fruit caused by a fungus or by improper conditions of growth or storage.

scale¹ (skāl), *n., v.,* **scaled, scal·ing.** —*n.* **1. a.** one of the thin flat horny plates forming the covering of certain animals, as snakes, lizards, and pangolins. **b.** one of the hard bony or dental plates, either flat or denticulate, forming the covering of other animals, as fishes. **2.** any thin platelike piece, lamina, or flake that peels off from a surface, as the skin. **3. a.** Also called **bud scale.** a specialized rudimentary leaf that protects an immature leaf bud. **b.** a thin, dry, membranous part of a plant, as the bract of a catkin. **4.** SCALE INSECT. **5.** a coating, as on the inside of a boiler, formed by the precipitation of salts from the water. **6.** an oxide, esp. an iron oxide, occurring in a scaly form on the surface of metal brought to a high temperature. —*v.t.* **7.** to remove the scales from: *to scale a fish.* **8.** to remove in scales or thin layers. **9.** to encrust with scale. **10.** to skip, as a stone over water. **11.** to remove (calculus) from teeth. —*v.i.* **12.** to come off in scales. **13.** to shed scales. **14.** to become coated with scale.

scale² (skāl), *n., v.,* **scaled, scal·ing.** —*n.* **1.** Often, **scales.** a balance or any of various other instruments or devices for weighing. **2.** either of the pans of a balance. **3. the Scales,** LIBRA. —*v.t.* **4.** to weigh in scales. —*Idiom.* **5. tip the scale(s), a.** to weigh, esp. a large amount: *to tip the scales at 300 lbs.* **b.** to be the crucial deciding factor.

scale³ (skāl), *n., v.,* **scaled, scal·ing.** —*n.* **1.** a progression of steps or degrees. **2.** a series of marks laid down at determinate distances, as along a line, for purposes of measurement or computation: *the scale of a thermometer.* **3. a.** a graduated line, as on a map, representing proportionate size. **b.** the ratio of distances on a map to corresponding values on the surface of the earth. **4.** Also called **union scale.** the minimum wage that can be paid to a particular category of employed persons, as established by a union contract. **5.** any measuring instrument with graduated markings. **6.** the proportion that a representation of an object bears to the object itself: *a model on a scale of one inch to one foot.* **7.** relative size or extent: *planning done on a grand scale.* **8.** a succession of tones ascending or descending according to fixed intervals. **9.** a graded series of tests or tasks for measuring intelligence, achievement, adjustment, etc. **10.** a system of numerical notation: *the decimal scale.* —*v.t.* **11.** to climb up or over. **12.** to make according to scale. **13.** to adjust proportionately; match or relate to some standard or measure. **14.** to measure by or as if by a scale. —*v.i.* **15.** to climb; ascend;

mount. **16.** to advance in a graduated series. **17. scale down** (or **up**), to decrease (or increase) in amount: *to scale down wages.*

scale·down (skāl'doun'), *n.* a reduction according to a fixed scale or proportion. Also called **scale'back'** (-bak').

scale' in'sect, *n.* any of numerous small plant-sucking insects of the superfamily Coccoidea, the males of which are winged and the females wingless and often covered by a waxy secretion resembling scales.

scale' moss', *n.* any of various branched leafy liverworts that grow in damp areas.

sca·lene (skā lēn'), *adj.* **1.** (of a cone or the like) having the axis inclined to the base. **2.** (of a triangle) having three unequal sides.

scale·up (skāl'up'), *n.* an increase according to a fixed scale or proportion: *a scaleup in wages.*

scal·lion (skal'yən), *n.* **1.** any onion that does not form a large bulb; green onion. **2.** SHALLOT. **3.** LEEK.

scal·lop (skol'əp, skal'-), *n.* **1.** any usu. ribbed bivalve mollusk of the family Pectinidae that swims by clapping the fluted shell valves together. **2.** the adductor muscle of certain species of such mollusks, used as food. **3.** one of the shells of such a mollusk, usu. having radial ribs and a wavy outer edge. **4.** a thin slice of meat, esp. veal, flattened by pounding. **5.** any of a series of curved projections cut along an edge, as of a fabric. —*v.t.* **6.** to finish (an edge) with scallops. **7.** to escallop. —*v.i.* **8.** to dredge for scallops.

scallop (def. 3), *Argopecten irradians,* width 2 to 3 in. (5 to 8 cm)

scal·lop·pi·ne or **scal·lo·pi·ni** (skä'lə pē'nē, skal'ə-), *n.* (*used with a sing. or pl. v.*) scallops of meat, esp. veal, floured and sautéed.

scalp (skalp), *n.* **1.** the skin of the upper part of the head, usu. covered with hair. **2.** a part of the human scalp taken from the head of an enemy as a sign of victory. **3.** any token of victory. —*v.t.* **4.** to cut or tear the scalp from. **5. a.** to resell at inflated price: *to scalp tickets.* **b.** to buy and sell (stocks) for quick profit. —*v.i.* **6.** to scalp tickets, stocks, or the like. —**scalp'er**, *n.*

scal·pel (skal'pəl), *n.* a small, light, usu. straight knife used in surgical and anatomical operations and dissections. —**scal·pel'lic** (-pel'ik), *adj.*

scal·y (skā'lē), *adj.,* **-i·er, -i·est. 1.** covered with or abounding in scales or scale. **2.** characterized by or consisting of scales. **3.** peeling or flaking in scales. **4.** shabby; despicable. —**scal'i·ness**, *n.*

scam (skam), *n., v.,* **scammed, scam·ming.** —*n.* **1.** a fraudulent scheme; swindle. —*v.t.* **2.** to cheat; defraud. —**scam'mer**, *n.*

scamp (skamp), *n.* **1.** an unscrupulous person; rascal. **2.** a playful or mischievous young person. —*v.t.* **3.** to do in a hasty, careless manner: *to scamp work.* —**scamp'ish**, *adj.*

scamp·er (skam'pər), *v.i.* **1.** to run or go hastily. **2.** to run playfully about; caper. —*n.* **3.** an act or instance of scampering.

scam·pi (skam'pē, skäm'-), *n., pl.* **-pi. 1.** a large shrimp or prawn. **2.** a dish of these cooked esp. in butter and garlic. [< Italian, pl. of *scampo* a type of shrimp]

scan (skan), *v.,* **scanned, scan·ning,** *n.* —*v.t.* **1.** to examine the particulars of minutely; scrutinize. **2.** to glance at or read hastily: *to scan a page.* **3.** to observe repeatedly or sweepingly: *to scan the horizon.* **4.** to analyze (verse) for its prosodic or metrical structure. **5.** to read (data) for use by a computer or computerized device, esp. using an optical scanner. **6.** to traverse (a surface) with a beam of electrons in order to reproduce or transmit a picture. **7.** to traverse (a region) with a beam from a radar transmitter. **8.** to examine (a body or body part) with a scanner. —*v.i.* **9.** to examine the meter of verse. **10.** (of verse) to conform to the rules of meter. —*n.* **11.** an act or instance of scanning. **12. a.** an examination of the body or a body part using a scanner. **b.** the image or display so obtained. —**scan'na·ble**, *adj.*

scan·dal (skan'dl), *n.* **1.** a disgraceful or discreditable action or circumstance. **2.** an offense caused by a fault or misdeed. **3.** damage to reputation; public disgrace. **4.** defamatory talk; malicious gossip. **5.** a person whose conduct brings disgrace or offense.

scan·dal·ize (skan'dl īz'), *v.t.,* **-ized, -iz·ing.** to shock or horrify by something scandalous.

scan·dal·ous (skan'dl əs), *adj.* **1.** disgraceful; improper or immoral: *scandalous behavior.* **2.** defamatory; libelous. **3.** attracted to scandal: *a scandalous gossip.* —**scan'dal·ous·ly**, *adv.* —**scan'dal·ous·ness**, *n.*

scan'dal sheet', *n.* a newspaper or magazine that emphasizes scandal and gossip.

scan·di·um (skan'dē əm), *n.* a gray, trivalent metallic element occurring in certain rare minerals. *Symbol:* Sc; *at. wt.:* 44.956; *at. no.:* 21; *sp. gr.:* 3.0. [after *Scandinavia*, where it is found]

scan·ner (skan'ər), *n.* **1.** a person or thing that scans. **2.** optical scanner. See under OPTICAL SCANNING. **3.** a radio receiver that continuously tunes to preselected frequencies, broadcasting any signal that it detects. **4.** a device for examining a body, organ, or tissue. Compare CAT SCANNER, PET SCANNER, SONOGRAM.

S

scan′ning elec′tron mi′croscope, *n.* a device in which electrons reflected by a specimen being examined under a moving beam are used to form a magnified, three-dimensional image on a television screen. *Abbr.:* SEM

scan′ning tun′neling mi′croscope, *n.* an electronic microscope that produces images of atomic structures by moving an extremely fine probe over the surface of a material. *Abbr:* STM

scan·sion (skan′shən), *n.* the metrical analysis of verse.

scant (skant), *adj.* **1.** barely sufficient in amount or quantity; meager. **2.** almost as much as indicated: *a scant cupful.* **3.** having an inadequate or limited supply (usu. fol. by *of*): *scant of breath.* **4.** to make scant; diminish. **5.** to stint the supply of; withhold. **6.** to treat slightly or inadequately. —*adv.* **7.** *Dial.* scarcely; barely; hardly. —**scant′ly,** *adv.* —**scant′ness,** *n.*

scant·ling (skant′ling), *n.* **1.** a timber of relatively slight width and thickness, as a stud or rafter in a house frame. **2.** such timbers collectively. **3.** the width and thickness of a timber.

scant·y (skan′tē), *adj.,* **scant·i·er, scant·i·est,** insufficient in amount, extent, or degree. —**scant′i·ly,** *adv.* —**scant′i·ness,** *n.*

-scape, a combining form extracted from LANDSCAPE, with the meaning "an extensive view, scenery," or "a picture or representation" of such a view, as specified by the initial element: *cityscape; moonscape; seascape.*

scape·goat (skāp′gōt′), *n.* **1.** a person or group made to bear the blame for others or to suffer in their place. **2.** a goat let loose in the wilderness on Yom Kippur after the high priest symbolically laid the sins of the people on its head. Lev. 16:8–22. —*v.t.* **3.** to make a scapegoat of. —**scape′goat·ism,** *n.*

scap·o·lite (skap′ə līt′), *n.* any of a group of tetragonal minerals consisting of various silicates of aluminum, calcium, and sodium with chlorine or carbonate, usu. occurring as aggregates in marble.

scap·u·la (skap′yə lə), *n., pl.* **-las, -lae** (-lē′) **1.** either of two flat triangular bones each forming the back part of a shoulder; shoulder blade. **2.** a dorsal bone of the pectoral girdle.

scap·u·lar¹ (skap′yə lər), *adj.* **1.** of or pertaining to the shoulders or the scapula or scapulas. —*n.* **2.** one of the feathers originating from a bird's shoulder.

scap·u·lar² (skap′yə lər), *n.* a loose, sleeveless monastic garment.

scar¹ (skär), *n., v.,* **scarred, scar·ring.** —*n.* **1.** a mark left by a healed wound, sore, or burn. **2.** a blemish remaining as a trace of damage or use. **3.** a mark indicating a former point of attachment, as where a leaf has fallen from a stem. **4.** a lasting aftereffect of a troubling experience. —*v.t.* **5.** to leave a scar on. —*v.i.* **6.** to form a scar in healing.

scar² (skär), *n.* **1.** a precipitous, rocky place; cliff. **2.** a low or submerged rock in the sea.

scar·ab (skar′əb), *n.* **1.** a large, dark beetle, esp. *Scarabaeus sacer.* **2.** a representation or image of a beetle, much used among the ancient Egyptians as a symbol, seal, or amulet. —**scar′a·boid′,** *adj.*

scarce (skârs), *adj.,* **scarc·er, scarc·est,** —*adj.* **1.** insufficient to satisfy the need or demand. **2.** rarely encountered. —*adv.* **3.** scarcely. —*Idiom.* **4. make oneself scarce, a.** to leave, esp. quickly. **b.** to stay away. —**scarce′ness,** *n.*

scarce·ly (skârs′lē), *adv.* **1.** barely; not quite: *We can scarcely see.* **2.** definitely not: *This is scarcely the time to raise such questions.* **3.** probably not: *You could scarcely have chosen better.* —**Usage.** See HARDLY.

scar·ci·ty (skâr′si tē), *n., pl.* **-ties. 1.** insufficiency or shortness of supply; dearth. **2.** rarity; infrequency.

scare (skâr), *v.,* **scared, scar·ing,** *n.* —*v.t.* **1.** to fill, esp. suddenly, with fear; frighten. —*v.i.* **2.** to become frightened. **3. scare up,** to find or procure in spite of difficulties: *Try to scare up some wood for the fire.* —*n.* **4.** a sudden fright or alarm. **5.** a time or condition of alarm or worry: *a war scare.* —**scar′er,** *n.*

scare·crow (skâr′krō′), *n.* **1.** an object, usu. a figure of a person in old clothes, set up to frighten crows or other birds away from crops. **2.** something frightening but not dangerous. **3.** a ragged or extremely thin person.

scared·y-cat (skâr′dē kat′), *n.* a needlessly fearful person.

scarf¹ (skärf), *n., pl.* **scarfs, scarves** (skärvz), *v.* —*n.* **1.** a long, sometimes broad strip of cloth worn about the neck, shoulders, or head for warmth or style. **2.** a long cover or ornamental cloth for a bureau, table, etc. —*v.t.* **3.** to cover or wrap with or as if with a scarf. **4.** to use in the manner of a scarf.

scarf² (skärf), *n., pl.* **scarfs,** *v.* —*n.* **1.** a tapered end on a piece to be assembled with a scarf joint. —*v.t.* **2.** to assemble with a scarf joint. **3.** to form a scarf on (timber). —**scarf′er,** *n.*

scarf³ (skärf), *v.t., v.i. Slang.* to eat, esp. voraciously (often fol. by *down* or *up*): *to scarf down junk food.*

scarf′ joint′, *n.* a joint in which two structural members are joined with long end laps and secured with bolts, straps, keys, fishplates, etc., to resist tension or compression.

scar·i·fy (skar′ə fī′), *v.t.,* **-fied, -fy·ing. 1.** to make scratches or superficial incisions in, as in vaccination. **2.** to wound with severe criticism. **3.** to hasten the sprouting of (hard-covered seeds) by making incisions in the seed coats. **4.** to loosen and break up the surface of (soil or pavement). —**scar′i·fi·ca′tion,** *n.*

scar·la·ti·na (skär′lə tē′nə), *n.* **1.** SCARLET FEVER. **2.** a mild form of scarlet fever. —**scar·la·ti′nal, scar·la·ti·nous** (skär′lə tē′nəs, skär lat′n əs), *adj.*

scar·let (skär′lit), *n.* **1.** a bright red color inclining toward orange. **2.** cloth or clothing of this color. —*adj.* **3.** of the color scarlet.

scar′let fe′ver, *n.* a contagious febrile disease caused by streptococci and characterized by a red rash.

scar′let let′ter, *n.* a scarlet letter "A," formerly worn by one convicted of adultery.

Scar′let Let′ter, The, a novel (1850) by Nathaniel Hawthorne.

scar′let pim′pernel, *n.* See under PIMPERNEL.

scar′let tan′ager, *n.* a tanager, *Piranga olivacea,* that breeds in E North America: the male in spring and summer is scarlet with black wings and tail.

scarp (skärp), *n.* **1.** a line of cliffs formed by the faulting or fracturing of the earth's crust; an escarpment. **2.** ESCARP. —*v.t.* **3.** to form or cut into a steep slope.

scar·ry (skär′ē), *adj.,* **-ri·er, -ri·est.** marked with scars.

scar′ tis′sue, *n.* connective tissue that has contracted and become dense and fibrous, forming a scar.

scarves (skärvz), *n.* a pl. of SCARF¹.

scar·y (skâr′ē), *adj.,* **scar·i·er, scar·i·est. 1.** causing fright or alarm. **2.** easily frightened; timid.

scat¹ (skat), *v.i.,* **scat·ted, scat·ting.** to move or go off hastily.

scat² (skat), *v.,* **scat·ted, scat·ting,** *n.* —*v.i.* **1.** to sing scat. —*n.* **2.** jazz singing using improvised nonsense syllables to imitate the phrasing or effect of a band instrument.

scat³ (skat), *n.* the excrement of an animal.

scathe (skā<u>th</u>), *v.,* **scathed, scath·ing,** *n.* —*v.t.* **1.** to attack with severe criticism. **2.** to injure, as by scorching. —*n.* **3.** harm; injury.

scath·ing (skā′<u>th</u>ing), *adj.* bitterly severe: *a scathing remark.* —**scath′ing·ly,** *adv.*

sca·tol·o·gy (skə tol′ə jē), *n.* **1.** the study of or preoccupation with excrement or obscenity. **2.** obscenity, esp. words or humor referring to excrement. —**scat·o·log·i·cal** (skat′l oj′i kəl), **scat′o·log′ic,** *adj.*

scat·ter (skat′ər), *v.t.* **1.** to throw loosely about: *to scatter seeds.* **2.** to cause to disperse: *to scatter a crowd.* **3.** *Physics.* to diffuse or deflect (a wave or beam of radiation) by collision with particles of the medium it traverses. —*v.i.* **4.** to separate and disperse. —*n.* **5.** the act of scattering. **6.** something that is scattered. —**scat′ter·a·ble,** *adj.*

scat·ter·brain (skat′ər brān′), *n.* a person incapable of serious, connected thought. —**scat′ter·brained′,** *adj.*

scat·ter·ing (skat′ər ing), *adj.* **1.** distributed or dispersing at irregular intervals. **2.** (of votes) cast in small numbers for various candidates. —*n.* **3.** a small, scattered number or quantity. **4.** *Physics.* the process in which a wave or beam of particles is diffused or deflected by collision with particles of the medium that it traverses. —**scat′ter·ing·ly,** *adv.*

scat′ter rug′, *n.* a small rug for random placement. Also called **throw rug.**

scat·ter·shot (skat′ər shot′), *adj.* generalized and indiscriminate: *a scattershot attack.*

scaup (skôp), *n.* any of several diving ducks esp. *A. marila,* of the Northern Hemisphere, having a bluish gray bill.

scav·enge (skav′inj), *v.,* **-enged, -eng·ing.** —*v.t.* **1.** to take or gather (something usable) from discarded material. **2.** to cleanse of filth, as a street. **3.** to expel burnt gases from (the cylinder of an internal-combustion engine). —*v.i.* **4.** to act as a scavenger.

scav·en·ger (skav′in jər), *n.* **1.** an animal or other organism that feeds on dead organic matter. **2.** a person who scavenges for useful material. **3.** a street cleaner. **4.** a chemical that consumes or renders inactive the impurities in a mixture.

scav′enger hunt′, *n.* a game in which individuals or teams are sent out to get without buying a series of objects, the winner being the person or team returning first with all the items.

Sc.D., Doctor of Science. [< L *Scientiae Doctor*]

sce·nar·i·o (si nâr′ē ō′, -när′-), *n., pl.* **-nar·i·os. 1.** an outline of the plot of a dramatic work, giving particulars of the scenes, characters, etc. **2.** the outline or sometimes the complete script of a motion picture or television program, often with directions for shooting. **3.** an imagined sequence of events, esp. any of several detailed plans or possibilities.

scene (sēn), *n.* **1.** the place where some action or event occurs or has occurred: *the scene of the accident.* **2.** any view or picture. **3.** an incident or situation in real life. **4.** an embarrassing display of anger, bad manners, or the like, esp. in public. **5.** a division of a play, film, novel, etc., representing a single episode. **6.** the place where the action of a story, drama, or dramatic episode is supposed to occur. **7.** SCENERY (def. 2). **8.** an area or sphere of activity, current interest, etc.: *the fashion scene.* —*Idiom.* **9. behind the scenes, a.** in secret or in private. **b.** where the full operations or activities of something take place.

scen·er·y (sē′nə rē), *n.* **1.** the general appearance of a place; the features that give character to a landscape. **2.** hangings, structures, etc., used on a stage to portray a locale or furnish decorative background.

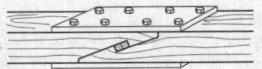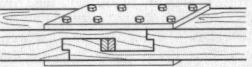

scarf joints

sce·nic (sē′nik, sen′ik) *adj.* **1.** of or pertaining to natural scenery. **2.** having pleasing or beautiful scenery. **3.** of or pertaining to the stage or to stage scenery. **4.** representing a scene, action, or the like.

scent (sent), *n.* **1.** a distinctive odor, esp. when agreeable. **2.** an odor left in passing, by means of which an animal or person may be traced. **3.** a track or trail indicated by such an odor. **4.** perfume. **5.** the sense of smell. —*v.t.* **6.** to perceive or recognize by or as if by the sense of smell: *to scent trouble.* **7.** to fill with an odor; perfume. —*v.i.* **8.** to hunt by the sense of smell, as a hound. —**scent′less,** *adj.*

scent′ mark′, *n.* a distinctive odor that an animal deposits on the ground or other surface as an identifying signal to others of its kind. —**scent′-mark′,** *v.i., v.t.*

scep·ter (sep′tər), *n.* **1.** a rod or wand borne in the hand as an emblem of regal or imperial power. **2.** royal or imperial power or authority; sovereignty. —*v.t.* **3.** to give a scepter to; invest with authority. Also, *esp. Brit.,* **sceptre.**

scepter

scepter (def. 1)

scep·tic (skep′tik), *n., adj.* SKEPTIC.
scep·tre (sep′tər), *n., v.t.,* **-tred, -tring.** *Chiefly Brit.* SCEPTER.
Schaff (shaf), *n.* **Philip,** 1818–93, U.S. theologian.
sched·ule (skej′ōōl, -ōol, -ōō əl; *Brit.* shed′yōol, shej′ōol), *n., v.,* **-uled, -ul·ing.** —*n.* **1.** a plan of procedure, usu. written, for a proposed objective, esp. with reference to the sequence of events and the time allotted for each. **2.** a series of things to be done or of events to occur at or during a particular time or period: *He always has a full schedule.* **3.** a timetable. **4.** a written or printed statement of details, often in tabular form, esp. as an addendum to another document. —*v.t.* **5.** to make a schedule of or enter in a schedule. **6.** to plan for a certain date: *to schedule publication for June.* —**sched′u·lar,** *adj.* —**sched′ul·er,** *n.*
Sche·her·a·za·de (shə her′ə zä′də, -zäd′, -her′-), *n.* (in *The Arabian Nights' Entertainments*) the wife of the sultan of India, who relates such interesting tales nightly that the sultan spares her life.
sche·ma (skē′mə), *n., pl.* **sche·ma·ta** (skē′mə tə *or, sometimes,* skē·mä′tə, ski-), **sche·mas. 1.** a diagram, plan, or scheme. **2.** an underlying organizational pattern or structure; conceptual framework.
sche·mat·ic (skē mat′ik, ski-), *adj.* **1.** pertaining to or of the nature of a schema, diagram, or scheme; diagrammatic. —*n.* **2.** a diagram, plan, or drawing. —**sche·mat′i·cal·ly,** *adv.*
sche·ma·tize (skē′mə tīz′), *v.t.,* **-tized, -tiz·ing.** to reduce to or arrange according to a scheme. —**sche′ma·ti·za′tion,** *n.*
scheme (skēm), *n., v.,* **schemed, schem·ing.** —*n.* **1.** a plan, design, or program of action; project. **2.** an underhand plot; intrigue. **3.** any system of correlated things, parts, etc., or the manner of its arrangement. **4.** an analytical or tabular statement. **5.** a diagram, map, or the like. —*v.t.* **6.** to devise as a scheme; plan; plot; contrive. —*v.i.* **7.** to lay schemes; devise plans; plot. —**schem′er,** *n.*
schem·ing (skē′ming), *adj.* given to making plans, esp. sly and underhand ones; crafty; calculating. —**schem′ing·ly,** *adv.*
scher·zo (skert′sō), *n., pl.* **scher·zos, scher·zi** (skert′sē). a musical movement of playful character, typically in *aba* form.
Schick′ test′, *n.* a diphtheria immunity test in which diphtheria toxoid is injected intracutaneously, nonimmunity being indicated by an inflammation at the site. [after B. *Schick* (1877–1967), U.S. pediatrician]
Schil·ler (shil′ər), *n.* **1. Johann Christoph Friedrich von,** 1759–1805, German poet, dramatist, and historian. **2.** *Astron.* an elliptical walled plain in the third quadrant of the face of the moon: about 112 miles (180 km) in length and 60 miles (96 km) in width.
schil·ling (shil′ing), *n.* the basic monetary unit of Austria.
schip·per·ke (skip′ər kē, -kə), *n.* one of a Belgian breed of small dogs with a foxlike head, erect ears, and a thick black coat.
schism (siz′əm, skiz′-), *n.* **1.** division or disunion, esp. into mutually opposed factions. **2.** the parties so formed. **3. a.** a formal division within, or separation from, a church or religious body over some doctrinal difference. **b.** the state of a sect or body formed by such division. **c.** the offense of causing or seeking to cause such a division.
schis·mat·ic (siz mat′ik, skiz-), *adj.* **1.** Also, **schis·mat′i·cal.** of, pertaining to, or of the nature of schism; guilty of schism. —*n.* **2.** a person who promotes or embraces schism. —**schis·mat′i·cal·ly,** *adv.*
schist (shist), *n.* any of a class of crystalline metamorphic rocks whose constituent mineral grains have a more or less parallel or foliated arrangement.
schizo-, a combining form meaning "split," "fission": *schizogenesis.* Also, *esp. before a vowel,* **schiz-.**
schiz·o·carp (skiz′ə kärp′, skit′sə-), *n.* a dry fruit that at maturity

splits into two or more one-seeded carpels. —**schiz′o·car′pous, schiz′o·car′pic,** *adj.*
schiz·oid (skit′soid), *adj.* **1.** *Psychiatry.* of or pertaining to a personality disorder marked by dissociation, passivity, and indifference to praise or criticism. **2.** of or pertaining to schizophrenia or to multiple personality. —*n.* **3.** a schizoid person.
schiz·o·phre·ni·a (skit′sə frē′nē ə, -frēn′yə), *n.* a severe mental disorder associated with brain abnormalities and typically evidenced by disorganized speech and behavior, delusions, and hallucinations. —**schiz′o·phren′ic** (-fren′ik), *adj., n.* —**schiz′o·phren′i·cal·ly,** *adv.*
Schle·gel (shlā′gəl), *n.* **Katharine von,** 18th century German religious leader and hymn writer.
Schlei·er·ma·cher (shlī′ər mä′kər, -кнаr), *n.* **Friedrich Ernst Daniel,** 1768–1834, German theologian and philosopher.
Schles·in·ger (shles′in jər, shlā′zing ər), *n.* **1. Arthur (Meier),** 1888–1965, U.S. historian. **2.** his son, **Arthur (Meier), Jr.,** born 1917, U.S. historian and writer.
Schles′wig-Hol′stein, *n.* a state of N Germany. 2,564,565; 6073 sq. mi. (15,728 sq. km). *Cap.:* Kiel.
schlock *or* **shlock** (shlok), *n. Slang.* something of cheap or inferior quality. —**schlock′y,** *adj.,* **schlock·i·er, schlock·i·est.**
schmaltz *or* **schmalz** *or* **shmaltz** (shmälts, shmôlts), *n. Informal.* exaggerated sentimentalism, as in music or writing. —**schmaltz′y,** *adj.*
schmear *or* **schmeer** (shmēr), *Slang.* —*n.* **1.** a number of related things, matters, etc.: *to go through the whole schmear.* **2.** a bribe. —*v.t.* **3.** to bribe.
schmooze (shmōōz), *v.,* **schmoozed, schmooz·ing,** *n. Slang.* —*v.i.* **1.** to chat idly; gossip. —*n.* **2.** an idle conversation; chat.
schnau·zer (shnou′zər, shnout′sər), *n.* any of three German breeds of dogs having a tight, wiry, usu. pepper-and-salt or black coat and a rectangular head with bristly eyebrows and beardlike whiskers: the breeds (miniature, standard, and giant) differ chiefly in size.
schnit·zel (shnit′səl), *n.* a cutlet, esp. of veal.
schnoz (shnoz) *also* **schnoz·zle** (shnoz′əl), *n. Slang.* a nose, esp. a large one.
scho·la can·to·rum (skō′lə kan tôr′əm, -tōr′-), *n., pl.* **scho·lae can·torum** (skō′lē). **1.** an ecclesiastical choir or choir school. **2.** a section of a church for use by the choir. [< Medieval Latin: school of singers]
schol·ar (skol′ər), *n.* **1.** a learned or erudite person, esp. one who has profound knowledge of a particular subject. **2.** a student who has been awarded a scholarship. **3.** a student; pupil.
schol·ar·ly (skol′ər lē), *adj.* **1.** of, like, or befitting a scholar. **2.** having the qualities of a scholar. **3.** concerned with academic learning. —*adv.* **4.** like a scholar. —**schol′ar·li·ness,** *n.*
schol·ar·ship (skol′ər ship′), *n.* **1.** the qualities, skills, or attainments of a scholar. **2.** a gift of money to enable a student to pursue his or her studies. **3.** the accumulated knowledge of a group of scholars.
scho·las·tic (skə las′tik), *adj.* Also, **scho·las′ti·cal. 1.** of or pertaining to schools, scholars, or education. **2.** of or pertaining to secondary schools: *a scholastic meet.* **3.** pedantic. —*n.* **4.** a pedantic person.
Scholas′tic Assess′ment Test′, a standardized academic assessment used for college admissions. *Abbr.:* SAT
scho·las·ti·cism (skə las′tə siz′əm), *n.* **1.** (*sometimes cap.*) the system of theological and philosophical teaching predominant in the Middle Ages, based chiefly upon the authority of the church fathers and of Aristotle and his commentators. **2.** narrow adherence to traditional teachings, doctrines, or methods.
Schön·berg (shœn′bûrg), *n.* **Arnold,** 1874–1951, U.S. composer, born in Austria.
school¹ (skōōl), *n.* **1.** an institution for teaching persons under college age. **2.** a college or university. **3.** an institution or academic department for instruction in a particular subject or field. **4.** a systematic program of studies: *summer school.* **5.** the activity of teaching or of learning under instruction: *No school today!* **6.** the body of persons belonging to an educational institution: *The whole school applauded.* **7.** a building, room, etc., housing an academic department or institution. **8.** any place, situation, etc., that instructs or indoctrinates. **9.** the body of pupils or followers of a master, system, etc.: *the Platonic school of philosophy.* **10. a.** a group of artists whose works reflect a common conceptual, regional, or personal influence. **b.** the art and artists of a geographical location considered independently of stylistic similarity. **11.** any group of persons having common beliefs. —*adj.* **12.** of or connected with a school or schools. —*v.t.* **13.** to educate in or as if in a school; teach; train.
school² (skōōl), *n.* **1.** a large number of fish, porpoises, whales, or the like, feeding or migrating together. —*v.i.* **2.** to form into, or go in, a school, as fish.
school′ age′, *n.* **1.** the age set by law for children to start school attendance. **2.** the period of school attendance required by law. —**school′-age′,** *adj.*
school′ board′, *n.* a local board or committee in charge of public education.
school′ day′, *n.* **1.** any day on which school is conducted. **2.** the daily hours during which school is conducted.
school′ fig′ure, *n.* one of a group of figures formerly required to be performed by ice skaters in a competition.
school·house (skōōl′hous′), *n., pl.* **-hous·es** (-hou′ziz). a building in which a school is conducted.

school·ing (skōō′ling), *n.* instruction, education, or training, esp. when received in a school.

school·mas·ter (skōōl′mas′tər, -mä′stər), *n.* **1.** a man who teaches in a school. **2.** anything that teaches or directs. **3.** a snapper, *Lutjanus apodus*, a food fish found in Florida, the West Indies, etc.

school·room (skōōl′rōōm′, -rŏŏm′), *n.* a room in which a class is conducted or pupils are taught.

school·teach·er (skōōl′tē′chər), *n.* a teacher in a school, esp. in one below the college level. —**school′teach′ing,** *n.*

school·work (skōōl′wûrk′), *n.* the material studied in or for school, comprising homework and work done in class.

school·yard (skōōl′yärd′), *n.* a playground or sports field near a school.

school′ year′, *n.* the months of the year during which school is open and attendance at school is required.

schoon·er (skōō′nər), *n.* **1.** any of various types of sailing vessel having a foremast and mainmast, with or without other masts, and having fore-and-aft sails on all lower masts. **2.** a very tall glass, as for beer.

schooner (def. 1)

schrod (skrod), *n.* SCROD.

schtick (shtik), *n. Slang.* SHTICK.

Schu·bert (shōō′bərt, -bert), *n.* **Franz,** 1797–1828, Austrian composer.

Schul·ler (shōō′lər), *n.* **Robert,** born 1916, U.S. evangelist.

Schulz (shŏŏlts), *n.* **Charles M(onroe),** born 1922, U.S. cartoonist.

Schu·mann (shōō′män), *n.* **1. Clara,** (*Clara Wieck*), 1819–96, German pianist and composer (wife of Robert Schumann). **2. Robert,** 1810–56, German composer.

schuss (shŏŏs, shōōs), *n.* **1.** a straight downhill ski run at high speed. —*v.i.* **2.** to execute a schuss. —*v.t.* **3.** to schuss over. —**schus′ser,** *n.*

Schuy·ler (skī′lər), *n.* **Philip John,** 1733–1804, American statesman and general in the Revolutionary War.

Schuy·ler·ville (skī′lər vil′), *n.* a village in E New York, on the Hudson: scene of Burgoyne's defeat and surrender in the Battle of Saratoga 1777. 1256. Formerly, **Saratoga.**

schwa or **shwa** (shwä), *n., pl.* **schwas** or **shwas. 1.** the mid-central, neutral vowel sound typically occurring in unstressed syllables in English, as the sound of *a* in *alone* and *sofa* or *u* in *circus.* **2.** the phonetic symbol ə, used to represent this sound.

Schweit·zer (shwīt′sər, shvīt′-), *n.* **Albert,** 1875–1965, Alsatian writer, missionary, doctor, and musician in Africa.

Schwenk·feld·er (shfengk′fel′dər, shvengk′-), *n.* a member of a Protestant group that emigrated in 1734 from Germany and settled in Pennsylvania, where they organized the Schwenkfelder Church. [< German, after Kaspar von *Schwenkfeld* (1490–1561), German mystic]

sci·at·ic (sī at′ik), *adj.* of, pertaining to, situated near, or affecting the ischium or back of the hip or the sciatic nerves.

sci·at·i·ca (sī at′i kə), *n.* pain involving the sacral plexus or sciatic nerve, often felt in the lower back and along the back of the thigh.

sciat′ic nerve′, *n.* either of a pair of nerves that originate in the sacral plexus of the lower back and extend down the buttocks to the back of the knees, where they divide into other nerves. [1735–45]

sci·ence (sī′əns), *n.* **1.** a branch of knowledge or study dealing with a body of facts or truths systematically arranged and showing the operation of general laws. **2.** systematic knowledge of the physical or material world gained through observation and experimentation. **3.** any of the branches of natural or physical science. **4.** systematized knowledge in general. **5.** knowledge, as of facts or principles; knowledge gained by systematic study. **6.** a particular branch of knowledge. **7.** any skill or technique that reflects a precise application of facts or principles.

sci′ence fic′tion, *n.* a form of fiction that draws imaginatively on scientific knowledge and speculation.

sci·en·tif·ic (sī′ən tif′ik), *adj.* **1.** of, pertaining to, or concerned with a science or the sciences. **2.** regulated by or conforming to the principles of exact science. **3.** systematic or accurate in the manner of an exact science. —**sci′en·tif′i·cal·ly,** *adv.*

scientif′ic meth′od, *n.* a method of research in which a problem is identified, relevant data are gathered, a hypothesis is formulated, and the hypothesis is empirically tested.

sci·en·tist (sī′ən tist), *n.* an expert in science, esp. one of the physical or natural sciences.

sci-fi (sī′fī′), *n., adj. Informal.* science fiction.

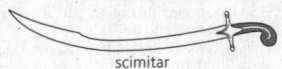
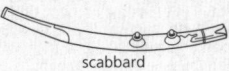

scimitar · · · · · · · · · · · · · · · scabbard

scimitar

scim·i·tar or **scim·i·ter** (sim′i tər), *n.* a curved, single-edged sword of Oriental origin.

scin·til·la (sin til′ə), *n., pl.* **-las.** a minute particle; spark; trace: *not a scintilla of remorse.*

scin·til·late (sin′tl āt′), *v.,* **-lat·ed, -lat·ing.** —*v.i.* **1.** to emit sparks. **2.** to be animated or witty; sparkle. **3.** to twinkle, as the stars. —*v.t.* **4.** to emit as sparks; flash. —**scin′til·lant,** *adj.* —**scin′til·lat′ing·ly,** *adv.*

scin·til·la·tion (sin′tl ā′shən), *n.* **1.** the act of scintillating. **2.** a spark or flash. **3.** the twinkling or tremulous effect of the light of the stars. **4.** a flash of light from the ionization of a phosphor struck by an energetic photon or particle.

sci·on (sī′ən), *n.* **1.** a descendant or offspring, esp. of an illustrious family. **2.** a shoot or twig, esp. one cut for grafting or planting.

scis·sion (sizh′ən, sish′-), *n.* **1.** a cutting, dividing, or splitting; division; separation.

scis·sor (siz′ər), *v.t.* **1.** to cut or clip out with scissors. —*v.i.* **2.** to move one's body or legs like the blades of scissors. —*n.* **3.** SCISSORS.

scis·sors (siz′ərz), *n.* **1.** (*used with a sing. or pl. v.*) a cutting instrument for paper, cloth, etc., consisting of two blades, each having a ring-shaped handle, that are so pivoted together that their sharp edges work one against the other (often used with *pair of*). **2.** (*used with a sing. v.*) **a.** any of several gymnastic feats in which the legs execute a scissorlike motion. **b.** a wrestling hold secured by clasping the legs around the body or head of the opponent. —**scis′sor·like′,** *adj.*

scis′sors kick′, *n.* a swimmer's scissorlike motion of the legs, as in the sidestroke.

SCLC or **S.C.L.C.,** Southern Christian Leadership Conference.

scle·ro·sis (skli rō′sis), *n., pl.* **-ses** (-sēz). **1.** a hardening of a body tissue or part, or an increase of connective tissue or the like at the expense of more active tissue. **2.** a hardening of a plant tissue or cell wall by thickening or becoming woody. —**scle·ro′sal,** *adj.*

Sc.M., Master of Science. [< Latin *Scientiae Magister*]

scoff¹ (skôf, skof), *n.* **1.** to speak derisively; mock; jeer (often fol. by *at*). —*v.t.* **2.** to mock at; deride. —*n.* **3.** an expression of mockery, derision, doubt, or derisive scorn. **4.** an object of mockery or derision. —**scoff′er,** *n.* —**scoff′ing·ly,** *adv.*

scoff² (skôf, skof), *Slang.* —*v.i., v.t.* **1.** to eat voraciously. —*n.* **2.** food; grub.

scoff·law (skôf′lô′, skof′-), *n.* a person who flouts the law, esp. one who fails to pay fines owed.

scold (skōld), *v.t.* **1.** to find fault with angrily; chide; reprimand. —*v.i.* **2.** to find fault angrily; reprove. **3.** to use abusive language. —*n.* **4.** a person who is constantly scolding, often with loud and abusive speech. —**scold′er,** *n.*

sconce¹ (skons), *n.* a bracket for candles or other lights, placed on a wall, mirror, picture frame, etc.

sconce² (skons), *n.* a small detached fort or defensive work, as to defend a gate or bridge.

scone (skōn, skon), *n.* **1.** a light, biscuitlike quick bread, often baked on a griddle. **2.** biscuit (def. 1).

Scone (skōōn, skōn), *n.* **1.** a village in central Scotland: site of coronation of Scottish kings. **2. Stone of,** a stone, formerly at Scone, Scotland, upon which Scottish kings sat at coronation, now placed beneath the coronation chair in Westminster Abbey.

scoop (skōōp), *n.* **1.** a ladle or ladlelike utensil, esp. a small shovel with a short handle, for taking up flour, sugar, etc. **2.** a utensil composed of a bowl attached to a handle, for dishing out ice cream or other soft foods. **3.** the bucket of a dredge, steam shovel, etc. **4.** the quantity held or taken up in a scoop. **5.** a hollow or hollowed-out place. **6.** the act of scooping; a scooping movement. **7.** a news item revealed in one newspaper, newscast, etc., before all others. **8.** *Informal.* current information; news: *What's the scoop on the new chairman?* **9.** *Informal.* a big haul, as of money. —*v.t.* **10.** to take up or out with or as if with a scoop. **11.** to empty with a scoop. **12.** to form a hollow or hollows in. **13.** to form with or as if with a scoop. **14.** to pick up or gather by a sweeping motion of one's arms or hands (often fol. by *up*). **15.** to reveal a news item before (one's competitors). —**scoop′er,** *n.*

scoot (skōōt), *v.i.* **1.** to go swiftly or hastily; dart. —*v.t.* **2.** to send or impel at high speed. —*n.* **3.** a swift, darting movement or course.

scoot·er (skōō′tər), *n.* **1.** a child's vehicle that typically has two wheels with a low footboard between them, is steered by a handlebar, and is propelled by pushing one foot against the ground while resting the other on the footboard. **2.** Also called **motor scooter.** a similar but larger and heavier vehicle for adults, propelled by a motor and having a saddlelike seat mounted on the footboard.

scope (skōp), *n., v.,* **scoped, scop·ing.** —*n.* **1.** extent or range of view, outlook, application, operation, effectiveness, etc.: *an investigation of wide scope.* **2.** opportunity or freedom for movement or activity: *to give one's fancy full scope.* **3.** extent in space; a tract or area. **4.** length: *a*

scope of cable. 5. (used as a short form of *microscope, periscope, radarscope,* etc.) **6.** *Ling., Logic.* the range of words or elements of an expression over which a modifier or operator can control: *In "old men and women," "old" may either take "men and women" or just "men" in its scope.* **7.** aim or purpose. —*v.t.* **8.** *Slang.* to look at or over; examine (often fol. by *out*).

-scope, a combining form meaning "instrument for viewing": *telescope.*

Scopes (skōps), *n.* **John Thomas,** 1901–70, U.S. high-school teacher whose teaching of the Darwinian theory of evolution became a cause célèbre **(Scopes/ Tri/al** or **Monkey Trial)** in 1925.

-scopy, a combining form meaning "examination," "measurement" (*cryoscopy; radioscopy*), also forming abstract nouns corresponding to nouns ending in -SCOPE (*spectroscopy; telescopy*).

scorch (skôrch), *v.t.* **1.** to burn slightly so as to affect color, taste, etc. **2.** to parch or shrivel with heat. **3.** to criticize severely. —*v.i.* **4.** to become scorched. **5.** *Informal.* to travel or drive at high speed. —*n.* **6.** a superficial burn.

scorched/-earth/ pol/icy, *n.* a military practice of devastating the property and agriculture of an area before abandoning it to an advancing enemy.

scorch•er (skôr/chər), *n.* **1.** a person or thing that scorches. **2.** *Informal.* a very hot day. **3.** something caustic or severe.

score (skōr, skôr), *n., pl.* **scores; score** for 10; *v.,* **scored, scor•ing.** —*n.* **1.** the record of points or strokes made by the competitors in a game or contest. **2.** the total points or strokes made by one side or competitor. **3.** the performance of an individual or group on an examination or test, expressed by a number or other symbol. **4.** a notch, scratch, or incision. **5.** a notch or mark for keeping an account or record. **6.** a reckoning or account so kept; tally. **7.** any account showing indebtedness. **8.** an amount recorded as due. **9.** a line drawn as a boundary, the starting point of a race, etc. **10.** a group or set of 20. **11. scores,** a great many. **12.** a reason, ground, or cause: *to complain on the score of low pay.* **13.** *Informal.* **a.** the basic facts of a situation: *What's the score on Saturday's picnic?* **b.** a successful move, remark, etc. **14. a.** a written or printed piece of music with the vocal and instrumental parts arranged on staves, one under the other. **b.** the music for a movie, play, or television show. **15.** *Slang.* **a.** a successful robbery. **b.** the victim of a robbery or swindle. —*v.t.* **16.** to make, gain, or earn in a game, as points or hits. **17.** to get a score of: *He scored 98 on the test.* **18.** to have as a specified value in points: *Four aces score 100.* **19.** to evaluate the responses a person has made on (a test or examination). **20.** *Music.* **a.** to orchestrate. **b.** to compose the music for (a movie, play, television show, etc.). **21.** to cut shallow ridges into (meat, fish, etc.), usu. in diamond patterns. **22.** to make notches, cuts, marks, or lines in or on. **23.** to keep a record of (points, items, etc.). **24.** to write down as a debt. **25.** to record as a debtor. **26.** to achieve or win: *The play scored a great success.* **27.** *Slang.* to steal. **28.** to berate or censure. **29.** to crease (paper or cardboard) in order to facilitate bending. —*v.i.* **30.** to make, gain, or earn points, hits, etc., in a game or contest. **31.** to keep score, as of a game. **32.** to achieve an advantage or success. **33.** to make notches, cuts, lines, etc. **34.** to run up a score or debt. —*Idiom.* **35. pay off** or **settle a score,** to avenge a wrong; retaliate. —**scor/er,** *n.*

score•board (skōr/bôrd/, skôr/bōrd/), *n.* a large board in a ballpark, sports arena, or the like that shows the score of a contest and other relevant information.

score•card (skōr/kärd/, skôr/-), *n.* a card for keeping score of a sports contest and, esp. in team sports, for identifying the players.

score•keep•er (skōr/kē/pər, skôr/-), *n.* an official of a sports contest who keeps record of the score.

scorn (skôrn), *n.* **1.** open or unqualified contempt; disdain. **2.** an object of derision or contempt. **3.** a derisive or contemptuous action or speech. —*v.t.* **4.** to treat or regard with contempt or disdain. **5.** to reject or refuse with contempt or disdain: *She scorned my help.* —*v.i.* **6.** to mock; jeer. —**scorn/er,** *n.*

scorn•ful (skôrn/fəl), *adj.* full of scorn; derisive; contemptuous. —**scorn/ful•ly,** *adv.* —**scorn/ful•ness,** *n.*

Scor•pi•o (skôr/pē ō/), *n.* **1.** SCORPIUS. **2.** the eighth sign of the zodiac. [< Latin: scorpion]

scor•pi•on (skôr/pē ən), *n.* **1.** any arachnid of the order Scorpiones, common in warm climates, having a front pair of pincers and a long, upcurved tail that ends in a venomous stinger. **2.** *Bible.* a whip or scourge. I Kings 12:11.

scorpion, *Centruroides sculpturatus,*
length ¼ in. (0.6 cm)

scor•pi•on•fish (skôr/pē ən fish/), *n., pl.* (*esp. collectively*) **-fish,** (*esp. for kinds or species*) **-fish•es.** any of several tropical and temperate marine fishes, esp. members of the genus *Scorpaena,* many having venomous dorsal spines. Also called **sea scorpion, rockfish.**

Scor•pi•us (skôr/pē əs) also **Scorpio,** *n., gen.* **-pi•i** (-pē ī/). the Scorpion, a zodiacal constellation between Libra and Sagittarius, containing the bright star Antares.

scot (skot), *n.* an assessment or tax.

Scot (skot), *n.* **1.** a native or inhabitant of Scotland. **2.** a member of a group of Irish raiders who shortly before A.D. 500 established a kingdom in the territory of modern Argyll, introducing Gaelic speech and Irish Christianity to the area that became Scotland.

Scot., 1. Scotland. **2.** Scottish.

scotch (skoch), *v.t.* **1.** to put an end to; crush; foil: *to scotch a rumor.* **2.** to cut, gash, or score. **3.** to injure so as to make harmless. **4.** to block or prop with a wedge or chock. —*n.* **5.** a cut, gash, or score. **6.** a block or wedge put under a wheel, barrel, etc., to prevent slipping.

Scotch (skoch), *adj.* **1.** of Scottish origin; regarded as characteristic of Scotland or the Scottish people. **2.** *Sometimes Offensive.* SCOTTISH (def. 1). **3.** (*usu. l.c.*) frugal; provident. —*n.* **4.** (*used with a pl. v.*) *Sometimes Offensive.* the inhabitants of Scotland; the Scots. **5.** (*often l.c.*) SCOTCH WHISKY.

Scotch/ broom/, *n.* the broom, *Cytisus scoparius.*

Scotch/ pine/, *n.* a pine, *Pinus sylvestris,* of Eurasia, having a reddish trunk and twisted, bluish green needles.

Scotch/ tape/, *Trademark.* a brand name for various transparent or semitransparent adhesive tapes made chiefly of cellulose acetate or cellophane.

Scotch/ ter/rier, *n.* SCOTTISH TERRIER.

Scotch/ whis/ky, *n.* whiskey distilled in Scotland, esp. from malted barley in a pot still.

Scotch/ wood/cock, *n.* toast spread with anchovy paste and topped with scrambled eggs.

sco•ter (skō/tər), *n., pl.* **-ters,** (*esp. collectively*) **-ter.** any of the large diving ducks of the genus *Melanitta,* inhabiting N parts of the Northern Hemisphere.

scot/-free/, *adj.* **1.** free from harm, restraint, punishment, or obligation. **2.** free from payment of scot.

Scot•land (skot/lənd), *n.* a division of the United Kingdom in the N part of Great Britain. 5,035,315; 30,412 sq. mi. (78,772 sq. km). *Cap.:* Edinburgh.

Scot/land Yard/, *n.* **1.** a street in London, England: formerly the site of the London police headquarters, which were removed in 1890 to a Thames embankment **(New Scotland Yard). 2.** the London police, esp. the branch engaged in crime detection.

Scots (skots), *n.* **1.** any of the dialects of English spoken historically in the Lowlands of Scotland: influenced increasingly by the English of S England since the late 16th century. —*adj.* **2.** SCOTTISH.

Scott (skot), *n.* **1. Dred,** 1795?–1858, a black slave whose suit for freedom (1857) was denied by the U.S. Supreme Court. **2. Robert Falcon,** 1868–1912, British naval officer and explorer. **3. Sir Walter,** 1771–1832, Scottish author. **4. Walter,** 1791–1861, U.S. religious leader, founder of the Christian Church (Disciples of Christ). **5. Winfield,** 1786–1866, U.S. general.

Scot•tish (skot/ish), *adj.* **1.** of or pertaining to Scotland or its inhabitants. —*n.* **2.** (*used with a pl. v.*) the inhabitants of Scotland; the Scots. **3.** SCOTS.

Scot/tish Gael/ic or **Scots Gaelic,** *n.* a Celtic language, closely related to Irish, spoken in the Hebrides and the Highlands of Scotland.

Scot/tish Psal/ter, *n.* a collection (1650) of metrical psalms published in Scotland.

Scot/tish ter/rier, *n.* one of a Scottish breed of small, stocky terriers having short legs, a large, square-jawed head with bushy eyebrows and whiskers, and a hard, wiry, often black coat.

Scottish terrier,
10 in. (25 cm) high at shoulder

Scotts•dale (skots/dāl/), *n.* a city in central Arizona. 152,439.

scoun•drel (skoun/drəl), *n.* **1.** an unprincipled, dishonorable person; villain. —*adj.* **2.** mean or base in nature; villainous; dishonorable. —**scoun/drel•ly,** *adj.*

scour¹ (skou²r, skou/ər), *v.t.* **1.** to cleanse or polish by hard rubbing, as with an abrasive material. **2.** to remove (dirt, grease, etc.) from something by hard rubbing. **3.** to clear or dig out (a channel, drain, etc.), as by the force of water. **4.** to purge thoroughly, as an animal. **5.** to clear or rid of what is undesirable. **6.** to remove by or as if by cleansing; get rid of. **7.** to clean or rid of debris, impurities, etc., by or as if by washing, as cotton or wool. —*v.i.* **8.** to cleanse or polish a surface by hard rubbing. **9.** to become clean and shiny when scoured. —*n.* **10.** the act of scouring. **11.** the place scoured. **12.** an implement or preparation used in scouring. **13.** the eroding force of moving water. **14.** Usu. **scours.** (*used with a sing. or pl. v.*) diarrhea in horses and cattle caused by intestinal infection. —**scour/er,** *n.*

scour² (skou²r, skou/ər), *v.t.* **1.** to range over, as in search: *to scour the countryside for a lost child.* **2.** to run or pass quickly over or along. —*v.i.* **3.** to range about, as in search of something. **4.** to move rapidly or energetically. —**scour/er,** *n.*

scourge (skûrj), *n., v.,* **scourged, scourg•ing.** —*n.* **1.** a whip or lash, esp. for the infliction of punishment. **2.** a person or thing that administers punishment or criticism. **3.** a cause of affliction or calamity: *the scourge of famine.* —*v.t.* **4.** to whip with a scourge. **5.** to punish, chastise, or criticize severely.

scout[1] (skout), *n.* **1.** a soldier, warship, airplane, etc., employed in reconnoitering. **2.** a person sent out to obtain information. **3.** a person employed to discover new talent, as in sports or the entertainment field. **4.** a person who observes and reports on the tactics, players, etc., of rival teams. **5.** the act of reconnoitering. **6.** (*sometimes cap.*) a Boy Scout or Girl Scout. **7.** *Informal.* a person: *a good scout.* **8.** a student's servant at Oxford University. —*v.i.* **9.** to act as a scout; reconnoiter. **10.** to make a search; hunt. **11.** to work as a talent scout. —*v.t.* **12.** to examine, inspect, or observe for the purpose of obtaining information; reconnoiter. **13.** to seek; search for (usu. fol. by *out* or *up*): *to scout up a date for Friday night.* **14.** to find by seeking or searching (usu. fol. by *out* or *up*): *Scout out a good book for me to read.* —**scout′er,** *n.*

scout[2] (skout), *v.t.* **1.** to reject or dismiss with scorn or derision. —*v.i.* **2.** to scoff; jeer.

scout•ing (skou′ting), *n.* **1.** the activities of a scout. **2.** (*often cap.*) the program of activities of the Boy Scouts or Girl Scouts.

scout•mas•ter (skout′mas′tər, -mä′stər), *n.* the adult leader of a troop of Boy Scouts.

scow (skou), *n.* any of various vessels having a flat-bottomed rectangular hull with sloping ends, as barges, rowboats, or sailboats.

scowl (skoul), *v.i.* **1.** to draw down or contract the brows in a sullen, displeased, or angry manner. **2.** to have a gloomy or threatening look. —*v.t.* **3.** to affect or express with a scowl. —*n.* **4.** a scowling expression, look, or aspect. —**scowl′er,** *n.*

scrab•ble (skrab′əl), *v.,* **-bled, -bling,** *n.* —*v.i.* **1.** to scratch or dig frantically with the hands or claws. **2.** to struggle in a disorderly way; scramble. —*v.t.* **3.** to scratch or scrape, as with the claws or hands. **4.** to gather hastily; scrape together. **5.** to scrawl; scribble. —*n.* **6.** a scratching or scraping, as with the claws or hands. **7.** a scrawled or scribbled writing. **8.** a disorderly struggle for possession of something; scramble. —**scrab′bler,** *n.*

Scrab•ble (skrab′əl), *Trademark.* a board game in which players form words with lettered tiles having various point values.

scrag (skrag), *n., v.,* **scragged, scrag•ging.** —*n.* **1.** a lean or scrawny person or animal. **2.** the lean end of a neck of veal or mutton. **3.** *Slang.* the neck of a human being. —*v.t.* **4.** *Slang.* to wring the neck of; hang; garrote.

scrag•gly (skrag′lē), *adj.,* **-gli•er, -gli•est.** **1.** irregular; uneven; jagged. **2.** shaggy; ragged; unkempt.

scram[1] (skram), *v.i.,* **scrammed, scram•ming.** *Informal.* to go away; get out (usu. used imperatively).

scram[2] (skram), *n.* the rapid shutdown of a nuclear reactor in an emergency.

scram•ble (skram′bəl), *v.,* **-bled, -bling,** *n.* —*v.i.* **1.** to climb or move quickly using one's hands and feet, as down a rough incline. **2.** to compete or struggle with others for possession or gain. **3.** to move hastily and with urgency. **4.** (of pilots or aircraft) to take off quickly to intercept enemy planes. —*v.t.* **5.** to collect or organize (things) in a hurried or disorderly manner. **6.** to mix together confusedly. **7.** to cause to move hastily. **8.** to fry (eggs) while constantly stirring together whites and yolks. **9.** to make (a radio or telephonic message) incomprehensible to interceptors by systematically changing the transmission frequencies. **10.** to mix the elements of (a television signal) so that only subscribers with a decoding box can receive the signal. **11.** to cause (an intercepting aircraft or pilot) to take off as quickly as possible. —*n.* **12.** a quick climb or progression over rough, irregular ground. **13.** a struggle for possession or gain. **14.** any disorderly or hasty struggle or proceeding. **15.** a quick emergency takeoff of an intercepting aircraft.

scram•bler (skram′blər), *n.* **1.** a person or thing that scrambles. **2.** an electronic device that mixes telecommunications signals to make them unintelligible without a corresponding device in the receiving apparatus.

scrap[1] (skrap), *n., adj., v.,* **scrapped, scrap•ping.** —*n.* **1.** a small piece or portion; fragment. **2. scraps, a.** bits of food, esp. of leftover food. **b.** the remains of animal fat after the oil has been tried out. **3.** a detached piece of something written or printed: *scraps of poetry.* **4.** discarded or leftover material that can be reused in some way, as metal that can be melted and reworked. —*adj.* **5.** consisting of scraps or scrap. **6.** discarded or left over. —*v.t.* **7.** to make into scrap; break up. **8.** to discard as useless or worthless.

scrap[2] (skrap), *n., v.,* **scrapped, scrap•ping.** *Informal.* —*n.* **1.** a fight or quarrel. —*v.i.* **2.** to engage in a fight or quarrel.

scrap•book (skrap′bo͝ok′), *n.* an album in which pictures, newspaper clippings, etc., may be pasted or mounted.

scrape (skrāp), *v.,* **scraped, scrap•ing,** *n.* —*v.t.* **1.** to rub (a surface) with something rough or sharp, as to clean or smooth it. **2.** to remove by rubbing with something rough or sharp. **3.** to scratch, injure, or mar by brushing against something rough or sharp. **4.** to produce by scratching or scraping. **5.** to gather laboriously or with difficulty (usu. fol. by *up* or *together*). **6.** to rub roughly on or across (something). **7.** to draw or rub (a thing) roughly across something. **8.** to level (an unpaved road) with a grader. —*v.i.* **9.** to scrape something. **10.** to rub against something gratingly. **11.** to produce a grating and unmusical tone from a string instrument. **12.** to manage or get by with difficulty. **13.** to economize or save by attention to even the slightest amounts. —*n.* **14.** an act or instance of scraping. **15.** a harsh, shrill, or scratching sound made by scraping. **16.** a scraped place. **17.** an embarrassing or distressing situation. **18.** a fight or quarrel; scrap. —**scrap′er,** *n.*

scrap′ heap′ or **scrap′heap′,** *n.* a pile of old, discarded material.

scrap•ing (skrā′ping), *n.* **1.** the act of a person or thing that scrapes. **2.** the sound of something being scraped. **3.** Usu., **scrapings.** something that is scraped off, up, or together.

scrap•per (skrap′ər), *n.* *Informal.* a person who is always ready and eager for a fight or argument.

scrap•ple (skrap′əl), *n.* cornmeal mush combined with pork bits, seasoned, and sliced for frying.

scrap•py[1] (skrap′ē), *adj.,* **-pi•er, -pi•est.** made up of scraps or of odds and ends; fragmentary; disconnected. —**scrap′pi•ly,** *adv.* —**scrap′pi•ness,** *n.*

scrap•py[2] (skrap′ē), *adj.,* **-pi•er, -pi•est.** *Informal.* fond of fighting or arguing.

scratch (skrach), *v.t.* **1.** to break, mar, or mark the surface of by rubbing, scraping, or tearing with something sharp or rough. **2.** to remove with a scraping or tearing action. **3.** to scrape slightly, as with the fingernails, to relieve itching. **4.** to rub or draw along a rough, grating surface. **5.** to strike out (something written) by or as if by drawing a line through it. **6.** to withdraw (an entry) from a race or contest. **7.** to strike out the name of (a candidate) on a party ticket, while predominantly supporting the ticket. **8.** to write or draw by cutting into a surface. —*v.i.* **9.** to use the nails, claws, etc., for tearing, digging, etc. **10.** to relieve itching by rubbing with the nails, etc. **11.** to make a slight grating noise; scrape. **12.** to earn a living or get along with difficulty. **13.** to withdraw from a race or contest. **14.** (in certain card games) to make no score; earn no points. **15.** *Billiards, Pool.* to make a shot that results in a penalty, esp. to pocket the cue ball without hitting the object ball. —*n.* **16.** a slight injury, mar, or mark caused by scratching. **17.** a rough mark made by a pen, pencil, etc.; scrawl. **18.** the act of scratching. **19.** a slight grating sound produced by scratching. **20.** the starting place, starting time, or status of a competitor in a handicap who has no allowance and no penalty. **21.** *Billiards, Pool.* **a.** a shot resulting in a penalty. **b.** a fluke or lucky shot. **22.** (in certain card games) a score of zero; nothing. **23.** *Slang.* MONEY. —*adj.* **24.** used for hasty writing, notes, etc.: *scratch paper.* **25.** without any allowance, penalty, or handicap, as a competitor. **26.** gathered hastily and indiscriminately: *a scratch crew.* —***Idiom.*** **27. from scratch, a.** from the very beginning or from nothing. **b.** using basic components or ingredients rather than prefabricated ones: *to bake a cake from scratch.* **28. up to scratch,** as good as the standard; satisfactory. —**scratch′er,** *n.*

scratch′ sheet′, *n.* a publication giving betting odds and other information on horse races.

scratch′ test′, *n.* a test for an allergy in which the skin is scratched and an allergen applied to the area.

scratch•y (skrach′ē), *adj.,* **-i•er, -i•est.** **1.** causing a slight grating noise. **2.** consisting of or marked by scratches: *a scratchy drawing.* **3.** uneven; haphazard. **4.** causing or liable to cause a scratch or minor irritation. —**scratch′i•ness,** *n.*

scrawl (skrôl), *v.t.* **1.** to write or draw in a sprawling, awkward manner. —*v.i.* **2.** to write awkwardly, carelessly, or illegibly. —*n.* **3.** awkward, careless, or illegible handwriting. **4.** something scrawled. —**scrawl′er,** *n.* —**scrawl′y,** *adj.*

scrawn•y (skrô′nē), *adj.,* **-i•er, -i•est.** excessively thin; lean. —**scrawn′i•ness,** *n.*

scream (skrēm), *v.i.* **1.** to utter a loud, sharp, piercing cry. **2.** to emit a shrill, piercing sound. **3.** to laugh immoderately or uncontrollably. **4.** to shout or speak shrilly. **5.** to be conspicuous or startling. —*v.t.* **6.** to utter with a scream. **7.** to make by screaming: *to scream oneself hoarse.* —*n.* **8.** a loud, sharp, piercing cry. **9.** a shrill, piercing sound. **10.** *Informal.* someone or something that is hilariously funny.

scream•er (skrē′mər), *n.* **1.** a person or thing that screams. **2.** *Informal.* something or someone causing screams of excitement, laughter, or the like. **3.** a sensational headline printed in very large type.

screech (skrēch), *v.i.* **1.** to utter or make a harsh, shrill cry or sound. —*v.t.* **2.** to utter with a screech. —*n.* **3.** a harsh, shrill cry or sound. —**screech′er,** *n.* —**screech•y,** *adj.,* **screech•i•er, screech•i•est.**

screech′ owl′, *n.* any of several small New World owls of the genus *Otus,* having hornlike tufts of feathers, as *O. asio,* of E North America.

screed (skrēd), *n.* **1.** a long discourse or essay, esp. a diatribe. **2.** a guide used in surfacing plasterwork or cement work.

screen (skrēn), *n.* **1.** a movable or fixed device, usu. consisting of a covered frame, that provides shelter, serves as a partition, etc. **2.** a permanent, usu. ornamental partition, as around the choir of a church. **3.** a specially prepared, light-reflecting surface on which motion pictures, slides, etc., may be projected. **4.** motion pictures collectively or the motion-picture industry. **5.** the part of a television or computer on which a picture is formed or information is displayed. **6.** anything that shelters, protects, or conceals. **7.** a frame holding a mesh of wire, cloth, or plastic, for placing in a window or doorway, around a porch, etc., to admit air but exclude insects. **8.** a sieve or other meshlike device used to separate smaller particles or objects from larger ones, as for grain or sand. **9.** a system for screening or grouping people, objects, etc. **10.** a body of troops sent out to protect the movement of an army. **11.** a protective formation of small vessels, as destroyers, around a larger ship or ships. **12.** a plate of ground glass or the like on which the image is brought into focus in a camera before being photographed. —*v.t.* **13.** to shelter, protect, or conceal with or as if with a screen. **14.** to select, reject, consider, or group (people, objects, ideas, etc.) by examining systematically. **15.** to provide with a screen or screens. **16.** to sift or sort by passing through a screen. **17. a.** to project (a motion picture, slide, etc.) on a screen. **b.** to photograph with a motion-picture camera; film. **c.** to adapt (a story, play, etc.) for presentation as a motion picture. **18.** to lighten (type or areas of a line engraving) by etching a regular pattern of dots or lines into the printing surface. —**screen′a•ble**, *adj.*

screen•ing (skrē′ning), *n.* **1.** the activity of a person who screens, as in ascertaining the qualifications of applicants. **2.** the showing of a motion picture. **3. screenings,** (*used with a sing. or pl. v.*) **a.** undesirable material that has been separated from usable material by means of a screen. **b.** extremely fine coal. **4.** the meshed material used in screens for windows and doors.

screen•play (skrēn′plā′), *n.* the outline or full script of a motion picture; scenario.

screen′ sav′er, *n. Computers.* a program that displays a constantly shifting pattern on a display screen, used to prevent damage to the screen through continuous display of the same image.

screen′ test′, *n.* a filmed audition to determine a person's suitability for acting in a motion picture. —**screen′-test′**, *v.t., v.i.*

screen•writ•er (skrēn′rī′tər), *n.* a person who writes screenplays as an occupation.

screw (skrōō), *n.* **1.** a metal fastener having a tapered shank with a helical thread, and topped with a slotted head, driven into wood or the like by rotating, as with a screwdriver. **2.** a threaded cylindrical rod, with a head at one end, that engages a threaded hole and is used as a fastener, clamp, etc. Compare BOLT¹ (def. 1). **3.** a tapped or threaded hole. **4.** something having a spiral form. **5.** PROPELLER (def. 1). **6.** a single turn of a screw. **7.** a twisting movement. —*v.t.* **8.** to turn or tighten (a screw). **9.** to fasten or attach with or as if with a screw or screws. **10.** to attach, detach, or adjust (a threaded part) by a twisting motion. **11.** to operate or adjust by a screw, as a press. **12.** to contort as by twisting; distort: *to screw one's face into a grimace.* **13.** to strengthen or intensify (usu. fol. by *up*): *I screwed up my courage and asked for a raise.* **14.** to coerce or threaten. **15.** to extract or extort. —*v.i.* **16.** to become attached, detached, or adjusted by being twisted: *The bottle top screws on.* **17. screw up,** *Slang.* **a.** to ruin or botch; make a mess of. **b.** to cause to become troubled, neurotic, or incapable of handling one's life. —*Idiom.* **18. have a screw loose,** to behave or think oddly. **19. put the screws on,** to use coercion on; force.

screw•ball (skrōō′bôl′), *n.* **1.** *Slang.* an eccentric or wildly whimsical person; a kook. **2.** a pitched baseball that veers toward the side from which it was thrown, counter to the motion of a curve ball. —*adj.* **3.** *Slang.* eccentric or whimsical: *screwball ideas.*

screw•driv•er (skrōō′drī′vər), *n.* **1.** a hand tool for tightening or loosening a screw, consisting of a handle attached to a long, metal shank, which tapers and flattens out to a tip that fits into the slotted head of a screw. **2.** a mixed drink of vodka and orange juice.

Screw′tape Let′ters, The, a work (1942) by C.S. Lewis that deals with Christian moral and theological issues.

screw′up′ or **screw′-up′**, *n. Slang.* **1.** a serious mistake or blunder; foul-up. **2.** a habitual blunderer.

screw•worm (skrōō′wûrm′), *n.* the larva of a blow fly, *Cochliomyia macellaria,* that is a pest of livestock.

screw′worm fly′, *n.* the adult screwworm.

screw•y (skrōō′ē), *adj.,* **screw•i•er, screw•i•est.** *Slang.* **1.** crazy; nutty. **2.** absurd or odd.

scrib•ble (skrib′əl), *v.,* **-bled, -bling,** *n.* —*v.t.* **1.** to write hastily or carelessly: *to scribble a letter.* **2.** to cover with meaningless marks. —*v.i.* **3.** to write or draw in a hasty or meaningless way. —*n.* **4.** a hasty or careless drawing or piece of writing. **5.** a series of meaningless marks or scrawls. —**scrib′bling•ly**, *adv.*

scribe¹ (skrīb), *n., v.,* **scribed, scrib•ing.** —*n.* **1.** a professional copyist, esp. one who made copies of manuscripts before the invention of printing. **2.** a public clerk or writer, esp. one with official status. **3.** one of a group of Palestinian scholars and teachers of Jewish law and tradition, active from the 5th century B.C. to the 1st century A.D., who transcribed, edited, and interpreted the Bible. **4.** a writer or author, esp. a journalist. —*v.i.* **5.** to act as a scribe; write. —*v.t.* **6.** to write down. —**scrib′al**, *adj.*

scribe² (skrīb), *v.t,* **scribed, scrib•ing.** to mark or score (wood or the like) with a pointed instrument as a guide to cutting or assembling.

scrim (skrim), *n.* **1.** a cotton or linen fabric of open weave used for bunting, curtains, etc. **2.** *Theat.* a piece of such fabric used as a drop, border, or the like, for creating the illusion of a solid wall or backdrop under certain lighting conditions or creating a semitransparent curtain when lit from behind.

scrim•mage (skrim′ij), *n., v.,* **-maged, -mag•ing.** —*n.* **1.** a rough or vigorous struggle. **2.** *Football.* **a.** the action from the snap of the ball to the end of the play. Compare LINE OF SCRIMMAGE. **b.** a practice session or informal game, as that played between two units of the same team. —*v.t., v.i.* **3.** to engage in a scrimmage. —**scrim′mag•er**, *n.*

scrim′mage line′, *n.* LINE OF SCRIMMAGE.

scrimp (skrimp), *v.i.* **1.** to be sparing or frugal; economize. —*v.t.* **2.** to be sparing of; limit severely. **3.** to provide sparingly for.

scrim•shaw (skrim′shô′), *n.* **1.** a carved or engraved article, esp. of

whale ivory or whalebone. **2.** the art or technique of producing such work. —*v.i.* **3.** to produce scrimshaw. —*v.t.* **4.** to carve or engrave (whale ivory or whalebone) into scrimshaw.

scrip (skrip), *n.* **1.** paper currency issued for temporary use in emergency situations, as by an occupying power. **2.** a certificate representing a fraction of a share of stock. **3.** a receipt, list, or other brief piece of writing. **4.** a scrap of paper. **5. a.** paper currency in denominations of less than one dollar, formerly issued in the U.S. **b.** such currency as a whole.

script (skript), *n.* **1.** the letters or characters used in writing by hand; handwriting. **2.** a manuscript or document. **3.** the written text of a play, motion picture, television program, or the like. **4.** any system of writing. **5.** *Print.* a type imitating handwriting. **6.** a plan. —*v.t.* **7.** to write a script for. **8.** to plan. —**script′er**, *n.*

scrip•tur•al (skrip′chər əl), *adj.* **1.** (*sometimes cap.*) of or pertaining to sacred writings, esp. the Scriptures. **2.** rendered in or related to writing. —**scrip′tur•al•ly**, *adv.*

Scrip•ture (skrip′chər), *n.* **1.** Often, **Scriptures.** Also called **Holy Scripture** (or **Scriptures**). the sacred writings of the Old or New Testaments or both together. **2.** (*often l.c.*) any writing or book, esp. when of a sacred or religious nature. **3.** (*sometimes l.c.*) a particular passage from the Bible. **4.** (*l.c.*) any collection of writings considered sacred.

Scrip′ture cake′, *n.* a cake whose recipe includes ingredients keyed to passages of scripture.

script•writ•er (skript′rī′tər), *n.* a person who writes scripts, as for movies or television. —**script′writ′ing**, *n.*

Scriv•en (skriv′ən), *n.* **Joseph,** 1819–86, Canadian hymn writer, born in Ireland.

scriv•ner (skriv′nər), *n.* **1.** SCRIBE¹ (defs. 1, 2). **2.** a notary.

scrod or **schrod** (skrod), *n.* a young Atlantic codfish or haddock.

scroll (skrōl), *n.* **1.** a roll of parchment, paper, or other material, esp. one with writing on it. **2.** a spiral or coiled ornament resembling a partly unrolled sheet of paper. **3.** a roll or roster. **4.** (in Japanese and Chinese art) a painting or text on silk or paper that is either displayed on a wall or held by the viewer and is rolled up when not in use. **5.** the curved head of a violin or other bowed instrument. —*v.t.* **6.** to cut into a curved form with a narrow-bladed saw. —*v.i.* **7.** to move a cursor smoothly, vertically or sideways, gradually causing new data to replace old on the display screen of a computer.

Scrooge (skrōōj), *n.* **1. Ebenezer,** a miserly curmudgeon in Dickens' *A Christmas Carol.* **2.** (*often l.c.*) any miserly person.

scro•tum (skrō′təm), *n., pl.* **-ta** (-tə), **-tums.** the pouch of skin that contains the testes. —**scro′tal**, *adj.*

scrounge (skrounj), *v.,* **scrounged, scroung•ing.** —*v.t.* **1.** to borrow with no intention of repaying. **2.** to assemble by foraging: *to scrounge enough food for supper.* —*v.i.* **3.** to borrow something small that one is not expected to return. —**scroung′er**, *n.*

scrub¹ (skrub), *v.,* **scrubbed, scrub•bing,** *n.* —*v.t.* **1.** to rub hard with a brush, cloth, etc., in washing. **2.** to remove (dirt, grime, etc.) from something by hard rubbing while washing. **3.** to remove (impurities or undesirable components) from a gas by chemical means, as sulfur dioxide from smokestack gas. **4.** *Informal.* to cancel or postpone, as a rocket launch. —*v.i.* **5.** to cleanse something by hard rubbing. **6.** to cleanse one's hands and arms as a preparation for performing surgery (often fol. by *up*). —*n.* **7.** an act or instance of scrubbing. **8.** a cosmetic preparation used for scrubbing. —**scrub′ba•ble**, *adj.*

scrub² (skrub), *n.* **1.** low trees or shrubs collectively. **2.** a large area covered with low trees and shrubs, as the Australian bush. **3.** a domestic animal of mixed or inferior breeding; mongrel. **4.** anything undersized or inferior. **5.** *Sports.* a player who is not on the regular, or first-string, team. —*adj.* **6.** small or stunted. **7.** inferior or insignificant.

scrub•ber (skrub′ər), *n.* **1.** a machine or appliance used in scrubbing. **2.** a device or process for removing pollutants from smoke or gas produced by burning high-sulfur fuels. **3.** a person who scrubs.

scrub′ brush′, *n.* a brush with stiff, short bristles.

scrub•by (skrub′ē), *adj.,* **-bi•er, -bi•est.** **1.** low or stunted, as trees. **2.** covered with scrub. **3.** undersized or stunted, as animals. **4.** wretched; shabby. —**scrub′bi•ly**, *adv.* —**scrub′bi•ness**, *n.*

scrub′ pine′, *n.* any of several pines, as the jack pine, characterized by a scrubby manner of growth, usu. found in dry, sandy soil.

scrub′ suit′, *n.* a loose-fitting, two-piece garment, often of green cotton, worn by surgeons.

scrub′ ty′phus, *n.* an infectious disease occurring chiefly in Japan and SE Asia, caused by the organism *Rickettsia tsutsugamushi,* transmitted by mites through biting.

scruff (skruf), *n.* the nape or back of the neck.

scruff•y (skruf′ē), *adj.,* **scruff•i•er, scruff•i•est.** untidy; shabby.

scrum (skrum), *n., v.,* **scrummed, scrum•ming.** —*n.* **1.** a rugby formation in which opposing forwards huddle and struggle for possession of the ball. **2.** *Brit.* a place or situation of confusion and racket; hubbub. —*v.i.* **3.** to engage in a scrum.

scrump•tious (skrump′shəs), *adj.* extremely pleasing, esp. to the taste; delectable. —**scrump′tious•ness**, *n.*

scrunch (skrunch, skrōōnch), *v.t.* **1.** to crunch or crush. **2.** to contract; squeeze together: *I scrunched my shoulders.* —*v.i.* **3.** to squat or hunker (often fol. by *down*). —*n.* **4.** the act or sound of scrunching.

scru•ple (skrōō′pəl), *n., v.,* **-pled, -pling.** —*n.* **1.** a moral or ethical

S

consideration that restrains one's behavior and inhibits certain actions. **2.** a very small portion or amount. **3.** a unit of apothecaries' weight equal to 20 grains (1.295 grams) or ⅓ of a dram. —*v.i.* **4.** to hesitate because of scruples; waver.

scru•pu•lous (skrōō′pyə ləs), *adj.* **1.** having scruples; principled. **2.** rigorously precise or exact: *scrupulous adherence to duty.* —**scru′pu•los′i•ty** (-los′i tē), **scru′pu•lous•ness,** *n.* —**scru′pu•lous•ly,** *adv.*

scru•ta•ble (skrōō′tə bəl), *adj.* capable of being understood by careful study or investigation; comprehensible. —**scru′ta•bil′i•ty,** *n.*

scru•ti•nize (skrōōt′n īz′), *v.,* **-nized, -niz•ing.** —*v.t.* **1.** to examine minutely. —*v.i.* **2.** to conduct a scrutiny. —**scru′ti•ni•za′tion,** *n.* —**scru′ti•niz′er,** *n.* —**scru′ti•niz′ing•ly,** *adv.*

scru•ti•ny (skrōōt′n ē), *n., pl.* **-nies. 1.** a searching examination; minute inquiry. **2.** continuous surveillance. **3.** a close and searching look.

scu•ba (skōō′bə), *n., pl.* **-bas,** *v.,* **-baed, -ba•ing.** —*n.* **1.** a portable breathing device for free-swimming divers, consisting of a mouthpiece joined by hoses to one or two tanks of compressed air that are strapped on the back. **2.** SCUBA DIVING. —*v.i.* **3.** to scuba-dive. [*s(elf)-c(ontained) u(nderwater) b(reathing) a(pparatus)*]

scu′ba div′ing, *n.* the activity or recreation of diving or exploring underwater through use of a scuba.

scud¹ (skud), *v.,* **scud•ded, scud•ding,** *n.* —*v.i.* **1.** to run or move quickly or hurriedly. **2.** *Naut.* to run before a gale with little or no sail set. —*n.* **3.** the act of scudding. **4. a.** clouds, spray, or mist driven by the wind. **b.** a driving shower. **c.** a gust of wind. **5.** low-drifting clouds appearing beneath a cloud from which precipitation is falling.

scud² (skud), *v.,* **scud•ded, scud•ding,** *n.* —*v.t.* **1.** to cleanse (a skin or hide) of remaining hairs or dirt. —*n.* **2.** the hairs or dirt removed by scudding.

Scud (skud), *n.* a surface-to-air missile, esp. one deployed on a mobile launcher.

scuff (skuf), *v.t.* **1.** to mar by scraping or hard use, as shoes or furniture. **2.** to scrape (something) with one's foot or feet. **3.** to rub or scrape (one's foot or feet) over something. —*v.i.* **4.** to shuffle. **5.** to scrape or rub one's foot back and forth over something. **6.** to be marred or scratched by scraping or wear. —*n.* **7.** the act or sound of scuffing. **8.** a flat-heeled slipper with an upper part covering only the front of the foot. **9.** a mar or scratch, as from scraping or wear.

scuf•fle (skuf′əl), *v.,* **-fled, -fling,** *n.* —*v.i.* **1.** to struggle or fight in a rough, confused manner. **2.** to go or move in hurried confusion. **3.** to move with a shuffle; scuff. —*n.* **4.** a rough, confused struggle or fight. **5.** a shuffling. **6.** Also called **scuf′fle hoe′.** a spadelike hoe that is pushed instead of pulled. —**scuf′fler,** *n.* —**scuf′fling•ly,** *adv.*

scull (skul), *n.* **1.** an oar mounted on a fulcrum at the stern of a small boat and moved from side to side to propel the boat forward. **2.** either of a pair of oars rowed by one rower. **3.** a boat propelled by an oar or oars. **4.** a light, narrow racing boat for one, two, or sometimes four rowers, each equipped with a pair of oars. —*v.t.* **5.** to propel or convey by means of a scull or sculls. —*v.i.* **6.** to scull a boat. —**scull′er,** *n.*

scul•ler•y (skul′ə rē, skul′rē), *n., pl.* **-ler•ies.** a small room off a kitchen where food is prepared and utensils are cleaned and stored.

sculpt (skulpt), *v.t., v.i.* **1.** to carve, model, or make by using the techniques of sculpture. **2.** to form or shape as in the manner of sculpture.

sculp•tor (skulp′tər), *n.* a person who sculptures.

sculp•ture (skulp′chər), *n.* **1.** the art of carving, modeling, welding, or otherwise producing figurative or abstract works of art in three dimensions, as in relief, intaglio, or in the round. **2.** such works of art collectively. **3.** an individual piece of such work. —*v.t.* **4.** to carve, model, weld, or otherwise produce (a piece of sculpture). **5.** to produce a portrait or image of in this way; represent in sculpture. **6.** to change the form of (the land surface) by erosion. —*v.i.* **7.** to work as a sculptor. —**sculp′tur•al,** *adj.* —**sculp′tur•al•ly,** *adv.*

sculp•tured (skulp′chərd), *adj.* having a surface or shape molded, carved, etc., by or as if by sculpture.

scum (skum), *n., v.,* **scummed, scum•ming.** —*n.* **1. a.** a film or layer of foul matter that forms on the surface of a liquid. **b.** a film of algae on still or stagnant water: *pond scum.* **2.** refuse or offscourings. **3.** a low, worthless person. **4.** such persons collectively; dregs. —*v.i.* **5.** to form scum; become covered with scum. —*v.t.* **6.** to remove the scum from.

scum•my (skum′ē), *adj.,* **-mi•er, -mi•est. 1.** consisting of or having scum. **2.** despicable; contemptible. —**scum′mi•ness,** *n.*

scup (skup), *n., pl.* **scups,** (*esp. collectively*) **scup.** an edible porgy, *Stenotomus chrysops,* of N Atlantic coastal waters, having a compressed body and a high back.

scup•per (skup′ər), *n.* **1.** an opening at the edge of a ship's deck that allows accumulated water to drain away into the sea or into the bilges. **2.** a drain, closed by one or two flaps, for allowing water from the sprinkler system of a factory or the like to run off a floor of the building to the exterior. **3.** any opening in the side of a building, as in a parapet, for draining off rainwater.

scup•per•nong (skup′ər nông′, -nong′), *n.* a silvery amber-green variety of muscadine grape.

scurf (skûrf), *n.* **1.** loose scales of skin. **2.** scaly matter on a surface. —**scurf′y,** *adj.,* **-i•er, -i•est.**

scur•ril•ous (skûr′ə ləs, skur′-), *adj.* **1.** grossly or obscenely abusive. **2.** coarsely jocular or derisive. —**scur′ril•ous•ly,** *adv.* —**scur′ril•ous•ness,** *n.*

scur•ry (skûr′ē, skur′ē), *v.,* **-ried, -ry•ing,** *n., pl.* **-ries.** —*v.i.* **1.** to move in haste. —*n.* **2.** a scurrying rush.

S-curve (es′kûrv′), *n.* a curve, esp. in a road, shaped like an S.

scur•vy (skûr′vē), *n., adj.,* **-vi•er, -vi•est.** —*n.* **1.** a disease marked by swollen and bleeding gums, livid spots on the skin, and prostration and caused by a lack of vitamin C. —*adj.* **2.** contemptible; despicable. —**scur′vi•ly,** *adv.* —**scur′vi•ness,** *n.*

scut (skut), *n.* a short tail, esp. of a hare, rabbit, or deer.

scutch (skuch), *v.t.* **1.** to dress (flax) by beating. —*n.* **2.** Also, **scutch′er.** a device for scutching flax fiber.

scut•tle¹ (skut′l), *n.* **1.** a deep bucket for carrying coal. **2.** a broad, shallow basket.

scut•tle² (skut′l), *v.,* **-tled, -tling.** —*v.i.* **1.** to run with short, quick steps; scurry. —*n.* **2.** a quick pace. **3.** a short, hurried run.

scut•tle³ (skut′l), *n., v.,* **-tled, -tling.** —*n.* **1. a.** a small hatch or port in the deck, side, or bottom of a vessel. **b.** a cover for this. **2.** a small hatchlike opening in a roof or ceiling. —*v.t.* **3.** to sink (a vessel) deliberately by making openings in the bottom. **4.** to abandon or destroy (plans, rumors, etc.).

scut•tle•butt (skut′l but′), *n.* **1.** *Informal.* rumor; gossip. **2.** a drinking fountain for use by the crew of a vessel.

scut′work′ or **scut′ work′,** *n.* menial, routine work.

scuzz (skuz), *Slang.* —*n.* **1.** Also called **scuzz•ball** (skuz′bôl′). a dirty or sordid person or thing. —*adj.* **2.** scuzzy.

scuzz•y (skuz′ē), *adj.,* **scuzz•i•er, scuzz•i•est.** *Slang.* dirty; repulsive; disgusting.

scythe (sīth), *n., v.,* **scythed, scyth•ing.** —*n.* **1.** a tool consisting of a long, curving blade fastened at an angle to a handle, for cutting grass, grain, etc., by hand. —*v.t.* **2.** to cut or mow with a scythe. —**scythe′less,** *adj.* —**scythe′like′,** *adj.*

scythe

Scyth•i•a (sith′ē ə), *n.* the ancient name of a region in SE Europe and Asia, between the Black and Aral seas. —**Scythian,** *adj., n.*

SD, 1. Also, **S.D.** South Dakota. **2.** Also, **S.D.** *Statistics.* standard deviation.

S.D., 1. Doctor of Science. [< Latin *Scientiae Doctor*] **2.** South Dakota. **3.** special delivery.

S. Dak., South Dakota.

SDI or **S.D.I.,** Strategic Defense Initiative.

SE, 1. southeast. **2.** southeastern. **3.** Standard English.

Se, *Chem. Symbol.* selenium.

se-, a prefix meaning "apart," occurring in loanwords from Latin: *seduce; select.*

sea (sē), *n.* **1.** the salt waters that cover the greater part of the earth's surface. **2.** a division of these waters, of considerable extent, marked off by land boundaries; ocean: *the North Sea.* **3.** a large, landlocked body of water. **4.** the turbulence of the ocean or other body of water, as caused by the wind. **5.** the waves. **6.** a large wave: *The heavy seas almost drowned us.* **7.** a widely extended or overwhelming quantity: *a sea of troubles.* **8.** the work, travel, and shipboard life of a sailor. —*adj.* **9.** pertaining to or adapted for use at sea. —*Idiom.* **10. at sea, a.** on the ocean. **b.** perplexed; uncertain. **11. follow the sea,** to pursue a nautical career. **12. go to sea, a.** to set out on a voyage. **b.** to embark on a nautical career. **13. put (out) to sea,** to embark on a sea voyage.

sea′ anem′one, *n.* any solitary, attached marine polyp of the order Actinaria, having a firm, gelatinous body topped with flowerlike tentacles.

sea′ bass′ (bas), *n.* **1.** any of numerous marine fishes of the family Serranidae, characterized by a large mouth and an exposed upper jaw. **2.** any of numerous related or similar marine food fishes.

sea•bed (sē′bed′), *n.* SEAFLOOR.

sea′ bis′cuit, *n.* ship biscuit; hardtack.

sea•board (sē′bôrd′, -bōrd′), *n.* **1.** the line where land and sea meet. **2.** a region bordering a seacoast: *the eastern seaboard.* —*adj.* **3.** bordering on the sea.

sea•borne (sē′bôrn′, -bōrn′), *adj.* carried on or over the sea.

sea′ breeze′, *n.* a thermally produced wind blowing from a cool ocean surface onto adjoining warm land.

sea′ cap′tain, *n.* the master of a seagoing vessel.

sea•coast (sē′kōst′), *n.* the land immediately adjacent to the sea.

sea′ cow′, *n.* the manatee or dugong.

sea′ cray′fish (or **craw′fish**), *n.* SPINY LOBSTER.

sea′ cu′cumber, *n.* any creeping echinoderm of the class Holothuroidea, having a long body and short tentacles around the mouth.

sea′ dog′, *n.* **1.** a sailor, esp. an old or experienced one. **2.** HARBOR SEAL. **3.** a pirate or privateer.

sea′ ea′gle, *n.* any of several large eagles of the genus *Haliaeetus,* that usu. feed on fish.

sea′ el′ephant, *n.* ELEPHANT SEAL.

sea·far·er (sē′fâr′ər), *n.* **1.** a sailor. **2.** a traveler on the sea.

sea·far·ing (sē′fâr′ing), *adj.* **1.** traveling by sea. **2.** following the sea as a trade, business, or calling. **3.** of, pertaining to, or occurring during a voyage on the sea. —*n.* **4.** the calling of a sailor.

sea·floor (sē′flôr′, -flōr′), *n.* the solid surface underlying a sea or ocean. Also called **seabed.**

sea·food (sē′fōod′), *n.* any fish or shellfish from the sea used for food.

sea′ front′, *n.* an area, including buildings, along the edge of the sea; waterfront.

sea′ gate′, *n.* a navigable channel giving access to the sea.

sea·go·ing (sē′gō′ing), *adj.* **1.** designed or fit for going to sea, as a vessel. **2.** seafaring.

sea′ grape′, *n.* **1.** a tropical American tree, *Coccoloba uvifera,* of the buckwheat family, bearing grapelike clusters of edible purple berries. **2.** the fruit itself.

sea′ green′, *n.* a clear, light, bluish green. —**sea′-green′,** *adj.*

sea′ gull′, *n.* a gull, esp. any of the marine species.

Sea·hawk (sē′hôk′), *n.* a twin-engine, four-seat U.S. Navy helicopter used for surveillance, targeting, and antisubmarine warfare.

sea′ horse′ or **sea′horse′,** *n.* **1.** any of various fishes of the genus *Hippocampus,* of the pipefish family, having a prehensile tail, an elongated snout, and a head bent at right angles to the body. **2.** a fabled marine animal with the foreparts of a horse and the hind parts of a fish.

sea horse, *Hippocampus hudsonius,*
length 3 to 4 in. (8 to 10 cm)

sea′-is′land (or **Sea′ Is′land**) **cot′ton,** *n.* a long-fibered cotton, *Gossypium barbadense,* raised orig. in the Sea Islands and now grown chiefly in the West Indies.

Sea′ Is′lands, *n.pl.* a group of islands in the Atlantic, along the coasts of South Carolina, Georgia, and N Florida.

sea′ kale′, *n.* a European broad-leaved maritime plant, *Crambe maritima,* of the mustard family: the young shoots are blanched and used like asparagus.

seal¹ (sēl), *n.* **1.** an embossed emblem, symbol, letter, etc., used as attestation or evidence of authenticity. **2.** a stamp, medallion, ring, etc., engraved with such a device, for impressing paper, wax, lead, or the like. **3.** the impression so obtained. **4.** an authenticating mark or symbol, orig. wax with an impression, attached to a legal document. **5.** a piece of wax or similar adhesive affixed to a document, envelope, door, etc., that must be broken when the object is opened. **6.** anything that tightly or completely closes or secures a thing. **7.** something that keeps a thing secret: *Her vow was the seal that kept her silent.* **8.** a stamplike label, esp. as given to contributors to a charity: *a Christmas seal.* **9.** a mark, sign, symbol, or the like, serving as visible evidence of something. **10.** anything that serves as assurance, confirmation, or bond: *She gave the plan her seal of approval.* **11.** a small amount of water held by a trap to exclude foul gases from a sewer or the like. —*v.t.* **12.** to affix a seal to in authorization, testimony, etc. **13.** to assure, confirm, or bind with or as if with a seal. **14.** to impress a seal upon as evidence of legal or standard exactness, measure, quality, etc. **15.** to close with a fastening that must be broken to gain access. **16.** to fasten or close tightly by or as if by a seal. **17.** to decide irrevocably: *to seal someone's fate.* **18.** *Mormon Ch.* to solemnize (a marriage or adoption). **19. seal off, a.** to close hermetically. **b.** to block all access to or from, as or as if with a police barricade. —*Idiom.* **20. set one's seal to,** to give one's approval to; authorize; endorse. —**seal′a·ble,** *adj.*

seal² (sēl), *n., pl.* **seals,** (*esp. collectively for 1*) **seal,** *v. n.* **1.** any of numerous marine carnivores of the order Pinnipedia, including the eared seals of the family Otariidae and the earless seals of the family Phocidae. **2.** the skin of such an animal. **3.** leather made from this skin. **4.** the fur of the fur seal; sealskin. **5.** a dark gray-brown. —*v.i.* **6.** to hunt, kill, or capture seals. —**seal′like′,** *adj.*

sea′ lam′prey, *n.* a parasitic marine lamprey, *Petromyzon marinus,* that spawns in fresh water along the Atlantic coast and in the Great Lakes.

seal·ant (sē′lənt), *n.* **1.** any of various liquids, paints, chemicals, or soft substances applied to a surface or circulated through pipes, that dry to form a watertight coating. **2.** any of various resins applied to the chewing surfaces of teeth to prevent decay.

sea′ legs′, *n.pl.* the ability to adjust one's balance to the motion of a ship at sea.

seal·er¹ (sē′lər), *n.* **1.** a substance applied to a porous surface as a basecoat for paint, varnish, etc. **2.** an officer who verifies that weights and measures are true to the standard.

seal·er² (sē′lər), *n.* a person or ship that hunts seals.

sea′ let′tuce, *n.* any seaweed of the genus *Ulva,* having large leaflike blades.

sea′ lev′el, *n.* the horizontal plane corresponding to the surface of the sea at mean level between high and low tide.

sea·lift (sē′lift′), *n.* **1.** a system for transporting persons or cargo by ship, esp. in an emergency. —*v.t.* **2.** to transport by sealift.

sea′ lil′y, *n.* a stalked, permanently attached crinoid.

seal′ing wax′, *n.* a resinous preparation, soft when heated, used for sealing letters, documents, etc.

sea′ li′on, *n.* any of several large eared seals, characterized by a blunt snout and a small amount of underfur, esp. *Zalophus californicus,* of the N Pacific.

seal′ point′, *n.* a Siamese cat having a cream- or fawn-colored body and dark brown points.

seal·skin (sēl′skin′), *n.* **1.** the skin or fur of the fur seal. **2.** a garment or article made of sealskin.

Sea′ly·ham ter′rier (sē′lē ham′, -lē əm), *n.* one of a Welsh breed of small, short-legged terriers having a long head with square jaws and whiskers and a hard, wiry mostly white coat. Also called **Sea′ly·ham.**

seam (sēm), *n.* **1.** the line formed by sewing together pieces of cloth, leather, or the like. **2.** the stitches used to make such a line. **3.** any line formed by abutting edges. **4.** any linear indentation or mark, as a wrinkle or scar. **5.** *Geol.* a comparatively thin stratum; a bed, as of coal. —*v.t.* **6.** to join with or as if with stitches. **7.** to furrow; mark with wrinkles, scars, etc. —*v.i.* **8.** to become cracked, fissured, or furrowed.

sea′-maid or **sea′-maid′en,** *n.* **1.** MERMAID. **2.** a goddess or nymph of the sea.

sea·man (sē′mən), *n., pl.* **-men. 1.** a person skilled in seamanship. **2.** a person who assists in the handling, sailing, and navigating of a vessel, esp. one below the rank of officer; sailor. **3.** an enlisted person in the U.S. Navy ranking below petty officer.

sea·man·ship (sē′mən ship′), *n.* knowledge and skill pertaining to the operation, navigation, safety, and maintenance of a ship.

seam·less (sēm′lis), *adj.* **1.** having no seams. **2.** smoothly continuous or uniform in quality: *a seamless blend of art and entertainment.* —**seam′less·ly,** *adv.* —**seam′less·ness,** *n.*

sea′ moss′, *n.* any of certain frondlike red algae.

sea·mount (sē′mount′), *n.* a mountain rising several hundred fathoms above the seafloor but having its summit well below the surface of the water.

seam·stress (sēm′stris; *esp. Brit.* sem′-), *n.* a woman who sews, esp. one whose occupation is sewing.

seam·y (sē′mē), *adj.,* **seam·i·er, seam·i·est. 1.** sordid; low; disagreeable: *the seamy side of life.* **2.** having or showing a seam, esp. the seam of the inside of a garment. —**seam′i·ness,** *n.*

sé·ance (sā′äns), *n.* **1.** a meeting in which a spiritualist attempts to communicate with the spirits of the dead. **2.** a session or sitting, as of a class or organization.

sea′ net′tle, *n.* any large stinging jellyfish.

sea′ oats′, *n.* a tall grass, *Uniola paniculata,* of coastal areas of SE North America, having as its inflorescence a densely crowded panicle.

sea′ on′ion, *n.* **1.** a Mediterranean plant, *Urginea maritima,* of the lily family, yielding medicinal squill. **2.** a squill, *Scilla verna,* of the Isle of Wight, having narrow leaves and clusters of violet flowers.

sea′ ot′ter, *n.* a marine otter, *Enhydra lutris,* of N Pacific coasts, with valuable fur.

sea′ palm′, *n.* a kelp, *Postelsia palmaeformis,* of the Pacific coast of North America, that resembles a miniature palm tree.

sea·plane (sē′plān′), *n.* an airplane with floats for water takeoffs and landings.

sea·port (sē′pôrt′, -pōrt′), *n.* **1.** a port or harbor that accommodates seagoing vessels. **2.** a town or city at such a place.

sea′ pow′er, *n.* **1.** naval strength. **2.** a nation that possesses formidable naval power.

sea·quake (sē′kwāk′), *n.* an agitation of the sea caused by a submarine eruption or earthquake.

sear¹ (sēr), *v.t.* **1.** to burn or char the surface of. **2.** to mark with a branding iron. **3.** to burn or scorch. **4.** to damage emotionally. **5.** to dry up or wither; parch. —*n.* **6.** a mark or scar made by searing. —*adj.* **7.** SERE.

sear² (sēr), *n.* a pivoted piece that holds the hammer at full or half cock in the firing mechanism of small arms.

search (sûrch), *v.t.* **1.** to look through (a place, area, etc.) carefully in order to find something missing or lost. **2.** to examine (a person, object, etc.) carefully in order to find something concealed. **3.** to explore or examine in order to discover: *They searched the hills for gold.* **4.** to examine (a record, writing, collection, repository, etc.) for information: *to* *search a property title.* **5.** to look into, question, or scrutinize: *to search one's conscience.* **6.** to pierce or penetrate: *The sunlight searched the room's dark corners.* **7.** to uncover by examination or exploration (often fol. by *out*): *to search out all the facts.* **8.** to command software to find specified characters or codes in (an electronic file): *to search a database for all instances of "U.S."* —*v.i.* **9.** to inquire, investigate, examine, or seek. **10.** to find specified characters or codes in an electronic file by means of software commands. —*n.* **11.** an act or instance of searching; careful examination or investigation. **12.** the wartime practice of boarding and searching any neutral vessel suspected of transporting contraband. —**search′a•ble,** *adj.* —**search′er,** *n.*

search•ing (sûr′ching), *adj.* **1.** examining carefully or thoroughly: *a searching inspection.* **2.** acutely observant or penetrating: *a searching glance; a searching mind.* **3.** piercing or sharp: *a searching wind.* —**search′ing•ly,** *adv.* —**search′ing•ness,** *n.*

search•light (sûrch′līt′), *n.* **1.** a device, usu. consisting of a light and reflector, for throwing a beam of light in any direction. **2.** a beam of light so thrown.

search′ war′rant, *n.* a court order authorizing police to search a premises for stolen goods, narcotics, etc.

Sears (sērz), *n.* **Edmund H(amilton),** 1810–76, U.S. clergyman and hymn writer.

sea′ salt′, *n.* table salt produced through the evaporation of seawater.

sea′ scal′lop, *n.* **1.** a large scallop, *Placopecten magellanicus,* of deep waters off the Atlantic coast of North America. **2.** the edible abductor muscle of this scallop.

sea•scape (sē′skāp′), *n.* **1.** a sketch, painting, or photograph of the sea. **2.** a view of the sea.

sea′ scor′pion, *n.* SCORPIONFISH.

sea′ ser′pent, *n.* **1.** an enormous, imaginary, snakelike or dragonlike marine animal. **2.** (*caps.*) the constellation Hydra.

sea′shell′ or **sea′ shell′,** *n.* the shell of a marine mollusk.

sea•shore (sē′shôr′, -shōr′), *n.* **1.** land along the sea. **2.** the ground between the ordinary high-water and low-water marks.

sea•sick (sē′sik′), *adj.* afflicted with seasickness.

sea•sick•ness (sē′sik′nis), *n.* nausea and dizziness, often accompanied by vomiting, induced by the motion of a vessel at sea.

sea•side (sē′sīd′), *n.* **1.** the land along the sea; seacoast. —*adj.* **2.** situated on or pertaining to the seaside.

sea•son (sē′zən), *n.* **1.** one of the four periods of the year (spring, summer, autumn, and winter), beginning astronomically at an equinox or solstice but geographically at different dates in different climates. **2.** a period of the year characterized by particular weather conditions: *the rainy season.* **3.** a period of the year when something is best or available: *the oyster season.* **4.** a period of the year marked by certain conditions, activities, etc.: *baseball season.* **5.** a period of the year immediately before and after a special holiday or occasion: *the Christmas season.* **6.** an athletic team's term of competitive play in terms of total games or overall success. **7.** period; time: *in the season of my youth.* —*v.t.* **8.** to give flavor to (food) by adding condiments, spices, or the like. **9.** to enhance: *conversation seasoned with wit.* **10.** to make fit or inure by experience. **11.** to prepare for use, as by drying: *to season timber.* —*v.i.* **12.** to become seasoned. —*Idiom.* **13. in good season,** in enough time; sufficiently early. **14. in season, a.** in the proper time or state for use: *Asparagus is now in season.* **b.** in the period regulated by law, as for hunting and fishing. **c.** (of an animal, esp. female) in heat. **15. out of season,** not in season. —*Proverb.* **16. To everything there is a season and a time to every purpose under the heaven,** everything that happens has its appointed time. Eccl. 3:1–8. —**sea′son•er,** *n.*

sea•son•a•ble (sē′zə nə bəl), *adj.* **1.** suitable to or characteristic of the season. **2.** timely: *a seasonable suggestion.* —**sea′son•a•bly,** *adv.*

sea•son•al (sē′zə nl), *adj.* **1.** pertaining to, dependent on, or accompanying the seasons of the year or some particular season; periodical: *seasonal work.* —*n.* **2.** a seasonal employee or product. —**sea′son•al•ly,** *adv.* —**sea′son•al•ness,** *n.* —**Usage.** In edited prose and in formal speech the adjectives SEASONAL and SEASONABLE are almost always distinguished. SEASONAL describes phenomena that occur with or depend upon a season or the seasons: *seasonal fluctuations in rainfall; seasonal sales.* SEASONABLE in reference to weather means "suitable to or characteristic of the season": *seasonable temperatures for July.* SEASONABLE also has the sense "timely": *a seasonable offer of financial assistance.*

sea′sonal affec′tive disor′der, *n.* recurrent winter depression characterized by oversleeping, overeating, and irritability and relieved by the arrival of spring or by light therapy. Abbr.: SAD

sea•son•ing (sē′zə ning), *n.* something, as salt or a spice, for enhancing the flavor of food.

sea′son tick′et, *n.* a ticket for a specified series of events or valid for a specified period of time.

sea′ squirt′, *n.* any of several attached tunicates of the class Ascidiacea, that, on contraction, eject a stream of water.

seat (sēt), *n.* **1.** something designed to support a person in a sitting position, as a chair or bench. **2.** the part of something on which one sits: *a chair seat.* **3.** the buttocks. **4.** the part of the garment covering the buttocks. **5.** a manner of or posture used in sitting on a horse. **6.** something on which the base of an object rests. **7.** the base itself. **8.** a place in which something occurs or is established: *a college as a seat of learning.* **9.** a place in which administrative power is centered: *Washington is the seat of the U.S. government.* **10.** accommodation for sitting, as in

a theater. **11.** a right to sit as a member in a legislative or similar body: *She was elected to a seat in the Senate.* **12.** a right to the privileges of membership in a stock exchange or the like. —*v.t.* **13.** to place on a seat; cause to sit down. **14.** to guide to a seat. **15.** to accommodate with seats: *a theater that seats 1200 people.* **16.** to put a seat on or into. **17.** to install in a position or office of authority. **18.** to fit (a valve) with a seat. **19.** to attach to or place firmly in or on something as a base: *Seat the telescope on the tripod.* —*v.i.* **20.** to fit properly in a seat.

seat′ belt′, *n.* a configuration of straps designed to keep a vehicle passenger firmly secure.

seat•ing (sē′ting), *n.* **1.** an act or instance of providing with seats. **2.** an arrangement of seats. **3.** material for seats.

seat•mate (sēt′māt′), *n.* a person who occupies an adjoining seat.

SEATO (sē′tō), *n.* Southeast Asia Treaty Organization.

seat′-of-the-pants′, *adj.* **1.** using or based on experience, instinct, or guesswork: *a seat-of-the-pants management style.* **2.** done without the aid of instruments: *The pilot made a seat-of-the-pants landing.*

sea′ trout′, *n.* any of various species of trout inhabiting salt water, as the salmon trout, *Salmo trutta.*

Se•at•tle (sē at′l), *n.* a seaport in W Washington, on Puget Sound. 520,947.

sea′ tur′tle, *n.* any of several large turtles of the families Cheloniidae and Dermochelyidae, widely distributed in tropical and subtropical seas, having the limbs modified into paddlelike flippers.

sea′ ur′chin, *n.* any echinoderm of the class Echinoidea, having a somewhat globular or discoid form and a shell composed of many calcareous plates covered with projecting spines.

sea′ wall′, *n.* a strong wall or embankment to prevent the encroachments of the sea.

sea•ward (sē′wərd), *adv.* **1.** Also, **sea′wards.** toward the sea. —*adj.* **2.** facing or tending toward the sea. **3.** coming from the sea: *a seaward wind.* —*n.* **4.** the direction toward the sea.

sea•way (sē′wā′), *n.* **1.** a way over the sea. **2.** the open sea. **3.** the progress of a ship through the waves. **4.** a more or less rough sea. **5.** a waterway giving access to a landlocked port by oceangoing vessels.

sea•weed (sē′wēd′), *n.* **1.** any of numerous leafy or branching marine algae. **2.** any of various marine plants.

sea•wor•thy (sē′wûr′thē), *adj.,* **-thi•er, -thi•est.** (of a vessel) fitted and safe for a voyage at sea. —**sea′wor′thi•ness,** *n.*

se•ba•ceous (si bā′shəs), *adj.* **1.** pertaining to, of the nature of, or resembling tallow or fat; fatty; greasy. **2.** secreting a fatty substance.

seba′ceous gland′, *n.* any of the cutaneous glands that secrete oily matter for lubricating hair and skin.

seb•or•rhe•a (seb′ə rē′ə), *n.* abnormally heavy discharge from the sebaceous glands. —**seb′or•rhe′ic,** *adj.*

SEC or **S.E.C.,** Securities and Exchange Commission.

sec, 1. secant. **2.** second. **3.** secondary. **4.** secretary. **5.** section. **6.** sector. **7.** according to.

se•cant (sē′kant, -kənt), *n.* **1.** an intersecting line, esp. one intersecting a curve at two or more points. **2.** (in a right triangle) the ratio of the hypotenuse to the side adjacent to a given angle; the reciprocal of its cosine. Abbr.: sec —**se′cant•ly,** *adv.*

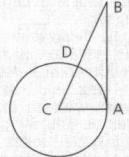

secant (def. 2) ACB being the angle, the ratio of BC to AC is the secant; or, AC being taken as unity, the secant is BC; BC secant of arc AD

se•cede (si sēd′), *v.i.,* **-ced•ed, -ced•ing.** to withdraw formally from an alliance, federation, or association. —**se•ced′er,** *n.*

se•ces•sion (si sesh′ən), *n.* **1.** an act or instance of seceding. **2.** (*often cap.*) the withdrawal from the Union of 11 southern states in the period 1860–61, which brought on the Civil War. —**se•ces′sion•al,** *adj.*

se•ces•sion•ist (si sesh′ə nist), *n.* **1.** one who secedes, advocates secession, or claims secession as a constitutional right. —*adj.* **2.** of secession or secessionists. —**se•ces′sion•ism,** *n.*

se•clude (si klōōd′), *v.t.,* **-clud•ed, -clud•ing. 1.** to remove from social contact and activity; isolate. **2.** to shut off; keep apart.

se•clud•ed (si klōō′did), *adj.* **1.** sheltered or screened from general activity or view. **2.** withdrawn from human contact: *a secluded life.* —**se•clud′ed•ly,** *adv.* —**se•clud′ed•ness,** *n.*

se•clu•sion (si klōō′zhən), *n.* **1.** an act of secluding. **2.** the state of being secluded; solitude. **3.** a secluded place. —**se•clu′sive,** *adj.* —**se•clu′sive•ly,** *adv.* —**se•clu′sive•ness,** *n.*

sec•o•bar•bi•tal (sek′ō bär′bi tôl′, -tal′), *n.* a white, odorless, slightly bitter powder, $C_{12}H_{18}N_2O_3$, used as a sedative and hypnotic.

sec•ond[1] (sek′ənd), *adj.* **1.** next after the first; being the ordinal number for two. **2.** being the latter of two equal parts. **3.** next after the first in place, time, or value. **4.** next after the first in rank: *the second in command.* **5.** alternate: *every second week.* **6.** inferior. **7.** being the lower of two parts for the same instrument or voice: *second alto.* **8.** another: *a second Solomon.* **9.** pertaining to the gear transmission ratio at which drive shaft speed is greater than that of low gear but not so great as that of other gears for a given engine crankshaft speed. —*n.* **10.** a second part. **11.** the second member of a series. **12.** a person who aids or supports another. **13.** a person who advises a boxer between rounds or attends a duelist. **14.** second gear. **15.** Usu., **seconds.** an additional helping of food. **16.** (in parliamentary procedure) **a.** a person who expresses formal support of a motion so that it may be discussed or put to a vote. **b.** an act or instance of expressing such support. **17.** Usu., **seconds.** goods of less than the highest quality. —*v.t.* **18.** to assist or support. **19.** to further or advance, as aims. **20.** (in parliamentary procedure) to express formal support of (a motion, etc.), as a preliminary to further discussion or to voting. —*adv.* **21.** in the second place; secondly: *The catcher is batting second.* —**sec′ond•er,** *n.* —**sec′ond•ly,** *adv.*

sec•ond² (sek′ənd), *n.* **1. a.** the sixtieth part of a minute of time. **b.** the base SI unit of time, equalling 9,192,631,770 cycles of radiation in a change in energy level of the cesium atom. *Symbol:* s; *Abbr.:* sec **2.** a moment or instant: *It takes only a second to phone.* **3.** the sixtieth part of a minute of angular measure, often represented by the sign ″, as in 30″, which is read as 30 seconds.

Sec′ond Amend′ment, *n.* an amendment to the U.S. Constitution, ratified in 1791 as part of the Bill of Rights, guaranteeing the right to keep and bear arms as necessary to maintain a state militia.

sec•ond•ar•y (sek′ən der′ē), *adj., n., pl.* **-ar•ies.** —*adj.* **1.** next after the first in order, rank, or time. **2.** not primary or original. **3.** of lesser importance. **4.** of or pertaining to secondary schools. **5.** *Chem.* involving or obtained by the replacement of two atoms or groups. **6.** noting or pertaining to the electrical current induced by a primary winding or to the winding in which the current is induced in an induction coil, transformer, or the like. **7.** pertaining to any of a set of flight feathers on the second segment of a bird's wing. —*n.* **8.** a subordinate, assistant, deputy, or agent. **9.** *Football.* the defensive unit that lines up behind the linemen. —**sec•ond•ar•i•ly** (sek′ən der′ə lē, sek′ən dâr′-), *adv.*

sec′ondary col′or, *n.* a color, as orange, green, or violet, produced by mixing two primary colors.

sec′ondary school′, *n.* a high school or a school of corresponding grade ranking between a primary school and a college or university. —**sec′ondary-school′,** *adj.*

sec′ondary sex′ characteris′tic, *n.* any of a number of manifestations, as breasts or a beard, specific to each sex and incipient at puberty but not essential to reproduction.

sec′ondary stress′, *n.* a degree of stress weaker than primary stress: indicated in this dictionary by the mark (′). Compare PRIMARY STRESS.

sec′ond banan′a, *n. Slang.* **1.** a comic who supports the leading comedian, esp. in burlesque or vaudeville. **2.** any person who plays a secondary role. Compare TOP BANANA.

sec′ond base′, *n.* **1.** the second in order of the bases from home plate in baseball. **2.** the position of the player covering the area of the infield between second and first bases. —**sec′ond base′man,** *n.*

sec′ond best′, *n.* a person or thing that is next after the best. —**sec′ond-best′,** *adj.*

sec′ond child′hood, *n.* senility; dotage.

sec′ond class′, *n.* **1.** the class of accommodations inferior to first class but superior to third class. **2.** the class of mail consisting of newspapers and periodicals not sealed against postal inspection.

sec′ond-class′, *adj.* **1.** of a secondary class or quality. **2.** second-rate. **3.** deprived of certain civil rights.

sec′ond-class cit′izen, *n.* **1.** a citizen, esp. a member of a minority group, who is denied the social, political, and economic benefits of citizenship. **2.** a person who is not accorded a fair share of respect, recognition, or consideration: *The boss treats us all like second-class citizens.*

Sec′ond Com′ing, *n.* the coming of Christ on Judgment Day.

Sec′ond Command′ment, *n.* "Thou shalt not make unto thee any graven image, or any likeness of any thing that is in heaven above, or that is in the earth beneath, or that is in the water under the earth; thou shalt not bow down unto them, nor serve them; for I the Lord thy God am a jealous God, visiting the iniquity of the fathers upon the children unto the third and fourth generation of them that hate Me; and showing mercy unto the thousandth generation of them that love Me and keep my commandments.": second of the Ten Commandments. Compare TEN COMMANDMENTS.

sec′ond cous′in, *n.* a child of a first cousin of one's parent.

sec′ond-degree′ burn′, *n.* See under BURN¹ (def. 26).

sec′ond-degree′ mur′der, *n.* See under MURDER (def. 1).

sec′ond estate′, *n.* the second of the three estates: the nobles in France; the Lords Temporal in England. Compare ESTATE (def. 5).

sec′ond fid′dle, *n.* a person serving in a subsidiary capacity.

sec′ond-guess′, *v.t.* **1.** to use hindsight in criticizing or correcting. **2.** to outguess. —**sec′ond-guess′er,** *n.*

sec•ond hand (sek′ənd hand′), *n.* the hand that indicates the seconds on a clock or watch.

sec•ond•hand (sek′ənd hand′), *adj.* **1.** not directly known or experienced: *secondhand knowledge.* **2.** previously used or owned: *secondhand clothes.* **3.** dealing in previously used goods: *a secondhand bookseller.* —*adv.* **4.** after another user or owner: *He bought it secondhand.* **5.** indirectly; at second hand: *heard the news secondhand.*

sec′ondhand smoke′, *n.* smoke from a cigarette, cigar, or pipe that is involuntarily inhaled, esp. by nonsmokers.

sec′ond lan′guage, *n.* a language learned by a person after his or her native language.

sec′ond lieuten′ant, *n.* an officer in the U.S. Army, Air Force, or Marines of the lowest commissioned rank. Compare ENSIGN (def. 4).

sec′ond mate′, *n.* the officer of a merchant vessel next in command beneath the first mate. Also called **sec′ond of′ficer.**

sec′ond na′ture, *n.* a habit or tendency that is so deeply ingrained as to appear automatic.

sec′ond per′son, *n.* **1.** the grammatical person used in an utterance in referring to the one or ones being addressed. **2.** a pronoun or verb form in the second person, as the pronoun *you.*

sec′ond-rate′, *adj.* of lesser or minor quality or importance.

sec′ond sight′, *n.* the faculty of seeing future events; clairvoyance.

sec′ond-sto′ry man′, *n.* a burglar who enters through an upstairs window.

sec′ond string′, *n.* the squad of players available either individually or as a team to replace or relieve those who start a game. —**sec′ond-string′,** *adj.* —**sec′ond-string′er,** *n.*

sec′ond thought′, *n.* Often, **second thoughts.** reservation about a previous action, position, decision, or judgment.

Sec′ond Vat′ican Coun′cil, *n.* the twenty-first Roman Catholic ecumenical council (1962–65) convened by Pope John XXIII. Its 16 documents redefined the nature of the church, gave bishops greater influence in church affairs, and increased lay participation in liturgy. Also called **Vatican II.**

sec′ond wind′ (wind), *n.* **1.** the return of ease in breathing after exhaustion caused by continued physical exertion, as in running. **2.** the energy for a renewed effort to continue an undertaking.

Sec′ond World′, *n.* (*sometimes l.c.*) **1.** the world's industrialized nations other than the U.S. and Russia. **2.** the Communist and socialist nations of the world.

Sec′ond World′ War′, *n.* WORLD WAR II.

se•cre•cy (sē′krə sē), *n., pl.* **-cies. 1.** the state or condition of being secret or concealed. **2.** privacy; retirement; seclusion. **3.** ability to keep a secret. **4.** the habit or characteristic of being secretive; reticence.

se•cret (sē′krit), *adj.* **1.** done, made, or conducted without the knowledge of others. **2.** kept from general knowledge: *a secret password.* **3.** carrying out activities in a manner that prevents them from being observed or detected: *a secret agent.* **4.** hidden from sight; concealed: *a secret entrance.* **5.** close-mouthed; secretive. **6.** beyond ordinary human understanding; esoteric. **7.** designating the security classification below top-secret, or a document so classified. —*n.* **8.** something that is secret, hidden, or concealed. **9.** a mystery: *the secrets of nature.* **10.** a reason or explanation not readily apparent: *the secret of her success.* **11.** a method, plan, etc., known only to the initiated: *a trade secret.* **12.** (*cap.*) an inaudible prayer said before the preface during the mass. —**Idiom. 13.** in secret, so as to remain hidden; secretly. —**se′cret•ly,** *adv.*

sec•re•tar•i•al (sek′ri târ′ē əl), *adj.* pertaining to a secretary or a secretary's skills and work.

sec•re•tar•i•at (sek′ri târ′ē ət), *n.* the office or the officials entrusted with administrative duties, maintaining records, and overseeing or performing secretarial duties, esp. for an international organization: *the secretariat of the United Nations.*

sec•re•tar•y (sek′ri ter′ē), *n., pl.* **-tar•ies. 1.** a person in charge of records, correspondence, and related affairs, as for a company. **2.** a person employed to do routine work in a business office, as typing, filing, and answering phones. **3.** PRIVATE SECRETARY. **4.** (*often cap.*) an officer of state charged with the superintendence and management of a particular department of government, as a member of the president's cabinet in the U.S.: *Secretary of the Treasury.* **5.** a diplomatic official who assists an ambassador or minister. **6.** a piece of furniture for use as a writing desk, esp. one with drawers below and a cabinet or bookshelves above an often enclosed writing surface. —**sec′re•tar′y•ship′,** *n.*

sec′retary-gen′eral, *n., pl.* **secretaries-general.** the chief administrative officer of a secretariat.

sec′retary of state′, *n.* (*often caps.*) **1.** the head and chief administrator of the U.S. Department of State. Compare FOREIGN MINISTER. **2.** (in the U.S.) the official in a state government whose chief function is to distribute statutes, administer elections, keep archives, etc.,

se•crete¹ (si krēt′), *v.t.* **-cret•ed, -cret•ing.** to discharge, generate, or release by secretion.

se•crete² (si krēt′), *v.t.* **-cret•ed, -cret•ing.** to place out of sight; hide.

Se′cret Gar′den, The, a children's novel (1909) by Frances H. Burnett.

se•cre•tion (si krē′shən), *n.* **1.** (in a cell or gland) the process of separating, elaborating, and releasing a substance that fulfills some function within the organism or undergoes excretion. **2.** the product of this process. —**se•cre′tion•ar′y** (-shə ner′ē), *adj.*

se•cre•tive (sē′kri tiv, si krē′-), *adj.* having or showing a disposition to secrecy; reticent; close-mouthed. —**se′cre•tive•ly,** *adv.* —**se′cre•tive•ness,** *n.*

se•cre•to•ry (si krē′tə rē), *adj.* **1.** pertaining to secretion. **2.** performing the process of secretion.

se′cret police′, *n.* a police force that operates secretly, esp. to suppress dissent against the government.

S

se′cret serv′ice, *n.* **1.** the branch of government service that conducts secret investigations, esp. regarding espionage. **2.** (*caps.*) a branch of the U.S. Department of the Treasury chiefly responsible for protecting the president and vice president and their families, and for apprehending counterfeiters. —**se′cret-serv′ice,** *adj.*

se′cret soci′ety, *n.* an organization, as a fraternal society, whose members share secret rites and promise to assist each other.

secs., **1.** seconds. **2.** sections.

sect (sekt), *n.* **1.** a body of persons adhering to a particular religious faith; denomination. **2.** a group regarded as heretical or as deviating from a generally accepted religious tradition. **3.** any group or faction united by a specific doctrine.

sec·tar·i·an (sek târ′ē ən), *adj.* **1.** of or pertaining to sectaries or sects. **2.** narrowly confined or devoted to a particular sect. **3.** narrowly confined or limited in interest, purpose, etc. —*n.* **4.** a member of a sect. **5.** a bigoted or narrow-minded person.

sec·tion (sek′shən), *n.* **1.** a distinct subdivision of anything, as an object or community. **2.** a distinct part of a newspaper, legal code, chapter, etc. **3.** a part that is separated. **4.** one of a number of parts that can be fitted together to make a whole. **5.** one of the 36 subdivisions of a township, being one square mile (2.59 sq. km or 640 acres) in area. **6.** an act or instance of cutting; separation by cutting. **7. a.** the making of a surgical incision. **b.** the incision itself. **8.** a thin slice of a tissue, mineral, or the like, as for microscopic examination. **9.** a representation of an object as it would appear if cut by a plane, showing its internal structure. **10. a.** a small military unit consisting of two or more squads. **b.** a small tactical division in naval and air units. **11.** any of two or more trains, buses, etc., running on the same route and considered as one unit. **12.** a segment of a naturally segmented fruit, as an orange. **13.** a division of an orchestra or band containing all the instruments of one class. **14.** a mark (§) used to indicate a subdivision of a text or a reference to a footnote. —*v.t.* **15.** to divide into sections. **16.** to cut through so as to show a section. **17.** to make a surgical incision.

sec·tion·al (sek′shə nl), *adj.* **1.** pertaining or limited to a particular section; local or regional. **2.** composed of sections: *a sectional sofa.* **3.** of or pertaining to a section: *a sectional view of the brain.* —*n.* **4.** a sofa composed of several sections that can be arranged in various combinations. —**sec′tion·al·ly,** *adv.*

sec·tor (sek′tər), *n.* **1. a.** a plane figure bounded by two radii and the included arc of a circle. **b.** a mathematical instrument consisting of two flat rulers hinged together at one end and bearing various scales. **2.** the area that a particular military unit is assigned to defend. **3.** a distinct part, esp. of society or of a nation's economy. **4.** a section or zone, as of a city. —*v.t.* **5.** to divide into sectors. —**sec·to′ri·al** (-tôr′ē əl, -tōr′-), *adj.*

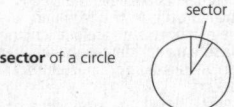

sector

sector of a circle

sec·u·lar (sek′yə lər), *adj.* **1.** of or pertaining to worldly things or to things not regarded as sacred; temporal. **2.** not relating to or concerned with religion (opposed to *sacred*): *secular music.* **3.** concerned with nonreligious subjects: *secular schools.* **4.** not belonging to a religious order. **5.** occurring or celebrated once in an age or century: *the secular games of Rome.* **6.** continuing throughout the ages. —*n.* **7.** a layperson. **8.** one of the secular clergy. —**sec′u·lar·ly,** *adv.*

sec′ular hu′manism, *n.* any set of beliefs that promotes human values without specific allusion to religious doctrines. —**sec′ular hu′manist,** *n.*

sec·u·lar·ism (sek′yə lə riz′əm), *n.* **1.** secular spirit or tendency, esp. a system of political or social philosophy that rejects all forms of religious faith and worship. **2.** the view that public education and other matters of civil policy should be conducted without the influence of religious beliefs. —**sec′u·lar·ist,** *n., adj.*

sec·u·lar·ize (sek′yə lə rīz′), *v.t.,* **-ized, -iz·ing.** **1.** to make secular; separate from religious connection or influences; make worldly. **2.** to change (clergy) from regular to secular. **3.** to transfer (property) from ecclesiastical to civil possession or use. —**sec′u·lar·i·za′tion,** *n.*

se·cure (si kyo͝or′), *adj.,* **-cur·er, -cur·est,** *v.,* **-cured, -cur·ing.** —*adj.* **1.** free from danger or harm; safe. **2.** not liable to fail, yield, etc., as a support or fastening; firm. **3.** affording safety, as a place. **4.** kept in safe custody. **5.** free from care or anxiety: *emotionally secure.* **6.** firmly established, as a reputation. **7.** certain; assured: *secure in his religious belief.* **8.** safe from penetration or interception by unauthorized persons: *secure radio communications.* —*v.t.* **9.** to get hold of; obtain. **10.** to free from danger or harm; make safe. **11.** to make certain of; ensure: *The novel secured his reputation.* **12.** to make fast: *to secure a rope.* **13. a.** to assure payment of (a debt) by pledging property. **b.** to assure (a creditor) of payment by a pledge. **14.** to lock or fasten against intruders. **15.** to capture (a person or animal). **16.** to tie up the arms or hands of; pinion. **17.** to guarantee the privacy or secrecy of. —*v.i.* **18.** to be or become safe; have security. **19.** *Naut.* **a.** to cover openings and make

movable objects fast. **b.** to be excused from duty: *All hands secure from general quarters.* —**se·cur′a·ble,** *adj.* —**se·cure′ly,** *adv.*

se·cu·ri·ty (si kyo͝or′i tē), *n., pl.* **-ties,** *adj.* —*n.* **1.** freedom from danger, risk, etc.; safety. **2.** freedom from anxiety. **3.** something that protects or makes safe. **4.** freedom from financial cares. **5.** precautions taken to guard against crime, sabotage, etc. **6.** a department or organization responsible for protection or safety. **7.** precautions taken against escape: *to be held in maximum security.* **8.** an assurance; guarantee. **9. a.** something given as surety for the fulfillment of an obligation. **b.** a person who becomes surety for another. **10. a.** evidence of property, as a bond or a certificate of stock. **b.** securities, stocks and bonds. —*adj.* **11.** pertaining to security: *strict security measures.*

secu′rity blan′ket, *n.* **1.** a blanket carried by a child to provide reassurance. **2.** any object whose presence gives a feeling of security.

Secu′rity Coun′cil, *n.* the committee of the United Nations charged with maintaining international peace and security.

secu′rity risk′, *n.* a person considered by authorities as likely to commit acts that might threaten the security of a country.

secy or **sec′y,** secretary.

se·dan (si dan′), *n.* **1.** an enclosed automobile body having two or four doors and seating four or more persons. **2.** SEDAN CHAIR.

sedan′ chair′ *n.* an enclosed vehicle for one person, borne on poles by two bearers.

se·date (si dāt′), *adj., v.,* **-dat·ed, -dat·ing.** —*adj.* **1.** calm, quiet, or composed; undisturbed. —*v.t.* **2.** to put under sedation. —**se·date′ly,** *adv.* —**se·date′ness,** *n.*

se·da·tion (si dā′shən), *n.* **1.** the bringing about of mental or physiological relaxation, esp. by the use of a drug. **2.** the state so induced.

sed·a·tive (sed′ə tiv), *adj.* **1.** tending to soothe. **2.** assuaging pain or allaying irritability or excitement. —*n.* **3.** a sedative drug or agent.

sed·en·tar·y (sed′n ter′ē), *adj.* **1.** characterized by or requiring a sitting posture: *a sedentary occupation.* **2.** characterized by inactivity and lack of exercise: *a sedentary life.* **3.** *Zool.* **a.** abiding in one place; not migratory. **b.** pertaining to animals that move about little or are permanently attached to something, as a barnacle.

Se·der (sā′dər), *n., pl.* **Se·ders, Se·da·rim** (sā′dä rēm′). *Judaism.* a ceremonial dinner, held on the first night or first two nights of Passover, that includes the reading of the haggadah and the eating of foods symbolic of the Israelites' slavery and the Exodus from Egypt. [< Hebrew *sēdher* lit., order, arrangement]

sedge (sej), *n.* any rushlike or grasslike plant of the genus *Carex,* growing in wet places.

sed·i·ment (sed′ə mənt), *n.* **1.** the matter that settles to the bottom of a liquid; lees; dregs. **2.** *Geol.* mineral or organic matter deposited by water, air, or ice. —**sed′i·men′tous,** *adj.*

sed·i·men·ta·ry (sed′ə men′tə rē) also **sed′i·men′tal,** *adj.* **1.** of or pertaining to sediment. **2.** formed by the deposition of sediment, as certain rocks.

sed·i·men·ta·tion (sed′ə mən tā′shən), *n.* the deposition or accumulation of sediment.

sed·i·men·tol·o·gy (sed′ə mən tol′ə jē), *n.* the study of sedimentary rocks. —**sed′i·men·tol′o·gist,** *n.*

se·di·tion (si dish′ən), *n.* **1.** incitement of discontent or rebellion against a government. **2.** any action promoting such discontent or rebellion.

se·di·tious (si dish′əs), *adj.* **1.** of, pertaining to, or of the nature of sedition. **2.** given to or guilty of sedition. —**se·di′tious·ly,** *adv.* —**se·di′tious·ness,** *n.*

se·duce (si do͞os′, -dyo͞os′), *v.t.,* **-duced, -duc·ing.** **1.** to lead astray, as from duty or principles; corrupt. **2.** to induce to have sexual intercourse. **3.** to win over; attract; entice. —**se·duce′ment,** *n.* —**se·duc′er,** *n.* —**se·duc′i·ble,** *adj.* —**se·duc′ing·ly,** *adv.*

se·duc·tion (si duk′shən), *n.* **1.** an act or instance of seducing, esp. sexually. **2.** the condition of being seduced. **3.** a means of seducing; enticement; lure.

se·duc·tive (si duk′tiv), *adj.* tending to seduce; enticing; alluring: *a seductive smile.* —**se·duc′tive·ly,** *adv.* —**se·duc′tive·ness,** *n.*

se·duc·tress (si duk′tris), *n.* a woman who seduces.

sed·u·lous (sej′ə ləs), *adj.* **1.** diligent in character or application; persevering. **2.** persistently or carefully maintained: *sedulous flattery.* —**sed′u·lous·ly,** *adv.* —**sed′u·lous·ness,** *n.*

see¹ (sē), *v.,* **saw, seen, see·ing.** —*v.t.* **1.** to perceive with the eyes; look at. **2.** to view; visit or attend as a spectator: *to see a play.* **3.** to perceive (things) mentally; understand. **4.** to construct a mental image of; visualize. **5.** to accept or imagine as acceptable: *I can't see him as president.* **6.** to be cognizant of; recognize: *to see one's mistake.* **7.** to scan or view, esp. by electronic means. **8.** to foresee: *He doesn't see us in a war.* **9.** to ascertain; find out: *See who is at the door.* **10.** to have experience of: *to see service in the Peace Corps.* **11.** to make sure: *See that the door is locked.* **12.** to meet and converse with. **13.** to receive as a visitor. **14.** to visit. **15.** to court or date frequently. **16.** to help or assist: *He's seeing his brother through college.* **17.** to escort or accompany: *to see someone home.* **18.** to match (a bet) or match the bet of (a bettor) by staking an equal sum; call: *I'll see your five and raise you five.* **19.** to read about: *I saw it in the newspaper.* —*v.i.* **20.** to have the power of sight. **21.** to understand intellectually or spiritually; have insight. **22.** to pay attention; heed: *See, here it comes.* **23.** to find out; ascertain: *See for yourself.* **24.** to think; consider: *Let me see, what was his name?* **25. see about, a.** to inquire about; investigate. **b.** Also, **see after.** to attend to; take care of. **26. see off,** to accompany (someone about to go on a journey) to the place of departure. **27. see out, a.** to work on until completion; finish; see through. **b.** to escort to an outer door. **28. see through, a.** to ascertain the true nature of, esp. to detect the sham or treachery in. **b.** to remain with until completion; see out. **29. see to,** to take care of; attend to; see about: *to see to the travel arrangements.* —*Idiom.* **30. see red,** *Informal.* to become enraged.

see² (sē), *n.* the seat, center of authority, office, or jurisdiction of a bishop.

seed (sēd), *n., pl.* **seeds,** (*esp. collectively*) **seed,** *v., adj.* —*n.* **1.** the fertilized, matured ovule of a flowering plant, containing an embryo or rudimentary plant. **2.** any propagative part of a plant, including tubers and bulbs. **3.** such parts collectively. **4.** any similar small part or fruit. **5.** the propagative source of anything: *the seeds of discord.* **6.** offspring; progeny. **7.** birth: *not of mortal seed.* **8.** sperm; semen. **9.** the ovum or ova of certain animals, as the lobster and the silkworm moth. **10.** SEED OYSTER. **11.** a small air bubble in a glass piece, caused by defective firing. **12.** *Crystall., Chem.* a small crystal added to a solution to promote crystallization. **13.** a player or team seeded in a tournament. —*v.t.* **14.** to sow (a field, lawn, etc.) with seed. **15.** to sow or scatter (seed). **16.** to sow or scatter (clouds) with crystals or particles of silver iodide, solid carbon dioxide, etc., to induce precipitation. **17.** to introduce in the hope of increase: *to seed a lake with trout.* **18.** to remove the seeds from (fruit). **19.** to rank (players or teams) by past performance in arranging tournament pairings, so that the most highly ranked competitors will not play each other until later rounds. **20.** to develop (a business), esp. by providing operating capital. —*v.i.* **21.** to sow seed. **22.** to produce or shed seed. —*adj.* **23.** producing seed; used for seed: *a seed potato.* —*Idiom.* **24. go** or **run to seed, a.** (of the flower of a plant) to pass to the stage of yielding seed. **b.** to deteriorate or decline, as in health or appearance. **25. in seed, a.** (of certain plants) in the state of bearing ripened seeds. **b.** (of a field, a lawn, etc.) sown with seed. —**seed′less,** *adj.* —**seed′like′,** *adj.*

seed·case (sēd′kās′), *n.* a seed capsule; pericarp.

seed′ coat′, *n.* the outer covering of a seed.

seed·ling (sēd′ling), *n.* **1.** a plant or tree grown from a seed. **2.** a tree not yet 3 ft. (1 m) high. **3.** any young plant, esp. one grown in a nursery for transplanting.

seed′ mon′ey, *n.* capital for the initial stages of a new business or other enterprise, esp. for the initial operating costs.

seed′ oy′ster, *n.* a very young oyster, esp. one suitable for transplanting to start an oyster bed.

seed′ pearl′, *n.* a small, sometimes irregularly shaped pearl weighing less than ¼ grain.

seed′ plant′, *n.* a seed-bearing plant; spermatophyte.

seed·pod (sēd′pod′), *n.* a seed vessel or dehiscent fruit that splits when ripe.

seed′stock′ or **seed′ stock′,** *n.* **1.** seed, tubers, or roots selected and kept for planting. **2.** the animals needed to replenish a population, as after hunting or fishing.

seed′ ves′sel, *n.* a pericarp.

seed·y (sē′dē), *adj.,* **seed·i·er, seed·i·est. 1.** containing many seeds. **2.** bearing seeds. **3.** poorly kept; run-down. **4.** shabbily dressed; unkempt. **5.** slightly ill. —**seed′i·ness,** *n.*

See·ger (sē′gər), *n.* **1. Alan,** 1888–1916, U.S. poet. **2. Peter** (*Pete*), born 1919, U.S. folk singer and folklorist.

see·ing (sē′ing), *conj.* considering; inasmuch as.

See′ing Eye′ dog′, *Trademark.* a guide dog trained by The Seeing Eye, Inc., of Morristown, N.J.

seek (sēk), *v.,* **sought, seek·ing.** —*v.t.* **1.** to go in search or quest of. **2.** to try to discover, as by studying. **3.** to try to obtain: *to seek fame.* **4.** to try or attempt (usu. fol. by an infinitive): *to seek to convince a person.* **5.** to ask for; request: *to seek advice.* —*v.i.* **6.** to make inquiry. —**seek′er,** *n.*

seem (sēm), *v.i.* **1.** to appear to be, feel, do, etc. **2.** to appear to one's own senses, judgment, etc. **3.** to appear to be true or probable: *It seems likely to rain.* **4.** to appear or pretend to be such: *to seem friendly.*

seem·ing (sē′ming), *adj.* **1.** apparent; ostensible: *a seeming advantage.* —*n.* **2.** outward appearance. —**seem′ing·ly,** *adv.*

seem·ly (sēm′lē), *adj.,* **-li·er, -li·est,** *adv.* —*adj.* **1.** fitting or proper; decorous: *Your outburst was hardly seemly.* **2.** suitable or appropriate: *a seemly gesture.* **3.** of pleasing appearance; handsome. —*adv.* **4.** in a seemly manner; fittingly; becomingly. —**seem′li·ness,** *n.*

seen (sēn), *v.* pp. of SEE¹.

seep (sēp), *v.i.* **1.** to pass, flow, or ooze gradually, as through a porous substance. **2.** to become diffused; permeate. —*v.t.* **3.** to cause to seep; filter. —*n.* **4.** moisture that seeps out; seepage. **5.** a small spring, pool, or the like, where liquid from the ground has oozed to the surface.

seep·age (sē′pij), *n.* **1.** the act or process of seeping. **2.** something that seeps. **3.** a quantity that has seeped out.

se·er (sē′ər for 1; sēr for 2–4), *n.* **1.** a person who sees; observer. **2.** a person who prophesies future events; prophet. **3.** a person endowed with moral and spiritual insight or knowledge. **4.** a person reputed to have powers of divination, as a crystal gazer.

seer·suck·er (sēr′suk′ər), *n.* a plain-weave cotton or cottonlike fabric, usu. striped and having a characteristic crinkled texture in the weave.

see·saw (sē′sô′), *n.* **1.** a recreational device on which two children alternately ride up and down while seated at opposite ends of a long plank balanced at the middle. **2.** any movement or procedure characterized by ups and downs or vacillation. —*adj.* **3.** moving up and down, back and forth, or alternately ahead and behind. —*v.i.* **4.** to move in a seesaw manner. **5.** to ride on a seesaw. **6.** to vacillate. —*v.t.* **7.** to cause to move in a seesaw manner.

seethe (sēth), *v.,* **seethed, seeth·ing,** *n.* —*v.i.* **1.** to surge or foam as if boiling. **2.** to be in a state of agitation or excitement. —*v.t.* **3.** to soak or steep. **4.** to cook by boiling or simmering; boil. —*n.* **5.** the act of seething. **6.** the state of being agitated or excited. —**seeth′ing·ly,** *adv.*

see′-through′, *adj.* **1.** Also **see′-thru′.** transparent. —*n.* **2.** a degree of transparency. **3.** a see-through item of clothing.

seg·ment (*n.* seg′mənt; *v.* seg′ment, seg ment′), *n.* **1.** one of the parts into which something is divided; a division, portion, or section. **2.** *Geom.* **a.** a part cut off from a figure, esp. a circular or spherical one, by a line or plane. **b.** a finite section of a line. **3.** an object, as a machine part, having the form of a segment or sector of a circle. —*v.t., v.i.* **4.** to separate or divide into segments. —**seg′men·tar′y** (-mən ter′ē), *adj.* —**seg′men·tate′,** *adj.*

seg·men·ta·tion (seg′mən tā′shən), *n.* **1.** division into segments. **2.** *Biol.* **a.** the subdivision of an organism or of an organ into more or less equivalent parts. **b.** cell division.

se·gno (sān′yō, sen′-), *n., pl.* **se·gni** (sān′yē, sen′-). a musical sign at the beginning or end of a section to be repeated.

seg·re·gate (*v.* seg′ri gāt′; *n.* -git, -gāt′), *v.,* **-gat·ed, -gat·ing,** *n.* —*v.t.* **1.** to separate or set apart from others; isolate. **2.** to require, often with force, the separation of (a specific racial, religious, or other group) from the body of society. —*v.i.* **3.** to become segregated. **4.** to practice or require segregation, esp. racial segregation. **5.** (of allelic genes) to separate during meiosis. —*n.* **6.** a segregated thing, person, or group. —**seg′re·ga·ble** (-gə bəl), *adj.* —**seg′re·ga′tive,** *adj.*

seg·re·gat·ed (seg′ri gā′tid), *adj.* **1.** characterized by or practicing racial segregation. **2.** restricted to one racial or other ethnic group. **3.** maintaining separate facilities for members of different ethnic groups. **4.** discriminating against a group, esp. on the basis of race. **5.** set apart.

seg·re·ga·tion (seg′ri gā′shən), *n.* **1.** the act or practice of segregating. **2.** the state of being segregated. **3.** something segregated. **4.** *Genetics.* the separation of allelic genes into different gametes during meiosis. —**seg′re·ga′tion·al,** *adj.*

seg·re·ga·tion·ist (seg′ri gā′shə nist), *n.* a person who advocates segregation, esp. racial segregation.

se·gue (sā′gwā, seg′wā), *v.,* **-gued, -gue·ing,** *n.* —*v.i.* **1.** to continue at once with the next musical section (used as a musical direction). **2.** to perform in the manner of the preceding section (used as a musical direction). **3.** to make a smooth transition from one item or topic to another. —*n.* **4.** an uninterrupted transition made between one musical section or composition and another.

seine (sān), *n., v.,* **seined, sein·ing.** —*n.* **1.** a fishing net that hangs vertically in the water, having floats at the upper edge and sinkers at the lower. —*v.t.* **2.** to fish for or catch with a seine. **3.** to use a seine in (water). —*v.i.* **4.** to fish with a seine. —**sein′er,** *n.*

Seine (sān, sen), *n.* a river in France, flowing NW through Paris to the English Channel. 480 mi. (773 km) long.

Seir *n.* a mountainous area between the Dead Sea and the Red Sea. Deut. 2:12, 29.

seis·mic (sīz′mik, sīs′-) also **seis′mal, seis′mi·cal,** *adj.* pertaining to, of the nature of, or caused by an earthquake or vibration of the earth, whether due to natural or artificial causes. —**seis′mi·cal·ly,** *adv.*

seismo-, a combining form meaning "earthquake": *seismograph.*

seis·mog·ra·phy (sīz mog′rə fē, sīs-), *n.* **1.** the scientific measuring and recording of the shock and vibrations of earthquakes. **2.** SEISMOLOGY. —**seis·mog′ra·pher,** *n.*

seis·mol·o·gy (sīz mol′ə jē, sīs-), *n.* the science or study of earthquakes and their phenomena. —**seis′mo·log′ic** (-mə loj′ik), **seis′mo·log′i·cal,** *adj.* —**seis′mo·log′i·cal·ly,** *adv.* —**seis·mol′o·gist,** *n.*

seize (sēz), *v.,* **seized, seiz·ing.** —*v.t.* **1.** to take hold of suddenly or forcibly; grasp: *to seize a weapon.* **2.** to grasp mentally; understand clearly and completely: *to seize an idea.* **3.** to take possession or control of as if by suddenly laying hold: *Panic seized the crowd.* **4.** to take possession of by legal authority; confiscate. **5.** to capture; take into custody. **6.** to take advantage of promptly: *to seize an opportunity.* **7.** to bind or fasten (rope) together with a seizing. —*v.i.* **8.** to grab or take hold suddenly or forcibly: *to seize on a rope.* **9.** to resort to a method, plan, etc., in desperation. **10.** to have moving parts bind and stop moving as a result of excessive pressure, temperature, or friction. —*Proverb.* **11. Seize the day,** take full advantage of each moment. —**seiz′a·ble,** *adj.* —**seiz′er,** *n.*

seiz·ing (sē′zing), *n.* **1.** the act of a person or thing that seizes. **2. a.** the binding or fastening of large rope by multiple turns of smaller cordage. **b.** the smaller cordage so used.

sei·zure (sē′zhər), *n.* **1.** an act or instance of seizing. **2.** the state of being seized. **3.** a taking possession of an item, property, or person legally or by force. **4.** a sudden attack, as of epilepsy.

se·lah (sē′lə, sel′ə), *n., interj.* an expression that occurs frequently in the Psalms and whose meaning is uncertain: thought to be a liturgical or musical note.

sel•dom (sel′dəm), *adv.* **1.** on only a few occasions; rarely; infrequently: *We seldom see them anymore.* —*adj.* **2.** rare; infrequent.

se•lect (si lekt′), *v.t.* **1.** to choose in preference to another or others. —*v.i.* **2.** to make a choice; pick. —*adj.* **3.** chosen in preference to another or others; preferred. **4.** choice; of special value or excellence. **5.** careful in choosing; discriminating. **6.** carefully chosen; exclusive: *a select group.* —**se•lect′ly,** *adv.* —**se•lect′ness,** *n.* —**se•lec′tor,** *n.*

se•lect•ee (si lek tē′), *n.* a person selected by draft for service in the armed forces.

se•lec•tion (si lek′shən), *n.* **1.** an act or instance of selecting or the state of being selected. **2.** a thing or a number of things selected. **3.** an aggregate of things displayed for choice, purchase, use, etc. **4.** a process that results in some members of a population having greater success in perpetuating their genetic traits.

se•lec•tive (si lek′tiv), *adj.* **1.** having the function or power of selecting; making a selection. **2.** characterized by careful selection. **3.** of or pertaining to selection. —**se•lec′tive•ly,** *adv.* —**se•lec′tive•ness,** *n.*

selec′tive serv′ice, *n.* compulsory military service.

se•lec•tiv•i•ty (si lek tiv′i tē, sē′lek-), *n.* **1.** the state or quality of being selective. **2.** the degree to which an electronic circuit or instrument, as a radio receiver, can distinguish particular frequencies.

se•lect•man (si lekt′mən), *n., pl.* **-men.** (in most New England states) one of a board of town officers chosen to manage certain public affairs.

sel•e•nite (sel′ə nīt′, si lē′nīt), *n.* a variety of gypsum, found in transparent crystals. —**sel′e•nit′ic** (-nit′ik), **sel′e•nit′i•cal,** *adj.*

se•le•ni•um (si lē′nē əm), *n.* a nonmetallic element occurring in several allotropic forms and having an electrical resistance that varies under the influence of light. *Symbol:* Se; *at. wt.:* 78.96; *at. no.:* 34; *sp. gr.:* (gray) 4.80 at 25°C, (red) 4.50 at 25°C.

seleno-, a combining form meaning "moon": *selenography.*

sel•e•nog•ra•phy (sel′ə nog′rə fē), *n.* the branch of astronomy that deals with the charting of the moon's surface. —**sel′e•nog′ra•pher,** *n.* —**se•le•no•graph•ic** (si lē′nə graf′ik), *adj.*

sel•e•nol•o•gy (sel′ə nol′ə jē), *n.* the branch of astronomy that deals with the nature and origin of the physical features of the moon. —**se•le•no•log•i•cal** (sə lēn′l oj′i kəl), *adj.* —**sel′e•nol′o•gist,** *n.*

Se•leu•cia (si lōō′shə), *n.* **1.** an ancient city in Iraq, on the Tigris River: capital of the Seleucid Empire. **2.** an ancient city in Asia Minor, near the mouth of the Orontes River: the port of Antioch.

Se•leu•cid (si lōō′sid), *n., pl.* **-cids, -ci•dae** (-si dē′), *adj.* —*n.* **1.** a member of a Macedonian dynasty, 312–64 B.C., ruling an empire that included much of Asia Minor, Syria, Persia, Bactria, and Babylonia. —*adj.* **2.** Also, **Se•leu′ci•dan.** of or pertaining to the Seleucids or their dynasty.

self (self), *n. and pron., pl.* **selves,** *adj.* —*n.* **1.** a person or thing referred to with respect to complete individuality: *one's own self.* **2.** a person's nature, character, etc.: *his better self.* **3.** personal interest. **4.** *Philos.* the subject of experience as contrasted with the object of experience; ego. —*pron.* **5.** myself, herself, etc.: *to make a check payable to self.* —*adj.* **6.** being the same throughout; uniform. **7.** being of one piece with the rest.

self′-abase′ment, *n.* humiliation of oneself, as from guilt or shame.

self′-absorbed′, *adj.* preoccupied with one's thoughts, interests, etc. —**self′-absorp′tion,** *n.*

self′-act′ing, *adj.* acting by itself; automatic.

self′-actualiza′tion, *n.* the achievement of one's full potential through creativity, independence, spontaneity, and a grasp of the real world. —**self′-ac′tualize,** *v.i.,* **-ized, -iz•ing.**

self′-addressed′, *adj.* addressed for return to the sender.

self′-aggran′dizement, *n.* increase of one's own power, wealth, etc., usu. aggressively. —**self′-aggran′dizing,** *adj.*

self′-anal′ysis, *n.* the application of psychoanalytic techniques to an analysis of one's own personality and behavior without the aid of another person.

self′-appoint′ed, *adj.* chosen by oneself to act or function in a certain capacity, esp. self-righteously.

self′-asser′tion, *n.* insistence on or an expression of one's own importance, opinions, or the like. —**self′-asser′tive,** *adj.* —**self′-asser′tively,** *adv.* —**self′-asser′tiveness,** *n.*

self′-assur′ance, *n.* self-confidence.

self′-assured′, *adj.* self-confident. —**self′-assur′edly,** *adv.* —**self′-assur′edness,** *n.*

self′-cen′tered, *adj.* **1.** engrossed in self; selfish; egotistical. **2.** centered in oneself or itself. Also, *esp. Brit.,* **self′-cen′tred.** —**self′-cen′tered•ly,** *adv.* —**self′-cen′tered•ness,** *n.*

self′-confessed′, *adj.* openly admitting to being a person of a specified type.

self′-con′fidence, *n.* faith in one's own judgment, ability, etc. —**self′-con′fident,** *adj.* —**self′-con′fidently,** *adv.*

self′-congratula′tion, *n.* the expression or feeling of uncritical satisfaction with oneself or one's own accomplishment, good fortune, etc.; complacency. —**self′-congrat′ulatory,** *adj.*

self′-con′scious, *adj.* **1.** excessively aware of being observed by others. **2.** conscious of oneself or one's own being. —**self′-con′sciously,** *adv.* —**self′-con′sciousness,** *n.*

self′-contained′, *adj.* **1.** containing in oneself or itself all that is necessary; independent. **2.** reserved or uncommunicative. **3.** self-possessed. —**self′-contain′edly,** *adv.* —**self′-contain′ment,** *n.*

self′-control′, *n.* restraint of oneself or one's actions, feelings, etc. —**self′-controlled′,** *adj.* —**self′-control′ling,** *adj.*

self′-crit′ical, *adj.* **1.** capable of criticizing oneself objectively. **2.** tending to find fault with one's own actions, motives, etc. —**self′-crit′ically,** *adv.* —**self′-crit′icism,** *n.*

self′-deceived′, *adj.* **1.** holding an erroneous opinion of oneself, one's own effort, or the like. **2.** being mistaken, as from careless or wishful thinking.

self′-decep′tion, *n.* the act or fact of deceiving oneself. Also called **self′-deceit′.** —**self′-decep′tive,** *adj.*

self′-defense′, *n.* **1.** the act of defending one's person by physical force. **2.** a claim or plea that the use of force was necessary in defending one's own person. **3.** an act or instance of protecting one's own interests, property, etc., as by argument. Also, *esp. Brit.,* **self′-defence′.** —**self′-defen′sive,** *adj.*

self′-delu′sion, *n.* the act or fact of deluding oneself. —**self′-delud′ed,** *adj.* —**self′-delud′ing,** *adj.*

self′-deni′al, *n.* **1.** the sacrifice of one's own desires; unselfishness. **2.** an act or instance of restraining or curbing one's desires. —**self′-deny′ing,** *adj.* —**self′-deny′ingly,** *adv.*

self′-dep′recating, *adj.* belittling or undervaluing oneself; excessively modest: *self-deprecating remarks.* —**self′-dep′recatingly,** *adv.* —**self′-depreca′tion,** *n.*

self′-destruct′, *v.i.* **1.** to destroy itself or oneself. —*adj.* **2.** causing something to self-destruct: *a self-destruct mechanism.*

self′-destruc′tion, *n.* **1.** the destruction or ruination of oneself or one's life. **2.** suicide.

self′-destruc′tive, *adj.* **1.** destructive to oneself. **2.** reflecting or exhibiting suicidal desires. —**self′-destruc′tively,** *adv.*

self′-determina′tion, *n.* **1.** freedom to live as one chooses, or to act or decide without consulting others. **2.** freedom of a people to determine the way in which they shall be governed. —**self′-deter′mined,** *adj.* —**self′-deter′mining,** *adj.*

self′-deter′minism, *n.* a philosophic doctrine that every present state or condition of the self is a result of previous states or conditions of the self.

self′-dis′cipline, *n.* discipline and training of oneself, usu. for improvement. —**self′-dis′ciplined,** *adj.*

self′-doubt′, *n.* lack of confidence in one's own motives, ability, etc. —**self′-doubt′ing,** *adj.*

self′-efface′ment, *n.* the act or fact of keeping oneself in the background, as in humility. —**self′-effac′ing,** *adj.* —**self′-effac′ingly,** *adv.*

self′-employed′, *adj.* earning one's living from one's own profession or business, esp. as a freelancer. —**self′-employ′ment,** *n.*

self′-esteem′, *n.* self-respect.

self′-ev′ident, *adj.* evident in itself without proof or demonstration; axiomatic. —**self′-ev′idently,** *adv.*

self′-examina′tion, *n.* **1.** examination into one's own state, motives, etc. **2.** examination of one's body for signs of illness or disease. —**self′-exam′ining,** *adj.*

self′-explan′atory, *adj.* needing no explanation; obvious.

self′-fulfill′ing, *adj.* **1.** characterized by or bringing about self-fulfillment. **2.** happening or brought about as a result of being foretold, expected, or talked about.

self′-fulfill′ment, *n.* the act or fact of fulfilling one's ambitions, desires, etc., through one's own efforts.

self′-gov′ernment, *n.* **1.** government of a state, community, or region by its own people; democratic government. **2.** the condition of being self-governed. **3.** self-control. —**self′-gov′erned,** *adj.* —**self′-gov′erning,** *adj.*

self′-help′, *adj.* (of a book, home study course, program, etc.) offering individuals information or counseling on how to help themselves attain certain goals. —**self′-help′er,** *n.* —**self′-help′ful, self′-help′ing,** *adj.*

self′-im′age, *n.* the conception or mental image one has of oneself.

self′-impor′tant, *adj.* having or showing an exaggerated opinion of one's own importance; pompously conceited or arrogant. —**self′-impor′tance,** *n.* —**self′-impor′tantly,** *adv.*

self′-improve′ment, *n.* improvement of one's mind, character, etc., through one's own efforts. —**self′-improv′ing,** *adj.*

self′-incrimina′tion, *n.* the act of incriminating oneself or exposing oneself to prosecution, esp. by giving evidence or testimony. —**self′-incrim′inating,** *adj.*

self′-induced′, *adj.* induced by oneself or itself.

self′-indul′gent, *adj.* **1.** indulging one's own desires, passions, whims, etc., esp. without restraint. **2.** characterized by such indulgence. —**self′-indul′gence,** *n.* —**self′-indul′gently,** *adv.*

self′-in′terest, *n.* **1.** regard for one's own interest or advantage, esp. with disregard for others. **2.** personal interest or advantage. —**self′-in′terested,** *adj.* —**self′-in′terestedness,** *n.*

self•ish (sel′fish), *adj.* **1.** caring only or chiefly for oneself; concerned with one's own interests, welfare, etc., regardless of others. **2.** characterized by or manifesting concern or care only for oneself: *selfish motives.* —**self′ish•ly,** *adv.* —**self′ish•ness,** *n.*

self′-knowl′edge, *n.* knowledge or understanding of oneself and one's character, abilities, motives, etc.

self′-less (self′lis), *adj.* having little concern for oneself and one's interests; unselfish. —**self′-less•ly,** *adv.* —**self′-less•ness,** *n.*

self′-made′, *adj.* **1.** having succeeded in life unaided: *a self-made man.* **2.** made by oneself.

self′-moti•va′tion, *n.* the initiative to undertake or continue a task without the prodding or supervision of others. —**self′-mo′tivated,** *adj.*

self′-op′erating or **self′-op′erative,** *adj.* automatic.

self′-paced′, *adj.* designed to proceed or be used at a student's own speed: *self-paced instruction.*

self′-perpet′uating, *adj.* **1.** capable of indefinite continuation or renewal of itself or oneself. **2.** continuing oneself in office, rank, etc., beyond the normal limit. —**self′-perpetua′tion,** *n.*

self′-pit′y, *n.* pity for oneself, esp. a self-indulgent attitude concerning one's own difficulties. —**self′-pit′ying,** *adj.*

self′-pollina′tion, *n.* the transfer of pollen from the anther to the stigma of the same flower, another flower on the same plant, or the flower of a plant of the same clone.

self′-por′trait, *n.* a portrait of oneself done by oneself.

self′-possessed′, *adj.* having or showing control of one's feelings, behavior, etc.; composed; poised. —**self′-possess′edly,** *adv.*

self′-posses′sion, *n.* control of one's feelings, behavior, etc., esp. when under pressure. —**self′-possessed′,** *adj.*

self′-preserva′tion, *n.* preservation of oneself from harm or destruction. —**self′-preserv′ing,** *adj.*

self′-propelled′ or **self′-propel′ling,** *adj.* **1.** propelled by itself. **2.** (of a vehicle) propelled by its own engine, motor, or the like. **3.** (of a gun or rocket launcher) having a vehicle as a base.

self′-protec′tion, *n.* protection of oneself or itself. —**self′-protect′ing,** *adj.* —**self′-protec′tive,** *adj.* —**self′-protec′tiveness,** *n.*

self′-pub′lished, *adj.* **1.** published independently by the author: *a self-published book.* **2.** having published one's own work independently: *a self-published author.*

self′-regard′, *n.* **1.** consideration of oneself or one's own interests. **2.** SELF-RESPECT. —**self′-regard′ing,** *adj.*

self′-reg′ulating, *adj.* **1.** adjusting or governing itself without outside interference, controls, or regulations: *a self-regulating economy.* **2.** functioning automatically: *a self-regulating machine.* —**self′-regula′tion,** *n.*

self′-reli′ance, *n.* reliance on oneself or one's own powers or resources. —**self′-reli′ant,** *adj.* —**self′-reli′antly,** *adv.*

self′-respect′, *n.* proper esteem or regard for the dignity of one's character. —**self′-respect′ful,** **self′-respect′ing,** *adj.*

self′-restraint′, *n.* restraint imposed on one by oneself; self-control. —**self′-restrained′,** *adj.* —**self′-restrain′ing,** *adj.*

Sel•fridge (sel′frij), *n.* **Harry Gordon,** 1857?–1947, British retail merchant, born in the U.S.

self′-right′eous, *adj.* confident of one's own righteousness, esp. when smugly moralistic and intolerant of the opinions of others. —**self′-right′eously,** *adv.* —**self′-right′eousness,** *n.*

self′-ris′ing, *adj.* containing a leavening agent.

self′-sac′rifice, *n.* sacrifice of oneself or one's interests for others. —**self′-sac′rificer,** *n.* —**self′-sacrifi′cial,** *adj.* —**self′-sac′rificing,** *adj.* —**self′-sac′rificingly,** *adv.*

self•same (self′sām′, -sām′), *adj.* being the very same; identical. —**self′same′ness,** *n.*

self′-satisfac′tion, *n.* a usu. smug satisfaction with oneself, one's achievements, etc.

self′-sat′isfied, *adj.* feeling or showing self-satisfaction.

self′-seal′ing, *adj.* capable of sealing itself automatically or without the application of adhesive, glue, or moisture.

self′-seek′ing, *n.* **1.** the seeking of one's own interest or selfish ends. —*adj.* **2.** characterized by self-seeking; selfish. —**self′-seek′er,** *n.*

self′-serve′, *adj.* SELF-SERVICE.

self′-serv′ice, *adj.* **1.** of or designating a restaurant, store, etc., in which customers serve themselves, as with items from a display counter, and pay upon leaving. **2.** of or pertaining to something designed to be used without the aid of an attendant: *self-service elevators.* —*n.* **3.** the system of serving oneself in a commercial establishment without the aid of a waiter, clerk, or other attendant.

self′-serv′ing, *adj.* **1.** preoccupied with one's own interests and often disregarding the truth or the interests, well-being, etc., of others. **2.** serving to further one's own selfish interests.

self′-start′er, *n.* **1.** STARTER (def. 3). **2.** a person who shows initiative in undertaking a project. —**self′-start′ing,** *adj.*

self′-stud′y, *n.,* *pl.* **-stud•ies. 1.** the study of something by oneself without direct supervision or attendance in a class. **2.** the study of oneself; self-examination.

self′-suffi′cient, *adj.* **1.** able to supply one's or its own needs without external assistance. **2.** having extreme confidence in one's own resources or powers. —**self′-suffi′ciency,** *n.* —**self′-suffi′ciently,** *adv.*

self′-sustain′ing, *adj.* able to support or sustain oneself or itself without outside aid. —**self′-sustained′,** *adj.*

self′-taught′, *adj.* **1.** taught by oneself without the aid of formal instruction: *a self-taught typist.* **2.** learned by oneself.

self′-will′, *n.* stubborn or obstinate willfulness, as in pursuing one's

own wishes or aims. —**self′-willed′,** *adj.* —**self′-willed′ly,** *adv.* —**self′-willed′ness,** *n.*

self′-wind′ing, *adj.* (of a timepiece) wound by a mechanism, as an electric motor or a system of weighted levers, so that winding by hand is not necessary.

self′-worth′, *n.* the sense of one's own value or worth as a person; self-esteem; self-respect. —**self′-wor′thiness,** *n.*

sell (sel), *v.,* **sold, sell•ing,** *n.* —*v.t.* **1.** to transfer (goods or property) or render (services) in exchange for money. **2.** to deal in; keep or offer for sale: *to sell insurance.* **3.** to persuade or induce to buy. **4.** to promote or effect the sale of. **5.** to achieve sales of. **6.** to cause to be accepted, esp. generally or widely: *to sell an idea to the public.* **7.** to cause or persuade to accept, approve of, or see the value of: *to sell the voters on a candidate.* **8.** to surrender or deliver dishonorably in return for advantage: *to sell one's soul for power; to sell votes.* **9.** to betray. **10.** to exact a price for: *They sold their lives dearly.* **11.** to cheat or hoax. —*v.i.* **12.** to make a sale of something; transfer goods or property in exchange for money. **13.** to offer something for sale. **14.** to be offered for sale at the price indicated (fol. by *at* or *for*). **15.** to engage or be employed in selling something. **16.** to promote sales. **17.** to be in demand by buyers. **18.** to win acceptance, approval, or adoption: *an idea that will sell.* **19. sell off,** to rid oneself of by selling, esp. at reduced prices: *to sell off last year's designs.* **20. sell out, a.** to dispose of entirely by selling. **b.** to betray (an associate, principles, a cause, etc.). **c.** to betray one's principles. —*n.* **21.** an act or method of selling. **22.** *Informal.* a cheat; hoax. —*Idiom.* **23. sell down the river,** to betray someone. —**sell′a•ble,** *adj.*

sell•er (sel′ər), *n.* **1.** a person who sells. **2.** an article considered with reference to its sales: *a poor seller.*

sell′ers′ mar′ket, *n.* a market in which goods and services are scarce and prices relatively high. Compare BUYERS′ MARKET.

sell′ing point′, *n.* a feature that appeals or is expected to appeal to prospective buyers.

sell′-off′ or **sell′ing-off′,** *n.* **1.** a sudden and marked decline in stock or bond prices resulting from widespread selling. **2.** an act or instance of liquidating assets or subsidiaries, as by divestiture.

sell•out (sel′out′), *n.* **1.** an entertainment for which all the seats are sold. **2.** a person who betrays a cause, organization, principles, etc., esp. for money or personal advantage; traitor.

selt•zer (selt′sər), *n.* **1.** naturally occurring mineral water that is effervescent or has been carbonated. **2.** carbonated tap water containing no added minerals or salts, flavorings, or sweeteners. Also called **selt′zer wa′ter.**

sel•vage or **sel•vedge** (sel′vij), *n.* **1.** the edge of woven fabric finished so as to prevent raveling, often in a narrow tape effect, different from the body of the fabric. **2.** any similar strip or part of surplus material, as around a sheet of postage stamps. **3.** a plate or surface through which a bolt of a lock passes. —**sel′vaged,** *adj.*

selves (selvz), *n.,* *pron.* pl. of SELF.

se•man•tic (si man′tik) also **se•man′ti•cal,** *adj.* **1.** of or pertaining to meaning or arising from the different meanings of words or other symbols: *semantic change; semantic confusion.* **2.** of or pertaining to semantics. —**se•man′ti•cal•ly,** *adv.*

se•man•tics (si man′tiks), *n.* (*used with a sing. v.*) **1.** a branch of linguistics dealing with the study of meaning, including the ways meaning is structured in language and changes in meaning and form over time. **2.** the branch of semiotics or logic dealing with the relationship between signs or symbols and what they denote. **3.** the meaning, or an interpretation of the meaning, of a word, sign, sentence, etc.: *Let's not argue about semantics.* —**se•man′ti•cist** (-tə sist), *n.*

sem•a•phore (sem′ə fôr′, -fōr′), *n.,* *v.,* **-phored, -phor•ing.** —*n.* **1.** an apparatus for conveying information by means of visual signals, as a light whose position may be changed. **2.** a system of signaling, esp. one by which a special flag is held in each hand and various positions of the arms indicate specific letters, numbers, etc. —*v.t., v.i.* **3.** to signal by semaphore or by a system of flags. —**sem′a•phor′ic** (-fôr′ik, -for′-), **sem′a•phor′i•cal,** *adj.* —**sem′a•phor′i•cal•ly,** *adv.*

sem•blance (sem′bləns), *n.* **1.** outward aspect or appearance. **2.** an assumed or unreal appearance; show. **3.** the slightest appearance or trace. **4.** a likeness, image, or copy. **5.** a spectral appearance; apparition.

se•men (sē′mən), *n.* a viscid, whitish fluid produced in the male reproductive organs, containing sperm.

se•mes•ter (si mes′tər), *n.* **1.** an academic session constituting half of the academic year, lasting typically from 15 to 18 weeks. **2.** (in German universities) a session, lasting about six months. —**se•mes′tral, se•mes′tri•al** (-trē əl), *adj.*

sem•i (sem′ē, sem′ī), *n.* **1.** a semitrailer. **2.** Often, **semis.** a semifinal contest or round.

semi-, a combining form meaning "half" (*semiannual*), "partially," "somewhat" (*semiautomatic; semidetached; semiformal*). —**Usage.** See BI-¹.

sem•i•ab•stract (sem′ē ab′strakt, -ab strakt′, sem′ī-), *adj.* having the subject recognizable although the forms are highly stylized: *semiabstract sculptures.* —**sem′i•ab•strac′tion,** *n.*

sem•i•am•a•teur (sem′ē am′ə choŏr′, -chər, -tər, -am′ə tûr′, sem′ī-), *adj.* **1.** retaining amateur status but receiving prize money or support. —*n.* **2.** a semiamateur athlete.

S

sem·i·an·nu·al (sem′ē an′yŏŏ əl, sem′ī-), *adj.* **1.** occurring, done, or published every half year or twice a year. **2.** lasting for half a year. —**sem′i·an′nu·al·ly,** *adv.*

sem·i·ar·id (sem′ē ar′id, sem′ī-), *adj.* (of a region, land, etc.) characterized by very little annual rainfall, usu. from 10 to 20 in. (25 to 50 cm). —**sem′i·a·rid′i·ty** (-ə rid′i tē), *n.*

sem·i·au·to·mat·ic (sem′ē ô′tə mat′ik, sem′ī-), *adj.* **1.** partly automatic. **2.** (of a firearm) automatically ejecting the spent cartridge case and loading the next cartridge but requiring a squeeze of the trigger to fire each shot. —*n.* **3.** a semiautomatic firearm. —**sem′i·au′to·mat′i·cal·ly,** *adv.*

sem·i·au·ton·o·mous (sem′ē ô ton′ə məs, sem′ī-), *adj.* partially self-governing, esp. with reference to internal affairs.

sem·i·cir·cle (sem′i sûr′kəl), *n.* **1.** half of a circle; the arc from one end of a diameter to the other. **2.** anything having or arranged in the form of a half of a circle. —**sem′i·cir′cu·lar** (-sûr′kyə lər), *adj.* —**sem′i·cir′cu·lar·ly,** *adv.* —**sem′i·cir′cu·lar·ness,** *n.*

semicir′cular canal′, *n.* any of the three curved tubular canals in the inner ear, associated with the sense of equilibrium.

sem·i·clas·si·cal (sem′ē klas′i kəl, sem′ī-), *adj.* intermediate in style between classical and popular music.

sem·i·co·lon (sem′i kō′lən), *n.* the punctuation mark (;) used to indicate a major division in a sentence where a more distinct separation is felt between clauses or items on a list than is indicated by a comma, as between the two clauses of a compound sentence.

sem·i·con·duc·tor (sem′ē kən duk′tər, sem′ī-), *n.* **1.** a substance, as silicon or germanium, with electrical conductivity intermediate between that of an insulator and a conductor. **2.** a basic electronic component incorporating such a substance, used in communications equipment and in computers. —**sem′i·con·duct′ing,** *adj.*

sem·i·con·scious (sem′ē kon′shəs, sem′ī-), *adj.* not fully conscious. —**sem′i·con′scious·ly,** *adv.* —**sem′i·con′scious·ness,** *n.*

sem·i·dark·ness (sem′ē därk′nis, sem′ī-), *n.* partial darkness.

sem·i·des·ert (sem′ē dez′ərt, sem′ī-), *n.* an extremely dry area characterized by sparse vegetation.

sem·i·de·tached (sem′ē di tacht′, sem′ī-), *adj.* **1.** partly detached. **2.** (of a house) joined to another house by a common wall.

sem·i·di·am·e·ter (sem′ē dī am′i tər, sem′ī-), *n.* half of a diameter; radius.

sem·i·di·ur·nal (sem′ē dī ûr′nl, sem′ī-), *adj.* **1.** pertaining to, consisting of, or accomplished in half a day. **2.** occurring every 12 hours or twice each day.

sem·i·fi·nal (sem′ē fīn′l, sem′ī-), *adj.* **1.** being the next to last round in an elimination tournament. **2.** being the second most important bout in a boxing tournament. —*n.* **3.** a semifinal round or bout. —**sem′i·fi′nal·ist,** *n.*

sem·i·for·mal (sem′ē fôr′məl, sem′ī-), *adj.* containing some formal elements: *semiformal attire.*

sem·i·lit·er·ate (sem′ē lit′ər it, sem′ī-), *adj.* **1.** barely able to read and write. **2.** able to read but not write. **3.** literate but poorly informed. —*n.* **4.** a person who is semiliterate. —**sem′i·lit′er·a·cy** (-ə sē), *n.*

sem·i·lu·nar (sem′ē lōō′nər, sem′ī-), *adj.* shaped like a half-moon.

sem′ilu′nar valve′, *n.* either of two heart valves situated at the ventricular openings to the aorta and the pulmonary artery, each containing three crescent-shaped flaps that prevent the reverse flow of blood.

sem·i·month·ly (sem′ē munth′lē, sem′ī-), *adj.,* *-lies,* *adv.* **1.** made, occurring, or published twice a month. —*n.* **2.** a semimonthly publication. —*adv.* **3.** twice a month.

sem·i·nal (sem′ə nl), *adj.* **1.** pertaining to, containing, or consisting of semen. **2.** highly original and influencing the development of future events: *a seminal artist.* —**sem′i·nal·ly,** *adv.*

sem·i·nar (sem′ə när′), *n.* **1.** a group of advanced students undertaking original research under the guidance of a faculty member and meeting regularly. **2.** a course or subject of study for advanced graduate students. **3.** any meeting for exchanging information and holding discussions.

sem·i·nar·i·an (sem′ə när′ē ən) also **sem·i·na·rist** (sem′ə nər ist), *n.* a student in a theological seminary.

sem·i·nar·y (sem′ə ner′ē), *n.,* *pl.* *-nar·ies.* **1.** a special school that prepares students for the priesthood, ministry, or rabbinate. **2.** a school, esp. one of higher grade. **3.** a school of secondary or higher level for young women. **4.** a place of origin and propagation: *a seminary of discontent.* —**sem′i·nar′i·al,** *adj.*

sem·i·na·tion (sem′ə nā′shən), *n.* a sowing or impregnating.

Sem·i·nole (sem′ə nōl′), *n.,* *pl.* *-noles,* (*esp. collectively*) *-nole.* **1.** a member of any of several groupings of American Indians comprising emigrants from the territories of the Creek confederacy to Florida, or their descendants in Florida and Oklahoma. **2.** either of the Muskogean languages spoken by the Seminoles, comprising Mikasuki and the Florida or Seminole dialect of Creek.

Sem′inole Wars′, *n.pl.* **1.** a series of conflicts in 1818–19 between American forces under Andrew Jackson and the Seminole Indians in Spanish-controlled eastern Florida. **2.** a series of conflicts from 1835 to 1842 between U.S. Army forces and the Seminole Indians over the Seminoles' refusal to move from Florida to designated Indian territories.

se·mi·ol·o·gy (sē′mē ol′ə jē, sem′ē-, sē′mī-), *n.* the study of signs and symbols; semiotics. —**se′mi·o·log′ic** (-ə loj′ik), **se′mi·o·log′i·cal,** *adj.* —**se′mi·ol′o·gist,** *n.*

se·mi·ot·ic (sē′mē ot′ik, sem′ē, sē′mī-), *adj.* Also, **se′mi·ot′i·cal.** **1.** of or pertaining to signs. **2.** of or pertaining to semiotics. **3.** of or pertaining to symptoms of disease; symptomatic. —*n.* **4.** semiotics.

se·mi·ot·ics (sē′mē ot′iks, sem′ē-, sē′mī-), *n.* (*used with a sing. v.*) the study of signs and symbols as elements of communicative behavior; the analysis of systems of communication, as language, gestures, or clothing. —**se′mi·o·ti′cian** (-ə tish′ən), *n.*

sem·i·per·ma·nent (sem′ē pûr′mə nənt, sem′ī-), *adj.* long-lasting but not permanent.

sem·i·pre·cious (sem′ē presh′əs, sem′ī-), *adj.* having commercial value as a gem but not classified as precious: *semiprecious minerals.*

sem·i·pri·vate (sem′ē prī′vit, sem′ī-), *adj.* having some degree of privacy but not fully private, as a hospital room with fewer beds than a ward.

sem·i·pro (*adj.* sem′ē prō′, sem′ī-; *n.* sem′ē prō′, sem′ī-), *adj., n., pl.* *-pros.* semiprofessional.

sem·i·pro·fes·sion·al (sem′ē prə fesh′ə nl, sem′ī-), *adj.* **1.** actively engaged in some field for pay but on a part-time basis: *semiprofessional ball players.* **2.** engaged in by semiprofessional people: *semiprofessional football.* —*n.* **3.** a person who is semiprofessional. —**sem′i·pro·fes′sion·al·ly,** *adv.*

sem·i·re·li·gious (sem′ē ri lij′əs, sem′ī-), *adj.* having a somewhat religious character.

sem·i·skilled (sem′ē skild′, sem′ī-), *adj.* having or requiring more training and skill than unskilled labor but less than skilled labor.

sem·i·sol·id (sem′ē sol′id, sem′ī-), *adj.* **1.** having a somewhat firm consistency. —*n.* **2.** a semisolid substance.

sem·i·sweet (sem′ē swēt′, sem′ī-), *adj.* somewhat sweet: *semisweet chocolate.*

Sem·ite (sem′īt; *esp. Brit.* sē′mīt), *n.* **1.** a member of a people speaking a Semitic language. **2.** a member of any of the peoples descended from Shem, the eldest son of Noah.

Se·mit·ic (sə mit′ik), *n.* **1.** a family of languages, a branch of the Afro-asiatic family, comprising a number of ancient and modern languages of SW Asia and Africa, as Akkadian, Aramaic, Hebrew, Arabic, and Amharic. —*adj.* **2.** of or pertaining to the Semitic languages.

---

sem′i·ac′tive, *adj.*
sem′i·an′i·mat·ed, *adj.*
sem′i·au·to·bi·o·graph′i·cal, *adj.; -ly, adv.*
sem′i·bald′, *adj.*
sem′i·bi′o·graph′i·cal, *adj.; -ly, adv.*
sem′i·closed′, *adj.*
sem′i·com·mer′cial, *adj.*
sem′i·con·di′tioned, *adj.*
sem′i·con·fine′ment, *n.*
sem′i·con·form′ist, *n.*
sem′i·con·ver′sion, *n.*
sem′i·cul′ti·vat·ed, *adj.*
sem′i·cul′tured, *adj.*
sem′i·dan′ger·ous, *adj.*
sem′i·def′i·nite, *adj.; -ly, adv.*
sem′i·de·pend′ent, *adj.; -ly, adv.*
sem′i·dis·a′bled, *adj.*
sem′i·dome′, *n.*
sem′i·do·mes′ti·cat·ed, *adj.*
sem′i·dry′, *adj.*
sem′i·ex·clu′sive, *adj.; -ly, adv.; -ness, n.*
sem′i·ex·posed′, *adj.*

sem′i·fic′tion·al, *adj.*
sem′i·fig′ur·a·tive, *adj.; -ly, adv.*
sem′i·fin′ished, *adj.*
sem′i·fit′ted, *adj.*
sem′i·flu′id, *adj.*
sem′i·flu·id′i·ty, *n.*
sem′i·fos′sil·ized′, *adj.*
sem′i·fur′nished, *adj.*
sem′i·gloss′, *adj.*
sem′i·gov′ern·men′tal, *adj.*
sem′i·his·tor′ic, *adj.*
sem′i·hos′tile, *adj.; -ly, adv.*
sem′i·hy′per·bol′ic, *adj.*
sem′i·il·lit′er·ate, *adj.*
sem′i·il·lu′mi·nat′ed, *adj.*
sem′i·in·dus′tri·al·ized′, *adj.*
sem′i·in·tox′i·cat′ed, *adj.*
sem′i·leg′end·ar′y, *adj.*
sem′i·liq′uid, *adj.; n.*
sem′i·log·a·rith′mic, *adj.*
sem′i·lu′mi·nous, *adj.; -ly, adv.; -ness, n.*
sem′i·mag′i·cal, *adj.; -ly, adv.*

sem′i·me·tal′lic, *adj.*
sem′i·mild′, *adj.; -ness, n.*
sem′i·moist′, *adj.*
sem′i·mys′ti·cal, *adj.*
sem′i·myth′ic, *adj.*
sem′i·noc·tur′nal, *adj.*
sem′i·no·mad′ic, *adj.*
sem′i·nor′mal, *adj.; -ly, adv.*
sem′i·o·paque′, *adj.*
sem′i·par′a·lyzed′, *adj.*
sem′i·path′o·log′i·cal, *adj.; -ly, adv.*
sem′i·peace′ful, *adj.; -ly, adv.*
sem′i·per′me·a·bil′i·ty, *n.*
sem′i·per′me·a·ble, *adj.*
sem′i·pet′ri·fied′, *adj.*
sem′i·plas′tic, *adj.*
sem′i·po·lit′i·cal, *adj.*
sem′i·pop′u·lar, *adj.; -ly, adv.*
sem′i·por′ce·lain, *n.*
sem′i·prim′i·tive, *adj.*
sem′i·pro·duc′tive, *adj.; -ly, adv.*
sem′i·pro·gres′sive, *adj.; n.; -ly, adv.; -ness, n.*

sem′i·pro·tect′ed, *adj.*
sem′i·prov′en, *adj.*
sem′i·pub′lic, *adj.*
sem′i·re′al·is′tic, *adj.*
sem′i·re·spect′a·ble, *adj.*
sem′i·re·tired′, *adj.*
sem′i·rig′id, *adj.*
sem′i·ru′ral, *adj.; -ly, adv.*
sem′i·sa·tir′i·cal, *adj.; -ly, adv.*
sem′i·se′ri·ous, *adj.*
sem′i·sub·merged′, *adj.*
sem′i·sub·ur′ban, *adj.*
sem′i·suc·cess′ful, *adj.; -ly, adv.*
sem′i·syn·thet′ic, *adj.*
sem′i·ter·res′tri·al, *adj.*
sem′i·tra·di′tion·al, *adj.; -ly, adv.*
sem′i·trained′, *adj.*
sem′i·trans·par′ent, *adj.*
sem′i·truth′ful, *adj.; -ly, adv.; -ness, n.*
sem′i·ur′ban, *adj.*
sem′i·vol′un·tar′y, *adj.*
sem′i·wild′, *adj.; -ly, adv.; -ness, n.*

sem•i•tone (sem′ē tōn′, sem′ī-), *n.* a musical pitch halfway between two whole tones. —**sem′i•ton′al,** *adj.*

sem•i•trail•er (sem′i trā′lər), *n.* a detachable trailer for hauling freight, with wheels at the rear end and the forward end supported by a tractor. Also called **semi.**

sem•i•trop•i•cal (sem′ē trop′i kəl, sem′ī-) also **sem′i•trop′ic,** *adj.* SUBTROPICAL. —**sem′i•trop′ics,** *n.pl.* —**sem′i•trop′i•cal•ly,** *adv.*

sem•i•vow•el (sem′i vou′əl), *n.* a speech sound of vowel quality used as a consonant, as (w) in *wet* or (y) in *yet.*

sem•i•week•ly (sem′ē wēk′lē, sem′ī-), *adj., n., pl.* **-lies,** *adv.* —*adj.* **1.** occurring, done, appearing, or published twice a week. —*n.* **2.** a semiweekly publication. —*adv.* **3.** twice a week.

sem•i•year•ly (sem′ē yēr′lē, sem′ī-), *adj.* **1.** SEMIANNUAL (def. 1). —*adv.* **2.** twice a year; semiannually.

sem•o•li•na (sem′ə lē′nə), *n.* a granular, milled product of durum wheat, used esp. in the making of pasta.

sem•per fi•de•lis (sem′pᴇʀ fi dā′lis; *Eng.* sem′pər fi dā′lis, -dē′-), *Latin.* always faithful: motto of the U.S. Marine Corps.

sen•ate (sen′it), *n.* **1.** an assembly or council having the highest deliberative functions in a government, esp. a legislative assembly. **2.** (*cap.*) the upper house of the U.S. Congress or of a state legislature. **3.** (*cap.*) the upper house of the legislature of other countries, as France and Canada. **4.** the room or building in which such a group meets. **5.** the supreme council of state of ancient Rome, the membership and functions of which varied at different periods. **6.** a governing, advisory, or disciplinary body, as at some universities.

sen•a•tor (sen′ə tər), *n.* a member of a senate. —**sen′a•tor•ship′,** *n.*

sen•a•to•ri•al (sen′ə tôr′ē əl, -tōr′-), *adj.* **1.** of, pertaining to, characteristic of, or befitting a senator or senate. **2.** consisting of senators. **3.** entitled to elect a senator: *a senatorial district.* —**sen′a•to′ri•al•ly,** *adv.*

senato′rial dis′trict, *n.* one of a fixed number of districts into which a state of the U.S. is divided, each electing one member to the state senate. Compare ASSEMBLY DISTRICT, CONGRESSIONAL DISTRICT.

send (send), *v.,* **sent, send•ing.** —*v.t.* **1.** to cause or enable to go: *to send a messenger.* **2.** to cause to be conveyed to a destination: *to send a letter.* **3.** to order or request to go: *sending troops to battle.* **4.** to propel or drive: *to send a punch to the jaw.* **5.** to emit or utter: *The lion sent a roar through the jungle.* **6.** to cause to occur. **7. a.** to transmit (a signal). **b.** to transmit (an electromagnetic wave or the like) in the form of pulses. —*v.i.* **8.** to dispatch a messenger, agent, message, etc. **9. send for,** to request the coming or delivery of; summon: *to send for a doctor.* **10. send forth,** to produce, emit, discharge, or cause to emerge. **11. send in,** to mail or otherwise dispatch to an authorized point of collection: *to send in one's taxes.* **12. send out,** to order delivery: *We sent out for coffee.* **13. send up, a.** to cause to rise up. **b.** *Informal.* to send to prison. **c.** to ridicule, as through parody. —***Idiom.*** **14. send packing,** to dismiss curtly. —**send′a•ble,** *adj.* —**send′er,** *n.*

Sen•dak (sen′dak), *n.* **Maurice (Bernard),** born 1928, U.S. author and illustrator of children's books.

send′-off′, *n.* **1.** a demonstration of good wishes for a person setting out on a new venture. **2.** a start; impetus.

send′-up′, *n.* a burlesque; parody; takeoff.

Sen•e•ca[1] (sen′i kə), *n., pl.* **-cas,** (*esp. collectively*) **-ca. 1.** a member of an American Indian people orig. residing in W central New York: the westernmost of the Iroquois Five Nations. **2.** the Iroquoian language of the Senecas.

Sen•e•ca[2] (sen′i kə), *n.* **Lucius Annaeus,** c4 B.C.–A.D. 65, Roman philosopher and dramatist.

Sen′eca Falls′ Conven′tion, *n.* a women's rights convention held at Seneca Falls, New York, in 1848, organized by Elizabeth Cady Stanton and Lucretia Mott. Also called **Sen′eca Falls′ Con′ference.**

Sen•e•gal (sen′i gôl′, -gäl′), *n.* **1.** a republic in W Africa: independent member of the French Community; formerly part of French West Africa. 9,403,546; 76,084 sq. mi. (197,057 sq. km). *Cap.:* Dakar. **2.** a river in W Africa, flowing NW from E Mali to the Atlantic. ab. 1000 mi. (1600 km) long. French, **Sé•né•gal** (sā nā gᴀl′). —**Sen′e•ga•lese′** (-gə lēz′, -lēs′), *adj., n., pl.* **-lese.**

se•nes•cent (si nes′ənt), *adj.* growing old; aging. —**se•nes′cence,** *n.*

se•nhor (sin yôr′, -yōr′), *n., pl.* **se•nhors, se•nho•res** (sin yôr′ās, -yōr′-). a Portuguese or Brazilian term of address for a man, equivalent to *sir* or *Mr. Abbr.:* Sr.

se•nile (sē′nīl, sen′īl), *adj.* **1.** showing a decline or deterioration of physical strength or mental functioning, esp. short-term memory and alertness, as a result of old age or disease. **2.** of or belonging to old age or aged persons; gerontological; geriatric. **3.** (of topography) having been leveled by peneplanation.

se•nil•i•ty (si nil′i tē), *n.* the state of being senile, esp. the weakness or mental infirmity of old age.

sen•ior (sēn′yər), *adj.* **1.** older or elder (typically identifying a father whose son is named after him; often abbreviated): *John Doe, Sr.* **2.** of earlier election, appointment, or admission: *the senior senator from New York.* **3.** of higher or the highest rank or standing. **4.** of or pertaining to seniors in high school or college. **5.** of, for, or pertaining to senior citizens. **6.** having a claim on assets, dividends, or the like prior to other stockholders, creditors, etc. —*n.* **7.** a person who is older than another. **8.** a person of higher rank or standing than another, esp. by virtue of longer service. **9.** a student in the final year at a high school, college, or university. **10.** a senior fellow at a college of an English university. **11.** a senior citizen.

sen′ior chief′ pet′ty of′ficer, *n.* an enlisted rating in the U.S. Navy and Coast Guard above chief petty officer.

sen′ior cit′izen, *n.* an older person, esp. one who is retired.

sen′ior high′ school′, *n.* a school usu. including grades 10 through 12.

sen•ior•i•ty (sēn yôr′i tē, -yor′-), *n., pl.* **-ties. 1.** the state of being senior; superior age. **2.** precedence or status obtained as the result of a person's length of service, as in a profession.

Sen•nach•er•ib (sə nak′ər ib), *n.* died 681 B.C., king of Assyria 705–681.

Sen•nett (sen′it), *n.* **Mack** (*Michael Sinnott*), 1884–1960, U.S. motion-picture director and producer, born in Canada.

se•ñor (sān yôr′, -yōr′), *n., pl.* **se•ñors, se•ño•res** (sān yôr′ās, -yōr′-). a Spanish term of address for a man, equivalent to *sir* or *Mr. Abbr.:* Sr.

se•ño•ra (sān yôr′ə, -yōr′ə), *n., pl.* **-ras.** a Spanish term of address for a married woman, equivalent to *Mrs. Abbr.:* Sra.

se•ño•ri•ta (sān′yə rē′tə), *n., pl.* **-tas. 1.** a Spanish term of address for a girl or unmarried woman, equivalent to *miss. Abbr.:* Srta. **2.** a cigar-shaped wrasse, *Oxyjulis californica,* of coastal waters of California.

sen•sate (sen′sāt), *adj.* perceiving or perceived through the senses. —**sen′sate•ly,** *adv.*

sen•sa•tion (sen sā′shən), *n.* **1.** perception of stimuli through the senses. **2.** a mental condition or physical feeling resulting from stimulation of a sense organ or from internal bodily change, as cold or pain. **3.** the faculty of perception of stimuli. **4.** a general feeling not directly attributable to any given stimulus, as discomfort or anxiety. **5.** widespread excitement or interest. **6.** a cause of such feeling or interest.

sen•sa•tion•al (sen sā′shə nl), *adj.* **1.** producing or intended to produce a startling or scandalous effect: *a sensational novel of betrayal and intrigue.* **2.** extraordinarily good: *a sensational performer.* **3.** of or pertaining to the senses or sensation. —**sen•sa′tion•al•ly,** *adv.*

sen•sa•tion•al•ism (sen sā′shə nl iz′əm), *n.* **1.** the use of sensational subject matter or style: *tabloids full of sensationalism.* **2.** the philosophic doctrine that the good is to be judged only by the gratification of the senses. —**sen•sa′tion•al•ist,** *n., adj.*

S

sense (sens), *n., v.,* **sensed, sens•ing.** —*n.* **1.** any of the faculties, as sight, hearing, smell, taste, or touch, by which humans and animals perceive stimuli originating from outside or inside the body. **2.** these faculties collectively. **3.** their operation or function; sensation. **4.** a feeling or perception produced through one of the senses: *a sense of cold.* **5.** a faculty or function of the mind analogous to a physical sense: *the moral sense.* **6.** any special capacity for perception, appreciation, etc.: *a sense of humor.* **7.** Usu., **senses.** sanity: *Have you taken leave of your senses?* **8.** a more or less vague perception or impression: *a sense of security.* **9.** a mental discernment, realization, or recognition: *a sense of value.* **10.** a motivating awareness: *a sense of duty.* **11.** sound practical intelligence. **12.** reasonable thought or discourse: *to talk sense.* **13.** substance or gist; content: *You missed the sense of his statement.* **14.** value; merit: *There's no sense in worrying.* **15.** a DNA sequence that is capable of coding for an amino acid (disting. from *nonsense*). **16.** the meaning of a word or phrase in a specific context, esp. as isolated in a dictionary or glossary. **17.** consensus: *the sense of a meeting.* —*v.t.* **18.** to perceive by the senses; become aware of. **19.** to grasp the meaning of; understand. **20.** to detect (physical phenomena, as light or temperature) mechanically, electrically, or photoelectrically. —***Idiom.*** **21. in a sense,** to some extent; in a way: *In a sense, the book was oddly gripping.*

Sense′ and Sensibil′ity, a novel (1811) by Jane Austen.

sense•less (sens′lis), *adj.* **1.** destitute or deprived of sensation; unconscious. **2.** stupid; foolish. **3.** lacking meaning; nonsensical: *senseless chattering.* —**sense′less•ly,** *adv.* —**sense′less•ness,** *n.*

sense′ or′gan, *n.* a specialized bodily structure that receives or is sensitive to internal or external stimuli; receptor.

sense′ percep′tion, *n.* perception by one or more of the senses rather than by the intellect.

sen•si•bil•i•ty (sen′sə bil′i tē), *n., pl.* **-ties. 1.** capacity for feeling; responsiveness to sensory stimuli. **2.** mental susceptibility or responsiveness. **3.** Often, **sensibilities.** acute capacity to respond to blame or praise. **4.** Often, **sensibilities.** capacity for intellectual and aesthetic discrimination: *a person of refined sensibilities.* **5.** the property, as in plants or instruments, of being readily affected by external influences.

sen•si•ble (sen′sə bəl), *adj.* **1.** having, using, or showing good sense or sound judgment: *a sensible young woman.* **2.** cognizant; aware: *sensible of his fault.* **3.** capable of being perceived by the senses or the mind: *the sensible universe.* **4.** capable of feeling or perceiving, as organs or parts of the body. **5.** conscious: *The patient was speechless but still sensible.* **6.** appreciable: *a sensible improvement.* —**sen′si•bly,** *adv.*

sen′sible hori′zon, *n.* See under HORIZON (def. 2a).

sen•si•tive (sen′si tiv), *adj.* **1.** endowed with sensation; having perception through the senses. **2.** readily or excessively affected by external influences. **3.** responsive to the feelings of others. **4.** easily hurt or offended. **5.** *Physiol.* having a low threshold of sensation or feeling. **6.** especially responsive to certain agents, as light: *sensitive photographic film.* **7.** highly secret or delicate; requiring prudence: *sensitive diplomatic issues.* **8.** constructed to measure small degrees of change: *a sensitive thermometer.* **9.** marked by high radio sensitivity. —*n.* **10.** a person who is sensitive. **11.** a person with psychic powers; medium. —**sen′si•tive•ly,** *adv.*

sen•si•tiv•i•ty (sen′si tiv′i tē), *n., pl.* **-ties. 1.** the state or quality of being sensitive. **2. a.** the ability of an organism or part of an organism to react to stimuli; irritability. **b.** degree of susceptibility to stimulation. **3.** the ability of a radio or television receiver to respond to incoming signals.

sen•si•tize (sen′si tīz′), *v.,* **-tized, -tiz•ing.** —*v.t.* **1.** to render sensitive. —*v.i.* **2.** to become sensitized. —**sen′si•tiz′er,** *n.*

sen•sor (sen′sôr, -sər), *n.* **1.** a mechanical device sensitive to light, temperature, radiation level, or the like, that transmits a signal to a measuring or control instrument. **2.** SENSE ORGAN.

sen•so•ri•mo•tor (sen′sə rē mō′tər), *adj.* **1.** of, pertaining to, or having both sensory and motor functions, as certain areas of the brain. **2.** of or pertaining to motor activity caused by sensory stimuli.

sen•so•ry (sen′sə rē) also **sen•so•ri•al** (sen sôr′ē əl, -sōr′-), *adj.* **1.** of or pertaining to the senses or sensation. **2.** of or noting a physiological structure for receiving or conveying an external stimulus.

sen′sory depriva′tion, *n.* extreme reduction of environmental stimuli, often leading to cognitive, perceptual, or behavioral disorientation or, in infants, developmental damage.

sen•su•al (sen′shōō əl), *adj.* **1.** arousing or preoccupied with gratification of the senses or appetites; carnal. **2.** lacking in moral restraints. **3.** worldly; materialistic; irreligious. **4.** sensory. —**sen′su•al′i•ty,** *n.* —**sen′su•al•ly,** *adv.*

sen•su•al•ize (sen′shōō ə līz′), *v.t.,* **-ized, -iz•ing.** to render sensual. —**sen′su•al•i•za′tion,** *n.*

sen•su•ous (sen′shōō əs), *adj.* **1.** perceived by or affecting the senses. **2.** readily affected through the senses: *a sensuous temperament.* **3.** of or pertaining to sensible objects or to the senses. —**sen′su•ous•ly,** *adv.* —**sen′su•ous•ness, sen′su•os′i•ty** (-os′i tē), *n.*

sent (sent), *v.* pt. and pp. of SEND.

sen•tence (sen′tns), *n., v.,* **-tenced, -tenc•ing.** —*n.* **1.** a grammatical unit of one or more words, typically consisting of a subject and a predicate containing a finite verb and expressing a statement, question, request, command, or exclamation, as *Summer is here.* or *Who is it?* or *Stop!* **2.** a judicial decision or decree, esp. one decreeing the punishment to be inflicted on a convicted criminal. **3.** to pronounce sentence upon; condemn to punishment. [< Old French < Latin *sententia* opinion, decision] —**sen′tenc•er,** *n.*

sen•ten•tious (sen ten′shəs), *adj.* **1.** given to or abounding in pithy aphorisms or maxims. **2.** given to excessive moralizing; self-righteous. **3.** of the nature of a maxim; pithy. —**sen•ten′tious•ly,** *adv.* —**sen•ten′tious•ness,** *n.*

sen•tient (sen′shənt), *adj.* **1.** having the power of perception by the senses; conscious. **2.** characterized by sensation and consciousness. —**sen′tient•ly,** *adv.*

sen•ti•ment (sen′tə mənt), *n.* **1.** an attitude or feeling toward something; opinion. **2.** refined or tender emotion, esp. as expressed in an artistic work. **3.** a thought influenced by emotion. **4.** the emotional content of something as distinguished from its verbal expression.

sen•ti•men•tal (sen′tə men′tl), *adj.* **1.** appealing to the tender emotions: *a sentimental song.* **2.** nostalgic: *a sentimental journey.* **3.** weakly emotional; mawkish. —**sen′ti•men′tal•ly,** *adv.*

sen•ti•men•tal•ism (sen′tə men′tl iz′əm), *n.* sentimental character or display. —**sen′ti•men′tal•ist,** *n.*

sen•ti•men•tal•i•ty (sen′tə men tal′i tē), *n., pl.* **-ties. 1.** the quality or state of being sentimental or excessively sentimental. **2.** a sentimental act, gesture, or expression.

sen•ti•men•tal•ize (sen′tə men′tl īz′), *v.,* **-ized, -iz•ing.** —*v.i.* **1.** to indulge in sentiment. —*v.t.* **2.** to view (someone or something) sentimentally. —**sen′ti•men′tal•i•za′tion,** *n.*

sen•ti•nel (sen′tn l, -tə nl), *n., v.,* **-neled, -nel•ing** or (*esp. Brit.*) **-nelled, -nel•ling.** —*n.* **1.** a person or thing that stands watch; sentry. —*v.t.* **2.** to watch over as a sentinel.

sen•try (sen′trē), *n., pl.* **-tries.** a guard, esp., a soldier stationed to prevent unauthorized passage.

Seoul (sōl), *n.* the capital of South Korea, in the W part. 9,645,824.

se•pal (sē′pəl), *n.* one of the individual leaves or parts of the calyx of a flower. —**se′paled, se′palled,** *adj.*

sep•a•ra•ble (sep′ər ə bəl, sep′rə-), *adj.* capable of being separated or dissociated. —**sep′a•ra•bil′i•ty, sep′a•ra•ble•ness,** *n.* —**sep′a•ra•bly,** *adv.*

sep•a•rate (*v.* sep′ə rāt′; *adj., n.* -ər it), *v.,* **-rat•ed, -rat•ing,** *adj., n.* —*v.t.* **1.** to keep apart; divide. **2.** to bring or force apart: *to separate two fighting boys.* **3.** to disconnect; dissociate: *to separate church and state.* **4.** to remove from active association: *separated from the army.* **5.** to sort or disperse into individual components. **6.** to extract: *to separate metal from ore.* —*v.i.* **7.** to withdraw from an association: *to separate from a church.* **8.** to stop living together but without divorce. **9.** to draw or come apart. **10.** to become parted from a mass or compound. **11.** to take or go in different directions. —*adj.* **12.** detached; distinct. **13.** existing or maintained independently. **14.** not shared; individual: *separate checks.* **15.** (*often cap.*) no longer associated with a parent organization, as a church. —*n.* **16.** Usu., **separates.** women's garments designed to be worn in various combinations. —**sep′a•rate•ly,** *adv.* —**sep′a•rate•ness,** *n.* —**Usage.** *separate* is often found with the spelling SEPERATE,

even in quite respectable publications. Despite this frequency, however, SEPERATE is almost universally considered a misspelling.

sep′arate but e′qual, *adj.* pertaining to a racial policy by which blacks may be segregated if granted equal opportunities and facilities, as for education, transportation, or jobs. Compare PLESSY V. FERGUSON.

sep•a•ra•tion (sep′ə rā′shən), *n.* **1.** an act or instance of separating or the state of being separated. **2.** a place, line, or point of parting. **3.** a gap; hole. **4.** something that separates or divides. **5.** cessation of conjugal cohabitation by mutual consent or by decree. **6.** the time or act of releasing a burned-out stage of a rocket or missile from the remainder.

separa′tion of pow′ers, *n.* the principle or system of vesting in separate branches the executive, legislative, and judicial powers of a government.

sep•a•ra•tist (sep′ər ə tist, -ə rā′-), *n.* **1.** a person who separates, as from a church. **2.** an advocate of ecclesiastical or political separation. —*adj.* **3.** of or pertaining to separatists. —**sep′a•ra•tism,** *n.*

sep•a•ra•tor (sep′ə rā′tər), *n.* **1.** a person or thing that separates. **2.** an apparatus for separating one thing from another, as cream from milk.

Se•phar•di (sə fär′dē, -fär dē′), *n., pl.* **-phar•dim** (-fär′dim, -fär dēm′). a Jew of Spanish or Portuguese origin or ancestry. Compare ASHKENAZI. [< Modern Hebrew *Səphāraddī* < Hebrew *Səphāradh* (Biblical region assumed to be Spain)] —**Se•phar′dic,** *adj.*

se•pi•a (sē′pē ə), *n.* **1.** a brown pigment obtained from the inklike secretion of various cuttlefish and used in drawing. **2.** a dark brown. —*adj.* **3.** of a brown, grayish brown, or olive brown similar to that of sepia ink.

sep•sis (sep′sis), *n.* local or generalized invasion of the body by pathogenic microorganisms or their toxins: *dental sepsis.*

Sep•tem•ber (sep tem′bər), *n.* the ninth month of the year, containing 30 days. *Abbr.:* Sept., Sep. —**Sep•tem′bral** (-brəl), *adj.*

sep•tet (sep tet′), *n.* **1.** any group of seven persons or things. **2.** a company of seven musicians. **3.** a musical composition for a septet.

sep•tic (sep′tik), *adj.* **1.** pertaining to or of the nature of sepsis; infected. **2.** putrefactive. —**sep′ti•cal•ly,** *adv.* —**sep•tic′i•ty** (-tis′i tē), *n.*

sep•ti•ce•mi•a (sep′tə sē′mē ə), *n.* the presence of pathogenic bacteria in the bloodstream. —**sep′ti•ce′mic,** *adj.*

sep′tic sore′ throat′, *n.* an acute toxic streptococcus infection of the throat producing fever, tonsillitis, and other serious effects.

sep′tic tank′, *n.* a tank in which solid organic sewage is decomposed and purified by anaerobic bacteria.

sep•tu•a•ge•nar•i•an (sep′chōō ə jə när′ē ən, -tōō-, -tyōō-), *adj.* **1.** of the age of 70 or between 70 and 80. —*n.* **2.** a septuagenarian person.

Sep•tu•a•ges•i•ma (sep′chōō ə jes′ə mə, -tōō-, -tyōō-), *n.* the third Sunday before Lent.

Sep•tu•a•gint (sep′chōō ə jint′, -tōō-, -tyōō-), *n.* the oldest Greek version of the Old Testament, traditionally said to have been translated by 70 or 72 Jewish scholars at the request of Ptolemy II. [< Latin *septuāgintā* seventy] —**Sep′tu•a•gint′al,** *adj.*

sep•ul•cher (sep′əl kər), *n., v.,* **-chered, -cher•ing.** —*n.* **1.** a tomb, grave, or burial place. **2. a.** a cavity in a mensa for containing relics of martyrs. **b.** a structure or a recess in some old churches in which the Eucharist was deposited with due ceremonies on Good Friday and taken out at Easter in commemoration of Christ's entombment and Resurrection. —*v.t.* **3.** to place in a sepulcher; bury. Also, *esp. Brit.,* **sep′ul•chre.**

se•pul•chral (sə pul′krəl), *adj.* **1.** of or pertaining to tombs or to burial. **2.** funereal; dismal. **3.** hollow and deep: *sepulchral tones.* —**se•pul′chral•ly,** *adv.*

seq., 1. sequel. **2.** the following (one). [< Latin *sequēns*]

seqq., the following (ones). [< Latin *sequentia*]

se•quel (sē′kwəl), *n.* **1.** a literary or filmic work that takes up and continues the narrative of a preceding work. **2.** a subsequent development. **3.** a result; consequence.

se•quence (sē′kwəns), *n., v.,* **-quenced, -quenc•ing.** —*n.* **1.** the following of one thing after another; succession. **2.** order of succession. **3.** a continuous connected series: *a sonnet sequence.* **4.** result; consequence. **5.** a melodic or harmonic pattern repeated three or more times at different pitches with or without modulation. **6.** a series of related scenes or shots that make up one episode of a film narrative. **7.** a series of three or more cards following one another in order of value, esp. of the same suit. —*v.t.* **8.** to place in a sequence. **9.** *Genetics, Biochem.* to determine the order of (chemical units in a polymer chain), esp. nucleotides in DNA or RNA.

se•quenc•ing (sē′kwən sing), *n.* the interruption of a career by a woman to bear and care for children until they reach an age that allows her to resume work.

se•quen•tial (si kwen′shəl), *adj.* **1.** characterized by regular sequence of parts. **2.** following; subsequent; consequent. —**se•quen′ti•al•i•ty** (-shē al′i tē), *n.* —**se•quen′tial•ly,** *adv.*

se•ques•ter (si kwes′tər), *v.t.* **1.** to remove or withdraw into solitude or retirement. **2.** to remove or separate. **3.** to seize and hold (property) until legal claims are satisfied. —*n.* **4.** an act or instance of sequestering. **5.** an across-the-board cut in government spending.

se•quin (sē′kwin), *n.* **1.** a small shiny disk used for ornamentation, as on clothing. **2.** a former gold coin of Turkey and Italy. —**se′quined,** *adj.*

se•quoi•a (si kwoi′ə), *n.* either of two large coniferous trees of California, *Sequoiadendron giganteum* or *Sequoia sempervirens*, of the bald cypress family, both having reddish bark and reaching heights of more than 300 ft. (91 m). Compare REDWOOD.

Sequoi•a Na′tional Park′, *n.* a national park in central California: giant sequoia trees. 604 sq. mi. (1565 sq. km).

se•ra•pe or **sa•ra•pe** (sə rä′pē), *n., pl.* **-pes.** a blanketlike shawl often of brightly colored wool worn esp. in Mexico.

ser•aph (ser′əf), *n., pl.* **-aphs, -a•phim** (-ə fim) **1.** one of the celestial beings hovering above God's throne in Isaiah's vision. Isa. 6. **2.** a member of the highest order of angels. Compare ANGEL (def. 1). —**se•raph•ic** (si raf′ik), **se•raph′i•cal,** *adj.* —**se•raph′i•cal•ly,** *adv.*

ser•a•phim (ser′ə fim), *n.* a pl. of SERAPH.

Se•ra•pis or **Sa•ra•pis** (sə rā′pis), *n.* a deity of Ptolemaic Egypt, later worshiped throughout the Greco-Roman world.

Serb (sûrb), *n.* **1.** a member of the Slavic people who comprise most of the population of Serbia. **2.** a native or inhabitant of Serbia.

Serb., 1. Serbia. **2.** Serbian.

Ser•bi•a (sûr′bē ə), *n.* a constituent republic of Yugoslavia, in the N part: includes the autonomous provinces of Kosovo and Vojvodina. 9,660,000; 34,116 sq. mi. (88,360 sq. km). *Cap.:* Belgrade. —**Ser′bi•an,** *adj., n.*

Ser•bo-Cro•a•tian (sûr′bō krō ā′shən, -shē ən), *n.* a South Slavic language spoken by most of the inhabitants of Serbia, Croatia, Bosnia, Herzegovina, and Montenegro.

sere (sēr), *adj.* dry; withered.

ser•e•nade (ser′ə nād′), *n., v.,* **-nad•ed, -nad•ing.** —*n.* **1.** a complimentary performance of music in the open air at night, as by a lover to his lady. **2.** an instrumental composition of several movements that is intermediate between the suite and the symphony. —*v.t.* **3.** to entertain with a serenade. —*v.i.* **4.** to perform a serenade. —**ser′e•nad′er,** *n.*

ser•en•dip•i•tous (ser′ən dip′i təs), *adj.* of, pertaining to, or suggesting serendipity. —**ser′en•dip′i•tous•ly,** *adv.*

ser•en•dip•i•ty (ser′ən dip′i tē), *n.* **1.** an aptitude for making desirable discoveries by accident. **2.** good fortune; luck.

se•rene (sə rēn′), *adj.* **1.** calm; peaceful; tranquil. **2.** clear; fair: *serene weather.* **3.** (*usu. cap.*) most high (used as a royal epithet): *His Serene Highness.* —*n.* **4.** serenity; tranquillity. **5.** a clear expanse of sea or sky. —**se•rene′ly,** *adv.* —**se•rene′ness,** *n.*

se•ren•i•ty (sə ren′i tē), *n.* the state or quality of being serene; tranquillity.

serf (sûrf), *n.* **1.** a person in a condition of feudal servitude, required to render services to a lord, commonly attached to the lord's land and transferred with it from one owner to another. **2.** a slave. [< Middle French < Latin *servus* slave] —**serf′dom, serf′hood, serf′age,** *n.*

ser•geant (sär′jənt), *n.* **1. a.** a noncommissioned officer in the U.S. Army and Marine Corps ranking above a corporal. **b.** an officer of similar rank in the armed services of other countries. **2.** any noncommissioned officer in the U.S. Air Force above the rank of airman first class. **3.** a police officer ranking immediately below a captain or a lieutenant in the U.S. and immediately below an inspector in Britain. **4.** SERGEANT AT ARMS.

ser′geant at arms′, *n.* an officer of a legislative, judicial, or other body, whose chief duty is to preserve order.

ser′geant first′ class′, *n.* a noncommissioned officer in the U.S. Army ranking above a staff sergeant.

ser•geant•fish (sär′jənt fish′), *n., pl.* (*esp. collectively*) **-fish,** (*esp. for kinds or species*) **-fish•es.** the cobia, *Rachycentron canadum.*

ser′geant ma′jor, *n.* **1.** a noncommissioned officer in the U.S. Army and Marine Corps ranking above a first sergeant. **2.** the chief administrative assistant in a military headquarters. **3.** a small damselfish, *Abudefduf saxatilis,* of warm Atlantic waters, having vertical black stripes on each side.

se•ri•al (sēr′ē əl), *n.* **1.** anything published, broadcast, etc., in short installments at regular intervals, as a novel appearing in successive issues of a magazine. **2.** a publication, as a periodical or annual report, issued in successive parts bearing numerical or chronological designations. —*adj.* **3.** published or presented in installments or successive parts: *a serial story.* **4.** pertaining to such publication or presentation: *serial rights to a novel.* **5.** of, pertaining to, or arranged in a series. **6.** occurring in a series: *serial murders.* **7.** responsible for a series of murders: *a serial killer.* —**se′ri•al•ly,** *adv.*

se•ri•al•ize (sēr′ē ə līz′), *v.t.,* **-ized, -iz•ing.** to create, publish, release, or broadcast in serial form. —**se′ri•al•i•za′tion,** *n.*

se′rial num′ber, *n.* a number, usu. one of a series, assigned for identification.

ser•i•cin (ser′ə sin), *n.* a gelatinous organic compound that holds the two strands of natural silk together.

ser•i•cul•ture (ser′i kul′chər), *n.* the raising of silkworms for the production of raw silk. —**ser′i•cul′tur•ist,** *n.*

se•ries (sēr′ēz), *n., pl.* **-ries. 1.** a group or a number of related or similar things, events, etc., arranged or occurring in temporal, spatial, or other order or succession; sequence. **2.** a number of games, contests, or sporting events, with the same participants, considered as a unit. **3.** a set, as of coins or postage stamps. **4.** a set of successive volumes or of issues of a periodical published in like form with similarity of subject or purpose. **5.** *Radio and Television.* **a.** a daily or weekly program with a set format, a regular cast of characters, and sometimes a continuing

story, as a situation comedy or a soap opera. **b.** two or more programs related by theme, format, or the like: *a series on African wildlife.* **6.** a sequence of terms combined by addition, as $1 + \frac{1}{2} + \frac{1}{4} + \frac{1}{8} + \ldots + \frac{1}{2}n$. **7.** a succession of coordinate sentence elements. **8.** a division of stratified rocks that is of next higher rank to a stage and next lower rank to a system, comprising deposits formed during part of a geological epoch. **9.** an arrangement of an electrical circuit in which the components are connected end-to-end, so that the same current flows through each component. **10.** a group of related chemical elements arranged in order of increasing atomic number.

se′ries com′ma, *n.* a comma placed after the next-to-last item in a series when the next-to-last and last items are separated by a conjunction, as the comma after *C* in the series *A, B, C,* or *D.* Also called **se′rial com′ma.**

ser•if (ser′if), *n.* a smaller line used to finish off a main stroke of a letter, as at the top and bottom of *E.* Compare SANS SERIF.

ser•i•graph (ser′i graf′, -gräf′), *n.* a print made by the silkscreen process. —**se•rig′ra•pher** (si rig′rə fər), *n.* —**se•rig′ra•phy,** *n.*

se•ri•o•com•ic (sēr′ē ō kom′ik) also **se′ri•o•com′i•cal,** *adj.* partly serious and partly comic: *a seriocomic play.*

se•ri•ous (sēr′ē əs), *adj.* **1.** of, showing, or characterized by deep thought. **2.** grave or somber, as in character, disposition, or mood. **3.** earnest; sincere; not trifling: *a serious proposal.* **4.** requiring thought, concentration, or application: *serious reading.* **5.** weighty, important, or significant: *Marriage is a serious matter.* **6.** giving cause for apprehension; critical or threatening: *a serious relapse.* **7.** arising from deep concern, perplexity, etc.: *serious questions.* —**se′ri•ous•ly,** *adv.* —**se′ri•ous•ness,** *n.*

Se′rious Call′ to a Devout′ and Ho′ly Life′, a devotional book (1728) by William Law.

se′rious-mind′ed, *adj.* characterized by seriousness of intention, purpose, thought, etc.; earnest. —**se′rious-mind′ed•ly,** *adv.* —**se′rious-mind′ed•ness,** *n.*

ser•mon (sûr′mən), *n.* **1.** a discourse for the purpose of religious instruction or exhortation, usu. delivered by a cleric during religious services. **2.** any serious speech, discourse, or exhortation, esp. on a moral issue; lecture. **3.** a long, tedious speech. —**ser•mon•ic** (sər-mon′ik), **ser•mon′i•cal,** *adj.* —**ser•mon′i•cal•ly,** *adv.*

ser•mon•ize (sûr′mə nīz′), *v.,* **-ized, -iz•ing.** —*v.i.* **1.** to deliver or compose a sermon; preach. —*v.t.* **2.** to give exhortation to; lecture. —**ser′mon•iz′er,** *n.*

Ser′mon on the Mount′, *n.* a discourse delivered by Jesus, containing fundamentals of Christian teachings, including the BEATITUDES, the GOLDEN RULE, and the LORD'S PRAYER. Matt. 5–7; Luke 6:20–49.

THE SERMON ON THE MOUNT

Matt. 5:1–2	The setting
Matt. 5:3–12	The Beatitudes
Matt. 5:13–16	The new community
Matt. 5:17–20	The abiding validity of the law
Matt. 5:21–48	On practicing righteousness toward others in matters of:
	Murder (5:21–26)
	Adultery (5:27–30)
	Divorce (5:31–32)
	Oaths (5:33–37)
	Retribution (5:38–42)
	Love of enemy (5:43–48)
Matt. 6:1–7:12	On practicing righteousness toward God:
	Almsgiving (6:1–4)
	Prayer (6:5–15)
	Fasting (6:16–18)
	On not laying up false treasure (6:19–24)
	On not being anxious (6:25–34)
	On not judging (7:1–5)
	On not squandering what is precious (7:6)
	On resting assured that God hears prayer (7:7–12)
Matt. 7:13–27	Concluding warnings and exhortations

sero-, a combining form representing SERUM: *serology.*

se•rol•o•gy (si rol′ə jē), *n.* the science dealing with the immunological properties and actions of serum. —**se•ro•log•ic** (sēr′ə loj′ik), **se′ro•log′i•cal,** *adj.* —**se′ro•log′i•cal•ly,** *adv.* —**se•rol′o•gist,** *n.*

ser•o•to•nin (ser′ə tō′nin, sēr′-), *n.* an amine, $C_{10}H_{12}N_2O$, that occurs esp. in blood and nervous tissue and functions as a vasoconstrictor and neurotransmitter.

se•rous (sēr′əs), *adj.* **1.** resembling serum; of a watery nature. **2.** of, pertaining to, or characterized by serum. —**se•ros•i•ty** (si ros′i tē), **se′rous•ness,** *n.*

ser•pent (sûr′pənt), *n.* **1.** a snake. **2.** a wily, treacherous, or malicious person. **3.** the Devil; Satan. Gen. 3:1–5. **4.** an obsolete wooden wind instrument having a serpentine shape and a deep tone.

ser•pen•tine[1] (sûr′pən tēn′, -tīn′), *adj., n., v.,* **-tined, -tin•ing.** —*adj.* **1.** of, characteristic of, or resembling a serpent, as in form or movement. **2.** having a winding course, as a road; sinuous. **3.** shrewd, wily, or cunning. **4.** (esp. of a furniture front) having a compound curve with a convex section between two concave ones. —*n.* **5.** something with a sinuous, snakelike form or movement. —*v.i.* **6.** to make or follow a winding course. —**ser′pen•tine′ly,** *adv.*

ser•pen•tine² (sûr′pən tēn′, -tīn′), *n.* a green mineral or rock composed of this mineral, hydrous magnesium silicate, $Mg_3Si_2O_5(OH)_4$, occurring in massive, platy, and fibrous varieties.

Ser•ra (ser′ə), *n.* **Ju•ní•pe•ro** (hōō nē′pə rō′) (*Miguel José Serra*), 1713–84, Spanish missionary in California and Mexico.

ser•rate (*adj.* ser′āt, -it; *v.* ser′āt, sə rāt′), *adj., v.,* **-rat•ed, -rat•ing.** —*adj.* **1.** notched on the edge like a saw: *a serrate leaf.* **2.** (of a coin) having a grooved edge. **3.** serrated. —*v.t.* **4.** to make serrate or serrated.

ser•rat•ed (ser′ā tid, sə rā′-), *adj.* having a notched edge or sawlike teeth, esp. for cutting; serrate.

se•rum (sēr′əm), *n., pl.* **se•rums, se•ra** (sēr′ə). **1.** the clear, pale yellow liquid that separates from the clot in the coagulation of blood. **2.** any watery animal fluid. **3.** milk whey. —**se′rum•al,** *adj.*

serv•ant (sûr′vənt), *n.* **1.** a person employed by another, esp. to perform domestic duties. **2.** a person in the service of another. **3.** a person employed by the government: *a public servant.* —**serv′ant•hood′,** *n.* —**serv′ant•less,** *adj.* —**serv′ant•like′,** *adj.*

serv′ant church′, *n.* the attitude or practices of a church whose avowed purpose is to serve the world.

serve (sûrv), *v.,* **served, serv•ing,** *n.* —*v.i.* **1.** to act as a servant. **2.** to wait on table, as a waiter. **3.** to have a meal or refreshments available, as for patrons or guests. **4.** to distribute a food or beverage, as a host or hostess. **5.** to render assistance; be of use; help. **6.** to go through a term of service as a senator, juror, etc. **7.** to have definite use: *This cup will serve as a sugar bowl.* **8.** to answer the purpose: *That will serve to explain my actions.* **9.** (in tennis, badminton, etc.) to put the ball or shuttlecock in play with a stroke, swing, or hit. **10.** to act as a server at mass. —*v.t.* **11.** to be in the service of; work for. **12.** to be useful or of service to; help. **13.** to go through (a term of service, imprisonment, etc.). **14.** to render active service, homage, or obedience to (God, a sovereign, commander, etc.). **15.** to perform the duties of (a position, an office, etc.). **16.** to answer the requirements of: *This will serve our needs for now.* **17.** to contribute to; promote: *to serve a cause.* **18.** to wait upon at table; act as a waiter or waitress to. **19.** to carry and distribute (food or drink) to a patron or a specific place, as a waiter or waitress. **20.** to act as a host or hostess in offering (a person) food or drink. **21.** to act as a host or hostess in offering or distributing (food or drink) to another. **22.** to provide with a regular or continuous supply of something. **23.** (in tennis, badminton, etc.) to put (the ball or shuttlecock) in play. **24.** to treat in a specified manner: *That served him ill.* **25.** *Law.* **a.** to make legal delivery of (a process or writ). **b.** to present (a person) with a writ. **26.** to gratify (wants, needs, etc.). **27.** (of a male animal) to mate with (a female animal); service. **28.** *Naut.* to wrap (a rope) tightly with light cordage, keeping the turns as close together as possible. —*n.* **29.** the act, manner, or right of serving, as in tennis. —***Idiom.*** **30. serve someone right,** to constitute someone's fair and just punishment, as for improper or stupid behavior. —**serv′a•ble, serve′a•ble,** *adj.*

serv•er (sûr′vər), *n.* **1.** a person who serves. **2.** something that serves or is used in serving, as a salver. **3.** a utensil for dishing out individual portions of vegetables, cake, etc. **4.** an attendant on the priest at mass. **5.** (in tennis, badminton, etc.) the player who puts the ball or shuttlecock in play. **6.** a computer that makes services, as access to data files, programs, etc., available to workstations on a network. Compare FILE SERVER.

Ser•ve•tus (sər vē′təs), *n.* **Michael** (*Miguel Serveto*), 1511–53, Spanish theologian, accused of heresy and burned at the stake.

serv•ice (sûr′vis), *n., adj., v.,* **-iced, -ic•ing.** —*n.* **1.** an act of helpful activity; help; aid. **2.** the supplying or supplier of utilities, commodities, or other facilities that meet a public need, as water, electricity, communication, or transportation. **3.** the providing or a provider of accommodation and activities required by the public, as maintenance or repair: *guaranteed service and parts.* **4.** the organized system of apparatus, appliances, employees, etc., for supplying some accommodation required by the public: *a television repair service.* **5.** the performance of duties or the duties performed as or by a waiter or servant. **6.** employment in any duties or work for a person, organization, government, etc. **7.** a department of public employment, or the body of public servants in it: *the diplomatic service.* **8.** the duty or work of public servants. **9. a.** the armed forces: *in the service.* **b.** a branch of the armed forces. **10.** the actions required in loading and firing a cannon. **11.** Often, **services.** the performance of any duties or work for another: *medical services.* **12.** something made or done by a commercial organization for the public benefit and without regard to direct profit. **13.** Also called **divine service.** public religious worship according to prescribed form and order. **14.** a ritual or form prescribed for public worship or for some particular occasion: *the marriage service.* **15.** the serving of God by obedience, piety, etc. **16.** a musical setting of the sung portions of a liturgy. **17.** a set of dishes, utensils, etc., for general table use or for particular use. **18.** ANSWERING SERVICE. **19.** *Law.* the serving of a process or writ upon a person. **20.** (in tennis, badminton, handball, etc.) **a.** the act or manner of putting the ball or shuttlecock into play; serve. **b.** the ball or shuttlecock as put into play. **21.** the mating of a female animal with the male. —*adj.* **22.** of service; useful. **23.** of, pertaining to, or used by servants, delivery people, etc., or in serving food. **24.** supplying services rather than products or goods: *the service professions.* **25.** supplying maintenance and repair: *a service center for electrical appliances.* **26.** of, for, or pertaining to the armed forces or one of them. **27.** providing, authorizing, or guaranteeing service: *a service contract.* —*v.t.* **28.** to make fit for use; repair or restore: *to service an automobile.* **29.** to supply with aid, information, or other incidental services. **30.** (of a male animal) to mate with (a female animal). **31.** to pay off (a debt) over a period of time, as by meeting periodic interest payments.

serv•ice•a•ble (sûr′və sə bəl), *adj.* **1.** being of service or help; useful. **2.** wearing well; durable: *serviceable cloth.* **3.** adequate; sufficient. —**serv′ice•a•bil′i•ty,** *n.* —**serv′ice•a•bly,** *adv.*

serv′ice ace′, *n.* ACE (def. 2).

serv′ice book′, *n.* a book containing the forms of worship used in religious services.

serv′ice break′, *n.* a game won against an opponent's service, as in tennis.

serv′ice cen′ter, *n.* an authorized commercial establishment for repairs and replacement parts for appliances or cars.

serv′ice charge′, *n.* a fee charged for a service, sometimes in addition to a basic charge. Also called **serv′ice fee′.**

serv′ice club′, *n.* **1.** an organization, esp. of businesspersons or professionals, dedicated to the general welfare of its members and the community. **2.** a recreational center for members of the armed forces.

serv′ice court′, *n.* the part of the court into which a player must serve in various games, as tennis, badminton, handball, or squash.

serv′ice line′, *n.* the boundary of a service court.

serv•ice•man (sûr′vis man′, -mən), *n., pl.* **-men** (-men′, -mən). **1.** a member of the armed forces of a country. **2.** a person whose occupation is to maintain or repair equipment.

serv′ice mark′, *n.* a proprietary term, similar to a trademark, that distinguishes the seller or provider of a service. *Abbr.:* SM

serv′ice med′al, *n.* a medal awarded for performance of specified service, usu. in time of war or national emergency.

serv•ice•per•son (sûr′vis pûr′sən), *n.* **1.** a person who is a member of the armed forces of a country. **2.** a person who maintains or repairs equipment.

serv′ice sta′tion, *n.* **1.** Also called **gas station.** a place equipped for servicing automobiles, as by selling gasoline or making repairs. **2.** a place that provides a service.

serv′ice stripe′, *n. Mil.* a stripe worn on the left sleeve by an enlisted person to indicate a specific period of time served on active duty.

serv•ice•wom•an (sûr′vis wŏŏm′ən), *n., pl.* **-wom•en.** a woman who is a member of the armed forces of a country.

ser•vile (sûr′vil, -vīl), *adj.* **1.** slavishly submissive or obsequious; fawning: *servile flatterers.* **2.** characteristic of, proper to, or customary for slaves; abject: *servile obedience.* **3.** of, pertaining to, or involving slaves, slavery, servants, or servitude. —**ser′vile•ly,** *adv.* —**ser•vil′i•ty,** *n.*

serv•ing (sûr′ving), *n.* **1.** the act of a person or thing that serves. **2.** a single portion of food or drink; helping. —*adj.* **3.** for use in distributing food to or at the table: *a serving tray.*

ser•vi•tude (sûr′vi tōōd′, -tyōōd′), *n.* **1.** bondage of any kind. **2.** compulsory service or labor as a punishment for criminals: *penal servitude.* **3.** *Law.* a right held by one person to use another's property.

ser•vo (sûr′vō), *adj., n., pl.* **-vos.** —*adj.* **1.** acting as part of a servomechanism: *a servo amplifier.* **2.** pertaining to or concerned with servomechanisms: *a servo engineer.* **3.** noting the action of certain mechanisms, as brakes, that are set in operation by other mechanisms but which themselves augment the force of that action by the way in which they operate. —*n.* **4.** SERVOMECHANISM.

servo-, a combining form used in the names of devices or operations that employ a servomechanism: *servocontrol.*

ser•vo•mech•an•ism (sûr′vō mek′ə niz′əm, sûr′vō mek′-), *n.* an electronic control system in which a hydraulic, pneumatic, or other type of controlling mechanism is actuated and controlled by a low-energy signal. —**ser′vo•me•chan′i•cal** (-mə kan′i kəl), *adj.*

ses•a•me (ses′ə mē), *n.* **1.** a tropical plant, *Sesamum indicum,* of the family Pedaliaceae, whose small oval seeds are edible and yield an oil. **2.** the seeds themselves, used to add flavor to bread, crackers, etc.

sesqui-, a combining form meaning "one and a half": *sesquicentennial.*

ses•qui•cen•ten•ni•al (ses′kwi sen ten′ē əl), *adj.* **1.** pertaining to or marking the completion of 150 years. —*n.* **2.** a 150th anniversary or its celebration. —**ses′qui•cen•ten′ni•al•ly,** *adv.*

ses•qui•pe•da•li•an (ses′kwi pi dā′lē ən, -dāl′yən), *adj.* Also, **ses•quip•e•dal** (ses kwip′i dl). **1.** given to using long words. **2.** (of a word) containing many syllables. —*n.* **3.** a sesquipedalian word. —**ses′qui•pe•dal′i•ty** (-dal′i tē), **ses′qui•pe•da′li•an•ism,** *n.*

ses•sile (ses′il, -īl), *adj.* **1.** *Bot.* attached by the base, or without any distinct projecting support, as a leaf issuing directly from the main stem. **2.** *Zool.* permanently attached; not freely moving. —**ses•sil•i•ty** (se sil′i-tē), *n.*

ses•sion (sesh′ən), *n.* **1.** the sitting together of a court, council, legislature, or the like, for conference or the transaction of business. **2.** a single continuous meeting or series of meetings of persons so assembled. **3.** the period or term of such meetings. **4. sessions,** (in English law) the sittings or a sitting of justices in court, usu. to deal with minor offenses, grant licenses, etc. **5.** a portion of the day or year into which instruction is organized at a school, college, or the like. **6.** the governing body of a local Presbyterian church, composed of the pastor and the elders. **7.** a period of time during which two or more persons meet to pursue a particular activity: *a study session.* —**ses′sion•al,** *adj.*

set (set), *v.*, **set, set•ting,** *n., adj.* **—***v.t.* **1.** to put (something or someone) in a particular place, position, or posture: *to set a vase on a table; Set the baby on her feet.* **2.** to put or cause to pass into some condition: *to set a house on fire; to set a prisoner free.* **3.** to put or apply: *to set fire to a house.* **4.** to fix definitely; establish or decide upon: *to set a time limit; to set a wedding date.* **5.** to put (a price or value) upon something. **6.** to fix the value of at a certain amount, rate, or point: *She sets honesty above everything else.* **7.** to post, station, or appoint for some duty or task: *to set guards at the door.* **8.** to place or plant firmly: *to set a flagpole in concrete.* **9.** to direct or settle resolutely or wishfully: *to set one's heart on a new bike.* **10.** to establish for others to follow. **11.** to prescribe or assign, as a task. **12.** to distribute or arrange china, silver, etc., for use on (a table). **13.** to style (the hair) by using rollers, clips, lotions, or other aids to induce curls, waves, fullness, etc. **14.** to put in the proper or desired order or condition for use: *to set a trap.* **15.** to adjust (a mechanism) so as to control its performance. **16.** to adjust the hands of (a clock or watch) to the desired position or according to a certain standard. **17.** to adjust (a timer, alarm, etc.) so as to sound when desired. **18.** to fix at a given point or calibration: *to set the dial on an oven.* **19.** to fix or mount (a gem or the like) in a frame or setting. **20.** to ornament or stud with gems or the like. **21.** to cause to sit; seat: *to set a child in a highchair.* **22.** to put (a hen) on eggs to hatch them. **23.** to place (eggs) under a hen or in an incubator for hatching. **24.** to cause to take a particular direction: *to set one's course to the south.* **25.** to put into a fixed, rigid, or settled state, as the face or muscles. **26.** to put (a broken or dislocated bone) back in position. **27.** to cause (glue, mortar, or the like) to become fixed or hard. **28.** to affix or apply, as by stamping: *The king set his seal to the decree.* **29.** to tighten (often fol. by *up*): *to set nuts well up.* **30.** (of a hunting dog) to indicate the position of (game) by standing stiffly and pointing with the muzzle. **31.** to urge, goad, or encourage to attack: *to set the hounds on a trespasser.* **32.** to put aside (dough with yeast in it) to permit rising. **33. a.** to fit, as words to music. **b.** to arrange for musical performance. **c.** to arrange (music) for certain voices or instruments. **34. a.** to arrange the scenery, properties, lights, etc., on (a stage) for an act or scene. **b.** to give decisive form to (an action, scene, etc.) in preparation for performance. **35.** to spread and secure (a sail) so as to catch the wind. **36. a.** to arrange (type) in the order required for printing. **b.** to arrange (a text) in type for printing. **37.** *Bridge.* to cause (the opponents or their contract) to fall short. **38.** to sink (a nail head) with a nail set. **—***v.i.* **39.** to pass below the horizon; sink: *The sun sets early in winter.* **40.** to decline; wane. **41.** to assume a fixed or rigid state, as the countenance or the muscles. **42.** (of mortar, glue, dye, or the like) to become firm, solid, or permanent. **43.** to sit on eggs to hatch them, as a hen. **44.** (of the hair) to assume a particular style as the result of having been temporarily rolled up, pinned, twisted, etc. **45.** (of a flower's ovary) to develop into a fruit. **46.** (of a hunting dog) to indicate the position of game. **47.** to have a certain direction or course, as a wind or current. **48.** (of a sail) to be spread so as to catch the wind. **49.** *Nonstandard.* to sit: *Come in and set a spell.* **50. set about,** to begin; undertake; start. **51. set aside, a.** to put to one side; reserve. **b.** to dismiss from the mind; reject. **c.** to prevail over; discard; annul: *to set aside a verdict.* **52. set back, a.** to hinder; impede. **b.** to fix at an earlier time or lower point on a scale: *Set back your clocks one hour.* **c.** *Informal.* to cause to pay; cost: *The house set them back $200,000.* **53. set by,** to save or keep for future use. **54. set down, a.** to record or copy in writing or printing. **b.** to land an airplane. **55. set forth, a.** to give an account of; state; describe. **b.** to begin a journey; start. **56. set in, a.** to begin to prevail; arrive: *Darkness set in.* **b.** (of winds or currents) to blow or flow toward the shore. **57. set off, a.** to cause to become ignited or to explode. **b.** to begin; start. **c.** to intensify or improve by contrast. **d.** to begin a journey or trip; depart. **58. set on, a.** Also, **set upon.** to attack or cause to attack. **b.** to instigate; incite. **59. set out, a.** to begin a journey or course. **b.** to undertake; attempt. **c.** to define; describe. **d.** to plant. **60. set to, a.** to begin work vigorously. **b.** to start to fight. **61. set up, a.** to put upright; raise. **b.** to put into a high or powerful position. **c.** to construct; assemble; erect. **d.** to inaugurate; establish. **e.** to enable to begin in business; provide with means. **f.** to make a gift of; treat, as to drinks. **g.** to bring about; cause. **h.** to lead or lure into a prearranged situation, esp. so as to embarrass or entrap. **—***n.* **62.** the act or state of setting, or the state of being set. **63.** a collection of articles designed for use together or in a complementary way: *a chess set; a set of carving knives.* **64.** a number, group, or combination of things of similar nature, design, or function: *a set of ideas.* **65.** a number or group of persons associated by common interests, occupations, conventions, or status: *the smart set.* **66.** fixed direction, bent, or inclination: *The set of his mind was obvious.* **67.** bearing or carriage: *the set of one's shoulders.* **68.** the assumption of a fixed, rigid, or hard state, as by mortar or glue. **69.** the fit, as of an article of clothing. **70.** the styling of the hair with rollers, pins, lotions, etc., or the hairstyle so formed. **71.** an apparatus for receiving radio or television programs; receiver. **72.** a construction representing the site of the action in a play, film, or the like. **73.** a young plant, or a slip, tuber, or the like, suitable for planting. **74.** *Tennis.* a unit of a match, consisting of a group of not fewer than six games with a margin of at least two games between the winner and loser. **75.** *Psychol.* a temporary state of readiness to respond to certain stimuli in a specific way. **76.** the number of couples required to execute a quadrille or the like. **77.** *Music.* **a.** a succession of pieces played by an ensemble, as a dance band or jazz group, before or after an intermission. **b.** the period during which these pieces are played. **78.** *Naut.* the direction of a wind, current, etc. **79.** *Math.* a collection of objects or elements classed together. **—***adj.* **80.** fixed or prescribed beforehand: *a set time.* **81.** specified; fixed: *The hall holds a set number of people.* **82.** deliberately composed; customary: *set phrases.* **83.** fixed; rigid: *a set smile.* **84.** resolved or determined; habitually or stubbornly fixed: *to be set in one's opinions.* **85.** completely prepared; ready: *Is everyone set?* **—*Idiom.*** **86. set one's face** or **heart against,** to become implacably opposed to. **—Usage.** The verbs SET and SIT are similar in form and meaning but different in grammatical use. SET is chiefly transitive and takes an object: *Set the dish on the shelf.* Its past tense and past participle are also SET: *The judge has set the date for the trial.* SET also has some standard intransitive uses, as "to pass below the horizon" and "to become firm, solid, etc." The intransitive use of SET for SIT, "to be seated," is nonstandard: *Pull up a chair and set by me.* SIT is chiefly intransitive and does not take an object: *Let's sit here in the shade.* Its past tense and past participle are SAT: *Have they sat down yet?* Transitive uses of SIT include "to cause to sit" (*Sit yourself on the sofa*) and "to provide seating for" (*The waiter sat us near the window*).

Set (set) also **Seth,** *n.* an ancient Egyptian god, the brother and murderer of Osiris, represented with the head of a donkey or other mammal.

se•ta (sē′tə), *n., pl.* **-tae** (-tē). a stiff hair; bristle or bristlelike part. —**se′tal,** *adj.*

set•back (set′bak′), *n.* **1.** a check to progress; a reverse or defeat. **2.** a recession of the upper part of a building from the building line, as to lighten the structure or to permit a desired amount of light and air to reach ground level. **3.** an act or instance of setting back.

Seth[1] (seth), *n.* the third son of Adam. Gen. 4:25.

Seth[2] (sāt), *n.* SET.

set′-in′, *adj.* **1.** made separately and placed within another unit: *set-in closets.* **2.** (of a sleeve) joined to the body of a garment at the shoulder and having a seam at that juncture.

set•off (set′ôf′, -of′), *n.* **1.** something that counterbalances or makes up for something else, as compensation for a loss. **2.** a counterbalancing claim that cancels an amount a debtor owes. **3.** something that enhances the effect of another thing by contrast, as an ornament. **4.** OFFSET (def. 7).

Se•ton (sēt′n), *n.* **1. Saint Elizabeth Ann (Bayley)** (*"Mother Seton"*), 1774–1821, U.S. religious leader: canonized 1975. **2. Ernest Thompson,** 1860–1946, English writer and illustrator in the U.S.

set′ piece′, *n.* **1.** a work of art, literature, music, etc., or a part of such a work having a conventionally prescribed thematic and formal structure. **2.** a piece of stage scenery built to stand independently on the floor and usu. forming part of a set. **3.** any sequence of rehearsed movements or maneuvers, as in sports.

set′ point′, *n.* **1.** *Tennis.* the point that if won would enable the scorer or the scorer's side to win the set. **2.** SETPOINT.

set•point (set′point′), *n.* the desired value in a closed-loop feedback system, as in regulation of temperature or pressure.

set•screw (set′skrōō′), *n.* a screw passing through a threaded hole in a part to tighten the contact of that part with another, as of a collar with the shaft on which it fits.

set′ shot′, *n.* a two-handed shot in basketball made from a standing position.

set•tee (se tē′), *n.* a seat for two or more persons, having a back and usu. arms, and often upholstered.

set•ter (set′ər), *n.* **1.** a person or thing that sets. **2.** any of several breeds of hunting dogs having long hair with feathering on the legs, chest, and tail, formerly trained to crouch when game was scented and now trained to point.

set•ting (set′ing), *n.* **1.** the act of a person or thing that sets. **2.** the point or position of something, as a thermostat, that has been set. **3.** the surroundings or environment of anything. **4.** the mounting in which a jewel is set. **5.** a group of all the articles, as of china or silver, required for setting a table or a single place at a table. **6.** the locale or period in which the action of a novel, play, film, etc., takes place. **7.** the scenery or locations, along with properties and other decorative elements, used in a theatrical or film production. **8.** a piece of music composed for certain words.

set•tle[1] (set′l), *v.*, **-tled, -tling.** **—***v.t.* **1.** to appoint, fix, or resolve definitely and conclusively; agree upon, as price or conditions. **2.** to place in a desired state or in order: *to settle one's affairs.* **3.** to pay, as a bill. **4.** to close (an account) by making full payment. **5.** to migrate to and organize (an area, territory, etc.); colonize. **6.** to cause to take up residence. **7.** to furnish (a place) with inhabitants or settlers. **8.** to quiet, calm, or bring to rest: *to settle one's nerves.* **9.** to relieve nausea or other distress in: *to settle a queasy stomach.* **10.** to stop from annoying or opposing. **11.** to conclude or resolve: *to settle a dispute.* **12.** to make stable; place in a permanent position or on a permanent basis. **13.** to cause (a liquid) to become clear by depositing dregs. **14.** to cause (dregs, sediment, etc.) to sink or be deposited. **15.** to cause to sink down gradually; make firm or compact. **16.** to dispose of finally; close out (sometimes fol. by *up*): *to settle an estate.* **17. a.** to secure (property, title, etc.) on or to a person by formal or legal process. **b.** to terminate (legal proceedings) by mutual consent of the parties. **—***v.i.* **18.** to decide, arrange, or agree (often fol. by *on* or *upon*): *to settle on a plan.* **19.** to arrange matters in dispute; come to an agreement: *to settle with a*

S

person. **20.** to pay a bill; make a financial arrangement (often fol. by *up*). **21.** to take up residence in a new country or place. **22.** to come to rest, as from flight: *a bird settling on a bough.* **23.** to gather, collect, or become fixed in a particular place, direction, etc. **24.** to become calm or composed (often fol. by *down*). **25.** to stop activity in order to rest or sleep (often fol. by *in* or *down*): *We settled in for the night at a country inn.* **26.** to sink down gradually; subside. **27.** to become clear by the sinking of suspended particles, as a liquid. **28.** to sink to the bottom, as sediment. **29.** to become firm or compact, as the ground. **30.** (of a female animal) to become pregnant; conceive. **31. settle down, a.** to achieve personal and professional stability, esp. upon marrying. **b.** to become calm or quiet. **c.** to apply oneself to serious work. **32. settle for,** to be satisfied with. **33. settle into,** to become established in.

settle²

set·tle² (set′l), *n.* a long seat or bench, usu. wooden, with arms and a high back.
set·tle·ment (set′l mənt), *n.* **1.** the act or state of settling or the state of being settled. **2.** the act of making stable or putting on a permanent basis. **3.** a state of stability or permanence. **4.** an arrangement or adjustment, as of business affairs or a disagreement. **5.** an agreement signed after labor negotiations between union and management. **6.** the settling of persons in a new country or place. **7.** a colony, esp. in its early stages. **8.** a small community, village, or group of houses in a thinly populated area. **9.** a community formed by members of a particular religious or ideological group. **10.** the satisfying of a claim or demand; a coming to terms. **11. a.** final disposition, through legal proceedings, of opposing claims, an estate, etc. **b.** the settling of property, title, etc., upon a person. **c.** the property so settled. **12.** Also called **set′tlement house′.** an establishment in an underprivileged area providing social services to local residents. **13.** a subsidence or sinking of all or part of a structure.
set·tler (set′lər, set′l ər), *n.* **1.** a person or thing that settles. **2.** a person who settles in a new country or area.
set·tling (set′ling, set′l ing), *n.* **1.** the act of a person or thing that settles. **2.** Usu., **settlings.** sediment.
set·up (set′up′), *n.* **1.** organization; arrangement. **2.** an act or instance of setting up or getting ready. **3.** the carriage of the body; bearing. **4.** a camera position, as for a particular shot. **5.** a service of glass, ice, soda water, etc., for patrons who provide their own liquor. **6. a.** an undertaking or contest deliberately made easy. **b.** a match or game against an opponent who can be defeated without difficulty. **c.** such an opponent. **7.** a pass, shot, play, etc., in a sport or game creating an advantageous opportunity for scoring, or the situation so created. **8.** an arrangement, collection, or package of all the items, parts, apparatus, etc., necessary for a specific activity or purpose. **9.** a plan or projected course of action. **10.** a prearranged situation or circumstance, usu. created to fool or trap someone; trick; scheme.
Seu·rat (soo rä′), *n.* **Georges,** 1859–91, French painter.
Seuss (soos), *n.* **Dr., Geisel,** Theodor Seuss.
sev·en (sev′ən), *n.* **1.** a cardinal number, 6 plus 1. **2.** a symbol for this number, as 7 or VII. **3.** a set of this many persons or things. —*adj.* **4.** amounting to seven in number.
Sev′en Church′es of A′sia, *n.pl.* the ancient Christian churches of Ephesus, Smyrna, Pergamum, Thyatira, Sardis, Philadelphia, and Laodicea. Rev. 1:2.
Sev′en Dead′ly Sins′, *n.pl.* **deadly sins.**
sev·en·fold (sev′ən fōld′), *adj.* **1.** comprising seven parts or members. **2.** seven times as great or as much. —*adv.* **3.** until seven times as many or as great: *multiplied sevenfold.*
Sev′en Gifts′ of the Spir′it, *n.pl.* wisdom, understanding, counsel, fortitude, knowledge, righteousness, and fear of the Lord.
Sev′en Hills′ of Rome′, *n.pl.* the seven hills (the Aventine, Caelian, Capitoline, Esquiline, Palatine, Quirinal, and Viminal) on and about which the ancient city of Rome was built.
sev·en-league boots′ (sev′ən lēg′), *n.pl.* fairy-tale boots enabling the wearer to reach seven leagues at a stride. [trans. of French *bottes de sept lieues* in the fairy tales of C. Perrault, esp. *Le petit Poucet* (English *Hop-o′-my-Thumb*)]
Sev′en Pil′lars of Wis′dom, a military chronicle (1926) by T.E. Lawrence. Prov. 9:1.
sev·en·teen (sev′ən tēn′), *n.* **1.** a cardinal number, 10 plus 7. **2.** a symbol for this number, as 17 or XVII. **3.** a set of this many persons or things. —*adj.* **4.** amounting to 17 in number.
sev·en·teenth (sev′ən tēnth′), *adj.* **1.** next after the sixteenth; being the ordinal number for 17. **2.** being one of 17 equal parts. —*n.* **3.** a seventeenth part, esp. of one (¹⁄₁₇). **4.** the seventeenth member of a series.
Sev′enteenth Amend′ment, *n.* an amendment to the U.S. Constitution, ratified in 1913, providing for the election of two U.S. senators from each state by popular vote and for a term of six years.
sev·enth (sev′ənth), *adj.* **1.** next after the sixth; being the ordinal num-

ber for seven. **2.** being one of seven equal parts. —*n.* **3.** a seventh part, esp. of one (¹⁄₇). **4.** the seventh member of a series. **5. a.** a musical interval encompassing seven diatonic degrees. **b.** a tone at this interval. **c.** the harmonic combination of two tones a seventh apart. —*adv.* **6.** in the seventh place.
Sev′enth Amend′ment, *n.* an amendment to the U.S. Constitution, ratified in 1791 as part of the Bill of Rights, guaranteeing trial by jury.
Sev′enth Command′ment, *n.* "Thou shalt not commit adultery": seventh of the Ten Commandments. Compare **ten commandments.**
Sev′enth-Day′, *adj.* (sometimes *l.c.*) designating certain Christian denominations that make Saturday their chief day of rest and religious observance: *Seventh-Day Adventists.*
sev′enth heav′en, *n.* **1.** (esp. in Islam and the cabala) the highest heaven, where God and the most exalted angels dwell. **2.** a state of intense happiness; bliss.
sev·en·ty (sev′ən tē), *n., pl.* **-ties,** *adj.* —*n.* **1.** a cardinal number, 10 times 7. **2.** a symbol for this number, as 70 or LXX. **3.** a set of this many persons or things. **4. seventies,** the numbers from 70 through 79, as in referring to the years of a lifetime or of a century or to degrees of temperature. **5. the Seventy,** the body of scholars who produced the Septuagint. —*adj.* **6.** amounting to 70 in number. —**sev′en·ti·eth,** *adj., n.*
78 (sev′ən tē āt′), *n., pl.* **78s, 78's.** an early type of shellac-based phonograph record that played at 78 revolutions per minute.
sev′en-up′, *n.* **all fours** (def. 2).
Sev′en Vir′tues, *n.pl.* the three Christian virtues of faith, hope, and charity, together with the four cardinal virtues of justice, fortitude, prudence, and temperance.
Sev′en Won′ders of the World′, *n.pl.* the seven structures considered the most remarkable of ancient times: the Egyptian pyramids, the Mausoleum at Halicarnassus, the Temple of Artemis at Ephesus, the Hanging Gardens of Babylon, the Colossus of Rhodes, the statue of Zeus by Phidias at Olympia, and the Pharos or lighthouse at Alexandria.
Sev′en Years′′ War′, *n.* the war (1756–63) in which England and Prussia defeated France, Austria, Russia, Sweden, and Saxony.
sev·er (sev′ər), *v.t.* **1.** to separate (a part) from the whole, as by cutting. **2.** to divide into parts, esp. forcibly; cleave. **3.** to break off or dissolve (ties, relations, etc.). —*v.i.* **4.** to become separated or divided.
sev·er·al (sev′ər əl, sev′rəl), *adj.* **1.** being more than two but fewer than many in number or kind: *several ways to do the same thing.* **2.** respective; individual: *They went their several ways.* **3.** separate; different: *several occasions.* **4.** single; particular. **5.** *Law.* binding two or more persons who may be sued separately on a common obligation. —*n.* **6.** several persons or things.
sev·er·ance (sev′ər əns, sev′rəns), *n.* **1.** the act of severing or the state of being severed. **2.** a breaking off, as of a friendship. **3.** *Law.* a division of liabilities, provisions, etc., into parts; removal of a part from the whole. **4.** Also called **sev′erance pay′.** an amount of money, exclusive of wages, fringe benefits, etc., paid to an employee who is dismissed for reasons beyond the employee's control.
se·vere (sə vēr′), *adj.* **-ver·er, -ver·est. 1.** harsh; unnecessarily extreme: *severe criticism.* **2.** serious or stern in manner or appearance. **3.** grave; critical: *a severe illness.* **4.** rigidly restrained in style, taste, etc.; plain; austere. **5.** of an extreme, intense, or violent character or nature: *severe thunderstorms; a severe shock.* **6.** difficult to endure, perform, fulfill, etc.: *a severe test of strength.* **7.** rigidly exact; demanding: *severe standards.* —**se·vere′ly,** *adv.*
se·ver·i·ty (sə ver′i tē), *n., pl.* **-ties. 1.** harshness, sternness, or rigor. **2.** austere simplicity, as of style or taste. **3.** intensity or sharpness, as of cold or pain. **4.** grievousness; hard or trying character or effect. **5.** rigid exactness or accuracy. **6.** an instance of strict or severe behavior, punishment, etc.
Se·ville (sə vil′), *n.* a port in SW Spain, on the Guadalquivir River. 668,356. Spanish, **Se·vi·lla** (se vē′lyä). —**Se·vil′lian** (-yən), *adj., n.*
sew (sō), *v.*, **sewed, sewn** or **sewed, sew·ing.** —*v.t.* **1.** to join or attach by stitches. **2.** to make, repair, etc., by such means: *She sewed her own wedding gown.* **3.** to enclose or secure with stitches: *to sew flour in a bag.* **4.** to close (a hole, wound, etc.) by means of stitches (usu. fol. by *up*). —*v.i.* **5.** to work with a needle and thread or with a sewing machine. **6. sew up,** *Informal.* to get, have, accomplish, or control successfully or completely: *to sew up a deal; to sew up votes at a convention.* —**sew′a·ble,** *adj.*
sew·age (soo′ij) also **sewerage,** *n.* the waste matter that passes through sewers.
Sew·all (soo′əl), *n.* **Samuel,** 1652–1730, American jurist, born in England.
Sew·ard (soo′ərd), *n.* **William Henry,** 1801–72, U.S. Secretary of State 1861–69.
Sew′ard's Fol′ly, *n.* the purchase of Alaska in 1867, through the negotiations of Secretary of State W. H. Seward. Compare **alaska purchase.** [so called because Alaska was regarded as worthless land]
sew·er¹ (soo′ər), *n.* an artificial conduit, usu. underground, for carrying off waste water and refuse, as in a town or city. —**sew′er·less,** *adj.* —**sew′er·like,** *adj.*
sew·er² (sō′ər), *n.* a person or thing that sews.
sew·ing (sō′ing), *n.* **1.** the act or work of one who sews. **2.** something sewn or to be sewn.

sew′ing cir′cle, *n.* a group, esp. of women, meeting regularly to sew.

sew′ing machine′, *n.* any of various foot-operated or electric machines for making stitches, ranging from machines for sewing garments to industrial machines for sewing leather, book pages, or the like.

sewn (sōn), *v.* a pp. of SEW.

sex (seks), *n.* **1.** either the female or male division of a species, esp. as differentiated with reference to the reproductive functions. **2.** the instinct or attraction drawing one sex toward another, or its manifestation in life and conduct. **3.** SEXUAL INTERCOURSE. **4.** GENITALIA. —*v.t.* **5.** to ascertain the sex of, esp. of newly hatched chicks. **6.** to arouse sexually (often fol. by *up*).

sex·a·ge·nar·i·an (sek′sə jə när′ē ən), *adj.* **1.** of the age of 60 years or between 60 and 70 years old. —*n.* **2.** a sexagenarian person.

sex·ag·e·nar·y (sek saj′ə ner′ē), *adj., n., pl.* **-nar·ies.** —*adj.* **1.** of or pertaining to the number 60. **2.** composed of or proceeding by sixties. **3.** sexagenarian. —*n.* **4.** a sexagenarian.

Sex·a·ges·i·ma (sek′sə jes′ə mə), *n.* the second Sunday before Lent.

sex′ appeal′, *n.* **1.** the ability to excite people sexually. **2.** a capacity to stimulate or attract interest or enthusiasm.

sex′ cell′, *n.* a spermatozoon or an ovum; gamete.

sex′ change′, *n.* the alteration, by surgery and hormone treatments, of a person's morphological sex characteristics to approximate those of the opposite sex.

sex′ hor′mone, *n.* any of a class of steroid hormones that regulate the growth and function of the reproductive organs or stimulate the development of the secondary sexual characteristics.

sex·ism (sek′siz əm), *n.* **1.** attitudes or behavior based on traditional stereotypes of sexual roles. **2.** discrimination or prejudice based on a person's sex, esp. discrimination against women.

sex·ist (sek′sist), *adj.* **1.** pertaining to, involving, or fostering sexism: *sexist advertising.* —*n.* **2.** a person with sexist attitudes or behavior.

sex·less (seks′lis), *adj.* **1.** having or seeming to have no sex; neuter. **2.** having or seeming to have no sexual desires. **3.** having no sexual interest or appeal. —**sex′less·ly,** *adv.* —**sex′less·ness,** *n.*

sex·ol·o·gy (sek sol′ə jē), *n.* the study of sexual behavior. —**sex′o·log′i·cal** (-sə loj′i kəl), *adj.* —**sex·ol′o·gist,** *n.*

sex·tant (sek′stənt), *n.* an astronomical instrument used to determine latitude and longitude at sea by measuring angular distances, esp. the altitudes of sun, moon, and stars.

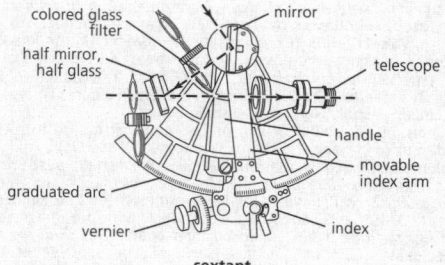

sextant

sex·tet or **sex·tette** (seks tet′), *n.* **1.** any group or set of six. **2. a.** a company of six singers or players. **b.** a musical composition for six voices or instruments.

sex·til·lion (seks til′yən), *n., adj.* **-lions,** (*as after a numeral*) **-lion,** *adj.* —*n.* **1.** a cardinal number represented in the U.S. by 1 followed by 21 zeros, and in Great Britain by 1 followed by 36 zeros. —*adj.* **2.** amounting to one sextillion in number. —**sex·til′lionth,** *adj., n.*

sex·ton (sek′stən), *n.* **1.** an official who maintains a church building and its contents, rings the bell, etc. **2.** an official whose main duty is to maintain a synagogue and its religious articles. —**sex′ton·ship,** *n.*

sex·tu·plet (seks tup′lit, -tōō′plit, -tyōō′-, seks′tōō plit, -tyōō-), *n.* **1.** a group or combination of six things. **2.** one of six offspring born at one birth. **3. sextuplets,** six children or offspring born of one pregnancy. **4.** *Music.* a group of six notes of equal value performed in the same time normally taken to perform four.

sex·u·al (sek′shōō əl), *adj.* **1.** of or pertaining to sex. **2.** occurring between or involving the sexes: *sexual relations.* **3.** having sexual organs, or reproducing by processes involving both sexes. —**sex′u·al·ly,** *adv.*

sex′ual harass′ment, *n.* unwelcome sexual advances, esp. when made by an employer or superior, usu. with compliance as a condition of continued employment or promotion.

sex′ual in′tercourse, *n.* genital contact or coupling between individuals, esp. one involving penetration of the penis into the vagina.

sex·u·al·i·ty (sek′shōō al′i tē), *n.* **1.** sexual character; possession of the structural and functional traits of sex. **2.** recognition of or emphasis upon sexual matters. **3.** involvement in sexual activity. **4.** an organism's preparedness for engaging in sexual activity.

sex′ually transmit′ted disease′, *n.* any disease characteristically transmitted by sexual contact, as gonorrhea, syphilis, genital herpes, and chlamydia. *Abbr.:* STD   Also called **venereal disease.**

sex′ual orienta′tion, *n.* one's natural preference in sexual partners; predilection for homosexuality, heterosexuality, or bisexuality.

sex′ual rela′tions, *n.* **1.** sexual intercourse; coitus. **2.** any sexual activity between individuals.

sex·y (sek′sē), *adj.,* **sex·i·er, sex·i·est. 1.** concerned predominantly or exclusively with sex; erotic: *a sexy novel.* **2.** sexually interesting or exciting; radiating sexuality. **3.** excitingly appealing; glamorous. —**sex′i·ly,** *adv.* —**sex′i·ness,** *n.*

Sey·chelles (sā shel′, -shelz′), *n.* (*used with a pl. v.*) a republic consisting of 115 islands in the Indian Ocean, NE of Madagascar: a member of the Commonwealth of Nations. 78,142; 175 sq. mi. (455 sq. km). *Cap.:* Victoria.

Sey·han (sā hän′), *n.* **1.** ADANA. **2.** a river in S central Turkey, flowing S from the Anatolia plateau to the Mediterranean Sea. 748 mi. (1204 km) long.

Sey·mour (sē′môr, -mōr), *n.* **Jane,** c1510–37, third wife of Henry VIII of England and mother of Edward VI.

SF or **s-f,** science fiction.

sf, 1. science fiction. **2.** sforzando.

Sfc, sergeant first class.

sfor·zan·do (sfôrt sän′dō) also **forzando,** *adj., adv. Music.* with force; emphatically. [< Italian *sforzare* to show strength]

sfu·ma·to (sfōō mä′tō), *n., pl.* **-tos.** gradation of tone used to blur the outlines of a form in painting.

SG, 1. senior grade. **2.** Secretary General. **3.** Solicitor General. **4.** Surgeon General.

s.g., specific gravity.

SGML, Standard Generalized Markup Language: a set of standards, approved by the ISO, enabling a user to create an appropriate markup scheme for tagging the elements of an electronic document.

sgraf·fi·to (skrä fē′tō; *It.* zgräf fē′tô), *n., pl.* **-ti** (-tē) **1.** a technique of ornamentation in which a surface layer of paint, plaster, slip, etc., is incised to reveal a ground of contrasting color. **2.** an object, esp. pottery, decorated by this technique. Compare GRAFFITO.

's Gra·ven·ha·ge (sкнrä′vən hä′кнə), *n.* a Dutch name of The HAGUE.

Sgt., Sergeant.

Sgt. Maj., Sergeant Major.

sh or **shh** (*usu. an extended* sh *sound*), *interj.* (used to urge silence.)

Shaan·xi (shän′shē′) also **Shensi,** *n.* a province in N central China. 30,430,000; 75,598 sq. mi. (195,799 sq. km). *Cap.:* Xian.

Sha·ban (shə bän′, shä-, shô-), *n.* the eighth month of the Islamic calendar.

Shab·bat (shä bät′), *n. Hebrew.* the Jewish Sabbath.

shab·by (shab′ē), *adj.,* **-bi·er, -bi·est. 1.** showing signs of wear or long use; worn. **2.** wearing worn clothes or having a slovenly appearance. **3.** run-down; dilapidated: *a shabby hotel.* **4.** meanly ungenerous or unfair; contemptible: *shabby behavior.* **5.** inferior; second-rate. —**shab′bi·ly,** *adv.* —**shab′bi·ness,** *n.*

Sha·bu·oth or **Sha·bu·ot** (shə vōō′ōs, shä vōō ôt′), *n.* SHAVUOTH.

shack (shak), *n.* **1.** a rough cabin; shanty. —*v.i.* **2. shack up,** *Slang.* to take up residence; dwell.

shack·le (shak′əl), *n., v.,* **-led, -ling.** —*n.* **1.** a ring or other fastening, as of iron, for securing the wrist, ankle, etc.; fetter. **2.** a hobble or fetter for a horse or other animal. **3.** the U-shaped bar of a padlock. **4.** any of various fastening or coupling devices. **5.** Often, **shackles.** anything that serves to inhibit freedom, thought, etc. —*v.t.* **6.** to confine or restrain by a shackle or shackles. **7.** to fasten together with a shackle. **8.** to restrict the freedom of. —**shack′ler,** *n.*

shad (shad), *n., pl.* (*esp. collectively*) **shad,** (*esp. for kinds or species*) **shads.** any of several herringlike marine fishes of the genus *Alosa* that spawn in rivers well upstream from the sea, as *A. sapidissima,* of Europe and North America.

shade (shād), *n., v.,* **shad·ed, shad·ing.** —*n.* **1.** the comparative darkness caused by the screening of rays of light from an object or area. **2.** a place or an area of comparative darkness, as one sheltered from the sun. **3.** WINDOW SHADE. **4.** LAMPSHADE. **5. shades. a.** darkness gathering at the close of day. **b.** *Informal.* sunglasses. **c.** a reminder of something: *shades of the Inquisition.* **6.** comparative obscurity. **7.** the disembodied spirit of a dead person, esp. an ancestor. **8.** the degree of darkness of a color, determined by the quantity of black or by the lack of illumination. **9.** a dark part of a picture or drawing. **10.** a slight amount or degree: *a shade of difference; coffee with a shade of cream.* **11.** anything used for protection against excessive light, heat, etc. **12.** a shadow. —*v.t.* **13.** to produce shade in or on. **14.** to obscure, dim, or darken. **15.** to screen or hide from view. **16.** to protect by or as if by a screen. **17. a.** to introduce degrees of darkness into (a drawing or painting) in order to render light and shadow or give the effect of color. **b.** to render the values of light and dark on (a drawn figure, object, etc.), esp. in order to create an illusion of three-dimensionality. **18.** to change by imperceptible degrees. **19.** to reduce (a price) by degrees. —*v.i.* **20.** to change by slight graduations. —**shad′er,** *n.* —**shade′less,** *adj.*

shade′ tree′, *n.* a tree planted or valued for its shade.

shad·ing (shā′ding), *n.* **1.** a slight variation or difference of color, character, etc. **2.** the representation of the different values of color or light and dark in a painting or drawing.

shad·ow (shad′ō), *n.* **1.** a dark figure or image cast on the ground or other surface by a body intercepting light. **2.** shade or comparative

S

darkness. **3. shadows,** darkness, esp. that coming after sunset. **4.** shelter or protection. **5.** a slight suggestion; trace: *beyond the shadow of a doubt.* **6.** a specter or ghost. **7.** a hint or intimation. **8.** a mere semblance: *the shadow of power.* **9.** a reflected image. **10.** (in painting, drawing, graphics, etc.) the dark part of a picture, esp. as representing the absence of illumination. **11.** a period or instance of gloom, unhappiness, or the like. **12.** a dominant or pervasive threat: *the shadow of war.* **13.** an inseparable companion. **14.** a spy or detective. *—v.t.* **15.** to cover with shadow; shade. **16.** to cast a gloom over; cloud. **17.** to screen or protect, as from light or heat. **18.** to follow the movements of (a person) secretly. **19.** to represent faintly, prophetically, etc. (often fol. by *forth*). *—adj.* **20.** of or pertaining to a shadow cabinet. **21.** without official authority: *a shadow government.* **—shad′ow•less,** *adj.*

shad′ow box′, *n.* a rectangular frame fronted with a glass panel, used to show and at the same time protect items on display.

shad•ow•box (shad′ō boks′), *v.i.* to go through the motions of boxing, without an opponent, as a training or conditioning procedure.

shad′ow cab′inet, *n.* (in the British Parliament) a group of prominent members of the opposition who are expected to hold positions in the cabinet when their party assumes power.

shad•ow•ing (shad′ō ing), *n.* a method of enhancing the visibility of the surface features of a specimen for electron-microscopic viewing by spraying it from one side with a coating of metal atoms.

shad′ow play′, *n.* a show in which shadows of puppets, flat figures, or live actors are projected onto a lighted screen. Also called **shad′ow show′, shad′ow the′ater.**

shad•ow•y (shad′ō ē), *adj.,* **-ow•i•er, -ow•i•est. 1.** resembling a shadow in faintness, slightness, etc. **2.** unsubstantial or illusory. **3.** abounding in shade or shadows; shady. —**shad′ow•i•ness,** *n.*

Shad•rach (shad′rak, shā′drak), *n.* a companion of Daniel who, with Meshach and Abednego, was thrown into the fiery furnace of Nebuchadnezzar and came out unharmed. Dan. 3:12–30.

shad•y (shā′dē), *adj.,* **shad•i•er, shad•i•est. 1.** abounding in shade; shaded. **2.** giving shade. **3.** shadowy; indistinct; spectral. **4.** of dubious character; disreputable. **—*Idiom.* 5. on the shady side of,** older than (a specified age, esp. beyond middle age). —**shad′i•ly,** *adv.*

shaft (shaft, shäft), *n.* **1.** a long pole forming the body of various weapons, as lances or arrows. **2.** something directed at someone or something in sharp attack: *shafts of sarcasm.* **3.** a ray or beam. **4.** a long handle serving to balance or manipulate a weapon or tool, as an ax or a golf club. **5.** a rotating or oscillating rod that transmits motion and torque, as a ship's propeller shaft or the drive shaft of an automobile. **6. a.** the part of a column or pier between the base and the capital. **b.** any distinct, slender vertical masonry feature engaged in a wall or pier and usu. supporting an arch or vault. **7.** a monument in the form of a column, obelisk, or the like. **8.** either of the parallel bars between which the animal drawing a vehicle is hitched. **9.** any well-like passage or vertical enclosed space, as in a building: *an elevator shaft.* **10.** a vertical or sloping passageway in a mine that leads to the surface. **11.** the trunk of a tree. **12.** the main stem or midrib of a feather. **13.** *Slang.* harsh or unfair treatment. *—v.t.* **14.** to push or propel with a pole. **15.** *Slang.* to treat in a harsh, unfair, or treacherous manner.

shaft•ing (shaf′ting, shäf′-), *n.* **1.** a number of shafts. **2.** a system of shafts, as the overhead shafts formerly used for driving the machinery of a mill.

shag¹ (shag), *n., v.,* **shagged, shag•ging.** *—n.* **1.** rough, matted hair, wool, or the like. **2.** a mass of this. **3.** a hairstyle in which the hair is cut in layers downward from the crown. **4.** a long, thick pile or nap. **5.** a rug or carpet with a thick, shaggy pile. **6.** a coarse tobacco cut into fine shreds. *—v.t., v.i.* **7.** to make or become rough or shaggy.

shag² (shag), *n.* any of several small cormorants, esp. *Phalacrocorax aristotelis,* of European coasts.

shag³ (shag), *v.t.,* **shagged, shag•ging. 1.** to chase or follow after; pursue. **2.** to go after and bring back; fetch. **3.** *Baseball.* to retrieve and throw back (fly balls) in batting practice.

shag•gy (shag′ē), *adj.,* **-gi•er, -gi•est. 1.** covered with or having long, rough hair. **2.** untidy; unkempt. **3.** forming a bushy mass, as the hair or mane. **4.** having a rough nap, as cloth. **5.** done in a sloppy manner. —**shag′gi•ly,** *adv.* —**shag′gi•ness,** *n.*

shag′gy-dog′ sto′ry, *n.* a long and involved story, regarded as humorous by the narrator, often told with extraneous detail that culminates in an absurd or irrelevant punch line.

shah (shä, shô), *n.* (*often cap.*) (formerly, in Iran) king; sovereign. [< Persian: king] —**shah′dom,** *n.*

Shai•tan or **Shei•tan** (shī tän′), *n.* (in Islam) Satan; the devil. [< Arabic *Shayṭān,* cognate of Hebrew *śāṭān* SATAN]

shake (shāk), *v.,* **shook, shak•en, shak•ing,** *n.* *—v.i.* **1.** to move with short, quick, vibratory movements. **2.** to tremble with emotion, cold, etc. **3.** to become dislodged and fall (often fol. by *off*). **4.** to move something, esp. in a bottle or container, briskly to and fro or up and down, as in mixing. **5.** to totter; become unsteady. **6.** to shake hands. **7.** to execute a trill. *—v.t.* **8.** to agitate (a container, bottle, etc.), as to mix the contents (sometimes fol. by *up*). **9.** to grasp and move (a person) back and forth violently. **10.** to brandish or flourish, esp. menacingly. **11.** to grasp firmly in an attempt to dislodge something by quick, vigorous movements. **12.** to dislodge (something) by quick, forcible movements: *to shake nuts from the tree.* **13.** to agitate or disturb profoundly. **14.** to cause to waver or weaken. **15.** to trill (a note). **16.** to get rid of; elude. **17. shake down, a.** to cause to descend by shaking; bring down. **b.** to cause to settle. **c.** (esp. of a ship) to cause to undergo a shakedown. **d.** to extort money from. **e.** to search for concealed weapons. **18. shake off, a.** to rid oneself of; reject. **b.** to get away from. **19. shake up, a.** to upset; jar. **b.** to trouble or distress. *—n.* **20.** an act or instance of rocking, swaying, etc. **21.** tremulous motion. **22.** a tremor. **23. shakes,** (*used with a sing. v.*) a state or spell of trembling, as caused by fear, fever, or cold (usu. prec. by *the*). **24.** MILK SHAKE. **25.** HANDSHAKE (def. 1). **26.** treatment; deal: *Everyone gets a fair shake.* **27.** something resulting from shaking. **28.** *Informal.* an earthquake. **29.** an internal crack or fissure in timber. **30.** TRILL (def. 1). **31.** a shingle or clapboard formed by splitting a short log into a number of tapered radial sections with a hatchet. **—*Idiom.* 32. no great shakes,** common; ordinary. **33. shake a leg,** *Informal.* **a.** to hurry. **b.** to dance. **34. shake hands,** to clasp another's hand or one another's hands, as in greeting. **35. two shakes** or **two shakes of a lamb's tail,** a very short time; a moment. —**shak′a•ble, shake′a•ble,** *adj.*

shake•down (shāk′doun′), *n.* **1.** extortion, as by blackmail. **2.** a thorough search. **3.** a makeshift bed, esp. one made up on the floor. **4.** the act or process of shaking down. **5.** a cruise or flight made in preparation for regular service by familiarizing the crew with a craft's operation, adjusting machinery, etc.

shak′en ba′by syn′drome, *n.* a condition occurring in infants less than one year old, caused by a violent shaking by the arms and shoulders that makes the brain whip back and forth in the skull, causing subdural hematomas and bleeding in the eyes.

shake•out (shāk′out′), *n.* an elimination of weaker businesses, esp. in a period of intense competition.

shak•er (shā′kər), *n.* **1.** a container with a perforated top from which a seasoning, condiment, sugar, flour, or the like is shaken onto food. **2.** any of various containers for shaking beverages to mix the ingredients. **3.** a dredger or caster. **4.** (*cap.*) a member of a religious sect originating in England in the middle of the 18th century and now extant only in the U.S., practicing celibacy, common ownership of property, and a strict and simple way of life. **5.** a person or thing that shakes. *—adj.* **6.** (*cap.*) of or pertaining to a style of furniture produced by Shakers in the U.S., characterized by simplicity of form, lack of ornamentation, and functionality. **7.** (*sometimes cap.*) of or designating a knitted fabric formed of parallel rows of ribbing, used for sweaters.

Shake•speare (shāk′spēr), *n.* **William,** 1564–1616, English poet and dramatist.

shake′-up′, *n.* a thorough change of administration in an organization, department, or the like, as by dismissals or reassignments.

Shak•ti or **Sak•ti** (shuk′tē), *n., pl.* **-tis.** *Hinduism.* **1.** the female principle or organ of generative power. **2.** the wife of a deity, esp. of Shiva.

shak•y (shā′kē), *adj.,* **shak•i•er, shak•i•est. 1.** tending to shake or tremble. **2.** liable to break down or give way; insecure. **3.** wavering, as in allegiance. —**shak′i•ly,** *adv.* —**shak′i•ness,** *n.*

shale (shāl), *n.* a rock of fissile or laminated structure formed by the consolidation of clay or argillaceous material.

shall (shal; *unstressed* shəl), *auxiliary v., pres.* **shall;** *past* **should;** *imperative, infinitive, and participles lacking.* **1.** plan to or intend to: *I shall go later.* **2.** will have to or is determined to: *You shall do it. He shall do it.* **3.** (in laws, directives, etc.) must; is or are obliged to: *Council meetings shall be public.* **4.** (used interrogatively): *Shall we go?*

shal•lot (shal′ət, shə lot′), *n.* **1.** a plant, *Allium ascalonicum,* related to the onion, having a divided bulb. **2.** the bulb of this plant, used in cooking.

shal•low (shal′ō), *adj.* **1.** of little depth: *shallow water.* **2.** lacking depth; superficial: *a shallow mind.* **3.** taking in a relatively small amount of air in each inhalation: *shallow breathing.* *—n.* **4.** Usu., **shallows.** (*used with a sing. or pl. v.*) a shallow part of a body of water; shoal. *—v.t., v.i.* **5.** to make or become shallow. —**shal′low•ly,** *adv.* —**shal′low•ness,** *n.*

Shal•ma•ne•ser (shal′mə nē′zər), *n.* an Assyrian king who defeated the northern kingdom of Israel. II Kings 17:3–6; 18:9–10.

sha•lom (shä lôm′; *Eng.* shə lōm′), *interj. Hebrew.* (used as a word of greeting or farewell.)

shalt (shalt), *v. Archaic.* 2nd pers. sing. of SHALL.

sham (sham), *n., adj., v.,* **shammed, sham•ming.** *—n.* **1.** a spurious imitation; fraud or hoax. **2.** a person who pretends or counterfeits. **3.** a cover or the like: *a pillow sham.* *—adj.* **4.** pretended; counterfeit: *sham attacks.* **5.** designed, made, or used as a sham. *—v.t.* **6.** to produce an imitation of. **7.** to feign: *to sham illness.* *—v.i.* **8.** to make a false show of something; pretend. —**sham′mer,** *n.*

sha•man (shä′mən, shā′-, sham′ən), *n.* (esp. among certain tribal peoples) a person who acts as intermediary between the natural and supernatural worlds, using magic to cure illness, control spiritual forces, etc. —**sha•man•ic** (shə man′ik), *adj.*

sham•ble (sham′bəl), *v.,* **-bled, -bling,** *n.* *—v.i.* **1.** to walk or move awkwardly; shuffle. *—n.* **2.** a shambling gait.

sham•bles (sham′bəlz), *n.* (*used with a sing. or pl. v.*) **1.** a slaughterhouse. **2.** any place of carnage. **3.** any scene of destruction. **4.** a place or condition of great disorder.

shame (shām), *n., v.,* **shamed, sham•ing.** *—n.* **1.** the painful feeling of having done or experienced something dishonorable, improper, foolish, etc. **2.** capacity to experience this feeling: *to be without shame.* **3.** disgrace; ignominy. **4.** a cause for regret, disappointment, etc.: *It was a* *shame you weren't there.* —*v.t.* **5.** to cause to feel shame. **6.** to activate or motivate through shame: *He shamed me into going.* **7.** to cause to suffer disgrace. —*Idiom.* **8. for shame,** (used to induce feelings of guilt in someone.) **9. put to shame, a.** to cause to suffer shame or disgrace. **b.** to outdo; surpass. —**sham′a•ble, shame′a•ble,** *adj.* —**sham′a•bly, shame′a•bly,** *adv.*

shame•faced (shām′fāst′), *adj.* **1.** feeling or showing shame: *shamefaced apologies.* **2.** modest or bashful. —**shame•fac•ed•ly** (shām′fā′sid-lē, shām′fāst′lē), *adv.* —**shame′fac′ed•ness,** *n.*

shame•ful (shām′fəl), *adj.* **1.** disgraceful or scandalous; vile: *shameful behavior.* **2.** causing shame; humiliating: *a shameful apology to his classmates.* —**shame′ful•ly,** *adv.* —**shame′ful•ness,** *n.*

shame•less (shām′lis), *adj.* **1.** lacking any sense of shame: una-shamed. **2.** showing no shame; brazen. —**shame′less•ly,** *adv.* —**shame′less•ness,** *n.*

Sham•gar (sham′gər), *n.* a judge of Israel who killed 600 Philistines with an ox goad. Judg. 3:31.

sham•mes or **sha•mes** (shä′məs), *n., pl.* **sham•mo•sim** or **sha•mo•sim** (shä mō′sim). **1.** SEXTON (def. 2). **2.** the candle used to kindle the other candles in the Hanukkah menorah. [< Hebrew *shammāsh* server, attendant]

sham•poo (sham pōō′), *n., pl.* **-poos.,** *v.* **-pooed, -pooing.** —*n.* **1.** a special cleansing preparation that produces suds. **2.** the act of washing the hair, a rug, etc., with such a preparation. —*v.t.* **3.** to wash (the hair), esp. with a shampoo. **4.** to wash the hair of. **5.** to clean (rugs, upholstery, etc.) with a shampoo. —**sham•poo′er,** *n.*

sham•rock (sham′rok), *n.* any of several trifoliate plants, esp. *Trifolium procumbens,* a small, yellow-flowered clover: the national emblem of Ireland.

shamrock, *Trifolium procumbens*

sha•mus (shä′məs, shā′-), *n., pl.* **-mus•es.** *Slang.* **1.** a private detective. **2.** a police officer.

shang•hai (shang′hī, shang hī′), *v.t.,* **-haied, -hai•ing.** to enroll or obtain (a sailor) for the crew of a ship by unscrupulous means, as by force.

Shang•hai (shang hī′), *n.* a seaport and municipality in Jiangsu province, in E China, near the mouth of the Chang Jiang. 6,980,000 (municipality 12,300,000).

Shan•gri-la (shang′grī lä′, shang′grī lä′), *n.* an imaginary paradise on earth, esp. a remote and exotic utopia. [after the fictional Tibetan land of eternal youth in the novel *Lost Horizon* (1933) by James Hilton]

shank (shangk), *n.* **1. a.** the part of the lower limb in humans between the knee and the ankle. **b.** the corresponding part in other vertebrates. **2.** the lower limb; the entire leg. **3.** a cut of meat from the top part of the front **(foreshank)** or backleg of an animal. **4. a.** a straight, narrow, shaftlike part of various objects usu. connecting two more important or complex parts, as the stem of a tobacco pipe. **b.** a knob or projection that allows a device to be attached to another object. **5.** *Informal.* the early part of a period of time. **6.** the narrow part of the sole of a shoe, lying beneath the instep. **7.** *Print.* the body of a type, between the shoulder and the foot. **8.** the part of a ring that surrounds the finger; hoop. **9.** *Slang.* a dagger fashioned from available materials by a prison inmate. —*v.t.* **10.** to mishit (a golf ball) with the club's shaft or heel, causing the ball to veer to the side.

shan't (shant, shänt), contraction of *shall not.*

shan•ty (shan′tē), *n., pl.* **-ties.** a crudely built hut, cabin, or house.

shan•ty•town (shan′tē toun′), *n.* a town or section of a town or city where there are many poor people living in shanties.

shape (shāp), *n., v.,* **shaped, shap•ing.** —*n.* **1.** the quality of a distinct object or body in having an external surface or outline of specific form or figure. **2.** something seen in outline, as in silhouette: *A vague shape appeared through the mist.* **3.** an imaginary form; phantom. **4.** an assumed appearance; guise. **5.** organized form or orderly arrangement: *He could give no shape to his ideas.* **6.** condition or state of repair: *The old house was in bad shape.* **7.** the collective conditions forming a way of life or mode of existence. **8.** the figure, physique, or body of a person, esp. of a woman. **9.** something used to give form, as a mold or a pattern. **10.** a flanged metal beam or bar of uniform section, as a channel or I-beam. —*v.t.* **11.** to give definite form, organization, or character to. **12.** to couch or express in words. **13.** to adjust; adapt. **14.** to direct (one's course, future, etc.). **15.** to teach (a behavior) by rewarding actions as they approximate the desired result. —*v.i.* **16.** to come to a desired conclusion or take place in a specified way. **17. shape up, a.** to evolve or develop, esp. favorably. **b.** to improve one's behavior, performance, or physical condition. —*Idiom.* **18. take shape,** to assume a fixed or more complete form; become defined.

shape•less (shāp′lis), *adj.* **1.** having no definite shape or form. **2.** lacking a pleasing shape. —**shape′less•ly,** *adv.* —**shape′less•ness,** *n.*

shape•ly (shāp′lē), *adj.,* **-li•er, -li•est.** having a pleasing shape, esp. with reference to a woman's figure. —**shape′li•ness,** *n.*

shape′-up′ or **shape′up′,** *n.* a former method of hiring longshore-men in which applicants appearing daily at the docks would be chosen for work.

shard (shärd) *n.* **1.** a fragment, esp. of broken earthenware. **2.** *Zool.* **a.** a scale. **b.** a shell, as of an egg or snail. **c.** the hardened forewing of a beetle.

share¹ (shâr), *n., v.,* **shared, shar•ing.** —*n.* **1.** a part of a whole, esp. a portion allotted or assigned to a member of a group. **2.** one of the equal fractional parts into which the capital stock of a corporation is divided. —*v.t.* **3.** to divide and distribute in shares; apportion. **4.** to use, participate in, receive, etc., jointly: *The two chemists shared the Nobel prize.* —*v.i.* **5.** to have a share or part; take part (often fol. by *in*). **6.** to receive equally. —*Idiom.* **7. go shares,** to engage in together, as a joint enterprise. —**shar′a•ble, share′a•ble,** *adj.* —**shar′er,** *n.*

share² (shâr), *n.* a plowshare.

share•crop•per (shâr′krop′ər), *n.* a tenant farmer who pays as rent a share of the crop. —**share′crop′,** *v.t., v.i.,* **-cropped, -crop•ping.**

share•hold•er (shâr′hōl′dər), *n.* a person, company, etc., that owns shares of stock in a company or corporation.

share•ware (shâr′wâr′), *n.* computer software distributed without initial charge but for which the user is encouraged to pay a nominal fee to cover support for continued use.

shark¹ (shärk), *n.* any of various predatory cartilaginous fishes of the order Selachii, having a rough scaleless skin, a wide mouth on the underside of the head, and five to seven gill slits on each side: some attack humans. —**shark′like′,** *adj.*

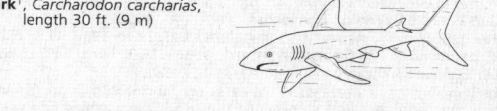

shark¹, *Carcharodon carcharias,*
length 30 ft. (9 m)

shark² (shärk), *n.* **1.** a person who preys greedily on others, as by cheating or usury. **2.** *Informal.* a person who has unusual ability in a particular field. [< German *Schurke* rascal]

shark•skin (shärk′skin′), *n.* **1.** a smooth fabric of acetate or rayon with a dull or chalklike appearance. **2.** a fine worsted fabric in twill weave, compact in texture and light to medium in weight.

shark•suck•er (shärk′suk′ər), *n.* any remora, esp. *Echeneis naucrates,* usu. found attached to sharks.

Shar•on (shar′ən), *n.* a fertile coastal plain in ancient Palestine: now a coastal region N of Tel Aviv in Israel.

sharp (shärp), *adj.* **1.** having a thin cutting edge or a fine point; well-adapted for cutting or piercing: *a sharp knife.* **2.** terminating in an edge or point; not blunt or rounded: *sharp corners.* **3.** involving an abrupt change in direction or course: *a sharp curve in the road.* **4.** clearly defined; distinct: *a sharp contrast.* **5.** pungent or biting in taste: *a sharp cheese.* **6.** piercing or shrill in sound: *a sharp cry.* **7.** keenly cold, as weather: *a sharp, biting wind.* **8.** felt acutely; intense: *sharp pain.* **9.** merciless, caustic, or harsh: *sharp words.* **10.** alert or vigilant: *a sharp watch.* **11.** mentally acute: *a sharp lad.* **12.** extremely sensitive; keen. **13.** shrewd or astute: *a sharp bargainer.* **14.** shrewd to the point of dishonesty: *sharp practice.* **15.** *Music.* **a.** (of a tone) raised a chromatic half step in pitch: *F sharp.* **b.** above an intended pitch, as a note; too high (opposed to *flat*). **16.** *Informal.* very stylish: *a sharp dresser.* —*v.t.* **17.** *Music.* to raise in pitch, esp. by one chromatic half step. —*v.i.* **18.** *Music.* to sound above the true pitch. —*adv.* **19.** keenly or acutely. **20.** abruptly or suddenly. **21.** punctually: *Meet me at one o'clock sharp.* **22.** *Music.* above the true pitch. —*n.* **23.** Usu., **sharps.** a medium-length, all-purpose sewing needle with a sharp point. **24.** SHARPER. **25.** *Informal.* an expert. **26.** *Music.* **a.** a tone one chromatic half step above a given tone. **b.** (in musical notation) the symbol indicating this. —**sharp′ly,** *adv.* —**sharp′ness,** *n.*

sharp′-edged′, *adj.* **1.** having a fine edge or edges. **2.** acute and caustic: *a sharp-edged wit.*

Shar-Pei (shär′pā′), *n.* one of a Chinese breed of medium-sized short-haired dogs with a squarish muzzle and wrinkly skin over the head and body.

sharp•en (shär′pən), *v.t., v.i.* to make or become sharp or sharper. —**sharp′en•er,** *n.*

sharp•er (shär′pər) also **sharpie,** *n.* **1.** a shrewd swindler. **2.** a professional gambler.

sharp•ie or **sharp•y** (shär′pē), *n., pl.* **sharp•ies.** *Informal.* **1.** SHARPER. **2.** a very alert person.

sharp•shoot•er (shärp′shōō′tər), *n.* **1.** a person skilled in shooting, esp. with a rifle. **2.** an athlete noted for accurate aim, as in basketball or archery. —**sharp′shoot′ing,** *n.*

sharp′-sight′ed, *adj.* having keen sight or perception. —**sharp′-sight′ed•ly,** *adv.* —**sharp′-sight′ed•ness,** *n.*

sharp′-tongued′, *adj.* harsh or sarcastic in speech.

sharp′-wit′ted, *adj.* having or showing mental acuity. —**sharp′-wit′ted•ly,** *adv.* —**sharp′-wit′ted•ness,** *n.*

Shas•ta (shas′tə), *n.* **Mount,** a volcanic peak in N California, in the Cascade Range. 14,161 ft. (4315 m).

Shas′ta dai′sy, *n.* any horticultural variety of the composite plant *Chrysanthemum maximum,* having large daisylike flowers.

shat•ter (shat′ər), *v.t.* **1.** to break (something) into pieces, as by a blow. **2.** to damage, as by breaking or crushing. **3.** to impair or destroy (health, nerves, etc.). **4.** to weaken or refute (ideas, opinions, etc.). —*v.i.* **5.** to be broken into fragments or become weak or insubstantial. **6.** to fall or scatter, as seeds, leaves, or fruits. —*n.* **7.** Usu., **shatters.** fragments made by shattering. —**shat′ter•ing•ly,** *adv.*

shave (shāv), *v.,* **shaved, shaved** or (*esp. in combination*) **shav•en, shav•ing,** *n.* —*v.i.* **1.** to remove a growth of hair or beard with a razor. —*v.t.* **2.** to remove hair from (the face, legs, etc.) by cutting it off close to the skin with a razor. **3.** to cut off (hair, esp. the beard) close to the skin with a razor (often fol. by *off* or *away*). **4.** to cut or scrape away the surface of with a sharp-edged tool. **5.** to reduce to shavings or thin slices. **6.** to cut or trim closely: *to shave a lawn.* **7.** to scrape, graze, or come very near to: *The car just shaved the garage door.* **8.** to purchase (a note) at a rate of discount greater than is legal or customary. **9.** to reduce or deduct from (a price). —*n.* **10.** the act, process, or an instance of shaving or being shaved. **11.** a thin slice; shaving. **12.** any of various tools for shaving, scraping, removing thin slices, etc.

shav•en (shā′vən), *v.* **1.** a pp. of SHAVE. —*adj.* **2.** closely trimmed.

shav•er (shā′vər), *n.* **1.** a person or thing that shaves. **2.** an electric razor. **3.** *Informal.* a small boy; youngster. **4.** a fellow. **5.** a person who makes close bargains or is extortionate.

shav•ing (shā′ving), *n.* **1.** Often, **shavings.** a very thin piece or slice, esp. of wood. **2.** the act of a person or thing that shaves.

Sha•vu•oth or **Sha•vu•ot** (shə vo͞o′ōs, shä vo͞o ôt′), *n.* a Jewish festival, celebrated on the sixth or sixth and seventh days of Sivan, that commemorates God's giving of the Ten Commandments to Moses. Also called **Feast of Weeks, Pentecost.**

Shaw (shô), *n.* **1. Artie** (*Arthur Arshawsky*), born 1910, U.S. clarinetist and bandleader. **2. George Bernard,** 1856–1950, Irish writer. **3. T(homas) E(dward),** LAWRENCE, T(homas) E(dward).

shawl (shôl), *n.* a piece of wool or other fabric worn, esp. by women, about the shoulders and sometimes the head, for warmth or for style.

shawl′ col′lar, *n.* a rolled collar and lapel in one piece that curves from the back of the neck down to the front closure of a garment.

Shaw•nee (shô nē′), *n., pl.* **-nees,** (*esp. collectively*) **-nee. 1.** a member of an American Indian people, probably orig. centered in the upper Ohio River valley, later fragmented, and confined to reservations in the Indian Territory in the 19th century. **2.** the Algonquian language of the Shawnee. [< Shawnee *ša·wano·ki,* lit., people of the south]

Shaw•wal (shə wäl′), *n.* the tenth month of the Islamic calendar.

Shays (shāz), *n.* **Daniel,** 1747–1825, American Revolutionary War soldier: leader of a popular insurrection **(Shays′′ Rebel′lion)** in Massachusetts 1786–87.

she (shē), *pron., sing. nom.* **she,** *poss.* **her** or **hers,** *obj.* **her;** *pl. nom.* **they,** *poss.* **their** or **theirs,** *obj.* **them;** *n., pl.* **shes.** —*pron.* **1.** the female person or animal being discussed or last mentioned; that female. **2.** the woman: *She who listens learns.* **3.** anything considered, as by personification, to be feminine: *spring, with all the memories she conjures up.* —*n.* **4.** a female person or animal. **5.** an object or device considered as female or feminine. —**Usage.** See HE[1], ME, THEY.

s/he (shē′ər hē′, shē′hē′), *pron.* she or he: used as an orthographic device to avoid *he* when the sex of the antecedent is unknown or irrelevant. Compare SHE/HE. —**Usage.** See HE[1].

Shea (shā), *n.* **George Beverly,** born 1909, singer in the Billy Graham Crusades.

sheaf (shēf), *n., pl.* **sheaves. 1.** one of the bundles in which cereal plants are bound after reaping. **2.** any bundle, cluster, or collection: *a sheaf of papers.* —**sheaf′like′,** *adj.*

shear (shēr), *v.,* **sheared, sheared** or **shorn, shear•ing,** *n.* —*v.t.* **1.** to cut (something). **2.** to remove by or as if by cutting or clipping: *to shear wool from sheep.* **3.** to cut or clip the hair, fleece, wool, etc., from: *to shear sheep.* **4.** to strip or deprive (usu. fol. by *of*): *to shear someone of power.* **5.** *Chiefly Scot.* to reap with a sickle. **6.** to travel through by or as if by cutting: *Chimney swifts sheared the air.* **7.** to subject (a solid body or structure) to shear. —*v.i.* **8.** to cut or cut through something with a sharp instrument. **9.** to break along an internal plane in response to a force parallel to the plane. —*n.* **10.** Usu., **shears.** (*sometimes used with a sing. v.*) **a.** scissors of large size (usu. used with *pair of*). **b.** any of various other cutting implements or machines having two blades that suggest those of scissors. **11.** the act or process of shearing or being sheared. **12.** the quantity, esp. of wool or fleece, cut off at one shearing. **13.** Usu., **shears.** (*usu. with a pl. v.*) Also, **sheers.** a framework for hoisting heavy weights, consisting of two or more spars with their legs separated, fastened together near the top and steadied by guys, which support a tackle. **14.** a machine for cutting rigid material by moving the edge of a blade through it. **15.** Also called **shearing stress.** the tendency of a force applied to a solid body or structure, as a rock stratum, to cause deformation or rupture along a plane parallel to the force. —**shear′er,** *n.*

shear′ing stress′ or **shear′ stress′,** *n.* SHEAR (def. 15).

shear•ling (shēr′ling), *n.* **1.** a yearling sheep that has been shorn once. **2.** the skin of a recently shorn sheep or lamb, tanned with the short wool still on it and used for coats, slippers, etc., with the wool on the inside.

sheath (shēth), *n., pl.* **sheaths** (shēthz). **1.** a case or close-fitting covering, esp. one for the blade of a sword, dagger, or the like. **2.** a closely enveloping part or structure in an animal or plant. **3.** a close-fitting dress, skirt, or coat, esp. an unbelted dress with a straight drape.

sheathe (shēth), *v.t.,* **sheathed, sheath•ing. 1.** to put (a sword, dagger, etc.) into a sheath. **2.** to plunge (a sword, dagger, etc.) into something as if in a sheath. **3.** to enclose in or as if in a casing or covering. **4.** to cover or provide with a protective layer or sheathing. **5.** to cover (a cable, electrical connector, etc.) with a metal sheath for grounding.

sheath′ knife′, *n.* a knife carried in a sheath.

sheave[1] (shēv), *v.t.,* **sheaved, sheav•ing.** to gather, collect, or bind into a sheaf or sheaves.

sheave[2] (shiv, shēv), *n.* **1.** a pulley for hoisting or hauling, having a grooved rim for retaining a rope or wire. **2.** a wheel with a grooved rim, for transmitting force to a cable or belt.

sheaves[1] (shēvz), *n.* pl. of SHEAF.

sheaves[2] (shivz, shēvz), *n.* pl. of SHEAVE[2].

She•ba (shē′bə), *n.* **1. Queen of,** the queen who visited Solomon to test his wisdom. I Kings 10:1–13. **2.** Biblical name of SABA.

she•bang (shə bang′), *n. Informal.* the structure of something, as of an organization, contrivance, or affair: *The whole shebang fell apart when the chairman quit.*

She•bat (shə vät′), *n.* SHEVAT.

She•chem (shē′kəm, shek′əm; *Heb.* shə KHEM′), *n.* Hebrew name of NABLUS.

shed[1] (shed), *n.* **1.** a slight or rude structure built for shelter, storage, etc. **2.** a large, strongly built structure, often open at the sides or end. —**shed′like′,** *adj.*

shed[2] (shed), *v.,* **shed, shed•ding,** *n.* —*v.t.* **1.** to pour forth; let fall: *to shed tears.* **2.** to give or send forth (light, influence, etc.). **3.** to resist being penetrated or affected by: *cloth that sheds water.* **4.** to cast off or lose (leaves, skin, etc.) by natural process. **5.** *Textiles.* to separate (the warp) in forming a shed. —*v.i.* **6.** to fall off, as leaves. **7.** to drop out, as hair or grain. **8.** to cast off hair, skin, or other covering or parts by natural process. —*n.* **9.** *Textiles.* (on a loom) a triangular, transverse opening created between raised and lowered warp threads through which the shuttle passes in depositing the loose pick. —**shed′a•ble, shed′da•ble,** *adj.*

she'd (shēd), **1.** contraction of *she had.* **2.** contraction of *she would.*

shed•der (shed′ər), *n.* **1.** a person or thing that sheds. **2.** a lobster, crab, etc., just before it molts.

she′-dev′il, *n.* a woman who resembles a devil, as in extreme wickedness, cruelty, or bad temper.

sheen (shēn), *n.* **1.** luster; brightness; radiance. **2.** gleaming attire. —*adj.* **3.** shining. **4.** beautiful. —*v.i.* **5.** *Scot.* to shine.

sheep (shēp), *n., pl.* **sheep. 1.** any of several ruminant mammals, esp. of the genus *Ovis,* closely related to goats, esp. *O. aries,* bred in a number of domesticated varieties. **2.** leather made from the skin of these animals. **3.** a meek, easily led person. —**sheep′like′,** *adj.*

sheep•ber•ry (shēp′ber′ē, -bə rē), *n., pl.* **-ries.** a North American shrub or small tree, *Viburnum lentago,* of the honeysuckle family, having small white flowers and edible, black berries. Also called **black haw.**

sheep′dog′ or **sheep′ dog′,** *n.* a dog trained to herd and guard sheep.

sheep•head (shēp′hed′), *n., pl.* (*esp. collectively*) **-head,** (*esp. for kinds or species*) **-heads.** a large California food fish, *Semicossyphus pulcher,* of the wrasse family. Also called **redfish, sheepshead.**

sheep•ish (shē′pish), *adj.* **1.** embarrassed or bashful, esp. for having done something wrong or foolish. **2.** like a sheep, as in meekness or docility. —**sheep′ish•ly,** *adv.* —**sheep′ish•ness,** *n.*

sheeps•head (shēps′hed′), *n., pl.* (*esp. collectively*) **-head,** (*esp. for kinds or species*). **-heads. 1.** a deep-bodied, black-banded food fish, *Archosargus probatocephalus,* inhabiting Atlantic coastal waters. **2.** a freshwater drum, *Aplodinotus grunniens,* of E North America. **3.** SHEEPHEAD.

sheep•skin (shēp′skin′), *n.* **1.** the skin of a sheep, esp. such a skin dressed with the wool on, as for a garment. **2.** leather, parchment, or the like, made from the skin of sheep. **3.** *Informal.* a diploma. —*adj.* **4.** made from the skin of a sheep. **5.** (of a garment) lined with the skin of a sheep dressed with the wool on.

sheep′tick′ or **sheep′ tick′,** *n.* a wingless, bloodsucking insect, *Melophagus ovinus,* that is parasitic on sheep.

sheer[1] (shēr), *adj.,* **-er, -est,** *adv., n.* —*adj.* **1.** transparently thin; diaphanous, as some fabrics: *sheer stockings.* **2.** unmixed with anything else; unadulterated: *sheer rock; sheer luck.* **3.** unqualified; utter: *sheer nonsense.* **4.** extending down or up very steeply; almost completely vertical: *a sheer descent.* —*adv.* **5.** completely; quite: *drove sheer off the road.* **6.** perpendicularly; vertically; down or up very steeply. —*n.* **7.** a thin, diaphanous fabric or garment. —**sheer′ly,** *adv.* —**sheer′ness,** *n.*

sheer[2] (shēr), *v.i.* **1.** to deviate from a course, as a ship; swerve. —*v.t.* **2.** to cause to sheer. —*n.* **3.** a deviation or divergence, as of a ship from its course. **4.** the fore-and-aft upward curve of the hull of a vessel at the main deck or bulwarks. **5.** the position in which a ship at anchor is placed to keep it clear of the anchor.

sheers (shērz), *n.* (*usu. with a pl. v.*) SHEAR (def. 16).

sheet¹ (shēt), *n.* **1.** a large rectangular piece of cotton or other fabric used as an article of bedding, commonly in pairs, with one below and one above the sleeper. **2.** a broad, relatively thin surface, layer, or covering: *a sheet of ice.* **3.** a relatively thin, usu. rectangular piece of material, as glass, metal, or photographic film. **4.** material, as metal or glass, in the form of broad, relatively thin pieces. **5.** a rectangular piece of paper, esp. one on which to write. **6.** a newspaper or periodical. **7.** a large, rectangular piece of printing paper, esp. one for printing a complete signature. **8. a.** the unseparated postage stamps on a single piece of paper containing a full impression of the printing plate or plates. **b.** PANE (def. 4). **9.** a sail, as on a ship or boat. **10.** an extent, stretch, or expanse, as of fire or water: *sheets of flame.* **11.** a thin, flat piece of metal or a very shallow pan on which to place food while baking. **12.** a more or less horizontal mass of rock, esp. volcanic rock intruded between strata or poured out over a surface. —*v.t.* **13.** to furnish with sheets. **14.** to wrap in a sheet. **15.** to cover with a sheet or layer of something. —**sheet′less,** *adj.* —**sheet′like′,** *adj.*
sheet² (shēt), *n.* a rope or wire used to secure or adjust a ship's sail.
sheet′ feed′er, *n.* a device that feeds paper into a printer one sheet at a time.
sheet•ing (shē′ting), *n.* **1.** the act of covering with or forming into sheets. **2.** any of various plain-weave cotton fabrics, esp. a firmly made muslin used for bedsheets.
sheet′ light′ning, *n.* lightning appearing as a general illumination over a broad area, usu. because the path of the flash is obscured by clouds.
sheet′ met′al, *n.* metal in sheets or thin plates.
sheet′ mu′sic, *n.* music printed on unbound sheets of paper.
she/he (shē′ər hē′, shē′hē′), *pron.* she or he: used to replace a singular nominative pronoun in denoting a person of either sex: *Each employee must sign the register when she/he enters or leaves.* Compare s/HE. —**Usage.** See HE¹.
sheik (shēk; *for 1 also* shāk), *n.* **1.** Also, **sheikh.** (in Arab countries) the patriarch of a tribe or family; chief: also used as a term of polite address. **2.** a man held to be irresistible to women.
sheik•dom or **sheikh•dom** (shēk′dəm, shāk′-), *n.* the land or territory under the control of a sheik.
shek•el (shek′əl), *n.* **1.** the basic monetary unit of Israel. **2.** an ancient, orig. Babylonian, unit of weight, equal to half an ounce or less. **3.** a coin of this weight, esp. the chief silver coin of the ancient Hebrews. **4. shekels,** *Slang.* money; cash.
She•khi•nah or **She•ki•nah** or **She•chi•nah** (shi kē′nə, -kī′-; *Heb.* shə khē nä′), *n. Judaism.* the presence of God on earth or a symbol or manifestation of His presence.
shel•drake (shel′drāk′), *n., pl.* **-drakes,** (*esp. collectively*) **-drake. 1.** any of several Old World ducks of the genus *Tadorna,* certain species of which have highly variegated plumage. **2.** any of various other ducks, esp. the merganser.
shel•duck (shel′duk′), *n., pl.* **-ducks,** (*esp. collectively*) **-duck.** SHELDRAKE.
shelf (shelf), *n., pl.* **shelves** (shelvz). **1.** a thin slab of wood, metal, etc., fixed horizontally to a wall or in a frame, for supporting objects. **2.** the contents of this: *a shelf of books.* **3.** a surface or projection resembling this; ledge. **4. a.** a sandbank or submerged extent of rock in the sea or river. **b.** the bedrock underlying an alluvial deposit or the like. **c.** CONTINENTAL SHELF. —*Idiom.* **5. off the shelf,** readily available from merchandise in stock. **6. on the shelf,** **a.** put aside temporarily; postponed. **b.** inactive; useless. —**shelf′like′,** *adj.*
shelf′ ice′, *n.* ice forming part of or broken from an ice shelf.
shelf′ life′, *n.* the term or period during which a stored commodity, as food, remains effective, useful, or suitable for consumption.
shell (shel), *n.* **1.** a hard outer covering of an animal, as of a clam, snail, lobster, or turtle. **2.** the material constituting any of various coverings of this kind. **3.** the hard exterior of an egg. **4.** the usu. hard outer covering of a seed, fruit, or the like. **5.** something resembling the shell of an animal, as in shape or hollowness. **6.** a hard, protecting or enclosing case or cover. **7.** a reserved attitude or manner. **8.** a hollow projectile, as for a cannon, filled with an explosive charge. **9.** a cartridge used in small arms. **10.** a cartridge for use in a shotgun. **11.** a cartridgelike pyrotechnic device that explodes in the air. **12.** an unfilled pastry crust, as for a pie. **13.** a light, long, narrow racing boat for rowing by one or more persons. **14.** the framework or external structure of a building. **15.** the outer part of a finished garment that has an often detachable lining. **16.** a woman's sleeveless blouse or sweater. **17.** the plating forming the exterior hull of a ship. **18.** TORTOISESHELL (def. 1). **19.** the curved solid forming a domed or arched roof. **20.** the metal, pressure-resistant outer casing of a fire-tube boiler. —*v.t.* **21.** to remove the shell of. **22.** to separate (corn, grain, etc.) from the ear, cob, or husk. **23.** to fire shells or explosive projectiles into, upon, or among; bombard. —*v.i.* **24.** to fall or come out of the shell, husk, or pod. **25.** to come away or fall off, as a shell or outer coat. **26.** to gather seashells. **27. shell out,** *Informal.* to pay (money). —**shell′-less,** *adj.* —**shell′-like′,** *adj.*
she'll (shēl; *unstressed* shil), contraction of *she will.*
shel•lac or **shel•lack** (shə lak′), *n., v.,* **-lacked, -lack•ing.** —*n.* **1.** lac that has been purified and formed into thin sheets, used for making varnish. **2.** a varnish made by dissolving this material in alcohol or a similar solvent. **3.** a phonograph record of a breakable material containing shellac, esp. one played at 78 r.p.m. —*v.t.* **4.** to coat or treat with shellac. **5.** *Slang.* **a.** to defeat; trounce. **b.** to thrash soundly.
shel•lack•ing (shə lak′ing), *n. Slang.* **1.** an utter defeat. **2.** a sound thrashing.
shell′ bean′, *n.* any bean grown chiefly for its edible seeds rather than its pods.
shelled (sheld), *adj.* **1.** having the shell removed: *shelled pecans.* **2.** removed from the ear or husk: *shelled corn.* **3.** having or enclosed in a shell, often of a specified kind: *soft-shelled crabs.*
Shel•ley (shel′ē), *n.* **1. Mary Wollstonecraft (Godwin),** 1797–1851, English author (wife of Percy Bysshe Shelley). **2. Percy Bysshe** (bish), 1792–1822, English poet. —**Shel′ley•an,** *adj., n.*
shell•fire (shel′fīᵊr′), *n.* **1.** the firing of explosive shells or projectiles. **2.** the explosions from such shells or projectiles.
shell•fish (shel′fish′), *n., pl.* (*esp. collectively*) **-fish,** (*esp. for kinds or species*) **-fish•es.** an aquatic animal having a shell, as the oyster or other mollusks or the lobster or other crustaceans.
shell′ game′, *n.* **1.** a swindling game in which a small object is supposedly hidden under one of three walnut shells or the like and bets are made. **2.** any swindle or fraud.
shell′ pink′, *n.* delicate whitish to yellow pink.
shell-proof (shel′proof′), *adj.* protected against the explosive effect of shells or bombs.
shell′ shock′, *n.* BATTLE FATIGUE. —**shell′-shocked′,** *adj.*
shell′ steak′, *n.* a porterhouse steak with the fillet removed.
shel•ter (shel′tər), *n.* **1.** something beneath, behind, or within which one is covered or protected, as from storms or danger; refuge. **2.** the protection or refuge afforded by such a thing: *We took shelter in a nearby barn.* **3.** a building serving as a temporary refuge or residence, as for homeless persons or abandoned animals. **4.** TAX SHELTER. —*v.t.* **5.** to act as a shelter for; afford shelter to. **6.** to provide with a shelter; place under cover. **7.** to take under one's protection; protect; shield. **8.** to invest (money) in a tax shelter. —*v.i.* **9.** to take shelter; find a refuge. —**shel′ter•er,** *n.* —**shel′ter•ing•ly,** *adv.* —**shel′ter•less,** *adj.*
shel•tered (shel′tərd), *adj.* **1.** protected from the weather. **2.** protected from unpleasant realities or wide experience: *a sheltered life.* **3.** of or pertaining to employment or housing, esp. for handicapped persons, in a noncompetitive, supervised environment.
Shel′ter in the Time′ of Storm′, A, a Christian hymn (1870) with music by Ira Sankey.
shelve¹ (shelv), *v.t.,* **shelved, shelv•ing. 1.** to place on a shelf. **2.** to put off or aside; defer: *to shelve a question.* **3.** to remove from active use or service; dismiss. **4.** to furnish with shelves. —**shelv′er,** *n.*
shelve² (shelv), *v.i.,* **shelved, shelv•ing.** to slope gradually.
shelves (shelvz), *n.* pl. of SHELF.
shelv•ing (shel′ving), *n.* **1.** material for shelves. **2.** shelves collectively.
Shem (shem), *n.* the eldest of the three sons of Noah. Gen. 10:21.
She•ma (shə mä′, shmä), *n. Judaism.* an important liturgical prayer recited at the morning and evening services, affirming the Jewish people's faith in God. [< Hebrew *shāma'* listen!]
She•mi•ni A•tze•reth (or **A•tze•ret**) (shə mē′nē at ser′es), *n.* a Jewish festival celebrated on the 8th day of Sukkoth, marked by a memorial service for the dead and a special prayer for rain.
Shen•an•do•ah (shen′ən dō′ə), *n.* a river flowing NE from N Virginia to the Potomac at Harpers Ferry, West Virginia. ab. 200 mi. (322 km) long.
she•nan•i•gan (shə nan′i gən), *n. Informal.* **1.** Usu., **shenanigans. a.** mischief; prankishness. **b.** deceit; trickery. **2.** a mischievous or deceitful trick.
She•ol (shē′ōl), *n. Judaism.* **1.** the abode of the dead or of departed spirits. **2.** (*l.c.*) hell.
Shep•ard (shep′ərd), *n.* **1. Alan Bartlett, Jr.,** born 1923, U.S. astronaut. **2. Sam,** born 1943, U.S. playwright, actor, and director.
shep•herd (shep′ərd), *n.* **1.** a person who herds, tends, and guards sheep. **2.** a person who protects, guides, or watches over other people. **3.** a cleric or pastor. **4. a.** SHEEPDOG. **b.** GERMAN SHEPHERD. —*v.t.* **5.** to tend or guard as a shepherd. **6.** to watch over, guide, or lead.
Shep′herd and the Sheep′, The, a parable of Jesus. John 10:1–8.
shep′herd's check′, *n.* **1.** a pattern of even checks, usu. of black and white, used in a variety of fabrics. **2.** a fabric having this pattern. Also called **shep′herd's plaid′.**
shep′herd's pie′, *n.* a baked dish of chopped meat with a crust of mashed potatoes.
shep′herd's-purse′, *n.* a weed, *Capsella bursa-pastoris,* of the mustard family, with white flowers and purselike pods.
Sher•a•ton (sher′ə tn), *n.* **1. Thomas,** 1751–1806, English cabinetmaker and furniture designer. —*adj.* **2.** of or in the style of furniture of Thomas Sheraton, characterized by straight lines, graceful shapes, and the use of contrasting veneers and inlay.
sher•bet (shûr′bit), *n.* **1.** Also, **sher′bert** (-bərt). a frozen fruit-flavored ice with milk, egg white, or gelatin added. **2.** *Brit.* a drink made of sweetened diluted fruit juice.
Sher•i•dan (sher′i dn), *n.* **1. Philip Henry,** 1831–88, U.S. general. **2. Richard Brinsley,** 1751–1816, Irish dramatist and political leader.
sher•iff (sher′if), *n.* **1.** the law-enforcement officer of a county or other civil subdivision of a state. **2.** (*formerly*) an important civil officer in an English shire. —**sher′iff•dom,** *n.*

S

sher•lock (shûr′lok), *n.* *(often cap.)* **1.** a detective. **2.** a person adept at solving mysteries, esp. by using insight and logical deduction. [after *Sherlock* Holmes, fictitious detective created by Arthur Conan Doyle] —**Sher•lock′i•an,** *adj.*

Sher•man (shûr′mən), *n.* **1. James Schoolcraft,** 1855–1912, vice president of the U.S. 1909–12. **2. John,** 1823–1900, U.S. statesman (brother of William T.). **3. Roger,** 1721–93, American statesman. **4. William Tecumseh,** 1820–91, Union general in the Civil War.

Sher′man Antitrust′ Act′, *n.* an act of Congress (1890) prohibiting any contract, conspiracy, or combination of business interests in restraint of foreign or interstate trade. Compare CLAYTON ANTITRUST ACT. [named after John SHERMAN, who introduced the bill in Congress]

Sher•pa (sher′pə, shûr′-), *n., pl.* **-pas,** *(esp. collectively)* **-pa. 1.** a member of a people of Tibetan stock living in the Nepalese Himalayas, who often serve as porters on mountain-climbing expeditions. **2.** *(sometimes l.c.)* an expert chosen by a chief executive to assist in preparations for a summit meeting.

sher•ry (sher′ē), *n., pl.* **-ries.** a fortified, amber-colored wine of S Spain or a similar wine made elsewhere. [< Spanish *(vino de) Xeres* (wine of) Xeres (now *Jerez*)]

Sher•wood (shûr′wo͝od′), *n.* **Robert Emmet,** 1896–1955, U.S. dramatist.

Sher′wood For′est, *n.* a forest in central England, chiefly in Nottinghamshire: the traditional haunt of Robin Hood.

she's (shēz), **1.** contraction of *she is.* **2.** contraction of *she has.*

Shet•land (shet′lənd), *n.* **1.** SHETLAND WOOL. **2.** a fabric or garment of Shetland wool. **3.** Formerly, **Zetland.** a region in NE Scotland, comprising the Shetland Islands.

Shet′land po′ny, *n.* one of a breed of small, sturdy, rough-coated ponies, raised orig. in the Shetland Islands.

Shet′land wool′, *n.* **1.** the fine wool undercoat pulled by hand from Shetland sheep. **2.** a fine yarn made from this.

She•vat (shə vät′, -vôt′) also **Shebat,** *n.* the fifth month of the Jewish calendar.

shew•bread or **show•bread** (shō′bred′), *n.* *Judaism.* the bread placed every Sabbath in the holy of holies of the tabernacle and the Temple as an offering by the priests to God.

SHF, superhigh frequency.

shh *(usu. an extended* sh *sound), interj.* SH.

shi•at•su or **shi•at•zu** (shē ät′so͞o), *n.* *(sometimes cap.)* a Japanese massage technique that includes the use of acupressure.

shib•bo•leth (shib′ə lith, -leth′), *n.* **1.** a peculiarity of pronunciation, usage, or behavior that distinguishes a particular group. **2.** a slogan; catchword. **3.** a common saying or belief with little current meaning or truth. [< Hebrew *shibbōleth* lit., freshet, a word used by the Gileadites as a test to detect the fleeing Ephraimites, who could not pronounce the sound *sh* (Judg. 12:4–6)]

shield (shēld), *n.* **1.** a device used as a defense against blows or hurled objects, esp. a broad piece of armor carried on the arm or in the hand. **2.** a person or thing that guards or defends. **3.** an emblem of trust and faith. Eph. 6:16. **4.** any of various devices or barriers for protection, as from injury. **5.** an escutcheon typically having a broad top and pointed bottom and displaying armorial bearings. **6.** something shaped like a shield. **7.** a police officer's, detective's, or sheriff's badge. **8.** a bulletproof screen attached to a gun to protect its crew, mechanism, etc. **9.** a protective plate or the like on the body of an animal, as an enlarged scale, etc. **10.** a pad worn or attached inside the underarm of a garment to protect it against perspiration stains. **11.** a lead or concrete structure around a nuclear reactor serving as a barrier against escaping radiation. —*v.t.* **12.** to protect with or as if with a shield. **13.** to serve as a protection for. **14.** to hide or conceal; protect by hiding. —*v.i.* **15.** to act or serve as a shield. —**shield′er,** *n.* —**shield′like′,** *adj.*

Shield′ of Da′vid, *n.* STAR OF DAVID.

shift (shift), *v.t.* **1.** to transfer from one place, position, person, etc., to another: *to shift the blame.* **2.** to put aside and replace by another; change or exchange: *to shift ideas.* **3.** to change (gears) from one ratio or arrangement to another in driving a motor vehicle. **4.** to change phonetically in a systematic way. —*v.i.* **5.** to move from one place, position, direction, etc., to another. **6.** to manage to get along or succeed by oneself. **7.** to use expedients, tricks, or evasion to get along or succeed. **8.** to change gears in driving a motor vehicle. **9.** (of sounds in a language) to undergo a systematic phonetic change. **10.** to press a shift key on a typewriter or computer as to type a capital letter. —*n.* **11.** a change or transfer from one place, position, direction, person, etc., to another: *a shift in the wind.* **12.** a person's scheduled period of work, esp. at a place of employment operating continuously during the day and night. **13.** a group of workers scheduled to work during such a period. **14.** *Baseball.* a repositioning by fielders as a strategy against batters who usu. hit the ball to the same side of the field. **15.** a gearshift. **16. a.** a straight, loose-fitting dress worn with or without a belt. **b.** a woman's chemise or slip. **17.** *Football.* a lateral or backward movement by offensive players just before the ball is put into play. **18.** a change or a system of parallel changes that affects the sound structure of a language. **19.** an expedient; ingenious device. **20.** an evasion, artifice, or trick. **21.** change or substitution. **22.** an act or instance of using the shift key, as on a typewriter or computer. —**shift′er,** *n.* —**shift′ing•ly,** *adv.*

shift′ key′, *n.* a key on a typewriter or computer that is pressed to enter capital letters and other symbols and on a computer, to control certain other functions.

shift•less (shift′lis), *adj.* **1.** lacking in resourcefulness; inefficient. **2.** lacking in incentive, ambition, or aspiration; lazy. —**shift′less•ly,** *adv.* —**shift′less•ness,** *n.*

shift•y (shif′tē), *adj.,* **shift•i•er, shift•i•est. 1.** resourceful; fertile in expedients. **2.** evasive; crafty. **3.** suggesting an evasive nature: *a shifty look.* —**shift′i•ly,** *adv.* —**shift′i•ness,** *n.*

shi•i•ta•ke (shē′ē tä′kā), *n., pl.* **-ke.** a large, meaty, black or dark brown mushroom, *Lentinus edodes,* native to E Asia and used in Japanese and Chinese cooking.

Shi•'ite or **Shi•ite** (shē′īt), also **Shi'ah, Shi•'i** (shē ē′, shē′ē), *n.* a member of one of the two great religious divisions of Islam that regards Ali, the son-in-law of Muhammad, as the legitimate successor of Muhammad, and disregards the three caliphs who succeeded him. Compare SUNNI (def. 1). —**Shi•'ism** (shē′iz əm), *n.* —**Shi•'it•ic** (shē it′ik), *adj.*

shill (shil), *n.* **1.** a person who poses as a customer in order to decoy others into participating, as at a gambling house. **2.** a person whose praises, endorsements, etc., are motivated by self-interest. —*v.i.* **3.** to work as a shill: *to shill for a large casino.*

shil•ling (shil′ing), *n.* **1.** a coin and former monetary unit of the United Kingdom, the 20th part of a pound, equal to 12 pence: discontinued in 1971. *Abbr.:* s. **2.** a former monetary unit of various other nations orig. settled or colonized by Great Britain. **3.** the basic monetary unit of Kenya, Somalia, Tanzania, and Uganda.

shil•ly-shal•ly (shil′ē shal′ē), *v.,* **-shal•lied, -shal•ly•ing,** *n., pl.* **-shal•lies,** *adj.* —*v.i.* **1.** to show indecision or hesitation; vacillate. **2.** to waste time. —*n.* **3.** indecision; vacillation. —*adj.* **4.** undecided; wavering.

Shi•loh (shī′lō), *n.* **1.** a military national park in SW Tennessee: Civil War battle 1862. **2.** an ancient town in central Palestine, west of the Jordan River.

shim (shim), *n., v.,* **shimmed, shim•ming.** —*n.* **1.** a thin slip or wedge of metal, wood, etc., for driving into crevices, as between machine parts to compensate for wear, or beneath bedplates, large stones, etc., to level them. —*v.t.* **2.** to fill out or bring to a level by inserting a shim.

Shimei *n.* a Benjamite who insulted David and disobeyed Solomon. II Sam. 16:5–13; I Kings 2:8.

shim•mer (shim′ər), *v.i.* **1.** to shine with a soft, tremulous light. **2.** to appear to quiver in faint light or while reflecting heat waves. —*n.* **3.** a soft, tremulous light or gleam. **4.** a quivering motion or image as produced by reflecting faint light or heat waves. —**shim′mer•ing•ly,** *adv.*

shim•mer•y (shim′ə rē), *adj.* shimmering; shining softly.

shim•my (shim′ē), *n., pl.* **-mies,** *v.,* **-mied, -my•ing.** —*n.* **1.** an American ragtime dance marked by rapid shaking of the hips and shoulders. **2.** excessive wobbling in the front wheels of a motor vehicle. **3.** a chemise. —*v.i.* **4.** to dance the shimmy. **5.** to shake, wobble, or vibrate.

shin (shin), *n., v.,* **shinned, shin•ning.** —*n.* **1.** the front part of the leg from the knee to the ankle. **2.** the lower part of the foreleg in cattle. **3.** the shinbone or tibia, esp. its sharp edge or front portion. —*v.t., v.i.* **4.** to climb (a pole or the like) by holding fast with the legs after drawing oneself up with the hands.

Shi•nar (shī′när), *n.* a land mentioned in the Bible, often identified with Sumer. Gen. 10:10; 11:2.

shin•bone (shin′bōn′), *n.* the tibia.

shin•dig (shin′dig′), *n.* *Informal.* an elaborate and usu. large dance, party, or other celebration.

shin•dy (shin′dē), *n., pl.* **-dies.** *Informal.* **1.** a row; rumpus. **2.** a shindig.

shine (shīn), *v.,* **shone** or, esp. for 8, 9, **shined; shin•ing;** *n.* —*v.i.* **1.** to give forth or glow with light. **2.** to be bright with reflected light; glisten; sparkle. **3.** (of light) to appear brightly or strongly; glare. **4.** to appear unusually animated, as the eyes or face. **5.** to excel: *to shine in algebra.* —*v.t.* **6.** to cause to shine. **7.** to direct the light of (a lamp, mirror, etc.). **8.** to polish (shoes, silverware, etc.). **9. shine up to,** *Informal.* **a.** to attempt to impress (a person), esp. in order to gain benefits for oneself. **b.** to become esp. attentive to. —*n.* **10.** radiance or brightness caused by emitted or reflected light. **11.** luster; polish. **12.** a polish or gloss given to shoes. **13.** an act or instance of polishing shoes. **14.** Often, **shines.** a prank or caper. —***Idiom.*** **15. take a shine to,** to develop a strong liking for (another person).

shin•er (shī′nər), *n.* **1.** *Informal.* BLACK EYE (def. 1). **2.** any of various small American freshwater fishes having glistening scales, esp. a minnow. **3.** a person or thing that shines.

shin•gle[1] (shing′gəl), *n., v.,* **-gled, -gling.** —*n.* **1.** a thin piece of wood, slate, metal, asbestos, or the like, usu. oblong, laid in overlapping rows to cover the roofs and walls of buildings. **2.** a woman's short hairstyle in which the hair is cropped close to the head from below the crown to the nape. **3.** a small signboard, esp. as hung before a doctor's or lawyer's office. —*v.t.* **4.** to cover with shingles, as a roof. **5.** to cut (hair) close to the head. —***Idiom.*** **6. hang out one's shingle,** to establish a professional practice, esp. in law or medicine. —**shin′gler,** *n.*

shin•gle[2] (shing′gəl), *n.* **1.** small, waterworn stones or pebbles lying loose esp. on a beach. **2.** a beach, riverbank, or other area covered with such small pebbles or stones. —**shin′gly,** *adj.*

shin•gles (shing′gəlz), *n.* *(used with a sing. or pl. v.)* a disease caused by the herpes zoster virus, characterized by skin eruptions and pain along the course of involved sensory nerves. Also called **herpes zoster.**

shin•ing (shī′ning), *adj.* **1.** radiant; gleaming. **2.** resplendent; brilliant: *a shining talent.* **3.** conspicuously fine: *a shining example.*

shin•ny[1] (shin′ē), *n., pl.* **-nies,** *v.,* **-nied, -ny•ing.** —*n.* **1.** a simple variety of hockey, played with a ball, block of wood, or the like, and clubs curved at one end. **2.** the club used. —*v.i.* **3.** to play shinny. **4.** to drive the ball at shinny.

shin•ny[2] (shin′ē), *v.i.,* **-nied, -ny•ing.** to shin (usu. fol. by *up*): *to shinny up a tree.*

shin′ splints′, *n.* (*used with a pl. v.*) a painful condition of the front lower leg associated with muscle strain or stress of the tibia from strenuous activity.

Shin•to (shin′tō), *n.* **1.** Also **Shin′to•ism.** the native religion of Japan, primarily a system of nature and ancestor worship. —*adj.* **2.** Also **Shin′-to•is′tic.** of, pertaining to, or characteristic of Shinto. [< Japanese *shintō,* earlier *shintau* < Chinese *shéndào* way of the gods] —**Shin′to•ist,** *n., adj.*

shin•y (shī′nē), *adj.,* **shin•i•er, shin•i•est. 1.** bright or glossy in appearance. **2.** filled with light, esp. sunshine. **3.** rubbed or worn to a glossy smoothness, as clothes. —**shin′i•ness,** *n.*

ship (ship), *n., v.,* **shipped, ship•ping.** —*n.* **1.** a vessel, esp. a large oceangoing one propelled by sails or engines. **2.** a sailing vessel square-rigged on all of three or more masts, having jibs, staysails, and a spanker on the aftermost mast. **3.** the crew and passengers of a vessel: *The ship was abuzz with the news.* **4.** an airship, airplane, or spacecraft. —*v.t.* **5.** to send or transport by ship, rail, truck, plane, etc. **6.** to take in (water) over the side, as a vessel does when waves break over it. **7.** to bring into a ship or boat: *Ship the anchor.* **8.** to engage (a person) for service on a ship. **9.** to fix in a ship or boat in the proper place for use: *Ship the oars.* **10.** to send away: *We shipped the kids off to camp.* —*v.i.* **11.** to go on board or travel by ship; embark. **12.** to engage to serve on a ship. **13. ship out, a.** to leave, esp. for another country or assignment. **b.** to send away, esp. to another country or assignment. **c.** to quit, resign, or be fired from a job: *Shape up or ship out!* **14. ship over,** to reenlist, esp. in the navy. —*Idiom.* **15. run a tight ship,** to exercise strict control over a company, organization, or the like. **16. when one's ship comes in,** when or if one finally becomes wealthy.

-ship, a noun-forming suffix denoting state or condition, usu. added to personal nouns: *friendship; kinship; statesmanship.*

ship′ bis′cuit, *n.* HARDTACK. Also called **ship′ bread′.**

ship•board (ship′bôrd′, -bōrd′), *adj.* **1.** done or used aboard ship, esp. while under way. —*n.* **2.** the deck or side of a ship. —*Idiom.* **3. on shipboard,** aboard a seagoing vessel.

ship•fit•ter (ship′fit′ər), *n.* a person who forms plates, shapes, etc., of ships according to plans, patterns, or molds.

ship•load (ship′lōd′), *n.* **1.** a full load for a ship. **2.** the cargo carried by a ship.

ship•mas•ter (ship′mas′tər, -mä′stər), *n.* a person who commands a ship; master; captain.

ship•mate (ship′māt′), *n.* a person who serves with another on the same vessel.

ship•ment (ship′mənt), *n.* **1.** an act or instance of shipping freight or cargo. **2.** a quantity of freight or cargo shipped at one time. **3.** something that is shipped.

ship′ of state′, *n.* a nation or its affairs likened to a ship under sail.

ship•per (ship′ər), *n.* a person who makes shipments.

ship•ping (ship′ing), *n.* **1.** the act or business of a person or thing that ships goods. **2.** a number of ships, esp. merchant ships, taken as a whole; tonnage.

ship′ping clerk′, *n.* a clerk who attends to the packing, dispatching, etc., of shipments.

ship′ping ton′, *n.* See under TON (def. 5).

ship•shape (ship′shāp′), *adj.* **1.** in good order; trim or tidy. —*adv.* **2.** in a shipshape manner.

ship•side (ship′sīd′), *n.* the area alongside a ship, as on a pier.

ship•wreck (ship′rek′), *n.* **1.** the destruction or loss of a ship, as by sinking. **2.** the remains of a wrecked ship. **3.** any ruin or destruction. —*v.t.* **4.** to cause to suffer shipwreck. **5.** to ruin; destroy. —*v.i.* **6.** to suffer shipwreck.

ship•wright (ship′rīt′), *n.* a person who builds and launches wooden vessels or does carpentry work on steel or iron vessels.

ship•yard (ship′yärd′), *n.* a yard or enclosure in which ships are built or repaired.

shire (shīr), *n.* **1.** one of the counties of Great Britain. **2. the Shires,** the counties in the Midlands in which hunting is esp. popular.

Shire (shīr), *n.* one of an English breed of large, strong draft horses having a usu. brown or bay coat with feathering on the legs.

shirk (shûrk), *v.t.* **1.** to evade (work, duty, etc.). —*v.i.* **2.** to evade work, duty, etc. —*n.* **3.** a shirker.

shirk•er (shûr′kər), *n.* a person who evades work, duty, responsibility, etc.

shirr (shûr), *v.t.* **1.** to draw up or gather (cloth or the like) on three or more parallel threads. **2.** to bake (eggs removed from the shell), esp. in individual dishes. —*n.* **3.** Also, **shirr′ing.** a shirred arrangement, as of cloth.

shirt (shûrt), *n.* **1.** a long- or short-sleeved garment for the upper part of the body, usu. lightweight and having a collar and a front opening. **2.** an undergarment of cotton, or other material, for the upper part of

the body. **3.** a shirtwaist. **4.** a nightshirt. —*Idiom.* **5. keep one's shirt on,** *Informal.* to refrain from becoming angry or impatient; remain calm. **6. lose one's shirt,** *Informal.* to suffer a severe financial reverse. —**shirt′less,** *adj.*

shirt•dress (shûrt′dres′), *n.* SHIRTWAIST (def. 2).

shirt′ front′ or **shirt′front′,** *n.* **1.** the front of a shirt, esp. the part exposed when a jacket or vest is worn. **2.** DICKEY (def. 1).

shirt•ing (shûr′ting), *n.* any shirt fabric, as broadcloth.

shirt′ jack′et, *n.* a shirtlike jacket. Also called **shirt′-jac′, shirt′ jac′** (jak).

shirt•mak•er (shûrt′mā′kər), *n.* a person who makes shirts. —**shirt′-mak′ing,** *n.*

shirt′-sleeve′ or **shirt′sleeve′,** also **shirt′-sleeved′, shirt′-sleeves′,** *adj.* **1.** not wearing a jacket; informally dressed. **2.** warm enough to not require a jacket or coat: *shirt-sleeve weather.* **3.** direct and straightforward in approach, manner, etc.: *shirt-sleeve diplomacy.* **4.** doing the actual work: *a shirt-sleeve editor.*

shirt•tail (shûrt′tāl′), *n.* **1.** the part of a shirt below the waistline. —*adj.* **2.** quite young and immature in behavior. **3.** of distant relation, esp. by marriage: *some shirttail cousins I'd never met.* —*v.t.* **4.** to append or add (an item) to a discussion or writing.

shirt•waist (shûrt′wāst′), *n.* **1.** a tailored blouse or shirt worn by women. **2.** Also called **shirtdress, shirt′waist′er.** a dress with a bodice and front opening like a tailored shirt.

shish ke•bab (shish′ kə bob′), *n.* small cubes of meat, esp. lamb, usu. marinated and broiled, often with vegetables, on a skewer.

Shi•va (shē′və) also **Siva,** *n.* "the Destroyer," the third member of the Hindu Trimurti, along with Brahma and Vishnu. —**Shi′va•ism,** *n.* —**Shi′va•ist,** *n.* —**Shi′va•is′tic,** *adj.*

shiv•a•ree (shiv′ə rē′), *n., v.,* **-reed, -ree•ing.** —*n.* **1.** a mock serenade with noisemakers given for a newly married couple; charivari. **2.** an elaborate, noisy celebration. —*v.t.* **3.** to serenade with a shivaree.

shiv•er[1] (shiv′ər), *v.i.* **1.** to shake or tremble with cold, fear, excitement, etc. **2. a.** (of a fore-and-aft sail) to shake when too close to the wind. **b.** (of a sailing vessel) to be headed so close to the wind that the sails shake. —*n.* **3.** a tremulous motion; a tremble or quiver. **4. the shivers,** an attack of shivering or chills. —**shiv′er•ing•ly,** *adv.*

shiv•er[2] (shiv′ər), *v.t., v.i.* **1.** to break or split into fragments. —*n.* **2.** a fragment; splinter.

shiv•er•y[1] (shiv′ə rē), *adj.* **1.** inclined to shiver; beset by shivers or tremors. **2.** causing shivering.

shiv•er•y[2] (shiv′ə rē), *adj.* readily breaking into shivers or fragments; brittle.

shoal[1] (shōl), *n.* **1.** a place where a sea, river, or other body of water is shallow. **2.** a sandbank or sand bar esp. one visible at low tide. —*adj.* **3.** (of water) shallow. —*v.i.* **4.** to become shallow or more shallow. —*v.t.* **5.** to make shallow. **6.** to sail so as to lessen the depth of (the water under a vessel).

shoal[2] (shōl), *n.* **1.** any large number of persons or things. **2.** a school of fish. —*v.i.* **3.** to collect in a shoal; throng.

shock[1] (shok), *n.* **1.** a sudden or violent disturbance of the emotions or sensibilities. **2.** a sudden and violent blow or impact. **3.** a sudden or violent commotion. **4.** gravely diminished blood circulation caused by severe injury or pain, blood loss, or certain diseases and characterized by pallor, weak pulse, and very low blood pressure. **5.** the physiological effect produced by the passage of an electric current through the body. **6. shocks,** shock absorbers, esp. in the suspension of an automobile. —*v.t.* **7.** to affect with intense surprise, horror, etc. **8.** to give an electric shock to. **9.** to strike against violently. —*v.i.* **10.** to undergo a shock. —*adj.* **11.** intended to scandalize or titillate an audience by breaking taboos, esp. by using vulgarity, obscenity, or ethnic slurs: *shock radio; shock art.* —**shock′a•ble,** *adj.* —**shock′a•bil′i•ty,** *n.*

shock[2] (shok), *n.* **1.** a thick, bushy mass, as of hair. —*adj.* **2.** shaggy, as hair.

shock′ absorb′er, *n.* a device for damping sudden and rapid motion, as the recoil of a spring-mounted object from shock.

shock•er (shok′ər), *n.* **1.** a person or thing that shocks. **2.** a sensational novel, play, etc.

shock•ing (shok′ing), *adj.* **1.** causing intense surprise, horror, etc. **2.** very bad: *shocking table manners.* —**shock′ing•ly,** *adv.*

shock′ing pink′, *n.* a vivid or intensely bright pink.

shock•proof (shok′prōōf′), *adj.* **1.** Also, **shock′-proof′.** (of timepieces, etc.) protected against damage from shocks. —*v.t.* **2.** to protect against damage from shocks.

shock′-resist′ant, *adj.* strong or resilient enough to sustain minor impacts without damage.

shock′ ther′apy, *n.* any of various therapies, as insulin shock therapy or electroconvulsive therapy, that induce convulsions or unconsciousness and are used for symptomatic relief in certain mental disorders. Also called **shock′ treat′ment.**

shock′ wave′, *n.* **1.** a region of abrupt change of pressure and density moving as a wave front at or above the velocity of sound. **2.** a repercussion from a startling event.

shod (shod), *v.* a pt. and pp. of SHOE.

shod•dy (shod′ē), *adj.,* **-di•er, -di•est,** *n., pl.* **-dies.** —*adj.* **1.** of inferior quality or workmanship. **2.** rude or inconsiderate; shabby. —*n.* **3. a.** a fiber made from reclaimed wool. **b.** a low-grade fabric made from this,

S

usu. in combination with other fibers. **4.** an inferior product, merchandise, etc. —**shod/di•ly,** *adv.* —**shod/di•ness,** *n.*

shoe (sho͞o), *n., pl.* **shoes,** (*esp. Brit. Dial.*) **shoon;** *v.,* **shod** or **shoed, shod** or **shoed** or **shod•den, shoe•ing.** —*n.* **1.** an external covering for the human foot, usu. of leather and consisting of a more or less stiff or heavy sole and a lighter upper part ending a short distance above, at, or below the ankle. **2.** a horseshoe or a similar plate for the hoof of some other animal. **3.** BRAKE SHOE. **4.** the outer casing of a pneumatic automobile tire. **5.** a part having a larger area than the end of an object on which it fits, serving to disperse or apply its weight or thrust. **6.** the sliding contact by which an electric car or locomotive takes its current from the third rail. **7.** a band of iron on the bottom of the runner of a sleigh. —*v.t.* **8.** to provide with a shoe or shoes. **9.** to protect or arm at the point, edge, or face with a ferrule, metal plate, or the like. —*Idiom.* **10.** **fill someone's shoes,** to take the place of another adequately, as by assuming that person's responsibilities. **11.** **in someone's shoes,** in the place or situation of another. —*Saying.* **12.** **The shoe is on the other foot,** relative positions or circumstances have been reversed, as of two competing people or groups. —**shoe/less,** *adj.*

shoe•black (sho͞o/blak/), *n.* BOOTBLACK.

shoe•horn (sho͞o/hôrn/), *n.* **1.** a shaped piece of horn, metal, or the like, inserted in the heel of a shoe to make it slip on more easily. —*v.t.* **2.** to force into a limited or tight space.

shoe•lace (sho͞o/lās/), *n.* a string or lace for fastening a shoe.

shoe•mak•er (sho͞o/mā/kər), *n.* a person who makes or mends shoes. —**shoe/mak/ing,** *n.*

shoe•shine (sho͞o/shīn/), *n.* **1.** an act or instance of cleaning and polishing a pair of shoes. **2.** the surface of polished shoes.

shoe•string (sho͞o/string/), *n.* **1.** SHOELACE. **2.** a very small amount of money. —*adj.* **3.** consisting of or characterized by a small amount of money: *living on a shoestring budget.*

shoe/string pota/toes, *n.pl.* long, thin, sticklike slices of raw potato deep-fried until crisp.

shoe/tree (sho͞o/trē/), *n.* a foot-shaped device, usu. of metal or wood, placed inside a shoe to support it when it is not being worn.

sho•far (shō/fär; *Heb.* shô fär/), *n., pl.* **-fars,** *Heb.* **-froth, -frot** (-frôt/). *Judaism.* a ram's horn used as a wind instrument, sounded in Biblical times as a signal and in modern times at synagogue services on Rosh Hashanah and Yom Kippur.

shofar

sho•gun (shō/gən, -gun), *n.* the title of the chief military commanders of Japan from the 8th to 12th centuries, later applied to the hereditary officials who governed Japan, with the emperor as nominal ruler, until 1868. —**sho/gun•ate** (-gə nit, -nāt/), *n.*

shone (shōn; *esp. Brit.* shon), *v.* a pt. and pp. of SHINE.

shoo (sho͞o), *interj., v.,* **shooed, shoo•ing.** —*interj.* **1.** (used to scare or drive away chickens, birds, etc.) —*v.t.* **2.** to drive away by saying or shouting "shoo." **3.** to request or force (a person) to leave. —*v.i.* **4.** to call out "shoo."

shoo/fly pie/, *n.* an open pie filled with a mixture of flour, butter, brown sugar, molasses, etc., and baked.

shoo/-in/, *n.* a candidate, competitor, etc., regarded as certain to win.

shook¹ (sho͝ok), *n.* **1.** a set of staves and headings sufficient for one hogshead, barrel, or the like. **2.** a set of the parts of a box, piece of furniture, or the like, ready to be put together.

shook² (sho͝ok), *v.* **1.** pt. of SHAKE. —*adj.* **2.** Also, **shook/ up/.** *Informal.* strongly affected by an event, circumstance, etc.; emotionally unsettled.

shoot¹ (sho͞ot), *v.,* **shot, shoot•ing,** *n.* —*v.t.* **1.** to hit, wound, damage, kill, or destroy with a missile discharged from a weapon. **2.** to send forth or discharge (a missile) from a weapon. **3.** to discharge (a weapon). **4.** to send forth (questions, ideas, etc.) rapidly. **5.** to fling; propel: *The volcano shot lava high into the air.* **6.** to direct suddenly or swiftly. **7.** to move suddenly; send swiftly along. **8.** to pass rapidly through, over, down, etc.: *to shoot the rapids.* **9.** to emit (a ray or rays, as of light) suddenly, briefly, or intermittently. **10.** to variegate by threads, streaks, etc., of another color. **11.** to cause to extend or project (often fol. by *out*): *He shot out his arm.* **12.** to put forth (buds, branches, etc.). **13.** to slide (a bolt or the like) into or out of its fastening. **14.** to pull (one's cuffs) abruptly toward one's hands. **15.** to take the altitude of (a heavenly body). **16.** to detonate; cause to explode. —*v.i.* **17.** to send forth missiles from a bow, firearm, or the like. **18.** to be discharged, as a firearm. **19.** to hunt with a gun for sport. **20.** to move or pass suddenly or swiftly. **21.** to put forth buds or shoots, as a plant; germinate. **22.** to take a photograph. **23.** to film or begin to film a scene or movie. **24.** to extend; jut. **25.** to propel a ball, puck, etc., toward a goal or in a particular way. **26.** to flow through the body. **27.** to carry by force of discharge or momentum. **28.** *Informal.* to begin to

talk. **29.** **shoot down, a.** to cause to fall by hitting with a shot. **b.** to disparage, reject, or expose as false or inadequate. **30.** **shoot for** or **at,** to attempt to obtain or accomplish. **31.** **shoot up, a.** to grow rapidly or suddenly. **b.** to damage or harass by reckless shooting. **c.** to wound by shooting. —*n.* **32.** the act of shooting with a bow, firearm, etc. **33.** a shooting expedition or contest. **34.** a growing or sprouting, as of a plant. **35.** a new or young growth that shoots off from some portion of a plant. **36.** a sprout that is not three feet high. **37.** a chute. **38.** the launching of a missile. **39.** a photographic assignment or session, as for a film or a television commercial. —*Idiom.* **40.** **shoot from the hip,** *Informal.* to act or speak without due consideration or deliberation. **41.** **shoot off one's mouth** or **face,** *Slang.* **a.** to talk indiscreetly, make thoughtless remarks, etc. **b.** to exaggerate; brag. **42.** **shoot one's wad** or **bolt,** *Informal.* **a.** to spend all one's money. **b.** Also, **shoot the works.** to spend and exhaust all one's energies or resources. **43.** **shoot the breeze,** *Informal.* to chat aimlessly. **44.** **shoot the messenger,** to blame the bearer of bad news. —**shoot/er,** *n.*

shoot² (sho͞ot), *interj.* (used to express irritation or astonishment.)

shoot/ing gal/lery, *n.* a place equipped with targets and used for practice in shooting.

shoot/ing star/, *n.* **1.** METEOR (def. 1b). **2.** any North American plant of the genus *Dodecatheon,* of the primrose family, esp. *D. media,* having pink or white flowers with reflexed petals and stamens forming a pointed beak.

shoot•out (sho͞ot/out/), *n.* a gunfight that must end in defeat for one side or the other.

shoot/-the-chute/, *n.* CHUTE-THE-CHUTE.

shop (shop), *n., v.,* **shopped, shop•ping.** —*n.* **1.** a retail store, esp. a small one. **2.** a department in a large store selling a specific type of goods. **3.** the workshop of an artisan. **4.** a place for doing specific, skilled manual work; workshop: *a carpenter's shop.* **5.** any factory, office, or business. **6.** a school course in a trade, as carpentry or printing, in which the use of tools is taught. —*v.i.* **7.** to visit shops and stores for the purpose of purchasing or examining goods. **8.** to purchase goods through the mail or by telephone. **9.** to search; hunt (often fol. by *for*). —*v.t.* **10.** to shop at (a particular store or stores). —*Idiom.* **11.** **set up shop,** to go into business; begin business operations. **12.** **talk shop,** to converse about a shared trade, profession, or business.

shop•keep•er (shop/kē/pər), *n.* a person who owns or operates a small store or shop. —**shop/keep/ing,** *n.*

shop•lift•er (shop/lif/tər), *n.* a person who steals goods from a retail store while posing as a customer. —**shop/lift/,** *v.t., v.i.*

shoppe (shop), *n.* a shop (used chiefly on store signs for quaint effect).

shop•per (shop/ər), *n.* **1.** a person who shops. **2.** a retail buyer for another person or a business concern. **3.** a locally distributed newspaper containing retail advertisements.

shop/ping bag/, *n.* a paper or plastic bag with handles, used to carry purchases or belongings.

shop/ping cen/ter, *n.* a group of stores, restaurants, etc., within a single architectural plan, esp. in suburban areas.

shop/ping mall/, *n.* MALL (def. 1).

shop/ stew/ard, *n.* a unionized employee elected to represent a shop, department, or the like, in dealings with an employer.

shop•talk (shop/tôk/), *n.* **1.** conversation about one's work or occupation, esp. after the workday is over. **2.** the specialized vocabulary having to do with work or a field of work.

shore¹ (shôr, shōr), *n.* **1.** the land along the edge of a sea, lake, broad river, etc. **2.** some particular country: *my native shore.* **3.** land, as opposed to water: *a marine serving on shore.* **4.** *Law.* SEASHORE (def. 2).

shore² (shôr, shōr), *n., v.,* **shored, shor•ing.** —*n.* **1.** a supporting post or beam, esp. one propped against the side of a building, a ship in drydock, etc.; prop; strut. —*v.t.* **2.** to support by or as if by a shore or shores; prop (usu. fol. by *up*).

shore•bird (shôr/bûrd/, shōr/-), *n.* a bird frequenting seashores, estuaries, etc., esp. birds of the order Charadriiformes, as sandpipers, plovers, oystercatchers, and avocets.

shore/ leave/, *n.* **1.** permission given to a sailor or ship's officer to spend time ashore. **2.** the time so spent.

shore•line (shôr/līn/, shōr/-), *n.* the line where shore and water meet.

shore/ patrol/, *n.* (*often caps.*) U.S. Navy personnel having duties similar to those performed by military police.

shore•ward (shôr/wərd, shōr/-), *adv.* **1.** Also, **shore/wards.** toward the shore. —*adj.* **2.** facing or moving toward the shore.

shorn (shôrn, shōrn), *v.* a pp. of SHEAR.

short (shôrt), *adj.* **1.** having little length; not long. **2.** having little height; not tall. **3.** extending or reaching only a little way: *a short path.* **4.** brief in duration; not extensive in time. **5.** concise, as writing. **6.** rudely brief; abrupt. **7.** low in amount; scanty: *short rations.* **8.** not reaching a mark, target, or the like. **9.** not reaching a standard, required level, etc.; deficient: *a short measure.* **10.** having an insufficient amount (often fol. by *in* or *on*). **11.** (of pastry) crisp and flaky from being made with a large proportion of butter or other shortening. **12.** (of metals) deficient in tenacity; friable; brittle. **13. a.** (of a speech sound) lasting a relatively short time. **b.** having the sound of the English vowels in *bat, bet, bit, hot, but,* and *put.* **14. a.** (of a syllable in quantitative verse) lasting a relatively short time. **b.** unstressed. **15.** (of an alcoholic drink) small. —*adv.* **16.** abruptly or suddenly: *to stop short.* **17.** briefly; curtly.

18. on the near side of an intended or particular point: *The arrow landed short.* —*n.* **19.** something that is short. **20.** the sum and substance of a matter; gist (usu. prec. by *the*). **21.** a deficiency or the amount of a deficiency; shortage. **22. shorts, a.** trousers, knee-length or shorter. **b.** short pants worn by men as underwear; drawers. **23. a.** a size of garments for persons who are shorter than average. **b.** a garment in this size. **24.** SHORT CIRCUIT. **25.** a short sound or syllable. **26.** SHORT SUBJECT. —*v.t.* **27.** to short-circuit. **28.** to shortchange. —*v.i.* **29.** to short-circuit. —*Idiom.* **30. come** or **fall short, a.** to fail to reach a particular standard. **b.** to prove insufficient; be lacking. **31. cut short,** to end abruptly; interrupt or terminate. **32. for short,** by way of abbreviation. **33. in short, a.** in summary. **b.** in brief. **34. sell short, a.** to sell stocks at a high price without actually possessing them, expecting to cover them later at a lower price and keeping the price difference as profit. **b.** to disparage or underestimate. **35. short and sweet,** pleasantly brief. **36. short for,** being a shorter form of: *"Phone" is short for "telephone."* **37. short of, a.** less than; inferior to. **b.** inadequately supplied with. **c.** without going to the length of: *Short of murder, there is nothing they wouldn't have tried.* —**short′ness,** *n.*

short•age (shôr′tij), *n.* **1.** a deficiency in quantity: *a shortage of cash.* **2.** the amount of such deficiency.

short•bread (shôrt′bred′), *n.* a type of butter cookie commonly made in rectangles or in thick, pie-shaped wheels.

short•cake (shôrt′kāk′), *n.* a short, sometimes sweetened biscuit, filled or topped with fruit and whipped cream.

short•change (shôrt′chānj′), *v.t.,* **-changed, -chang•ing. 1.** to give less than the correct change to. **2.** to cheat; defraud.

short′ cir′cuit, *n.* an abnormal condition of relatively low resistance between two points of differing potential in a circuit, usu. resulting in a flow of excess current.

short′-cir′cuit, *v.t.* **1. a.** to make (an appliance, switch, etc.) inoperable by establishing a short circuit in. **b.** to carry (a current) as a short circuit. **2.** to bypass, impede, hinder, or frustrate. —*v.i.* **3.** to form or become disabled by a short circuit.

short•com•ing (shôrt′kum′ing), *n.* a failure, defect, or deficiency in conduct, condition, thought, ability, etc.

short•cut (shôrt′kut′), *n.* **1.** a shorter or quicker way to get somewhere. **2.** a method, policy, etc., that reduces the time or energy needed to accomplish something.

short′ divi′sion, *n.* mathematical division, esp. by a one-digit divisor, in which the steps of the process are performed mentally and are not written down.

short•en (shôr′tn), *v.t.* **1.** to make short or shorter. **2.** to reduce, decrease, take in, etc.: *to shorten sail.* **3.** to make (pastry, bread, etc.) short, as with butter or other fat. —*v.i.* **4.** to become short or shorter. **5.** (of odds) to shorten. —**short′en•er,** *n.*

short•en•ing (shôrt′ning, shôr′tn ing), *n.* **1.** butter or other fat used to shorten pastry, bread, or the like. **2.** the act or process of making or becoming short or shorter. **3. a.** the act or process of dropping one or more syllables from a word or phrase to form a shorter word with the same meaning. **b.** CLIPPED FORM.

short•fall (shôrt′fôl′), *n.* **1.** the quantity or extent by which something falls short; deficiency; shortage. **2.** the act of falling short.

short•hair (shôrt′hâr′), *n.* a domestic cat having a short, dense coat.

short•haired (shôrt′hârd′), *adj.* (of an animal) having short hair lying close to the body.

short•hand (shôrt′hand′), *n.* **1.** a method of rapid handwriting using abbreviations or symbols that designate letters, words, or phrases. **2.** a simplified or abbreviated form or system of communicating. —*adj.* **3.** of, pertaining to, or using shorthand.

short′-hand′ed, *adj.* not having the usual or necessary number of workers, helpers, etc. —**short′-hand′ed•ness,** *n.*

short′-haul′, *adj.* pertaining to travel or transportation over short distances: *short-haul trucking.*

short′ list′ or **short′list′,** *n.* a list of those people or items preferred or most likely to be chosen, as winnowed from a longer list of possibilities. —**short′-list′,** *v.t.,* **-list•ed, -list•ing.**

short′-lived′ (līvd, livd), *adj.* living or lasting only a little while.

short•ly (shôrt′lē), *adv.* **1.** in a short time; soon. **2.** briefly; concisely. **3.** curtly; rudely.

short′ or′der, *n.* **1.** a serving of food that can be quickly prepared, as at a lunch counter. —*Idiom.* **2. in short order,** quickly; with dispatch. —**short′-or′der,** *adj.*

short′-range′, *adj.* having a limited extent, as in distance or time.

short′ shrift′, *n.* **1.** a brief time for confession or absolution given to a condemned prisoner before his or her execution. **2.** little attention or consideration in dealing with a person or matter.

short•sight•ed (shôrt′sī′tid), *adj.* **1.** unable to see far; nearsighted. **2.** lacking in foresight. —**short′sight′ed•ly,** *adv.* —**short′sight′ed•ness,** *n.*

short•stop (shôrt′stop′), *n. Baseball.* the player covering the area of the infield between second and third base.

short′ sto′ry, *n.* a piece of prose fiction, usu. under 10,000 words.

short′ sub′ject, *n.* a short film, as a documentary or travelogue, shown as part of a program with a feature-length film.

short′-tem′pered, *adj.* having a quick, hasty temper; irascible.

short′-term′, *adj.* **1.** covering or involving a relatively short period of time: *short-term memory.* **2.** maturing after a relatively short period of time: *a short-term loan.* **3.** (of a capital gain or loss) derived from the sale or exchange of an asset held for less than a specified time, as six months or one year.

short′ ton′, *n.* See under TON (def. 1). Also called **net ton.**

short′-waist′ed, *adj.* of less than average length between the shoulders and waistline; having a high waistline.

short•wave (shôrt′wāv′), *n., adj., v.,* **-waved, -wav•ing.** —*n.* **1.** a radio wave shorter than that used in AM broadcasting, corresponding to frequencies of over 1600 kHz: used for long-distance reception or transmission. **2.** SHORTWAVE RADIO. —*adj.* **3.** of, pertaining to, or using shortwaves. —*v.t., v.i.* **4.** to transmit by shortwaves.

short′wave ra′dio, *n.* a radio that transmits or receives shortwaves.

short′-wind′ed, *adj.* **1.** short of breath. **2.** brief or concise; to the point, as in speech or writing.

short•y or **short•ie** (shôr′tē), *n., pl.* **short•ies,** *adj.* —*n.* **1.** a person of less than average height. **2.** a garment designed to be of short length, as a nightgown. —*adj.* **3.** noting something designed to be of short length: *a shorty boot.*

Sho•sho•ne (shō shō′nē), *n., pl.* **-nes,** (*esp. collectively*) **-ne. 1.** a member of an American Indian people or group of peoples living mainly in Nevada, N Utah, Idaho, and W Wyoming. **2.** the Uto-Aztecan language of the Shoshones. **3.** a river in NW Wyoming, flowing NE into the Bighorn River. 120 mi. (193 km) long.

Sho•sta•ko•vich (shos′tə kō′vich), *n.* **Dimitri (Dimitrievich),** 1906–75, Russian composer.

shot¹ (shot), *n., pl.* **shots** or, for 6, 8, **shot;** *v.,* **shot•ted, shot•ting.** —*n.* **1.** a discharge of a firearm, bow, etc. **2.** an act or instance of shooting a firearm, bow, etc. **3.** the range of or the distance traveled by a missile in its flight. **4.** an aimed discharge of a missile. **5.** an attempt to hit a target with a missile. **6.** a small ball or pellet of lead, a number of which are loaded in a cartridge and used for one charge of a shotgun. **7.** such pellets collectively: *a charge of shot.* **8.** a projectile for discharge from a firearm or cannon. **9.** such projectiles collectively. **10.** a person who shoots; marksman: *a good shot.* **11.** anything like a shot, esp. in being sudden and forceful. **12.** a heavy metal ball used in shot-putting contests. **13.** an aimed stroke, throw, or the like, as in certain games, esp. in an attempt to score. **14.** an attempt or try. **15.** a remark aimed at some person or thing. **16.** a guess at something. **17.** a hypodermic injection, as of a serum or vaccine. **18.** a small quantity, esp. an ounce, of undiluted liquor. **19. a.** a photograph, esp. a snapshot. **b.** the act of taking a photograph. **20.** *Motion Pictures, Television.* a unit of action photographed without interruption and constituting a single camera view. **21.** an appearance as a guest, esp. on television. **22.** *Textiles.* **a.** a pick sent through the shed in a single throw of the shuttle. **b.** a defect in a fabric caused by an unusual color or size in the yarn. **23.** a chance with odds for and against; a bet: *a 20 to 1 shot.* —*v.t.* **24.** to load or supply with shot. **25.** to weight with shot. —*Idiom.* **26. have** or **take a shot at,** to make an attempt at. **27. like a shot,** instantly; quickly. **28. shot in the arm,** something that provides renewed vigor, confidence, etc. **29. shot in the dark,** a wild or random guess.

shot² (shot), *v.* **1.** pt. and pp. of SHOOT¹. —*adj.* **2.** woven so as to present a play of colors; variegated, as silk. **3.** spread or streaked with color. **4.** in hopelessly bad condition; ruined.

shot•gun (shot′gun′), *n., adj., v.,* **-gunned, -gun•ning.** —*n.* **1.** a smoothbore gun for firing small shot to kill birds and small quadrupeds, though often used with buckshot to kill larger animals. **2.** a football passing formation in which the quarterback lines up several yards behind the line of scrimmage. —*adj.* **3.** pertaining to, used in, or carried out with a shotgun. **4.** gained or characterized by coercive methods. **5.** tending to be wide-ranging, but haphazard: *the shotgun approach to buying stocks.* **6.** having all the rooms in a line from front to back: *a shotgun apartment.* —*v.t.* **7.** to fire a shotgun at.

shot′ put′, *n.* **1.** a field event in which a heavy ball or shot is thrown or put for distance. **2.** a single throw or put of the shot.

should (shŏŏd), *auxiliary v.* **1.** pt. of SHALL. **2.** (used to indicate duty, propriety, or expediency): *You should not do that.* **3.** (used to express condition): *Were he to arrive, I should be pleased.* **4.** (used to make a statement less direct or blunt): *I should think you would apologize.*

shoul•der (shōl′dər), *n.* **1.** the part on either side of the human body where the arm joins with the trunk, extending from the base of the neck to the upper arm. **2.** Usu., **shoulders.** these two parts together with the part of the back joining them. **3.** a corresponding part in animals. **4.** the upper foreleg and adjoining parts of a sheep, goat, etc. **5.** the part of a garment that fits over the shoulder. **6.** a shoulderlike part or projection. **7.** a cut of meat that includes the upper joint of the foreleg. **8.** Often, **shoulders.** capacity for bearing responsibility or blame. **9.** a step-

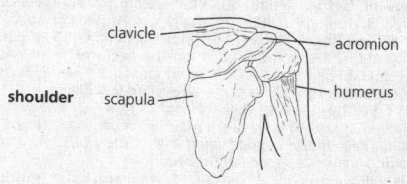

shoulder — clavicle — acromion — scapula — humerus

like change in the contour of an object. **10.** the flat surface on a type body extending beyond the base of the letter or character. **11.** a border alongside a roadway. —*v.t.* **12.** to push with or as if with the shoulder. **13.** to support or carry on the shoulder or shoulders. **14.** to assume as a responsibility. —*v.i.* **15.** to push with or as if with the shoulder. —*Idiom.* **16. shoulder to shoulder,** side by side; with united effort.

shoul·der bag′, *n.* a handbag with a shoulder strap.

shoul·der blade′, *n.* SCAPULA.

shoul·der strap′, *n.* a strap passing over the shoulder and supporting a garment or article.

should·n't (shŏŏd′nt), contraction of *should not.*

shout (shout), *v.i.* **1.** to call or cry out loudly. —*v.t.* **2.** to utter loudly. —*n.* **3.** a loud call or cry. —**shout′er,** *n.*

shove (shuv), *v.,* **shoved, shov·ing,** *n.* —*v.t.* **1.** to propel along. **2.** to push roughly or rudely; jostle. —*v.i.* **3.** to push. **4. shove off, a.** to push a boat from the shore. **b.** to go away; depart. —*n.* **5.** an act or instance of shoving. —**shov′er,** *n.*

shov·el (shuv′əl), *n., v.,* **-eled, -el·ing** or (*esp. Brit.*) **-elled, -el·ling.** —*n.* **1.** a hand implement consisting of a broad blade or scoop attached to a long handle, used for taking up or throwing loose matter. **2.** any fairly large contrivance or machine with a broad blade or scoop having a similar purpose: *a steam shovel.* —*v.t.* **3.** to take up and cast with a shovel. **4.** to gather up in large quantity energetically with or as if with a shovel: *to shovel food into one's mouth.* **5.** to dig or clear with or as if with a shovel. —*v.i.* **6.** to use a shovel. —**shov′el·er,** *n.*

shov·el-nosed′, *adj.* having the head, snout, or beak broad and flat like the blade of a shovel. —**shovelnose,** *n.*

show (shō), *v.,* **showed, shown, showed, show·ing,** *n.* —*v.t.* **1.** to cause or allow to be seen; exhibit; display. **2.** to present or perform as a public entertainment or spectacle. **3.** to indicate; point out: *to show the way.* **4.** to guide; escort: *Show her in.* **5.** to make known; explain: *He showed what he meant.* **6.** to reveal; demonstrate: *Your work shows promise.* **7.** to register; mark. **8.** to exhibit or offer for sale: *to show a house.* **9.** to allege, as in a legal document: *to show cause.* **10.** to produce, as facts in an affidavit or at a hearing. **11.** to offer; grant: *to show mercy.* —*v.i.* **12.** to be or become visible. **13.** to be manifested in a certain way: *to show to advantage.* **14.** to put on an exhibition or performance: *Several designers are showing now.* **15.** to make an appearance; show up. **16.** to finish third, as in a horse race. **17. show off, a.** to display to advantage: *The gold frame shows off the picture beautifully.* **b.** to present for admiration or approval: *young parents showing off their new baby.* **c.** to seek attention by ostentatious or insistent display of one's talent, possessions, achievements, etc. **18. show up, a.** to make known; reveal: *It showed up the flaws in the plan.* **b.** to appear as specified; be seen: *White shows up well against the blue.* **c.** to come to or arrive at a place. **d.** to make (another) seem inferior; outdo. —*n.* **19.** a theatrical production, performance, or company. **20.** a radio or television program. **21.** a motion picture. **22.** an exposition of products by various manufacturers in a particular industry. **23.** exhibition. **24.** ostentatious display. **25.** a display or demonstration. **26.** the position of the competitor who comes in third, as in a horse race. **27.** appearance; impression: *to make a sorry show.* **28.** a sight or spectacle. **29. a.** the first appearance of blood at the onset of menstruation. **b.** a blood-tinged mucous discharge from the vagina that indicates the onset of labor. —*Idiom.* **30. show the flag,** to make one's presence known.

show′ and tell′, *n.* **1.** an activity for young children, esp. in school, in which each participant produces an object of unusual interest and tells something about it. **2.** *Facetious.* any informative presentation or demonstration, as to introduce a new product or divulge and explain a special plan. —**show′-and-tell′,** *adj.* —**show′-and-tell′er,** *n.*

show′ biz′, *n. Informal.* SHOW BUSINESS.

show·boat (shō′bōt′), *n.* **1.** a boat, esp. a paddle-wheel steamer, used as a traveling theater. **2.** a show-off. —*v.i.* **3.** to perform or behave flamboyantly.

show·bread (shō′bred′), *n.* SHEWBREAD.

show′ busi′ness, *n.* the entertainment industry, as theater, motion pictures, television, radio, carnival, and circus.

show·case (shō′kās′), *n., v.,* **-cased, -cas·ing.** —*n.* **1.** a glass case for the display and protection of articles. **2.** an exhibit or display, usu. of an ideal or representative model of something. **3.** the setting, place, or vehicle for displaying something on a trial basis. —*v.t.* **4.** to exhibit or display. **5.** to present in or as if in an entertainment showcase. **6.** to present as a special event.

show·down (shō′doun′), *n.* **1.** (esp. in poker) the laying down of all the players' cards faceup to determine the winner in a hand. **2.** a conclusive confrontation or settlement of a matter of contention.

show·er (shou′ər), *n.* **1.** a brief fall of rain or of hail or snow. **2.** Also called **show′er bath′.** a bath in which water is sprayed on the body from above. **3.** the apparatus or space for providing such a bath. **4.** something resembling a shower: *a shower of sparks.* **5.** a party given to bestow presents of a specific kind upon the honoree. —*v.t.* **6.** to bestow liberally or lavishly. **7.** to give to in abundance. —*v.i.* **8.** to rain in a shower. **9.** to bathe in a shower. —**show′er·y,** *adj.*

show·ing (shō′ing), *n.* **1.** display; exhibition. **2.** the act of putting something on display. **3.** a performance or record considered for the impression it makes: *made a good showing at the polls.* **4.** a setting forth or presentation, as of facts or conditions.

show·man (shō′mən), *n., pl.* **-men. 1.** a person who produces theatri-

cal works. **2.** a person gifted in dramatic presentation. —**show′man·ly,** *adv.* —**show′man·ship′,** *n.*

show′-me′, *adj.* demanding proof or evidence.

shown (shōn), *v.* a pp. of SHOW.

show′-off′, *n.* **1.** a person given to pretentious display. **2.** the act of showing off. —**show′-off′ish,** *adj.*

show·place (shō′plās′), *n.* a place, as an estate or mansion, notable for its beauty, historical interest, etc.

show·room (shō′rōōm′, -rŏŏm′), *n.* a room used for the display of goods or merchandise.

show′-stop′per, *n.* **1.** a performer or performance that wins enthusiastic or prolonged applause. **2.** a spectacularly arresting person or thing. —**show′-stop′ping,** *adj.*

show·y (shō′ē), *adj.,* **show·i·er, show·i·est. 1.** making an imposing display: *showy flowers.* **2.** pompous; ostentatious; gaudy. —**show′i·ly,** *adv.* —**show′i·ness,** *n.*

shrank (shrangk), *v.* a pt. of SHRINK.

shrap·nel (shrap′nl), *n.* **1.** fragments scattered by a bursting artillery shell, mine, or bomb. **2.** a hollow projectile of the 19th century containing bullets and a bursting charge, designed to explode in the air and shower the target with missiles. [after its inventor, Henry *Shrapnel* (1761–1842), English army officer]

shred (shred), *n., v.,* **shred·ded** or **shred, shred·ding.** —*n.* **1.** a piece cut or torn off, esp. in a narrow strip. **2.** a bit; scrap: *not a shred of evidence.* —*v.t.* **3.** to cut or tear into small pieces. —*v.i.* **4.** to fragment into shreds.

shred′ded wheat′, *n.* a breakfast cereal made by shredding cooked, dried whole wheat and baking or toasting it as biscuits.

shred·der (shred′ər), *n.* **1.** a person or thing that shreds. **2.** a machine for shredding documents.

Shreve·port (shrēv′pôrt′, -pōrt′), *n.* a city in NW Louisiana, on the Red River. 196,982.

shrew[1] (shrōō), *n.* a woman of violent temper and speech; termagant.

shrew[2] (shrōō), *n.* any of several small, mouselike, insect-eating mammals of the family Soricidae, having a long, sharp snout and small, poorly developed eyes.

shrewd (shrōōd), *adj.* **1.** astute or sharp in practical matters: *a shrewd politician.* **2.** keen; piercing. **3.** artful; marked by cleverness, perceptiveness, etc. —**shrewd′ly,** *adv.* —**shrewd′ness,** *n.*

shrew·ish (shrōō′ish), *adj.* having the disposition of a shrew; nagging; ill-tempered. —**shrew′ish·ly,** *adv.* —**shrew′ish·ness,** *n.*

shriek (shrēk), *n.* **1.** a loud, sharp, shrill cry. **2.** any loud, shrill sound, as of a whistle. —*v.i.* **3.** to utter a loud, sharp, shrill cry. **4.** to give forth a loud, shrill sound. —*v.t.* **5.** to utter in a shriek: *to shriek defiance.* —**shriek′er,** *n.*

shrike (shrīk), *n.* any of various songbirds of the family Laniidae, mainly of the Old World, having a sharply hooked bill and feeding on large insects or small vertebrates: some species impale their prey on thorns or barbed wire.

shrill (shril), *adj.* **1.** high-pitched and piercing: *a shrill cry.* **2.** producing or marked by shrill sound. **3.** immoderate; strident. **4.** marked by great intensity: *shrill incandescent light.* —*v.t., v.i.* **5.** to cry shrilly. —*n.* **6.** a shrill sound. —*adv.* **7.** in a shrill manner; shrilly. —**shrill′ness,** *n.* —**shrill′ly,** *adv.*

shrimp (shrimp), *n., pl.* **shrimps,** (*esp. collectively*) **shrimp** for 1, *v.* —*n.* **1.** any of various small, long-tailed, chiefly marine decapod crustaceans of the suborder Natantia, certain species of which are used as food. **2.** a diminutive person. —*v.i.* **3.** to fish for shrimps.

shrimp·er (shrim′pər), *n.* **1.** a shrimp fisherman. **2.** a boat used for shrimping.

shrine (shrīn), *n., v.,* **shrined, shrin·ing.** —*n.* **1.** any structure or place consecrated or devoted to some saint, holy person, or deity, as an altar, chapel, church, or the like. **2.** a building enclosing the remains or relics of a saint. **3.** any place or object hallowed by its history or associations: *a historic shrine.* **4.** a receptacle for sacred relics; a reliquary. —*v.t.* **5.** to enshrine.

Shrin·er (shrī′nər), *n.* a member of a fraternal order that is an auxiliary of the Masonic order.

shrink (shringk), *v.,* **shrank** or, often, **shrunk, shrunk** or **shrunk·en, shrink·ing,** *n.* —*v.i.* **1.** to contract or lessen in size: *cloth that shrinks if washed.* **2.** to become reduced in extent, compass, or value. **3.** to draw back; recoil: *to shrink from danger.* —*v.t.* **4.** to cause to shrink or contract; reduce. **5.** PRESHRINK. —*n.* **6.** an act or instance of shrinking. **7.** SHRINKAGE. **8.** *Slang.* a psychotherapist, psychiatrist, or psychoanalyst. —**shrink′er,** *n.*

shrink·age (shring′kij), *n.* **1.** an act or process of shrinking. **2.** the amount or degree of shrinking. **3.** contraction of a fabric in finishing or washing. **4.** the difference between the original weight of livestock and that after it has been prepared for marketing.

shrink′ing vi′olet, *n.* a shy or self-effacing person.

shrink′-wrap′, *v.,* **-wrapped, -wrap·ping,** *n.* —*v.t.* **1.** to wrap and seal in a clear, flexible plastic sheet that when exposed to heat shrinks tightly around the thing it covers. —*n.* **2.** the plastic film used to shrink-wrap something.

shrive (shrīv), *v.,* **shrove** or **shrived, shriv·en** or **shrived, shriv·ing.** —*v.t.* **1.** to impose penance on (a sinner). **2.** to grant absolution to (a penitent).

shriv•el (shriv′əl), *v.t., v.i.,* **-eled, -el•ing** or (*esp. Brit.*) **-elled, -el•ling. 1.** to contract and wrinkle, as from great heat, cold, or dryness. **2.** to wither; make or become helpless or useless.

shroud (shroud), *n.* **1.** a cloth or sheet in which a corpse is wrapped for burial. **2.** something that covers, conceals, or protects: *a shroud of darkness.* **3.** any of a number of fixed ropes or wires that converge from the head of a ship's mast and keep it from swaying. **4.** Also called **shroud′ line′.** any of a number of suspension cords of a parachute attaching the load to the canopy. **—*v.t.* 5.** to wrap or clothe for burial; enshroud. **6.** to cover; hide from view. **7.** to veil in obscurity or mystery.

shrove (shrōv), *v.* a pt. of SHRIVE.

Shrove•tide (shrōv′tīd′), *n.* the three days before Ash Wednesday.

Shrove′ Tues′day, *n.* the last day of Shrovetide.

shrub[1] (shrub), *n.* a woody plant smaller than a tree, usu. having multiple permanent stems branching from or near the ground.

shrub[2] (shrub), *n.* **1.** an appetizer of sweetened fruit juice, often topped with sherbet. **2.** a drink of fruit juice, sugar, and alcohol.

shrub•ber•y (shrub′ə rē), *n., pl.* **-ber•ies. 1.** a planting of shrubs. **2.** shrubs collectively.

shrub•by (shrub′ē), *adj.,* **-bi•er, -bi•est. 1.** consisting of or abounding in shrubs. **2.** resembling a shrub. **—shrub′bi•ness,** *n.*

shrug (shrug), *v.,* **shrugged, shrug•ging,** *n.* **—*v.t.* 1.** to raise and contract (the shoulders), expressing ignorance, indifference, disdain, etc. **—*v.i.* 2.** to raise and contract the shoulders. **3. shrug off, a.** to disregard; minimize: *to shrug off an insult.* **b.** to rid oneself of: *to shrug off the effects of a drug.* **—*n.* 4.** the movement of raising and contracting the shoulders. **5.** a woman's shawllike sweater or jacket that ends above or at the waist.

shrunk (shrungk), *v.* a pp. and pt. of SHRINK.

shrunk•en (shrung′kən), *v.* a pp. of SHRINK.

shtetl (shtet′l, shtā′tl), *n., pl.* ***shtet•lach*** (shtet′läkн, -ləkн, shtāt′-), *Eng.* **shtetls.** *Yiddish.* (formerly) a Jewish village in E Europe.

shtick or **shtik** (shtik), *n. Slang.* **1.** a show-business routine or piece of business inserted to gain a laugh or draw attention to oneself. **2.** one's special interest, talent, etc.

shuck (shuk), *n.* **1.** a husk or pod, as the outer covering of corn, hickory nuts, chestnuts, etc. **2.** Usu., **shucks.** something useless or worthless. **3.** the shell of an oyster or clam. **—*v.t.* 4.** to remove the shucks from: *to shuck corn.* **5.** to remove or discard; peel off: *to shuck one's clothes.* **6.** to get rid of (often fol. by *off*): *to shuck off a bad habit.* **—*interj.* 7. shucks,** (used as a mild exclamation of disgust or regret.)

shud•der (shud′ər), *v.i.* **1.** to tremble with a sudden convulsive movement, as from horror, fear, or cold. **—*n.* 2.** a convulsive trembling, as from horror or cold.

shuf•fle (shuf′əl), *v.,* **-fled, -fling,** *n.* **—*v.i.* 1.** to walk without lifting the feet; shamble. **2.** to slide the feet lazily in dancing. **3.** to move clumsily (usu. fol. by *into*): *to shuffle into one's clothes.* **4.** to act evasively: *to shuffle out of one's responsibilities.* **5.** to intermix playing cards or the like. **—*v.t.* 6.** to move (one's feet) along the ground or floor without lifting them. **7.** to move (objects) this way and that. **8.** to rearrange in random order: *to shuffle playing cards.* **9. shuffle off, a.** to move or go away. **b.** to thrust aside. **—*n.* 10.** a scraping or sliding movement, esp. a dragging gait. **11.** an evasive trick; evasion. **12.** an act or instance of shuffling something, as cards. **13.** the right or turn to shuffle cards before dealing. **14.** a dance in which the feet are shuffled.

shuf•fle•board (shuf′əl bôrd′, -bōrd′), *n.* **1.** a game in which players use long cues to push disks toward numbered scoring sections marked on a floor or other surface. **2.** the marked surface on which this game is played.

Shu•ha (sho͞o′hä), *adj.* of or pertaining to any Shinto sect other than the Kokka.

shul or ***schul*** (sho͝ol, sho͞ol), *n., pl.* ***shuln*** (sho͝oln, sho͞oln), *Eng.* **shuls.** *Yiddish.* a synagogue.

Shu•lam•ite (sho͞o′lə mīt′), *n.* an epithet meaning "princess," applied to the bride in the Song of Solomon 6:13.

Shul•han A•rukh (or ***A•ruk*** or ***A•ruch***) (sho͞ol′кнän ô′rəкн, sho͞ol-кнän′ ä ro͞oкн′), *n.* an authoritative code of Jewish law and custom published in 1565.

shun (shun), *v.t.,* **shunned, shun•ning.** to keep away from; take pains to avoid. **—shun′na•ble,** *adj.* **—shun′ner,** *n.*

shunt (shunt), *v.t.* **1.** to force or turn aside or out of the way. **2. a.** to divert (a part of an electrical current) by connecting a circuit element in parallel with another. **b.** to place or furnish with a shunt. **3.** to shift (railroad rolling stock) from one track to another; switch. **4. a.** to divert blood or other fluid by means of a shunt. **b.** the tube or channel used for this purpose. **—*v.i.* 5. a.** to turn to the side. **b.** to move back and forth. **—*n.* 6.** the act of shunting; shift. **7.** a conducting element bridged across part of an electrical circuit so as to establish a parallel, alternative path for a portion of the current. **8.** a railroad switch. **9.** a channel through which blood or other bodily fluid is diverted from its normal path by surgical reconstruction or by a synthetic tube. **—shunt′er,** *n.*

shush (shush), *interj.* **1.** (used as a command to be quiet or silent.) **—*v.t.* 2.** to order to be silent; hush. **—shush′er,** *n.*

Shu•shan (sho͞o′shan, -shän), *n.* Biblical name of SUSA.

shut (shut), *v.,* **shut, shut•ting,** *adj., n.* **—*v.t.* 1.** to move into a closed position: *to shut a door.* **2.** to close the doors of (often fol. by *up*): *to shut up a house for the night.* **3.** to close by bringing together the parts of: *Shut your book.* **4.** to confine; enclose. **5.** to bar; exclude. **6.** to cause to end or suspend operations. **7.** to bolt; fasten. **—*v.i.* 8.** to become shut or closed; close. **9. shut down, a.** to settle over a place so as to envelop or darken. **b.** to cease or suspend operation. **10. shut in, a.** to enclose. **b.** to confine, as from illness. **11. shut off, a.** to stop the passage of. **b.** to isolate; separate. **12. shut out, a.** to keep from entering; exclude. **b.** to hide from view. **c.** to prevent (an opponent or opposing team) from scoring. **13. shut up, a.** to imprison; confine. **b.** to close entirely. **c.** to stop talking; become silent. **d.** to stop (someone) from talking; silence. **—*adj.* 14.** closed; fastened up: *a shut door.* **—*n.* 15.** the act or time of shutting. **—*Idiom.* 16. shut one's eyes to,** to refuse to acknowledge; disregard; ignore.

shut•down (shut′doun′), *n.* a suspension or stoppage of function or operation.

shut•eye (shut′ī′), *n.* sleep.

shut-in (*adj.* shut′in′; *n.* shut′in′), *adj.* **1.** confined to one's home, a hospital, etc., as from illness. **2.** disposed to desire solitude; withdrawn; asocial. **—*n.* 3.** a person confined by infirmity or disease to the house, a hospital, etc.

shut•off (shut′ôf′, -of′), *n.* **1.** an object or device that shuts something off. **2.** an interruption; stoppage.

shut•out (shut′out′), *n.* **1.** an act or instance of shutting out. **2.** the state of being shut out. **3.** any game in which one side does not score.

shut•ter (shut′ər), *n.* **1.** one that shuts. **2.** a solid or louvered movable cover for a window. **3.** a movable cover, slide, etc., for an opening. **4.** a mechanical device for opening and closing the aperture of a camera lens to expose film or the like. **—*v.t.* 5.** to close or provide with shutters. **—shut′ter•less,** *adj.*

shut•ter•bug (shut′ər bug′), *n.* an amateur photographer.

shut•tle (shut′l), *n., v.,* **-tled, -tling. —*n.* 1.** a device in a loom for passing or shooting the filling thread through the shed from one side of the web to the other, usu. consisting of a boat-shaped piece of wood containing a bobbin on which the filling is wound. **2.** the sliding container that carries the lower thread in a sewing machine. **3.** a public conveyance, as a train, airplane, or bus, that travels back and forth at regular intervals over a route. **4.** SHUTTLECOCK (def. 1). **5.** (*often cap.*) SPACE SHUTTLE. **—*v.t.* 6.** to cause to move to and fro by or as if by a shuttle. **—*v.i.* 7.** to move to and fro.

shut•tle•cock (shut′l kok′), *n.* **1.** the conical feathered cork device that is struck back and forth in badminton. **—*v.t.* 2.** to bandy to and fro like a shuttlecock.

shut′tle diplo′macy, *n.* diplomatic negotiations by a mediator who travels back and forth between the negotiating parties.

shy[1] (shī), *adj.,* **shy•er** or **shi•er, shy•est** or **shi•est,** *v.,* **shied, shy•ing,** *n., pl.* **shies. —*adj.* 1.** bashful; retiring. **2.** easily frightened away; timid. **3.** distrustful; wary. **4.** deficient: *shy of funds.* **5.** short of a full amount or number. **—*v.i.* 6.** (esp. of a horse) to start back or aside in alarm. **7.** to draw back; recoil. **—*n.* 8.** a sudden start aside, as in alarm. **—shy′er,** *n.* **—shy′ly,** *adv.* **—shy′ness,** *n.*

shy[2] (shī), *v.,* **shied, shy•ing,** *n., pl.* **shies. —*v.t., v.i.* 1.** to throw with a swift, sudden movement. **—*n.* 2.** a quick, sudden throw. **3.** a gibe or sneer. **—shy′er,** *n.*

Shy•lock (shī′lok), *n.* **1.** a relentless and vengeful moneylender in Shakespeare's *Merchant of Venice.* **2.** a hard-hearted moneylender. **—*v.i.* 3.** (*l.c.*) to lend money at extortionate rates of interest. **—Shy•lock′i•an,** *adj.* **—Shy′lock•y,** *adj.*

shy•ster (shī′stər), *n.* **1.** a lawyer who uses unprofessional or questionable methods. **2.** a person who gets along by petty, sharp practices.

Si, *Chem. Symbol.* silicon.

Si•am (sī am′, sī′am), *n.* **1.** former name of THAILAND (def. 1). **2. Gulf of,** THAILAND (def. 2).

Si•a•mese (sī′ə mēz′, -mēs′), *adj., n., pl.* **-mese. —*adj.* 1.** of or pertaining to Siam or its inhabitants. **2.** twin; closely connected; similar. **3.** twofold or two-way: *a Siamese sprinkler.* **—*n.* 4.** a native or inhabitant of Siam. **5.** THAI (def. 2). **6.** SIAMESE CAT. [1685–95]

Si′amese cat′, *n.* one of a breed of slender shorthaired cats, raised orig. in Thailand, having a wedge-shaped head, blue eyes, and a pale fawn or grayish body with darker mask, ears, feet, and tail.

Si′amese fight′ing fish′, *n.* a freshwater fish, *Betta splendens,* bred for centuries for brilliant color, very long fins, and pugnacity.

Si′amese twins′, *n.pl.* twins who are congenitally joined together. [alluding to Chang and Eng (1811–74), twins born in Siam who were joined in this way]

sib (sib), *adj.* **1.** related by blood; akin. **—*n.* 2.** a relative; kinsman or kinswoman. **3.** one's kin or kindred.

Si•be•li•us (si bā′lē əs, -bāl′yəs;), *n.* **Jean (Julius Christian),** 1865–1957, Finnish composer.

Si•be•ri•a (sī bēr′ē ə), *n.* a part of the Russian Federation in N Asia, from the Ural Mountains to the Pacific. **—Si•be′ri•an,** *adj., n.*

Sibe′rian husk′y, *n.* one of a Siberian breed of medium-sized dogs with a thick, soft coat, erect ears, and a bushy tail curved over the back, used as sled dogs.

sib•i•lant (sib′ə lənt), *adj.* **1.** hissing. **2.** of or pertaining to a consonant sound in which air is channeled through a narrow groove along the center of the tongue, producing a hissing sound. **—*n.* 3.** a sibilant consonant sound, as (s), (z), (sh), or (zh). **—sib′i•lance,** *n.* **—sib′i•lant•ly,** *adv.*

S

sib·i·late (sib′ə lāt′), v., **-lat·ed, -lat·ing.** —v.i. **1.** to hiss. —v.t. **2.** to utter or pronounce with a hissing sound. —**sib′i·la′tion,** n.

sib·ling (sib′ling), n. **1.** a brother or sister. **2.** Anthro. a member of a sib.

sib·yl (sib′əl), n. **1.** (sometimes cap.) any of a group of semilegendary women of the ancient world who possessed prophetic powers and were consulted as oracles. **2.** a female prophet or fortune-teller. —**sib′yl·line** (-ə lēn′, -līn′, -lin), **si·byl·ic, si·byl·lic** (si bil′ik), adj.

sic or **sick** (sik), v.t., **sicked** or **sicced** (sikt), **sick·ing** or **sic·cing. 1.** to attack (used esp. in commanding a dog): Sic 'em! **2.** to incite to attack (usu. fol. by on).

sic (sēk; Eng. sik), adv. Latin. so; thus: usu. placed within brackets to denote that a wording has been written intentionally or has been quoted verbatim: He signed his name as e. e. cummings [sic].

Si·chuan (sich′wän′, sich′ōō än′) also **Szechwan, Szechuan,** n. a province in S central China. 103,200,000; 219,691 sq. mi. (569,000 sq. km). Cap.: Chengdu.

Sic·i·ly (sis′ə lē), n. the largest island in the Mediterranean, constituting a region of Italy, and separated from the SW tip of the mainland by the Strait of Messina. 5,141,343; 9924 sq. mi. (25,705 sq. km). Cap.: Palermo. Italian, **Sicilia.** Ancient, **Sicilia, Trinacria.** —**Si·cil·ian** (si sil′yən, -sil′ē ən), adj., n.

sick¹ (sik), adj. **-er, -est** n. —adj. **1.** afflicted with ill health or disease; ailing. **2.** affected with nausea; inclined to vomit. **3.** deeply affected with some distressing feeling: sick at heart. **4.** mentally, morally, or emotionally deranged, corrupt, or unsound. **5.** characteristic of a sick mind: sick fancies. **6.** gruesome; sadistic: sick jokes. **7.** of, pertaining to, or for use during sickness: sick benefits. **8.** suggestive of sickness; sickly: a sick pallor. **9.** disgusted; chagrined. **10.** not in proper condition; impaired. —n. **11. the sick,** sick persons collectively. —**Idiom. 12. sick and tired,** exasperated and weary: sick and tired of working late.

sick² (sik), v.t. SIC¹.

sick′ bay′, n. a hospital or dispensary, esp. aboard ship.

sick·bed (sik′bed′), n. the bed used by a sick person.

sick′ call′, n. **1.** a military formation for those requiring medical attention. **2.** the period during which this formation is held.

sick′ day′, n. a day for which an employee will be paid while absent because of illness.

sick·en (sik′ən), v.t., v.i. to make or become sick. —**sick′en·er,** n.

sick·en·ing (sik′ə ning), adj. causing sickness or loathing: sickening arrogance. —**sick′en·ing·ly,** adv.

sick′ head′ache, n. MIGRAINE.

sick·ie (sik′ē), n. Slang. one who is deranged or perverted.

sick·le (sik′əl), n. **1.** an implement for cutting grain, grass, etc., consisting of a curved, hooklike blade mounted in a short handle. **2.** (cap.) a group of stars in the constellation Leo, likened to this implement in formation.

sickle (def. 1)

sick′ leave′, n. leave from duty, work, or the like, granted because of illness.

sick·le·bill (sik′əl bil′), n. any of various birds that have a long, curved bill, as the curlew.

sick′le cell′, n. an elongated, often sickle-shaped red blood cell, caused by defective hemoglobin.

sick′le cell′ ane′mia, n. a chronic hereditary blood disease, primarily affecting indigenous Africans and their descendants, in which an accumulation of oxygen-deficient sickle cells results in anemia, blood clotting, and joint pain. Also called **sicklemia.**

sick·ly (sik′lē), adj., **-li·er, -li·est,** adv., v., **-lied, -ly·ing.** —adj. **1.** not strong; unhealthy; ailing. **2.** arising from ill health: a sickly complexion. **3.** marked by the prevalence of ill health, as a region. **4.** causing sickness. **5.** nauseating. **6.** maudlin; mawkish. **7.** faint or feeble, as light or color. —adv. **8.** in a sick or sickly manner. —v.t. **9.** to cover with a sickly hue. —**sick′li·ness,** n.

sick·ness (sik′nis), n. **1.** a particular disease or malady. **2.** the state or an instance of being sick; illness. **3.** nausea; queasiness.

sick·o (sik′ō), n., pl. **sick·os.** Slang. SICKIE.

sick·out (sik′out′), n. an organized absence from work by employees on the pretext of sickness.

sick′ pay′, n. wages or other compensation received from an employer during an illness.

sick·room (sik′rōōm′, -rōŏm′), n. a room in which a sick person is confined.

sic sem·per ty·ran·nis (sēk sem′pɛʀ tɪ ʀăn′nis; Eng. sik sem′pər ti-ran′is), Latin. thus always to tyrants (motto of the State of Virginia).

sic tran·sit glo·ri·a mun·di (sēk trän′sit glō′ʀɪ ä′ mŏŏn′dē; Eng. sik tran′sit glôr′ē ə mun′dī, -dē, glôr′-, -zit), Latin. thus passes away the glory of this world.

sid·dur (sid′ər, si dŏŏr′; Heb. sē dŏŏʀ′), n., pl. **sid·du·rim** (si dŏŏr′im; Heb. sē dŏŏ rēm′), **sid·durs.** a Jewish prayer book designed for use chiefly on days other than festivals and holy days. Compare MAHZOR.

side (sīd), n., adj., v., **sid·ed, sid·ing.** —n. **1.** one of the surfaces forming the outside of something, or one of the lines bounding a geometric figure. **2.** either of the two broad surfaces of a thin flat object, as a door. **3.** one of the lateral surfaces of an object, as opposed to the front, back, top, and bottom. **4.** either of the two lateral parts or areas of a thing: the right side and the left side. **5.** either lateral half of the body, esp. of the trunk. **6.** the dressed, lengthwise half of an animal's body used for food. **7.** an aspect; phase: all sides of a problem. **8.** region, direction, or position with reference to a central line, space, or point: the east side of a city. **9.** a slope, as of a hill. **10.** one of two or more contesting teams or groups: Our side won the baseball game. **11.** the position, course, or part of a person or group opposing another: I am on your side. **12.** line of descent through either parent. **13.** the space immediately adjacent: Stand at my side. **14.** a side dish, esp. in a restaurant. **15.** Usu., **sides.** pages of a script containing only the lines and cues of a specific role. **16.** Billiards. ENGLISH (def. 5a). **17.** Chiefly Brit. affected manner; pretension. —adj. **18.** being at or on one side. **19.** coming from or directed toward one side. **20.** subordinate; incidental: a side issue. —v.i. **21. side with** (or **against**), to support (or oppose), as in an argument or other dispute. —**Idiom. 22. on the side,** in addition to some primary thing. **23. side by side. a.** next to one another; together. **b.** closely associated or related; in proximity. **24. take sides,** to support one participant in a dispute rather than another.

side′ arm′, n. a weapon, as a pistol or sword, carried at the side or in the belt.

side·arm (sīd′ärm′), adv. **1.** with a swinging motion of the arm moving to the side of the body at or below shoulder level and nearly parallel to the ground: to pitch sidearm. —adj. **2.** thrown or performed sidearm.

side·bar (sīd′bär′), n. **1.** a short news feature alongside and highlighting a longer story. **2.** a typographically distinct section of a page, as in a book or magazine, that amplifies or highlights the main text.

side·board (sīd′bôrd′, -bôrd′), n. a piece of furniture, as in a dining room, often with shelves and drawers for holding articles of table service.

side·burns (sīd′bûrnz′), n.pl. the projections of the hairline forming a border on the face in front of each ear. —**side′burned′,** adj.

side·car (sīd′kär′), n. **1.** a one-passenger car attached to the side of a motorcycle. **2.** a cocktail of brandy, orange liqueur, and lemon juice.

sid·ed (sī′did), adj. having a specified number or kind of sides (usu. used in combination): five-sided; plastic-sided.

side′ dish′, n. a portion of food that accompanies the main course, usu. served in a separate dish.

side′ effect′, n. an often adverse effect, as of a drug, that is secondary to the intended effect. Also called **side′ reac′tion.**

side·kick (sīd′kik′), n. **1.** a close friend. **2.** a confederate or assistant.

side·light (sīd′līt′), n. **1.** an item of incidental information. **2.** a red light on the port side or a green on the starboard carried by a vessel under way at night. **3.** light coming from the side. **4.** a window at the side of a door or another window.

side·line (sīd′līn′), n., v., **-lined, -lin·ing.** —n. **1.** a business or activity pursued in addition to one's primary business. **2.** an additional or auxiliary line of goods. **3. a.** either of the two lines defining the side boundaries of an athletic field or court. **b. sidelines,** the area immediately beyond either sideline. **c. sidelines,** a nonparticipant point of view. —v.t. **4.** to remove from action.

side·long (sīd′lông′, -long′), adj. **1.** directed to one side: a sidelong glance. **2.** slanting to one side; inclined. **3.** indirect; roundabout. —adv. **4.** toward the side; obliquely.

side·piece (sīd′pēs′), n. a piece forming a side or a part of a side of something.

si·de·re·al (sī dēr′ē əl), adj. **1.** determined by or from the stars. **2.** of or pertaining to the stars. —**si·de′re·al·ly,** adv. [< Latin sidus star, constellation]

side′real year′, n. YEAR (def. 4c).

side·sad·dle (sīd′sad′l), n. **1.** a saddle for women on which the rider sits, facing forward, usu. with both feet on the left side of the horse. —adv. **2.** seated on a sidesaddle.

side·show (sīd′shō′), n. **1.** a minor show or exhibition in connection with a principal one, as at a circus. **2.** any subordinate event.

side′ step′, n. a step to one side, as in dancing or boxing.

side·step (sīd′step′), v., **-stepped, -step·ping.** —v.i. **1.** to step to one side. **2.** to evade or avoid a decision or problem. —v.t. **3.** to dodge by stepping aside. **4.** to evade or avoid (a decision or problem). —**side′step′per,** n.

side′ street′, n. a street leading away from a main street.

side·stroke (sīd′strōk′), n., v., **-stroked, -strok·ing.** —n. **1.** a swimming stroke in which the body is turned sideways in the water, the hands pull alternately, and the legs perform a scissors kick. —v.i. **2.** to swim the sidestroke.

side·swipe (sīd′swīp′), v., **-swiped, -swip·ing,** n. —v.t. **1.** to strike with a glancing blow in passing. —n. **2.** a glancing blow in passing.

side·track (sīd′trak′), v.t., v.i. **1.** to move from a main track to a siding, as a train. **2.** to move or distract from the main subject or course. —n. **3.** a railroad siding.

side·walk (sīd′wôk′), n. a usu. paved walk at the side of a roadway.

side·wall (sīd′wôl′), n. the part of a pneumatic tire between the edge of the tread and the rim of the wheel.

side·ways (sīd′wāz′), adv. **1.** with a side foremost. **2.** facing to the side. **3.** toward or from one side. **4.** obliquely; askance. —adj. **5.** moving, facing, or directed toward one side. **6.** indirect; evasive.

side·wind·er (sīd′wīn′dər), n. **1.** a punch delivered with a wide swing from the side. **2.** a rattlesnake of the southwestern U.S. and N Mexico, that moves in loose sand by raising loops on the body and displacing them sideways. **3.** HORNED VIPER.

sid·ing (sī′ding), n. **1.** a short railroad track opening onto a main track at one or both ends. **2.** Also called **weatherboard.** any of several varieties of weatherproof facing for frame buildings.

si·dle (sīd′l), v., **-dled, -dling,** n. —v.i. **1.** to move sideways or obliquely. **2.** to edge along furtively. —n. **3.** a sidling movement.

Si·don (sīd′n), n. a city of ancient Phoenicia: site of modern Saida. —Si·do′ni·an (-dō′nē ən), adj., n.

SIDS, sudden infant death syndrome.

siege (sēj), n., v., **sieged, sieg·ing.** —n. **1.** the act or process of surrounding and attacking a fortified place in such a way as to compel the surrender of the defenders. **2.** any prolonged effort to overcome resistance. **3.** a series of besetting illnesses or troubles: a siege of head colds. **4.** a prolonged period of trouble. —v.t. **5.** to assail or assault; besiege. —Idiom. **6.** lay siege to, to besiege.

si·en·na (sē en′ə), n. **1.** a ferruginous earth used as a yellowish brown pigment or, after roasting in a furnace, as a reddish brown pigment. **2.** the color of such a pigment.

si·er·ra (sē er′ə), n., pl. **-ras. 1.** a chain of hills or mountains, the peaks of which suggest the teeth of a saw. **2.** any of several Spanish mackerels of the genus Scomberomorus, esp. S. sierra. [< Spanish: lit., saw < Latin serra]

Si·er·ra Le·o·ne (sē er′ə lē ō′nē, lē ōn′), n. a republic in W Africa: member of the Commonwealth; former British colony and protectorate. 4,891,546; 27,925 sq. mi. (72,326 sq. km). Cap.: Freetown.

si·es·ta (sē es′tə), n., pl. **-tas.** a midday or afternoon rest or nap, esp. as taken in Spain and Latin America.

sieve (siv), n., v., **sieved, siev·ing.** —n. **1.** a utensil with a meshed or perforated surface, used for separating coarse from fine parts of loose matter, for straining liquids, etc. —v.t., v.i. **2.** to put or force through a sieve; sift.

sieve′ tube′, n. Bot. a vertical series of cylindrical cells in the phloem, specialized for the conduction of food materials.

sift (sift), v.t. **1.** to separate and retain the coarse parts of (flour, ashes, etc.) with a sieve. **2.** to scatter by means of a sieve: to sift sugar onto a cake. **3.** to separate by or as if by a sieve. **4.** to examine closely. —v.i. **5.** to sift something. **6.** to pass or fall through or as if through a sieve. —sift′er, n.

sigh (sī), v.i. **1.** to let out one's breath audibly, as from sorrow, weariness, or relief. **2.** to yearn or long; pine. **3.** to make a sound suggesting a sigh: sighing wind. —v.t. **4.** to express or utter with a sigh. **5.** to lament with sighing. —n. **6.** the act or sound of sighing. —sigh′er, n.

sight (sīt), n. **1.** the power or faculty of seeing; perception of objects by use of the eyes; vision. **2.** the act or fact of seeing. **3.** one's range of vision on some specific occasion. **4.** a view; glimpse. **5.** mental perception or regard; judgment. **6.** something seen or worth seeing; spectacle: the sights of London. **7.** a person or thing that is unusual, shocking, or distressing to see. **8.** Chiefly Dial. a multitude; great deal: It's a sight better to work than to starve. **9.** an observation taken with a surveying, navigating, or other instrument to ascertain an exact position or direction. **10.** any of various mechanical or optical viewing devices, as on a firearm, for aiding the eye in aiming. —v.t. **11.** to see, glimpse, notice, or observe. **12.** to take a sight or observation of, esp. with surveying or navigating instruments. **13.** to direct or aim by a sight or sights, as a firearm. **14.** to provide with sights or adjust the sights of, as a gun. —v.i. **15.** to aim or observe through a sight. **16.** to look carefully in a certain direction. —Idiom. **17.** at first sight, after only one brief glimpse: love at first sight. **18.** at sight, a. immediately upon seeing. b. on presentation: a draft payable at sight. **19.** by a long sight, (usu. with a negative) to an extreme degree: You haven't finished yet by a long sight. **20.** catch sight of, to get a glimpse of; espy. **21.** on sight, immediately upon seeing. **22.** out of sight, a. beyond one's range of vision. b. Informal. exceedingly or extravagantly high: The price is out of sight. c. Slang. (often used as an interjection) fantastic; marvelous. **23.** sight for sore eyes, someone or something whose appearance is cause for relief or gladness. **24.** sight unseen, without previous examination: We bought it sight unseen. —Proverb. **25.** Out of sight, out of mind, one easily forgets persons or things that are not personally significant or constantly noticeable. —sight′er, n.

sight·ed (sī′tid), adj. **1.** having functional vision; not blind. **2.** having a particular type of eyesight or perception (used in combination): clear-sighted.

sight′ gag′, n. a comic effect produced by visual means rather than by spoken lines, as in a motion picture.

sight·less (sīt′lis), adj. **1.** unable to see; blind. **2.** invisible. —sight′-less·ly, adv. —sight′less·ness, n.

sight·ly (sīt′lē), adj., **-li·er, -li·est. 1.** pleasing to the sight; attractive; comely. **2.** affording a fine view. —sight′li·ness, n.

sight′-read′ (rēd), v.t., v.i., **-read** (red), **-read·ing.** to read, play, or sing without previous practice, rehearsal, or study of the material to be treated: to sight-read music. —sight′-read′er, n.

sight·see (sīt′sē′), v.i. to go about seeing places and things of interest: In Rome, we only had two days to sightsee. —sight′se·er, n.

sight·see·ing (sīt′sē′ing), n. **1.** the act of visiting and seeing places and things of interest. —adj. **2.** seeing, showing, or used for visiting sights: a sightseeing bus.

sign (sīn), n. **1.** a token; indication: Bowing is a sign of respect. **2.** a conventional figure or symbol used as an abbreviation for the word or words it represents. **3.** a gesture used to express or convey information, an idea, etc. **4.** an inscribed board, placard, or the like bearing a warning, advertisement, etc., and displayed for public view: a traffic sign. **5.** a trace; vestige. **6.** Usu., **signs,** traces, as footprints, of a wild animal. **7.** an omen; portent. **8.** an arbitrary or conventional symbol used in musical notation to indicate tonality, tempo, etc. **9.** an objective indication of a disease. **10.** any meaningful gestural unit belonging to a sign language. **11.** SIGN LANGUAGE (def. 1). **12.** SIGN OF THE ZODIAC. **13.** a symbol, as + or =, used to indicate a mathematical operation or relation. —v.t. **14.** to affix a signature to: to sign a letter. **15.** to write as a signature: to sign one's name. **16.** to engage or hire by written agreement (often fol. by on or up). **17.** to mark with a sign, esp. the sign of the cross. **18.** to communicate by means of a sign; signal. **19.** to convey (a message) in a sign language. —v.i. **20.** to write one's signature, as a token of agreement, receipt, etc. **21.** to make a sign or signal. **22.** to employ a sign language for communication. **23.** to obligate oneself by signature. **24. sign away** or **over,** to assign or dispose of by affixing one's signature to a document. **25. sign in** (or **out**), to record one's arrival (or departure) by signing a register. **26. sign off, a.** to cease radio or television broadcasting, esp. at the end of the day. **b.** to indicate one's approval explicitly if not formally. **27. sign up,** to enlist, as in an organization: to sign up for the navy. —Idiom. **28. sign of the times,** a typical or characteristic feature of the present. —sign′er, n.

sig·nal (sig′nl), n., adj., v., **-naled, -nal·ing** or (esp. Brit.) **-nalled, -nal·ling.** —n. **1.** anything that serves to indicate, warn, direct, command, or the like, as a light, a gesture, or an act. **2.** anything agreed upon or understood as the occasion for concerted action. **3.** an act, event, or the like that causes or incites some action. **4.** a token; indication. **5.** an electrical quantity or effect, as current, voltage, or electromagnetic waves, that can be varied in such a way as to convey information. **6.** (in cards) a play indicating to one's partner to continue or discontinue the suit led. —adj. **7.** serving as a signal. **8.** unusual; notable; outstanding. —v.t. **9.** to make a signal to. **10.** to communicate or make known by a signal. —v.i. **11.** to make communication by a signal or signals.

sig′nal corps′, n. (often caps.) a branch of the army responsible for military communications, meteorological studies, and related work.

sig·nal·ize (sig′nl īz′), v.t., **-ized, -iz·ing. 1.** to make notable or conspicuous. **2.** to point out or indicate particularly.

sig·nal·man (sig′nl mən), n., pl. **-men.** a person whose occupation or duty is signaling, as on a railroad or in the army.

sig·na·to·ry (sig′nə tôr′ē, -tōr′ē), adj., n., pl. **-ries.** —adj. **1.** having signed, or joined in signing, a document: the signatory powers to a treaty. —n. **2.** the signer, or one of the signers, of a document: The U.S. and British delegates were among the signatories.

sig·na·ture (sig′nə chər, -choor′), n. **1.** a person's name, or a mark representing it, as signed personally or by deputy, as in subscribing a letter or other document. **2.** the act of signing a document. **3.** Music. a sign or set of signs at the beginning of a staff to indicate the key or the time of a piece. **4.** a song, musical arrangement, etc., used as a theme identifying a radio or television program. **5.** any unique, distinguishing feature or mark. **6.** a printed sheet folded to page size for binding together, with other such sheets, to form a book, magazine, etc. —adj. **7.** serving to identify or distinguish a person, group, etc.: a signature tune.

sign·board (sīn′bôrd′, -bōrd′), n. a board bearing a sign, as an advertisement.

sign·ee (sī nē′, sī′nē), n. a person who signs a document, register, etc.

sig·net (sig′nit), n. **1.** a small seal, as on a finger ring. **2.** a small official seal for legal documents, contracts, etc. **3.** an impression made by or as if by a signet. —v.t. **4.** to stamp or mark with a signet.

sig′net ring′, n. a finger ring containing a small seal, one's initial, or the like.

sig·nif·i·cance (sig nif′i kəns), n. **1.** importance; consequence. **2.** meaning; import. **3.** the quality of being significant or meaningful. Sometimes, **sig·nif′i·can·cy.**

sig·nif·i·cant (sig nif′i kənt), adj. **1.** important; of consequence. **2.** having or expressing a meaning. **3.** having a special, secret, or disguised meaning: a significant wink. —n. **4.** something significant; a sign. —sig·nif′i·cant·ly, adv.

signif′icant oth′er, n. **1.** a person, as a parent or peer, who has great influence on one's behavior and self-esteem. **2.** a spouse or cohabiting lover.

sig·ni·fi·ca·tion (sig′nə fi kā′shən), n. **1.** meaning; import; sense. **2.** the act of signifying; indication.

sig·nif·i·ca·tive (sig nif′i kā′tiv), *adj.* **1.** serving to signify. **2.** significant; suggestive. —**sig·nif′i·ca′tive·ly,** *adv.*

sig·ni·fy (sig′nə fī′), *v.,* **-fied, -fy·ing.** —*v.t.* **1.** to make known by signs, speech, or action. **2.** to be a sign of; mean; portend. —*v.i.* **3.** to be of importance or consequence. —**sig·ni′fi·a·ble,** *adj.*

sig·ni·fy·ing (sig′nə fī′ing), *n.* a game or playful confrontation, as playing the dozens, in which witty insults are exchanged.

sign′ lan′guage, *n.* **1.** any of several visual-gestural systems of communication, esp. employing manual gestures, as used among deaf people. **2.** any means of communication, as between speakers of different languages, using gestures.

sign′ of the cross′, *n.* a movement of the hand to indicate a cross, as from forehead to breast and left shoulder to right or, in the Eastern Orthodox Church, from right shoulder to left.

sign′ of the zo′diac, *n.* **1.** one of the 12 constellations along the path of the ecliptic. **2.** (in contemporary Western astrology) one of the 12 divisions of the ecliptic, each consisting of 30 degrees, marked off from the point of the vernal equinox.

sign·post (sīn′pōst′), *n.* **1.** a post bearing a sign that gives information or guidance. **2.** any immediately perceptible indication, obvious clue, etc.

Si·hon (sī′hon), *n.* a king of the Amorites who was defeated by the Israelites. Num. 21:21–32.

Sikh (sēk), *n.* **1.** a member of a monotheistic religion, founded in the Punjab c1500 by the guru Nanak, that refuses to recognize the Hindu caste system and forbids magic, idolatry, and pilgrimages. —*adj.* **2.** of or pertaining to the Sikhs or to Sikhism.

Sikh·ism (sē′kiz əm), *n.* the religion of the Sikhs.

Si·kor·sky (si kôr′skē), *n.* **Igor,** 1889–1972, U.S. aeronautical engineer, born in Russia.

si·lage (sī′lij), *n.* fodder preserved through fermentation in a silo; ensilage.

Si·las (sī′ləs), *n.* a prophet who accompanied Barnabas and the Apostle Paul to Antioch. Acts 15:22–35.

si·lence (sī′ləns), *n., v.,* **-lenced, -lenc·ing,** *interj.* —*n.* **1.** absence of any sound or noise; stillness. **2.** the state of being silent. **3.** absence or omission of mention or comment. **4.** the state of being forgotten; oblivion. **5.** concealment; secrecy. —*v.t.* **6.** to bring to silence; still. **7.** to put (doubts, fears, etc.) to rest; quiet. —*interj.* **8.** be silent!

si·lenc·er (sī′lən sər), *n.* **1.** a person or thing that silences. **2.** a device for deadening the report of a firearm.

si·lent (sī′lənt), *adj.* **1.** making no sound; quiet; still. **2.** refraining from speech. **3.** speechless; mute. **4.** not inclined to speak. **5.** characterized by absence of speech or sound: *silent prayers.* **6.** unspoken; tacit: *a silent assent.* **7.** omitting mention of something, as in a narrative: *The records are silent about his crime.* **8.** inactive or quiescent, as a volcano. **9.** (of a film) not pronounced, as the *b* in *doubt.* **10.** (of a film) not having a soundtrack. **11.** producing no detectable symptoms: *silent heart irregularities.* —*n.* **12.** Usu., **silents.** silent films. —**si′lent·ly,** *adv.*

Si′lent Cal′ (kal), *n.* nickname of Calvin Coolidge.

si′lent major′ity, *n.* the majority of a country's citizens, regarded as not politically vocal, outspoken, or active.

Si′lent Night′! Ho′ly Night′!, a Christmas hymn (1818) with words by Joseph Mohr and music by Franz Gruber.

si′lent part′ner, *n.* a partner taking or allowed no active part in the conduct of a business.

si′lent vote′, *n.* the vote of persons who have not previously expressed or made evident a preference.

sil·hou·ette (sil′ōō et′), *n., v.,* **-et·ted, -et·ting.** —*n.* **1.** a two-dimensional representation of the outline of an object, as a person's profile, filled in with black or another color. **2.** the outline or general shape of something. **3.** a dark image outlined against a lighter background. —*v.t.* **4.** to show in or as if in a silhouette.

silhouette (def. 1)

sil·i·ca (sil′i kə), *n.* the dioxide form of silicon, SiO$_2$, occurring esp. as quartz sand, flint, and agate: used chiefly in the manufacture of glass, water glass, ceramics, and abrasives. Also called **silicon dioxide.**

sil′ica gel′, *n.* a highly adsorbent gelatinous form of silica, used chiefly as a dehumidifying and dehydrating agent.

sil·i·cate (sil′i kit, -kāt′), *n.* **1.** any of the largest group of minerals, as quartz, olivine, pyroxene, amphibole, mica, clay, and feldspar, consisting of silicon and oxygen with one or more metals: the basic building block is the silica tetrahedron, SiO$_4$. **2.** any salt derived from the silicic acids or from silica. —**sil′i·ca′tion,** *n.*

si·li·ceous or **si·li·cious** (sə lish′əs), *adj.* containing, consisting of, or resembling silica.

silic′ic ac′id, *n.* any of certain amorphous gelatinous masses, formed when alkaline silicates are treated with acids, used as a laboratory reagent.

sil·i·con (sil′i kən, -kon′), *n.* a nonmetallic element, having amorphous and crystalline forms, occurring in a combined state in minerals and rocks and constituting more than one fourth of the earth's crust: used in steelmaking, alloys, etc. *Symbol:* Si; *at. wt.:* 28.086; *at. no.:* 14; *sp. gr.:* 2.4 at 20°C.

sil′icon car′bide, *n.* a very hard, insoluble, crystalline compound, SiC, used as an abrasive and as an electrical resistor in objects exposed to high temperatures.

sil′icon diox′ide, *n.* SILICA.

sil·i·cone (sil′i kōn′), *n.* any of a number of polymers containing alternate silicon and oxygen atoms, whose properties are determined by the organic groups attached to the silicon atoms, and that are fluid, resinous, rubbery, extremely stable in high temperatures, and water-repellent: used as adhesives, lubricants, and hydraulic oils.

Sil′icon Val′ley, *n.* an area in N California, in the Santa Clara valley region, where many high-technology companies are located.

silk (silk), *n.* **1.** the soft, lustrous fiber obtained as a filament from the cocoon of the silkworm. **2.** thread or cloth made from this fiber. **3. silks,** the blouse and peaked cap, considered together, worn by a jockey or sulky driver. **4.** any fiber or filamentous matter resembling silk, as a filament produced by certain spiders. **5.** the hairlike styles on an ear of corn. —*adj.* **6.** made of silk. **7.** of, pertaining to, or resembling silk. —*v.i.* **8.** (of corn) to be in the course of developing silk. —*Idiom.* **9. hit the silk,** *Slang.* to parachute from an aircraft.

silk·en (sil′kən), *adj.* **1.** made of silk. **2.** like silk in appearance or texture. **3.** clad in silk. **4.** smoothly persuasive or ingratiating. **5.** elegant; luxurious.

silk·screen (silk′skrēn′), *n.* **1.** Also called **silk′screen proc′ess.** a printmaking technique in which a mesh cloth is stretched over a heavy wooden frame and the design, painted on the screen by tusche or affixed by stencil, is printed by having a squeegee force color through the pores of the material in areas not blocked out by a glue sizing. **2.** a print made by this technique. —*v.t.* **3.** to print by silkscreen.

silk′-stock′ing, *adj.* **1.** aristocratic or wealthy: *a silk-stocking district.* **2.** rich or luxurious in dress. —*n.* **3.** an aristocratic or wealthy person. **4.** a person who dresses richly or luxuriously.

silk·worm (silk′wûrm′), *n.* any of several moth caterpillars that spin a silken cocoon, esp. *Bombyx mori,* of China, which produces commercially valuable silk.

silk′worm moth′, *n.* any of several moths of the families Bombycidae and Saturniidae, the caterpillars of which are silkworms.

silk·y (sil′kē), *adj.,* **-i·er, -i·est.** **1.** of or like silk; smooth, lustrous, soft, or delicate: *silky skin.* **2.** covered with fine, soft, closely set hairs, as a leaf. —**silk′i·ly,** *adv.* —**silk′i·ness,** *n.*

silk′y ter′rier, *n.* one of an Australian breed of toy dogs with erect ears, a long, silky blue coat with tan markings, and a topknot.

sill (sil), *n.* **1.** a horizontal piece or member beneath a window, door, or other opening. **2.** a horizontal timber, block, etc., serving as a foundation of a wall, house, etc. **3.** a tabular body of intrusive igneous rock, ordinarily between beds of sedimentary rocks or layers of volcanic ejecta.

sil·la·bub (sil′ə bub′), *n.* SYLLABUB.

sil·ly (sil′ē), *adj.,* **-li·er, -li·est,** *n., pl.* **-lies.** —*adj.* **1.** weak-minded or lacking good sense; stupid or foolish. **2.** absurd; ridiculous; nonsensical. **3.** stunned; dazed: *He knocked me silly.* —*n.* **4.** *Informal.* a silly or foolish person. —**sil′li·ly,** *adv.* —**sil′li·ness,** *n.*

sil′ly sea′son, *n.* a time of year, usually in midsummer or during a holiday period, characterized by exaggerated news stories, frivolous entertainments, outlandish publicity stunts, etc.: *The new movie reminds us that the silly season is here.*

si·lo (sī′lō), *n., v.* **-loed, -loing** —*n.* **1.** a structure, typically cylindrical, in which fodder or forage is kept. **2.** a pit or underground space for storing grain, green feeds, etc. **3.** an underground installation constructed of concrete and steel, designed to house a ballistic missile. —*v.t.* **4.** to put into or preserve in a silo.

Si·lo·am (si lō′əm, sī-), *n.* a spring near Jerusalem. John 9:7.

silt (silt), *n.* **1.** earthy matter, fine sand, or the like carried by moving or running water and deposited as a sediment. —*v.i.* **2.** to become filled or choked up with silt. —*v.t.* **3.** to fill or choke up with silt. —**sil·ta′tion,** *n.* —**silt′y,** *adj.*

Si·lu·ri·an (si lŏŏr′ē ən, sī-), *adj.* **1.** of or designating a period of the Paleozoic Era, occurring from 425 million to 405 million years ago, marked by the advent of air-breathing animals and terrestrial plants. —*n.* **2.** the Silurian Period or System.

sil·van (sil′vən), *adj.* SYLVAN.

sil·ver (sil′vər), *n.* **1.** a white, ductile metallic element, used for making mirrors, coins, ornaments, table utensils, photographic chemicals, and conductors. *Symbol:* Ag; *at. wt.:* 107.870; *at. no.:* 47; *sp. gr.:* 10.5 at 20°C. **2.** coins made of this metal; specie; money: *a handful of silver.* **3.** this metal as a commodity or considered as a currency standard. **4.** table articles, as flatware, made of or plated with silver. **5.** flatware made of any metal. **6.** something resembling this metal in color, luster, etc. **7.** a lustrous grayish white or whitish gray. **8.** SILVER MEDAL. —*adj.* **9.** made of or plated with silver. **10.** of or pertaining to silver. **11.** producing or yielding silver. **12.** of the color silver; silvery. **13.** clear, soft, and ringing: *silver sounds.* **14.** eloquent; persuasive: *a silver tongue.* **15.** indicating the twenty-fifth event of a series, as a wedding anniversary. **16.** urging the use of silver as a currency standard. —*v.t.* **17.** to coat with silver or some silverlike substance. **18.** to give a silvery color to. —*v.i.* **19.** to become a silvery color. —*Idiom.* **20. thirty pieces of silver,** payment for a betrayal. Matt. 26:14–16. —**sil′ver•er,** *n.*

sil•ver•back (sil′vər bak′), *n.* an older male gorilla, usu. the leader of a troop, whose hairs along the back have turned gray.

sil•ver•ber•ry (sil′vər ber′ē), *n., pl.* **-ries.** a North American shrub, *Elaeagnus commutata* (or *E. argentea*), of the oleaster family, with silvery leaves and silvery berries.

sil′ver certif′icate, *n.* a former U.S. paper currency first issued in 1878, equal to and redeemable for silver to a stated value.

sil′ver chlo′ride, *n.* a white powder, AgCl, that darkens on exposure to light: used chiefly in photographic emulsions.

sil•ver•fish (sil′vər fish′), *n., pl.* (*esp. collectively*) **-fish,** (*esp. for kinds or species*) **-fish•es. 1.** any of various silvery fishes, as the tarpon or silversides. **2.** a wingless, silvery-gray insect, *Lepisma saccharina,* that feeds on starch, damaging books, wallpaper, etc.

sil′ver fox′, *n.* a red fox in the color phase in which the blackish fur has silver-gray tips.

sil′ver hake′, *n.* a common hake, *Merluccius bilinearis,* inhabiting Atlantic coastal waters of North America: valued as a food fish.

sil•ver•ing (sil′vər ing), *n.* **1.** a coating of silver or a silverlike substance. **2.** the act or process of coating with silver or a substance resembling silver. **3.** a silvery appearance or silvery highlights.

sil′ver i′odide, *n.* a pale yellow solid, AgI, that darkens on exposure to light: used chiefly in medicine, photography, and artificial rainmaking.

sil′ver lin′ing, *n.* a prospect of hope or comfort in an unfortunate or gloomy situation.

sil′ver ma′ple, *n.* **1.** a maple, *Acer saccharinum,* having leaves that are light green above and silvery white beneath. **2.** the hard, close-grained wood of this tree.

sil′ver med′al, *n.* a medal, traditionally of silver, awarded to a person or team finishing second in a competition. Compare BRONZE MEDAL, GOLD MEDAL. —**sil′ver med′alist,** *n.*

sil′ver perch′, *n.* **1.** Also called **mademoiselle.** a drum, *Bairdiella chrysoura,* of southern U.S. waters. **2.** any of various silvery, perchlike fishes, as the white perch.

sil′ver plate′, *n.* **1.** silver or silver-plated tableware. **2.** a coating of silver, esp. one electroplated on base metal. —**sil′ver-plate′,** *v.t.,* **-plat•ed, -plat•ing.**

sil′ver screen′, *n.* motion pictures; the motion-picture industry.

sil•ver•sides (sil′vər sīdz′), *n., pl.* **-sides.** any small fish of the worldwide family Atherinidae, having a silvery sheen, as *Menidia menidia,* of U.S. Atlantic coastal waters.

sil•ver•smith (sil′vər smith′), *n.* a person who makes and repairs articles of silver. —**sil•ver•smith′ing,** *n.*

sil•ver•ware (sil′vər wâr′), *n.* articles, esp. eating and serving utensils, made of silver, silver-plated metals, stainless steel, etc.

sil•ver•weed (sil′vər wēd′), *n.* **1.** a plant, *Potentilla anserina,* of the rose family, the leaves of which are silvery beneath. **2.** any tropical climbing plant of the genus *Argyreia* of the morning glory family having silvery leaves.

sil•ver•y (sil′və rē), *adj.* **1.** resembling silver; of a lustrous grayish white color. **2.** having a clear, ringing sound: *the silvery peal of bells.* **3.** containing or covered with silver. —**sil′ver•i•ness,** *n.*

Sim•e•on (sim′ē ən), *n.* **1.** a son of Jacob and Leah. Gen. 29:33. **2.** one of the 12 tribes of Israel, traditionally descended from him.

Sim′eon Sty•li′tes (stī lī′tēz), *n.* **Saint,** A.D. 390?–459, Syrian monk and stylite.

si•meth•i•cone (sī meth′i kōn′), *n.* an active ingredient in many antacid preparations that causes small mucus-entrapped air bubbles in the intestines to coalesce into larger bubbles that are more easily passed.

Sim•hath (or **Sim•chath**) **To•rah** (sim′KHäs tôr′ə, tōr′ə; *Heb.* sēm-KHät′ tô rä′) a Jewish festival, celebrated on the 23rd day of Tishri, being the 9th day of Sukkoth, that marks the completion of the annual cycle of the reading of the Torah in the synagogue and the beginning of the new cycle.

sim•i•an (sim′ē ən), *adj.* **1.** of, pertaining to, or characteristic of an ape or monkey. —*n.* **2.** an ape or monkey.

sim•i•lar (sim′ə lər), *adj.* **1.** having a likeness or resemblance, esp. in a general way; having qualities in common: *two similar houses.* **2.** (of geometric figures) having the same shape; having corresponding sides proportional and corresponding angles equal: *similar triangles.* —**sim′i•lar•ly,** *adv.*

sim•i•lar•i•ty (sim′ə lar′i tē), *n., pl.* **-ties. 1.** the state of being similar; likeness; resemblance. **2.** an aspect or feature like or resembling another: *similarities in their behavior.*

sim•i•le (sim′ə lē), *n.* a figure of speech in which two distinct things are compared by using "like" or "as," as in "She is like a rose." Compare METAPHOR. [< Latin: image, likeness]

si•mil•i•tude (si mil′i tōōd′, -tyōōd′), *n.* **1.** likeness; resemblance. **2.** a person or thing that is like or the counterpart of another. **3.** semblance; image. **4.** a likening or comparison; a simile, parable, or allegory.

Si•mi′ Val′ley (si mē′, sē′mē), *n.* a city in SW California. 106,949.

Sim•men•tal or **Sim•men•thal** (zim′ən täl′), also **Sim•men•tha•**

ler (-tä′lər), *n.* one of a large breed of cattle, yellowish brown to red and white, orig. of Switzerland, used for milk and beef.

sim•mer (sim′ər), *v.i.* **1.** to cook just at or below the boiling point. **2.** to be in a state of subdued or restrained activity, development, excitement, anger, etc. —*v.t.* **3.** to keep (liquid) in a state approaching boiling. **4.** to cook in a liquid kept just at or below the boiling point. **5. simmer down, a.** to become calm or quiet. **b.** to reduce in volume by simmering. —*n.* **6.** the state or process of simmering. —**sim′mer•ing•ly,** *adv.*

Si•mon¹ (sī′mən), *n.* **1.** the original name of the apostle Peter. Compare PETER¹ (def. 1). **2.** ("Simon the Canaanite" or "Simon the Zealot") one of the 12 apostles. Matt. 10:4; Mark 3:18; Luke 6:15. **3.** a relative, perhaps a brother, of Jesus: sometimes identified with Simon the Canaanite. Matt. 13:55; Mark 6:3. **4.** ("Simon Magus") a Samaritan sorcerer who was converted by the apostle Philip. Acts 8:9–24. **5.** ("Simon Magus") fl. 2nd century A.D.?, founder of a Gnostic sect and reputed prototype of the Faust legend: often identified with the Biblical Simon Magus.

Si•mon² (sī′mən; *Fr.* sē môn′ *for* 1), *n.* **1. Claude,** born 1913, French novelist. **2. Herbert Alexander,** born 1916, U.S. social scientist and economist. **3. Neil,** born 1927, U.S. playwright. **4. Paul,** born 1942, U.S. singer, songwriter, and actor.

si•mon•ize (sī′mə nīz′), *v.t.,* **-ized, -iz•ing.** to shine or polish to a high sheen, esp. with wax. [after *Simoniz,* trademark of an automobile wax]

Si′mon Le•gree′ (li grē′), *n.* **1.** a brutal slave dealer in the novel *Uncle Tom's Cabin,* by H. B. Stowe. **2.** any harsh, merciless taskmaster.

Si′mon Pe′ter, *n.* PETER¹ (def. 1).

sim•pa•ti•co (sim pä′ti kō′, -pat′i-), *adj.* congenial or like-minded; likable.

sim•ple (sim′pəl), *adj.,* **-pler, -plest,** *n.* —*adj.* **1.** easy to understand or deal with. **2.** not elaborate or complicated; plain; unembellished: *a simple design.* **3.** not ornate or luxurious; unadorned: *a simple dress.* **4.** unaffected; unassuming; modest. **5.** occurring or considered alone; mere; bare: *the simple truth.* **6.** free of deceit or guile; sincere; artless. **7.** common or ordinary: *a simple soldier.* **8.** not grand or sophisticated; unpretentious: *simple tastes.* **9.** humble or lowly: *simple folk.* **10.** unlearned; ignorant. **11.** lacking mental acuteness or sense. **12.** naive; credulous. **13.** mentally deficient; simpleminded. **14.** *Chem.* **a.** composed of only one substance or element: *a simple substance.* **b.** not mixed. **15.** *Bot.* not divided into parts: *a simple leaf.* **16.** *Zool.* not compound: *a simple ascidian.* **17. a.** (of a subject or predicate) having only the head without modifying elements included. Compare COMPLETE (def. 5). **b.** (of a verb tense) consisting of a main verb with no auxiliaries, as *takes* (simple present) or *stood* (simple past) (opposed to *compound*). **18.** *Math.* LINEAR (def. 7). **19.** (of a lens) having two optical surfaces only. —*n.* **20.** an ignorant, foolish, or gullible person. **21.** something simple, unmixed, or uncompounded. **22.** a person of humble origins; commoner. **23.** an herb or other plant used for medicinal purposes: *country simples.*

sim′ple frac′ture, *n.* a fracture in which the bone does not pierce the skin.

sim′ple fruit′, *n.* a fruit formed from one pistil.

sim′ple in′terest, *n.* interest payable only on the principal and not compounded.

sim′ple machine′, *n.* MACHINE (def. 2b).

sim•ple•mind•ed or **sim′ple-mind′ed,** *adj.* **1.** lacking in mental acuteness or sense. **2.** lacking in complexity or subtlety of thought. **3.** mentally deficient; feeble-minded. **4.** artless or unsophisticated. —**sim′ple•mind′ed•ly,** *adv.* —**sim′ple•mind′ed•ness,** *n.*

sim′ple sen′tence, *n.* a sentence having only one clause, as *I saw her the day before yesterday.* Compare COMPLEX SENTENCE, COMPOUND SENTENCE.

Sim′ple Si′mon, *n.* a simpleton. [after the nursery rhyme character]

sim′ple sug′ar, *n.* a monosaccharide.

sim•ple•ton (sim′pəl tən), *n.* an ignorant, foolish, or silly person.

sim•plex (sim′pleks), *adj.* (-ple sēs′). **1.** consisting of or characterized by a single element; simple. **2.** of or designating a telecommunications system permitting communication in only one direction at a time.

sim•plic•i•ty (sim plis′i tē), *n., pl.* **-ties. 1.** the state, quality, or an instance of being simple. **2.** freedom from complexity or intricacy. **3.** absence of luxury, pretentiousness, ornament, etc. **4.** freedom from deceit or guile; artlessness. **5.** lack of mental acuteness or shrewdness.

sim•pli•fy (sim′plə fī′), *v.t.,* **-fied, -fy•ing.** to make simple or simpler; make less complex, less complicated, plainer, or easier. —**sim′pli•fi•ca′tion,** *n.* —**sim′pli•fi′er,** *n.*

sim•plis•tic (sim plis′tik), *adj.* characterized by excessive simplification, esp. in ignoring complexities or subtleties; oversimplified. —**sim•plis′ti•cal•ly,** *adv.*

sim•ply (sim′plē), *adv.* **1.** in a simple manner; clearly. **2.** plainly; unaffectedly. **3.** sincerely; artlessly. **4.** merely; only: *It is simply a cold.* **5.** naively; foolishly. **6.** absolutely; really: *simply irresistible.*

Simp•son (simp′sən), *n.* **Albert Benjamin,** 1844–1919, U.S. clergyman, founder of the Christian and Missionary Alliance.

sim•u•late (sim′yə lāt′), *v.t.,* **-lat•ed, -lat•ing. 1.** to create a simulation or model of: *to simulate crisis conditions.* **2.** to make a pretense of; feign: *to simulate illness.* **3.** to assume or have the appearance or characteristics of: *simulated leather.* —**sim′u•la•tive,** *adj.* —**sim′u•la′-tive•ly,** *adv.*

sim•u•la•tion (sim′yə lā′shən), *n.* **1.** imitation or enactment, as of conditions anticipated. **2.** the act or process of pretending; feigning. **3.** an assumption or imitation of a particular appearance or form; counterfeit. **4.** the representation of the behavior or characteristics of one system through the use of another system, esp. using a computer. **5.** a conscious attempt to feign some mental or physical disorder.

sim•u•la•tor (sim′yə lā′tər), *n.* **1.** a person or thing that simulates. **2.** a machine that simulates environmental and other conditions for purposes of training or experimentation: *a flight simulator.*

si•mul•cast (sī′məl kast′, -käst′, sim′əl-), *n.* **1.** a program broadcast simultaneously on radio and television, or on more than one station, or in several languages, etc. **2.** a closed-circuit television broadcast of an event while it is taking place. —*v.t., v.i.* **3.** to broadcast in this manner.

si•mul•ta•ne•ous (sī′məl tā′nē əs, sim′əl-), *adj.* existing, occurring, or operating at the same time; concurrent. —**si′mul•ta′ne•ous•ly,** *adv.* —**si′mul•ta•ne′i•ty** (-tə nē′i tē), *n.*

sin (sin), *n., v.,* **sinned, sin•ning.** —*n.* **1.** transgression of divine law. **2.** any act regarded as such a transgression, esp. a willful violation of some religious or moral principle. **3.** any reprehensible action; serious fault or offense. —*v.i.* **4.** to commit a sinful act. **5.** to offend against a principle, standard, etc. —**sin′like′,** *adj.*

Si•nai (sī′nī, sī′nē ī′), *n.* **1.** Also called **Si′nai Penin′sula.** a peninsula in NE Egypt, at the N end of the Red Sea between the Gulf of Suez and the Gulf of Aqaba. **2. Mount,** the mountain, of uncertain identity, on which Moses received the Law. Ex. 19. —**Si′na•it′ic** (-nē it′ik), **Si•na•ic** (si nā′ik), *adj.*

Si•na•tra (si nä′trə), *n.* **Frank** (*Francis Albert*), born 1915, U.S. singer.

Sin•bad (sin′bad), *n.* SINDBAD.

since (sins), *adv.* **1.** from then till now (often prec. by *ever*): *Those elected in 1990 have been on the committee ever since.* **2.** between a particular past time and the present; subsequently: *She at first refused, but has since consented.* **3.** ago; before now: *long since.* —*prep.* **4.** continuously from or counting from: *It has been raining since noon.* **5.** between a past time or event and the present: *There have been many changes since the war.* —*conj.* **6.** in the period following the time when: *He has written once since he left.* **7.** continuously from or counting from the time when: *I've been busy since I arrived.* **8.** because; inasmuch as. —**Usage.** See AS[1].

sin•cere (sin sēr′), *adj.,* **-cer•er, -cer•est.** **1.** free of deceit, hypocrisy, or falseness: *a sincere apology.* **2.** genuine; real: *a sincere effort to improve.* **3.** pure; unmixed. —**sin•cere′ly,** *adv.*

sin•cer•i•ty (sin ser′i tē), *n., pl.* **-ties.** freedom from deceit, hypocrisy, or falseness; earnestness; probity.

Sind•bad (sin′bad, sind′-) also **Sinbad,** *n.* (in *The Arabian Nights' Entertainments*) a citizen of Baghdad who acquired great wealth in the course of seven fantastic voyages.

sine (sīn), *n.* a fundamental trigonometric function that, in a right triangle, is expressed as the ratio of the length of the side opposite an acute angle to the length of the hypotenuse. *Abbr.:* sin

si•ne•cure (sī′ni kyŏŏr′, sin′i-), *n.* an office or position requiring little or no work, esp. one yielding profitable returns.

si•ne qua non (sin′ā kwä nōn′, non′, kwā), *n.* an indispensable or essential condition, element, or factor.

sin•ew (sin′yōō), *n.* **1.** a tendon. **2.** Often, **sinews.** a source of strength, power, or vigor: *the sinews of the nation.* **3.** strength; power; resilience: *great moral sinew.* —*v.t.* **4.** to strengthen, as with sinews.

sin•ew•y (sin′yōō ē), *adj.* **1.** having strong or conspicuous sinews: *a sinewy back.* **2.** tough; firm: *a sinewy rope.* **3.** containing many sinews; stringy: *tough, sinewy meat.* **4.** vigorous or forceful, as language or style. —**sin′ew•i•ness,** *n.*

sin•ful (sin′fəl), *adj.* characterized by, guilty of, or full of sin; wicked; immoral. —**sin′ful•ly,** *adv.* —**sin′ful•ness,** *n.*

sing (sing), *v.,* **sang** or, often, **sung, sung, sing•ing,** *n.* —*v.i.* **1.** to utter words or sounds in succession with musical modulations of the voice; vocalize melodically. **2.** to perform songs or voice compositions. **3.** (of an animal) to produce a patterned vocal signal, as in courtship or territorial display. **4.** to tell about or praise someone or something in verse or song. **5.** to admit of being sung, as verses. **6.** to make a whistling, ringing, or whizzing sound. **7.** to give out a continuous murmuring, burbling, or other euphonious sound. **8.** to have the sensation of a ringing or humming sound, as the ears. **9.** *Slang.* to confess or act as an informer; squeal. —*v.t.* **10.** to utter with musical modulations of the voice, as a song. **11.** to proclaim enthusiastically. **12.** to bring, send, put, etc., with or by singing. **13.** to chant or intone: *to sing mass.* **14.** to escort or accompany with singing. **15.** to tell or praise in verse or song. **16. sing out,** to call in a loud voice; shout. —*n.* **17.** a gathering or meeting of people for the purpose of singing: *a community sing.* **18.** a singing, ringing, or whistling sound. —**sing′a•ble,** *adj.*

sing′-along′, *n.* SONGFEST.

Sin•ga•pore (sing′gə pôr′, -pōr′, sing′ə-), *n.* **1.** an island off the S tip of the Malay Peninsula. **2.** a republic comprising this and adjacent islets: member of the Commonwealth; formerly a British crown colony (1946–59) and a state of Malaysia (1963–65); independent since 1965. 3,461,929; 247 sq. mi. (639 sq. km). **3.** the capital of this republic, a port on the S coast. 206,500. —**Sin′ga•po′re•an,** *adj., n.*

singe (sinj), *v.,* **singed, singe•ing,** *n.* —*v.t.* **1.** to burn superficially or slightly; scorch. **2.** to burn the ends, nap, or the like, of (hair, cloth, etc.). **3.** to subject (a carcass) to flame in order to remove hair, bristles, feathers, etc. —*n.* **4.** a superficial burn. **5.** the act of singeing. —**singe′ing•ly,** *adv.*

sing•er (sing′ər), *n.* **1.** a person who sings, esp. a trained or professional vocalist. **2.** a poet. **3.** a singing bird.

Singh (siɴ′hᵊ), *n.* **Sadhu Sundar,** 1889–1929, Sikh Christian evangelist in India.

sin•gle (sing′gəl), *adj., v.,* **-gled, -gling,** *n.* —*adj.* **1.** only one in number; one only; unique; sole: *a single example.* **2.** of, pertaining to, or suitable for one person only: *a single room.* **3.** solitary or sole; lone: *He was the single survivor.* **4.** unmarried: *a single man.* **5.** pertaining to the unmarried state. **6.** of one against one: *single combat.* **7.** consisting of only one part, element, or member: *a single lens.* **8.** separate, particular, or distinct; individual: *every single one of you.* **9.** uniform; applicable to all. **10.** sincere and undivided: *single devotion.* **11.** (of a bed or bedclothes) twin-size. **12.** (of a flower) having only one set of petals. **13.** (of the eye) seeing rightly. —*v.t.* **14.** to pick or choose (one) from others (usu. fol. by *out*). **15.** (in baseball) **a.** to advance (a base runner) by a single. **b.** to cause (a run) to be scored by a single. —*v.i.* **16.** to hit a single in baseball. —*n.* **17.** one person or thing; a single one; individual. **18.** an accommodation, ticket, etc., for one person only. **19.** an unmarried person. **20.** a one-dollar bill. **21. a.** a phonograph record, compact disc, or audio tape, usu. with one popular song. **b.** a song so recorded. **22.** (in baseball) a base hit that enables a batter to reach first base safely. **23. singles,** (*used with a sing. v.*) a match with one player on each side, as a tennis match. **24.** *Golf.* TWOSOME (def. 4).

sin′gle-act′ing, *adj.* (of a reciprocating engine, pump, etc.) having pistons accomplishing work only in one direction.

sin′gle-ac′tion, *adj.* (of a firearm) requiring the cocking of the hammer before firing each shot.

sin′gle bond′, *n.* a chemical linkage consisting of one covalent bond between two atoms of a molecule, represented in chemical formulas by one line or two vertical dots, as C–H or C:H.

sin′gle-breast′ed, *adj.* **1.** (of a coat, jacket, etc.) having a front closure directly in the center with only a narrow overlap secured by a single button or row of buttons. **2.** (of a suit) having a jacket or coat of this type. Compare DOUBLE-BREASTED.

sin′gle cross′, *n.* *Genetics.* a first-generation hybrid produced by a cross between two inbred lines.

sin′gle-dig′it, *adj.* of a percentage smaller than ten: *single-digit inflation.*

sin′gle en′try, *n.* a simple accounting system noting only amounts owed by and due to a business. Compare DOUBLE ENTRY.

sin′gle file′, *n.* **1.** a line of persons or things arranged one behind the other. —*adv.* **2.** in such a line: *to walk single file.*

sin′gle-hand′ed, *adj.* **1.** accomplished or done by one person alone. **2.** by one's own effort; unaided. **3.** using only one hand. —*adv.* **4.** by oneself; alone; without aid. —**sin′gle-hand′ed•ly,** *adv.* —**sin′gle-hand′ed•ness,** *n.*

sin′gle-is′sue pol′itics, *n.* reduction of political discussion and debate to one issue.

sin′gle-mind′ed, *adj.* **1.** having or showing a single aim or purpose. **2.** dedicated; resolute; steadfast. —**sin′gle-mind′ed•ly,** *adv.* —**sin′gle-mind′ed•ness,** *n.*

sin′gles bar′, *n.* a bar frequented chiefly by unmarried people, esp. those seeking a lover or spouse.

sin′gle-space′, *v.t., v.i.,* **-spaced, -spac•ing.** to type or format so that there are no blank lines between lines of text.

sin•gle•ton (sing′gəl tən), *n.* **1.** a person or thing occurring or existing singly. **2.** a card that is the only one of a suit in a hand.

sin•gle•tree (sing′gəl trē′), *n.* WHIFFLETREE.

sin•gly (sing′glē), *adv.* **1.** apart from others; separately. **2.** one at a time; as single units. **3.** single-handed; alone.

sing•song (sing′sông′, -song′), *n.* **1.** a monotonous, rhythmical rising and falling in pitch of the voice when speaking. **2.** verse, or a piece of verse, that is monotonously jingly in rhythm and pattern of pitch. —*adj.* **3.** monotonous in rhythm and in pitch.

sin•gu•lar (sing′gyə lər), *adj.* **1.** extraordinary; remarkable; exceptional: *a singular success.* **2.** unusual or strange; odd; different: *singular behavior.* **3.** being the only one of its kind; unique: *a singular example.* **4.** separate; individual. **5.** of or belonging to the grammatical category of number used to indicate that a word has one referent or denotes one person, place, thing, or instance, as *child, it,* or *goes.* **6.** *Logic.* **a.** of or pertaining to something individual, specific, or not general. **b.** (of a proposition) containing no quantifiers. —*n.* **7.** the singular number. **8.** a word or other form in the singular. *Abbr.:* sing. —**sin′gu•lar•ly,** *adv.*

sin•gu•lar•i•ty (sing′gyə lar′i tē), *n., pl.* **-ties.** **1.** the state, fact, or quality of being singular. **2.** a singular, unusual, or unique quality or thing; peculiarity. **3.** a point at which a mathematical function of real or complex variables is not differentiable or analytic. **4.** a region of infinite density, as in a black hole.

sin•is•ter (sin′ə stər), *adj.* **1.** threatening or portending evil, harm, or trouble; ominous: *a sinister glance.* **2.** evil or malevolent; base: *sinister purposes.* **3.** unfortunate; disastrous; unfavorable. **4.** of or on the left side; left. **5.** being or pertaining to the side of a heraldic shield to the left of the bearer. Compare DEXTER (def. 2). —**sin′is•ter•ly,** *adv.*

sin•is•tral (sin′ə strəl), *adj.* **1.** of, pertaining to, or on the left side; left. **2.** having a preference for using the left hand or side; left-handed. **3.** (of certain gastropod shells) coiling counterclockwise, as seen from the apex. —**sin'is•tral•ly,** *adv.*

sink (singk), *v.,* **sank** or, often, **sunk, sunk** or **sunk•en, sink•ing,** *n.* —*v.i.* **1.** to fall, drop, or descend gradually to a lower level or position: *The ship sank to the bottom of the sea.* **2.** to settle or fall gradually: *The building is sinking.* **3.** to fall or collapse slowly from weakness, fatigue, etc. **4.** to penetrate or permeate; seep. **5.** to become engulfed in or gradually enter a state: *to sink into slumber.* **6.** to become deeply absorbed: *sunk in thought.* **7.** to pass or fall into some worse or lower state: *to sink into poverty.* **8.** to decline or deteriorate in quality or worth. **9.** to fail in physical strength or health. **10.** to become discouraged or depressed: *My heart sank.* **11.** to decrease in amount, extent, intensity, etc. **12.** to become lower in volume, tone, or pitch: *Her voice sank to a whisper.* **13.** to slope downward; dip. **14.** to disappear from sight, as below the horizon. **15.** to become or appear concave or hollow, as the cheeks. —*v.t.* **16.** to cause to become submerged; force into or below the surface. **17.** to cause to fall, drop, or descend gradually. **18.** to cause to penetrate: *to sink an ax into a tree.* **19.** to lower or depress the level of. **20.** to bury or lay in or as if in the ground. **21.** to dig, bore, or excavate (a hole, shaft, well, etc.). **22.** to bring to a worse or lower state or status. **23.** to bring to utter ruin or collapse. **24.** to reduce in amount, extent, intensity, etc. **25.** to lower in volume or pitch. **26.** to suppress; ignore. **27.** to invest with the hope of profit or other return. **28.** to lose (money) in an investment, enterprise, etc. **29.** to hit or propel (a ball) so that it goes through or into a basket, hole, pocket, etc. **30. sink in,** to enter or permeate the mind; become understood: *I repeated it till the words sank in.* —*n.* **31.** a basin, usu. connected with a water supply and drainage system, used for washing. **32.** a low-lying, poorly drained area where waters collect and sink into the ground or evaporate. **33.** SINKHOLE (def. 2). **34.** a place of vice or corruption. **35.** a drain or sewer. **36.** a device or place for disposing of energy within a system, as a power-consuming device in an electrical circuit or a condenser in a steam engine. **37.** any pond or pit for sewage or waste, as a cesspool or a pool for industrial wastes. —**sink'a•ble,** *adj.*

sink•er (sing'kər), *n.* **1.** a person or thing that sinks. **2.** a weight, as of lead, for sinking a fishing line or net below the surface of the water. **3.** *Slang.* a doughnut. **4.** (in baseball) a pitched ball that curves downward sharply as it reaches the plate. —**sink'er•less,** *adj.*

sink•hole (singk'hōl'), *n.* **1.** a hole formed in soluble rock by the action of water, serving to conduct surface water to an underground passage. **2.** a depressed area in which waste or drainage collects.

sin•ner (sin'ər), *n.* a person who sins; transgressor.

Sinn Fein (shin' fān'), *n.* an Irish nationalist organization founded about 1905, existing today as the political wing of the Irish Republican Army. [< Irish *sinn féin* we ourselves] —**Sinn' Fein'er,** *n.*

Sino-, a combining form meaning "China" or "Chinese": *Sinology; Sino-Tibetan.*

sin' tax', *n.* a tax levied on items, as cigarettes or liquor, considered neither luxuries nor necessities.

sin•ter (sin'tər), *n.* **1.** siliceous or calcareous matter deposited by springs, as that formed around the vent of a geyser. —*v.t.* **2.** to cause (metal particles) to bond together by pressing and heating.

sin•u•ate (*adj.* sin'yŏ̅ō̅ it, -āt'; *v.* -āt'), *adj., v.,* **-at•ed, -at•ing.** —*adj.* Also, **sin'u•at•ed. 1.** winding; sinuous. **2.** *Bot.* having the margin strongly or distinctly wavy, as a leaf. —*v.* **3.** to curve or wind in and out; creep in a winding path. —**sin'u•ate•ly,** *adv.*

sin•u•ous (sin'yŏ̅ō̅ əs), *adj.* **1.** having many curves or turns; winding: *a sinuous path.* **2.** characterized by graceful curving motions: *a sinuous dance.* **3.** *Bot.* sinuate, as a leaf. —**sin'u•ous•ly,** *adv.* —**sin'u•ous•ness,** *n.*

si•nus (sī'nəs), *n., pl.* **-nus•es. 1.** a curve; bend. **2.** a curving part or recess. **3. a.** any of various cavities, recesses, or passages in the body, as a hollow in a bone. **b.** one of the hollow cavities in the skull connecting with the nasal cavities. **4.** a narrow passage leading to an abscess or the like. **5.** a small, rounded depression between two projecting lobes, as of a leaf.

si•nus•i•tis (sī'nə sī'tis), *n.* inflammation of a sinus or the sinuses of the skull.

si•nus•oid (sī'nə soid'), *n.* a curve described by the equation $y = a \sin x$, the ordinate being proportional to the sine of the abscissa. —**si'nus•oi'dal,** *adj.* —**si'nus•oi'dal•ly,** *adv.*

-sion, var. of -TION.: *compulsion; explosion.*

Siou•an (sŏ̅ō̅'ən), *n.* a family of American Indian languages, including Dakota, Mandan, Hidatsa, Crow, Winnebago, Osage, and Catawba, spoken or formerly spoken by peoples dispersed over a large area of central and SE North America.

Sioux (sŏ̅ō̅), *n., pl.* **Sioux** (sŏ̅ō̅, sŏ̅ō̅z). DAKOTA (defs. 3, 5).

Sioux' Falls', *n.* a city in SE South Dakota. 109,174.

sip (sip), *v.,* **sipped, sip•ping,** *n.* —*v.t.* **1.** to drink (a liquid) a little at a time; take small tastes of. **2.** to drink from a little at a time. —*v.i.* **3.** to drink by sips. —*n.* **4.** an act or instance of sipping; a small taste of a liquid. **5.** a small quantity taken by sipping. —**sip'per,** *n.* —**sip'ping•ly,** *adv.*

si•phon or **sy•phon** (sī'fən), *n.* **1.** a U-shaped pipe that uses atmospheric pressure to draw liquid from one container, place, or level to another. **2.** a projecting tubular part of some animals, esp. certain mollusks, through which liquid enters or leaves the body. —*v.t., v.i.* **3.** to convey, draw, or pass through a siphon (sometimes fol. by *off*).

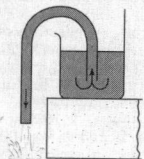

siphon (def. 1)

sir (sûr), *n.* **1. a.** a respectful or formal term of address used to a man: *No, sir.* **b.** a formal term of address used in the salutation of a letter. **2.** (*cap.*) the distinctive title of a knight or baronet: *Sir Walter Scott.* **3.** a lord or gentleman: *noble sirs and ladies.* **4.** an ironic or humorous title of respect: *sir critic.*

Si•rach (sī'rak), *n.* Son of, JESUS (def. 2).

sire (sīr), *n., v.,* **sired, sir•ing.** —*n.* **1.** the male parent of a quadruped. **2.** a respectful term of address, now used only to a male sovereign. —*v.t.* **3.** to beget; procreate as the male parent.

si•ren (sī'rən), *n.* **1.** (*sometimes cap.*) any of several supernatural beings in Greek legend who are part woman and part bird and who lure mariners to destruction with seductive singing. **2.** a seductively beautiful or charming woman, esp. one who beguiles men. **3.** an acoustical device that produces sound by means of a perforated, rotating disk that interrupts a jet of air or steam. **4.** an implement of this kind used as a whistle, fog signal, or warning device. **5.** any aquatic, eellike salamander of the family Sirenidae, having permanent external gills and no hind limbs. —*adj.* **6.** of or like a siren. **7.** seductive or tempting, esp. dangerously or harmfully. —**si'ren•like',** *adj.*

si•re•ni•an (sī rē'nē ən), *n.* an aquatic, herbivorous mammal of the order Sirenia, including the manatee and dugong.

Sir•i•us (sir'ē əs), *n.* the Dog Star, the brightest-appearing star in the heavens, located in the constellation Canis Major.

sir•loin (sûr'loin), *n.* the portion of the loin of beef in front of the rump.

si•roc•co (sə rok'ō), *n., pl.* **-cos. 1.** a hot, dry, dust-laden wind blowing from N Africa and affecting parts of S Europe. **2.** a warm, sultry south or southeast wind accompanied by rain, occurring in the same regions. **3.** any hot, oppressive wind, esp. one in the warm sector of a cyclone.

sis (sis), *n. Informal.* sister.

-sis, a suffix appearing in loanwords from Greek, where it was used to form from verbs abstract nouns of action, process, state, condition, etc.: *aphesis; thesis.*

si•sal (sī'səl, sis'əl), *n.* **1.** Also called **si'sal hemp'.** a fiber yielded by an agave, *Agave sisalana,* of Yucatán, used esp. for making rope or rugs. **2.** the plant itself.

Sis•er•a (sis'ər ə), *n.* a commander of the Canaanite army: killed by Jael. Judg. 4:14–22.

sis•kin (sis'kin), *n.* any of several small finches, esp. *Carduelis spinus,* of Eurasia. Compare PINE SISKIN.

sis•si•fied (sis'ə fīd'), *adj.* sissy.

sis•sy (sis'ē), *n., pl.* **-sies,** *adj.* —*n.* **1.** an effeminate boy or man. **2.** a timid or cowardly person. **3.** a little girl. —*adj.* **4.** (of a man or boy) effeminate. **5.** cowardly; timid. —**sis'sy•ish,** *adj.*

sis•ter (sis'tər), *n.* **1.** a female offspring having both parents in common with another offspring; female sibling. **2.** HALF SISTER. **3.** STEPSISTER. **4.** a sister-in-law. **5.** a woman or girl numbered in the same kinship group, nationality, race, church membership, society, etc., as another. **6.** a thing regarded as female and associated as if by kinship with something else: *The ships are sisters.* **7. a.** a woman member of a religious order whose vows are not as absolute as a nun's. **b.** (used as a title for a sister or a nun.) **8.** *Brit.* a nurse in charge of a hospital ward; head nurse. —*adj.* **9.** being or considered a sister; related by or as if by sisterhood. **10.** being in close relationship with another: *our sister city across the river.* **11.** being one of an identical pair. —**sis'ter•less,** *adj.* —**sis'ter•like',** *adj.*

sis•ter•hood (sis'tər hŏŏd'), *n.* **1.** the state of being a sister. **2.** a group of nuns or other females bound by religious ties. **3.** an organization of women with a common interest, as for social or charitable purposes. **4.** congenial relationship among women. **5.** the community or network of women who participate in or support feminism.

sis•ter-in-law (sis'tər in lô'), *n., pl.* **sis•ters-in-law. 1.** the sister of one's husband or wife. **2.** the wife of one's brother. **3.** the wife of the brother of one's husband or wife.

sis•ter•ly (sis'tər lē), *adj.* **1.** of, like, or befitting a sister: *sisterly affection.* —*adv.* **2.** in the manner of a sister; as a sister. —**sis'ter•li•ness,** *n.*

Sis'ter of Char'ity, *n.* **1.** a member of one of several congregations of Roman Catholic sisters founded in 1634 by St. Vincent de Paul. **2.** any of several other orders of nuns devoted to teaching, care of the sick, etc.

Sis'ter of Lo•ret'to (lə ret'ō), *n.* a member of a congregation of Roman Catholic sisters founded at Loretto, Ky., in 1812 and engaged in educational and missionary works.

Sis'tine Chap'el, *n.* the chapel of the pope in the Vatican at Rome,

S

built for Pope Sixtus IV and decorated with frescoes by Michelangelo and others.

Sis•y•phe•an (sis′ə fē′ən), *adj.* suggesting or resembling the punishment of Sisyphus in futility or hopelessness: *a Sisyphean task.*

Sis•y•phus (sis′ə fəs), *n.* a legendary ruler of Corinth punished in Tartarus by being compelled to roll to the top of a slope a stone that always escapes him and rolls back down again.

sit (sit), *v.*, **sat, sat, sit•ting.** —*v.i.* **1.** to rest with the body supported by the buttocks or thighs; be seated (often fol. by *down*). **2.** to be located or situated: *The house sits on a cliff.* **3.** to rest or lie (usu. fol. by *on* or *upon*): *An aura of greatness sits upon her.* **4.** to place oneself in position for an artist, photographer, etc.; pose. **5.** to remain quiet or inactive: *Let the matter sit.* **6.** (of a bird) to cover eggs with the body for hatching; brood. **7.** to fit or hang, as a garment. **8.** to occupy an official seat or have an official capacity, as a legislator. **9.** to be convened or in session, as an assembly. **10.** to take care of something or someone like a baby-sitter (usu. used in combination): *to plant-sit for the neighbors.* **11.** to blow from the indicated direction: *a wind sitting in the west.* **12.** to be accepted in the way indicated: *His answer didn't sit right with us.* **13.** to be acceptable to the stomach: *My breakfast didn't sit too well.* —*v.t.* **14.** to cause to sit; seat (often fol. by *down*): *Sit yourself down.* **15.** to sit astride or keep one's seat on (a horse or other animal). **16.** to provide seating accommodations; seat: *Our table only sits six people.* **17.** to baby-sit for. **18. sit in on,** to be a spectator, observer, or visitor at. **19. sit on** or **upon, a.** to inquire into or deliberate over: *A coroner's jury sat on the case.* **b.** to put off for a time; postpone. **c.** to check: *to sit on nasty rumors.* **20. sit out, a.** to stay to the end of. **b.** to stay, wait, or endure longer than: *to sit out one's rivals.* **c.** to keep one's seat during (a dance, competition, etc.); fail to participate in. **21. sit up, a.** to rise from a supine to a sitting position. **b.** to sit upright; hold oneself erect. **c.** to be awake and active during one's usual sleep time: *to sit up all night playing solitaire.* **d.** to take notice. —*Idiom.* **22. sit on one's hands, a.** to fail to applaud. **b.** to fail to take appropriate action. **23. sit tight,** to take no action; wait. —**Usage.** See SET.

si•tar (si tär′), *n.* a lute of India with a small, pear-shaped body and a long, broad, fretted neck. —**si•tar′ist,** *n.*

sit•com (sit′kom′), *n.* situation comedy.

sit′-down, *adj.* **1.** done or accomplished while sitting down. **2.** (of a meal or food) served to or intended for persons seated at a table. —*n.* **3.** SIT-DOWN STRIKE. **4.** SIT-IN. **5.** a period or instance of sitting, as to talk.

sit′-down′ strike′, *n.* a strike during which workers occupy their place of employment and refuse to work until the strike is settled. Also called **sit-down.**

site (sīt), *n., v.,* **sit•ed, sit•ing.** —*n.* **1.** the position or location of a town, building, etc., esp. as to its environment. **2.** the area or exact plot of ground on which anything is, has been, or is to be located: *the site of ancient Troy.* **3.** WEB SITE. —*v.t.* **4.** to place in or provide with a site; locate. **5.** to put in position for operation, as artillery.

sit′-in, *n.* any organized protest in which the demonstrators occupy and refuse to leave a public place. Also called **sit-down.**

sit′ spin′, *n.* a figure-skating spin performed on one skate, in which the skater slowly squats down into a sitting position, with the other leg extended out in front.

sit•ter (sit′ər), *n.* **1.** a person who sits. **2.** a brooding hen. **3.** a person who baby-sits; baby-sitter. **4.** a person who provides temporary or part-time care, as for a pet whose owner is away.

sit•ting (sit′ing), *n.* **1.** the act of a person or thing that sits. **2.** a period of being seated, as in posing for a portrait. **3.** a brooding, as of a hen upon eggs; incubation. **4.** a session, as of a court or legislature. **5.** the time allotted to the serving of a meal to a group, as aboard a ship. —*adj.* **6.** for, suited to, or accomplished while sitting: *sitting areas; a sitting catch.* **7.** (of a target) readily seen, approached, or hit. **8.** occupying an official position or office; incumbent. **9.** in session; active: *a sitting legislature.* **10.** (of a bird) occupying a nest of eggs for hatching. —*Idiom.* **11. sitting pretty,** in an auspicious position.

Sit′ting Bull′, *n.* 1834–90, Lakota Indian leader.

sit′ting duck′, *n.* a helpless or easy target or victim.

sit′ting room′, *n.* a small living room.

sit•u•ate (sich′o̅o̅ āt′), *v.t.* to put in or on a particular site or place; locate; establish.

sit•u•at•ed (sich′o̅o̅ ā′tid), *adj.* **1.** located; placed. **2.** being in a particular condition with reference to money and material possessions: *The inheritance leaves them well situated.*

sit•u•a•tion (sich′o̅o̅ ā′shən), *n.* **1.** manner of being situated; location or position with reference to environment. **2.** a place or locality. **3.** condition; case; plight: *in a desperate situation.* **4.** the state of affairs; combination of circumstances: *the international situation.* **5.** a position or post of employment; job. **6.** a state of affairs of special or critical significance in the course of a play, novel, etc. —**sit′u•a′tion•al,** *adj.* —**sit′u•a′tion•al•ly,** *adv.*

sit′ua′tion com′edy, *n.* a television series made up of independent episodes depicting the comic adventures of a fixed group of characters.

sit′ua′tion eth′ics, *n.* a view of ethics that deprecates general moral principles while emphasizing the source of moral judgments in the distinctive characters of specific situations.

situa′tion room′, *n.* a room at a military or political headquarters where the latest information on a situation is channeled.

sit′-up, *n.* an exercise in which a person lies flat on the back, lifts the

torso to a sitting position, and then lies flat again without changing the position of the legs.

sitz′ bath′ (sits, zits), *n.* **1.** a chairlike bathtub in which the thighs and hips are immersed in warm water. **2.** a therapeutic bath so taken.

Si•van (siv′ən, sē vän′), *n.* the ninth month of the Jewish calendar.

six (siks), *n.* **1.** a cardinal number, five plus one. **2.** a symbol for this number, as 6 or VI. **3.** a set of six persons or things. —*adj.* **4.** amounting to six in number. —*Idiom.* **5. at sixes and sevens, a.** in disorder or confusion. **b.** in disagreement or dispute. **6. six of one and a half dozen of the other,** both work out to be the same.

six•fold (siks′fōld′), *adj.* **1.** having six elements or parts. **2.** six times as great or as much. —*adv.* **3.** in sixfold measure.

six′-gun′, *n.* SIX-SHOOTER.

Six′ Na′tions, *n.pl.* the Five Nations of the Iroquois confederacy and the Tuscaroras.

six′-pack′, *n.* any package of six identical or closely related items sold as a unit, esp. six bottles or cans of beer or a soft drink.

six•pence (siks′pəns), *n., pl.* **-pence, -penc•es** for 2. **1.** (*used with a sing. or pl. v.*) *Brit.* a sum of six pennies. **2.** (*used with a sing. v.*) a cupronickel coin of the United Kingdom, the half of a shilling, formerly equal to six pennies: equal to two and one-half new pence after decimalization in 1971.

six-shoot•er (siks′sho̅o̅′tər, -sho̅o̅′-), *n.* a revolver that can fire six shots with one loading.

six•teen (siks′tēn′), *n.* **1.** a cardinal number, ten plus six. **2.** a symbol for this number, as 16 or XVI. **3.** a set of this many persons or things. —*adj.* **4.** amounting to 16 in number.

six•teenth (siks′tēnth′), *adj.* **1.** next after the fifteenth; being the ordinal number for 16. **2.** being one of 16 equal parts. —*n.* **3.** a sixteenth part ($\frac{1}{16}$). **4.** the sixteenth member of a series.

Six′teenth Amend′ment, *n.* an amendment to the U.S. Constitution, ratified in 1913, authorizing Congress to levy a tax on incomes.

six′teenth′ note′, *n.* a musical note having one sixteenth the time value of a whole note.

six′teenth′ rest′, *n.* a rest equal in time value to a sixteenth note.

sixth (siksth), *adj.* **1.** next after the fifth; being the ordinal number for six. **2.** being one of six equal parts. —*n.* **3.** a sixth part, esp. of one ($\frac{1}{6}$). **4.** the sixth member of a series. **5. a.** a musical interval encompassing six diatonic degrees. **b.** a tone at this interval. **c.** the harmonic combination of two tones a sixth apart. —*adv.* **6.** in the sixth place; sixthly. —**sixth′ly,** *adv.*

Sixth′ Amend′ment, *n.* an amendment to the U.S. Constitution, ratified in 1791 as part of the Bill of Rights, guaranteeing the right to a trial by jury in criminal cases.

Sixth′ Command′ment, *n.* "Thou shalt not kill": sixth of the Ten Commandments. Compare TEN COMMANDMENTS.

sixth′ sense′, *n.* a power of perception beyond the five senses; intuition.

six•ty (siks′tē), *n., pl.* **-ties,** *adj.* —*n.* **1.** a cardinal number, ten times six. **2.** a symbol for this number, as 60 or LX. **3.** a set of this many persons or things. **4. sixties,** the numbers from 60 through 69, as in referring to the years of a lifetime or of a century or to degrees of temperature. —*adj.* **5.** amounting to 60 in number. —*Idiom.* **6. like sixty,** with great speed, ease, energy, or zest. —**six′ti•eth,** *adj., n.*

six′ty-fourth′ note′, *n.* a musical note having one sixty-fourth the time value of a whole note.

six′ty-fourth′ rest′, *n.* a rest equal in time value to a sixty-fourth note.

siz•a•ble or **size•a•ble** (sī′zə bəl), *adj.* of considerable size; fairly large. —**siz′a•ble•ness,** *n.* —**siz′a•bly,** *adv.*

size¹ (sīz), *n., v.,* **sized, siz•ing.** —*n.* **1.** the spatial dimensions, proportions, or extent of anything. **2.** considerable or great magnitude: *size versus quality.* **3.** one of a series of graduated measures for articles of manufacture or trade: *shoe sizes.* **4.** extent; amount; range. **5.** actual condition, circumstance, or state of affairs: *That's about the size of it.* **6.** a number of population or contents. —*v.t.* **7.** to separate or sort according to size. **8.** to make of a certain size. **9. size up,** to form an estimate of; judge. —*Idiom.* **10. cut** or **chop down to size,** to reduce the stature or importance of. **11. of a size,** of the same or a similar size.

size² (sīz), *n., v.,* **sized, siz•ing.** —*n.* **1.** preparation made from glue, starch, etc., used for filling the pores of cloth, paper, or other material. —*v.t.* **2.** to coat or treat with size.

sized (sīzd), *adj.* having size as specified (often used in combination): *middle-sized.*

siz•ing (sī′zing), *n.* **1.** the act or process of applying size or preparing with size. **2.** size, as for strengthening fabric.

siz•zle (siz′əl), *v.,* **-zled, -zling,** *n.* —*v.i.* **1.** to make a hissing sound, as in frying; crackle. **2.** to be very hot. **3.** to be very angry. —*v.t.* **4.** to fry or burn with or as if with a hissing sound. —*n.* **5.** a sizzling sound. —**siz′zler,** *n.* —**siz′zling•ly,** *adv.*

skate¹ (skāt), *n., v.,* **skat•ed, skat•ing.** —*n.* **1.** ICE SKATE (def. 1). **2.** ROLLER SKATE. **3.** the blade of an ice skate. —*v.i.* **4.** to glide or propel oneself on skates. **5.** to glide or slide smoothly along. **6.** to do something, esp. one's work, in a lax or superficial way. —*v.t.* **7.** to perform by skating. —**skate′a•ble,** *adj.*

skate² (skāt), *n., pl.* (*esp. collectively*) **skate,** (*esp. for kinds or species*)

skates. any ray, esp. of the family Rajidae, having winglike pectoral fins.

skate·board (skāt′bôrd′, -bōrd′), *n.* **1.** a device consisting of an oblong board mounted on large roller-skate wheels and supporting a rider. —*v.i.* **2.** to ride a skateboard. —**skate′board′er,** *n.*

skat·er (skā′tər), *n.* a person who skates.

ske·dad·dle (ski dad′l), *v.,* **-dled, -dling,** *n. Informal.* —*v.i.* **1.** to run away hurriedly; flee. —*n.* **2.** a hasty flight. —**ske·dad′dler,** *n.*

skeet (skēt), *n.* a form of trapshooting in which targets are hurled at varying elevations and speeds so as to simulate the angles of flight taken by game birds. Also called **skeet′ shoot′ing.**

skein (skān), *n.* **1.** a length of yarn or thread wound on a reel or swift preparatory for use in manufacturing. **2. a.** a loose coil of thread or yarn in a package for retail sale. **b.** anything wound in or resembling such a coil: *a skein of hair.* **3.** something suggestive of the twistings of a skein. **4.** a flock of geese, ducks, or the like, in flight. **5.** a succession or series of similar or interrelated things.

skel·e·tal (skel′i tl), *adj.* of, pertaining to, or like a skeleton. —**skel′e·tal·ly,** *adv.*

skel′etal mus′cle, *n.* VOLUNTARY MUSCLE.

skel·e·ton (skel′i tn), *n.* **1.** the bones of a vertebrate considered as a whole, together forming the internal framework of the body. **2.** any of various structures forming a rigid framework in certain invertebrates. **3.** an emaciated person or animal. **4.** a supporting framework, as of a leaf, building, or ship. **5.** an outline, as of a literary work: *the skeleton of the plot.* **6.** something reduced to its essential parts. —*adj.* **7.** of or pertaining to a skeleton. **8.** reduced to the essential or minimal parts or numbers: *a skeleton staff.* —*Idiom.* **9. skeleton in the closet** or **cupboard,** any embarrassing, shameful, or damaging secret. [< Greek: mummy]

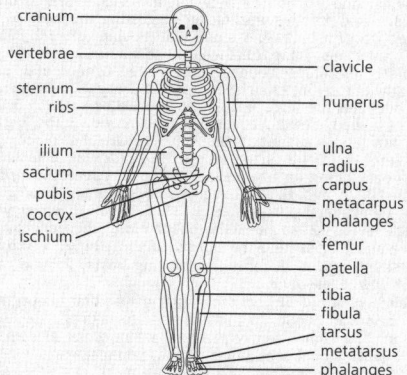

skeleton (human)

skel′eton key′, *n.* a key with nearly the whole substance of the bit filed away so that it opens various simple locks.

skep·tic or **scep·tic** (skep′tik), *n.* **1.** a person who questions the validity, authenticity, or truth of something purporting to be factual, esp. religion or religious tenets. **2.** a person who maintains a doubting attitude, as toward values, plans, or the character of others. **3.** (*cap.*) a member of a philosophical school of ancient Greece which maintained that real knowledge of things is impossible. —*adj.* **4.** SKEPTICAL. **5.** (*cap.*) pertaining to the Skeptics.

skep·ti·cal or **scep·ti·cal** (skep′ti kəl), *adj.* **1.** inclined to skepticism; having doubt. **2.** showing doubt: *a skeptical smile.* **3.** denying or questioning religion or the tenets of a religion. **4.** (*cap.*) of or pertaining to Skeptics or Skepticism. —**skep′ti·cal·ly,** *adv.*

skep·ti·cism or **scep·ti·cism** (skep′tə siz/əm), *n.* **1.** skeptical attitude or temper; doubt. **2.** doubt or unbelief regarding religion. **3.** (*cap.*) the doctrines or opinions of philosophical Skeptics; universal doubt.

sketch (skech), *n.* **1.** a simply or hastily executed drawing or painting, esp. a preliminary one, giving the essential features without the details. **2.** a rough design, plan, or draft, as of a book. **3.** a brief or hasty outline of facts, occurrences, etc. **4.** a short piece of writing, usu. descriptive. **5.** a short comic piece or routine or a brief dramatic scene. —*v.t.* **6.** to make a sketch of. **7.** to set forth in a brief or general account. —*v.i.* **8.** to make a sketch or sketches. —**sketch′er,** *n.*

sketch′book′ or **sketch′ book′,** *n.* **1.** a book or pad of drawing paper for sketches. **2.** a book of literary sketches.

sketch·y (skech′ē), *adj.,* **sketch·i·er, sketch·i·est. 1.** like a sketch; giving only outlines or essentials. **2.** imperfect; incomplete or slight. —**sketch′i·ly,** *adv.* —**sketch′i·ness,** *n.*

skew (skyōō), *v.i.* **1.** to turn aside or swerve; take an oblique course. **2.** to look obliquely or askance; squint. —*v.t.* **3.** to give an oblique direction to; shape, form, or cut obliquely. **4.** to distort; misrepresent: *to skew data.* —*adj.* **5.** having an oblique direction or position; slanting. **6.**

having a part that deviates from a straight line, right angle, etc.: *skew gearing.* **7.** *Statistics.* (of a distribution) having skewness. —*n.* **8.** an oblique movement, direction, or position. **9.** Also called **skew′ chis′el.** a wood chisel having a cutting edge set obliquely.

skew·er (skyōō′ər), *n.* **1.** a long pin for inserting through meat or other food to hold it while cooking. **2.** any similar pin for fastening or holding an item in place. —*v.t.* **3.** to fasten with or as if with a skewer.

skew·ness (skyōō′nis), *n. Statistics.* **1.** asymmetry in a frequency distribution. **2.** a measure of such asymmetry.

ski (skē), *n., pl.* **skis, ski,** *v.,* **skied, ski·ing.** —*n.* **1.** one of a pair of long, slender runners made of wood, plastic, or metal used in gliding over snow. **2.** WATER SKI. —*v.i.* **3.** to travel on skis, as for sport. —*v.t.* **4.** to use skis on; travel on skis over. —**ski′a·ble,** *adj.*

ski′ boot′, *n.* a heavy, thick-soled, ankle-high shoe for skiing, often having padding and supporting straps and laces around the ankle, with grooves on the heel for binding to a ski.

skid (skid), *n., v.,* **skid·ded, skid·ding.** —*n.* **1.** a plank, bar, log, or the like, esp. one of a pair, on which something heavy may be slid or rolled along. **2.** a low mobile platform on which goods are placed for ease in handling, moving, etc. **3.** a plank, log, low platform, etc., on or by which a load is supported. **4.** a shoe or some other choke or drag for preventing the wheel of a vehicle from rotating, as when descending a hill. **5.** an unexpected or uncontrollable slide on a smooth surface, esp. an oblique or wavering veer by a vehicle or its tires. —*v.t.* **6.** to place on or slide along a skid. **7.** to check the motion of with a skid. **8.** to cause to go into a skid: *to skid the car into a turn.* —*v.i.* **9.** to slide along without rotating, as a wheel to which a brake has been applied. **10.** to slip or slide sideways, as an automobile in turning a corner rapidly. **11.** to slide forward under the force of momentum after being braked, as a vehicle. **12.** (of an airplane when not banked sufficiently) to slide sideways, away from the center of the curve described in turning. **13.** to slip or slide; lose traction: *feet skidding on icy pavement.* **14.** to falter or fail; decline. —*Idiom.* **15. the skids,** the downward path to ruin, failure, depravity, etc. —**skid′ding·ly,** *adv.*

skid·doo (ski dōō′), *v.i.,* **-dooed, -doo·ing.** *Informal.* to go away; get out.

skid′ row′ (rō), *n.* an area of cheap barrooms and run-down hotels, frequented by alcoholics and vagrants. Also called **Skid′ Road′.**

skied[1] (skēd), *v.* pt. of SKI.

skied[2] (skīd), *v.* a pt. of SKY.

ski·er (skē′ər), *n.* a person who skis.

skies (skīz), *n.* **1.** pl. of SKY. —*v.* **2.** 3rd pers. sing. pres. of SKY.

skiff (skif), *n.* any of various types of boats small enough for sailing or rowing by one person. —**skiff′less,** *adj.*

ski·ing (skē′ing), *n.* the act or sport of gliding on skis.

ski′ jump′, *n.* **1.** a steep, snow-covered track with a platform at the lower end, from which a skier jumps into the air, soaring to a landing further downhill. **2.** a jump made by a skier from a ski jump. —*v.i.* **3.** to make a ski jump. —**ski′ jump′er,** *n.*

ski′ lift′, *n.* a device that carries skiers up a slope, consisting typically of chairs or bars suspended from a motor-driven cable.

skill (skil), *n.* **1.** the ability to do something well arising from talent, training, or practice. **2.** special competence in performance; expertness; dexterity. **3.** a craft, trade, or job requiring manual dexterity or special training.

skilled (skild), *adj.* **1.** having skill; trained or experienced in work that requires skill. **2.** showing, involving, or requiring skill.

skil·let (skil′it), *n.* a frying pan.

skill·ful (skil′fəl), *adj.* **1.** having or exercising skill: *a skillful juggler.* **2.** showing or involving skill. —**skill′ful·ly,** *adv.*

skill·less or **skil·less** (skil′lis), *adj.* without skill; unskilled or unskillful. —**skill′-less·ness,** *n.*

skim (skim), *v.,* **skimmed, skim·ming,** *n.* —*v.t.* **1.** to take up or remove (floating matter) from the surface of a liquid, as with a spoon. **2.** to clear (liquid) thus: *to skim milk.* **3.** to move or glide lightly over or along (a surface, as of water). **4.** to throw in a smooth, gliding path over a surface, or so as to bounce or ricochet along a surface: *skimmed a stone across the lake.* **5.** to read, study, consider, etc., in a superficial manner. **6.** to cover with a thin film or layer. **7.** to take the best or most available parts or items from. **8.** to take (the best parts or items) from something. **9.** to conceal a portion of (winnings, earnings, etc.) in order to avoid paying taxes, fees, and the like on the full amount (sometimes fol. by *off*). —*v.i.* **10.** to pass or glide lightly over or near a surface. **11.** to read, study, consider, etc., something in a superficial or cursory way. **12.** to become covered with a thin film or layer. **13.** to conceal some part of income or profits; practice skimming. —*n.* **14.** an act or instance of skimming. **15.** something that is skimmed off. **16.** a thin layer or film formed on the surface of something, esp. a liquid. **17.** the amount taken or concealed by skimming. **18.** SKIM MILK.

ski′ mask′, *n.* a one-piece pullover covering for the head and face, with holes for the eyes, the mouth, and sometimes the nose, orig. worn by skiers to protect the face from cold.

skim·mer (skim′ər), *n.* **1.** one that skims. **2.** a shallow utensil, usu. perforated, used in skimming liquids. **3.** any of several gull-like birds of the family Rynchopidae, that skim the water with the elongated lower bill immersed in search of food. **4.** a stiff, wide-brimmed hat with a shallow flat crown, usu. made of straw. **5.** an A-line dress with side darts that shape it slightly to the body.

(skateboard labels, cranium, vertebrae, sternum, ribs, ilium, sacrum, pubis, coccyx, ischium, clavicle, humerus, ulna, radius, carpus, metacarpus, phalanges, femur, patella, tibia, fibula, tarsus, metatarsus, phalanges)

S

skim′ milk′ or **skimmed′ milk′,** *n.* milk from which the cream has been skimmed.

skim•ming (skim′ing), *n.* **1.** Usu., **skimmings.** something that is removed by skimming. **2.** the practice of concealing income or profits so as to avoid paying taxes, fees, etc.

skimp (skimp), *v.i.* **1.** to scrimp. —*v.t.* **2.** to scrimp. **3.** to scamp. —*adj.* **4.** skimpy; scanty. —**skimp′ing•ly,** *adv.*

skimp•y (skim′pē), *adj.,* **-i•er, -i•est. 1.** lacking in size, fullness, etc.; scanty. **2.** too thrifty; stingy: *a skimpy housekeeper.* —**skimp′i•ly,** *adv.* —**skimp′i•ness,** *n.*

skin (skin), *n., v.,* **skinned, skin•ning.** —*n.* **1.** the external covering or integument of an animal body, esp. when soft and flexible. **2.** such an integument stripped from the body of an animal, esp. a small animal; pelt: *a beaver skin.* **3.** the tanned or treated hide of an animal; leather (usu. used in combination): *calfskin.* **4.** any integumentary covering, casing, outer coating, or surface layer, as an investing membrane, the rind of fruit, or a film on liquid. **5.** a casing, as of metal or plastic, around an object. **6.** a container made of animal skin, used for holding liquids, esp. wine. **7. skins,** *Slang.* drums. **8.** *Slang.* a dollar bill. **9.** to strip or deprive of skin; flay; peel; husk. **10.** to remove or strip off (any covering, surface layer, etc.). **11.** to scrape or rub a small piece of skin from (a part of the body), as in falling. **12.** to urge on, drive, or whip (a draft animal, as a mule or ox). **13.** to climb or jump. **14.** to cover with or as if with skin. **15.** to strip of money or belongings; fleece, as in gambling. —*Idiom.* **16. by the skin of one's teeth,** by an extremely narrow margin; just barely; scarcely. **17. get under one's skin, a.** to irritate; bother. **b.** to affect deeply; impress. **18. have a thick (or thin) skin,** to be remarkably insensitive (or sensitive), esp. to criticism. **19. no skin off one's back, nose,** or **teeth,** of no interest or concern or involving no risk to one. —*Proverb.* **20. There's more than one way to skin a cat,** a problem can be solved in different ways.

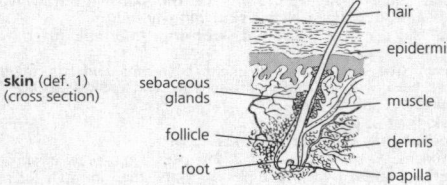

skin (def. 1)
(cross section)

hair
epidermis
sebaceous glands
muscle
follicle
dermis
root
papilla

skin′ and bones′ (or **bone′**), *n.* **1.** a condition or state of extreme thinness; emaciation. **2.** extremely thin and gaunt.

skin′-deep′, *adj.* superficial; not profound or substantial.

skin′-dive′, *v.i.,* **-dived** or **-dove** (-dōv′), **-div•ing.** to engage in skin diving. —**skin′ div′er,** *n.*

skin′ div′ing, *n.* underwater swimming and exploring with a face mask and flippers and sometimes with scuba.

skin′ game′, *n.* a dishonest or fraudulent scheme, operation, etc.; trick; swindle.

skin′ graft′, *n.* **1.** surgically transplanted skin, used for covering a burn or extensive wound. **2.** the site of such transplanted skin.

skin•head (skin′hed′), *n. Slang.* **1.** a person with a bald or shaved head or closely cropped hair. **2.** an antisocial person who affects a hairless head as a symbol of rebellion, racism, or anarchy.

skink (skingk), *n.* any lizard of the family Scincidae, common worldwide, usu. having a smooth, shiny body.

skin•less (skin′lis), *adj.* **1.** deprived of skin. **2.** (of frankfurters or sausages) having no casing.

skin•ner (skin′ər), *n.* **1.** one that skins. **2.** a person who prepares or deals in skins or hides. **3.** a person who drives draft animals, as mules.

Skin•ner (skin′ər), *n.* **1. B(urrhus) F(rederic),** 1904–90, U.S. psychologist. **2. Cornelia Otis,** 1901–79, U.S. actress. **3.** her father, **Otis,** 1858–1942, U.S. actor.

skin•ny (skin′ē), *adj.,* **-ni•er, -ni•est,** *n.* —*adj.* **1.** very lean or thin; emaciated. **2.** unusually low or reduced; meager. **3.** (of an object) narrow or slender. —*n.* **4.** *Slang.* **a.** accurate information; data; facts. **b.** news, esp. if confidential; gossip. —**skin′ni•ness,** *n.*

skin′ny-dip′, *v.,* **-dipped, -dip•ping,** *n. Informal.* —*v.i.* **1.** to swim in the nude. —*n.* **2.** a swim in the nude. —**skin′ny-dip′per,** *n.*

skin′ test′, *n.* a medical test in which a substance is introduced into the skin, as for the detection of an antibody reaction to an infectious disease.

skin•tight (skin′tīt′), *adj.* fitting almost as tightly as skin: *skintight trousers.*

skip¹ (skip), *v.,* **skipped, skip•ping,** *n.* —*v.i.* **1.** to move in a light, springy manner by bounding forward with alternate hops on each foot. **2.** to pass from one point, thing, etc., to another, disregarding or omitting what intervenes. **3.** to go away hastily and secretly. **4.** to be advanced two or more grades at once. **5.** to ricochet or bounce along a surface. —*v.t.* **6.** to jump lightly over: *to skip a fence.* **7.** to pass over without reading, noting, acting on, etc. **8.** to miss or omit (one of a repeated series of rhythmic actions). **9.** to be absent from; avoid attendance at: *to skip a party.* **10. a.** to advance (a student) by two or more

grades at once. **b.** to be advanced beyond (a grade) in school. **11.** to send (a missile) ricocheting along a surface. **12.** to leave hastily and secretly; flee from (a place). —*n.* **13.** a skipping movement; a light jump or bounce. **14.** a gait marked by such jumps. **15.** a passing from one point or thing to another, disregarding what intervenes. **16.** an instance of skipping or a thing skipped. **17.** a melodic interval greater than a second. —**skip′pa•ble,** *adj.* —**skip′ping•ly,** *adv.*

skip² (skip), *n., v.,* **skipped, skip•ping.** —*n.* **1.** the captain of a curling or bowling team. **2.** SKIPPER¹. —*v.t.* **3.** to serve as skip of (a curling or bowling team). **4.** SKIPPER¹.

ski′ pants′, *n.* (*used with a pl. v.*) pants worn for skiing, usu. with snug-fitting legs and often made of a stretch or waterproof fabric.

ski•plane (skē′plān′), *n.* an airplane equipped with skis to enable it to land on and take off from snow.

ski′ pole′, *n.* a slender pole or stick used by skiers for balance and propulsion, with a metal point below a ring at the lower end and a loop for the hand at the upper.

skip•per¹ (skip′ər), *n.* **1.** the master or captain of a vessel, esp. of a small trading or fishing vessel. **2.** a captain or leader, as of a team. —*v.t.* **3.** to act as skipper of.

skip•per² (skip′ər), *n.* **1.** one that skips. **2.** any of various insects that hop or fly with jerky motions.

skirl (skûrl), *v.i.* **1.** to play the bagpipe. —*n.* **2.** the sound of a bagpipe.

skir•mish (skûr′mish), *n.* **1.** a fight between small bodies of troops. **2.** any brisk conflict or encounter. —*v.i.* **3.** to engage in a skirmish. —**skir′mish•er,** *n.*

skirr (skûr), *v.i.* **1.** to go rapidly; fly; scurry. —*v.t.* **2.** to go rapidly over. —*n.* **3.** a grating or whirring sound.

skirt (skûrt), *n.* **1.** the part of a gown, dress, slip, or coat that extends downward from the waist. **2.** a one-piece garment extending downward from the waist and not joined between the legs, worn esp. by women and girls. **3.** some part resembling or suggesting the skirt of a garment, as the flared lip of a bell. **4.** a small leather flap on each side of a saddle, covering the metal bar from which the stirrup hangs. **5.** Also called **apron.** a flat, horizontal wooden piece, often ornamental, set immediately beneath a tabletop, chair seat, base of a chest of drawers, etc., and extending between the legs. **6.** a cloth flounce or valance fitting around the sides of a bed, couch, or chair, as to conceal the legs. **7.** Usu., **skirts.** the bordering, marginal, or outlying part of a place, group, etc.; outskirts. —*v.t.* **8.** to lie on or along the border of: *The hills skirt the town.* **9.** to pass along or around the border or edge of: *Traffic skirts the monument.* **10.** to avoid, go around the edge of, or keep distant from (something controversial, risky, etc.). **11.** to wrap or cover with or as if with a skirt. —*v.i.* **12.** to be or lie on or along the edge of something. **13.** to move along or around the border of something. —**skirt′like′,** *adj.*

skirt•ing (skûr′ting), *n.* **1.** fabric for making skirts. **2.** Also called **skirt′ing board′,** *Brit.* BASEBOARD.

skirt′ steak′, *n.* a cut of beef consisting of the diaphragm muscle.

ski′ run′, *n.* a trail, slope, or the like used for skiing.

skit (skit), *n.* **1.** a short literary piece of a humorous or satirical character. **2.** a short theatrical scene or act, usu. comical.

ski′ tow′, *n.* **1.** Also called **rope tow.** a type of ski lift in which skiers are hauled up a slope while grasping a looped, endless rope driven by a motor. **2.** SKI LIFT.

skit•tish (skit′ish), *adj.* **1.** apt to start or shy: *a skittish horse.* **2.** restlessly or excessively lively: *a skittish mood.* **3.** fickle; uncertain. **4.** shy; coy. —**skit′tish•ly,** *adv.* —**skit′tish•ness,** *n.*

skit•tle (skit′l), *n. Chiefly Brit.* **1. skittles,** (*used with a sing. v.*) ninepins in which a wooden ball or disk is used to knock down the pins. **2.** one of the pins used in this game.

skiv•vy (skiv′ē), *n., pl.* **-vies. 1.** Also called **skiv′vy shirt′.** a knit shirt with a small placket at the neck. **2. skivvies,** underwear consisting of this or a T-shirt and shorts.

Skop•je (skôp′ye), *n.* the capital of Macedonia, in the N part. 504,932. Serbo-Croatian, **Skop•lje** (skôp′lye).

skul•dug•ger•y or **skull•dug•gery** (skul dug′ə rē), *n., pl.* **-ger•ies. 1.** dishonorable proceedings; mean dishonesty or trickery. **2.** an instance of dishonest or deceitful behavior; a trick.

skulk (skulk), *v.i.* **1.** to lie or keep in hiding, as for some evil reason. **2.** to move stealthily; slink. —*n.* **3.** one that skulks. **4.** a pack or group of foxes. —**skulk′er,** *n.* —**skulk′ing•ly,** *adv.*

skull (skul), *n.* **1.** the bony or cartilaginous framework of the vertebrate head, enclosing the brain and sense organs and including the jaws. **2.** the head as the center of comprehension; mind. —**skull′-like′,** *adj.*

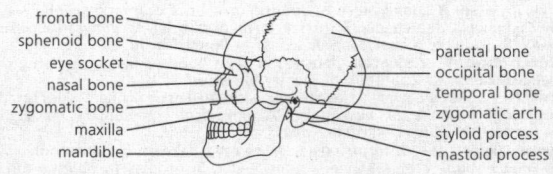

frontal bone
sphenoid bone
eye socket
nasal bone
zygomatic bone
maxilla
mandible
parietal bone
occipital bone
temporal bone
zygomatic arch
styloid process
mastoid process

human skull (lateral view)

skull′ and cross′bones, *n., pl.* **skulls and crossbones.** a representation of a front view of a human skull above two crossed bones, orig. used on pirates′ flags and now used as a warning sign, as in identifying poisons.

skull•cap (skul′kap′), *n.* **1.** a small, brimless, close-fitting cap, often made of silk or velvet, worn on the crown of the head. **2.** YARMULKE. **3.** the domelike roof of the skull.

skunk (skungk), *n., pl.* **skunks,** (*esp. collectively*) **skunk,** *v.* —*n.* **1.** any of several bushy-tailed New World members of the weasel family, having a black coat with white markings and spraying a fetid defensive fluid. **2.** a thoroughly contemptible person. —*v.t. Slang.* **3.** to defeat thoroughly in a game, esp. to keep scoreless. **4.** to cheat; swindle (usu. fol. by *out*).

skunk′ cab′bage, *n.* **1.** a low, fetid, broad-leaved North American plant, *Symplocarpus foetidus,* of the arum family, having a brownish purple and green mottled spathe surrounding a stout spadix, growing in moist ground. **2.** a related plant, *Lysichiton americanum,* of W North America, having a cluster of green leaves and a spike of flowers surrounded by a yellow spathe.

skunk•weed (skungk′wēd′), *n.* any of various plants having an unpleasant odor, as the skunk cabbage.

skunk′ works′ or **skunk′works′,** *n. Slang.* an often secret experimental laboratory, project, or the like, for producing innovative designs or products, as in computers or aerospace.

sky (skī), *n., pl.* **skies,** *v.,* **skied** or **skyed,** **sky•ing.** —*n.* Often, **skies** (for defs. 1–4). **1.** the region of the clouds or the upper air; upper atmosphere of the earth. **2.** the heavens or firmament, appearing as a great arch or vault. **3.** the supernal or celestial heaven. **4.** the climate: *the sunny skies of Italy.* —*v.t.* **5.** to raise, throw, or hit aloft or into the air. **6.** to hang (a painting) high on a wall, above the line of vision. —*Idiom.* **7. out of a** or **the clear (blue) sky,** without any advance warning. **8. The sky′s the limit,** potential and possibilities are limitless. —**sky′like′,** *adj.*

sky′ blue′, *n.* the color of the unclouded sky in daytime; azure. —**sky′-blue′,** *adj.*

sky•box (skī′boks′), *n.* a private compartment, usu. near the top of a stadium, for viewing a sports contest.

sky•bridge (skī′brij′), *n.* an elevated bridgelike walkway, esp. one built over a street to link two buildings. Also called **skywalk.**

sky•cap (skī′kap′), *n.* a porter who carries passenger baggage at an airport or airline terminal.

sky•div•ing or **sky′ div′ing,** *n.* the sport of jumping from an airplane and descending in free fall for a considerable distance before opening a parachute. —**sky′-dive′,** *v.i.,* **-dived** or **-dove, -dived, -div•ing.** —**sky′ div′er,** *n.*

Skye (skī), *n.* an island in the Hebrides, in NW Scotland. 7372; 670 sq. mi. (1735 sq. km).

Skye′ ter′rier, *n.* one of a Scottish breed of small terriers with short legs, a long body, and a long, straight coat.

sky′-high′, *adv., adj.* very high.

sky•hook (skī′hŏŏk′), *n.* **1.** a fanciful hook imagined to be suspended in the air. **2.** any of various lifting devices, as one hung from a helicopter, for hoisting heavy loads over a distance.

sky•jack (skī′jak′), *v.t.* to hijack (an airliner). —**sky′jack′er,** *n.*

Sky•lab (skī′lab′), *n.* a U.S. earth-orbiting space station that was periodically staffed by three separate crews of astronauts and remained in orbit 1973–79.

sky•lark (skī′lärk′), *n.* **1.** a brown-speckled Eurasian lark, *Alauda arvensis,* famed for its melodious song. —*v.i.* **2.** to frolic; sport.

sky•light (skī′līt′), *n.* an opening in a roof or ceiling, fitted with glass, for admitting daylight. —**sky′light′ed, sky′lit′** (-lit′), *adj.*

sky•line or **sky′ line′,** *n.* **1.** the boundary line between earth and sky; apparent horizon. **2.** the outline of something, as the buildings of a city, against the sky.

sky•rock•et (skī′rok′it), *n.* **1.** a rocket firework that explodes high in the air, usu. in brilliant and colorful sparks. —*v.i.* **2.** to rise or increase rapidly or suddenly, esp. to unprecedented levels. —*v.t.* **3.** to cause to rise or increase rapidly and usu. suddenly. **4.** to thrust or advance suddenly or dramatically; catapult.

sky•scrap•er (skī′skrā′pər), *n.* a tall building of many stories, esp. one for office or commercial use.

sky•walk (skī′wôk′), *n.* SKYBRIDGE.

sky•ward (skī′wərd), *adv.* **1.** Also, **sky′wards.** toward the sky. —*adj.* **2.** directed toward the sky.

sky•way (skī′wā′), *n.* an elevated highway, esp. one well above ground level and composed of a series of spans.

sky•writ•ing (skī′rī′ting), *n.* **1.** the act or technique of writing against the sky with chemically produced smoke released from a maneuvering airplane. **2.** the letters, designs, etc., so traced. —**sky′write′,** *v.i., v.t.,* **-wrote, -writ•ten, -writ•ing.** —**sky′writ′er,** *n.*

slab (slab), *n., v.,* **slabbed, slab•bing.** —*n.* **1.** a broad, flat, somewhat thick piece of stone, wood, or other solid material. **2.** a thick slice of anything. **3.** a rough outside piece cut from a log, as when sawing one into boards. —*v.t.* **4.** to make into a slab or slabs. **5.** to cover or lay with slabs. **6.** to put on in slabs or layers.

slack¹ (slak), *adj.* **1.** not tight, taut, firm, or tense; loose: *a slack rope.* **2.** negligent; careless; remiss. **3.** slow, sluggish, or indolent. **4.** not active

or busy; dull; not brisk. **5.** moving very slowly, as the tide, wind, or water. **6.** weak; lax. —*adv.* **7.** in a slack manner. —*n.* **8.** a slack condition or part. **9.** the part of a rope, sail, or the like, that hangs loose, without strain upon it. **10.** a decrease in activity, as in business or work. **11.** a period of decreased activity. **12.** a cessation in a strong flow, as of a current. —*v.t.* **13.** to be remiss in respect to (some matter, duty, right, etc.); shirk; leave undone. **14.** to make or allow to become less active, vigorous, intense, etc.; relax (efforts, labor, speed, etc.) (often fol. by *up*). **15.** to make loose, or less tense or taut, as a rope. —*v.i.* **16.** to be remiss; shirk one′s duty or part. **17.** to become less active, vigorous, rapid, etc. (often fol. by *up* or *off*). **18.** to become less tense or taut, as a rope; ease off. —**slack′ly,** *adv.* —**slack′ness,** *n.*

slack² (slak), *n.* a depression between hills, in a hillside, or in the land surface.

slack•en (slak′ən), *v.t., v.i.* **1.** to make or become less active, vigorous, intense, etc. **2.** to make or become looser or less taut.

slack•er¹ (slak′ər), *n.* **1.** a person who evades duty or work; shirker. **2.** a person who evades military service; dodger.

slack•er² (slak′ər), *n.* an esp. educated young person who is scornful of materialism, purposeless, apathetic, and usu. works in a dead-end job. [popularized by *Slackers* (1991), film by R. Linklater]

slacks (slaks), *n.* (*used with a pl. v.*) trousers for informal or casual wear.

slag (slag), *n., v.,* **slagged, slag•ging.** —*n.* **1.** the more or less completely fused and vitrified matter separated during the reduction of a metal from its ore. —*v.t.* **2.** to convert into slag. —*v.i.* **3.** to form slag. —**slag′gy,** *adj.,* **-gi•er, -gi•est.**

slain (slān), *v.* pp. of SLAY.

slake (slāk), *v.,* **slaked, slak•ing.** —*v.t.* **1.** to allay (thirst, desire, wrath, etc.) by satisfying; quench. **2.** to cool or refresh. **3.** to make less active, vigorous, intense, etc. **4.** to cause disintegration of (lime) by treatment with water. —*v.i.* **5.** (of lime) to become slaked.

sla•lom (slä′ləm, -lōm), *n.* **1.** a downhill ski race over a winding and zigzag course marked by poles or gates. **2.** any winding or zigzag course marked by obstacles or barriers. —*v.i.* **3.** to ski in or as if in a slalom. **4.** to move on or as if on a course with many twists and turns; zigzag; weave. —*adj.* **5.** pertaining to a zigzag course with obstacles.

slam¹ (slam), *v.,* **slammed, slam•ming,** *n.* —*v.t.* **1.** to shut with force and noise: *to slam the door.* **2.** to dash, strike, throw, etc., with violent, noisy impact: *She slammed the book on the table.* **3.** to hit, push, block, etc., so as to cause a violent noise (often fol. by *on): If you slam on the brakes, the car will skid.* **4.** to criticize harshly; attack verbally. —*v.i.* **5.** to shut, stop, or make an impact with force and noise. **6.** to move or act with a noisy vigor, force, or violence: *a hockey team slamming onto the ice.* —*n.* **7.** a violent, noisy closing, dashing, or impact. **8.** the noise so made. **9.** a harsh criticism.

slam² (slam), *n.* the winning or bidding of all the tricks or all the tricks but one in a deal of cards.

slam′-bang′, *adv.* **1.** with noisy violence. **2.** quickly and carelessly; slapdash. —*adj.* **3.** noisy and violent. **4.** excitingly fast-paced, esp. in a noisy and violent way: *a slam-bang movie.* **5.** slapdash. **6.** outstanding; excellent. —**slam′-bang′er,** *n.*

slam′ dance′, *n.* a dance performed to punk rock by groups of people who flail and toss themselves about and slam into one another. —**slam′-dance′,** *v.i.,* **-danced, -danc•ing.**

slam′ dunk′, *n.* a forceful, often dramatic dunk shot in basketball.

slan•der (slan′dər), *n.* **1.** defamation; calumny. **2.** a malicious, false, and defamatory statement or report. **3.** *Law.* defamation by oral utterance rather than by writing, pictures, etc. —*v.t.* **4.** to utter slander against; defame. —*v.i.* **5.** to utter or circulate slander. —**slan′der•er,** *n.* —**slan′der•ous,** *adj.* —**slan′der•ous•ly,** *adv.*

slang (slang), *n.* **1.** very informal usage in vocabulary and idiom that is characteristically more metaphorical, playful, elliptical, vivid, and ephemeral than ordinary language. **2.** speech or writing characterized by the use of vulgar and socially taboo vocabulary and idiomatic expressions. **3.** the jargon of a particular group, profession, etc. **4.** the special vocabulary of thieves, vagabonds, etc.; argot; cant. —*v.i.* **5.** to use slang or abusive language. —*v.t.* **6.** to assail with abusive language. —**slang′i•ness,** *n.* —**slang′y,** *adj.,* **-i•er, -i•est.**

slant (slant, slänt), *v.i.* **1.** to veer or angle away from a given level or line, esp. from a horizontal; slope. **2.** to have or be influenced by a subjective point of view, personal feeling or inclination, etc. (usu. fol. by *toward*). —*v.t.* **3.** to cause to slope. **4.** to distort (information), as by rendering it incompletely, esp. in order to reflect or favor a particular viewpoint. **5.** to present for the interest or amusement of a specific group: *a story slanted toward young adults.* —*n.* **6.** slanting or oblique direction; slope. **7.** a slanting line, surface, etc. **8.** a particular viewpoint, opinion, attitude, or perspective. **9.** a glance or look. —*adj.* **10.** sloping; oblique. —**slant′ing•ly,** *adv.*

slap (slap), *n., v.,* **slapped, slap•ping,** *adv.* —*n.* **1.** a sharp blow or smack, esp. with the open hand or with something flat. **2.** a sound made by or as if by such a blow or smack. **3.** a sharp or sarcastic rebuke or comment. —*v.t.* **4.** to strike sharply, esp. with the open hand or with something flat. **5.** to bring (the hand, something flat, etc.) with a sharp blow against something. **6.** to dash or cast forcibly: *He slapped the packages into a pile.* **7.** to put or place quickly and sometimes haphazardly (often fol. by *on): to slap mustard on a sandwich.* **8.** slap

down, a. to subdue, esp. by a blow or by force; suppress. **b.** to reject, oppose, or criticize sharply. *—adv.* **9.** directly; straight; smack.

slap•dash (slap′dash′), *adv.* **1.** in a hasty, haphazard manner. *—adj.* **2.** hasty and careless; offhand: *a slapdash answer.*

slap•hap•py (slap′hap′ē), *adj.*, **-pi•er, -pi•est.** **1.** severely befuddled; punch-drunk. **2.** agreeably giddy or foolish. **3.** cheerfully irresponsible.

slap′ shot′, *n.* a shot in ice hockey made with a full backswing and extended follow-through.

slap•stick (slap′stik′), *n.* **1.** broad comedy characterized by violently boisterous action. **2.** a stick or lath used by comic performers or characters for striking other persons, esp. a pair of laths that produce a loud noise without causing injury. *—adj.* **3.** using, or marked by the use of, broad farce and horseplay: *a slapstick routine.*

slash (slash), *v.t.* **1.** to cut with a violent sweeping stroke or by striking violently and at random, as with a knife or sword. **2.** to lash; whip. **3.** to cut, reduce, or alter: *to slash salaries.* **4.** to make slits in (a garment) to show an underlying fabric. **5.** to criticize or censure savagely. *—v.i.* **6.** to lay about one with sharp, sweeping strokes; make one's way by cutting. **7.** to make a sweeping, cutting stroke. *—n.* **8.** a sweeping stroke, as with a knife, sword, or pen. **9.** a cut, wound, or mark made with such a stroke. **10.** a curtailment, reduction, or alteration: *a slash in prices.* **11.** a decorative slit in a garment showing an underlying fabric. **12.** VIRGULE. **13.** (in forest land) **a.** an open area strewn with debris of trees from felling or from wind or fire. **b.** the debris itself.

slash′-and-burn′, *adj.* **1.** of or noting a method of agriculture in the tropics in which vegetation is felled and burned, the land is cropped for a few years, then the forest is allowed to reinvade. **2.** unnecessarily destructive or extreme.

slash•er (slash′ər), *n.* **1.** one that slashes. **2.** a person who criminally attacks others with a knife, razor, or the like. **3.** a horror film depicting such a criminal and featuring gory special effects.

slash•ing (slash′ing), *n.* **1.** a slash. **2.** the illegal swinging of the stick at an opponent, as in ice hockey or lacrosse. *—adj.* **3.** sweeping; cutting. **4.** violent; severe: *a slashing wind.* **5.** vivid; flashing; brilliant. —**slash′ing•ly,** *adv.*

slash′ pine′, *n.* a pine, *Pinus elliotii,* found in slashes or swamps in the southeastern U.S. and Central America.

slash′ pock′et, *n.* a pocket set into a garment, to which easy access is provided by an exterior slit.

slat (slat), *n., v.,* **slat•ted, slat•ting.** *—n.* **1.** a long, narrow strip of wood, metal, or the like used as a support for a bed, as one of the horizontal laths of a Venetian blind, etc. *—v.t.* **2.** to furnish or make with slats.

slat′-back′, *n.* a chair back having two or more horizontal slats between upright posts.

slate (slāt), *n., v.,* **slat•ed, slat•ing.** *—n.* **1.** a fine-grained rock formed by the metamorphosis of clay, shale, etc., that tends to split along parallel cleavage planes, usu. at an angle to the planes of stratification. **2.** a thin piece or plate of this rock or a similar material, used esp. for roofing or as a writing surface. **3.** a dull, dark bluish gray. **4.** a list of candidates, officers, etc., to be considered for nomination, appointment, or election. *—v.t.* **5.** to cover with or as if with slate. **6.** to write or set down for nomination or appointment. **7.** to plan or designate (something) for a particular place and time; schedule. *—**Idiom.*** **8. clean slate,** an unsullied record; a record marked by creditable conduct.

slate′ blue′, *n.* a moderate to dark grayish blue. —**slate′-blue′,** *adj.*

slath•er (slaŧħ′ər), *v.t.* **1.** to spread or apply thickly: *to slather butter on toast.* **2.** to spread something thickly on (usu. fol. by *with*): *to slather toast with butter.* **3.** to spend or use lavishly. *—n.* **4.** Often, **slathers.** a generous amount.

slat•tern (slat′ərn), *n.* **1.** a slovenly, untidy woman. **2.** a slut; harlot.

slat•tern•ly (slat′ərn lē), *adj.* **1.** slovenly and untidy. **2.** characteristic or suggestive of a slattern. *—adv.* **3.** in the manner of a slattern.

slaugh•ter (slô′tər), *n.* **1.** the killing or butchering of cattle, sheep, etc., esp. for food. **2.** a brutal or violent killing, esp. the killing of great numbers of people or animals indiscriminately; carnage. *—v.t.* **3.** to kill or butcher (animals), esp. for food. **4.** to kill in a brutal or violent manner. **5.** to slay in great numbers; massacre. —**slaugh′ter•er,** *n.*

slaugh•ter•house (slô′tər hous′), *n., pl.* **-hous•es** (-hou′ziz). a building or place where animals are butchered for food; abattoir.

Slaugh′ter of the In′nocents, *n.* the slaughter of male children in Bethlehem by order of Herod the Great. Matt. 2:16.

Slav (släv, slav), *n.* a member of a Slavic-speaking people.

Slav or **Slav.,** Slavic.

slave (slāv), *n., v.,* **slaved, slav•ing.** *—n.* **1.** a person who is the property of and wholly subject to another; bond servant. **2.** a person entirely under the domination of some influence or person. **3.** a drudge: *a housekeeping slave.* **4.** a mechanism under control of and repeating the actions of a similar mechanism. Compare MASTER (def. 17). *—v.i.* **5.** to work like a slave; drudge. **6.** to engage in the slave trade. —**slave′less,** *adj.* —**slave′like′,** *adj.*

Slave′ Coast′, *n.* the coast of W equatorial Africa, between the Benin and Volta rivers: a center of slavery traffic 16th–19th centuries.

slave′ driv′er, *n.* **1.** an overseer of slaves. **2.** a demanding, unyielding taskmaster.

slave′ la′bor, *n.* **1.** a labor force of slaves or slavelike prisoners. **2.** labor performed by such a force. **3.** any coerced or poorly paid work.

slav•er (slav′ər, slā′vər, slä′-), *v.i.* **1.** to let saliva run from the mouth; slobber; drool. **2.** to fawn. *—n.* **3.** saliva coming from the mouth.

slav•er•y (slā′və rē, slāv′rē), *n.* **1.** the condition of a slave; bondage. **2.** the keeping of slaves as a practice or institution. **3.** a state of subjection like that of a slave. **4.** severe toil; drudgery.

Slave′ State′, *n.* any of the 15 Southern states that permitted slavery before the Civil War.

slave′ trade′, *n.* the business of procuring, transporting, and selling slaves, esp. the bringing of black Africans to America.

Slav•ic (slä′vik, slav′ik), *n.* **1.** a family of languages, a branch of the Indo-European family, that includes Polish, Czech, Serbo-Croatian, Bulgarian, Ukrainian, and Russian. Compare EAST SLAVIC, SOUTH SLAVIC, WEST SLAVIC. *—adj.* **2.** of or pertaining to Slavic or its speakers. **3.** of or pertaining to the Slavs: *Slavic customs.*

slav•ish (slā′vish), *adj.* **1.** of or befitting a slave: *slavish subjection.* **2.** being or resembling a slave; abjectly submissive. **3.** deliberately imitative: *a slavish reproduction.* **4.** base; mean; ignoble: *slavish fears.* —**slav′ish•ly,** *adv.* —**slav′ish•ness,** *n.*

Slavo-, a combining form representing SLAV: *Slavophile.*

slaw (slô), *n.* coleslaw.

slay (slā), *v.,* **slew, slain, slay•ing.** *—v.t.* **1.** to kill by violence. **2.** to destroy; extinguish. *—v.i.* **3.** to kill or murder. —**slay′a•ble,** *adj.* —**slay′er,** *n.*

sleaze (slēz), *n.* **1.** sleazy quality, character, or content; sordidness, vulgarity, or squalor. **2.** *Slang.* **a.** a contemptible or vulgar person. **b.** a shabby or slovenly person.

slea•zy (slē′zē, slā′zē), *adj.,* **-zi•er, -zi•est.** **1.** contemptibly low or disreputable. **2.** squalid; filthy: *a sleazy hotel.* **3.** thin and limp in texture: *sleazy satin; a sleazy dress.* —**slea′zi•ness,** *n.*

sled (sled), *n., v.,* **sled•ded, sled•ding.** *—n.* **1.** a small vehicle consisting of a platform mounted on runners for use in traveling over snow or ice. **2.** a sledge. *—v.i.* **3.** to coast, ride, or be carried on a sled. *—v.t.* **4.** to convey by sled.

sled•der (sled′ər), *n.* **1.** a person who rides on or steers a sled. **2.** a horse or other animal for drawing a sled.

sled•ding (sled′ing), *n.* **1.** the state of the ground permitting use of a sled. **2.** the act of conveying or riding on a sled. **3.** a going, progress, or advance in any field: *The job won't be easy sledding.*

sled′ dog′, *n.* a dog trained to pull a sled, usu. working in a team.

sledge[1] (slej), *n., v.,* **sledged, sledg•ing.** *—n.* **1.** a vehicle mounted on runners and often drawn by draft animals, used for traveling or for conveying loads over snow, ice, rough ground, etc. **2.** a sled. **3.** *Brit.* a sleigh. *—v.t., v.i.* **4.** to convey or travel by sledge. *—v.i.* **5.** *Brit.* to ride in a sleigh.

sledge[2] (slej), *n., v.t., v.i.,* **sledged, sledg•ing.** SLEDGEHAMMER.

sledge•ham•mer (slej′ham′ər), *n.* **1.** a large heavy hammer wielded with both hands. *—v.t., v.i.* **2.** to hammer, beat, or strike with or as if with a sledgehammer. *—adj.* **3.** overly forceful.

sleek[1] (slēk), *adj.* **1.** smooth or glossy, as hair. **2.** well-fed or well-groomed. **3.** finely contoured; streamlined. **4.** smooth in manners, speech, etc.; suave. —**sleek′ly,** *adv.* —**sleek′ness,** *n.*

sleek[2] (slēk) also **sleek′en,** *v.t.* to make sleek; smooth; slick.

sleep (slēp), *v.,* **slept, sleep•ing,** *n.* *—v.i.* **1.** to take the rest afforded by a suspension of voluntary bodily functions and the natural suspension, complete or partial, of consciousness; to cease being awake. **2.** *Bot.* to assume, esp. at night, a state similar to the sleep of animals, marked by closing of petals, leaves, etc. **3.** to be dormant, quiescent, or inactive, as faculties. **4.** to allow one's alertness or attentiveness to lie dormant. **5.** to lie in death. *—v.t.* **6.** to take rest in (a specified kind of sleep): *to sleep the sleep of the innocent.* **7.** to have sleeping accommodations for. **8. sleep away, a.** to spend or pass (time) in sleep. **b.** Also, **sleep off.** to get rid of (a headache, etc.) by sleeping. **9. sleep in, a.** (of domestic help) to sleep where one is employed. **b.** to sleep beyond one's usual time of arising. **10. sleep on,** to postpone making a decision about for at least a day. **11. sleep over,** to sleep in another person's home. **12. sleep together,** to be sexual partners. **13. sleep with,** to have sexual relations with. *—n.* **14.** the state of a person, animal, or plant that sleeps. **15.** a period of sleeping. **16.** dormancy or inactivity. **17.** the repose of death.

sleep′ ap′nea, *n.* a brief suspension of breathing occurring repeatedly during sleep.

sleep•er (slē′pər), *n.* **1.** a person or thing that sleeps. **2.** a heavy horizontal timber for distributing loads. **3. a.** any long wooden, metal, or stone piece lying horizontally, as a sill or footing. **b.** any of a number of wooden pieces, laid upon the ground or upon masonry or concrete, to which floorboards are nailed. **4.** an unexpected success, esp. a film or play originally ignored or considered a failure. **5.** Often, **sleepers.** one-piece or two-piece pajamas with feet, esp. for children. **6.** a piece of furniture, as a sofa, that opens up or unfolds into a bed; convertible.

sleep′-in′, *adj.* LIVE-IN (def. 1).

sleep•ing (slē′ping), *n.* **1.** the condition of being asleep. *—adj.* **2.** asleep. **3.** concerning or having accommodations for sleeping: *a sleeping compartment.* **4.** used to sleep in or on: *a sleeping jacket.* **5.** used to induce or aid sleep or while asleep.

sleep′ing bag′, *n.* a warmly lined or padded body-length bag in which one or two persons can sleep outdoors, as when camping.

Sleep′ing Beau′ty, *n.* **1.** a beautiful princess, the heroine of a popular fairy tale, awakened from a charmed sleep by the kiss of the prince who is her true love. **2.** (*italics*) the fairy tale itself. **3.** (*italics*) a ballet (1889) by Peter Ilyich Tchaikovsky.

sleep′ing car′, *n.* a railroad car fitted with berths or compartments for passengers to sleep in.

sleep′ing gi′ant, *n.* an unrealized source of power and strength, esp. a group of nations.

sleep′ing pill′, *n.* a pill containing a drug for inducing sleep.

sleep′ing sick′ness, *n.* **1.** Also called **trypanosomiasis.** an infectious, usu. fatal disease of Africa, characterized by wasting and progressive lethargy, and caused by a trypanosome carried by the tsetse fly. **2.** a viral disease affecting the brain, characterized by apathy, sleepiness, extreme weakness, and impairment of vision.

sleep·less (slēp′lis), *adj.* **1.** without sleep: *a sleepless night.* **2.** watchful; alert: *sleepless devotion to duty.* **3.** always active: *the sleepless ocean.* —**sleep′less·ly,** *adv.* —**sleep′less·ness,** *n.*

sleep′ so′fa, *n.* a sofa that can be used as a bed; sofa bed.

sleep·walk·ing (slēp′wô′king), *n.* the act or state of walking while asleep; somnambulism. —**sleep′walk′,** *v.i.* —**sleep′walk′er,** *n.*

sleep·wear (slēp′wâr′), *n.* garments, as nightgowns or pajamas, worn for sleeping or at bedtime.

sleep·y (slē′pē), *adj.,* **sleep·i·er, sleep·i·est. 1.** ready or inclined to sleep; drowsy. **2.** of or showing drowsiness. **3.** lethargic; inactive: *a sleepy village.* **4.** inducing sleep; soporific: *sleepy warmth.* —**sleep′i·ly,** *adv.* —**sleep′i·ness,** *n.*

sleep·y·head (slē′pē hed′), *n.* a sleepy person.

sleet (slēt), *n.* **1.** precipitation in the form of ice pellets created by the freezing of rain as it falls (disting. from *hail*). —*v.i.* **2.** to send down sleet. **3.** to fall as or like sleet. —**sleet′y,** *adj.,* **sleet·i·er, sleet·i·est.**

sleeve (slēv), *n., v.,* **sleeved, sleev·ing.** —*n.* **1.** the part of a garment that covers all or part of the arm. **2.** an envelope for protecting a phonograph record. **3.** a tubular piece, as of metal, fitting over a rod, etc. —*v.t.* **4.** to furnish with sleeves. —*Idiom.* **5. up one's sleeve,** kept hidden, esp. for future use against another. —**sleeve′less,** *adj.*

sleigh (slā), *n.* **1.** a light vehicle on runners, usu. open and generally horse-drawn, used esp. for transporting persons over snow or ice. **2.** a sled. —*v.i.* **3.** to travel or ride in a sleigh.

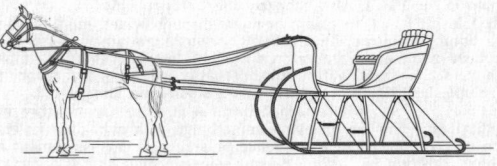

sleigh

sleight (slīt), *n.* **1.** skill; dexterity. **2.** an artifice; stratagem. **3.** cunning; craft.

sleight′ of hand′, *n.* **1.** skill in feats requiring quick and clever movements of the hands, esp. for entertainment or deception; legerdemain. **2.** a magic or conjuring trick. **3.** skill in deception.

slen·der (slen′dər), *adj.* **1.** having a circumference that is small in proportion to the height or length. **2.** thin or slight; light and graceful: *slender youths.* **3.** small in size, amount, extent, etc.; meager: *a slender income.* **4.** having little value, force, or justification: *slender prospects.* —**slen′der·ly,** *adv.* —**slen′der·ness,** *n.*

slen·der·ize (slen′də rīz′), *v.,* **-ized, -iz·ing.** —*v.t.* **1.** to make slender or more slender. **2.** to cause to appear slender. —*v.i.* **3.** to become slender.

slept (slept), *v.* pt. and pp. of SLEEP.

Sles·sor (sles′ər), *n.* **Mary,** 1848–1915, Scottish missionary in Africa.

sleuth (slōōth), *n.* **1.** a detective. **2.** a bloodhound. —*v.t., v.i.* **3.** to track or trail.

slew¹ (slōō), *v.* pt. of SLAY.

slew² (slōō), *n. Informal.* a large number or quantity: *a whole slew of people.*

slew³ (slōō), *n.* SLOUGH¹ (def. 3).

slice (slīs), *n., v.,* **sliced, slic·ing.** —*n.* **1.** a thin, flat piece cut from something: *a slice of bread.* **2.** a part or portion: *a slice of land.* **3.** any of various implements with a thin, broad blade or part; spatula. **4. a.** the path described by a baseball, golf ball, etc., that curves toward the side from which it was struck. **b.** a ball describing such a path. **5.** a stroke executed by hitting down on a tennis ball with an underhand motion and thus creating backspin. —*v.t.* **6.** to cut or divide into slices. **7.** to cut through or cleave with or as if with a knife. **8.** to cut off or remove as a slice or slices (sometimes fol. by *off, away,* etc.). **9.** to hit (a ball) so as to result in a slice. —*v.i.* **10. a.** (of a player) to slice the ball. **b.** (of a ball) to describe a slice in flight. —**slic′er,** *n.*

slice′-of-life′, *adj.* of or pertaining to a naturalistic, unembellished representation of real life: *a play with slice-of-life dialogue.*

slick¹ (slik), *adj.* **1.** smooth and glossy; sleek. **2.** smooth in manners, speech, etc.; suave. **3.** sly; shrewdly adroit. **4.** ingenious; cleverly devised. **5.** slippery, esp. from being covered with or as if with ice or oil. **6.** deftly executed and having surface appeal but shallow or glib in content: *slick writing.* **7.** *Slang.* wonderful; remarkable; first-rate. —*n.* **8.** a smooth or slippery place or spot or the substance causing it. **9.** *Informal.* a chic or sophisticated magazine printed on paper with a more or less glossy finish. —*adv.* **10.** smoothly; cleverly. —**slick′ly,** *adv.* —**slick′ness,** *n.*

slick² (slik), *v.t.* **1.** to make sleek or smooth. **2.** *Informal.* to make smart or spruce (usu. fol. by *up*). —*n.* **3.** any woodworking chisel having a blade more than 2 in. (5 cm) wide.

slick·er (slik′ər), *n.* **1.** a long, loose oilskin raincoat. **2.** any raincoat.

slide (slīd), *v.,* **slid** (slid), **slid·ing,** *n.* —*v.i.* **1.** to move along in continuous contact with a smooth or slippery surface. **2.** to slip or skid. **3.** to glide or pass smoothly. **4.** to slip easily or unobtrusively on or as if on a track or guide rail (usu. fol. by *in, out,* etc.). **5.** to pass or fall gradually into a specified state, character, practice, etc. **6.** to decline or decrease. **7.** to pursue a natural course without intervention. **8.** *Baseball.* (of a base runner) to cast oneself forward along the ground towards a base. —*v.t.* **9.** to cause to slide or coast, as over a surface or with a smooth, gliding motion. **10.** to hand, pass along, or slip (something) easily or quietly (usu. fol. by *in, into,* etc.). **11.** an act or instance of sliding. **12.** a smooth surface for sliding on, esp. a type of chute in a playground. **13.** an object intended to slide. **14. a.** a landslide or the like. **b.** the mass of matter sliding down. **15.** a transparency, as a frame of positive film, mounted for projection on a screen or magnification through a viewer. **16.** a usu. rectangular plate of glass on which objects are placed for microscopic examination. **17.** a shelf sliding into the body of a piece of furniture when not in use. **18.** a U-shaped section of the tube of an instrument of the trumpet class, as the trombone, that can be pushed in or out to change the pitch. **19.** (of a machine, mechanism, or device) **a.** a moving part working on a track, channel, or guide rails. **b.** the surface, track, channel, or guide rails on which the part moves. —**slid′a·ble,** *adj.*

slide′ fas′tener, *n.* ZIPPER (def. 1).

slid·er (slī′dər), *n.* **1.** a person or thing that slides. **2.** a fast-pitched baseball that curves slightly and sharply in front of a batter, away from the side from which it was thrown.

slide′ rule′, *n.* a mechanical calculator consisting of a ruler with a sliding section, both bearing logarithmic scales.

slid·ing (slī′ding), *adj.* **1.** rising or falling, increasing or decreasing, according to a standard or to a set of conditions. **2.** operated, adjusted, or moved by sliding: *a sliding door.*

slid′ing scale′, *n.* **1.** a wage scale that varies with the selling price of goods produced, the cost of living, or profits. **2.** a price scale, as of fees, that varies according to the ability of individuals to pay.

slight (slīt), *adj.* **1.** small in amount, degree, etc. **2.** of little importance, influence, etc.; trivial. **3.** slender or slim; not heavily built. **4.** frail; flimsy; delicate: *a slight fabric.* **5.** of little substance or strength. —*v.t.* **6.** to treat as of little importance. **7.** to treat (someone) with indifference; snub. **8.** to do negligently; scamp: *to slight one's studies.* —*n.* **9.** an instance of slighting indifference or treatment. **10.** a pointed and contemptuous discourtesy; affront. —**slight′ly,** *adv.* —**slight′ness,** *n.*

slight·ing (slī′ting), *adj.* derogatory and disparaging; belittling. —**slight′ing·ly,** *adv.*

slim (slim), *adj.,* **slim·mer, slim·mest,** *v.,* **slimmed, slim·ming.** —*adj.* **1.** slender, as in girth or form. **2.** poor or inferior; meager: *a slim chance; a slim excuse.* **3.** sized for the thinner than average person. —*v.t., v.i.* **4.** to make or become slim. —**slim′ly,** *adv.* —**slim′ness,** *n.*

slime (slīm), *n., v.,* **slimed, slim·ing.** —*n.* **1.** thin, glutinous mud. **2.** any ropy or viscous liquid matter, esp. of a foul kind. **3.** a viscous secretion of animal or vegetable origin. **4.** *Slang.* a repulsive or despicable person. —*v.t.* **5.** to cover or smear with or as if with slime.

slim·y (slī′mē), *adj.,* **slim·i·er, slim·i·est. 1.** of or like slime. **2.** abounding in or covered with slime. **3.** offensively foul or vile. —**slim′i·ly,** *adv.* —**slim′i·ness,** *n.*

sling (sling), *n., v.,* **slung, sling·ing.** —*n.* **1.** a device for hurling a missile by hand, usually consisting of a strap with a string at each end that is whirled around in a circle to gain momentum before the missile is released. **2.** a slingshot. **3.** a strap or band forming a loop by which something is suspended, supported, or carried, as a bandage for an injured arm. **4.** an act or instance of slinging. **5.** a rope, chain, net, etc., for hoisting or holding freight. —*v.t.* **6.** to throw or hurl; fling. **7.** to place in or move by a sling, as freight. **8.** to hang by a sling.

sling′-back′ or **sling′back′,** *n.* a woman's shoe with an open back and a strap or sling encircling the heel of the foot to keep the shoe secure. Also called **sling.**

sling·shot (sling′shot′), *n.* a Y-shaped stick with an elastic strip between the prongs for shooting small missiles.

slink (slingk), *v.,* **slunk, slink·ing,** *n., adj.* —*v.i.* **1.** to move or go in a furtive, abject manner, as from fear or shame. **2.** to walk or move in a sinuous, provocative way. —*v.t.* **3.** (esp. of cows) to bring forth (young) prematurely. —*n.* **4.** a prematurely born calf or other animal. —*adj.* **5.** born prematurely. —**slink′ing·ly,** *adv.*

slink·y (sling′kē), *adj.,* **slink·i·er, slink·i·est. 1.** characterized by or proceeding with slinking or stealthy movements. **2.** made of soft, often clinging material that follows the figure closely: *a slinky gown.* —**slink′i·ly,** *adv.* —**slink′i·ness,** *n.*

slip¹ (slip), *v.,* **slipped, slip·ping,** *n.* —*v.i.* **1.** to move or go smoothly or

S

easily; glide; slide. **2.** to slide suddenly and accidentally: *He slipped on the icy ground. The cup slipped from her hand.* **3.** to pass without having been acted upon or used, as an opportunity. **4.** to elapse or pass quickly or imperceptibly (often fol. by *away* or *by*): The years slipped by. **5.** to become involved or absorbed easily: *to slip into a new way of life.* **6.** to move or go quietly or unobtrusively: *to slip out of a room.* **7.** to put on or take off a garment easily or quickly. **8.** to make a mistake or error (often fol. by *up*). **9.** to decline; deteriorate: *His work slipped last year.* **10.** to be said or revealed inadvertently (often fol. by *out*): *The words just slipped out.* **—***v.t.* **11.** to cause to move, pass, go, etc., with a smooth or sliding motion. **12.** to put, pass, insert, etc., quickly or stealthily. **13.** to put on or take off (a garment) easily or quickly: *to slip a robe on.* **14.** to let or make (something) slide out of a fastening, hold, etc.: *I slipped the lock, and the door opened.* **15.** to release from a leash, harness, etc., as a hound or a hawk. **16.** to get away or free oneself from; escape (a pursuer, restraint, etc.): *The cow slipped its halter.* **17.** to untie or undo (a knot). **18.** to let go entirely, as an anchor cable or an anchor. **19.** to pass from or escape (one's memory, attention, etc.). **20.** to put out of joint or position: *I slipped a disk in my back.* **21.** to shed or cast, as a skin. **22.** (of animals) to bring forth (offspring) prematurely. **—***n.* **23.** an act or instance of slipping. **24.** a sudden, accidental slide. **25.** a mistake or blunder, as in speaking or writing, esp. a small, careless one. **26.** an error in conduct; indiscretion. **27.** a decline or fall in quantity, quality, extent, etc. **28.** a woman's undergarment, usu. having shoulder straps and extending down to the hemline of the outer dress. **29.** a pillowcase. **30.** an inclined plane, sloping to the water, on which vessels are built or repaired. **31.** a space between two wharves or in a dock for vessels to lie in. **32.** unintended movement or play between mechanical parts or the like. **33.** *Geol.* **a.** the relative displacement of formerly adjacent points on opposite sides of a fault. **b.** a small fault. **—*Idiom.*** **34. give someone the slip,** to elude a pursuer; escape from someone. **35. let slip,** to reveal unintentionally. **36. slip of the tongue,** a mistake in speaking, as an inadvertent remark.

slip[2] (slip), *n., v.,* **slipped, slip•ping.** **—***n.* **1.** a small paper form on which information is noted: *a correction slip.* **2.** a piece suitable for propagation cut from a plant; scion or cutting. **3.** any long, narrow piece or strip, as of wood, paper, or land. **4.** a young person, esp. one of slender form: *a mere slip of a girl.* **5.** a long seat or narrow pew in a church. **—***v.t.* **6.** to take slips or cuttings from (a plant).

slip[3] (slip), *n.* a creamy clay solution used for coating or decorating ceramic biscuit.

slip•cov•er (slip′kuv′ər), *n.* **1.** a cover, as for an upholstered chair or sofa, made so as to be easily removable. **2.** a book jacket. **—***v.t.* **3.** to cover with a slipcover.

slip′knot′ or **slip′ knot′,** *n.* a knot that slips easily along the cord or line around which it is made.

slip′-on′, *adj.* **1.** made without buttons, straps, zippers, etc., so as to be put on easily and quickly: *slip-on shoes.* **—***n.* **2.** something made this way, esp. an article of clothing.

slip•o•ver (slip′ō′vər), *n., adj.* PULLOVER.

slip•page (slip′ij), *n.* **1.** an act or instance of slipping. **2.** an amount or extent of slipping. **3.** (in machinery) the amount of work dissipated by slipping of parts, excess play, etc.

slipped′ disk′, *n.* HERNIATED DISK.

slip•per (slip′ər), *n.* any light, low-cut shoe into which the foot may be easily slipped, for wear in the home, for dancing, etc.

slip•per•y (slip′ə rē, slip′rē), *adj.,* **-per•i•er, -per•i•est.** **1.** tending or liable to cause slipping or sliding, as ice, oil, or a wet surface: *a slippery road.* **2.** tending to slip from the hold or grasp or from position: *a slippery rope.* **3.** likely to slip away or escape: *slippery prospects.* **4.** not to be depended on; shifty, tricky, or deceitful. **5.** unstable or insecure, as conditions: *a slippery situation.* **—slip′per•i•ness,** *n.*

slip′pery elm′, *n.* **1.** a North American elm, *Ulmus rubra,* having a mucilaginous inner bark. **2.** this bark.

slip•shod (slip′shod′), *adj.* **1.** careless, untidy, or slovenly: *slipshod work.* **2.** down-at-heel; seedy; shabby.

slip′ stitch′, *n.* a loose stitch taken between two layers of fabric, as on a facing or hem, so as to be invisible on the right or outer side. **—slip′-stitch′,** *v.t., v.i.*

slip′-up′, *n.* a mistake, blunder, or oversight.

slit (slit), *v.,* **slit, slit•ting,** *n.* **—***v.t.* **1.** to make a long cut or opening in. **2.** to cut or rend into strips; split. **—***n.* **3.** a straight, narrow cut or opening. **—slit′less,** *adj.* **—slit′like′,** *adj.*

slith•er (slith′ər), *v.i.* **1.** to move or walk with a sliding motion, as a snake. **2.** to slide down or along a surface, esp. unsteadily, from side to side. **—***v.t.* **3.** to cause to slither or slide. **—***n.* **4.** a slithering movement; slide. **—slith′er•y,** *adj.*

sliv•er (sliv′ər), *n.* **1.** a small, slender, often sharp piece, as of wood or glass; splinter. **2.** any small, narrow piece or portion. **3.** a strand of loose, untwisted fibers produced in carding. **—***v.t.* **4.** to split or cut into slivers. **5.** to form (textile fibers) into slivers. **—***v.i.* **6.** to split.

slob (slob), *n.* a slovenly or boorish person.

slob•ber (slob′ər), *v.i.* **1.** to drool; drivel. **2.** to indulge in mawkish sentimentality. **—***v.t.* **3.** to wet or make foul by slobbering. **4.** to let (saliva or liquid) run from the mouth. **—***n.* **5.** saliva or liquid dribbling from the mouth; slaver. **6.** mawkish speech or actions. **—slob′ber•er,** *n.* **—slob′ber•y,** *adj.*

sloe (slō), *n.* **1.** the small, sour, blackish fruit of the blackthorn, *Prunus spinosa,* of the rose family. **2.** the shrub itself.

sloe′-eyed′, *adj.* **1.** having very dark eyes. **2.** having slanted eyes.

slog (slog), *v.,* **slogged, slog•ging.** *n.* **—***v.t.* **1.** to hit hard, as in boxing; slug. **2.** to drive with blows. **—***v.i.* **3.** to deal heavy blows. **4.** to walk or plod heavily. **5.** to toil. **—***n.* **6.** a long, tiring walk or march. **7.** long, laborious work. **8.** a heavy blow. **—slog′ger,** *n.*

slo•gan (slō′gən), *n.* **1.** a distinctive phrase or motto identified with a particular party, product, etc.; catchword or catch phrase. **2.** a war cry or gathering cry formerly used among Scottish clans. [< Scottish Gaelic *sluagh-ghairm* army cry]

sloop (slo͞op), *n.* a single-masted, fore-and-aft-rigged sailing vessel.

slop[1] (slop), *v.,* **slopped, slop•ping,** *n.* **—***v.t.* **1.** to spill or splash (liquid). **2.** to spill liquid upon. **3.** to feed slop to (pigs or other livestock). **—***v.i.* **4.** to spill or splash liquid (sometimes fol. by *about*). **5.** (of liquid) to spill or splash out of a container (usu. fol. by *over*). **6.** to walk through mud, slush, or water. **7.** to be unduly effusive; gush (usu. fol. by *over*). **—***n.* **8.** bran from bolted cornmeal mixed with water and used as a feed for livestock. **9.** Often, **slops. a.** kitchen refuse; swill. **b.** the dirty water or liquid refuse of a household. **10.** unappetizing food or drink. **11.** liquid mud. **12.** gushing language.

slop[2] (slop), *n.* **1. slops, a.** clothing, bedding, etc., supplied to sailors from the ship's stores. **b.** cheap, ready-made clothing in general. **2.** a loose-fitting overgarment, as a tunic or smock.

slope (slōp), *v.,* **sloped, slop•ing,** *n.* **—***v.i.* **1.** to have an inclined or oblique direction or angle, esp. with reference to a horizontal plane; slant. **2.** to move at an inclination or obliquely. **—***v.t.* **3.** to cause to incline from the horizontal or vertical. **4.** to form with a slope or slant. **—***n.* **5.** ground that has a natural incline, as the side of a hill. **6.** inclination or slant, esp. downward or upward. **7.** the degree of deviation from the horizontal or vertical. **8.** an inclined surface. **9.** Usu., **slopes.** hills, esp. foothills. **—slop′er,** *n.*

slop•py (slop′ē), *adj.,* **-pi•er, -pi•est.** **1.** muddy, slushy, or very wet: *sloppy grounds.* **2.** splashed or soiled with liquid. **3.** untidy; slovenly: *a sloppy eater.* **4.** careless; slipshod: *sloppy writing.* **5.** overly emotional; gushy: *sloppy sentimentality.* **6.** (of clothes) loose-fitting; baggy. **—slop′pi•ly,** *adv.* **—slop′pi•ness,** *n.*

Slop′py Joe′, *n.* **1.** ground beef cooked with barbecue sauce and served on a bun. **2.** a baggy sweater orig. worn by girls and young women in the 1940s. Also, **slop′py Joe′, slop′py joe′.**

slosh (slosh), *v.i.* **1.** to splash or move through water, mud, or slush. **2.** (of a liquid) to move about actively within a container. **—***v.t.* **3.** to stir or splash (something) around in a fluid. **4.** to splash (liquid) clumsily or haphazardly. **—***n.* **5.** watery mire or partly melted snow; slush. **6.** the lap or splash of liquid. **—slosh′y,** *adj.,* **slosh•i•er, slosh•i•est.**

slot (slot), *n., v.,* **slot•ted, slot•ting.** **—***n.* **1.** a slit or other narrow opening, esp. one for receiving something, as a coin or a letter. **2.** a place or position, as in a sequence or series. **3.** an assignment or job opening; position. **4.** *Informal.* SLOT MACHINE (def. 1). **5.** a gap that is opened along the leading edge of an aircraft wing to improve airflow. **—***v.t.* **6.** to make a slot in; provide with a slot or slots. **7.** to place or fit into a slot: *You've been slotted for four o'clock.* **—***v.i.* **8.** to fit or be placed in a slot. **—slot′ter,** *n.*

sloth (slôth *or, esp. for 2,* slōth), *n.* **1.** indolence; laziness: one of the seven deadly sins. **2.** any slow-moving, arboreal tropical American edentate of the family Bradypodidae, having hooklike claws and usu. hanging upside down.

two-toed sloth, *Choloepus hoffmanni,* length 2 ft. (0.6 m)

sloth•ful (slôth′fəl, slōth′-), *adj.* indolent; lazy. **—sloth′ful•ly,** *adv.* **—sloth′ful•ness,** *n.*

slot′ machine′, *n.* **1.** a gambling machine operated by inserting coins into a slot and pulling down a long handle attached to its side. **2.** any machine operated by inserting coins into a slot, as a vending machine.

slouch (slouch), *v.i.* **1.** to sit or stand with an awkward, drooping posture. **2.** to move or walk with drooping body and shuffling gait. **3.** to have a droop or downward bend, as a hat. **—***v.t.* **4.** to cause to droop or bend down, as the shoulders or a hat. **—***n.* **5.** an awkward, drooping posture or carriage. **6.** an awkward person. **7.** a lazy, inept person. **8.** SLOUCH HAT. **—slouch′er,** *n.*

slouch′ hat′, *n.* a soft hat often made of felt and having a supple, usu. broad brim.

slouch•y (slou′chē), *adj.,* **slouch•i•er, slouch•i•est.** resembling a slouch or a slouching manner, posture, etc. **—slouch′i•ly,** *adv.*

slough[1] (slou *for 1, 2, 4;* slo͞o *for 3*), *n.* **1.** an area of soft, muddy ground; swamp or swamplike region. **2.** a hole full of mire, as in a road. **3.** a marshy pool, inlet, backwater, or the like. **4.** a condition of degradation or despair.

slough[2] (sluf), *n.* **1.** the outer layer of the skin of a snake, which is cast off periodically. **2.** a mass or layer of dead tissue separated from the surrounding or underlying tissue. **3.** anything that is shed or cast off. **4.** a discarded card. —*v.i.* **5.** to be shed, as the slough of a snake. **6.** to cast off a slough. **7.** to separate from the sound flesh, as a slough. **8.** to discard a card or cards. —*v.t.* **9.** to dispose or get rid of; cast (often fol. by *off*): *to slough off a bad habit.* **10.** to shed as or like a slough. **11.** to discard (a card). **12. slough over,** to treat as inconsequential.

slough′ of despond′ (slo͞o), *n.* extreme emotional depression: so called after the *Slough of Despond,* a deep bog into which Christian falls in John Bunyan's *Pilgrim's Progress.*

Slo•va•ki•a (slō vä′kē ə, -vak′ē ə), *n.* a republic in central Europe: formerly a part of Czechoslovakia; independent since 1993. 5,393,016; 18,931 sq. mi. (49,035 sq. km). *Cap.:* Bratislava. Also called **Slo′vak Repub′lic.** Slovak, **Slo•ven•sko** (slô′ven skô). —**Slo•va′ki•an,** *adj., n.*

slov•en (sluv′ən), *n.* **1.** a person who is habitually unclean or untidy in dress, appearance, or the like. **2.** a person who works, acts, speaks, etc., in a negligent, slipshod manner.

Slo•ve•ni•a (slō vē′nē ə, -vēn′yə), *n.* a republic in S Europe: formerly (1945–91) part of Yugoslavia. 1,945,998; 7819 sq. mi. (20,250 sq. km). *Cap.:* Ljubljana.

slov•en•ly (sluv′ən lē), *adj.,* **-li•er, li•est,** *adv.* —*adj.* **1.** untidy or unclean in appearance or habits. **2.** characteristic of a sloven; slipshod: *slovenly work.* —*adv.* **3.** in an untidy, careless, or slipshod manner. —**slov′en•li•ness,** *n.*

slow (slō), *adj.* and *adv.,* **slow•er, slow•est,** *v.* —*adj.* **1.** moving or proceeding with little or less than usual speed: *a slow train.* **2.** characterized by lack of speed: *a slow pace.* **3.** taking or requiring a comparatively long time. **4.** gradual: *slow growth.* **5.** mentally dull. **6.** not readily disposed (usu. fol. by *to* or an infinitive): *slow to anger.* **7.** burning or heating with little intensity: *a slow oven.* **8.** slack; not busy. **9.** progressing or allowing progress at less than the usual or desired rate of speed: *a slow worker; a slow road.* **10.** running at less than the proper rate of speed, as a clock. **11.** dull or tedious. **12.** *Photog.* requiring long exposure, as by having a small lens diameter or low film sensitivity. **13.** (of the surface of a racetrack) sticky from a recent rain and in the process of drying out. —*adv.* **14.** in a slow manner; slowly: *Drive slow.* —*v.t.* **15.** to make slow or slower (often fol. by *up* or *down*). **16.** to reduce the progress of. —*v.i.* **17.** to slacken in speed (often fol. by *up* or *down*). —***Proverb.*** **18. Slow but steady wins the race,** a task is best accomplished slowly and methodically. —**slow′ly,** *adv.* —**slow′ness,** *n.* —**Usage.** As an adverb, SLOW has two forms, SLOW and SLOWLY, and both are standard today. SLOW is now used chiefly in imperative constructions with short verbs of motion (*Drive slow. Don't walk so slow.*), more commonly in speech than in writing, though it occurs widely on traffic and road signs. SLOW also combines with present participles in forming adjectives: *slow-burning; slow-moving.* SLOWLY is by far the more common form of the adverb in writing. In both speech and writing it is the usual form following verbs that are not imperatives: *He drove slowly down the street.* See also QUICK, SURE.

slow′ cook′er, *n.* an electric ceramic cooking pot with a tight-fitting lid for cooking meats, casseroles, etc., for several hours at steady, relatively low temperatures. Compare CROCKPOT.

slow•down (slō′doun′), *n.* **1.** a slowing down or delay in progress, action, etc. **2.** a deliberate slowing of pace by workers to win demands from their employer.

slow′-foot′ed, *adj.* proceeding at a slow pace. —**slow′-foot′ed•ly,** *adv.* —**slow′-foot′ed•ness,** *n.*

slow′ mo′tion, *n.* the process or technique of filming or taping a motion-picture or television sequence at an accelerated rate of speed and then projecting or replaying it at normal speed so that the action appears to be slowed down.

slow′-mo′tion, *adj.* **1.** photographed or appearing in slow motion. **2.** proceeding at a strikingly slow rate.

slow′ (or **slo′**) **pitch′,** *n.* a variety of softball in which each pitch must make an arc at least six feet above the playing field.

slow•poke (slō′pōk′), *n. Informal.* a person who moves, works, etc., very slowly; dawdler.

slow′-release′, *adj.* (of a drug or fertilizer) capable of gradual release of an active agent, allowing for a sustained effect.

slow′-wit′ted, *adj.* slow in comprehension; dull-witted. —**slow′-wit′ted•ly,** *adv.* —**slow′-wit′ted•ness,** *n.*

sludge (sluj), *n.* **1.** mud, mire, or ooze; slush. **2.** a deposit of ooze at the bottom of a body of water. **3.** any of various mudlike deposits or mixtures. **4.** broken ice, as on the sea. **5.** sediment deposited during the treatment of sewage. —**sludg′y,** *adj.,* **sludg•i•er, sludg•i•est.**

slug¹ (slug), *n., v.,* **slugged, slug•ging.** —*n.* **1.** any of various snaillike terrestrial gastropod mollusks having no shell or only a rudimentary one, feeding on plants, and often a pest of leafy garden crops. **2.** a metal disk used as a coin or token, generally counterfeit. **3.** a piece of lead or other metal for firing from a gun. **4.** any heavy piece of crude metal. **5.** *Print.* a line of type in one piece, as produced by a Linotype. **6.** a shot of liquor taken neat; belt. **7.** *Slang.* a person who is lazy or slow-moving; sluggard. **8.** *Journalism.* **a.** a short phrase or title used to indicate the story content of a piece of copy. **b.** the line of type carrying this information. **9.** a unit of mass, of about 32.2 lbs. (15 kg), that is accelerated 1 ft per sec per sec by a force of 1 lb. —*v.t.* **10.** *Print.* to make (corrections) by replacing entire lines of type, esp. as set by a Linotype. **11.** *Journalism.* to furnish (copy) with a slug. —**slug′like′,** *adj.*

slug² (slug), *v.,* **slugged, slug•ging,** *n.* —*v.t.* **1.** to strike hard, esp. with the fist. **2.** to drive (a baseball) a great distance. **3.** to fight, esp. with fists. —*v.i.* **4.** to hit or be capable of hitting hard. **5.** to push onward, esp. through mud, snow, etc.; trudge. —*n.* **6.** a hard blow or hit, esp. with a fist or baseball bat.

slug•fest (slug′fest′), *n. Informal.* **1.** a baseball game in which both teams make many runs and extra-base hits. **2.** a boxing bout in which the boxers exchange powerful blows vigorously and aggressively. **3.** an intense conflict or combat.

slug•gard (slug′ərd), *n.* **1.** a person who is habitually inactive or lazy. —*adj.* **2.** lazy; sluggardly.

slug•ger (slug′ər), *n.* **1.** a boxer noted for delivering hard punches. **2.** (in baseball) a strong hitter.

slug•gish (slug′ish), *adj.* **1.** indisposed to action or exertion; lazy; indolent. **2.** not functioning with full vigor, as bodily organs. **3.** slow to act or respond: *a sluggish engine.* **4.** slow or slow-moving, as a stream. **5.** slack, as trade or sales. —**slug′gish•ly,** *adv.* —**slug′gish•ness,** *n.*

sluice (slo͞os), *n., v.,* **sluiced, sluic•ing.** —*n.* **1.** an artificial channel for conducting water, often fitted with a gate **(sluice′ gate′)** at the upper end for regulating the flow. **2.** the body of water held back or controlled by a sluice gate. **3.** a channel, esp. one carrying off surplus water. **4.** an artificial stream or channel of water for moving solid matter: *a lumbering sluice.* **5.** a long, sloping trough with grooves on the bottom, into which water is directed to separate gold from gravel or sand. —*v.t.* **6.** to let out (water) by opening a sluice. **7.** to drain (a pond, lake, etc.) by opening a sluice. **8.** to flush or cleanse with a rush of water: *to sluice the decks of a ship.* **9.** to wash in a sluice. —*v.i.* **10.** to flow or pour through a sluice.

slum (slum), *n., v.,* **slummed, slum•ming.** —*n.* **1.** Often, **slums.** a run-down part of a city, usu. thickly populated by poor people. **2.** any squalid, run-down place to live. —*v.i.* **3.** to visit slums, esp. out of curiosity. **4.** to visit or frequent a place, esp. an amusement spot, considered low in social status. —**slum′mer,** *n.*

slum•ber (slum′bər), *v.i.* **1.** to sleep, esp. lightly; doze. **2.** to be in a state of inactivity, quiescence, or calm. —*v.t.* **3.** to spend or pass (time) in slumbering (often fol. by *away*). —*n.* **4.** sleep, esp. light sleep. **5.** a period of light sleep. **6.** a state of inactivity, quiescence, etc. —**slum′ber•er,** *n.*

slum•ber•ous (slum′bər əs, slum′brəs) also **slum′brous,** *adj.* **1.** sleepy; heavy with drowsiness, as the eyelids. **2.** pertaining to slumber. **3.** inactive or sluggish; calm; quiescent. —**slum′ber•ous•ly,** *adv.*

slum′ber par′ty, *n.* a social gathering, typically of teenagers, held at the home of one of them for the purpose of sleeping there overnight.

slum•lord (slum′lôrd′), *n.* a landlord who owns poorly maintained buildings, esp. one who charges exorbitant rents.

slump (slump), *v.i.* **1.** to fall heavily; collapse. **2.** to assume a slouching or bent position or posture. **3.** to decrease suddenly and markedly, as prices or the market. **4.** to decline, as health, business, or efficiency. **5.** to sink heavily, as the spirits. —*n.* **6.** an act or instance of slumping. **7.** a decrease or decline. **8.** a period of decline or deterioration. **9.** a mild recession in the economy or in a particular industry. **10.** a period during which a person performs ineffectively. **11.** a slouching, bowed, or bent position or posture.

slung (slung), *v.* pt. and pp. of SLING¹.

slunk (slungk), *v.* a pt. and the pp. of SLINK.

slur¹ (slûr), *v.,* **slurred, slur•ring,** *n.* —*v.t.* **1.** to pronounce (a syllable, word, etc.) indistinctly by combining, reducing, or omitting sounds, as in hurried or careless utterance. **2.** to pass over without due mention or consideration (often fol. by *over*). **3.** to sing to a single syllable or play without a break (two or more tones of different pitch). —*v.i.* **4.** to read, speak, or sing hurriedly and carelessly. —*n.* **5.** a slurred utterance or sound. **6. a.** the combination of two or more tones of different pitch, sung to a single syllable or played without a break. **b.** a curved mark indicating this.

slur¹ (def. 6b)

slur² (slûr), *v.,* **slurred, slur•ring,** *n.* —*v.t.* **1.** to insult or disparage. —*n.* **2.** a disparaging remark; slight: *quick to take offense at a slur.* **3.** a blot or stain, as upon reputation.

slurp (slûrp), *v.t.* **1.** to ingest (food or drink) with loud sucking noises. —*v.i.* **2.** to make loud sucking noises while eating or drinking. —*n.* **3.** an intake of food or drink with a noisy sucking sound. **4.** any lapping or splashing sound.

slush (slush), *n.* **1.** partly melted snow. **2.** liquid mud; watery mire. **3.** refuse fat from the galley of a ship. **4.** a mixture of grease and other materials for lubricating. **5.** silly, sentimental talk or writing. —*v.t.* **6.** to splash with slush. **7.** to grease with slush. **8.** to fill or cover with mortar or cement. —**slush′i•ness,** *n.* —**slush′y,** *adj.,* **slush•i•er, slush•i•est.**

slush′ fund′, *n.* **1.** a sum of money used for illicit or corrupt political purposes, as for buying influence. **2.** a fund for a ship's crew for the purchase of small luxuries.

slut (slut), *n.* a dirty, slovenly woman.

sly (slī), *adj.*, **sly•er** or **sli•er, sly•est** or **sli•est,** *n.* —*adj.* **1.** cunning or wily. **2.** stealthy. **3.** mischievous or roguish: *sly humor.* —***Idiom.*** **4. on the sly,** secretly; furtively. —**sly′ly,** *adv.* —**sly′ness,** *n.*

Sm, *Chem. Symbol.* samarium.

smack[1] (smak), *n.* **1.** a taste or flavor, esp. a slight flavor distinctive or suggestive of something. **2.** a trace or suggestion of something. **3.** a taste or small quantity. —*v.i.* **4.** to have a trace or suggestion: *a compliment that smacks of condescension.*

smack[2] (smak), *v.t.* **1.** to strike sharply, esp. with the open hand; slap. **2.** to drive or send with a sharp, resounding blow. **3.** to close and open (the lips) smartly so as to produce a sharp sound, often as a sign of relish, as in eating. **4.** to kiss with a loud sound. —*v.i.* **5.** to smack the lips. **6.** to collide with or strike something forcibly. —*n.* **7.** a sharp blow; slap. **8.** a smacking of the lips, as in relish or anticipation. **9.** a loud kiss. —*adv.* **10.** suddenly and violently: *rode smack up against the side of the house.* **11.** directly; straight: *smack in the center of town.*

smack′-dab′, *adv. Informal.* directly; squarely.

small (smôl), *adj. and adv.* **-er, -est,** *n.* —*adj.* **1.** of limited size; not big; little: *a small box.* **2.** slender or narrow: *a small waist.* **3.** not large as compared with others of the same kind: *a small elephant.* **4.** (of an alphabetical letter) lowercase. **5.** not great in amount, extent, duration, etc.: *a small salary.* **6.** of low numerical value. **7.** carrying on some activity on a limited scale: *a small business.* **8.** of minor importance: *a small problem.* **9.** humble or modest: *small circumstances.* **10.** mean-spirited; petty: *a small, miserly man.* **11.** (of sound or the voice) having little volume. **12.** very young: *a small boy.* **13.** diluted; weak. —*adv.* **14.** in a small manner, esp. modestly or frugally. **15.** into small pieces. —*n.* **16.** a person or thing that is small. **17.** a small or narrow part, as of the back. **18. the small,** people without wealth or influence: *Democracy benefits the great and the small.* **19. smalls,** small goods or products. **20. a.** a size of garments for persons of less than average dimensions, weight, etc. **b.** a garment in this size. **21. smalls,** *Brit.* **a.** underclothes. **b.** household linen. —***Idiom.*** **22. feel small,** to be ashamed or mortified. —**small′ish,** *adj.* —**small′ness,** *n.*

small′ cal′orie, *n.* CALORIE (def. 1a).

small′ cap′ital, *n.* a capital letter of a particular font, having the height of a lowercase x. Also called **small′ cap′.**

small′ change′, *n.* **1.** coins of small denomination. **2.** an insignificant person or thing.

small′-claims′ court′, *n.* a special court established to handle small claims or debts, usu. without the services of lawyers.

small′ fry′, *n.pl.* **1.** very young children. **2.** unimportant persons or things. **3.** small or young fish. —**small′-fry′,** *adj.*

small′ game′, *n.* wild animals and birds hunted for sport, as rabbits or doves, that are smaller than animals classified as big game.

small′ intes′tine, *n.* INTESTINE (def. 2).

small′-mind′ed, *adj.* selfish, petty, or narrow-minded. —**small′-mind′ed•ly,** *adv.* —**small′-mind′ed•ness,** *n.*

small′ pota′toes, *n.* an insignificant person or thing.

small•pox (smôl′poks′), *n.* an acute, highly contagious, febrile disease, caused by a virus and characterized by a pustular eruption that often leaves permanent pits or scars: eradicated worldwide by vaccination programs.

small′ print′, *n.* FINE PRINT.

small′-scale′, *adj.* **1.** of limited extent or scope: *a small-scale enterprise.* **2.** (of a map, model, etc.) being a relatively small version of the original; showing relatively little detail.

small′ screen′, *n.* **1.** the medium of television. **2.** a television set.

small•sword (smôl′sôrd′, -sōrd′), *n.* a light, tapering sword for thrusting, formerly used in fencing or dueling.

small′ talk′, *n.* light conversation; chitchat. —**small′-talk′,** *v.i.*

small′-time′, *adj.* having little or no importance or influence: *a small-time politician.* —**small′-tim′er,** *n.*

small′-town′, *adj.* **1.** of, pertaining to, or characteristic of a town or village. **2.** provincial; unsophisticated. —**small′-town′er,** *n.*

smarm•y (smär′mē), *adj.*, **smarm•i•er, smarm•i•est.** excessively or unctuously flattering, ingratiating, servile, etc.

smart (smärt), *adj.*, **smart•er, smart•est,** *v.*, *adv.*, *n.* —*adj.* **1.** having or showing quick intelligence or ready mental capability: *a smart student.* **2.** quick or prompt in action, as a person. **3.** shrewd or sharp, as a person in dealing with others. **4.** clever or witty as a speaker, speech, or rejoinder. **5.** neat or trim in appearance, as a person or garment; spruce. **6.** socially elegant; sophisticated or fashionable: *the smart crowd.* **7.** saucy; pert: *smart remarks.* **8.** brisk or vigorous: *to walk with smart steps.* **9.** sharply severe, as a blow. **10.** sharp or keen: *a smart pain.* **11.** equipped with, using, or containing electronic control devices. **12.** *Computers.* INTELLIGENT (def. 4). —*v.i.* **13.** to be a source of sharp, local, and usu. superficial pain, as a wound. **14.** to be the cause of a sharp, stinging pain, as an irritating application or a blow. **15.** to feel a sharp, stinging pain, as in a wound. **16.** to suffer keenly from wounded feelings. **17.** to feel shame or remorse or to suffer in punishment or in return for something. —*v.t.* **18.** to cause a sharp pain to or in. —*adv.* **19.** in a smart manner; smartly. —*n.* **20.** a sharp local pain, usu. superficial, as from a wound, blow, or sting. **21.** keen mental suffering, as from wounded feelings, affliction, or grievous loss. **22. smarts,** *Informal.* intelligence; common sense. —**smart′ly,** *adv.* —**smart′ness,** *n.*

Smart (smärt), *n.* **Henry,** 1813–79, English writer and hymn writer.

smart′ al′eck (or **al′ec**) (al′ik), *n. Informal.* a conceited and impertinent person. —**smart′-al′eck•y, smart′-al′eck,** *adj.*

smart′ bomb′, *n.* an air-to-surface missile guided to its target visually by television or a laser beam.

smart•en (smär′tn), *v.t.* **1.** to improve in appearance (usu. fol. by *up*). **2.** to make brisker, as a pace. **3.** to sharpen the judgment or broaden the experience of (usu. fol. by *up*). **4. smarten up,** to become more aware, shrewd, or clever.

smart′ mon′ey, *n.* **1.** money invested or wagered by experienced investors or bettors. **2.** such knowledgeable investors or bettors. **3.** *Law.* punitive or exemplary damages.

smart′y-pants′, *n.* (*used with a sing. v.*) *Informal.* SMART ALECK.

smash (smash), *v.t.* **1.** to break to pieces with violence and often with a crashing sound, as by dashing against something; shatter. **2.** to destroy or defeat completely; crush; ruin. **3.** to hit or strike with force. **4.** (in racket sports) to hit (a ball or shuttlecock) with a powerful, downward overhand stroke. —*v.i.* **5.** to break to pieces from a violent blow or collision. **6.** to dash with a shattering force or with great violence; crash (usu. fol. by *against, into,* etc.). **7.** to be completely destroyed, defeated, or ruined. —*n.* **8.** an act or instance of smashing or shattering. **9.** the sound of such a smash. **10.** a blow, hit, or slap. **11.** a destructive collision, as between automobiles. **12.** a smashed or shattered condition. **13.** a process or state of collapse, ruin, or destruction. **14.** *Informal.* something achieving great success; hit. **15.** a drink made of brandy with sugar, water, mint, and ice. **16.** (in racket sports) a powerful, downward overhand stroke, or the ball or shuttlecock hit with such a stroke. —*adj.* **17.** *Informal.* of, pertaining to, or constituting a great success: *a smash hit on Broadway.*

smash•ing (smash′ing), *adj.* impressive or wonderful. —**smash′ing•ly,** *adv.*

smash′-up′, *n.* a complete smash, esp. a wreck of one or more vehicles.

smat•ter•ing (smat′ər ing), *n.* **1.** a slight, superficial, or introductory knowledge of something: *a smattering of Latin.* —*adj.* **2.** slight or superficial.

smear (smēr), *v.t.* **1.** to spread or daub (an oily, greasy, viscous, or wet substance) on or over something: *to smear butter on bread.* **2.** to spread or daub an oily, greasy, viscous, or wet substance on. **3.** to stain, spot, or make dirty with something oily, greasy, viscous, or wet. **4.** to sully, vilify, or soil (a reputation, good name, etc.). **5.** to smudge or blur, as by rubbing. **6.** *Slang.* to defeat decisively; overwhelm. —*n.* **7.** an oily, greasy, viscous, or wet substance, esp. a dab of such a substance. **8.** a stain, spot, or mark made by such a substance. **9.** a smudge. **10.** vilification; defamation. **11.** something smeared or to be smeared on a thing, as a glaze for pottery. **12.** a small quantity of something spread thinly on a slide for microscopic examination. —**smear′er,** *n.*

smear•case or **smier•case** (smēr′kās′), *n. Chiefly North Midland U.S.* any soft cheese suitable for spreading, esp. a sour cottage cheese.

smear•y (smēr′ē), *adj.*, **smear•i•er, smear•i•est. 1.** showing smears; smeared. **2.** tending to smear or soil. —**smear′i•ness,** *n.*

smell (smel), *v.*, **smelled** or **smelt, smelling,** *n.* —*v.t.* **1.** to perceive the odor or scent of through the nose by means of the olfactory nerves; inhale the odor of. **2.** to test by the sense of smell: *He smelled the meat to see if it was fresh.* **3.** to perceive, detect, or discover by shrewdness or sagacity: *The detective smelled foul play.* —*v.i.* **4.** to perceive the odor or scent of something. **5.** to give off or have an odor or scent. **6.** to have a particular odor or scent. **7.** to give out an offensive odor; stink. **8.** to have a trace or suggestion (fol. by *of*). **9.** to search or investigate (fol. by *around* or *about*). **10.** *Informal.* to be of inferior quality; stink. **11.** *Informal.* to appear to be guilty, corrupt, etc. **12. smell out,** to look for or detect by or as if by smelling. **13. smell up,** to fill with an offensive odor; stink up. —*n.* **14.** the sense of smell; faculty of smelling. **15.** that quality of a thing that is or may be smelled; odor; scent. **16.** a trace or suggestion. **17.** an act or instance of smelling. **18.** a pervading appearance, character, quality, or influence. —***Idiom.*** **19. smell a rat,** to suspect that something is wrong. —**smell′er,** *n.*

smell′ing salts′, *n.* (*used with a sing. or pl. v.*) a preparation for smelling, essentially an ammonia compound, used as a stimulant and restorative.

smell•y (smel′ē), *adj.*, **smell•i•er, smell•i•est.** emitting a strong or unpleasant odor. —**smell′i•ness,** *n.*

smelt[1] (smelt), *v.t.* **1.** to fuse or melt (ore) in order to separate the metal contained. **2.** to obtain or refine (metal) in this way.

smelt[2] (smelt), *n.*, *pl.* (*esp. collectively*) **smelt,** (*esp. for kinds or species*) **smelts.** any of various small, silvery food fishes of the family Osmeridae, inhabiting cold northern waters.

smelt[3] (smelt), *v.* a pt. and pp. of SMELL.

smid•gen or **smid•gin** or **smid•geon** (smij′ən), *n.* a very small amount.

smi•lax (smī′laks), *n.* any plant of the genus *Smilax,* of the lily family, growing in tropical and temperate zones, consisting mostly of woody-stemmed vines.

smile (smīl), *v.*, **smiled, smil•ing,** *n.* —*v.i.* **1.** to assume a facial expression usu. indicating pleasure, favor, or amusement, but sometimes derision or scorn, characterized by an upturning of the corners of the mouth. **2.** to regard with favor: *Luck smiled on us that night.* **3.** to have a pleasant or agreeable appearance or aspect, as natural scenes or objects. —*v.t.* **4.** to assume or give (a smile, esp. of a given kind). **5.** to express by a smile: *to smile approval.* **6.** to bring, put, drive, etc., by or as if by smiling. —*n.* **7.** an act or instance of smiling; a smiling expression of the face. **8.** favor or kindly regard: *fortune's smile.* **9.** a pleasant or agreeable appearance, look, or aspect. —**smil′ing•ly,** *adv.*

smile′ (or **smil′ey**) **face′,** *n.* a drawing of a face consisting of a usu. yellow circle with an upturned curve for a smile and two dots for eyes.

smirch (smûrch), *v.t.* **1.** to discolor or soil; spot or smudge with or as if with soot, dirt, etc. **2.** to sully or tarnish (a reputation, character, etc.); disgrace; discredit. —*n.* **3.** a dirty mark or smear. **4.** a stain or blot, as on reputation.

smirk (smûrk), *v.i.* **1.** to smile in an affected, smug, or offensively familiar way. —*n.* **2.** the facial expression of a person who smirks. —**smirk′er,** *n.* —**smirk′ing•ly,** *adv.*

smite (smīt), *v.,* **smote, smit•ten** or **smit** (smit) or **smote, smit•ing.** —*v.t.* **1.** to strike or hit hard, with or as if with the hand, a stick, or other weapon. **2.** to deliver or deal (a blow) by striking hard. **3.** to strike down, injure, or slay. **4.** to afflict or attack with deadly or disastrous effect. **5.** to affect mentally, morally, or emotionally with a strong and sudden feeling: *They were smitten with terror.* **6.** to impress favorably; enamor. —*v.i.* **7.** to strike; deal a blow. —**smit′er,** *n.*

smith (smith), *n.* **1.** a worker in metal. **2.** BLACKSMITH.

Smith (smith), *n.* **1. Adam,** 1723–90, Scottish economist. **2. Alfred E(manuel),** 1873–1944, U.S. political leader. **3. Edmond Kirby,** 1824–93, Confederate general in the Civil War. **4. John,** 1580–1631, English adventurer and colonist in Virginia. **5. Joseph,** 1805–44, U.S. religious leader: founded the Mormon Church. **6. Margaret Chase,** 1897–1995, U.S. politician. **7. Oswald,** 1890–1986, Canadian clergyman and hymn writer. **8. Samuel Francis,** 1808–95, U.S. clergyman and hymn writer.

smith•er•eens (smith′ə rēnz′), *n.pl.* small pieces; bits: *broken into smithereens.*

Smith•so′ni•an Institu′tion (smith sō′nē ən), *n.* an institution and national museum in Washington, D.C., founded in 1846 with a grant from James Smithson.

smith•y (smith′ē, smith′ē), *n., pl.* **smith•ies. 1.** the workshop of a smith, esp. a blacksmith. **2.** BLACKSMITH.

smit•ten (smit′n), *v.* a pp. of SMITE.

smock (smok), *n.* **1.** a loose, lightweight overgarment worn to protect the clothing. —*v.t.* **2.** to clothe in a smock. **3.** to draw (a fabric) by needlework into a honeycomb pattern with diamond-shaped recesses.

smock•ing (smok′ing), *n.* **1.** smocked needlework. **2.** embroidery stitches used to hold gathered cloth in even folds.

smog (smog, smôg), *n.* smoke or other atmospheric pollutants combined with fog in an unhealthy or irritating mixture. [*sm*(*oke*) + (*f*)*og*] —**smog′gy,** *adj.,* **-gi•er, -gi•est.**

smoke (smōk), *n., v.,* **smoked, smok•ing.** —*n.* **1.** the visible vapor and gases given off by a burning substance, esp. the mixture of gases and suspended carbon particles resulting from the combustion of wood or other organic matter. **2.** something resembling this, as vapor or mist. **3.** something unsubstantial, fleeting, or without result. **4.** an obscuring condition: *the smoke of controversy.* **5.** an act or spell of smoking something, esp. tobacco. **6.** something for smoking, as a cigarette. **7.** *Physics, Chem.* a system of solid particles suspended in a gaseous medium. **8.** a bluish or brownish gray. —*v.i.* **9.** to give off or emit smoke, as in burning. **10.** to give out smoke offensively, as a stove. **11.** to send forth steam or vapor, dust, or the like. **12.** to draw into the mouth and puff out the smoke of tobacco or the like, as from a pipe or cigarette. **13.** *Slang.* to move or travel with great speed. —*v.t.* **14.** to draw into the mouth and puff out the smoke of: *to smoke tobacco.* **15.** to use (a pipe, cigarette, etc.) in this process. **16.** to expose to smoke. **17.** to fumigate (rooms, furniture, etc.). **18.** to cure (meat, fish, etc.) by exposure to smoke. **19.** to color or darken by smoke. **20. smoke out, a.** to drive from a refuge by means of smoke. **b.** to force into public view or knowledge; expose. —***Idiom.*** **21. go up in smoke,** to terminate without producing a result; be unsuccessful. —***Proverb.*** **22. Where there's smoke, there's fire,** even if untrue, a rumor indicates that something is wrong.

smoke′ and mir′rors, *n.* (*used with a sing. or pl. v.*) something that distorts or blurs facts, figures, etc., like a magic or conjuring trick; artful deception.

smoke′ detec′tor, *n.* an electronic fire alarm that is activated by the presence of smoke. Also called **smoke′ alarm′.**

smoke′-filled′ room′, *n.* a place, as a hotel room, for conducting secret negotiations, devising strategy, etc.

smoke•house (smōk′hous′), *n., pl.* **-hous•es** (-hou′ziz). a building or place in which meat, fish, etc., are cured with smoke.

smoke•less (smōk′lis), *adj.* emitting, producing, or having little or no smoke.

smok•er (smō′kər), *n.* **1.** a person or thing that smokes. **2.** Also, **smok′ing car′.** a railroad passenger car or compartment for those who wish to smoke. **3.** an informal gathering of men for entertainment, discussion, or the like.

smoke′ screen′, *n.* **1.** a mass of dense smoke produced to conceal an area, vessel, or plane from the enemy. **2.** something intended to disguise, conceal, or deceive.

smoke•stack (smōk′stak′), *n.* **1.** a pipe for the escape of the smoke or gases of combustion, as on a steamboat, locomotive, or factory. —*adj.* **2.** pertaining to, engaged in, or dependent on a basic heavy industry, as steel or automaking: *smokestack companies.*

smok′ing gun′, *n.* indisputable proof or evidence, esp. of a crime.

smok′ing jack′et, *n.* a loose-fitting jacket for men, often of a heavy fabric worn indoors, esp. as a lounging jacket.

smok•y (smō′kē), *adj.,* **smok•i•er, smok•i•est. 1.** emitting smoke, esp. in large amounts. **2.** hazy; darkened or made grimy with smoke. **3.** having the character or appearance of smoke: *smoky colors.* **4.** pertaining to or suggestive of smoke: *a smoky haze.* **5.** of a dull or brownish gray; cloudy. —**smok′i•ly,** *adv.* —**smok′i•ness,** *n.*

smol•der or **smoul•der** (smōl′dər), *v.i.* **1.** to burn without flame; undergo slow or suppressed combustion. **2.** to exist or continue in a suppressed state or without outward demonstration: *Hatred smoldered beneath his smile.* **3.** to display repressed feelings, as of indignation, anger, or the like. —*n.* **4.** dense smoke resulting from slow or suppressed combustion. **5.** a smoldering fire.

smooch (smōōch), *v.i.* **1.** to kiss. **2.** to pet; caress. —*n.* **3.** a kiss. —**smooch′er,** *n.*

smooth (smōōth), *adj.,* **smooth•er, smooth•est,** *adv., v., n.* —*adj.* **1.** free from projections or unevenness of surface. **2.** generally flat or unruffled, as a calm sea. **3.** free from hairs or a hairy growth: *a smooth cheek.* **4.** of uniform consistency; free from lumps, as a sauce. **5.** allowing or having an even, uninterrupted movement or flow: *a smooth ride.* **6.** easy and uniform, as the working of a machine. **7.** having projections worn away: *a smooth tire.* **8.** free from hindrances or difficulties: *a smooth day at the office.* **9.** undisturbed, tranquil, or equable, as the temper; serene. **10.** elegant, easy, or polished: *a smooth manner.* **11.** ingratiatingly polite; suave: *a smooth talker.* **12.** free from harshness; mellow, as wine. **13.** not harsh to the ear, as sound. —*adv.* **14.** in a smooth manner; smoothly. —*v.t.* **15.** to make smooth of surface, as by scraping, planing, or pressing. **16.** to remove (projections, ridges, wrinkles, etc.) in making something smooth (often fol. by *away* or *out*). **17.** to free from difficulties. **18.** to remove (obstacles) from a path (often fol. by *away*). **19.** to make more polished, elegant, or agreeable. **20.** to tranquilize, calm, or soothe. **21.** *Math.* to simplify (an expression) by substituting approximate or certain known values for the variables. **22. smooth over,** to make seem less severe, disagreeable, or irreconcilable. —*n.* **23.** the act of smoothing. **24.** something that is smooth; a smooth part or place. —**smooth′er,** *n.* —**smooth′ly,** *adv.* —**smooth′ness,** *n.*

smooth•bore (smōōth′bôr′, -bōr′), *adj.* **1.** (of a firearm) having a smooth bore; not rifled. —*n.* **2.** a smoothbore gun.

smooth•ie or **smooth•y** (smōō′thē), *n., pl.* **smooth•ies.** *Informal.* a person, esp. a man, who has a winningly polished manner.

smooth′-tongued′, *adj.* fluent or convincing in speech; glib.

smor•gas•bord or **smör•gås•bord** (smôr′gəs bôrd′, -bōrd′ *or, often,* shmôr′-), *n.* **1.** a buffet meal of various hot and cold hors d'oeuvres, salads, casserole dishes, meats, cheeses, etc. **2.** an extensive array or variety. [< Swedish: sandwich table]

smote (smōt), *v.* a pt. of SMITE.

smoth•er (smuth′ər), *v.t.* **1.** to stifle or suffocate, as by smoke or other means of preventing free breathing. **2.** to extinguish or deaden (fire, coals, etc.) by covering so as to exclude air. **3.** to cover closely or thickly; envelop. **4.** to suppress or repress. **5.** to cook (food) slowly in a tightly covered pan with little liquid: *smothered onions.* —*v.i.* **6.** to become stifled or suffocated; be prevented from breathing freely. **7.** to be stifled; be suppressed or concealed. —*n.* **8.** dense, stifling smoke. **9.** a smoking or smoldering state, as of burning matter.

smudge (smuj), *n., v.,* **smudged, smudg•ing.** —*n.* **1.** a dirty mark or smear. **2.** a smeary state. **3.** a stifling smoke. **4.** a smoky fire, esp. one made for driving away mosquitoes or safeguarding fruit trees from frost. —*v.t.* **5.** to mark with dirty streaks or smears. **6.** to fill with smudge, as to drive away insects. —*v.i.* **7.** to form a smudge on something. **8.** to become smudged. **9.** to smolder or smoke; emit smoke, as a smudge pot. —**smudg′y,** *adj.,* **smudg•i•er, smudg•i•est.** —**smudg′i•ly,** *adv.* —**smudg′i•ness,** *n.*

smudge′ pot′, *n.* a container for burning oil or other fuels to produce smudge, as for protecting fruit trees from frost.

smug (smug), *adj.,* **smug•ger, smug•gest. 1.** contentedly confident of one's ability, superiority, or correctness; complacent. **2.** trim; spruce; smooth; sleek. —**smug′ly,** *adv.* —**smug′ness,** *n.*

smug•gle (smug′əl), *v.,* **-gled, -gling.** —*v.t.* **1.** to import or export (goods) secretly, in violation of the law, esp. without payment of legal duty. **2.** to bring, take, put, etc., surreptitiously. —*v.i.* **3.** to import, export, or convey goods surreptitiously or in violation of the law. —**smug′gler,** *n.*

smut (smut), *n., v.,* **smut•ted, smut•ting.** —*n.* **1.** a particle of soot; sooty matter. **2.** a black or dirty mark; smudge. **3.** indecent language or writing; obscenity. **4. a.** a disease of plants, esp. cereal grasses, characterized by the conversion of affected parts into black, powdery masses of spores, caused by fungi of the order Ustilaginales. **b.** a fungus causing this disease. —*v.t.* **5.** to soil or smudge. —*v.i.* **6.** to become affected with smut, as a plant.

smut•ty (smut′ē), *adj.,* **-ti•er, -ti•est. 1.** soiled with smut; grimy. **2.** indecent or obscene, as talk or writing. **3.** (of plants) affected with smut. —**smut′ti•ly,** *adv.* —**smut′ti•ness,** *n.*

Smyr•na (smûr′nə), *n.* **1.** former name of IZMIR: site of one of the seven churches of Asia (Rev. 1:11). **2. Gulf of,** former name of the Gulf of IZMIR.

Sn, *Chem. Symbol.* tin. [< Latin *stannum*]

snack (snak), *n.* **1.** a small portion of food or drink or a light meal, esp.

one eaten between regular meals. **2.** a share or portion. —*v.i.* **3.** to have a snack or light meal, esp. between regular meals.

snack′ bar′, *n.* a lunchroom or restaurant where light meals are sold.

snack′ ta·ble, *n.* a small portable folding table used for an individual serving of food or drink.

sna·fu (sna foo′, snaf′oo), *n., pl.* **-fus,** *adj.* **fu·ed, -fu·ing.** —*n.* **1.** a badly confused situation. —*adj.* **2.** in disorder; chaotic. —*v.t.* **3.** to muddle.

snag (snag), *n., v.,* **snagged, snag·ging.** —*n.* **1.** a tree or part of a tree held fast in the bottom of a river, lake, etc., and forming an impediment or danger to navigation. **2.** a short, projecting stump, as of a branch broken off. **3.** any sharp or rough projection. **4.** a hole, tear, or pull in a fabric, as caused by catching on a sharp projection. **5.** any obstacle or impediment. **6.** SNAGGLETOOTH. —*v.t.* **7.** to run or catch up on a snag. **8.** to damage by so doing. **9.** to obstruct or impede, as a snag does. **10.** to grab; seize. —*v.i.* **11.** to become entangled with some obstacle or hindrance. **12.** to become tangled, as twine or hair. **13.** (of a boat) to strike a snag. **14.** to form a snag. —**snag′gy,** *adj.,* **-gi·er, -gi·est.**

snag·gle·tooth (snag′əl tooth′), *n., pl.* **-teeth.** a tooth growing out beyond or apart from others. —**snag′gle-toothed′,** *adj.*

snail (snāl), *n.* **1.** any slow-moving gastropod mollusk, having a spirally coiled shell and a ventral muscular foot. **2.** a slow or lazy person. —**snail′like′,** *adj.*

snail′ dart′er, *n.* a tan, striped, snail-eating perch, *Percina tanasi,* 3 in. (7.5 cm) long, found only in the Tennessee River.

snail′s′ pace′, *n.* an extremely slow rate of progress. —**snail′-paced′,** *adj.*

snake (snāk), *n., v.,* **snaked, snak·ing.** —*n.* **1.** any limbless, scaly, elongate reptile of the suborder Serpentes, comprising venomous and nonvenomous species. **2.** a treacherous person; an insidious enemy. **3.** (in plumbing) a flexible metal device for dislodging obstructions in curved pipes. —*v.i.* **4.** to move, twist, or wind in the manner of a snake. —*v.t.* **5.** to wind or make (one's course, way, etc.) in the manner of a snake. **6.** to drag or haul, esp. by a chain or rope, as a log. **7.** to pull forcibly; yank. —**snake′like′,** *adj.*

snake′ charm′er, *n.* an entertainer who seems to charm venomous snakes, usu. by music.

snake′ dance′, *n.* **1.** any of various ceremonial dances of American Indian peoples in which snakes are handled or imitated by the dancers. **2.** a parade or procession in which the participants weave in single file in a serpentine course.

snake′ eyes′, *n.pl.* a cast of two in craps; two aces.

snake′ in the grass′, *n.* **1.** a treacherous person, esp. one who feigns friendship. **2.** a concealed danger.

snake′ oil′, *n.* any of various liquid concoctions of questionable medical value sold as an all-purpose curative, esp. by traveling hucksters.

snake′ pit′ or **snake′pit′,** *n.* **1.** a mental hospital marked by squalor and inhumane or indifferent care for the patients. **2.** an intensely chaotic or disagreeable place or situation.

snake·root (snāk′root′, -root′), *n.* any of various plants whose roots have been regarded as a remedy for snakebites, as *Aristolochia serpentaria,* of the birthwort family.

snak·y (snā′kē), *adj.,* **snak·i·er, snak·i·est. 1.** of or pertaining to snakes. **2.** infested with snakes: *a snaky cave.* **3.** twisting, winding, or sinuous; serpentine: *a snaky road.* **4.** treacherous or insidious. —**snak′i·ly,** *adv.* —**snak′i·ness,** *n.*

snap (snap), *v.,* **snapped, snap·ping,** *n., adj., adv.* —*v.i.* **1.** to make a sudden, sharp, distinct sound; crack, as a whip. **2.** to click, as a mechanism or the jaws coming together. **3.** to move, strike, shut, catch, etc., with a sharp sound, as a door or lid. **4.** to break suddenly, esp. with a sharp, cracking sound. **5.** to give way suddenly, as from strain. **6.** to act or move with quick or abrupt motions of the body. **7.** to take snapshots. **8.** to make a quick or sudden bite or grab (often fol. by *at*). **9.** to speak quickly and sharply (often fol. by *at*). **10.** to sparkle or flash, as the eyes. —*v.t.* **11.** to seize or obtain with or as if with a quick bite or grab (often fol. by *up*). **12.** to cause to make a sudden, sharp sound: *to snap one's fingers.* **13.** to strike, shut, open, operate, etc., with a sharp sound or movement: *to snap a lid down.* **14.** to say or utter in a quick, sharp manner (often fol. by *out*): *to snap out a complaint.* **15.** to break suddenly, esp. with a cracking sound. **16.** to take a snapshot of. **17.** *Football.* to put (the ball) into play by handing or tossing it from the line of scrimmage to the quarterback or another member of the offensive backfield. **18.** *Hunting.* to fire (a shot) quickly. **19. snap out of,** to recover from. —*n.* **20.** a quick, sudden action or movement, as the breaking of a twig. **21.** a short, sharp sound, as that caused by breaking a twig. **22.** a fastener in two pieces having a projection on one piece that snaps into a hole in the other, used esp. for holding parts of a garment together. **23.** *Informal.* briskness, vigor, or energy. **24.** a quick, sharp speech or manner of speaking. **25.** a quick or sudden bite or grab. **26.** something obtained by or as if by biting or grabbing. **27.** a brittle cookie. **28.** a short spell or period, as of cold weather. **29.** a snapshot. **30.** *Informal.* an easy task, duty, etc. **31.** *Football.* an act or instance of snapping the ball. **32.** SNAP BEAN. —*adj.* **33.** fastening or closing with a click or snap: *a snap lock.* **34.** made, done, taken, etc., suddenly or offhand: *a snap judgment.* **35.** easy or simple: *a snap course.* —*adv.* **36.** in a brisk, sudden manner. —*Idiom.* **37. snap one's fingers at,** to exhibit disdain for.

snap′ bean′, *n.* a crisp bean pod, as a green bean or a wax bean.

snap′ brim′, *n.* **1.** a hat brim that can be turned up or down. **2.** Also called **snap′-brim′ hat′.** a man's fedora, usu. of felt and often worn with the brim turned up in back and down in front.

snap·drag·on (snap′drag′ən), *n.* any plant belonging to the genus *Antirrhinum,* of the figwort family, esp. *A. majus,* cultivated for its spikes of showy flowers, each having a corolla supposed to resemble the mouth of a dragon.

snap·per (snap′ər), *n., pl.* (*esp. collectively*) **-per,** (*esp. for kinds or species*) **-pers** for 1, 2; **-pers** for 3. **1.** any of several marine food fishes of the family Lutjanidae, of tropical seas, having a large mouth with rows of small teeth. **2.** any of various other fishes, as the bluefish, *Pomatomus saltatrix.* **3.** SNAPPING TURTLE.

snap′ping bee′tle, *n.* CLICK BEETLE.

snap′ping tur′tle, *n.* either of two large freshwater American turtles of the family Chelydridae, having a massive nonretracting head and powerful jaws.

snap·pish (snap′ish), *adj.* **1.** apt to snap or bite, as a dog. **2.** disposed to speak or reply in an impatient or irritable manner. **3.** impatiently or irritably sharp; curt: *a snappish reply.* —**snap′pish·ly,** *adv.* —**snap′pish·ness,** *n.*

snap·py (snap′ē), *adj.,* **-pi·er, -pi·est. 1.** snappish. **2.** snapping or crackling in sound, as a fire. **3.** quick or sudden in action or performance. **4.** *Informal.* crisp, smart, lively, brisk, etc. —*Idiom.* **5. make it snappy,** *Informal.* to speed up; hurry. —**snap′pi·ly,** *adv.* —**snap′pi·ness,** *n.*

snap·shot (snap′shot′), *n.* **1.** an informal photograph, esp. one taken by a simple hand-held camera. **2.** a quick shot fired by a hunter without deliberate aim. **3.** a brief appraisal, summary, or profile.

snare¹ (snâr), *n., v.,* **snared, snar·ing.** —*n.* **1.** a device, often consisting of a noose, for capturing small game. **2.** anything serving to entrap, entangle, or catch unawares; trap. —*v.t.* **3.** to catch with a snare; entrap; entangle. **4.** to catch or involve by trickery or wile.

snare² (snâr), *n.* one of the strings of gut or of tightly spiraled metal stretched across the skin of a snare drum.

snare′ drum′, *n.* a small double-headed drum having snares across the lower head to produce a reverberant effect.

snarl¹ (snärl), *v.i.* **1.** to growl angrily or viciously, esp. with the teeth bared, as a dog. **2.** to speak in a sharp, angry, or quarrelsome manner. —*v.t.* **3.** to say by snarling: *to snarl a threat.* —*n.* **4.** the act of snarling. **5.** a snarling sound or utterance. —**snarl′ing·ly,** *adv.*

snarl² (snärl), *n.* **1.** a tangle, as of thread or hair. **2.** a complicated or confused condition or matter: *a traffic snarl.* **3.** a knot in wood. —*v.t.* **4.** to bring into a tangled condition, as thread or hair. **5.** to render complicated or confused. —*v.i.* **6.** to become tangled or confused. —**snarl′y,** *adj.,* **snarl·i·er, snarl·i·est.**

snatch (snach), *v.i.* **1.** to make a sudden effort to seize something, as with the hand; grab (usu. fol. by *at*). —*v.t.* **2.** to seize by a sudden or hasty grasp: *He snatched the woman's purse and ran.* **3.** to take, get, pull, etc., suddenly or hastily. **4.** *Slang.* to kidnap. —*n.* **5.** an act or instance of snatching. **6.** a sudden motion to seize something; grab. **7.** a bit, scrap, or fragment of something. **8.** a brief spell of effort, activity, or any experience. **9.** *Slang.* an act of kidnapping. **10.** *Weightlifting.* a lift in which the barbell is brought in a single motion from the floor to an arms-extended position overhead. —**snatch′er,** *n.*

snaz·zy (snaz′ē), *adj.,* **-zi·er, -zi·est.** *Slang.* extremely attractive or stylish; flashy. —**snaz′zi·ness,** *n.*

sneak (snēk), *v.,* **sneaked** or **snuck, sneaking,** *n., adj.* —*v.i.* **1.** to go in a stealthy or furtive manner; slink; skulk. **2.** to act in a furtive or underhand way. —*v.t.* **3.** to move, put, pass, etc., in a stealthy or furtive manner: *He sneaked the gun into his pocket.* **4.** to do, take, or have hurriedly or surreptitiously: *to sneak a cigarette.* —*n.* **5.** a sneaking, underhand, or contemptible person. **6.** a stealthy or furtive departure. **7.** SNEAKER (def. 1). —*adj.* **8.** stealthy; surreptitious: *a sneak raid.* —**Usage.** First recorded in writing near the end of the 19th century in the U.S., SNUCK has become in recent decades a standard variant past tense and past participle: *Bored by the lecture, we snuck out the side door.* SNUCK occurs frequently in fiction, in journalism, and on radio and television, whereas SNEAKED is more likely in formal writing. SNUCK is the only spoken past tense and past participle for many younger and middle-aged persons of all educational levels. It has occasionally been considered nonstandard but is so widely used by professional writers and educated speakers that it can no longer be so regarded.

sneak·er (snē′kər), *n.* **1.** a high or low shoe of canvas or other fabric, with a flat rubber or synthetic sole, worn for sports or recreation. **2.** any of various athletic shoes resembling this. **3.** one who sneaks.

sneak·ing (snē′king), *adj.* **1.** acting in a furtive or underhand way. **2.** deceitfully underhand, as actions; contemptible. **3.** secret; not generally avowed, as a feeling or suspicion. —**sneak′ing·ly,** *adv.*

sneak′ pre′view, *n.* a preview of a motion picture, often shown in addition to an announced film, in order to observe the reaction of the audience.

sneak·y (snē′kē), *adj.,* **sneak·i·er, sneak·i·est.** like or suggestive of a sneak; furtive; deceitful. —**sneak′i·ly,** *adv.* —**sneak′i·ness,** *n.*

sneer (snēr), *v.i.* **1.** to smile, laugh, or contort the face in a manner that shows scorn or contempt. **2.** to speak or write in a manner expressive of derision or scorn. —*v.t.* **3.** to utter or say in a sneering manner. —*n.* **4.** a look or expression of derision, scorn, or contempt. **5.** a derisive or scornful utterance or remark. **6.** an act of sneering. **—sneer′er,** *n.* **—sneer′ing•ly,** *adv.*

sneeze (snēz), *v.,* **sneezed, sneez•ing,** *n.* **—v.i. 1.** to emit air or breath suddenly, forcibly, and audibly through the nose and mouth by involuntary, spasmodic action. **2. sneeze at,** *Informal.* to treat with contempt; scorn: *$50,000 is nothing to sneeze at.* **—n. 3.** an act or sound of sneezing. **—sneez′er,** *n.* **—sneez′y,** *adj.*

snick•er (snik′ər) also **snigger,** *v., n.* **—v.i. 1.** to laugh in a half-suppressed, indecorous or disrespectful manner. **—v.t. 2.** to utter with a snicker. **—n. 3.** a snickering laugh. **—snick′er•ing•ly,** *adv.*

snide (snīd), *adj.,* **snid•er, snid•est.** derogatory in a nasty, insinuating manner: *snide remarks.*

sniff (snif), *v.i.* **1.** to draw air through the nose in short, audible inhalations. **2.** to clear the nose by so doing; sniffle. **3.** to smell by short inhalations. **4.** to show disdain, contempt, etc., by or as if by sniffing. **—v.t. 5.** to inhale through the nose: *to sniff the air.* **6.** to smell by sniffing. **7.** to perceive by or as if by sniffing: *to sniff a scandal.* **—n. 8.** an act of sniffing. **9.** the sound made by such an act. **10.** a barely perceptible scent or odor. **—sniff′er,** *n.*

snif•fle (snif′əl), *v.,* **-fled, -fling,** *n.* **—v.i. 1.** to sniff repeatedly, as from a head cold or in repressing tears. **—n. 2.** an act or sound of sniffling. **3. the sniffles,** a condition, as a cold, marked by sniffling. **—snif′fler,** *n.* **—snif′fly,** *adj.*

snif•ter (snif′tər), *n.* **1.** a pear-shaped glass, narrowing at the top to intensify the aroma of brandy, liqueur, etc. **2.** *Informal.* a very small drink of liquor.

snig•ger (snig′ər), *v.i., v.t., n.* SNICKER. **—snig′ger•er,** *n.* **—snig′ger•ing•ly,** *adv.*

snip (snip), *v.,* **snipped, snip•ping,** *n.* **—v.t. 1.** to cut with a small, quick stroke, or a succession of such strokes, with scissors or the like. **2.** to remove or cut off (something) by or as if by cutting in this manner: *to snip a rose.* **—v.i. 3.** to cut with small, quick strokes. **—n. 4.** the act of snipping, as with scissors. **5.** a small cut made by snipping. **6.** a small piece snipped off. **7.** any small piece; bit. **8.** *Informal.* **a.** a small or insignificant person. **b.** a presumptuous or impertinent person.

snipe (snīp), *n., pl.* **snipes,** (*esp. collectively*) **snipe** for 1; *v.,* **sniped, snip•ing.** **—n. 1.** any of several long-billed sandpipers of the genera *Gallinago* and *Limnocryptes,* inhabiting marshy areas. **2.** a shot from a hidden position. **—v.i. 3.** to shoot or hunt snipe. **4.** to shoot at individuals, esp. enemy soldiers, from a concealed or distant position. **5.** to attack a person or a person's work with petulant or snide criticism, esp. anonymously or from a safe distance. **—snip′er,** *n.*

snip•pet (snip′it), *n.* **1.** a small bit, scrap, or fragment: *snippets of information.* **2.** SNIP (def. 8).

snip•py (snip′ē), *adj.,* **-pi•er, -pi•est. 1.** sharp or curt, esp. in a contemptuous or haughty way. **2.** scrappy or fragmentary. Often, **snip′pe•ty** (-i tē). **—snip′pi•ness,** *n.*

snit (snit), *n.* an agitated or irritated state.

snitch¹ (snich), *v.t. Informal.* to snatch or steal; pilfer.

snitch² (snich), *Informal. v.i.* **1.** to turn informer; tattle. **—n. 2.** Also called **snitch′er.** an informer.

sniv•el (sniv′əl), *v.,* **-eled, -el•ing** or (*esp. Brit.*) **-elled, -el•ling,** *n.* **—v.i. 1.** to weep or cry with sniffling. **2.** to affect a tearful state; whine. **3.** to run at the nose; have a runny nose. **4.** to draw up mucus audibly through the nose. **—v.t. 5.** to utter with sniveling or sniffling. **—n. 6.** weak, whining, or pretended weeping. **7.** a light sniffle, as in weeping. **8.** mucus running from the nose. **—sniv′el•er;** *esp. Brit.,* **sniv′el•ler,** *n.*

snob (snob), *n.* **1.** a person who imitates, cultivates, or slavishly admires social superiors and is condescending to others. **2.** a person who believes himself or herself to have superior tastes and is condescending toward those with different tastes: *an intellectual snob.* **—snob′bish,** *adj.* **—snob′by,** *adj.,* **-bi•er, -bi•est.**

snob•ber•y (snob′ə rē), *n., pl.* **-ber•ies. 1.** snobbish character or conduct. **2.** an instance of this. Often, **snob′bism.**

snol•ly•gos•ter (snol′ē gos′tər), *n. Slang.* a clever, unscrupulous person.

snood (snood), *n.* **1.** the distinctive headband formerly worn by young unmarried women in Scotland and N England. **2.** a headband for the hair. **3.** a netlike hat or fabric that holds or covers the back of a woman's hair. **—v.t. 4.** to bind or confine (the hair) with a snood.

snook (snook, snook), *n.* **1.** a gesture of defiance, disrespect, or derision made by thumbing the nose. **—Idiom. 2. cock a snook,** to thumb the nose.

snook•er (snook′ər, snoo′kər), *n.* **1.** a variety of pool played with 15 red balls and 6 balls of other colors, in which a player must shoot one of the red balls, each with a point value of 1, into a pocket before shooting at one of the other balls, with point values of from 2 to 7. **—v.t. 2.** *Slang.* to deceive, cheat, or dupe: *snookered by a con man.*

snoop (snoop), *Informal. —v.i.* **1.** to prowl or pry; go about in a sneaking, prying way. **—n. 2.** an act or instance of snooping. **3.** Also, **snoop′er.** a person who snoops. **—snoop′y,** *adj.,* **snoop•i•er, snoop•i•est.**

snoot (snoot), *Informal. —n.* **1.** the nose. **2.** a snob. **—v.t. 3.** to behave condescendingly toward; snub.

snoot•y (snoo′tē), *adj.,* **snoot•i•er, snoot•i•est.** *Informal.* snobbish; condescending. **—snoot′i•ly,** *adv.* **—snoot′i•ness,** *n.*

snooze (snooz), *v.,* **snoozed, snooz•ing,** *n.* **—v.i. 1.** to sleep; doze; nap. **—n. 2.** a short sleep; nap. **—snooz′er,** *n.*

snore (snôr, snōr), *v.,* **snored, snor•ing,** *n.* **—v.i. 1.** to breathe during sleep with hoarse or harsh sounds caused by the vibrating of the soft palate. **—n. 2.** the act, instance, or sound of snoring. **—snor′er,** *n.*

snor•kel (snôr′kəl), *n., v.,* **-keled, -kel•ing. —n. 1.** a tube through which a swimmer can breathe while moving face down at or just below the surface of the water. **2.** either of the tubes extended above the surface of the water that allow a submarine to remain submerged by taking in air and venting gases. **—v.i. 3.** to swim while breathing by means of a snorkel. [< German] **—snor′kel•er,** *n.*

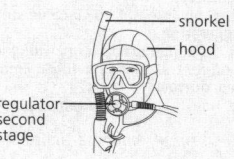

snorkel — snorkel, hood, regulator second stage

snorkel

snort (snôrt), *v.i.* **1.** to force the breath violently through the nostrils with a loud, harsh sound, as a horse. **2.** (of persons) to express contempt, indignation, etc., by a snort. **3.** to make sounds resembling snorts. **—v.t. 4.** to utter with a snort. **5.** to expel (air, sound, etc.) by or as if by snorting. **—n. 6.** the act or sound of snorting. **7.** *Slang.* a quick drink of liquor; shot. **—snort′er,** *n.*

snot (snot), *n. Informal.* an impudently disagreeable person, esp. a youth.

snot•ty (snot′ē), *adj.,* **-ti•er, -ti•est.** *Informal.* impudently disagreeable or offensive: *a snotty kid.* **—snot′ti•ly,** *adv.* **—snot′ti•ness,** *n.*

snout (snout), *n.* **1.** the part of an animal's head projecting forward and containing the nose and jaws; muzzle. **2.** anything that resembles or suggests an animal's snout in shape, function, etc. **3.** a nozzle or spout.

snout′ bee′tle, *n.* WEEVIL.

snow (snō), *n.* **1. a.** precipitation in the form of hexagonal crystals of ice, usu. grouped together as snowflakes, formed directly from water vapor freezing in air. **b.** these flakes as forming a layer on the ground. **c.** the fall of these flakes or a storm during which they fall. **2.** something resembling a layer of these flakes in whiteness, softness, or the like. **3.** *Literary.* **a.** white blossoms. **b.** the white color of snow. **4.** white spots or bands on a television screen caused by a weak signal. **—v.i. 5.** (of snow) to fall. **6.** to descend like snow. **—v.t. 7.** to let fall as or like snow. **8.** to cover, obstruct, confine, etc., with or as if with snow. **9.** *Slang.* to persuade or deceive by insincere talk or flattery. **10. snow under, a.** to cover with or bury in snow. **b.** to overwhelm. **c.** to defeat overwhelmingly.

snow•ball (snō′bôl′), *n.* **1.** a ball of snow pressed or rolled together, as for throwing. **2.** any of several shrubs of the honeysuckle family that bear large clusters of white flowers. **3.** a snow cone in which the crushed ice is shaped like a ball. **—v.i. 4.** to grow or become larger, greater, more intense, etc., at an accelerating rate. **—v.t. 5.** to throw snowballs at. **6.** to cause to grow or increase at an accelerating rate.

snow•bank (snō′bangk′), *n.* a mound or heap of snow, as a snowdrift.

snow•bell (snō′bel′), *n.* a small tree belonging to the genus *Styrax,* having showy white bell-shaped flowers.

Snow′belt′ or **Snow′ Belt′,** *n.* the northern parts of the U.S. that are subject to considerable snowfall.

snow•bird (snō′bûrd′), *n.* **1.** JUNCO. **2.** *Informal.* a person who vacations in or moves to a warmer climate during cold weather.

snow′ blind′ness, *n.* the usu. temporary dimming of the sight caused by the glare of reflected sunlight on snow. **—snow′-blind′,** *adj.*

snow′ blow′er or **snow′blow′er,** *n.* a motor-driven machine on wheels used to remove snow by throwing it into the air and to one side.

snow•board (snō′bôrd′, -bōrd′), *n.* a board for gliding on snow, resembling a wide ski, that one rides in an upright, standing position. **—snow′board′er,** *n.* **—snow′board′ing,** *n.*

snow•bound (snō′bound′), *adj.* shut in or immobilized by snow.

snow′ bunt′ing, *n.* a bunting, *Plectrophenax nivalis,* of the northern parts of the Northern Hemisphere, having white plumage.

snow•bush (snō′bŏosh′), *n.* any of several ornamental shrubs having a profusion of white flowers, as *Ceanothus cordulatus,* of the buckthorn family, native to W North America.

snow•cap (snō′kap′), *n.* a layer of snow forming a cap on or covering the top of something, as a mountain peak or ridge. **—snow′capped′,** *adj.*

snow′ cone′, *n.* a paper cup filled with crushed ice over which flavored syrup has been poured.

snow′ crab′, *n.* an edible spider crab of the N Pacific, *Chionoecetes opilio,* commercially important as a seafood product.

snow•drift (snō′drift′), *n.* **1.** a mound or bank of snow driven together by the wind. **2.** snow driven before the wind.

snow•drop (snō′drop′), *n.* any of several early-blooming bulbous Eurasian plants belonging to the genus *Galanthus,* of the amaryllis family, esp. *G. nivalis,* having drooping white flowers.

S

snow·fall (snō′fôl′), *n.* **1.** a fall of snow. **2.** the amount of snow at a particular place or in a given time.

snow′ fence′, *n.* a barrier erected on the windward side of a road, house, barn, etc., serving as a protection from drifting snow.

snow·field (snō′fēld′), *n.* a large and relatively permanent expanse of snow.

snow·flake (snō′flāk′), *n.* **1.** one of the small crystals, flakes, or masses in which snow falls. **2.** any of certain European plants of the amaryllis family, resembling the snowdrop.

snow′ goose′, *n.* a white North American goose, *Chen caerulescens,* with black primary feathers.

snow′ job′, *n. Slang.* an attempt to deceive or persuade through the use of flattery or exaggeration.

snow′ leop′ard, *n.* a longhaired, leopardlike cat, *Panthera (Uncia) uncia,* of mountains of central Asia, having a creamy gray coat with rosette spots. Also called **ounce.**

snow′ line′, *n.* the line, as on mountains, above which there is perpetual snow.

snow·man (snō′man′), *n., pl.* **-men.** a figure of a person made out of packed snow.

snow·mo·bile (snō′mə bēl′), *n., v.* **-biled, -bil·ing.** —*n.* **1.** a motor vehicle with a revolving tread in the rear and steerable skis in the front, for traveling over snow. —*v.i.* **2.** to operate or ride in a snowmobile. —**snow′mo·bil′er,** *n.*

snowmobile

snow′ pea′, *n.* a variety of the common pea, *Pisum sativum macrocarpon,* having thin, flat, edible pods. Also called **sugar pea.**

snow′ plant′, *n.* a leafless parasitic plant, *Sarcodes sanguinea,* of the wintergreen family, common in the Sierra Nevada in California and having a red flower spike and a thickly scaled stem.

snow·plow (snō′plou′), *n.* **1.** an implement or machine for clearing away snow from highways, railroad tracks, etc. **2.** a maneuver in which a skier pushes the heels of both skis outward so that they are far apart, as for turning, decelerating, or stopping. —*v.t.* **3.** to clear of snow using a snowplow. —*v.i.* **4.** to clear away snow with a snowplow. **5.** to execute a snowplow.

snow·shoe (snō′shōō′), *n., v.,* **-shoed, -shoe·ing.** —*n.* **1.** a racket-shaped contrivance for the foot for walking on deep snow without sinking. —*v.i.* **2.** to walk or travel on snowshoes. —**snow′sho′er,** *n.*

snow′shoe hare′, *n.* a large-footed North American hare, *Lepus americanus,* that is white in winter and dark brown in summer. Also called **snow′shoe rab′bit.**

snow·storm (snō′stôrm′), *n.* a storm accompanied by a heavy fall of snow.

snow·suit (snō′sōōt′), *n.* a child's outer garment for cold weather, consisting of warmly insulated long pants and a jacket, or top and pants in one piece, and often having a hood.

snow′ tire′, *n.* an automobile tire with a deep tread or protruding studs to give increased traction on snow or ice.

snow′-white′, *adj.* white as snow.

snow·y (snō′ē), *adj.,* **snow·i·er, snow·i·est. 1.** abounding in or covered with snow: *snowy fields.* **2.** characterized by snow, as the weather. **3.** of or resembling snow. **4.** of the color of snow; snow-white. **5.** immaculate. —**snow′i·ly,** *adv.* —**snow′i·ness,** *n.*

snow′y e′gret, *n.* a white egret, *Egretta thula,* of the warmer parts of the Western Hemisphere: formerly hunted for its plumes.

snow′y owl′, *n.* a diurnal arctic and subarctic owl, *Nyctea scandiaca,* having white plumage with dark brown markings.

snub (snub), *v.,* **snubbed, snub·bing,** *n., adj.* —*v.t.* **1.** to treat with disdain or contempt, esp. by ignoring. **2.** to check or reject with a sharp rebuke or cutting remark. **3.** to check or stop suddenly (a rope or cable that is running out). **4.** to check (a boat, an unbroken horse, etc.) by means of a rope or line made fast to a fixed object. —*n.* **5.** an act or instance of snubbing. **6.** an affront, slight, or rebuff. —*adj.* **7.** (of the nose) short and turned up at the tip. **8.** blunt. —**snub′ber,** *n.* —**snub′-bing·ly,** *adv.*

snub′-nosed′, *adj.* **1.** having a snub nose. **2.** having a blunt end: *snub-nosed pliers.*

snuck (snuk), *v.* a pp. and pt. of SNEAK.

snuff¹ (snuf), *v.t.* **1.** to draw in through the nose by inhaling. **2.** to per-

ceive by or as if by smelling; sniff. **3.** to examine by smelling, as an animal does. —*v.i.* **4.** to draw air into the nostrils by inhaling, as to smell something. **5.** to take snuff into the nostrils. —*n.* **6.** an act of snuffing; a sniff. **7.** smell, scent, or odor. **8.** a preparation of tobacco, either powdered and taken into the nostrils by inhalation or ground and placed between the cheek and gum. —*Idiom.* **9. up to snuff,** *Informal.* up to a certain standard; satisfactory. —**snuff′ing·ly,** *adv.*

snuff² (snuf), *n.* **1.** the charred or partly consumed portion of a candlewick. —*v.t.* **2.** to cut off or remove the snuff of (candles, tapers, etc.). **3. snuff out, a.** to extinguish. **b.** to suppress; crush. **c.** *Slang.* to kill or murder.

snuff·box (snuf′boks′), *n.* a box for holding snuff, esp. one small enough to be carried in the pocket.

snuff·er¹ (snuf′ər), *n.* **1.** a person who snuffs or sniffs. **2.** a person who takes snuff.

snuff·er² (snuf′ər), *n.* **1.** Usu. **snuffers.** a scissorlike instrument for removing the snuff of candles, tapers, etc. **2.** a small cup or cone with a handle used to smother a candle flame.

snuff·y (snuf′ē), *adj.,* **snuff·i·er, snuff·i·est. 1.** resembling snuff. **2.** soiled with snuff. **3.** given to the use of snuff. **4.** having an unpleasant appearance. —**snuff′i·ness,** *n.*

snug (snug), *adj.,* **snug·ger, snug·gest,** *v.,* **snugged, snug·ging,** *adv., n.* —*adj.* **1.** warmly comfortable or cozy, as a place, accommodations, etc.: *a snug little house.* **2.** fitting closely, as a garment. **3.** more or less compact or limited in size, and sheltered or warm: *a snug harbor.* **4.** trim or compactly arranged, as a ship or its parts. **5.** enabling one to live in comfort: *a snug fortune.* **6.** concealed; well-hidden: *a snug hideout.* —*v.i.* **7.** to lie closely or comfortably; nestle. —*v.t.* **8.** to make snug. **9.** to prepare for a storm by taking in sail, lashing deck gear, etc. (usu. fol. by *down*). —*adv.* **10.** in a snug manner. —*n.* **11.** *Brit.* a small, secluded room in a tavern, as for private parties. —**snug′ly,** *adv.* —**snug′ness,** *n.*

snug·gle (snug′əl), *v.,* **-gled, -gling,** *n.* —*v.i.* **1.** to lie or press closely, as for comfort or from affection; nestle; cuddle. —*v.t.* **2.** to draw or press closely against, as for comfort or from affection. —*n.* **3.** the act of snuggling.

so¹ (sō), *adv.* **1.** in the way or manner indicated: *Do it so.* **2.** in that or this manner or fashion; thus: *So it turned out.* **3.** in the aforesaid state or condition. **4.** to the extent or degree indicated or suggested: *Do not walk so fast.* **5.** very or extremely: *I'm so happy.* **6.** very greatly: *My head aches so!* **7.** (used before an adverb or an adverbial clause and fol. by *as*) to such a degree or extent: *so far as I know.* **8.** having the purpose of. **9.** hence; therefore. **10.** (used to emphasize or confirm a previous statement) most certainly: *I said I would come, and so I will.* **11.** (used to contradict a previous statement) indeed; truly; too: *I was so at the party!* **12.** likewise or correspondingly; also; too: *If he is going, then so am I.* **13.** in such manner as to follow or result from: *As he learned, so did he teach.* **14.** in the way that follows; in this way. **15.** in the way that precedes; in that way. **16.** in such way as to end in: *So live your life that old age will bring you no regrets.* **17.** then; subsequently: *and so to bed.* —*conj.* **18.** in order that (often fol. by *that*). **19.** with the result that (often fol. by *that*). **20.** on the condition that; if. —*pron.* **21.** such as has been stated: *to be good and stay so.* —*interj.* **22.** (used as an exclamation of surprise, shock, discovery, inquiry, indifference, etc., according to the manner of utterance.) —*adj.* **23.** true as stated or reported; conforming with reality or the fact: *Say it isn't so.*

so² (sō), *n. Music.* SOL¹.

soak (sōk), *v.i.* **1.** to lie in and become saturated or permeated with water or some other liquid. **2.** to pass, as a liquid, through pores, holes, or the like. **3.** to be thoroughly wet. **4.** to penetrate or become known to the mind or feelings (fol. by *in*): *The lesson didn't soak in.* —*v.t.* **5.** to place or keep in liquid in order to saturate thoroughly; steep. **6.** to wet thoroughly; saturate or drench. **7.** to permeate thoroughly, as liquid or moisture does. **8.** to extract or remove by or as if by soaking (often fol. by *out*). **9.** *Slang.* to overcharge. —*n.* **10.** the act or state of soaking or the state of being soaked. **11.** the liquid in which anything is soaked.

so′-and-so′, *n., pl.* **so-and-sos.** a person or thing not definitely named.

soap (sōp), *n.* **1.** a substance used for washing and cleansing purposes, usu. made by treating a fat with an alkali. **2.** any metallic salt of an acid derived from a fat. **3.** *Informal.* SOAP OPERA. —*v.t.* **4.** to rub, cover, lather, or treat with soap. —*Idiom.* **5. no soap,** *Informal.* the proposal, plan, etc., is not acceptable.

soap·bark (sōp′bärk′), *n.* **1.** a Chilean tree, *Quillaja saponaria,* of the rose family, having evergreen leaves and small white flowers. **2.** the inner bark of this tree, used as a substitute for soap.

soap·ber·ry (sōp′ber′ē, -bə rē), *n., pl.* **-ries. 1.** the fruit of any tropical or subtropical tree of the genus *Sapindus,* esp. *S. saponaria:* used as a substitute for soap. **2.** the tree itself.

soap′box′ or **soap′ box′,** *n.* an improvised platform, as one on a street, from which a speaker delivers an informal speech or political harangue.

soap′ bub′ble, *n.* **1.** a bubble of soapsuds. **2.** something that lacks substance or permanence.

soap·er (sō′pər), *n. Informal.* SOAP OPERA.

soap′ op′er·a (op′ər ə, op′rə), *n.* a radio or television series depicting the interconnected lives of many characters often in a sentimental, melodramatic way. [so called because soap manufacturers were among the original sponsors of such programs]

soap′ plant′, *n.* a California plant of the lily family, the bulb of which was used by the Indians as a soap.

soap•stone (sōp′stōn′), *n.* a massive variety of talc with a soapy feel, used for hearths, washtubs, etc. Also called **steatite.**

soap•suds (sōp′sudz′), *n.* (*used with a pl. v.*) suds made with water and soap. **—soap′suds′y,** *adj.*

soap•y (sō′pē), *adj.,* **soap•i•er, soap•i•est. 1.** containing or impregnated with soap: *soapy water.* **2.** covered with soap or lather. **3.** of or like soap: *a clean, soapy smell.* **4.** *Informal.* of or like a soap opera; melodramatic. **—soap′i•ly,** *adv.* **—soap′i•ness,** *n.*

soar (sôr, sōr), *v.i.* **1.** to fly upward, as a bird. **2.** to fly or glide high in the air with little effort or visible motion. **3.** to glide along at a height, as an airplane. **4.** to rise or ascend to a higher level, as a mountain. **5.** to rise or aspire to a higher level: *His hopes soared.* **—n. 6.** an act or instance of soaring. **7.** the height attained in soaring. **—soar′er,** *n.* **—soar′ing•ly,** *adv.*

so•a•ve (swä′vä, sō ä′-), *n.* a dry white wine produced in a region E of Verona in N Italy.

sob (sob), *v.,* **sobbed, sob•bing,** *n.* **—v.i. 1.** to weep with a convulsive catching of the breath. **2.** to make a sound resembling this. **—v.t. 3.** to utter with sobs. **4.** to put, send, etc., by sobbing or with sobs. **—n. 5.** the act of sobbing. **6.** any sound suggesting this. **—sob′ber,** *n.* **—sob′bing•ly,** *adv.* **—sob′ful,** *adj.*

so•ber (sō′bər), *adj.* **1.** not drunk. **2.** habitually temperate, esp. in the use of liquor. **3.** quiet or sedate in demeanor: *a serious, sober couple.* **4.** marked by seriousness, solemnity, etc.: *a sober occasion.* **5.** subdued in tone, as color; not flashy or showy, as clothes. **6.** free from excess, extravagance, or exaggeration: *sober facts.* **7.** showing self-control: *sober restraint.* **8.** rational. **—v.t., v.i. 9.** to make or become sober (often fol. by *up*). **—so′ber•ly,** *adv.* **—so′ber•ness,** *n.*

so•bri•e•ty (sə brī′i tē, sō-), *n.* **1.** the state or quality of being sober. **2.** temperance or moderation, esp. in the use of alcoholic beverages. **3.** seriousness or solemnity.

so•bri•quet or **sou•bri•quet** (sō′bri kā′, -ket′, sō′bri kā′, -ket′), *n.* a nickname.

sob′ sis′ter, *n.* **1.** a journalist who writes sentimental human-interest stories. **2.** a persistently sentimental do-gooder.

sob′ sto′ry, *n.* **1.** an excessively sentimental human-interest story. **2.** an alibi or excuse, esp. one designed to arouse sympathy.

so′-called′, *adj.* **1.** called or designated thus: *the so-called Southern bloc.* **2.** incorrectly called or styled thus: *so-called friends.*

soc•cer (sok′ər), *n.* a form of football played by two 11-member teams, in which the ball may be kicked or bounced off any part of the body but the arms and hands: only goalkeepers may use their hands to maneuver the ball.

so•cia•bil•i•ty (so′shə bil′i tē), *n., pl.* **-ties. 1.** the act or an instance of being sociable. **2.** the quality or state of being sociable.

so•cia•ble (sō′shə bəl), *adj.* **1.** inclined to associate with or be in the company of others. **2.** friendly or agreeable in company; companionable. **3.** characterized by agreeable companionship: *a sociable evening.* **—so′cia•ble•ness,** *n.* **—so′cia•bly,** *adv.*

so•cial (sō′shəl), *adj.* **1.** pertaining to, devoted to, or characterized by friendly companionship or relations: *a social club.* **2.** friendly or sociable, as persons or the disposition. **3.** pertaining to, connected with, or suited to polite or fashionable society: *a social event.* **4.** living or disposed to live in companionship with others or in a community, rather than in isolation. **5.** of or pertaining to human society, esp. as a body divided into classes according to status: *social rank.* **6.** of or pertaining to the life, welfare, and relations of human beings in a community: *social problems.* **7.** *Zool.* living habitually together in communities, as bees or ants. Compare SOLITARY (def. 4). **8.** pertaining to or between allies or confederates, as a war. **—n. 9.** a social gathering or party, esp. of or as given by an organized group: *a church social.* **—so′cial•ly,** *adv.*

so′cial climb′er, *n.* a person who attempts to gain admission into a group with a higher social standing. **—so′cial climb′ing,** *n.*

So′cial Cred′it, *n.* the doctrine that under capitalism there is an inadequate distribution of purchasing power, for which the remedy lies in governmental control of retail prices and the distribution of national dividends to consumers.

So′cial (or **so′cial**) **Dar′winism,** *n.* a 19th-century doctrine that the social order is a product of natural selection of those persons best suited to existing living conditions.

So′cial Democ′racy, *n.* the principles and policies of a Social Democratic Party. **—So′cial Dem′ocrat,** *n.*

So′cial Democrat′ic Par′ty, *n.* **1.** a German political party formed in 1875, orig. advocating a form of social organization based on Marxist ideology. **2.** any of several European political parties advocating a gradual transition to socialism by democratic processes. **3.** a centrist political party in Great Britain, formed in 1981.

so′cial gos′pel, *n.* Protestantism. a movement in America, chiefly in the early part of the 20th century, stressing the social teachings of Jesus and their applicability to public life.

so•cial•ism (sō′shə liz′əm), *n.* **1.** a theory or system of social organization in which the means of production and distribution of goods are owned and controlled collectively or by the government. **2.** (in Marxist theory) the stage following capitalism in the transition of a society to communism, characterized by the imperfect implementation of collectivist principles.

so•cial•ist (sō′shə list), *n.* **1.** an advocate or supporter of socialism. **2.** (*cap.*) a member of a Socialist Party.

so•cial•is•tic (sō′shə lis′tik), *adj.* **1.** of or pertaining to socialists or socialism. **2.** in accordance with socialism. **3.** advocating or supporting socialism. **—so′cial•is′ti•cal•ly,** *adv.*

So′cialist La′bor Par′ty, *n.* a U.S. political party, organized in 1874, advocating the peaceful introduction of socialism.

so•cial•ite (sō′shə līt′), *n.* a socially prominent person.

so•cial•i•za•tion (sō′shə lə zā′shən), *n.* **1.** a continuing process whereby an individual learns and assimilates the values and behavior patterns appropriate to his or her culture and social position. **2.** the act or process of making socialistic.

so•cial•ize (sō′shə līz′), *v.,* **-ized, -iz•ing. —v.t. 1.** to make social; make fit for life in companionship with others. **2.** to make socialistic; establish or regulate according to the theories of socialism. **3.** to require student participation in: *socialized instruction.* **—v.i. 4.** to associate or mingle sociably with others. **—so′cial•iz′er,** *n.*

so′cialized med′icine, *n.* any of various systems to provide a nation with complete medical care through government subsidization and regularization of medical and health services.

so′cial-mind′ed, *adj.* interested in or concerned with social conditions or the welfare of society.

so′cial psychol′ogy, *n.* the psychological study of social behavior, esp. of the reciprocal influence of the individual and the group with which the individual interacts.

so′cial sci′ence, *n.* **1.** the study of society and social behavior. **2.** a field of study, as history or economics, dealing with an aspect of society or forms of social activity. **—so′cial sci′entist,** *n.*

so′cial sec′retary, *n.* a personal secretary employed to make social appointments and handle personal correspondence.

so′cial secu′rity, *n.* **1.** (*often caps.*) a program of old age, unemployment, health, disability, and survivors' insurance maintained by the U.S. government through employer and employee payments. **2.** any public program providing for economic security and social welfare.

So′cial Secu′rity Act′, *n.* a law passed in 1935 providing old-age retirement insurance, a federal-state program of unemployment compensation, and federal grants for state welfare programs.

So′cial Secu′rity Administra′tion, *n.* a division of the Department of Health and Human Services, created in 1946, that administers federal Social Security programs. *Abbr.:* SSA

so′cial serv′ice, *n.* Often, **social services.** organized welfare efforts carried on under professional auspices by trained personnel. **—so′cial-serv′ice,** *adj.*

so′cial stud′ies, *n.* a school course comprising such subjects as history, geography, civics, sociology, and anthropology.

so′cial wasp′, *n.* any of several wasps, as the hornets or yellowjackets, that live together in a community.

so′cial wel′fare, *n.* social services provided by a government for its citizens.

so′cial work′, *n.* any organized service or activity designed to improve social conditions in a community, as assistance to poor persons or troubled families. **—so′cial work′er,** *n.*

so•ci•e•tal (sə sī′i tl), *adj.* noting or pertaining to large social groups, or to their activities, customs, etc. **—so•ci′e•tal•ly,** *adv.*

so•ci•e•ty (sə sī′i tē), *n., pl.* **-ties,** *adj.* **—n. 1.** an organized group of persons associated together for religious, benevolent, cultural, scientific, political or other purposes. **2.** a body of individuals living as members of a community. **3.** human beings collectively, viewed as members of a community: *the evolution of society.* **4.** a highly structured system of human organization for large-scale community living that normally furnishes protection, continuity, security, and a national identity for its members: *American society.* **5.** such a system characterized by its dominant economic class or form: *middle-class society; an industrial society.* **6.** those with whom one has companionship. **7.** companionship; company. **8.** the social life of wealthy, prominent, or fashionable persons. **9.** the social class that comprises such persons. **10.** the condition of those living in companionship with others, or in a community, rather than in isolation. **11.** *Biol.* a closely integrated group of social organisms of the same species exhibiting division of labor. **—adj. 12.** of, pertaining to, or characteristic of elegant society: *a society photographer.*

Soci′ety of Friends′, *n.* a sect founded by George Fox in England about 1650, opposed to oath-taking and war.

Soci′ety of Je′sus, *n.* See under JESUIT (def. 1).

So•ci•nus (sō sī′nəs), *n.* **Faustus** (*Fausto Sozzini*), 1539–1604, and his uncle **Laelius** (*Lelio Sozzini*), 1525–62, Italian Protestant theologians and reformers.

socio-, a combining form meaning "social," "sociological," "society": *socioeconomic; sociometry.*

so•ci•o•bi•ol•o•gy (sō′sē ō bī ol′ə jē, sō′shē-), *n.* the study of the biological, and esp. genetic and evolutionary, basis of social behavior in animals and humans. **—so′ci•o•bi′o•log′i•cal** (-bī′ə loj′i kəl), *adj.* **—so′ci•o•bi′o•log′i•cal•ly,** *adv.* **—so′ci•o•bi•ol′o•gist,** *n.*

so•ci•o•cul•tur•al (sō′sē ō kul′chər əl, sō′shē-), *adj.* of, pertaining to, or signifying the combination or interaction of social and cultural elements. **—so′ci•o•cul′tur•al•ly,** *adv.*

so•ci•o•ec•o•nom•ic (sō′sē ō ek′ə nom′ik, -ē′kə-, sō′shē-), *adj.* of, pertaining to, or signifying the combination or interaction of social and economic factors. —**so′ci•o•ec′o•nom′i•cal•ly,** adv.

so•ci•o•log•i•cal (sō′sē ə loj′i kəl, sō′shē-) also **so′ci•o•log′ic,** adj. **1.** of, pertaining to, or characteristic of sociology. **2.** dealing with social questions or problems. **3.** organized and structured into a society; social. —**so′ci•o•log′i•cal•ly,** adv.

so•ci•ol•o•gy (sō′sē ol′ə jē, sō′shē-), n. the science or study of the origin, development, organization, and functioning of human society; science of the fundamental laws of social relations, institutions, etc. —**so′ci•ol′o•gist,** n.

so•ci•o•path (sō′sē ə path′, sō′shē-), n. a person, as a psychopath, whose behavior is antisocial and who lacks a sense of moral responsibility or social conscience. —**so′ci•o•path′ic,** adj.

so•ci•o•po•lit•i•cal (sō′sē ō pə lit′i kəl, sō′shē-), adj. of or pertaining to the combination or interaction of social and political factors.

sock[1] (sok), n., pl. **socks** or, for 1, sometimes **sox. 1.** a short stocking usu. reaching to the calf or just above the ankle. **2.** a lightweight shoe worn by ancient Greek and Roman comic actors. **3.** comic writing for the theater; comedy or comic drama.

sock[2] (sok), v.t. **1.** to strike or hit hard. **2. sock away,** to put into savings or reserve. **3. sock in,** to close up, as an airport, or ground (an aircraft). —n. **4.** a hard blow. —adj. **5.** socko.

sock•et (sok′it), n. **1.** a hollow or concave part or piece that contains or fits a complementary part: *the eye socket; a socket for a light bulb.* —v.t. **2.** to place in or fit with a socket.

sock′eye salm′on (sok′ī′), n. a N Pacific salmon, *Oncorhynchus nerka:* an important food fish. Also called **red salmon, sock′eye′.**

sock•o (sok′ō), adj. Slang. extremely impressive or successful: *a socko performance.*

Soc•ra•tes (sok′rə tēz′), n. 469?–399 B.C., Athenian philosopher. —**So•crat•ic** (sə krat′ik), adj., n. —**So•crat′i•cal•ly,** adv.

Socrat′ic meth′od, the use of questions, as employed by Socrates, to develop a latent idea in the mind of a student or elicit an admission from an opponent.

sod (sod), n., v., **sod•ded, sod•ding.** —n. **1.** a section cut or torn from the surface of grassland, containing the matted roots of grass. **2.** the surface of the ground, esp. when covered with grass; turf. —v.t. **3.** to cover with sods or sod. —**sod′less,** adj.

so•da (sō′də), n. **1.** SODIUM HYDROXIDE. **2.** SODIUM CARBONATE (def. 2). **3.** sodium: *carbonate of soda.* **4.** SODA WATER. **5.** a drink made with soda water, flavored syrup, and often ice cream. **6.** SODA POP.

so′da ash′, n. SODIUM CARBONATE (def. 1).

so′da bis′cuit, n. **1.** a biscuit leavened with soda and sour milk or buttermilk. **2.** SODA CRACKER.

so′da crack′er, n. a thin, crisp cracker made with a yeast dough containing baking soda.

so′da foun′tain, n. **1.** a counter, as in a restaurant or drugstore, at which sodas, ice cream, light meals, etc., are served. **2.** an apparatus for dispensing soda water, usu. through faucets.

so′da jerk′ (or **jerk′er**), n. a person who prepares and serves sodas and ice cream at a soda fountain.

so′da lime′, n. a mixture of sodium hydroxide and calcium oxide. —**so′da-lime′,** adj.

so•dal•i•ty (sō dal′i tē, sə-), n., pl. **-ties. 1.** fellowship; comradeship. **2.** an association or society. **3.** a Roman Catholic lay society for religious and charitable purposes.

so′da ni′ter, n. a white or transparent mineral, sodium nitrate, NaNO₃, found as crusts and masses on surfaces, and used chiefly as a fertilizer.

so′da pop′, n. a carbonated, flavored, and sweetened soft drink.

so′da wa′ter, n. **1.** an effervescent beverage consisting of water charged with carbon dioxide. **2.** SODA POP. **3.** a weak solution of sodium bicarbonate, used to stimulate digestion.

sod•den (sod′n), adj. **1.** soaked with liquid or moisture; saturated. **2.** soggy or lumpy, as food that is poorly cooked. **3.** bloated, as the face. **4.** torpid or listless. —v.t., v.i. **5.** to make or become sodden. —**sod′den•ly,** adv. —**sod′den•ness,** n.

sod′ house′, n. a house built of strips of sod, laid like brickwork, and used esp. by settlers on the Great Plains.

so•di•um (sō′dē əm), n. **1.** a soft, silver-white, chemically active metallic element that occurs naturally only in combination: a necessary element in the body for the maintenance of normal fluid balance and other physiological functions. *Symbol:* Na; *at. wt.:* 22.9898; *at. no.:* 11; *sp. gr.:* 0.97 at 20°C. **2.** any salt of sodium, as sodium chloride or sodium bicarbonate.

so′dium ben′zoate, n. a white, water-soluble powder, C₇H₅NaO₂, used chiefly as a food preservative.

so′dium bicar′bonate, n. a white water-soluble powder, NaHCO₃, used chiefly as an antacid, a fire extinguisher, and a leavening agent in baking. Also called **bicarbonate of soda, baking soda.**

so′dium car′bonate, n. **1.** Also called **soda ash.** an anhydrous, grayish white, water-soluble powder, Na₂CO₃, used in the manufacture of glass, ceramics, soaps, paper, petroleum products, sodium salts, as a cleanser, for bleaching, and in water treatment. **2.** Also called **washing soda.** the hydrated form of this salt, Na₂CO₃·10H₂O, used similarly.

so′dium chlo′ride, n. SALT (def. 1).

so′dium fluor′ide, n. a colorless, crystalline, water-soluble, poison-

ous solid, NaF, used chiefly in the fluoridation of water, as an insecticide, and as a rodenticide.

so′dium hydrox′ide, n. a white, deliquescent solid, NaOH, used chiefly in the manufacture of other chemicals, rayon, film, soap, as a laboratory reagent, and in medicine as a caustic. Also called **caustic soda, soda.**

so′dium ni′trate, n. a crystalline, water-soluble compound, NaNO₃, that occurs naturally as soda niter: used in fertilizers, explosives, and glass, and as a color fixative in processed meats.

so′dium ni′trite, n. a yellowish or white crystalline compound, NaNO₂, used chiefly in dyeing and in electroplating. **2.** a water-soluble compound that in its anhydrous form, Na₃HPO₄, is used chiefly in the manufacture of ceramic glazes, enamels, baking powder, and cheeses, and that in its hydrated form, Na₃HPO₄·nH₂O, is used chiefly in the manufacture of dyes, fertilizers, detergents, and pharmaceuticals. **3.** a colorless water-soluble compound, Na₃PO₄·12H₂O, occurring as crystals: used chiefly in the manufacture of water-softening agents, detergents, paper, and textiles.

so′dium phos′phate, n. **1.** a white, crystalline, water-soluble powder, NaH₂PO₄, used chiefly in dyeing and in electroplating. **2.** a water-soluble compound that in its anhydrous form, Na₂HPO₄, is used chiefly in the manufacture of ceramic glazes, enamels, baking powder, and cheeses, and that in its hydrated form, Na₂HPO₄·nH₂O, is used chiefly in the manufacture of dyes, fertilizers, detergents, and pharmaceuticals. **3.** a colorless water-soluble compound, Na₃PO₄·12H₂O, occurring as crystals: used chiefly in the manufacture of water-softening agents, detergents, paper, and textiles.

so′dium sil′icate, n. any of several clear, white, or greenish water-soluble compounds of formulas varying in ratio from Na₂O·3.75SiO₂ to 2Na₂O·SiO₂, used chiefly in processing textiles and in the manufacture of paper products and cement. Also called **water glass.**

so′dium thiosul′fate, n. a white, crystalline, water-soluble powder, Na₂S₂O₃·5H₂O, used as a bleach and in photography as a fixing agent.

so′dium-va′por lamp′, n. an electric lamp in which sodium vapor is activated by current passing between two electrodes, producing a yellow, glareless light: used on streets and highways.

Sod•om (sod′əm), n. **1.** an ancient city destroyed because of its wickedness. Gen. 18–19. **2.** any corrupt, vice-ridden place.

Sod•om•ite (sod′ə mīt′), n. **1.** an inhabitant of Sodom. **2.** (l.c.) a person who engages in sodomy.

sod•om•ize (sod′ə mīz′), v.t., **-ized, -iz•ing. 1.** to engage in sodomy with. **2.** to force sodomy upon. —**sod′om•ist,** n.

sod•om•y (sod′ə mē), n. anal or oral copulation with a member of the same sex. **2.** enforced anal or oral copulation with a member of the opposite sex. —**sod′o•mit′i•cal** (-mit′i kəl), **sod′o•mit′ic,** adj.

so•fa (sō′fə), n., pl. **-fas.** a long upholstered couch with a back and two arms or raised ends.

so′fa bed′ or **so′fa•bed′,** n. a sofa that can be converted into a bed, either by folding out the seat or by lowering the back.

So•fi•a or **So•fi•ya** (sō′fē ə, sō fē′ə), n. the capital of Bulgaria, in the W part. 1,128,859.

soft (sôft, soft), adj. and adv., **-er, -est.** —adj. **1.** yielding readily to touch or pressure; not hard or stiff. **2.** relatively deficient in hardness, as metal or wood. **3.** smooth to the touch; not rough: *soft skin.* **4.** pleasant or comfortable: *a soft chair.* **5.** low or subdued in sound. **6.** not harsh or unpleasant to the eye: *soft light.* **7.** not hard or sharp: *soft outlines.* **8.** gentle or mild: *soft breezes.* **9.** not harsh or severe, as a penalty or demand. **10.** SOFT-HEARTED. **11.** not sturdy; delicate: *soft fabrics.* **12.** undemanding; easy, comfortable, etc.: *a soft job; a soft life.* **13.** weak, spiritless, etc., as from lack of effort or challenge: *We've grown soft with all these modern conveniences.* **14.** (of water) relatively free from mineral salts that interfere with the action of soap. **15.** (of paper money or a monetary system) not supported by sufficient gold reserves and, usu., not easily convertible into a foreign currency. **16.** (of a market, prices, etc.) declining in value, volume, etc.; weak. Compare FIRM[1] (def. 6). **17.** SOFT-CORE. **18.** *Photog.* **a.** (of a photographic image) having delicate gradations of tone. **b.** (of a focus) lacking in sharpness. **c.** (of a lens) unable to be focused sharply. **19. a.** (of c and g) pronounced as in *cent* and *gem.* **b.** (of consonants in Slavic languages) palatalized. Compare HARD (def. 34). **20.** (of the landing of a space vehicle) executed with deceleration; gentle. **21.** foolish or stupid: *soft in the head.* **22.** (of a detergent) readily biodegradable. —n. **23.** something that is soft or yielding; the soft part. **24.** softness. —adv. **25.** in a soft manner. —*Idiom.* **26. be soft on, a.** to feel affection for; be infatuated with. **b.** to be lenient or permissive with (something perceived as dangerous or threatening): *to be soft on crime.* —**soft′ly,** adv. —**soft′ness,** n.

soft•ball (sôft′bôl′, soft′-), n. **1.** a form of baseball played on a smaller diamond with a larger and softer ball. **2.** the ball itself.

soft′-boiled′, adj. (of an egg) boiled in the shell only until yolk and white are partially set.

soft•bound (sôft′bound′, soft′-), n., adj. PAPERBACK (defs. 1, 2).

soft′ coal′, n. BITUMINOUS COAL.

soft′-cov′er, n., adj. PAPERBACK (defs. 1, 2).

soft′ drink′, n. a beverage that is not alcoholic or intoxicating and is usu. carbonated, as root beer or ginger ale.

soft•en (sô′fən, sof′ən), v., **-ened, -en•ing.** —v.t. **1.** to make soft or softer. —v.i. **2.** to become soft or softer. —**soft′en•er,** n.

soft′ goods′, n.pl. the subclass of nondurable goods as represented esp. by textile products, as clothing and bedding; dry goods. Compare DURABLE GOODS.

soft′-heart′ed, adj. very sympathetic or responsive; generous in spirit. —**soft′-heart′ed•ly,** adv. —**soft′-heart′ed•ness,** n.

soft•ie (sôf′tē, sof′-), n. SOFTY.

soft′ land′ing, *n.* a slowing down of economic growth at a manageable rate relative to inflation and unemployment.

soft′ lens′, *n.* a nonrigid contact lens made of porous plastic, having a high water content that is replenished from eye surface moisture. Compare HARD LENS.

soft′ line′, *n.* a position or policy, as in politics, that is moderate and flexible. —**soft′-line′,** *adj.* —**soft′-lin′er,** *n.*

soft′ pal′ate, *n.* See under PALATE (def. 1).

soft′ ped′al, *n.* **1.** a pedal, as on a piano, for reducing tonal volume. **2.** something that restrains or dampens.

soft′-ped′al, *v.,* **-aled, -al•ing** or (*esp. Brit.*) **-alled, -al•ling.** —*v.i.* **1.** to use the soft pedal of a piano. —*v.t.* **2.** to attempt to make less obvious, important, or objectionable; downplay.

soft′ rock′, *n.* rock and roll that is relatively melodic in style with an underemphasized beat.

soft′ sculp′ture, *n.* sculpture using flexible material, as vinyl, to reproduce objects that are normally rigid in construction.

soft′ sell′, *n.* a method of advertising or selling that is quietly persuasive, indirect, and sophisticated (opposed to *hard sell*). —**soft′-sell′,** *v.t.,* **-sold, -sell•ing,** *adj.*

soft′-shell′, *adj.* **1.** Also, **soft′-shelled′.** having a soft, flexible, or fragile shell, as a crab that has recently molted. —*n.* **2.** a soft-shell animal, esp. a soft-shell crab.

soft′-shell′ clam′, *n.* any usu. oval edible clam of the genus *Mya,* esp. *M. arenaria,* inhabiting waters along both coasts of North America. Also called **steamer.**

soft′-shell′ crab′, *n.* a crab, esp. the blue crab, that has recently molted and therefore has a soft, edible shell.

soft′-shoe′, *adj.* of, pertaining to, or characteristic of tap dancing done in soft-soled shoes, without taps.

soft′ shoul′der, *n.* the unpaved edge of a road.

soft′ soap′, *n.* **1.** persuasive talk; flattery. **2.** the semifluid soap produced when potassium hydroxide is used in the saponification of a fat or an oil. —**soft′-soap′,** *v.t., v.i.* —**soft′-soap′er,** *n.*

soft′-spo′ken, *adj.* **1.** (of persons) speaking with a soft or gentle voice; mild. **2.** (of words) softly or mildly spoken; persuasive.

soft′ spot′, *n.* **1.** a weak or vulnerable position, place, condition, etc. **2.** emotional susceptibility: *a soft spot for kittens.*

soft′ touch′, *n.* **1.** a person who readily gives or lends money. **2.** a person who is easily duped or imposed upon.

soft•ware (sôft′wâr′, soft′-), *n.* **1. a.** programs for directing the operation of a computer or processing electronic data (disting. from *hardware*). **b.** DOCUMENTATION (def. 3). **2.** any material requiring the use of mechanical or electrical equipment, esp. audiovisual material such as film, tapes, or records.

soft•wood (sôft′wŏŏd′, soft′-), *n.* **1.** a coniferous tree or its wood. **2. a.** any wood that is relatively soft or easily cut. **b.** a tree yielding such a wood. —*adj.* **3.** of or pertaining to softwood.

soft•y or **soft•ie** (sôf′tē, sof′-), *n., pl.* **-ies.** *Informal.* **1.** a person easily stirred to sentiment. **2.** a weak or foolish person.

sog•gy (sog′ē), *adj.,* **-gi•er, -gi•est. 1.** thoroughly wet; soaked; sodden. **2.** damp and heavy, as poorly baked bread. **3.** ponderously dull; boring: *a soggy, sentimental play.* —**sog′gi•ness,** *n.*

soi•gné or **soi•gnée** (swän yā′; *Fr.* swA nyā′), *adj.* **1.** carefully or elegantly done. **2.** well-groomed.

soil¹ (soil), *n.* **1.** the portion of the earth's surface consisting of disintegrated rock and humus. **2.** the ground or earth. **3.** a particular kind of earth. **4.** a country, land, or region. **5.** any environment nurturing growth or development. —**soil′less,** *adj.*

soil² (soil), *v.t.* **1.** to make dirty or filthy. **2.** to smudge or stain. **3.** to sully or tarnish, as with disgrace. —*v.i.* **4.** to become soiled. —*n.* **5.** the act or fact of soiling. **6.** the state of being soiled. **7.** a spot or stain. **8.** foul matter; filth; sewage. **9.** dung; manure.

soil³ (soil), *v.t.* to feed (confined cattle, horses, etc.) freshly cut green fodder for roughage.

soi•ree or **soi•rée** (swä rā′), *n.* an evening party or social gathering.

so•journ (*n.* sō′jûrn; *v. also* sō jûrn′), *n.* **1.** a temporary stay: *a week's sojourn in Paris.* —*v.i.* **2.** to stay temporarily: *We sojourned at the beach for a month.* —**so′journ•er,** *n.*

sol¹ (sōl) also **so,** *n.* the musical syllable for the fifth tone of a diatonic scale.

sol² (sōl, sol; *Sp.* sôl), *n., pl.* **sols,** *Sp.* **so•les** (sô′les). the basic monetary unit of Peru.

sol³ (sôl, sol), *n.* a fluid colloidal solution.

Sol (sol), *n.* **1.** a personification of the sun. **2.** the Roman god of the sun, identified with the Greek god Helios.

-sol, a combining form meaning "soil" of the kind specified by the initial element: *spodosol.*

Sol., Solomon.

sol•ace (sol′is), *n., v.,* **-aced, -ac•ing.** —*n.* Also called **sol′ace•ment. 1.** comfort in sorrow or misfortune. **2.** a source of consolation or relief. —*v.t.* **3.** to console; cheer. **4.** to alleviate; relieve: *to solace sorrow.* —**sol′ac•er,** *n.*

so•lar¹ (sō′lər), *adj.* **1.** pertaining to the sun: *solar phenomena.* **2.** determined by the sun: *solar hour.* **3.** proceeding from the sun, as light or heat. **4.** utilizing, operated by, or depending on solar energy. **5.** indicating time by means of or with reference to the sun: *a solar chronometer.*

so•lar² (sol′ər, sō′lər), *n.* a private or upper chamber in a medieval English house.

so′lar bat′tery, *n.* an array of solar cells.

so′lar cell′, *n.* a photovoltaic cell that converts sunlight directly into electricity.

so′lar collec′tor, *n.* any of numerous devices or systems designed to capture and use solar radiation for heating air or water and for producing steam to generate electricity.

so′lar day′, *n.* DAY (def. 3b).

so′lar eclipse′, *n.* See under ECLIPSE (def. 1a).

so′lar en′ergy, *n.* energy derived from the sun in the form of solar radiation.

so•lar•i•um (sə lâr′ē əm, sō-), *n., pl.* **-lar•i•ums, -lar•i•a** (-lâr′ē ə). a glass-enclosed room or porch exposed to the sun's rays, as for convalescents in a hospital.

so′lar pan′el, *n.* a bank of solar cells.

so′lar plex′us, *n.* **1.** a network of nerves at the upper part of the abdomen, behind the stomach and in front of the aorta. **2.** a point on the stomach wall just below the sternum where a blow will affect this network.

so′lar sys′tem, *n.* the sun together with all the planets and other bodies that revolve around it.

so′lar wind′, *n.* the radial outflow of charged particles, mainly electrons and protons, from the sun.

so′lar year′, *n.* YEAR (def. 4b).

sold (sōld), *v.* pt. and pp. of SELL.

sol•der (sod′ər), *n.* **1.** any of various alloys fused and applied to the joint between metal objects to unite them without heating the objects to the melting point. **2.** anything that joins or unites. —*v.t.* **3.** to join (metal objects) with solder. **4.** to join closely and intimately. —*v.i.* **5.** to unite things with solder. **6.** to become united. —**sol′der•a•ble,** *adj.*

sol′dering i′ron, *n.* an instrument for melting and applying solder.

sol•dier (sōl′jər), *n.* **1.** a person engaged in military service. **2.** an enlisted man or woman, as distinguished from a commissioned officer. **3.** a person of military skill or experience. **4.** a person dedicated to a cause. **5.** a low-ranking member of a crime organization. **6.** a member of a caste of sexually underdeveloped female ants or termites specialized, as with powerful jaws, to defend the colony from invaders. —*v.i.* **7.** to act or serve as a soldier. **8.** to loaf while pretending to work. **9. soldier on,** to persist steadfastly. —**sol′dier•ly,** *adj.*

sol′dier of for′tune, *n.* a person who seeks riches or pleasure through adventurous, often military exploits.

sol′diers′ home′, *n.* an institution that provides care and shelter for military veterans.

Sol′dier's Med′al, *n.* a medal awarded by the U.S. Army for heroism not involving conflict with an enemy.

sol•dier•y (sōl′jə rē), *n., pl.* **-dier•ies. 1.** soldiers collectively. **2.** a body of soldiers. **3.** military training or skill.

sold′-out′, *adj.* having all tickets sold: *a sold-out matinee.*

sole¹ (sōl), *adj.* **1.** being the only one; only: *the sole living relative.* **2.** belonging or pertaining to one individual or group to the exclusion of all others; exclusive: *the sole right to the estate.* **3.** functioning automatically or with independent power: *the sole authority.* **4.** *Law.* (of a woman) unmarried. —**sole′ness,** *n.*

sole² (sōl), *n., v.,* **soled, sol•ing.** —*n.* **1.** the undersurface of a foot. **2.** the corresponding under part of a shoe or other footwear. **3.** the bottom or undersurface of anything. **4.** the part of the head of a golf club that touches the ground. —*v.t.* **5.** to furnish with a sole. **6.** to place the sole of (a golf club) on the ground.

sole³ (sōl), *n., pl.* (*esp. collectively*) **sole,** (*esp. for kinds or species*) **soles. 1.** any flatfish of the families Soleidae and Cynoglossidae, having a hooklike snout, esp. *Solea solea.* **2.** the market name of any of various other flatfishes resembling the sole.

sol•e•cism (sol′ə siz′əm, sō′lə-), *n.* **1.** a nonstandard or ungrammatical usage, as *unflammable* or *they was.* **2.** a breach of good manners or etiquette. —**sol′e•cist,** *n.* —**sol′e•cis′tic,** *adj.*

soled (sōld), *adj.* having a sole of a specified kind (usu. used in combination): *thick-soled; lug-soled.*

sole•ly (sōl′lē), *adv.* **1.** as the only one or ones: *solely responsible.* **2.** exclusively or only: *plants found solely in the tropics.* **3.** merely: *She wanted solely to be noticed.*

sol•emn (sol′əm), *adj.* **1.** grave; mirthless: *solemn remarks.* **2.** somberly sedate or profound: *solemn music.* **3.** serious; earnest: *solemn assurances.* **4.** of a formal or ceremonial character: *a solemn occasion.* **5.** made in due legal or other express form: *a solemn oath.* **6.** marked or observed with religious rites: *a solemn holy day.* —**sol′emn•ly,** *adv.*

so•lem•ni•fy (sə lem′nə fī′), *v.t.,* **-fied, -fy•ing.** to make solemn.

so•lem•ni•ty (sə lem′ni tē), *n., pl.* **-ties. 1.** the state or character of being solemn; gravity. **2.** Often, **solemnities.** solemn observance; ceremonial proceeding.

sol•em•nize (sol′əm nīz′), *v.,* **-nized, -niz•ing.** —*v.t.* **1.** to go through or observe with ceremony or formality. **2.** to perform the ceremony of (marriage). **3.** to render solemn; dignify. —*v.i.* **4.** to act or speak with solemnity. —**sol′em•ni•za′tion,** *n.*

Sol′emn League′ and Cov′enant, *n.* an agreement (1643) between the parliaments of Scotland and England permitting the promotion of

Presbyterianism in Scotland, England, and Ireland. Compare NATIONAL COVENANT.

sol′emn mass′, *n.* (*often caps.*) HIGH MASS.

so·le·noid (sō′lə noid′, sol′ə-), *n.* a coil of wire that, when carrying current, magnetically attracts a sliding iron core. —**so′le·noi′dal,** *adj.*

so·le·us (sō′lē əs), *n., pl.* **-le·i** (-lē ī′), **-le·us·es.** a muscle in the calf of the leg, behind the gastrocnemius muscle, that helps extend the foot forward.

sol-fa (sōl′fä′, sōl′fä′), *n., v.,* **-faed, -fa·ing.** —*n.* **1.** the musical syllables *do, re, me, fa, sol, la,* and *ti,* sung to the ascending tones of a diatonic scale. —*v.i.* **2.** to use sol-fa syllables in singing. —**sol′-fa′ist,** *n.*

so·lic·it (sə lis′it), *v.t.* **1.** to try to obtain by earnest plea or application: *to solicit aid.* **2.** to entreat; petition: *to solicit the committee for funds.* **3.** to seek to influence or incite to action, esp. unlawful or wrong action. —*v.i.* **4.** to make a petition or request for something desired. **5.** to solicit orders or trade: *No solicitation allowed in this building.*

so·lic·i·ta·tion (sə lis′i tā′shən), *n.* **1.** the act of soliciting. **2.** a petition or request; entreaty. **3.** enticement; allurement. **4. a.** the crime of asking another to commit or aid in a crime. **b.** the action of a prostitute who solicits in a public place.

so·lic·i·tor (sə lis′i tər), *n.* **1.** a person who solicits, as contributions or trade. **2.** an officer having charge of the legal business of a city, town, etc. **3.** (in England and Wales) a member of the legal profession who advises clients, represents them before the lower courts, and prepares cases for barristers to try in the higher courts.

solic′itor gen′eral, *n., pl.* **solicitors general. 1.** the chief legal officer in some states, charged with representing the state in suits affecting the public interest. **2.** (*caps.*) the law officer of the U.S. government next below the Attorney General, having charge of appeals.

so·lic·i·tous (sə lis′i təs), *adj.* **1.** anxious or concerned: *solicitous about a person's health.* **2.** anxiously desirous: *solicitous of the esteem of others.* **3.** eager: *always solicitous to please.* **4.** scrupulous; particular: *a solicitous housekeeper.* —**so·lic′i·tous·ly,** *adv.* —**so·lic′i·tous·ness,** *n.*

so·lic·i·tude (sə lis′i tōōd′, -tyōōd′), *n.* **1.** the state of being solicitous; deep concern. **2. solicitudes,** causes of anxiety or care. **3.** an attitude of extreme attentiveness.

sol·id (sol′id), *adj.* **1.** having the interior completely filled up; not hollow: *a piece of solid rock.* **2.** having the three dimensions of length, breadth, and thickness. **3.** having no openings or breaks: *a solid wall.* **4.** firm or compact in substance: *solid ground.* **5.** having relative firmness, coherence of particles, or persistence of form: *solid particles suspended in a liquid.* **6.** dense, thick, or heavy in nature or appearance: *solid masses of cloud.* **7.** firm in construction; substantial: *solid food.* **8.** without separation; continuous: *a solid row of buildings.* **9.** serious in character: *solid scholarship.* **10.** whole or entire: *one solid hour.* **11.** consisting entirely of one substance or material: *solid gold; a solid teak shelf.* **12.** uniform in tone: *a solid blue dress.* **13.** real; genuine: *solid comfort.* **14.** sound; reliable: *solid facts.* **15.** fully reliable or sensible: *a solid citizen.* **16.** financially sound: *a solid corporation.* **17.** cubic: *A solid foot contains 1728 solid inches.* **18.** written without a hyphen, as a compound word. **19.** having the lines not separated by leads, or having few open spaces, as type or printing. **20.** unanimous: *a solid majority.* **21.** on a friendly or favorable footing: *in solid with her parents.* —*n.* **22.** a body or object having the three dimensions of length, breadth, and thickness. **23.** a substance whose molecules are densely packed and that is usu. characterized by rigidity and resistance to deformation. **24.** something that is solid. —**sol′id·ly,** *adv.* —**sol′id·ness,** *n.*

sol′id an′gle, *n.* an angle formed by three or more planes intersecting in a common point or vertex at the vertex of a cone.

sol·i·dar·i·ty (sol′i dar′i tē), *n., pl.* **-ties.** unanimity of attitude or purpose, as between members of a group or class.

sol′id geom′etry, *n.* the geometry of solid figures; geometry of three dimensions.

so·lid·i·fy (sə lid′ə fī′), *v.,* **-fied, -fy·ing.** —*v.t.* **1.** to make solid; make into a hard or compact mass; change from a liquid or gaseous to a solid form. **2.** to unite firmly or consolidate. **3.** to form into crystals; make crystallized. —*v.i.* **4.** to become solid. **5.** to form into crystals; become crystallized. —**so·lid′i·fi·ca′tion,** *n.* —**so·lid′i·fi′er,** *n.*

so·lid·i·ty (sə lid′i tē), *n.* **1.** the state or quality of being solid. **2.** firmness; strength.

sol′id-state′, *adj.* being or pertaining to electronic devices, as transistors or crystals, that can control current without the use of moving parts, heated filaments, or vacuum gaps.

so·lil·o·quy (sə lil′ə kwē), *n., pl.* **-quies. 1.** a speech in a drama in which a character, alone or as if alone, discloses innermost thoughts. **2.** the act of talking while or as if alone.

sol·i·taire (sol′i târ′), *n.* **1.** any of various card games for one person in which the cards are arranged in predetermined patterns. **2.** a precious stone, esp. a diamond, set by itself, as in a ring.

sol·i·tar·y (sol′i ter′ē), *adj., n., pl.* **-tar·ies. 1.** without companions; sole: *a solitary passerby.* **2.** avoiding the society of others: *a solitary existence.* **3.** by itself; singular: *one solitary house.* **4.** marked by the absence of companions: *a solitary journey.* **5.** done in solitude: *solitary chores.* **6.** being the only one: *a solitary exception.* **7.** characterized by solitude; secluded: *a solitary cabin in the woods.* **8.** *Zool.* living habitually alone or in pairs, as certain wasps. Compare SOCIAL (def. 7). —*n.* **9.** a person who lives alone or in solitude. **10.** SOLITARY CONFINEMENT. —**sol′i·tar′i·ly,** *adv.* —**sol′i·tar′i·ness,** *n.*

sol′itary confine′ment, *n.* confinement of a prisoner in a cell or other place in isolation from others.

sol·i·tude (sol′i tōōd′, -tyōōd′), *n.* **1.** the state of being or living alone; seclusion. **2.** remoteness from habitations: *the solitude of the woods.* **3.** a lonely, unfrequented place. —**sol′i·tu′di·nous** (-n əs), *adj.*

sol·mi·za·tion (sol′mə zā′shən, sōl′-), *n.* the act, process, or system of using syllables to represent the tones of a musical scale.

so·lo (sō′lō), *n., pl.* **-los** or, for 1, **-li** (-lē), *adj., adv., v.,* **-loed, -lo·ing.** —*n.* **1.** a musical composition or a part in such a composition for one performer with or without accompaniment. **2.** any performance, as a dance, by one person. **3.** a flight in an airplane during which the pilot is unaccompanied by any other person. **4.** a person who works, acts, or performs alone. —*adj.* **5.** of, pertaining to, or being a solo. —*adv.* **6.** on one's own; alone: *flying solo.* —*v.i.* **7.** to perform or be a solo. **8.** to pilot an airplane by oneself. [< Italian < Latin *sōlus* alone]

so·lo·ist (sō′lō ist), *n.* a person who performs a solo.

Sol·o·mon (sol′ə mən), *n.* **1.** fl. 10th century B.C., king of Israel (son of David). **2.** an extraordinarily wise man; a sage.

Sol′omon Is′lands, *n.pl.* **1.** an archipelago in the W Pacific Ocean, E of New Guinea; politically divided between Papua New Guinea and the Solomon Islands. **2.** an independent country comprising the larger, SE part of this archipelago: a former British protectorate; gained independence in 1978. 426,855; 10,954 sq. mi. (28,370 sq. km). *Cap.:* Honiara. —**Sol′omon Is′lander,** *n.*

So·lon (sō′lən), *n.* c638–c558 B.C., Athenian statesman. **2.** (*often l.c.*) a wise lawgiver.

so′ long′, *interj.* (used to express farewell.)

sol·stice (sol′stis, sōl′-), *n.* **1. a.** either of the two times a year when the sun is at its greatest distance from the celestial equator: about June 21, when the sun reaches its northernmost point on the celestial sphere, or about Dec. 22, when it reaches its southernmost point. **b.** either of the two points in the ecliptic farthest from the equator. **2.** a furthest point.

sol·u·bil·i·ty (sol′yə bil′i tē), *n.* the quality or property of being soluble; relative capability of being dissolved.

sol·u·ble (sol′yōō bəl), *adj.* **1.** capable of being dissolved or liquefied: *a soluble powder.* **2.** capable of being solved or explained: *a soluble problem.* —*n.* **3.** something soluble. —**sol′u·bly,** *adv.*

sol·ute (sol′yōōt, sō′lōōt), *n.* the substance dissolved in a solution.

so·lu·tion (sə lōō′shən), *n.* **1.** the act or process of solving a problem. **2.** the state of being solved. **3.** an answer to a problem. **4. a.** the process by which a gas, liquid, or solid is dispersed homogeneously in a gas, liquid, or solid without chemical change. **b.** a homogeneous molecular mixture of two or more substances.

solv·a·ble (sol′və bəl), *adj.* capable of being solved, as a problem. —**solv′a·bil′i·ty,** *n.*

solve (solv), *v.t.,* **solved, solv·ing. 1.** to find the answer or explanation for; clear up; explain: *to solve a mystery or puzzle.* **2.** to work out the answer or solution to (a mathematical problem). —**solv′er,** *n.*

sol·ven·cy (sol′vən sē), *n.* the condition of being solvent.

sol·vent (sol′vənt), *adj.* **1.** able to pay all just debts. **2.** having the power of dissolving; causing solution. —*n.* **3.** a substance that dissolves another to form a solution: *Water is a solvent for sugar.* **4.** something that solves or explains. —**sol′vent·ly,** *adv.*

So·ma·li·a (sō mä′lē ə, -mäl′yə), *n.* a republic on the E coast of Africa, formed by the merger of British Somaliland and Italian Somaliland in 1960. 9,940,232; 246,201 sq. mi. (637,657 sq. km). *Cap.:* Mogadishu. —**So·ma′li·an,** *adj., n.*

so·mat·ic (sō mat′ik, sə-), *adj.* **1.** of the body; bodily; physical. **2.** of or pertaining to the body walls, as distinguished from the inner organs. **3.** of or pertaining to a somatic cell. —**so·mat′i·cal·ly,** *adv.*

somat′ic cell′, *n.* **1.** one of the cells that take part in the formation of the body, becoming differentiated into the various tissues, organs, etc. **2.** any cell of the body that is not a sexually reproductive cell (opposed to *germ cell*).

so·ma·tol·o·gy (sō′mə tol′ə jē), *n.* PHYSICAL ANTHROPOLOGY. —**so′ma·tol′o·gist,** *n.*

so·ma·to·stat·in (sə mat′ə stat′n), *n.* a polypeptide hormone, produced in the brain and pancreas, that inhibits secretion of somatotropin from the hypothalamus and inhibits insulin production by the pancreas.

som·ber (som′bər), *adj.* **1.** gloomily dark; shadowy. **2.** dark and dull in color or tone: *a somber dress.* **3.** downcast; glum: *a somber mood.* **4.** extremely serious; grave: *a somber expression on one's face.* Also, *esp. Brit.,* **som·bre.** —**som′ber·ly,** *adv.* —**som′ber·ness,** *n.*

som·bre·ro (som brâr′ō), *n.* a broad-brimmed, tall-crowned hat of straw or felt worn esp. in Mexico and the southwestern U.S. —**som·bre′roed,** *adj.*

sombrero

some (sum; *unstressed* səm), *adj.* **1.** being an undetermined or unspecified one: *Some person may object.* **2.** certain (used with plural nouns): *Some days I stay home.* **3.** unspecified in number, amount, degree, etc.: *to some extent.* **4.** unspecified in number but considerable in number, amount, degree, etc.: *We talked for some time.* **5.** *Informal.* remarkable of its type: *That was some storm.* —*pron.* **6.** certain persons, individuals, instances, etc., not specified: *Some think he is dead.* **7.** an unspecified number, amount, etc., as distinguished from the rest or in addition: *He paid a thousand dollars and then some.* —*adv.* **8.** approximately; about: *Some 300 were present.* **9.** to some degree or extent: *I like baseball some.*

-some[1], an adjective-forming suffix, now unproductive, with the meanings "like," "tending to": *burdensome; quarrelsome.*

-some[2], a collective suffix used with numerals: *threesome.*

-some[3], a combining form used in the names of structures or regions of a cell (*chromosome; ribosome*).

some·bod·y (sum'bod'ē, -bud'ē, -bə dē), *pron., n., pl.* **-bod·ies.** —*pron.* **1.** some person. —*n.* **2.** a person of some note or importance.

some·day (sum'dā'), *adv.* at an indefinite future time.

some·how (sum'hou'), *adv.* **1.** in some way not specified, apparent, or known. —*Idiom.* **2. somehow or other,** somehow.

some·one (sum'wun', -wən), *pron.* some person; somebody.

some·place (sum'plās'), *adv.* somewhere. —**Usage.** See ANYPLACE.

som·er·sault (sum'ər sôlt'), *n.* **1.** an acrobatic movement, either forward or backward, in which the body rolls end over end, making a complete revolution. **2.** such a movement performed in the air as part of a dive, tumbling routine, etc. —*v.i.* **3.** to perform a somersault.

some·thing (sum'thing'), *pron.* **1.** a certain undetermined or unspecified thing: *Something is wrong there. Tell me something.* **2.** (used esp. in combination to indicate an additional amount, as of years, that is unknown, unspecified, or forgotten): *twentysomething; fortysomething.* —*n.* **3.** a person or thing of some consequence. —*adv.* **4.** in some degree; to some extent; somewhat. **5.** *Informal.* to a high or extreme degree: *acted up something fierce.* —*Proverb.* **6. You can't get something for nothing,** everything has a cost.

some·time (sum'tīm'), *adv.* **1.** at some indefinite or indeterminate point of time: *We will arrive sometime next week.* **2.** at an indefinite future time: *Come to see us sometime.* —*adj.* **3.** having been formerly; former. **4.** being so only at times or to some extent: *a writer and sometime painter.* —**Usage.** The adverb SOMETIME is written as one word: *She promised to visit us sometime soon.* The two-word form SOME TIME means "an unspecified interval or period of time": *It will take some time for the wounds to heal.*

some·times (sum'tīmz'), *adv.* on some occasions; at times; now and then.

some·way (sum'wā') also **some'ways',** *adv.* in some way; somehow.

some·what (sum'hwut', -hwot', -hwət, -wut', -wot', -wət), *adv.* **1.** in some measure or degree; to some extent. —*pron.* **2.** some part or amount; something.

some·where (sum'hwâr', -wâr'), *adv.* **1.** in, at, or to some place not unspecified or unknown: *I've left the book somewhere.* **2.** in the neighborhood of; approximately: *somewhere around 60 years old.* —*n.* **3.** an unspecified or uncertain place. —**Usage.** See ANYPLACE.

som·me·lier (sum'əl yā'; *Fr.* sô mə lyā'), *n., pl.* **som·me·liers** (sum'əl yāz'; *Fr.* sô mə lyā'). a wine steward in a restaurant.

som·nam·bu·lism (som nam'byə liz'əm, səm-), *n.* SLEEPWALKING. —**som·nam'bu·list,** *n.* —**som·nam'bu·lis'tic,** *adj.*

som·ni·fa·cient (som'nə fā'shənt), *adj.* **1.** causing or inducing sleep. —*n.* **2.** a drug or other agent that induces sleep.

som·nif·ic (som nif'ik, səm-), *adj.* causing sleep; soporific.

som·no·lent (som'nə lənt), *adj.* **1.** sleepy; drowsy. **2.** tending to cause sleep. —**som'no·lence, som'no·len·cy,** *n.* —**som'no·lent·ly,** *adv.*

son (sun), *n.* **1.** a male child or person in relation to his parents. **2.** a male child or person adopted as a son. **3.** a son-in-law. **4.** a person related as if by ties of sonship. **5.** a male person looked upon as the product or result of a particular agent, force, or influence: *sons of the soil.* **6. the Son,** the second person of the Trinity; Jesus Christ. —**son'hood,** *n.*

so·nant (sō'nənt), *adj.* **1.** sounding; having sound. **2.** (of a speech sound) **a.** voiced (opposed to *surd*). **b.** capable of itself forming a syllable or the nucleus of a syllable; syllabic. —*n.* **3.** a speech sound that can itself form a syllable or the nucleus of a syllable, esp. a syllabic consonant. **4.** a voiced speech sound. —**so·nan'tal** (-nan'tl), *adj.*

so·nar (sō'när), *n.* **1.** a method for detecting and locating objects submerged in water by echolocation. **2.** the apparatus used in sonar. [*so(und) na(vigation) r(anging)*]

so·na·ta (sə nä'tə), *n., pl.* **-tas.** a musical composition for solo instrument or a small number of instruments typically in three or four movements in contrasting forms and keys.

sona'ta form', *n.* a musical form comprising an exposition stating the main themes, a development section, and a recapitulation of the exposition.

son·a·ti·na (son'ə tē'nə, sō'nə-), *n., pl.* **-nas, -ne** (-nā). a short or simplified sonata.

sonde (sond), *n.* a rocket or balloon used as a probe for observation of atmospheric phenomena.

Sond·heim (sond'hīm), *n.* **Stephen (Joshua),** born 1930, U.S. composer and lyricist.

song (sông, song), *n.* **1.** a short metrical composition intended or adapted for singing, esp. one in rhymed stanzas. **2.** poetical composition; poetry. **3.** the art or act of singing; vocal music. **4.** something that is sung. **5.** a patterned, sometimes elaborate vocal signal produced by an animal, as the distinctive sounds of male birds, frogs, etc., during the mating season. —*Idiom.* **6. for a song,** at a very low price: *I bought the rug for a song.* —**song'like',** *adj.*

Song (sông), *n.* SUNG.

song' and dance', *n. Informal.* an extended, often self-justifying explanation that may be irrelevant or untrue.

song·bird (sông'bûrd', song'-), *n.* **1.** a bird that sings. **2.** any passerine bird of the suborder Oscines. **3.** *Slang.* a woman vocalist.

song·book (sông'bŏŏk', song'-), *n.* a book of songs with words and music.

song·fest (sông'fest, song'-), *n.* an informal, often spontaneous gathering at which people sing folk songs, popular ballads, etc.

song·less (sông'lis, song'-), *adj.* devoid of song; lacking the power of a song, as a bird. —**song'less·ly,** *adv.*

Song' of Sol'omon, The, a book of the Bible, consisting of a series of love poems. Also called **Song' of Songs'.**

song' spar'row, *n.* a common North American sparrow, *Melospiza melodia,* that nests in brush and high grass.

song·ster (sông'stər, song'-), *n.* **1.** a person who sings; a singer. **2.** a writer of songs or poems; a poet. **3.** a songbird.

song' thrush', *n.* a common Eurasian thrush, *Turdus philomelos,* with a melodious song.

song·writ·er (sông'rī'tər, song'-), *n.* a person who writes the music and often the words for songs.

son·ic (son'ik), *adj.* **1.** of or pertaining to sound. **2.** noting or pertaining to a speed equal to that of sound in air at the same height above sea level.

son'ic bar'rier, *n.* SOUND BARRIER.

son'ic boom', *n.* a loud noise caused by the shock wave generated by an aircraft moving at supersonic speed.

son'-in-law', *n., pl.* **sons-in-law.** the husband of one's daughter.

son·net (son'it), *n.* a poem, properly expressive of a single idea or sentiment, of 14 lines, usu. in iambic pentameter, with rhymes arranged in a fixed scheme, being in the Italian form divided into a major group of eight lines followed by a minor group of six lines and in a common English form into three quatrains followed by a couplet.

son·ny (sun'ē), *n.* little son (often used as a familiar term of address to a boy).

son' of Ad'am, *n.* a man: *He had all the weaknesses to which a son of Adam is heir.*

son' of a gun', *n., pl.* **sons of guns.** *Slang.* rogue; rascal.

Son' of God', *n.* Jesus Christ, esp. as the Messiah.

Son' of Man', *n.* Jesus Christ, esp. at the Last Judgment.

Son' of Mar'y, *n.* Jesus.

son·o·gram (son'ə gram', sō'nə-), *n.* the visual image produced by reflected sound waves in a diagnostic ultrasound examination.

so·no·rous (sə nôr'əs, -nōr'-, son'ər əs), *adj.* **1.** resonant or resonating with sound: *a sonorous cavern.* **2.** loud and deep-toned: *a sonorous voice.* **3.** rich and full in sound, as language or verse. **4.** high-flown; grandiloquent: *a sonorous speech.* —**so·no'rous·ly,** *adv.* —**so·no'rous·ness,** *n.*

son·ship (sun'ship'), *n.* the state, fact, or relation of being a son.

Sons' of Lib'erty, *n.* **1.** any of several patriotic societies, originally secret, that opposed the Stamp Act and thereafter supported moves for American independence. **2.** (during the Civil War) a secret society of Copperheads.

soon (sōōn), *adv.* **1.** within a short period; before long: *soon after dark.* **2.** promptly; quickly: *Finish as soon as you can.* **3.** readily or willingly: *I would as soon walk as ride.* —*Idiom.* **4. sooner or later,** sometime; eventually. **5. would** or **had sooner,** to prefer to: *I would sooner not go.* Compare RATHER (def. 7).

soot (sŏŏt, sōōt), *n.* a black carbonaceous substance produced during incomplete combustion of coal, wood, oil, etc., rising in fine particles that adhere to and blacken surfaces on contact.

soothe (sōōth), *v.t.* **1.** to offer relief or comfort to: *to soothe someone with kind words.* **2.** to mitigate; assuage; allay: *to soothe sunburned skin.* —*v.i.* **3.** to exert a soothing influence. —**sooth'er,** *n.*

sooth·ing (sōō'thing), *adj.* tending to soothe: *a soothing voice.* —**sooth'ing·ly,** *adv.* —**sooth'ing·ness,** *n.*

sooth·say (sōōth'sā'), *v.i.,* **-said, -say·ing.** to foretell events; predict.

sooth·say·er (sōōth'sā'ər), *n.* a person who foretells events.

soot·y (sŏŏt'ē, sōō'tē), *adj.,* **soot·i·er, soot·i·est. 1.** covered or blackened with soot. **2.** consisting of or resembling soot. **3.** of a black, blackish, or dusky color. —**soot'i·ly,** *adv.* —**soot'i·ness,** *n.*

soot'y mold', *n.* a disease of plants caused by a dark fungus that grows on the honeydew secretions of certain insects.

sop (sop), *n., v.,* **sopped, sop·ping.** —*n.* **1.** a piece of solid food, as bread, for dipping in liquid food. **2.** something offered to conciliate, pacify, or bribe. —*v.t.* **3.** to dip or soak in liquid food: *to sop bread in gravy.* **4.** to drench. **5.** to take up (liquid) by absorption.

SOP, Standard Operating Procedure; Standing Operating Procedure.

soph·ism (sof'iz əm), *n.* **1.** a specious argument for displaying ingenuity in reasoning or for deceiving someone. **2.** any false argument.

S

soph•ist (sof′ist), *n.* **1.** (*often cap.*) any of a class of ancient Greek teachers of philosophy, rhetoric, etc., noted esp. for their ingenuity and speciousness in argumentation. **2.** a person who reasons adroitly and speciously rather than soundly.

so•phis•ti•cate (*n.*, sə fis′ti kit, -kāt′; *v.* -kāt′), *n.*, *v.*, **-cat•ed, -cat•ing.** —*n.* **1.** a sophisticated person. —*v.t.* **2.** to make less natural, simple, or ingenuous; make worldly-wise. **3.** to alter; pervert: *to sophisticate a meaning beyond recognition.*

so•phis•ti•cat•ed (sə fis′ti kā′tid), *adj.* **1.** worldly-wise; not naive: *sophisticated travelers.* **2.** appealing to cultivated tastes: *sophisticated music.* **3.** complex; intricate: *a sophisticated electronic control system.* **4.** deceptive; misleading. —**so•phis′ti•cat′ed•ly,** *adv.*

so•phis•ti•ca•tion (sə fis′ti kā′shən), *n.* **1.** the process or result of change from the natural or simple to the knowledgeable or cultured; worldliness. **2.** complexity, as in design or organization. **3.** impairment; disillusionment. **4.** the use of sophistry; a sophism, quibble, or fallacious argument.

soph•ist•ry (sof′ə strē), *n.*, *pl.* **-ries. 1.** a subtle, tricky, superficially plausible, but generally fallacious method of reasoning. **2.** a false argument; sophism.

Soph•o•cles (sof′ə klēz′), *n.* 495?–406? B.C., Greek dramatist. —**Soph′o•cle′an,** *adj.*

soph•o•more (sof′ə môr′, -mōr′; sof′môr, -mōr), *n.* a student in the second year at a high school, college, or university. [earlier *sophumer,* perh. = *sophum* sophism + -ER]

soph•o•mor•ic (sof′ə môr′ik, -mor′-), *adj.* **1.** of or pertaining to sophomores. **2.** intellectually pretentious and conceited but immature and ill-informed. —**soph′o•mor′i•cal•ly,** *adv.*

-sophy, a combining form meaning "wisdom," "knowledge": *philosophy; theosophy.*

sop•o•rif•ic (sop′ə rif′ik, sō′pə-), *adj.* **1.** Also, **sop′o•rif′er•ous. a.** causing or tending to cause sleep. **b.** pertaining to or characterized by sleep or sleepiness; sleepy; drowsy. —*n.* **2.** something that causes sleep, as a medicine or drug. —**sop′o•rif′i•cal•ly,** *adv.*

so•pran•o (sə pran′ō, -prä′nō), *n.*, *pl.* **-pran•os,** *adj.* —*n.* **1.** the highest singing voice in women and boys. **2.** a part for such a voice. **3.** a singer with such a voice. **4.** a musical instrument corresponding in compass to this voice. —*adj.* **5.** of or pertaining to a soprano; having the compass of a soprano.

sorb¹ (sôrb), *n.* **1.** any of several Old World trees of the genus *Sorbus,* as the service tree or the rowan. **2.** Also called **sorb′ ap′ple,** the fruit of any of these trees. —**sorb′ic,** *adj.*

sorb² (sôrb), *v.t. Chem.* to gather on a surface either by absorption, adsorption, or a combination of the two processes. —**sorb′a•ble,** *adj.* —**sorb′a•bil′i•ty,** *n.*

sor•bet (sôr bā′, sôr′bit; *Fr.* sôr be′), *n.* a fruit or vegetable ice, often served between courses to refresh the palate.

sor′bic ac′id (sôr′bik), *n.* a white, crystalline compound, $C_6H_8O_2$, used as a preservative in pharmaceuticals, cosmetics, and food.

sor•bi•tol (sôr′bi tôl′, -tol′), *n.* a sugar alcohol, $C_6H_{14}O_6$, naturally occurring in many fruits or synthesized, used as a sugar substitute and in the manufacture of vitamin C.

Sor•bonne (sôr bon′, -bun′; *Fr.* sôr bôn′), *n.* the seat of the faculties of arts and letters of the University of Paris.

sor•cer•er (sôr′sər ər), *n.* a person who practices sorcery.

sor•cer•ess (sôr′sər is), *n.* a woman who practices sorcery; witch.

sor•cer•y (sôr′sə rē), *n.*, *pl.* **-cer•ies.** the practices of a person who is thought to have supernatural powers granted by evil spirits; black magic; witchery.

sor•did (sôr′did), *adj.* **1.** morally ignoble or base; vile. **2.** meanly selfish or mercenary. **3.** filthy; squalid. —**sor′did•ly,** *adv.* —**sor′did•ness,** *n.*

sore (sôr, sōr), *adj.*, **sor•er, sor•est,** *n.* —*adj.* **1.** physically painful or sensitive, as a wound or diseased part: *a sore arm.* **2.** suffering bodily pain from wounds, bruises, etc. **3.** suffering mental pain; grieved or distressed: *to be sore at heart.* **4.** causing great mental pain, distress, or sorrow: *a sore loss.* **5.** causing very great misery, hardship, and the like: *in sore need.* **6.** annoyed; irritated; angered. **7.** causing annoyance or irritation: *a sore subject.* —*n.* **8.** a sore spot or place on the body. **9.** a source of grief, distress, etc. —**sore′ness,** *n.*

sore•head (sôr′hed′, sōr′-), *n. Informal.* a disgruntled or vindictive person, esp. an unsportsmanlike loser. —**sore′head′ed•ly,** *adv.*

sore•ly (sôr′lē, sōr′-), *adv.* **1.** in a painful manner. **2.** extremely; very: *I was sorely tempted to complain.*

sore′ throat′, *n.* **1.** a painful or sensitive condition of the throat due to pharyngitis. **2.** PHARYNGITIS.

sor•ghum (sôr′gəm), *n.* **1.** any cereal grass of the genus *Sorghum,* having broad leaves and a tall stem bearing grain in a dense terminal cluster. **2.** the syrup made from sorgo.

sor•go or **sor•gho** (sôr′gō), *n.*, *pl.* **-gos** or **-ghos.** any of several varieties of sorghum grown chiefly for the sweet juice yielded by the stems, used in making sugar and syrup and also for fodder. Also called **sweet sorghum.**

so•ror•i•ty (sə rôr′i tē, -ror′-), *n.*, *pl.* **-ties.** a society of women or girls, esp. in a college.

sor•rel¹ (sôr′əl, sor′-), *n.* **1.** light reddish brown. **2.** a horse of this color, often with a light-colored mane and tail.

sor•rel² (sôr′əl, sor′-), *n.* any of various plants belonging to the genus *Rumex,* of the buckwheat family, having edible acid leaves used in salads, sauces, etc.

sor•row (sor′ō, sôr′ō), *n.* **1.** distress caused by loss, disappointment, etc.; grief. **2.** a cause or occasion of grief, as a misfortune. **3.** the expression of grief: *muffled sorrow.* —*v.i.* **4.** to feel or express sorrow; grieve. —**sor′row•er,** *n.*

sor•row•ful (sor′ə fəl, sôr′-), *adj.* **1.** feeling sorrow; grieved; sad. **2.** expressing sorrow; mournful: *a sorrowful song.* **3.** causing sorrow; distressing. —**sor′row•ful•ly,** *adv.* —**sor′row•ful•ness,** *n.*

sor•ry (sor′ē, sôr′ē), *adj.*, **-ri•er, -ri•est. 1.** feeling regret, compunction, sympathy, pity, etc.: *sorry to leave one's friends.* **2.** regrettable or deplorable; unfortunate: *a sorry situation.* **3.** sorrowful; grieved. **4.** suggestive of grief; melancholy. **5.** wretched, poor, or useless. **6.** (used interjectionally as a conventional apology): *Did I bump you? Sorry.* —**sor′ri•ly,** *adv.* —**sor′ri•ness,** *n.*

sort (sôrt), *n.* **1.** a particular kind, class, or group; category: *two sorts of people—rich and poor.* **2.** character, quality, or nature: *friends of a nice sort.* **3.** an example of something that is undistinguished: *He is a sort of poet.* **4.** manner, fashion, or way. **5.** *Print.* any of the individual characters making up a font of type. **6.** an instance of sorting. —*v.t.* **7.** to arrange according to kind or class: *to sort socks.* **8.** to separate from other sorts (often fol. by *out*): *to sort the good from the bad.* **9.** to assign to a particular class, group, etc. (often fol. by *with, together,* etc.): *sorting people together indiscriminately.* **10.** to place (computerized data) in order, numerically or alphabetically. —*v.i.* **11. sort out, a.** evolve; turn out: *Wait and see how things sort out.* **b.** to put in order; clarify: *After I sort things out here, I can leave.* —**Idiom. 12. of sorts,** of a mediocre or poor kind: *a tennis player of sorts.* Also, **of a sort. 13. out of sorts, a.** irritable or depressed. **b.** indisposed; ill. **c.** *Print.* short of certain characters of a font of type. **14. sort of,** somewhat; rather. —**sort′a•ble,** *adj.* —**sort′er,** *n.* —**Usage.** See KIND².

sort•ed (sôr′tid), *adj.* (of sedimentary rock or particles) uniform in size.

sor•tie (sôr′tē), *n.*, *v.*, **-tied, -tie•ing.** —*n.* **1.** a rapid movement of troops from a besieged place to attack the besiegers. **2.** the flying of an airplane on a combat mission. **3.** any sudden attack or raid. —*v.i.* **4.** to go on a sortie.

sor•ti•lege (sôr′tl ij), *n.* **1.** divination by the drawing of lots. **2.** sorcery; magic. —**sor′ti•leg′ic** (-ej′ik), *adj.*

so•rus (sôr′əs, sōr′-), *n.*, *pl.* **so•ri** (sôr′ī, sōr′ī). **1.** one of the clusters of sporangia on the back of the fronds of ferns. **2.** a similar spore mass in certain fungi and lichens.

SOS (es′ō′es′), *n.*, *pl.* **SOSs, SOS's. 1.** an internationally recognized radiotelegraphic distress signal, used esp. by ships and consisting of the letters SOS spelled out in Morse Code (••• – – – •••). **2.** any call for help.

so′-so′ or **so′ so′,** *adj.* **1.** neither very good nor very bad; indifferent or mediocre. —*adv.* **2.** in a passable manner; tolerably.

sot•to vo•ce (sot′ō vō′chē; *It.* sôt′tô vô′che), *adv.* in a low, soft voice so as not to be overheard. [< Italian: lit., under (the) voice]

sou•brette (sōō bret′), *n.* **1.** a maidservant or lady's maid in a play, opera, or the like, esp. one displaying coquetry, pertness, and a tendency to engage in intrigue. **2.** an actress playing such a role. **3.** any lively or pert young woman. —**sou•bret′tish,** *adj.*

sou•bri•quet (sōō′brə kā′, -ket′, sōō′brə kā′, -ket′), *n.* SOBRIQUET.

sou•chong (sōō′shong′, -chong′), *n.* a variety of black tea grown in India and Sri Lanka.

souf•flé (sōō flā′, sōō′flā), *n.* **1.** a light, puffed-up baked dish, made fluffy by adding beaten egg whites to a thick sauce combined with other ingredients, as cheese or puréed vegetables. —*adj.* **2.** Also **souf•fléed′.** puffed up; made light, as by beating and cooking.

sough (sou, suf), *v.i.* **1.** to make a rushing, rustling, or murmuring sound: *the wind soughing through the pine trees.* —*n.* **2.** a sighing, rustling, or murmuring sound. —**sough′ful•ly,** *adv.*

sought (sôt), *v.* pt. and pp. of SEEK.

sought′-af′ter, *adj.* being in demand; desirable.

soul (sōl), *n.* **1.** the principle of life, feeling, thought, and action in humans, regarded as a distinct entity separate from the body; the spiritual part of humans as distinct from the physical. **2.** the spiritual part of humans regarded in its moral aspect, or as believed to survive death and be subject to happiness or misery in a life to come. **3.** the disembodied spirit of a deceased person. **4.** the seat of human feelings or sentiments. **5.** a person: *brave souls.* **6.** spirit or courage. **7.** the essential element or part of something. **8.** the embodiment of some quality: *He was the very soul of tact.* **9.** (*cap.*) (in Christian Science) God. **10.** (among black Americans) shared ethnic awareness and pride. **11.** deeply felt emotion, as conveyed by a performer or artist. **12.** SOUL MUSIC. —*adj.* **13.** of or pertaining to black Americans or their culture.

soul′ food′, *n.* traditional black American cuisine, orig. of the rural South. —**soul′-food′,** *adj.*

soul•ful (sōl′fəl), *adj.* pertaining to or expressive of deep feeling or emotion: *soulful eyes.* —**soul′ful•ly,** *adv.* —**soul′ful•ness,** *n.*

soul•less (sōl′lis), *adj.* **1.** having no soul. **2.** lacking nobility of soul; devoid of spirit or courage. —**soul′less•ly,** *adv.* —**soul′less•ness,** *n.*

soul′ mate′, *n.* a person with whom one has a strong affinity.

soul′ mu′sic, *n.* music deriving from the secularization of black American gospel music combined with rhythm and blues and marked by earthy expressiveness.

soul'-search'ing, *n.* a close and penetrating analysis of oneself, esp. in an effort to determine one's true feelings and desires.

sound¹ (sound), *n.* **1.** the sensation produced by stimulation of the organs of hearing by vibrations transmitted through the air or other medium. **2.** mechanical vibrations transmitted through an elastic medium, traveling in air at a speed of approximately 1087 ft. (331 m) per second at sea level and at other speeds in other media. **3.** the particular auditory effect produced by a given source: *the sound of fire engines.* **4.** a noise, vocal utterance, musical tone, or the like: *the sounds from the next room.* **5.** a distinctive, characteristic, or recognizable musical style: *the Motown sound.* **6. a.** SPEECH SOUND. **b.** the audible result of an articulation, utterance, or part of an utterance: *the* th*-sound in* there. **7.** the auditory effect of sound waves as transmitted or recorded by a particular system of sound reproduction. **8.** the quality of an event, letter, etc., as it affects a person: *I don't like the sound of that report.* **9.** the distance within which something can be heard. **10.** meaningless noise: *all sound and fury.* —*v.i.* **11.** to make or emit a sound. **12.** to give forth a signal, as a call or summons. **13.** to convey a certain impression when heard or read: *His voice sounded strange.* **14.** to give a specific sound: *to sound loud.* **15.** to appear; seem: *The report sounds true.* —*v.t.* **16.** to cause to sound: *Sound the alarm.* **17.** to give forth (a sound): *The oboe sounded an A.* **18.** to announce or order by a sound: *The bugle sounded retreat.* **19.** to utter audibly; pronounce: *to sound each letter.* **20.** to examine by percussion or auscultation: *to sound a patient's chest.* **21. sound off,** *Informal.* **a.** to call out one's name, as at military roll call. **b.** to call out the cadence as one marches in formation. **c.** to speak frankly or indiscreetly. **d.** to exaggerate; boast.

sound² (sound), *adj.,* **-er, -est,** *adv.* —*adj.* **1.** free from injury, damage, defect, disease, etc.; in good condition; healthy; robust: *a sound body.* **2.** financially strong, secure, or reliable: *a sound investment.* **3.** competent, sensible, or valid: *sound judgment.* **4.** of substantial or enduring character: *sound moral values.* **5.** having a logical basis: *sound reasoning.* **6.** uninterrupted and untroubled; deep: *sound sleep.* **7.** vigorous, thorough, or severe: *a sound thrashing.* **8.** upright; honorable. **9.** having no legal defect: *a sound title to the property.* —*adv.* **10.** deeply; thoroughly: *sound asleep.* —**sound'ly,** *adv.* —**sound'ness,** *n.*

sound³ (sound), *v.t.* **1.** to measure or try the depth of (water, a deep hole, etc.) by letting down a lead or plummet at the end of a line, or by some equivalent means. **2.** to measure (depth) in such a manner, as at sea. **3.** to examine or test (the bottom, as of the sea or a deep hole) with a lead that brings up adhering bits of matter. **4.** to seek to ascertain: *to sound a person's views.* **5.** to attempt to elicit the views of (a person) by indirect inquiries (often fol. by *out*). —*v.i.* **6.** to use the lead and line or some other device for measuring depth, as at sea. **7.** to go down or touch bottom, as a lead. **8.** to seek information, esp. by indirect inquiries.

sound⁴ (sound), *n.* **1.** a relatively narrow passage of water between larger bodies of water or between the mainland and an island: *Long Island Sound.* **2.** an inlet, arm, or recessed portion of the sea: *Puget Sound.* **3.** the air bladder of a fish.

sound·a·like (sound'ə līk'), *n.* a person or thing that sounds like another, esp. a better known or famous prototype.

sound'-and-light' show', *n.* a nighttime spectacle at which a building, historic site, or the like is illuminated and its historic significance imparted through narration, sound effects, and music.

sound' bar'rier, *n.* an abrupt increase in drag experienced by an aircraft approaching the speed of sound.

sound' bite', *n.* a brief, striking remark or statement excerpted from an audiotape or videotape for insertion in a broadcast news story.

sound·board (sound'bôrd', -bōrd'), *n.* SOUNDING BOARD (def. 1).

sound·box (sound'boks'), *n.* a chamber in a musical instrument, as the body of a violin, for increasing the sonority of its tone.

sound' effect', *n.* any sound, other than music or speech, artificially reproduced in a dramatic presentation.

sound' hole', *n.* an opening in the surface of a stringed instrument, as a violin or lute, for increasing vibration.

sound·ing¹ (soun'ding), *adj.* **1.** emitting or producing a sound or sounds. **2.** resounding or sonorous. **3.** grand; pompous. —*n.* **4.** SIGNIFYING. —**sound'ing·ly,** *adv.* —**sound'ing·ness,** *n.*

sound·ing² (soun'ding), *n.* **1.** Often, **soundings.** the act of measuring the depth of an area of water with or as if with a lead and line. **2. soundings, a.** an area of water that can be sounded with an ordinary lead and line, the depth being 100 fathoms (180 m) or less. **b.** the results or measurement obtained by sounding with a lead and line. **3.** any vertical penetration of the atmosphere for scientific measurement. —**sound'ing·ly,** *adv.* —**sound'ing·ness,** *n.*

sound'ing board', *n.* **1.** Also called **soundboard.** a thin, resonant plate of wood forming part of a musical instrument, and so placed as to enhance the power and quality of the tone. **2.** a person whose reactions serve as a measure of the acceptability of an idea or course of action.

sound'ing line', *n.* a line weighted with a lead or plummet (**sounding lead**) and bearing marks to show the length paid out, used for sounding, as at sea.

sound·less¹ (sound'lis), *adj.* without sound; silent; quiet. —**sound'less·ly,** *adv.* —**sound'less·ness,** *n.*

sound·less² (sound'lis), *adj.* unfathomable; very deep. —**sound'less·ly,** *adv.* —**sound'less·ness,** *n.*

Sound' of Mu'sic, The, a musical (1959) by Richard Rodgers and Oscar Hammerstein.

sound·proof (sound'prōōf'), *adj.* **1.** impervious to sound. —*v.t.* **2.** to make soundproof. —**sound'proof'ing,** *n.*

sound' stage' or **sound'stage',** *n.* a large, soundproof studio used for filming motion pictures.

sound'track' or **sound' track',** *n.* **1.** the narrow band on one or both sides of a strip of motion-picture film on which sound is recorded. **2.** the sound recorded on a film, esp. music or dialogue. **3.** a recording or tape of a stage musical.

sound' truck', *n.* a truck carrying a loudspeaker from which speeches, music, etc., are broadcast, as in political campaigning.

sound' wave', *n. Physics.* a longitudinal wave in an elastic medium, esp. a wave producing an audible sensation.

soup (sōōp), *n.* **1.** a liquid food made by simmering vegetables, seasonings, etc. **2.** *Slang.* a thick fog. **3.** *Slang.* added power, esp. horsepower. —*v.t.* **4. soup up,** *Slang.* **a.** to increase the power or top speed of (an engine or vehicle). **b.** to enliven. —*Idiom.* **5. from soup to nuts,** from beginning to end. **6. in the soup,** *Slang.* in trouble.

soup·çon (sōōp sôN', sōōp'sôN), *n.* a slight trace, as of a seasoning; hint.

soup du jour (sōōp' də zhōōr'), *n.* the soup featured by a restaurant on a particular day.

soup' kitch'en, *n.* a place where food, usu. soup, is served at little or no charge to the needy.

soup·spoon (sōōp'spōōn'), *n.* a large spoon, commonly having a rounded bowl, with which to eat soup.

soup·y (sōō'pē), *adj.,* **soup·i·er, soup·i·est. 1.** resembling soup in consistency. **2.** very thick; dense: *a soupy fog.* **3.** overly sentimental; maudlin.

sour (sou⁽ᵊ⁾r, sou'ər), *adj.* **1.** having an acid taste resembling that of vinegar or lemon juice; tart. **2.** rendered acid or affected by fermentation; fermented. **3.** producing the one of the four basic taste sensations that is not bitter, salt, or sweet. **4.** characteristic of something fermented: *a sour smell.* **5.** distasteful or disagreeable; unpleasant. **6.** cross; peevish: *a sour expression.* **7.** (of soil) having excessive acidity. **8.** (esp. of gasoline) contaminated by sulfur compounds. **9.** off-pitch: *a sour note.* —*n.* **10.** something that is sour. **11.** an acid or an acidic substance used in laundering and bleaching to neutralize alkalis and to decompose residual soap or bleach. —*v.i.* **12.** to become sour, rancid, etc.; spoil. **13.** (of relations) to become unpleasant or strained. **14.** to become bitter or disillusioned. —*v.t.* **15.** to make sour. **16.** to cause spoilage in; rot. **17.** to make bitter or disillusioned. —*Idiom.* **18. go sour,** to become unsatisfactory; fail: *a marriage gone sour.* **19. go sour on,** to become estranged from; turn against: *He went sour on his family.* —**sour'ly,** *adv.* —**sour'ness,** *n.*

sour·ball (sou⁽ᵊ⁾r'bôl', sou'ər-), *n.* **1.** a round piece of hard candy with a tart fruit flavoring. **2.** *Informal.* a chronic grouch.

source (sôrs, sōrs), *n., v.,* **sourced, sourc·ing.** —*n.* **1.** any thing or place from which something comes or is obtained; origin. **2.** the beginning or place of origin of a stream or river. **3.** a book, person, document, etc., supplying esp. firsthand information. **4.** a manufacturer or supplier. —*v.t.* **5.** to give as the source of, as a quotation. **6.** to obtain from a given supplier. —**source'ful,** *adj.*

source·book (sôrs'bŏŏk', sōrs'-), *n.* **1.** an original writing, as a document or diary, that serves as an authoritative basis for future study, writing, etc. **2.** a collection of such writings.

sour' cher'ry, *n.* **1.** a cherry tree, *Prunus cerasus,* characterized by gray bark and the spreading habit of its branches. **2.** the red, tart fruit of this tree, used in making pies and preserves.

sour' cream', *n.* cream soured by the lactic acid produced by a ferment.

sour·dough (sou⁽ᵊ⁾r'dō', sou'ər-), *n.* **1.** fermented dough, used as a leavening agent from one baking to the next. **2.** a veteran prospector in Alaska or NW Canada.

sour' grapes', *n.pl.* pretended disdain for something one does not or cannot have.

sour' mash', *n.* a blended grain mash used in the distilling of some whiskeys, consisting of new mash and a portion of mash from a preceding run and yielding a high rate of lactic acid.

sour·puss (sou⁽ᵊ⁾r'pŏŏs', sou'ər-), *n. Informal.* a grouchy, often scowling person.

sour·sop (sou⁽ᵊ⁾r'sop', sou'ər-), *n.* the large, dark green, slightly acid fruit of a small West Indian tree of the annona family.

Sou·sa (sōō'zə, -sə), *n.* **John Philip,** 1854–1932, U.S. band conductor and composer.

sou·sa·phone (sōō'zə fōn', -sə-), *n.* a form of bass tuba, similar to the helicon, used in brass bands.

sous-chef (sōō'shef'; *Fr.* sōō shef'), *n., pl.* **-chefs** (-shefs'; *Fr.* -shef'). the person ranking next after the head chef in a kitchen.

souse (sous), *v.,* **soused, sous·ing,** *n.* —*v.t.* **1.** to plunge into water or other liquid; immerse. **2.** to steep in pickling brine; pickle. —*v.i.* **3.** to plunge into water or other liquid. **4.** to be steeping or soaking in something. —*n.* **5.** an act of sousing. **6.** something kept or steeped in pickle, esp. the head, ears, and feet of a pig. **7.** a liquid used as a pickle.

S

south (south; *v. also* southˌ), *n.* **1.** a cardinal point of the compass lying directly opposite north. *Abbr.:* S **2.** the direction in which this point lies. **3.** (*usu. cap.*) a region or territory situated in this direction. **4. the South,** the general area south of Pennsylvania and the Ohio River and east of the Mississippi, consisting mainly of those states that formed the Confederacy. —*adj.* **5.** lying toward or situated in the south; directed or proceeding toward the south. **6.** coming from the south, as a wind. —*adv.* **7.** to, toward, or in the south. —*v.i.* **8.** to turn or move in a southerly direction.

South′ Af′rica, *n.* **Republic of,** a country in S Africa; member of the Commonwealth of Nations until 1961. 42,327,458; 472,000 sq. mi. (1,222,480 sq. km). *Caps.:* Pretoria and Cape Town. Formerly, **Union of South Africa.** —**South′ Af′rican,** *adj., n.*

South′ Amer′ica, *n.* a continent in the S part of the Western Hemisphere. 287,000,000; ab. 6,900,000 sq. mi. (17,871,000 sq. km). —**South′ Amer′ican,** *adj., n.*

South′ Bend′, *n.* a city in N Indiana. 105,092.

south•bound (south′bound′), *adj.* proceeding or headed south.

south′ by east′, *n.* a point on the compass 11°15′ east of south. *Abbr.:* SbE

south′ by west′, *n.* a point on the compass 11°15′ west of south. *Abbr.:* SbW

South′ Caroli′na, *n.* a state in the SE United States, on the Atlantic coast. 3,698,746; 31,055 sq. mi. (80,430 sq. km). *Cap.:* Columbia. *Abbr.:* SC, S.C. —**South′ Carolin′ian,** *adj., n.*

South′ Chi′na Sea′, *n.* a part of the W Pacific, bounded by SE China, Vietnam, the Malay Peninsula, Borneo, and the Philippines.

South′ Dako′ta, *n.* a state in the N central United States. 732,405; 77,047 sq. mi. (199,550 sq. km). *Cap.:* Pierre. *Abbr.:* SD, S. Dak. —**South′ Dako′tan,** *adj., n.*

south•east (south′ēst′; *Naut.* sou′-), *n.* **1.** the point or direction midway between south and east. *Abbr.:* SE **2.** a region in this direction. **3. the Southeast,** the southeast region of the United States. —*adj.* **4.** in, toward, or facing the southeast: *a southeast course.* **5.** coming from the southeast: *a southeast wind.* —*adv.* **6.** toward the southeast: *sailing southeast.* **7.** from the southeast. —**south′east′ern,** *adj.* —**south′east′ern•most′** (-mōst′), *adj.*

South′east A′sia, *n.* a region including Indochina, the Malay Peninsula, and the Malay Archipelago. —**South′east A′sian,** *adj., n.*

southeast′ by east′, *n.* a point on the compass 11°15′ east of southeast. *Abbr.:* SEbE

southeast′ by south′, *n.* a point on the compass 11°15′ south of southeast. *Abbr.:* SEbS

south•east•er (south′ē′stər; *Naut.* sou′-), *n.* a wind or storm from the southeast.

south•er•ly (suth′ər lē), *adj., adv., n., pl.* **-lies.** —*adj., adv.* **1.** toward the south: *a southerly course.* **2.** (esp. of a wind) coming from the south. —*n.* **3.** a wind that blows from the south. —**south′er•li•ness,** *n.*

south•ern (suth′ərn), *adj.* **1.** lying toward, situated in, or directed toward the south. **2.** coming from the south, as a wind. **3.** of or pertaining to the south. **4.** (*cap.*) of or pertaining to the South of the United States. **5.** being or located south of the celestial equator or of the zodiac: *a southern constellation.* —*n.* **6.** (*cap.*) American English spoken in the lowland southern U.S., from E Texas east to Georgia and Florida and north to Virginia and S Maryland.

South′ern Bap′tist, *n.* a member of the Southern Baptist Convention, founded in Augusta, Ga., in 1845, that is strictly Calvinistic and active in religious publishing and education.

South′ern Cross′, *n.* a southern constellation near Centaurus, having the form of a cross.

South′ern-fried′, *adj.* **1.** coated with flour, egg, and bread crumbs and fried in deep fat: *Southern-fried chicken.* **2.** (*often l.c.*) *Slang.* characteristic of or originating in the South: *a vocabulary full of southern-fried expressions.*

South′ern Hem′isphere, *n.* the half of the earth between the South Pole and the equator.

south′ern king′dom, *n.* Judah under King Rehoboam.

south′ern lights′, *n.pl.* AURORA AUSTRALIS.

South′ern Rhode′sia, *n.* a former name of ZIMBABWE (def. 1).

South′ Kore′a, *n.* a country in E Asia: formed 1948 after the division of the former country of Korea at 38° N. 45,948,811; 38,327 sq. mi. (99,263 sq. km). *Cap.:* Seoul. Compare KOREA. Official name, **Republic of Korea.** —**South′ Kore′an,** *adj., n.*

South′ Pacif′ic, a musical (1949) by Richard Rodgers and Oscar Hammerstein.

south•paw (south′pô′), *n. Informal.* **1.** a person who is left-handed. **2.** a baseball pitcher who throws with the left hand.

South′ Pole′, *n.* **1.** the southern end of the earth's axis, the southernmost point on earth. **2.** the point at which the axis of the earth extended cuts the southern half of the celestial sphere; the south celestial pole. **3.** (*l.c.*) See under MAGNETIC POLE (def. 1).

South′ Slav′ic, *n.* the branch of Slavic that includes Slovene, Serbo-Croatian, Macedonian, and Bulgarian.

south′-southeast′, *n.* **1.** the point on the compass midway between south and southeast. *Abbr.:* SSE —*adj.* **2.** coming from this point, as the wind. **3.** directed toward this point. —*adv.* **4.** in the direction of or toward this point.

south′-southwest′, *n.* **1.** the point on the compass midway between south and southwest. *Abbr.:* SSW —*adj.* **2.** coming from this point, as the wind. **3.** directed toward this point. —*adv.* **4.** in the direction of or toward this point.

South′ Vietnam′, *n.* a former country in SE Asia that comprised Vietnam south of the 17th parallel; a separate state 1954–75; now part of reunified Vietnam. *Cap.:* Ho Chi Minh City. Compare NORTH VIETNAM, VIETNAM.

south•ward (south′wərd; *Naut.* suth′ərd), *adj.* **1.** moving, bearing, facing, or situated toward the south. **2.** coming from the south, as a wind. —*adv.* **3.** Also, **south′wards.** toward the south; south. —*n.* **4.** the southward part, direction, or point. —**south′ward•ly,** *adj., adv.*

south•west (south′west′; *Naut.* sou′-), *n.* **1.** the point or direction midway between south and west. *Abbr.:* SW **2.** a region in this direction. **3. the Southwest,** the southwest region of the United States. —*adj.* **4.** in, toward, or facing the southwest. **5.** coming from the southwest: *a southwest wind.* —*adv.* **6.** toward the southwest. **7.** from the southwest. —**south′west′ern,** *adj.*

southwest′ by south′, *n.* a point on the compass 11°15′ south of southwest. *Abbr.:* SWbS

southwest′ by west′, *n.* a point on the compass 11°15′ west of southwest. *Abbr.:* SWbW

south•west•er (south′wes′tər; *Naut.* sou′-), *n.* **1.** a wind, gale, or storm from the southwest. **2.** SOU'WESTER (defs. 1, 2).

south•west•er•ly (south′wes′tər lē; *Naut.* sou′-), *adj., adv.* toward or from the southwest.

sou•ve•nir (sōō′və nēr′, sōō′və nēr′), *n.* **1.** a usu. small and relatively inexpensive article given or kept as a reminder of a place visited, an occasion, etc.; memento. **2.** a remembrance; memory.

souv•la•ki (sōōv lä′kē), *n.* a lamb dish similar to shish kebab.

sou′•west•er (sou′wes′tər), *n.* **1.** a waterproof hat, often of oilskin, having the brim very broad behind and slanted, worn esp. by seamen. **2.** an oilskin slicker, fastening with buckles, worn esp. by seamen in rough weather. **3.** SOUTHWESTER (def. 1).

sov•er•eign (sov′rin, sov′ər in, suv′-), *n.* **1.** a monarch or other supreme ruler. **2.** a person who has sovereign power or authority. **3.** a body of persons or a state having sovereign authority. **4.** a gold coin of the United Kingdom, equal to one pound sterling: went out of circulation after 1914. —*adj.* **5.** belonging to or characteristic of a sovereign or sovereignty; royal. **6.** having supreme rank, power, or authority. **7.** supreme; preeminent: *sovereign power; a sovereign right.* **8.** greatest in degree; utmost or extreme. **9.** being above all others in character, importance, excellence, etc. **10.** efficacious; potent: *a sovereign remedy.*

sov•er•eign•ty (sov′rin tē, suv′-), *n., pl.* **-ties. 1.** the quality or state of being sovereign. **2.** the status, dominion, power, or authority of a sovereign; royalty. **3.** supreme and independent power or authority in a state. **4.** rightful status, independence, or prerogative. **5.** a sovereign state, community, or political unit.

So•vi•et (sō′vē et′, -it, sōō′vē et′), *n.* **1.** a governing official or citizen of the former Soviet Union. **2.** (*l.c.*) (in the former Soviet Union) **a.** a governmental council, being part of a hierarchy of councils at various levels of government, culminating in the Supreme Soviet. **b.** a committee of workers, peasants, or soldiers during the revolutionary period. **3.** (*l.c.*) any similar council in a socialist system of government. —*adj.* **4.** pertaining to the former Soviet Union or the Soviets. **5.** (*l.c.*) pertaining to a soviet. [< Russian *sovét* council, advice.]

So′viet Un′ion, *n.* UNION OF SOVIET SOCIALIST REPUBLICS.

sow[1] (sō), *v.,* **sowed, sown** or **sowed, sow•ing.** —*v.t.* **1.** to scatter (seed) over land, earth, etc., for growth; plant. **2.** to scatter seed over (land, earth, etc.) for the purpose of growth. **3.** to implant, introduce, or promulgate; disseminate: *to sow distrust or dissension.* **4.** to strew or sprinkle with anything. —*v.i.* **5.** to sow seed, as for the production of a crop. —*Idiom.* **6. sow one's wild oats,** to have a youthful fling at reckless, indiscreet behavior. —*Proverb.* **7. As you sow, so shall you reap,** people bear responsibility for the results of their actions. Gal. 6:7. —**sow′a•ble,** *adj.* —**sow′er,** *n.*

sow[2] (sou), *n.* **1.** an adult female swine. **2.** the adult female of various other animals, as the bear.

sow′ bug′ (sou), *n.* any of several small terrestrial isopods, esp. of the genus *Oniscus;* wood louse.

Sow′er and the Seed′, The, a parable of Jesus. Matt. 13:3–23; Mark 4:1–20; Luke 8:4–15.

sown (sōn), *v.* a pp. of sow[1].

sox (soks), *n.* a pl. of SOCK[1].

soy (soi), *n.* the soybean.

soy•bean (soi′bēn′), *n.* **1.** a bushy Old World plant, *Glycine max,* of the legume family, grown in the U.S. chiefly for forage and soil improvement. **2.** the seed of this plant, used for food, as a livestock feed, and for a variety of other commercial uses.

soy′bean oil′, *n.* a pale yellow oil derived from soybeans: used in cooking and in the manufacture of soap, candles, paints, etc.

soy′ sauce′, *n.* a salty, fermented sauce from soybeans, used esp. as a flavoring in E Asian cuisine.

spa (spä), *n., pl.* **spas. 1.** a mineral spring, or a locality in which such springs exist. **2.** a luxurious resort or resort hotel. **3.** a hot tub or similar bathing facility, usu. for more than one person. **4.** *New England.* SODA FOUNTAIN.

space (spās), *n.*, *v.*, **spaced, spac·ing,** *adj.* —*n.* **1.** the unlimited three-dimensional realm or expanse in which all material objects are located and all events occur. **2.** the portion or extent of this in a given instance. **3.** extent or area in two dimensions; a particular extent of surface. **4. a.** OUTER SPACE. **b.** DEEP SPACE. **5.** a place available for a particular purpose: *a parking space.* **6.** a seat, berth, or room on a train, airplane, etc. **7.** linear distance, as between objects. **8. a.** the designed and structured surface of a picture. **b.** the illusion of depth on a two-dimensional surface. **9.** a set of points or mathematical elements that fulfills certain prescribed conditions: *Euclidean space; vector space.* **10.** extent, or particular extent, of time: *a space of two hours.* **11.** an interval of time; a while. **12.** an interval or blank area in text. **13.** an interval or blank area the width of one typed character. **14.** an area or time period allotted or available for a specific use, as advertising, in a publication or broadcasting medium. **15.** the interval between two adjacent lines of the musical staff. **16.** one of the blank pieces of metal, less than type-high, used in printing to separate words, sentences, etc. **17.** an interval during the transmitting of a telegraphic message when the key is not in contact. **18.** freedom or opportunity to express oneself, fulfill one's needs, have privacy, etc. —*v.t.* **19.** to fix the space or spaces of; divide into spaces. **20.** to set some distance apart. **21. a.** to separate (words, letters, or lines) by spaces. **b.** to extend by inserting more space or spaces (usu. fol. by *out*). **22. space out,** to become abstracted, forgetful, or dreamily inattentive. —*adj.* **23.** of, pertaining to, or suitable for use in outer space or deep space: *space travel; a space vehicle.*

Space′ Age′, *n.* (*sometimes l.c.*) the period marked by space exploration, considered as beginning Oct. 4, 1957, when the Soviet Union launched the first sputnik.

space′-age′, *adj.* **1.** of or pertaining to the Space Age. **2.** using the latest or most advanced technology or design. **3.** very modern; up-to-date; forward-looking: *space-age architecture.*

space′ bar′, *n.* a horizontal bar on a typewriter or computer keyboard that is pressed to insert a space.

space′ biol′ogy, *n.* EXOBIOLOGY.

space′ cadet′, *n. Slang.* a person who seems dazed or out of touch with reality, due or as if due to drugs.

space′ cap′sule, *n.* CAPSULE (def. 5).

space·craft (spās′kraft′, -kräft′), *n.*, *pl.* **-crafts, -craft.** a vehicle designed for travel or operation in space beyond the earth's atmosphere or in orbit around the earth.

spaced (spāst), *adj. Slang.* SPACED-OUT.

spaced′-out′, *adj. Slang.* dreamily or eerily out of touch with reality; disoriented.

space·flight (spās′flīt′), *n.* the flying of spacecraft into or in outer space.

space′ heat′ing, *n.* the heating of a limited area, as a room, by means of a heater (**space′ heat′er**) within the area.

space·less (spās′lis), *adj.* **1.** having no limits or dimensions in space; limitless; unbounded. **2.** occupying no space.

space·man (spās′man′, -mən), *n.*, *pl.* **-men** (-men′, -mən). **1.** an astronaut. **2.** a visitor to earth from outer space; extraterrestrial.

space′ mark′, *n.* a proofreader's symbol (#) used to indicate the need to insert space.

space′ med′icine, *n.* the branch of medicine dealing with the effects on humans of flying outside the earth's atmosphere.

space′ probe′, *n.* an unmanned spacecraft designed to explore the solar system and transmit data back to earth.

space′ sci′ence, *n.* any of the sciences involved in space travel or the exploration of space. —**space′ sci′entist,** *n.*

space·ship (spās′ship′), *n.* a spacecraft, esp. one that is manned.

space·shot (spās′shot′), *n.* a launch of a space vehicle beyond the earth's atmosphere.

space′ shut′tle, *n.* (*often caps.*) a reusable spacecraft, or orbiter, with two solid rocket boosters and an external fuel tank that are jettisoned after takeoff.

space′ sta′tion, *n.* a manned spacecraft or satellite orbiting the earth for an extended period of time, used for assembling and serving other spacecraft, for observation and research, etc.

space·suit (spās′sōot′), *n.* a sealed and pressurized suit designed to allow the wearer to leave a pressurized cabin in outer space.

space′-time′, *n.* **1.** Also called **space′-time′ contin′uum.** the four-dimensional continuum, having three coordinates of space and one coordinate of time, in which all physical quantities may be located. **2.** the physical reality that exists within this four-dimensional continuum.

space·walk (spās′wôk′), *n.* **1.** the act of performing a task or maneuvering in space outside a spacecraft. —*v.i.* **2.** to execute a spacewalk. —**space′walk′er,** *n.*

spac·ey or **spac·y** (spā′sē), *adj.*, **spac·i·er, spac·i·est. 1.** SPACED-OUT. **2.** eccentric; strange; eerie.

spa·cial (spā′shəl), *adj.* SPATIAL.

spac·ing (spā′sing), *n.* **1.** an act of someone or something that spaces. **2.** the arrangement of spaces or of objects in space.

spa·cious (spā′shəs), *adj.* **1.** containing much space, as a house or vehicle; roomy. **2.** occupying much space; vast. **3.** of a great extent or area; broad: *the spacious prairies.* **4.** broad in scope, range, inclusiveness, etc. —**spa′cious·ly,** *adv.* —**spa′cious·ness,** *n.*

spack·le (spak′əl), *v.*, **-led, -ling. 1.** (*cap.*) *Trademark.* a brand of quick-drying, plasterlike material for patching plasterwork. —*v.t.* **2.** to patch with Spackle. —*v.i.* **3.** to apply Spackle.

spade¹ (spād), *n.*, *v.*, **spad·ed, spad·ing.** —*n.* **1.** a tool for digging, typically having a long handle and a narrow, flat metal blade that can be pressed into the ground with the foot. **2.** an implement or part resembling this. —*v.t.* **3.** to dig, cut, or remove with a spade. —**Idiom. 4. call a spade a spade,** to speak plainly and bluntly. —**spade′like′,** *adj.*

spade² (spād), *n.* **1.** a black figure shaped like an inverted heart with a short stem at the cusp opposite the point, used on playing cards. **2.** a card of the suit bearing such figures. **3. spades, a.** (*used with a sing. or pl. v.*) the suit so marked. **b.** (*used with a pl. v.*) (in casino) the winning of seven spades or more. —**Idiom. 4. in spades,** *Informal.* **a.** in the extreme; to the utmost. **b.** without restraint.

spade·work (spād′wûrk′), *n.* preliminary work, as the gathering of data, on which further activity is to be based.

spa·dix (spā′diks), *n.*, *pl.* **spa·di·ces** (spā dī′sēz, spā′də sēz′). a fleshy or thickened spike of minute flowers, usu. enclosed in a spathe.

spa·ghet·ti (spə get′ē), *n.* **1.** pasta in the form of long strings, boiled, and usu. served with a sauce. **2.** an insulating tubing of small diameter into which bare wire can be slipped.

spaghet′ti squash′, *n.* a variety of squash, *Cucurbita pepo,* whose flesh forms spaghettilike strands when cooked.

spaghet′ti west′ern, *n.* a western movie made in Italy, usu. with Italian actors and an American star.

Spain (spān), *n.* a kingdom in SW Europe, on the Iberian Peninsula. 39,244,195; 194,984 sq. mi. (504,750 sq. km). *Cap.:* Madrid. Spanish, **España.**

spall (spôl), *n.* **1.** a chip or splinter, as of stone or ore. —*v.t.* **2.** to break into smaller pieces, as ore; split or chip. —*v.i.* **3.** to break or split off in chips or bits. —**spall·a′tion,** *n.* —**spall′er,** *n.*

span¹ (span), *n.*, *v.*, **spanned, span·ning.** —*n.* **1.** the full extent, stretch, or reach of something. **2.** a period of time during which something continues; duration. **3. a.** the distance or space between two supports of a structure, as an arch or a bridge. **b.** the part of the structure between the supports. **4.** the distance between the tip of the thumb and the tip of the little finger when the hand is fully extended. **5.** a unit of length corresponding to this distance, commonly taken as 9 inches (23 cm). **6.** a distance, amount, range, etc., of this length or of some small extent. **7.** WINGSPAN (def. 1). —*v.t.* **8.** to extend or reach over or across (space or time). **9.** to provide with something that extends over or across: *to span a river with a bridge.* **10.** to measure by the hand with the thumb and little finger extended. **11.** to encircle with the hand or hands. **12.** to bend (a bow) in preparation for shooting.

span² (span), *n.* a pair of horses or other animals harnessed and driven together.

span·dex (span′deks), *n.* a fabric made of or containing a polyurethane fiber with elastic properties.

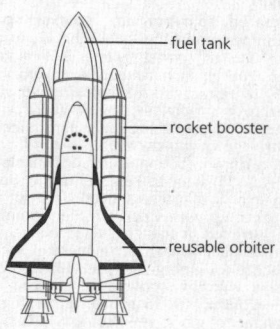

fuel tank

rocket booster

reusable orbiter

space shuttle

span·gle (spang′gəl), *n.*, *v.*, **-gled, -gling.** —*n.* **1.** a small, thin, often circular piece of glittering metal or other material, used esp. for decorating garments. **2.** any small, bright drop, object, or spot. —*v.t.* **3.** to decorate or sprinkle with or as if with spangles. —*v.i.* **4.** to glitter with or like spangles. —**span′gly,** *adj.*

span·iel (span′yəl), *n.* **1.** any of several breeds of small or medium-sized sporting dogs usu. having long, drooping ears and a long, silky coat with feathering on the legs and tail. **2.** a submissive, fawning, or cringing person. —**span′iel·like′,** *adj.*

Span·ish (span′ish), *n.* **1.** a Romance language spoken in Spain and in parts of the New World formerly under Spanish dominion, with official status in Mexico, most of Central and South America excluding Brazil, and several of the Antillean islands. *Abbr.:* Sp, Span. **2.** (*used with a pl. v.*) **a.** the inhabitants of Spain. **b.** natives of Spain or persons of Spanish ancestry outside Spain. —*adj.* **3.** of or pertaining to Spain or its inhabitants. **4.** of or pertaining to Spanish or its speakers.

Span′ish Amer′ica, *n.* the Spanish-speaking countries S of the U.S.:

Mexico, Central America (except Belize), South America (except Brazil, French Guiana, Guyana, and Suriname), and most of the West Indies.

Span'ish Amer'ican, *n.* **1.** a citizen or resident of the U.S. of Spanish birth or descent. **2.** a descendant of the Spanish-speaking population in parts of Mexico annexed by the U.S. as a result of the Texas revolt and the Mexican War. **3.** a native or inhabitant of Spanish America.

Span'ish-Amer'ican, *adj.* **1.** of or pertaining to Spanish America or its inhabitants. **2.** belonging to, pertaining to, or involving both Spain and the U.S., or the people of the two countries. **3.** of or pertaining to Spanish Americans.

Span'ish-Amer'ican War', *n.* the war between the U.S. and Spain in 1898.

Span'ish Arma'da, *n.* ARMADA (def. 1).

Span'ish bayonet', *n.* any of certain plants of the genus *Yucca,* of the agave family, having narrow, spine-tipped leaves.

Span'ish Civ'il War', *n.* the civil war in Spain 1936–39.

Span'ish Guin'ea, *n.* former name of EQUATORIAL GUINEA.

Span'ish mack'erel, *n.* **1.** any of various marine fishes, esp. of the genus *Scomberomorus,* as *S. maculatus,* of the Atlantic Ocean. **2.** (in California) the jack mackerel.

Span'ish moss', *n.* an epiphytic plant, *Tillandsia usneoides,* of the pineapple family, with narrow, drooping gray leaves, growing in long strands over trees, esp. in the southeastern U.S.

Span'ish om'elet, *n.* an omelet made with tomatoes, onions, and green peppers.

Span'ish on'ion, *n.* a large, mild, succulent onion, often eaten raw.

Span'ish rice', *n.* cooked rice flavored with tomato, onion, and green pepper.

spank[1] (spangk), *v.* **1.** to strike with the open hand, a slipper, etc., esp. on the buttocks, as in punishment. —*n.* **2.** a blow given in spanking.

spank[2] (spangk), *v.i.* to move rapidly, smartly, or briskly.

spank•ing (spang'king), *adj.* **1.** moving rapidly and smartly. **2.** quick and vigorous: *a spanking pace.* **3.** blowing briskly: *a spanking breeze.* **4.** unusually fine, great, large, etc.; remarkable; striking. —*adv.* **5.** extremely or strikingly; very: *spanking clean.* —**spank'ing•ly,** *adv.*

span•ner (span'ər), *n.* **1.** a person or thing that spans. **2.** a wrench having a curved head with a hook or pin at one end.

spar[1] (spär), *n., v.,* **sparred, spar•ring.** —*n.* **1.** a stout pole such as those used for masts; a mast, yard, boom, gaff, or the like. **2.** a principal lateral member of the framework of a wing of an airplane. —*v.t.* **3.** to provide or make with spars. —**spar'like',** *adj.*

spar[2] (spär), *v.,* **sparred, spar•ring,** *n.* —*v.i.* **1.** (of a boxer) to make the motions of attack and defense with the arms and fists, esp. as a part of training. **2.** to box, esp. with light blows. **3.** to strike or attack with the feet or spurs, as gamecocks do. **4.** to bandy words; dispute. —*n.* **5.** a motion of sparring. **6.** a boxing match. **7.** a dispute.

spar[3] (spär), *n.* any of various lustrous, nonmetallic, flaky minerals, as feldspar. —**spar'like',** *adj.*

spare (spâr), *v.,* **spared, spar•ing,** *adj.,* **spar•er, spar•est,** *n.* —*v.t.* **1.** to refrain from harming, punishing, or killing. **2.** to deal gently or leniently with: *His harsh review spared no one.* **3.** to save, as from strain or discomfort: *to spare you embarrassment.* **4.** to omit or withhold: *Spare the gory details.* **5.** to refrain from employing: *to spare the rod.* **6.** to give or lend, as from a supply, esp. without inconvenience: *Can you spare a cup of sugar?* **7.** to set aside for a particular purpose. **8.** to use frugally: *Don't spare the whipped cream!* —*v.i.* **9.** to use economy; be frugal. **10.** to refrain from inflicting injury or punishment; exercise lenience or mercy. —*adj.* **11.** kept in reserve, as for possible use: *a spare part.* **12.** being in excess of present need; free for other use: *a spare bedroom.* **13.** not taken up with work or other commitments; free: *spare time.* **14.** frugally restricted or meager: *a spare diet.* **15.** lean or thin, as a person. **16.** sparing, economical, or temperate. —*n.* **17.** a spare thing or part, as an extra tire for emergency use. **18. a.** the knocking down of all the bowling pins with two bowls. **b.** a score so made. Compare STRIKE (def. 56). —*Idiom.* **19. to spare,** remaining; left over: *We finished early, with time to spare.* —*Proverb.* **20. Spare the rod and spoil the child,** if one doesn't punish when necessary, a spoiled child may result. —**spare'a•ble,** *adj.* —**spare'ly,** *adv.* —**spare'ness,** *n.*

spare•ribs (spâr'ribz'), *n. (used with a pl. v.)* a cut of meat from the ribs, esp. of pork or beef, with some meat adhering to the bones, often barbecued with a pungent sauce.

spare' tire', *n.* **1.** a tire kept available as an emergency replacement on a vehicle. **2.** excess fat around the waistline.

spar•ing (spâr'ing), *adj.* **1.** economical; frugal (often fol. by *in* or *of*): *sparing in her praise.* **2.** lenient or merciful. **3.** scanty; meager; limited. —**spar'ing•ly,** *adv.* —**spar'ing•ness,** *n.*

spark (spärk), *n.* **1.** an ignited or fiery particle such as is thrown off by burning wood or produced by one hard body striking against another. **2. a.** the light produced by a sudden discontinuous discharge of electricity through air or another dielectric. **b.** the discharge itself. **c.** any electric arc of relatively small energy content. **d.** the electric discharge produced by a spark plug in an internal-combustion engine. **3.** anything that activates or stimulates; an inspiration or catalyst. **4.** a small amount or trace of something. **5.** a trace of life or vitality. **6.** animation; liveliness. **7. sparks,** *(used with a sing. v.) Slang.* a radio operator on a ship or aircraft. —*v.i.* **8.** to emit or produce sparks. **9.** to issue as or like sparks. **10.** to send forth gleams or flashes. **11.** (of the ignition of an in-

ternal-combustion engine) to function correctly in producing sparks. —*v.t.* **12.** to kindle, animate, or stimulate: *to spark someone's enthusiasm.* —**spark'er,** *n.* —**spark'less,** *adj.*

spark' gap', *n.* **1.** a space between two electrodes, across which a discharge of electricity may take place. **2.** the electrodes and the space between, considered as a unit: used in ignition systems.

spar•kle (spär'kəl), *v.,* **-kled, -kling,** *n.* —*v.i.* **1.** to shine or glisten with little gleams of light, as a brilliant gem; glitter. **2.** to be brilliant, lively, or vivacious. **3.** to emit little sparks, as burning matter. **4.** (of wine, soda water, etc.) to effervesce. —*v.t.* **5.** to cause to sparkle. —*n.* **6.** a sparkling appearance, luster, or play of light; glitter. **7.** brilliance, liveliness, or vivacity. **8.** a little spark or fiery particle. **9.** effervescence. —**spar'kly,** *adj.*

spar•kler (spär'klər), *n.* **1.** one that sparkles. **2.** a firework that emits little sparks. **3.** a sparkling gem, esp. a diamond.

spar'kling wa'ter, *n.* SODA WATER (def. 1).

spar'kling wine', *n.* a wine that is naturally carbonated by a second fermentation.

spark' plug', *n.* **1.** a device that ignites the fuel mixture in a cylinder of an internal-combustion engine. **2.** a person who leads, inspires, or animates. —**spark'plug',** *v.t.,* **-plugged, -plug•ging.**

spar'ring part'ner, *n.* **1.** a person who spars with and otherwise helps in training a boxer. **2.** a person with whom one engages in usu. friendly disputes.

spar•row (spar'ō), *n.* **1.** any of numerous small New World songbirds of the subfamily Emberizinae (family Emberizidae), typically dull graybrown with plain or streaked breasts of a lighter color, as the chipping sparrow and song sparrow. **2.** any of various similar songbirds of the Old World family Passeridae, as the house sparrow. —**spar'row•like',** *adj.*

sparse (spärs), *adj.,* **spars•er, spars•est.** **1.** thinly scattered or distributed. **2.** scanty; meager. —**sparse'ly,** *adv.*

Spar•ta (spär'tə), *n.* an ancient city in S Greece: the capital of Laconia and the chief city of the Peloponnesus, at one time the dominant city of Greece. Also called **Lacedaemon.**

Spar•ta•cus (spär'tə kəs), *n.* died 71 B.C., Thracian slave, gladiator, and insurrectionist against Rome.

Spar•tan (spär'tn), *adj.* Also, **Spar•tan•ic** (-tan'ik). **1.** of or pertaining to Sparta or its inhabitants. **2.** suggestive of the ancient Spartans; sternly disciplined and rigorously simple, frugal, or austere. **3.** brave; undaunted. —*n.* **4.** a native or inhabitant of Sparta. **5.** a person of Spartan characteristics. —**Spar'tan•ism,** *n.*

spasm (spaz'əm), *n.* **1.** a sudden, abnormal, involuntary muscular contraction, consisting of a continued muscular contraction or of a series of alternating muscular contractions and relaxations. **2.** any sudden, brief spell of great energy, activity, feeling, etc.

spas•mod•ic (spaz mod'ik) also **spas•mod'i•cal,** *adj.* **1.** pertaining to or of the nature of a spasm; characterized by spasms. **2.** resembling a spasm; sudden but brief; sporadic: *spasmodic efforts at reform.* **3.** characterized by bursts of excitement. —**spas•mod'i•cal•ly,** *adv.*

spas•tic (spas'tik), *adj.* **1.** pertaining to, of the nature of, characterized by, or afflicted with spasm or spastic paralysis. **2.** *Slang.* clumsy, inept, or stupid. —*n.* **3.** a person exhibiting or afflicted with spasms or spastic paralysis. —**spas'ti•cal•ly,** *adv.*

spat[1] (spat), *n., v.,* **spat•ted, spat•ting.** —*n.* **1.** a petty quarrel. **2.** a light blow; slap; smack. —*v.i.* **3.** to engage in a petty quarrel or dispute. **4.** to splash or spatter. —*v.t.* **5.** to strike lightly; slap.

spat[2] (spat), *v.* a pt. and pp. of SPIT[1].

spat[3] (spat), *n.* a short gaiter worn over the instep and usu. fastened under the foot with a strap.

spat[4] (spat), *n.* **1.** the spawn of an oyster or similar shellfish. **2.** young oysters collectively. **3.** a young oyster.

spate (spāt), *n.* **1.** a sudden, almost overwhelming outpouring. **2.** *Brit.* **a.** a flood. **b.** a sudden or heavy rainstorm.

spathe (spāth), *n.* a bract, often large and colored, enclosing a spadix or spike of flowers. —**spathed,** *adj.*

spa•tial (spā'shəl), *adj.* **1.** of or pertaining to space. **2.** existing or occurring in space; having extension in space. —**spa'ti•al'i•ty** (-shē al'i•tē), *n.* —**spa'tial•ly,** *adv.*

spat•ter (spat'ər), *v.t.* **1.** to scatter or dash in small particles or drops. **2.** to splash with something in small particles, esp. so as to soil or stain. —*v.i.* **3.** to send out small particles or drops, as falling water. **4.** to strike a surface in or as if in a shower, as bullets. —*n.* **5.** the act or the sound of spattering. **6.** a splash or spot of something spattered. —**spat'ter•ing•ly,** *adv.*

spat•u•la (spach'ə lə), *n., pl.* **-las.** an implement with a broad, flat, usu. flexible blade, used for blending or transferring foods, mixing drugs, spreading plaster, etc. —**spat'u•lar,** *adj.*

spawn (spôn), *n.* **1.** the mass of eggs deposited in the water by fishes, amphibians, and other aquatic creatures. **2.** the mycelium of mushrooms, esp. of the species grown for the market. **3.** a swarming brood; numerous progeny. **4.** *(used with a sing. or pl. v.)* any person or thing regarded as the offspring of some stock, idea, etc. —*v.i.* **5.** to deposit eggs or sperm directly into the water. —*v.t.* **6.** to produce (spawn). **7.** to give birth to; give rise to: *His disappearance spawned many rumors.* **8.** to produce in large number. **9.** to plant with mycelium.

spay[1] (spā), *v.t.* to remove the ovaries of (an animal).

spay² (spā), *n.* a three-year-old male red deer. Also called **spay•ad** (spā′əd), **spay′ard** (-ərd).

speak (spēk), *v.*, **spoke, spo•ken, speak•ing.** —*v.i.* **1.** to utter words or articulate sounds with the ordinary voice; talk. **2.** to communicate vocally; mention. **3.** to converse. **4.** to deliver an address, discourse, etc. **5.** to make a statement in written or printed words. **6.** to communicate, signify, or disclose by any means. **7.** to emit a sound, as a musical instrument; make a noise or report. —*v.t.* **8.** to utter vocally and articulately. **9.** to express or make known with the voice. **10.** to declare in writing or printing, or by any means of communication. **11.** to use, or be able to use, in oral utterance: *to speak French.* **12.** to communicate with (a passing vessel) at sea, as by voice or signal. **13. speak for,** to speak in behalf of. —***Idiom.*** **14. so to speak,** figuratively speaking: *We lost our shirt, so to speak.* **15. speak well for,** to be an indication or reflection of (something commendable). **16. to speak of,** worth mentioning: *no debts to speak of.* —***Proverb.*** **17. Speak softly and carry a big stick,** refrain from aggressiveness, but let it be known the strength is there: a saying popularized by Theodore Roosevelt.

-speak, a combining form extracted from NEWSPEAK, used in the formation of compound words, usu. derogatory, that denote the style or vocabulary of a field, person, era, etc., as specified by the initial element: *adspeak; artspeak; futurespeak.*

speak•eas•y (spēk′ē′zē), *n., pl.* **-eas•ies.** a saloon or nightclub selling alcoholic beverages illegally, esp. during Prohibition.

speak•er (spē′kər), *n.* **1.** a person who speaks. **2.** a person who speaks formally before an audience; lecturer; orator. **3.** (*usu. cap.*) the presiding officer of the U.S. House of Representatives, the British House of Commons, or other legislative assemblies. **4.** LOUDSPEAKER. **5.** a book of selections for practice in declamation.

speak•er•phone (spē′kər fōn′), *n.* a telephone with both a loudspeaker and microphone, for use without being held.

speak•ing (spē′king), *n.* **1.** the act, utterance, or discourse of a person who speaks. **2. speakings,** literary works composed for recitation. —*adj.* **3.** able to speak. **4.** used in, suited to, or involving speaking or talking. **5.** giving information as if by speech: *speaking proof of a thing.* **6.** highly expressive: *speaking eyes.* **7.** lifelike: *a speaking likeness.*

speak′ing in tongues′, *n.* a form of glossolalia in which a person experiencing religious ecstasy utters incomprehensible sounds believed to be of divine inspiration. Also called **gift of tongues.**

spear¹ (spēr), *n.* **1.** a weapon consisting of a long wooden shaft to which a sharp-pointed head, as of metal or stone, is attached. **2.** a similar weapon or stabbing implement, as one for use in fishing. **3.** the act of spearing. —*adj.* **4.** of or pertaining to the spear side. —*v.t.* **5.** to pierce with or as if with a spear. —*v.i.* **6.** to go or penetrate like a spear. —**spear′er,** *n.*

spear² (spēr), *n.* **1.** a sprout or shoot of a plant, as a blade of grass. —*v.i.* **2.** to sprout; shoot; rise up in a spear or spears.

spear•fish (spēr′fish′), *n., pl.* (*esp. collectively*) **-fish,** (*esp. for kinds or species*) **-fish•es,** *v.* —*n.* **1.** any of several large game fishes with a bill-like snout, esp. a marlin of the genus *Tetrapturus,* and sometimes including sailfish. —*v.i.* **2.** to fish underwater using a spearlike implement.

spear′ gun′, *n.* a device for shooting a barbed missile under water.

spear•head (spēr′hed′), *n.* **1.** the sharp-pointed head that forms the piercing end of a spear. **2.** any person, contingent, or force that leads an attack, undertaking, etc. —*v.t.* **3.** to act as a spearhead for.

spear•mint (spēr′mint′), *n.* an aromatic herb, *Mentha spicata,* of the mint family, with lance-shaped leaves used for flavoring.

spec (spek), *n., v.,* **spec'd** or **specked** or **specced, spec′•ing** or **speck•ing** or **spec•cing.** —*n.* **1.** Usu., **specs.** SPECIFICATION (defs. 2, 3). **2.** speculation. —*v.t.* **3.** to provide specifications for. —***Idiom.*** **4. on spec,** made, built, or done with hopes of but no assurance of payment or a sale.

spe•cial (spesh′əl), *adj.* **1.** of a distinct or particular kind or character: *a special key.* **2.** pertaining or peculiar to a particular person, thing, instance, etc.; distinctive: *the special features of a plan.* **3.** having a specific or particular function, purpose, etc.: *a special messenger.* **4.** distinguished from what is ordinary or usual: *a special occasion.* **5.** extraordinary; exceptional: *special importance.* **6.** particularly valued: *a special friend.* —*n.* **7.** a special person or thing. **8.** a train used for a particular purpose. **9.** a stage spotlight used for a particular area, actor, etc. **10.** a temporary reduction in the price of regularly stocked goods, esp. food. **11.** a single television program not forming part of a regular series. —**spe′cial•ly,** *adv.*

spe′cial assess′ment, *n.* a local tax levied on private property to pay for a public improvement that will increase the value of the property.

spe′cial deliv′ery, *n.* delivery of mail outside the regularly scheduled hours upon the payment of an extra fee.

spe′cial educa′tion, *n.* education modified for those with disabilities or exceptional needs, as handicapped people or gifted children.

spe′cial effects′, *n.pl.* unusual visual and sound effects created for motion pictures or television, as simulations of space travel, earthquakes, or supernatural phenomena.

Spe′cial Forc′es, *n.pl.* U.S. Army personnel trained to instruct non-U.S. forces in guerrilla warfare.

spe′cial han′dling, *n.* the handling of third- and fourth-class mail as first-class upon the payment of a fee.

spe′cial in′terest, *n.* a body of persons, a corporation, or an industry that seeks or receives benefits or privileged treatment, esp. through legislation. —**spe′cial-in′terest,** *adj.*

spe•cial•ist (spesh′ə list), *n.* **1.** a person devoted to one subject or to one particular branch of a subject or pursuit. **2.** a physician who deals only with a particular class of diseases, conditions, etc. **3.** an enlisted person in the U.S. Army holding a rank equivalent to that of corporal through sergeant first class but not requiring exercise of command.

spe•cial•ize (spesh′ə līz′), *v.,* **-ized, -iz•ing.** —*v.i.* **1.** to pursue some special line of study, work, etc.; have a specialty. **2.** (of an organism or one of its organs) to be adapted to a special function or environment. —*v.t.* **3.** to invest with a special character, function, etc. **4.** to adapt to special conditions; restrict to specific limits. **5.** to specify; particularize. —**spe′cial•i•za′tion,** *n.*

Spe′cial Olym′pics, *n.* an international athletic competition for the handicapped, founded in 1968 and featuring events and games modeled on the Olympics. —**Spe′cial Olym′pian,** *n.*

spec′ial relativ′ity, *n.* RELATIVITY (def. 2a).

spe•cial•ty (spesh′əl tē), *n., pl.* **-ties,** *adj.* —*n.* **1.** a special subject of study, line of work, skill, or the like on which one concentrates. **2.** an article or service particularly dealt in, manufactured, rendered, etc. **3.** an article of unusual or superior design or quality. **4.** a novelty; a new article. **5.** a special or particular point, item, matter, etc. **6.** special or distinctive quality or state. —*adj.* **7.** (in show business, esp. vaudeville) designating unusual or very specific routines, as juggling.

spe•ci•a•tion (spē′shē ā′shən, -sē ā′-), *n.* the formation of new species as a result of geographic, physiological, anatomical, or behavioral factors that prevent previously interbreeding populations from breeding with each other.

spe•cie (spē′shē, -sē), *n.* **1.** coined money; coin. —***Idiom.*** **2. in specie, a.** in the same kind. **b.** (of money) in coin. **c.** *Law.* in the identical shape, form, etc., as specified.

spe•cies (spē′shēz, -sēz), *n., pl.* **-cies. 1.** a class of individuals having some common characteristics or qualities; distinct sort or kind. **2.** the major subdivision of a genus or subgenus, regarded as the basic category of biological classification, composed of related individuals that resemble one another, are able to breed among themselves, but are not able to breed with members of another species. **3.** *Logic.* **a.** one of the classes of things included with other classes in a genus. **b.** the set of things within one of these classes. **4. the species,** the human race; humankind.

spe•cif•ic (spi sif′ik), *adj.* **1.** having a special application, bearing, or reference; explicit or definite. **2.** specified, precise, or particular. **3.** peculiar or proper to somebody or something, as characteristics or effects. **4.** of a special or particular kind. **5.** of or pertaining to a species. **6. a.** (of a disease) produced by a special cause or infection. **b.** (of a remedy) having special effect in the prevention or cure of a certain disease. **7.** (of an antibody or antigen) having a particular effect on only one antibody or antigen or affecting it in only one way. **8.** *Physics.* designating a physical quantity or property measured or considered in terms of a standard unit of mass. —*n.* **9.** something specific, as a statement, quality, or detail. —**spe•cif′i•cal•ly,** *adv.*

spec•i•fi•ca•tion (spes′ə fi kā′shən), *n.* **1.** the act of specifying. **2.** Usu., **specifications.** a detailed description of requirements, dimensions, materials, etc., as of a proposed building. **3.** something specified. **4.** an act of making specific. **5.** the state of having a specific character.

specif′ic grav′ity, *n.* the ratio of the density of any substance to the density of a standard substance, water being the standard for liquids and solids. —**spe•cif′ic-grav′i•ty,** *adj.*

specif′ic heat′, *n.* the number of calories required to raise the temperature of one gram of a substance 1°C, or the number of Btu's per pound per degree F.

spec•i•fic•i•ty (spes′ə fis′i tē), *n.* **1.** the quality or state of being specific. **2.** *Biol.* the selective attachment or influence of one substance on another, as of an antibiotic on its target organism.

spec•i•fy (spes′ə fī′), *v.,* **-fied, -fy•ing.** —*v.t.* **1.** to mention or name specifically or definitely; state in detail. **2.** to give a specific character to. **3.** to set forth as a specification. **4.** to name or state as a condition. —*v.i.* **5.** to make a specific mention or statement.

spec•i•men (spes′ə mən), *n.* **1.** a part or an individual taken as exemplifying a whole mass or number; a typical animal, mineral, etc. **2.** a sample of a substance or material for examination or study. **3.** a particular or peculiar kind of person.

spe•cious (spē′shəs), *adj.* **1.** apparently true or right though lacking real merit; not genuine. **2.** deceptively attractive. —**spe′cious•ly,** *adv.* —**spe′cious•ness,** *n.*

speck (spek), *n.* **1.** a small spot differing in color or substance from that of the surface or material upon which it appears or lies. **2.** a very little bit or particle. **3.** something appearing small by comparison or by reason of distance. —*v.t.* **4.** to mark with or as if with specks.

speck•le (spek′əl), *n., v.,* **-led, -ling.** —*n.* **1.** a small speck, spot, or mark. **2.** speckled coloring or marking. —*v.t.* **3.** to mark with or as if with speckles.

speck′led trout′, *n.* BROOK TROUT (def. 1).

specs (speks), *n.pl. Informal.* **1.** spectacles; eyeglasses. **2.** specifications.

spec•ta•cle (spek′tə kəl), *n.* **1.** anything presented to the sight or view, esp. something striking or impressive. **2.** a public show or display, esp. on a large scale. **3. spectacles,** GLASS (def. 5). **4.** Often, **spectacles.** something resembling eyeglasses in shape or function. —***Idiom.*** **5.**

make a spectacle of oneself, to behave badly or foolishly in public; be conspicuous for one's poor taste, rudeness, eccentricity, etc.
spec•tac•u•lar (spek tak′yə lər), *adj.* **1.** of or like a spectacle; impressive. **2.** dramatically daring or thrilling. —*n.* **3.** an impressive, large-scale display. —**spec•tac′u•lar•ly,** *adv.*
spec•ta•tor (spek′tā tər, spek tā′-), *n.* **1.** a person who looks on or watches; onlooker. **2.** a member of the audience at a public spectacle, display, or the like. **3.** Also called **spec′tator shoe′.** a white shoe with a wing tip and various trims, often perforated, in a contrasting color.
spec•ter (spek′tər), *n.* **1.** a visible incorporeal spirit, esp. one of a terrifying nature; ghost; phantom; apparition. **2.** some object or source of terror or dread: *the specter of disease.*
spec•tra (spek′trə), *n.* a pl. of SPECTRUM.
spec•tral (spek′trəl), *adj.* **1.** pertaining to or resembling a specter; ghostly. **2.** of, pertaining to, or produced by a spectrum or spectra. **3.** resembling or suggesting a spectrum or spectra. —**spec′tral•ly,** *adv.*
spectro-, a combining form representing SPECTRUM: *spectrometer.*
spec•tro•chem•is•try (spek′trō kem′ə strē), *n.* the branch of chemistry that deals with the chemical analysis of substances by means of the spectra of light they absorb or emit. —**spec′tro•chem′i•cal** (-kem′i-kəl), *adj.*
spec•trol•o•gy (spek trol′ə jē), *n.* the study of ghosts, phantoms, or apparitions. —**spec′tro•log′i•cal** (-trə loj′i kəl), *adj.*
spec•trom•e•ter (spek trom′i tər), *n.* an optical device for measuring wavelengths, deviation of refracted rays, and angles between faces of a prism, esp. an instrument consisting of a slit through which light passes, a collimator, a prism that deviates the light, and a telescope through which the deviated light is viewed and examined. —**spec′tro•met′ric** (-trə me′trik), *adj.* —**spec•trom′e•try,** *n.*
spec•tro•scope (spek′trə skōp′), *n.* an optical device consisting essentially of a collimating lens and a prism, for observing a spectrum of light or radiation. —**spec′tro•scop′ic** (-skop′ik), **spec′tro•scop′i•cal,** *adj.* —**spec′tro•scop′i•cal•ly,** *adv.*
spec•trum (spek′trəm), *n., pl.* **-tra** (-trə), **-trums. 1. a.** an array of entities, as light waves or particles, ordered in accordance with the magnitudes of a common physical property, as wavelength or mass. **b.** the band or series of colors, together with invisible extensions, produced by dispersion of radiant energy, as by a prism. **2.** a broad range of varied but related ideas, objects, etc., that form a continuous series or sequence: *the spectrum of political beliefs.*
spec•u•late (spek′yə lāt′), *v.,* **-lat•ed, -lat•ing.** —*v.i.* **1.** to engage in thought or reflection; meditate (often fol. by *on* or *upon*). **2.** to indulge in conjectural thought. **3.** to buy or sell commodities, property, stocks, etc., esp. at risk of a loss, in the expectation of making a profit through market fluctuations. —*v.t.* **4.** to consider or think curiously about; suppose, propose, or wonder: *to speculate that an agreement will be reached; to speculate whether a quarrel was serious.* —**spec′u•la′tor,** *n.*
spec•u•la•tion (spek′yə lā′shən), *n.* **1.** the contemplation or consideration of some subject. **2.** a single instance or process of consideration. **3.** a conclusion or opinion reached by such contemplation. **4.** conjectural consideration of a matter; conjecture or surmise. **5.** engagement in commercial transactions that involve risk with the hope of profiting as a result of market fluctuations.
spec•u•la•tive (spek′yə lā′tiv, -lə tiv), *adj.* **1.** pertaining to, of the nature of, or characterized by speculation, conjecture, or abstract reasoning. **2.** theoretical, rather than practical. **3.** given to speculation, as a person or the mind. **4.** of the nature of or involving financial speculation. —**spec′u•la′tive•ly,** *adv.*
spec•u•lum (spek′yə ləm), *n., pl.* **-la** (-lə), **-lums. 1.** a mirror or reflector, esp. one of polished metal, as on a reflecting telescope. **2.** a medical instrument for rendering a part accessible to observation, as by enlarging an orifice.
sped (sped), *v.* a pt. and pp. of SPEED.
speech (spēch), *n.* **1.** the faculty or power of speaking; ability to express one's thoughts and emotions by speech sounds. **2.** the act of speaking. **3.** something that is spoken; an utterance. **4.** a form of communication in spoken language, made by a speaker before an audience. **5.** any single utterance of an actor in the course of a play, film, etc. **6.** the form of utterance characteristic of a particular people or region; a language or dialect. **7.** manner of speaking, as of a person. **8.** a field of study devoted to the theory and practice of oral communication.
speech•i•fy (spē′chə fī′), *v.i.,* **-fied, -fy•ing.** to make a speech, esp. one that is ornate or pompous; orate. —**speech′i•fi•ca′tion,** *n.*
speech•less (spēch′lis), *adj.* **1.** temporarily deprived of speech by fear, exhaustion, astonishment, etc. **2.** lacking the faculty of speech; dumb. **3.** not able to be expressed in speech or words. **4.** refraining from speech. —**speech′less•ly,** *adv.* —**speech′less•ness,** *n.*
speech′ sound′, *n.* any of the minimal identifiable discrete segments of sound occurring in speech.
speed (spēd), *n., v.,* **sped** or **speed•ed, speed•ing.** —*n.* **1.** rapidity in moving, traveling, performing, etc.; swiftness. **2.** relative rate of motion or progress: *the speed of light.* **3.** a gear ratio in a motor vehicle or bicycle. **4. a.** the sensitivity of a photographic film or paper to light. **b.** the largest opening at which a lens can be used. **5.** a person, thing, activity, etc., that suits one's ability, inclinations, or personality: *Quiet, easygoing people are more my speed.* —*v.t.* **6.** to promote the success of; further, forward, or expedite. **7.** to direct (the course, way, etc.) with speed. **8.** to increase the rate of speed of (usu. fol. by *up*): *to speed up production.* **9.** to cause to move or go with speed. —*v.i.* **10.** to go or proceed with rapidity. **11.** to drive a vehicle at a rate that exceeds the legal limit. **12.** to increase the rate of speed (usu. fol. by *up*). **13.** to get on or fare in a specified or particular manner. —***Idiom.*** **14. at full** or **top speed, a.** at the greatest speed possible. **b.** to the maximum of one's capabilities. **15. up to speed, a.** operating at full or optimum speed. **b.** functioning at an anticipated or competitive level: *a new firm not yet up to speed.* —**speed′er,** *n.* —**speed′ing•ly,** *adv.* —**speed′less,** *adj.*
speed•boat (spēd′bōt′), *n.* a motorboat designed for high speeds. —**speed′boat′ing,** *n.*
speed′ bump′, *n.* a rounded ridge built crosswise into the pavement of a road to force vehicles to slow down.
speed•ing (spē′ding), *n.* the act or practice of exceeding the speed limit.
speed′ lim′it, *n.* the maximum speed at which a vehicle is legally permitted to travel.
speed•om•e•ter (spē dom′i tər, spi-), *n.* an instrument on an automobile or other vehicle for indicating the rate of travel in miles or kilometers per hour.
speed′-read′ or **speed′read′,** *v.t., v.i.,* **-read** (-red′), **-read•ing.** to read faster than normal, esp. by acquired techniques of skimming and controlled eye movements. —**speed′-read′er,** *n.*
speed′ skat′ing or **speed′skat′ing,** *n.* competitive racing on ice skates, usu. done on an oval course and against other skaters or the clock. —**speed′ skat′er,** *n.*
speed•ster (spēd′stər), *n.* a person who travels habitually at high speed.
speed′ trap′, *n.* a section of a road where hidden police, radar, etc., strictly enforce traffic regulations.
speed′-up′, *n.* **1.** an increase of speed. **2.** an increase in the quota of work demanded without a corresponding increase in pay.
speed•way (spēd′wā′), *n.* **1.** a track on which automobile or motorcycle races are held. **2.** a road or course for fast driving.
speed•writ•ing (spēd′rī′ting), *n.* a system of shorthand based on the sound of words and utilizing letters of the alphabet.
speed•y (spē′dē), *adj.,* **speed•i•er, speed•i•est. 1.** capable of or showing speed; fast; quick. **2.** accomplished quickly; prompt: *a speedy recovery.* —**speed′i•ly,** *adv.* —**speed′i•ness,** *n.*
Spiel•berg (spēl′bûrg), *n.* **Steven,** born 1947, U.S. film director.
spe•le•ol•o•gy or **spe•lae•ol•o•gy** (spē′lē ol′ə jē), *n.* the exploration and study of caves. —**spe′le•o•log′i•cal** (-ə loj′i kəl), *adj.* —**spe′le•ol′o•gist,** *n.*
spell¹ (spel), *v.,* **spelled** or **spelt, spell•ing.** —*v.t.* **1.** to name, write, or otherwise give the letters, in order, of (a word, syllable, etc.): *Did I spell your name right?* **2.** (of letters) to form (a word, syllable, etc.): *Y-e-s spells yes.* **3.** to read letter by letter or with difficulty (often fol. by *out*). **4.** to signify; amount to: *This delay spells disaster for us.* —*v.i.* **5.** to name, write, or give the letters of words, syllables, etc., esp. correctly. **6.** to express words by letters: *Sometimes we spell in front of the children.* **7. spell down,** to outspell others in a spelling bee. **8. spell out, a.** to explain something plainly, so that the meaning is unmistakable: *Must I spell it out for you?* **b.** to write out in full: *The title "Ph.D." is seldom spelled out.* **c.** to discern, as by study. —**spell′a•ble,** *adj.*
spell² (spel), *n.* **1.** a word or phrase supposed to have magic power; incantation. **2.** a state or period of enchantment: *living under a spell.* **3.** any dominating or irresistible influence; fascination: *the spell of fine music.* —**spell′-like′,** *adj.*
spell³ (spel), *n.* **1.** a continuous period of work or other activity: *to take a spell at the wheel.* **2.** a turn of work so taken. **3.** a bout, fit, or period of anything experienced: *a spell of coughing.* **4.** an indefinite period: *Come visit us for a spell.* **5.** a period of weather of a specified kind: *a hot spell.* —*v.t.* **6.** to take the place of for a time; relieve: *Let me spell you at the wheel.* —*v.i.* **7.** to take turns at a job.
spell•bind (spel′bīnd′), *v.t.,* **-bound, -bind•ing.** to hold by or as if by a spell; enchant. —**spell′bind′er,** *n.* —**spell′bind′ing•ly,** *adv.*
spell•bound (spel′bound′), *adj.* held by or as if by a spell; enchanted: *a spellbound audience.*
spell′ (or **spell′ing**) **check′er,** *n.* a computer program for checking the spelling of words in an electronic document.
spell•er (spel′ər), *n.* **1.** a person who spells words. **2.** Also called **spell′ing book′.** an elementary textbook or manual to teach spelling. **3.** SPELL CHECKER.
spell•ing (spel′ing), *n.* **1.** the manner in which words are spelled; orthography. **2.** a group of letters representing a word. **3.** the act of a speller.
spell′ing bee′, *n.* a spelling competition won by the individual or team spelling the greatest number of words correctly.
spell′ing pronuncia′tion, *n.* a pronunciation based on the spelling of a word, esp. one used in place of a traditional pronunciation, as (wāst′kōt′) instead of (wes′kət) for *waistcoat.*
spelt¹ (spelt), *v.* a pt. and pp. of SPELL[1].
spelt² (spelt), *n.* a primitive wheat, *Triticum spelta,* native to S Europe and W Asia: used chiefly for livestock feed.
spe•lunk•er (spi lung′kər), *n.* a person who explores caves, esp. as a hobby. —**spe•lunk′ing,** *n.*
spend (spend), *v.,* **spent, spend•ing.** —*v.t.* **1.** to pay out or otherwise dispose of (money, resources, etc.). **2.** to expend (time, labor, thought,

etc.) on some enterprise. **3.** to pass (time) in a particular manner, place, etc.: *to spend a few days in Boston.* **4.** to exhaust: *The storm had spent its fury.* **5.** to give (one's life, blood, etc.) for some cause; sacrifice. —*v.i.* **6.** to spend money, energy, time, etc. —**spend′a•ble,** *adj.*

spend•er (spen′dər), *n.* a person who spends, esp. habitually or excessively; spendthrift.

spend′ing cap′, *n.* an upper limit on expenditures, esp. by a government.

spend′ing mon′ey, *n.* POCKET MONEY.

spend•thrift (spend′thrift′), *n.* **1.** a person who spends money or wealth extravagantly and wastefully; prodigal. —*adj.* **2.** wastefully extravagant; prodigal.

Spe•ner (shpā′nər), *n.* **Phi•lipp Ja•kob** (fē′lēp yä′kôp), 1635–1705, German theologian: founder of Pietism. —**Spe•ner•ism** (shpā′nə riz′- əm, spā′-), *n.*

Speng•ler (speng′glər, shpeng′-), *n.* **Oswald,** 1880–1936, German philosopher. —**Speng•le′ri•an,** *adj., n.*

Spen•ser (spen′sər), *n.* **Edmund,** c1552–99, English poet. —**Spen•se′ri•an** (-sēr′ē ən), *adj., n.*

spent (spent), *v.* **1.** pt. and pp. of SPEND. —*adj.* **2.** used up; consumed. **3.** tired; worn-out; exhausted.

sperm (spûrm), *n., pl.* **sperm, sperms** for 1. **1.** a male reproductive cell; spermatozoon. **2.** semen. —**sper′mous,** *adj.*

sper•ma•cet•i (spûr′mə set′ē, -sē′tē), *n.* a pearly white, waxy, translucent solid, obtained from the oil of sperm whales and other cetaceans: formerly used chiefly in cosmetics and candles and as an emollient. —**sper′ma•cet′i•like′,** *adj.*

spermato-, a combining form meaning "seed"; used with this meaning and as a combining form of SPERM: *spermatocyte.*

sper•mat•o•cyte (spûr mat′ə sīt′), *n.* a male sex cell that gives rise by meiosis to a pair of haploid cells, which become the reproductive cells.

sper•mat•o•zo•id (spûr mat′ə zō′id), *n.* a motile male gamete of a plant or fungus, produced in an antheridium.

sper•mat•o•zo•on (spûr mat′ə zō′ən, -on), *n., pl.* **-zo•a** (-zō′ə). the mature male reproductive cell, actively motile in semen and serving to fertilize the ovum. —**sper•mat′o•zo′al, sper•mat′o•zo′an, sper•mat′o•zo′ic,** *adj.*

sperm′ bank′, *n.* a repository for storing sperm and keeping it viable under scientifically controlled conditions prior to its use in artificial insemination.

sperm′ cell′, *n.* **1.** SPERMATOZOON. **2.** any male gamete.

sper•mi•cide (spûr′mə sīd′), *n.* a sperm-killing agent, esp. a commercial birth-control preparation, usu. a cream or jelly. —**sper′mi•cid′al,** *adj.* —**sper′mi•cid′al•ly,** *adv.*

sperm′ oil′, *n.* a thin, yellow, water-insoluble liquid obtained from the sperm whale.

sperm′ whale′, *n.* a large, square-headed, toothed whale, *Physeter catodon,* having a cavity in the head that contains sperm oil and spermaceti.

spew (spyo̅o̅), *v.i.* **1.** to discharge the contents of the stomach through the mouth; vomit. **2.** to gush or pour out. —*v.t.* **3.** to eject from the stomach through the mouth; vomit. **4.** to pour out or hurl forth violently. —*n.* **5.** something that is spewed; vomit. Sometimes, **spue.**

SPF, sun protection factor: the effectiveness of suntanning preparations in protecting the skin from ultraviolet radiation.

sp. gr., specific gravity.

sphag•num (sfag′nəm), *n.* any spongy moss of the genus *Sphagnum,* occurring chiefly in bogs: used for potting and packing plants. —**sphag′nous,** *adj.*

sphe•noid (sfē′noid), *adj.* Also, **sphe•noi′dal.** **1.** wedge-shaped. **2.** of or pertaining to a compound bone at the base of the skull. —*n.* **3.** the sphenoid bone.

spher•al (sfēr′əl), *adj.* **1.** of or pertaining to a sphere. **2.** spherical. —**sphe•ral′i•ty,** *n.*

sphere (sfēr), *n., v.,* **sphered, spher•ing.** —*n.* **1. a.** a solid geometric figure generated by the revolution of a semicircle about its diameter; a round body whose surface is at all points equidistant from the center. **b.** the surface of such a figure; a spherical surface. **2.** any rounded, globular body. **3.** a planet or star; heavenly body. **4.** the environment within which a person or thing exists, acts, or operates. **5.** a field of something specified: *a sphere of knowledge.* —*v.t.* **6.** to enclose in a sphere. **7.** to form into a sphere. [< Latin *sphaera* globe < Greek *sphaîra*]

-sphere, a combining form meaning "sphere," "something spherical in shape" (*blastosphere; hemisphere*), used esp. in the names of the concentric layers of gases, water, rock, etc., characteristic of the earth or other celestial bodies (*ionosphere; lithosphere*).

sphere′ of in′fluence, *n.* any area in which one nation wields dominant power over another or others.

spher•i•cal (sfer′i kəl, sfēr′-) also **spher′ic,** *adj.* **1.** having the form of a sphere; globular. **2.** formed in or on a sphere, as a figure. **3.** pertaining to a sphere or spheres. **4.** pertaining to the heavenly bodies regarded astrologically as influencing human affairs. —**spher′i•cal′i•ty,** *n.* —**spher′i•cal•ly,** *adv.*

spher′ical geom′etry, *n.* the branch of geometry that deals with figures on spherical surfaces.

spher′ical trigonom′etry, *n.* the branch of trigonometry that deals with spherical triangles.

sphinc•ter (sfingk′tər), *n.* a circular band of voluntary or involuntary muscle that encircles and closes an orifice of the body or one of its hollow organs. —**sphinc′ter•al,** *adj.*

sphin•gid (sfin′jid), *n.* HAWK MOTH.

sphinx (sfingks), *n., pl.* **sphinx•es, sphin•ges** (sfin′jēz). **1. a.** an ancient Egyptian figure of an imaginary creature having the body of a lion and the head of a human or sometimes an animal. **b.** (*usu. cap.*) the colossal recumbent stone figure of this kind near the pyramids of Giza. **2.** (*cap.*) (in Greek myth) a monster, usu. represented as having the head and breasts of a woman, the body of a lion, and the wings of an eagle, who killed wayfarers unable to answer the riddle she posed to them. **3.** a mysterious, inscrutable person or thing.

sphinx (def. 1)

sphinx′ moth′, *n.* HAWK MOTH.

sphyg•mo•ma•nom•e•ter (sfig′mō mə nom′i tər), *n.* an instrument, often attached to an inflatable cuff and used with a stethoscope, for measuring blood pressure in an artery. —**sphyg′mo•man′o•met′ric** (-man′ə me′trik), *adj.* —**sphyg′mo•ma•nom′e•try,** *n.*

spi•ca (spī′kə), *n., pl.* **-cae** (-sē), **-cas** for 1, 2. **1.** SPIKE². **2.** a type of bandage in the shape of a figure eight, extending from an extremity to the trunk. **3.** (*cap.*) a first-magnitude star in the constellation Virgo.

spice (spīs), *n., v.,* **spiced, spic•ing.** —*n.* **1.** a pungent or aromatic vegetable substance, as pepper or cinnamon, used to season food. **2.** a spicy or aromatic odor or fragrance. **3.** something that gives zest or piquancy: *The anecdotes added spice to the speech.* —*v.t.* **4.** to season with spice. **5.** to give zest, piquancy, or interest to.

spice•bush (spīs′bo̅o̅sh′), *n.* an aromatic North American shrub, *Lindera benzoin,* of the laurel family, with small yellow flowers.

spick-and-span (spik′ən span′), *adj.* **1.** spotlessly clean and neat. **2.** perfectly new; fresh. —*adv.* **3.** in a spick-and-span manner.

spic•ule (spik′yo̅o̅l), *n.* **1.** a small, needlelike crystal, process, or the like. **2.** one of the small, hard, calcareous or siliceous bodies that serve as the skeletal elements of various marine and freshwater invertebrates. —**spic′u•late′** (-yə lāt′, -lit), **spic′u•lar,** *adj.*

spic•y (spī′sē), *adj.,* **spic•i•er, spic•i•est. 1.** seasoned, esp. strongly seasoned, with spice. **2.** of the nature of or resembling spice. **3.** abounding in or yielding spices. **4.** aromatic or fragrant. **5.** piquant or pungent: *spicy criticism.* **6.** slightly improper or risqué: *a spicy novel.* **7.** full of spirit; lively. —**spic′i•ness,** *n.*

spi•der (spī′dər), *n.* **1.** any of numerous predatory arachnids of the order Araneae, having a body divided into two parts, a cephalothorax bearing eight legs, and an abdomen with silk-secreting spinnerets: their webs serve as nests and as traps for prey. **2.** (*loosely*) any of various other arachnids resembling these. **3.** any of various devices with leglike extensions suggestive of a spider, as a tripod or trivet. **4.** a frying pan, orig. one with legs for cooking on a hearth. **5.** a machine part having a number of radiating spokes or arms.

spi′der crab′, *n.* any of various crabs of the family Majidae, having long, slender legs and a comparatively small, triangular body.

spi′der mite′, *n.* any of numerous, variously colored, web-spinning mites of the family Tetranychidae, many of which are pests of garden plants and fruit trees.

spi′der mon′key, *n.* any slender, long-limbed tropical American monkey of the genus *Ateles,* with a long, prehensile tail.

spi′der plant′, *n.* a plant, *Chlorophytum comosum,* of the lily family, native to S Africa, that has long, narrow leaves and clusters of white flowers: widely cultivated as a houseplant.

spi′der web′ or **spi′der•web′,** *n.* the web that is spun by a spider, made of interlaced threads of viscous fluid that harden on exposure to air.

spi•der•wort (spī′dər wûrt′, -wôrt′), *n.* any of various New World plants of the genus *Tradescantia,* having blue or rose-colored flowers.

spiel (spēl, shpēl), *Informal.* —*n.* **1.** a usu. high-flown talk or speech, esp. for the purpose of selling or persuading; pitch. —*v.i.* **2.** to speak extravagantly. —**spiel′er,** *n.*

Spiel•berg (spēl′bûrg), *n.* **Steven,** born 1947, U.S. film director.

spiff (spif), *v.t. Informal.* to make spiffy (usu. fol. by *up*): *Let's spiff up this office with new furniture.*

spiff•y (spif′ē), *adj.,* **spiff•i•er, spiff•i•est.** *Informal.* smart; fine; spruce: *a spiffy new convertible.* —**spiff′i•ness,** *n.*

spig•ot (spig′ət), *n.* **1.** a small peg or plug for stopping the vent of a cask. **2.** a peg or plug for stopping the passage of liquid in a faucet or cock. **3.** a faucet or cock for controlling the flow of liquid from a pipe or the like.

spike[1] (spīk), *n., v.,* **spiked, spik·ing. —***n.* **1.** a naillike fastener, 3 to 12 in. (7.6 to 30.5 cm) long and proportionately thicker than a common nail, for fastening together heavy timbers or railroad track. **2.** something resembling such a nail, as a sharp-pointed metal projection on a weapon. **3.** an abrupt increase or rise: *a spike of electrical current.* **4.** one of a number of rectangular or naillike metal projections on the heel and sole of a shoe for improving traction, as of a baseball player or a runner. **5. spikes, a.** shoes having metal projections on the heel and sole. **b.** shoes having spike heels. **6.** a pointed portion of a continuous curve or graph, usu. rising above the adjacent portion. **7.** the unbranched antler of a young deer. **8.** a young mackerel. —*v.t.* **9.** to fasten or secure with a spike or spikes. **10.** to provide or set with a spike or spikes. **11.** to pierce with or impale on a spike. **12.** to set or stud with something suggesting spikes. **13.** to injure (another player or a competitor) with the spikes of one's shoe, as in baseball. **14.** *Volleyball.* to hit (a ball in the air) from a position close to the net sharply downward into the opponent's court. **15.** to render (a muzzle-loading gun) useless by driving a spike into the breech. **16.** to suppress or thwart: *to spike a rumor.* **17.** *Informal.* **a.** to add alcoholic liquor to (a drink). **b.** to add (a chemical, poison, or other substance) to. —*v.i.* **18.** to rise or increase sharply (often fol. by *up*): *Interest rates have spiked up.*

spike[2] (spīk), *n.* **1.** an ear, as of wheat or other grain. **2.** an elongated flower cluster in which the flowers are arranged along an unbranched stalk.

spike′ heel′, *n.* a very high heel that tapers to a narrow base, used on women's shoes.

spike′ lav′ender, *n.* a lavender mint, *Lavandula latifolia,* having spikes of pale purple flowers: yields an oil used in paints.

spike·let (spīk′lit), *n.* a small or secondary spike in grasses.

spike·nard (spīk′nərd, -närd), *n.* **1.** an aromatic Indian plant, *Nardostachys jatamansi,* of the valerian family. **2.** any of various other plants, esp. an American plant, *Aralia racemosa,* of the ginseng family, having an aromatic root.

spik·y (spī′kē), *adj.,* **spik·i·er, spik·i·est. 1.** having a spike or spikes. **2.** resembling a spike; long and sharply pointed. **3.** acid or peevish in temper or mood; prickly. —**spik′i·ness,** *n.*

spile (spīl), *n., v.,* **spiled, spil·ing. —***n.* **1.** a peg or plug of wood, esp. one used as a spigot. **2.** a spout for conducting sap from the sugar maple. **3.** a heavy wooden stake or pile. —*v.t.* **4.** to stop up (a hole) with a spile. **5.** to tap by means of a spile.

spill[1] (spil), *v.,* **spilled** or **spilt, spill·ing,** *n.* —*v.t.* **1.** to cause or allow to run or fall from a container, esp. accidentally or wastefully: *to spill a glass of milk.* **2.** to shed (blood), as in killing or wounding. **3.** to scatter: *to spill papers all over the floor.* **4. a.** to let the wind out of (a sail). **b.** to lose (wind) from a sail. **5.** to cause to fall from a horse, vehicle, or the like. **6.** to divulge: *to spill a secret.* —*v.i.* **7.** (of a liquid, loose particles, etc.) to run or escape from a container, as by careless handling. **8.** to move in great numbers; pour out: *The children spilled into the playground.* —*n.* **9.** a spilling, as of liquid. **10.** a quantity spilled. **11.** Also called **spill′ light′.** superfluous or useless light rays, as from photographic lighting units. **12.** a throw or fall from a horse, vehicle, or the like. —**spill′a·ble,** *adj.*

spill[2] (spil), *n.* **1.** a splinter. **2.** a slender piece of wood or of twisted paper, for lighting candles, lamps, etc. **3.** a peg made of metal. **4.** a small pin for stopping a cask; spile.

spill·age (spil′ij), *n.* **1.** the act or process of spilling. **2.** an amount that spills or is spilled.

spill·o·ver (spil′ō′vər), *n.* **1.** the act of spilling over. **2.** a quantity of something spilled over; overflow.

spill·proof (spil′prōōf′), *adj.* (of a container) designed to prevent spilling.

spilt (spilt), *v.* a pt. and pp. of SPILL[1].

spin (spin), *v.,* **spun, spin·ning,** *n.* —*v.t.* **1.** to make (yarn) by drawing out, twisting, and winding fibers. **2.** to form (the fibers of any material) into thread or yarn. **3.** to produce (a thread, web, cocoon, etc.) by extruding from the body a viscous filament that hardens in the air. **4.** to cause to rotate rapidly; twirl; whirl: *to spin a coin on a table.* **5.** to produce, fabricate, or evolve in a manner suggestive of spinning thread: *to spin a tale.* **6.** to draw out, protract, or prolong (often fol. by *out*): *She spun the project out for over three years.* —*v.i.* **7.** to revolve or rotate rapidly, as the earth or a top. **8.** to produce a thread from the body, as a spider or silkworm. **9.** to produce yarn or thread by spinning. **10.** to move or travel rapidly. **11.** to have a sensation of whirling; reel: *My head began to spin.* **12.** to fish with a spinning or revolving bait. **13. spin off,** to create or derive, based on something already existing: *They took the character of the uncle and spun off another TV series.* —*n.* **14.** the act of causing a spinning or whirling motion. **15.** a spinning motion or movement. **16.** a downward movement or trend, esp. one that is sudden, alarming, etc. **17.** a short ride or drive for pleasure. **18.** *Slang.* a particular viewpoint or bias, esp. in the media; slant: *They tried to put a favorable spin on the news coverage of the controversial speech.* **19.** Also called **tailspin.** the descent of an aircraft, nose-down, in a helical path. **20.** *Physics.* the intrinsic angular momentum characterizing each kind of elementary particle. —*Idiom.* **21. spin one's wheels,** to waste one's efforts. —**spin′na·bil′i·ty,** *n.* —**spin′na·ble,** *adj.*

spin·ach (spin′ich), *n.* a plant, *Spinacia oleracea,* of the goosefoot family, cultivated for its edible, crinkly or flat leaves.

spi·nal (spīn′l), *adj.* **1.** of, pertaining to, or belonging to a spine or thornlike structure, esp. the backbone. —*n.* **2.** a spinal anesthetic. —**spi′nal·ly,** *adv.*

spi′nal anesthe′sia, *n.* injection of an anesthetic into the lumbar region of the spinal canal to reduce sensitivity to pain in the lower body. Also called **spi′nal block′.**

spi′nal col′umn, *n.* the series of vertebrae forming the axis of the skeleton in vertebrate animals; spine; backbone.

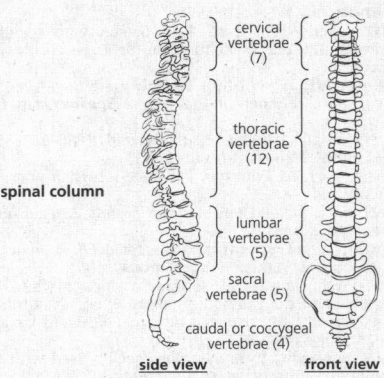

spinal column

cervical vertebrae (7)

thoracic vertebrae (12)

lumbar vertebrae (5)

sacral vertebrae (5)

caudal or coccygeal vertebrae (4)

side view   front view

spi′nal cord′, *n.* the cord of nerve tissue extending through the spinal canal of the spinal column.

spi′nal nerve′, *n.* any of a series of paired nerves that originate in the nerve roots of the spinal cord and emerge from the vertebrae on both sides of the spinal column, each branching out to innervate a specific region of the neck, trunk, or limbs.

spin′ control′, *n. Slang.* an attempt to give a bias to news coverage, esp. of a political candidate or event.

spin·dle (spin′dl), *n., v.,* **-dled, -dling.**—*n.* **1.** a rounded rod, usu. of wood, tapering toward each end, used in hand-spinning to twist into thread the fibers drawn from the mass on the distaff, and on which the thread is wound as it is spun. **2.** the rod on a spinning wheel by which the thread is twisted and on which it is wound. **3.** one of the rods of a spinning machine that bear the bobbins on which the spun thread is wound. **4.** any shaft, rod, or pin that turns around or on which something turns, as an axle, arbor, or mandrel. **5.** a vertical shaft that serves to center a phonograph record on a turntable. **6.** a measure of yarn containing, for cotton, 15,120 yards (13,825 m) and for linen, 14,400 yards (13,267 m). **7.** a spindle-shaped structure, composed of microtubules, that forms near the cell nucleus during mitosis or meiosis and, as it divides, draws the chromosomes to opposite poles of the cell. **8.** a short, turned or circular ornament, as in a baluster or stair rail. **9.** SPINDLE FILE. —*v.t.* **10.** to give the form of a spindle to. **11.** to provide or equip with a spindle or spindles. **12.** to impale (a card or paper) on a spindle, as for sorting purposes. —*v.i.* **13.** to shoot up or grow into a long, slender stalk or stem, as a plant. **14.** to grow tall and slender, often disproportionately so. —**spin′dle·like′,** *adj.*

spin′dle file′, *n.* a device for holding bills, memos, etc., having a projecting metal spike or hook on which to stick papers.

spin′dle tree′, *n.* EUONYMUS.

spin·dly (spind′lē), *adj.,* **-dli·er, -dli·est.** long or tall, thin, and usu. frail: *The colt wobbled on its spindly legs.*

spin′ doc′tor, *n. Slang.* a press agent skilled at spin control.

spin·drift (spin′drift′), *n.* spray swept by a violent wind along the surface of the sea.

spin′-dry′, *v.t.,* **-dried, -dry·ing.** to remove moisture from (laundry) by centrifugal force, as in an automatic washing machine.

spine (spīn), *n.* **1.** SPINAL COLUMN. **2.** a hard, sharp-pointed outgrowth on a plant; thorn. **3.** a stiff-pointed bone, process, or appendage, as the quill of a porcupine or the sharp rays in the fin of certain fishes. **4.** resolution or courage; backbone. **5.** a ridge, as of ground or rock. **6.** the back of a book binding, usu. indicating the title and author. —**spined,** *adj.* —**spine′like′,** *adj.*

spi·nel or **spi·nelle** (spi nel′, spin′l), *n.* **1.** any of a group of minerals composed of oxides of at least two metals (magnesium, aluminum, iron, zinc, manganese, etc.). **2.** a mineral of this group, magnesium aluminum oxide: some varieties are used as gems.

spine·less (spīn′lis), *adj.* **1.** having no spine or backbone. **2.** having no spines or quills. **3.** having a weak spine; limp. **4.** without resolution or courage. —**spine′less·ly,** *adv.* —**spine′less·ness,** *n.*

spin·et (spin′it), *n.* **1.** a small upright piano. **2.** any of various small harpsichords. **3.** a small electric organ.

spin·na·ker (spin′ə kər), *n.* a large, usu. triangular sail carried by a yacht when running before the wind or when the wind is abaft the beam.

spin·ner (spin′ər), *n.* **1.** a person or thing that spins. **2.** a fishing lure, as a spoon bait, that revolves in the water in trolling.

spin•ner•et (spin′ə ret′, spin′ə ret′), *n.* **1.** an organ or part by means of which a spider, insect larva, or the like spins a silky thread for its web or cocoon. **2.** Also, **spin′ner•ette**. a metal plate or cup with tiny holes through which a chemical solution is extruded to form continuous filaments, as of nylon or polyester.

spin•ning (spin′ing), *n.* **1. a.** the act or process of twisting fibers, as cotton or rayon, into yarn or thread. **b.** the extruding of a fiber-forming solution through a spinneret to form filaments. **2.** the act or process of secreting and placing silk or silklike filaments, as in the construction of a web by a spider or the formation of a cocoon by a caterpillar. **3.** the act or technique of fishing with a spinning reel and rod.

spin′ning jen′ny, *n.* an early spinning machine having more than one spindle, enabling a person to spin a number of yarns simultaneously.

spin′ning reel′, *n.* a fishing reel having a stationary spool mounted parallel to the rod and a revolving metal arm that winds the line onto the spool and disengages during casting.

spin′ning wheel′, *n.* a device formerly used for spinning wool, flax, etc., into yarn or thread, consisting essentially of a single spindle driven by a large wheel operated by hand or foot.

spin•off′ or **spin/off′,** *n.* **1.** a by-product or incidental outgrowth of something preexisting, as a program of research or technological development. **2.** a media product, as a television series, based on an idea or character in a preexisting product. **3.** the transfer to corporate stockholders of the stock of a subsidiary or newly acquired company.

spi•nose (spī′nōs, spī nōs′), *adj.* SPINY. **—spi′nose•ly,** *adv.* **—spi•nos′i•ty** (-nos′i tē), *n.*

spi•nous (spī′nəs), *adj.* **1.** covered with spines or thorns; spiny. **2.** resembling a spine or thorn.

spin•ster (spin′stər), *n.* **1.** a woman who has remained unmarried beyond the conventional age for marriage in her culture or society. **2.** *Chiefly Law.* a woman who has never married. **3.** a woman whose occupation is spinning. **—spin′ster•hood,** *n.* **—spin′ster•ish,** *adj.* **—spin′ster•ish•ly,** *adv.* **—spin′ster•like′,** *adj.*

spin•to (spin′tō, spēn′-), *adj.* having a lyric quality with a strong, dramatic element: *a spinto soprano voice.* [< Italian: lit., excessive]

spin•y (spī′nē), *adj.,* **spin•i•er, spin•i•est. 1.** abounding in or having spines; thorny, as a plant. **2.** covered with or having sharp-pointed processes, as an animal. **3.** resembling a spine; spinelike. **4.** difficult to handle; thorny: *a spiny problem.* **—spin′i•ness,** *n.*

spin′y ant′eater, *n.* ECHIDNA.

spin′y-head′ed worm′, *n.* any of a small group of intestinal parasites of the phylum Acanthocephala, having a proboscis covered with hooks used for attachment.

spin′y lob′ster, *n.* any of several edible crustaceans of the family Palinuridae, differing from true lobsters in having a spiny shell and lacking large pincers.

spi•ra•cle (spī′rə kəl, spir′ə-), *n.* **1.** a breathing hole; an opening by which a confined space has communication with the outer air; air hole; blowhole. **2.** one of the external orifices of the respiratory system in certain invertebrates. **—spi•rac′u•lar** (-rak′yə lər), *adj.*

spi•ral (spī′rəl), *n., adj., v.,* **-raled, -ral•ing** or (*esp. Brit.*) **-ralled, -ral•ling. —n. 1.** a plane curve generated by a point moving around a fixed point while constantly receding from or approaching it. **2.** a helix. **3.** a single circle or ring of a spiral or helical curve or object. **4.** a spiral or helical object, formation, or form. **5.** a football thrown or kicked so that the ball turns on its longer axis as it flies through the air. **6.** a continuous increase or decrease in wages, prices, etc. **—adj. 7.** of or of the nature of a spire or coil. **8.** bound with a spiral binding; spiral-bound: *a spiral notebook.* **—v.i. 9.** to take a spiral form or course. **10.** to rise or fall steadily. **—spi′ral•ly,** *adv.*

spirals (def. 4)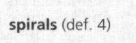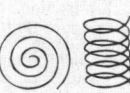

spi′ral bind′ing, *n.* a notebook binding in which the pages are fastened together by a spiral of wire that coils through holes at the side of each page.

spire¹ (spī^ər), *n., v.,* **spired, spir•ing. —n. 1.** a tall, acutely pointed pyramidal roof or rooflike construction upon a tower, roof, etc. **2.** a similar construction forming the upper part of a steeple. **3.** a tall, sharp-pointed summit, peak, or the like. **4.** the highest point or summit. **5.** a sprout or shoot of a plant. **—v.i. 6.** to shoot or rise into spirelike form. **—spired,** *adj.*

spire² (spī^ər), *n.* **1.** a coil or spiral. **2.** one of the series of convolutions of a coil or spiral. **3.** *Zool.* the upper, convoluted part of a spiral shell, above the aperture.

spi•re•a or **spi•rae•a** (spī rē′ə), *n., pl.* **-re•as** or **-rae•as.** any shrub of the genus *Spiraea,* of the rose family, having clusters of small white or pink flowers: some are cultivated as ornamentals.

spir•it (spir′it), *n.* **1.** the animating principle of life, esp. of humans; vital essence. **2.** the incorporeal part of humans, or an aspect of this, as the mind or soul. **3.** conscious, incorporeal being, as opposed to matter. **4.** a supernatural, incorporeal being, esp. one having a particular char-

acter: *evil spirits.* **5.** a fairy, sprite, or elf. **6.** an attitude or principle that pervades thought, stirs one to action, etc.: *the spirit of reform.* **7.** (*cap.*) the third person of the Trinity; Holy Spirit. **8.** the soul or heart as the seat of feelings or as prompting to action: *a man of broken spirit.* **9.** **spirits,** feelings or mood with regard to exaltation or depression: *high spirits.* **10.** a vigorous, courageous, or optimistic attitude: *That's the spirit!* **11.** temper or disposition: *meek in spirit.* **12.** an individual as characterized by a particular attitude, character, etc.: *a few brave spirits.* **13.** dominant tendency or character: *the spirit of the age.* **14.** vigorous sense of membership in a group: *college spirit.* **15.** general meaning or intent (opposed to *letter*): *the spirit of the law.* **16.** the essence or active principle of a substance as extracted in liquid form, esp. by distillation. **17.** Often, **spirits.** a strong distilled alcoholic liquor. **18.** a solution in alcohol of an essential or volatile principle; essence. **19. the Spirit,** God. **—adj. 20.** operating by burning alcoholic spirits: *a spirit stove.* **21.** of or pertaining to spiritualist bodies or activities. **—v.t. 22.** to carry off mysteriously or secretly (often fol. by *away* or *off*). **23.** to encourage; urge on or stir up. **—Proverb. 24. The spirit is willing, but the flesh is weak,** physical temptation may overcome virtue. Matt. 26:4.

spir•it•ed (spir′i tid), *adj.* **1.** having or showing mettle, courage, vigor, animation, etc. **2.** having a specified mood, disposition, or nature (used in combination): *high-spirited; meanspirited.* **—spir′it•ed•ly,** *adv.* **—spir′it•ed•ness,** *n.*

spir′it gum′, *n.* a glue used in fastening false hair, as a beard or mustache, to an actor's skin.

spir•it•less (spir′it lis), *adj.* without ardor, vigor, zeal, or the like. **—spir′it•less•ly,** *adv.* **—spir′it•less•ness,** *n.*

Spirit of '76, a patriotic painting (1876) of a boy, an old man, and Continental Army solider.

spir•it•u•al (spir′i chōō əl), *adj.* **1.** pertaining to the spirit or soul, as distinguished from the physical nature. **2.** of or pertaining to the spirit as the seat of the moral or religious nature. **3.** of or pertaining to sacred things or matters; religious. **4.** pertaining to or consisting of spirit; incorporeal. **5.** closely akin in interests, outlook, feeling, etc.: *the composer's spiritual heir.* **6.** pertaining to spirits or to spiritualists; supernatural or spiritualistic. **7.** of the church; ecclesiastical: *lords spiritual and temporal.* **8.** pertaining to the mind or intellect. **—n. 9.** an emotionally expressive religious song of a type originating among blacks in the southern U.S. **10.** a spiritual thing or matter. **—spir′it•u•al•ly,** *adv.*

spir•it•u•al•ism (spir′i chōō ə liz′əm), *n.* **1.** the belief that the spirits of the dead communicate with the living, esp. through a person (a medium) particularly susceptible to their influence. **2.** the practices or phenomena associated with this belief. **3.** the belief that all reality is spiritual. **—spir′it•u•al•ist,** *n.* **—spir′it•u•al•is′tic,** *adj.*

spir•it•u•al•i•ty (spir′i chōō al′i tē), *n., pl.* **-ties. 1.** the quality or fact of being spiritual. **2.** incorporeal or immaterial nature. **3.** Often, **spiritualities.** property or revenue belonging to the church or to an ecclesiastic.

spir•it•u•ous (spir′i chōō əs), *adj.* **1.** containing or of the nature of alcohol; alcoholic. **2.** (of alcoholic beverages) distilled, rather than fermented.

spiro-, a combining form meaning "coil," "spiral": *spirochete.*

spi•ro•chete (spī′rə kēt′), *n.* any of various mobile, very slender, tightly to loosely coiled bacteria of the family Spirochaetaceae, including pathogenic species that are the cause of syphilis.

spi•ru•li•na (spī′rə lī′nə), *n., pl.* **-nas.** any of the blue-green algae of the genus *Spirulina,* sometimes added to foods for its nutrient value.

spit¹ (spit), *v.,* **spit** or **spat, spit•ting,** *n.* **—v.i. 1.** to eject saliva from the mouth; expectorate. **2.** to sputter: *grease spitting in the fire.* **—v.t. 3.** to eject from the mouth: *to spit watermelon seeds.* **4.** to throw out or emit like saliva. **5.** spit up, to vomit; throw up. **—n. 6.** saliva, esp. when ejected. **7.** the act of spitting. **8.** SPITTLE (def. 2). **—Idiom. 9. spit and image,** exact likeness; counterpart. Also, **spitting image.**

spit² (spit), *n., v.,* **spit•ted, spit•ting. —n. 1.** a pointed rod for skewering and holding meat over a fire or other source of heat. **2.** any of various rods, pins, etc. **3.** a narrow point of land projecting into the water. **4.** a long, narrow shoal extending from the shore. **—v.t. 5.** to pierce, stab, or transfix with or as if with a spit; impale on something sharp.

spit′ and pol′ish, *n.* great care in maintaining smart appearance and crisp efficiency. **—spit′-and-pol′ish,** *adj.*

spit•ball (spit′bôl′), *n.* **1.** a small lump of chewed paper used as a missile. **2.** a baseball pitch, now illegal, made to curve by moistening the ball with saliva or another lubricant.

spit′ curl′, *n.* a tight curl of hair, usu. pressed against the forehead or cheek.

spite (spīt), *n., v.,* **spit•ed, spit•ing. —n. 1.** a malicious, usu. petty desire to harm, annoy, or humiliate another person; malice. **2.** a particular instance of such an attitude or action; grudge. **—v.t. 3.** to treat with spite or malice. **4.** to annoy or thwart, out of spite. **5.** to fill with spite; vex; offend. **—Idiom. 6. in spite of,** in disregard or defiance of; notwithstanding; despite.

spite•ful (spīt′fəl), *adj.* full of spite or malice; malicious. **—spite′ful•ly,** *adv.* **—spite′ful•ness,** *n.*

spit•fire (spit′fī^ər′), *n.* a person of fiery temper who is easily provoked to angry or impassioned outbursts.

spit′ting im′age, *n.* SPIT¹ (def. 9).

spit•tle (spit′l), *n.* **1.** saliva; spit. **2.** the frothy secretion exuded by spittlebugs.

spit·toon (spi tōōn′), *n.* a cuspidor.

spitz (spits), *n.* any of several dogs having a stocky body, a thick coat, erect, pointed ears, and a tail curved over the back, as a chow chow, Pomeranian, or Samoyed.

splash (splash), *v.t.* **1.** to wet or soil by dashing water, mud, or the like; spatter. **2.** to fall upon (something) in scattered masses or particles, as a liquid does. **3.** to dash (water, mud, etc.) about in scattered masses or particles. —*v.i.* **4.** to dash a liquid or semiliquid substance about. **5.** (of liquid) to dash with force in scattered masses or particles. **6.** to fall, move, or go with a splash or splashes. —*n.* **7.** the act of splashing. **8.** the sound of splashing. **9.** a quantity of a liquid or semi-liquid substance splashed. **10.** a spot caused by something splashed. **11.** a patch, as of color or light. **12.** a striking show or impression. **13.** a small amount of liquid. —**splash′er,** *n.* —**splash′ing·ly,** *adv.*

splash·down (splash′doun′), *n.* the landing of a space vehicle in a body of water, esp. the ocean.

splash′ guard′, *n.* a large flap behind a rear tire to prevent mud, water, etc., from being splashed on the following vehicle.

splash·y (splash′ē), *adj.,* **splash·i·er, splash·i·est. 1.** making a splash or splashes. **2.** full of or marked by splashes or irregular spots; spotty. **3.** making an ostentatious display; showy. —**splash′i·ly,** *adv.* —**splash′i·ness,** *n.*

splat¹ (splat), *n.* a broad, flat piece of wood, either pierced or solid, forming the center upright part of a chair back.

splat² (splat), *n.* a sound made by splattering or slapping.

splat·ter (splat′ər), *v.t., v.i.* **1.** to splash and scatter upon impact. —*n.* **2.** an act or instance of splattering. **3.** the quantity splattered. —*adj.* **4.** characterized by gory imagery: *splatter films.*

splay (splā), *v.t.* **1.** to spread out, expand, or extend. **2.** to form with an oblique angle; make slanting; bevel. **3.** to disjoin; dislocate. —*v.i.* **4.** to have an oblique or slanting direction. **5.** to spread or flare. —*n.* **6.** a surface that makes an oblique angle with another, as where the opening through a wall for a window or door widens from one side to the other. —*adj.* **7.** spread out; wide and flat; turned outward. **8.** oblique or awry.

splay·foot (splā′foot′), *n., pl.* **-feet. 1.** a broad foot that turns outward. **2.** FLATFOOT (def. 1).

spleen (splēn), *n.* **1.** a highly vascular, glandular, ductless organ, situated in humans at the cardiac end of the stomach, serving chiefly in the formation of mature lymphocytes, in the destruction of worn-out red blood cells, and as a reservoir for blood. **2.** (formerly) this organ conceived of as the seat of spirit and courage or of such emotions as mirth, ill humor, melancholy, etc. **3.** ill humor, peevish temper, or spite. —**spleen′ish,** *adj.*

splen·did (splen′did), *adj.* **1.** magnificent or sumptuous. **2.** distinguished or glorious: *a splendid achievement.* **3.** excellent or very good: *to have a splendid time.* **4.** brilliant in appearance, color, etc. —**splen′did·ly,** *adv.* —**splen′did·ness,** *n.*

splen·dif·er·ous (splen dif′ər əs), *adj.* splendid; magnificent; fine. —**splen·dif′er·ous·ly,** *adv.* —**splen·dif′er·ous·ness,** *n.*

splen·dor (splen′dər), *n.* **1.** brilliant or gorgeous appearance, coloring, etc.; grandeur; magnificence. **2.** an instance or display of imposing pomp or grandeur: *the splendor of the coronation.* **3.** great brightness; brilliant light or luster. Also, *esp. Brit.,* **splen′dour.** —**splen′dor·ous, splen′drous** (-drəs), *adj.*

sple·net·ic (spli net′ik), *adj.* Also, **sple·net′i·cal. 1.** of the spleen. **2.** irritable; peevish; spiteful. —*n.* **3.** a splenetic person. —**sple·net′i·cal·ly,** *adv.*

splice (splīs), *v.,* **spliced, splic·ing,** *n.* —*v.t.* **1.** to join together or unite (rope) by the interweaving of strands. **2.** to unite (timbers, spars, or the like) by overlapping and binding their ends. **3.** to unite (film, magnetic tape, etc.) by butting and cementing. **4.** to join or unite. **5.** to join (segments of DNA or RNA) together. **6.** *Informal.* to unite in marriage. **7.** a joining of two ropes or parts of a rope by splicing. **8.** the union or junction made by splicing. —**splice′a·ble,** *adj.* —**splic′er,** *n.*

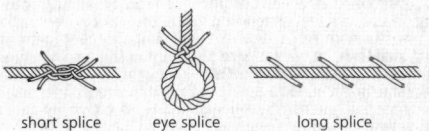

short splice   eye splice   long splice

splice (def. 7)

spline (splīn), *n.* **1.** a long, narrow, thin strip of wood, metal, etc.; slat. **2.** a long, flexible strip of wood or the like, used in drawing curves. **3.** any of a series of ridges on a shaft, parallel to its axis and fitting inside corresponding grooves in the hub of a gear, etc., to transmit torque. **4.** a thin strip of material inserted into the edges of two boards, acoustic tiles, etc., to make a butt joint.

splint (splint), *n.* **1.** a thin piece of wood or other rigid material used to immobilize a fractured or dislocated bone, or to maintain any part of the body in a fixed position. **2.** one of a number of thin strips of wood woven together to make a chair seat, basket, etc. —*v.t.* **3.** to secure, hold in position, or support by means of a splint, as a fractured bone. **4.** to support as if with splints.

splin·ter (splin′tər), *n.* **1.** a small, thin, sharp piece of wood, bone, or the like, split or broken off from the main body. **2.** SPLINTER GROUP. —*v.t.* **3.** to split or break into splinters. **4.** to break off (something) in splinters. **5.** to split or break (a larger group) into separate factions or independent groups. —*v.i.* **6.** to be split or broken into splinters. **7.** to break off in splinters. —**splin′ter·y,** *adj.*

splin′ter group′, *n.* a small organization that becomes separated from or acts apart from an original larger group.

split (split), *v.,* **split, split·ting,** *n., adj.* —*v.t.* **1.** to divide or separate from end to end or into layers: *to split a log in two.* **2.** to separate by cutting, chopping, etc.: *to split a piece from a block.* **3.** to divide into distinct parts or portions (often fol. by *up*). **4.** to divide into different groups, as by discord. **5.** to cast (a ballot or vote) for candidates of more than one political party. **6.** to divide between two or more persons, groups, etc.; share. **7.** to separate into parts by interposing something: *to split an infinitive.* **8.** to divide (molecules or atoms) by cleavage into smaller parts. **9.** to issue additional shares of (a stock) to stockholders without charge so that individual holdings are increased though the value per share is less. —*v.i.* **10.** to divide, break, or separate. **11.** to part or separate, as through disagreement. **12.** to divide or share something with another or others; apportion. **13.** *Slang.* to leave; depart. —*n.* **14.** the act of splitting. **15.** a crack, tear, or fissure caused by splitting. **16.** a piece or part separated by or as if by splitting. **17.** a breach or rupture, as between persons, in a party, organization, etc. **18.** a faction, party, etc., formed by a rupture or schism. **19.** an ice-cream dish made esp. with a split banana, flavored syrup, and chopped nuts. **20.** a bottle for wine containing from 6 to 6½ oz. (180 to 195 ml). **21.** Often, **splits.** the feat of separating the legs while sinking to the floor, until they extend at right angles to the body. **22.** an arrangement of bowling pins remaining after the first bowl in two separated groups, so that a spare is difficult. **23.** the act of splitting a stock. —*adj.* **24.** having been split; divided. **25.** parted lengthwise; cleft. **26.** (of a stock) having undergone a split. —*Idiom.* **27. split the difference,** to compromise, esp. to divide what remains equally. —**split′ta·ble,** *adj.*

split′ deci′sion, *n.* a decision in a boxing match that is not unanimously agreed upon by the judges and referee.

split′ end′, *n.* **1.** an offensive end in football who lines up some distance outside the formation. **2.** the end of a hair that has split into strands.

split′ infin′itive, *n.* an expression in which there is a word or phrase, usu. an adverb or adverbial phrase, between *to* and its accompanying verb form in an infinitive, as in *to readily understand.* —**Usage.** The traditional rule against the split infinitive is based on an analogy with Latin, in which infinitives are only one word and hence cannot be "split." In the past, Latin style was the model for good writing in English; criticism of the split infinitive was especially strong in 19th-century usage guides. In many sentences, however, the only natural place for an adverb or other word is between *to* and the verb: *To actually see the organisms you must use a microscope.* Many modern speakers and writers depend on their ear for a natural sentence rather than on an arbitrary rule. Those who ordinarily prefer not to split an infinitive will occasionally do so to avoid awkward or stilted language.

split′-lev′el, *adj.* **1.** (of a house) having a room or rooms that are somewhat above or below adjacent rooms, with the floor levels usu. differing by about half a story. —*n.* **2.** a split-level house.

split′ pea′, *n.* a dried green pea, split and used esp. for soup.

split′ personal′ity, *n.* MULTIPLE PERSONALITY.

split′ screen′, *n.* **1.** a mode of operation on a computer that uses windows to enable simultaneous viewing of two or more displays on the same screen. **2.** a motion-picture or television screen on which two or more images are projected at the same time.

split′ sec′ond, *n.* **1.** a fraction of a second. **2.** an infinitesimal amount of time; instant; twinkling. —**split′-sec′ond,** *adj.*

split′ tick′et, *n.* a ballot on which not all votes have been cast for candidates of the same political party.

split′-up′, *n.* **1.** a splitting or separating into two or more parts or groups. **2.** an exchange of all the capital stock and assets of a corporation for those of two or more newly formed companies, thus liquidating the parent corporation. Compare SPIN-OFF (def. 3).

splotch (sploch), *n.* **1.** a large, irregular spot; blot; stain; blotch. —*v.t.* **2.** to mark or cover with splotches. —*v.i.* **3.** to be susceptible to stains or blots. **4.** to cause or be liable to cause stains, blots, or spots.

splotch·y (sploch′ē), *adj.,* **splotch·i·er, splotch·i·est.** marked or covered with splotches.

splurge (splûrj), *v.,* **splurged, splurg·ing,** *n.* —*v.i.* **1.** to indulge oneself in some luxury or pleasure, esp. a costly one: *They splurged on a trip to Europe.* **2.** to show off. —*v.t.* **3.** to spend (money) lavishly or ostentatiously. —*n.* **4.** an ostentatious display. **5.** an instance or bout of extravagant spending.

splut·ter (splut′ər), *v.i.* **1.** to talk rapidly and somewhat incoherently, as when confused or excited. **2.** to make a sputtering sound, or emit particles of something explosively, as water on a hot griddle. **3.** to fly or fall in particles or drops; spatter, as a liquid. —*v.t.* **4.** to utter hastily and confusedly or incoherently; sputter. **5.** to spatter. —*n.* **6.** spluttering utterance or talk; noise or fuss. **7.** a sputtering or spattering.

Spock (spok), *n.* **Benjamin (McLane),** born 1903, U.S. physician.

spoil (spoil), *v.,* **spoiled** or **spoilt, spoil·ing,** *n.* —*v.t.* **1.** to damage or harm severely; ruin: *The tear spoiled the delicate fabric.* **2.** to impair the quality of; affect detrimentally: *Bad weather spoiled our vacation.* **3.** to impair the character of (someone) by excessive indulgence. —*v.i.* **4.** to become bad or unfit for use, as food or other perishable substances. **5.** to plunder, pillage, or rob. —*n.* **6.** Often, **spoils.** booty, loot, or plunder taken in war or robbery. **7. spoils,** the emoluments and advantages of public office viewed as won by a victorious political party. **8.** waste material, as that which is cast up in excavating. —***Idiom.* 9. be spoiling for,** *Informal.* to be very eager for: *They're spoiling for a fight.*

spoil•age (spoi′lij), *n.* **1.** the act of spoiling or the state of being spoiled. **2.** material or the amount of material that is spoiled.

spoil•er (spoi′lər), *n.* **1.** a person or thing that spoils. **2.** a person who robs or ravages; plunderer. **3.** a device used to break up the airflow around an aerodynamic surface, as an aircraft wing, to decrease lift and provide bank or descent control. **4.** a similar device on an automobile, designed to reduce lift and improve traction at high speeds. **5.** any candidate who has no chance of ultimate victory but does well enough to spoil the chances of another.

spoil•sport (spoil′spôrt′, -spōrt′), *n.* a person whose conduct spoils the pleasure of others, as in a game or social gathering.

spoils′ sys′tem, *n.* the process by which party loyalists are rewarded after their side has achieved electoral success.

spoilt (spoilt), *v.* a pt. and pp. of SPOIL.

Spo•kane (spō kan′), *n.* a city in E Washington. 192,781.

spoke[1] (spōk), *v.* a pt. of SPEAK.

spoke[2] (spōk), *n., v.,* **spoked, spok•ing.** —*n.* **1.** one of the bars, rods, or rungs radiating from the hub or nave of a wheel and supporting the rim. **2.** a handlelike projection from the rim of a wheel, as a ship's steering wheel. **3.** a rung of a ladder. —*v.t.* **4.** to fit or furnish with or as if with spokes.

spo•ken (spō′kən), *v.* **1.** a pp. of SPEAK. —*adj.* **2.** uttered or expressed by speaking; oral (disting. from *written*). **3.** speaking, or using speech, as specified (usu. used in combination): *plain-spoken; soft-spoken.* —***Idiom.* 4. spoken for,** claimed or reserved: *This seat is spoken for.*

spoke•shave (spōk′shāv′), *n.* a cutting tool having a blade set between two handles, used for dressing curved edges of wood.

spokes•per•son (spōks′pûr′sən), *n.* a person who speaks for another or for a group.

spo•li•ate (spō′lē āt′), *v.t., v.i.,* **-at•ed, -at•ing.** to plunder, rob, or ruin. —**spo′li•a′tion,** *n.* —**spo′li•a′tor,** *n.*

sponge (spunj), *n., v.,* **sponged, spong•ing.** —*n.* **1.** any porous, aquatic, sessile animal of the phylum Porifera, having a fibrous siliceous or calcareous internal skeleton and lacking tissue organization. **2.** the skeleton of certain sponges, readily absorbing water and becoming soft when wet while retaining toughness. **3.** a piece of any of various absorbent materials, as a block of porous cellulose or a surgical gauze pad. **4.** a person or thing that absorbs something freely. **5.** a person who lives at the expense of others. **6.** a porous mass of metallic particles, as of platinum, obtained by the reduction of an oxide or purified compound at a temperature below the melting point. **7. a.** yeast-raised bread dough, esp. before kneading. **b.** a light pudding made with gelatin, fruit juice, etc. **8.** a disposable piece of polyurethane foam impregnated with a spermicide for insertion into the vagina as a contraceptive. —*v.t.* **9.** to wipe or rub with or as if with a wet sponge. **10.** to wipe out or efface with or as if with a sponge (often fol. by *out*). **11.** to take up or absorb with or as if with a sponge (often fol. by *up*). **12.** to obtain by imposing on another's good nature. —*v.i.* **13.** to take in or soak up liquid by absorption. **14.** to live at the expense of others (often fol. by *on* or *off*). **15.** to gather sponges. —**spong′ing•ly,** *adv.* —**spong′er,** *n.*

sponge′ bath′, *n.* a bath in which the bather is cleaned by a wet sponge or washcloth, without getting into a tub of water.

sponge′ cake′, *n.* a light, sweet cake containing eggs but no shortening.

sponge′ rub′ber, *n.* a light, spongy rubber, usu. prepared by bubbling carbon dioxide through or whipping air into latex; foam rubber.

spon•gy (spun′jē), *adj.,* **-gi•er, -gi•est. 1.** of the nature of or resembling a sponge; light, porous, or readily compressible. **2.** having the absorbent characteristics of a sponge. **3.** of or pertaining to a sponge. **4.** porous but hard, as bone. —**spon′gi•ly,** *adv.* —**spon′gi•ness,** *n.*

spon•sor (spon′sər), *n.* **1.** a person who vouches for, is responsible for, or supports a person or thing. **2.** a person, firm, organization, etc., that supports the cost of a radio or television program by buying time for advertising or promotion during the broadcast. **3.** a person or group that provides or pledges money for an undertaking or event: *the corporate sponsors of a race.* **4.** a person who makes a pledge or promise on behalf of another. **5.** a person who answers for an infant at baptism, making the required professions and assuming responsibility for the child's religious upbringing; godparent. —*v.t.* **6.** to act as sponsor for. —**spon•so′ri•al** (-sôr′ē əl, -sōr′-), *adj.* —**spon′sor•ship′,** *n.*

spon•ta•ne•i•ty (spon′tə nē′i tē, -nā′-), *n., pl.* **-ties. 1.** the state, quality, or fact of being spontaneous. **2.** spontaneous activity. **3. spontaneities,** spontaneous impulses, movements, or actions.

spon•ta•ne•ous (spon tā′nē əs), *adj.* **1.** coming or resulting from a natural impulse or tendency; without effort or premeditation. **2.** (of a person) given to acting upon sudden impulses. **3.** (of natural phenomena) arising from internal forces or causes. **4.** growing naturally or without cultivation, as plants and fruits; indigenous. —**spon•ta′ne•ous•ly,** *adv.* —**spon•ta′ne•ous•ness,** *n.*

sponta′neous combus′tion, *n.* the ignition of a substance or body without heat from any external source.

sponta′neous genera′tion, *n.* ABIOGENESIS.

spoof (spo͞of), *n.* **1.** a light-hearted imitation of someone or something; lampoon or parody. **2.** a hoax; prank. —*v.t.* **3.** to mock (something or someone) lightly and good-humoredly; kid. **4.** to fool by a hoax. —*v.i.* **5.** to scoff at something lightly and good-humoredly; kid.

spook (spo͝ok), *n.* **1.** a ghost; specter. **2.** *Informal.* an espionage agent; spy. —*v.t.* **3.** to haunt; inhabit or appear in or to as a ghost or specter. **4.** to frighten; scare. —*v.i.* **5.** to become frightened or scared.

spook•y (spo͞o′kē), *adj.,* **spook•i•er, spook•i•est. 1.** like or befitting a spook; suggestive of spooks. **2.** eerie; scary. **3.** (esp. of horses) nervous; skittish. —**spook′i•ly,** *adv.* —**spook′i•ness,** *n.*

spool (spo͞ol), *n.* **1.** a cylindrical object or device on which something is wound, typically having a rim at each end and a hole for a spindle running lengthwise through the center. **2.** the material or quantity of material wound on such a device. **3.** a bobbin or reel. **4.** the cylindrical drum in a fishing reel that bears the line. —*v.t.* **5.** to wind on a spool. **6.** to unwind from a spool (usu. fol. by *off* or *out*). —*v.i.* **7.** to wind. **8.** to unwind. —**spool′er,** *n.*

spoon (spo͞on), *n.* **1.** a utensil for use in eating, stirring, measuring, ladling, etc., consisting of a small, shallow bowl with a handle. **2.** any of various implements, objects, or parts resembling or suggesting this. **3.** a spoonful. **4.** a fishing lure consisting of a bright spoon-shaped piece of metal. —*v.t.* **5.** to eat with, take up, or transfer in or as if in a spoon. **6.** to hollow out or shape like a spoon. **7.** to push or shove (a ball) with a lifting motion, as in golf. —*v.i.* **8.** *Informal.* to show affection or love, esp. in an openly sentimental way. **9.** to spoon a ball. **10.** to fish with a spoon. —***Idiom.* 11. born with a silver spoon in one's mouth,** born wealthy.

spoon•bill (spo͞on′bil′), *n.* **1.** any of several large wading birds of the ibis family, having a long, flat bill with a spoonlike tip. **2.** any of various other birds having a similar bill, as the shoveler. **3.** PADDLEFISH.

spoon′ bread′ or **spoon′bread′,** *n.* a baked dish of cornmeal, eggs, and shortening.

spoon•er•ism (spo͞o′nə riz′əm), *n.* the transposition of initial or other sounds of words, as in *a blushing crow* for *a crushing blow.* [after W. A. *Spooner* (1844–1930), English clergyman noted for such slips]

spoon′-feed′, *v.t.,* **-fed, -feed•ing. 1.** to feed with a spoon. **2.** to provide so fully with information or the like that one is prevented from thinking or acting independently. **3.** to provide someone with (information or the like) in this way. **4.** to pamper.

spoon•ful (spo͞on′fo͝ol), *n., pl.* **-fuls. 1.** as much as a spoon can hold. **2.** a small quantity. —**Usage.** See -FUL.

spoor (spo͝or, spôr, spōr), *n.* **1.** a track or trail, esp. of a wild animal. —*v.t.* **2.** to track by a spoor. —*v.i.* **3.** to track an animal by a spoor.

spo•rad•ic (spə rad′ik), *adj.* **1.** appearing or happening at irregular intervals in time; occasional. **2.** appearing in scattered or isolated instances. —**spo•rad′i•cal•ly,** *adv.*

spore (spôr, spōr), *n., v.,* **spored, spor•ing.** —*n.* **1.** the asexual reproductive body of a fungus or nonflowering plant. **2.** the resting or dormant stage of a bacterium or other microorganism. —*v.i.* **3.** to produce or shed spores. —**spo•ra•ceous** (spə rā′shəs), *adj.*

-spore, var. of SPORO-, as final element of compound words: *teliospore.*

spori-, var. of SPORO- before elements of Latin origin: *sporiferous.*

spo•rif•er•ous (spə rif′ər əs), *adj.* bearing spores.

sporo-, a combining form representing SPORE: *sporophyte.*

spo•ro•cyst (spôr′ə sist′, spōr′-), *n.* **1. a.** a case produced by a sporozoan. **b.** the sporozoan within such a case. **2.** a resting or dormant cell that produces spores. **3.** the first, saclike stage of many trematode worms, giving rise to cercariae by budding.

spo•ro•phore (spôr′ə fôr′, spōr′ə fōr′), *n.* a fungus hypha specialized to bear spores.

spo•ro•zo•an (spôr′ə zō′ən, spōr′-), *n.* any parasitic spore-forming protozoan of the class Sporozoa, several species of which cause malaria.

sport (spôrt, spōrt), *n.* **1.** an athletic activity requiring skill or physical prowess and often of a competitive nature. **2.** such activities collectively. **3.** diversion; recreation. **4.** jest; pleasantry. **5.** mockery; ridicule: *They made sport of his haircut.* **6.** LAUGHINGSTOCK. **7.** something tossed about like a plaything. **8.** SPORTSMAN. **9.** a person who behaves in a fair or admirable manner. **10.** a debonair person. **11.** *Biol.* an organism or part that shows an unusual or singular deviation from the normal or parent type; mutation. —*adj.* Also, **sports. 12.** of, pertaining to, or used in sports. **13.** suitable for informal wear: *sport clothes.* —*v.i.* **14.** to amuse oneself with some pleasant pastime. **15.** to frolic: *kittens sporting and playing.* **16.** to engage in athletic activity. **17.** to speak or act in jest. **18.** to mock something. **19.** *Bot.* to mutate. —*v.t.* **20.** to wear or display, esp. with ostentation: *sporting a new coat.* e

sport′ fish′, *n.* GAME FISH.

sport•fish•ing (spôrt′fish′ing, spōrt′-), *n.* fishing with a rod and reel for sport.

sport•ing (spôr′ting, spōr′-), *adj.* **1.** engaging in or favoring esp. outdoor sports. **2.** concerned with or suitable for such sports: *sporting equipment.* **3.** befitting a sportsman; fair. **4.** interested in or connected with gambling. —**sport′ing•ly,** *adv.*

sport′ing chance′, *n.* a fair opportunity for a favorable outcome in an enterprise.

sport′ing dog′, *n.* any of several breeds of dogs developed to assist a hunter by pointing, flushing, or retrieving game and including the pointers, setters, retrievers, and spaniels.

spor•tive (spôr′tiv, spōr′-), *adj.* **1.** playful; frolicsome. **2.** pertaining to or of the nature of a sport or sports. **3.** ardent; wanton. —**spor′tive•ly,** *adv.* —**spor′tive•ness,** *n.*

sports′ car′, *n.* a small, high-powered automobile with long, low lines, usu. seating two persons.

sports•cast (spôrts′kast′, -käst′, spōrts′-), *n.* a radio or television program consisting of sports news or commentary on a sports event. —**sports′cast′er,** *n.* —**sports′cast′ing,** *n.*

sport′ shirt′, *n.* a soft shirt for informal wear having a squared-off shirttail. Compare DRESS SHIRT.

sports′ jack′et, *n.* a jacket with a notched collar, long sleeves, and a somewhat full cut.

sports•man (spôrts′mən, spōrts′-), *n., pl.* **-men. 1.** a person who engages in sports, esp. hunting and fishing. **2.** a person who exhibits qualities of fairness, courtesy, and grace in winning and defeat. —**sports′man•like′, sports′man•ly,** *adj.*

sports•man•ship (spôrts′mən ship′, spōrts′-), *n.* **1.** the practice or skill of a sportsman. **2.** conduct befitting a sportsman.

sports′ med′icine, *n.* a field of medicine concerned with the functioning of the human body during physical activity and with the prevention and treatment of athletic injuries.

sports•wear (spôrts′wâr′, spōrts′-), *n.* **1.** clothing designed for recreational wear. **2.** clothing orig. designed for daytime or leisure activity but later adapted for more formal occasions.

sports•wom•an (spôrts′wo͝om′ən, spōrts′-), *n., pl.* **-wom•en.** a woman who engages in sports.

sports•writ•er (spôrts′rī′tər, spōrts′-), *n.* a journalist who reports on sporting events. —**sports′writ′ing,** *n.*

sport•y (spôr′tē, spōr′-), *adj.,* **sport•i•er, sport•i•est. 1.** flashy; showy: *a sporty costume.* **2.** smart in dress or behavior; dashing. **3.** like or befitting a sportsman. **4.** dissipated; fast. **5.** designed for or suitable for sport. —**sport′i•ly,** *adv.* —**sport′i•ness,** *n.*

spot (spot), *n., v.,* **spot•ted, spot•ting,** *adj.* —*n.* **1.** a rounded mark or stain made by foreign matter, as dirt. **2.** something that mars one's character or reputation; flaw. **3.** a small blemish, mole, or other circumscribed mark on the skin. **4.** a small part of a surface differing from the rest in color, texture, or character: *a bald spot.* **5.** a place; locality: *the spot where the explorers landed.* **6.** Also called **spot′ announce′ment.** a brief radio or television message inserted between programs or segments of a program. **7.** a position in a sequence or hierarchy: *an important spot in government.* **8. a.** one of various traditional, geometric drawings of a club, diamond, heart, or spade on a playing card for indicating suit and value. **b.** any playing card from a two through a ten. **9.** a pip, as on dice or dominoes. **10.** *Chiefly Brit. Informal.* a small quantity: *a spot of tea.* **11.** an awkward or difficult position: *in a bit of a spot.* **12.** SPOTLIGHT (def. 1). —*v.t.* **13.** to stain or mark with spots. **14.** to sully; blemish. **15.** to mark with spots. **16.** to remove a spot from. **17.** to locate or identify by seeing; notice or detect: *to spot an error; to spot a ship from afar.* **18.** to place or position on a particular place: *to spot a billiard ball.* **19.** to scatter; disperse: *to spot chairs here and there.* **20.** SPOTLIGHT (def. 5). **21. a.** to determine precisely: *to spot enemy movements.* **b.** to correct (gunfire) for accuracy. **22.** to grant an advantage to (an opponent). —*v.i.* **23.** to make a spot; stain: *Ink spots badly.* **24.** to become spotted. **25.** to act as a military spotter. —*adj.* **26. a.** pertaining to the point of origin of a local broadcast. **b.** broadcast between announced programs. **27.** made, paid, or delivered at once: *a spot sale; spot goods.* —***Idiom.* 28. on the spot, a.** without delay; at once; instantly. **b.** at the very place in question. **c.** in a difficult or embarrassing position. **d.** in a position of being held responsible.

spot′ check′, *n.* a random, quick sampling or investigation.

spot′-check′, *v.t.* **1.** to examine or investigate with a spot check. —*v.i.* **2.** to conduct a spot check. —**spot′-check′er,** *n.*

spot•less (spot′lis), *adj.* **1.** immaculately clean: *a spotless kitchen.* **2.** irreproachable; pure: *a spotless reputation.* —**spot′less•ly,** *adv.* —**spot′less•ness,** *n.*

spot•light (spot′līt′), *n., v.,* **-light•ed** or **-lit, -light•ing.** —*n.* **1.** an intense light focused so as to pick out an object, person, or group, as on a stage. **2.** a lamp for producing such a light. **3.** a brilliant narrowly focused light, as on an automobile, used for spotting objects. **4.** the area of immediate or conspicuous public attention. —*v.t.* **5.** to direct the beam of a spotlight upon. **6.** to make conspicuous; call attention to.

spot•ted (spot′id), *adj.* **1.** marked with or characterized by a spot or spots. **2.** sullied; blemished.

spot′ted fe′ver, *n.* **1.** any of several fevers characterized by spots on the skin, as Rocky Mountain spotted fever or typhus fever. **2.** TICK FEVER.

spot′ted hye′na, *n.* an African hyena, *Crocuta crocuta,* having a dark-spotted yellowish gray coat, noted for its distinctive howl. Also called **laughing hyena.**

spot′ted owl′, *n.* a medium-sized owl of the western U.S., having a barred breast and a white-spotted brown back.

spot′ted sand′piper, *n.* a common sandpiper, *Actitis macularia,* that breeds near fresh water in the northern U.S. and southern Canada.

spot•ter (spot′ər), *n.* **1.** a person who removes spots, as from clothing. **2.** a civilian who watches for enemy airplanes. **3.** a person employed to watch the activity of others, as for evidence of dishonesty. **4.** a military observer who spots targets. **5.** an assistant to a sportscaster who provides the names of the players in a game.

spot′ test′, *n.* an informal test for obtaining an immediate sample response.

spot•ty (spot′ē), *adj.* **-ti•er, -ti•est. 1.** marked with spots; spotted. **2.** distributed irregularly. **3.** uneven in quality or character: *a spotty performance.* —**spot′ti•ly,** *adv.* —**spot′ti•ness,** *n.*

spous•al (spou′zəl), *adj.* pertaining to one's spouse.

spouse (spous, spouz), *n.* one's husband or wife.

spout (spout), *v.t.* **1.** to discharge in a stream or jet: *volcanoes spouting ash and lava.* **2.** to state or declaim volubly or in a pompous manner: *spouting theories on foreign policy.* —*v.i.* **3.** to issue in a jet or continuous stream. **4.** to issue forth with force, as liquid through a narrow orifice. **5.** to speak volubly or pompously. —*n.* **6.** a pipe, tube, or liplike projection through or by which a liquid is discharged, poured, or conveyed. **7.** a trough or shoot for discharging or conveying grain, flour, etc. **8.** WATERSPOUT. **9.** a continuous stream of material discharged from or as if from a pipe. **10.** a spring of water. —**spout′er,** *n.*

sprain (sprān), *v.t.* **1.** to overstrain or wrench (the ligaments around a joint) so as to injure without fracture or dislocation. —*n.* **2.** a wrenching injury to ligaments around a joint. **3.** the condition of being sprained.

sprang[1] (sprang), *v.* a pt. of SPRING.

sprang[2] (sprang), *n.* a technique of plaiting or intertwining threads to form an openwork fabric.

sprat (sprat), *n., pl.* **sprats,** (*esp. collectively*) **sprat** for 1. **1.** a herring, *Clupea sprattus,* of the E North Atlantic. **2.** a young person or thing.

sprawl (sprôl), *v.i.* **1.** to be spread out awkwardly. **2.** to sit or lie with limbs spread out. **3.** to spread out or be distributed irregularly. **4.** to crawl or scramble awkwardly. —*v.t.* **5.** to stretch out (the limbs) as in sprawling. **6.** to spread out or distribute irregularly. —*n.* **7.** an act or instance of sprawling. —**sprawl′y,** *adj.,* **sprawl•i•er, sprawl•i•est.**

spray[1] (sprā), *n.* **1.** water or other liquid broken up into minute droplets and blown, ejected into, or falling through the air. **2.** a jet of fine particles of liquid discharged from an atomizer or other device. **3.** a liquid to be discharged or applied in such a jet. **4.** an apparatus or device for discharging such a liquid. **5.** a quantity of small objects, flying or discharged through the air: *a spray of shattered glass.* —*v.t.* **6.** to scatter in the form of fine particles. **7.** to apply or direct in a spray. **8.** to sprinkle or treat with a spray. —*v.i.* **9.** to scatter or discharge a spray. **10.** to issue forth in a spray. —**spray′er,** *n.*

spray[2] (sprā), *n.* **1.** a single, slender shoot, twig, or branch with its leaves, flowers, or berries. **2.** an arrangement of cut flowers or branches. **3.** an ornament resembling a spray of flowers.

spray′ can′, *n.* a can whose contents are in aerosol form.

spray′ gun′, *n.* a device consisting of a container from which paint or other liquid is sprayed through a nozzle by air pressure from a pump.

spray′ paint′, *n.* paint that is packaged in an aerosol container for spraying onto a surface. —**spray′-paint′,** *v.t.*

spread (spred), *v.,* **spread, spread•ing,** *n.* —*v.t.* **1.** to draw, stretch, or open out, esp. over a flat surface: *Spread out the blanket.* **2.** to extend out; move apart: *The bird spread its wings.* **3.** to distribute over an area of space or time: *to spread seed on the ground.* **4.** to apply in a thin layer or coating: *to spread butter on bread.* **5.** to extend as a covering: *to spread the sheet over the bed.* **6.** to set or prepare (a table) for a meal. **7.** to send out in various directions: *to spread light.* **8.** to cause to become widely known; disseminate: *to spread rumors.* **9.** —*v.i.* **10.** to become stretched out or extended; expand. **11.** to become broadly distributed. —*n.* **12.** an act or instance of spreading. **13.** expansion; diffusion: *the spread of suspicion.* **14.** the extent of spreading: *to measure the spread of branches.* **15. a.** the difference between the prices bid and asked of stock or a commodity. **b.** a commodities market transaction in which the call price is set above and the put price below the current market quotation. **c.** the difference between any two prices or rates for related costs. **16.** capacity for spreading. **17.** a distance or range between two points. **18.** WINGSPAN. **19.** an expanse of something: *a spread of timber.* **20.** a cloth covering for a bed, table, or the like, esp. a bedspread. **21.** *Informal.* an abundance of food set out on a table; feast. **22.** a food preparation for spreading, as jam or peanut butter. **23.** two facing pages, as of a book or newspaper. **24. a.** an extensive display treatment of a topic in a newspaper or magazine. **b.** an advertisement or story covering one or more pages. **25.** landed property, as a farm or ranch. **26.** POINT SPREAD. —***Idiom.* 27. spread oneself thin,** to undertake too many projects simultaneously. —**spread′a•ble,** *adj.* —**spread′a•bil′i•ty,** *n.*

spread′ ea′gle, *n.* **1.** a representation of an eagle with outspread wings: used as an emblem of the U.S. **2.** a skating figure performed with the skates touching heel-to-heel in a straight line and the arms outstretched.

spread′-ea′gle, *adj., v.,* **-gled, -gling.** —*adj.* **1.** having or suggesting the form of a spread eagle. **2.** lying with arms and legs outstretched. **3.** boastful or bombastic, esp. in the display of patriotic pride in the U.S. —*v.t.* **4.** to stretch out in a spread-eagle position. —*v.i.* **5.** to perform the skating figure of a spread eagle.

spread•er (spred′ər), *n.* **1.** a person or thing that spreads. **2.** a small knife or spatula for spreading butter or the like. **3.** a machine for dispersing bulk material: *manure spreader.* **4.** a device for spacing or keeping apart two objects, as electric wires. **5.** a strut for spreading shrouds on a mast.

spread·sheet (spred′shēt′), *n.* **1.** an outsize ledger sheet used by accountants. **2.** such a sheet simulated electronically by specialized computer software, used esp. for financial planning.

spree (sprē), *n.* **1.** a period, spell, or bout of indulgence, as of a particular craving or whim: *an eating spree; a spending spree.* **2.** a binge; carousal. **3.** a period or outburst of activity.

sprig (sprig), *n.*, *v.*, **sprigged, sprig·ging.** —*n.* **1.** a small spray of a plant with its leaves, flowers, etc. **2.** an ornament having the form of such a spray. **3.** a shoot, twig, or small branch. **4.** a scion; heir. **5.** a youth. —*v.t.* **6.** to mark or decorate with a design of sprigs. **7.** to fasten with brads. **8.** to remove a sprig or sprigs from (a plant).

spright·ly (sprīt′lē), *adj.*, **-li·er, -li·est,** *adv.* —*adj.* **1.** animated; buoyant; lively. —*adv.* **2.** in a sprightly manner. —**spright′li·ness,** *n.*

spring (spring), *v.*, **sprang** or, often, **sprung, sprung, spring·ing,** *n.* —*v.i.* **1.** to rise, leap, or move suddenly and swiftly: *a tiger about to spring.* **2.** to be released suddenly from a constrained position: *The door sprang open.* **3.** to issue forth suddenly or forcefully: *Oil sprang from the well.* **4.** to come into being; arise: *Industries sprang up in the suburbs.* **5.** to have as one's birth or lineage: *to spring from seafaring folk.* **6.** to extend upward. **7.** to take an upward course or curve from a point of support, as an arch. **8.** to occur suddenly: *An objection sprang to mind.* **9.** to become bent or warped. —*v.t.* **10.** to cause to spring. **11.** to cause the sudden operation of: *to spring a trap.* **12.** to cause to work loose, warp, or split: *Moisture sprang the board from the fence.* **13.** to undergo the development of: *sprang a leak.* **14.** to bend by force. **15.** to produce by surprise: *to spring a joke.* **16.** to leap over. **17.** *Slang.* to secure the release of from confinement. **18. spring for,** *Informal.* to pay for; treat someone to. —*n.* **19.** an act of springing; a sudden leap or bound. **20.** an elastic quality: *a spring in his walk.* **21.** an issue of water from the ground. **22.** the place of such an issue: *mineral springs.* **23.** a source; fountainhead: *a spring of inspiration.* **24.** an elastic contrivance or body, as a strip or wire of steel coiled spirally, that recovers its shape after being compressed, bent, or stretched. **25.** the season between winter and summer, marked by the budding and growth of plants and the onset of warmer weather: in the Northern Hemisphere from the March equinox to the June solstice; in the Southern Hemisphere from the September equinox to the December solstice. **26.** the first stage and freshest period: *the spring of life.* **27.** Also called **springing. a.** the point at which an arch or dome rises from its support. **b.** the rise or the angle of the rise of an arch.

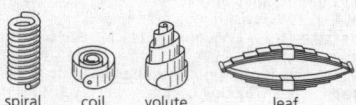

spiral   coil   volute   leaf

springs (def. 25)

spring·board (spring′bôrd′, -bōrd′), *n.* **1.** a flexible board anchored at one end and used in diving and gymnastics for gaining height and momentum. **2.** a starting point; point of departure, as for a discussion, argument, etc.

spring·bok (spring′bok′), *n., pl.* **-boks,** (*esp. collectively*) **-bok.** a gazelle, *Antidorcas marsupialis,* of S Africa, that leaps up high when alarmed.

spring′ chick′en, *n.* **1.** a young chicken, esp. a broiler or fryer. **2.** *Slang.* a young person.

spring′-clean′ing, *n.* a thorough cleaning of a place, done traditionally in the spring. —**spring′-clean′,** *v.t.*

spring′er span′iel, *n.* a dog of either of two breeds of medium-sized spaniels used for flushing and retrieving game. Compare ENGLISH SPRINGER SPANIEL, WELSH SPRINGER SPANIEL.

spring′ fe′ver, *n.* a listless, lazy, or restless feeling commonly associated with the beginning of spring.

Spring·field (spring′fēld′), *n.* **1.** a city in S Massachusetts, on the Connecticut River. 150,320. **2.** a city in SW Missouri. 149,164. **3.** the capital of Illinois, in the central part. 105,938.

spring′form pan′ (spring′fôrm′), *n.* a metal cake pan with sides that can be unfastened to release the cake when done.

spring·ing (spring′ing), *n.* **1.** the mechanical springs with which any of various devices are equipped. **2.** SPRING (def. 26).

spring′-load′ed, *adj.* (of a machine part) kept normally in a certain position by a spring.

spring′ roll′, *n.* an egg roll.

spring′ tide′, *n.* the large rise and fall of the tide at or soon after the new or the full moon.

spring·time (spring′tīm′), *n.* **1.** the season of spring. **2.** the first or earliest period. Also called **spring′tide** (-tīd′).

spring·wood (spring′wŏŏd′), *n.* the part of an annual ring of wood characterized by large, thin-walled cells formed during the first part of the growing season. Compare SUMMERWOOD.

spring·y (spring′ē), *adj.,* **spring·i·er, spring·i·est.** characterized by elasticity; resilient: *a springy step.* —**spring′i·ly,** *adv.*

sprin·kle (spring′kəl), *v.,* **-kled, -kling,** *n.* —*v.t.* **1.** to scatter in drops

or particles: *sprinkling water on the flowers.* **2.** to disperse or distribute here and there. **3.** to overspread with drops or particles of water, powder, or the like: *to sprinkle a lawn.* **4.** to diversify or intersperse with objects scattered here and there. —*v.i.* **5.** to scatter or disperse liquid, a powder, etc., in drops or particles. **6.** to rain slightly in scattered drops. —*n.* **7.** an act or instance of sprinkling. **8.** something used for sprinkling. **9.** Usu., **sprinkles.** small pieces of flavored candy used to decorate cakes, cookies, and ice cream. **10.** a light rain. **11.** a small quantity or number. —**sprin′kler,** *n.*

sprin′kler sys′tem, *n.* a system for automatically extinguishing fires in a building, consisting of overhead water pipes with outlet valves that open at a certain temperature.

sprin·kling (spring′kling), *n.* **1.** a small quantity or number scattered here and there. **2.** a small quantity sprinkled or to be sprinkled.

sprint (sprint), *v.i.* **1.** to race or move at full speed for a short distance, as in running or rowing. —*v.t.* **2.** to traverse in sprinting: *to sprint a half mile.* —*n.* **3.** a short race at full speed. **4.** a burst of speed, as during a race. —**sprint′er,** *n.*

sprite (sprīt), *n.* an elf, fairy, or goblin.

spritz (sprits, shprits), *v.t.* **1.** to spray briefly and quickly; squirt. —*n.* **2.** a brief spray; squirt.

spritz·er (sprit′sər, shprit′-), *n.* a drink made with wine and soda.

sprock·et (sprok′it), *n.* **1.** a toothed wheel engaging with a conveyor or power chain. **2.** a tooth on such a wheel.

sprout (sprout), *v.i.* **1.** to begin to grow; shoot forth. **2.** (of a seed or plant) to put forth buds or shoots. —*n.* **3.** a shoot of a plant. **4.** a new growth from a seed, rootstock, or the like. **5.** something suggesting a sprout, as a young person. **6. sprouts, a.** the young shoots of alfalfa, soybeans, etc., eaten, often raw, as a vegetable. **b.** BRUSSELS SPROUT.

spruce¹ (sprōōs), *n.* **1.** any evergreen, coniferous tree of the genus *Picea,* of the pine family, having short angular needle-shaped leaves attached singly around twigs. **2.** any of various allied trees, as the Douglas fir. **3.** the wood of any such tree.

spruce² (sprōōs), *adj.,* **spruc·er, spruc·est,** *v.,* **spruced, spruc·ing.** —*adj.* **1.** trim in dress or appearance; neat. —*v.t.* **2.** to make spruce (often fol. by *up*). —*v.i.* **3.** to make oneself spruce (usu. fol. by *up*).

spruce′ pine′, *n.* **1.** a tall pine tree, *Pinus glabra,* of the southeastern U.S., having furrowed gray bark and needles in bundles of two. **2.** any of several other pines, spruces, and hemlocks.

sprung (sprung), *v.* a pt. and pp. of SPRING.

spry (sprī), *adj.,* **spry·er** or **spri·er, spry·est** or **spri·est.** nimbly energetic; agile. —**spry′ly,** *adv.* —**spry′ness,** *n.*

spud (spud), *n., v.,* **spud·ded, spud·ding.** —*n.* **1.** *Informal.* a potato. **2.** a spadelike instrument, esp. one with a narrow blade, as for digging up or cutting the roots of weeds. **3.** a short pipe, as for connecting a water pipe with a meter. —*v.t.* **4.** to remove with a spud.

spume (spyōōm), *v.,* **spumed, spum·ing,** *n.* —*v.i.* **1.** to foam; froth. —*n.* **2.** foamy matter on a liquid; froth. —**spu′mous, spum′y,** *adj.*

spu·mo·ni or **spu·mo·ne** (spə mō′nē), *n.* variously flavored and colored ice cream containing candied fruit and nuts.

spun (spun), *v.* pt. and pp. of SPIN.

spun′ glass′, *n.* **1.** blown glass in which fine threads of glass form the surface texture. **2.** FIBERGLASS.

spunk (spungk), *n.* **1.** pluck; spirit; mettle. **2.** tinder; touchwood; punk.

spunk·y (spung′kē), *adj.,* **spunk·i·er, spunk·i·est.** plucky; spirited.

spun′ silk′, *n.* **1.** yarn produced by spinning silk waste and short broken filaments from which the sericin has been removed. **2.** a fabric woven from this yarn.

spun′ sug′ar, *n.* a fluffy confection made from threads of hot boiled sugar.

spun′ yarn′, *n.* **1.** yarn produced by spinning fibers into a continuous strand. **2.** cord formed of rope yarns loosely twisted together, for serving ropes, bending sails, etc.

spur (spûr), *n., v.,* **spurred, spur·ring.** —*n.* **1.** a U-shaped device fitted with a pointed projection, secured to the heel of a boot, and used by a rider to urge a horse forward. **2.** something that goads to action. **3.** a stiff, usu. sharp, horny process on the leg of various birds, esp. the domestic rooster. **4.** an abnormal bony growth. **5.** a gaff fastened to the leg of a gamecock. **6.** a ridge or line of elevation projecting from or subordinate to the main body of a mountain or mountain range. **7.** a short or stunted branch or shoot, as of a tree. **8.** a short shoot bearing flowers. **9.** *Archit.* a short wooden brace for strengthening a post or other part. —*v.t.* **10.** to prick with or as if with a spur or spurs; incite or urge on. **11.** to furnish with spurs or a spur. —*v.i.* **12.** to goad or urge one's horse with spurs. **13.** to proceed hurriedly; press forward. —*Idiom.* **14. win one's spurs,** to achieve distinction or success for the first time.

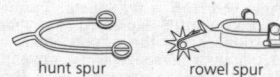

hunt spur   rowel spur

spurs (def. 1)

spurge (spûrj), *n.* any of numerous plants of the genus *Euphorbia,* having flowers with no petals or sepals.

Spur•geon (spûr′jən), *n.* **Charles Haddon,** 1834–92, English Baptist preacher.

spu•ri•ous (spyŏŏr′ē əs), *adj.* **1.** not genuine; not from the claimed or proper source; counterfeit. **2.** (of two or more parts, plants, etc.) having a similar appearance but a different structure. **3.** of illegitimate birth; bastard. —**spu′ri•ous•ly,** *adv.* —**spu′ri•ous•ness,** *n.*

spurn (spûrn), *v.t.* **1.** to reject with disdain; scorn. **2.** to kick or trample with the foot. —*n.* **3.** disdainful rejection. **4.** contemptuous treatment. **5.** a kick. —**spurn′er,** *n.*

spur′-of-the-mo′ment, *adj.* occurring or done without preparation or deliberation; impulsive: *a spur-of-the-moment decision.*

spurt (spûrt), *v.i.* **1.** to gush suddenly in a stream or jet. **2.** to show a sudden brief increase in activity. —*v.t.* **3.** to expel in a stream or jet; spout. —*n.* **4.** a sudden, forceful gush or jet. **5.** a marked increase of activity or effort for a short period or distance. —**spurt′er,** *n.*

sput•nik (spŏŏt′nik, sput′-), *n.* (*sometimes cap.*) any of a series of Soviet earth-orbiting satellites. [< Russian: satellite, traveling companion]

sput•ter (sput′ər), *v.i.* **1.** to make explosive popping or sizzling sounds. **2.** to emit particles, sparks, etc., explosively. **3.** to eject particles of saliva, food, etc., from the mouth, as when speaking angrily or excitedly. **4.** to utter words explosively or incoherently, as when angry or flustered. —*v.t.* **5.** to eject forcibly and in small particles, as if by spitting. **6.** to utter explosively and incoherently. —*n.* **7.** the act or sound of sputtering. **8.** explosive, incoherent utterance.

spu•tum (spyōō′təm), *n., pl.* **-ta** (-tə). matter, as saliva mixed with mucus or pus, expectorated from the lungs and respiratory passages.

spy (spī), *n., pl.* **spies,** *v.,* **spied, spy•ing.** —*n.* **1.** a person employed by a government to obtain secret information or intelligence about another, usu. hostile, country. **2.** a person who keeps close and secret watch on the actions and words of another or others. **3.** the act of spying. —*v.i.* **4.** to observe secretively, usu. with hostile intent (often fol. by *on* or *upon*). **5.** to act as a spy; engage in espionage. **6.** to search for or examine something closely or carefully. —*v.t.* **7.** to catch sight of; espy: *to spy a rare bird.* **8.** to discover by observation (often fol. by *out*). **9.** to observe secretively, usu. with hostile intent. **10.** to search or look for closely or carefully.

spy•glass (spī′glas′, -gläs′), *n.* a small telescope.

sq., **1.** sequence. **2.** the following one. **3.** squadron. **4.** square.

sqq., the following ones.

squab (skwob), *n., pl.* **squabs,** (*esp. collectively for 1*) **squab,** *adj.* —*n.* **1.** a nestling pigeon, marketed when fully grown but still unfledged. **2.** a short, stout person. —*adj.* **3.** short and broad. **4.** (of a bird) unfledged or newly hatched.

squab•ble (skwob′əl), *v.,* **-bled, -bling,** *n.* —*v.i.* **1.** to engage in a petty quarrel. —*n.* **2.** a petty quarrel. —**squab′bler,** *n.*

squad (skwod), *n., v.,* **squad•ded, squad•ding.** —*n.* **1.** the smallest military unit, consisting usu. of 10 privates, a staff sergeant, and a corporal. **2.** a group of police officers assigned esp. to a specific field: *the vice squad.* **3.** any small group of persons engaged in a common enterprise; team. —*v.t.* **4.** to form into squads. **5.** to assign to a squad.

squad′ car′, *n.* a police automobile equipped with a radiotelephone for communicating with police headquarters.

squad•ron (skwod′rən), *n.* **1.** a subdivision of a naval fleet usu. consisting of two or more divisions. **2.** an armored cavalry or cavalry unit consisting of two or more troops. **3.** (in the U.S. Air Force). **a.** the basic administrative and tactical unit, consisting of two or more flights. **b.** a flight formation.

squad′ room′, *n.* **1.** a room in a police station where police officers assemble. **2.** a room in a barracks in which soldiers are lodged.

squal•id (skwol′id, skwô′lid), *adj.* **1.** filthy and repulsive, as from neglect. **2.** degraded; sordid. —**squal′id•ly,** *adv.*

squall[1] (skwôl), *n.* **1.** a sudden, violent wind, often accompanied by rain, snow, or sleet. **2.** a sudden disturbance or commotion. —*v.i.* **3.** to blow as a squall.

squall[2] (skwôl), *v.i.* **1.** to cry or scream loudly and violently. —*v.t.* **2.** to utter in a screaming tone. —*n.* **3.** the act or sound of squalling. —**squall′er,** *n.*

squal•or (skwol′ər, skwô′lər), *n.* the condition of being squalid; filth and misery.

squan•der (skwon′dər), *v.t.* **1.** to spend or use extravagantly or wastefully. **2.** to scatter. —*n.* **3.** extravagant or wasteful expenditure. —**squan′der•er,** *n.*

Squan•to (skwon′tō), *n.* died 1622, North American Indian of the Narragansett tribe: interpreter for the Pilgrims. Also called **Tisquantum.**

square (skwâr), *n., v.,* **squared, squar•ing,** *adj.,* **squar•er, squar•est,** *adv.* —*n.* **1.** a rectangle having all four sides of equal length. **2.** something having or resembling this form, as a city block. **3.** an open area formed by the intersecting of two or more streets. **4.** a rectangularly shaped area on a game board. **5.** a try square, T square, or the like. **6. a.** the second power of a quantity, expressed as $a^2 = a \times a$, where a is the quantity. **b.** a quantity that is the second power of another: *Four is the square of two.* **7.** *Slang.* a person who is conventional or conservative. **8.** Usu., **squares.** *Informal.* a square meal: *three squares a day.* —*v.t.* **9.** to reduce to square, rectangular, or cubical form (often fol. by *off*). **10.** to mark out in one or more squares or rectangles. **11.** to test with measuring devices for deviation from a right angle, straight line, or plane surface. **12. a.** to multiply (a number or quantity) by itself; raise to the second power. **b.** to describe or find a square that is equivalent in area to: *to square a circle.* **13.** to set at right angles. **14.** to set (the shoulders and back) in an erect posture. **15.** to make straight, level, or even: *Square the cloth on the table.* **16.** to regulate, as by a standard. **17.** to adjust harmoniously or satisfactorily: *Can you square such actions with your conscience?* **18.** to balance; pay off; settle: *to square a debt.* —*v.i.* **19.** to accord; agree: *That theory does not square with the facts.* **20. square away, a.** to make preparations; get ready. **b.** to assume a fighting stance. **c.** to put in order. **21. square off,** to assume a fighting stance. **22. square up,** to settle an account. —*adj.* **23.** forming a right angle: *a square corner.* **24.** having four sides and four right angles or three pairs of parallel sides meeting at right angles: *a square box.* **25.** having the form of a square and designated by a unit of linear measurement forming a side of the square: *one square foot.* **26.** equal to a square of a specified length on a side: *five miles square.* **27.** having a solid, sturdy form. **28.** straight, level, or even, as a surface. **29.** having all accounts settled. **30.** fair; honest. **31.** straightforward; unequivocal. **32.** *Slang.* conventional or conservative in style or outlook. —*adv.* **33.** in square or rectangular form. **34.** at right angles. **35.** straightforwardly; fairly; honestly. —***Idiom.*** **36. on the square, a.** at right angles. **b.** *Informal.* straightforward; honest. **37. out of square, a.** not at right angles. **b.** not in agreement. —***Proverb.*** **38. You can't fit a square peg into a round hole,** a person should not be expected to do a task for which he or she is not suited. —**square′ness,** *n.*

square′ brack′et, *n.* BRACKET (def. 4).

square′ dance′, *n.* a dance by a set of four couples arranged in a square. —**square′ danc′er,** *n.* —**square′ danc′ing,** *n.*

square′-dance′, *v.i.,* **-danced, -danc•ing.** to perform or participate in a square dance.

square′ deal′, *n.* a fair and honest arrangement or transaction.

Square′ Deal′, *n.* the stated policy of President Theodore Roosevelt, originally promising fairness in all dealings with labor and management and later extended to include other groups.

square′ knot′, *n.* a knot in which the ends come out alongside the standing parts.

square•ly (skwâr′lē), *adv.* **1.** in a square shape, form, or manner. **2.** in an honest, straightforward manner: *faced problems squarely.* **3.** without equivocation. **4.** firmly; solidly: *feet squarely on the ground.*

square′ ma′trix, *n.* a mathematical matrix in which the number of rows is equal to the number of columns.

square′ meal′, *n.* a nourishing or filling meal.

square′ meas′ure, *n.* a system of units for the measurement of surfaces or areas.

square′ one′, *n.* the starting point; initial stage or step.

square′-rigged′, *adj.* having square sails as the principal sails. —**square′-rig′ger,** *n.*

square′ root′, *n.* a quantity of which a given quantity is the square: *The quantities +6 and −6 are square roots of 36 since* $(+6)\times(+6)=36$ *and* $(-6)\times(-6)=36$.

square′ sail′, *n.* a sail bent to a horizontal yard set from one side of a ship to another.

square′ shoot′er, *n.* an honest, fair person. —**square′ shoot′ing,** *n.*

square′-shoul′dered, *adj.* having the shoulders held back, giving a straight form to the upper part of the back.

square•toed (skwâr′tōd′), *adj.* **1.** having a square toe, as a shoe. **2.** old-fashioned; conservative. —**square′-toed′ness,** *n.*

squash[1] (skwosh, skwôsh), *v.t.* **1.** to press into a flat mass or pulp; crush. **2.** to suppress; quash. **3.** to press forcibly into a small space; cram. —*v.i.* **4.** to become pressed into a flat mass or pulp. **5.** to make a splashing sound; splash. **6.** to squeeze or crowd; crush. —*n.* **7.** an act or instance of squashing or being squashed. **8.** the sound of squashing. **9.** a squashed mass. **10.** Also called **squash′ rac′quets.** a game for two or four persons, similar to racquets but played on a smaller court and with a racket having a round head and a long handle. **11.** *Brit.* a beverage made from fruit juice and soda water: *lemon squash.*

squash[2] (skwosh, skwôsh), *n., pl.* **squash•es,** (*esp. collectively*) **squash. 1.** the fruit of any of various vinelike, tendril-bearing plants belonging to the genus *Curcurbita,* of the gourd family, as *C. moschata* or *C. pepo:* used as a vegetable. **2.** any of these plants.

squash•y (skwosh′ē, skwô′shē), *adj.,* **squash•i•er, squash•i•est. 1.** easily squashed; pulpy: *squashy fruit.* **2.** soft and wet: *squashy ground.* **3.** having a squashed appearance. —**squash′i•ly,** *adv.* —**squash′i•ness,** *n.*

squat (skwot), *v.,* **squat•ted, squat•ting,** *adj.,* **squat•ter, squat•test,** *n.* —*v.i.* **1.** to sit in a low or crouching position with the legs drawn up closely beneath or in front of the body. **2.** to crouch, as an animal. **3.** to occupy property or settle land as a squatter. —*v.t.* **4.** to cause to squat. **5.** to occupy or settle as a squatter. —*adj.* **6.** disproportionately short and thickset. **7.** assuming a squatting position; crouching. —*n.* **8.** the act of squatting. **9.** a squatting position or posture. **10.** a place occupied by squatters. —**squat′ly,** *adv.* —**squat′ness,** *n.*

squat•ter (skwot′ər), *n.* **1.** a person or thing that squats. **2.** a person who occupies property without permission, lease, or payment of rent. **3.** a person who settles on land under government regulation, in order to acquire title. —**squat′ter•dom,** *n.*

squat•ty (skwot′ē), *adj.*, **-ti•er, -ti•est. 1.** squat; dumpy. **2.** low to the ground. —**squat′ti•ly,** *adv.* —**squat′ti•ness,** *n.*
squawk (skwôk), *v.i.* **1.** to utter a loud, harsh cry, as a duck or other fowl when frightened. **2.** to complain loudly and vehemently. —*v.t.* **3.** to utter or give forth with a squawk. —*n.* **4.** a loud, harsh cry or sound. **5.** a loud, vehement complaint. —**squawk′er,** *n.*
squawk′ box′, *n. Informal.* the speaker of an intercom or public-address system.
squeak (skwēk), *n.* **1.** a sharp, shrill or high-pitched, usu. short cry or sound. **2.** an escape from danger, defeat, death, etc. (usu. prec. by *narrow* or *close*). —*v.i.* **3.** to utter or emit a squeak or squeaky sound. **4.** *Slang.* to confess or turn informer; squeal. —*v.t.* **5.** to utter or sound with a squeak. **6. squeak by** or **through,** to succeed, survive, win, etc., by a very narrow margin. —**squeak′ing•ly,** *adv.*
squeak•er (skwē′kər), *n.* **1.** a person or thing that squeaks. **2.** a contest or game won by a very small margin. **3.** a dangerous situation. **4.** a young bird, esp. a pigeon.
squeak•y (skwē′kē), *adj.*, **squeak•i•er, squeak•i•est.** squeaking; tending to squeak: *squeaky shoes.* —**squeak′i•ly,** *adv.* —**squeak′i•ness,** *n.*
squeak′y-clean′, *adj.* **1.** scrupulously clean. **2.** virtuous; wholesome; above reproach.
squeal (skwēl), *n.* **1.** a somewhat prolonged, sharp, shrill cry, as of pain, fear, or surprise. **2.** *Slang.* an instance of informing against someone. —*v.i.* **3.** to utter or emit a squeal or squealing sound. **4.** *Slang.* **a.** to turn informer; inform. **b.** to protest or complain. —*v.t.* **5.** to utter or produce with a squeal. —**squeal′er,** *n.*
squeam•ish (skwē′mish), *adj.* **1.** easily nauseated or disgusted. **2.** fastidious or dainty. **3.** easily shocked; prudish. **4.** excessively particular or scrupulous as to the moral aspect of things. —**squeam′ish•ly,** *adv.* —**squeam′ish•ness,** *n.*
squee•gee (skwē′jē, skwē jē′), *n.*, *v.*, **-geed, -gee•ing.** —*n.* **1.** an implement edged with rubber or the like, for removing water from windows after washing, sweeping water from wet decks, etc. **2.** a similar, smaller device, as for removing excess developer from photographic prints or for forcing paint, ink, etc., through a screen in serigraphy. —*v.t.* **3.** to sweep, scrape, or press with or as if with a squeegee.
squeeze (skwēz), *v.*, **squeezed, squeez•ing,** *n.* —*v.t.* **1.** to press forcibly together; compress. **2.** to apply pressure to in order to extract juice, sap, or the like: *to squeeze an orange.* **3.** to force out, extract, or procure by pressure. **4.** to force or thrust by pressure. **5.** to fit into a small or crowded space or time span. **6.** to press (another's hand or arm) within one's hand as a friendly or sympathetic gesture. **7.** to hug. **8.** to obtain by financial or emotional pressure, force, etc.; extort. **9.** to threaten, intimidate, or harass in order to obtain money, advantages, etc. **10.** to cause financial hardship to: *manufacturers squeezed by high tariffs.* **11. a.** *Baseball.* to enable (a runner on third base) to score on a squeeze play. **b.** to score (a run) in this way. **12.** to force (an opponent) to discard a potentially winning card in a hand of bridge. —*v.i.* **13.** to exert pressure or a compressing force. **14.** to force a way, as into some narrow or crowded place (usu. fol. by *through, in,* etc.). **15.** to merge or come together. —*n.* **16.** an act or instance of squeezing. **17.** the fact or state of being squeezed or crowded. **18.** a handclasp. **19.** a hug or close embrace. **20.** a troubled financial condition, esp. caused by a shortage or restriction, as of credit or funds. **21.** a small quantity of something obtained by squeezing. **22.** pressure or intimidation brought to bear to extort money or advantages, force compliance, etc.: *racketeers putting the squeeze on small businesses.* **23.** money or a favor obtained in such a way. **24.** SQUEEZE PLAY. **25.** a play or circumstance in bridge in which a player is forced to discard a potentially winning card. **26.** *Slang.* a sweetheart: *my main squeeze.* —**squeez′a•ble,** *adj.* —**squeez′a•bil′i•ty,** *n.* —**squeez′a•bly,** *adv.* —**squeez′er,** *n.*
squeeze′ bot′tle, *n.* a flexible plastic bottle the contents of which can be forced out by squeezing.
squeeze′ play′, *n.* **1.** a baseball play in which the batter bunts in an attempt to score a runner from third base, with the runner starting for home as the ball is pitched. **2.** the application of pressure in order to force compliance or gain an advantage.
squelch (skwelch), *v.t.* **1.** to strike or press with crushing force; squash. **2.** to put down or silence, as with a crushing retort. —*v.i.* **3.** to make a splashing sound. **4.** to tread heavily in water, mud, etc., with such a sound. —*n.* **5.** an act of squelching or suppressing. **6.** something that squelches, as a crushing retort. **7.** a splashing sound. **8.** a squelched or crushed mass of anything. —**squelch′er,** *n.*
squib (skwib), *n.*, *v.*, **squibbed, squib•bing.** —*n.* **1.** a short, witty or sarcastic saying or writing. **2.** a short news story, often used as a filler. **3.** a small firework, consisting of a tube or ball filled with powder, that burns with a hissing noise terminated usu. by a slight explosion. **4.** a firecracker broken in the middle so that it burns with a hissing noise but does not explode. —*v.i.* **5.** to write squibs. **6.** to shoot off or fire a squib. **7.** to explode with a small, sharp sound. **8.** to move swiftly and irregularly. —*v.t.* **9.** to assail in squibs or lampoons. **10.** to toss, shoot, or utilize as a squib. —**squib′bish,** *adj.*
squid (skwid), *n.*, *pl.* (*esp. collectively*) **squid,** (*esp. for kinds or species*) **squids.** any of several ten-armed cephalopods, as of the genera *Loligo* and *Ommastrephes,* having a slender body and a pair of rounded or triangular caudal fins and varying in length from 4–6 in. (10–15 cm) to 60–80 ft. (18–24 m).

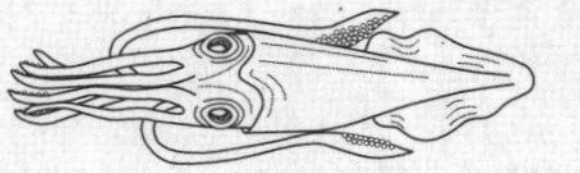

squid, *Loligo pealeii,* length 8 in. (20 cm); mantle 5 in. (13 cm)

squig•gle (skwig′əl), *n.*, *v.*, **-gled, -gling.** —*n.* **1.** a short, irregular curve or twist, as in writing or drawing. —*v.i.* **2.** to move in or appear as squiggles. —*v.t.* **3.** to form in or cause to appear as squiggles; scribble. —**squig′gly,** *adj.*
squill (skwil), *n.* **1.** the bulb of the sea onion, *Urginea maritima,* of the lily family, cut into thin slices and dried: used esp. as an expectorant. **2.** the plant itself. **3.** any related plant of the genus *Scilla.* —**squill′-like′,** *adj.*
squinch[1] (skwinch), *n.* a small arch, corbeling, etc., built across the interior angle between two walls, as in a square tower for supporting a superimposed octagonal spire.
squinch[2] (skwinch), *v.t.* **1.** to contort (the features) or squint. **2.** to squeeze together or contract. —*v.i.* **3.** to squeeze together or crouch down, as to fit into a smaller space.
squint (skwint), *v.i.* **1.** to look with the eyes partly closed. **2.** to be affected with strabismus; be cross-eyed. **3.** to look or glance obliquely or sidewise; look askance. **4.** to make or have an indirect reference or bearing (usu. fol. by *toward, at,* etc.). —*v.t.* **5.** to cause to squint. —*n.* **6.** an act or instance of squinting. **7.** a condition of the eye consisting in noncoincidence of the optic axes; strabismus. **8.** a quick glance. **9.** an indirect reference, inclination, or tendency. **10.** (in a church) a small opening in a wall giving a view of the altar. —*adj.* **11.** looking obliquely or with a side glance; looking askance. **12.** (of the eyes) affected with strabismus. —**squint′er,** *n.* —**squint′ing•ly,** *adv.* —**squint′y,** *adj.*, **squint•i•er, squint•i•est.**
squire (skwīᵊr), *n.*, *v.*, **squired, squir•ing.** —*n.* **1.** (in England) a country gentleman, esp. the chief landed proprietor in a district. **2.** a young man of noble birth who, as an aspirant to knighthood, served a knight. **3.** a personal attendant, as of a person of rank. **4.** a man who accompanies or escorts a woman. **5.** a title applied to a justice of the peace, local judge, or other local dignitary of a rural district or small town. —*v.t.* **6.** to attend or escort as, or in the manner of, a squire.
Squire′ of Hyde′ Park′, *n.* epithet for Franklin D. Roosevelt.
squirm (skwûrm), *v.i.* **1.** to wriggle or writhe. **2.** to feel or display discomfort or distress, as from embarrassment or pain. —*n.* **3.** the act of squirming; a squirming or wriggling movement. —**squirm′er,** *n.* —**squirm′ing•ly,** *adv.* —**squirm′y,** *adj.*, **squirm•i•er, squirm•i•est.**
squir•rel (skwûr′əl, skwur′-; *esp. Brit.* skwir′əl), *n.*, *pl.* **-rels,** (*esp. collectively*) **-rel,** *v.*, **-reled, -rel•ing** or (*esp. Brit.*) **-relled, -rel•ling.** —*n.* **1.** any arboreal, bushy-tailed rodent of the family Sciuridae, esp. of the genus *Sciurus.* **2.** any other member of the family Sciuridae, including ground squirrels, prairie dogs, and woodchucks. **3.** the meat of such an animal. **4.** the pelt or fur of such an animal. —*v.t.* **5.** to store or hide (money, valuables, etc.) for the future, as squirrels store nuts and seeds for winter (often fol. by *away*); hoard.
squir′rel cage′, *n.* **1.** a cage containing a cylindrical framework that is rotated by a squirrel or other small animal running inside of it. **2.** any situation that seems to continue endlessly without a goal.
squir•rel•ly or **squir•rel•y** (skwûr′ə lē, skwur′-; *esp. Brit.* skwir′-), *adj. Slang.* eccentric; flighty.
squir′rel mon′key, *n.* either of two small, long-tailed monkeys, *Saimiri oerstedii* of Central America and *S. sciureus* of South America, having a small white face with a black muzzle.
squirt (skwûrt), *v.i.* **1.** to eject liquid in a jet or spurt, as from a narrow orifice. —*v.t.* **2.** to cause (liquid or a viscous substance) to spurt or issue in a jet, as from a narrow orifice. **3.** to wet or spatter with a liquid or viscous substance so ejected. —*n.* **4.** the act of squirting. **5.** a small spurt or jetlike stream of liquid or viscous substance. **6.** *Informal.* **a.** a youngster, esp. a meddlesome or impudent one. **b.** a short person. **c.** an insignificant, self-assertive person, esp. one who is small or young. **7.** an instrument for squirting, as a syringe. —**squirt′er,** *n.*
squirt′ gun′, *n.* **1.** SPRAY GUN. **2.** WATER PISTOL.
squish (skwish), *v.t.* **1.** to squeeze or squash. —*v.i.* **2.** (of water, soft mud, etc.) to make a gushing or splashing sound when walked in or on. —*n.* **3.** a squishing sound.
squish•y (skwish′ē), *adj.*, **squish•i•er, squish•i•est. 1.** soft and moist. **2.** softly gurgling or splashing: *a squishy sound.* **3.** emotional or sentimental. —**squish′i•ness,** *n.*
sq. yd., square yard.
Sr, *Chem. Symbol.* strontium.
Sr., 1. Senhor. **2.** Senior. **3.** Señor. **4.** Sir. **5.** Sister.
Sri Lan•ka (srē′ läng′kə, lang′kə, shrē′), *n.* an island republic in the Indian Ocean, S of India: a member of the Commonwealth of Nations. 18,762,075; 25,332 sq. mi. (65,610 sq. km). *Cap.:* Colombo. Formerly, **Ceylon.** —**Sri′ Lan′kan,** *adj.*, *n.*
SRO, 1. single-room occupancy. **2.** standing room only.
ss or **ss.,** (in prescriptions) a half.
ss., 1. to wit; namely (used esp. on legal documents to verify the place of action). **2.** sections. **3.** shortstop.
SSA, Social Security Administration.
SSAE, stamped self-addressed envelope.

SSC, superconducting supercollider.
SSE, south-southeast.
SST, supersonic transport.
SSW, south-southwest.
-st, var. of -EST[2]: *dost; hadst; wouldst.*
St., **1.** Saint. **2.** statute. **3.** Strait. **4.** Street.
s.t., short ton.
stab (stab), *v.,* **stabbed, stab•bing,** *n.* —*v.t.* **1.** to pierce or wound with or as if with a pointed weapon. **2.** to thrust or plunge (a knife, pointed weapon, etc.) into something. **3.** to make a jabbing or thrusting motion at or in. —*v.i.* **4.** to thrust with or as if with a knife or other pointed weapon. **5.** to deliver a wound, as with a pointed weapon. —*n.* **6.** the act of stabbing. **7.** a thrust or blow with or as if with a pointed weapon. **8.** an attempt; try: *to make a stab at an answer.* **9.** a wound made by stabbing. **10.** a sudden, brief, and usu. painful sensation: *a stab of pain; a stab of pity.* —***Idiom.*** **11. stab in the back, a.** to betray (someone trusting). **b.** an act of betraying; treachery. —**stab′ber,** *n.*
Sta•bat Ma•ter (stä′bät mä′ter, stā′bat mā′tər), *n.* **1.** a Latin hymn, composed in the 13th century, commemorating the sorrows of the Virgin Mary at the Cross. **2.** a musical setting for this. [lit., (His) mother was standing, the first words of the hymn]
stab•bing (stab′ing), *adj.* **1.** penetrating; piercing: *a stabbing pain.* **2.** emotionally wounding. —**stab′bing•ly,** *adv.*
sta•bile (*adj.* stā′bil, -bəl; *n.* stā′bēl), *adj.* **1.** fixed in position; stable. **2.** resistant to physical or chemical change. —*n.* **3.** an abstract sculpture consisting of immobile units constructed of sheet metal, wire, etc., attached to fixed supports. Compare MOBILE (def. 8).
sta•bil•i•ty (stə bil′i tē), *n., pl.* **-ties. 1.** the state or quality of being stable. **2.** firmness in position. **3.** continuance without change; permanence. **4.** resistance to chemical change or disintegration. **5.** resistance to change, esp. sudden change or deterioration. **6.** constancy, as of character or purpose; steadiness: *emotional stability.* **7.** the ability of an aircraft to return to its original flying position when abruptly displaced. **8.** a vow, taken by a Benedictine, to stay in one monastery.
sta•bi•lize (stā′bə līz′), *v.,* **-lized, -liz•ing.** —*v.t.* **1.** to make or hold stable, firm, or steadfast. **2.** to maintain at a given or unfluctuating level or quantity: *to stabilize rents.* —*v.i.* **3.** to become stabilized. —**sta′bi•li•za′tion,** *n.*
sta•bi•liz•er (stā′bə lī′zər), *n.* **1.** a person or thing that stabilizes. **2.** a device for keeping an aircraft in stable equilibrium, as a horizontal tail surface. **3.** a device designed to counteract the roll of a vessel at sea by means of retractable fins. **4.** any of various substances added to foods, chemical compounds, etc., to prevent deterioration, the breaking down of an emulsion, or the loss of desirable properties. **5.** a comparatively large shock absorber for motor vehicles. **6. a.** a device or system for keeping a gun automatically trained on its target, as on a moving ship or aircraft. **b.** a mechanical or electronic device for keeping a rocket, shell, etc., aligned with its target. **7.** a device or system for keeping a submarine or a torpedo at the proper depth or in the proper position.
sta•ble¹ (stā′bəl), *n., v.,* **-bled, -bling.** —*n.* **1.** a building, usu. with stalls, for the lodging and feeding of horses, cattle, etc. **2.** a collection of animals housed in such a building. **3. a.** an establishment where racehorses are kept and trained. **b.** the horses belonging to, or the persons connected with, such an establishment. **4. a.** a number of people, as athletes, writers, or performers, who are employed, trained, or represented by the same company, agency, manager, etc. **b.** the establishment that trains or manages such a group. **c.** a collection of items produced by or belonging to an establishment, industry, etc. —*v.t.* **5.** to put or lodge in or as if in a stable. —*v.i.* **6.** to live in or as if in a stable.
sta•ble² (stā′bəl), *adj.,* **-bler, -blest. 1.** not likely to fall, give way, or overturn; firm; steady. **2.** able or likely to continue or last; firmly established; enduring or permanent: *a stable government.* **3.** resistant to sudden change or deterioration: *a stable currency.* **4.** not wavering or changeable in character or purpose; dependable; steadfast. **5.** not subject to emotional instability or illness; sane; mentally sound. **6.** having the ability to react to a disturbing force by maintaining or reestablishing position, form, etc. **7.** not readily decomposing, as a chemical compound; resisting chemical, molecular, or nuclear change. **8.** (of a patient's condition) exhibiting no significant change. —**sta′bly,** *adv.*
sta•ble•boy (stā′bəl boi′), *n.* a person who works in a stable.
sta•ble•man (stā′bəl mən, -man′), *n., pl.* **-men** (-mən, -men′). a person who works in a stable.
sta•ble•mate (stā′bəl māt′), *n.* **1.** a horse sharing a stable with another. **2.** one of several horses owned by the same person. **3.** a person belonging to the same establishment, field, etc., as another.
stac•ca•to (stə kä′tō), *adj., adv., n., pl.* **-tos, -ti** (-tē). —*adj.* **1. a.** shortened and detached when played or sung: *staccato notes.* **b.** characterized by performance in which the notes are abruptly disconnected: *a staccato style of playing.* Compare LEGATO. **2.** composed of or characterized by abruptly disconnected elements; disjointed: *rapid-fire, staccato speech.* —*adv.* **3.** in a staccato manner. —*n.* **4.** something done or performed in a staccato manner.
stacca′to mark′, *n.* a dot, wedge, or vertical stroke over or under a musical note to indicate that it should be played staccato.
stack (stak), *n.* **1.** a more or less orderly pile or heap. **2.** a large, usu. conical, circular, or rectangular pile of hay, straw, or the like. **3.** Often, **stacks.** a set of shelves for books ranged compactly one above the other, as in a library. **4. stacks,** the part of a library in which books and other holdings are stored. **5.** a number of chimneys or flues grouped together. **6.** SMOKESTACK. **7.** a great quantity or number. **8.** a radio antenna consisting of a number of components connected in a substantially vertical series. **9.** a linear list, as in a computer, arranged so that the last item stored is the first item retrieved. **10.** a conical, free-standing group of three rifles placed on their butts and hooked together. **11.** a group of airplanes circling over an airport awaiting their turns to land. **12.** an English measure for coal and wood, equal to 108 cubic feet (3 cu. m). **13. a.** a given quantity of chips that can be bought at one time, as in poker. **b.** the quantity of chips held by a player at a given point. —*v.t.* **14.** to pile, arrange, or place in a stack. **15.** to cover or load with something in stacks or piles. **16.** to arrange or select unfairly in order to force a desired result: *to stack a jury.* **17.** to keep (incoming airplanes) flying in circles over an airport where conditions prevent immediate landings. —*v.i.* **18.** to be arranged in or form a stack. **19. stack up, a.** to control the flight patterns of airplanes waiting to land at an airport so that each circles at a designated altitude. **b.** to compare; measure up (often fol. by *against*). **c.** to add up. —***Idiom.*** **20. stack the deck, a.** to arrange cards or a pack of cards so as to cheat. **b.** to manipulate events, information, etc., esp. unethically, in order to achieve a desired result. —**stack′er,** *n.* —**stack′less,** *adj.*
stack•a•ble (stak′ə bəl), *adj.* capable of being stacked, esp. easily. —**stack′a•bil′i•ty,** *n.*
stac•te (stak′tē), *n.* one of the sweet spices used in the holy incense of the ancient Hebrews. Ex. 30:34.
stad•hold•er also **stadt•hold•er** (stad′hōl′dər, stat′-) *n.* **1.** the chief magistrate of the former republic of the United Provinces of the Netherlands. **2.** (formerly, in the Netherlands) the viceroy or governor of a province. [partial trans. of Dutch *stadhouder* = *stad* place + *houder* holder]
sta•di•um (stā′dē əm), *n., pl.* **-di•ums, -di•a** (-dē ə). **1.** a sports arena, usu. oval or horseshoe-shaped, with tiers of seats for spectators. **2.** (in ancient Greece and Rome) a track for foot races. **3.** a stage in a process or in the life of an organism, as that between molts. [< Latin < Greek *stádion* running track]
staff¹ (staf, stäf), *n., pl.* **staffs** for 1–3, 7; **staves** (stāvz) or **staffs** for 4–6, 8; *adj., v.* —*n.* **1.** a group of people, esp. employees, who carry out the work of an establishment or perform a specific function. **2.** a group of assistants to a manager, superintendent, or executive. **3. a.** a body of military officers appointed to assist a commanding officer. **b.** the parts of an army concerned with administration rather than combat. **4.** a stick, pole, or rod for aid in walking or climbing, for use as a weapon, etc. **5.** a rod serving as a symbol of office or authority. **6.** a pole on which a flag is hung or displayed. **7.** something that supports or sustains. **8.** Also, **stave.** a set of usu. five horizontal lines, with the corresponding four spaces between them, on which music is written. —*adj.* **9.** of or pertaining to a military or organizational staff. **10.** employed on the staff of a corporation, publication, institution, etc.: *a staff writer.* —*v.t.* **11.** to provide with a staff of assistants or workers. **12.** to serve on the staff of. **13.** to send to a staff for study or further work (often fol. by *out*). —**staff′less,** *adj.* —**Usage.** See COLLECTIVE NOUN.
staff² (staf, stäf), *n.* a composition of plaster and fibrous material used for a temporary finish and in ornamental work.
staff•er (staf′ər, stä′fər), *n.* a member of a staff of employees, as at a newspaper.
staff′ of′ficer, *n.* a commissioned officer who is a member of a military staff.
staff′ of life′, *n.* bread, considered as the mainstay of the human diet.
Staf′fordshire bull′ ter′rier, *n.* one of an English breed of stocky, muscular dogs with a broad head and chest, wide-set forelegs, and a smooth coat, orig. raised for bullbaiting and dogfighting.
Staf′fordshire ter′rier, *n.* AMERICAN STAFFORDSHIRE TERRIER.
staff′ ser′geant, *n.* **1.** a noncommissioned officer in the U.S. Army ranking above a sergeant and below a sergeant first class. **2.** a noncommissioned officer in the U.S. Marine Corps ranking above a sergeant and below a gunnery sergeant. **3.** a noncommissioned officer in the U.S. Air Force ranking above a sergeant and below a technical sergeant.
stag (stag), *n., adj., adv., v.,* **stagged, stag•ging.** —*n.* **1.** an adult male deer. **2.** the male of various other animals. **3.** a man who attends a social gathering unaccompanied by a woman. **4.** STAG PARTY. **5.** a swine or bull castrated after maturation of the sex organs. —*adj.* **6.** of or for men only: *a stag dinner.* **7.** intended for male audiences and usu. pornographic in content: *a stag show.* —*adv.* **8.** without a companion or date: *to go stag.* —*v.i.* **9.** (of a man) to attend a social function without a female companion. —**stag′like′,** *adj.*
stage (stāj), *n., v.,* **staged, stag•ing.** —*n.* **1.** a phase, degree, or step in a process, development, or series. **2.** a raised platform, as for speakers or performers. **3. a.** the platform on which the actors perform in a theater. **b.** this platform with all the parts of the theater and all the apparatus back of the proscenium. **4. the stage,** the theater, esp. acting, as a profession. **5.** SOUND STAGE. **6.** the scene of any action. **7.** a stagecoach. **8.** a place of rest on a journey, esp. a regular stopping place of a stagecoach. **9.** the distance between two places of rest on a journey. **10.** a portion or period of a course of action or of life: *the pupal stage of an insect.* **11.** a division of stratified rocks corresponding to a single geologic age. **12.** the small platform of a microscope on which the object to be examined is placed. **13.** an element or functional unit of an elec-

tronic system, as a circuit containing a section of one of the tubes or transistors or an amplifier. **14.** a section of a rocket containing one or more engines, usu. designed to separate after burnout. —*v.t.* **15.** to represent, produce, or exhibit on or as if on a stage: *to stage a play.* **16.** to furnish with a stage, stage set, etc. **17.** to set (a play) in a specified locale or time. **18.** to plan, organize, or carry out, esp. for public or dramatic effect: *Workers staged a one-day strike.* **19.** to classify the natural progression of (a disease, esp. cancer). —*Idiom.* **20. by easy stages,** gradually; unhurriedly. **21. go on the stage,** to become an actor, esp. in the theater. **22. hold the stage,** to be the center of attention. **23. on stage,** performing, esp. as an actor. —**stage′a·ble,** *adj.*

stage·coach (stāj′kōch′), *n.* a horse-drawn coach that formerly traveled regularly over a fixed route with passengers, parcels, etc.

stage′ direc′tion, *n.* **1.** an instruction in the script of a play indicating performers' movements, production requirements, etc. **2.** the art or technique of a stage director.

stage′ direc′tor, *n.* **1.** a person who directs a theatrical production. **2.** (formerly) a stage manager.

stage′ door′, *n.* a door at the back or side of a theater, used by performers and theater personnel.

stage′ fright′, *n.* nervousness felt by a performer or speaker when appearing before an audience.

stage·hand (stāj′hand′), *n.* a person who moves properties, regulates lighting, etc., in a theatrical production.

stage′ left′, *n.* the part of the stage that is left of center as one faces the audience.

stage′ man′ager, *n.* a person responsible for the technical details of a theatrical production, for assisting the director at rehearsals, and for supervising the show during performance. *Abbr.:* SM

stage′ right′, *n.* the part of the stage that is right of center as one faces the audience.

stage′-struck′ or **stage′-struck′,** *adj.* **1.** obsessed with the desire to become an actor or actress. **2.** enthralled by the theater and the people, customs, traditions, etc., associated with it.

stag·fla·tion (stag flā′shən), *n.* an inflationary period accompanied by rising unemployment and lack of increase in business activity.

stag·ger (stag′ər), *v.i.* **1.** to walk, move, or stand unsteadily. **2.** to falter or begin to give way, as in an argument. **3.** to waver or hesitate, as in purpose or resolve. —*v.t.* **4.** to cause to reel, totter, or become unsteady. **5.** to astonish or shock: *a fact that staggers the mind.* **6.** to cause to waver or falter. **7.** to arrange in an alternating pattern: *to stagger lunch hours.* —*n.* **8.** the act of staggering; a reeling or tottering movement. **9.** a staggered order or arrangement. **10. staggers,** (*used with a sing. v.*) any of several severe diseases of livestock characterized by a staggering gait. —**stag′ger·er,** *n.*

stag·ger·ing (stag′ə ring), *adj.* tending to stagger or overwhelm: *a staggering amount of money.* —**stag′ger·ing·ly,** *adv.*

stag·ing (stā′jing), *n.* **1.** the act, process, or manner of presenting a play on the stage. **2.** a temporary platform or other structure used in building; scaffolding. **3.** the advancement of troops and supplies in a series of stages.

stag′ing ar′ea, *n.* **1.** an area, as a port of embarkation, where troops are assembled and readied for transit. **2.** any place serving as a point of assembly or preparation.

stag·nant (stag′nənt), *adj.* **1.** not flowing or running, as water or air. **2.** stale or foul from standing, as a pool of water. **3.** inactive or sluggish: *a stagnant economy.* —**stag′nan·cy,** *n.* —**stag′nant·ly,** *adv.*

stag·nate (stag′nāt), *v.i.,* **-nat·ed, -nat·ing. 1.** to cease to run or flow, as water or air. **2.** to become stale or foul from standing, as a pool of water. **3.** to stop developing or progressing. **4.** to become sluggish and dull. —**stag·na′tion,** *n.*

stag′ par′ty, *n.* **1.** a social gathering or outing for men only. **2.** a party given a bachelor by his male friends before his marriage, often on the night before the wedding.

staid (stād), *adj.* **1.** of decorous, sedate, or solemn character. **2.** fixed, settled, or permanent. —**staid′ly,** *adv.* —**staid′ness,** *n.*

stain (stān), *n.* **1.** a discoloration produced by foreign matter having penetrated into a material. **2.** a patch of color different from that of the basic color, as on the body of an animal. **3.** a cause of reproach; stigma: *a stain on one's reputation.* **4.** a dye made into a solution for coloring woods, textiles, etc. **5.** a reagent or dye used in treating a specimen for microscopic examination. —*v.t.* **6.** to discolor with spots or streaks of foreign matter. **7.** to color or dye (wood, cloth, etc.). **8.** to dye (a microscopic specimen) in order to give distinctness, produce contrast of tissues, etc. **9.** to bring reproach or dishonor upon; blemish. —*v.i.* **10.** to produce a stain. **11.** to become stained: *a fabric that stains easily.* —**stain′a·ble,** *adj.* —**stain′a·bil′i·ty, stain′a·ble·ness,** *n.*

stained′ glass′, *n.* glass that has been colored, esp. by having pigments baked onto its surface or by having various metallic oxides fused into it. —**stained′-glass′,** *adj.*

stain·less (stān′lis), *adj.* **1.** having no stain; spotless. **2.** made of stainless steel. **3.** resistant to staining or rusting. —*n.* **4.** flatware made of stainless steel. **5.** STAINLESS STEEL. —**stain′less·ly,** *adv.*

stain′less steel′, *n.* alloy steel containing 12 percent or more chromium, so as to be resistant to rust and attack from various chemicals.

stair (stâr), *n.* **1.** one of a flight or series of steps for going from one level to another, as in a building. **2. stairs,** such steps collectively, esp.

as forming a flight or a series of flights. **3.** a series or flight of steps; stairway. —**stair′less,** *adj.* —**stair′like′,** *adj.*

stair·case (stâr′kās′), *n.* a flight of stairs with its framework, banisters, etc., or a series of such flights.

stair′step′ or **stair′-step′,** *n., v.,* **-stepped, -step·ping,** *adj.* —*n.* **1.** a step in a staircase. **2. stairsteps,** stairs; a staircase. **3.** Often, **stairsteps.** a group of persons or things whose relative size, height, etc., suggests the graduated level of steps in a staircase. —*v.i.* **4.** to occur or move in a pattern suggesting the steps of a staircase. —*adj.* **5.** resembling the steps of a staircase.

stair·way (stâr′wā′), *n.* a passageway from one level, as of a building, to another by a series of stairs; staircase.

stair′well′ or **stair′ well′,** *n.* the vertical shaft or opening containing a stairway.

stake[1] (stāk), *n., v.,* **staked, stak·ing.** —*n.* **1.** a stick or post pointed at one end for driving into the ground as a boundary mark, part of a fence, support, etc. **2.** a post to which a person is bound for execution, usu. by burning. **3. the stake,** the punishment of death by burning. **4.** one of a number of vertical posts fitting into sockets or staples on the edge of the platform of a truck as to retain the load. —*v.t.* **5.** to mark with or as if with stakes (often fol. by *off* or *out*). **6.** to claim or reserve a share of (land, profit, etc.) as if by marking with stakes (usu. fol. by *out* or *off*). **7.** to support with a stake or stakes, as a plant. **8.** to tether or secure to a stake, as an animal. **9.** to fasten with a stake or stakes. **10. stake out, a.** to keep under police surveillance. **b.** to appoint (a police officer) to maintain watch over a suspect or place. **11. pull up stakes,** to leave one's job, place of residence, etc.; move.

stake[2] (stāk), *n., v.,* **staked, stak·ing.** —*n.* **1.** something that is wagered in a game or contest. **2.** a monetary or commercial investment in something, as in hope of gain. **3.** a personal interest or involvement. **4.** the funds with which a gambler operates. **5.** Often, **stakes.** a prize, reward, etc., in or as if in a contest. **6. stakes,** the cash values assigned in poker to various chips, bets, and raises. **7.** GRUBSTAKE. —*v.t.* **8.** to risk (something), as upon the outcome of an uncertain event, venture, etc. **9.** to furnish with necessities or resources, esp. money. —*Idiom.* **10. at stake,** in danger of being lost; at risk.

stake·out (stāk′out′), *n.* the surveillance of a location or a suspect by the police, as to intercept a wanted person.

stake′ (or **stakes′**) **race′,** *n.* a horse race in which part of the prize or purse is put up by the owners of the horses nominated to run.

sta·lac·tite (stə lak′tīt, stal′ək tīt′), *n.* a deposit, usu. of calcium carbonate, shaped like an icicle, hanging from the roof of a cave or the like.

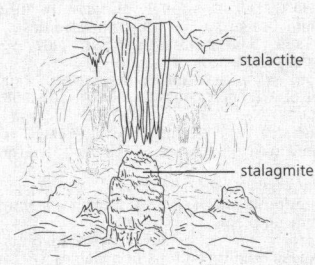

stalactite

stalagmite

stalactite

sta·lag·mite (stə lag′mīt, stal′əg mīt′), *n.* a deposit, usu. of calcium carbonate, resembling an inverted stalactite, formed on the floor of a cave or the like by the dripping of percolating calcareous water. —**stal′ag·mit′ic** (-mit′ik), **stal′ag·mit′i·cal,** *adj.* —**stal′ag·mit′i·cal·ly,** *adv.*

stale[1] (stāl), *adj.,* **stal·er, stal·est,** *v.,* **staled, stal·ing.** —*adj.* **1.** not fresh; vapid or flat, as beverages; dry or hardened, as bread. **2.** musty; stagnant: *stale air.* **3.** hackneyed; trite: *a stale joke.* **4.** having lost interest, initiative, or the like, as from overwork or boredom. **5.** *Law.* (of a claim) no longer in force through lack of action. —*v.t., v.i.* **6.** to make or become stale. —**stale′ly,** *adv.* —**stale′ness,** *n.*

stale[2] (stāl), *v.,* **staled, stal·ing,** *n.* —*v.i.* **1.** (of livestock, esp. horses) to urinate. —*n.* **2.** the urine of livestock.

stale·mate (stāl′māt′), *n., v.,* **-mat·ed, -mat·ing.** —*n.* **1.** a situation in which no action can be taken or progress made; deadlock. **2.** a position of the pieces on a chessboard in which a player cannot move any piece except the king and cannot move the king without putting it in check. —*v.t.* **3.** to subject to a stalemate. **4.** to bring to a standstill. —*v.i.* **5.** to be or result in a stalemate.

Sta·lin (stä′lin, -lēn, stal′in), *n.* **1. Joseph V.** (*Iosif Vissarionovich Dzhugashvili*), 1879–1953, premier of the U.S.S.R. 1941–53. **2.** a former name of DONETSK. **3.** former name of VARNA.

Sta·li·na·bad (stä′lə nə bäd′), *n.* a former name of DUSHANBE.

Sta·lin·grad (stä′lin grad′), *n.* former name of VOLGOGRAD.

Sta·lin·ism (stä′lə niz′əm), *n.* the principles and practice of communism associated with Stalin, characterized by the extreme suppression of

S

opposition, totalitarian rule, and an aggressive foreign policy. —**Sta′lin•ist,** *n., adj.*

stalk[1] (stôk), *n.* **1.** the stem or main axis of a plant. **2.** any slender supporting part of a plant, as a petiole or peduncle. **3.** a similar structural part of an animal. **4.** a stem, shaft, or slender supporting part of anything. —**stalked,** *adj.* —**stalk′less,** *adj.*

stalk[2] (stôk), *v.i.* **1.** to pursue prey, quarry, etc., stealthily. **2.** to walk with measured, stiff, or haughty strides (often fol. by *away, off,* etc.). **3.** to proceed in a steady, deliberate, or sinister manner. —*v.t.* **4.** to pursue (game, a person, etc.) stealthily. **5.** to proceed through (an area) in search of prey or quarry. **6.** to proceed or spread through in a steady or sinister manner. —*n.* **7.** an act or course of stalking prey. **8.** a slow, stiff stride or gait. —**stalk′er,** *n.* —**stalk′ing•ly,** *adv.*

stalk′ing-horse′, *n.* **1.** a horse, or a figure of a horse, behind which a hunter hides in stalking game. **2.** anything put forward to mask plans or efforts; pretext. **3.** a political candidate used to conceal the candidacy of a more important figure or to draw votes from a rival.

stall[1] (stôl), *n.* **1.** a compartment, as in a stable, for the accommodation of one animal. **2.** a stable or shed for horses or cattle. **3.** a booth or stand in which merchandise is displayed for sale (often used in combination): *a bookstall.* **4.** one of a number of enclosed seats in the choir or chancel of a church for the use of the clergy. **5.** a pew. **6.** any small compartment for a specific activity or housing a specific thing: *a shower stall.* **7.** a marked space for parking a car. **8. a.** an instance of causing an engine, or a vehicle powered by an engine, to stop, esp. by supplying it with a poor fuel mixture or by overloading it. **b.** the resulting condition. **9. a.** an instance of causing an airplane to fly at an angle of attack greater than the angle of maximum lift, causing loss of control and a downward spin. Compare CRITICAL ANGLE (def. 2). **b.** the resulting condition. **10.** *Brit.* a chairlike seat in a theater, esp. one in the front section of the parquet. —*v.t.* **11.** to put or keep in a stall, as an animal or a car. **12.** to cause (a motor or vehicle) to stop, esp. by supplying it with a poor fuel mixture or overloading it. **13.** to put (an airplane) into a stall. **14.** to bring to a standstill; check the progress or motion of. —*v.i.* **15.** (of an engine, car, airplane, etc.) to become stalled (sometimes fol. by *out*). **16.** to come to a standstill; be brought to a stop.

stall[2] (stôl), *v.i.* **1.** to delay, esp. by evasion or deception. **2.** *Sports.* to prolong holding the ball as a tactic to prevent the opponent from scoring, as when one's team has the lead. —*v.t.* **3.** to delay or put off, esp. by evasion or deception (often fol. by *off*). —*n.* **4.** a pretext, as a ruse or trick, used to delay or deceive. **5.** *Slang.* the member of a pickpocket's team who distracts the victim while the theft takes place.

stal•lion (stal′yən), *n.* an uncastrated adult male horse, esp. one used for breeding.

stal•wart (stôl′wərt), *adj.* **1.** strongly and stoutly built; sturdy and robust. **2.** strong and brave; valiant. **3.** firm; steadfast. —*n.* **4.** a physically stalwart person. **5.** a steadfast partisan: *party stalwarts.* —**stal′wart•ly,** *adv.* —**stal′wart•ness,** *n.*

sta•men (stā′mən), *n., pl.* **sta•mens, stam•i•na** (stam′ə nə). the pollen-bearing organ of a flower, consisting of the filament and the anther. —**sta′mened,** *adj.*

Stam•ford (stam′fərd), *n.* a city in SW Connecticut. 107,199.

stam•i•na[1] (stam′ə nə), *n.* strength or power to endure fatigue, stress, etc.; endurance.

stam•i•na[2] (stam′ə nə), *n.* a pl. of STAMEN.

stam•i•nate (stam′ə nit, -nāt′), *adj.* **1.** having a stamen or stamens. **2.** having stamens but no pistils.

stam•mer (stam′ər), *v.i.* **1.** to speak with involuntary breaks and pauses, or with spasmodic repetitions of syllables or sounds. —*v.t.* **2.** to say with a stammer (often fol. by *out*). —*n.* **3.** a stammering mode of utterance. **4.** a stammered utterance. —**stam′mer•er,** *n.* —**stam′mer•ing•ly,** *adv.*

stamp (stamp), *v.t.* **1.** to strike or beat with a forcible, downward thrust of the foot. **2.** to bring (the foot) down forcibly on the ground, floor, etc. **3.** to crush, extinguish, etc., by or as if by striking with a forcible downward thrust of the foot (often fol. by *out*): *to stamp out a fire; to stamp out crime.* **4.** to crush or pound with or as if with a pestle. **5.** to impress with a mark or device as an indication of genuineness, approval, etc. **6.** to mark with a distinguishing feature: *Age stamped his face with lines.* **7.** to imprint or impress on something: *Stamp the date on each page.* **8.** to affix a postage stamp to. **9.** to characterize; reveal: *His speech stamped him as a potential candidate.* —*v.i.* **10.** to bring the foot down forcibly, as in crushing something or expressing rage. **11.** to walk quickly with heavy, forcible steps. —*n.* **12.** POSTAGE STAMP. **13.** a die or block for impressing or imprinting. **14.** a design made for imprinting. **15.** an official mark or seal indicating genuineness, validity, etc., or payment of a duty or charge. **16.** a distinctive record or impression. **17.** an act or instance of stamping. **18.** TRADING STAMP. **19.** FOOD STAMP. **20.** an instrument for stamping, crushing, or pounding. —**stamp′a•ble,** *adj.*

Stamp′ Act′, *n.* an act of the British Parliament (1765) for raising revenue in the American colonies by requiring that documents, newspapers, etc., bear an official stamp.

stam•pede (stam pēd′), *n., v.,* **-ped•ed, -ped•ing.** —*n.* **1.** a sudden, frenzied rush or headlong flight of a herd of frightened animals, esp. cattle or horses. **2.** any headlong general flight or rush. **3.** *Western U.S., Canada.* a celebration, usu. held annually, combining a rodeo, contests, dancing, etc. —*v.i.* **4.** to scatter or flee in a stampede. **5.** to make a general rush. —*v.t.* **6.** to cause to stampede. **7.** to rush or overrun (a place). —**stam•ped′er,** *n.*

stamp•er (stam′pər), *n.* **1.** a person or thing that stamps. **2.** a pestle.

stamp′ing ground′, *n.* a habitual or favorite haunt.

stance (stans), *n.* **1.** the position or bearing of the body while standing. **2.** a mental or emotional position adopted with respect to something. **3.** *Sports.* the relative position of the feet, as in addressing a golf ball.

stanch[1] (stônch, stanch, stänch) also **staunch,** *v.t.* **1.** to stop the flow of (a liquid, esp. blood). **2.** to stop the flow of blood or other liquid from (a wound, leak, etc.). **3.** to check or stem (an outflow): *stanching the dollar drain.* —*v.i.* **4.** to stop flowing, as blood; be stanched. —**stanch′a•ble,** *adj.* —**stanch′er,** *n.*

stanch[2] (stônch, stänch, stanch), *adj.* STAUNCH[2]. —**stanch′ly,** *adv.* —**stanch′ness,** *n.*

stan•chion (stan′shən), *n.* **1.** an upright bar, beam, post, or support, as in a window, stall, or ship. —*v.t.* **2.** to furnish with stanchions. **3.** to secure by or to a stanchion or stanchions.

stand (stand), *v.,* **stood, stand•ing,** *n.* —*v.i.* **1.** to be in an upright position on the feet. **2.** to rise to one's feet (often fol. by *up*). **3.** to have a specified height when in this position: *He stands six feet.* **4.** to remain motionless on the feet. **5.** to take a position as indicated: *to stand aside.* **6.** to adhere to a certain policy or attitude: *We stand for free trade.* **7.** (of things) to rest in an upright or vertical position. **8.** to be located or situated: *The building stands upon the hill.* **9.** (of an account, score, etc.) to remain as indicated: *The score stands 18 to 14.* **10.** to continue in force; remain valid: *My offer still stands.* **11.** to be or remain in a specified state or condition: *I stand corrected. You stand in danger of losing your license.* **12.** to take or hold a particular course at sea. **13.** (of a male domestic animal, esp. a stud) to be available as a sire, usu. for a fee. —*v.t.* **14.** to cause to stand; set upright. **15.** to undergo or submit to: *to stand trial.* **16.** to endure or withstand: *My eyes can't stand the glare.* **17.** to treat (a person) to something. **18.** to perform one's job or duty as: *to stand watch aboard ship.* **19. stand by, a.** to uphold; support. **b.** to adhere to; remain firm regarding. **c.** to wait, esp. in anticipation. **d.** to be ready to board transport as an alternate passenger. **20. stand down, a.** *Law.* to leave the witness stand. **b.** to step aside; withdraw, as from a competition. **21. stand for, a.** to represent; symbolize: *P.S. stands for "postscript."* **b.** to advocate; favor. **c.** to tolerate; allow. **22. stand off, a.** to keep or stay at a distance. **b.** to put off; evade. **23. stand on,** to be based on; depend on; rest on. **24. stand out, a.** to project; protrude. **b.** to be conspicuous or prominent. **25. stand over, a.** to supervise constantly. **b.** to postpone or be postponed. **26. stand up, a.** to be or remain convincing: *The evidence won't stand up in court.* **b.** to be durable or serviceable: *Wool stands up better than silk.* **c.** to fail to keep an appointment with. **27. stand up for, a.** to defend; support. **b.** to serve (a bridegroom) as best man or (a bride) as maid or matron of honor. **28. stand up to,** to encounter fearlessly; confront. —*n.* **29.** the act of standing. **30.** a halt or stop. **31.** a final defensive effort: *Custer's last stand.* **32.** a determined policy, position, attitude, etc., taken or maintained: *We must take a stand on political issues.* **33.** WITNESS STAND. **34.** a raised platform, as for a speaker, a band, or the like. **35. stands,** a raised section of seats for spectators; grandstand. **36.** a framework on or in which articles are placed for support, exhibition, etc.: *a wig stand.* **37.** a piece of furniture of various forms, on or in which to put articles (often used in combination): *an umbrella stand; a washstand.* **38.** a small, light table. **39.** a stall, booth, or the like, where articles are displayed for sale: *a fruit stand.* **40.** NEWSSTAND. **41.** a site or location for business. **42.** a place or station occupied by vehicles available for hire: *a taxi stand.* **43.** a standing growth of trees. **44.** a stop on the tour of a theatrical company, rock group, etc., esp. for a single performance. **45.** HIVE (def. 2). —***Idiom.*** **46. stand firm,** to remain steadfast. **47. stand on your own two feet,** to be self-reliant. **48. stand pat,** to resist change; to remain in the same place. **49. stand to reason,** to be obvious, logical, or reasonable. **50. stand up and be counted,** to affirm one's position publicly. —***Proverb.*** **51. Here I stand, I can do no other, God help me,** I must obey my conscience: said by Martin Luther 1521.

stand•ard (stan′dərd), *n.* **1.** something considered by an authority or by general consent as a basis of comparison. **2.** an object regarded as the most common size or form of its kind. **3.** a rule or principle that is used as a basis for judgment. **4.** an average or normal quality, quantity, or level: *The work isn't up to his usual standard.* **5. standards,** the morals, ethics, customs, etc., regarded generally or by an individual as acceptable. **6.** the authorized exemplar of a unit of weight or measure. **7.** a certain commodity in or by which a basic monetary unit is stated: *gold standard.* **8.** the legally established content of full-weight coins. **9.** the prescribed degree of fineness for gold or silver. **10.** a musical piece of enduring popularity. **11.** a flag indicating the presence of a sovereign or public official. **12.** a flag or emblematic figure used as a rallying point for an army, fleet, etc. **13. a.** any of various military or naval flags. **b.** the colors of a mounted military unit. **14.** a long, narrow, tapering flag bearing heraldic devices and personal to an individual or group. **15.** something that stands or is placed upright. **16.** an upright support. **17.** a long candlestick or candelabrum used in a church. —*adj.* **18.** serving as a basis of weight, measure, value, comparison, or judgment. **19.** of recognized excellence or established authority: *a standard reference book.* **20.** usual or customary. **21.** manual; not electric or automatic: *standard transmission.* **22.** conforming in pronunciation, grammar, vocabulary, etc., to the usage of most educated native speakers and widely considered acceptable or correct. **23.** officially approved; authorized. **24.** (of meat, esp. beef or veal) of or designating a grade immediately below select or good.

stand′ard-bear′er, *n.* **1.** an officer or soldier of an army or military unit who bears a standard. **2.** the generally acknowledged leader of a movement, political party, or the like.

stand•ard•bred (stan′dərd bred′), *n.* (*often cap.*) any of an American breed of trotting and pacing horses used for harness racing. [1890–95]

stand′ard devia′tion, *n. Statistics.* a measure of dispersion in a frequency distribution, equal to the square root of the mean of the squares of the deviations from the arithmetic mean of the distribution.

Stand′ard Eng′lish, *n.* the English language in its most widely accepted form, as written and spoken by educated people in both formal and informal contexts, having universal currency while incorporating regional differences.

stand•ard•ize (stan′dər dīz′), *v.,* **-ized, -iz•ing.** —*v.t.* **1.** to make of a standard size, weight, etc. **2.** to test by a standard. **3.** to establish a standard for. —*v.i.* **4.** to become standardized. —**stand′ard•iz′a•ble,** *adj.* —**stand′ard•i•za′tion,** *n.* —**stand′ard•iz′er,** *n.*

stand′ard of liv′ing, *n.* a level of subsistence and comfort in daily life maintained by a community, class, or individual.

stand′ard op′erating proce′dure, *n.* a set of fixed instructions or steps for carrying out routine operations. *Abbr.:* SOP

stand′ard time′, *n.* the civil time officially adopted for a country or region, usu. the civil time of some specific meridian lying within the region, with a difference of exactly one hour between one zone and the next. The standard time zones in the U.S. are **Atlantic time, Eastern time, Central time, Mountain time, Pacific time, Yukon time, Alaska-Hawaii time,** and **Bering time.**

stand•by (stand′bī′), *n.* **1.** a staunch supporter or adherent. **2.** something upon which one can rely, as for regular use. **3.** something or someone held ready to serve as a substitute, as in an emergency. **4.** a traveler assured of transportation, as on a plane, only when another passenger cancels. —*adj.* **5.** kept ready for use as a substitute: *a standby player.* **6.** of, for, or traveling as a standby: *a standby flight.* —*adv.* **7.** as a standby: *to fly standby to Rome.* —*Idiom.* **8. on standby,** ready to act immediately when called upon.

stand′-in′, *n.* **1.** a substitute for a film or television performer on the set during the preparation of lighting, cameras, etc. **2.** any substitute.

stand•ing (stan′ding), *n.* **1.** rank or status, esp. with respect to social, economic, or personal position, reputation, etc. **2.** good position, reputation, or credit. **3.** length of continuance, residence, experience, etc. **4. standings,** a list of teams or contestants arranged according to their past records. **5.** a place where a person or thing stands. **6.** the right to initiate or participate in a legal action. —*adj.* **7.** having an erect or upright position: *a standing lamp.* **8.** performed in or from an erect position: *a standing jump.* **9.** still; not flowing or stagnant. **10.** lasting or permanent. **11.** continuing in force, use, etc.: *a standing rule.* **12.** out of use; idle. **13.** *Naut.* noting any of various objects or assemblages of objects fixed in place or position, unless moved for adjustment or repairs: *standing bowsprit.*

stand′ing ar′my, *n.* a permanently organized military force maintained by a nation.

Stand′ing by a Pur′pose True′, a Christian children's hymn with words by Philip Bliss.

stand′ing commit′tee, *n.* a permanent committee, as of a legislature, dealing with a designated subject.

Stand′ing in the Need′ of Prayer′, a traditional American spiritual.

Stand′ing on the Prom′ises, a Christian hymn (1886) with words and music by R. Kelso Carter; often sung in evangelistic crusades.

stand′ing or′der, *n.* **1.** a general order always in force in a military command. **2. standing orders,** the rules ensuring continuity of parliamentary procedure during the meetings of an assembly.

stand′ing room′, *n.* **1.** space in which to stand, as in a theater or stadium. **2.** accommodation for standing.

stand′ing wave′, *n. Physics.* a wave in which each point on the wave has a constant amplitude, ranging from zero at the nodes to a maximum, equal to the amplitude of the wave, at the antinodes.

Stan•dish (stan′dish), *n.* **Myles** or **Miles,** c1584–1656, American settler, born in England.

stand′off′ or **stand′-off′,** *n.* **1.** a tie or draw, as in a game. **2.** something that counterbalances. **3.** a standing apart; aloofness. —*adj.* **4.** aloof; reserved; standoffish.

stand′off′ish or **stand′-off′ish,** *adj.* tending to be aloof and unfriendly. —**stand′off′ish•ly,** *adv.* —**stand′off′ish•ness,** *n.*

stand′out′ or **stand′-out′,** *n.* **1.** a person, performance, etc., that is clearly superior to others. **2.** someone who is conspicuous because of a refusal to conform to the opinions, goals, etc., of the majority. —*adj.* **3.** outstanding; superior.

stand•point (stand′point′), *n.* **1.** the mental attitude from which a person views and judges things. **2.** the point or place at which a person stands to view something.

St. An′drew′s cross, *n.* a cross composed of four diagonal arms of equal length.

stand•still (stand′stil′), *n.* a state of cessation of movement or action; halt; stop.

stand′-up′ or **stand′up′,** *adj.* **1.** standing erect or upright, as a collar. **2.** taken, requiring, or performed in a standing position. **3.** characterized by an erect or bold stance: *a stand-up batter.* **4.** (of a comedian) delivering a comic monologue while standing alone in front of an audience or camera.

Stand′ Up′, Stand′ Up′ for Je′sus, a Christian hymn (1858) with words by George Duffield and music by George Webb.

Stan′ford-Binet′ test′ (stan′fərd), *n.* any of several revised versions of the Binet-Simon scale for testing intelligence.

Stan•i•slav•sky or **Stan•i•slav•ski** (stan′ə släv′skē, -släf′-), *n.* **Konstantin** (*Konstantin Sergeevich Alekseev*), 1863–1938, Russian actor, producer, and director.

Stanislav′sky Meth′od, *n.* METHOD (def. 4). Also called **Stanislav′-sky Sys′tem.**

stank (stangk), *v.* a pt. of STINK.

Stan•ley (stan′lē), *n.* **1. Edward George Geoffrey Smith, 14th Earl of Derby,** 1799–1869, British prime minister. **2. Sir Henry Morton** (*John Rowlands*), 1841–1904, British journalist and explorer in Africa. **3. Wendell M(eredith),** 1904–71, U.S. biochemist. **4.** the capital and principal harbor of the Falkland Islands, in the E part. 1200. **5. Mount,** former name of NGALIEMA, Mount.

stan•za (stan′zə), *n., pl.* **-zas.** an arrangement of a certain number of lines, usu. four or more, sometimes having a fixed length, meter, or rhyme scheme, forming a division of a poem. —**stan•za′ic** (-zā′ik), *adj.*

sta•pes (stā′pēz), *n., pl.* **sta•pes, sta•pe•des** (stə pē′dēz). a small, stirrup-shaped bone, the innermost of the chain of three small bones of the middle ear. Also called **stirrup.** —**sta•pe′di•al** (-dē əl), *adj.*

staph (staf), *n.* staphylococcus.

staph•y•lo•coc•cus (staf′ə lə kok′əs), *n., pl.* **-coc•ci** (-kok′sī). any of several spherical bacteria of the genus *Staphylococcus,* occurring in pairs, tetrads, and irregular clusters, certain species of which, as *S. aureus,* are pathogenic. —**staph′y•lo•coc′cal** (-kok′əl), **staph′y•lo•coc′cic** (-kok′sik), *adj.*

sta•ple¹ (stā′pəl), *n., v.,* **-pled, -pling.** —*n.* **1.** a short piece of wire bent so as to bind together papers or the like by driving the ends through the sheets and clinching them on the other side. **2.** a similar, often U-shaped piece of wire or metal with pointed ends for driving into a surface to hold a hasp, hook, pin, etc. —*v.t.* **3.** to secure or fasten by a staple or staples.

sta•ple² (stā′pəl), *n., adj., v.,* **-pled, -pling.** —*n.* **1.** a principal raw material or commodity grown or manufactured in a locality. **2.** a basic or necessary item of food: *flour, salt, and other staples.* **3.** a basic or principal item, feature, element, or part. **4.** the fiber of wool, cotton, flax, rayon, etc., considered with reference to length and fineness. **5.** a standard length of textile fibers, representing the average of such fibers taken collectively: *long-staple cotton.* —*adj.* **6.** chief or prominent among the products exported or produced by a country or district. **7.** basic, chief, or principal: *staple industries.* —*v.t.* **8.** to sort or classify according to the staple or fiber, as wool.

sta•pler (stā′plər), *n.* **1.** a machine for fastening together sheets of paper or the like with wire staples. **2.** Also called **sta′ple gun′.** a hand-powered tool used for driving heavy-duty wire staples into wood and other materials.

star (stär), *n., adj., v.,* **starred, star•ring.** —*n.* **1.** any of the various types of hot, gaseous, self-luminous celestial bodies, as the sun or Polaris, whose energy is derived from nuclear-fusion reactions. **2.** any celestial body, except the moon, that appears as a fixed point of light in the night sky: *the evening star.* **3.** Usu., **stars.** a heavenly body, esp. a planet, regarded as an astrological influence on human affairs. **4.** one's fortune in relation to advancement or decline: *Your star will rise someday.* **5.** a conventionalized figure usu. having five or six points radiating from or disposed about a center. **6.** this figure used as an ornament, badge, mark of excellence, etc. **7. a.** a prominent actor, singer, or the like, esp. one who plays the leading role in a production. **b.** a gifted or highly celebrated person in some art, profession, or field. **8.** an asterisk. **9. a.** the asterism in a crystal or a gemstone, as in a star sapphire. **b.** a crystal or a gemstone having such asterism. **10.** a gold or bronze star worn on the ribbon of a naval decoration to represent an additional award of the same decoration. **11.** a white spot on the forehead of a horse. —*adj.* **12.** celebrated, prominent, or distinguished; preeminent: *a star reporter.* **13.** of or pertaining to a star or stars. —*v.t.* **14.** to set with or as if with stars; spangle. **15.** to feature as a star. **16.** to mark with a star or asterisk, as for special notice. —*v.i.* **17.** to shine as a star; be brilliant. **18.** (of a performer) to appear as a star. —*Idiom.* **19. see stars,** to appear to see brilliant streaks of light before the eyes, as from a severe blow to the head. —**star′less,** *adj.* —**star′like′,** *adj.*

Star, *n.* **Belle,** 1848–89, U.S. outlaw.

star•board (stär′bərd, -bôrd′, -bōrd′), *n.* **1.** the right-hand side of or direction from a vessel or aircraft, facing forward. —*adj.* **2.** of, pertaining to, or located to the starboard. —*adv.* **3.** toward the right side.

starch (stärch), *n.* **1.** a white, tasteless, solid carbohydrate, $(C_6H_{10}O_5)_n$, occurring in the form of minute granules in the seeds, tubers, and other parts of plants, and forming an important constituent of rice, corn, wheat, beans, potatoes, and many other vegetable foods. **2.** a preparation of this substance used to stiffen fabrics in laundering. **3. starches,** foods rich in natural starch. **4.** stiffness or formality, as of manner. **5.**

(S)

vigor; energy; stamina; boldness. —*v.t.* **6.** to stiffen or treat with starch. **7.** to make stiff or rigidly formal (sometimes fol. by *up*).

starch′ block′er or **starch′block′,** *n.* a substance ingested in the belief that it inhibits the body's ability to metabolize starch and thereby promotes weight loss: declared illegal in the U.S. by the FDA. —**starch′-block′ing,** *adj.*

starch•y (stär′chē), *adj.*, **starch•i•er, starch•i•est. 1.** pertaining to or of the nature of starch. **2.** containing starch. **3.** stiffened with starch. **4.** stiff and formal, as in manner. —**starch′i•ly,** *adv.* —**starch′i•ness,** *n.*

star′-crossed′, *adj.* thwarted or opposed by the stars; ill-fated: *star-crossed lovers.*

star•dom (stär′dəm), *n.* the world or status of star performers or celebrities, as of the stage, motion pictures, or sports.

star′dust′ or **star′ dust′,** *n.* **1.** (not in technical use) a mass of distant stars appearing as tiny particles of dust. **2.** a naively romantic quality.

stare (stâr), *v.,* **stared, star•ing.** *n.* —*v.i.* **1.** to gaze fixedly and intently, esp. with the eyes wide open. **2.** to be boldly or obtrusively conspicuous. **3.** (of hair, feathers, etc.) to stand on end; bristle. —*v.t.* **4.** to stare at: *to stare a person up and down.* **5.** to effect or have a certain effect on by staring. **6. stare down,** to intimidate or discomfit with a stare. —*n.* **7.** a staring gaze; a fixed look with the eyes wide open. —*Idiom.* **8. stare one in the face,** to be urgent or impending, as a deadline. —**star′ing•ly,** *adv.*

star•fish (stär′fish′), *n., pl.* (*esp. collectively*) **-fish,** (*esp. for kinds or species*) **-fish•es.** any echinoderm of the class Asteroidea, having a radial body, usu. in the form of a star, with five or more arms radiating from a central disk.

starfish, *Asterias rubens,* diameter 3 ½ in. (8.9 cm)

star′ fruit′, *n.* CARAMBOLA (def. 2).

star•gaze (stär′gāz′), *v.i.,* **-gazed, -gaz•ing. 1.** to gaze at or observe the stars. **2.** to daydream.

stark (stärk), *adj.* **1.** sheer, utter, downright, or complete: *stark madness.* **2.** harsh, grim, or desolate, as a view or place. **3.** extremely simple or severe: *a stark interior.* **4.** bluntly or sternly plain: *the stark reality of our situation.* **5.** sharply or harshly distinct: *a stark contrast.* **6.** stiff or rigid, as in death. —*adv.* **7.** utterly, absolutely, or quite: *stark mad.* —**stark′ly,** *adv.* —**stark′ness,** *n.*

stark′-nak′ed, *adj.* absolutely naked.

star•let (stär′lit), *n.* **1.** a young actress promoted and publicized as a future motion picture star. **2.** a small star or other heavenly body.

star•light (stär′līt′), *n.* the light emanating from the stars.

star•ling (stär′ling), *n.* a stocky, medium-sized Eurasian songbird, *Sturnus vulgaris,* of the family Sturnidae, with iridescent black plumage, seasonally speckled: now established in North America, Australasia, and other parts of the world.

star′-nosed′ (or **star′nose**) **mole′,** *n.* a North American mole, *Condylura cristata,* having a starlike ring of fleshy processes around the end of the snout. Also called **star′nose′.**

Star′ of Beth′lehem, *n.* the star that guided the Magi to the manger of the infant Jesus in Bethlehem. Matt. 2:1–10.

star′-of-Beth′lehem, *n., pl.* **stars-of-Bethlehem. 1.** any plant of the genus *Ornithogalum,* of the lily family, having grasslike leaves and white, star-shaped flowers. **2.** any of various starflowers.

Star′ of Da′vid, *n.* a hexagram used as a symbol of Judaism. Also called **Magen David, Shield of David.**

Star of David

starred (stärd), *adj.* **1.** set or studded with or as if with stars. **2.** decorated with a star, as of an order. **3.** marked with a starlike figure or spot, esp. an asterisk.

star•ry (stär′ē), *adj.,* **-ri•er, -ri•est. 1.** abounding with stars: *a starry night.* **2.** of, pertaining to, or proceeding from the stars. **3.** of the nature of or consisting of stars: *starry worlds.* **4.** star-shaped. **5.** shining like stars. —**star′ri•ness,** *n.*

star′ry-eyed′, *adj.* overly romantic or idealistic.

Stars′ and Bars′, *n.* the flag adopted by the Confederate States of America.

Stars′ and Stripes′, *n.* the national flag of the U.S., consisting of 13 horizontal stripes that are alternately red and white, representing the original states, and of a blue field containing 50 white stars, representing the present states. Also called **Old Glory.**

star′ sap′phire, *n.* a sapphire, cut cabochon, exhibiting asterism in the form of a colorless six-rayed star.

star•ship (stär′ship′), *n.* a spaceship designed for intergalactic travel.

Star′-Span′gled Ban′ner, The, the national anthem of the U.S., based on a poem written by Francis Scott Key on September 14, 1814, and set by him to the melody of a popular English song: officially adopted by the U.S. Congress in 1931.

star′-stud′ded, *adj.* **1.** lighted by or full of stars; bright: *a star-studded night.* **2.** exhibiting or characterized by the presence of many preeminent performers: *a star-studded Hollywood party.*

star′ sys′tem, *n.* the practice of casting and promoting star performers for their ability to draw at the box office.

start (stärt), *v.i.* **1.** to begin or set out, as on a journey or activity. **2.** to become active, manifest, or operative; appear, issue forth, or come to life, esp. suddenly or abruptly: *The snowfall started at midnight. The engines started with a roar.* **3.** to spring, move, or dart suddenly from a position or place. **4.** to be among the entrants in a race or the initial participants in a game or contest. **5.** to give a sudden, involuntary jerk or jump, as from shock or pain. **6.** to protrude: *eyes seeming to start from their sockets.* **7.** to spring, slip, or work loose from place or fastenings, as timbers or other structural parts. —*v.t.* **8.** to set moving, going, or acting: *to start a car; to start a fire.* **9.** to establish or found: *to start a new business.* **10.** to begin work on. **11.** to enable or help (someone) set out on a journey, career, etc. **12.** to cause or choose to be an entrant in a game or contest: *He started his new pitcher in the crucial game.* **13.** to cause (an object) to work loose from place or fastenings. —*n.* **14.** a beginning of an action, journey, process, etc. **15.** a place or time from which something begins. **16.** the first part of anything: *We missed the start of the show.* **17.** a sudden, springing movement from a position. **18.** a sudden, involuntary jerk of the body. **19.** an instance of being an entrant in a race or an initial participant in a game or contest. **20.** a lead or advance, as over competitors or pursuers. **21.** a means of beginning or advancing something desired: *Her parents gave them a start by buying them a house.* **22.** a spurt of activity. **23.** a signal to move or begin, as on a course or in a race.

start•er (stär′tər), *n.* **1.** a person or thing that starts. **2.** a person who gives the signal to begin, as for a race or the running of a train, elevator, etc. **3.** a device that starts an internal-combustion engine without a need for cranking by hand. **4.** a person or thing that starts in a race or contest. **5.** a culture of bacteria used to start a particular fermentation, as in the manufacture of cheese. **6.** SOURDOUGH (def. 1). —*adj.* **7.** constituting a basis or beginning. —*Idiom.* **8. for starters,** as the first step, part, point, etc.; first.

start′ing gate′, *n.* a movable barrier for lining up and giving an equal start to the entries in a horse or dog race.

star•tle (stär′tl), *v.,* **-tled, -tling.** *n.* —*v.t.* **1.** to disturb or agitate suddenly and usu. briefly, as by surprise or alarm. —*v.i.* **2.** to start involuntarily, as from surprise or alarm. —*n.* **3.** a sudden shock of surprise, mild alarm, or the like. —**star′tler,** *n.*

star•tling (stärt′ling, stär′tl ing), *adj.* creating sudden alarm, surprise, or wonder; astonishing. —**star′tling•ly,** *adv.*

Star′ Trek′, a U.S. science-fiction television series, progenitor of other similarly named television named series.

start′-up′ or **start′up′,** *n.* **1.** the act or fact of starting something; a setting in motion. —*adj.* **2.** of or pertaining to the beginning of a new venture, esp. to the investment made for it.

star•va•tion (stär vā′shən), *n.* **1.** the act of starving or the state of being starved. —*adj.* **2.** seeming to cause starving: *a starvation diet.*

starve (stärv), *v.,* **starved, starv•ing.** —*v.i.* **1.** to weaken, waste, or die from lack of food. **2.** to be extremely hungry: *When do we eat? I'm starving.* **3.** to feel a strong need or desire: *a child starving for affection.* —*v.t.* **4.** to cause to starve; kill, weaken, or reduce by lack of food. **5.** to subdue, or force to some condition or action, by hunger. **6.** to cause to suffer for lack of something needed or craved.

Star′ Wars′, *n.* **1.** a research program begun by the U.S. in 1983 to explore technologies, including ground- and space-based lasers, for destroying incoming missiles and nuclear warheads over U.S. territory. Also called **Strategic Defense Initiative. 2.** (*italics*) a U.S. science-fiction film (1977) directed by George Lucas.

stash (stash), *v.t.* **1.** to put by or away as for safekeeping or future use, usu. in a secret place (usu. fol. by *away*). —*n.* **2.** something put away or hidden. **3.** a place in which something is stored secretly.

sta•sis (stā′sis, stas′is), *n., pl.* **sta•ses** (stā′sēz, stas′ēz). **1.** the state of equilibrium or inactivity caused by opposing equal forces. **2.** stagnation in the flow of any of the fluids of the body.

stat¹ (stat), *n.* **1.** Also, **'stat.** a thermostat. **2.** a photostat.

stat² (stat), *n.* a statistic.

state (stāt), *n., adj., v.,* **stat•ed, stat•ing. —***n.* **1.** the condition of a person or thing, as with respect to circumstances or attributes: *the state of one's health.* **2.** the condition of matter with respect to structure, form, phase, or the like: *water in a gaseous state.* **3.** status, rank, or position in life; station. **4.** the formal or elaborate style befitting a person of wealth and high rank: *to travel in state.* **5.** a particular condition of mind or feeling: *an excited state.* **6.** an abnormally tense, nervous, or perturbed condition: *in a state over losing one's job.* **7.** a politically unified people occupying a definite territory; nation. **8.** the territory or authority of a state. **9.** (*sometimes cap.*) any of the bodies politic or political units that together make up a federal union, as in the United States of America. **10.** the body politic as organized for civil rule and government: *separation of church and state.* **11.** the sphere of the highest civil authority and administration: *affairs of state.* **12. the States,** the United States (usu. used outside its borders). —*adj.* **13.** of or pertaining to the central civil government or authority. **14.** of, maintained by, or under the authority of a unit of a federal union: *a state highway.* **15.** characterized by, attended with, or involving ceremony: *a state dinner.* **16.** used on or reserved for occasions of ceremony. —*v.t.* **17.** to declare definitely or specifically. **18.** to set forth formally in speech or writing. **19.** to set forth in proper or definite form: *to state a problem.* **20.** to say. **21.** to fix or settle, as by authority. —*Idiom.* **22. lie in state,** (of a corpse) to be exhibited publicly with honors before burial.

state′ bird′, *n.* a bird chosen as an official symbol of a U.S. state.

stat•ed (stā′tid), *adj.* **1.** fixed or settled: *a stated price.* **2.** explicitly set forth; declared as fact. **3.** recognized or official.

state′ flow′er, *n.* a flower chosen as an official symbol of a U.S. state.

state•hood (stāt′hŏŏd), *n.* the status or condition of being a state, esp. a state of the U.S.

state•house (stāt′hous′), *n., pl.* **-hous•es** (-hou′ziz). the building in which the legislature of a state sits; the capitol of a state.

state•ly (stāt′lē), *adj.,* **-li•er, -li•est,** *adv.* —*adj.* **1.** majestic; imposing in magnificence, elegance, etc. **2.** dignified. —*adv.* **3.** in a stately manner. —**state′li•ness,** *n.*

state•ment (stāt′mənt), *n.* **1.** something stated. **2.** a communication or declaration in speech or writing, setting forth facts, particulars, etc. **3.** a single sentence or assertion: *I disagree with your last statement.* **4.** an abstract of a commercial account, as one rendered to show the balance due. **5.** an appearance of a theme, subject, or motif within a musical composition. **6.** the act or manner of stating something. **7.** the communication of an idea, position, mood, or the like through something other than words: *clothes that are statements of the owner's social position.*

state′ of the art′, *n.* the latest and most sophisticated or advanced stage of a technology, art, or science: *a camera considered the state of the art in design.* —**state′-of-the-art′,** *adj.*

State′ of the Un′ion address′, *n.* an annual message to Congress in which the President reports on the state of the nation and outlines a legislative program: required by the Constitution (Article II, Section 3). Also called **State′ of the Un′ion mes′sage.**

state′ reli′gion, *n.* the official religion of a state as established by law.

state•room (stāt′rŏŏm′, -rŏŏm′), *n.* a private room or compartment on a ship, train, etc.

state′s′ (or **state′**) **attor′ney,** *n.* (in judicial proceedings) the legal representative of the state.

state′s′ ev′idence, *n.* **1.** evidence for the prosecution given by an accomplice in a crime. —*Idiom.* **2. turn state's evidence,** to give evidence against one's accomplice or accomplices in a crime, usu. in exchange for a reduced sentence.

state•side or **State•side** (stāt′sīd′), *adj.* **1.** being in or toward the continental U.S. —*adv.* **2.** in or toward the continental U.S.

states•man (stāts′mən), *n., pl.* **-men. 1.** an experienced politician who holds a high office in government, esp. at the national level. **2.** a highly

S

STATES OF THE UNITED STATES

State	Postal Abbr.	Capital	Population (1990 census)	Total Area Sq. Mi.	Sq. Km	State Flower	State Nickname
Alabama	AL	Montgomery	4,040,587	51,609	133,670	Camellia	Cotton State
Alaska	AK	Juneau	550,043	586,400	1,519,000	Forget-me-not	Last Frontier
Arizona	AZ	Phoenix	3,665,228	113,909	295,025	Saguaro Cactus Blossom	Grand Canyon State
Arkansas	AR	Little Rock	2,350,725	53,103	137,537	Apple Blossom	Land of Opportunity
California	CA	Sacramento	29,760,021	158,693	411,015	Golden Poppy	Golden State
Colorado	CO	Denver	3,294,394	104,247	270,000	Columbine	Centennial State
Connecticut	CT	Hartford	3,287,116	5009	12,975	Mountain Laurel	Constitution State
Delaware	DE	Dover	666,168	2057	5330	Peach Blossom	First State
Florida	FL	Tallahassee	12,937,926	58,560	151,670	Orange Blossom	Sunshine State
Georgia	GA	Atlanta	6,478,216	58,876	152,489	Cherokee Rose	Empire State of the South
Hawaii	HI	Honolulu	1,108,229	6424	16,638	Hibiscus	Aloha State
Idaho	ID	Boise	1,006,749	83,557	216,415	Mock Orange	Gem State
Illinois	IL	Springfield	11,430,602	56,401)	146,075	Native Violet	Land of Lincoln
Indiana	IN	Indianapolis	5,544,159	36,291	93,995	Peony	Hoosier State
Iowa	IA	Des Moines	2,776,755	56,290	145,790	Wild Rose	Hawkeye State
Kansas	KS	Topeka	2,477,574	82,276	213,094	Sunflower	Sunflower State
Kentucky	KY	Frankfort	3,685,296	40,395	104,625	Goldenrod	Bluegrass State
Louisiana	LA	Baton Rouge	4,219,973	48,522	125,672	Magnolia	Pelican State
Maine	ME	Augusta	1,227,928	33,215	86,027	Pine Cone and Tassel	Pine Tree State
Maryland	MD	Annapolis	4,781,468	10,577	27,395	Black-eyed Susan	Old Line State
Massachusetts	MA	Boston	6,016,425	8257	21,385	Trailing Arbutus	Bay State
Michigan	MI	Lansing	9,295,297	58,216	150,780	Apple Blossom	Wolverine State
Minnesota	MN	St. Paul	4,375,099	84,068	217,735	Lady's-slipper	Gopher State
Mississippi	MS	Jackson	2,573,216	47,716	123,585	Magnolia	Magnolia State
Missouri	MO	Jefferson City	5,117,073	69,674	180,455	Hawthorn	Show Me State
Montana	MT	Helena	799,065	147,138	381,085	Bitterroot	Treasure State
Nebraska	NE	Lincoln	1,578,385	77,237	200,044	Goldenrod	Cornhusker State
Nevada	NV	Carson City	1,201,833	110,540	286,300	Sagebrush	Silver State
New Hampshire	NH	Concord	1,109,252	9304	24,100	Purple Lilac	Granite State
New Jersey	NJ	Trenton	7,730,188	7836	20,295	Purple Violet	Garden State
New Mexico	NM	Santa Fe	1,515,069	121,666	315,115	Yucca	Land of Enchantment
New York	NY	Albany	17,990,455	49,576	128,400	Rose	Empire State
North Carolina	NC	Raleigh	6,628,637	52,586	136,198	Dogwood	Tarheel State
North Dakota	ND	Bismarck	638,800	70,665	183,020	Prairie Rose	Flickertail State
Ohio	OH	Columbus	10,847,115	41,222	106,765	Scarlet Carnation	Buckeye State
Oklahoma	OK	Oklahoma City	3,145,585	69,919	181,090	Mistletoe	Sooner State
Oregon	OR	Salem	2,842,321	96,981	251,180	Oregon Grape	Beaver State
Pennsylvania	PA	Harrisburg	11,881,643	45,333	117,410	Mountain Laurel	Keystone State
Rhode Island	RI	Providence	1,003,464	1214	3145	Violet	Ocean State
South Carolina	SC	Columbia	3,486,703	31,055	80,430	Carolina Jessamine	Palmetto State
South Dakota	SD	Pierre	696,004	77,047	199,550	American Pasqueflower	Sunshine State
Tennessee	TN	Nashville	4,877,185	42,246	109,415	Iris	Volunteer State
Texas	TX	Austin	16,986,510	267,339	692,410	Bluebonnet	Lone Star State
Utah	UT	Salt Lake City	1,722,850	84,916	219,930	Sego Lily	Beehive State
Vermont	VT	Montpelier	562,758	9609	24,885	Red Clover	Green Mountain State
Virginia	VA	Richmond	6,187,358	40,815	105,710	American Dogwood	Old Dominion State
Washington	WA	Olympia	4,866,692	68,192	176,615	Rhododendron	Evergreen State
West Virginia	WV	Charleston	1,793,477	24,181	62,629	Rosebay Rhododendron	Mountain State
Wisconsin	WI	Madison	4,891,769	56,154	145,440	Wood Violet	Badger State
Wyoming	WY	Cheyenne	453,588	97,914	253,595	Indian Paintbrush	Equality State

FEDERAL DISTRICT

State	Postal Abbr.	Capital	Population (1990 census)	Total Area Sq. Mi.	Sq. Km	State Flower	State Nickname
Dist. of Columbia	DC	Washington	609,909	69	179	American Beauty Rose	

respected and influential political leader who exhibits great ability and devotion to public service. —**states′man•like′, states′man•ly,** *adj.* —**states′man•ship′,** *n.*

state′ so′cialism, *n.* the theory, doctrine, and movement advocating a planned economy controlled by the state, with state ownership of major industries and natural resources. —**state′ so′cialist,** *n.*

states′′ rights′, *n.pl.* the rights belonging to the states under the federal principle of government, esp. with reference to the strict construction of the Constitution by which all rights not delegated to the federal government belong to the states.

states•wom•an (stāts′wŏŏm′ən), *n., pl.* **-wom•en.** a woman who is an experienced and influential political leader, esp. one holding a high office in government.

state′ tree′, *n.* a tree chosen as an official symbol of a U.S. state.

state′ troop′er, *n.* a member of a state police force.

state′ univer′sity, *n.* a public university maintained by the government of a state.

state•wide (stāt′wīd′), *adj.* **1.** extending throughout all parts of a state: *statewide elections.* —*adv.* **2.** throughout a state.

stat•ic (stat′ik), *adj.* Also, **stat′i•cal. 1.** of or pertaining to bodies or forces at rest or in equilibrium. **2.** pertaining to or characterized by a fixed or stationary condition. **3.** showing little or no change: *a static relationship.* **4.** lacking movement, development, or vitality: *a novel marred by static characterizations.* **5.** pertaining to or noting static electricity. —*n.* **6. a.** static or atmospheric electricity. **b.** interference with radio broadcasts, etc., due to such electricity. **7.** resistance or hostility, as to one's actions or plans; opposition. —**stat′i•cal•ly,** *adv.*

stat′ic cling′, *n.* the adhering of clothing to other clothing or a person's body, caused by an accumulation of static electricity in the materials.

stat′ic electric′ity, *n.* an electrical charge, often created by friction, consisting of stationary ions that do not move in a current.

stat•ics (stat′iks), *n.* (*used with a sing. v.*) the branch of mechanics that deals with bodies at rest or forces in equilibrium.

sta•tion (stā′shən), *n.* **1.** a place or position in which a person or thing is normally located. **2.** a stopping place for trains or other land conveyances, for the transfer of freight or passengers. **3.** the building or buildings at such a stopping place. **4.** the district or municipal headquarters of certain public services: *a police station.* **5.** a place equipped for some particular kind of work, service, research, or activity: *a geophysical station.* **6.** the position, as of persons or things, in a scale of estimation, rank, or dignity; standing. **7.** a position, office, rank, calling, or the like. **8. a.** a studio or building from which radio or television broadcasts originate. **b.** a person or organization originating such broadcasts. **c.** a specific frequency or band of frequencies assigned to a regular or special broadcaster: *the Civil Defense station.* **d.** the complete equipment used in transmitting and receiving broadcasts. **9. a.** a military place of duty. **b.** a semipermanent army post. **10.** a place or region to which a ship or fleet is assigned for duty. **11.** a particular area or type of region where a given animal or plant is found. **12.** (in Australia) a ranch with its buildings, land, etc., esp. for raising sheep. **13.** *Survey.* **a.** a point where an observation is taken. **b.** a precisely located reference point. **14.** a section or area assigned for work or duty; post. **15.** one of the 14 stations of the cross. —*v.t.* **16.** to assign a station to.

sta•tion•ar•y (stā′shə ner′ē), *adj., n., pl.* **-ar•ies.** —*adj.* **1.** standing still; not moving. **2.** having a fixed position; not movable. **3.** established in one place; not itinerant or migratory. **4.** remaining in the same condition or state; not changing. —*n.* **5.** a person or thing that is stationary.

sta′tion break′, *n.* an interval during or after a radio or TV program for identifying the station, airing commercials, etc.

sta•tion•er (stā′shə nər), *n.* a seller of paper, pens, pencils, and other writing materials.

sta•tion•er•y (stā′shə ner′ē), *n.* **1.** writing paper. **2.** writing materials, as pens, pencils, paper, and envelopes.

sta′tion house′, *n.* a police station or fire station.

sta•tion•mas•ter (stā′shən mas′tər, -mä′stər), *n.* a person in charge of a railroad station.

sta′tions of the cross′ or **Sta′tions of the Cross′,** *n.pl.* a series of 14 representations of successive incidents from the Passion of Christ, each with a wooden cross, or a series of wooden crosses alone, set up in a church, or sometimes outdoors, and visited in sequence, for prayer and meditation.

sta′tion wag′on, *n.* an automobile with one or more rows of folding or removable seats behind the driver and an area behind these seats into which suitcases, parcels, etc., can be loaded through a tailgate.

stat•ism (stā′tiz əm), *n.* **1.** the principle or policy of concentrating extensive economic, political, and related controls in the state at the cost of individual liberty. **2.** support of or belief in the sovereignty of a state, usually a republic.

sta•tis•tic (stə tis′tik), *n.* a numerical fact or datum, esp. one computed from a sample.

sta•tis•ti•cal (stə tis′ti kəl), *adj.* of, pertaining to, consisting of, or based on statistics. —**sta•tis′ti•cal•ly,** *adv.*

stat•is•ti•cian (stat′i stish′ən), *n.* an expert in or compiler of statistics.

sta•tis•tics (stə tis′tiks), *n.* **1.** (*used with a sing. v.*) the science that deals with the collection, analysis, and interpretation of numerical data, often using probability theory. **2.** (*used with a pl. v.*) the data themselves.

stat•u•ar•y (stach′o͞o er′ē), *n., pl.* **-ar•ies,** *adj.* —*n.* **1.** statues collectively. **2.** a group or collection of statues. —*adj.* **3.** of, pertaining to, or suitable for statues.

stat•ue (stach′o͞o), *n.* a three-dimensional work of art, as a figure of a person or animal or an abstract form, carved in stone or wood, molded in a plastic material, cast in bronze, or the like. —**stat′ue•like′,** *adj.*

Stat′ue of Lib′erty, *n.* a large copper statue on Liberty Island in New York harbor depicting a woman holding a burning torch.

stat•u•esque (stach′o͞o esk′), *adj.* like or suggesting a statue, as in massive or majestic dignity, grace, or beauty. —**stat′u•esque′ly,** *adv.*

stat•u•ette (stach′o͞o et′), *n.* a small statue.

stat•ure (stach′ər), *n.* **1.** the height of a human or animal body. **2.** esteem or status based on one's positive qualities or achievements: *a person of stature in the community.*

sta•tus (stā′təs, stat′əs), *n., pl.* **-tus•es,** *adj.* —*n.* **1.** the position of an individual in relation to another or others; social or professional standing. **2.** high position or standing; prestige. **3.** state or condition of affairs: *What is the status of the contract negotiations?* **4.** the standing of a person before the law. —*adj.* **5.** conferring or believed to confer elevated status: *a status job.*

sta′tus quo′ (kwō), *n.* the existing state or condition. Also called **sta′tus in quo′.**

sta′tus sym′bol, *n.* an object, habit, etc., by which the social or economic status of the possessor may be determined, esp. something that indicates high social status or great affluence.

stat•ute (stach′o͞ot, -ŏŏt), *n.* **1. a.** a formal enactment by a legislature. **b.** a document setting forth such an enactment. **2.** an instrument annexed to an international agreement, as a treaty. **3.** a permanent rule established by an organization, corporation, etc., to govern its internal affairs.

stat′ute mile′, *n.* MILE (def. 1).

stat′ute of limita′tions, *n.* a statute defining the period within which legal action may be taken.

stat•u•to•ry (stach′o͞o tôr′ē, -tōr′ē), *adj.* **1.** of or pertaining to a statute. **2.** prescribed or authorized by statute. **3.** (of an offense) punishable by statute. —**stat′u•to′ri•ly,** *adv.*

stat′utory law′, *n.* the written law enacted by a legislature, as distinguished from unwritten law or common law.

stat′utory rape′, *n.* sexual intercourse with a girl under the legal age of consent.

St. Au•gus•tine (ô′gə stēn′), *n.* a seacoast city in NE Florida: founded by the Spanish 1565; oldest city in the U.S. 11,985.

staunch[1] (stônch), *v.t., v.i.* STANCH[1].

staunch[2] (stônch, stänch) also **stanch,** *adj.* **1.** firm or steadfast in principle, loyalty, etc.: *a staunch Democrat.* **2.** characterized by firmness, steadfastness, or loyalty: *a staunch defense of the government.* **3.** strong; substantial: *a staunch little cabin.* **4.** impervious to water or other liquids; watertight: *a staunch vessel.* —**staunch′ly,** *adv.* —**staunch′ness,** *n.*

stave (stāv), *n., v.,* **staved** or **stove, stav•ing.** —*n.* **1.** one of the thin, narrow, shaped pieces of wood that form the sides of a cask, tub, or similar vessel. **2.** a stick, rod, pole, or the like. **3.** a rung of a ladder, chair, etc. **4. a.** a verse or stanza of a poem or song. **b.** the alliterating sound in a line of verse, as the *w*-sound in *wind in the willows.* **5.** STAFF[1] (def. 8). —*v.t.* **6.** to break in a stave or staves of (a cask or barrel) so as to release the wine, liquor, or other contents. **7.** to break or crush (something) inward (often fol. by *in*). **8.** to break (a hole) in, esp. in the hull of a boat. **9.** to break to pieces; splinter; smash. **10.** to furnish with a stave or staves. **11.** to beat with a stave or staff. —*v.i.* **12.** to become staved in, as a boat; break in or up. **13.** to move along rapidly. **14. stave off, a.** to put, ward, or keep off, as by force or evasion. **b.** to prevent in time; forestall: *to stave off bankruptcy.*

staves (stāvz), *n.* **1.** a pl. of STAFF[1]. **2.** pl. of STAVE.

stay[1] (stā), *v.,* **stayed** or **staid, stay•ing,** *n.* —*v.i.* **1.** to remain or continue over a length of time, as in a place or situation: *to stay up late.* **2.** to dwell temporarily; lodge: *to stay at a friend's apartment.* **3.** to pause or wait briefly: *Stay inside until the taxi comes.* **4.** to continue to be as specified: *to stay clean.* **5.** to hold out or endure, as in a contest or at a task: *to stay with a project.* **6.** to keep up, as with a competitor. **7.** to stop or halt. **8.** to continue in a hand of poker by matching a bet or raise. —*v.t.* **9.** to stop or halt. **10.** to hold back, detain, or restrain. **11.** to suspend or delay (actions, proceedings, etc.). **12. a.** to appease temporarily the hunger of: *This sandwich will stay you till dinner.* **b.** to satisfy temporarily the cravings of (the stomach, appetite, etc.). **13.** to remain through or during (a period of time). **14.** to remain to the end of; remain beyond (usu. fol. by *out*). —*n.* **15.** the act of stopping or being stopped. **16.** a stop, halt, or pause. **17.** a sojourn or temporary residence: *a week's stay in Miami.* **18.** a suspension of a judicial proceeding: *a stay of execution.* **19.** staying power; endurance. —***Idiom.*** **20. stay put,** to remain in the same position or place. **21. stay the course,** to persevere; endure to completion.

stay[2] (stā), *n.* **1.** something used to support or steady a thing; prop; brace. **2.** a flat strip of firm material, as steel or whalebone, used esp. for stiffening corsets, collars, etc. **3. stays,** a corset. —*v.t.* **4.** to support, prop, or hold up (sometimes fol. by *up*). **5.** to sustain or strengthen mentally or spiritually. **6.** to attach to a foundation or base.

stay[3] (stā), *n.* **1.** any of various strong ropes or wires for steadying masts, funnels, etc. —*v.t.* **2.** to support or secure with stays: *to stay a mast.* **3.** to put (a ship) on the other tack. —*v.i.* **4.** (of a ship) to change to the other tack. —***Idiom.*** **5. in stays,** (of a fore-and-aft-rigged vessel) heading into the wind with sails shaking, as in coming about.

stay′-at-home′, *adj.* **1.** not inclined to venture outside one's residence, area, or country. **2.** of or pertaining to time spent at home. —*n.* **3.** a person who stays at or near home; homebody.

stay′ing pow′er, *n.* ability to endure; endurance; stamina.

stay•sail (stā′sāl′; *Naut.* -səl), *n.* any sail set on a stay, as a triangular sail between two masts.

St. Christopher-Nevis, *n.* St. Kitts-Nevis.

St. Clair (klâr), *n.* **1.** a river in the N central U.S. and S Canada, flowing S from Lake Huron to Lake St. Clair, forming part of the boundary between Michigan and Ontario. 41 mi. (66 km) long. **2. Lake,** a lake between SE Michigan and Ontario, Canada. 460 sq. mi. (1190 sq. km).

St. Croix (kroi), *n.* **1.** Also called **Santa Cruz.** a U.S. island in the N Lesser Antilles: the largest of the Virgin Islands. 55,300; 82 sq. mi. (212 sq. km). **2.** a river flowing from NW Wisconsin along the boundary between Wisconsin and Minnesota into the Mississippi. 164 mi. (264 km) long. **3.** a river in the northeast U.S. and SE Canada, forming a part of the boundary between Maine and New Brunswick, flowing into Passamaquoddy Bay. 75 mi. (121 km) long.

St. Den•is (sānt′ den′is; *for 2, 3 also Fr.* san də nē′), *n.* **1. Ruth,** 1880?–1968, U.S. dancer. **2.** a suburb of Paris in N France: famous abbey, the burial place of many French kings. 96,759. **3.** the capital of Réunion Island, in the Indian Ocean. 109,072.

Ste., (referring to a woman) Saint. [< French *Sainte*]

stead (sted), *n.* **1.** the place of a person or thing as occupied by a successor or substitute: *The nephew of the queen came in her stead.* —*v.t.* **2.** to be of service, advantage, or avail to. —***Idiom.*** **3. stand in good stead,** to prove useful to: *Her recommendation will stand you in good stead.*

stead•fast or **sted•fast** (sted′fast′, -fäst′, -fəst), *adj.* **1.** fixed in direction; steadily directed: *a steadfast gaze.* **2.** firm in purpose, resolution, faith, etc.: *a steadfast friend.* **3.** unwavering, as resolution, faith, or adherence. **4.** firmly established, as an institution or a state of affairs. **5.** firmly fixed in place or position; stable. —**stead′fast′ly,** *adv.* —**stead′fast′ness,** *n.*

stead•y (sted′ē), *adj.,* **stead•i•er, stead•i•est,** *interj., n., pl.* **stead•ies,** *v.,* **stead•ied, stead•y•ing,** *adv.* —*adj.* **1.** firmly placed or fixed; stable: *a steady ladder.* **2.** even or regular in movement: *a steady rhythm.* **3.** free from change, variation, or interruption; continuous. **4.** constant, regular, or habitual: *a steady job.* **5.** free from excitement or agitation; calm: *steady nerves.* **6.** firm; unfaltering: *a steady hand.* **7.** steadfast or unwavering; resolute: *a steady purpose.* **8.** settled, staid, or sober, as a person or habits. **9.** (of a vessel) keeping nearly upright, as in a heavy sea. —*interj.* **10.** (used to urge someone to calm down or be under control.) **11.** (a helm order to keep a vessel steady on its present heading.) —*n.* **12.** a person whom one dates exclusively; boyfriend or girlfriend. **13.** a steady visitor, customer, or the like; habitué. —*v.t.* **14.** to make or keep steady, as in position, movement, action, or character. —*v.i.* **15.** to become steady. —*adv.* **16.** steadily. —***Idiom.*** **17. go steady,** to date one person exclusively. —**stead′i•er,** *n.* —**stead′i•ly,** *adv.* —**stead′i•ness,** *n.*

steak (stāk), *n.* **1.** a slice of meat or fish, esp. beef, cooked by broiling, frying, or the like. **2.** chopped meat prepared in the same manner as a steak.

steak•house (stāk′hous′), *n., pl.* **-hous•es** (-hou′ziz). a restaurant specializing in beefsteak.

steak′ knife′, *n.* a sharp dinner knife the blade of which is made of steel and usu. serrated, used in cutting meat.

steak′ tar•tare′ (tär tär′), *n.* ground beefsteak served uncooked, often mixed with a raw egg, onions, and seasonings and garnished with capers. Also called **tartar steak.**

steal (stēl), *v.,* **stole, sto•len, steal•ing,** *n.* —*v.t.* **1.** to take (the property of another or others) without permission or right, esp. secretly or by force. **2.** to appropriate (ideas, credit, words, etc.) without right or acknowledgment. **3.** to take, get, or win insidiously, surreptitiously, subtly, or by chance: *He stole my girlfriend.* **4.** to move, bring, convey, or put secretly or quietly; smuggle: *She stole the dog upstairs at bedtime.* **5.** *Baseball.* (of a base runner) to reach (a base) safely by running while the ball is being pitched to the player at bat. —*v.i.* **6.** to commit or practice theft. **7.** to move, go, or come secretly, quietly, or unobserved: *to steal out of a room.* **8.** to pass, happen, etc., imperceptibly, gently, or gradually: *The years steal by.* **9.** *Baseball.* (of a base runner) to advance a base by running to it while the ball is being pitched to the player at bat. —*n.* **10.** an act of stealing; theft. **11.** the thing stolen. **12.** something acquired at a cost far below its real value; bargain. **13.** *Baseball.* the act of advancing a base by stealing. —***Idiom.*** **14. steal a march on,** to gain an advantage over, as by stealth. **15. steal someone's thunder, a.** to misappropriate the ideas or inventions of another. **b.** to spoil the effect of another's performance, remark, etc., by doing or saying it first. **16. steal the show, a.** to usurp the credit for something. **b.** to be more outstanding than anyone or anything else. —**steal′a•ble,** *adj.*

stealth (stelth), *n.* **1.** secret or surreptitious procedure or passage. —*adj.* **2.** (*often cap.*) having or providing the capacity to evade detection by radar: *Stealth planes; stealth technology.* —**stealth′ful,** *adj.* —**stealth′ful•ly,** *adv.*

stealth•y (stel′thē), *adj.,* **stealth•i•er, stealth•i•est.** done, characterized, or acting by stealth; furtive. —**stealth′i•ly,** *adv.*

steam (stēm), *n.* **1.** water in the form of an invisible gas or vapor. **2.** water changed to this form by boiling, extensively used for the generation of mechanical power, for heating purposes, etc. **3.** the mist formed when the gas or vapor from boiling water condenses in the air. **4.** an exhalation of a vapor or mist. **5.** power or energy. —*v.i.* **6.** to emit or give off steam or vapor. **7.** to rise or pass off in the form of steam or vapor. **8.** to become covered with condensed steam, as a window or other surface (often fol. by *up*). **9.** to generate or produce steam, as in a boiler. **10.** to move or travel by the agency of steam. **11.** to move rapidly or evenly: *He steamed out of the room.* **12.** to be angry or show anger. —*v.t.* **13.** to expose to or treat with steam, as in order to heat, cook, soften, or renovate. **14.** to emit or exhale (vapor, mist, etc.). **15.** to cause to become irked or angry (often fol. by *up*). **16.** to convey by the agency of steam: *to steam the ship safely into port.* —*adj.* **17.** employing or operated by steam: *a steam radiator.* **18.** conducting steam: *a steam line.* **19.** of or pertaining to steam. **20.** propelled by or propelling with a steam engine. —***Idiom.*** **21. blow** or **let off steam,** to give vent to emotion or energy previously suppressed or contained, esp. by talking or acting unrestrainedly.

steam′ bath′, *n.* **1.** a bath of steam, usu. in a specially equipped room or enclosure, for cleansing or refreshing oneself. **2.** the room or enclosure itself. **3.** an establishment with facilities for such a bath.

steam•boat (stēm′bōt′), *n.* a steam-driven vessel, esp. a small one or one used on inland waters.

steam′ en′gine, *n.* an engine worked by steam, typically one in which a sliding piston in a cylinder is moved by the expansive action of the steam generated in a boiler.

steam•er (stē′mər), *n.* **1.** something propelled or operated by steam, as a steamship. **2.** a person or thing that steams. **3.** a device, pot, or container in which something is steamed. **4.** soft-shell clam. —*v.i.* **5.** to travel by steamship.

steam′er trunk′, *n.* a rectangular traveling trunk low enough to slide under a bunk on a ship.

steam′fit′ter or **steam′ fit′ter,** *n.* a person who installs and repairs steam pipes and their accessories. —**steam′ fit′ting,** *n.*

steam′ heat′, *n.* heat obtained by the circulation of steam in pipes, radiators, etc.

steam′ i′ron, *n.* an electric iron with a chamber in which water is heated to steam, then directed onto the item being ironed.

steam′ point′, *n.* the temperature at which water vapor condenses at a pressure of one atmosphere, represented by 212°F (100°C). Compare ice point.

steam•roll•er (stēm′rō′lər), *n.* **1.** a heavy steam-powered vehicle having a roller for crushing, compacting, or leveling materials used for a road or the like. **2.** (not in technical use) any similar vehicle with a roller. **3.** an overpowering force, esp. a ruthless one. —*v.t.* **4.** to crush or flatten with a steamroller. **5.** to overcome with superior force. **6.** to bring about the adoption of by overwhelming pressure: *to steamroller the resolution through.* —*v.i.* **7.** to proceed with implacable force.

steam′ room′, *n.* a heated, steam-filled room for taking a steam bath.

steam•ship (stēm′ship′), *n.* a large commercial vessel, esp. one driven by steam.

steam′ shov′el, *n.* a machine for digging or excavating, operated by its own engine and boiler.

steam′ ta′ble, *n.* a boxlike table or counter with openings in the top into which containers of food may be fitted to be kept warm by steam or hot water in the compartment below.

steam•y (stē′mē), *adj.,* **steam•i•er, steam•i•est.** **1.** resembling, consisting of, or abounding in steam. **2.** covered with or as if with condensed steam. **3.** hot and humid. **4.** passionate or erotic. —**steam′i•ly,** *adv.* —**steam′i•ness,** *n.*

stear′ic ac′id, *n.* a colorless, waxlike, sparingly water-soluble fatty acid, $C_{18}H_{36}O_2$, occurring in animal fats and some vegetable oils: used in candles, cosmetics, and medicine.

ste•a•tite (stē′ə tīt′), *n.* soapstone. —**ste′a•tit′ic** (-tit′ik), *adj.*

Steb•bins (steb′inz), *n.* **George,** 1846–1945, U.S. musician and hymn writer, born in Canada.

steed (stēd), *n.* a horse, esp. a high-spirited one. —**steed′like′,** *adj.*

steel (stēl), *n.* **1.** any of various forms of refined iron containing less carbon than pig iron and more than wrought iron and possessing varying qualities of hardness, elasticity, and strength. **2.** a thing or things made of this metal. **3.** a flat strip of this metal used for stiffening, esp. in corsets; stay. **4.** a sword. **5.** a rounded rod of ridged steel, fitted with a handle and used esp. for sharpening knives. —*adj.* **6.** made of steel. **7.** of, pertaining to, or like steel. —*v.t.* **8.** to fit with steel, as by pointing, edging, or overlaying. **9.** to cause to resemble steel in some way. **10.** to render insensible, inflexible, unyielding, determined, etc.: *She steeled herself to open the door.* —**steel′like′,** *adj.*

steel′ band′, *n.* a band, native to Trinidad and common in other of the Caribbean islands, using steel oil drums cut to various heights and tuned to specific pitches.

steel′ blue′, *n.* dark bluish gray.

steel′ gray′, *n.* dark metallic gray with a bluish tinge.

steel′ guitar′, *n.* **1.** an acoustic, hand-held guitar having a metal resonator and producing a wailing, variable sound. **2.** PEDAL STEEL GUITAR. **3.** HAWAIIAN GUITAR.

steel′ mill′, *n.* a steelworks.

steel′ wool′, *n.* a tangled or matted mass of stringlike steel shavings, used for scouring, polishing, smoothing, etc.

steel·works (stēl′wûrks′), *n., pl.* **-works.** (*used with a sing. or pl. v.*) an establishment where steel and often steel parts are made.

steel·y (stē′lē), *adj.,* **steel·i·er, steel·i·est. 1.** consisting or made of steel. **2.** resembling or suggesting steel, as in color or hardness. **—steel′i·ness,** *n.*

steen·bok (stēn′bok′, stān′-) also **steinbok,** *n., pl.* **-boks,** (*esp. collectively*) **-bok.** a small African antelope, *Raphicerus campestris:* only males have spikes.

steep¹ (stēp), *adj.* **1.** having an almost vertical slope or pitch, or a relatively high gradient, as a hill, an ascent, or stairs. **2.** (of a price or amount) unduly high; exorbitant. **3.** high or lofty. —*n.* **4.** a steep place; declivity, as of a hill. **—steep′ly,** *adv.* **—steep′ness,** *n.*

steep² (stēp), *v.t.* **1.** to soak in water or other liquid, as to soften, cleanse, or extract some constituent. **2.** to wet thoroughly in or with a liquid; drench; saturate; imbue. **3.** to saturate with some pervading or absorbing influence or agency: *an incident steeped in mystery.* —*v.i.* **4.** to lie soaking in a liquid. —*n.* **5.** the act or process of steeping or the state of being steeped. **6.** a liquid in which something is steeped.

stee·ple (stē′pəl), *n.* **1.** an ornamental construction, usu. ending in a spire, erected on a roof or tower of a church, public building, etc. **2.** a tower terminating in such a construction. **3.** a spire. **—stee′pled,** *adj.* **—stee′ple·less,** *adj.* **—stee′ple·like′,** *adj.*

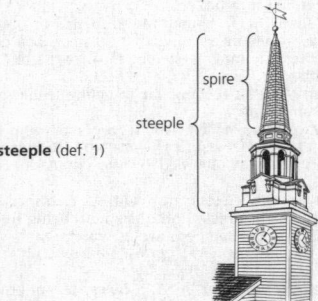

spire

steeple

steeple (def. 1)

stee·ple·bush (stē′pəl boֹosh′), *n.* HARDHACK.

stee·ple·chase (stē′pəl chās′), *n., v.,* **-chased, -chas·ing.** —*n.* **1.** a horse race over a turf course with artificial ditches, hedges, and other obstacles over which the horses must jump. **2.** a foot race run on a cross-country course or over a course with obstacles. —*v.i.* **3.** to ride or run in a steeplechase. **—stee′ple·chas′er,** *n.*

stee·ple·jack (stē′pəl jak′), *n.* a person who climbs steeples, towers, etc., to build or repair them.

steer¹ (stēr), *v.t.* **1.** to guide the course of (something in motion) by a rudder, helm, wheel, etc. **2.** to follow or pursue (a particular course). **3.** to direct the course of; guide. —*v.i.* **4.** to direct the course of a vessel, vehicle, airplane, etc., by the use of a rudder or other means. **5.** to pursue a course of action. **6.** (of a vessel, vehicle, airplane, etc.) to be steered or guided in a particular direction or manner. —*n.* **7.** a suggestion about a course of action; tip. **—Idiom. 8.** steer clear of, to stay away from purposely; avoid. **—steer′a·ble,** *adj.* **—steer′a·bil′i·ty,** *n.*

steer² (stēr), *n., pl.* **steers,** (*esp. collectively*) **steer.** a male bovine that is castrated before sexual maturity, esp. one raised for beef.

steer·age (stēr′ij), *n.* **1.** (in a passenger ship) the accommodations for travelers who pay the cheapest fare, usu. providing minimal comfort and convenience. **2. a.** the act or action of steering. **b.** management; direction.

steer·ing (stēr′ing), *n.* the discriminatory practice by a real estate agent of maneuvering a client from a minority group away from considering a home in a white neighborhood.

steer′ing col′umn, *n.* the shaft that connects the steering wheel to the steering gear assembly of an automotive vehicle.

steer′ing commit′tee, *n.* a committee, esp. of a deliberative or legislative body, that prepares the agenda of a session.

steer′ing gear′, *n.* the apparatus or mechanism for steering a ship, automobile, bicycle, airplane, etc.

steer′ing wheel′, *n.* a wheel held and turned by a driver, pilot, or the like, to steer an automobile, ship, etc.

steers·man (stērz′mən), *n., pl.* **-men.** a person who steers a ship; helmsman.

Stef·ans·son (stef′ən sən), *n.* **Vil·hjal·mur** (vil′hyoul′mər), 1879–1962, U.S. arctic explorer and author, born in Canada.

steg·o·saur (steg′ə sôr′), *n.* any plant-eating dinosaur of the Jurassic

and Cretaceous family Stegosauridae, having bony plates along the back.

stein (stīn), *n.* **1.** a mug, usu. earthenware, esp. for beer. **2.** the quantity contained in a stein.

Stein·beck (stīn′bek), *n.* **John (Ernst),** 1902–68, U.S. novelist.

stein·bok (stīn′bok), *n., pl.* **-boks,** (*esp. collectively*) **-bok.** STEENBOK.

Stei·ner (stī′nər, shtī′-), *n.* **Rudolf,** 1861–1925, Austrian social philosopher: teacher of the spiritual doctrines of anthroposophy.

Stein·metz (stīn′mets), *n.* **Charles Proteus,** 1865–1923, U.S. electrical engineer, born in Germany.

Stein·way (stīn′wā′), *n.* **Henry Engelhard,** (*Heinrich Engelhard Steinweg*), 1797–1871, U.S. piano manufacturer, born in Germany.

ste·la (stē′lə), *n., pl.* **ste·lae** (stē′lē). STELE (defs. 1, 2).

ste·le (stē′lē, stēl *for 1, 2;* stēl, stē′lē *for 3*), *n., pl.* **ste·lai** (stē′lī), **ste·les** (stē′lēz, stēlz). **1.** an upright stone slab or pillar bearing an inscription or design and serving as a monument, marker, etc. **2.** a prepared surface on the face of a building, a rock, etc., bearing an inscription or the like. **3.** the central cylinder of vascular tissue in the stems and roots of the higher plants. Also, **stela** (for defs. 1, 2). **—ste′lar,** *adj.*

stel·lar (stel′ər), *adj.* **1.** of or pertaining to the stars; consisting of stars. **2.** like a star, as in brilliance. **3.** pertaining to a preeminent performer, athlete, etc.

St. El·mo's fire (el′mōz), *n.* a form of luminous corona discharge that sometimes occurs during electrical storms.

stem¹ (stem), *n., v.,* **stemmed, stem·ming.** —*n.* **1.** the ascending axis of a plant, whether above or below ground, which ordinarily grows in an opposite direction to the root. **2.** the stalk that supports a leaf, flower, or fruit. **3.** a stalk of bananas. **4.** something resembling or suggesting a leaf or flower stalk. **5.** a long, slender part: *the stem of a tobacco pipe.* **6.** the slender, vertical part of a goblet, wineglass, etc., between the bowl and the base. **7.** a projection from the rim of a watch, having on its end a knob for winding the watch. **8.** the circular rod in some locks about which the key fits and rotates. **9.** the stock or line of descent of a family, esp. its original ancestry. **10.** the underlying form of a word, consisting of a root alone or a root plus an affix, to which inflectional endings may be added. **11.** the vertical line forming part of a musical note. **12.** the main or relatively thick stroke of a letter in printing. —*v.t.* **13.** to remove the stem from (a leaf, fruit, etc.). —*v.i.* **14.** to arise or originate (usu. fol. by *from*). **—stem′less,** *adj.*

stem² (stem), *v.,* **stemmed, stem·ming,** *n.* —*v.t.* **1.** to stop, check, or restrain. **2.** to dam up; stop the flow of (a stream, river, or the like). **3.** to tamp, plug, or make tight, as a hole or joint. **4.** to maneuver (a ski or skis) in executing a stem. **5.** to stanch (bleeding). —*v.i.* **6.** to execute a stem. —*n.* **7.** an act or instance whereby a skier pushes the heel of one or both skis outward, as in making certain turns or to slow down.

stem³ (stem), *n., v.,* **stemmed, stem·ming.** —*n.* **1.** (at the bow of a vessel) an upright into which the side timbers or plates are jointed. **2.** the forward part of a vessel (often opposed to *stern*). —*v.t.* **3.** to make headway against (a tide, current, gale, etc.). **4.** to make progress against (any opposition).

stem′ cell′, *n.* a cell that upon division replaces its own numbers and also gives rise to cells that differentiate further into one or more specialized types.

stem·ware (stem′wâr′), *n.* glass or crystal vessels, esp. for beverages and desserts, having rounded bowls on stems.

stem·wind·er (stem′wīn′dər), *n.* **1.** a stemwinding watch. **2.** *Older Slang.* **a.** something remarkable of its kind. **b.** a rousing speech, esp. a stirring political address. **c.** a stirring orator. Also, **stem′-wind′er.**

stem′wind′ing or **stem′-wind′ing,** *adj.* wound by turning a knob at the stem.

stench (stench), *n.* **1.** an offensive smell or odor; stink. **2.** a foul quality.

sten·cil (sten′səl), *n., v.,* **-ciled, -cil·ing** or (*esp. Brit.*) **-cilled, -cil·ling.** —*n.* **1.** a thin sheet of cardboard or other material in which letters, numbers, designs, etc., have been cut out so that they can be reproduced on another surface when ink, paint, or the like is applied over the cutout areas. **2.** the letters, designs, etc., produced. —*v.t.* **3.** to mark or paint (a surface) by means of a stencil. **4.** to produce (letters, designs, etc.) by means of a stencil. **—sten′cil·er;** *esp. Brit.,* **sten′cil·ler,** *n.*

Sten·dhal (sten däl′, stan-; *Fr.* stän dAl′), *n.* (*Marie Henri Beyle*), 1783–1842, French novelist and critic.

sten·o (sten′ō), *n., pl.* **sten·os. 1.** a stenographer. **2.** stenography.

ste·nog·ra·pher (stə nog′rə fər), *n.* a person who specializes in taking dictation in shorthand.

ste·nog·ra·phy (stə nog′rə fē), *n.* the art of writing in shorthand. **—sten·o·graph·ic** (sten′ə graf′ik), *adj.*

sten·o·type (sten′ə tīp′), *n., v.,* **-typed, -typ·ing.** —*n.* **1.** a keyboard machine resembling a typewriter, used in stenotypy. **2.** the symbols typed in one stroke on this machine. —*v.t.* **3.** to write or record with a stenotype. **—sten′o·typ′ist,** *n.*

sten·o·typ·y (sten′ə tī′pē), *n.* shorthand in which symbols are used to produce shortened forms of words or phrases. **—sten′o·typ′ic** (-tip′ik), *adj.*

sten·to·ri·an (sten tôr′ē ən, -tōr′-), *adj.* very loud or powerful in sound: *a stentorian voice.*

step (step), *n., v.,* **stepped, step·ping.** —*n.* **1.** a movement made by lifting the foot and setting it down again in a new position, accompanied by a shifting of the body in the direction of the new position, as in walking or dancing. **2.** the space passed over or the distance measured by one such movement of the foot. **3.** the sound made by the foot in making such a movement. **4.** a mark or impression made by the foot on the ground; footprint. **5.** the manner of stepping; gait; stride. **6.** pace or rhythm in marching: *double-quick step.* **7.** a pace or rhythm uniform with that of another or others, or in time with music. **8. steps,** movements or course in stepping or walking: *to retrace one's steps.* **9.** any of a series of successive stages in a process or the attainment of an end: *the five steps to success.* **10.** rank, degree, or grade, as on a vertical scale. **11.** a support for the foot in ascending or descending. **12.** a very short distance. **13.** a repeated pattern or unit of movement in a dance formed by a combination of foot and body motions. **14.** *Music.* **a.** a degree of the staff or of the scale. **b.** the interval between two adjacent scale degrees; second. —*v.i.* **15.** to move in steps. **16.** to walk, esp. for a few strides or a short distance: *Step over to the counter.* **17.** to move with measured steps, as in a dance. **18.** to go briskly or fast, as a horse. **19.** to come easily and naturally, as if by a step of the foot: *to step into a fortune.* **20.** to put the foot down; tread. **21.** to press with the foot, as on a lever or spring, in order to operate some mechanism. —*v.t.* **22.** to take (a step, pace, stride, etc.). **23.** to go through or perform the steps of (a dance). **24.** to move or set (the foot) in taking a step. **25.** to measure (a distance, ground, etc.) by steps (sometimes fol. by *off* or *out*). **26.** to make or arrange in the manner of a series of steps. **27.** to fix (a mast) in its step. **28. step down, a.** to lower or decrease by degrees. **b.** to relinquish one's authority or control; resign. **29. step in,** to become involved; intervene. **30. step out, a.** to leave a place, esp. for a short time. **b.** to walk or march at a more rapid pace. **c.** to go out socially. **31. step up, a.** to raise or increase by degrees. **b.** to be promoted; advance. **c.** to make progress; improve. —*Idiom.* **32. break step,** to cease or interrupt marching in step. **33. in** (or **out of**) **step, a.** in (or not in) time to a rhythm or beat, as while marching in unison. **b.** in (or not in) harmony or agreement with others. **34. keep step,** to stay in step; keep pace. **35. one step at a time,** slowly and cautiously. **36. step by step,** gradually; by stages. **37. step on it** or **on the gas,** *Informal.* to move more quickly; hurry. **38. take steps,** to employ necessary procedures. **39. watch one's step,** to proceed with caution.

step•broth•er (step′bruth′ər), *n.* one's stepfather's or stepmother's son by a previous marriage.

step•child (step′chīld′), *n., pl.* **-child•ren. 1.** a child of one's husband or wife by a previous marriage. **2.** any person, organization, project, etc., that is not properly supported or appreciated.

step′ dance′, *n.* a dance in which the focus of attention is on the steps rather than on body movement or gesture.

step•daugh•ter (step′dô′tər), *n.* a daughter of one's husband or wife by a previous marriage.

step•fa•ther (step′fä′thər), *n.* the husband of one's mother by a later marriage.

steph•a•no•tis (stef′ə nō′tis), *n.* any vine belonging to the genus *Stephanotis,* of the milkweed family, having fragrant, waxy, white flowers and leathery leaves.

Ste•phen (stē′vən), *n.* **1. Saint,** died A.D. c35, first Christian martyr. **2. Saint,** c975–1038, first king of Hungary 997–1038. **3.** (*Stephen of Blois*) 1097?–1154, king of England 1135–54. **4. Sir Leslie,** 1832–1904, English critic, biographer, and philosopher (father of Virginia Woolf).

Ste•phen•son (stē′vən sən), *n.* **1. George,** 1781–1848, English inventor and engineer. **2.** his son **Robert,** 1803–59, English engineer.

step•lad•der (step′lad′ər), *n.* a ladder having flat steps in place of rungs, esp. one with a hinged frame opening up to form four supporting legs.

step•moth•er (step′muth′ər), *n.* the wife of one's father by a later marriage.

step•par•ent (step′pâr′ənt, -par′-), *n.* a stepfather or stepmother. —**step′par•ent•ing,** *n.*

steppe (step), *n.* **1.** an extensive plain, esp. one without trees. **2. The Steppes,** the vast grasslands in the S and E European and W and SW Asian parts of Russia.

stepped′-up′, *adj.* increased; augmented; accelerated: *a stepped-up fundraising campaign.*

step′ping•stone′ or **step′ping stone′,** *n.* **1.** a stone for stepping on in crossing a stream, marsh, etc. **2.** any means or stage of advancement or improvement.

step•sis•ter (step′sis′tər), *n.* one's stepfather's or stepmother's daughter by a previous marriage.

step•son (step′sun′), *n.* a son of one's husband or wife by a previous marriage.

step•stool (step′stōōl′), *n.* a low set of hinged steps folding into or under a stool.

step•wise (step′wīz′), *adv.* **1.** in a steplike arrangement. —*adj.* **2.** *Music.* moving from one adjacent tone to another.

stere (stēr), *n.* a cubic meter, equivalent to 35.2 cubic feet, used to measure cordwood.

ster•e•o (ster′ē ō′, stēr′-), *n.* **1.** a system or equipment for reproducing stereophonic sound. **2.** stereophonic sound reproduction. **3.** stereoscopic photography. **4.** a stereoscopic photograph. **5.** STEREOTYPE (def. 1). —*adj.* **6.** pertaining to stereophonic sound, stereoscopic photography, etc.

stereo-, a combining form meaning "solid," "solid body or figure," "three-dimensions": *stereochemistry; stereoscope.* Also, *esp. before a vowel,* **stere-.**

ster•e•o•chem•is•try (ster′ē ō kem′ə strē, stēr′-), *n.* the branch of chemistry that deals with the determination of the relative positions in space of the atoms or groups of atoms in a compound and with the effects of these positions on the properties of the compound. —**ster′e•o•chem′ic, ster′e•o•chem′i•cal,** *adj.*

ster•e•og•ra•phy (ster′ē og′rə fē, stēr′-), *n.* **1.** the art of delineating the forms of solid bodies on a plane. **2.** a branch of solid geometry dealing with the construction of regularly defined solids. —**ster′e•o•graph′ic** (-ə graf′ik, stēr′-), **ster′e•o•graph′i•cal,** *adj.*

ster•e•o•phon•ic (ster′ē ə fon′ik, stēr′-), *adj.* pertaining to a system of recording and reproducing sound with enhanced realism by using two channels instead of one. —**ster′e•o•phon′i•cal•ly,** *adv.* —**ster′e•oph′o•ny** (-of′ə nē), *n.*

ster•e•o•scope (ster′ē ə skōp′, stēr′-), *n.* an optical instrument through which two pictures of the same object, taken from slightly different points of view, are viewed, one by each eye, producing the effect of a single picture of the object, with the appearance of depth or relief.

ster•e•o•scop•ic (ster′ē ə skop′ik, stēr′-) also **ster′e•o•scop′i•cal,** *adj.* **1.** of or pertaining to three-dimensional vision or any process or device for giving the illusion of three dimensions or depth from two-dimensional images. **2.** of or characterized by a stereoscope or stereoscopy. —**ster′e•o•scop′i•cal•ly,** *adv.*

ster•e•o•type (ster′ē ə tīp′, stēr′-), *n., v.,* **-typed, -typ•ing.** —*n.* **1. a.** a process for making printing plates by taking a mold of composed type and casting type metal from the mold. **b.** a plate made in this manner. **2.** an idea, expression, etc., lacking in originality or inventiveness; convention. **3.** a simplified and standardized conception or image of a person, group, etc., held in common by members of a group: *the stereotypes that society has of the mentally ill.* —*v.t.* **4.** to make a stereotype of. **5.** to give a fixed form to. —**ster′e•o•typ′er, ster′e•o•typ′ist,** *n.* —**ster′e•o•typ′ic** (-tip′ik), **ster′e•o•typ′i•cal,** *adj.*

ster•e•o•typed (ster′ē ə tīpt′, stēr′-), *adj.* **1.** reproduced in or by stereotype plates. **2.** fixed or settled in form; lacking freshness or originality; hackneyed; conventional.

ster•ile (ster′il; *esp. Brit.* -īl), *adj.* **1.** free from living germs or microorganisms; aseptic. **2.** incapable of producing offspring; infertile. **3.** barren; not producing vegetation: *sterile soil.* **4. a.** noting a plant in which reproductive structures fail to develop. **b.** bearing no stamens or pistils. **5.** not productive of results, ideas, etc.; fruitless. —**ster′ile•ly,** *adv.* —**ste•ril′i•ty** (stə ril′i tē), **ster′ile•ness,** *n.*

ster•i•lize (ster′ə līz′), *v.t.,* **-lized, -liz•ing. 1.** to cleanse by destroying microorganisms, parasites, etc., usu. by bringing to a high temperature. **2.** to render (a person or animal) infertile by removing or inhibiting the sex organs. **3.** to render (land, vegetation, etc.) barren or unproductive. **4.** to delete or remove compromising or damaging material from. —**ster′i•li•za′tion,** *n.*

ster•ling (stûr′ling), *adj.* **1.** of or denoting the currency of Great Britain. **2.** (of silver) having the standard fineness of 0.925. **3.** made of silver of this fineness. **4.** thoroughly excellent: *a person of sterling worth.* —*n.* **5.** British currency. **6.** the standard of fineness for gold and silver coin in the United Kingdom, 0.91666 for gold and 0.500 for silver. **7.** silver having a fineness of 0.925, now used esp. in the manufacture of table utensils, jewelry, etc. **8.** manufactured articles of sterling silver. **9.** sterling flatware.

Ster′ling Heights′, *n.* a city in SE Michigan, near Detroit. 119,505.

stern[1] (stûrn), *adj.* **1.** firm, strict, or uncompromising: *stern discipline.* **2.** hard, harsh, or severe. **3.** rigorous or austere; of an unpleasantly serious character: *stern times.* **4.** grim or forbidding in aspect: *a stern face.* —**stern′ly,** *adv.* —**stern′ness,** *n.*

stern[2] (stûrn), *n.* **1.** the after part of a vessel (often opposed to *stem*). **2.** the back or rear of anything.

Ster•no (stûr′nō), *Trademark.* flammable hydrocarbon jelly packaged in a small can for use as a portable heat source for cooking.

stern•post (stûrn′pōst′), *n.* an upright member rising from the after end of a keel; a rudderpost or propeller post.

ster•num (stûr′nəm), *n., pl.* **-na** (-nə), **-nums. 1.** the bony plate or series of bones to which the ribs are attached anteriorly or ventrally in most vertebrates; breastbone. **2.** the ventral surface of a body segment of an arthropod. —**ster′nal,** *adj.*

stern•wheel (stûrn′hwēl, -wēl′), *n.* a paddle wheel at the stern of a vessel.

ste•roid (stēr′oid, ster′-), *n.* any of a large group of fat-soluble organic compounds, as the sex hormones, most of which have specific physiological action. Compare ANABOLIC STEROID, CORTICOSTEROID. —**ste•roi′dal** (sti roid′l, ste-), *adj.*

ster•tor (stûr′tər), *n.* an abnormal snoring sound accompanying breathing.

ster•to•rous (stûr′tər əs), *adj.* **1.** characterized by stertor or heavy snoring. **2.** breathing in this manner. —**ster′to•rous•ly,** *adv.*

stet (stet), *v.i.* **1.** let it stand (used as a direction on a printer's proof or manuscript to retain material previously deleted). —*v.t.* **2.** to retain (material previously deleted) by marking it with the word "stet" or a row of dots.

steth•o•scope (steth′ə skōp′), *n.* an instrument used in auscultation to detect sounds in the chest or other parts of the body. **—ste•thos•co•py** (ste thos′kə pē, steth′ə skō′-), *n.* **—steth′o•scop′ic** (-skop′ik), *adj.*

Stet•son (stet′sən), *Trademark.* a brand of felt hat with a broad brim and high crown.

Steu•ben (sto͞o′bən, styo͞o′-, sto͞o ben′, styo͞o-; *Ger.* shtoi′bən), *n.* **Frie•drich Wil•helm Lu•dolf Ger•hard Au•gus•tin von** (frē′drĭkh vil′helm lo͞o′dôlf gär′härt ou′go͞os tēn′ fən), 1730–94, Prussian major general in the American Revolutionary army.

ste•ve•dore (stē′vi dôr′, -dōr′), *n., v.,* **-dored, -dor•ing.** **—***n.* **1.** a person or company engaged in the loading or unloading of ships. **—***v.t.* **2.** to load or unload the cargo of (a ship). **—***v.i.* **3.** to load or unload a ship.

Ste•vens (stē′vənz), *n.* **1. John Paul,** born 1920, associate justice of the U.S. Supreme Court since 1975. **2. Thaddeus,** 1792–1868, U.S. abolitionist and political leader. **3. Wallace,** 1879–1955, U.S. poet.

Ste•ven•son (stē′vən sən), *n.* **1. Ad•lai Ewing** (ad′lā), 1835–1914, vice president of the U.S. 1893–97. **2.** his grandson, **Adlai E(wing),** 1900–65, U.S. statesman and diplomat: ambassador to the U.N. 1960–65. **3. Robert Louis** (*Robert Lewis Balfour*), 1850–94, Scottish novelist, essayist, and poet.

stew (sto͞o, styo͞o), *v.t.* **1.** to cook (food) by simmering or slow boiling. **—***v.i.* **2.** to undergo cooking by simmering or slow boiling. **3.** to fret, worry, or fuss. **—***n.* **4.** a preparation of meat, fish, or other food cooked by stewing, esp. a mixture of meat and vegetables. **5.** a state of agitation, uneasiness, or worry. **—*Idiom.* 6. stew in one's own juice,** to suffer the consequences of one's own actions. **—stew′a•ble,** *adj.*

stew•ard (sto͞o′ərd, styo͞o′-), *n.* **1.** a person who manages another's property or financial affairs; one who administers anything as the agent of another or others. **2.** a person in charge of running the household of another. **3.** an employee who has charge of the table, wine, servants, etc., in a club, restaurant, or the like. **4.** an employee on a ship, train, or airplane who waits on and is responsible for the comfort of passengers. **5.** a person appointed by an organization or group to supervise the affairs of that group at certain functions. **6.** a petty officer in the U.S. Navy in charge of officer's quarters and mess. **—***v.t.* **7.** to act as steward of; manage. **—***v.i.* **8.** to act or serve as steward. **—stew′ard•ship′,** *n.*

stge., storage.

St. George's (jôr′jiz), *n.* the capital of Grenada, in the SW part. 6657.

St. He•le•na (hə lē′nə), *n.* **1.** a British island in the S Atlantic: Napoleon's place of exile 1815–21. 47 sq. mi. (122 sq. km). **2.** a British colony comprising this island, Ascension Island, and the Tristan da Cunha group. 5,564; 126 sq. mi. (326 sq. km). *Cap.:* Jamestown.

St. Hel•ens (hel′ənz), *n.* **Mount,** an active volcano in SW Washington, part of the Cascade Range: major eruptions 1980. 8364 ft. (2549 m).

St. Hel•ier (hel′yər), *n.* a seaport on and capital of the island of Jersey in the English Channel: resort. 28,135.

stick[1] (stik), *n.* **1.** a branch or shoot of a tree or shrub that has been cut or broken off. **2.** a relatively long and slender piece of wood. **3.** a long piece of wood for use as fuel, in carpentry, etc. **4.** a rod or wand. **5.** a baton. **6.** a club or cudgel. **7.** something that serves to goad or coerce. **8.** a long, slender piece or part of anything: *a stick of celery.* **9.** an implement used to drive or propel a ball or puck, as a crosse or a hockey stick. **10.** a lever by which the longitudinal and lateral motions of an airplane are controlled. **11.** a mast or spar. **12. the sticks,** *Informal.* any region distant from cities or towns, as rural districts; the country. **13. —***v.t.* **14.** to furnish (a plant, vine, etc.) with a stick or sticks in order to prop or support. **—*Saying.* 15. Sticks and stones may break my bones, but words will never hurt me,** insults are less injurious than a physical attack.

stick[2] (stik), *v.,* **stuck, stick•ing,** *n.* **—***v.t.* **1.** to pierce or puncture with something pointed; stab. **2.** to kill by stabbing. **3.** to thrust (something pointed) in, into, through, etc. **4.** to fasten in position by thrusting a point or end into something: *to stick a peg in a pegboard.* **5.** to fasten in position by or as if by something thrust through. **6.** to put on or hold with something pointed; impale. **7.** to decorate or furnish with things piercing the surface: *to stick a cushion full of pins.* **8.** to furnish or adorn with things attached or set here and there. **9.** to place upon a stick or pin for exhibit. **10.** to thrust or poke into a place or position indicated: *to stick one's head out of the window.* **11.** to place or set in a specified position; put: *Stick the chair in the corner.* **12.** to fasten or attach by causing to adhere: *to stick a stamp on a letter.* **13.** to bring to a standstill; render unable to proceed or go back (usu. used in the passive): *The car was stuck in the mud.* **14.** to confuse or puzzle; bewilder. **15.** *Informal.* to impose something disagreeable upon, as a large bill or a difficult task. **—***v.i.* **16.** to have the point piercing or embedded in something: *The arrow stuck in the tree.* **17.** to remain attached by adhesion. **18.** to hold, cleave, or cling. **19.** to remain persistently or permanently: *a fact that sticks in the mind.* **20.** to remain firm, as in resolution, opinion, etc. **21.** to keep or remain steadily or unremittingly, as to a task. **22.** to be rendered immovable by some obstruction: *The zipper stuck.* **23.** to be at a standstill, as from difficulties. **24.** to be embarrassed or puzzled; hesitate or scruple (usu. fol. by *at*). **25.** to be thrust or placed so as to extend, project, or protrude (usu. fol. by *through, out,* etc.). **26. stick around,** *Informal.* to wait in the vicinity; linger. **27. stick by** or **to,** to remain faithful to, esp. during difficulties. **28. stick up,** *Informal.* to rob, esp. at gunpoint. **29. stick up for,** to speak in favor of; come to the defense of; support. **—***n.* **30.** a thrust with a pointed instrument; stab. **31.** a stoppage or standstill. **32.** something causing delay or difficulty. **33.** the quality of adhering or of causing things to adhere. **34.** something causing adhesion. **—*Idiom.* 35. stick it out,** to endure something patiently to the end or its completion. **36. stick to one's guns.** See GUN[1] (def. 11). **37. stick to the** or **one's ribs,** to be substantial and nourishing, as a hearty meal. **—stick′a•ble,** *adj.*

stick•ball (stik′bôl′), *n.* a form of baseball played with a rubber ball and a broomstick or the like. **—stick′ball′er,** *n.*

stick•er (stik′ər), *n.* **1.** a person or thing that sticks. **2.** an adhesive label. **3.** something, as a problem or riddle, that puzzles or nonplusses one. **4.** a bur, thorn, or the like.

stick′er price′, *n.* a retailer's full asking price, esp. on a new automobile, from which a discount is usu. given.

stick′ fig′ure, *n.* **1.** a drawing of a human or animal, usu. made with one line each for the torso and appendages, and often a circle for the head. **2.** a one-dimensional character, as in a novel.

stick′-in-the-mud′, *n.* someone who avoids new activities, ideas, or attitudes; fogy.

stick•le (stik′əl), *v.i.,* **-led, -ling. 1.** to argue or haggle insistently, esp. on trivial matters. **2.** to raise objections; scruple; demur.

stick•le•back (stik′əl bak′), *n.* any of the small, pugnacious, spiny-backed fish of the family Gasterosteidae, inhabiting northern fresh waters and sea inlets.

stick•ler (stik′lər), *n.* **1.** a person who insists on something unyieldingly (usu. fol. by *for*). **2.** any puzzling or difficult problem.

stick•pin (stik′pin′), *n.* a straight pin with an ornamented head, used as a lapel ornament or for holding an ascot or a necktie in place.

stick′ shift′, *n.* a manual transmission for a motor vehicle, with the shift lever set either in the floor or on the steering column.

stick-to-it-ive (stik′to͞o′i tiv, -it iv), *adj. Informal.* tenaciously resolute; persevering. **—stick′-to′-it-ive•ness,** *n.*

stick•um (stik′əm), *n. Informal.* any adhesive substance.

stick•up (stik′up′), *n. Informal.* a holdup; robbery.

stick•y (stik′ē), *adj.,* **stick•i•er, stick•i•est. 1.** having the property of adhering, as glue; adhesive. **2.** covered with adhesive or viscid matter. **3.** (of the weather or climate) hot and humid. **4.** requiring careful treatment; awkwardly difficult: *a sticky problem.* **5.** *Informal.* unpleasant; unfortunate; nasty. **—stick′i•ly,** *adv.* **—stick′i•ness,** *n.*

stick′y fin′gers, *n.pl. Informal.* a propensity to steal. **—stick′y-fin′gered,** *adj.*

stiff (stif), *adj.* **1.** rigid or firm; difficult or impossible to bend or flex: *a stiff collar.* **2.** not moving or working easily. **3.** (of a person or animal) not supple; moving with difficulty, as from cold, age, etc. **4.** strong; forceful; powerful: *stiff winds.* **5.** strong or potent to the taste or system, as a beverage or medicine. **6.** resolute; firm in purpose; stubborn. **7.** stubbornly continued: *a stiff battle.* **8.** rigidly formal, as people or manners. **9.** lacking ease and grace; awkward. **10.** excessively regular or formal, as a design. **11.** laborious or difficult, as a task. **12.** severe or harsh, as a penalty or demand. **13.** excessive; unusually high or great: *a stiff price.* **14.** firm from tension; taut. **15.** relatively firm in consistency, as semisolid matter; thick. **16.** dense or compact; not friable: *stiff soil.* **17.** (of a vessel) having a high resistance to rolling; stable (opposed to *crank*). **—***n.* **18.** *Slang.* **a.** a dead body; corpse. **b.** a formal or priggish person. **c.** a poor tipper; tightwad. **d.** a fellow: *lucky stiff.* **—***adv.* **19.** in or to a firm or rigid state. **20.** completely, intensely, or extremely: *scared stiff.* **—***v.t.* **21.** *Slang.* to fail to tip or pay (a waiter, worker, etc.). **—stiff′ly,** *adv.* **—stiff′ness,** *n.*

stiff′-arm′, *v.t., n.* STRAIGHT-ARM.

stiff•en (stif′ən), *v.t.* **1.** to make stiff. **—***v.i.* **2.** to become stiff. **—stiff′en•er,** *n.*

sti•fle[1] (stī′fəl), *v.,* **-fled, -fling. —***v.t.* **1.** to quell, crush, or end by force. **2.** to suppress, curb, or withhold: *to stifle a yawn.* **3.** to kill by impeding respiration; smother. **—***v.i.* **4.** to suffer from difficulty in breathing, as in a close atmosphere. **5.** to become stifled or suffocated.

sti•fle[2] (stī′fəl), *n.* (in a horse or other quadruped) the joint between the femur and the tibia, corresponding to the human knee.

sti•fling (stī′fling), *adj.* suffocating; oppressively close: *a stifling atmosphere.* **—sti′fling•ly,** *adv.*

stig•ma (stig′mə), *n., pl.* **stig•ma•ta** (stig′mə tə, stig mä′tə, -mat′ə), **stig•mas. 1.** a stain or reproach, as on one's reputation. **2. a.** a mark or obvious trait that is characteristic of a defect or disease: *the stigmata of leprosy.* **b.** a place or point on the skin that bleeds during certain mental states, as in hysteria. **3.** a small mark, spot, or pore on an animal or organ. **4.** the part of a pistil that receives the pollen. **5. stigmata,** marks resembling the wounds of the crucified body of Christ, said to be supernaturally impressed on the bodies of certain holy persons.

stig•ma•tize (stig′mə tīz′), *v.t.,* **-tized, -tiz•ing. 1.** to set some mark of disgrace or infamy upon. **2.** to mark with a stigma or brand. **—stig′ma•ti•za′tion,** *n.* **—stig′ma•tiz′er,** *n.*

stile[1] (stīl), *n.* **1.** a step or steps for scaling a wall or fence. **2.** a turnstile.

stile[2] (stīl), *n.* any of various vertical members framing panels or the like, as in a paneled door or a window sash.

sti•let•to (sti let′ō), *n., pl.* **-tos, -toes,** *v.,* **-toed, -to•ing. —***n.* **1.** a short dagger with a slender, somewhat tapered blade. **2.** an awl used in sewing to make small holes in fabric. —*v.t.* **3.** to stab or kill with a stiletto.

stilet′to heel′, *n.* SPIKE HEEL.

still[1] (stil), *adj.* **1.** remaining in place or at rest; motionless; stationary: *to stand still.* **2.** free from sound or noise. **3.** subdued or low in sound; hushed. **4.** free from turbulence or commotion; calm. **5.** not flowing, as water. **6.** not effervescent, as wine. **7.** noting or used for making single photographs, as opposed to a motion picture. —*n.* **8.** calmness or silence: *the still of the night.* **9.** a single photographic print, as one of the frames of a motion-picture film. —*adv.* **10.** at this or that time; as previously: *Are you still here?* **11.** up to this or that time; as yet. **12.** in the future as in the past. **13.** even; in addition; yet (used to emphasize a comparative): *still greater riches.* **14.** even then; yet; nevertheless. **15.** without sound or movement; quietly: *Sit still!* **16.** at or to a greater distance or degree. —*conj.* **17.** and yet; but yet; nevertheless: *It was futile, still they fought.* —*v.t.* **18.** to silence or hush (sounds, voices, etc.). **19.** to calm, appease, or allay. **20.** to subdue or cause to subside. —*v.i.* **21.** to become still or quiet. —***Idiom.*** **22. still and all,** nonetheless. —***Saying.*** **23. Still waters run deep,** quietness may conceal complexity or passion. —**still′ness,** *n.*

still[2] (stil), *n.* **1.** a distilling apparatus. **2.** a distillery. —*v.t., v.i.* **3.** to distill.

still•birth (stil′bûrth′), *n.* **1.** the birth of a dead child or animal. **2.** a fetus dead at birth.

still•born (stil′bôrn′), *adj.* **1.** dead when born. **2.** ineffectual from the beginning; abortive; fruitless.

still′ life′, *n., pl.* **still lifes. 1.** a representation chiefly of inanimate objects, as a painting of a bowl of fruit. **2.** the category of subject matter in which inanimate objects are represented, as in painting or photography. —**still′-life′,** *adj.*

stilt (stilt), *n.* **1.** one of two poles, each with a support for the foot at some distance above the bottom end, enabling the wearer to walk above the ground. **2.** one of several posts supporting a structure built above the surface of land or water. **3.** any of several white-and-black wading birds having long, bright pink legs and a long, slender black bill. —*v.t.* **4.** to raise on or as if on stilts.

stilt•ed (stil′tid), *adj.* **1.** stiffly dignified or formal, as speech or literary style; pompous. **2.** (of an arch) resting on imposts treated in part as downward continuations of the arch.

Stil•ton (stil′tn), *n.* a rich white cheese, veined with mold: made principally in England. Also called **Stil′ton cheese′.**

Stil•well (stil′wel, -wəl), *n.* **Joseph W.** ("*Vinegar Joe*"), 1883–1946, U.S. general.

stim•u•lant (stim′yə lənt), *n.* **1.** a drug or other agent that temporarily quickens some vital process or the functional activity of some organ or part: *a heart stimulant.* **2.** any food or beverage that stimulates, esp. coffee, tea, or, in its initial effect, alcoholic liquor. **3.** a stimulus or incentive. —*adj.* **4.** temporarily quickening some vital process or functional activity. **5.** stimulating.

stim•u•late (stim′yə lāt′), *v.,* **-lat•ed, -lat•ing.** —*v.t.* **1.** to rouse to action or effort, as by encouragement or pressure; incite. **2.** to excite (a nerve, gland, etc.) to its functional activity. **3.** to invigorate (a person) by a food or beverage containing a stimulant. —*v.i.* **4.** to act as a stimulus or stimulant. —**stim′u•lat′ing•ly,** *adv.* —**stim′u•la′tion,** *n.* —**stim′u•la′tor, stim′u•lat′er,** *n.*

stim•u•lus (stim′yə ləs), *n., pl.* **-li** (-lī′). **1.** something that incites or quickens action, feeling, thought, etc. **2.** something that excites an organism or part to functional activity.

sting (sting), *v.,* **stung, sting•ing,** *n.* —*v.t.* **1.** to prick or wound with a sharp-pointed, often venom-bearing organ. **2.** to affect painfully or irritatingly as a result of contact, as certain plants do. **3.** to cause to smart or to feel a sharp pain. **4.** to cause mental or moral anguish. **5.** to goad or drive, as by sharp irritation. **6.** *Slang.* to cheat or take advantage of, esp. to overcharge; soak. —*v.i.* **7.** to use, have, or wound with a sting, as bees. **8.** to cause a sharp, smarting pain. **9.** to cause or feel acute mental pain or irritation: *The memory of that insult still stings.* **10.** to feel a smarting pain, as from a blow or the sting of an insect. —*n.* **11.** an act or an instance of stinging. **12.** a wound, pain, or smart caused by stinging. **13.** any sharp physical or mental wound, hurt, or pain. **14.** anything or an element in anything that wounds, pains, or irritates. **15.** capacity to wound or pain: *Satire has a sting.* **16.** a sharp stimulus or incitement. **17.** any of various sharp-pointed, often venom-bearing organs of insects or other animals. **18.** *Slang.* **a.** CONFIDENCE GAME. **b.** an ostensibly illegal operation, as the buying of stolen goods, used by undercover investigators to collect evidence of wrongdoing. —**sting′ing•ly,** *adv.* —**sting′less,** *adj.*

sting•er (sting′ər), *n.* **1.** one that stings. **2.** an animal having a stinging organ. **3.** the sting or stinging organ of an insect or other animal. **4.** *Informal.* a stinging blow, remark, or the like. **5.** (*cap.*) *Mil.* a U.S. Army shoulder-launched, heat-seeking antiaircraft missile, with a range of 3 miles (5 km).

sting′ing net′tle, *n.* a bristly, stinging Eurasian nettle, *Urtica dioica,* naturalized in North America, having forked clusters of greenish flowers.

sting•ray (sting′rā′), *n.* any ray of the family Dasyatidae, having a flexible tail armed with a bony, usu. poisonous spine.

stin•gy (stin′jē), *adj.,* **-gi•er, -gi•est. 1.** reluctant to give or spend; niggardly; penurious. **2.** scanty or meager. —**stin′gi•ly,** *adv.* —**stin′gi•ness,** *n.*

stink (stingk), *v.,* **stank** or, often, **stunk, stunk, stink•ing,** *n.* —*v.i.* **1.** to emit a strong offensive smell. **2.** to be offensive to propriety. **3.** *Informal.* to be disgustingly inferior. **4.** *Slang.* to have a large quantity of something (usu. fol. by *of* or *with*). —*v.t.* **5.** to cause to stink or be otherwise offensive (often fol. by *up*). —*n.* **6.** a strong offensive smell; stench. **7.** *Informal.* an unpleasant fuss; scandal.

stink′ bomb′, *n.* a small bomb made to emit a foul smell on exploding.

stink′ bug′, *n.* any of numerous broad, flat bugs of the family Pentatomidae, that emit a disagreeable odor.

stink•er (sting′kər), *n.* **1.** a person or thing that stinks. **2.** *Informal.* a mean or despicable person; louse. **3.** *Informal.* something, esp. some form of entertainment, of inferior quality. **4.** *Informal.* something difficult: *a stinker of a puzzle.*

stink′ing smut′, *n.* BUNT[3].

stink•pot (stingk′pot′), *n.* **1.** a jar containing combustibles or other materials that generate offensive and suffocating vapors, formerly used in warfare. **2.** *Informal.* a mean person; stinker.

stink•weed (stingk′wēd′), *n.* any of various rank-smelling plants, as the jimson weed.

stink•wood (stingk′wŏŏd′), *n.* **1.** any of several trees yielding fetid wood, esp. a South African tree, *Ocotea bullata,* of the laurel family. **2.** the wood of any of these trees.

stink•y (sting′kē), *adj.,* **stink•i•er, stink•i•est. 1.** foul-smelling; stinking. **2.** *Informal.* mean-spirited; nasty.

stint (stint), *v.i.* **1.** to be frugal; get along on a scanty allowance: *to stint on food.* —*v.t.* **2.** to limit to a certain amount, number, etc., often unduly. —*n.* **3.** a period of time spent doing something: *a stint in the army.* **4.** limitation, esp. as to amount. **5.** a limited, prescribed, or expected quantity, share, rate, etc. —**stint′ing•ly,** *adv.*

sti•pend (stī′pend), *n.* **1.** a periodic payment, esp. a scholarship or fellowship allowance granted to a student. **2.** fixed or regular pay; salary.

sti•pes (stī′pēz), *n., pl.* **stip•i•tes** (stip′i tēz′). the stalklike basal portion of the maxilla in crustaceans and insects. —**stip′i•tate′** (-tāt′), *adj.*

stip•ple (stip′əl), *v.,* **-pled, -pling,** *n.* —*v.t.* **1.** to paint, engrave, or draw by means of dots or small touches. —*n.* Also, **stip′pling. 2.** the method of painting, engraving, etc., by stippling. **3.** stippled work. —**stip′pler,** *n.*

stip•u•late (stip′yə lāt′), *v.,* **-lat•ed, -lat•ing.** —*v.t.* **1.** to arrange expressly or specify in terms of agreement: *to stipulate a price.* **2.** to require as an essential condition in making an agreement. **3.** to promise, in making an agreement. —*v.i.* **4.** to make an express demand as a condition of agreement (often fol. by *for*). —**stip′u•la•ble** (-lə bəl), *adj.* —**stip′u•la′tor,** *n.* —**stip′u•la•to′ry** (-tôr′ē, -tōr′ē), *adj.*

stip•u•la•tion (stip′yə lā′shən), *n.* **1.** a condition, demand, or promise in an agreement or contract. **2.** the act of stipulating.

stir[1] (stûr), *v.,* **stirred, stir•ring,** *n.* —*v.t.* **1.** to agitate (a liquid or other substance) with a continuous or repeated movement of an implement or one's hand. **2.** to set in tremulous, fluttering, or irregular motion. **3.** to affect strongly; excite: *to stir pity.* **4.** to incite, instigate, or prompt (usu. fol. by *up*): *likes to stir up trouble.* **5.** to move briskly: *to stir oneself.* **6.** to move, esp. in a slight way: *not stir a finger to help.* **7.** to rouse from inactivity, quiet, contentment, indifference, etc. (usu. fol. by *up*). —*v.i.* **8.** to move, esp. slightly or lightly. **9.** to move around, esp. briskly; be active. **10.** to become active, as from some rousing impulse. **11.** to be emotionally moved. **12.** to be in circulation, current, or afoot. —*n.* **13.** the act of stirring or moving. **14.** the sound made by stirring or moving slightly. **15.** a state or occasion of general excitement; commotion. **16.** a mental impulse, sensation, or feeling. **17.** a jog, poke, or thrust. **18.** movement, esp. brisk and busy movement. —**stir′ra•ble,** *adj.*

stir[2] (stûr), *n. Slang.* prison.

stir′-cra′zy, *adj. Slang.* restless or frantic from long confinement, as in prison. —**stir′-cra′ziness,** *n.*

stir′-fry′, *v.t.,* **-fried, -fry•ing,** to prepare (food) by cooking it quickly in a small amount of oil over high heat.

stirps (stûrps), *n., pl.* **stir•pes** (stûr′pēz). **1.** a stock; family or branch of a family; line of descent. **2.** *Law.* a person from whom a family is descended.

stir•ring (stûr′ing), *adj.* **1.** rousing, exciting, or thrilling. **2.** active, bustling, or lively. —**stir′ring•ly,** *adv.*

stir•rup (stûr′əp, stir′-, stur′-), *n.* **1.** a loop, ring, or other contrivance suspended from the saddle of a horse to support the rider's foot. **2.** any of various similar supports or clamps used for special purposes. **3.** a short rope with an eye at the end hung from a yard to support a footrope. **4.** STAPES. —**stir′rup•less,** *adj.* —**stir′rup•like′,** *adj.*

stitch (stich), *n.* **1.** one complete movement of a threaded needle through a fabric or material such as to leave behind a single loop or portion of thread, as in sewing or the surgical closing of wounds. **2.** the loop or portion of thread so left. **3.** one complete movement of the needle or other implement in knitting, crocheting, tatting, etc. **4. a.** a particular mode of disposing the thread or yarn in sewing, knitting, crocheting, etc. **b.** the style of work produced by this. **5.** a thread, bit, or piece of any fabric or of clothing: *not a stitch of clothes on.* **6.** the least bit of anything: *They wouldn't do a stitch of work.* **7.** a sudden, sharp pain, esp. in the intercostal muscles. —*v.t.* **8.** to work upon, join, mend, or fasten with or as if with stitches; sew. **9.** to ornament or embellish with stitches. —*v.i.* **10.** to make stitches, join together, or sew. —*Idiom.* **11. in stitches,** convulsed with laughter. —*Proverb.* **12. A stitch in time saves nine,** dealing with problems when they occur prevents future trouble. —**stitch′er,** *n.*

stitch•er•y (stich′ə rē), *n.* NEEDLEWORK.

St.-John's-wort, *n.* any of various plants or shrubs of the genus *Hypericum* and family Hypericaceae, typically having narrow, dotted leaves and five-petaled yellow flowers.

St. Kitts-Nevis, *n.* a twin-island state in the Leeward Islands, in the E West Indies, consisting of St. Kitts and Nevis: formerly a British colony; gained independence 1983. 41,803; 101 sq. mi. (261 sq. km). *Cap.:* Basseterre. Also called **St. Christopher-Nevis.**

St. Lawrence (sänt), *n.* **1.** a river in SE Canada, flowing NE from Lake Ontario, forming part of the boundary between New York and Ontario, and emptying into the Gulf of St. Lawrence. 760 mi. (1225 km) long. **2.** Gulf of, an arm of the Atlantic between SE Canada and Newfoundland.

St. Lawrence Seaway, *n.* a series of channels, locks, and canals between Montreal and the mouth of Lake Ontario, a distance of 182 miles (293 km), enabling most deep-draft vessels to travel from the Atlantic Ocean, up the St. Lawrence River, to all the Great Lakes ports: developed jointly by the U.S. and Canada.

St. Lou•is (sänt′ lŏŏ′is), *n.* a port in E Missouri, on the Mississippi. 368,215.

St. Lu•cia (lōō′shə, -sē ə), *n.* one of the Windward Islands, in the E West Indies: a former British colony. 159,639; 238 sq. mi. (616 sq. km). *Cap.:* Castries. —**St. Lucian,** *adj., n.*

sto•a (stō′ə), *n., pl.* **sto•as, sto•ai** (stō′ī), **sto•ae** (stō′ē) a portico, usu. detached and of considerable length, used as a promenade or meeting place in ancient Greece.

stoat (stōt), *n.* the European ermine, *Mustela erminea,* esp. in its brown summer coat.

stock (stok), *n.* **1.** a supply of goods kept on hand for sale to customers by a merchant, manufacturer, etc.; inventory. **2.** a quantity of something accumulated, as for future use. **3.** LIVESTOCK. **4. a.** a theatrical stock company. **b.** the work or business of such a company; repertory. **c.** SUMMER STOCK. **5. a.** the shares of a particular company or corporation. **b.** a stock certificate. **c.** (formerly) a tally or stick used in transactions between a debtor and a creditor. **6. a.** in grafting, a stem in which the bud or scion is inserted. **b.** a stem, tree, or plant that furnishes slips or cuttings. **7.** the trunk or main stem of a tree or other plant, as distinguished from roots and branches. **8.** the type from which a group of animals or plants has been derived. **9.** a race or other related group of animals or plants. **10.** the person from whom a given line of descent is derived; the original progenitor. **11.** a line of descent; a tribe, race, or ethnic group. **12. a.** a category consisting of language families that, because of resemblances in grammatical structure and vocabulary, are considered likely to be related by common origin. **b.** any grouping of related languages. **13.** the handle of a whip, fishing rod, etc. **14.** the wooden or metal piece to which the barrel and mechanism of a rifle are attached. **15.** a dull or stupid person. **16.** something lifeless or senseless. **17.** the main upright part of anything, esp. a supporting structure. **18. stocks, a.** a former instrument of punishment consisting of a framework with holes for securing the ankles and, sometimes, the wrists, used to expose an offender to public derision. Compare PILLORY (def. 1). **b.** a frame in which a horse or other animal is secured in a standing position for shoeing or for a veterinary operation. **c.** the frame on which a boat rests while under construction. **19. a.** a vertical shaft forming part of a rudder and controlling the rudder's movement. **b.** a transverse piece of wood or metal near the ring on some anchors. **20.** the raw material from which something is made. **21.** the broth from boiled meat, fish, or poultry, used in soups and sauces. **22.** any of several plants belonging to the genus *Matthiola,* of the mustard family, esp. *M. incana,* having fragrant flowers in a variety of colors. **23.** a bandlike collar or a neckcloth. **24.** the portion of a deck of cards left on the table to be drawn from as occasion requires. **25.** ROLLING STOCK. —*adj.* **26.** kept regularly on hand, as for use or sale; staple; standard. **27.** having as one's job the care of a concern's goods. **28.** of the common or ordinary type; commonplace. **29.** pertaining to or designating the breeding and raising of livestock. **30.** of or pertaining to the stock of a company or corporation. **31. a.** pertaining to a theatrical stock company or its repertoire. **b.** appearing in repertory: *stock players.* —*v.t.* **32.** to furnish with a stock or supply. **33.** to furnish with livestock. **34.** to lay up in store, as for future use. **35.** to fasten to or provide with a stock, as a rifle or plow. **36.** to put in the stocks as a punishment. —*v.i.* **37.** to lay in a stock of something (often fol. by *up*). —*Idiom.* **38. in stock,** on hand for use or sale. **39. out of stock,** lacking a supply, esp. temporarily. **40. take** or **put stock in,** to put confidence in or attach importance to; believe; trust. **41. take stock, a.** to make an inventory of stock on hand. **b.** to appraise resources or prospects.

stock•ade (sto kād′), *n., v.,* **-ad•ed, -ad•ing.** —*n.* **1.** a defensive barrier constructed from stakes or timbers driven upright into the ground one beside the other. **2.** an enclosure, as a fort or pen, consisting of such barriers. **3.** a prison for military personnel. —*v.t.* **4.** to protect, fortify, or encompass with a stockade.

stock•breed•ing (stok′brē′ding), *n.* the breeding and raising of livestock for marketing or exhibition. —**stock′breed′er,** *n.*

stock•brok•er (stok′brō′kər), *n.* a broker, esp. one employed by a member firm of a stock exchange, who buys and sells stocks and other securities for customers. —**stock′brok′er•age** (-ij), *n.*

stock′ car′, *n.* **1.** a standard model of automobile changed in various ways for racing purposes. **2.** a boxcar for carrying livestock. —**stock′-car′,** *adj.*

stock′ certif′icate, *n.* a certificate evidencing ownership of one or more shares of stock.

stock′ com′pany, *n.* **1.** a company or corporation whose capital is divided into shares represented by stock. **2.** a theatrical company acting a repertoire of plays, usu. at its own theater.

stock′ div′idend, *n.* **1.** a dividend given in extra shares of a corporation's stock rather than in cash. **2.** the stock thus received.

stock′ exchange′, *n.* **1.** a place where stocks and other securities are bought and sold. **2.** an association of brokers who transact business in stocks and bonds according to fixed rules.

stock′ farm′, *n.* a farm devoted to breeding livestock. —**stock′ farm′-er,** *n.* —**stock′ farm′ing,** *n.*

stock•hold•er (stok′hōl′dər), *n.* a holder or owner of stock in a corporation.

Stock•holm (stok′hōm, -hōlm), *n.* the chief seaport in and the capital of Sweden, in the SE part. 666,810; with suburbs 1,606,157.

stock′ horse′, *n.* a horse or pony used in herding cattle.

stock•ing (stok′ing), *n.* **1.** a close-fitting covering for the foot and part of the leg, usu. knitted, of wool, cotton, nylon, silk, or other material. **2.** something resembling this. —*Idiom.* **3. in one's stocking feet,** wearing stockings but no shoes. —**stock′inged,** *adj.*

stock′ing cap′, *n.* a long conical knitted cap, usu. with a tassel or pompom at the tip.

stock′ing stuff′er, *n.* a small, inexpensive gift given during the Christmas holidays.

stock•job•ber (stok′job′ər), *n.* a stockbroker, esp. one who sells or promotes worthless securities. —**stock′job′ber•y, stock′job′bing,** *n.*

stock′ mar′ket, *n.* **1.** a particular market where stocks and bonds are traded; stock exchange. **2.** the market for stocks throughout a nation.

stock′ op′tion, *n.* an option to buy stock at a specific price within a stated period.

stock•pile (stok′pīl′), *n., v.,* **-piled, -pil•ing.** —*n.* **1.** a supply of an essential material held in reserve, esp. for use during a shortage. —*v.t.* **2.** to accumulate for future use; put or store in a stockpile. —*v.i.* **3.** to accumulate in a stockpile. —**stock′pil′er,** *n.*

stock•pot (stok′pot′), *n.* a pot in which stock for soup, sauces, etc., is made and kept.

stock•room (stok′rōōm′, -rŏŏm′), *n.* a room in which a stock of materials or goods is kept for use or sale.

Stock•ton (stok′tən), *n.* a city in central California, on the San Joaquin River. 222,503.

stock•y (stok′ē), *adj.,* **stock•i•er, stock•i•est. 1.** of sturdy form or build and, usu., short; thickset. **2.** having a strong, stout stem, as a plant. —**stock′i•ly,** *adv.* —**stock′i•ness,** *n.*

stock•yard (stok′yärd′), *n.* **1.** an enclosure with pens, sheds, etc., connected with a slaughterhouse, railroad, market, etc., for the temporary housing of livestock. **2.** a yard for livestock.

stodg•y (stoj′ē), *adj.,* **stodg•i•er, stodg•i•est. 1.** dull or uninteresting; boring. **2.** heavy, as food. **3.** stocky; thickset. **4.** unduly formal and traditional. **5.** dull; graceless; inelegant: *a stodgy business suit.* —**stodg′i•ly,** *adv.* —**stodg′i•ness,** *n.*

sto•gy or **sto•gie** (stō′gē), *n., pl.* **-gies. 1.** a long, slender, roughly made, inexpensive cigar. **2.** a coarse, heavy boot or shoe.

Sto•ic (stō′ik), *adj.* **1.** of or pertaining to the school of philosophy founded by Zeno, who taught that people should be free from passion, unmoved by joy or grief, and submit without complaint to unavoidable necessity. **2.** (*l.c.*) stoical. —*n.* **3.** a member or adherent of the Stoic school of philosophy. **4.** (*l.c.*) a person who maintains or affects the mental attitude advocated by the Stoics.

sto•i•cal (stō′i kəl), *adj.* **1.** impassive; characterized by a calm, austere fortitude befitting the Stoics. **2.** (*cap.*) of or pertaining to the Stoics. —**sto′i•cal•ly,** *adv.* —**sto′i•cal•ness,** *n.*

stoi•chi•om•e•try (stoi′kē om′i trē) also **stoi•chei•om•e•try** (-kī om′-); *n.* **1.** the calculation of the quantities of chemical elements or compounds involved in chemical reactions. **2.** the branch of chemistry dealing with relationships of combining elements, esp. quantitatively. —**stoi′chi•o•met′ric** (-ə me′trik), *adj.*

Sto•i•cism (stō′ə siz′əm), *n.* **1.** the philosophy of the Stoics. **2.** (*l.c.*) conduct conforming to the precepts of the Stoics, as repression of emotion and indifference to pleasure or pain.

stoke (stōk), *v.,* **stoked, stok•ing.** —*v.t.* **1.** to poke, stir up, and feed (a fire). **2.** to tend the fire of (a furnace); supply with fuel. —*v.i.* **3.** to shake up the coals of a fire. **4.** to tend a fire or furnace.

stok•er (stō′kər), *n.* **1.** a laborer employed to tend and fuel a furnace, esp. a furnace that generates steam, as on a steamship. **2.** a mechanical device for supplying coal or other solid fuel to a furnace.

STOL (es′tôl′), *n.* a convertiplane that can become airborne after a short takeoff run and has forward speeds comparable to those of conventional aircraft. [*s(hort) t(ake)o(ff and) l(anding)*]

stole¹ (stōl), *v.* pt. of STEAL.

stole² (stōl), *n.* **1.** an ecclesiastical vestment consisting of a narrow strip of silk or other material worn over the shoulders or, by deacons, over the left shoulder only. **2.** a woman's shoulder scarf of fur, marabou, silk, or other material. **3.** a long robe, esp. one worn by the matrons of ancient Rome.

sto•len (stō′lən), *v.* pp. of STEAL.

stol•id (stol′id), *adj.* not easily stirred or moved mentally or emotionally; unemotional. —**sto•lid•i•ty** (stə lid′i tē), *n.* —**stol′id•ly,** *adv.*

stol•len (stō′lən; *Ger.* shtô′lən), *n.* a sweetened German bread made from raised dough, usu. containing nuts, raisins, and citron.

sto•ma (stō′mə), *n., pl.* **sto•ma•ta** (stō′mə tə, stom′ə-, stō mä′tə), **sto•mas. 1.** a minute opening in leaves, stems, etc., through which gases are exchanged. **2.** a primitive mouth or simple ingestive organ of an invertebrate animal. —**sto′mal,** *adj.*

stom•ach (stum′ək), *n.* **1.** a saclike enlargement of the vertebrate alimentary canal, forming an organ for storing and partially digesting food. **2.** any analogous digestive cavity or tract in invertebrates. **3.** the part of the body containing the stomach; belly or abdomen. **4.** appetite for food. **5.** desire; inclination; liking: *I have no stomach for this trip.* —*v.t.* **6.** to endure or tolerate; bear.

stom′ach pump′, *n.* a suction pump for removing the contents of the stomach, used esp. in cases of poisoning.

-stome, a combining form meaning "organism having a mouth or mouthlike organ" of the kind specified (*cyclostome*), "mouthlike organ" (*peristome*).

stomp (stomp), *v.t.* **1.** to tread on heavily; trample; stamp. —*v.i.* **2.** to step heavily; trample; stamp. —*n.* **3.** the act of stomping; stamp. **4.** a jazz dance marked by stamping to a driving rhythm. —**stomp′er,** *n.*

stone (stōn), *n., pl.* **stones** for 1–5, 7–16, **stone** for 6, *adj., adv., v.,* —*n.* **1.** the hard substance, formed of mineral matter, of which rocks consist. **2.** a rock or particular piece or kind of rock. **3.** a piece of rock quarried and worked into a specific size and shape for a particular purpose: *paving stones.* **4.** a small piece of rock, as a pebble. **5.** a mineral used in jewelry; gemstone. **6.** one of various units of weight, esp. the British unit equivalent to 14 pounds (6.4 kg). **7.** something resembling a small piece of rock in size, shape, or hardness. **8.** any small, hard seed, as of a date; pit. **9.** the hard endocarp of a drupe, as of a peach. **10.** a calculous concretion in the body, as in the kidney, gallbladder, or urinary bladder. **11.** a gravestone or tombstone. **12.** GRINDSTONE (def. 1). **13.** MILLSTONE (def. 1). **14.** HAILSTONE. **15.** any of various artificial building materials imitating cut stone or rubble. **16. a.** *Print.* a table with a smooth surface, formerly made of stone, on which page forms are composed. **b.** any surface on which a picture or design is drawn or etched in the process of making a lithograph. —*adj.* **17.** made of or pertaining to stone or stoneware. —*adv.* **18.** completely; totally: *stone cold.* —*v.t.* **19.** to throw stones at. **20.** to put to death by pelting with stones. **21.** to provide, pave, line, face, or fortify with stones. **22.** to rub with or on a stone, as to sharpen, polish, or smooth. **23.** to remove stones from (fruit). —*Idiom.* **24. leave no stone unturned,** to explore every possibility; spare no effort. —*Proverb.* **25. A rolling stone gathers no moss,** a wanderer acquires no responsibilities. **26. Let him who is without sin cast the first stone,** one should examine one's own faults before condemning others. John 8:7. —**ston′er,** *n.*

Stone (stōn), *n.* **1. Lucy,** 1818–93, U.S. suffragist. **2. Samuel,** 1810–76, English clergyman and hymn writer.

Stone′ Age′, *n.* the early period of human history preceding the Bronze and Iron ages and characterized by the use of stone implements and weapons: subdivided into the Paleolithic, Mesolithic, and Neolithic periods.

stone′-broke′, *adj.* having no money whatsoever.

stone′ chi′na, *n.* hard ceramic ware containing feldspar; stoneware.

stone′ crab′, *n.* an edible crab, *Menippe mercenaria,* of rocky shores from the southern U.S. to Mexico and certain areas of the Caribbean: prized for the meat of its claws.

stone•crop (stōn′krop′), *n.* any plant of the genus *Sedum,* esp. a mosslike herb, *S. acre,* having small, fleshy leaves and yellow flowers, frequently growing on rocks and walls.

stone′-deaf′, *adj.* totally deaf.

stone•fly (stōn′flī′), *n., pl.* **-flies.** any of numerous dull-colored primitive aquatic insects of the order Plecoptera, having a distinctive flattened body shape: a major food source for game fish.

stone′ fruit′, *n.* a fruit with a stone or hard endocarp, as a peach or plum; drupe.

stone′-ground′, *adj.* (of wheat or other grain) ground between millstones, esp. those made of burstone.

Stone•henge (stōn′henj), *n.* a prehistoric megalithic monument on Salisbury Plain, in S England, dating to late Neolithic and early Bronze Age times (3rd to 2nd millennium B.C.): believed to have had religious or astronomical functions.

stone′ mar′ten, *n.* a Eurasian marten, *Martes foina,* having light-colored underfur. Also called **beech marten.**

stone•ma•son (stōn′mā′sən), *n.* a person who builds with or dresses stone. —**stone′ma′son•ry,** *n.*

stone′ pars′ley, *n.* a parsley, *Sison amomum,* of Eurasia, bearing aromatic seeds that are used as a condiment.

stone•roll•er (stōn′rō′lər), *n.* an American minnow, *Campostoma anomalum,* that moves stones as it feeds.

stone's′ throw′, *n.* a short distance.

stone•wall (stōn′wôl′), *v.i.* **1.** to be evasive or uncooperative; use obstructive tactics: *to stonewall on the arms control issue.* **2.** *Chiefly Brit.* to filibuster. —*v.t.* **3.** to obstruct or evade; refuse to cooperate with. **4.** *Chiefly Brit.* to filibuster. —**stone′wall′er,** *n.*

stone•ware (stōn′wâr′), *n.* a hard, opaque, vitrified ceramic ware.

stone•wash (stōn′wosh′, -wôsh′), *v.t.* to wash (cloth) with pebbles or stones so as to give the appearance of wear.

stone•work (stōn′wûrk′), *n.* **1.** a construction built of stone; stone masonry. **2.** the process, technique, or art of dressing, setting, or designing in stone. **3.** Usu., **stoneworks.** (*usu. with a sing. v.*) a place where stone is dressed, as for building. —**stone′work′er,** *n.*

ston•y or **ston•ey** (stō′nē), *adj.,* **ston•i•er, ston•i•est. 1.** full of or abounding in stones or rock. **2.** pertaining to or characteristic of stone. **3.** resembling or suggesting stone, esp. in its hardness. **4.** unfeeling; merciless; obdurate. **5.** coldly inexpressive: *a stony stare.* **6.** petrifying; stupefying: *stony fear.* **7.** having stones, as fruit. **8.** *Slang.* stone-broke. —**ston′i•ly,** *adv.* —**ston′i•ness,** *n.*

stood (stŏŏd), *v.* pt. and pp. of STAND.

stooge (stōōj), *n., v.,* **stooged, stoog•ing.** —*n.* **1.** an entertainer who feeds lines to the main comedian and usu. serves as the butt of jokes. **2.** an underling, assistant, or accomplice. **3.** a stool pigeon. —*v.i.* **4.** to act as a stooge.

stool (stōōl), *n.* **1.** a simple armless and usu. backless seat on legs or a pedestal. **2.** a short, low support on which to step, kneel, or rest the feet while sitting. **3. a.** a stump, base, or root of a plant that produces new stems or shoots. **b.** a shoot or cluster of shoots springing up from such a base. **4.** the fecal matter evacuated at each movement of the bowels. **5.** a privy or toilet seat. **6.** an artificial duck or other bird used as a decoy. **7.** the sill of a window. **8.** a seat considered symbolic of authority. —*v.i.* **9.** to put forth shoots from the base or root, as a plant; form a stool. **10.** *Slang.* to act as a stool pigeon. —**stool′like′,** *adj.*

stool′ pi′geon, *n.* **1.** a pigeon used as a decoy. **2.** Also called **stool•ie** (stōō′lē). *Slang.* a person employed or acting as a decoy or informer, esp. for the police.

stoop[1] (stōōp), *v.i.* **1.** to bend the head and shoulders, or the body generally, forward and downward from an erect position. **2.** to carry the head and shoulders habitually bowed forward. **3.** to descend from one's level of dignity; condescend; deign. **4.** to swoop down, as a hawk at prey. **5.** to submit; yield. —*v.t.* **6.** to bend (oneself, one's head, etc.) forward and downward. —*n.* **7.** an act or instance of stooping. **8.** a stooping position or carriage of the body: *to walk with a stoop.* **9.** a descent from dignity or superiority. **10.** a downward swoop, as of a hawk.

stoop[2] (stōōp), *n.* a raised platform or porch, esp. a small porch with steps, at the entrance of a house.

stoop[3] (stōōp), *n.* STOUP.

stop (stop), *v.,* **stopped, stop•ping,** *n.* —*v.t.* **1.** to cease from or discontinue: *to stop running.* **2.** to cause to cease: *to stop crime.* **3.** to interrupt or check. **4.** to cut off, intercept, or withhold: *to stop supplies.* **5.** to restrain or prevent: *I couldn't stop him from going.* **6.** to prevent from proceeding, acting, or operating: *to stop a car.* **7.** to block or close off (often fol. by *up*): *to stop up a sink.* **8.** to fill holes in (a wall, a decayed tooth, etc.). **9.** to close (a container, tube, etc.) with a cork, plug, or the like. **10.** to close the external orifice of (the ears, nose, mouth, etc.). **11.** to check (a stroke, blow, etc.); parry; ward off. **12. a.** to defeat (an opposing player or team). **b.** to defeat in a boxing match by a knockout or technical knockout. **13.** to notify a bank to refuse payment of (a check) upon presentation. **14.** (in bridge) to have an honor card and a sufficient number of protecting cards to keep an opponent from continuing to win in (a suit). **15. a.** to close (a fingerhole) in order to produce a particular note from a wind instrument. **b.** to press down (a string of a violin, viola, etc.) in order to alter the pitch of the tone produced. **c.** to produce (a particular note) by so doing. —*v.i.* **16.** to come to a stand, as in a course or journey; halt. **17.** to cease moving, proceeding, operating, etc.; pause or desist. **18.** to cease; come to an end. **19.** to halt for a stay or visit: *They're stopping at a nice hotel.* **20. stop by** or **in,** to make a brief visit. **21. stop down,** (on a camera) to reduce (the diaphragm opening of a lens). **22. stop off,** to halt for a brief stay at some point on the way elsewhere. **23. stop out, a.** to withdraw temporarily from school. **b.** to mask (areas of an etching plate, photographic negative, etc.) to prevent their being etched, printed, etc. **24. stop over, a.** to stop briefly, as overnight, in the course of a journey. **b.** to make a brief visit. —*n.* **25.** the act of stopping. **26.** a cessation or arrest of movement, activity, or operation; end: *Put a stop to that!* **27.** a stay made at a place, as in the course of a journey. **28.** a place where trains or other vehicles halt to take on and discharge passengers: *a bus stop.* **29.** a closing or filling up, as of a hole. **30.** a blocking or obstructing, as of a passage or channel. **31.** a plug or other stopper for an opening. **32.** an obstacle, impediment, or hindrance. **33.** a piece or device that serves to check or control movement or action in a mechanism. **34. a.** an order to refuse payment of a check. **b.** STOP ORDER. **35. a.** the act of closing a fingerhole or pressing a string of an instrument in order to produce a particular note. **b.** a device, as on an instrument, for accomplishing this. **c.** a graduated set of organ pipes of the same kind giving tones of the same quality. **d.** a knob or handle that controls the sounding of such a set of pipes. **e.** a set of jacks on a harpsichord or reeds in a reed organ functioning like a pipe-organ stop. **36.** a piece of small line used to lash or fasten something, as a furled sail. **37.** a consonant sound made with complete closure at some part of the vocal tract, usu. followed by sudden release of the interrupted air, as in the sounds (p, b, t, d, k, g). Compare CONTINUANT. **38.** the diaphragm opening of a camera lens, esp. as indicated by an f-number. **39.** any of various marks used as punctuation at the end of a sentence, esp. a period. **40.** the word "stop" printed in the body of a telegram or cablegram to indicate a period. **41.** a depression in the face of certain animals, esp. dogs, marking the division between the forehead and the projecting part of the muzzle. —*Idiom.* **42. pull out all the stops,** to use every means available, as to accomplish something. —**stop′pa·ble,** *adj.*

stop′-and-go′, *adj.* characterized by periodically enforced stops, as caused by heavy traffic or traffic signals.

stop′ bath′, *n.* an acid bath or rinse for stopping the action of a developer before fixing a photographic negative or print.

stop·cock (stop′kok′), *n.* COCK¹ (def. 3).

stope (stōp), *n., v.,* **stoped, stop·ing.** —*n.* **1.** an excavation made in a mine, esp. from a steeply inclined vein, to remove the ore that has been rendered accessible by the shafts and drifts. —*v.i., v.t.* **2.** to mine by stopes. —**stop′er,** *n.*

stop·gap (stop′gap′), *n.* **1.** something that fills the place of something else that is lacking; temporary substitute; makeshift. —*adj.* **2.** serving as a stopgap: *a stopgap solution.*

stop·light (stop′līt′), *n.* **1.** a taillight that lights up as the driver of a vehicle steps on the brake pedal to slow down or stop. **2.** TRAFFIC LIGHT.

stop′-off′ or **stop′off′,** *n.* STOPOVER.

stop′ or′der, *n.* an order from a customer to a broker to buy or to sell a security if the market price goes above or below a designated level.

stop·o·ver (stop′ō′vər), *n.* **1.** a stop or brief stay in the course of a journey. **2.** such a stop made with the privilege of proceeding at a later time on the ticket orig. issued.

stop·page (stop′ij), *n.* **1.** an act or instance of stopping. **2.** the state of being stopped or obstructed. **3.** a cessation of activity, esp. work; strike.

stop′ pay′ment, *n.* an order by the drawer of a check to his or her bank not to pay a specified check.

stop·per (stop′ər), *n.* **1.** a person or thing that stops. **2.** a plug, cork, bung, or other piece for closing a bottle, tube, drain, etc. —*v.t.* **3.** to close or secure with a stopper.

stop′ sign′, *n.* a traffic sign requiring a motorist to stop before continuing.

stop′ street′, *n.* a street at the intersections of which all traffic must stop before continuing. Compare THROUGH STREET.

stop·watch (stop′woch′), *n.* a watch with a hand that can be stopped or started at any instant, used for precise timing, as in races.

stor·age (stôr′ij, stōr′-), *n.* **1.** the act of storing; the state or fact of being stored. **2.** capacity or space for storing. **3.** a place, as a room or building, for storing. **4.** MEMORY (def. 10). **5.** the price charged for storing goods.

stor′age bat′tery, *n.* a voltaic battery consisting of two or more storage cells. **2.** STORAGE CELL.

stor′age cell′, *n.* a cell whose energy can be renewed by passing a current through it in the direction opposite to that of the flow of current generated by the cell.

sto·rax (stôr′aks, stōr′-), *n.* **1.** a solid resin with a vanillalike odor, obtained from a small tree, *Styrax officinalis:* formerly used in medicine and perfumery. **2.** a liquid balsam obtained from certain liquidambar trees, used chiefly in medicine and perfumery.

store (stôr, stōr), *n., v.,* **stored, stor·ing,** *adj.* —*n.* **1.** an establishment where merchandise is sold, usu. on a retail basis. **2.** a grocery. **3.** a supply or stock of something, esp. for future use. **4. stores,** supplies of food, clothing, arms, or other requisites. **5.** *Chiefly Brit.* a storehouse or warehouse. **6.** quantity, esp. great quantity; abundance: *a rich store of grain.* —*v.t.* **7.** to supply or stock with something, as for future use. **8.** to accumulate or put away, for future use. **9.** to deposit in a storehouse or other place for keeping. **10.** to put or retain (data) in a computer memory unit. —*v.i.* **11.** to remain fresh and usable for considerable time on being stored. **12.** to take in or hold supplies or articles, as for future use. —*adj.* **13.** bought from a store; commercial: *store bread.* —*Idiom.* **14. in store, a.** in readiness or reserve. **b.** about to happen. **15. set** or **lay store by,** to have regard for; value; esteem. —**stor′a·ble,** *adj.* —**stor′er,** *n.*

store′-bought′, *adj.* commercially made rather than homemade.

store·front (stôr′frunt′, stōr′-), *n.* **1.** the side of a store facing a street, usu. containing display windows. **2.** a room, set of rooms, or establishment at street level with frontage on a street or thoroughfare. —*adj.* **3.** of or located in a storefront: *a storefront community center.*

store·house (stôr′hous′, stōr′-), *n., pl.* **-hous·es** (-hou′ziz). **1.** a building in which things are stored; warehouse. **2.** a repository or source of abundant supplies, as of facts or knowledge.

store·keep·er (stôr′kē′pər, stōr′-), *n.* **1.** a person who owns or operates a store. **2.** a petty officer in the U.S. Navy in charge of a supply of office afloat or ashore. —**store′keep′ing,** *n.*

store·room (stôr′rōōm′, -rŏŏm′, stōr′-), *n.* a room in which supplies or other articles are stored.

store·wide (stôr′wīd′, stōr′-), *adj.* applying to all the merchandise or all the departments within a store: *a storewide clearance sale.*

sto·rey (stôr′ē, stōr′ē), *n., pl.* **-reys.** *Chiefly Brit.* STORY².

sto·ried¹ (stôr′ēd, stōr′-), *adj.* **1.** recorded or celebrated in history or story. **2.** ornamented with designs representing historical, legendary, or similar subjects.

sto·ried² (stôr′ēd, stōr′-), *adj.* having stories (often used in combination): *a two-storied house.* Also, *esp. Brit.,* **sto′reyed.**

stork (stôrk), *n., pl.* **storks,** (*esp. collectively*) **stork. 1.** any of several wading birds of the family Ciconiidae, having long legs and a long neck and bill. **2. the stork,** this bird as the symbolic deliverer of a new baby: *a visit from the stork.* —**stork′like′,** *adj.*

storm (stôrm), *n.* **1.** a disturbance of normal atmospheric conditions, manifesting itself by strong winds and often accompanied by rain, thunder and lightning, snow, hail, or sleet. **2.** an instance of heavy precipitation unaccompanied by strong winds. **3.** a wind of 64–72 mph (29–32 m/sec). **4.** a violent military assault, esp. on a fortified place or strong position. **5.** a heavy or sudden volley or discharge: *a storm of bullets.* **6.** a tumultuous condition; commotion. **7.** a violent outburst or outbreak of expression: *a storm of abuse.* **8.** STORM WINDOW. —*v.i.* **9.** (of the wind or weather) to blow with unusual force, or to rain, snow, hail, etc., esp. heavily (usu. used impersonally with *it* as subject): *It stormed all day.* **10.** to rage or complain with violence or fury. **11.** to rush angrily: *He stormed out of the room.* **12.** to deliver a violent attack or fire, as with artillery. **13.** to rush to an assault or attack. —*v.t.* **14.** to subject to or as if to a storm. **15.** to attack or assault: *to storm a fortress.* —*Proverb.* **16. After a storm comes a calm,** a lull follows an uproar or upheaval. —**storm′less,** *adj.* —**storm′like′,** *adj.*

storm′ cel′lar, *n.* a cellar or underground chamber for refuge during violent storms; cyclone cellar.

storm′ cen′ter, *n.* **1.** the center of a cyclonic storm, the area of lowest pressure and of comparative calm. **2.** a center of disturbance, tumult, or trouble.

storm′ door′, *n.* a supplementary outside door, usu. glazed, for protecting the entrance door against wind, rain, etc.

storm′ pet′rel or **storm′-pet′rel,** *n.* any of several small, tube-nosed seabirds of the family Hydrobatidae, usu. having black or sooty-brown plumage with a white rump.

storm·proof (stôrm′prōōf′), *adj.* protected from or not affected by storms.

storm′ sew′er, *n.* a sewer for carrying off rainfall drained from paved surfaces, roofs, etc. Also called **storm′ drain′.**

storm′ troop′er, *n.* **1.** a member of the Sturmabteilung of Nazi Germany. **2.** a member of a similar brutal or terroristic group.

storm′ win′dow, *n.* a supplementary window sash for protecting a window against bad weather. Also called **storm′ sash′.**

storm·y (stôr′mē), *adj.,* **storm·i·er, storm·i·est. 1.** indicative of or characterized by storms; tempestuous: *stormy seas.* **2.** full of turmoil or strife: *stormy debate; stormy relationships.* —**storm′i·ly,** *adv.*

storm′y pet′rel, *n.* the storm petrel, *Hydrobates pelagicus,* of the E Atlantic Ocean, Mediterranean Sea, and Indian Ocean.

sto·ry¹ (stôr′ē, stōr′ē), *n., pl.* **-ries 1.** a narrative, either true or fictitious, in prose or verse; tale. **2.** a fictitious tale, shorter and less elaborate than a novel. **3.** such narratives or tales as a branch of literature: *song and story.* **4.** the plot or succession of incidents of a novel, poem, drama, etc. **5.** a narration of incidents or events. **6.** a report of the facts concerning a matter in question. **7.** a lie; fabrication.

sto·ry² (stôr′ē, stōr′ē), *n., pl.* **-ries. 1.** a complete horizontal section of a building, having one continuous or practically continuous floor. **2.** the set of rooms on the same floor or level of a building. **3.** any major horizontal architectural division, as of a facade or the wall of a nave. **4.** a layer. Also, *esp. Brit.,* **storey.**

sto·ry·board (stôr′ē bôrd′, stōr′ē bōrd′), *n.* a panel or series of panels with sketches depicting changes of action and scene, as for a motion picture or a television show.

sto·ry·book (stôr′ē bŏŏk′, stōr′-), *n.* **1.** a book that contains a story or stories, esp. for children. —*adj.* **2.** idealized in the manner of a storybook: *a storybook romance.*

sto′ry line′, *n.* PLOT (def. 2).

sto·ry·tell·er (stôr′ē tel′ər, stōr′-), *n.* **1.** a person who tells or writes stories. **2.** a person who tells trivial falsehoods; fibber.

Stott (stot), *n.* **John,** born 1921, English clergyman.

stoup (stōōp), *n.* **1.** a basin for holy water, as at the entrance of a church. **2.** *Scot.* a pail or bucket.

stout (stout), *adj.* **-er, -est,** *n.* —*adj.* **1.** overweight; corpulent; fat. **2.** courageous; brave: *stout warriors.* **3.** firm; stubborn; resolute: *stout resistance.* **4.** forceful; vigorous: *a stout wind.* **5.** strong of body; sturdy: *stout seamen.* **6.** substantial; solid: *a stout cudgel.* —*n.* **7.** a dark, sweet ale having a higher percentage of hops than porter. **8.** a fat person. **9.** a clothing size for persons of ample figure. —**stout′ish,** *adj.* —**stout′ly,** *adv.* —**stout′ness,** *n.*

stove¹ (stōv), *n.* **1.** a portable or fixed apparatus that furnishes heat for warmth or cooking and uses coal, oil, gas, wood, or electricity for fuel or power. **2.** a heated chamber or box for some special purpose, as firing pottery.

stove² (stōv), *v.* a pt. and pp. of STAVE.

stove·pipe (stōv′pīp′), *n.* **1.** a pipe, as of sheet metal, serving as a stove chimney or to connect a stove with a chimney flue. **2.** a tall silk hat.

stow (stō), *v.t.* **1.** to put away in an orderly fashion. **2.** to put away for future use. **3.** to fill; load: *to stow a carton with books.* **4.** to have room for; hold. **5.** *Slang.* to stop; break off: *Stow the talk.* **6.** to lodge; house.

7. stow away, to conceal oneself aboard a conveyance as a means of getting free transportation. —**stow′a·ble,** adj.

stow·age (stō′ij), n. **1.** an act or process of stowing. **2.** the state of being stowed. **3.** capacity for stowing something. **4.** a place for stowing something. **5.** something that is stowed or to be stowed. **6.** a charge for stowing something.

stow·a·way (stō′ə wā′), n. a person who stows away.

Stowe (stō), n. **Harriet (Elizabeth) Beecher,** 1811–96, U.S. abolitionist and novelist.

St. Paul, n. a port in and the capital of Minnesota, in the SE part, on the Mississippi. 262,071.

St. Petersburg, n. **1.** Formerly, **Leningrad** (1924–91); **Petrograd** (1914–24). a seaport in the NW Russian Federation in Europe, in the Gulf of Finland: capital of the Russian Empire (1712–1917). 5,020,000. **2.** a city in W Florida, on Tampa Bay: 238,585.

St. Pierre and Miq·ue·lon (sănt′ pyâr′; Fr. saN pyer′; mik′ə lon′; Fr. mēk lôN′), n.pl. two small groups of islands off the S coast of Newfoundland: an overseas territory of France. 6041; 93 sq. mi. (240 sq. km).

stra·bis·mus (strə biz′məs), n. a deviation from normal orientation of one or both eyes so that both cannot be directed at the same object at the same time; squint; crossed eyes. —**stra·bis′mal, stra·bis′mic, stra·bis′mi·cal,** adj. —**stra·bis′mal·ly,** adv.

strad·dle (strad′l), v., **-dled, -dling,** n. —v.i. **1.** to walk, stand, or sit with the legs wide apart; stand or sit astride. **2.** to be positioned wide apart, as the legs. **3.** to favor or appear to favor both of two opposite sides; equivocate. —v.t. **4.** to stand or sit astride of: to straddle a horse. **5.** to favor or appear to favor both sides of: straddle an issue. —n. **6.** an act or instance of straddling. **7.** the taking of a noncommittal position. **8.** the simultaneous purchase of a stock option to buy and one to sell, in an effort to hedge one's risk. —**strad′dler,** n.

Stra·di·va·ri (strad′ə vâr′ē, -vâr′ē), n. **Antonio,** 1644?–1737, Italian violinmaker of Cremona.

Strad·i·var·i·us (strad′ə vâr′ē əs), n. a violin or other instrument made by Stradivari or his family.

strafe (strāf, sträf), v., **strafed, straf·ing,** n. —v.t. **1.** to attack (ground troops or installations) with fire from low-flying airplanes. —n. **2.** a strafing attack. [< German propaganda slogan Gott strafe England may God punish England] —**straf′er,** n.

strag·gle (strag′əl), v.i., **-gled, -gling. 1.** to stray from the road, course, or line of march. **2.** to wander about; ramble. **3.** to spread at irregular intervals: trees straggling over the hillside. —**strag′gler,** n. —**strag′gling·ly,** adv.

strag·gly (strag′lē), adj., **-gli·er, -gli·est.** sparsely scattered; irregular.

straight (strāt), adj. **1.** without a bend, angle, wave, or curve: a straight path; straight hair. **2.** exactly vertical or horizontal. **3.** (of a line) generated by a point moving at a constant velocity with respect to another point. **4.** evenly or uprightly formed or set: straight shoulders. **5.** direct in character; candid: straight talk. **6.** honest; honorable; upright. **7.** reliable; factual; objective: straight reportage. **8.** cogent; rational: straight thinking. **9.** being in the proper order or condition. **10.** continuous; unbroken: in straight succession. **11.** thoroughgoing; complete: a straight liberal. **12.** supporting all candidates of one political party: voted a straight ticket. **13.** adhering to the suitable conventions: a straight comedy. **14.** Informal. **a.** heterosexual. **b.** traditional; conventional. **c.** not engaged in crime; law-abiding; reformed. —adv. **15.** in a straight line: to walk straight. **16.** in or into an even or proper condition or position: pictures hung straight. **17.** in an erect posture: Stand straight. **18.** directly: Go straight home. **19.** frankly; candidly (often fol. by out). **20.** honestly; virtuously: to live straight. **21.** in possession of truth or facts: to set someone straight. **22.** without embellishment: Tell the story straight. —n. **23.** the condition of being straight. **24.** a straight form, part, or position. **25.** Informal. **a.** a heterosexual. **b.** a person who follows conventional mores. **26.** a sequence of five consecutive cards of various suits. —**Idiom. 27.** straight off or away, without delay; immediately. —**straight′ly,** adv. —**straight′ness,** n.

straight′-a·head′, adj. not deviating from what is usual or expected.

straight′ and nar′row, n. the way of virtuous or proper conduct: follow the straight and narrow.

straight′ an′gle, n. an angle of 180°.

straight′-arm′, v.t. **1.** to deflect (an opponent) by pushing away with the arm held out straight; stiff-arm. —n. **2.** Also called **stiff-arm.** an act or instance of straight-arming.

straight′ ar′row, n. a person righteously devoted to clean or conventional living. —**straight′-ar′row,** adj.

straight·a·way (adj., n. strāt′ə wā′; adv. -wā′), adj. **1.** straight onward in course. —n. **2.** a straightaway stretch. —adv. **3.** immediately; right away.

straight·edge (strāt′ej′), n. a bar or strip of wood, plastic, or metal having at least one long edge for use in drawing or testing straight lines, plane surfaces, etc.

straight′-edge′, adj. advocating abstinence from alcohol, cigarettes, drugs, and sex and sometimes advocating vegetarianism.

straight·en (strāt′n), v.t., v.i. **1.** to make or become straight or orderly (often fol. by up or out). **2. straighten out, a.** to free or become free of confusion or difficulties. **b.** to improve in conduct or character.

straight′ face′, n. an impassive facial expression that conceals one's true feelings, esp. a desire to laugh. —**straight′-faced′,** adj.

straight′ flush′, n. a poker hand containing five consecutive cards of the same suit.

straight·for·ward (strāt′fôr′wərd), adj. **1.** going or directed straight ahead. **2.** direct; not roundabout: straightforward criticism. **3.** free from deceit; honest. —adv. **4.** Also, **straight′for′wards.** straight ahead; directly or continuously forward. —**straight′for′ward·ly,** adv. —**straight′for′ward·ness,** n.

straight′-from-the-shoul′der, adj. STRAIGHT (def. 5).

straight·jack·et (strāt′jak′it), n., v.t. STRAITJACKET.

straight′-laced′, adj. STRAIT-LACED. —**straight′-lac′ed·ly,** adv. —**straight′-lac′ed·ness,** n.

straight′ man′, n. an entertainer who plays the part of a foil for a comic partner.

straight′-out′, adj. **1.** thoroughgoing; complete. **2.** frank; aboveboard.

straight′ ra′zor, n. a razor having a stiff blade of steel that is hinged to a handle into which it folds.

straight′ time′, n. **1.** a standardized work period of a set number of hours. **2.** the rate of pay for such a period. —**straight′-time′,** adj.

strain¹ (strān), v.t. **1.** to draw tight; make taut: to strain a rope. **2.** to exert to the utmost: to strain one's reach. **3.** to injure (a muscle, tendon, etc.) by stretching or overexertion. **4.** to cause mechanical deformation in by stress. **5.** to stretch beyond the proper limit: to strain the meaning of a word. **6.** to make excessive demands upon: to strain one's resources. **7.** to cause to pass through a strainer. **8.** to draw off by means of a strainer: to strain the water from spinach. —v.i. **9.** to pull forcibly: a dog straining at a leash. **10.** to make strenuous efforts; exert oneself. **11.** to resist strongly; balk. **12.** to undergo strain. **13.** to filter, percolate, or ooze. —n. **14.** any force or pressure tending to alter shape, cause a fracture, etc. **15.** strong muscular or physical effort. **16.** great effort in pursuit of a goal. **17.** an injury to a muscle, tendon, etc., due to excessive tension or use; sprain. **18.** deformation of a solid body or structure in response to application of a force. **19.** condition of being strained or stretched. **20.** severe or fatiguing pressure: the strain of hard work. —**Saying. 21. strain at a gnat and swallow a camel,** to pay attention to small wrongs but neglect big ones. Matt. 23:24.

strain² (strān), n. **1.** the body of descendants of a common ancestor, as a family or stock. **2.** any of the different lines of ancestry united in a family or an individual. **3.** an artificial variety of a species of domestic animal or cultivated plant. **4.** a variety, esp. of microorganisms. **5.** ancestry or descent. **6.** hereditary or natural character, tendency, or trait: a strain of insanity in a family. **7.** a streak or trace. **8.** a kind or sort.

strain³ (strān), n. **1.** a flow or burst of language, eloquence, etc.: the lofty strain of Cicero. **2.** a melody; tune. **3.** a passage or piece of poetry. **4.** a pervading style; spirit: a humorous strain.

strained (strānd), adj. produced by effort; not natural or spontaneous; forced: strained hospitality. —**strained′ly,** adv.

strain·er (strā′nər), n. **1.** one that strains. **2.** a filter or sieve for straining liquids. **3.** a device for stretching or tightening.

strait (strāt), n. **1.** Often, **straits.** (used with a sing. v.) a narrow passage of water connecting two large bodies of water. **2.** Often, **straits.** a position of difficulty, distress, or need. **3.** ISTHMUS.

strait·en (strāt′n), v.t., **-ened, -en·ing. 1.** to put into esp. financial difficulties. **2. a.** to make narrow. **b.** to confine within narrow limits.

strait·jack·et or **straight·jack·et** (strāt′jak′it), n. **1.** a garment made of strong material and designed to bind the arms, as of a violent person. **2.** anything that severely confines, constricts, or hinders. —v.t. **3.** to put in or as if in a straitjacket.

strait′-laced′ or **straight′-laced′,** adj. excessively strict in conduct or morality; puritanical.

strand¹ (strand), v.t. **1.** to drive or cause to run onto a shore; run aground. **2.** to leave in a helpless position: stranded in the middle of nowhere. —v.i. **3.** to become stranded. —n. **4.** the land bordering a body of water; shore; beach.

strand² (strand), n. **1.** one of the larger elements, each consisting of a bundle of yarns, that are plaited together to form a rope. **2.** a similar part of a wire rope or cable. **3.** any fiber or thread twisted or plaited into cord, string, etc. **4.** a fiber or filament, as in animal or plant tissue. **5.** an interwoven element in a larger structure: the strands of a plot. **6.** a filament of hair. **7.** any particular length of cord or string upon which pearls, beads, etc., are threaded. —v.t. **8.** to form by twisting strands together. **9.** to break one or more strands of (a rope).

strange (strānj), adj., **strang·er, strang·est,** adv. —adj. **1.** exciting curiosity or wonder; odd: a strange remark to make. **2.** estranged; alienated: felt strange in the foreign city. **3.** being outside of one's experience; unfamiliar; foreign: moving to a strange place. **4.** unaccustomed; inexperienced: I'm strange to his ways. **5.** reserved; aloof. —adv. **6.** in a strange manner. —**strange′ly,** adv.

strange′ bed′fellows, n.pl. Informal. odd or incongruous allies.

stran·ger (strān′jər), n. **1.** a person with whom one has had no personal acquaintance. **2.** a newcomer in a place: a stranger in town. **3.** a person who does not belong to the family, group, or community; an outsider: Our town shows hospitality to strangers. **4.** a person unacquainted with or unaccustomed to something: no stranger to poverty. **5.** Law. a person not legally party to an act, proceeding, etc.

stran·gle (strang′gəl), v., **-gled, -gling.** —v.t. **1.** to kill by squeezing the throat in order to compress the windpipe and prevent the intake of air; throttle. **2.** to obstruct seriously or fatally the breathing of in any manner; choke; stifle; suffocate. **3.** to prevent the continuance, growth, or action of; suppress: *Censorship strangles a free press.* —*v.i.* **4.** to be choked, stifled, or suffocated. —**stran′gler,** *n.*

stran•gle•hold (strang′gəl hōld′), *n.* **1.** an illegal wrestling hold by which an opponent's breath is choked off. **2.** any force or influence that restricts free actions or development.

stran•gu•late (strang′gyə lāt′), *v.t.,* **-lat•ed, -lat•ing.** to compress or constrict (a duct, intestine, vessel, etc.) so as to prevent circulation or suppress function. —**stran′gu•la′tion,** *n.*

strap (strap), *n., v.,* **strapped, strap•ping.** —*n.* **1.** a narrow strip of flexible material, esp. leather, as for fastening or holding things together. **2.** a looped band by which an item may be held, pulled, or lifted. **3.** a long, narrow piece of something. **4.** SHOULDER STRAP. **5.** WATCHBAND. **6. a.** a metal fitting that surrounds and retains other parts of a mechanism. **b.** STROP. **c.** a leather strip for flogging. —*v.t.* **7.** to secure with a strap. **8.** to fasten around something in the manner of a strap. **9.** to strop: *to strap a razor.* **10.** to flog with a strap. —**strap′pa•ble,** *adj.* —**strap′like′,** *adj.*

strap•hang•er (strap′hang′ər), *n.* **1.** a standing passenger in a bus or subway train who holds onto a strap or other support suspended from above. **2.** a commuter using public transportation.

strap•less (strap′lis), *adj.* **1.** lacking a strap or straps. **2.** having no shoulder straps to hold it in place; bare-shouldered: *a strapless gown.* —*n.* **3.** a woman's gown or other garment that exposes the shoulders and has no shoulder straps.

strapped (strapt), *adj.* needy; wanting: *strapped for funds.*

strap•ping[1] (strap′ing), *adj.* **1.** powerfully built; robust. **2.** large; whopping.

strap•ping[2] (strap′ing), *n.* **1.** straps collectively. **2.** material used to make straps.

stra•ta (strā′tə, strat′ə, strä′tə), *n.* a pl. of STRATUM.

strat•a•gem (strat′ə jəm), *n.* **1.** a scheme or trick for surprising or deceiving an enemy. **2.** any artifice or ruse devised to attain a goal or gain an advantage.

stra•te•gic (strə tē′jik) also **stra•te′gi•cal,** *adj.* **1.** pertaining to or marked by strategy: *strategic maneuvers.* **2.** important in or essential to strategy. **3.** forming an integral part of a stratagem: *a strategic move in chess.* **4. a.** intended to destroy an enemy's warmaking capacity: *strategic bombing.* **b.** essential to the conduct of a war: *a strategic metal.* —**stra•te′gi•cal•ly,** *adv.*

Strate′gic Arms′ Limita′tion Trea′ty, *n.* either of two preliminary five-year agreements between the U.S. and the Soviet Union for the control of certain nuclear weapons, the first concluded in 1972 **(Salt I)** and the second drafted in 1979 **(Salt II)** but not ratified.

Strate′gic Defense′ Ini′tiative, *n.* STAR WARS.

strat•e•gist (strat′i jist), *n.* an expert in strategy.

strat•e•gy (strat′i jē), *n., pl.* **-gies. 1.** the science or art of planning and directing large-scale military movements and operations. **2.** the use of or an instance of using this science or art. **3.** the use of a stratagem. **4.** a plan or method for achieving a specific goal: *a strategy for getting ahead in the world.*

Strat′ford-upon-A′von or **Strat′ford-on-A′von,** *n.* a town in SW Warwickshire, in central England, on the Avon River: birthplace and burial place of Shakespeare. 107,200.

strati-, a combining form representing STRATUM: *stratiform.*

strat•i•fi•ca•tion (strat′ə fi kā′shən), *n.* **1.** the act or process of stratifying. **2.** a stratified state or appearance. **3.** the hierarchal division of society according to rank, caste, or class. **4.** a stratified geological formation.

strat•i•form (strat′ə fôrm′), *adj.* **1.** occurring or arranged in strata, as rock. **2.** formed or occurring in thin layers, as bone.

strat•i•fy (strat′ə fī′), *v.,* **-fied, -fy•ing.** —*v.t.* **1.** to form or place in strata. **2.** to preserve or germinate (seeds) by placing them between layers of earth. **3.** to arrange or divide (society) into a hierarchy of graded status levels. —*v.i.* **4.** to become arranged into strata.

stra•tig•ra•phy (strə tig′rə fē), *n.* a branch of geology dealing with the classification, nomenclature, correlation, and interpretation of stratified rocks. —**stra•tig′ra•pher,** *n.* —**strat•i•graph•ic** (strat′i graf′ik), *adj.*

stra•to•cu•mu•lus (strā′tō kyōō′myə ləs, strat′ō-), *n., pl.* **-li** (-lī′). a cloud of a class characterized by large dark, rounded masses, usu. in groups, lines, or waves.

strat•o•sphere (strat′ə sfēr′), *n.* **1.** the region of the upper atmosphere extending upward from the tropopause to about 30 miles (50 km) above the earth, characterized by little vertical change in temperature. **2.** any great height or degree. —**strat′o•spher′ic** (-sfer′ik), *adj.*

Strat•ton (strat′n), *n.* **Charles Sherwood** (*"General Tom Thumb"*), 1838–83, U.S. midget who performed in the circus of P. T. Barnum.

stra•tum (strā′təm, strat′əm), *n., pl.* **stra•ta** (strā′tə, strat′ə), **stra•tums. 1.** a layer of material, naturally or artificially formed, often formed one upon another. **2.** layer; level: *an allegory with many strata of meaning.* **3.** a single bed of sedimentary rock, generally consisting of one kind of matter representing continuous deposition. **4.** a layer of tissue; lamella. **5.** a layer of vegetation in a plant community. **6.** a layer of the ocean or the atmosphere distinguished by natural or arbitrary limits. **7.** a level or grade of a people or population esp. with reference to social position and education: *the lowest stratum of society.*

Strauss (strous, shtrous), *n.* **1. Johann,** 1804–49, Austrian composer. **2.** his son **Johann** (*"The Waltz King"*), 1825–99, Austrian composer. **3. Richard** (riᴋʜ′ärt), 1864–1949, German composer.

Stra•vin•sky (strə vin′skē), *n.* **Igor (Fëdorovich),** 1882–1971, U.S. composer, born in Russia.

straw (strô), *n.* **1.** a single stalk or stem esp. of a cereal grass, as wheat, rye, oats, or barley. **2.** a mass of such stalks, esp. after drying and threshing, used as fodder. **3.** material made from such stalks and used to fashion hats or baskets. **4.** something of negligible value: *not to care a straw.* **5.** a paper, plastic, or glass tube for sucking up a beverage from a container. **6.** STRAW MAN (def. 1). **7.** something made of straw, esp. a hat. —*adj.* **8.** of, pertaining to, or made of straw: *a straw hat.* **9.** of the color of straw; pale yellow. **10.** of little value or consequence; worthless. **11.** sham; fictitious. —***Idiom.*** **12. catch, clutch,** or **grasp at a straw** or **at straws,** to pursue even the slightest hope or possibility out of desperation. **13. straw in the wind,** a piece of information foreshadowing future events. **14. straw that breaks the camel's back,** a final burden that makes a situation intolerable. —**straw′y,** *adj.*

straw•ber•ry (strô′ber′ē, -bə rē), *n., pl.* **-ries. 1.** the fruit of any stemless plant belonging to the genus *Fragaria,* of the rose family, consisting of an enlarged fleshy receptacle bearing achenes on its exterior. **2.** the plant itself.

straw′berry blond′, *adj.* reddish blond.

straw′berry mark′, *n.* a small, reddish, slightly raised birthmark.

straw′berry roan′, *n.* a horse with a reddish coat that is liberally flecked with white hairs.

straw′berry tree′, *n.* an evergreen shrub or tree, *Arbutus unedo,* of the heath family, native to S Europe, bearing a scarlet, strawberrylike fruit.

straw•flow•er (strô′flou′ər), *n.* any of several everlasting flowers, esp. an Australian composite plant, *Helichrysum bracteatum,* having heads of chaffy yellow, orange, red, or white flowers.

straw′ man′, *n.* **1.** a mass of straw formed to resemble a man, as for a doll or scarecrow. **2.** a person whose importance or function is only nominal, as to cover another's activities; front. **3.** a fabricated or conveniently weak or innocuous person, object, matter, etc., used as a seeming adversary or argument: *The issue she railed about was no more than a straw man.*

straw′ vote′, *n.* an unofficial vote taken to determine the general trend of opinion on a given issue. Also called **straw′ poll′.**

stray (strā), *v.i.* **1.** to deviate from the direct or proper course: *to stray from the main road.* **2.** to wander; roam: *straying from room to room.* **3.** to deviate, as from a moral course. **4.** to become distracted; digress. —*n.* **5.** a domestic animal found wandering at large or without an owner. **6.** any homeless or friendless person or animal. —*adj.* **7.** straying or having strayed. **8.** found or occurring apart from others or as an isolated or casual instance; incidental; occasional.

streak (strēk), *n.* **1.** a long, narrow mark, smear, band of color, or the like. **2.** a vein; stratum: *streaks of fat in meat.* **3.** a slight ingredient; trace: *a streak of humor.* **4. a.** a spell; run: *a streak of good luck.* **b.** an uninterrupted series: *a losing streak of ten games.* **5.** a flash leaving a visible line, as of lightning; bolt. —*v.t.* **6.** to mark with streaks; form streaks on. **7.** to lighten or color (strands of hair). **8.** to spread in streaks. —*v.i.* **9.** to become streaked. **10.** to run, go, or work rapidly.

stream (strēm), *n.* **1.** a body of water flowing in a channel or watercourse, as a river, rivulet, or brook. **2.** any flow or current of liquid, fluid, or gas. **3.** a trail of light; beam: *a stream of moonlight.* **4.** a continuous succession: *a stream of words.* **5.** prevailing direction; drift: *the stream of opinion.* —*v.i.* **6.** to flow, pass, or issue in a stream. **7.** to emit a fluid copiously: *eyes streaming with tears.* **8.** to extend in rays: *Sunlight streamed in.* **9.** to proceed continuously: *traffic streaming by.* **10.** to wave, as a flag in the wind. **11.** to hang in a flowing manner: *streaming hair.* —*v.t.* **12.** to discharge in a stream: *The wound streamed blood.* **13.** to cause to float outward, as a flag. —***Idiom.*** **14. on stream,** in or into operation: *The factory will be on stream in a month.*

stream•er (strē′mər), *n.* **1.** something that streams: *streamers of flame.* **2.** a long, narrow flag; pennant. **3.** any long narrow piece or thing, as a paper ribbon, a spray of a plant, or a strip of cloud. **4.** BANNER (def. 6).

stream•ing (strē′ming), *n.* **1.** an act or instance of flowing. **2.** *Biol.* rapid flowing of cytoplasm within a cell.

stream•line (strēm′līn′), *n., v.,* **-lined, -lin•ing.** *adj.* —*n.* **1.** a teardrop line of contour offering the least resistance to a current, as of air or water. **2.** the path of a particle that is flowing steadily and without turbulence in a fluid past an object. —*v.t.* **3.** to make streamlined. **4.** to alter so as to make more efficient or simple. —*adj.* **5.** STREAMLINED.

stream•lined (strēm′līnd′), *adj.* **1.** contoured to offer the least resistance to a current, as of air or water; optimally shaped for motion or conductivity. **2.** designed or organized for maximum efficiency. **3.** modernized; up-to-date.

stream′ of con′sciousness, *n.* **1.** thought regarded as a succession of ideas and images constantly moving forward in time. **2.** a style of writing in which a character's random thoughts are represented by disregarding logical sequence, normal syntax, or distinctions in the levels of reality. —**stream′-of-con′sciousness,** *adj.*

street (strēt), *n.* **1.** a usu. paved public thoroughfare, as in a town or city, including sidewalks. **2.** such a thoroughfare together with adjacent property. **3.** the roadway of such a thoroughfare distinguished from the sidewalk. **4.** the inhabitants or frequenters of a street: *The whole street is talking.* **5. the Street,** the section of a city associated with a given profession or trade, as Wall Street. —*adj.* **6.** of or adjoining a street: *a street door.* **7.** taking place or appearing on the street: *street fight; street musicians.* **8.** coarse; vulgar: *street language.* **9.** suitable for everyday wear in public: *street clothes.* **10.** retail: *the street price of a new computer.* —*Idiom.* **11. on** or **in the street, a.** without a home. **b.** without a job or occupation. **c.** out of prison or police custody; at liberty.

street•car (strēt′kär′), *n.* a public vehicle on rails running regularly along city streets.

street′ Chris′tian, *n.* (esp. in the 1960s) a Christian whose religious life centers more in social or communal groups than in institutional churches.

street•light (strēt′līt′), *n.* a light, usu. supported by a lamppost, for illuminating a street or road.

street′ mon′ey, *n. Slang.* WALKING-AROUND MONEY.

street′ peo′ple, *n.pl.* **1.** persons whose home is in the streets of a city; the homeless. **2.** people who make their living in the streets, esp. of large cities, as vendors or performers. **3.** the people of a neighborhood, esp. a crowded big-city neighborhood or ghetto, who frequent the streets of their area.

street′ smarts′, *n.pl.* shrewd awareness of how to survive in an urban environment. —**street′-smart′,** *adj.*

street′ the′ater, *n.* the outdoor presentation of drama or entertainment dealing esp. with political or social issues.

street•wise (strēt′wīz′), *adj.* possessing street smarts.

strength (strengkth, strength, strenth), *n.* **1.** the quality or state of being strong; physical power; vigor. **2.** intellectual or moral force. **3.** power by reason of influence, authority, or resources. **4.** the full force in numbers of an organization or body. **5.** effective force or cogency: *the strength of his plea.* **6.** power of resistance. **7.** vigor of action, language, feeling, etc. **8.** degree of concentration; intensity, as of light, color, sound, flavor, or odor. **9.** a strong or valuable attribute: *He was asked to list his strengths and weaknesses.* **10.** a source of power or encouragement; sustenance: *The Bible was her strength and joy.* —*Idiom.* **11. on the strength of,** on the basis of.

strength•en (strengk′thən, streng′-, stren′-), *v.t.* **1.** to make stronger; give strength to. —*v.i.* **2.** to grow stronger. —**strength′en•er,** *n.* —**strength′en•ing•ly,** *adv.*

stren•u•ous (stren′yōō əs), *adj.* **1.** characterized by or calling for vigorous exertion: *strenuous tasks.* **2.** intensely active; energetic: *a strenuous intellect.* —**stren′u•ous•ly,** *adv.* —**stren′u•ous•ness,** *n.*

strep (strep), *n.* **1.** streptococcus. —*adj.* **2.** streptococcal.

strep′ throat′, *n.* an acute sore throat caused by hemolytic streptococci.

strep•to•coc•cus (strep′tə kok′əs), *n., pl.* **-coc•ci** (-kok′sī, -sē). any of several spherical bacteria of the genus *Streptococcus,* occurring in pairs or chains, species of which cause such diseases as tonsillitis, pneumonia, and scarlet fever. —**strep′to•coc′cal** (-kok′əl), **strep′to•coc′cic** (-kok′sik), *adj.*

strep•to•my•cin (strep′tə mī′sin), *n.* an antibiotic, $C_{21}H_{39}N_7O_{12}$, produced by a streptomyces and used chiefly to treat tuberculosis.

stress (stres), *n.* **1.** importance or significance attached to a thing; emphasis: *to lay stress upon good manners.* **2.** emphasis in the form of prominent relative loudness of a speech sound, syllable, or word as a result of special effort in utterance. **3.** accent or emphasis on syllables in a metrical pattern; beat. **4.** *Music.* ACCENT (def. 7). **5.** the physical pressure, pull, or other force exerted on one thing by another; strain. **6. a.** the action on a body of any system of balanced forces whereby strain or deformation results. **b.** the intensity of such action, as measured in pounds per square inch or pascals. **7.** a specific response by the body to a stimulus, as fear or pain, that disturbs or interferes with the normal physiological equilibrium. **8.** physical, mental, or emotional strain or tension. —*v.t.* **9.** to emphasize. **10.** to pronounce (a speech sound, syllable, or word) with prominent loudness; accent. **11.** to subject to stress. —**stress′ful,** *adj.* —**stress′ful•ly,** *adv.*

stressed′-out′, *adj.* afflicted with or incapacitated by stress.

stress′ mark′, *n.* a mark placed before, after, or over a syllable to indicate stress in pronunciation; accent mark.

stress′ test′, *n.* a test of cardiovascular health made by recording heart rate, blood pressure, electrocardiogram, and other parameters while a person undergoes physical exertion.

stretch (strech), *v.t.* **1.** to spread out fully: *to stretch oneself out on the ground.* **2.** to extend to the limit: *stretched out her arms.* **3.** to cause to extend from one point or place to another: *to stretch a rope across a road.* **4.** to draw tight or taut: *to stretch the strings of a violin.* **5.** to distend or enlarge by tension: *to stretch a rubber band.* **6.** to draw out, extend, or enlarge unduly: *The jacket was stretched at the elbows.* **7.** to extend, force, or make serve beyond the normal or proper limits; strain: *to stretch the facts.* **8.** to exert (oneself) to the utmost. —*v.i.* **9.** to recline at full length: *to stretch out on a couch.* **10.** to extend one's limbs or body. **11.** to extend over a distance: *The forest stretches for miles.* **12.** to extend in time: *His memory stretches back to his early childhood.* **13.** to become stretched without breaking. —*n.* **14.** an act or instance of stretching. **15.** the state of being stretched. **16.** a continuous length: *a stretch of meadow.* **17.** the backstretch or homestretch of a racetrack. **18.** an extent in time: *a stretch of ten years.* **19.** ELASTICITY. **20.** a term of

imprisonment. —*adj.* **21.** (of yarn) having high elasticity. **22.** made from such yarn: *stretch denim.* **23.** longer than standard: *stretch limousine.* —**stretch′a•ble,** *adj.* —**stretch′a•bil′i•ty,** *n.*

stretch•er (strech′ər), *n.* **1.** a litter, as of canvas, for carrying a sick or dead person. **2.** a person or thing that stretches. **3.** any of various instruments for extending, widening, or distending. **4.** a bar, beam, or framework serving as a tie or brace.

stretch′ mark′, *n.* a silvery streak occurring typically on the abdomen or thighs and caused by stretching of the skin over a short period of time, as during rapid weight gain.

stretch•y (strech′ē), *adj.,* **stretch•i•er, stretch•i•est. 1.** stretching unduly. **2.** elastic; stretchable. —**stretch′i•ness,** *n.*

streu•sel (strōō′zəl, stroi′-, shtroi′-), *n.* a mixture of flour, butter, sugar, nuts, and cinnamon used as a topping esp. on coffeecake.

strew (strōō), *v.t.,* **strewed, strewn** (strōōn) or **strewed, strew•ing. 1.** to scatter freely: *to strew seed in a garden bed.* **2.** to overspread with something scattered: *to strew a floor with sawdust.* **3.** to be scattered over: *Flowers strewed the meadow.* **4.** to disseminate: *to strew rumors.*

stri•ate (*v.* strī′āt; *adj.* strī′it, -āt), *v.,* **-at•ed, -at•ing,** *adj.* —*v.t.* **1.** to mark with striae; furrow; streak. —*adj.* **2.** striated.

stri•at•ed (strī′ā tid), *adj.* marked with striae; furrowed; streaked.

strick•en (strik′ən), *v.* **1.** a pp. of STRIKE. —*adj.* **2.** wounded by or as if by a missile. **3.** beset or afflicted, as with disease, trouble, or sorrow. **4.** characterized by or showing the effects of affliction: *stricken features.* —**strick′en•ly,** *adv.*

strict (strikt), *adj.* **1.** closely conforming to requirements or principles: *a strict observance of rituals.* **2.** stringent; exacting: *strict laws; a strict judge.* **3.** rigorously enforced: *strict silence.* **4.** exact; precise: *It wasn't robbery in the strict sense of the word.* **5.** narrowly or carefully limited: *a strict construction of the Constitution.* **6.** absolute; complete: *strict confidence.* —**strict′ly,** *adv.* —**strict′ness,** *n.*

strict′ construc′tionist, *n.* one who interprets the Constitution narrowly. Compare LOOSE CONSTRUCTIONIST.

stric•ture (strik′chər), *n.* **1.** an abnormal contraction of any passage or duct of the body. **2.** limitation; restriction. **3.** an adverse criticism. —**stric′tured,** *adj.*

stride (strīd), *v.,* **strode, strid•den** (strid′n), **strid•ing,** *n.* —*v.i.* **1.** to walk with long steps. **2.** to take a long step: *to stride across a puddle.* **3.** to straddle. —*v.t.* **4.** to walk with long steps over or along: *to stride the deck.* **5.** to pass over in one long step: *to stride a ditch.* **6.** to straddle. —*n.* **7.** a striding manner or gait. **8.** a long step in walking. **9.** a progressive movement, as of a horse, composed of characteristic steps in which each foot is returned to its relative starting position. **10.** the distance covered in a stride. **11.** a steady natural pace. **12.** a step forward in development or progress. —*Idiom.* **13. hit one's stride, a.** to achieve a steady pace. **b.** to reach the level at which one functions most competently. **14. take in stride,** to deal with calmly or acceptingly. —**strid′er,** *n.* —**strid′ing•ly,** *adv.*

stri•dent (strīd′nt), *adj.* **1.** harsh in sound; grating: *strident voices.* **2.** having an obtrusive, insistent character: *strident opinions.* —**stri′dence, stri′den•cy,** *n.* —**stri′dent•ly,** *adv.*

stri•dor (strī′dər), *n.* **1.** a harsh, grating, or creaking sound. **2.** a harsh respiratory sound due to obstruction of the breathing passages. —**strid•u•lous** (strij′ə ləs), **strid′u•lant,** *adj.*

strid•u•late (strij′ə lāt′), *v.i.,* **-lat•ed, -lat•ing.** to produce a shrill, grating sound by rubbing together certain parts of the body: *crickets stridulating.* —**strid′u•la′tion,** *n.*

strife (strīf), *n.* **1.** violent or bitter conflict or enmity. **2.** a struggle; clash: *armed strife.* **3.** competition; rivalry. —**strife′ful,** *adj.*

strike (strīk), *v.,* **struck, struck** or (*esp. for 22–25*) **strick•en, strik•ing,** *n.* —*v.t.* **1.** to deal a blow to, as with the fist, a weapon, or a hammer; hit. **2.** to inflict; deliver: *struck a blow.* **3.** to drive so as to cause impact: *to strike the hands together.* **4.** to thrust forcibly: *struck a pike into the earth.* **5.** to produce by percussion or friction: *to strike sparks.* **6.** to cause (a match) to ignite by friction. **7.** to come into forcible contact with: *The ship struck a rock.* **8.** to reach or fall upon, as light or sound. **9.** to enter the mind of: *A happy thought struck him.* **10.** to arrest the faculty of: *That painting struck my eye.* **11.** to impress in a particular manner: *How does it strike you?* **12.** to happen upon; find: *struck oil.* **13.** to send down or put forth (a root), as a plant. **14.** to arrive at; achieve: *to strike a compromise.* **15.** to take apart; pull down: *to strike a tent.* **16.** to lower: *to strike a sail.* **17.** (of a fish) to snatch at (bait). **18.** to cancel; cross out: *to strike a passage from a speech.* **19.** to stamp: *to strike a medal.* **20.** to separate by or as if by a blow: *struck chips from a log.* **21.** to mark by or as if by chimes: *The clock struck 12.* **22.** to afflict suddenly: *stricken with fever.* **23.** to overwhelm emotionally: *struck with awe.* **24.** to cause to become a certain way: *struck me dumb.* **25.** to implant; induce: *to strike fear into someone.* **26.** to assume the formal character of: *struck a pose.* **27.** to conclude: *struck a bargain.* **28.** to go on strike against (an employer). —*v.i.* **29.** to deal a blow or stroke. **30.** to make an attack, esp. a planned military assault. **31.** to knock; rap. **32.** to come into forcible contact; collide. **33.** to run aground. **34.** to make an impression. **35.** to come suddenly: *struck on a new way of doing it.* **36.** to sound by percussion: *The clock strikes.* **37.** to be indicated by or as if by such percussion: *The hour has struck.* **38.** to ignite by friction. **39.** to take root, as a slip of a plant. **40.** to make one's way: *They struck for the woods.* **41.** to go on strike against an employer. **42.** to lower the flag or colors, esp. in salute or surrender. **43.** (of fish) to take bait. **44. strike off, a.** to remove: *to strike names off a list.* **b.** to produce rapidly and easily. **45. strike out, a.** to put out or be put out by a strike-out in baseball. **b.** to fail. **c.** to cross out. **d.** to set forth; venture forth. **46. strike up, a.** to cause to begin performing: *struck up a tune.* **b.** to bring into being: *to strike up an acquaintance.* —*n.* **47.** an act or instance of striking. **48.** a group work stoppage to compel an employer to accede to workers' demands or to protest an employer's conditions. **49.** a baseball pitch that is either swung at and missed, in the strike zone but not swung at, or hit into foul territory with less than two strikes against the batter. **50.** the knocking down of all the bowling pins with the first bowl. **51.** the discovery of a rich mineral deposit. **52.** a planned attack, esp. by military aircraft. **53.** the striking mechanism of a timepiece. **54. a.** a sharp jerk made on a fishing line to set the hook in the fish's mouth. **b.** a pull on the line by a fish taking bait. **55.** a quantity of coins struck at one time. **56.** the direction of the line formed by the intersection of each intervening surface of a bed or stratum of sedimentary rock with a horizontal plane. —*Idiom.* **57.** have **two strikes against one,** to be at a critical disadvantage: *Without a job or a bank account, I'll have two strikes against me.* **58. strike a blow for,** to further the cause of. **59. strike home, a.** to deal an effective blow. **b.** to have the intended effect. **60. strike it rich,** to have sudden or unexpected success. **61. strike while the iron is hot,** to act vigorously at the right time.

strike•bound (strīk′bound′), *adj.* closed by a strike: *a strikebound factory.*

strike•break•er (strīk′brā′kər), *n.* a person who takes part in breaking up a strike of workers, as by furnishing workers.

strike•out (strīk′out′), *n.* an out in baseball made by a batter to whom three strikes have been charged.

strike•o•ver (strīk′ō′vər), *n.* **1.** an act or instance of typing over a character without erasing it. **2.** the typed-over character.

strik•er (strī′kər), *n.* **1.** a person or thing that strikes. **2.** a worker who is on strike. **3.** the clapper in a clock that strikes the hours or rings an alarm. **4.** a naval enlisted person working toward a technical rating. **5.** an attacking forward in soccer.

strike′ zone′, *n. Baseball.* the area above home plate extending from the batter's knees to the armpits.

strik•ing (strī′king), *adj.* **1.** conspicuously attractive or impressive. **2.** noticeable: *a striking lack of enthusiasm.* —**strik′ing•ly,** *adv.*

string (string), *n., v.,* **strung, string•ing.** —*n.* **1.** a slender cord used for binding or tying. **2.** a narrow strip of flexible material for tying parts together: *bonnet strings.* **3.** a collection of objects threaded on a string: *a string of pearls.* **4.** a series of things arranged in or as if in a line: *a string of questions.* **5.** a group of animals, businesses, etc., owned or managed by one person or group: *a string of race horses; a string of hotels.* **6.** the tightly stretched cord or wire of a musical instrument that produces a tone when caused to vibrate, as by plucking, striking, or the friction of a bow. **7. strings, a.** stringed instruments, esp. those played with a bow. **b.** players of strings in an orchestra or band. **8.** a cord or fiber in a plant. **9.** one of the sloping sides of a stair, supporting the treads and risers. **10.** a linear sequence of symbols, words, or bits that is treated as a unit. **11.** **12.** a complement of contestants or players grouped as a squad according to their skill. **13.** Usu., **strings.** conditions or limitations on a proposal: *a generous offer with no strings attached.* —*v.t.* **14.** to furnish with or as if with a string: *to string a bow.* **15.** to extend or stretch like a string: *strung lights on the tree.* **16.** to adorn with strung objects: *a room strung with lights.* **17.** to thread on or as if on a string: *to string beads.* **18.** to arrange in a series or succession: *stringing words together.* **19.** to equip (a bow or instrument) with new strings. **20.** to strip the strings from: *to string beans.* **21.** to make tense: *My nerves are strung.* **22.** to kill by hanging (usu. fol. by *up*). **23.** to fool; deceive (often fol. by *along*). —*v.i.* **24.** to lie or move in a string. **25.** to form into a string or strings. **26. string along, a.** to be in agreement; go along. **b.** to keep in a state of uncertainty. **27. string out, a.** to extend; stretch out. **b.** to prolong. —*Idiom.* **28. on a** or **the string,** subject to the whim of another. —**string′less,** *adj.* —**string′like′,** *adj.*

string′ bass′ (bās), *n.* DOUBLE BASS.

string′ bean′, *n.* **1.** any of various kinds of bean, as the green bean, the unripe pods of which are used as food. **2.** SNAP BEAN. **3.** a tall, thin person.

stringed (stringd), *adj.* **1.** fitted with strings: *violins, banjos, and other stringed instruments.* **2.** produced by strings: *stringed melodies.*

strin•gen•cy (strin′jən sē), *n.* the quality or state of being stringent.

strin•gent (strin′jənt), *adj.* **1.** rigorously binding or exacting; strict: *stringent laws.* **2.** compelling; urgent: *stringent necessity.* **3.** convincing; forcible: *stringent arguments.* **4.** (of the money market) making little money available for loans or investments; tight. —**strin′gent•ly,** *adv.*

string•er (string′ər), *n.* **1.** a person or thing that strings. **2.** a long horizontal timber connecting upright posts. **3.** a longitudinal bridge girder for supporting part of a deck or railroad track between bents or piers. **4.** a longitudinal reinforcement in the fuselage or wing of an airplane. **5.** a part-time correspondent covering a local area for a newspaper, magazine, etc. **6.** a performer ranked according to skill or accomplishment (used in combination): *first-stringers.*

string′ quartet′, *n.* **1.** a musical composition for four stringed instruments, typically two violins, viola, and cello. **2.** the musicians performing string quartets.

string′ tie′, *n.* a narrow necktie usu. tied in a bow.

string•y (string′ē), *adj.,* **string•i•er, string•i•est. 1.** resembling or consisting of strings or stringlike pieces: *stringy weeds.* **2.** toughly fibrous: *stringy meat.* **3.** lean and sinewy; wiry: *a stringy build.* **4.** ropy, as a glutinous liquid. —**string′i•ness,** *n.*

strip[1] (strip), *v.,* **stripped** or **stript, strip•ping,** *n.* —*v.t.* **1.** to deprive of covering: *to strip a fruit of its rind.* **2.** to deprive of clothing. **3.** to remove: *to strip sheets from a bed.* **4.** to deprive; divest: *stripped of one's rights.* **5.** to clear out; empty: *to strip a house of its contents.* **6.** to deprive of equipment or possessions. **7.** to remove varnish, paint, wax, or the like from. **8.** to separate the leaves from the stalks of (tobacco). **9.** to remove the midrib from (tobacco leaves). **10.** to shear or damage the thread or the teeth of: *to strip gears.* **11.** to draw the last milk from (a cow), esp. by a stroking and compressing movement. **12.** to remove (color) from a cloth or yarn. **13.** *Chem.* to remove the most volatile components from, as by distillation or evaporation. —*v.i.* **14.** to remove one's clothes. **15.** to become stripped: *Bananas strip easily.* —*n.*

strip[2] (strip), *n., v.,* **stripped, strip•ping.** —*n.* **1.** a long narrow piece of material. **2.** a narrow expanse of water or land. **3.** COMIC STRIP. **4.** an airstrip; runway. **5.** an area of commercial development along a thoroughfare. **6.** DRAG STRIP. —*v.t.* **7.** to cut, tear, or form into strips.

stripe[1] (strīp), *n., v.,* **striped, strip•ing.** —*n.* **1.** a narrow band differing in color, material, or texture from the background parts. **2.** a fabric or material containing such bands. **3.** a strip of braid, tape, or the like. **4.** variety; sort: *a person of a different stripe.* —*v.t.* **5.** to mark or furnish with stripes. —*Idiom.* **6. earn one's stripes,** to gain experience. —**stripe′less,** *adj.*

stripe[2] (strīp), *n.* a stroke with a whip or rod.

striped (strīpt, strī′pid), *adj.* having stripes or bands.

striped′ bass′ (bas), *n.* an important American game fish, *Morone saxatilis,* having blackish stripes along each side.

strip′-mine′, *v.t., v.i.,* **-mined, -min•ing.** to excavate by open-cut methods. —**strip′ mine′,** *n.*

stripped′-down′, *adj.* having only essential features; lacking any special appointments or accessories.

strip•per (strip′ər), *n.* a chemical solution that removes varnish, paint, etc., from a surface.

strip•y (strī′pē), *adj.,* **strip•i•er, strip•i•est.** having or marked with stripes.

strive (strīv), *v.i.,* **strove** or **strived, striv•en** (striv′ən) or **strived, striv•ing. 1.** to exert oneself vigorously; try hard. **2.** to make strenuous efforts toward any goal: *to strive for success.* **3.** to contend in opposition, battle, or any conflict; compete. **4.** to struggle vigorously, as in opposition or resistance: *to strive against fate.* **5.** to rival; vie. —**striv′er,** *n.*

strobe (strōb), *n.* **1.** Also called **strobe′ light′.** an electronic flash that produces rapid, brilliant bursts of light, used for high-speed photography, special lighting effects, etc. —*adj.* **2.** pertaining to or using a strobe.

strode (strōd), *v.* pt. of STRIDE.

stroke[1] (strōk), *n., v.,* **stroked, strok•ing.** —*n.* **1.** an act or instance of striking, as with the fist or a hammer; blow. **2.** a hitting of or upon anything. **3.** a striking of a clapper or hammer, as on a bell, or the sound produced by this. **4.** a throb or pulsation, as of the heart. **5.** a blockage or hemorrhage of a blood vessel leading to the brain, causing an inadequate oxygen supply and often long-term impairment of sensation, movement, or functioning of part of the body. **6.** a sudden, vigorous action or movement likened to a blow in its effect. **7.** a hitting of the ball in tennis, pool, etc. **8.** a single complete movement, esp. one continuously repeated in some process. **9. a.** a movement of a pen, pencil, brush, or the like. **b.** a mark made by such a movement. **10.** a distinctive or effective touch in a literary composition. **11.** a piece or portion of work. **12.** an attempt to attain some object: *a bold stroke for liberty.* **13.** a feat; achievement: *a stroke of genius.* **14.** a sudden or chance happening: *a stroke of luck.* **15. a.** a type or method of swimming: *The crawl is a rapid stroke.* **b.** any of the successive movements of the arms and legs in swimming. **16. a.** a single pull of the oar. **b.** the manner or style of moving the oars. **c.** Also called **stroke′ oar′.** the crew member nearest to the stern of the boat, to whose strokes those of the other crew members must conform. **17. a.** one of a series of alternating continuous movements of a mechanical component back and forth over or through the same line. **b.** the complete movement of a moving part, esp. a reciprocating part, in one direction. —*v.t.* **18.** to mark with a stroke or strokes; cancel, as by a stroke of a pen. **19. a.** to row as a stroke oar of (a boat or crew). **b.** to set the stroke for the crew of (a boat). **20.** to hit (a ball), as with a smooth swing of a bat. —*Saying.* **21. different strokes for different folks,** people have different tastes.

stroke[2] (strōk), *v.,* **stroked, strok•ing,** *n.* —*v.t.* **1.** to pass the hand or an instrument over gently, or with little pressure, as in soothing or caressing. **2.** to promote feelings of self-approval in, as by praise or flattery. —*n.* **3.** an act or instance of stroking.

stroll (strōl), *v.i.* **1.** to walk leisurely as inclination directs; ramble: *to stroll along the beach.* **2.** to wander or rove from place to place; roam: *strolling troubadours.* —*v.t.* **3.** to walk leisurely along or through: *to stroll the countryside.* —*n.* **4.** a leisurely walk.

stroll•er (strō′lər), *n.* **1.** one who takes a leisurely walk. **2.** a wanderer; vagrant. **3.** an itinerant performer. **4.** a four-wheeled, often collapsible, chairlike carriage in which small children are pushed.

strong (strông, strong), *adj.* **1.** having, showing, or involving great bodily or muscular power; physically vigorous or robust. **2.** mentally powerful or vigorous. **3.** very competent or powerful in a specific field or respect: *She is strong in mathematics.* **4.** of great moral power, firmness, or courage. **5.** powerful in influence, authority, resources, or means of prevailing: *a strong nation.* **6.** aggressive; willful: *a strong personality.* **7.** of great force, effectiveness, potency, or cogency: *strong arguments.* **8.** clear and firm; loud: *a strong voice.* **9.** well-supplied or rich in something specified: *a strong hand in trumps.* **10.** able to resist strain, force, wear, etc.: *strong cloth.* **11.** firm or unfaltering under trial: *strong faith.* **12.** fervent; zealous: *a strong liberal.* **13.** strenuous or energetic; vigorous: *strong efforts.* **14.** moving or acting with force or vigor: *strong winds.* **15.** distinct or marked, as an impression or a resemblance. **16.** intense, as light or color. **17.** having a large proportion of the effective or essential properties or ingredients: *strong tea.* **18.** (of a beverage or food) containing much alcohol. **19.** having a high degree of flavor or odor: *strong cheese.* **20.** having an unpleasant or offensive flavor or odor. **21.** of a designated number: *an army 20,000 strong.* **22.** characterized by steady or advancing prices: *a strong market.* **23. a.** (of verbs in Germanic languages) forming the past tense and usu. the past participle by a vowel change in the root, as *sing, sang, sung; ride, rode, ridden.* Compare WEAK (def. 12). **b.** (of Germanic nouns and adjectives) inflected with endings that are generally distinctive of case, number, and gender, as German *alter Mann* "old man." **24.** (of a word or syllable) stressed. **25.** having great magnifying or refractive power: *a strong microscope.* —*adv.* **26.** in a strong manner. —***Idiom.* 27. come on strong,** *Informal.* to behave too aggressively. —**strong′ly,** *adv.*

strong′-arm′, *adj.* **1.** using, involving, or threatening the use of physical force or violence. —*v.t.* **2.** to use violent methods upon; assault. **3.** to rob by force.

strong•box (strông′boks′, strong′-), *n.* a strongly made, lockable box or chest for safeguarding valuables or money.

strong•hold (strông′hōld′, strong′-), *n.* **1.** a well-fortified place; fortress. **2.** a place that serves as the center of a group sharing certain opinions or attitudes: *That campus is a stronghold of liberalism.*

strong•man (strông′man′, strong′-), *n., pl.* **-men. 1.** a person who performs remarkable feats of strength, as in a circus. **2.** a political leader who controls by force; dictator.

strong′-willed′, *adj.* **1.** having a powerful will; resolute. **2.** stubborn; obstinate.

stron•ti•um (stron′shē əm, -shəm, -tē əm), *n.* a bivalent, metallic chemical element whose compounds resemble those of calcium, found in nature only in the combined state: used in fireworks, flares, and tracer bullets. *Symbol:* Sr; *at. wt.:* 87.62; *at. no.:* 38; *sp. gr.:* 2.6. —**stron′tic** (-tik), *adj.*

strontium 90, *n.* a harmful radioactive isotope of strontium, produced in certain nuclear reactions and present in their fallout.

strop (strop), *n., v.,* **stropped, strop•ping.** —*n.* **1.** a device for sharpening razors, esp. a strip of leather or other flexible material. **2. a.** a rope or a band of metal surrounding and supporting a block, etc. **b.** a metal band surrounding the pulley of a block to transmit the load on the pulley to its hook or shackle. —*v.t.* **3.** to sharpen on or as if on a strop. —**strop′per,** *n.*

stro•phe (strō′fē), *n., pl.* **-phes. 1. a.** the part of an ancient Greek choral ode sung by the chorus when moving from right to left. **b.** the movement performed by the chorus while singing the strophe. **2.** the first of the three series of lines forming the divisions of each section of a Pindaric ode. **3.** (in modern poetry) any separate section or extended movement in a poem, distinguished from a stanza in that it does not follow a regularly repeated pattern.

strove (strōv), *v.* a pt. of STRIVE.

struck (struk), *v.* **1.** pt. and a pp. of STRIKE. —*adj.* **2.** (of a factory, industry, etc.) closed or otherwise affected by a strike of workers.

struc•tur•al (struk′chər əl), *adj.* **1.** of or pertaining to structure, structures, or construction. **2.** pertaining to organic structure; morphological. **3.** of or pertaining to geological structure, as of rock. **4.** pertaining to or showing the arrangement or mode of attachment of the atoms that constitute a molecule of a substance. —**struc′tur•al•ly,** *adv.*

struc′tural anthropol′ogy, *n.* a school of anthropology founded by Claude Lévi-Strauss, based upon discovery and analysis of the structures inherent in various cultural forms.

struc′tural for′mula, *n.* a chemical formula showing the linkage of the atoms in a molecule diagrammatically, as H–O–H.

struc•tur•al•ism (struk′chər ə liz′əm), *n.* **1.** any study or theory that embodies structural principles. **2.** STRUCTURAL ANTHROPOLOGY. **3.** a school of psychology that analyzes conscious mental activity by studying the hierarchical association of structures, or complex ideas, with simpler ideas, perceptions, and sensations. —**struc′tur•al•ist,** *n., adj.* —**struc′tur•al•is′tic,** *adj.*

struc•ture (struk′chər), *n., v.,* **-tured, -tur•ing.** —*n.* **1.** the manner in which something is constructed. **2.** the manner in which the elements of anything are organized or interrelated: *the structure of a poem; the structure of protein.* **3.** something constructed, as a building or bridge. **4.** anything composed of organized or interrelated elements. **5.** the construction and arrangement of body parts, tissues, or organs. **6. a.** the attitude of a bed or stratum or of beds or strata of sedimentary rocks, as indicated by the dip and strike. **b.** the coarser composition of a rock, as contrasted with its texture. **7.** the manner in which atoms in a molecule are joined to each other, esp. as represented in organic chemistry. **8.** the pattern or system of beliefs, relationships, institutions, etc., in a social group or society. —*v.t.* **9.** to give a structure to; organize. —**struc′ture•less,** *adj.*

stru•del (strōōd′l; *Ger.* shtrōōd′l), *n.* a pastry usu. consisting of a fruit, cheese, or other mixture rolled in a paper-thin sheet of dough and baked. [< German: lit., eddy, whirlpool]

strug•gle (strug′əl), *v.,* **-gled, -gling,** *n.* —*v.i.* **1.** to contend vigorously with an adversary or adverse conditions. **2.** to contend resolutely with a task or problem. **3.** to make strenuous efforts; strive. **4.** to advance with great effort: *to struggle through heavy snow.* —*v.t.* **5.** to bring, put, etc., by struggling. **6.** to make (one's way) with great effort. —*n.* **7.** an act or instance of struggling. **8.** a war, fight, conflict, or contest of any kind. —**strug′gler,** *n.*

strum (strum), *v.,* **strummed, strum•ming,** *n.* —*v.t.* **1.** to play on (a stringed musical instrument) by running the fingers lightly across the strings. **2.** to produce by such playing: *to strum a tune.* —*v.i.* **3.** to strum a stringed instrument. —*n.* **4.** an act, instance, or sound of strumming. —**strum′mer,** *n.*

strung (strung), *v.* pt. and pp. of STRING.

strung′-out′, *adj. Slang.* physically or emotionally exhausted.

strut[1] (strut), *v.,* **strut•ted, strut•ting,** *n.* —*v.i.* **1.** to walk with a vain, pompous bearing, as with the chest thrown out. —*n.* **2.** the act of strutting. **3.** a strutting walk or gait. —**strut′ter,** *n.*

strut[2] (strut), *n., v.,* **strut•ted, strut•ting.** —*n.* **1.** any of various structural members, as in trusses, primarily intended to resist longitudinal compression. —*v.t.* **2.** to brace or support by means of a strut or struts.

strych•nine (strik′nin, -nēn, -nīn), *n.* a colorless, crystalline poison, $C_{21}H_{22}N_2O_2$, formerly used as a central nervous system stimulant.

St. Thomas, *n.* **1.** an island in the Virgin Islands of the U.S. 52,660; 32 sq. mi. (83 sq. km). **2.** former name of CHARLOTTE AMALIE.

Stu•art (stōō′ərt, styōō′-), *n.* **1.** a member of the royal family that ruled in Scotland from 1371 to 1714 and in England from 1603 to 1714. **2. Charles Edward** (*"the Young Pretender"* or *"Bonnie Prince Charlie"*), 1720–80, grandson of James II. **3. Gilbert (Charles),** 1755–1828, U.S. painter. **4. James Ewell Brown** (*"Jeb"*), 1833–64, Confederate general in the Civil War. **5. James Francis Edward.** Also called **James III.** (*"the Old Pretender"*), 1688–1766, English prince.

stub (stub), *n., v.,* **stubbed, stub•bing.** —*n.* **1.** a short projecting piece or part. **2.** a short remaining piece, as of a pencil or cigar. **3.** (in a checkbook, etc.) the inner end of each leaf, for keeping a record of the content of the part filled out and torn away. **4.** the returned portion of a ticket. **5.** the end of a fallen tree, shrub, or plant left fixed in the ground; stump. **6.** something having a short, blunt shape, esp. a short-pointed, blunt pen. —*v.t.* **7.** to strike (one's toe or foot) accidentally against a projecting object. **8.** to extinguish the burning end of (a cigarette or cigar) by crushing it against a solid object (often fol. by *out*).

stub•ble (stub′əl), *n.* **1.** Usu., **stubbles.** the stumps of grain and other stalks left in the ground when the crop is cut. **2.** any short, rough growth, as of beard. —**stub′bled, stub′bly,** *adj.*

stub•born (stub′ərn), *adj.* **1.** unreasonably or perversely obstinate; unyielding. **2.** fixed or set in purpose or opinion. **3.** obstinately maintained, as a course of action: *stubborn resistance.* **4.** difficult to handle, treat, etc.: *a stubborn pain.* —**stub′born•ly,** *adv.* —**stub′born•ness,** *n.*

stub•by (stub′ē), *adj.,* **-bi•er, -bi•est. 1.** of the nature of or resembling a stub. **2.** short and thick or broad; thickset or squat: *stubby fingers.* **3.** consisting of or abounding in stubs. **4.** bristly, as the hair or beard. —**stub′bi•ness,** *n.*

stuc•co (stuk′ō), *n., pl.* **-coes, -cos,** *v.,* **-coed, -co•ing.** —*n.* **1.** an exterior finish for masonry or frame walls, usu. composed of cement, sand, and hydrated lime mixed with water and laid on wet. **2.** any of various fine plasters for decorative work, moldings, etc. —*v.t.* **3.** to cover or ornament with stucco.

stuck (stuk), *v.* **1.** pt. and pp. of STICK[2]. —***Idiom.* 2. stuck on,** *Informal.* infatuated with.

stuck′-up′, *adj. Informal.* snobbishly conceited.

stud[1] (stud), *n., v.,* **stud•ded, stud•ding,** *adj.* —*n.* **1.** a boss, knob, nailhead, or other protuberance projecting from a surface or part, esp. as an ornament. **2.** any buttonlike, usu. ornamental object mounted on a shank that is passed through an article of clothing to fasten it: *a collar stud.* **3.** any of a number of slender, upright members of wood, steel, etc., forming the frame of a wall or partition and covered with plasterwork, siding, etc. **4.** any of various projecting pins, lugs, or the like on machines or other implements. **5.** an earring consisting of a small, buttonlike ornament mounted on a metal post designed to pass through a pierced ear lobe. —*v.t.* **6.** to set with or as if with studs or the like. **7.** to be scattered over the surface of: *Stars studded the sky.* **8.** to set or scatter (objects) at intervals over a surface: *to stud raisins over a cake.* **9.** to furnish with or support by studs. —*adj.* **10.** ornamented with rivets, nailheads, or other buttonlike, usu. metallic objects: *a stud belt.*

stud[2] (stud), *n.* **1.** a studhorse or stallion. **2.** any male animal kept for breeding. **3.** a group of horses or other animals kept for breeding. **4.** a farm where horses are kept for breeding. **5.** a number of horses or other animals bred or kept by one owner. **6.** STUD POKER. —*adj.* **7.** of or pertaining to studhorses. **8.** kept for breeding purposes. —***Idiom.* 9. at stud,** (of a male animal) offered for the purpose of breeding.

stud•ding (stud′ing), *n.* **1.** a number of studs, as in a wall or partition. **2.** timbers or manufactured objects for use as studs.

stu•dent (stōōd′nt, styōōd′-), *n.* **1.** a person formally engaged in learning, esp. one enrolled in an institution of secondary or higher education.

2. any person who studies, investigates, or examines thoughtfully: *a student of human nature.*

stu′dent teach′er, *n.* a person studying to be a teacher who does closely supervised teaching in an elementary or secondary school. Also called **intern, practice teacher.**

stu′dent un′ion, *n.* a building on a college campus set aside for recreational, social, and governmental activities of the students.

stud•horse (stud′hôrs′), *n.* a stallion kept for breeding.

stud•ied (stud′ēd), *adj.* **1.** marked by or suggestive of conscious effort; not spontaneous or natural: *studied simplicity.* **2.** carefully deliberated: *a studied approval.* **3.** learned. —**stud′ied•ly,** *adv.*

stu•di•o (stōō′dē ō′, styōō′-), *n., pl.* **-di•os. 1.** the workroom or atelier of an artist, as a painter or sculptor. **2.** a room or place for instruction or experimentation in one of the performing arts: *a dance studio.* **3.** a room or set of rooms specially equipped for broadcasting radio or television programs, making recordings, filming motion pictures, etc. **4. a.** all the buildings and adjacent land required or used by a company engaged in the production of motion pictures. **b.** the company itself: *The studio produced lavish musicals during the thirties.* **5.** STUDIO APARTMENT.

stu′dio apart′ment, *n.* an apartment consisting of one main room, a kitchen or kitchenette, and a bathroom.

stu•di•ous (stōō′dē əs, styōō′-), *adj.* **1.** disposed or given to diligent study. **2.** concerned with or pertaining to study: *studious interests.* **3.** zealous, assiduous, or painstaking: *studious care.* **4.** carefully planned; studied. **5.** devoted to or favorable for study. —**stu′di•ous•ly,** *adv.* —**stu′di•ous•ness,** *n.*

stud′ pok′er, *n.* **1.** a variety of poker in which each player is dealt one card facedown in the first round and one card faceup in each of the next four rounds, each of the last four rounds being followed by a betting interval. **2.** any similar variety of poker.

stud•y (stud′ē), *n., pl.* **stud•ies,** *v.,* **stud•ied, stud•y•ing.** —*n.* **1.** application of the mind to the acquisition of knowledge, as by reading, investigation, or reflection. **2.** the acquisition of knowledge or skill in a particular branch of learning, science, or art: *the study of law.* **3.** Often, **studies,** a student's work at school or college: *to pursue one's studies.* **4.** something studied or to be studied. **5.** a detailed investigation and analysis of a subject, phenomenon, etc. **6.** a well-defined, organized branch of learning or knowledge. **7.** zealous endeavor or assiduous effort. **8.** the object of such endeavor or effort. **9.** deep thought; reverie. **10.** a room set apart for private study, reading, writing, or the like. **11.** a musical composition whose purpose is to improve a player's technique. **12.** a literary composition executed for exercise or as an experiment in a particular method of treatment. **13.** a work of art produced esp. as a guide for a finished work. **14.** a person in relation to the speed at which he or she can memorize something, esp. an actor in regard to learning lines: *a quick study.* —*v.i.* **15.** to apply oneself to the acquisition of knowledge, as by reading or investigation. **16.** to apply oneself; endeavor. **17.** to think deeply, reflect, or consider. **18.** to take a course of study, as at a college. —*v.t.* **19.** to apply oneself to acquiring a knowledge of (a subject). **20.** to examine or investigate carefully and in detail. **21.** to observe attentively; scrutinize: *to study a person's face.* **22.** to read carefully or intently. **23.** to endeavor to learn or memorize, as a part in a play. **24.** to give thought to; consider.

stud′y hall′, *n.* **1.** (in some schools) a room used chiefly for studying. **2.** a period of time in a school day set aside for study.

stuff (stuf), *n.* **1.** the material of which anything is made. **2.** material to be worked upon or to be used in making something. **3.** material, objects, or items of some unspecified kind. **4.** property, as personal belongings or equipment. **5.** something to be swallowed, as food, drink, or medicine. **6.** inward character, qualities, or capabilities: *to have the right stuff in one.* **7.** action or talk of a particular kind: *kid stuff.* **8.** a specialty or special skill: *to do one's stuff.* **9.** worthless things or matter. **10.** worthless or foolish ideas, talk, or writing: *a lot of stuff and nonsense.* **11.** *Informal.* spin or speed imparted to a ball, as by a baseball pitcher or tennis player. **12.** *Informal.* one's trade, skill, subject, etc.: *She knows her stuff.* —*v.t.* **13.** to fill (a receptacle, aperture, etc.), esp. by packing the contents closely together. **14.** to thrust or cram (something) into a receptacle, cavity, or the like. **15.** to fill or line with some kind of material as a padding or packing. **16.** to fill or cram with food. **17.** to fill (poultry, vegetables, etc.) with a stuffing. **18.** to fill the preserved skin of (a dead animal) with material, retaining its natural form and appearance for display. **19.** to put fraudulent votes into (a ballot box). **20.** to pack tightly in a confined place; crowd together. **21.** to fill (the mind) with facts, details, etc. **22.** to stop up or plug; block or choke (usu. fol. by *up*). —*v.i.* **23.** to cram oneself with food; gorge.

stuffed′ shirt′, *n.* a pompous, self-satisfied, and inflexible person.

stuff•er (stuf′ər), *n.* **1.** a person or thing that stuffs. **2.** an advertisement, announcement, or reminder inserted in an envelope and mailed with something else, as a bill or bank statement.

stuff•ing (stuf′ing), *n.* **1.** the act of a person or thing that stuffs. **2.** a material or substance used to stuff something. **3.** seasoned bread crumbs or other filling used to stuff poultry, vegetables, etc., before cooking.

stuff•y (stuf′ē), *adj.,* **stuff•i•er, stuff•i•est. 1.** close; poorly ventilated. **2.** oppressive from lack of freshness: *stuffy air.* **3.** blocked or stopped up: *a stuffy nose.* **4.** dull or tedious. **5.** self-important; pompous. **6.** rigid or old-fashioned in attitudes, esp. in matters of personal behavior. —**stuff′i•ly,** *adv.* —**stuff′i•ness,** *n.*

stul•ti•fy (stul′tə fī′), *v.t.,* **-fied, -fy•ing. 1.** to make, or cause to appear, foolish or ridiculous. **2.** to render futile or ineffectual, esp. by degrading or frustrating means. —**stul′ti•fi•ca′tion,** *n.*

stum•ble (stum′bəl), *v.,* **-bled, -bling,** *n.* —*v.i.* **1.** to strike the foot against something, as in walking or running, so as to stagger or fall. **2.** to walk or go unsteadily. **3.** to make a mistake or blunder, esp. a sinful one. **4.** to proceed in a hesitating or blundering manner, as in action or speech (often fol. by *along*). **5.** to discover or meet with accidentally or unexpectedly (usu. fol. by *on, upon,* or *across*): *They stumbled on a little village.* —*v.t.* **6.** to cause to stumble; trip. **7.** to give pause to; puzzle or perplex. —*n.* **8.** the act of stumbling. **9.** a moral lapse or error. **10.** a slip or blunder. —**stum′bler,** *n.* —**stum′bling•ly,** *adv.*

stum•ble•bum (stum′bəl bum′), *n. Informal.* **1.** a clumsy, second-rate prizefighter. **2.** a clumsy, incompetent person.

stum′bling block′, *n.* an obstacle or hindrance to progress, belief, or understanding.

stump (stump), *n.* **1.** the lower end of a tree trunk or plant left standing after the upper part falls or is cut off. **2.** the part of a limb of the body remaining after the rest has been cut off. **3.** a part of a broken or decayed tooth left in the gum. **4.** any base part or short remnant remaining after the main part has been removed; stub. **5.** an artificial leg. **6.** Usu., **stumps.** *Informal.* the legs. **7.** a short, stocky person. **8.** a heavy, sometimes uneven step or gait. **9.** the figurative place of political speechmaking: *to go on the stump.* **10.** a short, thick roll of paper, leather, etc., usu. having a blunt point, for rubbing a pencil, charcoal, or crayon drawing in order to achieve subtle gradations of tone in representing light and shade. —*v.t.* **11.** to reduce to a stump; truncate; lop. **12.** to clear of stumps, as land. **13.** to nonplus or render completely at a loss: *The question stumped me.* **14.** to challenge or dare to do something. **15.** to make political campaign speeches to or in: *to stump a state.* **16.** *Southern U.S.* to stub, as one's toe. **17.** to tone or modify (a drawing) with a stump. —*v.i.* **18.** to walk heavily or clumsily, as if with a wooden leg. **19.** to make political campaign speeches; electioneer.

stump•y (stum′pē), *adj.,* **stump•i•er, stump•i•est. 1.** of the nature of or resembling a stump. **2.** short and thick; stubby; stocky. **3.** abounding in stumps: *a stumpy field.* —**stump′i•ness,** *n.*

stun (stun), *v.,* **stunned, stun•ning,** *n.* —*v.t.* **1.** to deprive of consciousness, feeling, or strength by or as if by a blow, fall, etc. **2.** to astonish; astound; amaze. **3.** to shock; overwhelm. **4.** to daze or bewilder by noise. —*n.* **5.** the act of stunning. **6.** the condition of being stunned.

stung (stung), *v.* a pt. and pp. of STING.

stun′ gun′, *n.* a hand-held weapon that releases an electric charge or a tranquilizer dart to immobilize a person or animal.

stunk (stungk), *v.* a pt. and pp. of STINK.

stun•ner (stun′ər), *n.* **1.** a person or thing that stuns. **2.** a person or thing of striking excellence, beauty, etc.

stun•ning (stun′ing), *adj.* of striking beauty or excellence. —**stun′ning•ly,** *adv.*

stunt¹ (stunt), *v.t.* **1.** to stop, slow down, or hinder the growth or development of. —*n.* **2.** a stop or hindrance in growth or development. **3.** arrested development. **4.** a plant or animal hindered from attaining its proper growth. **5.** a disease of plants, characterized by a dwarfing or stunting of the plant. —**stunt′ed•ness,** *n.* —**stunt′ing•ly,** *adv.*

stunt² (stunt), *n.* **1.** a performance displaying a person's skill, dexterity, or daring; feat. **2.** a feat performed chiefly to attract attention: *a publicity stunt.* —*v.i.* **3.** to do a stunt or stunts.

stunt′ man′ or **stunt′man′,** *n.* a man who substitutes for an actor in film scenes requiring hazardous or acrobatic feats.

stunt′ wom′an or **stunt′wom′an,** *n.* a woman who substitutes for an actor in film scenes requiring hazardous or acrobatic feats.

stu•pe•fa•cient (stōō′pə fā′shənt, styōō′-), *adj.* **1.** stupefying; producing stupor. —*n.* **2.** a drug or agent that produces stupor.

stu•pe•fac•tion (stōō′pə fak′shən, styōō′-), *n.* **1.** the state of being stupefied; stupor. **2.** overwhelming amazement.

stu•pe•fy (stōō′pə fī′, styōō′-), *v.t.,* **-fied, -fy•ing. 1.** to numb the faculties of; put into a stupor. **2.** to stun, as with strong emotion. **3.** to overwhelm with amazement; astound; astonish. —**stu′pe•fy′ing•ly,** *adv.*

stu•pen•dous (stōō pen′dəs, styōō-), *adj.* **1.** causing amazement; astounding; marvelous. **2.** amazingly large or great; immense. —**stu•pen′dous•ly,** *adv.* —**stu•pen′dous•ness,** *n.*

stu•pid (stōō′pid, styōō′-), *adj.,* **-er, -est,** *n.* —*adj.* **1.** lacking ordinary quickness and keenness of mind; dull. **2.** characterized by or proceeding from mental dullness; foolish: *a stupid question.* **3.** tediously dull, esp. due to lack of meaning or sense; inane; pointless: *a stupid party.* **4.** annoying or irritating. **5.** in a state of stupor; stupefied: *stupid from fatigue.* —*n.* **6.** *Informal.* a stupid person. —**stu′pid•ly,** *adv.*

stu•pid•i•ty (stōō pid′i tē, styōō-), *n., pl.* **-ties. 1.** the state, quality, or fact of being stupid. **2.** a stupid act, notion, speech, etc.

stu•por (stōō′pər, styōō′-), *n.* **1.** suspension or great diminution of sensibility, as in disease or as caused by narcotics, intoxicants, etc. **2.** mental torpor; apathy; stupefaction.

stur•dy (stûr′dē), *adj.,* **-di•er, -di•est. 1.** strongly built; robust; hardy. **2.** strong, as in substance, construction, or texture: *a sturdy table.* **3.** firm; courageous; indomitable: *the sturdy defenders of the fort.* **4.** of strong or hardy growth, as a plant. —**stur′di•ly,** *adv.* —**stur′di•ness,** *n.*

stur·geon (stûr′jən), *n.*, *pl.* (*esp. collectively*) **-geon**, (*esp. for kinds or species*) **-geons**. any of the large fresh- and saltwater fishes of the family Acipenseridae, valued for their flesh and as a source of caviar and isinglass.

Sturm·ab·tei·lung (shtŏŏRM′äp′tī′lŏŏng), *n.* a Nazi militia organized about 1923, notorious for its violence and terrorism; storm troopers; Brownshirts. [< German, = *Sturm* storm, unit of storm troopers + *Abteilung* division, department]

Sturm und Drang (shtŏŏRM′ ŏŏnt dräng′), *n.* **1.** a romantic movement in German literature of the late 18th century, characterized chiefly by exaltation of the individual, rejection of established forms, and nationalism. **2.** turmoil; upheaval. [< German: lit., storm and stress]

stut·ter (stut′ər), *v.i.* **1.** to speak with the rhythm interrupted by repetitions, blocks or spasms, or prolongations of sounds or syllables. **2.** to proceed or operate with spasmodic interruptions or repetitions. —*v.t.* **3.** to say with a stutter. —*n.* **4.** an act or instance of stuttering. **5.** speech characterized by blocks or spasms interrupting the rhythm. —**stut′ter·er**, *n.* —**stut′ter·ing·ly**, *adv.*

Stuy·ve·sant (stī′və sənt), *n.* **Peter,** 1592–1672, last Dutch governor of New Netherland 1646–64.

St. Vin·cent (vin′sənt), *n.* **1.** an island in the S Windward Islands, in the SE West Indies: part of the state of St. Vincent and the Grenadines. 133 sq. mi. (345 sq. km). **2. Cape,** the SW tip of Portugal.

St. Vin′cent and the Gren′a·dines, *n.* a country in the S Windward Islands, in the SE West Indies, comprising St. Vincent island and the N Grenadines: a former British colony; gained independence 1979. 119,092; 150 sq. mi. (388 sq. km). *Cap.*: Kingstown.

St. Vi′tus's dance (vī′tə siz) also **St. Vi′tus dance** (vī′təs), **St. Vi′tus' dance** (vī′təs, -tə siz), *n.* CHOREA (def. 2).

sty¹ (stī), *n.*, *pl.* **sties,** *v.*, **stied, sty·ing.** —*n.* **1.** an enclosure for swine; pigpen. **2.** a filthy place or abode. —*v.t.* **3.** to keep or lodge in or as if in a sty. —*v.i.* **4.** to live in or as if in a sty.

sty² or **stye** (stī), *n.*, *pl.* **sties** or **styes.** abscess caused by bacterial infection of the glands on the edge of the eyelid.

style (stīl), *n.*, *v.* **styled, styl·ing.** —*n.* **1.** a particular type or sort, with reference to form, appearance, or character. **2.** a particular, distinctive, or characteristic mode or manner of acting: *to do things in a grand style.* **3.** prevailing fashion, as in dress, esp. approved fashion; smartness: *out of style.* **4.** an elegant, fashionable, or luxurious mode of living: *to live in style.* **5.** a mode of expressing thought in writing or speaking, esp. as characteristic of a group, person, etc. **6.** a mode or form of design, construction, or execution in any art or work, esp. as characteristic of a person, group, period, etc.: *the baroque style; the Georgian style of architecture.* **7.** a distinctive quality of originality, elegance, or flair: *a person with style.* **8.** a person's characteristic tastes, attitudes, and mode of behavior: *It's not his style to flatter people.* **9.** a descriptive or distinguishing appellation, esp. a legal, official, or recognized title. **10.** the gnomon of a sundial. **11.** a method of reckoning time. **12.** a narrow, cylindrical extension of the pistil that, when present, bears the stigma at its apex. **13.** *Zool.* a small, pointed process or part. **14.** the rules or customs of spelling, punctuation, and the like, observed by a publisher. —*v.t.* **15.** to call by a given title or appellation; designate; name. **16.** to design or arrange in accordance with a given or new style: *to style one's hair.* **17.** to bring into conformity with a specific style: *to style a manuscript.* —**style′less,** *adj.* —**style′less·ness,** *n.*

-style¹, a combining form of STYLE (defs. 12, 13). Compare STYLO-¹.

-style², a combining form with the meanings "column," "having columns (of the kind specified)": *urostyle.* Compare STYLO-².

style·book (stīl′bŏŏk′), *n.* **1.** a book containing the rules of usage in punctuation, typography, and the like, used by editors, writers, typographers, etc. **2.** a book of styles and fashions.

styl·ish (stī′lish), *adj.* characterized by or conforming to the current style or fashion; smart or chic. —**styl′ish·ly,** *adv.* —**styl′ish·ness,** *n.*

styl·ist (stī′list), *n.* **1.** a writer or speaker who is skilled in or cultivates a literary style. **2.** a designer or consultant on style, esp. in hairdressing, clothing, or interior decoration.

sty·lis·tic (stī lis′tik) also **sty·lis′ti·cal,** *adj.* of or pertaining to style. —**sty·lis′ti·cal·ly,** *adv.*

sty·lis·tics (stī lis′tiks), *n.* (*used with a sing. v.*) the study, esp. in literary works, of characteristic choices of linguistic expression and the effects they create. —**sty·lis·ti′cian** (-li stish′ən), *n.*

styl·ize (stī′līz), *v.t.*, **-ized, -iz·ing.** to design in or cause to conform to a particular or conventionalized style, as of representation in art. —**styl′i·za′tion,** *n.* —**styl′iz·er,** *n.*

stylo-¹, a combining form representing STYLE or STYLUS: *stylography; stylopodium.*

stylo-², a combining form meaning "column," "pillar," "tube": *stylobate.*

sty·lus (stī′ləs), *n.*, *pl.* **-li** (-lī), **-lus·es.** **1.** a pointed instrument used by the ancients for writing on wax tablets. **2.** any of various pointed, pen-shaped instruments used in drawing, artwork, etc. **3.** a needle for reproducing the sounds of a phonograph record. **4.** any of various pointed wedges used to punch holes in paper or other material, as in writing Braille. **5.** any of various pens for tracing a line automatically, as on an electrocardiograph.

sty·mie or **sty·my** or **sti·my** (stī′mē), *v.*, **-mied, -mie·ing** or **-my·ing,** *n.*, *pl.* **-mies.** —*v.t.* **1.** to hinder, block, or thwart. —*n.* **2.** a situa-

tion or problem presenting such difficulties as to discourage or defeat attempts to deal with or resolve it.

styp·tic (stip′tik), *adj.* Also, **styp′ti·cal. 1.** serving to contract organic tissue; astringent; binding. **2.** serving to check hemorrhage or bleeding, as a drug. —*n.* **3.** a styptic agent or substance.

styp′tic pen′cil, *n.* a pencil-shaped stick of alum or a similar styptic agent, used to stanch the bleeding of minor cuts.

Sty·ro·foam (stī′rə fōm′), *Trademark.* an expanded plastic made from polystyrene.

su·a·ble (sōō′ə bəl), *adj.* liable to be sued; capable of being sued. —**su′a·bil′i·ty,** *n.* —**su′a·bly,** *adv.*

sua·sion (swā′zhən), *n.* the act of attempting to persuade; persuasion. —**sua′sive** (-siv), *adj.* —**sua′sive·ly,** *adv.* —**sua′sive·ness,** *n.*

suave (swäv), *adj.*, **suav·er, suav·est.** smoothly agreeable or polite; agreeably or blandly urbane. —**suave′ly,** *adv.* —**suave′ness, suav′i·ty,** *n.*

sub (sub), *n.*, *v.*, **subbed, sub·bing.** —*n.* **1.** a submarine. **2.** a substitute. **3.** a submarine sandwich. **4.** a subordinate. **5.** a subaltern. —*v.i.* **6.** to act as a substitute for another.

sub-, a prefix, occurring orig. in loanwords from Latin, with the meanings "under," "below," "beneath" (*subsoil*), "just outside of," "near" (*subtropical*), "less than," "not quite" (*subhuman; suboscine*), "secondary," "at a lower point in a hierarchy" (*subcommittee; subplot*).

sub·al·pine (sub al′pīn, -pin), *adj.* **1.** pertaining to the regions at the foot of the Alps. **2.** growing on mountains below the limit of tree growth, and above the foothill, or montane, zone.

sub·al·tern (sub ôl′tərn *or, esp. for 3,* sub′əl tûrn′), *n.* **1.** a person who has a subordinate position. **2.** a commissioned officer in the British army below the rank of captain. **3.** *Logic.* a particular proposition inferred from a corresponding universal proposition. —*adj.* **4.** lower in rank; subordinate. —**sub′al·ter′ni·ty,** *n.*

sub·al·ter·nate (sub ôl′tər nit, -al′-), *adj.* **1.** subordinate. **2.** *Bot.* placed singly along an axis, but tending to become grouped oppositely. —**sub·al′ter·na′tion** (-nā′shən), *n.*

sub·a·que·ous (sub ā′kwē əs, -ak′wē-), *adj.* **1.** existing or situated under water. **2.** used or performed under water.

sub·arc·tic (sub ärk′tik, -är′tik), *adj.* of, pertaining to, or resembling the region immediately S of the Arctic Circle.

sub·as·sem·bly (sub′ə sem′blē), *n.*, *pl.* **-blies.** a structural assembly, as of electronic parts, forming part of a larger assembly.

sub·a·tom·ic (sub′ə tom′ik), *adj.* **1.** of or pertaining to a process that occurs within an atom. **2.** of or pertaining to particles contained in an atom, as electrons, protons, or neutrons.

sub·base·ment (sub′bās′mənt), *n.* a basement below the main basement of a building.

sub·branch (sub′branch′, -bränch′), *n.* a subordinate branch or a division of a branch, as of a bank or business.

sub·class (sub′klas′, -kläs′), *n.* **1.** a primary division of a class. **2.** a subordinate class, as of people. **3.** *Biol.* a category of related orders within a class.

sub·clas·si·fy (sub klas′ə fī′), *v.t.*, **-fied, -fy·ing.** to arrange in subclasses. —**sub′clas·si·fi·ca′tion,** *n.*

sub·clin·i·cal (sub klin′i kəl), *adj.* pertaining to an early stage of a disease; having no noticeable clinical symptoms.

sub·com·mit·tee (sub′kə mit′ē), *n.* a secondary committee appointed out of a main committee, usu. to deal with a specific matter.

sub·com·pact (sub kom′pakt), *n.* an automobile that is smaller than a compact.

sub·con·scious (sub kon′shəs), *adj.* **1.** existing or operating in the mind beneath or beyond consciousness. **2.** imperfectly or not wholly conscious: *subconscious motivations.* —*n.* **3.** the totality of mental processes of which the individual is not aware. —**sub·con′scious·ly,** *adv.* —**sub·con′scious·ness,** *n.*

sub·con·ti·nent (sub kon′tn ənt, sub′kon′-), *n.* **1.** a large, relatively self-contained landmass forming a subdivision of a continent: *the subcontinent of India.* **2.** a large landmass, as Greenland, that is smaller than any of the usu. recognized continents.

sub·con·tract (sub kon′trakt, sub′kon′-; *v. also* sub′kən trakt′), *n.* **1.** a contract by which one agrees to provide services or materials necessary to fulfill another's contract. —*v.t.* **2.** to make a subcontract for. —*v.i.* **3.** to make a subcontract.

sub·con·trac·tor (sub kon′trak tər, sub′kon′-, sub′kən trak′tər), *n.* a person or business that contracts to provide a service, materials, etc., necessary to fulfill another's contract, esp. a person or business that contracts to do part of another's work.

sub·cul·ture (*n.* sub′kul′chər; *v.* sub kul′chər), *n.*, *v.*, **-cul·tured, -cul·tur·ing.** —*n.* **1.** a group having social, economic, ethnic, or other traits distinctive enough to distinguish it from others within the same culture or society. **2.** a bacterial culture derived from a strain that has been recultivated on a different medium. —*v.t.* **3.** to cultivate (a bacterial strain) again on a different medium. —**sub·cul′tur·al,** *adj.* —**sub·cul′tur·al·ly,** *adv.*

sub·cu·ta·ne·ous (sub′kyōō tā′nē əs), *adj.* situated or introduced under the skin; subdermal. —**sub′cu·ta′ne·ous·ly,** *adv.*

sub·di·vide (sub′di vīd′, sub′di vīd′), *v.*, **-vid·ed, -vid·ing.** —*v.t.* **1.** to divide (something already divided) into smaller parts. **2.** to divide into parts. **3.** to divide (a tract of land) into building lots. —*v.i.* **4.** to be-

S

come separated into divisions or subdivisions. —**sub′di•vid′a•ble**, *adj.* —**sub′di•vid′er**, *n.*

sub•di•vi•sion (sub′di vizh′ən), *n.* **1.** the act or fact of subdividing. **2.** a division of a larger division. **3.** a portion of land divided into lots for real-estate development.

sub•duc•tion (səb duk′shən), *n.* *Geol.* the process by which collision of the earth's crustal plates results in one plate's being drawn down or overridden by another, localized along the juncture (**subduc′tion zone′**) of two plates.

sub•due (səb doō′, -dyoō′), *v.t.*, **-dued, -du•ing. 1.** to conquer and bring into subjection: *Rome subdued Gaul.* **2.** to overpower by superior force; overcome. **3.** to bring under mental or emotional control, as by persuasion or intimidation. **4.** to repress (feelings, impulses, etc.). **5.** to bring (land) under cultivation. **6.** to reduce the intensity, force, or vividness of (sound, light, color, etc.); tone down; soften. **7.** to allay (inflammation, infection, etc.). —**sub•du′ing•ly**, *adv.*

sub•dued (səb doōd′, -dyoōd′), *adj.* **1.** quiet; repressed; controlled. **2.** reduced in fullness of tone, as a color or sound; muted. —**sub•dued′ly**, *adv.* —**sub•dued′ness**, *n.*

sub•fam•i•ly (sub fam′ə lē, -fam′lē, sub′fam′ə lē, -fam′lē), *n., pl.* **-lies. 1.** *Biol.* a category of related genera within a family. **2.** *Ling.* a group of related languages within a family, constituting a higher order than a branch.

sub•floor (sub′flôr′, -flōr′), *n.* a rough floor beneath a finished floor.

sub•freez•ing (sub′frē′zing), *adj.* below the freezing point.

sub•ge•nus (sub jē′nəs), *n., pl.* **-gen•er•a** (-jen′ər ə), **-ge•nus•es.** *Biol.* a category of related species within a genus. —**sub′ge•ner′ic** (-jə ner′ik), *adj.*

sub•gla•cial (sub glā′shəl), *adj.* occurring or situated beneath a glacier, either at the present time or at some time in the past. —**sub•gla′cial•ly**, *adv.*

sub•grade (sub′grād′), *n.* the prepared earth surface on which a pavement or the ballast of a railroad track is placed or upon which the foundation of a structure is built.

sub•group (sub′groōp′), *n.* **1.** a subordinate group or a division of a group. **2.** *Math.* a subset of a group that is closed under the group operation and in which every element has an inverse in the subset.

sub•gum (sub′gum′), *adj.* (of various Chinese-style dishes) prepared with a mixed variety of vegetables, diced meat, and seafood.

sub•head (sub′hed′) also **sub′head′ing**, *n.* a title or heading of a subdivision, as in a chapter, essay, or newspaper article.

sub•hu•man (sub hyoō′mən; *often* -yoō′-), *adj.* less than or not quite human.

sub•in•dex (sub in′deks), *n., pl.* **-dex•es, -di•ces** (-də sēz′). **1.** an index to a part or subdivision of a larger category. **2.** SUBSCRIPT.

sub•ir•ri•gate (sub ir′i gāt′), *v.t.*, **-gat•ed, -gat•ing.** to irrigate beneath ground level, as with a system of buried pipes. —**sub′ir•ri•ga′tion**, *n.*

sub•ja•cent (sub jā′sənt), *adj.* **1.** situated or occurring underneath or below; underlying. **2.** forming a basis. **3.** lower than but not directly under something. —**sub•ja′cent•ly**, *adv.*

sub•ject (*n., adj.* sub′jikt; *v.* səb jekt′), *n.* **1.** that which forms a basic matter of thought, discussion, investigation, etc. **2.** a branch of knowledge as a course of study. **3.** a motive, cause, or ground: *a subject for complaint.* **4.** something or someone treated or represented in a literary composition, work of art, etc. **5.** the principal melodic motif or phrase in a musical composition, esp. in a fugue. **6.** a person who owes allegiance to, or is under the domination of, a sovereign or state. **7.** a syntactic unit that functions as one of the two main constituents of a sentence, the other being the predicate, and that consists of a noun, noun phrase, or noun substitute typically referring to the one performing the action or being in the state expressed by the predicate, as *I* in *I gave no-*

tice. **8.** a person or thing that undergoes some kind of treatment at the hands of others. **9.** a person, animal, or corpse as an object of medical or scientific treatment or experiment. **10.** *Philos.* **a.** that which thinks, feels, perceives, intends, etc., as contrasted with the objects of thought, feeling, etc. **b.** the self or ego. —*adj.* **11.** being under the domination, control, or influence of something (often fol. by *to*). **12.** being under the dominion, rule, or authority of a sovereign, state, etc. (often fol. by *to*). **13.** open or exposed (usu. fol. by *to*): *subject to ridicule.* **14.** dependent upon something (usu. fol. by *to*): *His consent is subject to your approval.* **15.** being under the necessity of undergoing something (usu. fol. by *to*): *All beings are subject to death.* **16.** liable; prone (usu. fol. by *to*): *subject to headaches.* —*v.t.* **17.** to bring under domination, control, or influence (usu. fol. by *to*). **18.** to cause to undergo the action of something specified; expose (usu. fol. by *to*): *to subject metal to intense heat.* **19.** to make liable or vulnerable; expose (usu. fol. by *to*): *to subject oneself to ridicule.* —**sub•jec′tion**, *n.*

sub′ject com•ple′ment, *n.* a word or group of words, usu. functioning as an adjective or noun, that is used in the predicate following a copula and describes or is identified with the subject of the sentence, as *sleepy* in *The travelers were sleepy.* Also called **subjec′tive com′plement.**

sub•jec•tive (səb jek′tiv), *adj.* **1.** existing in the mind; belonging to the thinking subject rather than to the object of thought (opposed to *objective*). **2.** pertaining to or characteristic of an individual; personal: *a subjective evaluation.* **3.** placing excessive emphasis on one's own moods, attitudes, opinions, etc. **4.** *Philos.* relating to or of the nature of an object as it is known in the mind as distinct from a thing in itself. **5.** relating to properties or specific conditions of the mind as distinguished from general or universal experience. **6.** pertaining to the subject or substance in which attributes inhere; essential. **7. a.** of or designating a grammatical case that typically indicates the subject of a finite verb; nominative (contrasted with *objective*). **b.** of or pertaining to the subject of a sentence. —**sub•jec′tive•ly**, *adv.* —**sub′jec•tiv′i•ty**, *n.*

sub•jec•tiv•ism (səb jek′tə viz′əm), *n.* **1.** the doctrine that all knowledge is limited to experiences by the self, and that transcendent knowledge is impossible. **2.** any of several theories holding that certain states of thought or feeling are the highest good. —**sub•jec′tiv•ist**, *n.* —**sub•jec′ti•vis′tic**, *adj.*

sub′ject mat′ter, *n.* the substance of a discussion, book, writing, etc., as distinguished from its form or style.

sub•join (səb join′), *v.t.* to add at the end, as of something said or written; append.

sub•ju•gate (sub′jə gāt′), *v.t.*, **-gat•ed, -gat•ing. 1.** to bring under complete control or subjection; conquer; master. **2.** to make submissive or subservient; enslave. —**sub′ju•ga•ble** (-gə bəl), *adj.* —**sub′ju•ga′tion**, *n.* —**sub′ju•ga′tor**, *n.*

sub•junc•tive (səb jungk′tiv), *adj.* **1.** of or designating a grammatical mood typically used for subjective, doubtful, hypothetical, or grammatically subordinate statements or questions, as the mood of *be* in *if this be treason.* —*n.* **2.** the subjunctive mood. **3.** a verb form in the subjunctive mood. —**sub•junc′tive•ly**, *adv.* —**Usage.** The subjunctive mood has largely disappeared in English. It survives, though inconsistently, in sentences with conditional clauses contrary to fact and in subordinate clauses after verbs like *wish: If the house were nearer to the road, we would hear more traffic noise. I wish I were in Florida.* The subjunctive also occurs in subordinate *that* clauses after a main clause expressing recommendation, resolution, demand, etc.: *We ask that each tenant take* (not *takes*) *responsibility for keeping the front door locked. It is important that only fresh spinach be* (not *is*) *used.* The subjunctive occurs too in some established or idiomatic expressions: *So be it. Heaven help us. God rest ye merry, gentlemen.*

---

sub′ad•min′is•tra′tor, *n.*
sub′a′gent, *n.*
sub′ag′gre•gate, *adj., n.*
sub′al•li′ance, *n.*
sub•an′gu•lar, *adj.; -ly, adv.*
sub•ant•arc′tic, *adj.*
sub•ap′ical, *adj.*
sub•a•quat′ic, *adj.*
sub•ar•bo′re•al, *adj.*
sub•ar′chi•tect′, *n.*
sub•ar′e•a, *n.*
sub•ar′id, *adj.*
sub•ar′ti•cle, *n.*
sub′as•so′ci•a′tion, *n.*
sub•as′tral, *adj.*
sub′at•mos•pher′ic, *adj.*
sub•at′om, *n.*
sub•au′di•ble, *adj.; -bly, adv.*
sub•au′ral, *adj.; -ly, adv.*
sub•au•ric′u•lar, *adj.*
sub•au′to•mat′ic, *adj.*
sub•av′er•age, *adj.*
sub•ax′i•al, *adj.*
sub•ax′il•la•ry, *adj.*

sub′ba′sin, *n.*
sub•cab′i•net, *n.*
sub•cal′i•ber, *adj.*
sub•cap′su•lar, *adj.*
sub•car′di•nal, *adj.*
sub•caste′, *n.*
sub•cat′e•go•ri•za′tion, *n.*
sub•cat′e•go•ry, *n., pl.* -ries.
sub•cav′i•ty, *n., pl.* -ties.
sub•ceil′ing, *n.*
sub′ce•les′ti•al, *adj.*
sub•cel′lu•lar, *adj.*
sub•cen′ter, *n.*
sub•cen′tral, *adj.*
sub•chap′ter, *n.*
sub•chief′, *n.*
sub•civ′i•lized′, *adj.*
sub•claim′, *n.*
sub•clan′, *n.*
sub•clause′, *n.*
sub•cla′vi•an, *adj.*
sub•cli′max, *n.*
sub•code′, *n.*
sub•col′le•giate, *adj.*

sub′com•mand′er, *n.*
sub′com•mis′sion, *n.*
sub′com•pen•sa′tion, *n.*
sub′con•stel•la′tion, *n.*
sub•con′sul, *n.*
sub•coun′cil, *n.*
sub•cra′ni•al, *adj.; -ly, adv.*
sub•cur′rent, *n.*
sub•deal′er, *n.*
sub•dean′, *n.*
sub′def•i•ni′tion, *n.*
sub•del′e•gate, *n.*
sub•de•part′ment, *n.*
sub•de′pot, *n.*
sub•dep′u•ty, *n., pl.* -ties.
sub•di′a•lect′, *n.*
sub•di•rec′tor, *n.*
sub•dis′trict, *n., v.t.*
sub•dom′i•nant, *n.*
sub•ed′i•tor, *n.*
sub•el′e•ment, *n.*
sub•en′try, *n., pl.* -tries.
sub•frac′tion, *n.*
sub•func′tion, *n.*

sub•le′thal, *adj.*
sub•lin′gual, *adj.*
sub•man′ag•er, *n.*
sub′man•dib′u•lar, *adj.*
sub•mar′gin•al, *adj.*
sub′mi•cro•scop′ic, *adj.*
sub•mol′e•cule′, *n.*
sub•mon′tane, *adj.*
sub•mul′ti•ple, *n.*
sub′pop•u•la′tion, *n.*
sub•re′gion, *n.*
sub•rule′, *n.*
sub•sec′tion, *n.*
sub•seg′ment, *n.*
sub•state′, *n.*
sub•stel′lar, *adj.*
sub•sys′tem, *n.*
sub•teen′, *n.*
sub•tem′per•ate, *adj.*
sub•ten′ant, *n.*
sub•ter′ri•to•ry, *n., pl.* -ries.
sub•theme′, *n.*
sub•top′ic, *n.*
sub•treas′ur•y, *n., pl.,* -ur•ies.

sub•king•dom (sub king′dəm, sub′king′-), *n. Biol.* a category of related phyla within a kingdom.

sub•lease (*n.* sub′lēs′; *v.* sub lēs′), *n., v.,* **-leased, -leas•ing.** —*n.* **1.** a lease granted to another person by the lessee of a property. —*v.t.* **2.** to grant a sublease of. **3.** to take or hold a sublease of. —*v.i.* **4.** to grant or hold a sublease; sublet. —**sub′les•see′** (-le sē′), *n.* —**sub•les•sor** (sub-les′ôr, sub′le sôr′), *n.*

sub•let (*v.* sub let′, sub′let′; *n.* sub′let′), *v.,* **-let, -let•ting,** *n.* —*v.t., v.i.* **1.** to sublease. **2.** to subcontract. —*n.* **3.** SUBLEASE. **4.** a property, as an apartment, obtained by subleasing.

sub•li•mate (*v.* sub′lə māt′; *n., adj.* -mit, -māt′), *v.,* **-mat•ed, -mat•ing,** *n., adj.* —*v.t.* **1.** *Psychol.* to divert the energy of (a sexual or other biological impulse) from its immediate goal to one of a more acceptable social, moral, or aesthetic nature or use. **2.** to refine or purify (a substance). **3.** to make nobler or purer. —*v.i.* **4.** to become sublimated; undergo sublimation. —*n.* **5.** the crystals, deposit, or material obtained when a substance is sublimated. —*adj.* **6.** purified or exalted; sublimated. —**sub′li•ma′tion,** *n.*

sub•lime (sə blīm′), *adj., n., v.,* **-limed, -lim•ing.** —*adj.* **1.** elevated or lofty in thought, language, etc. **2.** impressing the mind with a sense of grandeur or power; inspiring awe, veneration, etc. **3.** supreme or outstanding: *a sublime dinner.* —*n.* **4. the sublime, a.** the realm of things that are sublime. **b.** the quality of sublimity. **c.** the greatest or supreme degree. —*v.t.* **5.** to make higher, nobler, or purer. **6.** to convert (a solid substance) by heat into a vapor, which on cooling condenses again to solid form, without apparent liquefaction. —*v.i.* **7.** to volatilize from the solid state to a gas, and then condense again as a solid without passing through the liquid state. —***Proverb.*** **8. From the sublime to the ridiculous is but a step,** only a small detail may separate the great and the laughable. —**sub•lime′ly,** *adv.* —**sub•lime′ness,** *n.* —**sub•lim′er,** *n.*

sub•lim•i•nal (sub lim′ə nl), *adj.* existing or operating below the threshold of consciousness; insufficiently intense to produce a discrete sensation but influencing or designed to influence mental processes or behavior: *subliminal advertising.* —**sub•lim′i•nal•ly,** *adv.*

sub•lim•i•ty (sə blim′i tē), *n., pl.* **-ties. 1.** the state or quality of being sublime. **2.** a sublime person or thing.

sub•lit•to•ral (sub lit′ər əl), *adj.* **1.** of or pertaining to the region of the ocean extending from the lowest shoreline to the edge of the continental shelf. **2.** of or pertaining to the region of a lake extending from the deepest rooted plants to the end of the warmer, oxygen-rich layer of water. —*n.* **3.** a sublittoral zone or region.

sub•lu•nar•y (sub′lo͞o ner′ē, sub lo͞o′nə rē) also **sub•lu•nar** (sub lo͞o′-nər), *adj.* **1.** situated beneath the moon or between the earth and the moon. **2.** characteristic of or pertaining to the earth; terrestrial. **3.** mundane or worldly.

sub•ma•chine′ gun′ (sub′mə shēn′), *n.* an automatic firearm using small-caliber ammunition and fired from the shoulder or hip.

sub•ma•rine (sub′mə rēn′, sub′mə rēn′), *n., adj., v.,* **-rined, -rin•ing.** —*n.* **1.** a vessel that can be submerged and navigated under water. **2.** something situated or living under the surface of the sea, as a plant or animal. **3.** *Northeastern U.S.* a hero sandwich. —*adj.* **4.** situated, occurring, operating, or living under the surface of the sea. **5.** of, pertaining to, or carried on by a submarine. —*v.i.* **6.** to participate in the operating of a submarine.

sub•max•il•lar•y (sub mak′sə ler′ē, sub′mak sil′ə rē), *adj.* of or pertaining to the lower jaw or lower jawbone.

sub•merge (səb mûrj′), *v.,* **-merged, -merg•ing.** —*v.t.* **1.** to put or sink below the surface of water or any other enveloping medium. **2.** to cover or overflow with water; immerse. **3.** to cover; suppress. —*v.i.* **4.** to sink or plunge under water or beneath the surface of any enveloping medium. **5.** to be covered or lost from sight. —**sub•mer′gence,** *n.*

sub•merged (səb mûrjd′), *adj.* **1.** under the surface of water or any other enveloping medium; inundated. **2.** hidden, covered, or unknown. **3.** poverty-stricken; destitute; impoverished.

sub•merse (səb mûrs′), *v.t.,* **-mersed, -mers•ing.** to submerge. —**sub•mer•sion** (səb mûr′zhən, -shən), *n.*

sub•mersed (səb mûrst′), *adj.* **1.** submerged. **2.** *Bot.* growing under water.

sub•mers•i•ble (səb mûr′sə bəl), *adj.* **1.** capable of being submersed. **2.** capable of functioning while submersed. —*n.* **3.** a small submarine equipped to carry out underwater research at great depths. —**sub•mers′i•bil′i•ty,** *n.*

sub•min•i•a•ture (sub min′ē ə chər, -cho͝or′, -min′ə chər), *adj.* smaller than miniature, as certain electronic components.

sub•min•i•a•tur•ize (sub min′ē ə chə rīz′, -min′ə chə-), *v.t.,* **-ized, -iz•ing.** to design or manufacture (equipment, esp. electronic equipment) in a greatly reduced scale. —**sub•min′i•a•tur•i•za′tion,** *n.*

sub•mis•sion (səb mish′ən), *n.* **1.** an act or instance of submitting. **2.** the condition of having submitted. **3.** submissive conduct or attitude. **4.** something submitted, as for consideration. **5.** an agreement between disputing parties to abide by the decision of an arbitrator.

sub•mis•sive (səb mis′iv), *adj.* **1.** inclined or ready to submit; unresistingly or humbly obedient. **2.** marked by or indicating submission. —**sub•mis′sive•ly,** *adv.* —**sub•mis′sive•ness,** *n.*

sub•mit (səb mit′), *v.,* **-mit•ted, -mit•ting.** —*v.t.* **1.** to give over or yield to the power or authority of another (often used reflexively). **2.** to subject to some kind of treatment or influence. **3.** to present for approval or consideration. **4.** to state or urge with deference; suggest or propose: *I submit that full proof should be required.* —*v.i.* **5.** to yield oneself to the power or authority of another. **6.** to allow oneself to be subjected to some kind of treatment. **7.** to defer to another's judgment, opinion, decision, etc. —**sub•mit′ta•ble, sub•mis′si•ble** (-mis′ə bel), *adj.* —**sub•mit′ter,** *n.*

sub•nor•mal (sub nôr′məl), *adj.* below the normal or average; less than or inferior to the normal, as in intelligence. —**sub′nor•mal′i•ty,** *n.*

sub•or•der (sub′ôr′dər), *n. Biol.* a category of related families within an order.

sub•or•di•nate (*adj., n.* sə bôr′dn it; *v.* -dn āt′), *adj., n., v.,* **-nat•ed, -nat•ing.** —*adj.* **1.** placed in or belonging to a lower order or rank. **2.** of less importance; secondary. **3.** subject to or under the authority of a superior. **4.** subservient or inferior. **5.** subject; dependent. **6. a.** acting as a modifier in a grammatical construction, as *when I finished* in *They were glad when I finished.* **b.** pertaining to a subordinating conjunction. —*n.* **7.** a subordinate person or thing. —*v.t.* **8.** to place in a lower order or rank. **9.** to make secondary (usu. fol. by *to*). **10.** to make subservient or dependent (usu. fol. by *to*). —**sub•or′di•nate•ly,** *adv.* —**sub•or′di•na′tion,** *n.* —**sub•or′di•na′tive** (-ā′tiv, -ə tiv), *adj.*

subor′dinate clause′, *n.* a clause that modifies the principal clause or some part of it or that serves a noun function in the principal clause, as *when she arrived* in the sentence *I was there when she arrived* or *that she has arrived* in the sentence *I doubt that she has arrived.* Compare MAIN CLAUSE.

subor′dinating conjunc′tion, *n.* a conjunction introducing a subordinate clause, as *when* in *They were glad when I finished.* Also called **sub•or′di•na′tor.** Compare COORDINATING CONJUNCTION.

sub•orn (sə bôrn′), *v.t.* **1.** to induce, as by bribe, to commit a crime. **2.** to induce (a person, esp. a witness) to give false testimony. —**sub•or•na•tion** (sub′ôr nā′shən), *n.* —**sub•orn′er,** *n.*

sub•phy•lum (sub fī′ləm), *n., pl.* **-la** (-lə). *Biol.* a category of related classes within a phylum. —**sub•phy′lar,** *adj.*

sub•plot (sub′plot′), *n.* a secondary plot, as in a novel or play; underplot.

sub•poe•na or **sub•pe•na** (sə pē′nə, səb-), *n., pl.* **-nas,** *v.,* **-naed, -na•ing.** *Law.* —*n.* **1.** a writ to summon witnesses or evidence before a court. —*v.t.* **2.** to serve with a subpoena.

sub ro•sa (sub rō′zə), *adv.* confidentially; secretly; privately.

sub•rou•tine (sub′ro͞o tēn′), *n.* a prepared instruction sequence that a programmer can insert into a computer program as needed.

sub•scribe (səb skrīb′), *v.,* **-scribed, -scrib•ing.** —*v.t.* **1.** to give, pay, or pledge (a sum of money) as a contribution, gift, or investment. **2.** to append one's signature or mark to (a document), as in approval or attestation of its contents. **3.** to append, as one's signature, at the bottom of a document or the like; sign. **4.** to agree or assent to. —*v.i.* **5.** to give, pay, or pledge money as a contribution, gift, or investment. **6.** to obtain a subscription to a publication, series of concerts, cable television service, etc. **7.** to give one's consent; sanction: *I will not subscribe to popular fallacies.* **8.** to sign one's name to a document, as to show approval. —**sub•scrib′er,** *n.* —**sub•scrib′er•ship′,** *n.*

sub•script (sub′skript), *adj.* **1.** written below (disting. from *superscript*). **2.** INFERIOR (def. 7). —*n.* **3.** Also called **inferior.** a letter, number, or symbol written or printed low on a line of text.

sub•scrip•tion (səb skrip′shən), *n.* **1.** a sum of money given or pledged as a contribution, payment, investment, etc. **2.** a fund raised through sums of money subscribed. **3.** the right to receive a periodical or cable television service, attend a series of concerts or plays, etc., for a sum paid. **4.** the act of appending one's signature or mark, as to a document. **5.** a signature or mark thus appended. **6.** something written beneath or at the end of a document or the like. **7.** assent, agreement, or approval. **8.** *Eccles.* assent to or acceptance of a body of principles or doctrines. —**sub•scrip′tive** (-tiv), *adj.* —**sub•scrip′tive•ly,** *adv.*

subscrip′tion tel′evision, *n.* PAY TELEVISION. Also called **subscription TV.**

sub•se•quent (sub′si kwənt), *adj.* **1.** occurring or coming later or after. **2.** following in order or succession; succeeding. —**sub′se•quent•ly,** *adv.*

sub•serve (səb sûrv′), *v.t.,* **-served, -serv•ing.** to be useful or instrumental in promoting (a purpose, action, etc.).

sub•ser•vi•ent (səb sûr′vē ənt), *adj.* **1.** serving or acting in a subordinate capacity; subordinate. **2.** servile; excessively submissive; obsequious. **3.** useful in promoting a purpose or end. —**sub•ser′vi•ence, sub•ser′vi•en•cy,** *n.* —**sub•ser′vi•ent•ly,** *adv.*

sub•set (sub′set′), *n.* **1.** a set that is a part of a larger set. **2.** *Math.* a set consisting of elements of a given set that can be the same as the given set or smaller.

sub•side (səb sīd′), *v.i.,* **-sid•ed, -sid•ing. 1.** to sink to a low or lower level. **2.** to become quiet, less active, or less violent; abate. **3.** to sink or fall to the bottom, as sediment; settle; precipitate. —**sub•sid•ence** (səb-sīd′ns, sub′si dns), *n.* —**sub•sid′er,** *n.*

sub•sid•i•ar•y (səb sid′ē er′ē), *adj., n., pl.* **-ar•ies.** —*adj.* **1.** serving to assist or supplement. **2.** subordinate or secondary: *subsidiary issues.* —*n.* **3.** a subsidiary thing or person. **4.** a company whose controlling interest is owned by another company. —**sub•sid′i•ar′i•ly** (-sid′ē âr′ə lē, -sid′ē er′-), *adv.*

subsid′iary rights′, *n.pl.* rights to publish or produce in different formats or media a work based on an original literary property.

sub•si•dize (sub′si dīz′), *v.t.,* **-dized, -diz•ing. 1.** to furnish or aid with a subsidy. **2.** to purchase the assistance of by the payment of a subsidy. **3.** to secure the cooperation of by bribery; buy over. —**sub′si•diz′a•ble,** adj. —**sub′si•di•za′tion,** n. —**sub′si•diz′er,** n.

sub•si•dy (sub′si dē), n., pl. **-dies. 1.** a direct financial aid furnished by a government, as to a private commercial enterprise, an individual, or another government. **2.** any grant or contribution of money.

sub•sist (səb sist′), v.i. **1.** to exist; continue in existence. **2.** to remain alive; live, as on food, resources, etc. **3.** to have existence in, or by reason of, something. **4.** to reside, lie, or consist (usu. fol. by in). —v.t. **5.** to provide sustenance or support for; maintain. —**sub•sist′ing•ly,** adv.

sub•sist•ence (səb sis′təns), n. **1.** the state or fact of subsisting or existing. **2.** the providing of sustenance or support. **3.** means of supporting life; a living or livelihood. **4.** the source from which food and other items necessary to exist are obtained.

subsist′ence farm′ing, n. farming that provides for the farm family's needs with little surplus for marketing.

sub•sist•ent (səb sis′tənt), adj. **1.** subsisting, existing, or continuing in existence. **2.** inherent: subsistent qualities of character.

sub•soil (sub′soil′), n. the bed or stratum of earth immediately under the surface soil. Also called **undersoil.**

sub•spe•cies (sub′spē′shēz, sub spē′-), n., pl. **-cies.** a subdivision of a species, esp. a geographical or ecological subdivision. —**sub′spe•cif′ic** (-spə sif′ik), adj.

sub•stance (sub′stəns), n. **1.** that of which a thing consists; physical matter or material: form and substance. **2.** a kind of matter of definite chemical composition: a metallic substance. **3.** the actual matter of a thing, as opposed to the appearance; reality. **4.** substantial or solid character or quality: claims lacking in substance. **5.** consistency; body. **6.** the meaning or gist, as of speech or writing. **7.** possessions, means, or wealth. **8.** CONTROLLED SUBSTANCE. **9.** Philos. that which exists by itself and in which accidents or attributes inhere. —**Idiom. 10. in substance, a.** concerning the essentials; substantially. **b.** actually; really.

sub′stance abuse′, n. long-term use of an addictive or behavior-altering drug when not needed for medical treatment.

sub•stand•ard (sub stan′dərd), adj. **1.** below standard or less than adequate. **2.** of or pertaining to a dialect or variety of a language or a feature of usage often considered by others to mark its user as uneducated; nonstandard.

sub•stan•tial (səb stan′shəl), adj. **1.** of ample or considerable amount, quantity, size, etc. **2.** of a corporeal or material nature; real or actual. **3.** of solid character or quality; firm, stout, or strong: a substantial fabric. **4.** being such with respect to essentials: two stories in substantial agreement. **5.** wealthy or influential. **6.** of real worth, value, or effect: substantial reasons. **7.** pertaining to the substance, matter, or material of a thing. **8.** pertaining to the essence of a thing. **9.** Philos. pertaining to or of the nature of substance rather than an accident or attribute. —n. **10.** something substantial. —**sub•stan′ti•al•i•ty, sub•stan′tial•ness,** n. —**sub•stan′tial•ly,** adv.

sub•stan•ti•ate (səb stan′shē āt′), v.t., **-at•ed, -at•ing. 1.** to establish by proof or competent evidence: to substantiate a charge. **2.** to give substantial existence to. **3.** to affirm as having substance; strengthen: to substantiate a friendship. —**sub•stan′ti•a′tion,** n. —**sub•stan′ti•a′tive,** adj. —**sub•stan′ti•a′tor,** n.

sub•stan•tive (sub′stən tiv), adj. **1.** having independent existence; independent. **2.** belonging to the real nature or essential part of a thing; essential. **3.** real or actual. **4.** of considerable amount or quantity. **5.** possessing substance; having practical importance, value, or effect: substantive issues. **6. a.** of, pertaining to, or functioning as a noun: a substantive adjective. **b.** expressing existence: To be is a substantive verb. —n. **7.** a noun. **8.** a pronoun, adjective, or other word or phrase functioning as a noun. —**sub′stan•tive•ly,** adv. —**sub′stan•tive•ness,** n.

sub•sta•tion (sub′stā′shən), n. **1.** a branch of a main post office. **2.** an auxiliary power station where electrical current is converted, as from AC to DC, voltage is stepped up or down, etc.

sub•sti•tute (sub′sti tōōt′, -tyōōt′), n., v., **-tut•ed, -tut•ing,** adj. —n. **1.** a person or thing acting or serving in place of another. **2.** a word that functions as a replacement for any member of a class of words or constructions, as do in He doesn't know but I do. —v.t. **3.** to put (a person or thing) in the place of another. **4.** to take the place of; replace. **5.** to replace (one or more elements or groups in a chemical compound) by other elements or groups. —v.i. **6.** to act as a substitute. —adj. **7.** of or pertaining to a substitute or substitutes. **8.** composed of substitutes. —**sub′sti•tut′a•ble,** adj. —**sub′sti•tu′tion,** n.

sub•sti•tu•tive (sub′sti tōō′tiv, -tyōō′-), adj. **1.** serving as a substitute. **2.** involving substitution. —**sub′sti•tu′tive•ly,** adv.

sub•strate (sub′strāt), n. **1.** the surface or medium on which an organism lives or grows. **2.** the substance acted upon by an enzyme. **3.** the foundation on which an integrated electronic circuit is formed or fabricated.

sub•stra•tum (sub′strā′təm, -strat′əm, sub strā′təm, -strat′əm), n., pl. **-stra•ta** (-strā′tə, -strat′ə, -strā′tə, -strat′ə), **-stra•tums. 1.** something that is spread or laid under something else; a stratum or layer lying under another. **2.** something that underlies or serves as a basis or foundation. **3.** the subsoil. **4.** Philos. substance, considered as that which supports accidents or attributes. **5.** a set of features of a language traceable to the influence of a language that it has replaced, esp. among a subjugated population. Compare SUPERSTRATUM (def. 2). —**sub•stra′tive,** adj.

sub•struc•ture (sub struk′chər, sub′struk′-), n. **1.** a structure forming the foundation of a building or other construction. **2.** any foundation or supporting structure; basis. —**sub•struc′tur•al,** adj.

sub•sume (səb sōōm′), v.t., **-sumed, -sum•ing. 1.** to consider or include (an idea, term, etc.) as part of a more comprehensive one. **2.** to bring (a case, instance, etc.) under a rule. **3.** to take up into a more inclusive classification. —**sub•sum′a•ble,** adj.

sub•sump•tion (səb sump′shən), n. **1.** the act of subsuming. **2.** the state of being subsumed. **3.** something subsumed.

sub•tend (səb tend′, sub-), v.t. **1.** Geom. to extend under or be opposite to: a chord subtending an arc. **2.** (of a leaf, bract, etc.) to occur beneath or close to. **3.** to form or mark the outline or boundary of.

subtends (def. 1)   chord AC subtends arc ABC

sub•ter•fuge (sub′tər fyōōj′), n. an artifice or expedient used to evade a rule, escape a consequence, hide something, etc.

sub•ter•ra•ne•an (sub′tə rā′nē ən), adj. Also, **sub′ter•ra′ne•ous. 1.** existing, situated, or operating below the earth's surface; underground. **2.** existing or operating out of sight or secretly. —n. **3.** a person or thing that is subterranean. —**sub′ter•ra′ne•an•ly,** adv.

sub•text (sub′tekst′), n. the underlying or implicit meaning, as of a literary work.

sub•ti•tle (sub′tīt′l), n., v., **-tled, -tling.** —n. **1.** a secondary or subordinate title of a literary work, usu. of explanatory character. **2.** a repetition of the leading words in the full title of a book at the head of the first page of text. **3. a.** (in motion pictures and television) the text of dialogue, speeches, etc., translated into another language and projected onto the bottom of the screen. **b.** (in silent motion pictures) a caption. —v.t. **4.** to give a subtitle or subtitles to.

sub•tle (sut′l), adj., **-tler, -tlest. 1.** thin, tenuous, or rarefied, as a fluid or an odor. **2.** fine or delicate in meaning or intent; difficult to perceive or understand: subtle irony. **3.** delicate or faint and mysterious: a subtle smile. **4.** characterized by or requiring mental acuteness, penetration, or discernment. **5.** cunning, wily, or crafty. **6.** insidious in operation: a subtle poison. **7.** skillful, clever, or ingenious. —**sub′tle•ness,** n. —**sub′tly,** adv.

sub•tle•ty (sut′l tē), n., pl. **-ties. 1.** the state or quality of being subtle. **2.** acuteness or penetration of mind; delicacy of discrimination. **3.** a fine-drawn distinction; refinement of reasoning. **4.** something subtle.

sub•to•tal (sub′tōt′l, sub tōt′-), n., v., **-taled, -tal•ing** or (esp. Brit.) **-talled, -tal•ling.** —n. **1.** the sum or total of a part of a group or column of figures, as in an accounting statement. —v.t. **2.** to determine a subtotal for. —v.i. **3.** to determine a subtotal.

sub•tract (səb trakt′), v.t. **1.** to withdraw or take away, as a part from a whole. **2.** to take (one number or quantity) from another; deduct. —v.i. **3.** to take away something or a part, as from a whole.

sub•trac•tion (səb trak′shən), n. **1.** an act or instance of subtracting. **2.** the operation or process of finding the difference between two numbers or quantities, denoted by a minus sign (−).

sub•trac•tive (səb trak′tiv), adj. **1.** tending to or having power to subtract. **2.** (of a quantity) to be subtracted; having the minus sign (−).

sub•tra•hend (sub′trə hend′), n. a number that is subtracted from another. Compare MINUEND.

sub•trop•i•cal (sub trop′i kəl), adj. **1.** bordering on the tropics; nearly tropical. **2.** pertaining to or occurring in a region between tropical and temperate; semitropical.

sub•trop•ics (sub trop′iks), n.pl. subtropical regions.

sub•type (sub′tīp′), n. **1.** a subordinate type. **2.** a special type included within a more general type. —**sub•typ′i•cal** (-tip′i kəl), adj.

sub•urb (sub′ûrb), n. **1.** a district lying immediately outside a city or town, esp. a smaller residential community. **2. the suburbs,** the area composed of such districts.

sub•ur•ban (sə bûr′bən), adj. **1.** pertaining to, inhabiting, or being in a suburb or the suburbs. **2.** characteristic of a suburb or suburbs. —n. **3.** a suburbanite. **4.** a short overcoat for casual wear.

sub•ur•ban•ite (sə bûr′bə nīt′), n. a person who lives in a suburb of a city or large town.

sub•ur•bi•a (sə bûr′bē ə), n. **1.** suburbs or suburbanites collectively. **2.** the social or cultural aspects of life in suburbs.

sub•vene (səb vēn′), v.i., **-vened, -ven•ing.** to arrive or occur as a support or relief.

sub•ven•tion (səb ven′shən), n. **1.** a grant of money, as by a government or other authority, in aid or support of an institution or undertaking. **2.** the furnishing of aid or relief.

sub•ver•sion (səb vûr′zhən, -shən), n. **1.** an act or instance of subverting. **2.** the state of being subverted; destruction. **3.** something that subverts or overthrows.

sub•ver•sive (səb vûr′siv), adj. **1.** advocating subversion, esp. in an attempt to overthrow or undermine a legally constituted government. —n. **2.** a person who adopts subversive principles or policies. —**sub•ver′sive•ly,** adv. —**sub•ver′sive•ness,** n.

sub•vert (səb vûrt′), v.t. **1.** to overthrow (something established or existing). **2.** to cause the downfall or ruin of. **3.** to undermine the principles of; corrupt. —**sub•vert′er,** n.

sub•way (sub′wā′), *n.* **1.** an underground electric railroad, usu. in a large city. **2.** *Chiefly Brit.* an underground passageway; underpass.

suc•cah (so͞o kä′, so͝ok′ə), *n., pl.* ***suc•coth, suc•cot*** (so͞o kôt′), *Eng.* **suc•cahs.** *Hebrew.* SUKKAH.

suc•ceed (sək sēd′), *v.i.* **1.** to happen or terminate according to desire; turn out successfully: *Our efforts succeeded.* **2.** to thrive, prosper, grow, or the like. **3.** to accomplish what is attempted or intended: *We succeeded in our efforts to start the car.* **4.** to attain success in some popularly recognized form, as wealth or standing. **5.** to follow or replace another by descent, election, appointment, etc. (often fol. by *to*). **6.** to come next after something else in an order or series. —*v.t.* **7.** to come after and take the place of, as in an office or estate. **8.** to come next after in an order or series, or in the course of events; follow. —***Proverb.*** **9. If at first you don't succeed, try, try again,** keep trying instead of accepting defeat.

suc•cess (sək ses′), *n.* **1.** the favorable or prosperous termination of attempts or endeavors. **2.** the attainment of wealth, position, honors, or the like. **3.** a successful performance or achievement. **4.** a person or thing that is successful.

suc•cess•ful (sək ses′fəl), *adj.* **1.** achieving or having achieved success. **2.** having attained wealth, position, honors, or the like. **3.** resulting in or attended with success. —**suc•cess′ful•ly,** *adv.*

suc•ces•sion (sək sesh′ən), *n.* **1.** the coming of one person or thing after another in order, sequence, or in the course of events. **2.** a number of persons or things following one another in order or sequence. **3.** the right, act, or process by which one person succeeds to the office, rank, estate, or the like of another. **4.** the order or line of those entitled to succeed one another. **5.** the descent or transmission of a throne, dignity, estate, or the like. **6.** the progressive replacement of one ecological community by another until a climax community is established. —**suc•ces′sion•al,** *adj.*

suc•ces•sive (sək ses′iv), *adj.* **1.** following in order or in uninterrupted sequence; consecutive: *three successive days.* **2.** following another in a regular sequence: *the second successive day.* **3.** characterized by or involving succession. —**suc•ces′sive•ly,** *adv.*

suc•ces•sor (sək ses′ər), *n.* **1.** a person or thing that succeeds or follows. **2.** a person who succeeds another in an office, position, etc.

success′ sto′ry, *n.* an account of the achievement of success, fortune, or fame by someone or some enterprise.

suc•cinct (sək singkt′), *adj.* **1.** expressed in few words; concise; terse. **2.** characterized by conciseness or verbal brevity. **3.** compressed into a small area, scope, etc. —**suc•cinct′ly,** *adv.* —**suc•cinct′ness,** *n.*

suc•cor (suk′ər), *n.* **1.** help; relief; aid. **2.** a person or thing that gives help, relief, or aid. —*v.t.* **3.** to help or relieve in difficulty, need, or distress. Also, *esp. Brit.,* **suc′cour.** —**suc′cor•er,** *n.*

suc•co•tash (suk′ə tash′), *n.* a cooked dish of beans, esp. lima beans, and kernels of corn. [< Algonquin]

Suc•coth (so͝ok′əs, so͞o kôt′, -kōs′), *n.* SUKKOTH.

suc•cu•lent (suk′yə lənt), *adj.* **1.** full of juice; juicy. **2.** rich in desirable qualities. **3.** affording mental nourishment. **4.** (of a plant) having fleshy and juicy tissues. —*n.* **5.** a succulent plant, as a sedum or cactus. —**suc′cu•lence,** *n.* —**suc′cu•lent•ly,** *adv.*

suc•cumb (sə kum′), *v.i.* **1.** to give way to superior force; yield. **2.** to yield to disease, wounds, old age, etc.; die.

such (such), *adj.* **1.** of the kind, character, degree, etc., indicated or implied: *Such a man is dangerous.* **2.** like or similar: *tea, coffee, and such commodities.* **3.** of so extreme a kind; so good, bad, etc.: *He is such a liar.* **4.** being as stated or indicated: *Such is the case.* **5.** being the person or thing indicated: *If any member be late, such member shall be suspended.* **6.** definite but not specified: *Allow such an amount for rent, and the rest for other things.* —*adv.* **7.** so; to such a degree: *such nice people.* **8.** in such a way or manner. —*pron.* **9.** such a person or thing or such persons or things: *kings, princes, and such.* —***Idiom.*** **10. such as, a.** of the kind specified: *A plan such as you propose will succeed.* **b.** for example: *pastimes, such as reading and chess.*

such′ and such′, *adj.* **1.** definite or particular but not named or specified: *at such and such a place.* —*pron.* **2.** something or someone not specified: *if such and such should happen.*

such•like (such′līk′), *adj.* **1.** of any such kind; similar. —*pron.* **2.** persons or things of such a kind.

suck (suk), *v.t.* **1.** to draw into the mouth by producing a partial vacuum by action of the lips and tongue: *to suck lemonade through a straw.* **2.** to draw (water, moisture, air, etc.) by or as if by suction. **3.** to apply the lips or mouth to and draw the liquid from: *to suck an orange.* **4.** to put into the mouth and draw upon: *to suck one's thumb.* **5.** to take into the mouth and dissolve by the action of the tongue, saliva, etc.: *to suck a piece of candy.* —*v.i.* **6.** to draw something in by producing a partial vacuum in the mouth, esp. to draw milk from the breast. **7.** to draw or be drawn by or as if by suction. **8.** (of a pump) to draw air instead of water, as when the water is low or a valve is defective. **9.** *Slang.* to behave in a fawning manner (usu. fol. by *around*). **10.** *Slang.* to be repellent or disgusting. **11. suck in,** *Informal.* to deceive; cheat; defraud. **12. suck up,** *Slang.* to be obsequious; toady. —*n.* **13.** an act or instance of sucking. **14.** a sucking force. **15.** the sound produced by sucking. **16.** that which is sucked. **17.** a small drink; sip.

suck•er (suk′ər), *n.* **1.** a person or thing that sucks. **2.** *Informal.* a person easily cheated, deceived, or imposed upon. **3.** a suckling pig. **4.** a part or organ that is adapted for sucking, or for clinging by suction. **5.** any freshwater food fish of the family Catostomidae, mainly of North America, having thick lips. **6.** a lollipop. **7. a.** the piston or valve of a suction pump. **b.** a pipe or tube through which something is drawn or sucked. **8.** a shoot rising from an underground stem or root. **9. a.** *Informal.* a person attracted to something as indicated: *He's a sucker for new clothes.* **b.** any person or thing. —*v.t.* **10.** *Informal.* to make a sucker of; fool. —*v.i.* **11.** to send out suckers or shoots, as a plant.

suck•er•fish (suk′ər fish′), *n., pl.* **-fish•es,** (*esp. collectively*) **-fish.** REMORA.

suck•le (suk′əl), *v.,* **-led, -ling.** —*v.t.* **1.** to nurse at the breast or udder. **2.** to nourish or bring up. —*v.i.* **3.** to suck at the breast or udder.

Su•cre (so͞o′krā), *n., pl.* **-cres** for . **1. Antonio José de,** 1793–1830, Venezuelan general and South American liberator: 1st president of Bolivia 1826–28. **2.** the official capital of Bolivia, in the S part. 86,609.

su•crose (so͞o′krōs), *n.* SUGAR (def. 1).

suc•tion (suk′shən), *n.* **1.** the act, process, or condition of sucking. **2. a.** the force that, owing to a pressure differential, attracts a fluid or a solid to where the pressure is lowest. **b.** the act or process of creating such a force. —*v.t.* **3.** to draw out or remove by aspiration.

suc′tion pump′, *n.* a pump for raising water or other fluids by suction, consisting of a valved cylinder with a vertically moving piston.

suc•to•ri•al (suk tôr′ē əl, -tōr′-), *adj.* **1.** adapted for sucking or suction, as an organ; functioning as a sucker for imbibing or adhering. **2.** having sucking organs; imbibing or adhering by suckers.

Su•dan (so͞o dan′), *n.* **1.** a region in N Africa, S of the Sahara and Libyan deserts, extending from the Atlantic to the Red Sea. **2. Republic of the.** Formerly, **Anglo-Egyptian Sudan.** a republic in NE Africa, S of Egypt and bordering on the Red Sea: a former condominium of Egypt and Great Britain; gained independence 1956. 32,594,128; 967,500 sq. mi. (2,505,825 sq. km). *Cap.:* Khartoum. —**Su•da•nese** (so͞od′n ēz′, -ēs′), *adj., n., pl.* **-nese.**

sud•den (sud′n), *adj.* **1.** happening, coming, made, or done quickly, without warning, or unexpectedly: *a sudden attack.* **2.** occurring without transition from the previous form, state, etc.; abrupt: *a sudden turn.* **3.** impetuous; rash. —*adv.* **4.** *Literary.* suddenly. —***Idiom.*** **5. all of a sudden,** without warning; unexpectedly; suddenly. —**sud′den•ly,** *adv.* —**sud′den•ness,** *n.*

sud′den death′, *n.* an overtime period in which a tied contest is won and play is stopped immediately after one of the contestants scores, as in football, or goes ahead, as in golf.

sud′den in′fant death′ syn′drome, *n.* death from cessation of breathing in a seemingly healthy infant, almost always during sleep. *Abbr.:* SIDS Also called **crib death.**

Su•de•ten•land (so͞o dāt′n land′, -länt′), *n.* a mountainous region in the N Czech Republic, including the Sudeten and the Erzgebirge: annexed by Germany 1938; returned to Czechoslovakia 1945. Also called **Sudeten.**

suds (sudz), *n.* (*used with a sing. or pl. v.*) **1.** water containing soap or detergent and having bubbles or froth on the surface. **2.** foam; lather. —*v.t.* **3.** to wash in suds (often fol. by *out*). —*v.i.* **4.** to produce suds.

suds•y (sud′zē), *adj.,* **suds•i•er, suds•i•est. 1.** consisting of, containing, or producing suds. **2.** resembling or suggesting suds.

sue (so͞o), *v.,* **sued, su•ing.** —*v.t.* **1.** to bring civil action against: *to sue someone for damages.* **2.** to make petition or appeal to. —*v.i.* **3.** to institute legal proceedings. **4.** to make petition or appeal: *to sue for peace.*

suede or **suède** (swād), *n., v.,* **sued•ed** or **suèd•ed, sued•ing** or **suèd•ing.** —*n.* **1.** kid or other leather finished with a soft, napped surface. **2.** Also called **suede′ cloth′.** a fabric with a napped surface suggesting this. —*v.t.* **3.** to treat so as to raise a nap on (leather, cloth, etc.). —*v.i.* **4.** to raise a nap on leather, cloth, etc.

su•et (so͞o′it), *n.* the hard fatty tissue about the loins and kidneys of beef, sheep, etc., used in cooking and for tallow. —**su′et•y,** *adj.*

Su′ez Canal′, *n.* a canal in NE Egypt, crossing the Isthmus of Suez and connecting the Mediterranean and Red seas. 107 mi. (172 km) long.

suf•fer (suf′ər), *v.i.* **1.** to undergo or feel pain or great distress. **2.** to sustain injury, disadvantage, or loss. **3.** to endure or be afflicted with something temporarily or chronically: *to suffer with a cold; to suffer from parkinsonism.* **4.** to undergo a penalty, as of death. —*v.t.* **5.** to undergo, be subjected to, or endure (pain, distress, injury, loss, or anything unpleasant). **6.** to undergo or experience (any action, process, or condition): *to suffer change.* **7.** to tolerate or allow: *I do not suffer fools gladly.* —**suf′fer•a•ble,** *adj.* —**suf′fer•a•bly,** *adv.* —**suf′fer•er,** *n.*

suf•fer•ance (suf′ər əns, suf′rəns), *n.* **1.** passive permission resulting from lack of interference; tolerance, esp. of something wrong or illegal (usu. prec. by *on* or *by*). **2.** capacity to endure pain, hardship, etc.; endurance.

suf•fer•ing (suf′ər ing, suf′ring), *n.* **1.** the state of a person or thing that suffers. **2.** Often, **sufferings.** something suffered; pain: *the sufferings of the slaves.* —**suf′fer•ing•ly,** *adv.*

suf•fice (sə fīs′, -fīz′), *v.,* **-ficed, -fic•ing.** —*v.i.* **1.** to be enough or adequate, as for needs or purposes. —*v.t.* **2.** to be enough or adequate for; satisfy.

suf•fi•cien•cy (sə fish′ən sē), *n., pl.* **-cies. 1.** the state or fact of being sufficient; adequacy. **2.** a sufficient number or amount; enough. **3.** adequate provision or supply, esp. of wealth.

suf•fi•cient (sə fish′ənt), *adj.* **1.** adequate for the purpose; enough. **2.** *Logic.* (of a condition) such that its existence leads to the occurrence of a given event or the existence of a given thing. Compare NECESSARY (def. 4c). —**suf•fi′cient•ly,** *adv.*

suf•fix (*n.* suf′iks; *v.* suf′iks, sə fiks′), *n* **1.** an affix that follows the element to which it is added, as *-ly* in *kindly.* **2.** something added to the end of something else. —*v.t.* **3.** to add as a suffix.

suf•fo•cate (suf′ə kāt′), *v.,* **-cat•ed, -cat•ing.** —*v.t.* **1.** to kill by preventing the access of air to the blood through the lungs or analogous organs, as gills; strangle. **2.** to impede the respiration of. **3.** to discomfort by a lack of fresh or cool air. **4.** to smother or stifle; suppress: *students suffocated by rigid discipline.* —*v.i.* **5.** to become suffocated; stifle; smother. **6.** to be uncomfortable due to a lack of fresh or cool air. —**suf′fo•cat′ing•ly,** *adv.* —**suf′fo•ca′tion,** *n.* —**suf′fo•ca′tive,** *adj.*

Suf•folk (suf′ək), *n.* **1.** a county in E England. 635,100; 1470 sq. mi. (3805 sq. km). **2.** a city in SE Virginia. 52,141. **3.** one of an English breed of sheep having a black face and legs. **4.** one of an English breed of chestnut draft horses having a deep body and short legs.

suf•fra•gan (suf′rə gən), *adj.* **1.** assisting or auxiliary to, as applied to any bishop in relation to the archbishop or metropolitan who is his or her superior. **2.** (of a see or diocese) subordinate to an archiepiscopal or metropolitan see. —*n.* **3.** a suffragan bishop.

suf•frage (suf′rij), *n.* **1.** the right to vote, esp. in a political election. **2.** a vote given in favor of a proposed measure, candidate, or the like. **3.** a prayer, esp. a short intercessory prayer or petition.

suf•fra•gette (suf′rə jet′), *n.* a woman who advocates female suffrage. —**suf′fra•get′tism,** *n.*

suf•fra•gist (suf′rə jist), *n.* an advocate of the grant or extension of political suffrage, esp. to women. —**suf′fra•gism,** *n.*

suf•fuse (sə fyōōz′), *v.t.,* **-fused, -fus•ing.** to overspread with or as if with a liquid, color, etc.; pervade. —**suf•fu′sion** (-zhən), *n.* —**suf•fu′sive** (-siv), *adj.*

Su•fi (sōō′fē), *n., pl.* **-fis,** *adj.* —*n.* **1.** a member of an ascetic, mystical Muslim sect. —*adj.* **2.** of or pertaining to Sufis or Sufism. —**Su′fism** (-fiz əm), **Su′fi•ism,** *n.*

sug•ar (shŏŏg′ər), *n.* **1.** a sweet, crystalline substance, $C_{12}H_{22}O_{11}$, obtained from the juice or sap of many plants, esp. commercially from sugarcane and the sugar beet; sucrose. **2.** any other plant or animal substance of the same class of carbohydrates, as fructose or glucose. **3.** (*sometimes cap.*) an affectionate or familiar term of address (sometimes offensive when used to strangers, subordinates, etc.). —*v.t.* **4.** to cover, sprinkle, mix, or sweeten with sugar. **5.** to make agreeable. —*v.i.* **6.** to form sugar or sugar crystals. **7.** to make maple sugar. **8. sugar off,** (in making maple sugar) to complete the boiling down of the syrup in preparation for granulation. —**sug′ar•less,** *adj.* —**sug′ar•like′,** *adj.*

Sug′ar Act′, *n.* a law passed by the British Parliament in 1764 raising duties on foreign refined sugar imported by the colonies so as to give British sugar growers in the West Indies a monopoly on the colonial market.

sug′ar ap′ple, *n.* SWEETSOP.

sug′ar beet′, *n.* a variety of the common beet, *Beta vulgaris,* having a white root, cultivated for the sugar it yields.

sug•ar•bush (shŏŏg′ər bŏŏsh′), *n.* a grove of sugar maples.

sug′ar•cane′ or **sug′ar cane′,** *n.* a tall grass, *Saccharum officinarum,* of tropical and warm regions, having a stout, jointed stalk and constituting the chief source of sugar.

sug•ar•coat (shŏŏg′ər kōt′), *v.t.* **1.** to cover with sugar. **2.** to cause to appear more pleasant or acceptable.

sug•ar•loaf (shŏŏg′ər lōf′), *n., pl.* **-loaves** (-lōvz′). **1.** a large, usu. conical mass of hard refined sugar. **2.** anything resembling this in shape. —**sug′ar-loaf′, sug′ar-loafed′,** *adj.*

sug′ar ma′ple, *n.* any of several maples having a sweet sap, esp. *Acer saccharum,* yielding a valuable hard wood and being the chief source of maple syrup and maple sugar. —**sug′ar-ma′ple,** *adj.*

sug′ar pea′, *n.* SNOW PEA.

sug′ar pine′, *n.* the tallest American pine, *Pinus lambertiana,* of California, Oregon, etc., having cones 20 in. (51 cm) long.

sug•ar•plum (shŏŏg′ər plum′), *n.* a sweetmeat or bonbon.

sug•ar•y (shŏŏg′ə rē), *adj.* **1.** of, containing, or resembling sugar. **2.** sweet; excessively sweet. **3.** insincerely agreeable; honeyed.

sug•gest (səg jest′, sə-), *v.t.* **1.** to mention, introduce, or propose (an idea, plan, person, etc.) for consideration, possible action, or some purpose or use. **2.** (of things) to prompt the consideration, making, doing, etc., of: *The open door suggests a hasty exit.* **3.** to indicate indirectly or without plain expression; imply: *Your question suggests that you doubt my sincerity.* **4.** to call (something) up in the mind through association or natural connection of ideas: *The music suggests a still night.*

sug•gest•i•ble (səg jes′tə bəl, sə-), *adj.* **1.** subject to or easily influenced by suggestion. **2.** able to be suggested. —**sug•gest′i•bil′i•ty, sug•gest′i•ble•ness,** *n.* —**sug•gest′i•bly,** *adv.*

sug•ges•tion (səg jes′chən, sə-), *n.* **1.** the act of suggesting or the state of being suggested. **2.** something suggested, as a piece of advice. **3.** a slight trace: *a suggestion of tears in his eyes.* **4.** the calling up in the mind of one idea by another by virtue of some association or of some natural connection between the ideas. **5.** the idea thus called up. **6. a.** the process of inducing a thought, sensation, or action in a receptive person without using persuasion and without giving rise to reflection in the recipient. **b.** the thought, sensation, or action so induced.

sug•ges•tive (səg jes′tiv, sə-), *adj.* **1.** suggesting; referring to other thoughts, persons, etc.: *a recommendation suggestive of her current mood.* **2.** rich in suggestions or ideas: *a suggestive critical essay.* **3.** evocative; presented partially rather than in detail. **4.** implying or hinting at something improper or indecent; risqué: *suggestive remarks.* —**sug•ges′tive•ly,** *adv.* —**sug•ges′tive•ness,** *n.*

su•i•cid•al (sōō′ə sīd′l), *adj.* **1.** pertaining to, involving, or suggesting suicide. **2.** tending or leading to suicide. **3.** foolishly or rashly dangerous. —**su′i•cid′al•ly,** *adv.*

su•i•cide (sōō′ə sīd′), *n., v.,* **-cid•ed, -cid•ing.** —*n.* **1.** the intentional taking of one's own life. **2.** destruction of one's own interests or prospects: *financial suicide.* **3.** a person who intentionally takes his or her own life. —*v.i.* **4.** to commit suicide. —*v.t.* **5.** to kill (oneself).

su•i ge•ne•ris (sōō′ē jen′ər is, sōō′ī), *adj.* of his, her, its, or their own kind; unique.

su•i ju•ris (sōō′ē jŏŏr′is, sōō′ī), *adj. Law.* capable of managing one's affairs or assuming legal responsibility.

suit (sōōt), *n.* **1.** a set of clothing, armor, or the like, intended for wear together. **2.** a set of garments of the same color and fabric, consisting typically of trousers or a skirt, a jacket, and sometimes a vest. **3.** any costume worn for some special activity. **4.** *Law.* an act or instance of suing in a court of law; lawsuit. **5.** one of the classes into which cards are divided, as spades, clubs, diamonds, and hearts for a deck of playing cards. **6.** the wooing or courting of a woman. **7.** a petition, as to a person of rank or station. **8.** SUITE (defs. 1–3, 5). **9.** *Slang.* a business executive. —*v.t.* **10.** to make appropriate, adapt, or accommodate, as one thing to another: *to suit the punishment to the crime.* **11.** to be appropriate or becoming to: *Blue suits you very well.* **12.** to be acceptable or agreeable to; satisfy or please: *The arrangements suit me.* **13.** to provide with a suit, as of clothing or armor; clothe; array. —*v.i.* **14.** to be appropriate or suitable; accord. **15.** to be satisfactory, agreeable, or acceptable. **16. suit up,** to put on a uniform or special suit. —***Idiom.*** **17. follow suit, a.** to play a card of the same suit as that led. **b.** to follow the example of another. —**suit′like′,** *adj.*

suit•a•ble (sōō′tə bəl), *adj.* such as to suit; appropriate; acceptable; fitting. —**suit′a•bil′i•ty, suit′a•ble•ness,** *n.* —**suit′a•bly,** *adv.*

suit•case (sōōt′kās′), *n.* a usu. rectangular piece of luggage, esp. for carrying clothes while traveling.

suite (swēt; *for 3 often* sōōt), *n.* **1.** a number of things forming a series or set. **2.** a connected series of rooms to be used together: *a hotel suite.* **3.** a set of matching furniture for one room. **4.** a company of followers or attendants; train or retinue. **5. a.** an ordered series of instrumental dances, in the same or related keys, commonly preceded by a prelude. **b.** an ordered series of instrumental movements of any character.

suit•or (sōō′tər), *n.* **1.** a man who courts or woos a woman. **2.** *Law.* a petitioner or plaintiff. **3.** a person who sues or petitions for anything. **4.** an individual or company that seeks to buy another company.

su•ki•ya•ki (sōō′kē yä′kē, sŏŏk′ē-, skē yä′kē), *n.* a Japanese dish containing slices of meat, vegetables, and soy sauce cooked together, often at the table.

suk•kah (sōō kä′, sŏŏk′ə), *n., pl.* ***suk•koth, suk•kot*** (sōō kôt′), *Eng.* **suk•kahs.** *Hebrew.* a booth or hut roofed with branches, used during Sukkoth as a temporary dining or living area.

Suk•koth or **Suk•kot** or **Suk•kos** (sŏŏk′əs, sōō kôt′, -kōs′), *n.* a Jewish festival beginning on the 15th day of Tishri that celebrates the harvest and commemorates the temporary huts used by the Israelites in the wilderness. [< Hebrew *sukkōth* lit., booths]

Su•lei•man I (sōō′lə män′, -lā-, sōō′lā män′), *n.* (*"the Magnificent"*) 1495?–1566, sultan of the Ottoman Empire 1520–66.

sul•fa (sul′fə), *adj.* **1.** related chemically to sulfanilamide. **2.** pertaining to, consisting of, or involving a sulfa drug or drugs. —*n.* **3.** SULFA DRUG.

sul′fa drug′, *n.* any of a group of drugs closely related in chemical structure to sulfanilamide: used in the treatment of various wounds, burns, and bacterial infections. Also called **sulfonamide.**

sul•fa•nil•a•mide (sul′fə nil′ə mīd′, -mid), *n.* a crystalline sulfur-containing compound formerly used to treat bacterial infections.

sul•fate (sul′fāt), *n., v.,* **-fat•ed, -fat•ing.** —*n.* **1.** a salt or ester of sulfuric acid. —*v.t.* **2.** to combine, treat, or impregnate with sulfuric acid, a sulfate, or sulfates. **3.** to convert into a sulfate.

sul•fide (sul′fīd, -fid), *n.* a compound of sulfur with a more electropositive element or, less often, group.

sul•fite (sul′fīt), *n.* **1.** a salt or ester of sulfurous acid. **2.** any sulfite-containing compound, esp. one that is used in foods or drug products as a preservative. —**sul•fit′ic** (-fit′ik), *adj.*

sul•fur (sul′fər), *n.* **1.** Also, *esp. Brit.,* **sulphur.** a nonmetallic element, ordinarily a flammable yellow solid, of widespread occurrence in combined form, as in sulfide and sulfate compounds and cellular protein: used esp. in making gunpowder and matches, in medicine, and in vulcanizing rubber. *Symbol:* S; *at. wt.:* 32.064; *at. no.:* 16; *sp. gr.:* 2.07 at 20° C. **2.** SULPHUR (def. 2).

sul′fur diox′ide, *n.* a colorless, nonflammable, water-soluble, suffocating gas, SO_2, formed when sulfur burns: used chiefly in the manufacture of chemicals such as sulfuric acid, in preserving fruits and vegetables, and in bleaching, disinfecting, and fumigating.

sulfu′ric ac′id, *n.* a clear, colorless to brownish, dense, oily, corrosive, water-miscible liquid, H_2SO_4, used chiefly in the manufacture of fertilizers, chemicals, explosives, and dyestuffs and in petroleum refining. Also called **oil of vitriol.**

sul•fur•ous (sul′fər əs, sul fyŏŏr′əs), *adj.* **1.** of, pertaining to, or containing sulfur, esp. in the tetravalent state. **2.** of the yellow color of sulfur. **3.** SULPHUROUS. —**sul′fur•ous•ly,** *adv.* —**sul′fur•ous•ness,** *n.*

sul′furous ac′id, *n.* a colorless liquid, H_2SO_3, having a suffocating odor, used chiefly in organic synthesis and as a bleach.

sul′fur spring′, *n.* a spring whose water contains naturally occurring sulfur compounds.

sulk (sulk), *v.i.* **1.** to remain silent or hold oneself aloof in a sullen, ill-humored, or offended mood. —*n.* **2.** a state of sulking. **3. the sulks,** ill-humor shown by sulking. **4.** Also, **sulk′er.** a person who sulks.

sulk•y (sul′kē), *adj.,* **sulk•i•er, sulk•i•est,** *n., pl.* **sulk•ies.** —*adj.* **1.** marked by or given to sulking; sullen; moody. **2.** gloomy or dull: *sulky weather.* —*n.* **3.** a light, two-wheeled, one-horse carriage for one person. —**sulk′i•ly,** *adv.* —**sulk′i•ness,** *n.*

sul•len (sul′ən), *adj.* **1.** showing irritation or ill humor by a gloomy silence or reserve. **2.** persistently and silently ill-humored; morose. **3.** indicative of gloomy ill humor. **4.** gloomy or dismal, as weather or a sound. **5.** sluggish, as a stream; slow. —**sul′len•ly,** *adv.*

Sul•li•van (sul′ə vən), *n.* **1. Annie** (*Anne Mansfield Sullivan Macy*), 1866–1936, U.S. teacher of Helen Keller. **2. Sir Arthur (Seymour),** 1842–1900, English composer. **3. Harry Stack,** 1892–1949, U.S. psychiatrist. **4. John L(awrence),** 1858–1918, U.S. boxer. **5. Louis Hen•ri** (hen′rē), 1856–1924, U.S. architect.

sul•phur (sul′fər), *n.* **1.** *Chiefly Brit.* SULFUR (def. 1). **2.** Also, **sulfur.** yellow with a greenish tinge.

sul•phur•ous (sul′fər əs, sul fyŏŏr′əs), *adj.* **1.** pertaining to the fires of hell; hellish or satanic. **2.** fiery or heated. —**sul′phur•ous•ly,** *adv.* —**sul′phur•ous•ness,** *n.*

sul•tan (sul′tn), *n.* **1.** the sovereign of an Islamic country. **2.** (*often cap.*) any of the former sovereigns of Turkey. **3.** an absolute ruler or despot. —**sul•tan•ic** (sul tan′ik), *adj.* —**sul′tan•like′,** *adj.*

sul•tan•a (sul tan′ə, -tä′nə), *n., pl.* **-tan•as. 1.** a small, seedless raisin. **2.** a wife, concubine, or female relative of a sultan. **3.** a mistress of a king or other royal personage.

sul•tan•ate (sul′tn āt′), *n.* **1.** the office or rule of a sultan. **2.** the territory ruled over by a sultan.

sul•try (sul′trē), *adj.,* **-tri•er, -tri•est. 1.** oppressively hot and close or humid; sweltering: *a sultry day.* **2.** oppressively hot; emitting great heat: *the sultry sun.* **3.** characterized by or arousing passion: *sultry eyes.* —**sul′tri•ness,** *n.*

sum (sum), *n., v.,* **summed, sum•ming.** —*n.* **1.** the aggregate of two or more numbers, magnitudes, quantities, or particulars as determined by or as if by the mathematical process of addition: *The sum of 6 and 8 is 14.* **2.** an amount or quantity, esp. of money: *to lend small sums.* **3.** a series of numbers or quantities to be added up. **4.** an arithmetical problem to be solved, or such a problem worked out and having the various steps shown. **5.** the full amount, or the whole: *the sum of our knowledge.* **6.** the main idea, gist, or point: *the sum and substance of his argument.* **7.** a summary. —*v.t.* **8.** to combine into an aggregate or total (often fol. by *up*). **9.** to ascertain the sum of, as by addition. **10.** to bring into or contain in a small compass (often fol. by *up*). —*v.i.* **11.** to amount. **12. sum up, a.** to express in a brief and comprehensive statement; summarize. **b.** to form a quick estimate or judgment of. —*Idiom.* **13. in sum,** in concise or brief form.

su•mac or **su•mach** (sŏŏ′mak, shŏŏ′-), *n.* **1.** any shrub or small tree of the genus *Rhus,* of the cashew family, having pinnately compound leaves and clusters of red, fleshy fruit. **2.** a preparation of the dried and powdered leaves, bark, etc., of certain species of *Rhus,* esp. *R. coriaria* of S Europe, used esp. in tanning.

Su•ma•tra (sŏŏ mä′trə), *n.* an island in the W part of Indonesia. 28,016,160; 164,147 sq. mi. (425,141 sq. km). —**Su•ma′tran,** *adj., n.*

Su•mer (sŏŏ′mər), *n.* an ancient region in S Mesopotamia containing a number of independent cities and city-states, fl. c3200–2000 B.C.

Su•me•ri•an (sŏŏ mēr′ē ən, -mer′-), *n.* **1.** a native or inhabitant of Sumer. **2.** the extinct language of the Sumerians, of uncertain affiliation, attested in pictographic and later in cuneiform writing. —*adj.* **3.** of or pertaining to Sumer, its people, or their language.

sum•ma (sŏŏm′ə, sum′ə), *n., pl.* **sum•mae** (sŏŏm′ī, sum′ē), **sum•mas.** a comprehensive work, esp. a philosophical or theological treatise, covering, synthesizing, or summarizing a field or subject.

sum•ma cum lau•de (sŏŏm′ə kŏŏm lou′dä, -də, -dē; sum′ə kum lô′dē), *adv.* with highest praise: used in diplomas to grant the highest of three special honors for grades above the average. Compare CUM LAUDE, MAGNA CUM LAUDE.

sum•mar•i•ly (sə mâr′ə lē), *adv.* **1.** in a prompt or direct manner; immediately; straightaway. **2.** without notice; precipitately: *to be dismissed summarily.*

sum•ma•rize (sum′ə rīz′), *v.,* **-rized, -riz•ing.** —*v.t.* **1.** to make a summary of; state or express in a concise form. **2.** to constitute a summary of. —*v.i.* **3.** to provide a summary. —**sum′ma•riz′a•ble,** *adj.* —**sum′ma•ri•za′tion,** *n.* —**sum′ma•riz′er, sum′mar•ist,** *n.*

sum•ma•ry (sum′ə rē), *n., pl.* **-ries,** *adj.* —*n.* **1.** a comprehensive and usu. brief abstract, recapitulation, or compendium of things previously stated. —*adj.* **2.** brief and comprehensive; concise. **3.** direct and prompt; unceremoniously fast: *treated with summary dispatch.* **4.** (of legal proceedings) conducted without a formal trial. —**sum•mar•i•ness** (sə mâr′i nis), *n.*

sum′mary proceed′ing, *n.* a mode of trial authorized by statute to be held before a judge without the usual full hearing.

sum•mate (sum′āt), *v.t.,* **-mat•ed, -mat•ing.** to add together; total; sum up.

Sum•ma The•o•log•i•ca (sŏŏm′ə thē′ə loj′i kə, sum′ə), a philosophical and theological work (1265–74) by St. Thomas Aquinas, consisting of an exposition of Christian doctrine.

sum•ma•tion (sə mā′shən), *n.* **1.** the act or process of summing. **2.** the result of this; an aggregate or total. **3.** a review or recapitulation of previously stated facts or statements, often with final conclusions drawn from them. **4.** the final arguments of opposing attorneys before a case goes to the jury. **5.** the arousal of nerve impulses by a rapid succession of sensory stimuli. —**sum•ma′tion•al,** *adj.*

sum•mer (sum′ər), *n.* **1.** the warm season between spring and autumn, in the Northern Hemisphere from the June solstice to the September equinox, and in the Southern Hemisphere from the December solstice to the March equinox. **2.** hot, usu. sunny weather. **3.** the hotter half of the year (opposed to *winter*). **4.** the period of greatest development, perfection, beauty, etc.: *the summer of life.* **5.** a year: *a girl of fifteen summers.* —*adj.* **6.** of or characteristic of summer. **7.** suitable for or done during the summer: *summer sports.* —*v.i.* **8.** to spend or pass the summer. —*v.t.* **9.** to keep, feed, or manage during the summer: *to summer sheep in high pastures.* —**sum′mer•like,** *adj.*

sum′mer camp′, *n.* a camp, esp. one for children, operated during the summer and providing facilities for sleeping, eating, and recreation.

sum′mer cy′press, *n.* BURNING BUSH (def. 2).

sum•mer•house (sum′ər hous′), *n., pl.* **-hous•es** (-hou′ziz). a simple, often rustic structure in a park or garden, intended to provide shade in the summer.

sum′mer sa′vory, *n.* See under SAVORY[2].

sum′mer school′, *n.* **1.** study programs offered during the summer to those who wish to obtain their degrees more quickly, supplement their education, etc. **2.** a school offering such programs.

sum′mer sol′stice, *n.* the solstice on or about June 21 that marks the beginning of summer in the Northern Hemisphere.

sum′mer squash′, *n.* any of several squashes of the variety *Cucurbita pepo melopepo* that mature in the late summer or early autumn: used as a vegetable in its unripe state.

sum′mer stock′, *n.* **1.** the production of plays, musicals, etc., during the summer, esp. in a resort area, often by a repertory company. **2.** summer theaters collectively or their productions.

sum′mer the′ater, *n.* **1.** a theater that operates during the summer, esp. in a resort area, usu. offering a different play or musical each week. **2.** SUMMER STOCK.

sum•mer•wood (sum′ər wŏŏd′), *n.* the part of an annual ring of wood, characterized by compact, thick-walled cells, formed during the later part of the growing season. Compare SPRINGWOOD.

sum•mer•y (sum′ə rē), *adj.* of, like, or appropriate for summer: *a summery dress.* —**sum′mer•i•ness,** *n.*

sum′ming-up′, *n., pl.* **sum•mings-up.** a concluding summation or statement reviewing the basic ideas or principles of an argument, explanation, testimony, etc.

sum•mit (sum′it), *n.* **1.** the highest point or part, as of a hill; top; apex. **2.** the highest point of attainment: *the summit of one's ambition.* **3.** the highest state or degree; acme; zenith. **4.** the highest level of diplomatic or other government officials: *negotiations at the summit.* **5.** Also called **sum′mit meet′ing, sum′mit con′ference.** a conference between heads of state or other top-level government officials. —**sum′mit•al,** *adj.* —**sum′mit•less,** *adj.*

sum•mit•ry (sum′i trē), *n.* **1.** the act or practice of holding a summit meeting, esp. to conduct diplomatic negotiations. **2.** the art or technique of conducting summit meetings. **3.** summit meetings collectively.

sum•mon (sum′ən), *v.t.* **1.** to call for the presence of, as by command, message, or signal. **2.** to call upon to do something specified. **3.** to call or notify to appear at a specified place, esp. before a court: *to summon a witness.* **4.** to call together by authority, as for deliberation or action: *to summon parliament.* **5.** to call into action; rouse; call forth (often fol. by *up*): *to summon all one's courage.* —**sum′mon•a•ble,** *adj.*

sum•mons (sum′ənz), *n., pl.* **-mons•es,** *v.* —*n.* **1.** a command, message, or signal by which one is summoned. **2. a.** a call or citation by authority to appear before a court or a judicial officer. **b.** the writ by which the call is made. **3.** an authoritative call or notice to appear at a specified place for a particular purpose or duty. **4.** a request, demand, or call to do something: *a summons to surrender.* —*v.t.* **5.** to serve with a summons; summon.

sum•mum bo•num (sŏŏm′ŏŏm bō′nŏŏm; Eng. sum′əm bō′nəm), *n. Latin.* the highest or chief good.

su•mo (sŏŏ′mō), *n.* a form of wrestling in Japan in which a contestant wins by forcing his opponent out of the ring or by causing him to touch the ground with any part of his body other than the soles of his feet, contestants usu. being men of great height and weight. —**su′mo•ist,** *n.*

sump (sump), *n.* **1.** a pit, basin, cesspool, etc., in which liquid is collected or into which it drains. **2.** a chamber at the bottom of a machine, pump, etc., into which a fluid drains before recirculation or in which wastes gather before disposal. **3.** *Brit.* CRANKCASE.

sump′ pump′, *n.* a pump for removing liquid or wastes from a sump.

sump•tu•ar•y (sump′chŏŏ er′ē), *adj.* **1.** pertaining to or regulating expense or personal expenditure, esp. with the intent of restraining extrav-

S

agance. **2.** intended to regulate personal habits on moral or religious grounds.

sump·tu·ous (sump′choo əs), *adj.* **1.** entailing great expense, as from choice materials, fine work, etc.; costly. **2.** luxuriously fine or large; lavish; splendid: *a sumptuous feast.* —**sump′tu·ous·ly,** *adv.* —**sump′tu·ous·ness,** *n.*

sum′ to′tal, *n.* **1.** the complete numerical total. **2.** the substance or totality: *the sum total of our knowledge.*

sum′-up′, *n.* the act or result of summing up; summary.

sun (sun), *n., v.,* **sunned, sun·ning.** —*n.* **1.** (*often cap.*) the star that is the central body of the solar system, around which the planets revolve and from which they receive light and heat: its mean distance from the earth is about 93 million miles (150 million km), its diameter about 864,000 miles (1.4 million km), and its mass about 330,000 times that of the earth. **2.** this star with reference to its position in the sky, the temperature it produces, the time when it is seen, etc. **3.** the heat and light from the sun; sunshine: *to be exposed to the sun.* **4.** a self-luminous heavenly body; star. **5.** a figure or representation of the sun, as a heraldic bearing surrounded with rays and marked with human facial features. **6.** something likened to the sun in brightness, splendor, etc. **7.** sunrise or sunset: *to travel from sun to sun.* —*v.t.* **8.** to expose to the sun's rays. **9.** to warm, dry, etc., in the sunshine. —*v.i.* **10.** to expose oneself or be exposed to the rays of the sun. —*Idiom.* **11. under the sun,** on earth; anywhere. —**sun′like′,** *adj.*

sun·baked (sun′bākt′), *adj.* **1.** baked by exposure to the sun, as bricks. **2.** heated, dried, or hardened by the heat of the sun.

sun·bath (sun′bath′, -bäth′), *n., pl.* **-baths** (-baᴛʜz′, -bäᴛʜz′, -baths′, -bäths′). deliberate exposure of the body to the direct rays of the sun or a sunlamp, esp. while sitting or lying down.

sun·bathe (sun′bāᴛʜ′), *v.i.,* **-bathed, -bath·ing.** to take a sunbath. —**sun′bath′er,** *n.*

sun·beam (sun′bēm′), *n.* a beam or ray of sunlight.

Sun′belt′ or **Sun′ Belt′,** *n.* (*sometimes l.c.*) the southern and southwestern region of the U.S.

sun′ bit′tern, *n.* a graceful tropical wading bird, *Eurypyga helias,* related to the cranes and rails, having variegated plumage that produces a sunburst effect when spread in display.

sun′block′ or **sun′ block′,** *n.* **1.** a substance that provides a high degree of protection against sunburn, often preventing most tanning as well. **2.** a lotion, cream, etc., containing such a substance.

sun·bow (sun′bō′), *n.* a bow or arc of prismatic colors like a rainbow, appearing in the spray of waterfalls, fountains, etc.

sun·burn (sun′bûrn′), *n., v.,* **-burned** or **-burnt, -burn·ing.** —*n.* **1.** inflammation of the skin caused by overexposure to the sun or a sunlamp. **2.** SUNTAN (def. 1). —*v.i., v.t.* **3.** to become or cause to become sunburned.

sun·burst (sun′bûrst′), *n.* **1.** a sudden burst of sunlight, esp. through a rift in the clouds. **2.** something that suggests the sun and its radiating beams, esp. a brooch with gemstones encircled by raylike projections. —*adj.* **3.** (in sewing, needlepoint, etc.) having the parts or lines of the design flared from a central point: *sunburst pleats.*

sun′-cured′, *adj.* cured or preserved by exposure to the rays of the sun, as meat or tobacco.

sun·dae (sun′dā, -dē), *n.* a dish of ice cream topped with syrup, nuts, whipped cream, etc.

Sun·day¹ (sun′dā, -dē), *n.* **1.** the first day of the week, observed as the Sabbath by most Christian denominations. —*adj.* **2.** of, pertaining to, or characteristic of Sunday. **3.** used, done, taking place, or being as indicated only on or as if on Sundays: *a Sunday driver.* [< Old English *sunnandæg,* trans. of Latin *diēs sōlis*] —**Sun′day·like′,** *adj.*

Sun·day² (sun′dā, -dē), *n.* **William Ashley** ("*Billy Sunday*"), 1862–1935, U.S. evangelist.

Sun·day-go-to-meet·ing (sun′dā gō′tə mēt′n, -mē′ting, -dē-). *adj. Informal.* most presentable; best: *Sunday-go-to-meeting clothes.*

Sun′day school′, *n.* **1.** a school for religious instruction on Sunday. **2.** the members of such a school.

sun′ deck′ or **sun′deck′,** *n.* a raised, open area, as a roof, terrace, or ship's deck, that is exposed to the sun.

sun·der (sun′dər), *v.t.* **1.** to separate; part; divide; sever. —*v.i.* **2.** to become separated; part. —**sun′der·a·ble,** *adj.* —**sun′der·ance,** *n.*

sun·dew (sun′doo′, -dyoo′), *n.* any of several small bog or aquatic plants of the sundew family, esp. of the genus *Drosera.*

sun·di·al (sun′dī′əl, -dīl′), *n.* an instrument that indicates the time of day by means of the position, on a graduated plate or surface, of the shadow of the gnomon as cast by the sun.

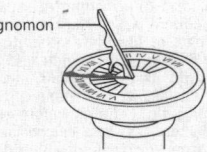

gnomon

sundial

sun·down (sun′doun′), *n.* **1.** sunset, esp. the time of sunset. —*v.i.* **2.** to experience nighttime confusion, esp. as a result of strange surroundings, drug effects, or decreased sensory input.

sun·dress (sun′dres′), *n.* a dress with a bodice styled to expose the arms, shoulders, and back, for wear during hot weather.

sun′-dried′, *adj.* **1.** dried in the sun, as bricks or raisins. **2.** dried up or withered by the sun.

sun·dries (sun′drēz), *n.pl.* small, miscellaneous items of little value.

sun·drops (sun′drops′), *n., pl.* **-drops.** any of various plants of the genus *Oenothera,* of the evening primrose family, having flowers that open near sunrise.

sun·dry (sun′drē), *adj.* **1.** various or diverse. —*Idiom.* **2. all and sundry,** everybody, collectively and individually: *gave free samples to all and sundry.* —**sun′dri·ly,** *adv.* —**sun′dri·ness,** *n.*

sun·fish (sun′fish′), *n., pl.* (*esp. collectively*) **-fish,** (*esp. for kinds or species*) **-fish·es.** any freshwater fish of the North American family Centrarchidae, having a deep, compressed body.

sun·flow·er (sun′flou′ər), *n.* any of various composite plants of the genus *Helianthus* having showy, yellow-rayed flower heads often 12 in. (30 cm) wide, and edible seeds that yield an oil.

sung (sung), *v.* a pt. and pp. of SING.

Sung (soong) also **Song,** *n.* a dynasty in China, A.D. 960–1279.

sun·glass (sun′glas′, -gläs′), *n.* **sunglasses,** eyeglasses with tinted lenses to protect the eyes against sunlight.

sun′ god′ or **sun′-god′,** *n.* **1.** the sun considered or personified as a deity. **2.** a god identified or associated with the sun.

sunk (sungk), *v.* **1.** a pt. and pp. of SINK. —*adj.* **2.** beyond help; done for; undone.

sunk·en (sung′kən), *adj.* **1.** having sunk or been sunk beneath the surface; submerged. **2.** having settled to a lower level, as walls. **3.** situated on a lower level: *a sunken living room.* **4.** hollow: *sunken cheeks.*

sun·lamp (sun′lamp′), *n.* **1.** a lamp that generates ultraviolet rays, used therapeutically or for suntanning. **2.** a lamp used in motion-picture photography, having parabolic mirrors arranged to direct and concentrate the light.

sun·light (sun′līt′), *n.* the light of the sun; sunshine.

Sun·na or **Sun·nah** (soon′ə), *n.* the traditional portion of Muslim law, based on words and acts of Muhammad not recorded in the Koran. [< Arabic *sunnah* lit., way, path, rule]

Sun·ni (soon′ē), *n., pl.* **-ni, -nis. 1.** Also called **Sun·nite** (soon′īt). a member of one of the two great religious divisions of Islam, regarding the first four caliphs as legitimate successors of Muhammad and stressing the importance of Sunna as a basis for law. Compare SHI′ITE. **2.** (*used with a pl. v.*) the Sunni Muslims. —**Sun′nism,** *n.*

sun·ny (sun′ē), *adj.,* **-ni·er, -ni·est. 1.** abounding in sunshine. **2.** exposed to, lighted, or warmed by the direct rays of the sun: *a sunny room.* **3.** cheery, cheerful, or joyous: *a sunny disposition.* **4.** of or resembling the sun. —**sun′ni·ly,** *adv.* —**sun′ni·ness,** *n.*

sun′ny side′, *n.* **1.** a pleasant or hopeful aspect or part. **2.** some age less than that specified: *on the sunny side of thirty.*

sun′ny·side up′ (sun′ē sīd′), *adj., adv.* (of an egg) fried on one side only, with the unbroken yolk on the upper side.

Sun·ny·vale (sun′ē vāl′), *n.* a city in central California. 119,584.

sun′ par′lor, *n.* a room or porch with many large windows exposed to sunshine; sun porch; solarium. Also called **sunroom.**

sun′ porch′, *n.* a windowed porch having more window than wall area, intended to receive large amounts of sunlight.

sun·proof (sun′proof′), *adj.* impervious to sunlight or damage by the rays of the sun.

sun′ protec′tion fac′tor, *n.* See SPF.

sun·rise (sun′rīz′), *n.* **1.** the rise or ascent of the sun above the horizon in the morning. **2.** the atmospheric and scenic phenomena accompanying this. **3.** the time when half the sun has risen above the horizon. **4.** (of an industry, technology, etc.) new and growing; developing; emerging: *high-technology sunrise industries.*

sun·roof (sun′roof′, -roof′), *n., pl.* **roofs.** a section of an automobile roof that can be slid or lifted open.

sun·room (sun′room′, -room′), *n.* SUN PARLOR.

sun′screen′ or **sun′ screen′,** *n.* **1.** a substance that protects the skin from excessive exposure to the ultraviolet radiation of the sun. **2.** a lotion, cream, etc., containing this.

sun·set (sun′set′), *n.* **1.** the setting or descent of the sun below the horizon in the evening. **2.** the atmospheric and scenic phenomena accompanying this. **3.** the time when the sun sets. —*adj.* **4.** (of an industry, technology, etc.) old; declining. **5.** of or denoting a law requiring the termination of a government program or agency at the end of a specified period unless it is reauthorized by the legislature.

sun·shade (sun′shād′), *n.* something used as a protection from the rays of the sun, as an awning or a parasol.

sun·shine (sun′shīn′), *n.* **1.** the shining of the sun; direct light of the sun. **2.** cheerfulness or happiness. **3.** a source of cheer or happiness. **4.** the effect of the sun in lighting and heating a place. **5.** a place where the direct rays of the sun fall. —*adj.* **6.** denoting a law requiring a government agency to open its official meetings and records to the public.

sun·spot (sun′spot′), *n.* one of the relatively dark patches that appear periodically on the surface of the sun and affect terrestrial magnetism and certain other terrestrial phenomena.

sun·stroke (sun'strōk'), *n.* a sudden and sometimes fatal condition caused by overexposure to the sun's rays, marked by prostration with or without fever, convulsion, and coma. —**sun'struck'**, *adj.*

sun·suit (sun'soot'), *n.* any of various brief one- or two-piece garments worn for leisure or play in warm weather, esp. by children.

sun·tan (sun'tan'), *n., v.,* **-tanned, -tan·ning.** —*n.* **1.** a darkening of the skin caused by exposure to sunlight or a sunlamp. **2.** a light to medium yellow-brown. —*v.t., v.i.* **3.** TAN¹ (defs. 2, 4).

sun·up (sun'up'), *n.* sunrise, esp. the time of sunrise.

Sun Yat-sen (soon' yät'sen'), *n.* 1866–1925, Chinese political and revolutionary leader.

sup¹ (sup), *v.,* **supped, sup·ping.** —*v.i.* **1.** to eat the evening meal; have supper. —*v.t.* **2.** to provide with or entertain at supper.

sup² (sup), *v.,* **supped, sup·ping,** *n.* —*v.t.* **1.** to take (liquid food or any liquid) into the mouth in small quantities; sip. —*v.i.* **2.** to take liquid into the mouth in small quantities, as by spoonfuls or sips. —*n.* **3.** a mouthful or small portion of drink or liquid food; sip.

su·per (soo'pər), *n.* **1.** a superintendent, esp. of an apartment house. **2.** a supernumerary. **3.** a supervisor. **4.** an article of a superior quality, grade, size, etc. **5.** (in beekeeping) the portion of a hive in which honey is stored. —*adj.* **6.** of the highest degree, power, etc.: *a super council.* **7.** of an extreme or excessive degree: *super haste.* **8.** very good; first-rate; excellent. —*adv.* **9.** very; extremely or excessively: *super cooperative.*

super-, a prefix occurring orig. in loanwords from Latin, with the basic meaning "above, beyond." Words formed with **super-** have the following general senses: "to place or be placed above or over" (*superimpose*), "a thing placed over another" (*superstructure*), "situated over" (*superficial; superlunary*) and, more figuratively, "an individual, thing, or property that exceeds customary norms or levels" (*superconductivity; superman*), "something larger, more powerful, or with wider application than others of its kind" (*supercomputer; superhighway*), "exceeding norms or limits" (*superhuman; superplastic*), "having the specified property to a great or excessive degree" (*supercritical; superfine*), "to subject to (a physical process) to an extreme degree" (*supercharge; supercool*), "a category that embraces a number of lesser items of the specified kind" (*superfamily; supergalaxy*), "a chemical compound with a higher proportion than usual of a given constituent" (*superphosphate*).

su·per·a·ble (soo'pər ə bəl), *adj.* capable of being overcome; surmountable. —**su'per·a·bil'i·ty, su'per·a·ble·ness,** *n.*

su·per·a·bun·dant (soo'pər ə bun'dənt), *adj.* exceedingly or excessively abundant; excessive. —**su'per·a·bun'dance,** *n.* —**su'per·a·bun'dant·ly,** *adv.*

su·per·an·nu·at·ed (soo'pər an'yoo ā'tid), *adj.* **1.** retired because of age or infirmity. **2.** too old for use, work, service, etc. **3.** antiquated or obsolete: *superannuated ideas.* —**su'per·an'nu·a'tion,** *n.*

su·perb (soo pûrb'), *adj.* **1.** admirably fine or excellent. **2.** sumptuous; rich; grand. **3.** of a proudly imposing appearance or kind; majestic. —**su·perb'ly,** *adv.* —**su·perb'ness,** *n.*

Su'per Bowl', *n.* the annual championship football game between the best team of the National Football Conference and that of the American Football Conference.

su·per·cal·en·der (soo'pər kal'ən dər), *n.* **1.** a roll or set of rolls for giving a high, smooth finish to paper. —*v.t.* **2.** to finish (paper) in a supercalender.

su·per·charge (soo'pər chärj'), *v.t.,* **-charged, -charg·ing. 1.** to charge with an abundant or excessive amount, as of energy, emotion, or tension. **2.** to supply air to (an internal-combustion engine) at greater than atmospheric pressure.

su·per·charg·er (soo'pər chär'jər), *n.* a mechanism for forcing air into an internal-combustion engine in order to increase engine power.

su·per·church (soo'pər chûrch'), *n.* a church housed in an extremely large structure and containing elaborate facilities.

su·per·cil·i·ar·y (soo'pər sil'ē er'ē), *adj.* **1.** of or pertaining to the eyebrow. **2.** having a marking over the eye, as certain birds. **3.** situated on the frontal bone at the level of the eyebrow.

su·per·cil·i·ous (soo'pər sil'ē əs), *adj.* haughtily disdainful or contemptuous, as a person or a look. —**su'per·cil'i·ous·ly,** *adv.* —**su'per·cil'i·ous·ness,** *n.*

su·per·class (soo'pər klas', -kläs'), *n. Biol.* **1.** a category of related classes within a phylum or subphylum. **2.** a subphylum.

su·per·com·put·er (soo'pər kəm pyoo'tər, soo'pər kəm pyoo'tər), *n.* a very fast, powerful mainframe computer, used in advanced military and scientific applications.

su·per·con·duc·tiv·i·ty (soo'pər kon'dək tiv'i tē), *n.* the disappearance of electrical resistance in certain metals at temperatures near absolute zero and in new classes of ceramic oxides at temperatures well above this. —**su'per·con·duc'tive, su'per·con·duct'ing,** *adj.* —**su'per·con·duc'tor,** *n.*

su·per·cool (soo'pər kool'), *v.t.* **1.** to cool (a liquid) below its freezing point without producing solidification or crystallization; undercool. —*v.i.* **2.** to become supercooled.

su·per·e·go (soo'pər ē'gō, -eg'ō), *n., pl.* **-gos.** *Psychoanal.* the part of the personality representing the conscience, formed in early life by internalization of the standards of parents and other models of behavior. Compare EGO, ID.

su·per·e·ro·gate (soo'pər er'ə gāt'), *v.i.,* **-gat·ed, -gat·ing.** to do more than duty requires. —**su'per·er'o·ga'tion,** *n.* —**su'per·er'o·ga'tor,** *n.*

su·per·e·rog·a·to·ry (soo'pər ə rog'ə tôr'ē, -tōr'ē), *adj.* **1.** going beyond the requirements of duty. **2.** greater than that required or needed; superfluous. —**su'per·e·rog'a·to'ri·ly,** *adv.*

su·per·fect·a (soo'pər fek'tə), *n., pl.* **-fect·as.** a type of bet, esp. on horse races, in which the bettor must select the first four finishers in exact order.

su·per·fi·cial (soo'pər fish'əl), *adj.* **1.** being at, on, or near the surface: *a superficial wound.* **2.** external or outward; apparent rather than real: *a superficial resemblance.* **3.** concerned with or comprehending only what is on the surface or obvious. **4.** shallow; not profound or thorough. **5.** insubstantial or insignificant. **6.** of or pertaining to the surface: *superficial measurement.* —**su'per·fi'ci·al'i·ty** (-ē al'i tē), **su'per·fi'cial·ness,** *n.* —**su'per·fi'cial·ly,** *adv.*

su·per·fine (soo'pər fīn'), *adj.* **1.** extra fine, as in grain or texture: *superfine sugar.* **2.** excessively refined; overnice.

su·per·flu·id (soo'pər floo'id), *n.* a fluid having frictionless flow, high heat conductivity, and other unusual physical properties: helium below 2.186 K is the only known example. —**su'per·flu·id'i·ty,** *n.*

su·per·flu·i·ty (soo'pər floo'i tē), *n., pl.* **-ties. 1.** the state of being superfluous. **2.** a superabundant or excessive amount. **3.** something superfluous, as a luxury.

su·per·flu·ous (soo pûr'floo əs), *adj.* **1.** being more than is sufficient or required; excessive. **2.** unnecessary or needless. —**su·per'flu·ous·ly,** *adv.* —**su·per'flu·ous·ness,** *n.*

su·per·gal·ax·y (soo'pər gal'ək sē), *n., pl.* **-ax·ies.** a system of galaxies. —**su'per·ga·lac'tic** (-gə lak'tik), *adj.*

su·per·graph·ics (soo'pər graf'iks), *n.* (*used with a sing. or pl. v.*) large-scale graphic art in bold colors and in geometric or typographic designs.

su·per·heat (*n.* soo'pər hēt'; *v.* soo'pər hēt'), *n.* **1.** the state of being superheated. **2.** the amount of superheating. —*v.t.* **3.** to heat to an extreme degree or to a very high temperature. **4.** to heat (a liquid) above its boiling point without the formation of bubbles of vapor. **5.** to heat (a gas, as steam not in contact with water) to such a degree that its temperature may be lowered or its pressure increased without the conversion of any of the gas into liquid. —**su'per·heat'er,** *n.*

su·per·he·ro (soo'pər hēr'ō), *n., pl.* **-roes.** a hero, esp. in children's comic books and television cartoons, possessing extraordinary, often magical powers.

su'per·high fre'quency (soo'pər hī'), *n.* any radio frequency between 3000 and 30,000 megahertz. *Abbr.:* SHF

su·per·high·way (soo'pər hī'wā, soo'pər hī'wā'), *n.* a highway designed for travel at high speeds, having more than one lane for each direction of traffic; expressway.

su·per·hu·man (soo'pər hyoo'mən; *often* -yoo'-), *adj.* **1.** above or beyond what is human; having a higher nature or greater powers than humans have: *a superhuman being.* **2.** exceeding ordinary human power, achievement, experience, etc.: *a superhuman effort.* —**su'per·hu·man'i·ty** (-man'i tē), **su'per·hu'man·ness,** *n.* —**su'per·hu'man·ly,** *adv.*

su·per·im·pose (soo'pər im pōz'), *v.t.,* **-posed, -pos·ing. 1.** to impose, place, or set over, above, or on something else. **2.** to put or join as an addition (usu. fol. by *on* or *upon*). —**su'per·im'po·si'tion** (-pə zish'ən), *n.*

su·per·in·cum·bent (soo'pər in kum'bənt), *adj.* **1.** lying or resting on something else. **2.** situated above; overhanging. **3.** exerted from above. —**su'per·in·cum'bent·ly, su'per·in·cum'ben·cy,** *n.*

su·per·in·tend (soo'pər in tend', soo'prin-), *v.t.* **1.** to oversee and direct (work, processes, etc.). **2.** to exercise supervision over (an institution, district, place, etc.).

su·per·in·tend·ent (soo'pər in ten'dənt, soo'prin-), *n.* **1.** a person who oversees or directs some work, establishment, district, etc.; supervisor. **2.** a person who is in charge of maintenance and repairs of an apartment house; custodian. —*adj.* **3.** superintending.

su·pe·ri·or (sə pēr'ē ər, soo-), *adj.* **1.** higher in station, rank, degree, etc. **2.** above the average in excellence, merit, intelligence, etc. **3.** of higher grade or quality. **4.** greater in quantity or amount. **5.** showing a consciousness or feeling of being better than or above others. **6.** not yielding or susceptible (usu. fol. by *to*): *to be superior to temptation.* **7.** higher in place or position: *superior ground.* **8.** *Bot.* situated above some other organ. **9.** *Anat.* (of an organ or part) **a.** higher in place or position; situated above another. **b.** being toward the head. **10.** (of a planet) having an orbit outside that of the earth, as Mars and Jupiter. **11.** written or printed high on a line of text, as the "2" in a^2b; superscript. Compare INFERIOR (def. 7). —*n.* **12.** one superior to another. **13.** SUPERSCRIPT. **14.** the head of a monastery, convent, or the like.

supe'rior court', *n.* **1.** the court of general jurisdiction in many states of the U.S., often intermediate between trial courts and the chief appellate court. **2.** any court having jurisdiction over other courts.

su·pe·ri·or·i·ty (sə pēr'ē ôr'i tē, -or'-, soo-), *n.* the quality or condition of being superior.

superior'ity com'plex, *n.* an exaggerated feeling of one's own superiority.

su·per·ja·cent (soo'pər jā'sənt), *adj.* lying above or upon something else.

S

su•per•jet (soo′pər jet′), *n.* a jet aircraft, esp. a large one, capable of supersonic flight.

su•per•la•tive (sə pûr′lə tiv, soo-), *adj.* **1.** of the highest kind or order. **2.** of or designating the highest degree of comparison of adjectives and adverbs, used to show the extreme or greatest in quality, quantity, or intensity, as in *smallest, best,* and *most carefully,* the superlative forms of *small, good,* and *carefully.* —*n.* **3.** a superlative person or thing. **4.** the utmost degree; acme. **5.** the superlative form of an adjective or adverb. —**su•per′la•tive•ly,** *adv.* —**su•per′la•tive•ness,** *n.*

su•per•lu•na•ry (soo′pər loo′nə rē) also **su′per•lu′nar,** *adj.* **1.** situated above or beyond the moon. **2.** celestial, rather than earthly.

su•per•man (soo′pər man′), *n., pl.* **-men. 1.** a person of superhuman powers. **2.** an ideal superior being conceived by Nietzsche as attaining happiness and dominance through creativity and integrity.

su•per•mar•ket (soo′pər mär′kit), *n.* a large self-service retail store that sells food and other household goods.

su•per•nal (soo pûr′nl), *adj.* **1.** heavenly, celestial, or divine. **2.** lofty; of more than human excellence, powers, etc. **3.** being on high or in the sky or visible heavens. —**su•per′nal•ly,** *adv.*

su•per•nat•u•ral (soo′pər nach′ər əl, -nach′rəl), *adj.* **1.** of, pertaining to, or being above or beyond what is natural or explainable by natural law. **2.** of, pertaining to, or attributed to God or a deity. **3.** of a superlative degree; preternatural. **4.** pertaining to or attributed to ghosts, goblins, or other unearthly beings; eerie; occult. —*n.* **5.** a being, place, object, occurrence, etc., considered as supernatural or of supernatural origin. **6. the supernatural, a.** supernatural beings, behavior, and occurrences collectively. **b.** supernatural forces and the supernatural plane of existence. —**su•per•nat′u•ral•ly,** *adv.* —**su•per•nat′u•ral•ness,** *n.*

su•per•nor•mal (soo′pər nôr′məl), *adj.* **1.** in excess of the normal or average. **2.** lying beyond normal or natural powers of comprehension. —**su•per•nor•mal′i•ty,** *n.* —**su•per•nor′mal•ly,** *adv.*

su•per•no•va (soo′pər nō′və), *n., pl.* **-vas, -vae** (-vē). a nova millions of times brighter than the sun.

su•per•nu•mer•ar•y (soo′pər noo′mə rer′ē, -nyoo′-), *adj., n., pl.* **-ar•ies.** —*adj.* **1.** being in excess of the usual, proper, or prescribed number; additional; extra. **2.** associated with a regular body or staff as an assistant or substitute in case of necessity. —*n.* **3.** a supernumerary or extra person or thing. **4.** a supernumerary official or employee. **5.** a person who appears in a play, opera, etc., without speaking lines or as part of a crowd; extra.

su•per•or•di•nate (*adj., n.* soo′pər ôr′dn it; *v.* -āt′), *adj., n., v.,* **-nat•ed, -nat•ing.** —*adj.* **1.** of higher degree in condition or rank. —*n.* **2.** a superordinate person or thing. **3.** a word that denotes a general class under which a set of subcategories is subsumed. —*v.t.* **4.** to elevate to superordinate position.

su•per•pa•tri•ot (soo′pər pā′trē ət, soo′pər pā′-; *esp. Brit.,* soo′pər pa′trē ət, soo′pər pa′-), *n.* a person who is patriotic to an extreme. —**su•per•pa•tri•ot•ic** (soo′pər pā′trē ot′ik; *esp. Brit.,* soo′pər pa′trē ot′ik), *adj.* —**su′per•pa′tri•ot′i•cal•ly,** *adv.* —**su′per•pa′tri•ot•ism,** *n.*

su•per•pose (soo′pər pōz′), *v.t.,* **-posed, -pos•ing. 1.** to place above or upon something else, or one upon another. **2.** *Geom.* to place (one figure) in the space occupied by another, so that the two figures coincide throughout their whole extent.

su•per•po•si•tion (soo′pər pə zish′ən), *n.* the order in which sedimentary strata are superposed one above another.

su•per•pow•er (soo′pər pou′ər), *n.* **1.** a very powerful nation, esp. one with significant interests and influence outside its own region. **2.** power greater in scope or magnitude than that which is considered natural or has previously existed. **3.** power, esp. mechanical or electric power, on an extremely large scale secured by the linking together of a number of separate power systems. —**su′per•pow′ered,** *adj.*

su•per•saur (soo′pər sôr′), *n.* a huge sauropod dinosaur of the genus *Supersaurus,* of W North America, that reached a length of about 130 ft. (40 m).

su•per•sav•er (soo′pər sā′vər), *n.* **1.** a specially reduced fare, as for travel on an airplane or train. **2.** an item offered at a specially reduced price, as in a food market.

su•per•script (soo′pər skript′), *adj.* **1.** written above (disting. from *subscript*). **2.** superior (def. 11). —*n.* **3.** Also called **superior.** a letter, number, or symbol written or printed high on a line of text.

su•per•sede (soo′pər sēd′), *v.t.,* **-sed•ed, -sed•ing. 1.** to replace in power, authority, effectiveness, acceptance, use, etc., as by another person or thing. **2.** to set aside or cause to be set aside as void, useless, or obsolete, usu. in favor of something mentioned; make obsolete. **3.** to

succeed to the position, function, office, etc., of; supplant. —**su′per•sed′a•ble,** *adj.* —**su′per•sed′er,** *n.*

su•per•sen•si•tive (soo′pər sen′si tiv), *adj.* extremely or excessively sensitive, esp. (of devices, materials, etc.) by design or treatment. —**su′per•sen′si•tive•ly,** *adv.* — **su′per•sen′si•tiv′i•ty,** *n.*

su•per•son•ic (soo′pər son′ik), *adj.* **1.** greater than the speed of sound waves through air. **2.** capable of achieving such speed: *a supersonic plane.* **3.** ULTRASONIC. —**su′per•son′i•cal•ly,** *adv.*

su•per•son•ics (soo′pər son′iks), *n.* (*used with a sing. v.*) the branch of science that deals with supersonic phenomena.

su′person′ic trans′port, *n.* a commercial jet airplane that can fly faster than the speed of sound. *Abbr.:* SST

su•per•star (soo′pər stär′), *n.* a very prominent or successful person or thing, esp. a performer or athlete who enjoys great renown and admiration and commands extremely high fees for services.

su•per•sta•tion (soo′pər stā′shən), *n.* a television station whose signal is transmitted by satellite to subscribers on a cable system.

su•per•sti•tion (soo′pər stish′ən), *n.* **1.** an irrational belief in or notion of the ominous significance of a particular thing, circumstance, occurrence, etc. **2.** a system or collection of such beliefs. **3.** a custom or act based on such a belief. **4.** irrational fear of what is unknown or mysterious, esp. in connection with religion. **5.** any blindly accepted belief or notion.

su•per•sti•tious (soo′pər stish′əs), *adj.* **1.** characterized by or proceeding from superstition: *superstitious fears.* **2.** pertaining to or connected with superstition: *superstitious legends.* **3.** believing in or full of superstition. —**su′per•sti′tious•ly,** *adv.*

su•per•store (soo′pər stôr′, -stōr′), *n.* a very large store, esp. one stocking a wide variety of merchandise.

su•per•stra•tum (soo′pər strā′təm, -strat′əm), *n., pl.* **-stra•ta** (-strā′tə, -strat′ə), **-stra•tums. 1.** an overlying stratum or layer. **2.** a set of features of a language traceable to the influence of a language formerly spoken in the society by a dominant or conquering group. Compare SUBSTRATUM (def. 5).

su•per•struc•ture (soo′pər struk′chər), *n.* **1.** the part of a building or construction entirely above its foundation or basement. **2.** any structure built on something else. **3.** anything based on, arising from, or superimposed on a more fundamental construct, concept, system, etc. **4.** any construction built above the main deck of a vessel. —**su′per•struc′tur•al,** *adj.*

su•per•tank•er (soo′pər tang′kər), *n.* a tanker with a deadweight capacity of over 75,000 tons.

su•per•vene (soo′pər vēn′), *v.i.,* **-vened, -ven•ing. 1.** to take place or occur as something additional or extraneous (sometimes fol. by *on* or *upon*). **2.** to ensue. —**su′per•ven′ience** (-vēn′yəns), **su′per•ven′tion** (-ven′shən), *n.* —**su′per•ven′ient,** *adj.*

su•per•vise (soo′pər vīz′), *v.t.,* **-vised, -vis•ing.** to watch over and direct (a process, work, workers, etc.); oversee; superintend. —**su′per•vi′sion** (-vizh′ən), *n.*

su•per•vi•sor (soo′pər vī′zər), *n.* **1.** a person who supervises workers or the work done by others; superintendent. **2.** an official responsible for assisting teachers in the preparation of syllabuses, in devising teaching methods, etc., esp. in public schools. **3.** the chief elective officer of a township. —**su′per•vi′sor•ship′,** *n.*

su•per•vi•so•ry (soo′pər vī′zə rē), *adj.* of, pertaining to, or having supervision.

su•per•wom•an (soo′pər woom′ən), *n., pl.* **-wom•en. 1.** a woman of superhuman powers. **2.** a woman who copes successfully with the simultaneous demands of a career, marriage, and motherhood.

su•pi•na•tor (soo′pə nā′tər), *n.* a muscle in the forearm that rotates the radius outward.

su•pine (*adj.* soo pīn′; *n.* soo′pīn), *adj.* **1.** lying on the back, face upward. **2. a.** (of the hand) having the palm turned forward or upward. **b.** (of the foot) having the sole turned upward or outward. **3.** inactive, passive, or inert, esp. from indolence or indifference. —*n.* **4.** (in English) the infinitive of a verb preceded by *to.* —**su•pine′ly,** *adv.* —**su•pine′ness,** *n.*

sup•per (sup′ər), *n.* **1.** the evening meal, often the principal meal of the day. **2.** any light evening meal, esp. one taken late in the evening. **3.** an evening social event at which a supper is served to raise money for a church, charity, etc. —**sup′per•less,** *adj.*

sup′per club′, *n.* a nightclub, esp. a small, luxurious one.

sup•plant (sə plant′, -plänt′), *v.t.* **1.** to take the place of (another), as through force, scheming, or strategy. **2.** to replace (one thing) by something else. —**sup•plan•ta•tion** (sup′lən tā′shən), *n.* —**sup•plant′er,** *n.*

---

sup•ple (sup′əl), *adj.,* **-pler, -plest,** *v.,* **-pled, -pling.** —*adj.* **1.** bending readily without breaking, splitting, etc.; pliant; flexible. **2.** characterized by ease in bending; limber; lithe: *supple movements.* **3.** characterized by mental responsiveness and adaptability. **4.** compliant or yielding. **5.** obsequious. —*v.t., v.i.* **6.** to make or become supple. —**sup′ple•ness,** *n.*

sup•ple•ment (*n.* sup′lə mənt; *v.* -ment′), *n.* **1.** something added to complete a thing, supply a deficiency, or reinforce or extend a whole. **2.** something added to or issued after a publication, as a book or periodical, that supplies further information or treats special subjects. **3.** *Geom.* the quantity by which an angle or an arc falls short of 180° or a semicircle. —*v.t.* **4.** to complete, add to, or extend by a supplement. **5.** to form a supplement or addition to. —**sup′ple•ment′er,** *n.*

sup•ple•men•tal (sup′lə men′tl), *adj.* **1.** SUPPLEMENTARY. **2.** NONSCHEDULED. —*n.* **3.** anything that is supplemental. —**sup′ple•men′tal•ly,** *adv.*

sup•ple•men•ta•ry (sup′lə men′tə rē), *adj., n., pl.* **-ries.** —*adj.* **1.** Also, **supplemental.** of the nature of or forming a supplement; additional. —*n.* **2.** a person or thing that is supplementary.

sup′plemen′tary an′gle, *n. Geom.* either of two angles that added together produce an angle of 180°. Compare COMPLEMENTARY ANGLE.

sup•ple•men•ta•tion (sup′lə men tā′shən, -mən-), *n.* **1.** the act or process of supplementing. **2.** the state of being supplemented. **3.** something that supplements.

sup•pli•cate (sup′li kāt′), *v.,* **-cat•ed, -cat•ing.** —*v.i.* **1.** to make humble and earnest entreaty. —*v.t.* **2.** to pray humbly to; entreat or petition humbly. **3.** to ask for by humble entreaty. —**sup′pli•cat′ing•ly,** *adv.* —**sup′pli•ca•to′ry** (-kə tôr′ē, -tōr′ē), *adj.*

sup•ply¹ (sə plī′), *v.,* **-plied, -ply•ing,** *n., pl.* **-plies.** —*v.t.* **1.** to furnish or provide (a person, establishment, etc.) with what is lacking or requisite: *supplying the poor with clothing.* **2.** to furnish or provide (something wanting or requisite): *supplied needed water to the region.* **3.** to make up, compensate for, or satisfy (a deficiency, loss, need, etc.). **4.** to fill or occupy as a substitute, as a vacancy or a pulpit. —*v.i.* **5.** to substitute for another, esp. in the pulpit of a church. —*n.* **6.** the act of supplying, furnishing, satisfying, etc. **7.** something that is supplied: *the city's water supply.* **8.** a quantity of something on hand or available; stock or store: *a large supply of swimwear.* **9.** Usu., **supplies.** a provision, stock, or store of food or other things necessary for maintenance. **10.** the quantity of a commodity that is in the market and available for purchase or that is available for purchase at a particular price. **11.** **supplies, a.** the food, clothing, arms, etc., necessary to equip a military command. **b.** the department, officers, etc., in charge of procuring supplies. **12.** a person who fills a vacancy or takes the place of another, esp. temporarily. —**sup•pli′er,** *n.*

sup•ply² (sup′lē), *adv.* in a supple manner or way.

supply′-side′, *adj.* of or denoting the hypothesis in economics that reduced taxes will stimulate investment and economic growth. Compare DEMAND-SIDE. —**supply′-sid′er,** *n.*

sup•port (sə pôrt′, -pōrt′), *v.t.* **1.** to bear or hold up (a load, mass, structure, part, etc.). **2.** to sustain or withstand (weight, pressure, strain, etc.) without giving way. **3.** to maintain (a person, family, institution, etc.) with the necessities of existence; provide for. **4.** to sustain (a person, the spirits, etc.) under trial or affliction. **5.** to uphold or advocate (a person, cause, principle, etc.); back. **6.** to corroborate (a statement, opinion, etc.). **7.** to undergo or endure, esp. patiently; tolerate. **8.** to perform with (a leading actor or performer) in a secondary role. —*n.* **9.** an act or instance of supporting. **10.** the state of being supported. **11.** something that serves as a foundation, prop, brace, or stay. **12.** maintenance, as of a person or family, with necessaries, means, or funds. **13.** a person or thing that supports, esp. financially: *The pension was her only support.* **14.** backup or assistance in combat, as by naval gunfire or air cover. —*adj.* **15.** (of hosiery) made with elasticized fibers that exert a degree of tension on the legs, thereby aiding circulation, relieving fatigue, etc. —**sup•port′ing•ly,** *adv.*

sup•port•er (sə pôr′tər, -pōr′-), *n.* **1.** a person or thing that supports. **2.** a follower, backer, or advocate. **3.** a jockstrap. **4.** a garter.

support′ group′, *n.* a group of people who meet regularly to support or sustain each other by discussing problems affecting them in common, as alcoholism or bereavement.

sup•port•ive (sə pôr′tiv, -pōr′-), *adj.* **1.** giving support. **2.** providing sympathy or encouragement. **3.** providing additional help; auxiliary. —**sup•port′ive•ness,** *n.*

sup•pose (sə pōz′), *v.,* **-posed, -pos•ing.** —*v.t.* **1.** to assume (something), as for the sake of argument: *Suppose you won a million dollars in the lottery.* **2.** to consider (something) as a possibility or plan: *Suppose we wait until tomorrow.* **3.** to believe or assume as true; take for granted. **4.** to think or hold as an opinion: *What do you suppose he will do?* **5.** to require logically; imply; presuppose. **6.** (used in the passive) to expect or require (fol. by an infinitive verb): *She was supposed to meet me here.* —*v.i.* **7.** to assume something; presume; think. —**sup•pos′a•ble,** *adj.* —**sup•pos′a•bly,** *adv.*

sup•posed (sə pōzd′, -pō′zid), *adj.* **1.** assumed as true; hypothetical: *a supposed case.* **2.** accepted as true, without positive knowledge: *the supposed site of an ancient temple.* **3.** merely thought to be such; imagined: *supposed gains.* —**sup•pos′ed•ly,** *adv.*

sup•pos•ing (sə pō′zing), *conj.* upon the supposition or premise that; in the event that.

sup•po•si•tion (sup′ə zish′ən), *n.* **1.** the act of supposing. **2.** some-

thing that is supposed; assumption; hypothesis. —**sup′po•si′tion•al,** *adj.* —**sup′po•si′tion•al•ly,** *adv.*

sup•pos•i•ti•tious (sə poz′i tish′əs), *adj.* **1.** fraudulently substituted or pretended; spurious; not genuine. **2.** based on supposition; hypothetical. —**sup•pos′i•ti′tious•ly,** *adv.* —**sup•pos′i•ti′tious•ness,** *n.*

sup•pos•i•tive (sə poz′i tiv), *adj.* **1.** of the nature of or involving supposition. **2.** spurious or false. —**sup•pos′i•tive•ly,** *adv.*

sup•pos•i•to•ry (sə poz′i tôr′ē, -tōr′ē), *n., pl.* **-ries.** a solid mass of medicinal substance that melts upon insertion into the rectum or vagina.

sup•press (sə pres′), *v.t.* **1.** to put an end to the activities of (a person, group, etc.). **2.** to do away with by or as if by authority; abolish; stop (a practice, custom, etc.). **3.** to inhibit (an impulse or action) consciously. **4.** to withhold from disclosure or publication (evidence, a book, etc.). **5.** to stop or arrest (a cough, hemorrhage, etc.). **6.** to subdue (a revolt, rebellion, etc.); crush. **7.** to keep (a thought, memory, etc.) out of conscious awareness. —**sup•press′i•ble,** *adj.* —**sup•pres′sor, sup•press′er,** *n.*

sup•pres•sant (sə pres′ənt), *n.* a substance that suppresses an undesirable action or condition: *a cough suppressant.*

sup•pres•sion (sə presh′ən), *n.* **1.** the act of suppressing. **2.** the state of being suppressed. **3.** *Psychoanal.* **a.** conscious or unconscious inhibition of a painful memory or idea. **b.** conscious inhibition of an impulse.

sup•pu•rate (sup′yə rāt′), *v.i.,* **-rat•ed, -rat•ing.** to produce or discharge pus. —**sup′pu•ra′tion,** *n.* —**sup′pu•ra′tive,** *n., adj.*

su•pra (sōō′prə), *adv.* above, esp. when used in referring to parts of a text. Compare INFRA.

supra-, a prefix meaning "above, over" (*supraorbital*) or "beyond the limits of, outside of" (*suprasegmental*). Compare SUPER-.

su•pra•lap•sar•i•an•ism (sōō′prə lap sâr′ē ə niz′əm), *n. Theol.* the doctrine that the decree of election preceded human creation and the Fall (opposed to *infralapsarianism*). —**su′pra•lap•sar′i•an,** *n., adj.*

su•pra•lit•to•ral (sōō′prə lit′ər əl), *adj.* **1.** of or pertaining to the region of a lake or ocean shore that is above the shoreline but is often damp from spray or capillary action of the water. —*n.* **2.** a supralittoral zone or region.

su•pra•na•tion•al (sōō′prə nash′ə nl), *adj.* above the authority or scope of one national government, as a project or policy. —**su′pra•na′tion•al•ism,** *n.* —**su′pra•na′tion•al′i•ty,** *n.*

su•prem•a•cist (sə prem′ə sist, sōō-), *n.* a person who believes in or advocates the supremacy of a particular group, esp. a racial group: *a white supremacist.*

su•prem•a•cy (sə prem′ə sē, sōō-), *n.* **1.** the state of being supreme. **2.** supreme authority or power.

su•preme (sə prēm′, sōō-), *adj.* **1.** highest in rank or authority; paramount; sovereign; chief. **2.** of the highest quality, degree, character, importance, etc. **3.** greatest, utmost, or extreme. **4.** last or final; ultimate. —**su•preme′ly,** *adv.* —**su•preme′ness,** *n.*

su•prême (sə prēm′, -prâm′, sōō-; *Fr.* sy prem′), *n.* **1.** a velouté sauce made with chicken stock. **2.** a dish prepared with this sauce, esp. boned chicken breast.

Supreme′ Court′, *n.* **1.** the highest court of the U.S. **2.** (*l.c.*) the highest court of a state or, in some states, a court of general jurisdiction subordinate to an appeals court.

CHIEF JUSTICES OF THE UNITED STATES SUPREME COURT

Name	Born	Died	Term
John Jay	1745	1829	1789-1795
John Rutledge	1739	1800	1795
Oliver Ellsworth	1745	1807	1796-1800
John Marshall	1755	1835	1801-1835
Roger B. Taney	1777	1864	1836-1864
Salmon P. Chase	1808	1873	1864-1873
Morrison R. Waite	1816	1888	1874-1888
Melville W. Fuller	1833	1910	1888-1910
Edward D. White	1845	1921	1910-1921
William H. Taft	1857	1930	1921-1930
Charles E. Hughes	1862	1948	1930-1941
Harlan F. Stone	1872	1946	1941-1946
Frederick M. Vinson	1890	1953	1946-1953
Earl Warren	1891	1974	1953-1969
Warren E. Burger	1907	1995	1969-1986
William H. Rehnquist	1924		1986-

supreme′ sac′rifice, *n.* the sacrifice of one's own life: *Many made the supreme sacrifice during the war.*

Supt. or **supt.,** superintendent.

Sur (sōōr), *n.* a town in S Lebanon, on the Mediterranean Sea: site of the ancient port of Tyre.

sur-, a prefix meaning "over, above," "in addition": *surcharge; surname; surrender.*

sur•cease (sûr sēs′), *v.,* **-ceased, -ceas•ing,** *n.* —*v.i.* **1.** to cease from some action; desist. **2.** to come to an end. —*n.* **3.** cessation; end.

sur•charge (*n.* sûr′chärj′; *v.* sûr chärj′, sûr′chärj′), *n., v.,* **-charged, -charg•ing.** —*n.* **1.** an additional charge, tax, or cost. **2.** an excessive sum or price charged. **3.** an additional or excessive load or burden. **4.** an overprint that alters or restates the face value of a postage or revenue stamp to which it has been applied. **5.** the act of surcharging. —*v.t.* **6.** to subject to an additional or extra charge, tax, cost, etc. **7.** to overcharge for goods. **8.** to print a surcharge on (a stamp). **9.** to put an additional or excessive burden upon. —**sur·charg′er,** *n.*

surd (sûrd), *adj.* **1.** (of a speech sound) voiceless (opposed to *sonant*). **2.** (of a quantity) not capable of being expressed in rational numbers; irrational. —*n.* **3.** a voiceless consonant. **4.** a surd quantity.

sure (shŏŏr, shûr), *adj.,* **sur·er, sur·est,** *adv.* —*adj.* **1.** free from doubt as to the reliability, character, action, etc., of something: *to be sure of one's facts.* **2.** confident, as of something expected: *sure of success.* **3.** convinced, fully persuaded, or positive: *to be sure of a person's honesty.* **4.** assured or certain beyond question: *a sure victory.* **5.** worthy of confidence; reliable: *a sure messenger.* **6.** unfailing; never disappointing expectations: *a sure cure.* **7.** unerring; never missing, slipping, etc.: *a sure aim.* **8.** admitting of no doubt or question: *sure proof.* **9.** destined; certain: *It is sure to happen.* —*adv.* **10.** certainly; surely. —*Idiom.* **11.** **be** or **make sure,** to take care (to be or do as specified): *Be sure to close the windows.* **12. for sure,** without a doubt; surely; for certain. **13. sure enough,** *Informal.* as might have been expected; certainly. **14. to be sure,** admittedly; without doubt or dispute. —**sure′ness,** *n.* —**Usage.** Both SURE and SURELY are used as intensifying adverbs with the sense "undoubtedly, certainly." In this use, SURE is generally informal and occurs mainly in speech and written representations of speech: *It sure is hot in here. I sure wouldn't want to be in your place.* SURELY is used in this sense in all varieties of speech and writing, even the most formal: *The law was surely meant to apply to both rich and poor.* See also QUICK, SLOW.

sure·fire (shŏŏr′fīᵊr′, shûr′-), *adj. Informal.* sure to work.

sure·foot·ed (shŏŏr′fŏŏt′id, shûr′-), *adj.* **1.** not likely to stumble, slip, or fall. **2.** proceeding surely; unerring: *a surefooted pursuit of success.* —**sure′foot′ed·ly,** *adv.* —**sure′foot′ed·ness,** *n.*

sure·ly (shŏŏr′lē, shûr′-), *adv.* **1.** firmly; unerringly. **2.** undoubtedly, assuredly, or certainly. **3.** (in emphatic utterances that are not necessarily sustained by fact) assuredly: *Surely you are mistaken.* **4.** inevitably or without fail. **5.** yes, indeed. —**Usage.** See SURE.

sure′ thing′, *Informal.* —*n.* **1.** something that is or should be a certain success, as a bet. —*interj.* **2.** surely; for sure; OK.

sur·e·ty (shŏŏr′i tē, shŏŏr′tē, shûr′-), *n., pl.* **-ties. 1.** security against loss or damage or for the payment of a debt or fulfillment of an obligation; a pledge, guaranty, or bond. **2.** a person who has made himself or herself responsible for another, as a sponsor or bondsman. **3.** the state or quality of being sure; certainty. **4.** something that makes sure; ground of confidence or safety. **5.** a person legally responsible for the debts of another. **6.** assurance, esp. self-assurance.

surf (sûrf), *n.* **1.** the swell of the sea that breaks upon a shore or upon shoals. **2.** the mass or line of foamy water caused by the breaking of the sea upon a shore, esp. a shallow or sloping shore. —*v.i.* **3.** to ride a surfboard. **4.** to float on the crest of a wave toward shore. **5.** to swim, play, or bathe in the surf. **6.** to search haphazardly, as for information on a computer network or an interesting program on television. —*v.t.* **7.** to ride a surfboard on: *We surfed every big wave in sight.* **8.** to search through (a computer network or TV channels) for information or entertainment. —**surf′a·ble,** *adj.* —**surf′er,** *n.* —**surf′like′,** *adj.*

sur·face (sûr′fis), *n., adj., v.,* **-faced, -fac·ing.** —*n.* **1.** the outer face, outside, or exterior boundary of a thing; outermost ŏr uppermost layer or area. **2.** any face of a body or thing: *the six surfaces of a cube.* **3.** extent or area of outer face; superficial area. **4.** the outward appearance, esp. as distinguished from the inner nature. **5.** any geometric figure having only two dimensions; part or all of the boundary of a solid. **6.** land or sea transportation, rather than air, underground, or undersea transportation. **7.** an airfoil. —*adj.* **8.** of, on, or pertaining to the surface; external. **9.** apparent rather than real; superficial. **10.** of, pertaining to, or via land or sea: *surface mail.* **11.** of or pertaining to the surface structure of a sentence. —*v.t.* **12.** to finish the surface of; give a particular kind of surface to. **13.** to bring to the surface; cause to appear openly. —*v.i.* **14.** to rise to the surface. **15.** to work on or at the surface. **16.** to appear or emerge; turn up: *New evidence has surfaced.* —**sur′face·less,** *adj.* —**sur′fac·er,** *n.*

sur′face struc′ture, *n.* (in transformational grammar) **1.** a structural representation of the final syntactic form of a sentence, as it exists after the transformational component has modified a deep structure. Compare DEEP STRUCTURE. **2.** the string of words that is actually produced.

sur′face ten′sion, *n.* the elasticlike force existing in the surface of a body, esp. a liquid, tending to minimize the area of the surface and manifested in capillarity, constriction of the surface, etc.

sur′face-to-air′, *adj.* (of a missile) capable of traveling from the surface of the earth to a target in the atmosphere.

surf·board (sûrf′bôrd′, -bōrd′), *n.* **1.** a long, narrow board on which a person stands or lies prone and rides the crest of a breaking wave toward the shore in surfing. —*v.i.* **2.** to ride a surfboard. —**surf′board′er,** *n.*

surf′ cast′ing, *n.* the act, technique, or sport of fishing by casting from the shoreline into the sea, usu. using heavy-duty tackle. —**surf′cast′er,** *n.*

sur·feit (sûr′fit), *n.* **1.** excess; an excessive amount. **2.** excess or overindulgence in eating or drinking. **3.** an uncomfortably full feeling due to excessive eating or drinking. **4.** general disgust caused by excess or sati-

ety. —*v.t.* **5.** to supply or feed to excess or satiety; satiate. —*v.i.* **6.** to indulge in something, as food or drink, to excess. —**sur′feit·er,** *n.*

surf·ing (sûr′fing), *n.* the act or sport of riding the crest of a breaking wave toward the shore, esp. on a surfboard.

surge (sûrj), *n., v.,* **surged, surg·ing.** —*n.* **1.** a strong, wavelike forward movement, rush, or sweep: *the surge of the crowd.* **2.** a sudden, strong rush or burst: *a surge of energy.* **3.** a strong, swelling, wavelike volume or body of something. **4.** the rolling swell of the sea. **5.** a swelling wave; billow. **6.** the swelling and rolling sea. **7. a.** a sudden rush or burst of electric current or voltage. **b.** a violent oscillatory disturbance. **8.** a slackening or slipping back, as of a rope or cable. —*v.i.* **9.** (of a ship) to rise and fall, toss about, or move along on the waves. **10.** to rise, roll, move, or swell forward in or like waves. **11.** to rise as if by a heaving or swelling force: *Blood surged to his face.* **12.** (esp. of electric current or voltage) **a.** to increase suddenly. **b.** to oscillate violently. **13.** to slack off or loosen, as a rope. —*v.t.* **14.** to cause to surge or roll in or as if in waves. **15.** to slacken (a rope).

sur·geon (sûr′jan), *n.* a physician who specializes in surgery.

sur′geon gen′eral, *n., pl.,* **surgeons general. 1.** the chief of medical services in one of the armed forces. **2.** (*caps.*) the head of the U.S. Bureau of Public Health or, in some states, of a state health agency.

sur·ger·y (sûr′jə rē), *n., pl.* **-ger·ies** for 3, 4. **1.** the art, practice, or work of treating diseases, injuries, or deformities by manual or operative procedures. **2.** the branch of medicine concerned with such treatment. **3.** treatment, as an operation, performed by a surgeon. **4.** a room or place for surgical operations. **5.** any major repair or alteration produced as if by a surgical operation. **6.** *Brit.* a doctor's office.

sur·gi·cal (sûr′ji kal), *adj.* **1.** pertaining to or involving surgery or surgeons. **2.** used in surgery. **3.** characterized by extreme precision or incisiveness: *a surgical air strike.* —**sur′gi·cal·ly,** *adv.*

sur′gical strike′, *n.* a bombing raid that is intended to attack a military target and avoid civilian centers.

su·ri·cate (sŏŏr′i kāt′), *n.* a small burrowing South African colonial viverrid, *Suricata suricatta,* related to the mongooses. Also called meerkat.

Su·ri·na·me (sŏŏr′ə nä′mə) also **Su·ri·nam** (sŏŏr′ə näm′, -nam′), *n.* a republic on the NE coast of South America: formerly a territory of the Netherlands; gained independence 1975. 443,446; 63,251 sq. mi. (163,820 sq. km). *Cap.:* Paramaribo. Formerly, **Dutch Guiana, Netherlands Guiana.** —**Su′ri·nam′er,** *n.* —**Su′ri·na·mese′** (-nə mēz′, -mēs′), *n., pl.* **-mese,** *adj.*

sur·ly (sûr′lē), *adj.,* **-li·er, -li·est. 1.** sullenly rude or bad-tempered. **2.** unfriendly or hostile; menacingly irritable: *a surly old lion.* **3.** dark or dismal: *a surly sky.* —**sur′li·ly,** *adv.* —**sur′li·ness,** *n.*

sur·mise (sər mīz′; *n. also* sûr′mīz), *v.,* **-mised, -mis·ing,** *n.* —*v.t.* **1.** to think or infer without certain or strong evidence; conjecture; guess. —*v.i.* **2.** to conjecture or guess. —*n.* **3.** an idea or thought of something as being possible; conjecture. —**sur·mis′a·ble,** *adj.* —**sur·mis′er,** *n.*

sur·mount (sər mount′), *v.t.* **1.** to get over or across (barriers, obstacles, etc.). **2.** to prevail over; overcome: *to surmount difficulties.* **3.** to get to the top of; mount upon. **4.** to be on top of or above. **5.** to furnish with something placed on top or above. —**sur·mount′a·ble,** *adj.* —**sur·mount′er,** *n.*

sur·name (sûr′nām′; *v. also* sûr nām′), *n., v.,* **-named, -nam·ing.** —*n.* **1.** the name that a person has in common with other family members, as distinguished from a given name; family name. **2.** a name added to a person's name, as one indicating a circumstance of birth or some characteristic or achievement; epithet. —*v.t.* **3.** to give a surname to; call by a surname.

sur·pass (sər pas′, -päs′), *v.t.* **1.** to go beyond in amount, extent, or degree; be greater than; exceed. **2.** to go beyond in excellence or achievement; be superior to; excel. **3.** to be beyond the range or capacity of; transcend: *misery that surpasses description.* —**sur·pass′a·ble,** *adj.* —**sur·pass′er,** *n.*

sur·plice (sûr′plis), *n.* **1.** a loose-fitting, broad-sleeved white vestment worn over a cassock. **2.** a garment in which the two halves of the front cross diagonally. —*adj.* **3.** designating, forming, or having a closure with diagonally crossing halves: *a surplice neckline.* —**sur′pliced,** *adj.*

surplice

sur·plus (sûr′plus, -pləs), *n., adj., v.,* **-plussed** or **-plused, -plus·sing** or **-plus·ing.** —*n.* **1.** something that remains above what is used or needed. **2.** an amount, quantity, etc., greater than needed. **3.** the excess of assets over liabilities, esp. the excess of net worth over capital-stock value. —*adj.* **4.** being a surplus; being in excess of what is required or used: *surplus wheat.* —*v.t.* **5.** to treat as surplus; sell off.

sur•prise (sər prīz′, sə-), *v.,* **-prised, -pris•ing,** *n.* —*v.t.* **1.** to strike with a sudden feeling of wonder or astonishment, esp. by being unexpected. **2.** to come upon or discover suddenly and unexpectedly. **3.** to make an unexpected assault on (an unprepared fort, person, etc.). **4.** to lead or bring unawares into doing something unintended: *to surprise someone into telling the truth.* **5.** to elicit suddenly and without warning. —*n.* **6.** the state of being surprised; a feeling of sudden wonder or astonishment, esp. at something unexpected. **7.** something that surprises; an unexpected event, appearance, or gift. **8.** an act or instance of surprising or taking unawares. **9.** an attack or assault made without warning. —*Idiom.* **10.** take by surprise, **a.** to come upon unawares. **b.** to astonish; amaze. —**sur•pris′ed•ly,** *adv.* —**sur•pris′er,** *n.*

sur•pris•ing (sər prī′zing, sə-), *adj.* causing surprise; unexpected or unusual. —**sur•pris′ing•ly,** *adv.*

sur•re•al (sə rē′əl, -rēl′), *adj.* **1.** SURREALISTIC. **2.** having the disorienting, hallucinatory quality of a dream; unreal; fantastic. —**sur•re′al•ly,** *adv.* —**sur•re•al′i•ty** (-al′i tē), *n.*

sur•re•al•ism (sə rē′ə liz′əm), *n.* (*sometimes cap.*) a style of art and literature developed principally in the 20th century, stressing the subconscious or nonrational significance of imagery arrived at by automatism or the exploitation of chance effects, unexpected juxtapositions, etc. —**sur•re′al•ist,** *n., adj.*

sur•re•al•is•tic (sə rē′ə lis′tik), *adj.* **1.** of, pertaining to, or characteristic of surrealism. **2.** having features typical or reminiscent of those depicted in surrealistic painting or drawing: *the moon's surrealistic landscape.* —**sur•re′al•is′ti•cal•ly,** *adv.*

sur•ren•der (sə ren′dər), *v.t.* **1.** to deliver up or yield (something) to the possession or power of another on demand or under duress: *to surrender the fort to the enemy.* **2.** to give (oneself) up, as to the police. **3.** to give (oneself) up to some influence, course, emotion, etc.: *surrendered himself to despair.* **4.** to give up, abandon, or relinquish (comfort, hope, etc.). **5.** to yield or resign (an office, privilege, etc.) in favor of another. —*v.i.* **6.** to give oneself up, as into the power of another; submit or yield. —*n.* **7.** an act or instance of surrendering.

sur•rep•ti•tious (sûr′əp tish′əs), *adj.* **1.** obtained, done, made, etc., by stealth; clandestine; secret: *a surreptitious glance.* **2.** acting in a stealthy way. —**sur′rep•ti′tious•ly,** *adv.* —**sur′rep•ti′tious•ness,** *n.*

sur•rey (sûr′ē, sur′ē), *n.* a light, four-wheeled, two-seated horse-drawn carriage, with or without a top, for four persons.

surrey

sur•ro•ga•cy (sûr′ə gə sē, sur′-), *n.* the fact or state of being a surrogate.

sur•ro•gate (*n., adj.* sûr′ə gāt′, -git, sur′-; *v.* -gāt′), *n., adj., v.,* **-gat•ed, -gat•ing.** —*n.* **1.** a person appointed to act for another; deputy. **2.** a substitute. **3.** (in some states) a judicial officer having jurisdiction over the probate of wills, the administration of estates, etc. **4.** SURROGATE MOTHER. —*adj.* **5.** pertaining to, acting as, or involving a surrogate. —*v.t.* **6.** to put into the place of another as a successor, substitute, or deputy. —**sur′ro•gate•ship′,** *n.* —**sur′ro•ga′tion,** *n.*

sur′rogate moth′er, *n.* **1.** a person who acts in the place of another person's biological mother. **2. a.** a woman who helps a couple to have a child by carrying to term an embryo conceived by the couple and transferred to her uterus; gestational carrier. **b.** a woman who helps a couple to have a child by being inseminated with the man's sperm and either donating the embryo for transfer to the woman's uterus or carrying it to term.

sur•round (sə round′), *v.t.* **1.** to enclose on all sides; encompass: *surrounded by admirers.* **2.** to form an enclosure round; encircle. **3.** to exist around or accompany; attend: *An aura of mystery surrounds her.* **4.** to enclose so as to cut off communication or retreat. **5.** to cause to be enclosed, encircled, or attended: *surrounding himself with friends.* —*n.* **6.** something that surrounds, as the area, border, etc., around an object or central space. **7.** environment or setting.

sur•round•ing (sə roun′ding), *n.* **1.** something that surrounds. **2.** surroundings, environing things, circumstances, conditions, etc.; environment. —*adj.* **3.** enclosing or encircling. **4.** being the environment or adjacent area.

sur•sum cor•da (soor′soom kôr′dä, kōr′-), the words "Lift up your hearts," addressed by the celebrant of the mass to the congregation just before the preface.

sur•tax (*n., v.* sûr′taks′; *v. also* sûr taks′), *n.* **1.** an additional or extra tax on something already taxed. **2.** one of a graded series of additional

taxes levied on incomes exceeding a certain amount. —*v.t.* **3.** to charge with a surtax.

sur•veil•lance (sər vā′ləns, -vāl′yəns), *n.* **1.** a watch kept over someone or something, esp. over a suspect, prisoner, etc.: *under police surveillance.* **2.** supervision or superintendence.

sur•vey (*v.* sər vā′; *n.* sûr′vā, sər vā′), *v.t.* **1.** to view, consider, or study in a general or comprehensive way: *to survey a situation.* **2.** to view in detail, esp. to inspect, examine, or appraise in order to ascertain condition, value, etc. **3.** to conduct a survey of or among: *to survey TV viewers.* **4.** to determine the exact dimensions and position of (a tract of land) by measurements and the application of geometric and trigonometric principles. —*v.i.* **5.** to survey land; practice surveying. —*n.* **6.** a general or comprehensive view, description, course of study, etc.: *a survey of Italian painting.* **7.** a sampling, or partial collection, of facts, figures, or opinions taken and used to indicate what a complete collection and analysis might reveal. **8.** a detailed formal or official examination, as to ascertain condition, character, etc. **9. a.** the act of surveying a tract of land. **b.** a plan or description resulting from this. **c.** an agency that makes such determinations. —**sur•vey′a•ble,** *adj.*

sur•vey•ing (sər vā′ing), *n.* **1.** the science or scientific method of making surveys of land. **2.** the occupation of one who makes land surveys. **3.** the act of one who surveys.

sur•vey•or (sər vā′ər), *n.* **1.** a person whose occupation is surveying. **2.** an overseer or supervisor. —**sur•vey′or•ship′,** *n.*

sur•viv•al (sər vī′vəl), *n.* **1.** the act or fact of surviving, esp. under adverse or unusual circumstances. **2.** a person or thing that survives or endures, esp. an ancient custom, observance, belief, etc. —*adj.* **3.** of or for use in surviving, esp. under adverse or unusual circumstances: *survival techniques.*

sur•viv•al•ist (sər vī′və list), *n.* a person who makes preparations to survive a widespread catastrophe, as an atomic war, esp. by storing food and weapons in a safe place. —**sur•viv′al•ism,** *n.*

surviv′al of the fit′test, *n.* **1.** (not in technical use) natural selection. **2.** a 19th-century concept of human society, inspired by the principle of natural selection, postulating that those who are eliminated in the struggle for existence are the unfit.

sur•vive (sər vīv′), *v.,* **-vived, -viv•ing.** —*v.i.* **1.** to remain alive, as after the death of another or the occurrence of some event; continue to live. **2.** to remain or continue in existence or use. **3.** to continue to function or manage in spite of some adverse circumstance or hardship; hold up; endure. —*v.t.* **4.** to continue to live or exist after the death, cessation, or occurrence of. **5.** to endure or live through (an affliction, adversity, misery, etc.).

sur•vi•vor (sər vī′vər), *n.* **1.** a person or thing that survives. **2.** *Law.* the one of two or more designated persons, as joint tenants or others having a joint interest, who outlives the other or others.

Su•sa (soo′sə, -sä), *n.* a ruined city in W Iran: the capital of ancient Elam. Biblical name, **Shushan.** —**Su′si•an** (-zē ən), *adj., n.*

Su•san•na (soo zan′ə), *n.* a book of the Apocrypha, constituting the 13th chapter of Daniel in the Douay Bible.

sus•cep•tance (sə sep′təns), *n.* (in electricity) the imaginary component of admittance, equal to the quotient of the negative of the reactance divided by the sum of the squares of the reactance and resistance.

sus•cep•ti•bil•i•ty (sə sep′tə bil′i tē), *n., pl.* **-ties. 1.** the state or character of being susceptible. **2.** capacity for receiving mental or moral impressions; tendency to be emotionally affected. **3.** susceptibilities, capacities for emotion; feelings. **4.** the degree to which a substance can become magnetized, expressed as the ratio of magnetization to the strength of the magnetizing force.

sus•cep•ti•ble (sə sep′tə bəl), *adj.* **1.** admitting or capable of some specified treatment: *susceptible to various interpretations.* **2.** accessible, liable, or subject to some influence, agency, etc.: *susceptible to colds; susceptible to flattery.* **3.** capable of being affected emotionally. —**sus•cep′ti•ble•ness,** *n.* —**sus•cep′ti•bly,** *adv.*

su•shi (soo′shē), *n.* a Japanese dish of bite-sized cakes of cold boiled rice flavored with rice vinegar and rolled in seaweed with or topped with raw fish, vegetables, or egg.

sus•pect (*v.* sə spekt′; *n.* sus′pekt; *adj.* sus′pekt, sə spekt′), *v.t.* **1.** to believe to be guilty, with little or no proof: *to suspect a person of murder.* **2.** to doubt or mistrust: *I suspect his motives.* **3.** to believe to be the case or to be likely or probable; surmise. —*v.i.* **4.** to believe something, esp. something evil or wrong, to be the case; have suspicion. —*n.* **5.** a person who is suspected, esp. one suspected of a crime or offense. —*adj.* **6.** suspected; open to or under suspicion.

sus•pend (sə spend′), *v.t.* **1.** to hang by attachment to something above, esp. so as to allow free movement. **2.** to keep from falling or sinking, as if by hanging: *to suspend particles in a liquid.* **3.** to keep undetermined; refrain from concluding definitely: *to suspend judgment.* **4.** to defer or postpone: *to suspend a sentence for robbery.* **5.** to bring to a stop, usu. for a time: *to suspend payment.* **6.** to cause to cease for a time from operation or effect, as a law, privilege, or service: *to suspend ferry service.* **7.** to debar, usu. for a limited time, from office, membership, school attendance, etc., esp. as a punishment. **8.** to keep in a state of expectation or suspense. —*v.i.* **9.** to come to a stop or cease from operation, usu. temporarily. **10.** to stop payment; be unable to meet financial obligations. **11.** to hang or be suspended. —**sus•pend′i•ble,** *adj.* —**sus•pend′i•bil′i•ty,** *n.*

S

suspend′ed anima′tion, *n.* a state of temporary cessation of the vital functions.

sus•pend•er (sə spen′dər), *n.* **1.** Usu., **suspenders.** Also called, *esp. Brit.,* **braces.** adjustable straps or bands worn over the shoulders with the ends secured to the waistband of a pair of trousers or a skirt to support it. **2.** a person or thing that suspends.

sus•pense (sə spens′), *n.* **1.** a state of mental uncertainty, as in awaiting a decision or outcome, accompanied by anxiety or excitement. **2.** a state of mental indecision. **3.** doubtful condition, as of affairs. **4.** the state or condition of being suspended. —**sus•pense′ful,** *adj.*

sus•pen•sion (sə spen′shən), *n.* **1.** the act of suspending. **2.** the state of being suspended. **3.** temporary abrogation, as of a law or rule. **4.** temporary withholding, as of a decision or belief. **5.** temporary debarring, as from an office, school, or privilege. **6.** stoppage of payment of debts or claims because of financial inability or insolvency. **7. a.** a state in which the particles of a chemical substance are mixed with a fluid but are undissolved. **b.** a substance in such a state. **8.** something on or by which something else is suspended or hung. **9.** something that is suspended or hung. **10.** Also called **suspen′sion sys′tem.** the arrangement of springs, shock absorbers, etc., in a vehicle, connecting the wheel-suspension units or axles to the chassis frame.

suspen′sion bridge′, *n.* a bridge having a deck suspended from cables anchored at their extremities and usu. raised on towers.

sus•pi•cion (sə spish′ən), *n.* **1.** the act of suspecting, esp. something wrong or evil. **2.** the state of mind or feeling of one who suspects; doubt; misgiving. **3.** an instance of suspecting something or someone. **4.** the state of being suspected: *under suspicion; above suspicion.* **5.** imagination of something to be the case or to be likely; notion. **6.** a slight trace, hint, or suggestion: *a suspicion of a smile.* —*v.t.* **7.** *Nonstandard.* to suspect. —**sus•pi′cion•al,** *adj.* —**sus•pi′cion•less,** *adj.*

sus•pi•cious (sə spish′əs), *adj.* **1.** tending to cause or excite suspicion; questionable: *suspicious behavior.* **2.** inclined to suspect, esp. inclined to suspect evil; distrustful. **3.** full of or feeling suspicion. **4.** expressing or indicating suspicion: *a suspicious glance.* —**sus•pi′cious•ly,** *adv.* —**sus•pi′cious•ness,** *n.*

sus•pire (sə spīr′), *v.,* **-pired, -pir•ing.** —*v.i.* **1.** to sigh. **2.** to breathe. —*v.t.* **3.** to utter with sighing breaths. —**sus•pi•ra•tion** (sus′pə rā′shən), *n.*

Sus•que•han•na (sus′kwə han′ə), *n.* a river flowing S from central New York through E Pennsylvania and NE Maryland into Chesapeake Bay. 444 mi. (715 km) long.

sus•tain (sə stān′), *v.t.* **1.** to support, hold, or bear up from below; bear the weight of. **2.** to bear (a burden, charge, etc.). **3.** to undergo or suffer (injury, loss, etc.). **4.** to endure without giving way or yielding. **5.** to keep (a person, the spirits, etc.) from giving way, as under trial or affliction. **6.** to keep up or keep going, as an action or process; maintain: *to sustain a conversation.* **7.** to supply with food, drink, and other necessities of life. **8.** to provide for by furnishing means or funds. **9.** to support by aid or approval. **10.** to uphold as valid, just, or correct: *The judge sustained the lawyer's objection.* **11.** to confirm or corroborate. —**sus•tain′a•ble,** *adj.* —**sus•tain′er,** *n.*

sus•te•nance (sus′tə nəns), *n.* **1.** means of sustaining life; nourishment. **2.** means of livelihood. **3.** the process of sustaining. **4.** the state of being sustained.

Suth•er•land (suth′ər lənd), *n.* **1. Earl Wilbur, Jr.,** 1915–74, U.S. biochemist. **2. Dame Joan,** born 1926, Australian soprano.

su•tra (sōō′trə), *n., pl.* **-tras.** a collection of Hindu aphorisms relating to some aspect of the conduct of life.

Sut•ter (sut′ər), *n.* **John Augustus,** 1803–80, U.S. frontiersman.

Sut′ter's Mill′, *n.* the location of John Sutter's mill in California, NE of Sacramento, near which gold was discovered, precipitating the gold rush of 1849.

Sut′ton Hoo′ (hōō), *n.* an archaeological site in Suffolk, England: a rowing boat, 80 feet (24 m) long, discovered here and believed to have been buried A.D. c670 by Anglo-Saxons, possibly as a cenotaph in honor of a king.

su•ture (sōō′chər), *n., v.,* **-tured, -tur•ing.** —*n.* **1. a.** a joining of the edges of a wound or the like by stitching or some similar process. **b.** one of the stitches or fastenings employed. **2.** the seam where two bones are fused, as at the top of the skull. **3.** the seam where any two parts join, as the halves of a walnut. **4.** a seam formed in sewing; line of junction between two parts. **5.** a sewing together or a joining as if by sewing. —*v.t.* **6.** to unite by a suture. —**su′tur•al,** *adj.*

Su•va (sōō′vä), *n.* the capital of Fiji, on Viti Levu island. 71,608.

su•ze•rain (sōō′zə rin, -rān′), *n.* **1.** a sovereign or a state exercising political control over a dependent state. **2.** a feudal overlord. —*adj.* **3.** characteristic of or being a suzerain.

su•ze•rain•ty (sōō′zə rin tē, -rān′-), *n., pl.* **-ties. 1.** the position or power of a suzerain. **2.** the domain subject to a suzerain.

svc. or **svce.,** service.

svelte (svelt, sfelt), *adj.,* **svelt•er, svelt•est. 1.** slender, esp. gracefully slender in figure; lithe. **2.** suave; urbane. —**svelte′ly,** *adv.* —**svelte′ness,** *n.*

SW or **S.W., 1.** southwest. **2.** southwestern.

Sw or **Sw., 1.** Sweden. **2.** Swedish.

swab or **swob** (swob), *n., v.,* **swabbed, swab•bing.** —*n.* **1.** a large mop used on shipboard for cleaning decks, living quarters, etc. **2.** a bit

of cotton, sponge, or the like, often fixed to a stick, for applying medicaments, cleansing the mouth, etc. **3.** material collected with a swab as a specimen. **4.** a wad of absorbent material for cleaning the bore of a firearm. **5.** *Slang.* a sailor; swabby. **6.** *Slang.* a clumsy oaf. —*v.t.* **7.** to clean with or as if with a swab. **8.** to take up or apply (moisture, etc.) with or as if with a swab.

swab•by (swob′ē), *n., pl.* **-bies.** *Slang.* (in the Navy or Coast Guard) a seaman, esp. a new recruit.

swad•dle (swod′l), *v.,* **-dled, -dling,** *n.* —*v.t.* **1.** to bind (a newborn infant) with swaddling clothes to prevent free movement. **2.** to wrap (anything) round with bandages. —*n.* **3.** a long, narrow strip of cloth used for swaddling.

swad′dling clothes′, *n.pl.* **1.** Also called **swad′dling bands′.** long, narrow strips of cloth formerly used for swaddling an infant. **2.** a period of infancy or immaturity. **3.** rigid supervision, as of the immature.

swag¹ (swag), *n., v.,* **swagged, swag•ging.** —*n.* **1.** a suspended garland, drapery, etc., fastened at each end and hanging down in the middle; festoon. **2.** a wreath or cluster of foliage, flowers, or fruit. **3.** a swale. **4.** a swaying or lurching movement. —*v.i.* **5.** to sway or lurch. **6.** to hang loosely and heavily; sag. —*v.t.* **7.** to cause to sway or sag. **8.** to adorn with swags.

swag² (swag), *n., v.,* **swagged, swag•ging.** —*n.* **1.** *Slang.* **a.** plunder; booty. **b.** money; valuables. **2.** *Australian.* a traveler's bundle containing food and belongings. —*v.i.* **3.** *Australian.* to travel about carrying one's bundle of belongings.

swag•ger (swag′ər), *v.i.* **1.** to strut about with an insolent air. **2.** to boast noisily; bluster. —*v.t.* **3.** to force by blustering; bully. —*n.* **4.** a swaggering manner; ostentatious display of arrogance. —**swag′ger•er,** *n.*

swain (swān), *n.* **1.** a male admirer or lover. **2.** a country lad. —**swain′ish,** *adj.* —**swain′ish•ness,** *n.*

swale (swāl), *n. Chiefly Northeastern U.S.* a low place in a tract of land, usu. producing ranker vegetation than the adjacent higher ground.

swal•low¹ (swol′ō), *v.t.* **1.** to take into the stomach by drawing through the throat and esophagus with a voluntary muscular action. **2.** to take in so as to envelop; assimilate or absorb (often fol. by *up*): *to be swallowed up in a crowd.* **3.** to accept without question or suspicion. **4.** to accept without resentment; put up with. **5.** to suppress (emotion, pride, etc.) as if by drawing it down one's throat. **6.** to take back; retract: *to swallow one's words.* **7.** to enunciate poorly; mutter: *to swallow one's words.* —*v.i.* **8.** to perform the act of swallowing. —*n.* **9.** an act or instance of swallowing. **10.** a quantity swallowed at one time. —**swal′low•a•ble,** *adj.* —**swal′low•er,** *n.*

swal•low² (swol′ō), *n.* **1.** any of numerous small, long-winged, fork-tailed songbirds of the family Hirundinidae, noted for their swift, graceful flight and for the extent and regularity of their migrations. Compare BARN SWALLOW, MARTIN. **2.** any of several unrelated, swallowlike birds, as the chimney swift. —*Proverb.* **3. One swallow does not make a summer,** a single fact is not enough with which to reach a conclusion.

swal•low•tail (swol′ō tāl′), *n.* **1.** the tail of a swallow or a deeply forked tail like that of a swallow. **2.** any of several butterflies of the genus *Papilio,* characterized by elongated hind wings. **3.** TAIL COAT.

swal′low-tailed′ coat′, *n.* TAIL COAT.

swam (swam), *v.* pt. of SWIM.

swa•mi (swä′mē), *n., pl.* **-mis. 1.** an honorific title given to a Hindu religious teacher. **2.** a person resembling a swami, esp. in authority or judgment. [< Sanskrit, < *svāmin* master]

swamp (swomp), *n.* **1.** a tract of wet, spongy land, usu. with abundant vegetation. —*v.t.* **2.** to flood or drench, esp. with water. **3.** to sink or fill (a boat) with water. **4.** to overwhelm, esp. to overwhelm with an excess of something: *swamped with work.* **5.** to clear underbrush from, esp. to make a trail. —*v.i.* **6.** to fill with water and sink, as a boat. —**swamp′ish,** *adj.*

swamp′ fe′ver, *n.* MALARIA.

swamp′ gas′, *n.* MARSH GAS.

swamp•land (swomp′land′), *n.* land or an area covered with swamps.

swan (swon), *n.* **1.** any of several large, stately aquatic birds of the goose family, having a long, slender neck and usu. pure-white plumage in the adult. **2.** a person of unusual beauty, talent, or excellence. **3.** (*cap.*) the constellation Cygnus. —**swan′like′,** *adj.*

swank (swangk), *n.* **1.** dashing smartness, as in dress or appearance; style. **2.** pretentiousness; swagger. —*adj.* **3.** stylish or elegant. **4.** pretentiously stylish. —*v.i.* **5.** to swagger; show off.

swank•y (swang′kē), *adj.,* **swank•i•er, swank•i•est.** elegant or stylish; swank. —**swank′i•ly,** *adv.* —**swank′i•ness,** *n.*

swan′ song′, *n.* a final act or farewell appearance.

swap (swop), *v.,* **swapped, swap•ping.** —*v.t.* **1.** to trade or barter, as one thing for another. —*v.i.* **2.** to make an exchange. —*n.* **3.** an exchange: *He got the radio in a swap.* —**swap′per,** *n.*

sward (swôrd), *n.* **1.** the grassy surface of land; turf. **2.** a stretch of turf; a growth of grass.

swarm¹ (swôrm), *n.* **1.** a body of honeybees that emigrate from a hive and fly off together, accompanied by a queen, to start a new colony. **2.** a body of bees settled together, as in a hive. **3.** a great number of things or persons moving together. **4.** an aggregation of free-floating or free-swimming cells or organisms. **5.** a cluster of similar geologic phenomena or features, as a series of earthquakes of nearly equal intensity.

—*v.i.* **6.** to fly off together in a swarm, as bees. **7.** to move about or along in great numbers. **8.** to congregate or occur in large groups or multitudes. **9.** (of a place) to abound or teem: *a beach swarming with children.* —*v.t.* **10.** to swarm over or in; overrun. —**swarm′er,** *n.*

swarm² (swôrm), *v.t., v.i.* to climb by clasping with the legs and drawing oneself up with the hands; shin.

swarth•y (swôr′thē, -thē), *adj.,* **swarth•i•er, swarth•i•est.** (of skin color, complexion, etc.) dark or darkish. —**swarth′i•ness,** *n.*

swash (swosh, swôsh), *v.i.* **1.** to splash, as things in water, or as water does. **2.** to dash around, as things in violent motion. **3.** to swagger. —*v.t.* **4.** to dash (water or other liquid) around, down, etc. —*n.* **5.** the surging or dashing of water, waves, etc. **6.** a swagger.

swash•buck•ler (swosh′buk′lər, swôsh′-), *n.* a swaggering swordsman, soldier, or adventurer. Also called **swash′er.**

swas•ti•ka (swos′ti kə), *n.* **1.** a symbolic or ornamental figure of ancient origin, consisting of a cross with arms of equal length, each arm having a continuation at right angles in a uniformly clockwise or counterclockwise direction. **2.** this figure as the emblem of the Nazi Party and the Third Reich. —**swas′ti•kaed,** *adj.*

swat (swot), *v.,* **swat•ted, swat•ting,** *n.* —*v.t.* **1.** to hit sharply; slap; smack: *to swat a fly.* —*n.* **2.** a smart blow; slap; smack.

SWAT or **S.W.A.T.** (*as initials or* swot), *n.* a special section of some law enforcement agencies trained and equipped to deal with esp. dangerous or violent situations, as when hostages are being held (often used attributively): *a SWAT team.*

swatch (swoch), *n.* **1.** a sample of cloth or other material. **2.** a sample, patch, or characteristic specimen of anything.

swath (swoth, swôth) also **swathe,** *n.* **1.** the space covered by the stroke of a scythe or the cut of a mowing machine. **2.** the piece or strip so cut. **3.** a line or ridge of grass, grain, or the like, cut and thrown together by a scythe or mowing machine. **4.** a strip, belt, or long and relatively narrow extent of anything. —***Idiom.*** **5. cut a (wide) swath,** to make a conspicuous or striking impression.

swathe (swoth, swāth), *v.,* **swathed, swath•ing,** *n.* —*v.t.* **1.** to wrap, bind, or swaddle with bands of some material. **2.** to bandage. **3.** to enfold or envelop, as wrappings do. —*n.* **4.** a wrapping or bandage.

swat•ter (swot′ər), *n.* a person or thing that swats.

sway (swā), *v.i.* **1.** to move or swing to and fro, as something fastened at one end. **2.** to move or incline to one side. **3.** to incline in opinion, sympathy, etc. **4.** to fluctuate or vacillate, as in opinion. **5.** to wield power; exercise rule. —*v.t.* **6.** to cause to move to and fro. **7.** to cause to move to one side. **8.** *Naut.* to hoist or raise (a yard, topmast, or the like) (usu. fol. by *up*). **9.** to cause to fluctuate or vacillate. **10.** to influence (the mind, emotions, etc., or a person). **11.** to cause to swerve, as from a purpose or a course of action. **12.** to dominate; rule or govern. —*n.* **13.** the act of swaying; swaying movement. **14.** dominating power or influence. **15.** rule; dominion. —**sway′a•ble,** *adj.* —**sway′er,** *n.*

sway•back (swā′bak′), *n.* an excessive downward curvature of the spinal column in the dorsal region, esp. of horses. —**sway′backed′,** *adj.*

Swa•zi•land (swä′zē land′), *n.* a kingdom in SE Africa between Mozambique and the Republic of South Africa: formerly a British protectorate. 1,031,600; 6704 sq. mi. (17,363 sq. km). *Cap.:* Mbabane.

swear (swâr), *v.,* **swore, sworn, swear•ing.** —*v.i.* **1.** to make a solemn declaration or affirmation by some sacred being or object, as a deity or the Bible. **2.** to bind oneself by oath; vow. **3.** to give evidence or make a statement on oath. **4.** to use profane oaths or language. —*v.t.* **5.** to declare, affirm, etc., by swearing by a deity or a sacred object. **6.** to testify or state on oath. **7.** to affirm, assert, or say with solemn earnestness. **8.** to promise on oath; vow. **9.** to take (an oath). **10.** to bind by an oath: *swore them to secrecy.* **11. swear by, a.** to name (a sacred being or object) as one's witness or guarantee in swearing. **b.** to have great confidence in. **12. swear in,** to admit to office or service by administering an oath. **13. swear off,** to promise to give up (something, esp. intoxicating beverages). **14. swear out,** to secure (a warrant for arrest) by making an accusation under oath. —**swear′er,** *n.*

swear′ing-in′, *n.* an official ceremony in which a person takes an oath of office, allegiance, etc.

swear•word (swâr′wûrd′), *n.* a word used in swearing or cursing; a profane or obscene word.

sweat (swet), *v.,* **sweat** or **sweat•ed, sweat•ing,** *n.* —*v.i.* **1.** to perspire, esp. freely. **2.** to exude moisture, as green plants. **3.** to gather moisture from the surrounding air by condensation. **4.** (of moisture or liquid) to ooze or be exuded. **5.** *Informal.* **a.** to work hard. **b.** to be anxious or distressed. —*v.t.* **6.** to excrete (moisture) through the pores of the skin. **7.** to exude in drops or small particles. **8.** to wet or stain with perspiration. **9.** to cause (a person, a horse, etc.) to perspire. **10.** to earn or obtain by hard work. **11.** to force (a person, an animal, etc.) to work hard; overwork. **12. a.** to heat (an alloy) in order to remove a constituent that melts at a lower temperature than the alloy as a whole. **b.** to heat (solder or the like) to melting. **c.** to join (metal objects) by heating and pressing together, usu. with solder. **13. sweat off,** to get rid of (weight) by or as if by sweating. **14. sweat out,** *Informal.* **a.** to await anxiously the outcome of. **b.** to work arduously at. —*n.* **15.** that which is secreted from sweat glands; perspiration. **16.** a state or a period of sweating. **17.** hard work. **18.** *Informal.* a state of anxiety or impatience. **19.** moisture exuded from something or gathered on a surface. **20.** an exuding of moisture, as by a substance. **21.** a run given to a horse for exercise, as before a race. **22. sweats,** sweatpants, sweatshirts, sweat suits, or the like. —***Idiom.*** **23. sweat blood,** *Informal.* **a.** to be under a strain; work strenuously. **b.** to wait anxiously; worry. **24. sweat it,** *Informal.* to wait anxiously; worry.

sweat•band (swet′band′), *n.* **1.** a band lining the inside of a hat or cap to protect it against sweat from the head. **2.** a band of fabric worn, as around the head, to absorb sweat.

sweat•box (swet′boks′), *n.* **1.** a sauna or other enclosure for sweating. **2.** any uncomfortably warm room or place. **3.** a box or cell, exposed to the sun, in which a prisoner is confined as punishment.

sweat′ eq′uity, *n.* unreimbursed labor that increases the value of a property or is invested to establish a business or other enterprise.

sweat•er (swet′ər), *n.* **1.** a knitted jacket or jersey, in pullover or cardigan style, with or without sleeves. **2.** a person or thing that sweats. **3.** an employer who underpays and overworks employees. —*adj.* **4.** of, for, or pertaining to a sweater: *sweater yarn; sweater fashions.* **5.** made like a sweater: *a sweater dress.*

sweat′ gland′, *n.* one of the minute, coiled, tubular glands of the skin that secrete sweat.

sweat′pants′ or **sweat′ pants′,** *n.* (*used with a pl. v.*) loose-fitting pants of soft, absorbent fabric, as cotton jersey, commonly worn during athletic activity for warmth or to induce sweating.

sweat•shirt (swet′shûrt′), *n.* a loose, long-sleeved, collarless pullover of soft, absorbent fabric, commonly worn during athletic activity for warmth or to induce sweating.

sweat•shop (swet′shop′), *n.* a shop employing workers at low wages, for long hours, and under poor conditions.

sweat′ suit′, *n.* an outfit consisting of sweatpants and a sweatshirt or matching jacket.

sweat•y (swet′ē), *adj.,* **sweat•i•er, sweat•i•est. 1.** covered, moist, or stained with sweat. **2.** causing sweat. —**sweat′i•ly,** *adv.* —**sweat′i•ness,** *n.*

Swe•den (swēd′n), *n.* a kingdom in N Europe, in the E part of the Scandinavian Peninsula. 8,946,193; 173,732 sq. mi. (449,964 sq. km). *Cap.:* Stockholm. Swedish, **Sverige.**

Swe•den•borg (swēd′n bôrg′), *n.* **Emanuel** (*Emanuel Swedberg*), 1688–1772, Swedish scientist, philosopher, and mystic.

Swe•den•bor•gi•an (swēd′n bôr′jē ən, -gē-), *adj.* **1.** of or pertaining to Emanuel Swedenborg, his religious doctrines, or the body of followers adhering to these doctrines and constituting the New Jerusalem Church. —*n.* **2.** a believer in the religious doctrines of Swedenborg. —**Swe′den•bor′gi•an•ism, Swe′den•borg′ism,** *n.*

Swed•ish (swē′dish), *adj.* **1.** of or pertaining to Sweden, the Swedes, or the language Swedish. —*n.* **2.** the North Germanic language of the Swedes, spoken also in parts of Finland. *Abbr.:* Sw

Swed′ish massage′, *n.* a massage employing techniques systematized in Sweden in the 19th century.

sweep¹ (swēp), *v.,* **swept, sweep•ing,** *n.* —*v.t.* **1.** to remove (dust, dirt, etc.) with a broom, brush, or the like. **2.** to clear (a floor, room, chimney, etc.) of dirt, litter, or the like, using a broom or brush. **3.** to drive or carry by some steady force, as of a wind or wave. **4.** to pass or draw over a surface with a continuous stroke or movement: *The painter swept a brush over his canvas.* **5.** to make (a path, opening, etc.) with or as if with a broom. **6.** to clear (a surface, place, etc.) (often fol. by *of*): *to sweep the sea of enemy ships.* **7.** (of winds, a flood, etc.) to pass over (a surface, region, etc.) with a steady, driving movement. **8.** to search (an area or building) thoroughly. **9.** to direct a gaze, the eyes, etc., over (a region, area, etc.). **10.** to win decisively in (a contest or series of contests). —*v.i.* **11.** to sweep a floor, room, etc., with or as if with a broom. **12.** to move swiftly and forcefully (usu. fol. by *along, into,* etc.). **13.** to move or extend in a wide curve or circuit: *His glance swept around the room.* **14.** to conduct an underwater search by towing a drag under the surface of the water. —*n.* **15.** the act of sweeping with or as if with a broom. **16.** the steady, driving motion of something: *the sweep of the wind.* **17.** a swinging or curving movement or stroke, as of the arm or an oar. **18.** a continuous extent or stretch. **19.** a large oar used in small vessels. **20.** an overwhelming victory in a contest. **21.** a winning of all the games, prizes, etc., in a contest by one contestant. **22.** END RUN (def. 1). **23.** CHIMNEY SWEEP.

sweep² (swēp), *n.* SWEEPS (def. 1).

sweep′ hand′, *n.* a hand, usu. a second hand, centrally mounted with the minute and hour hands of a timepiece and reaching to the edge of the dial.

sweep•ing (swē′ping), *adj.* **1.** of wide range or scope. **2.** moving or passing over a wide area: *a sweeping glance.* **3.** moving or driving steadily and forcibly on. **4.** (of the outcome of a contest) decisive; overwhelming: *a sweeping victory.* —*n.* **5.** the act of a person or thing that sweeps. **6. sweepings,** matter swept out or up, as dust or refuse. —**sweep′ing•ly,** *adv.*

sweeps (swēps), *n.* (*used with a sing. or pl. v.*) **1.** a sweepstakes. **2.** a period when the audience level for television or radio shows is determined in order to set advertising rates.

sweep•stakes (swēp′stāks′) also **sweep′stake′,** *n.* (*used with a sing. or pl. v.*) **1.** a race or other contest for which the prize consists of the stakes contributed by the various competitors. **2.** the prize itself. **3.** a lottery in which winning tickets are selected at random, and the amounts paid the winners being determined by the finishing order of the horses that run.

sweet (swēt), *adj.* **1.** having the taste or flavor of sugar, honey, or the like. **2.** producing the one of the four basic taste sensations that is not bitter, sour, or salt. **3.** not rancid or stale; fresh. **4.** not salt or salted: *sweet butter.* **5.** pleasing to the ear; making an agreeable sound. **6.** fragrant; perfumed. **7.** pleasing or agreeable; delightful. **8.** amiable; kind or gracious, as a person or action. **9.** dear; beloved. **10.** easily managed; done or effected without effort. **11.** (of wine) not dry; containing unfermented, natural sugar. **12.** free from acidity or sourness, as soil. **13.** *Chem.* **a.** devoid of corrosive or acidic substances. **b.** (of fuel oil or gas) containing no sulfur compounds. **14.** performed with an emphasis on warm tone and clearly outlined melody: *sweet jazz.* **15.** in a sweet manner; sweetly. —*n.* **16.** a sweet flavor, smell, or sound; sweetness. **17.** something that is sweet or causes or gives a sweet flavor, smell, or sound. **18.** **sweets,** very sweet foods, as pie, cake, or candy. **19.** *Brit.* **a.** a piece of candy. **b.** a sweet dish or dessert. **20.** a beloved person. **21.** (in direct address) darling; sweetheart. —**Idiom.** **22.** **sweet on,** *Informal.* infatuated with; in love with. —**sweet′ly,** *adv.* —**sweet′ness,** *n.*

sweet′ alys′sum, *n.* a garden plant, *Lobularia maritima,* of the mustard family, having narrow leaves and small, white or violet flowers.

sweet′-and-sour′, *adj.* cooked with sugar and vinegar or lemon juice and often other seasonings.

sweet′ bas′il, *n.* See under BASIL.

sweet′ bay′, *n.* **1.** LAUREL (def. 1). **2.** a North American magnolia, *Magnolia virginiana,* of the Atlantic coast, having large, fragrant, white flowers.

sweet·bread (swēt′bred′), *n.* the thymus or, sometimes, the pancreas of a young animal, esp. a calf or lamb, used for food.

sweet·bri·er or **sweet·bri·ar** (swēt′brī′ər), *n.* a Eurasian rose, *Rosa eglanteria,* naturalized in the U.S., having a tall stem with stout, hooked prickles and single, pink flowers. Also called **eglantine.**

Sweet′ By′ and By′, a Christian hymn (1868) with words by Sanford F. Bennett and music by Joseph P. Webster: often sung at funerals.

sweet′ cher′ry, *n.* **1.** an Old World cherry tree, *Prunus avium,* the ancestor of many cultivated varieties. **2.** the red, purplish black, or yellow, edible, sweet fruit of this tree.

sweet′ ci′der, *n.* See under CIDER.

sweet′ corn′, *n.* **1.** any of several varieties of corn, esp. *Zea mays rugosa,* the grain or kernels of which are sweet and suitable for eating. **2.** the young and tender ears of such corn.

sweet·en (swēt′n), *v.t.* **1.** to make sweet, as by adding sugar. **2.** to make mild or kind; soften. **3.** to make (the breath, room air, etc.) sweet or fresh, as with a mouthwash or spray. **4.** to make (the stomach, soil, etc.) less acidic, as by means of certain preparations or chemicals. **5.** to remove sulfur and its compounds from (oil or gas). **6.** *Informal.* **a.** to enhance the value of (loan collateral) by including additional or esp. valuable securities. **b.** to add to the value or attractiveness of (a proposition, holding, etc.). **7.** to add stakes to (a pot) before opening in a game of poker. —*v.i.* **8.** to become sweet or sweeter.

sweet·en·er (swēt′n ər), *n.* something that sweetens, as sugar or a low-calorie sugar substitute.

sweet·en·ing (swēt′n ing, swēt′ning), *n.* something that sweetens.

sweet′ gale′, *n.* an aromatic marsh shrub, *Myrica gale,* of the bayberry family, with lance-shaped leaves.

sweet′ gum′, *n.* **1.** a tall, aromatic tree, *Liquidambar styraciflua,* of the witch hazel family, native to the eastern U.S., with star-shaped leaves and fruits in rounded, burlike clusters. **2.** the hard reddish brown wood of this tree, used for making furniture. **3.** the amber balsam exuded by this tree, used in perfumes and medicines.

sweet·heart (swēt′härt′), *n.* **1.** either of a pair of lovers in relation to the other. **2.** (*sometimes cap.*) an affectionate or familiar term of address (sometimes offensive when used to strangers, subordinates, etc.). **3.** *Informal.* a generous, friendly person. **4.** *Informal.* anything that arouses loyal affection.

sweet′heart con′tract, *n.* a contract made through collusion between management and labor representatives having terms detrimental to union workers. Also called **sweet′heart agree′ment.**

Sweet′ Hour′ of Prayer′, a Christian hymn (1842) with words by William Walford and music by William B. Bradbury.

sweet·ie (swē′tē), *n.* **1.** Also, **sweet′ie pie′.** *Informal.* sweetheart; dear. **2.** *Usu.* **sweeties.** *Brit.* candy; sweets.

sweet·ish (swē′tish), *adj.* somewhat sweet. [1570–80]

sweet′ mar′joram, *n.* See under MARJORAM.

sweet·meat (swēt′mēt′), *n.* **1.** (formerly) a sweetened cake or pastry. **2.** any confection or candy, as a bonbon, sugarplum, or candied fruit.

sweet′ness and light′, *n.* **1.** extreme or excessive pleasantness or amiability. **2.** decorous charm combined with intelligence.

sweet′ pea′, *n.* a climbing plant, *Lathyrus odoratus,* of the legume family, having sweet-scented flowers.

sweet′ pep′per, *n.* **1.** a variety of pepper, *Capsicum annuum grossum,* having a mild-flavored, bell-shaped or somewhat oblong fruit. **2.** the fruit itself, used as a vegetable. Also called **bell pepper.**

sweet′ pota′to, *n.* **1.** a Central American trailing vine, *Ipomoea batatas,* of the morning glory family, grown widely for its sweet tuberous roots. **2.** the root itself, used as a vegetable. Compare YAM (def. 1). **3.** OCARINA.

sweet′ roll′, *n.* a roll made of sweet dough, often containing spices, raisins, nuts, candied fruit, etc., and sometimes iced on top.

sweet·sop (swēt′sop′), *n.* **1.** a sweet, pulpy fruit having a thin, tuberculate rind, borne by a tropical American tree or shrub, *Annona squamosa,* of the annona family. **2.** the tree or shrub. Also called **sugar apple.**

sweet′ sor′ghum, *n.* SORGO.

sweet′ talk′, *n. Informal.* cajolery; flattery.

sweet′-talk′, *Informal.* —*v.t.* **1.** to use cajoling words on in order to persuade; flatter. —*v.i.* **2.** to use cajoling words.

sweet′ tooth′, *n.* a liking or craving for sweets.

sweet′ wil′liam (or **Wil′liam**), *n.* a pink, *Dianthus barbatus,* having clusters of small, variously colored flowers.

swell (swel), *v.,* **swelled, swol·len** or **swelled, swell·ing,** *n., adj.* —*v.i.* **1.** to enlarge in bulk, as by growth, absorption of fluid, or engorgement. **2.** (of a body part or area) to enlarge abnormally without growth of tissue. **3.** to rise in waves, as the sea. **4.** to well up, as a spring or as tears. **5.** to bulge out, as a sail. **6.** to grow in amount, degree, force, etc. **7.** to increase gradually in volume or intensity, as sound. **8.** to arise and grow within one, as a feeling or emotion. **9.** to become puffed up with pride. —*v.t.* **10.** to cause to grow in bulk. **11.** to cause to increase gradually in loudness: *to swell a musical tone.* **12.** to cause to bulge out or be protuberant. **13.** to increase in amount, degree, force, etc. **14.** to affect with a strong, expansive emotion. **15.** to puff up with pride. —*n.* **16.** the act of swelling or the condition of being swollen. **17.** inflation or distention. **18.** a protuberant part. **19.** a wave, esp. when long and unbroken, or a series of such waves. **20.** a gradually rising elevation of the land. **21.** an increase in amount, degree, force, etc. **22.** a gradual increase in loudness of sound. **23. a.** a gradual increase and then decrease in musical volume. **b.** the sign (< >) for indicating this. **c.** a device, as in an organ, by which the loudness of tones may be varied. **24.** a swelling of emotion within one. **25.** *Informal.* **a.** a fashionably dressed person; dandy. **b.** a socially prominent person. —*adj. Informal.* **26.** (of things) stylish; elegant. **27.** (of persons) fashionably dressed or socially prominent. **28.** first-rate; fine.

swelled′ head′, *n.* an inordinately grand opinion of oneself; conceit.

swell·ing (swel′ing), *n.* **1.** the act of a person or thing that swells. **2.** a swollen part. **3.** an abnormal enlargement or protuberance, as that resulting from edema.

swel·ter (swel′tar), *v.i.* **1.** to suffer from oppressive heat. —*v.t.* **2.** to oppress with heat. —*n.* **3.** a sweltering condition.

swel·ter·ing (swel′tar ing), *adj.* **1.** suffering from oppressive heat. **2.** characterized by oppressive heat. —**swel′ter·ing·ly,** *adv.*

swept (swept), *v.* pt. and pp. of SWEEP[1].

swept·back (swept′bak′), *adj.* **1.** (of the leading edge of an airfoil) forming a markedly obtuse angle with the fuselage. **2.** (of an aircraft or winged missile) having wings of this type.

swept·wing (swept′wing′), *adj.* (of an aircraft or winged missile) having sweptback wings.

swerve (swûrv), *v.,* **swerved, swerv·ing,** *n.* —*v.i.* **1.** to turn aside abruptly in movement or direction; deviate suddenly from the straight or direct course. —*v.t.* **2.** to cause to turn aside. —*n.* **3.** the act of swerving.

swift (swift), *adj.* **-er, -est,** *adv., n.* —*adj.* **1.** moving or capable of moving with great speed or velocity: *a swift boat.* **2.** coming, happening, or performed quickly or without delay: *a swift decision.* **3.** quick to act or respond. **4.** *Slang.* smart; clever. —*adv.* **5.** in a swift manner. —*n.* **6.** any of numerous long-winged, swallowlike birds of the family Apodidae, related to the hummingbirds and noted for their rapid flight. —**swift′ly,** *adv.* —**swift′ness,** *n.*

Swift (swift), *n.* **Jonathan,** 1667–1745, English satirist and clergyman, born in Ireland.

swift′-foot′ed, *adj.* swift in running.

swig (swig), *n., v.,* **swigged, swig·ging.** *Informal.* —*n.* **1.** an amount of liquid, esp. liquor, taken in one swallow. —*v.t., v.i.* **2.** to drink heartily or greedily. —**swig′ger,** *n.*

swill (swil), *n.* **1.** liquid or partly liquid food for animals, esp. kitchen refuse given to swine. **2.** kitchen refuse; garbage. **3.** any liquid mess or refuse; slop. **4.** a deep draught of liquor. —*v.i.* **5.** to drink greedily or excessively. —*v.t.* **6.** to drink greedily or to excess. **7.** to feed (animals) with swill.

swim (swim), *v.,* **swam, swum, swim·ming,** *n.* —*v.i.* **1.** to move in water by using the limbs, fins, tail, etc. **2.** to float on the surface of water or some other liquid. **3.** to move, rest, or be suspended in air as if swimming in water. **4.** to move, glide, or go smoothly over a surface. **5.** to be flooded with a liquid: *eyes swimming with tears.* **6.** to be dizzy; seem to whirl: *My head began to swim.* —*v.t.* **7.** to move along in or cross (a body of water) by swimming. **8.** to perform (a particular stroke) in swimming. **9.** to cause to swim or float. —*n.* **10.** an act, instance, or period of swimming. —**Idiom.** **11. in the swim,** alert to or actively engaged in current affairs, social activities, etc. —**swim′ma·ble,** *adj.* —**swim′mer,** *n.*

swim′ blad′der, *n.* AIR BLADDER (def. 2).

swim·mer·et (swim′ə ret′), *n.* (in certain crustaceans) any of the small paired paddlelike abdominal appendages used for swimming and carrying eggs.

swim·ming (swim′ing), *n.* **1.** the act of a person or thing that swims. **2.** the skill or technique of a person who swims. **3.** a sport based on the ability to swim. —*adj.* **4.** capable of swimming. **5.** used in or for swimming. **6.** immersed in or overflowing with water or some other liquid. **7.** dizzy or giddy.

swim′ming hole′, *n.* a place, as in a stream, where there is water deep enough for swimming.

swim•ming•ly (swim′ing lē), *adv.* without difficulty; with great success.

swim′ming pool′, *n.* a tank or large artificial basin, as of concrete, for filling with water for swimming.

swim•suit (swim′so͞ot′), *n.* BATHING SUIT.

swim•wear (swim′wâr′), *n.* clothing designed to be worn for swimming or at a beach.

swin•dle (swin′dl), *v.,* **-dled, -dling,** *n.* —*v.t.* **1.** to cheat out of money or other assets. **2.** to obtain by fraud or deceit. —*v.i.* **3.** to defraud others; cheat. —*n.* **4.** the act of swindling or a fraudulent transaction or scheme. **5.** anything deceptive; a fraud. —**swin′dler,** *n.*

swine (swīn), *n., pl.* **swine. 1.** any stout artiodactyl mammal of the Old World family Suidae, having a disklike snout and a thick hide usu. sparsely covered with coarse hair. Compare HOG, PIG, WILD BOAR. **2.** the domestic hog, *Sus scrofa.* **3.** a coarse, gross, or brutishly sensual person. **4.** a contemptible person.

swine′ fe′ver, *n.* HOG CHOLERA.

swing (swing), *v.,* **swung, swing•ing,** *n., adj.* —*v.t.* **1.** to cause to move to and fro or oscillate, as something suspended from above. **2.** to cause to move or turn in alternate directions or in either direction on a fixed point or axis, as a door on hinges. **3.** to move (the hand or something held) with an oscillating or rotary movement. **4.** to cause to move in a curve: *I swung the car into the driveway.* **5.** to suspend so as to hang freely, as a hammock. **6.** *Informal.* to sway, influence, or manage as desired: *to swing a business deal.* **7.** to change or shift (one's interest, opinion, support, etc.). **8.** to play (a piece of music) in the style of swing. **9.** to pull or turn (the propeller of an aircraft) by hand, esp. in order to start the engine. —*v.i.* **10.** to move or sway to and fro, as a pendulum or other suspended object. **11.** to move to and fro in a swing. **12.** to move or turn in alternate directions or in either direction on a fixed point or axis. **13.** to move in a curve, as around a corner. **14.** to move with a free, swaying motion. **15.** to be suspended so as to hang freely, as a hammock. **16.** to move by grasping a support with the hands and drawing up the arms. **17.** to change or shift one's attention, interest, opinion, etc. **18.** to hit at with the hand or something grasped in the hand. **19.** *Slang.* to be lively, fashionable, or trendy. **20.** *Informal.* to die by hanging. —*n.* **21.** the act or manner of swinging. **22.** the amount or extent of such movement. **23.** a curving movement or course. **24.** a moving of the body with a free, swaying motion. **25.** a blow or stroke with the hand or an object grasped in the hands. **26.** a change or shift in attitude, opinion, behavior, etc. **27.** a steady, marked rhythm or movement, as of verse. **28.** a regular upward or downward movement in the price of a security or in any business activity. **29.** freedom of action. **30.** active operation; progression: *to get into the swing of things.* **31.** something that is swung or that swings. **32.** a seat suspended from above by means of a loop of rope or between ropes or rods, on which one may sit and swing to and fro for recreation. **33.** a style of jazz often played by a large dance band and marked by a smooth beat and flowing phrasing. —*adj.* **34.** capable of determining the outcome, as of an election: *the swing vote.* —***Idiom.* 35. in full swing,** operating at normal capacity; in full operation.

swing′ by′, *n.* a trajectory that uses the gravitational field of one celestial body to alter the course of a spacecraft destined for another body.

swing•er (swing′ər), *n.* **1.** a person or thing that swings. **2.** *Slang.* a lively, fashionable, or trendy person.

swing′ing door′, *n.* a door that swings open on being pushed or pulled from either side and then swings closed by itself.

swing′ loan′, *n.* BRIDGE LOAN.

Swing′ Low′, Sweet′ Char′iot, a traditional American spiritual.

swing•man (swing′man′), *n., pl.* **-men.** a basketball player who can play either of two positions, usu. guard and forward.

swing′ shift′, *n.* **1.** a work shift in industry from midafternoon until midnight. **2.** the group of workers on such a shift.

swin•ish (swī′nish), *adj.* **1.** like or befitting swine; hoggish. **2.** brutishly coarse, gross, or sensual. —**swin′ish•ly,** *adv.* —**swin′ish•ness,** *n.*

swipe (swīp), *n., v.,* **swiped, swip•ing.** —*n.* **1.** a strong, sweeping blow, as with a golf club. **2.** a sideswipe. **3.** *Informal.* a critical or cutting remark. **4.** a person who rubs down horses in a stable; groom. —*v.t.* **5.** to strike with a sweeping blow. **6.** to slide (a magnetic card) quickly through an electronic device that reads data. **7.** *Informal.* to steal. —*v.i.* **8.** to make a sweeping blow or stroke.

swirl (swûrl), *v.i.* **1.** to move around or along with a whirling motion; whirl; eddy. **2.** to be dizzy or giddy, as the head. —*v.t.* **3.** to cause to whirl; twist. —*n.* **4.** a swirling movement; whirl; eddy. **5.** a twist, as of hair around the head. **6.** any curving, twisting line, shape, or form. **7.** confusion; disorder. —**swirl′ing•ly,** *adv.* —**swirl′y,** *adj.,* **swirl•i•er, swirl•i•est.**

swish (swish), *v.i.* **1.** to move with or make a sibilant sound, as a slender rod cutting sharply through the air. **2.** to rustle, as silk. —*v.t.* **3.** to flourish, whisk, etc., with a swishing movement or sound. **4.** to bring, take, cut, etc., with such a movement or sound. **5.** to flog or whip. —*n.* **6.** a swishing movement or sound. **7.** a stick or rod for flogging, or a stroke with this.

swish•y (swish′ē), *adj.,* **swish•i•er, swish•i•est.** causing, giving rise to, or characterized by a swishing sound or motion.

Swiss (swis), *n., pl.* **Swiss,** *adj.* —*n.* **1.** a native or inhabitant of Switzerland. **2.** (*sometimes l.c.*) SWISS MUSLIN. **3.** SWISS CHEESE. —*adj.* **4.** of or pertaining to Switzerland or its inhabitants.

Swiss′ cheese′, *n.* a firm, pale yellow cheese typically made from cow's milk and having many holes.

Swiss′ Fam′ily Rob′inson, a children's novel (1813) by Johann David Wyss.

Swiss′ mus′lin, *n.* a crisp, sheer muslin often woven or printed with raised dots or figures **(dotted swiss),** used esp. for curtains and summer clothing.

Swiss′ steak′, *n.* steak that is floured and pounded, then browned and braised with tomatoes, onions, etc.

switch (swich), *n.* **1.** a slender, flexible shoot, rod, etc., used esp. in whipping or disciplining. **2.** the act of whipping or beating with or as if with such an object; a stroke, lash, or whisking movement. **3.** a tress of long hair or some substitute, worn by women to supplement their own hair. **4.** a device for turning on or off or directing an electric current or for making or breaking a circuit. **5.** a track structure for diverting moving trains or rolling stock from one track to another. **6.** a turning, shifting, or changing. **7.** a tuft of hair at the end of the tail of some animals. —*v.t.* **8.** to whip or beat with a switch or the like. **9.** to move, swing, or whisk (a cane, a fishing line, etc.) with a swift, lashing stroke. **10.** to change or exchange. **11.** to turn, shift, or divert: *to switch the subject.* **12.** to connect, disconnect, or redirect (an electric circuit or the device it serves) by operating a switch (often fol. by *off* or *on*). **13. a.** to move or transfer (a train, car, etc.) from one set of tracks to another. **b.** to drop or add (cars) or to make up (a train). —*v.i.* **14.** to strike with or as if with a switch. **15.** to change, as direction or course; turn or shift: *to switch to another road.* **16.** to exchange or replace something with another. **17.** to move back and forth briskly, as a cat's tail. **18.** to be shifted, turned, etc., by means of a switch. —**switch′er,** *n.*

switch•back (swich′bak′), *n., v.,* **-backed, -back•ing.** —*n.* **1.** a highway, as in a mountainous area, having many hairpin curves. **2.** a zigzag railroad track arrangement for climbing a steep grade. —*v.i.* **3.** (of a road, railroad track, etc.) to progress through a series of hairpin curves; zigzag.

switch•blade (swich′blād′), *n.* a pocketknife, the blade of which is held by a spring and can be released suddenly, as by pressing a button. Also called **switch′blade knife′.**

switch•board (swich′bôrd′, -bōrd′), *n.* a structural unit on which are mounted switches and instruments necessary to complete telephone circuits manually.

switch′ grass′, *n.* a North American grass, *Panicum virgatum,* having an open, branching inflorescence.

switch′-hit′, *v.i.,* **-hit, -hit•ting.** *Baseball.* to be able to bat from either side of the plate, or both as a left-handed and as a right-handed batter.

switch′-hit′ter, *n.* a baseball player who switch-hits.

Switz•er•land (swit′sər lənd), *n.* a republic in central Europe. 7,248,984; 15,944 sq. mi. (41,295 sq. km). *Cap.:* Bern. French, **Suisse.** German, **Schweiz.** Italian, **Svizzera.** Latin, **Helvetia.**

swiv•el (swiv′əl), *n., v.,* **-eled, -el•ing** or (*esp. Brit.*) **-elled, -el•ling.** —*n.* **1.** a fastening device that allows the thing fastened to turn around freely upon it. **2.** such a device consisting of two parts, each of which turns around independently, as a compound link of a chain. **3.** a pivoted support allowing something to turn around in a horizontal plane. —*v.t.* **4.** to turn or pivot on or as if on a swivel: *He swiveled his chair around.* **5.** to fasten by a swivel; furnish with a swivel. —*v.i.* **6.** to turn on or if as on a swivel.

swiz•zle (swiz′əl), *n., v.,* **-zled, -zling.** —*n.* **1.** a tall drink of dark rum, lime juice, crushed ice, and sugar: typically served with a swizzle stick. —*v.t.* **2.** to agitate (a beverage) with a swizzle stick. **3.** to gulp down.

swiz′zle stick′, *n.* a small wand or straw for stirring highballs and cocktails in the glass.

swol•len (swō′lən), *v.* **1.** a pp. of SWELL. —*adj.* **2.** enlarged by or as if by swelling; tumid. **3.** turgid or bombastic. —**swol′len•ness,** *n.*

swoon (swo͞on), *v.i.* **1.** to faint; lose consciousness. **2.** to enter a state of hysterical rapture or ecstasy. —*n.* **3.** a faint or fainting fit; syncope. —**swoon′ing•ly,** *adv.*

swoop (swo͞op), *v.i.* **1.** to sweep down through the air, as a bird upon prey. **2.** to come down upon something in a sudden, swift attack (often fol. by *down* and *on* or *upon*): *The army swooped down on the town.* —*v.t.* **3.** to take, lift, scoop up, or remove with or as if with one sweeping motion (often fol. by *up, away,* or *off*): *He swooped her up in his arms.* —*n.* **4.** an act or instance of swooping.

swoosh (swo͝osh), *v.i.* **1.** to move with or make a rustling, swirling, or brushing sound. **2.** to pour out swiftly. —*v.t.* **3.** to cause to make or move with a rustling, swirling, or brushing sound. —*n.* **4.** a swirling or rustling sound or movement.

sword (sôrd, sōrd), *n.* **1.** a weapon, typically having a long, sharp-edged blade affixed to a hilt or handle. **2.** this weapon as a symbol of military power, punitive justice, etc.: *The pen is mightier than the sword.* **3.** a cause of death or destruction. **4.** military force or aggression, esp. war: *to perish by the sword.* —***Idiom.* 5. at swords' points,** mutually ready to fight or argue; opposed. **6. cross swords, a.** to engage in combat; fight. **b.** to disagree violently; argue. **7. put to the sword,** to slay; execute. —**sword′like′,** *adj.*

sword·fish (sôrd′fish′, sōrd′-), *n., pl.* **-fish·es,** (*esp. collectively*) **-fish.** a large marine food fish, *Xiphias gladius,* having the upper jaw elongated into a bladelike structure.

swordfish, *Xiphias gladius,* length to 15 ft. (4.6 m)

sword′ of Dam′o·cles, *n.* any situation threatening imminent harm or disaster.

sword·play (sôrd′plā′, sōrd′-), *n.* the action or technique of wielding a sword; fencing. **—sword′play′er,** *n.*

swords·man (sôrdz′mən, sōrdz′-) also **swordman,** *n., pl.* **-men. 1.** a person who uses or is skilled in the use of a sword. **2.** a fencer. **3.** a soldier. **—swords′man·ship′,** *n.*

swore (swôr, swōr), *v.* pt. of SWEAR.

sworn (swôrn, swōrn), *v.* **1.** pp. of SWEAR. **—adj. 2.** having taken an oath. **3.** bound by or as if by an oath or pledge. **4.** avowed; affirmed.

swum (swum), *v.* pp. of SWIM.

swung (swung), *v.* pt. and pp. of SWING.

swung′ dash′, *n.* a mark of punctuation (~) used in place of a word or part of a word previously spelled out.

-sy, a suffix forming nouns or adjectives, sometimes a diminutive of the base word and usu. confined to informal and jocular use (*bitsy; footsies*); adjectives formed with **-sy** may be ironic, implying that the quality in question is self-consciously assumed or feigned (*artsy; cutesy; folksy*).

Syb·a·ris (sib′ə ris), *n.* an ancient Greek city in S Italy: noted for its wealth and luxury; destroyed 510 B.C.

Syb·a·rite (sib′ə rīt′), *n.* **1.** (*usu. l.c.*) a person devoted to luxury and pleasure. **2.** a native or resident of Sybaris. **—syb′a·rit·ism,** *n.*

Syb·a·rit·ic (sib′ə rit′ik) also **Syb′a·rit′i·cal,** *adj.* **1.** (*usu. l.c.*) pertaining to or characteristic of a sybarite. **2.** of or pertaining to Sybaris or its residents. **—syb′a·rit′i·cal·ly,** *adv.*

syc·a·mine (sik′ə min, -mīn′), *n.* a tree mentioned in the New Testament, probably the black mulberry, *Morus nigra.* Luke 17:6.

syc·a·more (sik′ə môr′, -mōr′), *n.* **1.** Also called **buttonwood.** any plane tree, esp. *Platanus occidentalis,* of E North America, having palmately lobed leaves, globular seed heads, and wood valued as timber. **2.** *Brit.* the sycamore maple. a tree, *Ficus sycomorus,* of the Near East, related to the common fig, bearing an edible fruit: the sycamore of the Bible.

syc′amore ma′ple, *n.* a Eurasian maple, *Acer pseudoplatanus,* having gray bark and opposite, lobed leaves: grown as a shade tree.

Sy·char (sī′kär), *n.* a city in Samaria where Jesus visited Jacob's Well. John 4:5.

syc·o·phant (sik′ə fənt, -fant′, sī′kə-), *n.* a self-seeking, servile flatterer; fawning parasite. **—syc′o·phan′tic, syc′o·phan′ti·cal, syc′o·phant′ish,** *adj.* **—syc′o·phan′ti·cal·ly, syc′o·phant′ish·ly,** *adv.* **—syc′o·phant·ism,** *n.*

Syd·ney (sid′nē), *n.* the capital of New South Wales, in SE Australia. 3,430,600.

syl·la·bar·y (sil′ə ber′ē), *n., pl.* **-bar·ies. 1.** a set of written symbols, each of which represents a syllable, used in writing certain languages, as Japanese. **2.** a list or catalog of syllables.

syl·lab·ic (si lab′ik), *adj.* **1.** of, pertaining to, or consisting of a syllable or syllables. **2.** based on or pertaining to a specific number of syllables, as opposed to vowel length or number of stresses: *syllabic verse.* **3. a.** (of a consonant) forming a syllable by itself, as the (n) in *button* (but′n) or the (l) in *bottle* (bot′l). **b.** (of a vowel) dominating the other sounds in a syllable; sonantal. **4.** pronounced with careful distinction of syllables. **—n. 5.** a syllabic sound or character. **—syl·lab′i·cal·ly,** *adv.*

syl·lab·i·cate (si lab′i kāt′), *v.t.,* **-cat·ed, -cat·ing.** to syllabify. **—syl·lab′i·ca′tion,** *n.*

syl·lab·i·fy (si lab′ə fī′), *v.t.,* **-fied, -fy·ing.** to form or divide into syllables. **—syl·lab′i·fi·ca′tion,** *n.*

syl·la·ble (sil′ə bəl), *n., v.,* **-bled, -bling. —n. 1.** an uninterrupted segment of speech consisting of a center of relatively great sonority with or without one or more accompanying sounds of relatively less sonority: *"Dog," "eye," "strength," and "sixths" are English words of one syllable; "doghouse" has two syllables.* **2.** one or more written letters or characters representing more or less exactly such an element of speech. **3.** the slightest portion or amount of speech or writing; the least mention. **—v.t. 4.** to utter in syllables; articulate.

syl·la·bub (sil′ə bub′), *n.* **1.** a drink of milk or cream sweetened, flavored, and mixed with wine or cider. **2.** a dessert of whipped cream thickened with gelatin and flavored with wine or liquor.

syl·la·bus (sil′ə bəs), *n., pl.* **-bus·es, -bi** (-bī′). an outline or other brief statement of the main points of a discourse, the subjects of a course of lectures, the contents of a curriculum, etc.

syl·lep·sis (si lep′sis), *n., pl.* **-ses** (-sēz). the use of a word or expression to perform two syntactic functions, esp. to modify or govern two or more words of which at least one does not agree in number, case, or gender, as the use of *are* in *Neither he nor we are willing.* **—syl·lep′tic** (-tik), *adj.* **—syl·lep′ti·cal·ly,** *adv.*

syl·lo·gism (sil′ə jiz′əm), *n.* **1.** an argument of a form containing a major premise and a minor premise connected with a middle term and a conclusion, as "All A is C; all B is A; therefore, all B is C." **2.** deductive reasoning. **3.** an extremely subtle, sophisticated, or deceptive argument. **—syl′lo·gis′tic, syl′lo·gis′ti·cal,** *adj.* **—syl′lo·gis′ti·cal·ly,** *adv.*

syl·lo·gize (sil′ə jīz′), *v.i., v.t.,* **-gized, -giz·ing.** to argue or reason by syllogism.

sylph (silf), *n.* a slender, graceful woman or girl. **—sylph′ic,** *adj.*

syl·van or **sil·van** (sil′vən), *adj.* **1.** of, pertaining to, or inhabiting the woods. **2.** consisting of or abounding in woods or trees; wooded; woody. **3.** made of trees, branches, boughs, etc.

syl·van·ite (sil′və nīt′), *n.* a silvery-yellowish ore mineral, gold silver telluride, (AuAg)Te$_4$.

syl·vite (sil′vīt), *n.* a transparent mineral, potassium chloride, KCl, mined for its potassium content.

sym·bi·o·sis (sim′bē ō′sis, -bī-), *n., pl.* **-ses** (-sēz). **1.** the living together of two dissimilar organisms, as in mutualism, commensalism, or parasitism. **2.** any interdependent or mutually beneficial relationship between two persons, groups, etc. **—sym′bi·ot′ic** (-ot′ik), *adj.* **—sym′bi·ot′i·cal·ly,** *adv.*

sym·bol (sim′bəl), *n., v.,* **-boled, -bol·ing** or (*esp. Brit.*) **-bolled, -bol·ling. —n. 1.** something used for or regarded as representing something else, esp. a material object representing something immaterial; emblem or sign. **2.** a letter, figure, or other conventional mark designating an object, quantity, operation, function, etc., as in mathematics or chemistry. **3.** *Psychoanal.* any object or idea that represents or disguises a repressed wish or impulse: *dream symbols.* **—v.t. 4.** to symbolize.

sym·bol·ic (sim bol′ik), *adj.* **1.** serving as a symbol of something (often fol. by *of*). **2.** of, pertaining to, or expressed by a symbol. **3.** characterized by or involving the use of symbols: *a highly symbolic poem.* Often, **sym·bol′i·cal. —sym·bol′i·cal·ly,** *adv.*

symbol′ic log′ic, *n.* a modern development of formal logic employing a special notation or symbolism capable of manipulation in accordance with precise rules.

sym·bol·ism (sim′bə liz′əm), *n.* **1.** the practice of representing things by symbols, or of investing things with a symbolic meaning or character. **2.** a set or system of symbols. **3.** symbolic meaning or character. **4.** the principles and practice of symbolists in literature or art. **5.** (*cap.*) the literary movement of the Symbolists of the late 19th century.

sym·bol·ist (sim′bə list), *n.* **1. a.** a writer or artist who seeks to express or evoke emotions, ideas, etc., by the use of symbolic language, imagery, color, etc. **b.** (*usu. cap.*) any of a group of chiefly French and Belgian poets and writers of the late 19th century who rejected naturalism and used evocative, suggestive, or synesthetic images. **2.** a person who uses symbols or symbolism. **3.** a person versed in the study or interpretation of symbols. **4.** *Fine Arts.* **a.** an artist who seeks to symbolize or suggest ideas or emotions by the objects represented, the colors used, etc. **b.** (*usu. cap.*) a member of a group of late 19th-century artists who rejected realism and sought to express subjective visions rather than objective reality through the use of evocative images. **—adj. 5.** of or pertaining to symbolists or symbolism. **—sym′bol·is′tic,** *adj.*

sym·bol·ize (sim′bə līz′), *v.,* **-ized, -iz·ing. —v.t. 1.** to be a symbol of; stand for or represent in the manner of a symbol: *The fox often symbolizes slyness and cunning.* **2.** to represent by a symbol or symbols. **3.** to regard or treat as symbolic. **—v.i. 4.** to use symbols.

sym·bol·o·gy (sim bol′ə jē), *n.* **1.** the study of symbols. **2.** the use of symbols; symbolism. **—sym′bo·log′i·cal** (-bə loj′i kəl), *adj.* **—sym·bol′o·gist,** *n.*

sym·met·ri·cal (si me′tri kəl) also **sym·met′ric,** *adj.* **1.** characterized by or exhibiting symmetry; regular in form or arrangement of corresponding parts. **2. a.** noting two points in a plane such that the line segment joining them is bisected by an axis. **b.** noting a set consisting of pairs of points with this relation to the same axis. **c.** noting an equation whose terms can be interchanged without altering its validity. **d.** noting a set consisting of pairs of points having this relation with respect to the same center. **3.** having a chemical structure that exhibits a regular repeated pattern of the component parts. **—sym·met′ri·cal·ly,** *adv.* **—sym·met′ri·cal·ness,** *n.*

sym·me·try (sim′i trē), *n., pl.* **-tries. 1.** the correspondence in size, form, and arrangement of parts on opposite sides of a plane, line, or point; regularity of form or arrangement in terms of like, reciprocal, or corresponding parts. **2.** the proper or due proportion of the parts of a body or whole to one another with regard to size and form; excellence of proportion. **3.** beauty based on or characterized by such excellence of proportion. **4.** a type of regularity, as of a circle or other plane figure, that is characterized by the geometric operations, as rotation or reflection, that leave a figure unchanged.

sym·pa·thet·ic (sim′pə thet′ik), *adj.* **1.** characterized by, proceeding from, exhibiting, or feeling sympathy; sympathizing; compassionate: *a sympathetic listener.* **2.** in harmony with one's tastes, mood, or disposition; congenial: *a sympathetic companion.* **3.** looking upon with favor (often fol. by *to* or *toward*): *She is sympathetic to the project.* **4.** pertaining to that part of the autonomic nervous system that originates in the thoracic and lumbar region of the spinal cord and that regulates involuntary reactions to stress, stimulating the heartbeat, breathing rate, sweating, and other physiological processes. **5.** noting or pertaining to vibrations, sounds, etc., produced by a body as the direct result of similar vibrations in a different body. —**sym′pa•thet′i•cal•ly,** *adv.*

sym•pa•thize (sim′pə thīz′), *v.i.,* **-thized, -thiz•ing. 1.** to be in sympathy or agreement of feeling; share in a feeling (often fol. by *with*). **2.** to feel a compassionate sympathy, as for suffering or trouble (often fol. by *with*). **3.** to express sympathy or condole (often fol. by *with*). **4.** to be in approving accord, as with a person or cause. **5.** to agree, correspond, or accord. —**sym′pa•thiz′er,** *n.* —**sym′pa•thiz′ing•ly,** *adv.*

sym•pa•thy (sim′pə thē), *n., pl.* **-thies,** *adj.* —*n.* **1.** harmony of or agreement in feeling, as between persons or on the part of one person with respect to another. **2.** the harmony of feeling existing between persons of like tastes or opinion or of congenial dispositions. **3.** the ability to share the feelings of another, esp. in sorrow or trouble; compassion. **4. sympathies,** feelings or impulses of compassion or support. **5.** favorable or approving accord; favor or approval. **6.** agreement, consonance, or accord. **7.** *Physiol.* the relation between parts or organs whereby a condition or disorder of one part induces some effect in another. —*adj.* **8.** acting out of or expressing sympathy: *a sympathy vote.*

sym•phon•ic (sim fon′ik), *adj.* **1.** of, for, pertaining to, or having the character of a symphony or symphony orchestra. **2.** of or pertaining to symphony or harmony of sounds. **3.** characterized by similarity of sound, as words. —**sym•phon′i•cal•ly,** *adv.*

sym•pho•nist (sim′fə nist), *n.* a composer who writes symphonies.

sym•pho•ny (sim′fə nē), *n., pl.* **-nies. 1.** an extended sonatalike musical composition for large orchestra. **2.** SYMPHONY ORCHESTRA. **3.** a concert performed by a symphony orchestra. **4.** anything characterized by a harmonious combination of elements, esp. an effective combination of colors. **5.** harmony of sounds.

sym′phony or′chestra, *n.* a large orchestra composed of wind, string, and percussion instruments and organized to perform symphonic compositions.

sym•phy•sis (sim′fə sis), *n., pl.* **-ses** (-sēz′). **1.** a joining of two complementary bones along the midline of the body, as at the halves of the lower jaw. **2.** a similar joining of parts in a plant. —**sym•phys′tic** (-fis′tik), **sym•phys′i•al** (-fiz′ē əl), *adj.*

sym•po•si•um (sim pō′zē əm), *n., pl.* **-si•ums, -si•a** (-zē ə). **1.** a conference for the discussion of some subject, esp. a meeting at which several speakers discuss a topic before an audience. **2.** a collection of opinions expressed or articles contributed by several persons on a given subject or topic. **3.** (in ancient Greece) **a.** a drinking party following the evening meal, attended only by men, and typically featuring songs, games, and entertainment by hired performers. **b.** such a party as the frame for a literary work that purports to be a record of the guests' conversation. **4.** (*cap., italics*) a philosophical dialogue (4th century B.C.) by Plato, dealing with ideal love and the vision of absolute beauty.

symp•tom (simp′təm), *n.* **1.** any phenomenon or circumstance accompanying something and serving as evidence of it. **2.** a sign or indication of something. **3.** a phenomenon that arises from and accompanies a particular disease or disorder and serves as an indication of it.

symp•to•mat•ic (simp′tə mat′ik) *adj.* **1.** pertaining to a symptom or symptoms. **2.** of the nature of or constituting a symptom; indicative (often fol. by *of*): *a condition symptomatic of cholera.* **3.** according to symptoms: *a symptomatic classification of disease.* —**symp′to•mat′i•cal•ly,** *adv.*

syn-, a prefix occurring orig. in loanwords from Greek, meaning "with," "together": *syncarpous; synchronous; synthesis.* For variants before certain consonants, see SY-.

syn•a•gogue or **syn•a•gog** (sin′ə gog′, -gôg′), *n.* **1.** a Jewish house of worship, often having facilities for religious instruction or serving as a community center. **2.** a congregation of Jews for the purpose of religious worship. —**syn′a•gog′i•cal** (-goj′i kəl), **syn′a•gog′al** (-gog′əl, -gô′gəl), *adj.*

syn•apse (sin′aps, si naps′), *n., v.,* **-apsed, -aps•ing.** —*n.* **1. a.** a region where nerve impulses are transmitted across a small gap from an axon terminal to an adjacent structure, as another axon. **b.** Also called **synap′tic gap′.** the gap itself. —*v.i.* **2.** to form a synapse.

sync or **synch** (singk), *n., v.,* **synced** or **synched** (singkt), **sync•ing** or **synch•ing** (sing′king). —*n.* **1.** synchronization: *The images and sound were out of sync.* **2.** harmony or harmonious relationship: *in sync with the times.* —*v.t., v.i.* **3.** to synchronize.

synchro-, a combining form representing SYNCHRONIZED or SYNCHRONOUS: *synchroscope; synchrotron.*

syn•chro•nal (sing′krə nl), *adj.* SYNCHRONOUS.

syn•chron•ic (sin kron′ik, sing-), *adj.* of or pertaining to the study of a language as it exists at one point in time without reference to its history: *synchronic linguistics.* Compare DIACHRONIC. [1825–35]

syn•chro•nic•i•ty (sing′krə nis′i tē), *n.* synchronism of events that appear to be connected but have no demonstrable causal relationship.

syn•chro•nize (sing′krə nīz′), *v.,* **-nized, -niz•ing.** —*v.t.* **1.** to cause to indicate the same time, as one timepiece with another. **2.** to cause to go on, move, operate, work, etc., at the same rate and exactly together. **3. a.** to cause (sound and action) to match precisely in the making of a film or videotape. **b.** to match the sound and action in (a filmed or taped scene). **4.** to cause to agree in time of occurrence; assign to the same time or period, as in a history. —*v.i.* **5.** to occur at the same time or coincide or agree in time. **6.** to go on, move, operate, work, etc., at the same rate and exactly together; recur together. —**syn′chro•ni•za′tion,** *n.* —**syn′chro•niz′er,** *n.*

syn′chronized swim′ming, *n.* a sport in which swimmers complete various figures and synchronized movements to music and are judged for body position, control, and the degree of difficulty of the moves.

syn•chro•nous (sing′krə nəs), *adj.* **1.** occurring at the same time; coinciding in time; contemporaneous; simultaneous. **2.** going on at the same rate and exactly together; recurring together. **3.** (of two or more electrical devices) having the same frequency or period; in phase. **4.** GEOSTATIONARY. —**syn′chro•nous•ly,** *adv.*

syn•co•pat•ed (sing′kə pā′tid, sin′-), *adj.* **1.** marked by syncopation: *syncopated rhythm.* **2.** cut short; abbreviated.

syn•co•pa•tion (sing′kə pā′shən, sin′-), *n.* **1.** a shifting of a normal musical accent, usu. by stressing the normally unaccented beats. **2.** something, as a rhythm or a passage of music, that is syncopated. **3.** SYNCOPE.

syn•co•pe (sing′kə pē′, sin′-), *n.* **1.** the shortening of a word by omitting one or more sounds from the middle, as in the reduction of *never* to *ne'er.* **2.** brief loss of consciousness associated with an inadequate flow of oxygenated blood to the brain. —**syn•cop•ic** (sin kop′ik), **syn′co•pal,** *adj.*

syn•cre•tism (sing′kri tiz′əm, sin′-), *n.* **1.** the attempted reconciliation or union of different or opposing principles, practices, or parties, as in philosophy or religion. **2.** the merging, as by historical change in a language, of two or more inflectional categories into one, as the use in nonstandard English of *was* with both singular and plural subjects. —**syn•cret•ic** (sin kret′ik), **syn•cret′i•cal, syn′cre•tis′tic** (-tis′tik), *adj.* —**syn′cre•tist,** *n.*

syn•det•ic (sin det′ik) also **syn•det′i•cal,** *adj.* **1.** serving to unite or connect; connective; copulative. **2.** connected by a conjunction: *syndetic clauses.* —**syn•det′i•cal•ly,** *adv.*

syn•dic (sin′dik), *n.* **1.** a person chosen to represent and transact business for a corporation, as a university. **2.** a civil magistrate having different powers in different countries. [< Late Latin *syndicus* city official < Greek *sýndikos* advocate, lawyer] —**syn′dic•ship′,** *n.*

syn•di•cate (*n.* sin′di kit; *v.* -kāt′), *n., v.,* **-cat•ed, -cat•ing.** —*n.* **1.** a group of individuals or organizations combined or cooperating to undertake some specific duty, transactions, or negotiations. **2. a.** an agency that buys articles, stories, photographs, etc., and distributes them for simultaneous publication in a number of newspapers or periodicals. **b.** a chain of newspapers. **3.** a group or association of gangsters controlling organized crime or one type of crime. **4.** a council or body of syndics. —*v.t.* **5.** to combine into a syndicate. **6.** to publish simultaneously in a number of newspapers or periodicals. **7.** to sell (a radio or television program, series, etc.) directly to independent stations. —*v.i.* **8.** to combine to form a syndicate. —**syn′di•cat′a•ble,** *adj.* —**syn′di•ca′tion,** *n.*

syn•drome (sin′drōm, -drəm), *n.* **1.** a group of symptoms that together are characteristic of a specific disorder, disease, or the like. **2.** a predictable, characteristic condition or pattern of behavior that tends to occur under certain circumstances: *the empty nest syndrome.* —**syn•drom′ic** (-drom′ik), *adj.*

syn•ec•do•che (si nek′də kē), *n.* a figure of speech in which a part is used for the whole as in *ten sails* for *ten ships* —**syn•ec•doch•ic** (sin′ik-dok′ik), *adj.* —**syn′ec•doch′i•cal•ly,** *adv.*

syn•er•get•ic (sin′ər jet′ik), *adj.* working together; cooperative.

syn•er•gism (sin′ər jiz′əm, si nûr′jiz-), *n.* **1.** the interaction of elements that when combined produce a total effect that is greater than the sum of the individual elements, contributions, etc. **2.** the joint action of agents, as drugs, that when taken together increase each other's effectiveness (contrasted with *antagonism*). —**syn′er•gis′tic,** *adj.*

syn•er•gy (sin′ər jē), *n., pl.* **-gies.** combined action or functioning; synergism. —**syn•er•gic** (si nûr′jik), *adj.*

syn•fu•el (sin′fyo͞o′əl), *n.* SYNTHETIC FUEL.

Synge (sing), *n.* **1. John Millington,** 1871–1909, Irish dramatist. **2. Richard Laurence Millington,** 1914–96, English biochemist.

syn•od (sin′əd), *n.* **1.** an assembly of ecclesiastics or other church delegates that discusses and decides upon church affairs; ecclesiastical council. **2.** any council. —**syn′od•al,** *adj.*

syn•o•nym (sin′ə nim), *n.* **1.** a word having the same or nearly the same meaning as another in the language, as *joyful* in relation to *elated* and *glad.* **2.** a word or expression accepted as another name for something, as *Arcadia* for *pastoral simplicity;* metonym. —**syn′o•nym′ic, syn′o•nym′i•cal,** *adj.* —**syn′o•nym′i•ty,** *n.*

syn•on•y•mous (si non′ə məs), *adj.* having the character of synonyms or a synonym; expressing or implying the same idea. —**syn•on′y•mous•ly,** *adv.* —**syn•on′y•mous•ness,** *n.*

syn•on•y•my (si non′ə mē), *n., pl.* **-mies** for 3, 4. **1.** the quality of being synonymous; equivalence in meaning. **2.** the study of synonyms. **3.** a set, list, or system of synonyms. **4.** *Biol.* a list of the scientific names, with explanatory matter and location of type or types, for a particular taxonomic group.

syn•op•sis (si nop′sis), *n., pl.* **-ses** (-sēz). **1.** a brief or condensed statement giving a general view of some subject. **2.** a compendium of heads or short paragraphs giving a view of the whole. **3.** a brief summary of the plot of a novel, motion picture, play, etc.

syn•op•tic (si nop′tik) also **syn•op′ti•cal,** *adj.* **1.** pertaining to or constituting a synopsis; affording or taking a general view of the principal parts of a subject. **2.** (*often cap.*) taking a common view: used chiefly in reference to the first three Gospels. **3.** (*often cap.*) pertaining to the synoptic Gospels. [< Greek *synoptikos*, der. of *synopsis* view] —**syn•op′ti•cal•ly,** *adv.*

syn•tac•tic (sin tak′tik) also **syn•tac′ti•cal,** *adj.* of or pertaining to syntax. —**syn•tac′ti•cal•ly,** *adv.*

syn•tax (sin′taks), *n.* **1. a.** the study of the patterns of formation of sentences and phrases from words and of the rules for the formation of grammatical sentences in a language. **b.** the patterns or rules so studied: *English syntax.* **2. a.** the study of the formulas of a logical system. **b.** the set of rules that generate such a system. **3.** *Computers.* the grammatical rules and structural patterns governing the ordered use of appropriate words and symbols for issuing commands, writing code, etc., in a particular software application or programming language.

syn•the•sis (sin′thə sis), *n., pl.* **-ses** (-sēz′). **1.** the combining of the constituent elements of separate material or abstract entities into a single or unified entity (opposed to *analysis*). **2.** a complex whole formed by combining. **3.** the forming or building of a more complex chemical substance or compound from elements or simpler compounds. —**syn′the•sist,** *n.*

syn•the•size (sin′thə sīz′) *v.,* **-sized, -siz•ing.** —*v.t.* **1.** to form (a material or abstract entity) by combining parts or elements (opposed to *analyze*). **2.** to combine (constituent elements) into a single or unified chemical entity. —*v.i.* **3.** to make or form a synthesis. —**syn′the•si•za′tion,** *n.*

syn•the•siz•er (sin′thə sī′zər), *n.* **1.** a person or thing that synthesizes. **2.** an electronic, usu. computerized console or module for creating or modifying the sounds of musical instruments.

syn•thet•ic (sin thet′ik), *adj.* **1.** of, pertaining to, proceeding by, or involving synthesis (opposed to *analytic*). **2.** pertaining to or denoting compounds, materials, etc., formed through a chemical process by human agency, as opposed to those of natural origin: *synthetic fiber; synthetic drugs.* **3.** not real or genuine; artificial; feigned: *a synthetic chuckle.* **4.** (of a language) characterized by the use of affixes, rather than separate words, to express syntactic relationships, as Latin. Compare ANALYTIC (def. 3), POLYSYNTHETIC. **5.** Also, **syn•thet′i•cal.** *Logic.* of or pertaining to a noncontradictory proposition in which the predicate is not included in, or entailed by, the subject. **6.** noting a gem mineral manufactured so as to be physically, chemically, and optically identical with the mineral as found in nature. —*n.* **7.** something made by a synthetic, or chemical, process. —**syn•thet′i•cal•ly,** *adv.*

synthet′ic fu′el, *n.* liquid or gaseous fuel manufactured from coal or in the form of oil extracted from shale or tar sands.

synthet′ic rub′ber, *n.* any of several substances similar to natural rubber in properties and uses, produced by the polymerization or the copolymerization of unsaturated hydrocarbons.

syph•i•lis (sif′ə lis), *n.* a chronic infectious disease caused by a spirochete, *Treponema pallidum,* usu. venereal in origin but often congenital, affecting almost any body organ, esp. the genitals.

sy•phon (sī′fən), *n., v.t., v.i.* SIPHON.

Syr•a•cuse (sir′ə kyōōs′, -kyōōz′), *n.* **1.** a city in central New York. 159,985. **2.** Italian, **Siracusa.** a seaport in SE Sicily: ancient city founded by the Carthaginians 734 B.C.; battles 413 B.C., 212 B.C. 121,134. —**Syr′a•cu′san,** *adj., n.*

Syr•i•a (sēr′ē ə), *n.* **1.** Official name, **Syr′ian Ar′ab Repub′lic.** a republic in SW Asia at the E end of the Mediterranean. 16,137,899; 71,498 sq. mi. (185,180 sq. km). *Cap.:* Damascus. **2.** an ancient country in W Asia, including modern Syria, Lebanon, and Israel: a part of the Roman Empire 64 B.C.–A.D. 636. —**Syr′i•an,** *adj., n.*

sy•ringe (sə rinj′, sir′inj), *n., v.,* **-ringed, -ring•ing.** —*n.* **1.** a small tube with a narrow outlet and fitted with a piston or rubber bulb for drawing in or ejecting fluid. **2.** any similar device for pumping and spraying liquids through a small aperture. —*v.t.* **3.** to cleanse, wash, inject, etc., by means of a syringe.

syr•up (sir′əp, sûr′-), *n.* **1.** any of various thick, sweet liquids prepared for table use from molasses, glucose, etc. **2.** any of various preparations consisting of fruit juices, water, etc., boiled with sugar. —*v.t.* **3.** to bring to the form of syrup. **4.** to cover or sweeten with syrup.

syr•up•y (sir′ə pē, sûr′-), *adj.* **1.** having the appearance or quality of syrup; thick or sweet. **2.** sentimental or saccharine; mawkish.

sys•tal•tic (si stôl′tik, -stal′-), *adj.* rhythmically contracting, as the heart.

sys•tem (sis′təm), *n.* **1.** an assemblage or combination of things or parts forming a complex or unitary whole. **2.** any assemblage or set of correlated members. **3.** an ordered and comprehensive assemblage of facts, principles, doctrines, or the like in a particular field. **4.** a coordinated body of methods or a scheme or plan of procedure: *a system of government.* **5.** any formulated, regular, or special method or plan of procedure. **6. a.** an assemblage of organs or related tissues concerned with the same function: *the digestive system.* **b.** the entire human or animal body considered as a functioning unit: *an ingredient toxic to the system.* **7. a.** a number of heavenly bodies associated and acting together according to certain natural laws, as the solar system. **b.** a hypothesis or theory of the characteristics of heavenly bodies by which their phenomena, changes, etc., are explained: *the Copernican system.* **8.** one's psychological makeup, esp. with reference to desires or preoccupations: *to get something out of one's system.* **9.** a method or scheme of classification: *the Linnaean system.* **10.** (*sometimes cap.*) the prevailing structure or organization of society, business, or politics or of society in general; establishment (usu. prec. by *the*): *to work within the system.* **11.** a major division of rocks comprising sedimentary deposits and igneous masses formed during a single geologic period. **12.** a working combination of computer hardware, software, and data communications devices. —*Idiom.* **13. all systems go,** everything is ready for action.

sys•tem•at•ic (sis′tə mat′ik) also **sys′tem•at′i•cal,** *adj.* **1.** having, showing, or involving a system, method, or plan: *systematic efforts.* **2.** given to or using a system or method; methodical: *a systematic person.* **3.** arranged in or comprising an ordered system: *systematic theology.* **4.** concerned with classification: *systematic botany.* **5.** pertaining to, based on, or in accordance with a system of classification: *the systematic names of plants.* —**sys′tem•at′ic•ness,** *n.* —**sys′tem•at′i•cal•ly,** *adv.*

sys•tem•at•ics (sis′tə mat′iks), *n.* (*used with a sing. v.*) **1.** the study of systems or of classification. **2.** any system of classification. **3.** the classification of organisms into hierarchical groups; taxonomy.

sys•tem•a•tize (sis′tə mə tīz′), *v.t.,* **-tized, -tiz•ing.** to arrange in or according to a system; reduce to a system; make systematic. —**sys′tem•a•ti•za′tion,** *n.* —**sys′tem•a•tiz′er,** *n.*

sys•tem•ic (si stem′ik), *adj.* **1.** of or pertaining to a system. **2.** pertaining to, affecting, or circulating through the entire body: *systemic disease; systemic pesticide.* —**sys•tem′i•cal•ly,** *adv.*

system′ic lu′pus er•y•the•ma•to′sus (er′ə thē′mə tō′səs, -them′ə-), *n.* an autoimmune inflammatory disease of the connective tissues, chiefly characterized by skin eruptions, joint pain, recurrent pleurisy, and kidney disease.

sys•tem•ize (sis′tə mīz′), *v.t.,* **-ized, -iz•ing.** SYSTEMATIZE. —**sys′tem•i•za′tion,** *n.* —**sys′tem•iz′er,** *n.*

sys′tem (or **sys′tems**) **pro′gram,** *n.* a program, as an operating system, compiler, or utility program, that controls some aspect of the operation of a computer (disting. from *application program*). —**sys′tem pro′grammer,** *n.* —**sys′tem pro′gramming,** *n.*

sys′tems anal′ysis, *n.* the methodical study of the data-processing needs of a business or project. —**sys′tems an′alyst,** *n.*

sys′tems engineer′, *n.* an engineer who specializes in the design and implementation of production systems. —**sys′tems engineer′ing,** *n.*

sys•to•le (sis′tə lē′, -lē), *n.* **1.** the normal rhythmical contraction of the heart, during which the blood in the chambers is forced onward. Compare DIASTOLE. **2.** (in classical prosody) the shortening of a syllable regularly long. —**sys•tol•ic** (si stol′ik), *adj.*

syz•y•gy (siz′i jē), *n., pl.* **-gies. 1.** an alignment of three celestial objects, as the sun, the earth, and either the moon or a planet. **2.** a measure in classical verse consisting of two feet, often of different kinds. **3.** any two related things, either alike or opposite. —**sy•zyg•i•al** (si zij′ē-əl), **syz′y•get′ic** (-jet′ik), **syz′y•gal** (-gəl), *adj.*

Sze•chwan or **Sze•chuan** (sech′wän′, sech′ōō än′), *n.* SICHUAN.

T

T, t (tē), *n.*, *pl.* **Ts** or **T's, ts** or **t's.** **1.** the 20th letter of the English alphabet, a consonant. **2.** any spoken sound represented by this letter. **3.** something shaped like a T. **4.** a written or printed representation of the letter *T* or *t.* —*Idiom.* **5. to a T** or **tee,** exactly; perfectly.

T, **1.** temperature. **2.** tera-. **3.** tesla.

T, *Symbol.* **1.** the 20th in order or in a series. **2.** surface tension. **3. a.** threonine. **b.** thymine. **4.** the launching time of a rocket or missile: *T minus two.*

TA, **1.** transactional analysis. **2.** transit authority.

Ta, *Chem. Symbol.* tantalum.

tab¹ (tab), *n.*, *v.*, **tabbed, tab·bing.** —*n.* **1.** a small flap, strap, loop, etc., as on a garment, used for pulling, hanging, or decoration. **2.** a tag or label. **3.** a small projection from a card, paper, or folder, used as an aid in filing. **4.** *Informal.* a bill; check. **5.** a small piece attached or intended to be attached, as to an automobile license plate. **6. a.** a typewriter stop or computer command that moves the carriage, cursor, or printing element a predetermined number of spaces. **b.** the key that activates such a stop or command. **7.** a small airfoil hinged to the rear portion of a control surface, as to an elevator, aileron, or rudder. —*v.t.* **8.** to furnish or ornament with tabs. **9.** to name or designate. —*v.i.* **10.** to operate the tab function on a typewriter or computer. —*Idiom.* **11. keep tab(s) on,** to maintain a watch over; record the activities of.

tab² (tab), *n. Informal.* **1.** TABLOID (def. 1). **2.** a tablet, as of a drug.

tab·a·nid (tab′ə nid, tə bā′nid, -ban′id), *n.* any bloodsucking fly of the family Tabanidae, comprising the deer flies and horse flies.

tab·ard (tab′ərd), *n.* **1.** a loose outer garment, sleeveless or with short sleeves, esp. one worn by a knight over his armor. **2.** an official garment of a herald, emblazoned with the arms of his master. **3.** a coarse, heavy, short coat, with or without sleeves, formerly worn outdoors.

tab·by (tab′ē), *n.*, *pl.* **-bies,** *adj.*, *v.*, **-bied, -by·ing.** —*n.* **1.** a cat with a striped or brindled coat. **2.** a domestic cat, esp. a female one. **3. a.** PLAIN WEAVE. **b.** any of various plain-weave fabrics, esp. a watered silk or taffeta. —*adj.* **4.** striped or brindled. **5.** made of or resembling tabby. —*v.t.* **6.** to give a wavy or watered appearance to, as silk.

tab·er·na·cle (tab′ər nak′əl), *n.*, *v.*, **-led, -ling.** —*n.* **1.** a place or house of worship, esp. one designed for a large congregation. **2.** (*often cap.*) the portable tentlike structure used as a place of worship by the Israelites during their wandering in the wilderness. Ex. 25–27. **3.** an ornamental receptacle for the reserved Eucharist. **4.** a canopied niche or recess, as for an image or icon. —*v.t.*, *v.i.* **5.** to place or dwell in or as if in a tabernacle. [< Late Latin *tabernāculum,* Latin: tent < *tabern(a)* hut, stall, inn] —**tab′er·nac′u·lar** (-yə lər), *adj.*

tab·la·ture (tab′lə chər, -chŏŏr′), *n.* any of various systems of music notation using letters, numbers, or other signs to indicate the strings, frets, keys, etc., to be played.

ta·ble (tā′bəl), *n.*, *v.*, **-bled, -bling,** *adj.* —*n.* **1.** an article of furniture consisting of a flat, slablike top supported on one or more legs or other supports. **2.** such a piece of furniture used for serving food to those seated at it. **3.** the food served at a table. **4.** a group of people at a table, as for a meal or game. **5.** a gaming table. **6.** a flat or plane surface; a level area. **7.** a tableland or plateau. **8.** a concise list or guide: *a table of contents.* **9.** an arrangement of words, numbers, or signs, usu. in parallel columns, displaying a set of facts or relations in a compact and comprehensive form. **10.** a smooth, flat board or slab on which inscriptions may be put. **11. tables, a.** the tablets on which certain collections of laws were anciently inscribed. **b.** the laws themselves. —*v.t.* **12.** to lay aside (a bill, motion, etc.) for future discussion, or for an indefinite period of time. **13.** to place (a card, money, etc.) on a table. **14.** to enter in or form into a table or list. —*adj.* **15.** of, pertaining to, or suitable for a table: *a table lamp.* —*Idiom.* **16. on the table,** (of a bill, motion, etc.) postponed; shelved. **17. turn the tables,** to reverse an unfavorable situation, esp. by gaining the advantage over an opponent. **18. under the table,** covertly.

tab·leau (ta blō′, tab′lō), *n.*, *pl.* **tab·leaux** (ta blōz′, tab′lōz), **tab·leaus.** **1.** a picture, as of a scene. **2.** a picturesque grouping of people or objects. **3.** a representation of a picture, scene, etc., by one or more persons suitably costumed and posed.

ta·ble·cloth (tā′bəl klôth′, -kloth′), *n.*, *pl.* **-cloths** (-klôt͟hz′, -kloth͟z′, -klôths′, -kloths′). a cloth for covering the top of a table during a meal.

ta·ble d'hôte (tā′bəl dōt′, tab′əl), *n.*, *pl.* **ta·bles d'hôte** (tā′bəlz, tab′-əlz). a meal of preselected courses served at a fixed time and price to the guests at a hotel or restaurant.

ta′ble-hop′, *v.i.,* **-hopped, -hop·ping.** to move about in a restaurant, nightclub, etc., chatting with people at various tables. —**ta′ble-hop′per,** *n.*

ta·ble·land (tā′bəl land′), *n.* PLATEAU (def. 1).

ta′ble lin′en, *n.* tablecloths, napkins, etc.

ta·ble·spoon (tā′bəl spoon′), *n.* **1.** a large spoon used in serving food and as a measuring unit in recipes. **2.** a tablespoonful.

ta·ble·spoon·ful (tā′bəl spoon fool′), *n.*, *pl.* **-fuls.** **1.** the amount a tablespoon can hold. **2.** a volumetric measure equal to ½ fluid ounce (14.8 ml), or three teaspoonfuls.

tab·let (tab′lit), *n.* **1.** a small, flattish cake or piece of some solid or solidified substance, as a drug. **2.** a number of sheets of writing paper, forms, etc., fastened together at the edge; pad. **3.** a flat slab or surface, esp. one intended for or bearing an inscription or carving; plaque. **4.** a thin, flat sheet of slate, wood, or the like, used for writing on, esp. one of a pair or set fastened together. **5. tablets,** such a set as a whole.

ta′ble ten′nis, *n.* a game resembling tennis, played on a table with small paddles and a hollow celluloid or plastic ball.

ta·ble·top (tā′bəl top′), *n.* **1.** a surface forming or suggesting the top of a table. —*adj.* **2.** intended for use on a tabletop.

ta·ble·ware (tā′bəl wâr′), *n.* the dishes, utensils, etc., used at the table.

ta′ble wine′, *n.* wine that is usu. served with food and contains not more than 14 percent alcohol.

tab·loid (tab′loid), *n.* **1.** a newspaper about half the size of an ordinary newspaper, usu. heavily illustrated, and often concentrating on sensational or lurid news. **2.** a condensation or summary. —*adj.* **3.** compressed; condensed. **4.** luridly or vulgarly sensational. —**tab′loid·ism,** *n.*

ta·boo (tə boo′, ta-), *adj.*, *n.*, *pl.* **-boos,** *v.*, **-booed, -boo·ing.** —*adj.* **1.** proscribed by society as improper or unacceptable: *taboo words.* **2.** set apart as sacred; forbidden for general use; placed under a prohibition or bar. —*n.* **3.** a prohibition or interdiction of something; exclusion from use or practice. **4.** the system or practice of setting things apart as sacred or forbidden for general use. **5.** exclusion from social relations; ostracism. —*v.t.* **6.** to put under a taboo; prohibit or forbid.

ta·bor or **ta·bour** (tā′bər), *n.* a small drum used to accompany oneself on a pipe or fife. —**ta′bor·er,** *n.*

Ta·bor (tā′bər), *n.* **Mount,** a mountain in N Israel. 1929 ft. (588 m). Judg. 4:6; 8:18.

ta·bu (tə boo′, ta-), *adj.*, *n.*, *pl.* **-bus,** *v.t.*, **-bued, -bu·ing.** TABOO.

tab·u·lar (tab′yə lər), *adj.* **1.** of or arranged in a table, as in columns and rows. **2.** ascertained from or computed by the use of tables. **3.** shaped like a table or tablet. —**tab′u·lar·ly,** *adv.*

ta·bu·la ra·sa (tab′yə lə rä′sə, -zə), *n.*, *pl.* **ta·bu·lae ra·sae** (tab′yə-lē′ rä′sē, -zē). **1.** a mind not yet affected by experiences, impressions, etc. **2.** anything existing undisturbed in its original pure state. [< Latin: scraped tablet, clean slate]

tab·u·late (*v.* tab′yə lāt′; *adj.* -lit, -lāt′), *v.*, **-lat·ed, -lat·ing,** *adj.* —*v.t.* **1.** to put or arrange in a tabular form. —*v.i.* **2.** TAB¹ (def. 10). —*adj.* **3.** TABULAR (def. 3). —**tab′u·la·ble,** *adj.* —**tab′u·la′tion,** *n.*

tach (tak), *n.* a tachometer.

tach′i·na fly′ (tak′ə nə), *n.* a bristly fly of the family Tachinidae, with larvae parasitic on other insects. —**tach′i·nid,** *adj.*

ta·chom·e·ter (ta kom′i tər, tə-), *n.* an instrument for measuring or indicating speed, esp. of rotation. —**tach·o·met·ri·cal·ly** (tak′ə me′trik-lē), *adv.* —**ta·chom′e·try,** *n.*

tac·it (tas′it), *adj.* **1.** understood without being openly expressed; implied: *tacit approval.* **2.** silent; saying nothing: *a tacit partner.* **3.** unvoiced or unspoken: *a tacit prayer.* —**tac′it·ly,** *adv.*

tac·i·turn (tas′i tûrn′), *adj.* **1.** inclined to silence; reserved in speech; uncommunicative. **2.** dour, stern, and silent in expression and manner. —**tac′i·tur′ni·ty,** *n.* —**tac′i·turn′ly,** *adv.*

tack¹ (tak), *n.* **1.** a short, sharp-pointed nail, usu. with a broad, flat head. **2.** a course of action, esp. one differing from some preceding or other course: *took the wrong tack.* **3.** the heading of a sailing vessel, when sailing close-hauled, with reference to the wind direction. **4.** one of the movements of a zigzag course on land. **5.** a stitch, esp. a long stitch used in fastening seams, preparatory to a more thorough sewing. **6.** a fastening, esp. of a slight or temporary kind. **7.** stickiness, as of nearly dry paint or glue; adhesiveness. **8.** the gear used in equipping a horse. —*v.t.* **9.** to fasten with tacks. **10.** to secure by some slight or temporary fastening. **11.** to join together. **12.** to attach as something supplementary; append; annex (often fol. by *on*). **13. a.** to change the course of (a sailing vessel) to the opposite tack. **b.** to navigate (a sailing vessel) by a series of tacks. **14.** to put a saddle, bridle, etc., on (a horse). —*v.i.* **15. a.** to tack a sailing vessel. **b.** (of a sailing vessel) to change course in this way. **16.** to take or follow a zigzag course or route. **17.** to change one's course of action, ideas, etc. **18.** to put a saddle, bridle, etc., on a horse (usu. fol. by *up*). —*Idiom.* **19. get down to brass tacks,** to concentrate on essentials.

tack² (tak), *n.* food; fare.

tack′ ham′mer, *n.* a light hammer for driving tacks.

tack·le (tak′əl; *for* 2, 3 tā′kəl), *n.*, *v.*, **-led, -ling.** —*n.* **1.** equipment, apparatus, or gear, esp. for fishing: *fishing tackle.* **2.** any system of leverage using pulleys, as a combination of ropes and blocks for hoisting, lowering, and shifting objects. **3.** the gear and running rigging of a ship. **4.** an act of tackling, as in football. **5.** either of the linemen stationed between a guard and an end in football. —*v.t.* **6.** to undertake to handle, master, solve, etc.: *to tackle a problem.* **7.** to deal with (a person) on some problem, issue, etc. **8.** to seize, stop, or throw down (a ball-carrier) in football. **9.** to seize suddenly, esp. in order to stop. **10.** to harness (a horse). —*v.i.* **11.** to tackle a ballcarrier in football.

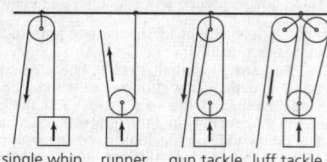

single whip   runner   gun tackle luff tackle

tackles (def. 2)

tack•y¹ (tak′ē), *adj.*, **tack•i•er, tack•i•est.** sticky to the touch; adhesive: *a tacky liquid.* —**tack′i•ness,** *n.*

tack•y² (tak′ē), *adj.*, **tack•i•er, tack•i•est.** **1.** not tasteful or fashionable; dowdy: *a tacky outfit.* **2.** in poor taste; vulgar; crass: *tacky jokes.* **3.** of poor quality; cheaply made; shoddy: *a tacky car.* **4.** shabby; seedy. —**tack′i•ness,** *n.*

ta•co (tä′kō), *n.* a usu. crisply fried tortilla folded over and filled, as with seasoned chopped meat, tomatoes, cheese, lettuce, and hot sauce.

Ta•co•ma (tə kō′mə), *n.* a seaport in W Washington, on Puget Sound. 183,060. —**Ta•co′man,** *n.*

tact (takt), *n.* **1.** a keen sense of what to say or do to avoid giving offense; skill in dealing with difficult or delicate situations; diplomacy. **2.** a keen sense of what is appropriate, tasteful, or aesthetically pleasing; taste; discrimination.

tact•ful (takt′fəl), *adj.* having or manifesting tact. —**tact′ful•ly,** *adv.*

tac•tic (tak′tik), *n.* **1.** TACTICS (def. 1). **2.** a system or a detail of tactics. **3.** a plan, procedure, or expedient for promoting a desired end. —*adj.* **4.** of or pertaining to arrangement or order; tactical.

tac•ti•cal (tak′ti kəl), *adj.* **1.** of or pertaining to tactics, esp. military or naval tactics. **2.** characterized by skillful tactics or adroit maneuvering or procedure. —**tac′ti•cal•ly,** *adv.*

tac•ti•cian (tak tish′ən), *n.* a person who is adept in planning tactics.

tac•tics (tak′tiks), *n.* **1.** (*used with a sing. v.*) the science or art of deploying military or naval forces and maneuvering them in battle. **2.** (*used with a pl. v.*) the maneuvers themselves. **3.** (*used with a pl. v.*) any maneuvers for gaining advantage or success.

tac•tile (tak′til, -tīl), *adj.* **1.** of, pertaining to, or affecting the sense of touch. **2.** perceptible to the touch; tangible.

tact•less (takt′lis), *adj.* lacking in tact; offendingly blunt; undiplomatic. —**tact′less•ly,** *adv.* —**tact′less•ness,** *n.*

tad (tad), *n. Informal.* **1.** a small child, esp. a boy. **2.** a small amount or degree; bit: *Add a tad more vanilla.*

Tad•mor (tad′môr, täd′-), *n.* Biblical name of PALMYRA.

tad•pole (tad′pōl), *n.* the aquatic larva of frogs and toads, having internal gills and a tail.

tadpoles in early stages of growth

Ta•dzhik•i•stan (tə jik′ə stan′, -stän′, -jē•kə-), *n.* TAJIKISTAN. Former official name, **Tadzhik′ So′viet So′cialist Repub′lic.**

tae kwon do or **tae•kwon•do** (tī′ kwon′ dō′), *n.* a Korean martial art similar to karate.

taf•fe•ta (taf′i tə), *n.* **1.** a smooth, crisp fabric of silk, rayon, acetate, or various other fibers, in plain weave, with a fine horizontal rib. —*adj.* **2.** of or resembling taffeta.

taf•fy (taf′ē), *n., pl.* **-fies.** **1.** a chewy candy made of sugar or molasses boiled down, often with butter, nuts, etc. **2.** *Informal.* flattery.

Taft (taft), *n.* **1. Lorado,** 1860–1936, U.S. sculptor. **2. Robert A(l•phon•so)** (al fon′sō), 1889–1953, U.S. lawyer and politician (son of William Howard). **3. William Howard,** 1857–1930, 27th president of the U.S. 1909–13.

Taft′-Hart′ley Act′ (härt′lē), *n.* an act of the U.S. Congress (1947) that supersedes but continues most of the provisions of the National Labor Relations Act and that, in addition, provides for an 80-day injunction against strikes that endanger public health and safety and bans closed shops, featherbedding, secondary boycotts, jurisdictional strikes, and certain other union practices. [after R.A. *Taft* and Fred Allen *Hartley,* Jr., 1902–69, U.S. politician]

tag¹ (tag), *n., v.,* **tagged, tag•ging.** —*n.* **1.** a piece of paper, plastic, etc., attached to something as a marker or label: *a price tag.* **2.** any small hanging or loosely attached part or piece; tatter. **3.** a loop of material sewn on a garment so that it can be hung up. **4.** a metal or plastic tip at the end of a shoelace or cord. **5.** a small piece of tinsel or the like tied to the shank of a fishhook at the body of an artificial fly. **6.** the tail

end or concluding part, as of a proceeding. **7.** a symbol or other labeling device indicating the beginning or end of a unit of information in an electronic document. **8.** an addition to a speech or writing, as the moral of a fable. **9.** a quotation added for special effect. **10.** a descriptive word or phrase applied to a person, group, etc., as a label or identifier; epithet. **11.** a lock of hair. **12.** a matted lock of wool on a sheep. —*v.t.* **13.** to furnish with a tag; attach a tag to. **14.** to append as a tag, addition, or afterthought. **15.** to attach or give an epithet to; label. **16.** to give a traffic ticket to. **17.** to hold accountable for something; attach blame to. **18.** to set a price on; fix the cost of. **19.** to follow closely. —*v.i.* **20.** to follow closely: *to tag along behind someone.* —**tag′ger,** *n.*

tag² (tag), *n., v.,* **tagged, tag•ging.** —*n.* **1.** a children's game in which one player chases the others in an effort to touch one of them, who then becomes the pursuer. **2.** an act or instance of tagging a runner in baseball. —*v.t.* **3.** to touch in or as if in the game of tag. **4.** to put out (a runner) in baseball by a touch with the ball held in the hand or glove. **5.** to make a hit or run in batting against (a baseball pitcher). **6. tag up,** (of a runner in baseball) to touch the base before attempting to advance after the catch of a fly ball.

tag•a•long (tag′ə lông′, -long′), *n.* a person that follows the lead or initiative of another.

tag′ line′ or **tag′line′,** *n.* **1.** the last line of a play, story, etc., used to clarify or dramatize a point. **2.** a catchword or slogan.

tag′ ques′tion, *n.* **1.** a short interrogative structure appended to a statement or command, often inviting confirmation or assent, as *isn't it* in *It's raining, isn't it?* **2.** the question formed by appending such a structure to a statement or command.

tag′ team′, *n.* a team of two wrestlers who compete one at a time against either member of another such team.

ta•hi•ni (tə hē′nē, tä-), *n.* a food paste made of ground sesame seeds.

t'ai chi ch'uan or **tai chi chuan** (tī′ jē′ chwän′, chē′), *n.* a Chinese system of meditative exercises, characterized by methodically slow circular and stretching movements. Also called **t'ai′ chi′, tai′ chi′.**

tai•ga (tī′gə, tī gä′), *n.* any of the coniferous evergreen forests of subarctic lands, covering vast areas of N North America and Eurasia.

tail¹ (tāl), *n.* **1.** the hindmost part of an animal, esp. that forming a distinct, flexible appendage to the trunk. **2.** something resembling or suggesting this in shape or position: *a kite tail.* **3.** the luminous stream extending from the head of a comet. **4.** Also, **tails.** the reverse of a coin (opposed to *head*). **5.** the rear portion of an airplane or the like. **6. tails, a.** TAIL COAT. **b.** the tapering skirts or ends at the back of a coat, esp. a tail coat. **c.** men's full-dress attire. **7.** a person who trails or keeps a close surveillance of another, as a detective or spy. **8.** the trail of a fleeing person or animal. **9.** the hinder, bottom, or end part of something. **10.** a final or concluding part; end. **11.** the inferior or unwanted part of something. **12.** a long braid or tress of hair. **13.** a retinue; train. **14.** the lower part of a pool or stream. **15.** the exposed portion of a piece of roofing, as a slate. **16.** the bottom part of a page or book. **17.** the lower portion of a printer's type, as of *g, y,* or *Q.* —*adj.* **18.** coming from behind: *a tail breeze.* **19.** being in the back or rear: *a tail gun on an aircraft.* —*v.t.* **20.** to follow in order to hinder escape or to observe. **21.** to form or furnish with a tail. **22.** to form or constitute the tail or end of. **23.** to join or attach (one thing) at the tail or end of another. **24.** to fasten (a beam, stone, etc.) by one end (usu. fol. by *in*). **25.** to dock the tail of (a horse, dog, etc.). —*v.i.* **26.** to follow close behind; tag. **27.** to disappear gradually or merge into. —**Idiom.** **28. turn tail,** to run away from difficulty, opposition, etc.; flee. **29. with one's tail between one's legs,** utterly defeated or humiliated. —**tail′less,** *adj.*

tail² (tāl), *n.* **1.** limitation of the passage of an estate; entail. —*adj.* **2.** limited to a specified line of heirs; entailed. —**tail′less,** *adj.*

tail•back (tāl′bak′), *n.* the offensive football back who lines up farthest behind the line of scrimmage.

tail•bone (tāl′bōn′), *n.* COCCYX.

tail′ coat′ or **tail′coat′,** *n.* a man's formal fitted coat, with a pair of tapering skirts behind. Also called **tails.**

tail′ end′, *n.* **1.** REAR END. **2.** the concluding or final part: *the tail end of a lecture.*

tail•gate (tāl′gāt′), *n., v.,* **-gat•ed, -gat•ing,** *adj.* —*n.* **1.** a board or gate at the back of a wagon, truck, station wagon, etc., that can be removed or let down for loading or unloading. **2.** a style of playing the trombone, esp. in Dixieland jazz, distinguished esp. by the use of melodic counterpoint and long glissandi. —*v.i.* **3.** to drive hazardously close to the rear of another vehicle. **4.** to have a picnic on a tailgate, esp. of a station wagon. —*v.t.* **5.** to drive hazardously close to the rear of (another vehicle). —*adj.* **6.** set up on a tailgate or near an automobile, as in a parking lot: *a tailgate picnic before a football game.*

tail•light (tāl′līt′), *n.* a light, usu. red, at the rear of an automobile, train, etc. Also called **tail′ lamp′.**

tai•lor (tā′lər), *n.* **1.** a person whose occupation is the making, mending, or altering of clothes, esp. suits, coats, and other outer garments. —*v.t.* **2.** to make by tailor's work. **3.** to fashion or adapt to a particular taste, purpose, need, etc. **4.** to fit or furnish with clothing. —*v.i.* **5.** to do the work of a tailor.

tai•lor•bird (tā′lər bûrd′), *n.* any of several warblers of tropical Asia, esp. of the genus *Orthotomus,* that stitch leaves together to form and conceal their nests.

tai•lored (tā′lərd), *adj.* **1.** (of a woman's garment) in a simple or plain style with fitted lines. **2.** having simple, straight lines and a neat appearance: *tailored slipcovers.*

tai•lor•ing (tā′lər ing), *n.* **1.** the business or work of a tailor. **2.** the skill or craftsmanship of a tailor.

tai•lor-made (*adj.* tā′lər mād′; *n.* -mād′), *adj.* **1.** tailored. **2.** custom-made; made-to-order: *an expensive tailor-made suit.* **3.** fashioned to a particular taste, purpose, demand, etc.: *tailor-made books.* —*n.* **4.** something, as a garment, that is tailor-made.

tail•piece (tāl′pēs′), *n.* **1.** a piece added at the end; appendage. **2.** a small decorative design at the end of a chapter or a page.

tail•pipe (tāl′pīp′), *n.* an exhaust pipe at the rear of a vehicle or aircraft powered by an internal-combustion engine.

tails (tālz), *adj., adv.* **1.** (of a coin) with the reverse facing up. Compare HEADS. —*n.* **2.** TAIL (def. 6).

tail•spin (tāl′spin′), *n., v.,* **-spinned, -spin•ning.** —*n.* **1.** SPIN (def. 19). **2.** a sudden collapse into failure or confusion. —*v.i.* **3.** to take or experience a sudden and dramatic downturn.

tail•wind (tāl′wind′), *n.* a wind from directly behind a moving object (opposed to *headwind*).

Tai•no (tī′nō), *n., pl.* **-nos,** (*esp. collectively*) **-no. 1.** a member of an American Indian people of the Greater Antilles and the Bahamas. **2.** the extinct Arawakan language of the Taino.

taint (tānt), *n.* **1.** a trace of something bad or offensive. **2.** a trace of infection or contamination. —*v.t.* **3.** to modify by a trace of something bad or offensive. **4.** to infect or contaminate. **5.** to sully or tarnish (a person's name, reputation, etc.). —*v.i.* **6.** to become tainted; spoil.

Tai•pei (tī′pā′, -bā′), *n.* a city in the N part of Taiwan: the capital of the Republic of China. 2,640,000.

Tai•wan (tī′wän′), *n.* an island off the SE coast of China: seat of the Republic of China since 1949. 13,900 sq. mi. (36,000 sq. km). Also called **Formosa.** —**Tai′wan•ese′** (-wä nēz′, -nēs′), *adj., n., pl.* **-ese.**

Ta•jik or **Ta•dzhik** (tä jik′, -jēk′), *n., pl.* **-jiks** or **-dzhiks,** (*esp. collectively*) **-jik** or **-dzhik. 1.** a member of a people of Central Asia, living mainly in Tadzhikistan, Uzbekistan, and N Afghanistan. **2.** the form of Persian spoken by the Tajiks.

Ta•jik•i•stan or **Ta•dzik•i•stan** (tə jik′ə stan′, –jē′kə), *n.* a republic in S central Asia, S of Kyrgyzstan: a former constituent republic of the U.S.S.R. 6,013,855; 55,240 sq. mi. (143,100 sq. km). *Cap.:* Dushanbe.

Taj Ma•hal (täzh′ mə häl′, täj′), *n.* a white marble mausoleum built at Agra, India, by Shah Jahan (fl. 1628–58).

take (tāk), *v.,* **took, tak•en, tak•ing,** *n.* —*v.t.* **1.** to get into one's hands or possession by voluntary action: *Take the book, please.* **2.** to hold, grasp, or grip: *to take a child by the hand.* **3.** to get into one's possession or control by force or artifice: *took the bone from the snarling dog.* **4.** to seize or capture: *to take a prisoner.* **5.** to catch or get (fish, game, etc.), esp. by killing. **6.** to pick from a number; select. **7.** to receive and accept willingly (something given or offered): *to take a bribe.* **8.** to accept and act upon or comply with: *Take my advice.* **9.** to receive or accept (a person) into some relation: *to take someone in marriage.* **10.** to receive or react to in a specified manner: *She took his death hard.* **11.** to receive as a payment or charge. **12.** to get or obtain from a source; derive: *The book takes its title from Dante.* **13.** to extract or quote. **14.** to obtain or exact as compensation for a wrong: *to take revenge.* **15.** to receive into the body, as by swallowing or inhaling: *to take a pill; to take a deep breath.* **16.** to have for one's benefit or use: *to take a nap; to take a bath.* **17.** to use as a flavoring agent: *to take sugar in one's coffee.* **18.** to endure or submit to with equanimity or without weakening: *unable to take punishment.* **19.** to enter into the enjoyment of: *Let's take a vacation.* **20.** to carry off without permission; steal: *to take someone's wallet.* **21.** to remove: *to take a coat from the closet.* **22.** to remove by death: *The flood took many victims.* **23.** to subtract or deduct: *to take 2 from 5.* **24.** to carry with one: *Are you taking an umbrella?* **25.** to convey or transport: *We took them for a drive.* **26.** to serve as a means of conducting: *These stairs take you to the attic.* **27.** to bring about a change in the condition of: *Her talent took her to the top.* **28.** to escort or accompany. **29.** to attempt or succeed in getting over, through, or around; clear; negotiate: *The horse took the fence easily.* **30.** to come upon suddenly; catch: *to take a thief by surprise.* **31.** to attack or affect with or as if with a disease: *taken with a fit of laughter.* **32.** to be capable of attaining: *This leather takes a high polish.* **33.** to absorb or become impregnated with; be susceptible to: *The cloth will not take a dye.* **34.** to require: *It takes courage to do that.* **35.** to employ for some purpose: *to take measures to curb drugs.* **36.** to use as a means of transportation: *to take the bus to work.* **37.** to proceed to occupy: *Take a seat.* **38.** to fill (time, space, etc.); occupy: *His hobby takes most of his spare time.* **39.** to use up; consume: *It took ten minutes to solve the problem.* **40.** to avail oneself of: *I took the opportunity to leave.* **41.** to do, perform, execute, etc.: *to take a walk.* **42.** to go into or enter: *Take the road to the left.* **43.** to adopt and enter upon (a way, course, etc.): *to take the path of least resistance.* **44.** to make (a reproduction, picture, or photograph): *to take home movies.* **45.** to make a picture, esp. a photograph, of: *The photographer took us sitting down.* **46.** to write down: *to take notes.* **47.** to apply oneself to; study: *to take a history course.* **48.** to deal with; treat: *to take a matter under consideration.* **49.** to assume the obligation of; be bound by: *to take an oath.* **50.** to assume or adopt as one's own: *to take someone's side in an argument.* **51.** to determine by inquiry, examination, measurement, etc.: *to take someone's pulse; to take a census.* **52.** to have or experience (a feeling or state of mind): *to take pride in one's appearance.* **53.** to form and hold in the mind: *to take a gloomy view.* **54.** to grasp or apprehend mentally; understand: *Do you take my meaning?* **55.** to accept the statements of: *She took him at his word.* **56.** to assume as a fact: *I take it that you won't be there.* **57.** to regard or consider: *They were taken to be wealthy.* **58.** to capture or win (a piece, trick, etc.) in a game. **59.** *Informal.* to cheat, swindle, or victimize: *The museum got taken on that painting.* **60.** to win or obtain money from: *He took me for $10 in the poker game.* **61.** to be used with (a certain grammatical form, accent, case, etc.): *a verb that takes an object.* **62.** (of a baseball batter) to allow (a pitch) to go by without swinging at it. —*v.i.* **63.** to catch or engage, as a mechanical device. **64.** to strike root or begin to grow, as a plant. **65.** to adhere, as ink, dye, or color. **66.** to win favor or acceptance. **67.** to have the intended result or effect: *The vaccination took.* **68.** to detract (usu. fol. by *from*). **69.** to fall or become: *to take sick.* **70. take after, a.** to resemble (another person, as a parent). **b.** to follow or chase. **71. take apart, a.** to disassemble: *to take a clock apart.* **b.** to criticize severely; attack. **c.** to examine or analyze closely; dissect. **72. take back, a.** to regain possession of. **b.** to return, as for exchange. **c.** to allow to return; resume a relationship with. **d.** to cause to remember: *It takes me back to the old days.* **e.** to retract: *to take back a statement.* **73. take down, a.** to write down; record. **b.** to reduce the pride or arrogance of; humble: *to take someone down a peg.* **74. take in, a.** to alter (a garment) so as to make smaller or tighter. **b.** to provide lodging for. **c.** to include; encompass. **d.** to grasp the meaning of; comprehend. **e.** to deceive; trick; cheat. **f.** to observe; notice. **g.** to visit or attend: *to take in a show.* **h.** to furl (a sail). **i.** to receive as proceeds, as from business activity. **75. take off, a.** to remove: *Take off your coat.* **b.** to lead away. **c.** to leave the ground, as an airplane. **d.** to depart; leave. **e.** to move onward or forward with a burst of speed. **f.** to withdraw or remove from: *She was taken off the night shift.* **g.** to subtract, as a discount; deduct: *The store took off 20 percent.* **h.** to imitate; mimic; burlesque. **i.** to achieve sudden, marked growth, success, etc.: *Sales took off just before Christmas.* **76. take on, a.** to hire; employ. **b.** to undertake; assume. **c.** to acquire. **d.** to accept as a challenge or opponent. **e.** *Informal.* to show great emotion; become excited. **77. take out, a.** to withdraw; remove. **b.** to deduct. **c.** to procure by application: *to take out insurance.* **d.** to carry out for use or consumption elsewhere. **e.** to escort, as on a date. **f.** to set out; start. **g.** *Slang.* to kill or destroy. **78. take over,** to assume management or possession of or responsibility for. **79. take up, a.** to occupy oneself with the study or practice of. **b.** to lift or pick up. **c.** to fill, occupy, or consume (space, time, etc.). **d.** to begin to advocate or support; sponsor. **e.** to continue; resume. **f.** to raise for discussion or consideration. **g.** to undertake; assume. **h.** to absorb (a liquid). **i.** to make shorter, as by hemming. **j.** to make tighter, as by winding in. **k.** to deal with: *to take up an issue.* **l.** to adopt seriously: *to take up an idea.* **m.** to accept, as an offer or challenge. **80. take up with,** to become friendly with; keep company with. —*n.* **81.** the act of taking. **82.** something that is taken. **83.** the quantity of fish, game, etc., taken at one time. **84.** *Informal.* money taken in, esp. profits. **85.** a scene in a movie or television program photographed without any interruption or break. **86.** *Informal.* a visual and mental response: *She did a slow take.* **87.** a recording of a musical performance. —***Idiom.*** **88. on the take,** *Slang.* **a.** accepting bribes. **b.** in search of personal profit at the expense of others. **89. take five, ten,** etc., *Informal.* to rest briefly, esp. for the approximate time specified. **90. take for, a.** to assume to be: *I took it for a fact.* **b.** to assume falsely to be; mistake for: *to be taken for a foreigner.* **91. take it, a.** to believe, assume, or accept something: *Take it from me.* **b.** to be able to resist or endure hardship, abuse, etc. **92. take it out on,** to cause (another) to suffer for one's own misfortune, frustration, anger, etc. **93. take place,** to happen; occur. **94. take to, a.** to devote or apply oneself to; become habituated to: *to take to drink.* **b.** to respond favorably to; begin to like: *They took to each other at once.* **c.** to go to: *to take to one's bed.* **d.** to have recourse to; resort to. **95. take upon oneself,** to assume as a responsibility or obligation. —**tak′er,** *n.*

take′down′ or **take′-down′,** *adj.* **1.** constructed to be easily dismantled. —*n.* **2.** the act of taking down or being taken down. **3.** a firearm made to be swiftly disassembled. **4.** a move in wrestling that brings a standing opponent down onto the mat.

take′-home′ pay′, *n.* the amount of salary less deductions.

Take′ My Life′ and Let′ It Be′, a hymn (1874) with words by Frances Havergal.

tak•en (tā′kən), *v.* **1.** pp. of TAKE. —***Idiom.*** **2. taken with,** charmed or captivated by.

take′-no′-pris′oners, *adj.* wholeheartedly aggressive; zealous: *a businessman with a take-no-prisoners attitude toward dealmaking.*

take•off (tāk′ôf′, -of′), *n.* **1.** the leaving of the ground, as in beginning an airplane flight. **2.** a departure from a starting point, as in beginning a race. **3.** the place or point at which a person or thing takes off. **4.** a humorous imitation; parody; send-up.

take•out (tāk′out′), *n.* **1.** something made to be taken out. **2.** a store or restaurant preparing food to be eaten elsewhere. —*adj.* **3.** intended to be taken from the point of sale and consumed elsewhere.

take•o•ver (tāk′ō′vər), *n.* **1.** the act of seizing or appropriating authority or control. **2.** the acquisition of a corporation through the purchase or exchange of stock.

ta•kin (tä′kin, -kēn), *n.* a massive, goatlike bovid, *Budorcas taxicolor,* of the E Himalayas, China, and N Burma.

talc (talk), *n.* **1.** a soft green-to-gray mineral, hydrous magnesium silicate, $Mg_3(Si_4O_{10})(OH)_2$. **2.** TALCUM POWDER.

tal′cum pow′der (tal′kəm), *n.* a powder for the skin made of purified, usu. perfumed talc.

tale (tāl), *n.* **1.** a narrative that relates some real or imaginary incident; story. **2.** a literary composition in the form of such a narrative. **3.** a falsehood; lie. **4.** a malicious rumor.

tale•bear•er (tāl′bâr′ər), *n.* a person who spreads gossip.

tal•ent (tal′ənt), *n.* **1.** a special, often creative natural ability or aptitude: *a talent for drawing.* **2.** a person or persons with special ability: *the theater's major talents; the local talent.* **3.** a power of mind or body considered as given to a person. Matt. 25:14-30. —**tal′ent•ed,** *adj.*

tal′ent scout′, *n.* a person who searches for people of special aptitude, as in entertainment or sports.

tal′ent show′, *n.* a theatrical show in which a series of usu. amateur entertainers perform in the hope of gaining recognition.

Talents, The, a parable of Jesus. Matt. 25:14-30; Luke 19:11-17.

tal•is•man (tal′is mən, -iz-), *n., pl.* **-mans. 1.** an object engraved with figures supposed to possess occult powers, worn as a charm. **2.** anything that exercises a powerful or magical influence. —**tal•is•man•ic** (-man′ik) *adj.*

talk (tôk), *v.i.* **1.** to communicate or exchange ideas or information by speaking. **2.** to consult or confer: *Talk with your adviser.* **3.** to spread a rumor; gossip. **4.** to chatter or prate. **5.** to use speech; perform the act of speaking. **6.** to deliver a speech or lecture: *The professor talked on modern physics.* **7.** to give confidential or incriminating information: *The spy talked during interrogation.* **8.** to communicate by means other than speech, as by writing, signs, or signals. **9.** to make sounds imitative or suggestive of speech. —*v.t.* **10.** to express in words; utter: *to talk sense.* **11.** to use (a specified language or idiom) in speaking or conversing: *They talk French together.* **12.** to discuss: *to talk politics.* **13.** to drive or influence by talk: *to talk a person to sleep.* **14. talk around,** to avoid discussion of. **15. talk back,** to reply in a disrespectful manner. **16. talk down, a.** to subdue by talking, as by argument. **b.** to speak condescendingly. **c.** Also, **talk in** to give landing instructions to (a pilot) by radio. **17. talk out,** to try to clarify or resolve by discussion. **18. talk out of,** to dissuade, as from doing, using, etc. **19. talk over,** to consider; discuss. **20. talk up, a.** to promote with enthusiastic description. **b.** to speak openly or distinctly. —*n.* **21.** the act of talking; speech. **22.** an informal speech or lecture. **23.** a conference or negotiating session: *peace talks.* **24.** rumor; gossip. **25.** empty speech: *all talk and no results.* —**talk′er,** *n.*

talk•a•tive (tô′kə tiv), *adj.* inclined to talk a great deal.

talk′ing book′, *n.* a sound recording of readings of a book, magazine, or newspaper, often for use by the blind.

talk′ing head′, *n.* a television or film closeup of a person who is talking, as in a documentary or interview.

talk′ing-to′, *n., pl.* **-tos.** a scolding.

talk′ ra′dio, *n.* a radio format with talk shows and listener call-ins.

talk′ show′, *n.* a radio or television show in which a host interviews or chats with guests, esp. celebrity guests.

talk•y (tô′kē), *adj.,* **talk•i•er, talk•i•est. 1.** having superfluous talk: *a talky play.* **2.** TALKATIVE. —**talk′i•ness,** *n.*

tall (tôl), *adj.* **-er, -est,** *adv., n.* —*adj.* **1.** having a relatively great height or stature. **2.** having stature or height as specified: *a man six feet tall.* **3.** large in amount or degree: *a tall price.* **4.** exaggerated; improbable: *a tall tale.* **5.** high-flown; grandiloquent: *tall talk.* —*adv.* **6.** in a proud, erect manner: *to stand tall.* —*n.* **7.** a garment size for tall persons. **8.** a garment in this size. —**tall′ness,** *n.*

Tal•la•has•see (tal′ə has′ē), *n.* the capital of Florida, in the N part. 133,718.

Tal•ley•rand-Pé•ri•gord (tal′ə rand/per′i gôr/), *n.* **Charles Maurice de, Prince de Bénévent,** 1754–1838, French statesman.

Tal•linn or **Tal•lin** (tä′lin, tal′in), *n.* the capital of Estonia, on the Gulf of Finland. 499,800.

Tal•lis or **Tal•lys** or **Tal•ys** (tal′is), *n.* **Thomas,** c1505–85, English organist and composer, esp. of church music.

tal•lith or **tal•lit** (tä′lis; *Heb.* tä lēt′), *n., pl.* **tal•li•thim, tal•li•tim** (tä-lā′sim, tä′ sim′; *Heb.* tä lē tēm′). a shawl with fringes at the four corners, worn over the shoulders or head by Jews during prayer.

tallith

tal•low (tal′ō), *n.* **1.** the hard, rendered fat of sheep and cattle, used to make candles and soap. **2.** any similar fatty substances, esp. vegetable tallow. —*v.t.* **3.** to smear with tallow.

tal•ly (tal′ē), *n., pl.* **-lies,** *v.,* **-lied, -ly•ing.** —*n.* **1.** an account; reckoning. **2.** a stick of wood with notches cut to indicate the amount of a debt or payment. **3.** anything on which a score or account is kept. **4.** a notch or mark made on or in a tally. **5.** a number recorded, as of points in a game. **6.** a number of objects used as a unit of computation. **7.** anything corresponding to another thing as a counterpart or duplicate. —*v.t.* **8.** to mark on a tally; record. **9.** to count; reckon. **10.** to cause to correspond or agree. —*v.i.* **11.** to correspond; agree: *Both accounts tally.* **12.** to score a point or goal, as in a game. —**tal′li•er,** *n.*

tal•ly•ho (tal′ē hō′), *interj.* (used as a cry in fox hunting on sighting the fox.)

Tal•mage (tal′mij), *n.* **Thomas DeWitt,** 1832–1902, U.S. clergyman and lecturer.

Tal•mud (täl′mŏŏd, tal′məd), *n.* **1.** the collection of Jewish law and tradition: the Mishnah and the Gemara. [< Hebrew *talmūdh* lit., instruction] —**Tal•mud′ic,** *adj.* —**Tal′mud•ism,** *n.*

Tal•mud•ist (täl′mŏŏ dist, tal′mə-), *n.* **1.** a person versed in the Talmud. **2.** one of the writers or compilers of the Talmud. **3.** a person who accepts or supports the doctrines of the Talmud.

tal•on (tal′ən), *n.* **1.** a claw, esp. of a bird of prey. **2.** the shoulder on the bolt of a lock against which the key presses in sliding the bolt. **3.** the cards left over after the deal; stock. —**tal′oned,** *adj.*

ta•luk (tä′lŏŏk, tä lŏŏk′), *n.* (in India) **1.** a hereditary estate. **2.** a subdivision of a revenue district. Also, **ta•lu•ka, ta•loo•ka** (tä lŏŏ′kə).

ta•lus[1] (tā′ləs), *n., pl.* **-li** (-lī). the uppermost bone of the proximal row of bones of the tarsus; anklebone.

ta•lus[2] (tā′ləs, tal′əs), *n., pl.* **-lus•es. 1.** a slope. **2.** a sloping mass of rocky fragments at the base of a cliff.

ta•ma•le (tə mä′lē), *n., pl.* **-les.** minced and seasoned meat packed in cornmeal dough, wrapped in corn husks, and steamed.

Ta•mar (tā′mər, tä′-), *n.* the daughter of David and half-sister of Absalom. II Sam. 13.

tam•a•rack (tam′ə rak′), *n.* **1.** a North American larch, *Larix laricina,* of the pine family, having reddish brown bark and blue-green needles. **2.** its wood.

tam•a•rind (tam′ə rind), *n.* **1.** the pod of a large tropical tree, *Tamarindus indica,* of the legume family, containing seeds in a juicy acid pulp used in beverages and food. **2.** the tree itself.

tam•bour (tam′bŏŏr, tam bŏŏr′), *n.* **1.** DRUM¹ (def. 1). **2.** a circular frame consisting of two interlocking hoops in which cloth is stretched for embroidering. **3.** embroidery done on such a frame. **4.** a flexible shutter used as a desk top or door, composed of closely set wood strips attached to a piece of cloth, the whole sliding along in grooves. **5.** DRUM¹ (def. 9). —*v.t., v.i.* **6.** to embroider on a tambour.

tam•bou•rine (tam′bə rēn′), *n.* a small drum having a circular frame with several pairs of metal jingles attached, played by striking with the knuckles and shaking.

Tam•bur•laine (tam′bər lān′), *n.* TAMERLANE.

tame (tām), *adj.,* **tam•er, tam•est,** *v.,* **tamed, tam•ing.** —*adj.* **1.** changed from the wild or savage state; domesticated. **2.** docile or submissive. **3.** lacking in excitement; dull: *a very tame party.* **4.** spiritless; pusillanimous. **5.** rendered useful and manageable: *tame natural resources.* **6.** cultivated or improved by cultivation, as a plant or its fruit. —*v.t.* **7.** to make tame; domesticate. **8.** to deprive of courage, ardor, or zest. **9.** to deprive of interest or excitement; make dull. **10.** to harness or control, as a source of power. **11.** to cultivate, as land or plants. —*v.i.* **12.** to become tame. —**tam′a•ble, tame′a•ble,** *adj.* —**tame′ly,** *adv.* —**tame′ness,** *n.* —**tam′er,** *n.*

Tam•er•lane (tam′ər lān′) also **Tamburlaine,** *n.* (*Timur Lenk*) 1336?–1405, Tartar conqueror in S and W Asia. Also called **Timur.**

Tam•il (tam′əl, tum′-, tä′məl), *n.* **1.** a member of a people of S Asia, living mainly in S India and in N and E Sri Lanka. **2.** the Dravidian language of the Tamils.

Tam′ma•ny Hall′ (tam′ə nē), *n.* a Democratic political organization in New York City, founded in 1789 as a fraternal society (**Tam′many Soci′ety**) and associated with corruption and abuse of power. Also called **Tam′ma•ny.** [after *Tammany,* 17th-cent. Delaware Indian chief, facetiously canonized as patron saint of America, c1770]

Tam•muz (tä′mŏŏz, tä mŏŏz′), *n.* the tenth month of the Jewish calendar.

tam-o′-shan•ter (tam′ə shan′tər), *n.* a cap of Scottish origin, usu. of wool, having a round, flat, projecting top with a pompom at its center. Also called **tam.**

tamp (tamp), *v.t.* **1.** to force in or down by repeated, rather light, strokes: *to tamp tobacco into a pipe.* **2.** (in blasting) to fill (a drilled hole) with earth or the like after the charge has been inserted.

Tam•pa (tam′pə), *n.* a city in W Florida, on Tampa Bay. 285,523. —**Tam′pan,** *n., adj.*

tam•per[1] (tam′pər), *v.i.* **1.** to meddle, esp. in order to alter or misuse (usu. fol. by *with*): *to tamper with a lock.* **2.** to make changes, esp. in order to falsify (usu. fol. by *with*): *to tamper with official records.* **3.** to engage secretly or improperly in something. **4.** to engage in underhand dealings, esp. in order to influence improperly (usu. fol. by *with*): *to tamper with a jury.* —**tam′per•er,** *n.*

tam·per² (tam′pər), *n.* a person or thing that tamps.

tam·pi·on (tam′pē ən), *n.* a plug placed in the muzzle of a piece of ordnance to keep it free of moisture and dirt when not in use.

tam·pon (tam′pon), *n.* **1.** a plug of cotton or the like for insertion into a wound, body cavity, etc., chiefly for absorbing blood or stopping hemorrhages. **2.** a two-headed drumstick for playing rolls. —*v.t.* **3.** to fill or plug with a tampon.

tan¹ (tan), *v.,* **tanned, tan·ning,** *n., adj.,* **tan·ner, tan·nest.** —*v.t.* **1.** to convert (a hide) into leather, esp. by steeping in a bath prepared from tanbark. **2.** to brown by exposure to ultraviolet rays, as of the sun. **3.** to thrash; spank. —*v.i.* **4.** to become tanned. —*n.* **5.** a brown color imparted to the skin by exposure to the sun or open air. **6.** yellowish brown; light brown. **7.** TANBARK. —*adj.* **8.** yellowish brown; light brown. **9.** used in or relating to tanning. —*Idiom.* **10. tan someone's hide,** to beat someone soundly. —**tan′na·ble,** *adj.*

tan² (tan), *n.* TANGENT (def. 2).

Ta·nach (tä näкн′), *n. Hebrew.* the Old Testament, divided into the Law or Torah, the Prophets, and the Hagiographa.

tan·a·ger (tan′ə jər), *n.* any of numerous New World songbirds of the subfamily Thraupinae (family Emberizidae), the males of which are usu. brightly colored.

Ta·na·na·rive (tə nan′ə rēv′), *n.* former name of ANTANANARIVO.

tan·bark (tan′bärk′), *n.* **1.** the bark of the oak, hemlock, etc., bruised and broken by a mill and used esp. in tanning hides. **2.** a surface covered with pieces of tanbark, esp. a circus ring.

tan·dem (tan′dəm), *adv.* **1.** one following or behind the other: *to drive horses tandem.* —*adj.* **2.** having animals, seats, parts, etc., arranged one behind another. —*n.* **3.** a vehicle, as a truck or tractor, in which a pair or pairs of axles are arranged in tandem. **4.** TANDEM BICYCLE. **5.** a team of horses harnessed one behind the other. **6.** a two-wheeled carriage drawn by horses so harnessed. —*Idiom.* **7. in tandem, a.** in single file; one behind the other. **b.** in association or partnership.

tan′dem bi′cycle, *n.* a bicycle for two or more persons, having seats and corresponding pedals arranged in tandem.

tan·door (tän dŏŏr′), *n., pl.* **-doors, -door·i** (-dŏŏr′ē). a clay oven used esp. in the cooking of N India and Pakistan for roasting and baking at high heat.

tan·door·i (tän dŏŏr′ē), *adj.* **1.** baked or roasted in a tandoor: *tandoori chicken.* —*n.* **2.** a pl. of TANDOOR.

tang (tang), *n.* **1.** a strong taste or flavor. **2.** a pungent or distinctive odor. **3.** the distinctive character of a thing. **4.** a suggestion of something; trace; hint. **5.** a slender projection from an object, as a chisel or knife, serving as attachment for a handle, stock, etc. —*v.t.* **6.** to provide with a tang.

T′ang or **Tang** (täng), *n.* a dynasty in China, A.D. 618–907, marked by territorial expansion, the invention of printing, and the development of the arts.

Tan·gan·yi·ka (tan′gən yē′kə, -gə nē′-, tang′-), *n.* **1.** a former country in E Africa: the larger part of German East Africa; British trusteeship **(Tan′ganyi′ka Ter′ritory)** 1946–61; became independent 1961; now part of Tanzania. 361,800 sq. mi. (937,062 sq. km). **2. Lake,** a lake in central Africa, between Zaire and Tanzania: longest freshwater lake in the world. 12,700 sq. mi. (32,893 sq. km). —**Tan′gan·yi′kan,** *adj., n.*

tan·ge·lo (tan′jə lō′), *n., pl.* **-los.** a hybrid citrus fruit that is a cross between a grapefruit and a tangerine.

tan·gent (tan′jənt), *n.* **1.** a line or plane touching but not intersecting a curve or surface at a point so that it is closer to the curve or surface in the vicinity of the point than any other line or plane drawn through the point. **2.** Also called **tan.** a fundamental trigonometric function that, in a right triangle, is expressed as the ratio of the side opposite an acute angle to the side adjacent to that angle. —*adj.* **3.** in immediate physical contact; touching; abutting. **4.** touching at a single point, as a tangent in relation to a curve or surface. **5.** TANGENTIAL (def. 3). —*Idiom.* **6. off on** or **at a tangent,** digressing suddenly from one course of action or thought and turning to another. —**tan′gen·cy** (-jən sē), *n.*

tangent (def. 2) ACB being the angle, the ratio of AB to AC is the tangent, or AC is the tangent, or AC being taken equal to unity, the tangent is AB

tan·gen·tial (tan jen′shəl), *adj.* **1.** pertaining to or of the nature of a tangent; being or moving in the direction of a tangent. **2.** incidental; peripheral. **3.** divergent or digressive: *tangential remarks.* —**tan·gen′ti·al′i·ty** (-shē al′i tē), *n.* —**tan·gen′tial·ly,** *adv.*

tan·ge·rine (tan′jə rēn′, tan′jə rēn′), *n.* **1.** any of several varieties of mandarin, cultivated widely, esp. in the U.S. **2.** deep orange; reddish orange. —*adj.* **3.** of the color tangerine; reddish orange.

tan·gi·ble (tan′jə bəl), *adj.* **1.** capable of being touched; discernible by touch; material or substantial. **2.** actual, rather than imaginary or visionary. **3.** definite; not vague or elusive: *no tangible grounds for suspicion.* **4.** (of an asset) having physical existence, as real estate, and

therefore capable of being assigned a monetary value. —*n.* **5.** something tangible, esp. a tangible asset. —**tan′gi·bil′i·ty,** *n.* —**tan′gi·bly,** *adv.*

Tan·gier (tan jēr′) also **Tan·giers** (-jērz′), *n.* a seaport in N Morocco, on the W Strait of Gibraltar: capital of the former Tangier Zone. 266,346. French, **Tan·ger** (tän zha′).

tan·gle (tang′gəl), *v.,* **-gled, -gling,** *n.* —*v.t.* **1.** to bring together into a mass of confusedly interlaced or intertwisted strands; snarl. **2.** to involve in something that hampers, obstructs, or overgrows. **3.** to catch and hold in or as if in a net or snare. —*v.i.* **4.** to be or become tangled. **5.** to come into conflict; fight or argue. —*n.* **6.** a tangled condition or situation. **7.** a tangled mass; snarl. **8.** a confused jumble; maze. **9.** a conflict; disagreement. —**tan′gle·ment,** *n.* —**tan′gler,** *n.* —**tan′gly,** *adv.*

tan·gled (tang′gəld), *adj.* **1.** snarled, interlaced, or mixed up: *tangled thread.* **2.** very complicated, intricate, or involved.

tan·go (tang′gō), *n., pl.* **-gos,** *v.,* **-goed, -go·ing.** —*n.* **1.** a ballroom dance of Latin-American origin, danced by couples, and having many varied, often quite elaborate or dramatic steps, figures, and poses. **2.** music for this dance. —*v.i.* **3.** to dance the tango. —*Proverb.* **4. It takes two to tango,** some activities require a partner.

tang·y (tang′ē), *adj.,* **tang·i·er, tang·i·est.** having a tang.

Ta·nis (tā′nis), *n.* an ancient city in Lower Egypt, in the Nile delta. Biblical, **Zoan.**

tank (tangk), *n.* **1.** a large container or structure for holding a liquid or gas. **2.** an armored combat vehicle, moving on caterpillar treads and usu. armed with a cannon mounted inside a rotating turret. **3.** a prison cell for more than one occupant, esp. for groups of new prisoners. **4.** a natural or artificial pond, esp. for storing water. **5.** TANK TOP. —*v.t.* **6.** to put or store in a tank. —**tank′less,** *adj.* —**tank′like′,** *adj.*

tank·age (tang′kij), *n.* **1.** the capacity of a tank or tanks. **2.** the act or process of storing liquid in a tank. **3.** the fee for such storage. **4.** the residue from tanks in which animal carcasses have been steamed and the fat rendered, used as a fertilizer.

tan·kard (tang′kərd), *n.* a large drinking cup, usu. with a handle and a hinged cover.

tank′ car′, *n.* a car containing one or more tanks for the transportation of liquids, gases, or granular solids.

tank·er (tang′kər), *n.* a ship, airplane, or truck designed for bulk shipment of liquids or gases.

tank′ suit′, *n.* a one-piece bathing suit for women, with a scoop neck, shoulder straps, and usu. no inner construction; maillot.

tank′ top′, *n.* a low-cut, sleeveless, pullover shirt with shoulder straps, often made of lightweight knitted fabric.

tank′ truck′, *n.* a truck with a tank body, suitable for transporting gases or liquids in bulk.

tan·nage (tan′ij), *n.* **1.** the act or process of tanning. **2.** the product of tanning; something tanned.

tan·ner (tan′ər), *n.* a person whose occupation is the tanning of hides.

tan·ner·y (tan′ə rē), *n., pl.* **-ner·ies.** a place where tanning is carried on.

tan·nic (tan′ik), *adj.* **1.** of, pertaining to, or derived from tan or tannin. **2.** (of wine) having an astringent taste due to the presence of tannin.

tan·nin (tan′in), *n.* any of a group of astringent vegetable principles or compounds, as the reddish compound that gives the tanning properties to oak bark or the whitish compound that occurs in large quantities in nutgalls. Also called **tan′nic ac′id.**

tan·ning (tan′ing), *n.* **1.** the process or art of converting hides or skins into leather. **2.** a browning or darkening of the skin, as by exposure to the sun. **3.** a thrashing; whipping.

tan·sy (tan′zē), *n., pl.* **-sies.** any of several composite plants of the genus *Tanacetum,* esp. an Old World herb, *T. vulgare,* having clusters of tubular yellow flowers.

tan·ta·lize (tan′tl īz′), *v.t.,* **-lized, -liz·ing.** to torment with, or as if with, the sight of something desired but out of reach; tease by arousing expectations. —**tan′ta·li·za′tion,** *n.* —**tan′ta·liz′er,** *n.*

tan·ta·liz·ing (tan′tl ī′zing), *adj.* provoking or arousing desire, esp. for what is or seems unobtainable or unreachable.

tan·ta·lum (tan′tl əm), *n.* a hard, rare metallic element that resists corrosion by most acids: used for chemical, dental, and surgical instruments. *Symbol:* Ta; *at. wt.:* 180.948; *at. no.:* 73; *sp. gr.:* 16.6.

Tan·ta·lus (tan′tl əs), *n., pl.* **-lus·es. 1.** a legendary king of Phrygia who was condemned to remain in Tartarus, chin deep in water, with fruit-laden branches above his head: whenever he tried to drink or eat, the water and fruit receded out of reach. **2.** (*l.c.*) a rack containing visible decanters secured by a lock.

tan·ta·mount (tan′tə mount′), *adj.* equivalent, as in value, force, effect, or signification: *an insult tantamount to a slap in the face.*

Tan·tra (tun′trə, tän′-), *n., pl.* **-tras. 1.** (*italics*) any of several books of esoteric Hindu doctrine regarding rituals, meditation, etc., composed in the form of dialogues between Shiva and his Shakti. **2.** (*l.c.*) the esoteric philosophy or practice based on these writings: influential in Buddhism, esp. in Tibet. —**Tan′tric,** *adj.*

tan·trum (tan′trəm), *n.* a violent demonstration of rage or frustration; a sudden burst of ill temper.

Tan·za·ni·a (tan′zə nē′ə), *n.* a republic in E Africa formed in 1964 by the merger of Tanganyika and Zanzibar. 29,460,753; 364,881 sq. mi. (945,037 sq. km). *Cap.:* Dodoma. —**Tan′za·ni′an,** *adj., n.*

T

Tao (dou, tou), *n.* **1.** (*sometimes l.c.*) (in Taoism) the dynamic principle of life by which all things happen or exist. **2.** (*often l.c.*) (in Confucianism) the rational basis of human conduct. [< Chinese *dào*: lit., way]

Tao·ism (dou′iz əm, tou′-), *n.* **1.** a Chinese philosophic tradition founded by Lao-tzu, advocating a life of simplicity and naturalness and of noninterference with the course of natural events, in order to attain a happy existence in harmony with the Tao. **2.** a pantheistic religion based on this tradition, whose practitioners seek longevity and immortality. —**Tao′ist,** *n., adj.* —**Tao·is′tic,** *adj.*

tap¹ (tap), *v.,* **tapped, tap·ping,** *—v.t.* **1.** to strike with a light but audible blow or blows; hit with repeated, slight blows. **2.** to make, put, etc., by tapping: *to tap a nail into a wall.* **3.** to strike (the fingers, a foot, a pencil, etc.) upon or against something, esp. with repeated light blows. **4.** to add a metal or leather piece to the sole or heel of (a boot or shoe). —*v.i.* **5.** to strike lightly but audibly. **6.** to strike light blows. **7.** to tap-dance. —*n.* **8.** a light but audible blow. **9.** the sound made by this. **10.** a piece of metal attached to the toe or heel of a shoe, as for reinforcement or for making the tapping of a dancer more audible.

tap² (tap), *n., v.,* **tapped, tap·ping.** —*n.* **1.** a cylindrical plug or stopper for closing an opening through which liquid is drawn, as in a cask; spigot. **2.** a faucet or cock. **3.** the liquor drawn through a particular tap. **4.** a connection made at an intermediate point on an electrical circuit or device. **5.** an act or instance of wiretapping. **6.** the surgical withdrawal of fluid: *spinal tap.* **7.** a tool for cutting screw threads into the cylindrical surface of a round opening. **8.** a hole made in tapping, as one in a pipe to furnish connection for a branch pipe. —*v.t.* **9.** to draw liquid from (a vessel or container). **10.** to draw off (liquid), as by removing a tap or piercing a container. **11.** to draw the tap from or pierce (a cask or other container). **12.** to draw upon; begin to use: *to tap one's resources.* **13.** to connect into secretly so as to receive what is being transmitted: *to tap a telephone.* **14.** to furnish (a cask, pipe, etc.) with a tap. **15.** to cut a screw thread into the surface of (an opening). **16.** to open outlets from (power lines, highways, pipes, etc.). **17. tap off,** to remove (liquid, molten metal, etc.) from a keg, furnace, or the like. —*Idiom.* **18. on tap, a.** ready to be drawn and served, as liquor from a cask. **b.** furnished with a tap or cock, as a barrel of liquor. **c.** ready for immediate use; available.

tap′ dance′, *n.* a dance in which the rhythm or rhythmical variation is audibly tapped out with the toe or heel by a dancer wearing shoes with special hard soles or with taps. —**tap′-dance′,** *v.i.,* **-danced, -danc·ing.** —**tap′-danc′er,** *n.*

tape (tāp), *n., v.,* **taped, tap·ing,** *adj.* —*n.* **1.** a long, narrow strip of fabric, as for tying garments or binding seams or edges. **2.** a long, narrow strip of paper, metal, etc. **3.** a strip of material with an adhesive surface, used for sealing, binding, etc.; adhesive tape or masking tape. **4.** a magnetic tape, esp. an audiotape or a videotape. **5.** a string stretched across the finish line of a race and broken by the winner on crossing the line. **6.** TAPE MEASURE. —*v.t.* **7.** to tie up, bind, or attach with tape. **8.** to record or prerecord on magnetic tape. **9.** to measure with or as if with a tape measure. **10.** to furnish with a tape or tapes. —*v.i.* **11.** to record something on magnetic tape. —*adj.* **12.** of, for, or recorded on magnetic tape. —**tape′less,** *adj.* —**tape′like′,** *adj.*

tape′ deck′, *n.* a component of an audio system for playing tapes, using an external amplifier and speakers.

tape′ meas′ure, *n.* a long, flexible strip or ribbon, as of cloth or metal, marked with subdivisions of the foot or meter and used for measuring. Also called **tape·line** (tāp′līn′).

tape′ play′er, *n.* a device for playing magnetic tape recordings.

ta·per¹ (tā′pər), *v.i.* **1.** to become smaller or thinner toward one end. **2.** to grow gradually lean. —*v.t.* **3.** to make gradually smaller toward one end. **4.** to reduce gradually. **5. taper off, a.** to become gradually more slender toward one end. **b.** to cease by degrees; decrease; diminish. —*n.* **6.** gradual diminution of width or thickness in an elongated object. **7.** gradual decrease of force, capacity, etc. **8.** a candle, esp. a very slender one. **9.** a long wick coated with wax, tallow, or the like, as for use in lighting candles or gas. —**ta′per·er,** *n.* —**ta′per·ing·ly,** *adv.*

tap·er² (tā′pər), *n.* a person who records or edits magnetic tape.

tape′ record′er, *n.* an electrical device for recording or playing back something recorded on magnetic tape, usu. sound.

tape′ record′ing, *n.* **1.** a magnetic tape on which speech, music, etc., has been recorded. **2.** the act of recording on magnetic tape.

tap·es·try (tap′ə strē), *n., pl.* **-tries,** *v.,* **-tried, -try·ing.** —*n.* **1.** a fabric consisting of a warp upon which colored threads are woven by hand to produce a reversible design, often pictorial, used for wall hangings, furniture coverings, etc. **2.** a machine-woven, nonreversible reproduction of this. —*v.t.* **3.** to furnish, cover, or adorn with tapestry. **4.** to represent or depict in a tapestry. —**tap′es·try·like′,** *adj.*

tap′estry car′pet, *n.* a carpet in which the design is printed on the pile warp before weaving. Also called **tap′estry Brus′sels.**

tap′estry weave′, *n.* a weave structure in which the filling threads conceal the warp threads.

tape·worm (tāp′wûrm′), *n.* any of various flat, ribbony worms of the class Cestoda, parasitic in the digestive tract of humans and other vertebrates.

tap·i·o·ca (tap′ē ō′kə), *n.* a cassava preparation, usu. in granular or pellet (**pearl tapioca**) form, used in puddings and as a thickener.

ta·pir (tā′pər, tə pēr′), *n., pl.* **-pirs,** (*esp. collectively*) **-pir.** any stout,

odd-toed, hoofed mammal of the genus *Tapirus* of tropical America and SE Asia, having a short, fleshy proboscis.

tap′ pants′, *n.* (*used with a pl. v.*) **1.** women's loose-fitting underpants. **2.** women's loose-fitting shorts worn for exercising, dancing, etc.

tap·pet (tap′it), *n.* a sliding rod that moves another machine part, as a valve, when intermittently struck by a cam.

tap·room (tap′rōōm′, -rŏŏm′), *n.* a barroom, esp. in an inn or hotel.

tap·root (tap′rōōt′, -rŏŏt′), *n.* a main root descending downward and giving off small lateral roots.

taps (taps), *n.* (*used with a sing. or pl. v.*) a bugle signal sounded in a camp or military post at night as an order to extinguish all lights.

tap′ wa′ter, *n.* water obtained via a plumbing system directly from a faucet or tap.

tar¹ (tär), *n., v.,* **tarred, tar·ring,** *adj.* —*n.* **1.** any of various dark-colored viscid products obtained by the destructive distillation of certain organic substances, as coal or wood. **2.** coal-tar pitch. **3.** smoke solids or components: *cigarette tar.* —*v.t.* **4.** to smear or cover with or as if with tar. —*adj.* **5.** of or characteristic of tar. **6.** covered or smeared with tar; tarred. —*Idiom.* **7. beat, knock,** or **whale the tar out of,** to beat mercilessly. **8. tar and feather,** to coat (a person) with tar and feathers as a punishment or humiliation. **9. tar with the same brush,** to regard as having the same unfavorable qualities as another whose shortcomings are known.

tar² (tär), *n.* a sailor.

tar·an·tel·la (tar′ən tel′ə), *n., pl.* **-las.** **1.** a rapid, whirling dance of S Italy in ⁶⁄₈ time. **2.** music in the rhythm of a tarantella.

ta·ran·tu·la (tə ran′chə lə), *n., pl.* **-las, -lae** (-lē′). a large, hairy spider of the family Theraphosidae, as *Aphonopelma chalcodes,* of the southwestern U.S., having a painful but not highly venomous bite.

tarantula, *Aphonopelma chalcodes,*
body length 2 in. (5 cm)

tar·dy (tär′dē), *adj.,* **-di·er, -di·est.** **1.** late; behind time; not on time. **2.** moving or acting slowly; sluggish. **3.** delaying through reluctance. —**tar′di·ly,** *adv.* —**tar′di·ness,** *n.*

tare (târ), *n.* **1.** any of various vetches, esp. *Vicia sativa.* **2.** (in the Bible) a noxious weed, probably the darnel. Matt. 13:25–30.

tar·get (tär′git), *n.* **1.** an object, usu. marked with concentric circles, to be aimed at in shooting practice or contests. **2.** any object used for this purpose. **3.** anything fired at. **4.** a goal or aim. **5.** an object of abuse, scorn, derision, etc.; butt. —*adj.* **6.** being or indicating a target or goal. —*v.t.* **7.** to use, set up, or designate as a target or goal. **8.** to direct toward a target. **9.** to make a target of, as for attack or abuse. —*Idiom.* **10. on target,** accurate or correct; precisely right. —**tar′get·a·ble,** *adj.*

tar′get date′, *n.* the date set or aimed at for the commencement or completion of some effort.

Tar·gum (tär′gŏŏm; *Heb.* tär gōōm′), *n., pl.* **Tar·gums,** *Heb.* **Tar·gu·mim** (tär gŏŏ mēm′). a translation or paraphrase in Aramaic of a book or division of the Old Testament. —**Tar·gum′ic,** *adj.* —**Tar′gum·ist,** *n.*

tar·iff (tar′if), *n.* **1.** a schedule or system of duties imposed by a government on imports or exports. **2.** a duty or rate of duty in such a schedule. **3.** any table of charges or fares. **4.** bill; cost; charge. —*v.t.* **5.** to subject to a tariff. **6.** to put a valuation on according to a tariff.

Tar·mac (tär′mak), **1.** *Trademark.* a bituminous binder, similar to tarmacadam, for surfacing roads, airport runways, etc. —*n.* **2.** (*l.c.*) a road or runway paved with Tarmac or tarmacadam.

tar·mac·ad·am (tär′mə kad′əm), *n.* a paving material consisting of coarse crushed stone covered with tar and bitumen.

tarn (tärn), *n.* a small mountain lake or pool, esp. one in a cirque.

tar·na·tion (tär nā′shən), *interj., n.* damnation; hell (used as a euphemism).

tar·nish (tär′nish), *v.t.* **1.** to dull the luster of or discolor (a metallic surface), esp. by oxidation. **2.** to diminish or destroy the purity of; stain; sully: *to tarnish a reputation.* —*v.i.* **3.** to become tarnished. —*n.* **4.** a tarnished coating. **5.** tarnished condition; discoloration. **6.** a stain or blemish. —**tar′nish·a·ble,** *adj.*

ta·ro (tär′ō, târ′ō, tar′ō), *n., pl.* **-ros.** **1.** a stemless plant, *Colocasia esculenta,* of the arum family, cultivated in tropical regions for its edible tuber. **2.** the tuber itself. [< Polynesian]

ta·rot (tar′ō, ta rō′), *n.* any of a set of 22 playing cards bearing allegorical representations, used for fortune-telling.

tarp (tärp), *n. Informal.* a tarpaulin.

tar·pa·per (tär′pā′pər), *n.* a heavy, tar-coated paper used as a waterproofing material in building construction.

tar·pau·lin (tär pô′lin, tär′pə lin), *n.* **1.** a sheet of waterproofed canvas or other material used as a protective covering for objects exposed to the weather. **2.** a sailor.

tar′ pit′, *n.* a seepage of natural tar or asphalt, esp. an accumulation that has acted as a natural trap for animals, whose bones have become preserved within it.

tar•pon (tär′pən), *n., pl.* **-pons,** (*esp. collectively*) **-pon.** a powerful game fish, *Megalops atlanticus,* of warm W Atlantic waters, having large, silvery scales.

tar•ra•gon (tar′ə gon′, -gən), *n.* **1.** an Old World composite plant, *Artemisia dracunculus,* with aromatic leaves used for seasoning. **2.** the leaves themselves.

tar•ry[1] (tar′ē), *v.,* **-ried, -ry•ing,** *n., pl.* **-ries.** —*v.i.* **1.** to stay in a place; sojourn. **2.** to delay or be tardy in acting, starting, etc.; linger or loiter. **3.** to wait. —*n.* **4.** a stay; sojourn. —**tar′ri•er,** *n.*

tar•ry[2] (tär′ē), *adj.,* **-ri•er, -ri•est.** of, like, or smeared with tar.

tar•sal (tär′səl), *adj.* **1.** of or pertaining to the tarsus of the foot. **2.** pertaining to the tarsi of the eyelids. —*n.* **3.** a tarsal bone, joint, etc.

Tar•shish (tär′shish), *n.* an ancient country of uncertain location mentioned in the Bible. I Kings 10:22.

tar•si•er (tär′sē ər, -sē ā′), *n.* any small tree-dwelling SE Asian primate of the genus *Tarsius,* suborder Tarsioideae, having a long naked tail and very large eyes.

tar•sus (tär′səs), *n., pl.* **-si** (-sī, -sē). **1.** the bones between the tibia and metatarsus of the foot, forming the ankle joint. **2.** the small plate of connective tissue along the border of an eyelid. **3.** the distal part of the limb of an arthropod, as the fifth segment of an insect leg.

Tar•sus (tär′səs), *n.* a city in S Turkey, near the Cilician Gates: important seaport of ancient Cilicia; birthplace of Saint Paul. 121,074.

tart[1] (tärt), *adj.* **1.** sharp to the taste; sour or acid: *tart apples.* **2.** sharp in character, spirit, or expression; cutting; caustic: *a tart remark.* —**tart′ly,** *adv.* —**tart′ness,** *n.*

tart[2] (tärt), *n.* a usu. small, shallow pie, without a top crust, filled with fruit, custard, or the like.

tar•tan (tär′tn), *n.* **1.** a woolen or worsted cloth woven with stripes of different colors and widths crossing at right angles, worn chiefly by the Scottish Highlanders, each clan having its own distinctive pattern. **2.** such a pattern known by the name of the clan wearing it; plaid. **3.** any plaid or plaid fabric. —*adj.* **4.** of, resembling, or made of tartan.

tar•tar (tär′tər), *n.* **1.** CALCULUS (def. 3). **2.** the deposit from wines, cream of tartar. **3.** the intermediate product of cream of tartar, obtained from the crude form, argol. —**tar•tar′ic** (-tar′ik, -tär′-), *adj.*

Tar•tar (tär′tər), *n.* **1.** a member of any of various Mongolian and Turkic peoples who, under Genghis Khan and his successors, ruled parts of central and W Asia and E Europe until the 18th century. **2.** TATAR (defs. 1, 2). **3.** (*often l.c.*) a savage, intractable, or ill-tempered person.

tar′tar emet′ic, *n.* a poisonous powder, $C_4H_4KO_7Sb$, used as a mordant for dyeing and in medicine as an expectorant, emetic, etc.

tar•tar′ic ac′id (tär tar′ik, -tär′-), *n.* an organic compound, $C_4H_6O_6$, occurring in four isomeric forms: used in effervescent beverages, baking powder, photography, and tanning.

tar′tar sauce′, *n.* a mayonnaise sauce containing chopped pickles, olives, capers, etc., served with fish.

tar′tar steak′, *n.* STEAK TARTARE.

Tar•ta•rus (tär′tər əs), *n.* (in Greek myth) **1.** UNDERWORLD (def. 2). **2.** a region of the underworld in which evildoers were eternally punished.

Tar•ta•ry (tär′tə rē) *n.* TATARY.

tart•let (tärt′lit), *n.* a small tart.

Tar•tuffe or **Tar•tufe** (tär to͝of′, -to͞of′), *n.* (*often l.c.*) a hypocritical pretender to piety. [after the title character in a Molière play (1664)]

Tar•zan (tär′zan, -zan), *n.* **1.** the hero of a series of jungle stories by Edgar Rice Burroughs. **2.** a person of superior or superhuman physical strength, agility, and prowess.

Tash•kent (täsh kent′, tash-), *n.* the capital of Uzbekistan, in the NE part. 2,073,000.

task (task, täsk), *n.* **1.** a piece of work assigned to or expected of a person. **2.** any piece of work. **3.** a matter of considerable labor or difficulty. —*v.t.* **4.** to subject to severe or excessive labor or exertion; strain. **5.** to impose a task on. —***Idiom.*** **6. take** or **bring to task,** to reprimand; chide; censure.

task′ force′, *n.* **1.** a group of military units brought together under one command for a specific operation. **2.** a group or committee, as of experts, formed to examine or solve a specific problem.

task•mas•ter (task′mas′tər, täsk′mä′stər), *n.* a person who assigns tasks, esp. burdensome ones, to others or who supervises others' work rigorously. —**task′mas′ter•ship′,** *n.*

Tas•man (taz′mən), *n.* **Abel Janszoon,** 1602?–59, Dutch explorer.

Tas•ma•ni•a (taz mā′nē ə, -mān′yə), *n.* an island S of Australia: a state of the commonwealth of Australia. 436,353; 26,382 sq. mi. (68,330 sq. km). *Cap.:* Hobart. Formerly, **Van Diemen's Land.** —**Tas•ma′ni•an,** *adj., n.*

Tasma′nian dev′il, *n.* a small, massive-headed, predatory Tasmanian marsupial, *Sarcophilus harrisii.*

tas•sel (tas′əl), *n., v.,* **-seled, -sel•ing** or (*esp. Brit.*) **-selled, -sel•ling.** —*n.* **1.** a pendent ornament consisting of a bunch of threads, cords, or other strands hanging from a roundish knob or head, used on clothing, in jewelry, etc. **2.** something resembling this, as at the top of a stalk of corn. —*v.t.* **3.** to furnish or adorn with tassels. —*v.i.* **4.** (of corn) to put forth tassels. —**tas′sel•y,** *adj.*

Tas•so (tas′ō, tä′sō), *n.* **Torquato,** 1544–95, Italian poet.

taste (tāst), *v.,* **tast•ed, tast•ing,** *n.* —*v.t.* **1.** to test the flavor or quality of by taking some into the mouth. **2.** to eat or drink a little of. **3.** to eat or drink: *He hadn't tasted food for three days.* **4.** to perceive or distinguish the flavor of: *to taste the wine in a sauce.* **5.** to experience, esp. to only a slight degree. —*v.i.* **6.** to try the flavor or quality of something. **7.** to eat or drink a little (usu. fol. by *of*). **8.** to perceive or distinguish the flavor of anything. **9.** to have a particular flavor: *The coffee tastes bitter.* **10.** to have experience, however limited (usu. fol. by *of*): *to taste of victory even in defeat.* —*n.* **11.** the sense by which the flavor or savor of things is perceived when they are brought into contact with the tongue. **12.** the sensation or quality as perceived by this sense; flavor. **13.** the act of tasting food or drink. **14.** a small quantity tasted. **15.** a relish, liking, or partiality for something: *a taste for music.* **16.** a sense of what is fitting, harmonious, or beautiful. **17.** a sense of what is polite, tactful, etc., to say or do in a given social situation. **18.** one's attitude toward or display of aesthetic or social values, regarded as good or bad: *elegant taste in clothes; jokes in poor taste.* **19.** the ideas or preferences typical of a culture or an individual in regard to what is beautiful or harmonious: *a sample of Victorian taste.* **20.** a slight experience of something: *a taste of adventure.* **21.** a feeling or sensation resulting from an experience: *a compromise that had left her with a bad taste.*

taste′ bud′, *n.* one of numerous small flask-shaped bodies, chiefly in the epithelium of the tongue, that are the sense organs of taste.

taste•ful (tāst′fəl), *adj.* having, displaying, or in accordance with good taste. —**taste′ful•ly,** *adv.* —**taste′ful•ness,** *n.*

taste•less (tāst′lis), *adj.* **1.** having no taste or flavor; insipid. **2.** dull; uninteresting. **3.** having or displaying bad taste; devoid of good taste. —**taste′less•ly,** *adv.* —**taste′less•ness,** *n.*

tast•er (tā′stər), *n.* **1.** a person who tastes, esp. one skilled in distinguishing the qualities of wines, teas, etc., by the taste. **2.** a cup or other container for taking samples to be tasted. **3.** a person employed to taste food and drink prepared for a king, dictator, etc., to test for poison.

tast•y (tā′stē), *adj.,* **tast•i•er, tast•i•est. 1.** good-tasting; savory. **2.** very appealing or intriguing. **3.** TASTEFUL. —**tast′i•ly,** *adv.* —**tast′i•ness,** *n.*

ta•ta•mi (tə tä′mē), *n., pl.* **-mi, -mis.** a thick, woven straw mat of uniform dimensions used in Japanese houses as a floor covering.

Ta•tar (tä′tər), *n.* **1.** a member of a modern Turkic-speaking people living in the Tatar Autonomous Republic and adjacent regions of E European Russia and in scattered communities in W Siberia and central Asia. **2.** the language of this people. **3.** TARTAR (def. 1).

Ta•ta•ry (tä′tə rē) also **Tartary,** *n.* a historic region of indefinite extent in E Europe and Asia: designates the area overrun by the Tartars in the Middle Ages, from the Dnieper River to the Pacific.

Tate (tāt), *n.* **1. (John Orley) Allen,** 1899–1979, U.S. poet and critic. **2. Nahum,** 1652–1715, English poet and playwright, born in Ireland: poet laureate 1692–1715.

ta•ter (tā′tər), *n. Dial.* potato.

tat•ter (tat′ər), *n.* **1.** a torn piece hanging from the main part, as of a garment or flag. **2.** a separate piece; shred. **3. tatters,** torn or ragged clothing. —*v.t.* **4.** to tear or wear to tatters. —*v.i.* **5.** to become ragged.

tat•ter•de•mal•ion (tat′ər di māl′yən, -mal′-), *n.* **1.** a person in tattered clothing; shabby person. —*adj.* **2.** ragged; unkempt or dilapidated.

tat•tered (tat′ərd), *adj.* **1.** torn to tatters; ragged: *a tattered flag.* **2.** wearing ragged clothing: *a tattered old man.*

tat•ter•sall (tat′ər sôl′, -səl), *n.* **1.** a pattern of squares formed by colored crossbars on a solid-color, usu. light background. **2.** a fabric with this pattern. —*adj.* **3.** having this pattern.

tat•tle (tat′l), *v.,* **-tled, -tling,** *n.* —*v.i.* **1.** to tell something secret or private about another, often out of spite. **2.** to chatter, prate, or gossip. —*v.t.* **3.** to utter idly; disclose by gossiping. **4. tattle on,** to betray by tattling. —*n.* **5.** the act of tattling. **6.** idle talk; chatter; gossip.

tat•tler (tat′lər), *n.* **1.** a person who tattles. **2.** either of two shorebirds of the genus *Heteroscelus,* having a loud, whistling cry.

tat•tle•tale (tat′l tāl′), *n.* **1.** a talebearer or informer, esp. among children. —*adj.* **2.** telltale; revealing: *tattletale crumbs.*

tat•too[1] (ta to͞o′), *n.* **1.** a bugle call or other signal preceding taps and ordering soldiers to go to their quarters. **2.** a knocking or strong pulsation: *My heart beat a tattoo on my ribs.* **3.** *Brit.* an outdoor military pageant or display.

tat•too[2] (ta to͞o′), *n., pl.* **-toos,** *v.* **-tooed, -too•ing.** —*n.* **1.** the act or practice of marking the skin with indelible designs, legends, etc., by making punctures in it and inserting pigments. **2.** any mark or markings so made. —*v.t.* **3.** to mark with tattoos, as a person or a part of the body. **4.** to put (a design, legend, etc.) on the skin.

Ta•tum (tā′təm), *n.* **1. Art,** 1910–56, U.S. jazz pianist. **2. Edward Lawrie,** 1909–75, U.S. biochemist.

tau′ cross′, *n.* a T-shaped cross.

taught (tôt), *v.* pt. and pp. of TEACH.

tau′ lep′ton, *Physics.* an unstable lepton with a mass approximately 3500 times that of the electron. *Symbol:* T Also called **tau, tauon.**

taunt (tônt, tänt), *v.t.* **1.** to reproach in a sarcastic or insulting manner; mock. **2.** to provoke by taunts; twit. —*n.* **3.** a scornful or sarcastic reproach or challenge; gibe; insult. —**taunt′er,** *n.* —**taunt′ing•ly,** *adv.*

tau•on (tô′on, tou′-), *n.* TAU LEPTON.

taupe (tōp), *n.* a moderate to dark brownish gray.

tau•rine (tôr′īn, -in), *adj.* **1.** of or resembling a bull. **2.** pertaining to the zodiacal sign Taurus.

Tau•rus[1] (tôr′əs), *n.* **1.** the Bull, a zodiacal constellation between Aries and Gemini, containing the bright star Aldebaran. **2.** the second sign of the zodiac, between Aries and Gemini. [< Latin: bull]

Tau·rus² (tôr′əs), *n.* a mountain range in S Turkey. Highest peak, 12,251 ft. (3734 m).

taut (tôt), *adj.* **1.** tightly drawn; tense; not slack. **2.** emotionally or mentally strained or tense: *taut nerves.* **3.** in good order or condition; tidy; neat; trim. —**taut′ly,** *adv.* —**taut′ness,** *n.*

tau·tol·o·gy (tô tol′ə jē), *n., pl.* -**gies. 1.** needless repetition of an idea in different words, as in "widow woman." **2.** an instance of such repetition. **3.** *Logic.* a compound proposition or propositional form all of whose instances are true, as "A or not A" or "The candidate will win or lose." —**tau·to·log·i·cal** (tôt′l oj′i kəl), *adj.* —**tau′to·log′i·cal·ly,** *adv.*

tav·ern (tav′ərn), *n.* **1.** a place where liquors are sold to be consumed on the premises. **2.** a public house for travelers and others; inn. [< Old French < Latin *taberna* hut, inn, shop]

taw¹ (tô), *n.* **1.** a playing marble used as a shooter. **2.** a game in which marbles are knocked out of a circle drawn on the ground by using a marble as a shooter. **3.** Also called **taw′ line′.** the line from which the players shoot. —*v.i.* **4.** to shoot a marble.

taw² (tô), *v.t.* **1.** to prepare or dress (a raw material) for use or further manipulation. **2.** to convert (animal skin) into white leather by the application of minerals, emulsions, etc. —**taw′er,** *n.*

taw·dry (tô′drē), *adj.,* -**dri·er, -dri·est,** *n.* —*adj.* **1.** showy and cheap; gaudy. **2.** low or mean; base. —*n.* **3.** cheap, gaudy apparel. —**taw′dri·ly,** *adv.* —**taw′dri·ness,** *n.*

taw·ny (tô′nē), *adj.,* -**ni·er, -ni·est.** —*adj.* **1.** of a dark yellowish or yellowish brown color; yellowish or dullish golden brown. —*n.* **2.** tawny color. —**taw′ni·ly,** *adv.* —**taw′ni·ness,** *n.*

tax (taks), *n.* **1.** a sum of money levied on incomes, property, sales, etc., by a government for its support or for specific services. **2.** a burdensome charge, obligation, or demand. —*v.t.* **3.** (of a government) **a.** to impose a tax on (a person or business). **b.** to levy a tax on (income, goods, etc.), usu. in proportion to the value of money involved. **4.** to make serious demands on or of; burden; strain: *to tax one's resources.* **5.** to reprove or accuse; censure or charge: *to tax a person with laziness.*

tax·a·ble (tak′sə bəl), *adj.* **1.** capable of being taxed; subject to tax: *a taxable gain.* —*n.* **2.** Usu. **taxables.** persons or things that are subject to tax. —**tax′a·bil′i·ty, tax′a·ble·ness,** *n.*

tax·a·tion (tak sā′shən), *n.* **1.** the act of taxing. **2.** the fact of being taxed. **3.** a tax imposed. **4.** the revenue raised by taxes. —**tax·a′tion·al,** *adj.*

taxa′tion without′ representa′tion, a phrase, generally attributed to James Otis about 1761, that reflected the resentment of American colonists at being taxed by a British Parliament without elected representatives; the phrase became an anti-British slogan before the American Revolution: in full, "Taxation without representation is tyranny."

tax′-deduct′ible, *adj.* noting an item the value or cost of which is deductible from the gross amount on which a tax is calculated.

tax′-deferred′ annu′ity, *n.* an annuity to which teachers and other employees of nonprofit organizations may contribute, taxes to be deferred until withdrawal, usually at retirement. *Abbr.:* TDA

tax′-exempt′, *adj.* **1.** not subject or liable to taxation. **2.** providing income that is not taxable: *tax-exempt municipal bonds.* —*n.* **3.** a tax-exempt security.

tax′ ex′ile, *n.* a person who moves outside the jurisdiction of a country to avoid paying taxes. Also called **tax′ expa′triate.**

tax′-free′, *adj.* TAX-EXEMPT.

tax·i (tak′sē), *n., pl.* **tax·is** or **tax·ies,** *v.,* **tax·ied, tax·i·ing** or **tax·y·ing.** —*n.* **1.** a taxicab. —*v.i.* **2.** to travel in a taxicab. **3.** (of an airplane) to move over the surface of the ground or water at slow speed, as in preparing for takeoff. —*v.t.* **4.** to cause (an airplane) to taxi.

tax·i·cab (tak′si kab′), *n.* a public passenger vehicle, esp. an automobile, usu. fitted with a taximeter.

tax·i·der·my (tak′si dûr′mē), *n.* the art of preparing, preserving, and stuffing the skins of animals and mounting them in lifelike form. —**tax′i·der′mal, tax′i·der′mic,** *adj.* —**tax′i·der′mist,** *n.*

tax·i·me·ter (tak′sē mē′tər), *n.* a device fitted to a taxicab or other vehicle, for automatically computing and indicating the fare due.

tax·ing (tak′sing), *adj.* wearingly burdensome: *the taxing duties of a hotel manager.* —**tax′ing·ly,** *adv.*

tax·is¹ (tak′sis), *n., pl.* **tax·es** (tak′sēz). **1.** arrangement or order, as in the physical sciences. **2.** oriented movement of a motile organism in response to an external stimulus, as toward or away from light. **3.** the repositioning of a displaced body part without cutting.

tax·is² (tak′sēz), *n.* a pl. of TAXIS.

tax·i·way (tak′sē wā′), *n.* any surface area of an airport used for taxiing airplanes, as to and from a runway.

tax·on (tak′son), *n., pl.* **tax·a** (tak′sə). a taxonomic category, as a species or genus.

tax·on·o·my (tak son′ə mē), *n.* **1.** the science or technique of classification. **2.** the science dealing with the description, identification, naming, and classification of organisms. **3.** any classification, esp. the systematic classification of organisms into hierarchical groups or taxa. —**tax′o·nom′ic** (-sə nom′ik), *adj.* —**tax′o·nom′i·cal·ly,** *adv.* —**tax·on′o·mist, tax·on′o·mer,** *n.*

TAXONOMIC CLASSIFICATION

Taxon	Animal	Plant
	human being	white oak
Kingdom	Animalia	Plantae
Phylum	Chordata	Magnoliophyta
Class	Mammalia	Magnoliopsida
Order	Primates	Fagales
Family	Hominidae	Fagaceae (beech)
Genus	Homo	Quercus
Species	*Homo sapiens*	*Quercus alba*

tax·pay·er (taks′pā′ər), *n.* a person who pays a tax or is subject to taxation. —**tax′pay′ing,** *adj., n.*

tax′ rate′, *n.* the percentage of the value of a property to be paid as a tax.

tax′ return′, *n.* RETURN (def. 22).

tax′ revolt′, *n.* a movement by taxpayers to rescind increases in property taxes.

tax′ shar′ing, *n.* REVENUE SHARING.

tax′ shel′ter, *n.* any financial arrangement, as an investment or allowance, that reduces or eliminates the taxes due. —**tax′-shel′tered,** *adj.*

Tay·lor (tā′lər), *n.* **1. Elizabeth,** born 1932, U.S. film actress, born in England. **2. Jeremy,** 1613–67, English prelate and theological writer. **3. Kenneth (Nathaniel),** born 1917, U.S. Bible editor and publisher. **4. Maxwell (Davenport),** 1901–87, U.S. army general. **5. Paul (Belville),** born 1930, U.S. choreographer. **6. Zachary** ("Old Rough and Ready"), 1784–1850, 12th president of the U.S. 1849–50. **7.** a city in SE Michigan. 71,640.

Tay′-Sachs′ disease′ (tā′saks′), *n.* a degenerative brain disorder caused by lack of or deficiency in an essential enzyme, usu. resulting in mental and physical deterioration and death in early childhood. [after Warren *Tay* (1843–1927), British ophthalmologist, and Bernard *Sachs* (1858–1944), U.S. neurologist, who described it independently]

TB or **tb, 1.** tubercle bacillus. **2.** tuberculosis.

Tb, *Chem. Symbol.* terbium.

TBA or **t.b.a.,** to be announced.

T-bar (tē′bär′), *n.* **1.** a metal bar or beam with a cross section resembling a T. **2.** Also called **T-bar lift.** a ski lift having an upside-down T-shaped bar against which two skiers may lean while being pulled uphill.

Tbi·li·si (tə bə lē′sē, -bil′ə-), *n.* the capital of the Georgian Republic, in the SE part, on the Kura. 1,194,000. Formerly, **Tiflis.**

T-bill (tē′bil′), *n.* TREASURY BILL.

T-bond (tē′bond′), *n.* TREASURY BOND.

T-bone steak (tē′bōn′), *n.* a loin steak with a small piece of tenderloin, characterized by its T-shaped bone.

tbs. or **tbsp., 1.** tablespoon. **2.** tablespoonful.

Tc, *Chem. Symbol.* technetium.

T cell, *n.* any of several closely related lymphocytes, developed in the thymus, that circulate in the blood and lymph and regulate the immune system's response to infected or malignant cells. Also called **T lymphocyte.**

Tchai·kov·sky (chī kôf′skē, -kof′-, chi-), *n.* **Peter Ilyich** or **Pëtr Ilich,** 1840–93, Russian composer.

TD, Also, **T.D.** Treasury Department.

T/D, time deposit.

TDA, tax-deferred annuity.

Te, *Chem. Symbol.* tellurium.

tea (tē), *n.* **1.** the dried and prepared leaves of a shrub, *Thea (Camellia) sinensis,* of the family Theaceade. **2.** the shrub itself, extensively cultivated in China, Japan, India, etc., and having fragrant white flowers. **3.** a somewhat bitter, aromatic beverage prepared by infusing tea leaves in boiling water, served hot or iced. **4.** any leaves, flowers, etc., so used, or any plant yielding them. **5.** an infusion prepared from the leaves, flowers, etc., of other plants, used as a beverage or medicine. **6.** a snack or light meal, usu. including tea, sandwiches, and cakes, eaten in the late afternoon. **7.** *Brit.* any meal eaten in the late afternoon or evening. **8.** an afternoon reception at which tea is served. —*Idiom.* **9.** one's cup of tea, something suitable, appropriate, or attractive to one.

Tea′ Act′, *n.* an act of the British Parliament (1773) that created a monopoly unfair to American tea merchants: the chief cause of the Boston Tea Party.

tea′ bag′, *n.* a small sack of thin paper or cloth holding a measured amount of tea leaves for making an individual serving of tea.

tea′ ball′, *n.* a small ball of perforated metal in which tea leaves are placed for immersion in hot water to make tea.

tea·ber·ry (tē′ber′ē, -bə rē), *n., pl.* -**ries.** the spicy red fruit of the American wintergreen, *Gaultheria procumbens.*

tea′ bis′cuit, *n.* a small, round, soft biscuit, usually shortened and sweetened.

tea′ cad′dy, *n.* a small box, can, or chest for holding tea leaves.

tea·cake (tē′kāk′), *n.* **1.** *Brit.* a light, flat cake with raisins, usu. buttered and served hot. **2.** any small cake or cookie.

teach (tēch), *v.,* **taught, teach·ing.** —*v.t.* **1.** to impart knowledge of or skill in; give instruction in: *She teaches mathematics.* **2.** to impart knowledge or skill to; give instruction to: *He teaches a large class.* —*v.i.* **3.** to impart knowledge or skill; give instruction, esp. as one's profession or vocation.

teach·a·ble (tē′chə bəl), *adj.* **1.** capable of being instructed, as a person. **2.** capable of being taught, as a subject. —**teach′a·bil′i·ty, teach′·a·ble·ness,** *n.* —**teach′a·bly,** *adv.*

teach·er (tē′chər), *n.* a person who teaches, esp. as a profession; instructor.

teach′ers col′lege, *n.* a college offering courses for the training of teachers.

teach·ing (tē′ching), *n.* **1.** the act or profession of a person who teaches. **2.** Often, **teachings.** something that is taught, esp. a doctrine or precept.

teach′ing fel′lowship, *n.* a fellowship stipulating that the student who receives it must perform some teaching duties.

teach′ing hos′pital, *n.* a hospital associated with a medical college and offering practical experience to students, interns, and residents.

tea·cup (tē′kup′), *n.* **1.** a cup in which tea is served, usu. of small or moderate size. **2.** the amount a teacup will hold.

tea′ fam′ily, *n.* a plant family, Theaceae, of evergreen shrubs and vines of warm climates, with simple alternate leaves and often showy flowers: includes camellias, certain bays, and tea.

tea′ gar′den, *n.* **1.** a tea plantation. **2.** an outdoor restaurant serving tea and other refreshments.

tea·house (tē′hous′), *n., pl.* **-hous·es** (-hou′ziz). an establishment, esp. in the Far East, where tea and refreshments are served.

teak (tēk), *n.* **1.** a large East Indian tree, *Tectona grandis,* of the verbena family, yielding a hard, medium brown wood. **2.** the wood of this tree, used in shipbuilding, furniture-making, etc.

tea·ket·tle (tē′ket′l), *n.* a portable kettle with a cover, spout, and handle, used for boiling water.

teak·wood (tēk′wood′), *n.* TEAK (def. 2).

teal (tēl), *n., pl.* **teals,** (*esp. collectively*) **teal** for 1. **1.** any of several small dabbling ducks, esp. of the genus *Anas.* **2.** Also called **teal′ blue′.** a medium to dark greenish blue.

team (tēm), *n.* **1.** a number of persons forming one of the sides in a game or contest: *a debating team.* **2.** a number of persons associated in some joint action: *a team of experts.* **3.** two or more horses, oxen, or other animals harnessed together to draw a vehicle, plow, or the like. **4.** a brood or litter of young, esp. of ducklings or piglets. —*v.t.* **5.** to join together in a team. —*v.i.* **6.** to drive a team. **7.** to gather or join in a team (usu. fol. by *up, together,* etc.). —*adj.* **8.** pertaining to or performed by a team: *a team effort.* —**Usage.** See COLLECTIVE NOUN.

team·mate (tēm′māt′), *n.* a member of the same team.

team′ play′er, *n.* a person who willingly cooperates with others.

team·ster (tēm′stər), *n.* a person who drives a team or a truck for hauling, esp. as an occupation.

Team′sters U′nion, *n.* the unofficial name of the International Brotherhood of Teamsters, Chauffeurs, Warehousemen, and Helpers of America.

team·work (tēm′wûrk′), *n.* **1.** cooperative effort on the part of a group of persons acting together as a team or in the interests of a common cause. **2.** work done with a team.

tea′ par′ty, *n.* a social gathering, usu. in the afternoon, at which tea and light refreshments are served.

tea·pot (tē′pot′), *n.* a container with a lid, spout, and handle, in which tea is made and from which it is poured.

Tea′pot Dome′, *n.* a federal oil reserve in Wyoming, leased to private producer Harry F. Sinclair by Secretary of the Interior Albert B. Fall in 1922, leading to a major government scandal and the tarnishing of the reputation of President Warren G. Harding's administration (1921–23).

tear[1] (tēr), *n.* **1.** a drop of the saline, watery fluid continually secreted by the lacrimal glands between the surface of the eye and the eyelid. **2.** a drop of this fluid appearing in or flowing from the eye as the result of emotion, esp. grief. **3.** something resembling a tear, as a drop of a liquid or a tearlike mass of a solid substance. **4.** tears, **a.** grief; sorrow. **b.** an act of weeping: *bored to tears.* —*v.i.* **5.** (of the eyes) to fill up and overflow with tears. —**Idiom. 6.** in tears, weeping.

tear[2] (târ), *v.,* **tore, torn, tear·ing,** *n.* —*v.t.* **1.** to pull apart or in pieces by force; rend. **2.** to pull or snatch violently; wrench away with force: *to tear a book from someone's hands.* **3.** to divide or disrupt: *a country torn by civil war.* **4.** to produce by rending: *to tear a hole in one's coat.* **5.** to wound or injure by or as if by rending; lacerate: *grief that tears the heart.* **6.** to remove by force or effort (often fol. by *away*): *It was such an exciting lecture, I couldn't tear myself away.* —*v.i.* **7.** to become torn: *The fabric tears easily.* **8.** to move or behave with force, violent haste, or energy: *The wind tore through the trees; cars tearing up and down the highway.* **9. tear at, a.** to pluck violently at. **b.** to distress; afflict. **10. tear down, a.** to pull down; demolish. **b.** to disparage or discredit. **11. tear into,** to attack impulsively or viciously. **12. tear up, a.** to tear into small shreds. **b.** to cancel or annul: *to tear up a contract.* —*n.* **13.** the act of tearing. **14.** a rent or fissure. **15.** a rage or passionate outburst. **16.** *Informal.* a spree. —**Idiom. 17. tear it,** *Slang.* to ruin all chances for a successful outcome. —**tear′er,** *n.*

tear·a·way (târ′ə wā′), *adj.* **1.** designed to be easily separated or opened by tearing: *a box with a tearaway seal.* —*n.* **2.** *Brit.* a wild, reckless person.

tear·drop (tēr′drop′), *n.* **1.** a tear. **2.** something shaped like a falling drop of a thin liquid, having a globular form at the bottom tapering to a point at the top.

tear·ful (tēr′fal), *adj.* **1.** full of tears; weeping. **2.** causing tears: *a tearful story of poverty.* —**tear′ful·ly,** *adv.* —**tear′ful·ness,** *n.*

tear′ gas′, *n.* a gas that makes the eyes smart and water, thus producing a temporary blindness, used in warfare, to quell riots, etc. —**tear′-gas′, tear′gas′,** *v.t.*

tear·ing (târ′ing), *adj.* violent or hasty: *with tearing speed.*

tear·jerk·er (tēr′jûr′kər), *n. Informal.* a sentimental story, play, movie, or the like, designed to elicit tears. —**tear′jerk′ing,** *adj.*

tea·room (tē′rōōm′, -rōōm′), *n.* a restaurant or shop where tea and other refreshments are served.

tea′ rose′, *n.* any of several hybrid varieties of roses descended from a Chinese rose, *Rosa odorata,* having a scent resembling that of tea.

tear′ sheet′, *n.* a page torn from a magazine, journal, or the like, esp. one containing an advertisement and sent to the advertiser as proof of publication.

tear′-stained′ (tēr′), *adj.* marked or wet with tears: *a tear-stained letter.*

tear′ strip′ or **tear′strip′** (târ′), *n.* a strip, string, etc., that is pulled to open a box, wrapper, or the like.

tear·y (tēr′ē), *adj.,* **tear·i·er, tear·i·est. 1.** tearful: *a teary farewell.* **2.** of or like tears. —**tear′i·ly,** *adv.* —**tear′i·ness,** *n.*

tease (tēz), *v.,* **teased, teas·ing.** —*v.t.* **1.** to irritate or provoke with petty taunts, playful mockery, pretended offers, persistent requests, or other annoyances, often in sport. **2.** to comb or card (wool or the like). **3.** to ruffle (the hair) by holding at the ends and combing toward the scalp so as to give body to a hairdo. —*v.i.* **4.** to tease a person or animal. —*n.* **5.** a person who teases. **6.** Also, **teaser.** a short scene or highlight shown at the beginning of a film or television show to engage the audience's attention. —**teas′a·ble,** *adj.* —**teas′ing·ly,** *adv.*

tea·sel (tē′zəl), *n., v.,* **-seled, -sel·ing** or (*esp. Brit.*) **-selled, -sel·ling.** —*n.* **1.** any of several plants of the genus *Dipsacus,* of the teasel family, having prickly leaves and flower heads. **2.** the dried flower head or burr of the plant *D. fullonum,* used for teaseling cloth. **3.** any mechanical contrivance used for teaseling cloth. —*v.t.* **4.** to raise a nap on (cloth) with teasels; dress by means of teasels. Often, **teazel, teazle.**

teas·er (tē′zər), *n.* **1.** a person or thing that teases. **2.** a drapery or flat piece across the top of the proscenium arch that masks the flies and that, together with the tormentors, forms a frame for the stage opening. **3.** an advertisement that lures customers or clients by offering a bonus, gift, or the like. **4.** TEASE (def. 6).

tea′ serv′ice, *n.* a set of chinaware, silver, etc., for preparing and serving hot beverages, esp. tea. Also called **tea′ set′.**

tea·spoon (tē′spōōn′), *n.* **1.** a small spoon used to stir tea and coffee, eat desserts, etc. **2.** a teaspoonful.

tea·spoon·ful (tē′spōōn fōōl′), *n., pl.* **-fuls. 1.** the amount a teaspoon can hold. **2.** a volumetric measure equal to $\frac{1}{6}$ fluid ounce (4.9 ml); $\frac{1}{3}$ tablespoonful. *Abbr.:* t., tsp.

teat (tēt, tit), *n.* the protuberance on the breast or udder in female mammals, through which the milk ducts discharge; nipple.

tea·time (tē′tīm′), *n.* the time at which tea is served or taken, usu. in the late afternoon.

tea′ tow′el, *n.* a dishtowel.

Te·bet (te vet′, tā-, tā′vās), *n.* TEVET.

tech (tek), *Informal.* —*adj.* **1.** technical: *tech talk.* —*n.* **2.** a technician: *the techs on a film crew.* **3.** technology: *computer tech.* **4.** technical work.

tech·ie or **tek·kie** (tek′ē), *n. Informal.* **1.** a technical expert, student, or enthusiast, esp. in the field of electronics. **2.** a technician, as for a stage crew.

tech·ne·ti·um (tek nē′shē əm, -shəm), *n.* a synthetic element obtained in the fission of uranium or by the bombardment of molybdenum. *Symbol:* Tc; *at. wt.:* 99; *at. no.:* 43; *sp. gr.:* 11.5.

tech·ni·cal (tek′ni kəl), *adj.* **1.** pertaining to an art, science, or the like: *technical skill.* **2.** peculiar to or characteristic of a particular art, science, profession, trade, etc.: *technical details.* **3.** meaningful or of interest to persons of specialized knowledge: *a technical article; a technical journal.* **4.** of, pertaining to, or showing technique. **5.** concerned with the mechanical or industrial arts and the applied sciences: *a technical school.* **6.** considered so by a stringent interpretation of the rules: *a technical defeat.* **7.** concerned merely with technicalities. **8.** concerned with or coordinating those practical functions or tasks that help to create a theatrical or film production, as lighting, costuming, and scene design: *a technical rehearsal.* **9.** noting a market in which prices are determined largely by supply and demand rather than by chance economic factors. —**tech′ni·cal·ly,** *adv.*

tech′nical foul′, *n.* a foul called in a game, as basketball, for unsportsmanlike conduct or delay of the game.

tech·ni·cal·i·ty (tek′ni kal′i tē), *n., pl.* **-ties. 1.** a technical point, detail, or expression. **2.** technical character. **3.** the use of technical methods or terms.

tech′nical knock′out, *n.* the termination of a boxing bout by officials when the losing boxer's safety or health is deemed to be at risk. *Abbr.:* TKO, T.K.O.

tech·ni·cal ser·geant, *n.* a noncommissioned officer in the U.S. Air Force ranking above a staff sergeant. *Abbr.:* tech. sgt.

tech·ni·cian (tek nish′ən), *n.* **1.** a person who is trained or skillled in the technicalities of a field, esp. one engaged in mechanical or in applied scientific work. **2.** a person skilled in the technique of an art, as music or painting.

Tech·ni·col·or (tek′ni kul′ər), **1.** *Trademark.* a brand name for a system of making color motion pictures by means of superimposing the three primary colors to produce a final colored print. —*adj.* **2.** (*often l.c.*) flamboyant or lurid, as in color, meaning, or detail.

tech·nique (tek nēk′), *n.* **1.** the manner and ability with which an artist, writer, athlete, etc., employs the technical skills of a particular art or field. **2.** the body of specialized procedures and methods used in any specific field. **3.** any method used to accomplish something. **4.** technical skill; degree to which one is able to apply procedures or methods.

tech·noc·ra·cy (tek nok′rə sē), *n.,* *pl.* **-cies. 1.** a theory or movement advocating management and control of the economy, government, and social system by technological experts. **2.** a system of government in which this theory is applied.

tech·nol·o·gy (tek nol′ə jē), *n.,* *pl.* **-gies. 1.** the branch of knowledge that deals with applied science, engineering, the industrial arts, etc. **2.** the application of knowledge for practical ends. **3.** a technological process, invention, or method. **4.** the sum of the ways in which social groups provide themselves with the material objects of their civilization. **5.** the terminology of a field; technical nomenclature. —**tech′no·log′i·cal** (-nə loj′i kəl), *adj.* —**tech′no·log′i·cal·ly,** *adv.*

tech·no·struc·ture (tek′nō struk′chər), *n.* the group of technically skilled administrators, engineers, and scientists who manage or control business, the economy, or government affairs.

tech·no·thrill·er (tek′nō thril′ər), *n.* a suspense novel in which the manipulation of sophisticated technology, as of aircraft or weapons systems, plays a prominent part.

tech. sgt., technical sergeant.

tec·ton·ic (tek ton′ik), *adj.* **1.** pertaining to building or construction; constructive; architectural. **2. a.** pertaining to the structure of the earth's crust. **b.** referring to the forces or conditions within the earth that cause movements of the crust. **c.** designating the results of such movements: *tectonic valleys.* —**tec·ton′i·cal·ly,** *adv.*

tec·ton·ics (tek ton′iks), *n.* (*used with a sing. v.*) the branch of geology that studies structural features of regional extent for the clues they provide regarding diastrophism and its causes.

ted·dy (ted′ē), *n.,* *pl.* **-dies. 1.** Often, **teddies.** a woman's one-piece undergarment combining a chemise and underpants. **2.** TEDDY BEAR.

ted′dy bear′, *n.* a toy bear, esp. a stuffed one.

Te De·um (tā dā′ōōm, -əm, tē dē′əm), *n.* a Christian hymn of praise to God, composed in Latin c400. [< Late Latin, the first two words of the hymn (*Tē Deum laudāmus* we praise thee God)]

te·di·ous (tē′dē əs, tē′jəs), *adj.* **1.** marked by tedium; long and tiresome. **2.** tiresomely wordy, as a speaker or writer. —**te′di·ous·ly,** *adv.*

te·di·um (tē′dē əm), *n.* the quality or state of being wearisome; tediousness.

tee¹ (tē), *n.* **1.** the letter *T* or *t.* **2.** something shaped like a T, as a three-way pipe joint. **3.** T-BAR (def. 1). **4.** T-SHIRT. **5.** the mark aimed at in various games, as curling. —*adj.* **6.** shaped like a T, esp. with a crosspiece at the top.

tee² (tē), *n.,* *v.,* **teed, tee·ing.** —*n.* **1. a.** Also called **teeing ground.** the area from which the first stroke on each hole of a golf course is played. **b.** a small peg or a mound of earth from which a golf ball is driven at the tee. **2.** a stand on which a football is rested to position it for kicking prior to a kickoff. —*v.t.* **3.** to place (a ball) on a tee. **4. tee off, a.** to strike a golf ball from a tee. **b.** to begin. **c.** *Slang.* to make angry or irritated.

teem¹ (tēm), *v.i.* to abound or swarm (usu. fol. by *with*).

teem² (tēm), *v.t., v.i.* **1.** to empty or pour out; discharge. **2.** (of molten metal) to pour or be poured into a mold.

teem·ing¹ (tē′ming), *adj.* **1.** abounding or swarming, as with people. **2.** prolific or fertile. —**teem′ing·ly,** *adv.* —**teem′ing·ness,** *n.*

teem·ing² (tē′ming), *adj.* falling in torrents: *a teeming rain.*

teen (tēn), *adj.* **1.** teenage. —*n.* **2.** a teenager.

teen·age (tēn′āj′) also **teen′aged′,** *adj.* pertaining to or characteristic of a teenager.

teen·ag·er (tēn′ā′jər), *n.* a person 13 through 19 years of age.

teens (tēnz), *n.pl.* the numbers 13 through 19, esp. the 13th through 19th years of a lifetime or a century.

teen·sy (tēn′sē), *adj.,* **-si·er, -si·est.** teeny; tiny.

tee·ny (tē′nē), *adj.,* **-ni·er, -ni·est.** TINY.

tee·pee (tē′pē), *n.* TEPEE.

tee′ shirt′, *n.* T-SHIRT.

tee·ter (tē′tər), *v.i.* **1.** to move unsteadily. **2.** to waver; fluctuate. **3.** to ride a seesaw; teetertotter. —*n.* **4.** a seesaw; teetertotter.

tee·ter-tot·ter or **tee′ter-tot′ter,** *n.* **1.** a seesaw. —*v.i.* **2.** to ride a seesaw.

teeth (tēth), *n.* pl. of TOOTH. —**teeth′less,** *adj.*

teethe (tēth), *v.i.,* **teethed, teeth·ing.** to grow teeth; cut one's teeth.

teeth·er (tē′thər), *n.* **1.** a device, as a teething ring, for a baby to bite on during teething. **2.** a baby who is teething.

teeth·ing (tē′thing), *n.* eruption of the deciduous teeth, esp. the phenomena associated with their eruption.

teeth′ing ring′, *n.* a circular ring, usu. of plastic, ivory, bone, etc., on which a teething baby can bite.

tee·to·tal (tē tōt′l, tē′tōt′l), *adj., v.* **-taled, -tal·ing** or (*esp. Brit.*) **-talled, -tal·ling.** —*adj.* **1.** pledged to or advocating total abstinence from intoxicating drink. **2.** *Informal.* absolute; complete. —*v.i.* **3.** to practice teetotalism. —**tee·to′tal·ly,** *adv.*

tee·to·tal·er (tē tōt′l ər, tē′tōt′-) also **tee·to′tal·ist,** *n.* a person who abstains from intoxicating drink. Also, *esp. Brit.,* **tee·to′tal·ler.**

te·fil·lin (tə fil′in; *Heb.* tə fē lēn′), *n.pl. Judaism.* the phylacteries.

TEFL, teaching English as a foreign language.

Tef·lon (tef′lon), **1.** *Trademark.* a fluorocarbon polymer with slippery, nonsticking properties: used in the manufacture of electrical insulation, cookware coatings, etc. —*adj.* **2.** characterized by imperviousness to blame or criticism: *a Teflon politician.*

teg·men (teg′mən), *n.,* *pl.* **-mi·na** (-mə nə). **1.** a covering or integument, esp. of a plant or animal. **2.** the delicate inner coat of a seed. **3.** either of a pair of leathery forewings extending over the hind wings in certain insects. —**teg′mi·nal,** *adj.*

Te·gu·ci·gal·pa (tə gōō′si gal′pə, -gäl′pä), *n.* the capital of Honduras, in the S part. 604,600.

Te·haph·ne·hes (ti haf′ni hēz′) also **Tah·pan·hes** (tä′pən hēz′), *n.* a city in eastern Egypt that was a refuge for the Jews. Jer. 2:16; Ezek. 30:18.

Te·he·ran or **Teh·ran** (te ran′, -rän′, tā′ə-), *n.* the capital of Iran, in the N part. 6,042,584.

Teil·hard de Char·din (te yAR də shAR dan′), *n.* **Pierre,** 1881–1955, French Jesuit priest, paleontologist, and philosopher.

Te·ko·a or **Te·ko·ah** (ti kō′ə), *n.* the home of the prophet Amos. Amos. 1:1.

tel·a·mon (tel′ə mən, -mon′), *n.,* *pl.* **tel·a·mo·nes** (tel′ə mō′nēz). AT-LAS (def. 4).

Tel A·viv (tel′ ə vēv′), *n.* a city in W central Israel. 334,900. Official name, **Tel′ Aviv′-Jaf′fa** (-yä′fə), **Tel′ Aviv′-Ya′fo** (-yä′fō). —**Tel′ A·viv′an,** *n.*

tele-, 1. a combining form meaning "reaching over a distance," "carried out between two remote points," "performed or operating through electronic transmissions": *telegraph; telekinesis; teletypewriter.* **2.** a combining form representing TELEVISION: *telegenic; telethon.* Also, *esp. before a vowel,* **tel-.**

tel·e·cast (tel′i kast′, -käst′), *v.,* **-cast** or **-cast·ed, -cast·ing,** *n.* —*v.t., v.i.* **1.** to broadcast by television. —*n.* **2.** a television broadcast. —**tel′e·cast′er,** *n.*

tel·e·com·mu·ni·ca·tions (tel′i kə myōō′ni kā′shənz), *n.* **1.** Sometimes, **telecommunication.** (*used with a sing. v.*) the science and technology of transmitting information, as words, sounds, or images, over great distances, in the form of electromagnetic signals, as by telegraph, telephone, radio, or television. **2.** Usu., **telecommunication.** the act or fact of communicating in such a manner: *We are in constant telecommunication with London.*

tel·e·con·fer·ence (tel′i kon′fər əns, -frəns), *n.,* *v.,* **-enced, -enc·ing.** —*n.* **1.** a business meeting, educational session, etc., conducted among participants in different locations via telecommunications equipment. —*v.i.* **2.** to participate in such a meeting.

tel·e·course (tel′i kôrs′, -kōrs′), *n.* a course of study given on television for home viewers, esp. those receiving college credit.

tel·e·gen·ic (tel′i jen′ik), *adj.* having physical qualities or characteristics that televise well. —**tel′e·gen′i·cal·ly,** *adv.*

tel·e·gram (tel′i gram′), *n.* a message or communication sent by telegraph; a telegraphic dispatch. —**tel′e·gram′mic, tel′e·gram·ma′tic** (-grə mat′ik), *adj.*

tel·e·graph (tel′i graf′, -gräf′), *n.* **1.** a system or apparatus for transmitting messages or signals to a distant place, esp. between two electric devices connected by a conducting wire or other communications channel. —*v.t.* **2.** to transmit (a message) by telegraph. **3.** to send a message to (a person) by telegraph. **4.** to divulge unwittingly (one's intention, next offensive move, etc.), as to an opponent or to an audience. —*v.i.* **5.** to send a message by telegraph. —**te·leg·ra·pher** (tə leg′rə fər), *n.*

tel·e·graph·ic (tel′i graf′ik), *adj.* **1.** of or pertaining to the telegraph. **2.** concise, clipped, or elliptical in style: *telegraphic speech.* —**tel′e·graph′i·cal·ly,** *adv.*

te·leg·ra·phy (tə leg′rə fē), *n.* the technique or practice of constructing or operating telegraphs.

tel·e·ki·ne·sis (tel′i ki nē′sis, -kī-), *n.* the purported ability to move or deform inanimate objects by mental power. Also called **psychokinesis.** —**tel′e·ki·net′ic** (-net′ik), *adj.*

tel·e·mark (tel′ə märk′), *n.* (*sometimes cap.*) a skier's turn in which the tip of the forward ski is gradually angled inward.

tel·e·mar·ket·ing (tel′ə mär′ki ting), *n.* selling or advertising by telephone. —**tel′e·mar′ket·er,** *n.*

tel·en·ceph·a·lon (tel′en sef′ə lon′, -lən), *n.,* *pl.* **-lons, -la** (-lə). the anterior section of the forebrain comprising the cerebrum and olfactory lobes. —**tel′en·ce·phal′ic** (-sə fal′ik), *adj.*

tel·e·ol·o·gy (tel′ē ol′ə jē, tēl′ē-), *n.* **1.** the doctrine that final causes exist. **2.** the study of the evidences of design or purpose in nature. **3.** such design or purpose. **4.** the belief that purpose and design are a part of or are apparent in nature. **5.** (in vitalist philosophy) the doctrine that phenomena are guided not only by mechanical forces but that they also move toward certain goals of self-realization. —**tel′e•o•log′i•cal** (-ə loj′i kəl), *adj.* —**tel′e•o•log′i•cal•ly,** *adv.* —**tel′e•ol′o•gist,** *n.*

te•lep•a•thy (tə lep′ə thē), *n.* communication between minds by some means other than sensory perception. —**tel•e•path•ic** (tel′ə path′ik), *adj.* —**tel′e•path′i•cal•ly,** *adv.* —**te•lep′a•thist,** *n.* —**te•lep′a•thize′** (-thīz′), *v.t., v.i.,* **-thized, -thiz•ing.**

tel•e•phone (tel′ə fōn′), *n., v.,* **-phoned, -phon•ing.** —*n.* **1.** Also called **phone.** an apparatus, system, or process for transmission of sound or speech to a distant point, esp. by an electric device. —*v.t.* **2.** to speak to (a person) by telephone; phone. **3.** to send (a message) by telephone; phone. —*v.i.* **4.** to send a message or speak by telephone; phone. —**tel′e•phon′er,** *n.*

tel′ephone book′, *n.* a directory containing an alphabetical list of telephone subscribers in a particular area, together with their addresses and telephone numbers. Also called **tel′ephone direc′tory.**

tel′ephone booth′, *n.* an enclosed booth containing a public telephone. Also called, *esp. Brit.,* **tel′ephone box′.**

tel′ephone num′ber, *n.* NUMBER (def. 12).

tel•e•phon•ic (tel′ə fon′ik), *adj.* **1.** of, pertaining to, or happening by means of a telephone system. **2.** carrying sound to a distance by artificial means. —**tel′e•phon′i•cal•ly,** *adv.*

tel•e•pho•tog•ra•phy (tel′ə tog′rə fē), *n.* photography of distant objects, using a telephoto lens. —**tel′e•pho′to•graph′ic** (-fō′tə graf′ik), *adj.*

tel′epho′to lens′, *n.* a camera lens that produces a relatively large image with a focal length shorter than that required by an ordinary lens to produce an image of the same size: used to photograph small or distant objects.

tel•e•play (tel′ə plā′), *n.* a play written or adapted for television.

tel•e•port (tel′ə pôrt′, -pōrt′), *n.* a regional telecommunications network that provides access to communications satellites and other long-distance media; telecommunications hub.

tel•e•print•er (tel′ə prin′tər), *n.* a teletypewriter.

Tel•e•Promp•Ter (tel′ə promp′tər), *Trademark.* an off-camera device that displays a magnified script to the performers or speakers on a television program.

tel•e•ran (tel′ə ran′), *n.* (*sometimes cap.*) a navigational aid that uses radar to map the sky above an airfield which, with a map of the airfield itself, is transmitted by television to aircraft approaching the field.

tel•e•scope (tel′ə skōp′), *n., adj., v.,* **-scoped, -scop•ing.** —*n.* **1.** an optical instrument for making distant objects appear larger and therefore nearer when viewed directly through lenses (**refracting telescope**) or indirectly as through images focused by a concave mirror (**reflecting telescope**). —*adj.* **2.** consisting of parts that fit and slide one within another. —*v.t.* **3.** to force together, one into another, in the manner of the sliding tubes of a jointed telescope. **4.** to shorten or condense; compress. —*v.i.* **5.** to slide together in the manner of the tubes of a telescope. **6.** to be driven one into another, as railroad cars in a collision. **7.** to become condensed.

tel•e•scop•ic (tel′ə skop′ik) also **tel′e•scop′i•cal,** *adj.* **1.** pertaining to or of the nature of a telescope. **2.** capable of magnifying distant objects: *a telescopic lens.* **3.** obtained by means of a telescope: *a telescopic view of the moon.* **4.** visible only through a telescope. **5.** capable of viewing objects from a distance; farseeing: *a telescopic eye.* **6.** (of an object) constructed of parts that slide one within another and permit lengthening or shortening. —**tel′e•scop′i•cal•ly,** *adv.*

tel•e•shop•ping (tel′ə shop′ing), *n.* electronic shopping via videotex or other interactive information service. —**tel′e•shop′,** *v.i.,* **-shopped, -shop•ping.** —**tel′e•shop′per,** *n.*

tel•e•text (tel′i tekst′), *n.* a data-broadcasting system that displays printed information as well as graphics on television screens. Compare VIDEOTEX.

tel•e•thon (tel′ə thon′), *n.* a television broadcast extended over many hours, usu. to raise money for a charity or cause.

Tel•e•type (tel′ə tīp′), *Trademark.* a brand of teletypewriter.

tel•e•type•writ•er (tel′i tīp′rī′tər, tel′i tīp′-), *n.* a telegraphic apparatus by which signals are sent by striking the keys of a typewriterlike instrument and received and reproduced by a similar instrument.

tel•e•van•ge•list (tel′i van′jə list), *n.* an evangelist who regularly conducts religious services on television. —**tel′e•van′ge•lism,** *n.*

tel•e•vise (tel′ə vīz′), *v.t., v.i.,* **-vised, -vis•ing.** to broadcast by television.

tel•e•vi•sion (tel′ə vizh′ən), *n.* **1.** the broadcasting of a still or moving image via radiowaves to receivers that project a view of the image on a picture tube or screen. **2.** the process involved. **3.** a set for receiving television broadcasts. **4.** the field of television broadcasting.

tel•ex (tel′eks), *n.* **1.** (*sometimes cap.*) a two-way teletypewriter service channeled through a public telecommunications system for direct communication between subscribers at remote locations. **2.** a message transmitted by telex. —*v.t.* **3.** to send (a message) by telex. [*tel*(*eprinter*) + *ex*(*change*)]

tell[1] (tel), *v.,* **told, tell•ing.** —*v.t.* **1.** to narrate or relate (a story, tale, etc.). **2.** to make known (news, information, etc.); communicate. **3.** to announce or proclaim. **4.** to utter (the truth, a lie, etc.); speak. **5.** to express in words (thoughts, feelings, etc.). **6.** to reveal or divulge (some-

thing secret or private). **7.** to say positively: *I can't tell just when I'll be done.* **8.** to discern or recognize; identify: *to tell twins apart.* **9.** to inform (a person) of something: *He told me his name.* **10.** to order or command: *Tell her to stop.* **11.** to enumerate; count. —*v.i.* **12.** to give an account or report. **13.** to give evidence; be an indication. **14.** to disclose something secret or private: *Will you hate me if I tell?* **15.** to say positively; determine or predict: *It may be the same shade, but I can't tell.* **16.** to produce a marked effect. **17. tell off,** to rebuke severely; scold. **18. tell on,** to tattle on. —*Idiom.* **19. tell it like it is,** *Informal.* to be blunt and forthright. **20. tell tales out of school,** to betray a confidence.

tell[2] (tel), *n.* an artificial mound consisting of the accumulated remains of one or more ancient settlements (often used in Egypt and the Middle East as part of a place name).

Tell (tel), *n.* **William,** WILLIAM TELL.

tell′-all′, *adj.* thoroughly revealing; candid; personal: *a tell-all biography of the movie star.*

tell•er (tel′ər), *n.* **1.** a person employed in a bank to receive or pay out money over the counter. **2.** one that tells, relates, or communicates; narrator. **3.** a person who counts or enumerates, as one appointed to count votes in a legislative body. —**tell′er•ship′,** *n.*

Tell′ Me′ the Old′, Old′ Sto′ry, a Christian children's hymn with words by Katherine Hankey.

tell•tale (tel′tāl′), *n.* **1.** a person who reveals confidential matters; tattler; talebearer. **2.** a thing serving to reveal something. **3.** any of various devices for indicating or registering, as a time clock. **4.** a row of strips hung over a track to warn train crew members on freight trains that a low bridge, tunnel, or the like, is approaching. **5.** (on a sailboat) a string or ribbon hung aloft to indicate the direction of the wind. —*adj.* **6.** revealing what is not intended to be known: *a telltale blush.* **7.** giving notice or warning of something, as a mechanical device.

tel•lu•ri•an (te lŏor′ē ən), *adj.* **1.** pertaining to the earth or its inhabitants; terrestrial. —*n.* **2.** an inhabitant of the earth.

tel•lu•ride (tel′yə rīd′, -rid), *n.* a binary compound of tellurium with an electropositive element or group.

tel•lu•ri•um (te lŏor′ē əm), *n.* a rare, lustrous, brittle, crystalline, silver-white element: used in the manufacture of alloys and as a coloring agent in glass and ceramics. *Symbol:* Te; *at. wt.:* 127.60; *at. no.:* 52; *sp. gr.:* 6.24. —**tel•lu′ric,** (te lŏor′ik), *adj.*

tel•o•phase (tel′ə fāz′, tē′lə-), *n.* the final stage of meiosis or mitosis in cell division, during which the two sets of chromosomes reach opposite poles and nuclei form around them as the cell divides in midsection. —**tel′o•pha′sic,** *adj.*

Tel•star (tel′stär′), *Trademark.* one of a series of privately financed communications satellites providing domestic television, telephone, and data exchange transmission to the U.S.

Tel•u•gu or **Tel•e•gu** (tel′ə gōō′), *n.* a Dravidian language spoken mainly in the state of Andhra Pradesh in SE India.

tem•blor (tem′blər, -blôr), *n.* a tremor; earthquake.

tem•er•ar•i•ous (tem′ə râr′ē əs), *adj.* reckless; rash. —**tem′er•ar′i•ous•ly,** *adv.* —**tem′er•ar′i•ous•ness,** *n.*

te•mer•i•ty (tə mer′i tē), *n., pl.* **-ties. 1.** reckless boldness; rashness. **2.** an instance of this.

temp (temp), *n. Informal.* a temporary.

Tem•pe (tem′pē), *n.* **1.** Vale of, a valley in E Greece, in Thessaly, between Mounts Olympus and Ossa. **2.** a city in central Arizona, near Phoenix. 144,289.

tem•per (tem′pər), *n.* **1.** a particular state of mind or feelings. **2.** habit of mind, esp. with respect to irritability or patience; disposition: *an even temper.* **3.** heat of mind or passion, shown in outbursts of anger, resentment, etc. **4.** calm disposition; composure: *to lose one's temper.* **5.** a substance added to modify other properties. **6. a.** the degree of hardness and strength imparted to a metal, as by quenching or heat treatment. **b.** the operation of tempering metal. —*v.t.* **7.** to moderate: *to temper justice with mercy.* **8.** to soften or tone down. **9.** to make suitable by or as if by blending. **10.** to work into proper consistency, as clay or mortar. **11.** to impart strength or toughness to (steel or cast iron) by heating and cooling. —*v.i.* **12.** to be or become tempered. —**tem′per•a•ble,** *adj.* —**tem′per•a•bil′i•ty,** *n.* —**tem′per•er,** *n.*

tem•per•a (tem′pər ə), *n.* **1.** a technique of painting in which an emulsion consisting of water and pure egg yolk or a mixture of egg and oil is used as a binder or medium, characterized by its lean film-forming properties and rapid drying rate. **2.** a painting executed in this technique. **3.** a water paint used in this technique in which the egg-water or egg-oil emulsion is used as a binder.

tem•per•a•ment (tem′pər ə mənt, -prə mənt, -pər mənt), *n.* **1.** the combination of mental and emotional traits of a person; natural predisposition. **2.** unusual personal nature as manifested by peculiarities of feeling, temper, action, etc., often with a disinclination to submit to conventional rules or restraints: *a display of temperament.*

tem•per•a•men•tal (tem′pər ə men′tl, -prə men′-, -pər men′-), *adj.* **1.** having or exhibiting a strongly marked, individual temperament. **2.** moody, irritable, or excitable. **3.** given to erratic behavior; unpredictable. **4.** pertaining to temperament; constitutional: *temperamental differences.* —**tem′per•a•men′tal•ly,** *adv.*

tem•per•ance (tem′pər əns, tem′prəns), *n.* **1.** moderation or self-restraint; self-control. **2.** habitual moderation in any indulgence, appetite, etc. **3.** total abstinence from alcoholic liquors.

T

tem·per·ate (tem′pər it, tem′prit), *adj.* **1.** moderate or self-restrained; not extreme in opinion, statement, etc. **2.** moderate in any indulgence, as in the use of alcoholic liquors. **3.** (of things) not excessive in degree. **4.** moderate in respect to temperature; not subject to prolonged extremes of hot or cold weather. **5.** (of a virus) existing in infected host cells but rarely causing lysis. —**tem′per·ate·ly,** *adv.*

Tem′perate Zone′, *n.* the part of the earth between the tropic of Cancer and the Arctic Circle in the Northern Hemisphere or between the tropic of Capricorn and the Antarctic Circle in the Southern Hemisphere, having a climate that is warm in the summer, cold in the winter, and moderate in the spring and fall.

tem·per·a·ture (tem′pər ə chər, -chŏŏr′, -prə-, -pər chər, -chŏŏr′), *n.* **1.** a measure of the warmth or coldness of an object or substance with reference to some standard value. **2. a.** the degree of heat in a living body, normally about 98.6°F (37°C) in humans. **b.** a level of such heat above the normal; fever: *running a temperature.*

tem·pered (tem′pərd), *adj.* **1.** having a temper or disposition as specified (usu. used in combination): *a good-tempered child.* **2.** *Music.* tuned in accordance with some temperament, esp. equal temperament. **3.** made less intense or violent, esp. by the influence of something else. **4.** properly mixed, as clay. **5.** of or pertaining to steel or cast iron that has been tempered.

tem′per tan′trum, *n.* TANTRUM.

tem·pest (tem′pist), *n.* **1.** a violent windstorm, esp. one with rain. **2.** a violent commotion, disturbance, or tumult. —*v.t.* **3.** to affect by a tempest; disturb violently. —**Idiom.** **4.** tempest in a teacup or teapot, an uproar over something minor.

Tempest, The, a comedy (1611) by William Shakespeare.

tem·pes·tu·ous (tem pes′chŏŏ əs), *adj.* **1.** characterized by or subject to tempests. **2.** resembling a tempest. **3.** tumultuous; turbulent —**tem·pes′tu·ous·ly,** *adv.* —**tem·pes′tu·ous·ness,** *n.*

tem·plate or **tem·plet** (tem′plit), *n.* **1.** a pattern, mold, etc., usu. consisting of a thin plate of wood or metal, serving as a gauge or guide in mechanical work. **2.** a horizontal piece, as of timber or stone, in a wall, to receive and distribute the pressure of a girder, beam, or the like. **3.** *Genetics.* a strand of DNA that serves as pattern for the formation of a complementary strand. **4.** a flat strip, as of cardboard, placed on a computer keyboard to provide ready reference to software commands.

tem·ple¹ (tem′pəl), *n.* **1.** an edifice or place dedicated to the service or worship of a deity or deities. **2.** (*usu. cap.*) any of the three successive houses of worship in Jerusalem used in law by the Jews in Biblical times. **3.** a synagogue, usu. a Reform or Conservative one. **4.** a church, esp. a large or imposing one. **5.** any place or object in which God dwells, as the body of a Christian. I Cor. 6:19. **6.** a Mormon building for sacred ordinances, esp. marriage. **7.** any large or pretentious public building. **8.** (*cap.*) either of two groups of buildings on the site of the Templars' former establishment in London, occupied by two of the Inns of Court. **9.** a building used by a fraternal order. —**tem′pled,** *adj.*

tem·ple² (tem′pəl), *n.* **1.** the region of the face that lies on either side of the forehead. **2.** either of the sidepieces of a pair of eyeglasses extending back above the ears.

tem′ple or′ange, *n.* a hybrid citrus fruit that is a cross between a sweet orange and a tangerine.

tem·po (tem′pō), *n., pl.* **-pos, -pi** (-pē). **1.** the rate of speed of a musical passage or work, typically indicated by printed direction, as *largo* or *presto,* or by a metronome setting. **2.** any characteristic rate, rhythm, or pattern: *the tempo of city life.* [< Italian < Latin *tempus* time]

tem·po·ral¹ (tem′pər əl, tem′prəl), *adj.* **1.** of or pertaining to time. **2.** pertaining to the present life; worldly: *temporal joys.* **3.** temporary or transitory, as opposed to eternal. **4.** of or pertaining to verb tenses or the expression of time: *a temporal adverb.* **5.** secular, lay, or civil, as opposed to ecclesiastical. —*n.* Usu. **temporals. 6.** a temporal possession, estate, or the like; temporality. **7.** a temporal matter or affair. —**tem′po·ral·ly,** *adv.* —**tem′po·ral·ness,** *n.*

tem·po·ral² (tem′pər əl, tem′prəl), *adj.* **1.** of, pertaining to, or situated near the temple or a temporal bone. —*n.* **2.** any of several parts in the temporal region, esp. the temporal bone.

tem′poral bone′, *n.* either of a pair of compound bones forming the sides of the primate skull.

tem·po·ral·ize (tem′pər ə līz′, tem′prə-), *v.t.,* **-ized, -iz·ing. 1.** to make temporal; place in time. **2.** to secularize.

tem·po·rar·y (tem′pə rer′ē), *adj., n., pl.* **-rar·ies.** —*adj.* **1.** lasting or effective for a time only; not permanent. —*n.* **2.** an office worker hired, usu. through an agency on a per diem basis, for a short period of time. —**tem′po·rar′i·ly,** *adv.* —**tem′po·rar′i·ness,** *n.*

tem·po·rize (tem′pə rīz′), *v.i.,* **-rized, -riz·ing. 1.** to be indecisive or evasive to gain time or delay acting. **2.** to comply with the time or occasion. **3.** to treat or parley so as to gain time (usu. fol. by *with*). **4.** to come to terms (usu. fol. by *with*). **5.** to effect a compromise (usu. fol. by *between*). —**tem′po·ri·za′tion,** *n.*

tempt (tempt), *v.t.* **1.** to entice or allure to do something often regarded as unwise, wrong, or immoral. **2.** to attract, appeal strongly to, or invite: *The offer tempts me.* **3.** to put to the test in a venturesome way; provoke: *to tempt one's fate.* —**tempt′a·ble,** *adj.*

temp·ta·tion (temp tā′shən), *n.* **1.** the act of tempting; enticement or allurement. **2.** something that tempts, entices, or allures. **3.** the fact or state of being tempted, esp. to evil. **4.** an instance of this. **5.** (*cap.*) the temptation of Christ by Satan. Matt. 4. —**temp·ta′tion·al,** *adj.*

tempt·er (temp′tər), *n.* **1.** a person or thing that tempts, esp. to evil. **2. the Tempter,** Satan; the devil.

tem·pu·ra (tem pŏŏr′ə), *n.* a Japanese dish of seafood or vegetables dipped in batter and deep-fried. [< Japanese < Portuguese]

ten (ten), *n.* **1.** a cardinal number, nine plus one. **2.** a symbol for this number, as 10 or X. **3.** a set of this many persons or things. **4.** a ten-dollar bill. **5.** Also called **ten's place. a.** (in a mixed number) the position of the second digit to the left of the decimal point. **b.** (in a whole number) the position of the second digit from the right. —*adj.* **6.** amounting to ten in number.

ten·a·ble (ten′ə bəl), *adj.* capable of being held, maintained, or defended. —**ten′a·bil′i·ty, ten′a·ble·ness,** *n.* —**ten′a·bly,** *adv.*

te·na·cious (tə nā′shəs), *adj.* **1.** holding fast; characterized by keeping a firm hold (often fol. by *of*): *a tenacious grip; tenacious of old habits.* **2.** highly retentive: *a tenacious memory.* **3.** persistent, stubborn, or obstinate. **4.** adhesive or sticky. **5.** holding together; cohesive; tough. —**te·na′cious·ly,** *adv.*

te·nac·i·ty (tə nas′i tē), *n.* the quality or property of being tenacious.

ten·an·cy (ten′ən sē), *n., pl.* **-cies. 1.** a holding, as of lands, by any kind of title; occupancy of land, a house, or the like, under a lease or on payment of rent; tenure. **2.** the period of a tenant's occupancy. **3.** occupancy or enjoyment of a position, post, situation, etc.

ten·ant (ten′ənt), *n.* **1.** a person or group that rents and occupies land, a house, an office, or the like, usu. under the terms of a lease; lessee. **2.** an occupant or inhabitant of any place. —*v.t.* **3.** to hold or occupy as a tenant; dwell in; inhabit. —*v.i.* **4.** to dwell or live (usu. fol. by *in*).

ten′ant farm′er, *n.* a person who farms the land of another and pays rent with cash or with a portion of the crops.

Ten Boom (ten bōōm′), *n.* **Corrie,** 1892–1983, Dutch Christian writer who sheltered Jews during the Nazi occupation of The Netherlands.

Ten′ Command′ments, *n.pl.* the precepts spoken by God to Israel, delivered to Moses on Mount Sinai; the Decalogue. Ex. 20; 24:12, 34; Deut. 5.

tend¹ (tend), *v.i.* **1.** to be disposed or inclined in action, operation, or effect to do something: *The particles tend to unite.* **2.** to be disposed toward an idea, emotion, way of thinking, etc. **3.** to lead (to some result or condition): *measures tending to safer working conditions.* **4.** to be inclined or have a tendency toward a particular quality, state, or degree: *This wine tends toward the sweet side.* **5.** (of a course, road, etc.) to lead in a particular direction (usu. fol. by *to, toward,* etc.).

tend² (tend), *v.t.* **1.** to attend to by work or services, care, etc.: *to tend a fire.* **2.** to watch over and care for; minister to: *to tend the sick.* **3.** to handle or attend to (a rope). —*v.i.* **4.** to attend by action, care, etc. (usu. fol. by *to*).

ten·den·cy (ten′dən sē), *n., pl.* **-cies. 1.** a natural or prevailing disposition to move, proceed, or act in some direction or toward some point, end, or result. **2.** an inclination, bent, or predisposition to something. **3.** a special and definite purpose in a novel or other literary work.

THE TEN COMMANDMENTS

1. I am the Lord thy God, who brought thee out of the land of Egypt, out of the house of bondage. Thou shalt have no other gods before me.
2. Thou shalt not make unto thee any graven image, or any likeness of any thing that is in heaven above, or that is in the earth beneath, or that is in the water under the earth; thou shalt not bow down unto them, nor serve them; for I the Lord thy God am a jealous God, visiting the iniquity of the fathers upon the children unto the third and fourth generation of them that hate Me; and showing mercy unto the thousandth generation of them that love Me and keep my commandments.
3. Thou shalt not take the name of the Lord thy God in vain; for the Lord will not hold him guiltless that taketh His name in vain.
4. Remember the Sabbath day, to keep it holy. Six days shalt thou labor, and do all thy work; but the seventh day is a sabbath unto the Lord thy God, in it thou shalt not do any manner of work, thou, nor thy son, nor thy daughter, nor thy man-servant, nor thy maid-servant, nor thy cattle, nor thy stranger that is within thy gates; for in six days the Lord made heaven and earth, the sea, and all that in them is, and rested on the seventh day; wherefore the Lord blessed the Sabbath day, and hallowed it.
5. Honor thy father and thy mother, that thy days may be long upon the land which the Lord thy God giveth thee.
6. Thou shalt not murder.
7. Thou shalt not commit adultery.
8. Thou shalt not steal.
9. Thou shalt not bear false witness against thy neighbor.
10. Thou shalt not covet thy neighbor's house, thou shalt not covet thy neighbor's wife, nor his manservant, nor his maidservant, nor his ox, nor his ass, nor any thing that is thy neighbor's.

ten•den•tious or **ten•den•cious** (ten den′shəs), also **ten•den•tial** (-shəl), *adj.* having or showing a tendency to favor or promote a point of view; biased: *a tendentious novel.* —**ten•den′tious•ly,** *adv.* —**ten•den′tious•ness,** *n.*

ten•der[1] (ten′dər), *adj.* **1.** soft or delicate in substance; not hard or tough: *a tender steak.* **2.** weak or delicate in constitution; not strong or hardy. **3.** (of plants) unable to withstand freezing temperatures. **4.** young or immature: *children of tender age.* **5.** delicate or gentle: *the tender touch of her hand.* **6.** easily moved to sympathy or compassion; kind: *a tender heart.* **7.** affectionate or sentimental: *a tender glance.* **8.** acutely or painfully sensitive: *a tender bruise.* **9.** easily distressed; readily made uneasy: *a tender conscience.* **10.** of a delicate or ticklish nature; requiring careful handling: *a tender subject.* —*v.t.* **11.** to make tender. —**ten′der•ly,** *adv.* —**ten′der•ness,** *n.*

ten•der[2] (ten′dər), *v.t.* **1.** to present formally for acceptance; make formal offer of: *to tender one's resignation.* **2.** to offer or proffer. **3.** *Law.* to offer (money, goods, etc.) in payment of an obligation and in exact accordance with its terms. —*v.i.* **4.** to make or submit a bid (often fol. by *for*). —*n.* **5.** the act of tendering; an offer of something for acceptance. **6.** something tendered or offered, esp. money, as in payment. **7.** an offer made in writing by one party to another to execute certain work, supply certain commodities, etc., at a given cost; bid. **8.** *Law.* an offer of money, goods, etc., in satisfaction of a debt. —**ten′der•er,** *n.*

tend•er[3] (ten′dər), *n.* **1.** a person who tends; a person who attends to or takes charge of someone or something. **2.** an auxiliary ship employed to attend one or more other ships, as for supplying provisions. **3.** a dinghy carried or towed by a yacht. **4.** a railroad car attached to a steam locomotive for carrying fuel and water.

ten•der•foot (ten′dər fo͝ot′), *n., pl.* **-foots, -feet** (-fēt′). **1.** a raw, inexperienced person; novice. **2.** a newcomer to the ranching and mining regions of the western U.S., unused to hardships. **3.** one in the lowest rank of the Boy Scouts or Girl Scouts of America.

ten•der•ize (ten′də rīz′), *v.t.,* **-ized, -iz•ing.** to make (meat) tender, as by pounding or by a chemical treatment. —**ten′der•iz′er,** *n.*

ten•der•loin (ten′dər loin′), *n.* **1.** (in beef or pork) the tender meat of the muscle running through the sirloin and terminating before the ribs. **2.** (*cap.*) **a.** (formerly) a district in New York City noted for corruption and vice: so called because police there could eat well from their bribes. **b.** a similar district in any U.S. city.

ten′der of′fer, *n.* a public offer to purchase stock of a corporation from its shareholders at a stated price within a limited time, usu. in an effort to take control of the corporation.

ten•di•ni•tis or **ten•do•ni•tis** (ten′də nī′tis), *n.* inflammation of a tendon.

ten•don (ten′dən), *n.* a cord or band of dense, tough, inelastic, white, fibrous tissue, serving to connect a muscle with a bone or part; sinew.

ten•dril (ten′dril), *n.* a threadlike, leafless organ of climbing plants, often growing in spiral form, which attaches itself to or twines round some other body, so as to support the plant.

Ten•e•brae (ten′ə brā′), *n.* (*used with a sing. or pl. v.*) any of various liturgical services in the Western Church during Holy Week, in which all candles are gradually extinguished, to commemorate the darkness at the Crucifixion. [< Latin: lit., darkness]

ten•e•brif•ic (ten′ə brif′ik), *adj.* producing darkness.

ten•e•brous (ten′ə brəs) also **te•neb•ri•ous** (tə neb′rē əs), *adj.* dark; gloomy; obscure. —**ten′e•brous•ness,** *n.*

ten•e•ment (ten′ə mənt), *n.* **1.** Also called **ten′ement house′.** a rundown and often overcrowded apartment house, esp. in a poor section of a large city. **2.** *Law.* property of a permanent or fixed nature, whether corporeal or incorporeal, as lands or rent. —**ten′e•men′tal, ten′e•men′ta•ry,** *adj.* —**ten′e•ment•ed,** *adj.*

ten•et (ten′it; *Brit. also* tē′nit), *n.* any opinion, principle, doctrine, dogma, etc., esp. one held as true by members of a profession, group, or movement.

ten•fold (*adj.* ten′fōld′; *adv.* -fōld′), *adj.* **1.** having ten parts or members. **2.** ten times as great or as much. —*adv.* **3.** in tenfold measure.

10-gauge (ten′gāj′), *n.* **1.** Also called **10-gauge shotgun.** a shotgun using a shell of approx. 0.775 in. (1.97 cm) in diameter. **2.** this shell.

Ten•nes•see (ten′ə sē′), *n.* **1.** a state in the SE United States. 5,319,654; 42,246 sq. mi. (109,415 sq. km). *Cap.:* Nashville. *Abbr.:* TN, Tenn. **2.** a river flowing from E Tennessee through N Alabama, W Tennessee, and SW Kentucky into the Ohio near Paducah. 652 mi. (1050 km) long. —**Ten′nes•se′an,** *n., adj.*

Ten′nessee Val′ley Author′ity, *n.* a U.S. government-owned corporation created in 1933 to develop the Tennessee River and its tributaries as sources of cheap electric power, irrigation, etc. *Abbr.:* TVA

Ten′nessee walk′ing horse′, *n.* one of a breed of saddle horses developed largely from Standardbred and Morgan stock.

ten•nis (ten′is), *n.* a game played on a rectangular court by two players or two pairs of players equipped with rackets, in which a ball is driven back and forth over a low net that divides the court in half. Compare LAWN TENNIS.

ten′nis ball′, *n.* a hollow ball used in tennis, made of rubber with a fuzzy covering of woven Dacron, nylon, or wool.

ten′nis el′bow, *n.* inflammation and pain at the elbow caused by strong, repetitive movements of the forearm and wrist, as while playing tennis.

ten′nis shoe′, *n.* a low sports shoe with a flat rubber sole and a canvas or leather upper that laces over the instep; sneaker.

Ten•ny•son (ten′ə sən), *n.* **Alfred, Lord** (*1st Baron*), 1809–92, English poet: poet laureate 1850–92.

ten•on (ten′ən), *n.* **1.** a projection formed on the end of a timber or the like for insertion into a mortise of the same dimensions. —*v.t.* **2.** to provide with a tenon. **3.** to join by or as if by a tenon. **4.** to join securely.

ten•or (ten′ər), *n.* **1.** the course of thought or meaning that runs through something written or spoken; drift. **2.** continuous course, progress, or movement: *nothing to disturb the even tenor of our lives.* **3. a.** the adult male voice intermediate between the bass and the alto or countertenor. **b.** a part sung by or written for such a voice. **c.** a singer with such a voice. **d.** an instrument corresponding in compass to this voice. **4.** quality, character, or condition. —*adj.* **5.** pertaining to, or having the compass of a tenor.

ten•pen•ny (ten′pen′ē, -pə nē), *adj.* **1.** denoting a nail 3 in. (7.6 cm) in length. *Symbol:* 10d. **2.** worth or costing ten cents.

ten•pins (ten′pinz′), *n.* **1.** (*used with a sing. v.*) a form of bowling, played with ten wooden pins. **2. tenpin,** a pin used in this game.

tense[1] (tens), *adj.,* **tens•er, tens•est,** *v.,* **tensed, tens•ing.** —*adj.* **1.** stretched tight, as a cord, fiber, etc.; drawn taut; rigid. **2.** in a state of mental or nervous strain; high-strung: *a tense person.* **3.** characterized by a strain upon the nerves or feelings: *a tense moment.* **4.** (of a speech sound) pronounced with the muscles of the speech organs relatively tense, as the vowel (ē) in *seat.* Compare LAX (def. 7). —*v.t., v.i.* **5.** to make or become tense. —**tense′ly,** *adv.* —**tense′ness,** *n.*

tense[2] (tens), *n.* **1.** a category of verbs or verbal inflection serving chiefly to specify the time of the action or state expressed by the verb. **2.** a set of such categories or constructions in a particular language. **3.** the time, as past, present, or future, expressed by such a category.

ten•sile (ten′səl, -sil, -sīl), *adj.* **1.** of or pertaining to tension: *tensile strain.* **2.** capable of being stretched or drawn out; ductile.

ten′sile strength′, *n.* the resistance of a material to longitudinal stress, measured by the minimum amount of longitudinal stress required to rupture the material.

ten•sion (ten′shən), *n.* **1.** the act of stretching or straining. **2.** the state of being stretched or strained. **3.** mental or emotional strain. **4.** intense, suppressed suspense, anxiety, or excitement. **5.** a strained relationship between individuals, groups, nations, etc. **6. a.** the longitudinal deformation of an elastic body that results in its elongation. **b.** the force producing such deformation. **7.** electromotive force; potential. **8.** a device for extending or maintaining tension, as on material in a loom. —*v.t.* **9.** to subject (a cable, belt, tendon, or the like) to tension.

ten•sor (ten′sər, -sôr), *n.* **1.** a muscle that stretches or tightens some part of the body. **2.** a mathematical entity with components that change in a particular way in a transformation from one coordinate system to another. —**ten•so′ri•al** (-sôr′ē əl, -sōr′-), *adj.*

ten′-speed′, *n.* **1.** a bicycle whose gear system comprises ten forward gear ratios. —*adj.* **2.** having ten forward gear ratios.

ten′-spot′, *n.* **1.** a playing card the face of which bears ten pips. **2.** *Slang.* a ten-dollar bill.

tent[1] (tent), *n.* **1.** a portable shelter or temporary structure of fabric or skins supported by poles and usu. secured by stakes in the ground. **2.** something that resembles a tent. —*v.t.* **3.** to provide with or lodge in tents. —*v.i.* **4.** to live in a tent; encamp. —**tent′like′,** *adj.*

tent[2] (tent), *n.* **1.** a surgical probe. **2.** a plug of soft absorbent material, as lint or gauze, for dilating an orifice, keeping a wound open, etc. —*v.t.* **3.** to keep (a wound) open with a tent.

ten•ta•cle (ten′tə kəl), *n.* **1.** any of various slender, flexible processes or appendages in animals, esp. invertebrates, that serve as organs of touch, prehension, etc.; feeler. **2.** a sensitive filament or hair on a plant, as one of the hairs of the sundew. —**ten′ta•cled,** *adj.* —**ten•tac′u•lar** (-tak′yə lər), *adj.*

ten•ta•tive (ten′tə tiv), *adj.* **1.** of the nature of or made or done as a trial, experiment, or attempt: *a tentative agreement.* **2.** unsure; not definite or positive; hesitant: *a tentative smile.* —**ten′ta•tive•ly,** *adv.*

tent′ cat′erpillar, *n.* any of the larvae of several moths of the genus *Malacosoma,* which feed on the leaves of deciduous trees and live colonially in a tentlike silken web.

ten•ter•hook (ten′tər ho͝ok′), *n.* **1.** one of the hooks or bent nails that hold cloth stretched on a framework. —***Idiom.*** **2. on tenterhooks,** in a state of uneasy suspense or painful anxiety.

tenth (tenth), *adj.* **1.** next after ninth; being the ordinal number for ten. **2.** being one of ten equal parts. —*n.* **3.** a tenth part, esp. of one (1/10). **4.** the tenth member of a series. **5. a.** a musical interval encompassing an octave and a third. **b.** the harmonic combination of two tones a tenth apart. **6.** Also called **tenth's′ place′.** (in decimal notation) the position of the first digit to the right of the decimal point. —*adv.* **7.** in the tenth place; tenthly. —**tenth′ly,** *adv.*

Tenth′ Amend′ment, *n.* an amendment to the U.S. Constitution, ratified in 1791 as part of the Bill of Rights, guaranteeing to the states and the people those rights that are not delegated to the federal government by the Constitution.

Tenth′ Command′ment, *n.* "Thou shalt not covet thy neighbor's house, thou shalt not covet thy neighbor's wife, nor his manservant, nor his maidservant, nor his ox, nor his ass, nor any thing that is thy neighbor's": tenth of the Ten Commandments. Compare TEN COMMANDMENTS.

ten·u·ous (ten′yōō əs), *adj.* **1.** lacking a sound basis; unsubstantiated; weak. **2.** thin or slender in form. **3.** thin in consistency; rarefied. **4.** of slight importance or significance; unsubstantial. —**ten′u·ous·ly,** *adv.*

ten·ure (ten′yər), *n., v.,* **-ured, -ur·ing.** —*n.* **1.** the holding or possessing of anything: *the tenure of an office.* **2.** the holding of property, esp. real property, of a superior in return for services to be rendered. **3.** the period or term of holding something. **4.** status granted to an employee indicating that the position or employment is permanent. —*v.t.* **5.** to give tenure to. —**ten·u′ri·al** (-yŏŏr′ē əl), *adj.* —**ten·u′ri·al·ly,** *adv.*

tep′a·ry bean′ (tep′ə rē), *n.* a twining or bushy plant, *Phaseolus acutifolius latifolius,* of the legume family, cultivated in the southwestern U.S. and N Mexico for its edible seeds.

tee·pee or **tee·pee** (tē′pē), *n.* a Plains Indian tent made from animal skins laid on a conical frame of long poles.

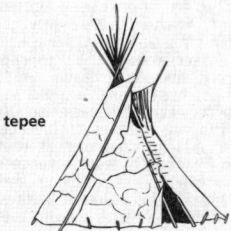

tepee

tep·id (tep′id), *adj.* **1.** moderately warm; lukewarm: *tepid water.* **2.** characterized by a lack of force or enthusiasm. —**te·pid′i·ty, tep′id·ness,** *n.* —**tep′id·ly,** *adv.*

te·qui·la (tə kē′lə), *n.* a strong liquor from Mexico, distilled from fermented mash of the agave.

tera-, 1. a combining form used in the names of units of measure equal to one trillion of a given base unit: *terahertz.* **2.** a combining form of like function with the value 2⁴⁰ (= 1,099,511,627,766). *Abbr.:* T

ter·a·flops (ter′ə flops′), *n.* a measure of computer speed, equal to one trillion floating-point operations per second.

terato-, a combining form meaning "monster," "malformation": *teratology.*

ter·a·tol·o·gy (ter′ə tol′ə jē), *n.* the science or study of monstrosities or abnormal formations in organisms. —**ter′a·to·log′i·cal** (-tl oj′i kəl), *adj.* —**ter′a·tol′o·gist,** *n.*

ter·bi·um (tûr′bē əm), *n.* a rare-earth, metallic element present in certain minerals and yielding colorless salts. *Symbol:* Tb; *at. no.:* 65; *at. wt.:* 158.924; *sp. gr.:* 8.25. —**ter′bic,** *adj.*

ter·cel (tûr′səl) also **terce·let** (tûrs′lit), **tiercel,** *n.* the male of a hawk, esp. of a gyrfalcon or peregrine.

ter·cen·ten·ni·al (tûr′sen ten′ē əl), *adj.* **1.** pertaining to a period of 300 years. **2.** marking the completion of such a period. —*n.* **3.** a 300th anniversary or its celebration.

Ter·ence (ter′əns), *n.* (*Publius Terentius Afer*) c190–159? B.C., Roman playwright.

Te·re·sa (tə rē′sə, -zə, -rā′-; *for 2 also Sp.* te re′sä), *n.* **1. Mother** (*Agnes Gonxha Bojaxhiu*), 1910–97, Albanian nun: Nobel peace prize 1979 for work in the slums of Calcutta, India. **2. Saint. Theresa, Saint.**

ter·gi·ver·sate (tûr′ji vər sāt′, tər jiv′ər-), *v.i.,* **-sat·ed, -sat·ing. 1.** to change repeatedly one's attitude or opinions with respect to a cause, subject, etc.; equivocate. **2.** to turn renegade. —**ter′gi·ver·sa′tion,** *n.* —**ter′gi·ver·sa′tor, ter′gi·ver′sant** (-vûr′sənt), *n.*

ter·i·ya·ki (ter′ē yä′kē), *n.* **1.** a Japanese dish of grilled slices of meat or fish that have been marinated in soy sauce, sake, ginger, and sugar. —*adj.* **2.** prepared in this manner: *chicken teriyaki.*

term (tûrm), *n.* **1.** a word or group of words designating something, esp. in a particular field: *the term* atom *in physics.* **2.** any word or group of words considered as a member of a construction or utterance. **3.** the time or period through which something lasts. **4.** a period of time to which limits have been set: *a one-year term of office.* **5.** one of two or more divisions of a school year, during which instruction is regularly provided. **6.** an appointed or set time or date, as for the payment of rent, interest, etc. **7. terms, a.** conditions with regard to payment, price, rates, etc.: *reasonable terms.* **b.** conditions or stipulations limiting what is proposed to be granted or done: *the terms of a treaty.* **c.** footing or standing; relations: *on good terms with someone.* **8.** each of the members of which a mathematical expression, a series of quantities, or the like, is composed. **9.** (in logic) **a.** the subject or predicate of a categorical proposition. **b.** the word or expression denoting such a subject or predicate. **10.** a herm. **11.** *Law.* **a.** an estate, property, etc., to be enjoyed for a specified period. **b.** the duration of such a period. **c.** the period when a court is in session. **12.** completion of pregnancy; parturition. —*v.t.* **13.** to apply a particular term or name to; call; designate. —*Idiom.* **14. bring to terms,** to force to agree to stated demands or conditions. **15. come to terms,** to reach an agreement. **16. in terms of,** with regard to; concerning.

ter·ma·gant (tûr′mə gənt), *n.* **1.** a violent, turbulent, or brawling woman. **2.** (*cap.*) a mythical deity believed in the Middle Ages to be worshiped by the Muslims: portrayed in morality plays as a violent, overbearing personage. —*adj.* **3.** violent; turbulent; brawling; shrewish.

ter·mi·na·ble (tûr′mə nə bəl), *adj.* **1.** capable of being terminated. **2.** (of an annuity) coming to an end after a certain term. —**ter′mi·na·bil′i·ty, ter′mi·na·ble·ness,** *n.* —**ter′mi·na·bly,** *adv.*

ter·mi·nal (tûr′mə nl), *adj.* **1.** situated at or forming the end or extremity of something: *a terminal bud.* **2.** occurring at or forming the end of a series, succession, or the like; closing; concluding. **3.** pertaining to or lasting for a term or definite period; occurring at fixed terms or in every term: *terminal payments.* **4.** pertaining to or placed at a boundary, as a landmark. **5.** occurring at or causing the end of life: *a terminal disease.* —*n.* **6.** a terminal part of a structure; end or extremity. **7. a.** a point of termination or a major junction within a transportation system. **b.** the structures and service facilities located at a terminal. **8.** any device for entering information into a computer or receiving information from it, as a keyboard with video display unit. **9. a.** the mechanical device by which an electric connection to an apparatus is established. **b.** the point where current enters or leaves any conducting component in an electric circuit. **10.** a carving or the like at the end of something, as a finial. —**ter′mi·nal·ly,** *adv.*

ter·mi·nate (tûr′mə nāt′), *v.,* **-nat·ed, -nat·ing.** —*v.t.* **1.** to bring to an end; put an end to. **2.** to occur at or form the conclusion of. **3.** to bound or limit spatially; form or be situated at the extremity of. **4.** to dismiss from a job; fire. —*v.i.* **5.** to end, conclude, or cease. **6.** (of a public conveyance) to end a scheduled run or flight at a certain place. **7.** to come to an end (often fol. by *at, in,* or *with*). **8.** to issue or result (usu. fol. by *in*). —**ter′mi·na′tive,** *adj.* —**ter′mi·na′tive·ly,** *adv.*

ter·mi·na·tion (tûr′mə nā′shən), *n.* **1.** the act of terminating. **2.** the fact of being terminated. **3.** the place or part where anything terminates; bound. **4.** an end or extremity; close or conclusion. **5.** an issue or result. **6.** a suffix or word ending. **7.** an ending of employment with a specific employer. —**ter′mi·na′tion·al,** *adj.*

ter·mi·na·tor (tûr′mə nā′tər), *n.* **1.** one that terminates. **2.** the dividing line between the bright side and the dark side of a moon or planet.

ter·mi·nol·o·gy (tûr′mə nol′ə jē), *n., pl.* **-gies. 1.** the system of terms belonging or peculiar to a specialized subject; nomenclature. **2.** the science of terms, as in particular sciences or arts. —**ter′mi·no·log′i·cal** (-nl oj′i kal), *adj.* —**ter′mi·nol′o·gist,** *n.*

term′ insur′ance, an insurance policy that provides coverage for a limited period, the value payable only if a loss occurs within the term, and without value upon expiration.

ter·mi·nus (tûr′mə nəs), *n., pl.* **-ni** (-nī′), **-nus·es. 1.** the end or extremity of anything. **2.** either end of a railroad line. **3.** the station at the end of a railway or bus route. **4.** the point toward which anything tends; goal or end. **5.** a boundary or limit.

ter·mite (tûr′mīt), *n.* any of numerous pale, soft-bodied, chiefly tropical, social insects of the order Isoptera that feed on wood, some highly destructive to buildings, furniture, etc. Also called **white ant.**

term·less (tûrm′lis), *adj.* **1.** unconditional. **2.** boundless; endless.

term′ pa′per, a long essay, report, or the like, written by a student as a major assignment over the span of a term or semester.

tern¹ (tûrn), *n.* any of various web-footed aquatic birds of the subfamily Sterninae (family Laridae), resembling gulls, though typically smaller, slimmer, and more graceful in flight.

tern² (tûrn), *n.* three winning numbers drawn together in a lottery.

ter·na·ry (tûr′nə rē), *adj., n., pl.* **-ries.** —*adj.* **1.** consisting of or involving three; threefold; triple. **2.** third in order or rank. **3.** based on the number three. **4.** consisting of three different chemical elements or groups. —*n.* **5.** a group of three.

ter·ra (ter′ə), *n.* earth; land.

ter·race (ter′əs), *n., v.,* **-raced, -rac·ing.** —*n.* **1.** a raised level with a vertical or sloping front or sides faced with masonry, turf, or the like, esp. one of a series of levels rising one above another. **2.** the top of such a construction, used as a platform, garden, road, etc. **3.** a nearly level strip of land with a more or less abrupt descent along the margin of the sea, a lake, or a river. **4.** an open, often paved area connected to a house or apartment building and serving as an outdoor living area; patio. **5.** a platform projecting from an outside wall, as of an apartment; balcony. **6.** the flat roof of a house. **7.** a row of houses on or near the top of a slope. **8.** a residential street following the top of a slope. —*v.t.* **9.** to form into or furnish with a terrace or terraces.

ter′ra cot′ta (kot′ə), *n., pl.* **terra cot·tas. 1.** a hard, brownish red fired clay, usu. unglazed, that is used for architectural ornaments, pottery, and as a material for sculpture. **2.** something made of terra cotta. [< Italian: lit., baked earth] —**ter′ra-cot′ta,** *adj.*

ter′ra fir′ma (fûr′mə), *n.* firm or solid earth; dry land (as opposed to water or air). [< Latin]

ter·rain (tə rān′), *n.* **1.** a tract of land, esp. as considered with reference to its natural features, military advantages, etc. **2. terrane.**

ter·rane or **ter·rain** (tə rān′, ter′ān), *n.* a distinctive geologic formation or group of rocks or the area in which such features occur.

ter·ra·pin (ter′ə pin), *n.* any of several edible North American turtles of the family Emydidae, inhabiting fresh or brackish waters, esp. the diamondback terrapin.

ter·rar·i·um (tə râr′ē əm), *n., pl.* **-rar·i·ums, -rar·i·a** (-râr′ē ə). **1.** a glass container, chiefly or wholly enclosed, for growing and displaying plants. **2.** a vivarium for land animals.

ter·raz·zo (tə rä′tsō, -raz′ō), *n.* a mosaic flooring or paving composed of chips of broken stone, usu. marble, and cement.

ter·rene (te rēn′, tə-, tĕr′ēn), *adj.* **1.** earthly; worldly. **2.** earthy. —*n.* **3.** the earth. **4.** a land or region. —**ter·rene′ly,** *adv.*

ter·res·tri·al (tə res′trē əl), *adj.* **1.** pertaining to, consisting of, or representing the earth as distinct from other planets. **2.** of or pertaining to land as distinct from water. **3. a.** growing or living on land or on the ground; not aquatic, arboreal, etc. **b.** growing in the ground; not epiphytic or aerial. **4.** of or pertaining to the earth or this world; worldly; mundane. —*n.* **5.** an inhabitant of the earth, esp. a human being. —**ter·res′tri·al·ly,** *adv.*

ter·ri·ble (ter′ə bəl), *adj.* **1.** distressing; severe. **2.** extremely bad; horrible. **3.** exciting terror or great fear; dreadful; awful. **4.** formidably great: *a terrible responsibility.* —**ter′ri·ble·ness,** *n.*

ter·ri·bly (ter′ə blē), *adv.* **1.** in a terrible manner. **2.** extremely; very: *It's terribly late. I'm terribly sorry.*

ter·ri·er (ter′ē ər), *n.* any of several breeds of usu. small dogs, used orig. to pursue game and drive it out of its hole or burrow.

ter·rif·ic (tə rif′ik), *adj.* **1.** extraordinarily great or intense: *terrific speed.* **2.** extremely good; wonderful: *a terrific vacation.* **3.** causing terror; terrifying. —**ter·rif′i·cal·ly,** *adv.*

ter·ri·fy (ter′ə fī′), *v.t.,* **-fied, -fy·ing.** to fill with terror or alarm; make greatly afraid. —**ter′ri·fi·er,** *n.* —**ter′ri·fy′ing·ly,** *adv.*

ter·rine (tə rēn′), *n.* **1.** a casserole dish made of pottery. **2.** a paté baked in such a dish and served cold.

ter·ri·to·ri·al (ter′i tôr′ē əl, -tōr′-), *adj.* **1.** of or pertaining to territory or land. **2.** of, pertaining to, associated with, or restricted to a particular territory or district. **3.** (of an animal) characterized by territoriality. **4.** (*usu. cap.*) of or pertaining to a U.S. Territory. **5.** (*often cap.*) organized for home defense: *the British Territorial Army.* —*n.* **6.** (*often cap.*) a soldier in a territorial army. —**ter′ri·to′ri·al·ly,** *adv.*

ter·ri·to·ri·al·i·ty (ter′i tôr′ē al′i tē, -tōr′-), *n.* **1.** territorial quality or condition. **2.** the behavior of an animal in defining and defending its territory. **3.** attachment to or protection of a territory or domain.

ter·ri·to·ri·al·ize (ter′i tôr′ē ə līz′, -tōr′-), *v.t.,* **-ized, -iz·ing. 1.** to extend by adding new territory. **2.** to reduce to the status of a territory. **3.** to make territorial. —**ter′ri·to′ri·al·i·za′tion,** *n.*

ter′rito′rial wa′ters, *n.pl.* the waters of a littoral state that are regarded as under the jurisdiction of the state: traditionally, those waters within three miles (4.8 km) of the shore.

ter·ri·to·ry (ter′i tôr′ē, -tōr′ē), *n., pl.* **-ries. 1.** any tract of land; region; district. **2.** the land and waters belonging to or under the jurisdiction of a state, sovereign, etc. **3.** any separate tract of land belonging to a state. **4.** (*usu. cap.*) a region of the U.S. not admitted as a state but having its own legislature and an appointed governor. **5.** a field or sphere of action, thought, etc. **6.** the region or district assigned to a representative, agent, or the like, as for making sales. **7.** the area that an animal defends against intruders, esp. of the same species. —*Saying.* **8. It comes with the territory,** certain consequences follow from a situation or circumstance.

ter·ror (ter′ər), *n.* **1.** intense, sharp, overmastering fear. **2.** a person or thing that causes such fear. **3.** violence or threats of violence used as a means of intimidation or coercion. **4.** *Informal.* a person or thing that is especially annoying or unpleasant.

ter·ror·ism (ter′ə riz′əm), *n.* **1.** the use of violence and threats to intimidate or coerce, esp. for political purposes. **2.** the state of fear and submission so produced. **3.** government or resistance to government by means of terror. —**ter′ror·ist,** *n., adj.*

ter·ror·ize (ter′ə rīz′), *v.t.,* **-ized, -iz·ing. 1.** to fill or overcome with terror. **2.** to dominate or coerce by intimidation.

ter·ry (ter′ē), *n., pl.* **-ries, adj.** —*n.* **1.** the loop formed by the pile of a fabric when left uncut. **2.** Also called **ter′ry cloth′.** a pile fabric, usu. of cotton, with uncut loops on one or both sides, often used for toweling. —*adj.* **3.** made of terry fabric: *a terry towel.* **4.** having the pile loops uncut: *terry velvet.*

terse (tûrs), *adj.* **ters·er, ters·est. 1.** neatly or effectively concise; brief, as language. **2.** abruptly concise; curt; brusque. —**terse′ly,** *adv.*

ter·ti·ar·y (tûr′shē er′ē, -shə rē), *adj., n., pl.* **-ar·ies.** —*adj.* **1.** of the third order, rank, stage, formation, etc.; third. **2. a.** noting or containing a carbon atom united to three other carbon atoms. **b.** formed by replacement of three atoms or groups. **3.** (*cap.*) noting or pertaining to the earlier period of the Cenozoic Era, beginning about 65 million years ago, during which mammals gained ascendancy. —*n.* **4.** (*cap.*) the Tertiary Period or System. **5.** *Roman Catholic Church.* (*often cap.*) a member of a Third Order.

ter′tiary col′or, *n.* a color, as brown, produced by mixing two secondary colors.

Ter·tul·li·an (tər tul′ē ən, -tul′yən), *n.* (*Quintus Septimius Florens Tertullianus*) A.D. c160–c230, Carthaginian theologian.

TESL, teaching English as a second language.

tes·la (tes′lə), *n.* a unit of magnetic induction equal to one weber per square meter. *Abbr.:* T [named after N. TESLA]

Tes·la (tes′lə), *n.* Nikola, 1856–1943, U.S. physicist, electrical engineer, and inventor, born in Croatia.

TESOL (tē′sôl, tes′əl), **1.** teaching English to speakers of other languages. **2.** Teachers of English to Speakers of Other Languages.

tes·sel·late or **tes·se·late** (tes′ə lāt′), *v.t.,* **-lat·ed, -lat·ing.** to form of small squares or blocks, as floors or pavements; form or arrange in a checkered or mosaic pattern.

tes·ser·a (tes′ər ə), *n., pl.* **tes·ser·ae** (tes′ə rē′). **1.** one of the small pieces used in mosaic work. **2.** a small square of bone, wood, or the like, used in ancient Rome as a token, tally, ticket, etc.

test (test), *n.* **1.** the means by which the presence, quality, or genuineness of anything is determined; a trial: *a test of a new product.* **2.** the trial of the quality of something: *to put to the test.* **3.** a particular process or method for trying or assessing. **4.** a set of problems, questions, etc., for evaluating abilities, aptitudes, skills, or performance. **5. a.** a reaction used to identify or detect the presence of a chemical constituent. **b.** an indication obtained by means of such reactions. **6.** an oath or other confirmation of one's loyalty, religious beliefs, etc. —*v.t.* **7.** to subject to a test of any kind. —*v.i.* **8.** to undergo a test or trial. **9.** to perform on a test: *People test better in a relaxed environment.* **10.** to conduct a test: *to test for diabetes.* —**test′a·ble,** *adj.*

tes·ta (tes′tə), *n., pl.* **-tae** (-tē) the outer, usu. hard, integument or coat of a seed.

tes·ta·cy (tes′tə sē), *n.* the state of being testate.

tes·ta·ment (tes′tə mənt), *n.* **1. a.** a legal document disposing of one's personal property after death. **b.** a will. **2.** (*cap.*) either the New Testament or the Old Testament. **3.** a covenant, esp. between God and humans. **4.** a proof; testimony. —**tes′ta·men′ta·ry** (-men′tə rē, -men′trē), *adj.*

tes·tate (tes′tāt), *adj.* having made and left a valid will.

tes·ta·tor (tes′tā tər, te stā′tər), *n.* a person who makes a will, esp. one who has died leaving a valid will.

tes·ta·trix (te stā′triks), *n., pl.* **tes·ta·tri·ces** (te stā′trə sēz′, tes′tə trī′sēz). a woman who makes a will, esp. one who has died leaving a valid will.

test′ ban′, *n.* an agreement by nations producing nuclear weapons to refrain from testing them in the atmosphere.

test′ case′, *n.* **1.** a case that serves afterward as a precedent for similar cases. **2.** a suit used to test a legal principle, the constitutionality of a statute, etc.

test′-drive′, *v.t.,* **-drove, -driv·en, -driv·ing.** to drive (a vehicle) in order to evaluate performance and reliability.

tes·tes (tes′tēz), *n.* pl. of TESTIS.

test′-fly′, *v.t.,* **-flew, -flown, -fly·ing.** to fly (an aircraft or spacecraft) in order to evaluate performance.

tes·ti·cle (tes′ti kəl), *n.* a testis, esp. of a human being.

tes·ti·fy (tes′tə fī′), *v.,* **-fied, -fy·ing.** —*v.i.* **1.** to bear witness; give or afford evidence. **2.** to give testimony under oath, usu. in court. **3.** to make solemn declaration. —*v.t.* **4.** to bear witness to; affirm as fact or truth; attest. **5.** to give or afford evidence of in any manner. **6.** to state or declare under oath, usu. in court. **7.** to declare, profess, or acknowledge openly. —**tes′ti·fi·er,** *n.*

tes·ti·mo·ni·al (tes′tə mō′nē əl), *n.* **1.** a written declaration certifying to a person's character, conduct, or qualifications, or to the value, excellence, etc., of a thing; letter or written statement of recommendation. **2.** something given or done as an expression of esteem, admiration, or gratitude. —*adj.* **3.** pertaining to or serving as a testimonial: *a testimonial dinner for the retiring dean.*

tes·ti·mo·ny (tes′tə mō′nē; *esp. Brit.* -mə nē), *n., pl.* **-nies. 1.** the statement or declaration of a witness under oath, usu. in court. **2.** evidence in support of a fact or statement; proof. **3.** open declaration or profession, as of faith.

tes·tis (tes′tis), *n., pl.* **-tes** (-tēz). the male gonad or reproductive gland, either of two oval glands located in the scrotum.

tes·tos·ter·one (tes tos′tə rōn′), *n.* the sex hormone, $C_{19}H_{28}O_2$, secreted by the testes, that stimulates the development of male sex organs, secondary sexual traits, and sperm: isolated from animal testes or produced synthetically for use in medicine.

test′ pa′per, *n.* **1.** a paper bearing a student's answers on an examination. **2.** paper impregnated with a reagent, as litmus, that changes color when acted upon by certain substances.

test′ pat′tern, *n.* a geometric design used to test the quality of television transmission, often identifying the station and channel.

test′ pi′lot, *n.* a pilot employed to test-fly newly built aircraft.

test′ tube′, *n.* a hollow cylinder of thin glass with one end closed, used to hold chemicals, specimens, etc., in laboratory experimentation and analysis.

test′-tube′, *adj.* produced in or as if in a test tube; synthetic or experimental.

test′-tube′ ba′by, *n.* an infant developed from an ovum fertilized in vitro and implanted into a woman's uterus.

tes·tu·di·nate (te stōōd′n it, -āt′, -styōōd′-), *adj.* **1.** formed like the carapace of a tortoise; arched; vaulted. **2.** of or pertaining to turtles. —*n.* **3.** any member of the order Testudines, comprising turtles, tortoises, and terrapins.

tes·ty (tes′tē), *adj.,* **-ti·er, -ti·est.** irritably impatient; touchy: *a testy mood; a testy reply.* —**tes′ti·ly,** *adv.* —**tes′ti·ness,** *n.*

Tet (tet), *n.* the Vietnamese New Year celebration, occurring during the first seven days of the first month of the lunar calendar.

tet·a·nus (tet′n əs), *n.* an infectious disease characterized by tonic spasms and rigidity of muscles, esp. of the lower jaw and neck, sometimes leading to respiratory paralysis and death, caused by a bacterium,

Clostridium tetani, which commonly enters the body through wounds and cuts. Compare LOCKJAW.

tetched or **teched** (techt), *adj.* touched; slightly crazy.

tetch•y or **tech•y** (tech′ē), *adj.,* **tetch•i•er, tetch•i•est.** irritable; touchy. **—tetch′i•ly,** *adv.* **—tetch′i•ness,** *n.*

tête-à-tête (tāt′ə tāt′, tet′ə tet′), *n., pl.* **tête-à-têtes,** *adj., adv.* **—n. 1.** a private conversation or interview, usu. between two people. **2.** Also called **vis-à-vis.** a small sofa shaped like an S so that two people can converse face to face. **—adj. 3.** of, between, or for two persons privately. **—adv. 4.** (of two persons) together in private: *to sit tête-à-tête.*

teth•er (teth′ər), *n.* **1.** a rope, chain, or the like, by which an animal is fastened to a fixed object so as to limit its range of movement. **2.** the utmost length to which one can go in action; the utmost extent or limit of ability or resources. **—v.t. 3.** to fasten or confine with or as if with a tether. **—Idiom. 4. at the end of one's tether,** at the end of one's resources, patience, or strength.

teth•er•ball (teth′ər bôl′), *n.* a game in which two players hit in opposite directions a ball attached by a cord to a post, the object being to coil the cord completely around the post.

Tet′ offen′sive, *n.* an offensive by Vietcong and North Vietnamese forces against South Vietnamese and U.S. positions in South Vietnam, beginning on Jan. 31, 1968, the start of Tet.

tet•ra (te′trə), *n., pl.* **-ras.** any of several small, brightly colored characin fishes, of tropical American waters.

tetra-, a combining form meaning "four": *tetrabasic.* Also, *esp. before a vowel,* **tetr-.**

tet•ra•chlo•ride (te′trə klôr′īd, -id, -klôr′-), *n.* a chloride containing four atoms of chlorine.

tet•ra•cy•cline (te′trə sī′klēn, -klin), *n.* an antibiotic, $C_{22}H_{24}H_2O_8$, derived from a streptomyces, used to treat a variety of infections.

tet•rad (te′trad), *n.* **1.** a group of four. **2.** *Biol.* a group of four chromatids formed by synapsis at the beginning of meiosis.

tet•ra•eth•yl•lead or **tet•ra•eth•yl lead** (te′trə eth′əl led′), *n.* a colorless, oily, water-insoluble, poisonous liquid, $(C_2H_5)_4Pb$, used as an antiknock agent in gasoline.

tet•ra•gon (te′trə gon′), *n.* a polygon having four angles or sides; a quadrangle or quadrilateral. **—te•trag′o•nal,** *adj.*

Tet•ra•gram•ma•ton (te′trə gram′ə ton′), *n.* the Hebrew word for God, consisting of the four letters *yod, he, vav,* and *he,* transliterated consonantally usu. as *YHVH,* now pronounced as *Adonai* in substitution for the original pronunciation forbidden since the 2nd or 3rd century B.C. Compare YAHWEH.

tet•ra•he•dral (te′trə hē′drəl), *adj.* **1.** pertaining to or having the form of a tetrahedron. **2.** having four lateral planes in addition to the top and bottom. **—tet′ra•he′dral•ly,** *adv.*

tet•ra•he•dron (te′trə hē′drən), *n., pl.* **-drons, -dra** (-drə). **1.** a solid contained by four plane faces; a triangular pyramid. **2.** an object resembling a tetrahedron in the distribution of its faces or apexes.

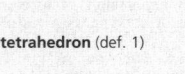

tetrahedron (def. 1)

tet•ra•pod (te′trə pod′), *n.* **1.** any vertebrate having four limbs or, as in the snake and whale, having had four-limbed ancestors. **—adj. 2.** having four limbs or descended from four-limbed ancestors.

Te•traz•zi•ni (te′trə zē′nē), *adj.* (*often l.c.*) served over pasta with a cream sauce, often flavored with sherry, sprinkled with cheese, and browned in the oven: *chicken Tetrazzini.*

Tet•zel or **Te•zel** (tet′səl), *n.* **Johann,** 1465?–1519, German monk: antagonist of Martin Luther.

Teu•ton (tōōt′n, tyōōt′n), *n.* **1.** a member of any people speaking a Germanic language, esp. a language of the West Germanic group. **2.** GERMAN (def. 1). [< Latin *Teutonī* (pl.) a people, presumed to be Germanic, who migrated from Jutland to Gaul and were destroyed by the Romans in 102 B.C.] **—Teu•ton′ic,** *adj.*

Te•vet or **Te•bet** (te vet′, tā-, tā′vās), *n.* the fourth month of the Jewish calendar.

Tex•as (tek′səs), *n.* a state in the S United States. 19,128,261; 267,339 sq. mi. (692,410 sq. km). *Cap.:* Austin. *Abbr.:* Tex., TX **—Tex′an,** *adj., n.*

Tex′as Independ′ence Day′, *n.* March 2, observed in Texas as the anniversary of the declaration in 1836 of the independence of Texas from Mexico and also as the birthday of Sam Houston.

Tex′as lea′guer, *n.* a pop fly in baseball that falls safely between converging infielders and outfielders.

Tex′as long′horn, *n.* one of a breed of long-horned beef cattle of the southwestern U.S., developed from Spanish stock.

Tex′as Rang′er, *n.* a member of a special branch of the Texas state police force, orig. a semiofficial group of mounted settlers organized to fight Indians and maintain order.

Tex′as Revolu′tion, *n.* a revolutionary movement, 1832–36, in which

U.S. settlers asserted their independence from Mexico and established the republic of Texas.

Tex-Mex (teks′meks′), *adj.* of or denoting aspects of Texan or southwestern U.S. culture originating with or influenced by Mexicans or Mexican-Americans: *Tex-Mex cooking.*

text (tekst), *n.* **1.** the main body of matter in a manuscript, book, etc., as distinguished from notes, appendixes, illustrations, etc. **2.** the actual, original words of an author or speaker, as opposed to a translation, paraphrase, or the like. **3.** any of the various forms in which a writing exists: *The text is a medieval transcription.* **4.** the wording adopted by an editor as representing the original words of an author: *the authoritative text of Catullus.* **5.** any theme or topic. **6.** the words of a song or the like. **7.** a textbook. **8.** a short passage of Scripture, esp. one chosen in proof of a doctrine or as the subject of a sermon. **9. a.** BLACK LETTER. **b.** type, as distinguished from illustrations, margins, etc. **10.** *Ling.* a unit of connected speech or writing that forms a cohesive whole.

text•book (tekst′bŏok′), *n.* **1.** a book used by students as a standard work for a particular branch of study. **—adj. 2.** pertaining to, characteristic of, or seemingly suitable for inclusion in a textbook; typical; classic: *a textbook example of administrative competence.*

tex•tile (teks′tīl, -til), *n.* **1.** any cloth or goods produced by weaving, knitting, or felting. **2.** a material, as a fiber or yarn, used in or suitable for weaving. **—adj. 3.** woven or capable of being woven: *textile fabrics.* **4.** of or pertaining to weaving. **5.** of or pertaining to textiles or their production: *the textile industry.*

tex•tu•al (teks′chōo əl), *adj.* **1.** of or pertaining to a text. **2.** based on or conforming to a text, as of the Scriptures. **—tex′tu•al•ly,** *adv.*

tex′tual crit′icism, *n.* LOWER CRITICISM.

tex•ture (teks′chər), *n., v.,* **-tured, -tur•ing. —n. 1.** the characteristic physical structure given to a material, an object, etc., by the size, shape, and arrangement of its parts: *soil of a sandy texture.* **2.** the characteristic structure of the threads, fibers, etc., that make up a textile fabric: *coarse texture.* **3.** essential or characteristic quality; essence. **4.** the visual and tactile quality of the surface of a work of art resulting from the way in which the materials are used. **5.** the quality given, as to a musical work, by the combination or interrelation of parts or elements. **6.** a rough or grainy surface quality. **7.** anything produced by weaving; woven fabric. **—v.t. 8.** to give texture or a particular texture to. **9.** to make by or as if by weaving. **—tex′tur•al,** *adj.* **—tex′tur•al•ly,** *adv.*

tex•tur•ize (teks′chə rīz′), *v.t.,* **-ized, -iz•ing.** TEXTURE.

T formation, *n.* an offensive football formation with the quarterback and fullback lined up behind the center and a halfback on each side of the fullback.

Th, *Chem. Symbol.* thorium.

Thack•er•ay (thak′ə rē), *n.* **William Makepeace,** 1811–63, English novelist, born in India.

Thad•de•us (thad′ē əs), *n.* one of the twelve apostles. Matt. 10:3.

Thai (tī), *n., pl.* **Thais.** **1.** Also called **Thai′land′er** (-lan′dər, -lən-). a native or inhabitant of Thailand. **2. a.** a member of the dominant ethnic group of Thailand, living mainly in the S and E parts of the country. **b.** the Tai language of this group.

Thai•land (tī′land′, -lənd), *n.* **1.** Formerly, **Siam.** a kingdom in SE Asia. 59,450,115; 198,115 sq. mi. (513,445 sq. km). *Cap.:* Bangkok. **2. Gulf of.** Also, **Gulf of Siam.** an arm of the South China Sea, S of Thailand.

thal•a•mus (thal′ə məs), *n., pl.* **-mi** (-mī′). **1.** the middle part of the diencephalon of the brain, serving to transmit and integrate sensory impulses. **2.** *Bot.* a receptacle or torus. **—tha•lam′ic** (thə lam′ik), *adj.*

tha•las•sic (thə las′ik), *adj.* **1.** of or pertaining to seas and oceans. **2.** growing, living, or found in the sea; marine.

tha•lid•o•mide (thə lid′ə mīd′), *n.* a crystalline, slightly water-soluble solid, $C_{13}H_{10}N_2O_4$, formerly used as a sedative: if taken during pregnancy, it may cause severe abnormalities in the limbs of the fetus.

thal•lic (thal′ik), *adj.* of or containing thallium, esp. in the trivalent state.

thal•li•um (thal′ē əm), *n.* a soft, malleable, rare, bluish white metallic element: used in the manufacture of alloys and, in its salts, in rodenticides. *Symbol:* Tl; *at. wt.:* 204.37; *at. no.:* 81; *sp. gr.:* 11.85 at 20°C.

thal•lus (thal′əs), *n., pl.* **thal•li** (thal′ī), **thal•lus•es.** a simple vegetative body undifferentiated into true leaves, stem, and root, ranging from an aggregation of filaments to a complex plantlike form.

Thames (temz; *for 3 also* thāmz, tāmz), *n.* **1.** a river in S England, flowing E through London to the North Sea. 209 mi. (336 km) long. **2.** a river in SE Canada, in Ontario province, flowing SW to Lake St. Clair. 160 mi. (260 km) long. **3.** an estuary in SE Connecticut, flowing S past New London to Long Island Sound. 15 mi. (24 km) long.

than (than, then; *unstressed* thən, ən), *conj.* **1.** (used after comparative adjectives and adverbs and certain other words, such as *other, otherwise, else,* etc., to introduce the second member of a comparison): *She's taller than I am.* **2.** (used after some adverbs and adjectives expressing choice or diversity, such as *other, otherwise, else, anywhere, different,* etc., to introduce an alternative or denote a difference in kind, place, style, identity, etc.): *I had no choice other than that.* **3.** when: *We barely arrived than it was time to leave.* **—Usage.** Whether THAN is to be followed by the objective or subjective case of a pronoun is much discussed in usage guides. When, as a conjunction, THAN introduces a subordinate clause, the case of any pronouns following THAN is determined by their function in that clause: *He is younger than I am. I like her better than I like him.* When THAN is followed only by a pronoun or pronouns, with no verb expressed, the usual advice for determining the case is to form a clause mentally after THAN to see whether the pronoun would be a subject or an object. Thus, the sentences *He was more upset than I* and *She gave him more sympathy than I* are to be understood, respectively, as *He was more upset than I was* and *She gave him more sympathy than I gave him.* This method is generally employed in formal speech and writing. In informal speech and writing THAN is usu. treated like a preposition and followed by the objective case of the pronoun: *He is younger than me.* See also BUT[1], DIFFERENT, ME.

thanato-, a combining form meaning "death": *thanatophobia.*

than•a•tol•o•gy (than′ə tol′ə jē), *n.* **1.** the study of death and its circumstances, as in forensic medicine. **2.** the branches of medicine and psychiatry concerned with the terminally ill and their survivors. —**than′a•to•log′i•cal** (-tl oj′i kəl), *adj.* —**than′a•tol′o•gist,** *n.*

Than•a•tos (than′ə tos′, -tōs), *n.* **1.** (among the ancient Greeks) a personification of death. **2.** *Psychoanal.* (*usu. l.c.*) the death instinct, esp. as expressed in violent aggression. —**Than′a•tot′ic** (-tot′ik), *adj.*

thank (thangk), *v.t.* **1.** to express gratitude or appreciation to. **2.** to hold personally responsible; blame: *We have him to thank for this lawsuit.* —*n.* **3. thanks,** a grateful feeling or acknowledgment of a kindness, favor, or the like, expressed by words or otherwise. —*interj.* **4. thanks,** I thank you. —***Idiom.*** **5. thanks to,** because of; owing to. **6. thank you,** (a common elliptical expression used to express gratitude or appreciation, as for a gift or favor.) —**Usage.** See WELCOME.

thank•ful (thangk′fəl), *adj.* feeling or expressing gratitude or appreciation. —**thank′ful•ly,** *adv.* —**thank′ful•ness,** *n.*

thank•less (thangk′lis), *adj.* **1.** not likely to be appreciated or rewarded: *a thankless job.* **2.** not feeling or expressing gratitude; ungrateful: *a thankless child.* —**thank′less•ly,** *adv.* —**thank′less•ness,** *n.*

thanks•giv•ing (thangks′giv′ing), *n.* **1.** the act of giving thanks. **2.** an expression of thanks, esp. to God. **3.** a public celebration in acknowledgment of divine favor. **4.** (*cap.*) THANKSGIVING DAY.

Thanksgiv′ing Day′, *n.* a national holiday celebrated as a day of feasting and giving thanks for divine goodness, observed on the fourth Thursday of November in the U.S. and on the second Monday of October in Canada.

thank′-you′, *adj., n., pl.* **-yous.** —*adj.* **1.** expressing thanks: *a thank-you note.* —*n.* **2.** an expression of thanks.

that (t͟hat; *unstressed* t͟hət), *pron.* and *adj., pl.* **those,** *adv., conj.* —*pron.* **1.** (used to indicate a person or thing as pointed out or present, mentioned before, supposed to be understood, or by way of emphasis): *That is her mother.* **2.** (used to indicate one of two or more persons or things already mentioned, referring to the one more remote in place, time, or thought; opposed to *this*): *This is my sister and that's my cousin.* **3.** (used to indicate one of two or more persons or things already mentioned, implying a contrast or contradistinction; opposed to *this*): *This suit fits better than that.* **4.** (used as the subject or object of a relative clause, esp. one defining or restricting the antecedent, sometimes replaceable by *who, whom,* or *which*): *the horse that he bought.* **5.** (used as the object of a preposition, the preposition standing at the end of a relative clause): *the farm that I spoke of.* **6.** (used in various special or elliptical constructions): *fool that he is.* —*adj.* **7.** (used to indicate a person, place, thing, or degree as indicated, mentioned before, present, or as well-known or characteristic): *That woman is her mother.* **8.** (used to indicate the more remote in time, place, or thought of two persons or things already mentioned; opposed to *this*): *This room is his and that one is mine.* **9.** (used to imply mere contradistinction; opposed to *this*): *not this house, but that one.* —*adv.* **10.** (used with adjectives and adverbs of quantity or extent) to the extent or degree indicated: *Don't take that much.* **11.** to a great extent or degree: *It's not that important.* **12.** *Dial.* (used to modify an adjective or another adverb) to such an extent: *He was that weak he could hardly stand.* —*conj.* **13.** (used to introduce a subordinate clause as the subject or object of the principal verb or as the necessary complement to a statement made, or a clause expressing cause or reason, purpose or aim, result or consequence, etc.): *I'm sure that you'll like it. That he will come is certain.* **14.** (used elliptically to introduce an exclamation expressing desire, indignation, or other strong feeling): *Oh, that I had never been born!* —***Idiom.*** **15. at that, a.** nevertheless. **b.** in addition; besides. **16. that is,** to be more accurate: *I read the book, that is, I read most of it.* **17. that's that,** *Informal.* there is no more to be said or done: *I'm not going, and that's that!* **18. with that,** following that; thereupon.

thatch (thach), *n.* **1.** Also, **thatch′ing.** a material, as straw, rushes, leaves, or the like, used to cover roofs, grain stacks, etc. **2.** a covering of such a material. **3.** any of various palms having leaves used for thatch. **4.** something resembling thatch on a roof, esp. thick hair covering the head. **5.** a matted layer of dead vegetation at the base of lawn grasses or other plantings. —*v.t.* **6.** to cover with or as if with thatch. **7.** to remove thatch from (a lawn, etc.); dethatch. —**thatch′er,** *n.*

Thatch•er (thach′ər), *n.* **Margaret (Hilda),** born 1925, British prime minister 1979–90.

that's (t͟hats; *unstressed* t͟həts), **1.** contraction of *that is: That's mine.* **2.** contraction of *that has: That's got more leaves.*

thaumato-, a combining form meaning "miracle," "wonder": *thaumatology.*

thau•ma•tol•o•gy (thô′mə tol′ə jē), *n.* the study or description of miracles.

thau•ma•turge (thô′mə tûrj′) also **thau′ma•tur′gist,** *n.* a worker of wonders or miracles.

thau•ma•tur•gy (thô′mə tûr′jē), *n.* the working of wonders or miracles; magic. —**thau′ma•tur′gic, thau′ma•tur′gi•cal,** *adj.*

thaw (thô), *v.i.* **1.** to pass or change from a frozen to a liquid or semiliquid state; melt. **2.** to be freed from the physical effect of frost or extreme cold (sometimes fol. by *out*): *Sit by the fire and thaw out.* **3.** (of the weather) to become warm enough to melt ice and snow. **4.** to become less hostile, tense, or aloof: *International relations thawed.* —*v.t.* **5.** to cause to thaw. **6.** to make less hostile, tense, or aloof. —*n.* **7.** the act or process of thawing. **8.** a reduction or easing in tension or hostility. **9.** (in winter or in areas where freezing weather is the norm) weather warm enough to melt ice and snow. **10.** a period of such weather. **11. the thaw,** the period in spring when ice in waterways breaks up enough to allow navigation.

Thay•er (thā′ər, thâr), *n.* **1. Ernest Lawrence,** 1863–1940, U.S. journalist, author of *Casey at the Bat.* **2. Sylvanus,** 1785–1872, U.S. army officer and educator.

Th.D., Doctor of Theology. [< New Latin *Theologicae Doctor*]

the[1] (*stressed* t͟hē; *unstressed before a consonant* t͟hə, *unstressed before a vowel* t͟hē), *definite article.* **1.** (used, esp. before a noun, with a specifying or particularizing effect, as opposed to the indefinite or generalizing force of the indefinite article *a* or *an*): *the book you gave me.* **2.** (used to mark a noun as indicating something well-known or unique): *the Alps.* **3.** (used with or as part of a title): *the Duke of Wellington.* **4.** (used to mark a noun as indicating the best-known, most approved, most important, etc.): *the place to ski.* **5.** (used to mark a noun as being used generically): *The dog is a quadruped.* **6.** (used in place of a possessive pronoun, to note a part of the body or a personal belonging): *He was shot in the arm.* **7.** (used before adjectives that are used substantively, to note an individual, a class or number of individuals, or an abstract idea): *to visit the sick; from the sublime to the ridiculous.*

the[2] (*before a consonant* t͟hə; *before a vowel* t͟hē), *adv.* **1.** (used to modify an adjective or adverb in the comparative degree and to signify "in or by that," "on that account," "in or by so much," or "in some or any degree"): *He's been on vacation and looks the better for it.* **2.** (used in correlative constructions to modify an adjective or adverb in the comparative degree, in one instance with relative force and in the other with demonstrative force, and signifying "by how much ... by so much"): *the more the merrier.*

the•a•ter or **thea•tre** (thē′ə tər, thēə′-), *n.* **1.** a building, part of a building, or an outdoor area for dramatic presentations, stage entertainments, or motion-picture shows. **2.** a room or hall with tiers of seats, used for lectures, surgical demonstrations, etc. **3. a. the theater,** dramatic performances as a branch of art; the drama, esp. as a profession. **b.** a particular type, style, or category of this art: *musical theater.* **4.** dramatic works collectively, as of literature, a nation, or an author (often prec. by *the*): *the Elizabethan theater.* **5.** the quality or effectiveness of dramatic performance. **6.** a place of action; area of activity.

the•a•ter•go•er or **the•a•tre•go•er** (thē′ə tər gō′ər, thēə′-), *n.* a person who goes to the theater, esp. often or regularly.

the′ater-in-the-round′, *n.* a style of theatrical presentation in which the audience is seated on all sides of the performance area.

the′ater of the absurd′, *n.* theater in which naturalistic conventions of plot and characterization are ignored or distorted to convey the irrationality of existence and the isolation and impotence of humanity.

the•at•ri•cal (thē a′tri kəl), *adj.* Also, **the•at′ric. 1.** of or pertaining to the theater or dramatic presentations. **2.** suggestive of the theater or of acting; artificial, spectacular, or extravagantly histrionic. —*n.* **3. theatricals,** dramatic performances, esp. as given by amateurs. **4.** a professional actor. —**the•at′ri•cal′i•ty,** *n.* —**the•at′ri•cal•ly,** *adv.*

the•at•rics (thē a′triks), *n.* **1.** (*used with a sing. v.*) the art of staging plays and other stage performances. **2.** (*used with a pl. v.*) exaggerated, artificial, or histrionic mannerisms, actions, or words.

Thebes (thēbz), *n.* **1.** an ancient city in S Egypt, on the Nile, on the site of the modern towns of Karnak and Luxor. **2.** a city of ancient Greece, in Boeotia. —**The′ban,** *adj., n.*

the•ca (thē′kə), *n., pl.* **-cae** (-sē). **1.** a case or sheath enclosing an animal organ, structure, etc., as the horny covering of an insect pupa. **2.** a sac, cell, capsule, or sporangium of a plant or mushroom. —**the′cal, the′cate** (-kit, -kāt), *adj.*

thee (t͟hē), *pron.* **1.** the objective case of THOU: *With this ring, I thee wed.* **2.** thou (now used chiefly by the Friends).

theft (theft), *n.* **1.** the act of stealing; larceny. **2.** an instance of this.

their (t͟hâr; *unstressed* t͟hər), *pron.* **1.** a form of the possessive case of THEY used as an attributive adjective, before a noun: *their home; their rights as citizens.* **2.** (used after an indefinite singular antecedent in place of the definite form *his* or *her*): *Someone left their book on the table.* Compare THEIRS. —**Usage.** See HE[1], ME, THEY.

theirs (t͟hârz), *pron.* **1.** a form of the possessive case of THEY used as a predicate adjective, after a noun or without a noun: *Are you a friend of theirs? It is theirs.* **2.** (used after an indefinite singular antecedent in place of the definite form *his* or *hers*): *I have my book; does everyone else have theirs?* **3.** that which belongs to them.

the•ism (thē′iz əm), *n.* **1.** belief in one God as the creator and ruler of the universe, without rejection of revelation (disting. from *deism*). **2.** belief in the existence of a god or gods (opposed to *atheism*). —**the′ist,** *n., adj.* —**the•is′tic, the•is′ti•cal,** *adj.*

them (*th*em; *unstressed* *th*əm, əm), *pron.* **1.** the objective case of THEY, used as a direct or indirect object: *We saw them yesterday. I gave them the books.* **2.** (used instead of the pronoun *they* in the predicate after the verb *to be*): *It's them, across the street. It isn't them.* **3.** (used instead of the pronoun *their* before a gerund or present participle): *The boys' parents objected to them hiking without supervision.* **—Usage.** See HE[1], ME, THEY.

the•mat•ic (thē mat′ik), *adj.* **1.** of or pertaining to a theme. **2. a.** of or pertaining to the theme or stem of a word. **b.** (of a vowel) occurring at the end of the stem and before the inflectional ending of a word form, as *i* in Latin *audiō* "I hear." **c.** (of a noun or verb form) containing a thematic vowel. **—the•mat′i•cal•ly,** *adv.*

theme (thēm), *n.* **1.** a subject of discourse, discussion, meditation, or composition; topic. **2.** a unifying or dominant idea, motif, etc., as in a work of art. **3.** a short essay, esp. a school composition. **4. a.** a principal melodic subject in a musical composition. **b.** a short melodic subject from which variations are developed. **5.** STEM[1] (def. 10). **6.** TOPIC (def. 3).

theme′ park′, *n.* an amusement park whose attractions are based on one or several themes, as fairy tales or the Old West.

theme′ song′, *n.* **1.** a song or melody in an operetta or musical comedy so emphasized by repetition as to dominate the presentation. **2.** a song or melody identifying or identified with a radio or television program, dance band, etc.

The•mis•to•cles (thə mis′tə klēz′), *n.* 527?–460? B.C., Athenian statesman.

them•selves (*th*əm selvz′, *th*em′-), *pron.pl.* **1.** a reflexive form of THEY: *They washed themselves quickly.* **2.** (used as an intensive): *The authors themselves left the theater.* **3.** (used after an indefinite singular antecedent in place of the definite form *himself* or *herself*): *No one who ignores the law can call themselves a good citizen.* **4.** their normal or customary selves. **—Usage.** See MYSELF.

then (*th*en), *adv.* **1.** at that time: *Prices were lower then.* **2.** immediately or soon afterward: *The rain stopped and then started again.* **3.** next in order of time or place: *We ate, then we started home.* **4.** at the same time: *At first the water seemed blue, then gray.* **5.** in addition; besides: *I love my job, and then it pays so well.* **6.** in that case; as a consequence; in those circumstances. **7.** since that is so; as it appears; therefore. **—***adj.* **8.** existing or being at the time indicated: *the then prime minister.* **—***n.* **9.** that time: *We haven't been back since then.* **—*Idiom.* 10. but then,** but on the other hand. **11. then and there,** at that precise time and place; at once.

thence (*th*ens), *adv.* **1.** from that place: *I went to Paris and thence to Rome.* **2.** from that time; thenceforth. **3.** from that source.

thence•forth (*th*ens′fôrth′, -fōrth′, *th*ens′fôrth′, -fōrth′), *adv.* from that time onward.

thence•for•ward (*th*ens′fôr′wərd) also **thence′for′wards,** *adv.* THENCEFORTH.

theo-, a combining form meaning "god": *theocracy.* Also, *esp. before a vowel,* **the-.**

the•o•cen•tric (thē′ə sen′trik), *adj.* having God as the focal point of thoughts, interests, and feelings.

the•oc•ra•cy (thē ok′rə sē), *n., pl.* **-cies.** **1.** a form of government in which God or a deity is recognized as the supreme ruler. **2.** a system of government by priests claiming a divine commission. **3.** a commonwealth or state under such a form of government. **—the′o•crat′** (-ə krat′), *n.* **—the′o•crat′ic,** *adj.* **—the′o•crat′i•cal•ly,** *adv.*

The•oc•ri•tus (thē ok′ri təs), *n.* fl. c270 B.C., Greek poet.

the•od•i•cy (thē od′ə sē), *n., pl.* **-cies.** a vindication of God's justice in tolerating the existence of evil. **—the•od′i•ce′an,** *adj.*

the•od•o•lite (thē od′l īt′), *n.* a precision instrument having a telescopic sight for establishing horizontal and sometimes vertical angles. Compare TRANSIT (def. 7). **—the•od′o•lit′ic** (-it′ik), *adj.*

The•o•do•sian (thē′ə dō′shən, -shē ən), *adj.* **1.** of or pertaining to Theodosius I, who made Christianity the official state religion of the Roman Empire. **2.** of or pertaining to Theodosius II, who issued the earliest collection of the imperial laws **(Theodo′sian Code′).**

The•o•do•si•us I (thē′ə dō′shē əs, -shəs), *n.* (*"the Great"*) A.D. 346?–395, Roman emperor of the Eastern Roman Empire 379–395.

Theodosius II, A.D.401–450, emperor of the Eastern Roman Empire 408–450.

the•o•lo•gian (thē′ə lō′jən, -jē ən), *n.* a person versed in theology.

the•o•log•i•cal (thē′ə loj′i kəl) also **the′o•log′ic,** *adj.* **1.** of or pertaining to theology: *a theological argument.* **2.** of or pertaining to religious studies: *a theological seminary.* **—the′o•log′i•cal•ly,** *adv.*

theolog′ical vir′tue, *n.* one of the three graces: faith, hope, or charity, infused into the human intellect and will by a special grace of God. Compare NATURAL VIRTUE.

the•ol•o•gy (thē ol′ə jē), *n., pl.* **-gies.** **1.** the field of study and analysis that treats of God and of God's attributes and relations to the universe; the study of divine things or religious truth; divinity. **2.** a particular form, system, or branch of this study.

the•o•rem (thē′ər əm, thēr′əm), *n.* **1.** *Math.* a theoretical proposition, statement, or formula embodying something to be proved from other propositions or formulas. **2.** a rule or law, esp. one expressed by an equation or formula. **3.** *Logic.* a proposition that can be deduced from the premises or assumptions of a system. **4.** an idea, method, or statement generally accepted as true or worthwhile without proof. **—the′o•re•mat′ic** (-ə mat′ik), *adj.* **—the′o•re•mat′i•cal•ly,** *adv.*

the•o•ret•i•cal (thē′ə ret′i kəl) also **the′o•ret′ic,** *adj.* **1.** of, pertaining to, or consisting in theory; not practical. **2.** existing only in theory; hypothetical. **3.** given to, forming, or dealing with theories; speculative. **—the′o•ret′i•cal•ly,** *adv.*

the•o•re•ti•cian (thē′ər i tish′ən, thēr′i-), *n.* a person who deals with or is expert in the theoretical part of a subject.

the•o•rist (thē′ər ist, thēr′-), *n.* **1.** a person who theorizes. **2.** a person who deals mainly with the theory of a subject.

the•o•rize (thē′ə rīz′, thēr′īz), *v.i.,* **-rized, -riz•ing.** to form a theory or theories. **—the′o•ri•za′tion,** *n.* **—the′o•riz′er,** *n.*

the•o•ry (thē′ə rē, thēr′ē), *n., pl.* **-ries.** **1.** a coherent group of general propositions used as principles of explanation for a class of phenomena: *Darwin's theory of evolution.* **2.** a proposed explanation whose status is still conjectural. **3.** a body of mathematical principles, theorems, or the like, belonging to one subject: *number theory.* **4.** the branch of a science or art that deals with its principles or methods, as distinguished from its practice: *music theory.* **5.** a particular conception or view of something to be done or of the method of doing it. **6.** a guess or conjecture. **7.** contemplation or speculation. **—*Idiom.* 8. in theory,** under hypothetical or ideal conditions; theoretically.

Theosoph′ical Soci′ety, *n.* a society founded in New York in 1875 by Madame Blavatsky and others, advocating a worldwide eclectic religion based largely on Brahmanic and Buddhistic teachings.

the•os•o•phy (thē os′ə fē), *n.* **1.** any of various forms of philosophical or religious thought based on a mystical insight into the divine nature. **2.** (*often caps.*) the system of belief and practice of the Theosophical Society. **—the′o•soph′i•cal** (-ə sof′i kəl), **the′o•soph′ic,** *adj.* **—the′o•soph′i•cal•ly,** *adv.* **—the•os′o•phism,** *n.* **—the•os′o•phist,** *n.*

ther•a•peu•tic (ther′ə pyōō′tik), *adj.* Also, **ther′a•peu′ti•cal.** **1.** pertaining to the treating or curing of disease or disorders; curative; rehabilitative. **2.** serving to maintain or restore health: *therapeutic abortion.* **3.** having a beneficial effect on one's mental state; serving to relax or calm. **—***n.* **4.** a therapeutic substance. **—ther′a•peu′ti•cal•ly,** *adv.*

ther•a•peu•tics (ther′ə pyōō′tiks), *n.* (*used with a sing. v.*) the branch of medicine concerned with the use of remedies to treat disease.

ther•a•pist (ther′ə pist), *n.* **1.** a person trained in the use of physical methods, as exercise or massage, for the treatment of disease, injury, or disability. **2.** a person trained in the use of psychological methods for the treatment of mental or emotional problems; psychotherapist. **3.** Also, **ther•a•peu•tist** (ther′ə pyōō′tist). a person, as a physician, skilled in therapeutics.

ther•a•py (ther′ə pē), *n., pl.* **-pies.** **1.** the treatment of disease or disorders, as by some remedial, rehabilitative, or curative process: *speech therapy.* **2.** PSYCHOTHERAPY. **3.** a curative power or quality. **4.** any act, task, program, etc., that relieves tension.

there (*th*âr; *unstressed* *th*ər), *adv.* **1.** in or at that place (opposed to *here*): *She is there now.* **2.** at that point in an action, speech, etc.: *He stopped there for applause.* **3.** in that matter, particular, or respect: *Your anger was justified there.* **4.** into or to that place; thither: *We went there last year.* **5.** (used by way of calling attention to something or someone): *There they go.* **—***pron.* **6.** (used in place of a noun of address): *Hello, there.* **—***n.* **7.** that place or point: *I come from there, too.* **—***adj.* **8.** (used for emphasis, esp. after a noun modified by a demonstrative adjective): *Ask that man there.* **—***interj.* **9.** (used to express satisfaction, relief, encouragement, approval, consolation, etc.): *There! It's done.* **—Usage.** The verb following the pronoun THERE is singular or plural according to the number of the subject that follows the verb: *There is a message for you. There are patients in the waiting room.* With compound subjects in which all the coordinate words are singular, a singular verb often occurs, although the plural may also be used: *There was* (or *were*) *a horse and a cow in the pasture.* When a compound subject contains both singular and plural words, the verb usu. agrees with the subject closest to the verb, although a plural verb sometimes occurs regardless, esp. if the compound has more than two elements: *There were staff meetings and a press conference daily. There was* (or *were*) *a glass, two plates, two cups, and a teapot on the shelf.* It is nonstandard usage to place THERE between a demonstrative adjective and the noun it modifies: *that there car.* The same is true of HERE: *these here nails.* Placed after the noun, both THERE and HERE are entirely standard: *that car there; these nails here.*

there•a•bout (*th*âr′ə bout′, *th*âr′ə bout′) also **there′a•bouts′,** *adv.* **1.** about or near that place or time: *last June or thereabout.* **2.** about that number, amount, etc.: *a dozen or thereabout.*

there•af•ter (*th*âr′af′tər, -äf′-), *adv.* after that in time or sequence; afterward; subsequently.

there•at (*th*âr′at′), *adv.* **1.** at that place or time; there. **2.** because of that; thereupon.

there•by (*th*âr′bī′, *th*âr′bī′), *adv.* **1.** by that; by means of that. **2.** in that relation: *Thereby hangs a tale.* **3.** by or near that place.

there•for (*th*âr′fôr′), *adv.* for or in exchange for that or this; for it: *a refund therefor.*

there•fore (*th*âr′fôr′, -fōr′), *adv.* in consequence of that; as a result; consequently; hence.

there•from (*th*âr′frum′, -from′), *adv.* from that place, thing, etc.

there•in (*th*âr′in′), *adv.* **1.** in or into that place or thing. **2.** in that matter, circumstance, etc.

there·in·af·ter (t͟hâr′in af′tər, -äf′-), *adv.* afterward in that document, statement, etc.

there·in·to (t͟hâr′in′tōō, -in tōō′), *adv.* **1.** into that place or thing. **2.** into that matter, circumstance, etc.

There′ Is′ a Green′ Hill′ Far′ Away′, a Christian hymn (1848) with words by Cecil Alexander.

there·of (t͟hâr′uv′, -ov′), *adv.* **1.** of that or it. **2.** from or out of that origin or cause.

there·on (t͟hâr′on′, -ôn′), *adv.* **1.** on or upon that or it. **2.** immediately after that; thereupon.

there's (t͟hârz), **1.** contraction of *there is.* **2.** contraction of *there has.*

The·re·sa (tə rē′sə, -zə; *Sp.* te ʀe′sä), *n.* Saint. Also, **Teresa.** Also called **There′sa of A′vi·la** (ä′vē lä′). 1515–82, Spanish Carmelite nun, mystic, and writer.

there·to (t͟hâr′tōō′) also **there·un·to** (t͟hâr′un′tōō, -un tōō′), *adv.* **1.** to that place or thing. **2.** to that matter, circumstance, etc.

there·to·fore (t͟hâr′tə fôr′, -fōr′), *adv.* before or until that time.

there·un·der (t͟hâr′un′dər), *adv.* **1.** under or beneath that. **2.** under the authority of or in accordance with that.

there·up·on (t͟hâr′ə pon′, -pôn′, t͟hâr′ə pon′, -pôn′), *adv.* **1.** immediately following that. **2.** in consequence of that. **3.** upon that or it. **4.** with reference to that.

There′ Were′ Nine′ty and Nine′, a Christian hymn with words by Elizabeth Cecilia Clephane.

there·with (t͟hâr′with′, -wit͟h′), *adv.* **1.** with that. **2.** in addition to that. **3.** following upon that; thereupon.

there·with·al (t͟hâr′with ôl′, -wit͟h-, t͟hâr′wit͟h ôl′, -with-), *adv.* **1.** together with that; in addition to that. **2.** following upon that.

ther·mae (thûr′mē), *n.pl.* hot springs or baths, esp. the public baths of ancient Rome.

ther·mal (thûr′məl), *adj.* **1.** Also, **thermic.** of, pertaining to, or caused by heat or temperature: *thermal energy.* **2.** of, pertaining to, or of the nature of hot or warm springs: *thermal waters.* **3.** designed to aid in or promote the retention of body heat: *a thermal blanket; thermal underwear.* —*n.* **4.** a rising air current caused by heating from the underlying surface. **5.** thermals, clothing, esp. underwear, designed to help retain body heat. —**ther′mal·ly,** *adv.*

thermo-, a combining form meaning "heat," "hot": *thermoplastic.* Also, *esp. before a vowel,* **therm-.**

ther·mo·chem·is·try (thûr′mō kem′ə strē), *n.* the branch of chemistry dealing with the relationship between chemical action and heat. —**ther′mo·chem′i·cal** (-kem′i kəl), *adj.* —**ther′mo·chem′i·cal·ly,** *adv.* —**ther′mo·chem′ist,** *n.*

ther·mo·cou·ple (thûr′mə kup′əl), *n.* a device that measures temperature as a function of the electromotive force induced when heat is applied to two dissimilar metal wires joined at both ends.

ther·mo·dy·nam·ic (thûr′mō dī nam′ik) also **ther′mo·dy·nam′i·cal,** *adj.* **1.** of or pertaining to thermodynamics. **2.** using or producing heat. —**ther′mo·dy·nam′i·cal·ly,** *adv.*

ther·mo·dy·nam·ics (thûr′mō dī nam′iks), *n.* (*used with a sing. v.*) the science concerned with the relations between heat and mechanical energy or work, and the conversion of one into the other.

ther·mo·e·lec·tric (thûr′mō i lek′trik) also **ther′mo·e·lec′tri·cal,** *adj.* of, pertaining to, or involving the direct relationship between heat and electricity. —**ther′mo·e·lec′tri·cal·ly,** *adv.*

ther·mog·ra·phy (thər mog′rə fē), *n.* **1.** a technique for imitating an embossed appearance, as on stationery, by fusing wet ink and an adhesive powder to the paper by heat. **2.** a technique for measuring regional skin temperatures, used esp. as a screening method for detection of breast cancer. —**ther·mog′ra·pher,** *n.* —**ther·mo·graph·ic** (thûr′mə graf′ik), *adj.* —**ther′mo·graph′i·cal·ly,** *adv.*

ther·mo·lu·mi·nes·cence (thûr′mō lōō′mə nes′əns), *n.* phosphorescence produced by the heating of a substance.

ther·mo·mag·net·ic (thûr′mō mag net′ik), *adj.* **1.** of or pertaining to the effect of heat on the magnetic properties of a substance. **2.** of or pertaining to the effect of a magnetic field on a conductor of heat.

ther·mom·e·ter (thər mom′i tər), *n.* an instrument for measuring temperature, often a sealed glass tube containing a column of liquid, as mercury, that expands and contracts with temperature changes, the temperature being read where the top of the column coincides with a calibrated scale on the tube or frame. —**ther·mo·met·ric** (thûr′mə me′trik), **ther′mo·met′ri·cal,** *adj.* —**ther′mo·met′ri·cal·ly,** *adv.*

ther·mo·nu·cle·ar (thûr′mō nōō′klē ər, -nyōō′- or, *by metathesis,* -kyə lər), *adj.* **1.** of, pertaining to, or involving fusion reactions between nuclei of a light element, as hydrogen, that require temperatures of several million degrees to occur: *thermonuclear power.* **2.** pertaining to or using energy from such reactions: *thermonuclear weapons systems.*

ther·mo·plas·tic (thûr′mə plas′tik), *adj.* **1.** soft and pliable when heated, as some plastics, without any change of the inherent properties. —*n.* **2.** a plastic of this type. —**ther′mo·plas·tic′i·ty** (-pla stis′i tē), *n.*

Ther·mop·y·lae (thər mop′ə lē′), *n.* a pass in E Greece, in Locris, near an arm of the Aegean: Persian defeat of the Spartans 480 B.C.

ther·mos (thûr′məs), *n.* a vacuum bottle or insulated container, used for keeping liquids hot or cold. Also called **ther′mos bot′tle.**

ther·mo·sphere (thûr′mə sfēr′), *n.* the region of the upper atmosphere in which temperature increases continuously with altitude, encompassing essentially the atmosphere above the mesosphere.

ther·mo·stat (thûr′mə stat′), *n., v.,* **-stat·ted** or **-stat·ed, -stat·ting** or **-stat·ing.** —*n.* **1.** a device that functions to establish and maintain a desired temperature automatically or signals a change in temperature for manual adjustment. **2.** a similar device that activates or controls an apparatus, as a fire alarm, based on the temperature of the environment. —*v.t.* **3.** to equip or control with a thermostat. —**ther′mo·stat′ic,** *adj.* —**ther′mo·stat′i·cal·ly,** *adv.*

-thermy, a combining form meaning "heat": *diathermy.*

the·sau·rus (thi sôr′əs), *n., pl.* **-sau·rus·es, -sau·ri** (-sôr′ī). **1.** a dictionary of synonyms and antonyms. **2.** any dictionary, encyclopedia, or other reference book. **3.** a storehouse, repository, or treasury.

these (t͟hēz), *pron., adj.* pl. of THIS.

The·se·us (thē′sē əs, -syōōs), *n.* a legendary hero of Attica and king of ancient Athens, renowned for the slaying of the Minotaur.

the·sis (thē′sis), *n., pl.* **-ses** (-sēz). **1.** a proposition stated or put forward for consideration, esp. one to be discussed and proved or to be maintained against objections. **2.** a subject for a composition or essay. **3.** a formal paper incorporating original research on a subject, esp. one presented by a candidate for a degree, as a master's degree. **4.** the downward stroke in conducting music; downbeat. Compare ARSIS (def. 1). **5. a.** a part of a metrical foot that does not bear the ictus or stress. **b.** (less commonly) the part of a metrical foot that bears the ictus.

Thes·pi·an (thes′pē ən), *adj.* **1.** (*often l.c.*) pertaining to tragedy or to the dramatic art in general. **2.** of or characteristic of Thespis. —*n.* **3.** (*usu. l.c.*) an actor or actress.

Thes·pis (thes′pis), *n.* fl. 6th century B.C., Greek poet.

Thess., Thessalonians.

Thes·sa·lo·ni·ans (thes′ə lō′nē ənz), *n.* (*used with a sing. v.*) either of two books of the New Testament, I Thessalonians or II Thessalonians, written by Paul.

the′ta rhythm′, *n.* a pattern of brain waves (**the′ta waves′**) with a regular frequency of 4 to 7 hertz per second, during light sleep.

thew (thyōō), *n.* **1.** Usu., **thews.** muscle or sinew. **2.** thews, physical strength. —**thew′y,** *adj.*

they (t͟hā), *pron.pl., poss.* **their** or **theirs,** *obj.* **them. 1.** nominative plural of HE, SHE, and IT. **2.** people in general: *They say he's rich.* **3.** (used with an indefinite singular antecedent: *Whoever is of voting age, whether they are interested in politics or not, should vote.*

they'd (t͟hād), **1.** contraction of *they had.* **2.** contraction of *they would.*

they'll (t͟hāl), contraction of *they will.*

they're (t͟hâr; *unstressed* t͟hər), contraction of *they are.*

they've (t͟hāv), contraction of *they have.*

thi·a·mine (thī′ə min, -mēn′) also **thi·a·min** (-min), *n.* a crystalline, water-soluble vitamin-B compound, $C_{12}H_{17}ClN_4OS$, abundant in liver, legumes, and cereal grains. Also called **vitamin B₁.**

thick (thik), *adj.* **1.** having relatively great extent from one surface to the opposite: *a thick slice of bread.* **2.** measured as specified between opposite surfaces: *a board one inch thick.* **3.** composed of objects close together; dense: *a thick fog.* **4.** filled or covered: *thick with dust.* **5.** not distinctly articulated: *thick speech.* **6.** marked; pronounced: *a thick foreign accent.* **7.** deep or profound: *thick darkness.* **8.** heavy or viscous: *a thick syrup.* **9.** close in friendship; intimate. **10.** mentally slow; stupid. **11.** disagreeably excessive or exaggerated. —*adv.* **12.** in a thick manner. **13.** close together; closely packed: *vines grow thick.* **14.** so as to produce something thick: *cheese sliced thick.* —*n.* **15.** the densest or most crowded part: *in the thick of the fight.* —*Idiom.* **16. through thick and thin,** under favorable and unfavorable conditions; steadfastly. —**thick′ish,** *adj.* —**thick′ly,** *adv.*

thick·en (thik′ən), *v.t., v.i.* to make or become thick or thicker. **2.** to make or grow more profound or intricate: *The plot thickens in the next chapter.* —**thick′en·er,** *n.*

thick·en·ing (thik′ə ning), *n.* **1.** making or becoming thick. **2.** a thickened part or area; swelling. **3.** something used to thicken; thickener.

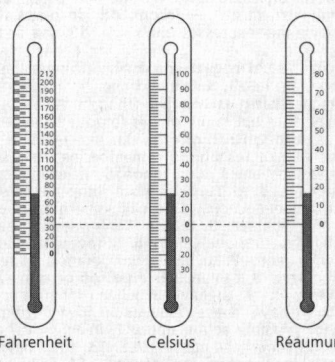

Fahrenheit   Celsius   Réaumur

thermometers

T

thick•et (thik′it), *n.* a dense growth of shrubs, bushes, or small trees. —**thick′et•ed, thick′et•y,** *adj.*
thick•head•ed (thik′hed′id), *adj.* **1.** dull-witted; stupid. **2.** (of an animal) having a thick head. —**thick′head′ed•ly,** *adv.*
thick•ness (thik′nis), *n.* **1.** the state or quality of being thick. **2.** the measure of the smallest dimension of a solid figure: *a board of two-inch thickness.* **3.** the thick part of something. **4.** layer; ply: *three thicknesses of cloth.*
thick•set (*adj.* thik′set′; *n.* -set′), *adj.* **1.** heavily or solidly built; stocky: *a thickset wrestler.* **2.** set in close arrangement; dense: *a thickset hedge.* —*n.* **3.** a thicket.
thick′-skinned′, *adj.* **1.** having a thick skin. **2.** insensitive or hardened to criticism; obtuse; callous.
thick′-wit′ted, *adj.* stupid; dull. —**thick′-wit′ted•ly,** *adv.* —**thick′-wit′ted•ness,** *n.*
thief (thēf), *n., pl.* **thieves.** a person who steals, esp. secretly.
thieve (thēv), *v.t., v.i.,* **thieved, thiev•ing.** to steal.
thiev•er•y (thē′və rē), *n., pl.* **-er•ies.** the act or practice of stealing; theft.
thigh (thī), *n.* **1.** the part of the lower limb in humans between the hip and the knee. **2.** the corresponding part of the hind limb of other animals; the femoral region.
thigh•bone (thī′bōn′), *n.* FEMUR (def. 1).
thim•ble (thim′bəl), *n.* **1.** a small cap worn over the fingertip to protect it when pushing a needle through cloth in sewing. **2.** a metal ring with a concave groove on the outside, used to line the outside of a ring of rope to prevent chafing. —**thim′ble•like′,** *adj.*
thim•ble•weed (thim′bəl wēd′), *n.* any of several plants that have a thimble-shaped fruiting head, esp. either of two white-flowered buttercups, *Anemone riparia* or *A. virginiana.*
Thim•phu (tim po͞o′) also **Thim•bu** (-bo͞o′), *n.* the capital of Bhutan, in the W part. 15,000.
thin (thin), *adj.,* **thin•ner, thin•nest,** *adv., v.,* **thinned, thin•ning.** —*adj.* **1.** having relatively little extent from one surface to the opposite: *thin ice.* **2.** of small cross section in comparison with the length: *a thin wire.* **3.** having little flesh; lean: *a thin man.* **4.** composed of objects widely separated; sparse: *thin vegetation.* **5.** scant. **6.** of slight consistency: *thin soup.* **7.** rarefied, as air. **8.** lacking solidity; flimsy: *a thin excuse.* **9.** lacking volume; weak and shrill: *a thin voice.* **10.** lacking force or a sincere effort: *a thin smile.* **11.** lacking body or richness: *a thin wine.* **12.** of light tint. **13.** (of a photographic negative) lacking in contrast through underdevelopment or underexposure. —*adv.* **14.** in a thin manner. **15.** sparsely; not densely. **16.** so as to produce something thin: *ham sliced thin.* —*v.t.* **17.** to make thin or thinner (often fol. by *down* or *out*). —*v.i.* **18.** to become reduced or diminished (often fol. by *down, out,* or *off*): *The crowd thinned out.* —**thin′ly,** *adv.* —**thin′ness,** *n.*
thine (t͟hīn), *pron.* **1.** the possessive case of THOU used as a predicate adjective, after a noun or without a noun. **2.** the possessive case of THOU used as an attributive adjective before a noun beginning with a vowel or vowel sound: *thine honor.* Compare THY. **3.** that which belongs to thee: *Thine is the glory.*
thing (thing), *n.* **1.** an inanimate object: *a person, animal, or thing.* **2.** some object that is not or cannot be specifically designated: *Hand me that thing.* **3.** anything that is or may become an object of thought. **4.** **things,** matters; affairs: *How are things?* **5.** a fact, circumstance, or state of affairs: *It is a curious thing.* **6.** an action, event, or performance: *Biking is a fun thing.* **7.** a particular; detail: *You left out some things.* **8.** aim; objective: *The thing is to enjoy it.* **9.** an article of clothing: *not a thing to wear.* **10.** **things, a.** utensils: *the breakfast things.* **b.** personal possessions: *Pack your things!* **11.** a task; chore: *things to do.* **12.** a living being; creature. **13.** a thought; observation: *a thing or two to say.* **14.** a peculiar attitude toward something: *She has a thing about cats.* **15.** something represented, as distinguished from a word, symbol, or idea representing it. **16.** *Informal.* issue; subject; topic (*usu. preceded by a noun*): *the leadership thing; the peace thing.* **17.** **the thing, a.** something that is correct or fashionable: *it's the new thing.* **b.** that which is expedient: *Do the right thing.* —***Idiom.*** **18.** **do one's thing,** *Informal.* to pursue a lifestyle that expresses one's self. **19.** **see** or **hear things,** to hallucinate.
thing•a•ma•bob or **thing•u•ma•bob** (thing′ə mə bob′), also **thing•um•bob** (-əm bob′), *n.* THINGAMAJIG.
thing•a•ma•jig or **thing•u•ma•jig** (thing′ə mə jig′), *n.* a thing for which the speaker does not know or has forgotten the name.
think (thingk), *v.,* **thought, think•ing,** *adj., n.* —*v.i.* **1.** to have a conscious mind, capable of reasoning, remembering, and making rational decisions. **2.** to employ one's mind rationally in evaluating a given situation: *Think carefully.* **3.** to have a certain thing as the subject of one's thoughts: *thinking about school.* **4.** to call something to one's conscious mind: *to think of a number.* **5.** to consider something as a possible action: *to think about cutting one's hair.* **6.** to invent or conceive of something: *to think of a plan.* **7.** to have consideration or regard for someone: *to think of others.* **8.** to consider a person or thing as indicated: *to think well of someone.* **9.** to have a belief or opinion: *I think she is funny.* —*v.t.* **10.** to have in the mind as an idea: *thinking nice things.* **11.** to evaluate for possible action upon: *Think the deal over.* **12.** to regard as specified: *He thought me unkind.* **13.** to believe to be true of someone or something: *to think evil of them.* **14.** to have as a plan: *We think that we will go.* **15.** to anticipate or expect: *I did not think to call you.* **16.** **think out** or **through, a.** to understand or solve by thinking. **b.** to devise; contrive: *to think out a plan.* —*adj.* **17.** pertaining to thinking or thought. —*n.* **18.** the act or a period of thinking: *First, give it a good think.* —***Idiom.*** **19.** **think better of,** to reconsider. **20.** **think fit,** to consider appropriate. **21.** **think little** or **nothing of,** to regard as insignificant. **22.** **think the world of,** to like or admire greatly. **23.** **think twice,** to consider carefully before acting.
think•a•ble (thing′kə bəl), *adj.* **1.** conceivable. **2.** possible.
think•er (thing′kər), *n.* **1.** a person who thinks, as in a specified way or manner: *a slow thinker.* **2.** a person with a well-developed faculty for thinking, as a philosopher, theorist, or scholar: *great thinkers.*
think•ing (thing′king), *adj.* **1.** rational; reasoning: *Humans are thinking animals.* **2.** thoughtful; reflective: *Any thinking person would approve.* —*n.* **3.** thought; judgment: *clear thinking.*
think′ing cap′, *n.* a state of mind marked by concentration: *We'll need our thinking caps to solve this one.*
think′ piece′, *n.* a journalistic article analyzing a news event, often giving the writer's opinions about its significance.
think′ tank′, *n.* a research organization employed to analyze problems and plan future developments, as in military, political, or social areas. Also called **think′ fac′tory.**
thin•ner[1] (thin′ər), *n.* a volatile liquid, as turpentine, used to dilute paint, varnish, etc., to a desired consistency.
thin•ner[2] (thin′ər), *adj.* comparative of THIN.
thin′-skinned′, *adj.* **1.** having a thin skin. **2.** sensitive to criticism; easily offended; touchy.
thi′o•pen′tal so′dium (thī′ə pen′tl, -tal, -tôl, thī′-), *n.* a barbiturate, $C_{11}H_{18}N_2NaO_2S$, used as an anesthetic.
third (thûrd), *adj.* **1.** next after the second; being the ordinal number for three. **2.** being one of three equal parts. **3.** pertaining to the gear transmission ratio at which the drive shaft speed is next greater than that of second gear. **4.** graded or ranked one level below the second: *third mate.* —*n.* **5.** a third part, esp. of one ($\frac{1}{3}$). **6.** the third member of a series. **7.** third gear. **8.** a person or thing next after second in rank or precedence. **9. a.** a musical interval encompassing three diatonic degrees. **b.** a tone at this interval. **c.** the harmonic combination of two tones a third apart. **10.** Usu., **thirds.** a product or goods below second quality. —*adv.* **11.** in the third place; thirdly. —**third′ly,** *adv.*
Third′ Amend′ment, *n.* an amendment to the U.S. Constitution, ratified in 1791 as part of the Bill of Rights, guaranteeing that the forced quartering of soldiers in private homes would be prohibited in peacetime and allowed only by prescribed law during wartime.
third′ base′, *n.* **1.** the third of the bases in baseball, in counterclockwise order from home plate. **2.** the position of the fielder covering this base. —**third′ base′man,** *n.*
third′ class′, *n.* **1.** the class, grade, or rank immediately below the second. **2.** the least costly class of accommodations, as on trains. Compare TOURIST CLASS. **3.** (in the U.S. Postal Service) the class of mail consisting of merchandise weighing up to 16 ounces, and printed material not sealed against postal inspection.
third′-class′, *adj.* of the lowest class or quality; inferior.
Third′ Command′ment, *n.* "Thou shalt not take the name of the Lord thy God in vain": third of the Ten Commandments. Compare TEN COMMANDMENTS.
third′ degree′, *n.* intensive questioning and rough treatment in order to get a confession.
third′-degree′, *v.t.,* **-greed, -gree•ing.** to subject to the third degree.
third′-degree′ burn′, *n.* See under BURN[1] (def. 26).
third′ dimen′sion, *n.* **1.** the additional dimension by which a solid object is distinguished from a planar object; depth. **2.** an aspect that heightens the reality or vividness of something.
third′ estate′, *n.* the third of the three estates: the commons in France or England. Compare ESTATE (def. 5).
third′ fin′ger, *n.* the finger next to the little finger; ring finger.
third•hand (thûrd′hand′), *adj.* **1.** previously owned by two successive people. **2.** secondhand, esp. in poor condition. **3.** twice removed. —*adv.* **4.** after two other users or owners. **5.** by way of intermediate sources; indirectly.
Third′ Or′der, *n. Roman Catholic Church.* **1.** a branch of a religious order whose members are lay people following the avocations of a secular life. **2.** a member of a Third Order who follows its rule in the community under ordinary simple vows.
third′ par′ty, *n.* **1.** any party to a case or quarrel who is incidentally involved. **2.** (in a two-party system) a usu. temporary political party composed of independents. —**third′-par′ty,** *adj.*
third′ per′son, *n.* **1.** the grammatical person used in an utterance in referring to anyone or anything other than the speaker or the one or ones being addressed. **2.** a pronoun or verb form in the third person, as *it, they,* or *goes,* or a set of such forms.
third′ rail′, *n.* a rail in an electrified railroad that provides current to a car or locomotive.
third′-rate′, *adj.* **1.** of the third rate, quality, or class. **2.** distinctly inferior. —**third′-rat′er,** *n.*
Third′ Reich′, *n.* Germany during the Nazi regime 1933–45. [partial trans. of German *drittes Reich*]
Third′ Repub′lic, *n.* the republic established in France in 1870 and terminating with the Nazi occupation in 1940.

Third′ World′, *n.* (*sometimes l.c.*) the developing nations of Africa, Asia, and Latin America. [trans. of French *tiers monde*]

thirst (thûrst), *n.* **1.** a sensation of dryness in the mouth and throat caused by need of liquid. **2.** a need for liquid or moisture. **3.** eager desire; craving: *a thirst for knowledge.* —*v.i.* **4.** to feel thirst; be thirsty. **5.** to have a strong desire. —**thirst′er,** *n.*

thirst·y (thûr′stē), *adj.*, **thirst·i·er, thirst·i·est. 1.** having thirst; craving liquid. **2.** needing moisture; parched: *the thirsty soil.* **3.** eagerly desirous: *thirsty for news.* **4.** causing thirst: *Digging is thirsty work.* —**thirst′i·ly,** *adv.* —**thirst′i·ness,** *n.*

thir·teen (thûr′tēn′), *n.* **1.** a cardinal number, 10 plus 3. **2.** a symbol for this number, as 13 or XIII. **3.** a set of this many persons or things. —*adj.* **4.** amounting to 13 in number.

Thir′teen Col′onies, *n.pl.* the American colonies that joined the revolution against British rule in 1776: New Hampshire, Massachusetts, Rhode Island, Connecticut, New York, New Jersey, Pennsylvania, Delaware, Maryland, Virginia, North Carolina, South Carolina, and Georgia.

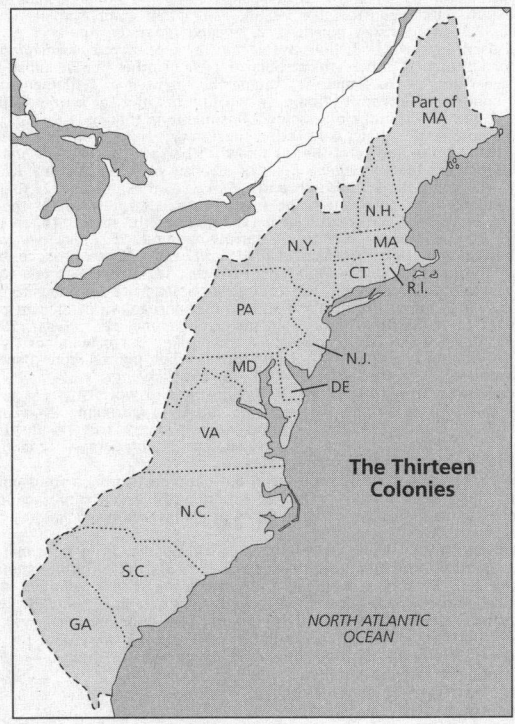

The Thirteen Colonies

thir·teenth (thûr′tēnth′), *adj.* **1.** next after the twelfth; being the ordinal number for 13. **2.** being one of 13 equal parts. —*n.* **3.** a thirteenth part, esp. of one (¹⁄₁₃). **4.** the thirteenth member of a series.

Thir′teenth Amend′ment, *n.* an amendment to the U.S. Constitution, ratified in 1865, abolishing slavery.

thir·ty (thûr′tē), *n.*, *pl.* **-ties,** *adj.* —*n.* **1.** a cardinal number, 10 times 3. **2.** a symbol for this number, as 30 or XXX. **3.** a set of this many persons or things. **4. thirties,** the numbers from 30 through 39, as in referring to the years of a lifetime or of a century or to degrees of temperature. —*adj.* **5.** amounting to 30 in number. —**thir′ti·eth,** *adj.*, *n.*

Thir′ty-Nine′ Ar′ticles, *n.pl.* a set of statements (1563) defining the Church of England's position on matters of doctrine that were controversial in the 16th century.

thir′ty-sec′ond note′, *n.* a musical note having ¹⁄₃₂ the time value of a whole note.

thir′ty-sec′ond rest′, *n.* a rest equal in value to a thirty-second note.

Thir′ty Years′ War′, *n.* a series of wars (1618–48) that began as a conflict between German Protestants and Catholics and developed into a struggle for power among most European nations.

this (ŧẖis), *pron.* and *adj.*, *pl.* **these** (ŧẖēz); *adv.* —*pron.* **1.** (used to indicate a person, thing, idea, or event as present, near, just mentioned, or by way of emphasis): *This is my coat.* **2.** (used to indicate one of two or more persons, things, etc., referring to the one nearer in place, time, or thought; opposed to *that*): *This is Liza and that is Amy.* **3.** (used to indicate one or more persons, things, etc., implying a contrast or contradistinction; opposed to *that*): *Do this, not that.* **4.** what is about to follow: *Watch this!* —*adj.* **5.** (used to indicate a person, place, thing, or degree as present, near, or characteristic): *This book is mine.* **6.**

(used to indicate the nearer in time, place, or thought of two persons, things, etc.; opposed to *that*). **7.** (used to imply mere contradistinction; opposed to *that*). **8.** (used in place of an indefinite article for emphasis): *I heard this funny noise.* —*adv.* **9.** (used with adjectives and adverbs of quantity or extent) to the extent indicated: *this far.* —**Idiom. 10. with this,** following this; hereupon: *With this, he wept.*

This′ Is′ My′ Fa′ther's World′, a Christian hymn with words by Maltbie Babcock and music by Franklin Sheppard.

this·tle (this′əl), *n.* any of various prickly composite plants usu. having showy purple flower heads, esp. of the genera *Cirsium, Carduus,* and *Onopordum.* **2.** any of various other prickly plants.

this·tle·down (this′əl doun′), *n.* the mature silky pappus of a thistle.

this·tly (this′lē, -ə lē), *adj.* **1.** filled with or having many thistles. **2.** suggesting a growth of thistles, esp. in being troublesome.

thith·er (thith′ər, thiŧẖ′-), *adv.* **1.** Also, **thith·er·ward** (-wərd), **thith′er·wards.** to or toward that place or point; there. —*adj.* **2.** on the farther or other side; farther; more remote.

Th.M., Master of Theology.

tho or **tho′** (ŧẖō), *conj.*, *adv.* an informal or poetic simplified spelling of THOUGH.

Thom·as (tom′əs), *n.* **1.** an apostle who demanded proof of Christ's Resurrection. John 20:24–29. **2. Clarence,** born 1948, associate justice of the U.S. Supreme Court since 1991. **3. Dylan (Marlais),** 1914–53, Welsh poet. **4. George Henry,** 1816–70, Union general in the U.S. Civil War. **5. Isaiah,** 1749–1831, U.S. printer of the first American Bible. **6. Lowell (Jackson),** 1892–1981, U.S. newscaster, traveler, and writer. **7. Martha Carey,** 1857–1935, U.S. educator and women's-rights advocate. **8. Norman (Mattoon),** 1884–1968, U.S. socialist leader. **9. Seth,** 1785–1859, U.S. clock designer. **10. William Henry Griffith,** U.S. clergyman and educator.

Thom′as à Beck′et, *n.* BECKET, Saint Thomas à.

Thom′as à Kem′pis, *n.* KEMPIS, Thomas à.

Thom′as Aqui′nas, *n.* AQUINAS, Saint Thomas.

Tho·mism (tō′miz əm), *n.* the theological and philosophical system of Thomas Aquinas. —**Tho′mist,** *n.*, *adj.* —**Tho·mis′tic,** *adj.*

Thomp·son (tomp′sən, tom′-), *n.* **1. Dorothy,** 1894–1961, U.S. journalist. **2. Sir John Sparrow David,** 1844–94, Canadian statesman: prime minister 1892–94. **3. Randall,** 1899–1984, U.S. composer and teacher. **4. Will,** 1847–1909, U.S. hymn writer.

Thomp′son submachine′ gun′, *n.* a portable, .45-caliber, automatic weapon designed to be fired from the shoulder or hip. Also called **Tommy gun.** [named after J. T. *Thompson* (1860–1940), American army officer who aided in its invention]

Thom·son (tom′sən), *n.* **1. Sir George Paget,** 1892–1975, English physicist (son of Sir Joseph John). **2. John Arthur,** 1861–1933, Scottish scientist and author. **3. Sir Joseph John,** 1856–1940, English physicist. **4. Virgil,** 1896–1989, U.S. composer and music critic. **5. Sir William,** KELVIN, 1st Baron.

Thom′son's gazelle′, *n.* an E African gazelle, *Gazella thomsoni.*

thong (thông, thong), *n.* **1.** a narrow strip, esp. of leather or hide, used to fasten or secure something. **2.** a strip of leather or hide used for whipping; whiplash. **3.** a shoe or slipper fastened to the foot by a strip of leather or the like that passes between the first two toes and is often attached to another strip, as across the instep. **4.** a brief garment for the lower body that exposes the buttocks, consisting of a strip of fabric passing between the thighs and attached to a band around the waist.

Thor (thôr), *n.* the Norse god of thunder and the sky, armed with a magical hammer.

tho·rac·ic (thô ras′ik, thō-), *adj.* of, pertaining to, or involving the thorax.

tho·rax (thôr′aks, thōr′-), *n.*, *pl.* **tho·rax·es, tho·ra·ces** (thôr′ə sēz′, thōr′-). **1.** the part of the trunk between the neck and the abdomen, containing the heart and lungs in a bony cage of vertebrae, ribs, and sternum; chest: in mammals separated from the lower trunk by the diaphragm. **2.** the portion of the body of an insect between the head and the abdomen.

Tho·reau (thə rō′, thôr′ō, thōr′ō), *n.* Henry David, 1817–62, U.S. naturalist and author. —**Tho·reau′vi·an,** *adj.*

tho·ri·um (thôr′ē əm, thōr′-), *n.* a grayish white, lustrous, radioactive metallic element: used as a source of nuclear energy, in sun-lamp and vacuum-tube filaments, and in alloys. Symbol: Th; *at. wt.:* 232.038; *at. no.:* 90; *sp. gr.:* 11.7. —**thor·ic** (thôr′ik, thōr′-), *adj.*

thorn (thôrn), *n.* **1.** a hard, sharp outgrowth on a plant, esp. a sharp-pointed aborted branch. **2.** a thorny tree or shrub, as the hawthorne. **3.** the wood of such a tree. **4.** a runic character (Þ), borrowed into the Latin alphabet and used to represent the initial *th* sounds of *thin* and *they* in Old English and of *thin* in modern Icelandic. **5.** a source of continual irritation, trouble, or discomfort (esp. in the phrase *thorn in one's side* or *flesh*). —*v.t.* **6.** to prick with a thorn; vex. —**thorn′less,** *adj.*

thorn′ ap′ple (thôrn), *n.* **1.** the jimsonweed or a related plant bearing prickly fruit. **2.** the bright red or yellow fruit of certain hawthorns.

thorn·y (thôr′nē), *adj.*, **thorn·i·er, thorn·i·est. 1.** abounding in or characterized by thorns; spiny; prickly. **2.** thornlike. **3.** painful; vexatious: *a thorny predicament.* **4.** full of difficulties, complexities, or controversial points: *a thorny question.* —**thorn′i·ly,** *adv.*

thor·ough (thûr′ō, thur′ō), *adj.* **1.** executed without negligence or omissions: *a thorough search.* **2.** complete; perfect; utter: *thorough en-*

T

joyment. **3.** extremely attentive to accuracy and detail; painstaking: *a thorough worker.* **4.** having full command or mastery of an art, talent, etc. **5.** extending or passing through. **—thor′ough•ly,** *adv.* **—thor′ough•ness,** *n.*

thor•ough•bred (thûr′ō bred′, -ə bred′, thur′-), *adj.* **1.** of pure or unmixed breed or stock, as a horse or other animal; purebred. **2.** (*often cap.*) of or pertaining to the Thoroughbred breed of horses. **3.** (of a person) well-bred or well-educated; cultivated. **—n. 4.** (*usu. cap.*) one of a breed of horses, to which all racehorses belong, orig. developed in England by crossing Arabian stallions with European mares. **5.** a thoroughbred animal. **6.** a well-bred or well-educated person.

thor•ough•fare (thûr′ō fâr′, -ə fâr′, thur′-), *n.* **1.** a road, street, etc., that leads at each end into another street. **2.** a major road or highway. **3.** a passage or way through: *no thoroughfare.* **4.** a strait, river, etc., affording passage.

thor•ough•go•ing (thûr′ō gō′ing, -ə gō′-, thur′-), *adj.* **1.** doing things thoroughly. **2.** carried out to the full extent; thorough. **3.** complete; unqualified: *a thoroughgoing knave.* **—thor′ough•go′ing•ly,** *adv.*

Thorpe (thôrp), *n.* **James Francis** ("Jim"), 1888–1953, U.S. athlete.

those (thōz), *pron., adj.* pl. of THAT.

Thoth (thōth, tōt), *n. Egyptian Religion.* the god of wisdom, learning, and magic represented as a man with the head of an ibis or a baboon.

thou¹ (thou), *pron., sing., nom.* **thou;** *poss.* **thy** or **thine;** *obj.* **thee;** *pl., nom.* **you** or **ye;** *poss.* **your** or **yours;** *obj.* **you** or **ye;** *v.,* **thoued, thou•ing.** *—pron.* **1.** *Archaic* (*except in elevated or ecclesiastical prose or as used by the Friends*). the second person singular personal pronoun in the nominative case (used to denote the person addressed): *Thou shalt not kill.* **—v.t. 2.** to address as *thou.* **—v.i. 3.** to use *thou* in discourse.

thou² (thou), *n., pl.* **thous,** (*as after a numeral*) **thou.** *Slang.* one thousand dollars, pounds, etc.

though (thō), *conj.* **1.** notwithstanding that; in spite of the fact that; although: *Though we tried hard, we lost the game.* **2.** even if; granting that (often prec. by *even*). **—adv. 3.** for all that; however. **—Idiom. 4. as though,** as if: *It seemed as though the place was deserted.*

thought (thôt), *n.* **1.** the product of mental activity; that which one thinks: *a body of thought.* **2.** an act or product of thinking; idea or notion: *to collect one's thoughts.* **3.** the process of thinking; mental activity; reflection or cogitation. **4.** the capacity or faculty of thinking, reasoning, imagining, etc. **5.** meditation, contemplation, or recollection: *deep in thought.* **6.** intention, design, or purpose: *We had some thought of going.* **7.** anticipation or expectation: *I had no thought of seeing you here.* **8.** consideration, attention, care, or regard: *to take no thought of one's appearance.* **9.** a judgment, opinion, or belief: *According to his thought, all violence is evil.* **10.** the intellectual activity or the ideas, opinions, etc., characteristic of a place, group, or time: *Greek thought.*

thought•ful (thôt′fəl), *adj.* **1.** showing consideration for others; considerate. **2.** characterized by or manifesting careful thought: *a thoughtful essay.* **3.** occupied with or given to thought; contemplative; meditative; reflective: *in a thoughtful mood.* **4.** careful, heedful, or mindful. **—thought′ful•ly,** *adv.* **—thought′ful•ness,** *n.*

thought•less (thôt′lis), *adj.* **1.** lacking in consideration for others; inconsiderate; tactless: *a thoughtless remark.* **2.** not thinking enough; careless or heedless: *thoughtless of his health.* **3.** devoid of or lacking capacity for thought. **4.** characterized by or showing lack of thought. **—thought′less•ly,** *adv.* **—thought′less•ness,** *n.*

thought′-out′, *adj.* produced by or showing the results of much thought: *a carefully thought-out argument.*

thou•sand (thou′zənd), *n., pl.* **-sands,** (*as after a numeral*) **-sand,** *adj.* **—n. 1.** a cardinal number, 10 times 100. **2.** a symbol for this number, as 1000 or M. **3.** a set of this many persons or things. **4. thousands, a.** the numbers between 1000 and 999,999, as in referring to money. **b.** a great number or amount. **5.** Also called **thou′sand's place′. a.** (in a mixed number) the position of the fourth digit to the left of the decimal point. **b.** (in a whole number) the position of the fourth digit from the right. **—adj. 6.** amounting to 1000 in number.

thou′sand days′, *n.* (*sometimes caps.*) the presidential administration of John F. Kennedy, which lasted 1037 days (January 20, 1961, to November 22, 1963).

thou•sand•fold (adj. thou′zənd fōld′; adv. -fōld′), *adj.* **1.** having a thousand elements or parts. **2.** a thousand times as great or as much. **—adv. 3.** in a thousandfold manner or measure.

Thou′sand Is′land dress′ing, *n.* mayonnaise seasoned with chopped pickles, pimientos, hard-boiled eggs, etc.

Thou′sand Is′lands, *n.pl.* a group of about 1500 islands in S Ontario, Canada, and N New York State, in the St. Lawrence River at the outlet of Lake Ontario: summer resorts.

Thou′sand Oaks′, *n.* a town in S California. 110,981.

thou•sandth (thou′zəndth, -zəntth, -zənth), *adj.* **1.** last in order of a series of a thousand. **2.** being one of a thousand equal parts. **—n. 3.** a thousandth part, esp. of one (¹/₁₀₀₀). **4.** the thousandth member of a series. **5.** (in decimal notation) the position of the third digit to the right of the decimal point.

Thrace (thrās), *n.* **1.** an ancient region of varying extent in the E part of the Balkan Peninsula: later a Roman province; now in Bulgaria, Turkey, and Greece. **2.** a modern region corresponding to the S part of the Roman province: now divided between Greece **(Western Thrace)** and Turkey **(Eastern Thrace).**

Thra•cian (thrā′shən), *adj.* **1.** of or pertaining to Thrace, its inhabitants, or their language. **—n. 2.** a native or inhabitant of Thrace. **3.** an Indo-European language of ancient Thrace.

thrall (thrôl), *n.* **1.** a person who is in bondage; slave. **2.** a person who is morally or mentally enslaved by some power, influence, etc. **3.** slavery; thralldom. **—Idiom. 4. in thrall,** in the power of someone or something; in a state of subjugation or rapt absorption: *The speaker held us in thrall.*

thrash (thrash), *v.t.* **1.** to beat soundly in punishment; flog. **2.** to defeat thoroughly. **3.** to beat or move wildly or violently; flail. **4.** THRESH. **—v.i. 5.** to toss or plunge about wildly or violently. **6. thrash out** or **over,** to talk over thoroughly in order to reach a decision or understanding. **—n. 7.** an act or instance of thrashing; beating. **8.** THRESH. **9.** the upward and downward movement of the legs in swimming.

thrash•er (thrash′ər), *n.* **1.** a person or thing that thrashes. **2.** any of several long-tailed, thrushlike birds, esp. of the genus *Toxostoma,* related to the mockingbirds.

thrash•ing (thrash′ing), *n.* a flogging; whipping.

thread (thred), *n.* **1.** a fine cord of flax, cotton, or other fibrous material spun out to considerable length, esp. when composed of two or more filaments twisted together. **2.** twisted filaments or fibers of any kind used for sewing. **3.** (loosely) yarn or a piece of yarn used in weaving or knitting. **4.** a filament or fiber of glass or other ductile substance. **5.** YARN (def. 3). **6.** something having the fineness of a filament, as a thin continuous stream of liquid, a thin line of color, or a thin seam of ore. **7.** the helical ridge of a screw. **8.** something that runs through the whole course of a thing, connecting successive parts: *I lost the thread of the story.* **9.** the course of life, as fabled to be spun, measured, and cut by the Fates. **10.** *Computers.* a series of posts on a newsgroup dealing with the same subject. **11. threads,** *Slang.* clothes. **—v.t. 12.** to pass the end of a thread through the eye of (a needle). **13.** to fix (beads, pearls, etc.) upon a thread that is passed through; string. **14.** to pass (tape, film, etc.) through or into a narrow opening. **15.** to interweave or ornament with threads: *silk threaded with gold.* **16.** to pass continuously through the whole course of; pervade. **17.** to make (one's way), as past or around obstacles or through a passage: *He threaded his way through the crowd.* **18.** to place and arrange thread, yarn, etc., in position on (a sewing machine, loom, textile machine, etc.). **—v.i. 19.** to thread one's way. **20.** to move in a threadlike course; wind or twine. **21.** (of boiling syrup) to form a fine thread when poured from a spoon. **—thread′er,** *n.* **—thread′less,** *adj.* **—thread′like′,** *adj.*

thread•bare (thred′bâr′), *adj.* **1.** having the nap worn off so as to lay bare the threads of the weave, as a fabric or garment. **2.** wearing threadbare clothes; shabby or poor. **3.** hackneyed; trite; ineffectively stale: *threadbare arguments.* **4.** meager, scanty, or poor: *a threadbare account or report.* **—thread′bare′ness,** *n.*

threat (thret), *n.* **1.** a declaration of an intention to inflict punishment, injury, etc., as in retaliation for, or conditionally upon, some action or course. **2.** an indication or warning of probable trouble. **3.** a person or thing that threatens.

threat•en (thret′n), *v.t.* **1.** to utter a threat against. **2.** to be a menace or danger to: *to threaten one's peace of mind.* **3.** to offer (a punishment, injury, etc.) by way of a threat: *They threatened swift retaliation.* **4.** to give an ominous indication of: *The clouds threaten rain.* **—v.i. 5.** to utter or use threats. **6.** to indicate impending evil, difficulty, etc.

three (thrē), *n.* **1.** a cardinal number, 2 plus 1. **2.** a symbol for this number, as 3 or III. **3.** a set of this many persons or things. **—adj. 4.** amounting to three in number.

three′-bag′ger, *n.* TRIPLE (def. 6).

three′-base′ hit′, *n.* TRIPLE (def. 6).

three′-card′ mon′te, *n.* a swindling game in which a bettor must identify a stipulated card from among three cards after they have been moved around facedown: played illegally on the street using shills.

three′-col′or, *adj.* **1.** having or characterized by the use of three colors. **2.** of or pertaining to a photomechanical process for making reproductions, usu. by making three printing plates, each corresponding to a primary color.

three′-cor′nered, *adj.* **1.** having three points or corners, as a hat. **2.** pertaining to or involving three persons, items, etc.

3-D (thrē′dē′), *adj.* **1.** of, pertaining to, or representing something in three dimensions; three-dimensional: *3-D movies.* **—n. 2.** a three-dimensional form or appearance.

three′-deck′er, *n.* **1.** something having three layers, levels, decks, or tiers. **2.** TRIPLE-DECKER.

three′-dimen′sional, *adj.* **1.** having, or seeming to have, the dimension of depth as well as width and height. **2.** (esp. in a literary work) fully developed; lifelike: *three-dimensional characters.* **—three′-dimensional′ity,** *n.*

three′-fold (thrē′fōld′), *adj.* **1.** having three elements or parts; triple. **2.** three times as great or as much; treble; triple. **—adv. 3.** in threefold manner or measure; triply; trebly.

three′-hand′ed, *adj.* involving three hands or players, as a game at cards.

three′-leg′ged, *adj.* having three legs, as a stool.

three′-leg′ged race′, *n.* a race among paired contestants, with each contestant having one leg tied to the adjacent leg of his or her partner.

Three′ Mile′ Is′land, *n.* an island in the Susquehanna River, SE of Harrisburg, Pennsylvania: nuclear plant accident in 1979.

three′-mile′ lim′it, *n.* the outer limit of a three-mile belt of waters adjacent to a coast, regarded as under the jurisdiction of the state possessing the coast. Compare TWELVE-MILE LIMIT.

Three′ Musketeers′, The, (French, *Les Trois Mousquetaires*), a historical novel (1844) by Alexandre Dumas père.

three′-piece′, *adj.* 1. (of clothing) consisting of three matching or harmonious pieces. 2. having three parts.

three′-ply′, *adj.* consisting of three thicknesses, strands, etc.

three′-point′ land′ing, *n.* an aircraft landing in which the two wheels of the main landing gear and the tail or nose wheel touch the ground simultaneously.

three′-quar′ter, *adj.* 1. consisting of or involving three quarters of a whole or of the usual length: *a three-quarter sleeve.* 2. showing the face or an object as seen from in front and somewhat to the side: *a three-quarter view.*

three′-ring′ (or **three′-ringed′**) **cir′cus,** *n.* 1. a circus having three adjacent rings with simultaneous performances. 2. something spectacular, tumultuous, entertaining, or full of confused action.

three R′s, *n.pl.* 1. reading, writing, and arithmetic, regarded as the fundamentals of education. 2. the fundamentals or basic skills of any field.

three•some (thrē′səm), *n.* 1. three forming a group. 2. something in which three persons participate, as certain games. 3. a golf match in which two players, playing alternately with one ball, compete against a third player who also plays with one ball. —*adj.* 4. performed or played by three persons.

three′-speed′, *n.* 1. a system of gears having three forward gear ratios, esp. on a bicycle. 2. a bicycle having such a system of gears. —*adj.* 3. having three forward gear ratios.

three′-star′, *adj.* ranked as being in the second highest, third highest, or sometimes the highest category of excellence.

three′-way′ bulb′, *n.* a light bulb that can be switched to three successive degrees of illumination.

three′-wheel′er, *n.* a vehicle equipped with three wheels, as a tricycle, a motorcycle with a sidecar, or some early-model cars.

thren•o•dy (thren′ə dē), *n., pl.* **-dies.** a poem, speech, or song of lamentation, esp. for the dead; dirge; funeral song. —**thre•no•di•al** (thrinō′dē əl), **thre•nod′ic** (-nod′ik), *adj.* —**thren′o•dist,** *n.*

thre•o•nine (thrē′ə nēn′, -nin), *n.* an essential amino acid, CH₃CHOHCH(NH₂)COOH, obtained by the hydrolysis of proteins. *Symbol:* T *Abbr.:* Thr

thresh (thresh), *v.t.* 1. to separate the grain or seeds from (a cereal plant or the like), as by beating with a flail or by the action of a threshing machine. 2. to beat as if with a flail. —*v.i.* 3. to thresh wheat, grain, etc. 4. to deliver blows as if with a flail. —*n.* 5. the act of threshing. Sometimes, **thrash.**

thresh•er (thresh′ər), *n.* 1. a person or thing that threshes. 2. a large shark of the genus *Alopias,* esp. *A. vulpinus,* which herds small fish by flailing its tail.

thresh′ing machine′, *n.* a machine for removing grains and seeds from straw and chaff.

thresh•old (thresh′ōld, thresh′hōld), *n.* 1. the sill of a doorway. 2. the entrance to a house or building. 3. any point of entering or beginning: *the threshold of a new career.* 4. Also called **limen.** the point at which a stimulus is of sufficient intensity to begin to produce an effect: *the threshold of consciousness; a low threshold of pain.*

thrice (thrīs), *adv.* 1. three times, as in succession. 2. in threefold quantity or degree. 3. very; extremely.

thrift (thrift), *n.* 1. economical management; economy. 2. Also called **thrift′ institu′tion.** a savings and loan association, savings bank, or credit union. 3. any alpine and maritime plant belonging to the genus *Armeria,* of the leadwort family, having pink or white flowers, esp. *A. maritima,* noted for its vigorous growth. 4. vigorous growth, as of a plant. [< Old Norse]

thrift•less (thrift′lis), *adj.* improvident; wasteful.

thrift•shop (thrift′shop′), *n.* a retail store that sells secondhand goods at reduced prices.

thrift•y (thrif′tē), *adj.,* **thrift•i•er, thrift•i•est.** 1. practicing thrift or economical management; frugal: *a thrifty shopper.* 2. (of an enterprise) prosperous or successful. 3. thriving physically. —**thrift′i•ly,** *adv.*

thrill (thril), *v.t.* 1. to affect with a sudden wave of excitement, as to produce a tingling sensation through the body: *I was thrilled by the good news.* —*v.i.* 2. to experience a wave of emotion or excitement: *to thrill at the thought of home.* 3. to move tremulously; vibrate or throb. —*n.* 4. a sudden wave of keen emotion or excitement. 5. something that produces such a sensation. 6. a thrilling experience. 7. an abnormal tremor within the body, as in the throat or heart.

thrill•er (thril′ər), *n.* 1. an exciting, suspenseful play or story, esp. a mystery story. 2. a person or thing that thrills.

thrill•ing (thril′ing), *adj.* producing a thrill or thrills; exciting: *a thrilling experience.* —**thrill′ing•ly,** *adv.*

thrips (thrips), *n., pl.* **thrips.** any of several minute insects of the order Thysanoptera, that have long, narrow wings fringed with hairs and that infest and feed on weeds and crop plants.

thrive (thrīv), *v.i.,* **thrived** or **throve, thrived** or **thriv•en** (thriv′ən), **thriv•ing.** 1. to prosper; be successful. 2. to grow or develop vigorously; flourish. —**thriv′er,** *n.* —**thriv′ing•ly,** *adv.*

throat (thrōt), *n.* 1. the first part of the passage from the mouth to the stomach and lungs, including the pharynx, larynx, and upper parts of

the trachea and esophagus. 2. some analogous or similar narrowed part or passage. 3. the front of the neck below the chin and above the collarbones. 4. the narrow opening between a fireplace and its flue or smoke chamber. —*v.t.* 5. to speak or sing throatily. —**Idiom.** 6. **cut one's own throat,** to bring about one's own ruin. 7. **jump down someone's throat,** to disagree with overhastily. 8. **ram something down someone's throat,** to force someone to accept something. 9. **stick in one's throat,** to be difficult or impossible to express.

throat•ed (thrō′tid), *adj.* having a throat of a specified kind (usu. used in combination): *a yellow-throated warbler.*

throat•y (thrō′tē), *adj.,* **throat•i•er, throat•i•est.** (of sound) husky; hoarse; guttural. —**throat′i•ly,** *adv.* —**throat′i•ness,** *n.*

throb (throb), *v.,* **throbbed, throb•bing,** *n.* —*v.i.* 1. to beat with increased force or rapidity, as the heart under the influence of emotion or excitement; palpitate. 2. to feel or exhibit emotion. 3. to pulsate or vibrate, as a sound. —*n.* 4. a violent beat or pulsation, as of the heart. 5. any pulsing or vibrating sound. 6. the act of throbbing. —**throb′ber,** *n.*

throe (thrō), *n.* 1. a violent spasm or pang; paroxysm. 2. **throes, a.** any violent convulsion or struggle. **b.** the agony of death.

throm•bo•sis (throm bō′sis), *n.* coagulation of the blood within a blood vessel in any part of the circulatory system. —**throm•bot′ic** (-bot′ik), *adj.*

throm•bus (throm′bəs), *n., pl.* **-bi** (-bī). a fibrinous clot that forms in and obstructs a blood vessel, or that forms in one of the chambers of the heart.

throne (thrōn), *n., v.,* **throned, thron•ing.** —*n.* 1. the chair or seat occupied by a sovereign or other exalted personage on ceremonial occasions. 2. the occupant of a throne; sovereign. 3. the office or dignity of a sovereign. 4. sovereign power or authority. 5. **thrones,** an order of angels. Compare ANGEL (def. 1). —*v.t., v.i* 6. to sit on or as if on a throne. —**throne′less,** *adj.* —**throne′like,** *adj.*

throng (thrông, throng), *n.* 1. a multitude of people crowded together. 2. a great number of things crowded or considered together. —*v.i.* 3. to assemble in large numbers; crowd. —*v.t.* 4. to crowd or press upon; jostle. 5. to fill or occupy with or as if with a crowd.

throt•tle (throt′l), *n., v.,* **-tled, -tling.** —*n.* 1. **a.** the valve in an internal-combustion engine that regulates the amount of fuel entering the cylinders. **b.** a lever that controls this valve. 2. the throat, gullet, or windpipe, as of a horse. —*v.t.* 3. to stop the breath of by compressing the throat; strangle. 4. to choke or suffocate in any way. 5. to silence or check as if by choking. 6. **a.** to obstruct or check the flow of (a fluid), as to control the speed of an engine. **b.** to reduce the pressure of (a fluid) by passing it from a smaller area to a larger one. —**Idiom.** 7. **at full throttle,** at maximum speed or effort. —**throt′tler,** *n.*

through (thrōō), *prep.* 1. in at one end, side, or surface and out at the other: *to pass through a tunnel.* 2. past; beyond: *went through a red light.* 3. from one to the other of: *swinging through the trees.* 4. across the extent of: *traveled through several countries.* 5. during the whole period of; throughout: *worked through the night.* 6. done with: *What time are you through work?* 7. to and including: *from 1900 through 1950.* 8. by the means of: *I found out through him.* 9. by reason of: *He ran away through fear.* 10. from the first to final stage of: *to get through a performance on time.* —*adv.* 11. in at one end, side, or surface and out at the other: *to push a needle through.* 12. all the way: *This train goes through to Boston.* 13. throughout: *soaking wet through.* 14. from beginning to end: *to read a letter through.* —*adj.* 15. at a point or in a state of completion of an action, process, etc.; finished: *Please be quiet until I'm through.* 16. at the end of all relations or dealings: *She's through with her boyfriend.* 17. extending from one end to the other. 18. proceeding to a destination, goal, etc., without a change, break, or deviation: *a through flight; the through line of a story.* 19. (of a road, route, etc.) permitting continuous or uninterrupted passage. 20. of no further use or value; washed-up: *Critics say he's through as a writer.* —**Idiom.** 21. **through and through, a.** throughout every part; thoroughly: *cold through and through.* **b.** in all respects: *an aristocrat through and through.*

through•out (thrōō out′), *prep.* 1. in or to every part of: *throughout the house.* 2. from beginning to end of: *nodding throughout the sermon.* —*adv.* 3. in every part or place: *rotten throughout.* 4. at every moment or point: *Follow the text throughout.*

through′ street′, *n.* a street on which traffic can move without interruption. Compare STOP STREET.

Through′ the Look′ing-Glass, a story for children (1871) by Lewis Carroll; the sequel to *Alice's Adventures in Wonderland.*

through•way (thrōō′wā′), *n.* THRUWAY.

throw (thrō), *v.,* **threw, thrown, throw•ing,** *n.* —*v.t.* 1. to propel from the hand by a sudden forward motion: *to throw a ball.* 2. to hurl or project (a missile), as a gun does. 3. to project or cast (light, a shadow, etc.). 4. to project (the voice). 5. to direct (one's voice) so as to appear to come from a different source, as in ventriloquism. 6. to direct or send forth (words, a glance, etc.). 7. to put into some place, condition, etc., as if by hurling: *to throw someone into prison.* 8. **a.** to move (a lever or the like) in order to turn on, disconnect, etc., an apparatus or mechanism: *to throw the switch.* **b.** to connect, engage, disconnect, or disengage by such a procedure: *to throw the current.* 9. to shape on a potter's wheel. 10. to deliver (a blow or punch). 11. (in wrestling) to hurl (an opponent) to the ground. 12. to play (a card). 13. to lose (a game, race, or other contest) intentionally, as for a bribe. 14. **a.** to cast

T

(dice). **b.** to make (a cast) at dice. **15.** (of an animal, as a horse) to cause (someone) to fall off; unseat. **16.** to give or host: *to throw a lavish party.* **17.** (of domestic animals) to bring forth (young). **18.** to amaze or confuse: *The dark glasses really threw me.* —*v.i.* **19.** to cast, fling, or hurl a missile or the like. **20. throw away, a.** to dispose of; discard. **b.** to employ wastefully; squander. **c.** to fail to use; miss (a chance, opportunity, etc.). **d.** (of an actor) to speak (lines, a joke, etc.) casually or indifferently. **21. throw in, a.** to add as a bonus or gratuity. **b.** to interject, as a comment. **c.** to abandon (a hand) in a card game. **22. throw off, a.** to free oneself of; cast aside. **b.** to escape from or delay, as a pursuer. **c.** to give off; discharge. **d.** to perform or produce with ease: *to throw off a few jokes.* **e.** to confuse; fluster. **f.** *Australian Slang.* to criticize or ridicule (usu. fol. by *at*). **23. throw out, a.** to cast away; discard; reject. **b.** to cause (a runner in baseball) to be out by throwing the ball to a teammate who prevents the runner from reaching base safely. **c.** to eject from a place, esp. forcibly. **d.** to expel, as from membership in a club. **24. throw over,** to forsake; abandon. **25. throw together, a.** to make hurriedly and haphazardly. **b.** to cause to associate: *bitter enemies thrown together by circumstance.* **26. throw up, a.** to give up; relinquish. **b.** to build hastily. **c.** to vomit. **d.** to point out, as an error. **e.** (of a hawk) to fly suddenly upward. —*n.* **27.** an act or instance of throwing or casting; cast; fling. **28.** the distance to which something can be thrown: *a stone's throw.* **29. a.** the distance between the center of a crankshaft and the center of the crankpins, equal to one half of the piston stroke. **b.** the distance between the center of a crankshaft and the center of an eccentric. **c.** the movement of a reciprocating part in one direction. **30.** the length of a beam of light: *a spotlight with a throw of 500 feet.* **31.** a scarf, boa, shawl, or the like. **32.** a lightweight blanket; afghan. **33.** a cast of dice or the number thrown. **34.** the act, method, or an instance of throwing an opponent in wrestling. —***Idiom.*** **35. a throw,** each: *ordered four suits at $300 a throw.* **36. throw in the sponge** or **towel,** to concede defeat; give up. **37. throw oneself at,** to strive to attract the interest or affections of. **38. throw oneself into,** to engage in with energy and enthusiasm. —**throw′er,** *n.*

throw•a•way (thrō′ə wā′), *adj.* **1.** made or intended to be discarded after use or quick examination: *a throwaway container.* **2.** delivered or expressed casually: *a throwaway line that always gets a laugh.* —*n.* **3.** something that is intended to be discarded after use, reading, etc.

throw•back (thrō′bak′), *n.* **1.** an act of throwing back. **2.** a setback or check. **3.** the reversion to an ancestral or earlier type or character; atavism. **4.** an example of this.

throw′ pil′low, *n.* a small pillow placed on a chair, couch, etc., primarily for decoration.

throw′ rug′, *n.* SCATTER RUG.

thru (thro͞o), *prep., adv., adj.* an informal simplified spelling of THROUGH.

thrum[1] (thrum), *v.,* **thrummed, thrum•ming,** *n.* —*v.i.* **1.** to pluck the strings of a guitar or other stringed instrument, esp. idly; strum. **2.** to sound when thrummed on, as a guitar. **3.** to drum or tap idly with the fingers. —*v.t.* **4.** to play (a stringed instrument or a melody) by plucking the strings, esp. idly; strum. **5.** to drum or tap idly on. —*n.* **6.** an act or sound of thrumming; a dull, monotonous sound.

thrum[2] (thrum), *n., v.,* **thrummed, thrum•ming.** —*n.* **1.** one of the ends of the warp threads in a loom, left unwoven and remaining attached to the loom when the web is cut off. **2. thrums,** the row or fringe of such threads. **3. a.** any short piece of waste thread or yarn. **b.** a tuft or fringe of such pieces. —*v.t.* **4.** to furnish or cover with thrums, ends of thread, or tufts.

thrush[1] (thrush), *n.* **1.** any of various typically dull-plumaged songbirds of the subfamily Turdinae (family Muscicapidae), of nearly worldwide distribution: many species are outstanding singers. **2.** any of various superficially similar birds, as the waterthrushes. —**thrush′like′,** *adj.*

thrush[2] (thrush), *n.* **1.** a disease of the mouth marked by a whitish growth and ulcerations, caused by a fungus of the genus *Candida,* esp. *C albicans.* **2.** (in horses) a diseased condition of the frog of the foot.

thrust (thrust), *v.,* **thrust, thrust•ing,** *n.* —*v.t.* **1.** to push forcibly; shove. **2.** to put boldly forth or force acceptance of: *to thrust oneself into a conversation.* —*v.i.* **3.** to make a lunge or stab at something. **4.** to push or force one's way. **5.** to push against something. —*n.* **6.** an act or instance of thrusting. **7.** a lunge or stab, as with a sword. **8.** a linear reactive force exerted by a propeller, propulsive gases, etc., to propel a missile, ship, aircraft, or the like. **9.** the main point; essence. **10.** a pushing force or pressure exerted by a thing or a part against a contiguous one. **11.** the downward and outward force exerted by an arch on each side. **12.** a military assault; offensive.

thrust•er (thrus′tər), *n.* **1.** a small rocket attached to a spacecraft and used for producting thrust to control attitude or translational motion. **2.** a propeller located in a ship's bow or stern to provide added maneuverability, as when docking. **3.** a person or thing that thrusts.

thru•way or **through•way** (thro͞o′wā′), *n.* an expressway providing a means of direct transportation between distant areas for high-speed automobile traffic.

Thu•cyd•i•des (tho͞o sid′i dēz′), *n.* c460–c400 B.C., Greek historian.

thud (thud), *n., v.,* **thud•ded, thud•ding.** —*n.* **1.** a dull sound, as of a heavy blow or fall. **2.** a blow causing such a sound. —*v.i.* **3.** to strike or fall with a dull sound of heavy impact. —**thud′ding•ly,** *adv.*

thug (thug), *n.* **1.** a vicious criminal; ruffian. **2.** (*sometimes cap.*) a member of a fraternity of professional robbers and murderers in India, suppressed by the British in the 19th century. —**thug′gish,** *adj.*

Thu•le (tho͞o′lē *for 1;* to͞o′- *for 2, 3*), *n.* **1.** Also called **ultima Thule.** an island or region believed by the ancient Greeks and Romans to be the northernmost part of the inhabited world: variously identified as Iceland, Norway, or one of the Shetland Islands. **2.** a settlement in NW Greenland: site of U.S. air base. 749. —*adj.* **3.** of or designating an Eskimo culture flourishing from A.D. 500 to 1400, and extending throughout the Arctic from Greenland to Alaska.

thu•li•um (tho͞o′lē əm), *n.* a rare-earth metallic element found in gadolinite and other uncommon minerals. *Symbol:* Tm; *at. wt.*: 168.934; *at. no.:* 69; *sp. gr.:* 9.32.

thumb (thum), *n.* **1.** the short, thick, inner digit of the human hand, next to the forefinger. **2.** the corresponding digit in other animals; pollex. **3.** the part of a glove or mitten for containing this digit. —*v.t.* **4.** to soil or wear with the thumbs in handling, as the pages of a book. **5.** to glance through (pages) (usu. fol. by *through*): *to thumb through a brochure.* **6.** (of a hitchhiker) to solicit or get (a ride) by pointing the thumb in the desired direction of travel. —***Idiom.*** **7. be all thumbs,** to be clumsy. **8. thumb one's nose, a.** to raise the hand with fingers extended and touch the thumb to the nose as a gesture of scorn, defiance, etc. **b.** to manifest defiance or contempt (usu. fol. by *at*): *to thumb one's nose at convention.*

thumb′ in′dex, *n.* a series of labeled notches cut along the fore edge of a book, to indicate the divisions or sections. —**thumb′-in′dex,** *v.t.*

thumb•nail (thum′nāl′), *n.* **1.** the nail of the thumb. **2.** anything quite small or brief, as a biographical sketch. —*adj.* **3.** brief and concise: *a thumbnail description of Corsica.*

thumb•print (thum′print′), *n.* a mark or impression of the ventral surface of the last joint of the thumb.

thumb•screw (thum′skro͞o′), *n.* **1.** a screw having a flat head that may be turned easily with the thumb and forefinger. **2.** Often, **thumbscrews.** an old instrument of torture by which one or both thumbs were compressed.

thumbs′-down′, *n.* an act or gesture of disapproval or rejection.

thumbs′-up′, *n.* an act, instance, or gesture of approval or support.

thumb•tack (thum′tak′), *n.* **1.** a tack with a large, flat head, designed to be thrust into a board or other fairly soft object or surface by the pressure of the thumb. —*v.t.* **2.** to attach by means of a thumbtack.

thump (thump), *n.* **1.** a blow or knock with a heavy object, producing a dull sound. **2.** the sound made by or as if by such a blow. —*v.t.* **3.** to strike or beat with a heavy object, so as to produce a dull sound; pound. **4.** (of an object) to strike against (something) heavily and noisily. **5.** to thrash severely. —*v.i.* **6.** to strike or fall heavily, with a dull sound. **7.** to palpitate or beat violently, as the heart. —**thump′er,** *n.*

thump•ing (thum′ping), *adj.* **1.** exceptional or impressive; resounding: *a thumping victory.* **2.** of, like, or pertaining to a thump.

thun•der (thun′dər), *n.* **1.** a loud, explosive, resounding noise produced by the explosive expansion of air heated by a lightning discharge. **2.** any loud, resounding noise: *the thunder of applause.* —*v.i.* **3.** to give forth thunder (often used impersonally with *it* as the subject): *It thundered all night.* **4.** to make a loud, resounding noise like thunder: *artillery thundering in the hills.* **5.** to speak in a very loud or vehement, esp. denunciatory, tone; shout. —*v.t.* **6.** to strike, drive, etc., with loud noise or violent action. **7.** to express loudly or vehemently. —**thun′der•er,** *n.* —**thun′der•less,** *adj.*

thun•der•a•tion (thun′də rā′shən), *interj.* (used as an exclamation of impatience or annoyance.)

thun•der•bolt (thun′dər bōlt′), *n.* **1.** a flash of lightning with the accompanying thunder. **2.** an imaginary destructive missile cast to earth in a flash of lightning: *the thunderbolts of Jove.* **3.** a person or thing that acts with destructive force, speed, or suddenness.

thun•der•clap (thun′dər klap′), *n.* **1.** a crash of thunder. **2.** something resembling a thunderclap, as in loudness or suddenness.

thun•der•ing (thun′dər ing), *adj.* very great; extraordinary: *a thundering lie.* —**thun′der•ing•ly,** *adv.*

thun•der•ous (thun′dər əs, -drəs), *adj.* producing thunder or a loud noise like thunder. —**thun′der•ous•ly,** *adv.*

thun•der•show•er (thun′dər shou′ər), *n.* a shower accompanied by thunder and lightning.

thun•der•storm (thun′dər stôrm′), *n.* a transient storm of lightning and thunder, usu. with rain and gusty winds.

thun•der•struck (thun′dər struk′) also **thun•der•strick•en** (-strik′-ən), *adj.* astonished; dumbfounded.

Thur•ber (thûr′bər), *n.* **James (Grover),** 1894–1961, U.S. writer, caricaturist, and illustrator.

thu•ri•ble (tho͝or′ə bəl), *n.* CENSER.

thu•ri•fer (tho͝or′ə fər), *n.* a person who carries the thurible in religious ceremonies.

Thur•mond (thûr′mənd), *n.* **Strom,** born 1902, U.S. politician.

Thurs•day (thûrz′dā, -dē), *n.* the fifth day of the week, following Wednesday.

thus (t͟hus), *adv.* **1.** in the way just indicated; in this way: *Managed thus, the business will succeed.* **2.** in the following manner; so: *Thus it came to pass that a child was born.* **3.** accordingly; consequently. **4.** to this extent or degree: *thus far.* **5.** for instance.

thus•ly (t͟hus′lē), *adv.* THUS.

thwack (thwak), *v.t.* **1.** to strike or beat vigorously with something flat; whack. —*n.* **2.** a sharp blow with something flat. —**thwack′er,** *n.*

thwart¹ (thwôrt), *v.t.* **1.** to oppose successfully; prevent from accomplishing a purpose. **2.** to frustrate or baffle (a plan, purpose, etc.). —*adj.* **3.** set crosswise or across; transverse. —*prep., adv.* **4.** ATHWART.

thwart² (thwôrt), *n.* **1.** a seat across a boat, esp. one used by a rower. **2.** a transverse member spreading the gunwales of a canoe or the like.

thy (t̶hī), *pron.* the possessive case of THOU (used as an attributive adjective before a noun beginning with a consonant sound): *thy table.* Compare THINE.

Thy•a•ti•ra (thī′ə tī′rə), *n.* ancient name of AKHISAR: site of one of the seven churches of Asia (Rev. 1:11).

thyme (tīm; *spelling pron.* thīm), *n.* any plant of the genus *Thymus,* of the mint family, esp. *T. vulgaris,* an herb having narrow, aromatic leaves used for seasoning.

thy•mine (thī′mēn, -min), *n.* a pyrimidine base, $C_5H_6N_2O_2$, that is one of the principal components of DNA, in which it is paired with adenine. *Symbol:* T

thy•mus (thī′məs), *n., pl.* **-mus•es, -mi** (-mī). a ductless, butterfly-shaped gland lying at the base of the neck, formed mostly of lymphatic tissue and aiding in the production of T cells of the immune system: after puberty, the lymphatic tissue gradually degenerates. Also called **thy′mus gland′.**

thy•roid (thī′roid), *adj.* **1.** of or pertaining to the thyroid gland. **2.** of or pertaining to the largest cartilage of the larynx, forming the projection known in humans as the Adam's apple. —*n.* **3.** THYROID GLAND. **4.** the thyroid cartilage.. **5.** an artery, vein, etc., in the thyroid region. —**thy•roi′dal,** *adj.* —**thy′roid•less,** *adj.*

thy′roid gland′, *n.* a two-lobed endocrine gland located at the base of the neck and secreting two hormones that regulate the rates of metabolism, growth, and development.

thy′roid-stim′ulating hor′mone, *n.* THYROTROPIN. *Abbr.:* TSH

thy•ro•tro•pin (thī′rə trō′pin, thī ro′trə-) also **thy•ro•tro•phin** (-fin), *n.* an anterior pituitary hormone that regulates the activity of the thyroid gland. Also called **thyroid-stimulating hormone.**

thyrotro′pin-releas′ing hor′mone, *n.* See TRH.

thy•rox•ine (thī rok′sēn, -sin) also **thy•rox•in** (-sin), *n.* a hormone of the thyroid gland that regulates the metabolic rate of the body: preparations of it used for treating hypothyroidism.

ti (tē), *n., pl.* **tis.** the musical syllable used for the seventh tone of the ascending diatonic scale.

Ti, *Chem. Symbol.* titanium.

Tian′an•men Square′ (tyän′än men′) also **Tienanmen Square,** *n.* a large plaza in Beijing, China, noted esp. as the site of major student demonstrations in 1989, suppressed by the government.

ti•ar•a (tē ar′ə, -är′ə, -âr′ə), *n., pl.* **-ar•as. 1.** a jeweled, ornamental coronet worn by women. **2.** the pope's crown, consisting of three coronets on top of which are an orb and a cross. [< Latin < Greek *tiā́ra* a headdress worn by Asians] —**ti•ar′aed,** *adj.*

Ti•ber (tī′bər), *n.* a river in central Italy, flowing through Rome into the Mediterranean. 244 mi. (395 km) long. Italian, **Tevere.**

Ti•be•ri•as (tī bēr′ē əs), *n.* **Lake.** GALILEE, SEA OF.

Ti•be•ri•us (tī bēr′ē əs), *n.* (*Tiberius Claudius Nero Caesar*) 42 B.C.–A.D. 37, Roman emperor 14–37.

Ti•bet (ti bet′), *n.* an autonomous region in SW China, on a plateau N of the Himalayas: average elevation ab. 16,000 ft. (4877 m). 2,030,000; 471,660 sq. mi. (1,221,600 sq. km). *Cap.:* Lhasa. Chinese, **Xizang.**

Ti•bet•an (ti bet′n), *n.* **1.** a native or inhabitant of Tibet. **2.** a Tibeto-Burman language comprising a broad range of dialects spoken in Tibet and adjacent parts of S and E Asia. **3.** a member of any Tibetan-speaking ethnic group. —*adj.* **4.** of or pertaining to Tibet, its inhabitants, or Tibetan.

tib•i•a (tib′ē ə), *n., pl.* **tib•i•ae** (tib′ē ē′), **tib•i•as. 1.** the inner of the two bones of the leg, extending from the knee to the ankle and articulating with the femur and the talus; shinbone. **2.** a corresponding bone in a horse or other hoofed quadruped, extending from the stifle to the hock. **3.** the fourth segment of an insect leg, between the femur and tarsus. —**tib′i•al,** *adj.*

tic (tik), *n.* **1.** a sudden, spasmodic, painless, involuntary muscular contraction, as of the face. **2.** a persistent behavioral trait; personal quirk.

tick¹ (tik), *n.* **1.** a slight, sharp, recurring click, tap, or beat, as of a clock. **2.** *Brit. Informal.* a moment or instant. **3.** a small dot, mark, check, or electronic signal, used to mark off an item on a list, serve as a reminder, or call attention to something. **4.** a small contrasting spot of color on the coat of a mammal or the feathers of a bird. —*v.i.* **5.** to emit a tick, like that of a clock. **6.** to pass as with ticks of a clock: *The hours ticked by.* —*v.t.* **7.** to sound or announce by a tick or ticks: *The clock ticked the minutes.* **8.** to mark with a check (usu. fol. by *off*): *to tick off the items on the memo.* **9. tick off,** *Slang.* to make angry. —***Idiom.*** **10. what makes one tick,** one's underlying motives, needs, etc.

tick² (tik), *n.* **1.** any of numerous bloodsucking arachnids of the order Acarina, related to but larger than mites, having a barbed proboscis for attachment to the skin: some are disease vectors. **2.** SHEEPTICK.

tick³ (tik), *n.* **1.** the cloth case of a mattress, pillow, etc., containing hair, feathers, or the like. **2.** TICKING.

ticked (tikt), *adj.* **1.** *Slang.* angry; miffed. **2.** (of fur or feathers) tipped or banded with a contrasting color.

tick•er (tik′ər), *n.* **1.** formerly, a telegraphic receiving instrument that automatically prints stock prices, market reports, etc., on a paper tape. **2.** a person or thing that ticks. **3.** *Slang.* **a.** a watch. **b.** the heart.

tick′er tape′, *n.* the ribbon of paper on which a ticker prints quotations or news.

tick′er-tape′ parade′, *n.* a parade in which a celebrity is showered with confetti (formerly with ticker tape) thrown into the streets from buildings along the parade route.

tick•et (tik′it), *n.* **1.** a slip, usu. of paper or cardboard, serving as evidence that the holder has paid a fare or admission or is entitled to some service: *a train ticket.* **2.** a summons issued for a traffic or parking violation. **3.** a label or tag affixed to something to indicate its price, content, etc. **4.** a slate of candidates nominated by a particular party or faction and running together in an election. **5.** the license of a ship's officer or of an aviation pilot. **6.** a preliminary recording of transactions prior to their entry in more permanent books of account. **7. the ticket,** *Informal.* the proper or advisable thing: *Put it down gently—that's the ticket!* —*v.t.* **8.** to attach a ticket to; label. **9.** to furnish with a ticket. **10.** to serve with a summons for a traffic or parking violation. **11.** to attach such a summons to: *to ticket illegally parked cars.*

tick′et a′gency, *n.* an agency where tickets, esp. theater tickets, are sold. —**tick′et a′gent,** *n.*

tick′ fe′ver, *n.* any infectious disease transmitted by ticks, as Rocky Mountain spotted fever. Compare LYME DISEASE.

tick•ing (tik′ing), *n.* any of various strong, durable fabrics in plain, twill, or satin weave, constructed or printed in striped or floral patterns and used esp. to cover mattresses and pillows.

tick•le (tik′əl), *v.,* **-led, -ling,** *n.* —*v.t.* **1.** to touch or stroke lightly with the fingers, a feather, etc., so as to excite a tingling or itching sensation in; titillate. **2.** to poke some sensitive part of the body so as to excite spasmodic laughter. **3.** to excite agreeably; gratify: *to tickle someone's vanity.* **4.** to amuse or delight: *The clown's antics tickled the kids.* —*v.i.* **5.** to be affected with a tingling or itching sensation. **6.** to produce such a sensation. —*n.* **7.** an act or instance of tickling. **8.** a tickling sensation. —***Idiom.*** **9. tickled pink,** greatly pleased.

tick•lish (tik′lish), *adj.* **1.** sensitive to tickling. **2.** requiring delicate or tactful handling: *a ticklish situation.* **3.** hypersensitive; touchy. **4.** easily upset, as a boat. —**tick′lish•ly,** *adv.* —**tick′lish•ness,** *n.*

tick-tack-toe or **tic-tac-toe** (tik′tak tō′), *n.* a simple game, played on a grid with nine compartments, in which one player marking X's and one marking O's take turns filling the grid until one has placed three markers in a horizontal, vertical, or diagonal row.

tick•tock (tik′tok′), *n.* **1.** an alternating ticking sound, as that made by a clock. —*v.i.* **2.** to emit or produce a ticking sound, as that of a clock.

Ti•con•der•o•ga (tī′kon də rō′gə), *n.* a village in NE New York, on Lake Champlain: site of fort captured by the English 1759 and by Americans under Ethan Allen 1775. 2938.

tic-tac-toe (tik′tak tō′), *n.* TICK-TACK-TOE.

tid•al (tīd′l), *adj.* **1.** pertaining to, characterized by, or subject to tides. **2.** dependent on the state of the tide as to time of departure: *a tidal steamer.* —**tid′al•ly,** *adv.*

tid′al ba′sin, *n.* an artificial body of water open to a river, stream, etc., subject to tidal action.

tid′al flat′, *n.* flat or nearly flat tideland, often muddy or marshy.

tid′al wave′, *n.* **1.** (not in technical use) a large, destructive ocean wave, produced by a seaquake, hurricane, or strong wind. Compare TSUNAMI. **2.** either of the two great wavelike swellings of the ocean surface that move around the earth on opposite sides and give rise to tide, caused by the attraction of the moon and sun. **3.** any powerful or widespread movement, opinion, etc.

tid•bit (tid′bit′), *n.* **1.** a delicate bit or morsel of food. **2.** a choice or pleasing bit of anything, as gossip. Also, *esp. Brit.,* **titbit.**

tid•dly•winks (tid′lē wingks′) also **tid•dle•dy•winks** (tid′l dē-), *n.* (*used with a sing. v.*) a game in which small plastic disks are snapped with larger disks against a flat surface into a cup.

tide (tīd), *n., v.,* **tid•ed, tid•ing.** —*n.* **1.** the periodic rise and fall of the waters of the ocean and its inlets, produced by the attraction of the moon and sun, and occurring about every 12 hours. **2.** the inflow, outflow, or current of water at any given place resulting from the waves of tides. **3.** FLOOD TIDE. **4.** a stream or current. **5.** anything that alternately rises and falls, increases and decreases, etc. **6.** tendency or drift, as of events. **7.** a season or period (usu. used in combination): *Eastertide; eventide.* —*v.i.* **8.** to flow as the tide. **9.** to float or drift with the tide. —*v.t.* **10.** to carry, as the tide does. **11. tide over,** to assist in getting over a period of difficulty or distress. —***Idiom.*** **12. turn the tide,** to reverse the course of events, esp. from one extreme to another: *The Battle of Saratoga turned the tide of the American Revolution.* —***Proverb.*** **13. A rising tide lifts all boats,** improvement in one part of society will benefit other parts. —**tide′less,** *adj.* —**tide′less•ness,** *n.*

tide•land (tīd′land′), *n.* **1.** land alternately exposed and covered by the ordinary ebb and flow of the tide. **2.** Often, **tidelands.** submerged offshore land within the territorial waters of a state or nation.

tide•mark (tīd′märk′), *n.* **1.** the point reached or risen above: *the tidemark of our prosperity.* **2.** a mark left by the highest or lowest point of a tide. **3.** a mark indicating such a point.

tide′ ta′ble, *n.* a table listing the predicted times and heights of the tides for specific dates and places.

tide•wa•ter (tīd′wô′tər, -wot′ər), *n.* **1.** water affected by the ebb and flow of the tide. **2.** the water covering tideland at flood tide. **3.** SEACOAST.

ti•dings (tī′dingz), *n.* (*sometimes used with a sing. v.*) news, information, or notification: *sad tidings.*

ti•dy (tī′dē), *adj.,* **-di•er, -di•est,** *v.,* **-died, -dy•ing,** *n., pl.* **-dies.** —*adj.* **1.** neat, orderly, or trim, as in appearance or dress. **2.** clearly organized and systematic. **3.** tolerably good; acceptable: *They worked out a tidy arrangement.* **4.** fairly large; considerable: *a tidy sum.* —*v.t., v.i.* **5.** to make tidy (often fol. by *up*). —*n.* **6.** a place for keeping miscellaneous articles, as a box with small drawers and compartments. **7.** ANTIMACASSAR. —**ti′di•ly,** *adv.* —**ti′di•ness,** *n.*

tie (tī), *v.,* **tied, ty•ing,** *n.* —*v.t.* **1.** to bind or fasten with a cord, string, or the like: *to tie a bundle.* **2.** to fasten by tightening and knotting the string or strings of: *to tie one's shoes.* **3.** to draw or fasten together into a knot or bow: *to tie one's shoelaces.* **4.** to form by looping and interlacing, as a knot or bow. **5.** to bind or join closely or firmly: *Great affection tied them.* **6.** to confine or restrict: *The weather tied us to the house.* **7.** to oblige to do something. **8.** to make the same score as; equal in a contest. **9.** to connect (musical notes) by a tie. **10.** to design and make (an artificial fly) for fishing. —*v.i.* **11.** to make a tie, bond, or connection. **12.** to make the same score; be equal in a contest: *to tie for first place.* **13. tie down,** to curtail the activities of; confine: *The desk job ties him down.* **14. tie in, a.** to connect coherently; be consistent: *His story ties in with the facts.* **b.** to make or form a tie-in. **15. tie off,** to tie a cord or suture around (a blood vessel or the like) so as to stop the flow within. **16. tie up, a.** to fasten securely by tying. **b.** to wrap and secure, as with string; bind. **c.** to hinder or bring to a stop; impede. **d.** to render (money or property) unavailable for further disposition, investment, etc. **e.** to moor (a ship). **f.** to engage or occupy completely: *The boss is tied up till noon.* —*n.* **17.** a cord, string, or the like, used for tying, fastening, or wrapping something. **18.** that with which anything is tied. **19.** a necktie. **20.** a low shoe fastened with a lace. **21.** an ornamental knot; bow. **22.** a bond, as of affection, kinship, or mutual interest: *family ties.* **23.** a state of equality in points scored, votes obtained, etc., among competitors. **24.** any of various structural members, as beams or rods, for keeping two objects, as rafters or the haunches of an arch, from spreading or separating. **25.** a curved line connecting two musical notes on the same line or space to indicate that the sound is to be sustained for their joint value, not repeated. **26.** one of the wooden beams laid across the bed of a railroad to support the rails and keep them in place; crosstie. **27.** BAR[1] (def. 19). —***Idiom.*** **28. tie the knot,** *Informal.* to marry.

tie•back (tī′bak′), *n.* **1.** a strip of material, heavy braid, or the like, used for holding a curtain back to one side. **2.** Often, **tiebacks.** a curtain having such a device.

tie′ beam′, *n.* a horizontal timber or the like for connecting two structural members to keep them from spreading apart.

tie•break•er (tī′brā′kər), *n.* a short period of additional play for deciding a tie score, as in tennis and soccer.

tie′ clasp′, *n.* an ornamental metal clasp for securing the two ends of a necktie to a shirt front. Also called **tie′ clip′.**

tie′-dye′ing, *n.* a process of hand-dyeing fabric, in which sections of the fabric are tightly bound to resist the dye solution, thereby producing a variegated pattern. Also, **tie-and-dye, tie-dye.** —**tie-dyed,** *adj.*

tie′-in′, *adj.* **1.** designating a sale in which the buyer, in order to get the item desired, must also purchase one or more other items. **2.** pertaining to two or more products advertised or sold together. —*n.* **3.** a marketing strategy or campaign in which related products are promoted or sold together: *a book and movie tie-in.* **4.** an item in a tie-in sale or advertisement. **5.** any direct or indirect link or relationship.

tie′ line′, *n.* **1.** a line that connects two or more extensions in a PBX telephone system. **2.** a private telephone channel, leased from a telephone company, that connects two or more PBX systems.

tie•pin (tī′pin′), *n.* a straight pin, usu. with an ornamented head and a small metal sheath for its point, for holding together the ends of a necktie or to pin them to a shirt front.

Tie•po•lo (tē ep′ə lō′), *n.* **Giovanni Battista,** 1696–1770, and his son, **Giovanni Domenico,** 1727–1804, Italian painters.

tier[1] (tēr), *n.* **1.** one of a series of rows or ranks rising one behind or above another, as of seats in an amphitheater. **2.** one of a number of galleries, as in a theater. **3.** a layer; level; stratum: *a wedding cake with six tiers.* —*v.t.* **4.** to arrange in tiers. —*v.i.* **5.** to rise in tiers.

ti•er[2] (tī′ər), *n.* a person or thing that ties.

tiered (tērd), *adj.* set in tiers or layers (usu. used in combination): *a two-tiered garden.*

tie′ rod′, *n.* **1.** an iron or steel rod serving as a structural tie, esp. one keeping the lower ends of a roof truss, arch, etc., from spreading. **2.** a rod that serves as part of the linkage in the steering system of a motor vehicle.

tie′ tack′ (or **tac′**), *n.* a pin having an ornamental head, pinned through the ends of a necktie to hold it against a shirt.

tie′-up′, *n.* **1.** a temporary stoppage or slowing of traffic, telephone service, etc., as due to an accident or storm. **2.** the act of tying up or the state of being tied up. **3.** a connection or involvement. **4.** a mooring place.

tiff (tif), *n.* **1.** a slight or petty quarrel. —*v.i.* **2.** to have a petty quarrel.

tif•fa•ny (tif′ə nē), *n., pl.* **-nies.** a sheer, mesh fabric constructed in plain weave.

Tif•fa•ny (tif′ə nē), *n.* **1. Charles Lewis,** 1812–1902, U.S. jeweler. **2.** his son **Louis Comfort,** 1848–1933, U.S. painter and decorator, esp. of glass.

Tif′fany glass′, *n.* an iridescent art glass, introduced by L. C. Tiffany c1890 and used by him for blown vases, flower holders, etc.

Tif•lis (tif′lis), *n.* former name of TBILISI.

ti•ger (tī′gər), *n., pl.* **-gers,** (*esp. collectively for 1*) **-ger. 1.** a large, powerful, tawny-colored and black-striped cat, *Panthera tigris,* of Asia. **2.** a person resembling a tiger in fierceness, courage, etc.

ti′ger bee′tle, *n.* any of numerous active, usu. brightly colored beetles, of the family Cicindelidae, that prey on other insects.

ti′ger cat′, *n.* **1.** any of various striped or spotted wildcats smaller than but resembling the tiger, as the serval. **2.** a domestic cat having a striped coat resembling that of a tiger.

ti•ger•fish (tī′gər fish′), *n., pl.* (*esp. collectively*) **-fish,** (*esp. for kinds or species*) **-fish•es.** a large, African freshwater game fish, *Hydrocyenus goliath.*

ti′ger lil′y, *n.* **1.** a lily, *Lilium tigrinum,* having dull orange flowers spotted with black. **2.** any lily of similar coloration.

ti′ger moth′, *n.* any of numerous moths of the family Arctiidae, many of which have conspicuously striped or spotted wings.

ti′ger's-eye′ also **tigereye,** *n.* a golden-brown chatoyant stone used for ornament, consisting essentially of quartz colored by iron oxide.

ti′ger shark′, *n.* a large, voracious shark, *Galeocerdo cuvieri,* of warm seas.

tight (tīt), *adj.* **1.** firmly or closely fixed in place; secure: *a tight knot.* **2.** drawn or stretched so as to be tense; taut. **3.** fitting closely, esp. too closely: *a tight collar.* **4.** difficult to deal with or manage: *a tight situation.* **5.** of such close texture or fit as to be impervious to water, air, etc.: *a tight roof.* **6.** concise; terse. **7.** firm; rigid: *tight control.* **8.** affording little leeway; full: *a tight schedule.* **9.** nearly even; close: *a tight race.* **10.** parsimonious; stingy. **11.** characterized by scarcity or demand that exceeds supply: *a tight job market; tight money.* **12.** tidy; orderly. **13.** neatly or well built or made. —*adv.* **14.** in a tight manner; closely; securely: *Shut the door tight.* **15.** soundly or deeply: *to sleep tight.* —***Idiom.*** **16. run a tight ship,** to maintain smooth efficiency, as in a company. —**tight′ly,** *adv.* —**tight′ness,** *n.*

tight′ end′, *n.* an offensive end in football positioned directly beside a tackle and used as both a blocker and a pass receiver.

tight′-fist′ed or **tight′fist′ed,** *adj.* parsimonious; stingy. —**tight′-fist′ed•ness,** *n.*

tight′-knit′, *adj.* well-organized or closely integrated.

tight′-lipped′, *adj.* **1.** speaking very little; taciturn; closemouthed. **2.** having the lips drawn tight.

tight•rope (tīt′rōp′), *n.* **1.** a tightly stretched cable on which acrobats perform feats of balancing. **2.** a risky or delicate situation.

tights (tīts), *n.* (*used with a pl. v.*) **1.** a skin-tight, one-piece garment for the lower part of the body and the legs, orig. worn by dancers, acrobats, gymnasts, etc. **2.** a leotard with legs and, sometimes, feet.

tight•wad (tīt′wod′), *n.* a stingy person.

Tig•lath-Pi•le•ser (tig′lath pī lē′zər), *n.* a king of Assyria (745–727 B.C.) who greatly expanded the empire. II Kings 15:29; 16:7–10. Also called **Pul.** II Kings 15:19–20.

ti•glon (tī′glən) also **ti•gon** (-gən), *n.* the offspring of a male tiger and a female lion. Compare LIGER.

ti•gress (tī′gris), *n.* **1.** a female tiger. **2.** a woman likened to a tiger, as in fierceness or courage.

Ti•gris (tī′gris), *n.* a river in SW Asia, flowing SE from SE Turkey through Iraq, joining the Euphrates to form the Shatt-al-Arab. 1150 mi. (1850 km) long.

tike (tīk), *n.* TYKE.

til (til, tēl) also **teel,** *n.* the sesame plant.

'til (til), *prep., conj.* till; until. —**Usage.** See TILL[1].

til•de (til′də), *n., pl.* **-des. 1.** a diacritic (˜) placed over an *n,* as in Spanish *mañana,* to indicate a palatal nasal sound or over a vowel, as in Portuguese *são,* to indicate nasalization. **2.** SWUNG DASH.

Til•den (til′dən), *n.* **1. Samuel (Jones),** 1814–86, U.S. statesman. **2. William Tatem, Jr.,** 1893–1953, U.S. tennis player.

tile (tīl), *n., v.,* **tiled, til•ing.** —*n.* **1.** a thin slab or bent piece of baked clay, sometimes painted or glazed, used for various purposes, as in forming a roof covering or floor. **2.** any of various similar slabs or pieces, as of linoleum, stone, or metal. **3.** tiles collectively. **4.** a pottery tube or pipe used as a drain. **5.** any of various hollow or cellular units of burnt clay or other materials, as gypsum or cinder concrete, for building walls, partitions, floors, and roofs, or for fireproofing steelwork or the like. **6.** a high silk hat. —*v.t.* **7.** to cover with or as if with tiles. **8.** to install drainage tile in. —**tile′like′,** *adj.* —**til′er,** *n.*

-tile, an adjective-forming suffix occurring orig. in loanwords from Latin, with the sense "obtained by, produced by" the action of the base verb (*textile*) or "characterized by" the action of the base verb (*missile; motile; sessile; versatile*); esp. in later formations identical in sense with -ILE[1] (*ductile; erectile*).

till[1] (til), *prep.* **1.** up to the time of; until: *to fight till death.* **2.** before (used in negative constructions): *They didn't come till today.* **3.** before; to: *My watch says ten till four.* **4.** *Chiefly Scot.* to. —*conj.* **5.** UNTIL. —**Usage.** TILL and UNTIL are both old in the language and are interchangeable as both prepositions and conjunctions: *It rained till* (or *un-*

til) nearly midnight. The savannah remained brown and lifeless until (or *till*) *the rains began.* TILL is not a shortened form of UNTIL and is not spelled *'till.* 'TIL is usu. considered a spelling error, though commonly used in business and advertising: *Open 'til ten.*

till[2] (til), *v.t.* **1.** to labor, as by plowing or harrowing, upon (land) for the raising of crops; cultivate. *—v.i.* **2.** to cultivate the soil.

till[3] (til), *n.* **1.** a drawer, box, or the like, in which money is kept, as in a shop. **2.** a drawer, tray, or the like, as in a cabinet, chest, or desk, for keeping valuables.

till•age (til′ij), *n.* **1.** the operation, practice, or art of tilling land. **2.** tilled land.

till•er[1] (til′ər), *n.* **1.** a person who tills; farmer. **2.** a thing that tills; cultivator.

til•ler[2] (til′ər), *n.* a bar or lever fitted to the head of a rudder, for turning the rudder in steering.

til•ler[3] (til′ər), *n.* **1.** a plant shoot that springs from the root or bottom of the original stalk. *—v.i.* **2.** (of a plant) to put forth new shoots from the root or around the bottom of the original stalk.

Til•lich (til′ik, -ɪᴋʜ), *n.* **Paul (Johannes),** 1886–1965, U.S. philosopher and theologian, born in Germany.

tilt (tilt), *v.t.* **1.** to cause to lean, incline, slope, or slant. **2.** to rush at or charge, as in a joust. **3.** to hold poised for attack, as a lance. *—v.i.* **4.** to assume a sloping position or direction. **5.** to strike, thrust, or charge with a lance or the like (usu. fol. by *at*). **6.** to engage in a joust, tournament, or similar contest. **7.** to incline in opinion, feeling, etc.; lean. *—n.* **8.** an act or instance of tilting. **9.** the state of being tilted; a sloping position. **10.** an incline or slope. **11.** a joust or similar contest. **12.** a dispute; controversy. **13.** a thrust of a weapon, as at a tilt or joust. *—**Idiom.*** **14. (at) full tilt,** at maximum speed; with great energy. **15. tilt at windmills,** to contend against imaginary opponents or injustices.

Tim., Timothy.

tim•bal (tim′bəl), *n.* **1.** KETTLEDRUM. **2.** Also, **tymbal.** a vibrating membrane in certain insects, as the cicada.

tim•bale (tim′bəl; *Fr.* taɴ bᴀʟ′), *n., pl.* **-bales** (-bəlz; *Fr.* -bᴀʟ′). **1.** a preparation, as of minced meat, fish, or vegetables, in a custardlike sauce, baked in a small cylindrical mold. **2.** a small shell of deep-fried batter, usu. filled with a similar preparation.

tim•ber (tim′bər), *n.* **1.** the wood of growing trees suitable for construction purposes. **2.** growing trees themselves. **3.** wooded land. **4.** wood, esp. when adapted for various building purposes. **5.** a single piece of wood forming part of a structure: *A timber fell from the roof.* **6.** (in a ship's frame) one of the curved pieces of wood that spring upward and outward from the keel; rib. **7.** a person regarded as having exceptional qualifications: *He's presidential timber.* *—v.t.* **8.** to furnish or support with timber. *—v.i.* **9.** to fell timber, esp. as an occupation. *—interj.* **10.** (used as a lumberjack's call to warn others that a cut tree is about to fall.) **—tim′ber•less,** *adj.* **—tim′ber•y,** *adj.*

tim•bered (tim′bərd), *adj.* **1.** made of or furnished with timber. **2.** covered with growing trees; wooded.

tim•ber•ing (tim′bər ing), *n.* building material of wood.

tim•ber•land (tim′bər land′), *n.* land covered with timber-producing forests.

tim•ber•line (tim′bər līn′), *n.* **1.** the altitude above sea level at which timber ceases to grow. **2.** the arctic or antarctic limit of tree growth.

tim′ber rat′tlesnake, *n.* a rattlesnake, *Crotalus horridus,* of the eastern U.S., usu. having dark crossbands.

tim′ber wolf′, *n.* the gray wolf, *Canis lupus,* esp. the North American populations, sometimes considered a subspecies, *C. lupus occidentalis.*

tim•bre (tam′bər, tim′-; *Fr.* taɴ′brᵊ), *n.* **1.** the characteristic quality of a sound, independent of pitch and loudness, depending on the number and relative strengths of its component frequencies, as determined by resonance. **2.** the characteristic quality of sound produced by a particular instrument or voice; tone color.

tim•brel (tim′brəl), *n.* a tambourine or similar instrument.

time (tīm), *n., adj., v.,* **timed, tim•ing.** *—n.* **1.** the system of those sequential relations that any event has to any other, as past, present, or future; indefinite and continuous duration regarded as that in which events succeed one another. **2.** duration regarded as an aspect of the present life as distinct from the life to come or from eternity; finite duration. **3.** (*sometimes cap.*) a system or method of measuring or reckoning the passage of time: *Greenwich Time.* **4.** a limited period or interval, as between two events: *a long time.* **5.** a particular period: *Youth is the best time of life.* **6.** Often, **times. a.** a period in history, or one contemporaneous with a notable person: *prehistoric times; in Lincoln's time.* **b.** the period or era now or previously present: *a sign of the times.* **c.** a period with reference to its conditions: *hard times.* **7.** the end of a prescribed or allotted period, as of one's life or a pregnancy. **8.** a period experienced in a particular way: *Have a good time.* **9.** a period of work of an employee, or the pay for it. **10.** *Informal.* a term of enforced duty or imprisonment. **11.** leisure or spare time: *I hope to take some time in August.* **12.** a definite point in time, as indicated by a clock: *What time is it?* **13.** a particular period in a day, year, etc.: *breakfast time.* **14.** an appointed or proper instant or period: *There is a time for everything.* **15.** an indefinite period extending into the future: *Time will tell.* **16.** each occasion of a recurring action or event: *to do something five times.* **17. times,** the number of instances a quantity or factor are taken together: *Two goes into six three times; five times faster.* **18.** a unit or a group of units in the measurement of poetic meter. **19.** *Music.* **a.** tempo; relative rapidity of movement. **b.** meter; rhythm. **c.** the metrical duration of a note or rest. **d.** proper or characteristic rhythm or tempo. **20.** rate of marching, calculated on the number of paces taken per minute: *double time.* *—adj.* **21.** of, pertaining to, or showing the passage of time. **22.** (of an explosive device) containing a clock so that it will detonate at the desired moment: *a time bomb.* **23.** of or pertaining to an installment plan: *time payments.* *—v.t.* **24.** to measure or record the speed, duration, or rate of: *to time a race.* **25.** to fix the duration of: *She timed the test at 15 minutes.* **26.** to fix the interval between (actions, events, etc.): *They timed their strokes at six per minute.* **27.** to regulate (a train, clock, etc.) as to time. **28.** to choose the moment or occasion for; schedule: *He timed the attack perfectly.* *—v.i.* **29.** to keep time; sound or move in unison. *—**Idiom.*** **30. against time,** in an effort to finish within a limited period. **31. ahead of time,** before the time due; early. **32. at one time, a.** once; formerly. **b.** at the same time; simultaneously. **33. at the same time,** nevertheless; yet: *He's young; at the same time, he's quite responsible.* **34. at times,** at intervals; occasionally. **35. behind the times,** old-fashioned; dated. **36. for the time being,** temporarily; for the present. **37. from time to time,** occasionally; at intervals. **38. gain time,** to achieve a delay or postponement. **39. in good time,** at or in advance of the appointed time; punctually. **40. in no time,** in a very brief time. **41. in time, a.** early enough: *Come in time for dinner.* **b.** in the future; eventually: *In time he'll understand.* **c.** in the correct rhythm or tempo. **42. keep time, a.** to record time, as a watch or clock does. **b.** to mark or observe the tempo, as by performing rhythmic movements. **43. kill time,** to occupy oneself with some activity to make time pass more quickly. **44. make time,** to move or travel quickly. **45. many a time,** again and again; frequently. **46. mark time, a.** to suspend progress temporarily, as to await developments; fail to advance. **b.** to move the feet alternately as in marching, but without advancing. **47. on one's own time,** during one's free time; while not being paid. **48. on time, a.** at the specified time; punctually. **b.** to be paid for within a designated period of time, as in installments. **49. take one's time,** to act without hurry; be slow; dawdle. **50. the time of one's life,** an extremely enjoyable experience. **51. time after time,** again and again; repeatedly. **52. time and (time) again,** repeatedly; often. **53. time of life,** (one's) age: *At my time of life I must rest frequently.* *—**Proverb.*** **54. Time heals all wounds,** hurt fades as time passes. **55. Time will tell,** the truth will become known in the future.

time′ and a half′, *n.* a rate of pay for overtime work equal to one and one half times the regular hourly wage.

time′ bomb′, *n.* **1.** a bomb containing a clock or timer that can be set to explode at a certain time. **2.** a situation, condition, etc., that may have disastrous consequences in the near future.

time′ cap′sule, *n.* a receptacle containing documents or objects typical of the current period, placed in the earth, in a cornerstone, etc., for discovery in the future.

time•card (tīm′kärd′), *n.* a card for recording the time at which an employee arrives at and departs from a job.

time′ clock′, *n.* a clock with an attachment that records the exact time on a card or tape, used to keep a record of the time of something, as the arrival and departure of employees.

time′-consum′ing, *adj.* requiring or wasting much time.

time′ depos′it, *n.* a bank deposit that can be withdrawn without penalty only after a specified period of time.

timed′-release′ also **time-release,** *adj.* SLOW-RELEASE.

time′ expo′sure, *n.* **1.** exposure of photographic film for a period longer than the slowest automatic shutter speed of the camera. **2.** a photograph taken by means of such an exposure.

time′ frame′, *n.* a period of time during which something has taken or will take place.

time′-hon′ored, *adj.* revered or respected because of long observance or continuance: *a time-honored custom.* Also, *esp. Brit.,* **time′-hon′oured.**

time′ immemo′rial, *n.* time in the distant past beyond memory or record.

time•keep•er (tīm′kē′pər), *n.* **1.** an official who times, regulates, and records the duration of a sports contest or its parts. **2.** TIMEPIECE. **3.** a person employed to keep account of the hours of work done by others.

time′ kill′er, *n.* **1.** an activity that helps the time to go by agreeably or tolerably; pastime. **2.** a person with free time to spend.

time′-lag′ or **time′ lag′,** *n.* the period of time between two closely related events, phenomena, etc., as between stimulus and response or between cause and effect.

time′-lapse′ photog′raphy, *n.* the photographing on motion-picture film of a slow, continuous process, as the growth of a plant, at regular intervals, esp. by exposing a single frame at a time, for projection at a higher speed.

time•less (tīm′lis), *adj.* **1.** without beginning or end; eternal. **2.** referring or restricted to no particular time: *timeless beauty.*

time′ lim′it, *n.* a period of time within which something must be done or completed.

time′ line′ or **time′line′,** *n.* **1.** a linear, chronological representation of important events. **2.** a schedule; timetable.

time′ lock′, *n.* a lock, as for the door of a bank vault, equipped with a mechanism that makes it impossible to operate within certain hours.

time•ly (tīm′lē), *adj.,* **-li•er, -li•est,** *adv.* *—adj.* **1.** occurring at a suitable time; opportune: *a timely warning.* *—adv.* **2.** seasonably; opportunely.

time′ machine′, *n.* a theoretical apparatus that would convey a person or object to the past or future.

time′ of day′, *n.* **1.** a definite time as shown by a timepiece; the hour. **2.** (in negative constructions) a minimum of attention: *I wouldn't give her the time of day.*

time′-out′ or **time′out′,** *n., pl.* **-outs.** **1.** a brief suspension of activity; break. **2.** an interruption of play in a sports contest.

time•piece (tīm′pēs′), *n.* **1.** an apparatus for measuring and recording the progress of time; chronometer. **2.** a clock or a watch.

tim•er (tī′mər), *n.* **1.** a person who measures or records time; timekeeper. **2.** a device for indicating or measuring elapsed time, as a stopwatch. **3.** a device for controlling machinery, appliances, or the like, in a specified way at a predetermined time. **4.** (in an internal-combustion engine) a set of points actuated by a cam, which causes the spark for igniting the charge at the instant required.

time′-release′, *adj.* SLOW-RELEASE.

times (tīmz), *prep.* multiplied by: *Two times four is eight.*

time•sav•ing (tīm′sā′ving), *adj.* (of methods, devices, etc.) reducing the time spent or required to do something. —**time′sav′er,** *n.*

time′-shar′ing, *n.* **1.** a plan in which several persons share ownership or rental costs of a vacation home, entitling each to use the residence for a specified time each year. **2.** a computer system or service in which users at different terminals simultaneously use a single computer.

time′ sheet′, *n.* a sheet or card recording the hours worked by an employee, made esp. for payroll purposes.

times′ sign′, *n.* MULTIPLICATION SIGN.

time•ta•ble (tīm′tā′bəl), *n.* **1.** a schedule showing the times at which trains, airplanes, etc., arrive and depart. **2.** any schedule or plan designating the times when certain things occur or are scheduled to occur.

time′-test′ed, *adj.* tested and proven valid, workable, etc., over a long period of time.

time′ warp′, *n.* a hypothetical eccentricity in the progress of time that would allow movement back and forth between eras.

time•worn (tīm′wôrn′, -wōrn′), *adj.* **1.** worn or impaired by time. **2.** showing the effects of age; antiquated: *timeworn methods.*

time′ zone′, *n.* one of the 24 regions or divisions of the globe approximately coinciding with meridians at successive hours from the observatory at Greenwich, England.

tim•id (tim′id), *adj.* **1.** lacking in self-assurance, courage, or boldness; timorous; shy. **2.** indicating fear or lack of assurance: *a timid manner.* —**ti•mid′i•ty, tim′id•ness,** *n.* —**tim′id•ly,** *adv.*

tim•ing (tī′ming), *n.* **1.** the selecting of the best time for doing or saying something in order to achieve the desired effect. **2.** *Sports.* the control of the speed of a stroke, blow, etc., in order that it may reach its maximum at the proper moment. **3.** an act or instance of observing and recording the elapsed time of an act, contest, process, etc.

tim•or•ous (tim′ər əs), *adj.* **1.** full of or subject to fear; fearful. **2.** characterized by or indicating fear or timidity: *a timorous approach to a serious problem.* —**tim′or•ous•ly,** *adv.* —**tim′or•ous•ness,** *n.*

tim•o•thy (tim′ə thē), *n., pl.* **-thies.** a coarse grass, *Phleum pratense,* having cylindrical spikes: used as fodder. [after *Timothy* Hanson, American farmer who cultivated it in the early 18th cent.]

Tim•o•thy (tim′ə thē), *n.* **1.** a disciple and companion of the apostle Paul, to whom Paul is supposed to have addressed two Epistles. **2.** either of these Epistles, I Timothy or II Timothy.

tim•pa•ni or **tym•pa•ni** (tim′pə nē), *n.* (*used with a sing. or pl. v.*) a set of kettledrums, esp. as used in an orchestra or band. —**tim′pa•nist, tympanist,** *n.*

Ti•mur (ti mo͝or′), *n.* TAMERLANE.

tin (tin), *n., adj., v.,* **tinned, tin•ning.** —*n.* **1.** a low-melting, malleable, ductile metallic element with a silvery color and luster: used in plating and in making alloys, tinfoil, and soft solders. *Symbol:* Sn; *at. wt.:* 118.69; *at. no.:* 50; *sp. gr.:* 7.31 at 20°C. **2.** TIN PLATE. **3.** any shallow pan, esp. one used in baking: *a pie tin.* **4.** any pot, box, can, or other container or vessel made of tin or tin plate. **5.** *Chiefly Brit.* a hermetically sealed can containing food. —*adj.* **6.** made of tin or tin plate. **7.** false; worthless: *a set of tin values.* **8.** indicating the tenth event of a series, as a wedding anniversary. —*v.t.* **9. a.** to cover or coat with tin. **b.** to coat with soft solder. **10.** *Chiefly Brit.* to preserve or pack (food, etc.) in cans; can. —**tin′like′,** *adj.*

tinct (tingkt), *v.t.* **1.** to tinge or tint, as with color. —*adj.* **2.** tinged; colored. —*n.* **3.** a tint or tinge.

tinc•ture (tingk′chər), *n., v.,* **-tured, -tur•ing.** —*n.* **1.** a solution of alcohol or of alcohol and water, containing animal, vegetable, or chemical drugs. **2.** a slight infusion, as of some element or quality; smattering; trace; tinge: *a tincture of irony.* **3.** any of various heraldic colors, metals, or furs. **4.** a dye or pigment. —*v.t.* **5.** to impart a tint or color to; tinge. **6.** to imbue or infuse with something.

tin•der (tin′dər), *n.* **1.** a highly flammable material formerly used for starting a fire by catching the spark from a flint and steel struck together. **2.** any dry, easily ignitable substance. —**tin′der•y,** *adj.*

tin•der•box (tin′dər boks′), *n.* **1.** a box for holding tinder, usu. fitted with a flint and steel. **2.** a person or thing that is highly volatile; any potential source of violence.

tine (tīn), *n.* a sharp, projecting point or prong, as of a fork.

tin′ ear′, *n.* **1.** an insensitivity to or inability to distinguish differences in musical sound. **2.** an insensitivity to subtlety in verbal expression.

tin•foil (tin′foil′), *n.* tin, or an alloy of tin and lead, in the form of a thin sheet, used as a wrapping for foods, drugs, etc.

tinge (tinj), *v.,* **tinged, tinge•ing** or **ting•ing,** *n.* —*v.t.* **1.** to impart a slight degree of some color to; tint. **2.** to impart a slight taste or smell to. —*n.* **3.** a slight degree of coloration. **4.** a slight admixture; trace: *a tinge of garlic.*

tin•gle (ting′gəl), *v.,* **-gled, -gling,** *n.* —*v.i.* **1.** to have a sensation of slight prickles, stings, or tremors, as from cold. **2.** to cause such a sensation. —*n.* **3.** a tingling sensation. **4.** the tingling action of cold, excitement, etc. —**tin′gler,** *n.* —**tin′gling•ly,** *adv.* —**tin′gly,** *adj.*

tin•ker (ting′kər), *n.* **1.** a mender of pots and pans, usu. an itinerant. **2.** an unskillful or clumsy worker; bungler. **3.** a jack-of-all-trades. **4.** an act or instance of tinkering. **5.** a young mackerel. —*v.i.* **6.** to busy oneself with a thing without useful results. **7.** to work unskillfully or clumsily at anything. **8.** to do the work of a tinker. —*v.t.* **9.** to mend as a tinker. **10.** to repair in a clumsy or makeshift way. —**tin′ker•er,** *n.*

tin′ker's damn′ (or **dam′**), *n.* the least bit; hoot; damn: *not worth a tinker's damn.*

tin•kle (ting′kəl), *v.,* **-kled, -kling,** *n.* —*v.i.* **1.** to make light ringing sounds, as a small bell. —*v.t.* **2.** to cause to tinkle. **3.** to make known by tinkling: *to tinkle the time.* —*n.* **4.** a tinkling sound. **5.** an act or instance of tinkling. —**tin′kly,** *adj.,* **-kli•er, -kli•est.**

tin•ni•tus (ti nī′təs, tin′i-), *n.* a sensation of sound, as ringing, in the ears.

tin•ny (tin′ē), *adj.,* **-ni•er, -ni•est.** **1.** of or like tin. **2.** containing tin. **3.** lacking in timbre or resonance: *a tinny piano.* **4.** not durable; flimsy. **5.** having the taste of tin. —**tin′ni•ly,** *adv.*

Tin′ Pan′ Al′ley, *n.* **1.** an urban district regarded as a center for the composition and publication of popular music. **2.** the composers and publishers of popular music.

tin′ plate′ or **tin′plate′,** *n.* thin iron or steel sheet coated with tin. Also called **tin.**

tin•sel (tin′səl), *n., adj., v.,* **-seled, -sel•ing** or (*esp. Brit.*) **-selled, -sel•ling.** —*n.* **1.** a thin sheet, strip, or thread of glittering metal, paper, or plastic, used to produce a sparkling effect in threads and decorations. **2.** a metallic yarn for weaving brocade or lamé. **3.** showy pretense. —*adj.* **4.** consisting of tinsel. **5.** gaudy; tawdry. —*v.t.* **6.** to adorn with tinsel. **7.** to adorn with anything glittering. **8.** to make showy or gaudy. —**tin′sel•like′,** *adj.* —**tin′sel•ly,** *adj.*

Tin•sel•town (tin′səl toun′), *n.* (*sometimes l.c.*) a nickname for Hollywood, Calif.

tin•smith (tin′smith′), *n.* a person who makes or repairs tinware or items of other light metals.

tint (tint), *n.* **1.** a variety of a color; hue. **2.** a color diluted with white. **3.** a delicate or pale color. **4.** any of various commercial dyes for the hair. **5.** a uniform shading, as in an engraving. —*v.t.* **6.** to color slightly; tinge. —**tint′er,** *n.*

tin•tin•nab•u•lar (tin′ti nab′yə lər) also **tin•tin•nab•u•lar•y** (-ler′ē), **tin′tin•nab′u•lous,** *adj.* of or pertaining to bells or ringing.

tin•tin•nab•u•la•tion (tin′ti nab′yə lā′shən), *n.* the ringing or sound of bells. [< Latin *tintinnābul(um)* bell]

Tin•to•ret•to (tin′tə ret′ō), *n.* **Il** (ēl), (*Jacopo Robusti*), 1518–94, Venetian painter.

tin•type (tin′tīp′), *n.* FERROTYPE (def. 2).

ti•ny (tī′nē), *adj.,* **-ni•er, -ni•est.** very small; minute. —**ti′ni•ly,** *adv.* —**ti′ni•ness,** *n.*

-tion or **-sion,** a suffix occurring in Latin loanwords, orig. nouns of action or state formed from verbs: *relation; section; station; temptation.* Compare -ION.

tip[1] (tip), *n., v.,* **tipped, tip•ping.** —*n.* **1.** a pointed end, esp. of something long or tapered: *the tips of the fingers.* **2.** the top; apex: *the tip of a steeple.* **3.** a small piece covering the extremity of something: *a cane with a rubber tip.* —*v.t.* **4.** to furnish with a tip. **5.** to serve as or form the tip of. **6.** to mark or adorn the tip of. **7.** to remove the tip or stem of. **8.** to frost the ends of (hair strands). **9. tip in,** to insert (an extra sheet, as a list of errata) into the signature of a book before binding.

tip[2] (tip), *v.,* **tipped, tip•ping,** *n.* —*v.t.* **1.** to cause to assume a slanting position; tilt. **2.** to overturn; upset: *to tip the basket over.* **3.** to lift (one's hat) in salutation. —*v.i.* **4.** to assume a slanting position; incline. **5.** to tilt up; slant. **6.** to become overturned; upset: *The car tipped into the ditch.* **7.** to tumble; topple: *The lamp tipped over.* —*n.* **8.** the act of tipping. **9.** the state of being tipped. —***Idiom.*** **10. tip one's hand,** to reveal one's plans or feelings, often unintentionally. —**tip′pa•ble,** *adj.*

tip[3] (tip), *n., v.,* **tipped, tip•ping.** —*n.* **1.** GRATUITY. **2.** a piece of confidential information, as for use in betting, speculating, or writing a news story. **3.** a useful hint or idea; a basic, practical fact: *tips on painting.* —*v.t.* **4.** to give a gratuity to: *tipping a waiter.* —*v.i.* **5.** to give a gratuity: *She tipped lavishly.* **6. tip off, a.** to supply with confidential information. **b.** to warn of impending trouble. —**tip′pa•ble,** *adj.*

tip[4] (tip), *n., v.,* **tipped, tip•ping.** —*n.* **1.** a light blow. **2.** a batted baseball that glances off the bat. —*v.t.* **3.** to hit with a light, smart blow. **4.** to strike (a baseball) with a glancing blow.

tip′-off′, *n.* a tip; warning: *They got a tip-off on the raid.*

tip•off (tip′ôf′, -of′), *n.* a jump ball that begins each period of a basketball game.

Tippecanoe and Tyler Too, a political slogan of the 1840 presidential campaign, referring to the Whig candidate for president, William Henry

Harrison, who had led U.S. troops against the Shawnee at the battle of Tippecanoe (1811), and to the Democratic vice presidential candidate, John Tyler.

tip•pet (tip′it), *n.* **1.** a scarf, usu. of fur or wool, for covering the neck and shoulders, and usu. having ends hanging down in front. **2.** a band of silk or the like worn by Anglican clergy around the neck with the ends pendent in front.

tip•ple (tip′əl), *n.* **1.** a device that tilts a freight car to dump its contents. **2.** a place where loaded cars are emptied by tipping.

tip•py (tip′ē), *adj.,* **-pi•er, -pi•est.** liable to tip over.

tip•py•toe (tip′ē tō′), *n., v.i.* **-toed, -toe•ing,** *adj., adv. Informal.* TIPTOE.

tip′ sheet′, *n.* a publication containing the latest information, tips, and predictions, as on the stock market or horse racing.

tip•ster (tip′stər), *n.* a person who sells tips, as for betting.

tip•sy (tip′sē), *adj.,* **-si•er, -si•est. 1.** slightly intoxicated. **2.** caused by intoxication: *a tipsy lurch.* **3.** unsteady; tippy. —**tip′si•ly,** *adv.*

tip•toe (tip′tō′), *n., v.* **-toed, -toe•ing,** *adj., adv.* —*n.* **1.** the tip or end of a toe. —*v.i.* **2.** to go on tiptoe, as with stealth. —*adj.* **3.** characterized by standing or walking on tiptoe. **4.** straining upward. **5.** eagerly expectant. **6.** cautious; stealthy. —*adv.* **7.** eagerly or cautiously; on tiptoe. —*Idiom.* **8. on tiptoe, a.** on the tips of one's toes. **b.** expectant; eager. **c.** stealthily; cautiously.

tip•top (tip′top′, -top′), *n.* **1.** the extreme top or summit. **2.** the highest point or degree, as of excellence. —*adj.* **3.** situated at the very top. **4.** of the highest quality, rank, etc.: *an athlete in tiptop shape.* —*adv.* **5.** very well: *It's shaping up tiptop.*

tip′-up′, *adj.* designed to tip or fold up, as when not in use: *tip-up seats.*

ti•rade (tī′rād, tī rād′), *n.* **1.** a prolonged outburst of bitter denunciation. **2.** a long, vehement speech. **3.** a passage dealing with a single theme, as in poetry: *the stately tirades of Corneille.*

Ti•ra•në or **Ti•ra•na** (ti rä′nə), *n.* the capital of Albania, in the central part. 206,000.

tire[1] (tīər), *v.,* **tired, tir•ing.** —*v.t.* **1.** to reduce or exhaust the strength of; make weary. **2.** to exhaust the interest or patience of; bore. —*v.i.* **3.** to have the strength reduced or exhausted; be or become weary or fatigued. **4.** to have one's interest or patience exhausted; become bored: *to tire of playing cards.*

tire[2] (tīər), *n.* a ring or band of rubber, either solid or hollow and inflated, or of metal, placed over the rim of a wheel to provide traction or resistance to wear.

tire′ chain′, *n.* a chain fitting over the tire of a vehicle to increase traction on icy or snow-covered roads.

tired (tīərd), *adj.* **1.** exhausted; fatigued; wearied. **2.** weary or bored: *tired of the same routine.* **3.** hackneyed; stale, as a joke. **4.** impatient or disgusted: *You make me tired.*

tire′ i′ron, *n.* a short length of steel with one end flattened to form a blade, used to remove tires from wheel rims.

tire•less (tīər′lis), *adj.* untiring; indefatigable: *a tireless worker.* —**tire′less•ly,** *adv.* —**tire′less•ness,** *n.*

Ti•re•si•as or **Tei•re•si•as** (tī rē′sē əs), *n.* (in Greek myth) a blind prophet of Thebes.

tire•some (tīər′səm), *adj.* **1.** causing a person to tire; wearisome. **2.** annoying or vexatious. —**tire′some•ly,** *adv.*

ti•ro (tī′rō), *n., pl.* **-ros.** TYRO.

'tis (tiz), a contraction of *it is.*

ti•sane (ti zan′, -zän′), *n.* a decoction of herbs usu. drunk for medicinal purposes.

Tish•ah b'Av or **Tish•ah b'Ab** (tish′ə bôv′, tē shä′ bə äv′), *n.* a Jewish fast day observed on the ninth day of Av in memory of the destruction of the First and Second Temples in Jerusalem.

Tish•bite (tish′bīt), *n.* **The,** an epithet of Elijah. I Kings 17:1; 21:17; II Kings 9:36.

Tish•ri (tish′rē, -rä), *n.* the first month of the Jewish calendar.

Tis•quan•tum (ti skwon′təm), *n.* SQUANTO.

tis•sue (tish′ōō; *esp. Brit.* tis′yōō), *n., v.,* **-sued, -su•ing.** —*n.* **1.** an aggregate of similar cells and cell products forming one of the structural materials of an organism. **2.** TISSUE PAPER. **3.** any of several kinds of soft gauzy papers used for various purposes: *toilet tissue.* **4.** an interconnected series or mass: *a tissue of falsehoods.* **5.** a piece of thin writing paper on which carbon copies are made. **6.** a woven fabric, esp. one of light or gauzy texture, orig. woven with gold or silver. —*v.t.* **7.** to cover or clothe with tissue. **8.** to remove with facial or other tissues.

tis′sue cul′ture, *n.* the technique or process of growing living tissue in a prepared medium outside the body.

tis′sue pa′per, *n.* a very thin, nearly transparent paper used for wrapping, packing, etc.

tit (tit), *n.* **1.** a titmouse. **2.** any of various other small birds.

Tit., Titus.

tit., title.

Ti•tan (tīt′n), *n.* **1. a.** (in Greek myth) any of a race of gods, the children of Uranus and Gaea, who lost their supremacy over the world after a great battle with the Olympian gods. **b.** any of several figures of Greek myth sometimes represented as offspring of the Titans. **2.** a moon of the planet Saturn: the largest moon in the solar system. **3.** (*usu. l.c.*) one of great size, strength, or influence: *a titan of industry.* **4.** *Mil.* a

two-stage, liquid-fueled U.S. intercontinental ballistic missile in service since the late 1950s and designed for launch from underground silos. —*adj.* **5.** (*l.c.*) TITANIC.

ti•tan•ate (tīt′n āt′), *n.* a salt of titanic acid.

ti•tan•ic[1] (tī tan′ik, ti-), *adj.* containing tetravalent titanium.

ti•tan•ic[2] (tī tan′ik) also **titan,** *adj.* of great size, strength, or power.

ti•tan′ic ac′id (tī tan′ik, ti-), *n.* any of various acids derived from titanium dioxide, esp. H_2TiO_3 or $Ti(OH)_4$.

ti•ta•ni•um (tī tā′nē əm), *n.* a dark gray or silvery, lustrous, very hard, light, corrosion-resistant, metallic element, used to toughen steel. Symbol: Ti; *at. wt.:* 47.90; *at. no.:* 22; *sp. gr.:* 4.5 at 20°C.

tita′nium diox′ide, *n.* a white water-insoluble powder, TiO_2, used in white pigments and plastics.

tit for tat (tit′ fər tat′), *n.* an equivalent given in retaliation.

tithe (tīth), *n., v.,* **tithed, tith•ing.** —*n.* **1.** Sometimes, **tithes.** the tenth part of goods or income paid as a tax for the support of the church. **2.** any tax or levy esp. of one-tenth. **3.** a tenth part or small part of something. —*v.t.* **4.** to give or pay a tithe of (goods or money). **5.** to give or pay tithes on, as income. **6.** to exact a tithe from. **7.** to levy a tithe on, as money. —*v.i.* **8.** to give or pay a tithe. —**tith′a•ble,** *adj.*

tith•er (tī′thər), *n.* **1.** a person who gives or pays tithes, as to a church. **2.** a person who advocates payment of tithes. **3.** a person who collects tithes.

Ti•tian (tish′ən), *n.* **1.** (*Tiziano Vecellio*) c1477–1576, Italian painter. **2.** (*l.c.*) a bright golden brown color. —*adj.* **3.** (*l.c.*) bright golden brown: *titian hair.* —**Ti′tian•esque′,** *adj.*

tit•il•late (tit′l āt′), *v.t.,* **-lat•ed, -lat•ing. 1.** to excite agreeably: *to titillate one's curiosity.* **2.** to excite a tingling sensation in, as by touching lightly; tickle. —**tit′il•lat′ing•ly,** *adv.* —**tit′il•la′tion,** *n.*

tit•i•vate or **tit•ti•vate** (tit′ə vāt′), *v.,* **-vat•ed, -vat•ing.** —*v.t.* **1.** to make smart; spruce up. —*v.i.* **2.** to make oneself smart or spruce. —**tit′i•va′tion,** *n.* —**tit′i•va′tor,** *n.*

ti•tle (tīt′l), *n., adj., v.,* **-tled, -tling.** —*n.* **1.** the distinguishing name of a work, as a book or a piece of music. **2.** a descriptive heading, as of a chapter of a book. **3.** TITLE PAGE. **4.** a book, magazine, or other publication: *We published 25 titles last year.* **5.** a descriptive appellation, esp. one belonging to a person by right of rank or office: *the title of Lord Mayor.* **6.** a championship: *to win a tennis title.* **7.** an established right to something. **8.** anything that provides a basis for a claim. **9. a.** a legal right to the possession of property, esp. real estate. **b.** the instrument constituting evidence of such right. **10.** Usu., **titles.** any written matter inserted into a motion picture or television program, as credits or subtitles. —*adj.* **11.** of or pertaining to a title: *the title story in a collection.* **12.** that decides a championship: *a title bout.* —*v.t.* **13.** to furnish with a title; entitle.

ti′tle deed′, *n.* a document constituting evidence of property ownership.

ti•tle•hold•er (tīt′l hōl′dər), *n.* **1.** a person who holds a title. **2.** a person who holds a championship.

ti′tle page′, *n.* the page at the beginning of a volume that bears the title, author's name, and publication information.

ti•tlist (tīt′list, -l ist), *n.* TITLEHOLDER (def. 2).

tit•mouse (tit′mous′), *n., pl.* **-mice** (-mīs′). any of various small, stout-billed songbirds of the family Paridae, esp. of the genus *Parus,* found in most of the world outside of Australasia and South America.

Ti•to (tē′tō), *n.* Marshal (*Josip Broz*), 1891–1980, president of Yugoslavia 1953–80.

ti•trate (tī′trāt), *v.t., v.i.,* **-trat•ed, -trat•ing.** to ascertain the quantity of a given constituent by adding a liquid reagent of known strength and measuring the volume necessary to convert the constituent through a given reaction. —**ti′tra•ta•ble, ti′tra•ble** (-trə bəl), *adj.*

tit•ter (tit′ər), *v.i.* **1.** to laugh in a half-restrained, self-conscious, or affected way, as from nervousness. —*n.* **2.** a tittering laugh. —**tit′ter•er,** *n.* —**tit′ter•ing•ly,** *adv.*

tit•tle (tit′l), *n.* **1.** a dot or other small mark in writing or printing, used as a diacritic or punctuation. **2.** a very small thing; particle, jot, or whit: *I don't care a tittle.*

tit•u•lar (tich′ə lər, tit′yə-), *adj.* **1.** in title only; nominal. **2.** bearing the same name as the title: *the titular hero of the novel.* **3.** of, pertaining to, or of the nature of a title. **4.** having a title, as of rank. —*n.* **5.** a person who bears a title. **6.** a person from whom or thing from which a title or name is taken. **7.** an ecclesiastic entitled to a benefice but not required to perform its duties. —**tit′u•lar′i•ty,** *n.* —**tit′u•lar•ly,** *adv.*

Ti•tus (tī′təs), *n.* **1.** a disciple and companion of the apostle Paul, to whom Paul is supposed to have addressed an Epistle. **2.** this New Testament Epistle. **3.** (*Titus Flavius Sabinus Vespasianus*) A.D. 40?–81, Roman emperor 79–81.

tiz•zy (tiz′ē), *n., pl.* **-zies.** *Slang.* a dither; nervous, excited, or distracted state.

tkt., ticket.

Tl, *Chem. Symbol.* thallium.

TLC or **T.L.C.** or **t.l.c.,** tender loving care.

Tlin•git (tling′git), *n., pl.* **-gits,** (*esp. collectively*) **-git. 1.** a member of an American Indian people of the Alaskan panhandle and adjacent areas of Canada. **2.** the language of the Tlingit.

T lymphocyte, *n.* T CELL.

TM, 1. trademark. **2.** transcendental meditation.

Tm, *Chem. Symbol.* thulium.
TN, Tennessee.
Tn, *Chem. Symbol.* thoron.
T-note (tē′nōt′), *n.* TREASURY NOTE.
TNT, a flammable toluene derivative, $C_7H_5N_3O_6$, used as a high explosive and in the manufacture of dyestuffs and photographic chemicals. Also called **trinitrotoluene.** [*t(ri)n(itro)t(oluene)*]
T number, *n.* one of a series of calibrations of the lens openings of a camera according to the intensity of transmitted light.
to (to͞o; *unstressed* to͝o, tə), *prep.* **1.** (used for expressing motion or direction toward a place, person, or thing approached and reached): *Come to the house.* **2.** (used for expressing motion or direction toward something): *from north to south.* **3.** (used for expressing limit of movement or extension): *He grew to six feet.* **4.** (used for expressing a point of limit in time) before; until: *ten minutes to six.* **5.** (used for expressing destination or appointed end): *sentenced to jail.* **6.** (used for expressing a resulting state or condition): *He tore it to pieces.* **7.** (used for expressing the object of inclination or desire): *They drank to her health.* **8.** (used for expressing the object of a right or claim): *claimants to an estate.* **9.** (used for expressing limit in degree, condition, or amount): *wet to the skin.* **10.** (used for expressing comparison or opposition): *inferior to last year's crop.* **11.** (used for expressing agreement or accordance) according to; by: *a room to your liking.* **12.** (used for expressing reference, reaction, or relation): *What will he say to this?* **13.** (used for expressing a relative position): *parallel to the roof; the woman standing to the left of the car.* **14.** (used for expressing a proportion) in; making up: *12 to the dozen.* **15.** (used for indicating the indirect object of a verb or for connecting a verb with its complement): *Give it to me.* **16.** (used as the ordinary sign of the infinitive, as in expressing motion, direction, or purpose.) **17.** *Math.* raised to the power indicated: *Three to the fourth is 81* ($3^4 = 81$). —*adv.* **18.** toward a point, person, place, or thing. **19.** toward a closed position: *Pull the door to.* **20.** toward a matter, action, or work. **21.** into a state of consciousness: *after he came to.* —***Idiom.* 22. to and fro,** alternately in opposite directions; back and forth: *trees swaying to and fro in the wind.*
toad (tōd), *n.* **1.** any of various mostly terrestrial, tailless amphibians that are close relatives of frogs in the order Anura, typically having dry, warty skin. Compare FROG[1] (def. 1). **2.** Also called **true toad.** a toad of the widespread and chiefly terrestrial family Bufonidae, having relatively short hind legs and warty skins. Compare FROG[1] (def. 2). **3.** a disgusting person or thing.
toad•fish (tōd′fish′), *n., pl.* (*esp. collectively*) **-fish,** (*esp. for kinds or species*) **-fish•es.** any bottom-dwelling fish of the family Batrachoididae, of U.S. Atlantic coasts, having a froglike head.
toad•stone (tōd′stōn′), *n.* any of various stonelike objects, usu. fossilized animal parts, formerly supposed to have been formed in the body of a toad, worn esp. as amulets to protect against poison.
toad•stool (tōd′sto͞ol′), *n.* **1.** any of various mushrooms having a stalk with an umbrellalike cap, esp. the agarics. **2.** a poisonous mushroom, as distinguished from an edible one. **3.** any of various other fleshy fungi, as the puffballs and coral fungi.
toad•y (tō′dē), *n., pl.* **toad•ies,** *v.,* **toad•ied, toad•y•ing.** —*n.* **1.** an obsequious flatterer; sycophant. —*v.i.* **2.** to be a toady. —**toad′y•ish,** *adj.* —**toad′y•ism,** *n.*
to′-and-fro′, *adj., n., pl.* **to-and-fros, tos-and-fros,** *v., pres. part.* **to•ing-and-fro•ing.** —*adj.* **1.** back-and-forth: *to-and-fro motion.* —*n.* **2.** a continuous or regular movement backward and forward: *the to-and-fro of the surf.* —*v.i.* **3.** to move or go back and forth (used only in present participle): *soldiers toing-and-froing; toing and froing on policy decisions.*
toast[1] (tōst), *n.* **1.** sliced bread that has been browned by dry heat. —*v.t.* **2.** to brown (bread, cheese, etc.) by exposure to heat. **3.** to heat or warm thoroughly at a fire: *to toast one's feet at the fireplace.* —*v.i.* **4.** to become toasted. —***Idiom.* 5. be toast,** *Slang.* to be doomed, ruined, or in trouble: *If you come here again, you're toast!*
toast[2] (tōst), *n.* **1.** a few words of welcome, congratulation, etc., uttered immediately before drinking to a person, event, etc. **2.** a person, event, etc., honored with raised glasses before drinking. **3.** an act or instance of thus drinking: *to drink a toast to the queen.* **4.** a person, esp. an entertainer, who is widely celebrated: *She was the toast of five continents.* —*v.t.* **5.** to propose or drink a toast to or in honor of. —*v.i.* **6.** to propose or drink a toast.
toast•er (tō′stər), *n.* **1.** an instrument or appliance for toasting bread, muffins, etc. **2.** a person who toasts something.
toast′er ov′en, *n.* an electrical appliance that functions as both an oven and a toaster.
toast•mas•ter (tōst′mas′tər, -mä′stər), *n.* **1.** a person who presides at a dinner and introduces the after-dinner speakers. **2.** a person who proposes or announces toasts.
toast•mis•tress (tōst′mis′trəs), *n.* a woman who assumes the duties of toastmaster.
toast•y (tō′stē), *adj.,* **toast•i•er, toast•i•est. 1.** cozily warm. **2.** of or resembling toast: *toasty aromas.* —**toast′i•ness,** *n.*
Tob., Tobit.
to•bac•co (tə bak′ō), *n., pl.* **-cos, -coes. 1.** any plant of the genus *Nicotiana,* of the nightshade family, esp. any of the species, as *N. tabacum,* whose leaves are prepared for smoking or chewing or as snuff. **2.** the prepared leaves, as used in cigarettes, cigars, and pipes. **3.** any product made from such leaves. —**to•bac′co•less,** *adj.*
to•bac•co•nist (tə bak′ə nist), *n.* a dealer in tobacco, esp. the owner of a store that sells pipe tobaccos, cigarettes, and cigars.
To•ba•go (tə bā′gō), *n.* an island in the SE West Indies, off the NE coast of Venezuela: formerly a British colony, now part of Trinidad and Tobago. 45,000; 117 sq. mi. (303 sq. km). —**To•ba•go•ni•an** (tō′bə gō′nē ən, -gōn′yən), *n.*
to-be′, *adj.* future; soon to be (used in combination): *bride-to-be.*
To•bi•as (tə bī′əs), *n.* the son of Tobit.
To•bit (tō′bit), *n.* **1.** a book of the Apocrypha. **2.** a devout Jew whose story is recorded in this book.
to•bog•gan (tə bog′ən), *n.* **1.** a long, narrow, flat-bottomed sled made of a thin board curved upward and backward at the front, used esp. in downhill coasting. —*v.i.* **2.** to coast on a toboggan. **3.** to plummet, as prices. —**to•bog′gan•er, to•bog′gan•ist,** *n.*
toc•ca•ta (tə kä′tə), *n. pl.* **-tas, -te** (-tē, -tā). a composition in the style of an improvisation, for the piano, organ, or other keyboard instrument, intended to exhibit the player's technique.
Tocque•ville (tōk′vil, tok′-), *n.* **Alexis Charles Henri Maurice Clérel de,** 1805–59, French statesman and author.
toc•sin (tok′sin), *n.* **1.** a signal, esp. of alarm, sounded on a bell or bells. **2.** a bell used to sound an alarm.
to•day (tə dā′), *n.* **1.** this present day. **2.** this present age: *the world of today.* —*adv.* **3.** on this present day: *Call me today.* **4.** at the present time; in these days. —*adj.* **5.** up-to-date: *the today look.*
tod•dle (tod′l), *v.,* **-dled, -dling,** *n.* —*v.i.* **1.** to move with short, unsteady steps, as a young child. —*n.* **2.** the act of toddling. **3.** an unsteady gait.
tod•dler (tod′lər), *n.* a person who toddles, esp. a young child learning to walk. —**tod′dler•hood′,** *n.*
tod•dy (tod′ē), *n., pl.* **-dies.** a drink of liquor and usu. hot water, sweetened and sometimes spiced.
to-do′, *n., pl.* **-dos.** bustle; fuss: *to make a big to-do over dinner.*
toe (tō), *n., v.,* **toed, toe•ing.** —*n.* **1.** one of the terminal digits of the foot. **2.** the forepart of a hoof. **3.** the forepart of a shoe or stocking. **4.** a part resembling a toe in shape or position. **5. a.** a journal or part placed vertically in a bearing, as the lower end of a vertical shaft. **b.** a curved partial cam lifting the flat surface of a follower and letting it drop; wiper. **6.** the outer end of the head of a golf club. —*v.t.* **7.** to furnish with a toe or toes. **8.** to touch with the toes. **9.** to kick with the toe. **10.** to strike (a golf ball) with the toe of the club. —*v.i.* **11.** to stand, walk, etc., with the toes in a specified position: *to toe in.* **12.** to tap with the toe, as in dancing. —***Idiom.* 13. on one's toes,** energetic; alert; ready: *Competition will keep you on your toes.* **14. step** or **tread on someone's toes,** to offend a person by encroaching on his or her rights or responsibilities. **15. toe the line** or **mark, a.** to conform strictly to a rule, command, etc. **b.** to do one's duty. —**toe′less,** *adj.* —**toe′like′,** *adj.*
toe′ dance′, *n.* a dance performed on the tips of the toes. —**toe′-dance′,** *v.i.,* **-danced, -danc•ing.** —**toe′ danc′er,** *n.*
toe′hold′ or **toe′-hold′,** *n.* **1.** a small ledge or niche just large enough to support the toes, as in climbing. **2.** any slight advantage, support, or the like, that aids progress. **3.** an illegal wrestling hold in which the foot or toes are twisted.
toe′ loop′, *n.* a figure-skating jump in which the skater takes off from the back outer edge of one skate, makes one full rotation in the air, and lands on the back outer edge of the same skate.
toe•nail (tō′nāl′), *n.* **1.** the nail of a toe. **2.** a nail driven obliquely to secure a piece of wood to a beam. —*v.t.* **3.** to secure with oblique nailing.
toe•shoe (tō′sho͞o′), *n.* a dance slipper fitted with a thick, reinforced toe to enable a person to toe-dance.
toe′-to-toe′, *adj.* **1.** being in direct confrontation or opposition. —*adv.* **2.** in a position or attitude of direct confrontation: *slugging it out toe-to-toe.*
tof•fee or **tof•fy** (tô′fē, tof′ē), *n.* a brittle confection made by boiling together brown sugar, butter, and vinegar.
to•fu (tō′fo͞o), *n.* a soft cheeselike food made from curdled soybean milk. [< Japanese]
tog (tog), *n., v.,* **togged, tog•ging.** —*n.* **1.** a coat. **2.** Usu., **togs.** clothes. —*v.t.* **3.** to dress (often fol. by *out* or *up*).
to•ga (tō′gə), *n., pl.* **-gas, -gae** (-jē, -gē). **1.** (in ancient Rome) the traditional formal outer garment of white wool worn by freeborn men. **2.** a robe of office or other distinctive garment. —**to′gaed,** *adj.*
to•geth•er (tə geth′ər), *adv.* **1.** into or in one gathering, company, or body: *Call the people together.* **2.** into or in union, proximity, collision, etc., as two or more things: *to sew things together.* **3.** into relationship, agreement, etc., as two or more persons: *to bring strangers together.* **4.** considered collectively: *to cost more than all the others together.* **5.** (of a single thing) into a condition of compactness or coherence: *to squeeze a thing together.* **6.** at the same time; simultaneously. **7.** continuously; uninterruptedly: *for days together.* **8.** in cooperation; with united action; conjointly: *to undertake a task together.* **9.** with mutual action; reciprocally: *conferring together.* —*adj.* **10.** *Informal.* emotionally stable and well organized: *a very together person.* —**Usage.** See ALTOGETHER.
to•geth•er•ness (tə geth′ər nis), *n.* **1.** warm fellowship, as among members of a family. **2.** the quality or condition of being together.
tog•gle (tog′əl), *n., v.,* **-gled, -gling.** —*n.* **1.** a pin, bolt, or rod placed transversely through a chain, an eye or loop in a rope, etc., as to bind it

temporarily to another chain or rope similarly treated. **2.** a toggle joint, or a device having one. **3.** an ornamental, rod-shaped button for inserting into a large buttonhole, loop, or frog, used esp. on sports clothes. —*v.t.* **4.** to furnish with a toggle. **5.** to bind or fasten with a toggle. **6.** to control or manipulate with a toggle switch. —*v.i.* **7.** to shift back and forth between two settings or modes of computer operation by means of a key or programmed keystroke. —**tog′gler,** *n.*

tog′gle bolt′, *n.* a bolt anchored to a hole drilled through a hollow wall by two hinged wings fixed to its end and opened by a spring.

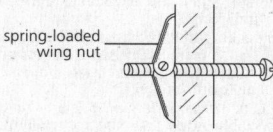

spring-loaded wing nut

toggle bolt

tog′gle joint′, *n.* any of various devices consisting basically of a rod that can be inserted into an object and then manipulated so that the inserted part spreads or becomes offset, allowing it to be used as a support, handle, linkage, lever, etc.

tog′gle switch′, *n.* an electrical switch controlled by a projecting knob or arm that can be moved through a small arc.

To•go (tō′gō), *n.* **Republic of,** a country in W Africa on the Gulf of Guinea: formerly a French mandate; gained independence in 1960. 4,735,610; 21,925 sq. mi. (56,785 sq. km). *Cap.:* Lomé. —**To′go•lese′** (-gə lēz′, -lēs′), *adj., n., pl.* **-lese.**

toil[1] (toil), *n.* **1.** exhausting labor or effort. **2.** a laborious task. —*v.i.* **3.** to labor arduously. **4.** to move or travel with great effort or weariness. —*v.t.* **5.** to accomplish by unremitting labor. —**toil′er,** *n.*

toil[2] (toil), *n.* Usu., **toils.** a net or series of nets in which game is trapped. **2.** a trap or snare.

toile (twäl), *n.* any of various transparent linens and cottons.

toi•let (toi′lit), *n.* **1.** a bathroom fixture consisting of a bowl, usu. with a hinged seat and lid, and a device for flushing with water, used for defecation and urination. **2.** a bathroom or washroom; lavatory. **3.** a dressing room, esp. one containing a bath. **4.** the act or process of dressing or grooming oneself. **5.** the dress or costume of a person. Also, **toilette** (for defs. 4, 5).

toi′let pa′per, *n.* a soft, lightweight paper used in bathrooms for personal cleansing after defecation or urination. Also called **toi′let tis′sue.**

toi•let•ry (toi′li trē), *n., pl.* **-ries.** any article or preparation used in cleaning or grooming oneself, as soap or deodorant.

toi′let set′, *n.* a set of articles used in grooming, as a mirror, brush, and comb.

toi′let soap′, *n.* a mild and usu. perfumed soap for washing the skin.

toi•lette (twä let′), *n.* TOILET (defs. 4, 5).

toi′let train′ing, *n.* the training of a very young child to control bowel and bladder movements and use the toilet. —**toi′let-train′,** *v.t.*

toi′let wa′ter, *n.* a scented liquid used as a cologne or light perfume.

toil•some (toil′səm), *adj.* demanding toil; laborious or fatiguing.

to•kay (tō kā′), *n.* a large gecko, *Gekko gecko,* of SE Asia.

To•kay (tō kā′), *n.* **1.** an aromatic wine made near the town of Tokay in NE Hungary. **2.** a large, red variety of grape, grown for table use. **3.** a strong, sweet white wine of California.

to•ken (tō′kən), *n.* **1.** something serving to represent or indicate some feeling, event, fact, etc.; sign: *Black is a token of mourning.* **2.** something offered or taken as evidence or proof: *This badge will be the token of your authority.* **3.** a memento; souvenir. **4.** a stamped piece of metal, issued as a limited medium of exchange, as for bus fares or bridge tolls. **5.** an item, idea, etc., representing a group; a part as representing the whole; sample. **6.** a person who has been hired, admitted, enrolled, etc., to forestall charges of prejudice or discrimination, as against a minority. **7.** a particular instance in speech or writing of a word, symbol, or linguistic expression. —*v.t.* **8.** to be a token of; signify; symbolize. —*adj.* **9.** serving as a token: *a token male on an all-female staff.* **10.** slight; minimal: *token resistance.* —*Idiom.* **11. by the same token,** for similar reasons; furthermore. **12. in token of,** as a sign of; in evidence of: *a ring in token of one's love.*

to•ken•ism (tō′kə niz′əm), *n.* the practice or policy of making no more than a minimal effort to offer opportunities to minorities equal to those of the majority. —**to′ken•is′tic,** *adj.*

to′ken pay′ment, *n.* a small payment binding an agreement or partially repaying a debt.

To•kyo (tō′kē ō′), *n.* the capital of Japan, on Tokyo Bay in SE Honshu. 11,618,281. Formerly, **Edo, Yedo.** —**To′kyo•ite′,** *n.*

told (tōld), *v.* pt. and pp. of TELL. —*Idiom.* **2. all told,** counting everyone or everything; in all.

tole (tōl), *n.* **1.** enameled or lacquered metal, often gilded, used esp. in the 18th century for trays, boxes, etc. **2.** articles made of this.

To•le•do (tə lē′dō; *for 2, 3 also* -lā′-), *n., pl.* **-dos** *for 3.* **1.** a port in NW Ohio, on Lake Erie. 322,550. **2.** a city in central Spain, on the Ta-

gus River. 57,769. **3.** a sword or sword blade of finely tempered steel, as formerly made in Toledo, Spain.

tol•er•a•ble (tol′ər ə bəl), *adj.* **1.** capable of being tolerated; endurable. **2.** fairly good; not bad. **3.** *Chiefly Dial.* in fair health. —**tol′er•a•ble•ness, tol′er•a•bil′i•ty,** *n.* —**tol′er•a•bly,** *adv.*

tol•er•ance (tol′ər əns), *n.* **1.** a fair and permissive attitude toward those whose race, religion, nationality, etc., differ from one's own; freedom from bigotry. **2.** a fair and permissive attitude toward opinions and practices that differ from one's own. **3.** any liberal, undogmatic viewpoint. **4.** the act or capacity of enduring; endurance: *My tolerance of noise is limited.* **5. a.** the power of enduring or resisting the action of a drug, poison, etc. **b.** the lack of, or low levels of, immune response to transplanted tissue or other foreign substance. **6.** *Mach.* **a.** the permissible range of variation in a dimension of an object. **b.** the permissible variation of an object or objects in some characteristic such as hardness, weight, or quantity. **7.** a permissible deviation in the fineness and weight of coin.

tol•er•ant (tol′ər ənt), *adj.* **1.** inclined or disposed to tolerate; showing tolerance; forbearing: *tolerant of errors.* **2.** favoring toleration: *a tolerant church.* **3. a.** able to endure or resist the action of a drug, poison, etc. **b.** lacking, or exhibiting low levels of, immune response to a normally immunogenic substance. —**tol′er•ant•ly,** *adv.*

tol•er•ate (tol′ə rāt′), *v.t.,* **-at•ed, -at•ing. 1.** to allow the existence, presence, practice, or act of without prohibition or hindrance; permit. **2.** to endure without repugnance; put up with: *I cannot tolerate incompetence.* **3.** to experience, undergo, or sustain, as pain or hardship. **4.** *Med.* to endure or resist the action of (a drug, invasive procedure, etc.).

tol•er•a•tion (tol′ə rā′shən), *n.* **1.** an act or instance of tolerating, esp. of allowing, enduring, or accepting what is not actually approved; forbearance. **2.** allowance by law or government of the exercise of religions other than an established one. —**tol′er•a′tion•ism,** *n.* —**tol′er•a′tion•ist,** *n.*

toll[1] (tōl), *n.* **1.** a payment or fee exacted, as by the state, for some right or privilege, as for passage along a road or over a bridge. **2.** the extent of loss, damage, suffering, etc., resulting from some action or calamity: *The toll was 300 persons dead or missing.* **3.** a tax, duty, or tribute, as for services or use of facilities. **4.** a payment made for a long-distance telephone call. **5.** a compensation for services, as for transportation or transmission. —*v.t.* **6.** to collect (something) as toll. **7.** to impose a tax or toll on (a person). —*v.i.* **8.** to collect toll; levy toll.

toll[2] (tōl), *v.t.* **1.** to cause (a large bell) to sound with single strokes slowly and regularly repeated. **2.** to sound or strike (a knell, the hour, etc.) by such strokes. **3.** to announce by this means; ring a knell for (a dying or dead person). **4.** to summon or dismiss by tolling. **5.** Also, **tole.** to allure; entice. —*v.i.* **6.** to sound with single strokes slowly and regularly repeated, as a bell. —*n.* **7.** the act of tolling a bell. **8.** one of the strokes made in tolling a bell. **9.** the sound made. —**toll′er,** *n.*

toll•booth (tōl′bōōth′, -bōōth′), *n., pl.* **-booths** (-bōōthz′, -bōōths′). a booth, as at a bridge or the entrance to a toll road, where a toll is collected.

toll′ bridge′, *n.* a bridge at which a toll is charged.

toll′ call′, *n.* any telephone call involving a higher base rate than that fixed for a local message.

toll′-free′, *adj.* **1.** made, used, provided, etc., without tolls or a charge. —*adv.* **2.** free of charge.

toll•gate (tōl′gāt′), *n.* a gate where a toll is collected.

toll•house (tōl′hous′), *n., pl.* **-hous•es** (-hou′ziz). a house or booth at a tollgate.

toll′house cook′ie, *n.* a crisp cookie containing bits of chocolate and sometimes chopped nuts.

toll′ road′, *n.* a road or highway on which a toll is exacted.

Tol•stoy or **Tol•stoi** (tōl′stoi, tol′-, tōl stoi′, tol-), *n.* **Leo** or **Lev Nikolaevich, Count,** 1828–1910, Russian novelist and social critic. —**Tol′stoy•an,** *adj., n.*

tom (tom), *n.* **1.** the male of various animals, as the turkey. **2.** a tomcat.

tom•a•hawk (tom′ə hôk′), *n.* **1.** a light ax used by American Indians as a weapon or tool. **2.** any similar weapon or implement. **3.** (in Australia) a stone hatchet of the Aborigines. —*v.t.* **4.** to attack, wound, or kill with or as if with a tomahawk. [< Algonquian]

to•ma•til•lo (tō′mə tē′ō, -tēl′yō), *n., pl.* **-los, -los.** a plant of Mexico and the southern U.S., *Physalis ixocarpa,* of the nightshade family, one variety of which produces a small, green, tomatolike fruit used in cooking.

to•ma•to (tə mā′tō, -mä′-), *n., pl.* **-toes. 1.** a large, mildly acid, pulpy berry, red to red-yellow when ripe, eaten raw or cooked as a vegetable. **2.** the plant bearing this berry, *Lycopersicon esculentum,* of the nightshade family.

tomb (tōōm), *n.* **1.** an excavation in earth or rock for the burial of a corpse; grave. **2.** a mausoleum, burial chamber, or the like. **3.** a monument for housing or commemorating a dead person. **4.** any sepulchral structure. —*v.t.* **5.** to place in or as if in a tomb; entomb; bury.

Tom•baugh (tom′bô), *n.* **Clyde William,** born 1906, U.S. astronomer: discovered the planet Pluto 1930.

tom•boy (tom′boi′), *n.* an energetic, boisterous girl whose behavior and pursuits are considered typical of boys. —**tom′boy•ish,** *adj.*

T

tomb•stone (to͞om′stōn′), *n.* a stone marker, usu. inscribed, on a tomb or grave.
tom•cat (tom′kat′), *n.* a male cat.
Tom′, Dick′, and Har′ry, *n.* the ordinary person; people generally; everyone: *They invited every Tom, Dick, and Harry to the party.*
tome (tōm), *n.* **1.** a book, esp. a very heavy, large, or learned book. **2.** a volume forming a part of a larger work.
-tome, a combining form with the meanings "cutting instrument" (*microtome*), "segment, somite" (*dermatome*).
tom•fool (tom′fo͞ol′), *n.* **1.** a grossly foolish or stupid person; a silly fool. **—***adj.* **2.** being or characteristic of a tomfool. —**tom′fool′ish,** *adj.* —**tom′fool′ish•ness,** *n.*
tom•fool•er•y (tom′fo͞o′lə rē), *n., pl.* **-er•ies. 1.** foolish or silly behavior. **2.** a silly act, matter, or thing.
Tom′my gun′, *n.* **1.** Thompson submachine gun. **2.** any submachine gun.
tom•my•rot (tom′ē rot′), *n.* nonsense; utter foolishness.
tomo-, a combining form meaning "a cut, section": *tomography.*
to•mog•ra•phy (tə mog′rə fē), *n.* a method of making x-ray photographs of a selected plane of the body. **—to•mo•graph•ic** (tō′mə-graf′ik), *adj.* —**to′mo•graph′i•cal•ly,** *adv.*
to•mor•row (tə môr′ō, -mor′ō), *n.* **1.** the day following today. **2.** a future period or time. **—***adv.* **3.** on the day following today. **4.** at some future time. **—*Saying.* 5. Tomorrow is another day,** life may be better tomorrow: popularized by Margaret Mitchell's novel and the motion picture *Gone With the Wind.*
Tomp•kins (tomp′kinz), *n.* **Daniel D.,** 1774–1825, vice president of the U.S. 1817–25.
Tom′ Saw′yer, (*The Adventures of Tom Sawyer*) a novel (1876) by Mark Twain.
Tom′ Thumb′, *n.* **1.** a diminutive hero of folk tales. **2.** a very small person; dwarf. **3. General,** nickname of Charles Sherwood Stratton.
tom-tom (tom′tom′), *n.* **1.** a drum of American Indian or Asian origin, commonly played with the hands. **2.** a dully repetitious drumbeat or similar sound.
-tomy, a combining form meaning "cutting, dissection" (*zootomy*), "division" (*trichotomy*), "surgical incision" into an organ (*lobotomy*), "excision" of an object (*lithotomy*).
ton (tun), *n.* **1.** a unit of weight, equivalent to 2000 pounds (0.907 metric ton) avoirdupois **(short ton)** in the U.S. and 2240 pounds (1.016 metric tons) avoirdupois **(long ton)** in Great Britain. **2.** Also called **freight ton.** a unit of volume for freight that weighs one ton, varying with the type of freight measured, as 40 cubic feet of oak timber or 20 bushels of wheat. **3.** METRIC TON. **4.** DISPLACEMENT TON. **5.** a unit of volume used in transportation by sea, commonly equal to 40 cubic feet (1.13 cu. m) **(shipping ton** or **measurement ton). 6.** a unit of internal capacity of ships, equal to 100 cubic feet (2.83 cu. m) **(register ton). 7.** Often, **tons.** a great quantity; a lot: *a ton of jokes.*
ton•al (tōn′l), *adj.* pertaining to or having tonality. —**ton′al•ly,** *adv.*
to•nal•i•ty (tō nal′i tē), *n., pl.* **-ties. 1. a.** the sum of relations, melodic and harmonic, existing between the tones of a scale or musical system. **b.** a particular scale or system of tones; a key. **2.** (in painting, graphics, etc.) the system of tones or tints, or the color scheme, of a picture. **3.** the quality of tones.
tone (tōn), *n., v.,* **toned, ton•ing. —***n.* **1.** any sound considered with reference to its quality, pitch, strength, source, etc.: *shrill tones.* **2.** quality or character of sound. **3.** vocal sound; the sound made by vibrating muscular bands in the larynx. **4.** a particular quality, way of sounding, modulation, or intonation of the voice. **5.** an accent peculiar to a person, people, locality, etc., or a characteristic mode of sounding words in speech. **6.** a pitch or movement in pitch serving to distinguish two words otherwise composed of the same sounds, as in Chinese. **7.** the pitch, relative pitch, or change in pitch of a syllable, word, phrase, etc. **8. a.** a musical sound of definite pitch, consisting of several partial tones, the lowest being the fundamental and the others the harmonics or overtones. **b.** WHOLE STEP. **9.** a quality of color with reference to the degree of absorption or reflection of light; a tint or shade; value. **10.** a slight modification of a given color; hue. **11.** the prevailing effect of harmony of color and values. **12. a.** the normal state of tension or responsiveness of the organs or tissues of the body. **b.** that state of the body or of an organ in which all its functions are performed with healthy vigor. **13. a.** a normal healthy mental condition. **b.** a particular mental state or disposition. **14.** a particular style or manner, as of writing or speech; mood. **15.** prevailing character or style, as of manners, morals, or philosophical outlook: *the liberal tone of the 1960s.* **16.** style, distinction, or elegance. **—***v.t.* **17.** to sound with a particular tone. **18.** to give the proper tone to (a musical instrument). **19.** to modify the tone or general coloring of. **20.** to give the desired tone to (a painting, drawing, etc.). **21.** to render as specified in tone or coloring. **22.** to modify the tone or character of. **23.** to give or restore physical or mental tone to. **—***v.i.* **24.** to take on a particular tone; assume color or tint. **25. tone down, a.** to become or cause to become softened or moderated. **b.** to make (a painted color) less intense in hue; subdue. **26. tone up, a.** to give a higher or stronger tone to. **b.** to gain or cause to gain in tone or strength. **27. tone (in) with,** to harmonize or blend well with. —**tone′less,** *adj.* —**tone′less•ly,** *adv.* —**tone′less•ness,** *n.*
tone′-deaf′, *adj.* unable to distinguish differences in pitch in musical sounds when producing or hearing them. —**tone′ deaf′ness,** *n.*
ton•er (tō′nər), *n.* **1.** a highly concentrated organic pigment. **2.** a powder, either dry or dispersed in an organic liquid, used in xerography to produce the final image. **3.** a cosmetic preparation for restoring firmness to the skin.
tong[1] (tông, tong), *n.* **1.** TONGS. **—***v.t.* **2.** to lift, seize, gather, hold, or handle with tongs, as logs or oysters. **—***v.i.* **3.** to use or work with tongs.
tong[2] (tông, tong), *n.* **1.** (in China) an association, society, or political party. **2.** (among Chinese living in the U.S.) a fraternal or secret society, often associated with criminal activities.
ton•ga (tong′gə), *n., pl.* **-gas.** (in S Asia) a light two-wheeled horse-drawn vehicle. [< Hindi *tāṅgā*]
Ton•ga (tong′gə), *n.* a kingdom consisting of three groups of islands in the SW Pacific, E of Fiji: a former British protectorate. 100,105; 289 sq. mi. (748 sq. km). *Cap.:* Nukualofa. Also called **Ton′ga Is′lands, Friendly Islands.** —**Ton′gan,** *adj., n.*
tongs (tôngz, tongz), *n.* (*usu. with a pl. v.*) any of various implements consisting of two movable arms fastened together, used for picking up an object (usu. used with *pair of*).
tongue (tung), *n., v.* **tongued, tongu•ing. —***n.* **1.** a movable organ in the floor of the mouth, functioning in tasting, eating, and, in humans, speaking. **2.** the tongue of an animal, as an ox, beef, or sheep, used for food, often prepared by smoking or pickling. **3.** the faculty or power of speech. **4.** manner or character of speech: *a flattering tongue.* **5.** the language of a particular people, region, or nation. **6.** (in the Bible) a people or nation distinguished by its language. **7. tongues,** speech, often incomprehensible, typically uttered during moments of religious ecstasy. **8.** a strip of leather or other material under the lacing or fastening of a shoe. **9.** a piece of metal suspended inside a bell that strikes against the side, producing a sound; clapper. **10.** a vibrating reed or similar structure in a musical instrument. **11.** the pole extending from a carriage or other vehicle between the animals drawing it. **12.** a projecting strip along the center of the edge or end of a board, for fitting into a groove in another board. **13.** a narrow strip of land extending into a body of water; cape. **14.** the pin of a buckle, brooch, etc. **—***v.t.* **15.** to articulate (tones played on a clarinet, trumpet, etc.) by strokes of the tongue. **16. a.** to cut a tongue on (a board). **b.** to join or fit together by a tongue-and-groove joint. **17.** to touch with the tongue. **18.** to articulate or pronounce. **—***v.i.* **19.** to tongue tones played on a clarinet, trumpet, etc. **20.** to project like a tongue. **—*Idiom.* 21. at** or **on the tip of one's** or **the tongue, a.** on the verge of being said. **b.** eluding the memory but about to be recalled: *The answer is on the tip of my tongue.* **22. give tongue,** (of a hound in fox hunting) to bay while following a scent. **23. give tongue to,** to utter; speak. **24. hold one's tongue,** to remain silent; refrain from speaking. **25. (with) tongue in cheek,** as a joke; ironically. —**tongue′less,** *adj.* —**tongue′like′,** *adj.*
tongue′-lash′, *v.t., v.i.* to scold severely.
tongue′-tie′, *n., v.,* **-tied, -ty•ing. —***n.* **1.** impeded motion of the tongue caused esp. by shortness of the frenum, which binds it to the floor of the mouth. **—***v.t.* **2.** to make tongue-tied.
tongue′-tied′, *adj.* **1.** unable to speak, as from shyness, embarrassment, or surprise. **2.** affected with tongue-tie.
tongue′ twist′er, *n.* a word or sequence of words difficult to pronounce, esp. rapidly, because of alliteration or a slight variation of consonant sounds, as "She sells seashells by the seashore."
ton•ic (ton′ik), *n.* **1.** a medicine that invigorates or strengthens. **2.** anything invigorating physically, mentally, or morally. **3.** TONIC WATER. **4.** the first degree of a musical scale; keynote. **5.** *Chiefly Eastern New Eng.* soda pop. **6.** a tonic syllable or accent. **—***adj.* **7.** pertaining to, maintaining, increasing, or restoring the tone or health of the body or an organ, as a medicine. **8.** invigorating physically, mentally, or morally. **9. a.** pertaining to tension, as of the muscles. **b.** marked by continued muscular tension: *a tonic spasm.* **10.** of or pertaining to tone or accent in speech. **11.** pertaining to or being a tone language. **12.** (of a syllable) bearing the principal stress or accent, usu. accompanied by a change in pitch. **13.** pertaining to or based on the first tone of a musical scale: *a tonic chord.* —**ton′i•cal•ly,** *adv.*
to•nic•i•ty (tō nis′i tē), *n.* **1.** tonic quality or condition. **2.** the state of bodily tone.
ton′ic wa′ter, *n.* carbonated water containing lemon, lime, sweetener, and quinine, often used as a mixer. Also called **tonic, quinine water.**
to•night (tə nīt′), *n.* **1.** the present or coming night; the night of the present day. **—***adv.* **2.** on the present night; on the night of the present day.
ton′ka bean′ (tong′kə), *n.* the fragrant black seed of a tropical American tree, *Dipteryx odorata,* or related species: used in perfumes and as a vanilla substitute.
ton′-mile′, *n.* a unit of measurement equivalent to a ton of freight transported one mile. —**ton′-mile′age,** *n.*
ton•nage (tun′ij), *n.* **1.** the capacity of a merchant vessel, expressed either in units of weight, as deadweight tons, or of volume, as gross tons. **2.** ships collectively considered with reference to their carrying capacity or together with their cargoes. **3.** a duty on ships or boats at so much per ton of cargo or freight, or according to the capacity in tons.
tonne (tun), *n.* METRIC TON.
ton•neau (tu nō′), *n., pl.* **-neaus, -neaux** (-nōz′). a rear part or compartment of an automobile body, containing seats for passengers.

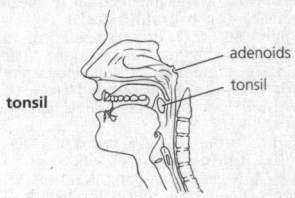

tonsil

ton·sil (ton′səl), *n.* a prominent oval mass of lymphoid tissue on each side of the throat. —**ton′sil·lar,** *adj.*

ton·sil·lec·to·my (ton′sə lek′tə mē), *n., pl.* **-mies.** the operation of excising or removing one or both tonsils.

ton·sil·li·tis (ton′sə lī′tis), *n.* inflammation of a tonsil or the tonsils.

ton·so·ri·al (ton sôr′ē əl, -sōr′-), *adj.* of or pertaining to a barber or barbering.

ton·sure (ton′shər), *n., v.,* **-sured, -sur·ing.** —*n.* **1.** the shaving of the head or of a part of it, as upon entering the priestood or a monastic order. **2.** the part of a cleric's head, usu. the crown, left bare by shaving the hair. **3.** the state of being shorn. —*v.t.* **4.** to subject to tonsure.

ton·tine (ton′tēn, ton tēn′), *n.* an annuity scheme in which subscribers share a common fund with the benefit of survivorship, the survivors' shares being increased as the subscribers die, until the whole goes to the last survivor. [< French, after Lorenzo *Tonti,* Neapolitan banker who started the scheme in France c1653]

ton·y (tō′nē), *adj.,* **ton·i·er, ton·i·est.** stylish; swank: *a tony nightclub.*

To·ny (tō′nē), *n., pl.* **-nys.** one of a group of awards given annually by the American Theatre Wing for superior achievements in production and performance in the Broadway theater.

too (tōō), *adv.* **1.** in addition; also; moreover: *young, clever, and rich too.* **2.** to an excessive or marked degree; beyond what is usual, desirable, fitting, etc.: *too sick to travel; too suprised for words.* **3.** more, as specified, than should be: *too near the fire.* **4.** (used as an emphatic affirmative to contradict a negative statement): *I am too!* **5.** extremely; very (usu. with a negative): *none too pleased with the results.*

took (tŏŏk), *v.* pt. of TAKE.

tool (tōōl), *n.* **1.** an implement, esp. one held in the hand, as a hammer, saw, or file, for performing or facilitating mechanical operations. **2.** any instrument of manual operation. **3.** the cutting or machining part of a lathe, planer, drill, or similar machine. **4.** the machine itself; a machine tool. **5.** anything used as a means of accomplishing a task or purpose: *Education is a tool for success.* **6.** a person manipulated by another for the latter's own ends; cat's-paw. —*v.t.* **7.** to work or shape with a tool. **8.** to work decoratively with a hand tool. **9.** to ornament (a book cover) with a bookbinder's tool. **10.** to drive (a vehicle). **11.** to equip with tools or machinery. —*v.i.* **12.** to work with a tool. **13.** to drive or ride in a vehicle: *tooling along the freeway.* **14. tool up,** to install machinery and tools for performing a job. —**tool′er,** *n.*

tool·box (tōōl′boks′), *n.* a box or case in which tools are kept. Also called **tool′ chest′.**

tool·ing (tōō′ling), *n.* **1.** work or ornamentation done with a tool, as on wood, stone, or leather. **2. a.** the process of equipping a factory with machinery and tools for a particular manufacturing process. **b.** a number of tools, as in a particular factory.

tool·mak·er (tōōl′mā′kər), *n.* **1.** a machinist skilled in the building and reconditioning of tools, jigs, and related devices used in a machine shop. **2.** one that fashions tools. —**tool′mak′ing,** *n.*

tool·room (tōōl′rōōm′, -rŏŏm′), *n.* a room, as in a machine shop, in which tools are stored, repaired, produced, etc.

tool·shed (tōōl′shed′), *n.* a small building where tools are stored, often in the backyard of a house.

Too′ner·ville trol′ley (tōō′nər vil′), *n.* a dilapidated, outmoded trolley line or railway. [after the train in the comic strip *Toonerville Trolley* by U.S. cartoonist Fontaine T. Fox (1884–1964)]

toot (tōōt), *v.i.* **1.** (of a horn or whistle) to give forth its characteristic sound. **2.** to make a sound resembling that of a horn or whistle. **3.** to sound or blow a horn, whistle, or wind instrument. —*v.t.* **4.** to cause (a horn, whistle, or wind instrument) to sound. **5.** to sound (notes, music, etc.) on a horn or the like. —*n.* **6.** an act or sound of tooting.

tooth (tōōth), *n., pl.* **teeth,** *v.,* **toothed** (tōōtht, tōōthd), **tooth·ing** (tōō′thing, -thing). —*n.* **1.** (in most vertebrates) one of the hard bodies or processes usu. attached in a row to each jaw, serving for the prehension and mastication of food, as weapons of attack or defense, etc., and in mammals typically composed chiefly of dentin surrounding a sensitive pulp and covered on the crown with enamel. **2.** (in invertebrates) any of various similar or analogous processes occurring in the mouth or alimentary canal, or on a shell. **3.** any projection resembling or suggesting a tooth. **4.** one of the projections of a comb, rake, saw, etc. **5. a.** any of the uniform projections on a gear or rack by which it drives or is driven by a gear, rack, or worm. **b.** any of the uniform projections on a sprocket by which it drives or is driven by a chain. **6.** taste, relish, or liking. **7. teeth,** effective power, esp. to enforce or accomplish something: *to put teeth into a law.* **8.** to furnish with teeth. —*v.i.* **9.** to interlock, as cogwheels. —***Idiom.* 10. cast** or **throw in someone's**

teeth, to reproach someone for, esp. aggressively. **11. in the teeth of,** straight into, against, or in defiance of. **12. long in the tooth,** noticeably old; elderly. **13. set** or **put one's teeth on edge,** to induce great discomfort or irritation in one: *The noise of the machine set my teeth on edge.* **14. set one's teeth,** to become resolute; prepare for difficulty. **15. show one's teeth,** to become menacing; reveal one's hostility. **16. sink** or **get one's teeth into,** to work on earnestly and enthusiastically. **17. to the teeth,** to the fullest extent; fully; entirely: *armed to the teeth.*

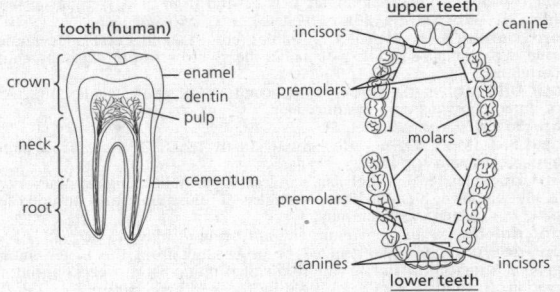

tooth (def. 1)

tooth·ache (tōōth′āk′), *n.* a pain in or about a tooth.

tooth′ and nail′, *adv.* with all one's resources or energy; fiercely: *We fought tooth and nail.*

tooth·brush (tōōth′brush′), *n.* a small brush with a long handle, for cleaning the teeth.

tooth′ decay′, *n.* DENTAL CARIES.

tooth′ fair′y, *n.* a fairy credited with leaving a child money or a small gift in exchange for a baby tooth placed under the child's pillow.

tooth·less (tōōth′lis), *adj.* **1.** lacking teeth. **2.** without a serrated edge: *a toothless saw.* **3.** lacking in force or sharpness; dull or ineffectual.

tooth·paste (tōōth′pāst′), *n.* a dentifrice in the form of paste.

tooth·pick (tōōth′pik′), *n.* a small pointed piece of wood, plastic, etc., for removing food particles from between the teeth.

tooth′ pow′der, *n.* a dentifrice in the form of a powder.

tooth·some (tōōth′səm), *adj.* **1.** pleasing to the taste; delicious; appetizing. **2.** pleasing or desirable.

tooth·wort (tōōth′wûrt′, -wôrt′), *n.* **1.** any parasitic plant of the genus *Lathraea,* of the broomrape family, having a rootstock covered with toothlike scales. **2.** any plant of the genus *Dentaria,* of the mustard family, having toothlike projections on the creeping rootstock.

tooth·y (tōō′thē, -thē), *adj.,* **-i·er, -i·est.** having or displaying conspicuous teeth: *a toothy smile.* —**tooth′i·ly,** *adv.* —**tooth′i·ness,** *n.*

too·tle (tōōt′l), *v.,* **-tled, -tling,** —*v.i.* **1.** to toot gently or repeatedly on a flute or the like. **2.** to proceed in a leisurely way. —*n.* **3.** the sound made by tooting on a flute or the like. —**too′tler,** *n.*

toots (tōōts), *n.* (*sometimes cap.*) an affectionate or familiar term of address (sometimes offensive when used to strangers, subordinates, etc.).

top[1] (top), *n., adj., v.,* **topped, top·ping.** —*n.* **1.** the highest point, part, or level of anything; summit. **2.** the uppermost or upper part, surface, end, etc., of anything. **3.** a lid or covering of a container. **4.** the highest or leading position or rank: *at the top of the class.* **5.** a person or thing occupying such a position. **6.** the highest pitch or degree: *at the top of one's voice.* **7.** the first or foremost part; beginning: *Take it from the top.* **8.** a garment for the upper body. **9.** a rooflike upper part or cover on a vehicle. **10. tops,** the part of a plant that grows above ground, esp. of an edible root. **11.** the head or crown of the head: *from top to toe.* **12.** the best or choicest part: *the top of the lot.* **13.** a platform surrounding the head of a lower mast on a ship and serving as a foothold, a means of extending the upper rigging, etc. **14.** (in bridge) the best card of a suit in a player's hand. **15.** the first half of an inning in baseball. **16.** *Chem.* the part of a mixture under distillation that volatilizes first. —*adj.* **17.** of, situated at, or forming the top; highest; uppermost; upper. **18.** highest in degree; greatest: *to pay top prices.* **19.** foremost, chief, or principal: *the top players.* **20.** highest in rank, quality, or popularity: *the top ten movies.* —*v.t.* **21.** to furnish with a top; put a top on. **22.** to be at or constitute the top of. **23.** to reach the top of. **24.** to rise above. **25.** to exceed in height, amount, number, etc. **26.** to surpass, excel, or outdo: *That tops everything.* **27.** to surmount with something specified. **28.** to remove the top of; crop; prune: *to top a tree.* **29.** to get or leap over the top of (a fence, barrier, etc.). **30.** *Chem.* to distill off only the most volatile part of (a mixture). **31.** to strike (a ball) above its center, giving it a forward spin. —*v.i.* **32.** to rise aloft. **33. top off, a.** to climax or complete, esp. in an exceptional manner; finish. **b.** to fill (a partly filled container, as a gas tank) to capacity. **34. top out, a.** to finish the top (of a structure). **b.** to reach the highest level. —***Idiom.* 35. at the top of one's lungs,** as loudly as possible; with full voice. **36. off the top of one's head,** without thought or preparation; extemporaneously. **37. on top,** successful; victorious; dominant. **38. on top of, a.** over or upon. **b.** in addition to; over and above. **c.** in

T

complete control: *on top of the problem.* **d.** very or overly close to: *living on top of each other.* **e.** close upon; following upon. **f.** aware of; informed about. **39. on top of the world,** elated; exuberant. **40. over the top, a.** over the top of a trench, as in charging the enemy. **b.** surpassing a goal, quota, or limit. —*Saying.* **41. There's always room at the top,** effort will be rewarded by success.

top² (top), *n.* **1.** a toy, often inversely conical, with a point on which it is made to spin. —*Idiom.* **2. sleep like a top,** to sleep soundly.

to•paz (tō′paz), *n.* **1.** a mineral, $Al_2(SiO_4)(OH,F)_2$, occurring in transparent crystal prisms and granular masses and used as a gem. **2.** CITRINE (def. 2). —**to′paz•ine′** (-pə zēn′, -zin), *adj.*

top′ banan′a, *n. Slang.* **1.** a leading comedian in burlesque, vaudeville, etc. Compare SECOND BANANA. **2.** the chief person in a group or undertaking.

top′ bill′ing, *n.* the first or most prominent position in a list of actors or entertainers, as on a marquee.

top′ brass′, *n.* BRASS (def. 5).

top•coat (top′kōt′), *n.* **1.** a lightweight overcoat. **2.** the coat of paint applied last to a surface.

top′ dog′, *n.* **1.** one that has acquired a position of highest authority. **2.** the winner of a competition or rivalry. **3.** the alpha male or alpha female in a dominance hierarchy.

top′ dol′lar, *n.* the maximum amount being or likely to be paid.

top′-down′, *adj.* **1.** organized or proceeding from the larger, more general structure to smaller, more detailed units, as in processing information. **2.** coming from or directed by those of highest rank.

top′ drawer′, *n.* the highest level in status, excellence, or importance. —**top′-drawer′,** *adj.*

tope (tōp), *n.* a small shark, *Galeorhinus galeus,* of European coasts.

To•pe•ka (tə pē′kə), *n.* the capital of Kansas, in the NE part, on the Kansas River. 120,646.

top′ flight′, *n.* the highest or most outstanding level, as in achievement or development. —**top′flight′, top′-flight′,** *adj.*

top•gal•lant (top′gal′ənt; *Naut.* tə gal′-), *n.* **1.** Also called **topgal′lant mast′.** a mast fixed to the head of a topmast on a square-rigged vessel. **2.** Also called **topgal′lant sail′.** a sail or either of two sails set on the yard or yards of a topgallant mast. —*adj.* **3.** of or pertaining to a topgallant mast or sail: *a topgallant spar.*

top′ hat′, *n.* a man's tall, cylindrical hat with a stiff, slightly curved brim, for formal occasions.

top′-heav′y, *adj.* **1.** having the top disproportionately heavy or large. **2.** (of an organization) having a disproportionately large number of people in the upper ranks. **3.** (of a company) having a financial structure overburdened with dividend-paying securities; overcapitalized.

To•phel (tō′fel), *n.* the place where Moses addressed the Israelites in the wilderness. Deut. 1:1.

To•phet or **To•pheth** (tō′fit, -fet), *n.* **1.** a place near Jerusalem where children were offered as sacrifices to Moloch. II Kings 23:10. **2.** the place of punishment for the wicked after death; hell.

to•pi•ar•y (tō′pē er′ē), *adj., n., pl.* **-ar•ies.** —*adj.* **1.** (of a tree or shrub) clipped or trimmed into fantastic or ornamental shapes. **2.** of or pertaining to such trimming. —*n.* **3.** topiary work; the topiary art. **4.** a garden containing such work.

top•ic (top′ik), *n.* **1.** a subject of conversation or discussion. **2.** the subject or theme of a discourse or of one of its parts. **3.** Also called **theme.** the part of a sentence that announces the item about which the rest of the sentence communicates information. Compare COMMENT (def. 5).

top•i•cal (top′i kəl), *adj.* **1.** pertaining to or dealing with matters of current or local interest. **2.** pertaining to the subject of a discourse, composition, etc. **3.** of a place; local. **4.** *Med.* on the skin or external surface: *a topical ointment.* —**top′i•cal•ly,** *adv.*

top′ic sen′tence, *n.* a sentence that expresses the essential idea of a paragraph or larger section, usu. appearing at the beginning.

top•knot (top′not′), *n.* **1.** a tuft of hair or feathers growing on the top of the head. **2.** hair fashioned into a knob or bun on top of the head. **3.** a knot or bow of ribbon worn on top of the head.

Top•la•dy (top′lā′dē), *n.* **Augustus,** 1740–78, English clergyman and hymn writer.

top′-lev′el, *adj.* of or involving those at the highest level, as of rank or authority; high-level: *a top-level conference.*

top•mast (top′mast′, -məst′; *Naut.* -məst), *n.* the mast next above a lower mast, usu. formed as a separate spar from the lower mast and used to support the yards or rigging of a topsail or topsails.

top•most (top′mōst′), *adj.* highest; uppermost.

top′notch′ or **top′-notch′,** *adj.* first-rate.

topo-, a combining form meaning "place": *topography; topology.* Also, *esp. before a vowel,* **top-.**

top′-of-the-line′, *adj.* being the best or most expensive of its kind.

to•pog•ra•pher (tə pog′rə fər), *n.* a specialist in topography.

top′ograph′ic map′, *n.* a map showing topographic features, usu. by means of contour lines. Compare CONTOUR MAP.

to•pog•ra•phy (tə pog′rə fē), *n., pl.* **-phies. 1.** the detailed mapping or charting of the features of a relatively small area or district. **2.** the detailed description, esp. by means of surveying, of particular localities, as cities, towns, or estates. **3.** the relief features or surface configuration of an area. **4.** the features, relations, or configuration of a structural entity, as the mind. **5.** a schema of a structural entity reflecting a division

into distinct areas having a specific relation to one another. —**top•o•graph•ic** (top′ə graf′ik), **top′o•graph′i•cal,** *adj.*

to•pol•o•gy (tə pol′ə jē), *n.* **1.** the mathematical study of those properties of geometric forms that remain invariant under certain transformations, as bending or stretching. **2.** the topography of a place or entity. —**top•o•log•ic** (top′ə loj′ik), **top′o•log′i•cal,** *adj.*

top•o•nym (top′ə nim), *n.* **1.** a place name. **2.** a name derived from the name of a place.

to•pon•y•my (tə pon′ə mē), *n.* the study of place names. —**top•o•nym•ic** (top′ə nim′ik), **top′o•nym′i•cal,** *adj.*

top•per (top′ər), *n.* **1.** a person or thing that tops. **2.** a woman's loose, usu. lightweight topcoat, esp. one that is hip-length. **3.** TOP HAT.

top•ping (top′ing), *n.* **1.** a distinct part forming a top to something. **2.** a sauce or garnish placed on food before serving. **3. toppings,** the parts removed in topping plants. —*adj.* **4.** rising above something else. **5.** very high in rank, degree, etc.

top•ple (top′əl), *v.,* **-pled, -pling.** —*v.i.* **1.** to fall forward, as from topheaviness or weakness; pitch. **2.** to lean over or totter, as if threatening to fall. —*v.t.* **3.** to cause to topple. **4.** to overthrow, as from a position of authority: *to topple a king.*

top′ round′, *n.* a cut of beef taken from the inner part of the round.

tops (tops), *adj.* **1.** ranked among the highest, as in ability, performance, quality, or favor; outstanding. —*n.* **2. the tops,** a person or thing that is tops.

top•sail (top′sāl′; *Naut.* -səl), *n.* a sail or one of a pair of sails set immediately above the lowermost sail of a mast and supported by a topmast.

top′-se′cret, *adj.* of or designating the highest category of security classification, or a document assigned to this category.

top•side (top′sīd′), *n.* **1.** the upper side. **2.** Usu., **topsides.** the outer surface of a hull above the water. **3.** the most authoritative position or level. —*adj.* **4.** of, pertaining to, or located on the topside. **5.** of the most authoritative rank. —*adv.* **6.** Also, **top′sides′.** up on the deck.

top•soil (top′soil′), *n.* the fertile, upper part of the soil.

top•spin (top′spin′), *n.* a spinning motion imparted to a ball that causes it to rotate forward.

top•stitch (top′stich′), *v.t.* **1.** to sew a line of stitches on the face side of (a garment or the like) alongside a seam. —*n.* **2.** a line of such stitches.

top•sy-tur•vy (top′sē tûr′vē), *adv., adj., n., pl.* **-vies.** —*adv.* **1.** with the top where the bottom should be; upside down. **2.** in or into a state of confusion or disorder. —*adj.* **3.** turned upside down; inverted; reversed. **4.** confused or disorderly. —*n.* **5.** inversion of the natural order. **6.** a state of confusion or disorder.

toque (tōk), *n.* **1.** a soft, brimless, close-fitting hat for women, in any of several shapes. **2.** a velvet hat with a narrow brim, a full crown, and usu. a plume, worn by men and women in the 16th century.

tor (tôr), *n.* a rocky pinnacle; a peak of a rocky mountain or hill.

-tor, a suffix found in words from Latin, forming personal agent nouns from verbs and, less commonly, from nouns: *janitor; orator; victor.*

To•rah or **To•ra** (tôr′ə, tôr′ə; *Heb.* tō rä′), *n., pl.* **-rahs** or **-ras** for 2. (*sometimes l.c.*) **1.** the Pentateuch. **2.** a parchment scroll on which the Pentateuch is written, used in synagogue services. **3.** the entire body of Jewish religious literature, law, and teaching as contained chiefly in the Old Testament and the Talmud. **4.** law or instruction. [< Hebrew *tōrāh* instruction, law]

torah scroll

torc (tôrk), *n.* TORQUE².

torch (tôrch), *n.* **1.** a light, usu. carried in the hand, consisting of a stick of resinous wood, tallow-soaked flax, or some other flammable substance, ignited at the upper end. **2.** something considered as a source of illumination, enlightenment, or guidance: *the torch of learning.*

3. any of various lamplike devices producing a hot flame, used for soldering, burning off paint, etc. **4.** *Slang.* an arsonist. **5.** *Chiefly Brit.* FLASHLIGHT (def. 1). —*v.t.* **6.** to subject to the flame or light of a torch. **7.** to set fire to, esp. maliciously. —**Idiom. 8. carry a** or **the torch for,** to be in love with, esp. without being loved in return. —**torch′a•ble,** *adj.* —**torch′less,** *adj.* —**torch′like′,** *adj.*

tor•chiere or **tor•chier** (tôr chēr′, -shēr′), *n.* a floor lamp for indirect lighting, having its source of light within a reflecting bowl that directs the light upward.

torch•light (tôrch′līt′), *n.* the light of a torch or torches.

torch′ song′, *n.* a plaintive popular ballad expressing unhappiness in love. —**torch′ sing′er,** *n.*

tore[1] (tôr, tōr), *v.* pt. of TEAR[2].

tore[2] (tôr, tōr), *n.* a torus.

tor•e•a•dor (tôr′ē ə dôr′), *n.* a bullfighter; torero.

to•re•ro (tə râr′ō; *Sp.* tô Re′Rô), *n.*, *pl.* **-re•ros** (-râr′ōz; *Sp.* -Re′Rôs). a bullfighter, esp. a matador.

tor•ic (tôr′ik, tor′-), *adj.* **1.** of or designating a lens with a surface forming a portion of a torus, used for eyeglasses and contact lenses that correct astigmatism. —*n.* **2.** a toric contact lens.

to•ri•i (tôr′ē ē′, tōr′-), *n.*, *pl.* **-ri•i.** a Japanese gateway or portal, as at a Shinto temple, consisting of two upright wooden posts connected at the top by two horizontal crosspieces.

torii

tor•ment (*v.* tôr ment′, tôr′ment; *n.* tôr′ment), *v.t.* **1.** to afflict with great, usu. incessant or repeated bodily or mental suffering. **2.** to worry or annoy excessively; plague. **3.** to throw into commotion; stir up; disturb. —*n.* **4.** a state of great bodily or mental suffering; agony; misery. **5.** something that causes pain or suffering. **6.** a source of much trouble, worry, or annoyance. **7.** an instrument of torture, as the rack. **8.** the infliction of torture. —**tor•ment′ed•ly,** *adv.* —**tor•ment′ing•ly,** *adv.*

tor•men•tor or **tor•ment•er** (tôr men′tər, tôr′men-), *n.* **1.** a person or thing that torments. **2.** a curtain or framed structure behind the proscenium at both sides of the stage, for screening the wings from the audience. Compare TEASER (def. 2).

torn (tôrn, tōrn), *v.* pp. of TEAR[2].

tor•na•do (tôr nā′dō), *n.*, *pl.* **-does, -dos. 1.** a localized, violently destructive windstorm occurring over land, esp. in the Middle West, and characterized by a long, funnel-shaped cloud that extends to the ground. **2.** a violent squall or whirlwind of small extent, as one of those occurring during the summer on the W coast of Africa. **3.** a violent outburst, as of emotion or activity. [< Spanish *tronada* thunderstorm < Latin *tonāre* to thunder] —**tor•nad′ic** (-nad′ik, -nā′dik), *adj.*

to•roid (tôr′oid, tōr′-), *n. Geom.* **1.** a surface generated by the revolution of any closed plane curve or contour about an axis lying in its plane. **2.** the solid enclosed by such a surface. —**to•roi′dal,** *adj.*

To•ron•to (tə ron′tō), *n.* the capital of Ontario, in SE Canada, on Lake Ontario. 612,289. —**To•ron•to•ni•an** (tôr′ən tō′nē ən, tor′-, tə ron-), *adj., n.*

Toron′to bless′ing, *n.* in some charismatic Protestant churches, the manifestation of the Holy Spirit as giggling or laughter: named after Toronto, Canada, where the phenomenon occurred.

tor•pe•do (tôr pē′dō), *n.*, *pl.* **-does**, *v.*, **-doed, -do•ing.** —*n.* **1.** a self-propelled underwater missile containing a high explosive and often a guidance system, usu. launched from a submarine or other warship against surface vessels. **2.** any of various submarine explosive devices for destroying hostile ships, as a mine. **3.** any of various other explosive devices, as a firework that consists of an explosive wrapped up with gravel in a piece of tissue paper and that detonates when thrown against a hard surface. —*v.t.* **4.** to attack, hit, damage, or destroy with or as if with torpedoes.

torpe′do boat′, *n.* a small, fast, highly maneuverable boat used for torpedoing enemy shipping.

tor•pid (tôr′pid), *adj.* **1.** inactive or sluggish, as a bodily organ. **2.** slow; dull; apathetic; lethargic. **3.** dormant, as a hibernating or estivating animal. —**tor•pid′i•ty, tor′pid•ness,** *n.* —**tor′pid•ly,** *adv.*

tor•por (tôr′pər), *n.* **1.** sluggish inactivity or inertia. **2.** lethargic indifference; apathy. **3.** a state of suspended physical powers and activities. **4.** dormancy, as of a hibernating animal.

torque[1] (tôrk), *n.*, *v.*, **torqued, torqu•ing.** —*n.* **1.** something that produces or tends to produce torsion or rotation. **2.** the measured ability of a rotating element, as of a gear or shaft, to overcome turning resistance. **3.** the rotational effect on plane-polarized light passing through certain liquids or crystals. —*v.i., v.t.* **4.** to rotate or cause to rotate or twist.

torque[2] (tôrk), *n.* a collar, necklace, or similar ornament consisting of a twisted narrow band, usu. of precious metal, worn esp. by the ancient Gauls and Britons.

Tor•rance (tôr′əns, tor′-), *n.* a city in SW California, SW of Los Angeles. 138,219.

tor•rent (tôr′ənt, tor′-), *n.* **1.** a stream of water flowing with great rapidity and violence. **2.** a rushing, violent, or abundant stream of anything. **3.** a violent downpour of rain. —*adj.* **4.** torrential.

tor•ren•tial (tô ren′shəl, tō-, tə-), *adj.* **1.** pertaining to or having the nature of a torrent. **2.** resembling a torrent in rapidity or violence. **3.** falling in torrents: *torrential rains.* **4.** produced by the action of a torrent. **5.** violent, vehement, or impassioned. —**tor•ren′tial•ly,** *adv.*

Tor•rey (tôr′ē), *n.* **Reuben Archer,** 1865–1928, U.S. clergyman and writer.

tor•rid (tôr′id, tor′-), *adj.* **1.** subject to parching or burning heat, esp. of the sun, as a geographical area. **2.** oppressively hot, parching, or burning, as climate, weather, or air. **3.** ardent; passionate: *a torrid love story.* —**tor•rid′i•ty, tor′rid•ness,** *n.* —**tor′rid•ly,** *adv.*

Tor′rid Zone′, *n.* the part of the earth between the tropics of Cancer and Capricorn, characterized by a climate that is hot year-round.

tor•sion (tôr′shən), *n.* **1.** the act of twisting. **2.** the state of being twisted. **3. a.** the twisting of an object by two equal and opposite torques. **b.** the internal torque so produced. —**tor′sion•al,** *adj.*

tor′sion bar′, *n.* a metal bar having elasticity when subjected to torsion: used as a spring in machines and in automobile suspensions.

tor•so (tôr′sō), *n.*, *pl.* **-sos, -si** (-sē). **1.** the trunk of the human body. **2.** a sculptured form representing the trunk of a nude figure.

tort (tôrt), *n. Law.* a wrongful act resulting in injury to another's person, property, or reputation, for which the injured party is entitled to seek compensation.

torte (tôrt), *n.*, *pl.* **tortes** (tôrts), *Ger.* **tor•ten** (tôr′tn). a rich cake made with eggs, ground nuts, and usu. no flour.

tor•tel•li•ni (tôr′tl ē′nē), *n.* (*used with a sing. or pl. v.*) small rounds of pasta, filled with meat, cheese, etc., folded and shaped into rings.

tor•ti•col•lis (tôr′ti kol′is), *n.* a condition in which the neck is twisted and the head inclined to one side, caused by spasmodic contraction of the muscles of the neck. Also called **wryneck.**

tor•til•la (tôr tē′ə), *n.* a thin, round, unleavened bread made from cornmeal or wheat flour, and baked on a griddle or stone.

tor•toise (tôr′təs), *n.* **1.** a turtle, esp. a terrestrial turtle. **2.** a very slow person or thing.

tor•toise•shell (tôr′təs shel′), *n.* Also, **tor′toise shell′. 1.** the horny brown and yellow layer on the outer surface of the hawksbill turtle's carapace, used for making combs and ornamental articles. **2.** any synthetic substance made to look like natural tortoiseshell. **3.** any of several butterflies of the genus *Nymphalis,* typically with bright, variegated markings. —*adj.* Also, **tor′toise-shell′. 4.** mottled or variegated like tortoiseshell, esp. with yellow and brown and sometimes other colors. **5.** made of tortoiseshell. **6.** (of a domestic cat) having a variegated black, orange, and cream coat.

tor•to•ni (tôr tō′nē), *n.* rich ice cream of eggs, heavy cream, chopped cherries, etc., often topped with crushed almonds or macaroons.

tor•tu•os•i•ty (tôr′chōō os′i tē), *n.*, *pl.* **-ties. 1.** the state of being tortuous; twisted form or course; crookedness. **2.** a twist, bend, or crook.

tor•tu•ous (tôr′chōō əs), *adj.* **1.** full of twists, turns, or bends; twisting, winding, or crooked. **2.** not direct or straightforward, as in procedure or speech; circuitous: *tortuous negotiations.* **3.** deceitfully indirect or morally crooked; devious. —**tor′tu•ous•ly,** *adv.* —**tor′tu•ous•ness,** *n.* —**Usage.** See TORTUROUS.

tor•ture (tôr′chər), *n.*, *v.*, **-tured, -tur•ing.** —*n.* **1.** the act of inflicting excruciating pain, as punishment or revenge, as a means of getting a confession or information, or for sheer cruelty. **2.** a method of inflicting such pain. **3.** Often, **tortures.** the pain or suffering caused or undergone. **4.** extreme anguish of body or mind; agony. **5.** a cause of severe pain or anguish. —*v.t.* **6.** to subject to torture. **7.** to afflict with severe pain of body or mind. **8.** to twist, force, or bring into some unnatural shape. —**tor′tured•ly,** *adv.* —**tor′tur•er,** *n.* —**tor′tur•ing•ly,** *adv.*

tor•tur•ous (tôr′chər əs), *adj.* pertaining to, involving, or causing torture or suffering. —**tor′tur•ous•ly,** *adv.* —**Usage.** TORTUROUS refers specifically to what involves or causes pain or suffering: *prisoners working in the torturous heat; torturous memories of past injustice.* Some speakers and writers use TORTUROUS for TORTUOUS, esp. in the senses "twisting, winding" and "convoluted": *a torturous road; torturous descriptions.* Others, however, keep the two adjectives (and their corresponding adverbs) separate in all senses: *a tortuous* (twisting) *road; tortuous* (convoluted) *descriptions; torturous* (painful) *treatments.*

to•rus (tôr′əs, tōr′-), *n.*, *pl.* **to•ri** (tôr′ī, tōr′ī). *Bot.* the receptacle of a flower.

To•ry (tôr′ē, tōr′ē), *n.*, *pl.* **-ries,** *adj.* —*n.* **1.** a member of the Conservative Party in Great Britain or Canada. **2.** a member of a British political party formed in the late 17th century, favoring royal authority and opposing reform: succeeded by the Conservative Party about 1832. **3.** (*often l.c.*) an advocate of conservative principles. **4.** a person who supported the British cause in the American Revolution; a loyalist. **5.** (in the 17th century) one of a class of dispossessed Irish, nominally royalists, who became outlaws. —*adj.* **6.** of, belonging to, or characteristic of the Tories. **7.** being a Tory. **8.** (*often l.c.*) conservative. —**To′ry•ism,** *n.*

-tory[1], a suffix occurring in loanwords from Latin, orig. adjectival derivatives of agent nouns ending in -TOR (*predatory*); also forming adjectival derivatives directly from verbs (*obligatory; transitory*).

-tory², a suffix occurring in loanwords from Latin, usu. derivatives from agent nouns ending in -TOR or directly from verbs, denoting a place or object appropriate for the activity of the verb: *dormitory; repository.*

toss (tôs, tos), *v.,* **tossed** or **tost, toss•ing,** *n.* —*v.t.* **1.** to throw, pitch, or fling, esp. to throw lightly or carelessly. **2.** to throw or send from one to another, as in play: *to toss a ball.* **3.** to pitch with irregular or careless motions; jerk about. **4.** to agitate, disturb, or disquiet. **5.** to throw, raise, or jerk upward suddenly, as the head. **6.** to interject (a remark, comment, etc.) in a sudden, offhand manner. **7.** to throw (a coin) into the air in order to decide something by the side turned up when it falls (sometimes fol. by *up*). **8.** to toss a coin with (someone). **9.** to stir or mix (a salad) lightly until the ingredients are coated with the dressing. —*v.i.* **10.** to pitch, sway, or move irregularly, as a ship on a rough sea. **11.** to fling or jerk oneself or move restlessly about, esp. on a bed or couch. **12.** to throw something. **13.** to throw a coin into the air in order to decide something by the way it falls (sometimes fol. by *up*). **14.** to go with a fling of the body. **15. toss off, a.** to accomplish quickly or easily. **b.** to consume rapidly, esp. to drink up in one swallow. —*n.* **16.** an act or instance of tossing. **17.** a pitching about or up and down. **18.** a throw or pitch. **19.** TOSSUP (def. 1). **20.** a sudden fling or jerk, esp. of the head. —**toss′er,** *n.*

toss•up (tôs′up′, tos′-), *n.* **1.** the tossing of a coin to decide something by its fall. **2.** an even choice or chance.

tos•ta•da (tō stä′də), *n.* a tortilla fried until crisp, topped with cheese, chopped meat, refried beans, etc.

tot¹ (tot), *n.* **1.** a small child. **2.** a small portion, as of liquor.

tot² (tot), *v.,* **tot•ted, tot•ting,** *n.* —*v.t., v.i.* **1.** to add; total (often fol. by *up*). —*n.* **2.** a total.

to•tal (tōt′l), *adj., n., v.,* **-taled, -tal•ing** or (*esp. Brit.*) **-talled, -tal•ling.** —*adj.* **1.** constituting or comprising the whole; entire: *the total expenditure.* **2.** of or pertaining to the whole of something: *the total effect of a play.* **3.** complete in extent or degree; utter: *a total failure.* —*n.* **4.** the total amount; sum; aggregate. **5.** the whole; an entirety. —*v.t.* **6.** to bring to a total; add up. **7.** to reach a total of; amount to. **8.** to wreck or demolish beyond repair: *He totaled his car in the accident.* —*v.i.* **9.** to amount (often fol. by *to*).

to′tal deprav′ity, *n.* the Calvinistic doctrine that humanity's entire nature is corrupt as a result of the Fall.

to′tal eclipse′, *n.* an eclipse in which the surface of the eclipsed body is completely obscured.

to•tal•i•tar•i•an (tō tal′i târ′ē ən), *adj.* **1.** noting or pertaining to a centralized government that does not tolerate parties of differing opinion and that exercises dictatorial control over many aspects of life. **2.** exercising control over the freedom, will, or thought of others; authoritarian; autocratic. —*n.* **3.** an adherent of totalitarian principles or government. —**to•tal′i•tar′i•an•ism,** *n.*

to•tal•i•ty (tō tal′i tē), *n., pl.* **-ties. 1.** something that is total or constitutes a total; the total amount; a whole. **2.** the state of being total; entirety. **3.** *Astron.* total obscuration in an eclipse.

to•tal•ly (tōt′l ē), *adv.* wholly; entirely; completely.

to′tal re•call′, *n.* the ability to remember with complete accuracy.

total war, *n.* warfare that fully involves all citizens, civilians and military personnel alike.

tote¹ (tōt), *v.,* **tot•ed, tot•ing,** *n.* —*v.t.* **1.** to carry, as on one's back or in one's arms. **2.** to carry on one's person: *to tote a gun.* **3.** to transport or convey, as on a vehicle or boat. —*n.* **4.** something that is toted. **5.** TOTE BAG. —**tot′a•ble, tote′a•ble,** *adj.* —**tot′er,** *n.*

tote² (tōt), *v.t.,* **tot•ed, tot•ing.** *Informal.* to add up; total.

tote′ bag′, *n.* an open handbag or shopping bag used esp. for carrying packages or small items.

to•tem (tō′təm), *n.* **1.** a natural object or an animate being, as an animal or bird, assumed as the emblem of a clan, family, or group. **2.** a representation of such an object or being serving as the distinctive mark of the clan or group. **3.** anything serving as a distinctive, often venerated, emblem or symbol. —**to•tem′ic** (-tem′ik), *adj.*

to′tem pole′, *n.* a pole or post carved and painted with totemic figures, erected by Indians of the NW coast of North America.

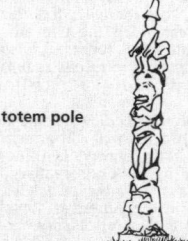
totem pole

tot•ter (tot′ər), *v.i.* **1.** to walk with faltering steps, as if from extreme weakness. **2.** to sway or rock on the base or ground, as if about to fall. **3.** to shake; tremble. —*n.* **4.** the act of tottering; an unsteady gait.

tou•can (tōō′kan, -kän, tōō kän′), *n.* any of several brightly colored, fruit-eating birds of the family Ramphastidae, of the New World tropics, having a very large bill.

red-billed toucan, *Ramphastos monilis,*
length 22 in. (56 cm)

touch (tuch), *v.t.* **1.** to put the hand, finger, etc., on or into contact with (something) so as to feel it. **2.** to bring (the hand, finger, etc., or something held) into contact with something: *She touched a match to the papers.* **3.** to pat or tap as with the hand or an instrument. **4.** to come into contact with; be adjacent to. **5.** (of a line or surface) to be tangent to. **6.** to attain equality with; compare with (usu. with a negative): *a style that can't touch that of Shakespeare.* **7.** to mark slightly with a brush, pencil, or a color. **8.** to treat or affect in some way by contact. **9.** to move to tenderness or sympathy. **10.** to handle, use, or have to do with in any way (usu. with a negative): *She can't touch the money until she's 21.* **11.** to eat or drink; consume; taste (usu. with a negative): *He won't touch another drink.* **12.** to lay hands on, often in a violent manner. **13.** to deal with or allude to in speech or writing. **14.** to pertain or relate to. **15.** to be a matter of importance to; affect. **16.** *Slang.* to apply to for money, or succeed in getting money from: *He touched me for a loan.* —*v.i.* **17.** to place the hand, finger, etc., on or in contact with something. **18.** to come into or be in contact. **19. touch down,** (of an aircraft or spacecraft) to land. **20. touch off, a.** to cause to ignite or explode. **b.** to start or initiate. **21. touch on** or **upon,** to mention (a subject) briefly or casually. **22. touch up, a.** to make minor changes or improvements in the appearance of. **b.** to rouse by or as if by striking. —*n.* **23.** the act of touching; state or fact of being touched. **24.** that sense by which anything material is perceived by means of physical contact; feel. **25.** the quality of something touched that imparts a sensation; feel. **26.** a coming into or being in contact. **27.** ability, skill, or dexterity; knack: *to lose one's touch.* **28.** (in fencing) the contact of the point of a foil or épée or the point or edge of the blade of a saber with a specified portion of the opponent's body, counting one point for the scorer. **29.** relationship or close communication: *Let's keep in touch.* **30.** a slight stroke or blow. **31.** a slight attack, as of illness or disease. **32.** a slight added action or effort in completing any piece of work: *finishing touches.* **33.** manner of execution in artistic work. **34.** the act or manner of touching or fingering a keyboard instrument. **35.** the mode of action of the keys of an instrument, as of a piano or typewriter. **36.** a slight amount of some quality, attribute, etc. **37.** a slight quantity or degree: *a touch of salt.* **38.** *Slang.* **a.** the act of approaching someone for money as a gift or a loan. **b.** the obtaining of money in this manner. **c.** the money obtained. **d.** a person considered from the standpoint of the relative ease with which he or she will lend money. **39. a.** the area outside the touchlines in soccer. **b.** either of the touchlines or the area outside them in Rugby. —**touch′a•ble,** *adj.* —**touch′er,** *n.*

touch′ and go′, *n.* a precarious or delicate state of affairs. —**touch′-and-go′,** *adj.*

touch•back (tuch′bak′), *n.* a deliberate downing of the ball by a football team in its own end zone or possession assumed by that team when the ball lands beyond the end zone.

touch•down (tuch′doun′), *n.* **1.** an act or instance of scoring six points in football by being in possession of the ball on or behind the opponent's goal line. **2.** the act of a Rugby player who touches the ball on or to the ground behind his own goal line. **3.** the act or the moment of landing, as of an aircraft.

tou•ché (tōō shā′), *interj.* **1.** (an expression used to indicate a hit or touch in fencing.) **2.** (an expression used for acknowledging a telling remark or rejoinder.)

touched (tucht), *adj.* **1.** moved; stirred. **2.** slightly crazy; unbalanced: *touched in the head.*

touch′ foot′ball, *n.* a kind of football in which a touch is used instead of a tackle to stop the ballcarrier.

touch•ing (tuch′ing), *adj.* **1.** affecting; moving; pathetic. **2.** being in contact; tangent. —*prep.* **3.** in reference or relation to; concerning; about. —**touch′ing•ly,** *adv.* —**touch′ing•ness,** *n.*

touch′-me-not′, *n.* JEWELWEED.

touch′ screen′ or **touch′ screen′,** *n.* a computer display that can detect and respond to the presence and location of a finger or instrument on or near its surface.

touch•stone (tuch′stōn′), *n.* **1.** a test or criterion for the qualities of a thing. **2.** a black stone once used to test gold and silver by rubbing them on it.

touch′ sys′tem, *n.* a system of typing in which each finger is assigned to particular keys, thereby enabling a person to type without looking at the keyboard.

touch′-tone′ or **touch′tone′,** *n.* a telephone dialing system using

push buttons to generate ten tones of different pitch, each tone corresponding to a digit of a telephone number.
touch′-type′, *v.i.,* **-typed, -typ•ing.** to type by means of the touch system. —**touch′-typ′ist,** *n.*
touch′-up′, *n.* an act or instance of touching up: *Her makeup needed a touch-up.*
touch•y (tuch′ē), *adj.,* **touch•i•er, touch•i•est. 1.** apt to take offense on slight provocation; irritable. **2.** requiring caution, tactfulness, or expert handling; precarious; risky. **3.** sensitive to touch. **4.** easily ignited, as tinder. —**touch′i•ly,** *adv.* —**touch′i•ness,** *n.*
touch•y-feel•y (tuch′ē fē′lē), *adj. Informal.* emphasizing or marked by emotional openness and enthusiastic physicality: *a touchy-feely encounter group.*
tough (tuf), *adj.* **1.** strong and durable; not easily broken or cut. **2.** not brittle or tender. **3.** difficult to chew: *a tough steak.* **4.** capable of great endurance; sturdy; hardy: *tough troops.* **5.** not easily influenced, as a person; unyielding; stubborn. **6.** hardened; incorrigible: *a tough criminal.* **7.** difficult to perform, accomplish, or deal with. **8.** hard to bear or endure (often used ironically): *tough luck.* **9.** vigorous; severe; violent: *a tough struggle.* **10.** vicious; rough; rowdy: *a tough neighborhood.* —*adv.* **11.** in a tough manner. —*n.* **12.** a ruffian; rowdy. —***Idiom.* 13. tough it out,** *Informal.* to endure or resist hardship or adversity. —***Proverb.* 14. When the going gets tough, the tough get going,** people who are strong don't give up in a crisis. —**tough′ly,** *adv.* —**tough′ness,** *n.*
tough•en (tuf′ən), *v.t., v.i.* to make or become tough or tougher.
tough•ie or **tough•y** (tuf′ē), *n., pl.* **tough•ies.** *Informal.* **1.** a tough person; rowdy. **2.** a difficult problem or situation.
tough′ love′, *n.* a mixture of toughness and warmth used in a relationship, esp. with an adolescent.
tough′-mind′ed, *adj.* **1.** characterized by a practical, unsentimental attitude or point of view. **2.** strong-willed; vigorous; not easily swayed.
Tou•louse-Lau•trec (to͞o lo͞oz′lō trek′; *often* -lo͞os′-), *n.* **Henri Marie Raymond de,** 1864–1901, French painter and lithographer.
tou•pee (to͞o pā′), *n.* **1.** a man's wig. **2.** a patch of false hair for covering a bald spot.
tour (to͝or), *n.* **1.** a traveling around from place to place. **2.** a long journey including the visiting of a number of places, esp. with a group led by a guide. **3.** a brief trip through a place in order to view or inspect it. **4.** a journey from town to town, as by a theatrical company or performer. **5.** a period of duty at one place or in one job. —*v.i.* **6.** to travel from place to place. **7.** to travel from town to town giving performances. —*v.t.* **8.** to travel through (a place). **9.** to send or take (a theatrical company, its production, etc.) from town to town.
tour de force (to͝or′ də fôrs′, -fōrs′), *n., pl.* **tours de force** (to͝orz). **1.** an exceptional achievement by an artist, author, or the like, unlikely to be equaled by that person or anyone else; stroke of genius. **2.** a particularly adroit maneuver or technique in handling a difficult situation.
Tourette's′ syn′drome (to͞o rets′), *n.* a neurological disorder characterized by recurrent involuntary movements and sometimes vocal tics, as grunts or words, esp. obscenities. [after Georges Gilles de la *Tourette* (1857–1904), French neurologist, who described it in 1885]
tour′ing car′, *n.* **1.** an early type of open automobile designed for five or more passengers. **2.** a modern two-door coupe. Compare GT.
tour•ism (to͝or′iz əm), *n.* **1.** the occupation of providing information, accommodations, transportation, and other services to tourists. **2.** the promotion of tourist travel, esp. for commercial purposes.
tour•ist (to͝or′ist), *n.* **1.** a person who makes a tour, esp. for pleasure. **2.** TOURIST CLASS. —*adv.* **3.** in tourist-class accommodations, or by tourist-class conveyance: *to travel tourist.*
tour•is•ta or **tu•ris•ta** (to͞o rē′stə), *n.* traveler's diarrhea, esp. as experienced in Latin America.
tour′ist class′, *n.* the least costly class of accommodations on regularly scheduled ships and airplanes. Compare THIRD CLASS (def. 2).
tour′ist home′, *n.* a private home with rooms for rent, usu. for one night, to tourists, travelers, etc.
tour′ist trap′, *n.* a place, as a restaurant, shop, or hotel, that exploits tourists by overcharging.
tour•ist•y (to͝or′i stē), *adj.* **1.** pertaining to or characteristic of tourists. **2.** appealing to or frequented by tourists.
tour•ma•line (to͝or′mə lin, -lēn′), *n.* a complex silicate mineral occurring in variously colored transparent gem varieties.
tour•na•ment (to͝or′nə mənt, tûr′-), *n.* **1.** a trial of skill in some game, in which competitors play a series of contests: *a chess tournament.* **2.** a meeting for contests in a variety of sports, as between teams of different nations. **3.** a medieval contest or martial sport in which mounted knights fought with blunted lances for a prize.
tour•ne•dos (to͝or′ni dō′, to͝or′ni dō′), *n., pl.* **-dos.** a small, thick beef fillet, served with a sauce and garnished.
tour•ney (to͝or′nē, tûr′-), *n., pl.* **-neys,** *v.,* **-neyed, -ney•ing.** —*n.* **1.** a tournament. —*v.i.* **2.** to contend or engage in a tournament.
tour•ni•quet (tûr′ni kit, to͝or′-), *n.* any device for arresting bleeding by forcibly compressing a blood vessel, as a bandage tightened by twisting.
tour′ of du′ty, *n.* TOUR (def. 5).
tou•sle (tou′zəl, -səl), *v.,* **-sled, -sling,** *n.* —*v.t.* **1.** to disorder or dishevel. **2.** to handle roughly. —*n.* **3.** a disheveled or rumpled mass, esp. of hair. **4.** a disordered, disheveled, or tangled condition.
Tous•saint L'Ou•ver•ture (*Fr.* to͞o saN′ lo͞o ver tyr′), *n.* (*Francis Dominique Toussaint*) 1743–1803, Haitian military and political leader.
tout (tout), *v.i.* **1.** to solicit business, employment, votes, or the like, importunately. **2.** to act as a tout. —*v.t.* **3.** to solicit importunately. **4.** to describe or advertise boastfully; praise extravagantly: *a highly touted nightclub.* **5.** to provide information on (a racehorse), esp. for a fee. **6.** to watch; spy on. —*n.* **7.** a person who solicits business, employment, or the like, importunately. **8.** a person who gives information on a racehorse, esp. for a fee.
tow[1] (tō), *v.t.* **1.** to pull or haul (a car, barge, trailer, etc.) by a rope, chain, or other device. —*n.* **2.** an act or instance of towing. **3.** something being towed. **4.** something, as a boat or truck, that tows. **5.** a rope, chain, metal bar, or other device for towing. —***Idiom.* 6. in tow, a.** in the state of being towed. **b.** under one's guidance; in one's charge. **c.** as a follower, admirer, or companion. **7. under tow,** in the condition of being towed; in tow. —**tow′er,** *n.*
tow[2] (tō), *n.* **1.** the fiber of flax, hemp, or jute prepared for spinning by scutching. **2. a.** the shorter, less desirable fibers of flax, hemp, or jute separated in scutching or hackling and used for twine, yarn, etc. **b.** yarn or fabric made from this.
TOW (tō), *n.* a U.S. Army antitank missile, steered by two wires connected to a computerized launcher, which is mounted on a vehicle or helicopter. [*t*(*ube-launched,*) *o*(*ptically-guided,*) *w*(*ire-tracked missile*)]
to•ward (*prep.* tôrd, tōrd, twôrd, twōrd; *adj.* tôrd, tōrd), *prep.* Also, **to•wards′. 1.** in the direction of: *to walk toward the river.* **2.** with a view to obtaining or having; for: *They're saving money toward a new house.* **3.** in the area or vicinity of; near. **4.** turned to; facing. **5.** shortly before; close to: *toward midnight.* **6.** as a help or contribution to: *to give money toward a person's expenses.* **7.** with respect to; as regards. —*adj.* **8.** coming soon; imminent. **9.** going on; in progress; afoot.
tow•a•way (tō′ə wā′), *n.* **1.** an act or instance of towing away a vehicle that has been illegally parked. **2.** the vehicle towed away. —*adj.* **3.** designated as an area from which such vehicles are towed away.
tow•boat (tō′bōt′), *n.* **1.** a boat used to push groups of barges, esp. in inland waterways. **2.** TUGBOAT.
tow•el (tou′əl, toul), *n., v.,* **-eled, -el•ing** or (*esp. Brit.*) **-elled, -el•ling.** —*n.* **1.** an absorbent cloth or paper for wiping and drying something wet, esp. the hands, face, or body. —*v.t.* **2.** to wipe or dry with a towel.
tow•el•ette (tou′ə let′, tou′let′), *n.* a small paper towel, usu. premoistened in a sealed package.
tow•el•ing (tou′ə ling, tou′ling), *n.* a narrow fabric of cotton or linen, in plain, twill, or huck weave, used for hand towels or dishtowels. Also, *esp. Brit.,* **tow′el•ling.**
tow•er (tou′ər), *n.* **1.** a building or structure higher than it is wide, either isolated or forming part of a building. **2.** such a structure used as or intended for a stronghold, fortress, prison, etc. **3.** any of various fully enclosed fireproof housings, as staircases, between the stories of a building. **4.** any structure, contrivance, or object that resembles or suggests a tower. **5.** a tall, movable structure used in ancient and medieval warfare in storming a fortified place. —*v.i.* **6.** to rise or extend far upward, as a tower; reach or stand high.
Tow•er (tou′ər), *n.* **Daniel B(rink),** 1850–1919, U.S. musician and hymn writer.
tow•er•ing (tou′ər ing), *adj.* **1.** very high or tall; lofty: *a towering oak.* **2.** surpassing others; very great. **3.** rising to an extreme degree of violence or intensity: *a towering rage.* **4.** beyond the proper or usual limits; inordinate; excessive. —**tow′er•ing•ly,** *adv.*
Tow′er of Ba′bel (tou′ər), *n.* See under BABEL (def. 1).
Tow′er of Lon′don (tou′ər), *n.* a historic fortress in London, England: orig. a royal palace, later a prison, now an arsenal and museum.
tow•head (tō′hed′), *n.* **1.** a head of very light blond, almost white hair. **2.** a person with such hair. —**tow′-head′ed,** *adj.*
tow•hee (tou′hē, tō′hē, tō′ē), *n.* any of several long-tailed North American finches of the genera *Pipilo* and *Chlorura* with a black back, rust-colored sides, and a white breast.
town (toun), *n.* **1.** a thickly populated area, usu. smaller than a city and larger than a village, having fixed boundaries and certain local powers of government. **2.** a densely populated area of considerable size, as a city or borough. **3.** (esp. in New England) a municipal corporation with less elaborate organization and powers than a city. **4.** (in most U.S. states except those of New England) a township. **5.** the inhabitants of a town; townspeople; citizenry. **6.** the particular town or city in mind or referred to: *to be out of town.* **7.** the main business or shopping area in a town or city; downtown. —*adj.* **8.** of, pertaining to, or characteristic of a town. —***Idiom.* 9. go to town,** *Informal.* **a.** to accomplish something with great speed and efficiency. **b.** to indulge oneself in a fling or binge. **10. on the town,** *Informal.* in quest of entertainment in a city's nightclubs, bars, etc.; out to have a good time.
town′ clerk′, *n.* a town official who keeps records and issues licenses.
town′ cri′er, *n.* a person formerly employed by a town to make public announcements or proclamations, usu. by shouting in the streets.
town′ hall′, *n.* a building used for the transaction of a town's business and often as a place of public assembly.
town′ house′ or **town′house′,** *n.* **1.** a house in the city, esp. a luxurious one or one distinguished from a house in the country owned by the same person. **2.** one of a group of two- or three-story houses of uniform architectural treatment, usu. joined by common sidewalls.

T

town•ie or **town•y** (tou′nē), *n., pl.* **town•ies.** *Informal.* a resident of a town, esp. a nonstudent resident of a college town.
town′ meet′ing, *n.* **1.** a general meeting of the inhabitants of a town. **2.** (esp. in New England) a legislative assembly of the qualified voters of a town.
Town′shend Acts′ (toun′zənd), *n.* acts of the British Parliament in 1767, esp. the act that placed duties on tea, paper, lead, paint, etc., imported into the American colonies. [after Charles *Townshend* (1725–67), English statesman, their sponsor]
town•ship (toun′ship), *n.* **1.** a unit of local government, usu. a subdivision of a county, found in most midwestern and northeastern states of the U.S. and in most Canadian provinces. **2.** (in U.S. surveys of public land) a region or district approximately 6 sq. mi. (93.2 sq. km), containing 36 sections. **3. a.** one of the local divisions or districts of a large parish in ancient England. **b.** the parish itself. **4.** (in South Africa) a segregated residential settlement for blacks outside a city or town.
towns•peo•ple (tounz′pē′pəl), *n.pl.* **1.** the inhabitants or citizenry of a town. **2.** people who were raised in a town or city. Also called **towns′folk′** (-fōk′).
tow•rope (tō′rōp′), *n.* a rope or hawser used in towing boats.
tow′ truck′, *n.* WRECKER (def. 3).
tox•e•mi•a (tok sē′mē ə), *n.* blood poisoning resulting from the presence of toxins, as bacterial toxins, in the blood. **—tox•e′mic,** *adj.*
tox•ic (tok′sik), *adj.* **1.** of, pertaining to, affected with, or caused by a toxin or poison: *a toxic condition.* **2.** acting as or having the effect of a poison; poisonous: *a toxic drug.* **—tox′i•cal•ly,** *adv.*
tox•ic•i•ty (tok sis′i tē), *n., pl.* **-ties.** the quality, relative degree, or specific degree of being toxic or poisonous.
toxico- or **toxo-,** a combining form meaning “toxin,” “poison”: *toxicology.*
tox•i•col•o•gy (tok′si kol′ə jē), *n.* the branch of pharmacology dealing with the effects, antidotes, detection, etc., of poisons. **—tox′i•co•log′i•cal** (-kə loj′i kəl), *adj.* **—tox′i•col′o•gist,** *n.*
tox′ic shock′ syn′drome, *n.* a rapidly developing toxemia caused by the bacterium *Staphylococcus aureus,* occurring esp. in menstruating women using high-absorbency tampons. *Abbr.:*TSS
tox•in (tok′sin), *n.* any poison produced by an organism, including the bacterial toxins that are the causative agents of tetanus, diphtheria, etc., and such plant and animal toxins as ricin and snake venom.
tox•oid (tok′soid), *n.* a bacterial toxin rendered harmless by chemicals and used for inducing immunity.
toy (toi), *n.* **1.** an object, often a small representation of something familiar, as an animal or person, for children to play with. **2.** a thing or matter of little or no value or importance; trifle. **3.** something diminutive, esp. in comparison with like objects. **4.** an animal, esp. a dog, of a breed or variety noted for smallness of size, as a Yorkshire terrier. *—adj.* **5.** made or designed for use as a toy: *a toy gun.* **6.** of or resembling a toy, esp. diminutive in size. *—v.i.* **7.** to amuse oneself; play. **8.** to act idly or with indifference; trifle. **9.** to dally amorously; flirt.
Toyn•bee (toin′bē), *n.* **Arnold J(oseph),** 1889–1975, English historian.
To•zer (tō′zər), *n.* **Aiden Wilson,** 1897–1963, U.S. clergyman and writer.
trace[1] (trās), *n., v.,* **traced, trac•ing,** *—n.* **1.** a surviving mark, sign, or evidence of the former existence, influence, or action of some agent or event; vestige. **2.** a barely discernible indication or evidence of some quantity, quality, characteristic, expression, etc. **3.** an extremely small amount of some chemical component: *a trace of copper in its composition.* **4. traces,** the series of footprints left by an animal. **5.** the track left by the passage of a person, animal, or object. **6.** precipitation of less than 0.005 in. (0.127 mm). **7.** a trail or path, esp. through wild or open territory, made by the passage of people, animals, or vehicles. **8.** a tracing, drawing, or sketch of something. **9.** a lightly drawn line, as the record drawn by a self-registering instrument. **10.** *Math.* **a.** the intersection of two planes, or of a plane and a surface. **b.** the sum of the elements along the principal diagonal of a square matrix. *—v.t.* **11.** to follow the footprints, track, or traces of. **12.** to follow (footprints, evidence, the history or course of something, etc.). **13.** to follow the course, development, or history of: *to trace a political movement.* **14.** to ascertain by investigation; find out; discover. **15.** to draw (a line, outline, figure, etc.). **16.** to make a plan, diagram, or map of. **17.** to copy (a drawing, plan, etc.) by following the lines of the original on a superimposed transparent sheet. **18.** to make an impression or imprinting of (a design, pattern, etc.). *—v.i.* **19.** to go back in history, ancestry, or origin; date back in time. **20.** to follow a course, trail, etc.; make one’s way.
trace[2] (trās), *n.* **1.** either of the two straps, ropes, or chains by which a carriage or wagon is drawn by a harnessed animal. *—Idiom.* **2. kick over the traces,** to throw off restraint; become independent.
trace′ el′ement, *n.* **1.** any chemical element required in minute quantities for physiological functioning. **2.** a substance that occurs naturally only in minute amounts in the earth’s crust. Also, **trace′ min′eral.**
trac•er (trā′sər), *n.* **1.** a person or thing that traces. **2.** a person whose business or work is the tracing of missing property, parcels, persons, etc. **3.** an inquiry sent from point to point to trace a missing shipment, parcel, or the like. **4.** a projectile, as a bullet, containing a chemical substance that leaves a trail of fire or smoke. **5.** a substance, esp. a radioactive one, traced through a biological, chemical, or physical system in order to study the system.
trac•er•y (trā′sə rē), *n., pl.* **-er•ies.** **1.** ornamental work consisting of ramified ribs, bars, or the like, as in the upper part of a Gothic window, in panels, screens, etc. **2.** any delicate, interlacing work of lines, threads, etc., as in carving or embroidery; network.
tra•che•a (trā′kē ə), *n., pl.* **-che•ae** (-kē ē′), **-che•as.** **1.** (in air-breathing vertebrates) a tube that extends from the larynx to the bronchi, serving as the principal passageway of air to and from the lungs; windpipe. **2.** (in insects and certain other invertebrates) any of a network of air-conveying tubules throughout the body.
tra•che•id (trā′kē id), *n.* an elongated, tapering xylem cell having woody, pitted, intact walls, adapted for conduction and support. Compare VESSEL (def. 4).
tra•che•ole (trā′kē ōl′), *n.* any of the smallest branches of an insect trachea.
tra•che•ot•o•my (trā′kē ot′ə mē), *n., pl.* **-mies.** the operation of cutting into the trachea. **—tra′che•ot′o•mist,** *n.*
trac•ing (trā′sing), *n.* **1.** the act of a person or thing that traces. **2.** something that is produced by tracing. **3.** a copy of a drawing, map, etc., made by tracing on a transparent sheet placed over the original.
trac′ing pa′per, *n.* a thin, transparent paper for making tracings.
track (trak), *n.* **1.** a pair of parallel lines of rails with their crossties, on which a railroad train, trolley, or the like runs. **2.** a wheel rut. **3.** evidence, as a mark or a series of marks, that something has passed. **4.** Usu., **tracks.** footprints or other marks left by an animal, person, or vehicle. **5.** a path made or beaten by or as if by the feet of people or animals; trail. **6.** a course or route followed; line of travel. **7.** a course of action, conduct, or procedure. **8.** a series or sequence of events or ideas. **9.** a caterpillar tread. **10. a.** a course laid out for running or racing. **b.** the group of sports performed on such a course, as running or hurdling, as distinguished from field events. **11. a.** a band of recorded sound laid along the length of a magnetic tape. **b.** a discrete, separate recording that is combined with other parts of a musical recording to produce the final aural version. **12.** the distance between the centers of the treads of either the front or rear wheels of a motor vehicle. **13.** a metal strip or rail along which something, as lighting or a curtain, can be mounted or moved. **14.** a study program or level of curriculum to which a student is assigned on the basis of aptitude or need; academic course or path. *—v.t.* **15.** to follow or pursue the track, traces, or footprints of. **16.** to follow (a track, course, etc.). **17.** to leave footprints on (often fol. by *up*): *to track the floor with muddy shoes.* **18.** to make a trail of footprints with (dirt, snow, or the like). **19.** to monitor the course or path of (an aircraft, satellite, star, etc.), as by radar or radio signals. **20.** to follow the course of progress of; keep track of. *—v.i.* **21.** to follow or pursue a track or trail. **22.** to run in the same track, as the wheels of a vehicle. **23.** to be in alignment, as one gearwheel with another. **24.** to have a specified span between wheels or runners. **25. track down,** to pursue until caught or captured; follow. *—Idiom.* **26. keep track,** to remain aware; keep informed. **27. lose track,** to fail to keep informed; neglect to keep a record. **28. make tracks,** *Informal.* to hurry. **29. off the track,** departing from the objective or the subject at hand; astray. **30. on the track of,** in search or pursuit of; close upon. **31. the wrong** (or **right**) **side of the tracks,** the unfashionable, unacceptable (or fashionable, acceptable) part of a city or other community.
track′ and field′, *n.* a sport performed indoors or outdoors and made up of several events, as running, pole-vaulting, shot-putting, and broad-jumping. **—track′-and-field′,** *adj.*
track′ing shot′, *n.* a camera shot taken from a moving dolly.
track′ing sta′tion, *n.* a facility with equipment for following the flight of a rocket or spacecraft.
track′ light′ing, *n.* an interior lighting system using spotlight fixtures positioned along an electrified track attached to the wall or ceiling. —**track′ light′,** *n.*
track′ meet′, *n.* a series of athletic contests such as running and jumping, usu. including most track-and-field events.
track′ rec′ord, *n.* a record of achievements or performance: *an outstanding track record in publishing.*
track′ shoe′, *n.* a light, heelless, usu. leather shoe with steel spikes or a rubber sole, worn for racing or running on a sports track.
track′ suit′ or **track′suit′,** *n.* a sweat suit worn by athletes.
track′ sys′tem, *n.* a system of separating students into groups or classes according to scholastic ability.
tract[1] (trakt), *n.* **1.** an expanse or area of land, water, etc.; region; stretch. **2. a.** a definite region or area of the body, esp. a system of elongated parts or organs: *the digestive tract.* **b.** a bundle of nerve fibers having a common origin and destination. **3.** a stretch or period of time; interval; lapse.
tract[2] (trakt), *n.* an anthem of scriptural verses, usu. from a psalm, sung after the gradual, esp. during the pre-Lenten and Lenten seasons.
tract[3] (trakt), *n.* a brief treatise or pamphlet for general distribution, usu. on a religious or political topic.
trac•ta•ble (trak′tə bəl), *adj.* **1.** easily managed or controlled; docile; yielding. **2.** easily worked, shaped, or otherwise handled; malleable. **—trac′ta•bil′i•ty, trac′ta•ble•ness,** *n.*
Trac•tar•i•an•ism (trak târ′ē ə niz′əm), *n.* the High Church doctrine of the Oxford movement as given in a series of 90 tracts published in Oxford, England, 1833–41. **—Trac•tar′i•an,** *adj., n.*
tract′ house′, *n.* a house forming part of a real-estate development, usu. having a plan and appearance common to some or all of the houses in the development.

trac·tile (trak′til, -tīl), *adj.* **1.** capable of being drawn out in length; ductile. **2.** capable of being drawn. —**trac·til′i·ty** (-til′i tē), *n.*

trac·tion (trak′shən), *n.* **1.** the adhesive friction of a body on some surface, as a wheel on a rail or a tire on a road. **2.** the action of drawing a body, vehicle, train, or the like, along a surface, as a road, track, railroad, or waterway. **3.** the deliberate and prolonged pulling of a muscle, organ, or the like, as by weights, to correct dislocation, relieve pressure, etc. **4.** the act of drawing or pulling. **5.** the state of being drawn.

trac·tor (trak′tər), *n.* **1.** a powerful motor-driven vehicle with large, heavy treads, used for pulling farm machinery, other vehicles, etc. **2.** a short truck with a driver's cab but no body, designed for hauling a trailer or semitrailer. **3.** something used for drawing or pulling.

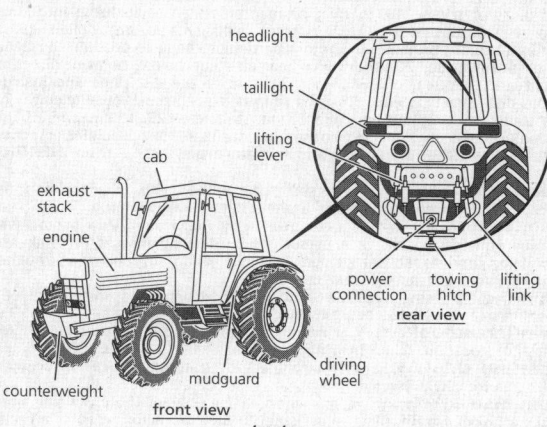

front view

tractor

trac′tor feed′, *n.* a mechanism for moving paper in a computer printer by means of pins that catch in perforations along the paper's sides.

trac′tor pull′, *n.* a contest in which tractors compete to pull the heaviest load.

trac′tor-trail′er, *n.* a trucking unit consisting of a tractor hooked up to a full trailer or a semitrailer.

trade (trād), *n., v.,* **trad·ed, trad·ing,** *adj.* —*n.* **1.** the act or process of buying, selling, or exchanging commodities, at either wholesale or retail, within a country or between countries: *domestic trade; foreign trade.* **2.** a purchase or sale; business deal or transaction. **3.** an exchange of items, usu. without payment of money. **4.** any occupation pursued as a business or livelihood. **5.** some line of skilled manual or mechanical work; craft. **6.** people engaged in a particular line of business: *a show open to the trade.* **7.** market: *an increase in the tourist trade.* **8.** a field of business activity. **9.** the customers of a business establishment. **10. trades,** TRADE WIND. —*v.t.* **11.** to buy and sell; barter; traffic in. **12.** to exchange: *to trade seats.* —*v.i.* **13.** to carry on trade: *trading in silver and gold.* **14.** to traffic (usu. fol. by *in*): *a tyrant who trades in human lives.* **15.** to make an exchange. **16.** to make one's purchases; shop; buy. **17. trade in,** to give (a used article) as payment to be credited toward a purchase. **18. trade off,** to exchange something for or with another. **19. trade on** or **upon,** to turn to one's advantage, esp. selfishly or unfairly; exploit: *to trade on the weaknesses of others.* —*adj.* **20.** of or pertaining to trade or commerce. **21.** used by, serving, or intended for a particular trade: *trade journals.* **22.** Also, **trades.** of, composed of, or serving the members of a trade: *a trade club.*

trade′ accept′ance, *n.* a bill of exchange drawn by the seller of goods and accepted by the buyer for payment at a future date.

trade′ bal′ance, *n.* BALANCE OF TRADE.

trade′ book′, *n.* a book of general interest available through an ordinary book dealer, as distinguished from a limited-edition book or textbook.

trade′ dis′count, *n.* a discount given by a manufacturer or wholesaler to a retailer.

trade′-in′, *n.* **1.** goods given in whole or, usu., part payment of a purchase: *We used our old car as a trade-in for the new one.* **2.** a business transaction involving a trade-in. —*adj.* **3.** of or pertaining to a trade-in. **4.** of or pertaining to the valuation of goods used in a trade-in: *trade-in price.* **4.** of or pertaining to such a business transaction: *trade-in terms.*

trade′ lan′guage, *n.* a lingua franca, esp. one used primarily for trade and conducting business.

trade·mark (trād′märk′), *n.* **1.** any name, symbol, figure, letter, word, or mark adopted and used by a manufacturer or merchant to distinguish a product or products from the ones manufactured or sold by others: a trademark must be registered with a government patent office to assure its exclusive use by its owner. **2.** a distinctive mark or feature particularly characteristic of or identified with a person or thing. —*v.t.* **3.** to

stamp or otherwise place a trademark designation upon. **4.** to register the trademark of.

trade′ name′, *n.* **1.** a word or phrase used in a trade to designate a business, service, or a particular class of goods. **2.** a brand name. **3.** the name or style under which a firm does business.

trade′-off′ or **trade′off′,** *n.* the exchange of one thing for another of more or less equal value, esp. to effect a compromise.

trad·er (trā′dər), *n.* **1.** a person who trades; a merchant or businessperson. **2.** a ship used in trade, esp. foreign trade. **3.** a member of a stock exchange trading privately and not on behalf of customers.

trade′ route′, *n.* any route usu. taken by merchant ships, caravans, etc.

trade′ school′, *n.* a high school giving instruction chiefly in the skilled trades.

trade′ se′cret, *n.* a secret method, device, process, or formula, used to competitive advantage in a business.

trade′ show′, *n.* SHOW (def. 22).

trades·peo·ple (trādz′pē′pəl), *n.pl.* those persons who are engaged in trade; tradesmen. Also called **trades′folk′** (-fōk′).

trade′ un′ion, *n.* **1.** a labor union of workers in related crafts, as distinguished from general workers or a union including all workers in an industry. **2.** LABOR UNION. —**trade′-un′ion,** *adj.* —**trade′ un′ionism,** *n.* —**trade′ un′ionist,** *n.*

trade′ wind′ (wind), *n.* Often, **trade winds.** any of the nearly constant easterly winds that dominate most of the tropics and subtropics throughout the world, blowing mainly from the northeast in the Northern Hemisphere, and from the southeast in the Southern Hemisphere.

trad′ing post′, *n.* a general store established in a remote area, orig. by a trading company to obtain furs, etc., in exchange for food, clothing, and other supplies.

trad′ing stamp′, *n.* a stamp given as a premium to a customer, specified quantities of these stamps being exchangeable for various articles.

tra·di·tion (trə dish′ən), *n.* **1.** the handing down of statements, beliefs, legends, customs, etc., from generation to generation, esp. by word of mouth or by practice. **2.** something that is so handed down: *the traditions of the Eskimos.*

tra·di·tion·al (trə dish′ə nl), *adj.* **1.** of or pertaining to tradition. **2.** handed down by tradition. **3.** in accordance with tradition. Sometimes, **tra·di·tion·ar·y** (-ner′ē). —**tra·di·tion·al·ly,** *adv.*

tra·di·tion·al·ism (trə dish′ə nl iz′əm), *n.* **1.** adherence to tradition as authority, esp. in matters of religion. **2.** a system of philosophy according to which all knowledge of religious truth is derived from divine revelation and received by traditional instruction. —**tra·di·tion·al·ist,** *n., adj.* —**tra·di·tion·al·is′tic,** *adj.*

tra·duce (trə dōos′, -dyōos′), *v.t.,* **-duced, -duc·ing.** to speak maliciously and falsely of; slander; defame. —**tra·duce′ment,** *n.* —**tra·duc′er,** *n.* —**tra·duc′ing·ly,** *adv.*

tra·du·cian·ism (trə dōo′shə niz′əm, -dyōo′-), *n.* the doctrine that the human soul is propagated along with the body. Compare **creationism** (def. 3).

Tra·fal·gar (trə fal′gər; *Sp.* trä′fäl gär′), *n.* **Cape,** a cape on the SW coast of Spain, W of Gibraltar: British naval victory over the French and Spanish fleets 1805.

traf·fic (traf′ik), *n., v.,* **-ficked, -fick·ing.** —*n.* **1.** the movement of vehicles, ships, aircraft, persons, etc., in an area or over a route. **2.** the vehicles, persons, etc., moving in an area or over a route. **3.** the transportation of goods for trade, by sea, land, or air: *ships of traffic.* **4.** trade; buying and selling; commercial dealings. **5.** trade between different countries or places; commerce. **6.** the business done by a railroad or other carrier in the transportation of freight or passengers. **7.** the aggregate of freight, passengers, telephone messages, etc., handled, esp. in a given period. **8.** communication, dealings, or contact between persons or groups. **9.** mutual exchange or communication: *traffic in ideas.* **10.** trade in some specific commodity or service, often of an illegal nature: *drug traffic.* —*v.i.* **11.** to carry on traffic, trade, or commercial dealings. **12.** to trade or deal in a specific commodity or service, often of an illegal nature (usu. fol. by *in*): *to traffic in opium.* —**traf′fick·er,** *n.*

traf′fic cir′cle, *n.* a circular arrangement built at the intersection of two or more roads in order to facilitate the passage of vehicles from one road to another. Also called **rotary;** *Brit.,* **roundabout.**

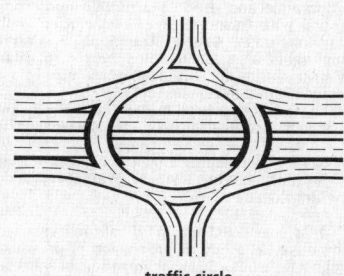

traffic circle

traf′fic court′, *n.* a court that passes on alleged violations of traffic laws.

traf′fic is′land, *n.* a raised or marked-off area between lanes of a roadway, used by pedestrians as a safety island, for separating lanes, etc.

traf′fic light′, *n.* a set of electrically operated signal lights to direct or control traffic at intersections. Also called **stoplight, traf′fic sig′nal.**

traf′fic man′ager, *n.* **1.** an employee responsible for scheduling transportation for freight or passengers. **2.** an office employee, usu. an executive, responsible for routing items of business within a company for appropriate action by various departments.

traf′fic pat′tern, *n.* **1.** a system of courses about an airfield that aircraft are assigned to fly when taking off, landing, or preparing to land. **2.** any systematic movement of people or vehicles. **3.** the flow of air traffic prescribed for aircraft landing at or taking off from an airport.

trag•a•canth (trag′ə kanth′, traj′-), *n.* a gum of various Asian shrubs belonging to the genus *Astragalus,* of the legume family, used as a filler, as in pills, and to stiffen calico.

tra•ge•di•an (trə jē′dē ən), *n.* **1.** an actor noted for performing tragic roles. **2.** a writer of tragedy.

trag•e•dy (traj′i dē), *n.,* *pl.* **-dies. 1.** a lamentable, dreadful, or fatal event or affair; calamity; disaster: *a family tragedy.* **2.** the tragic element of drama, of literature generally, or of life: *the tragedy of poverty.* **3.** a literary composition, as a novel, dealing with a somber theme carried to a tragic conclusion. **4.** a dramatic composition, often in verse, dealing with a serious or somber theme, typically that of a great person destined through a flaw of character or conflict with some overpowering force, as fate or society, to suffer downfall or destruction. **5.** the branch of the drama that is concerned with this form of composition.

trag•ic (traj′ik) also **trag′i•cal,** *adj.* **1.** dreadful, calamitous, disastrous, or fatal: *a tragic event.* **2.** extremely mournful, melancholy, or pathetic. **3.** of, pertaining to, or characteristic of tragedy: *a tragic actor; tragic solemnity.* —**trag′i•cal•ly,** *adv.*

trag′ic flaw′, *n.* a character defect that causes the downfall of the protagonist of a tragedy.

trag•i•com•e•dy (traj′i kom′i dē), *n.,* *pl.* **-dies. 1.** a dramatic or other literary composition combining elements of both tragedy and comedy. **2.** an incident, or series of incidents, of mixed tragic and comic character. —**trag′i•com′ic** (-kom′ik), *adj.* —**trag′i•com′i•cal•ly,** *adv.*

tra•gus (trā′gəs), *n.,* *pl.* **-gi** (-jī) a small projection of cartilage at the front of the ear.

trail (trāl), *v.t.* **1.** to drag or let drag along the ground or other surface; draw or drag along behind. **2.** to bring or have floating after itself or oneself: *a racing car trailing clouds of dust.* **3.** to follow the track, trail, or scent of; track. **4.** to follow along behind (another), as in a race. —*v.i.* **5.** to be drawn or dragged along the ground or some other surface: *The bridal gown trailed across the floor.* **6.** to hang down loosely from something. **7.** to stream from or float after something moving, as dust, smoke, and sparks do. **8.** to follow as if drawn along. **9.** to go slowly, lazily, or wearily along. **10.** to pass or extend in a straggling line. **11.** to change gradually or wander from a course, so as to become weak, ineffectual, etc. (usu. fol. by *off* or *away*): *Her voice trailed off into silence.* **12.** to arrive or be last. **13.** to be losing in a contest. **14.** to follow a track or scent, as of game. **15.** (of a plant) to extend itself in growth along the ground rather than taking root or clinging by tendrils, etc. —*n.* **16.** a path or track made in overgrown or rough terrain by the passage of people or animals. **17.** the track, scent, or the like, left by an animal, person, or thing. **18.** something that is trailed or that trails behind, as the train of a skirt or robe. **19.** a stream of dust, smoke, light, people, vehicles, etc., behind something moving. **20.** either of two rearward-facing parts of an artillery piece, spread out on the ground for support when the piece is fired. —**trail′ing•ly,** *adv.* —**trail′less,** *adj.*

trail′ bike′, *n.* a small motorcycle designed and built with special tires and suspension for riding on unpaved roads and over rough terrain. Also called **dirt bike.**

trail•blaz•er (trāl′blā′zər), *n.* **1.** a person who blazes a trail for others to follow through unsettled country or wilderness; pathfinder. **2.** a pioneer in any field of endeavor. Also called **trail•break•er** (trāl′brā′kər). —**trail′blaze′,** *v.t., v.i.,* **-blazed, -blaz•ing.**

trail•er (trā′lər), *n.* **1.** a large van or wagon drawn by an automobile, truck, or tractor, used esp. in hauling freight by road. **2.** a vehicle attached to an automobile and used as a mobile home or place of business, usu. equipped with furniture, kitchen facilities, bathroom, etc. **3.** a person or thing that trails. **4.** a trailing plant. **5.** a short promotional film showing highlights of a forthcoming movie. **6.** blank film at the end of a reel or strip of film, for winding off the film in a motion-picture camera or projector. Compare LEADER (def. 6).

trail′er camp′, *n.* an area where house trailers may be parked, usu. having running water, electrical outlets, etc. Also called **trail′er court′, trail′er park′.**

trail′ing arbu′tus, *n.* a creeping E North American plant, *Epigaea repens,* of the heath family, having leathery oval leaves and terminal clusters of pink or white flowers.

trail′ mix′, *n.* GORP.

train (trān), *n.* **1.** a connected group of railroad cars, usu. pushed or pulled by a locomotive. **2.** a line or procession of persons, vehicles, animals, etc., traveling together. **3.** an aggregation of vehicles and personnel used to carry supplies for an army. **4.** a series or row of objects or

parts. **5.** POWER TRAIN. **6.** an elongated part of a skirt or robe trailing behind on the ground. **7.** a line or succession of persons or things following one after the other. **8.** a body of followers or attendants; retinue. **9.** a series of proceedings, events, ideas, etc. **10.** a series of resulting circumstances; aftermath: *Disease came in the train of war.* **11.** a course of reasoning: *to lose one's train of thought.* **12.** a line of combustible material, as gunpowder, for leading fire to an explosive charge. **13.** *Physics.* a succession of wave fronts, oscillations, or the like. —*v.t.* **14.** to develop or form the habits, thoughts, or behavior of (a child or other person) by discipline and instruction. **15.** to make proficient by instruction and practice, as in some art, profession, or work. **16.** to make (a person) fit by exercise, diet, practice, etc., as for an athletic performance. **17.** to discipline and instruct (an animal), as in the performance of tasks or tricks. **18.** to treat or manipulate so as to bring into some desired form, position, etc.: *to train one's hair to stay down.* **19.** to bring (a plant, branch, etc.) into a particular shape or position, by bending, pruning, etc. **20.** to bring to bear on some object; point or direct, as a firearm, camera, or eye. —*v.i.* **21.** to give the discipline and instruction, drill, practice, etc., designed to impart proficiency or efficiency. **22.** to undergo discipline and instruction, drill, etc. **23.** to get oneself into condition for an athletic performance through exercise, diet, practice, etc. **24.** to travel or go by train. —**train′a•ble,** *adj.* —**train′a•bil′i•ty,** *n.*

train•ee (trā nē′), *n.* **1.** a person being trained, esp. in a vocation; apprentice. **2.** an enlisted person undergoing military training.

train•er (trā′nər), *n.* **1.** a person or thing that trains. **2.** a person who trains athletes; coach. **3.** a person who trains racehorses or other animals for contests, shows, or performances. **4.** an airplane or a simulated aircraft used in training crew members.

train•ing (trā′ning), *n.* the education, instruction, or discipline of a person or thing that is being trained.

train′ing school′, *n.* **1.** a school providing training in an art, profession, or vocation. **2.** an institution for the care of juvenile delinquents.

train′ing ship′, *n.* a ship equipped for training novices in seamanship, as for naval service.

train•man (trān′mən), *n.,* *pl.* **-men.** a member of the crew that operates a railroad train, usu. an assistant to the conductor, such as a brakeman or flagman.

traipse (trāps), *v.,* **traipsed, traips•ing,** *n.* —*v.i.* **1.** to walk or go aimlessly or idly or without finding or reaching one's goal. —*v.t.* **2.** to walk over; tramp: *to traipse the fields.* —*n.* **3.** a tiring walk.

trait (trāt; *Brit. also* trā), *n.* **1.** a distinguishing characteristic or quality, esp. of one's personal nature: *bad traits.* **2.** an inherited feature or characteristic: *a recessive trait.*

trai•tor (trā′tər), *n.* **1.** a person who betrays another, a cause, or any trust. **2.** a person who commits treason by betraying his or her country.

trai•tor•ous (trā′tər əs), *adj.* **1.** having the character of a traitor; treacherous; perfidious. **2.** characteristic of a traitor. **3.** of the nature of treason; treasonable. —**trai′tor•ous•ly,** *adv.*

Tra•jan (trā′jən), *n.* (*Marcus Ulpius Nerva Trajanus*) A.D. 53?–117, Roman emperor 98–117.

tra•ject (trə jekt′), *v.t.* to transmit.

tra•jec•to•ry (trə jek′tə rē), *n.,* *pl.* **-ries. 1.** the curve described by a projectile, rocket, etc., in its flight. **2.** any path or course. **3.** a geometric curve or surface that cuts all the curves or surfaces of a given system at a constant angle. —**tra•jec′tile** (-til, -tīl), *adj.* —**tra•jec′tion,** *n.*

tram (tram), *n., v.,* **trammed, tram•ming.** —*n.* **1.** *Brit.* a streetcar. **2.** a tramway or tramroad. **3.** a truck or car on rails for carrying loads in a mine. **4.** the vehicle or cage of an overhead carrier. —*v.t., v.i.* **5.** to convey or travel by tram.

tram•mel (tram′əl), *n., v.,* **-meled, -mel•ing** or (*esp. Brit.*) **-melled, -mel•ling.** —*n.* **1.** Usu., **trammels.** a hindrance or impediment to free action; restraint. **2.** an instrument for drawing ellipses. **3.** a device used to align or adjust parts of a machine. **4.** a net for catching birds or fish, esp. a three-layered net in which fish are trapped in two or more layers of mesh. —*v.t.* **5.** to involve or hold in trammels; restrain. **6.** to catch or entangle in or as if in a net.

tra•mon•tane (trə mon′tān, tram′ən tān′), *adj.* Also, **transmontane. 1.** being or situated beyond the mountains, esp. the Alps, as viewed in Italy. **2.** foreign. —*n.* **3.** a person who lives beyond the mountains. **4.** a foreigner.

tramp (tramp), *v.i.* **1.** to tread or walk with a firm, heavy step. **2.** to tread heavily or trample (usu. fol. by *on* or *upon*). **3.** to walk steadily; march; trudge. **4.** to go on a walking excursion; hike. **5.** to go about as a vagabond or tramp. **6.** to make a voyage on a tramp steamer. —*v.t.* **7.** to walk heavily or steadily through or over. **8.** to traverse on foot: *to tramp the streets.* **9.** to tread or trample underfoot: *to tramp grapes.* **10.** to travel over as a tramp. —*n.* **11.** the act of tramping. **12.** a firm, heavy, resounding tread. **13.** the sound made by such a tread. **14.** a long, steady walk; trudge; hike. **15.** a person who travels about on foot, esp. a vagabond living on occasional jobs or gifts of money or food. **16.** a freight vessel that does not run regularly between fixed ports, but takes a cargo wherever shippers desire. —**tramp′ish•ly,** *adv.*

tram•ple (tram′pəl), *v.,* **-pled, -pling,** *n.* —*v.i.* **1.** to tread or step heavily and noisily; stamp. **2.** to tread heavily, roughly, or crushingly (usu. fol. by *on, upon,* or *over*). —*v.t.* **3.** to tread heavily, roughly, or carelessly on or over; tread underfoot. **4.** to domineer harshly over; crush.

5. to put out or extinguish by trampling (usu. fol. by *out*). —*n.* **6.** the act or sound of trampling. —**tram′pler,** *n.*

tram•po•line (tram′pə lēn′, tram′pə lēn′, -lin), *n.* a sheet, usu. of canvas, attached by resilient cords or springs to a horizontal frame several feet above the floor, used as a springboard in tumbling. —**tram′po•lin′er, tram′po•lin′ist,** *n.*

trampoline

trance (trans, träns), *n., v.,* **tranced, tranc•ing.** —*n.* **1.** a half-conscious state, seemingly between sleeping and waking, in which ability to function voluntarily may be suspended, esp. a state produced by hypnosis or religious ecstasy. **2.** a dazed or bewildered condition. **3.** a state of complete mental absorption or deep musing. —*v.t.* **4.** to entrance; enrapture. —**trance′like′,** *adj.*

tran•quil (trang′kwil), *adj.* **1.** free from commotion or tumult; peaceful; quiet; calm: *a tranquil village.* **2.** unaffected by disturbing emotions; serene; placid: *a tranquil life.* —**tran′quil•ly,** *adv.* —**tran′quil•ness,** *n.*

tran•quil•ize or **tran•quil•lize** (trang′kwə līz′), *v.t., v.i.,* **-ized** or **-lized, -iz•ing** or **-liz•ing.** to make or become tranquil.

tran•quil•iz•er or **tran•quil•liz•er** (trang′kwə lī′zər), *n.* **1.** a person or thing that tranquilizes. **2.** Also called **anxiolytic, minor tranquilizer.** any of various drugs, as the benzodiazepines, that have a mildly sedative, calming, or muscle-relaxing effect.

tran•quil•li•ty or **tran•quil•i•ty** (trang kwil′i tē), *n.* the quality or state of being tranquil.

trans-, 1. a prefix meaning "across," "through," occurring orig. in loanwords from Latin, used in particular to form verbs denoting movement or conveyance from place to place (*transfer; transmit; transplant*) or complete change (*transform; transmute*), or to form adjectives meaning "crossing," "on the other side of," or "going beyond" the place named (*transmontane; transnational; trans-Siberian*). **2.** a prefix used in the names of chemical compounds that are geometric isomers having two identical atoms or groups attached on opposite sides of a molecule divided by a given plane of symmetry. Compare CIS- (def. 2).

trans•act (tran sakt′, -zakt′), *v.t.* **1.** to carry on or conduct (business, negotiations, etc.) to a conclusion or settlement. —*v.i.* **2.** to carry on or conduct business, negotiations, etc. —**trans•ac′tor,** *n.*

trans•ac•tion (tran sak′shən, -zak′-), *n.* **1.** the act or process of transacting; the fact of being transacted. **2.** something that is transacted, esp. a business agreement. **3. transactions,** the published record of the proceedings at a meeting of a learned society or other association. **4.** *Psychol.* an interaction of an individual with one or more other persons, esp. as influenced by their assumed relational roles of parent, child, or adult. —**trans•ac′tion•al,** *adj.*

transac′tional anal′ysis, *n.* a form of psychotherapy focusing on social interactions and analysis of relationships as individuals shift among the roles of parent, child, and adult. *Abbr.:* TA

trans•at•lan•tic (trans′ət lan′tik, tranz′-), *adj.* **1.** crossing or reaching across the Atlantic: *a transatlantic liner.* **2.** situated beyond the Atlantic.

Trans•cau•ca•sia (trans′kô kā′zhə, -shə), *n.* a region in SE Europe, S of the Caucasus Mountains, between the Black and Caspian seas: includes the republics of Armenia, Azerbaijan, and Georgia. —**Trans′cau•ca′sian** (-kā′zhən, -shən, -kazh′ən, -kash′-), *adj., n.*

trans•ceiv•er (tran sē′vər), *n.* a radio transmitter and receiver combined in one unit.

tran•scend (tran send′), *v.t.* **1.** to rise above or go beyond the ordinary limits of; overpass; exceed. **2.** to outdo or exceed in excellence, extent, degree, etc.; surpass; excel. **3.** to be independent of or prior to (the universe, time, etc.). —*v.i.* **4.** to be transcendent or superior; excel.

tran•scend•ence (tran sen′dəns) also **tran•scend′en•cy,** *n.* the quality or state of being transcendent.

tran•scend•ent (tran sen′dənt), *adj.* **1.** going beyond ordinary limits; surpassing; exceeding. **2.** superior or supreme. **3.** (of the Deity) transcending the universe, time, etc. Compare IMMANENT (def. 3). **4. a.** (in Kantian philosophy) transcending experience; not realizable in human experience. **b.** (in modern realism) referred to, but beyond, direct apprehension; outside consciousness. —**tran•scend′ent•ly,** *adv.*

tran•scen•den•tal (tran′sen den′tl, -sən-), *adj.* **1.** transcendent, surpassing, or superior. **2.** being beyond ordinary or common experience, thought, or belief; supernatural. **3.** abstract or metaphysical. **4.** idealistic, lofty, or visionary. **5.** beyond the contingent and accidental in human experience, but not beyond all human knowledge. —**tran′scen•den′tal•i•ty,** *n.* —**tran′scen•den′tal•ly,** *adv.*

tran•scen•den•tal•ism (tran′sen den′tl iz′əm, -sən-), *n.* **1.** transcendental character, thought, or language. **2.** Also called **transcenden′tal**

philos′ophy. any philosophy based upon the doctrine that the principles of reality are to be discovered by the study of the processes of thought, or a philosophy emphasizing the intuitive and spiritual above the empirical: in the U.S., associated with Ralph Waldo Emerson. —**tran′scen•den′tal•ist,** *n., adj.*

transcenden′tal medita′tion, *n.* a technique, based on Hindu practices, for seeking serenity through regular meditation centered upon the repetition of a mantra. *Abbr.:* TM

trans•con•ti•nen•tal (trans′kon tn en′tl), *adj.* **1.** passing or extending across a continent: *a transcontinental railroad.* **2.** on the other, or far, side of a continent. —**trans′con•ti•nen′tal•ly,** *adv.*

tran•scribe (tran skrīb′), *v.t.,* **-scribed, -scrib•ing. 1.** to make a written or typed copy of (dictated material, lecture notes, or other spoken material). **2.** to make an exact copy of (a document, text, etc.). **3.** to write out in another language or alphabet; translate or transliterate. **4.** to represent (speech sounds) in written phonetic symbols. **5.** to make a recording of (a program, announcement, etc.) for broadcasting. **6.** to make a musical transcription of. **7.** to cause to undergo genetic transcription. —**tran•scrib′er,** *n.*

tran•script (tran′skript), *n.* **1.** a written, typewritten, or printed copy; something transcribed or made by transcribing. **2.** an exact copy or reproduction, esp. one having an official status. **3.** an official school report on a student's record, listing subjects studied, grades received, etc.

tran•scrip•tion (tran skrip′shən), *n.* **1.** the act or process of transcribing. **2.** something transcribed. **3.** a transcript; copy. **4.** the arrangement of a musical composition for a medium other than that for which it was orig. written. **5.** a recording made esp. for broadcasting on radio or television. **6.** the process by which messenger RNA is synthesized on a template of DNA. —**tran•scrip′tion•al,** *adj.* —**tran•scrip′tive,** *adj.*

trans•duce (trans dōōs′, -dyōōs′, tranz-), *v.t.,* **-duced, -duc•ing. 1.** to convert (energy) from one form into another. **2.** to cause transduction in (a cell).

tran•sect (tran sekt′), *v.t.* to cut across; dissect transversely.

tran•sept (tran′sept), *n.* **1.** any major transverse part of the body of a church, usu. crossing the nave, at right angles, at the entrance to the choir. **2.** an arm of this, on either side of the central aisle of a church. —**tran•sep′tal,** *adj.*

trans•e•unt (tran′sē ənt) also **transient,** *adj. Philos.* (of a mental act) producing an effect outside of the mind. Compare IMMANENT (def. 2).

trans•fer (*v.* trans fûr′, trans′fər; *n.* trans′fər), *v.,* **-ferred, -fer•ring,** *n.* —*v.t.* **1.** to convey or remove from one place, person, or position to another. **2.** to cause to pass from one person to another, as thought or power; transmit. **3.** *Law.* to make over the possession or control of: *to transfer a title to land.* **4.** to imprint, impress, or otherwise convey (a drawing, design, etc.) from one surface to another. —*v.i.* **5.** to remove oneself or be moved from one place, position, or job to another. **6.** to withdraw from one school, college, etc., and enter another. **7.** to change from one bus, train, etc., to another. —*n.* **8.** a means or system of transferring. **9.** an act of transferring. **10.** the fact of being transferred. **11.** a point or place for transferring. **12.** a ticket entitling a passenger to continue a journey on another bus, train, or the like. **13.** a drawing, design, etc., that is or may be transferred from one surface to another, usu. by direct contact. **14.** a person who has transferred, as from one college to another. **15.** *Law.* the conveyance to another, as by sale or gift, of real or personal property. **16.** the positive or negative influence of prior learning on subsequent learning. —**trans•fer′a•ble, trans•fer′ra•ble,** *adj.* —**trans•fer′a•bil′i•ty,** *n.* —**trans•fer′rer,** *n.*

trans•fer•al or **trans•fer•ral** (trans fûr′əl), *n.* transference; transfer.

trans•fer•ee (trans′fə rē′), *n.* **1.** a person to whom property is transferred. **2.** a person who is transferred.

trans•fer•ence (trans fûr′əns, trans′fər əns), *n.* **1.** the act or process of transferring. **2.** the fact of being transferred. **3.** *Psychoanal.* **a.** the shift of emotions, esp. those experienced in childhood, from one person or object to another, esp. the transfer of feelings about a parent to an analyst. **b.** DISPLACEMENT (def. 7). —**trans•fer•en′tial** (-fə ren′shəl), *adj.*

trans′fer pay′ment, *n.* payment made by a government for a purpose other than purchasing goods or services, as for welfare benefits.

transfer RNA, *n.* any of a class of small, cloverleaf forms of RNA that transfer unattached amino acids in the cell cytoplasm to the ribosomes for protein synthesis. *Abbr.:* tRNA

trans•fig•u•ra•tion (trans′fig yə rā′shən, trans fig′-), *n.* **1.** the act of transfiguring. **2.** the state of being transfigured. **3.** (*cap.*) **a.** the supernatural and glorified change in the appearance of Jesus on the mountain. Matt. 17:1–9. **b.** the festival commemorating this, observed by the Roman Catholic Church on August 6 and by Protestant churches in the U.S. on the last Sunday after Epiphany.

trans•fig•ure (trans fig′yər; *esp. Brit.* -fig′ər), *v.t.,* **-ured, -ur•ing. 1.** to change in outward form or appearance; transform. **2.** to change so as to glorify or exalt. —**trans•fig′ure•ment,** *n.*

trans•fix (trans fiks′), *v.t.,* **-fixed** or **fixt, fix•ing. 1.** to make or hold motionless with amazement, awe, terror, etc. **2.** to pierce through with or as if with a pointed weapon; impale. **3.** to hold or fasten with or on something that pierces.

trans•form (*v.* trans fôrm′; *n.* trans′fôrm), *v.t.* **1.** to change in form, appearance, or structure; metamorphose. **2.** to change in condition, nature, or character; convert. **3.** to change into another substance; transmute. **4.** to alter (voltage and current) by means of an electrical transformer. **5.** *Math.* to change the form of (a figure, expression, etc.)

without in general changing the value. —*v.i.* **6.** to undergo a change in form, appearance, or character; become transformed. —*n.* **7. a.** a mathematical quantity obtained from a given quantity by an algebraic, geometric, or functional transformation. **b.** the transformation itself.

trans•for•ma•tion (trans′fər mā′shən), *n.* **1.** the act or process of transforming. **2.** the state of being transformed. **3.** change in form, appearance, nature, or character. **4.** *Logic.* a mapping between equivalent expressions. **5.** FUNCTION (def. 4a). **6.** the transfer of genetic material from one cell to another resulting in a genetic change in the recipient cell. —**trans′for•ma′tion•al,** *adj.*

transforma′tional gram′mar, *n.* a system of grammatical analysis, esp. a form of generative grammar, that posits the existence of deep structure and surface structure and uses a set of transformational rules to derive surface structure forms from deep structure.

trans•form•er (trans fôr′mər), *n.* **1.** a person or thing that transforms. **2.** a device that uses electromagnetic induction to transfer electrical energy from one circuit to another with a change in voltage and current.

trans•fuse (trans fyōōz′), *v.t.,* **-fused, -fus•ing. 1.** to transfer or pass from one to another; transmit; instill. **2.** to diffuse into or through; permeate; infuse. **3. a.** to transfer (blood, saline solution, etc.) by injection into a vein or artery. **b.** to give a transfusion to. —**trans•fus′er,** *n.* —**trans•fus′i•ble, trans•fus′a•ble,** *adj.*

trans•fu•sion (trans fyōō′zhən), *n.* **1.** the act or process of transfusing. **2.** the direct transferring of blood, plasma, etc., into a blood vessel.

trans•gress (trans gres′, tranz-), *v.,* **-gressed, -gress•ing.** —*v.i.* **1.** to violate a law, command, moral code, etc.; offend; sin. —*v.t.* **2.** to pass over or go beyond (a limit, boundary, etc.): *to transgress the bounds of prudence.* **3.** to go beyond the limits imposed by (a law, command, etc.); violate; infringe. —**trans•gres′sive,** *adj.* —**trans•gres′sor,** *n.*

trans•gres•sion (trans gresh′ən, tranz-), *n.* an act of transgressing; violation of a law, command, etc.; sin.

tran•sient (tran′shənt, -zhənt, -zē ənt), *adj.* **1.** not lasting, enduring, or permanent; transitory. **2.** lasting only a short time; existing briefly; temporary: *transient authority.* **3.** staying only a short time: *transient guests at a hotel.* —*n.* **4.** a person or thing that is transient, esp. a temporary guest, boarder, or laborer. **5.** *Physics.* **a.** a nonperiodic signal of short duration. **b.** a decaying signal, wave, or oscillation. **6.** a sudden pulse of voltage or current. —**tran′science,** *n.* —**tran′sient•ly,** *adv.*

tran•sil•i•ent (tran sil′ē ənt, -sil′yənt), *adj.* leaping or passing from one thing or state to another. —**tran•sil′i•ence,** *n.*

tran•sis•tor (tran zis′tər), *n.* a compact solid-state device consisting of a semiconductor with three or more electrodes: performs the primary functions of an electron tube, as amplification, switching, and detection, but uses less power.

tran•sit (tran′sit, -zit), *n.* **1.** the act or fact of passing across or through; passage from one place to another. **2.** conveyance or transportation from one place to another, as of persons or goods. **3.** a means or system of local public transportation, esp. in an urban area. **4.** a transition or change. **5.** *Astron.* **a.** the passage of a heavenly body across the meridian of a given location or through the field of a telescope. **b.** the passage of Mercury or Venus across the disk of the sun, or of a satellite or its shadow across the face of its primary. **6.** *Astrol.* the passage of a planet in aspect to another planet or a specific point in a horoscope. **7.** a surveyor's instrument, as a theodolite, having a telescope that can be transited, used for measuring horizontal and sometimes vertical angles. —*v.t.* **8.** to pass across or through. **9.** to turn (the telescope of a surveyor's transit) in a vertical plane in order to reverse direction. **10.** *Astron.* to cross (a meridian, celestial body, etc.). —*v.i.* **11.** to pass over or through something; make a transit. **12.** *Astron.* to make a transit across a meridian, celestial body, etc.

tran•si•tion (tran zish′ən, -sish′-), *n.* **1.** movement, passage, or change from one position, state, stage, subject, concept, etc., to another. **2.** a period during which such change takes place. **3. a.** a modulation in music. **b.** a modulating passage from one part of a musical composition to another. **4.** a passage that links one scene or topic to another, as in a piece of writing. —*v.i.* **5.** to make a transition. —**tran•si′tion•al, tran•si′tion•a′ry** (-ə ner′ē), *adj.* —**tran•si′tion•al•ly,** *adv.*

tran•si•tive (tran′si tiv, -zi-), *adj.* **1.** of or designating a verb that is accompanied by a direct object and from which a passive can be formed, as *deny, put,* or *elect.* —*n.* **2.** a transitive verb. —**tran′si•tive•ly,** *adv.*

tran•si•to•ry (tran′si tôr′ē, -tōr′ē, -zi-), *adj.* **1.** not lasting, enduring, permanent, or eternal. **2.** lasting only a short time; brief; short-lived; temporary. —**tran′si•to′ri•ly** (-tôr′ə lē, -tōr′-), *adv.*

Trans•jor•dan (trans jôr′dn, tranz-), *n.* an area E of the Jordan River, in SW Asia: a British mandate (1921–23); an emirate (1923–49); now the major part of the kingdom of Jordan.

Trans•kei (trans kā′, -kī′), *n.* a self-governing black homeland in SE South Africa, on the Indian Ocean: granted independence in 1976. 2,876,122; 16,910 sq. mi. (43,798 sq. km). *Cap.* Umtata. —**Trans•kei′an,** *adj., n.*

trans•late (trans lāt′, tranz-, trans′lāt, tranz′-), *v.,* **-lat•ed, -lat•ing.** —*v.t.* **1.** to turn from one language into another or from a foreign language into one's own. **2.** to change the form, condition, or nature of; transform; convert: *to translate thought into action.* **3.** to explain in terms that can be more easily understood; interpret. **4.** to bear, carry, or move from one place or position to another; transfer. **5.** to cause (a body) to move without rotation or angular displacement. **6.** to exalt in spiritual or emotional ecstasy; enrapture. **7.** to cause to undergo genetic

translation. —*v.i.* **8.** to provide or make a translation; act as translator. **9.** to admit of translation. —**trans•lat′a•ble,** *adj.* —**trans•la′tor,** *n.*

trans•la•tion (trans lā′shən, tranz-), *n.* **1.** a rendering of something into another language or into one's own language from another. **2.** a version in a different language: *an English translation of Plato.* **3.** the act or process of translating. **4.** the state of being translated. **5.** motion in which all particles of a body move with the same velocity along parallel paths. **6.** the process by which messenger RNA specifies the sequence of amino acids that line up on a ribosome for protein synthesis. —**trans•la′tion•al,** *adj.*

trans•lit•er•ate (trans lit′ə rāt′, tranz-), *v.t.,* **-at•ed, -at•ing.** to change (letters, words, etc.) into corresponding characters of another alphabet or language. —**trans•lit′er•a′tion,** *n.* —**trans•lit′er•a′tor,** *n.*

trans•lu•cent (trans lōō′sənt, tranz-), *adj.* **1.** permitting light to pass through but diffusing it so that objects on the opposite side are not clearly visible: *Frosted window glass is translucent.* **2.** easily understandable; lucid. **3.** clear; transparent: *translucent seawater.* —**trans•lu′cence,** *n.* —**trans•lu′cent•ly,** *adv.*

trans•mi•grant (trans mī′grənt, tranz-), *n.* **1.** a person passing through a country or place on the way to the place in which he or she intends to settle. —*adj.* **2.** passing from one place or state to another.

trans•mi•grate (trans mī′grāt, tranz-), *v.,* **-grat•ed, -grat•ing.** —*v.i.* **1.** (of the soul) to be reborn after death in another body. **2.** to move from one place to another. **3.** to migrate from one country to another in order to settle there. —*v.t.* **4.** to cause to transmigrate. —**trans•mi′gra•tor,** *n.* —**trans•mi′gra•to•ry** (-grə tôr′ē, -tōr′ē), *adj.*

trans•mi•gra•tion (trans′mī grā′shən, tranz′-), *n.* **1.** the act of transmigrating. **2.** the passage of a soul after death into another body; metempsychosis. Compare REINCARNATION.

trans•mis•sion (trans mish′ən, tranz-), *n.* **1.** the act or process of transmitting. **2.** the fact of being transmitted. **3.** something that is transmitted. **4. a.** the transference of force between machines or mechanisms, often with changes of torque and speed. **b.** a compact, enclosed unit of gears or the like for this purpose, as in an automobile. **5.** the broadcasting of radio waves from one location to another, as from a transmitter to a receiver. —**trans•mis′sive** (-mis′iv), *adj.* —**trans•mis′sive•ly,** *adv.* —**trans•mis•siv′i•ty,** *n.*

trans•mit (trans mit′, tranz-), *v.,* **-mit•ted, -mit•ting.** —*v.t.* **1.** to send or forward, as to a recipient or destination; dispatch; convey. **2.** to communicate, as information or news. **3.** to pass or spread (disease, infection, etc.) to another. **4.** to pass on (a genetic characteristic) from parent to offspring. **5. a.** to cause (light, heat, sound, etc.) to pass through a medium. **b.** to permit (light, heat, etc.) to pass through: *Glass transmits light.* **c.** to convey or pass along (an impulse, force, motion, etc.). **6.** *Radio and Television.* to emit (electromagnetic waves). —*v.i.* **7.** to send a signal by radio waves or by wire. —**trans•mit′ta•ble,** *adj.* —**trans•mit′tal,** *n.*

trans•mit•ter (trans mit′ər, tranz-), *n.* **1.** a person or thing that transmits. **2.** a device for sending radio waves; the part of a broadcasting apparatus that generates and modulates radiofrequency current, conveying it to the antenna. **3.** the part of a telephonic or telegraphic apparatus that converts sound waves or mechanical movements into corresponding electric waves or impulses.

trans•mog•ri•fy (trans mog′rə fī′, tranz-), *v.t.,* **-fied, -fy•ing.** to change in appearance or form, esp. strangely or grotesquely; transform. —**trans•mog′ri•fi•ca′tion,** *n.*

trans•mute (trans myōōt′, tranz-), *v.t., v.i.,* **-mut•ed, -mut•ing.** to change from one nature, substance, form, or condition into another; transform. —**trans•mut′a•ble,** *adj.* —**trans•mut•a•bil′i•ty,** *n.* —**trans•mut′a•bly,** *adv.* —**trans•mut′er,** *n.*

trans•o•ce•an•ic (trans′ō shē an′ik, tranz′-), *adj.* **1.** extending across or traversing the ocean: *a transoceanic cable.* **2.** situated or living beyond the ocean.

tran•som (tran′səm), *n.* **1.** a crosspiece separating a door or the like from a window above it. **2.** a window above such a crosspiece. **3.** a crossbar of wood or stone, dividing a window horizontally.

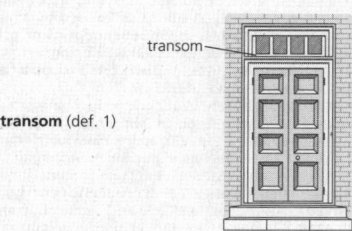

transom (def. 1)

trans•pa•cif•ic (trans′pə sif′ik), *adj.* **1.** crossing or extending across the Pacific. **2.** beyond or on the other side of the Pacific.

trans•par•en•cy (trans pâr′ən sē, -par′-), *n., pl.* **-cies. 1.** Also, **trans•par′ence.** the quality or state of being transparent. **2.** something transparent, esp. a picture or design on glass or some translucent substance, made visible by light shining through from behind. **3.** a photographic print on a clear base for viewing by transmitted light.

trans•par•ent (trans pâr′ənt, -par′-), *adj.* **1.** having the property of transmitting rays of light through its substance so that bodies situated beyond or behind can be distinctly seen. **2.** admitting the passage of light through interstices. **3.** so sheer as to permit light to pass through; diaphanous. **4.** easily seen through, recognized, or detected: *transparent excuses.* **5.** easily understood; manifest; obvious. **6.** candid; frank; open. —**trans•par′ent•ly,** *adv.* —**trans•par′ent•ness,** *n.*

tran•spire (tran spīər′), *v.,* **-spired, -spir•ing.** —*v.i.* **1.** to occur; happen; take place. **2.** to emit or give off waste matter, watery vapor, etc., through the surface, as of leaves or the body. **3.** to escape, as moisture or odor, through or as if through pores. **4.** to be revealed or become known. —*v.t.* **5.** to emit or give off (watery vapor, an odor, etc.) through the surface, as of leaves or the body. —**tran•spir′a•ble,** *adj.*

trans•plant (*v.* trans plant′, -plänt′; *n.* trans′plant′, -plänt′), *v.t.* **1.** to remove (a plant) from one place and plant it in another. **2.** to transfer (an organ, tissue, etc.) from one part of the body to another or from one person or animal to another. **3.** to move from one place to another. **4.** to bring from one country, region, etc., to another for settlement; relocate. —*v.i.* **5.** to undergo or accept transplanting. —*n.* **6.** the act or process of transplanting. **7.** a plant, organ, person, etc., that has been transplanted. —**trans•plant′a•ble,** *adj.* —**trans′plan•ta′tion,** *n.*

tran•spon•der (tran spon′dər), *n.* a radio, radar, or sonar transceiver that automatically transmits a signal upon reception of a designated incoming signal.

trans•port (*v.* trans pôrt′, -pōrt′; *n.* trans′pôrt, -pōrt), *v.t.* **1.** to carry, move, or convey from one place to another. **2.** to carry away by strong emotion; enrapture. **3.** to send into banishment, esp. to a penal colony. —*n.* **4.** the act of transporting or conveying; conveyance. **5.** a means of transporting or conveying, as a truck or bus. **6.** a ship or plane for transporting soldiers, military stores, etc. **7.** a plane carrying freight or passengers as part of a transportation system. **8.** a system of public travel. **9.** strong emotion, esp. ecstasy, bliss, etc.; rapture. **10.** a convict sent into banishment, esp. to a penal colony. —**trans•port′a•ble,** *adj.*

trans•por•ta•tion (trans′pər tā′shən), *n.* **1.** the act of transporting. **2.** the state of being transported. **3.** the means of transport or conveyance. **4.** the business of conveying people, goods, etc. **5.** fare or tickets for transport or travel. **6.** banishment, as of a criminal to a penal colony; deportation.

trans•pose (*v.* trans pōz′; *n.* trans′pōz), *v.,* **-posed, -pos•ing,** —*v.t.* **1.** to change or reverse the relative position, order, or sequence of; interchange: *to transpose the third and fourth letters of a word.* **2.** to transfer or transport. **3.** to write or perform (a musical composition) in a different key. **4.** to bring (a term) from one side of an algebraic equation to the other, with corresponding change of sign. **5.** to transform; transmute. —*v.i.* **6.** to transpose music. —**trans•pos′a•ble,** *adj.* —**trans•pos′a•bil′i•ty,** *n.* —**trans•pos′er,** *n.*

trans•po•si•tion (trans′pə zish′ən), *n.* **1.** an act of transposing. **2.** the state of being transposed. **3.** a transposed form of something. **4.** the movement of a gene or set of genes from one DNA site to another. —**trans′po•si′tion•al, trans•pos′i•tive** (-poz′i tiv), *adj.*

tran•sub•stan•ti•a•tion (tran′səb stan′shē ā′shən), *n.* **1.** the changing of one substance into another. **2.** (in the Eucharist) the conversion of the whole substance of the bread and wine into the body and blood of Christ, only the appearance of bread and wine remaining.

trans′u•ran′ic el′ement (trans′yo͝o ran′ik, tranz′-, trans′-, tranz′-) also **trans•u•ra′ni•um el′ement** (trans′yo͝o rā′nē əm, tranz′-), *n.* any element having an atomic number greater than 92, the atomic number of uranium.

Trans•vaal (trans väl′, tranz-), *n.* a province in the NE Republic of South Africa. 11,885,000; 110,450 sq. mi. (286,066 sq. km). *Cap.:* Pretoria. —**Trans•vaal′er,** *n.* —**Trans•vaal′i•an,** *adj.*

trans•ver•sal (trans vûr′səl, tranz-), *adj.* **1.** transverse. —*n.* **2.** a line intersecting two or more other lines. —**trans•ver′sal•ly,** *adv.*

trans•verse (trans vûrs′, tranz-; trans′vûrs, tranz′-), *adj.* **1.** lying or extending across or in a cross direction; cross. **2.** (of a flute) having a mouth hole in the side of the tube, near its end, across which the player's breath is directed. Compare END-BLOWN. —*n.* **3.** something that is transverse. —**trans•verse′ly,** *adv.*

Tran•syl•va•nia (tran′sil vān′yə, -vā′nē ə), *n.* a region in central Romania: formerly part of Hungary. 24,027 sq. mi. (62,230 sq. km). —**Tran′syl•va′nian,** *adj., n.*

trap[1] (trap), *n., v.,* **trapped, trap•ping.** —*n.* **1.** a contrivance for catching game or other animals, as a mechanical device that springs shut suddenly. **2.** a device, stratagem, or trick for catching a person unawares. **3.** an unpleasant or confining situation from which it is difficult to escape. **4.** any of various devices for removing undesirable substances from a moving fluid, vapor, etc., or for preventing passage of a substance. **5.** an arrangement in a pipe, as a double curve or a U-shaped section, in which liquid remains and forms a seal for preventing the passage or escape of air or gases through the pipe. **6.** TRAPDOOR. **7.** *Slang.* mouth: *Keep your trap shut.* **8. traps,** the percussion instruments of a jazz or dance band. **9.** a device for hurling clay pigeons into the air in trapshooting. **10.** an act or instance of trapping a ball. **11.** a horse-drawn carriage, esp. a light, two-wheeled one. —*v.t.* **12.** to catch in or as if in a trap; ensnare. **13.** to catch by stratagem, artifice, or trickery. **14.** to stop and hold by or as if by a trap. **15.** to confine or hold without possibility of escape. **16.** to provide with a trap or traps. **17.** to catch (a ball) as it rises after having just hit the ground. —*v.i.* **18.** to set traps for game. **19.** to engage in the business of trapping animals for their furs. **20.** to work the trap in trapshooting.

trap[2] (trap), *v.,* **trapped, trap•ping,** *n.* —*v.t.* **1.** to furnish with or as if with trappings; caparison. —*n.* **2. traps,** personal belongings; baggage.

trap•door (trap′dôr′, -dōr′), *n.* **1.** a door flush with the surface of a floor, ceiling, or roof. **2.** the opening that it covers.

trap′-door′ spi′der, *n.* any of several burrowing spiders, esp. of the family Ctenizidae, that construct a tubular nest with a hinged lid.

tra•peze (tra pēz′; *esp. Brit.* trə-), *n.* an apparatus, used in gymnastics and acrobatics, consisting of a short horizontal bar attached to the ends of two suspended ropes.

trapeze′ art′ist, *n.* a person who performs, esp. professionally, on a trapeze. Also called **tra•pez′ist.**

tra•pe•zi•um (trə pē′zē əm), *n., pl.* **-zi•ums, -zi•a** (-zē ə). **1.** (in Euclidean geometry) any rectilinear quadrilateral plane figure not a parallelogram. **2.** a quadrilateral plane figure of which no two sides are parallel. ca **3.** *Brit.* TRAPEZOID (def. 1a). —**tra•pe′zi•al,** *adj.*

tra•pe•zi•us (trə pē′zē əs), *n., pl.* **-us•es.** a broad, flat muscle on each side of the upper back.

trap•e•zoid (trap′ə zoid′), *n.* **1. a.** a quadrilateral plane figure having two parallel and two nonparallel sides. **b.** *Brit.* TRAPEZIUM (def. 1b). **2.** the mammalian wrist bone that articulates with the metacarpal of the second digit or forefinger. —*adj.* **3.** Also, **trap′e•zoi′dal.** of, pertaining to, or having the form of a trapezoid.

trapezoid (def. 1a)
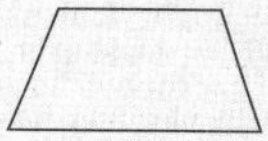

trap•pings (trap′ingz), *n.pl.* **1.** articles of equipment or dress, esp. of an ornamental or symbolic character. **2.** conventional outward forms or symbols; characteristic signs: *the trappings of democracy.* **3.** Sometimes, **trapping.** an ornamental covering for a horse; caparison.

Trap•pist (trap′ist), *n.* **1.** a member of a branch of the Cistercian order, observing the austere reformed rule established at the abbey of La Trappe in France in 1664. —*adj.* **2.** of or pertaining to the Trappists.

trap•shoot•ing (trap′sho͞o′ting), *n.* the sport of shooting at clay pigeons hurled into the air from a trap. Compare SKEET.

trash (trash), *n.* **1.** anything worthless, useless, or discarded; rubbish. **2.** foolish or pointless ideas or talk; nonsense. **3.** a worthless or disreputable person. **4.** such persons collectively. **5.** literary or artistic material of poor or inferior quality. **6.** broken or torn bits, as twigs, splinters, or rags. **7.** something that is broken or lopped off from anything in preparing it for use. **8.** the refuse of sugarcane after the juice has been expressed. —*v.t.* **9.** to destroy, damage, or vandalize, as in anger or protest. **10.** to criticize, dismiss, or condemn as worthless. **11.** to remove the outer leaves of (a growing sugarcane plant). **12.** to free from superfluous twigs or branches. —**trash′er,** *n.*

trash•y (trash′ē), *adj.,* **trash•i•er, trash•i•est.** of the nature of trash; of inferior quality or worth. —**trash′i•ly,** *adv.* —**trash′i•ness,** *n.*

trat•to•ri•a (trä′tə rē′ə), *n., pl.* **-ri•as.** a restaurant or café serving Italian food.

trau•ma (trou′mə, trô′-), *n., pl.* **-mas, -ma•ta** (-mə tə). **1. a.** a body wound or shock produced by physical injury, as from violence or an accident. **b.** the condition produced by this; traumatism. **2.** *Psychiatry.* psychological shock or severe distress from experiencing a disastrous event outside the range of usual experience, as rape, military combat, or an airplane crash. **3.** any wrenching or distressing experience, esp. one causing a disturbance in normal functioning. —**trau•mat•ic** (trə mat′ik, trô-, trou-), *adj.* —**trau•mat′i•cal•ly,** *adv.*

trau•ma•tize (trou′mə tīz′, trô′-), *v.t.,* **-tized, -tiz•ing.** **1.** to cause a trauma in or to: *to be traumatized by a childhood experience.* **2.** to injure (tissues) by force or by thermal, chemical, etc., agents. —**trau′ma•ti•za′tion,** *n.*

tra•vail (trə vāl′, trav′āl), *n.* **1.** painfully difficult or burdensome work; toil. **2.** pain, anguish, or suffering resulting from mental or physical hardship. **3.** the pain of childbirth; labor. —*v.i.* **4.** to toil or exert oneself. **5.** to suffer the pangs of childbirth; be in labor.

trav•el (trav′əl), *v.,* **-eled, -el•ing** or (*esp. Brit.*) **-elled, -el•ling,** *n., adj.* —*v.i.* **1.** to go from one place to another, as by car, train, plane, or ship; take a trip; journey. **2.** to move or pass from one place or point to another. **3.** to proceed or advance. **4.** to pass or be transmitted, as light, sound, or information: *The news traveled quickly.* **5.** to go from place to place as a representative of a business firm. **6.** to associate or consort: *to travel with a wealthy crowd.* **7.** to admit of being transported or transmitted, esp. without suffering harm: *a wine that does not travel well.* **8.** *Informal.* to move with speed. **9.** to move in a fixed course, as a piece of mechanism. —*v.t.* **10.** to travel, journey, or pass through or over. **11.** to journey or traverse (a specified distance). **12.** to cause to travel or journey: *to travel logs downriver.* —*n.* **13.** the act of traveling; journeying, esp. to distant places. **14. travels, a.** journeys; wanderings. **b.** a written work describing such journeys. **15.** the coming and going of people or conveyances along a route; traffic. **16. a.** the complete movement of a moving mechanical part, esp. a reciprocating part, in one direction, or the distance traversed; stroke. **b.** length of stroke. **17.** movement or passage in general. —*adj.* **18.** designed for use while traveling: *a travel alarm clock.*

trav·el a′gency, *n.* a business that provides information and makes arrangements for travelers, as the securing of tickets and accommodations. —**trav′el a′gent,** *n.*

trav·eled (trav′əld), *adj.* **1.** having traveled, esp. to distant places; experienced in travel. **2.** used by travelers: *a heavily traveled road.*

trav·el·er (trav′ə lər, trav′lər), *n.* **1.** a person or thing that travels. **2.** a person who travels or has traveled in distant places or foreign lands. **3.** TRAVELING SALESMAN. **4.** a part of a mechanism constructed to move in a fixed course. **5. a.** a metal ring or thimble fitted to move freely on a rope, spar, or rod. **b.** the rope, spar, or rod itself. **6.** Also called **trav′eler cur′tain,** a transverse curtain opened by being drawn from both sides of the proscenium. Also, *esp. Brit.,* **trav′el·ler.**

trav·el·er's check′, *n.* a check issued in any of various denominations by a bank, travel agency, etc., that is signed by the purchaser upon purchase and again when being cashed or used.

trav′eling sales′man, *n.* a representative of a business firm who travels in an assigned territory soliciting orders for the company.

trav·e·logue or **trav·e·log** (trav′ə lôg′, -log′), *n.* a lecture, slide show, film, etc., describing a person's travels or depicting travels in a particular, often distant or exotic, place.

tra·verse (*v.* trə vûrs′, trav′ərs; *n., adj.* trav′ərs, trə vûrs′), *v.,* **-versed, -vers·ing,** *n., adj.* —*v.t.* **1.** to pass or move over, along, or through; cross. **2.** to go to and fro over or along. **3.** to extend across or over: *A bridge traverses the stream.* **4.** to go up, down, or across (a mountain, hill, rope, etc.) at an angle. **5.** to ski across (a hill or slope). **6.** to cause to move laterally. **7.** to look over, examine, or consider carefully; review; survey. **8.** to go counter to; obstruct; thwart. **9.** to contradict or deny. **10.** *Law.* **a.** (in pleading) to deny formally (an allegation). **b.** to enter into controversy on (a matter). **11.** to turn and point (a gun) in any direction. —*v.i.* **12.** to pass along or go across something; cross. **13.** to ski or climb across a hill or slope on a diagonal. **14.** to turn laterally, as a gun. **15.** (in fencing) to glide the blade toward the hilt of the contestant's foil while applying pressure to the blade. —*n.* **trav·erse 16.** the act of passing across, over, or through. **17.** something that crosses or extends across. **18.** a transversal or similar line. **19.** a place where one may traverse or cross; crossing. **20.** a lateral or oblique course or movement. **21.** something that obstructs or thwarts; obstacle. **22.** a transverse gallery or loft in a church or other large building. **23.** a bar, strip, rod, or other structural part placed or extending across; crosspiece; crossbar. **24.** a railing, lattice, or screen serving as a barrier. **25.** the zigzag track of a vessel compelled by contrary winds or currents to sail on different courses. **26.** a defensive barrier, parapet, or the like, placed transversely. **27.** the horizontal turning of a mounted gun to change direction of fire. **28. a.** the motion of a lathe tool or grinding wheel along a piece of work. **b.** a part moving along a piece of work in this way, as the carriage of a lathe. **29.** a series of intersecting surveyed lines whose lengths and angles of intersection, measured at instrument stations, are recorded graphically on a map and in numerical form in data tables. —*adj.* **trav·erse 30.** lying, extending, or passing across; transverse. —**tra·vers′a·ble,** *adj.* —**tra·vers′al,** *n.* —**tra·vers′er,** *n.*

trav′erse rod′, *n.* a horizontal rod upon which drapes slide to open or close when pulled by cords.

trav·er·tine (trav′ər tēn′, -tin), *n.* a form of limestone deposited by springs, esp. hot springs, used in Italy for building.

trav·es·ty (trav′ə stē), *n., pl.* **-ties,** *v.,* **-tied, -ty·ing.** —*n.* **1.** a grotesque or debased likeness or imitation of something: *a travesty of justice.* **2.** a literary or artistic burlesque of a serious work or subject, characterized by grotesque or ludicrous incongruity of style, treatment, or subject matter. —*v.t.* **3.** to make a travesty of or on; burlesque; mock.

trawl (trôl), *n.* **1.** Also called **trawl′ net′.** a strong fishing net dragged along the sea bottom to catch the fish living there. **2.** Also called **trawl′ line′.** a buoyed line used in sea fishing, having numerous short lines with baited hooks attached at intervals. —*v.i.* **3.** to fish with a trawl. **4.** to troll. —*v.t.* **5.** to catch with a trawl. **6.** to drag (a trawl net). **7.** to troll. —**trawl′a·ble,** *adj.*

trawl·er (trô′lər), *n.* **1.** any of various types of vessels used in fishing with a trawl net. **2.** a person who trawls.

tray (trā), *n.* **1.** a flat, shallow container or receptacle, usu. with slightly raised edges, used for carrying, holding, or displaying articles. **2.** a removable receptacle of this shape in a cabinet, box, trunk, etc., sometimes forming a drawer. **3.** a tray and its contents: *a breakfast tray.*

treach·er·ous (trech′ər əs), *adj.* **1.** characterized by faithlessness or readiness to betray trust; traitorous. **2.** deceptive, untrustworthy, or unreliable. **3.** unstable or insecure, as footing. **4.** dangerous; hazardous: *a treacherous climb.* —**treach′er·ous·ly,** *adv.* —**treach′er·ous·ness,** *n.*

treach·er·y (trech′ə rē), *n., pl.* **-er·ies.** **1.** violation of faith; betrayal of trust; treason. **2.** an act of perfidy, faithlessness, or treason.

trea·cle (trē′kəl), *n.* **1.** something that is excessively sweet or sentimental. **2.** *Brit.* MOLASSES. —**trea′cly** (-klē), *adj.*

tread (tred), *v.,* **trod, trod·den** or **trod, tread·ing,** *n.* —*v.i.* **1.** to set down the foot or feet in walking; step; walk. **2.** to step or walk, esp. so as to press, crush, or injure something; trample (usu. fol. by *on* or *upon*). —*v.t.* **3.** to step or walk on, about, in, or along. **4.** to trample or crush underfoot. **5.** to form by the action of walking or trampling: *to tread a path.* **6.** to treat with disdainful harshness or cruelty; crush; op-

press. **7.** to perform by walking or dancing: *to tread a measure.* **8.** (of a male bird) to copulate with (a female bird). —*n.* **9.** the action of treading. **10.** the sound of footsteps. **11.** manner of treading or walking. **12.** a single step. **13.** any of various things or parts on which a person or thing treads, stands, or moves. **14.** the horizontal upper surface of a step in a stair. **15.** the part of a wheel, tire, or runner that bears on the road, rail, etc. **16.** the pattern raised on or cut into the face of a rubber tire. **17.** the part of the undersurface of the foot or of a shoe that touches the ground. —*Idiom.* **18. tread on someone's toes,** to offend or irritate someone. **19. tread water, a.** to maintain the body erect in the water with the head above the surface, usu. by a pumping up-and-down movement of the legs and sometimes the arms. **b.** to maintain one's position without making any progress. —**tread′er,** *n.*

trea·dle (tred′l), *n., v.,* **-dled, -dling.** —*n.* **1.** a lever or the like worked by continual action of the foot to impart motion to a machine. —*v.i.* **2.** to work a treadle. —**tread′ler** (-lər), *n.*

tread·mill (tred′mil′), *n.* **1.** a mill powered by people or animals treading on a succession of moving steps or on a belt that forms a continuous path. **2.** any monotonous, wearisome routine in which there is little or no satisfactory progress.

trea·son (trē′zən), *n.* **1.** the offense of acting to overthrow one's government or to harm or kill its sovereign. **2.** a violation of allegiance to one's sovereign or state. **3.** the betrayal of trust; treachery.

trea·son·ous (trē′zə nəs), *adj.* treasonable. —**trea′son·ous·ly,** *adv.*

treas·ure (trezh′ər), *n., v.,* **-ured, -ur·ing.** —*n.* **1.** wealth or riches stored or accumulated, esp. in the form of precious metals, money, or jewels. **2.** wealth, rich materials, or valuable things. **3.** any thing or person greatly valued or highly prized. —*v.t.* **4.** to retain carefully or keep in store, as in the mind. **5.** to regard or treat as precious; cherish. **6.** to put away for security or future use, as money; hoard. [< Old French < Latin *thēsaurus* storehouse, hoard]

treas′ure hunt′, *n.* a game in which one attempts to be first in finding hidden objects, using written directions or clues.

Treas′ure Is′land, *n.* **1.** (*italics*) a novel (1883) by R. L. Stevenson. **2.** an artificial island in San Francisco Bay, in W California; naval base.

treas·ur·er (trezh′ər ər), *n.* **1.** an officer of a government, corporation, association, etc., in charge of the receipt, care, and disbursement of money. **2.** a person who is in charge of treasure or a treasury.

treas′ure-trove′, *n.* **1.** anything of the nature of treasure that one finds. **2.** money, bullion, or the like, of unknown ownership, found hidden in the earth or elsewhere: considered the property of the finder.

treas·ur·y (trezh′ə rē), *n., pl.* **-ur·ies. 1.** a place where the funds of the government, a corporation, etc., are deposited, kept, and disbursed. **2.** funds or revenue of a government, public or private corporation, etc. **3.** (*cap.*) the department of government that has control over the collection, management, and disbursement of the public revenue. **4.** a building, room, chest, or other place for the preservation of treasure or valuable objects. **5.** a collection or supply of excellent or highly prized writings, works of art, etc.

Treas′ury bill′, *n.* a promissory note issued by the U.S. government, bearing no interest and maturing in one year or less.

Treas′ury bond′, *n.* any of various interest-bearing bonds issued by the U.S. government in amounts of $1000 or more and maturing in 10 to 30 years.

Treas′ury note′, *n.* an interest-bearing note issued by the U.S. Treasury in amounts of $1000 or more and maturing in ten years or less.

treat (trēt), *v.t.* **1.** to act or behave toward in some specified way: *to treat someone with respect.* **2.** to consider or regard in a specified way: *to treat a matter as unimportant.* **3.** to deal with in a specified way; handle. **4.** to deal with (a disease, patient, etc.) in order to relieve or cure. **5.** to subject to some agent or action in order to bring about a particular result: *to treat a substance with an acid.* **6.** to provide with food, entertainment, gifts, etc., at one's own expense. **7.** to provide with as a source of pleasure or enjoyment. **8.** to deal with in speech or writing; discuss. **9.** to deal with or represent artistically, esp. in some specified manner or style: *to treat a theme realistically.* —*v.i.* **10.** to deal with a subject in speech or writing; discourse (usu. fol. by *of*). **11.** to give, or bear the expense of, a treat. **12.** to carry on negotiations with a view to a settlement; negotiate. —*n.* **13.** entertainment, food, drink, etc., given by way of compliment or as an expression of friendly regard. **14.** anything that affords particular pleasure or enjoyment. **15.** the act of treating. **16.** one's turn to treat. —**treat′er,** *n.*

treat·a·ble (trē′tə bəl), *adj.* able to be treated, esp. medically. —**treat′a·bil′i·ty,** *n.*

trea·tise (trē′tis), *n.* a formal and systematic exposition in writing of the principles of a subject, usu. longer and more detailed than an essay.

treat·ment (trēt′mənt), *n.* **1.** the act, manner, or process of treating. **2.** the application of medicines, surgery, therapy, etc., in treating a disease or disorder. **3.** a substance, procedure, or course of such substances or procedures used in treating medically. **4.** literary or artistic handling, esp. with reference to style. **5.** subjection to some agent or action. **6.** a preliminary outline of a film or teleplay laying out the key scenes, characters, and locales.

trea·ty (trē′tē), *n., pl.* **-ties. 1.** a formal agreement between two or more states with reference to peace, alliance, commerce, or other international relations. **2.** the formal document embodying such an international agreement. **3.** any agreement or compact.

tre·ble (treb′əl), *adj., n., v.,* **-bled, -bling.** —*adj.* **1.** threefold; triple. **2.**

a. of or pertaining to the highest part in harmonized music; soprano. **b.** of the highest pitch or range, as a voice part, voice, singer, or instrument. **c.** high in pitch; shrill. **—***n.* **3. a.** the treble or soprano part. **b.** a treble voice, singer, or instrument. **4.** the upper portion of the range of audio frequencies. **—***v.t., v.i.* **5.** to make or become three times as much or as many; triple. —**tre′bly** (-lē), *adv.*

tre′ble clef′, *n.* a musical sign that locates the G above middle C, placed on the second line of the staff, counting up; G clef.

tree (trē), *n., v.,* **treed, tree•ing.** **—***n.* **1.** a plant having a permanently woody main stem or trunk, ordinarily growing to a considerable height, and usu. developing branches at some distance from the ground. **2.** any of various shrubs, bushes, and plants, as the banana, resembling a tree in form and size. **3.** something resembling a tree in shape, as a clothes tree. **4.** FAMILY TREE. **5.** a pole, post, beam, bar, handle, or the like, as one forming part of some structure. **6.** SHOETREE. **7.** a treelike group of crystals, as one forming in an electrolytic cell. **8.** the cross on which Christ was crucified. **—***v.t.* **9.** to drive into or up a tree, as one pursued. **10.** to put into a difficult position; corner. **11.** to stretch or shape on a tree, as a boot. **—*Idiom.*** **12. up a tree,** in a difficult or embarrassing situation; stumped. **—*Proverb.*** **13. The tree is known by its fruit,** parents can be judged by their children's character. Matt. 12:33.

treed (trēd), *adj.* **1.** planted with trees; wooded. **2.** driven up a tree.

tree′ ear′, *n.* a thin, stemless, rubbery, edible fungus, *Auricularia auricula,* that grows on tree bark.

tree′ farm′, *n.* a tree-covered area managed as a business using reforestation to make continuous production of timber possible.

tree′ fern′, *n.* any of various mostly tropical ferns, chiefly of the family Cyatheaceae, that attain the size of trees, sending up a straight trunklike stem with fronds at the summit.

tree′ frog′, *n.* any frog, esp. of the family Hylidae, that climbs into trees, usu. with the aid of disks at the toes.

tree′ house′, *n.* a small house, esp. one for children to play in, set in the branches of a tree.

tree′ line′, *n.* TIMBERLINE.

tree•lined (trē′līnd′), *adj.* lined with trees, as a street.

tree′ of heav′en, *n.* See under AILANTHUS.

tree′ of knowl′edge of good′ and e′vil, *n.* the tree in the Garden of Eden bearing the forbidden fruit that was tasted by Adam and Eve. Gen. 2:17; 3:6–24. Also called **tree′ of knowl′edge.**

tree′ of life′, *n.* **1.** a tree in the Garden of Eden that yielded food giving everlasting life. Gen 2:9; 3:22. **2.** a tree in the heavenly Jerusalem with leaves for the healing of the nations. Rev. 22:2.

tree′ ring′, *n.* ANNUAL RING.

tree′ shrew′, *n.* any S Asian tree-dwelling mammal of the family Tupaiidae, resembling a squirrel with a long snout and taxonomically combining the characteristics of a primate and insectivore.

tree′ snail′, *n.* any tree-dwelling snail of the family Bulimulidae, of warm climates, usu. having a brightly colored banded shell.

tree′ squir′rel, *n.* any bushy-tailed arboreal squirrel, esp. of the genus *Sciurus.*

tree′ sur′gery, *n.* the repair of damaged trees, as by the removal of diseased parts, filling of cavities, and bracing of branches. —**tree′ sur′geon,** *n.*

tree•top (trē′top′), *n.* the top or uppermost part of a tree.

tref (trāf), *adj.* unfit to be eaten, according to the Jewish dietary laws; not kosher.

tre•foil (trē′foil, tref′oil), *n.* **1.** CLOVER (def. 1). **2.** a three-lobed flower or leaf. **3.** an architectural ornament composed of three lobes, separated by cusps, radiating from a common center. **4.** any three-lobed figure, design, or emblem resembling a clover leaf.

trek (trek), *v.,* **trekked, trek•king,** *n.* **—***v.i.* **1.** to travel or migrate, esp. slowly or with difficulty. **2.** *South Africa.* to travel by ox wagon. **—***n.* **3.** a journey or trip, esp. one involving difficulty or hardship. **4.** *South Africa.* a migration or expedition, esp. by ox wagon. —**trek′ker,** *n.*

trel•lis (trel′is), *n.* **1.** a frame or structure of latticework; lattice. **2.** such a framework used as a support for growing vines or plants. **3.** a summerhouse, arch, etc., made chiefly or completely of latticework. **4.** something with interwoven or interconnected parts suggesting a latticework. **—***v.t.* **5.** to furnish with a trellis. **6.** to enclose in a trellis. **7.** to train or support on a trellis. **8.** to form into or like a trellis.

trem•a•tode (trem′ə tōd′, trē′mə-), *n.* any of various parasitic flatworms of the class Trematoda, having external suckers.

trem•ble (trem′bəl), *v.,* **-bled, -bling,** *n.* **—***v.i.* **1.** to shake involuntarily with quick, short movements, as from fear, excitement, or cold; quake; quiver. **2.** to be troubled with fear or apprehension. **3.** (of things) to be affected with vibratory motion; oscillate. **4.** to be tremulous, as light or sound: *His voice trembled.* **—***n.* **5.** the act of trembling. **6.** a state or fit of trembling. —**trem′bler,** *n.* —**trem′bling•ly,** *adv.*

tre•men•dous (tri men′dəs), *adj.* **1.** extraordinarily great in size, amount, or intensity: *a tremendous ocean liner.* **2.** extraordinary in excellence: *a tremendous movie.* **3.** dreadful or awful; exciting fear; frightening; terrifying. —**tre•men′dous•ly,** *adv.* —**tre•men′dous•ness,** *n.*

trem•o•lo (trem′ə lō′), *n., pl.* **-los.** **1.** a tremulous or vibrating effect produced on certain instruments and in the human voice, as to express emotion. **2.** a mechanical device in an organ by which such an effect is produced.

trem•or (trem′ər, trē′mər), *n.* **1.** involuntary shaking of the body or limbs, as from disease, fear, or excitement; shudder; shiver. **2.** any tremulous or vibratory movement; vibration: *tremors following an earthquake.* **3.** a trembling or quivering effect, as of light. **4.** a quavering sound, as of the voice. —**trem′or•ous,** *adj.*

trem•u•lous (trem′yə ləs), *adj.* **1.** (of persons, the body, etc.) characterized by trembling, as from fear, nervousness, or weakness. **2.** timid; timorous; fearful. **3.** (of things) vibratory, shaking, or quivering. **4.** (of writing) done with a trembling hand. —**trem′u•lous•ly,** *adv.*

trench (trench), *n.* **1.** a long, narrow excavation in the ground dug by soldiers as a defense against enemy fire or attack. **2.** a deep furrow, ditch, or cut. **3.** a long, narrow depression in the deep-sea floor, site of one or more ocean deeps. **—***v.t.* **4.** to surround or fortify with trenches; entrench. **5.** to cut a trench in. **6.** to set or place in a trench. **7.** to form (a furrow, ditch, etc.) by cutting into or through something. **8.** to make a cut in; carve. **—***v.i.* **9.** to dig a trench. **10. trench on** or **upon, a.** to encroach or infringe on. **b.** to come close to; verge on: *His remarks were trenching on poor taste.*

trench•ant (tren′chənt), *adj.* **1.** incisive or keen, as language or a person; caustic; cutting: *trenchant wit.* **2.** vigorous; effective; energetic: *a trenchant policy of reform.* **3.** clearly or sharply defined; clear-cut; distinct. —**trench′an•cy,** *n.* —**trench′ant•ly,** *adv.*

trench′ coat′, *n.* a waterproof coat, usu. double-breasted, with a belt, epaulets, and a strap near the bottom of each sleeve.

trench′ fe′ver, *n.* a recurrent fever and pain in the muscles and joints, often suffered by soldiers serving in trenches, caused by a rickettsia transmitted by the body louse.

trench′ foot′, *n.* injury of the skin, blood vessels, and nerves of the feet due to prolonged exposure to cold and moisture, common among soldiers serving in trenches.

trench′ mouth′, *n.* an acute ulcerating infection of the gums and throat, caused by a combination of bacilli and spirochetes. Also called **Vincent's angina, acute necrotizing gingivitis.**

trend (trend), *n.* **1.** the general course or prevailing tendency; drift: *the trend of events.* **2.** style; vogue: *the new trend in women's apparel.* **3.** the general direction followed by a road, river, coastline, or the like. **—***v.i.* **4.** to have a general tendency, as events or conditions; incline. **5.** to tend to take a particular direction; extend in some direction indicated.

trend•set•ter (trend′set′ər), *n.* a person or thing that establishes a new trend or fashion. —**trend′set′ting,** *adj.*

trend•y (tren′dē), *adj.,* **trend•i•er, trend•i•est.** **1.** of, in, or pertaining to the latest trend or style. **2.** following the latest trends or fashions; up-to-date, chic, or faddish: *the trendy young generation; a trendy resort hotel.* —**trend′i•ly,** *adv.* —**trend′i•ness,** *n.*

Trent (trent), *n.* **1.** a river in central England, flowing NE from Staffordshire to the Humber. 170 mi. (275 km) long. **2.** Italian, **Trento.** a city in N Italy, on the Adige River. 100,677. **3. Council of,** the ecumenical council of the Roman Catholic Church that met at Trent from 1545 to 1563 and defined church doctrine and condemned the Reformation.

Tren•ton (tren′tn), *n.* the capital of New Jersey, in the W part, on the Delaware River. 90,790. —**Tren•to′ni•an** (-tō′nē ən), *n.*

tre•pan (tri pan′), *n., v.,* **-panned, -pan•ning.** **—***n.* **1.** a tool for cutting shallow holes by removing a core. **—***v.t.* **2.** to cut round disks from (plate stock) using a rotating cutter. —**trep•a•na•tion** (trep′ə nā′shən), *n.*

tre•pang (tri pang′), *n.* any of various sea cucumbers, as *Holothuria edulis,* used as food in Asia.

trep•id (trep′id), *adj.* fearful or apprehensive.

trep•i•da•tion (trep′i dā′shən), *n.* **1.** tremulous fear, alarm, or agitation; perturbation. **2.** a trembling or quivering movement; tremor.

tres•pass (tres′pəs, -pas), *n.* **1. a.** wrongful entry upon the lands of another. **b.** an unlawful act causing injury to the person, property, or rights of another. **c.** the action to recover damages for such injury. **2.** an encroachment or intrusion. **3.** an offense, sin, or wrong. **—***v.i.* **4.** to commit a trespass. **5.** to encroach on a person's privacy, time, etc.; infringe (usu. fol. by *on* or *upon*). **6.** to commit a transgression or offense; transgress; offend; sin. —**tres′pass•er,** *n.*

tress (tres), *n.* Usu., **tresses.** long locks or curls of hair, esp. those of a woman.

tressed (trest), *adj.* **1.** (of the hair) arranged or formed into tresses; braided; plaited. **2.** having tresses (usu. used in combination): *golden-tressed schoolgirls.*

tres•tle (tres′əl), *n.* **1.** a frame typically composed of a horizontal member rigidly attached at each end to the top of a transverse A-frame, used as a barrier, a support for planking, etc.; horse. **2. a.** one of a number of transverse frames joined together to support a bridge. **b.** a bridge made of these.

tres′tle ta′ble, *n.* a table composed of a top supported by trestles, often strengthened by a long stretcher.

TRH, thyrotropin-releasing hormone: a hormone of the hypothalamus that controls the release of thyrotropin by the pituitary gland.

tri-, a combining form meaning "three": *triatomic; trilateral.*

tri•ac•e•tate (trī as′i tāt′), *n.* **1.** a compound containing three acetate groups. **2.** a textile fiber made of cellulose triacetate or a fabric made from this fiber.

tri•ad (trī′ad, -əd), *n.* **1.** a group of three, esp. of three closely related persons or things. **2. a.** an element, atom, or group having a valence of three. **b.** a group of three closely related compounds or elements, as isomers or halides. **3.** the basic chord of a musical tonality, consisting of a tonic, a third, and a fifth. —**tri•ad′ic,** *adj.*

tri•age (trē äzh′), *n., adj., v.,* **-aged, ag•ing.** —*n.* **1.** the process of sorting victims, as of a battle or disaster, to determine priority of medical treatment, with highest priority usu. given to those having the greatest likelihood of survival. **2.** the determination of priorities for action in an emergency. —*adj.* **3.** of, pertaining to, or performing the task of triage: *a triage officer.* —*v.t.* **4.** to act on or in by triage: *to triage a crisis.*

tri•al (trī′əl, trīl), *n.* **1. a.** the examination of a cause before a court of law, often involving issues both of law and of fact. **b.** the use of due process to determine a person's guilt or innocence. **2.** the act of trying, testing, or putting to the proof. **3.** an attempt or effort to do something. **4.** a tentative or experimental action in order to ascertain results; experiment. **5.** the state or position of a person or thing being tried or tested; probation. **6.** subjection to suffering or grief; tribulation; distress. **7.** an affliction or trouble. **8.** a troublesome, wearying, or annoying thing or person. —*adj.* **9.** of, pertaining to, or employed in a trial. **10.** done or made by way of trial, proof, or experiment. **11.** used in or for testing, experimenting, sampling, etc.

tri′al and er′ror, *n.* experimentation or investigation in which various means are tried and faulty ones eliminated in order to find the correct solution or achieve the desired result.

tri′al bal′ance, *n.* a statement of open debit and credit items, made before balancing a double-entry ledger.

tri′al balloon′, *n.* a preliminary announcement or other effort made to determine the likely success of a proposed project.

tri′al court′, *n.* the court in which a controversy is first adjudicated, as opposed to an appellate court.

tri′al exam′iner, *n.* a person appointed to hold hearings and report findings to an administrative agency.

tri′al ju′ry, *n.* PETTY JURY.

tri′al law′yer, *n.* a lawyer who specializes in appearing before trial courts.

tri′al run′, *n.* a preliminary performance or test.

Trial, The, (German, *Der Prozess*), a novel (1925) by Franz Kafka.

tri•an•gle (trī′ang′gəl), *n.* **1.** a closed plane figure having three sides and three angles. **2.** a flat triangular piece with straight edges, used in connection with a T square for drawing perpendicular lines, geometric figures, etc. **3.** any three-cornered or three-sided figure, object, or piece: *a triangle of land.* **4.** a musical percussion instrument that consists of a steel triangle, open at one corner, that is struck with a steel rod. **5.** a group of three; triad. **6.** a situation involving three persons, esp. one in which two of them are in love with the third. —**tri′an′gled,** *adj.*

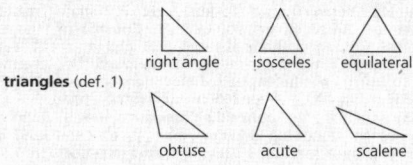

right angle   isosceles   equilateral

triangles (def. 1)

obtuse   acute   scalene

tri•an•gu•lar (trī ang′gyə lər), *adj.* **1.** pertaining to or having the form of a triangle; three-cornered. **2.** having a triangle as base or cross section: *a triangular prism.* **3.** comprising three parts or elements; triple. **4.** pertaining to or involving a group of three persons, parties, or things. —**tri′an′gu•lar′i•ty,** *n.* —**tri•an′gu•lar•ly,** *adv.*

tri•an•gu•late (*adj.* trī ang′gyə lit, -lāt′; *v.* -lāt′), *adj., v.,* **-lat•ed, -lat•ing.** —*adj.* **1.** composed of or marked with triangles. —*v.t.* **2.** to make triangular. **3.** to divide into triangles. **4.** to survey by triangulation.

tri•an•gu•la•tion (trī ang′gyə lā′shən), *n.* **1.** a technique for establishing the distance between any two points, or the relative position of two or more points, by calculations based on the vertices of a triangle and the length of side of measurable length (**base** or **baseline**). **2.** the triangles thus formed and measured.

tri•an•nu•al (trī an′yōō əl), *adj.* **1.** done, occurring, issued, etc., three times a year. **2.** TRIENNIAL. —*n.* **3.** a triannual publication, event, etc. **4.** TRIENNIAL. —**tri•an′nu•al•ly,** *adv.*

tri•ar•chy (trī′är kē), *n., pl.* **-chies. 1.** government by three persons. **2.** a set of three joint rulers; triumvirate. **3.** a country divided into three governments. **4.** a group of three countries or districts, each under its own ruler.

Tri•as•sic (trī as′ik), *adj.* **1.** noting or pertaining to a period of the Mesozoic Era, occurring from 230 million to 190 million years ago and characterized by the advent of dinosaurs and coniferous forests. —*n.* **2.** Also, **Tri•as** (trī′əs). the Triassic Period or System.

tri•ath•lon (trī ath′lon), *n.* **1.** an athletic contest comprising three consecutive events, usu. swimming, bicycling, and distance running, and won by the contestant finishing the entire contest in the least time. **2.** a women's track-and-field competition comprising the 100-meter dash, high jump, and shot put.

trib•al (trī′bəl), *adj.* of, pertaining to, or characteristic of a tribe. —**trib′al•ly,** *adv.*

trib•al•ism (trī′bə liz′əm), *n.* **1.** the customs and beliefs of tribal life and society. **2.** strong loyalty to one's own group. —**trib′al•ist,** *n.*

tribe (trīb), *n.* **1.** any aggregate of people united by ties of descent from a common ancestor, community of customs and traditions, adherence to a leader, etc. **2.** a local division of an aboriginal people. **3. a.** a category in the classification of organisms usu. between a subfamily and a genus or sometimes between a suborder and a family. **b.** any group of plants or animals. **c.** a group of animals, esp. cattle, descended through the female line from a common female ancestor. **4.** a company, group, or set of persons, esp. one with strong common traits or interests. **5.** a large family. **6.** (in ancient Rome) **a.** any one of three divisions of the people representing the Latin, Sabine, and Etruscan settlements. **b.** one of the later political divisions of the people, reaching a total of 35 in number.

tribes•man (trībz′mən), *n., pl.* **-men.** a member of a tribe.

tribes•peo•ple (trībz′pē′pəl), *n.pl.* the members of a tribe.

trib•u•la•tion (trib′yə lā′shən), *n.* **1.** grievous trouble; severe trial or suffering. **2.** an instance of this; an affliction, trouble, or woe.

tri•bu•nal (trī byōon′l, tri-), *n.* **1.** a court of justice. **2.** a place or seat of judgment. **3.** Also called **tribune.** a raised platform for the seats of magistrates, as in an ancient Roman basilica.

trib•une[1] (trib′yōon, tri byōon′), *n.* **1.** a person who upholds or defends the rights of the people. **2.** (in ancient Rome) any of various administrative officers, esp. one of ten officers elected to protect the interests and rights of the plebeians from the patricians.

trib•une[2] (trib′yōon, tri byōon′), *n.* **1.** a raised platform for a speaker; a dais, rostrum, or pulpit. **2.** a raised part, or gallery, with seats, as in a church. **3.** the apse of a church. **4.** TRIBUNAL (def. 3).

trib•u•tar•y (trib′yə ter′ē), *n., pl.* **-tar•ies,** *adj.* —*n.* **1.** a stream that flows to a larger stream or other body of water. **2.** a person or nation that pays tribute. —*adj.* **3.** (of a stream) flowing into a larger stream or other body of water. **4.** furnishing subsidiary aid; contributory. **5.** paying tribute. **6.** paid as tribute. —**trib′u•tar′i•ly,** *adv.*

trib•ute (trib′yōot), *n.* **1.** a gift, testimonial, compliment, or the like, given as due or as an expression of gratitude or esteem. **2.** a stated sum or other valuable consideration paid by one sovereign or state to another in acknowledgment of subjugation or as the price of peace. **3.** a rent, tax, or the like, as that paid by a subject to a sovereign. **4.** any enforced payment or contribution. **5.** obligation to make such payment. —*adj.* **6.** of or pertaining to a band or individual who performs songs made famous by another.

tri•cam•er•al (trī kam′ər əl), *adj.* (of a legislative body) consisting of three chambers or houses.

tri•cen•ten•ni•al (trī′sen ten′ē əl), *adj., n.* TERCENTENNIAL.

tri•ceps (trī′seps), *n., pl.* **-ceps•es** (-sep siz), **-ceps.** any muscle with three heads, esp. the one at the back of the upper arm, extending the forearm when contracted.

tri•cer•a•tops (trī ser′ə tops′), *n.* any massive, plant-eating Cretaceous dinosaur of the genus *Triceratops,* having a bony crest on the neck, a horn over each eye, and a horn on the nose.

triceratops, *Triceratops elatus,*
8 ft. (2.4 m) high at shoulder;
length 20 ft. (6 m); horns 3 ¼ ft. (1 m);
skull 8 ft. (2.4 m)

tri•chi•na (tri kī′nə), *n., pl.* **-nae** (-nē). a nematode, *Trichinella spiralis,* parasitic esp. in humans, pigs, and rats.

trich•i•no•sis (trik′ə nō′sis) also **trich•i•ni•a•sis** (-nī′ə sis), *n.* infestation of the intestines and muscle tissue with trichinae, usu. by eating infected meat, esp. undercooked pork.

tri•chop•ter•an (trī kop′tər ən), *n.* CADDISFLY. —**tri•chop′ter•ous,** *adj.*

tri•chot•o•my (tri kot′ə mē), *n., pl.* **-mies. 1.** division into three parts, classes, elements, etc. **2.** an instance of this. —**trich•o•tom•ic** (trik′ə tom′ik), **tri•chot′o•mous,** *adj.* —**tri•chot′o•mous•ly,** *adv.*

tri•chro•mat•ic (trī′krō mat′ik, -krə-), *adj.* **1.** pertaining to the use or combination of three colors, as in printing or in color photography. **2.** pertaining to, characterized by, or involving three colors. **3.** of, pertaining to, or exhibiting normal color vision.

tri•cit•y (trī′sit′ē, -sit′ē), *adj.* of or pertaining to a metropolitan area consisting of three separate but interdependent cities.

trick (trik), *n.* **1.** a crafty or underhanded device, maneuver, or stratagem intended to deceive or cheat; artifice; ruse; wile. **2.** a roguish or mischievous act; practical joke; prank. **3.** a clever or ingenious device or expedient; adroit technique: *the tricks of the trade.* **4.** the art or knack of doing something skillfully: *the trick of making others laugh.* **5.** a clever or dexterous feat intended to entertain, amuse, etc.: *This bird can do some amazing tricks.* **6.** a feat of magic or legerdemain: *card tricks.* **7.** an optical illusion: *a trick played by the flickering lights.* **8.** a mean, foolish, or childish action. **9.** a behavioral peculiarity; trait; habit; mannerism. **10.** a period or tour of duty; turn; stint. **11. a.** the group or set of cards played and won in one round. **b.** a point or scoring unit based on this. **c.** a card that is a potential winner. **12.** a child or young girl: *a pretty little trick.* —*adj.* **13.** of, pertaining to, characterized by, or involving tricks: *trick shooting.* **14.** specially made or used for tricks: *a trick chair.* **15.** (of a joint) inclined to stiffen or weaken suddenly and unexpectedly: *a trick shoulder.* —*v.t.* **16.** to deceive by trickery. **17.** to cheat or swindle (usu. fol. by *out of*): *to trick someone out of an inheritance.* **18.** to beguile by trickery (usu. fol. by *into*). —*v.i.* **19.** to practice trickery or deception; cheat. **20.** to play tricks; trifle (usu. fol. by *with*). **21. trick out,** to adorn with fancy ornaments; bedeck. —***Idiom.*** **22. do** or **turn the trick,** to produce the desired effect.

trick•er•y (trik′ə rē), *n., pl.* **-er•ies. 1.** the use of tricks or stratagems to deceive; artifice; deception. **2.** a trick so used.

trick•le (trik′əl), *v.,* **-led, -ling,** *n.* —*v.i.* **1.** to flow or fall by drops, or in a small, gentle stream: *Tears trickled down her cheeks.* **2.** to come, go, or pass bit by bit, slowly, or irregularly: *The guests trickled out of the room.* —*v.t.* **3.** to cause to trickle. —*n.* **4.** a trickling flow or stream. **5.** a small, slow, or irregular quantity of anything coming, going, or proceeding. —**trick′ling•ly,** *adv.*

trick′le-down′ the′ory, *n.* an economic theory that monetary benefits directed esp. by the government to big business will in turn pass down to and profit smaller businesses and the general public.

trick′ or treat′, *n.* a Halloween custom in which children call on neighbors, local merchants, etc., to ask for a small treat, ritualistically threatening to play a trick if refused. —**trick′-or-treat′,** *v.i.* —**trick′-or-treat′er,** *n.*

trick•ster (trik′stər), *n.* **1.** a deceiver; cheat; fraud. **2.** a person who plays tricks. **3.** a mischievous, knavish figure of myth and folklore, often a being with supernatural powers as well as a culture hero.

trick•y (trik′ē), *adj.,* **trick•i•er, trick•i•est. 1.** given to or characterized by deceitful tricks; crafty; wily; sly. **2.** unpredictably difficult or troublesome; unreliable or uncooperative: *a tricky light switch.* **3.** having, using, or involving clever, intricate, or demanding maneuvers: *a tricky dance step.* —**trick′i•ly,** *adv.* —**trick′i•ness,** *n.*

tri•col•or (trī′kul′ər; *esp. Brit.* trik′ə lər), *adj.* **1.** Also, **tri′col′ored;** *esp. Brit.,* **tri′col′oured.** having three colors. —*n.* **2.** a flag with three colors, esp. the national flag of France, adopted during the French Revolution, having one vertical band each of blue, white, and red. Also, *esp. Brit.,* **tri′col′our.**

tri•cor•nered (trī′kôr′nərd), *adj.* three-cornered; tricorn.

tri•cot (trē′kō), *n.* **1.** a warp-knit fabric of various natural or synthetic fibers, as silk or nylon, having fine vertical ribs on the face and horizontal ribs on the back, used esp. for garments. **2.** a woolen or worsted fabric with horizontal or vertical ribbing.

tri•cus•pid (trī kus′pid), *adj.* **1.** Also, **tri•cus′pi•dal.** having three cusps or points, as a tooth. Compare BICUSPID. **2.** of, pertaining to, or affecting the tricuspid valve. —*n.* **3.** a tricuspid part, as a tooth.

tri•cy•cle (trī′si kəl, -sik′əl), *n.* **1.** a vehicle, esp. one for children, with one large front wheel and two small rear wheels, propelled by pedals. **2.** a velocipede with three wheels propelled by pedals or hand levers.

tri•dent (trīd′nt), *n.* **1.** a three-pronged instrument or weapon. **2.** the three-pronged spear forming a characteristic attribute of the sea god Poseidon, or Neptune. **3.** (*cap.*) *Mil.* a 34-ft (10-m) submarine-launched U.S. ballistic missile with eight to ten warheads and a range of 6500 mi. (10,459 km). —*adj.* **4.** Also, **tri•den•tal** (trī den′tl). having three prongs or tines.

Tri•den•tine (trī den′tin, -tīn, -tēn), *adj.* of or pertaining to the Council of Trent or its decrees.

tried (trīd), *v.* **1.** pt. and pp. of TRY. —*adj.* **2.** tested and proved good, reliable, or trustworthy. **3.** subjected to hardship, worry, trouble, etc.

tried′-and-true′, *adj.* tested and found to be reliable or workable.

tri•en•ni•al (trī en′ē əl), *adj.* **1.** occurring every three years. **2.** lasting three years. —*n.* **3.** a third anniversary. **4.** something that appears or occurs every three years. **5.** a period of three years; triennium. —**tri•en′ni•al•ly,** *adv.*

tri•en•ni•um (trī en′ē əm), *n., pl.* **-en•ni•ums, -en•ni•a** (-en′ē ə). a period of three years.

tries (trīz), *n.* **1.** pl. of TRY. —*v.* **2.** 3rd pers. sing. pres. indic. of TRY.

Tri•este (trē est′, -es′tā, -tē), *n.* **1.** a seaport in NE Italy, on the Gulf of Trieste. 237,191. **2. Free Territory of,** an area bordering the N Adriatic: designated a free territory by the U.N. 1947; N zone, including the city of Trieste, turned over to Italy in 1954; S zone incorporated into Yugoslavia. **3. Gulf of,** an inlet in the N Adriatic, in NE Italy.

tri•fect•a (trī′fek′tə), *n., pl.* **-fect•as.** a type of bet, esp. on horse races, in which the bettor must select the first three finishers in exact order. Also called **triple.**

tri•fle (trī′fəl), *n., v.,* **-fled, -fling.** —*n.* **1.** something of very little value, importance, or consequence. **2.** a small, inconsiderable, or trifling amount of anything. **3.** a dessert of cake soaked in liqueur, then combined with custard, fruit, jam, etc., and topped with whipped cream. —*v.i.* **4.** to deal lightly or without due seriousness or respect (usu. fol. by *with*): *Don't trifle with me!* **5.** to play or toy by handling or fingering (usu. fol. by *with*): *He sat trifling with a pen.* **6.** to act or talk idly or frivolously. **7.** to waste time; idle. —*v.t.* **8.** to pass or spend (time) idly or frivolously (usu. fol. by *away*); fritter. —***Idiom.*** **9. a trifle,** to a small degree; somewhat: *still a trifle angry.* —**tri′fler,** *n.*

tri•fling (trī′fling), *adj.* **1.** of very small importance, value, or amount; trivial; insignificant: *a trifling matter; a trifling sum.* **2.** frivolous; shallow; light: *trifling conversation.* **3.** shiftless; worthless. —*n.* **4.** idle or frivolous conduct, talk, etc. **5.** foolish delay or waste of time. —**tri′fling•ly,** *adv.* —**tri′fling•ness,** *n.*

tri•fo•cal (trī fō′kəl, trī′fō′-), *adj.* **1.** (of a lens) having three foci. **2.** (of an eyeglass lens) having three portions, one for near, one for intermediate, and one for far vision. —*n.* **3. trifocals,** eyeglasses with trifocal lenses.

tri•fur•cate (trī fûr′kāt, trī′fər kāt′; *adj. also* -kit), *v.,* **-cat•ed, -cat•ing,** *adj.* —*v.i.* **1.** to divide into three forks or branches. —*adj.* **2.** Also, **tri•fur′cat•ed.** divided into three forks or branches. —**tri′fur•ca′tion,** *n.*

trig (trig), *n.* trigonometry.

trig•ger (trig′ər), *n.* **1.** a small projecting tongue in a firearm that, when pressed by the finger, actuates the mechanism that discharges the weapon. **2.** a device, as a lever, the pulling or pressing of which releases a detent or spring. **3.** anything, as an act or event, that initiates or precipitates a reaction or series of reactions. —*v.t.* **4.** to initiate or precipitate (a reaction, process, or chain of events). **5.** to fire or explode (a gun, missile, etc.) by pulling a trigger or releasing a triggering device. —*v.i.* **6.** to release a trigger. **7.** to become active; activate. —***Idiom.*** **8. quick on the trigger, a.** quick to act or respond; impetuous; volatile. **b.** ready to act; sensitive; alert.

trig′ger fin′ger, *n.* any finger, usu. the forefinger, that presses the trigger of a gun.

trig′ger-hap′py, *adj.* **1.** ready to fire a gun at the least provocation, regardless of the situation or probable consequences. **2.** reckless in advocating action that can result in war.

tri•glyc•er•ide (trī glis′ə rīd′, -ər id), *n.* an ester obtained from glycerol, forming much of the fats and oils stored in tissues.

trig•o•nom•e•try (trig′ə nom′i trē), *n.* the branch of mathematics that deals with the relations between the sides and angles of plane or spherical triangles, and the calculations based on them. —**trig′o•no•met′ric** (-nə me′trik), *adj.* —**trig′o•no•met′ri•cal•ly,** *adv.*

tri•lat•er•al (trī lat′ər əl), *adj.* having three sides. —**tri•lat′er•al′i•ty,** *n.* —**tri•lat′er•al•ly,** *adv.*

tri•lin•e•ar (trī lin′ē ər), *adj.* of or bounded by three lines.

tri•lin•gual (trī ling′gwəl), *adj.* expressed in, using, or able to use three languages. —**tri•lin′gual•ism,** *n.* —**tri•lin′gual•ly,** *adv.*

trill (tril), *n.* **1.** a rapid alternation of two adjacent musical tones; shake. **2.** a similar quavering sound, as that made by a bird or a person laughing. **3. a.** a sequence of rapid vibratory movements produced in a speech organ, as the tongue or uvula. **b.** a speech sound produced by a trill. —*v.t.* **4.** to sing, utter, or play with a trill. **5.** to pronounce with a trill: *to trill an* r. —*v.i.* **6.** to perform or utter a trill.

Tril•ling (tril′ing), *n.* **Lionel,** 1905–75, U.S. critic and author.

tril•lion (tril′yən), *n., pl.* **-lions,** (*as after a numeral*) **-lion,** *adj.* —*n.* **1.** a cardinal number represented in the U.S. by 1 followed by 12 zeros, and in Great Britain by 1 followed by 18 zeros. —*adj.* **2.** amounting to one trillion in number. —**tril′lionth,** *n., adj.*

tril•li•um (tril′ē əm), *n.* any of several plants belonging to the genus *Trillium,* of the lily family, having on the stem a whorl of three leaves and a solitary flower with three sepals and three petals.

tri•lo•bite (trī′lə bīt′), *n.* any marine arthropod of the extinct class Trilobita, from the Paleozoic Era, having a flattened oval body in three vertical segments. —**tri′lo•bit′ic** (-bit′ik), *adj.*

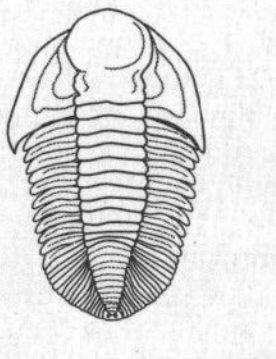

trilobite, *Griffithides bufo,* length 1 1/4 in. (3.2 cm)

tril•o•gy (tril′ə jē), *n., pl.* **-gies.** a series or group of three plays, novels, operas, etc., that, although individually complete, are closely related in theme, sequence, or the like.

trim (trim), *v.,* **trimmed, trim•ming,** *n., adj.,* **trim•mer, trim•mest,** *adv.* —*v.t.* **1.** to put into a neat or orderly condition by clipping, paring, pruning, etc.: *to trim a hedge.* **2.** to remove (something superfluous or dispensable) by or as if by cutting (often fol. by *off*): *to trim off loose threads.* **3.** to cut down to required size or shape. **4.** to level off (an airship or airplane) in flight. **5. a.** to distribute the load of (a ship) so that it sits well in the water. **b.** to adjust (the sails or yards) with reference to the direction of the wind and the course of the ship. **6.** to decorate or adorn with ornaments or embellishments. **7.** to arrange goods in (a store window, showcase, etc.) as a display. **8.** to prepare or adjust (a lamp, fire, etc.) for proper burning. **9.** to beat or thrash. **10.** to defeat. —*v.i.* **11. a.** to assume a particular position or trim in the water, as a vessel. **b.** to adjust the sails or yards with reference to the direction of the wind and the course of the ship. **12.** to accommodate one's views to the prevailing opinion for reasons of expediency. —*n.* **13.** the condition, order, or fitness of a person or thing for action, work, use, etc. **14. a.** the set of a ship in the water, esp. the most advantageous one. **b.** the condition of a ship with reference to its fitness for sailing. **c.** the adjustment of sails, rigging, etc., with reference to wind direction and the course of the ship. **15.** a person's dress, adornment, or appearance. **16.** material used for decoration or embellishment. **17.** decoration of a store window for the display of merchandise. **18.** a trimming by cutting, clipping, or the like. **19.** something that is or is intended to be cut off or eliminated, esp. the outer edges of a page of a book, magazine, or the

T

like before folding or binding. **20.** the attitude of an airplane with respect to all three axes, at which balance occurs in forward flight under no controls. **21.** finished woodwork or the like, as cornices, baseboards, or moldings, used as a decoration or border. **22.** ornamentation on the exterior of an automobile, esp. in metal or a contrasting color. *—adj.* **23.** pleasingly neat or smart in appearance: *trim lawns.* **24.** in good condition or order. **25.** (of a person) in excellent physical condition. **26.** slim; lean: *a trim figure.* *—adv.* **27.** trimly. *—Idiom.* **28. trim one's sails,** to cut expenses; economize. **—trim′ly,** *adv.* **—trim′ness,** *n.*

tri•ma•ran (trī′mə ran′), *n.* a boat similar to a catamaran but having three separate hulls.

tri•mes•ter (trī mes′tər, trī′mes-), *n.* **1.** a term or period of three months: *the first trimester of pregnancy.* **2.** one of the three approximately equal terms into which the academic year is divided. **—tri•mes′tral** (-trəl), **tri•mes′tri•al,** *adj.*

trim•ming (trim′ing), *n.* **1.** anything used or serving to decorate or complete: *the trimming on a uniform.* **2.** Usu., **trimmings.** an accompaniment or garnish to a main dish: *roast turkey with all the trimmings.* **3. trimmings,** pieces cut off in trimming, clipping, paring, or pruning. **4.** the act of a person or thing that trims. **5.** a beating or thrashing. **6.** a defeat: *Our team took quite a trimming.*

tri•month•ly (trī munth′lē), *adj.* occurring, taking place, done, or acted upon every three months.

Tri•mur•ti (tri mo͝or′tē), *n.* (in later Hinduism) a trinity consisting of Brahma the Creator, Vishnu the Preserver, and Shiva the Destroyer. [< Sanskrit *trimūrti* = *tri* THREE + *mūrti* shape]

trine (trīn), *adj.* **1.** threefold; triple. **2.** *Astrol.* pertaining to the positive aspect of two of the zodiac planets distant from each other 120°. *—n.* **3.** a set or group of three; triad. **4.** (*cap.*) the Trinity.

Trin•i•dad (trin′i dad′), *n.* an island in the SE West Indies, off the NE coast of Venezuela: formerly a British colony, now part of Trinidad and Tobago. 1,198,000; 1864 sq. mi. (4828 sq. km). **—Trin′i•da′di•an** (-dā′dē ən, -dad′ē-), *adj., n.*

Trin′idad and Toba′go, *n.* a republic in the West Indies, comprising the islands of Trinidad and Tobago: member of the Commonwealth of Nations. 1,273,141; 1980 sq. mi. (5128 sq. km). *Cap.:* Port-of-Spain.

Trin•i•tar•i•an (trin′i târ′ē ən), *adj.* **1.** believing in the doctrine of the Trinity. **2.** of or pertaining to the Trinity or Trinitarians. *—n.* **3.** a person who believes in the doctrine of the Trinity.

Trin•i•ty (trin′i tē), *n., pl.* **-ties** for 3. **1.** the union of three persons (Father, Son, and Holy Ghost) in one Godhead, or the threefold personality of the one Divine Being. **2.** TRINITY SUNDAY. **3.** (*l.c.*) a group of three; triad. **4.** (*l.c.*) the state of being threefold or triple. [< Old French < Late Latin *trīnitās* triad, the Trinity, der. of Latin *trīn(ī)* by threes]

Trin′ity Sun′day, *n.* the Sunday after Pentecost, observed as a festival in honor of the Trinity.

trin•ket (tring′kit), *n.* **1.** a small ornament, piece of jewelry, etc., usu. of little value. **2.** anything of trivial value.

tri•no•mi•al (trī nō′mē əl), *adj.* **1.** consisting of or pertaining to three algebraic terms. **2. a.** pertaining to a scientific name comprising three terms, as of genus, species, and subspecies. **b.** characterized by the use of such names. *—n.* **3.** an expression that is a sum or difference of three terms, as $3x + 2y + z$ or $3x^3 + 2x^2 + x$. **—tri•no′mi•al•ly,** *adv.*

tri•o (trē′ō), *n.* **1.** any group of three persons or things. **2.** a musical composition for three voices or instruments. **3.** a company of three singers or players. **4.** the middle section of a minuet, scherzo, or march.

trip (trip), *n., v.,* **tripped, trip•ping.** *—n.* **1.** a traveling from one place to another; journey or voyage. **2.** a journey or run made by a boat, train, or the like, between two points. **3.** a single course of travel taken as part of one's duty, work, etc.: *my weekly trip to the bank.* **4.** a stumble; misstep. **5.** a sudden impeding or catching of a person's foot so as to throw the person down. **6.** a slip, error, or blunder. **7.** a light, nimble step or movement of the feet. **8.** a projection on a moving part that strikes a control lever to stop, reverse, or control a machine, as a printing press. **9.** *Slang.* a stimulating or exciting experience. *—v.i.* **10.** to stumble: *to trip on a toy.* **11.** to make a slip or mistake, as in conversation or conduct. **12.** to step lightly or nimbly; skip. **13.** to tip or tilt. *—v.t.* **14.** to cause to stumble (often fol. by *up*). **15.** to cause to fail; obstruct or overthrow. **16.** to cause to make a slip or error (often fol. by *up*). **17.** to catch in a slip or error. **18.** to tip or tilt. **19.** to break out (a ship's anchor) by turning over or lifting from the bottom by a line attached to the crown of the anchor. **20.** to operate, start, or set free (a mechanism, weight, etc.) by suddenly releasing a catch, clutch, or the like. **21.** to release or operate suddenly (a catch, clutch, etc.). *—Idiom.* **22. trip the light fantastic,** to go dancing.

tri•par•tite (trī pär′tīt), *adj.* **1.** divided into or consisting of three parts: *a tripartite leaf.* **2.** involving, participated in, or made by three parties: *a tripartite treaty.* **—tri′par•ti′tion** (-pär tish′ən, -pər-), *n.*

tripe (trīp), *n.* **1.** the first and second divisions of the stomach of a ruminant, esp. oxen, sheep, or goats, used as food. **2.** *Informal.* something, esp. speech or writing, that is false or worthless.

tri•ped•al (trī′ped′l, trip′i dl), *adj.* having three feet.

trip′ham′mer or **trip′ ham′mer,** *n.* a heavy hammer raised and then let fall by some tripping device, as a cam.

tri•phib•i•ous (trī fib′ē əs), *adj.* of or pertaining to combined military operations by land, air, and naval forces.

triph•thong (trif′thông, -thong, trip′-), *n.* a monosyllabic speech-sound sequence made up of three differing vowel qualities, as in some pronunciations of *our.* **—triph•thong′al** (-gəl), *adj.*

tri•ple (trip′əl), *adj., n., v.,* **-pled, -pling.** *—adj.* **1.** threefold; having three parts. **2.** of three kinds; threefold in character or relationship. **3.** three times as great. *—n.* **4.** an amount, number, etc., three times as great as another. **5.** a group or series of three; triad. **6.** Also called **three-base hit.** a hit in baseball that enables a batter to reach third base safely. **7.** (in bowling) three strikes in succession. **8.** TRIFECTA. *—v.t.* **9.** to make triple. **10.** to cause (a base runner) to come into home plate by a triple. *—v.i.* **11.** to become triple. **12.** to make a triple in baseball.

Tri′ple Alli′ance, *n.* **1.** the alliance (1882–1915) of Germany, Austria-Hungary, and Italy. **2.** a league (1717) of France, Great Britain, and the Netherlands against Spain. **3.** a league (1668) of England, Sweden, and the Netherlands against France.

Tri′ple Crown′, *n.* **1.** an unofficial title held by a horse that wins the Kentucky Derby, the Preakness, and the Belmont Stakes. **2.** a usu. unofficial title held by someone who wins three major awards or championships in the same year.

tri′ple-deck′er, *n.* a sandwich made of three slices of bread with two layers of filling; club sandwich.

Tri′ple Entente′, *n.* an understanding among Great Britain, France, and Russia before World War I to counterbalance the Triple Alliance.

tri′ple jump′, *n.* (in track and field) a jumping event for distance in which a participant leaps on one foot from a takeoff point, lands on the same foot, steps forward on the other foot, leaps, and lands on both feet.

tri′ple play′, *n.* a baseball play resulting in three putouts.

tri′ple-space′, *v.t., v.i.,* **-spaced, -spac•ing.** to type so as to have two blank lines after each typed line.

tri•plet (trip′lit), *n.* **1.** one of three children or offspring born at the same birth. **2. triplets,** three offspring born at one birth. **3.** any group or combination of three. **4.** a group of three lines of verse, usu. rhyming. **5.** a group of three musical notes to be performed in the same time of two notes of the same value.

tri′ple threat′, *n.* an expert in three different fields or in three different skills in the same field.

tri•plex (trip′leks, trī′pleks), *adj.* **1.** threefold; triple. *—n.* **2.** something triple. **3.** an apartment having three floors. **4.** a multiplex of three theaters or movie houses.

trip•li•cate (*n., adj.* trip′li kit, -kāt′; *v.* -kāt′), *n., v.,* **-cat•ed, -cat•ing,** *adj. —n.* **1.** one of three identical items. *—v.t.* **2.** to make threefold; triple. **3.** to make three identical copies of. *—adj.* **4.** having or consisting of three identical copies or parts; threefold. *—Idiom.* **5. in triplicate,** in three identical copies. **—trip′li•ca′tion,** *n.*

tri•pod (trī′pod), *n.* **1.** a three-legged stand or support, as for a camera or telescope. **2.** a stool, table, pedestal, etc., with three legs.

Trip•o•li (trip′ə lē), *n.* **1.** Also, **Trip•o•li•ta•ni•a** (trip′ə li tā′nē ə, -tān′yə, tri pol′i-). one of the Barbary States of N Africa: later a province of Turkey; now a part of Libya. **2.** the capital of Libya, in the NW part. 858,000. **3.** a seaport in NW Lebanon, on the Mediterranean. 175,000. —**Tri•pol•i•tan** (tri pol′i tn), *adj., n.*

trip•per (trip′ər), *n.* **1.** a person or thing that trips. **2.** an apparatus causing a signal or other operating device to be tripped or activated. **3.** a person who goes on a pleasure trip or excursion.

trip•tych (trip′tik), *n.* **1.** a set of three panels or compartments side by side, bearing pictures, carvings, or the like. **2.** a set of three hinged writing tablets, used in antiquity for letters, etc., usu. by inscribing the wax-coated inner surfaces with a stylus.

trip•wire (trip′wīər′), *n.* a wire that activates something hidden or distant, as explosives or a camera, when tripped on or otherwise disturbed.

tri•reme (trī′rēm), *n.* an ancient galley, used chiefly as a warship, having three banks or tiers of oars on each side.

tri•sect (trī sekt′, trī′sekt), *v.t.,* **-sect•ed, -sect•ing.** to divide into three parts, esp. into three equal parts. **—tri•sec′tion,** *n.* **—tri•sec′tor,** *n.*

Tris•tan da Cu•nha (tris′tən də ko͞o′nə, ko͞on′yə), *n.* a group of volcanic islands in the S Atlantic, belonging to St. Helena. 40 sq. mi. (104 sq. km).

tri′state′ or **tri′-state′,** *adj.* pertaining to a territory made up of three adjoining states or to the three adjoining parts of such states.

Tris•tram (tris′trəm) also **Tris•tan** (-tən), **Tris•tam** (-təm), *n.* one of the knights of the Round Table, whose love for Iseult, wife of King Mark, is the subject of many romances.

tri•sul•fide (trī sul′fīd, -fid), *n.* a sulfide containing three sulfur atoms.

tri•syl•lab•ic (trī′si lab′ik), *adj.* consisting of three syllables: *a trisyllabic metrical foot.* **—tri′syl•lab′i•cal•ly,** *adv.*

tri•syl•la•ble (trī′sil′ə bəl, trī sil′-), *n.* a word or metrical unit of three syllables.

trite (trīt), *adj.,* **trit•er, trit•est. 1.** lacking in freshness or effectiveness because of constant use or excessive repetition; hackneyed. **2.** characterized by hackneyed expressions, ideas, etc. [< Latin *trītus* worn, common] **—trite′ly,** *adv.* **—trite′ness,** *n.*

tri•ton (trī′ton), *n.* a positively charged particle consisting of a proton and two neutrons, equivalent to the nucleus of an atom of tritium.

Tri•ton (trīt′n), *n.* **1.** (in Greek myth) a sea god, or one of a group of gods, usu. represented as a merman blowing a conch-shell trumpet. **2.**

(*l.c.*) any of various marine gastropods of the family Cymatiidae, having a large, spiral shell. **3.** (*l.c.*) the shell of a triton.

trit•u•rate (*v.* trich′ə rāt′; *n.* -ər it), *v.*, **-rat•ed, -rat•ing,** *n.* —*v.t.* **1.** to reduce to fine particles or powder by rubbing, grinding, bruising, or the like; pulverize. —*n.* **2.** a triturated substance.

tri•umph (trī′əmf, -umf), *n.* **1.** the act, fact, or condition of being victorious or highly successful; victory; success: *a military triumph; medical triumphs.* **2.** exultation resulting from victory or success. **3.** the ceremonial entrance into ancient Rome of a victorious commander with his army, captives, etc., authorized by the senate in honor of the victory. **4.** a public pageant, spectacle, etc. —*v.i.* **5.** to gain a victory or be highly successful. **6.** to gain mastery; prevail: *to triumph over fear.* **7.** to exult over victory; rejoice over success. **8.** to be elated or glad; rejoice proudly; glory. **9.** to celebrate a triumph, as a victorious Roman commander.

tri•um•phal (trī um′fəl), *adj.* of, pertaining to, celebrating, or commemorating a triumph or victory.

tri•um•phant (trī um′fənt), *adj.* **1.** having achieved victory or success; victorious; successful. **2.** exulting over victory; rejoicing over success; exultant. —**tri•um′phant•ly,** *adv.*

tri•um•vir (trī um′vər), *n., pl.* **-virs, -vi•ri** (-və rī′). **1.** one of three officers or magistrates of ancient Rome jointly exercising the same public function. **2.** one of three persons associated in any office or position of authority. —**tri•um′vi•ral,** *adj.*

tri•um•vi•rate (trī um′vər it, -və rāt′), *n.* **1.** the office or magistracy of a triumvir in ancient Rome. **2.** a board or government of three officials or magistrates functioning jointly. **3.** a coalition of three magistrates or rulers for joint administration. **4.** any association of three in office or authority. **5.** any group or set of three.

tri•une (trī′yo͞on), *adj.* **1.** three in one; constituting a trinity in unity, as the Godhead. —*n.* **2.** (*cap.*) the Trinity. —**tri•u′ni•ty,** *n., pl.* **-ties.**

tri•va•lent (trī vā′lənt, triv′ə lənt), *adj.* **1.** having a chemical valence of three. **2.** having three binding sites, as certain antigens. —**tri•va′lence, tri•va′len•cy,** *n.*

triv•et (triv′it), *n.* **1.** a small metal or ceramic plate with short legs, used under a hot platter or dish to protect a table. **2.** a three-legged stand placed over a fire to support cooking vessels.

triv•i•a (triv′ē ə), *n.* (*used with a sing. or pl. v.*) unimportant, inconsequential, or nonessential matters or things; trifles; trivialities.

triv•i•al (triv′ē əl), *adj.* **1.** of very little importance or value; insignificant. **2.** commonplace; ordinary. —**triv′i•al•ly,** *adv.*

triv•i•al•i•ty (triv′ē al′i tē), *n., pl.* **-ties. 1.** something trivial; a trivial matter, remark, etc. **2.** trivial quality or character.

triv•i•al•ize (triv′ē ə līz′), *v.t.,* **-ized, -iz•ing.** to make trivial; cause to appear unimportant, insignificant, etc. —**triv′i•al•i•za′tion,** *n.*

triv′ial name′, *n.* **1.** the species name that follows the genus name in taxonomic classification. **2.** the common or unscientific name of an organism or a chemical compound.

tri•week•ly (trī wēk′lē), *adv., adj., n., pl.* **-lies.** —*adv.* **1.** every three weeks. **2.** three times a week. —*adj.* **3.** occurring or appearing every three weeks. **4.** occurring or appearing three times a week. —*n.* **5.** a triweekly publication.

-trix, a suffix occurring in words from Latin, where it formed feminine nouns or adjectives corresponding to agent nouns ending in -TOR; on this model, **-trix** is used in English to form feminine nouns (*aviatrix; executrix*) and geometrical terms denoting straight lines (*directrix*). Also, **-trice.** —**Usage.** Most English nouns in -TRIX have dropped from general use and occur rarely or not at all in present-day English. The forms in *-tor* are applied to both men and women. When relevant, sex is specified with the generic term: *Amelia Earhart was a pioneer woman aviator.* Legal documents still use *administratrix, executrix, inheritrix,* etc., but these forms too are giving way to the *-tor* forms. See also -ESS.

TRM, trademark.

tRNA, TRANSFER RNA.

tro•cha•ic (trō kā′ik), *adj.* **1.** pertaining to the trochee. **2.** consisting of or employing a trochee or trochees. —*n.* **3.** TROCHEE. **4.** Usu., **trochaics.** a verse or poem written in trochees.

tro•chan•ter (trō kan′tər), *n.* **1.** (in humans) either of two knobs at the top of the femur that serve for the attachment of muscles between the thigh and pelvis. **2.** (in other vertebrates) any of two or more similar knobs at the top of the femur. **3.** the second segment of an insect leg, between the coxa and femur. —**tro′chan•ter′ic** (-kən ter′ik), **tro•chan′ter•al,** *adj.*

tro•che (trō′kē), *n., pl.* **-ches.** a small tablet or lozenge, usu. a circular one, made of medicinal substance worked into a paste with sugar and mucilage or the like and dried.

tro•chee (trō′kē), *n.* a foot of two syllables, a long followed by a short in quantitative meter, or a stressed followed by an unstressed in accentual meter.

troch•le•a (trok′lē ə), *n., pl.* **-le•ae** (-lē ē′), **-le•as.** a pulleylike anatomical structure or arrangement of parts.

trod (trod), *v.* a pt. and pp. of TREAD.

trod•den (trod′n), *v.* a pp. of TREAD.

trog•lo•dyte (trog′lə dīt′), *n.* **1.** a prehistoric cave dweller. **2.** a person of degraded, primitive, or brutal character. **3.** a person living in seclusion; hermit. **4.** an extremely old-fashioned or conservative person; a reactionary. **5.** an animal living underground. —**trog′lo•dyt′ic** (-dit′ik), **trog′lo•dyt′i•cal,** *adj.*

troi•ka (troi′kə), *n.* **1.** a Russian carriage, wagon, or sleigh drawn by a team of three horses abreast. **2.** a team of three horses driven abreast. **3.** a ruling group of three; triumvirate. **4.** any group of three. [< Russian]

Tro•jan (trō′jən), *adj.* **1.** of or pertaining to ancient Troy or its inhabitants. —*n.* **2.** a native or inhabitant of Troy. **3.** a person who shows determination or energy.

Tro′jan horse′, *n.* **1.** a gigantic hollow wooden horse that the Greeks left at the gates of Troy as a feigned tribute: once the horse was within the walls, soldiers emerging from it allowed the Greek army to enter and conquer the city. **2.** a person or thing intended to undermine or destroy from within. **3.** a nonreplicating computer program planted illegally in another program to do damage locally when the software is activated. Compare VIRUS (def. 4).

Tro′jan War′, *n.* a legendary war between a confederation of Greeks and the city of Troy as a result of the abduction of Helen by Paris.

troll[1] (trōl), *v.t.* **1.** to sing or utter in a full, rolling voice. **2.** to sing in the manner of a round or catch. **3.** to fish in (a body of water) by trailing a line behind a slow-moving boat. **4.** to cause to turn round and round; roll. —*v.i.* **5.** to sing with a full, rolling voice; give forth full, rolling tones. **6.** to be uttered or sounded in such tones. **7.** to fish by trolling. **8.** to roll; turn round and round. **9.** to move nimbly, as the tongue in speaking. —*n.* **10.** a song whose parts are sung in succession; a round. **11.** the act of trolling. **12.** the lure or hook, with or without the attached line, used in trolling. —**troll′er,** *n.*

troll[2] (trōl), *n.* (in Scandinavian folklore) any of a race of supernatural beings, usu. hostile to humans, who live underground or in caves.

trol•ley or **trol•ly** (trol′ē), *n., pl.* **-leys** or **-lies,** *v.,* **-leyed** or **-lied, -ley•ing** or **-ly•ing.** —*n.* **1.** TROLLEY CAR. **2.** a pulley or truck traveling on an overhead track and serving to support and move a suspended object. **3. a.** a grooved wheel or pulley on the end of a pole, used by an electric streetcar or locomotive to draw current from an overhead conductor. **b.** any of various other devices for collecting current for propulsion. **4.** a small truck or car operated on a track, as in a mine or factory. **5.** a serving cart, as one used to serve desserts. **6.** *Chiefly Brit.* any of various low carts. —*v.t., v.i.* **7.** to convey or go by trolley. —***Idiom.*** **8. off one's trolley,** *Slang.* mentally unstable; insane.

trol′ley bus′, *n.* a passenger bus operating on tires and having an electric motor that draws power from overhead wires.

trol′ley car′, *n.* a streetcar propelled electrically by current taken by means of a trolley from a conducting wire strung overhead or running beneath a slot between the tracks.

Trol•lope (trol′əp), *n.* **Anthony,** 1815–82, English novelist. —**Trol•lop•i•an, Trol•lop•e•an** (trə lop′ē ən, -lō′pē-, trol′ə pē′-), *adj., n.*

trom•bone (trom bōn′, trom′bōn), *n.* a musical wind instrument having a cylindrical metal tube expanding into a bell and bent twice into a U shape, with a slide for varying the tone. —**trom•bon′ist,** *n.*

trompe l'oeil (*Fr.* trôɴp lœ′yᵊ; *Eng.* trômp′ lā′, loi′), *n.* **1.** visual deception, esp. in paintings, in which objects are rendered in extremely fine detail emphasizing the illusion of tactile and spatial qualities. **2.** a painting, mural, or panel of wallpaper designed to create such an effect. [< French: lit., (it) fools the eye]

-tron, a combining form extracted from ELECTRON, used in the names of electron tubes (*magnetron*) and of devices for accelerating subatomic particles (*cyclotron*); also, more generally, in the names of any kind of chamber or apparatus for conducting experiments (*biotron*).

troop (tro͞op), *n.* **1.** an assemblage of persons or things; company; band. **2.** a cavalry unit corresponding in size to a company of infantry. **3. troops, a.** a body of soldiers, police, etc. **b.** soldiers, esp. enlisted persons. **4.** a unit of Boy Scouts or Girl Scouts usu. having a maximum of 32 members under an adult leader. **5.** a herd, flock, or swarm. —*v.i.* **6.** to gather in a company; flock together. **7.** to come, go, or pass in great numbers; throng. **8.** to walk, as if in a march; go: *trooping down to breakfast.* **9.** to associate or consort (usu. fol. by *with*). **10.** *Chiefly Brit.* to carry (the flag or colors) in a ceremonial way before troops.

troop•er (tro͞o′pər), *n.* **1.** a mounted police officer. **2.** STATE TROOPER. **3.** a cavalry soldier. **4.** a cavalry horse.

trope (trōp), *n.* **1. a.** any literary or rhetorical device, as metaphor, metonymy, synecdoche, and irony, that consists in the use of words in other than their literal sense. **b.** an instance of this. **2.** a phrase, sentence, or verse formerly interpolated in a liturgical text to amplify or embellish.

-trope, a combining form meaning "one turned toward" that specified by the initial element (*heliotrope*); also occurring in concrete nouns that correspond to abstract nouns ending in -TROPY or -TROPISM: *allotrope.*

-troph, a combining form meaning "an organism with nutritional requirements" of the kind specified: *heterotroph.*

troph•ic (trof′ik, trō′fik), *adj.* of or pertaining to nutrition; involving nutritive processes: *a trophic disease.* —**troph′i•cal•ly,** *adv.*

-trophic, a combining form with the meanings "deriving nourishment" from the source or in the manner specified (*autotrophic; eutrophic*), "affecting the activity of, maintaining" that specified (*thyrotrophic*) (in this sense often interchangeable with -TROPIC); also forming adjectives corresponding to nouns ending in -TROPH or -TROPHY (*hypertrophic*).

Troph•i•mus (trof′ə məs), *n.* a Gentile Christian of Ephesus who accompanied the Apostle Paul to Jerusalem. Acts 20:1–5; 21:27–29; II Tim. 4:20.

tropho-, a combining form meaning "nourishment": *trophosome.* Also, *esp. before a vowel,* **troph-.**

tro•phy (trō′fē), *n., pl.* **-phies. 1.** anything taken in war, hunting, competition, etc., esp. when preserved as a memento; spoil, prize, or award. **2.** anything won or awarded as a token or evidence of victory, valor, skill, etc.: *athletic trophies.* **3.** a carving, painting, or other representation of objects associated with victory or achievement. **4.** (in ancient Greece and Rome) a memorial to a military victory, orig. captured armor and weapons hung at the site of a rout.

-trophy, a combining form meaning "nutrition," "growth, development" (*dystrophy; hypertrophy*); also forming abstract nouns corresponding to adjectives ending in -TROPHIC.

trop•ic (trop′ik), *n.* **1. a.** either of two corresponding parallels of latitude on the terrestrial globe, one (**tropic of Cancer**) about 23½° N, the other (**tropic of Capricorn**) about 23½° S of the equator, being the boundaries of the Torrid Zone. **b. the tropics,** the regions lying between and near these parallels of latitude; the Torrid Zone and neighboring regions. **2.** either of two circles on the celestial sphere, one lying in the same plane as the tropic of Cancer, the other in the same plane as the tropic of Capricorn. —*adj.* **3.** pertaining to the tropics; tropical.

-tropic, a combining form with the meanings "turned toward, with an orientation toward" that specified by the initial element (*geotropic*), "having an affinity for, affecting" what is specified (*lipotropic*), "affecting the activity of, maintaining" a specified organ (*thyrotropic*). Compare -TROPHIC.

trop•i•cal (trop′i kəl *for 1–3;* trō′pi kəl *for 4*), *adj.* **1.** pertaining to, characteristic of, occurring in, or inhabiting the tropics. **2.** very hot and humid. **3.** used in or suitable for the tropics. **4.** pertaining to, characterized by, or of the nature of a trope or tropes; metaphorical. —**trop′i•cal•ly,** *adv.*

trop′ical cy′clone, *n.* a cyclone that begins in the tropics and can develop into a hurricane or typhoon.

trop′ical fish′, *n.* any of numerous small, usu. brightly colored fishes native to the tropics and often kept in home aquariums.

trop′ical storm′, *n.* a tropical cyclone of less than hurricane force.

trop′ic bird′ or **trop′ic•bird′,** *n.* any of several web-footed seabirds of the family Phaethontidae, chiefly of tropical seas, having white plumage with black markings and two elongated central tail feathers.

trop′ic of Can′cer, *n.* See under TROPIC (def. 1a).

trop′ic of Cap′ricorn, *n.* See under TROPIC (def. 1a).

tro•pism (trō′piz əm), *n.* the orientation of an organism toward or away from a stimulus, as light. —**tro•pis′tic** (-pis′tik), *adj.*

-tropism, var. of -TROPY.

tropo-, a combining form meaning "turn, reaction," "response," "change," "troposphere": *tropophilous.*

tro•pol•o•gy (trō pol′ə jē), *n., pl.* **-gies. 1.** the use of figurative language in speech or writing. **2.** a treatise on figures of speech or tropes. **3.** the use of a Scriptural text so as to give it a moral interpretation or significance apart from its direct meaning. —**trop•o•log•ic** (trop′ə loj′ik), **trop′o•log′i•cal,** *adj.*

trop•o•pause (trop′ə pôz′, trō′pə-), *n.* the boundary, or transitional layer, between the troposphere and the stratosphere.

trop•o•sphere (trop′ə sfēr′, trō′pə-), *n.* the lowest layer of the atmosphere, varying in height from 6 to 12 mi. (10 to 20 km), within which nearly all clouds and weather conditions occur. —**trop′o•spher′ic** (-sfer′ik), *adj.*

-tropous, a combining form meaning "turned, curved" in the direction specified by the initial element: *orthotropous.*

-tropy or **-tropism,** a combining form occurring in abstract nouns that correspond to adjectives ending in -TROPIC or -TROPOUS: *isotropy.*

trot (trot), *v.,* **trot•ted, trot•ting,** *n.* —*v.i.* **1.** (of a horse or other quadruped) to go at a gait between a walk and a run, in which the legs move in diagonal pairs, but not quite simultaneously. **2.** to go at a quick, steady pace; hurry. —*v.t.* **3.** to cause to trot. **4. trot out,** *Informal.* **a.** to bring forward for inspection. **b.** to bring to the attention of others. —*n.* **5.** the gait of a horse, dog, or other quadruped, when trotting. **6.** the jogging gait of a human being, between a walk and a run. **7.** a horse race for trotters. **8.** brisk, continuous movement or activity: *I've been on the trot all afternoon.* **9.** *Slang.* a literal translation used illicitly in doing schoolwork; crib; pony.

Trot•sky (trot′skē), *n.* **Leon** (*Lev* or *Leib Davidovich Bronstein*), 1879–1940, Russian Communist revolutionary.

trot•ter (trot′ər), *n.* **1.** an animal that trots, esp. a horse bred and trained for harness racing. **2.** a person who moves about briskly. **3.** the foot of an animal, as a pig, used as food.

trou•ba•dour (trōō′bə dôr′, -dōr′, -dōōr′), *n.* **1.** one of a class of lyric poets who lived principally in S France from the 11th to 13th centuries and wrote songs and poems, chiefly on themes of courtly love. **2.** any wandering singer or minstrel.

trou•ble (trub′əl), *v.,* **-bled, -bling,** *n.* —*v.t.* **1.** to disturb the mental calm and contentment of; worry; distress: *The sufferings of the poor troubled him.* **2.** to put to inconvenience, exertion, pains, or the like: *May I trouble you to shut the door?* **3.** to cause bodily pain or discomfort to; afflict: *to be troubled by arthritis.* **4.** to annoy, vex, or bother. **5.** to disturb or agitate so as to make turbid, as water. —*v.i.* **6.** to put oneself

to inconvenience, extra effort, or the like. **7.** to be distressed; worry. —*n.* **8.** difficulty, annoyance, or harassment: *to make trouble for someone.* **9.** an unfortunate or distressing position, circumstance, or occurrence; misfortune: *financial trouble.* **10.** civil disorder, disturbance, or conflict. **11.** a physical disease, ailment, etc.: *heart trouble.* **12.** mental or emotional distress; worry. **13.** effort, exertion, or inconvenience in accomplishing something: *not worth the trouble.* **14.** an objectionable feature or characteristic; drawback: *the trouble with the proposal.* **15.** a cause or source of disturbance, annoyance, difficulty, etc. **16.** a mechanical defect or breakdown: *trouble with the washing machine.*

trou•ble•mak•er (trub′əl mā′kər), *n.* a person who causes trouble for others, esp. one who does so habitually out of malice.

trou•ble•shoot•er (trub′əl shōō′tər), *n.* **1.** a person with special skill in resolving disputes, impasses, etc., as in business or international affairs. **2.** an expert in discovering and eliminating the cause of trouble in mechanical equipment, etc. —**troubleshoot,** *v.*

trou•ble•some (trub′əl səm), *adj.* causing trouble, annoyance, or difficulty. —**trou′ble•some•ly,** *adv.* —**trou′ble•some•ness,** *n.*

trough (trôf, trof *or, sometimes,* trôth, troth), *n.* **1.** a long, narrow, open receptacle, usu. boxlike in shape, used chiefly to hold water or food for animals. **2.** any of several similarly shaped receptacles used for various commercial or household purposes. **3.** a channel or conduit for conveying water, as a gutter under the eaves of a building. **4.** any long depression or hollow, as between two ridges on a weather chart. **5.** a long, wide, and deep depression in the ocean floor having gently sloping sides, wider and shallower than a trench. **6.** an elongated area of relatively low barometric pressure.

trounce (trouns), *v.t.,* **trounced, trounc•ing. 1.** to beat severely; thrash. **2.** to defeat decisively. —**trounc′er,** *n.*

troupe (trōōp), *n., v.,* **trouped, troup•ing.** —*n.* **1.** a company or group of actors or other performers, esp. one that travels about. —*v.i.* **2.** to travel as a member of a troupe.

troup•er (trōō′pər), *n.* **1.** an actor, esp. a member of a touring company. **2.** an experienced, devoted, and dependable performer, esp. a veteran actor. **3.** a loyal, dependable worker or participant in an undertaking.

troup•i•al (trōō′pē əl), *n.* any bird of the New World subfamily Icterinae (family Emberizidae), including the orioles and blackbirds.

trou•ser (trou′zər), *adj.* **1.** of or pertaining to trousers: *trouser cuffs.* —*n.* **2.** TROUSERS.

trou•sers (trou′zərz), *n.* (*used with a pl. v.*) Sometimes, **trouser.** a loose-fitting outer garment for the lower part of the body, having individual leg portions, usu. full length. Also called **pants.** Compare SLACKS.

trous•seau (trōō′sō, trōō sō′), *n., pl.* **-seaux** (-sōz, -sōz′), **-seaus.** an outfit of clothing, household linen, etc., for a bride.

trout (trout), *n., pl.* (*esp. collectively*) **trout,** (*esp. for kinds or species*) **trouts.** any of various usu. speckled freshwater game fishes belonging to the genera *Salmo* and *Salvelinus,* of the salmon family, as the brook trout, rainbow trout, and lake trout.

trout′ lil′y, *n.* DOGTOOTH VIOLET.

trout•perch (trout′pûrch′), *n., pl.* **-perch•es,** (*esp. collectively*) **-perch.** a North American freshwater fish, *Percopsis omiscomaycus,* exhibiting characteristics of both trouts and perches.

trove (trōv), *n.* **1.** a collection of objects, esp. a valuable one. **2.** any valuable discovery.

trow•el (trou′əl), *n., v.,* **-eled, -el•ing** or (*esp. Brit.*) **-elled, -el•ling.** —*n.* **1.** any of various tools having a flat blade with a handle, used for depositing and working mortar, plaster, etc. **2.** a similar tool with a curved, scooplike blade, used in gardening for taking up plants, turning up earth, etc. —*v.t.* **3.** to apply, shape, smooth, or dig with or as if with a trowel. —**trow′el•er;** *esp. Brit.,* **trow′el•ler,** *n.*

troy (troi), *adj.* expressed or computed in troy weight. [after *Troyes,* France, where it was standard]

Troy (troi), *n.* **1.** Latin, **Ilium.** Greek, **Ilion.** an ancient ruined city in NW Asia Minor: the seventh of nine settlements on the site is commonly identified as the Troy of the *Iliad.* **2.** a city in SE Michigan, near Detroit. 68,700. **3.** a city in E New York, on the Hudson River. 52,150.

troy′ weight′, *n.* a system of weights in use for precious metals and gems, in which a pound equals 12 ounces (0.373 kg) and an ounce equals 20 pennyweights or 480 grains (31.103 grams).

Trp, tryptophan.

tru•an•cy (trōō′ən sē), *n., pl.* **-cies. 1.** the act or state of being truant. **2.** an instance of being truant.

tru•ant (trōō′ənt), *n.* **1.** a student who stays away from school without permission. **2.** a person who shirks or neglects his or her duty. —*adj.* **3.** absent from school without permission. **4.** neglectful of duty or responsibility; idle. **5.** of, pertaining to, or characteristic of a truant. —*v.i.* **6.** to be truant. [< Old French: beggar < Celtic] —**tru′ant•ly,** *adv.*

tru′ant of′ficer, *n.* a school official who investigates unauthorized student absences.

truce (trōōs), *n.* **1.** a suspension of hostilities for a specified period of time by mutual agreement of the warring parties; cease-fire; armistice. **2.** an agreement or treaty establishing this. **3.** a temporary respite, as from trouble or pain. —**truce′less,** *adj.*

truck¹ (truk), *n.* **1.** a large motor vehicle for carrying goods and materials, consisting either of a single self-propelled unit or of a trailer vehicle hauled by a tractor unit. **2.** any of various wheeled frames, platforms, or carts used for transporting heavy objects. **3.** HAND TRUCK. **4.** a group of two or more pairs of wheels in one frame, for supporting one end of a railroad car, locomotive, etc. **5.** a small wooden wheel, cylinder, or roller, as on certain old-style gun carriages. **6.** a popular dance with shuffling, jitterbuglike steps. *—v.t.* **7.** to transport by truck. **8.** to put on a truck. *—v.i.* **9.** to convey articles or goods on a truck. **10.** to drive a truck. **11.** to dance with jitterbuglike steps. **12.** *Informal.* to proceed, esp. in an unhurried or jaunty manner: *trucking down the avenue.*

truck² (truk), *n.* **1.** vegetables raised for the market. **2.** miscellaneous articles of little worth; odds and ends. **3.** *Informal.* rubbish; trash: *That's a lot of truck.* **4.** dealings: *I'll have no truck with him.* **5.** barter. **6.** a bargain or deal. **7.** the payment of wages in goods instead of money. *—v.t.* **8.** to exchange; trade; barter. *—v.i.* **9.** to exchange commodities; barter. **10.** to traffic; have dealings.

truck•driv•er (truk′drī′vər), *n.* a person who drives a truck.

truck•er¹ (truk′ər), *n.* **1.** a person who drives a truck; truckdriver. **2.** a person whose business is trucking goods.

truck•er² (truk′ər), *n.* a truck farmer.

truck′ farm′, *n.* a farm for the growing of vegetables for the market. —**truck′ farm′er,** *n.* —**truck′ farm′ing,** *n.*

truck•ing (truk′ing), *n.* the process or business of conveying articles or goods on trucks.

truck•le (truk′əl), *v.i.*, **-led, -ling.** to submit or yield obsequiously or tamely (usu. fol. by *to*). —**truck′ler,** *n.* —**truck′ling•ly,** *adv.*

truck•load (truk′lōd′), *n.* **1.** the amount that a truck can carry. **2.** the minimum weight legally required for making shipments at a rate **(truck′load rate′)** below that charged for shipments under this minimum.

truck′ stop′, *n.* a restaurant, often combined with a gas station and other facilities, located along a major highway and frequented esp. by truckdrivers.

truc•u•lent (truk′yə lənt, trōō′kyə-), *adj.* **1.** aggressively hostile; belligerent: *a truculent attitude.* **2.** brutally harsh; vitriolic; scathing: *truculent criticism.* **3.** fierce; cruel; savagely brutal. —**truc′u•lence, truc′u•len•cy,** *n.* —**truc′u•lent•ly,** *adv.*

Tru•deau (trōō dō′), *n.* **Pierre Elliott,** born 1919, Canadian prime minister 1968–79 and 1980–84.

trudge (truj), *v.*, **trudged, trudg•ing,** *n.* *—v.i.* **1.** to walk, esp. laboriously or wearily. *—v.t.* **2.** to walk laboriously or wearily along or over. *—n.* **3.** a laborious or tiring walk; tramp. —**trudg′er,** *n.*

true (trōō), *adj.*, **tru•er, tru•est,** *n.*, *adv.*, *v.*, **trued, tru•ing** or **true•ing.** *—adj.* **1.** being in accordance with the actual state or conditions; conforming to reality or fact: *a true story.* **2.** real; genuine; authentic: *true gold.* **3.** sincere; not deceitful: *a true interest in others.* **4.** loyal; faithful; steadfast: *a true friend.* **5.** being or reflecting the essential or genuine character: *the true meaning of his statement.* **6.** conforming to or consistent with a standard, pattern, etc.: *a true copy.* **7.** exact; precise; accurate; correct: *a true balance.* **8.** such as it should be; proper: *to arrange things in their true order.* **9.** properly so called; rightly answering to a description: *true statesmanship.* **10.** legitimate or rightful: *the true heir.* **11.** reliable, unfailing, or sure: *a true sign.* **12.** exactly or accurately shaped, formed, fitted, or placed, as a surface or instrument. **13.** honest; honorable; upright. **14.** conforming to the type, structural standards, or norm of a particular group: *The lion is a true cat.* **15.** PUREBRED. **16.** (of a bearing, course, etc.) determined in relation to true north. *—n.* **17.** exact or accurate formation, position, or adjustment: *to be out of true.* *—adv.* **18.** in a true manner; truly; truthfully. **19.** exactly or accurately. *—v.t.* **20.** to adjust, shape, place, etc., exactly or accurately; make true. **21.** (esp. in carpentry) to make even, symmetrical, level, etc. (often fol. by *up*). —***Idiom.*** **22. come true,** (of a wish, dream, etc.) to become a reality. —**true′ness,** *n.*

true′ believ′er, *n.* **1.** a person who has been thoroughly convinced of something. **2.** a fanatic, esp. a religious or political one.

true′-blue′, *adj.* unwaveringly loyal or faithful.

true′-false′ test′, *n.* a test requiring one to mark statements as either true or false.

true′-life′, *adj.* resembling or depicting everyday life; true to life; realistic: *true-life stories.*

true•love (trōō′luv′), *n.* a sweetheart.

true′ north′, *n.* the direction of the north pole from a given point.

true′ rib′, *n.* one of the upper seven pairs of ribs in humans, which are attached by cartilage to the sternum. Compare FLOATING RIB.

Tru•ett (trōō′it), *n.* **George Washington,** 1867–1944, U.S. evangelist.

True′ Vine′, *n.* Jesus. John 15:1.

truf•fle (truf′əl, trōō′fəl), *n.* **1.** any of several subterranean, edible, ascomycetous fungi of the genus *Tuber.* **2.** any similar fungi of other genera. **3.** a ball-shaped candy of soft chocolate dusted with cocoa.

tru•ism (trōō′iz əm), *n.* a self-evident, obvious truth, esp. a cliché. —**tru•is′tic,** *adj.*

Tru•ji•llo (trōō hē′ō), *n.* **1. Rafael Leonidas** (*Rafael Leonidas Trujillo Molina*), 1891–1961, Dominican president 1930–38, 1942–52. **2.** a seaport in NW Peru. 491,100.

tru•ly (trōō′lē), *adv.* **1.** in accordance with fact or truth; truthfully. **2.** exactly; accurately; correctly. **3.** rightly; properly; duly. **4.** legitimately; by right. **5.** really; genuinely; authentically. **6.** indeed; verily. **7.** sincerely: *yours truly.*

Tru•man (trōō′mən), *n.* **Harry S,** 1884–1972, 33rd president of the U.S. 1945–53.

Tru′man Doc′trine, *n.* the policy of President Truman, as advocated in his address to Congress on March 12, 1947, to provide military and economic aid to Greece and Turkey and, by extension, to any country threatened by Communism or any totalitarian ideology.

trump (trump), *n.* **1. a.** any playing card of a suit that for the time outranks the other suits, such a card being able to take any card of another suit. **b.** Often, **trumps.** (*used with a sing. v.*) the suit itself. **2.** *Informal.* a fine person; brick. *—v.t.* **3.** to take with a trump. **4.** to excel; surpass; outdo. *—v.i.* **5. a.** to play a trump. **b.** to take a trick with a trump. **6. trump up,** to devise or invent (an accusation, excuse, etc.), esp. deceitfully; fabricate.

trump′ card′, *n.* **1.** TRUMP (def. 1a). **2.** something that gives a person or group a decisive or winning advantage.

trumped′-up′, *adj.* spuriously devised; fraudulent; fabricated: *arrested on some trumped-up charge.*

trump•er•y (trum′pə rē), *n.*, *pl.* **-ries,** *adj.* *—n.* **1.** something without use or value. **2.** nonsense; twaddle. *—adj.* **3.** of little or no value; worthless; rubbishy.

trum•pet (trum′pit), *n.* **1. a.** any of a family of brass wind instruments with a powerful, penetrating tone, consisting of a tube commonly curved once or twice around on itself and having a cup-shaped mouthpiece at one end and a flaring bell at the other. **b.** TRUMPETER (def. 1). **2.** something used as or resembling a trumpet, esp. in sound. **3.** a sound like that of a trumpet. **4.** the loud piercing or blaring cry of an animal, esp. an elephant. **5.** EAR TRUMPET. *—v.i.* **6.** to blow a trumpet. **7.** to emit a loud, trumpetlike cry. *—v.t.* **8.** to sound on a trumpet. **9.** to utter with a sound like that of a trumpet. **10.** to proclaim loudly or widely.

trum′pet creep′er, *n.* **1.** a climbing vine, *Campsis radicans,* of the southern U.S., having large, red trumpet-shaped flowers. **2.** a related Chinese vine, *C. chinensis.*

trum•pet•er (trum′pi tər), *n.* **1.** a person who plays a trumpet. **2.** a soldier who sounds calls on a trumpet. **3.** a person who proclaims or extols something loudly or widely. **4.** any of several large South American birds of the family Psophiidae, related to the cranes, having a loud cry. **5.** TRUMPETER SWAN.

trum′peter swan′, *n.* a large wild swan, *Cygnus buccinator,* of North America, having a sonorous cry.

trum′pet flow′er, *n.* **1.** any of various plants with pendent flowers shaped like a trumpet. **2.** TRUMPET CREEPER. **3.** TRUMPET HONEYSUCKLE. **4.** the flower of any of these plants.

trum′pet hon′eysuckle, *n.* an American honeysuckle, *Lonicera sempervirens,* having spikes of large red flowers.

trum′pet vine′, *n.* TRUMPET CREEPER.

T

trun•cate (trung′kāt), *v.*, **-cat•ed, -cat•ing,** *adj.* *—v.t.* **1.** to shorten by or as if by cutting off a part; cut short. *—adj.* **2.** truncated. **3.** *Biol.* **a.** square or broad at the end, as if cut off transversely. **b.** lacking the apex, as certain spiral shells. —**trun′cate•ly,** *adv.*

trun•cat•ed (trung′kā tid), *adj.* **1.** shortened by or as if by having a part cut off; cut short. **2.** (of a geometric figure or solid) having the apex, vertex, or end cut off by a plane: *a truncated cone or pyramid.* **3.** (of a crystal) having corners, angles, or edges cut off or replaced by a single plane. **4.** TRUNCATE (def. 3).

trun•ca•tion (trung kā′shən), *n.* **1.** the act or process of truncating. **2.** the quality or state of being truncated. **3.** the omission of one or more unaccented syllables at the beginning or the end of a line of verse.

trun•cheon (trun′chən), *n.* **1.** the club carried by a police officer; billy. **2.** a staff representing an office or authority; baton. **3.** the shattered shaft of a spear.

trun•dle (trun′dl), *v.*, **-dled, -dling,** *n.* *—v.t.* **1.** to cause (a circular object) to roll along; roll. **2.** to convey or move in a wagon, cart, or other wheeled vehicle; wheel. *—v.i.* **3.** to roll along. **4.** to move or run on a wheel or wheels. **5.** to move or walk with a rolling gait. *—n.* **6.** a small wheel, roller, or the like. **7.** a truck or carriage on low wheels.

trun′dle bed′, *n.* a low bed on casters, usu. pushed under another bed when not in use. Also called **truckle bed.**

trunk (trungk), *n.* **1.** the main stem of a tree, as distinct from the branches and roots. **2.** a large sturdy box or case for holding or transporting clothes, personal effects, etc. **3.** a large compartment, usu. in the rear of an automobile, for holding luggage, a spare tire, etc. **4.** the body of a person or an animal excluding the head and appendages; torso. **5.** the long, flexible cylindrical nasal appendage of the elephant. **6.** the main channel, artery, or line in a river, railroad, highway, canal, or other tributary system. **7. a.** a telephone line or channel between two central offices or switching devices, used in providing telephone connections between subscribers. **b.** a telegraph line or channel between two main or central offices. **8. trunks,** brief shorts, loose-fitting or tight, worn by men chiefly for boxing, swimming, and track. **9.** the shaft of a column. —**trunk′ful,** *n.* —**trunk′less,** *adj.*

trunk•fish (trungk′fish′), *n.*, *pl.* (*esp. collectively*) **-fish,** (*esp. for kinds or species*) **-fish•es.** any of various fishes of the family Ostraciidae, of warm seas, having a boxlike body encased in bony plates. Also, **boxfish.**

trunk′ line′, *n.* **1.** a major long-distance transportation line. **2.** TRUNK (def. 7).

truss (trus), *v.t.* **1.** to tie, bind, or fasten (often fol. by *up*). **2.** to make fast with skewers, thread, or the like, as the wings and legs of a fowl in preparation for cooking. **3.** to furnish or support with a truss or trusses. —*n.* **4.** any of various structural frames designed to function as a beam or cantilever for supporting bridges, roofs, etc. **5.** a device consisting of a pad usu. supported by a belt for maintaining a hernia in a reduced state. **6.** a compact terminal cluster or head of flowers growing upon one stalk. **7.** a device for supporting a standing yard on a ship's mast, having a pivot permitting the yard to swing horizontally when braced. **8.** a bundle or pack. —**truss′er,** *n.*

truss•ing (trus′ing), *n.* **1.** the members that form a truss. **2.** a structure consisting of trusses. **3.** trusses collectively.

trust (trust), *n.* **1.** reliance on the integrity, strength, ability, surety, etc., of a person or thing; confidence. **2.** confident expectation of something; hope. **3.** confidence in the certainty of future payment for property or goods received; credit: *to sell merchandise on trust.* **4.** one upon which a person relies: *God is my trust.* **5.** the condition of one to whom something has been entrusted. **6.** the obligation or responsibility imposed on a person in whom confidence or authority is placed: *a position of trust.* **7.** charge, custody, or care: *leaving valuables in someone's trust.* **8.** something committed or entrusted to one's care for use or safekeeping; charge. **9. a.** a fiduciary relationship in which a trustee holds title to property for the beneficiary. **b.** the property so held. **10. a.** an illegal combination of industrial or commercial companies in which the stock of the constituent companies is controlled by a central board of trustees, thus making it possible to minimize production costs, control prices, eliminate competition, etc. **b.** any large corporation or combination having monopolistic or semimonopolistic control over the production of a commodity or service. —*v.t.* **11.** to have trust or confidence in; rely or depend on. **12.** to believe. **13.** to expect confidently; hope: *I trust that the job will soon be finished.* **14.** to commit or consign with trust or confidence. **15.** to permit to stay or go somewhere or to do something without fear of consequences: *He doesn't trust them out of his sight.* **16.** to invest with a trust; entrust with something. **17.** to give credit to (a person) for goods, services, etc., supplied. —*v.i.* **18.** to place confidence; rely (usu. fol. by *in* or *to*): *trusting to luck.* **19.** to have confidence; hope. **20.** to sell merchandise on credit. —***Idiom.*** **21. in trust,** in the care or guardianship of another, esp. a trustee. —**trust′a•ble,** *adj.* —**trust′a•bil′i•ty,** *n.* —**trust′er,** *n.*

Trust′ and Obey′, a Christian hymn (1886) with words by John Sammis and music by Daniel B. Tower.

trust′ com′pany, *n.* a company or corporation organized to exercise the functions of a trustee, but also engaging in the usual activities of a bank or financial institution.

trust•ee (tru stē′), *n., v.,* **-eed, -ee•ing.** —*n.* **1.** a person appointed to administer the affairs of a company, institution, etc. **2.** a person who holds title to property for the benefit of another. **3.** a country that administers a trust territory. —*v.i.* **4.** to serve as a trustee. —*v.t.* **5.** to place in the hands of a trustee.

trust•ee•ship (tru stē′ship), *n.* **1.** the office or function of a trustee. **2.** the administrative control of a territory granted to a country by the United Nations. **3.** TRUST TERRITORY.

trust′ fund′, *n.* money, securities, etc., held in trust.

trust•ing (trus′ting), *adj.* inclined to trust; confiding; trustful. —**trust′ing•ly,** *adv.* —**trust′ing•ness,** *n.*

trust′ ter′ritory, *n.* a territory placed under the administrative control of a country by the United Nations.

trust•wor•thy (trust′wûr′thē), *adj.* deserving of trust or confidence; reliable. —**trust′wor′thi•ly,** *adv.* —**trust′wor′thi•ness,** *n.*

trust•y (trus′tē), *adj.,* **trust•i•er, trust•i•est,** *n., pl.* **trust•ies.** —*adj.* **1.** able to be trusted or relied on; trustworthy. —*n.* **2.** one that is trusted, esp. a convict considered trustworthy and granted special privileges. —**trust′i•ly,** *adv.* —**trust′i•ness,** *n.*

truth (trōōth), *n., pl.* **truths** (trōōthz, trōōths). **1.** the true or actual state of a matter: *to tell the truth.* **2.** conformity with fact or reality; verity: *to check the truth of a statement.* **3.** a verified or indisputable fact, proposition, principle, or the like: *mathematical truths.* **4.** the state or character of being true. **5.** actuality or actual existence. **6.** an obvious or accepted fact; truism; platitude. **7.** honesty; integrity; truthfulness. **8.** (*often cap.*) ideal or fundamental reality apart from and transcending perceived experience. **9.** agreement with a standard or original. **10.** accuracy, as of position or adjustment. **11.** (*cap.*) Jesus. John 14:6. —***Idiom.*** **12. in truth,** in reality; in fact; actually. —***Proverb.*** **13. The truth shall make you free,** to be truly free, one must know and accept the truth. John 8:32. —**truth′less,** *adj.* —**truth′less•ness,** *n.*

Truth (trōōth), *n.* **Sojourner** (*Isabella Van Wagener*), 1797?–1883, U.S. abolitionist and women's-rights advocate, born a slave.

truth•ful (trōōth′fəl), *adj.* **1.** telling the truth, esp. habitually. **2.** conforming to truth. **3.** corresponding with reality: *a truthful portrait.* —**truth′ful•ly,** *adv.* —**truth′ful•ness,** *n.*

truth′ se′rum, *n.* a drug, as the barbiturate thiopental sodium, considered to induce an inclination to talk freely and to reveal repressed or consciously withheld information. Also called **truth′ drug′.**

try (trī), *v.,* **tried, try•ing,** *n., pl.* **tries.** —*v.t.* **1.** to attempt to do or accomplish: *Try running a mile a day.* **2.** to test the effect or result of (often fol. by *out*): *tried a new recipe.* **3.** to endeavor to evaluate by experiment or experience: *to try a new field.* **4.** to sample, taste, or test, as in order to evaluate. **5.** to examine and determine judicially, esp. to determine the guilt or innocence of (a person). **6.** to put to a severe test; subject to strain, as of endurance: *trying one's patience.* **7.** to attempt to open (a door, window, etc.) in order to find out whether it is locked. **8.** to melt down (fat, blubber, etc.) to obtain the oil; render (usu. fol. by *out*). —*v.i.* **9.** to make an attempt or effort; strive: *You must try harder.* **10. try on,** to put on an article of clothing in order to judge its appearance and fit. **11. try out, a.** to use experimentally; test. **b.** to compete for a position or role, as by taking part in a test or trial. —*n.* **12.** an attempt or effort. **13.** a score of three points in rugby earned by advancing the ball to or beyond the opponent's goal line.

try•ing (trī′ing), *adj.* straining one's patience and goodwill; annoying, difficult, or irritating. —**try′ing•ly,** *adv.* —**try′ing•ness,** *n.*

try•out (trī′out′), *n.* **1.** a trial or test to ascertain fitness for some purpose. **2.** the performance of a play in preparation for an official opening, often taking place away from a major theatrical center.

try•pan•o•some (tri pan′ə sōm′, trip′ə nə-), *n.* any of various flagellated protozoans of the genus *Trypanosoma,* transmitted by insect bite and parasitic in the blood and tissue of humans, domestic animals, and other vertebrates. —**try•pan′o•som′ic** (-som′ik), *adj.*

try•pan•o•so•mi•a•sis (tri pan′ə sō mī′ə sis, trip′ə nə-), *n.* an infectious disease caused by a trypanosome.

tryp•sin (trip′sin), *n.* an enzyme of the pancreatic juice, capable of converting proteins into peptone. —**tryp′tic** (-tik), *adj.*

tryp•to•phan (trip′tə fan′) also **tryp•to•phane** (-fān′), *n.* an essential amino acid, $(C_8H_6N)CH_2CH(NH_2)COOH$, released from proteins by the enzyme trypsin during digestion. *Abbr:* Trp; *Symbol:* W

tryst (trist, trīst), *n.* **1.** an appointment to meet at a certain time and place, esp. one made secretly by lovers. **2.** an appointed meeting. **3.** Also called **tryst′ing place′.** an appointed place of meeting; rendezvous. —*v.i.* **4.** to arrange a tryst. —**tryst′er,** *n.*

tsar (zär, tsär), *n.* CZAR. —**tsar′dom,** *n.* —**tsar′ism,** *n.* —**tsar′ist,** *adj., n.* —**tsar•is′tic,** *adj.*

tset′se (or **tzet′ze**) **fly′** (tset′sē, tet′-, tsē′tsē, tē′-), *n.* any of several bloodsucking African flies of the genus *Glossina,* including some that are vectors of trypanosomes that cause sleeping sickness and other diseases. Also called **tset′se.**

TSH, thyroid-stimulating hormone. Compare THYROTROPIN.

T-shirt or **tee shirt** (tē′shûrt′), *n.* a lightweight, usu. knitted, pullover shirt, typically with short sleeves and a collarless round neckline, worn as an undershirt or outer garment. Also called **tee.**

tsk (*pronounced as an alveolar click; spelling pron.* tisk), *interj.* (used, often in quick repetition, as an exclamation of impatience, annoyance, disapproval, commiseration, etc.)

tsp., **1.** teaspoon. **2.** teaspoonful.

T square, *n.* a T-shaped ruler having a short crosspiece that slides along the edge of a drawing board as a guide to the perpendicular longer section in making parallel lines, right angles, etc.

TSS, toxic shock syndrome.

tsu•na•mi (tsōō nä′mē), *n., pl.* **-mis.** an unusually large sea wave produced by a seaquake or undersea volcanic eruption. [< Japanese: harbor wave] —**tsu•na′mic** (-nä′mik, -nam′ik), *adj.*

tu•a•ta•ra (tōō′ə tär′ə) also **tu•a•te•ra** (-târ′ə), *n., pl.* **-ras.** a large lizardlike reptile, *Sphenodon punctatus,* of New Zealand: the only surviving rhynchocephalian.

tub (tub), *n., v.,* **tubbed, tub•bing.** —*n.* **1.** a bathtub. **2.** a broad, round, open container, orig. one made of wooden staves held together by hoops and fitted around a flat bottom. **3.** any of various small, usu. round containers: *a tub of butter.* **4.** the amount a tub will hold. **5.** an old, slow, or clumsy boat. **6.** *Informal.* a short and fat person. **7.** a bath in a bathtub. —*v.t.* **8.** to place or keep in a tub. **9.** to bathe. —*v.i.* **10.** to undergo washing. —**tub′ba•ble,** *adj.* —**tub′ber,** *n.* —**tub′like′,** *adj.*

tu•ba (tōō′bə, tyōō′-), *n.* **1.** a valved brass musical wind instrument having a low range. **2.** FUNNEL CLOUD.

tub•al (tōō′bəl, tyōō′-), *adj.* pertaining to a tube, as a fallopian tube.

tub′al liga′tion, *n.* a method of permanent sterilization for women, involving the surgical sealing of the fallopian tubes to prevent the ovum from passing from the ovary to the uterus.

tub•by (tub′ē), *adj.,* **-bi•er, -bi•est.** **1.** short and fat. **2.** having a dull, thumping sound; lacking resonance. —**tub′bi•ness,** *n.*

tube (tōōb, tyōōb), *n., v.,* **tubed, tub•ing.** —*n.* **1.** a hollow, usu. cylindrical body of metal, glass, rubber, etc., used esp. for conveying or containing liquids or gases. **2.** a small collapsible cylinder of metal or plastic sealed at one end and having a capped opening at the other from which a semifluid substance, as paint or toothpaste, may be squeezed. **3.** any hollow, cylindrical vessel or organ: *the bronchial tubes.* **4.** the elongated lower part of a united sepal or corolla of a flower. **5.** INNER TUBE. **6.** ELECTRON TUBE. **7. the tube,** *Informal.* television. **8.** a cylindrical garment without sleeves, pockets, or closures, usu. of stretch fabric, worn as a blouse, dress, skirt, etc. **9.** the tubular tunnel in which an underground railroad runs. **10.** the railroad itself. **11.** *Brit.* SUBWAY (def. 1). —*v.t.* **12.** to furnish with a tube. **13.** to convey or enclose in a tube. **14.** to form into the shape of a tube; make tubular. —*v.i.* **15.** to float down a river on an inner tube. —***Idiom.*** **16. down the tube(s),** into a wasted or abandoned state. —**tube′like′,** *adj.*

tube′ foot′, *n.* one of many small, tubular processes on the ventral body surface of most echinoderms, used for locomotion and grasping.

tube′less tire′, *n.* a rubber balloon tire made as a single piece without an inner tube.

tube′-nosed′, *adj.* **1.** having a long, tubelike beak or snout. **2.** (of a petrel or similar bird) having extended tubelike nostrils.

tube′ pan′, *n.* a circular cake pan with a hollow cone-shaped centerpiece, used for baking ring-shaped cakes.

tu•ber (to͞o′bər, tyo͞o′-), *n.* **1.** a thick, fleshy underground stem, as the potato, that bears buds from which new plants may arise. **2.** TUBERCLE. —**tu′ber•oid′,** *adj.*

tu•ber•cle (to͞o′bər kəl, tyo͞o′-), *n.* **1.** a small rounded projection, as on a bone or on the surface of the body. **2. a.** a small, firm, rounded nodule or swelling. **b.** such a swelling as the characteristic lesion of tuberculosis. **3.** a tuberlike swelling or nodule on a plant.

tu′bercle bacil′lus, *n.* the bacterium, *Mycobacterium tuberculosis,* causing tuberculosis. ABBR.: TB

tu•ber•cu•lar (to͞o bûr′kyə lər, tyo͞o-), *adj.* Also, **tuberculous. 1.** pertaining to or infected with tuberculosis. **2.** of, pertaining to, or of the nature of a tubercle or tubercles. **—***n.* **3.** a person affected with tuberculosis. —**tu•ber′cu•lar•ly,** *adv.*

tu•ber•cu•late (to͞o bûr′kyə lit, -lāt′, tyo͞o-), *adj.* **1.** Also, **tu•ber′cu•lat′ed.** having tubercles. **2.** TUBERCULAR. —**tu•ber′cu•la′tion,** *n.*

tu•ber•cu•lin (to͞o bûr′kyə lin, tyo͞o-), *n.* a sterile liquid prepared from cultures of the tubercle bacillus, used in a scratch test for tuberculosis.

tu•ber•cu•lo•sis (to͞o bûr′kyə lō′sis, tyo͞o-), *n.* **1.** an infectious disease that may affect almost any tissue of the body, esp. the lungs, caused by the organism *Mycobacterium tuberculosis,* and characterized by tubercles. **2.** this disease when affecting the lungs. *Abbr.:* TB

tube•rose (to͞ob′rōz′, tyo͞ob′-, to͞o′bə rōz′, tyo͞o′-), *n.* a bulbous plant, *Polianthes tuberosa,* of the agave family, cultivated for its spike of fragrant, creamy white, lilylike flowers.

tu•ber•ous (to͞o′bər əs, tyo͞o′-), *adj.* **1.** characterized by the presence of rounded or wartlike prominences or tubers. **2.** (of a plant) bearing tubers. **3.** of or resembling a tuber.

tu′berous root′, *n.* a true root so thickened as to resemble a tuber, but bearing no buds or eyes. —**tu′berous-root′ed,** *adj.*

tube′ sock′, *n.* a casual sock that is not shaped at the heel.

tube′worm′ or **tube′ worm′,** *n.* any of various marine worms that produce and inhabit a tube.

tub•ing (to͞o′bing, tyo͞o′-), *n.* **1.** material in the form of a tube: *glass tubing.* **2.** tubes collectively. **3.** a piece of tube. **4.** the sport or recreation of floating down a river or stream on an inner tube.

Tu Bi•she•vat or **Tu Bi•she•bat** (to͞o′ bi shə vät′, -shvät′), *n. Judaism.* the 15th day of Shevat, observed as a new year for trees by planting trees and by eating fruits.

Tub•man (tub′mən), *n.* **1. Harriet** (*Araminta*), 1820?–1913, U.S. abolitionist: escaped slave. **2. William Vacanarat Shadrach,** 1895–1971, president of Liberia 1944–71.

tu•bu•lar (to͞o′byə lər, tyo͞o′-), *adj.* **1.** having the form or shape of a tube. **2.** of or pertaining to a tube or tubes. **3.** characterized by or consisting of tubes. —**tu′bu•lar′i•ty,** *n.* —**tu′bu•lar•ly,** *adv.*

tuck (tuk), *v.t.* **1.** to put into a small, close, or concealing place: *Tuck the money into your wallet; a house tucked away in the woods.* **2.** to thrust in the loose end or edge of so as to hold in place: *Tuck in your blouse.* **3.** to cover snugly in or as if in this manner: *She tucked the children into bed.* **4.** to draw into a fold or a folded arrangement: *to tuck up one's skirts.* **5.** to sew tucks in. **6.** *Informal.* to eat or drink: *to tuck away a big meal.* **—***v.i.* **7.** to draw together; contract; pucker. **8.** to make tucks. **9.** to fit securely or snugly. **10. tuck into,** to eat or start to eat with enthusiasm. **—***n.* **11.** something tucked or folded in. **12.** a fold, or one of a series of folds, made by doubling cloth upon itself and stitching parallel with the edge of the fold. **13.** a body position in diving and gymnastics in which the head is lowered and the knees and thighs held against the chest. **14.** a crouching position in skiing in which the ski poles are held close to the chest. **15.** *Informal.* a plastic surgery operation: *an ear tuck; a tummy tuck.* **16.** *Brit.* food, esp. sweets.

tuck•er[1] (tuk′ər), *n.* **1.** a person or thing that tucks. **2.** a piece of fine fabric, as linen or lace, formerly worn by women around the neck and shoulders. ca **3.** *Australian.* food.

tuck•er[2] (tuk′ər), *v.t. Informal.* to tire; exhaust (often fol. by *out*).

Tuc•son (to͞o′son, to͞o son′), *n.* a city in S Arizona. 434,726.

-tude, a suffix occurring primarily in words from Latin or French, usu. abstract nouns formed from adjectives: *altitude; gratitude; exactitude.*

Tu•dor (to͞o′dər, tyo͞o′-), *n.* **1.** a member of the royal family that ruled in England from 1485 to 1603. **—***adj.* **2.** pertaining or belonging to the English royal house of Tudor. **3.** of or characteristic of the periods of the reigns of the Tudor sovereigns: *Tudor architecture.*

Tues•day (to͞oz′dā, -dē, tyo͞oz′-), *n.* the third day of the week, following Monday.

tuff (tuf), *n.* a fragmental rock consisting of the smaller kinds of volcanic detritus, as ash or cinder, usu. more or less stratified. —**tuff•a′ceous,** *adj.*

tuft (tuft), *n.* **1.** a bunch or cluster of small, usu. upright but flexible parts, as hair, feathers, flowers, or leaves, that are attached or close together at the base. **2.** a cluster of cut threads used decoratively on garments, upholstery, curtains, mattresses, etc. **3.** a small clump of bushes, trees, etc. **—***v.t.* **4.** to furnish or decorate with a tuft or tufts. **5.** to arrange in a tuft or tufts. **6.** to draw together (a cushion, mattress, etc.) by passing a thread through at regular intervals, the depressions thus produced usu. being ornamented with tufts or buttons. **—***v.i.* **7.** to form into or grow in a tuft or tufts. —**tuft′er,** *n.* —**tuft′y,** *adj.*

tuft•ed (tuf′tid), *adj.* **1.** furnished or decorated with tufts. **2.** formed into or growing in a tuft or tufts.

tuft′ed tit′mouse, *n.* a gray titmouse, *Parus bicolor,* of the E and midwestern U.S., having a crested head.

tug (tug), *v.,* **tugged, tug•ging,** *n.* **—***v.t.* **1.** to pull at with force, vigor, or effort. **2.** to move by pulling forcibly; drag; haul. **3.** to tow (a vessel) by means of a tugboat. **—***v.i.* **4.** to pull with force or effort. **5.** to strive hard; labor; toil. **—***n.* **6.** an act or instance of tugging; pull. **7.** a strenuous contest; struggle. **8.** TUGBOAT. **9.** that by which something is tugged, as a rope or chain. **10.** TRACE[2] (def. 1). —**tug′ger,** *n.*

tug•boat (tug′bōt′), *n.* a small, powerful boat for towing or pushing ships, barges, etc.

tug′ of war′, *n.* **1.** an athletic contest between two teams at opposite ends of a rope, each team trying to drag the other over a line. **2.** a hard-fought, critical struggle for supremacy.

tu•i•tion (to͞o ish′ən, tyo͞o-), *n.* **1.** the charge or fee for instruction, as at a private school or a college or university. **2.** teaching or instruction. —**tu•i′tion•al,** *adj.* —**tu•i′tion•less,** *adj.*

tu•la•re•mi•a or **tu•la•rae•mi•a** (to͞o′lə rē′mē ə), *n.* a plaguelike disease of rabbits, squirrels, etc., caused by a bacterium, *Francisella tularensis,* transmitted to humans by insects or ticks or by the handling of infected animals.

tu•lip (to͞o′lip, tyo͞o′-), *n.* **1.** any of various plants belonging to the genus *Tulipa,* of the lily family, having lance-shaped leaves and large, showy, cup-shaped or bell-shaped flowers in a variety of colors. **2.** a flower or bulb of such a plant. —**tu′lip•like′,** *adj.*

tu′lip tree′, *n.* a tall tree, *Liriodendron tulipifera,* of the magnolia family, native to the eastern U.S., having large, cup-shaped, green and orange flowers. Also called **yellow poplar.**

tu•lip•wood (to͞o′lip wo͝od′, tyo͞o′-), *n.* **1.** the wood of the tulip tree. **2.** any of various striped or variegated woods of other trees.

tulle (to͞ol; *Fr.* tyl), *n.* a thin, fine, machine-made net of acetate, nylon, rayon, or silk.

Tul•sa (tul′sə), *n.* a city in NE Oklahoma, on the Arkansas River. 374,851. —**Tul′san,** *n., adj.*

tum•ble (tum′bəl), *v.,* **-bled, -bling,** *n.* **—***v.i.* **1.** to fall helplessly down, esp. headfirst. **2.** to roll end over end, as in falling. **3.** to fall or decline rapidly; drop: *Prices on the stock exchange tumbled.* **4.** to perform gymnastic feats of skill, as leaps and somersaults. **5.** to fall suddenly from a position of power or authority. **6.** to fall in ruins; collapse; topple. **7.** to roll about by turning one way and another; pitch about; toss. **8.** to stumble or fall (usu. fol. by *over*). **9.** to go, come, get, etc., in a hasty and confused way. **10.** *Informal.* to understand or become aware of some fact or circumstance (often fol. by *to*). **—***v.t.* **11.** to cause to fall or roll end over end. **12.** to put in a disordered or rumpled condition; throw or toss about. **13.** to cause to fall from power; overthrow; topple. **14.** to cause to collapse in ruins. **15.** to subject to the action of a tumbling barrel. **—***n.* **16.** an act of tumbling or falling. **17.** a gymnastic or acrobatic feat. **18.** an accidental fall; spill. **19.** a drop in value, as of stocks. **20.** a fall from a position of power or authority. **21.** a response indicating interest, affection, etc.: *She wouldn't give me a tumble.* **22.** tumbled condition; disorder or confusion. **23.** a confused heap.

tum′ble-down′, *adj.* dilapidated; ruined; run-down.

tum•bler (tum′blər), *n.* **1.** a person who performs leaps, somersaults, and other acrobatic feats. **2.** a part of a lock that, when lifted or released by the action of a key or the like, allows the bolt to move. **3.** a stemless drinking glass having a flat, often thick bottom. **4.** (in a gunlock) a leverlike piece that by the action of a spring forces the hammer forward when released by the trigger. **5.** a part moving a gear into place in a selective transmission. **6.** Also called **roller.** one of a breed of pigeons that can roll over in flight.

tum•ble•weed (tum′bəl wēd′), *n.* any of various plants whose branching upper parts become detached from the roots and are driven about by the wind, as the amaranth *Amaranthus albus* or the Russian thistle *Salsola kali.*

tu•me•fa•ci•ent (to͞o′mə fā′shənt, tyo͞o′-), *adj.* becoming swollen; swelling.

tu•mes•cent (to͞o mes′ənt, tyo͞o-), *adj.* **1.** swelling; slightly tumid. **2.** exhibiting or affected with many ideas or emotions; teeming. **3.** pompous and pretentious, esp. in the use of language; bombastic. —**tu•mes′cence,** *n.*

tu•mid (to͞o′mid, tyo͞o′-), *adj.* **1.** swollen, or affected with swelling, as a part of the body. **2.** pompous or inflated, as language; turgid; bombastic. **3.** seeming to swell; bulging. —**tu•mid′i•ty,** *n.* —**tu′mid•ly,** *adv.*

tum•my (tum′ē), *n., pl.* **-mies.** *Informal.* the stomach or abdomen.

tu•mor (to͞o′mər, tyo͞o′-), *n.* **1.** a swollen part; swelling; protuberance. **2.** an uncontrolled, abnormal, circumscribed growth of cells in any animal or plant tissue; neoplasm. Also, *esp. Brit.,* **tu′mour.** —**tu′mor•like′,** *adj.* —**tu′mor•ous, tu′mor•al,** *adj.*

tu•mult (to͞o′mult, -məlt, tyo͞o′-), *n.* **1.** violent and noisy commotion or disturbance of a crowd or mob; uproar. **2.** a general outbreak, riot, uprising, or other disorder. **3.** highly distressing agitation of mind or feeling; turbulent mental or emotional disturbance.

tu•mul•tu•ous (to͞o mul′cho͞o əs, tyo͞o-), *adj.* **1.** full of tumult or riotousness; uproarious; disorderly. **2.** highly agitated; distraught; turbulent.

tun (tun), *n.*, *v.*, **tunned, tun·ning.** —*n.* **1.** a large cask for holding liquids, esp. wine, ale, or beer. **2.** a measure of liquid capacity, usu. equivalent to 252 gallons. —*v.t.* **3.** to put into or store in a tun or tuns.

tu·na (tōō′nə, tyōō′-), *n.*, *pl.* (*esp. collectively*) **-na,** (*esp. for kinds or species*) **-nas. 1.** any of several large marine food and game fishes of the family Scombridae, including the albacore, bluefin tuna, and yellowfin tuna. **2.** any of various related fishes. **3.** Also called **tu′na fish′.** the flesh of the tuna, used as food.

tun·a·ble (tōō′nə bəl, tyōō′-), *adj.* capable of being tuned. —**tun′a·bil′i·ty, tun′a·ble·ness,** *n.* —**tun′a·bly,** *adv.*

tun·dra (tun′drə, tōōn′-), *n.*, *pl.* **-dras.** any of the vast, nearly level, treeless plains of the arctic regions of Europe, Asia, and North America.

tune (tōōn, tyōōn), *n.*, *v.*, **tuned, tun·ing.** —*n.* **1.** a succession of musical sounds forming an air or melody. **2.** the state of being in the proper pitch: *to be in tune.* **3.** agreement in pitch; unison; harmony. **4.** proper adjustment, as of radio instruments or circuits with respect to frequency. **5.** harmonious relationship; accord; agreement. —*v.t.* **6.** to adjust (a musical instrument) to a correct or given standard of pitch (often fol. by *up*). **7.** to bring (someone or something) into harmony or agreement. **8.** to adjust (a motor, mechanism, or the like) for proper functioning. **9.** to adjust (a radio or television) so as to receive signals from a particular transmitting station. **10.** to put into or cause to be in a receptive condition, mood, etc. —*v.i.* **11.** to be in harmony or accord; become responsive. **12. tune in,** to adjust a radio or television so as to receive (signals, a station, etc.). **13. tune out, a.** to adjust a radio or television so as to avoid (static, interference, etc.). **b.** *Slang.* to stop paying attention to. **14. tune up, a.** to cause a group of musical instruments to be brought to the same pitch. **b.** to bring into proper operating order, as a motor. —*Idiom.* **15. change one's tune,** to reverse one's opinions; change one's mind. **16. sing** or **whistle a different tune,** to contradict one's previous opinions in response to changes in one's circumstances. **17. to the tune of,** in the amount of; for the cost of.

tune·ful (tōōn′fəl, tyōōn′-), *adj.* **1.** full of melody; melodious. **2.** producing musical sounds or melody. —**tune′ful·ly,** *adv.*

tun·er (tōō′nər, tyōō′-), *n.* **1.** a person or thing that tunes. **2.** the portion of a radio or television receiver that captures the broadcast signal and feeds it to other circuits in the set for further processing.

tune′-up′, *n.* an adjustment, as of a motor, to improve working order or condition.

tung·state (tung′stāt), *n.* a salt of any tungstic acid.

tung·sten (tung′stən), *n.* a rare, bright gray, lustrous metallic element having a high melting point, 3410°C: used in electric-lamp filaments. *Symbol:* W; *at. wt.:* 183.85; *at. no.:* 74; *sp. gr.:* 19.3. Also called **wolfram.** —**tung·sten′ic** (-sten′ik), *adj.*

tung′sten lamp′, *n.* an incandescent electric lamp with a tungsten filament.

tung′stic ac′id, *n.* **1.** a hydrate of tungsten trioxide, $H_2WO_4 \cdot H_2O$, used in the manufacture of filaments for tungsten lamps. **2.** any of a group of acids derived from tungsten by the addition of acid to a soluble tungstate or to a mixture of a tungstate and a silicate, phosphate, etc.

tu·nic (tōō′nik, tyōō′-), *n.* **1.** a coat worn as part of a military or other uniform. **2.** a gownlike outer garment worn by the ancient Greeks and Romans. **3. a.** a woman's straight, usu. sleeveless upper garment, loose or fitted, extending over the skirt to the hips or below. **b.** Also called **tu′nic dress′.** any of various dresses styled like this or incorporating this as one element. **4.** a covering membrane, layer, or integument over an organ or part.

tu·ni·cate (tōō′ni kit, -kāt′, tyōō′-), *n.* **1.** any marine chordate of the subphylum Tunicata (or Urochordata), having a saclike body enclosed in a thick membrane or tunic: includes ascidians and salps. —*adj.* Also, **tu′ni·cat′ed. 2.** (esp. of the Tunicata) having a tunic or covering. **3.** of or pertaining to the tunicates. **4.** *Bot.* having or consisting of a series of concentric layers, as a bulb.

tun′ing fork′, *n.* a steel instrument consisting of a stem with two prongs, producing a musical tone of definite, constant pitch when struck, and serving as a standard for tuning musical instruments, making acoustical experiments, and the like.

Tu·nis (tōō′nis, tyōō′-), *n.* **1.** the capital of Tunisia, in the NE part. 596,654. **2.** one of the former Barbary States in N Africa: constitutes modern Tunisia.

Tu·ni·sia (tōō nē′zhə, -shə, -nizh′ə, -nish′ə, tyōō′-), *n.* a republic in N Africa, on the Mediterranean: a French protectorate until 1956. 9,183,097. 63,379 sq. mi. (164,150 sq. km). *Cap.:* Tunis. —**Tu·ni′sian,** *adj.*, *n.*

tun·nel (tun′l), *n.*, *v.*, **-neled, -nel·ing** or (*esp. Brit.*) **-nelled, -nel·ling.** —*n.* **1.** an underground passage. **2.** a passageway, as for trains or automobiles, through or under a mountain, river, or other obstruction. **3.** an approximately horizontal gallery or corridor in a mine. **4.** the burrow of an animal. **5.** *Dial.* a funnel. —*v.t.* **6.** to construct a passageway through or under. **7.** to make or excavate (a tunnel or underground passage). —*v.i.* **8.** to make a tunnel or tunnels. —**tun′nel·er,** *n.*

tun·nel·ing (tun′l ing), *n.* a quantum-mechanical process, forbidden in classical mechanics, in which an atomic particle passes through a region where its potential energy is higher than its total energy. Also, *esp. Brit.* **tun′nel·ling.** Also called **tun′nel effect′.**

Tun·ney (tun′ē), *n.* **James Joseph** ("Gene"), 1898–1978, U.S. boxer: world heavyweight champion 1926–28.

tu·pe·lo (tōō′pə lō′, tyōō′-), *n.* any tall North American swamp tree of

the genus *Nyssa,* family Nyssaceae, having ovate leaves, purple berry-like fruit, and a soft, light wood with a variety of commercial uses.

tur·ban (tûr′bən), *n.* **1.** a man's headdress worn chiefly by Muslims in S Asia, consisting of a long cloth of silk, linen, cotton, etc., wound either about a cap or directly around the head. **2.** any headdress resembling this, esp. a woman's close-fitting, brimless hat of soft fabric.

turban

tur·bid (tûr′bid), *adj.* **1.** not clear or transparent because of stirred-up sediment or the like; clouded; opaque; obscured: *turbid water.* **2.** thick or dense, as smoke or clouds. **3.** confused; muddled; disturbed. —**tur·bid′i·ty, tur′bid·ness,** *n.* —**tur′bid·ly,** *adv.*

tur·bi·nate (tûr′bə nit, -nāt′), *adj.* Also, **tur′bi·nat′ed. 1.** having the shape of an inverted cone; scroll-like; whorled; spiraled. **2.** of or pertaining to certain scroll-like, spongy bones of the nasal passages. —*n.* **3.** a turbinate shell. —**tur′bi·na′tion,** *n.*

tur·bine (tûr′bin, -bīn), *n.* any of various machines having a group of rotor, usu. with vanes or blades, driven by the pressure or thrust of a moving fluid, as steam, water, hot gases, or air, either in the form of free jets or as a fluid filling a housing around the rotor.

tur·bit (tûr′bit), *n.* one of a breed of domestic pigeons having a stout, roundish body, a short head and beak, and a ruffled breast and neck.

tur·bo (tûr′bō), *n.* **1.** TURBINE. **2.** *Informal.* TURBOCHARGER.

turbo-, a combining form representing TURBINE: *turbojet.*

tur·bo·charg·er (tûr′bō chär′jər), *n.* a supercharger that is driven by a turbine turned by exhaust gases from the engine.

tur′bojet en′gine, *n.* a jet-propulsion engine in which air is compressed for combustion by a turbine-driven compressor.

tur′bo-propel′ler en′gine, *n.* a jet engine with a turbine-driven propeller that produces the principal thrust, augmented by the thrust of the jet exhaust. Also called **propjet engine, tur′boprop en′gine.**

tur·bo·shaft (tûr′bō shaft′, -shäft′), *n.* a gas turbine used to deliver shaft power, as to a helicopter rotor. Also called **tur′boshaft en′gine.**

tur·bot (tûr′bət), *n.*, *pl.* (*esp. collectively*) **-bot,** (*esp. for kinds or species*) **-bots. 1.** a European flatfish, *Psetta maxima,* having a diamond-shaped body. **2.** any of several other flatfishes.

tur·bu·lence (tûr′byə ləns) also **tur′bu·len·cy,** *n.* **1.** the quality or state of being turbulent; violent disorder or commotion. **2.** the haphazard secondary motion caused by eddies within a moving fluid. **3.** irregular motion of the atmosphere, as that indicated by gusts and lulls in the wind.

tur·bu·lent (tûr′byə lənt), *adj.* **1.** being in a state of agitation or tumult; disturbed. **2.** characterized by, showing, or causing disturbance, disorder, etc. **3.** characterized by turbulence; tempestuous: *turbulent waters.* —**tur′bu·lent·ly,** *adv.*

tu·reen (tōō rēn′, tyōō-), *n.* a large, deep, covered dish for serving soup, stew, etc.

turf (tûrf), *n.*, *pl.* **turfs,** (*esp. Brit.*) **turves,** *v.* —*n.* **1. a.** a layer of matted earth formed by grass and plant roots. **b.** *Chiefly Brit.* a piece cut or torn from this; sod. **2.** peat or a block of peat, esp. as material for fuel. **3. the turf, a.** the track over which horse races are run. **b.** the practice or sport of racing horses. **4. a.** the neighborhood over which a street gang asserts its authority. **b.** a familiar area, as of residence or expertise. —*v.t.* **5.** to cover with turf or sod. —**turf′like′,** *adj.*

Tur·ge·nev or **Tur·ge·niev** (tûr gen′yəf, -gän′-), *n.* **Ivan Sergeevich,** 1818–83, Russian novelist.

tur·gid (tûr′jid), *adj.* **1.** swollen; distended; tumid. **2.** inflated, overblown, or pompous; bombastic: *turgid language.* —**tur·gid′i·ty, tur′gid·ness,** *n.* —**tur′gid·ly,** *adv.*

tu·ris·ta (tōō rē′stə), *n.* TOURISTA.

Turk (tûrk), *n.* **1.** a native or inhabitant of Turkey. **2.** a Turkish-speaking citizen of the Ottoman Empire. **3.** a member of any Turkic-speaking people. **4. a.** one of a breed of Turkish horses closely related to the Arabian horse. **b.** any Turkish horse. **5.** YOUNG TURK.

tur·key (tûr′kē), *n.*, *pl.* **-keys,** (*esp. collectively*) **-key** for 1. **1.** either of two large North American gallinaceous birds of the pheasant family, esp. *Meleagris gallopavo,* with brownish, iridescent plumage and a bare head and neck: domestic forms now kept in many parts of the world. **2.** the flesh of this bird, used as food. **3.** *Slang.* **a.** a person or thing of little appeal; dud; loser. **b.** a naive, stupid, or inept person. **c.** a poor and unsuccessful theatrical production; flop. —*Idiom.* **4. talk turkey,** *Informal.* to talk frankly and directly.

Tur·key (tûr′kē), *n.* a republic in W Asia and SE Europe. 63,528,225; 300,948 sq. mi. (779,452 sq. km). *Cap.:* Ankara. Compare OTTOMAN EMPIRE.

tur′key cock′, *n.* **1.** the male of the turkey. **2.** a strutting, pompous, conceited person.

tur′key shoot′, *n.* **1.** a marksmanship contest in which rifles are fired at moving targets, orig. live turkeys. **2.** an easy destruction of enemy troops, esp. of flying aircraft.

tur′key trot′, *n.* a ragtime dance marked by a springy walk, shoulder movements, and little bending of the knees.

tur′key vul′ture, *n.* a blackish brown New World vulture, *Cathartes aura,* with a bare, wrinkled red head and neck. Also called **tur′key buz′zard.**

Tur•kic (tûr′kik), *n.* **1.** a family of closely related languages of SW, central, and N Asia and E Europe, including Turkish, Azerbaijani, Turkmen, Uzbek, Uighur, and Yakut. —*adj.* **2.** of or pertaining to Turkic or Turkic-speaking peoples.

Turk•ish (tûr′kish), *adj.* **1.** of or pertaining to Turkey, its inhabitants, or the language Turkish. **2.** TURKIC. —*n.* **3.** the Turkic language of Turkey. **4.** TURKIC. —**Turk′ish•ness,** *n.*

Turk′ish bath′, *n.* a bath in which the bather, after copious perspiration in a steam room, showers and has a rubdown.

Turk′ish cof′fee, *n.* a strong, usu. sweetened coffee, made by boiling pulverized coffee beans.

Turk•me•ni•stan (tûrk′me nə stan′, -stän′), *n.* a republic in central Asia, E of the Caspian Sea: a former constituent republic of the U.S.S.R. 4,225,351; 188,456 sq. mi. (488,100 sq. km). *Cap.:* Ashgabat.

tur•mer•ic (tûr′mər ik), *n.* **1.** the aromatic rhizome of an Asian plant, *Curcuma longa,* of the ginger family. **2.** a powder prepared from it, used as a condiment, a yellow dye, a medicine, etc. **3.** the plant itself. **4.** any of various similar substances or plants.

tur•moil (tûr′moil), *n.* a state of great commotion, confusion, or disturbance; tumult; agitation; disquiet.

turn (tûrn), *v.t.* **1.** to cause to move around on an axis or about a center; rotate: *to turn a wheel.* **2.** to cause to move around or partly around, as for the purpose of opening, closing, or tightening: *to turn a key.* **3.** to reverse the position or placement of: *to turn a page.* **4.** to bring the lower layers of (sod, soil, etc.) to the surface, as in plowing. **5.** to change the position of, by or as if by rotating; move into a different position: *to turn the handle one notch.* **6.** to change or reverse the course of; divert; deflect. **7.** to change the focus or tendency of. **8.** to change or alter the nature, character, or appearance of. **9.** to change or convert (usu. fol. by *into* or *to*): *to turn water into ice.* **10.** to render or make by some change. **11.** to cause to become sour, to ferment, or the like. **12.** to affect (the stomach) with nausea. **13.** to change from one form of expression to another; translate. **14.** to put or apply to some use or purpose. **15.** to go or pass around or to the other side of: *to turn a street corner.* **16.** to reach or pass (a certain age, amount, etc.). **17.** to direct, aim, or set toward, away from, or in a specified direction. **18.** to shape (a piece of metal, wood, etc.) into rounded form with a cutting tool while rotating on a lathe. **19.** to bring into a rounded or curved form in any way. **20.** to form or express gracefully: *to turn a phrase.* **21.** to cause to go; send; drive. **22.** to revolve in the mind; ponder (often fol. by *over*). **23.** to persuade (a person) to change or reorder the course of his or her life. **24.** to cause to be antagonistic toward: *turning children against their parents.* **25.** to maintain a steady flow or circulation of (money or merchandise). **26.** to earn or gain: *She turned a profit on the sale.* **27.** to reverse (a garment, collar, etc.) so that the inner side becomes the outer. **28.** to curve, bend, or twist. **29.** to twist out of position; wrench: *He turned his ankle.* **30.** to disturb the mental balance of; distract; derange. **31.** to disorder or upset the placement or condition of. —*v.i.* **32.** to move around on an axis or about a center; rotate. **33.** to move partly around through the arc of a circle, as a door on a hinge. **34.** to hinge or depend (usu. fol. by *on* or *upon*): *The question turns on this point.* **35.** to direct or set one's course toward, away from, or in a particular direction. **36.** to direct one's thought, gaze, attention, etc., toward or away from someone or something. **37.** to give or apply one's interest, effort, etc., to something; pursue: *to turn to crime.* **38.** to change or reverse a course so as to face or go in a different or the opposite direction: *to turn to the right.* **39.** to shift the body about as if on an axis. **40.** to assume a curved form; bend. **41.** to become blunted or dulled by bending, as the cutting edge of a knife or saw. **42.** to be affected with nausea, as the stomach. **43.** to be affected with giddiness or dizziness. **44.** to change or transfer one's loyalties; defect. **45.** to change an attitude or policy: *to turn against a person.* **46.** to change or alter, as in nature, character, or appearance. **47.** to become sour, rancid, or fermented, as milk or butter. **48.** to change color: *The leaves turn in October.* **49.** to change so as to be; become: *to turn pale.* **50.** to have recourse for help or information: *to turn to a friend for a loan.* **51.** to become mentally unbalanced or distracted. **52.** to put about or tack, as a ship. **53. turn down, a.** to turn over; fold down. **b.** to lower in intensity; lessen. **c.** to refuse or reject (a person, request, etc.). **54. turn in, a.** to hand in; submit. **b.** to inform on or deliver up. **c.** to go to bed; retire. **55. turn off, a.** to stop the flow of (water, gas, etc.), as by closing a faucet or valve. **b.** to extinguish (a light). **c.** to divert; deflect. **d.** to drive a vehicle or walk onto (a side road) from a main road. **e.** *Slang.* to disaffect, alienate, or disgust. **56. turn on, a.** to cause (water, gas, etc.) to flow, as by opening a valve. **b.** to switch on (a light). **c.** to put into operation; activate. **d.** to start suddenly to affect or show: *turned on the charm.* **e.** *Slang.* to arouse the interest of; engage. **f.** Also, **turn upon.** to become suddenly hostile to. **57. turn out, a.** to extinguish (a light). **b.** to produce as the result of labor. **c.** to drive out; dismiss; discharge. **d.** to come to be; become ultimately. **e.** to be found or known; prove. **58. turn over, a.** to move or be moved from one side to another. **b.** to put in reverse position; invert. **c.** to transfer; give. **d.** to start (an engine). **e.** (of an engine) to start. **59. turn up, a.** to fold (material, a hem, cuffs, etc.) up or over in order to alter a garment. **b.** to bring to the surface by digging. **c.** to uncover; find. **d.** to intensify or increase. **e.** to happen; occur. **f.** to appear; arrive. **g.** to be recovered. **h.** to come to notice; be seen. —*n.* **60.** a movement of partial or total rotation: *a turn of the handle.* **61.** an act of changing position or posture, as by a rotary movement: *a turn of the head.* **62.** a time or opportunity for action that comes in due order. **63.** an act of changing or reversing the course or direction. **64.** a place or point at which such a change occurs. **65.** a place where a road, river, or the like turns; bend. **66.** a single revolution, as of a wheel. **67.** an act of turning so as to face or go in a different direction. **68.** direction, drift, or trend. **69.** any change, as in nature, condition, or circumstances. **70.** the point or time of change. **71.** rounded or curved form. **72.** a passing or twisting of one thing around another, as of a rope around a mast. **73.** the state or manner of being twisted. **74.** a small latch operated by a turning knob or lever. **75.** a distinctive form or style of expression or language. **76.** a short walk, ride, or the like out and back, esp. by different routes. **77.** a natural inclination, bent, tendency, or aptitude: *one's turn of mind.* **78.** a spell or period of work; shift. **79.** an attack of illness or the like. **80.** an act of service or disservice. **81.** requirement, exigency, or need: *This will serve your turn.* **82.** treatment or rendering, esp. with reference to the form or content of a work of literature, art, etc.; twist. **83.** a nervous shock, as from fright or astonishment. **84.** *Music.* a melodic embellishment or grace, commonly consisting of a principal tone with two auxiliary tones, one above and the other below it. **85.** an individual stage performance. —***Idiom.*** **86. at every turn,** in every case or instance; constantly. **87. by turns,** one after another; alternately. **88. in turn,** in due order of succession. **89. out of turn, a.** not in the correct succession; out of proper order. **b.** at an unsuitable time; imprudently; indiscreetly: *He spoke out of turn.* **90. take turns,** to succeed one another in order; rotate; alternate. **91. to a turn,** to just the proper degree; to perfection. **92. turn one's back on,** to abandon, ignore, or reject. **93. turn the corner,** to pass through a crisis safely. **94. turn the other cheek,** to refuse to retaliate for an injury. Matt. 5:39; Luke 6:29. **95. turn the tide,** to reverse the course of events, esp. from one extreme to another.

turn•a•bout (tûrn′ə bout′), *n.* **1.** the act of turning in a different or opposite direction. **2.** a change of opinion, loyalty, etc. **3.** *Chiefly Brit.* MERRY-GO-ROUND.

turn•a•round (tûrn′ə round′), *n.* **1.** the total time consumed in the round trip of a ship, aircraft, vehicle, etc. **2.** turnabout. **3.** change of allegiance, opinion, mood, policy, etc. **4.** a place or area having sufficient room for a vehicle to turn around. **5.** a recovery, as in business sales; change from loss to profit.

turn•coat (tûrn′kōt′), *n.* a person who changes to the opposite party or faction, reverses principles, etc.; renegade.

turn•down (tûrn′doun′), *adj.* **1.** that is or may be turned down; folded or doubled down: *a turndown collar.* —*n.* **2.** an act or instance of being refused or rejected.

turn•er (tûr′nər), *n.* **1.** one that turns or is employed in turning. **2.** a person who fashions or shapes objects on a lathe.

Tur•ner (tûr′nər), *n.* **1. Frederick Jackson,** 1861–1932, U.S. historian. **2. Joseph Mallord William,** 1775–1851, English painter. **3. Nat,** 1800–31, U.S. leader of uprising of slaves.

turn•er•y (tûr′nə rē), *n., pl.* **-er•ies. 1.** the process or art of forming or shaping objects on a lathe. **2.** objects or articles fashioned on a lathe collectively. **3.** a workshop where such work is done.

turn•ing (tûr′ning), *n.* **1.** the act of a person or thing that turns. **2.** an act of reversing position. **3.** the place or point at which anything bends or changes direction. **4.** the forming of objects on a lathe. **5.** an object, as a spindle, turned on a lathe. **6.** an act of shaping something: *the turning of verses.*

turn′ing point′, *n.* a point at which a decisive change takes place; critical point; crisis.

tur•nip (tûr′nip), *n.* **1.** the thick, fleshy root of either of two plants of the mustard family, the white *Brassica rapa,* or the yellow rutabaga, *B. napobrassica,* eaten as a vegetable. **2.** either of these two plants, the leaves of which are sometimes eaten as a vegetable. —**tur′nip•like′,** *adj.*

turn•key (tûrn′kē′), *n.* **1.** a person who has charge of the keys of a prison; jailer. —*adj.* **2.** ready for occupancy when turned over to the owner: *turnkey housing.* **3.** fully equipped; ready to go into operation: *a turnkey power plant.*

turn•off (tûrn′ôf′, -of′), *n.* **1.** a small road that branches off from a larger one, esp. an exit off a major highway. **2.** a place at which one changes from a former course. **3.** an act of turning off. **4.** *Slang.* something or someone that makes one lose interest or excitement.

turn•on (tûrn′on′, -ôn′), *n. Slang.* something or someone that arouses one's interest or excitement.

turn•out (tûrn′out′), *n.* **1.** the gathering of persons who come to an exhibition, party, spectacle, or the like. **2.** quantity of production; output. **3.** an act of turning out. **4.** equipment; outfit. **5.** a short side track, space, spur, etc., that enables trains, automobiles, etc., to pass one another or park.

turn•o•ver (tûrn′ō′vər), *n.* **1.** an act or result of turning over; upset. **2.** change or movement of people, as tenants or customers, in, out, or through a place. **3.** the rate at which workers are replaced in a given period. **4.** the amount of business done in a given time. **5.** the rate at which items are sold and inventory replaced. **6.** a change from one position, opinion, etc., to another. **7.** a reorganization of a political organization, business, etc. **8.** a baked pastry in which half the dough is turned over the filling and sealed. —*adj.* **9.** capable of being turned over.

turn•pike (tûrn′pīk′), *n.* **1.** a high-speed highway, esp. one maintained by tolls. **2.** (formerly) a barrier set across such a highway to stop passage until a toll has been paid; tollgate.

turn′ sig′nal, *n.* a signal light on a motor vehicle that can be made to flash on the side toward which the driver intends to steer; directional.

turn•stile (tûrn′stīl′), *n.* **1.** a structure of usu. four horizontally revolving arms pivoted atop a post and set in a passageway to control the flow of people or animals. **2.** a similar device set up in an entrance to bar passage until a charge is paid; to record the number of persons passing through, etc.

turn•stone (tûrn′stōn′), *n.* any of several shorebirds of the genus *Arenaria*, of the sandpiper family, having a slender, upturned bill used for turning over pebbles in search of food.

turn•ta•ble (tûrn′tā′bəl), *n.* **1.** the rotating disk that spins the record on a phonograph. **2.** a rotating, track-bearing platform pivoted in the center, used for turning railroad locomotives and cars around. **3.** a rotating stand used in sculpture, metalwork, and ceramics.

tur•pen•tine (tûr′pən tīn′), *n.*, *v.*, **-tined, -tin•ing.** —*n.* **1.** an oleoresin derived from coniferous trees and yielding a volatile oil and a resin when distilled. **2.** a distilled form of this oleoresin, having a penetrating odor and a pungent, bitter taste, used as a paint thinner and solvent and in medicine. —*v.t.* **3.** to treat with turpentine; apply turpentine to. **4.** to gather or take crude turpentine from (trees). —**tur′pen•tin′ic** (-tin′ik), **tur′pen•tin′ous** (-tin′əs, -tī′nəs), **tur′pen•tin′y** (-tī′nē), *adj.*

tur•pi•tude (tûr′pi tōōd′, -tyōōd′), *n.* **1.** vile or base character; depravity. **2.** a vile or depraved act.

tur•quoise (tûr′koiz, -kwoiz), *n.* **1.** an opaque mineral, a basic hydrous copper aluminum phosphate often containing a small amount of iron, sky-blue or greenish blue in color, cut cabochon as a gem. **2.** Also called **tur′quoise blue′.** a greenish blue or bluish green.

tur•ret (tûr′it, tur′-), *n.* **1.** a small tower, usu. one forming part of a larger structure. **2.** a small tower at an angle of a building, as of a castle or fortress, frequently beginning some distance above the ground. **3.** a domelike structure, usu. revolving horizontally, in which a gun is mounted, as on an armored vehicle, ship, or aircraft. **4.** Also called **tur′ret•head′** (-hed′). a pivoted attachment on a lathe or the like for holding a number of tools. —**turreted** *adj.*

tur•tle¹ (tûr′tl), *n.*, *pl.* **-tles,** (*esp. collectively*) **-tle,** *v.*, **-tled, -tling.** —*n.* **1.** any reptile of the worldwide order Testudines, comprising aquatic and terrestrial species having the trunk enclosed in a shell consisting of a dorsal carapace and a ventral plastron. —*v.i.* **2.** to catch turtles, esp. as a business. —*Idiom.* **3. turn turtle,** to capsize or turn over completely. —**tur′tler,** *n.*

tur•tle² (tûr′tl), *n. Archaic.* a turtledove. Song of Solomon 2:12.

tur•tle•dove (tûr′tl duv′), *n.* **1.** any of several small to medium-sized Old World doves of the genus *Streptopelia*, esp. *S. turtur*, of Europe, having a long, graduated tail. **2.** MOURNING DOVE.

tur•tle•head (tûr′tl hed′), *n.* any North American plant of the genus *Chelone*, of the figwort family, having spikes of white or purple two-lipped flowers.

tur•tle•neck (tûr′tl nek′), *n.* **1.** a high, close-fitting collar, often rolled or turned down, appearing esp. on pullover sweaters. **2.** a garment with such a neck, esp. a sweater.

Tus•ca•ny (tus′kə nē), *n.* a region in W central Italy: formerly a grand duchy. 3,578,814; 8879 sq. mi. (22,995 sq. km). Italian, **Toscana**.

Tus•ca•ro•ra (tus′kə rôr′ə, -rōr′ə), *n.*, *pl.* **-ras,** (*esp. collectively*) **-ra. 1.** a member of an Indian people living originally in North Carolina and later, after their admission into the Iroquois confederacy, in New York. **2.** an Iroquoian language, the language of the Tuscarora people.

tusch•e (tōōsh′ə), *n.* a greaselike liquid used in lithography as a medium receptive to lithographic ink, and in etching and silkscreen as a resist.

tush (tōōsh), *n. Slang.* TUSHIE.

tush•ie or **tush•y** (tōōsh′ē), *n.*, *pl.* **tush•ies.** *Slang.* the buttocks.

tusk (tusk), *n.* **1.** an animal tooth developed to great length, usu. one of a pair, as in the elephant, walrus, and wild boar, but singly in the narwhal. **2.** a long, pointed, or protruding tooth. **3.** a projection resembling the tusk of an animal. —*v.t.* **4.** to dig, tear, or gore with the tusks.

Tus•ke•gee (tus kē′gē), *n.* a city in E Alabama: location of Tuskegee Institute. 12,716.

tus•sive (tus′iv), *adj.* of or pertaining to a cough.

tus•sle (tus′əl), *v.*, **-sled, -sling,** *n.* —*v.i.* **1.** to struggle or fight roughly or vigorously; wrestle; scuffle. —*n.* **2.** a rough physical contest or struggle; scuffle. **3.** any vigorous or determined struggle, conflict, etc.

tus•sock (tus′ək), *n.* a tuft or clump of growing grass or the like. —**tus′socked,** *adj.* —**tus•sock•y,** *adj.*

tus′sock grass′, *n.* any of various grasses that grow in tuftlike clumps.

tus′sock moth′, *n.* any of several moths of the family Lymantriidae, the larvae of which have characteristic tufts of hair on the body and feed on the leaves of various deciduous trees.

tut (*pronounced as an alveolar click; spelling pron.* tut) also **tut-tut,** *interj.*, *n.*, *v.*, **tut•ted, tut•ting.** —*interj.* **1.** (used as an exclamation of contempt, disdain, impatience, etc.) **2.** for shame! —*n.* **3.** an exclamation of "tut." —*v.i.* **4.** to utter the exclamation "tut."

Tut•ankh•a•men or **Tut•ankh•a•mon** or **Tut•ankh•a•mun** (tōōt′äng kä′mən), *n.* fl. c1350 B.C., king of Egypt.

tu•te•lage (tōōt′l ij, tyōōt′-), *n.* **1.** the act of protecting or guiding; office or function of a guardian; guardianship. **2.** instruction; teaching; guidance. **3.** the state of being under a guardian or a tutor.

tu•te•lar•y (tōōt′l er′ē, tyōōt′-) also **tu•te•lar** (-l ər), *adj.*, *n.*, *pl.* **-lar•ies.** —*adj.* **1.** having the position of guardian or protector of a person, place, or thing: *a tutelary spirit.* **2.** of or pertaining to a guardian or guardianship. —*n.* **3.** a person who has tutelary powers, as a saint, deity, or guardian.

tu•tor (tōō′tər, tyōō′-), *n.* **1.** a person employed to instruct another, esp. privately. **2.** a teacher of academic rank lower than instructor in some American universities and colleges. **3.** esp. at Oxford and Cambridge) a university officer responsible for teaching and supervising a number of undergraduates. —*v.t.* **4.** to act as a tutor to; teach or instruct, esp. privately; coach. **5.** to have the guardianship, instruction, or care of. —*v.i.* **6.** to act as a tutor or private instructor. **7.** to study privately with a tutor. —**tu′tor•ship′,** *n.*

tu•tor•age (tōō′tər ij, tyōō′-), *n.* **1.** the office, authority, or care of a tutor. **2.** the charge for instruction by a tutor.

tu•to•ri•al (tōō tôr′ē əl, -tōr′-; tyōō-), *adj.* **1.** pertaining to or·exercised by a tutor. —*n.* **2.** a session of intensive instruction by a tutor.

tut•ti (tōō′tē), *adj.*, *n.*, *pl.* **-tis.** —*adj.* **1.** all (used as a musical direction for voices or instruments to perform together). —*n.* **2.** a musical passage or movement performed by all players together.

tut•ti-frut•ti (tōō′tē frōō′tē), *n.* **1.** a confection, esp. ice cream, flavored with a variety of fruits, usu. candied and minced. **2.** a synthetic flavoring combining the flavors of a variety of fruits.

tut-tut (*pronounced as two alveolar clicks; spelling pron.* tut′tut′), *interj.*, *n.*, *v.i.*, **-tut•ted, -tut•ting.** TUT.

tu•tu (tōō′tōō), *n.*, *pl.* **-tus.** a short, full skirt, usu. made of several layers of tarlatan or tulle, worn by ballerinas. —**tu′tued′,** *adj.*

tutu

Tu•tu (tōō′tōō), *n.* **Desmond (Mpilo),** born 1931, South African Anglican bishop and civil-rights activist.

Tu•va•lu (tōō′və lōō′, tōō vä′lōō), *n.* a parliamentary state consisting of a group of islands in the central Pacific, S of the equator: a former British colony; gained independence 1978. 8229; 10 sq. mi. (26 sq. km). *Cap.* Funafuti. Formerly, **Ellice Islands.** —**Tu′va•lu′an,** *adj.*, *n.*

tux (tuks), *n. Informal.* a tuxedo. Often, **tuck.**

tux•e•do (tuk sē′dō), *n.* **1.** Also called **dinner jacket.** a man's jacket for semiformal evening dress, traditionally of black or dark blue color and characteristically having satin or grosgrain facing on the lapels. **2.** the complete semiformal outfit, including this jacket, dark trousers, often with silk stripes down the sides, a bow tie, and usu. a cummerbund. —**tux•e′doed,** *adj.*

TV or **tv,** television.

TVA, Tennessee Valley Authority.

twad•dle (twod′l), *n.*, *v.*, **-dled, -dling.** —*n.* **1.** silly or tedious talk or writing. —*v.i.* **2.** to talk in a silly or tedious manner; prate. —*v.t.* **3.** to utter as twaddle. —**twad′dler,** *n.* —**twad′dly,** *adj.*

twain (twān), *adj.*, *n.* two.

Twain (twān), *n.* **Mark,** pen name of Samuel Langhorne CLEMENS.

twang (twang), *v.i.* **1.** to give out a sharp, vibrating sound, as the string of a musical instrument when plucked. **2.** to have or produce a sharp, nasal tone, as the human voice. —*v.t.* **3.** to cause to make a sharp, vibrating sound, as a string of a musical instrument. **4.** to pluck the strings of (a musical instrument). **5.** to speak with a sharp, nasal tone. **6.** to pull the string of (an archer's bow). —*n.* **7.** a sharp, ringing sound, esp. one produced by plucking or suddenly releasing a tense string. **8.** an act of plucking or picking. **9.** a sharp, nasal tone. —**twang′y,** *adj.*, **twang•i•er, twang•i•est.**

'twas (twuz, twoz; *unstressed* twəz), contraction of *it was.*

'Twas′ the Night′ Before′ Christ′mas, popular name for *A Visit from St. Nicholas* (1823), a children's poem by Clement Clarke Moore (1779–1863).

tweak (twēk), *v.t.* **1.** to pinch and pull with a jerk and twist: *to tweak someone's ear; to tweak someone's nose.* **2.** to pull or pinch the nose of, esp. gently: *He tweaked the baby on greeting.* **3.** to make a minor adjustment to: *to tweak a computer program.* —*n.* **4.** an act or instance of tweaking; a sharp, twisting pull or jerk.

tweed (twēd), *n.* **1.** a coarse wool cloth in a variety of weaves and colors, produced esp. in Scotland. **2. tweeds,** garments made of this cloth.

Tweed (twēd), *n.* **1. William Marcy** (*"Boss Tweed"*), 1823–78, U.S. politician. **2.** a river flowing E from S Scotland along part of the NE boundary of England into the North Sea. 97 mi. (156 km) long.

twee·dle (twēd′l), *v.i.*, **-dled, -dling. 1.** to produce high-pitched, modulated sounds, as a singer, bird, or musical instrument. **2.** to perform lightly upon a musical instrument.

Twee·dle·dum and Twee·dle·dee (twēd′l dum′ ən twēd′l dē′), *n.pl.* two persons or things nominally different but practically the same; a nearly identical pair.

tweed·y (twē′dē), *adj.,* **tweed·i·er, tweed·i·est. 1.** made of or resembling tweed, as in texture or appearance. **2.** wearing tweeds, esp. as a mark of a casual or outdoor life. **3.** accustomed to, preferring, or characterized by the wearing of tweeds, as in genteel country life or academia: *a large and tweedy colony of civil servants and government officials.*

'tween (twēn), *prep.* contraction of *between.*

tweet (twēt), *n.* **1.** a chirping sound, as of a small bird. —*v.i.* **2.** to chirp.

tweet·er (twē′tər), *n.* a small loudspeaker designed for the reproduction of high-frequency sounds.

tweeze (twēz), *v.t., v.i.,* **tweezed, tweez·ing.** to pluck with tweezers.

tweez·ers (twē′zərz), *n.* (*used with a sing. or pl. v.*) small pincers or nippers for plucking out hairs, extracting splinters, picking up small objects, etc.

twelfth (twelfth), *adj.* **1.** next after the eleventh; being the ordinal number for 12. **2.** being one of 12 equal parts. —*n.* **3.** a twelfth part, esp. of one ($^1/_{12}$). **4.** the twelfth member of a series.

Twelfth′ Amend′ment, *n.* an amendment to the U.S. Constitution, ratified in 1804, providing for election of the president and vice president by the electoral college: should there be no majority vote for one person, the House of Representatives (one vote per state) chooses the president and Senate the vice president.

Twelfth′ Day′, *n.* Epiphany; formerly observed as the last day of the Christmas festivities.

Twelfth′ Night′, *n.* **1.** the evening before Twelfth Day or the evening of Twelfth Day itself. **2.** (*italics*) a comedy (1602) by William Shakespeare.

twelve (twelv), *n.* **1.** a cardinal number, 10 plus 2. **2.** a symbol for this number, as 12 or XII. **3.** a set of this many persons or things. **4. a. the Twelve,** the 12 apostles chosen by Christ. **b.** the 12 books of the Minor Prophets. —*adj.* **5.** amounting to 12 in number.

twelve′-mile′ lim′it, *n.* the offshore boundary of a state, extending 12 miles (19 km) at sea. Compare THREE-MILE LIMIT.

Twelve′ Step′ or **12-step,** *adj.* of or based on a program for recovery from addiction originating with Alcoholics Anonymous and providing 12 progressive levels toward attainment. —**12-stepper,** *n.*

twen·ti·eth (twen′tē ith, twun′-), *adj.* **1.** next after the nineteenth; being the ordinal number for 20. **2.** being one of 20 equal parts. —*n.* **3.** a twentieth part, esp. of one ($^1/_{20}$). **4.** the twentieth member of a series.

Twen′tieth Amend′ment, *n.* an amendment to the U.S. Constitution, ratified in 1933, that abolished the December to March session of those Congressmen defeated for reelection in November. Also called **Lame Duck Amendment.**

twen·ty (twen′tē, twun′-), *n., pl.* **-ties,** *adj.* —*n.* **1.** a cardinal number, 10 times 2. **2.** a symbol for this number, as 20 or XX. **3.** a set of this many persons or things. **4.** a twenty-dollar bill. **5. twenties,** the numbers from 20 through 29, as in reference to the years of a lifetime or century or to degrees of temperature. —*adj.* **6.** amounting to 20 in number.

Twen′ty-fifth′ Amend′ment, *n.* an amendment to the U.S. Constitution, ratified in 1967, establishing the succession to the presidency in the event of the president's death, resignation, or incapacity.

Twen′ty-first′ Amend′ment, *n.* an amendment to the U.S. Constitution, ratified in 1933, providing for the repeal of the Eighteenth Amendment, which had outlawed the manufacture, sale, and transportation of alcoholic beverages.

Twen′ty-fourth′ Amend′ment, *n.* an amendment to the U.S. Constitution, ratified in 1964, forbidding the use of the poll tax as a requirement for voting in national or U.S. Congressional elections.

twen′ty-one′, *n.* **1.** a cardinal number, 20 plus 1. **2.** a symbol for this number, as 21 or XXI. **3.** BLACKJACK (def. 2a).

Twen′ty-sec′ond Amend′ment, *n.* an amendment to the U.S. Constitution, ratified in 1951, limiting presidential terms to two for any one person, or to one elected term if the person has completed more than two years of another's term.

Twen′ty-sev′enth Amend′ment, *n.* an amendment to the U.S. constitution, ratified in 1992, providing that no law to vary the compensation for senators or represenatives can take effect until an election of representatives has intervened.

Twen′ty-sixth′ Amend′ment, *n.* an amendment to the U.S. Constitution, ratified in 1971, lowering the voting age to 18.

Twen′ty-third′ Amend′ment, *n.* an amendment to the U.S. Consti-

tution, ratified in 1961, allowing District of Columbia residents to vote in presidential elections.

twen′ty-twen′ty or **20-20,** *adj.* having normal visual acuity.

twen′ty-two′, *n.* **1.** a cardinal number, 20 plus 2. **2.** a symbol for this number, as 22 or XXII. **3.** a set of this many persons or things. **4.** a .22-caliber handgun or its cartridge (often written as *.22*).

'twere (twûr; *unstressed* twər), contraction of *it were.*

twerp or **twirp** (twûrp), *n. Informal.* an insignificant or despicable person.

twice (twīs), *adv.* **1.** two times. **2.** on two occasions. **3.** in twofold quantity or degree.

twice-born (twīs′bôrn′), *adj.* **1.** *Hinduism.* of or pertaining to members of the Indian castes of Brahmins, Kshatriyas, and Vaisyas, who undergo a spiritual rebirth and initiation in adolescence. **2.** having undergone reincarnation. **3.** born-again (def. 1). **4.** denoting any moral or religious experience that brings about a major reorientation of a person's character or personality.

twice′-told′, *adj.* having been told before; well-known.

twid·dle (twid′l), *v.,* **-dled, -dling,** *n.* —*v.t.* **1.** to turn about or play with lightly or idly, esp. with the fingers; twirl. —*v.i.* **2.** to play or trifle idly with something; fiddle. **3.** to turn about lightly; twirl. —*n.* **4.** the act of twiddling; turn; twirl. —*Idiom.* **5. twiddle one's thumbs,** to do nothing; be idle. —**twid′dler,** *n.*

twig (twig), *n.* a small, thin offshoot of a wooden branch or stem.

twi·light (twī′līt′), *n.* **1.** the soft, diffused light from the sky when the sun is below the horizon, either from daybreak to sunrise or, more commonly, from sunset to nightfall. **2.** the period in the morning or, more commonly, in the evening during which this light prevails. **3.** a terminal period, esp. after full development, success, etc. **4.** a state of uncertainty, vagueness, or gloom. —*adj.* **5.** of, pertaining to, or resembling twilight; dim; obscure. **6.** appearing or flying at twilight; crepuscular.

twi′light zone′, *n.* an ill-defined area between two distinct conditions, categories, etc.; an indefinite boundary.

twill (twil), *n.* **1.** a fabric constructed in twill weave. **2.** a garment, as a suit or trousers, of this fabric. **3.** TWILL WEAVE. —*v.t.* **4.** to weave in the manner of a twill. **5.** to weave in twill construction.

'twill (twil), contraction of *it will.*

twill′ weave′, *n.* one of the three basic weave structures, in which the filling threads are woven over and under two or more warp yarns, producing a characteristic diagonal pattern. Compare PLAIN WEAVE, SATIN WEAVE. Also called **twill.**

twin (twin), *n., adj., v.,* **twinned, twin·ning.** —*n.* **1.** either of two children or animals brought forth at a birth. **2.** either of two persons or things closely related to or closely resembling each other. **3. the Twins,** GEMINI (def. 1). —*adj.* **4.** being a twin or twins: *twin sisters.* **5.** being two persons or things closely related to or closely resembling each other. **6.** being one of a pair; identical. **7.** consisting of two similar parts or elements joined or connected: *a twin vase.* **8.** *Zool., Bot.* occurring in pairs. **9.** twofold or double. —*v.t.* **10.** to bring together in close relationship; pair; couple. **11.** to furnish a counterpart to; match. —*v.i.* **12.** to give birth to twins. **13.** to be paired or coupled.

twin′ bed′, *n.* a twin-size bed, esp. one of a matching pair in a bedroom; single bed.

Twin′ Cit′ies, *n.pl.* the cities of St. Paul and Minneapolis.

twine (twīn), *n., v.,* **twined, twin·ing.** —*n.* **1.** a strong thread or string composed of two or more strands twisted together. **2.** an act of twining, twisting, or interweaving. **3.** a coiled or twisted object or part; convolution. **4.** a twist or turn in anything. **5.** a knot or tangle. —*v.t.* **6.** to twist together; interweave. **7.** to form by or as if by twisting together: *to twine a wreath.* **8.** to twist (one strand, thread, or the like) with another; interlace. **9.** to insert with a twisting or winding motion (usu. fol. by *in* or *into*): *He twined his fingers in his hair.* **10.** to clasp or enfold (something) around something else; place by or as if by winding (usu. fol. by *about, around,* etc.). **11.** to wreathe or wrap: *They twined the arch with flowers.* —*v.i.* **12.** to wind about something; twist itself in spirals (usu. fol. by *about, around,* etc.). **13.** to wind in a sinuous or meandering course. —**twine′a·ble,** *adj.* —**twin′er,** *n.*

twin′-en′gine, *adj.* having two engines of equal power as prime movers: *a twin-engine airplane.*

twinge (twinj), *n., v.,* **twinged, twing·ing.** —*n.* **1.** a sudden, sharp pain. **2.** a mental or emotional pang. —*v.t.* **3.** to affect (the body or mind) with a sudden, sharp pain or pang. **4.** to pinch; tweak; twitch. —*v.i.* **5.** to have or feel a sudden, sharp pain.

twi-night (twī′nīt′), *adj.* of or denoting a baseball doubleheader begun late in the afternoon and continued into the evening.

twin·kle (twing′kəl), *v.,* **-kled, -kling,** *n.* —*v.i.* **1.** to shine with a flickering gleam of light, as a star or distant light. **2.** to sparkle in the light. **3.** (of the eyes) to be bright with amusement, pleasure, etc. **4.** to move flutteringly and quickly, as flashes of light; flit. —*v.t.* **5.** to emit (light) in intermittent gleams or flashes. —*n.* **6.** a flickering or intermittent brightness or light. **7.** a scintillating brightness in the eyes; sparkle. **8.** the time required for a wink; twinkling. —**twin′kler,** *n.*

twin·kling (twing′kling), *n.* **1.** an act of shining with intermittent gleams of light. **2.** the time required for a wink; an instant.

twin′-size′ or **twin′-sized′,** *adj.* **1.** (of a bed) approximately 39 in. (99 cm) wide and 75–76 in. (191–3 cm) long. **2.** of or for a twin bed.

twirl (twûrl), *v.t.* **1.** to cause to rotate rapidly; spin; whirl: *to twirl a ba-*

T

ton. **2.** to twiddle. **3.** to wind idly, as about something. **4.** *Baseball.* to pitch. —*v.i.* **5.** to rotate rapidly; whirl. **6.** to turn quickly so as to face or point in another direction. —*n.* **7.** an act or instance of twirling; spin; whirl. **8.** something having a spiral shape; coil; curl; convolution.

twist (twist), *v.t.* **1.** to combine, as two or more strands or threads, by winding together; intertwine. **2.** to form by or as if by winding strands together. **3.** to entwine (one thing) with another. **4.** to wind or coil (something) about something else. **5.** to alter in shape, as by turning the ends in opposite directions. **6.** to turn sharply or wrench out of place; sprain: *twisted his ankle.* **7.** to pull, tear, or break off by turning forcibly. **8.** to contort. **9.** to distort the meaning or form of; pervert. **10.** to cause to become mentally or emotionally distorted; warp. **11.** to form into a coil or knot by winding, rolling, etc. **12.** to bend tortuously. **13.** to cause to move with a rotary motion, as a ball pitched in a curve. **14.** to turn (something) from one direction to another, as by rotating. —*v.i.* **15.** to be or become intertwined. **16.** to wind or twine about something. **17.** to writhe or squirm. **18.** to take a spiral form or course. **19.** to turn so as to face in another direction. **20.** to turn, coil, or bend into a spiral shape. **21.** to change shape under forcible turning or twisting. **22.** to move with a progressive rotary motion, as a ball pitched in a curve. —*n.* **23.** a deviation in direction; curve; bend; turn. **24.** a rotary motion or spin. **25.** anything formed by or as if by twisting. **26.** the act or process of twining strands together. **27.** a twisting awry or askew. **28.** distortion or perversion, as of meaning or form. **29.** an eccentric turn or bent of mind. **30.** spiral arrangement or form. **31.** spiral movement or course. **32.** an irregular bend; crook; kink. **33.** a sudden, unanticipated change of course, as of events. **34.** a novel treatment, method, etc. **35.** the changing of the shape of anything by or as if by turning the ends in opposite directions. **36.** the stress causing this alteration; torque. **37.** a twisting or torsional action, force, or stress; torsion. **38.** a full rotation of the body performed during a dive or vault. **39.** a strong, twisted silk thread, heavier than ordinary sewing silk, for working buttonholes and for other purposes. **40.** the direction of twisting in weaving yarn. **41.** a loaf or roll of dough twisted and baked. **42.** a strip of citrus peel added to a drink as a flavoring. **43.** a dance characterized by strongly rhythmic turns and twists of body. —***Idiom.*** **44. twist someone's arm,** to use force or coercion on someone. —**twist′a•ble,** *adj.* —**twist′a•bil′i•ty,** *n.* —**twist′ed•ly,** *adv.* —**twist′ing•ly,** *adv.*

twist•er (twis′tər), *n.* **1.** a person or thing that twists. **2.** *Informal.* a whirlwind or tornado.

twit[1] (twit), *v.,* **twit•ted, twit•ting,** *n.* —*v.t.* **1.** to taunt or ridicule with reference to anything embarrassing; gibe at. **2.** to reproach or upbraid. —*n.* **3.** an act of twitting. **4.** a derisive reproach; taunt.

twit[2] (twit), *n. Informal.* an insignificant or bothersome person.

twitch (twich), *v.t.* **1.** to tug or pull at with a quick, short movement; pluck. **2.** to jerk rapidly. **3.** to move (body part) with a sudden, jerking motion. **4.** to pinch or pull at sharply and painfully; give a smarting pinch to; nip. —*v.i.* **5.** to move spasmodically or convulsively; jerk; jump. **6.** to give a sharp, sudden pull; tug; pluck (usu. fol. by *at*). **7.** to ache or hurt with a sharp, shooting pain; twinge. —*n.* **8.** a quick, jerky movement of the body or of some part of it. **9.** involuntary, spasmodic movement of a muscle; tic. **10.** a bodily or mental twinge, as of pain, conscience, etc.; pang. —**twitch′ing•ly,** *adv.* —**twitch′y,** *adj.*

twit•ter (twit′ər), *v.i.* **1.** to utter a succession of small, tremulous sounds, as a bird. **2.** to talk lightly and rapidly, esp. of trivial matters; chatter. **3.** to titter; giggle. —*v.t.* **4.** to express or utter by twittering. —*n.* **5.** an act of twittering. **6.** a twittering sound. **7.** a state of tremulous excitement. —**twit′ter•ing•ly,** *adv.* —**twit′ter•y,** *adj.*

′twixt (twikst), *prep.* contraction of *betwixt.*

two (to͞o), *n.* **1.** a cardinal number, 1 plus 1. **2.** a symbol for this number, as 2 or II. **3.** a set of this many persons or things. —*adj.* **4.** amounting to two in number. —***Idiom.*** **5. in two,** into two separate parts, as halves. **6. put two and two together,** to reach the correct and obvious conclusion.

two′-bag′ger, *n.* DOUBLE (def. 19).

two′-bit′, *adj. Informal.* **1.** costing 25 cents. **2.** inferior or unimportant; small-time: *a two-bit actor.*

two′ bits′, *n. Informal.* 25 cents.

Two′ Build′ers, The, a parable of Jesus. Matt. 7:24–27; Luke 6:47–49.

two′-by-four′, *adj.* **1.** two units thick and four units wide, esp. in inches. **2.** *Informal.* unimportant; insignificant. —*n.* **3.** a timber measuring 2 by 4 in. (5 × 10 cm) in cross section, when untrimmed: equivalent to 1⅝ by 3⅝ in. (4.5 × 9 cm) when trimmed.

two′ cents′, *n.* **1.** (*used with a sing. or pl. v.*) something of little value; a paltry amount. **2. two cents worth,** an opinion, usu. unsolicited and unwelcome.

two′-dimen′sional, *adj.* **1.** having the dimensions of height and width only: *a two-dimensional surface.* **2.** (of a work of art) having its elements organized in terms of a flat surface. **3.** (of a literary work) superficial, as in character development. —**two′-dimensional′ity,** *n.* —**two′-dimen′sionally,** *adv.*

two′-edged′, *adj.* **1.** having two edges, as a sword. **2.** cutting or effective both ways: *a two-edged remark.*

two′-faced′, *adj.* **1.** having two faces. **2.** deceitful or hypocritical. —**two′-fac′ed•ly,** *adv.* —**two′-fac′ed•ness,** *n.*

two•fer (to͞o′fər), *n.* **1.** a coupon redeemable for two tickets to a theatrical performance at a reduced price. **2.** a coupon or offer for the purchase of two items or services for approximately the price of one.

two′-fist′ed, *adj.* **1.** ready for or inclined to physical combat. **2.** strong and vigorous.

two′-fold′, *n.* a unit of stage scenery consisting of two flats hinged together.

two•fold (*adj.* to͞o′fōld′; *adv.* -fōld′), *adj.* **1.** having two elements or parts. **2.** twice as great or as much; double. —*adv.* **3.** in twofold measure; doubly. —**two′fold′ness,** *n.*

two′-hand′ed, *adj.* **1.** having two hands. **2.** ambidextrous. **3.** involving or requiring the use of both hands. **4.** requiring or engaged in by two persons. —**two′-hand′ed•ly,** *adv.* —**two′-hand′ed•ness,** *n.*

two′-piece′, *adj.* **1.** having or consisting of two parts or pieces, esp. two matching pieces of a clothing ensemble. —*n.* **2.** Also, **two′-piec′er.** a two-piece garment.

two′-ply′, *adj.* consisting of two thicknesses, layers, strands, or the like: *two-ply knitting yarn.*

two′-seat′er, *n.* a vehicle accommodating two persons.

two′-sid′ed, *adj.* **1.** having two sides; bilateral. **2.** having two aspects or characters. —**two′-sid′ed•ness,** *n.*

two•some (to͞o′səm), *adj.* **1.** consisting of two; twofold. **2.** performed or played by two persons. —*n.* **3.** two together or in company; couple; duo. **4.** a golf match between two persons.

Two′ Sons′, The, a parable of Jesus. Matt. 21:28–32.

two′-spot′, *n.* **1.** a playing card or the upward face of a die that bears two pips, or a domino one half of which bears two pips. **2.** *Informal.* a two-dollar bill.

two′-step′, *n., v.,* **-stepped, -step•ping.** —*n.* **1.** a ballroom dance in duple meter, marked by sliding steps. **2.** a piece of music for, or in the rhythm of, this dance. —*v.i.* **3.** to dance the two-step.

two′-time′, *v.t.,* **-timed, -tim•ing.** *Informal.* **1.** to be unfaithful to (a lover or spouse). **2.** to double-cross. —**two′-tim′er,** *n.*

′twould (twŏŏd), contraction of *it would.*

two′-way′, *adj.* **1.** providing for or allowing movement in opposite directions: *two-way traffic.* **2.** involving two parties or participants: *a two-way political race.* **3.** entailing responsibilities or obligations on both parties. **4.** capable of receiving and sending signals: *a two-way radio.*

twp., township.

TX, Texas.

-ty, a suffix occurring in loanwords from Latin and French, forming mainly from adjectives nouns denoting state or condition: *ability; certainty; chastity; unity.*

ty•coon (tī ko͞on′), *n.* **1.** a businessperson of great wealth and power; magnate. **2.** a title used by foreigners to refer to the Japanese shogun. [< Japanese]

ty•ing (tī′ing), *v.* pres. part. of TIE.

tyke or **tike** (tīk), *n.* a child, esp. a small boy.

Ty•ler (tī′lər), *n.* **1. Anne,** born 1931, U.S. novelist. **2. John,** 1790–1862, 10th president of the U.S. 1841–45. **3. Wat** or **Walter,** died 1381, English leader of the peasants' revolt of 1381. **4.** a city in E Texas. 74,740.

tym•bal (tim′bəl), *n.* TIMBAL.

tym•pa•ni (tim′pə nē), *n.* (*used with a sing. or pl. v.*) TIMPANI. —**tym′pa•nist,** *n.*

tym•pa•num (tim′pə nəm), *n., pl.* **-nums, -na** (-nə). **1. a.** MIDDLE EAR. **b.** EARDRUM. **2.** (in certain insects) a drumlike vibrating structure in the body wall, functioning as a hearing organ. **3.** the diaphragm of a telephone. **4.** a drum or similar instrument.

Tyn•dale or **Tindale** or **Tindal** (tin′dl), *n.* **William,** c1492–1536, English religious reformer, translator of the Bible, and martyr.

typ•al (tī′pəl), *adj.* **1.** of, pertaining to, or constituting a type. **2.** serving as a type; representative; typical.

type (tīp), *n., v.,* **typed, typ•ing.** —*n.* **1.** a class, group, or category of things or persons sharing one or more characteristics: *people of a criminal type; a car of the luxury type.* **2.** a thing or person regarded as a member of a class or category; kind; sort (usu. fol. by *of*): *This is a type of mushroom.* **3.** a thing or person that represents perfectly or in the best way a class or category; model. **4.** a person regarded as typifying a certain line of work, behavior, environment, etc.: *a civil service type.* **5. a.** a wood or metal block with a raised character on its surface that, when fixed into a press and coated with ink, prints an impression of the character on paper or a similar absorbent surface. **b.** such pieces or blocks collectively. **c.** FACE (defs. 19b, c). **6.** *Biol.* **a.** a genus or species that most nearly exemplifies the essential characteristics of a higher group. **b.** the one or more specimens on which the description and naming of a species is based. **7. a.** the inherited features of an animal or breed that are favorable for any given purpose: *dairy type.* **b.** a strain, breed, or variety of animal, or a single animal, belonging to a specific kind. **8.** the pattern or model from which something is made. **9.** an image or figure produced by impressing or stamping. **10.** a distinctive or characteristic mark or sign. —*v.t.* **11.** to write on a typewriter; typewrite. **12.** to reproduce in type or in print. **13.** to ascertain the type of (a blood or tissue sample). **14.** to typecast. **15.** to typify or symbolize; represent. **16.** to represent prophetically; foreshadow; prefigure. —*v.i.* **17.** to write using a typewriter; typewrite. —**Usage.** When preceded by a modifier, TYPE meaning "kind, sort" is sometimes used without a following *of: This type furnace uses very little current. We have a magnetic-type holder for the rack.* Frequently criticized by usage guides, this construction occurs rarely in formal contexts. It can usu. be remedied by inserting *of* (*this type of furnace*) or by dropping TYPE altogether (*a magnetic holder*).

Type A, *n.* a personality type characterized by competitiveness, perfectionism, and a sense of urgency, believed to be associated with susceptibility to heart attack.

Type B, *n.* a personality type characterized by amiability, tolerance of imperfection, and an unhurried manner, believed to be associated with decreased risk of heart attack.

type•cast (tīp′kast′, -käst′), *v.t.,* **-cast, -cast•ing. 1.** to cast (an actor) in a role that seems to match the actor's physique, personality, etc. **2.** to cast (an actor) repeatedly or exclusively in the same kind of role: *She became typecast as a socialite.*

type•face (tīp′fās′), *n.* FACE (defs. 17b, c).

type′ ge′nus, *n. Biol.* the genus that is formally held to be typical of the family or other higher group to which it belongs.

type•script (tīp′skript′), *n.* **1.** a typewritten copy of a literary composition. **2.** typewritten matter.

type•set (tīp′set′), *v.,* **-set, -set•ting,** *adj.* —*v.t.* **1.** to set (textual matter) in type. —*adj.* **2.** (of written, textual matter) set in type.

type•set•ter (tīp′set′ər), *n.* **1.** a person who sets or composes type; compositor. **2.** a typesetting machine.

type•set•ting (tīp′set′ing), *n.* **1.** the process or action of setting type. —*adj.* **2.** used or intended for setting type.

type•write (tīp′rīt′), *v.t., v.i.,* **-wrote, -writ•ten, -writ•ing.** to write by means of a typewriter; type.

type•writ•er (tīp′rī′tər), *n.* **1.** a machine for writing in characters similar to printers' types by manually pressing the letters of a keyboard. **2.** a style of printers' type that gives the appearance of typewritten copy. **3.** (formerly) a typist. —**type′writ′er•like′,** *adj.*

type•writ•ing (tīp′rī′ting), *n.* **1.** the act or skill of using a typewriter. **2.** printed work done on a typewriter.

ty•phoid (tī′foid), *n.* **1.** Also called **ty′phoid fe′ver.** an acute infectious disease characterized by high fever and intestinal inflammation, spread by food or water contaminated with the bacillus *Salmonella typhosa.* —*adj.* **2.** resembling typhus.

Ty′phoid Mar′y, *n.* a carrier or transmitter of anything undesirable, harmful, or catastrophic. [after *Mary Mallon* (d. 1938), Irish-born cook in the U.S., who was found to be a typhoid carrier]

ty•phoon (tī fōōn′), *n.* **1.** a tropical cyclone or hurricane of the W Pacific area and the China seas. **2.** a violent storm or tempest of India.

ty•phus (tī′fəs), *n.* an acute infectious disease caused by several species of rickettsias, esp. *Rickettsia prowazekii,* transmitted by lice and fleas, and characterized by acute prostration, headache, and a peculiar eruption of reddish spots on the body. Also called **ty′phus fe′ver.**

typ•i•cal (tip′i kəl), *adj.* **1.** of the nature of or serving as a type or representative specimen: *a typical family.* **2.** conforming to a particular type. **3.** exemplifying most nearly the essential characteristics of a higher group of organisms and forming the type: *the typical genus of a family.* **4.** characteristic or distinctive: *typical mannerisms.* **5.** pertaining to, of the nature of, or serving as a type or emblem; symbolic. —**typ′i•cal•ly,** *adv.* —**typ′i•cal•ness, typ′i•cal′i•ty,** *n.*

typ•i•fy (tip′ə fī′), *v.t.,* **-fied, -fy•ing. 1.** to serve as a typical example of; exemplify: *a hero who typified courage.* **2.** to serve as a symbol or emblem of; symbolize: *The dog appropriately typifies loyalty.* —**typ′i•fi•ca′tion,** *n.* —**typ′i•fi′er,** *n.*

typ•ist (tī′pist), *n.* a person who operates a typewriter.

ty•po (tī′pō), *n., pl.* **-pos.** a typographical error.

typo-, a combining form representing TYPE: *typography; typology.*

ty•pog•ra•pher (tī pog′rə fər), *n.* a person skilled or engaged in typography.

ty•po•graph•ic (tī′pə graf′ik) also **ty′po•graph′i•cal,** *adj.* of or pertaining to typography. —**ty′po•graph′i•cal•ly,** *adv.*

typograph′ical er′ror, *n.* an error in printed or typewritten matter resulting from a mistake in typing, mechanical failure, etc.

ty•pog•ra•phy (tī pog′rə fē), *n.* **1.** the art or process of printing with type. **2.** the work of setting and arranging types and of printing from them. **3.** the general character or appearance of printed matter.

ty•pol•o•gy (tī pol′ə jē), *n.* **1.** the study of types or prefigurative symbols in scriptural literature. **2.** a systematic classification or study of types. —**ty′po•log′i•cal** (-pə loj′i kəl), *adj.* —**ty′po•log′i•cal•ly,** *adv.*

ty•ran•ni•cal (ti ran′i kəl, tī-) also **ty•ran′nic,** *adj.* **1.** unjustly cruel or severe; arbitrary or oppressive; despotic. **2.** of or characteristic of a tyrant. —**ty•ran′ni•cal•ly,** *adv.*

tyr•an•nize (tir′ə nīz′), *v.,* **-nized, -niz•ing.** —*v.t.* **1.** to rule or govern tyrannically; treat oppressively. —*v.i.* **2.** to exercise absolute power or control, esp. cruelly or oppressively (often fol. by *over*). **3.** to govern or reign as a tyrant. —**tyr′an•niz′er,** *n.*

ty•ran•no•saur (ti ran′ə sôr′, tī-), *n.* any of several large carniverous dinosaurs of the late Cretaceous Period of North America and Asia of the genus *Tyrannosaurus,* esp. *T. rex.*

tyr•an•ny (tir′ə nē), *n., pl.* **-nies. 1.** arbitrary or unrestrained exercise of power; despotic abuse of authority. **2.** the government or rule of a tyrant. **3.** a state ruled by a tyrant. **4.** oppressive or unjust government. **5.** undue severity or harshness. **6.** a tyrannical act or proceeding.

ty•rant (tī′rənt), *n.* **1.** a sovereign or other ruler who uses power oppressively or unjustly. **2.** any person in a position of authority who exercises power oppressively or despotically. **3.** a tyrannical or compulsory influence. **4.** an absolute ruler, esp. one in ancient Greece or Sicily.

Tyre (tīᵊr), *n.* an ancient seaport and trading center of Phoenicia: site of modern Sur. —**Tyr•i•an** (tir′i an), *adj., n.*

ty•ro or **ti•ro** (tī′rō), *n.* a beginner in learning anything; novice. —**ty•ron′ic** (-ron′ik), *adj.*

Ty•rol or **Ti•rol** (ti rōl′, tī-, tī′rōl; *Ger.* tē rōl′), *n.* an alpine region in W Austria and N Italy: a former Austrian crown land. —**Ty•ro′le•an,** *adj., n.*

ty•ro•sine (tī′rə sēn′, -sin, tir′ə-), *n.* a crystalline amino acid, $HOC_6H_4CH_2CH(NH_2)COOH$, abundant in ripe cheese, that acts as a precursor of norepinephrine and dopamine. *Abbr.:* Tyr; *Symbol:* Y

tzad•dik (tsä′dik; *Heb.* tsä dēk′), *n., pl.* **tzad•di•kim** (tsä dik′im; *Heb.* tsä dē kēm′). ZADDIK.

tzar (zär, tsär), *n.* CZAR. —**tzar′dom,** *n.* —**tzar′ism,** *n.* —**tzar′ist,** *adj., n.* —**tzar•is′tic,** *adj.*

T

U

U, u (yo͞o), _n., pl._ **U's** or **Us, u's** or **us.** **1.** the 21st letter of the English alphabet, a vowel. **2.** any spoken sound represented by this letter. **3.** something shaped like a U. **4.** a written or printed representation of the letter _U_ or _u._

U, _Symbol._ **1.** the 21st in order or in a series. **2.** uranium. **3.** uracil. **4.** kosher (label).

u. & l.c., _Print._ upper and lower case.

UAW or **U.A.W.,** United Automobile Workers (full name: International Union of United Automobile, Aerospace, and Agricultural Implement Workers of America).

u·biq·ui·tous (yo͞o bik/wi təs), _adj._ existing or being everywhere, esp. at the same time; omnipresent. —**u·biq/ui·tous·ly,** _adv._ —**u·biq/ui·tous·ness, u·biq/ui·ty,** _n._

U-boat (yo͞o/bōt/), _n._ a German submarine. [< German _U-Boot,_ short for _Unterseeboot_ lit., undersea boat]

u.c., _Print._ upper case.

Uc·cel·lo (o͞o chel/ō), _n._ **Paolo** (_Paolo di Dono_), 1397–1475, Italian painter.

ud·der (ud/ər), _n._ a mamma or mammary gland, esp. when baggy and with more than one teat, as in cows.

UFO (yo͞o/ef/ō/; _sometimes_ yo͞o/fō), _n., pl._ **UFOs, UFO's.** unidentified flying object: any unexplained moving object observed in the sky, esp. one assumed to be of extraterrestrial origin.

U·gan·da (yo͞o gan/də, o͞o gän/-), _n._ a republic in E Africa, between NE Democratic Republic of the Congo and Kenya: member of the Commonwealth of Nations; formerly a British protectorate. 20,604,874; 91,343 sq. mi. (236,860 sq. km). _Cap.:_ Kampala. —**U·gan/dan,** _adj., n._

U·ga·rit (o͞o/gə rēt/, yo͞o/-), _n._ an ancient city in Syria, N of Latakia, on the site of modern Ras Shamra: destroyed by an earthquake early in the 13th century B.C.; excavations have yielded tablets written in cuneiform and hieroglyphic script that provide information on Canaanite mythology.

ugh (o͞oкн, uкн, u, o͞o; _spelling pron._ ug), _interj._ **1.** (used as an exclamation of disgust, aversion, horror, or the like.) —_n._ **2.** the sound of a cough, grunt, or the like.

ug·li (ug/lē), _n., pl._ **ug·lis, ug·lies.** a large, sweet variety of tangelo, of Jamaican origin, having rough, wrinkled, yellowish skin. Also called **ug/li fruit/.**

ug·li·fy (ug/lə fī/), _v.t.,_ **-fied, -fy·ing.** to make ugly. —**ug/li·fi·ca/tion,** _n._ —**ug/li·fi/er,** _n._

ug·ly (ug/lē), _adj._, **-li·er, -li·est.** **1.** very unattractive or displeasing in appearance. **2.** disagreeable; objectionable: _ugly weather._ **3.** morally revolting: _an ugly crime._ **4.** threatening trouble or danger: _an ugly wound._ **5.** hostile; quarrelsome: _an ugly mood._ —**ug/li·ly,** _adv._ —**ug/li·ness,** _n._

ug/ly Amer/ican, _n._ an insensitive American resident or traveler in a foreign country. [from a 1965 novel by that name by William J. Lederer and Eugene Burdick]

ug/ly duck/ling, _n._ an unattractive or unpromising child who becomes a beautiful or much-admired adult. [after the bird in the story of the same name by Hans Christian Andersen]

uh (u, uɴ), _interj._ **1.** (used to indicate hesitation, doubt, or a pause.) **2.** HUH.

UHF or **uhf,** ultrahigh frequency.

U.K. or **UK,** United Kingdom.

u·kase (yo͞o kās/, -kāz/, yo͞o/kās, -kāz), _n._ **1.** (in czarist Russia) an edict or order of the czar having the force of law. **2.** any order or proclamation by an absolute or arbitrary authority.

uke (yo͞ok), _n._ UKULELE.

U·kraine (yo͞o krān/, -krīn/, yo͞o/krān), _n._ a republic in S central Europe: a former constituent republic of the U.S.S.R. 50,684,635; 231,990 sq. mi. (603,700 sq. km). _Cap.:_ Kiev. Ukrainian, **U·kra··na** (o͞o kru-yē/nə). Formerly, **Ukrain/ian So/viet So/cialist Repub/lic.**

U·krain·i·an (yo͞o krā/nē ən, -krī/-), _n._ **1.** a member of a Slavic people who are the principal inhabitants of Ukraine. **2.** any native or inhabitant of Ukraine. **3.** an East Slavic language spoken in Ukraine and adjacent parts of the Carpathian Mountains. —_adj._ **4.** of or pertaining to Ukraine, Ukrainians, or the language Ukrainian.

u·ku·le·le or **u·ke·le·le** (yo͞o/kə lā/lē, o͞o/-), _n., pl._ **-les.** a small, guitarlike musical instrument associated chiefly with Hawaiian music.

UL, Underwriters' Laboratories (used esp. on labels for electrical appliances approved by this nonprofit safety-testing organization).

'u·la·ma or **u·le·ma** (o͞o/lə mä/), _n.pl._ the body of scholars who are authorities on Muslim religion and law.

U·lan Ba·tor (o͞o/län bä/tôr), _n._ the capital of the Mongolian People's Republic, in the N central part. 500,000. Formerly, **Urga.**

ul·cer (ul/sər), _n._ **1.** a sore on the skin or a mucous membrane, accompanied by the disintegration of tissue, the formation of pus, etc. **2.** PEPTIC ULCER. **3.** any corrupting or disrupting condition.

ul·cer·ate (ul/sə rāt/), _v._, **-at·ed, -at·ing.** —_v.i._ **1.** to form an ulcer. —_v.t._ **2.** to cause an ulcer on or in. —**ul/cer·a/tion,** _n._

ul·cer·ous (ul/sər əs), _adj._ **1.** of the nature of an ulcer; characterized by the formation of ulcers. **2.** affected with an ulcer.

-ule, a suffix occurring in loanwords from Latin, orig. diminutive nouns (_capsule; globule; nodule_) or noun derivatives of verbs (_ligule_).

-ulent or **-lent,** a suffix occurring in adjectives borrowed from Latin, with the meaning "having in quantity, full of" that specified by the initial element: _corpulent; fraudulent; opulent; purulent._

ul·na (ul/nə), _n., pl._ **-nae** (-nē), **-nas.** **1.** the bone of the forearm on the side opposite to the thumb. **2.** a corresponding bone in the forelimb of other vertebrates. —**ul/nar,** _adj._

-ulous, a suffix occurring in adjectives borrowed from Latin, with the meaning "inclined to do, habitually engaging in" the action specified by the initial element: _bibulous; credulous; garrulous; tremulous._

Ul·ster (ul/stər), _n._ **1.** a former province in Ireland, now comprising Northern Ireland and a part of the Republic of Ireland. **2.** a province in N Republic of Ireland. 235,641; 3123 sq. mi. (8090 sq. km). **3.** NORTHERN IRELAND. **4.** (_l.c._) a long, loose, heavy overcoat, orig. of Irish frieze, now also of any of various other woolen cloths. —**Ul/ster·ite/,** _n._

ul·te·ri·or (ul tēr/ē ər), _adj._ **1.** intentionally kept concealed: _an ulterior motive._ **2.** subsequent; future. **3.** lying beyond or some specified boundary: _a suggestion ulterior to this discussion._ —**ul·te/ri·or·ly,** _adv._

ul·ti·ma·cy (ul/tə mə sē), _n., pl._ **-cies.** **1.** the state or quality of being ultimate. **2.** a fundamental quality.

ul·ti·mate (ul/tə mit), _adj._ **1.** last; furthest or farthest: _the ultimate destination._ **2.** decisive; conclusive: _the ultimate authority._ **3.** highest; most desirable: _one's ultimate goal._ **4.** basic; fundamental: _ultimate principles._ **5.** final; total: _the ultimate cost; ultimate consequences._ **6.** unequaled or unsurpassed: _the ultimate vacation._ —_n._ **7.** the final point or result. **8.** a fundamental fact or principle. **9.** the finest or most superior of its kind. —**ul/ti·mate·ly,** _adv._

ul·ti·ma Thu·le (ul/tə mə tho͞o/lē), _n._ **1.** (_italics_) _Latin._ the highest degree attainable. **2.** the farthest point; the limit of any journey. **3.** THULE (def. 1). [lit., farthest Thule]

ul·ti·ma·tum (ul/tə mā/təm, -mä/-), _n., pl._ **-tums, -ta** (-tə). a final, uncompromising demand or set of terms issued by a party to a dispute, the rejection of which may lead to a severance of relations or to the use of force.

ul·tra (ul/trə), _adj., n., pl._ **-tras.** —_adj._ **1.** going beyond what is usual or ordinary; excessive; extreme. —_n._ **2.** an extremist, as in politics, religion, or fashion.

ultra-, a prefix occurring orig. in loanwords from Latin, with the basic meaning "on the far side of, beyond." In relation to the base to which it is prefixed, ultra- has the senses "located beyond, on the far side of" (_ultramontane; ultraviolet_), "carrying to the furthest degree possible, on the fringe of" (_ultraleft; ultramodern_), "extremely" (_ultralight_); nouns to which it is added denote objects, properties, etc., that surpass customary norms, or instruments designed to produce or deal with such things (_ultramicroscope; ultrasound; ultrastructure_).

ul·tra·ba·sic (ul/trə bā/sik), _adj._ (of rocks) containing iron and magnesium, with little or no silica.

ul·tra·clean (ul/trə klēn/), _adj._ extremely clean, esp. free of germs.

ul·tra·con·ser·va·tive (ul/trə kən sûr/və tiv), _adj._ **1.** extremely conservative, esp. in politics. —_n._ **2.** an ultraconservative person.

ul·tra·crit·i·cal (ul/trə krit/i kəl), _adj._ HYPERCRITICAL. —**ul/tra·crit/i·cal·ly,** _adv._

ul·tra·fil·ter (ul/trə fil/tər), _n._ **1.** a filter for purifying sols, having a membrane with pores sufficiently small to prevent the passage of the suspended particles. —_v.t._ **2.** to purify by means of an ultrafilter. —**ul/tra·fil·tra/tion** (-trā/shən), _n._

ul·tra·fine (ul/trə fīn/), _adj._ too small to be visible under a light microscope: _ultrafine cell structure._

ul·tra·high (ul/trə hī/), _adj._ extremely high.

ul/trahigh fre/quency, _n._ any radio frequency between 300 and 3000 megahertz. _Abbr.:_ UHF, uhf **—ul/trahigh-fre/quency,** _adj._

ul·tra·light (_adj._ ul/trə līt/, ul/trə līt/; _n._ ul/trə līt/), _adj._ **1.** extremely lightweight in comparison with others of its kind. —_n._ **2.** something that is ultralight. **3.** a light single-seat airplane that is essentially a motorized hang glider.

ul·tra·ma·rine (ul/trə mə rēn/), _adj._ **1.** of a deep blue color. **2.** beyond the sea. —_n._ **3.** a blue pigment consisting of powdered lapis lazuli. **4.** a similar artificial blue pigment. **5.** any of various related pigments. **6.** a deep blue color.

ul·tra·min·i·a·ture (ul/trə min/ē ə chər, -cho͞or/, -min/ə chər), _adj._ SUBMINIATURE.

ul·tra·mod·ern (ul/trə mod/ərn), _adj._ very advanced in ideas, design, etc. —**ul/tra·mod/ern·ism,** _n._ —**ul/tra·mod/ern·ist,** _n._

ul·tra·mon·tane (ul/trə mon tān/, -mon/tān), _adj._ **1.** beyond the mountains. **2.** of or pertaining to the area south of the Alps, esp. to Italy. **3.** —_n._ **4.** a person who lives beyond the mountains. **5.** a person living south of the Alps.

ul·tra·mun·dane (ul'trə mun dān', -mun'dān), *adj.* **1.** beyond the earth or the orbits of the planets. **2.** outside the sphere of physical existence.

ul·tra·pure (ul'trə pyŏor'), *adj.* extremely pure, esp. without any impurities. —**ul'tra·pure'ly**, *adv.* —**ul'tra·pu'ri·ty**, *n.*

ul·tra·short (ul'trə shôrt'), *adj.* **1.** extremely short, esp. in duration. **2.** (of a wavelength) smaller than 10 meters.

ul·tra·son·ic (ul'trə son'ik), *adj.* of, pertaining to, or utilizing ultrasound. —**ul'tra·son'i·cal·ly**, *adv.*

ul·tra·son·ics (ul'trə son'iks), *n.* (*used with a sing. v.*) the study of the effects of sound waves having wavelengths above the limits of human perception.

ul·tra·sound (ul'trə sound'), *n.* **1.** sound with a frequency greater than 20,000 Hz, approximately the upper limit of human hearing. **2.** *Med.* the application of ultrasonic waves to therapy or diagnostics, as in deep-heat treatment of a joint or in ultrasonography.

ul·tra·struc·ture (ul'trə struk'chər), *n.* the aggregate of structures within a cell that are revealed by electron microscopy. —**ul'tra·struc'tur·al**, *adj.*

ul·tra·vi·o·let (ul'trə vī'ə lit), *adj.* **1.** pertaining to electromagnetic radiation having wavelengths in the range of approximately 5–400 nm, shorter than visible light but longer than x-rays. **2.** pertaining to, producing, or using light having such wavelengths: *an ultraviolet lamp.* Compare INFRARED. —*n.* **3.** ultraviolet radiation.

ul·u·lant (ul'yə lənt, yŏol'-), *adj.* ululating; howling or wailing.

ul·u·late (ul'yə lāt', yŏol'-), *v.i.*, **-lat·ed, -lat·ing. 1.** to howl, hoot, or wail. **2.** to lament loudly and shrilly. —**ul'u·la'tion**, *n.*

U·lys·ses (yŏo lis'ēz; *Brit. also* yŏo'lə sēz'), *n.* ODYSSEUS.

um (um, UN, əm, əN), *interj.* (used as an expression of doubt, hesitation, deliberation, etc.)

um·bel (um'bəl), *n.* an inflorescence in which a number of flower stalks or pedicels, nearly equal in length, spread from a common center.

um·ber (um'bər), *n.* **1.** a brown earth, largely oxides of iron and manganese, used as a pigment. **2.** the color of such a pigment; dark dusky brown or dark reddish brown. **3.** the European grayling, *Thymallus thymallus.* —*adj.* **4.** of the color umber. —*v.t.* **5.** to color with umber.

um·bil·i·cal (um bil'i kəl), *adj.* **1.** of, pertaining to, or characteristic of an umbilicus or umbilical cord. **2.** joined together by or as if by an umbilical cord. **3.** adjacent to or located near the navel. —*n.* **4.** UMBILICAL CORD. —**um·bil'i·cal·ly**, *adv.*

umbil'ical cord', n. 1. a cordlike structure connecting the fetus with the placenta during pregnancy, conveying nourishment from the mother and removing wastes. **2.** a disconnectable connection for servicing, operating, or testing equipment, as in a rocket. **3.** a strong line that supplies air, communications, etc., as to an astronaut on a space walk.

um·bil·i·cus (um bil'i kəs, um'bə lī'kəs), *n., pl.* **-bil·i·ci** (-bil'ə sī', -bə lī'sī). **1.** NAVEL (def. 1). **2.** a navellike formation.

um·bra (um'brə), *n., pl.* **-bras, -brae** (-brē). **1.** shade; shadow. **2.** the usual accompaniment or companion of a person or thing. **3.** *Astron.* the complete or perfect shadow of an opaque body, as a planet, where the direct light from the source of illumination is completely cut off. **4.** a phantom or ghost. —**um'bral**, *adj.*

um·brage (um'brij), *n.* **1.** offense; displeasure: *to take umbrage at* someone's rudeness. **2.** the slightest feeling of suspicion, doubt, hostility, or the like. **3.** leafy shade, as tree foliage.

um·brel·la (um brel'ə), *n.* **1.** a light, portable, circular cover for protection from inclement weather, consisting of a collapsible, fabric-covered frame of thin ribs radiating from the top of a carrying stick or handle. **2.** Also, **bell.** the bell-shaped body of a jellyfish. **3.** something that protects from above, as military aircraft safeguarding surface forces: *an air umbrella.* **4.** something, as an organization or policy, that encompasses a number of groups or elements. —*adj.* **5.** functioning or shaped like an umbrella. **6.** applying to or covering simultaneously a number of similar items, elements, or groups: *the umbrella coverage of an insurance policy.* [< Italian < Latin *umbella* sunshade]

umbrel'la tree', n. an American magnolia, *Magnolia tripetala,* having large leaves in umbrellalike clusters.

um·laut (ōom'lout), *n.* **1.** a mark (¨) used as a diacritic over a vowel, as ä, ö, ü, to indicate a vowel sound different from that of the letter without the diacritic, esp. as so used in German. Compare DIERESIS. —*v.t.* **2.** to modify by umlaut. **3.** to write an umlaut over.

um·mah (um'ə), *n. Islam.* the Islamic community. Also, **um'ma.** [< Arabic: lit., nation]

ump (ump), *n., v.t., v.i.* UMPIRE.

umph (əm, əmf; *spelling pron.* umf), *interj., v.i., v.t.* HUMPH.

um·pire (um'pī°r), *n., v.,* **-pired, -pir·ing.** —*n.* **1.** a person selected to rule on the plays in a game. **2.** one selected to settle disputes about rules or usages; a person agreed on by disputing parties to arbitrate their differences. —*v.t.* **3.** to act as umpire in (a game). **4.** to decide or settle (a dispute) as umpire; arbitrate. —*v.i.* **5.** to act as umpire.

ump·teen (ump'tēn'), *adj. Informal.* innumerable; many.

ump·teenth (ump'tēnth'), *adj. Informal.* of an indefinitely large number in succession: *For the umpteenth time, no!*

'um·rah (ōom'rə), *n. Islam.* the pilgrimage, consisting of rituals performed at various shrines, made by a Muslim upon entering Mecca: often part of the hajj. Also, ' **um'ra.** Also called **lesser pilgrimage.** [< Ar: lit., visit]

Um·ta·ta (ōom tä'tə), *n.* the capital of Transkei, SE Africa. 24,805.

UMW or **U.M.W.,** United Mine Workers.

un or **'un** (ən), *pron. Dial.* one: *young uns; He's a bad un.*

UN or **U.N.,** United Nations.

un-¹, a prefix meaning "not," freely used as an English formative, giving negative or opposite force in adjectives and their derivative adverbs and nouns (*unfair; unfairly; unfairness; unfelt; unseen; unfitting; unformed; unheard-of; un-get-at-able*), and less freely used in certain other nouns (*unrest; unemployment*).

un-², a prefix freely used in English to form verbs expressing a reversal of some action or state, or removal, deprivation, release, etc. (*unbend; uncork; unfasten;* etc.), or to intensify the force of a verb already having such a meaning (*unloose*).

un·a·bat·ed (un'ə bā'tid), *adj.* with undiminished force, power, or vigor. —**un'a·bat'ed·ly**, *adv.*

un·a·ble (un ā'bəl), *adj.* lacking the necessary power, competence, etc., to accomplish some specified act: *unable to swim.*

un·a·bridged (un'ə brijd'), *adj.* **1.** not abridged or shortened, as a book. —*n.* **2.** a dictionary that has not been reduced in size by omission of terms or definitions; the comprehensive edition.

---

un'·a·ban'doned, *adj.*
un'·a·bashed', *adj.*
un'·ab·bre'vi·at'ed, *adj.*
un'·ab·solved', *adj.*
un'·ab·sorb'ent, *adj.*
un'·a·bu'sive, *adj.; -ly, adv.; -ness, n.*
un'·ac·cen'tu·at'ed, *adj.*
un'·ac·cept'a·ble, *adj.; -ble·ness, n.; -bly, adv.*
un'·ac·cli'ma·tized', *adj.*
un'·ac·com'mo·dat'ing, *adj.; -ly, adv.*
un'·ac·com'plished, *adj.*
un'·ac·cred'it·ed, *adj.*
un'·ac·cu'mu·lat'ed, *adj.*
un'·a·cer'bic, *adj.*
un'·a·chiev'a·ble, *adj.*
un'·a·cous'tic, *adj.*
un'·ac·quaint'ed, *adj.*
un'·ac·quis'i·tive, *adj.; -ly, adv.; -ness, n.*
un'·ac·quit'ted, *adj.*
un'·ac'tion·a·ble, *adj.*
un'·ac'ti·vat·ed, *adj.*
un'·ac'tu·at'ed, *adj.*
un'·a·dapt'a·ble, *adj.; -ness, n.*
un'·ad·dressed', *adj.*
un'·a·dept', *adj.; -ly, adv.; -ness, n.*
un'·ad·journed', *adj.*
un'·ad·ju'di·cat'ed, *adj.*
un'·ad·just'a·ble, *adj.; -bly, adv.*

un'·ad·mired', *adj.*
un'·ad·mis'si·ble, *adj.; -ble·ness, n.; -bly, adv.*
un'·ad·mit'ted, *adj.; -ly, adv.*
un'·a·dopt'a·ble, *adj.*
un'·a·dopt'ed, *adj.*
un'·a·dorned', *adj.*
un'·ad·van'taged, *adj.*
un'·ad·van·ta'geous, *adj.; -ly, adv.; -ness, n.*
un'·ad·ven'tur·ous, *adj.; -ly, adv.; -ness, n.*
un'·ad·ver'tised', *adj.*
un'·ad·vis'a·ble, *adj.; -ble·ness, n.; -bly, adv.*
un'·aes·thet'ic, *adj.*
un'·af·fil'i·at'ed, *adj.*
un'·af·firmed', *adj.*
un'·a·ford'a·ble, *adj.*
un'·a·fraid', *adj.*
un'·ag·gra·vat'ing, *adj.*
un'·a·greed', *adj.*
un'·aid'ed, *adj.; -ly, adv.*
un'·aired', *adj.*
un'·a·larmed', *adj.*
un'·a·larm'ing, *adj.; -ly, adv.*
un'·al'ien·at·ed, *adj.*
un'·a·ligned', *adj.*
un'·a·like', *adj., adv.*
un'·al'layed, *adj.*
un'·al·leged', *adj.*
un'·al·leg'ed·ly, *adv.*

un'·al·ler'gic, *adj.*
un'·al·le'vi·at'ed, *adj.; -ble·ness, n.; -ly, adv.*
un'·al·lied', *adj.*
un'·al·lit'er·a'tive, *adj.*
un'·al·lot'ted, *adj.*
un'·al·low'a·ble, *adj.*
un'·al·lowed', *adj.*
un'·al·loyed', *adj.*
un'·al'pha·bet·ized', *adj.*
un'·a·massed', *adj.*
un'·a·mazed', *adj.*
un'·am·big'u·ous, *adj.; -ly, adv.; -ness, n.*
un'·am·bi'tious, *adj.; -ly, adv.*
un'·a·me'na·ble, *adj.; -bly, adv.*
un'·a·mend'ed, *adj.*
un'·a·mi·a·ble, *adj.; -ble·ness, n.; -bly, adv.*
un'·am·pli·fied', *adj.*
un'·a·mused', *adj.*
un'·an·a·lyt'ic, *adj.*
un'·an·a·lyzed', *adj.*
un'·an'chored, *adj.*
un'·an·i·mat'ed, *adj.; -ly, adv.*
un'·an·nexed', *adj.*
un'·an·nounced', *adj.*
un'·an·noyed', *adj.*
un'·an·nulled', *adj.*
un'·a·noint'ed, *adj.*
un'·an'swered, *adj.*
un'·an·tic'i·pat'ed, *adj.*
un'·a·pol'o·get'ic, *adj.*

un'·ap·par'ent, *adj.; -ly, adv.*
un'·ap·peal'ing, *adj.; -ly, adv.*
un'·ap·peased', *adj.*
un'·ap·pe·tiz'ing, *adj.; -ly, adv.*
un'·ap·plied', *adj.*
un'·ap·point'ed, *adj.*
un'·ap·por'tioned, *adj.*
un'·ap·praised', *adj.*
un'·ap·pre'ci·at'ed, *adj.*
un'·ap·pre'cia·tive, *adj.; -ly, adv.; -ness, n.*
un'·ap·pre·hend'ing, *adj.*
un'·ar'gu·a·ble, *adj.; -bly, adv.*
un'·a·ris'to·crat'ic, *adj.*
un'·ar·o·mat'ic, *adj.*
un'·a·roused', *adj.*
un'·ar·raigned', *adj.*
un'·ar·ranged', *adj.*
un'·ar·tic'u·lat'ed, *adj.*
un'·ar·tis'tic, *adj.*
un'·ar·tis'ti·cal·ly, *adv.*
un'·as·cer·tain'a·ble, *adj.; -bly, adv.*
un'·as·cribed', *adj.*
un'·as·pir'ing, *adj.; -ly, adv.*
un'·as·sailed', *adj.*
un'·as·sem'bled, *adj.*
un'·as·ser'tive, *adj.; -ly, adv.; -ness, n.*
un'·as·sim'i·lat'ed, *adj.*
un'·as·sist'ed, *adj.*
un'·as·suage'a·ble, *adj.*
un'·ath·let'ic, *adj.*

un·ac·cent·ed (un ak′sen tid, un′ak sen′-), *adj.* not accented; unstressed.

un·ac·com·pa·nied (un′ə kum′pə nēd), *adj.* **1.** not accompanied; alone. **2.** without accompaniment by a musical instrument.

un·ac·count·a·ble (un′ə koun′tə bəl), *adj.* **1.** impossible to account for; inexplicable. **2.** exempt from being called to account; not answerable. **—un′ac·count′a·ble·ness, un′ac·count′a·bil′i·ty,** *n.* **—un′ac·count′a·bly,** *adv.*

un·ac·count′ed-for′ (un′ə coun′tid), *adj.* unexplained.

un·ac·cus·tomed (un′ə kus′təmd), *adj.* **1.** not accustomed or habituated: *unaccustomed to hardships.* **2.** uncommon; unexpected: *an unaccustomed delay.* **—un′ac·cus′tomed·ness,** *n.*

u·na cor·da (ōō′nä kôr′də, -dä), *adv., adj.* with the soft pedal depressed (a musical direction in piano playing).

un·a·dul·ter·at·ed (un′ə dul′tə rā′tid), *adj.* **1.** not diluted or made impure by adulterating; pure: *unadulterated maple syrup.* **2.** utter; absolute: *unadulterated nonsense.* **—un′a·dul′ter·at·ed·ly,** *adv.*

un·ad·vised (un′ad vīzd′), *adj.* **1.** without advice or counsel; uninformed. **2.** imprudent; ill-advised. **—un′ad·vis′ed·ly,** *adv.* **—un′ad·vis′ed·ness,** *n.*

un·af·fect·ed[1] (un′ə fek′tid), *adj.* **1.** free from affectation; sincere; genuine: *unaffected grief.* **2.** unpretentious, as a personality or literary style. **—un′af·fect′ed·ly,** *adv.* **—un′af·fect′ed·ness,** *n.*

un·af·fect·ed[2] (un′ə fek′tid), *adj.* not changed, altered, or influenced.

un·al·ien·a·ble (un āl′yə nə bəl, -āl′ē ə-), *adj.* INALIENABLE.

un·al·ter·a·ble (un ôl′tər ə bəl) also **inalterable,** *adj.* not capable of being altered, changed, or modified. **—un·al′ter·a·ble·ness, un·al′ter·a·bil′i·ty,** *n.* **—un·al′ter·a·bly,** *adv.*

un·al·tered (un ôl′tərd), *adj.* **1.** not altered, changed, or modified. **2.** (of an animal) not neutered.

un·am·biv·a·lent (un′am biv′ə lənt), *adj.* not ambivalent; definite; certain.

un-A·mer·i·can (un′ə mer′i kən), *adj.* not typifying or contrary to American values, standards, goals, etc. **—un′-A·mer′i·can·ism,** *n.*

U·na·mu·no (ōō′nä mōō′nō), *n.* **Miguel de,** 1864–1936, Spanish philosopher and writer.

u·na·nim·i·ty (yōō′nə nim′i tē), *n.* the state or quality of being unanimous; a consensus or undivided opinion.

u·nan·i·mous (yōō nan′ə məs), *adj.* **1.** in complete agreement; of one mind. **2.** showing complete agreement: *a unanimous vote.* **—u·nan′i·mous·ly,** *adv.*

un·an·swer·a·ble (un an′sər ə bəl, -än′-), *adj.* **1.** not capable of being answered: *an unanswerable question.* **2.** not open to dispute or rebuttal; irrefutable: *an unanswerable proof.* **—un·an′swer·a·bly,** *adv.*

un·ap·peal·a·ble (un′ə pē′lə bəl), *adj.* **1.** not appealable to a higher court, as a case. **2.** incapable of being appealed from, as a judgment. **—un′ap·peal′a·ble·ness,** *n.* **—un′ap·peal′a·bly,** *adv.*

un·ap·proach·a·ble (un′ə prō′chə bəl), *adj.* **1.** not capable of being approached; remote; unreachable. **2.** impossible to equal or rival. **—un′ap·proach′a·bil′i·ty, un′ap·proach′a·ble·ness,** *n.* **—un′ap·proach′a·bly,** *adv.*

un·ap·pro·pri·at·ed (un′ə prō′prē ā′tid), *adj.* **1.** not set apart or voted for some purpose, as money or revenues. **2.** not taken into possession by any person: *Some land remains unappropriated.*

un·apt (un apt′), *adj.* **1.** not appropriate; unfit or unsuitable. **2.** not prone, likely, or disposed: *unapt to waste money.* **3.** deficient in aptitude or capacity; slow; dull. **—un·apt′ly,** *adv.* **—un·apt′ness,** *n.*

un·arm (un ärm′), *v.t.* to deprive or relieve of arms; disarm.

un·armed (un ärmd′), *adj.* **1.** without weapons or armor. **2.** not having claws, thorns, scales, etc., as animals or plants.

un·a·shamed (un′ə shāmd′), *adj.* **1.** not ashamed; not embarrassed by actions or conscious of moral guilt. **2.** unconcealed; unabashed. **—un′a·sham′ed·ly,** *adv.* **—un′a·sham′ed·ness,** *n.*

un·asked (un askt′, -äskt′), *adj.* **1.** not asked: *questions left unasked.* **2.** not asked for: *unasked advice.* **3.** uninvited.

un·as·sail·a·ble (un′ə sā′lə bəl), *adj.* **1.** not vulnerable to attack or assault, as by military force or argument. **2.** not subject to denial or dispute: *an unassailable position in world literature.* **—un′as·sail′a·ble·ness,** *n.* **—un′as·sail′a·bly,** *adv.*

un·as·sum·ing (un′ə sōō′ming), *adj.* modest; unpretentious. **—un′as·sum′ing·ly,** *adv.* **—un′as·sum′ing·ness,** *n.*

un·at·tached (un′ə tacht′), *adj.* **1.** not attached. **2.** not associated with any particular group, organization, or the like; independent. **3.** not engaged, married, or involved with another.

un·at·tend·ed (un′ə ten′did), *adj.* **1.** not attended by an audience, spectators, etc. **2.** not cared for or ministered to. **3.** not accompanied by a companion, attendant, or the like; alone. **4.** unheeded; disregarded. **5.** not done or completed, as a task (usu. fol. by *to*): *several chores still unattended to.*

un·a·vail·ing (un′ə vā′ling), *adj.* ineffectual; futile: *unavailing efforts.* **—un′a·vail′ing·ly,** *adv.*

un·a·void·a·ble (un′ə voi′də bəl), *adj.* unable to be avoided; inescapable: *an unavoidable delay.* **—un′a·void′a·bly,** *adv.*

un·a·ware (un′ə wâr′), *adj.* **1.** not aware or conscious; unconscious. **—adv.** **2.** UNAWARES. **—un′a·ware′ness,** *n.*

un·a·wares (un′ə wârz′), *adv.* **1.** unknowingly or inadvertently. **2.** without warning; unexpectedly: *to find someone unawares.*

un·bal·ance (un bal′əns), *v.,* **-anced, -anc·ing,** *n.* **—v.t.** **1.** to put out of balance. **2.** to disorder or derange, as the mind. **—n.** **3.** IMBALANCE. **—un·bal′ance·a·ble,** *adj.*

un·bal·anced (un bal′ənst), *adj.* **1.** lacking balance or the proper balance. **2.** lacking steadiness and soundness of judgment. **3.** mentally disordered; disturbed or deranged. **4.** (of an account) not adjusted; not brought to an equality of debits and credits.

un·bal·last·ed (un bal′ə stid), *adj.* not ballasted; not properly steadied or regulated.

un·bar (un bär′), *v.t.,* **-barred, -bar·ring.** to remove a bar or bars from; unbolt; open: *Unbar the gate.*

un·bat·ed (un bā′tid), *adj.* undiminished; unabated.

un·bear·a·ble (un bâr′ə bəl), *adj.* unendurable; intolerable. **—un·bear′a·ble·ness,** *n.* **—un·bear′a·bly,** *adv.*

un·beat·a·ble (un bē′tə bəl), *adj.* **1.** incapable of being beaten; impossible to defeat. **2.** of surpassingly good quality; superlative: *an unbeatable product.* **—un·beat′a·bly,** *adv.*

un·beat·en (un bēt′n), *adj.* **1.** not beaten, pounded, or whipped. **2.** not defeated or never defeated. **3.** untrodden: *unbeaten paths.*

un·be·com·ing (un′bi kum′ing), *adj.* detracting from one's appear-

---

un·at′ro·phied, *adj.*
un′at·tain′a·ble, *adj.;* -ble·ness, *n.;*
  -bly, *adv.*
un′at·tempt′ed, *adj.*
un′at·test′ed, *adj.*
un′at·tract′ed, *adj.*
un′at·trac′tive, *adj.;* -ly, *adv.;*
  -ness, *n.*
un′at·trib′ut·ed, *adj.*
un′at·tuned′, *adj.*
un′au·dit′ed, *adj.*
un′aug·ment′ed, *adj.*
un′au·thor′i·ta·tive, *adj.;* -ly, *adv.;*
  -ness, *n.*
un′au·thor·ized′, *adj.*
un′a·vail′a·ble, *adj.;* -ble·ness, *n.;*
  -bly, *adv.*
un′a·venged′, *adj.*
un·av′er·aged, *adj.*
un′a·vert′ed, *adj.*
un′a·vowed′, *adj.*
un′a·wake′, *adj.*
un·awed′, *adj.*
un·ax′i·o·mat′ic, *adj.*
un·baked′, *adj.*
un·band′aged, *v.t.,* -aged, -ag·ing.
un·bap′tized, *adj.*
un·bar′bered, *adj.*
un·bathed′, *adj.*
un·bat′tered, *adj.*
un·beau′ti·fied′, *adj.*
un′be·decked′, *adj.*

un′be·fit′ting, *adj.*
un′be·friend′ed, *adj.*
un′be·hold′en, *adj.*
un·bel·lig′er·ent, *adj.;* -ly, *adv.*
un·belt′ed, *adj.*
un′be·reaved′, *adj.*
un′be·seech′ing, *adj.;* -ly, *adv.*
un′be·trayed′, *adj.*
un·big′ot·ed, *adj.*
un·bill′a·ble, *adj.*
un·billed′, *adj.*
un′bi·o·log′i·cal, *adj.;* -ly, *adv.*
un·bleached′, *adj.*
un·blem′ished, *adj.*
un·blend′ed, *adj.*
un·blind′ed, *adj.*
un·blocked′, *adj.*
un·blood′ied, *adj.*
un·blos′som·ing, *adj.*
un·boiled′, *adj.*
un·book′ish, *adj.;* -ly, *adv.;* -ness, *n.*
un·both′ered, *adj.*
un·box′, *v.t.*
un·branched′, *adj.*
un·break′a·ble, *adj.;* -bly, *adv.*
un·brib′a·ble, *adj.;* -bly, *adv.*
un·bridge′a·ble, *adj.*
un·bris′tled, *adj.*
un·broached′, *adj.*
un·bruised′, *adj.*
un·brushed′, *adj.*
un·budg′et·ed, *adj.*

un·burn′a·ble, *adj.*
un·burned′, *adj.*
un·burnt′, *adj.*
un·busi′ness·like′, *adj.*
un·but′tered, *adj.*
un·but′tressed, *adj.*
un·cal′cu·lat′ing, *adj.;* -ly, *adv.*
un·cal′i·brat′ed, *adj.*
un·cam′ou·flaged′, *adj.*
un·canned′, *adj.*
un′cap·i·tal·is′tic, *adj.*
un·cap′i·tal·ized′, *adj.*
un·cap′siz·a·ble, *adj.*
un·cap′tioned, *adj.*
un·cap′ti·vat′ing, *adj.*
un·car′bon·at′ed, *adj.*
un·car′ing, *adj.*
un·car′pet·ed, *adj.*
un·carved′, *adj.*
un·cashed′, *adj.*
un·cas′trat·ed, *adj.*
un·cat′a·loged′, *adj.*
un·cat′a·logued′, *adj.*
un·catch′a·ble, *adj.*
un·cat′e·go·rized′, *adj.*
un·ca′tered, *adj.*
un·cau′ter·ized′, *adj.*
un·ced′ed, *adj.*
un·cen′sored, *adj.*
un·cen′tered, *adj.*
un·cen′tral·ized′, *adj.*
un·cer′e·mo′ni·al, *adj.;* -ly, *adv.*

un·cer′ti·fi′a·ble, *adj.;* -bly, *adv.*
un·cer′ti·fied′, *adj.*
un·chal′lenged, *adj.*
un·change′a·ble, *adj.;* -bly, *adv.*
un·changed′, *adj.*
un·chang′ing, *adj.;* -ly, *adv.;*
  -ness, *n.*
un·chap′er·oned′, *adj.*
un′char·ac·ter·is′tic, *adj.*
un′char·ac·ter·is′ti·cal·ly, *adv.*
un·checked′, *adj.*
un·cher′ished, *adj.*
un·chew′a·ble, *adj.*
un·chlo′ri·nat′ed, *adj.*
un·chris′tened, *adj.*
un·chron′i·cled, *adj.*
un′chron·o·log′i·cal, *adj.;* -ly, *adv.*
un′cin·e·mat′ic, *adj.*
un·cir′cu·lat′ed, *adj.*
un·cir′cu·lat′ing, *adj.*
un·claimed′, *adj.*
un·clar′i·fied′, *adj.*
un·class′i·fi′a·ble, *adj.;*
  -ble·ness, *n.;* -bly, *adv.*
un·clean′a·ble, *adj.*
un·cleaned′, *adj.*
un·clear′, *adj.;* -ly, *adv.*
un·cleared′, *adj.*
un·clois′tered, *adj.*
un·clos′et·ed, *adj.*
un·cloud′ed, *adj.*
un·cloud′y, *adj.*

ance, character, or reputation; unattractive or unseemly: *an unbecoming hat; unbecoming language.* —**un′be•com′ing•ly,** *adv.*

un•be•known (un′bi nōn′) also **un•be•knownst** (-nōnst′), *adj.* unknown; without one's knowledge (usu. fol. by *to*).

un•be•lief (un′bi lēf′), *n.* incredulity or skepticism, esp. in matters of religious faith.

un•be•liev•a•ble (un′bi lē′və bəl), *adj.* **1.** too improbable to be believed. **2.** extraordinarily impressive of its kind: *an unbelievable performance.* —**un′be•liev′a•bly,** *adv.*

un•be•liev•er (un′bi lē′vər), *n.* **1.** a person who does not believe. **2.** NONBELIEVER.

un•be•liev•ing (un′bi lē′ving), *adj.* **1.** not believing; skeptical. **2.** not accepting any, or some particular, religious belief; nonbelieving. —**un′be•liev′ing•ly,** *adv.* —**un′be•liev′ing•ness,** *n.*

un•bend (un bend′), *v.,* -**bent**, -**bend•ing.** —*v.t.* **1.** to straighten from a bent form or position. **2.** to ease from the strain of formality, intense effort, etc.; relax. **3.** to release from tension, as a bow. **4.** *Naut.* **a.** to loose or untie, as a sail or rope. **b.** to unfasten from spars or stays, as sails. —*v.i.* **5.** to act in an easy, genial manner. **6.** to become unbent; straighten. —**un•bend′a•ble,** *adj.*

un•bend•ing (un ben′ding), *adj.* **1.** not bending; inflexible; rigid. **2.** refusing to yield or compromise; resolute. **3.** austere or formal; aloof. —**un•bend′ing•ly,** *adv.* —**un•bend′ing•ness,** *n.*

un•bent (un bent′), *v.* **1.** pt. and pp. of UNBEND. —*adj.* **2.** not bent; unbowed. **3.** not having yielded or submitted.

un•bi•ased (un bī′əst), *adj.* not biased or prejudiced; impartial. Also, *esp. Brit.,* **un•bi′assed.** —**un•bi′ased•ly,** *adv.*

un•bid•den (un bid′n) also **un•bid′,** *adj.* **1.** not ordered or commanded; spontaneous. **2.** not asked or summoned; uninvited.

un•bind (un bīnd′), *v.t.,* -**bound**, -**bind•ing. 1.** to release from bonds or restraint, as a prisoner; free. **2.** to unfasten or loose.

un•blessed or **un•blest** (un blest′), *adj.* **1.** not given a blessing. **2.** not sanctified or hallowed. **3.** wicked; evil.

un•blink•ing (un bling′king), *adj.* **1.** not blinking. **2.** without displaying surprise, confusion, or chagrin. **3.** not varying or wavering: *an unblinking faith in the future.* —**un•blink′ing•ly,** *adv.*

un•block (un blok′), *v.t.* to remove a block or obstruction from.

un•blush•ing (un blush′ing), *adj.* **1.** showing no remorse; shameless: *unblushing servility.* **2.** not blushing. —**un•blush′ing•ly,** *adv.*

un•bolt (un bōlt′), *v.t.* **1.** to open (a door, window, etc.) by or as if by removing a bolt; unlock. **2.** to unfasten, as by the removal of threaded bolts. —*v.i.* **3.** to become unbolted or unfastened.

un•born (un bôrn′), *adj.* **1.** not yet born; future: *unborn generations.* **2.** not yet delivered; still existing in the mother's womb. **3.** existing without birth or beginning.

un•bos•om (un bŏŏz′əm, -bōō′zəm), *v.t.* **1.** to disclose (a confidence, secret, etc.). —*v.i.* **2.** to disclose one's thoughts, feelings, or the like, esp. in confidence. —*Idiom.* **3.** unbosom oneself, to reveal one's innermost thoughts.

un•bound (un bound′), *v.* **1.** pt. and pp. of UNBIND. —*adj.* **2.** not bound, as a book. **3.** free; not attached, as by a chemical bond: *unbound electrons.*

un•bound•ed (un boun′did), *adj.* **1.** having no limits or bounds. **2.**

unrestrained; unfettered: *unbounded enthusiasm.* —**un•bound′ed•ly,** *adv.* —**un•bound′ed•ness,** *n.*

un•brace (un brās′), *v.t.,* -**braced**, -**brac•ing. 1.** to remove the braces or bonds of. **2.** to weaken.

un•braid (un brād′), *v.t.* to separate (anything braided, as hair) into the several strands.

un•brand•ed (un bran′did), *adj.* **1.** not branded or marked to show ownership. **2.** carrying no commercial brand or trademark.

un•bred (un bred′), *adj.* **1.** not taught or trained. **2.** not mated, as a stock animal.

un•bri•dle (un brīd′l), *v.t.,* -**dled**, -**dling. 1.** to remove the bridle from (a horse, mule, etc.). **2.** to free from restraint.

un•bri•dled (un brīd′ld), *adj.* **1.** not restrained; uninhibited: *unbridled enthusiasm.* **2.** not fitted with a bridle.

un•bro•ken (un brō′kən), *adj.* **1.** not broken; whole; intact. **2.** uninterrupted; undisturbed: *unbroken sleep.* **3.** not tamed, as a horse. —**un•bro′ken•ly,** *adv.* —**un•bro′ken•ness,** *n.*

un•buck•le (un buk′əl), *v.,* -**led**, -**ling.** —*v.i.* **1.** to unfasten the buckle or buckles of. —*v.i.* **2.** to undo a buckle.

un•bun•dle (un bun′dl), *v.,* -**dled**, -**dling.** —*v.t.* **1.** to separate the charges for (related products or services usu. offered as a package). —*v.i.* **2.** to specify separate charges for related products or services.

un•bun•dled (un bun′dld), *adj.* (of related products or services) sold separately rather than as a package.

un•bur•den (un bûr′dn), *v.t.* **1.** to free from a burden. **2.** to relieve (one's mind, conscience, etc.) by confessing something. **3.** to cast off or get rid of, as a burden; disclose.

un•but•ton (un but′n), *v.t.* **1.** to free (buttons) from buttonholes; unfasten or undo. **2.** to unfasten by or as if by unbuttoning: *to unbutton a jacket.* **3.** to disclose (one's feelings, thoughts, etc.) after deliberate or prolonged silence. —*v.i.* **4.** to unfasten a button or one's buttons.

un•but•toned (un but′nd), *adj.* **1.** not buttoned. **2.** free, open, or informal; unrestrained: *unbuttoned humor.*

un•cage (un kāj′), *v.t.,* -**caged**, -**cag•ing.** to set free from or as if from a cage; free from confinement.

un•called-for (un kôld′fôr′), *adj.* **1.** not required or expected; unwanted. **2.** unwarranted; improper: *an uncalled-for criticism.*

un•can•ny (un kan′ē), *adj.* **1.** having or seeming to have a supernatural or inexplicable basis; extraordinary: *uncanny accuracy.* **2.** mysterious; arousing fear or dread: *Uncanny sounds filled the house.* —**un•can′ni•ly,** *adv.* —**un•can′ni•ness,** *n.*

un•cap (un kap′), *v.,* -**capped**, -**cap•ping.** —*v.t.* **1.** to remove a cap or cover from (a bottle, container, etc.). **2.** to free from restrictions. —*v.i.* **3.** to remove the cap or hat from the head.

un•cared-for (un kârd′fôr′), *adj.* **1.** untended; neglected. **2.** not liked or favored.

un•ceas•ing (un sē′sing), *adj.* not stopping; continuous. —**un•ceas′ing•ly,** *adv.* —**un•ceas′ing•ness,** *n.*

un•cer•e•mo•ni•ous (un′ser ə mō′nē əs), *adj.* **1.** abrupt; hasty or rude: *an unceremonious departure.* **2.** without formalities; informal. —**un′cer•e•mo′ni•ous•ly,** *adv.*

un•cer•tain (un sûr′tn), *adj.* **1.** not known precisely; not fixed, as in time of occurrence, number, or size. **2.** not confident or assured; hesi-

---

un•clut′tered, *adj.*
un•co•ag′u•lat′ed, *adj.*
un•cod′i•fied, *adj.*
un•coiled′, *adj.*
un•col•lat′ed, *adj.*
un•col•lect′ed, *adj.*
un•col•lect′i•ble, *adj., n.*
un•col′ored, *adj.; -ly, adv.; -ness, n.*
un•com•bat′ive, *adj.*
un•combed′, *adj.*
un•com•bin′a•ble, *adj.; -bly, adv.*
un•com•bined′, *adj.*
un•come′ly, *adj.*
un•com′fort•ed, *adj.*
un•com•mem′o•rat′ed, *adj.*
un•com•mer′cial•ized′, *adj.*
un•com•mis′sioned, *adj.*
un•com•pan′ion•a•ble, *adj.*
un•com•pas′sion•ate, *adj.; -ly, adv.; -ness, n.*
un•com•pel′ling, *adj.*
un•com•pen•sat′ed, *adj.*
un•com•plain′ing, *adj.; -ly, adv.*
un•com•plet′ed, *adj.*
un•com•pli•cat′ed, *adj.*
un•com•pli•men′ta•ry, *adj.*
un•com•pound′ed, *adj.*
un•com•pre•hend′ed, *adj.*
un•com•pre•hend′ing, *adj.; -ly, adv.*
un•com•pressed′, *adj.*
un•com•put′er•ized′, *adj.*
un•con•cealed′, *adj.*
un•con•ceit′ed, *adj.; -ly, adv.*

un•con•clud′ed, *adj.*
un•con•densed′, *adj.*
un•con•du′cive, *adj.; -ly, adv.; -ness, n.*
un•con•fessed′, *adj.*
un•con•fined′, *adj.*
un•con•firmed′, *adj.*
un•con•formed′, *adj.*
un•con•gen′ial, *adj.*
un•con′quer•a•ble, *adj.; -bly, adv.*
un•con′quered, *adj.*
un•con•sci•en′tious, *adj.; -ly, adv.; -ness, n.*
un•con′se•crat′ed, *adj.*
un•con•sec′u•tive, *adj.; -ly, adv.*
un•con•sent′ing, *adj.*
un•con•sid′ered, *adj.*
un•con•sol′a•ble, *adj.; -bly, adv.*
un•con•soled′, *adj.*
un•con•sol′i•dat′ed, *adj.*
un•con•strict′ed, *adj.*
un•con•sumed′, *adj.*
un•con•sum′mat′ed, *adj.*
un•con•tam′i•nat′ed, *adj.*
un•con•tem•plat′ed, *adj.*
un•con•test′a•ble, *adj.; -bly, adv.*
un•con•test′ed, *adj.; -ly, adv.*
un•con•tra•dict′ed, *adj.; -ly, adv.*
un•con•trol′la•ble, *adj.*
un•con•trolled′, *adj.*
un•con•tro•ver′sial, *adj.; -ly, adv.*
un•con•vert′ed, *adj.*
un•con•vinced′, *adj.*

un•con•vin′ci•ble, *adj.*
un•con•vinc′ing, *adj.; -ly, adv.*
un•cooked′, *adj.*
un•co•op′er•a•tive, *adj.; -ly, adv.; -ness, n.*
un•cop′y•right′ed, *adj.*
un•cor•rect′ed, *adj.*
un•cor•rob′o•rat′ed, *adj.*
un•cor•rupt′ed, *adj.; -ly, adv.*
un•count′a•ble, *adj.*
un•crate′, *v.t.,* -crat•ed, -crat•ing.
un•cre•a′tive, *adj.; -ly, adv.*
un•cred′it•a•ble, *adj.; -ble•ness, n.; -bly, adv.*
un•cred′it•ed, *adj.*
un•crip′pled, *adj.*
un•cropped′, *adj.*
un•crowd′ed, *adj.*
un•crush′a•ble, *adj.*
un•crys′tal•lized′, *adj.*
un•cuffed′, *adj.*
un•cul′ti•vat′ed, *adj.*
un•cul′tured, *adj.*
un•cur′a•ble, *adj.; -ble•ness, n.; -bly, adv.*
un•curbed′, *adj.*
un•cured′, *adj.*
un•cu′ri•ous, *adj.; -ly, adv.*
un•cur′tained, *adj.*
un•cus′tom•ar′y, *adj.*
un•cyn′i•cal, *adj.; -ly, adv.*
un•dam′aged, *adj.*
un•dat′ed, *adj.*

un•de•bat′a•ble, *adj.*
un•de•bat′ed, *adj.*
un•de•cayed′, *adj.*
un•de•ci′pher•a•ble, *adj.*
un•de•ci′phered, *adj.*
un•de•clared′, *adj.*
un•dec′o•rat′ed, *adj.*
un•ded′i•cat′ed, *adj.*
un•de•duct′ed, *adj.*
un•de•feat′ed, *adj.; -ly, adv.; -ness, n.*
un•de•fend′ed, *adj.*
un•de•fen′si•ble, *adj.; -ble•ness, n.; -bly, adv.*
un•de•filed′, *adj.*
un•de•fin′a•ble, *adj.*
un•de•flect′ed, *adj.*
un•de•formed′, *adj.*
un•del′e•gat′ed, *adj.*
un•de•let′ed, *adj.*
un•de•liv′er•a•ble, *adj.*
un•de•liv′ered, *adj.*
un•de•lud′ed, *adj.; -ly, adv.*
un•de•mand′ing, *adj.*
un•dem•o•crat′ic, *adj.*
un•dem•o•crat′i•cal•ly, *adv.*
un•dem′on•strat′ed, *adj.*
un•de•nied′, *adj.*
un•dent′ed, *adj.*
un•de•part′ed, *adj.*
un•de•pend′a•ble, *adj.; -ble•ness, n.; -bly, adv.*
un•de•pos′it•ed, *adj.*

tant: *an uncertain smile.* **3.** not clearly determined. —**un·cer′tain·ly,** *adv.* —**un·cer′tain·ness,** *n.*

un·cer·tain·ty (un sûr′tn tē), *n., pl.* **-ties. 1.** the state of being uncertain; doubt; hesitancy. **2.** an instance of doubt or hesitancy. **3.** unpredictability; indefiniteness.

un·chain (un chān′), *v.t.* to free from or as if from chains; set free. —**un·chain′a·ble,** *adj.*

un·charged (un chärjd′), *adj.* not charged, esp. with electricity; electrically neutral: *an uncharged battery; an uncharged particle.*

un·char·i·ta·ble (ŭm char′i tə bəl), *adj.* deficient in charity; unforgiving. —**un·char′i·ta·ble·ness,** *n.* —**un·char′i·ta·bly,** *adv.*

un·chart·ed (un chär′tid), *adj.* not shown or located on a map; unexplored.

un·char·tered (un chär′tərd), *adj.* **1.** without a charter. **2.** without regulation; lawless.

un·chris·tian (un kris′chən), *adj.* **1.** not conforming to Christian teaching or principles. **2.** not of the Christian religion. **3.** uncivilized; unconscionable. —**un·chris′tian·ly,** *adv.*

un·ci·al (un′shē əl, -shəl), *adj.* **1.** pertaining to a form of majuscule writing having a curved or rounded shape and used chiefly in Greek and Latin manuscripts from about the 3rd to the 9th century A.D. —*n.* **2.** an uncial letter. **3.** uncial writing. —**un′ci·al·ly,** *adv.*

uncial

uncials (Latin)
(8th century)

un·cir·cum·cised (un sûr′kəm sīzd′), *adj.* **1.** not circumcised. **2.** not Jewish; gentile. **3.** heathen; unregenerate.

un·civ·il (un siv′əl), *adj.* **1.** impolite; rude. **2.** uncivilized. —**un′ci·vil′i·ty** (-sə vil′i tē), **un·civ′il·ness,** *n.* —**un·civ′il·ly,** *adv.*

un·civ·i·lized (un siv′ə līzd′), *adj.* not civilized or cultured; barbarous. —**un·civ′i·liz′ed·ly,** *adv.* —**un·civ′i·liz′ed·ness,** *n.*

un·clad (un klad′), *v.* **1.** a pt. and pp. of UNCLOTHE. —*adj.* **2.** naked; nude; undressed.

un·clasp (un klasp′, -kläsp′), *v.t.* **1.** to undo the clasp or clasps of; unfasten. **2.** to release from the grasp. —*v.i.* **3.** to release or relax the grasp.

un·clas·si·fied (un klas′ə fīd′), *adj.* **1.** not assigned to a class or category. **2.** (of data, documents, etc.) not requiring a security clearance; not secret or confidential.

un·cle (ung′kəl), *n.* **1.** a brother of one's father or mother. **2.** an aunt's husband. **3.** a familiar title or term of address for any elderly man. **4.** (*cap.*) UNCLE SAM. —*Idiom.* **5.** say or cry uncle, to concede defeat.

un·clean (un klēn′), *adj.* **1.** not clean; dirty. **2.** morally impure; vile. **3.** having a physical or moral blemish so as to make impure according to Biblical laws. —**un·clean′ness,** *n.*

un·clean·ly¹ (un klēn′lē), *adv.* in an unclean manner.

un·clean·ly² (un klen′lē), *adj.,* **-li·er, -li·est.** unclean. —**un·clean′li·ness,** *n.*

Un′cle Sam′, *n.* a personification of the government or people of the U.S.: represented as a tall, lean man with white chin whiskers, wearing a blue tailcoat, red-and-white-striped trousers, and a top hat with a band of stars.

Un′cle Tom′s′ Cab′in, an antislavery novel (1852) by Harriet Beecher Stowe.

un·cloak (un klōk′), *v.t.* **1.** to remove the cloak from. **2.** to reveal; expose. —*v.i.* **3.** to take off one's cloak.

un·clog (un klog′, -klôg′), *v.,* **-clogged, -clog·ging.** —*v.t.* **1.** to free of an obstruction: *to unclog a drain.* —*v.i.* **2.** to become unclogged. —**un·clog′ger,** *n.*

un·closed (un klōzd′), *adj.* **1.** not closed: *an unclosed door.* **2.** not concluded or settled.

un·clothe (un klōth′), *v.t.,* **-clothed** or **-clad** (-klad′), **-cloth·ing. 1.** to strip of clothes. **2.** to uncover; lay bare.

un·cod·ed (un kō′did), *adj.* **1.** not coded or encoded. **2.** (of mail) addressed without a ZIP code.

un·coil (un koil′), *v.t., v.i.* to unwind from a coiled position.

un·com·fort·a·ble (un kumf′tə bəl, -kum′fər tə-), *adj.* **1.** causing discomfort or distress; irritating; painful. **2.** experiencing discomfort caused by stress or strain; uneasy. —**un·com′fort·a·bly,** *adv.*

un·com·mer·cial (un′kə mûr′shəl), *adj.* **1.** not engaged in or involved with commerce or trade. **2.** not producing or likely to produce a profit: *an artistic but uncommercial film.*

un·com·mit·ted (un′kə mit′id), *adj.* not pledged or bound, as to a specific course of action or cause.

un·com·mon (un kom′ən), *adj.* **1.** not common; unusual; rare. **2.** more than the usual in amount or degree. **3.** exceptional; outstanding. —**un·com′mon·ly,** *adv.* —**un·com′mon·ness,** *n.*

un·com·mu·ni·ca·ble (un′kə myōō′ni kə bəl), *adj.* INCOMMUNICABLE.

un·com·mu·ni·ca·tive (un′kə myōō′ni kə tiv, -kā′tiv), *adj.* not inclined to talk or communicate; reserved; reticent. —**un′com·mu′ni·ca·tive·ly,** *adv.* —**un′com·mu′ni·ca·tive·ness,** *n.*

un·com·pro·mis·ing (un kom′prə mī′zing), *adj.* **1.** not admitting of compromise; making no concessions; unyielding. **2.** undeviating in one's belief or adherence to a principle, point of view, etc. —**un·com′pro·mis′ing·ly,** *adv.* —**un·com′pro·mis′ing·ness,** *n.*

un·con·cern (un′kən sûrn′), *n.* **1.** absence of feeling or concern; indifference. **2.** freedom from anxiety. —**un′con·cerned′,** *adj.* —**un′con·cern′ed·ly,** *adv.* —**un′con·cern′ed·ness,** *n.*

un·con·di·tion·al (un′kən dish′ə nl), *adj.* not limited by conditions; absolute. —**un′con·di′tion·al·ly,** *adv.*

uncondi′tional surren′der, *n.* a statement by a warring side that warfare will continue until the other side surrenders without conditions: first used by U.S. Grant.

un·con·di·tioned (un′kən dish′ənd), *adj.* **1.** not subject to conditions; absolute. **2.** not learned or taught: *an unconditioned response.*

un·con·form·a·ble (un′kən fôr′mə bəl), *adj.* **1.** not conformable; not conforming. **2.** *Geol.* indicating discontinuity in a stratigraphic sequence. —**un′con·form′a·bly,** *adv.*

un·con·form·i·ty (un′kən fôr′mi tē), *n., pl.* **-ties. 1.** lack of conformity; incongruity; inconsistency. **2.** *Geol.* a discontinuity in a stratigraphic sequence.

un·con·nec·ted (un′kə nek′tid), *adj.* **1.** not connected; not joined together or attached. **2.** lacking coherence or continuity. —**un′con·nect′ed·ly,** *adv.* —**un′con·nect′ed·ness,** *n.*

un·con·scion·a·ble (un kon′shə nə bəl), *adj.* **1.** not restrained by conscience; unscrupulous. **2.** excessive; extortionate. —**un·con′scion·a·ble·ness,** *n.* —**un·con′scion·a·bly,** *adv.*

un·con·scious (un kon′shəs), *adj.* **1.** not conscious; without awareness, sensation, or cognition. **2.** temporarily devoid of consciousness. **3.** not perceived at the level of awareness: *an unconscious impulse.* **4.** done unintentionally. —*n.* **5. the unconscious,** *Psychoanal.* the part of the psyche that is rarely accessible to awareness but that has a pronounced influence on behavior. —**un·con′scious·ly,** *adv.* —**un·con′scious·ness,** *n.*

un·con·sti·tu·tion·al (un′kon sti tōō′shə nl, -tyōō′-), *adj.* not constitutional; unauthorized by or inconsistent with a constitution, esp. the U.S. Constitution. —**un′con·sti·tu′tion·al·ly,** *adv.*

un·con·struct·ed (un′kən struk′tid), *adj.* (of clothing) made with little or no padding, interfacing, or lining, so as to fit loosely or softly on the body.

un·con·ven·tion·al (un′kən ven′shə nl), *adj.* not conventional; not bound by or conforming to convention: *an unconventional use of color.* —**un′con·ven′tion·al·ist,** *n.* —**un′con·ven′tion·al·i·ty,** *n., pl.* **-ties.** —**un′con·ven′tion·al·ly,** *adv.*

un·cool (un kōōl′), *adj. Slang.* **1.** not self-assured or relaxed. **2.** not sophisticated or practical.

un·cork (un kôrk′), *v.t.* **1.** to draw the cork from. **2.** *Informal.* to release or unleash.

un·count·ed (un koun′tid), *adj.* **1.** not counted. **2.** innumerable.

un·cou·ple (un kup′əl), *v.,* **-pled, -pling.** —*v.t.* **1.** to release the coupling or link between; disconnect. —*v.i.* **2.** to become unfastened; let go. **3.** *Informal.* to divorce or separate.

un·court·ly (un kôrt′lē, -kōrt′-), *adj.* **1.** not courtly; rude. **2.** not conforming to the customs or usage of a royal court. —**un·court′li·ness,** *n.*

un·couth (un kōōth′), *adj.* **1.** lacking manners or grace; clumsy; oafish. **2.** rude, uncivil, or boorish. **3.** strange and ungraceful in appearance or form. —**un·couth′ly,** *adv.* —**un·couth′ness,** *n.*

un·cov·er (un kuv′ər), *v.t.* **1.** to remove the cover or covering from. **2.** to lay bare; disclose; reveal. —*v.i.* **3.** to remove a cover or covering. **4.** to take off one's hat as a gesture of respect.

un·cov·ered (un kuv′ərd), *adj.* **1.** having no cover or covering. **2.** having the head bare. **3.** not protected by collateral or other security, as a loan. **4.** not protected by insurance.

un·crit·i·cal (un krit′i kəl), *adj.* **1.** not inclined or able to judge or evaluate: *an uncritical reader.* **2.** undiscriminating; not able or inclined to analyze: *an uncritical acceptance of traditional values.* —**un·crit′i·cal·ly,** *adv.*

un·cross (un krôs′, -kros′), *v.t.* to change from a crossed position, as the legs.

un·crown (un kroun′), *v.t.* **1.** to deprive or divest of a crown. **2.** to reduce from dignity or preeminence.

unc·tion (ungk′shən), *n.* **1.** the act of anointing, esp. as a medical treatment or religious rite. **2.** the oil used in religious rites, as in anointing the sick or dying. **3.** an affected or excessive earnestness in manner or utterance; unctuousness.

unc·tu·ous (ungk′chōō əs), *adj.* **1.** characterized by affected earnestness or moralistic fervor; excessively suave or smug. **2.** characteristic of an unguent or ointment; oily; greasy. **3.** having an oily or soapy feel, as certain minerals. —**unc′tu·ous·ly,** *adv.* —**unc′tu·ous·ness,** *n.*

un·curl (un kûrl′), *v.t., v.i.* to straighten out from a curled position.

un·cut (un kut′), *adj.* **1.** not cut. **2.** not shortened or condensed; unabridged. **3.** in the original form; neither reduced in size nor given shape, as a diamond. **4.** not diluted or adulterated.

un·daunt·ed (un dôn′tid, -dän′-), *adj.* **1.** not discouraged; undismayed. **2.** undiminished in courage or valor; intrepid. —**un·daunt′ed·ly,** *adv.* —**un·daunt′ed·ness,** *n.*

un·de·ceive (un′di sēv′), *v.t.,* **-ceived, -ceiv·ing.** to free from deception. —**un′de·ceiv′a·ble,** *adj.* —**un′de·ceiv′er,** *n.*

un•de•cid•ed (un′di sī′did), *adj.* **1.** not yet decided or determined. **2.** not having one's mind made up. **—***n.* **3.** a person who is undecided. —**un′de•cid′ed•ly,** *adv.* —**un′de•cid′ed•ness,** *n.*

un•de•fined (un′di fīnd′), *adj.* **1.** not defined or explained. **2.** indefinite in form or extent: *an undefined feeling of sadness.* **—un′de•fin′ed•ly,** *adv.* —**un′de•fin′ed•ness,** *n.*

un•de•mon•stra•tive (un′də mon′strə tiv), *adj.* not given to open expression of emotion, esp. of affection; reserved or unresponsive. —**un′de•mon′stra•tive•ly,** *adv.* —**un′de•mon′stra•tive•ness,** *n.*

un•de•ni•a•ble (un′di nī′ə bəl), *adj.* **1.** incapable of being denied or disputed. **2.** not open to refusal. **3.** unquestioned as to quality or merit; indisputably good: *undeniable talent.* —**un′de•ni′a•ble•ness,** *n.* —**un′de•ni′a•bly,** *adv.*

un•der (un′dər), *prep.* **1.** beneath and covered by: *under a tree.* **2.** below the surface of: *under water.* **3.** at a point lower than: *a bump just under his eye.* **4.** in the position of sustaining, enduring, etc.: *to sink under a heavy load.* **5.** beneath the cover or disguise of: *registered under a pseudonym.* **6.** beneath the heading of: *Classify the books under "Fiction."* **7.** below in degree, amount, etc.; less than: *purchased under cost.* **8.** below in rank. **9.** subject to the authority, influence, effect, or guidance of: *a bureau under the prime minister; to study violin under Heifetz.* **10.** in accordance with: *under the provisions of the law.* **11.** during the administration or reign of: *laws passed under President Lincoln.* **12.** in the state or process of: *under construction.* **—***adv.* **13.** below or beneath something: *Go over the fence, not under.* **14.** beneath the surface. **15.** in a lower degree, amount, etc.: *selling shirts for $25 and under.* **16.** in a subordinate position or condition. **17. go under, a.** to give in; succumb; yield. **b.** to fail in business. **—***adj.* **18.** located beneath or on the underside. **19.** lower in position. **20.** lower in degree, amount, rank, etc. **21.** subject to the control, effect, etc., as of a person, drug, or force.

under-, a prefixal use of UNDER, as to indicate place or situation below or beneath (*underbrush; undertow*); lower in grade or dignity (*undersheriff; understudy*); of lesser degree, extent, or amount (*undersized*); or insufficiency (*underfeed*).

un•der•a•chieve (un′dər ə chēv′), *v.i.,* **-a•chieved, -a•chiev•ing. 1.** to perform below the potential indicated by tests of one's mental ability or aptitude. **2.** to achieve less than expected. —**un′der•a•chieve′ment,** *n.* —**un′der•a•chiev′er,** *n.*

un•der•ac•tive (un′dər ak′tiv), *adj.* insufficiently active: *an underactive thyroid gland.* —**un′der•ac•tiv′i•ty, un′der•ac′tive•ness,** *n.*

un•der•age[1] (un′dər āj′), *adj.* being below the legal or required age.

un•der•age[2] (un′dər ij), *n.* shortage; deficiency.

un•der•arm (un′dər ärm′), *adj.* **1.** of, situated, or for use under the arm or in the armpit: *an underarm deodorant.* **2.** UNDERHAND (def. 2). **—***n.* **3.** ARMPIT. **—***adv.* **4.** UNDERHAND (def. 3).

un•der•bel•ly (un′dər bel′ē), *n., pl.* **-lies. 1.** the lower abdomen. **2.** the underneath part of an animal behind the chest. **3.** the lower surface or underside: *the underbelly of an airplane.* **4.** a vulnerable area; weak point: *the soft underbelly of Europe.* **5.** a dark, seamy, often hidden area or side: *the underbelly of society.*

un•der•bid (un′dər bid′), *v.,* **-bid, -bid•ding. —***v.t.* **1.** to bid less than (another bid) or less than the bid of (another bidder), esp. in seeking a contract. **2.** to bid less than the value or worth of (a contract or hand) at cards. **—***v.i.* **3.** to bid lower than another, esp. too low to gain something. —**un′der•bid′der,** *n.*

un•der•bite (un′dər bīt′), *n.* (not in technical use) occlusion in which the lower incisor teeth overlap the upper.

un•der•bod•y (un′dər bod′ē), *n., pl.* **-bod•ies.** the bottom or underneath part, as of a mechanism or animal.

un•der•bred (un′dər bred′), *adj.* **1.** not of pure breed, as a horse. **2.** ill-bred; vulgar. —**un′der•breed′ing** (-brē′ding), *n.*

un•der•brush (un′dər brush′), *n.* shrubs, saplings, low vines, etc., growing under the large trees in a wood or forest.

un•der•cap•i•tal•ize (un′dər kap′i tl īz′), *v.t.,* **-ized, -iz•ing.** to provide an insufficient amount of capital for (a business enterprise). —**un′der•cap′i•tal•i•za′tion,** *n.*

un•der•card (un′dər kärd′), *n.* an event or group of events preceding and supporting a featured event: *the undercard of tonight's boxing match.*

un•der•car•riage (un′dər kar′ij), *n.* **1.** the supporting framework underneath a vehicle, as an automobile or trailer; the structure to which the wheels, tracks, or the like are attached or fitted. **2.** the portions of an aircraft that are below the body.

un•der•charge (*v.* un′dər chärj′; *n.* un′dər chärj′), *v.,* **-charged, -charg•ing,** *n.* **—***v.t.* **1.** to charge (a purchaser) less than the proper or fair price. **2.** to charge (a stated amount) less than the proper price. **—***v.i.* **3.** to charge too little. **—***n.* **4.** a charge or price less than is proper or customary.

un•der•class (un′dər klas′, -kläs′), *n.* a social stratum consisting of impoverished persons with very low social status.

un•der•class•man (un′dər klas′mən, -kläs′-), *n., pl.* **-men.** a freshman or sophomore in a secondary school or college.

un•der•clothes (un′dər klōz′, -klōthz′) also **un•der•cloth•ing** (-klō′thing), *n.* (*used with a pl. v.*) **1.** UNDERWEAR. **2.** clothes worn under outer clothes.

un•der•coat (un′dər kōt′), *n.* **1.** a coat or jacket worn under another. **2.** *Zool.* a growth of short fur or hair lying beneath a longer growth. **3.** an undercoating. **4. a.** a paint, sealer, or the like specially prepared for use underneath a finishing coat. **b.** a coat of such paint or sealer applied under the finishing coat.

un•der•coat•ing (un′dər kō′ting), *n.* a protective seal applied to the underside of an automobile to reduce corrosion and vibration.

un•der•com•pen•sate (un′dər kom′pən sāt′), *v.t.,* **-sat•ed, -sat•ing.** to compensate or pay less than is fair, customary, or the like.

un•der•count (*v.* un′dər kount′; *n.* un′dər kount′), *v.t.* **1.** to count less than the full number or amount of, esp. in an attempt to falsify records, returns, etc. **—***n.* **2.** a count or total that is less than the actual number or amount.

un•der•cov•er (un′dər kuv′ər, un′dər kuv′-), *adj.* **1.** clandestine or secret: *an undercover investigation.* **2.** engaged in securing confidential information: *an undercover agent.*

un•der•cur•rent (un′dər kûr′ənt, -kur′-), *n.* **1.** a hidden tendency or feeling underlying and often at variance with someone's words, actions, etc. **2.** a current, as of air or water, that flows below the upper currents or surface.

un•der•cut (*v.* un′dər kut′; *n., adj.,* un′dər kut′), *v.,* **-cut, -cut•ting,** *n., adj.* **—***v.t.* **1.** to cut under or beneath. **2.** to weaken or destroy the impact or effectiveness of; undermine. **3.** to offer goods or services at a lower price or rate than (a competitor). **4.** to cut away material from so as to leave a portion overhanging, as in carving or sculpture. **5.** to hit (a ball) underhand so as to cause backspin; slice. **6.** to cut a notch in (a tree) in order to control the direction in which the tree is to fall. **—***v.i.* **7.** to undercut material, a competitor, etc. **—***n.* **8.** a cut or a cutting away underneath. **9.** a notch cut in a tree to determine its direction of fall. **10.** a hitting of a ball underhand so as to cause backspin; slice. **—***adj.* **11.** having or resulting from an undercut.

un•der•de•vel•op (un′dər di vel′əp), *v.t.* to develop (something) partially, esp. short of the required amount. —**un′der•de•vel′op•ment,** *n.*

un•der•de•vel•oped (un′dər di vel′əpt), *adj.* **1.** improperly or insufficiently developed. **2.** (of a photographic negative) less developed than is normal, so as to produce a relatively dark positive lacking in contrast. **3.** DEVELOPING (def. 2).

un•der•do (un′dər do͞o′), *v.i., v.t.,* **-did, -done, -do•ing.** to do less than is usual or necessary.

un•der•dog (un′dər dôg′, -dog′), *n.* **1.** a person who is expected to lose in a contest or conflict. **2.** a victim of social or political injustice.

un•der•done (un′dər dun′), *adj.* **1.** not cooked enough. **2.** *Chiefly Brit.* (of meat) rare.

un•der•draw•ers (un′dər drôrz′), *n.* (*used with a pl. v.*) underpants typically covering at least part of the legs.

un•der•dress (un′dər dres&prim), *v.i.* to clothe oneself less formally than is usual or fitting for the circumstances. **—***n.*

un•der•em•pha•size (un′dər em′fə sīz′), *v.t.,* **-sized, -siz•ing.** to give less than sufficient emphasis to; minimize.

un•der•em•ployed (un′dər em ploid′), *adj.* **1.** employed at a job that does not fully use one's skills or abilities. **2.** employed only part-time when one is available for full-time work. **3.** not utilized fully, as machinery or facilities. —**un′der•em•ploy′ment,** *n.*

un•der•en•dowed (un′dər en doud′), *adj.* **1.** (of a school, hospital, or other institution) lacking sufficient income from an endowment. **2.** lacking certain desirable traits, skills, or the like.

un•der•es•ti•mate (*v.* un′dər es′tə māt′; *n.* -mit, -māt′), *v.,* **-mat•ed, -mat•ing,** *n.* **—***v.t.* **1.** to estimate at too low a value, rate, or the like. **—***v.i.* **2.** to make an estimate lower than the correct one. **—***n.* **3.** an estimate that is too low.

un•der•ex•pose (un′dər ik spōz′), *v.t.,* **-posed, -pos•ing.** to expose either to insufficient light or to sufficient light for too short a period, as in photography. —**un•der•ex•po•sure,** *n*

un•der•feed (un′dər fēd′ *for 1;* un′der fēd′ *for 2*), *v.t.,* **-fed, -feed•ing. 1.** to feed insufficiently. **2.** to feed with fuel from beneath.

un•der•foot (un′dər fo͝ot′), *adv.* **1.** under the foot or feet; on the ground or underneath. **2.** in the way: *Our dog is always getting underfoot.* **—***adj.* **3.** lying under the foot; in a position to be stepped on.

un•der•gar•ment (un′dər gär′mənt), *n.* an article of underwear.

un•der•gird (un′dər gûrd′), *v.t.,* **-gird•ed** or **-girt, -gird•ing. 1.** to strengthen or secure, as by passing a rope or chain under and around. **2.** to give fundamental support; provide with a sound basis: *ethics undergirded by faith.*

un•der•go (un′dər gō′), *v.t.,* **-went, -gone, -go•ing. 1.** to be subjected to; experience: *has undergone surgery.* **2.** to endure or sustain; suffer: *underwent starvation.* —**un′der•go′er,** *n.*

un•der•grad (un′dər grad′), *n. Informal.* an undergraduate.

un•der•grad•u•ate (un′dər graj′o͞o it, -āt′), *n.* **1.** a college-level student who has not received a first, esp. a bachelor's, degree. **—***adj.* **2.** having the standing of an undergraduate.

un•der•ground (*adv.* un′dər ground′; *adj., n.* -ground′), *adv.* **1.** beneath the surface of the ground. **2.** in concealment or secrecy; not openly. **—***adj.* **3.** existing, situated, or operating beneath the surface of the ground. **4.** hidden or secret; not open: *underground political activities.* **5.** published or produced by political or social radicals: *an underground newspaper.* **6.** done by or for nonconformists; avant-garde; experimental: *an underground movie.* **—***n.* **7.** the place or region beneath the surface of the ground. **8.** a secret organization fighting the established government or occupation forces. **9.** (*often cap.*) a movement or

U

group existing outside the establishment and usu. reflecting unorthodox, avant-garde, or radical views. **10.** *Brit.* a subway system.

un·der·ground rail·road, *n.* (*often caps.*) (before the abolition of slavery in the U.S.) a system for helping fugitive slaves escape into Canada and other places of safety.

un·der·grown (un′dər grōn′, un′dər grōn′), *adj.* not grown to normal size or height: *sickly and undergrown cattle.*

un·der·growth (un′dər grōth′), *n.* **1.** UNDERBRUSH. **2.** the condition of being undergrown or undersized. **3.** UNDERCOAT (def. 2).

un·der·hand (un′dər hand′), *adj.* **1.** not open and aboveboard; secret and crafty. **2.** executed with the hand below the level of the shoulder and the palm turned upward and forward: *an underhand pitch.* —*adv.* **3.** with the hand below the level of the shoulder and the palm turned upward and forward. **4.** secretly; stealthily.

un·der·hand·ed (un′dər han′did), *adj.* **1.** UNDERHAND. **2.** SHORT-HANDED. —**un′der·hand′ed·ly,** *adv.* —**un′der·hand′ed·ness,** *n.*

un·der·hung (un′dər hung′), *adj.* **1.** (of the lower jaw) projecting beyond the upper jaw. **2.** resting on a track beneath instead of being overhung, as a sliding door.

un·der·in·sure (un′dər in shoor′, -shûr′), *v.t.,* **-sured, -sur·ing.** to insure for an amount less than the true or replacement value. —**un′der·in·sured′,** *adj.*

un·der·laid (un′dər lād′), *adj.* **1.** placed or laid underneath, as a foundation or substratum. **2.** having an underneath layer (often fol. by *with*): *lace underlaid with satin.* —*v.* **3.** pt. and pp. of UNDERLAY.

un·der·lay (*v.* un′dər lā′; *n.* un′dər lā′), *v.,* **-laid, -lay·ing,** *n.* —*v.t.* **1.** to lay under or beneath. **2.** to provide with something laid underneath, as for support. **3.** to extend across the bottom of. —*n.* **4.** something underlaid. **5.** paper put under type or cuts to bring them to the proper height for printing.

un·der·lie (un′dər lī′), *v.t.,* **-lay, -lain, -ly·ing. 1.** to lie under or beneath. **2.** to form the foundation of.

un·der·line (un′dər līn′), *v.t.,* **-lined, -lin·ing,** *n.* —*v.t.* **1.** to mark with a line or lines underneath; underscore. **2.** to indicate the importance of; emphasize. —*n.* **3.** a caption under an illustration. **4.** a line drawn beneath; underscore. —**un′der·lin′er,** *n.*

un·der·ling (un′dər ling), *n.* a subordinate, esp. one of slight importance.

un·der·ly·ing (un′dər lī′ing), *adj.* **1.** lying beneath something else, as a substratum. **2.** fundamental; basic: *the underlying cause.* **3.** discoverable only by close scrutiny or analysis; implicit. **4.** (of a claim, mortgage, etc.) taking precedence; prior.

un·der·manned (un′dər mand′), *adj.* UNDERSTAFFED.

un·der·mine (un′dər mīn′ or, esp. for 1, 3, un′dər mīn′), *v.t.,* **-mined, -min·ing. 1.** to impair, weaken, or destroy (health, morale, etc.) by imperceptible stages. **2.** to make an excavation under; dig or tunnel beneath. **3.** to weaken or cause to collapse by removing underlying supports. —**un′der·min′er,** *n.*

un·der·neath (un′dər nēth′, -nēth′), *prep.* **1.** below the surface of; directly beneath. **2.** at the bottom of: *exploration underneath the sea.* **3.** under the control of; in a lower position than, esp. in a hierarchy of authority. **4.** hidden, disguised, or misrepresented by, as a false appearance or pretense. —*adv.* **5.** below; at a lower level or position; on the underside. —*adj.* **6.** situated below or under something else; lower. —*n.* **7.** the bottom; underside.

un·der·nour·ished (un′dər nûr′isht, -nur′-), *adj.* **1.** not nourished with sufficient or proper food to maintain health or normal growth. **2.** lacking the essential elements for proper development: *emotionally undernourished.* —**un′der·nour′ish·ment,** *n.*

un·der·pants (un′dər pants′), *n.* (*used with a pl. v.*) drawers or shorts worn under outer clothing, usu. next to the skin.

un·der·pass (un′dər pas′, -päs′), *n.* a passage running underneath, esp. a passage for pedestrians or vehicles under a railroad or street.

un·der·pay (un′dər pā′), *v.t.,* **-paid, -pay·ing.** to pay (a person) less than is customary or deserved. —**un·der·pay·ment** (un′dər pā′mənt, un′dər pā′-), *n.*

un·der·per·form (un′dər pər fôrm′), *v.t., v.i.* to perform less well than (others of its kind) or less well than expected.

un·der·pin (un′dər pin′), *v.t.,* **-pinned, -pin·ning. 1.** to prop up or support from below; strengthen. **2.** to replace or strengthen the foundation of. **3.** to substantiate or corroborate.

un·der·pin·ning (un′dər pin′ing), *n.* **1.** a system of supports beneath a wall or the like. **2.** Often, **underpinnings.** a foundation or basis: *to strengthen the underpinnings of a friendship.*

un·der·play (un′dər plā′, un′dər plā′), *v.t.* **1.** to play (a part or scene)

subtly and with restraint. **2.** to play (a part) sketchily. **3.** to understate or de-emphasize; downplay. —*v.i.* **4.** to underplay a part or scene.

un·der·price (un′dər prīs′), *v.t.,* **-priced, -pric·ing. 1.** to price (goods or merchandise) lower than the standard price. **2.** to undercut (a competitor) by setting prices below actual cost.

un·der·priv·i·leged (un′dər priv′ə lijd, -priv′lijd), *adj.* denied the enjoyment of the normal privileges or rights of a society because of low economic and social status.

un·der·pro·duc·tion (un′dər prə duk′shən), *n.* production that is less than normal or than is required by the demand. —**un′der·pro·duc′tiv′i·ty** (-prō′duk tiv′i tē, -prod′ək-), *n.*

un·der·rate (un′dər rāt′), *v.t.,* **-rat·ed, -rat·ing.** to rate or evaluate too low; underestimate.

un·der·re·port (un′dər ri pôrt′, -pōrt′), *v.t., v.i.* to report as less or fewer than is correct: *to underreport the enemy's strength.*

un·der·run (un′dər run′), *v.,* **-ran, -run, -run·ning,** *n.* —*v.t.* **1.** to run, pass, or go under. —*n.* **2.** something that runs or passes underneath, as a current. **3.** an instance of costing less than estimated. **4.** a production run below the quantity ordered.

un·der·score (un′dər skôr′, -skōr′), *v.,* **-scored, -scor·ing,** *n.* —*v.t.* **1.** to mark with a line or lines underneath; underline, as for emphasis. **2.** to stress; emphasize. **3.** to provide music or a musical soundtrack for (a film). —*n.* **4.** a line drawn beneath something written or printed. **5.** music for a film soundtrack.

un·der·sea (un′dər sē′), *adj.* **1.** located, carried on, or used under the surface of the sea. —*adv.* **2.** UNDERSEAS.

un·der·seas (un′dər sēz′), *adv.* beneath the surface of the sea.

un′der sec′retary or **un′der·sec′re·tar·y,** *n.* (*often caps.*) a government official who is subordinate to a principal secretary.

un·der·sell (un′dər sel′), *v.t.,* **-sold, -sell·ing. 1.** to sell more cheaply than (a competitor). **2.** to sell (something) for less than the actual value. —**un′der·sell′er,** *n.*

un·der·shirt (un′dər shûrt′), *n.* a collarless, usu. pullover undergarment for the torso, typically of lightweight fabric, as cotton, with or without sleeves.

un·der·shoot (un′dər shoot′, un′dər shoot′), *v.,* **-shot, -shoot·ing.** —*v.t.* **1.** to shoot or launch a projectile that falls short of (a target). **2.** (of an aircraft or pilot) to land before reaching (a landing strip) because of a too rapid loss of altitude. —*v.i.* **3.** to shoot or launch a projectile that falls short of a target.

un·der·shorts (un′dər shôrts′), *n.* (*used with a pl. v.*) short underpants for men and boys.

un·der·shot (un′dər shot′; *for 3 also* un′dər shot′), *adj.* **1.** having the front teeth of the lower jaw projecting in front of the upper teeth, as a bulldog. **2.** driven by water passing beneath: *an undershot vertical water wheel.* —*v.* **3.** pt. and pp. of UNDERSHOOT.

un·der·side (un′dər sīd′), *n.* an under or lower side.

un·der·sign (un′dər sīn′), *v.t.* to sign one's name at the end of (a letter or document).

un·der·signed (un′dər sīnd′), *adj.* **1.** being the one or ones whose signatures appear at the end of a letter or document. **2.** signed at the bottom or end, as a letter or document. —*n.* **3. the undersigned,** the person or persons signing a letter or document.

un·der·size (un′dər sīz′), *adj.* **1.** UNDERSIZED. **2.** (of screened minerals) passing through a sieve of given mesh.

un·der·sized (un′dər sīzd′), *adj.* smaller than the usual or normal size.

un·der·staffed (un′dər staft′, -stäft′), *adj.* having an insufficient number of personnel.

un·der·stand (un′dər stand′), *v.,* **-stood, -stand·ing.** —*v.t.* **1.** to perceive the meaning of; comprehend: *to understand a poem.* **2.** to be familiar with; have a thorough knowledge of: *to understand a trade.* **3.** to interpret or comprehend in a specified way: *She understood his suggestion as a complaint.* **4.** to grasp the significance or importance of: *He doesn't understand responsibility.* **5.** to regard as agreed or settled; assume: *We understand that you will repay this loan in 30 days.* **6.** to learn or hear: *I understand you were ill.* **7.** to infer (something not stated). —*v.i.* **8.** to perceive what is meant; comprehend. **9.** to accept something tolerantly or sympathetically: *If you can't do it, I will understand.* **10.** to have knowledge about a particular subject.

un·der·stand·a·ble (un′dər stan′də bəl), *adj.* capable of being understood; comprehensible. —**un′der·stand′a·bly,** *adv.*

un·der·stand·ing (un′dər stan′ding), *n.* **1.** the mental process of a person who understands; comprehension; personal interpretation. **2.** intellectual faculties; intelligence. **3.** knowledge of a particular thing. **4.** a state of cooperation between people, nations, factions, etc. **5.** a mutual

---

agreement, esp. of a private or tacit kind. —*adj.* **6.** characterized by comprehension, empathy, or the like. —**un·der·stand′ing·ly,** *adv.*

un·der·state (un′dər stāt′), *v.t.,* **-stat·ed, -stat·ing.** to state or represent less strongly or strikingly than the facts would indicate; set forth in restrained terms: *The report understates the magnitude of the disaster.* —**un·der·state·ment** (un′dər stāt′mənt, un′dər stāt′-), *n.*

un·der·stat·ed (un′dər stā′tid), *adj.* restrained; de-emphasized; low-key: *understated elegance.* —**un′der·stat′ed·ness,** *n.*

un·der·stood (un′dər stŏŏd′), *v.* **1.** pt. and pp. of UNDERSTAND. —*adj.* **2.** agreed upon by all parties. **3.** implied but not stated: *The understood meaning of a danger sign is "Keep away."*

un·der·struc·ture (un′dər struk′chər), *n.* **1.** a structure serving as a support; base or foundation. **2.** any thing, condition, etc., establishing support or providing a basis.

un·der·stud·y (un′dər stud′ē), *n., pl.* **-stud·ies,** *v.,* **-stud·ied, -stud·y·ing.** —*n.* **1.** a performer who learns the role of another in order to serve as a replacement if necessary. —*v.t.* **2.** to learn (a role) in order to replace the regular performer when necessary. **3.** to act as understudy to (a performer): *to understudy the lead.* —*v.i.* **4.** to act or work as an understudy.

un·der·sur·face (un′dər sûr′fis), *n.* **1.** a bottom surface; underside. —*adj.* **2.** submerged; under the surface, as of water.

un·der·take (un′dər tāk′), *v.,* **-took, -tak·en, -tak·ing.** —*v.t.* **1.** to take upon oneself, as a task or performance; attempt: *He undertook the job of answering the mail.* **2.** to obligate oneself (fol. by an infinitive). **3.** to warrant or guarantee (fol. by a clause): *to undertake that a loan is fully secured.* **4.** to take in charge.

un·der·tak·er (un′dər tā′kər for 1; un′dər tā′kər for 2), *n.* **1.** FUNERAL DIRECTOR. **2.** a person who undertakes something.

un·der·tak·ing (un′dər tā′king, un′dər tā′- for 1–3; un′dər tā′king for 4, 5), *n.* **1.** the act of a person who undertakes any task or responsibility. **2.** a task, enterprise, etc., undertaken. **3.** a pledge or guarantee. **4.** the business of an undertaker or funeral director. —*adj.* **5.** pertaining to such a business.

un′der-the-count′er, *adj.* **1.** (of merchandise) sold clandestinely. **2.** illegal; unauthorized: *under-the-counter payments.*

un′der-the-ta′ble, *adj.* transacted in secret or in an underhand manner.

un·der·things (un′dər thingz′), *n.pl.* women's underclothes.

un·der·tone (un′dər tōn′), *n.* **1.** a low or subdued tone. **2.** an unobtrusive or background sound. **3.** an underlying quality or element; undercurrent: *an undertone of regret in his voice.* **4.** a subdued color; a color modified by an underlying color.

un·der·tow (un′dər tō′), *n.* **1.** the seaward subsurface flow of water from waves breaking on a beach. **2.** any strong subsurface current, moving in a direction different from that of the surface current.

un·der·trick (un′dər trik′), *n.* a trick in bridge that the declarer failed to win as part of the contract. Compare OVERTRICK.

un·der·val·ue (un′dər val′yŏŏ), *v.t.,* **-ued, -u·ing. 1.** to put too low a value on. **2.** to have insufficient regard or esteem for. —**un′der·val′u·a′tion,** *n.*

un·der·wa·ter (un′dər wô′tər, -wot′ər), *adj.* **1.** existing or occurring under water. **2.** designed to be used under water. **3.** located below a ship's waterline. —*adv.* **4.** beneath the water: *to travel underwater.* —*n.* **5.** the water beneath the surface. **6. underwaters,** the depths, as of a sea or lake.

un·der·way (un′dər wā′, -wā′), *adj.* **1.** occurring while under way. **2.** (of a ship) no longer in port or at anchor; moving.

un·der·wear (un′dər wâr′), *n.* clothing worn next to the skin under outer clothes. Also called **underclothes.**

un·der·weight (*adj.* un′dər wāt′; *n.* un′dər wāt′), *adj.* **1.** weighing less than is usual or proper. —*n.* **2.** deficiency in weight below a standard or requirement.

un·der·went (un′dər went′), *v.* pt. of UNDERGO.

un·der·whelm (un′dər hwelm′, -welm′), *v.t. Informal.* to fail to interest or astonish.

un·der·wire (un′dər wīʳr′), *n.* **1.** a wire sewn into the underside of each cup of a brassiere, used for support and shape. **2.** a brassiere with such wires.

un·der·world (un′dər wûrld′), *n.* **1.** the criminal element of human society. **2.** (in the religious beliefs of various cultures, esp. the ancient Greeks and Romans) a realm below the surface of the earth in which the spirits of the dead reside.

un·der·write (un′dər rīt′, un′dər rīt′), *v.,* **-wrote, -writ·ten, -writ·ing.** —*v.t.* **1.** to contribute a sum of money to guarantee the success of (an undertaking). **2.** to guarantee the sale of (a security to be offered for public subscription). **3.** *Insurance.* **a.** to write one's name at the end of (a policy), thereby becoming liable in case of specified losses. **b.** to insure. **c.** to assume liability to the extent of (a specified sum). **4.** to write under other written matter. **5.** to sign one's name to. **6.** to show agreement with; support. —*v.i.* **7.** to underwrite something. **8.** to work as an underwriter.

un·der·writ·er (un′dər rī′tər), *n.* **1.** a person or company that underwrites insurance policies or investment securities. **2.** a sponsor.

un·de·sir·a·ble (un′di zīʳr′ə bəl), *adj.* **1.** not desirable or attractive; objectionable. —*n.* **2.** an undesirable person or thing. —**un′de·sir′a·bil′i·ty, un′de·sir′a·ble·ness,** *n.* —**un′de·sir′a·bly,** *adv.*

un·de·vel·oped (un′di vel′əpt), *adj.* not developed.

un·dies (un′dēz), *n.pl.* women's or children's underwear.

un·di·gest·i·ble (un′di jes′tə bəl, -dī-), *adj.* INDIGESTIBLE.

un·di·rect·ed (un′di rek′tid, -dī-), *adj.* **1.** not directed or guided. **2.** bearing no address, as a letter.

un·dis·posed (un′di spōzd′), *adj.* **1.** not disposed of. **2.** not willing or inclined.

un·dis·tin·guished (un′di sting′gwisht), *adj.* **1.** having no distinguishing marks or features. **2.** without any claim to distinction. **3.** not separated or categorized.

un·do (un dŏŏ′), *v.t.,* **-did, -done, -do·ing. 1.** to reverse the doing of. **2.** to repair or erase: *to undo the damage.* **3.** to bring to ruin; destroy. **4.** to unfasten or unlatch. **5.** to untie. —**un·do′a·ble,** *adj.*

un·dock (un dok′), *v.t.* **1.** to uncouple (two spacecraft modules or a spacecraft and space station). —*v.i.* **2.** (of a spacecraft module or spacecraft) to uncouple.

un·do·ing (un dŏŏ′ing), *n.* **1.** the reversing of what has been done; annulling. **2.** the action of ruining or destroying. **3.** a cause of destruction or ruin. **4.** the act of unfastening or loosing.

un·done¹ (un dun′), *adj.* not done; not accomplished or completed.

un·done² (un dun′), *v.* **1.** pp. of UNDO. —*adj.* **2.** brought to destruction or ruin. **3.** unfastened.

un·doubt·ed (un dou′tid), *adj.* not doubted or disputed; accepted as true or authentic. —**un·doubt′ed·ly,** *adv.*

un·draw (un drô′), *v.,* **-drew, -drawn, -draw·ing.** —*v.t.* **1.** to draw open or aside. —*v.i.* **2.** to be drawn open or aside.

un·dress (un dres′), *v.t.* **1.** to take the clothes off (a person); disrobe. **2.** to remove the dressing from (a wound, sore, etc.). **3.** to strip or expose. —*v.i.* **4.** to take off one's clothes. —*n.* **5.** dress of a style designed to be worn on other than highly formal or ceremonial occasions; informal dress, as opposed to full dress. **6.** dress of a style not designed to be worn in public; negligee. **7.** the condition of being unclothed; nakedness. —*adj.* **8.** of or pertaining to clothing of a style less formal than full dress: *undress uniform.*

un·dressed (un drest′), *adj.* **1.** wearing few or no clothes. **2.** wearing informal clothing or clothing not meant to be worn in public. **3.** not dressed; not specially prepared: *undressed poultry.* **4.** (of leather) having a napped finish on the flesh side.

un·due (un dŏŏ′, -dyŏŏ′), *adj.* **1.** unwarranted; excessive. **2.** inappropriate; unjustifiable or improper: *undue influence.* **3.** not owed or currently payable.

un·du·lant (un′jə lənt, un′dyə-, -də-), *adj.* undulating; wavelike in motion or pattern. —**un′du·lance,** *n.*

un·du·late (*v.* un′jə lāt′, un′dyə-, -də-; *adj.* -lit, -lāt′), *v.,* **-lat·ed, -lat·ing,** *adj.* —*v.i.* **1.** to move with a wavelike motion, as with a smooth rising-and-falling or side-to-side movement. **2.** to have a wavy form or surface. **3.** (of a sound) to rise and fall in pitch: *a siren undulating in the distance.* —*v.t.* **4.** to cause to move in waves. **5.** to give a wavy form to. —*adj.* **6.** Also, **un′du·lat′ed.** having a wavelike form or surface; wavy. —**un′du·la′tor,** *n.*

un·du·la·tion (un′jə lā′shən, un′dyə-, -də-), *n.* **1.** the act of undulating; a wavelike motion. **2.** a wavy form or outline. **3.** a wavelike bend or curve. **4.** *Physics.* **a.** a wave. **b.** the motion of waves.

un·du·la·to·ry (un′jə lə tôr′ē, -tōr′ē, un′dyə-, -də-) also **un·du·la·tive** (-lā′tiv), *adj.* **1.** Also, **un′du·lar.** moving in undulations. **2.** resembling waves.

un·du·ly (un dŏŏ′lē, -dyŏŏ′-), *adv.* **1.** excessively. **2.** inappropriately or unjustifiably.

un·dy·ing (un dī′ing), *adj.* deathless; eternal: *undying fame; undying gratitude.* —**un·dy′ing·ly,** *adv.*

un·earned (un ûrnd′), *adj.* **1.** not received in exchange for labor or services. **2.** unmerited; undeserved: *unearned punishment.* **3.** not yet earned. **4.** (of income) derived from investments.

un·earth (un ûrth′), *v.t.* **1.** to dig out of the earth. **2.** to bring to light by search, inquiry, etc.; uncover.

un·earth·ly (un ûrth′lē), *adj.* **1.** seeming not to belong to this earth or world. **2.** supernatural; ghostly; weird: *an unearthly cry.* **3.** unreasonable or absurd. —**un·earth′li·ness,** *n.*

un·eas·y (un ē′zē), *adj.,* **-eas·i·er, -eas·i·est. 1.** not easy in body or mind; restless; perturbed. **2.** not easy in manner; awkward; constrained. **3.** not conducive to ease. **4.** insecure; uncertain or risky. —**un·ease′,** *n.* —**un·eas′i·ly,** *adv.* —**un·eas′i·ness,** *n.*

un·em·ploy·a·ble (un′em ploi′ə bəl), *adj.* **1.** unsuitable for employment; unable to find or keep a job. —*n.* **2.** an unemployable individual. —**un′em·ploy′a·bil′i·ty,** *n.*

un·em·ployed (un′em ploid′), *adj.* **1.** not employed; without a job. **2.** not currently in use. **3.** not productively used: *unemployed capital.* —*n.* **4. the unemployed,** unemployed persons collectively.

un·em·ploy·ment (un′em ploi′mənt), *n.* **1.** the state of being unemployed. **2.** the number of unemployed persons, usu. expressed as a percentage: *Unemployment went up two-tenths of a percent in April.* **3.** *Informal.* UNEMPLOYMENT BENEFIT.

unemploy′ment ben′efit, *n.* a usu. weekly payment of money to an unemployed worker under an unemployment insurance program. Also called **unemploy′ment compensa′tion.**

unemploy′ment insur′ance, *n.* a government program that provides a limited number of payments to eligible workers who are involuntarily unemployed.

un·e·qual (un ē′kwəl), *adj.* **1.** not equal; not of the same rank, ability, etc. **2.** not adequate, as in amount, power, or ability (usu. fol. by *to*). **3.** uneven or variable in character, quality, etc. —*n.* **4. unequals,** persons or things not equal to each other. —**un·e′qual·ly,** *adv.* —**un·e′qual·ness,** *n.*

un·e·qualed (un ē′kwəld), *adj.* not equaled or surpassed; matchless; peerless. Also, *esp. Brit.,* **un·e′qualled.**

un·e·quiv·o·cal (un′i kwiv′ə kəl), *adj.* **1.** having only one possible meaning or interpretation; unambiguous; clear. **2.** absolute; unqualified. —**un′e·quiv′o·cal·ly,** *adv.* —**un′e·quiv′o·cal·ness,** *n.*

un·err·ing (un ûr′ing, -er′-), *adj.* **1.** not erring; not going astray or missing the mark: *to chart an unerring course for home.* **2.** undeviatingly accurate; without error. **3.** invariably right or apt; infallible: *unerring good taste.* —**un·err′ing·ly,** *adv.*

UNESCO (yōō nes′kō), *n.* United Nations Educational, Scientific, and Cultural Organization.

un·e·ven (un ē′vən), *adj.* **1.** not level or flat; rough. **2.** not uniform; varying, as in quality. **3.** not equitable or fair; one-sided. **4.** not balanced; not symmetrical or parallel. **5.** (of a number) odd; not divisible into two equal integers: *The numerals 3, 5, and 7 are uneven.* —**un·e′ven·ly,** *adv.* —**un·e′ven·ness,** *n.*

un·e·vent·ful (un′i vent′fəl), *adj.* lacking in important or interesting occurrences; routine. —**un′e·vent′ful·ly,** *adv.*

un·ex·cep·tion·al (un′ik sep′shə nl), *adj.* **1.** not exceptional; not unusual or extraordinary. **2.** admitting of no exception to the general rule. —**un′ex·cep′tion·al·ly,** *adv.*

un·ex·pend·a·ble (un′ik spen′də bəl), *adj.* **1.** essential; absolutely required. **2.** not capable of being expended; inexhaustible.

un·fail·ing (un fā′ling), *adj.* **1.** fulfilling all expectations; completely dependable. **2.** endless: *unfailing good humor.* —**un·fail′ing·ly,** *adv.*

un·fair (un fâr′), *adj.* **1.** not fair; not conforming to standards of justice, honesty, or the like. **2.** beyond what is proper or fitting; disproportionate. —**un·fair′ly,** *adv.* —**un·fair′ness,** *n.*

un′fair prac′tice, *n.* any business practice involving the general public or competing parties that is prohibited by statute and regulated by an appropriate government agency.

un·faith·ful (un fāth′fəl), *adj.* **1.** not faithful; false to duty, obligation, or promises; disloyal. **2.** not sexually faithful to a spouse or lover. **3.** not accurate or reliable; inexact: *an unfaithful translation.* —**un·faith′ful·ly,** *adv.* —**un·faith′ful·ness,** *n.*

un·fa·mil·iar (un′fə mil′yər), *adj.* **1.** not familiar; not acquainted or conversant with: *to be unfamiliar with modern art.* **2.** unaccustomed; different, unusual, or novel: *an unfamiliar treat.* —**un′fa·mil·i·ar′i·ty** (-ē ar′i tē), *n.* —**un′fa·mil′iar·ly,** *adv.*

un·fas·ten (un fas′ən, -fä′sən), *v.t.* **1.** to release from or as if from fastenings; detach. **2.** to undo or open (something fastened). —*v.i.* **3.** to become unfastened.

un·fa·thered (un fā′thərd), *adj.* **1.** having no father; fatherless. **2.** of illegitimate or unknown paternity; bastard.

un·fa·vor·a·ble (un fā′vər ə bəl), *adj.* **1.** not favorable; adverse; disadvantageous: *an unfavorable wind.* **2.** not propitious: *unfavorable omens.* —**un·fa′vor·a·ble·ness,** *n.* —**un·fa′vor·a·bly,** *adv.*

un·feel·ing (un fē′ling), *adj.* **1.** having no feeling; insensible or insensate. **2.** unsympathetic; callous; hardhearted. —**un·feel′ing·ly,** *adv.* —**un·feel′ing·ness,** *n.*

un·feigned (un fānd′), *adj.* not feigned; sincere; genuine. —**un·feign′ed·ly,** *adv.*

un·fet·ter (un fet′ər), *v.t.* **1.** to release from fetters. **2.** to free from restraint; liberate.

un·fil·i·al (un fil′ē əl), *adj.* not fulfilling the customary obligation of a child to a parent. —**un·fil′i·al·ly,** *adv.*

un·fin·ished (un fin′isht), *adj.* **1.** not finished; incomplete or unaccomplished. **2.** lacking some special finish or surface treatment, as polish or paint. **3.** (of cloth) not sheared, dyed, etc., following the looming process. **4.** (of worsted) given a slight nap.

Unfin′ished Tow′er, The, a parable of Jesus. Luke 14:28–30.

un·fit (un fit′), *adj., v., -*fit·ted, -fit·ting. —*adj.* **1.** not adapted or suited; unsuitable or inappropriate: *an office unfit for more than two occupants.* **2.** incompetent or unqualified: *unfit parents.* **3.** not physically fit or well. **4.** *Biol.* not producing offspring in sufficient numbers to maintain a genetic contribution to succeeding generations. —*v.t.* **5.** to render unfit or unsuitable; disqualify. —**un·fit′ness,** *n.*

un·flap·pa·ble (un flap′ə bəl), *adj.* not easily upset or confused, esp. in a crisis; imperturbable. —**un·flap′pa·bil′i·ty,** *n.* —**un·flap′pa·bly,** *adv.*

un·fledged (un flejd′), *adj.* **1.** not fledged; without sufficient feathers for flight, as a young bird. **2.** immature; callow.

un·flinch·ing (un flin′ching), *adj.* not flinching; unshrinking; unfaltering. —**un·flinch′ing·ly,** *adv.*

un·fo·cused (un fō′kəst), *adj.* **1.** not brought into focus; lacking proper focus: *an unfocused camera.* **2.** lacking a clear purpose, direction, or target. Also, *esp. Brit.,* **un·fo′cussed.**

un·fold (un fōld′), *v.t.* **1.** to bring out of a folded state; spread or open out. **2.** to spread out or lay open to view. **3.** to reveal or display. **4.** to disclose in words, esp. by careful exposition; set forth; explain. —*v.i.* **5.** to become unfolded; open. **6.** to develop. **7.** to become clear, apparent, or known. —**un·fold′a·ble,** *adj.* —**un·fold′er,** *n.* —**un·fold′ment,** *n.*

un·for·get·ta·ble (un′fər get′ə bəl), *adj.* impossible to forget; indelibly impressed on the memory. —**un·for·get′ta·bly,** *adv.*

un·for·giv·ing (un′fər giv′ing), *adj.* **1.** not disposed or able to forgive; unrelenting; unyielding. **2.** not allowing for carelessness or weakness. —**un′for·giv′ing·ness,** *n.*

Un′forgiv′ing Serv′ant, The, a parable of Jesus. Matt. 18:21–35.

un·formed (un fôrmd′), *adj.* **1.** not definitely shaped; shapeless or formless. **2.** undeveloped; crude. **3.** not formed; not created.

un·for·tu·nate (un fôr′chə nit), *adj.* **1.** suffering from bad luck; hapless. **2.** unfavorable or inauspicious: *an unfortunate beginning.* **3.** regrettable or deplorable: *an unfortunate remark.* **4.** lamentable; sad. —*n.* **5.** an unfortunate person, esp. one who is poor or disabled. —**un·for′tu·nate·ly,** *adv.* —**un·for′tu·nate·ness,** *n.*

un·found·ed (un foun′did), *adj.* **1.** not based on fact or reality; without foundation; groundless. **2.** not established; not founded.

un·freeze (un frēz′), *v., -*froze, -fro·zen, -freez·ing. —*v.t.* **1.** to cause to thaw; melt. **2.** to remove or relax controls or restrictions on (funds, prices, rents, etc.). —*v.i.* **3.** to become unfrozen; thaw.

un·friend·ly (un frend′lē), *adj., -*li·er, -li·est, *adv.* —*adj.* **1.** not friendly or kind; unsympathetic; aloof. **2.** hostile; antagonistic. **3.** unfavorable; inhospitable, as an environment. —*adv.* **4.** in an unfriendly manner. —**un·friend′li·ness,** *n.*

un·frock (un frok′), *v.t.* to deprive of ecclesiastical rank, authority, and function; depose: *an unfrocked priest.*

un·fruit·ful (un frōōt′fəl), *adj.* **1.** not providing satisfaction; unprofitable; unrewarding: *an unfruitful search for gold.* **2.** not producing offspring; sterile. **3.** not bearing fruit or harvest; barren: *an unfruitful tree.* —**un·fruit′ful·ly,** *adv.* —**un·fruit′ful·ness,** *n.*

un·fund·ed (un fun′did), *adj.* **1.** not provided with a fund or money; not financed. **2.** FLOATING (def. 4b).

un·furl (un fûrl′), *v.t.* to spread or shake out from a furled state, as a sail or a flag; unfold. —*v.i.* **2.** to become unfurled. —**un·furl′a·ble,** *adj.*

---

un′de·scend′ed, *adj.*	un′dis·bursed′, *adj.*	un·doc′u·ment·ed, *adj.*	un′em·bel′lished, *adj.*
un′de·scribed′, *adj.*	un′dis·cern′ing, *adj.;* -ly, *adv.*	un′dog·mat′ic, *adj.*	un′em·bit′tered, *adj.*
un′de·served′, *adj.*	un′dis·charged′, *adj.*	un′do·mes′ti·cat·ed, *adj.*	un′em·broi′dered, *adj.*
un′de·serv′ing, *adj.;* -ly, *adv.;* -ness, *n.*	un′dis·ci′plined, *adj.*	un′doubt′ing, *adj.*	un·e′mo′tion·al, *adj.;* -ly, *adv.*
un′des·ig′nat·ed, *adj.*	un′dis·closed′, *adj.*	un·drained′, *adj.*	un′em′pha·sized′, *adj.*
un′de·sired′, *adj.*	un′dis·cour′aged, *adj.*	un′dra·mat′ic, *adj.*	un′em·phat′ic, *adj.*
un′de·tach′a·ble, *adj.*	un′dis·cov′ered, *adj.*	un·drape′, *v.t.,* -draped, -drap·ing.	un′em·pow′ered, *adj.*
un′de·tached′, *adj.*	un′dis·crim′i·nat′ing, *adj.;* -ly, *adv.*	un·dreamed′, *adj.*	un′en·closed′, *adj.*
un′de·tect′a·ble, *adj.;* -bly, *adv.*	un′dis·cussed′, *adj.*	un·dried′, *adj.*	un′en·cour′ag·ing, *adj.*
un′de·tect′ed, *adj.*	un′dis·guised′, *adj.*	un·drink′a·ble, *adj.*	un′en·cum′bered, *adj.*
un′de·tect′i·ble, *adj.*	un′dis·mayed′, *adj.*	un·du′pli·cat·ed, *adj.*	un·end′ed, *adj.*
un′de·ter′mined, *adj.*	un′dis·pelled′, *adj.*	un·du′ti·ful, *adj.;* -ly, *adv.*	un·end′ing, *adj.;* -ly, *adv.*
un′de·terred′, *adj.*	un′dis·played′, *adj.*	un′dy·nam′ic, *adj.*	un′en·dorsed′, *adj.*
un′de′vi·at′ing, *adj.;* -ly, *adv.*	un′dis·proved′, *adj.*	un·eat′en, *adj.*	un′en·dowed′, *adj.*
un·di′ag·nosed′, *adj.*	un′dis·put′a·ble, *adj.*	un′ec·o·log′i·cal, *adj.;* -ly, *adv.*	un′en·dur′a·ble, *adj.;* -ble·ness, *n.;* -bly, *adv.*
un′dif·fer·en′ti·at′ed, *adj.*	un′dis·put′ed, *adj.;* -ly, *adv.*	un·ed′i·ble, *adj.*	un′en·er·get′ic, *adj.*
un·di·gest′ed, *adj.*	un′dis·solved′, *adj.*	un·ed′i·fy′ing, *adj.*	un′en·force′a·ble, *adj.*
un·dig′ni·fied′, *adj.;* -ly, *adv.*	un′dis·tilled′, *adj.*	un·ed′it·ed, *adj.*	un′en·forced′, *adj.*
un·di·lut′ed, *adj.*	un′dis·tin′guish·a·ble, *adj.*	un·ed′u·cat·ed, *adj.*	un′en·gaged′, *adj.*
un′di·min′ished, *adj.*	un′dis·tort′ed, *adj.;* -ly, *adv.*	un′e·lect′a·ble, *adj.*	un-Eng′lish, *adj.*
un·dimmed′, *adj.*	un′dis·trib′ut·ed, *adj.*	un′e·lect′ed, *adj.*	un′en·joy′a·ble, *adj.;* -ble·ness, *n.;* -bly, *adv.*
un′dip·lo·mat′ic, *adj.*	un′dis·turbed′, *adj.*	un′e·lec′tri·fied′, *adj.*	
un′dip·lo·mat′i·cal·ly, *adv.*	un′di·ver′si·fied′, *adj.*	un′e·lic′it·ed, *adj.*	un′en·light′ened, *adj.*
	un′di·vid′ed, *adj.*	un′e·man′ci·pat′ed, *adj.*	un′en·riched′, *adj.*
	un′di·vulged′, *adj.*	un′em·bar′rassed, *adj.*	

un·gain·ly (un gān′lē), *adj.*, **-li·er, li·est,** *adv.* —*adj.* **1.** not graceful; awkward; unwieldy; clumsy. —*adv.* **2.** in an awkward manner. —**un·gain′li·ness,** *n.*

un·gen·er·ous (un jen′ər əs), *adj.* **1.** stingy; niggardly; miserly. **2.** uncharitable; petty: *ungenerous criticism.* —**un′gen·er·os′i·ty** (-ə ros′i tē), *n.* —**un·gen′er·ous·ly,** *adv.*

un·gird (un gûrd′), *v.t.*, **-gird·ed** or **-girt, -gird·ing. 1.** to loosen or remove a girdle or belt from. **2.** to loosen or remove by unfastening a belt: *to ungird a sword.*

un·glued (un glōod′), *adj.* **1.** separated or detached; not glued. —*Idiom.* **2. come unglued,** *Informal.* **a.** to lose emotional control. **b.** to disintegrate; fall apart: *Negotiations have come unglued.*

un·god·ly (un god′lē), *adj.*, **-li·er, -li·est. 1.** not accepting God or a particular religious doctrine; irreligious; atheistic. **2.** sinful; wicked; impious: *an ungodly life.* **3.** outrageous; shocking; dreadful: *an ungodly hour to drop in.* —**un·god′li·ness,** *n.*

un·gra·cious (un grā′shəs), *adj.* **1.** discourteous; ill-mannered. **2.** unpleasant; disagreeable; unrewarding: *an ungracious task.* —**un·gra′cious·ly,** *adv.* —**un·gra′cious·ness,** *n.*

un·gram·mat·i·cal (un′grə mat′i kəl), *adj.* not conforming to the rules or principles of grammar or accepted usage: *an ungrammatical sentence.* —**un′gram·mat′i·cal·ly,** *adv.*

un·grate·ful (un grāt′fəl), *adj.* **1.** unappreciative; not displaying gratitude; not giving due return or acknowledgment. **2.** unpleasant or unrewarding; distasteful; thankless: *an ungrateful task.* —**un·grate′ful·ly,** *adv.* —**un·grate′ful·ness,** *n.*

un·grudg·ing (un gruj′ing), *adj.* not begrudging; not reluctant or resentful; wholehearted. —**un·grudg′ing·ly,** *adv.*

un·guard·ed (un gär′did), *adj.* **1.** not guarded; unprotected; undefended. **2.** open; frank; guileless: *an unguarded manner.* **3.** not cautious or discreet; careless. —**un·guard′ed·ly,** *adv.* —**un·guard′ed·ness,** *n.*

un·guent (ung′gwənt), *n.* an ointment or salve, esp. when liquid or semiliquid. —**un′guen·tar′y,** *adj.*

un·gu·late (ung′gyə lit, -lāt′), *adj.* **1.** having hoofs. **2.** belonging or pertaining to the former order Ungulata, comprising all hoofed mammals, now divided into the odd-toed perissodactyls and the even-toed artiodactyls. **3.** hooflike. —*n.* **4.** a hoofed mammal.

Unh, *Chem. Symbol.* unnilhexium.

un·hand (un hand′), *v.t.* to take the hand or hands from; release from a grasp; let go.

un·hand·y (un han′dē), *adj.*, **-hand·i·er, -hand·i·est. 1.** not skillful in manual work; clumsy; inept. **2.** inconveniently placed or arranged. **3.** difficult to handle or use, as tools or objects. —**un·hand′i·ly,** *adv.* —**un·hand′i·ness,** *n.*

un·hap·py (un hap′ē), *adj.*, **-pi·er, -pi·est. 1.** sad; miserable; wretched. **2.** unfortunate; unlucky. **3.** unfavorable; inauspicious: *an unhappy omen.* **4.** infelicitous; unsuitable: *an unhappy choice of words.* —**un·hap′pi·ly,** *adv.* —**un·hap′pi·ness,** *n.*

un·har·ness (un här′nis), *v.t.* **1.** to detach the harness from (a horse, mule, etc.). **2.** to divest of armor, as a knight.

un·health·ful (un helth′fəl), *adj.* not conducive to good health; unwholesome. —**un·health′ful·ness,** *n.*

un·health·y (un hel′thē), *adj.*, **-health·i·er, -health·i·est. 1.** not in a state of good or normal health; unsound or abnormal; diseased: *unhealthy tissue.* **2.** symptomatic of or resulting from bad health. **3.** unhealthful: *unhealthy weather.* **4.** morally harmful; corrupt; debased: *unhealthy examples for the young.* **5.** dangerous; risky. —**un·health′i·ly,** *adv.* —**un·health′i·ness,** *n.*

un·heard (un hûrd′), *adj.* **1.** not heard; not perceived by the ear. **2.** not given a hearing or audience.

unheard′-of′, *adj.* **1.** unprecedented: *an unheard-of scientific advance.*

2. outrageous: *unheard-of extravagance.* **3.** not previously known: *the debut of an unheard-of singer.*

un·hes·i·tat·ing (un hez′i tā′ting), *adj.* **1.** without hesitation or uncertainty. **2.** unwavering; unfaltering; steady: *unhesitating loyalty.* —**un·hes′i·tat′ing·ly,** *adv.*

un·hinge (un hinj′), *v.t.*, **-hinged, -hing·ing. 1.** to remove from hinges: *to unhinge a door.* **2.** to open or separate by disengaging or releasing the hinges or hingelike parts: *to unhinge one's jaws.* **3.** to throw into confusion or turmoil; upset. —**un·hinge′ment,** *n.*

un·ho·ly (un hō′lē), *adj.*, **-li·er, -li·est. 1.** not holy; not sacred or hallowed. **2.** impious; sinful; wicked. **3.** dreadful; outrageous; ungodly: *neighbors making an unholy racket.* —**un·ho′li·ness,** *n.*

un·hook (un hŏŏk′), *v.t.* **1.** to unfasten or detach by or as if by undoing a hook or hooks: *to unhook railroad cars.* **2.** to detach from a hook. **3.** to rid of an undesirable attachment, habit, etc. —*v.i.* **4.** to become unhooked.

unhoped′-for′, *adj.* unexpected; unanticipated.

un·horse (un hôrs′), *v.t.*, **-horsed, -hors·ing. 1.** to cause to fall from a horse. **2.** to dislodge, as from office; unseat.

un·hur·ried (un hûr′ēd, -hur′-), *adj.* not hurried; leisurely; deliberate. —**un·hur′ried·ly,** *adv.* —**un·hur′ried·ness,** *n.*

uni-, a combining form occurring in loanwords from Latin (*universe*), used with the meaning "one" (*unicycle*).

U·ni·ate (yōō′nē it, -āt′) also **U·ni·at** (-at′), *n.* a member of an Eastern church that is in union with the Roman Catholic Church, acknowledges the Roman pope as supreme in matters of faith, but maintains its own liturgy, discipline, and rite. —**U′ni·at·ism,** *n.*

u·ni·cam·er·al (yōō′ni kam′ər əl), *adj.* (of a legislative body) consisting of a single chamber or house. —**u′ni·cam′er·al·ism,** *n.*

UNICEF (yōō′nə sef′), *n.* an agency of the United Nations (**United Nations Children's Fund**) concerned with the health and nutrition of mothers and children worldwide. [U(*nited*) N(*ations*) I(*nternational*) C(*hildren's*) E(*mergency*) F(*und*) (an earlier name)]

u·ni·cel·lu·lar (yōō′nə sel′yə lər), *adj.* having or consisting of a single cell. —**u′ni·cel′lu·lar′i·ty,** *n.*

u·ni·corn (yōō′ni kôrn′), *n.* a mythical creature resembling a horse, with a single horn in the center of its forehead: often symbolic of chastity or purity.

unicorn

u·ni·cy·cle (yōō′nə sī′kəl), *n., v.,* **-cled, -cling.** —*n.* **1.** a vehicle with one wheel, esp. a pedal-driven device kept upright and steered by body balance. —*v.i.* **2.** to ride a unicycle. —**u′ni·cy′clist,** *n.*

uniden′tified fly′ing ob′ject, *n.* See UFO.

u·ni·fi·ca·tion (yōō′nə fi kā′shən), *n.* **1.** the act or process of unifying; union. **2.** the state of being unified; consolidation.

U′nifica′tion Church′, *n.* an eclectic religious sect founded by the Rev. Sun Myung Moon in 1954.

u·ni·form (yōō′nə fôrm′), *adj.* **1.** identical or consistent, as from exam-

---

un·en·rolled′, *adj.*
un′en·thu′si·as′tic, *adj.*
un′en·thu′si·as′ti·cal·ly, *adv.*
un·en′vi·a·ble, *adj.; -bly, adv.*
un′e·quipped′, *adj.*
un′e·quiv′a·lent, *adj.; -ly, adv.*
un′es·cap′a·ble, *adj.; -bly, adv.*
un′es·cort′ed, *adj.*
un′es·tab′lished, *adj.*
un′es·thet′ic, *adj.*
un·eth′i·cal, *adj.; -ly, adv.*
un·e′val′u·at′ed, *adj.*
un·e′vap′o·rat′ed, *adj.*
un′ex·ag′ger·at′ed, *adj.*
un′ex·am′ined, *adj.*
un′ex·celled′, *adj.*
un′ex·cept′ing, *adj.*
un′ex·cep′tion·a·ble, *adj. -bly.; adv.*
un′ex·change′a·ble, *adj.; -ness, n.*
un′ex·cit′ed, *adj.*
un′ex·cit′ing, *adj.*
un′ex·cused′, *adj.*
un·ex′e·cut′ed, *adj.*
un′ex·hib′it·ed, *adj.*
un′ex·pand′ed, *adj.*

un′ex·pend′ed, *adj.*
un′ex·pired′, *adj.*
un′ex·plained′, *adj.*
un′ex·plod′ed, *adj.*
un′ex·plored′, *adj.*
un′ex·posed′, *adj.*
un′ex·pressed′, *adj.*
un·ex′pur·gat′ed, *adj.*
un′ex·tend′ed, *adj.; -ly, adv.*
un′ex·tin′guished, *adj.*
un·fad′ed, *adj.*
un·fal′ter·ing, *adj.; -ly, adv.*
un·fash′ion·a·ble, *adj.; -bly, adv.*
un·fath′om·a·ble, *adj.; -ness, n.*
un·fath′omed, *adj.*
un·fa′vored, *adj.*
un·fazed′, *adj.*
un·fea′si·ble, *adj.; -bly, adv.*
un·feath′ered, *adj.*
un·fed′, *adj.*
un·fem′i·nine, *adj.; -ly, adv.*
un·fer·ment′ed, *adj.*
un·fer′ti·lized′, *adj.*
un·filled′, *adj.*
un·filmed′, *adj.*

un·fil′tered, *adj.*
un′fi·nanced′, *adj.*
un·fit′ting, *adj.; -ly, adv.*
unfix, *v.t.,* -fixed, -fixing.
un·flag′ging, *adj.; -ly, adv.*
un·flam′ma·ble, *adj.*
un·flat′ter·ing, *adj.; -ly, adv.*
un·fla′vored, *adj.*
un·flus′tered, *adj.*
un·forced′, *adj.*
un′fore·see′a·ble, *adj.;* -ble·ness, *n.; -bly, adv.*
un′fore·seen′, *adj.*
un·for·est′ed, *adj.*
un′for·giv′a·ble, *adj.; -bly, adv.*
un′for·giv′en, *adj.*
un′for·got′ten, *adj.*
un·for′mu·lat′ed, *adj.*
un′for·sak′en, *adj.*
un′forth·com′ing, *adj.*
un·for′ti·fied′, *adj.*
un·frag′ment·ed, *adj.*
un·framed′, *adj.*
un·fran′chised, *adj.*
un·fre′quent·ed, *adj.*

un′ful·filled′, *adj.*
un′ful·fill′ing, *adj.*
un·fun′ny, *adj.*
un·fur′nished, *adj.*
un·gen′tle·man·ly, *adj.*
un·glo′ri·fied′, *adj.*
un·gov′erned, *adj.*
un·grace′ful, *adj.; -ly, adv.;* -ness, *n.*
un·grad′ed, *adj.*
un·grasp′a·ble, *adj.*
un·grat′i·fy′ing, *adj.*
un·greased′, *adj.*
un·groomed′, *adj.*
un·ground′ed, *adj.*
un·grouped′, *adj.*
un·guid′ed, *adj.; -ly, adv.*
un·hal′lowed, *adj.*
un·ham′pered, *adj.*
un·harmed′, *adj.*
un·harm′ful, *adj.; -ly, adv.*
un′har·mo′ni·ous, *adj.; -ly, adv.*
un·har′ried, *adj.*
un·har′vest·ed, *adj.*
un·healed′, *adj.*

ple to example or place to place: *a uniform building code.* **2.** without variations in detail: *a uniform surface.* **3.** constant; unvarying: *uniform fairness.* —*n.* **4.** an identifying outfit or style of dress worn by the members of a given profession, organization, or rank. —*v.t.* **5.** to make uniform or standard. **6.** to clothe in or furnish with a uniform. —**u′ni•form′ly,** *adv.* —**u′ni•form′ness,** *n.*

u•ni•form•i•ty (yōō′nə fôr′mi tē), *n., pl.* **-ties. 1.** the state or quality of being uniform; overall sameness or regularity. **2.** something uniform.

u•ni•fy (yōō′nə fī′), *v.t., v.i.,* **-fied, -fy•ing.** to make or become a single unit; unite; merge. —**u′ni•fi′a•ble,** *adj.* —**u′ni•fi′er,** *n.*

u•ni•lat•er•al (yōō′nə lat′ər əl), *adj.* **1.** relating to, occurring on, or involving one side only. **2.** undertaken or done by or on behalf of one side, party, or faction only; not mutual: *unilateral disarmament.* **3.** *Law.* pertaining to a contract in which obligation rests on one party only. **4.** *Bot.* having all the parts disposed on one side of an axis, as an inflorescence. **5.** through forebears of one sex only, as through either the mother's or father's line. —**u′ni•lat′er•al•i•ty,** *n.* —**u′ni•lat′er•al•ly,** *adv.*

u•ni•lin•e•ar (yōō′nə lin′ē ər), *adj.* developing or evolving in a steady, consistent, and undeviating way.

un•im•peach•a•ble (un′im pē′chə bəl), *adj.* above suspicion; impossible to discredit; impeccable. —**un′im•peach′a•bil′i•ty, un′im•peach′a•ble•ness,** *n.* —**un′im•peach′a•bly,** *adv.*

un•im•proved (un′im prōōvd′), *adj.* **1.** not developed to full potential, as the mind. **2.** not showing improvement, as one's health. **3.** not used to advantage; neglected: *an unimproved opportunity.* **4.** not made more useful, productive, or attractive, as land by clearing or cultivation or animal species by selective breeding.

un•in•hib•it•ed (un′in hib′i tid), *adj.* **1.** not inhibited or restricted; unhampered. **2.** not restrained by or mindful of social convention or usage; free; candid or spontaneous. —**un′in•hib′it•ed•ly,** *adv.* —**un′in•hib′it•ed•ness,** *n.*

un•in•spired (un′in spī[r]d′), *adj.* not inspired; not creative or spirited: *an uninspired performance.*

un•in•tel•li•gent (un′in tel′i jənt), *adj.* **1.** deficient in intelligence; dull; stupid. **2.** not endowed with intelligence. —**un′in•tel′li•gence,** *n.* —**un′in•tel′li•gent•ly,** *adv.*

un•in•tel•li•gi•ble (un′in tel′i jə bəl), *adj.* not intelligible; not capable of being understood. —**un′in•tel′li•gi•bil′i•ty, un′in•tel′li•gi•ble•ness,** *n.* —**un′in•tel′li•gi•bly,** *adv.*

un•in•ten•tion•al (un′in ten′shə nl), *adj.* not intentional or deliberate; unplanned. —**un′in•ten′tion•al•ly,** *adv.*

un•in•ter•est•ed (un in′tər ə stid, -trə stid, -tə res′tid), *adj.* **1.** having or showing no feeling of interest; indifferent. **2.** not personally concerned in something. —**un•in′ter•est•ed•ly,** *adv.* —**un•in′ter•est•ed•ness,** *n.* —**Usage.** See DISINTERESTED.

un•ion (yōōn′yən), *n.* **1.** the act of uniting or the state of being united: *promoted the union between the two families.* **2.** something formed by uniting two or more things; combination. **3.** a number of persons, states, etc., joined or associated together for some common purpose. **4.** a uniting of states or nations into one political body, as that of England and Scotland in 1707. **5. the Union,** the United States, esp. during the Civil War. **6.** LABOR UNION. **7.** the act of uniting or an instance of being united in marriage. **8.** *Math.* **a.** Also called **join.** the set consisting of elements each of which is in at least one of two or more given sets. *Symbol:* ∪ **b.** the least upper bound of two elements in a lattice. **9.** any of various contrivances for connecting parts of machinery or the like.

un′ion card′, *n.* a card identifying one as a member of a particular labor union.

un•ion•ism (yōōn′yə niz′əm), *n.* **1.** the principle of union, esp. trade unionism. **2.** (*cap.*) loyalty to the federal union of the U.S., esp. during the Civil War. —**un′ion•ist,** *n., adj.* —**un′ion•is′tic,** *adj.*

un•ion•ize (yōōn′yə nīz′), *v.,* **-ized, -iz•ing.** —*v.t.* **1.** to organize (workers) into a labor union. —*v.i.* **2.** to join in or form a labor union. —**un′ion•i•za′tion,** *n.* —**un′ion•iz′er,** *n.*

Un′ion of So′viet So′cialist Repub′lics, *n.* a former federal union of 15 constituent republics, in E Europe and N Asia, comprising the larger part of the earlier Russian Empire: dissolved in December 1991. 286,717,000; 8,650,069 sq. mi. (22,402,200 sq. km). *Cap.:* Moscow. Also called **Soviet Union.** *Abbr.:* U.S.S.R., USSR

un′ion shop′, *n.* a shop, business, etc., in which membership in a union is made a condition of employment.

un′ion suit′, *n.* a close-fitting, knitted undergarment combining shirt and drawers in one piece and often having a drop seat.

u•nique (yōō nēk′), *adj.* **1.** existing as the only one or as the sole example; single; solitary in type or characteristics. **2.** having no like or equal; unparalleled; incomparable. **3.** limited in occurrence to a given class, situation, or area: *a species unique to Australia.* **4.** not typical; unusual: *She has a very unique ability to inspire people.* —*n.* **5.** the embodiment of unique characteristics; the only one of a given kind. —**u•nique′ly,** *adv.* —**u•nique′ness,** *n.*

u•ni•sex (yōō′nə seks′), *adj.* **1.** designed or suitable for both sexes; not distinguishing between male and female: *unisex clothes.* —*n.* **2.** the state or quality of being unisex. **3.** unisex styles or fashions.

u•ni•sex•u•al (yōō′nə sek′shōō əl), *adj.* **1.** of or pertaining to one sex only. **2.** having only male or female organs in one individual, as an animal or a flower. **3.** unisex.

u•ni•son (yōō′nə sən, -zən), *n.* **1.** coincidence in pitch of two or more musical tones, voices, etc. **2.** the performance of musical parts at the same pitch or at the octave. **3.** a sounding together in octaves, esp. of male and female voices or of higher and lower instruments of the same class. **4.** a state or process in which all members or elements behave in the same way at the same time. —*Idiom.* **5. in unison, a.** in perfect accord: *to march in unison; My feelings are in unison with yours.* **b.** at the same time; all at once: *students shouting answers in unison.* —**u•nis′o•nous** (-nis′ə nəs), **u•nis′o•nal, u•nis′o•nant,** *adj.*

u•nit (yōō′nit), *n.* **1.** a single entity; one person or thing. **2.** any group of things or persons regarded as an entity: *They formed a cohesive unit.* **3.** one of the individuals, parts, or elements into which a whole may be divided or analyzed. **4.** one of a number of things, organizations, etc., identical or equivalent in function or form: *a rental unit.* **5.** any specified amount of a quantity, as of length, volume, or time, by comparison with which any other quantity of the same kind is measured. **6.** the least positive integer; one. **7.** Also called **unit's place.** (in a mixed or whole number) the position of the first digit to the left of the decimal point. **8.** a machine, part, or system of machines having a specified purpose; apparatus: *a heating unit.* **9.** a quantity of educational instruction, usu. determined by the number of hours of classroom or laboratory work. **10.** a subdivision of an organized body of soldiers.

U•ni•tar•i•an (yōō′ni târ′ē ən), *n.* **1.** a member of a liberal religious denomination founded upon the doctrine that God is one being, and giving each congregation complete control over its affairs. Compare UNITARIAN UNIVERSALIST. **2.** (*l.c.*) a person who maintains that God is one being, rejecting the doctrine of the Trinity. **3.** (*l.c.*) an advocate of unity or centralization, as in government. —*adj.* **4.** of or pertaining to the Unitarians or their doctrines. **5.** (*l.c.*) unitary. [< New Latin *ūnitārius,* der. of Latin *ūnitās* UNITY] —**U′ni•tar′i•an•ism,** *n.*

Unitar′ian Univer′salist, *n.* **1.** a member of a liberal religious denomination (**Unitar′ian Univer′salist Associa′tion**) formed in 1961 by the merger of the Unitarians and the Universalists. —*adj.* **2.** of or pertaining to the Unitarian Universalists or their doctrines. —**Unitar′ian Univer′salism,** *n.*

---

un•heat′ed, *adj.*
un•heed′ed, *adj.;* -ly, *adv.*
un•heed′ful, *adj.;* -ly, *adv.;* -ness, *n.*
un•heed′ing, *adj.;* -ly, *adv.*
un•helped′, *adj.*
un•help′ful, *adj.;* -ly, *adv.*
un•her′ald•ed, *adj.*
un•he•ro′ic, *adj.;* -ness, *n.*
un•hes′i•tant, *adj.;* -ly, *adv.*
un•hin′dered, *adj.*
un•hired′, *adj.*
un•hitch′, *v.,* -hitched, -hitch•ing.
un•hon′ored, *adj.*
un•housed′, *adj.*
un•hy•gi•en′ic, *adj.*
un•hy′phen•at•ed, *adj.*
un′i•den′ti•fi′a•ble, *adj.;* -bly, *adv.*
un′i•den′ti•fied′, *adj.*
un′id•i•o•mat′ic, *adj.*
un′i•mag′i•na•ble, *adj.*
un′i•mag′i•na•tive, *adj.;* -ly, *adv.*
un′i•mag′ined, *adj.*
un′im•i•tat′ed, *adj.*
un′im•paired′, *adj.*
un′im•pas′sioned, *adj.*

un′im•ped′ed, *adj.*
un′im•por′tant, *adj.;* -ly, *adv.*
un′im•pos′ing, *adj.*
un′im•pressed′, *adj.*
un′im•pres′sion•a•ble, *adj.*
un′im•pres′sive, *adj.;* -ly, *adv.*
un′in•clined′, *adj.*
un′in•fect′ed, *adj.*
un′in•fest′ed, *adj.*
un′in•flat′ed, *adj.*
un′in•flect′ed, *adj.*
un′in•flu•en′tial, *adj.;* -ly, *adv.*
un′in•form′a•tive, *adj.;* -ly, *adv.*
un′in•formed′, *adj.*
un′in•hab′it•ed, *adj.*
un′in•i′ti•at′ed, *adj.*
un′in•jured, *adj.*
un•in•spir′ing, *adj.;* -ly, *adv.*
un′in•sur′a•ble, *adj.,n.*
un′in•sured′, *adj.*
un•in′ter•est•ing, *adj.;* -ly, *adv.*
un′in•ter•rupt′ed, *adj.;* -ly, *adv.;* -ness, *n.*
un′in•tim′i•dat′ed, *adj.*

un′in•tru′sive, *adj.;* -ly, *adv.*
un′in•ven′tive, *adj.;* -ly, *adv.*
un′in•vest′ed, *adj.*
un′in•vit′ed, *adj.*
un′in•vit′ing, *adj.;* -ly, *adv.*
un′in•volved′, *adj.*
un•i′roned, *adj.*
un•ir′ri•gat′ed, *adj.*
un•i′tem•ized′, *adj.*
un•jad′ed, *adj.*
un•jus′ti•fi′a•ble, *adj.;* -ble•ness, *n.;* -bly, *adv.*
un•jus′ti•fied′, *adj.*
un•kin′dled, *adj.*
un•knot′, *v.t.*
un•knowl′edge•a•ble, *adj.*
un•la′beled, *adj.*
un•lad′en, *adj.*
un•la•ment′ed, *adj.*
un•lash′, *v.t.,* -lashed, -lash•ing.
un•laun′dered, *adj.*
un•leased′, *adj.*
un•lev′ied, *adj.*
un•lib′er•at′ed, *adj.*
un•life′like′, *adj.*

un•light′ed, *adj.*
un•lik′a•ble, *adj.;* -ble•ness, *n.*
un•like′a•ble, *adj.;* -ble•ness, *n.*
un•liked′, *adj.*
un•lined′, *adj.*
un•lit′, *adj.*
un•lived′-in′, *adj.*
un•loose′, *v.t.,* -loosed, -loos•ing.
un•loos′en, *v.t.,* -ened, -en•ing.
un•lov′a•ble, *adj.;* -ble•ness, *n.;* -bly, *adv.*
un•loved′, *adj.*
un•lov′ing, *adj.*
un•mailed′, *adj.*
un•man′age•a•ble, *adj.;* -ble•ness, *n.;* -bly, *adv.*
un•mapped′, *adj.*
un•marked′, *adj.*
un•mar′ket•a•ble, *adj.*
un•mar′ried, *adj., n.*
un•mas′cu•line, *adj.;* -ly, *adv.*
un•masked′, *adj.*
un•matched′, *adj.*
un•men′tioned, *adj.*
un•mer′it•ed, *adj.;* -ly, *adv.*

u·ni·tar·y (yōō′ni ter′ē), *adj.* **1.** of or pertaining to a unit or units. **2.** of the nature of a unit; indivisible; whole. —**u′ni·tar′i·ly** (-târ′-), *adv.*

u′nit cell′, *n.* the simplest unit of a regular crystal lattice.

u·nite (yōō nīt′), *v.*, **u·nit·ed, u·nit·ing.** —*v.t.* **1.** to join, combine, or incorporate so as to form a single whole or unit. **2.** to cause to adhere. **3.** to cause to be in a state of mutual sympathy, or to have a common opinion or attitude. **4.** to have or exhibit in combination, as qualities. —*v.i.* **5.** to become or form a single whole. **6.** to be or act in agreement; have a common goal, attitude, etc. **7.** to be joined by or as if by adhesion. —**u·nit′a·ble, u·nite′a·ble,** *adj.* —**u·nit′er,** *n.*

u·nit·ed (yōō nī′tid), *adj.* **1.** made into or caused to act as a single entity. **2.** formed or produced by the uniting of persons or things: *a united effort.* **3.** agreed; in harmony. —*Saying.* **4. United we stand, divided we fall,** cooperation is essential to the success of an endeavor: from *The Liberty Song* (1768) by John Dickinson, a member of the First Continental Congress. —**u·nit′ed·ly,** *adv.*

Unit′ed Ar′ab Em′irates, *n.* (*used with a sing. or pl. v.*) an independent federation in E Arabia, formed in 1971, now comprising seven emirates on the S coast of the Persian Gulf, formerly under British protection. 2,262,309; ab. 32,300 sq. mi. (83,657 sq. km). *Cap.:* Abu Dhabi. *Abbr.:* U.A.E. Formerly, **Trucial Coast, Trucial Oman, Trucial States.**

Unit′ed Breth′ren, *n.* a Protestant denomination, of Wesleyan beliefs and practices, founded in 1800.

Unit′ed Church′ of Can′ada, *n.* a Christian denomination founded in 1924–25 by members of the Presbyterian, Methodist, and Congregationalist churches, now the largest Protestant group in Canada.

Unit′ed Church′ of Christ′, *n.* an American Protestant denomination formed in 1957 as the result of a union of the Congregational-Christian Church with the Evangelical and Reformed Church.

unit′ed front′, *n.* a coalition formed to oppose a force that threatens the interests of all the members.

Unit′ed King′dom, *n.* a kingdom in NW Europe, consisting of Great Britain and Northern Ireland: formerly comprising Great Britain and Ireland 1801–1922. 58,610,182; 94,242 sq. mi. (244,100 sq. km). *Cap.:* London. *Abbr.:* U.K. Official name, **Unit′ed King′dom of Great′ Brit′ain and North′ern Ire′land.**

Unit′ed Meth′odist Church′, *n.* **1.** the largest denomination of the Methodist church in the U.S., formed in 1939 from the merger of the Methodist Episcopal Church, the Methodist Episcopal Church, South, and the Methodist Protestant Church, with the addition in 1968 of the Evangelical United Brethren. **2.** a British Methodist church formed in 1907 by a union of three Methodist churches and united in 1932 with the Wesleyan Methodist Church and the Primitive Methodist Church to form the Methodist Church in Great Britain.

Unit′ed Na′tions, *n.* (*used with a sing. v.*) an international organization with headquarters in New York City, formed in 1945 to promote peace, security, and cooperation. *Abbr.:* UN, U.N. **2.** (*used with a pl. v.*) the nations that signed a joint declaration in 1942, pledging to employ full resources against the Axis powers.

Unit′ed Presbyte′rian, *n.* **1.** a member of the United Presbyterian Church of North America, founded in Pittsburgh in 1858 by a union of two Presbyterian groups. **2.** a member of the United Presbyterian

MEMBER NATIONS OF THE UNITED NATIONS

Afghanistan (1946)	Ghana (1957)	Oman (1971)
Albania (1955)	Greece*	Pakistan (1947)
Algeria (1962)	Grenada (1974)	Patau (1994)
Andorra (1993)	Guatemala*	Panama*
Angola (1976)	Guinea (1958)	Papua New Guinea (1975)
Antigua and Barbuda (1981)	Guinea-Bissau (1974)	Paraguay*
Argentina*	Guyana (1966)	Peru*
Armenia (1992)	Haiti*	Philippines*
Australia*	Honduras*	Poland*
Austria (1955)	Hungary (1955)	Portugal (1955)
Azerbaijan (1992)	Iceland (1946)	Qatar (1971)
Bahamas (1973)	India*	Republic of Korea (1991)
Bahrain (1971)	Indonesia (1950)	Rumania (1955)
Bangladesh (1974)	Iran*	Russian Federation*
Barbados (1966)	Iraq*	Rwanda (1962)
Belarus (1974)	Ireland (1955)	St. Kitts-Nevis (1983)
Belgium*	Israel (1949)	St. Lucia (1979)
Belize (1981)	Italy (1955)	St. Vincent and the Grenadines (1980)
Benin (1960)	Ivory Coast (1960)	Samoa (1976)
Bhutan (1971)	Jamaica (1962)	San Marino (1990)
Bolivia*	Japan (1956)	Sao Tome and Principe (1975)
Bosnia and Herzegovina (1992)	Jordan (1955)	Saudi Arabia*
Botswana (1966)	Kazakhstan (1992)	Senegal (1960)
Brazil *	Kenya (1963)	Seychelles (1976)
Brunei (1984)	Kirghizia (1992)	Sierra Leone (1961)
Bulgaria (1955)	Kuwait (1963)	Singapore (1965)
Burkina Faso (1960)	Laos (1955)	Slovakia (1993)
Burundi (1962)	Latvia (1991)	Slovenia (1992)
Cambodia (1955)	Lebanon*	Solomon Islands (1978)
Cameroon (1960)	Lesotho (1966)	Somalia (1960)
Canada*	Liberia*	South Africa*
Cape Verde (1975)	Libya (1955)	South Korea (1991)
Central African Republic (1960)	Liechtenstein (1990)	Spain (1955)
Chad (1960)	Lithuania (1991)	Sri Lanka (1955)
Chile*	Luxembourg*	Sudan (1956)
China*(1)	Macedonia (1993)	Suriname (1975)
Colombia*	Madagascar (1960)	Swaziland (1968)
Comoros (1975)	Malawi (1964)	Sweden (1946)
Congo (1960)	Malaysia (1957)	Syria*
Costa Rica*	Maldives (1965)	Tadzhikistan (1992)
Croatia (1992)	Mali (1960)	Tanzania (1961)
Cuba*	Malta (1964)	Thailand (1946)
Cyprus (1960)	Marshall Islands (1991)	Togo (1960)
Czech Republic (1993)	Mauritania (1961)	Trinidad and Tobago (1962)
Denmark*	Mauritius (1968)	Tunisia (1956)
Djibouti (1977)	Mexico*	Turkey*
Dominica (1978)	Micronesia (1991)	Turkmenistan (1992)
Dominican Republic*	Moldavia (1992)	Uganda (1962)
Ecuador*	Monaco (1993)	Ukraine*
Egypt*	Mongolia (1961)	United Arab Emirates (1971)
El Salvador*	Morocco (1956)	United Kingdom*
Equatorial Guinea (1968)	Mozambique (1975)	United States*
Eritrea (1993)	Myanmar (1948)	Uruguay (1945)
Estonia (1991)	Namibia (1990)	Uzbekistan (1992)
Ethiopia*	Nepal (1955)	Vanuatu (1981)
Fiji (1970)	Netherlands*	Venezuela*
Finland (1955)	New Zealand*	Vietnam (1977)
France*	Nicaragua*	Yemen (1947)
Gabon (1960)	Niger (1960)	Yugoslavia*
Gambia (1965)	Nigeria (1960)	Zaire (1960)
Georgia (1992)	North Korea (1991)	Zambia (1964)
Germany (1973)	Norway*	Zimbabwe (1980)

*Indicates charter member in 1945. (Year in parentheses shows date of admission.)
(1) The People's Republic of China replaced the Republic of China in 1971.

Church in the U.S.A., founded in Pittsburgh in 1958 by combining the United Presbyterian Church of North America with another Presbyterian body.

Unit′ed States′, *n.* a republic in the N Western Hemisphere comprising 48 conterminous states, the District of Columbia, and Alaska in North America, and Hawaii in the N Pacific. 267,954,767; conterminous United States, 3,022,387 sq. mi. (7,827,982 sq. km); with Alaska and Hawaii, 3,615,122 sq. mi. (9,363,166 sq. km). *Cap.:* Washington, D.C. *Abbr.:* U.S., US Also called **United States of America, America.**

Unit′ed States′ Air′ Force′, *n.* the permanent military air force of the U.S., established in 1947 as a separate service under the Department of Defense. *Abbr.:* USAF

Unit′ed States′ Air′ Force′ Acad′emy, *n.* an institution at Colorado Springs, Colorado, for the training of U.S. air force officers.

Unit′ed States′ Ar′my, *n.* the permanent military land force of the U.S., under the authority of the Department of Defense. *Abbr.:* USA

Unit′ed States′ Cus′toms Serv′ice, *n.* the division of the Department of the Treasury that collects customs and enforces laws dealing with smuggling.

Unit′ed States′ Employ′ment Serv′ice, *n.* the division of the Department of Labor that supervises and coordinates the activities of state employment agencies. *Abbr.:* USES

Unit′ed States′ Informa′tion A′gency, *n.* an independent agency, created in 1953 and known from 1978 to 1982 as the International Communication Agency, that administers the government's overseas information and cultural programs. *Abbr.:* USIA

Unit′ed States′ Interna′tional Devel′opment Coopera′tion A′gency, *n.* an independent agency, created in 1979, that administers government programs for economic relations with developing countries.

Unit′ed States′ Interna′tional Trade′ Commis′sion, *n.* a federal agency, created in 1916, that conducts research, makes reports, and resolves problems in international trade and tariffs.

Unit′ed States′ Marine′ Corps′, *n.* MARINE CORPS. *Abbr.:* USMC

Unit′ed States′ Mil′itary Acad′emy, *n.* an institution in SE New York for the training of U.S. army officers; West Point. *Abbr.:* USMA

Unit′ed States′ Na′val Acad′emy, *n.* an institution at Annapolis, Maryland, for the training of U.S. naval officers. *Abbr.:* USNA

Unit′ed States′ Na′vy, *n.* the permanent naval force of the U.S., under the authority of the Department of Defense. *Abbr.:* USN

Unit′ed States′ of Amer′ica, *n.* UNITED STATES. *Abbr.:* U.S.A., USA

Unit′ed States′ Post′al Serv′ice, *n.* an independent federal agency created in 1971 by the Postal Reorganization Act to replace the Post Office Department as the division of the federal government responsible for postal services. *Abbr.:* USPS

Unit′ed Way′, *n.* **1.** a nationwide civic organization **(Unit′ed Way′ of Amer′ica)** or any of its affiliated local groups that raise funds through individual contributions and allocate them to benefit civic and charitable programs and organizations, as the YMCA and Red Cross. **2.** a·similar and related organization **(Unit′ed Way′ of Can′ada)** in Canada.

u·nit·ize (yōō′ni tīz′), *v.t.,* **-ized, -iz·ing. 1.** to form or combine into one unit, as by welding parts together. **2.** to divide or separate into units. —**u′nit·i·za′tion,** *n.* —**u′nit·iz′er,** *n.*

u′nit trust′, *n.* **1.** an investment company having a fixed portfolio of securities that are held to maturity, each investor sharing in the profits proportionately. **2.** a type of mutual fund in which an investor must invest a specified amount of money each month or quarter.

u·ni·ty (yōō′ni tē), *n., pl.* **-ties. 1.** the state of being one; oneness. **2.** a whole or totality as combining all its parts into one. **3.** the state or fact of being united or combined into one, as of the parts of a whole; unification. **4.** absence of diversity; unvaried or uniform character. **5.** oneness of mind, feeling, etc., as among a number of persons; concord, harmony, or agreement. **6.** *Math.* the number one; a quantity regarded as one. **7.** (in literature and art) harmony among the parts or elements of a work producing a single major effect. —*Proverb.* **8. In unity there is strength,** a group can accomplish more than individuals working separately.

u·ni·va·lent (yōō′nə vā′lənt, yōō niv′ə-), *adj.* **1.** having a chemical valence of one; monovalent. **2.** *Biol.* **a.** having one binding site, as an antibody. **b.** unpaired, as a chromosome.

u·ni·valve (yōō′nə valv′), *adj.* Also, **u′ni·valved′, u·ni·val·vu·lar** (yōō′nə val′vyə lər). **1.** having a single shell, as a gastropod mollusk. **2.** (of a mollusk shell) composed of a single valve or piece. —*n.* **3.** a univalve mollusk or its shell.

u·ni·ver·sal (yōō′nə vûr′səl), *adj.* **1.** of, pertaining to, or characteristic of all or the whole. **2.** applicable everywhere or in all cases: *a universal cure.* **3.** affecting, concerning, or involving all: *universal military service.* **4.** used or understood by all: *a universal language.* **5.** present or existing everywhere. **6.** versed in or embracing many or all skills, branches of learning, etc. **7.** of or pertaining to the universe, all nature, or all existing things. **8.** *Logic.* (of a proposition) asserted of every member of a class. **9.** noting any of various machines, tools, or devices widely adaptable in position, range of use, etc. —*n.* **10.** a cultural pattern or trait found in every known society or common to all members of a particular culture. **11.** *Logic.* a universal proposition. **12.** *Philos.* **a.** a general term or concept or the generic nature that such a term signifies; a Platonic idea or Aristotelian form. **b.** an entity that remains unchanged in character in a series of changes or changing relations. **13.** UNIVERSAL JOINT. —**u′ni·ver′sal·ly,** *adv.*

u′niver′sal do′nor, *n.* a person with blood type O.

u·ni·ver·sal·ist (yōō′nə vûr′sə list), *n.* **1.** a person characterized by universalism, as in knowledge, interests, or activities. **2.** (*cap.*) a member of a liberal religious denomination advocating Universalism. Compare UNITARIAN UNIVERSALIST. —*adj.* **3.** (*cap.*) Also, **U′ni·ver′sal·is′tic.** of or pertaining to Universalism or Universalists.

u·ni·ver·sal·i·ty (yōō′nə vər sal′i tē), *n., pl.* **-ties. 1.** the character or state of being universal; existence or prevalence everywhere. **2.** relation, extension, or applicability to all. **3.** universal character or range of knowledge, interests, etc.

u′niver′sal joint′, *n. Mach.* a coupling between rotating shafts set at an angle to one another, allowing for rotation in three planes.

U′niver′sal Prod′uct Code′, *n.* a standardized bar code in widespread use in retail sales, as in ringing up purchases at supermarket checkout counters.

u·ni·verse (yōō′nə vûrs′), *n.* **1.** the totality of known or supposed objects and phenomena throughout space; the cosmos; macrocosm. **2.** the whole world, esp. with reference to humanity. **3.** a world or sphere in which something exists or prevails. **4.** Also called **u′niverse of dis′course.** *Logic.* the aggregate of all the objects, attributes, and relations assumed or implied in a given discussion.

u·ni·ver·si·ty (yōō′nə vûr′si tē), *n., pl.* **-ties.** an institution of learning of the highest level, comprising a college of liberal arts, a program of graduate studies, and several professional schools, and authorized to confer both undergraduate and graduate degrees.

u·niv·o·cal (yōō niv′ə kəl, yōō′nə vō′-), *adj.* having only one meaning; unambiguous. —**u·niv′o·cal·ly,** *adv.*

un·just (un just′), *adj.* not just; lacking in justice or fairness. —**un·just′ly,** *adv.* —**un·just′ness,** *n.*

Un′just Stew′ard, The, a parable of Jesus. Luke 16:1–13.

un·kempt (un kempt′), *adj.* **1.** not combed: *unkempt hair.* **2.** uncared-for or neglected; disheveled; messy. **3.** unpolished; rough; crude. —**un·kempt′ly,** *adv.* —**un·kempt′ness,** *n.*

un·ken·nel (un ken′l), *v.t.,* **-neled, -nel·ing** or (*esp. Brit.*) **-nelled, -nel·ling. 1.** to drive (a fox or other animal) from a den or lair. **2.** to release from or as if from a kennel. **3.** to make known; disclose.

un·kind (un kīnd′), *adj.* lacking in kindness or mercy; severe. —**un·kind′ness,** *n.*

un·kind·ly (un kīnd′lē), *adj.,* **-li·er, -li·est. 1.** not kindly; unkind; ill-natured; mean. **2.** inclement or bleak, as weather or climate. —*adv.* **3.** in an unkind manner. **4.** as being unkind: *to take a comment unkindly.* —**un·kind′li·ness,** *n.*

un·knit (un nit′), *v.,* **-knit·ted** or **-knit, -knit·ting.** —*v.t.* **1.** to untie, unfasten, or unravel; undo. **2.** to weaken, undo, or destroy. **3.** to smooth out (something wrinkled). —*v.i.* **4.** to become undone. —**un·knit′ta·ble,** *adj.*

un·know·a·ble (un nō′ə bəl), *adj.* **1.** not knowable; incapable of being known or understood. —*n.* **2.** something that is unknowable.

un·know·ing (un nō′ing), *adj.* ignorant or unaware. —**un·know′ing·ly,** *adv.*

un·known (un nōn′), *adj.* **1.** not known; not within the range of knowledge, experience, or understanding; strange; unfamiliar. **2.** not discovered, explored, identified, or ascertained. **3.** not widely known; not famous; obscure. —*n.* **4.** a person or thing that is unknown. **5.** a symbol representing an unknown quantity in algebra, analysis, etc., frequently x, y, or z.

Un′known Sol′dier, *n.* (*sometimes l.c.*) an unidentified soldier killed in battle and buried with honors, the tomb serving as a memorial to all the unidentified dead of a nation's armed forces.

un·lace (un lās′), *v.t.,* **-laced, -lac·ing. 1.** to loosen or undo the lacing or laces of (shoes, a corset, etc.). **2.** to loosen or remove the garments of (a person) by or as if by undoing laces.

un·law·ful (un lô′fəl), *adj.* **1.** not lawful; contrary to law; illegal. **2.** born out of wedlock; illegitimate. —**un·law′ful·ly,** *adv.* —**un·law′ful·ness,** *n.*

un·lay (un lā′), *v.t.,* **-laid, -lay·ing. 1.** to separate (a strand) from a rope. **2.** to untwist (a rope) in order to separate its strands.

un·lead·ed (un led′id), *adj.* **1.** (of gasoline) containing no tetraethyl-lead. **2.** not separated or spaced with leads, as lines of type. —*n.* **3.** an unleaded product, esp. gasoline.

un·learn (un lûrn′), *v.t.* **1.** to forget or lose knowledge of. **2.** to discard (ideas or behavior) as being false or harmful. —*v.i.* **3.** to lose or discard knowledge.

un·learn·ed (un lûr′nid *for 1, 2;* un lûrnd′ *for 3*), *adj.* **1.** uneducated; ignorant. **2.** not scholarly or erudite; not learned. **3.** not having been learned: *an unlearned lesson.*

un·leash (un lēsh′), *v.t.* to release from or as if from a leash or restraint; let loose.

un·leav·ened (un lev′ənd), *adj.* containing no leaven.

un·less (un les′, ən-), *conj.* **1.** except under the circumstances that: *We'll be there at nine, unless the train is late.* —*prep.* **2.** except; but; save: *Nothing will come of it, unless disaster.*

un·let·tered (un let′ərd), *adj.* **1.** uneducated; untutored; ignorant. **2.** illiterate. **3.** not marked with letters, as a tombstone.

un·li·censed (un lī′sənst), *adj.* **1.** having no license. **2.** done or undertaken without license or permission; unauthorized. **3.** unrestrained; unbridled.

un·like (un līk′), *adj.* **1.** different, dissimilar, or unequal; not alike: *They gave unlike accounts of the incident.* —*prep.* **2.** dissimilar to; different from: *She is unlike my sister in many ways.* **3.** not typical or characteristic of. —**un·like′ness,** *n.*

un·like·ly (un līk′lē), *adj.*, **-li·er, -li·est,** *adv.* —*adj.* **1.** not likely to be or occur; improbable; doubtful. **2.** holding little prospect of success; unpromising. —*adv.* **3.** in an unlikely way. —**un·like′li·hood′,** *n.* —**un·like′li·ness,** *n.*

un·lim·ber[1] (un lim′bər), *adj.* **1.** not limber; inflexible; stiff. —*v.i., v.t.* **2.** LIMBER[1].

un·lim·ber[2] (un lim′bər), *v.t.* **1.** to detach (a gun) from its limber or prime mover. **2.** to make ready for use or action. —*v.i.* **3.** to prepare for action.

un·lim·it·ed (un lim′i tid), *adj.* **1.** without limitations or restrictions. **2.** boundless; infinite; vast: *the unlimited skies.* **3.** without any qualification or exception; unconditional. —**un·lim′it·ed·ly,** *adv.*

un·link (un lingk′), *v.t.* **1.** to separate the links of (a chain, bracelet, etc.); unfasten. **2.** to detach or release as if by undoing a link or links: *to unlink hands.* —*v.i.* **3.** to become detached.

un·list·ed (un lis′tid), *adj.* **1.** not listed; not entered in a list or directory: *an unlisted phone number.* **2.** (of a security) not admitted to trading privileges on an exchange.

un·load (un lōd′), *v.t.* **1.** to take the load or cargo from. **2.** to remove or discharge (cargo, passengers, etc.). **3.** to remove the charge from (a firearm). **4.** to relieve of anything burdensome, oppressive, etc. **5.** to express freely, as feelings or grievances; pour out. **6.** to get rid of (goods, shares of stock, etc.) by sale in large quantities. —*v.i.* **7.** to unload something. —**un·load′er,** *n.*

un·lock (un lok′), *v.t.* **1.** to undo the lock of (a door, chest, etc.), esp. with a key. **2.** to open or release by or as if by undoing a lock. **3.** to lay open; disclose: *to unlock the secrets of one's heart.* —*v.i.* **4.** to become unlocked. —**un·lock′a·ble,** *adj.*

un·luck·y (un luk′ē), *adj.*, **i·er, i·est. 1.** (of a person) not lucky; lacking good fortune; ill-fated. **2.** (of an event or circumstance) inauspicious or characterized by misfortune; ominous. —**un·luck′i·ly,** *adv.* —**un·luck′i·ness,** *n.*

un·made (un mād′), *adj.* **1.** not made. **2.** UNMANNED (def. 2).

un·make (un māk′), *v.t.*, **-made, -mak·ing. 1.** to cause to be as if never made; reduce to the original elements or condition; undo; destroy. **2.** to depose from office or authority; demote in rank. **3.** to change the character of. **4.** to alter the opinion of (one's mind).

un·man (un man′), *v.t.*, **-manned, -man·ning. 1.** to deprive of courage or fortitude; break down the manly spirit of. **2.** to deprive of virility; emasculate; castrate.

un·man·ly (un man′lē), *adj.*, **-li·er, -li·est. 1.** not manly; not characteristic of or befitting a man. **2.** effeminate. —**un·man′li·ness,** *n.*

un·manned (un mand′), *adj.* **1.** without the physical presence of people in control: *an unmanned spacecraft.* **2.** (of a captured hawk) untrained for hunting with a master; unmade.

un·man·nered (un man′ərd), *adj.* **1.** lacking good manners; rude or ill-bred. **2.** without affectation or insincerity; ingenuous. —**un·man′nered·ly,** *adv.*

un·man·ner·ly (un man′ər lē), *adj.* **1.** not mannerly; impolite; discourteous. —*adv.* **2.** with bad manners; impolitely. —**un·man′ner·li·ness,** *n.*

un·mask (un mask′, -mäsk′), *v.t.* **1.** to strip a mask or disguise from. **2.** to reveal the true character of; disclose; expose. —*v.i.* **3.** to put off one's mask; appear in true nature. —**un·mask′er,** *n.*

un·mean·ing (un mē′ning), *adj.* **1.** not meaning anything; devoid of sense or significance, as words or actions; empty. **2.** expressionless or unintelligent, as the face. —**un·mean′ing·ly,** *adv.*

un·meas·ured (un mezh′ərd), *adj.* of undetermined or indefinitely great extent or amount; unlimited; measureless. —**un·meas′ur·a·ble,** *adj.* —**un·meas′ur·a·bly,** *adv.*

un·men·tion·a·ble (un men′shə nə bəl), *adj.* **1.** inappropriate, unfit, or improper to be mentioned; unspeakable. —*n.* **2.** something that is not to be mentioned. **3. unmentionables,** undergarments. —**un·men′tion·a·ble·ness,** *n.*

un·mer·ci·ful (un mûr′si fəl), *adj.* **1.** merciless; relentless; severe; cruel; pitiless. **2.** unsparingly great, extreme, or excessive: *to talk for an unmerciful length of time.* —**un·mer′ci·ful·ly,** *adv.* —**un·mer′ci·ful·ness,** *n.*

un·mind·ful (un mīnd′fəl), *adj.* not mindful; unaware; forgetful; neglectful. —**un·mind′ful·ly,** *adv.* —**un·mind′ful·ness,** *n.*

un·mis·tak·a·ble (un′mi stā′kə bəl), *adj.* not mistakable; clear; obvious. —**un′mis·tak′a·bly,** *adv.*

un·mit·i·gat·ed (un mit′i gā′tid), *adj.* **1.** not mitigated; not softened or lessened. **2.** unqualified or absolute: *an unmitigated bore.* —**un·mit′i·gat′ed·ly,** *adv.*

un·mixed or **un·mixt** (un mikst′), *adj.* not mixed; pure. —**un·mix′ed·ly,** *adv.*

un·mor·al (un môr′əl, -mor′-), *adj.* **1.** neither moral nor immoral; amoral. **2.** lacking or unaffected by moral sense or principles. —**un′mo·ral′i·ty** (-mə ral′i tē, -mô-), *n.* —**un·mor′al·ly,** *adv.*

un·mov·ing (un moo′ving), *adj.* **1.** not moving; still; motionless. **2.** not stirring the emotions.

un·mu·si·cal (un myoo′zi kəl), *adj.* **1.** not musical; deficient in melody, harmony, rhythm, or tone. **2.** not fond of or skilled in music. —**un·mu′si·cal·ly,** *adv.* —**un′mu·si·cal·ness,** *n.*

un·muz·zle (un muz′əl), *v.t.*, **-zled, zling. 1.** to remove a muzzle from (a dog, cat, etc.). **2.** to free from restraint, as speech.

un·named (un nāmd′), *adj.* **1.** without a name; nameless. **2.** not indicated or mentioned by name; unidentified.

un·nat·u·ral (un nach′ər əl, -nach′rəl), *adj.* **1.** contrary to the laws or course of nature. **2.** at variance with the character or nature of a person, animal, or plant. **3.** at variance with what is normal or to be expected. **4.** lacking human qualities or sympathies; monstrous; inhuman. **5.** not genuine or spontaneous; artificial or contrived: *a stiff, unnatural manner.* —**un·nat′u·ral·ly,** *adv.* —**un·nat′u·ral·ness,** *n.*

un·nec·es·sar·y (un nes′ə ser′ē), *adj.* not necessary; needless; unessential. —**un·nec′es·sar·i·ly** (-nes′ə sâr′ə lē, -nes′ə ser′-), *adv.* —**un·nec′es·sar·i·ness,** *n.*

un·nerve (un nûrv′), *v.t.*, **-nerved, -nerv·ing.** to deprive of courage, strength, determination, or confidence; upset.

un·nil·hex·i·um (yoo′nil hek′sē əm), *n.* provisional name for the transuranic element with atomic number 106. *Symbol:* Unh

un·nil·pen·ti·um (yoo′nil pen′tē əm), *n.* provisional name for the transuranic element with atomic number 105. *Symbol:* Unp Also called **hahnium.**

un·nil·qua·di·um (yoo′nil kwod′ē əm), *n.* provisional name for the transuranic element with atomic number 104. *Symbol:* Unq Also called **rutherfordium.**

un·nil·sep·ti·um (yoo′nil sep′tē əm), *n.* provisional name for the transuranic element with atomic number 107. *Symbol:* Uns

un·num·bered (un num′bərd), *adj.* **1.** having or bearing no number or numbers. **2.** countless; innumerable. **3.** uncounted.

un·oc·cu·pied (un ok′yə pīd′), *adj.* **1.** without occupants; empty; vacant. **2.** not held or controlled by invading forces: *unoccupied nations.* **3.** not busy or active; idle; not employed.

un·or·gan·ized (un ôr′gə nīzd′), *adj.* **1.** not organized; without organic structure. **2.** not formed into a systematized whole; haphazard. **3.**

---

not thinking or acting methodically. **4.** not belonging to or represented by a labor union.

Unp, *Chem. Symbol.* unnilpentium.

un•pack (un pak′), *v.t.* **1.** to undo or remove the contents from (a box, trunk, etc.). **2.** to remove (something) from a container, suitcase, etc. **3.** to unburden, as the mind; reveal. **4.** to remove a pack or load from (a horse, vehicle, etc.). —*v.i.* **5.** to remove the contents of a container. —**un•pack′er,** *n.*

un•paged (un pājd′), *adj.* (of a publication) having unnumbered pages.

un•pal•at•a•ble (un pal′ə tə bəl), *adj.* **1.** not palatable; unpleasant to the taste. **2.** disagreeable; unacceptable: *unpalatable behavior.* —**un•pal′at•a•bil′i•ty,** *n.* —**un•pal′at•a•bly,** *adv.*

un•par•al•leled (un par′ə leld′), *adj.* not paralleled; unequaled or unmatched; peerless. Also, *esp. Brit.,* **un•par′al•lelled′.**

un•par•lia•men•ta•ry (un′pär lə men′tə rē, -trē), *adj.* not in accordance with parliamentary law or practice.

un•pile (un pīl′), *v.,* **-piled, -pil•ing.** —*v.t.* **1.** to disentangle or remove from a pile or a piled condition: *to unpile boxes.* —*v.i.* **2.** to become removed or separated from a pile or piled condition.

un•pin (un pin′), *v.t.,* **-pinned, -pin•ning. 1.** to remove pins from. **2.** to unfasten or loosen by or as if by removing a pin; detach.

un•pleas•ant (un plez′ənt), *adj.* not pleasant; displeasing; disagreeable; offensive. —**un•pleas′ant•ly,** *adv.*

un•pleas•ant•ness (un plez′ənt nis), *n.* **1.** the quality or state of being unpleasant. **2.** something that is displeasing or offensive, as an experience or situation.

un•plug (un plug′), *v.,* **-plugged, -plug•ging.** —*v.t.* **1.** to remove a plug or stopper from. **2.** to free of an obstruction; unclog. **3.** to disconnect (an appliance, a telephone, etc.) by removing a plug. **4.** to remove (an electric plug) from an outlet. —*v.i.* **5.** to become unplugged. —**un•plug′ga•ble,** *adj.*

un•plumbed (un plumd′), *adj.* **1.** not plumbed; not measured with a plumb line. **2.** not understood or explored in depth, as an idea or experience.

un•pop•u•lar (un pop′yə lər), *adj.* **1.** not popular; disliked, disapproved, or ignored by the public. **2.** in disfavor with a particular person or group. —**un′pop•u•lar′i•ty,** *n.* —**un•pop′u•lar•ly,** *adv.*

un•prac•ti•cal (un prak′ti kəl), *adj.* IMPRACTICAL. —**un′prac•ti•cal′i•ty, un•prac′ti•cal•ness,** *n.* —**un•prac′ti•cal•ly,** *adv.*

un•prac•ticed (un prak′tist), *adj.* **1.** not trained or skilled. **2.** not practiced; not usually or generally done.

un•prec•e•dent•ed (un pres′i den′tid), *adj.* never before known or experienced; unparalleled. —**un•prec′e•dent•ed•ly,** *adv.*

un•pre•dict•a•ble (un′pri dik′tə bəl), *adj.* **1.** not predictable; variable, uncertain, or erratic. —*n.* **2.** something that is unpredictable. —**un′pre•dict′a•bly,** *adv.*

un•prin•ci•pled (un prin′sə pəld), *adj.* **1.** lacking or not based on moral scruples or principles; dishonest. **2.** not instructed in the principles of something (usu. fol. by *in*). —**un•prin′ci•pled•ness,** *n.*

un•print•a•ble (un prin′tə bəl), *adj.* improper or unfit for print, esp. because of obscenity or offensiveness. —**un•print′a•ble•ness,** *n.* —**un•print′a•bly,** *adv.*

un•pro•fes•sion•al (un′prə fesh′ə nl), *adj.* **1.** not professional; not pertaining to or characteristic of a profession. **2.** at variance with professional standards or ethics: *unprofessional conduct.* **3.** not belonging to a profession; nonprofessional. **4.** not done with professional competence; amateurish. —*n.* **5.** a person who is not a professional; nonprofessional; amateur. —**un′pro•fes′sion•al•ly,** *adv.*

un•prof•it•a•ble (un prof′i tə bəl), *adj.* **1.** not showing or turning a profit. **2.** pointless or futile. —**un•prof′it•a•ble•ness, un•prof′it•a•bil′i•ty,** *n.* —**un•prof′it•a•bly,** *adv.*

un•prom•is•ing (un prom′ə sing), *adj.* unlikely to be favorable or successful. —**un•prom′is•ing•ly,** *adv.*

Unq, *Chem. Symbol.* unnilquadium.

un•qual•i•fied (un kwol′ə fīd′), *adj.* **1.** not qualified; not fit; lacking the necessary qualifications. **2.** not modified or limited; without reservations or restrictions: *unqualified praise.* **3.** absolute; complete; out-and-out: *an unqualified disaster.* —**un•qual′i•fi′a•ble,** *adj.* —**un•qual′i•fied′ly,** *adv.* —**un•qual′i•fied′ness,** *n.*

un•ques•tion•a•ble (un kwes′chə nə bəl), *adj.* **1.** not open to question; beyond doubt or dispute; certain. **2.** above criticism; unexceptionable: *a person of unquestionable principles.* —**un•ques′tion•a•ble•ness,** *n.* —**un•ques′tion•a•bly,** *adv.*

un•ques•tioned (un kwes′chənd), *adj.* **1.** not open to doubt or question; undisputed. **2.** investigated or interrogated.

un•qui•et (un kwī′it), *adj.* **1.** agitated; restless; disordered; turbulent: *unquiet times.* **2.** unsettled, as in one's thoughts or feelings; vexed or perturbed; uneasy. —*n.* **3.** a state of agitation, turbulence, disturbance, etc. —**un•qui′et•ly,** *adv.* —**un•qui′et•ness,** *n.*

un•rav•el (un rav′əl), *v.,* **-eled, -el•ing** or (*esp. Brit.*) **-elled, -el•ling.** —*v.t.* **1.** to separate or disentangle the threads of (a fabric, rope, etc.). **2.** to free from complications; make plain or clear; solve: *to unravel a mystery.* **3.** to take apart; undo; destroy (a plan, agreement, or arrangement). —*v.i.* **4.** to become unraveled. —**un•rav′el•er;** *esp. Brit.,* **un•rav′el•ler,** *n.* —**un•rav′el•ment,** *n.*

un•read (un red′), *adj.* **1.** not read, as a letter or newspaper. **2.** lacking in knowledge gained by reading. **3.** having little knowledge of a specific field.

un•read•a•ble (un rē′də bəl), *adj.* **1.** not readable; undecipherable; illegible. **2.** not interesting to read; dull; tedious. **3.** extraordinarily difficult to understand or interpret; obscure; incomprehensible. —**un•read′a•bly,** *adv.*

un•re•al (un rē′əl, -rēl′), *adj.* **1.** not real or actual. **2.** imaginary; fanciful; illusory; fantastic. **3.** not genuine; false; artificial.

un•re•al•i•ty (un′rē al′i tē), *n., pl.* **-ties. 1.** lack of reality; quality of being unreal. **2.** something that is unreal, invalid, imaginary, or illusory. **3.** incompetence or impracticality.

un•re•al•iz•a•ble (un rē′ə lī′zə bəl), *adj.* **1.** incapable of being made actual or real, as an ideal or ambition. **2.** incapable of being sensed or understood; unthinkable.

un•re•al•ized (un rē′ə līzd′), *adj.* **1.** not made real or actual; not resulting in accomplishment, as a task or aim: *unrealized ambitions.* **2.** not known or suspected: *unrealized talent.*

un•rea•son (un rē′zən), *n.* **1.** inability or unwillingness to think or act rationally, reasonably, or sensibly; irrationality. **2.** lack of reason or sanity; madness; confusion; disorder; chaos.

un•rea•son•a•ble (un rē′zə nə bəl, -rēz′nə-), *adj.* **1.** not reasonable or rational; not guided by reason or sound judgment; irrational. **2.** not in accordance with practical realities, as attitude or behavior; inappropriate. **3.** excessive, immoderate, or exorbitant; unconscionable: *unreasonable demands.* **4.** not having the faculty of reason. —**un•rea′son•a•ble•ness,** *n.* —**un•rea′son•a•bly,** *adv.*

un•rea•son•ing (un rē′zə ning), *adj.* not reasoning or exercising reason; thoughtless; irrational. —**un•rea′son•ing•ly,** *adv.*

un•re•flec•tive (un′ri flek′tiv), *adj.* not reflective; thoughtless; lacking in due deliberation; rash. —**un•re•flec′tive•ly,** *adv.*

un•re•gen•er•ate (un′ri jen′ər it), *adj.* Also, **un′re•gen′er•at′ed** (-ə rā′tid). **1.** not regenerate; unrepentant: *an unregenerate sinner.* **2.** unconvinced by or unconverted to a particular religion, sect, or movement. **3.** opposing new ideas, causes, etc.; obstinate; unyielding. **4.** wicked;

---

sinful; dissolute: *an unregenerate life.* —*n.* **5.** an unregenerate person. —**un′re·gen′er·ate·ly,** *adv.*

un·re·lent·ing (un′ri len′ting), *adj.* **1.** not relenting; not swerving in determination or resolution; inflexible. **2.** not easing or slackening, as in intensity, speed, or vigor: *unrelenting poverty; an unrelenting attack.* —**un′re·lent′ing·ly,** *adv.* —**un′re·lent′ing·ness,** *n.*

un·re·mit·ting (un′ri mit′ing), *adj.* not slackening or abating; incessant: *unremitting noise.* —**un′re·mit′ting·ly,** *adv.*

un·re·quit·ed (un′ri kwī′tid), *adj.* **1.** not returned or reciprocated: *unrequited love.* **2.** not avenged or retaliated: *an unrequited wrong.* **3.** not repaid or satisfied.

un·rest (un rest′), *n.* **1.** lack of rest; uneasiness. **2.** disturbance or turmoil; agitation: *political unrest.* —**un·rest′ing,** *adj.*

un·rig (un rig′), *v.t.,* **-rigged, -rig·ging. 1.** to strip of rigging, as a ship. **2.** to strip of equipment.

un·right·eous (un rī′chəs), *adj.* **1.** not righteous; sinful; evil. **2.** unfair or unjust: *an unrighteous law.* —**un·right′eous·ly,** *adv.*

un·ripe (un rīp′), *adj.* **1.** not ripe; immature; not fully developed: *unripe fruit.* **2.** too early; premature. —**un·ripe′ness,** *n.*

un·ri·valed (un rī′vəld), *adj.* having no rival or competitor; having no equal; incomparable; peerless. Also, *esp. Brit.,* **un·ri′valled.**

un·roll (un rōl′), *v.t.* **1.** to open or spread out (something rolled or coiled). **2.** to lay open; display; reveal. —*v.i.* **3.** to become unrolled or spread out. **4.** to become continuously visible or apparent: *The landscape unrolled before our eyes.*

un·ruf·fled (un ruf′əld), *adj.* **1.** calm; composed; unflustered. **2.** not ruffled, as a surface; smooth. —**un·ruf′fled·ness,** *n.*

un·ru·ly (un rōō′lē), *adj.,* **-li·er, -li·est.** not submissive or cooperative; ungovernable; unmanageable; disorderly. —**un·ru′li·ness,** *n.*

Uns, *Chem. Symbol.* unnilseptium.

un·sad·dle (un sad′l), *v.,* **-dled, -dling.** —*v.t.* **1.** to take the saddle from. **2.** to cause to fall or dismount from a saddle; unhorse. —*v.i.* **3.** to take the saddle from a horse.

un·said (un sed′), *adj.* not said; thought but not mentioned or discussed; unstated.

un·sat·is·fac·to·ry (un′sat is fak′tə rē), *adj.* not satisfactory; not satisfying or meeting one's demands; inadequate. —**un′sat·is·fac′to·ri·ly,** *adv.* —**un′sat·is·fac′to·ri·ness,** *n.*

un·sat·u·rat·ed (un sach′ə rā′tid), *adj.* **1.** not saturated; having the power to dissolve still more of a substance. **2.** (of an organic compound) having a double or triple bond and capable of forming new compounds by addition. —**un·sat′u·rate** (-ər it, -ə rāt′), *n.* —**un′sat·u·ra′tion,** *n.*

un·sa·vor·y (un sā′və rē), *adj.* **1.** not savory; tasteless or insipid: *an unsavory meal.* **2.** unpleasant in taste or smell; distasteful. **3.** unappealing or disagreeable, as a pursuit or task. **4.** socially or morally objectionable or offensive: *an unsavory past.* Also, *esp. Brit.,* **un·sa′vour·y.** —**un·sa′vor·i·ly,** *adv.* —**un·sa′vor·i·ness,** *n.*

un·scathed (un skāthd′), *adj.* not scathed; unharmed.

un·schooled (un skōōld′), *adj.* not schooled, taught, or trained. **2.** not acquired or artificial; natural: *an unschooled ability.*

un·sci·en·tif·ic (un′sī ən tif′ik), *adj.* **1.** not scientific; not employed in science. **2.** not conforming to the principles or methods of science. **3.** not demonstrating scientific knowledge or scientific methods. —**un′sci·en·tif′i·cal·ly,** *adv.*

un·scram·ble (un skram′bəl), *v.t.,* **-bled, -bling. 1.** to bring out of a scrambled condition; reduce to order or intelligibility. **2.** to make (a scrambled radio or telephonic message) comprehensible.

un·screw (un skrōō′), *v.t.* **1.** to draw or loosen a screw from (a hinge, bracket, etc.). **2.** to unfasten or withdraw by turning, as a screw or lid. **3.** to open (a jar, bottle, etc.) by turning the lid or cover. —*v.i.* **4.** to permit of being unscrewed.

un·script·ed (un skrip′tid), *adj.* **1.** not scripted; lacking or not made into a script: *an unscripted idea for a movie.* **2.** not coming from or as if from a script; unprepared or unplanned for.

un·scru·pu·lous (un skrōō′pyə ləs), *adj.* not scrupulous; not restrained by scruples; unprincipled: *unscrupulous business dealings.* —**un·scru′pu·lous·ly,** *adv.* —**un·scru′pu·lous·ness,** *n.*

un·seal (un sēl′), *v.t.* to break or remove the seal of; open. —**un·seal′a·ble,** *adj.*

un·search·a·ble (un sûr′chə bəl), *adj.* not lending itself to research or exploration; unfathomable; mysterious. —**un·search′a·ble·ness,** *n.* —**un·search′a·bly,** *adv.*

un·sea·son·a·ble (un sē′zə nə bəl), *adj.* **1.** not seasonable; being out of season: *unseasonable weather.* **2.** untimely; inopportune. —**un·sea′son·a·ble·ness,** *n.* —**un·sea′son·a·bly,** *adv.*

un·sea·son·al (un sē′zə nl), *adj.* not characteristic or typical of a particular season: *unseasonal April snows.*

un·sea·soned (un sē′zənd), *adj.* **1.** (of things) not matured, dried, etc., by due seasoning: *unseasoned wood.* **2.** (of persons) not inured to a climate, work, etc.; inexperienced: *an unseasoned crew.* **3.** (of food) not flavored with seasoning.

un·seat (un sēt′), *v.t.* **1.** to dislodge from a seat, esp. to throw from a saddle. **2.** to remove from political office by an elective process, by force, or by legal action.

un·seem·ly (un sēm′lē), *adj.,* **-li·er, -li·est,** *adv.* —*adj.* **1.** not seemly; not in keeping with accepted standards of taste or proper form. **2.** inappropriate for time or place: *an unseemly hour.* —*adv.* **3.** in an unseemly manner. —**un·seem′li·ness,** *n.*

un·seen (un sēn′), *adj.* **1.** not seen; unperceived; unobserved; invisible. **2.** read, interpreted, played, etc., without prior examination or rehearsal, as a text or musical score.

un·self·ish (un self′ish), *adj.* not selfish; disinterested; generous; altruistic. —**un·self′ish·ly,** *adv.* —**un·self′ish·ness,** *n.*

un·set (un set′), *adj.* **1.** not set; not solidified or made firm, as concrete or asphalt. **2.** (of a gemstone) not mounted in a setting.

un·set·tle (un set′l), *v.,* **-tled, -tling.** —*v.t.* **1.** to alter from a settled state; render unstable; disturb. **2.** to shake or weaken (beliefs, feelings, etc.); cause doubt or uncertainty about. **3.** to vex or agitate the mind or emotions of; upset. —*v.i.* **4.** to become unfixed or disordered. —**un·set′tle·ment,** *n.*

un·set·tled (un set′ld), *adj.* **1.** not settled; not fixed or stable; lacking order: *an unsettled situation.* **2.** continuously moving or changing; not situated in one place: *an unsettled life.* **3.** wavering or uncertain, as in opinions or behavior; unstable; erratic. **4.** not populated or settled: *an unsettled wilderness.* **5.** undetermined, as a point at issue; undecided; doubtful. **6.** not adjusted, closed, or disposed of, as an account, estate, or law case: *unsettled claims.* **7.** liable to change; inconstant; variable: *unsettled weather.*

un·shack·le (un shak′əl), *v.t.,* **-led, -ling.** to free from or as if from shackles; unfetter.

un·shaped (un shāpt′), *adj.* not shaped or definitely formed.

un·shap·en (un shā′pən), *adj.* **1.** not shaped or definitely formed; shapeless. **2.** not shapely; ill-formed. **3.** misshapen or deformed.

un·sight·ly (un sīt′lē), *adj.,* **-li·er, -li·est.** distasteful or unpleasant to look at; unattractive; ugly. —**un·sight′li·ness,** *n.*

un·skilled (un skild′), *adj.* **1.** of or pertaining to workers who lack technical training or skill. **2.** not demanding special training or skill: *unskilled jobs.* **3.** showing a lack of skill or competence: *an unskilled painting.* **4.** not skilled or expert.

un·skill·ful (un skil′fəl), *adj.* not skillful; clumsy or bungling; inept. Also, *esp. Brit.,* **un·skil′ful.** —**un·skill′ful·ly,** *adv.*

un·snap (un snap′), *v.t.,* **-snapped, -snap·ping.** to open or release by or as if by undoing a snap fastener.

un·snarl (un snärl′), *v.t.* to disentangle.

un·so·cia·ble (un sō′shə bəl), *adj.* **1.** not sociable; having or marked

---

un·stress′ful, *adj.*
un·stretch′a·ble, *adj.*
un·styl′ish, *adj.; -ly, adv.; -ness, n.*
un·sub·dued′, *adj.*
un·sub′si·dized′, *adj.*
un·sub·stan′ti·at·ed, *adj.*
un·suc·cess′ful, *adj.; -ly, adv.*
un·suit′a·ble, *adj.; -ble·ness, n.; -bly, adv.*
un·suit′ed, *adj.*
un·sul′lied, *adj.*
un·su′per·vised′, *adj.*
un′sup·port′ed, *adj.*
un·sure′, *adj.*
un·sur·mount′a·ble, *adj.*
un′sur·passed′, *adj.*
un′sur·prised′, *adj.*
un·sus·cep′ti·ble, *adj.*
un·sus·pect′ing, *adj.; -ly, adv.*
un·sus·tained′, *adj.*
un·sweet′ened, *adj.*
un·swerv′ing, *adj.*

un′sym·pa·thet′ic, *adj.*
un′syn·chro·nized′, *adj.*
un·sys·tem·at′ic, *adj.*
un·sys′tem·a·tized′, *adj.*
un·tact′ful, *adj.; -ly, adv.*
un·taint′ed, *adj.*
un·tal′ent·ed, *adj.*
un·tamed′, *adj.*
un·tapped′, *adj.*
un·tast′ed, *adj.*
un·tend′ed, *adj.*
un·test′ed, *adj.*
un·tex′tured, *adj.*
un·thank′ful, *adj.*
un·thought′ful, *adj.; -ly, adv.*
un·thread′, *v.t.*
un·threat′en·ing, *adj.*
un·timed′, *adj.*
un·tir′ing, *adj.; -ly, adv.*
un·torn′, *adj.*
un·touched′, *adj.*
un·trace′a·ble, *adj.*

un′tra·di′tion·al, *adj.; -ly, adv.*
un·trained′, *adj.*
un·tram′meled, *adj.*
un′trans·fer′a·ble, *adj.*
un′trans·formed′, *adj.*
un′trans·lat′ed, *adj.*
un·treat′ed, *adj.*
un·trimmed′, *adj.*
un·trou′bled, *adj.*
un·trust′ing, *adj.*
un·trust′wor′thy, *adj.*
un·turned′, *adj.*
un·twine′, *v.,* -twined, -twin·ing.
un·twist′, *v.*
un·typ′i·cal, *adj.; -ly, adv.*
un·us′a·ble, *adj.*
un·u′ti·lized′, *adj.*
un·ut′tered, *adj.*
un·van′quished, *adj.*
un·var′ied, *adj.*
un·var′y·ing, *adj.; -ly, adv.*
un·ven′ti·lat′ed, *adj.*

un·versed′, *adj.*
un·vi′a·ble, *adj.*
un·want′ed, *adj.*
un·warmed′, *adj.*
un·war′rant·a·ble, *adj.; -bly, adv.*
un·war′rant·ed, *adj.; -ly, adv.*
un·wa′ver·ing, *adj.; -ly, adv.*
un·waxed′, *adj.*
un·weaned′, *adj.*
un·wed′, *adj.*
un·weed′ed, *adj.*
un·wel′come, *adj.*
un·willed′, *adj.*
un·win′na·ble, *adj.*
un·wit′nessed, *adj.*
un·won′, *adj.*
un·word′ly, *adj.*
un·worn′, *adj.*
un·wor′ried, *adj.*
un·wound′ed, *adj.*
un·wo′ven, *adj.*
un·yield′ing, *adj.; -ly, adv.*

by a disinclination to friendly social relations. **2.** lacking or preventing social relationships. —**un·so′cia·bly,** *adv.*

un·so·phis·ti·cat·ed (un′sə fis′ti kā′tid), *adj.* **1.** not sophisticated; simple; artless; naive. **2.** without complexity or refinements. **3.** unadulterated; pure; genuine. —**un′so·phis′ti·cat′ed·ly,** *adv.*

un·sound (un sound′), *adj.* **1.** not sound; unhealthy or diseased, as the body or mind. **2.** decayed or impaired, as timber or foods; defective. **3.** not solid or firm, as foundations. **4.** not well-founded or valid; fallacious: *an unsound argument.* **5.** easily broken; light: *unsound slumber.* **6.** not financially strong or secure: *an unsound investment.* —**un·sound′ly,** *adv.* —**un·sound′ness,** *n.*

un·spar·ing (un spâr′ing), *adj.* **1.** not sparing; liberal or profuse. **2.** unmerciful; harsh; severe. —**un·spar′ing·ly,** *adv.*

un·speak·a·ble (un spē′kə bəl), *adj.* **1.** not speakable; not able or allowed to be spoken. **2.** exceeding the power of speech; not expressible; indescribable. **3.** inexpressibly bad or objectionable. —**un·speak′a·ble·ness,** *n.* —**un·speak′a·bly,** *adv.*

un·spo·ken (un spō′kən), *adj.* implied or understood without being spoken or uttered: *unspoken truths.*

un·sta·ble (un stā′bəl), *adj.* **1.** not stable; not firm or firmly fixed; unsteady. **2.** liable to change or fluctuate quickly: *an unstable weather pattern.* **3.** marked by emotional instability. **4.** inconstant; inconsistant; wavering. **5.** irregular in movement: *an unstable heartbeat.* **6.** noting chemical compounds that readily decompose or change into other compounds. —**un·sta′ble·ness,** *n.*

un·stead·y (un sted′ē), *adj., v.,* **-stead·ied, -stead·y·ing.** —*adj.* **1.** not steady or firm; unstable; shaky. **2.** fluctuating or wavering: *an unsteady flame.* **3.** irregular or uneven: *an unsteady development.* —*v.t.* **4.** to make unsteady. —**un·stead′i·ly,** *adv.*

un·stick (un stik′), *v.,* **-stuck, -stick·ing.** —*v.t.* **1.** to free, as one thing stuck to another. —*v.i.* **2.** to become unstuck.

un·stop (un stop′), *v.t.,* **-stopped, -stop·ping. 1.** to remove the stopper from. **2.** to free from any obstruction; open.

un·stop·pa·ble (un stop′ə bəl), *adj.* not able to be stopped or stemmed: *an unstoppable team.* —**un·stop′pa·bly,** *adv.*

un·stressed (un strest′), *adj.* **1.** without stress or emphasis, as a syllable in a word. **2.** not receiving or subjected to stress.

un·string (un string′), *v.t.,* **-strung, -string·ing. 1.** to loosen or remove the strings of: *to unstring a bow.* **2.** to take from a string: *to string beads.* **3.** to relax the tension of. **4.** to relax unduly or weaken (the nerves). **5.** to weaken the nerves of.

un·struc·tured (un struk′chərd), *adj.* lacking a clearly defined structure or organization: *unstructured classes.*

un·strung (un strung′), *v.* **1.** pt. and pp. of UNSTRING. —*adj.* **2.** weakened or nervously upset, as a person or a person's nerves; unnerved.

un·stuck (un stuk′), *v.* **1.** pt. and pp. of UNSTICK. —*adj.* **2.** out of order, control, or coherence; undone: *to come unstuck.*

un·stud·ied (un stud′ēd), *adj.* **1.** not studied; not premeditated or labored; natural; unaffected. **2.** not having studied; not possessing knowledge in a specific field; unversed.

un·sub·stan·tial (un′səb stan′shəl), *adj.* **1.** having no foundation in fact. **2.** without material substance. **3.** materially paltry. **4.** lacking strength or solidity; flimsy. —**un′sub·stan′tial·ly,** *adv.*

un·sung (un sung′), *adj.* **1.** not sung; not uttered or rendered by singing. **2.** not celebrated in song or verse; not praised or acclaimed: *unsung heroes.*

un·sus·pect·ed (un′sə spek′tid), *adj.* **1.** not regarded with suspicion. **2.** not imagined to exist. —**un′sus·pect′ed·ly,** *adv.*

un·tan·gle (un tang′gəl), *v.t.,* **-gled, -gling. 1.** to bring out of a tangled state; disentangle; unsnarl. **2.** to straighten out or clear up (something confused or perplexing).

un·taught (un tôt′), *v.* **1.** pt. and pp. of UNTEACH. —*adj.* **2.** not taught; natural. **3.** not instructed or educated; naive; ignorant.

un·teach (un tēch′), *v.t.,* **-taught, -teach·ing. 1.** to cause to be forgotten or disbelieved, as by contrary teaching. **2.** to cause to forget or disbelieve something previously taught.

un·ten·a·ble (un ten′ə bəl), *adj.* **1.** incapable of being defended, as an argument or thesis; indefensible. **2.** not fit to be occupied or lived in. —**un′ten·a·bil′i·ty, un·ten′a·ble·ness,** *n.*

un·think (un thingk′), *v.t.,* **-thought, -think·ing.** to dispel from the mind.

un·think·a·ble (un thing′kə bəl), *adj.* **1.** inconceivable; unimaginable. **2.** not to be considered; out of the question. —**un·think′a·bly,** *adv.*

un·think·ing (un thing′king), *adj.* **1.** thoughtless; heedless; inconsiderate. **2.** indicating lack of thought or reflection. **3.** not endowed with the faculty of thought. **4.** not exercising thought; not given to reflection. **5.** not thinking; unmindful. —**un·think′ing·ly,** *adv.*

un·thought (un thôt′), *v.* **1.** pt. and pp. of UNTHINK. —*adj.* **2.** not expected; not anticipated (often fol. by *of*).

un·ti·dy (un tī′dē), *adj.,* **-di·er, -di·est. 1.** not tidy or neat; slovenly; disordered: *an untidy room.* **2.** not well-organized or carried out: *an untidy plan.* —**un·ti′di·ly,** *adv.* —**un·ti′di·ness,** *n.*

un·tie (un tī′), *v.,* **-tied, -ty·ing.** —*v.t.* **1.** to loose or unfasten (anything tied); let or set loose by undoing a knot. **2.** to undo the string or cords of. **3.** to undo, as a cord or a knot. **4.** to free from restraint. **5.** to resolve, as perplexities. —*v.i.* **6.** to become untied.

un·til (un til′), *conj.* **1.** up to the time that or when; till. **2.** before (usu.

used in negative constructions): *I didn't remember it until the meeting was over.* —*prep.* **3.** onward to or till (a specified time or occurrence): *to work until 6 P.M.* —**Usage.** See TILL[1].

un·time·ly (un tīm′lē), *adj.,* **-li·er, -li·est,** *adv.* —*adj.* **1.** not timely; not occurring at a suitable time or season; ill-timed or inopportune. **2.** happening too soon or too early; premature. —*adv.* **3.** prematurely. **4.** unseasonably. —**un·time′li·ness,** *n.*

un·ti·tled (un tīt′ld), *adj.* **1.** without a title: *an untitled painting; an untitled nobleman.* **2.** having no right or claim.

un·to (un′tōō; *unstressed* -tə), *prep.* **1.** to (except to indicate the infinitive). **2.** until; till.

un·told (un tōld′), *adj.* **1.** not told; not related; not revealed. **2.** not numbered or enumerated; uncounted. **3.** inexpressible; incalculable: *untold suffering.*

Un′to the Hills′ Around′ Do′ I′ Lift′ Up′, a Christian hymn based on Psalm 121.

un·touch·a·ble (un tuch′ə bəl), *adj.* **1.** that may not be touched; not palpable; intangible. **2.** too distant to be touched. **3.** vile or loathsome to the touch. **4.** beyond criticism, control, or suspicion. —*n.* **5.** a member of a lower caste in India whose touch was formerly believed to defile a high-caste Hindu. **6.** a social outcast. **7.** a person or thing considered or beyond criticism.

un·to·ward (un tôrd′, -tōrd′), *adj.* **1.** unfavorable or unfortunate: *Untoward circumstances forced him into bankruptcy.* **2.** improper: *untoward social behavior.*

un·trav·eled (un trav′əld), *adj.* **1.** not having traveled, esp. to distant places. **2.** not traveled through or over; not frequented by travelers. Also, *esp. Brit.,* **un·trav′elled.**

un·tried (un trīd′), *adj.* **1.** not tried; not attempted, proved, or tested. **2.** not tried in a law court.

un·true (un trōō′), *adj.,* **-tru·er, -tru·est. 1.** not true to fact; incorrect or inaccurate; false. **2.** unfaithful; disloyal. **3.** not true to a standard.

un·truth (un trōōth′), *n., pl.* **-truths** (-trōōthz′, -trōōths′). **1.** the state or character of being untrue. **2.** want of veracity; divergence from truth. **3.** something untrue; a falsehood or lie.

un·truth·ful (un trōōth′fəl), *adj.* not truthful; lacking in veracity; false. —**un·truth′ful·ly,** *adv.* —**un·truth′ful·ness,** *n.*

un·tu·tored (un tōō′tərd, -tyōō′-), *adj.* **1.** not tutored; untaught. **2.** naive, ignorant, or unsophisticated.

un·used (un yōōzd′ *for 1, 2;* un yōōst′ *for 3*), *adj.* **1.** not used; not put to use: *an unused room.* **2.** never having been used. **3.** not accustomed: *unused to cold winters.*

un·u·su·al (un yōō′zhōō əl, -yōōzh′wəl), *adj.* not usual or ordinary; uncommon; exceptional. —**un·u′su·al·ly,** *adv.*

un·ut·ter·a·ble (un ut′ər ə bəl), *adj.* not communicable by utterance; unspeakable; beyond expression: *unutterable joy.*

un·var·nished (un vär′nisht), *adj.* **1.** straightforward; without vagueness or subterfuge; frank: *the unvarnished truth.* **2.** not coated with or as if with varnish.

un·veil (un vāl′), *v.t.* **1.** to remove a veil or other covering from. **2.** to reveal by or as if by removing a veil. —*v.i.* **3.** to become revealed by or as if by removing a veil.

un·veil·ing (un vā′ling), *n.* a ceremony in which a new statue, monument, tombstone, etc., is publicly or formally unveiled.

un·voiced (un voist′), *adj.* **1.** not voiced; not uttered: *unvoiced complaints.* **2.** VOICELESS (def. 4).

un·war·y (un wâr′ē), *adj.,* **-war·i·er, -war·i·est.** not wary; not cautious or watchful; as against danger or misfortune. —**un·war′i·ly,** *adv.* —**un·war′i·ness,** *n.*

un·washed (un wosht′, -wôsht′), *adj.* **1.** not cleaned or purified by or as if by washing. **2.** untutored, unsophisticated, or ignorant; plebeian. —*n.* **3. the (great) unwashed,** the masses; the rabble.

un·well (un wel′), *adj.* not well; ailing; ill.

un·whole·some (un hōl′səm), *adj.* **1.** not wholesome; unhealthful; deleterious to physical or mental health. **2.** unhealthy, esp. in appearance: *an unwholesome pallor.* **3.** morally harmful; depraved. —**un·whole′some·ly,** *adv.* —**un·whole′some·ness,** *n.*

un·wield·y (un wēl′dē), *adj.,* **-wield·i·er, -wield·i·est.** wielded with difficulty; not readily handled or managed in use or action, as from size, shape, or weight. —**un·wield′i·ness,** *n.*

un·will·ing (un wil′ing), *adj.* **1.** not willing; reluctant; loath; averse. **2.** opposed; offering resistance; stubborn or obstinate. —**un·will′ing·ly,** *adv.* —**un·will′ing·ness,** *n.*

un·wind (un wīnd′), *v.,* **-wound, -wind·ing.** —*v.t.* **1.** to undo or loosen from or as if from a coiled condition. **2.** to relieve of tension; relax. **3.** to disentangle or disengage; untwist. —*v.i.* **4.** to become unwound. **5.** to become relieved of tension; relax.

un·wise (un wīz′), *adj.,* **-wis·er, -wis·est.** not wise; foolish; imprudent; lacking in good sense or judgment. —**un·wise′ly,** *adv.*

unwished′-for′ or **unwished,** *adj.* undesired; unwelcome.

un·wit·ting (un wit′ing), *adj.* **1.** inadvertent; unintentional; accidental. **2.** not knowing; unaware. —**un·wit′ting·ly,** *adv.*

un·wont·ed (un wôn′tid, -wōn′-, -wun′-), *adj.* not customary, habitual, or usual; rare. —**un·wont′ed·ly,** *adv.*

un·wor·thy (un wûr′thē), *adj.,* **-thi·er, -thi·est,** *n., pl.* **-thies.** —*adj.* **1.** not worthy; lacking worth or excellence. **2.** beneath the dignity (usu. fol. by *of*): *behavior unworthy of a leader.* **3.** of a kind not worthy (often fol. by *of*). **4.** not of adequate merit or character. **5.** not commendable or creditable. **6.** not deserving. **—*n.*** **7.** an unworthy person. **—un•wor′thi•ly,** *adv.* **—un•wor′thi•ness,** *n.*

un•wound (un wound′), *v.* pt. and pp. of UNWIND.

un•wrap (un rap′), *v.*, **-wrapped, -wrap•ping.** **—*v.t.*** **1.** to remove or open the wrapping of. **2.** to open (something wrapped). **—*v.i.*** **3.** to become unwrapped.

un•writ•ten (un rit′n), *adj.* **1.** not actually formulated or expressed; customary; traditional. **2.** not written; not put in writing or print; oral: *an unwritten agreement.* **3.** containing no writing.

unwrit′ten law′, *n.* a law that derives its authority from custom, judicial decision, etc., rather than statute or decree.

un•zip (un zip′), *v.*, **-zipped, -zip•ping.** **—*v.t.*** **1.** to open or unfasten by or as if by means of a zipper. **2.** to open (a zipper). **—*v.i.*** **3.** to become unzipped.

up (up), *adv., prep., adj., n., v.,* **upped, up•ping.** **—*adv.*** **1.** to, toward, or in a more elevated position. **2.** to or in an erect position: *to stand up.* **3.** out of bed: *to get up.* **4.** above the horizon: *The moon came up.* **5.** to or at any point that is considered higher. **6.** to or at a source, origin, center, or the like. **7.** to or at a higher point or degree, as of rank, size, value, volume, or intensity: *Prices went up. Speak up!* **8.** to or at a point of equal advance, extent, etc.: *to catch up in a race.* **9.** in continuing contact, esp. as reflecting continuing awareness or knowledge: *to keep up with the news.* **10.** into or in activity, operation, etc.: *to set up shop* **11.** entirely: *to be used up.* **12.** to a halt: *The car pulled up.* **13.** (used with a verb for additional emphasis): *Go wake your brother up.* **14.** at bat in baseball. **15.** ahead; in a leading position in a competition. **16.** each; apiece: *The score was seven up.* **17.** *Naut.* toward the wind: *Put the helm up.* **—*prep.*** **18.** to, toward, or at a higher place on or in: *to go up the stairs.* **19.** to, toward, or at a higher station, condition, or rank on or in: *being well up the social ladder.* **20.** at or to a farther point or higher place on or in: *The store is up the street.* **21.** toward the source, origin, etc., of: *to float up a stream.* **22.** toward or in the interior of (a region, etc.). **23.** in a direction contrary to that of: *to row up the current.* **—*adj.*** **24.** moving in or related to a direction that is up or is regarded as up: *the up elevator.* **25.** informed; familiar; aware (usu. fol. by *on* or *in*): *I'm not up on current events.* **26.** concluded; ended: *Your time is up.* **27.** going on or happening: *What's up over there?* **28.** having a high position or station: *to be up in society.* **29.** in an erect, vertical, or raised position: *The tent is up.* **30.** above the ground: *The corn is up.* **31.** (of heavenly bodies) risen above the horizon. **32.** awake or out of bed. **33.** (of water in natural bodies) high with relation to the banks or shore. **34.** built; constructed. **35.** facing upward. **36.** SUNNYSIDE UP. **37.** in a state of agitation. **38.** cheerful or optimistic; exuberant; upbeat. **39.** afoot or amiss: *Her nervous manner told me that something was up.* **40.** higher than formerly in amount, degree, etc.: *The price of meat is up.* **41.** in a state of enthusiastic or confident readiness (usu. fol. by *for*). **42.** being or due to be prosecuted: *to be up for fraud.* **43.** ahead of an opponent in a competition: *He's two sets up.* **44.** considered or under consideration: *a candidate up for reelection.* **45.** wagered; bet. **46.** living or located inland or on elevated ground. **—*n.*** **47.** an upward movement; ascent. **48.** a time of good fortune, prosperity, etc.: *the ups and downs in a career.* **49.** *Informal.* a feeling or state of happiness or exuberance. **50.** an upward slope; elevation. **51.** an upward course or rise, as in price or value. **—*v.t.*** **52.** to put or take up. **53.** to make larger; step up: *to up output.* **54.** to raise; go better than (a preceding wager). **—*v.i.*** **55.** *Informal.* to start up; begin something abruptly (usu. fol. by *and* and another verb): *Then he upped and ran away from home.* **56.** (often used imperatively or hortatively) to stand or rise up: *Up, men, and fight!* **—*Idiom.*** **57. on the up and up,** worth believing; honest; trustworthy. **58. up against,** confronted with; faced with. **59. up and around** or **about,** recovered from an illness; able to leave one's bed. **60. up and doing,** busily engaged in activities. **61. up for grabs,** *Informal.* freely available to whoever can acquire it first. **62. up to, a.** as far as: *I am up to the eighth lesson.* **b.** in fulfillment of: *I couldn't live up to their expectations.* **c.** as many as; to the limit of: *up to five persons.* **d.** capable of; equal to: *Is he up to the job?* **e.** incumbent upon: *It's up to you to tell her.* **f.** engaged in; doing: *What have you been up to lately?*

up′-and-com′ing, *adj.* likely to succeed; bright and industrious: *an up-and-coming young executive.*

up′-and-down′, *adj.* **1.** moving alternately up and down. **2.** having an uneven surface. **3.** changeable: *up-and-down luck.* **4.** perpendicular or nearly so: *a straight up-and-down hillside.*

U•pan•i•shad (o͞o pan′i shad′, o͞o pä′ni shäd′), *n. Hinduism.* any of a class of speculative prose treatises composed between the 8th and 6th centuriesB.C.and first writtenA.D.c1300: they represent a philosophical development beyond the Vedas, having as their principal message the unity of Brahman and Atman. [< Skt *upaniṣad,* equiv. to *upa* near + *ni-* down + *-ṣad,* sandhi variant of *sad-* SIT[1]] **—U•pan′i•shad′ic,** *adj.*

up•beat (up′bēt′), *n.* **1.** an unaccented beat in music. **2.** the upward stroke with which a conductor indicates such a beat. **—*adj.*** **3.** optimistic; happy; cheerful.

up•braid (up brād′), *v.t.* **1.** to find fault with or reproach severely; censure. **2.** (of things) to bring reproach on; serve as a reproach to. **—up•braid′er,** *n.*

up•bring•ing (up′bring′ing), *n.* the care and training of children or a particular type of such care and training: *the proper upbringing of the young; He had a religious upbringing.*

UPC, Universal Product Code.

up•cast (up′kast′, -käst′), *n.* **1.** something that is cast or thrown up, as soil in digging. **—*adj.*** **2.** directed or thrown upward: *upcast eyes.*

up•chuck (up′chuk′), *v.i., v.t. Informal.* to vomit.

up•com•ing (up′kum′ing), *adj.* coming up; about to take place, appear, or be presented: *the upcoming spring fashions.*

up•coun•try (*adj., n.* up′kun′trē; *adv.* up kun′trē), *adj.* **1.** of, relating to, residing in, or situated in the interior of a region or country; inland. **—*n.*** **2.** the interior of a region or country. **—*adv.*** **3.** toward, into, or in the interior of a country.

up•date (up′dāt′; *v. also* up′dāt′), *v.*, **-dat•ed, -dat•ing,** *n.* **—*v.t.*** **1.** to bring up to date; incorporate new information in. **—*n.*** **2.** an act or instance of updating. **3.** new or current information used in updating. **4.** an updated version, account, or the like.

Up•dike (up′dīk′), *n.* **John,** born 1932, U.S. author.

up•draft (up′draft′, -dräft′), *n.* the movement upward of air or other gas.

up•end (up end′), *v.t.* **1.** to set on end, as a barrel or ship. **2.** to affect drastically or radically, as tastes, opinions, or reputations. **3.** to defeat in competition. **—*v.i.*** **4.** to become upended. **5.** to place the body back-end up, as a dabbling duck.

up•field (up′fēld′), *adv., adj. Football.* in or toward the part of the field nearest the goal line of the defensive team.

up′-front′, *adj.* Also, **up′front′.** **1.** invested or paid in advance or as beginning capital: *an up-front fee of five percent.* **2.** honest; candid; straightforward. **3.** conspicuous or prominent. **—*adv.*** Also, **up′ front′.** **4.** in advance; initially: *They asked for $1,000 up-front.*

up•grade (*n.* up′grād′; *adj., adv.* up′grād′; *v.* up grād′, up′grād′), *n., adj., adv., v.,* **-grad•ed, -grad•ing.** **—*n.*** **1.** an incline going up in the direction of movement. **2.** an increase, rise, or improvement: *Production is on the upgrade.* **—*adj.*** **3.** uphill; of, pertaining to, on, or along an upgrade. **—*adv.*** **4.** up a slope. **—*v.t.*** **5.** to raise in rank, position, importance, etc.: *upgraded to senior vice president.* **6.** to improve or enhance the quality or value of.

up•heav•al (up hē′vəl), *n.* **1.** strong or violent change or disturbance, as in a society. **2.** an act of upheaving, esp. of a part of the earth's crust. **3.** the state of being upheaved.

up•hill (*adv., adj.* up′hil′; *n.* up′hil′), *adv.* **1.** up or as if up the slope of a hill or other incline; upward: *The soldiers marched uphill.* **—*adj.*** **2.** going or tending upward on or as if on a hill: *an uphill road.* **3.** at a high place or point: *an uphill village.* **4.** laboriously fatiguing or difficult: *an uphill struggle.* **—*n.*** **5.** a rising terrain; ascent.

up•hold (up hōld′), *v.t.*, **-held, -hold•ing.** **1.** to support or defend, as against opposition or criticism: *to uphold the family's good name.* **2.** to keep up or keep from sinking; support. **3.** to lift upward; raise. **—up•hold′er,** *n.*

up•hol•ster (up hōl′stər, ə pōl′-), *v.t.* to provide (chairs, sofas, etc.) with coverings, cushions, stuffing, springs, etc.

up•hol•ster•er (up hōl′stər ər, ə pōl′-), *n.* a person whose business it is to upholster furniture.

up•hol•ster•y (up hōl′stə rē, -strē, ə pōl′-), *n., pl.* **-ster•ies.** **1.** the materials used to cushion and cover furniture. **2.** the business of an upholsterer.

up•keep (up′kēp′), *n.* **1.** the maintenance, repairs, etc., necessary for the proper functioning of a machine, building, household, etc. **2.** the cost of this: *Upkeep is one quarter of our budget.*

up•land (up′lənd, -land′), *n.* **1.** land elevated above other land. **2.** the higher ground of a region or district; an elevated region. **3.** land above the level where water flows or where flooding occurs. **—*adj.*** **4.** of or pertaining to uplands or elevated regions.

up•lift (*v.* up lift′; *n.* up′lift′), *v.t.* **1.** to lift up; raise; elevate. **2.** to improve socially, culturally, morally, or the like. **3.** to exalt emotionally or spiritually. **—*v.i.*** **4.** to become uplifted. **—*n.*** **5.** an act of lifting up or raising; elevation. **6.** the process or work of improving, as socially, intellectually, or morally. **7.** emotional or spiritual exaltation.

up•link (up′lingk′), *n.* a transmission path for data or other signals from an earth station to a communications satellite.

up•load (up′lōd′), *v.t.* to transfer (software or data) from a smaller to a larger computer.

up•man•ship (up′mən ship′), *n.* ONE-UPMANSHIP.

up•mar•ket (up′mär′kit), *adj.* appealing or catering to high-income consumers; upscale: *upmarket fashions.*

up•most (up′mōst′), *adj.* UPPERMOST.

up•on (ə pon′, ə pôn′), *prep.* **1.** up and on; upward so as to get or be on: *She climbed upon her horse.* **2.** in an elevated position on: *a flag upon the roof.* **3.** in or into complete or approximate contact with: *The enemy was upon us. The holidays will soon be upon us.* **4.** on the occasion of, at the time of, or immediately after: *She was joyful upon seeing her child take his first steps.*

up•per (up′ər), *adj.* **1.** higher, as in place, position, pitch, or in a scale: *the upper stories of a house; the upper register of a singer's voice.* **2.** superior, as in rank, dignity, or station. **3.** (of places) at a higher level, more northerly, or farther from the sea: *upper New York State.* **4.** (*often cap.*) denoting a later division of a geologic period, system, or the like: *the Upper Devonian.* **—*n.*** **5.** the part of a shoe or boot above the sole, comprising the quarter, vamp, counter, and lining. **6.** an upper berth. **7.**

Usu., **uppers. a.** an upper dental plate. **b.** an upper tooth. —*Idiom.* **8. on one's uppers,** *Informal.* poor; without means.

up′per at′mosphere, *n.* the portion of the atmosphere above the troposphere.

up′per case′, *n.* See under CASE² (def. 8).

up•per•case (up′ər kās′), *adj., v.,* **-cased, -cas•ing,** *n.* —*adj.* **1.** (of an alphabetical character) capital. **2.** pertaining to or belonging in the upper case. —*v.t.* **3.** to print or write with an uppercase letter or letters. —*n.* **4.** a capital letter. Compare LOWERCASE.

up′per cham′ber, *n.* UPPER HOUSE.

up′per class′, *n.* a class of people above the middle class, characterized by wealth and social prestige. —**up′per-class′,** *adj.*

up•per•class•man (up′ər klas′mən, -kläs′-), *n., pl.* **-men.** a junior or senior in a secondary school or college.

up′per crust′, *n. Informal.* the highest social class.

up•per•cut (up′ər kut′), *n., v.,* **-cut, -cut•ting.** —*n.* **1.** a swinging blow directed upward, as to an adversary's chin. —*v.t.* **2.** to strike (an opponent) with an uppercut. —*v.i.* **3.** to deliver an uppercut.

up′per hand′, *n.* the dominating or controlling position; advantage.

up′per house′, *n.* one of two branches of a legislature, generally smaller and less representative than the lower branch.

up•per•most (up′ər mōst′), *adj.* Also, **upmost. 1.** highest in place, order, rank, power, etc. **2.** topmost; predominant: *a subject of uppermost concern.* —*adv.* **3.** in or into the uppermost place, rank, or predominance.

Up′per Vol′ta, *n.* former name of BURKINA FASO. —**Up′per Vol′tan,** *adj., n.*

up•pi•ty (up′i tē) *adj. Informal.* inclined to be haughty, snobbish, or arrogant. —**up′pi•ty•ness,** *n.*

up•right (up′rīt′, up rīt′), *adj.* **1.** erect or vertical, as in position or posture. **2.** raised or directed vertically or upward. **3.** adhering to rectitude; righteous, honest, or just. **4.** being in accord with what is right. —*n.* **5.** the state of being upright or vertical. **6.** something standing erect or vertical, as a piece of timber. **7.** Usu., **uprights.** goalposts, as on a football field. **8.** an upright piano. —*adv.* **9.** in an upright position or direction. —*v.t.* **10.** to make upright. —**up′right′ly,** *adv.* —**up′right′ness,** *n.*

up′right pian′o, *n.* a piano with an upright rectangular body and with its strings running vertically.

up•rise (*v.* up rīz′; *n.* up′rīz′), *v.,* **-rose, -ris•en, -ris•ing,** *n.* —*v.i.* **1.** to rise up; get up. **2.** to rise into view. **3.** to rise in revolt. **4.** to come into existence or prominence. **5.** to move upward; ascend. **6.** to come above the horizon. **7.** to slope upward. **8.** to swell or grow, as a sound. —*n.* **9.** an act of rising up. —**up′ris•er,** *n.*

up•ris•ing (up′rī′zing, up rī′zing), *n.* **1.** an insurrection or revolt. **2.** an act of rising up. **3.** an ascent or acclivity.

up•riv•er (up′riv′ər), *adv., adj.* in the direction of or nearer the source of a river.

up•roar (up′rôr′, -rōr′), *n.* **1.** a state of violent and noisy disturbance, as of a multitude; turmoil. **2.** an instance of this.

up•roar•i•ous (up rôr′ē əs, -rōr′-), *adj.* **1.** characterized by or in a state of uproar; tumultuous. **2.** making an uproar; confused and noisy. **3.** very funny, as a person or situation. **4.** very loud, as sounds or utterances. **5.** expressed by or producing uproar. —**up•roar′i•ous•ly,** *adv.* —**up•roar′i•ous•ness,** *n.*

up•root (up rōōt′, -rŏŏt′), *v.t.* **1.** to pull out by or as if by the roots. **2.** to destroy or eradicate as if by pulling out roots. **3.** to displace or remove violently, as from a home, country, customs, or way of life. —*v.i.* **4.** to become uprooted.

ups′ and downs′, *n.pl.* rises and falls of fortune.

up•scale (up′skāl′), *adj.* of, for, or designating people at the upper end of a social or economic scale.

up•set (*v., adj.* up set′; *n.* up′set′), *v.,* **-set, -set•ting,** *n., adj.* —*v.t.* **1.** to overturn: *to upset a glass of milk.* **2.** to disturb mentally or emotionally; distress: *The accident upset her.* **3.** to disturb completely; throw into disorder: *to upset a plan.* **4.** to disturb physically: *The food upset his stomach.* **5.** to defeat (an opponent that is favored), as in politics or sports. —*v.i.* **6.** to become upset or overturned. —*n.* **7.** an upsetting or instance of being upset; overturn; overthrow. **8.** the unexpected defeat of an opponent that is favored. **9.** a nervous, irritable state of mind. **10.** a disturbance or disorder. —*adj.* **11.** overturned. **12.** disordered; disorganized. **13.** distressed; disturbed. —**up•set′ter,** *n.*

up•shift (up′shift′), *v.t.* to shift (an automotive transmission or vehicle) into a higher gear.

up•shot (up′shot′), *n.* **1.** the final outcome; conclusion; result: *The upshot of the disagreement was that they broke up the partnership.* **2.** the gist, as of an argument or thesis.

up•side (up′sīd′), *n.* **1.** the upper side or part. **2.** an upward trend, as in stock prices.

up′side down′, *adv.* **1.** with the upper part undermost. **2.** in or into complete disorder; topsy-turvy: *to turn the house upside down.* —**up′side-down′,** *adj.*

up′side-down′ cake′, *n.* a cake that is baked on a layer of fruit, then turned before serving so that the fruit is on top.

up•stage (up′stāj′), *adv., adj., v.,* **-staged, -stag•ing,** *n.* —*adv.* **1.** at or toward the back of the stage. —*adj.* **2.** of, pertaining to, or located at the back of the stage. **3.** haughtily aloof; supercilious. —*v.t.* **4. a.** to move upstage of (another actor), forcing him or her to act with back to

the audience. **b.** to draw attention away from (another actor) by some activity. **5.** to outdo professionally, socially, etc. **6.** to behave snobbishly toward. —*n.* **7.** the rear half of the stage. **8.** any stage position to the rear of another.

up•stairs (up′stârz′), *adv., adj., n., pl.* **-stairs.** —*adv.* **1.** up the stairs; to or on an upper floor. **2.** to or at a higher level of authority. **3.** *Mil. Slang.* to or at a higher level in the air. —*adj.* **4.** of, pertaining to, or situated on an upper floor: *an upstairs apartment.* —*n.* **5.** (*usu. with a sing. v.*) an upper story or stories; the part of a building or house that is above the ground floor. —*Idiom.* **6. kick upstairs,** to promote to a higher but less influential position.

up•stand•ing (up stan′ding), *adj.* **1.** upright; honorable; straightforward. **2.** standing erect; erect and tall.

up•start (*n., adj.* up′stärt′; *v.* up stärt′), *n.* **1.** a person who has risen suddenly from a humble position to wealth, power, or importance, esp. one who is presumptuous or arrogant; parvenu. —*adj.* **2.** being, resembling, or characteristic of an upstart. —*v.i.* **3.** to spring into existence or into view. **4.** to start up; spring up, as to one's feet. —*v.t.* **5.** to cause to start up.

up•state (up′stāt′), *n.* **1.** the part of a state that is farther north or farther from the chief city, esp. the northerly part of New York State. —*adj.* **2.** of or coming from such an area. —*adv.* **3.** in, to, or toward an upstate area. —**up′stat′er,** *n.*

up•stream (up′strēm′), *adv.* **1.** toward or in the higher part of a stream; against the current. —*adj.* **2.** directed or situated upstream. **3.** against or opposite to the direction of transcription, translation, or synthesis of a DNA, RNA, or protein molecule.

up•stroke (up′strōk′), *n.* **1.** an upward stroke, esp. of a pen or pencil, or of a piston in a vertical cylinder.

up•surge (*v.* up sûrj′; *n.* up′sûrj′), *v.,* **-surged, -surg•ing,** *n.* —*v.i.* **1.** to surge up; increase; rise. —*n.* **2.** the act of surging up; a large or rapid increase.

up•sweep (*v.* up swēp′; *n.* up′swēp′), *v.,* **-swept, -sweep•ing,** *n.* —*v.t., v.i.* **1.** to sweep upward. —*n.* **2.** a sweeping upward, as an increase in elevation or a rise in activity. **3.** an upswept hairdo.

up•swept (up′swept′), *adj.* **1.** curved or sloped upward: *upswept automobile fenders.* **2.** combed or brushed upward to the top of the head: *an upswept hairdo.*

up•swing (*n.* up′swing′; *v.* up swing′), *n., v.,* **-swung, -swing•ing.** —*n.* **1.** an upward swing or swinging movement, as of a pendulum. **2.** a marked increase or improvement: *an upswing in stock prices.* —*v.i.* **3.** to make or undergo an upswing.

up′sy-dai′sy (up′sē), *interj.* (used, as for reassurance, at the moment of lifting a baby up.)

up•take (up′tāk′), *n.* **1.** understanding or comprehension; mental grasp: *quick on the uptake.* **2.** an act or instance of taking up. **3.** a pipe or passage leading upward from below, as for conducting a current of air. **4.** the absorption of substances, as nutrients, by the tissues.

up′-tem′po, *n., pl.* **-pos.** a fast, bouncy tempo, esp. in jazz.

up•tight (up′tīt′), *adj. Informal.* **1.** tense, nervous, or jittery. **2.** stiffly conventional in manner or attitudes.

up•time (up′tīm′), *n.* the time during which a machine is operating or an employee is working.

up′-to-date′, *adj.* **1.** keeping up with the times, as in outlook, ideas, appearance, or style. **2.** in accordance with the latest or newest ideas, standards, techniques, styles, etc.; modern. **3.** extending to the present time; current; including the latest information or facts: *an up-to-date report.* —**up′-to-date′ness,** *n.*

up•town (*adv., n.* up′toun′; *adj.* -toun′), *adv.* **1.** to, toward, or in the upper part of a town or city, usu. the part away from the main business section. —*adj.* **2.** moving toward, situated in, or pertaining to the upper part of a town or city: *Take the uptown bus.* —*n.* **3.** the uptown section of a town or city.

up•turn (*v.* up tûrn′, up′tûrn′; *n.* up′tûrn′), *v.t.* **1.** to turn up or over. **2.** to direct or turn upward. —*v.i.* **3.** to turn up or upward. —*n.* **4.** an upward turn, as in prices or business.

up•ward (up′wərd), *adv.* Also, **up′wards. 1.** toward a higher place or position: *birds flying upward.* **2.** toward a higher or more distinguished condition, rank, level, etc. **3.** beyond; more: *30 years old and upward.* **4.** toward a large city, the source or origin of a stream, or the interior of a country or region. **5.** in the upper parts; above. —*adj.* **6.** moving or tending upward; directed at or situated in a higher place or position. —*Idiom.* **7. upward(s) of,** more than: *My vacation cost me upwards of a thousand dollars.* —**up′ward•ly,** *adv.*

up•wind (up′wind′), *adv.* **1.** toward or against the wind or the direction from which it is blowing. —*adj.* **2.** moving or situated toward or in the direction from which the wind is blowing.

Ur (ûr, ŏŏr), *n.* an ancient Sumerian city on the Euphrates, in what is now S Iraq.

ur-¹, var. of URO-¹: *uremia.*

ur-², (*sometimes cap.*) a combining form meaning "earliest, original," used in words denoting the primal stage of a historical or cultural entity or phenomenon: *ur-civilization; urtext.*

u•ra•cil (yŏŏr′ə sil), *n.* a pyrimidine base, $C_4H_4N_2O_2$, that is one of the fundamental components of RNA, in which it forms base pairs with adenine. *Symbol:* U

u•rae•us (yŏŏ rē′əs), *n., pl.* **-us•es.** a representation of the sacred asp upon the headdress of rulers in ancient Egypt, symbolizing supreme power.

U′ral Moun′tains, *n.pl.* a mountain range in the W Russian Federation, extending N and S from the Arctic Ocean to near the Caspian Sea, forming a natural boundary between Europe and Asia. Highest peak, 6214 ft. (1894 m). Also called **U′rals.**

u·ra·ni·um (yŏŏ rā′nē əm), *n.* a white, lustrous, radioactive, metallic element, isotopes of which are used in atomic and hydrogen bombs and as a fuel in nuclear reactors. *Symbol:* U; *at. wt.:* 238.03; *at. no.:* 92; *sp. gr.:* 19.07.

uranium 235, *n.* the radioactive uranium isotope having a mass number of 235 and that undergoes fission with a release of energy when bombarded with neutrons.

uranium 238, *n.* the radioactive uranium isotope having a mass number of 238, used chiefly in nuclear reactors as a source of the fissionable isotope plutonium 239.

U·ra·nus (yŏŏr′ə nəs, yŏŏ rā′-), *n.* **1.** the planet seventh in order from the sun, having an equatorial diameter of 32,600 miles (56,460 km), a mean distance from the sun of 1,784 million miles (2871 million km), a period of revolution of 84.07 years, and 15 known moons. **2.** (in Greek myth) a personification of the sky, engendered by Gaea, with whom Uranus mates to produce the Cyclopes and Titans. [< Greek *ouranós* sky]

ur·ban (ûr′bən), *adj.* **1.** of, pertaining to, or comprising a city or town. **2.** living in a city. **3.** characteristic of or accustomed to cities; citified. [< Latin *urbānus* < *urbs* city]

ur·bane (ûr bān′), *adj.* having polish and suavity in manner or style; sophisticated. —**ur·bane′ly,** *adv.* —**ur·bane′ness,** *n.*

ur·ban·ite (ûr′bə nīt′), *n.* a resident of a city or urban community.

ur·ban·i·ty (ûr ban′i tē), *n., pl.* **-ties. 1.** the quality of being urbane; refined courtesy or politeness; suavity. **2. urbanities,** civilities or amenities.

ur·ban·ol·o·gy (ûr′bə nol′ə jē), *n.* the study of urban problems, esp. as a social science. —**ur·ban·ol′o·gist,** *n.*

ur′ban plan′ning, *n.* CITY PLANNING. —**ur′ban plan′ner,** *n.*

ur′ban renew′al, *n.* the rehabilitation of substandard city areas by renovating buildings or demolishing and replacing them with new ones. Also called **ur′ban redevel′opment.**

ur·chin (ûr′chin), *n.* **1.** a mischievous boy. **2.** any small boy or youngster. **3.** SEA URCHIN. **4.** *Chiefly Brit. Dial.* HEDGEHOG.

Ur·du (ŏŏr′dŏŏ, ûr′-), *n.* a standardized form of Hindi, written in Arabic script, used by Muslims in India and Pakistan: the official language of Pakistan.

-ure, an abstract-noun suffix of action, result, and instrument, occurring in loanwords from French and Latin: *pressure; legislature.*

u·re·a (yŏŏ rē′ə, yŏŏr′ē ə), *n.* **1.** a compound, CO(NH₂)₂, occurring in urine and other body fluids as a product of protein metabolism. **2.** a water-soluble powder form of this compound, used as a fertilizer, animal feed, in the synthesis of plastics, resins, and barbiturates, and in medicine as a diuretic. —**u·re′al, u·re′ic,** *adj.*

u·re·mi·a (yŏŏ rē′mē ə), *n.* the presence in the blood of excessive urea and other products normally excreted in the urine. —**u·re′mic,** *adj.*

u·re·ter (yŏŏ rē′tər), *n.* a duct that conveys urine from a kidney to the bladder in mammals or to the cloaca in other vertebrates. —**u·re′ter·al, u·re·ter·ic** (yŏŏr′i ter′ik), *adj.*

u·re·thane (yŏŏr′ə thān′), *n.* **1.** any derivative of carbamic acid having the formula CH₃NO₂R. **2.** a white, crystalline, water-soluble powder, C₃H₇NO₂, used chiefly as a solvent, in organic synthesis, as a fungicide and pesticide, and formerly in cancer treatment.

u·re·thra (yŏŏ rē′thrə), *n., pl.* **-thrae** (-thrē), **-thras.** a duct that conveys urine from the bladder to the exterior and, in most male mammals, also conveys semen. —**u·re′thral,** *adj.*

urge (ûrj), *v.,* **urged, urg·ing,** *n.* —*v.t.* **1.** to push or force along; impel with force or vigor. **2.** to drive with incitement to speed or effort: *to urge dogs on with shouts.* **3.** to press, push, or hasten (the course, activities, etc.): *to urge one's escape.* **4.** to impel or move to some action: *urged by necessity.* **5.** to endeavor to induce or persuade, as by entreaties; exhort: *to urge a person to greater caution.* **6.** to press (something) upon the attention: *to urge a claim.* **7.** to insist on or assert with earnestness: *to urge the need of haste.* **8.** to recommend earnestly: *to urge a plan of action.* —*v.i.* **9.** to exert a driving or impelling force; give an impulse to haste or action. **10.** to make entreaties or earnest recommendations. **11.** to press arguments or allegations, as against a person. —*n.* **12.** an act of urging; impelling action, influence, or force; impulse. **13.** an involuntary or instinctive impulse. —**urg′er,** *n.*

ur·gen·cy (ûr′jən sē), *n., pl.* **-cies. 1.** urgent character; imperativeness; insistence. **2. urgencies,** urgent requirements or needs.

ur·gent (ûr′jənt), *adj.* **1.** compelling or requiring immediate action or attention; imperative; pressing. **2.** insistent or earnest in solicitation; importunate. **3.** expressed with insistence. —**ur′gent·ly,** *adv.*

Uri′ah Heep′ (hēp), *n.* the hypocritical and villainous clerk in Charles Dickens's *David Copperfield.*

U·ri′ah the Hit′tite (yŏŏ rī′ə), *n.* the husband of Bathsheba and an officer in David's army. II Sam. 11.

u′ric ac′id, *n.* a compound, C₅H₄N₄O₃, that is present in mammalian urine in small amounts and is the principal nitrogenous component of the excrement of reptiles and birds.

U·ri·el (yŏŏr′ē əl), *n.* one of the archangels. II Esdras 4.

U·ri·jah (yŏŏ rī′jə), *n.* a priest in Jerusalem who built a heathen altar for King Ahaz. II Kings 16:10–16.

U·rim and Thum·mim (yŏŏr′im, ŏŏr′-; thum′im, tŏŏm′-), *n. Judaism.* objects, possibly made of metal or precious stones and inscribed with symbols, worn in the breastplate of the high priest and used, perhaps like lots, to determine God's response to a question answerable by "yes" or "no." Ex. 28:30.

u·ri·nal (yŏŏr′ə nl), *n.* **1.** a flushable wall fixture, as in a public lavatory, used by men for urinating. **2.** a building or enclosure containing such fixtures. **3.** a receptacle to receive the urine of a person with urinary incontinence or that of a bedridden person.

u·ri·nal·y·sis (yŏŏr′ə nal′ə sis), *n., pl.* **-ses** (-sēz′). a diagnostic analysis of urine.

u·ri·nar·y (yŏŏr′ə ner′ē), *adj.* **1.** of or pertaining to urine. **2.** pertaining to the organs secreting and discharging urine.

u′rinary blad′der, *n.* a distensible, muscular sac in most vertebrates, in which urine is retained until discharged from the body. Also called **bladder.**

u·ri·nate (yŏŏr′ə nāt′), *v.i.,* **-nat·ed, -nat·ing.** to discharge urine. —**u′ri·na′tion,** *n.* —**u′ri·na′tive,** *adj.*

u·rine (yŏŏr′in), *n.* the waste matter excreted by the kidneys, in mammals as a slightly acid yellowish liquid, in birds and reptiles as a semisolid consisting mostly of uric acid.

URL, *Computers.* Uniform Resource Locater: a protocol for specifying addresses on the Internet.

urn (ûrn), *n.* **1.** a large or decorative vase, esp. one with an ornamental foot or pedestal. **2.** a vase for holding the ashes of the cremated dead. **3.** a large metal container with a spigot, used for making or serving tea or coffee in quantity. **4.** the spore-bearing part of the capsule of a moss, between lid and seta.

uro-¹, a combining form meaning "urine": *urology.* Also, *esp. before a vowel,* **ur-.**

uro-², a combining form meaning "tail": *uropod.*

Ur′ of the Chal·dees′ (kal dēz′, kal′dēz), *n.* the city where Abraham was born, sometimes identified with the Sumerian city of Ur. Gen. 11:28, 31; 15:7; Neh. 9:7.

u·rol·o·gy (yŏŏ rol′ə jē), *n.* the scientific, clinical, and esp. surgical aspects of the study of the urinary and the genitourinary tract. —**u·ro·log·ic** (yŏŏr′ə loj′ik), **u·ro·log′i·cal,** *adj.* —**u·rol′o·gist,** *n.*

Ur·sa Ma·jor (ûr′sə mā′jər), *n., gen.* **Ur·sae Ma·jor·is** (ûr′sē mə jôr′is, -jôr′-). the Great Bear, the most prominent northern constellation, containing the seven stars that form the Big Dipper.

Ur·sa Mi·nor (ûr′sə mī′nər), *n., gen.* **Ur·sae Mi·nor·is** (ûr′sē mī nôr′is, -nôr′-). the Little or Lesser Bear, the northernmost constellation, containing the stars that form the Little Dipper, the outermost of which, at the end of the handle, is Polaris.

ur·sine (ûr′sīn, -sin), *adj.* of or pertaining to a bear or bears; bearlike.

Ur·su·la (ûr′sə lə), *n.* **Saint,** a legendary British princess who, with 11,000 virgins, is said to have been martyred by the Huns at Cologne.

Ur·su·line (ûr′sə lin, -līn′, -lēn′), *n.* a member of an order of nuns founded at Brescia, Italy, about 1537, devoted to teaching. —*adj.* **2.** of or pertaining to the Ursulines.

U·ru·guay (yŏŏr′ə gwā′, -gwī′, ŏŏr′-), *n.* **1.** a republic in SE South America. 3,261,707; 68,037 sq. mi. (176,215 sq. km). *Cap.:* Montevideo. **2.** a river in SE South America, flowing from S Brazil into the Río de la Plata. 981 mi. (1580 km) long. —**U′ru·guay′an,** *adj., n.*

us (us), *pron.* **1.** the objective case of WE, used as a direct or indirect object: *They took us to the circus. She asked us the way.* **2.** (used in place of the pronoun *we* in the predicate after the verb *to be*): *It's us!* **3.** (used instead of the pronoun *our* before a gerund or present participle): *She graciously forgave us spilling the gravy on the tablecloth.* —**Usage.** See ME.

U.S. or **US,** United States.

USA or **U.S.A., 1.** United States of America. **2.** United States Army.

us·a·ble or **use·a·ble** (yŏŏ′zə bəl), *adj.* **1.** available or convenient for use. **2.** capable of being used. —**us′a·bil′i·ty, us′a·ble·ness,** *n.* —**us′a·bly,** *adv.*

us·age (yŏŏ′sij, -zij), *n.* **1.** a customary way of doing something; a custom or practice. **2.** the customary manner in which a language or a form of a language is spoken or written: *a grammar based on usage rather than on arbitrary notions of correctness.* **3.** a particular instance of this: *a usage borrowed from French.* **4.** any manner of doing or handling something; treatment: *rough usage.* **5.** habitual or customary use; long-continued practice. **6.** an act of using or employing; use.

USDA or **U.S.D.A.,** United States Department of Agriculture.

use (*v.* yŏŏz or, *for pt. form of 7,* yŏŏst; *n.* yŏŏs), *v.,* **used, us·ing,** *n.* —*v.t.* **1.** to employ for some purpose; put into service: *to use a knife.* **2.** to avail oneself of; apply to one's own purposes: *to use the facilities.* **3.** to consume, expend, or exhaust (often fol. by *up*). **4.** to treat or behave toward: *He used his employees well.* **5.** to take unfair advantage of; exploit. **6.** to habituate or accustom. —*v.i.* **7.** to be accustomed, wont, or customarily found (used with an infinitive expressed or understood, and, except in archaic use, now only in the past): *He used to go every day.* —*n.* **8.** the act of using or the state of being used. **9.** an instance or way of using something: *a painter's use of color.* **10.** a way of being used; a purpose for which something is used. **11.** the power, right, or privilege of using something: *to lose the use of an eye.* **12.** service or advantage in or for being used; utility or usefulness: *of no practical use.* **13.** help; profit; resulting good: *What's the use of complaining?* **14.** occasion or need, as for something to be used: *Have you any use for another calendar?* **15.** continued, habitual, or customary employment or practice; custom. **16.** *Law.* **a.** the enjoyment of property, as by occupation or employment of it. **b.** the benefits or profits of property held by another for the beneficiary. **17.** the distinctive form of ritual or of any liturgical observance used in a particular church, diocese, community, etc. —*Idiom.* **18. have no use for, a.** to have no need for. **b.** to feel intolerant of or indifferent to: *to have no use for one's employees.* **c.** to have a strong distaste for; dislike intensely: *to have no use for cheating.* **19. make use of,** to use, esp. effectively; employ. **20. put to use,** to find a function for; utilize.

use•a•ble (yo͞o′zə bəl), *adj.* USABLE. —**use′a•bil′i•ty, use′a•ble•ness,** *n.* —**use′a•bly,** *adv.*

used (yo͞ozd *or, for 3,* yo͞ost), *adj.* **1.** previously used or owned; secondhand: *a used car.* **2.** employed for a purpose; utilized. —*Idiom.* **3. used to,** accustomed or habituated to.

use•ful (yo͞os′fəl), *adj.* **1.** being of use or service; serving some purpose; advantageous, helpful, or of good effect: *a useful member of society.* **2.** of practical use; producing material results; supplying common needs. —**use′ful•ly,** *adv.* —**use′ful•ness,** *n.*

use•less (yo͞os′lis), *adj.* **1.** of no use; not serving the purpose or any purpose; unavailing. **2.** without useful qualities; of no practical good. —**use′less•ly,** *adv.* —**use′less•ness,** *n.*

Use•net or **USENET** (yo͞oz′net′, yo͞os′-), *n. Computers.* an extensive system of newsgroups: a branch of the Internet.

us•er (yo͞o′zər), *n.* **1.** a person or thing that uses. **2.** a person who uses a computer.

us′er-friend′ly, *adj.* easy to operate, understand, etc.: *a user-friendly computer.* —**us′er-friend′liness,** *n.*

us′er (or **us′er's**) **group′,** *n.* a club for the exchange of information and services among computer users.

ush•er (ush′ər), *n.* **1.** a person who escorts people to seats in a theater, church, etc. **2.** an official doorkeeper, as in a courtroom. **3.** a male attendant of a bridegroom at a wedding. **4.** an officer whose business it is to introduce strangers or to walk before a person of rank. —*v.t.* **5.** to act as an usher to: *She ushered them to their seats.* **6.** to precede or herald (usu. fol. by *in*). —*v.i.* **7.** to act as an usher.

USIA or **U.S.I.A.,** United States Information Agency.

USPS or **U.S.P.S.,** United States Postal Service.

U.S. RDA, *n.* United States recommended daily allowance: the daily amount of a protein, vitamin, or mineral that the FDA has established as sufficient to maintain the nutritional health of persons in various age groups and categories, derived from the RDA developed by the Food and Nutrition Board of the National Academy of Sciences and used in the labeling of food. Compare RECOMMENDED DIETARY ALLOWANCE.

USS or **U.S.S., 1.** United States Senate. **2.** United States Service. **3.** United States Ship. **4.** United States Steamer. **5.** United States Steamship.

Ussh•er (ush′ər), *n.* **James,** 1581–1656, Irish ecclesiastic who calculated a system of Biblical chronology, dating the creation at 4004 B.C.

u•su•al (yo͞o′zho͞o əl, yo͞ozh′wəl), *adj.* **1.** expected by reason of previous experience with the same occurrence, situation, person, etc.: *her usual skill.* **2.** commonly met with or observed in experience; ordinary: *the usual January weather.* **3.** commonplace; everyday: *He says the usual things.* —*n.* **4.** something that is usual. —*Idiom.* **5. as usual,** in the customary or habitual way. —**u′su•al•ly,** *adv.* —**u′su•al•ness,** *n.*

U•sum•bu•ra (o͞o′so͞om bo͞or′ə), *n.* former name of BUJUMBURA.

u•su•rer (yo͞o′zhər ər), *n.* a person who lends money and charges interest, esp. at an exorbitant or unlawful rate.

u•surp (yo͞o sûrp′, -zûrp′), *v.t.* **1.** to seize and hold (a position, office, power, etc.) by force or without legal right. **2.** to use without authority or right; employ wrongfully: *The magazine usurped copyrighted material.* —*v.i.* **3.** to commit forcible or illegal seizure of an office, power, etc.; encroach. —**u•surp′er,** *n.* —**u•surp′ing•ly,** *adv.*

u•su•ry (yo͞o′zhə rē), *n., pl.* **-ries. 1.** the practice of lending money at an exorbitant interest rate. **2.** an exorbitant amount or rate of interest.

UT or **Ut.,** Utah.

U•tah (yo͞o′tô, -tä), *n.* a state in the W United States. 2,000,494; 84,916 sq. mi. (219,930 sq. km). *Cap.:* Salt Lake City. *Abbr.:* UT, Ut. —**U•tah•an, U•tahn** (yo͞o′tôn, -tän), *adj., n.*

u•ten•sil (yo͞o ten′səl), *n.* **1.** any of the instruments or vessels commonly used in a kitchen, dairy, etc.: *eating utensils.* **2.** any instrument, vessel, or tool serving a useful purpose: *farming utensils.*

u•ter•ine (yo͞o′tər in, -tə rīn′), *adj.* **1.** of or pertaining to the uterus or womb. **2.** related through having the same mother.

u•ter•us (yo͞o′tər əs), *n., pl.* **u•ter•i** (yo͞o′tə rī′), **u•ter•us•es.** a hollow expandable organ of female placental mammals in which the fertilized egg develops during pregnancy; womb.

u•tile (yo͞o′til, -tīl), *adj.* USEFUL.

u•til•i•tar•i•an (yo͞o til′i târ′ē ən), *adj.* **1.** of, pertaining to, or characterized by utility. **2.** designed for or concerned with utility or usefulness

rather than beauty, ornamentation, etc. **3.** of, pertaining to, or adhering to the doctrine of utilitarianism. —*n.* **4.** an adherent of utilitarianism.

u•til•i•tar•i•an•ism (yo͞o til′i târ′ē ə niz′əm), *n.* **1.** the ethical doctrine that virtue is based on utility, and that conduct should be directed toward promoting the greatest happiness of the greatest number of persons. **2.** utilitarian quality or character.

u•til•i•ty (yo͞o til′i tē), *n., pl.* **-ties,** *adj.* —*n.* **1.** the state or quality of being useful; usefulness. **2.** something useful; a useful thing. **3.** a public service, as the providing of electricity, gas, water, a telephone system, or bus and railroad lines. **4.** PUBLIC UTILITY. **5.** Often, **utilities.** a useful or advantageous factor or feature. **6.** the capacity of a commodity or a service to satisfy some human want. **7.** UTILITY PROGRAM. **8. utilities,** stocks or bonds of public utilities. —*adj.* **9.** (of domestic animals) raised or kept as potentially profitable products rather than for show or as pets. **10.** designed for a number of practical purposes rather than a single, specialized one: *a utility knife.* **11.** capable of serving in any of various capacities or positions when called on: *a utility player on a baseball team.* **12.** designed chiefly for use or service rather than beauty, high quality, etc. **13.** of or designating a low-quality grade of meat.

util′ity pole′, *n.* one of a series of large, upright poles used to support telephone wires, electric cables, or the like.

util′ity pro′gram, *n.* a system program used esp. to simplify standard computer operations, as sorting, copying, or deleting files.

util′ity room′, *n.* a room, esp. in a house, reserved for a washing machine, furnace, or other large appliances.

u•ti•lize (yo͞ot′l īz′), *v.t.,* **-lized, -liz•ing.** to put to use; turn to profitable or practical account. —**u′ti•li•za′tion,** *n.*

ut•most (ut′mōst′), *adj.* **1.** of the greatest or highest degree, quantity, etc.; greatest: *of the utmost importance.* **2.** being at the farthest point or extremity; farthest. —*n.* **3.** the greatest degree or amount: *providing the utmost in comfort.* **4.** the most or best of one's abilities, powers, etc.: *He did his utmost to win.* **5.** the extreme limit or extent: *patience taxed to the utmost.*

U•to-Az•tec•an (yo͞o′tō az′tek ən), *n.* **1.** a family of American Indian languages spoken or formerly spoken in the U.S. Great Basin, the U.S. Southwest and S California, and NW and W Mexico, including as well the Nahuatl language of central Mexico and Central America. —*adj.* **2.** of or pertaining to Uto-Aztecan.

U•to•pi•a (yo͞o tō′pē ə), *n., pl.* **-pi•as. 1.** an imaginary island described in Sir Thomas More's *Utopia* (1516) as enjoying perfection in law, politics, etc. **2.** (*usu. l.c.*) any ideal place or state. **3.** (*usu. l.c.*) any visionary system of political or social perfection. [< New Latin < Greek *ou* not + *tóp(os)* a place]

ut•ter[1] (ut′ər), *v.t.* **1.** to give audible, esp. verbal, expression to; speak or pronounce: *unable to utter a word.* **2.** to emit (cries, notes, etc.) with the voice: *to utter a sigh.* **3.** to give forth (a sound) otherwise than with the voice: *The engine uttered a shriek.* **4.** to express by written or printed words. **5.** to make publicly known; publish: *to utter a libel.* **6.** to put into circulation, as coins, notes, and esp. counterfeit money or forged checks. **7.** to expel; emit. —*v.i.* **8.** to use the voice to talk, make sounds, etc.; speak. —**ut′ter•a•ble,** *adj.* —**ut′ter•er,** *n.*

ut•ter[2] (ut′ər), *adj.* **1.** complete; total; absolute: *utter abandonment to grief.* **2.** unconditional; unqualified: *an utter denial.* —**ut′ter•ly,** *adv.* —**ut′ter•ness,** *n.*

ut•ter•ance (ut′ər əns), *n.* **1.** an act of uttering; vocal expression. **2.** something uttered, esp. a word or words. **3.** manner or power of speaking. **4.** *Ling.* any speech sequence consisting of one or more words and preceded and followed by silence.

ut•ter•most (ut′ər mōst′), *adj., n.* UTMOST.

U-turn (yo͞o′tûrn′), *n.* **1.** a U-shaped turn made by a vehicle so as to head in the opposite direction from its original course. **2.** a reversal of policy, tactics, etc., resembling such a maneuver. —*v.i.* **3.** to execute a U-turn.

UV, ultraviolet.

U-val•ue (yo͞o′val′yo͞o), *n.* a measure of the flow of heat through an insulating or building material: the lower the U-value, the better the insulating ability. Compare R-VALUE.

u•vu•la (yo͞o′vyə lə), *n., pl.* **-las, -lae** (-lē′). the small, fleshy, conical body projecting downward from the middle of the soft palate.

u•vu•lar (yo͞o′vyə lər), *adj.* **1.** of or pertaining to the uvula. **2.** (of a consonant) articulated with the back of the tongue close to or touching the uvula, as the *r*-sound of Parisian French. —*n.* **3.** a uvular consonant. —**u′vu•lar•ly,** *adv.*

ux•o•ri•al (uk sôr′ē əl, -sōr′-, ug zôr′-, -zōr′-), *adj.* of, pertaining to, or characteristic of a wife. —**ux•o′ri•al•ly,** *adv.*

Uz•bek•i•stan (o͞oz bek′ə stan′, -stän′, uz-), *n.* a republic in S central Asia, S. of Kazakhstan: a former constituent republic of the U.S.S.R.. 23,860,452; 172,741 sq. mi. (447,400 sq. km). *Cap.:* Tashkent. Former official name, **Uz′bek So′viet So′cialist Repub′lic.**

U•zi (o͞o′zē), *n., pl.* **U•zis.** a compact 9mm submachine gun of Israeli design. [after *Uzi* (el Gal), Israeli army officer who designed it]

Uz•zi•ah (ə zī′ə), *n.* the son and successor of Amaziah as king of Judah, reigned 783?–742? B.C. II Kings 15:13, 30–34. Also, **Azariah.**

V

V, v (vē), *n., pl.* **Vs** or **V's, vs** or **v's.** **1.** the 22nd letter of the English alphabet, a consonant. **2.** any spoken sound represented by this letter. **3.** something shaped like a V. **4.** a written or printed representation of the letter *V* or *v*.

V, 1. velocity. **2.** verb. **3.** victory (by the Allies in WWII). **4.** volt. **5.** vowel.

V, *Symbol.* **1.** the 22nd in order or in a series. **2.** (*sometimes l.c.*) the Roman numeral for five. Compare ROMAN NUMERALS. **3.** *Chem.* vanadium.

v, 1. variable. **2.** velocity. **3.** volt.

v., (*in legal contexts pronounced* vē *or* vûr′səs), versus.

V-6 (vē′siks′), *n., pl.* **V-6's.** V-SIX.

V-8 (vē′āt′), *n., pl.* **V-8's.** V-EIGHT.

VA, 1. Also, **V.A.** Veterans Administration. **2.** Virginia. **3.** Also, **va** volt-ampere.

Va., Virginia.

va·can·cy (vā′kən sē), *n., pl.* **-cies.** **1.** the state of being vacant; emptiness. **2.** a vacant or unoccupied place, esp. one for rent. **3.** an unoccupied position or office. **4.** a gap; opening; breach. **5.** lack of thought or intelligence; vacuity. **6.** (in a crystal) an imperfection resulting from an unoccupied lattice position.

va·cant (vā′kənt), *adj.* **1.** having no contents; empty; void. **2.** having no occupant; unoccupied: *no vacant seats on this train.* **3.** not in use: *a vacant warehouse.* **4.** lacking in thought or intelligence: *a vacant expression.* **5.** not occupied by an incumbent, official, or the like, as a benefice or office. **6.** free from work, business, activity, etc.: *vacant hours.* —**va′cant·ly,** *adv.* —**va′cant·ness,** *n.*

va·cate (vā′kāt; *esp. Brit.* və kāt′, vā-), *v.,* **-cat·ed, -cat·ing.** —*v.t.* **1.** to give up possession or occupancy of: *to vacate an apartment.* **2.** to give up or relinquish (an office, position, etc.). **3.** to render inoperative; deprive of validity; annul: *to vacate a contract.* **4.** to cause to be empty or unoccupied; make vacant. —*v.i.* **5.** to withdraw from occupancy; surrender possession. **6.** to give up or leave a position, office, etc.

va·ca·tion (vā kā′shən, və-), *n.* **1.** a period of suspension of regular work, study, or other activity, usu. used for rest, recreation, or travel. **2.** freedom or release from duty, business, or activity. **3.** an act or instance of vacating. —*v.i.* **4.** to take or have a vacation. —**va·ca′tion·er,** *n.*

vac·ci·nate (vak′sə nāt′), *v.,* **-nat·ed, -nat·ing.** —*v.t.* **1.** to inoculate with a vaccine. —*v.i.* **2.** to perform or practice vaccination.

vac·ci·na·tion (vak′sə nā′shən), *n.* **1.** the act or practice of inoculating with vaccine. **2.** the scar where a vaccine was administered.

vac·cine (vak sēn′; *esp. Brit.* vak′sēn), *n.* **1.** any preparation introduced into the body to prevent a disease by stimulating antibodies against it. **2.** a software program that helps to protect against computer viruses, as by detecting them and warning the user.

vac·il·late (vas′ə lāt′), *v.i.,* **-lat·ed, -lat·ing.** **1.** to waver in mind or opinion; be indecisive or irresolute. **2.** to sway unsteadily; totter. **3.** to oscillate or fluctuate. —**vac·il·la′tion,** *n.* —**vac′il·la′tor,** *n.*

vac·il·lat·ing (vas′ə lā′ting), *adj.* **1.** not resolute; wavering; indecisive. **2.** oscillating; swaying; fluctuating. —**vac′il·lat′ing·ly,** *adv.*

va·cu·i·ty (va kyōō′i tē, və-), *n., pl.* **-ties.** **1.** the state of being vacuous or without contents. **2.** absence of thought or intelligence. **3.** something inane, senseless, or stupid. **4.** an empty space; void.

vac·u·ole (vak′yōō ōl′), *n.* **1.** a membrane-bound cavity within a cell, often containing a watery liquid or secretion.. **2.** a minute cavity or vesicle in organic tissue. —**vac·u·o·lar** (vak′yōō ō′lər, vak′yōō ə-, vak′yə-lər), *adj.*

vac·u·ous (vak′yōō əs), *adj.* **1.** without contents; empty. **2.** lacking in or showing a lack of ideas or intelligence: *a vacuous mind.* **3.** purposeless; idle. —**vac′u·ous·ly,** *adv.* —**vac′u·ous·ness,** *n.*

vac·u·um (vak′yōōm, -yōō əm, -yəm), *n., pl.* **-u·ums** for 1, 2, 4, 5, **-u·a** (-yōō ə) for 1, 2, 4; *adj.; v.* —*n.* **1.** a space entirely devoid of matter. **2.** an enclosed space from which matter, esp. air, has been partially removed so that the matter or gas remaining in the space exerts less pressure than the atmosphere (opposed to *plenum*). **3.** the state or degree of exhaustion in such an enclosed space. **4.** a space not filled or occupied; emptiness; void: *The loss left a vacuum in his life.* **5.** VACUUM CLEANER. —*adj.* **6.** of, pertaining to, employing, or producing a vacuum. **7.** (of a hollow container) partly exhausted of gas or air. **8.** noting or pertaining to canning or packaging in which air is removed from the container to prevent deterioration of the contents. —*v.t.* **9.** to clean with a vacuum cleaner. **10.** to treat with any vacuum device, as a vacuum drier. —*v.i.* **11.** to use a vacuum cleaner.

vac′uum bot′tle, *n.* a bottle or flask having a double wall enclosing a vacuum to retard heat transfer; thermos.

vac′uum clean′er, *n.* an electrical appliance for cleaning carpets, floors, etc., by suction. Also called **vac′uum sweep′er.**

vac′uum-packed′, *adj.* packed, as in a can, with as much air as possible evacuated before sealing.

vac′uum tube′, *n.* an electron tube from which almost all air or gas has been evacuated: formerly used extensively in radio and electronics.

va·de me·cum (vā′dē mē′kəm, vä′-), *n., pl.* **vade me·cums.** **1.** something a person carries about for frequent or regular use. **2.** a book for ready reference; manual; handbook. [< Latin *vāde mēcum* lit., go with me]

V. Adm., Vice-Admiral.

Va·duz (fä dōōts′), *n.* the capital of Liechtenstein, on the upper Rhine. 4891.

vag·a·bond (vag′ə bond′), *adj.* **1.** wandering from place to place without any settled home; nomadic. **2.** leading an unsettled or carefree life. **3.** disreputable; worthless; shiftless. **4.** of, pertaining to, or characteristic of a vagabond. **5.** having an uncertain or irregular course or direction: *a vagabond voyage.* —*n.* **6.** a person, usu. without a permanent home, who wanders from place to place; nomad. **7.** an idle wanderer without a permanent home or visible means of support; tramp; vagrant. **8.** a carefree, worthless, or irresponsible person; rogue.

va·gar·y (və gâr′ē, vā′gə rē), *n., pl.* **-gar·ies.** **1.** an unpredictable, capricious, or erratic action, occurrence, or course. **2.** a whimsical, wild, or unusual idea or notion.

va·gi·na (və jī′nə), *n., pl.* **-nas, -nae** (-nē). **1. a.** the passage leading from the uterus to the vulva in female mammals. **b.** a sheathlike part or organ. **2.** the sheath at the base of a leaf where it surrounds the stalk.

vag·i·nal (vaj′ə nl), *adj.* **1.** pertaining to or involving the vagina. **2.** pertaining to or resembling a sheath. —**vag′i·nal·ly,** *adv.*

va·gran·cy (vā′grən sē), *n., pl.* **-cies.** **1.** the state or condition of being a vagrant. **2.** the conduct of a vagrant. **3.** mental wandering; reverie.

va·grant (vā′grənt), *n.* **1.** a person who wanders about idly and has no permanent home or employment; vagabond. **2.** *Law.* an idle person without visible means of support, as a tramp or beggar. **3.** a person who wanders from place to place; wanderer; rover. —*adj.* **4.** wandering or roaming from place to place. **5.** of or characteristic of a vagrant. **6.** wandering idly without a permanent home or employment: *vagrant beggars.* **7.** (of plants) straggling in growth. **8.** not fixed or settled, esp. in course: *a vagrant leaf blown by the wind.* —**va′grant·ly,** *adv.*

vague (vāg), *adj.,* **va·guer, va·guest.** **1.** not clearly or explicitly stated or expressed: *vague promises.* **2.** indefinite or indistinct in nature or character, as ideas or feelings: *a vague premonition of disaster.* **3.** not clearly perceptible: *vague murmurs.* **4.** not definitely established, confirmed, or known: *a vague rumor.* **5.** (of persons) not clear or definite in thought, understanding, or expression. **6.** showing lack of understanding: *a vague stare.* —**vague′ly,** *adv.* —**vague′ness,** *n.*

va·gus (vā′gəs), *n., pl.* **-gi** (-jī, -gī). either of the tenth pair of cranial nerves, composed of long sensory and motor neurons that innervate the body from the throat to the abdominal viscera and that function in speech, swallowing, breathing, heart rate, and digestion. Also called **va′gus nerve′.**

vail (vāl), *v.t.* to let sink; lower.

vain (vān), *adj.,* **-er, -est.** **1.** excessively proud of or concerned about one's own appearance, qualities, achievements, etc. **2.** proceeding from or showing personal vanity. **3.** ineffectual or unsuccessful; futile: *vain efforts.* **4.** without real significance, value, or importance. —*Idiom.* **5. in vain, a.** without effect or avail; to no purpose. **b.** in an improper or irreverent manner: *to take God's name in vain.* —**vain′ly,** *adv.*

vain·glo·ri·ous (vān glôr′ē əs, -glōr′-), *adj.* **1.** filled with or given to vainglory. **2.** characterized by, showing, or proceeding from vainglory. —**vain·glo′ri·ous·ly,** *adv.* —**vain·glo′ri·ous·ness,** *n.*

vain·glo·ry (vān′glôr′ē, -glōr′ē, vān glôr′ē, -glōr′ē), *n.* **1.** excessive elation or pride over one's own achievements, abilities, etc.; boastful vanity. **2.** empty pomp or show.

val·ance (val′əns, vā′ləns), *n.* **1.** a short ornamental piece of drapery, wood, metal, etc., placed across the top of a window. **2.** a short curtain or piece of drapery hung from the edge of a canopy, the frame of a bed, etc. —**val′anced,** *adj.*

vale (vāl), *n.* **1.** VALLEY. **2.** the world, or mortal or earthly life: *this vale of tears.*

val·e·dic·tion (val′i dik′shən), *n.* **1.** an act of bidding farewell or taking leave. **2.** an utterance made in bidding farewell or taking leave; valedictory.

val·e·dic·to·ri·an (val′i dik tôr′ē ən, -tōr′-), *n.* a student, usu. the one ranking highest academically in a graduating class, who delivers the valedictory.

val·e·dic·to·ry (val′i dik′tə rē), *adj., pl.* **-ries.** —*adj.* **1.** bidding good-bye; saying farewell: *a valedictory speech.* **2.** of or pertaining to an occasion of leave-taking: *a valedictory ceremony.* —*n.* **3.** an address delivered at the commencement exercises of a college or school on behalf of the graduating class. **4.** any farewell address or oration.

va·lence (vā′ləns) also **valency,** *n.* **1. a.** the quality that determines the number of atoms or groups with which any single atom or group will unite chemically. **b.** the relative combining capacity of an atom or group compared with that of the standard hydrogen atom. **2.** the number of binding sites on a molecule, as an antibody or antigen.

va′lence elec′tron, *n.* an electron of an atom, located in the outermost shell **(va′lence shell′)** of the atom, that can be transferred to or shared with another atom.

-valent, a combining form with the meanings "having a valence" (*quadrivalent*), "having homologous chromosomes" (*univalent*), "having antibodies" (*multivalent*), of the number specified by the initial element.

val•en•tine (val′ən tīn′), *n.* **1.** a card or message, usu. amatory or sentimental, or a gift sent by one person to another on Valentine's Day, sometimes anonymously. **2.** a sweetheart chosen or greeted on this day. **3.** a written or other artistic work, message, etc., expressing affection.

Val•en•tine (val′ən tīn′), *n.* **Saint,** died A.D. c270, Christian martyr at Rome.

Val′entine's (or **Val′entine**) **Day′,** *n.* February 14, observed in honor of St. Valentine as a day for the exchange of valentines and other tokens of affection. Also called **Saint Valentine's Day.**

Val•en•ti•no (val′ən tē′nō), *n.* **Rudolph** (*Rodolpho d'Antonguolla*), 1895–1926, U.S. motion-picture actor, born in Italy.

va•le•ri•an (və lēr′ē ən), *n.* **1.** any plant of the genus *Valeriana,* as the common valerian *V. officinalis,* having white, lavender, or pink flowers and a root that is used medicinally. **2.** a drug consisting of or made from the root, formerly used as a nerve sedative and antispasmodic.

val•et (va lā′, val′it, val′ā), *n., v.,* **-et•ed, -et•ing.** —*n.* **1.** a male servant who attends to the personal needs of his employer, as by taking care of clothing; manservant. **2.** an employee who cares for the clothing of patrons of a hotel, passengers on a ship, etc. **3.** an attendant who parks cars for patrons at a hotel, restaurant, etc. **4.** a stand or rack for holding coats, hats, etc. —*v.t., v.i.* **5.** to serve as a valet.

val•e•tu•di•nar•i•an (val′i to͞od′n âr′ē ən, -tyo͞od′-), *n.* **1.** an invalid. **2.** a person who is excessively concerned about his or her health. —*adj.* **3.** in poor health; sickly. **4.** excessively concerned about one's health.

Val•hal•la (val hal′ə, väl hä′lə), *n.* (in Norse myth) the hall of Odin into which the souls of those fallen in battle are received. [> Old Norse *Valhǫll* = *val(r)* the slain in battle, slaughter + *hǫll* HALL]

val•iant (val′yənt), *adj.* **1.** boldly courageous; brave. **2.** marked by or showing bravery or valor; heroic: *a valiant effort.* —**val′ian•cy** (-yən sē), **val′iance,** *n.* —**val′iant•ly,** *adv.*

val•id (val′id), *adj.* **1.** sound; just; well-founded. **2.** producing the desired result; effective: *a valid remedy.* **3.** having force, weight, or cogency; authoritative. **4.** legally sound, effective, or binding: *a valid contract.* **5.** (of an argument) so constructed that if the premises are jointly asserted, the conclusion cannot be denied without contradiction. —**val′id•ly,** *adv.* —**val′id•ness,** *n.*

val•i•date (val′i dāt′), *v.t.,* **-dat•ed, -dat•ing.** **1.** to make valid; substantiate; confirm. **2.** to give legal force to; legalize. **3.** to give official sanction, confirmation, or approval to: *to validate a passport.* —**val′i•da′tion,** *n.*

va•lid•i•ty (və lid′i tē), *n.* **1.** the state or quality of being valid. **2.** legal soundness or force.

va•lise (və lēs′; *esp. Brit.* -lēz′), *n.* a small piece of hand luggage; suitcase.

Val•i•um (val′ē əm), *Trademark.* a brand of diazepam.

Val•kyr•ie (val kēr′ē, -kī′rē, väl-, val′kə rē), *n.* (in Norse myth) any of the female spirits who bring the souls of slain warriors to Valhalla. —**Val•kyr′i•an,** *adj.*

Val•le•jo (və lā′ō, -yā′hō), *n.* **1. César,** 1895–1938, Peruvian poet. **2.** a city in W California, on San Pablo Bay, NE of San Francisco. 111,484.

Val•let•ta (və let′ə), *n.* the capital of Malta, on the NE coast. 14,049.

val•ley (val′ē), *n.* **1.** an elongated depression between uplands, hills, or mountains, esp. one following the course of a stream. **2.** an extensive, more or less flat, and relatively low region drained by a great river system. **3.** any depression or hollow resembling a valley. **4.** a low point or interval in any process, representation, or situation. **5.** any place, period, or situation that is filled with fear, gloom, or the like.

Val′ley Forge′, *n.* a village in SE Pennsylvania: winter quarters of Washington's army 1777–78.

val•or (val′ər), *n.* boldness or determination in facing danger. Also, *esp. Brit.,* **val′our.** —**val′or•ous,** *adj.*

val•or•ize (val′ə rīz′), *v.t.,* **-ized, -iz•ing.** to maintain the value or price of (a commodity), esp. by subsidies or the government's purchase at a fixed price. —**val′or•i•za′tion,** *n.*

Val•po•li•cel•la (val′pō li chel′ə, väl′-), *n.* a light, dry red table wine of N Italy.

val•u•a•ble (val′yo͞o ə bəl, -yə bəl), *adj.* **1.** having considerable monetary worth. **2.** having qualities worthy of esteem. **3.** of considerable use or importance. —*n.* **4.** Usu., **valuables.** personal articles, as jewelry, of great value. —**val′u•a•ble•ness,** *n.* —**val′u•a•bly,** *adv.*

val•u•ate (val′yo͞o āt′), *v.t.,* **-at•ed, -at•ing.** to set a value on. —**val′u•a′tor,** *n.*

val•u•a•tion (val′yo͞o ā′shən), *n.* **1.** the act of appraisal. **2.** an estimated value. **3.** the estimation or acknowledgment of the worth of something: *to set a high valuation on heroism.* —**val′u•a′tion•al,** *adj.* —**val′u•a′tion•al•ly,** *adv.*

val•ue (val′yo͞o), *n., v.t.,* **-ued, -u•ing.** —*n.* **1.** relative worth or importance. **2.** monetary or material worth, as in commerce. **3.** the worth of something in terms of some medium of exchange. **4.** equivalent worth in money, material, or services. **5.** estimated or assigned worth. **6.** denomination, as of a monetary issue. **7. a.** magnitude; quantity: *the value of an angle.* **b.** a point in the range of a function: *The value of* x^2 *at 2 is 4.* **8.** import; significance: *the value of a word.* **9.** favorable regard. **10.** Often, **values.** the abstract concepts of what is right, worthwhile, or desirable; moral and ethical principles: *The ultimate determinant in the struggle now going on for the world will not be bombs and rockets but...the values we hold, the beliefs we cherish, and the ideals to which we are dedicated* (Ronald Reagan). **11.** any object or quality desirable as a means or as an end in itself. **12. a.** degree of lightness or darkness in a color. **b.** the relation of light and shade, as in a drawing. **13.** the relative duration of a musical note as expressed by a particular notation symbol. **14.** quality. —*v.t.* **15.** to calculate the monetary value of. **16.** to consider with respect to worth or importance. **17.** to regard highly; esteem.

val′ue-add′ed, *n.* **1.** something, as an item of equipment, added to a product by a marketer to warrant a markup in the retail price. —*adj.* **2.** of, pertaining to, or supplying value-added.

val′ue-add′ed tax′, *n.* an excise tax based on the value added to a product at each stage of production. *Abbrev.:* VAT

val′ue judg′ment, *n.* a usu. subjective estimate of the worth, quality, or goodness of something or someone.

valve (valv), *n., v.,* **valved, valv•ing.** —*n.* **1.** any device for halting or controlling the flow of something, as a liquid, through a pipe or other passage. **2.** a hinged lid or other movable part that closes or modifies the passage in such a device. **3.** a membranous structure that permits the flow of a fluid, as blood, in one direction only. **4.** (in musical wind instruments of the trumpet class) a device for changing the length of the air column to alter the pitch of a tone. **5.** one of the two or more separable pieces composing certain shells: *the valves of a clamshell.* **6.** *Bot.* **a.** one of the segments into which a fruit capsule dehisces. **b.** a flap or lidlike part of certain anthers. **7.** *Chiefly Brit.* VACUUM TUBE. —*v.t.* **8.** to provide with a valve. —**val′vu•lar, val′val, val′var,** *adj.*

va•moose (va mo͞os′), *v.,* **-moosed, -moos•ing.** *Slang.* —*v.i.* **1.** to leave hurriedly; decamp. —*v.t.* **2.** to leave hurriedly from; decamp from.

vamp (vamp), *n.* **1.** the portion of a shoe or boot upper that covers the instep and toes. **2.** something patched up or pieced together. **3.** an introductory musical passage commonly consisting of a repeated succession of chords played before the start of a solo. —*v.t.* **4.** to repair (a shoe) with a new vamp. **5.** to patch; repair. **6.** to give (something) a new appearance by adding a patch. **7.** to concoct or invent: *to vamp up ugly rumors.* —*v.i.* **8.** to play a musical vamp. —**vamp′ish,** *adj.*

vam•pire (vam′pīər), *n.* **1. a.** (in E European folklore) a corpse, animated by an undeparted soul or a demon, that periodically leaves the grave and disturbs the living. **b.** any of various popular or literary representations of the folkloric vampire, typically a being that sucks the blood of sleeping persons at night. **2.** a person who preys ruthlessly upon others. **3.** a woman who seduces and exploits men. —**vam•pir′ic** (-pir′ik), **vam′pir•ish,** *adj.*

vam′pire bat′, *n.* **1.** any small New World tropical bat of the family Desmodontidae, having specialized front teeth for drawing blood from resting animals. **2.** any of several other bats, esp. those of the family Megadermatidae, erroneously believed to feed on blood.

van (van), *n.* **1.** a covered vehicle, usu. a large truck or trailer, used for moving goods or animals. **2.** a smaller boxlike vehicle, resembling a panel truck, that can be used as a truck or for passengers or camping. **3.** Also called **van′ conver′sion.** a van whose cargo area has been equipped with living facilities.

va•na•di•um (və nā′dē əm), *n.* a rare element occurring in certain minerals and obtained as a light gray powder or as a ductile metal: used to toughen steel. *Symbol:* V; *at. wt.:* 50.942; *at. no.:* 23; *sp. gr.:* 5.96.

Van Al′len belt′ (van al′ən), *n.* either of two atmospheric regions of high-energy charged particles, one at an altitude of about 2000 mi. (3200 km) and the other at from 9000 to 12,000 mi. (14,500 to 19,000 km). [after J. A. *Van Allen* (b. 1914), U.S. physicist]

Van Bu•ren (van byo͝or′ən), *n.* **Martin,** 1782–1862, 8th president of the U.S. 1837–41.

Van•cou•ver (van ko͞o′vər), *n.* **1. George,** 1758–98, English explorer. **2.** a large island in SW Canada, off the SW coast of British Columbia. 12,408 sq. mi. (32,135 sq. km). **3.** a seaport in SW British Columbia, on the Strait of Georgia opposite SE Vancouver island. 431,147; with suburbs 1,226,152. **4. Mount,** a mountain on the boundary between Alaska and Canada, in the St. Elias Mountains. 15,700 ft. (4785 m).

van•dal (van′dl), *n.* **1.** (*cap.*) a member of a Germanic people who shortly after A.D. 400 moved from E Europe through Gaul and Spain to Africa, established a kingdom there, and raided the W Mediterranean by sea, sacking Rome in 455. **2.** a person who willfully or ignorantly destroys or mars public or private property.

van•dal•ism (van′dl iz′əm), *n.* **1.** deliberate destruction or damage of property. **2.** the conduct or spirit characteristic of the Vandals.

van•dal•ize (van′dl īz′), *v.t.,* **-ized, -iz•ing.** to destroy or deface by vandalism. —**van′dal•i•za′tion,** *n.*

Van Do•ren (van dôr′ən, dōr′-), *n.* **1. Carl,** 1885–1950, U.S. writer. **2.** his brother, **Mark,** 1894–1972, U.S. writer and critic.

Van Dyck or **Van•dyke** (van dīk′), *n.* **Sir Anthony,** 1599–1641, Flemish painter.

Van Dyke (van′ dīk′), *n.* **Henry,** 1852–1933, U.S. clergyman and hymn writer.

Vandyke′ beard′, *n.* a short, pointed beard.

vane (vān), *n.* **1.** WEATHER VANE. **2.** any of a number of blades or plates attached radially to a rotating cylinder or shaft, as in a turbine or windmill, that move or are moved by a fluid, as steam or air. **3.** a person who is readily changeable or fickle. **4. a.** (on a rocket) any fixed or movable surface providing directional control for atmospheric flight. **b.** a similar plane surface in the exhaust jet of a reaction engine, providing directional control while the engine is firing. **5.** the web of a feather. **6.** FEATHER (def. 6). **—vaned,** *adj.* **—vane′less,** *adj.*

van Gogh (van gō′, gôkh′; *Du.* vän khôkh′), *n.* **Vincent,** 1853–90, Dutch painter.

van•guard (van′gärd′), *n.* **1.** the front part of an advancing army. **2.** the forefront in any movement or field. **3.** the leaders of any intellectual or political movement. **—van′guard•ism,** *n.* **—van′guard•ist,** *n.*

va•nil•la (və nil′ə *or, often,* -nel′ə), *n., pl.* **-las. 1.** any tropical climbing orchid of the genus *Vanilla,* esp. *V. planifolia,* bearing podlike fruit yielding an extract used in flavoring food and in perfumery. **2.** Also called **vanil′la bean′.** the fruit or bean of this orchid. **3.** the extract of this fruit. **—*adj.* 4.** containing or flavored with vanilla. **5. a.** ordinary; commonplace. **b.** bland; dull: *a vanilla personality.* **c.** PLAIN-VANILLA.

van•ish (van′ish), *v.i.* **1.** to disappear quickly from sight; become invisible. **2.** to go away, esp. furtively. **3.** to come to an end. **4.** (of a number, quantity, or function) to become zero. **—*v.t.* 5.** to cause to disappear. **—van′ish•ing•ly,** *adv.*

van•i•ty (van′i tē), *n., pl.* **-ties,** *adj.* **—*n.* 1.** excessive pride in oneself or one's appearance; character or quality of being vain. **2.** an instance of this quality or feeling. **3.** something about which one is vain. **4.** lack of real value; worthlessness. **5.** something worthless, trivial, or pointless. **6.** VANITY CASE. **7.** DRESSING TABLE. **8.** a cabinet built around or below a bathroom sink. **9.** COMPACT[1] (def. 10). **—*adj.* 10.** produced as a showcase for one's own performing talents. **11.** of, pertaining to, or issued by a vanity press: *vanity books.* **—*Proverb.* 12. Vanity of vanities, all is vanity,** all earthly strivings are ultimately futile and worthless. Eccl. 12:8. **—van′i•tied,** *adj.*

van′ity case′, *n.* a small bag or case for cosmetics. Also called **van′ity bag′, van′ity box′.**

Van′ity Fair′, *n.* **1.** (in Bunyan's *Pilgrim's Progress*) a fair that goes on perpetually in the town of Vanity and symbolizes worldly ostentation and frivolity. **2.** (*often l.c.*) any place or group, as the world or fashionable society, characterized by or displaying a preoccupation with idle pleasures or ostentation. **3.** (*italics*) a novel (1847–48) by William Makepeace Thackeray.

van′ity plate′, *n.* a vehicle license plate bearing a combination of letters or numbers requested by the licensee.

van′ity press′, *n.* a printing house that publishes books for which the authors pay the costs. Also called **van′ity pub′lisher.**

van•quish (vang′kwish, van′-), *v.t.* **1.** to conquer by superior force, as in battle. **2.** to defeat in any contest or conflict. **3.** to overcome. **—van′quish•a•ble,** *adj.* **—van′quish•er,** *n.*

Van Rens•se•laer (van ren′sə lēr′, ren′sə lər), *n.* **Stephen,** 1765–1839, U.S. political leader and major general.

van•tage (van′tij, vän′-), *n.* **1.** a position affording some strategic advantage or a commanding view. **2.** an advantage or superiority. **3.** *Brit.* ADVANTAGE (def. 4).

van′tage point′, *n.* a position that affords a wide perspective.

Va•nu•a•tu (vä′no͞o ä′to͞o), *n.* a republic consisting of a group of islands in the SW Pacific, W of Fiji: formerly under joint British and French administration; gained independence in 1980. 181,358; ab. 4707 sq. mi. (12,190 sq. km). *Cap.:* Vila. Formerly, New Hebrides. **—Va′nu•a′tu•an,** *adj., n.*

Van•zet•ti (van zet′ē), *n.* **Bartolomeo,** 1888–1927, Italian anarchist, in the U.S. after 1908. Compare SACCO, Nicola.

vap•id (vap′id), *adj.* **1.** lacking spirit or interest; dull: *vapid conversation.* **2.** lacking sharpness or flavor. **—va•pid′i•ty, vap′id•ness,** *n.* **—vap′id•ly,** *adv.*

va•por (vā′pər), *n.* **1.** a visible exhalation, as fog or smoke, suspended in the air. **2.** a substance in gaseous form that is below its critical temperature. **3.** a substance converted into vapor for technical or medicinal uses. **4.** a combination of a vaporized substance and air. **5.** gaseous particles of drugs that can be inhaled as a therapeutic agent. **—*v.i.* 6.** to rise in the form of vapor. **7.** to emit vapor. **8.** to talk pompously. Also, *esp. Brit.,* **vapour. —va′por•y,** *adj.*

va•por•ize (vā′pə rīz′), *v.,* **-ized, -iz•ing. —*v.t.* 1.** to cause to change into vapor. **—*v.i.* 2.** to become converted into vapor. **—va′por•iz′a•ble,** *adj.* **—va′por•i•za′tion,** *n.* **—va′por•iz′er,** *n.*

va•por•ous (vā′pər əs), *adj.* **1.** having the form of vapor: *a vaporous cloud.* **2.** full of vapor; foggy. **3.** giving off or obscured by vapor. **4.** diaphanous: *vaporous fabrics.* **5.** vaguely formed, fanciful, or unsubstantial. **—va′por•ous•ly,** *adv.* **—va′por•ous•ness,** *n.*

va′por pres′sure, *n.* the pressure exerted by the molecules of a vapor.

va′por trail′, *n.* CONTRAIL.

Va•ra•na•si (və rä′nə sē), *n.* a city in SE Uttar Pradesh, in NE India, on the Ganges River. 794,000. Formerly, **Benares.**

var•i•a•ble (vâr′ē ə bəl), *adj.* **1.** apt to vary; changeable. **2.** capable of being varied; alterable. **3.** inconstant; fickle. **4.** having much variation or diversity. **5.** deviating from the usual type, as a species. **6.** (of a star) changing in brightness. **7.** (of wind) tending to change in direction. **8.** having the characteristics of a variable. **—*n.* 9.** something that may or does vary. **10.** a quantity or function that may assume any given value or set of values. **11.** a shifting wind, esp. as distinguished from a trade wind. **—var′i•a•bil′i•ty, var′i•a•ble•ness,** *n.* **—var′i•a•bly,** *adv.*

var′iable-rate′, *adj.* adjusted periodically to a rate in accordance with market conditions: *a variable-rate mortgage.*

var•i•ance (vâr′ē əns), *n.* **1.** the state of being variable or different. **2.** an instance of varying. **3.** *Statistics.* the square of the standard deviation. **4.** the number of degrees of freedom of a physical system. **5.** *Law.* **a.** a discrepancy, as between two sworn statements. **b.** a departure from the cause of action originally stated in a legal complaint. **6.** a permit to do something normally regulated by law, esp. to build in a way forbidden by a zoning law. **7.** a disagreement or dispute. **—*Idiom.* 8. at variance,** in a state of disagreement.

var•i•ant (vâr′ē ənt), *adj.* **1.** tending to change; exhibiting variety. **2.** differing, esp. from something of the same general kind. **3.** not definitive; alternative: *a variant reading.* **4.** not universally accepted. **—*n.* 5.** a person or thing that varies. **6.** a different spelling, pronunciation, or form of the same word: Vehemency *is a variant of* vehemence.

var•i•ate (vâr′ē it, -āt′), *n.* RANDOM VARIABLE.

var•i•a•tion (vâr′ē ā′shən), *n.* **1.** the act or process of varying: *prices subject to variation.* **2.** an instance of this: *a variation in quality.* **3.** amount or degree of change: *a temperature variation of 20°.* **4.** a different form of something. **5.** the transformation of a melody or theme with changes or elaborations in harmony, rhythm, and melody. **6.** a solo dance, esp. one forming a section of a pas de deux. **7.** any deviation from the mean orbit of a heavenly body. **8.** the angle between the geographic and the magnetic meridian at a given point. **9.** a deviation in structure or character from others of the same species. **—var′i•a′tion•al,** *adj.* **—var′i•a′tion•al•ly,** *adv.*

var•i•col•ored (vâr′i kul′ərd), *adj.* having various colors.

var•i•cose (var′i kōs′), *adj.* **1.** abnormally enlarged or swollen: *a varicose vein.* **2.** pertaining to or affected with varices.

var•ied (vâr′ēd), *adj.* **1.** characterized by or exhibiting variety; diverse. **2.** changed; altered. **3.** having several different colors.

var•i•e•gate (vâr′ē i gāt′, vâr′i gāt′), *v.t.,* **-gat•ed, -gat•ing. 1.** to make varied in appearance, as by adding different colors. **2.** to give variety to; diversify. **—var′i•e•ga′tion,** *n.* **—var′i•e•ga′tor,** *n.*

var•i•e•gat•ed (vâr′ē i gā′tid, vâr′i gā′-), *adj.* **1.** marked with patches or spots of different colors. **2.** varied; diverse.

va•ri•e•tal (və rī′i tl), *adj.* **1.** of or pertaining to a variety. **2.** constituting a variety. **3.** of or designating a wine made entirely or chiefly from one variety of grape. **—*n.* 4.** a varietal wine. **—va•ri′e•tal•ly,** *adv.*

va•ri•e•ty (və rī′i tē), *n., pl.* **-ties. 1.** the state of being diversified: *to give variety to one's diet.* **2.** difference; discrepancy. **3.** a number of different types of things, esp. ones in the same general category: *a large variety of fruits.* **4.** a kind or sort. **5.** a different form or phase of something: *varieties of experience.* **6.** a category within a species, based on some hereditary difference. **7.** a type of animal or plant produced by artificial selection. **8. a.** Also called **vari′ety show′.** an entertainment consisting of a series of brief performances, as of singing, dancing, and comedy. **b.** VAUDEVILLE (def. 1). **c.** MUSIC HALL (def. 3). **—*Proverb.* 9. Variety is the spice of life,** different activities make life more pleasurable. **—Usage.** As a collective noun, VARIETY, when preceded by *a,* is often treated as a plural: *A variety of inexpensive goods are sold here.* When preceded by *the,* it is usu. treated as a singular: *The variety of products is small.* See also COLLECTIVE NOUN, NUMBER.

vari′ety store′, *n.* a retail store with a wide variety of low-priced articles, as a five-and-ten.

var•i•o•rum (vâr′ē ôr′əm, -ōr′-), *adj.* **1.** containing different versions of a certain text. **2.** containing notes and commentaries by a number of scholars or critics. **—*n.* 3.** a variorum edition or text.

var•i•ous (vâr′ē əs), *adj.* **1.** of different kinds, as two or more things: *various cheeses for sale.* **2.** exhibiting diversity: *houses of various designs.* **3.** different from each other; dissimilar. **4.** several; many: *stayed at various hotels.* **5.** individual; separate: *We spoke to the various officials.* **6.** having many different qualities: *a woman of various talent.* **7.** having a variety of colors. **—var′i•ous•ly,** *adv.* **—var′i•ous•ness,** *n.*

var•mint or **var•ment** (vär′mənt), *n.* **1.** an undesirable, usu. predatory or verminous animal. **2.** an obnoxious or annoying person.

Var•na (vär′nə), *n.* a seaport in NE Bulgaria, on the Black Sea. 305,891. Formerly, **Stalin.**

var•nish (vär′nish), *n.* **1.** a preparation for coating surfaces, as of wood, consisting of resinous matter dissolved in oil, alcohol, or the like. **2.** the sap of certain trees, used for the same purpose. **3.** any of various other preparations similarly used, as one having India rubber as its chief constituent. **4.** a coating or surface of varnish. **5.** something suggesting this; gloss. **6.** superficial polish, esp. to conceal some inadequacy. **7.** NAIL POLISH. **—*v.t.* 8.** to coat with varnish. **9.** to give a glossy appearance to. **10.** to give an improved appearance to; adorn. **11.** to give a superficially pleasing appearance to, esp. in order to deceive: *to varnish the truth.* **—var′nish•er,** *n.* **—var′nish•y,** *adj.*

va•room (və ro͞om′, -ro͝om′, vä-), *n., v.* VROOM.

var•si•ty (vär′si tē), *n., pl.* **-ties,** *adj.* **—*n.* 1.** a first-string team, esp. in sports, representing a school, college, or university. **2.** *Chiefly Brit.* UNIVERSITY. **—*adj.* 3.** of or pertaining to a school or university team, activity, or competition. [British var. of *(uni)versity*]

var•y (vâr′ē), *v.,* **var•ied, var•y•ing. —*v.t.* 1.** to alter, as in form, appearance, character, or substance; to make different in some way: *to*

V

vary the program each night. **2.** to relieve from uniformity; diversify: to vary one's diet. **3.** to alter (a melody or theme) by modification or embellishments. —v.i. **4.** to show diversity; differ: Opinions vary. **5.** to undergo change, as in appearance or form. **6.** to change periodically or in succession: Demand varies with the season. **7.** to diverge; deviate: vary from the norm. **8.** to be subject to change, as a mathematical function. **9.** to exhibit biological variation. —**var'i•er,** n. —**var'y•ing•ly,** adv.

Va•sa•ri (və zär'ē, -sär'ē), n. **Giorgio,** 1511–74, Italian painter, architect, and art historian.

Vas•co da Ga•ma (vas'kō də gam'ə, gä'mə), n. **Gama,** Vasco da.

vas•cu•lar (vas'kyə lər), adj. pertaining to, composed of, or provided with vessels that convey fluids, as blood or sap. —**vas'cu•lar'i•ty,** n.

vas'cular bun'dle, n. any of the strands of the conducting channels in vascular plants composed of xylem and phloem in various structural arrangements.

vas•cu•lar•ize (vas'kyə lə rīz'), v., **-ized, -iz•ing.** —v.i. **1.** (of a tissue) to develop or extend blood vessels or other fluid-bearing vessels or ducts. —v.t. **2.** to supply (an organ or tissue) with blood vessels. —**vas'•cu•lar•i•za'tion,** n.

vas'cular tis'sue, n. plant tissue consisting of ducts or vessels that in the higher plants forms the system (**vas'cular sys'tem**) by which sap is conveyed through the plant.

vas def•e•rens (vas' def'ə renz', -ər ənz), n., pl. **va•sa de•fe•ren•ti•a** (vā'sə def'ə ren'shē ə, -shə) a duct that transports sperm from the epididymis to the penis.

vase (vās, vāz, väz), n. a vessel, as of glass or porcelain, usu. higher than it is wide, used to hold cut flowers or for decoration. —**vase'like',** adj.

va•sec•to•my (va sek'tə mē, vā zek'-), n., pl. **-mies.** surgical excision of part or all of the vas deferens to effect sterility in men. —**va•sec'to•mize',** v.t., **-mized, -miz•ing.**

Vas•e•line (vas'ə lēn', vas'ə lēn'), Trademark. a brand of petrolatum.

Vash•ti (vash'tē, -tī), n. the queen of Ahasuerus, banished by him for refusing to appear before his guests. Esther 1:9–22.

vaso-, a combining form meaning "vessel": vasoconstrictor.

vas•o•con•stric•tor (vas'ō kən strik'tər, vā'zō-), n. any of various agents, as certain nerves or drugs, that narrow blood vessels and thereby maintain or increase blood pressure. —**vas'o•con•stric'tion,** n. —**vas'o•con•stric'tive,** adj.

vas•o•di•la•tor (vas'ō dī lā'tər, -di-, -dī'lā-, vā'zō-), n. any of various agents, as certain nerves or drugs, that relax or widen blood vessels and thereby maintain or lower blood pressure. —**vas'o•di•la'tion,** n., —**vas'o•di•la'tive,** adj.

vas•o•mo•tor (vas'ō mō'tər, vā'zō-), adj. regulating the diameter of blood vessels, as certain nerves.

vas•sal (vas'əl), n. **1.** (in the feudal system) a person granted the use of land in return for rendering homage, fealty, and usu. military service to a lord or other superior; feudal tenant. **2.** a person holding some similar relation to a superior; a subject or subordinate. **3.** a servant or slave. —adj. **4.** of or characteristic of a vassal. **5.** having the status or position of a vassal.

vas•sal•age (vas'ə lij), n. **1.** the state of being a vassal. **2.** homage or service required of a vassal.

vast (vast, väst), adj. **1.** of very great area or extent. **2.** of very great size or proportions. **3.** very great in number, quantity, or amount. **4.** very great in degree or intensity. —n. **5.** Literary. an immense expanse or space. —**vast'ly,** adv. —**vast'ness,** n.

vas•ti•tude (vas'ti tōōd', -tyōōd', vä'sti-), n. **1.** vastness; immensity. **2.** a vast expanse or space.

vat (vat), n., v., **vat•ted, vat•ting.** —n. **1.** a large container, as a tank, used for holding liquids: a wine vat. **2. a.** a preparation containing an insoluble dye that is converted by reduction to a water-soluble form. **b.** a vessel containing such a preparation. —v.t. **3.** to put into or treat in a vat.

VAT, value-added tax.

vat' dye', n. any of a class of water-insoluble dyes that are taken up by textile fibers and then fixed by oxidation.

Vat•i•can (vat'i kən), n. **1.** Also called **Vat'ican Pal'ace.** the chief residence of the popes in Vatican City. **2.** the authority and government of the pope. [< Latin vātīcānus (mōns) Vatican (hill)]

Vatican II, n. Second Vatican Council.

Vat'ican Cit'y, n. an independent state within the city of Rome, on the right bank of the Tiber: established in 1929. 1000; 109 acres (44 hectares). Italian, Città del Vaticano.

va•tu (vä'tōō), n., pl. **-tus.** the basic monetary unit of Vanuatu.

vaude•ville (vôd'vil, vōd'-, vô'də-), n. **1.** a form of popular entertainment in the U.S. from the late 1800s to the mid 1920s, having a program of separate and varied acts. **2.** a light theatrical piece interspersed with songs and dances. —**vaude•vil'lian,** n., adj.

Vaughan' Wil'liams, n. Ralph (usu. rāf), 1872–1958, English composer.

vault¹ (vôlt), n. **1.** an arched structure, usu. of stones, concrete, or bricks, forming a ceiling or roof. **2.** a space, chamber, or passage enclosed by a vault or vaultlike structure, esp. one located underground. **3.** a room or compartment for the safekeeping of valuables. **4.** a burial chamber. **5.** something likened to an arched roof: the vault of heaven.

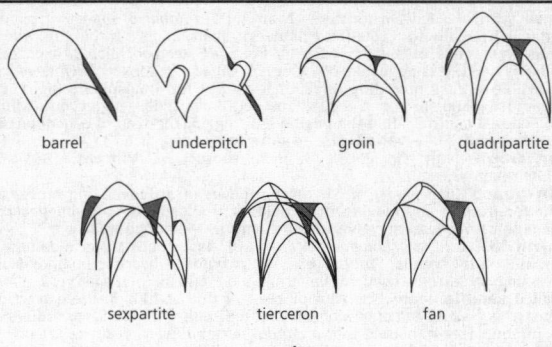

barrel   underpitch   groin   quadripartite

sexpartite   tierceron   fan

vault

—v.t. **6.** to construct or cover with or as if with a vault. **7.** to store in a vault. —v.i. **8.** to curve in the form of a vault.

vault² (vôlt), v.i. **1.** to leap, as to or from a position or over something: to vault over the tennis net. **2.** to leap with the hands supported by something, as by a horizontal pole. **3.** to leap over a horse in gymnastics, using the hands for pushing off. **4.** to achieve something as if by a leap: to vault into prominence. —v.t. **5.** to leap over. **6.** to cause to leap over or surpass others. —n. **7.** the act of vaulting. **8.** a leap of a horse; curvet. —**vault'er,** n.

vault•ing¹ (vôl'ting), n. **1.** the act or process of constructing vaults. **2.** the structure forming a vault. **3.** such structures collectively.

vault•ing² (vôl'ting), adj. **1.** leaping up or over. **2.** used in vaulting: a vaulting pole. **3.** excessive in presumption; overweening: vaulting ambition.

vault'ing horse', n. a padded, somewhat cylindrical, floor-supported gymnastic apparatus braced horizontally at an adjustable height, used in vaulting. Also called **long horse.**

vaunt (vônt, vänt), v.t. **1.** to boast of: to vaunt one's achievements. —v.i. **2.** to speak boastfully; brag. —n. **3.** a boastful action or utterance. —**vaunt'er,** n. —**vaunt'ing•ly,** adv.

vb., **1.** verb. **2.** verbal.

VC, 1. venture capital. **2.** vice-chancellor. **3.** vice-consul. **4.** Victoria Cross. **5.** Vietcong. **6.** vital capacity.

V-chip (vē'chip'), n. a computer chip or other electronic device that blocks the reception of violent or sexually explicit television shows.

VCR, videocassette recorder: an electronic device capable of recording television programs or other signals onto videocassettes and playing them, or prerecorded cassettes, back through a television receiver.

VD, 1. Also, **v.d.** various dates. **2.** venereal disease.

V-Day (vē'dā'), n. a day of final military victory.

VDT, video display terminal.

've, contraction of have: I've got it.

Ve•a•dar (vē'ə där', vē'ə där'), n. Adar Sheni.

veal (vēl), n. **1.** the flesh of a calf as used for food. **2.** Also, **veal'er.** a calf raised for its meat.

vec•tor (vek'tər), n. **1.** a quantity possessing both magnitude and direction, as force or velocity. Compare scalar (def. 4). **2.** the direction or course followed by something, as an airplane. **3. a.** something or someone, as a person or an insect, that carries and transmits a disease-causing organism. **b.** any agent, as a mutated virus, that acts as a carrier or transporter. —v.t. **4. a.** to guide (an aircraft) in flight by issuing appropriate headings. **b.** to change direction of (the thrust of a jet or rocket engine) in order to steer the craft.

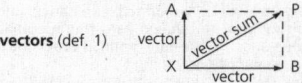

vectors (def. 1)

Ve•da (vā'də, vē'-), n., pl. **-das. 1.** Sometimes, **Vedas.** the sacred scriptures of Hinduism, esp. as comprising the hymns and formulas in the Rig-Veda, the Sama-Veda, the Atharva-Veda, and the Yajur-Veda. **2.** Also called **Samhita.** any of these individual writings. —**Ve•da•ic** (vi-dā'ik), adj. —**Ve'da•ism,** n.

Ve•dan•ta (vi dän'tə, -dan'-), n. the chief Hindu philosophy, dealing mainly with the Upanishadic doctrine of the identity of Brahman and Atman. —**Ve•dan'tic,** adj. —**Ve•dan'tism,** n. —**Ve•dan'tist,** n.

V-E Day, n. May 8, 1945, the day of victory in Europe for the Allies in World War II.

Ve•dic (vā'dik, vē'-), adj. **1.** of or pertaining to the Veda or Vedas. —n. **2.** Also called **Ve'dic San'skrit.** the language of the Vedas, closely related to classical Sanskrit.

vee (vē), adj. **1.** shaped like the letter V: a vee neckline. —n. **2.** anything shaped like or suggesting a V.

veep (vēp), *n. Informal.* a vice president.

veer (vēr), *v.i.* **1.** to change direction or turn aside; shift or change from one course, position, etc., to another. **2.** (of the wind) **a.** to change direction clockwise (opposed to *back*). **b.** *Naut.* to shift to a direction more nearly astern (opposed to *haul*). —*v.t.* **3.** to alter the direction or course of; turn. **4.** to turn (a vessel) away from the wind; wear. —*n.* **5.** a change of direction, position, course, etc.

veg (vej), *n., pl.* **veg,** *v.,* **vegged, veg·ging.** *Informal.* —*n.* **1.** *Chiefly Brit.* a vegetable. —*v.i.* **2.** to relax passively, esp. while watching television; vegetate (often fol. by *out*).

Ve·ga[1] (vē′gə, vā′-), *n.* a star of the first magnitude in the constellation Lyra.

Ve·ga[2] (vā′gə), *n.* **Lo·pe de** (lō′pā), (*Lope Félix de Vega Carpio*), 1562–1635, Spanish dramatist and poet.

ve·gan (vē′gən, vej′ən), *n.* a vegetarian who omits all animal products from the diet. —**ve′gan·ism,** *n.*

veg·e·ta·ble (vej′tə bəl, vej′i tə-), *n.* **1.** any plant whose fruit, seeds, roots, tubers, stems, leaves, or flower parts are used as food. **2.** any part of a plant that is customarily eaten and is not developed from a flower. Compare FRUIT (def. 1). **3.** any member of the vegetable kingdom; plant. **4.** a person who is severely impaired mentally or physically. **5.** an inactive, dull, or spiritless person. —*adj.* **6.** of, consisting of, or made from edible vegetables. **7.** of, pertaining to, or characteristic of plants. **8.** derived from plants. **9.** comprising or containing the substance or remains of plants: *vegetable matter.*

veg′etable king′dom, *n.* the plants of the world collectively (contrasted with *animal kingdom, mineral kingdom*).

veg′etable oil′, *n.* any of various liquid oils derived from the fruit or seeds of plants.

veg·e·tal (vej′i tl), *adj.* **1.** of, pertaining to, or of the nature of plants or vegetables. **2.** VEGETATIVE (def. 7).

veg·e·tar·i·an (vej′i târ′ē ən), *n.* **1.** a person who does not eat or does not believe in eating meat, fish, fowl, or, in some cases, any food derived from animals. —*adj.* **2.** of or pertaining to vegetarianism or vegetarians. **3.** consisting solely of vegetables.

veg·e·tar·i·an·ism (vej′i târ′ē ə niz′əm), *n.* the beliefs or practices of a vegetarian.

veg·e·tate (vej′i tāt′), *v.i.,* **-tat·ed, -tat·ing. 1.** to grow as or like a plant. **2.** to lead an inactive life without much physical, mental, or social activity.

veg·e·ta·tion (vej′i tā′shən), *n.* **1.** all the plants or plant life of a place. **2.** the act or process of vegetating. **3.** a dull or passive existence. —**veg′e·ta′tion·al,** *adj.*

veg·e·ta·tive (vej′i tā′tiv), *adj.* **1.** growing or developing as or like plants; vegetating. **2.** of, pertaining to, or concerned with vegetation or vegetable growth. **3.** noting the parts of a plant not specialized for reproduction. **4.** (of reproduction) asexual. **5.** noting or pertaining to unconscious or involuntary bodily functions. **6.** having the power to produce or support growth in plants: *vegetative mold.* **7.** inactive; passive: *a vegetative existence.* Sometimes, **veg′e·tive.** —**veg′e·ta′tive·ly,** *adv.*

veg·gie or **veg·ie** (vej′ē), *n. Informal.* **1.** a vegetable. **2.** a vegetarian.

ve·he·mence (vē′ə məns) also **ve′he·men·cy,** *n.* **1.** the quality of being vehement. **2.** vigorous impetuosity; fury.

ve·he·ment (vē′ə mənt), *adj.* **1.** zealous; ardent; impassioned: *a vehement defense.* **2.** characterized by rancor or anger: *vehement opposition.* **3.** marked by great energy or vigor: *a vehement shake of the head.* —**ve′he·ment·ly,** *adv.*

ve·hi·cle (vē′i kəl *or, sometimes,* vē′hi-), *n.* **1.** any means in or by which someone or something is carried or conveyed; means of conveyance or transport: *a motor vehicle.* **2.** a conveyance moving on wheels, runners, or the like, as an automobile. **3.** a means of transmission or passage: *Air is the vehicle of sound.* **4.** a medium of communication, expression, or display: *Language is the vehicle of thought.* **5.** a play, screenplay, or other work with a role designed or especially well-suited to display the talents of a particular performer. **6.** a chemically inert substance used as a medium for active remedies. **7.** a liquid, as oil, in which a paint pigment is mixed before being applied to a surface.

ve·hic·u·lar (vē hik′yə lər), *adj.* **1.** of, pertaining to, or for vehicles. **2.** serving as a vehicle. **3.** caused by a vehicle: *vehicular homicide.*

V-eight or **V-8** (vē′āt′), *n.* a V-engine having eight cylinders.

veil (vāl), *n.* **1.** a piece of opaque, transparent, or mesh material worn over the face for concealment or protection. **2.** a piece of material worn so as to fall over the head and shoulders on each side of the face, forming a part of a headdress, as of a nun or a bride. **3.** something that covers, screens, or conceals. **4.** VELUM (def. 1). **5.** a caul. —*v.t.* **6.** to cover or conceal with or as if with a veil. —*v.i.* **7.** to don or wear a veil. —*Idiom.* **8. take the veil,** to become a nun.

veiled (vāld), *adj.* **1.** having or wearing a veil. **2.** not openly or directly revealed or expressed: *a veiled threat.*

veil·ing (vā′ling), *n.* **1.** a veil. **2.** a thin net for veils.

vein (vān), *n.* **1.** one of the system of branching vessels or tubes conveying blood from various parts of the body to the heart. **2.** (loosely) any blood vessel. **3.** one of the riblike thickenings that form the framework of the wing of an insect. **4.** one of the strands or bundles of vascular tissue forming the principal framework of a leaf. **5. a.** a body or mass of mineral deposit, igneous rock, or the like occupying a crevice or fissure in rock; lode. **b.** any body or stratum of ore, coal, etc., clearly separated or defined. **6.** a streak or marking, as of a different color, running through marble, wood, etc. **7.** a temporary attitude, mood, or temper: *spoke in a serious vein.* **8.** a tendency, quality, or strain traceable in conduct, writing, etc.: *a vein of pessimism.* —*v.t.* **9.** to furnish with veins. **10.** to mark with lines or streaks suggesting veins. **11.** to extend over or through in the manner of veins.

ve·lar (vē′lər), *adj.* **1.** of or pertaining to a velum, esp. the soft palate. **2.** (of a consonant) articulated with the tongue close to or touching the soft palate, as the sounds (k), (g), or (ng). —*n.* **3.** a velar consonant.

Ve·láz·quez (və läs′kes, -läs′kəs), *n.* **Diego Rodríguez de Silva y,** 1599–1660, Spanish painter.

Vel·cro (vel′krō), *Trademark.* a fastening tape consisting of opposing pieces of nylon fabric, one with tiny hooks and the other with a dense pile, that interlock when pressed together, used as a closure on garments, luggage, etc.

vel·lum (vel′əm), *n.* **1.** calfskin, lambskin, kidskin, etc., treated for use as a writing surface. **2.** a manuscript or the like on vellum. **3.** a texture of paper or cloth resembling vellum. —*adj.* **4.** made of or resembling vellum. **5.** bound in vellum.

ve·loc·i·pede (və los′ə pēd′), *n.* an early kind of bicycle or tricycle.

ve·loc·i·ty (və los′i tē), *n., pl.* **-ties. 1.** rapidity of motion, action, or operation; swiftness; speed. **2.** *Mech.* the time rate of change of position of a body in a specified direction.

ve·lo·drome (vē′lə drōm′, vel′ə-), *n.* a sports arena equipped with a banked track for cycling.

ve·lour or **ve·lours** (və lŏŏr′), *n.* **1.** a velvetlike fabric of rayon, wool, or any of several other natural or synthetic fibers, used for clothing and upholstery. **2.** a velvety fur felt, as of beaver, for hats.

ve·lou·té (və lŏŏ tā′), *n.* a smooth white sauce made with meat, poultry, or fish stock. Also called **velouté′ sauce′.**

ve·lum (vē′ləm), *n., pl.* **-la** (-lə). **1.** *Biol.* any of various veillike or curtainlike membranous partitions. **2.** the soft palate. See under PALATE (def. 1). **3.** the frontal ciliated swimming organ of gastropod larvae.

ve·lure (və lŏŏr′), *n.* velvet or a substance resembling it.

vel·vet (vel′vit), *n.* **1.** a fabric of silk, nylon, acetate, rayon, etc., sometimes having a cotton backing, with a thick, soft pile formed of loops of the warp thread, either cut at the end or left uncut. **2.** something likened to this fabric, as in softness or texture. **3.** the soft, deciduous covering of a growing antler. **4.** *Informal.* **a.** winnings. **b.** clear gain or profit. —*adj.* **5.** Also, **vel′vet·ed.** made of or covered with velvet. **6.** resembling or suggesting velvet; smooth; soft.

vel′vet ant′, *n.* any of several fuzzy, often brightly colored wasps of the family Mutillidae, the wingless, antlike female of which inflicts a severe sting.

vel′vet bean′, *n.* a vine, *Stizolobium deeringianum,* of the legume family, having long clusters of purplish flowers and densely hairy pods, grown in warm regions for forage or as an ornamental.

vel·vet·een (vel′vi tēn′), *n.* **1.** a cotton pile fabric with short, velvetlike pile. **2.** velveteens, trousers of this fabric.

vel·vet·y (vel′vi tē), *adj.* **1.** suggestive of or resembling velvet; smooth; soft. **2.** (of liquor) smooth-tasting; mild; mellow.

ve·na ca·va (vē′nə kā′və), *n., pl.* **ve·nae ca·vae** (vē′nē kā′vē). either of two large veins discharging blood into the right atrium of the heart.

ve·nal (vēn′l), *adj.* **1.** open to bribery or corruption: *a venal judge.* **2.** able to be purchased, as by a bribe: *venal acquittals.* **3.** associated with or characterized by bribery. —**ve·nal′i·ty,** *n.* —**ve′nal·ly,** *adv.*

ve·na·tion (vē nā′shən, və-), *n.* **1.** the arrangement of veins, as in a leaf or in the wing of an insect. **2.** these veins collectively.

pinnate   palmate   parallel

venation of leaves

vend (vend), *v.t.* **1.** to sell as one's occupation, esp. by peddling: *to vend flowers at a sidewalk stand.* **2.** to give utterance to (opinions, ideas, etc.); publish. —*v.i.* **3.** to engage in selling merchandise. **4.** to be sold.

vend·er (ven′dər), *n.* VENDOR.

ven·det·ta (ven det′ə), *n., pl.* **-tas. 1.** a private feud, as formerly in Corsica and Italy, in which the family of a murdered person seeks vengeance by killing the slayer or one of the slayer's relatives. **2.** any prolonged and bitter feud, rivalry, or the like. —**ven·det′tist,** *n.*

vend·i·ble (ven′də bəl), *adj.* **1.** capable of being vended; salable. —*n.* **2.** Usu., **vendibles.** vendible articles. —**vend′i·bil′i·ty,** *n.* —**vend′i·bly,** *adv.*

vend′ing machine′, *n.* a coin-operated machine for selling small articles, as candy bars or soft drinks.

ven·dor (ven′dər; *esp. contrastively* ven dôr′), *n.* **1.** a person or agency that sells. **2.** VENDING MACHINE.

ve·neer (və nēr′), *n.* **1.** a thin layer of wood or other material for facing or inlaying wood. **2.** any of the thin layers of wood glued together to form plywood. **3.** a facing of a certain material applied to a different one or to a type of construction not ordinarily associated with it. **4.** a superficially good or pleasing appearance. —*v.t.* **5.** to overlay or face (wood) with thin sheets of some material, as a fine wood, ivory, or tortoiseshell. **6.** to face or cover (an object) with a more desirable material than the existing basic one. **7.** to cement (layers of wood veneer) to form plywood.

ven·er·a·ble (ven′ər ə bəl), *adj.* **1.** worthy of respect or reverence, as because of great age, high office, or noble character. **2.** a title given to an Anglican archdeacon, or to a person proclaimed by the Roman Catholic Church to have attained the first degree of sanctity. **3.** hallowed by religious, historic, or other lofty associations: *the venerable halls of the abbey.* —*n.* **4.** a venerable person. —**ven′er·a·bil′i·ty, ven′er·a·ble·ness,** *n.* —**ven′er·a·bly,** *adv.*

ven·er·ate (ven′ə rāt′), *v.t.,* **-at·ed, -at·ing.** to regard or treat with reverence; revere. —**ven′er·a′tor,** *n.*

ven·er·a·tion (ven′ə rā′shən), *n.* **1.** the act of venerating or the state of being venerated. **2.** the feeling of a person who venerates.

ve·ne·re·al (və nēr′ē əl), *adj.* **1.** arising from, connected with, or transmitted through sexual intercourse, as an infection. **2.** pertaining to conditions so arising. **3.** infected with or suffering from a sexually transmitted disease. **4.** adapted to the cure of such disease. **5.** of or pertaining to sexual desire or intercourse.

vene′real disease′, *n.* SEXUALLY TRANSMITTED DISEASE. *Abbr.:* VD

Ve·ne·tian (və nē′shən), *adj.* **1.** of or pertaining to Venice, its residents, or their speech. —*n.* **2.** a native or resident of Venice. **3.** the form of Upper Italian spoken in Venice and its environs. **4.** (*l.c.*) VENETIAN BLIND. **5.** Also called **Vene′tian cloth′. a.** a wool or worsted fabric made in satin or twill weave and sometimes napped, used in the manufacture of coats, suits, skirts, and dresses. **b.** a cotton fabric constructed in satin or twill weave, used chiefly for linings.

vene′tian blind′, *n.* a window blind having overlapping horizontal slats that may be opened, closed, or set at an angle, esp. one in which the slats may be raised and drawn together by pulling a cord.

Vene′tian glass′, *n.* ornamental glassware of the type made at Venice.

Ven·e·zue·la (ven′ə zwā′lə, -zwē′-), *n.* **1.** a republic in N South America. 22,396,407; 352,143 sq. mi. (912,050 sq. km). *Cap.:* Caracas. **2. Gulf of,** a gulf on the NW coast of Venezuela. —**Ven′e·zue′lan,** *adj., n.*

venge·ance (ven′jəns), *n.* **1.** infliction of injury, harm, humiliation, or the like in return for an injury or other offense received; revenge. **2.** an opportunity for or an instance of this. **3.** the desire for revenge: *to be full of vengeance.* —**Idiom. 4. with a vengeance, a.** with violent force and rage. **b.** with extreme or excessive energy: *to set to work with a vengeance.*

venge·ful (venj′fəl), *adj.* **1.** desiring or seeking vengeance; vindictive. **2.** characterized by or showing a vindictive spirit. —**venge′ful·ly,** *adv.* —**venge′ful·ness,** *n.*

V-en·gine (vē′jən), *n.* an internal-combustion engine having two opposed banks of cylinders inclined so that they form a V-shaped angle.

ve·ni·al (vē′nē əl, vēn′yəl), *adj.* **1.** able to be forgiven or pardoned: *venial offenses.* **2.** excusable; trifling; minor: *a venial error.* —**ve′ni·al′i·ty,** *n.* —**ve′ni·al·ly,** *adv.*

ve′nial sin′, *n.* Rom. Cath. Ch. a sin that does not deprive the soul of divine grace either because it is a minor offense or because it was committed without full consent or understanding of its seriousness. Compare MORTAL SIN.

Ven·ice (ven′is), *n.* **1.** Italian, **Venezia.** a seaport in NE Italy, built on numerous small islands in the Lagoon of Venice. 361,722. **2. Gulf of,** the N arm of the Adriatic Sea. **3. Lagoon of,** an inlet of the Gulf of Venice.

ven·i·son (ven′ə sən, -zən), *n.* the flesh of a deer or similar animal as used for food.

Ve·ni·te (vi nī′tē, ve nē′tā), *n.* **1.** the 95th Psalm (94th in the Vulgate and Douay), used as a canticle at matins or morning prayers. **2.** a musical setting of this psalm. [< Latin: come ye; so called from the first word of Vulgate text]

ve·ni, vi·di, vi·ci (wā′nē wē′dē wē′kē; *Eng.* vē′nī vī′dī vī′sī, ven′ē vē′dē vē′chē, -sē), *Latin.* I came, I saw, I conquered.

Venn′ di′agram (ven), *n.* Math., Logic. a diagram that uses circles to represent sets and their relationships.

ve·nog·ra·phy (vē nog′rə fē), *n.* x-ray examination of a vein or veins following injection of a radiopaque substance.

ve·nol·o·gy (vē nol′ə jē), *n.* PHLEBOLOGY.

ven·om (ven′əm), *n.* **1.** the poisonous fluid that some animals, as certain snakes and spiders, secrete and introduce into the bodies of their victims by biting, stinging, etc. **2.** something suggesting poison in its effect, as malice or jealousy. —*v.t.* **3.** to apply venom to.

ven·om·ous (ven′ə məs), *adj.* **1.** (of an animal) having a gland or glands for secreting venom; able to inflict a poisonous bite or sting. **2.** full of or containing venom; poisonous. **3.** spiteful; malignant. —**ven′om·ous·ly,** *adv.* —**ven′om·ous·ness,** *n.*

ve·nous (vē′nəs), *adj.* **1.** of or pertaining to a vein or veins. **2.** having or composed of veins. **3.** pertaining to or designating the oxygen-poor, dark red blood that is carried back to the heart by the veins and by the

pulmonary artery. —**ve′nous·ly,** *adv.* —**ve′nous·ness, ve·nos·i·ty** (vi nos′i tē), *n.*

vent[1] (vent), *n.* **1.** an opening, as in a wall, serving as an outlet for air, fumes, or the like. **2.** an opening at the earth's surface from which volcanic material, as lava or gas, is emitted. **3.** a means of exit or escape; an outlet, as from confinement. **4.** expression; utterance; release: *giving vent to one's emotions.* **5.** the small opening at the breech of a gun by which fire is communicated to the charge. **6.** Zool. the external opening of the cloaca. —*v.t.* **7.** to give free play or expression to (an emotion). **8.** to relieve through such expression: *to vent one's disappointment.* **9.** to release or discharge (liquid, smoke, etc.). **10.** to furnish or provide with a vent or vents. —*v.i.* **11.** to be relieved of pressure or discharged by means of a vent. **12.** (of a marine animal) to rise to the surface of the water to breathe.

vent[2] (vent), *n.* a slit in the back or side of a coat, jacket, or other garment, at the bottom part of a seam.

ven·ter (ven′tər), *n.* **1.** Anat., Zool. **a.** the abdomen or belly. **b.** a bellylike cavity. **c.** a bellylike protuberance. **2.** Law. **a.** the womb. **b.** a wife as a source of offspring.

ven·ti·late (ven′tl āt′), *v.,* **-lat·ed, -lat·ing.** —*v.t.* **1.** to provide (a room, mine, etc.) with fresh air in place of air that has been used or contaminated. **2.** (of air or wind) to circulate through or blow on, so as to cool or freshen the air of: *Cool breezes ventilated the house.* **3.** to expose to the action of air or wind: *to ventilate floor timbers.* **4.** to submit (a question, problem, etc.) to open, full examination and discussion. **5.** to give utterance or expression to (an opinion, complaint, etc.). **6.** to furnish with a vent or opening, as for the escape of air or gas. **7. a.** to oxygenate (blood) by exposure to air in the lungs or gills. **b.** to assist the breathing of (a person), as with a respirator. —*v.i.* **8.** to give utterance or expression to one's emotions, opinions, etc.

ven·ti·la·tion (ven′tl ā′shən), *n.* **1.** the act of ventilating or the state of being ventilated. **2.** facilities or equipment for providing ventilation. —**ven′ti·la·tive, ven′ti·la·to·ry** (-ə tôr′ē, -tōr′ē), *adj.*

ven·ti·la·tor (ven′tl ā′tər), *n.* **1.** one that ventilates. **2.** a contrivance or opening for replacing foul or stagnant air with fresh air.

ven·tral (ven′trəl), *adj.* **1.** of or pertaining to the venter or belly; abdominal. **2.** situated on or toward the lower, abdominal plane of an animal's body, equivalent to the front in humans. **3.** of or designating the lower or inner surface of a plant structure. —**ven′tral·ly,** *adv.*

ven·tri·cle (ven′tri kəl), *n.* **1.** any of various hollow organs or parts in an animal body. **2.** either of the two lower chambers of the heart that receive blood from the atria and in turn force it into the arteries. **3.** one of a series of connecting cavities of the brain.

ven·tri·cose (ven′tri kōs′), *adj.* **1.** protuberant on one side. **2.** having a large abdomen.

ven·tric·u·lar (ven trik′yə lər), *adj.* **1.** of, pertaining to, or of the nature of a ventricle. **2.** of or pertaining to a belly or to something resembling one.

ven·tril·o·quism (ven tril′ə kwiz′əm) also **ven·tril·o·quy** (-kwē), *n.* the art or practice of speaking with little or no lip movement so that the voice does not appear to come from the speaker but from another source. —**ven′tri·lo′qui·al** (-trə lō′kwē əl), **ven·tril′o·qual,** *adj.* —**ven′tri·lo/qui·al·ly,** *adv.*

ven·tril·o·quist (ven tril′ə kwist), *n.* a person who performs or is skilled in ventriloquism.

ven·ture (ven′chər), *n., v.,* **-tured, -tur·ing.** —*n.* **1.** an undertaking involving risk or uncertainty. **2.** a business enterprise in which something is risked in the hope of profit. **3.** the money or property risked in such an enterprise. —*v.t.* **4.** to expose to hazard; risk. **5.** to take the risk of; brave: *to venture a voyage.* **6.** to undertake to express, in spite of possible contradiction or opposition: *to venture a guess.* —*v.i.* **7.** to undertake or embark upon a venture: *We ventured deep into the jungle; to venture upon an ambitious program of reform.* **8.** to invest venture capital. —**Idiom. 9. at a venture,** according to chance; at random. —**ven′tur·er,** *n.*

ven′ture cap′ital, *n.* funds invested or available for investment in a new business enterprise. —**ven′ture cap′italism,** *n.* —**ven′ture cap′italist,** *n.*

ven·ture·some (ven′chər səm), *adj.* **1.** having or showing a disposition to undertake ventures; adventurous. **2.** attended with risk; hazardous. —**ven′ture·some·ly,** *adv.* —**ven′ture·some·ness,** *n.*

ven·tu′ri tube′ (ven toōr′ē), *n.* **1.** a device for measuring fluid flow, consisting of a tube constricted in such a way that a pressure differential is created between the center and the ends. **2.** an alteration in the shape of the throat of a carburetor for controlling the flow of fuel. [after G. B. *Venturi* (1746–1822), Italian physicist]

ven·tur·ous (ven′chər əs), *adj.* VENTURESOME. —**ven′tur·ous·ly,** *adv.* —**ven′tur·ous·ness,** *n.*

ven·ue (ven′yoō), *n.* **1.** Law. **a.** the place of a crime or cause of action. **b.** the county or place where the jury is gathered and the case tried. **c.** the designation of the place where a trial will be held. **2.** the scene or locale of any action or event.

Ve·nus (vē′nəs), *n., pl.* **-us·es. 1.** The Roman goddess of love and beauty, identified with Aphrodite. **2.** an exceptionally beautiful woman. **3.** the most brilliant planet, second in order from the sun, having an equatorial diameter of 7521 miles (12,104 km), a mean distance from the sun of 67.2 million miles (108.2 million km), a period of revolution of 224.68 days, and no moons. **4.** Also called **Ve′nus fig′ure.** (*some-*

times l.c.) a statuette of a female figure, usu. carved of ivory and typically having exaggerated breasts, belly, or buttocks, often found in Upper Paleolithic cultures from Siberia to France.

Ve′nus's-fly′trap, *n.* an insectivorous bog plant, *Dionaea muscipula,* of the sundew family, native to the Carolinas, having spiny-edged leaves divided in halves that snap shut when sensitive hairs on their inner surface are touched.

Venus's-flytrap, *Dionaea muscipula,*
height about 1 ft. (0.3 m)

ve•ra•cious (və rā′shəs), *adj.* **1.** habitually truthful. **2.** characterized by truthfulness. —**ve•ra′cious•ly,** *adv.* —**ve•ra′cious•ness,** *n.*

ve•rac•i•ty (və ras′i tē), *n., pl.* **-ties. 1.** habitual observance of truth in speech or statement; truthfulness. **2.** conformity to truth or fact; accuracy. **3.** correctness or accuracy. **4.** something veracious; a truth.

ve•ran•da or **ve•ran•dah** (və ran′də), *n., pl.* **-das** or **-dahs.** a porch, usu. roofed and partly enclosed, often extending across the front and sides of a house. —**ve•ran′daed, ve•ran′dahed,** *adj.*

verb (vûrb), *n.* a member of a class of words that function as the main elements of predicates, typically express action, state, or a relation between two things, and are often formally distinguished, as by being inflected for tense, aspect, voice, mood, or agreement with the subject or object. *Abbr.:* v.

ver•bal (vûr′bəl), *adj.* **1.** of or consisting of words: *verbal ability.* **2.** spoken rather than written; oral: *verbal communication.* **3.** pertaining to or concerned with words only, rather than with the ideas, facts, or realities expressed: *a purely verbal distinction.* **4.** corresponding word for word; verbatim: *a verbal translation.* **5. a.** of, pertaining to, or derived from a verb: *a verbal adjective.* **b.** used in a sentence as or like a verb. —*n.* **6.** a word, esp. a noun or adjective, derived from a verb, as a gerund, infinitive, or participle. **7.** a word or group of words functioning as or like a verb. —**ver′bal•ly,** *adv.* —**Usage.** VERBAL has had the meaning "spoken" since the late 16th century and is thus synonymous with ORAL: *I wrote a memorandum to confirm the verbal agreement.* Although some say this use produces ambiguity, the context usu. makes the meaning clear: *No documents are necessary; a verbal order will suffice.* ORAL can be used if the context demands: *My lawyer insists on a written contract because oral agreements are too difficult to enforce.*

ver•bal•ism (vûr′bə liz′əm), *n.* **1.** a verbal expression, as a word or phrase. **2.** a phrase or sentence having little or no meaning. **3.** a use of words considered as obscuring the ideas or facts; verbiage.

ver•bal•ist (vûr′bə list), *n.* **1.** a person skilled in the use of words. **2.** a person who is more concerned with words than with ideas or facts. —**ver′bal•is′tic,** *adj.*

ver•bal•ize (vûr′bə līz′), *v.,* **-ized, -iz•ing.** —*v.t.* **1.** to express in words. **2.** to convert into or use as a verb. —*v.i.* **3.** to use many words; be verbose. **4.** to express something verbally. —**ver′bal•i•za′tion,** *n.*

ver′bal noun′, *n.* a noun derived from a verb, esp. by a regular process, as the *-ing* form in *Smoking is forbidden.*

ver•ba•tim (vər bā′tim), *adv.* **1.** in exactly the same words; word for word. —*adj.* **2.** corresponding word for word to the original source or text: *a verbatim record of the proceedings.*

ver•be•na (vər bē′nə), *n., pl.* **-nas.** any plant of the genus *Verbena,* esp. any of several hybrid species cultivated for their showy flower clusters.

ver•bi•age (vûr′bē ij), *n.* **1.** overabundance or superfluity of words, as in writing or speech. **2.** manner or style of expressing something in words; wording.

ver•bose (vər bōs′), *adj.* expressed in or characterized by the use of many or too many words; wordy: *a verbose report; a verbose speaker.* —**ver•bose′ly,** *adv.* —**ver•bos′i•ty** (-bos′i tē), **ver•bose′ness,** *n.*

ver•bo•ten (vər bōt′n; *Ger.* fɛʀ bōt′n), *adj.* forbidden, as by law; prohibited.

verb′ phrase′, *n.* **1.** a grammatical construction consisting of a verb and its complements, objects, or other modifiers that combines with a noun or noun phrase acting as subject to form a sentence. *Abbr.:* VP **2.** a phrase that functions syntactically as a verb, consisting of a main verb and any auxiliaries.

ver•dant (vûr′dnt), *adj.* **1.** green with vegetation; covered with growing plants or grass. **2.** of the color green. **3.** inexperienced; unsophisticated. —**ver′dan•cy,** *n.* —**ver′dant•ly,** *adv.*

Ver•di (vâr′dē), *n.* **Giuseppe,** 1813–1901, Italian composer.

ver•dict (vûr′dikt), *n.* **1.** the finding of a jury in a matter submitted to their judgment. **2.** any judgment or decision.

ver•di•gris (vûr′di grēs′, -gris), *n.* a green or bluish patina formed on copper, brass, or bronze surfaces exposed to the atmosphere for long periods of time, consisting principally of basic copper sulfate.

ver•dure (vûr′jər), *n.* **1.** greenness, esp. of fresh, flourishing vegetation. **2.** green vegetation, esp. grass or herbage. **3.** freshness in general; flourishing condition; vigor. —**ver′dured, ver′dur•ous** *adj.*

verge[1] (vûrj), *n., v.,* **verged, verg•ing.** —*n.* **1.** the limit or point beyond which something begins or occurs; brink: *on the verge of a nervous breakdown.* **2.** the edge, rim, or margin of something: *the verge of a desert.* **3.** a limiting belt, strip, or border of something. **4.** a strip of turf bordering a walk or roadway. **5.** the part of a sloping roof that projects beyond the gable wall. **6.** a rod or staff, esp. one carried as a symbol of office of a bishop, dean, etc. —*v.i.* **7.** to be on the verge or margin; border: *Our property verges on theirs.* **8.** to come close to or approach some state, quality, etc.: *a scientific mind verging on genius.*

verge[2] (vûrj), *v.i.,* **verged, verg•ing. 1.** to incline; tend (usu. fol. by *to* or *toward*): *The economy verges toward inflation.* **2.** to slope or sink.

ve•rid•i•cal (və rid′i kəl) also **ve•rid′ic,** *adj.* **1.** truthful; veracious. **2.** corresponding to facts; actual; genuine. —**ve•rid′i•cal•ly,** *adv.*

ver•i•fi•ca•tion (ver′ə fi kā′shən), *n.* **1.** the act of verifying. **2.** the state of being verified. **3.** evidence that verifies something.

ver•i•fy (ver′ə fī′), *v.t.,* **-fied, -fy•ing. 1.** to prove the truth of, as by evidence or testimony; confirm. **2.** to ascertain the truth, authenticity, or correctness of, as by examination, research, or comparison. **3.** to act as ultimate proof or evidence of; serve to confirm. —**ver′i•fi•a•bil′i•ty,** *n.* —**ver′i•fi•a•ble,** *adj.* —**ver′i•fi•er,** *n.*

ver•i•sim•i•lar (ver′ə sim′ə lər), *adj.* having the appearance of truth; likely; probable. —**ver′i•sim′i•lar•ly,** *adv.*

ver•i•si•mil•i•tude (ver′ə si mil′i tōōd′, -tyōōd′), *n.* **1.** the appearance or semblance of truth; likelihood; probability. **2.** something, as an assertion, having merely the appearance of truth.

ver•i•ta•ble (ver′i tə bəl), *adj.* being truly or very much so; genuine or real: *a veritable triumph.* —**ver′i•ta•bly,** *adv.*

ver•i•ty (ver′i tē), *n., pl.* **-ties. 1.** the state or quality of being true. **2.** something that is true, as a principle, belief, or statement.

Ver•meer (vər mēr′), *n.* **Jan** (yän), (*Jan van der Meer van Delft*), 1632–75, Dutch painter.

ver•meil (vûr′mil, -māl *or, esp. for 2,* vər mā′), *n.* **1.** vermilion red. **2.** metal, as silver or bronze, that has been gilded. —*adj.* **3.** of the color vermilion.

ver•mi•cel•li (vûr′mi chel′ē, -sel′ē), *n.* (*used with a sing. or pl. v.*) pasta in the form of long and very fine threads.

ver•mic•u•lar (vər mik′yə lər), *adj.* **1.** of, pertaining to, or done by worms. **2.** consisting of or characterized by sinuous or wavy outlines, tunnels, or markings resembling the form or tracks of a worm. —**ver•mic′u•lar•ly,** *adv.*

ver•mic•u•late (*v.* vər mik′yə lāt′; *adj.* -lit, -lāt′), *v.,* **-lat•ed, -lat•ing,** *adj.* —*v.t.* **1.** to work or ornament with wavy lines or markings resembling the form or tracks of a worm. —*adj.* Also, **ver•mic′u•lat′ed. 2.** worm-eaten. **3.** VERMICULAR. **4.** sinuous; tortuous; intricate. —**ver•mic′u•la′tion,** *n.*

ver•mil•ion (vər mil′yən), *n.* **1.** a brilliant scarlet red. **2.** a bright red, water-insoluble pigment consisting of mercuric sulfide. —*adj.* **3.** of the color vermilion.

ver•min (vûr′min), *n., pl.* **ver•min. 1.** noxious or objectionable animals collectively, esp. those of small size that appear commonly and are difficult to control, as flies, lice, cockroaches, and rats. **2.** an objectionable or obnoxious person, or such persons collectively. **3.** animals that prey upon game, as coyotes or weasels.

Ver•mont (vər mont′), *n.* a state of the NE United States: a part of New England. 588,654; 9609 sq. mi. (24,885 sq. km). *Cap.:* Montpelier. *Abbr.:* VT, Vt. —**Ver•mont′er,** *n.*

ver•mouth (vər mōōth′), *n.* a white wine in which herbs and other flavorings have been steeped.

ver•nac•u•lar (vər nak′yə lər, və nak′-), *adj.* **1.** (of language) native or indigenous (opposed to *literary* or *learned*). **2.** expressed or written in the native language of a place. **3.** of, pertaining to, or using such a language. **4.** using plain, everyday, ordinary language. **5.** of or pertaining to the common name for a plant, animal, or other organism. —*n.* **6.** the native speech or language of a place. **7.** the distinctive language or vocabulary of a class or profession. **8.** the plain variety of language in everyday use by ordinary people. **9.** the common name of a plant, animal, or other organism as distinguished from its Latin scientific name. —**ver•nac′u•lar•ly,** *adv.*

ver•nal (vûr′nl), *adj.* **1.** of, pertaining to, or occurring in spring. **2.** appropriate to or suggesting spring. **3.** belonging to or characteristic of youth. —**ver′nal•ly,** *adv.*

ver′nal e′quinox, *n.* See under EQUINOX (def. 1).

Verne (vûrn), *n.* **Jules,** 1828–1905, French novelist.

Ve•ro•ne•se (ver′ə nā′zē), *n.* **Paolo** (*Paolo Cagliari*), 1528–88, Venetian painter.

ve•ron•i•ca[1] (və ron′i kə), *n., pl.* **-cas.** (*sometimes cap.*) **1. a.** a handkerchief said to have been given to Christ while on the way to Calvary by St. Veronica and to have borne the image of His face thereafter. **b.** the image itself. **2.** any handkerchief, veil, or cloth bearing a representation of the face of Christ.

ve•ron•i•ca[2] (və ron′i kə), *n., pl.* **-cas.** any plant of the genus *Veronica,* of the figwort family, having opposite leaves and clusters of small flowers, as the speedwell.

V

Ver·ra·za·no or **Ver·raz·za·no** (ver′ə zä′nō, -əd zä′-, -ət sä′-), *n.* Giovanni da, c1480–1527?, Italian navigator and explorer.

Ver·sailles (ver sī′, vər-), *n.* a city in N France, near Paris: palace of the French kings; peace treaty between the Allies and Germany 1919. 95,240.

ver·sa·tile (vûr′sə tl; *esp. Brit.* -tīl′), *adj.* **1.** capable of or adapted for turning easily from one to another of various tasks, fields of endeavor, etc. **2.** having or capable of many uses or applications: *a versatile tool.* **3.** *Bot.* attached at or near the middle so as to swing freely, as an anther. **4.** *Zool.* turning either forward or backward: *a versatile toe.* **5.** variable or changeable, as in feeling, purpose, or policy. —**ver′sa·tile·ly,** *adv.* —**ver′sa·til′i·ty,** *n.*

verse (vûrs), *n., v.,* **versed, vers·ing.** —*n.* **1.** one of the lines of a poem. **2.** a particular type of metrical line or composition: *hexameter verse; elegaic verse.* **3.** a poem or a piece of poetry. **4.** metrical composition; poetry, esp. as involving metrical form. **5.** a stanza. **6.** one of the short conventional divisions of a chapter of the Bible. **7.** the part of a song following the introduction and preceding the chorus. —*v.t.* **8.** to express in verse. —*v.i.* **9.** to versify.

versed (vûrst), *adj.* experienced or practiced; skilled; learned (usu. fol. by *in*): *well versed in Greek and Latin.*

ver·si·fi·ca·tion (vûr′sə fi kā′shən), *n.* **1.** the act of versifying. **2.** verse form; metrical structure. **3.** a metrical version of something. **4.** the art of composing verses.

ver·si·fy (vûr′sə fī′), *v.,* **-fied, -fy·ing.** —*v.t.* **1.** to put into verse. —*v.i.* **2.** to compose verses. —**ver′si·fi′er,** *n.*

ver·sion (vûr′zhən, -shən), *n.* **1.** a particular account of some matter, esp. as contrasted with some other account: *two different versions of the accident.* **2.** a particular form or variant of something: *an updated version of a computer program.* **3.** a translation. **4.** (*often cap.*) a translation of the Bible or a part of it. **5.** the act of turning a fetus in the uterus so as to bring it into a more favorable position for delivery. **6.** an abnormal direction of the axis of the uterus or other organ. —**ver′sion·al,** *adj.*

ver·so (vûr′sō), *n., pl.* **-sos.** a left-hand page of an open book or manuscript (opposed to *recto*).

ver·sus (vûr′səs, -səz), *prep.* **1.** against (used esp. to join names of parties in a legal case or competing teams or players in a sports contest): *Smith versus Jones; Army versus Navy.* **2.** as compared to; in contrast with: *traveling by plane versus traveling by train. Abbr.:* v., vs.

ver·te·bra (vûr′tə brə), *n., pl.* **-brae** (-brē′, -brā′), **-bras.** any of the bones or segments of the spinal column, consisting in higher vertebrates of a cylindrical body with two projections, forming an arch surrounding the spinal cord.

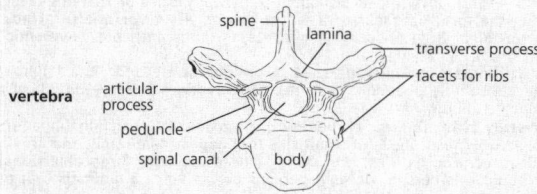

spine
lamina
transverse process
facets for ribs
articular process
vertebra
peduncle
spinal canal
body

ver·te·bral (vûr′tə brəl), *adj.* of, pertaining to, or composed of vertebrae; spinal.

ver·te·brate (vûr′tə brit, -brāt′), *adj.* **1.** having vertebrae; having a segmented backbone. **2.** belonging or pertaining to the Vertebrata, a subphylum of chordate animals having an internal skeleton of bone or cartilage that includes a braincase and a spinal column, and comprising mammals, birds, reptiles, amphibians, and fishes. —*n.* **3.** a vertebrate animal.

ver·tex (vûr′teks), *n., pl.* **-tex·es, -ti·ces** (-tə sēz′). **1.** the highest point of something; apex. **2.** the crown or top of the head. **3.** a point in the celestial sphere toward which or from which the common motion of a group of stars is directed. **4.** *Geom.* **a.** the point farthest from the base. **b.** a point in a geometrical solid common to three or more sides. **c.** the intersection of two sides of a plane figure.

ver·ti·cal (vûr′ti kəl), *adj.* **1.** being in a position or direction perpendicular to the plane of the horizon; upright; plumb. **2.** of, pertaining to, or situated at the vertex. **3.** *Bot.* being in the same direction as the axis; lengthwise. **4.** pertaining to vertical merger. **5.** pertaining to vertical integration. **6.** pertaining to or noting a stratified society, nation, etc. —*n.* **7.** something vertical, as a line or plane. **8.** a vertical or upright position. —**ver′ti·cal′i·ty,** *n.* —**ver′ti·cal·ly,** *adv.*

ver′ti·cal an′gle, *n.* one of two opposite and equal angles formed by the intersection of two lines.

ver′ti·cal file′, *n.* **1.** a collection of pamphlets, pictures, clippings, or other materials stored upright, as in a filing cabinet or cabinets. **2.** a cabinet for such storage.

ver′ti·cal integra′tion, *n.* the means whereby a company can control all aspects of designing, manufacturing, and selling a product.

ver′ti·cal merg′er, *n.* the purchase by a company of a supplier or a distributor. Compare HORIZONTAL MERGER.

ver·ti·ces (vûr′tə sēz′), *n.* a pl. of VERTEX.

ver·tig·i·nous (vər tij′ə nəs), *adj.* **1.** whirling; spinning; rotary. **2.** affected with vertigo. **3.** liable or threatening to cause vertigo: *a vertiginous climb.* **4.** apt to change quickly; unstable. —**ver·tig′i·nous·ly,** *adv.* —**ver·tig′i·nous·ness,** *n.*

ver·ti·go (vûr′ti gō′), *n., pl.* **ver·ti·goes, ver·tig·i·nes** (vər tij′ə nēz′). **1.** a disordered condition in which one feels oneself or one's surroundings whirling about. **2.** the dizzying sensation caused by this. **3.** a disease marked by vertigo.

verve (vûrv), *n.* **1.** vivaciousness or liveliness; animation. **2.** enthusiasm or vigor, as in literary or artistic work; spirit.

ver·y (ver′ē), *adv., adj.,* **ver·i·er, ver·i·est.** —*adv.* **1.** in a high degree; extremely; exceedingly: *a very clever person.* **2.** (used as an intensive emphasizing superlatives or stressing identity or oppositeness): *the very best thing; in the very same place.* —*adj.* **3.** precise; particular: *That is the very item we want.* **4.** mere: *The very thought of it is distressing.* **5.** sheer; utter: *the very joy of living.* **6.** actual: *caught in the very act of stealing.* **7.** being such in the true or fullest sense of the term: *the very heart of the matter.*

ver′y high′ fre′quency, *n.* any frequency between 30 and 300 megahertz. *Abbr.:* VHF, vhf, V.H.F.

ver′y low′ fre′quency, *n.* any frequency between 3 and 30 kilohertz. *Abbr.:* VLF, vlf

Ve·sa·li·us (vi sā′lē əs, -sāl′yəs), *n.* **Andreas,** 1514–64, Flemish anatomist.

ves·i·cant (ves′i kənt), *adj.* **1.** producing a blister or blisters, as a medicinal substance. —*n.* **2.** a vesicant agent or substance. **3.** a chemical agent that causes burns and destruction of tissue.

ves·i·cate (ves′i kāt′), *v.t.,* **-cat·ed, -cat·ing.** to raise vesicles or blisters on; blister. —**ves′i·ca′tion,** *n.*

ves·i·cle (ves′i kəl), *n.* **1. a.** a small sac, cyst, or cavity, esp. one filled with fluid. **b.** BLISTER (def. 1). **2.** a small, usu. spherical cavity in a rock or mineral.

Ves·pa·sian (ve spā′zhən, -zhē ən), *n.* (*Titus Flavius Sabinus Vespasianus*), A.D. 9–79, Roman emperor 70–79.

ves·per (ves′pər), *n.* **1.** (*cap.*) the evening star, esp. Venus. **2.** Also called **ves′per bell′.** a bell rung at evening. **3. vespers,** (*often cap.*) **a.** a religious service in the late afternoon or evening; the sixth of the seven canonical hours. **b.** EVENSONG. **c.** a part of the Roman Catholic office to be said in the afternoon or evening. —*adj.* **4.** pertaining to, appearing in, or proper to the evening. **5.** of or pertaining to vespers. [< Latin: evening, evening star; pl. form < Old French *vespres* < Middle Latin *vespera*; cognate Greek *hésperos*; akin to WEST]

ves·per·al (ves′pər əl), *n.* **1.** the part of an antiphonary containing the chants for vespers. **2.** a cloth used between offices to cover the altar cloth.

ves·per·tine (ves′pər tin, -tīn′) also **ves·per·ti·nal** (ves′pər tīn′l), *adj.* **1.** of, pertaining to, or occurring in the evening. **2.** *Bot.* opening or expanding in the evening, as certain flowers. **3.** *Zool.* appearing or flying in the early evening; crepuscular.

Ves·puc·ci (ve spōō′chē, -spyōō′-), *n.* **Amerigo** (*Americus Vespucius*), 1451–1512, Italian explorer after whom America was named.

ves·sel (ves′əl), *n.* **1.** a craft for traveling on water, esp. a fairly large one; a ship or boat. **2.** a hollow or concave utensil, as a cup, bowl, or pitcher, used for holding liquids or other contents. **3.** a tube or duct, as an artery or vein, containing or conveying blood or some other body fluid. **4.** a water-conducting duct within the xylem of vascular plants, composed of connected cells without intervening partitions. **5.** a person regarded as a holder of a particular trait or quality: *a vessel of grace.*

vest (vest), *n.* **1.** a fitted, waist-length, sleeveless garment with buttons down the front, usu. worn under a jacket. **2.** a part or trimming simulating the front of such a garment. **3.** any of various sleeveless garments for the upper body, having a front opening and worn for style, warmth, or protection: *a down vest; a bulletproof vest.* —*v.t.* **4.** to dress or clothe, as in ecclesiastical vestments. **5.** to place or settle in the possession or control of someone (usu. fol. by *in*): *to vest authority in a new official.* **6.** to invest or endow with something, as powers, functions, or rights: *to vest the board with power to increase production.* —*v.i.* **7.** to put on vestments. **8.** to become vested in a person, as a right. **9.** to devolve upon a person as possessor.

Ves·ta (ves′tə), *n.* **1.** the Roman goddess of the hearth: identified with the Greek goddess Hestia. **2.** (*l.c.*) *Brit.* a short friction match.

ves′tal vir′gin, *n.* (in ancient Rome) any of the women, pledged to remain virgins, who tended the sacred fire in Vesta's sanctuary.

vest·ed (ves′tid), *adj.* **1.** held completely, permanently, and inalienably: *vested rights.* **2.** protected or established by law, tradition, etc.: *vested contributions to a fund.* **3.** clothed or robed, esp. in ecclesiastical vestments. **4.** having a vest; sold with a vest: *a vested suit.*

vest′ed in′terest, *n.* **1.** a special interest in an existing system, arrangement, or institution for particular personal reasons. **2.** a permanent right given to an employee under a pension plan. **3. vested interests,** the persons, groups, etc., who benefit most from existing systems.

ves·ti·ar·y (ves′tē er′ē), *adj.* of or pertaining to garments or vestments.

ves·ti·bule (ves′tə byōōl′), *n., v.,* **-buled, -bul·ing.** —*n.* **1.** a passage, hall, or antechamber between the outer door and the interior parts of a house or building. **2.** an enclosed entrance at the end of a railroad passenger car, serving also as a passage to the next car. **3.** any hollow part in the body serving as an approach to another hollow part, esp. the front part of the inner ear leading to the cochlea. —*v.t.* **4.** to provide with a vestibule.

ves•tige (ves′tij), *n.* **1.** a mark, trace, or visible evidence of something that is no longer present or in existence. **2.** a very slight trace or amount of something: *the last vestige of hope.* **3.** a degenerate or imperfectly developed biological structure that performed a useful function at an earlier stage in the development of the individual or evolution of the species. —**ves•tig•i•al** (ve stij′ē əl, -stij′əl), *adj.* —**ves•tig′i•al•ly,** *adv.*

vest•ing (ves′ting), *n.* the granting to an employee of the right to pension benefits despite retirement before the usual time or age.

vest•ment (vest′mənt), *n.* **1.** a garment, esp. an outer garment. **2.** **vestments,** attire; clothing. **3.** an official or ceremonial robe. **4.** one of the garments worn by the clergy and their assistants, choristers, etc., during divine service and on other occasions.

vest′-pock′et, *adj.* **1.** designed to be carried in or as if in the pocket of a vest: *a vest-pocket dictionary.* **2.** contained in a small space; compact: *a vest-pocket park.*

ves•try (ves′trē), *n., pl.* **-tries. 1.** a room in or a building attached to a church, in which the vestments, and sometimes liturgical objects, are kept; sacristy. **2.** a room in or a building attached to a church, used as a chapel, for prayer meetings, for the Sunday school, etc. **3.** (in the Episcopal Church) a committee elected by members of a congregation to manage the temporal affairs of the church. —**ves′tral,** *adj.*

Ve•su•vi•us (və sōō′vē əs), *n.* **Mount,** an active volcano in SW Italy, near Naples: its eruption destroyed the ancient cities of Pompeii and Herculaneum A.D. 79. ab. 3900 ft. (1190 m). —**Ve•su′vi•an,** *adj.*

vet¹ (vet), *n., v.,* **vet•ted, vet•ting.** *Informal.* —*n.* **1.** a veterinarian. —*v.t.* **2.** to examine or treat in one's capacity as a veterinarian or physician. **3.** to appraise, verify, or check for accuracy, authenticity, etc. —*v.i.* **4.** to work as a veterinarian.

vet² (vet), *n., adj. Informal.* veteran.

vetch (vech), *n.* any of several climbing plants of the legume family, bearing pealike flowers, esp. *Vicia sativa,* cultivated for forage and soil improvement.

vet•er•an (vet′ər ən, ve′trən), *n.* **1.** a person who has had long service or experience in an occupation, office, or the like: *a veteran of the police force.* **2.** a person who has served in a military force, esp. during a war. —*adj.* **3.** (of a soldier) having served in a military force, esp. during a war. **4.** experienced through long service or practice. **5.** of or pertaining to veterans.

Vet′erans Administra′tion, *n.* a federal agency that administers benefits provided by law for veterans of the armed forces. *Abbr.:* VA, V.A.

Vet′erans Day′, *n.* November 11, a legal holiday in the U.S. in commemoration of the end of World War I and in honor of veterans of the armed forces. Formerly, **Armistice Day.**

vet•er•i•nar•i•an (vet′ər ə nâr′ē ən, ve′trə-), *n.* a person who practices veterinary medicine.

vet•er•i•nar•y (vet′ər ə ner′ē, ve′trə-), *n., pl.* **-nar•ies,** *adj.* —*n.* **1.** a veterinarian. —*adj.* **2.** of or pertaining to the medical and surgical treatment of animals, esp. domesticated animals.

vet′erinary med′icine, *n.* the branch of medicine dealing with the study, prevention, and treatment of diseases in animals, esp. domesticated animals.

ve•to (vē′tō), *n., pl.* **-toes,** *v.* —*n.* **1.** the power vested in one branch of a government to cancel or postpone the decisions or actions of another branch, esp. the right of a president or other chief executive to reject bills passed by the legislature. **2.** the exercise of this power. **3.** Also called **ve′to mes′sage.** a document exercising such power and setting forth the reasons for its use. **4.** the power of any of the five permanent members of the UN Security Council to overrule actions or decisions by a nonconcurring vote. **5.** an emphatic prohibition of any sort. —*v.t.* **6.** to reject (a proposed bill or enactment) by exercising a veto. **7.** to prohibit emphatically; disapprove: *to veto a plan.* —**ve′to•er,** *n.*

vex (veks), *v.t.* **1.** to irritate; annoy; provoke. **2.** to torment; trouble; distress; worry: *vexed by many problems.* **3.** to discuss or debate (a subject, question, etc.) with vigor or at great length. **4.** to disturb by motion; stir up; toss about. —**vex′er,** *n.*

vex•a•tion (vek sā′shən), *n.* **1.** the act of vexing. **2.** the state of being vexed; irritation; annoyance. **3.** something that vexes; a cause of annoyance.

vex•a•tious (vek sā′shəs), *adj.* **1.** causing vexation; troublesome; annoying. **2.** disorderly; confused; troubled. —**vex•a′tious•ly,** *adv.* —**vex•a′tious•ness,** *n.*

vexed (vekst), *adj.* **1.** irritated; annoyed. **2.** much discussed or disputed: *a vexed question.* —**vex′ed•ly,** *adv.* —**vex′ed•ness,** *n.*

VFW or **V.F.W.,** Veterans of Foreign Wars.

VHF or **vhf** or **V.H.F.,** very high frequency.

VHS, *Trademark.* a videocassette tape format.

VI or **V.I.,** Virgin Islands.

v.i., **1.** intransitive verb. **2.** see below. [< Latin *vidē infrā*]

vi•a (vī′ə, vē′ə), *prep.* **1.** by a route that touches or passes through; by way of. **2.** by the agency or instrumentality of; by means of: *to communicate via sign language.*

vi•a•ble (vī′ə bəl), *adj.* **1.** capable of living. **2.** (of a fetus) sufficiently developed to be capable of living outside the uterus. **3.** having the ability to grow or develop: *a viable country; a viable seedling.* **4.** practicable; workable: *a viable alternative.* **5.** capable of winning elections: *a viable political party.* —**vi′a•bil′i•ty,** *n.* —**vi′a•bly,** *adv.*

vi•a•duct (vī′ə dukt′), *n.* a bridge for carrying a road, railroad, etc., over a valley or the like, consisting of a number of short spans.

viaduct

vi•al (vī′əl, vīl), *n., v.,* **-aled, -al•ing** or (*esp. Brit.*) **-alled, -al•ling.** —*n.* **1.** Also, **phial.** a small container, as of glass, for holding liquids. —*v.t.* **2.** to put into or keep in a vial.

vi•and (vī′ənd), *n.* **1.** an article of food. **2.** **viands,** dishes of food, esp. delicacies.

vibes¹ (vībz), *n.pl. Slang.* VIBRATION (def. 5).

vibes² (vībz), *n.pl.* vibraphone. —**vib′ist,** *n.*

vi•brant (vī′brənt), *adj.* **1.** moving to and fro rapidly; vibrating. **2.** (of sounds) characterized by perceptible vibration; resonant. **3.** pulsating with vigor and energy; lively: *the vibrant life of a large city.* **4.** vigorous; energetic; vital: *a vibrant personality.* —**vi′bran•cy,** *n.* —**vi′brant•ly,** *adv.*

vi•bra•phone (vī′brə fōn′), *n.* a musical percussion instrument resembling a xylophone and having metal bars struck with mallets and electrically powered resonators to sustain the tone and create a vibrato. Also called **vibraharp.** —**vi•bra•phon•ist,** vī brä fō′nist, vī brof′ə-), *n.*

vi•brate (vī′brāt), *v.,* **-brat•ed, -brat•ing.** —*v.i.* **1.** to move to and fro, as a pendulum; oscillate. **2.** to move to and fro or up and down quickly and repeatedly; quiver; tremble. **3.** (of sounds) to produce or have a quivering or vibratory effect; resound. **4.** to thrill, as in emotional response. **5.** to move between alternatives; vacillate. —*v.t.* **6.** to cause to move to and fro, swing, or oscillate. **7.** to cause to quiver or tremble. **8.** to give forth or emit by or as if by vibration.

vi•bra•tion (vī brā′shən), *n.* **1.** the act of vibrating or the state of being vibrated. **2.** *Physics.* **a.** the oscillating, reciprocating, or other periodic motion of a rigid or elastic body or medium forced from a position or state of equilibrium. **b.** the analogous motion of the particles of a mass of air or the like, whose state of equilibrium has been disturbed, as in transmitting sound. **3.** an instance of vibratory motion; oscillation; quiver. **4.** a supernatural emanation that is sensed by or revealed to those attuned to the occult. **5.** **vibrations,** *Informal.* general emotional feelings one has from another person or a place, situation, etc. —**vi•bra′tion•al,** *adj.*

vi•bra•to (vi brä′tō, vī-), *n., pl.* **-tos.** a pulsating effect produced in vocal or instrumental music by rapid but slight alternations in pitch.

vi•bra•tor (vī′brā tər), *n.* **1.** a person or thing that vibrates or causes vibration. **2.** any of various machines or devices causing a vibratory motion or action, esp. one used in massage. **3. a.** an electrical device in which, by continually repeated impulses, a steady current is changed into an oscillating current. **b.** a device for producing electric oscillations.

vi•bur•num (vī bûr′nəm), *n.* any shrub of the genus *Viburnum,* of the honeysuckle family, many having showy white flower clusters, as the snowball.

vic•ar (vik′ər), *n.* **1.** a cleric in the Anglican Church acting as priest of a parish in place of the rector. **2.** a cleric in the Episcopal Church whose charge is a chapel in a parish. **3.** a Roman Catholic ecclesiastic representing a bishop. **4.** a person who is authorized to perform the functions of another; deputy. —**vic′ar•ship′,** *n.*

vic•ar•age (vik′ər ij), *n.* **1.** the residence of a vicar. **2.** the office, benefice, or duties of a vicar.

vi•car•i•ous (vī kâr′ē əs, vi-), *adj.* **1.** performed, exercised, received, or suffered in place of another. **2.** taking the place of another person or thing. **3.** felt or enjoyed through imagined participation in the experience of others: *a vicarious thrill.* —**vi•car′i•ous•ly,** *adv.* —**vi•car′i•ous•ness,** *n.*

Vic′ar of Christ′, *n.* the pope. Also called **Vic′ar of Je′sus Christ′.**

vice¹ (vīs), *n.* **1.** an immoral or evil habit or practice. **2.** immoral conduct; depraved behavior. **3.** sexual immorality, esp. prostitution. **4.** a personal shortcoming; foible. **5.** a fault, defect, or flaw. **6.** a physical defect or infirmity. **7.** a bad habit, as in a horse.

vice² (vīs), *n., v.t.,* **viced, vic•ing.** VISE.

vi·ce³ (vī′sē, -sə, vīs), *prep.* instead of; in the place of.

vice-, a combining form meaning "deputy," used esp. in the titles of officials who serve in the absence of the official denoted by the base word: *viceroy; vice-chancellor; vice-chairman.*

vice-ad·mi·ral (vīs′ad′mər əl), *n.* a commissioned officer in the U.S. Navy or Coast Guard ranking above a rear admiral. —**vice′-ad′mi·ral·ty,** *n.*

vice-chan·cel·lor (vīs′chan′sə lər, -chän′-), *n.* **1.** a substitute, deputy, or subordinate chancellor. **2.** the chief administrator of certain British universities. Compare CHANCELLOR (def. 7).

vice′-con′sul or **vice′ con′sul** (vīs), *n.* a consular officer of a grade below that of consul. —**vice′-con′sular,** *adj.*

vice·ge·rent (vīs jēr′ənt), *n.* an officer appointed to serve as a deputy, esp. to a sovereign or supreme chief.

vice′ pres′ident or **vice′-pres′ident** (vīs), *n.* **1.** (often caps.) a governmental officer next in rank to a president, serving as president in the event of the president's death, disability, removal, or resignation. **2.** an officer who serves as a deputy to a president or oversees a special division or function, as in a corporation. —**vice′ pres′idency,** *n.* —**vice′-presiden′tial,** *adj.*

vice-re·gent (*n.* vīs′rē′jənt; *adj.* vīs rē′jənt), *n.* a deputy regent. —**vice′-re′gen·cy,** *n.*

vice·reine (vīs′rān), *n.* the wife of a viceroy.

vice·roy (vīs′roi), *n.* **1.** a person appointed to rule a country or province as the deputy of the sovereign. **2.** a brightly marked American butterfly, *Basilarchia archippus,* closely mimicking the monarch butterfly in coloration.

vice·roy·al·ty (vīs roi′əl tē, vīs′roi′-) also **vice·roy·ship** (vīs′roi-ship′), *n., pl.* **-al·ties** also **-ships. 1.** the position, office, or period of office of a viceroy. **2.** a country or province ruled by a viceroy.

vice′ squad′ (vīs), *n.* a police squad charged with enforcing laws dealing with gambling, prostitution, narcotics, etc.

vi·ce ver·sa (vī′sə vûr′sə, vīs′, vī′sē), *adv.* in reverse order from that of a preceding statement; conversely: *She likes me, and vice versa.*

Vi·chy (vish′ē, vē′shē), *n.* a city in central France: provisional capital of unoccupied France 1940–42; hot springs. 32,251.

vi·chys·soise (vish′ē swäz′, vē′shē swäz′), *n.* a thick cream soup made with potatoes and leeks, usu. served cold.

vi′chy (or **Vi′chy**) **wa′ter** (vish′ē), *n.* **1.** a natural mineral water from springs at Vichy, containing sodium bicarbonate and other alkaline salts. **2.** any of various mineral waters of similar composition. Also called **vi′chy, Vi′chy.**

vic·i·nage (vis′ə nij), *n.* **1.** the region near or about a place; vicinity. **2.** a particular neighborhood or district, or the people belonging to it. **3.** proximity.

vic·i·nal (vis′ə nl), *adj.* **1.** of, pertaining to, or belonging to a neighborhood or district. **2.** neighboring; adjacent.

vi·cin·i·ty (vi sin′i tē), *n., pl.* **-ties. 1.** the area or region near a place; neighborhood. **2.** the state or fact of being near; proximity; propinquity. —*Idiom.* **3. in the vicinity of,** in the neighborhood of; approximately.

vi·cious (vish′əs), *adj.* **1.** addicted to or characterized by vice; immoral or evil; depraved. **2.** spiteful; malicious: *vicious gossip.* **3.** unpleasantly severe or intense: *a vicious headache.* **4.** savage; ferocious: *a vicious temper.* **5.** (of an animal) unruly, fierce, or of a violent disposition. **6.** characterized by faults or defects; unsound: *vicious reasoning.* **7.** morbid, foul, or noxious. —**vi′cious·ly,** *adv.* —**vi′cious·ness,** *n.*

vi′cious cir′cle, 1. Sometimes, **vi′cious cy′cle.** a situation in which effort to solve a given problem results in aggravation of the problem or the creation of a worse one. **2.** *Logic.* **a.** (in demonstration) the use of each of two propositions to establish the other. **b.** (in definition) the use of each of two terms to define the other.

vi·cis·si·tude (vi sis′i tōōd′, -tyōōd′), *n.* **1.** regular change or succession of one state or thing to another. **2.** change or variation; mutation; mutability. **3.** vicissitudes, successive or changing phases or conditions, as of life or fortune; ups and downs. —**vi·cis′si·tu′di·nar′y** (-n er′ē), **vi·cis′si·tu′di·nous,** *adj.*

Vicks·burg (viks′bûrg), *n.* a city in W Mississippi, on the Mississippi River: Civil War siege and Confederate surrender 1863. 25,500.

Vi·co (vik′ō, vē′kō), *n.* **Giovanni Battista,** 1668–1744, Italian philosopher and jurist.

vic·tim (vik′təm), *n.* **1.** a person who suffers from a destructive or injurious action or agency: *war victims.* **2.** a person who is deceived or cheated: *the victims of a fraudulent scheme.* **3.** a living creature sacrificed in religious rites.

vic·tim·ize (vik′tə mīz′), *v.t.,* **-ized, -iz·ing. 1.** to make a victim of. **2.** to dupe, swindle, or cheat. —**vic′tim·i·za′tion,** *n.* —**vic′tim·iz′er,** *n.*

vic′tim·less crime′ (vik′təm lis), *n.* a legal offense, as prostitution or gambling, to which all participating parties have consented.

vic·tor (vik′tər), *n.* **1.** a person who has overcome or defeated an adversary; conqueror. **2.** a winner in any struggle or contest. —*Proverb.* **3. To the victor belong the spoils,** a winner gains all.

Vic′tor Emman′uel (vik′tər), *n.* **1. Victor Emmanuel II,** 1820–78, king of Sardinia 1849–78; first king of Italy 1861–78. **2. Victor Emmanuel III,** 1869–1947, king of Italy 1900–46.

Vic·to·ri·a (vik tôr′ē ə, -tōr′-), *n.* **1.** 1819–1901, queen of Great Britain 1837–1901; empress of India 1876–1901. **2.** Also called **Hong Kong.** the capital of Hong Kong, on the N coast of Hong Kong island. 1,100,000. **3.**

a state in SE Australia. 4,183,500; 87,884 sq. mi. (227,620 sq. km). *Cap.:* Melbourne. **4.** the capital of British Columbia, on Vancouver Island, in SW Canada. 66,303. **5.** a city in S Texas. 55,330. **6.** the capital of the Seychelles. 23,000. **7.** *Lake.* Also called **Victoria Nyanza.** a lake in E central Africa, in Uganda, Tanzania, and Kenya: second largest freshwater lake in the world. 26,828 sq. mi. (69,485 sq. km). **8.** (*l.c.*) a low, light, four-wheeled carriage with a calash top, a seat for two passengers, and a perch in front for the driver.

victoria (def.8)

Victo′ria Cross′, *n.* a British decoration awarded to soldiers and sailors for conspicuous bravery in combat. *Abbr.:* VC

Victo′ria Day′, *n.* (in Canada) the first Monday preceding May 25, observed as a national holiday; formerly May 24, birthday of Queen Victoria.

Victo′ria Falls′, *n.* falls of the Zambezi River in S Africa, between Zambia and Zimbabwe, near Livingstone. 350 ft. (107 m) high; more than 1 mi. (1.6 km) wide.

Vic·to·ri·an (vik tôr′ē ən, -tōr′-), *adj.* **1.** of or pertaining to Queen Victoria or the period of her reign: *Victorian poets.* **2.** having the characteristics usu. attributed to the Victorians, esp. prudishness and observance of the conventionalities. **3.** of or pertaining to a style of architecture, furniture, and decoration between c1840 and c1900, characterized by massiveness and lavish ornamentation. —*n.* **4.** a person, esp. a famous one, who lived during the Victorian period. —**Vic·to′ri·an·ism,** *n.*

vic·to·ri·ous (vik tôr′ē əs, -tōr′-), *adj.* **1.** having achieved a victory; conquering; triumphant. **2.** of, pertaining to, or characterized by victory. —**vic·to′ri·ous·ly,** *adv.*

vic·to·ry (vik′tə rē, vik′trē), *n., pl.* **-ries. 1.** a success or triumph over an enemy in battle or war. **2.** a military engagement ending in such triumph. **3.** a success or superior position achieved against any opponent, opposition, difficulty, etc.: *a moral victory.*

vict·ual (vit′l), *n., v.,* **-ualed, -ual·ing** or (*esp. Brit.*) **-ualled, -ual·ling.** —*n.* **1.** victuals, food supplies; provisions. **2.** food or provisions for human beings. —*v.t.* **3.** to supply with victuals. —*v.i.* **4.** to take or obtain victuals.

vi·cu·na or **vi·cu·ña** (vī kōō′nə, -kyōō′-, vi-, vi kōō′nyə), *n., pl.* **-nas** or **-ñas. 1.** a wild Andean ruminant, *Vicugna vicugna,* closely related to the llama. **2.** a fabric of the soft wool of this animal.

vi·de (wē′de; *Eng.* vī′dē, vē′dā), *v. Latin.* see (used esp. to refer a reader to parts of a text).

vi·de·li·cet (wi dā′li ket′; *Eng.* vi del′ə sit), *adv. Latin.* that is to say; namely (used esp. to introduce examples, etc.). *Abbr.:* viz.

vid·e·o (vid′ē ō′), *n.* **1. a.** the elements of television, as in a program or script, pertaining to the transmission or reception of the image (disting. from *audio*). **b.** the video part of a television broadcast. **2.** television: *a star of stage and video.* **3.** videotape. **4.** a program, movie, or the like, recorded on videotape, esp. one that is available commercially on videocassette. **5.** MUSIC VIDEO. —*adj.* **6.** of or pertaining to the electronic apparatus for producing the television picture. **7.** of or pertaining to television, esp. the visual elements: *video journalism.* **8.** of or pertaining to videocassettes, videocassette recorders, music videos, etc.

vid·e·o·cas·sette (vid′ē ō kə set′, -ka-), *n.* a cassette enclosing a length of tape for video recording or reproduction.

vid′eocassette′ record′er, *n.* See VCR.

vid·e·o·con·fer·ence (vid′ē ō kon′fər əns, -frəns), *n.* a teleconference conducted via television equipment.

vid·e·o·disc (vid′ē ō disk′), *n.* an optical disc on which a motion picture or television program is recorded for playback on a television set. Also called **laser videodisc.**

vid′eo display′ ter′minal, *n.* a computer terminal consisting of a screen on which data or graphics can be displayed. *Abbr.:* VDT

vid′eo game′, *n.* **1.** any of various games played on a video screen or television set with a microcomputer. **2.** any of various games played on a microchip-controlled device, as a toy or arcade machine.

vid·e·o·re·cord·er or **vid′eo record′er,** *n.* an electronic device for recording video signals on magnetic tape or on videodiscs.

vid·e·o·tape (vid′ē ō tāp′), *n., v.,* **-taped, -tap·ing.** —*n.* **1.** magnetic tape on which a television program, motion picture, etc., can be recorded. —*v.t.* **2.** to record (programs, etc.) on videotape.

vid′eotape record′er, *n.* a device for recording television programs on magnetic tape for delayed playback or for storage. *Abbr.:* VTR

vid·e·o·tex (vid′ē ō teks′), *n.* an information transmission and retrieval system that provides interactive communication via telephone or television for such purposes as data processing and electronic banking and shopping.

vie (vī), *v.i.,* **vied, vy•ing.** to strive in competition or rivalry with another; contend for superiority: *The two teams were vying for the championship.* —**vi′er,** *n.*

Vi•en•na (vē en′ə), *n.* the capital of Austria, in the NE part, on the Danube. 1,482,800. German, **Wien.** —**Vi′en•nese′** (-ə nēz′, -nēs′), *adj., n., pl.* **-nese.**

Vien′na (or **vien′na) sau′sage,** *n.* a small frankfurter, often served as an hors d'oeuvre.

Vien•tiane (vyen tyän′), *n.* the capital of Laos, on the Mekong River, in the NW part. 377,409.

Vi•et•cong or **Vi•et Cong** (vē et′kong′, -kông′, vyet′-, vē′it-), *n., pl.* **-cong.** **1.** a Communist-led army and guerrilla force in South Vietnam during the Vietnam War, supported largely by North Vietnam. **2.** a member of this force.

Vi•et•nam or **Vi•et Nam** (vē et′näm′, -nam′, vē′it-), *n.* a country in SE Asia, comprising the former states of Annam, Tonkin, and Cochin-China: formerly in French Indochina; divided into North Vietnam and South Vietnam in 1954 and reunified in 1976. 75,123,880; 127,246 sq. mi. (329,565 sq. km). *Cap.:* Hanoi. Official name, **Socialist Republic of Vietnam.** Compare NORTH VIETNAM, SOUTH VIETNAM.

Vi•et•nam•ese (vē et′nä mēz′, -mēs′, -nə-, vyet′-, vē′it-), *n., pl.* **-ese,** *adj.* —*n.* **1.** a native or inhabitant of Vietnam. **2.** a member of the dominant ethnic group of Vietnam, living mainly in the lowland parts of the country. **3.** the Austroasiatic language of this ethnic group: the official language of Vietnam. —*adj.* **4.** of or pertaining to Vietnam, its inhabitants, or the language Vietnamese.

Vi•et•nam•i•za•tion (vē et′nə mə zā′shən, vyet′-, vē′it-), *n.* a U.S. policy during the Vietnam War of giving the South Vietnamese government responsibility for carrying on the war, so as to allow for the withdrawal of American troops.

Vietnam′ syn′drome, *n.* the belief that foreign military involvement has no enduring chance of success.

Viet′nam War′, *n.* a conflict (1954–75) between South Vietnam, aided by the U.S. and other nations, and the Vietcong and North Vietnam, aided by the Soviet Union, Communist China, and other nations, ending in Communist victory.

view (vyōō), *n.* **1.** an instance of seeing or beholding; visual inspection. **2.** sight or vision. **3.** range of sight or vision: *objects in view.* **4.** a sight or prospect of a landscape, the sea, etc. **5.** a picture or photograph of a scene. **6.** a particular manner of looking at something: *from a practical view.* **7.** mental contemplation or examination; a mental survey. **8.** aim, intention, or purpose. **9.** prospect or expectation: *the view for the future.* **10.** a sight afforded of something from a position stated or qualified: *a bird's-eye view.* **11.** a general account or survey of a subject. **12.** a personal attitude; opinion; judgment. —*v.t.* **13.** to see; watch; behold. **14.** to look at; survey; inspect. **15.** to contemplate mentally; consider. **16.** to regard in a particular light or as specified: *Experts viewed the situation with alarm.* —*Idiom.* **17. in view of,** because of; in thinking about; considering. **18. on view,** in a place for public inspection; on exhibition. **19. with a view to, a.** with the aim or intention of: *to work hard with a view to getting promoted.* **b.** with the expectation or hope of. —**view′a•ble,** *adj.*

view′ cam′era, *n.* a camera with an extensible bellows and a ground glass for focusing, used esp. for portraits and landscapes.

view•er (vyōō′ər), *n.* **1.** a person who views something: *viewers of the spectacle.* **2.** a person who watches television. **3.** any of various optical devices to facilitate viewing, as of a photographic transparency. **4.** an eyepiece or viewfinder.

view•er•ship (vyōō′ər ship′), *n.* **1.** an audience of television viewers. **2.** the number or makeup of such viewers.

view•find•er (vyōō′fīn′dər), *n.* a camera attachment, as a lens and mirror that enables the operator to determine visually what will appear in the picture.

view•ing (vyōō′ing), *n.* **1.** an act or occasion of seeing, watching, or inspecting. **2.** an act or instance of watching television: *Which channel offers the best viewing?*

view•point (vyōō′point′), *n.* **1.** a place affording a view of something. **2.** an attitude of mind, or the circumstances of an individual that lead to such an attitude.

vig•il (vij′əl), *n.* **1.** wakefulness maintained for any reason during the normal hours for sleeping. **2.** a watch or a period of watchful attention maintained at night or at other times. **3.** Sometimes, **vigils.** a nocturnal devotional exercise or service, esp. on the eve of a church festival. **b.** the eve or day and night before a church festival, esp. an eve that is a fast.

vig•i•lance (vij′ə ləns), *n.* the state or quality of being vigilant; watchfulness.

vig′ilance commit′tee, *n.* **1.** an unauthorized committee of citizens organized for the maintenance of order and the summary punishment of crime in the absence of regular or efficient courts. **2.** (in the South) an organization of citizens using extralegal means to control or intimidate blacks and abolitionists, and, during the Civil War, to suppress Union loyalists.

vig•i•lant (vij′ə lənt), *adj.* **1.** keenly watchful to detect danger or trouble; wary. **2.** ever awake and alert; sleeplessly watchful. —**vig′i•lant•ly,** *adv.*

vig•i•lan•te (vij′ə lan′tē), *n., pl.* **-tes.** **1.** a member of a vigilance com-

mittee. **2.** any person who assumes the authority of the law, as by avenging a crime. —**vig′i•lan′tism,** *n.*

vig′il light′, *n.* a small candle lighted as a devotional act before a shrine, icon, etc., esp. in a church.

vi•gnette (vin yet′), *n.* **1.** a decorative design or small illustration used on the title page of a book or at the beginning or end of a chapter. **2.** an engraving, drawing, photograph, or the like that is shaded off gradually at the edges so as to leave no definite line at the border. **3.** a decorative design representing branches, leaves, grapes, or the like, as in a manuscript. **4.** a short, graceful literary sketch. **5.** a brief, quietly touching or appealing scene or episode in a play, movie, or the like. —**vi•gnet′tist,** *n.*

vig•or (vig′ər), *n.* **1.** active strength or force; intensity; energy. **2.** healthy physical or mental energy; vitality. **3.** healthy growth in any living matter or organism, as a plant. **4.** effective force, esp. legal validity.

vig•or•ous (vig′ər əs), *adj.* **1.** full of or characterized by vigor: *a vigorous effort.* **2.** strong or active; robust. **3.** energetic; forceful: *a vigorous personality.* **4.** powerful in action or effect: *vigorous law enforcement.* **5.** growing well, as a plant. —**vig′or•ous•ly,** *adv.* —**vig′or•ous•ness,** *n.*

Vi•king (vī′king), *n.* **1.** (*sometimes l.c.*) any of the Scandinavians who from the late 8th to the 11th centuries engaged in raiding, trade, and colonization throughout Europe and the islands of the N Atlantic. **2.** *Informal.* a Scandinavian. **3.** one of a series of U.S. space probes in 1975–76 that obtained scientific information about Mars.

Vi•la (vē′lə), *n.* a seaport in and the capital of Vanuatu. 15,000.

vile (vīl), *adj.,* **vil•er, vil•est. 1.** wretchedly bad: *vile weather.* **2.** highly offensive, unpleasant, or objectionable: *a vile odor.* **3.** morally debased, depraved, or despicable. **4.** menial; lowly: *vile tasks.* **5.** of little value or account; paltry. —**vile′ly,** *adv.* —**vile′ness,** *n.*

vil•i•fy (vil′ə fī′), *v.t.,* **-fied, -fy•ing.** to speak ill of; defame; slander. —**vil′i•fi•ca′tion,** *n.* —**vil′i•fi′er,** *n.*

vil•la (vil′ə), *n., pl.* **-las. 1.** a country residence or estate. **2.** an imposing country or suburban home of a wealthy person. **3.** *Brit.* a detached or semidetached house.

vil•lage (vil′ij), *n.* **1.** a small community or group of houses in a rural area, larger than a hamlet and usu. smaller than a town, sometimes incorporated as a municipality. **2.** the inhabitants of such a community collectively. **3.** a group of animal dwellings resembling a village. —*adj.* **4.** of, pertaining to, or characteristic of a village.

vil•lag•er (vil′i jər), *n.* an inhabitant of a village.

vil•lain (vil′ən), *n.* **1.** a cruelly malicious person who is involved in or devoted to wickedness or crime; scoundrel. **2.** a character in a play, novel, or the like, who constitutes an important evil agency in the plot. **3.** VILLEIN.

vil•lain•ess (vil′ə nis), *n.* a woman who is a villain.

vil•lain•ous (vil′ə nəs), *adj.* **1.** having a cruel, wicked, malicious nature or character. **2.** of, pertaining to, or befitting a villain. **3.** very objectionable or unpleasant; bad; wretched. —**vil′lain•ous•ly,** *adv.*

vil•lain•y (vil′ə nē), *n., pl.* **-lain•ies. 1.** the actions or conduct of a villain; outrageous wickedness. **2.** a villainous act or deed.

Vil•la-Lo•bos (vē′lä lō′bōs, -bōs, vil′ə-), *n.* **Hei•tor** (ā′tŏŏr), 1881–1959, Brazilian composer.

vil•lein (vil′ən, -ān, vi lān′), *n.* (in the feudal system) a member of a class of persons who were serfs with respect to their lord but had the rights and privileges of freemen with respect to others.

vil•lein•age or **vil•len•age** (vil′ə nij), *n.* **1.** the tenure by which a villein held land from a lord. **2.** the condition or status of a villein.

Vil•lon (vē yôn′), *n.* **1. François,** 1431–63?, French poet. **2. Jacques** (*Gaston Duchamp*), 1875–1963, French painter.

vil•lus (vil′əs), *n., pl.* **vil•li** (vil′ī). **1.** any of the fingerlike projections on the surface of certain membranes, esp. on the mucous membrane of the small intestine, functioning to increase the area for the absorption, secretion, or exchange of materials. **2.** any of the long, soft, straight hairs covering the fruit, flowers, and other parts of certain plants.

Vil•ni•us (vil′nē ŏŏs′), *n.* the capital of Lithuania, in the SE part. 582,000. Russian, **Vil•na** (vyēl′nə; *Eng.* vil′nə).

vim (vim), *n.* lively or energetic spirit; enthusiasm; vitality.

vin•ai•grette (vin′ə gret′), *adj.* **1.** (of food) served with vinaigrette sauce: *asparagus vinaigrette.* —*n.* **2.** a small ornamental bottle or box for aromatic vinegar, smelling salts, or the like. **3.** VINAIGRETTE SAUCE.

vinaigrette′ sauce′, *n.* a tart sauce or dressing of oil, vinegar, and seasonings, used esp. on salads and cold meats.

Vin•cent de Paul (vin′sənt də pôl′), *n.* **Saint,** 1576–1660, French priest noted for his aid to the poor.

vin•ci•ble (vin′sə bəl), *adj.* capable of being conquered or overcome. —**vin′ci•bil′i•ty,** *n.*

vin•cu•lum (ving′kyə ləm), *n., pl.* **-la** (-lə). **1.** a bond signifying union or unity; tie. **2.** *Math.* a stroke or brace drawn over a quantity consisting of several members or terms, as $\overline{a+b}$, in order to show that they are to be considered together.

vin•di•ca•ble (vin′di kə bəl), *adj.* capable of being vindicated.

vin•di•cate (vin′di kāt′), *v.t.,* **-cat•ed, -cat•ing. 1.** to clear, as from an accusation or suspicion: *to vindicate someone's honor.* **2.** to afford justification for; justify. **3.** to uphold or justify by argument or evidence. **4.** to maintain or defend against opposition. **5.** to claim for oneself or another. —**vin′di•ca′tor,** *n.*

vin•di•ca•tion (vin′di kā′shən), *n.* **1.** the act of vindicating or the state of being vindicated. **2.** an excuse or justification. **3.** something that vindicates.

vin·dic·tive (vin dik′tiv), *adj.* **1.** disposed to revenge; vengeful. **2.** proceeding from or showing a revengeful spirit. —**vin·dic′tive·ly,** *adv.* —**vin·dic′tive·ness,** *n.*

vine (vīn), *n.* **1.** any plant with a long stem that grows along the ground or that climbs a support by winding or by clinging with tendrils or claspers. **2.** the stem of such a plant. **3.** a grape plant.

Vine′ and the Branch′es, The, a parable of Jesus. John 15:1–8.

vine·dress·er (vīn′dres′ər), *n.* a person who tends or cultivates vines, esp. grapevines.

vin·e·gar (vin′i gər), *n.* **1.** a sour liquid consisting of dilute and impure acetic acid, obtained by acetous fermentation from wine, cider, beer, ale, or the like: used as a condiment, preservative, etc. **2.** sour or irritable speech, manner, or countenance. **3.** vigor; high spirits; vim. [< Old French: sour wine]

vin·e·gar·y (vin′i gə rē), *adj.* **1.** resembling vinegar; sour; acid. **2.** having a disagreeable character or manner; ill-tempered.

vin·er·y (vī′na rē), *n.,* *pl.* **-er·ies. 1.** a place or enclosure in which vines, esp. grapevines, are grown. **2.** vines collectively.

vine·yard (vin′yərd), *n.* **1.** a plantation of grapevines, esp. one producing grapes for winemaking. **2.** a sphere of activity, esp. on a high spiritual plane.

vini-, a combining form meaning "wine": *viniculture.*

vin·i·cul·ture (vin′i kul′chər, vī′ni-), *n.* WINEMAKING —**vin·i·cul·tur·al,** *adj.* —**vin′i·cul′tur·ist,** *n.*

vi·nif·er·a (vī nif′ər ə, vi-), *adj.* of, pertaining to, or derived from a European grape, *Vitis vinifera,* widely cultivated for making wine and raisins.

Vin·land (vin′lənd), *n.* a region in E North America variously identified as a place between Newfoundland and Virginia: visited and described by Norsemen ab. A.D. 1000.

vi·no (vē′nō), *n.* wine; specifically, red Italian wine, as chianti.

vin·tage (vin′tij), *n.* **1.** the wine from a particular harvest or crop. **2.** the annual produce of a grape harvest, esp. with reference to the wine obtained. **3.** an exceptionally fine wine from the crop of a good year. **4.** the act or season of gathering grapes or of making wine. **5.** the output of a particular time; a collection of things manufactured or in use at the same time: *a car of 1917 vintage.* —*adj.* **6.** being of a specified vintage: *vintage wine.* **7.** representing the high quality of a past time; classic: *vintage movies.* **8.** being the best of its kind; choice: *vintage Shakespeare.* **9.** old-fashioned or obsolete.

vin′tage year′, *n.* **1.** the year of production of a vintage wine. **2.** any year that was esp. happy or successful.

vint·ner (vint′nər), *n.* a person who makes wine or sells wines.

vin·y (vī′nē), *adj.,* **vin·i·er, vin·i·est. 1.** of, pertaining to, of the nature of, or resembling vines. **2.** abounding in or producing vines.

vi·nyl (vīn′l), *n.* **1.** the univalent group C₂H₃, derived from ethylene. **2.** any resin formed by polymerizing vinyl compounds or any plastic made from such resins.

vi′nyl ac′etate, *n.* a colorless, easily polymerized, water-insoluble liquid, C₄H₆O₂, produced by the reaction of acetylene and acetic acid: used chiefly in making plastics, films, paints, and adhesives.

vi′nyl chlo′ride, *n.* a colorless gas, C₂H₃Cl, used in making plastics and polyvinyl chloride and as a refrigerant.

vi′nyl res′in, *n.* any of a series of thermoplastic polymers of vinyl compounds, as polyvinyl chloride.

vi·ol (vī′əl), *n.* a bowed musical instrument, differing from the violin in having deeper ribs, sloping shoulders, a greater number of strings, usu. six, and frets: common in the 16th and 17th centuries in various sizes from the treble viol to the bass viol. —**vi′ol·ist,** *n.*

vi·o·la¹ (vē ō′lə), *n.* a four-stringed musical instrument of the violin family, slightly larger than the violin. —**vi′ol·ist,** *n.*

vi·o·la² (vī′ə lə, vī ō′-, vē-), *n.* any plant of the genus *Viola,* esp. any cultivated violet developed from a pansy.

vi·o·la·ble (vī′ə lə bəl), *adj.* capable of being violated. —**vi·o·la·bil·i·ty, vī′o·la·ble·ness,** *n.* —**vi′o·la·bly,** *adv.*

vi·o·la·ceous (vī′ə lā′shəs), *adj.* **1.** of or belonging to the violet family. **2.** of a violet color; reddish blue.

vi·o·la da gam·ba (vē ō′lə də gäm′bə, gam′-), *n.,* *pl.* **viola da gambas.** an old instrument of the viol family, held on or between the knees; bass viol.

vi·o·la d'a·mo·re (vē ō′lə dä môr′ā, -mōr′ā, də-), *n.,* *pl.* **viola d'amores.** a treble viol with numerous sympathetic strings and several gut strings, producing a resonant sound.

vi·o·late (vī′ə lāt′), *v.t.,* **-lat·ed, -lat·ing. 1.** to break or infringe (a law, promise, instructions, etc.). **2.** to break in upon or disturb rudely: *to violate someone's privacy.* **3.** to assault sexually, esp. to rape. **4.** to treat irreverently or disrespectfully; desecrate: *to violate a church.* —**vi′o·la′tor,** *n.*

vi·o·la·tion (vī′ə lā′shən), *n.* **1.** the act of violating or the state of being violated. **2.** a breach or infringement, as of a law or promise. **3.** a sexual assault, esp. rape. **4.** desecration; profanation. **5.** a distortion of meaning or fact.

vi·o·lence (vī′ə ləns), *n.* **1.** swift and intense force. **2.** rough or injurious physical force, action, or treatment. **3.** an unjust or unwarranted exertion of force or power. **4.** a violent act or proceeding. **5.** rough or immoderate vehemence, as of feeling or language; fury. **6.** damage, as through distortion of meaning or fact: *to do violence to a translation.*

vi·o·lent (vī′ə lənt), *adj.* **1.** acting with or characterized by uncontrolled, strong, rough force. **2.** characterized by or caused by injurious or destructive force: *a violent death.* **3.** intense in force, effect, etc.; severe; extreme: *violent pain.* **4.** roughly or immoderately vehement or ardent; furious: *violent passions.* —**vi′o·lent·ly,** *adv.*

vi·o·let (vī′ə lit), *n.* **1.** any chiefly low, stemless or leafy-stemmed plant of the genus *Viola,* of the violet family, having purple, blue, yellow, white, or variegated flowers. **2.** any of various other plants, as the dogtooth violet or the African violet. **3.** the flower of any native, wild species of violet, as distinguished from the cultivated pansy: the state flower of Illinois, New Jersey, and Rhode Island. **4.** a reddish blue color at the opposite end of the visible spectrum from red, an effect of light with a wavelength between 400 and 450 nm. —*adj.* **5.** of the color violet; reddish blue.

vi·o·lin (vī′ə lin′), *n.* the treble instrument of the family of modern bowed stringed instruments, held nearly horizontal by the player's arm with the lower part supported against the collarbone or shoulder. —**vi·o·lin′ist,** *n.*

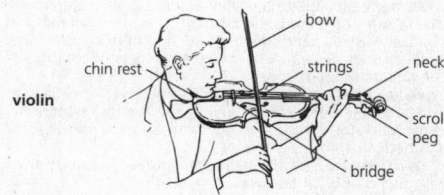

violin

bow
chin rest
strings
neck
scroll
peg
bridge

vi·o·lon·cel·lo (vē′ə lən chel′ō, vī′-), *n.,* *pl.* **-los.** CELLO. —**vi·o·lon·cel′list,** *n.*

VIP or **V.I.P.** (vē′ī′pē′), *n. Informal.* very important person.

vi·per (vī′pər), *n.* **1.** any venomous snake of the cosmopolitan family Viperidae, characterized by a pair of hollow fangs that can be erected for biting and injecting venom: includes the adders, puff adders, and pit vipers. **2.** a malignant or spiteful person. **3.** a false or treacherous person. —**vi′per·ish,** *adj.* —**vi′per·ish·ly,** *adv.*

vi·per·ous (vī′pər əs), *adj.* **1.** resembling a viper. **2.** pertaining to or characteristic of vipers. **3.** venomous. —**vi′per·ous·ly,** *adv.*

vi·ra·go (vi rä′gō, -rā′-), *n.,* *pl.* **-goes, -gos. 1.** a loud-voiced, ill-tempered, scolding woman; shrew. **2.** *Archaic.* a woman of strength or spirit.

vi·ral (vī′rəl), *adj.* of, pertaining to, or caused by a virus.

vir·e·o (vir′ē ō′), *n.* any of various small, insectivorous, typically dull-plumaged songbirds of the family Vireonidae, of the New World, having a slightly hooked bill.

Vir·gil (vûr′jəl), *n.* (Publius Vergilius Maro) 70–19 B.C., Roman poet: author of *The Aeneid,* an epic poem recounting the adventure of Aeneas after the fall of Troy. —**Vir·gil·i·an** (vər jil′ē ən, -jil′yən), *adj.*

vir·gin (vûr′jin), *n.* **1.** a person who has never had sexual intercourse. **2.** an unmarried girl or woman. **3.** the Virgin, Mary, the mother of Jesus. **4.** *Informal.* any person who is uninitiated, uninformed, or the like. **5.** an animal, esp. a female, that has not copulated. **6. a.** a female insect that lays viable eggs without male fertilization. **b.** the female resulting from such an egg. **7.** (cap.) VIRGO. —*adj.* **8.** being a virgin. **9.** of, pertaining to, or characteristic of a virgin. **10.** pure; unsullied. **11.** first: *the senator's virgin speech.* **12.** without alloy or modification: *virgin gold.* **13.** not previously exploited or used: *virgin timberlands.* **14.** *Zool.* not fertilized. **15.** (esp. of olive oil) obtained by the first light pressing and without the application of heat.

vir·gin·al¹ (vûr′jə nl), *adj.* **1.** pertaining to, characteristic of, or befitting a virgin. **2.** continuing in a state of virginity. **3.** pure; unsullied. **4.** *Zool.* not fertilized. —**vir′gin·al·ly,** *adv.*

vir·gin·al² (vûr′jə nl), *n.* Often, **virginals.** a rectangular harpsichord with the strings stretched parallel to the keyboard, the earlier types placed on a table: popular in the 16th and 17th centuries. —**vir′gin·al·ist,** *n.*

vir′gin birth′, *n.* **1.** *Theology.* the doctrine or dogma that, by the miraculous agency of God, the birth of Christ did not impair or prejudice the virginity of Mary. Compare IMMACULATE CONCEPTION. **2.** *Zoology.* parthenogenesis; parturition by a female who has not copulated.

Vir·gin·ia (vər jin′yə), *n.* **1.** a state in the E United States, on the Atlantic coast: part of the historical South. 6,675,451; 40,815 sq. mi. (105,710 sq. km). *Cap.:* Richmond. *Abbr.:* VA, Va. **2.** (italics) MERRIMACK (def. 2). —**Vir·gin′ian,** *n., adj.*

Virgin′ia Beach′, *n.* a city in SE Virginia. 430,295.

Virgin′ia creep′er, *n.* a North American climbing plant, *Parthenocissus quinquefolia,* of the grape family, having palmate leaves, usu. with five leaflets, and bluish black berries. Also called **American ivy.**

Virgin′ia ham′, *n.* a ham from a hog fed on corn and peanuts, cured in hickory smoke.

Virgin′ia pine′, *n.* a pine, *Pinus virginiana,* of the eastern U.S., that grows in poor soil and has needles in groups of two. Also called **Jersey pine.**

Vir·gin'ia plan', *n.* a plan, unsuccessfully proposed at the Constitutional Convention, providing for a legislature of two houses with proportional representation in each house and executive and judicial branches to be chosen by the legislature. Compare CONNECTICUT COMPROMISE, NEW JERSEY PLAN.

Virgin'ia reel', *n.* an American country dance in which the partners start by facing each other in two lines.

Vir'gin Is'lands, *n.pl.* a group of islands in the West Indies, E of Puerto Rico: comprises the Virgin Islands of the United States and the British Virgin Islands. *Abbr.:* VI, V.I.

Vir'gin Is'lands of the Unit'ed States', *n.pl.* a group of islands in the West Indies, including St. Thomas, St. John, and St. Croix: purchased from Denmark 1917. 110,000; 133 sq. mi. (345 sq. km). *Cap.:* Charlotte Amalie. Formerly, **Danish West Indies.**

vir·gin·i·ty (vər jin'i tē), *n.* **1.** the condition of being a virgin. **2.** the condition of being pure or unused. **3.** *Informal.* any naive or uninformed state.

Vir'gin Mar'y, *n.* MARY (def. 1).

Vir·go (vûr'gō), *n.* **1.** the Virgin, a zodiacal constellation between Leo and Libra, containing the bright star Spica. **2.** the sixth sign of the zodiac. [< Latin: *maiden*]

vir·gule (vûr'gyōol), *n.* **1.** a short oblique stroke (/) between two words indicating that the appropriate one may be chosen to complete the sense of the text: *The defendant and/or his/her attorney must appear in court.* **2.** a dividing line, as in dates, fractions, a run-in passage of poetry to show verse division, etc. Also called **diagonal.**

vir·ile (vir'əl; *esp. Brit.* -īl), *adj.* **1.** having or exhibiting masculine strength; masculine; manly. **2.** characterized by a vigorous, masculine spirit. **3.** pertaining to or characteristic of a man.

vi·ril·i·ty (və ril'i tē), *n.* the state or quality of being virile; manly character, vigor, or spirit; masculinity.

vi·rol·o·gy (vī rol'ə jē, vi-), *n.* the study of viruses and viral diseases. —**vi'ro·log'i·cal** (-rə loj'i kal), *adj.* —**vi·rol'o·gist,** *n.*

vir·tu or **ver·tu** (vər tōō', vûr'tōō), *n.* **1.** excellence or merit in objects of art, curios, and the like. **2.** (*used with a pl. v.*) such objects or articles collectively. **3.** a taste for or knowledge of such objects.

vir·tu·al (vûr'chōo əl), *adj.* **1.** being such in force or effect, though not actually or expressly such: *reduced to virtual poverty.* **2.** noting an optical image formed by the apparent convergence of rays geometrically, but not actually, prolonged, as the image formed by a mirror (opposed to *real*). **3.** temporarily simulated or extended by computer software: *a virtual disk in RAM; virtual memory on a hard disk.* —**vir'tu·al'i·ty,** *n.*

vir·tu·al·ly (vûr'chōo ə lē), *adv.* for the most part; almost wholly; just about.

vir'tual real'ity, *n.* a realistic simulation of an environment, including three-dimensional graphics, by a computer system using interactive software and hardware.

vir·tue (vûr'chōo), *n.* **1.** moral excellence; goodness; righteousness. **2.** conformity of one's life and conduct to moral and ethical principles; moral excellence; rectitude. **3.** a particular moral or ethical characteristic: *The vast majority of Americans share a respect for certain fundamental traits of character: honesty, compassion, courage, and perseverance. These are virtues* (William J. Bennett). Compare CARDINAL VIRTUE, THEOLOGICAL VIRTUE. **4.** chastity; virginity: *to lose one's virtue.* **5.** a good or admirable quality or property. **6.** effective force; power or potency. **7.** **virtues,** an order of angels. Compare ANGEL (def. 1). **8.** manly excellence; valor. —*Idiom.* **9. by** or **in virtue of,** by reason of; because of. —*Proverb.* **10. make a virtue of necessity,** to make the best of a difficult or unsatisfactory situation.

vir·tu·o·sa (vûr'chōo ō'sə), *n.* a woman who is a virtuoso.

vir·tu·os·i·ty (vûr'chōo os'i tē), *n.* **1.** the character, ability, or skill of a virtuoso. **2.** a fondness for or interest in virtu.

vir·tu·o·so (vûr'chōo ō'sō), *n., pl.* **-sos, -si** (-sē) *adj.* —*n.* **1.** a person who has special knowledge or skill in a field. **2.** a person who excels in musical technique or execution. **3.** a person who has a cultivated appreciation of artistic excellence. —*adj.* **4.** of, pertaining to, or characteristic of a virtuoso: *a virtuoso performance.* —**vir'tu·os'ic** (-os'ik), *adj.*

vir·tu·ous (vûr'chōo əs), *adj.* **1.** conforming to moral and ethical principles; morally excellent; upright. **2.** chaste: *a virtuous young person.* —**vir'tu·ous·ly,** *adv.* —**vir'tu·ous·ness,** *n.*

vir·u·lence (vir'yə ləns, vir'ə-) also **vir'u·len·cy,** *n.* **1.** the quality of being virulent. **2.** the relative ability of a microorganism to cause disease. **3.** venomous hostility. **4.** intense sharpness of temper.

vir·u·lent (vir'yə lənt, vir'ə-), *adj.* **1.** actively poisonous; intensely noxious. **2.** highly infectious; malignant or deadly: *a virulent disease.* **3.** violently or spitefully hostile. **4.** intensely bitter, spiteful, or malicious. —**vir'u·lent·ly,** *adv.*

vi·rus (vī'rəs), *n., pl.* **-rus·es. 1.** an ultramicroscopic (20 to 300 nm in diameter), metabolically inert, infectious agent that replicates only within the cells of living hosts, mainly bacteria, plants, and animals: composed of an RNA or DNA core, a protein coat, and, in more complex types, a surrounding envelope. **2.** a disease caused by a virus. **3.** a corrupting influence on morals or the intellect; poison. **4.** a segment of self-replicating code planted illegally in a computer program, often to damage or shut down a system or network. —**vi'rus·like',** *adj.*

vi·sa (vē'zə), *n., pl.* **-sas,** *v.* **-saed, -saing.** —*n.* **1.** an official endorsement made on a passport, permitting the bearer to enter the country making the endorsement. —*v.t.* **2.** to give a visa to; approve a visa for. **3.** to put a visa on (a passport).

vis·age (viz'ij), *n.* **1.** the face, usu. with reference to shape, features, expression, etc.; countenance: *a sad visage.* **2.** aspect; appearance: *a ghost town's desolate visage.* —**vis'aged,** *adj.*

vis-à-vis (vē'zə vē'; *Fr.* vē ZA vē'), *adv., adj., prep., n., pl.* **-vis** (-vēz'; *Fr.* -vē'). —*adv.* **1.** face to face. —*adj.* **2.** face-to-face. —*prep.* **3.** in relation to; compared with: *income vis-à-vis expenditures.* **4.** facing; opposite. —*n.* **5.** a person face-to-face with or situated opposite to another. **6.** a person of equal authority, rank, or the like. **7.** a carriage in which the occupants sit face to face. **8.** TÊTE-À-TÊTE (def. 2).

vis·cer·a (vis'ər ə), *n.pl., sing.* **vis·cus** (vis'kəs). **1.** the organs in the cavities of the body, esp. those in the abdominal cavity. **2.** (not in technical use) the intestines.

vis·cer·al (vis'ər əl), *adj.* **1.** of, pertaining to, or affecting the viscera. **2.** characterized by or proceeding from instinct rather than intellect: *a visceral reaction.* **3.** characterized by or dealing with coarse or base emotions; earthy. —**vis'cer·al·ly,** *adv.*

vis·cid (vis'id), *adj.* **1.** having a glutinous consistency; sticky; adhesive; viscous. **2.** *Bot.* covered by a sticky substance. —**vis·cid'i·ty, vis'cid·ness,** *n.* —**vis'cid·ly,** *adv.*

vis·cose (vis'kōs), *n.* **1.** a viscous solution prepared by treating cellulose with caustic soda and carbon bisulfide: used in manufacturing regenerated cellulose fibers, sheets, or tubes, as rayon or cellophane. **2.** viscose rayon. —*adj.* **3.** of, pertaining to, or made from viscose.

vis·cos·i·ty (vi skos'i tē), *n., pl.* **-ties. 1.** the state or quality of being viscous. **2. a.** the property of a fluid that resists the force tending to cause the fluid to flow. **b.** the measure of the extent to which a fluid possesses this property.

vis·count (vī'kount), *n.* a nobleman next below an earl or count and next above a baron. —**vis'count·cy,** *n., pl.* **-cies.** —**vis'count·ship',** *n.*

vis·count·ess (vī'koun'tis), *n.* **1.** the wife or widow of a viscount. **2.** a woman holding in her own right a rank equivalent to that of a viscount.

vis·cous (vis'kəs), *adj.* **1.** of a glutinous nature or consistency; sticky; thick; adhesive. **2.** having the property of viscosity. —**vis'cous·ly,** *adv.* —**vis'cous·ness,** *n.*

vise or **vice** (vīs), *n., v.,* **vised, vis·ing.** —*n.* **1.** any of various devices, usu. having two jaws adjusted by means of a screw, lever, or the like, used to hold an object firmly while work is being done on it. —*v.t.* **2.** to hold, press, or squeeze with or as if with a vise. —**vise'like',** *adj.*

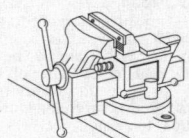

vise

Vish·nu (vish'nōo), *n.* "the Preserver," the second member of the Hindu Trimurti, along with Brahma the Creator and Shiva the Destroyer, believed to have descended from heaven to earth in several incarnations. [< Sanskrit *viṣṇu*] —**Vish'nu·ism,** *n.*

vis·i·bil·i·ty (viz'ə bil'i tē), *n.* **1.** the quality, state, or fact of being visible. **2.** the greatest distance it is possible to see under given atmospheric conditions. **3.** the relative capacity to be seen under given conditions of distance, light, etc.

vis·i·ble (viz'ə bəl), *adj.* **1.** capable of being seen; perceptible to the eye. **2.** apparent; manifest; obvious: *no visible means of support.* **3.** being constantly or frequently in the public view; conspicuous. **4.** noting or pertaining to a system of keeping records or information that can be brought instantly to view: *a visible index.* **5.** available or accessible; already existing, as goods in a warehouse. **6.** prepared for visual presentation; represented visually. —**vis'i·ble·ness,** *n.* —**vis'i·bly,** *adv.*

Vis·i·goth (viz'i goth'), *n.* a member of the western division of the Goths, who, after sacking Rome in A.D. 410, formed a kingdom in SW Europe, maintaining it in S Gaul until 507 and in Spain until 711. —**Vis'i·goth'ic,** *adj.*

vi·sion (vizh'ən), *n.* **1.** the act or power of sensing with the eyes; sight. **2.** the act or power of anticipating that which will or may come to be; foresight: *entrepreneurial vision.* **3. a.** something seen in or as if in a dream or trance, often attributed to divine agency. **b.** the experience of such a perception. **4.** a vivid, imaginative conception or anticipation: *visions of wealth and glory.* **5.** something seen; an object of sight. **6.** a scene, person, etc., of extraordinary beauty. —*v.t.* **7.** to envision. —*Proverb.* **8. Where there is no vision, the people perish,** people must foresee a better life for themselves. Prov. 29:18. —**vi'sion·less,** *adj.*

vi·sion·ar·y (vizh'ə ner'ē), *adj., n., pl.* **-ar·ies.** —*adj.* **1.** given to or concerned with seeing visions. **2.** belonging to or seen in a vision. **3.** unreal; imaginary. **4.** purely idealistic or speculative; impractical: *a vi-*

sionary scheme. **5.** given to or characterized by fanciful or impractical ideas. **6.** of, pertaining to, or proper to a vision. —*n.* **7.** a person of unusually keen foresight. **8.** a person who sees visions. **9.** a person who is given to highly speculative or impractical ideas or schemes; dreamer.

vi'sion quest', *n.* (esp. among some North American Indians) the ritual seeking of personal communication with the spirit world through visions that are induced by fasting, prayer, and other measures during a time of isolation: typically undertaken by an adolescent male.

vis•it (viz'it), *v.t.* **1.** to go to and stay with (a person or family) or at (a place) for a short time. **2.** to stay with as a guest. **3.** to go to for the purpose of official inspection or examination. **4.** to come upon; afflict: *The plague visited London in 1665.* **5.** to inflict, as punishment, vengeance, etc. (often fol. by *on* or *upon*). **6.** to cause trouble, suffering, etc, to: *to visit one with sorrows.* —*v.i.* **7.** to make a visit. **8.** to talk or chat casually. **9.** to inflict punishment. —*n.* **10.** the act of or an instance of visiting: *a long visit.* **11.** a chat or talk. **12.** a call paid to a person, family, etc. **13.** a stay or sojourn as a guest. **14.** an official inspection or examination. **15.** the boarding by a naval officer onto a neutral vessel to determine if it is carrying contraband. —**vis'it•a•ble**, *adj.*

vis•it•ant (viz'i tant), *n.* **1.** a temporary resident; visitor; guest. **2.** a being believed to come from the spirit world: *a ghostly visitant.* **3.** a migratory bird that has come to a place temporarily. —*adj.* **4.** visiting; paying a visit.

vis•it•a•tion (viz'i tā'shən), *n.* **1.** the act of visiting. **2.** a formal visit, as one granted by a court to a divorced parent to visit a child in custody of the other parent. **3.** a visit for the purpose of making an official examination or inspection, as of a bishop to a diocese. **4.** the administration of comfort or aid, or of affliction or punishment: *a visitation of the plague.* **5.** an affliction or punishment, as from God. **6.** the appearance or coming of a supernatural influence or spirit. —**vis'it•a'tion•al**, *adj.*

vis'iting card', *n.* CALLING CARD (def. 1).

vis'iting nurse', *n.* a registered nurse employed by a social service agency to give medical care to the sick in their homes.

vis'iting profes'sor, *n.* a professor invited from another college or university to teach for a limited period.

vis•i•tor (viz'i tər), *n.* a person who visits, as for reasons of friendship, business, duty, travel, or the like.

vi•sor or **vi•zor** (vī'zər), *n.* **1.** the projecting front brim of a cap. **2.** a flap, mounted on the inside of an automobile, used to shield one's eyes from glare. **3.** the front piece on a medieval helmet, often being movable and having slits for vision. —*v.t.* **4.** to protect or mask with a visor; shield. —**vi'sored**, *adj.*

vis•ta (vis'tə), *n.*, *pl.* **-tas. 1.** a view or prospect, esp. one seen through a long, narrow passage, as between rows of trees or houses. **2.** a far-reaching mental view. —**vis'taed**, *adj.*

vis•u•al (vizh'ळ əl), *adj.* **1.** of or pertaining to seeing or sight: *a visual image.* **2.** used in seeing: *the visual sense.* **3.** optical. **4.** perceptible by the sense of sight; visible. **5.** perceptible by the mind: *a visual impression captured in a line of verse.* **6.** of or involving the use of pictures, charts, maps, models, etc. for education or informative purposes: *visual aids.* —*n.* **7.** Usu., **visuals.** the picture elements, as distinguished from the sound elements, in films, television, etc.

vis'ual acu'ity, *n.* acuteness of the vision as determined by a comparison with the normal ability to identify certain letters at a given distance, usu. 20 ft. (6 m).

vis'ual arts', *n.pl.* the arts created primarily for visual perception, as drawing, graphics, painting, sculpture, and the decorative arts.

vis•u•al•ize (vizh'ळ ə līz'), *v.*, **-ized, -iz•ing. 1.** to recall or form mental images or pictures. —*v.t.* **2.** to form a mental image of. **3.** to make perceptible to the mind or imagination. —**vis'u•al•iz'a•ble**, *adj.* —**vis'u•al•i•za'tion**, *n.* —**vis'u•al•iz'er**, *n.*

vis•u•al•ly (vizh'ळ ə lē), *adv.* in a visual manner; with respect to sight; by sight: *to be visually impaired.*

vi•tal (vīt'l), *adj.* **1.** of, pertaining to, or necessary to life: *vital processes.* **2.** energetic, lively, or forceful: *a vital leader.* **3.** necessary to the existence, continuance, or well-being of something; indispensable; essential. **4.** of critical importance: *vital decisions.* **5.** destructive to life; deadly: *a vital wound.* —**vi'tal•ly**, *adv.*

vi'tal capac'ity, *n.* the greatest amount of air that can be forced from the lungs after maximum inhalation.

vi'tal force', *n.* **1.** Also called **vi'tal prin'ciple.** the force that animates and perpetuates living beings and organisms. **2.** ÉLAN VITAL.

vi•tal•ism (vīt'l iz'əm), *n.* **1.** the doctrine that phenomena are only partly controlled by mechanical forces, and are in some measure self-determining. Compare DYNAMISM (def. 1), MECHANISM (def. 6). **2.** *Biol.* a doctrine that attributes the viability of a living organism to a vital principle distinct from the physical and chemical processes of life. —**vi'tal•ist**, *n.*, *adj.* —**vi'tal•is'tic**, *adj.* —**vi'tal•is'ti•cal•ly**, *adv.*

vi•tal•i•ty (vī tal'i tē), *n.* **1.** exuberant physical or mental vigor: *a person of great vitality.* **2.** capacity for survival or for the continuation of a meaningful or purposeful existence: *the vitality of an institution.* **3.** power to live or grow. **4.** vital force or principle.

vi•tals (vīt'lz), *n.pl.* **1.** those bodily organs that are essential to life, as the brain, heart, liver, lungs, and stomach. **2.** the essential parts of something.

vi'tal signs', *n.pl.* essential body functions, comprising pulse rate, body temperature, and respiration.

vi'tal statis'tics, *n.pl.* statistics concerning human life or the

conditions affecting human life and the maintenance of population, as deaths, births, and marriages.

vi•ta•min (vī'tə min; *Brit. also* vit'ə-) also **vi•ta•mine** (-min, -mēn'), *n.* any of a group of organic substances essential in small quantities to normal metabolism, found in minute amounts in natural foodstuffs and also produced synthetically: deficiencies of vitamins produce specific disorders. —**vi'ta•min'ic**, *adj.*

vitamin A, *n.* a yellow, fat-soluble terpene alcohol, $C_{20}H_{30}O$, obtained from carotene and occurring in green and yellow vegetables, egg yolk, etc.: essential to growth, the protection of epithelial tissue, and the prevention of night blindness. Also called **vitamin A$_1$, retinol.**

vitamin A$_2$, *n.* a yellow oil, $C_{20}H_{28}O$, similar to vitamin A, obtained from fish liver.

vitamin B$_1$, *n.* THIAMINE.

vitamin B$_2$, *n.* RIBOFLAVIN.

vitamin B$_3$, *n.* NICOTINIC ACID.

vitamin B$_6$, *n.* PYRIDOXINE.

vitamin B$_{12}$, *n.* a complex water-soluble solid, $C_{63}H_{88}N_{14}O_{14}PCo$, obtained from liver, milk, eggs, fish, oysters, and clams: a deficiency causes pernicious anemia and disorders of the nervous system. Also called **cyanocobalamin, cobalamin, extrinsic factor.**

vitamin B complex, *n.* an important group of water-soluble vitamins containing vitamin B$_1$, vitamin B$_2$, etc.

vitamin C, *n.* ASCORBIC ACID.

vitamin D, *n.* any of the several fat-soluble, antirachitic vitamins D$_1$, D$_2$, D$_3$, occurring in milk and fish-liver oils, esp. cod and halibut: essential for the formation of normal bones and teeth.

vitamin D$_1$, *n.* a form of vitamin D obtained by ultraviolet irradiation of ergosterol.

vitamin D$_2$, *n.* CALCIFEROL.

vitamin D$_3$, *n.* a form of vitamin D, $C_{27}H_{43}OH$, occurring in fish-liver oils, that differs from vitamin D$_2$ by slight structural differences in the molecule.

vitamin E, *n.* a pale yellow, viscous fluid, abundant in vegetable oils, cereal grains, butter, and eggs, important as an antioxidant.

vitamin G, *n.* RIBOFLAVIN.

vitamin H, *n.* BIOTIN.

vitamin K$_1$, *n.* a yellowish, oily, viscous liquid, $C_{31}H_{46}O_2$, that occurs in leafy vegetables, rice, bran, and hog liver or is obtained esp. from alfalfa or putrefied sardine meat or synthesized and that promotes blood clotting by increasing the prothrombin content of the blood.

vitamin K$_2$, *n.* a light yellow, crystalline solid, $C_{41}H_{56}O_2$, having properties similar to those of vitamin K$_1$.

vitamin K$_3$, *n.* MENADIONE.

vitamin M, *n.* FOLIC ACID.

vitamin P, *n.* BIOFLAVONOID.

vi•ti•ate (vish'ē āt'), *v.t.*, **-at•ed, -at•ing. 1.** to impair the quality of; make faulty; spoil. **2.** to impair or weaken the effectiveness of. **3.** to debase; corrupt; pervert. **4.** to make legally invalid; invalidate: *to vitiate a claim.* —**vi'ti•a'tion**, *n.* —**vi'ti•a'tor**, *n.*

vit•i•cul•ture (vit'i kul'chər, vī'ti-), *n.* the cultivation of grapes and grapevines. —**vit'i•cul'tur•al**, *adj.* —**vit'i•cul'tur•ist**, *n.*

vit•re•ous (vi'trē əs), *adj.* **1.** of the nature of or resembling glass, as in transparency, brittleness, hardness, or glossiness: *vitreous china.* **2.** of or pertaining to glass. **3.** obtained from or containing glass. —**vit're•ous•ly**, *adv.* —**vit're•ous•ness**, *n.*

vit'reous hu'mor, *n.* the transparent gelatinous substance that fills the eyeball behind the crystalline lens.

vitri-, a combining form meaning "glass": *vitriform.*

vit•ric (vi'trik), *adj.* of, having the nature of, or resembling glass.

vit•ri•fy (vi'trə fī'), *v.t.*, *v.i.*, **-fied, -fy•ing. 1.** to convert or be converted into glass. **2.** to make or become vitreous. —**vit'ri•fi'a•bil'i•ty**, *n.* —**vit'ri•fi'a•ble**, *adj.* —**vit'ri•fi•ca'tion**, *n.*

vit•ri•ol (vi'trē əl), *n.* **1.** any of various glassy metallic sulfates, as copper sulfate or iron sulfate. **2.** oil of vitriol; sulfuric acid. **3.** something highly caustic or severe in effect, as criticism.

vit•ri•ol•ic (vi'trē ol'ik), *adj.* **1.** of, pertaining to, or resembling vitriol. **2.** very caustic or bitter; scathing: *a vitriolic denunciation.*

vit•tle (vit'l), *n.*, *v.t.*, *v.i.*, **-tled, -tling.** VICTUAL.

vi•tu•per•ate (vī too'pə rāt', -tyoo'-, vi-), *v.*, **-at•ed, -at•ing.** —*v.i.* **1.** to use harsh or abusive language. —*v.t.* **2.** to censure harshly; revile. —**vi•tu'per•a'tion**, *n.*

vi•tu•per•a•tive (vī too'pər ə tiv, -pə rā'tiv, -tyoo'-, vi-), *adj.* given to, characterized by, or of the nature of vituperation. —**vi•tu'per•a•tive•ly**, *adv.*

vi•va (vē'və, -vä), *interj.* (used as an exclamation of acclaim or approval): *Viva Zapata!*

vi•va•cious (vi vā'shəs, vī-), *adj.* lively; animated; spirited. —**vi•va'cious•ly**, *adv.* —**vi•va'cious•ness**, *n.*

vi•vac•i•ty (vi vas'i tē, vī-), *n.*, *pl.* **-ties. 1.** the quality or state of being vivacious. **2.** a vivacious act or statement.

Vi•val•di (vi väl'dē), *n.* **Antonio,** 1678–1741, Italian composer.

vi•var•i•um (vī vâr'ē əm, vi-), *n.*, *pl.* **-var•i•ums, -var•i•a** (-vâr'ē ə). a place, as a laboratory, where live animals or plants are kept under conditions simulating their natural environment, as for research.

vi•va vo•ce (vī'və vō'sē, vē'və), *adv.* **1.** by word of mouth; orally.

—*n.* **2.** (in British and European universities) an oral examination. [< Medieval Latin: with living voice] —**vi′va-vo′ce,** *adj.*

vivi-, a combining form meaning "living," "alive": *vivisection.*

viv•id (viv′id), *adj.* **1.** (of color, light, etc.) strikingly bright or intense; brilliant. **2.** having bright or striking colors. **3.** presenting the appearance, freshness, spirit, etc., of life; realistic: *a vivid account.* **4.** strong, distinct, or clearly perceptible: *a vivid recollection.* **5.** forming distinct and striking mental images: *a vivid imagination.* **6.** full of life; lively; animated: *a vivid personality.* —**viv′id•ly,** *adv.* —**viv′id•ness,** *n.*

viv•i•fy (viv′ə fī′), *v.t.,* **-fied, -fy•ing. 1.** to give life to; animate. **2.** to enliven; brighten. —**viv′i•fi•ca′tion,** *n.* —**viv′i•fi′er,** *n.*

vi•vip•a•rous (vī vip′ər əs, vi-), *adj.* **1.** bringing forth living young rather than eggs. **2.** producing seeds that germinate on the plant. —**viv•i•par•i•ty** (viv′ə par′i tē, vī′və-), *n.* —**vi•vip′a•rous•ly,** *adv.*

viv•i•sec•tion (viv′ə sek′shən), *n.* **1.** the action of cutting into or dissecting a living body. **2.** the practice of subjecting living animals to cutting operations, esp. in order to advance physiological and pathological knowledge. —**viv′i•sec′tion•al,** *adj.*

vix•en (vik′sən), *n.* **1.** a female fox. **2.** an ill-tempered or quarrelsome woman. —**vix′en•ish, vix′en•ly,** *adj.*

viz., videlicet.

vi•zier (vi zēr′, viz′yər) also **vi•zir′,** *n.* a high governmental official in certain Muslim countries, esp. in the former Ottoman Empire. —**vi•zier′ate** (-it, -āt), **vi•zier′ship,** *n.* —**vi•zier′i•al,** *adj.*

V-J Day (vē′jā′), *n.* August 14, 1945, the day Japan accepted the Allied surrender terms in World War II, or September 2, 1945, the day the surrender was signed.

Vlad•i•mir (vlad′ə mēr′, vlə dē′mir), *n.* **1. Saint.** Also, **Vladimir I.** (*"Vladimir the Great"*) A.D. c956-1015, grand prince of Kiev 980-1015: first Christian ruler of Russia. **2.** a city in the W Russian Federation, E of Moscow. 343,000.

Vla•di•vos•tok (vlad′ə vos′tok, -və stok′), *n.* a seaport in the SE Russian Federation in Asia, on the Sea of Japan: eastern terminus of the Trans-Siberian Railroad. 648,000.

VLF or **vlf,** very low frequency.

V.M.D., Doctor of Veterinary Medicine. [< New Latin *Veterināriae Medicīnae Doctor*]

V neck, *n.* a neckline V-shaped in front. —**V-necked,** *adj.*

vo•cab•u•lar•y (vō kab′yə ler′ē), *n., pl.* **-lar•ies. 1.** the stock of words used by or known to a particular person or group. **2.** a list or collection of words and often phrases, usu. arranged in alphabetical order and defined. **3.** the words of a language. **4.** any collection of signs or symbols constituting a means or system of nonverbal communication. **5.** the set of forms, techniques, or other means of expression available to or characteristic of an artist, art form, etc. —**vo•cab′u•lar′ied,** *adj.*

vo•cal (vō′kəl), *adj.* **1.** of, pertaining to, or uttered with the voice. **2.** rendered by or intended for singing: *vocal music.* **3.** having a voice. **4.** giving forth sound with or as if with a voice. **5.** inclined to express oneself in words, esp. insistently; outspoken: *a vocal advocate of reform.* **6.** VOICED (def. 3). —*n.* **7.** a vocal sound. **8. a.** a musical piece for a singer; song. **b.** a performer of such a piece. —**vo′cal•ly,** *adv.*

vo′cal cords′, *n.pl.* either of two pairs of folds of mucous membrane stretched across the larynx, the lower pair of which produces sound or voice as it is made to vibrate by the passage of air from the lungs.

vo•cal•ist (vō′kə list), *n.* a singer.

vo•cal•ize (vō′kə līz′), *v.,* **-ized, -iz•ing.** —*v.t.* **1.** to make vocal; utter; articulate. **2.** to endow with a voice; cause to utter. **3. a.** to change into a vowel sound. **b.** to voice. —*v.i.* **4.** to utter sounds using the vocal organs. **5. a.** to sing. **b.** to sing without uttering words. —**vo′cal•i•za′tion,** *n.* —**vo′cal•iz′er,** *n.*

vo•ca•tion (vō kā′shən), *n.* **1.** a particular occupation, business, or profession; calling. **2.** a strong impulse or inclination to follow a particular activity or career. **3.** a divine call to a religious life.

vo•ca•tion•al (vō kā′shə nl), *adj.* **1.** of, pertaining to, or connected with a vocation or occupation. **2.** of, pertaining to, or providing instruction or training in an occupation or trade. **3.** of or pertaining to guidance in the choice of an occupation: *a vocational counselor.* —**vo•ca′tion•al•ly,** *adv.*

voc•a•tive (vok′ə tiv), *adj.* **1.** of or designating a grammatical case, as in Latin, used to indicate that a noun or pronoun refers to the person or thing being addressed. **2.** of or used in calling or addressing. —*n.* **3.** the vocative case. **4.** a word in this case, as Latin *Paule* "O Paul." —**voc′a•tive•ly,** *adv.*

vo•cif•er•ate (vō sif′ə rāt′), *v.i., v.t.,* **-at•ed, -at•ing.** to speak or cry out loudly, noisily, or vehemently, as in protest or complaint; shout; clamor. —**vo•cif′er•a′tion,** *n.* —**vo•cif′er•a′tor,** *n.*

vo•cif•er•ous (vō sif′ər əs), *adj.* **1.** crying out noisily. **2.** characterized by noisy or vehement outcry: *vociferous protests.* —**vo•cif′er•ous•ly,** *adv.* —**vo•cif′er•ous•ness,** *n.*

vod•ka (vod′kə), *n.* a colorless distilled alcoholic spirit made esp. from rye or wheat mash.

vogue (vōg), *n.* **1.** the prevailing fashion at a particular time; mode. **2.** popular currency, acceptance, or favor; popularity. —*adj.* **3.** currently fashionable or popular: *vogue words.* —**vogu′ish,** *adj.*

voice (vois), *n., v.,* **voiced, voic•ing.** —*n.* **1.** the sound or sounds uttered through the mouth of living creatures, esp. of human beings in speaking, singing, etc. **2.** the faculty or power of uttering sounds through the mouth by the controlled expulsion of air; speech: *to lose one's voice.* **3.** such sounds as distinctive to an individual. **4.** such sounds with reference to their character or quality. **5.** the condition or effectiveness of the voice for speaking or singing: *to be in poor voice.* **6.** a sound likened to or resembling vocal utterance. **7.** something likened to speech as conveying impressions to the mind: *the voice of one's conscience.* **8.** expression in words or by other means: *to give voice to one's disapproval.* **9.** the right to present and receive consideration of one's desires or opinions: *to have a voice in company policy.* **10.** an expressed opinion, choice, or desire: *the voice of the people.* **11.** a person or other agency through which something is expressed or revealed: *the voice of doom.* **12.** a person or other agency through which the views of another person or a group are expressed: *the voice of the opposition.* **13.** a singer: *He is one of the great voices in opera.* **14.** a melodic part in a musical composition: *a fugue with three voices.* **15.** the audible result produced by vibration of the vocal cords as air is expelled from the lungs. **16.** a category of the verb used to indicate the relation of the subject to the verb as performer or beneficiary of its action: *the active voice; the passive voice.* **17.** the finer regulation, as of intensity and color, in tuning, esp. of a piano or organ. —*v.t.* **18.** to give expression to; declare; proclaim. **19.** to regulate the tone of, as the pipes of an organ. **20.** to utter with the voice. **21.** to pronounce with vibration of the vocal cords. —*Idiom.* **22. with one voice,** in accord; unanimously.

voice′ box′, *n.* the larynx.

voiced (voist), *adj.* **1.** having a voice of a specified kind (usu. used in combination): *shrill-voiced.* **2.** expressed vocally: *his voiced opinion.* **3.** (of a speech sound) pronounced with vibration of the vocal cords, as the consonants (b), (v), and (n). —**voic′ed•ness,** *n.*

voice•less (vois′lis), *adj.* **1.** having no voice; mute. **2.** uttering no words; silent. **3.** having an unmusical voice. **4.** unspoken; unuttered. **5.** having no vote or right of choice. **6.** (of a speech sound) pronounced without vibration of the vocal cords, as the consonants (p), (f), and (s). —**voice′less•ly,** *adv.* —**voice′less•ness,** *n.*

voice′ mail′, *n.* an electronic communications system that routes voice messages interactively to appropriate recipients, stores the messages in digitized form, and notifies the recipients that the messages are available for playback through the system.

voice′-o′ver, *n.* **1.** the voice of an offscreen narrator, announcer, or the like, in television or motion pictures. **2.** a televised sequence, as in a commercial, narrated by voice-over.

voice′ vote′, *n.* a vote based on estimation of the relative strength of ayes and noes called out by voters.

void (void), *adj.* **1.** having no legal force or effect; not legally binding or enforceable. **2.** useless; ineffectual; vain. **3.** devoid; destitute (usu. fol. by *of*): *a life void of meaning.* **4.** without contents; empty. **5.** without an incumbent, as an office; vacant. **6.** (in cards) having no cards in a suit. —*n.* **7.** an empty space; emptiness: *He disappeared into the void.* **8.** a state or feeling of loss or privation: *His death left a great void in her life.* **9.** a gap or opening. **10.** a vacancy; vacuum. **11.** (in cards) lack of cards in a suit: *a void in clubs.* —*v.t.* **12.** to make ineffectual; invalidate; nullify: *to void a check.* **13.** to empty; discharge; evacuate. **14.** to clear or empty (often fol. by *of*). —*v.i.* **15.** to defecate or urinate. —**void′a•ble,** *adj.* —**void′er,** *n.* —**void′ness,** *n.*

void•ed (voi′did), *adj.* **1.** having a void. **2.** having been made void.

voi•là or **voi•la** (vwä lä′; *Fr.* VWA LA′), *interj.* (used to express success or satisfaction.)

voile (voil), *n.* a lightweight, semisheer fabric of wool, silk, rayon, or cotton constructed in plain weave.

voir dire (vwär′ dēr′), *n.* the examination of a proposed witness or juror to ascertain the person's competence to give or hear testimony. [< Old French *voir* true, truly + *dire* to say]

vol•a•tile (vol′ə tl, -til; *esp. Brit.* -tīl′), *adj.* **1.** evaporating rapidly; passing off readily in the form of vapor: *Acetone is a volatile solvent.* **2.** tending or threatening to break out into open violence; explosive: *a volatile political situation.* **3.** characterized by or liable to sharp or sudden changes; unstable: *a volatile stock market.* **4.** changeable, as in mood or temper; mercurial; flighty. **5.** fleeting; transient. **6.** (of computer storage) not retaining data when electrical power is turned off. —*n.* **7.** a volatile substance, as a gas or solvent. —**vol′a•til′i•ty** (-til′i tē), *n.*

vol′atile oil′, *n.* a distilled oil, esp. one obtained from plant tissue, as distinguished from glyceride oils by their volatility and failure to saponify.

vol•a•til•ize (vol′ə tl īz′), *v.,* **-ized, -iz•ing.** —*v.i.* **1.** to become volatile; pass off as vapor. —*v.t.* **2.** to make volatile. —**vol′a•til•iz′a•ble,** *adj.* —**vol′a•til•i•za′tion,** *n.* —**vol′a•til•iz′er,** *n.*

vol-au-vent (vô lō väN′), *n.* a shell of light pastry filled with chicken, meat, or fish in a sauce.

vol•can•ic (vol kan′ik), *adj.* **1.** of or pertaining to a volcano. **2.** discharged from or produced by volcanoes: *volcanic ash.* **3.** characterized by the presence of volcanoes. **4.** suggestive of or resembling a volcano; potentially explosive; volatile. —**vol•can′i•cal•ly,** *adv.* —**vol′can•ic′i•ty** (-kə nis′i tē), *n.*

volcan′ic glass′, *n.* a natural glass produced when molten lava cools very rapidly; obsidian.

vol•ca•no (vol kā′nō), *n., pl.* **-noes, -nos. 1.** a vent in the earth's crust through which lava, steam, ashes, etc., are expelled, either continuously or at irregular intervals. **2.** a mountain or hill, usu. having a cuplike crater at the summit, formed around such a vent from the ash and lava expelled through it.

vol·can·ol·o·gy (vol′kə nol′ə jē) also **vulcanology**, *n.* the scientific study of volcanoes and volcanic phenomena. —**vol′can·ol′o·gist**, *n.*

vole (vōl), *n.* any of several short-tailed, stocky cricetid rodents, esp. of the genus *Microtus.*

Vol·ga (vol′gə, vōl′-), *n.* a river flowing from the Valdai Hills in the W Russian Federation, E and then S to the Caspian Sea: the longest river in Europe. 2325 mi. (3745 km) long.

Vol·go·grad (vol′gə grad′, vōl′-; *Russ.* vəl gu grät′), *n.* a city in the SW Russian Federation in Europe, on the Volga River: battles in World War II, September 1942–February 1943. 999,000. Formerly, **Stalingrad, Tsaritsyn.**

vo·li·tion (vō lish′ən, və-), *n.* **1.** the act of willing, choosing, or resolving; exercise of the will: *She left of her own volition.* **2.** the power of willing, choosing, or deciding; will. **3.** a choice or decision made by the will. —**vo·li′tion·al, vo·li′tion·ar′y,** *adj.* —**vo·li′tion·al·ly,** *adv.*

vol·ley (vol′ē), *n.* **1.** the simultaneous discharge of a number of missiles or firearms. **2.** the missiles so discharged. **3.** a burst or outpouring of many things at once or in quick succession: *a volley of protests.* **4. a.** the return of a ball or shuttlecock, as in tennis or badminton, before it hits the ground. **b.** the flight of the ball before it hits the ground. **c.** a series of such returns; rally. **5.** a kick of the ball in soccer before it bounces on the ground. —*v.t.* **6.** to discharge in or as if in a volley. **7.** to return (a ball) before it hits the ground, as in tennis. **8.** to kick (the ball) in soccer before it bounces on the ground. —*v.i.* **9.** to be discharged together, as missiles. **10.** to move or proceed with great rapidity, as in a volley. **11.** to fire a volley; sound together, as firearms. **12.** to return a ball, as in tennis or soccer, before it touches the ground. —**vol′ley·er,** *n.*

vol·ley·ball (vol′ē bôl′), *n.* **1.** a game for two teams in which the object is to keep a large ball in motion, from side to side over a high net, by striking it with the hands before it touches the ground. **2.** the ball used in this game.

vols., volumes.

volt¹ (vōlt), *n.* the SI unit of potential difference and electromotive force, equal to the difference of electric potential between two points of a conductor carrying a constant current of one ampere, when the power dissipated between these points is equal to one watt. *Abbr.:* V —**vol·ta·ic** (vol tā′ik, vōl-), *adj.*

volt² (vōlt), *n.* **1.** a circular movement or gait in manège in which a horse going sideways turns around a center with its head facing outward. **2.** a sudden movement or leap in fencing to avoid a thrust.

volt·age (vōl′tij), *n.* electromotive force or potential difference expressed in volts.

volta′ic pile′, *n.* an early battery cell consisting of disks of dissimilar metals separated by electrolytic pads.

vol·tam·e·ter (vol tam′i tər, vōl-), *n.* a device that measures the flow of electricity through a conductor in relation to electrolytic decomposition. —**vol′ta·met′ric** (-tə me′trik), *adj.*

volt′-am′pere, *n.* an electric measurement unit, equal to the product of one volt and one ampere, equivalent to one watt for direct current systems and a unit of apparent power for alternating current systems. *Abbr.:* VA, va

volte-face (volt fäs′, vōlt-; *Fr.* vôlt′ fᴀs′), *n.* a turnabout, esp. a reversal of opinion or policy. [< Italian *volta* turn + *faccia* face]

vol·u·ble (vol′yə bəl), *adj.* characterized by a ready and continuous flow of words; fluent; glib; talkative. —**vol′u·bil′i·ty, vol′u·ble·ness,** *n.* —**vol′u·bly,** *adv.*

vol·ume (vol′yŏŏm, -yəm), *n.* **1. a.** the amount of space, measured in cubic units, that an object or substance occupies. **b.** the measured amount that a container or other object can hold; cubic capacity. **2.** a mass or quantity, esp. a large quantity, of something: *a volume of mail.* **3.** amount; total: *the volume of sales.* **4.** mass; bulk. **5.** the degree of sound intensity or audibility; loudness: *to turn up the volume on a radio.* **6.** fullness or quantity of tone. **7.** a book, esp. as a separately bound portion of a larger work, or as one of a series of works. **8.** a set of issues of a periodical, often covering one year. **9.** a roll of papyrus, parchment, etc.; scroll. —*Idiom.* **10. speak volumes,** to be expressive or full of meaning. —**vol′umed,** *adj.*

vol·u·met·ric (vol′yə me′trik) also **vol·u·met′ri·cal,** *adj.* of, pertaining to, or involving measurement by volume. —**vol′u·met′ri·cal·ly,** *adv.* —**vo·lu·me·try** (və lōō′mi trē), *n.*

vo·lu·mi·nous (və lōō′mə nəs), *adj.* **1.** filling or sufficient to fill a volume or volumes: *a voluminous correspondence.* **2.** writing copiously or at great length: *a voluminous writer.* **3.** of great volume, size, or extent.

MAJOR VOLCANOES OF THE WORLD

Volcano	Location	Height		Last Major Eruption
		ft.	m	
Guallatiri	Northern Chile	19,882	6060	1959
Lascar	Northern Chile	19,652	5990	1951
Cotopaxi	Northern Central Ecuador	19,498	5943	Active
El Misti	Southern Peru	19,200	5880	Active
Demavend	Northern Iran	18,606	5670	Active
Tupungatito	Central Chile	18,504	5640	1959
Nevado del Ruiz	West Central Colombia	17,720	5401	1985
Sangay	Central Ecuador	17,159	5230	1946
Cotacachi	Northern Ecuador	16,197	4937	1955
Klyuchevskaya	Russian Federation, Kamchatka Peninsula	15,912	4850	1946
Purace	Southern Colombia	15,420	4700	1950
Pasto	Southwestern Colombia	13,990	4265	Active
Mauna Loa	United States, Central Hawaii	13,680	4170	1984
Colima	Western Mexico	12,631	3850	Active
Fuji	Japan, Central Honshu	12,395	3778	1707
Nyiragongo	Zaire, Eastern Edge	11,385	3470	1948
Koryaksky	Russian Federation, Kamchatka Peninsula	11,339	3456	1957
Spurr	United States, South Central Alaska	11,069	3374	1992
Etna	Italy, Eastern Sicily	10,758	3280	1985
Torbert	United States, South Central Alaska	10,600	3231	1953
Lassen	United States, Northeastern California	10,465	3190	1921
Dempo	Indonesia, Southwestern Sumatra	10,364	3159	Active
Shishaldin	United States, Southwestern Alaska	9500	2896	Active
Poas	Central Costa Rica	8930	2722	Active
Pavlof	United States, Soutwestern Alaska	8900	2712	1982
St. Helens	United States, Southwestern Washington	8364	2549	1990
Hualalai	United States, Western Hawaii	8269	2520	1800-01
Paricutin	West Central, Mexico	8200	2500	1943-52
Katmai	United States, Southern Alaska	7500	2286	1962
Martin	United States, Alaska Peninsula	6100	1859	1960
Trident	United States, Alaska Peninsula	6010	1832	1960
Great Sitkin	United States, Aleutians	5740	1750	Active
Cleveland	United States, Aleutians	5675	1730	1944
Mount Pinatubo	Philippine Islands	4795	1462	1991
Taal	Phillipine Islands	4752	1448	1968
Pelee	Martinique	4583	1397	1902
Hubok Hibok	Phillippine Islands	4363	1330	1951
Kilauea	United States, South Central Hawaii	4040	1231	Active
Vesuvius	Italy, Bay of Naples	3900	1189	1944
El Chichon	Southern Mexico	3478	1060	1982
Capelinhos	Faial Island, Azores	3351	1021	Active
Stromboli	Italy, Lipari Islands	3040	927	1956
Ascuncion	Marianas	2923	891	Active
Krakata	Indonesia	2667	813	1883
Therra	Greece, Cyclades, Aegean Sea	1858	566	1866
Barren Island	Andaman Islands	1160	354	early 19th c.
White Island	New Zealand, Northern North Island	1075	328	Active
Surtsey	North Atlantic	568	173	1967

4. having ample folds or fullness: *voluminous skirts.* **5.** having many coils, convolutions, or windings. —**vo•lu′mi•nous•ly,** *adv.* —**vo•lu′mi•nous•ness,** *n.*

vol•un•tar•y (vol′ən ter′ē), *adj., n., pl.* **-tar•ies.** —*adj.* **1.** done, made, brought about, or undertaken of one's own accord or by free choice: *a voluntary contribution.* **2.** of, pertaining to, or acting in accord with the will. **3.** of, pertaining to, or depending on voluntary action: *voluntary hospitals.* **4.** done by or composed of volunteers. **5.** *Law.* **a.** acting or done without compulsion or obligation. **b.** done by intention, and not by accident: *voluntary manslaughter.* **c.** made without valuable consideration: *a voluntary settlement.* **6.** subject to or controlled by the will. **7.** having the power of willing or choosing: *a voluntary agent.* **8.** proceeding from a natural impulse; spontaneous. —*n.* **9.** someone or something voluntary. **10.** a piece of music performed as a prelude to a larger work, esp. an organ piece performed before, during, or after a church service. —**vol•un•tar•i•ly** (vol′ən târ′ə lē, vol′ən ter′-), *adv.*

vol′untary mus′cle, *n.* any muscle moved at will and composed of bundles of striated fibers.

vol•un•teer (vol′ən tēr′), *n.* **1.** a person who voluntarily offers himself or herself for a service or undertaking. **2.** a person who performs a service willingly and without pay. **3.** a person who enters military service voluntarily rather than through conscription. **4.** a person who acts without legal obligation to do so, esp. such a person who pays the debt of another. **5.** a plant that has sprung up spontaneously from seed rather than having been planted or cultivated. —*adj.* **6.** of, pertaining to, or serving as a volunteer. **7.** consisting of or performed by volunteers: *a volunteer army.* —*v.i.* **8.** to offer oneself for some service or undertaking. **9.** to enter service or enlist as a volunteer. —*v.t.* **10.** to offer (oneself or one's services) for some undertaking or purpose. **11.** to give, bestow, or perform voluntarily. **12.** to say, tell, or communicate voluntarily: *to volunteer an explanation.*

vo•lup•tu•ar•y (və lup′cho͞o er′ē), *n., pl.* **-ar•ies,** *adj.* —*n.* **1.** a person devoted to the pursuit and enjoyment of luxury and sensual pleasure. —*adj.* **2.** of, pertaining to, or characterized by preoccupation with luxury and sensual pleasure.

vo•lup•tu•ous (və lup′cho͞o əs), *adj.* **1.** derived from gratification of the senses: *voluptuous pleasure.* **2.** sensuously pleasing or delightful. **3.** full and shapely: *a voluptuous figure.* **4.** characterized by or ministering to indulgence in luxury, pleasure, and sensuous enjoyment. —**vo•lup′tu•ous•ly,** *adv.* —**vo•lup′tu•ous•ness,** *n.*

vo•lute (və lo͞ot′), *n.* **1.** a spiral or twisted formation or object. **2.** a spiral ornament, found esp. on the capitals of the Ionic, Corinthian, and Composite orders. **3.** a horizontal scrolled termination to the handrail of a stair. **4.** a turn or whorl of a spiral shell. —*adj.* **5.** having a volute or rolled-up form. **6.** spirally shaped or having a part so shaped. —**vo•lut′ed,** *adj.* —**vo•lu′tion,** *n.*

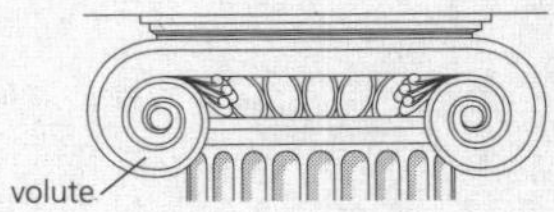

volute (def. 2) (on an Ionic capital)

vom•it (vom′it), *v.i.* **1.** to eject the contents of the stomach through the mouth; regurgitate; throw up. **2.** to belch or spew with force or violence. —*v.t.* **3.** to eject from the stomach through the mouth; spew. **4.** to eject forcefully or violently: *The volcano vomited flames and molten rock.* **5.** to cause (a person) to vomit. —*n.* **6.** the act of vomiting. **7.** the matter ejected in vomiting. —**vom′i•tive,** *adj.*

vom•i•to•ry (vom′i tôr′ē, -tōr′ē), *adj., n., pl.* **-ries.** —*adj.* **1.** inducing vomiting; emetic. **2.** of or pertaining to vomiting. —*n.* **3.** an opening through which something is ejected or discharged. **4.** an opening, as in an ancient Roman theater or stadium, permitting large numbers of people to enter or leave.

vom•i•tous (vom′i təs), *adj.* **1.** of, pertaining to, or causing vomiting. **2.** repugnant; disgusting; nauseating. —**vom′i•tous•ly,** *adv.*

Von Neu•mann (von noi′män, -mən), *n.* **John,** 1903–57, U.S. mathematician, born in Hungary.

voo•doo (vo͞o′do͞o), *n., pl.* **-doos,** *adj., v.* **-dooed, -dooing.** —*n.* **1.** a polytheistic religion practiced chiefly by West Indians, deriving principally from African cult worship and containing elements borrowed from the Catholic religion. **2.** a person who practices this religion. **3.** a fetish or other object of voodoo worship. **4.** a group of magical and ecstatic rites associated with voodoo. **5.** black magic; sorcery. —*adj.* **6.** of, associated with, or practicing voodoo. **7.** characterized by deceptively simple, almost magical, solutions or ideas: *voodoo economics.* —*v.t.* **8.** to affect by voodoo sorcery.

voo•doo•ism (vo͞o′do͞o iz′əm), *n.* **1.** voodoo religious rites and practices. **2.** the practice of sorcery. —**voo′doo•is′tic,** *adj.*

vo•ra•cious (vô rā′shəs, vō-, və-), *adj.* **1.** craving or consuming large quantities of food: *a voracious appetite.* **2.** exceedingly eager or avid; insatiable: *a voracious reader.* —**vo•ra′cious•ly,** *adv.* —**vo•ra′cious•ness, vo•rac′i•ty** (-ras′i tē), *n.*

-vore, a combining form meaning "one that eats" what is specified by the initial element: *carnivore.* Compare -VOROUS.

-vorous, a combining form meaning "eating, gaining sustenance from" that specified by the initial element: *carnivorous.*

vor•tex (vôr′teks), *n., pl.* **-tex•es, -ti•ces** (-tə sēz′). **1.** a whirling mass of water, esp. one in which a force of suction operates, as a whirlpool. **2.** a whirling mass of air, esp. one in the form of a visible column or spiral, as a tornado. **3.** something likened to a whirlpool, as in violent activity or the tendency to draw into its current everything that surrounds it: *the vortex of war.*

vor•ti•cal (vôr′ti kəl), *adj.* **1.** of, pertaining to, or resembling a vortex. **2.** moving in a vortex. —**vor′ti•cal•ly,** *adv.*

vor•ti•ces (vôr′tə sēz′), *n.* a pl. of VORTEX.

vot•a•ble or **vote•a•ble** (vō′tə bəl), *adj.* capable of being voted upon; subject to a vote.

vo•ta•ry (vō′tə rē) also **vo′ta•rist,** *n., pl.* **-ries** also **-rists.** **1.** a devoted worshiper of a deity, saint, etc., or a devout adherent of a religion. **2.** a person who is devoted to some subject or pursuit; devotee: *a votary of jazz.* **3.** a devoted follower or admirer. **4.** a person who is bound by solemn religious vows, as a nun.

vote (vōt), *n., v.,* **vot•ed, vot•ing.** —*n.* **1.** a formal expression of positive or negative opinion or choice made by an individual or a body of individuals. **2.** the right to such expression: *to give women the vote.* **3.** the total number of votes cast. **4.** the decision reached by voting. **5.** a collective expression of will as inferred from a number of votes. **6.** a particular group of voters. **7.** an expression of approval, agreement, or judgment: *a vote of confidence.* —*v.i.* **8.** to express or signify will or choice in a matter, as by casting a ballot. —*v.t.* **9.** to enact, establish, or determine by vote: *to vote a bill into law.* **10.** to support by one's vote: *to vote the Republican ticket.* **11.** to advocate by or as if by one's vote. **12.** to declare or decide by general consent. —***Idiom.*** **13. vote with one's feet,** to reject something by leaving it. [< Latin *vōtum* a vow]

vot•er (vō′tər), *n.* **1.** a person who votes. **2.** a person who has a right to vote; elector.

vot′ing machine′, *n.* a mechanical or electronic apparatus used in a polling place to register and count the votes.

vo•tive (vō′tiv), *adj.* **1.** offered, dedicated, performed, etc., in accordance with a vow, often as an act of veneration or of gratitude for a favor granted: *a votive offering.* **2.** of the nature of or expressive of a wish or desire. —**vo′tive•ly,** *adv.* —**vo′tive•ness,** *n.*

vouch (vouch), *v.i.* **1.** to provide proof, supporting evidence, or assurance (usu. fol. by *for*): *to vouch for someone's integrity.* **2.** to give a guarantee or act as surety or sponsor; take responsibility (usu. fol. by *for*). —*v.t.* **3.** to sustain or uphold by or as if by practical proof or demonstration. **4.** to cite (an authority, fact, etc.) in support or justification.

vouch•er (vou′chər), *n.* **1.** a person or thing that vouches. **2.** a document, receipt, stamp, etc., that gives evidence of an expenditure. **3.** a form authorizing a disbursement of cash or a credit against a future purchase or expense. **4.** written authorization; credential. **5.** a piece of evidence or proof. —*v.t.* **6.** to pay for or authorize by voucher. **7.** to prepare a voucher for.

vouch•safe (vouch sāf′), *v.t.,* **-safed, -saf•ing.** **1.** to grant or give, as by favor, graciousness, or condescension: *to vouchsafe a reply.* **2.** to allow or permit, as by favor or graciousness.

vow (vou), *n.* **1.** a solemn promise, pledge, or personal commitment: *marriage vows; a vow of secrecy.* **2.** a solemn promise made to a deity or saint committing oneself to an act, service, or condition. **3.** a solemn declaration. —*v.t.* **4.** to make a vow of; promise by a vow, as to a deity or a saint. **5.** to pledge or resolve solemnly to do, make, give, etc.: *They vowed revenge.* **6.** to declare solemnly or earnestly; assert emphatically. **7.** to dedicate or devote by a vow. —*v.i.* **8.** to make a vow. —***Idiom.*** **9. take vows,** to make an official commitment to a religious order.

vow•el (vou′əl), *n.* **1.** a speech sound, as (ē), (o͞o), or (a), produced without occluding, diverting, or obstructing the flow of air from the lungs, and usu. constituting the sound of greatest sonority in a syllable (opposed to *consonant*). **2.** a letter or other symbol representing a vowel sound, as, in English, *a, e, i, o, u,* and sometimes *y* or *w.*

vox po•pu•li (voks′ pop′yə lī′), *n.* the voice of the people; popular opinion. [< Latin]

voy•age (voi′ij), *n., v.,* **-aged, -ag•ing.** —*n.* **1.** a course of travel or passage, esp. a long journey by water to a distant place. **2.** a passage or journey through air or space. **3.** a journey or expedition by land. **4.** Often, **voyages.** journeys or travels as the subject of a written account, or the account itself. —*v.i.* **5.** to make or take a voyage; travel; journey. —*v.t.* **6.** to traverse by a voyage. —**voy′ag•er,** *n.*

Voy•ag•er (voi′ə jər), *n.* one of a series of U.S. space probes between 1977 and 1989 that obtained scientific information while flying by the planets Jupiter, Saturn, Uranus, and Neptune.

vo•yeur (vwä yûr′, voi ûr′), *n.* **1.** a person who obtains sexual gratification by looking at sexual objects or acts, esp. secretively. **2.** a person who derives exaggerated or unseemly enjoyment from being an observer. —**vo•yeur•ism** (vwä yûr′iz əm, voi ûr′-, voi′ə riz′-), *n.* —**voy′eur•is′tic,** *adj.* —**voy′eur•is′ti•cal•ly,** *adv.*

VP, 1. verb phrase. **2.** Also, **vp, v-p** vice president.

V.P. or **V. Pres.,** Vice President.

V. Rev., Very Reverend.

vroom (vro͞om, vro͝om), *n.* **1.** the roaring sound made by a motor at high speed. —*v.i.* **2.** to make or move with such a sound. —*v.t.* **3.** to cause to make such a sound.

vs. or **vs, 1.** verse. **2.** versus.

v.s., see above [< Latin *vidē suprā*].

V sign, *n.* **1.** a sign of victory formed by raising the index and middle fingers in the shape of a V. **2.** this sign used as an indication of approval.

V-six or **V-6** (vē′siks′), *n.* a V-engine having six cylinders.

V/STOL (vē′stôl′), *n.* a convertiplane capable of taking off and landing vertically or on a short runway.

VT or **Vt.,** Vermont.

v.t., transitive verb.

VTO, vertical takeoff.

VTOL (vē′tôl′), *n.* a convertiplane capable of taking off and landing vertically, having forward speeds comparable to those of conventional aircraft.

Vul•can (vul′kən), *n.* **1.** the Roman god of fire and metalworking: identified with the Greek god Hephaestus. **2.** a hypothetical planet nearest the sun whose existence was erroneously postulated to account for perturbations in Mercury's orbit.

vul•can•ite (vul′kə nīt′), *n.* a hard, polished vulcanized rubber used for combs, buttons, and electrical insulation.

vul•can•ize (vul′kə nīz′), *v.t.,* **-ized, -iz•ing. 1.** to treat (rubber) with sulfur and heat, thereby imparting greater strength, elasticity, and durability. **2.** to subject (a substance other than rubber) to some analogous process, as to harden it. —**vul′can•iz′a•ble,** *adj.* —**vul′can•i•za′tion,** *n.* —**vul′can•iz′er,** *n.*

vul•can•ol•o•gy (vul′kə nol′ə jē), *n.* VOLCANOLOGY. —**vul′can•o•log′i•cal** (-nl oj′i kəl), *adj.* —**vul′can•ol′o•gist,** *n.*

vul•gar (vul′gər), *adj.* **1.** characterized by lack of good breeding or taste: *vulgar ostentation.* **2.** indecent; obscene; lewd. **3.** lacking in refinement; crude; coarse; boorish. **4.** of, pertaining to, or constituting the ordinary people in a society. **5.** spoken by, or being in the language spoken by, the people generally; vernacular. **6.** current; popular; common: *vulgar beliefs.* **7.** lacking in distinction or aesthetic value; banal; ordinary. —**vul′gar•ly,** *adv.*

vul•gar•ism (vul′gə riz′əm), *n.* **1.** vulgar behavior or character; vulgarity. **2.** a vulgar word or phrase.

vul•gar•i•ty (vul gar′i tē), *n., pl.* **-ties. 1.** the state or quality of being vulgar. **2.** something vulgar, as an act or expression.

vul•gar•ize (vul′gə rīz′), *v.t.,* **-ized, -iz•ing. 1.** to make vulgar or coarse; lower; debase. **2.** to make (a technical or abstruse work) easier to understand and more widely known; popularize. —**vul′gar•i•za′tion,** *n.*

Vul′gar Lat′in, *n.* popular Latin, as distinguished from literary or standard Latin, esp. those spoken forms of Latin from which the Romance languages developed.

Vul•gate (vul′gāt, -git), *n.* **1.** a Latin version of the Bible prepared chiefly by Saint Jerome at the end of the 4th century A.D. and used as an authorized version of the Roman Catholic Church. **2.** (*l.c.*) any commonly recognized text or version of a work. —*adj.* **3.** of or pertaining to the Vulgate. **4.** (*l.c.*) commonly used or accepted; common. [< Late Latin *vulgāta (editiō)* popular (edition); *vulgāta,* fem. ptp. of *vulgāre* to make common, publish, der. of *vulgus* the public]

vul•ner•a•ble (vul′nər ə bəl), *adj.* **1.** capable of or susceptible to being hurt physically or emotionally. **2.** susceptible to temptation or corrupt influence. **3.** open to or defenseless against criticism or moral attack. **4.** (of a place) open to assault; difficult to defend. **5.** having won one of the games of a rubber of bridge. —**vul′ner•a•bil′i•ty,** *n.*

vul•pine (vul′pīn, -pin), *adj.* **1.** of, pertaining to, or resembling a fox. **2.** cunning or crafty.

vul•ture (vul′chər), *n.* **1.** any of several superficially similar Old World birds of the family Accipitridae. **2.** a person or thing that preys, esp. greedily or unscrupulously.

vul•tur•ine (vul′chə rīn′, -chər in) also **vul•tur•ous** (-chər əs), *adj.* **1.** of, pertaining to, or characteristic of a vulture. **2.** resembling a vulture, esp. in rapacious or predatory qualities.

vul•va (vul′və), *n., pl.* **-vae** (-vē), **-vas.** the external female genitalia. —**vul′val, vul′var,** *adj.* —**vul′vi•form′** (-və fôrm′), **vul′vate** (-vāt, -vit), *adj.*

v.v., vice versa.

vy•ing (vī′ing), *v.* pres. part. of VIE.

W

W, w (dub′əl yōō′, -yŏŏ; *rapidly* dub′yə), *n., pl.* **Ws** or **W's, ws** or **w's.**
1. the 23rd letter of the English alphabet, a semivowel. **2.** any spoken sound represented by this letter. **3.** something shaped like a W. **4.** a written or printed representation of the letter *W* or *w.*

W, *Symbol.* **1.** the 23rd in order or in a series. **2.** *Chem.* tungsten. [< German *Wolfram*] **3.** *Biochem.* tryptophan.

W⁺, *Symbol.* the positively charged W particle.

W⁻, *Symbol.* the negatively charged W particle.

w/, with.

WA, Washington.

Wac (wak), *n.* a member of the Women's Army Corps, formerly an auxiliary of the U.S. Army.

wack•o (wak′ō), *n., pl.* **wack•os,** *adj. Slang.* —*n.* **1.** Also, **wack.** an eccentric person. —*adj.* **2.** WACKY.

wack•y (wak′ē) also **whacky,** *adj.,* **wack•i•er, wack•i•est.** *Slang.* odd or irrational; crazy. —**wack′i•ly,** *adv.* —**wack′i•ness,** *n.*

Wa•co (wā′kō), *n.* a city in central Texas, on the Brazos River. 105,892.

wad¹ (wod), *n., v.,* **wad•ded, wad•ding.** —*n.* **1.** a small mass or ball of anything. **2.** a small mass of cotton, wool, or the like, used for padding, packing, etc. **3.** a roll of something, esp. of bank notes. **4.** a comparatively large stock or quantity of something, esp. money. **5.** a plug of cloth, paper, or the like, used to hold the powder or shot, or both, in place in a muzzleloading gun or a cartridge. —*v.t.* **6.** to form (material) into a wad. **7.** to roll tightly (often fol. by *up*): *He wadded up his cap.* **8.** to stuff with a wad. **9.** to fill out with or as if with wadding. —*v.i.* **10.** to become formed into a wad. —**wad′der,** *n.*

wad² (wod), *n.* a soft, earthy, black to dark brown mass of manganese oxide minerals.

wad•a•ble or **wade•a•ble** (wā′də bəl), *adj.* shallow or calm enough to be waded: *a wadable stream.*

wad•ding (wod′ing), *n.* **1.** any fibrous or soft material for stuffing, padding, packing, etc., esp. carded cotton in specially prepared sheets. **2.** material used as wads for guns, cartridges, etc. **3.** a wad or lump.

wad•dle (wod′l), *v.,* **-dled, -dling.** —*v.i.* **1.** to walk with short steps, swaying from side to side in the manner of a duck. **2.** to move in any similar, slow, rocking manner; wobble. —*n.* **3.** a waddling gait. —**wad′dler,** *n.* —**wad′dling•ly,** *adv.* —**wad′dly,** *adj.*

wade (wād), *v.,* **wad•ed, wad•ing.** —*v.i.* **1.** to walk while partially immersed in water. **2.** to walk through a substance, as snow or sand, that impedes motion. **3.** to make one's way slowly or laboriously: *to wade through a dull book.* —*v.t.* **4.** to cross by wading; ford: *to wade a stream.* **5. wade in,** to begin a task energetically. **6. wade into,** to attack with vigor and energy. —*n.* **7.** an act or instance of wading.

wad•er (wā′dər), *n.* **1.** a person or thing that wades. **2.** WADING BIRD. **3.** any of the shorebirds that wade in shallow waters. **4. waders,** high, waterproof boots or pants with attached boots, worn for wading while fishing, hunting, etc.

wad′ing bird′, *n.* any of various long-legged, long-billed, and long-necked birds that wade in shallow waters for live food, as the crane, heron, ibis, stork, spoonbill, and flamingo.

wad′ing pool′, *n.* a small, shallow pool for children to wade in.

wa•fer (wā′fər), *n.* **1.** a thin, crisp cake or biscuit, often sweetened and flavored. **2.** a thin disk of unleavened bread, used in the Eucharist. **3.** a thin disk, esp. of dried paste, used esp. for sealing letters. **4.** any small, thin disk, as a washer or piece of insulation. **5.** a thin slice of semiconductor used as a base material on which single transistors or integrated-circuit components are formed. —*v.t.* **6.** to seal, close, or attach by means of a wafer. —**wa′fer•like′, wa′fer•y,** *adj.*

waf•fle¹ (wof′əl), *n.* **1.** a batter cake baked in a hinged appliance (**waf′fle i′ron**) that forms a gridlike pattern on each side. —*adj.* **2.** Also, **waf′fled.** having a gridlike or indented lattice shape or design.

waf•fle² (wof′əl), *v.,* **-fled, -fling,** *n.* —*v.i.* **1.** to speak or write equivocally: *to waffle on fundamental issues.* —*v.t.* **2.** to speak or write equivocally about. —*n.* **3.** waffling language. —**waf′fler,** *n.* —**waf′fly,** *adj.*

waf•fle³ (wof′əl), *v.i.,* **-fled, -fling.** to talk tiresomely; blather.

waf•fle•stomp•er (wof′əl stom′pər), *n.* an ankle boot with a ridged sole used esp. for hiking.

waft (wäft, waft), *v.t.* **1.** to carry lightly and smoothly through the air or over water: *A breeze wafted the music across the lake.* **2.** to send or convey lightly: *wafting kisses across the footlights.* —*v.i.* **3.** to float or be carried, esp. through the air. —*n.* **4.** a sound, odor, etc., faintly perceived. **5.** a wafting motion, as a light current or gust: *a waft of air.* **6.** the act of wafting. —**waft′er,** *n.*

wag (wag), *v.,* **wagged, wag•ging,** *n.* —*v.t.* **1.** to move from side to side, esp. rapidly and repeatedly: *a dog wagging its tail.* **2.** to move (the tongue), as in idle chatter. **3.** to shake (a finger) at someone, as in reproach. —*v.i.* **4.** to be moved from side to side, esp. rapidly and repeatedly, as the head or tail. **5.** to move constantly, esp. in idle chatter: *Local tongues are wagging.* —*n.* **6.** the act of wagging: *a wag of the tail.* **7.** a witty person. —**wag′ger,** *n.*

wage (wāj), *n., v.,* **waged, wag•ing.** —*n.* **1.** Often, **wages.** money paid or received for work or services. Compare LIVING WAGE, MINIMUM WAGE. **2. wages,** recompense or return: *The wages of sin is death.* —*v.t.* **3.** to carry on (a battle or argument): *to wage war.* —*v.i.* —**wage′less,** *adj.*

wage′ earn′er, *n.* a person who works for wages.

wa•ger (wā′jər), *n.* **1.** something risked or staked on an uncertain event; bet. **2.** the act of betting. **3.** the subject or terms of a bet. —*v.t.* **4.** to risk (something) on the outcome of a contest, event, etc.; bet. —*v.i.* **5.** to make or offer a wager; bet.

wage′ scale′, *n.* a schedule of wages paid workers performing related tasks in an industry or shop.

wage′ slave′, *n.* a person who works for a wage, being totally dependent on such income. —**wage′ slav′ery,** *n.*

wag•gish (wag′ish), *adj.* **1.** full of roguish good humor. **2.** characteristic of or befitting a wag: *waggish humor.* —**wag′gish•ly,** *adv.*

wag•gle (wag′əl), *v.,* **-gled, -gling,** *n.* —*v.i.* **1.** to wobble or shake, esp. while in motion. —*v.t.* **2.** to move up and down or from side to side: *to waggle one's head.* —*n.* **3.** a waggling motion.

Wag•ner (väg′nər *for* 1; wag′nər *for* 2;), *n.* **1. Richard,** 1813–83, German composer. **2. Robert F(erdinand),** 1877–1953, U.S. politician.

Wag′ner Act′ (wag′nər), *n.* NATIONAL LABOR RELATIONS ACT. [named after the legislation's sponsor, R. F. WAGNER]

Wag•ne•ri•an (väg nēr′ē ən), *adj.* **1.** of, pertaining to, or characteristic of Richard Wagner and his works. —*n.* **2.** a follower or admirer of the music or theories of Richard Wagner.

wag•on (wag′ən), *n.* **1.** a four-wheeled vehicle designed to be pulled or having its own motor and ranging from a child's toy to a commercial vehicle for the transport of heavy loads, delivery, etc. **2.** *Informal.* STATION WAGON. **3.** a patrol wagon. **4.** *Brit.* a railway freight car or flatcar. —*v.t.* **5.** to transport or convey by wagon. —*v.i.* **6.** to proceed or haul goods by wagon. —*Idiom.* **7. fix someone's wagon,** *Informal.* to get even with or punish someone. Also, *esp. Brit.,* **waggon.**

wag•on•er (wag′ə nər), *n.* **1.** a person who drives a wagon. **2.** (*cap.*) the northern constellation Auriga.

wag′on mas′ter, *n.* **1.** a person in charge of a wagon train. **2.** someone leading a caravan of recreational vehicles, as on a camping trip.

wag′on train′, *n.* a train of wagons and horses, as one transporting settlers in the westward migration.

wag•tail (wag′tāl′), *n.* **1.** any of various slim, usu. boldly patterned songbirds of the family Motacillidae, mainly of Eurasia and Africa, having a long tail that wags up and down when the bird is still. **2.** any of several similar birds, as the water thrushes of the genus *Seiurus.*

waif (wāf), *n.* **1.** a person, esp. a child, who has no home. **2.** a stray animal, whose owner is not known. **3.** a stray item or article.

wail (wāl), *v.i.* **1.** to utter a prolonged, mournful cry, as in grief or suffering. **2.** to make mournful sounds, as music or the wind. **3.** to lament or mourn bitterly. **4.** *Slang.* to express emotion musically or verbally in an exciting, satisfying way. —*v.t.* **5.** to express deep sorrow for; mourn. **6.** to express in wailing or in lamentation. —*n.* **7.** the act of wailing. **8.** a wailing cry. **9.** any similar mournful sound. —**wail′ing•ly,** *adv.*

Wail′ing Wall′, *n.* WESTERN WALL.

wain•scot (wān′skət, -skot, -skōt), *n., v.,* **-scot•ed, -scot•ing** or (*esp. Brit.*) **-scot•ted, -scot•ting.** —*n.* **1.** a lining, esp. of wood paneling, for covering interior walls or often only the lower portion of the walls. **2.** the dado of an interior wall esp. when finished with wood paneling. **3.** *Brit.* oak of superior quality imported for fine woodwork. —*v.t.* **4.** to line the walls of with wainscoting.

wain•scot•ing (wān′skō ting, -skot ing, -skə ting), *n.* **1.** paneling or woodwork with which rooms, hallways, etc., are wainscoted. **2.** wainscots collectively. Also, *esp. Brit.,* **wain′scot•ting.**

wain•wright (wān′rīt′), *n.* a wagon maker.

waist (wāst), *n.* **1.** the part of the human body between the ribs and the hips, usu. the narrowest part of the torso. **2.** the part of a garment covering this part of the body. **3.** BLOUSE (def. 1). **4.** the part of a one-piece garment covering the body from the neck or shoulders more or less to the waistline, esp. this part of a woman's or child's garment. **5.** a child's undergarment to which other articles of apparel may be attached. **6.** the central or middle part of an object: *the waist of a violin.*

waist•coat (wes′kət, wāst′kōt′), *n.* **1.** *Chiefly Brit.* VEST (def. 1). **2.** an 18th-century garment for women that is similar to a man's vest, usu. worn with a riding habit. **3.** a man's body garment, often quilted and embroidered and having sleeves, worn under the doublet in the 16th and 17th centuries. —**waist′coat•ed,** *adj.*

waist•ed (wā′stid), *adj.* **1.** having a waist of a specified kind (usu. used in combination): *long-waisted.* **2.** (of an object, a container, etc.) shaped like a waist; having concave sides: *a waisted vase.*

waist•line (wāst′līn′), *n.* **1.** the circumference of the body at the waist: *exercises to reduce the waistline.* **2.** the part of a garment that lies at or near the natural waistline, as the seam where the skirt and bodice of a dress are joined. **3.** an imaginary line encircling the waist.

wait (wāt), *v.i.* **1.** to remain inactive or in a state of repose, as until something expected happens (often fol. by *for* or *until*): *to wait for the bus.* **2.** (of things) to be available or in readiness: *A letter is waiting for you.* **3.** to remain neglected for a time: *a matter that can wait.* **4.** to postpone or delay something or to be postponed or delayed: *Your vacation will have to wait.* **5.** to look forward to eagerly: *to wait for a chance to get even.* **6.** to work or serve as a waiter. **—*v.t.* 7.** to await: *You'll have to wait your turn.* **8.** to postpone or delay: *Don't wait supper for me.* **9.** to serve as waiter for: *to wait tables.* **10. wait on, a.** to serve food or drink to. **b.** to attend to the purchasing needs of (a customer) in a store. **c.** to be an attendant or servant for. **d.** to call upon or visit (a person, esp. a superior). **e.** to wait for (a person); await. **f.** Also, **wait upon.** to await (an event). **11. wait out,** to postpone action until the end of: *to wait out a storm.* **12. wait up, a.** to postpone going to bed in anticipation of an expected person or event. **b.** *Informal.* to halt one's walking, running, etc., to allow someone to overtake one. **—*n.* 13.** an act or instance of waiting; delay. **14.** a period or interval of waiting. **—*Idiom.* 15. lie in wait,** to wait in ambush. **—*Proverb.* 16. Good things come to those who wait,** patience is a key factor in success.

wait•er (wā′tər), *n.* **1.** a person, esp. a man, who waits on tables, as in a restaurant. **2.** a tray for carrying dishes or a tea service; salver. **3.** a person who waits or awaits.

wait•ing (wā′ting), *n.* **1.** a period during which one waits; a pause or delay. **—*adj.* 2.** serving or being in attendance: *waiting maid.* **—*Idiom.* 3. in waiting,** in attendance, esp. upon a royal personage: *ladies in waiting.*

wait′ing game′, *n.* a stratagem in which decisive action is postponed to a later date, allowing one to gain a possible advantage by the delay.

wait′ing list′ or **waitlist,** *n.* a list of persons waiting, as for reservations or admission.

wait′ing room′, *n.* a room for the use of persons waiting, as in a railroad station or a physician's office.

wait•ress (wā′tris), *n.* **1.** a woman who waits on tables, as in a restaurant. **—*v.i.* 2.** to work or serve as a waitress.

wait•ron (wā′tron, -trən), *n.* a person of either sex who waits on tables; waiter or waitress.

waive (wāv), *v.t.*, **waived, waiv•ing. 1.** to refrain from claiming or insisting on; forgo: *to waive one's rank.* **2.** to relinquish (a right) intentionally: *to waive an option.* **3.** to put aside; defer or dispense with: *to waive formalities.* **4.** to dismiss from consideration or discussion.

waiv•er (wā′vər), *n.* **1.** the intentional relinquishment of a right. **2.** an express or written statement specifying this.

wake¹ (wāk), *v.*, **waked** or **woke, waked** or **wok•en, wak•ing,** *n.* **—*v.i.* 1.** to become roused from sleep; awake; awaken; waken (often fol. by *up*). **2.** to become roused from a tranquil or inactive state; awake: *to wake from one's daydreams.* **3.** to become cognizant or aware of something: *to wake to the true situation.* **4.** to be or continue to be awake. **5.** to hold a wake over a corpse. **6.** to keep watch or vigil. **—*v.t.* 7.** to rouse from sleep; awake; awaken (often fol. by *up*): *Wake me at six o'clock.* **8.** to rouse from lethargy, apathy, etc. (often fol. by *up*): *It woke us up to the need for conservation.* **9.** to hold a wake for. **10.** to keep watch or vigil over. **—*n.* 11.** a watch kept, esp. for some solemn purpose. **12.** a watch or vigil by the body of a dead person before burial. **13.** the state of being awake: *between sleep and wake.*

wake² (wāk), *n.* **1.** the track of waves left by a ship or boat moving through the water. **2.** the path or course of anything that has passed or preceded: *The tornado left ruin in its wake.* **—*Idiom.* 3. in the wake of, a.** as a result of. **b.** closely behind.

wake•ful (wāk′fəl), *adj.* **1.** unable to sleep. **2.** sleepless: *a wakeful night.* —**wake′ful•ly,** *adv.* —**wake′ful•ness,** *n.*

wak•en (wā′kən), *v.t.* **1.** to rouse from sleep; wake. **2.** to stir up or excite; arouse; awaken: *to waken the reader's interest.* **—*v.i.* 3.** to awake; awaken; wake. —**wak′en•er,** *n.*

wak•en•ing (wā′kə ning), *n.* AWAKENING.

wake′-up′, *n.* **1.** an act or instance of waking up. **2.** an act or instance of being awakened: *I'd like a wake-up at 6.* **3.** FLICKER². **—*adj.* 4.** serving to wake one from sleep: *a wake-up call.*

Wal′den Pond′ (wôl′dən), *n.* a pond in NE Massachusetts, near Concord: site of Thoreau's cottage.

Wal•den•ses (wôl den′sēz, wol-), *n.pl.* members of a Christian sect that arose in 1170 in S France under the leadership of Pierre Waldo and that joined the Reformation in the 16th century. —**Wal•den′si•an** (-sē-ən, -shən), *adj.*, *n.*

Wald•heim (wôld′hīm′, vält′-), *n.* **Kurt,** born 1918, secretary-general of the United Nations 1972–82; president of Austria 1986–92.

Wal•do (wôl′dō, wol′-), *n.* **Pierre** or **Peter,** died c1217, French religious reformer, declared a heretic.

Wal′dorf sal′ad (wôl′dôrf), *n.* a salad of celery, diced apples, nuts, and mayonnaise. [after the *Waldorf*-Astoria Hotel in New York City]

wale (wāl), *n.*, *v.*, **waled, wal•ing. —*n.* 1.** a ridge or stripe produced on the skin by the stroke of a rod or whip; welt. **2.** the vertical rib or cord in woven cloth. **3.** the texture or weave of a fabric. **4.** any of certain strakes of thick outside planking on the sides of a wooden ship. **5.** a horizontal timber or other support for reinforcing various upright members. **—*v.t.* 6.** to mark with wales. **7.** to weave with wales. **8.** to reinforce with a wale or wales.

Wales (wālz), *n.* a division of the United Kingdom, in SW Great Britain. 2,791,851; 8018 sq. mi. (20,768 sq. km). Medieval, **Cambria.**

Wa•łę•sa (və wen′sə), *n.* **Lech** (lek), born 1943, president of Poland 1990–96.

Walford *n.* **William,** 1772–1850, English hymn writer.

walk (wôk), *v.i.* **1.** to advance or travel on foot at a moderate speed or pace; proceed by advancing the feet alternately so that there is always one foot on the ground in bipedal locomotion and two or more feet on the ground in quadrupedal locomotion. **2.** to move about or travel on foot for exercise or pleasure: *to walk in the park.* **3.** (of things) to move in a manner suggestive of walking, as through repeated vibrations. **4.** (in baseball) to receive a walk. **5.** *Slang.* **a.** to go on strike; stage a walkout. **b.** to be acquitted. **6.** (of spirits) to go about on the earth. **7.** to conduct one's life in a particular manner. **8.** (of a basketball player in possession of the ball) to take more than two steps without dribbling or passing the ball. **—*v.t.* 9.** to proceed through, over, etc., on foot: *walking London streets by night.* **10.** to lead, drive, or ride at a walk, as an animal: *to walk one's horse.* **11.** to force or help to walk, as a person. **12.** to conduct or accompany on a walk: *He walked us about the park.* **13.** to move (a box, trunk, or other object) by a rocking motion suggestive of walking. **14.** (of a baseball pitcher) to give a base on balls to (a batter). **15.** to spend or pass (time) in walking (often fol. by *away*): *We walked the morning away.* **16.** to accomplish by walking: *to walk guard.* **17.** to examine, measure, etc., by traversing on foot: *to walk the boundaries of a property.* **18. walk off,** to get rid of by walking: *to walk off a headache.* **19. walk off** or **away with, a.** to take away; steal. **b.** to win, as a prize or a competition, esp. with ease. **20. walk out, a.** to go on strike. **b.** to leave in protest. **21. walk out on,** to desert; forsake. **22. walk out with,** *Brit.* to court or be courted by. **23. walk through, a.** to rehearse (a play or the like) by reading the lines aloud while doing the designated physical movements. **b.** to perform in a perfunctory manner. **c.** to guide (someone) carefully, one step at a time. **—*n.* 24.** an act or instance of walking. **25.** a period of walking for exercise or pleasure. **26.** a distance walked or to be walked, often in terms of the time required: *a ten-minute walk from here.* **27.** the gait or pace of a person or an animal that walks. **28.** a characteristic manner of walking. **29.** (in baseball) the awarding of first base to a batter to whom four balls have been pitched. **30.** a sidewalk. **31.** a place or path prepared or set apart for walking. **32.** an enclosed yard, pen, or the like where domestic animals are fed and left to exercise. **33.** a branch of activity, line of work, or position in society: *in every walk of life.* **—*Idiom.* 34. walk on water,** to perform miracles. Matt. 14:25–33. **35. walk the plank, a.** to go to one's death by being forced to walk off the end of a board that extends from the side of a ship. **b.** to be forced to resign from one's job.

walk•a•ble (wô′kə bəl), *adj.* capable of being reached or traveled by walking. —**walk′a•bil′i•ty,** *n.*

walk•a•bout (wôk′ə bout′), *n.* *Chiefly Brit.* an informal public stroll taken by members of the royal family or by a political figure for the purpose of greeting and being seen by the public.

walk•a•thon (wô′kə thon′), *n.* **1.** a long-distance walking race. **2.** such a race held to raise funds for a charity or special cause.

walk•a•way (wôk′ə wā′), *n.* **1.** an easy victory or conquest. **2.** a patient or inmate of an institution who unobtrusively leaves while unsupervised.

walk•er (wô′kər), *n.* **1.** an enclosing framework on casters or wheels for supporting a baby who is learning to walk. **2.** a similar device, usu. a waist-high four-legged framework of lightweight metal, for use by an infirm or disabled person as a support while walking. **3.** one that walks or likes to walk. **4.** a man who makes himself available as public escort for a society woman.

Walk•er (wô′kər), *n.* **1. Alice,** born 1944, U.S. novelist and short-story writer. **2. David,** 1785–1830, U.S. abolitionist, author of *Walker's Appeal* (1829). **3. James John** (*Jimmy*), 1881–1946, U.S. politician: mayor of New York City 1926–32.

walk•ie-talk•ie or **walk•y-talk•y** (wô′kē tô′kē), *n.*, *pl.* **-talk•ies.** a combined voice transmitter and receiver light enough to be carried by one person.

walk′-in′, *adj.* **1.** of or pertaining to persons who walk into an office or store from the street without an appointment. **2.** large enough to be walked into: *a walk-in closet.* **—*n.* 3.** a customer, patient, etc., who arrives without an appointment. **4.** something large enough to be walked into, as a refrigerator. **5.** an assured victory.

walk•ing (wô′king), *adj.* **1.** able to walk; ambulatory: *walking patients.* **2.** living; live: *He's walking proof that people can lose weight quickly.* **3.** designed esp. for walking: *walking shoes.* **4.** characterized or accomplished by walking: *a walking tour of Spain.* **5.** (of an implement or machine) drawn by a draft animal: *a walking plow.* **6.** of or pertaining to a mechanical part that moves back and forth. **—*n.* 7.** the act or action of a person or thing that walks: *Walking is good exercise.* **8.** the manner or way in which a person walks. **9.** the condition of the surface on which a person walks. **10.** RACE WALKING.

walk′ing-a•round′ mon′ey (wô′king ə round′), *n.* **1.** money that is carried on the person for routine expenses and minor emergencies; pocket money. **2.** Also called **street money.** *Political Slang.* cash sums given by political managers, district leaders, or the like, to grass-roots workers and others for expenses incurred while canvassing for votes or doing other chores before an election.

walk′ing cat′fish, *n.* an Asian catfish, *Clarias batrachus,* that can move overland between bodies of water: introduced into Florida.

walk′ing pa′pers, *n.pl. Informal.* a notification of dismissal.

walk′ing stick′, *n.* **1.** a stick held in the hand and used to help support oneself while walking. **2.** Also, **walk′ing•stick′.** any of several insects of the family Phasmatidae, having a long, slender, twiglike body.

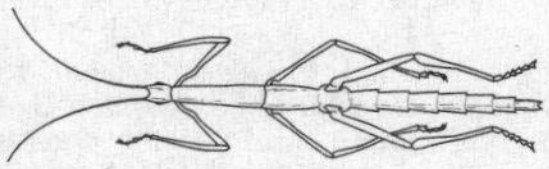

walking stick (def. 2), *Diapheromera femorata,* length 2 1/2 to 4 in. (6.5 to 10 cm)

Walk•man (wôk′mən, -man′), *Trademark.* a small portable stereo cassette player, radio, or cassette player and radio used with headphones.

walk′-on′, *n.* **1.** a small part in a play or other entertainment, esp. a part without speaking lines. Compare BIT[2] (def. 4). **2.** an athlete trying out for a team who has not been drafted, specifically invited, or awarded a scholarship.

walk′out′ or **walk′-out′,** *n.* **1.** a strike by workers. **2.** the act of leaving or being absent from a meeting, esp. as a protest.

walk•o•ver (wôk′ō′vər), *n.* **1.** a horse race having only one starter because the other entrants have been scratched or withdrawn. **2.** an unopposed or easy victory. **3.** a gymnastic feat performed by leaning forward to a brief handstand and bringing the legs over and back down to the floor one at a time or by arching backward to a similar handstand and returning the feet to the floor.

walk′-through′, *n.* **1. a.** a rehearsal of a play or other script in which the lines are read aloud while the actions are performed. **b.** a rehearsal of a motion-picture scene without cameras and often dialogue. **c.** a perfunctory performance of a role, play, or the like. **2.** a step-by-step demonstration of a procedure or process. **—*adj.*** **3.** designed to be walked through: *a walk-through aviary.* **4.** activated by a person passing through: *a walk-through electronic scanner.*

walk′-up′, *n.* **1.** an apartment above the ground floor in a building with no elevator. **2.** a building, esp. an apartment house, that has no elevator. **—*adj.*** **3.** located above the ground floor in a building that has no elevator. **4.** (of a building) having no elevator. **5.** accessible to pedestrians from the outside of a building: *a walk-up teller's window.*

walk•way (wôk′wā′), *n.* **1.** any passage for walking, esp. one connecting the various areas of a factory or shopping area. **2.** a garden path or walk. **3.** the front walk of a house, leading to the sidewalk or road.

wall (wôl), *n.* **1.** any of various permanent upright constructions having a length much greater than the thickness and presenting a continuous surface except where pierced by doors, windows, etc.: used for shelter, protection, or privacy. **2.** an immaterial or intangible barrier, obstruction, etc., suggesting a wall: *a wall of prejudice.* **3.** a wall-like enclosing part, thing, mass, etc.: *a wall of fire; a wall of troops.* **4.** an embankment to prevent flooding, as a levee or sea wall. **5.** Usu., **walls.** a rampart raised for defensive purposes. **6.** the outermost film or layer of structural material protecting, surrounding, and defining the physical limits of an object: *the wall of a blood cell.* **—*adj.*** **7.** of or pertaining to a wall. **8.** growing against or on a wall: *wall plants.* **9.** situated or installed in or on a wall: *a wall oven.* **—*v.t.*** **10.** to enclose, border, etc., with or as if with a wall (often fol. by *in* or *off*): *to wall in the playground.* **11.** to seal or fill (a doorway or other opening) with a wall: *to wall an unused entrance.* **12.** to seal or entomb (something or someone) within a wall; immure (usu. fol. by *up*). **—*Idiom.*** **13. climb the walls,** *Informal.* to become tense or frantic. **14. drive** or **push to the wall,** to force into a desperate situation. **15. go to the wall, a.** to be defeated; yield. **b.** to fail in business; be forced into bankruptcy. **c.** to risk one's own position to defend or protect another. **16. hit the wall,** to reach a point in a long-distance race when the body's fuels are virtually depleted and willpower becomes crucial to the ability to finish. **17. off the wall,** *Slang.* **a.** unreasonable; crazy. **b.** eccentric; bizarre. **18. up the wall,** *Informal.* into a state of frantic frustration. **19. The walls have ears,** no matter how careful one is, one may be overheard.

wal•la•by (wol′ə bē), *n., pl.* **-bies,** (*esp. collectively*) **-by.** any of certain small to medium-sized plant-eating marsupials of the kangaroo family, Macropodidae. [< Dharuk (Australian Aboriginal language)]

Wal•lace (wol′is, wô′lis), *n.* **1. George (Corley),** born 1919, U.S. politician: governor of Alabama 1963–67, 1971–79, and 1983–87. **2. Henry (Agard),** 1888–1965, U.S. agriculturalist, author, and statesman: Secretary of Agriculture 1933–40; vice president of the U.S. 1941–45; Secretary of Commerce 1945–46. **3. (William Roy) DeWitt,** 1889–1981, and his wife, **Lila Bell (Acheson),** 1889–1984, U.S. magazine publishers.

wall•board (wôl′bôrd′, -bōrd′), *n.* material manufactured in large sheets for use in making or covering walls, ceilings, etc., as a substitute for wooden boards or plaster.

wall′cov′er•ing or **wall′ cov′ering,** *n.* wallpaper or other sheets of fabric, vinyl, etc., for pasting on walls as decoration and protection.

walled (wôld), *adj.* **1.** having walls (often used in combination): *a high-walled prison.* **2.** enclosed or fortified with a wall: *a walled village.*

Wal•ler (wol′ər, wô′lər), *n.* **Thomas** (*"Fats"*), 1904–43, U.S. jazz pianist and songwriter.

wal•let (wol′it, wô′lit), *n.* **1.** a flat, folding case with compartments for paper money and other items, as credit cards, driver's license, and sometimes coins, carried in a pocket or handbag. **2.** *Brit.* a bag for carrying articles during a journey.

wall•eye (wôl′ī′), *n., pl.* **-eyes,** (*esp. collectively for 1*) **-eye. 1.** Also called **walleyed pike.** a large game fish, *Stizostedion vitreum,* of lakes and rivers in NE North America, having large eyes. **2.** a condition in which the eye or eyes are turned outward.

wall′eyed pike′, *n.* WALLEYE (def. 1).

wall•flow•er (wôl′flou′ər), *n.* **1.** a person who, because of shyness, lack of a partner, etc., remains at the side at a party or dance. **2.** any person, organization, etc., that remains on the sidelines of any activity. **3.** a European plant of the mustard family, that has sweet-scented yellow or orange flowers when growing wild on walls or cliffs.

wall′ hang′ing, *n.* a tapestry, carpet, or similar object hung against a wall as decoration; arras.

wal•lop (wol′əp), *v.t.* **1.** to beat soundly; thrash. **2.** to strike with a vigorous blow; belt; sock: *to wallop the ball out of the park.* **3.** to defeat thoroughly, as in a game. **—*v.i.*** **4.** to move clumsily. **5.** (of a liquid) to boil violently. **—*n.*** **6.** a vigorous blow. **7.** the ability to deliver vigorous blows, as in boxing. **8.** *Informal.* **a.** the ability to make a forceful impression; punch: *an ad that packs a wallop.* **b.** a pleasurable thrill; kick.

wal•lop•ing (wol′ə ping), *Informal.* **—*n.*** **1.** a sound beating or thrashing. **2.** a thorough defeat. **—*adj.*** **3.** very large; whopping. **4.** very fine; impressive. **—*adv.*** **5.** extremely; immensely: *a walloping big bill.*

wal•low (wol′ō), *v.i.* **1.** to roll about or lie in water, mud, dust, etc., as for refreshment: *goats wallowing in the dust.* **2.** to indulge oneself; luxuriate; revel: *to wallow in luxury; to wallow in sentimentality.* **3.** to flounder about; move or proceed clumsily. **4.** to billow forth, as smoke. **—*n.*** **5.** an act or instance of wallowing. **6.** a place in which animals wallow.

wall•pa•per (wôl′pā′pər), *n.* **1.** paper, usu. on rolls and with printed decorative patterns, for pasting on and covering walls or ceilings. **2.** any fabric, foil, vinyl material, etc., used as a wall or ceiling covering. **—*v.t.*** **3.** to put wallpaper on or in.

Wall′ Street′, *n.* **1.** a street in New York City, in S Manhattan: the major financial center of the U.S. **2.** the money market or the financiers of the U.S.

wall′ u′nit, *n.* a modular system of shelves, often including cabinets or other storage space, either mounted on a wall or arranged in freestanding units. Also called **wall′ sys′tem.**

wall′-to-wall′, *adj.* **1.** covering the entire floor from one wall to another. **2.** *Informal.* occupying a space or period of time completely: *a dance floor with wall-to-wall dancers.* **3.** *Informal.* being available everywhere; full of something specified: *a town with wall-to-wall gambling.* **—*adv.*** **4.** from one side to the other; to overflowing: *a store jammed wall-to-wall with shoppers.* **—*n.*** **5.** a wall-to-wall carpet.

wal•ly•ball (wol′ē bôl′, wô′lē-), *n.* a game similar to volleyball played in a walled court so that the ball may be bounced against the walls.

wal•nut (wôl′nut′, -nət), *n.* **1.** the edible nut of trees of the genus *Juglans,* of the North Temperate Zone. **2.** the tree itself. **3.** the wood of this tree, used in making furniture. **4.** a somewhat reddish shade of brown, as that of the heartwood of the black walnut tree.

Wal•pole (wôl′pōl′, wol′-), *n.* **1. Horace, 4th Earl of Orford** (*Horatio Walpole*), 1717–97, English author (son of Sir Robert Walpole). **2. Sir Hugh Seymour,** 1884–1941, English novelist, born in New Zealand. **3. Sir Robert, 1st Earl of Orford,** 1676–1745, British prime minister 1715–17; 1721–42.

Wal•pur′gis Night′ (väl po͝or′gis), *n.* (in German folklore and literature) the evening preceding the 1st of May, when a witches' Sabbath was held on the Brocken. German, ***Wal•pur•gis•nacht*** (väl po͝or′gis-näKHt′). [after St. *Walpurgis* (c710–780), Anglo-Saxon abbess in Germany, whose relics were enshrined on May 1]

wal•rus (wôl′rəs, wol′-), *n., pl.* **-rus•es,** (*esp. collectively*) **-rus.** a large marine mammal, *Odobenus rosmarus,* of arctic seas, related to eared seals, having large tusks and a tough, wrinkled hide. [< Dutch: lit., whale horse]

wal′rus mus′tache, *n.* a thick, shaggy mustache hanging down loosely at both ends.

Wal′ter Mit′ty (wôl′tər), *n., pl.* **Walter Mit•tys.** an ordinary, timid person who is given to adventurous and self-aggrandizing daydreams. [from the title character of James Thurber's short story "The Secret Life of Walter Mitty" (1939)] **—Wal′ter Mit′ty•ish,** *adj.*

Wal•ton (wôl′tn), *n.* **1. Ernest Thomas Sinton,** 1903–95, Irish physicist. **2. Izaak,** 1593–1683, English writer. **3. Sir William (Turner),** 1902–83, English composer.

waltz (wôlts), *n.* **1.** a ballroom dance, in moderately fast triple meter, in which the dancers revolve in perpetual circles, taking one step to each beat. **2.** a piece of music for, or in the rhythm of, this dance. **3.** an easy victory or accomplishment. **—*adj.*** **4.** of, pertaining to, or characteristic of the waltz. **—*v.i.*** **5.** to dance a waltz. **6.** to move or progress easily or directly: *to waltz through an exam.* **—*v.t.*** **7.** to lead (a partner) in dancing a waltz. **8.** to move or lead briskly and easily. **—waltz′er,** *n.*

wam•pum (wom′pəm, wôm′-), *n.* **1.** cylindrical beads made from shells, pierced and strung, used by North American Indians as a medium of exchange, for ornaments, and for ceremonial and sometimes spiritual purposes. **2.** *Informal.* MONEY.

wan (won), *adj.,* **wan•ner, wan•nest,** *v.,* **wanned, wan•ning. —*adj.*** **1.** of an unnatural or sickly pallor; pallid. **2.** showing or suggesting ill health, fatigue, etc.: *a wan smile.* **3.** lacking in forcefulness or effectiveness: *wan attempts to organize the alumni.* —*v.i., v.t.* **4.** to become or make wan. —**wan′ly,** *adv.* —**wan′ness,** *n.*

Wan·a·ma·ker (won′ə mā′kər), *n.* **John,** 1838–1922, U.S. merchant.

wand (wond), *n.* **1.** a slender stick or rod, esp. one used by a magician or conjurer. **2.** a rod or staff carried as an emblem of one's office or authority. **3.** a slender shoot, stem, or branch of a shrub or tree. **4.** a small applicator for cosmetics, usu. having a brush at the tip. **5.** an electronic device, in the form of a hand-held rod, that can optically read coded or printed data, as on a merchandise label or in a document.

wan·der (won′dər), *v.i.* **1.** to ramble without a definite purpose or objective; roam. **2.** to go aimlessly or indirectly; meander: *The river wanders among the rocks.* **3.** to extend in an irregular course or direction: *Foothills wandered off to the south.* **4.** to move, pass, or turn idly, as the hand or the eyes. **5.** (of the mind, thoughts, desires, etc.) to take one direction or another without conscious control. **6.** to stray from a path, place, companions, etc.: *The ship wandered from its course.* **7.** to deviate in conduct, belief, etc.; err; go astray. —*v.t.* **8.** to travel about, on, or through: *He wandered the streets.* —**wan′der·er,** *n.*

wan·der·ing (won′dər ing), *adj.* **1.** moving from place to place without a fixed plan; roaming. **2.** having no permanent residence; nomadic. **3.** meandering; winding: *a wandering river.* —*n.* **4.** an aimless roving about; leisurely traveling from place to place: *a summer of delightful wandering through Italy.* **5.** Usu., **wanderings. a.** aimless travels; meanderings: *Her wanderings took her all over the world.* **b.** disordered thoughts or utterances; incoherencies: *mental wanderings.* —**wan′der·ing·ly,** *adv.*

Wan′dering Jew′, *n.* **1.** a legendary character condemned to roam without rest because he struck Christ on the day of the Crucifixion. **2.** any of various creeping plants of the spiderwort family, with green or variegated leaves, as *Zebrina pendula.*

wan·der·lust (won′dər lust′), *n.* a strong desire or impulse to travel about.

wane (wān), *v.*, **waned, wan·ing,** *n.* —*v.i.* **1.** to decrease in strength, intensity, etc.: *My enthusiasm is waning.* **2.** to decline in power, importance, etc.: *Colonialism began to wane after World War II.* **3.** to draw to a close: *Summer is waning.* **4.** (of the moon) to decrease periodically in the extent of its illuminated portion after the full moon. Compare WAX² (def. 2). —*n.* **5.** a gradual decrease or decline. **6.** the drawing to a close of life, an era, etc. **7.** the waning of the moon. **8.** a defect in lumber characterized by bark or insufficient wood at a corner or along an edge. —*Idiom.* **9.** **on the wane,** decreasing; diminishing.

wan·gle (wang′gəl), *v.*, **-gled, -gling,** *n.* —*v.t.* **1.** to bring about or obtain by scheming or underhand methods: *to wangle an invitation.* **2.** to falsify or manipulate for dishonest ends. —*v.i.* **3.** to use contrivance or scheming to achieve some goal. **4.** to manipulate something for dishonest ends. —*n.* **5.** an act or instance of wangling. —**wan′gler,** *n.*

wan·i·gan or **wan·ni·gan** (won′i gən), also **wan·gan, wan·gun** (wang′gən), *n.* **1.** a small portable house, used as an office or shelter in temporary lumber camps. **2.** (esp. in Alaska and the Pacific Northwest) a lean-to or other small addition built onto a house.

wan·na (won′ə, wô′nə), *Pron. Spelling.* **1.** want to: *I wanna get out of here.* **2.** want a: *Wanna beer?*

wan·na·be or **wan·na·bee** (won′ə bē′, wô′nə-), *n., pl.* **-bes** or **-bees.** *Informal.* one who aspires, often vainly, to emulate another's success or attain eminence in some area.

want (wont, wônt), *v.t.* **1.** to feel a need or a desire for; wish for: *to want a new dress.* **2.** to wish or need (often fol. by an infinitive): *I want to see you.* **3.** to be deficient in: *to want judgment.* **4.** to require or need: *The house wants painting.* **5.** to have an arrest warrant for: *They want him in Arizona for armed robbery.* —*v.i.* **6.** to feel inclined; wish (often fol. by *to*): *We can stay home if you want.* **7.** to be deficient; have a need (sometimes fol. by *for*): *He did not want for abilities.* **8.** to be in a state of neediness or poverty: *She would never allow her parents to want.* **9.** to be lacking or absent: *All that wants is your signature.* —*n.* **10.** something wanted or needed: *My wants are few.* **11.** something desired or demanded: *a person of childish wants.* **12.** absence or deficiency; lack: *for want of rain.* **13.** a state of need: *to be in want of an assistant.* **14.** a state of destitution; poverty: *a country where want is virtually unknown.* —*Idiom.* **15.** **want in** (or **out**), *Informal.* to desire admission or inclusion (or withdrawal).

want′ ad′, *n.* CLASSIFIED AD.

want·ing (won′ting, wôn′-), *adj.* **1.** lacking or absent: *a motor with some of the parts wanting.* **2.** deficient in some part or respect: *to be wanting in courtesy.* —*prep.* **3.** lacking; without: *a box wanting a lid.* **4.** less; minus: *a century wanting three years.*

wan·ton (won′tn), *adj.* **1.** done maliciously or unjustifiably: *wanton cruelty.* **2.** deliberate and without motive; unprovoked: *a wanton attack.* **3.** without regard for what is right, just, etc.; reckless: *wanton assassination of a person's character.* **4.** lascivious; lewd: *wanton behavior.* **5.** extravagant or excessive: *living in wanton luxury.* **6.** luxuriant, as vegetation. —*n.* **7.** a wanton or lascivious person, esp. a woman. —*v.i.* **8.** to behave in a wanton manner. —*v.t.* **9.** to squander (often fol. by *away*): *to wanton away one's inheritance.* —**wan′ton·ly,** *adv.* —**wan′ton·ness,** *n.*

wap·i·ti (wop′i tē), *n., pl.* **-tis,** (*esp. collectively*) **-ti.** ELK (def. 1).

war (wôr), *n., v.,* **warred, war·ring,** *adj.* —*n.* **1.** armed conflict between nations or factions within a nation; warfare. **2.** a state or period of active military operations. **3.** (*often cap.*) a particular armed conflict

consisting of a series of battles or campaigns: *the War of 1812.* **4.** armed fighting as a science or profession. **5.** active hostility or contention; conflict: *a war of words.* **6.** aggressive competition in business: *a fare war among airlines.* **7.** a struggle to achieve a particular goal: *a war against poverty.* —*v.i.* **8.** to make or carry on war. **9.** to carry on active hostility or feel strong opposition. —*adj.* **10.** of or resulting from war.

War′ and Peace′, a novel (1862–69) by Leo Tolstoy.

War′ Between′ the States′, *n.* the American Civil War: used esp. in the South.

war·ble¹ (wôr′bəl), *v.,* **-bled, -bling,** *n.* —*v.i.* **1.** to sing or whistle with trills, quavers, or melodic embellishments, as a bird. **2.** to yodel. **3.** (of electronic equipment) to produce a continuous sound varying regularly in pitch and frequency. —*v.t.* **4.** to sing (an aria or other selection) with trills, quavers, or melodious turns. **5.** to express or celebrate in or as if in song; carol. —*n.* **6.** a warbled song or succession of melodic trills, quavers, etc. **7.** the act of warbling.

war·ble² (wôr′bəl), *n.* **1.** a small, hard tumor on a horse's back, produced by the galling of the saddle. **2.** a lump in the skin of an animal's back, containing the larva of a warble fly. —**war′bled,** *adj.*

war′ble fly′, *n.* any of several stout, woolly flies of the family Oestridae, the larvae of which produce warbles in cattle and other animals.

war·bler (wôr′blər), *n.* **1.** Also called **wood warbler.** any of numerous small New World songbirds of the subfamily Parulinae (family Emberizidae), many species of which are brightly colored. **2.** any of numerous small, chiefly Old World songbirds of the subfamily Sylviinae (family Muscicapidae). **3.** a person or thing that warbles.

war′bon·net or **war′ bon′net,** *n.* an American Indian headdress consisting of a headband with a tail of ornamental feathers.

warbonnet

war′ bride′, *n.* **1.** a woman who marries a serviceman about to go overseas in wartime. **2.** a woman who marries a foreign serviceman and goes to live in his country.

war′ chest′, *n.* money set aside for a particular purpose, as a political campaign.

war′ cloud′, *n.* something that threatens war; a harbinger of conflict.

war′ correspond′ent, *n.* a reporter or commentator assigned to send news or opinions directly from battle areas.

war′ crime′, *n.* Usu., **war crimes.** crimes committed against an enemy, prisoners of war, or subjects in wartime that violate international agreements or, as in the case of genocide, are offenses against humanity. —**war′ crim′inal,** *n.*

war′ cry′, *n.* **1.** a word or phrase shouted in charging; battle cry. **2.** a slogan, phrase, or motto used to unite a political party, rally support for a cause, etc.

ward (wôrd), *n.* **1.** a division or district of a city or town, as for administrative or political purposes. **2.** one of the districts into which certain English and Scottish boroughs are divided. **3.** a division or large room of a hospital for a particular class of patients: *a convalescent ward.* **4.** any of the separate divisions of a prison. **5.** one of the subdivisions of a stake in the Mormon Church, presided over by a bishop. **6.** an open space within or between the walls of a castle. **7.** a person, esp. a minor, who has been legally placed under the care of a guardian or a court. **8.** the state of being under restraining guard or in custody. **9.** a movement or posture of defense, as in fencing. **10.** a curved ridge of metal in a lock, fitting only a key with a corresponding notch. **11.** the notch or slot on a key into which such a ridge fits. **12.** the act of keeping guard or protective watch: *watch and ward.* —*v.t.* **13.** to avert or turn aside (danger, an attack, etc.) (usu. fol. by *off*): *to ward off a blow.* **14.** to place in a ward, as of a hospital. —**ward′less,** *adj.*

Ward (wôrd), *n.* **1. (Aaron) Montgomery,** 1843–1913, U.S. mail-order retailer. **2. Ar·te·mas** (är′tə məs), 1727–1800, American general in the American Revolution. **3. Ar·te·mus** (är′tə məs), (*Charles Farrar Browne*), 1834–67, U.S. humorist. **4. Barbara** (*Baroness Jackson of Lodsworth*), 1914–81, English economist. **5. Mrs. Humphry** (*Mary Augusta Arnold*), 1851–1920, English novelist, born in Tasmania. **6. Nathaniel** (*"Theodore de la Guard"*), 1578?–1652, English clergyman, lawyer, and author in America.

-ward, a suffix denoting spatial or temporal direction, as specified by the initial element: *afterward; backward; seaward.* Also, **-wards.**

war′ dance′, *n.* (formerly among American Indians) a dance prior to going into battle or in celebration of a victory.

war·den (wôr′dn), *n.* **1.** a person charged with the care and custody of something; keeper. **2.** the chief administrative officer in charge of a prison. **3.** any of various public officials charged with superintendence or with enforcement of regulations, as a fire warden or game warden. **4.**

(in Connecticut) the chief executive officer of a borough. **5.** (formerly) the principal official in a region, town, etc. **6.** the president or governor of certain British schools and colleges. **7.** a member of the governing body of a guild. **8.** a gatekeeper. —**ward′en•ship′**, *n.*

War′ Depart′ment, *n.* the department of the federal government responsible for defense and the military establishment from 1789 until 1947: in 1947 it became the Department of the Army, which became part of the Department of Defense when it was established in 1949.

ward•er¹ (wôr′dər), *n.* **1.** a person who guards something, as a doorkeeper. **2.** a soldier or other person set to guard an entrance. —**ward′er•ship′**, *n.*

ward•er² (wôr′dər), *n.* a truncheon or staff of office or authority, esp. one carried by a monarch to signal commands.

ward′ heel′er, *n.* a minor politician who canvasses voters and does other chores for a political machine or party boss.

ward•robe (wôr′drōb), *n., v.,* **-robed, -rob•ing.** —*n.* **1.** a collection or stock of clothes or costumes. **2.** a piece of furniture for holding clothes, usu. a tall, upright case fitted with a rail or hooks for hanging clothes. **3.** a room or place in which to keep clothes or costumes. **4. a.** the department of a royal or other great household charged with the care of wearing apparel. **b.** a department in a motion-picture or television studio that supplies and maintains costumes. **5.** WARDROBE TRUNK. —*v.t.* **6.** to provide with a wardrobe.

ward′robe trunk′, *n.* a large, upright trunk, usu. with space on one side for hanging clothes and drawers or compartments on the other for small articles, shoes, etc.

ward•ship (wôrd′ship), *n.* **1.** guardianship; custody. **2.** *Law.* the guardianship over a ward, esp. a minor.

ware (wâr), *n.* **1.** Usu., **wares. a.** articles of merchandise or manufacture; goods. **b.** any intangible items, as artistic skills or intellectual accomplishments, that are salable. **2.** a specified kind of merchandise (usu. used in combination): *silverware; glassware.* **3.** pottery, or a particular kind of pottery: *delft ware.*

ware•house (*n.* wâr′hous′; *v.* -houz′, -hous′), *n., pl.* **-hous•es** (-hou′ziz), *v.,* **-housed, -hous•ing.** —*n.* **1.** a building for the storage of goods, merchandise, etc. **2.** any large and usu. public custodial institution for the confinement of the mentally ill, the aged, etc. —*v.t.* **3.** to place, deposit, or store in a warehouse. **4.** to set aside or accumulate, as for future use. **5.** to place in a government or bonded warehouse, to be kept until duties are paid. **6.** to confine (the mentally ill, the aged, etc.) in large custodial institutions. **7.** (of a landlord) to keep (an apartment) vacant prior to a conversion to cooperative or condominium so as to bring a higher price from a nonresident.

war•fare (wôr′fâr′), *n.* **1.** the process of military struggle between two nations or groups of nations; war. **2.** armed conflict between two massed enemies, armies, or the like. **3.** conflict, esp. when vicious and unrelenting, between competitors, political rivals, etc.

war′ game′, *n.* Often, **war games.** a simulated military operation carried out to test the validity of a plan or theory.

war′ hawk′, *n.* **1.** HAWK¹ (def. 4). **2.** (*caps.*) any of the members of Congress who wanted war against Britain in the period leading up to the War of 1812.

war•head (wôr′hed′), *n.* the forward section of a missile, bomb, torpedo, or the like, containing the explosive or payload.

war′-horse′, *n.* **1.** a horse used in war; charger. **2.** *Informal.* a veteran of many conflicts, as a soldier or politician. **3.** *Informal.* a musical composition, play, etc., that has been seen, heard, or performed excessively.

war•like (wôr′līk′), *adj.* **1.** fit, qualified, or ready for war; martial. **2.** threatening or indicating war. **3.** pertaining to or waging war.

war•lock (wôr′lok′), *n.* **1.** a man who is a witch, esp. a practitioner of black magic; sorcerer. **2.** a fortuneteller or conjurer.

war•lord (wôr′lôrd′), *n.* **1.** a military commander, esp. of a warlike nation. **2.** (esp. formerly in China) a military commander who has seized control of a region in a country. —**war′lord′ism,** *n.*

warm (wôrm), *adj.* **1.** having or giving out a moderate degree of heat, as perceived by the senses: *a warm bath.* **2.** characterized by a moderately or comparatively high temperature: *a warm oven; a warm climate.* **3.** having a sensation of bodily heat. **4.** conserving or maintaining warmth or heat: *warm clothes.* **5.** (of colors) suggestive of warmth; inclining toward red or orange rather than green or blue. **6.** characterized by or showing affection, kindliness, or sympathy: *a warm heart.* **7.** strongly attached; intimate: *warm friends.* **8.** cordial or hearty: *a warm welcome.* **9.** heated, irritated, or angry. **10.** animated; vigorous: *a warm debate.* **11.** strong or fresh: *a warm scent.* **12.** close to something sought, as in a game. **13.** uncomfortable or unpleasant: *His opponents made things so warm that he decided to quit.* —*v.t.* **14.** to make warm; heat (often fol. by *up*): *to warm one's hands.* **15.** to heat or cook (something) for reuse, as leftovers (usu. fol. by *over* or *up*): *Warm up the stew.* **16.** to excite enthusiasm, cheerfulness, vitality, etc., in (someone): *a little wine to warm the company.* **17.** to inspire with kindly feeling; affect with lively pleasure: *It warms my soul to hear you say that.* **18.** to fill (a person, crowd, etc.) with strong feelings, as hatred or anger. —*v.i.* **19.** to become warm or warmer (often fol. by *up*). **20.** to become enthusiastic, animated, etc. (often fol. by *up* or *to*): *The speaker quickly warmed to her subject.* **21.** to grow kindly or sympathetically disposed (often fol. by *to* or *toward*): *My heart warmed toward him.* **22. warm up, a.** to prepare one's body for strenuous exercise by engaging in moderate exercise. **b.** to increase in excitement, intensity, violence, etc. **c.** to become friendlier or more receptive. **d.** to entertain (an audience) prior to a broadcast to increase receptiveness. —*n.* **23.** *Informal.* a warming. —**warm′er,** *n.* —**warm′ish,** *adj.* —**warm′ly,** *adv.*

warm′-blood′ed or **warm′blood′ed,** *adj.* **1.** of or designating animals, as mammals and birds, having a body temperature that is relatively constant and independent of the environment. **2.** ardent; impetuous: *warm-blooded valor.* —**warm′-blood′ed•ness,** *n.*

warmed′-o′ver, *adj.* **1.** (of cooked foods) reheated: *warmed-over stew.* **2.** reworked or repeated without enthusiasm or introduction of new ideas; stale: *a warmed-over version of an old plot.*

warm′ front′, *n.* a transition zone between a mass of warm air and the colder air it is replacing.

warm′-heart′ed or **warm′heart′ed,** *adj.* having or showing affection or cordiality: *a warm-hearted welcome.* —**warm′-heart′ed•ly,** *adv.*

warm′ing pan′, *n.* a long-handled, covered pan filled with live coals or hot water, formerly used for warming a bed.

war•mon•ger (wôr′mung′gər, -mong′-), *n.* a person who advocates war. —**war′mon′ger•ing,** *n.*

warmth (wôrmth), *n.* **1.** the quality or state of being warm; moderate or gentle heat. **2.** the sensation of moderate heat. **3.** ardor or fervor; enthusiasm. **4.** the quality of being intimate and attached: *the warmth and affection of a large family.* **5.** an effect of brightness, cheerfulness, etc., achieved esp. by the use of warm colors: *a room of great warmth.* **6.** the ability to produce a sensation of heat: *a jacket with little warmth.* **7.** slight anger or irritation.

warm′up′ or **warm′-up′,** *n.* **1.** an act of warming up: *dancers going through a quick warmup.* **2.** the time lapse between turning on the power in an electronic component or device and the time it is operable. **3.** Often, **warmups.** any apparel, esp. a sweat suit, worn over other clothing for warmth, chiefly in sports or during preliminary exercise.

warn (wôrn), *v.t.* **1.** to give notice, advice, or intimation to (a person, group, etc.) of impending danger, possible harm, or the like: *They warned the dictator of a plot against his life.* **2.** to urge or advise to be careful; caution: *to warn a careless driver.* **3.** to admonish or exhort, as to action or conduct: *Employees are warned to be on time.* **4.** to notify; inform: *to warn a person of an intended visit.* **5.** to notify to go away, keep at a distance, etc. (often fol. by *away, off,* etc.): *A sign warned boats away from the island.* **6.** to order; summon: *to warn a person to appear in court.* —*v.i.* **7.** to give a warning; caution. —**warn′er,** *n.*

War•ner (wär′nər), *n.* **Anna Bartlett,** 1820–1915, U.S. novelist and hymn writer.

warn•ing (wôr′ning), *n.* **1.** the act or utterance of one who warns; the appearance, sound, etc., of a thing that warns. **2.** something that serves to warn, give notice, or caution: *We fired a warning at the intruders.* **3.** *Meteorol.* an announcement from the U.S. National Weather Service alerting the public that a storm or other weather-related hazard is imminent and that immediate steps should be taken to protect lives and property. Compare ADVISORY (def. 5), WATCH (def. 21). —*adj.* **4.** serving to warn or caution: *a warning bell.* —**warn′ing•ly,** *adv.*

War′ of Amer′ican Independ′ence, *n. Brit.* AMERICAN REVOLUTION.

War of 1812, *n.* the war between the United States and Great Britain from 1812 to 1815.

War′ of Independ′ence, *n.* AMERICAN REVOLUTION.

war′ of nerves′, *n.* a campaign of propaganda, false rumors, or the like, in an attempt to confuse and demoralize the enemy without resorting to direct violence.

War′ of Seces′sion, *n.* AMERICAN CIVIL WAR.

War′ of the Span′ish Succes′sion, *n.* a war (1701–14) in which Austria, England, the Netherlands, and Prussia opposed France and Spain over the succession to the Spanish throne.

warp (wôrp), *v.t.* **1.** to bend or twist out of shape, esp. from a straight or flat form, as timbers or flooring. **2.** to bend or turn from the natural or true direction or course. **3.** to distort or cause to distort from the truth, fact, etc.; bias; falsify: *Prejudice warps the mind.* **4.** to move (a vessel) into a desired place or position by hauling on a rope that has been fastened to something fixed, as a buoy. —*v.i.* **5.** to become bent or twisted out of shape, esp. out of a straight or flat form: *The wood warped in drying.* **6.** to hold or change an opinion due to prejudice, influence, etc. —*n.* **7.** a bend or other variation from a straight or flat form. **8.** a mental twist, bias, or quirk. **9.** the set of yarns placed lengthwise in a loom, crossed by and interlaced with the filling, and forming the lengthwise threads in a woven fabric. **10.** a situation, environment, etc., that seems characteristic of another era and out of touch with contemporary life. **11.** a rope for warping or hauling a ship or boat along or into position. —**warp′age,** *n.* —**warp′er,** *n.*

war′ paint′, *n.* **1.** paint applied by American Indians to their faces and bodies before going to war. **2.** *Informal.* makeup; cosmetics. **3.** *Informal.* full dress; regalia.

war′ par′ty, *n.* **1.** a group of American Indians prepared for war. **2.** any political party or group that advocates war.

war•path (wôr′path′, -päth′), *n., pl.* **-paths** (-pathz′, -päthz′, -paths′, -päths′). **1.** the path or course taken by American Indians on a warlike expedition. —***Idiom.*** **2. on the warpath, a.** ready for or engaged in fighting. **b.** extremely hostile.

war•plane (wôr′plān′), *n.* a military aircraft, esp. one equipped for combat.

War′ Produc′tion Board′, *n.* the board (1942–45) that supervised and regulated the production and sale of matériel essential to the logistics of World War II. *Abbr.:* WPB, W.P.B.

war·rant (wôr′ənt, wor′-), *n.* **1.** authorization, sanction, or justification. **2.** something that serves to give formal assurance of something; a guarantee. **3.** something regarded as offering a guarantee or positive assurance of a thing: *The cavalry and artillery were sure warrants of success.* **4.** a document certifying or authorizing something, as a receipt or license. **5.** *Law.* an instrument authorizing an officer to make an arrest, search or seize property, etc. **6.** the certificate of authority issued to an officer of the armed forces immediately below the rank of a commissioned officer. **7.** a written authorization for the payment or receipt of money. —*v.t.* **8.** to authorize. **9.** to give reason or sanction for; justify. **10.** to vouch for (often used with a clause): *I'll warrant he did!* **11.** to give a formal assurance to or for; guarantee: *to warrant payment.* **12.** to guarantee the quantity, quality, and other representations of (a product), as to a purchaser. **13.** to assure indemnification against loss to. **14.** *Law.* to guarantee title of property to (a grantee).

war′rant of′ficer, *n.* **1.** (in the U.S. armed forces) an officer of one of four grades ranking above enlisted personnel and below commissioned officers. **2.** a similar officer in other countries.

war·ran·ty (wôr′ən tē, wor′-; *v.* wôr′ən tēd, wor′-), *n., pl.* **-ties,** *v.,* **-tied, -ty·ing.** —*n.* **1.** a written guarantee given to the purchaser of a new appliance, automobile, or other item by the manufacturer or dealer, usu. specifying that the manufacturer will make any repairs or replace defective parts free of charge for a stated period. **2.** *Law.* **a.** written or implied assurance that specific aspects of a contract, sale, etc., will be as represented. **b.** a covenant in a deed guaranteeing clear and unencumbered title to property. **c.** a judicial document, as a warrant or writ. —*v.t.* **3.** to provide a manufacturer's or dealer's warranty for.

war′ranty deed′, *n. Law.* a deed containing a warranty that the property is free of any encumbrance. Compare QUITCLAIM DEED.

war·ren (wôr′ən, wor′-), *n.* **1.** a place where rabbits breed or abound. **2.** a building or area containing many inhabitants in crowded quarters. **3.** a mazelike place containing many passageways or small rooms.

War·ren (wôr′ən, wor′-), *n.* **1. Earl,** 1891–1974, Chief Justice of the U.S. Supreme Court 1953–69. **2. Robert Penn,** 1905–89, U.S. novelist and poet: named the first U.S. poet laureate 1986–87. **3.** a city in SE Michigan, near Detroit. 142,625.

war·ri·or (wôr′ē ər, wôr′yər, wor′ē ər, wor′yər), *n.* **1.** a person engaged or experienced in warfare; soldier. **2.** a person who has shown great vigor, courage, or aggressiveness, as in politics.

war·saw (wôr′sô), *n.* a large grouper, *Epinephelus nigritus,* found in the warmer waters of the Atlantic Ocean. Also called **war′saw group′er.**

War·saw (wôr′sô), *n.* the capital of Poland, in the E central part, on the Vistula River. 2,432,000. Polish, **War·sza·wa** (vär shä′vä).

war·ship (wôr′ship′), *n.* a ship built or armed for combat purposes.

Wars′ of the Ros′es, *n.pl.* the conflict (1455–85) between the English royal houses of Lancaster and York, ending with the accession of Henry VII and the union of the two houses.

wart (wôrt), *n.* **1.** a small, hard growth in the skin, usu. caused by a virus. **2.** any small protuberance, as on the surface of certain plants, the skin of certain animals, etc. **3.** any unattractive detrimental feature or aspect. —*Idiom.* **4. warts and all,** including all imperfections.

Wart·burg (värt′bŏŏrk′), *n.* a castle in Thuringia, Germany: Luther translated the New Testament here 1521–22.

wart·hog (wôrt′hôg′, -hog′), *n.* a wild African swine, *Phacochoerus aethiopicus,* having large tusks and facial outgrowths.

warthog, *Phacochoerus aethiopicus,*
2 ½ ft. (0.8 m) high at shoulder;
head and body 4 ½ ft. (1.4 m);
tail 1 ½ ft. (0.5 m)

war·time (wôr′tīm′), *n.* **1.** a time or period of war: *travel restrictions in wartime.* —*adj.* **2.** characteristic of or occurring during war.

war′ to end′ all′ wars′, *n.* epithet for World War I.

war·y (wâr′ē), *adj.,* **war·i·er, war·i·est. 1.** watchful; being on one's guard against danger. **2.** arising from or characterized by caution: *a wary look.* —**war′i·ly,** *adv.* —**war′i·ness,** *n.*

war′ zone′, *n.* (during wartime) a combat area, esp. on the high seas, where neutral ships are subject to attack the same as enemy vessels.

was (wuz, woz; *unstressed* wəz), *v.* 1st and 3rd pers. sing. past indic. of BE.

wash (wosh, wôsh), *v.t.* **1.** to cleanse by dipping, rubbing, or scrubbing in water or some other liquid. **2.** to remove (dirt or other matter) by or as if by the action of water: *She washed the stain out of her dress.* **3.** to free from spiritual defilement or from sin, guilt, etc. **4.** to moisten with water or other liquid: *a meadow newly washed with dew.* **5.** to flow through, over, or against: *a beach washed by waves.* **6.** to carry, remove, or deposit by means of water or any liquid: *A sailor was washed overboard.* **7.** (of water) to form by flowing over and eroding a surface.

8. a. to subject (earth or ore) to the action or force of water in order to separate valuable material. **b.** to separate (valuable material) in this way. **9.** to cover with a watery or thin coat of color. **10.** to overlay with a thin coat or deposit of metal: *to wash brass with gold.* —*v.i.* **11.** to wash oneself. **12.** to wash clothes. **13.** to cleanse anything in a liquid. **14.** to undergo washing without shrinking, fading, etc. **15.** *Informal.* to prove true when subjected to testing: *His alibi simply won't wash.* **16.** to be carried or driven by water. **17.** to flow or beat with a lapping sound, as waves. **18.** to move along in or as if in waves. **19.** to be removed by the action of water (often fol. by *away*): *Much of the topsoil washes away each spring.* **20. wash down, a.** to clean completely by washing. **b.** to facilitate the swallowing of (food or medicine) by drinking liquid. **21. wash out, a.** to be removed by washing. **b.** to damage or demolish by the action of water. **c.** *Informal.* to fail to qualify or continue; be eliminated: *to wash out of graduate school.* **22. wash up, a.** to wash one's face and hands: *to wash up before dinner.* **b.** to wash dishes, flatware, etc. —*n.* **23.** the act or process of washing with water or other liquid: *Give the car a wash.* **24.** a quantity of clothes, linens, etc., washed, or to be washed, at one time: *a heavy wash.* **25.** a liquid with which something is colored, overspread, etc.: *She gave the room a wash of pale blue.* **26.** the flow, sweep, or breaking of water. **27.** the sound made by this. **28.** water moving along in waves or with a rushing movement: *the wash of the incoming tide.* **29.** the rough or broken water left behind a moving ship, boat, etc.; wake. **30.** the disturbance in the air left behind by a moving airplane or any of its parts: *wing wash.* **31.** any of various liquids for grooming: *a hair wash.* **32.** a lotion or other liquid having medicinal properties (often used in combination): *to apply wash to a skinned knee; mouthwash.* **33.** a shallow arm of the sea or a shallow part of a river. **34.** a depression or channel formed by flowing water. **35.** *Western U.S.* the dry bed of a stream. **36.** a broad, thin layer of color applied by a continuous movement of the brush, as in watercolor painting. **37.** Also, **washing.** a thin coat of metal applied in liquid form: *a gold wash.* **38.** waste liquid matter, refuse, food, etc., from the kitchen, as for hogs; swill (often used in combination): *hogwash.* **39.** weak or watered liquor. —*adj.* **40.** capable of being washed without shrinking, fading, etc.; washable: *a wash dress.* —*Idiom.* **41. come out in the wash, a.** to result eventually in something satisfactory. **b.** to be made known eventually.

wash·a·ble (wosh′ə bəl, wô′shə-), *adj.* **1.** capable of being washed without shrinking, fading, or the like. —*n.* **2.** a washable garment.

wash′-and-wear′, *adj.* noting or pertaining to a garment or fabric that can be washed, that dries quickly, and that requires little or no ironing.

wash·board (wosh′bôrd′, -bōrd′, wôsh′-), *n.* **1.** a rectangular board or frame, typically with a corrugated metallic surface, on which clothes are rubbed in the process of washing. **2.** a baseboard around the walls of a room. **3.** a thin, broad plank fastened to and projecting above the gunwale or side of a boat to keep out the spray and sea. —*adj.* **4.** resembling a washboard in being rough and bumpy: *a washboard roadbed.*

wash·bowl (wosh′bōl′, wôsh′-), *n.* a large bowl or basin used for washing one's hands and face, small articles of clothing, etc. Also called **wash′ba′sin** (-bā′sən).

wash·cloth (wosh′klôth′, -kloth′, wôsh′-), *n., pl.* **-cloths** (-klôthz′, -kloth̸z′, -klôths′, -kloths′). a small cloth for washing one's face or body.

washed′-out′, *adj.* **1.** faded, esp. from washing. **2.** *Informal.* **a.** weary; exhausted. **b.** tired-looking; wan.

washed′-up′, *adj. Informal.* done for; having failed.

wash·er (wosh′ər, wô′shər), *n.* **1.** a person or thing that washes. **2.** WASHING MACHINE. **3.** a flat ring or perforated piece of leather, rubber, metal, etc., used to give tightness to a joint, to prevent leakage, to distribute pressure, etc., as under the head of a nut or bolt.

wash′er-dry′er, *n.* a washing machine and a clothes dryer combined in one unit.

wash·ing (wosh′ing, wô′shing), *n.* **1.** the act of one that washes; ablution. **2.** clothes, linens, etc., washed or to be washed at one time; wash. **3.** Often, **washings.** any liquid that has been used to wash something. **4.** matter removed or carried off in washing.

wash′ing machine′, *n.* an apparatus, esp. a household appliance, for washing clothing, linens, etc. Also called **washer.**

wash′ing so′da, *n.* SODIUM CARBONATE (def. 2).

Wash·ing·ton (wosh′ing tən, wô′shing-), *n.* **1. Booker T(al·ia·fer·ro)** (tol′ə vər), 1856–1915, U.S. reformer and educator. **2. George,** 1732–99, U.S. general: 1st president of the U.S. 1789–97. **3. Martha** (*Martha Dandridge*), 1732–1802, wife of George. **4.** Also called **Washington, D.C.** the capital of the United States, on the Potomac: coextensive with the District of Columbia. 567,094. **5.** a state in the NW United States, on the Pacific coast. 5,532,939; 68,192 sq. mi. (176,615 sq. km). *Cap.:* Olympia. *Abbr.:* WA, Wash. **6. Mount,** a mountain in N New Hampshire, in the White Mountains: highest peak in the northeastern U.S. 6293 ft. (1918 m). **7. Lake,** a lake in W Washington, near Seattle. 20 mi. (32 km) long.

Wash′ington pie′, *n.* a Boston cream pie with raspberry jam instead of custard between the layers.

Wash′ington's Birth′day, *n.* **1.** February 22, formerly observed as a legal holiday in most states of the U.S. in honor of the birth of George Washington. **2.** PRESIDENTS' DAY.

Wash′ington State′, *n.* the state of Washington, esp. as distinguished from Washington, D.C.

wash•out (wosh′out′, wôsh′-), *n.* **1.** a washing out of earth, gravel, etc., by water, as from an embankment or a roadway by heavy rain. **2.** the hole, break, or erosion produced by such a washing out. **3.** *Informal.* **a.** a complete failure or disappointment. **b.** a person who has failed a course of training or study: *air force washouts.*

wash•rag (wosh′rag′, wôsh′-), *n.* WASHCLOTH.

wash•room (wosh′ro͞om′, -ro͝om′, wôsh′-), *n.* a room having washbowls and other toilet facilities.

wash•stand (wosh′stand′, wôsh′-), *n.* **1.** a piece of furniture holding a basin, pitcher, etc., for use in washing one's hands and face. **2.** a stationary fixture having faucets with running water, for the same purpose.

wash•tub (wosh′tub′, wôsh′-), *n.* a tub for use in washing clothes, linens, etc.

wash′up′ or **wash′-up′,** *n.* **1.** an act of washing, esp. of the face and hands. **2.** a place, as a bathroom, for washing.

wash•y (wosh′ē, wô′shē), *adj.,* **wash•i•er, wash•i•est. 1.** diluted too much; weak: *washy coffee.* **2.** pale, thin, or weak, as if from excessive dilution; pallid: *washy coloring.* —**wash′i•ness,** *n.*

was•n't (wuz′ənt, woz′-), contraction of *was not.*

wasp (wosp), *n.* **1.** any of numerous winged hymenopterous insects with a slender body and a narrow stalk between the abdomen and thorax, the female having a harsh stinger that can strike repeatedly. **2.** a person who is snappish or petulant. —**wasp′like′,** *adj.*

WASP or **Wasp** (wosp), *n.* **1.** a white Anglo-Saxon Protestant. **2.** a member of the privileged, established white upper middle class in the U.S. —**wasp′y,** *adj.*

wasp•ish (wos′pish), *adj.* **1.** like or suggesting a wasp, esp. in behavior. **2.** snappish or peevish; petulant; testy. **3.** having a slight or slender build. —**wasp′ish•ly,** *adv.* —**wasp′ish•ness,** *n.*

wasp•y (wos′pē), *adj.,* **wasp•i•er, wasp•i•est.** resembling a wasp; waspish. —**wasp′i•ly,** *adv.* —**wasp′i•ness,** *n.*

was•sail (wos′əl, -āl, was′-, wo sāl′), *n.* **1.** (in early England) a salutation offered when presenting a cup of drink to a person or when drinking that person's health. **2.** a festivity or revel with drinking of healths. **3.** liquor, as hot spiced ale or wine, used in drinking another's health, esp. at Christmastime. —*v.i.* **4.** to revel with drinking. —*v.t.* **5.** to toast (a person). —**was′sail•er,** *n.*

wast•age (wā′stij), *n.* **1.** loss by use, decay, etc. **2.** losses resulting from wastefulness. **3.** the action or process of wasting: *the steady wastage of erosion.* **4.** something that is wasted; waste or waste materials.

waste (wāst), *v.,* **wast•ed, wast•ing,** *n., adj.* —*v.t.* **1.** to consume or use to no avail or profit; squander: *to waste natural resources; to waste words.* **2.** to fail or neglect to use: *to waste an opportunity.* **3.** to destroy or consume gradually; wear away: *waves wasting the rocky shore.* **4.** to wear down or reduce in bodily substance or strength; emaciate; enfeeble: *to be wasted by disease.* **5.** to devastate or ruin. **6.** *Slang.* to kill or murder. —*v.i.* **7.** to be consumed or employed uselessly or inadequately. **8.** to become gradually used up or worn away. **9.** to become physically worn, esp. emaciated or enfeebled. **10.** to diminish gradually, as wealth or power; dwindle. —*n.* **11.** useless consumption or expenditure; an act or instance of wasting. **12.** neglect, instead of use. **13.** gradual impairment or decay. **14.** devastation or ruin. **15.** an area devastated or ruined. **16.** anything unused, inadequately used, or unproductive. **17.** desolate country, as desert. **18.** something left over or superfluous. **19.** material derived by mechanical and chemical disintegration of rock, as the detritus transported by streams, rivers, etc. **20.** garbage; refuse. **21. wastes,** excrement. —*adj.* **22.** not used or in use: *waste energy.* **23.** (of land, regions, etc.) wild; desolate. **24.** (of regions, towns, etc.) in a state of desolation and ruin. **25.** left over; superfluous. **26.** rejected as useless or worthless; refuse. **27.** *Physiol.* pertaining to material unused by or unusable to the organism. **28.** designed or used to receive or carry away useless material (often in combination): *a waste pipe.* —***Idiom.* 29. go to waste,** to be wasted, rather than used or consumed. **30. lay waste,** to devastate; destroy. —***Proverb.* 31. Waste not, want not,** no waste today means no scarcity in the future.

waste•bas•ket (wāst′bas′kit, -bä′skit), *n.* a standing basket or other open receptacle for wastepaper, small items of trash, etc. Also called **waste′paper bas′ket.**

wast•ed (wā′stid), *adj.* **1.** useless; unavailing: *wasted efforts.* **2.** physically debilitated; enfeebled: *the wasted bodies of the hostages.*

waste•ful (wāst′fəl), *adj.* **1.** given to or characterized by useless consumption or expenditure: *a wasteful way of living.* **2.** grossly extravagant; prodigal: *a wasteful party.* **3.** devastating or destructive: *wasteful war.* —**waste′ful•ly,** *adv.* —**waste′ful•ness,** *n.*

waste•land (wāst′land′), *n.* **1.** land that is uncultivated or barren. **2.** an area that is devastated, as by flood or war. **3.** something, as a period of history or locality, that is spiritually or intellectually barren.

waste•pa•per (wāst′pā′pər), *n.* paper discarded as useless.

waste′ pipe′, *n.* **1.** a pipe for draining liquid waste or excess liquids. **2.** a pipe for draining away the wastes of a building other than those from water closets.

waste•wa•ter (wāst′wô′tər, -wot′ər), *n.* water that has been used in washing, flushing, etc.; sewage.

wast•ing (wā′sting), *adj.* **1.** gradually reducing the fullness and strength of the body: *a wasting disease.* **2.** laying waste; devastating: *a wasting war.* —**wast′ing•ly,** *adv.* —**wast′ing•ness,** *n.*

wast•rel (wā′strəl), *n.* a wasteful person; spendthrift.

watch (woch), *v.i.* **1.** to look attentively, as to see what is done or happens; observe. **2.** to wait attentively and expectantly (usu. fol. by *for*): *to watch for a signal.* **3.** to be careful or cautious. **4.** to keep awake, esp. for a purpose; remain vigilant: *to watch with a sick person.* **5.** to keep vigil, as for devotional purposes. **6.** to keep guard: *to watch at the door.* —*v.t.* **7.** to view attentively or with interest. **8.** to contemplate or regard mentally: *to watch a student's progress.* **9.** to wait attentively and expectantly for. **10.** to guard or tend: *to watch the baby.* **11. watch out,** to be cautious. **12. watch over,** to safeguard; protect. —*n.* **13.** close, continuous observation for the purpose of seeing or discovering something. **14.** vigilant guard, as for protection or restraint: *to keep watch for prowlers.* **15.** a keeping awake for some special purpose: *a watch beside a sickbed.* **16.** a small, portable timepiece, as a wristwatch or pocket watch. **17.** a chronometer. **18. a.** a period of time, usu. four hours, during which one part of a ship's crew is on duty, taking turns with another part. **b.** the officers and crew who attend to the working of a ship for an allotted period of time. **19.** one of the periods, usu. three or four, into which the night was divided in ancient times. **20.** a lookout, guard, or sentinel: *A watch was posted at sunset.* **21.** Also called **storm watch.** *Meteorol.* an announcement from the U.S. National Weather Service alerting the public that dangerous weather conditions are a possibility and that vigilance and precautionary preparations are advised: *hurricane watch, tornado watch.* Compare ADVISORY (def. 5), **warning** (def. 3). —***Idiom.* 22. on the watch,** vigilant; alert: *a hunter on the watch for game.* **23. watch oneself,** to practice caution, discretion, or self-restraint. —***Proverb.* 24. A watched pot never boils,** impatient hovering only seems to make something take longer.

watch•a•ble (woch′ə bəl), *adj.* interesting or enjoyable to watch: *a watchable TV talk show.* —**watch′a•bil′i•ty,** *n.*

watch•band (woch′band′), *n.* a leather, metal, fabric, or plastic bracelet or strap for holding a wristwatch on the wrist.

watch′ cap′, *n.* a usu. dark blue, knitted woolen cap with a turned-up cuff, worn esp. by naval enlisted personnel.

watch•dog (woch′dôg′, -dog′), *n., v.,* **-dogged, -dog•ging.** —*n.* **1.** a dog kept to guard property. **2.** a watchful guardian: *a watchdog of the public morals.* —*v.t.* **3.** to watch carefully, esp. so as to detect illegal or unethical conduct.

watch′dog commit′tee, *n.* a legislative committee that investigates government expenditures.

watch•ful (woch′fəl), *adj.* vigilant or alert; closely observant. —**watch′ful•ly,** *adv.* —**watch′ful•ness,** *n.*

Watch′ful Door′keeper, The, a parable of Jesus. Mark 13:32–37.

watch′ful wait′ing, *n.* alert attention to a problem with a view to taking action at the right time.

watch′ list′ or **watch′list′,** *n.* a list of persons or things to watch for possible action in the future: *a watch list of possible growth stocks.*

watch•man (woch′mən), *n., pl.* **-men. 1.** a person who keeps guard over a building at night. **2.** (formerly) a person who guards or patrols the streets at night.

watch•tow•er (woch′tou′ər), *n.* a tower for a sentinel.

Watch•tower, The (woch′tou′ər), a magazine published by the Jehovah's Witnesses. Is. 21:5.

watch•word (woch′wûrd′), *n.* **1.** a word or short phrase to be communicated, on challenge, to a sentinel; password. **2.** a word or phrase expressive of a principle or rule of action; slogan. **3.** a rallying cry of a party, club, team, etc.

wa•ter (wô′tər, wot′ər), *n.* **1.** a transparent, odorless, tasteless liquid, a compound of hydrogen and oxygen, H_2O, freezing at 32°F or 0°C and boiling at 212°F or 100°C, that in a more or less impure state constitutes rain, oceans, lakes, rivers, etc. **2.** a special form or variety of this liquid, as rain. **3.** Often, **waters.** this liquid in an impure state as obtained from a mineral spring. **4.** the liquid content of a river, inlet, etc., with reference to its relative height, esp. as dependent on tide. **5.** the surface of a stream, river, ocean, etc.: *boats on the water.* **6. waters, a.** flowing water, or water moving in waves. **b.** the sea or seas bordering a particular country or continent. **7.** a liquid preparation, esp. one used for cosmetic purposes: *lavender water.* **8.** Often, **waters. a.** AMNIOTIC FLUID. **b.** the bag of waters; amnion. **9.** any of various solutions of volatile or gaseous substances in water: *ammonia water.* **10.** any liquid or aqueous organic secretion, exudation, humor, or the like, as tears, perspiration, or urine. **11.** fictitious assets or the inflated values given to the stock of a corporation. **12.** a wavy, lustrous pattern or marking, as on silk. **13.** (formerly) the degree of transparency and brilliancy of a diamond or other precious stone. —*v.t.* **14.** to sprinkle or drench with water. **15.** to supply with water, as a ship. **16.** to supply (animals) with drinking water. **17.** to supply (land, a region, etc.) with water, as by streams or irrigation. **18.** to dilute, weaken, or adulterate with or as if with water (often fol. by *down*). **19.** to issue or increase the par value of (shares of stock) without having the necessary assets (often fol. by *down*). **20.** to produce a wavy, lustrous pattern, marking, or finish on (fabrics, metals, etc.). —*v.i.* **21.** to fill with, or secrete water or liquid, as the eyes when irritated. **22.** to drink water, as an animal. —*adj.* **23.** of or pertaining to water in any way. **24.** holding, or designed to hold, water. **25.** worked or powered by water. **26.** heating, pumping, or circulating water (often used in combination): *a hot-water furnace.* **27.** used in or on water: *water skis.* **28.** containing or prepared with water. **29.** located or occurring on or by water. **30.** residing by or in, or ruling

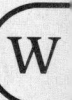

over, water: *water people; water deities.* **—Idiom. 31. by water,** by ship or boat: *to send goods by water.* **32. hold water,** to be able to be substantiated or defended: *That accusation won't hold water.* **33. in deep water,** in great distress or difficulty. **34. keep one's head above water,** to stay out of financial difficulties. **35. like water,** freely; abundantly; lavishly: *The champagne flowed like water.* **36. make one's mouth water,** to excite a desire or appetite for something: *a sports car that makes your mouth water.* **37. make water,** to urinate. **38. water under the bridge** or **over the dam,** something irrelevant because it is past.

wa′ter ballet′, *n.* synchronized movements, patterns, and other visual effects performed in the water by swimmers, usu. to a musical accompaniment.

Wa′ter Bear′er, *n.* AQUARIUS.

wa·ter·bed (wô′tər bed′, wot′ər-), *n.* a bed with a liquid-filled rubber or plastic mattress in a rigid, often heated, waterproof frame.

wa′ter bee′tle, *n.* any of various aquatic beetles, as a predaceous diving beetle of the family Dytiscidae.

wa′ter bis′cuit, *n.* an unsalted cracker made with flour and water.

wa′ter blis′ter, *n.* a blister containing a clear, serous fluid.

wa′ter boy′, *n.* **1.** a person who brings drinking water to those unable to fetch it, as soldiers or laborers. **2.** a person who supplies livestock with water.

wa·ter·buck (wô′tər buk′, wot′ər-), *n.* any large swamp-dwelling African antelope of the genus *Kobus,* esp. *K. ellipsiprymnus.*

wa′ter buf′falo, *n.* a widely domesticated Asian buffalo, *Bubalus bubalis,* having large, flattened, curved horns.

wa′ter bug′, *n.* **1.** any of various aquatic bugs, as of the family Belostomatidae. **2.** (loosely) a very large, relatively slow cockroach, as the American cockroach.

Wa·ter·bur·y (wô′tər ber′ē, -bə rē, wot′ər-), *n.* a city in W Connecticut. 103,523.

wa′ter chest′nut, *n.* **1.** any of several aquatic plants of the genus *Trapa,* family Trapaceae, with an edible, nutlike fruit, esp. *T. natans* of the Old World. **2.** the fruit itself. Also called **wa′ter cal′trop.**

wa′ter clos′et, *n.* **1.** an enclosed room or compartment containing a toilet bowl fitted with a mechanism for flushing. **2.** a privy or bathroom. *Abbr.:* WC, wc

wa·ter·col·or (wô′tər kul′ər, wot′ər-), *n.* **1.** a pigment for which water and not oil is used as the vehicle. **2.** the art or technique of painting with such pigments. **3.** a painting or design using such pigments. —*adj.* **4.** of, done in, or using watercolor. **—wa′ter·col′or·ist,** *n.*

wa′ter cool′er, *n.* **1.** a container for holding drinking water that is drawn off by a faucet or spigot. **2.** a drinking fountain in which water is cooled by mechanical refrigeration.

wa·ter·course (wô′tər kôrs′, -kōrs′, wot′ər-), *n.* **1.** a stream of water, as a river or brook. **2.** the bed of a stream that flows only seasonally. **3.** a natural channel conveying water. **4.** a channel or canal made for the conveyance of water.

wa·ter·craft (wô′tər kraft′, -kräft′, wot′ər-), *n.* **1.** skill in boating and water sports. **2.** a boat or ship. **3.** CRAFT (def. 6).

wa·ter·cress (wô′tər kres′, wot′ər-), *n.* **1.** a cress, *Nasturtium officinale,* of the mustard family, usu. growing in clear, running streams and having pungent leaves. **2.** the leaves, used for salads, soups, and as a garnish.

wa·tered (wô′tərd, wot′ərd), *adj.* **1.** having rivers or streams. **2.** sprinkled, irrigated, etc., with water. **3.** having a wavy, lustrous pattern or marking: *watered silk.* **4.** (of stock) issued in excess of a company's true worth.

wa′tered-down′, *adj.* made weaker from or as if from dilution with water: *a watered-down cocktail; a watered-down version of the play for television.*

wa·ter·fall (wô′tər fôl′, wot′ər-), *n.* **1.** a steep fall or flow of water in a watercourse from a height, as over a precipice; cascade. **2.** a simulation of this, as in a garden or hotel lobby.

wa·ter·fowl (wô′tər foul′, wot′ər-), *n., pl.* **-fowls,** (*esp. collectively*) **-fowl. 1.** a water bird, esp. a swimming bird. **2.** such birds collectively, esp. the swans, geese, and ducks.

wa·ter·front (wô′tər frunt′, wot′ər-), *n.* **1.** a part of a city on the edge of a body of water, esp. an ocean; wharf or dock section. **—Idiom. 2. cover the waterfront,** to be informed about, research, or deal with all aspects of a topic or area.

wa′ter gas′, *n.* a toxic mixture of carbon monoxide and hydrogen; an illuminant and fuel and in organic synthesis. **—wa′ter-gas′,** *adj.*

wa′ter gate′, *n.* **1.** FLOODGATE. **2.** a gateway leading to the edge of a body of water, as at a landing.

Wa·ter·gate (wô′tər gāt′, wot′ər-), *n.* **1.** a political scandal during the 1972 presidential campaign, arising from a break-in at Democratic Party headquarters at the Watergate building complex in Washington, D.C., and culminating in the resignation of President Nixon. **2.** any scandal involving corruption and other abuses of power, and an attempt to conceal these activities from the public.

wa′ter glass′ or **wa′ter·glass′,** *n.* **1.** a drinking glass; tumbler. **2.** a glass container for holding water, as for growing bulbs, plants, or the

NOTED WATERFALLS OF THE WORLD

Waterfall	Location (and Nearby City or Community)	River or Other Source of Water	Height: ft.	m
Angel	Southeastern Venezuela (Canaima)	Tributary of the Caroni	3212	979
Tugela	Natal, South Africa (Durban)	Tugela	2810	856
Yosemite	Yosemite National Park	Yosemite Creek	2526	770
Cuquenan	Guyana-Venezuela Border (Santa Elena)	Tributary of the Arabopo	2000	610
Sutherland	Southwest South Island, N.Z. (Milford Sound)	Into Arthur R.	1904	580
Kile	Western Norway (Bergen)	Kile	1840	561
Wollomombi	New South Wales, Australia (Armidale)	Macleay	1700	518
Takakkaw	Yoho National Park, B.C., Canada (Lake Louise)	Into Yoho R.	1650	503
Ribbon	Yosemite National Park	Ribbon Creek	1612	491
Upper Yosemite	Yosemite National Park	Yosemite Creek	1436	438
Gavarnie	Southern France (Lourdes)	Pyrenees Glaciers	1385	422
Krimmler	West Central Austria (Innsbruck)	Krimmler	1246	380
Vettisfos	South Central Norway	Morkedola	1200	366
Silver Strand	Yosemite National Park	(Stream)	1170	357
Staubbach	South Central Switzerland (Lauterbrunnen)	Staubbach	1000	305
Rjukan	Southern Norway (Skien)	Mane	983	300
Giessbach	South Central Switzerland (Brienz)	Giessbach	980	299
Trummelbach	South Central Switzerland (Lauterbrunnen)	Jungfrau Glaciers	950	290
Kalambo	Zambia-Tanzania Border (Mbala)	Kalambo	704	215
Bridalveil	Yosemite National Park	Bridalveil Creek	620	189
Multnomah	Northwestern Oregon (Bonneville)	Into Columbia R.	620	189
Nevada	Yosemite National Park	(Stream)	594	181
Toce	Northern Italy (Domodossola)	Toce	540	165
Voring	Southwestern Norway (Eidfjord)	Bjoreia	535	163
Skjaggedals	Southwestern Norway (Odda)	Ringdal Lake	525	160
Tequendama	Central Columbia (Bogota)	Bogota	482	147
Victoria	Zambia-Zimbabwe Border (Livingstone)	Zambezi	420	128
Kabalega	Northwestern Uganda (Butiaba)	Victoria Nile	400	122
Glomach	Scotland (Inverness)	Elchaig	370	113
Illilouette	Yosemite National Park	Illilouette Creek	370	113
Granite	Northwestern Washington (Everett)	Stillaguamish	350	107
Lower Yosemite	Yosemite National Park	Yosemite Creek	320	98
Churchill	Western Labrador (Goose Bay)	Upper Hamilton	316	96
Lower Yellowstone	Yellowstone National Park	Yellowstone	308	94
Reichenbach, Upper	Central Switzerland (Grindelwald)	Rosenlaui Glacier	300	91
Iguassu	Argentina-Brazil Border (Puerto Iguassu)	Iguassu	210	64
Shoshone	Southern Idaho (Twin Falls)	Snake	210	64
Twin	Southern Idaho (Twin Falls)	Snake	180	55
Niagara	Western New York and Southern Ontario (Niagara Falls)	Niagara	167	51
Manitou	Northwestern Wisconsin (La Crosse)	Black	165	50
Pistyll Cain	Northern Wales (Dolgelley)	Cain	150	46
Tower	Yellowstone National Park	Yellowstone	132	40
Upper Yellowstone	Yellowstone National Park	Yellowstone	109	33
Rheinfall (Schaffhausen)	Northern Switzerland (Schaffhausen)	Rhine	100	30

like. **3.** a device, as a tube or a box with a glass bottom, for observing objects beneath the surface of water. **4.** SODIUM SILICATE.

wa′ter gun′, *n.* WATER PISTOL.

wa′ter ham′mer, *n.* the concussion and accompanying noise that result when a volume of water moving in a pipe suddenly stops or loses momentum.

wa′ter heat′er, *n.* a household appliance consisting of a gas or electric heating unit under a tank in which water is heated and stored.

wa′ter hole′, *n.* **1.** a depression in the surface of the ground containing water; pond or pool. **2.** a source of drinking water, as a spring or well in the desert. **3.** a hole in the frozen surface of water.

wa′ter hy′acinth, *n.* a floating freshwater plant, *Eichornia crassipes*, related to the pickerelweed, that grows so prolifically it often hinders the passage of boats.

wa′ter-inch′, *n.* the quantity of water (approx. 500 cu. ft.) discharged in 24 hours through a circular opening of one inch diameter leading from a reservoir in which the water is constantly only high enough to cover the orifice.

wa′tering can′, *n.* a hand-held container for water, typically having a spout with a perforated nozzle, used for watering flowers or plants. Also called **wa′tering pot′.**

wa′tering hole′, *n.* **1.** a pool where animals go to drink; water hole. **2.** Also called **watering place, wa′tering spot′.** a bar, nightclub, or other social gathering place where alcoholic drinks are sold.

wa′tering place′, *n.* **1.** a seaside or lakeside vacation resort. **2.** a health resort near mineral springs, a lake, or the sea, featuring therapeutic baths, water cures, or the like; spa. **3.** a spring or water hole containing drinking water. **4.** WATERING HOLE (def. 2).

wa•ter•jet (wô′tər jet′, wot′ər-), *n.* **1.** a stream of water forced out through a small aperture. **2.** Also, **wa′ter jet′.** WATERPICK. —*adj.* **3.** of, pertaining to, or operated by a waterjet: *a waterjet pump.*

wa•ter•leaf (wô′tər lēf′, wot′ər-), *n.* any of several North American plants of the genus *Hydrophyllum*, having clusters of bluish or white flowers and leaves often bearing marks resembling water stains.

wa′ter lev′el, *n.* **1.** the surface level of any body of water. **2.** the level to which a vessel is immersed; water line.

wa′ter lil′y, *n.* any of various aquatic plants of the genus *Nymphaea*, species of which have large, disklike, floating leaves and showy flowers, esp. *N. odorata*, of America, or *N. alba*, of Europe.

wa′ter line′ or **wa′ter•line′,** *n.* **1.** the part of the outside of a ship's hull that is just at the water level. **2.** any of a series of lines on the hull plans of a vessel representing the level to which the vessel is immersed or the bottom of the keel. **3.** the line in which water at its surface borders upon a floating body. **4.** WATER LEVEL (def. 2). **5.** Also called **watermark,** a line indicating the former level or passage of water.

wa•ter•locked (wô′tər lokt′, wot′ər-), *adj.* enclosed entirely, or almost entirely, by water: *a waterlocked nation.*

wa•ter•logged (wô′tər lôgd′, -logd′, wot′ər-), *adj.* **1.** so filled with water as to be heavy or unmanageable, as a ship. **2.** excessively saturated with water: *waterlogged ground.*

Wa•ter•loo (wô′tər lōō′, wô′tər lōō′, wot′ər-), *n.* **1.** a village in central Belgium, S of Brussels: Napoleon decisively defeated here on June 18, 1815. **2.** any decisive or crushing defeat.n

wa′ter main′, *n.* a main pipe or conduit in a system for conveying water.

wa•ter•mark (wô′tər märk′, wot′ər-), *n.* **1.** a design impressed in some paper during manufacture, visible when the paper is held to the light. **2.** WATER LINE (def. 5). —*v.t.* **3.** to mark (paper) with a watermark.

wa•ter•mel•on (wô′tər mel′ən, wot′ər-), *n.* **1.** the large, roundish or elongated fruit of a trailing vine, *Citrullus lanata*, of the gourd family, having a hard, green rind and a sweet, juicy, usu. pink or red pulp. **2.** the vine itself.

wa′ter mil′foil, *n.* any of various aquatic plants, chiefly of the genus *Myriophyllum*, family Haloragaceae, the submerged leaves of which are finely divided and feathery: used in aquariums.

wa′ter mill′, *n.* a mill with machinery driven by water.

wa′ter moc′casin, *n.* **1.** the cottonmouth. **2.** any of various similar but harmless snakes, as a water snake of the genus *Nerodia*.

wa′ter mold′, *n.* any of various aquatic fungi of the phylum Oomycota, free-living or parasitic in fish and other aquatic organisms.

wa′ter oak′, *n.* **1.** an oak, *Quercus nigra*, of the southern U.S., growing chiefly along streams and swamps. **2.** any of several other American oaks of similar habit.

wa•ter•pick (wô′tər pik′, wot′ər-), *n.* an electric appliance that uses a pressurized stream of water to remove food particles from between the teeth and to massage the gums. Also called **waterjet.**

wa′ter pill′, *n.* a diuretic pill.

wa′ter pipe′, *n.* **1.** a pipe for conveying water. **2.** a smoking apparatus, as a hookah, in which the smoke is drawn through a container of water and cooled before reaching the mouth.

wa′ter pis′tol, *n.* a toy gun that shoots a stream of water or other liquid. Also called **water gun, squirt gun.**

wa′ter po′lo, *n.* an aquatic game played by two teams of seven swimmers each, the object being to score goals by pushing, carrying, or passing an inflated ball and tossing it into the opponent's goal, defended by a goalkeeper.

wa′ter pow′er or **wa′ter•pow′er,** *n.* **1.** the power of water used to drive machinery. **2.** a waterfall or descent in a watercourse capable of being so used. **3.** a water right possessed by a mill.

wa•ter•proof (wô′tər prōōf′, wot′ər-), *adj.* **1.** impervious to water. **2.** rendered impervious to water by some special process, as coating with rubber. —*n.* **3.** *Chiefly Brit.* a raincoat or other outer coat impervious to water. **4.** any fabric specially processed to be impervious to water. —*v.t.* **5.** to make waterproof.

wa′ter rat′, *n.* **1.** any of various aquatic rodents, as the muskrat. **2.** *Slang.* a vagrant or thief who frequents a waterfront.

wa′ter-repel′lent, *adj.* having a finish that resists but does not entirely prevent the penetration of water. Also **wa′ter resist′ant,** *adj.*

wa•ter•scape (wô′tər skāp′, wot′ər-), *n.* a picture or view of the sea or other body of water.

wa•ter•scor•pi•on (wô′tər skôr′pē ən, wot′ər-), *n.* any of several predatory aquatic bugs of the family Nepidae, having a long respiratory tube at the end of the abdomen.

wa•ter•shed (wô′tər shed′, wot′ər-), *n.* **1.** the region or area drained by a river, stream, etc. **2.** the ridge or crest line dividing two drainage areas. **3.** an important point of division or transition.

wa•ter•side (wô′tər sīd′, wot′ər-), *n.* **1.** the bank or shore of a river, lake, ocean, etc. —*adj.* **2.** of, pertaining to, or situated at the waterside. **3.** working by the waterside: *waterside police.*

wa′ter ski′, *n.* a ski on which to water-ski, designed to plane over water: it is shorter and broader than the ski used on snow.

wa′ter-ski′, *v.i.*, **-skied, -ski•ing.** to plane over water on water skis or a water ski by grasping a towing rope pulled by a speedboat.

wa′ter snake′, *n.* **1.** any of numerous and widely distributed harmless snakes of the genus *Natrix*, inhabiting areas in or near fresh water. **2.** any of various other snakes living in or frequenting water.

wa′ter sof′tener, *n.* any of a group of substances that when added to water containing calcium and magnesium ions cause the ions to precipitate or change their usual properties: used to purify water and increase its sudsing ability.

wa′ter span′iel, *n.* either of two breeds of spaniels used for retrieving waterfowl. Compare AMERICAN WATER SPANIEL, IRISH WATER SPANIEL.

wa•ter•sport (wô′tər spôrt′, -spōrt′, wot′ər-), *n.* a sport played or practiced on or in water, as swimming, water polo, or surfing.

wa•ter•spout (wô′tər spout′, wot′ər-), *n.* **1.** a spout, duct, or the like, from which water is discharged. **2.** DOWNSPOUT. **3.** a whirling, funnel-shaped cloud that touches the surface of a body of water, drawing upward spray and mist.

wa′ter supply′, *n.* **1.** the supply of purified water available to a community. **2.** the facilities for supplying this water.

wa′ter sys′tem, *n.* **1.** a river and all its branches. **2.** a system of supplying water, as throughout a metropolitan area.

wa′ter ta′ble or **wa′ter•ta′ble,** *n.* the planar, underground surface beneath which earth materials, as soil or rock, are saturated with water.

wa′ter tax′i, *n.* a motorboat that transports passengers, as between waterfront resorts or communities, for a fare.

wa•ter•tight (wô′tər tīt′, wot′ər-), *adj.* **1.** constructed or fitted so tightly as to be impervious to water. **2.** so devised as to be impossible to nullify or discredit: *a watertight contract; a watertight alibi.*

Wa′ter•ton-Gla′cier Interna′tional Peace′ Park′ (wô′tər tən, wot′ər-), *n.* a park in S Alberta and NW Montana, jointly administered by Canada and the U.S., encompassing Waterton Lakes National Park (Canada) and Glacier National Park (U.S.). 1584 sq. mi. (4102 sq. km).

wa′ter tow′er, *n.* **1.** a hollow vertical structure into which water is pumped high enough to maintain pressure required for firefighting, distribution, etc. **2.** a fire-extinguishing apparatus for throwing a stream of water on the upper parts of a tall burning building.

wa′ter va′por, *n.* water in the gaseous state, esp. as produced by evaporation at temperatures below the boiling point.

wa′ter wag′on, *n.* a wagon used to transport water, as in military field operations or on a construction site.

wa′ter wave′, *n.* a wave combed or pressed into wet hair and then dried. —**wa′ter-wave′,** *v.t.*, **-waved, -wav•ing.**

wa•ter•way (wô′tər wā′, wot′ər-), *n.* a river, canal, or other body of water serving as a route or way of travel or transport.

wa′ter wheel′ or **wa′ter wheel′,** *n.* **1.** a wheel or turbine turned by the weight or momentum of water and used to operate machinery. **2.** the paddle wheel of a steamboat.

wa′ter wings′, *n.pl.* an inflatable contrivance shaped like a pair of wings, usu. worn under the arms to keep the body afloat, esp. while one learns to swim.

wa′ter witch′ing, *n.* the search for or discovery of underground water sources by means of a divining rod.

wa•ter•works (wô′tər wûrks′, wot′ər-), *n.*, *pl.* **-works. 1.** (*used with a sing. or pl. v.*) a complete system of reservoirs, pipelines, conduits, etc., by which water is collected, purified, stored, and pumped to urban users. **2.** (*used with a sing. v.*) a pumping station or a purifying station of such a system. **3.** Sometimes, **waterwork.** a spectacular display of water, mechanically produced, as for a pageant. **4.** (*used with a sing. or pl. v.*) *Slang.* tears, or the source of tears: *to turn on the waterworks.* **5.** (*used with a pl. v.*) *Slang.* the urinary system.

wa•ter•y (wô′tə rē, wot′ə-), *adj.* **1.** consisting of or pertaining to water. **2.** full of or abounding in water, as soil; boggy. **3.** containing too much water: *a watery lemonade.* **4.** soft, soggy, tasteless, etc., due to excessive water or overcooking: *watery vegetables.* **5.** tearful: *a watery farewell.* **6.** resembling water in appearance or color: *a watery blue.* **7.** resembling water in fluidity and absence of viscosity. **8.** thin, weak, or vapid: *watery prose.* **9.** filled with or secreting a waterlike substance.

WATS (wots), *n.* a service providing unlimited long-distance telephone calls for a fixed monthly charge.

Wat•son (wot′sən), *n.* **1. James Dewey,** born 1928, U.S. biologist. **2. John (Broadus),** 1878–1958, U.S. psychologist.

watt (wot), *n.* the SI unit of power, equivalent to one joule per second and equal to the power in a circuit in which a current of one ampere flows across a potential difference of one volt. *Abbr.:* W, w [after J. WATT]

Watt (wot), *n.* **James,** 1736–1819, Scottish engineer and inventor.

watt•age (wot′ij), *n.* **1.** power, as measured in watts. **2.** the amount of power required to operate an electrical appliance or device.

Wat•teau[1] (wo tō′, vä-), *n.* **Jean Antoine,** 1684–1721, French painter.

Wat•teau[2] (wo tō′, vä-), *adj.* **1.** designating the loose, full back of a woman's gown, formed by wide box pleats extending from shoulder to hem in an unbroken line. **2.** designating a low-crowned straw hat with the brim turned up at the back and trimmed with flowers. [alluding to articles of clothing depicted in paintings by J. A. WATTEAU]

watt′-hour′ or **watt′hour′,** *n.* a unit of energy equal to the energy of one watt operating for one hour, equivalent to 3600 joules. *Abbr.:* Wh, whr, whr.

wat•tle[1] (wot′l), *n., v.,* **-tled, -tling,** *adj.* **—***n.* **1.** Often, **wattles.** a number of rods or stakes interwoven with twigs or tree branches for making fences, walls, etc. **2. wattles,** a number of poles laid on a roof to hold thatch. **3.** (in Australia) any of various acacias whose shoots and branches were used by the early colonists for wattles, now valued esp. for their bark, which is used in tanning. **—***v.t.* **4.** to bind, wall, fence, etc., with wattle or wattles. **5.** to make or construct by interweaving twigs or branches: *to wattle a fence.* **—***adj.* **6.** built or roofed with wattle or wattles.

wat•tle[2] (wot′l), *n.* a fleshy lobe hanging down from the throat or chin of certain birds, as the domestic chicken or turkey.

wat′tle and daub′ (or **dab′**), *n.* a building technique employing wattles plastered with clay and mud.

Watts (wots), *n.* **Isaac,** 1674–1748, English theologian and hymn writer.

Waugh (wô), *n.* **Eve•lyn (Arthur St. John)** (ēv′lin, ē′və-), 1903–66, English novelist.

wave (wāv), *n., v.,* **waved, wav•ing.** **—***n.* **1.** a disturbance on the surface of a liquid body, as the sea or a lake, in the form of a moving ridge or swell. **2.** any surging or progressing movement or part resembling a wave of the sea. **3.** a swell, surge, or rush: *a wave of disgust; a wave of cholera.* **4.** a widespread attitude, tendency, etc.: *a wave of anti-intellectualism.* **5.** a mass movement: *a wave of settlers.* **6.** an outward curve in a surface or line; undulation. **7.** an act or instance of waving. **8.** a waviness of the hair. **9.** a period of unusually hot or cold weather. **10.** *Physics.* a progressive disturbance propagated from point to point in a medium or space without progress or advance by the points themselves, as in the transmission of sound or light. **—***v.i.* **11.** to move freely and gently back and forth or up and down, as by the action of air currents, sea swells, etc.: *flags waving in the wind.* **12.** to curve alternately in opposite directions; have an undulating form. **13.** to bend or sway up and down or to and fro. **14.** to be moved alternately in opposite directions: *a handkerchief waving in the distance.* **15.** to signal, esp. in greeting, by raising the hand and moving the fingers up and down. **—***v.t.* **16.** to cause to have a waving motion in: *A breeze waved the tattered banners.* **17.** to cause to bend or sway up and down or to and fro. **18.** to cause to curve up and down or in and out. **19.** to give a wavy appearance or pattern to, as silk. **20.** to impart a wave to (the hair). **21.** to greet or signal someone by raising and moving (the hand), esp. alternately in opposite directions. **22.** to direct by a waving movement: *to wave traffic around an obstacle.* **23.** to signify or express by a waving movement: *to wave a last good-bye.* **—*Idiom.* 24. make waves,** *Informal.* to disturb the status quo. **—wave′less,** *adj.* **—wave′like′,** *adj.*

wave′ band′, *n.* BAND[2] (def. 6).

wave•guide (wāv′gīd′), *n.* a conduit, as a metal tube, coaxial cable, or strand of glass fibers, used as a conductor or directional transmitter for various kinds of electromagnetic waves.

wave′length′ or **wave′ length′,** *n.* **1.** the distance, measured in the direction of propagation of a wave, between two successive points in the wave that are characterized by the same phase of oscillation. **—*Idiom.* 2. on the same wavelength,** sharing values, ideas, or impulses; thinking and acting in harmony.

wave′ of the fu′ture, *n.* a trend or development that may influence or become a significant part of the future: *Computerization is the wave of the future.* [phrase popularized as the title of an essay (1940) by Anne Morrow Lindbergh]

wa•ver[1] (wā′vər), *v.i.* **1.** to sway to and fro; flutter. **2.** to flicker or quiver, as light. **3.** to become unsteady; begin to fail or give way: *At the news my courage wavered.* **4.** to shake or tremble, as the hands or voice. **5.** to feel or show doubt, indecision, etc.; vacillate: *to waver in one's determination.* **6.** (of things) to fluctuate or vary. **7.** to totter or reel: *The tower wavered during the earthquake.* **—***n.* **8.** an act of wavering; vacillation. **—wa′ver•er,** *n.* **—wa′ver•ing•ly,** *adv.*

wav•er[2] (wā′vər), *n.* a person or thing that waves.

wav•y (wā′vē), *adj.,* **wav•i•er, wav•i•est.** **1.** curving alternately in opposite directions; undulating: *wavy hair.* **2.** abounding in or characterized by waves. **3.** resembling waves: *fabric with a wavy pattern.* **4.** vibrating or tremulous; wavering. **—wav′i•ly,** *adv.* **—wav′i•ness,** *n.*

wax[1] (waks), *n.* **1.** Also called **beeswax.** a solid, yellowish, nonglycerine substance allied to fats and oils, secreted by bees in constructing their honeycomb, used in making candles, casts, ointments, etc. **2.** any of various similar substances, as spermaceti or the secretions of certain insects and plants. **3.** any of a group of substances composed of hydrocarbons, alcohols, fatty acids, and esters that are solid at ordinary temperatures. **4.** cerumen; earwax. **5.** a resinous substance used by shoemakers for rubbing thread. **6.** SEALING WAX. **—***v.t.* **7.** to rub, polish, etc., with wax. **8.** *Slang.* to defeat decisively; drub. **—***adj.* **9.** pertaining to, made of, or resembling wax. **—wax′a•ble,** *adj.* **—wax′like′,** *adj.*

wax[2] (waks), *v.i.* **1.** to increase in extent, quantity, intensity, power, etc. **2.** (of the moon) to increase in the extent of its illuminated portion before the full moon. Compare WANE (def. 4). **3.** to grow or become: *to wax resentful.*

wax′ bean′, *n.* **1.** a variety of string bean bearing yellowish, waxy pods. **2.** the edible pod itself, used as a vegetable.

waxed′ pa′per, *n.* WAX PAPER.

wax•en (wak′sən), *adj.* **1.** made of or covered, polished, or treated with wax. **2.** pallid: *the waxen face of illness.* **3.** malleable; pliable; impressionable.

wax•ing (wak′sing), *n.* **1.** the act or process of applying wax, as in polishing or filling. **2.** the act or technique of applying a depilatory wax to the body.

wax′ light′, *n.* a candle made of wax.

wax′ muse′um, *n.* a museum containing wax effigies of famous persons, esp. historical figures.

wax′ myr′tle, *n.* a bayberry, *Myrica cerifera,* of the southeastern U.S., having waxy berries used in candlemaking.

wax′ palm′, *n.* **1.** a tall, pinnate-leaved palm, *Ceroxylon alpinum* (or *C. andicola*), of the Andes, yielding a resinous wax. **2.** any of several other palms that are the source of wax, as the carnauba.

wax′ pa′per, *n.* a whitish, translucent wrapping paper made moistureproof by a paraffin coating.

wax•wing (waks′wing′), *n.* any of several crested songbirds of the family Bombycillidae, of the Northern Hemisphere, having certain feathers tipped with a red, waxy substance.

wax•work (waks′wûrk′), *n.* an artistic object made of wax, esp. a life-size effigy of a person. **—wax′work′er,** *n.*

wax•works (waks′wûrks′), *n., pl.* **-works.** (*usu. used with a sing. v.*) an exhibition of or a museum for displaying wax figures.

wax•y (wak′sē), *adj.,* **wax•i•er, wax•i•est.** **1.** resembling wax, esp. in appearance: *a waxy shine on his face.* **2.** abounding in, covered with, or made of wax: *Be careful, the floor is waxy.* **3.** pliable or impressionable: *a waxy personality.* **—wax′i•ly,** *adv.* **—wax′i•ness,** *n.*

way[1] (wā), *n.* **1.** manner, mode, or fashion: *to reply in a polite way.* **2.** characteristic or habitual manner. **3.** a method, plan, or means for attaining a goal. **4.** a respect or particular: *defective in several ways.* **5.** a direction or vicinity: *There's a drought out our way.* **6.** passage or progress on a course: *Lead the way.* **7.** Often, **ways.** distance: *They've come a long way.* **8.** a path or course: *the shortest way to town.* **9.** a road, passage, or channel (usu. used in combination): *highway; waterway.* **10.** Often, **ways.** a habit or custom. **11.** one's preferred manner of acting or doing: *He always gets his own way.* **12.** condition; state: *He's in a bad way.* **13.** the range or extent of one's experience or notice. **14.** space for passing or advancing: *to clear a way through the crowd.* **15.** a course of life, action, or experience: *the way of transgressors.* **16. the Way,** Jesus. John 14:6. **17.** *Naut.* **a. ways,** two or more ramps that a hull slides along in being launched. **b.** movement or passage through the water. **18.** *Mach.* a longitudinal strip, as in a planer, guiding a moving part along a surface. **—*Idiom.* 19. by the way,** incidentally (used to introduce information that has just come to mind). **20. by way of, a.** by the route of; through; via. **b.** as a method or means of. **21. give way, a.** to withdraw or retreat. **b.** to collapse; break down. **22. give way to, a.** to yield to: *He gave way to their entreaties.* **b.** to lose control of (one's temper, emotions, etc.). **23. go all the way, a.** to do or finish something completely. **b.** *Informal.* to be in complete agreement with someone or something. **24. go out of one's way,** to make an extra or unusual effort, as to do someone a favor. **25. have a way with,** to have a charming, persuasive, or effective manner of dealing with: *He has a way with children; to have a way with words.* **26. in a way,** after a fashion; to some extent. **27. in someone's** or **the way,** forming a hindrance, impediment, or obstruction: *Look out, you're in my way.* **28. lead the way, a.** to go along a course in advance of others, as a guide. **b.** to take the initiative; be first or most prominent: *In fashion she has always led the way.* **29. make one's way, a.** to go forward along a course; proceed. **b.** to achieve recognition or success; advance. **30. make way, a.** to remove obstructions to passage. **b.** to relinquish a place or position; stand aside: *Make way for the motorcade.* **31. no way,** *Informal.* not under any circumstances; no: *Apologize? No way!* **32. out of the way, a.** in a state or condition so as not to obstruct or hinder. **b.** dealt with; disposed of. **c.** at a distance from the usual route. **d.** improper; amiss. **e.** extraordinary; unusual. **33. see one's way (clear),** to discern no impediment to doing something: *Can you see your way clear to giving me $100?* **34. under way, a.** in motion; traveling: *The ship is under way.* **b.** proceeding; in progress. **—*Saying.* 35. You can't have it both**

ways, only one alternative is possible regardless of the difficulty of making a choice.

way² (wā), *adv.* **1.** Also, **'way.** away; from this or that place: *Go way.* **2.** to a great degree or at quite a distance; far: *way too heavy; way down the road.*

way•far•er (wā/fâr′ər), *n.* a traveler, esp. on foot.

way•far•ing (wā/fâr′ing), *adj., n.* traveling, esp. on foot.

way•laid (wā/lād′, wā lād′), *v.* pt. and pp. of WAYLAY.

way•lay (wā/lā′, wā lā′), *v.t.,* **-laid, -lay•ing. 1.** to intercept or attack from ambush, as in order to rob, seize, or slay. **2.** to await and accost unexpectedly. **—way/lay′er,** *n.*

Wayne (wān), *n.* **1. Anthony** (*"Mad Anthony"*), 1745–96, American Revolutionary War general. **2. John** (*Marion Michael Morrison*) (*"Duke"*), 1907–79, U.S. film actor.

Way′ of the Cross′, *n.* STATIONS OF THE CROSS.

way′-out′, *adj. Informal.* **1.** advanced in style or technique: *way-out jazz.* **2.** exotic or esoteric in character: *way-out theories on nutrition.*

ways′ and means′, *n.* **1.** legislation and other methods for raising revenue for the use of the government. **2.** methods and means of accomplishing or paying for something.

way•side (wā/sīd′), *n.* **1.** the side of the way; land immediately adjacent to a road, highway, etc.; roadside. **—adj. 2.** located at or along the wayside: *a wayside inn.*

way•ward (wā/wərd), *adj.* **1.** disregarding or rejecting what is right or proper; willful; disobedient: *a wayward son.* **2.** prompted by caprice; capricious: *a wayward impulse.* **3.** changing unpredictably; erratic: *a wayward breeze.* **—way/ward•ly,** *adv.* **—way/ward•ness,** *n.*

Wb, weber.

WC or **wc,** water closet.

we (wē), *pron.pl., poss.* **our** or **ours,** *obj.* **us. 1.** nominative plural of I. **2.** (used to denote oneself and another or others, specifically or generally): *We have two children. We often take good health for granted.* **3.** (used in the predicate following a linking verb): *It is we who should thank you.* **4.** Also called the **royal we.** (used by a sovereign or other high officials and dignitaries in place of *I* in formal speech.) **5.** Also called the **editorial we.** (used by editors, writers, etc., to avoid the personal *I* or to represent a collective viewpoint.) **6.** you (used familiarly, often with mild condescension or sarcasm): *We know we've been naughty, don't we?*

weak (wēk), *adj.* **1.** not strong; liable to give way under pressure or strain; fragile; frail. **2.** lacking in bodily strength or healthy vigor, as from age or sickness; feeble; infirm. **3.** lacking in force, potency, or efficacy; impotent, ineffectual, or inadequate: *weak sunlight; a weak president.* **4.** lacking in rhetorical or creative force or effectiveness: *one of the author's weakest novels.* **5.** lacking in logical or legal force or soundness: *a weak argument.* **6.** deficient in mental power, intelligence, or judgment: *a weak mind.* **7.** not having much moral strength or force of character: *to prove weak under temptation.* **8.** deficient in amount, volume, intensity, etc.; faint; slight: *a weak electrical current; a weak pulse.* **9.** deficient, lacking, or poor in something specified: *I'm weak in spelling.* **10.** deficient in the essential or usual properties or characteristics: *weak tea.* **11.** unstressed, as a syllable, vowel, or word. **12.** (of verbs in Germanic languages) forming the past tense and past participle by the addition of a suffix without change of the root vowel, as *work, worked,* or having a preterit ending in a dental, as *bring, brought.* Compare STRONG (def. 23). **13.** (of Germanic nouns and adjectives) inflected with endings orig. appropriate to stems terminating in *-n,* as the adjective *alte* in German *der alte Mann* (*"the old man"*). **14.** (of wheat or flour) having a low gluten content or having a poor quality of gluten. **15.** characterized by a decline in prices: *a weak stock market.*

weak•en (wē/kən), *v.t., v.i.* to make or become weak or weaker; lessen; diminish. **—weak/en•er,** *n.*

weak′-kneed′, *adj.* yielding readily to opposition, pressure, intimidation, etc.

weak•ling (wēk/ling), *n.* **1.** a person who is physically or morally weak. **—adj. 2.** weak; not strong.

weak•ly (wēk/lē), *adj.,* **-li•er, -li•est,** *adv.* **—adj. 1.** weak or feeble in constitution; not robust; sickly. **—adv. 2.** in a weak manner.

weak′-mind′ed, *adj.* **1.** having or showing a lack of mental firmness; irresolute; vacillating. **2.** feeble-minded; foolish. **—weak′-mind/ed•ly,** *adv.* **—weak′-mind/ed•ness,** *n.*

weak•ness (wēk/nis), *n.* **1.** the state or quality of being weak; lack of strength, firmness, vigor, or the like; feebleness. **2.** an inadequate or defective quality, as in a person's character; slight fault or defect. **3.** a self-indulgent liking or special fondness: *a weakness for the opera.* **4.** an object of such liking or fondness.

weak′ sis′ter, *n.* **1.** a vacillating person; coward. **2.** a part or element that undermines the whole of something; weak link.

weal (wēl), *n.* well-being, prosperity, or happiness: *the public weal.*

wealth (welth), *n.* **1.** a great quantity or store of money, property, or other riches. **2.** plentiful amount; abundance: *a wealth of imagery.* **3.** any or all things with monetary or exchange value. **4.** rich or valuable contents or produce: *the wealth of the soil.* **5.** the state of being rich; prosperity; affluence. **—wealth/less,** *adj.*

wealth•y (wel/thē), *adj.,* **-i•er, -i•est. 1.** having great wealth; rich; affluent. **2.** marked by or suggesting wealth: *wealthy furnishings.* **3.** rich in something stated or implied; abundant. **—wealth/i•ly,** *adv.*

wean (wēn), *v.t.* **1.** to cause (a child or young animal) to lose the need to suckle; accustom to food other than the mother's milk. **2.** to withdraw (a person, the affections, etc.) from some object or practice deemed undesirable: *to wean oneself from rich desserts.*

wean•ling (wēn/ling), *n.* **1.** a child or animal newly weaned. **—adj. 2.** newly weaned.

weap•on (wep/ən), *n.* **1.** any instrument or device used for attack or defense in a fight or in combat. **2.** anything used against an opponent, adversary, or victim: *the weapon of satire.* **3.** any part or organ serving for attack or defense, as claws, horns, teeth, or stings. **—v.t. 4.** to supply or equip with a weapon or weapons. **—weap/oned,** *adj.*

weap•on•ry (wep/ən rē), *n.* **1.** weapons or weaponlike instruments collectively. **2.** the invention and production of weapons.

wear (wâr), *v.,* **wore, worn, wear•ing,** *n.* **—v.t. 1.** to carry or have on the body or about the person as a covering, support, ornament, or the like. **2.** to bear or have in one's aspect or appearance: *to wear a smile.* **3.** to cause to deteriorate, diminish, or waste by some constant or repetitive action: *The waves have worn these rocks.* **4.** to make (a hole, channel, way, etc.) by such action. **5.** to consume gradually by use or any continued process. **6.** to weary; fatigue; exhaust. **7.** to pass (time) gradually or tediously (usu. fol. by *away* or *out*). **8.** *Naut.* to bring (a vessel) on another tack by turning until the wind is on the stern. **—v.i. 9.** to undergo gradual impairment, diminution, reduction, etc., from use, attrition, or other causes. **10.** to retain shape, color, firmness, etc., under continued use or strain: *a strong fabric that will wear.* **11.** (of time) to pass, esp. slowly or tediously (often fol. by *on* or *away*). **12. wear down, a.** to make or become shabbier, smaller, or more aged by wearing. **b.** to make or become weary; tire. **c.** to prevail upon or over by persistence; overcome: *to wear down the opposition.* **13. wear off,** to diminish slowly or gradually or to diminish in effect; disappear: *The drug began to wear off.* **14. wear out, a.** to make or become unfit or useless through hard or extended use: *to wear out clothes.* **b.** to expend, consume, or remove, esp. slowly or gradually. **c.** to exhaust, as by continued strain; weary. **—n. 15.** the act of wearing; use, as of a garment: *articles for winter wear.* **16.** the state of being worn, as on the person. **17.** clothing or other articles for wearing, esp. for a particular function, fashion, or type of person (often used in combination): *sleepwear; sportswear.* **18.** gradual impairment, wasting, diminution, etc., as from use. **19.** the quality of resisting deterioration with use; durability. **—*Idiom.* 20. wear thin, a.** to diminish; weaken. **b.** to become less appealing, interesting, tolerable, etc. **—wear/er,** *n.*

wear•a•ble (wâr/ə bəl), *adj.* **1.** capable of being worn; appropriate, suitable, or ready for wearing. **—n. 2.** Usu., **wearables.** something that may be worn; clothing. **—wear/a•bil/i•ty,** *n.*

wear′ and tear′, (târ), *n.* damage or deterioration resulting from ordinary use; normal depreciation.

wear•ing (wâr/ing), *adj.* **1.** causing or producing wear; eroding or wasting. **2.** wearying or exhausting: *a wearing task.* **3.** relating to or made for wear. **—wear/ing•ly,** *adv.*

wea•ri•some (wēr/ē sam), *adj.* **1.** causing weariness; fatiguing. **2.** tiresome; tedious. **—wea/ri•some•ly,** *adv.*

wea•ry (wēr/ē), *adj.,* **-ri•er, -ri•est,** *v.,* **-ried, -ry•ing. —adj. 1.** physically or mentally exhausted; fatigued; tired. **2.** characterized by or causing fatigue: *a weary journey.* **3.** impatient or dissatisfied with something (often fol. by *of*): *weary of excuses.* **4.** characterized by or causing impatience or dissatisfaction; tedious; irksome: *a weary wait.* **—v.t., v.i. 5.** to make or become weary; fatigue or tire. **6.** to make or grow impatient or dissatisfied with something (often fol. by *of*): *He wearied of living in hotel rooms.* **—wea/ri•ly,** *adv.* **—wea/ri•ness,** *n.*

wea•sel (wē/zəl), *n., pl.* **-sels,** (*esp. collectively*) **-sel,** *v.,* **-seled, -sel•ing. —n. 1.** any small carnivore of the genus *Mustela,* of the family Mustelidae, having a long, slender body and feeding chiefly on small rodents and birds: includes ferrets, stoats, minks, and ermines. **2.** any of various similar carnivores of the family Mustelidae. **3.** a cunning, sneaky person. **—v.i. 4.** to evade an obligation, duty, or the like; renege (often fol. by *out*). **5.** to use weasel words; be ambiguous; mislead. **—wea/sel•ly,** *adj.*

weasel (def. 1), *Mustela frenata,*
head and body 10 in. (25 cm);
tail 5 in. (13 cm)

wea/sel word/, *n.* a word used to avoid stating something forthrightly or directly; a word that makes one's views misleading or confusing. **—wea/sel-word/ed,** *adj.*

weath•er (weth/ər), *n.* **1.** the state of the atmosphere with respect to wind, temperature, cloudiness, moisture, pressure, etc. **2.** a strong wind or storm, or strong winds and storms collectively. **3.** a report on the weather broadcast on radio or television. **4.** Usu., **weathers.** changes or vicissitudes in one's lot or fortunes. **—v.t. 5.** to dry, season, or otherwise affect by exposure to the air or atmosphere. **6.** to discolor, disintegrate, or affect injuriously, as by the effects of weather. **7.** to bear up against and come safely through (a storm, danger, trouble, etc.). **8.** to cause (a roof, sill, etc.) to slope, so as to shed water. —*v.i.* **9.** to undergo change, esp. discoloration or disintegration, as the result of exposure to atmospheric conditions. **10.** to endure or resist exposure to the weather. **11.** to go or come safely through a storm, danger, trouble, etc. (usu. fol. by *through*). —**Idiom.** **12. under the weather,** not feeling well; somewhat ill. —**weath′er•er,** *n.*

weath•er•a•bil•i•ty (weᵗʰ′ər ə bil′i tē) *n.* the property, as of a material, of tolerating the effects of exposure to the weather.

weath′er-beat′en, *adj.* **1.** worn or damaged as a result of exposure to the weather. **2.** tanned, hardened, or otherwise affected by exposure to weather: *a weather-beaten face.*

weath•er•cast (weᵗʰ′ər kast′, -käst′) *n.* a forecast of weather conditions, esp. on radio or television. —**weath′er•cast′er,** *n.* —**weath′er•cast′ing,** *n.*

weath•er•cock (weᵗʰ′ər kok′) *n.* **1.** a weather vane with the figure of a rooster on it. **2.** (loosely) any weather vane. **3.** a person who readily adopts the latest fads, opinions, etc.

weath•ered (weᵗʰ′ərd) *adj.* **1.** seasoned or otherwise affected by exposure to the weather. **2.** (of wood) artificially treated to seem discolored or stained by the action of air, rain, etc. **3.** made sloping or inclined, as a windowsill, to prevent the lodging of water.

weath′er eye′, *n.* **1.** sensitivity and alertness to signs of change in the weather. **2.** a steady and astute watchfulness, esp. alertness to change.

weath•er•glass (weᵗʰ′ər glas′, -gläs′) *n.* any of various instruments, as a barometer, designed to indicate the state of the atmosphere.

weath•er•ing (weᵗʰ′ər ing) *n.* the process by which various natural agents, as wind and water, act upon exposed rock, causing it to disintegrate to sand and soil.

weath•er•ize (weᵗʰ′ə rīz′) *v.t.,* **-ized, -iz•ing.** to make (a house or other building) secure against cold or stormy weather, as by adding insulation and storm windows. —**weath′er•i•za′tion,** *n.*

weath•er•man (weᵗʰ′ər man′) *n., pl.* **-men.** a meteorologist or weathercaster.

weath′er map′, *n.* a map or chart showing weather conditions over a wide area at a particular time.

weath•er•per•son (weᵗʰ′ər pûr′sən) *n.* a meteorologist or weathercaster.

weath•er•proof (weᵗʰ′ər prōōf′) *adj.* **1.** able to withstand exposure to all kinds of weather. —*v.t.* **2.** to make weatherproof.

weath′er sta′tion, *n.* an installation equipped and used for meteorological observation.

weath•er•strip or **weath′er strip′,** *n.* a narrow strip of metal, wood, rubber, or the like placed between a door or window sash and its frame to exclude rain, wind, etc. —**weath′er-strip′,** *v.t.,* **-stripped, -strip•ping.**

weath′er•strip′ping or **weath′er strip′ping,** *n.* **1.** WEATHERSTRIP. **2.** weatherstrips collectively.

weath•er•tight (weᵗʰ′ər tīt′) *adj.* secure against wind, rain, etc.

weath′er vane′ or **weath′er•vane′,** *n.* a device to which a freely rotating pointer is attached, for indicating the direction of the wind.

weave (wēv) *v.,* **wove** or (*esp. for 7, 9*) **weaved, wo•ven** or **wove, weav•ing,** *n.* —*v.t.* **1.** to interlace (threads, yarns, fibrous material, etc.) so as to form a fabric or material. **2.** to form by such interlacing: *to weave a basket.* **3.** (of a spider or larva) to spin (a web or cocoon). **4.** to form by combining various elements or details into a connected whole: *to weave a tale.* **5.** to introduce as an element into a connected whole (usu. fol. by *in* or *into*). **6.** to combine (two or more things) to form a whole. **7.** to make or move by winding or zigzagging, esp. to avoid obstructions: *to weave one's way across a crowded room.* —*v.i.* **8.** to form or construct something by interlacing materials or combining elements. **9.** to move or proceed in a winding course or from side to side. —*n.* **10.** a pattern or method for interlacing yarns.

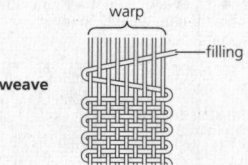

weave — warp, filling

weav•er (wē′vər) *n.* **1.** a person who weaves. **2.** a person whose occupation is weaving. **3.** Also called **weav′er•bird′** (-bûrd′). any of numerous finchlike African and Asian birds of the family Ploceidae, noted for their elaborately woven nests and colonial habits.

web (web) *n., v.,* **webbed, web•bing.** —*n.* **1.** something formed by or as if by weaving or interweaving. **2.** a woven, silky network spun by spiders and the larvae of some insects; cobweb. **3. a.** a woven fabric, esp. a whole piece of cloth in the course of being woven or after it comes from the loom. **b.** the flat woven strip, without pile, often found at one or both ends of an Oriental rug. **4.** something interlaced or latticelike: *a web of branches.* **5.** an intricate set or pattern of circumstances, facts, etc.: *a web of evidence; the web of life.* **6.** something that snares or entangles; a trap. **7.** WEBBING (def. 1). **8.** a membrane connecting the

digits of an animal, as the toes of aquatic birds. **9.** the series of barbs on each side of the shaft of a feather. **10.** a broad section connecting the flanges of a metal beam, rail, or truss. **11.** an arm of a crank, usu. one of a pair, holding one end of a crankpin at its outer end. **12.** *Archit.* (in a vault) any surface framed by ribbing. **13.** a large roll of paper, as for continuous feeding of a web press. **14.** a network of interlinked stations, services, communications, etc., covering a region or country. —*v.t.* **15.** to cover with or as if with a web; envelop. **16.** to ensnare or entrap. —*v.i.* **17.** to make or form a web. —**web′like′,** *adj.*

Webb (web) *n.* **George,** 1803–87, U.S. musician.

webbed (webd) *adj.* **1.** having the fingers or toes connected by a membrane: *a webbed foot.* **2.** connected by a web, as the fingers or toes. **3.** formed like or with a web: *a webbed roof.*

web•bing (web′ing) *n.* **1.** a strong, woven material of hemp, cotton, or jute, in bands of various widths, used for belts, carrying straps, harness, etc., or for support under upholstery or springs. **2.** the membrane of a web-footed animal. **3.** something resembling this, as the material connecting the thumb and forefinger in a baseball glove. **4.** any interlaced or latticelike material or part, as the face of a tennis racket.

web•er (web′ər, vā′bər) *n.* the SI unit of magnetic flux and magnetic pole strength, equal to a flux that produces an electromotive force of one volt in a single turn of wire when the flux is uniformly reduced to zero in a period of one second; 10^8 maxwells. *Abbr.:* Wb [after W. E. WEBER]

We•ber (vā′bər *for 1–3, 5;* web′ər *for 4*) *n.* **1. Ernst Heinrich,** 1795–1878, German physiologist. **2. Baron Karl Maria (Friedrich Ernst) von,** 1786–1826, German composer. **3. Max,** 1864–1920, German sociologist and political economist. **4. Max,** 1881–1961, U.S. painter, born in Russia. **5. Wilhelm Eduard,** 1804–91, German physicist (brother of E. H.).

web•foot (web′fŏŏt′) *n., pl.* **-feet. 1.** a foot with the toes joined by a web. **2.** an animal with webbed feet. —**web′-foot′ed,** *adj.*

Web′ page′, *n.* a single, usu. hypertext document on the World Wide Web that can incorporate text, graphics, sounds, etc.

Web′ site′, *n.* a connected group of pages on the World Wide Web regarded as a single entity, usu. maintained by one person or organization and devoted to one single topic or several closely related topics.

Web•ster (web′stər) *n.* **1. Daniel,** 1782–1852, U.S. statesman and orator. **2. John,** c1580–1625?, English dramatist. **3. Joseph P(hilbrick),** 1819–75, U.S. musician and hymn writer. **4. Noah,** 1758–1843, U.S. lexicographer and essayist. **5.** *Informal.* Also, **Web′ster's.** a dictionary of the English language. —**Web•ste′ri•an** (-stĕr′ē ən), *adj.*

Web′ster-Ash′bur•ton Trea′ty (ash′bûr tn) *n.* an agreement between the U.S. and England (1842) defining the boundary between British and American territory from Maine to present-day Minnesota. [named after D. WEBSTER and A. Baring, 1st Baron *Ashburton,* who negotiated it]

web′-toed′, *adj.* having webbed toes; web-footed.

wed (wed) *v.,* **wed•ded** or **wed, wed•ding.** —*v.t.* **1.** to marry (another person) in a formal ceremony; take as one's husband or wife. **2.** to unite (a couple) in marriage or wedlock; marry. **3.** to bind; attach firmly: *to wed oneself to the cause of the poor.* **4.** to blend; unite. —*v.i.* **5.** to contract marriage; marry. **6.** to become united or to blend.

we'd (wēd) contraction of *we had, we should,* or *we would.*

wed•ding (wed′ing) *n.* **1.** the act or ceremony of marrying; marriage; nuptials. **2.** the anniversary of a marriage, or its celebration: *They observed their silver wedding.* **3.** an act of blending or joining. —*adj.* **4.** of or pertaining to a wedding: *a wedding cake; one's wedding day.*

Wed′ding Feast′, The, a parable of Jesus. Matt. 22:1–14.

wed′ding march′, *n.* a stately march played to accompany the bridal procession during a wedding.

wed′ding ring′, *n.* **1.** a ring, usu. of precious metal, given by the groom to the bride during a marriage ceremony. **2.** a ring similarly given by the bride to the groom. Also called **wed′ding band′.**

wedge (wej) *n., v.,* **wedged, wedg•ing.** —*n.* **1.** a piece of hard material with two principal faces meeting in a sharply acute angle, for raising, holding, or splitting objects by applying a pounding or driving force. Compare MACHINE (def. 2b). **2.** a piece of anything of like shape: *a wedge of pie.* **3.** a cuneiform character or stroke of this shape. **4.** something that serves to part, split, divide, etc.: *The quarrel drove a wedge between them.* **5.** an iron-headed golf club with a nearly horizontal face, used for lofting the ball. **6.** a wedge heel or shoe with such a heel. **7.** a V-shaped formation of infantry or cavalry, with the point directed toward the enemy. **8.** FLYING WEDGE. **9.** *Chiefly Coastal Connecticut and Rhode Island.* a hero sandwich. —*v.t.* **10.** to separate or split with or as if with a wedge (often fol. by *open, apart,* etc.). **11.** to insert or fix with a wedge. **12.** to pack or fix tightly; stuff. **13.** to thrust, drive, fix, etc., like a wedge. **14.** to pound (clay) in order to remove air bubbles. —*v.i.* **15.** to force a way like a wedge (usu. fol. by *in, into, through,* etc.). —**wedge′like′,** *adj.*

wedged (wejd) *adj.* having the shape of a wedge.

wedge′ is′sue, *n.* an issue that divides or causes conflict in an otherwise unified group: *Abortion is a wedge issue for the Republican Party.*

Wedg•wood (wej′wŏŏd′) *Trademark.* a ceramic ware, typically bluegray with raised white decoration, made by Josiah Wedgwood (1730–95), English potter, and his successors.

wed•lock (wed′lok′) *n.* the state of marriage; matrimony: *joined in wedlock; born out of wedlock.*

Wednes•day (wenz′dā, -dē), *n.* the fourth day of the week, following Tuesday.

wee (wē), *adj.,* **we•er, we•est. 1.** little; very small; tiny. **2.** very early: *the wee hours of the morning.*

weed[1] (wēd), *n.* **1.** an undesirable plant growing wild, esp. one growing on cultivated ground to the disadvantage of a crop, lawn, or flower bed. **2.** something unattractive, wretched, or useless, esp. a horse unfit for breeding purposes. **3.** *Informal.* a cigarette or cigar. **4. the weed,** *Informal.* tobacco. **—*v.t.* 5.** to free from weeds or troublesome plants: *to weed a garden.* **6.** to root out or remove (a weed or weeds), as from a garden (often fol. by *out*). **7.** to remove as being undesirable, inefficient, or superfluous (often fol. by *out*). **8.** to rid (something) of undesirable or superfluous elements. **—*v.i.* 9.** to remove weeds or the like. —**weed′less,** *adj.* —**weed′like′,** *adj.*

weed[2] (wēd), *n.* **1. weeds,** mourning garments: *widow's weeds.* **2.** a mourning band of black crepe or cloth, as worn on a coat sleeve. **3.** Often, **weeds.** *Archaic.* **a.** a garment: *clad in rustic weeds.* **b.** clothing.

weed•kill•er (wēd′kil′ər), *n.* a herbicide.

weed•y (wē′dē), *adj.,* **weed•i•er, weed•i•est. 1.** consisting of, abounding in, or pertaining to weeds. **2.** (of a plant, flower, etc.) growing poorly or in a straggling manner. **3.** (of a person or animal) scrawny or ungainly. —**weed′i•ly,** *adv.* —**weed′i•ness,** *n.*

week (wēk), *n.* **1.** a period of seven successive days, usu. understood as beginning with Sunday and ending with Saturday. **2.** a period of seven successive days that begins with or includes an indicated day: *the week of June 3; Christmas week.* **3.** (*often cap.*) a period of seven successive days devoted to celebrating or honoring something: *National Book Week.* **4.** the working portion of the seven-day period; workweek: *a 35-hour week.* **—*adv.* 5.** seven days before or after a specified day: *I shall come Tuesday week.*

week•day (wēk′dā′), *n.* **1.** any day of the week except Sunday or, often, Saturday and Sunday. **—*adj.* 2.** of, on, or for a weekday: *weekday occupations.*

week•days (wēk′dāz′), *adv.* every day, esp. Monday through Friday, during the workweek.

week•end (wēk′end′, -end′), *n.* **1.** the end of a week, esp. the period of time between Friday evening and Monday morning. **2.** this period as extended by one or more days immediately before or after: *a three-day holiday weekend.* **3.** any two-day period taken or given regularly as a weekly rest period from one's work. **—*adj.* 4.** of, for, or on a weekend. **—*v.i.* 5.** to pass the weekend.

week′end bag′, *n.* WEEKENDER (def. 3).

week•end•er (wēk′en′dər), *n.* **1.** a person who goes on a weekend vacation. **2.** a weekend guest. **3.** a traveling bag large enough to carry the clothing and personal items needed for a weekend trip.

week•ends (wēk′endz′), *adv.* every weekend; on weekends.

week•ly (wēk′lē), *adj., adv., n., pl.* **-lies. —*adj.* 1.** done, happening, appearing, etc., once a week, or every week. **2.** computed or determined by the week: *the weekly rate.* **3.** of or pertaining to a week or the working days in a week. **—*adv.* 4.** once a week; by the week. **—*n.* 5.** a publication appearing once a week.

week•night (wēk′nīt′), *n.* **1.** any night of the week except Sunday or, often, except Saturday and Sunday. **—*adj.* 2.** Also, **week′night′ly.** of, on, or for a weeknight.

wee•nie or **wie•nie** (wē′nē), *n.* WIENER.

wee•ny (wē′nē), *adj.,* **-ni•er, -ni•est.** *Informal.* tiny; small.

weep (wēp), *v.,* **wept, weep•ing,** *n.* **—*v.i.* 1.** to express an overpowering emotion, esp. grief, by shedding tears; shed tears; cry. **2.** to let fall drops of water or other liquid; drip; leak. **3.** to exude water or liquid, as a plant stem or a sore. **—*v.t.* 4.** to weep for (someone or something); mourn with tears; bewail: *He wept his dead brother.* **5.** to shed (tears); pour forth in weeping. **6.** to let fall or give forth in drops: *trees weeping an odorous gum.* **7.** to pass, bring, put, etc., to or into a specified condition with the shedding of tears (usu. fol. by *away, out,* etc.). **—*n.* 8.** weeping, or a fit of weeping. **9.** the exudation of water or liquid.

weep•ing (wē′ping), *adj.* **1.** expressing grief or other overwhelming emotion by shedding tears. **2.** marked by tears; tearful; weepy: *a weeping fit.* **3.** dripping or oozing liquid. **4.** (of trees, shrubs, etc.) having slender, drooping branches. —**weep′ing•ly,** *adv.*

weep′ing wil′low, *n.* an Asian willow, *Salix babylonica,* characterized by the drooping habit of its branches.

weep•y (wē′pē), *adj.,* **weep•i•er, weep•i•est. 1.** easily moved to tears; tearful; lachrymose. **2.** marked or accompanied by weeping: *a weepy account.* **3.** tending to cause weeping; sad: *a weepy novel.* **4.** exuding water or other moisture. —**weep′i•ness,** *n.*

wee•vil (wē′vəl), *n.* any of numerous beetles of the family Curculionidae, having the head prolonged into a snout, and destructive to nuts, grain, fruit, etc. Also called **snout beetle.**

weft (weft), *n.* **1.** FILLING (def. 4). **2.** a woven fabric or garment.

wei•ge•la (wī gē′lə, -jē′-, wī′gə lə), *n., pl.* **-las.** any of various shrubby, E Asian plants belonging to the genus *Weigela,* of the honeysuckle family, having funnel-shaped white, pink, or crimson flowers.

weigh (wā), *v.t.* **1.** to determine or ascertain the force that gravitation exerts upon (a person or thing) by use of a balance, scale, or other mechanical device. **2.** to measure or apportion (a certain quantity of something) according to weight (usu. fol. by *out*): *weighed out five pounds of sugar.* **3.** to make heavy; increase the weight or bulk of; weight. **4.** to evaluate in the mind; consider carefully in order to reach an opinion, decision, or choice: *Let's weigh the facts.* **—*v.i.* 5.** to have weight or a specified amount of weight: *to weigh less; to weigh a ton.* **6.** to have importance, moment, or consequence. **7.** to bear down as a weight or burden (usu. fol. by *on* or *upon*). **8.** to consider carefully or judicially: *to weigh well before deciding.* **9. weigh down, a.** to cause to become bowed under a weight. **b.** to lower the spirits of; burden; depress. **10. weigh in, a.** (of a boxer or wrestler) to be weighed by a medical examiner on the day of a bout. **b.** (of a jockey) to be weighed with the saddle and weights after a race. **c.** to be of the weight determined by such a weighing. **11. weigh out,** (of a jockey) **a.** to be weighed with the saddle and weights before a race. **b.** to be of the weight determined by such a weighing. **—*Idiom.* 12. weigh anchor,** to heave up a ship's anchor in preparation for getting under way. —**weigh′a•ble,** *adj.*

weight (wāt), *n., v.,* **weight•ed, weight•ing. —*n.* 1.** the amount or quantity of heaviness or mass; amount a thing weighs. **2.** the force that gravitation exerts upon a body, equal to the mass of the body times the local acceleration of gravity. **3.** a system of units for expressing heaviness or mass: *avoirdupois weight.* **4.** a unit of heaviness or mass, as the pound. **5.** a body of determinate mass, as of metal, for using on a balance or scale in weighing objects, substances, etc. **6.** a specific quantity of a substance that is determined by weighing or that weighs a fixed amount. **7.** any heavy load, mass, or object. **8.** excess fat; corpulence. **9.** an object used or useful solely because of its heaviness. **10.** a mental or moral burden, as of care, sorrow, or responsibility. **11.** importance, moment, consequence, or effective influence. **12. a.** a barbell, dumbbell, or similar heavy apparatus lifted or held for exercise, body building, or in athletic competition. **b.** a replaceable metal disk of specific heaviness fastened to each end of a barbell. **13.** a measure of the relative importance of an item in a statistical population. **14.** (of clothing, textiles, etc.) relative heaviness or thickness as related to general or seasonal use (often used in combination): *a winter-weight jacket.* **15.** (of type) the degree of blackness or boldness. **16.** (esp. in boxing) a division or class to which a contestant or competitor belongs according to body weight. **17.** the total amount the jockey, saddle, and leads must weigh on a racehorse during a race. **—*v.t.* 18.** to add weight to; load with additional weight. **19.** to load (fabrics, threads, etc.) with mineral or other matter to increase the weight or bulk. **20.** to burden with or as if with weight (often fol. by *down*). **21.** to give a statistical weight to. **22.** to bias or slant toward a particular goal or direction; manipulate. **23.** to assign (a racehorse) a specific weight to carry in a race. **—*Idiom.* 24. carry weight,** to have importance or significance; influence. **25. pull one's (own) weight,** to contribute one's share of work to a project or job. **26. throw one's weight around** or **about,** to use one's power and influence, esp. improperly for personal gain.

weight•ed (wā′tid), *adj.* **1.** having additional weight. **2.** loaded or burdened: *weighted with sorrow.* **3.** adjusted to a representative value, as a statistic. —**weight′ed•ly,** *adv.* —**weight′ed•ness,** *n.*

weight•less (wāt′lis), *adj.* being without apparent weight, as a freely falling body. —**weight′less•ly,** *adv.* —**weight′less•ness,** *n.*

weight•lift•ing (wāt′lif′ting), *n.* the act, art, or sport of lifting barbells of given weights in a prescribed manner, as a conditioning exercise or in a competitive event. —**weight′lift′er,** *n.*

weight•y (wā′tē), *adj.,* **weight•i•er, weight•i•est. 1.** having considerable weight; heavy; ponderous. **2.** burdensome or troublesome. **3.** important or momentous: *weighty negotiations.* **4.** having or exerting influence, power, etc. —**weight′i•ly,** *adv.* —**weight′i•ness,** *n.*

Wei•mar (vī′mär, wī′-), *n.* a city in Thuringia, in central Germany. 64,000. —**Wei•mar′i•an,** *adj., n.*

Wei′mar Repub′lic, *n.* the German republic (1919–33), founded at Weimar.

weir (wēr), *n.* **1.** a small dam in a river or stream. **2.** a fence, as of brush, or a net set in a stream, channel, etc., for catching fish.

weird (wērd), *adj.* **1.** involving or suggesting the supernatural; unearthly or uncanny: *a weird sound.* **2.** strange; unusual; peculiar: *a weird costume.* —**weird′ly,** *adv.* —**weird′ness,** *n.*

weird•o (wēr′dō), *n., pl.* **weird•os.** *Slang.* an odd, or abnormal person.

Weiss•mul•ler (wīs′mul′ər), *n.* **Peter John** (*Johnny*), 1904–84, U.S. swimmer and film actor.

Weiz•mann (vīts′män′, wīts′mən), *n.* **Cha•im** (KHī′im), 1874–1952, 1st president of Israel 1948–52, born in Russia.

wel•come (wel′kəm), *interj., n., v.,* **-comed, -com•ing,** *adj.* **—*interj.* 1.** (a word of kindly greeting, as to one whose arrival gives pleasure): *Welcome, stranger!* **—*n.* 2.** a kindly greeting or reception: *to give someone a warm welcome.* **—*v.t.* 3.** to greet the arrival of (a person, guests, etc.) with pleasure or kindly courtesy. **4.** to receive or accept with pleasure: *to welcome a change.* **5.** to meet, accept, or receive (an action, challenge, person, etc.) in a specified, esp. unfriendly, manner: *They welcomed him with hisses and catcalls.* **—*adj.* 6.** gladly received: *a welcome visitor.* **7.** agreeable: *a welcome rest.* **8.** given permission or consent: *She is welcome to try it.* **9.** without obligation for the courtesy or favor received (used as a conventional response to expressions of thanks): *You're quite welcome.* **—*Idiom.* 10. wear out one's welcome,** to make one's presence undesirable, as by visiting too often or by misbehaving. —**wel′come•ly,** *adv.* —**wel′come•ness,** *n.* —**wel′com•er,** *n.* **—Usage.** "You're welcome," the customary polite response to "thank you," has been falling out of favor in recent years. More common replies are now an emphatic "Thank *you,*" or an outright denial of the favor such as "It's nothing," or in especially informal use, "No problem." The decline of "You're welcome" is apparently the result of a courteous desire on the part of the thanked person to minimize the importance of the favor done.

weld (weld), *v.t.* **1.** to unite or fuse (pieces, as of metal or plastic) by hammering, compressing, or the like, esp. after rendering soft or pasty by heat. **2.** to bring into complete union, harmony, agreement, etc. —*v.i.* **3.** to undergo welding; be capable of being welded: *a metal that welds easily.* —*n.* **4.** a welded junction or joint. **5.** the act of welding or the state of being welded. —**weld′a•ble,** *adj.* —**weld′a•bil′i•ty,** *n.* —**weld′er, weld′or,** *n.*

wel•fare (wel′fâr′), *n.* **1.** the good fortune, health, happiness, prosperity, etc., of a person, group, or organization; well-being. **2.** WELFARE WORK. **3.** financial or other assistance given to those in poverty or need; public relief. —*Idiom.* **4. on welfare,** receiving financial or other assistance from the government because of poverty or need.

wel′fare state′, *n.* a state in which the welfare of the people in such matters as social security, health, education, housing, and working conditions is the responsibility of the government. —**wel′fare stat′ism,** *n.*

wel′fare work′, *n.* the efforts or programs of a community or a public or private agency to improve the living conditions of needy persons. —**wel′fare work′er,** *n.*

well[1] (wel), *adv., adj., compar.* **bet•ter,** *superl.* **best,** *interj., n.* —*adv.* **1.** in a good or satisfactory manner: *Our plans are going well.* **2.** thoroughly, carefully, or soundly: *Shake well before using.* **3.** in a moral or proper manner: *to behave well.* **4.** commendably, meritoriously, or excellently. **5.** with propriety, justice, or reason: *I could not well refuse.* **6.** with favor or approval: *to think well of someone.* **7.** comfortably or prosperously: *to live well.* **8.** to a considerable extent or degree. **9.** with great or intimate knowledge: *to know a person well.* **10.** certainly; without doubt: *I cry easily, as you well know.* **11.** with good nature; without rancor: *He took the joke well.* —*adj.* **12.** in good health; sound in body and mind: *He is not a well man.* **13.** satisfactory, pleasing, or good: *All is well with us.* **14.** proper, fitting, or gratifying: *It is well that you didn't go.* **15.** in a satisfactory position; well-off: *I am very well as I am.* —*interj.* **16.** (used to express surprise, reproof, etc.): *Well! There's no need to shout.* **17.** (used to introduce a sentence, resume a conversation, etc.): *Well, it's time to go home.* —*n.* **18.** well-being; good fortune; success. —*Idiom.* **19. as well,** in addition; also; too. **20. as well as,** as much or as truly as; equally as: *witty as well as kind.* **21. leave well enough alone,** to avoid changing something that is satisfactory. —**well′ness,** *n.*

well[2] (wel), *n.* **1.** a hole drilled or bored into the earth to obtain water, petroleum, natural gas, brine, or sulfur. **2.** a spring or natural source of water. **3.** an apparent reservoir or a source of human feelings, emotions, energy, etc.: *a well of compassion.* **4.** a container, receptacle, or reservoir for a liquid, as ink. **5.** any sunken or deep enclosed space, as a shaft for air or light, stairs, or an elevator, extending vertically through the floors of a building. **6.** a hollow compartment, recessed area, or depression for holding a specific item or items, as fish in the bottom of a boat or the retracted wheels of an airplane in flight. **7.** *Naut.* a part of a weather deck between two superstructures, extending from one side of a vessel to the other. —*v.i.* **8.** to rise, spring, or gush, as water, from the earth or some other source (often fol. by *up, out,* or *forth*): *Tears welled up in my eyes.* —*v.t.* **9.** to send welling up or forth: *a fountain welling its water.* —*adj.* **10.** like, of, resembling, from, or used in connection with a well.

we'll (wēl; *unstressed* wil), contraction of *we shall* or *we will.*

well′-ad•vised′, *adj.* **1.** acting with caution, care, or wisdom: *well-advised to sell the stock now.* **2.** based on or showing wise consideration: *a well-advised delay.*

well′-ap•point′ed, *adj.* attractively or conveniently equipped, arranged, or furnished: *a well-appointed room.*

well′-bal′anced, *adj.* **1.** rightly balanced, adjusted, or regulated: *a well-balanced diet.* **2.** sensible; sane: *a well-balanced mind.*

well′-be′ing, *n.* a good or satisfactory condition of existence; a state characterized by health, happiness, and prosperity; welfare.

well′-bred′, *adj.* **1.** showing good breeding, as in behavior or manners. **2.** (of animals) of a desirable breed or pedigree.

well′-de•fined′, *adj.* **1.** sharply or clearly stated, outlined, described, etc.: *a well-defined character; a well-defined boundary.*

well′-dis•posed′, *adj.* **1.** feeling favorable, sympathetic, or kind: *well-disposed toward our plan.* **2.** of pleasant disposition.

well′-done′, *adj.* **1.** performed accurately and diligently; executed with skill and efficiency. **2.** (of meat) thoroughly cooked, esp. until all redness is gone.

Welles (welz), *n.* **(George) Orson,** 1915–85, U.S. actor, director, and producer.

well′-fed′, *adj.* fat; plump.

well′-formed′, *adj.* rightly or pleasingly formed: *a well-formed contour.*

well′-found′ed, *adj.* having a foundation in fact; based on good reasons, information, etc.

well′-groomed′, *adj.* **1.** having the hair, skin, etc., well cared for; well-dressed, clean, and neat: *a well-groomed young man.* **2.** (of an animal) tended, cleaned, combed, etc., with great care. **3.** carefully cared for; neat; tidy: *a well-groomed lawn.*

well′-ground′ed, *adj.* **1.** based on good reasons; well-founded. **2.** well or thoroughly instructed in the basic principles of a subject.

well′-han′dled, *adj.* **1.** managed, directed, or treated with skill, efficiency, taste, etc. **2.** having been handled or used much: *a sale of well-handled goods.*

well•head (wel′hed′), *n.* **1.** a fountainhead; source. **2.** Also, **well-house.** a shelter for a well. **3.** the top of the opening of a well.

well′-heeled′, *adj.* well-off; rich.

well′-in•formed′, *adj.* having extensive knowledge, as in one particular subject or in a variety of subjects.

Wel•ling•ton (wel′ing tan), *n.* **1. 1st Duke of** (*Arthur Wellesley*), 1769–1852, British general and statesman, born in Ireland: prime minister 1828–30. **2.** the capital of New Zealand, on S North Island. 325,200. **3.** (*sometimes l.c.*) WELLINGTON BOOT.

Wel′lington (or **wel′lington**) **boot′,** *n.* **1.** a leather boot with the front part of the top extending above the knee. **2.** a rubber or water-repellent leather boot usu. extending to the knee.

well′-in•ten′tioned, *adj.* well-meaning.

well′-known′, *adj.* **1.** clearly, fully, or thoroughly known: *to hear the well-known voice of a loved one.* **2.** generally or widely known; famous: *a well-known painting.*

well′-made′, *adj.* **1.** skillfully built or put together. **2.** characterized by a carefully constructed or contrived plot: *a well-made play.*

well′-man′nered, *adj.* polite; courteous.

well′-mean′ing, *adj.* **1.** meaning or intending well; having good intentions: *a well-meaning but tactless person.* **2.** Also, **well′-meant′.** proceeding from good intentions: *well-meaning words.*

well•ness (wel′nis), *n.* **1.** the fact or condition of being in maximum physical and mental health. **2.** the quality or state of being healthy, esp. as the result of deliberate effort; health.

well′-nigh′, *adv.* very nearly; almost: *It's well-nigh bedtime.*

well′-off′, *adj.* **1.** well-to-do; prosperous. **2.** in a satisfactory, favorable, or good position or condition.

well′-or′dered, *adj.* arranged, planned, or occurring in a desirable way, sequence, etc.

well′-read′, *adj.* having read extensively (sometimes fol. by *in*): *well-read in oceanography.*

well′-round′ed, *adj.* **1.** having desirably varied abilities or attainments. **2.** desirably varied: *a well-rounded curriculum.* **3.** fully developed; well-balanced.

Wells (welz), *n.* **H(erbert) G(eorge),** 1866–1946, English novelist and historian.

well′-spo′ken, *adj.* **1.** speaking well, fittingly, or pleasingly: *a well-spoken diplomat.* **2.** spoken in an apt, fitting, or pleasing manner: *a few well-spoken words on civic pride.*

well•spring (wel′spring′), *n.* **1.** the head or source of a spring, stream, river, or the like; fountainhead. **2.** a continuous, seemingly inexhaustible source or supply of something.

well′-tak′en, *adj.* soundly logical; worthy of consideration.

well′-thought′-of′, *adj.* highly esteemed; of good repute.

well′-timed′, *adj.* fittingly or appropriately timed; opportune; timely: *a well-timed request for a promotion.*

well′-to-do′, *adj.* prosperous; rich; affluent.

well′-turned′, *adj.* **1.** gracefully shaped: *a well-turned ankle.* **2.** gracefully and concisely expressed: *a well-turned phrase.* **3.** turned or contoured skillfully or smoothly: *a well-turned archway.*

well′-wish′er, *n.* a person who wishes well to another person, a cause, etc. —**well′-wish′ing,** *adj., n.*

well′-worn′, *adj.* **1.** showing the effects of extensive use or wear: *well-worn carpets.* **2.** trite; hackneyed; stale: *a well-worn saying.* **3.** becomingly worn or borne: *a well-worn modesty.*

welsh (welsh, welch) also **welch,** *v.i. Sometimes Offensive.* **1.** to fail to pay what is owed (often fol. by *on*): *welshed on his gambling debts.* **2.** to go back on one's word (often fol. by *on*): *to welsh on a promise.*

Welsh (welsh, welch), *n.* **1.** (*used with a pl. v.*) **a.** the inhabitants of Wales. **b.** natives of Wales or persons of Welsh ancestry living outside Wales. **2.** the Celtic language of Wales, now spoken mainly in the W and N parts. —*adj.* **3.** of or pertaining to Wales, its inhabitants, or the language Welsh.

Welsh′ cor′gi, *n.* either of two Welsh breeds of dogs having short legs, erect ears, and a foxlike head, one breed **(Cardigan)** having slightly rounded ears and a long tail and the other **(Pembroke)** having pointed ears and a short or docked tail.

Welsh′ rab′bit, *n.* a dish of melted cheese, usu. mixed with ale or beer, served over toast. Also called **Welsh′ rare′bit.**

Welsh′ spring′er span′iel, *n.* one of a Welsh breed of springer spaniels having a red and white coat.

Welsh′ ter′rier, *n.* one of a Welsh breed of terriers with a wiry black-and-tan coat, resembling an Airedale but smaller.

welt (welt), *n.* **1.** a ridge or wale on the surface of the body, as from a blow of a stick or whip. **2.** a blow producing such a ridge or wale. **3. a.** a strip, as of leather, to which the edges of the insole and upper of a shoe are attached, the whole then being joined to the outsole. **b.** a strip, usu. of leather, that ornaments a shoe. **4.** a strip of material sewn along a seam, the edge of a garment, etc., for strength or as decoration. —*v.t.* **5.** to beat soundly, as with a stick or whip. **6.** to furnish or supply (a shoe or garment) with a welt or welts; sew a welt on or to.

Welt·an·schau·ung (velt/än/shou/ŏŏng), *n. German.* a comprehensive conception or image of the universe and of humanity's relation to it. [lit., world-view]

wel·ter (wel/tər), *v.i.* **1.** to roll, toss, or heave, as waves or the sea. **2.** to roll, writhe, or tumble about; wallow (often fol. by *about*): *pigs weltering about in the mud.* **3.** to lie bathed in or be drenched in something, esp. blood. **4.** to become deeply or extensively involved, associated, entangled, etc.: *to welter in confusion.* —*n.* **5.** a confused mass; a jumble or muddle. **6.** a state of commotion, turmoil, or upheaval; tumult. **7.** a rolling, tossing, or tumbling about, as or as if by the sea, waves, or wind.

wel·ter·weight (wel/tər wāt/), *n.* a boxer intermediate in weight between a lightweight and a middleweight, esp. a professional boxer weighing up to 147 lb. (67 kg).

Welt·schmerz (velt/shmеRтs/), *n. German.* sorrow that one feels and accepts as one's necessary portion in life. [lit., world-pain]

Wen·ces·laus (wen/sis lôs/), *n.* **1.** 1361–1419, emperor of the Holy Roman Empire 1378–1400; as Wenceslaus IV, king of Bohemia 1378–1419. **2. Saint** ("*Good King Wenceslaus*"), A.D. 903?–c935, duke of Bohemia 928–935. German, **Wenzel.**

wench (wench), *n.* **1.** a girl or young woman. —*v.i.* **2.** to associate, esp. habitually, with promiscuous women. —**wench/er,** *n.*

wend (wend), *v.t.* **1.** to pursue or direct (one's way). —*v.i.* **2.** to proceed or go; travel.

went (went), *v.* pt. of GO¹.

wept (wept), *v.* pt. and pp. of WEEP.

were (wûr; *unstressed* wər), *v.* a 2nd pers. sing. past indic.; 1st, 2nd, and 3rd pers. pl. past indic.; and past subj. of BE.

we're (wēr), contraction of *we are.*

were·n't (wûrnt, wûr/ənt), contraction of *were not.*

were·wolf or **wer·wolf** (wâr/wŏŏlf/, wēr/-, wûr/-), *n., pl.* **-wolves** (-wŏŏlvz/). (in folklore) a person who has assumed the form of a wolf.

Were/ You/ There?/, a traditional American spiritual.

We/ Shall/ Overcome/, a song of the U.S. civil rights movement of the 1960s.

Wes·ley (wes/lē, wez/-), *n.* **1. Charles,** 1707–88, English evangelist and hymnist. **2.** his brother **John,** 1703–91, English theologian and evangelist: founder of Methodism.

Wes·ley·an (wes/lē ən, wez/-), *adj.* **1.** of or pertaining to John Wesley, founder of Methodism. **2.** pertaining to Methodism. —*n.* **3.** a follower of John Wesley. **4.** *Chiefly Brit.* a Methodist. —**Wes/ley·an·ism,** *n.*

west (west), *n.* **1.** a cardinal point of the compass, 90° to the left of north. *Abbr.:* W **2.** the direction in which this point lies. **3.** (*often cap.*) a region or territory situated in this direction. **4. the West, a.** the western part of the world, as distinguished from the East or Orient; the Occident. **b.** the non-Communist countries of Europe and the Americas. **c.** the part of the U.S. west of the Mississippi River. **d.** the part of the U.S. west of the Allegheny Mountains. —*adj.* **5.** directed or proceeding toward the west. **6.** coming from the west: *a west wind.* **7.** lying toward or situated in the west: *the west side.* —*adv.* **8.** to, toward, or in the west: *The car headed west.*

West (west), *n.* **1. Benjamin,** 1738–1820, U.S. painter, in England after 1763. **2. Mae,** 1892?–1980, U.S. actress. **3. Nathanael** (*Nathan Wallenstein Weinstein*), 1902?–40, U.S. novelist. **4. Dame Rebecca** (*Cicily Isabel Fairfield Andrews*), 1892–1983, English novelist, journalist, and critic, born in Ireland.

West. or **west.,** western.

West/ Bank/, *n.* a region in the Middle East, between the W bank of the Jordan River and the E frontier of Israel: occupied in 1967 by Israel; formerly held by Jordan.

West/ Bengal/, *n.* a state in E India: formerly part of the province of Bengal. 54,485,560; 33,805 sq. mi. (87,555 sq. km). *Cap.:* Calcutta.

west·bound (west/bound/), *adj.* proceeding or headed west.

west/ by north/, *n.* a point on the compass 11°15′ north of west. *Abbr.:* WbN

west/ by south/, *n.* a point on the compass 11°15′ south of west. *Abbr.:* WbS

West/ Co·vi/na (kə vē/nə), *n.* a city in SW California, E of Los Angeles. 103,298.

west·er·ly (wes/tər lē), *adj., adv., n., pl.* **-lies.** —*adj.* **1.** moving, directed, or situated toward the west. **2.** (esp. of a wind) coming from the west. —*adv.* **3.** toward the west. **4.** from the west. —*n.* **5.** a wind that blows from the west. **6. westerlies,** (*used with a pl. v.*) any semipermanent belt of westerly winds, esp. those that prevail at latitudes lying between the tropical and polar regions of the earth. —**west/er·li·ness,** *n.*

west·ern (wes/tərn), *adj.* **1.** lying toward or situated in the west. **2.** directed or proceeding toward the west: *a western migration.* **3.** coming or originating from the west, as a wind. **4.** (*often cap.*) of or pertaining to the West in the U.S. **5.** (*usu. cap.*) Occidental. **6.** (*usu. cap.*) of or pertaining to the non-Communist countries of Europe and the Americas. —*n.* **7.** (*often cap.*) a story, movie, or radio or television play about the U.S. West of the 19th century. **8.** a person or thing from a western region or country.

West/ern Church/, *n.* the Roman Catholic Church, sometimes with the Anglican Church, or the Christian churches of the West.

West/ern Hem/isphere, *n.* **1.** the part of the globe west of the Atlantic, including North and South America, their islands, and the surround-

ing waters. **2.** that half of the earth traversed in passing westward from the prime meridian to 180° longitude.

west·ern·ize (wes/tər nīz/), *v.t.* **-ized, -iz·ing.** to influence with or convert to ideas, customs, practices, etc., characteristic of the Occident or of the western U.S. —**west/ern·i·za/tion,** *n.*

west/ern om/elet, *n.* an omelet containing chopped ham, onions, and green peppers.

West/ern Reserve/, *n.* a tract of land in NE Ohio reserved by Connecticut (1786) when its rights to other land in the western U.S. were ceded to the federal government: relinquished in 1800.

West/ern sad/dle, *n.* a heavy saddle having a deep seat, high cantle and pommel, pommel horn, wide leather flaps for protecting the rider's legs, and little padding.

West/ern Samo/a, *n.* an independent country in the S Pacific, comprising the W part of Samoa: formerly a trust territory of New Zealand. 219,509; 1093 sq. mi. (2831 sq. km). *Cap.:* Apia. —**West/ern Samo/an,** *adj., n.*

west/ern tan/ager, *n.* a tanager, *Piranga ludoviciana,* of W North America, the male of which is black, yellow, and orange-red.

West/ern Wall/, *n.* a wall in Jerusalem where Jews, on certain occasions, assemble for prayer and lamentation: traditionally believed to be the remains of the western wall of Herod's Temple, destroyed by the Romans in A.D. 70. Also called **Wailing Wall.**

West/ In/dies, *n.* **1.** (*used with a pl. v.*) Also called **the Indies.** an archipelago in the N Atlantic between North and South America, comprising the Greater Antilles, the Lesser Antilles, and the Bahamas. **2. Federation of.** Also called **West/ In/dies Federa/tion.** a former federation (1958–62) of the British islands in the Caribbean, comprising Barbados, Jamaica, Trinidad, Tobago, and the Windward and Leeward island colonies. —**West/ In/dian,** *adj., n.*

West·ing·house (wes/ting hous/), *n.* **George,** 1846–1914, U.S. inventor and manufacturer.

West·min·ster (west/min/stər), *n.* **1.** a central borough (officially a city) of Greater London, England: Westminster Abbey, Houses of Parliament, Buckingham Palace. 173,400. **2.** a city in SW California. 73,320. **3.** a city in NE Colorado. 73,890.

west/-northwest/, *n.* **1.** a point on the compass midway between west and northwest. —*adj.* **2.** coming from this point: *a west-northwest wind.* **3.** directed toward this point. —*adv.* **4.** toward this point. *Abbr.:* WNW

West/ Point/, *n.* a military reservation in SE New York, on the Hudson: U.S. Military Academy.

West/ Prus/sia, *n.* a former province of Prussia: since 1945 part of Poland. German, **West·preus·sen** (vest/pROi/sən). —**West/ Prus/sian,** *adj., n.*

West/ Side/ Sto/ry, a musical (1957) with lyrics by Stephen Sondheim and music by Leonard Bernstein.

West/ Slav/ic, *n.* the branch of Slavic that includes Polish, Czech, Slovak, and Sorbian.

west/-southwest/, *n.* **1.** a point on the compass midway between west and southwest. —*adj.* **2.** coming from this point: *a west-southwest wind.* **3.** directed toward this point. —*adv.* **4.** toward this point. *Abbr.:* WSW

West/ Virgin/ia, *n.* a state in the E United States. 1,825,754; 24,181 sq. mi. (62,629 sq. km). *Cap.:* Charleston. *Abbr.:* WV, W.Va. —**West/ Virgin/ian,** *n., adj.*

west·ward (west/wərd), *adj.* **1.** moving, bearing, facing, or situated toward the west. —*adv.* **2.** Also, **west/wards.** toward the west. —*n.* **3.** a westward part, direction, or point.

wet (wet), *adj.,* **wet·ter, wet·test,** *n., v.,* **wet** or **wet·ted, wet·ting.** —*adj.* **1.** moistened, covered, or soaked with water or some other liquid. **2.** in a liquid form or state: *wet paint.* **3.** characterized by the presence or use of water or other liquid. **4.** moistened or dampened with rain; rainy. **5.** allowing or favoring the sale of alcoholic beverages: *a wet town.* **6.** characterized by frequent rain, mist, etc.: *the wet season.* **7.** laden with moisture or vapor, esp. water vapor: *a wet breeze from the west.* —*n.* **8.** something that is or makes wet, as water or other liquid; moisture. **9.** damp weather; rain. **10.** a person in favor of allowing the manufacture and sale of alcoholic beverages. —*v.t.* **11.** to make (something) wet, as by moistening or soaking (sometimes fol. by *through* or *down*). **12.** to urinate on or in: *The dog had wet the carpet.* —*v.i.* **13.** to become wet (sometimes fol. by *through* or *down*): *My jacket has wet through.* **14.** (of animals and children) to urinate. —*Idiom.* **15. all wet,** completely mistaken; in error. **16. wet behind the ears,** immature; naive; green. —**wet/ly,** *adv.* —**wet/ness,** *n.* —**wet/ter,** *n.*

wet/ bar/, *n.* a small bar, as in the home or a hotel suite, equipped with a sink and running water.

wet/ blan/ket, *n.* a person or thing that dampens or discourages one's enthusiasm or enjoyment.

wet/ dream/, *n.* an erotic dream accompanied by a nocturnal emission.

wet·land (wet/land/), *n.* Often, **wetlands.** land that has a wet and spongy soil, as a marsh, swamp, or bog.

wet/ mop/, *n.* a long-handled mop for cleaning floors with water. —**wet/-mop/,** *v.t.,* **-mopped, -mop·ping.**

wet/ nurse/, *n.* a woman hired to suckle another's infant.

wet′-nurse′, *v.t.,* **-nursed, -nurs•ing. 1.** to act as a wet nurse to (an infant). **2.** to give excessive care or attention to.
wet′ suit′, *n.* a close-fitting rubber or rubberlike suit worn for body warmth, as by scuba divers or surfers.
we've (wēv), contraction of *we have.*
Wey•mouth (wā′məth), *n.* **Richard Francis,** 1822–1902, English Bible scholar.
Wh or **wh,** watt-hour.
whack (hwak, wak), *v.t.* **1.** to strike with a smart, resounding blow or blows. **2.** to cut or chop vigorously: *He whacked the vines from his path with a hunting knife.* —*v.i.* **3.** to strike a smart, resounding blow or blows. **4. whack off,** to cut off or separate with a blow: *The cook whacked off the fish's head.* —*n.* **5.** a smart, resounding blow. **6.** a trial or attempt: *to take a whack at a job.* **7.** a portion or share. —***Idiom.*** **8. out of whack,** out of order or alignment; not in proper condition.
whacked′-out′ or **wacked′-out′,** *adj. Slang.* **1.** exhausted; worn-out. **2.** wacky; crazy.
whale[1] (hwāl, wāl), *n., pl.* **whales,** (*esp. collectively*) **whale,** *v.,* **whaled, whal•ing.** —*n.* **1.** any of the larger marine mammals of the order Cetacea, esp. as distinguished from the smaller dolphins, having a fishlike body, forelimbs modified into flippers, and a horizontally flattened head. **2.** something big, great, or fine of its kind: *I had a whale of a time in Europe.* **3.** (*cap.*) the constellation Cetus. —*v.i.* **4.** to engage in whaling or whale fishing. —**whale′like′,** *adj.*
whale[2] (hwāl, wāl), *v.t., v.i.,* **whaled, whal•ing.** to hit, thrash, or beat soundly.
whale•boat (hwāl′bōt′, wāl′-), *n.* a long, narrow boat designed for quick turning and use in rough seas: formerly used in whaling, now mainly for sea rescue.
whale•bone (hwāl′bōn′, wāl′-), *n.* **1.** Also called **baleen.** an elastic, horny substance hanging in fringed platelike sheets from the upper jaws of whalebone whales and serving to strain plankton. **2.** something made of this substance, as corset stays.
whal•er (hwā′lər, wā′-), *n.* a person or vessel employed in whaling.
whale′ shark′, *n.* a tropical shark, *Rhincodon typus,* ranging in size from 30 to 60 ft. (9 to 18 m) and having small teeth and a sievelike structure over the gills for catching plankton.
whal•ing (hwā′ling, wā′-), *n.* the work or industry of capturing and rendering whales; whale fishing.
wham (hwam, wam), *n., v.,* **whammed, wham•ming.** —*n.* **1.** a loud sound produced by an explosion or sharp impact. **2.** a forcible impact. —*v.t., v.i.* **3.** to hit or make a forcible impact, producing a loud sound.
wham•my (hwam′ē, wam′ē), *n., pl.* **-mies.** *Slang.* **1.** the evil eye; hex. **2.** a devastating blow, setback, or catastrophe.
whang (hwang, wang), *n.* **1.** a resounding blow. **2.** the sound produced by such a blow. —*v.t.* **3.** to strike with a resounding blow. —*v.i.* **4.** to resound with such a blow.
wharf (hwôrf, wôrf), *n., pl.* **wharves** (hwôrvz, wôrvz), **wharfs,** *v.* —*n.* **1.** a structure built on the shore of or projecting into a harbor, stream, etc., so that vessels may be moored alongside to load or unload or to lie at rest; quay; pier. —*v.t.* **2.** to provide with a wharf or wharves. **3.** to place or store on a wharf. **4.** to accommodate at or bring to a wharf. —*v.i.* **5.** to tie up at a wharf; dock.
Whar•ton (hwôr′tn, wôr′-), *n.* **Edith,** 1862–1937, U.S. novelist.
wharves (hwôrvz, wôrvz), *n.* a pl. of WHARF.
what (hwut, hwot, wut, wot; *unstressed* hwət, wət), *pron.* **1.** (used interrogatively as a request for specific information): *What is the matter?* **2.** (used interrogatively to inquire about the character, occupation, etc., of a person): *What does he do?* **3.** (used interrogatively to inquire as to the origin, identity, etc., of something): *What are those birds?* **4.** (used interrogatively to inquire as to the worth, usefulness, force, or importance of something): *What is wealth without friends?* **5.** (used interrogatively to request a repetition of words or information not fully understood, usu. used in elliptical constructions): *You need what?* **6.** (used interrogatively to inquire the reason or purpose of something, usu. used in elliptical constructions): *What of it?* **7.** how much?: *What does it cost?* **8.** (used relatively to indicate that which): *I will send what was promised.* **9.** whatever; anything that: *Come what may.* **10.** the kind of thing or person that: *She said just what I was expecting she would.* **11.** as much as; as many as: *We should each give what we can.* **12.** the thing or fact that (used in parenthetic clauses): *He went to the meeting and, what was worse, insisted on speaking.* **13.** (used to indicate more to follow, additional possibilities, alternatives, etc.): *You know what? Shall we go or what?* **14.** (used as an intensifier in exclamatory phrases, often fol. by an indefinite article): *What luck! What an idea!* **15.** *Brit.* don't you agree?: *An unusual chap, what?* **16.** *Nonstandard.* that; which; who: *She's the one what told me.* —*n.* **17.** the true nature or identity of something, or the sum of its characteristics: *a lecture on the whats and hows of crop rotation.* —*adj.* **18.** (used interrogatively before nouns): *What clothes shall I pack?* **19.** whatever: *Take what supplies you need.* —*adv.* **20.** to what extent or degree? how much?: *What does it matter?* **21.** (used to introduce a prepositional phrase beginning with *with*): *What with storms and all, their return was delayed.* —*interj.* **22.** (used in exclamatory expressions, often fol. by a question): *What, no kiss?* —***Idiom.*** **23. but what,** *Informal.* but that: *Who knows but what the sun may still shine.* **24. so what,** (an expression of disinterest, disinclination, or contempt.) **25. what for, a.** why: *What are you doing that for?* **b.** a punishment or scolding: *My mother will give me what for if I come home late again.* **26. what have you,** other things of the same kind; so forth: *money, jewels, and what have you.* **27. what if,** what would be the outcome if; suppose that: *What if we get lost?* **28. what it takes,** whatever characteristics or aids will insure one's success, as intelligence, talent, good looks, or wealth. **29. what's what,** the true situation; all the facts: *Ask someone who knows what's what.*
What′ a Friend′ We′ Have′ in Je′sus, a Christian hymn (1857) with words by Joseph Scriven.
what•e'er (hwut âr′, hwot-, hwət-, wut-, wot-, wət-), *pron., adj. Literary.* WHATEVER.
what•ev•er (hwut ev′ər, hwot-, hwət-, wut-, wot-, wət-), *pron.* **1.** anything that (usu. used in relative clauses): *Do whatever you like.* **2.** (used relatively to indicate a quantity of a specified or implied antecedent). **3.** no matter what: *Do it, whatever happens.* **4.** any of a number of things whether specifically known or not: *papers, magazines, or whatever.* **5.** what (used interrogatively): *Whatever do you mean?* —*adj.* **6.** in any amount; to any extent: *whatever merit the work has.* **7.** no matter what. **8.** being what or who it may be. **9.** of any kind (used as an intensifier following the noun or pronoun it modifies): *any person whatever.*
What′ hath′ God′ wrought!′, a statement sent by Samuel Morse as the first telegraph transmission.
what-if (hwut′if′, hwot′-, wut′-, wot′-), *adj.* **1.** hypothetical: *a what-if scenario.* —*n.* **2.** a hypothetical case or situation; conjecture: *a series of what-ifs.*
what'll (hwut′l, hwot′l, wut′l, wot′l), contraction of *what will* or *what shall: What'll I do and what'll she say?*
what•not (hwut′not′, hwot′-, wut′-, wot′-), *n.* **1.** a stand with shelves for bric-a-brac, books, etc. **2.** anything of the same or similar kind: *sheets, towels, and whatnot.*
what's (hwuts, hwots, wuts, wots; *unstressed* hwəts, wəts), **1.** contraction of *what is* or *what has: What's the matter? What's been done?* **2.** contraction of *what does: What's she do for a living?*
what•so•e'er (hwut′sō âr′, hwot′-, wut′-, wot′-), *pron., adj. Literary.* WHATSOEVER.
what•so•ev•er (hwut′sō ev′ər, hwot′-, wut′-, wot′-), *pron., adj.* (an intensive form of WHATEVER): *whatsoever it be; in any place whatsoever.*
wheal (hwēl, wēl) also **weal,** *n.* **1.** a small, burning or itching swelling on the skin, as from a mosquito bite or from hives. **2.** a wale or welt.
wheat (hwēt, wēt), *n.* **1.** the grain of any cereal grass of the genus *Triticum,* esp. *T. aestivum,* used in the form of flour. **2.** the plant itself.
wheat′ ber′ry, *n.* the whole kernel of wheat, sometimes cracked or ground and made into bread or used as a cereal.
wheat•ear (hwēt′ēr′, wēt′-), *n.* any of several small thrushes of the genus *Oenanthe,* having a distinctive white rump, esp. *O. oenanthe,* of Eurasia and N North America.
wheat′ germ′, *n.* the embryo of the wheat kernel, used in or on foods as a concentrated source of vitamins.
whee (hwē, wē), *interj.* (used to express joy or delight.)
whee•dle (hwēd′l, wēd′l), *v.,* **-dled, -dling.** —*v.t.* **1.** to try to influence (a person) by flattering or beguiling words or acts; cajole. **2.** to persuade (a person) by such words or acts: *She wheedled him into going with her.* **3.** to obtain (something) by artful persuasions: *I wheedled a new car out of my father.* —*v.i.* **4.** to use beguiling or artful persuasions. —**whee′dler,** *n.* —**whee′dling•ly,** *adv.*
wheel (hwēl, wēl), *n.* **1.** a circular frame or disk arranged to revolve on an axis, as on or in vehicles or machinery. **2.** any machine, apparatus, instrument, etc., shaped like this or having a circular frame, disk, or revolving drum as an essential feature: *a potter's wheel.* **3.** STEERING WHEEL. **4.** *Naut.* **a.** a circular frame with an axle connecting to the rudder of a ship, for steering. **b.** PADDLE WHEEL. **5.** a bicycle. **6.** a round object, decoration, etc.: *a wheel of cheese.* **7.** an old instrument of torture in the form of a circular frame on which the victim was stretched until disjointed. **8.** PINWHEEL (def. 2). **9.** a rotating instrument that Fortune is represented as turning so as to bring about changes or reverses in human affairs. **10. wheels, a.** moving, propelling, or animating agencies: *the wheels of commerce.* **b.** *Slang.* a personal means of transportation, esp. a car. **11.** a cycle, recurring action, or steady progression: *the wheel of days and nights.* **12.** a wheeling or circular movement: *the intricate wheels of the folk dances.* **13.** someone active and influential, as in business or politics; an important person: *a big wheel.* —*v.t.* **14.** to cause to turn, rotate, or revolve, as on an axis. **15.** to perform (a movement) in a circular or curving direction. **16.** to move, roll, or convey on wheels, casters, etc.: *The waiters wheeled the tables out.* —*v.i.* **17.** to turn on or as if on an axis or about a center; revolve, rotate, or pivot. **18.** to move in a circular or curving course: *pigeons wheeling above.* **19.** to change direction or course by turning or seeming to turn the opposite way (often fol. by *about* or *around*): *He wheeled about and glared at us. She wheeled around and argued for the opposition.* **20.** to roll on or as if on wheels; travel smoothly: *The car wheeled along the highway.* —***Idiom.*** **21. at the wheel, a.** at the helm of a ship, the steering wheel of a motor vehicle, etc. **b.** in command or control. **22. wheel and deal,** to operate dynamically and esp. craftily for one's own profit or benefit. **23. wheels within wheels,** involved, interacting motives and schemes. —***Proverb.*** **24. The squeaky wheel gets the grease,** outspoken complaints are heeded.
wheel′ and ax′le, *n.* a simple machine consisting typically of a cylindrical drum to which a concentric wheel is firmly fastened: ropes are so

applied that as one rope unwinds from the wheel, another is wound onto the drum.

wheel·bar·row (hwēl′bar′ō, wēl′-), *n.* **1.** a frame or box for conveying a load, supported at one end by a wheel or wheels, and lifted and pushed at the other by two horizontal shafts. —*v.t.* **2.** to move or convey in a wheelbarrow.

wheel·base (hwēl′bās′, wēl′-), *n.* the distance from the center of the front-wheel spindle of a vehicle to the center of the rear-wheel axle.

wheel·chair (hwēl′châr′, wēl′-), *n.* a chair mounted on wheels for use by persons who cannot walk.

wheeled (hwēld, wēld), *adj.* **1.** equipped with or having wheels (often used in combination): *a four-wheeled carriage.* **2.** moving or traveling on wheels: *wheeled transportation.*

Whee·ler (hwē′lər, wē′-), *n.* **William Almon,** 1819–87, vice president of the U.S. 1877–81.

wheel′er-deal′er or **wheel′er and deal′er,** *n.* a clever or crafty person who devises intricate, highly profitable schemes and transactions, as in business or politics.

wheel′ horse′ or **wheel′-horse′,** *n.* **1.** Also called **wheeler.** a horse, or one of the horses, harnessed behind others and nearest the front wheels of a vehicle. **2.** *Chiefly South Midland and Southern U.S.* a reliable, diligent, and strong worker.

wheel·house (hwēl′hous′, wēl′-), *n., pl.* **-hous·es** (-hou′ziz). PILOT-HOUSE.

wheel′ lock′, *n.* **1.** an old type of gunlock in which sparks are produced by the friction of a small steel wheel against a piece of iron pyrites. **2.** a gun having such a gunlock.

wheel·wright (hwēl′rīt′, wēl′-), *n.* a person whose trade is making or repairing wheels, wheeled carriages, etc.

wheeze (hwēz, wēz), *v.,* **wheezed, wheez·ing,** *n.* —*v.i.* **1.** to breathe with difficulty and with a whistling sound: *Asthma caused him to wheeze.* **2.** to make a sound resembling difficult breathing. —*n.* **3.** a wheezing breath or sound. **4.** an old and frequently used joke, saying, story, etc. —**wheez′er,** *n.* —**wheez′ing·ly,** *adv.*

wheez·y (hwē′zē, wē′-), *adj.,* **wheez·i·er, wheez·i·est.** afflicted with or characterized by wheezing. —**wheez′i·ly,** *adv.* —**wheez′i·ness,** *n.*

whelk¹ (hwelk, welk), *n.* any of various medium- to large-sized, spiral-shelled marine gastropods of the family Buccinidae, as *Buccinum undatum,* used for food.

whelk¹, *Buccinum undatum,*
length 3 in. (8 cm)

whelk² (hwelk, welk), *n.* a pimple or pustule.

whelm (hwelm, welm), *v.t.* **1.** to submerge; engulf. **2.** to overcome utterly; overwhelm: *whelmed by misfortune.* —*v.i.* **3.** to roll or surge over something, as in causing it to submerge.

whelp (hwelp, welp), *n.* **1.** the young of the dog, or of the wolf, bear, lion, tiger, seal, etc. **2.** a youth, esp. one regarded as impudent or reckless; brat. —*v.t.* **3.** (of a female dog, bear, lion, etc.) to give birth to (young). —*v.i.* **4.** (of a female dog, bear, etc.) to give birth to young.

when (hwen, wen; *unstressed* hwən, wən), *adv.* **1.** at what time or period: *How long ago? how soon?* **2.** under what circumstances? upon what occasion?: *When is a letter of condolence in order? When did you ever see such a crowd?* —*conj.* **3.** at what time: *to know when to be silent.* **4.** at the time or in the event that. **5.** at any time; whenever: *The dogs always bark when anyone approaches the house.* **6.** upon or after which; and then. **7.** while on the contrary; whereas: *Why are you here when you should be in school?* —*pron.* **8.** what time: *Till when is the store open?* **9.** which time: *They left on Monday, since when we have heard nothing.* —*n.* **10.** the time of anything.

whence (hwens, wens), *adv.* **1.** from what place?: *Whence comest thou?* **2.** from what source, origin, or cause?: *Whence has he wisdom?* —*conj.* **3.** from what place, source, cause, etc.: *He told whence he came.*

when·e′er (hwen âr′, wen-, hwən-, wən-), *conj. Literary.* WHENEVER.

when·ev·er (hwen ev′ər, wen-, hwən-, wən-), *conj.* **1.** at whatever time; at any time when: *Come whenever you like.* —*adv.* **2.** when? (used emphatically): *Whenever did he say that?*

When′ He′ Com′eth, a Christian children's hymn (1846) with words by William O. Cushing and music by George F. Root.

When′ I′ Survey′ the Won′drous Cross′, a Christian hymn (1707) with words by Isaac Watts.

when′ll (hwen′l, wen′l), contraction of *when shall* or *when will: When'll we meet again?*

when·so·ev·er (hwen′sō ev′ər, wen′-), *conj., adv.* at whatsoever time; whenever.

When′ the Roll′ Is′ Called′ Up′ Yon′der, a Christian hymn (1894) with words and music by James M. Black.

where (hwâr, wâr), *adv.* **1.** in or at what place?: *Where is he? Where do you live?* **2.** in what position or circumstances?: *Where do you stand on this question? Without money, where are you?* **3.** in what particular re-

spect, way, etc.?: *Where does this affect us?* **4.** to what place, point, or end? whither?: *Where are you going?* **5.** from what source? whence?: *Where did you get such a notion?* —*conj.* **6.** in or at what place, part, point, etc.: *Find where the trouble is.* **7.** in or at the place, part, point, etc., in or at which: *The cup is where you left it.* **8.** in a position, case, etc., in which: *Where ignorance is bliss, 'tis folly to be wise.* **9.** in any place, position, case, etc., in which; wherever: *Use the ointment where pain is felt.* **10.** to what or whatever place; to the place or any place to which: *I will go where you go.* **11.** in or at which place; and there: *They came to the town, where they lodged for the night.* —*pron.* **12.** what place?: *Where did you come from?* **13.** the place in which; point at which: *This is where the boat docks. That was where the phone rang.* —*n.* **14.** a place; that place in which something is located or occurs: *the wheres and hows of job hunting.* —*Idiom.* **15. where it's at,** where the most exciting, prestigious, or profitable activity or circumstance is to be found. —*Usage.* The constructions WHERE ... AT (*Where was he at?*) and WHERE ... TO (*Where is this leading to?*) are often criticized on the grounds that neither *at* nor *to* adds anything to the meaning of WHERE, and that sentences like those above are perfectly clear without the final *at* or *to.* Both constructions occur in the speech of educated people but are rare in formal speech and edited writing.

where·a·bout (hwâr′ə bout′, wâr′-), *adv., conj.* WHEREABOUTS.

where·a·bouts (hwâr′ə bouts′, wâr′-), *adv.* **1.** about where? where? —*conj.* **2.** near or in what place: *trying to find whereabouts in the world we were.* —*n.* **3.** (*used with a sing. or pl. v.*) the place where a person or thing is; locality: *no clue as to his whereabouts.*

where·as (hwâr az′, wâr-), *conj., n., pl.* **where·as·es.** —*conj.* **1.** while on the contrary: *One came forward immediately, whereas the others hung back.* **2.** it being the case that, or considering that (used esp. in formal preambles). —*n.* **3.** a qualifying or introductory statement, esp. one having "whereas" as the first word.

where·at (hwâr at′, wâr-), *conj.* **1.** at which: *a reception whereat many were present.* **2.** to which; whereupon: *a remark whereat she quickly angered.*

where·by (hwâr bī′, wâr-), *conj.* by what or by which; under the terms of which.

wher·e·er (hwâr âr′, wâr-), *conj. Literary.* WHEREVER.

where·fore (hwâr′fôr′, -fōr′, wâr′-), *adv.* **1.** for that cause or reason: *Wherefore let us be grateful.* **2.** *Archaic.* for what? why? —*n.* **3.** the cause or reason: *the whys and wherefores of a situation.*

where·in (hwâr in′, wâr-), *conj.* **1.** in what or in which. —*adv.* **2.** in what way or respect?

where′ll (hwârl, wârl), contraction of *where shall* or *where will: Where'll I be ten years from now?*

where·of (hwâr uv′, -ov′, wâr-), *adv., conj.* of what, which, or whom.

where·on (hwâr on′, -ôn′, wâr-), *conj.* on what or which.

where·so·ev·er (hwâr′sō ev′ər, wâr′-), *conj.* in or to whatsoever place; wherever.

where·to (hwâr tōō′, wâr-), *conj., adv.* **1.** to what or what place or end. **2.** to which.

where·up·on (hwâr′ə pon′, -pôn′, wâr′-; hwâr′ə pon′, -pôn′, wâr′-), *conj.* **1.** upon what or upon which. **2.** at or after which.

wher·ev·er (hwâr ev′ər, wâr-), *conj.* **1.** in, at, or to whatever place. **2.** in any case or condition: *wherever it is heard of.* —*adv.* **3.** where? (used emphatically): *Wherever did you find that?*

where·with (hwâr with′, -with′, wâr-), *adv., conj.* with which; by means of which.

where·with·al (hwâr′with ôl′, -with-, wâr′-), *n.* **1.** that with which to do something; means or supplies for the purpose or need, esp. money: *the wherewithal to pay my rent.* —*adv.* **2.** by means of which; out of which. —*pron.* **3.** wherewith.

whet (hwet, wet), *v.,* **whet·ted, whet·ting,** *n.* —*v.t.* **1.** to sharpen (a knife, tool, etc.) by grinding or friction. **2.** to make keen or eager; stimulate: *to whet the appetite; to whet the curiosity.* —*n.* **3.** the act of whetting. **4.** something that whets; stimulus, esp. an appetizer or drink.

wheth·er (hweth′ər, weth′-), *conj.* **1.** (used to introduce the first of two or more alternatives, and sometimes repeated before the second or later alternative, usu. with the correlative *or*): *It matters little whether we go or stay. Whether we go or whether we stay, the result is the same.* **2.** (used to introduce a single alternative, the other being implied or understood, or some clause or element not involving alternatives): *I doubt whether we can do anything now.* —*Idiom.* **3. whether or no,** under whatever circumstances; regardless: *He threatens to go whether or no.*

whet·stone (hwet′stōn′, wet′-), *n.* a stone for sharpening cutlery or tools by friction.

whew (hwyōō), *interj.* (a whistling exclamation or sound expressing astonishment, dismay, relief, etc.)

whey (hwā, wā), *n.* (in cheese making) the liquid that separates from the curd in coagulated milk. —**whey′ey,** *adj.* —**whey′like′,** *adj.*

which (hwich, wich), *pron.* **1.** what one?: *Which of these do you want? Which do you want?* **2.** whichever: *Choose which appeals to you.* **3.** (used relatively in restrictive and nonrestrictive clauses to represent a specified antecedent): *This book, which I read last night, was exciting. The socialism which Owen preached was unpalatable to many. The lawyer represented five families, of which ours was the largest.* **4.** (used relatively in restrictive clauses having *that* as the antecedent): *Damaged goods constituted part of that which was sold at the auction.* **5.** (used after a preposition to represent a specified antecedent): *the house in which*

I lived. **6.** (used relatively to represent a specified or implied antecedent) the one that; a particular one that: *You may choose which you like.* **7.** (used in parenthetic clauses) the thing or fact that: *He hung around for hours and, which was worse, kept me from doing my work.* —*adj.* **8.** what one of (a certain number or group mentioned or implied)?: *Which book do you want?* **9.** whichever; any that: *Go which way you please, you'll end up here.* **10.** being previously mentioned: *It rained all day, during which time we played cards.*

which•ev•er (hwich ev′ər, wich-), *pron.* **1.** any one that: *Take whichever you like.* **2.** no matter which: *Whichever you choose, the others will be offended.* —*adj.* **3.** no matter which: *whichever day.*

which•so•ev•er (hwich′sō ev′ər, wich′-), *pron., adj.* WHICHEVER.

which′ way′, *adv.* EVERY (def. 5).

whiff (hwif, wif), *n.* **1.** a slight gust or puff of wind, air, vapor, smoke, or the like. **2.** a slight trace of odor or smell: *a whiff of onions.* **3.** a single inhalation or exhalation of air, tobacco smoke, etc. **4.** a trace or hint: *a whiff of scandal.* —*v.i.* **5.** to blow or come in whiffs or puffs, as wind or smoke. **6.** to inhale or exhale whiffs, as in smoking tobacco. **7.** *Baseball.* FAN[1] (def. 15). —*v.t.* **8.** to blow or drive with a whiff or puff, as the wind does. **9.** to inhale or exhale (air, tobacco smoke, etc.) in whiffs. **10.** to smoke (a pipe, cigar, etc.). **11.** *Baseball.* FAN[1] (def. 11).

whif•fle (hwif′əl, wif′-), *v.,* **-fled, -fling.** —*v.i.* **1.** to blow in light shifting gusts, as the wind. **2.** to shift about; vacillate. —*v.t.* **3.** to blow with light shifting gusts. —**whif′fler,** *n.*

whif•fle•tree (hwif′əl trē′, wif′-), *n.* *Northern U.S.* a crossbar, pivoted at the middle, to which the traces of a harness are fastened for pulling a vehicle or a plow. Also called **singletree.** Compare DOUBLETREE.

Whig (hwig, wig), *n.* **1.** a member of a political party in Great Britain (c1679–1832) that favored reforms and parliamentary authority. **2.** a member of a U.S. political party (c1834–55) formed in opposition to the Democratic Party and favoring high tariffs and a weak presidency. **3.** an American colonist who supported the American Revolution. —*adj.* **4.** of, pertaining to, or characteristic of Whigs. —**Whig′gish,** *adj.*

while (hwīl, wīl), *n., conj., v.,* **whiled, whil•ing.** —*n.* **1.** an interval of time: *a long while ago.* —*conj.* **2.** during or in the time that: *He ate ice cream while he waited.* **3.** throughout the time that; as long as. **4.** even though; although: *While they are related, they don't get along.* **5.** at the same time that: *She exercises while he grows fat.* —*v.t.* **6.** to cause (time) to pass, esp. in some pleasant manner: *to while away the hours.* —***Idiom.*** **7. worth one's while,** worth one's time, trouble, or expense.

While′ Shep′herds Watched′ Their′ Flocks′ By′ Night′, a Christmas hymn (1700) with words by Nahum Tate.

whil•li•kers (hwil′i kərz, wil′-) also **whil•li•kins** (-kinz), *interj.* (used as an intensive esp. after *gee* to express astonishment or delight.)

whilst (hwīlst, wīlst), *conj. Chiefly Brit.* WHILE.

whim (hwim, wim), *n.* **1.** a capricious notion; fancy: *a party thrown on a whim.* **2.** capricious humor.

whim•per (hwim′pər, wim′-), *v.i.* **1.** to cry with low plaintive sounds. —*v.t.* **2.** to utter in a whimper. —*n.* **3.** a whimpering sound. —**whim′per•er,** *n.* —**whim′per•ing•ly,** *adv.*

whim•si•cal (hwim′zi kəl, wim′-), *adj.* **1.** given to fanciful notions; capricious. **2.** of the nature of or proceeding from whimsy, as thoughts or actions: *whimsical inventions.* **3.** erratic; unpredictable. —**whim′si•cal′i•ty,** *n.* —**whim′si•cal•ly,** *adv.*

whim•sy or **whim•sey** (hwim′zē, wim′-), *n., pl.* **-sies** or **-seys. 1.** capricious humor; playfulness: *a comedy with an air of whimsy.* **2.** an odd or fanciful notion. **3.** anything odd or fanciful, as an artistic creation.

whine (hwīn, wīn), *v.,* **whined, whin•ing,** *n.* —*v.i.* **1.** to utter a low, nasal complaining sound: *The puppies whined from hunger.* **2.** to complain in a peevish, self-pitying way. —*v.t.* **3.** to utter with or as if with a whine: *to whine complaints.* —*n.* **4.** a whining utterance or sound. **5.** a feeble, peevish complaint. —**whin′er,** *n.* —**whin′ing•ly,** *adv.*

whin•ny (hwin′ē, win′ē), *n., pl.* **-nies,** *v.,* **-nied, -ny•ing.** —*n.* **1.** a subdued gentle neigh of a horse. —*v.i.* **2.** to utter a whinny or similar sound.

whin•y or **whin•ey** (hwī′nē, wī′-), *adj.,* **whin•i•er, whin•i•est.** complaining; cranky. —**whin′i•ness,** *n.*

whip (hwip, wip), *v.,* **whipped** or **whipt, whip•ping,** *n.* —*v.t.* **1.** to beat with a flexible implement, as a strap, lash, or rod, esp. as punishment; flog. **2.** to spank. **3.** to urge on with or as if with lashes. **4.** to castigate with words. **5.** to train or organize forcefully: *to whip the team into shape.* **6.** to defeat; overcome: *to whip a bad habit.* **7.** to hoist or haul by means of a whip. **8.** to move, pull, or seize with a sudden movement: *She whipped out her camera.* **9.** to fish (a body of water) with rod and line, esp. by making repeated casts. **10.** to beat, as eggs, to a froth with an implement. **11.** to overlay or cover (cord or rope) with cord, thread, or the like. **12.** to wind (cord, twine, or thread) about something. **13.** to sew with a light overcasting stitch. —*v.i.* **14.** to go quickly and suddenly; dart. **15.** to lash about: *flags that whip in the wind.* **16. whip off,** to write hurriedly: *to whip off a book report.* **17. whip up, a.** to prepare quickly: *to whip up dinner in ten minutes.* **b.** to incite; arouse: *to whip up the mob.* —*n.* **18.** an instrument for striking, as in driving animals or in punishing, typically consisting of a lash or other flexible part with a more rigid handle. **19.** a lashing stroke or motion. **20.** a utensil for whipping; whisk. **21.** a dessert of beaten egg whites or cream, flavoring, and often chopped fruit: *pineapple whip.* **22. a.** a party manager in a legislative body who secures attendance for voting and directs other members. **b.** (in Britain) a written call made on members of a party to be in attendance for voting. **23.** a windmill vane. **24.** a tackle consisting of a fall rove through a single standing block, or a fall secured at one end and rove through a single running and a single standing block. **25.** the wrapping around the end of a whipped cord or the like. **26.** Also called **whirl.** eccentric rotation of a shaft having its center line slightly curved between supporting bearings. **27.** a branchless shoot of a woody plant, esp. one resulting from the first year's growth of a bud or graft. —**whip′like′,** *adj.* —**whip′per,** *n.*

whip•cord (hwip′kôrd′, wip′-), *n.* a cotton, woolen, or worsted fabric with a steep, diagonally ribbed surface.

whip•lash (hwip′lash′, wip′-), *n.* **1.** the lash of a whip. **2.** an abrupt snapping motion resembling the lash of a whip. **3.** a neck injury caused by a sudden jerking of the head backward, forward, or both.

whip•per•snap•per (hwip′ər snap′ər, wip′-), *n.* an unimportant but offensively presumptuous person, esp. a young one.

whip•pet (whip′it, wip′-), *n.* any of a breed of slender swift dogs resembling a small greyhound.

whip•ping (hwip′ing, wip′-), *n.* **1.** a beating, esp. one administered with a whip or the like in punishment. **2.** a defeat, as in sports. **3.** an arrangement of cord, twine, or thread wound about something.

whip′ping boy′, *n.* **1.** a person who is made to bear the blame for another's mistake; scapegoat. **2.** (formerly) a boy educated along with and taking punishment in place of a young prince or nobleman.

whip•poor•will or **whip-poor-will** (hwip′ər wil′, wip′-; hwip′ər-wil′, wip′-), *n.* a North American nightjar of woodlands, *Caprimulgus vociferus,* with an insistently repeated call.

whip•saw (hwip′sô′, wip′-), *n., v.,* **-sawed, -sawed** or **-sawn, -saw•ing.** —*n.* **1.** a saw for two persons, used to divide timbers lengthwise. —*v.t.* **2.** to cut with a whipsaw. **3.** to win two bets from (a person) at one turn or play, as at faro. **4.** to subject to two opposing forces at the same time.

whip′snake′ or **whip′ snake′,** *n.* **1.** any of various long, slender, fast-moving snakes of the genus *Masticophis,* common in W North America. **2.** any of various similar or related snakes.

whip•stitch (hwip′stich′, wip′-), *v.t.* **1.** to sew with stitches passing over an edge in joining, finishing, or gathering. —*n.* **2.** one such stitch.

whir or **whirr** (hwûr, wûr), *v.,* **whirred, whir•ring,** *n.* —*v.i.* **1.** to go, revolve, or otherwise move quickly with a humming sound. —*v.t.* **2.** to move or transport with a whirring sound: *A limousine whirred him away.* —*n.* **3.** an act or sound of whirring: *the whir of wings.*

whirl (hwûrl, wûrl), *v.i.* **1.** to spin or rotate rapidly. **2.** to turn about or aside quickly. **3.** to move or be carried rapidly along: *to whirl down the freeway.* **4.** to experience confusion or dizziness: *My head is whirling.* —*v.t.* **5.** to cause to spin or rotate rapidly. **6.** to drive or carry in a circular or curving course. **7.** to drive or carry along rapidly. **8.** *Obs.* to throw or hurl. —*n.* **9.** the act of whirling. **10.** a whirling movement; quick turn. **11.** a short trip, as a drive or walk: *a whirl around the block.* **12.** something that whirls; a whirling mass. **13.** a rapid round of events: *a whirl of graduation parties.* **14.** a state marked by dizziness or a dizzying succession of feelings or thoughts: *My head is in a whirl.* **15.** an attempt; trial: *He gave the diet a whirl.* **16.** WHIP (def. 26).

whirl•i•gig (hwûr′li gig′, wûr′-), *n.* **1.** something that whirls or revolves. **2.** a whirling motion or course. **3.** a flighty person. **4.** a merry-go-round; carousel. **5.** a toy for whirling or spinning, as a top. Also called **whirl•a•bout** (hwûrl′ə bout′).

whirl•pool (hwûrl′po͞ol′, wûrl′-), *n.* **1.** water in swift circular motion, as that produced by the meeting of opposing currents, often causing a downward spiraling action. **2.** WHIRLPOOL BATH.

whirl′pool bath′, *n.* **1.** a bath in which the body is immersed in swirling water as therapy or for relaxation. **2.** a device that swirls and often heats the water in such a bath. **3.** a tub or pool containing or equipped with such a device.

whirl•wind (hwûrl′wind′, wûrl′-), *n.* **1.** a small mass of air, as a tornado, rotating rapidly and advancing over land or sea. **2.** something resembling a whirlwind, as in destructive force. **3.** any circling rush or violent onward course. —*adj.* **4.** like a whirlwind, as in speed or force: *a whirlwind visit.* —***Proverb.*** **5. They that sow the wind shall reap the whirlwind,** violent deeds bring disastrous results. Hosea 8:7.

whirl•y•bird (hwûr′lē bûrd′, wûr′-), *n.* HELICOPTER.

whirr (hwûr, wûr), *v.i., v.t.,* **whirred, whirr•ing,** *n.* WHIR.

whisk (hwisk, wisk), *v.t.* **1.** to move with a rapid sweeping stroke: *to whisk the dishes off the table.* **2.** to sweep with a whisk broom or brush. **3.** to draw, snatch, etc., lightly and rapidly: *to whisk a child from danger.* **4.** to whip to a froth, as eggs, or blend, as a sauce, using a whisk. —*v.i.* **5.** to sweep or pass lightly and rapidly. —*n.* **6.** an act of whisking. **7.** a rapid sweeping stroke. **8.** WHISK BROOM. **9.** a small bunch of grass, straw, hair, or the like, esp. for use in brushing. **10.** an implement, usu. wire loops held together in a handle, for beating or whipping eggs, cream, etc.

whisk′ broom′, *n.* a small short-handled broom used to brush clothes.

whisk•er (hwis′kər, wis′-), *n.* **1. whiskers,** a beard. **2.** Usu., **whiskers.** the hair growing on the sides of a man's face, esp. when worn long and with the chin clean-shaven. **3.** a single hair of the beard. **4.** one of the long stiff bristly hairs growing about the mouth of certain animals, as the cat or rat. **5.** any spar for extending the clew or clews of a sail so that it can catch more wind. —***Idiom.*** **6. by a whisker,** by the narrowest margin. —**whisk′ered,** *adj.* —**whisk′er•y,** *adj.*

whis·key or **whis·ky** (hwis′kē, wis′-), *n., pl.* **-keys** or **-kies. 1.** an alcoholic liquor distilled from a fermented mash of grain, as barley, rye, or corn. **2.** a drink of whiskey.

Whis′key Rebel′lion, *n.* a revolt of settlers in western Pennsylvania in 1794 against a federal excise tax on whiskey: suppressed by militia called out by President George Washington to establish the authority of the federal government.

whis′key sour′, *n.* a cocktail made with whiskey, lemon juice, and sugar.

whis·ky (hwis′kē, wis′-), *n., pl.* **-kies.** WHISKEY (used esp. for Scotch or Canadian whiskey).

whis·per (hwis′pər, wis′pər), *v.i.* **1.** to speak with soft hushed sounds using the breath but with no vibration of the vocal cords. **2.** to talk softly and privately, often implying gossip: *The town whispered about the rumors.* **3.** to make a soft rustling sound like that of whispering: *The breeze whispers in the leaves.* —*v.t.* **4.** to utter with soft low sounds using the breath. **5.** to say in a whisper; tell privately. **6.** to speak to or tell (a person) in a whisper or privately. —*n.* **7.** the mode of utterance, or the voice, of one who whispers: *to speak in a whisper.* **8.** a word or remark uttered by whispering. **9.** a rumor or insinuation. **10.** a soft rustling sound like a whisper. —**whis′per·y,** *adj.*

whis·per·ing (hwis′pər ing, wis′-), *n.* **1.** whispered talk or conversation. **2.** rumor or gossip. **3.** a whispered sound. —*adj.* **4.** making a sound like a whisper. **5.** like a whisper. **6.** gossipy. **7.** conversing in whispers. —**whis′per·ing·ly,** *adv.*

whis′pering campaign′, *n.* the organized spreading of insinuations or rumors to destroy the reputation of a person, organization, etc.

whist[1] (hwist, wist), *n.* a card game, a form of bridge without bidding.

whist[2] (hwist, wist) also **whisht,** *interj.* **1.** (used to urge silence.) —*adj.* **2.** hushed; silent.

whis·tle (hwis′əl, wis′-), *v.,* **-tled, -tling,** *n.* —*v.i.* **1.** to make a high clear musical sound or a series of such sounds by forcing the breath through puckered lips or through the teeth. **2.** to produce sounds resembling a whistle, as by blowing on some device. **3.** to emit a call like a whistle: *birds whistling in the shrubbery.* **4.** to produce a similar sound when actuated by steam or the like: *The teapot whistles.* **5.** to move with a whistling sound, as a bullet or the wind. —*v.t.* **6.** to produce by whistling: *to whistle a tune.* **7.** to call, direct, or signal by or as if by whistling: *He whistled his dog over.* **8.** to send with a whistling or whizzing sound. —*n.* **9.** an instrument for producing whistling sounds by various means, as by the breath through a small tin or plastic tube or through a device with an air chamber containing a small ball. **10.** a sound produced by whistling. —*Idiom.* **11. blow the whistle on,** to expose (wrongdoing or wrongdoers). **12. wet one's whistle,** to take a drink. **13. whistle Dixie,** to indulge in unrealistically optimistic fantasies. **14. whistle in the dark,** to try to remain brave in the face of danger or adversity. —**whis′tle·a·ble,** *adj.*

whis·tle-blow′er or **whis′tle blow′er,** *n.* a person who informs on another or makes public disclosure of corruption or wrongdoing. —**whis′tle-blow′ing,** *n.*

Whis′tler's Moth′er, popular name for a painting (1871) by James McNeil Whistler: full name *Arrangement in Grey and Black: Portrait of the Painter's Mother.*

whis′tle stop′, *n.* **1.** a small unimportant town, esp. one along a railroad line. **2.** a short talk from the rear platform of a train, esp. during a political campaign. **3.** a brief appearance, single performance, or the like in a small town, as during a theatrical tour.

whis·tle-stop′, *v.i.,* **-stopped, -stop·ping. 1.** to campaign for political office by traveling, orig. by train, through small communities to address voters. **2.** to take a trip consisting of several brief usu. overnight stops.

whit (hwit, wit), *n.* the smallest amount: *I don't care a whit.*

white (hwīt, wīt), *adj.,* **whit·er, whit·est,** *n., v.,* **whit·ed, whit·ing.** —*adj.* **1.** of the color of pure snow; reflecting nearly all the rays of sunlight or a similar light. **2.** light or comparatively light in color. **3.** marked by slight pigmentation of the skin. **4.** for, limited to, or predominantly made up of persons whose racial heritage is Caucasian: *a white neighborhood.* **5.** pallid or pale, as from fear or other strong emotion. **6.** silvery; gray: *white hair.* **7.** snowy: *a white Christmas.* **8.** lacking color; transparent. **9.** politically conservative or reactionary. **10.** blank, as part of a page. **11.** lustrously shiny: *a knight in white armor.* **12.** wearing white clothing: *a white monk.* **13.** auspicious; fortunate. **14.** morally pure; innocent. **15.** lacking malice; harmless: *white magic.* **16.** (of wine) light-colored or yellowish. —*n.* **17.** a color without hue at one extreme end of the scale of grays, opposite to black, that reflects light of all hues completely and diffusely. **18.** a hue completely desaturated by admixture with white. **19.** quality or state of being white. **20.** lightness of skin pigment. **21.** a person whose racial heritage is Caucasian. **22.** a white material or substance. **23.** the white part of something. **24.** a pellucid, viscous fluid that surrounds the yolk of an egg; albumen. **25.** the white part of the eyeball. **26. whites,** **a.** white or nearly white clothing. **b.** top-grade white flour. **27.** white wine. **28.** a type or breed that is white in color. **29. a.** a hog of any of several breeds having a white coat, as a Chester White. **30. a.** the outermost ring of a target. **b.** an arrow that hits this portion of the target. **c.** the central part of the target, formerly painted white but now painted gold or yellow. **31.** the pieces in chess or checkers that are light-colored. **32.** (*often cap.*) a member of a royalist, conservative, or reactionary political party. —*v.t.* **33.** to make white; whiten. **34. white out,** to cover (errors in copy) with a white

correction fluid. —*Idiom.* **35. bleed white,** to deprive of all resources: *Corruption bled the country white.*

White (hwīt, wīt), *n.* **1. Byron R(aymond)** (*"Whizzer"*), born 1917, associate justice of the U.S. Supreme Court 1962–93. **2. Edmund,** born 1940, U.S. novelist. **3. Edward Douglass,** 1845–1921, Chief Justice of the U.S. Supreme Court 1910–21. **4. Edward H(iggins), II,** 1930–67, U.S. astronaut: first American to walk in space 1965. **5. E(lwyn) B(rooks),** 1899–1985, U.S. humorist and essayist. **6. Patrick (Victor Martindale),** 1912–90, Australian writer. **7. Stanford,** 1853–1906, U.S. architect. **8. Theodore H.,** 1915–86, U.S. journalist and writer.

white′ ant′, *n.* TERMITE.

white′ belt′, *n.* **1.** a white cloth waistband worn by a beginner in a martial art. **2.** a beginner in a martial art. Compare BLACK BELT (def. 1), BROWN BELT. —**white′-belt′,** *adj.*

white′ birch′, *n.* **1.** the European birch, *Betula pendula,* yielding a hard wood. **2.** PAPER BIRCH.

white′ blood′ cell′, *n.* any of various nearly colorless cells of the immune system that circulate mainly in the blood and lymph, including the B cells, T cells, and macrophages. Also called **leukocyte, white′ blood′ cor′puscle, white′ cell′.**

white·board (hwīt′bôrd′, -bōrd′, wīt′-), *n.* a smooth, glossy sheet of white plastic that can be written on with a colored pen or marker in the manner of a blackboard.

white′ bread′, *n.* any white or light-colored bread made from finely ground, usu. bleached, flour.

white′-bread′, *adj. Informal (disparaging).* **1.** pertaining to or characteristic of the white middle class; bourgeois: *white-bread attitudes.* **2.** bland; conventional.

white·cap (hwīt′kap′, wīt′-), *n.* a wave with a broken and foaming white crest.

white′ clo′ver, *n.* a clover, *Trifolium repens,* having white flowers, common in pastures and meadows.

white′-col′lar, *adj.* pertaining to or designating professional or clerical workers whose jobs are usu. salaried and do not involve manual labor. Compare BLUE-COLLAR.

white′ cor′puscle, *n.* WHITE BLOOD CELL.

whit′ed sep′ulcher, *n.* an evil person who feigns goodness; hypocrite. Matt. 23:27.

white′ dwarf′, *n.* a star that is approximately the size of the earth, has undergone gravitational collapse, and is in the final stage of evolution for low-mass stars.

white′ el′ephant, *n.* **1.** a possession unwanted by the owner but difficult to dispose of. **2.** a possession entailing great expense out of proportion to its value to the owner. **3.** an albino Indian elephant.

white·face (hwīt′fās′, wīt′-), *n.* white facial makeup, esp. as worn by clowns and mimes.

White·field (hwit′fēld′, wit′-), *n.* **George,** 1714–70, English Methodist evangelist. —**White′field·i·an, White′field·ite′,** *n.*

white′ fir′, *n.* **1.** a tall narrow fir, *Abies concolor,* of W North America. **2.** the soft wood of this tree, used for lumber and pulp.

white·fish (hwīt′fish′, wīt′-), *n., pl.* (*esp. collectively*) **-fish,** (*esp. for kinds or species*) **-fish·es. 1.** any of several fishes of the genera *Coregonus* and *Prosopium,* inhabiting northern waters of North America and Eurasia, similar to the trout but having a smaller mouth and larger scales. **2.** any of various similar or related fishes.

white′ flag′, *n.* **1.** an all-white banner or piece of cloth used as a symbol of surrender or truce. —*Idiom.* **2. hoist, show,** or **wave the white flag,** to give up; yield. —**white′-flag′,** *adj.*

white·fly (hwīt′flī′, wīt′-), *n., pl.* **-flies.** any of several widespread plant-sucking insects of the family Aleyrodidae, having the body and wings dusted with a white, powdery wax.

white′-foot′ed mouse′, *n.* any North or Central American mouse of the genus *Peromyscus,* usu. having white feet and undersides.

white′ fox′, *n.* the Arctic fox, *Alopex lagopus,* in its white-coated winter phase.

white′ gasoline′, *n.* unleaded and uncracked gasoline esp. for use in motorboats. Also called **white′ gas′.**

white′ gold′, *n.* any of several gold alloys colored white by the presence of nickel, palladium, or platinum.

white′ goods′, *n.pl.* **1.** household goods, as bed sheets and towels, formerly white but now often colored. **2.** bleached goods, esp. cotton or linen fabrics. **3.** large household appliances, as refrigerators, that are often finished in white.

white·head (hwīt′hed′, wīt′-), *n.* MILIUM.

White·head (hwīt′hed′, wīt′-), *n.* **Alfred North,** 1861–1947, English philosopher and mathematician, in the U.S. after 1924.

white′ heat′, *n.* **1.** an intense heat at which a substance glows with white light. **2.** a stage of intense activity or excitement.

white′ hope′, *n.* **1.** a person who is expected to accomplish much in a given field. **2.** a white boxer at one time thought to have a good chance of winning a title held by a black.

white′-hot′, *adj.* **1.** extremely hot. **2.** showing white heat. **3.** exceedingly enthusiastic; impassioned.

White′ House′, the, *n.* **1.** the official residence of the president of the U.S.: a white mansion in Washington, D.C. **2.** the executive branch of the U.S. government.

W

white′ knight′, *n.* **1.** a hero who comes to the rescue. **2.** a beleaguered champion who fights for a cause. **3.** a company that comes to the rescue of another, as to prevent a takeover.

white′ lead′, (led), *n.* **1.** a white heavy powder of basic lead carbonate, $2PbCO_3 \cdot Pb(OH)_2$, used as a pigment, in putty, and in ointments for burns. **2.** putty made from white lead in oil.

white′ lie′, *n.* a minor or harmless lie; fib.

white′ light′ning, *n.* MOONSHINE (def. 1).

white′ list′, *n.* a list of persons or things that are approved or considered acceptable.

white′ mat′ter, *n.* nerve tissue, esp. of the brain and spinal cord, that primarily contains myelinated fibers and is nearly white in color. Compare GRAY MATTER (def. 1).

white′ met′al, *n.* any of various light-colored alloys, as Babbitt metal or Britannia metal.

white′ mus′tard, *n.* a Eurasian mustard plant, *Sinapis alba*, grown for its seeds for use in mustard and mustard oil.

whit•en (hwīt′n, wīt′n), *v.t., v.i.* to make or become white or whiter.

white′ noise′, *n.* random noise with a uniform frequency spectrum over a wide range of frequencies.

white′ oak′, *n.* any of a group of oak trees characterized by leaves with round lobes and acorns that mature in one season, as *Quercus alba*, of E North America.

white•out (hwīt′out′, wīt′-), *n.* **1. a.** a condition of polar regions in which illumination from snow on the ground and a low cloud layer obscure the landscape. **b.** a condition of heavily falling or blowing snow in which visibility is poor. **2.** a quick-drying white fluid used for blotting out written or printed errors.

white′ pa′per, *n.* **1.** an official government report. **2.** an authoritative report issued by any organization.

white′ pep′per, *n.* a condiment prepared from the husked dried berries of the pepper plant.

white′ pine′, *n.* **1.** a large irregularly branched pine, *Pinus strobus*, of E North America with a gray bark. **2.** the soft light-colored wood of this pine. **3.** any of various other similar species of pine.

white′ pop′lar, *n.* **1.** Also called **abele.** an Old World poplar, *Populus alba*, widely cultivated in the U.S. and having the underside of the leaves covered with a dense silvery white down. **2.** the soft straight-grained wood of this tree.

white′ pota′to, *n.* POTATO (def. 1).

white′ sale′, *n.* a sale of sheets and other linens.

white′ sauce′, *n.* a sauce of butter, flour, milk, and seasonings.

white′-shoe′, *adj.* of members of the upper class who own or run large corporations: *white-shoe bankers; a conservative white-shoe image.*

white′ slave′, *n.* a woman who is sold or forced into prostitution. —**white′ slav′er,** *n.* —**white′ slav′ery,** *n.*

white′ spruce′, *n.* **1.** a spruce, *Picea glauca*, of N North America, having bluish green needles and silvery brown bark. **2.** the light soft wood of this tree.

white′ stork′, *n.* a large Eurasian stork, *Ciconia ciconia*, having white plumage with black in the wings and a red bill.

white′ suprem′acy, *n.* a belief that the white race is superior to other races, esp. the black race. —**white′ suprem′acist,** *n.*

white′-tailed′ (or **white′tail′**) **deer′,** *n.* a North American deer, *Odocoileus virginianus*, having a tail with a white underside. Also called **white′tail′.**

white′ tie′, *n.* **1.** a white bow tie, worn with formal evening dress. **2.** formal evening dress for men Compare TAIL COAT. —**white′-tie′,** *adj.*

white•wall (hwīt′wôl′, wīt′-), *n.* an automobile tire with a white sidewall.

white•wash (hwīt′wosh′, -wôsh′, wīt′-), *n.* **1.** a composition, as of lime and water or of whiting, size, and water, used for whitening walls and woodwork. **2.** something that glosses over faults or absolves one from blame. **3.** a defeat in which the loser fails to score. —*v.t.* **4.** to whiten with whitewash. **5.** to cover up the faults or errors of; absolve from blame. **6.** to defeat by keeping the opponent from scoring.

white′ wa′ter, *n.* **1.** frothy water, as in whitecaps and rapids. **2.** light-colored seawater over a shoal or sandy bottom.

white′ whale′, *n.* BELUGA (def. 2).

white′ wine′, *n.* wine having a yellowish to amber color derived esp. from light-colored grapes.

whith•er (hwith′ər, with′-), *adv.* **1.** to what place; where. **2.** to what end or point; to what. —*conj.* **3.** to which place. **4.** to whatever place.

whit•ing[1] (hwīt′ing, wī′-), *n., pl.* (*esp. collectively*) **-ing,** (*esp. for kinds or species*) **-ings.** **1.** any of several kingfishes of the genus *Menticirrhus.* **2.** any of various hakes of the genus *Merluccius.*

whit•ing[2] (hwīt′ing, wī′-), *n.* pure-white chalk ground and washed and used in making putty, whitewash, and silver polish.

whit•low (hwit′lō, wit′-), *n.* FELON[2].

Whit•man (hwit′mən, wit′-), *n.* **Walt(er),** 1819–92, U.S. poet.

Whit•ney (hwit′nē, wit′-), *n.* **1. Eli,** 1765–1825, U.S. manufacturer and inventor. **2. Mount,** a mountain in E California, in the Sierra Nevada: highest peak in the U.S. outside Alaska. 14,495 ft. (4418 m).

Whit•sun•day (hwit′sun′dā, -dē, -sən dā′, wit′-), *n.* the Christian festival of Pentecost. [< Middle English *whitsonenday*, Old English *Hwīta*

Sunnandæg white Sunday; prob. so called because the newly baptized wore white robes on that day]

Whit•ti•er (hwit′ē ər, wit′-), *n.* **1. John Greenleaf,** 1807–92, U.S. poet. **2.** a city in SW California, E of Los Angeles. 73,630.

whit•tle (hwit′l, wit′l), *v.,* **-tled, -tling,** —*v.t.* **1.** to cut, trim, or shape (a piece of wood or bone) by carving off bits with a knife. **2.** to form by whittling: *to whittle a figure.* **3.** to cut off (a bit). **4.** to reduce the amount of gradually (usu. fol. by *down, away,* etc.): *to whittle away an inheritance.* —*v.i.* **5.** to whittle wood or the like with a knife. **6.** to tire oneself or another by worrying. —**whit′tler,** *n.*

whit•tling (hwit′ling, wit′-), *n.* **1.** the act of a person who whittles. **2.** Often, **whittlings.** a bit or chip whittled off.

whiz or **whizz** (hwiz, wiz), *v.,* **whizzed, whiz•zing,** *n.* —*v.i.* **1.** to make a humming, buzzing, or hissing sound, as an object passing swiftly through the air. **2.** to move with such a sound: *A cloud of hornets whizzed by.* —*v.t.* **3.** to cause to whiz. **4.** to treat with a whizzer. —*n.* **5.** *Informal.* a person who is very good at a particular activity or in a specific field: *a whiz at math.* **6.** the sound of a whizzing object. **7.** a swift movement producing such a sound.

whiz′-bang′ or **whiz′bang′** or **whizz′-bang′,** *adj.* first-rate; top-notch: *a whiz-bang slam dunk.*

whiz′ kid′, *n. Informal.* a youthful and exceptionally intelligent, talented, or successful person. —**whiz′-kid′,** *adj.*

who (hōō), *pron., possessive* **whose,** *objective* **whom. 1.** what person or persons?: *Who is he?* **2.** (of a person) of what character or importance: *Who does she think she is?* **3.** the person that or any person that (used relatively to represent a specified or implied antecedent): *It was who you thought.* **4.** (used relatively in restrictive and nonrestrictive clauses to represent a specified antecedent, the antecedent being a person or sometimes an animal or personified thing): *Any kid who wants to can learn to swim.*

WHO, World Health Organization.

whoa (hwō, wō), *interj.* (used to command an animal, esp. a horse, to stop.)

who′d (hōōd), contraction of *who would.*

who•dun•it (hōō dun′it), *n.* a narrative of a murder or a series of murders and the detection of the criminal; detective story.

who•e′er (hōō âr′), *pron. Literary.* WHOEVER.

who•ev•er (hōō ev′ər), *pron., possessive* **whos•ev•er,** *objective* **whom•ev•er. 1.** whatever person; anyone that: *Whoever did it should be proud.* **2.** no matter who: *I won't do it, whoever asks.* **3.** who? what person? (used to express astonishment): *Whoever told you that?*

whole (hōl), *adj.* **1.** comprising the full quantity or amount; entire or total: *He ate the whole pie.* **2.** complete: *a whole set of china.* **3.** undivided; in one piece: *to swallow a thing whole.* **4.** not fractional; integral. **5.** not broken, damaged, or impaired; intact: *The vase arrived whole.* **6.** uninjured or unharmed; sound. **7.** pertaining to all aspects of human nature: *education for the whole person.* —*n.* **8.** the entire quantity, extent, or number: *to accept some of the teachings but reject the whole.* **9.** a thing complete in itself or comprising all its parts or elements. **10.** an assemblage of parts associated together as one thing; a unitary system. —*Idiom.* **11. as a whole,** as a unit; considered together. **12. on** or **upon the whole,** in all of the most significant ways; in general. **13. out of whole cloth,** without foundation in fact; fictitious. —**whole′ness,** *n.*

whole′ blood′, *n.* blood for transfusion that has not been separated into its components.

whole′-grain′, *adj.* of or being natural or unprocessed grain containing the germ and bran.

whole•heart•ed (hōl′här′tid), *adj.* completely sincere or enthusiastic; earnest: *She made a wholehearted attempt to comply.* —**whole′heart′ed•ly,** *adv.* —**whole′heart′ed•ness,** *n.*

whole′ hog′, *n.* **1.** the furthest extent; everything. —*Idiom.* **2. go (the) whole hog,** to do something completely or thoroughly: *to go whole hog for the celebration.* —**whole′-hog′,** *adj.*

whole′ milk′, *n.* milk from which none of the components, as fat or water, has been removed.

whole′ note′, *n.* a musical note equivalent to four quarter notes.

whole′ num′ber, *n.* INTEGER (def. 1).

whole′ rest′, *n.* a musical rest equivalent in duration to a whole note.

whole•sale (hōl′sāl′), *n., adj., adv., v.,* **-saled, -sal•ing.** —*n.* **1.** the sale of goods in quantity, as to retailers. —*adj.* **2.** of, pertaining to, or engaged in sale by wholesale. **3.** extensive; broadly indiscriminate: *wholesale discharge of workers.* —*adv.* **4.** on wholesale terms. **5.** in large quantities; on a large scale, esp. without discrimination. —*v.t., v.i.* **6.** to sell by wholesale. —**whole′sal′er,** *n.*

whole•some (hōl′səm), *adj.* **1.** conducive to moral or general wellbeing: *a wholesome environment.* **2.** healthful: *wholesome food.* **3.** suggestive of physical or moral health, esp. in appearance. **4.** healthy or sound. —**whole′some•ly,** *adv.* —**whole′some•ness,** *n.*

whole′ step′, *n.* a musical interval, as A–B or B–C, encompassing two semitones. Also called **whole′ tone′.**

whole′-tone′ scale′, *n.* a musical scale progressing entirely by whole tones, as C, D, E, F sharp, G sharp, A sharp, C.

whole′-wheat′, *adj.* prepared with the complete wheat kernel: *wholewheat flour.*

who′ll (hōōl), contraction of *who will* or *who shall.*

whol·ly (hō′lē, hōl′lē), *adv.* **1.** entirely; totally. **2.** to the whole amount, extent, etc.

whom (hōōm), *pron.* the objective case of WHO, used as a direct or indirect object: *Whom did you call? You gave whom the book?*

whom·ev·er (hōōm ev′ər), *pron.* the objective case of WHOEVER: *Whomever she spoke to, she was always polite.*

whomp (hwomp, womp), *n. Informal.* **1.** a loud, heavy blow, slap, bang, or the like: *He fell with an awful whomp.* —*v.t.* **2.** to defeat (a person, opposing team, etc.) decisively. **3.** to slap or strike. —*v.i.* **4.** to make a banging or slapping noise. **5. whomp up, a.** to make or create quickly: *to whomp up a new recipe.* **b.** to stir up; rouse: *to whomp up public approval.*

whom·so·ev·er (hōōm′sō ev′ər), *pron.* the objective case of WHOSO-EVER: *Ask whomsoever you like.*

whoop (hwōōp, hwŏŏp, wōōp, wŏŏp; *esp. for 3* hōōp, hŏŏp), *n.* **1.** a loud cry or shout, as of excitement or joy. **2.** a loud, hollow call or hoot, as of an owl or baboon. **3.** a deep intake of air with a hollow gasping sound, as brought on by choking or rapidly repetitive coughing. —*v.i.* **4.** to utter a loud cry or shout in expressing enthusiasm, excitement, etc. **5.** to utter the cry of an owl or crane. —*v.t.* **6.** to utter with or as if with a whoop. **7.** to whoop to or at. **8.** to urge, pursue, or drive with whoops: *to whoop the dogs on.* —*interj.* **9.** (used as a cry to attract attention from afar, or to show excitement, encouragement, enthusiasm, etc.) —*Idiom.* **10. whoop it up,** *Informal.* **a.** to celebrate noisily. **b.** to stir up enthusiasm.

whoop-de-do or **whoop-de-doo** (hōōp′dē dōō′, hŏŏp′-, hwōōp′-, hwŏŏp′-, wōōp′-, wŏŏp′-), *n., pl.* **-dos** or **-doos.** *Informal.* **1.** lively and noisy festivities; merrymaking: *the annual New Year's Eve whoop-de-do.* **2.** heated discussion or debate, esp. in public: *a whoop-de-do over the new tax bill.* **3.** extravagant publicity or fanfare: *the whoop-de-do of a movie premiere.*

whoop·ee or **whoop·ie** (*interj.* hwŏŏp′ē′, wŏŏp′ē′, hwŏŏ′pē′, wŏŏ′-); *n.* hwŏŏp′ē, wŏŏp′ē, hwŏŏ′pē, wŏŏ′-), *Informal.* —*interj.* **1.** (used as a shout of exuberant joy.) —*Idiom.* **2. make whoopee,** to engage in uproarious merrymaking.

whoop·er (hōō′pər, hwŏŏ′-, wŏŏ′-), *n.* **1.** a person or thing that whoops. **2.** WHOOPING CRANE.

whoop′ing cough′ (hōō′ping, hōōp′ing), *n.* an infectious disease of the respiratory mucous membrane caused by the bacterium *Bordetella pertussis* and characterized by a series of short, convulsive coughs followed by a whooping intake of breath.

whoop′ing crane′, *n.* a white North American crane, *Grus americana,* having a loud, whooping call.

whoops (hwŏŏps, hwŏŏps, wŏŏps, wŏŏps), *interj.* (used to express surprise, mild embarrassment, etc., or as a casual apology.)

whoosh (hwŏŏsh, hwŏŏsh, wŏŏsh, wŏŏsh) also **woosh,** *n.* **1.** a loud, rushing noise, as of air or water: *a great whoosh as the door opened.* —*v.i.* **2.** to move swiftly with a gushing or hissing noise: *gusts of wind whooshing down the street.* —*v.t.* **3.** to move (an object, a person, etc.) with a whooshing motion or sound.

whop (hwop, wop) also **whap,** *v.,* **whopped, whop·ping,** *n.* or **whapped, whap·ping,** *n. Informal.* —*v.t.* **1.** to strike forcibly. **2.** to defeat soundly. **3.** to pull violently; whip: *to whop out a book.* —*v.i.* **4.** to drop; flop (usu. fol. by *down*): *to whop down on the sofa.* —*n.* **5.** a forcible blow. **6.** the sound made by it. **7.** a bump; heavy fall.

whop·per (hwop′ər, wop′-), *n. Informal.* **1.** something uncommonly large of its kind. **2.** a big lie.

whop·ping (hwop′ing, wop′-), *adj. Informal.* **1.** very large of its kind; thumping: *We caught four whopping trout.* —*adv.* **2.** extremely; exceedingly: *a whopping big lie.*

whore (hôr, hōr; *often* hŏŏr), *n., v.,* **whored, whor·ing.** —*n.* **1.** a prostitute. —*v.i.* **2.** to act as a whore. **3.** to consort with whores.

who′re (hōō′ər), contraction of *who are: Who're the people at the next table?*

whorl (hwûrl, hwôrl, wûrl, wôrl), *n.* **1.** a circular arrangement of like parts, as leaves or flowers, around a point on an axis. **2.** one of the turns or volutions of a spiral shell. **3.** anything shaped like a coil. **4.** one of the ridges of a fingerprint forming at least one complete circle.

whorled (hwûrld, hwôrld, wûrld, wôrld), *adj.* **1.** having a whorl or whorls. **2.** disposed in the form of a whorl, as leaves.

whor·tle·ber·ry (hwûr′tl ber′ē, wûr′-), *n., pl.* **-ries. 1.** BILBERRY. **2.** BLUEBERRY.

who's (hōōz), **1.** contraction of *who is.* **2.** contraction of *who has.*

whose (hōōz), *pron.* **1.** the possessive case of WHO used as an adjective: *someone whose faith is strong.* **2.** the possessive case of WHICH used as an adjective: *a word whose meaning escapes me; a cat whose fur is white.* **3.** the one or ones belonging to what person or persons: *Whose umbrella is that?*

who·so·ev·er (hōō′sō ev′ər), *pron., possessive* **whose·so·ev·er,** *objective* **whom·so·ev·er.** whoever; whatever person: *Whosoever violates this law will be prosecuted.*

who's′ who′, *n.* **1.** a reference work containing short biographical entries on the outstanding persons in a country, industry, profession, etc.: *a who's who in science.* **2.** the outstanding or influential persons in a community, industry, profession, or other group: *The who's who of racing will be there.*

whr or **whr.,** watt-hour.

whup (hwup, wup), *v.t.,* **whupped, whup·ping.** *Southern U.S.* to defeat decisively; whip: *He whupped his opponent in three straight sets.*

why (hwī, wī), *adv., conj., n., pl.* **whys,** *interj.* —*adv.* **1.** for what reason or purpose: *Why do you ask?* —*conj.* **2.** for what cause or reason: *I don't know why he left.* **3.** for which; on account of which (usu. after *reason* to introduce a relative clause): *the reason why she refused to go.* **4.** the reason for which: *That is why he returned.* —*n.* **5.** a question concerning the cause or reason for which something is done, achieved, etc.: *a child's unending whys.* **6.** the cause or reason: *the whys and wherefores of the Cold War.* —*interj.* **7.** (used as an expression of surprise, hesitation, etc., or sometimes a mere expletive): *Why, it's all gone!*

why′ll (hwī′əl), contraction of *why will* or *why shall.*

why′re (hwī′ər), contraction of *why are.*

why′s (hwīz), contraction of *why is.*

Whyte (hwīt, wīt), *n.* **Alexander,** 1836–1921, Scottish clergyman.

WI, Wisconsin.

wic·ca (wik′ə), *n.* (*sometimes cap.*) witchcraft, esp. benevolent, nature-oriented practices derived from pre-Christian religions.

Wich·i·ta (wich′i tô′), *n.* a city in S Kansas, on the Arkansas River. 310,236.

wick (wik), *n.* **1.** a twist or braid of soft threads or a woven strip, as of cotton, that in a candle, lamp, etc., serves to draw up the flammable liquid to be burned. —*v.t.* **2.** to draw off (liquid) by capillary action.

wick·ed (wik′id), *adj.* **1.** evil or morally bad; sinful; iniquitous. **2.** mischievous or playfully malicious. **3.** distressingly severe, as weather. **4.** unjustifiable; dreadful; beastly: *wicked prices.* **5.** having a bad disposition; ill-natured; mean. **6.** spiteful; vicious: *a wicked tongue.* **7.** hazardous; dangerous: *wicked roads.* **8.** unpleasant; foul: *a wicked odor.* **9.** *Slang.* wonderful; great. —*adv.* **10.** *Slang.* very; totally: *a wicked cool shirt.* —**wick′ed·ly,** *adv.*

wick·ed·ness (wik′id nis), *n.* **1.** the quality or state of being wicked. **2.** wicked conduct. **3.** a wicked act or thing.

Wick′ed One′, the, *n.* Satan; the devil. Matt. 13:19.

Wick′ed Vine′dressers, The, a parable of Jesus. Matt. 21:33–41; Mark 12:1–12; Luke 20:9–18.

wick·er (wik′ər), *n.* **1.** a slender, pliant twig; osier. **2.** plaited or woven twigs or osiers as the material of baskets, chairs, etc.; wickerwork. **3.** something made of wickerwork, as a basket. —*adj.* **4.** consisting or made of wicker: *a wicker chair.* **5.** covered with wicker: *a wicker jug.*

wick·er·work (wik′ər wûrk′), *n.* material or products consisting of plaited or woven twigs or osiers; articles made of wicker.

wick·et (wik′it), *n.* **1.** a window or opening, often closed by a grating, as in a door, or forming a place of communication in a ticket office, a teller's cage in a bank, etc. **2.** a croquet hoop or arch. **3.** a small door or gate, esp. one beside, or forming part of, a larger one. **4.** a turnstile. **5.** *Cricket.* **a.** either of the two frameworks, each consisting of three stumps with two bails in grooves across the tops, at which the bowler aims the ball. **b.** the area between the wickets; the playing field. **c.** one batsman's turn at the wicket. **d.** the period during which two players bat together. **e.** a batsman's inning that is not completed or not begun.

wick·ing (wik′ing), *n.* **1.** material for wicks. **2.** the process whereby the fibers in a cloth garment draw perspiration from the skin and to the surface of the fabric, allowing the moisture to evaporate quickly.

wick·i·up or **wick·y·up** or **wik·i·up** (wik′ē up′), *n.* (in Nevada, Arizona, etc.) an American Indian hut made of brushwood or covered with mats.

wide (wīd), *adj.,* **wid·er, wid·est,** *adv.* —*adj.* **1.** of great extent from side to side; broad: *a wide street.* **2.** having a specified extent from side to side: *three feet wide.* **3.** vast; spacious: *the wide plains.* **4.** of great range or scope: *a person of wide experience.* **5.** expanded; distended: *to stare with wide eyes.* **6.** apart or remote from a specified objective: *wide of the truth.* **7.** too far to one side: *a shot wide of the mark.* **8.** Baseball. OUTSIDE (def. 14). **9.** full or roomy, as clothing: *wide, flowing robes.* **10.** (of a speech sound) LAX (def. 7). —*adv.* **11.** to the utmost, or fully: *to be wide awake.* **12.** away from a point or mark; astray: *The shot went wide.* **13.** over an extensive area: *scattered far and wide.* **14.** to a great extent from side to side: *The river runs wide here.* —**wide′ness,** *n.*

-wide, a combining form of WIDE, forming from nouns adjectives with the sense "extending or applying throughout a given space," as specified by the noun: *communitywide; countrywide; worldwide.*

wide′-an′gle, *adj.* **1.** of or pertaining to a lens having a relatively wide angle of view, generally 45° or more. **2.** employing or made with a wide-angle lens: *a wide-angle camera; a wide-angle shot.*

wide′-awake′, *adj.* **1.** fully awake; with the eyes wide open. **2.** alert or observant; sharp: *a wide-awake young woman.* —*n.* **3.** a soft, low-crowned felt hat. —**wide′-awake′ness,** *n.*

wide′bod′y or **wide′-bod′y,** *n., pl.* **-bod·ies.** a jet airliner with a cabin wide enough for passenger seating to be divided by two aisles rather than one.

wide′-eyed′, *adj.* having the eyes open wide, as in amazement, innocence, or sleeplessness.

wide·ly (wīd′lē), *adv.* **1.** to a wide extent. **2.** over a wide area: *a widely distributed plant.* **3.** by or among a large number of persons: *a widely known artist.* **4.** in many subjects: *to be widely read.* **5.** greatly or very: *widely differing accounts of the incident.*

wide·mouthed (wīd′mouthd′, -moutht′), *adj.* **1.** (of a person, object, body of water, etc.) having a wide mouth: *a widemouthed river.* **2.** (of a person) having the mouth opened wide, as in astonishment.

wid·en (wīd′n), *v.t., v.i.* to make or become wide or wider; broaden.

wide′-o′pen, *adj.* **1.** opened to the full extent: *a wide-open window.* **2.** lacking laws or strict enforcement of laws concerning liquor, vice, gambling, etc.: *a wide-open town.*

wide′-rang′ing, *adj.* extending over a large area; extensive or diversified in scope: *wide-ranging lands; a wide-ranging discussion.*

wide′ receiv′er, *n.* an offensive player in football, as a split end, who lines up wide of the formation and is used primarily as a pass receiver.

wide′-screen′, *adj.* **1.** of, noting, or pertaining to motion pictures projected on a screen having greater width than height, in an average ratio of 2.5 to 1. **2.** of, noting, or pertaining to a television screen that is larger than average.

wide·spread (wīd′spred′), *adj.* **1.** spread over a wide area. **2.** in many places or among many persons; far-reaching: *widespread poverty.*

widg·eon (wij′ən), *n., pl.* **-eons,** (*esp. collectively*) **-eon.** WIGEON.

widg·et (wij′it), *n.* **1.** a small mechanical device, as a knob or switch, esp. one whose name is not known or cannot be recalled; gadget. **2.** something typical or representative, as of a manufacturer's products.

wid·ow (wid′ō), *n.* **1.** a woman who has lost her husband by death and has not remarried. **2.** (in cards) an additional hand or part of a hand, as one dealt to the table. **3. a.** a short last line of a paragraph, esp. one less than half of the full measure or one consisting of only a single word. **b.** (esp. in word processing) the last line of a paragraph when it is carried over to the top of the following page. Compare OR-PHAN (def. 4). **4.** a woman often left alone because her husband devotes his free time to a hobby or sport: *a golf widow.* —*v.t.* **5.** to make (someone) a widow. **6.** to deprive of anything cherished or needed.

wid·ow·er (wid′ō ər), *n.* a man who has lost his wife by death and has not remarried. —**wid′ow·ered,** *adj.* —**wid′ow·er·hood′,** *n.*

wid·ow·hood (wid′ō hŏŏd′), *n.* the state or a period of being a widow or, sometimes, a widower.

wid′ow's mite′, *n.* a small contribution given by one who can ill afford it. Mark 12:41–44.

wid′ow's peak′, *n.* a point formed in the hairline in the middle of the forehead.

wid′ow's walk′, *n.* a platform or walk atop a roof, as on coastal New England houses of the 18th and 19th centuries, often used as a lookout for incoming ships.

width (width, witth; *often* with), *n.* **1.** extent from side to side; breadth. **2.** a piece of the full wideness of something, as cloth.

wield (wēld), *v.t.* **1.** to exercise (power, influence, etc.). **2.** to use (a weapon, instrument, etc.) effectively; handle or employ actively. —**wield′a·ble,** *adj.* —**wield′er,** *n.*

wield·y (wēl′dē), *adj.,* **wield·i·er, wield·i·est.** readily wielded or managed, as in use or action.

wie·ner (wē′nər), *n.* **1.** FRANKFURTER. **2.** VIENNA SAUSAGE. Also called **wie′ner·wurst′** (-wûrst′, -wŏŏrst′).

Wie·ner schnit·zel (vē′nər shnit′səl, shnit′səl), *n.* a breaded veal cutlet variously seasoned or garnished. [< German, *Wiener* Viennese + *Schnitzel* cutlet, chop]

wie·nie or **wee·nie** (wē′nē), *n.* WIENER.

Wies·ba·den (vēs′bäd′n), *n.* the capital of Hesse in W Germany: health resort; mineral springs. 251,800.

wife (wīf), *n., pl.* **wives** (wīvz). **1.** a woman joined in marriage to a man and considered as his spouse. **2.** a woman (*archaic* or *dial.,* except in idioms): *old wives' tales.* —**Idiom. 3. take to wife,** to marry (a particular woman): *And he took to wife a woman of the next village.* —**wife′dom,** *n.* —**wife′less,** *adj.*

wife·ly (wīf′lē) also **wifelike,** *adj.,* **-li·er, -li·est.** of, like, or befitting a wife. —**wife′li·ness,** *n.*

wig (wig), *n., v.,* **wigged, wig·ging.** —*n.* **1.** an artificial covering of hair or all or most of the head. **2.** a similar head covering, worn in one's official capacity, as part of a costume or disguise. **3.** a toupee or hairpiece. —*v.t.* **4.** to furnish with a wig. **5.** *Brit. Informal.* to reprimand severely; scold. **6. wig out,** *Slang.* to make or become wildly excited or enthusiastic. —**wig′less,** *adj.* —**wig′like′,** *adj.*

wig·eon (wij′ən), *n., pl.* **-eons,** (*esp. collectively*) **-eon.** either of two dabbling ducks, *Anas americana,* of North America, and *A. penelope,* of Eurasia, having prominent white patches on the forewings.

wig·gle (wig′əl), *v.,* **-gled, -gling,** *n.* —*v.i.* **1.** to move or go with quick, irregular state-to-side movements: *The puppies wiggled with delight.* —*v.t.* **2.** to cause to wiggle; move quickly and irregularly from side to side. —*n.* **3.** a wiggling movement or course. **4.** a wiggly line. —**Idiom. 5. get a wiggle on,** *Informal.* to hurry up; get a move on.

wig·gler (wig′lər), *n.* **1.** a person or thing that wiggles. **2.** WRIGGLER (def. 2). **3.** *Southern U.S.* an earthworm.

wig′gle room′, *n.* room to maneuver; latitude.

wig·gly (wig′lē), *adj.,* **-gli·er, -gli·est. 1.** wiggling: *a wiggly child.* **2.** undulating; wavy: *a wiggly line.*

wig·let (wig′lit), *n.* a small wig, esp. one used to supplement the existing hair.

wig·wam (wig′wom, -wôm), *n.* an American Indian dwelling of rounded or oval shape, formed of poles overlaid with bark, mats, or skins.

wigwam

Wil·ber·force (wil′bər fôrs′, -fōrs′), *n.* **William,** 1759–1833, British statesman, philanthropist, and writer.

wil·co (wil′kō′), *interj.* (esp. in radio transmission) an indication that the message just received will be complied with. [short for *will comply*]

wild (wīld), *adj.* **1.** living in a state of nature; not tamed or domesticated: *a wild animal.* **2.** growing or produced without cultivation, as flowers, fruit, or honey. **3.** uninhabited; undeveloped: *wild country.* **4.** uncivilized; barbarous: *wild tribes.* **5.** of unrestrained violence or intensity, etc.: *wild storms.* **6.** characterized by violent feelings or excitement: *a wild look.* **7.** frantic; distracted: *to drive someone wild.* **8.** unruly or lawless: *a gang of wild boys.* **9.** unrestrained by reason or prudence: *to regret one's wild youth.* **10.** amazing; incredible: *It's wild that he's suing for divorce.* **11.** disheveled: *wild hair.* **12.** wide of the mark: *a wild throw.* **13.** *Informal.* intensely eager or enthusiastic: *I'm wild about your new hairstyle.* **14.** (of a card) having its value decided by the wishes of the players. —*adv.* **15.** in an unrestrained manner; wildly. —*n.* **16.** Often, **wilds.** an uncultivated, uninhabited region or tract; wilderness: *a safari to the wilds of Africa.* —*v.t.* **17.** *Slang.* to attack or assault violently: *The gang wilded some runners.* —**wild′ly,** *adv.* —**wild′ness,** *n.*

wild′ boar′, *n.* a wild Old World swine, *Sus scrofa,* the ancestor of domestic breeds of hogs.

wild′ card′, *n.* **1.** a playing card having its value decided by the wishes of the players. **2.** a person or thing whose qualities are unknown or unpredictable but could be decisive. **3.** a character, as an asterisk, set aside by a computer operating system to represent one or more other characters of a file name, as in the DOS command "DEL *.DOC," which would delete all files with names ending in ".DOC."

wild′-card′, *adj.* of, being, or including an unseeded or unproven participant or team, as a team in a championship tournament that has not placed first in its league or area.

wild·cat (wīld′kat′), *n., pl.* **-cats,** (*esp. collectively*) **-cat** for 1, *adj., v.,* **-cat·ted, -cat·ting.** —*n.* **1. a.** a small striped Eurasian cat, *Felis sylvestris,* related to the domestic cat. **b.** any of several small- to medium-sized wild cats, as the bobcat or ocelot. **c.** a domestic cat that has become feral. **2.** a quick-tempered or savage person. **3.** a single locomotive operating without a train, as one switching cars. **4.** an exploratory well drilled in an effort to discover deposits of oil or gas; a prospect well. **5.** a reckless or unsound enterprise, business, etc. **6.** WILDCATTER (def. 2). **7.** WILDCAT STRIKE. —*adj.* **8.** characterized by or proceeding from unsafe business methods: *wildcat stocks.* **9.** of or pertaining to an illicit enterprise or product. **10.** running without control or regulation, as a locomotive, or apart from the regular schedule, as a train. —*v.i.* **11.** to search an area for oil, gas, ore, etc., esp. as an independent prospector. —*v.t.* **12.** to search (an area of unknown or doubtful productivity) for oil, ore, or the like.

wild′cat strike′, *n.* a labor strike that has not been called or sanctioned by the officials of the union.

wild·cat·ter (wīld′kat′ər), *n.* **1.** an oil prospector. **2.** a person who promotes risky or unsound business ventures. **3.** a person who participates in a wildcat strike.

Wilde (wīld), *n.* **Oscar (Fingal O'Flahertie Wills),** 1854–1900, Irish writer. —**Wild·e·an** (wīl′dē ən), *adj.*

wil·de·beest (wil′də bēst′, vil′-), *n., pl.* **-beests,** (*esp. collectively*) **-beest.** GNU.

Wil·der (wīl′dər), *n.* **1. Billy** (*Samuel Wilder*), born 1906, U.S. film director, producer, and writer; born in Austria. **2. Laura Ingalls,** 1867–1957, U.S. writer of children's books. **3. Thornton (Niven),** 1897–1975, U.S. novelist and playwright.

wil·der·ness (wil′dər nis), *n.* **1.** a wild, uncultivated, uninhabited region, as of forest or desert. **2.** a part of a garden set apart for plants to grow unchecked. **3.** a bewildering mass or collection.

Wil·der·ness (wil′dər nis), *n.* a wooded area in NE Virginia: several battles fought here in 1864 between the armies of Grant and Lee.

wil′derness ar′ea, *n.* a region whose natural growth is protected by legislation and whose recreational and industrial use is restricted.

Wil′derness Road′, *n.* a 300-mile (500-km) route from eastern Virginia through the Cumberland Gap into Kentucky, explored by Daniel Boone in 1769 and marked as a trail by him and other pioneers in 1775: a major route for early settlers moving west.

wild′-eyed′, *adj.* **1.** having an angry, distressed, or distraught expression in the eyes. **2.** so extreme or radical as to seem irrational or senseless: *a wild-eyed scheme.*

wild·fire (wīld′fīᵊr′), *n.* **1.** a highly flammable composition, difficult to extinguish when ignited, formerly used in warfare. **2.** any large fire that spreads rapidly and is hard to extinguish. —**Idiom. 3. like wildfire,** very rapidly and with unchecked force: *The rumor spread like wildfire.*

wild′flow′er or **wild′ flow′er,** *n.* the flower of a plant that normally grows without cultivation in fields, woods, etc.

wild·fowl (wīld′foul′), *n.* a game bird; a wild duck, goose, or swan.

wild′ gin′ger, *n.* any of various plants of the genus *Asarum,* of the birthwort family, esp. *A. canadense,* of E North America, having two heart-shaped leaves, a single red-brown flower, and a pungent rhizome.

wild′-goose′ chase′, *n.* a wild or absurd search for something nonexistent or unobtainable; a senseless pursuit.

wild′ hy′acinth, *n.* a plant having flowers resembling those of a hyacinth, as the camass, *Camassia scilloides,* of the central U.S.

wild·ing (wīl′ding), *n.* **1.** a wild apple tree. **2.** its fruit. **3.** any plant that grows wild. **4.** a plant originally cultivated that now grows wild; an escape. **5.** a wild animal. **6.** a spree of violent criminal activity, as by a group of youths. —*adj.* **7.** not cultivated or domesticated; wild.

wild·life (wīld′līf′), *n.* undomesticated animals living in the wild, including those hunted for food, sport, or profit.

wild′ oat′, *n.* any uncultivated species of *Avena,* esp. a common weedy grass, *A. fatua,* resembling the cultivated oat.

wild′ pitch′, *n.* a pitched baseball that the catcher misses and could not be expected to catch, resulting in a base runner's or runners' advancing. Compare PASSED BALL.

wild′ rice′, *n.* **1.** a tall aquatic grass, *Zizania aquatica,* of N North America. **2.** the grain of this plant, used for food.

wild′ rose′, *n.* an Old World roses growing wild, as the sweetbrier.

wild′ sarsaparil′la, *n.* SARSAPARILLA (def. 5).

wild′ tur′key, *n.* the ancestral species of the domesticated turkey. Compare TURKEY (def. 1).

wild′ type′, *n.* **1.** an organism having an appearance that is characteristic of the species in a natural breeding population. **2.** the form or forms of a gene commonly occurring in nature in a given species.

Wild′ West′, *n.* the western frontier region of the U.S., before the establishment of stable government.

Wild′ West′ show′, *n.* a show depicting scenes from the early history of the western U.S. and displaying feats of marksmanship, horsemanship, rope twirling, and the like.

wild·wood (wīld′wŏod′), *n.* a wood growing in the wild or natural state; forest.

wile (wīl), *n., v.,* **wiled, wil·ing.** —*n.* **1.** a trick, artifice, or stratagem to fool, trap, or entice. **2.** wiles, artful or beguiling behavior. **3.** deceitful cunning; trickery. —*v.t.* **4.** to beguile, entice, or lure (usu. fol. by *away, from, into,* etc.): *The music wiled him from his study.* **5. wile away,** to spend or pass (time), esp. in a leisurely or pleasurable fashion.

wil·ful (wil′fəl), *adj.* WILLFUL.

Wilkes (wilks), *n.* **1. Charles,** 1798–1877, U.S. rear admiral and explorer. **2. John,** 1727–97, English political leader.

Wil·kins (wil′kinz), *n.* **1. Sir George Hubert,** 1888–1958, Australian Antarctic explorer. **2. Maurice Hugh Frederick,** born 1916, English biophysicist, born in New Zealand. **3. Roy,** 1901–81, U.S. civil-rights leader.

will[1] (wil), *auxiliary v.* and *v., pres.* **will**; *past* **would**; *imperative, infinitive, and participles lacking.* —*auxiliary verb.* **1.** am (is, are, etc.) about or going to: *I will be there tomorrow. She will see you at dinner.* **2.** am (is, are, etc.) disposed or willing to: *People will do right.* **3.** am (is, are, etc.) expected or required to: *You will report to the principal at once.* **4.** may be expected or supposed to: *You will not have forgotten him.* **5.** am (is, are, etc.) determined or sure to (used emphatically): *People will talk.* **6.** am (is, are, etc.) accustomed to, or do usually or often: *She would write for hours at a time.* **7.** am (is, are, etc.) habitually disposed or inclined to: *Tyrants will be tyrants.* **8.** am (is, are, etc.) capable of; can: *This tree will live without water for three months.* —*v.t., v.i.* **9.** to wish; desire; like: *Take what you will. Ask, if you will, who the owner is.*

will[2] (wil), *n.* **1.** the faculty of conscious and particularly of deliberate action: *the freedom of the will.* **2.** power of choosing one's own actions: *to have a strong will.* **3.** the act or process of using or asserting one's choice; volition: *My hands are obedient to my will.* **4.** wish or desire: *to submit against one's will.* **5.** purpose or determination: *to have the will to succeed.* **6.** the wish or purpose as carried out, or to be carried out: *to work one's will.* **7.** disposition, whether good or ill, toward another. **8.** a legal document in which a person specifies the disposition of his or her property after death. Compare TESTAMENT. —*v.t.* **9.** to decide upon, bring about, or attempt to effect or bring about by an act of will: *He can walk if he wills it.* **10.** to purpose, determine on, or elect by act of will: *If you will success, you can find it.* **11.** to dispose of (property) by a will; bequeath. **12.** to influence by or as if by exerting will power: *I willed her to survive the crisis.* —*v.i.* **13.** to exercise the will. **14.** to decide or determine: *Others debate, but the king wills.* —**Idiom. 15. at will,** as one desires; whenever one chooses: *to wander off at will.* —*Proverb.* **16. Where there's a will, there's a way,** determination can make anything happen. —**will′er,** *n.*

will·a·ble (wil′ə bəl), *adj.* capable of being willed or fixed by will.

Wil·lard (wil′ərd), *n.* **1. Emma (Hart),** 1787–1870, U.S. educator. **2. Frances Elizabeth Caroline,** 1839–98, U.S. educator, reformer, and author.

will′-call′, *n.* **1.** a department in a store where merchandise is held for a customer until payment has been completed. **2.** LAYAWAY PLAN.

willed (wild), *adj.* having a will (usu. used in combination): *strong-willed; weak-willed.*

wil·let (wil′it), *n., pl.* **-lets,** (*esp. collectively*) **-let.** a large North American sandpiper with a striking black-and-white wing pattern.

will·ful or **wil·ful** (wil′fəl), *adj.* **1.** deliberate, voluntary, or intentional: *willful murder.* **2.** unreasonably stubborn or headstrong; perversely obstinate. —**will′ful·ly,** *adv.* —**will′ful·ness,** *n.*

Wil·liam (wil′yəm), *n.* **1. William I, a.** ("the Conqueror") 1027–87, duke of Normandy 1035–87; king of England 1066–87. **b.** (*William I of Orange*) ("the Silent") 1533–84, Dutch leader born in Germany: 1st stadholder of the Netherlands 1578–84. **c.** (*Wilhelm Friedrich Ludwig*) 1797–1888, king of Prussia 1861–88; emperor of Germany 1871–88. **2. William II, a.** (*William Rufus*) ("the Red") 1056?–1100, king of England 1087–1100 (son of William I, duke of Normandy). **b.** (*Frederick Wilhelm Viktor Albert*) 1859–1941, king of Prussia and emperor of Germany 1888–1918. **3. William III,** (*William III of Orange*) 1650–1702, stadholder of the Netherlands 1672–1702; king of England 1689–1702, joint ruler with his wife, Mary II. **4. William IV,** 1765–1837, king of Great Britain and Ireland 1830–37 (brother of George IV).

Wil·liams (wil′yəmz), *n.* **1. John Towner,** born 1932, U.S. composer and conductor. **2.** VAUGHAN WILLIAMS, Ralph. **3. Roger,** 1603?–83, English clergyman in America: founder of Rhode Island colony 1636. **4. Tennessee** (*Thomas Lanier Williams*), 1911–83, U.S. dramatist. **5. William,** 1717–91, Welsh clergyman and hymnwriter. **6. William Car·los** (kär′lōs), 1883–1963, U.S. poet and novelist.

Wil′liam Tell′, *n.* a legendary Swiss patriot of c1300 forced by the Austrian governor to shoot an apple off his son's head with a crossbow.

wil·lies (wil′ēz), *n.pl.* nervousness or fright; jitters (usu. prec. by *the*).

will·ing (wil′ing), *adj.* **1.** disposed or consenting; inclined: *willing to go along.* **2.** cheerfully consenting or ready: *a willing worker.* **3.** done, given, borne, used, etc., with cheerful readiness. —**will′ing·ly,** *adv.* —**will′ing·ness,** *n.*

wil·li·waw (wil′ē wô′), *n.* a violent squall that blows in near-polar latitudes, as in the Strait of Magellan, Alaska, and the Aleutian Islands.

will-o'-the-wisp (wil′ə thə wisp′), *n.* **1.** IGNIS FATUUS (def. 1). **2.** anything that deludes or misleads by luring on; an elusive thing or person.

wil·low (wil′ō), *n.* any tree or shrub of the genus *Salix,* of the willow family, characterized by narrow, lance-shaped leaves and dense catkins bearing small flowers, many species having tough, pliable twigs or branches used for wickerwork, etc.

wil′low herb′, *n.* any plant of the genus *Epilobium,* of the evening primrose family, having terminal clusters of purplish or white flowers. Compare FIREWEED.

wil′low oak′, *n.* a narrow-leafed North American oak, *Quercus phellos,* yielding a hard, heavy wood.

wil′low pat′tern, *n.* a decorative design in English ceramics, derived from Chinese sources, usu. executed in blue and white and depicting a willow tree, small bridge, and two birds.

will′pow′er or **will′ pow′er,** *n.* control of one's impulses and actions; determination; self-control.

Wil·son (wil′sən), *n.* **1. August,** born 1945, U.S. playwright. **2. Charles Thomson Rees,** 1869–1959, Scottish physicist. **3. Edmund,** 1895–1972, U.S. literary and social critic. **4. Henry** (*Jeremiah Jones Colbath* or *Colbaith*), 1812–75, vice president of the U.S. 1873–75. **5. Sir (James) Harold,** 1916–95, British prime minister 1964–70, 1974–76. **6. Lan·ford** (lan′fərd), born 1937, U.S. playwright. **7. Robert W(oodrow),** born 1936, U.S. radio astronomer. **8. (Thomas) Woodrow,** 1856–1924, 28th president of the U.S. 1913–21. **9. Mount,** a mountain in SW California, near Pasadena: astronomical observatory. 5710 ft. (1740 m).

wilt (wilt), *v.i.* **1.** to become limp and drooping, as a fading flower or parched plant; wither. **2.** to lose strength, vigor, assurance, etc. —*v.t.* **3.** to cause to wilt. —*n.* **4.** the act of wilting or the state of being wilted.

wil·y (wī′lē), *adj.,* **wil·i·er, wil·i·est.** full of, marked by, or proceeding from wiles; crafty; cunning. —**wil′i·ness,** *n.*

wim·ble (wim′bəl), *n., v.,* **-bled, -bling.** —*n.* **1.** a marbleworker's brace for drilling. **2.** any of various instruments for boring. —*v.t.* **3.** to bore or perforate with or as if with a wimble.

Wim·ble·don (wim′bəl dən), *n.* a former borough, now part of Merton, in SE England, near London: international tennis tournaments.

wimp (wimp), *n. Informal.* **1.** a weak, ineffectual, timid person. —*v.* **2. wimp out, a.** to be or act like a wimp. **b.** to show timidity or cowardice; chicken out. —**wimp′y,** *adj.,* **wimp·i·er, wimp·i·est.**

wim·ple (wim′pəl), *n., v.,* **-pled, -pling.** —*n.* **1.** a woman's headcloth drawn in folds about the chin, formerly worn out of doors, esp. in the Middle Ages, and still in use by some nuns. —*v.t.* **2.** to cover or muffle with or as if with a wimple. **3.** to cause to ripple or undulate, as water. —*v.i.* **4.** to ripple.

wimple

win (win), *v.,* **won, win·ning,** *n.* —*v.i.* **1.** to finish first in a race, contest, or the like. **2.** to succeed by striving or effort (sometimes fol. by *out*): *His finer nature won out.* **3.** to gain the victory; overcome an adversary: *The home team won.* —*v.t.* **4.** to succeed in reaching (a place, condition, etc.), esp. by great effort: *They won the shore through a violent storm.* **5.** to get by effort, as through labor or competition: *She won the post after years of striving.* **6.** to gain (a prize, fame, etc.). **7.** to be successful in (a game, battle, etc.). **8.** to make (one's way), as by effort or ability. **9.** to attain or reach (a point, goal, etc.). **10.** to gain (favor, love, consent, etc.), as by qualities or influence. **11.** to gain the favor, regard, or adherence of. **12.** to gain the consent or support of; persuade (often fol. by *over*): *The speech won them over to our side.* **13.** to persuade to marry one. **—***n.* **14.** a victory, as in a game or horse race. **15.** the position of the competitor who comes in first, esp. in a horse race. **—*Saying.*** **16. Win this one for the Gipper,** win for the sake of an admired figure: saying attributed to U.S. football coach Knute Rockne and associated with Ronald Reagan. —**win′na•ble,** *adj.*

wince (wins), *v.,* **winced, winc•ing,** *n.* **—***v.i.* **1.** to draw back or tense the body, as from pain or from a blow; start; flinch. **—***n.* **2.** a wincing or shrinking movement; slight start. —**winc′er,** *n.*

winch (winch), *n.* **1.** the crank or handle of a revolving machine. **2.** a windlass turned by a crank, for hoisting or hauling. **3.** any of various devices for cranking. **—***v.t.* **4.** to hoist or haul by means of a winch.

Win•ches•ter (win′ches′tər, -chə stər), *n.* **1.** a city in Hampshire, in S England: cathedral; capital of the early Wessex kingdom and of medieval England. 95,600. **2.** WINCHESTER RIFLE. **3.** WINCHESTER DISK.

Win′chester disk′, *n.* a hard disk permanently mounted in a hermetically sealed unit that is housed either within a computer's CPU or in an external disk drive case. [from the designation for the prototype, 3030 (two disks of 30 megabytes each), the same as a well-known Winchester rifle]

Win′chester ri′fle, *n.* a .44-caliber magazine rifle, first produced in 1866. [after D. F. *Winchester* (1810–80), U.S. manufacturer]

wind¹ (*n.* wind, *Literary* wīnd; *v.* wind), *n.* **1.** air in natural motion, as that moving horizontally at any velocity along the earth's surface, caused by temperature differentials in air. **2.** a gale; storm; hurricane. **3.** any stream of air, as that produced by a bellows or fan. **4.** WIND INSTRUMENT. **5.** wind instruments collectively, as distinguished from percussion and strings. **6. winds,** the members of a band or orchestra playing wind instruments. **7.** breath or breathing: *to catch one's wind.* **8.** the power of breathing freely, as during continued exertion. **9.** any influential force or trend: *the winds of public opinion.* **10.** a hint or intimation. **11.** air carrying an animal's odor or scent. **12.** empty talk; mere words. **13.** vanity; conceit. **14.** gas generated in the stomach and intestines. **—***v.t.* **15.** to expose to wind or air. **16.** to follow by the scent. **17.** to make short of wind or breath, as by vigorous exercise. **18.** to let recover breath, as by resting after exertion. **—***v.i.* **19.** to catch the scent or odor of game. **—*Idiom.*** **20. how** or **which way the wind blows** or **lies,** what the tendency or probability is. **21. in the teeth** or **eye of the wind,** directly into or against the wind. **22. in the wind,** about to occur; impending. **23. off the wind, a.** away from the wind; with the wind at one's back. **b.** (of a sailing vessel) headed into the wind with sails shaking or aback. **24. on the** or **a wind,** as close as possible to the wind. **25. sail close to the wind, a.** to sail as nearly as possible in the direction from which the wind is blowing. **b.** to practice economy in one's affairs. **c.** to verge on a breach of propriety or decency. **d.** to take a risk. **26. take the wind out of one's sails,** to destroy one's self-assurance; disconcert or deflate one. **—*Proverb.*** **27. It's an ill wind that blows no good,** one person's misfortune generally brings benefits to someone else.

wind² (wīnd), *v.,* **wound** (wound) or (*Rare*) **wind•ed** (wīn′did); **wind•ing;** *n.* **—***v.i.* **1.** to take a frequently bending course; change direction; meander: *The stream winds through the forest.* **2.** to have a circular or spiral course or direction. **3.** to coil or twine about something. **4.** to proceed circuitously or indirectly. **5.** to undergo winding or winding up. **6.** to be twisted or warped, as a board. **—***v.t.* **7.** to encircle or wreathe, as with something twined, wrapped, or placed about. **8.** to roll or coil (thread, string, etc.) into a ball, on a spool, or the like (often fol. by *up*). **9.** to remove or take off by unwinding (usu. fol. by *off* or *from*): *to wind thread off a bobbin.* **10.** to twine, fold, wrap, or place about something. **11.** to make (a mechanism) operational by turning a key, crank, etc. (often fol. by *up*): *to wind a clock.* **12.** to haul or hoist by means of a winch, windlass, or the like (often fol. by *up*). **13.** to make (one's or its way) in a bending or curving course. **14.** to make (one's or its way) by indirect, stealthy, or devious procedure: *wound his way into our confidence.* **15. wind down, a.** to bring or come to a gradual conclusion. **b.** to calm down; relax. **16. wind up, a.** to bring or come to a conclusion: *to wind up a campaign.* **b.** to end up: *to wind up in jail.* **c.** to make tense or nervous; excite: *She got all wound up before the game.* **—***n.* **17.** the act of winding. **18.** a single turn, twist, or bend of something wound. **19.** a twist producing an uneven surface.

wind³ (wīnd, wind), *v.t.,* **wind•ed** or **wound** (wound), **wind•ing. 1.** to blow (a horn, etc.). **2.** to sound by blowing.

wind•bag (wind′bag′), *n.* an empty, voluble, pretentious talker.

wind•blown (wind′blōn′), *adj.* **1.** blown by the wind: *windblown hair.* **2.** (of trees) growing in a certain shape because of strong prevailing winds. **3.** (of a woman's hairstyle) cut short in layers and combed forward so as to seem tousled by the wind: *a windblown bob.*

wind′-borne′ (wind), *adj.* carried by the wind, as pollen or seed.

wind•break (wind′brāk′), *n.* a growth of trees, a structure of boards, or the like serving as a shelter from the wind.

Wind•break•er (wind′brā′kər), *Trademark.* a jacket of wind-resistant material with close-fitting elastic hip band and cuffs.

wind•burn (wind′bûrn′), *n.* an inflammation of the skin caused by overexposure to the wind. —**wind′burned′,** *adj.*

Wind′ Cave′ Na′tional Park′ (wind), *n.* a national park in SW South Dakota. 41½ sq. mi. (107 sq. km).

wind′chill fac′tor (wind′chil′), *n.* the apparent temperature felt on the exposed human body owing to the combination of temperature and wind speed.

wind′ chimes′ (wind), *n.pl.* an arrangement of small pieces of glass, metal, bamboo, or the like, hung so as to strike each other and tinkle, as when moved by the wind.

wind•ed (win′did), *adj.* **1.** out of breath. **2.** having wind or breath of a specified kind (usu. used in combination): *short-winded.*

wind•er (wīn′dər), *n.* **1.** one that winds. **2.** a step that narrows toward one end: used in a spiral staircase. Compare FLIER (def. 8). **3.** an instrument or a machine for winding thread or the like.

wind•fall (wind′fôl′), *n.* **1.** an unexpected gain, piece of good fortune, or the like. **2.** something blown down by the wind, as fruit.

Wind•hoek (vint′ho͝ok′), *n.* the capital of Namibia, in the central part. 114,500.

wind•ing (wīn′ding), *n.* **1.** the act of a person or thing that winds. **2.** a bend, turn, or flexure. **3.** a coiling, folding, or wrapping, as of one thing about another. **4.** something that is wound or coiled, or a single round of it. **5. a.** a symmetrically laid, electrically conducting current path in any device. **b.** the manner in which wires are coiled to produce such a path: *a series winding.* **—***adj.* **6.** bending or turning; sinuous. **7.** spiral, as stairs. —**wind′ing•ly,** *adv.*

wind′ in′strument (wind), *n.* a musical instrument sounded by the breath or other air current, as the trumpet, oboe, or flute.

Wind′ in the Wil′lows, The, a children's novel (1908) by Kenneth Grahame.

wind•jam•mer (wind′jam′ər, win′-), *n.* any large sailing ship. —**wind′jam′ming,** *n.*

wind•lass (wind′ləs), *n.* **1.** a device for hauling or hoisting, usu. having a horizontal drum on which a rope attached to the load is wound; winch. **—***v.t.* **2.** to raise, haul, or move by means of a windlass.

wind•mill (wind′mil′), *n.* **1.** any of various machines for grinding, pumping, etc., driven by the force of the wind acting upon a number of vanes or sails. **2.** an imaginary opponent, wrong, etc. (in allusion to Cervantes' *Don Quixote*): *to tilt at windmills.* **—***v.i.* **3.** to move like a windmill. **4.** (of a propeller) to turn by itself, unpowered, driven only by the force of the airstream. **—***v.t.* **5.** to cause to move like a windmill.

win•dow (win′dō), *n.* **1.** an opening in the wall of a building, the side of a vehicle, etc., for the admission of air or light, or both, commonly fitted with a frame in which are set movable sashes containing panes of glass. **2.** such an opening with the frame, sashes, and panes of glass or any other device by which it is closed. **3.** a windowpane. **4.** a framed or bracketed opening in a wall, above a counter, etc., where some service or product may be obtained, as in a bank or post office. **5.** anything likened to a window in appearance or function, as a transparent section in an envelope. **6.** a period of time available or highly favorable for doing something. **7. a.** LAUNCH WINDOW. **b.** a specific area at the outer limits of the earth's atmosphere through which a spacecraft must reenter to arrive safely at its planned destination. **8.** a portion of the screen of a computer terminal on which data can be displayed independently of the rest of the screen. **—***v.t.* **9.** to furnish with a window or windows. —**win′dow•less,** *adj.* —**win′dow•y,** *adj.*

win′dow blind′, *n.* WINDOW SHADE.

win′dow box′, *n.* a box for growing plants, placed at or in a window.

win′dow dress′ing, *n.* **1.** the art, act, or technique of trimming the display windows of a store. **2.** anything used or done only to create a favorable impression. —**win′dow dress′er,** *n.* —**win′dow-dress′,** *v.t.*

win′dow en′velope, *n.* an envelope with a transparent opening through which the address on the enclosure may be read.

win•dow•pane (win′dō pān′), *n.* **1.** a plate of glass for filling a window sash within the frame. **—***adj.* **2.** being or having a large, regular design of intersecting lines suggesting windowpanes: *a windowpane plaid.*

win′dowpane shell′, *n.* CAPIZ (def. 2).

win′dow seat′, *n.* a seat built beneath the sill of a window.

win′dow shade′, *n.* a shade or blind for a window, as a sheet of cloth or paper on a spring roller.

win′dow-shop′, *v.i.,* **-shopped, -shop•ping.** to look at articles in store windows without purchasing any. —**win′dow-shop′per,** *n.*

win•dow•sill (win′dō sil′), *n.* the sill under a window.

wind•pipe (wind′pīp′), *n.* the trachea of an air-breathing vertebrate.

wind•proof (wind′pro͞of′), *adj.* resisting penetration by the wind, as fabric or a coat.

wind•row (wind′rō′, win′-), *n.* **1.** a row or line of hay left to dry before being raked into heaps. **2.** any similar row, as of sheaves of grain, for drying. **3.** a row of dry leaves, dust, etc., swept together by the wind. **—***v.t.* **4.** to arrange in a windrow.

wind′ sail′ (wind), *n.* a sail rigged over a hatchway, ventilator, or the like, to divert moving air downward into the vessel.

wind′ scale′ (wind), *n.* a numerical scale, as the Beaufort scale, for designating relative wind intensities.

wind′ shear′ (wind), *n.* **1.** the rate at which wind velocity changes from point to point in a given direction. **2.** a condition, dangerous to aircraft, in which the speed or direction of the wind changes abruptly.

wind·shield (wind′shēld′, win′-), *n.* a shield of glass, in one or more sections, projecting above and across the dashboard of an automobile.

wind′shield wip′er, *n.* an electrically or pneumatically operated device on a vehicle or craft consisting of a squeegee on a mechanical arm for wiping rain, snow, etc., from a windshield or window.

wind·sock (wind′sok′), *n.* a tapered, tubular cloth vane, pivoted to catch the wind and swing freely so as to indicate the direction toward which the wind is blowing.

winds′ of change′, *n.pl.* a decisive shift in political power or policies.

Wind·sor (win′zər), *n.* **1.** Duke of, EDWARD VIII. **2. Wallis Warfield, Duchess of** (*Bessie Wallis Warfield Spencer Simpson*), 1896–1986, U.S. socialite: wife of Edward VIII of England. **3.** Official name, **Wind′sor and Maid′enhead.** a city in E Berkshire, in S England, on the Thames: the site of the residence (**Wind′sor Cas′tle**) of English sovereigns since William the Conqueror. 129,900. **4.** a city in S Ontario, in SE Canada, opposite Detroit, Michigan. 193,111.

Wind′sor chair′, *n.* any of various wooden chairs of 18th-century England and America, having a spindle back and legs slanting outward.

Windsor chairs

wind·storm (wind′stôrm′), *n.* a storm with heavy wind but little or no precipitation.

wind·surf·ing (wind′sûr′fing), *n.* a form of sailing in which a person stands on a surfboard mounted with a flexible sail and guides the craft by maneuvering the sail. —**wind′surf′,** *v.i.* —**wind′surf′er,** *n.*

windsurfing

wind′-swept′ (wind), *adj.* exposed to or blown by the wind.

wind′ tun′nel (wind), *n.* a tubular chamber in which scale-model aircraft or other objects can be suspended and studied to determine their aerodynamic response to airflow of controlled velocity.

wind·up (wīnd′up′), *n.* **1.** the conclusion of any action, activity, etc.; end or close. **2.** *Baseball.* the preparatory movements of the pitcher's arm before pitching a ball. —*adj.* **3.** made to function by the manual winding of an internal spring or the like: *windup toys.*

wind·ward (wind′wərd), *adv.* **1.** toward the wind; toward the point from which the wind blows. —*adj.* **2.** pertaining to, situated in, or moving toward the quarter from which the wind blows (opposed to *leeward*). —*n.* **3.** the point or quarter from which the wind blows. **4.** the side toward the wind. —*Idiom.* **5. to (the) windward,** in or into a favorable or secure position: *to get to windward of a difficulty.*

Wind′ward Is′lands, *n.pl.* a group of islands in the SE West Indies, consisting of the S part of the Lesser Antilles: includes British, French, and independent territories.

wind·y (win′dē), *adj.,* **wind·i·er, wind·i·est. 1.** accompanied or characterized by wind: *a windy day.* **2.** exposed to or swept by the wind: *a windy hill.* **3.** unsubstantial; empty: *windy promises.* **4.** characterized by or given to prolonged, empty talk; voluble; bombastic. **5.** characterized by or causing flatulence. —**wind′i·ly,** *adv.* —**wind′i·ness,** *n.*

wine (wīn), *n., adj., v.,* **wined, win·ing.** —*n.* **1.** the fermented juice of grapes used esp. as a beverage, made in many varieties, as red or white, sweet or dry, and still or sparkling, and containing no more than 14 percent alcohol. **2.** the juice, fermented or unfermented, of various other fruits, used esp. as a beverage. **3.** a dark reddish color. **4.** something that invigorates, cheers, or intoxicates like wine. **5. new wine in old bottles,** something new placed in or superimposed on an old or existing form, system, etc. Matt. 9:17. —*adj.* **6.** dark red in color. —*v.t.* **7.**

to supply with wine. —*v.i.* **8.** to drink wine. —*Idiom.* **9. wine and dine,** to entertain lavishly. [< Latin *vīnum*] —**win′ish,** *adj.*

wine′ cel′lar, *n.* **1.** a cellar for storing wine. **2.** the wine stored there.

wine′ cool′er, *n.* **1.** a bucket for holding ice to chill a bottle of wine. **2.** a drink of wine, fruit juice, soda, and often flavorings.

wine·glass (wīn′glas′, -gläs′), *n.* a stemmed drinking glass in which wine is served.

wine·mak·ing (wīn′mā′king), *n.* the procedures and processes carried out in the making and maturing of wine; viniculture; oenology. —**wine′mak′er,** *n.*

win·er·y (wī′nə rē), *n., pl.* **-er·ies.** an establishment for making wine.

wine·skin (wīn′skin′), *n.* a bag, usu. of goatskin, for carrying wine.

wine′ stew′ard, *n.* a waiter in a restaurant or club who is in charge of wine; sommelier.

wine·tast·er (wīn′tā′stər), *n.* **1.** a critic or other professional who tests the quality of wine by tasting. **2.** a small bowl, often of silver, from which wine is tasted.

wine·tast·ing (wīn′tā′sting), *n.* a gathering of critics, buyers, friends, etc., to taste a group of wines for comparative purposes.

wing (wing), *n.* **1.** either of the two forelimbs of birds and some mammals, corresponding to the human arms, that are specialized for flight or may be rudimentary, as in flightless birds, and sometimes adapted for swimming, as in penguins. **2.** one of the paired thin, lateral extensions·of the body wall on the thorax of an insect, by means of which it flies. **3.** a means or instrument of flight, travel, or progress. **4.** the act or manner of flying. **5.** any winglike part or extension, as the vane of a windmill, the feather of an arrow, or the ala of a bone. **6. a.** one of a pair of airfoils attached transversely to the fuselage of an aircraft and providing lift. **b.** both airfoils, taken collectively. **7.** a part of a building projecting on one side of, or subordinate to, a central or main part. **8.** either of two forward extensions of the sides of the back of an easy chair. **9.** either of the two side portions of an army or fleet; flank. **10.** an administrative and tactical unit of the U.S. Air Force consisting of two or more groups, a headquarters, and various support units. **11.** a faction within a political party or other organization, usu. at one extreme or the other: *the liberal wing.* **12.** *Sports.* (in some team games) any one of the positions, or a player in such a position, on the far side of the center position, known as the left or right wing with reference to the direction of the opposite goal. **13.** *Theat.* Usu., **wings.** the space at the right or left side of the playing area of a stage, ordinarily not seen by the audience. **14.** *Bot.* any leaflike expansion, as of a samara. **15. wings,** any of various insignia representing outspread wings and usu. signifying achievement, acceptance, etc., esp. the successful completion of flight training. **16.** *Slang.* an arm of a human being. —*v.t.* **17.** to equip with wings or a winglike part or parts. **18.** to lend speed or celerity to. **19.** to transport on or as if on wings. **20.** to perform or accomplish by wings or by flight. **21.** to traverse in flight. **22.** to wound or disable in the wing: *to wing a bird.* **23.** to wound (a person) in an arm or other nonvital part. **24.** to deliver with or by the arm; throw or lob: *to wing a ball through a window.* —*v.i.* **25.** to travel on or as if on wings; fly; soar. —*Idiom.* **26. in the wings, a.** in the concealed side area of a stage; offstage. **b.** ready to be called or put into action, as a person or thing intended to replace another. **27. on the wing, a.** in flight, or flying: *a bird on the wing.* **b.** active; traveling. **28. take wing,** to begin to fly; take to the air. **29. under one's wing,** under one's protection, care, or patronage. **30. wing it,** to engage in something with little or no preparation or experience; improvise. —**wing′like′,** *adj.* —**wing′y,** *adj.,* **wing·i·er, wing·i·est.**

wing·back (wing′bak′), *n.* **1.** an offensive back in football who lines up outside an end. **2.** the position played by this back.

wing′ bolt′, *n.* a bolt with a head like a wing nut.

wing′ chair′, *n.* a large upholstered chair having a high back with wings.

wing′ col′lar, *n.* a stand-up collar having the front edges or corners folded down, worn by men for formal or evening dress.

wing′ command′er, *n.* a British air force officer equivalent in rank to an army lieutenant colonel.

wing′ding′ or **wing′-ding′,** *n. Slang.* a noisy, exciting party.

winged (wingd; *esp. Literary* wing′id), *adj.* **1.** having wings or a winglike part or parts: *the winged ants; a winged seed.* **2.** having a certain kind of wing (used in combination): *the white-winged dove.* **3.** moving on or as if on wings: *winged words.* **4.** rapid; swift. **5.** elevated or lofty: *winged sentiments.*

wing·er (wing′ər), *n.* (in Rugby, soccer, etc.) a person who plays a wing position.

wing·less (wing′lis), *adj.* **1.** having no wings. **2.** having only rudimentary wings, as a kiwi. —**wing′less·ness,** *n.*

wing′ nut′, *n.* a nut having two flat, widely projecting pieces such that it can be readily tightened with the thumb and forefinger.

wing·span (wing′span′), *n.* **1.** the distance between the wingtips of an airplane. **2.** WINGSPREAD.

wing·spread (wing′spred′), *n.* the distance between the outermost tips of the wings of a bird, insect, etc., when the wings are extended as far as possible.

wing′tip′ or **wing′ tip′,** *n.* **1.** the far or outer end of an airplane wing, wing of a bird, or the like. **2.** the portion of a bird's folded wing formed by the part of the·primary feathers extending beyond the secondary feathers. **3.** a toecap, often with a perforated pattern, having a

W

point at the center and side pieces that extend backward. **4.** a style of shoe with such a toe.

wink (wingk), *v.i.* **1.** to close and open one or both eyes quickly. **2.** to close and open one eye quickly as a hint or signal or with some sly or humorous intent. **3.** (of the eyes) to close and open quickly; blink. **4.** to shine with little flashes of light; twinkle: *city lights winking in the distance.* —*v.t.* **5.** to close and open (one or both eyes) quickly. **6.** to drive or force by winking (usu. fol. by *back* or *away*): *to wink back tears.* **7.** to signal or convey by a wink: *to wink hello.* **8. wink at,** to ignore (misdeeds or wrongdoing) deliberately. —*n.* **9.** an act of winking. **10.** a winking movement, esp. of one eye. **11.** a hint or signal given by winking. **12.** the time taken by one wink; an instant; a twinkling. **13.** a little flash of light; twinkle. **14.** the least bit. —**wink′ing•ly,** *adv.*

Win•ne•ba•go (win′ə bā′gō), *n.* **Lake,** a lake in E Wisconsin. 30 mi. (48 km) long.

win•ner (win′ər), *n.* a person or thing that wins; victor.

win′ner's cir′cle, *n.* a small, usu. circular area at a racetrack where awards are bestowed on winning mounts and their jockeys.

Win•nie-the-Pooh (win′ē thə pōō′), a collection of children's stories (1926) by A. A. Milne.

win•ning (win′ing), *n.* **1.** the act of a person or thing that wins. **2.** Usu., **winnings.** something that is won, esp. money. —*adj.* **3.** successful or victorious: *the winning team.* **4.** charming; engaging; pleasing: *a winning personality.* —**win′ning•ly,** *adv.*

Win•ni•peg (win′ə peg′), *n.* **1.** the capital of Manitoba, in S Canada, on the Red River. 594,551. **2. Lake,** a lake in S Canada, in Manitoba. 9465 sq. mi. (24,514 sq. km). **3.** a river in S Canada, flowing NW from the Lake of the Woods to Lake Winnipeg. ab. 200 mi. (320 km) long. —**Win′ni•peg′ger,** *n.*

win•now (win′ō), *v.t.* **1.** to free (grain) of chaff by fanning with wind or a forced current of air. **2.** to drive or blow (chaff, dirt, etc.) away by fanning. **3.** to blow upon; fan. **4.** to subject to some process of separating or distinguishing; analyze critically; sift: *to winnow a mass of statements.* **5.** to separate or distinguish (valuable from worthless parts) (sometimes fol. by *out*): *to winnow fact from fiction.* —*v.i.* **6.** to free grain from chaff by wind or driven air. —*n.* **7.** a device used for winnowing. **8.** an act of winnowing. —**win′now•er,** *n.*

win•some (win′səm), *adj.* sweetly or innocently charming; winning; engaging: *a winsome smile.* —**win′some•ly,** *adv.* —**win′some•ness,** *n.*

Win′ston-Sa′lem (win′stən), *n.* a city in N North Carolina. 155,128.

win•ter (win′tər), *n.* **1.** the cold season between autumn and spring, in the Northern Hemisphere from the December solstice to the March equinox, and in the Southern Hemisphere from the June solstice to the September equinox. **2.** the months of December, January, and February in the U.S., and of November, December, and January in Great Britain. **3.** cold weather. **4.** the colder half of the year (opposed to *summer*). **5.** a year. **6.** a period like winter; a period of decline, dreariness, or adversity. —*adj.* **7.** of, pertaining to, or characteristic of winter. **8.** (of fruit and vegetables) of a kind that may be kept for use during the winter. **9.** planted in the autumn to be harvested in the spring or early summer: *winter rye.* —*v.i.* **10.** to spend or pass the winter. —*v.t.* **11.** to keep, feed, or manage during the winter, as plants or cattle. —**win′ter•er,** *n.* —**win′ter•ish,** *adj.* —**win′ter•less,** *adj.*

Win′ter Games′, *n.pl.* Olympic Games held every fourth winter and including skiing, ice-skating, bobsledding, and other primarily winter sports. Compare SUMMER GAMES.

win•ter•green (win′tər grēn′), *n.* **1.** a creeping evergreen shrub, *Gaultheria procumbens,* of the heath family, bearing white flowers, red berries, and oval leaves that yield an aromatic oil. **2.** the oil itself. **3.** the flavor of this oil. **4.** any of various other plants of the same genus.

win•ter•ize (win′tə rīz′), *v.t.,* **-ized, -iz•ing.** to prepare (something) by various measures to be functional in or to withstand cold weather. —**win′ter•i•za′tion,** *n.* —**win′ter•iz′er,** *n.*

win•ter•kill (win′tər kil′), *v.t., v.i.* **1.** to kill by or die from exposure to the cold of winter, as wheat. —*n.* **2.** an act or instance of winterkilling. **3.** death resulting from winterkilling.

win′ter mel′on, *n.* a variety of late-keeping muskmelon, *Cucumis melo inodorus,* having sweet, edible flesh.

Win′ter Olym′pics, *n.pl.* WINTER GAMES.

win′ter sol′stice, *n.* the solstice on or about December 21 that marks the beginning of winter in the Northern Hemisphere.

win′ter squash′, *n.* any of several squash varieties that mature in late autumn and can be kept for an extended time.

win•ter•time (win′tər tīm′), *n.* the season of winter.

win′ter wheat′, *n.* any variety of wheat that is planted in the autumn to be harvested in the spring or early summer.

win•ter•y (win′tə rē, -trē), *adj.,* **-ter•i•er, -ter•i•est.** WINTRY.

Win•throp (win′thrəp), *n.* **1. John,** 1588–1649, English colonist in America: 1st governor of the Massachusetts Bay colony. **2.** his son, **John,** 1606–76, colonial governor of Connecticut 1657, 1659–76.

win•try (win′trē) also **wintery,** *adj.,* **-tri•er, -tri•est. 1.** of or characteristic of winter: *wintry skies.* **2.** suggestive of winter, as in lack of warmth or cheer; bleak. —**win′tri•ness,** *n.*

win′-win′, *adj.* advantageous to both sides, as in a negotiation: *a win-win proposal; a win-win situation.*

WIP, 1. work in process. **2.** work in progress.

wipe (wīp), *v.,* **wiped, wip•ing,** *n.* —*v.t.* **1.** to rub lightly with something in order to clean or dry the surface. **2.** to clean or dry by patting or rubbing on or with something. **3.** to rub or draw (something) over a surface, as in cleaning or drying. **4.** to remove by or as if by rubbing with or on something (usu. fol. by *away, off, out,* etc.). **5.** to erase, as from existence or memory: *to wipe a thought from one's mind.* **6.** to erase (magnetic tape, a recording, etc.). **7.** to seal (a pipe joint) with solder spread by a piece of cloth or leather. **8. wipe out, a.** to destroy completely; demolish. **b.** to murder; kill. **c.** *Slang.* to be forced out of competition by a fall, collision, etc. **d.** *Slang.* to fail decisively, as in one's training or in an enterprise. **9. wipe up,** to clean completely by wiping. —*n.* **10.** an act of wiping. **11.** a rub or one thing over another. **12.** a piece of absorbent material, as of paper or cloth, used for wiping. **13.** a sweeping stroke or blow. **14.** a gibe.

wiped′-out′, *adj. Slang.* completely exhausted.

wipe′out′ or **wipe′-out′,** *n.* **1.** destruction, annihilation, or murder. **2.** a fall from a surfboard.

wip•er (wī′pər), *n.* **1.** a person or thing that wipes. **2.** the thing with which something is wiped, as a towel, handkerchief, or squeegee. **3.** WINDSHIELD WIPER. **4.** a thin strip of metal providing electrical contact with a moving coil, as in a rheostat.

wire (wīr), *n., adj., v.,* **wired, wir•ing.** —*n.* **1.** a slender, stringlike piece or filament of metal. **2.** such pieces as a material. **3.** a length of such material used as a conductor of current in electrical, cable, telegraph, or telephone systems. **4.** a cross hair. **5. a.** a telegram. **b.** the telegraphic system: *to send a message by wire.* **6. wires,** a system of wires by which puppets are moved. **7.** *Naut.* a wire rope. **8.** a wire stretched across and above the track at the finish line of a racetrack. **9.** the woven wire mesh over which the wet pulp is spread in a papermaking machine. **10. the wire,** the telephone: *There's someone on the wire for you.* —*adj.* **11.** made of wire; consisting of or constructed with wires. —*v.t.* **12.** to furnish, fit, fasten, or bind with wire or wires. **13.** to install an electric system of wiring in, as for lighting. **14.** to send by telegraph. **15.** to send a message to by telegraph. **16.** to connect (a receiver, area, or building) to a television cable and other equipment so that cable television programs may be received. —*v.i.* **17.** to send a telegraphic message; telegraph: *Don't write; wire.* —*Idiom.* **18. down to the wire,** to the very last moment or the very end. **19. under the wire,** just within the limit or deadline; scarcely; barely. —**wir′a•ble,** *adj.*

wired (wīrd), *adj.* **1.** equipped with wires, as for electricity or telephone service. **2.** tied or secured with wires. **3.** strengthened or supported with wires. **4.** *Slang.* tense with excitement or anticipation. **5.** equipped so as to receive cable television.

wire′ fox′ ter′rier, *n.* one of a breed of fox terriers having a wiry coat. Also called **wire•hair** (wī^ər′hâr′), **wire′haired ter′rier.**

wire′ gauge′, *n.* a gauge calibrated for determining the diameter of wire.

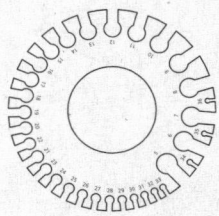

wire gauge

wire′haired′ or **wire′-haired′,** *adj.* having coarse, stiff, wirelike hair.

wire•less (wī^ər′lis), *adj.* **1.** having no wire. **2.** noting or pertaining to any of various devices that are operated with or actuated by electromagnetic waves. **3.** *Chiefly Brit.* radio. —*n.* **4.** wireless telegraphy or telephony. **5.** a wireless telegraph or telephone. **6.** a wireless message. **7.** *Chiefly Brit.* radio.

Wire•pho•to (wī^ər′fō′tō), *pl.* **-tos.** *Trademark.* **1.** a device for transmitting photographs by wire. **2.** a photograph so transmitted.

wire′ serv′ice, *n.* a business organization that sends syndicated news, usu. by teletypewriter, to its subscribers. Also called **wire agency.**

wire•tap (wī^ər′tap′), *n., v.,* **-tapped, -tap•ping.** —*n.* **1.** an act or instance of tapping telephone or telegraph wires for evidence or other information. —*v.t.* **2.** to listen in on by means of a wiretap: *to wiretap a conversation.* —*v.i.* **3.** to tap telephone or telegraph wires for evidence, information, etc. —**wire′tap′per,** *n.*

wire wheel (wī^ər′ hwēl′, wēl′ *for* 1; hwēl′, wēl′ *for* 2), *n.* **1.** a wheel-like brush having stiff wire bristles and used esp. for finishing or cleaning metal. **2.** a wheel, as on a sports car, having wire spokes.

wir•ing (wī^ər′ing), *n.* **1.** an act or instance of using, applying, or working with wire. **2.** the aggregate of wires in a lighting system, switchboard, radio, etc.

wir•y (wī^ər′ē), *adj.,* **wir•i•er, wir•i•est. 1.** made of wire. **2.** resembling wire, as in form, stiffness, etc. **3.** lean and sinewy: *a wiry little person.*

4. produced by or resembling the sound of a vibrating wire: *wiry tones.* —**wir′i•ly,** *adv.* —**wir′i•ness,** *n.*

Wis. or **Wisc.,** Wisconsin.

Wis•con•sin (wis kon′sən), *n.* **1.** a state in the N central United States. 5,159,795; 56,154 sq. mi. (145,440 sq. km). *Cap.:* Madison. *Abbr.:* WI, Wis., Wisc. **2.** a river flowing SW from N Wisconsin to the Mississippi. 430 mi. (690 km) long. —**Wis•con′sin•ite′,** *n.*

wis•dom (wiz′dəm), *n.* **1.** the quality or state of being wise; sagacity, discernment, or insight. **2.** scholarly knowledge or learning. **3.** wise sayings or teachings; precepts. **4.** a wise act or saying. —***Idiom.*** **5. the wisdom of Solomon,** exceptional wisdom. I Kings 4:34.

Wis′dom of Je′sus, Son′ of Si′rach, *n.* ECCLESIASTICUS.

Wis′dom of Sol′omon, *n.* a book of the Apocrypha.

wis′dom tooth′, *n.* **1.** the third molar on each side of the upper and lower jaws: the last tooth to erupt. —***Idiom.*** **2. cut one's wisdom teeth,** to attain maturity or discretion.

wise[1] (wīz), *adj.,* **wis•er, wis•est,** *v.,* **wised, wis•ing.** —*adj.* **1.** having the power of discerning and judging properly as to what is true or right; possessing discernment, judgment, or discretion. **2.** characterized by or showing such power; judicious or prudent: *a wise decision.* **3.** possessed of or characterized by scholarly knowledge or learning; learned; erudite: *wise in the law.* **4.** knowing; informed: *to be the wiser for it.* —*v.* **5. wise up,** *Slang.* to make or become aware or enlightened. —***Idiom.*** **6. be** or **get wise to,** *Slang.* to be or become cognizant of; learn. **7. get wise,** *Slang.* **a.** to become informed. **b.** to be presumptuous or impertinent. **8. put** or **set someone wise,** *Slang.* to inform someone, esp. about confidential information. **9. be wise after the event,** to understand a situation in hindsight. —**wise′ly,** *adv.*

wise[2] (wīz), *n.* way of proceeding or considering; manner; fashion (usu. used in combination or in certain phrases): *otherwise; in no wise.*

-wise, a suffixal use of WISE[2] in adverbs denoting manner, position, direction, reference, etc.: *clockwise; edgewise; marketwise.*

wise•a•cre (wīz′ā′kər), *n.* WISE GUY.

Wise′ and Fool′ish Vir′gins, The, a parable of Jesus. Matt. 25:1–13.

wise•crack (wīz′krak′), *n.* **1.** a smart or facetious remark. —*v.i.* **2.** to make a wisecrack. —*v.t.* **3.** to say as a wisecrack. —**wise′crack′er,** *n.*

wise′ guy′, *n. Informal.* a cocksure, conceited, and often insolent person; smart aleck.

Wise′ Men′, *n.pl.* the MAGI.

wish (wish), *v.t.* **1.** to want; desire; long for (usu. fol. by an infinitive or a clause): *I wish to travel. I wish that it were morning.* **2.** to desire (a person or thing) to be (as specified): *to wish the matter settled.* **3.** to entertain hopes or desires regarding the fortunes of: *to wish someone well.* **4.** to bid, as in greeting or leave-taking. **5.** to request or charge: *I wish him to come.* —*v.i.* **6.** to desire; long; yearn (often fol. by *for*): *to wish for a friend.* **7.** to make a wish. **8. wish on, a.** Also, **wish off on.** to pass or desire to pass (something undesirable) to another (often used negatively): *I wouldn't wish this weather on my worst enemy.* **b.** Also, **wish upon.** to use as a magical charm while making a wish. —*n.* **9.** an act or instance of wishing. **10.** a request or command: *to disregard someone's wishes.* **11.** an expression of a hope or desire toward another, usu. of a kindly or courteous nature: *to send one's best wishes.* **12.** something wished or desired. —***Proverb.*** **13. If wishes were horses, beggars would ride,** wishing doesn't make things happen.

wish•bone (wish′bōn′), *n.* **1.** a forked bone, formed by the fusion of the two clavicles, in front of the breastbone in most birds; furcula. **2.** a football offensive formation in which the fullback is directly behind the quarterback and two halfbacks are farther behind to either side.

wish•ful (wish′fəl), *adj.* having or showing a wish; desirous; longing. —**wish′ful•ly,** *adv.* —**wish′ful•ness,** *n.*

wish′ful think′ing, *n.* interpretation of facts, actions, words, etc., as one would like them to be rather than as they really are.

wish′ing well′, *n.* a well or pool of water supposed to grant the wish of one who tosses a coin into it.

wish′ list′, *n.* a usu. unwritten list of things one wishes for.

wish•y-wash•y (wish′ē wosh′ē, -wô′shē), *adj.* **1.** lacking in decisiveness; without strength or character; irresolute. **2.** washy or watery, as a liquid; thin and weak. —**wish′y-wash′i•ness,** *n.*

wisp (wisp), *n.* **1.** a handful or small bundle of straw, hay, or the like. **2.** any thin tuft, lock, mass, etc.: *wisps of hair.* **3.** a thin puff or streak, as of smoke; slender trace. **4.** a person or thing that is small, delicate, or barely discernible. **5.** WILL-O'-THE-WISP. —*v.t., v.i.* **6.** to twist into a wisp. —**wisp′like′,** *adj.*

wisp•y (wis′pē) also **wisp′ish,** *adj.,* **wisp•i•er, wisp•i•est.** being a wisp or in wisps; wisplike. —**wisp′i•ly,** *adv.* —**wisp′i•ness,** *n.*

wis•te•ri•a (wi stēr′ē ə) also **wis•tar•i•a** (-stēr′-, -stâr′-), *n.* any climbing shrub of the genus *Wisteria,* with pendent flower clusters in white, pale purple, blue-violet, or pink.

wist•ful (wist′fəl), *adj.* **1.** characterized by a pensive longing or yearning. **2.** pensive, esp. in a melancholy way. —**wist′ful•ly,** *adv.* —**wist′ful•ness,** *n.*

wit[1] (wit), *n.* **1.** the keen perception and clever expression of those connections between ideas that awaken amusement and pleasure. **2.** a person having or noted for such perception and expression. **3.** witty speech or writing. **4.** understanding, intelligence, or sagacity; astuteness. **5.** Usu., **wits. a.** shrewdness; resourcefulness; ingenuity. **b.** mental faculties; senses: *to have one's wits about one.* —***Idiom.*** **6. at one's wit's** or **wits' end,** drained of all ideas or mental resources; utterly confused or frustrated.

wit[2] (wit), *v.t., v.i., pres. sing. 1st pers.* **wot,** *2nd* **wost,** *3rd* **wot,** *pres. pl.* **wit** or **wite,** *past* and *past part.* **wist;** *pres. part.* **wit•ting. 1.** *Archaic.* to know. —***Idiom.*** **2. to wit,** that is to say; namely: *an overwhelming victory, to wit, a landslide.*

witch (wich), *n.* **1.** a person, now esp. a woman, who professes or is believed to practice magic, esp. black magic; sorceress. **2.** an ugly or mean old woman; hag. **3.** a person who uses a divining rod; dowser. —*v.t.* **4.** to subject to or bring about by or as if by witchcraft. —*v.i.* **5.** DOWSE[2] (def. 1). —**witch′hood,** *n.* —**witch′like′,** *adj.* —**witch′y,** *adj.,* **witch•i•er, witch•i•est.**

witch•craft (wich′kraft′, -kräft′), *n.* **1.** the art or practices of a witch; sorcery; magic. **2.** magical influence; witchery.

witch′ doc′tor, *n.* a person in some societies who attempts to cure sickness and to exorcise evil spirits by the use of magic.

witch•er•y (wich′ə rē), *n., pl.* **-er•ies. 1.** witchcraft; magic. **2.** magical influence; fascination; charm.

witch′es' brew′, *n.* a harmful or threatening mixture; diabolical concoction: *a witches' brew of innuendo and rumor.*

witch′es'-broom′, *n.* an abnormal, brushlike growth of small, thin branches on woody plants, caused esp. by fungi and viruses.

witch ha•zel (wich′ hā′zəl; *for 2 also* wich′ hā′-), *n.* **1.** a tree or shrub of the genus *Hamamelis,* esp. *H. virginiana,* of E North America, having toothed, egg-shaped leaves and small, yellow flowers. **2.** an extract from the leaves or bark of this plant mixed with water and alcohol, used as a liniment for inflammations and bruises and as an astringent.

witch′ hunt′ or **witch′-hunt′,** *n.* an intensive, often highly publicized effort to discover and expose those who are disloyal, subversive, etc., as in a government or political party, usu. on the basis of slight or doubtful evidence. —**witch′ hunt′er,** *n.* —**witch′-hunt′ing,** *n.*

witch′ing hour′, *n.* midnight.

with (with, wiŧh), *prep.* **1.** accompanied by; accompanying: *I will go with you.* **2.** in some particular relation to (esp. implying interaction, company, association, conjunction, or connection): *I dealt with the problem. She agreed with me.* **3.** characterized by or having: *a person with initiative.* **4.** by the use of as a means or instrument; using: *to line a coat with silk; to cut with a knife.* **5.** in a manner using or showing: *to work with diligence.* **6.** in correspondence, comparison, or proportion to: *Their power increased with their number. How does their plan compare with ours?* **7.** in regard to: *to be pleased with a gift.* **8.** owing to: *to shake with fear.* **9.** in the region, sphere, or view of: *It is day with us while it is night with the Chinese.* **10.** from: *to part with a thing.* **11.** against, as in opposition or competition: *Don't fight with your brother.* **12.** in the keeping or service of: *to leave something with a friend.* **13.** in affecting the judgment, estimation, or consideration of: *Her argument carried a lot of weight with the trustees.* **14.** at the same time as or immediately after; upon: *And with that last remark, she turned and left.* **15.** of the same opinion or conviction as: *Are you with me on this issue?* **16.** in proximity to or in the same household as: *He lives with his parents.* **17.** (used as a function word to specify an additional circumstance or condition): *We climbed the hill, with Jeff following behind.* —***Idiom.*** **18. with child,** pregnant. **19. with it,** aware of and participating in up-to-date trends. —***Proverb.*** **20. He that is not with me is against me,** anything less than active support is almost as damaging as direct opposition. Luke 11:23.

with•al (wiŧh ôl′, with-), *adv.* **1.** with it all; as well; besides. **2.** in spite of all; nevertheless.

with•draw (wiŧh drô′, with-), *v.,* **-drew, -drawn, -draw•ing.** —*v.t.* **1.** to draw back, away, or aside; take or pull back: *to withdraw one's support; She withdrew her hand.* **2.** to take out or away, as from a place or from consideration or circulation; remove: *to withdraw a product from the market.* **3.** to remove (money) from deposit. **4.** to retract or recall: *to withdraw an untrue charge.* **5.** to cause (a person) to undergo withdrawal from addiction to a substance. —*v.i.* **6.** to go or move back, away, or aside; retire; retreat: *to withdraw from the room.* **7.** to remove oneself from some activity, competition, etc. **8.** to cease using or consuming an addictive narcotic (fol. by *from*): *to withdraw from heroin.* **9.** (in parliamentary procedure) to remove a motion, amendment, etc., from consideration. —**with•draw′a•ble,** *adj.* —**with•draw′er,** *n.*

with•draw•al (wiŧh drô′əl, -drôl′, with-), *n.* **1.** the act of withdrawing. **2.** the state of being withdrawn. **3.** retirement or removal, as to a more peaceful or protected situation. **4.** something withdrawn, esp. a sum of money from a fund, account, or the like. **5.** the act or process of ceasing to use an addictive drug.

with•drawn (wiŧh drôn′, with-), *v.* **1.** pp. of WITHDRAW. —*adj.* **2.** removed from circulation, contact, competition, etc. **3.** shy and introverted; retiring; remote. —**with•drawn′ness,** *n.*

with•er (wiŧh′ər), *v.i.* **1.** to shrivel; fade; decay. **2.** to lose the freshness of youth (often fol. by *away*). —*v.t.* **3.** to cause to shrivel, fade, or lose vigor or bloom. **4.** to abash, as by a scathing glance; humiliate; shame.

with•er•ite (wiŧh′ə rīt′), *n.* a white to grayish mineral, barium carbonate, $BaCO_3$, occurring in crystals and masses.

with•ers (wiŧh′ərz), *n.* (*used with a pl. v.*) the highest part of the back at the base of the neck of a horse, cow, sheep, etc.

With•er•spoon (wiŧh′ər spo͞on′), *n.* **John,** 1723–94, U.S. theologian and statesman, born in Scotland.

with·hold (with hōld′), v., **-held, -hold·ing.** —v.t. **1.** to hold back; restrain or check. **2.** to refrain from giving or granting: *to withhold payment.* **3.** to collect (taxes) at the source of income, esp. as a deduction from salary or wages. —v.i. **4.** to hold back; refrain. Also called **with·hold′ing.**

withhold′ing tax′, n. that part of an employee's tax liability withheld by the employer from wages or salary and paid directly to the government. Also called **with·hold′ing.**

with·in (with in′, with-), prep. **1.** in or into the interior of or the parts or space enclosed by: *within city walls.* **2.** inside of; in: *the love within my heart.* **3.** in the compass or limits of; not beyond: *within view; to live within one's income.* **4.** at or to some point not beyond, as in length or distance; not farther than: *within a radius of a mile.* **5.** at or to some amount or degree not exceeding: *within two degrees of freezing.* **6.** in the course or period of, as in time: *within the year.* **7.** inside of the limits fixed or required by; not transgressing: *within the law.* **8.** in the field, sphere, or scope of: *within the family.* —adv. **9.** in or into an interior or inner part; inside. **10.** in or into a house, building, etc.; indoors. **11.** as regards the inside; internally. **12.** in the mind, heart, or soul; inwardly. —n. **13.** the inside of a place, space, or building.

with·out (with out′, with-), prep. **1.** with the absence, omission, or avoidance of; not with; with no or none of; lacking: *without help; without shoes; without you to help.* **2.** free from; excluding: *a world without hunger.* **3.** not accompanied by: *Don't go without me.* **4.** at, on, or to the outside of; outside of: *both within and without the city.* **5.** beyond the compass, limits, range, or scope of (now used chiefly in opposition to *within*): *either within or without the law.* —adv. **6.** in or into an exterior or outer place; outside. **7.** outside a house, building, etc. **8.** lacking something implied or understood: *We must take this or go without.* **9.** as regards the outside; externally. —n. **10.** the outside of a place, area, room, etc. —conj. **11.** *Midland and Southern U.S.* unless.

with·stand (with stand′, with-), v., **-stood, -stand·ing.** —v.t. **1.** to resist or oppose, esp. successfully: *to withstand the invaders; to withstand temptation.* **2.** to bear; tolerate the effects of: *to withstand pain; to withstand rejection.* —v.i. **3.** to stand in opposition; resist.

wit·less (wit′lis), adj. lacking wit or intelligence; stupid; foolish. —**wit′less·ly,** adv. —**wit′less·ness,** n.

wit·ness (wit′nis), v.t. **1.** to see, hear, or know by personal presence and perception: *to witness an accident.* **2.** to be present at (an occurrence) as a formal witness, spectator, bystander, etc.: *She witnessed our wedding.* **3.** to bear witness to; testify to; give or afford evidence of. **4.** to attest by one's signature. —v.i. **5.** to bear witness; testify; give or afford evidence. —n. **6.** a person who is present at an occurrence, esp. one who is able to attest as to what took place. **7.** a person who gives testimony, as in a court of law. **8.** a person or thing serving as evidence. **9.** a person who signs a document attesting the genuineness of its execution. **10.** testimony or evidence: *to bear witness to her suffering.* —**wit′ness·a·ble,** adj. —**wit′ness·er,** n.

wit′ness stand′, n. the place occupied by a person giving testimony in a court.

wit·ted (wit′id), adj. having wit or wits (usu. used in combination): *quick-witted; dull-witted.* —**wit′ted·ness,** n.

Wit·ten·berg (wit′n bûrg′, vit′-), n. a city in E central Germany, on the Elbe: Luther taught in the university here; beginnings of the Reformation 1517. 54,190.

Witt·gen·stein (vit′gən shtīn′, -stīn′), n. **Ludwig (Josef Johann),** 1889–1951, Austrian philosopher.

wit·ti·cism (wit′ə siz′əm), n. a witty remark or sentence; jest; quip.

wit·ty (wit′ē), adj., **-ti·er, -ti·est. 1.** amusingly clever in perception and expression; possessing wit: *a witty writer.* **2.** characterized by wit: *a witty remark.* —**wit′ti·ly,** adv. —**wit′ti·ness,** n.

Wit·wa·ters·rand (wit′wô′tərz rand′, -wot′ərz-), n. a rocky ridge in S Transvaal, in the Republic of South Africa, near Johannesburg: gold mining. Also called **The Rand.**

wive (wīv), v., **wived, wiv·ing.** —v.i. **1.** to take a wife; marry. —v.t. **2.** to take as wife; marry. **3.** to provide with a wife.

wives (wīvz), n. pl. of **wife.**

wiz (wiz), n. **wizard** (def. 2).

wiz·ard (wiz′ərd), n. **1.** a person who practices magic; magician or sorcerer. **2.** a person of amazing skill or accomplishment: *a wizard at chemistry.* —adj. **3.** of or pertaining to a wizard or wizardry; magic; enchanted. **4.** *Brit. Slang.* superb; excellent; wonderful.

wiz·ard·ry (wiz′ər drē), n. the art or skill of a wizard.

wiz·en (wiz′ən, wē′zən), v.i., v.t. **1.** to wither; shrivel. —adj. **2.** wizened.

wiz·ened (wiz′ənd, wē′zənd), adj. withered; shriveled: *wizened features.*

wk., **1.** week. **2.** work.

wkly., weekly.

WNW, west-northwest.

WO or **W.O.,** Warrant Officer.

w/o, without.

woad (wōd), n. **1.** any Old World plant of the genus *Isatis,* of the mustard family, esp. *I. tinctoria,* formerly cultivated for a blue dye extracted from its leaves. **2.** this dye.

wob·ble (wob′əl), v., **-bled, -bling,** n. —v.i. **1.** to incline to one side and to the other alternately, as a wheel, top, or other rotating body when not properly balanced. **2.** to move, walk, etc., unsteadily with a

side-to-side motion. **3.** to show unsteadiness; tremble; quaver: *His voice wobbled.* **4.** to vacillate; waver. —v.t. **5.** to cause to wobble. —n. **6.** a wobbling movement or effect. —**wob′bler,** n. —**wob′bli·ness,** n. —**wob′bly,** adj., **-bli·er, -bli·est.**

Wode·house (wŏŏd′hous′), n. **Sir P(elham) G(renville).** 1881–1975, U.S. novelist and humorist, born in England.

woe (wō), n. **1.** grievous distress, affliction, or trouble. **2.** an affliction: *She suffered a fall, among her other woes.* —interj. **3.** (used to express grief, distress, or lamentation.)

woe·be·gone (wō′bi gôn′, -gon′), adj. **1.** beset with woe. **2.** showing or indicating woe; forlorn: *a woebegone look on his face.*

woe·ful (wō′fəl), adj. **1.** full of woe; wretched; unhappy: *a woeful situation.* **2.** affected with, characterized by, or indicating woe. **3.** of wretched quality; sorry; poor: *a woeful collection of paintings.* Sometimes, **wo′ful.** —**woe′ful·ly,** adv. —**woe′ful·ness,** n.

wok (wok), n. a large bowl-shaped pan used in cooking Chinese food.

wok

woke (wōk), v. a pt. of **wake**[1].

wok·en (wō′kən), v. a pp. of **wake**[1].

wolf (wŏŏlf), n., pl. **wolves** (wŏŏlvz), v. —n. **1.** any of several carnivorous mammals of the genus *Canus,* esp. the gray wolf, *Canis lupus,* formerly common throughout the Northern Hemisphere. **2.** any of several other large canids, as the maned wolf. **3.** the fur of such an animal. **4.** any of various unrelated wolflike animals, as the thylacine. **5.** a cruelly rapacious person. **6.** a man who makes amorous advances to many women. **7.** a pitch of unstable quality or loudness sometimes occurring in a bowed musical instrument. —v.t. **8.** to devour voraciously (often fol. by *down*): *to wolf one's food.* —v.i. **9.** to hunt for wolves. —**Idiom. 10. cry wolf,** to give a false alarm. **11. keep the wolf from the door,** to avert poverty or starvation. **12. wolf in sheep's clothing,** a person who conceals evil beneath an innocent exterior. Matt. 7:15

wolf·ber·ry (wŏŏlf′ber′ē, -bə rē), n., pl. **-ries.** a North American shrub, *Symphoricarpos occidentalis,* of the honeysuckle family, with bell-shaped pink flowers and white berries.

Wolfe (wŏŏlf), n. **1. James,** 1727–59, English general. **2. Thomas (Clayton),** 1900–38, U.S. novelist. **3. Tom** (*Thomas Kennerly Wolfe, Jr.*), born 1931, U.S. novelist and journalist.

wolf·hound (wŏŏlf′hound′), n. any of several large dogs, as the borzoi or Irish wolfhound, formerly used in hunting wolves.

wolf·ish (wŏŏl′fish), adj. **1.** resembling a wolf, as in form or characteristics. **2.** characteristic of or befitting a wolf; fiercely rapacious. —**wolf′ish·ly,** adv. —**wolf′ish·ness,** n.

wolf′ pack′, n. **1.** a group of submarines operating as a unit to detect and destroy enemy convoys. **2.** a group of wolves that live and hunt together.

wolf·ram·ite (wŏŏl′frə mīt′, vôl′-), n. a mineral, iron manganese tungstate, $(Fe,Mn)WO_4$, occurring in heavy grayish black to brownish black tabular or bladed crystals: an important ore of tungsten.

wolfs·bane (wŏŏlfs′bān′), n. **1.** any of several plants of the genus *Aconitum,* of the buttercup family, esp. *A. lycoctonum,* bearing hood-shaped purplish blue flowers. **2. monkshood.**

wolf′ whis′tle, n. a whistle consisting of two gliding tones, uttered by a male to express appreciation of a female's appearance.

wol·ver·ine (wŏŏl′və rēn′, wŏŏl′və rēn′), n. **1.** a strong, stocky Northern Hemisphere carnivore, *Gulo luscus,* of the weasel family. **2.** (*cap.*) a native or inhabitant of Michigan (used as a nickname).

wolves (wŏŏlvz), n. pl. of **wolf.**

wom·an (wŏŏm′ən), n., pl. **wom·en** (wim′in), adj. —n. **1.** an adult female person, as distinguished from a girl or a man. **2.** a wife. **3.** a female lover or sweetheart. **4.** a female servant or attendant. **5.** women collectively; womankind. **6.** the nature, characteristics, or feelings often attributed to women; womanliness. —adj. **7.** female: *a woman plumber.* —**wom′an·less,** adj. —**Usage.** Although formerly **woman** was sometimes regarded as demeaning and **lady** was the term of courtesy, **woman** is the designation preferred by most modern female adults: *League of Women Voters; American Association of University Women.* **woman** is the standard parallel to **man.** When modifying a plural noun, **woman,** like **man,** becomes plural: *women athletes; women students.* The use of **lady** as a term of courtesy has diminished somewhat in recent years, although it still survives in a few set phrases (*ladies' room; Ladies' Day*). **lady** is also used, but decreasingly, as a term of reference for women engaged in occupations considered by some to be menial or routine: *cleaning lady; saleslady.* See also **girl, lady.**

-woman, a combining form of **woman**: *chairwoman; forewoman; spokes-*

woman. **—Usage.** Compounds ending in -WOMAN commonly correspond to the masculine compounds in -MAN: *councilman, councilwoman; congressman, congresswoman.* The current practice, esp. in edited written English, is to avoid the -MAN form in reference to a woman or the plural -MEN when members of both sexes are involved. Often, a sex-neutral term is used; for example, *council member* rather than either *councilman* or *councilwoman; representatives* or *legislators* rather than *congressmen.* See also -MAN, -PERSON.

wom•an•hood (wŏŏm′ən hŏŏd′), *n.* **1.** the state or time of being a woman. **2.** traditional womanly qualities. **3.** women collectively.

wom•an•ish (wŏŏm′ə nish), *adj.* **1.** characteristic of a woman; womanlike. **2.** weakly feminine; effeminate. **—wom′an•ish•ly,** *adv.*

wom•an•ize (wŏŏm′ə nīz′), *v.,* **-ized, -iz•ing.** **—v.t. 1.** to make effeminate. **—v.i.** to pursue or court women habitually.

wom•an•iz•er (wŏŏm′ə nī′zər), *n.* a philanderer.

wom•an•kind (wŏŏm′ən kīnd′), *n.* women as distinguished from men.

wom•an•ly (wŏŏm′ən lē), *adj.* **1.** having qualities traditionally ascribed to women; feminine; not masculine or girlish. **—adv. 2.** in the manner of, or befitting, a woman. **—wom′an•li•ness,** *n.*

wom•an•pow•er (wŏŏm′ən pou′ər), *n.* **1.** the women who make up a potential or actual labor force. **2.** the influence exerted by women as a group, as in social and political activities.

wom′an's rights′, *n.pl.* WOMEN'S RIGHTS.

wom′an suf′frage, *n.* the right of women to vote. **—wom′an-suf′-fra•gist,** *n.*

womb (wŏŏm), *n.* **1.** UTERUS. **2.** the place in which anything is formed or produced: *the womb of time.* **3.** the interior of anything. **—wombed,** *adj.*

wom•bat (wom′bat), *n.* a stocky, burrowing, herbivorous marsupial of the family Vombatidae, of Australia, about the size of a badger.

wom•en (wim′in), *n.* pl. of WOMAN.

wom•en•folk (wim′in fōk′) also **wom′en•folks′,** *n.pl.* **1.** women in general; all women. **2.** a particular group of women.

wom•en•kind (wim′in kīnd′), *n.* WOMANKIND.

wom•en's (wim′inz), *n., pl.* **-en's. 1.** a range of sizes usu. from 38 to 44 for garments that fit larger-than-average women. **2.** a garment in this size range.

wom′en's libera′tion, *n.* a movement to combat sexism and to gain full political, social, and other rights and opportunities for women equal to those of men. Also called **wom′en's libera′tion move′ment, wom′-en's move′ment.** **—wom′en's libera′tionist,** *n.*

wom′en's (or **wom′an's**) **rights′,** *n.pl.* the rights claimed for women, equal to those of men, with respect to suffrage, property, employment, etc.

wom′en's room′, *n.* LADIES' ROOM.

wom′en's stud′ies, *n.* a program of studies concentrating on the role of women in history, learning, and culture.

wom′en's wear′, *n.* apparel and accessories for women.

won (wun), *v.* pt. and pp. of WIN.

won•der (wun′dər), *v.i.* **1.** to think or speculate curiously and sometimes doubtfully: *to wonder about the future; to wonder about the truth of a statement.* **2.** to be filled with awe; marvel (often fol. by *at*): *We wondered at her skill and daring.* **—v.t. 3.** to speculate curiously; be curious to know: *I wonder what happened.* **4.** to feel wonder at: *We wondered that you went.* **—n. 5.** a cause of surprise, astonishment, or admiration: *It is a wonder he declined such an offer.* **6.** a feeling of amazement, puzzled interest, or reverent admiration: *a sense of wonder at seeing the Grand Canyon.* **7.** a remarkable or extraordinary phenomenon, deed, or event; marvel or miracle. **—won′der•er,** *n.*

won′der drug′, *n.* a new drug that is noted for its striking curative effect.

won•der•ful (wun′dər fəl), *adj.* **1.** excellent; grand; marvelous: *a wonderful vacation.* **2.** exciting wonder; marvelous; extraordinary: *a scene wonderful to behold.* **—won′der•ful•ly,** *adv.* **—won′der•ful•ness,** *n.*

Won′derful Wiz′ard of Oz′, The, a U.S. children's novel (1900) by Frank L. Baum, later made into a film, *The Wizard of Oz* (1939).

won•der•land (wun′dər land′), *n.* **1.** a land of wonders or marvels. **2.** a scene or place of special beauty or delight: *a winter wonderland.*

won•der•ment (wun′dər mənt), *n.* **1.** an expression or state of wonder. **2.** a cause or occasion of wonder.

won•drous (wun′drəs), *adj.* wonderful; remarkable. **—won′drous•ly,** *adv.* **—won′drous•ness,** *n.*

wonk (wongk), *n. Slang.* **1.** a student who studies intensively; grind. **2.** a person who studies a subject or issue in an excessively assiduous and thorough manner: *a policy wonk.* **—wonk′y,** *adj.*

wont (wônt, wōnt, wunt), *adj., n., v.,* **wont, wont** or **wont•ed, wont•ing.** **—adj. 1.** accustomed; used (usu. fol. by an infinitive): *She is wont to rise at dawn.* **—n. 2.** custom; habit; practice: *It was his wont to meditate daily.* **—v.t. 3.** to accustom (a person), as to a thing. **4.** to render (a thing) customary or usual (usu. used passively). **—v.i. 5.** to be wont.

won't (wōnt), contraction of *will not.*

wont•ed (wôn′tid, wōn′-, wun′-), *adj.* **1.** WONT. **2.** customary, habitual, or usual. **—wont′ed•ly,** *adv.* **—wont′ed•ness,** *n.*

won ton or **won•ton** (won′ ton′), *n.* a Chinese dumpling filled with minced pork and seasonings, usu. boiled and served in soup. [< dial. Chinese]

woo (wŏŏ), *v.,* **wooed, woo•ing.** **—v.t. 1.** to seek the favor, affection, or love of, esp. with a view to marriage. **2.** to seek or invite: *to woo fame; to woo one's own destruction.* **3.** to seek to persuade (a person, group, etc.), as to do something; solicit; importune. **4.** to court a woman: *He went wooing.* **—woo′er,** *n.* **—woo′ing•ly,** *adv.*

wood (wŏŏd), *n.* **1.** the hard, fibrous substance composing most of the stem and branches of a tree or shrub, and lying beneath the bark; the xylem. **2.** the trunks or main stems of trees as suitable for building and other purposes; timber or lumber. **3.** FIREWOOD. **4.** Often, **woods.** a large and thick collection of growing trees; a grove or forest. **5.** a cask or keg, as distinguished from a bottle: *aged in the wood.* **6.** any of a set of four golf clubs, orig. with wooden heads, used for hitting long shots. Compare IRON (def. 5). **—adj. 7.** made of wood; wooden. **8.** used to store, work, or carry wood: *a wood chisel.* **9.** dwelling or growing in woods: *a wood bird.* **—v.t. 10.** to cover or plant with trees. **—v.i. 11.** to take in or get supplies of wood (often fol. by *up*): *to wood up before winter comes.* **—Idiom. 12. out of the woods,** no longer in a dangerous, critical, or difficult situation or condition; safe. **—wood′less,** *adj.*

Wood (wŏŏd), *n.* **Grant,** 1892–1942, U.S. painter.

wood′ al′cohol, *n.* METHYL ALCOHOL.

wood′ anem′one, *n.* any of several anemones, esp. *Anemone nemorosa,* of the Old World, or *A. quinquefolia,* of the U.S.

wood•bine (wŏŏd′bīn′), *n.* any of several climbing vines, as a European honeysuckle or the Virginia creeper.

wood•block (wŏŏd′blok′), *n.* **1.** WOODCUT. **2.** a hollow block of hard wood struck with a stick or mallet and used in the percussion section of an orchestra. **—adj. 3.** made from a woodcut: *woodblock prints.*

wood•bor•er (wŏŏd′bôr′ər, -bōr′-), *n.* **1.** a tool, operated by compressed air, for boring wood. **2.** any of various beetles, worms, mollusks, etc., that bore into wood. **—wood′bor′ing,** *adj.*

wood•carv•ing (wŏŏd′kär′ving), *n.* **1.** the art of carving objects by hand from wood or of carving decorations into wood. **2.** something made or decorated in such a manner. **—wood′carv′er,** *n.*

wood•chuck (wŏŏd′chuk′), *n.* a stocky North American burrowing rodent, *Marmota monax,* that hibernates in the winter. Also called **groundhog.**

wood′ coal′, *n.* **1.** brown coal; lignite. **2.** charcoal.

wood•cock (wŏŏd′kok′), *n., pl.* **-cocks,** (*esp. collectively*) **-cock.** either of two plump, short-legged woodland birds of the sandpiper family, a North American species *Scolopax minor* and a larger Eurasian species *S. rusticola,* having variegated brown plumage.

wood•craft (wŏŏd′kraft′, -kräft′), *n.* **1.** skill in anything that pertains to the woods or forest, esp. in making one's way through the woods or in hunting, trapping, etc. **2.** the art of making or carving wooden objects. **—wood′crafts′man,** *n., pl.* **-men.**

wood•creep•er (wŏŏd′krē′pər), *n.* any of various suboscine birds of the family Dendrocolaptidae, of New World tropical and subtropical regions, having stiffened tail feathers and primarily brown or rufous plumage: most seek insects by climbing up tree trunks.

wood•cut (wŏŏd′kut′), *n.* **1.** a block of wood engraved in relief, from which prints are made; woodblock. **2.** a print or impression from such a block.

wood•ed (wŏŏd′id), *adj.* covered with or abounding in woods or trees.

wood•en (wŏŏd′n), *adj.* **1.** consisting or made of wood; wood. **2.** stiff, ungainly, or awkward: *a wooden gait.* **3.** without spirit, animation, or awareness. **—Saying. 4. Don't take any wooden nickels,** don't let anyone cheat or deceive you. **—wood′en•ly,** *adv.* **—wood′en•ness,** *n.*

wood′ engrav′ing, *n.* **1.** the art or process of engraving designs in relief with a burin on wood cut against the grain, for printing. **2.** a block of wood so engraved. **3.** a print or impression from it.

wood′en In′dian, *n.* a carved wooden statue of a standing American Indian, formerly placed before a cigar store as an advertisement.

wood•grain (wŏŏd′grān′), *n.* **1.** a material or finish that imitates the natural grain of wood in pattern, color, and sometimes texture. **—adj. 2.** of or pertaining to woodgrain. **—wood′grain′ing,** *n.*

wood′ i′bis, *n.* WOOD STORK.

wood•land (*n.* wŏŏd′land′, -lənd; *adj.* -lənd), *n.* **1.** land covered with woods or trees. **—adj. 2.** of, pertaining to, or inhabiting the woods; sylvan: *a woodland nymph.* **—wood′land•er,** *n.*

wood′ lot′ or **wood′lot′,** *n.* a tract, esp. on a farm, set aside for trees.

wood′ louse′, *n.* any of various tiny isopod crustaceans, often of damp shady habitats, as the pill bug and the sow bug.

wood′ nymph′, *n.* **1.** a nymph of the woods; dryad. **2.** a brown satyr butterfly, *Cercyonis pegala,* having a broad yellow band and black-and-white eyelike spots on each front wing.

wood•peck•er (wŏŏd′pek′ər), *n.* any of numerous climbing birds of the family Picidae, of nearly worldwide distribution, having a chisellike bill that is hammered repeatedly into wood in search of insects and stiff tail feathers that assist in climbing: often boldly patterned.

wood′ pi′geon, *n.* a Eurasian pigeon, *Columba palumbus,* having a whitish patch on each side of the neck.

wood′ pulp′, *n.* wood reduced to pulp through various treatments for use in manufacturing certain kinds of paper.

wood•ruff (wŏŏd′rəf, -ruf′), *n.* any of several plants of the genus *Asperula,* of the madder family, as *A. odorata,* a fragrant plant with small white flowers.

wood·shed (wŏŏd/shed/), *n., v.,* **-shed·ded, -shed·ding.** —*n.* **1.** a shed for storing wood for fuel. —*v.i.* **2.** *Informal.* to practice a musical instrument assiduously and with a specific goal in mind: *He's woodshedding for next week's show.*

woods·man (wŏŏdz/mən), *n., pl.* **-men. 1.** Also, **woodman.** a person accustomed to life in the woods and skilled in the arts of the woods, as hunting or trapping. **2.** a lumberman.

wood′ sor′rel, *n.* any woodland plant of the genus *Oxalis,* of the family Oxalidaceae, having three heart-shaped leaflets and colorful flowers.

Wood·stock (wŏŏd/stok/), *n.* a rock music festival held in August 1969 near Bethel, a village in SE New York: orig. to have been held near Woodstock, a town in SE New York.

wood′ stork′, *n.* a large white stork, *Mycteria americana,* inhabiting warmer parts of the New World, with a naked head and neck and black flight feathers.

wood′ sug′ar, *n.* a white, crystalline, water-soluble powder, $C_5H_{10}O_5$, the dextrorotatory form of xylose: used chiefly in dyeing and tanning.

woods·y (wŏŏd/zē), *adj.,* **woods·i·er, woods·i·est.** of, or characteristic or suggestive of, the woods: *a woodsy fragrance.*

wood′ tar′, *n.* a dark, viscid wood product used to preserve timber, rope, etc., or distilled to yield creosote, oils, and pitch.

wood′ thrush′, *n.* a large, melodious thrush, *Hylocichla mustelina,* breeding in woodlands of E North America.

wood·tone (wŏŏd/tōn/), *adj.* **1.** having a finish painted, dyed, printed, etc., to imitate the pattern or color of wood; woodgrain. —*n.* **2.** a woodtone finish.

wood′ turn′ing, *n.* the forming of wood articles upon a lathe. —**wood′turn′er,** *n.* —**wood′-turn′ing,** *adj.*

wood′ tur′pentine, *n.* turpentine obtained from pine trees.

wood·wind (wŏŏd/wind/), *n.* **1.** a musical wind instrument of the group comprising the flutes, clarinets, oboes, bassoons, and sometimes the saxophones. **2. woodwinds,** the section of an orchestra or band comprising the woodwind instruments.

wood·work (wŏŏd/wûrk/), *n.* **1.** objects or parts made of wood. **2.** interior wooden fittings, esp. of a house, as doors, stairways, or moldings. —*Idiom.* **3. come out of the woodwork,** to emerge, as from a hiding place.

wood·work·er (wŏŏd/wûr/kər), *n.* a worker in wood, as a carpenter, joiner, or cabinetmaker.

wood·work·ing (wŏŏd/wûr/king), *n.* **1.** the act or art of working wood. —*adj.* **2.** of or used for shaping wood: *woodworking tools.*

wood·y¹ (wŏŏd/ē), *adj.,* **wood·i·er, wood·i·est. 1.** abounding with woods; wooded. **2.** belonging or pertaining to the woods; sylvan. **3.** consisting of or containing wood; ligneous. **4.** resembling wood, as in appearance, texture, or toughness: *a woody vegetable.*

wood·y² or **wood·ie** (wŏŏd/ē), *n., pl.* **wood·ies.** *Informal.* a station wagon having wood panels on the outside of the body.

woof¹ (wŏŏf, wŏŏf), *n.* **1.** FILLING (def. 4). **2.** texture; fabric.

woof² (wŏŏf), *n.* **1.** the bark of a dog, esp. when low-pitched. —*v.i.* **2.** to make this sound. —*interj.* **3.** (used to imitate the bark of a dog.)

woof·er (wŏŏf/ər), *n.* a loudspeaker designed for the reproduction of low-frequency sounds.

wool (wŏŏl), *n.* **1.** the fine, soft, curly hair that forms the fleece of sheep and certain other animals. **2.** yarn made of such wool. **3.** a fabric or garment of such wool. **4.** any finely fibrous or filamentous matter suggestive of the wool of sheep: *steel wool.* **5.** any coating of short, fine hairs or hairlike processes, as on a caterpillar or a plant; pubescence. —*Idiom.* **6. pull the wool over someone's eyes,** to deceive or delude someone. —**wool/like/,** *adj.*

wool·en (wŏŏl/ən), *n.* **1.** any cloth of carded wool yarn of which the fibers vary in length: bulkier, looser, and less regular than worsted. **2. woolens,** wool cloth or clothing. —*adj.* **3.** made or consisting of wool: *woolen cloth.* **4.** of or pertaining to wool or woolen fabrics. Also, *esp. Brit.,* **wool/len.**

Woolf (wŏŏlf), *n.* **Virginia** (*Adeline Virginia Stephen Woolf*), 1882–1941, English novelist, essayist, and critic.

wool·gath·er·ing (wŏŏl/gath/ər ing), *n.* **1.** indulgence in idle fancies and in daydreaming; absentmindedness. **2.** gathering of the tufts of wool shed by sheep and caught on bushes. —**wool/gath/er,** *v.i.*

wool·ly or **wool·y** (wŏŏl/ē), *adj.,* **wool·li·er** or **wool·i·er, wool·li·est** or **wool·i·est,** *n., pl.* **wool·lies** or **wool·ies.** —*adj.* **1.** consisting of or resembling wool: *a woolly fleece; woolly hair.* **2.** clothed or covered with wool or something like it: *a woolly caterpillar.* **3.** like the rough, vigorous atmosphere of the early West in the U.S.: *wild and woolly.* **4.** fuzzy; unclear; disorganized: *woolly thinking.* —*n.* **5.** *Western U.S.* a wool-bearing animal; sheep. **6.** Also, **wool/ie.** Usu. **woollies** or **wool·ies.** a woolen garment, esp. a knitted undergarment. —**wool/li·ness,** *n.*

wool′ly mam′moth, *n.* a shaggy-coated Pleistocene mammoth, *Mammuthus primigenius,* that lived in cold regions across Eurasia and North America.

Wool·man (wŏŏl/mən), *n.* **John,** 1720–72, American Quaker leader.

wool·pack (wŏŏl/pak/), *n.* **1.** a coarse fabric, usu. of jute, in which raw wool is packed for transport. **2.** the package in which raw wool is done up for transport. **3.** a cumulus cloud of fleecy appearance with a horizontal base.

Wool·worth (wŏŏl/wûrth/), *n.* **Frank Winfield,** 1852–1919, U.S. merchant.

wool·y (wŏŏl/ē), *adj.,* **wool·i·er, wool·i·est,** *n., pl.* **wool·ies.** WOOLLY. —**wool/i·ness,** *n.*

wooz·y (wŏŏ/zē, wŏŏz/ē), *adj.,* **wooz·i·er, wooz·i·est. 1.** stupidly confused; muddled. **2.** physically unsettled, as with dizziness, faintness, or slight nausea. —**wooz/i·ly,** *adv.* —**wooz/i·ness,** *n.*

Worces·ter (wŏŏs/tər), *n.* **1. Joseph Emerson,** 1784–1865, U.S. lexicographer. **2.** a city in central Massachusetts. 165,387. **3.** a city in Hereford and Worcester, in W England, on the Severn. 74,300. **4.** WORCESTERSHIRE.

Worces·ter·shire (wŏŏs/tər shēr/, -shər), *n.* a former county in W central England, now part of Hereford and Worcester.

Worces′ter·shire sauce′, (wŏŏs/tər shēr/), *n.* a sharp sauce of soy, vinegar, spices, etc., orig. made in Worcester, England.

word (wûrd), *n.* **1.** a unit of language, consisting of one or more spoken sounds or their written representation, that functions as a principal carrier of meaning, is typically seen as the smallest such unit capable of independent use, is separated from other such units by spaces in writing, and is often distinguished phonologically, as by accent or pause. **2. words, a.** verbal expression, esp. speech or talk: *to express one's emotions in words.* **b.** the text or lyrics of a song as distinguished from the music. **c.** contentious or angry speech; a quarrel. **3.** a short talk or conversation. **4.** an expression or utterance: *a word of warning.* **5.** warrant, assurance, or promise. **6.** news; tidings; information. **7.** a verbal signal, as a password, watchword, or countersign. **8.** an authoritative utterance or command: *His word was law.* **9.** a string of bits or bytes of fixed length treated as a unit for storage and processing by a computer. **10.** (*cap.*) Also called **the Word, the Word′ of God′. a.** the Scriptures; the Bible. **b.** the Logos. **c.** the message of the gospel of Christ. **d.** Jesus Christ. 1 John 1:1–14; Rev. 19:13. **11.** a proverb or motto. —*v.t.* **12.** to select words to express; phrase: *to word a contract carefully.* —*interj.* **13.** Sometimes, **word up.** *Slang.* (used to express satisfaction, approval, or agreement): *You got a job? Word!* —*Idiom.* **14. be as good as one's word,** to do what one has promised. **15. eat one's words,** to retract one's statement, esp. with humility. **16. in a word,** in summary; in short. **17. in so many words,** in unequivocal terms; explicitly: *She told them in so many words to get out.* **18. man of his word** or **woman of her word,** a trustworthy, reliable person. **19. my word!** or **upon my word!** (used as an exclamation of surprise or astonishment.) **20. of few words,** not talkative; laconic; taciturn. **21. of many words,** talkative; loquacious; wordy. **22. put in a (good) word for,** to speak favorably on behalf of; commend. **23. take one at one's word,** to take a statement to be literal and true. **24. take the words out of someone's mouth,** to say exactly what another person was about to say. —*Proverb.* **25. A word to the wise (is sufficient),** intelligent people need to be told something only once.

word·book (wûrd/bŏŏk/), *n.* a book of words, usu. with definitions, explanations, etc.; a dictionary.

word′ for word′, *adv.* **1.** in exactly the same words; verbatim. **2.** one word at a time, without regard for the sense of the whole: *to translate a book word for word.* —**word′-for-word′,** *adj.*

word·ing (wûr/ding), *n.* **1.** the act or manner of expressing in words; phrasing. **2.** the particular choice of words in which a thing is expressed: *I like the thought but not the wording.*

word·less (wûrd/lis), *adj.* **1.** speechless; silent. **2.** not put into words; unexpressed. —**word/less·ly,** *adv.* —**word/less·ness,** *n.*

word′ of mouth′, *n.* informal oral communication: *rumors spreading by word of mouth.* —**word′-of-mouth′,** *adj.*

word′ or′der, *n.* the way in which words are arranged in sequence in a sentence or smaller construction.

word·play (wûrd/plā/), *n.* **1.** clever or subtle repartee; verbal wit. **2.** a play on words; pun.

word′ proc′essing, *n.* the automated production and storage of documents using computers, electronic printers, and text-editing software.

word′ proc′essor, *n.* a computer program or computer system designed for word processing.

word·smith (wûrd/smith/), *n.* an expert in the use of words, esp. a professional writer.

word′ square′, *n.* a set of words that when arranged one beneath another in the form of a square read alike horizontally and vertically: *The words* sated, atone, toast, ensue, deter *form a word square.*

word′ stress′, *n.* the pattern of stress given to an individual word, esp. when said in isolation.

Words·worth (wûrdz/wûrth/), *n.* **William,** 1770–1850, English poet: poet laureate 1843–50.

word·y (wûr/dē), *adj.,* **word·i·er, word·i·est. 1.** characterized by or given to the use of many, or too many, words; verbose. **2.** pertaining to or consisting of words; verbal. —**word/i·ly,** *adv.* —**word/i·ness,** *n.*

wore (wôr, wōr), *v.* pt. of WEAR.

work (wûrk), *n., adj., v.,* **worked** or (*Archaic except in some senses, esp.* 24, 26, 29) **wrought, working.** —*n.* **1.** exertion or effort directed to produce or accomplish something; labor; toil. **2.** something on which exertion or labor is expended; a task or undertaking. **3.** productive or operative activity, esp. employment to earn one's living: *to look for work.* **4.** one's place of employment. **5.** materials, things, etc., on which one is working or is to work. **6.** the result of exertion, labor, or activity; a deed, performance, or product. **7.** an engineering structure, as a building or bridge. **8.** a building, wall, trench, or the like, constructed or made as a means of fortification. **9. works, a.** (*used with a sing. or pl.*

v.) a place or establishment for manufacturing (often used in combination): *ironworks.* **b.** the working parts of a machine: *the works of a watch.* **c.** *Theol.* righteous deeds. **10.** *Physics.* the transfer of energy, as measured by the scalar product of a force and the distance through which it acts. **11. the works, a.** everything; all related items or matters: *a hamburger with the works.* **b.** harsh or cruel treatment: *to give someone the works.* —*adj.* **12.** of, for, or concerning work: *work clothes.* —*v.i.* **13.** to do work; labor. **14.** to be employed, esp. as a means of earning one's livelihood. **15.** to be in operation; be functional, as a machine or system. **16.** to act or operate effectively: *This plan works.* **17.** to attain a specified condition, as by repeated movement: *The nails worked loose.* **18.** to have an effect or influence, as on a person or on a person's mind or feelings. **19.** to move in agitation, as the features under strong emotion. **20.** to make way with effort or under stress: *The ship works to windward.* **21.** to ferment, as a liquid. **22.** *Naut.* to give slightly at the joints, as a vessel under strain at sea. —*v.t.* **23.** to use, manage, or operate (an apparatus, contrivance, etc.). **24.** to bring about (any result) by or as if by work or effort: *to work a change.* **25.** to manipulate or treat by labor: *to work butter.* **26.** to put into effective operation. **27.** to make (a mine, farm, etc.) productive. **28.** to carry on operations or activity in (a district or region). **29.** to make, fashion, or execute by work. **30.** to achieve or win by work or effort: *to work one's passage.* **31.** to keep at work: *to work one's employees hard.* **32.** to solve (a puzzle or arithmetic problem). **33.** to cause a strong emotion in: *to work a crowd into a frenzy.* **34.** to influence or persuade, esp. insidiously: *to work other people to one's will.* **35.** to use to one's advantage: *He worked his charm in landing a new job.* **36.** to make or decorate by needlework or embroidery. **37.** to cause fermentation in. **38. work in** or **into, a.** to blend in. **b.** to include after some effort: *Try to work me into your schedule.* **39. work off, a.** to lose or dispose of, as by exercise or labor. **b.** to pay or fulfill by working: *to work off a debt.* **40. work on** or, **upon,** to exercise influence on; persuade. **41. work out, a.** to bring about by work, effort, or action. **b.** to solve, as a problem. **c.** to arrive at by or as if by calculation. **d.** to pay or fulfill by working; work off. **e.** to exhaust, as a mine. **f.** to issue in a result. **g.** to evolve; elaborate. **h.** (of a total, specified figure, etc.) to amount; add up: *The total works out to 176.* **i.** to prove effective or successful. **j.** to practice, exercise, or train, esp. in an athletic sport: *boxers working out at a gym.* **42. work over, a.** to study or examine thoroughly. **b.** to beat unsparingly. **43. work through,** to deal with successfully; come to terms with. **44. work up, a.** to move or stir the feelings of; excite. **b.** to prepare; elaborate: *Work up a proposal.* **c.** to cause to develop by exertion: *to work up an appetite.* —*Idiom.* **45. at work, a.** working, as at one's job. **b.** in action or operation: *machines at work.* **46. in the works,** in preparation or being planned. **47. out of work,** unemployed; jobless. —*Proverb.* **48. He who does not work, neither should he eat,** idleness should not be rewarded. II Thess. 3:10. **49. Work never hurt anybody,** honest labor is not harmful.

work•a•ble (wûrk′kə bəl), *adj.* **1.** practicable; feasible: *a workable schedule.* **2.** capable of or suitable for being worked. —**work′a•bil′i•ty,** *n.*

work•a•day (wûr′kə dā′), *adj.* **1.** characteristic of or befitting working days or the workday. **2.** ordinary; everyday; prosaic.

work•a•hol•ic (wûrk′ə hô′lik, -hol′ik), *n.* a person who works compulsively at the expense of other pursuits. [WORK + -AHOLIC]

work•bench (wûrk′bench′), *n.* a table at which an artisan works.

work•book (wûrk′bŏŏk′), *n.* **1.** a book designed to guide the work of a student by inclusion of questions, exercises, etc. **2.** a manual of operating instructions. **3.** a book with a record of work completed or planned.

work′ camp′, *n.* **1.** a camp for prisoners sentenced to labor, esp. to outdoor labor. **2.** a volunteer project in which members of a church, service organization, etc., work together in aid of some worthy cause.

work•day (wûrk′dā′), *n.* **1.** a day on which work is done; working day. **2.** the part of a day during which one works. **3.** the length of time during a day on which one works: *a seven-hour workday.*

worked (wûrkt), *adj.* having undergone working.

worked′-up′, *adj.* WROUGHT-UP.

work•er (wûr′kər), *n.* **1.** a person or thing that works. **2.** a laborer or employee: *steel workers.* **3.** a member of a caste of sexually underdeveloped, nonreproductive bees, ants, wasps, or termites, specialized to collect food and maintain the colony.

work′ers′ compensa′tion insur′ance, *n.* insurance required by law from employers for the protection of employees while engaged in the employer's business.

Work′ers in the Vine′yard, The, a parable of Jesus. Matt. 20:1–16.

work′ eth′ic, *n.* a belief in the moral benefit and importance of work and its inherent ability to strengthen character.

work•fare (wurk′fâr′), *n.* a governmental plan under which welfare recipients are required to accept public-service jobs or to participate in job training.

work′ farm′, *n.* a farm to which juvenile or minor offenders are sent to work for a short period.

work′ force′ or **work′force′,** *n.* **1.** the total number of workers in a specific undertaking: *a holiday for the company's work force.* **2.** the total number of persons employed or employable, as in a country. Also called **labor force.**

work•horse (wûrk′hôrs′), *n.* **1.** a horse used for plowing, hauling, and

other heavy labor, as distinguished from a riding horse, racehorse, etc. **2.** a person who works tirelessly at a task, assumes extra duties, etc.

work′-hour′ or **work′hour′,** *n.* any of the hours of a day during which work is done.

work•ing (wûr′king), *n.* **1.** the act of a person or thing that works. **2.** operation; action: *the involuted workings of his mind.* **3.** the process of shaping a material: *the working of damp clay.* **4.** Usu., **workings.** a part of a mine, quarry, or the like in which work is carried on. **5.** the process of fermenting, as of yeasts. **6.** a slow advance involving exertion. **7.** twitching, flexing, or twisting motions: *the agitated working of his jaw muscles.* **8.** repeated movement or strain tending to loosen a structural assembly or part. —*adj.* **9. a.** engaged in some form of work, esp. manual labor, for a living: *the working people of this community.* **b.** employed outside the home while fulfilling major domestic responsibilities: *working wives and mothers.* **10.** serving to permit or facilitate continued work: *a working model; a working majority.* **11.** adequate for usual or customary needs: *a working knowledge of Spanish.* **12.** organized for some kind of work, as for a cause or project: *a working party.* **13.** done, taken, etc., while conducting or discussing business: *a working lunch.*

work′ing as′set, *n.* invested capital that is comparatively liquid.

work′ing cap′ital, *n.* **1.** the amount of capital needed to carry on a business. **2.** *Accounting.* current assets minus current liabilities.

work′ing class′, *n.* **1.** those persons working for wages, esp. in manual labor. **2.** the social or economic class composed of these workers. —**work′ing-class′,** *adj.*

work′ing dog′, *n.* any of several breeds of usu. large dogs developed to perform a practical function, as herding, guarding, or pulling heavy loads, as the collie, Doberman pinscher, and Siberian husky.

work′ing group′, *n.* a small body of people organized to engage in a single project or to support a cause.

work′ing hypoth′esis, *n.* See under HYPOTHESIS (def. 1).

work•ing•man (wûr′king man′), *n., pl.* **-men.** a man of the working class; a man, whether skilled or unskilled, who earns his living at some manual or industrial work. —**Usage.** See -MAN.

work′ing or′der, *n.* the condition of a mechanism, system, etc., when functioning properly.

work′ing pa′pers, *n.pl.* legal papers required for or permitting employment, as of an alien or minor.

work•ing•per•son (wûr′king pûr′sən), *n.* a workingman or workingwoman. —**Usage.** See -PERSON.

work•ing•wom•an (wûr′king wŏŏm′ən), *n., pl.* **-wom•en. 1.** a woman who earns a salary, wages, or other income through regular employment, usu. outside the home. **2.** a woman employed in manual or industrial labor. —**Usage.** See -WOMAN.

work′ load′ or **work′load′,** *n.* the amount of work that a machine, employee, or group of employees is expected to perform.

work•man (wûrk′mən), *n., pl.* **-men.** a man employed or skilled in some form of manual, mechanical, or industrial work.

work•man•ship (wûrk′mən ship′), *n.* **1.** the art or skill of a workman or workwoman. **2.** the quality or mode of execution, as of a thing made. **3.** the work executed.

work′men's compensa′tion insur′ance, *n.* WORKERS' COMPENSATION INSURANCE.

work′ of art′, *n.* **1.** a piece of creative work in the arts, esp. a painting or sculpture. **2.** a product that gives aesthetic pleasure apart from any utilitarian considerations.

work•out (wûrk′out′), *n.* **1.** any trial or practice session to determine or maintain ability, endurance, etc., esp. in athletics. **2.** a structured regime of physical exercise.

work•place (wûrk′plās′), *n.* the place where one is employed or customarily does one's work; one's office, station, laboratory, etc.

work′-release′, *adj.* of or designating a program under which prisoners may work outside of prison while serving their sentences.

work•room (wûrk′rŏŏm′, -rŏŏm′), *n.* a room in which work is done.

work′ sheet′, *n.* **1.** a sheet of paper on which work schedules, special instructions, etc., are recorded. **2.** a piece of paper on which problems, ideas, or the like are set down in tentative form.

work•shop (wûrk′shop′), *n.* **1.** a room, group of rooms, or building in which work, esp. mechanical work, is carried on. **2.** a seminar or small group that meets to explore some subject, develop a skill or technique, carry out a creative project, etc.

work′ sta′tion or **work′sta′tion,** *n.* **1.** a work or office area assigned to one person, often one accommodating a computer terminal or other electronic equipment. **2.** a computer terminal or microcomputer connected to a mainframe, minicomputer, or data-processing network. **3.** a powerful microcomputer, often with a high-resolution display, used for computer-aided design, electronic publishing, or other graphics-intensive processing.

work′ stop′page, *n.* the collective stoppage of work by employees in a business or industry to protest working conditions.

work•ta•ble (wûrk′tā′bəl), *n.* a table for working at, often with drawers or receptacles for materials, tools, etc.

work•up (wûrk′up′), *n.* a thorough medical diagnostic examination including laboratory tests and x-rays.

work•week (wûrk′wēk′), *n.* the total number of regular working hours or days in a week.

work·wom·an (wûrk′wŏŏm′ən), *n.*, *pl.* **-wom·en.** a woman employed or skilled in some manual, mechanical, or industrial work.

world (wûrld), *n.* **1.** the earth or globe, considered as a planet. **2.** (*often cap.*) a particular division of the earth: *the Western world.* **3.** the earth or a part of it, with its inhabitants, affairs, etc., during a particular period: *the ancient world.* **4.** humankind; the human race; humanity. **5.** the public generally: *The whole world knows it.* **6.** the class of persons devoted to the affairs, interests, or pursuits of this life: *The world worships success.* **7.** a particular class of people, with common interests, aims, etc.: *the fashionable world.* **8.** any sphere, realm, or domain, with all pertaining to it: *the world of dreams.* **9.** everything that exists; the universe; the macrocosm. **10.** one of the three general groupings of physical nature: *animal world; mineral world; vegetable world.* **11.** any period, state, or sphere of existence: *this world; the world to come.* **12.** Often, **worlds.** a great deal: *That trip was worlds of fun.* **13.** any indefinitely great expanse. **14.** any heavenly body: *the starry worlds.* —*Idiom.* **15. bring into the world, a.** to give birth to; bear. **b.** to deliver (a baby). **16. come into the world,** to be born. **17. for all the world, a.** for any consideration, however great: *She wouldn't visit them for all the world.* **b.** in every respect; precisely: *You look for all the world like my friend Mary.* **18. in the world, a.** at all: *without a care in the world.* **b.** (used as an intensifier after interrogative words): *What in the world do you mean by that?* **19. out of this world,** extraordinary; wonderful; fantastic. **20. world without end,** for all eternity; forever.

World′ Bank′, *n.* an international bank established in 1944 to help member nations reconstruct and develop, esp. by guaranteeing loans: a specialized agency of the United Nations. Official name, **International Bank for Reconstruction and Development.**

world′beat′er or **world′-beat′er,** *n.* a person or thing that surpasses all others of like kind, as in quality or endurance.

world′-class′ or **world′ class′,** *adj.* **1.** ranked among the world's best; of the highest caliber: *a world-class orchestra.* **2.** attracting or comprising first-rank players, performers, etc.: *a world-class tennis tournament.*

World′ Commun′ion Sun′day, *n.* the first Sunday in October, during which members of ecumenical churches throughout the world celebrate Holy Communion, esp. to affirm their unity in Christ.

World′ Coun′cil of Church′es, *n.* an ecumenical organization formed in 1948 in Amsterdam, the Netherlands, comprising more than 160 Protestant and Eastern churches in over 48 countries, for cooperative, coordinated, theological, ecclesiastical, and secular action.

World′ Court′, *n.* **1.** Permanent Court of International Justice. **2.** International Court of Justice.

World′ Cup′, *n.* the trophy for the world championship in soccer, or the quadrennial international competition for this trophy.

World′ Day′ of Prayer′ (prâr), *n.* the first Friday in Lent, during which Christians belonging to ecumenical communions pray for foreign missions.

World′ Health′ Organiza′tion, *n.* an agency of the United Nations, established in 1948, concerned with improving the health of the world's people and preventing or controlling communicable diseases on a worldwide basis through various technical projects and programs. *Abbr.:* WHO

world·ly (wûrld′lē), *adj.*, **-li·er, -li·est,** *adv.* —*adj.* **1.** of or pertaining to this world as contrasted with heaven, spiritual life, etc.; earthly; mundane. **2.** experienced; knowing; sophisticated. **3.** devoted to or connected with the material or sensual pleasures of this world: *a worldly clergy; worldly temptations.* —*adv.* **4.** in a worldly manner (archaic except in combination): *worldly-wise; worldly-minded.* —**world′li·ness,** *n.*

world′ly-wise′, *adj.* wise as to the affairs of this world.

world′ pow′er, *n.* a nation so powerful that it is capable of influencing or changing the course of world events.

world′ premiere′, *n.* the first public performance of a play, motion picture, musical work, etc.

World′ Se′ries, *n.* an annual series of games between the champions of baseball's two major leagues, won by the first team to win four games.

world′s′ fair′, *n.* a large international exposition of arts, crafts, industrial products, scientific achievements, etc.

world′ war′, *n.* a war that involves most of the principal nations of the world.

World War I, *n.* the war fought mainly in Europe and the Middle East, between the Central Powers and the Allies, beginning on July 28, 1914, and ending on Nov. 11, 1918, with the collapse of the Central Powers.

World War II, *n.* the war between the Axis and the Allies, beginning on Sept. 1, 1939, with the German invasion of Poland, and ending with the surrender of Germany on May 8, 1945, and of Japan on Aug. 14, 1945.

world′-wea′ry, *adj.* weary of the world; bored with existence, material pleasures, etc. —**world′-wea′ri·ness,** *n.*

world′wide′ or **world′-wide′,** *adj.*, *adv.* throughout the world.

World′ Wide′ Web′, *n.* a system of extensively interlinked hypertext documents: a branch of the Internet. *Abbr.:* WWW

worm (wûrm), *n.* **1.** any of numerous long, slender, soft-bodied, legless invertebrates, including the roundworms, nemerteans, and annelids. **2.** something resembling or suggesting a worm in appearance, movement, etc. **3.** a groveling, abject, or contemptible person. **4.** the thread of a screw. **5.** a rotating cylinder or shaft, cut with one or more helical

threads, that engages with and drives a worm gear. **6.** something that penetrates, injures, or consumes slowly or insidiously. **7. worms,** (*used with a sing. v.*) any disease or disorder arising from the presence of parasitic worms in the intestines or other tissues. **8.** computer code planted illegally in a software program so as to destroy data in any system that downloads the program, as by reformatting the hard disk. —*v.i.* **9.** to move or act like a worm; creep, crawl, or advance slowly, stealthily, or insidiously. —*v.t.* **10.** to cause to move in a devious or stealthy manner: *a thief worming his hand into a coat pocket.* **11.** to get by persistent, insidious efforts (usu. fol. by *out* or *from*). **12.** to insinuate (oneself or one's way) into another's favor, confidence, etc.: *He wormed his way into the king's favor.* **13.** to free from worms: *to worm puppies.*

worm′ gear′ or **worm′gear′,** *n.* **1.** a mechanism consisting of a worm engaging with and driving a worm wheel. **2.** Also called **worm wheel.** a gear wheel driven by a worm.

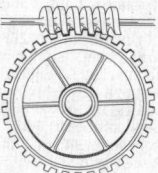

worm gear (def. 2)

Worms (wûrmz; *Ger.* vôrms), *n.* **1.** a city in E Rhineland-Palatinate, in SW Germany. 71,827. **2. Diet of,** the council, or diet, held here (1521) at which Luther was condemned as a heretic.

worm·wood (wûrm′wŏŏd′), *n.* **1.** any composite plant of the genus *Artemisia,* esp. the bitter, aromatic plant, *A. absinthium,* of Eurasia, used as a vermifuge and a tonic, and as an ingredient in absinthe. **2.** a plant mentioned in the Bible, symbolizing the bitterness of sorrow. Jer. 9:15; Lam. 3:15, 19. **3.** something bitter, grievous, or extremely unpleasant.

worm·y (wûr′mē), *adj.*, **worm·i·er, worm·i·est. 1.** containing a worm or worms; contaminated with worms. **2.** damaged or bored into by worms; worm-eaten. **3.** wormlike; groveling; low. —**worm′i·ness,** *n.*

worn (wôrn, wōrn), *v.* **1.** pp. of WEAR. —*adj.* **2.** diminished in value or usefulness through wear, use, handling, etc.: *worn clothing; worn tires.* **3.** wearied; exhausted; spent. —**worn′ness,** *n.*

worn′-out′, *adj.* **1.** worn or used beyond repair. **2.** depleted of energy, strength, or enthusiasm; exhausted; fatigued.

wor·ried (wûr′ēd, wur′-), *adj.* **1.** having or characterized by worry; concerned; anxious. **2.** indicating, expressing, or attended by worry: *worried looks.* —**wor′ried·ly,** *adv.*

wor·ri·some (wûr′ē səm, wur′-), *adj.* **1.** causing worry; trying, annoying, or disturbing: *a worrisome problem.* **2.** inclined to worry. —**wor′ri·some·ly,** *adv.* —**wor′ri·some·ness,** *n.*

wor·ry (wûr′ē, wur′ē), *v.*, **-ried, -ry·ing,** *n.*, *pl.* **-ries.** —*v.i.* **1.** to feel uneasy or anxious; torment oneself with or suffer from disturbing thoughts; fret. **2.** to move with effort: *an old car worrying uphill.* —*v.t.* **3.** to make uneasy or anxious; cause anxiety, apprehension, or care. **4.** to disturb with annoyances; plague. **5.** to seize, esp. by the throat, with the teeth and shake or mangle, as one animal does another. **6.** to harass by repeated biting, snapping, etc. **7.** to examine, adjust, or handle continually or repeatedly. —*n.* **8.** a worried condition or feeling; uneasiness or anxiety. **9.** a cause of uneasiness or anxiety; trouble. **10.** the act of worrying. —**wor′ri·er,** *n.* —**wor′ry·ing·ly,** *adv.*

wor′ry beads′, *n.pl.* a string of beads manipulated to relieve worry and tension.

wor·ry·wart (wûr′ē wôrt′, wur′-), *n.* a person who tends to worry habitually and often needlessly.

worse (wûrs), *adj.*, *comparative of* **bad** *and* **ill. 1.** bad or ill in a greater or higher degree; inferior in excellence, quality, or character. **2.** more unfavorable or injurious. **3.** in less good condition; in poorer health. —*n.* **4.** that which is worse. —*adv.* **5.** in a more evil, wicked, severe, or disadvantageous manner. **6.** with more severity, intensity, etc.; in a greater degree.

wors·en (wûr′sən), *v.t.*, *v.i.* to make or become worse.

wor·ship (wûr′ship), *n.*, *v.*, **-shiped** or **shipped, -ship·ing** or **-ship·ping.** —*n.* **1.** reverent honor and homage paid to God or a sacred personage, or to any object regarded as sacred. **2.** formal or ceremonious rendering of such honor and homage: *to attend worship on Sundays.* **3.** adoring reverence or regard. **4.** the object of adoring reverence or regard. **5.** (*cap.*) *Brit.* a title of honor used of certain magistrates and others of high rank or station (usu. prec. by *Your, His,* or *Her*). —*v.t.* **6.** to render religious reverence and homage to. **7.** to feel an adoring reverence or regard for (any person or thing). —*v.i.* **8.** to render religious reverence and homage, as to a deity. **9.** to attend services of divine worship. **10.** to feel an adoring reverence or regard. —**wor′ship·er,** *n.*

wor·ship·ful (wûr′ship fəl), *adj.* **1.** feeling or showing worship. **2.** (*cap.*) *Brit.* a formal title of honor used of certain highly regarded or respected persons or groups (usu. prec. by *the*).

worst (wûrst), *adj., superlative of* **bad** *and* **ill,** *n., adv., v.* **—***adj.* **1.** bad or ill in the highest, greatest, or most extreme degree: *the worst person.* **2.** most faulty or unsatisfactory. **3.** most unfavorable or injurious: *the worst rating.* **4.** in the poorest condition: *the worst house on the block.* **5.** most unpleasant, unattractive, or disagreeable. **6.** most lacking in skill; least skilled: *the worst typist in the group.* **—***n.* **7.** that which is worst. **—***adv.* **8.** in the most evil, wicked, severe, or disadvantageous manner. **9.** with the most severity, intensity, etc.; in the greatest degree. **—***v.t.* **10.** to defeat; beat. **—*Idiom.* 11. at (the) worst,** if the worst happens; under the worst conditions. **12. if worst comes to worst,** if the very worst happens. **13. in the worst way,** very much; extremely.

worst′-case′, *adj.* of the worst possibility; being the worst result that could be expected: *a worst-case scenario.*

wor•sted (wo͝os′tid, wûr′stid), *n.* **1.** firmly twisted yarn or thread spun from combed, stapled wool fibers of the same length, for weaving, knitting, etc. Compare WOOLEN. **2.** wool cloth woven from such yarns, having a hard, smooth surface and no nap. **—***adj.* **3.** made of worsted.

wort[1] (wûrt, wôrt), *n.* the infusion of malt or meal that after fermentation becomes beer or whiskey.

wort[2] (wûrt, wôrt), *n.* a plant, herb, or vegetable (now usu. only in combination): *figwort.*

worth (wûrth), *prep.* **1.** good or important enough to justify (what is specified): *advice worth taking.* **2.** having a value of, or equal in value to, as in money. **3.** having property to the value or amount of. **—***n.* **4.** excellence of character or quality as commanding esteem: *people of worth.* **5.** usefulness or importance, as to the world, to a person, or for a purpose. **6.** value, as in money. **7.** a quantity of something of a specified value: *50 cents' worth of candy.* **8.** wealth; riches; property or possessions: *net worth.* **—*Idiom.* 9. for all one is worth,** to the utmost. **—*Proverb.* 10. If a thing is worth doing, it's worth doing well,** something worthwhile should be done as completely as possible.

worth•less (wûrth′lis), *adj.* without worth; of no use, importance, or value. —**worth′less•ly,** *adv.* —**worth′less•ness,** *n.*

worth•while (wûrth′hwīl′, -wīl′), *adj.* such as to repay one's time, attention, interest, work, trouble, etc.: *a worthwhile project.* —**worth′-while′ness,** *n.*

wor•thy (wûr′thē), *adj.,* **-thi•er, -thi•est,** *n., pl.* **-thies.** **—***adj.* **1.** having adequate or great merit, character, or value: *a worthy successor.* **2.** of commendable excellence or merit; deserving; meritorious: *an effort worthy of praise.* **—***n.* **3.** a person of eminent worth, merit, or position. —**wor′thi•ly,** *adv.* —**wor′thi•ness,** *n.*

-worthy, a combining form of WORTHY, used with the meanings "deserving of, fit for" (*newsworthy; trustworthy*), "capable of travel in or on" (*roadworthy; seaworthy*) the thing specified by the initial element.

would (wo͝od; *unstressed* wəd), *v.* **1.** a pt. of WILL[1]. **2.** (used to express the future in past sentences): *He said he would go tomorrow.* **3.** (used in place of *will,* to make a statement or form a question less direct or blunt): *That would scarcely be fair. Would you be so kind?* **4.** (used to express repeated or habitual action in the past): *We would visit Grandma every morning up at the farm.* **5.** (used to express an intention or inclination): *Nutritionists would have us all eat whole grains.* **6.** (used to express a wish): *Would that she were here!* **7.** (used to express an uncertainty): *It would appear that he is guilty.* **8.** (used in conditional sentences to express choice or possibility): *They would come if they had the fare. If the temperature were higher, the water would evaporate.* **9.** (used with the present perfect to express unfulfilled intention or preference): *I would have saved you some but the children took it all.* **—*Idiom.* 10. would like,** (used to express desire): *I would like to go next year.*

would′-be′, *adj.* **1.** wishing or pretending to be: *a would-be wit.* **2.** intended to be: *a would-be kindness.*

would•n't (wo͝od′nt), contraction of *would not.*

wouldst (wo͝odst, wo͝otst) also **would•est** (wo͝od′ist), *v. Archaic.* 2nd pers. sing. past of WILL[1].

wound[1] (wo͞ond; *Older Use and Literary* wound), *n., v.,* **wound•ed, wound•ing.** **—***n.* **1.** an injury, usu. involving division of tissue or rupture of the integument or mucous membrane, due to external violence or some mechanical agency rather than disease. **2.** a similar injury to the tissue of a plant. **3.** an injury or hurt to feelings, sensibilities, reputation, etc. **—***v.t.* **4.** to inflict a wound upon; injure; hurt. **—***v.i.* **5.** to inflict a wound. —**wound′ed•ly,** *adv.* —**wound′ing•ly,** *adv.*

wound[2] (wound), *v.* a pt. and pp. of WIND[2] and WIND[3].

wound•ed (wo͞on′did), *adj.* **1.** suffering from a wound or wounds. **2.** hurt; impaired; damaged: *a wounded reputation.* **—***n.* **3.** wounded persons collectively (often prec. by *the*).

Wound′ed Knee′, *n.* a village in SW South Dakota: site of a massacre of about 300 Oglala Sioux Indians on Dec. 29, 1890.

wove (wōv), *v.* a pt. and pp. of WEAVE.

wo•ven (wō′vən), *v.* a pp. of WEAVE.

wow[1] (wou), *interj.* **1.** (an exclamation of surprise, wonder, or pleasure.) **—***v.t.* **2.** to gain an enthusiastic response from; thrill. **—***n.* **3.** an extraordinary success. **4.** excitement, interest, great pleasure, or the like.

wow[2] (wou), *n.* a slow wavering of pitch in sound recording or reproducing equipment caused by uneven speed of the turntable or the tape. Compare FLUTTER (def. 12).

WP, word processing.

WPA, Work Projects Administration: the former federal agency (1935–43) charged with instituting and administering public works in order to relieve national unemployment. Orig., **Works Progress Administration.**

W particle, *n.* either of two types of charged intermediate vector boson, one positively charged and the other negatively charged. *Symbols:* W^+, W^-

WPB or **W.P.B.,** War Production Board.

wpm, words per minute.

wrack[1] (rak), *n.* **1.** damage or destruction: *wrack and ruin.* **2.** wreck or wreckage. **3.** a trace of something destroyed: *leaving not a wrack behind.* **4.** seaweed or other vegetation cast on the shore. **—***v.t.* **5.** to wreck.

wrack[2] (rak), *n., v.i.* RACK[4].

wraith (rāth), *n.* **1.** an apparition of a living person supposed to portend his or her death. **2.** a visible spirit. —**wraith′like′,** *adj.*

Wran•gell-St. E•li•as National Park (rang′gəl sānt′ i lī′əs), *n.* a national park in E Alaska. 12,730 sq. mi. (32,970 sq km).

wran•gle (rang′gəl), *v.,* **-gled, -gling,** *n.* **—***v.i.* **1.** to argue or dispute, esp. in a noisy or angry manner. **—***v.t.* **2.** to argue or dispute. **3.** to tend or round up (cattle, horses, or other livestock). **4.** to obtain by badgering or scheming; wangle. **—***n.* **5.** a noisy or angry dispute; altercation.

wran•gler (rang′glər), *n.* **1.** a cowboy, esp. one in charge of saddle horses. **2.** a person who wrangles or disputes.

wrap (rap), *v.,* **wrapped** or **wrapt, wrap•ping,** *n., adj.* **—***v.t.* **1.** to enclose in something wound or folded about (often fol. by *up*): *She wrapped her head in a scarf.* **2.** to enclose and make fast within a covering of paper or the like (often fol. by *up*): *Wrap the box up in brown paper.* **3.** to wind, fold, or bind (something) about as a covering. **4.** to protect with coverings, outer garments, etc. (usu. fol. by *up*). **5.** to surround, envelop, or hide. **6.** to fold or roll up. **7.** to finish the filming of (a motion picture). **—***v.i.* **8.** to wrap oneself (usu. fol. by *up*). **9.** to become wrapped, as about something; fold. **10.** to complete the filming of a motion picture. **11. a. wrap up,** to conclude; finish work on: *to wrap up a project.* **b.** to give a summary of. **—***n.* **12.** something to be wrapped about the person, esp. in addition to the usual indoor clothing, as a shawl, scarf, or sweater: *an evening wrap.* **13.** a beauty treatment in which a part or all of the body is covered with cream, lotion, herbs, or the like and then wrapped snugly with cloth. **14. a.** the completion of photography on a motion picture or an individual scene. **b.** the termination of a working day during the shooting of a motion picture. **—***adj.* **15.** Also, **wrapped.** wraparound in style: *a wrap skirt.* **—*Idiom.* 16. under wraps,** *Informal.* secret: *The army wants this research project kept under wraps.* **17. wrapped up in, a.** intensely absorbed in: *wrapped up in one's work.* **b.** involved in; bound up with: *Peace is wrapped up in compromise.*

wrap′a•round′ or **wrap′-a•round′,** *adj.* **1.** (of a garment) made to fold around or across the body so that one side of the fabric overlaps the other, forming the closure. **2.** extending in a curve from the front around to the sides: *a wraparound windshield.* **3.** all-inclusive; comprehensive: *a wraparound insurance plan.* **—***n.* **4.** a wraparound object.

wrap•per (rap′ər), *n.* **1.** a person or thing that wraps. **2.** something in which a thing is wrapped. **3.** a long, loose garment, esp. a woman's bathrobe or negligee. **4.** *Brit.* JACKET (def. 5). **5.** the tobacco leaf used for covering a cigar.

wrap•ping (rap′ing), *n.* Often, **wrappings.** the covering in which something is wrapped.

wrap′-up′, *n.* **1.** a final report or summary: *a wrap-up of the evening news.* **2.** the conclusion or final result.

wrasse (ras), *n.* any tropical marine fish of the family Labridae, esp. of the genus *Labrus,* having fleshy lips and powerful teeth.

wrath (rath, räth; *esp. Brit.* rôth), *n.* **1.** stern or fierce anger; deep indignation; ire: one of the seven deadly sins. **2.** vengeance or punishment as the consequence of anger.

wrath•ful (rath′fəl, räth′-; *esp. Brit.* rôth′-), *adj.* **1.** extremely angry; enraged. **2.** characterized by or showing wrath: *wrathful words.* —**wrath′ful•ly,** *adv.* —**wrath′ful•ness,** *n.*

wreak (rēk), *v.t.* **1.** to inflict or execute (punishment, vengeance, etc.): *to wreak havoc on the enemy.* **2.** to carry out the promptings of (one's rage, ill humor, etc.), as on a victim or object: *to wreak one's anger on subordinates.* —**wreak′er,** *n.*

wreath (rēth), *n., pl.* **wreaths** (rēthz, rēths), *v.* **—***n.* **1.** a circular band of flowers, foliage, etc., for adorning the head or for decoration; garland or chaplet. **2.** any ringlike, curving, or curling mass or formation: *a wreath of clouds.* **—***v.t., v.i.* **3.** to wreathe. —**wreath′like′,** *adj.*

wreathe (rēth), *v.,* **wreathed, wreath•ing.** **—***v.t.* **1.** to encircle or adorn with or as if with a wreath. **2.** to form as a wreath by twisting or twining. **3.** to envelop: *a face wreathed in smiles.* **—***v.i.* **4.** to take the form of a wreath or wreaths. **5.** to move in curving or curling masses, as smoke. —**wreath′er,** *n.*

wreck (rek), *n.* **1.** any building, structure, or thing reduced to ruin. **2. a.** wreckage, goods, etc., remaining above water after a shipwreck, esp. when cast ashore. **b.** the ruin or destruction of a vessel in the course of navigation; shipwreck. **c.** a vessel in a state of ruin from disaster at sea, on rocks, etc. **3.** the ruin or destruction of anything. **4.** a person of ruined mental or physical health. **—***v.t.* **5.** to cause the wreck of (a vessel); shipwreck. **6.** to cause the ruin or destruction of: *to wreck a car.* **7.** to tear down; demolish. **—***v.i.* **8.** to be involved in a wreck; become wrecked. **9.** to work as a wrecker; engage in wrecking.

wreck•age (rek′ij), *n.* **1.** the act of wrecking, or the state of being wrecked. **2.** remains or fragments of something that has been wrecked: *They searched the wreckage for survivors.*

wreck•er (rek′ər), *n.* **1.** a person or thing that wrecks. **2.** a person, car, or train employed in removing wreckage, debris, etc., as from railroad tracks. **3.** Also called **tow car, tow truck.** a vehicle equipped with a mechanical apparatus for hoisting and pulling, used to tow wrecked, disabled, or stalled automobiles. **4.** a person or business that demolishes and removes houses or other buildings, as in clearing sites for other use. **5.** a person or vessel employed in recovering salvage from wrecked or disabled vessels.

wreck′er's (or **wreck′ing**) **ball′,** *n.* a heavy metal ball swung on a cable from a crane and used in demolition work.

wreck•ing (rek′ing), *n.* **1.** the act, work, or business of a wrecker. *—adj.* **2.** employed or for use in wrecking: *a wrecking crew.*

wren (ren), *n.* **1.** any of various small, active songbirds of the family Troglodytidae, with streaked or spotted brown-gray plumage, a slender bill, and, in many species, elaborate vocal repertoires: found only in the New World with the exception of *Troglodytes troglodytes,* of North America, Eurasia, and NW Africa. **2.** any of various similar, unrelated songbirds, as Australasian flycatchers of the subfamily Malurinae and New Zealand birds of the family Acanthisittidae.

Wren (ren), *n.* **Sir Christopher,** 1632–1723, English architect.

wrench (rench), *v.t.* **1.** to twist suddenly and forcibly; pull, jerk, or force by a violent twist. **2.** to overstrain or injure (the ankle, knee, etc.) by a sudden, violent twist. **3.** to affect distressingly as if by a wrench. **4.** to wrest, as from the right use or meaning; distort: *to wrench the facts out of context.* *—v.i.* **5.** to give a wrench or twist at something. **6.** to twist, turn, or move suddenly aside. *—n.* **7.** a wrenching movement; a sudden, violent twist. **8.** a sharp, distressing strain, as to the feelings. **9.** a twisting or distortion, as of meaning. **10.** a tool for gripping and turning or twisting the head of a bolt, a nut, a pipe, or the like, commonly consisting of a bar of metal with fixed or adjustable jaws. —**wrench′er,** *n.* —**wrench′ing•ly,** *adv.*

wrenches (def. 10)

wrest (rest), *v.t.* **1.** to pull, jerk, or force by a violent twist. **2.** to take away by force: *to wrest a knife from a child.* **3.** to get by effort: *to wrest a living from the soil.* **4.** to twist or turn from the proper course, meaning, etc.; wrench. *—n.* **5.** a wresting; twist or wrench. **6.** a key or small wrench for tuning stringed musical instruments, as the harp or piano, by turning the pins to which the strings are fastened. —**wrest′er,** *n.*

wres•tle (res′əl), *v.,* **-tled, -tling,** *n.* *—v.i.* **1.** to engage in wrestling. **2.** to contend or struggle, as for mastery; grapple: *to wrestle with one's conscience.* *—v.t.* **3.** to contend with in wrestling. **4.** to force by or as if by wrestling. **5.** to throw (a calf or other animal) for branding. *—n.* **6.** an act of or a bout at wrestling. **7.** a struggle. —**wres′tler,** *n.*

wres•tling (res′ling), *n.* **1.** a sport in which two opponents struggle hand to hand in order to pin or press each other's shoulders to the mat or ground, with the style and rules differing greatly between amateur and professional matches. **2.** the act of a person who wrestles.

wretch (rech), *n.* **1.** a deplorably unfortunate or unhappy person. **2.** a person of despicable or base character.

wretch•ed (rech′id), *adj.* **1.** very unfortunate in condition or circumstances; pitiable. **2.** characterized by or attended with misery and sorrow; miserable. **3.** despicable, contemptible, or mean: *a wretched miser.* **4.** pitiful or worthless; inferior: *a wretched job of sewing.* —**wretch′ed•ly,** *adv.* —**wretch′ed•ness,** *n.*

wrig•gle (rig′əl), *v.,* **-gled, -gling,** *n.* *—v.i.* **1.** to twist to and fro; writhe; squirm. **2.** to move along by twisting and turning the body, as a worm or snake. **3.** to make one's way by shifts or expedients (often fol. by *out*): *to wriggle out of a difficulty.* *—v.t.* **4.** to cause to wriggle: *to wriggle one's hips.* **5.** to bring, get, make, etc., by wriggling: *to wriggle one's way through a tunnel.* *—n.* **6.** the act of wriggling; a wriggling movement. —**wrig′gling•ly,** *adv.*

wrig•gler (rig′lər), *n.* **1.** a person or thing that wriggles. **2.** Also called **wiggler.** the larva of a mosquito.

wrig•gly (rig′lē), *adj.,* **-gli•er, -gli•est. 1.** twisting; squirming: *a wriggly caterpillar.* **2.** evasive; shifty: *a wriggly character.*

wright (rīt), *n.* a worker, esp. a constructive worker (used chiefly in combination): *a wheelwright; a playwright.* [Old English *wryhta,* var. of *wyrhta* worker]

Wright (rīt), *n.* **1. Frances** or **Fanny,** 1795–1852, U.S. abolitionist and social reformer, born in Scotland. **2. Frank Lloyd,** 1867–1959, U.S. architect. **3. Orville,** 1871–1948, and his brother **Wilbur,** 1867–1912, U.S. aeronautical inventors. **4. Richard,** 1908–60, U.S. novelist.

wring (ring), *v.,* **wrung, wring•ing,** *n.* *—v.t.* **1.** to twist forcibly. **2.** to twist or compress in order to force out water or other liquid (often fol. by *out*): *to wring out a washcloth.* **3.** to extract by or as if by twisting or compression. **4.** to affect painfully by or as if by some contorting or compressing action. **5.** to clasp tightly, usu. with twisting: *to wring one's hands in pain.* *—v.i.* **6.** to writhe, as in anguish. *—n.* **7.** a wringing; forcible twist or squeeze.

wring•er (ring′ər), *n.* **1.** a person or thing that wrings. **2.** an apparatus for squeezing out liquid, as two rollers through which an article of wet clothing may be squeezed. *—Idiom.* **3. put through the wringer,** to subject to a difficult or exhausting experience.

wrin•kle[1] (ring′kəl), *n., v.,* **-kled, -kling.** *—n.* **1.** a small furrow or crease in the skin, esp. of the face, as from aging or frowning. **2.** a slight ridge or furrow, esp. in a fabric, due to folding or crushing. **3.** problem; fault. *—v.t.* **4.** to form wrinkles in. *—v.i.* **5.** to become wrinkled. —**wrin′kly,** *adj.,* **-kli•er, -kli•est.**

wrin•kle[2] (ring′kəl), *n.* innovation; trick: *a new advertising wrinkle.*

wrist (rist), *n.* **1.** Also called **carpus. a.** the lower part of the forearm, where it joins the hand. **b.** the joint or articulation between the forearm and the hand. **2.** the part of a garment that fits around the wrist.

wrist′watch′ or **wrist′ watch′,** *n.* a watch attached to a strap or band worn about the wrist.

writ (rit), *n.* **1. a.** a sealed document, issued in the name of a court, government, sovereign, etc., directing an officer or official to do or refrain from doing some specified act. **b.** (in early English law) any formal document in letter form, under seal, and in the sovereign's name. **2.** something written; a writing: *sacred writ.*

write (rīt), *v.,* **wrote, writ•ten, writ•ing.** *—v.t.* **1.** to trace or form (characters, letters, words, etc.), esp. on paper, with a pen, pencil, or other instrument or means. **2.** to express or communicate in writing: *He wrote that he would be visiting soon.* **3.** to communicate with by letter or note. **4.** to fill in the blank spaces of (a printed form) with writing: *to write a check.* **5.** to execute or produce by setting down words, figures, etc.: *to write two copies of a letter.* **6.** to produce as a written message. **7.** to be the author or originator of; compose. **8.** to impress the marks or indications of: *Honesty is written on his face.* **9.** to transfer (data, text, etc.) from computer memory to an output medium. **10.** to underwrite. *—v.i.* **11.** to trace or form characters, words, etc., with a pen, pencil, or other instrument or means, or as a pen or the like does. **12.** to express ideas in writing. **13.** to write a letter or letters, or communicate by letter: *Write whenever you can.* **14.** to compose or work as a writer or author: *to write for a living.* **15. write down, a.** to set down in writing; record; note. **b.** to direct one's writing to a less intelligent reader or audience: *He writes down to the public.* **16. write in, a.** to vote for (a candidate not listed on the ballot) by writing his or her name on the ballot. **b.** to include in or add to a text by writing: *Do not write in corrections on the galley.* **c.** to request something by mail: *If interested, please write in for details.* **17. write off, a.** to cancel (an unpaid or uncollectible debt). **b.** to regard as worthless or irreparable; decide to forget: *to write off a bad experience.* **c.** to amortize. **18. write out, a.** to put into writing. **b.** to write in full form; state completely. **c.** to exhaust the capacity or resources of (oneself) by excessive writing: *another author who has written herself out.* **19. write up, a.** to put into writing, esp. in full detail: *Write up a report.* **b.** to present to public notice in a written description or account. *—Idiom.* **20. nothing** (or **something**) **to write home about,** nothing (or something) worth one's notice. **21. write the book,** to be the originator or recognized authority: *I'd trust their judgment about nuclear energy; they practically wrote the book.*

write′-in′, *n.* a candidate or vote for a candidate not listed on the printed ballot but written onto it by the voter.

write′-off′, *n.* **1.** a cancellation from the accounts as a loss. **2.** a reduction in book value; depreciation. **3.** a person or thing that is given up as hopeless or pointless.

writ•er (rī′tər), *n.* **1.** a person engaged in writing books, articles, stories, etc., esp. as an occupation or profession. **2.** a person who commits thoughts to writing: *an expert letter writer.*

writ′er's cramp′, *n.* spasmodic, painful contractions of the muscles of the hand and forearm from constant writing.

write′-up′, *n.* **1.** a written description or account, as in a newspaper or magazine: *The play got a terrible write-up.* **2.** an increase in the book value of an asset, as to compensate for inflation.

writhe (rīth), *v.,* **writhed, writh•ing,** *n.* *—v.i.* **1.** to twist the body about, as in pain or effort. **2.** to suffer acute embarrassment. *—v.t.* **3.** to twist or bend out of shape or position; contort. **4.** to twist (oneself, the body, etc.) about, as in pain. *—n.* **5.** a twisting of the body, as in pain. —**writh′er,** *n.* —**writh′ing•ly,** *adv.*

writ•ing (rī′ting), *n.* **1.** the act of a person or thing that writes. **2.** matter written with a pen or the like: *His writing is illegible.* **3.** written form: *Put the agreement in writing.* **4.** a legal document, as a contract or deed. **5.** an inscription. **6.** literary or musical composition. **7.** the style, form, quality, etc., of such composition: *I find her writing stilted.* **8.** the profession of a writer: *He turned to writing at an early age.* **9. the Writings,** Hagiographa.

writ′ing desk′, *n.* **1.** a piece of furniture with a surface for writing on, usu. with drawers and compartments for writing materials. **2.** a portable case that holds writing materials and that when opened forms a surface on which to write.

writ′ing pa′per, *n.* paper suitable for writing on in ink; stationery.

writ′ of assist′ance, *n.* (before the American Revolution) a writ authorizing officers of the British crown to search any premises for smuggled goods.

writ•ten (rit′n), *v.* **1.** a pp. of write. *—adj.* **2.** expressed in writing (disting. from *spoken*).

wrong (rông, rong), *adj.* **1.** not in accordance with what is morally right or good: *a wrong deed.* **2.** deviating from truth or fact; erroneous: *a wrong answer.* **3.** not correct in action, judgment, opinion, etc., as a person; in error. **4.** not proper or usual; not in accordance with rules or practice. **5.** out of order; awry; amiss: *Something is wrong with the machine.* **6.** not suitable or appropriate: *the wrong shoes with that dress.* **7.** of or designating the side ordinarily kept inward or under: *to wear a sweater wrong side out.* —*n.* **8.** something improper or not in accordance with morality, goodness, or truth; evil. **9.** an injustice. **10.** *Law.* **a.** an invasion of another's right, resulting in that person's suffering or damage. **b.** a tort. —*adv.* **11.** in a wrong manner; not rightly; amiss. —*v.t.* **12.** to do wrong to; treat unfairly or unjustly; harm. **13.** to impute evil to (someone) unjustly; malign. —*Idiom.* **14. go wrong, a.** to go amiss; fail. **b.** to pursue an immoral course; become depraved. **15. in the wrong,** to blame; in error. —*Proverb.* **16. Two wrongs don't make a right,** responding to evil behavior with an equally reprehensible act makes the situation worse, not better. —**wrong′er,** *n.* —**wrong′ly,** *adv.*

wrong·do·er (rông′dōō′ər, -dōō′-, rong′-), *n.* a person who does wrong, esp. a sinner or transgressor.

wrong·do·ing (rông′dōō′ing, -dōō′-, rong′-), *n.* **1.** wrong, evil, or blameworthy behavior. **2.** a misdeed; sin.

wronged (rôngd, rongd), *adj.* treated unfairly or unjustly.

wrong·ful (rông′fəl, rong′-), *adj.* **1.** unjust or unfair: *a wrongful act.* **2.** having no legal right; unlawful: *a wrongful diversion of trust income.* —**wrong′ful·ly,** *adv.* —**wrong′ful·ness,** *n.*

wrote (rōt), *v.* a pt. of WRITE.

wrought (rôt), *v.* **1.** *Archaic except in some senses.* a pt. and pp. of WORK. —*adj.* **2.** worked. **3.** elaborated; embellished. **4.** not rough or crude. **5.** produced or shaped by beating with a hammer, as iron or silver articles.

wrought′ i′ron, *n.* a form of iron, almost entirely free of carbon and having a fibrous structure including a uniformly distributed slag content, that is readily forged and welded. —**wrought′-i′ron,** *adj.*

wrought′-up′, *adj.* excited; perturbed; worked up.

wry (rī), *adj.,* **wri·er, wri·est. 1.** distorted; lopsided: *a wry grin.* **2.** ab- normally bent or turned to one side; twisted. **3.** devious in course or purpose; misdirected. **4.** contrary; perverse. **5.** bitingly ironic or amusing: *a wry remark.* —**wry′ly,** *adv.* —**wry′ness,** *n.*

wry·neck (rī′nek′), *n.* **1.** *Informal.* **a.** TORTICOLLIS. **b.** a person having torticollis. **2.** either of two small birds of the woodpecker family, with mottled gray-brown plumage: noted for their snakelike contortions of the neck when disturbed on the nest.

WSW, west-southwest.

wt., weight.

wun·der·kind (vōōn′dər kind′, wun′-; *Ger.* vōōn′dər kint′), *n., pl.* **-kinds,** *Ger.* **-kin·der** (-kin′dər). **1.** a child prodigy. **2.** a person who succeeds, esp. in business, at a comparatively early age.

wurst (wûrst, wōōrst), *n.* SAUSAGE.

wuss (wōōs), *n.* *Slang.* a weakling; wimp.

Wuth′er·ing Heights′ (wuth′ər ing), a novel (1846) by Emily Brontë.

WV or **W.Va.,** West Virginia.

WWW, World Wide Web.

WY or **Wy.,** Wyoming.

Wy·att or **Wy·at** (wī′ət), *n.* **Sir Thomas,** 1503?–42, English poet and diplomat.

Wych·er·ley (wich′ər lē), *n.* **William,** c1640–1716, English dramatist.

Wyc·liffe or **Wyc·lif** (wik′lif), *n.* **John,** c1320–84, English religious reformer and Bible translator. —**Wyc′liff·ism,** *n.* —**Wyc′liff·ite′,** *n.*

Wycliffe's Bible, *n.* either of two translations of the Vulgate (1384, 1395–97) done wholly or partly by John Wycliffe.

Wy·eth (wī′əth), *n.* **1. Andrew (Newell),** born 1917, U.S. painter. **2.** his father, **Newell Convers,** 1882–1945, U.S. illustrator and painter.

Wyo., Wyoming.

Wy·o·ming (wī ō′ming), *n.* **1.** a state in the NW United States. 481,400; 97,914 sq. mi. (253,595 sq. km). *Cap.:* Cheyenne. *Abbr.:* WY, Wyo., Wy. **2.** a city in W Michigan, near Grand Rapids. 62,410. —**Wy·o′ming·ite′,** *n.*

WYSIWYG (wiz′ē wig′), *adj.* what you see is what you get: pertaining to a computer screen display that shows text exactly as it will appear when printed.

Wyss (vēs), *n.* **Johann David,** 1743–1818, Swiss writer.

X

X, x (eks), *n., pl.* **Xs** or **X's, xs** or **x's. 1.** the 24th letter of the English alphabet, a consonant. **2.** any spoken sound represented by this letter. **3.** something shaped like an X. **4.** a written or printed representation of the letter *X* or *x.*

x (eks), *v.t.,* **x-ed** or **x'd** (ekst), **x-ing** or **x'ing** (ek'sing). **1.** to cross out or mark with an *x* (often fol. by *out*): *to x out an error.* **2.** to indicate choice, as on a ballot or examination (often fol. by *in*): *to x in the candidate of your choice.*

X, 1. experimental. **2.** extra.

X, *Symbol.* **1.** the 24th letter in order or in a series. **2.** (*sometimes l.c.*) the Roman numeral for 10. Compare ROMAN NUMERALS. **3.** Christ. **4.** Christian. **5.** cross. **6.** reactance. **7. a.** a motion-picture rating applied to sexually graphic or explicit films. **b.** (formerly) such a rating advising that persons under the age of 17 would not be admitted to the film. Compare G (def. 2), PG, PG-13, R (def. 4). **8.** a person, thing, agency, factor, etc., of unknown identity.

x, 1. EX[1] (def. 1). **2.** experimental. **3.** extra.

x, *Symbol.* **1.** an unknown quantity or a variable. **2.** (used at the end of letters, telegrams, etc., to indicate a kiss.) **3.** (used to indicate multiplication) times: $8 \times 8 = 64$. **4.** (used between figures indicating dimensions) by: $3'' \times 4''$ (read: "three inches by four inches"). **5.** power of magnification: *a 50x telescope.* **6.** (used as a signature by an illiterate person.) **7.** cross. **8.** (used to indicate a particular place or point on a map or diagram.) **9.** (used to indicate choice, as on a ballot or examination.) **10.** (used to indicate an error or incorrect answer, as on a test.) **11.** a person or thing of unknown identity.

Xan•a•du (zan'ə dōō′, -dyōō′), *n.* a place of great beauty, luxury, and contentment.

xan•thene (zan'thēn), *n.* a yellow, crystalline substance, $C_{13}H_{10}O$, used in organic synthesis and as a fungicide.

xan•thine (zan'thēn, -thin), *n.* a crystalline, nitrogenous compound, $C_5H_4N_4O_2$, related to uric acid, occurring in urine, blood, and certain animal and vegetable tissues.

xantho-, a combining form meaning "yellow": *xanthophyll.*

Xa•vi•er (zā'vē ər, zav'ē-, zā'vyər), *n.* **Saint Francis** (*Francisco Javier*), 1506–52, Spanish Jesuit missionary.

x-ax•is (eks'ak'sis), *n., pl.* **x-ax•es** (eks'ak'sēz). **1.** (in a plane Cartesian coordinate system) the axis, usu. horizontal, along which the abscissa is measured and from which the ordinate is measured. **2.** (in a three-dimensional Cartesian coordinate system) the axis along which values of *x* are measured and at which both *y* and *z* equal zero.

xc or **xcp,** *Stock Exchange.* without coupon.

X-C, cross-country: *X-C skiing.*

X chromosome, *n.* a sex chromosome of humans and most mammals that determines femaleness when paired with another X chromosome and that occurs singly in males.

xd or **xdiv.,** *Stock Exchange.* ex dividend; without dividend.

Xe, *Chem. Symbol.* xenon.

xeno-, a combining form meaning "foreign," "strange": *xenolith.*

xe•non (zē'non, zen'on), *n.* a heavy, colorless, chemically inactive, monatomic gaseous element used for filling radio, television, and luminescent tubes. *Symbol:* Xe; *at. wt.:* 131.30; *at. no.:* 54.

xen•o•phile (zen'ə fīl′, zē'nə-), *n.* a person who is attracted to foreign peoples, cultures, or customs.

xen•o•phobe (zen'ə fōb′, zē'nə-), *n.* a person who fears or hates foreigners, strange customs, etc.

xen•o•pho•bi•a (zen'ə fō'bē ə, zē'nə-), *n.* an unreasonable fear or hatred of foreigners or strangers or of that which is foreign or strange. —**xen′o•pho′bic,** *adj.*

Xen•o•phon (zen'ə fən, -fon′), *n.* 434?–355? B.C., Greek historian.

xero-, a combining form meaning "dry": *xerophyte.* Also, *esp. before a vowel,* **xer-.**

xe•rog•ra•phy (zi rog'rə fē), *n.* a copying process in which areas on a sheet of paper corresponding to those on the original are sensitized by static electricity and then sprinkled with black or colored resin that adheres and is fused to the paper. —**xe•ro•graph•ic** (zēr'ə graf'ik), *adj.* —**xe′ro•graph′i•cal•ly,** *adv.*

Xe•rox (zēr'oks), **1.** *Trademark.* a brand name for a copying machine for reproducing printed, written, or pictorial matter by xerography. —*n.* **2.** (*sometimes l.c.*) a copy made on a xerographic copying machine. —*v.t., v.i.* **3.** (*sometimes l.c.*) to reproduce by xerography.

Xerx•es I (zûrk'sēz), *n.* 519?–465 B.C., king of Persia 486?–465 (son of Darius I).

Xi•an or **Xi′•an** or **Si•an** (shē'än′), *n.* the capital of Shaanxi province, in central China: a capital of China under the Han and T'ang dynasties. 2,330,000. Formerly, **Changan.**

x in, *Stock Exchange.* ex interest; without interest.

Xing or **xing** (usu. krô'sing, kros'ing), crossing (used esp. on road signs): *deer Xing.*

xiph•o•su•ran (zif'ə sŏŏr'ən), *adj.* **1.** belonging or pertaining to the arthropod order Xiphosura, comprising the horseshoe crabs. —*n.* **2.** an arthropod of the order Xiphosura.

XL, 1. extra large. **2.** extra long.

X-linked (eks'lingkt′), *adj.* **1.** of or pertaining to a trait controlled by a gene or genes on the X chromosome. **2.** of or pertaining to a gene on an X chromosome.

Xmas (kris'məs; *often* eks'məs), Christmas. —**Usage.** The abbreviation XMAS for Christmas dates from the mid-16th cent. The X is the Greek letter chi, the initial in the word Χριστός (*Christos*) "Christ." In spite of a long and respectable history, today XMAS is objectionable to many, perhaps because of its associations with advertising. It is not used in formal writing.

x-ra•di•a•tion (eks'rā'dē ā'shən), *n.* radiation in the form of x-rays.

X-rat•ed (eks'rā'tid), *adj.* **1.** (of a motion picture) having a rating of X. **2.** sexually explicit; obscene: *X-rated language.*

x-ray or **X-ray** (eks'rā′), *n.* Also, **x ray, X ray. 1.** Often, **x-rays.** electromagnetic radiation having wavelengths in the range of approximately 0.1–10 nm, between ultraviolet radiation and gamma rays, and capable of penetrating solids and of ionizing gases. **2.** a radiograph made by x-rays. —*v.t.* **3.** to photograph, examine, or treat with x-rays. —*adj.* **4.** of or pertaining to x-rays.

x-ray crystallography, *n.* the determination of the structure of a crystal by the use of x-ray diffraction.

x-ray diffraction, *n.* diffraction of x-rays by the regularly spaced atoms of a crystal, useful for determining the arrangement of the atoms.

x-ray therapy, *n.* treatment of a disease using controlled quantities of x-rays.

x-ray tube, *n.* an electronic tube for producing x-rays, essentially a cathode-ray tube in which a metal target is bombarded with high-energy electrons.

XS, extra small.

XX, *Symbol.* powdered sugar.

XXXX, *Symbol.* confectioners' sugar.

xy•lem (zī'ləm, -lem), *n.* a compound tissue in vascular plants that helps provide support and that conducts water and nutrients upward from the roots, consisting of tracheids, vessels, parenchyma cells, and woody fibers.

xylo-, a combining form meaning "wood": *xylophagous.*

xy•log•ra•phy (zī log'rə fē), *n.* the art of engraving on wood, or of printing from such engravings. —**xy′lo•graph′** (-lə graf′, -gräf′), *n.* —**xy•log′ra•pher,** *n.* —**xy′lo•graph′ic** (-graf′ik), **xy′lo•graph′i•cal,** *adj.*

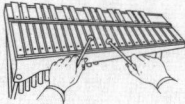

xylophone

xy•lo•phone (zī'lə fōn′), *n.* a musical instrument consisting of a graduated series of wooden bars, usu. sounded by striking with small wooden hammers. —**xy′lo•phon′ist,** *n.*

Y

Y, y (wī), *n., pl.* **Ys** or **Y's, ys** or **y's. 1.** the 25th letter of the English alphabet, a semivowel. **2.** any spoken sound represented by this letter. **3.** something shaped like a Y. **4.** a written or printed representation of the letter Y or y.

Y (wī), **the Y,** *Informal.* the YMCA, YWCA, YMHA, or YWHA.

Y, *Symbol.* **1.** the 25th in order or in a series. **2.** (*sometimes l.c.*) *Elect.* admittance. **3.** *Chem.* yttrium. **4.** *Biochem.* tyrosine.

y, *Math. Symbol.* an unknown quantity or a variable.

y- or **i-,** a prefix occurring in certain obsolete words (*iwis*) and esp. in archaic past participles (*yclad; yclept*).

-y¹ or **-ey,** an adjective-forming suffix meaning "characterized by or inclined to" the substance or action of the word or stem to which the suffix is attached: *bloody; cloudy; sexy; squeaky.*

-y² or **-ie,** a noun-forming suffix, added to monosyllabic bases, occurring in endearing or familiar names or common nouns formed from personal names, other nouns, and adjectives (*Billy; Susie; birdie; granny; sweetie; tummy*) and in various other usu. informal coinages, sometimes pejorative (*boonies; goalie; groupie; Okie; preemie; rookie*). This suffix also forms from adjectives nouns that denote exemplary or extreme instances of the quality specified (*baddie; biggie; toughie*), sometimes focusing on a restricted, usu. unfavorable sense of the adjective (*sharpie; sickie; whitey*). Compare -O, -SY.

-y³, a suffix of various origins used in the formation of action nouns from verbs (*inquiry*), and also found in other abstract nouns (*infamy*).

yacht (yot), *n.* **1.** a vessel used for private cruising, racing, or other noncommercial purposes. —*v.i.* **2.** to sail or voyage in a yacht.

yachts•man (yots′mən), *n., pl.* **-men.** a person who owns or sails a yacht. —**yachts′man•ship′,** *n.*

yachts•wom•an (yots′wŏŏm′ən), *n., pl.* **-wom•en.** a woman who owns or sails a yacht.

yack•e•ty-yack (yak′i tē yak′), *n. Slang.* YAK².

Ya•hoo (yä′hŏŏ, yā′-, yä hŏŏ′), *n., pl.* **-hoos. 1.** (in Jonathan Swift's *Gulliver's Travels*) one of a race of brutes, having the form and all the vices of humans, who are subject to the Houyhnhnms. **2.** (*l.c.*) a boorish person; lout. —**ya′hoo•ism,** *n.*

Yahr•zeit (yär′tsīt, yôr′-), *n. Judaism.* the anniversary of the death of a parent or other close relative, observed by lighting a candle and reciting the Kaddish.

Yah•weh or **Jah•weh** (yä′we), also **Yah•veh, Jah•veh** (-ve), *n.* a name of God, transliterated by scholars from the Tetragrammaton and commonly rendered Jehovah.

Yah•wism (yä′wiz əm) also **Yah•vism** (-viz-), *n.* the worship of Yahweh or the religious system based on such worship.

Yah•wist (yä′wist) also **Yah•vist** (-vist), *n.* a writer of the earliest major source of the Hexateuch, in which God is characteristically referred to as *Yahweh* rather than *Elohim.* Compare ELOHIST. —**Yah•wis′tic,** *adj.*

yak¹ (yak), *n.* **1.** a large, shaggy-haired wild ox, *Bos grunniens,* of the Tibetan highlands, having long, curved horns. **2.** a domesticated variety of this animal.

yak² or **yack** (yak), *v.,* **yakked** or **yacked, yak•king** or **yack•ing,** *n. Slang.* —*v.i.* **1.** to gab; chatter. —*n.* **2.** incessant idle or gossipy talk. —**yak′ker,** *n.*

yak³ (yak), *n., v.i., yakked, yak•king. Slang.* YUK¹.

yak•e•ty-yak or **yack•e•ty-yak** (yak′i tē yak′), *v.i.,* **-yakked** or **-yacked, -yak•king** or **-yack•ing,** *n. Slang.* YAK².

ya•ki•to•ri (yä′ki tôr′ē, -tōr′ē), *n.* small pieces of boneless chicken marinated and then broiled and served on skewers.

y'all (yôl), *pron.* YOU-ALL.

Yal•ta (yôl′tə, yäl′-), *n.* a seaport in the Crimea, in S Ukraine, on the Black Sea: site of wartime conference of Roosevelt, Churchill, and Stalin 1945. 83,000.

yam (yam), *n.* **1.** the starchy, tuberous root of any of various African climbing vines of the genus *Dioscorea,* family Dioscoreaceae, cultivated for food in warm regions: resembling but botanically unrelated to the sweet potato. **2.** any of these plants. **3.** the sweet potato.

yam•mer (yam′ər), *Informal.* —*v.i.* **1.** to whine or complain. **2.** to talk loudly and persistently. —*v.t.* **3.** to utter clamorously and persistently, esp. in complaint. —*n.* **4.** the act or noise of yammering. —**yam′mer•er,** *n.* —**yam′mer•ing•ly,** *adv.*

Ya•mous•sou•kro (yä′mə s′ŏŏ′krō), *n.* the capital of the Ivory Coast, in the S central part. 120,000.

yang (yäng, yang), *n.* See under YIN AND YANG.

Yan•gon (yang gon′, -gôn′), *n.* the capital of Burma, in the S part. 2,459,000. Formerly, **Rangoon.**

yank (yangk), *v.i.* **1.** to pull or tug sharply: *Yank on the bell rope.* —*v.t.* **2.** to pull abruptly. **3.** to remove abruptly and unceremoniously. —*n.* **4.** an abrupt, vigorous pull; jerk.

Yank (yangk), *n., adj. Informal.* Yankee.

Yan•kee (yang′kē), *n.* **1.** a native or inhabitant of the United States. **2.** a native or inhabitant of New England. **3.** a native or inhabitant of a Northern state. **4.** a Federal soldier in the Civil War. —*adj.* **5.** of, pertaining to, or characteristic of a Yankee or Yankees: *Yankee ingenuity.* [perh. < Dutch *Jan Kees* John Cheese, Dutch nickname for English colonial settlers] —**Yan′kee•dom,** *n.*

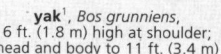
yak¹, *Bos grunniens,*
6 ft. (1.8 m) high at shoulder;
head and body to 11 ft. (3.4 m)

Yan′kee bond′, *n.* a bond issued by a foreign corporation or country designed for sale in the U.S.

Yan′kee Clip′per, *n.* epithet of Joe DiMaggio.

Yan′kee Doo′dle (dŏŏd′l), *n.* **1.** (*italics*) a song with a melody of apparent British origin, popular with American troops during the Revolutionary War. **2.** a Yankee.

Ya•oun•dé (youn′dā, youn dā′), *n.* the capital of Cameroon, in the SW part. 436,000.

yap (yap), *v.,* **yapped, yap•ping,** *n.* —*v.i.* **1.** to bark sharply, shrilly, or snappishly; yelp. **2.** *Slang.* to talk shrilly, noisily, or foolishly. —*v.t.* **3.** to utter by yapping. —*n.* **4.** a shrill, snappish bark; yelp. **5.** *Slang.* **a.** shrill, noisy, or foolish talk. **b.** mouth: *Keep your yap shut.* **6.** *Slang.* a stupid or uncouth person; fool; bumpkin. —**yap′per,** *n.* —**yap′ping•ly,** *adv.*

yard¹ (yärd), *n.* **1. a.** a unit of linear measure in English-speaking countries, equal to 3 feet or 36 inches (0.9144 meter). **b.** a cubic yard: *a yard of topsoil.* **2.** a long spar, supported more or less at its center, to which the head of a square sail, lateen sail, or lugsail is bent. **3.** *Informal.* a large quantity or extent. **4.** *Slang.* one hundred or, usu., one thousand dollars. —*Idiom.* **5. the whole nine yards,** *Informal.* in every respect; without limits.

yard² (yärd), *n.* **1.** the ground that immediately adjoins or surrounds a house, public building, etc. **2.** a courtyard. **3.** an outdoor enclosure for exercise, as by students or inmates. **4.** an outdoor space surrounded by a group of buildings, as on a college campus. **5.** an enclosure for livestock. **6.** an enclosure within which any work or business is carried on (often used in combination): *a lumberyard.* **7.** an outside area used for storage, assembly, etc. **8.** a system of parallel tracks, crossovers, switches, etc., where rail cars are made up into trains and where rolling stock is kept when not in use or when awaiting repairs. **9.** the winter pasture or browsing ground of moose and deer. —*v.t.* **10.** to put into, enclose, or store in a yard.

yard•age¹ (yär′dij), *n.* measurement, or the amount measured, in yards; length or extent in yards.

yard•age² (yär′dij), *n.* **1.** the use of a yard or enclosure, as in loading or unloading livestock at a railroad station. **2.** the charge for such use.

yard•arm (yärd′ärm′), *n.* either of the outer portions of the yard of a square sail.

yard′ goods′, *n.pl.* PIECE GOODS.

yard•man (yärd′mən), *n., pl.* **-men. 1.** a person who works in a railroad yard, lumberyard, or the like. **2.** a person employed to care for the yard of a house, public building, etc.

yard′ sale′, *n.* GARAGE SALE.

yard•stick (yärd′stik′), *n.* **1.** a stick a yard long, commonly marked with subdivisions, used for measuring. **2.** any standard of measurement or judgment: *Tests are not the only yardstick of academic achievement.*

yar•mul•ke (yär′məl kə, -mə-, yä′-), *n., pl.* **-kes.** a skullcap worn by Jewish Orthodox or Conservative males, esp. during meals, prayer, and religious study.

yarn (yärn), *n.* **1.** thread made of natural or synthetic fibers and used for knitting and weaving. **2.** a continuous strand or thread made from glass, metal, plastic, etc. **3.** an aggregate of fibers, as of hemp, that forms one of the small elements composing a strand of rope. **4.** a tale, esp. a long story of adventure or incredible happenings. —*v.i.* **5.** to tell a yarn.

yarn′-dyed′, *adj.* (of fabric) made from yarns previously dyed (opposed to *piece-dyed*).

yaw (yô), *v.i.* **1.** to deviate temporarily from a straight course, as a ship. **2.** (of an aircraft) to have a motion about its vertical axis. **3.** (of a rocket or guided missile) to deviate from a stable flight attitude by oscillation of the longitudinal axis in the horizontal plane. —*v.t.* **4.** to cause to yaw. —*n.* **5.** the movement of yawing. **6.** a motion of an aircraft about its vertical axis. **7.** a right or left angle determined by the direction of motion of an aircraft or spacecraft and its vertical and longitudinal plane of symmetry.

yawl (yôl), *n.* **1.** a ship's small boat, rowed by a crew of four or six. **2.** a two-masted, fore-and-aft-rigged sailing vessel having a large mainmast and a smaller jiggermast or mizzenmast stepped abaft the sternpost. Compare KETCH.

yawl (def. 2)

yawn (yôn), *v.i.* **1.** to open the mouth somewhat involuntarily with a prolonged, deep inhalation and sighing or heavy exhalation, as from drowsiness or boredom. **2.** to extend or stretch wide, as an open and deep space. —*v.t.* **3.** to say with a yawn. —*n.* **4.** an act or instance of yawning. **5.** a deep, open space; chasm. **6. a.** a bored reaction. **b.** Also called **yawner**. something so boring as to make one yawn. —**yawn′ing•ly,** *adv.*

yawp or **yaup** (yôp, yäp), *v.i.* **1.** to utter a loud, harsh cry; yelp; squawk. **2.** to talk noisily and complainingly. —*n.* **3.** a harsh cry. **4. a.** raucous or querulous talk. **b.** a noisy, foolish utterance. —**yawp′er,** *n.*

yaws (yôz), *n.* (*used with a sing. v.*) an infectious tropical disease, primarily of children, characterized by raspberrylike eruptions of the skin and caused by a spirochete, *Treponema pertenue.* —**yaw′ey,** *adj.*

y-ax•is (wī′ak′sis), *n., pl.* **y-ax•es** (wī′ak′sēz). **1.** (in a plane Cartesian coordinate system) the axis, usu. vertical, along which the ordinate is measured and from which the abscissa is measured. **2.** (in a three-dimensional Cartesian coordinate system) the axis along which values of *y* are measured and at which both *x* and *z* equal zero.

Yb, *Chem. Symbol.* ytterbium.

YB or **Y.B.,** yearbook.

Y chromosome, *n.* a sex chromosome of humans and most mammals that is present only in males and is paired with an X chromosome.

yd., yard.

ye (yē), *pron.* **1.** *Archaic* (*except in ecclesiastical prose*) *or Brit. Dial.* **a.** (used nominatively as the plural of THOU): *O ye of little faith; ye brooks and hills.* **b.** (used nominatively for the second person singular, esp. in polite address): *Do ye not know me?* **c.** (used objectively in the second person singular or plural): *I have something to tell ye.* **2.** (used with mock seriousness in an invocation, mild oath, or the like): *Ye gods and little fishes!*

yea (yā), *adv.* **1.** yes (used in affirmation or assent). **2.** indeed: *Yea, and she did hear.* **3.** moreover: *a good, yea, a noble man.* —*n.* **4.** an affirmative reply or vote: *The yeas have it.* **5.** a person who votes in the affirmative.

yeah (yà), *adv., n. Informal.* yes.

yean (yēn), *v.i.* (of a sheep or goat) to bring forth young.

yean•ling (yēn′ling), *n.* **1.** the young of a sheep or goat; a lamb or kid. —*adj.* **2.** just born; infant.

year (yēr), *n.* **1.** a period of 365 or 366 days, in the Gregorian calendar, divided into 12 calendar months, now reckoned as beginning Jan. 1 and ending Dec. 31 (**calendar year**). Compare COMMON YEAR, LEAP YEAR. **2.** a period of approximately the same length in other calendars. **3. a.** a space of 12 calendar months calculated from any point: *We expect to finish in a year.* **b.** FISCAL YEAR. **4.** *Astron.* **a.** Also called **lunar year**. a division of time equal to 12 lunar months. **b.** Also called **solar year**. a division of time equal to 365 days, 5 hours, 48 minutes, and 46 seconds, representing the interval between one vernal equinox and the next. **c.** Also called **sidereal year**. a division of time equal to the solar year plus 20 minutes, the time it takes the earth to complete one revolution around the sun. **5.** the time in which any planet completes a revolution around the sun: *the Martian year.* **6.** a full round of the seasons. **7.** a period out of every 12 months devoted to a certain pursuit, activity, or the like: *the academic year.* **8. years, a.** age: *a person of her years.* **b.** old age: *a man of years.* **c.** time; period: *the years of hardship.* **d.** an unusually or markedly long time: *We haven't spoken in years.* **9.** a group of students entering school or college, or those graduating in the same year; class. —*Idiom.* **10. year in and year out,** regularly through the years; continually. Also, **year in, year out.**

year′-around′, *adj.* YEAR-ROUND.

year•book (yēr′bŏŏk′), *n.* **1.** a book published annually, containing information, statistics, etc., about the past year: *an encyclopedia yearbook.* **2.** a book published by the graduating class of a high school or college,

containing photographs of class members and commemorating school activities.

year′-end′ or **year′end′,** *n.* **1.** the end of a calendar year. —*adj.* **2.** occurring at the year-end: *a year-end sale.*

year•ling (yēr′ling), *n.* **1.** an animal in its second year. **2.** a horse one year old, dating from January 1 of the year after the year of foaling. —*adj.* **3.** being a year old. **4.** of a year's standing: *a yearling bride.*

year•long (yēr′lông′, -long′), *adj.* lasting for a year.

year•ly (yēr′lē), *adj., adv., n., pl.* **-lies.** —*adj.* **1.** done, occurring, appearing, etc., once each year: *a yearly report.* **2.** computed or determined by the year: *yearly interest.* **3.** pertaining to a year or to each year. —*adv.* **4.** once a year; annually. —*n.* **5.** a publication issued once a year.

yearn (yûrn), *v.i.* **1.** to have an earnest or strong desire; long. **2.** to feel tenderness; be moved or concerned. —**yearn′er,** *n.*

yearn•ing (yûr′ning), *n.* **1.** deep longing, esp. when accompanied by tenderness or sadness. **2.** an instance of this. —**yearn′ing•ly,** *adv.*

year′ of grace′, *n.* a specified year of the Christian era: *the year of grace 1992.*

year′-round′, *adj.* **1.** continuing, available, used, etc., throughout the year: *a year-round vacation spot.* —*adv.* **2.** throughout the year. —**year′-round′er,** *n.*

yea•say•er (yā′sā′ər), *n.* **1.** an undaunted optimist. **2.** a toady; sycophant.

yeast (yēst), *n.* **1.** any of various small, single-celled fungi of the phylum Ascomycota that reproduce by fission or budding, the daughter cells often remaining attached, and that are capable of fermenting carbohydrates into alcohol and carbon dioxide. **2.** any of several yeasts of the genus *Saccharomyces,* used in brewing alcoholic beverages, as a leaven in baking breads, and in pharmacology as a source of vitamins and proteins. **3.** something that causes ferment or agitation. —*v.i.* **4.** to ferment. **5.** to froth.

yeast•y (yē′stē), *adj.,* **yeast•i•er, yeast•i•est. 1.** of, containing, or resembling yeast. **2.** characterized by agitation, excitement, change, etc. **3.** frothy; foamy. **4.** youthful; ebullient. **5.** trifling; frivolous. —**yeast′i•ness,** *n.*

Yeats (yāts), *n.* **William Butler,** 1865–1939, Irish poet and dramatist.

yech or **yecch** (yɛкн, yek, yuкн, yuk), *interj. Slang.* YUCK[1].

yell (yel), *v.i.* **1.** to cry out; shout. **2.** to scream with pain, fright, etc. —*v.t.* **3.** to say by yelling: *to yell an order to the troops.* —*n.* **4.** a cry uttered by yelling. **5.** a cheer or shout, as one adopted by a school to encourage a team.

yel•low (yel′ō), *n.* **1.** a color like that of egg yolk, ripe lemons, etc.; the primary color between green and orange in the visible spectrum, an effect of light with a wavelength between 570 and 590 nm. **2.** the yolk of an egg. **3.** a yellow pigment or dye. **4.** YELLOW LIGHT. —*adj.* **5.** of the color yellow. **6.** having a sallow or yellowish complexion. **7.** having a yellowish cast due to age or deterioration: *a stack of yellow newspapers.* **8.** cowardly. **9.** (of a newspaper, reporting, etc.) emphasizing sensational or lurid details, often by distorting the facts: *yellow journalism.* —*v.t., v.i.* **10.** to make or become yellow. —**yel′low•ness,** *n.*

yel•low-bel•lied, *adj.* **1.** having a yellow abdomen or underside. **2.** *Slang.* cowardly; lily-livered.

yel•low-bel•ly (yel′ō bel′ē), *n., pl.* **-lies.** *Slang.* a cowardly person; craven.

yel′low bile′, *n.* one of the four elemental bodily humors of medieval physiology, regarded as causing anger; choler.

yel′low birch′, *n.* **1.** a North American birch, *Betula alleghaniensis,* having yellowish or bronze bark. **2.** the hard, light, reddish brown wood of this tree, used for furniture, buildings, boxes, etc.

yel′low dog′, *n.* a cowardly, despicable person; craven.

yel′low fe′ver, *n.* an acute, often fatal, infectious febrile disease of warm climates, caused by a virus transmitted by a mosquito, esp. *Aedes aegypti,* and characterized by liver damage and jaundice. Also called **yellow jack.**

yel′low•fin tu′na (yel′ō fin′), *n.* an important food fish, *Thunnus albacares,* inhabiting warm seas. Also called **yellowfin.**

yel•low•ham•mer (yel′ō ham′ər), *n. Southern U.S.* a flicker, *Colaptes auratus auratus,* having yellow wing and tail linings.

yel•low•ish (yel′ō ish), *adj.* somewhat yellow; yellowy.

yel′low jack′, *n., pl.* (*esp. collectively*) **-jack,** (*esp. for kinds or species*) **-jacks** for 3. **1.** YELLOW FEVER. **2.** a yellow flag signaling quarantine. **3.** a silvery and yellowish Caribbean food fish, *Caranx bartholomaei.*

yel′low jack′et, *n.* any of several paper wasps of the family Vespidae, having black and bright yellow bands.

yel•low•legs (yel′ō legz′), *n.* (*used with a sing. v.*) either of two large New World sandpipers having yellow legs, *Tringa melanoleuca* or *T. flavipes.*

yel′low light′, *n.* a yellow or amber traffic light indicating caution, usu. preceding a signal halting traffic in a particular direction.

yel′low pag′es, *n.pl.* (*often caps.*) a classified telephone directory or section of a directory, listing subscribers by the type of business or service they offer, usu. printed on yellow paper.

yel′low perch′, *n.* a North American perch, *Perca flavescens,* having a yellowish body with dark brown vertical bars.

yel′low pine′, *n.* **1.** any of several North American pines yielding a strong, yellowish wood. **2.** the wood of any such tree.

yel′low pop′lar, *n.* **1.** TULIP TREE. **2.** the wood of the tulip tree.

yel′low rain′, *n.* powdery yellow deposits containing a fungal toxin, tricothecene, identified in SE Asia and claimed by some to be a chemical weapon and by others to be contaminated bee excrement.

yel′low rib′bon, *n.* a yellow-colored ribbon displayed as a symbol of solidarity with soldiers in combat, political hostages, etc.

yel′low spot′, *n.* MACULA (def. 2b).

Yel′lowstone Na′tional Park′, *n.* a park in NW Wyoming and adjacent parts of Montana and Idaho: geysers, hot springs, falls, canyon. 3458 sq. mi. (8955 sq. km).

yel′low streak′, *n.* a strain of cowardice.

yel·low·tail (yel′ō tāl′), *n.*, *pl.* **-tails,** (*esp. collectively*) **-tail. 1.** a game fish, *Seriola lalandei,* of California. **2.** Also called **yel′lowtail snap′per.** a small West Indian snapper, *Ocyurus chrysurus.* **3.** YELLOWTAIL FLOUNDER.

yel′lowtail floun′der, *n.* a spotted flounder, *Limanda ferruginea,* of the Atlantic coast of North America, having a yellowish tail fin.

yel·low·throat (yel′ō thrōt′), *n.* any of various New World wood warblers of the genus *Geothlypis,* typically nesting in dense undergrowth, esp. the common North American species *G. trichas,* with a yellow throat and breast, and, in the male, a black mask.

yel′low war′bler, *n.* a common North American wood warbler of thickets and gardens, *Dendroica petechia aestiva,* having bright yellow plumage.

yel·low·wood (yel′ō wŏŏd′), *n.* **1.** a tree, *Cladrastis lutea,* of the legume family, of the southeastern U.S., having clusters of fragrant white flowers and wood that yields a yellow dye. **2.** any of several other trees having yellowish wood or yielding a yellow dye.

yel·low·y (yel′ō ē), *adj.* tinged with yellow; yellowish.

yelp (yelp), *v.i.* **1.** to give a sharp, shrill cry, as a dog or fox. **2.** to call or cry out sharply, as in pain. —*v.t.* **3.** to utter by or as if by yelping. —*n.* **4.** a quick, sharp bark or cry. —**yelp′er,** *n.*

Yel·tsin (yelt′sin), *n.* **Boris (Nikolayevich),** born 1931, president of the Russian Federation since 1991.

Yem·en (yem′ən, yā′mən), *n.* **Republic of,** a country in S Arabia, formed in 1990 by the merger of the Yemen Arab Republic and the People's Democratic Republic of Yemen. 13,972,477; 207,000 sq. mi. (536,130 sq. km). *Cap.* (*political*) San'a. *Cap.* (*economic*) Aden.

yen[1] (yen), *n.*, *pl.* **yen.** the basic monetary unit of Japan.

yen[2] (yen), *n.*, *v.*, **yenned, yen·ning.** —*n.* **1.** a desire or craving. —*v.i.* **2.** to have a craving; yearn.

yen·ta (yen′tə), *n.*, *pl.* **-tas.** *Slang.* a gossipy woman; busybody.

yeo·man (yō′mən), *n.*, *pl.* **-men,** *adj.* —*n.* **1.** an enlisted person in the U.S. Navy whose duties are chiefly clerical. **2.** *Brit.* a farmer who cultivates his own land. **3.** (formerly, in England) **a.** one of a class of lesser freeholders, below the gentry, who cultivated their own land. **b.** an attendant in a royal or other great household. **c.** an assistant, as of a sheriff or other official. —*adj.* **4.** of or pertaining to yeomen. **5.** (esp. of an arduous task) performed in a loyal, valiant, or workmanlike manner.

yep (yep), *adv.*, *n.* *Informal.* yes.

-yer, var. of -ER[1] after *w: bowyer; lawyer.*

Ye·re·van (yer′ə vän′), *n.* a city in and the capital of Armenia, in the W part. 1,199,000.

yes (yes), *adv.*, *n.*, *pl.* **yes·es,** *v.*, **yessed, yes·sing.** —*adv.* **1.** (used to express affirmation or agreement or to emphasize a previous statement): *Do you want that? Yes, I do.* **2.** (used to express disagreement with a negative statement or command): *You can't do that! Oh yes I can!* **3.** (used interrogatively to express uncertainty, curiosity, etc.): *"Yes?" he said as he opened the door.* **4.** (used to express polite interest or attention.) —*n.* **5.** an affirmative reply or vote. —*v.t.* **6.** to give an affirmative reply to; give assent or approval to.

ye·shi·va or **ye·shi·vah** (yə shē′və), *n.*, *pl.* **-vas** or **-vahs. 1.** an Orthodox Jewish school for the religious and secular education of children of elementary school age. **2.** an Orthodox Jewish school of higher instruction in Jewish learning, chiefly for students preparing to enter the rabbinate.

yes′-man′, *n.*, *pl.* **-men.** a person who always agrees with superiors, regardless of personal convictions; sycophant.

yes′-no′ ques′tion, *n.* a question calling for an answer of *yes* or *no,* as *Has the plane left yet?*

yes·ter·day (yes′tər dā′, -dē), *adv.* **1.** on the day before this day. **2.** in the or a previous era: *Yesterday your money went further.* —*n.* **3.** the day before this day. **4.** time in the immediate past. —*adj.* **5.** belonging or pertaining to the day before or to an immediate past time: *yesterday morning.*

yes·ter·year (yes′tər yēr′, -yēr′), *n.* **1.** last year. **2.** the recent years; time not long past. —*adv.* **3.** during the recent past; in past generations.

Yes′, Virgin′ia, there′ is′ a San′ta Claus′, part of a *New York Sun* editorial (1897) by Francis Pharcellus Church, affirming the existence of Santa Claus to a little girl whose friends had told her he did not exist.

yet (yet), *adv.* **1.** at the present time; now: *Are they here yet?* **2.** up to a particular time; thus far: *They had not yet come.* **3.** in the time remaining; still: *There is yet time.* **4.** at the present moment; as previously; still: *He came this morning, and he is here yet.* **5.** in addition; again: *The mail brought yet another reply.* **6.** moreover: *I've never read it nor yet intend to.* **7.** even to a larger extent (used to emphasize a comparative): *yet greater power.* **8.** nevertheless: *strange and yet very true.* —*conj.* **9.** though; still; nevertheless: *The essay is good, yet it could be improved.* —**Idiom. 10. as yet,** so far; until this moment.

yet·i (yet′ē), *n.* (*sometimes cap.*) ABOMINABLE SNOWMAN.

yew[1] (yōō), *n.* **1.** any of several evergreen trees or shrubs of the genus *Taxus,* of the family Taxaceae, having needlelike foliage and seeds enclosed in a fleshy aril. **2.** the fine-grained, elastic wood of any of these trees. **3.** an archer's bow made of this wood.

yew[2] (yōō; *unstressed* yōō), *pron.* Eye Dial. you.

Yid·dish (yid′ish), *n.* **1.** a language of central and E European Jews and their descendants elsewhere: based on Rhenish dialects of Middle High German with an admixture of vocabulary from Hebrew and Aramaic, the Slavic languages, and other sources, and written in the Hebrew alphabet. —*adj.* **2.** of or pertaining to Yiddish.

yield (yēld), *v.t.* **1.** to give forth or produce by a natural process or in return for cultivation: *to yield 40 bushels to the acre.* **2.** to produce or furnish (profit). **3.** to give up, as to superior power or authority: *yielded the fort to the enemy.* **4.** to relinquish or resign: *to yield the floor to the senator from Ohio.* **5.** to give as due or required: *to yield obedience.* —*v.i.* **6.** to give a return, as for labor expended; produce or bear. **7.** to surrender to superior power. **8.** to give way to influence, entreaty, or the like: *to yield to outrageous demands.* **9.** to give place or precedence (usu. fol. by *to*): *to yield to the next speaker.* **10.** to give way to force, pressure, etc.; collapse. —*n.* **11.** the act of yielding or producing. **12.** the quantity or amount yielded. **13.** the income produced by a financial investment, usu. shown as a percentage of cost. **14.** *Chem.* the quantity of product formed by the interaction of two or more substances, generally expressed as a percentage of the quantity obtained to that theoretically obtainable. **15.** something given up or relinquished. **16.** a measure of the destructive energy of a nuclear explosion, expressed in kilotons of the amount of TNT that would produce the same destruction. —**yield′er,** *n.*

yield·ing (yēl′ding), *adj.* **1.** submissive; compliant. **2.** tending to give way, esp. under pressure; flexible. **3.** (of a crop, soil, etc.) producing a yield; productive.

yield′ man′agement, *n.* the process of frequently adjusting the price of a product in response to various market factors, as demand or competition.

yin (yin), *n.* See under YIN AND YANG.

yin′ and yang′, *n.* (in Chinese philosophy and religion) two principles, one negative, dark, and feminine **(yin)**, and one positive, bright, and masculine **(yang)**, whose interaction influences the destinies of creatures and things.

symbol for **yin and yang**

yip (yip), *v.*, **yipped, yip·ping,** *n.* —*v.i.* **1.** to bark sharply, as a young dog. —*n.* **2.** a sharp bark; yelp.

yipe (yīp), *interj.* (used as an expression or exclamation of fright, surprise, pain, etc.)

yip·pee (yip′ē, yip′ē′), *interj.* (used as an exclamation to express joy, exultation, or the like.)

yip·pie (yip′ē), *n.* (*sometimes cap.*) a member of a group of radical, politically active hippies.

-yl, a suffix used in the names of chemical groups: *ethyl.*

YMCA or **Y.M.C.A.,** Young Men's Christian Association.

YMHA or **Y.M.H.A.,** Young Men's Hebrew Association.

yo (yō), *interj.* (used as an exclamation to get someone's attention, express excitement, etc.)

yo·del (yōd′l), *v.*, **-deled, -del·ing,** or (*esp. Brit.*) **-delled, -del·ling,** *n.* —*v.t., v.i.* **1.** to sing or call out with frequent changes from the ordinary voice to falsetto and back again, in the manner of Swiss and Tyrolean mountaineers. —*n.* **2.** a song, refrain, etc., so sung or called out. **3.** an act of yodeling. —**yo′del·er,** *n.*

yo·ga (yō′gə), *n.* (*sometimes cap.*) **1.** a system of physical and mental disciplines practiced to attain control of body and mind, tranquillity, etc., esp. a series of postures and breathing exercises. **2.** a school of Hindu philosophy using such a system to unify the self with the Supreme Being or ultimate principle. [< Sanskrit] —**yo′gic,** *adj.* —**yo′gism,** *n.*

yo·gi (yō′gē) also **yo·gin** (-gin), *n.*, *pl.* **-gis** also **-gins.** a person who practices yoga.

yo·gi·ni (yō′gə nē), *n.*, *pl.* **-nis.** a woman who practices yoga.

yo·gurt or **yo·ghurt** or **yo·ghourt** (yō′gərt), *n.* a tart, custardlike food made from milk curdled by the action of bacterial cultures and sometimes sweetened or flavored.

yo-ho (yō hō′), *interj.* (used as a call or shout to attract attention, accompany effort, etc.)

yoke (yōk), *n.*, *pl.* **yokes** for 1, 3–13, **yoke** for 2, *v.* —*n.* **1.** a device for joining together a pair of draft animals, esp. oxen, usu. consisting of a crosspiece with two bow-shaped pieces, each enclosing the head of an animal. Compare HARNESS (def. 1). **2.** a pair of draft animals fastened together by a yoke. **3.** something resembling a yoke in form or use. **4.** a frame fitting a person's neck and shoulders, for carrying a pair of buckets or the like, one at each end. **5.** an agency of oppression, subjection, servitude, etc. **6.** an emblem or symbol of subjection, servitude, etc., as an archway under which prisoners of war were compelled to pass by the ancient Romans and others. **7.** something that couples or binds together; bond or tie. **8.** a viselike piece gripping two parts firmly together. **9.** a fitting for the neck of a draft animal for suspending the tongue of a cart, carriage, etc., from a harness. **10.** a shaped and fitted piece in a garment, as at the shoulders or the hips, from which the rest of the garment hangs. —*v.t.* **11.** to put a yoke on. **12.** to attach (a draft animal) to a plow or vehicle. **13.** to harness a draft animal to (a plow or vehicle). **14.** to join, couple, link, or unite. —*v.i.* **15.** to be or become joined, linked, or united.

yoke

yoke[1] (def. 1)

yo·kel (yō′kəl), *n.* a rustic; country bumpkin.
Yo·ko·ha·ma (yō′kə hä′mə), *n.* a seaport on SE Honshu, in central Japan, on Tokyo Bay. 3,072,000.
yolk (yōk, yōlk), *n.* **1.** the yellow and principal substance of an egg, as distinguished from the white. **2.** the part of the contents of the egg of an animal that enters directly into the formation of the embryo, together with any material that nourishes the embryo during its formation. **3.** a natural grease exuded from the skin of sheep. —**yolked,** *adj.* —**yolk′y,** *adj.*
Yom Kip·pur (yom kip′ər, yōm; *Heb.* yôm′ kē pŏŏr′), *n.* the holiest Jewish holiday, observed on the 10th day of Tishri by fasting and by recitation of prayers of repentance in the synagogue. Also called **Day of Atonement.** [< Hebrew = *yōm* day + *kippūr* atonement]
yon·der (yon′dər), *adj.* **1.** being in that place or over there; being that or those over there: *Do you see yonder hut?* **2.** being the more distant or farther: *the yonder side of the hill.* —*adv.* **3.** at, in, or to that specified place; over there: *Look yonder!*
Yon·kers (yong′kərz), *n.* a city in SE New York, on the Hudson, N of New York City. 183,490.
yoo-hoo (yōō′hōō′), *interj.* (used as an exclamation to get someone's attention, in calling to another person, or the like.)
yore (yôr, yōr), *n. Chiefly Literary.* time past: *knights of yore.*
York (yôrk), *n.* **1.** a member of the royal house of England that ruled from 1461 to 1485. **2. 1st Duke of** (*Edmund of Langley*), 1341–1402, progenitor of the house of York (son of Edward III). **3. Alvin Cullum** (*Sergeant*), 1887–1964, U.S. soldier. **4.** YORKSHIRE (def. 1). **5.** Ancient, **Eboracum.** a city in North Yorkshire, in NE England, on the Ouse: the capital of Roman Britain. 102,700. **6.** a city in SE Pennsylvania: meeting of the Continental Congress 1777–78. 44,619. **7.** an estuary in E Virginia, flowing SE into Chesapeake Bay. 40 mi. (64 km) long. **8. Cape,** a cape at the NE extremity of Australia.
York·shire (yôrk′shēr, -shər), *n.* **1.** Also called **York.** a former county in N England, now part of Humberside, North Yorkshire, South Yorkshire, Cleveland, and Durham. **2.** one of an English breed of white hogs having erect ears.
York′shire pud′ding, *n.* a batter of flour, salt, eggs, and milk baked in hot drippings, esp. of roast beef.
York′shire ter′rier, *n.* one of an English breed of toy terriers having a long, silky, straight coat that is dark steel-blue with tan on the head, chest, and legs.
York·town (yôrk′toun′), *n.* a village in SE Virginia: surrender in 1781 of Cornwallis to Washington in the American Revolution.
Yosem′ite Na′tional Park′, *n.* a national park in E California, in the Sierra Nevada: granite peaks, waterfalls, giant sequoias, and a steepwalled valley (**Yosem′ite Val′ley**). 1182 sq. mi. (3060 sq. km).
you (yōō; *unstressed* yōō, yə), *pron., poss.* **your** or **yours,** *obj.* **you,** *pl.* **you;** *n., pl.* **yous.** —*pron.* **1.** the pronoun of the second person singular or plural, used of the person or persons being addressed, in the nominative or objective case: *You are the highest bidder. We can't help you.* **2.** one; anyone; people in general: *a tiny animal you can't even see.* **3.** (used in apposition with the subject of a sentence, sometimes repeated for emphasis following the subject): *You rascal, you!* **4.** (used in place of the pronoun *your* before a gerund or present participle): *There's no sense in you getting upset.* —*n.* **5.** something or someone closely identified with or resembling the person addressed: *That bright red shirt just isn't you.* **6.** the nature or character of the person addressed: *Try to discover the hidden you.*
you-all (yōō ôl′, yôl), *pron. Chiefly South Midland and Southern U.S.* (used in direct address to two or more people, or to one person who represents a family, organization, etc.): *You-all come back now, hear?*

you'd (yōōd; *unstressed* yōōd, yəd), contraction of *you had* or *you would.*
you'll (yōōl; *unstressed* yōōl, yəl), contraction of *you will* or *you shall.*
young (yung), *adj.,* **young·er** (yung′gər), **young·est** (yung′gist), *n.* —*adj.* **1.** being in the first or early stage of life or growth. **2.** having the appearance, vigor, or other qualities of youth. **3.** of or pertaining to youth. **4.** not far advanced in years or experience in comparison with others. **5.** junior: *the young Mr. Smith.* **6.** being in an early stage, as of existence, development, or maturity: *a young wine.* **7.** representing or advocating recent or progressive tendencies, policies, or the like. —*n.* **8.** young persons collectively. **9.** young offspring: *a mother hen protecting her young.* —*Idiom.* **10. with young,** (of an animal) pregnant. —**young′ish,** *adj.*
Young (yung), *n.* **1.** Andrew (Jackson, Jr.), born 1932, U.S. clergyman, civil-rights leader, politician, and diplomat: mayor of Atlanta, Georgia, since 1981. **2. Brigham,** 1801–77, U.S. Mormon leader. **3. Edward,** 1683–1765, English poet. **4. Thomas,** 1773–1829, English physician, physicist, and Egyptologist. **5. Whitney M., Jr.,** 1921–71, U.S. social worker and educator.
young′ blood′, *n.* **1.** youthful people. **2.** fresh new ideas, practices, etc.; vigor.
young′-eyed′, *adj.* **1.** clear-eyed; bright-eyed. **2.** having a youthful outlook; enthusiastic; fresh.
young·ling (yung′ling), *n.* **1.** a young person. **2.** anything young, as a young animal. **3.** a novice; beginner. —*adj.* **4.** young; youthful.
young·ster (yung′stər), *n.* **1.** a child. **2.** a young person. **3.** a young horse or other animal.
Young′ Turk′, *n.* **1.** a member of a reformist and nationalist group in Turkey that was politically dominant from 1908 to 1918. **2.** Also, **young′ Turk′.** a member of an insurgent, usu. liberal faction within a political party or other organization.
your (yōōr, yôr, yōr; *unstressed* yər), *pron.* **1.** a form of the possessive case of *you* used as an attributive adjective: *I like your idea.* Compare YOURS. **2.** (used to indicate that one belonging or relevant to oneself or to any person): *The library is on your left.* **3.** (used to indicate all members of a group, occupation, etc., or things of a particular type): *Take your factory worker, for instance.*
you're (yōōr; *unstressed* yər), contraction of *you are.*
yours (yōōrz, yôrz, yōrz), *pron.* **1.** a form of the possessive case of *you* used as a predicate adjective: *Which cup is yours? Is she a friend of yours?* **2.** that which belongs to you: *Yours was the first face I recognized.*
your·self (yōōr self′, yôr-, yōr-, yər-), *pron., pl.* **-selves** (-selvz′). **1.** a reflexive form of *you* (used as the direct or indirect object of a verb or the object of a preposition): *Did you ever ask yourself, "Why"? You can think for yourself.* **2.** (used as an intensifier): *a letter you yourself wrote.* **3.** (used in absolute constructions): *Yourself so sensitive, how can you ignore my feelings?* **4.** (used in place of *you* in various compound and comparative constructions): *Ted and yourself have been elected; a small gift for your mother and yourself; a girl no older than yourself.* **5.** your normal or customary self: *You'll soon be yourself again.* **6.** oneself: *The surest way is to do it yourself.*
yours′ tru′ly, 1. (a conventional phrase used at the end of a letter.) —*pron.* **2.** I; myself; me.
youth (yōōth), *n., pl.* **youths** (yōōths, yōōthz), (*collectively*) **youth. 1.** the condition of being young. **2.** the appearance, freshness, vigor, spirit, etc., characteristic of the young. **3.** the time of being young; early life. **4.** the period of life from puberty to the attainment of full growth; adolescence. **5.** the first or early period of anything. **6.** young persons collectively. **7.** a young person, esp. a young man.
youth·ful (yōōth′fəl), *adj.* **1.** characterized by youth; young. **2.** of, pertaining to, or suggesting youth or its vitality: *youthful enthusiasm.* **3.** in an early period of existence; early in time. **4.** (of topographical features) having undergone erosion to a slight extent only; immature. —**youth′ful·ly,** *adv.* —**youth′ful·ness,** *n.*
youth′ hos′tel, *n.* HOSTEL (def. 1).
you've (yōōv; *unstressed* yōōv, yəv), contraction of *you have.*
yow (you), *interj.* (used as an exclamation or shout of pain, dismay, etc.)
yowl (youl), *v.i.* **1.** to utter a long, distressful or dismal cry, as an animal or a person; howl. —*n.* **2.** a yowling cry; a howl. —**yowl′er,** *n.*
yo-yo (yō′yō), *n.* **1.** a spoollike toy that is spun out and reeled in by an attached string that loops around the player's finger. **2.** something that fluctuates or moves up and down, esp. suddenly or repeatedly. **3.** *Slang.* a stupid, foolish, or incompetent person. —*v.i.* **4.** to move up and down or back and forth; fluctuate or vacillate.
Y·pres (*Fr.* ē′pR°), *n.* a town in W Belgium: battles 1914–18. 34,758. Flemish, **Ieper.**
yr., 1. year. **2.** your.
yrs., 1. years. **2.** yours.
YT or **Y.T.,** Yukon Territory, Canada.
YTD, *Accounting.* year to date.
yt·ter·bi·um (i tûr′bē əm), *n.* a rare metallic element forming compounds resembling those of yttrium. Symbol: Yb; at. wt.: 173.04; at. no.: 70; sp. gr.: 6.96. —**yt·ter′bic, yt·ter′bous,** *adj.*
yt·tri·um (i′trē əm), *n.* a rare metallic element, found in gadolinite

and other minerals. *Symbol:* Y; *at. wt.:* 88.905; *at. no.:* 39; *sp. gr.:* 4.47. —**yt′tric,** *adj.*

yu•an (yōō än′; *Chin.* yvän), *n., pl.* **-an.** the basic monetary unit of China.

Yu•ca•tán or **Yu•ca•tan** (yōō′kə tan′, -tän′), *n.* **1.** a peninsula in SE Mexico and N Central America comprising parts of SE Mexico, N Guatemala, and Belize. **2.** a state in SE Mexico, in N Yucatán Peninsula. 1,302,600; 14,868 sq. mi. (38,510 sq. km). *Cap.:* Mérida.

Yu•ca•tec (yōō′kə tek′), *n., pl.* **-tecs,** (*esp. collectively*) **-tec. 1.** a member of an American Indian people of the Yucatán Peninsula in Mexico. **2.** Also called **Yu′catec Ma′yan.** the Mayan language of these people. —**Yu′ca•tec′an,** *adj.*

yuc•ca (yuk′ə), *n., pl.* **-cas.** any New World plant of the genus *Yucca,* of the agave family, having rigid sword-shaped leaves and white flowers borne in a dense terminal cluster.

yuck (yuk), *interj. Slang.* (used as an expression of disgust or repugnance.)

yuck•y (yuk′ē), *adj.,* **yuck•i•er, yuck•i•est.** *Slang.* thoroughly unappetizing, disgusting, or repugnant.

Yu•go•slav or **Ju•go•slav** (yōō′gō släv′, -slav′), *n.* **1.** a native or inhabitant of Yugoslavia. **2.** any member of a South Slavic–speaking people.

Yu•go•sla•vi•a or **Ju•go•sla•vi•a** (yōō′gō slä′vē ə), *n.* a federal republic in S Europe on the Adriatic: formed 1918 from the kingdoms of Serbia and Montenegro and part of Austria-Hungary; a federal republic 1945–91 comprised of Bosnia and Herzegovina, Croatia, Macedonia, Montenegro, Serbia, and Slovenia; since 1992 comprised of Serbia and Montenegro. 10,515,000; 39,449 sq. mi. (102,173 sq. km). *Cap.:* Belgrade. Formerly (1918–29), **Kingdom of the Serbs, Croats, and Slovenes.** —**Yu′go•sla′vi•an,** *adj., n.* —**Yu′go•slav′ic,** *adj.*

yuk or **yuck** (yuk), *n., v.,* **yukked** or **yucked, yuk•king** or **yuck•ing.** *Slang.* —*n.* **1.** a loud, hearty laugh. **2.** a joke or circumstance evoking such a laugh. —*v.i., v.t.* **3.** to laugh or joke: *yukking it up.*

yuk•ky (yuk′ē), *adj.,* **-ki•er, -ki•est.** *Slang.* YUCKY.

Yu•kon (yōō′kon), *n.* **1.** a river flowing NW and then SW from NW Canada through Alaska to the Bering Sea. ab. 2000 mi. (3220 km) long. **2.** Also called **Yu′kon Ter′ritory.** a territory in NW Canada. 23,504; 207,076 sq. mi. (536,325 sq. km). *Cap.:* Whitehorse.

yule (yōōl), *n.* Christmas, or the Christmas season. [< Old English *geōl(a)*, cognate Old Norse *jōl* orig., a pagan festival held near midwinter]

yule′ log′, *n.* a large log of wood that traditionally formed the backlog of the fire at Christmas.

yule•tide (yōōl′tīd′), *n.* the Christmas season.

yum•my (yum′ē), *adj.,* **-mi•er, -mi•est.** very pleasing to the senses, esp. to the taste; delicious.

yup (yup) also **yep,** *adv., n. Informal.* yes.

yup•pie or **yup•py** (yup′ē), *n., pl.* **-pies.** (*sometimes cap.*) a young, ambitious, educated city dweller who has a professional career and an affluent lifestyle. [*y(oung) u(rban) p(rofessional)* + -IE]

yup′pie flu′, *n. Informal.* CHRONIC FATIGUE SYNDROME.

YWCA or **Y.W.C.A.,** Young Women's Christian Association.

YWHA or **Y.W.H.A.,** Young Women's Hebrew Association.

Y

Z

Z, z (zē; *esp. Brit.* zed), *n., pl.* **Zs** or **Z's, zs** or **z's. 1.** the 26th letter of the English alphabet, a consonant. **2.** any spoken sound represented by this letter. **3.** something shaped like a Z. **4.** a written or printed representation of the letter *Z* or *z*.

Z, *Symbol.* **1.** the 26th in order or in a series. **2.** atomic number.

z, *Math. Symbol.* an unknown quantity or a variable.

za (zä), *n. Slang.* pizza.

za·ba·glio·ne (zä′bəl yō′nē, -bäl-), *n.* a custardlike dessert of egg yolks beaten to a froth with sugar and Marsala and served either hot or chilled.

Zac·chae·us (za kē′əs), *n.* a tax collector in Jericho whom Jesus invited to dine with him. Luke 19:1–10.

Zach·a·ri·ah (zak′ə rī′ə) also **Zach·a·ri·as** (-rī′əs), *n.* the father of John the Baptist. Luke 1:5.

zad·dik or **tzad·dik** (tsä′dik; *Heb.* tsä dēk′), *n., pl.* **zad·di·kim** or **tzad·di·kim** (tsä dik′im; *Heb.* tsä dē kēm′). **1.** a person of outstanding virtue and piety. **2.** the leader of a Hasidic group.

Za·dok (zā′dok), *n.* a priest at the time of David and Solomon. I Sam. 15:34–37; I Kings 1:7, 8.

zaf·tig or **zof·tig** (zäf′tik, -tig), *adj. Slang.* (of a woman) having a pleasantly plump figure. [< Yiddish *zaftik* lit., juicy]

zag (zag), *v.i.,* **zagged, zag·ging.** to move in one of the two directions followed in a zigzag course.

Za·greb (zä′greb), *n.* the capital of Croatia, in the NW part. 1,174,512.

Za·ire or **Za·ïre** (zä ēr′, zä′ēr), *n.* **1. Republic of.** a former name of the DEMOCRATIC REPUBLIC OF THE CONGO. **2.** official name within the Democratic Republic of the Congo of the CONGO River. —**Za·ir′i·an, Za·ir′e·an,** *adj.*

Zam·bi·a (zam′bē ə), *n.* a republic in S central Africa: formerly a British protectorate; gained independence 1964. 9,349,975; 290,586 sq. mi. (752,614 sq. km). *Cap.:* Lusaka. Formerly, **Northern Rhodesia.** —**Zam′bi·an,** *adj., n.*

Zam·bo·ni (zam bō′nē), *Trademark.* a brand of machine that smooths the surface of the ice on a rink. [after Frank J. *Zamboni,* 1901–88, U.S. inventor]

za·mi·a (zā′mē ə), *n., pl.* **-mi·as.** any of various plants of the genus *Zamia,* chiefly of tropical and subtropical America, having a short, tuberous stem and a crown of palmlike pinnate leaves.

za·ny (zā′nē), *adj.,* **-ni·er, -ni·est,** *n., pl.* **-nies.** —*adj.* **1.** absurdly or whimsically comical; clownishly crazy: *a zany comedian.* —*n.* **2.** a comically wild or eccentric person. **3.** a secondary character in old comedies, usu. a bungling imitator, derived from the male servant figures of commedia dell'arte. **4.** a buffoon; clown. [orig. the name for a character in early Italian comedy; perh. a form of *Gianni* John] —**za′ni·ly,** *adv.* —**za′ni·ness,** *n.*

Zan·zi·bar (zan′zə bär′, zan′zə bär′), *n.* **1.** an island off the E coast of Africa: with Pemba and adjacent small islands it formerly comprised a British protectorate that became independent in 1963; now part of Tanzania. 640 sq. mi. (1658 sq. km). **2.** a seaport on W Zanzibar. 110,669.

zap (zap), *v.,* **zapped, zap·ping,** *n. Informal.* —*v.t.* **1.** to attack, defeat, destroy, or kill with sudden speed and force. **2.** to bombard with electrical current, radiation, laser beams, gunfire, etc. **3.** to strike or jolt suddenly and forcefully. **4.** to skip over or delete (TV commercials), as by switching channels or fast-forwarding a VCR. —*v.i.* **5.** to move quickly, forcefully, or destructively. —*n.* **6.** force, energy, or drive; zip. **7.** a jolt or charge, as of electricity. **8.** a forceful and sudden blow, hit, or attack. **9.** a handbill, esp. one used in political activism. —**zap′per,** *n.*

Za·po·tec (zap′ə tek′, zä′pə-), *n., pl.* **-tecs,** (*esp. collectively*) **-tec,** *adj.* —*n.* **1.** a member of an American Indian people living primarily in central and E Oaxaca in Mexico. **2.** the complex of languages spoken by the Zapotecs, varying in degree of mutual intelligibility. —*adj.* **3.** Also, **Za/po·tec′an.** of or designating a Mesoamerican civilization of the Oaxaca region of Mexico c600 B.C.–A.D. c1000.

zap·py (zap′ē), *adj.,* **-pi·er, -pi·est.** *Informal.* energetic, lively, or fast-moving; zippy.

Zar·a·thus·tra (zar′ə thōō′strə), *n.* ZOROASTER. —**Zar′a·thus′tri·an** (-thōō′strē ən), *adj., n.* —**Zar′a·thus′tric,** *adj.*

z-ax·is (zē′ak′sis), *n., pl.* **z-ax·es** (zē′ak′sēz). (in a three-dimensional Cartesian coordinate system) the axis along which values of *z* are measured and at which both *x* and *y* equal zero.

ZBB, zero-base budgeting.

zeal (zēl), *n.* fervor for a person, cause, or object; eager desire or endeavor; enthusiastic diligence; ardor.

zeal·ot (zel′ət), *n.* **1.** a person who shows zeal. **2.** an excessively zealous person; fanatic. **3.** (*cap.*) a member of a radical, warlike group of Jews in Judea during the 1st century A.D., advocating the overthrow of Roman rule.

zeal·ous (zel′əs), *adj.* full of, characterized by, or due to zeal; ardently active, devoted, or diligent. —**zeal′ous·ly,** *adv.* —**zeal′ous·ness,** *n.*

Zeb·e·dee (zeb′i dē′), *n.* the father of the apostles James and John. Matt. 4:21.

ze·bra (zē′brə; *Brit. also* zeb′rə), *n., pl.* **-bras,** (*esp. collectively*) **-bra. 1.** any of several horselike African mammals of the genus *Equus,* each species having a characteristic pattern of black or dark brown stripes on a whitish background. **2.** *Slang.* a football official, who usu. wears a black-and-white striped shirt. —**ze·bra·ic** (zi brā′ik), *adj.* —**ze′brine** (-brīn, -brin), *adj.*

ze·bra·fish (zē′brə fish′; *Brit. also* zeb′rə-), *n., pl.* **-fish·es,** (*esp. collectively*) **-fish.** a thin freshwater minnow, *Brachydanio rerio,* of India, having luminous blue and gold horizontal stripes.

ze·bra·wood (zē′brə wŏŏd′; *Brit. also* zeb′rə-), *n.* **1.** a tropical American shrub, *Connarus guianensis,* yielding a hard, striped wood. **2.** the wood itself, used in making furniture.

ze·bu (zē′byōō, -bōō), *n.* one of a domesticated variety of cattle, *Bos taurus indicus,* of India, having a large hump over the shoulders and a large dewlap.

Zeb·u·lun (zeb′yŏŏ lən), *n.* **1.** a son of Jacob and Leah. Gen. 30:20. **2.** one of the 12 tribes of Israel, traditionally descended from him.

Zech., Zechariah.

Zech·a·ri·ah (zek′ə rī′ə), *n.* **1.** a Minor Prophet of the 6th century B.C. **2.** a book of the Bible bearing his name.

Zed·e·ki·ah (zed′i kī′ə), *n.* the last king of Judah. II Kings 24, 25; Jer. 52:1–11.

zed·o·a·ry (zed′ō er′ē), *n., pl.* **-ries.** any of several curcuma plants, as *Curcuma zedoaria* or *C. pallida,* having an aromatic rhizome that resembles ginger and is used as a tonic, flavoring, or perfume.

zee (zē), *n.* the letter Z or z.

ze·in (zē′in), *n.* a soft, yellow powder of simple proteins obtained from corn, used chiefly in the manufacture of textile fibers, plastics, and paper coatings.

zeit·ge·ber (tsīt′gā′bər), *n.* an environmental cue, as the length of daylight or the degree of temperature, that helps to regulate the cycles of an organism's biological clock.

Zeit·geist (tsīt′gīst′), *n. German.* the spirit of the time; general trend of thought or feeling characteristic of a particular period of time.

Zen (zen), *n.* **1.** a Mahayana movement of Buddhism, introduced into China in the 6th century A.D. and into Japan in the 12th century, that emphasizes enlightenment by means of meditation and direct, intuitive insights. **2.** the discipline and practice of this sect. —**Zen′ic,** *adj.*

Zen′ Bud′dhism, *n.* ZEN. —**Zen′ Bud′dhist,** *n., adj.*

ze′ner (or **Ze′ner**) **di′ode** (zē′nər), *n.* a semiconductor diode across which the reverse voltage remains almost constant over a wide range of currents, used esp. to regulate voltage.

ze·nith (zē′nith; *esp. Brit.* zen′ith), *n.* **1.** the point on the celestial sphere vertically above a given position or observer. Compare NADIR. **2.** the highest point or state; culmination; peak.

Ze′no's par′adox (zē′nōz), *n. Math.* any of various versions of a paradox regarding the relation of the discrete to the continuous and requiring the concept of limit for its satisfactory explanation. [after *Zeno* of Elea, c490–c430 B.C., Greek philosopher]

ze·o·lite (zē′ə līt′), *n.* any of a group of hydrated aluminosilicate minerals, used as molecular sieves. —**ze′o·lit′ic** (-lit′ik), *adj.*

Zeph., Zephaniah.

Zeph·a·ni·ah (zef′ə nī′ə), *n.* **1.** a Minor Prophet of the 7th century B.C. **2.** a book of the Bible bearing his name.

zeph·yr (zef′ər), *n.* **1.** a gentle, mild breeze. **2.** (*often cap.*) *Literary.* the west wind. **3.** any of various things of fine, light quality, as fabric or yarn.

zep·pe·lin (zep′ə lin), *n.* (*often cap.*) a large, rigid airship consisting of a long cylindrical covered framework, suspended from which is a compartment holding the engines, passengers, etc. [after Count von ZEPPELIN]

Zep·pe·lin (zep′ə lin), *n.* Count Ferdinand von, 1838–1917, German general and manufacturer of the zeppelin.

ze·ro (zēr′ō), *n., pl.* **-ros, -roes,** *v.,* **-roed, -ro·ing,** *adj.* —*n.* **1.** the figure or symbol 0, which in the Arabic notation for numbers stands for the absence of quantity; cipher. **2.** an origin from which values are calibrated, as on a temperature scale. **3.** a mathematical value intermediate between positive and negative values. **4.** naught; nothing. **5.** the lowest point or degree. **6.** the absence of a linguistic element, as a morpheme, in a position in which one previously existed or might by analogy be expected to exist. **7.** a sight setting on a firearm or artillery piece for striking the center of a target at any particular range. **8.** *Math.* **a.** the identity element of a group in which the operation is addition. **b.** an argument at which the value of a function vanishes. —*v.t.* **9.** to adjust (an instrument or apparatus) to a zero point or to an arbitrary reading from which other readings are to be measured. **10. zero in,** to aim (a rifle, etc.) at the precise center or range of a target. **11. zero in on, a.** to aim directly at (a target). **b.** to direct one's attention to; focus on. **c.** to converge on; close in on. —*adj.* **12.** amounting to zero. **13.** having no measurable quantity or magnitude; not any: *zero economic growth.* **14.** of or designating a hypothetical morphological element that is posited as existing by analogy with some regular pattern in a language but has no physical realization: *Deer has a zero plural.* **15.** *Meteorol.* **a.** (of an atmospheric ceiling) pertaining to or limiting vertical visibility to 50 ft. (15.2 m) or less. **b.** of, pertaining to, or limiting horizontal visibility to 165 ft. (50.3 m) or less.

ze·ro-base′ or **ze·ro-based′,** *adj.* according to present needs only, without reference to previous practice: *zero-base planning; zero-base budgeting.*

ze′ro-base (or **ze′ro-based**) **budg′et·ing,** *n.* a process in government and corporate finance of justifying an overall budget or individual budgeted items each fiscal year or each review period rather than dealing only with proposed changes from a previous budget. *Abbr.:* ZBB

ze′ro grav′ity, *n.* the condition in which the apparent effect of gravity is zero, as on a body in free fall or in orbit. Also called **ze·ro-g, ze·ro-G** (zēr′ō jē′).

ze′ro hour′, *n.* **1.** the time set for the beginning of a military attack or operation. **2.** the time set for the beginning of any event or action. **3.** a decisive or critical time.

ze′ro popula′tion growth′, *n.* a condition in which the population is maintained at a constant level by a balance between the number of births and deaths.

ze′ro-sum′, *adj.* denoting an element of game theory in which the amount lost is always equal to the amount gained: *a zero-sum economy.*

ze′ro-ze′ro, *adj.* (of atmospheric conditions) having or characterized by zero visibility in both horizontal and vertical directions.

Ze·rub·ba·bel (za rub′ə bəl), *n.* a leader of the Jews on their return to Jerusalem after the Babylonian captivity. Ezra 2:1, 2; 3:2–13.

zest (zest), *n.* **1.** keen relish; hearty enjoyment; gusto. **2.** an agreeable or piquant flavor imparted to something. **3.** anything added to impart flavor or relish. **4.** piquancy; interest; charm. **5.** a small strip of citrus peel, esp. lemon, used for flavoring. —**zest′ful,** *adj.* —**zest′ful·ly,** *adv.* —**zest′ful·ness,** *n.* —**zest′y,** *adj.,* **zest·i·er, zest·i·est.**

Zeus (zōōs), *n.* the god of the heavens and supreme deity of the ancient Greeks: identified by the Romans with Jupiter.

Zhou En·lai or **Chou En·lai** (jō′ en lī′), *n.* 1898–1976, Chinese Communist leader: premier 1949–76.

Zi·ba (zī′bə), *n.* a servant of King Saul who befriended him after Absalom's revolt. II Sam. 9:2–11; 16:1–4; 19:17, 29.

zig (zig), *v.i.,* **zigged, zig·ging.** to move in one of the two directions followed in a zigzag course.

zig·gu·rat (zig′ŏō rat′) also **zik·ku·rat** (zik′-), *n.* a brick temple tower built by the Sumerians, Babylonians, and Assyrians, consisting of a number of successively receding stories giving the appearance of a series of terraces.

zig·zag (zig′zag′), *n., adj., adv., v.,* **-zagged, -zag·ging.** —*n.* **1.** a line, course, or progression characterized by sharp turns first to one side and then to the other. **2.** one of a series of such turns, as in a line or path. —*adj.* **3.** formed or formed in a zigzag: *zigzag stitches.* —*adv.* **4.** in a zigzag manner. —*v.t.* **5.** to make (something) zigzag, as in form or course; move in a zigzag direction. —*v.i.* **6.** to proceed in a zigzag line or course. —**zig′zag′ger,** *n.*

zilch (zilch), *n. Slang.* zero; nothing.

zil·lion (zil′yən), *n., pl.* **-lions,** (*as after a numeral*) **-lion.** *Informal.* an extremely large, indeterminate number.

Zil·pah (zil′pə), *n.* the mother of Gad and Asher. Gen. 30:10–13.

Zim·bab·we (zim bäb′wā, -wē), *n.* **1.** Formerly, (until 1964) **Southern Rhodesia,** (1964–80) **Rhodesia.** a republic in S Africa: a former British colony; unilaterally declared independence in 1965; gained independence in 1980. 11,423,175; 150,873 sq. mi. (390,759 sq. km). *Cap.:* Harare. **2.** **GREAT ZIMBABWE.** —**Zim·bab′we·an,** *adj., n.*

Zim·ri (zim′rē, -rī), *n.* a king of Israel who killed himself after his capital city was seized. I Kings 16:8–20.

zinc (zingk), *n., v.,* **zincked** or **zinced** (zingkt), **zinck·ing** or **zinc·ing** (zing′king). —*n.* **1.** a ductile, bluish white metallic element: used in making galvanized iron, brass, and other alloys, and as an element in voltaic cells. *Symbol:* Zn; *at. wt.:* 65.37; *at. no.:* 30; *sp. gr.:* 7.14 at 20°C. —*v.t.* **2.** to coat or cover with zinc.

zinc′ chlo′ride, *n.* a poisonous solid substance, $ZnCl_2$, used as a wood preservative, in deodorants and antiseptics, and in a variety of manufacturing processes.

zin·cog·ra·phy (zing kog′rə fē), *n.* the art or process of producing a printing surface on a zinc plate, esp. of producing it in relief by etching away unprotected parts with acid. —**zin·cog′ra·pher,** *n.* —**zin′co·graph′ic** (-kə graf′ik), **zin′co·graph′i·cal,** *adj.*

zinc′ oint′ment, *n.* an ointment composed of mineral oil and zinc oxide, used as a sunblock and to treat skin conditions.

zinc′ ox′ide, *n.* a white powder, ZnO, used as a pigment and in cosmetics, dental cement, matches, printing inks, and glass, and in medicine for treatment of skin conditions.

zinc′ sul′fate, *n.* a colorless powder, $ZnSO_4 \cdot 7H_2O$, used for preserving skins and wood, in the bleaching of paper, as a mordant, and as an astringent.

zinc′ sul′fide, *n.* a white powder, ZnS, used as a pigment and as a phosphor on x-ray and television screens.

zin·fan·del (zin′fən del′), *n.* **1.** a black vinifera grape, grown in California. **2.** a dry red wine made from this grape.

zing (zing), *n.* **1.** a sharp singing or whining noise, as of a bullet passing through the air. **2.** vitality, animation, or zest. —*v.i.* **3.** to move or proceed with a sharp singing or whining noise. —*v.t.* **4.** to cause to move with or as if with a sharp singing or whining noise. **5.** to blame or criticize severely. —**zing′y,** *adj.* **zing·i·er, zing·i·est.**

zing·er (zing′ər), *n.* **1.** a quick, witty, or pointed remark or retort. **2.** something that surprises or shocks, as a piece of news.

zin·ni·a (zin′ē ə), *n., pl.* **-ni·as.** any New World composite plant of the genus *Zinnia,* having dense, colorful flower heads.

Zin·zen·dorf (tsin′tsən dôrf′), *n.* **Count Ni·ko·laus Lud·wig von** (nē′kō lous′ lōōt′vikh fän, lōōd′-), 1700–60, German religious leader: reformer and organizer of the Moravian Church.

Zi·on (zī′ən) also **Sion,** *n.* **1.** a hill in Jerusalem, on which the Temple was built: used to symbolize the city itself, esp. as a religious or spiritual center. **2.** the Jewish people. **3.** Palestine as the Jewish homeland and symbol of Judaism. **4.** heaven as the final gathering place of true believers. [Old English *Sion* < Late Latin *Siōn* < Greek *Seiṓn* < Hebrew *ṣīyyōn*]

Zi·on·ism (zī′ə niz′əm), *n.* a worldwide Jewish movement for the establishment and development of the state of Israel. —**Zi′on·ist,** *n., adj.* —**Zi′on·is′tic,** *adj.*

Zi′on Na′tional Park′, *n.* a park in SW Utah. 148 sq. mi. (383 sq. km).

zip[1] (zip), *n., v.,* **zipped, zip·ping.** —*n.* **1.** a sudden, brief hissing sound, as of a bullet. **2.** energy; vim; vigor. —*v.i.* **3.** to move with a sudden, brief hissing sound. **4.** to act or move with speed and energy. —*v.t.* **5.** to convey with speed and energy. **6.** to add vitality or zest to (usu. fol. by *up*).

zip[2] (zip), *v.,* **zipped, zip·ping.** —*v.t.* **1.** to fasten or unfasten with a zipper. **2.** to close or open (a zipper). —*v.i.* **3.** to become fastened or unfastened by means of a zipper. —*n.* **4.** *Chiefly Brit.* a zipper.

zip[3] (zip), *n., v.,* **zipped, zip·ping.** *Slang.* —*n.* **1.** zero; nothing, esp. as a score. —*v.t.* **2.** (in sports) to defeat by keeping from scoring.

zip[4] (zip), *n.* a ZIP-code number.

ZIP′ code′, *Trademark.* a system used in the U.S. to facilitate delivery of mail, consisting of a numerical code of five or nine digits printed directly after the address. [*Z(one) I(mprovement) P(rogram)*]

zip′ gun′, *n.* a homemade pistol, typically consisting of a metal tube taped to a wooden stock and firing a .22-caliber bullet.

zip·per (zip′ər), *n.* **1.** Also called **slide fastener.** a device for fastening clothing, luggage, etc., consisting of two parallel tracks of teeth or coils that can be interlocked or separated by the pulling of a slide between them. **2.** a large illuminated display of news bulletins or advertisements that rapidly and continously flash by on an upper part of a building. **3.** a person or thing that zips. —*v.t., v.i.* **4.** zip[2].

Zip·po·rah (zi pôr′ə, -pōr′ə, zip′ər ə), *n.* the wife of Moses. Ex. 2:21.

zip·py (zip′ē), *adj.,* **-pi·er, -pi·est.** full of energy and vim; lively; peppy.

zir·con (zûr′kon), *n.* a mineral, zirconium silicate, $ZrSiO_4$, occurring in small tetragonal crystals or grains of various colors, usu. opaque: used as a gem when transparent.

zir·co·ni·um (zûr kō′nē əm), *n.* a metallic element resembling titanium chemically: used in steel metallurgy, as a scavenger and refractory, and to make vitreous enamels opaque. *Symbol:* Zr; *at. wt.:* 91.22; *at. no.:* 40; *sp. gr.:* 6.49 at 20°C. —**zir·con′ic** (-kon′ik), *adj.*

zit (zit), *n. Slang.* a pimple; skin blemish.

zith·er (zith′ər, zith′-), *n.* a musical instrument, consisting of a flat sounding box with numerous strings stretched over it, that is placed on a horizontal surface and played with a plectrum and the fingertips. —**zith′er·ist,** *n.*

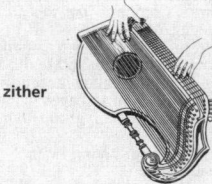

zither

zi·ti (zē′tē), *n.* (*used with a sing. or pl. v.*) a tubular pasta in short pieces, often baked in a tomato sauce.

zi·zith or **zi·zit** or **tzi·tzith** (tsit′sis, tsē tsēt′), *n.pl. Judaism.* the fringes or tassels formerly worn on the outer garment and now worn at the four corners of the tallith.

zlo·ty (zlô′tē), *n., pl.* **-tys,** (*collectively*) **-ty.** the basic monetary unit of Poland.

Zn, *Chem.* Symbol. zinc.

Zo·an (zō′an, -ən), *n.* Biblical name of TANIS.

Zo·ar (zō′ər, -är), *n.* the city where Lot and his family took refuge during the destruction of Sodom and Gomorrah. Gen. 19:20–30.

zo·di·ac (zō′dē ak′), *n.* **1.** an imaginary belt extending about 8° on each side of the ecliptic and containing the apparent paths of the sun, moon, and principal planets through 12 constellations or signs. **2.** a diagram representing this and often containing the symbol for each sign of the zodiac. **3.** a circuit or round. —**zo·di·a·cal** (zō dī′ə kəl), *adj.*

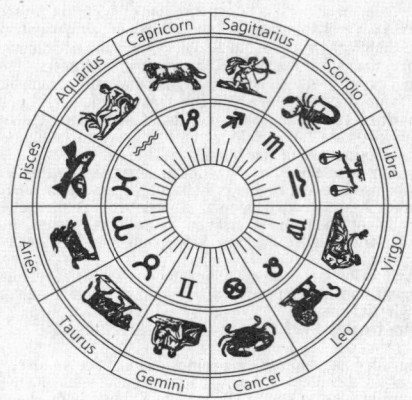

zodiac (def. 2)

Zo·har (zō′här), *n.* a medieval mystical work, consisting chiefly of interpretations of and commentaries on the Pentateuch: the definitive work of Jewish cabala.

Zo·la (zō′lə, -lä), *n.* **É·mile** (ā mēl′), 1840–1902, French novelist.

zom·bie (zom′bē), *n.* **1.** (in voodoo) **a.** the body of a dead person supernaturally imbued with the semblance of life and set to perform tasks as a mute, will-less slave. **b.** a living person enslaved in the same manner after the soul has been magically removed. **2. a.** a person whose behavior or responses are wooden, listless, or mechanical; automaton. **b.** an eccentric or peculiar person. —**zom′bi·ism,** *n.*

zon·al (zōn′l) also **zon′ar·y,** *adj.* **1.** of or pertaining to a zone or zones. **2.** of the nature of a zone. —**zon′al·ly,** *adv.*

zone (zōn), *n., v.,* **zoned, zon·ing.** —*n.* **1.** an area that differs in some respect, or is distinguished for some purpose, from adjoining areas, or within which distinctive circumstances exist or are established. **2.** any of five great divisions of the earth's surface, bounded by lines parallel to the equator and named according to the prevailing temperature. **3.** an area characterized by a particular set of organisms whose presence is determined by environmental conditions, as an altitudinal belt on a mountain. **4.** a specific district, area, etc., within which a uniform charge is made for transportation or other service. **5.** an area or district in a city or town under special restrictions as to the type of buildings that may be erected. **6.** TIME ZONE. **7.** any of the numbered districts into which a U.S. city or metropolitan area was formerly divided for expediting mail delivery. **8.** a particular portion of a football field or other playing area: *defensive zone.* —*v.t.* **9.** to divide into zones. **10.** to divide (a city or town) into zones in order to enforce building restrictions. **11.** to mark with zones or bands. **12.** to encircle or surround with a zone. —*v.i.* **13.** to be formed into zones. **14. zone out,** *Slang.* to become inattentive or dazed. [< Latin *zōna* belt, girdle < Greek *zṓnē*]

zone′ de·fense′, *n.* a method of defense, esp. in basketball and football, in which each member of the defensive team guards a specified portion of the playing area. Compare MAN-TO-MAN DEFENSE.

zonk (zongk, zôngk), *Slang.* —*v.i.* (often fol. by *out*) **1.** to become exhausted or fall asleep from fatigue. —*v.t.* (often fol. by *out*) **2.** to stupefy, sedate, or intoxicate. **3.** to strike suddenly; knock out.

zoo (zōō), *n., pl.* **zoos. 1.** Also called **zoological garden.** a parklike area in which live animals are kept in cages or large enclosures for public exhibition. **2.** a place, activity, or group marked by chaos or unrestrained behavior.

zoo-, a combining form meaning "living being," "animal": *zooplankton.* Also, *esp. before a vowel,* **zo-.**

zo·o·ge·og·ra·phy (zō′ə jē og′rə fē), *n.* the scientific study of the distribution of animals around the world and their interactions with the environment in the regions they inhabit. —**zo′o·ge·og′ra·pher,** *n.* —**zo′o·ge′o·graph′ic, zo′o·ge′o·graph′i·cal,** *adj.*

zo·og·ra·phy (zō og′rə fē), *n.* the branch of zoology dealing with the description of animals. —**zo·og′ra·pher,** *n.* —**zo′o·graph·ic,** (zō′ə graf′ik), **zo′o·graph′i·cal,** *adj.*

zo·oid (zō′oid), *n.* **1.** any of the distinct individuals of an animallike compound or colonial organism, as a polyp of a bryozoan. —*adj.* **2.** Also, **zo·oi′dal.** pertaining to, resembling, or of the nature of an animal.

zoo·keep·er (zōō′kē′pər), *n.* a person who feeds and tends animals in a zoo.

zo·o·log·i·cal (zō′ə loj′i kəl) also **zo′o·log′ic,** *adj.* **1.** of or pertain-

ing to zoology. **2.** relating to or concerned with animals. —**zo′o·log′i·cal·ly,** *adv.*

zoolog′ical gar′den, *n.* zoo (def. 1).

zo·ol·o·gist (zō ol′ə jist), *n.* a specialist in zoology.

zo·ol·o·gy (zō ol′ə jē), *n.* the scientific study of animals, including characteristics, physiology, development, classification, etc.

zoom (zōōm), *v.i.* **1.** to move quickly or suddenly with a loud humming or buzzing sound. **2.** to fly a plane suddenly and sharply upward at great speed for a short distance. **3.** to move or go rapidly. **4.** to bring a photographic subject, movie scene, etc., into closeup or cause it to recede by using a zoom lens (often fol. by *in* or *out*). **5.** to increase or rise suddenly and sharply. —*v.t.* **6.** to cause to zoom or be zoomed. **7. zoom in on, a.** to bring (a subject, scene, etc.) into closeup by using a zoom lens. **b.** to examine more closely; focus on. —*n.* **8.** the act or process of zooming. **9.** a zooming sound. **10.** ZOOM LENS. **11.** a camera shot using a zoom lens.

zoom′ lens′, *n.* (in a camera or motion-picture projector) a lens assembly whose focal length can be continuously adjusted to provide various degrees of magnification with no loss of focus.

zo·o·mor·phic (zō′ə môr′fik), *adj.* **1.** of or pertaining to a deity or other being conceived of as having the form of an animal. **2.** characterized by a highly stylized or conventionalized representation of animal forms. **3.** representing or using animal forms. —**zo′o·morph′,** *n.*

zo·on (zō′on), *n., pl.* **zo·a** (zō′ə). **1.** ZOOID. **2.** any individual, or the individuals collectively, produced from a single egg. —**zo′on·al** (-ə nl), *adj.*

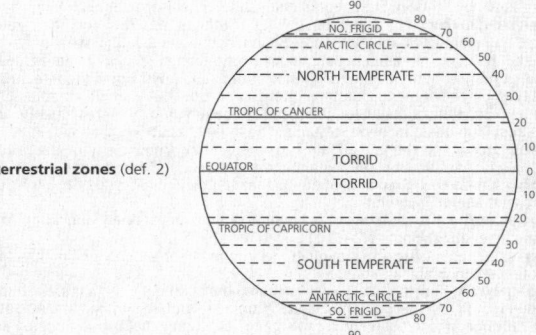

terrestrial zones (def. 2)

-zoon, a combining form meaning "animal," "organism" of the kind specified by the initial element, often corresponding to zoological taxa ending in *-zoa,* with **-zoon** used to name a single member of such a class: *protozoon.*

zo·o·phyte (zō′ə fīt′), *n.* any of various invertebrate animals resembling a plant, as a coral or a sea anemone. —**zo′o·phyt′ic** (-fit′ik), **zo′o·phyt′i·cal,** *adj.*

zo·o·plank·ton (zō′ə plangk′tən), *n.* the aggregate of animal or animallike organisms in plankton. Compare PHYTOPLANKTON.

zo·o·spore (zō′ə spôr′, -spōr′), *n.* **1.** an asexual spore of certain algae or fungi that moves by cilia or flagella. **2.** an ameboid or flagellate reproductive form that emerges from the sporocyst in certain protozoans. —**zo′o·spor′ic** (-spôr′ik, -spōr′-), **zo·os·po·rous** (zō os′pər əs, zō′ə spôr′-, -spōr′-), *adj.*

zo·ot·o·my (zō ot′ə mē), *n.* the anatomy, esp. the dissection, of animals other than humans. —**zo′o·tom′ic** (-ə tom′ik), **zo′o·tom′i·cal,** *adj.* —**zo·ot′o·mist,** *n.*

Zo·phar (zō′fär), *n.* a friend of Job. Job 2:11.

zo·ri (zôr′ē), *n., pl.* **-ri, -ris.** a Japanese sandal, often made of straw or rubber and consisting of a flat sole held on the foot by a thong passing between the first and second toes.

Zo·ro·as·ter (zôr′ō as′tər, zōr′-, zôr′ō as′tər, zōr′-), *n.* fl. 6th century B.C., Persian religious teacher. Also called **Zarathustra.**

Zo·ro·as·tri·an·ism (zôr′ō as′trē ə niz′əm, zōr′-) also **Zo′ro·as′trism,** *n.* an Iranian religion, founded c600 B.C. by Zoroaster, based on beliefs in a supreme deity, Ahura Mazda, and a cosmic struggle between a spirit of good and a spirit of evil.

zos·ter (zos′tər), *n.* SHINGLES.

zoy·si·a (zoi′sē ə, -zē ə, -shə, -zhə), *n.* any low-growing grass of the genus *Zoysia,* esp. *Z. matrella,* of tropical Asia, now widely used for lawns.

Zr, *Chem. Symbol.* zirconium.

zuc·chi·ni (zōō kē′nē), *n., pl.* **-ni, -nis. 1.** a cucumber-shaped summer squash having a smooth, dark green skin. **2.** the plant bearing this fruit.

zwie·back (zwī′bak′, -bäk′, zwē′-, swī′-, swē′-), *n.* an egg bread, often sweetened, that is baked, sliced and dried, then baked again until crisp.

Zwing·li (zwing′glē, swing′-, tsving′-), *n.* **Ulrich** or **Huldreich,** 1484–1531, Swiss Protestant reformer.

zy•de•co (zī′di kō′), *n.* a blues-influenced type of Cajun dance music popular in Louisiana and Texas, usu. played on accordion, guitar, and violin.

zyg•a•poph•y•sis (zig′ə pof′ə sis, zī′gə-), *n., pl.* **-ses** (-sēz′). one of the four processes of a vertebra, occurring in pairs that interlock each vertebra with the vertebrae above and below. —**zyg•ap•o•phys•e•al, zyg•ap•o•phys•i•al** (zig′ap ə fiz′ē əl, zī′gap-), *adj.*

zygo-, a combining form meaning "yoke," "zygote": *zygomorphism.* Also, *esp. before a vowel,* **zyg-.**

zy•go•dac•tyl (zī′gə dak′til, zig′ə-), *adj.* **1.** (of a bird) having the toes of the foot arranged in pairs, with two toes pointed forward and two turned rearward, as woodpeckers. **2.** of or pertaining to a zygodactyl bird. —*n.* **3.** a zygodactyl bird. —**zy•go•dac′tyl•ism,** *n.*

zy′gomat′ic arch′, *n.* the bony arch at the outer border of the eye socket, formed by the union of the cheekbone and the zygomatic process of the temporal bone.

zygomat′ic proc′ess, *n.* any of several bony processes that articulate with the cheekbone.

zy•go•my•cete (zī′gə mī′sēt, -mī sēt′, zig′ə-), *n.* any of a wide variety of common fungi constituting the phylum Zygomycota, of the kingdom Fungi, in which sexual reproduction is by the formation of zygospores.

zy•go•spore (zī′gə spôr′, -spōr′, zig′ə-), *n.* a cell formed by fusion of two similar gametes, as in certain algae and fungi. —**zy′go•spor′ic** (-spôr′ik, -spor′-), *adj.*

zy•gote (zī′gōt, zig′ōt), *n.* the cell produced by the union of two gametes, before it undergoes cleavage. —**zy•got′ic** (zī got′ik, zi-), *adj.* —**zy•got′i•cal•ly,** *adv.*

zymo-, a combining form meaning "ferment," "leaven": *zymology.* Also, *esp. before a vowel,* **zym-.**

zy•mo•sis (zī mō′sis), *n., pl.* **-ses** (-sēz). an infectious or contagious disease. —**zy•mot′ic** (-mot′ik), *adj.*

zy•mur•gy (zī′mûr jē), *n.* the branch of applied chemistry dealing with fermentation, as in winemaking or brewing.

ZZZ or **zzz,** (used to represent the sound of a person snoring.)

GUIDE FOR WRITERS

PUNCTUATION

There is a considerable amount of variation in punctuation practices. At one extreme are writers who use as little punctuation as possible. At the other extreme are writers who use too much punctuation in an effort to make their meaning clear. The principles presented here represent a middle road. As in all writing, consistency of style is essential.

The punctuation system is presented in six charts. Since punctuation marks are frequently used in more than one way, some marks appear on more than one chart. Readers who are interested in the various uses of a particular mark can scan the left column of each chart to locate relevant sections.

1. SENTENCE-LEVEL PUNCTUATION

	Guidelines	**Examples**
■	Ordinarily an independent clause is made into a sentence by beginning it with a capital letter and ending it with a period.	Some of us still support the mayor. Others think he should retire. There's only one solution. We must reduce next year's budget.
▮	Independent clauses may be combined into one sentence by using the words *and, but, yet, or, not, for,* and *so.* The first clause is usually followed by a comma.	The forecast promised beautiful weather, but it rained every day. Take six cooking apples and put them into a flameproof dish.
■ ▮	The writer can indicate that independent clauses are closely connected by joining them with a semicolon.	Some of us still support the mayor; others think he should retire. There was silence in the room; even the children were still.
■ ■	When one independent clause is followed by another that explains or exemplifies it, they can be separated by a colon. The second clause may or may not begin with a capital letter.	There's only one solution: we must reduce next year's budget. The conference addresses a basic question: How can we take the steps needed to protect the environment?
?	Sentences that ask a question should be followed by a question mark.	Are they still planning to move to Houston? What is the population of Norway?
!	Sentences that express strong feeling may be followed by an exclamation mark.	Watch out! That's a stupid thing to say!
. **?** **!**	End-of-sentence punctuation is sometimes used after groups of words that are not independent clauses. This is especially common in advertising and other writing that seeks to reflect the rhythms of speech.	Somerset Estates has all the features you've been looking for. Like state-of-the-art facilities. A friendly atmosphere. And a very reasonable price. Sound interesting? Phone today!

2. SEPARATING ELEMENTS IN CLAUSES

When one of the elements in a clause is compounded, that is, when there are two or more subjects, predicates, objects, and so forth, punctuation is necessary.

Guidelines	Examples
When two elements are compounded, they are usually joined together with a word such as *and* or *or* without any punctuation. Occasionally more than two elements are joined in this way.	Haiti and the Dominican Republic share the island of Hispaniola. Tuition may be paid by check or charged to a major credit card. I'm taking history and English and biology this semester.
Compounds that contain more than two elements are called series. Commas are used to separate items in a series, with a word such as *and* or *or* usually occurring between the last two items.	England, Scotland, and Wales share the island of Great Britain. Environmentally-conscious businesses use recycled paper, photocopy on both sides of a sheet, and use ceramic cups. We frequently hear references to government of the people, by the people, for the people.
When the items in a series are very long or have internal punctuation, separation by commas can be confusing, and semicolons may be used instead. Note: Some writers omit the final comma when punctuating a series, and newspapers and magazines often follow this practice. Book publishers and educators, however, usually follow the practice recommended above.	Next year, they plan to open stores in Pittsburgh, Pennsylvania; Cincinnati, Ohio; and Baltimore, Maryland. Students were selected on the basis of grades; tests of vocabulary, memory, and reading; and teacher recommendations.

3. SETTING OFF MODIFIERS

Another way that sentences become more complex is by the addition of free modifiers. Free modifiers can ordinarily be omitted without affecting the meaning or basic structure of the sentence.

Guidelines	Examples
Words that precede the subject are potentially confusing, so they are often set off by a comma that shows where the main part of the sentence begins.	Born to wealthy parents, he was able to pursue his career without financial worries. Since the team was in last place, the attendance for the final game was less than two thousand.
When the introductory modifier is short, the comma is often omitted.	In this article I will demonstrate that we have chosen the wrong policy. At the present time the number of cigarette smokers is declining.
Certain kinds of introductory modifiers are followed by a comma even though they are short.	Thoroughly chilled, he decided to set out for home. Yes, we are prepared for any mishaps. However, it is important to understand his point of view.
Free modifiers that occur in the middle of the sentence require two commas to set them off.	It is important, however, to understand his point of view. Our distinguished colleague, the president of the guild, will be our speaker tonight.
When free modifiers occur at the end of a sentence, they should be preceded by a comma.	It is important to understand his point of view, however. She was much influenced by the impressionist painters, especially Monet and Renoir.
If the sentence can be read without pauses before and after the modifier, the commas may be omitted.	We can therefore conclude that the defendant is innocent. The applicant must understand before sending in the forms that the deposit fee is not refundable.

It is important to distinguish between free modifiers and other modifiers that may look very much the same but are part of the basic sentence structure. The latter should not be set off by commas.	This admirable woman, who started out on the assembly line thirty years ago, became president of the company last week. An employee who started out on the assembly line thirty years ago became president of the company last week. We congratulate the Senate whip, who organized the filibuster. We congratulate the senator who organized the filibuster.
When dates and addresses are used in sentences, each part except the first is treated as a free modifier and set off by commas. When only the month and year are given, the comma is usually omitted.	She was born on Tuesday, December 20, 1901, in a log cabin near Casey Creek, Kentucky. We took our first trip to Alaska in August 1988.
— When a free modifier has internal punctuation or produces an emphatic break in the sentence, commas may not seem strong enough, and dashes can be used instead. A dash can also be used to set off a free modifier that comes at the end of a sentence.	The challenges of raising children—disciplinary, financial, emotional—are getting more formidable. These families had a median income of $55,000—$35,000 earned by the husband and $20,000 by the wife.
( ) Parentheses provide another method for setting off extra elements from the rest of the sentence. They are used in a variety of ways.	The Federal Trade Commission (FTC) has issued regulations on the advertising of many products (see Appendix B). The community didn't feel (and why should they?) that there was adequate police protection.

4. QUOTATIONS

Quotations are used for making clear to a reader which words are the writer's and which have been borrowed from someone else.

Guidelines	**Examples**
" " When writers use the exact words of someone else, they must use quotation marks to set them off from the rest of the text.	In 1841, Ralph Waldo Emerson wrote, "I hate quotations. Tell me what you know."
Indirect quotations—in which writers report what someone else said without using the exact words—should not be set off by quotation marks.	Emerson said that he hated quotations and that writers should instead tell the reader what they themselves know.

When quotations are longer than two or three lines, they are often placed on separate lines. Sometimes shorter line length and/or smaller type is also used. When this is done, quotation marks are not used.	In his essay "Notes on Punctuation," Lewis Thomas* gives the following advice to writers using quotations:
	    If something is to be quoted, the exact
	    words must be used.
	If part of it must be left out because of space limitations, it is good manners to insert three dots to indicate the omission, but it is unethical to do this if it means connecting two thoughts which the original author did not intend to have tied together.

· · · **· · · ·** If part of a quotation is omitted, the omission must be marked with points of ellipsis. When the omission comes in the middle of a sentence, three points are used. When the omission includes the end of one or more sentences, four points are used.	Lewis Thomas offers this advice:
	    If something is to be quoted, the exact
	    words must be used.
	If part of it must be left out...insert three dots to indicate the omission, but it is unethical to do this if it means connecting two thoughts which the original author did not intend to have tied together.

* *New England Journal of Medicine,* Vol. 296, pp. 1103–05 (May 12, 1977). Quoted by permission.

[ ]	When writers insert something within a quoted passage, the insertion should be set off with brackets. Insertions are sometimes used to supply words that make a quotation easier to understand.	Lewis Thomas warns that "it is unethical to [omit words in a quotation] ... if it means connecting two thoughts which the original author did not intend to have tied together."
	Writers can make clear that a mistake in the quotation has been carried over from the original by using the word *sic*, meaning "thus."	As Senator Claghorne wrote to his constituents, "My fundamental political principals [*sic*] make it impossible for me to support the bill in its present form."
▮	Text that reports the source of quoted material is usually separated from it by a comma.	Mark said, "I've decided not to apply to law school until next year." "I think we should encourage people to vote," said the mayor.
	When quoted words are woven into a text so that they perform a basic grammatical function in the sentence, no introductory punctuation is used.	According to Thoreau, most of us "lead lives of quiet desperation."
▮ ▮	Quotations that are included within other quotations are set off by single quotation marks.	The witness made the same damaging statement under cross-examination: "As I entered the room, I heard him say, 'I'm determined to get even.'"
▮▮ ▮▮	Final quotation marks follow other punctuation marks, except for semicolons and colons.	Ed began reading Williams's "The Glass Menagerie"; then he turned to "A Streetcar Named Desire."
	Question marks and exclamation marks precede final quotation marks when they refer to the quoted words. They follow when they refer to the sentence as a whole.	Once more she asked, "What do you think we should do about this?" What did Carol mean when she said, "I'm going to do something about this"? "Get out of here!" he yelled.

5. WORD-LEVEL PUNCTUATION

The punctuation covered so far is used to clarify the structure of sentences. There are also punctuation marks that are used with words.

Guidelines	**Examples**
▮ The apostrophe is used with nouns to show possession:	The company's management resisted the union's demands. She found it impossible to decipher the students' handwriting.
(1) An apostrophe plus *s* is added to all words—singular or plural—that do not end in *-s*.	the boy's hat children's literature a week's vacation
(2) Just an apostrophe is added at the end of plural words that end in *-s*.	the boys' hats two weeks' vacation
(3) An apostrophe plus *s* is usually added at the end of singular words that end in *-s*. Just an apostrophe is added to names of classical or biblical derivation that end in *-s*.	the countess's daughter Dickens's novels Achilles' heel Moses' brother
An apostrophe is used in contractions to show where letters or numerals have been omitted.	he's didn't let's ma'am four o'clock readin', writin', and 'rithmetic the class of '55

An apostrophe is sometimes used when making letters or numbers plural.	45's ABC's	

■ A period is used to mark shortened forms like abbreviations and initials.	Prof. M. L. Smith 14 ft. 4:00 p.m. U.S.A. or USA etc.		

▬ A hyphen is used to end a line of text when part of a word must be carried over to the next line.	... insta- bility

Hyphens are sometimes used to form compound words.	twenty-five self-confidence

In certain situations, hyphens are used between prefixes or suffixes and root words.	catlike *but* bull-like preschool *but* pre-Christian recover *vs.* re-cover

Hyphens are often used to indicate that a group of words is to be understood as a unit.	a scholar-athlete hand-to-hand combat

When two modifiers containing hyphens are joined together, common elements are often not repeated.	The study included fourth- and twelfth-grade students.

Note: It is important not to confuse the hyphen (-) with the dash (—), which is more than twice as long. The hyphen is used to group words and parts of words together, while the dash is used to clarify sentence structure. With a typewriter, a dash is formed by typing two successive hyphens(--). Many word-processing programs have both a hyphen and a dash on the keyboard.

6. OTHER USES OF PUNCTUATION MARKS

Guidelines	**Examples**
' Commas are used to indicate that a word or words used elsewhere in the sentence have been omitted.	Our company has found it difficult to find and keep skilled workers: the supply is limited; the demand, heavy; the turnover, high.
A comma is used after the complimentary close in a letter. In a personal letter, a comma is also used after the salutation.	Very truly yours, Love, Dear Sally,
In numbers used primarily to express quantity, commas are used to divide the digits into groups of three. Commas are not ordinarily used in numbers that are used for identification.	The attendance at this year's convention was 12,347. Norma lived at 18325 Sunset Boulevard.
" " Quotation marks are used occasionally to indicate that a word or phrase is used in a special way. For other special uses of quotation marks, see the Italics section below.	People still speak of "typing," even when they are seated in front of a computer screen.
▪ A colon can be used generally to call attention to what follows.	There were originally five Marx brothers: Groucho, Chico, Harpo, Zeppo, and Gummo. The senior citizens demanded the following: better police protection, more convenient medical facilities, and a new recreational center.
A colon is used after the salutation in a business letter.	Dear Ms. McFadden: Dear Valued Customer: Dear Frank:
▬ The dash can be used to indicate hesitations in speech.	"Well—uh—I'd like to try again—if you'll let me," he offered.

When a list precedes a general statement about the items listed, it is followed by a dash.	Strength, endurance, flexibility—these three goals should guide your quest for overall physical fitness.
─ The hyphen can be used as a substitute for *to,* with the meaning "up to and including." It should not, however, be used in conjunction with *from.*	The text of the Constitution can be found on pages 679–87. The period between 1890–1914 was a particularly tranquil time in Europe. The Civil War lasted from 1861 to 1865. (not from 1861–1865)

ITALICS

Guidelines	**Examples**
Titles of newspapers, magazines, and books should be put in italics. Articles, essays, stories, chapters, and poems should be enclosed in quotation marks.	*The New York Times* *Consumer Reports* Whitman's "Song of Myself"
Titles of plays and movies should be put in italics. Television and radio programs should be enclosed in quotation marks.	Shakespeare's *Hamlet* the movie *High Noon* "Sesame Street"
Titles of works of art and long musical works should be put into italics. Shorter works such as songs should be enclosed in quotation marks. When the form of a musical work is used as its title, neither italics nor quotation marks are used.	Leonardo da Vinci's *Last Supper* Handel's *Messiah* "Summertime" Beethoven's Ninth Symphony
The names of ships and airplanes should be put in italics.	the aircraft carrier *Intrepid* Lindbergh's *The Spirit of St. Louis*
Words and phrases from a foreign language should be put in italics. Accompanying translations are often enclosed in quotation marks. Words of foreign origin that have become familiar in an English context should not be italicized.	As a group, these artists are in the avant-garde. They are not, however, to be thought of as *enfants terribles,* or "terrible children," people whose work is so outrageous as to shock or embarrass.
Words used as words, and letters used as letters, should be put in italics.	I can never remember how to spell *broccoli.* Your handwriting is hard to read; the *o*'s and *a*'s look alike.
Italics are sometimes used to indicate that a word or words should be pronounced with extra emphasis.	The boss is *very* hard to get along with today. John loaned the tape to Robert, and *he* gave it to Sally.

CAPITALIZATION

Guidelines	**Examples**
The important words in titles are capitalized. This includes the first and last words and all other words except articles, prepositions, and coordinating conjunctions, such as *and, but,* and *or.*	*The Cat in the Hat* *Gone with the Wind*
Proper nouns—names of specific people, places, organizations, groups, events, etc.—are capitalized, as are the proper adjectives derived from them.	Martin Luther King, Jr. Civil War United States Coast Guard Canada Canadian

When proper nouns and adjectives have taken on a specialized meaning, they are often no longer capitalized.	My brother ordered a bologna sandwich and french fries.
Titles of people are capitalized when they precede the name, but not usually when they follow or when they are used alone.	Queen Victoria Victoria, queen of England the queen of England
Kinship terms are capitalized when they are used before a name or alone in place of a name. They are not capitalized when they are preceded by modifiers.	I'm expecting Aunt Alice to drop by this weekend. I forgot to call Mother on her birthday. I forgot to call my mother on her birthday.
Geographical features are capitalized when they are part of the official name. In the plural, they are capitalized when they precede names, but not when they follow.	The Pacific Ocean is the world's largest ocean. In recent years, Lakes Erie and Ontario have been cleaned up. The Hudson and Mohawk rivers are both in New York State.
Points of the compass are capitalized only when they are used as the name of a section of the country.	We've been driving east for over two hours. We visited the South last summer.

AVOIDING INSENSITIVE AND OFFENSIVE LANGUAGE

This essay is intended as a general guide to language that can, intentionally or not, cause offense or perpetuate discriminatory values and practices by emphasizing the differences between people or implying that one group is superior to another. Its purpose is to make readers aware of the possible consequences of the words they choose. Before looking at the words themselves, it is important to note that offensive or insensitive speech is not limited to a specific group of words. One can be hurtful and insulting by using any type of vocabulary, if that is one's intent. While in most cases it is easy to avoid blatantly offensive slurs and comments, more subtle bias that is an inherent part of our language or that is the habit of a lifetime is much harder to change.

Several factors complicate the question. A group may disagree within itself as to what is acceptable and what is not. Many seemingly inoffensive terms develop negative connotations over time and become dated or go out of style as awareness changes. A "within the group" rule often applies, which allows a member of a group to use terms freely that would be considered offensive if used by a non-member of the group.

What is considered acceptable shifts constantly as people become more aware of language and its power. The rapid changes of the last few decades have left many people puzzled and afraid of unintentionally insulting someone. At the same time, these changes have angered others, who decry what they see as extremes of "political correctness" in rules and locutions that alter language to the point of obscuring, even destroying, its meaning. The abandonment of traditional usages has also upset many people. But while it is true that some of the more extreme attempts to avoid offending language have resulted in ludicrous obfuscation, it is also true that heightened sensitivity in language is a statement of respect, indicates a precision of thought and is a positive move toward rectifying the unequal social status between one group and another.

Suggestions for avoiding offensive language are given in the following pages. The suggested terms are given on the right. While these suggestions can reflect trends, they cannot dictate or predict the preferences of each individual.

Sexism

Sexism is the most difficult bias to avoid, in part because of the convention of using man or men and he or his to refer to people of either sex. Other, more disrespectful conventions include giving descriptions of women in terms of age and appearance while describing men in terms of accomplishment and neglecting to use parallel terms to refer to men and women.

Replacing man or men

Man may refer to a male or to a human in general. This ambiguity is often thought to be slighting of women.

mankind, man	human beings, humans, humankind, humanity, people, human race, human species, *homo sapiens*, society, men and women
a man who	someone who, anyone who
man-made	synthetic, artificial
man in the street	average person, ordinary person

Using gender-neutral terms for occupations, positions, roles, etc.

Terms that specify a particular sex can unnecessarily perpetuate certain stereotypes when used generically.

anchorman	anchor
bellman, bellboy	bellhop

businessman	businessperson, business executive, manager, business owner, retailer, etc.
chairman	chair, chairperson
cleaning lady, girl, maid	housecleaner, housekeeper, cleaning person, office cleaner
clergyman	member of the clergy, minister, rabbi, priest, pastor, etc.
clergymen	the clergy
congressman	representative, member of Congress, legislator
fireman	firefighter
forefather	ancestor
girl/gal Friday	assistant
housewife	homemaker
insurance man	insurance agent
layman	layperson, nonspecialist, nonprofessional
mailman, postman	mail carrier, letter carrier
policeman	police officer, law enforcement officer
salesman, saleswoman, saleslady, salesgirl	salesperson, sales representative, sales associate, clerk
spokesman	spokesperson, representative
stewardess, steward	flight attendant
weatherman	weather reporter, weathercaster, meteorologist
workman	worker
actress	actor

Replacing the pronoun *he*

Like *man*, *he* can be used both generically and in reference to males. The generic use can be seen to exclude women.

When a driver approaches a red light, he must prepare to stop	When drivers approach a red light, they must prepare to stop.
	When a driver approaches a red light, he or she must prepare to stop. ("She/he" or "s/he" are sometimes used in business or legal writing, but many people consider them distracting.)
	When approaching a red light, a driver must prepare to stop.
	A driver must prepare to stop when approaching a red light.

Referring to members of both sexes with parallel names, titles, or descriptions.

Don't be inconsistent unless you are trying to make a specific point.

men and ladies	men and women, ladies and gentlemen
10 men and 13 females	10 men and 13 women
Betty Schmidt, an attractive 49-year-old physician, and her husband, Alan Schmidt, a noted editor	Betty Schmidt, a physician, and her husband, Alan Schmidt, an editor
Mr. David Kim and Mrs. Betty Harrow	Mr. David Kim and Ms. Betty Harrow (unless *Mrs.* is her known preference)
man and wife	husband and wife
Dear Sir:	Dear Sir/Madam: Dear Madam or Sir: To whom it may concern:
Mrs. Whitman and President Clinton	Governor Whitman and President Clinton

Race, Ethnicity, and National Origin

Some words and phrases that refer to racial and ethnic groups are clearly offensive. Other words (e.g., *Indian, Oriental, colored*) are outdated or inaccurate. *Hispanic* is generally accepted as a broad term for Spanish-speaking people of the Western Hemisphere, but more specific terms (*Latino, Mexican American*) are also acceptable and in some cases preferred. *Mixed race* and *multiracial* are acceptable terms for people who identify with more than one race.

Negro, colored, Afro-American	black, African-American (generally preferred to Afro-American)
Oriental, Asiatic	Asian, or more specific designations such as Pacific Islander, Chinese American, Korean
Indian	*Indian* properly refers to people who live in or hail from India.
	American Indian, Native American, or more specific designations (*Chinook, Hopi*), are usually preferred when referring to the native peoples of the Western Hemisphere. *First Nation* is the preferred term in Canada. *Red man* and *Red Indian* are considered offensive.
Eskimo	Inuit, Alaska Natives
native (n.)	native peoples, early inhabitants, aboriginal peoples (but not *aborigines*)

Age

The concept of aging is changing in our society as people are living longer and more active lives. Be aware of word choices that reinforce stereotypes (*decrepit, senile*) and avoid mentioning age unless it is relevant to the subject at hand. As with other groups, preferred terms for referring to older people are changing, and individual preferences may vary.

elderly, aged, old, geriatric, the elderly, the aged	older person, senior citizen, older people, senior citizens, seniors

Avoiding Depersonalization of Persons with Disabilities or Illnesses

Terminology that emphasizes the person rather than the disability is generally preferred. *Handicap* is used to refer to the environmental barrier that affects the person. (Stairs handicap a person who uses a wheelchair.) While words such as *crazy, demented,* and *insane* are used in facetious or informal contexts, these terms are not used to describe people with clinical diagnoses of mental illness. The euphemisms *challenged, differently abled,* and *special* are preferred by some people, but are often ridiculed and are best avoided.

Mongoloid	person with Down syndrome
wheelchair-bound	a person who uses a wheelchair
polio victim	has/had polio
the handicapped, the disabled, cripple	persons with disabilities, person with a disability or person who uses crutches *or* other more specific description
deaf-mute, deaf and dumb	deaf person

Avoiding Patronizing or Demeaning Expressions

girls (when referring to adult women), the fair sex	women
sweetie, dear, dearie, honey	(usually not appropriate with strangers or in public situations)
old maid, spinster, bachelorette	single woman, woman, divorced woman (but only if one would specify "divorced man" in the same context)

| the little woman, old lady, ball and chain | wife |
| boy (when referring to or addressing an adult man) | man, sir |

Avoiding Language that Excludes or Unnecessarily Emphasizes Differences

References to age, sex, religion, race, and the like should only be included if they are relevant.

| lawyers and their wives | lawyers and their spouses |
| a secretary and her boss | a secretary and boss, a secretary and his or her boss |

a good female surgeon	a good surgeon
the male nurse	the nurse
Arab man denies assault charge	Man denies assault charge
the articulate black student	the articulate student
Marie Curie was a great woman scientist	Marie Curie was a great scientist. (unless the intent is to compare her only with other women in the sciences)
Christian name	given name, personal name, first name

FORMS OF ADDRESS

The forms of address shown below cover most of the commonly encountered problems in correspondence. Although there are many alternative forms, the ones given here are generally preferred in conventional usage.

As a complimentary close, use "Sincerely yours," but, when particular formality is preferred, use "Very truly yours."

Government (United States)

President
Address: The President
The White House
Washington, D.C. 20500
Salutation: Dear Mr. *or* Madam President:

Vice President
Address: The Vice President
United States Senate
Washington, D.C. 20510
Salutation: Dear Mr. *or* Madam Vice President:

Cabinet Member
Address: The Honorable *(full name)*
Secretary of *(name of Department)*
Washington, D.C. *(zip code)*
Salutation: Dear Mr. *or* Madam Secretary:

Attorney General
Address: The Honorable *(full name)*
Attorney General
Washington, D.C. 20530
Salutation: Dear Mr. *or* Madam Attorney General:

Senator
Address: The Honorable *(full name)*
United States Senate
Washington, D.C. 20510
Salutation: Dear Senator *(surname)*:

Representative
Address: The Honorable *(full name)*
House of Representatives
Washington, D.C. 20515
Salutation: Dear Mr. *or* Madam *(surname)*:

Chief Justice
Address: The Chief Justice of the United States
The Supreme Court of the United States
Washington, D.C. 20543
Salutation: Dear Mr. *or* Madam Chief Justice:

Associate Justice
Address: Mr. *or* Madam Justice *(surname)*
The Supreme Court of the United States
Washington, D.C. 20543
Salutation: Dear Mr. *or* Madam Justice:

Judge of a Federal Court
Address: The Honorable *(full name)*
Judge of the *(name of court; if a district court, give district)*
(Local address)
Salutation: Dear Judge *(surname)*:

American Ambassador
Address: The Honorable *(full name)*
American Ambassador
(City), (Country)
Salutation: *Formal:* Sir: *or* Madam:
Informal: Dear Mr. *or* Madam Ambassador:

Governor
Address: The Honorable *(full name)*
Governor of *(name of state)*
(City), (State)
Salutation: Dear Governor *(surname)*:

State Senator

Address: The Honorable *(full name)*
            (Name of state) Senate
            (City), (State)
Salutation: Dear (Mr., Ms., Miss, *or* Mrs.)
            (surname):

State Representative; Assemblyman (or -woman); Delegate

Address: The Honorable *(full name)*
            (Name of state) House of
                Representatives *(or* Assembly *or*
                House of Delegates)
            (City), (State)
Salutation: Dear (Mr., Ms., Miss, *or* Mrs.)
            (surname):

Mayor

Address: The Honorable *(full name)*
            Mayor of *(name of city)*
            (City), (State)
Salutation: Dear Mayor *(surname)*:

Government (Canada)

Governor General

Address: (His *or* Her) Excellency *(full
                name)*
            Government House
            Ottawa, Ontario K1A 0A1
Salutation: *Formal:* Sir: *or* Madam:
            Informal: Dear Governor General:

Prime Minister

Address: The Right Honourable *(full name)*,
                P.C., M.P.
            Prime Minister of Canada
            Prime Minister's Office
            Ottawa, Ontario K1A 0A2
Salutation: *Formal:* Dear Sir: *or* Madam:
            Informal: Dear Mr. *or* Madam Prime
                Minister:

Cabinet Member

Address: The Honourable *(full name)*
            Minister of *(function)*
            House of Commons
            Parliament Buildings
            Ottawa, Ontario K1A 0A2
Salutation: *Formal:* Dear Sir: *or* Madam:
            Informal: Dear (Mr., Ms., Miss, *or*
                Mrs.) *(surname)*:

Senator

Address: The Honourable *(full name)*
            The Senate
            Parliament Buildings
            Ottawa, Ontario K1A 0A4
Salutation: *Formal:* Dear Sir: *or* Madam:
            Informal: Dear Senator:

Member of House of Commons

Address: (Mr., Ms., Miss, *or* Mrs.) *(full name)*,
                M.P.
            House of Commons
            Parliament Buildings
            Ottawa, Ontario K1A 0A6
Salutation: *Formal:* Dear Sir: *or* Madam:
            Informal: Dear (Mr., Ms., Miss, *or*
                Mrs.) *(surname)*:

Canadian Ambassador

Address: (Mr., Ms., Miss, *or* Mrs.) *(full
                name)*
            Canadian Ambassador to *(name of
                country)*
            (City), (Country)
Salutation: *Formal:* Dear Sir: *or* Madam:
            Informal: Dear (Mr., Ms., Miss, *or*
                Mrs.) *(surname)*:

Premier of a Province

Address: The Honourable *(full name)*,
                M.L.A.*
            Premier of the Province of *(name)***
            (City), (Province)
Salutation: *Formal:* Dear Sir: *or* Madam:
            Informal: Dear (Mr., Ms., Miss, *or*
                Mrs.) *(surname)*:

Mayor

Address: His *or* Her Worship Mayor *(full
                name)*
            City Hall
            (City), (Province)
Salutation: Dear Sir: *or* Madam:

Religious Leaders

Minister, Pastor or Rector

Address: The Reverend *(full name)*
            (Title), (name of church)
            (Local address)
Salutation: Dear (Mr., Ms., Miss, *or* Mrs.)
                (surname):

*For Ontario, use M.P.P.; for Quebec, use M.N.A. **For Quebec, use "Prime Minister."

Rabbi
Address: Rabbi *(full name)*
              (Local address)
Salutation: Dear Rabbi *(surname):*

Catholic Cardinal
Address: His Eminence *(Christian name)*
              Cardinal *(surname)*
              Archbishop of (province)
              (Local address)
Salutation: *Formal:* Your Eminence:
              Informal: Dear Cardinal *(surname):*

Catholic Archbishop
Address: The Most Reverend *(full name)*
              Archbishop of *(province)*
              (Local address)
Salutation: *Formal:* Your Excellency:
              Informal: Dear Archbishop *(surname):*

Catholic Bishop
Address: The Most Reverend *(full name)*
              Bishop of *(province)*
              (Local address)
Salutation: *Formal:* Your Excellency:
              Informal: Dear Bishop *(surname):*

Catholic Monsignor
Address: The Right Reverend Monsignor
                  (full name)
              (Local address)
Salutation: *Formal:* Right Reverend Monsignor:
              Informal: Dear Monsignor *(surname):*

Catholic Priest
Address: The Reverend *(full name), (initials
                  of order, if any)*
              (Local address)
Salutation: *Formal:* Reverend Sir:
              Informal: Dear Father *(surname):*

Catholic Sister
Address: Sister *(full name)*
              (Name of organization)
              (Local address)
Salutation: Dear Sister *(full name):*

Catholic Brother
Address: Brother *(full name)*
              (Name of organization)
              (Local address)
Salutation: Dear Brother *(given name):*

Protestant Episcopal Bishop
Address: The Right Reverend *(full name)*
              Bishop of *(name)*
              (Local address)
Salutation: *Formal:* Right Reverend Sir *or* Madam:
              Informal: Dear Bishop *(surname):*

Protestant Episcopal Dean
Address: The Very Reverend *(full name)*
              Dean of *(church)*
              (Local address)
Salutation: *Formal:* Very Reverend Sir *or* Madam:
              Informal: Dear Dean *(surname):*

Methodist Bishop
Address: The Reverend *(full name)*
              Methodist Bishop
              (Local address)
Salutation: *Formal:* Reverend Sir or Madam:
              Informal: Dear Bishop *(surname):*

Mormon Bishop
Address: Bishop *(full name)*
              Church of Jesus Christ of Latter-day
                  Saints
              (Local address)
Salutation: *Formal:* Sir:
              Informal: Dear Bishop
                  (surname):

Miscellaneous

President of a university or college
Address: (Dr., Mr., Ms., Miss, *or* Mrs.) *(full
                  name)*
              President, *(name of institution)*
              (Local address)
Salutation: Dear (Dr., Mr., Ms., Miss, *or* Mrs.)
                  (surname):

Dean of a college or school
Address: Dean *(full name)*
              School of *(name)*
              (Name of institution)
              (Local address)
Salutation: Dear Dean *(surname):*

Professor
Address: Professor (full name)
              Department of *(name)*
              (Name of institution)
              (Local address)
Salutation: Dear Professor *(surname):*

FROM SOUNDS TO SPELLINGS

These lists of words are given to provide help in the fundamental task of looking up words in the dictionary when you know how a word sounds but not how to spell it. By presenting a variety of possible spellings for each basic sound in English (these spellings are shown in boldface in the sample words), the lists can enable you to figure out where to look for the word you need in the alphabetical dictionary listings. It is especially useful to notice where in a word a particular spelling can occur—whether at the beginning, the middle, or the end, so that you can refine your search using the sample words as models.

Vowels and Diphthongs

(a) "short" a
at, hat, ma'am, drachm, diaphragm, dahlia, plaid, half, laugh, guarantor, guimpe, ingenue, lingerie, timbre

(ā) "long" a
ate, hate, Gaelic, champagne, rain, straight, arraign, gaol, gauge, vague, ray, étude, exposé, suede, steak, matinee, eh, veil, feign, eight, weight, weigh, Marseilles, dossier, demesne, beret, obey

(âr)
air, chair, doctrinaire, chary, dare, prayer, wear, Mynheer, ne'er, their, mal de mer, there, they're

(ä) "broad" a
ah, hurrah, father, à la mode, bazaar, half, calm, faux pas, éclat, laugh, sergeant, hearth, reservoir, guard, ingenue, lingerie

(e) "short" e
ebb, any, many, aesthete, said, says, leather, phlegm, heifer, jeopardy, friend, foetid

(ē) "long" e
keep, Aesop, Caesar, quay, equal, secret, strophe, each, team, tea, league, e'en, precede, receive, receipt, people, key, rani, machine, field, debris, intrigue, antique, amoeba, quay, city

(i) "short" i
if, damage, anaesthetic, England, been, counterfeit, carriage, sieve, women, business, build, guilt, sympathetic

(ī) "long" i
ice, faille, aisle, kayak, aye, stein, height, eye, pie, high, island, buy, cycle, sky, lye

(o) "short" o
box, wander, quadrant, yacht, astronaut, bureaucracy, cough, honor

(ō) "long" o
lo, mauve, hautboy, faux pas, beau, Bordeaux, yeoman, Seoul, sew, rote, road, toe, oh, yolk, brooch, depot, soul, flow, owe

(ô)
paw, tall, warrant, Utah, walk, Arkansas, author, vault, caught, alcohol, broad, floor, sought

(oi)
boy, lawyer, Freud, oil, boil, Iroquois, buoy

(oo̅) "short" double o
look, wolf, would, pull

(ōō) "long" double o
ooze, mood, ahchoo, maneuver, grew, lieu, who, move, canoe, manoeuvre, troup, rule, flue, impugn, suit

(ou)
brow, Frau, landau, out, shout, bough

(u) "short" u
up, pup, other, son, does, love, blood, trouble

(ûr)
urn, turn, earn, learn, ermine, term, err, poseur, herb, thirsty, fir, work, scourge, purr, myrtle

(ōō) "long" u
unique, future; beauty, feud, few, human, huge, purlieu, view, use, cue, queue, yew, you, Yukon, yule

(ə)

alone, system, easily, gallop, circus, tête-à-tête, mountain, mullein, dungeon, parliament, legion, porpoise, curious, martyr

(ər)

father; liar, elixir, labor, labour, augur, future, martyr

Consonants

(b)

bed, amber, rub; hobby, ebb, lobe, bhakti

(ch)

chief, ahchoo, rich; cello, niche, hatchet, catch, righteous, question, natural

(d)

do, odor, red; we'd, ladder, odd, fade, dhurrie, pulled, should

(f)

feed, safer; life, muffin, off, soften, tough, calf, pfennig, physics, staphylococcus, staph

(g)

give, agate, fog; egg, ghost, guard, plague

(h)

hit, ahoy; who

(hw)

where

(hyo͞o)

huge

(j)

just; Greenwich, graduate, judgment, bridge, soldier, sage, exaggerate, gem, agent, gin, agile, Hajji

(k)

keep, making; car, become, account, bacchanal, character, back, acquaint, lacquer, sacque, biscuit, lough, rake, Sikh, walk, qadi, Iraq, liquor, plaque

(l)

live, alive, sail; mile, call, faille, lisle, aisle

(m)

more, amount, ham; drachm, paradigm, calm, limb, home, mho, hammer, hymn

(n)

not, center, can; gnat, knife, mnemonic, done, runner, pneumatic

(ng)

ringing, ring; pink, mahjongg, tongue

(p)

pen, super, stop; hope, supper, lagniappe

(r)

red, arise, four; pure, rhythm, carrot, catarrh, wrong

(s)

see, beside, alas; center, racer, city, acid, mice, psychology, scene, schism, mouse, messenger, loss

(sh)

ship, ashamed, wash; ocean, chaise, machine, fuchsia, special, pshaw, sugar, schist, conscience, nauseous, mansion, tissue, mission, caption

(t)

toe, atom, hat; doubt, yacht, ctenophore, talked, bought, 'twas, bite, thyme, bottom, two

(th)

thin, ether, path; chthonian

(t͡h)

then, other, smooth; bathe

(v)

visit, over, luv; of, Stephen, have, flivver

(w)

well, away; marijuana, choir, ouija, quiet, where

(y)

yet; union, hallelujah, tortilla

(z)

zone, Bizet; has, discern, rise, xylem, fuze, buzzard, fuzz

(zh)

brazier; garage, measure, division, azure

SIGNS AND SYMBOLS

Business

@	at; as in: eggs @ 99¢ per dozen
a/c	account
B/E	bill of exchange
B/L	bill of lading
B/P	bills payable
B/R	bills receivable
B/S	bill of sale
c&f.	cost and freight
c/o	care of
L/C	letter of credit
O/S	out of stock
P&L	profit and loss
w/	with
w/o	without
#	**1.** (before a figure or figures) number; numbered; as in: #40 thread. **2.** (after a figure or figures) pound(s); as in: 20#

Mathematics

Arithmetic and Algebra

+	**1.** plus; add. **2.** positive; positive value; as: +64. **3.** denoting underestimated approximate accuracy, with some figures omitted at the end; as in: $\pi = 3.14159+$.
−	**1.** minus; subtract. **2.** negative; negative value; as: −64. **3.** denoting overestimated approximate accuracy, with some figures omitted at the end; as in: $\pi = 3.1416-$.
±	**1.** plus or minus; add or subtract; as in: $4 \pm 2 = 6$ or 2. **2.** positive or negative; as in: $\sqrt{a^2} = \pm a$. **3.** denoting the probable error associated with a figure derived by experiment and observation, approximate calculation, etc.
×	times; multiplied by; as in: $2 \times 4 = 2 \cdot 4$
÷/−	divided by; as in: $8 \div 2 = 8/2 = \frac{8}{2} = 4$
:/−	denoting the ratio of (in proportion)
=	equals; is equal to
: :	equals; is equal to (in proportion); as in $6 : 3 : : 8 : 4$
≠ ≠	is not equal to
≡	is identical with
≢ ≢	is not identical with
≈	is approximately equal to
~	**1.** is equivalent to. **2.** is similar to
>	is greater than
≫	is much greater than
<	is less than
≪	is much less than
≯	is not greater than
≮	is not less than
≥ ≧	is equal to or greater than
≤ ≦	is equal to or less than
∝	varies directly as; is directly proportional to; as in: $x \propto y$
√ √	the radical sign, indicating the square root of; as in: $\sqrt{81} = 9$
( )	parentheses; as in: $2(a + b)$
[ ]	brackets; as in: $4 + 3 [a(a + b)]$
{ }	braces; as in: $5 + b\{(a + b)[2 - a(a + b)] - 3\}$
Note:	Parentheses, brackets, and braces are used with quantities consisting of more than one member or term, to group them and show they are to be considered together.
∞	infinity
%	percent; per hundred
′ ″ ‴	prime, double prime, triple prime
etc.	etc., used to indicate: a. constants, as distinguished from the variable denoted by a letter alone. b. a variable under different conditions, at different times, etc.
∪	union
∩	intersection
⊂	is a subset of
⊃	contains as a subset
⊄	is not a subset of
⊅	does not contain as a subset
∅ ∧○	set containing no numbers; empty set

∈   is a member of
∉   is not a member of

Geometry

∠   angle (pl. ∠s); as in: ∠ ABC
⊥   **1.** a perpendicular (pl. ⊥s). **2.** is
      perpendicular to; as in: AB ⊥ CD
|| **1.** a parallel (pl. ||s). **2.** is parallel to; as in:
      AB || CD
△   triangle (pl. △s); as in: △ ABC
▭   rectangle; as in: ▭ ABCD
□   square; as in: □ ABCD
▱   parallelogram; as in: ▱ ABCD
○   circle (pl. ○s)
≅ ≡   is congruent to; as in: △ ABD ≅ △ CEF
~   is similar to; as in: △ ACE ~ △ CEF
∴   therefore; hence
∵   since, because
π   the Greek letter pi, representing the ratio
      (3.14159+) of the circumference of a circle
      to its diameter
⌒   (over a group of letters) indicating an arc
      of a circle; as: GH, the arc between points
      G and H
°   degree(s) of arc; as in: 90°
'   minute(s) of arc; as in: 90°30'
"   second(s) of arc; as in: 90°30'15"

Miscellaneous

&   the ampersand, meaning and
&c.   et cetera; and others; and so forth; and
      so on

'   foot; feet; as in: 6' = six feet
"   inch; inches as in: 6' 2" = six feet, two
      inches
×   **1.** by: used in stating dimensions; as in:
      2' × 4' × 1'; a 2" × 4" board. **2.** a sign
      (the cross) made in place of a signature
      by a person who cannot write; as in:

                       his
            George × Walsh
                      mark

†   **1.** dagger. **2.** died
‡   double dagger
©   copyright; copyrighted
®   registered; registered trademark
*   **1.** asterisk. **2.** born
/   slash; diagonal
¶   paragraph mark
§   section mark
"   ditto; indicating the same as the aforesaid:
      used in lists, etc.
...   ellipsis: used to show the omission of
      words, letters, etc.
~   tilde
^   circumflex
¸   cedilla; as in: ç
´   acute accent
`   grave accent
¨   **1.** dieresis. **2.** umlaut
¯   macron
˘   breve
℞   take (Latin *recipe*)
°   degree(s) of temperature; as in: 99°F, 36°C

NATIONS OF THE WORLD

Nation	Population	Area (sq. mi.)	Area (sq. km.)	Capital
Afghanistan	23,738,085	252,000	652,680	Kabul
Albania	3,293,252	10,362	27,536	Tirana
Algeria	29,830,370	919,352	2,381,121	Algiers
American Samoa	61,819	76	197	Pago Pago
Andorra	74,839	181	468	Andorra La Vella
Angola	10,623,994	481,226	1,246,375	Luanda
Argentina	35,797,536	1,084,120	2,807,870	Buenos Aires
Armenia	3,465,611	11,490	29,759	Yerevan
Australia	18,438,824	2,974,581	7,704164	Canberra
Austria	8,054,078	32,381	83,866	Vienna
Azerbaijan	7,735,918	33,430	86,583	Baku
Bahamas, The	262,034	5,353	13,864	Nassau
Bahrain	603,318	266	688	Manama
Bangladesh	125,340,261	54,501	141,157	Dhaka
Barbados	257,731	166	429	Bridgetown
Belarus	10,439,916	80,154	207,598	Minsk
Belgium	10,203,683	11,800	30,562	Brussels
Belize	224,663	8,866	22,962	Belmopan
Bermuda	62,569	20	53	Hamilton
Bhutan	1,865,191	19,300	49,987	Thimphu
Bolivia	7,669,868	404,388	1,047,364	La Paz
Bosnia & Herzegovina	2,607,734	19,741	51,129	Sarajevo
Botswana	1,500,765	275,00	712,250	Gaborone
Brazil	164,511,366	3,286,170	8,511,180	Brasilia
Brunei	307,616	2,226	5,765	Bandar Seri Begawan
Bulgaria	8,652,745	42,800	110,852	Sofia
Burkina Faso	10,891,159	106,111	274,827	Ouagadougou
Burma	46,821,943	261,228	676,577	Rangoon
Burundi	6,052,614	10,747	27,834	Bujumbura
Cambodia	11,163,861	69,866	180,952	Phnom Penh
Cameroon	14,677,510	179,558	465,055	Yaounde
Canada	29,123,194	3,690,410	9,558,161	Ottawa
Cape Verde	393,843	1,557	4,032	Praia
Central African Rep.	3,342,051	238,000	616,420	Bangui
Chad	7,166,023	501,000	1,297,590	N'Djamena
Chile	14,508,168	286,396	741,765	Santiago
China	1,221,591,778	3,691,502	9,560,990	Beijing
Colombia	37,418,290	439,828	1,139,154	Bogota
Comoros	589,797	719	1,862	Moroni
Congo	2,583,198	132,000	341,880	Brazzaville
Costa Rica	3,534,174	19,238	49,826	San Jose
Cote d'Ivoire	14,986,218	123,854	320,783	Yamoussoukro
Croatia	5,026,995	21,835	56,552	Zagreb
Cuba	10,999,041	44,200	114,478	Havana
Cyprus	752,808	3,572	9,251	Nicosia
Czech Republic	10,318,958	30,449	78,862	Prague
Denmark	5,268,775	16,576	42,931	Copenhagen
Djibouti	434,116	8,960	23,206	Djibouti

NATIONS OF THE WORLD
(CONTINUED)

Nation	Population	Area (sq. mi.)	Area (sq. km.)	Capital
Dominica	83,226	290	751	Roseau
Dominican Rep.	8,228,151	19,129	49,544	Santo Domingo
Ecuador	11,690,535	109,483	283,560	Quito
Egypt	64,791,891	386,659	1,001,449	Cairo
El Salvador	5,661,827	13,176	34,125	San Salvador
Equatorial Guinea	442,516	10,824	28,034	Malabo
Eritrea	3,589,687	47,076	121,926	Asmara
Estonia	1,444,721	17,413	45,099	Tallinn
Ethiopia	58,732,577	424,724	1,100,035	Addis Ababa
Fiji	792,441	7,078	18,332	Sulva
Finland	5,109,148	130,119	337,008	Helsinki
France	58,470,421	212,736	550,986	Paris
Gabon	1,190,159	102,290	264,931	Libreville
Gambia, The	1,248,085	4,003	10,367	Banjul
Georgia	5,174,642	26,872	69,598	Tbilisi
Germany	84,068,216	137,852	357,036	Berlin
Ghana	18,100,703	91,843	237,873	Accra
Greece	10,583,126	50,147	129,880	Athens
Grenada	95,537	133	344	St. George's
Guatemala	11,558,407	42,042	108,888	Guatemala City
Guinea	7,405,375	96,900	250,971	Conakry
Guinea-Bissau	1,178,584	13,948	36,125	Bissau
Guyana	706,116	82,978	214,913	Georgetown
Haiti	6,611,407	10,714	27,749	Port-au-Prince
Honduras	5,751,384	43,277	112,087	Tegucigalpa
Hungary	9,935,774	35,926	93,048	Budapest
Iceland	272,550	39,709	102,846	Reykjavik
India	967,612,804	1,246,880	3,229,419	New Delhi
Indonesia	209,774,138	741,100	1,919,449	Jakarta
Iran	67,540,002	635,000	1,644,650	Tehran
Iraq	22,219,289	172,000	445,480	Baghdad
Ireland	3,555,500	27,136	70,282	Dublin
Israel	5,534,672	7,984	20,678	Jerusalem
Italy	57,534,088	116,294	301,201	Rome
Jamaica	2,615,582	4,413	11,429	Kingston
Japan	125,716,637	141,529	366,560	Tokyo
Jersey	88,510	44	116	St. Helier
Jordan	4,324,638	37,264	96,513	Amman
Kazakstan	16,898,572	1,049,155	2,717,311	Alma-Ata
Kenya	28,803,085	223,478	578,808	Nairobi
Kuwait	2,076,805	8,000	20,720	Kuwait
Kyrgyzstan	4,540,185	76,460	198,031	Bishkek
Laos	5,116,959	91,500	236,985	Vientiane
Latvia	2,437,649	25,395	65,773	Riga
Lebanon	3,858,736	3,927	10,170	Beirut
Lesotho	2,007,814	11,716	30,344	Maseru
Liberia	2,602,068	43,000	111,370	Monrovia

NATIONS OF THE WORLD
(CONTINUED)

Nation	Population	Area (sq. mi.)	Area (sq. km.)	Capital
Libya	5,648,359	679,400	1,759,646	Tripoli
Liechtenstein	31,461	65	168	Vaduz
Lithuania	3,635,932	25,174	65,200	Vilnius
Luxembourg	422,474	999	2,587	Luxembourg
Macedonia	2,113,866	9,928	25,713	Skopje
Madagascar	14,061,627	226,657	587,041	Antananarivo
Malawi	9,609,081	49,177	127,368	Lilongwe
Malaysia	20,376,235	127,3117	329,751	Kuala Lumpur
Maldives	280,391	115	297	Male
Mali	9,945,383	478,841	1,240,198	Bamako
Malta	379,365	122	315	Valletta
Marshall Islands	60,652	70	181	Majuro
Mauritania	2,411,317	398,000	1,030,820	Nouakchott
Mauritius	1,154,272	788	2,040	Port Louis
Mexico	97,563,374	756,198	1,966,322	Mexico City
Micronesia, Federated States of	127,616	271	701	
Moldova	4,475,232	13,000	33,700	Chisinau
Monaco	31,892	1/2	1.29	Monaco
Mongolia	2,538,211	600,000	1,554,000	Ulan Bator
Morocco	30,391,423	172,104	445,749	Rabat
Mozambique	18,165,476	297,731	771,123	Maputo
Namibia	1,727,183	318,249	824,268	Windhoek
Nepal	22,641,061	54,000	139,860	Katmandu
Netherlands	15,653,091	16,163	41,862	Amsterdam
New Zealand	3,587,275	103,416	267,847	Wellington
Nicaragua	4,386,399	57,143	148,000	Managua
Niger	9,388,859	458,976	1,188,747	Niamey
Nigeria	107,129,469	356,669	923,772	Abuja
North Korea	24,317,004	50,000	12,950	Pyongyang
Norway	4,404,456	124,555	322,597	Oslo
Oman	2,264,590	82,800	214,452	Muscat
Pakistan	132,185,299	310,403	803,943	Islamabad
Panama	2,693,417	28,575	74,009	Panama City
Papua New Guinea	4,496,221	178,260	461,693	Port Moresby
Paraguay	5,651,634	157,047	406,751	Ascuncion
Peru	24,949,512	496,222	1,285,214	Lima
Philippines	76,103,564	114,830	297,409	Manila
Poland	38,700,291	121,000	313,390	Warsaw
Portugal	9,867,654	35,414	91,722	Lisbon
Qatar	665,485	8,500	22,015	Doha
Reunion	692,204	970	2,512	St. Denis
Romania	21,399,114	91,654	237,383	Bucharest
Russian Federation	147,987,101	6,593,000	17,075,870	Moscow
Rwanda	7,737,537	10,169	26,337	Kigali
Saint Kitts-Nevis	41,803	104	269	Basseterre
Saint Lucia	159,639	238	616	Castries

NATIONS OF THE WORLD
(CONTINUED)

Nation	Population	Area (sq. mi.)	Area (sq. km.)	Capital
Saint Vincent and the Grenadines	119,092	150	388	Kingstown
San Marino	24,714	24	62	San Marino
São Tomé and Principe	147,865	387	1,002	São Tomé
Saudi Arabia	20,087,965	830,000	2,149,700	Riyadh
Senegal	9,403,546	76,084	197,057	Dakar
Seychelles	78,142	175	453	Victoria
Sierra Leone	4,891,546	27,925	72,325	Freetown
Singapore	3,461,929	240	621	Singapore
Slovakia	5,393,016	18,932	49,033	Bratislava
Slovenia	1,945,998	7,819	20,251	Ljubljana
Solomon Islands	426,855	11,458	29,676	Honiara
Somalia	9,940,232	246,198	637,652	Mogadishu
South Africa	42,327,458	472,000	1,222,480	Pretoria/Cape Town
South Korea	45,948,811	38,232	99,020	Seoul
Spain	39,244,195	194,988	505,018	Madrid
Sri Lanka	18,762,075	25,332	65,609	Colombo
Sudan	32,594,128	967,500	2,505,825	Khartoum
Suriname	443,446	63,251	163,820	Paramaribo
Swaziland	1,031,600	6,704	17,363	Mbabane
Sweden	8,946,193	173,394	449,090	Stockholm
Switzerland	7,248,984	15,994	41,294	Bern
Syria	16,137,899	71,227	184,477	Damascus
Tajikistan	6,013,855	55,240	143,071	Dushanbe
Tanzania	29,460,753	363,950	942,630	Dodoma
Thailand	59,450,818	198,242	513,446	Bangkok
Togo	4,735,610	21,830	56,539	Lome
Trinidad and Tobago	1,273,141	1,980	5,128	Port-of-Spain
Tunisia	9,183,097	48,330	125,174	Tunis
Turkey	63,528,225	300,948	779,455	Ankara
Turkmenistan	4,225,351	188,417	488,000	Ashkhabad
Uganda	20,604,874	93,065	241,038	Kampala
Ukraine	50,684,635	233,090	603,703	Kiev
United Arab Emirates	2,262,309	32,300	83,657	Abu Dhabi
United Kingdom	58,610,182	94,242	244,086	London
United States	267,954,767	3,615,122	9,363,165	Washington, D.C.
Uruguay	3,261,707	172,172	445,925	Montevideo
Uzbekistan	23,860,452	172,741	447,399	Tashkent
Vanuatu	181,358	5,700	14,763	Vila
Venezuela	22,396,407	352,143	912,050	Caracas
Vietnam	75,123,880	126,104	326,609	Hanoi
Western Samoa	219,509	1,133	2,934	Apia
Yemen	13,972,477	207,000	536,130	Sanaa
Zaire	47,440,362	905,063	2,344,113	Kinshasa
Zambia	9,349,975	290,585	752,615	Lusaka
Zimbabwe	11,423,175	150,804	390,582	Harare

Source: U.S. Bureau of the Census, International Data Base. (Total midyear population, 1997 estimates.)

MAJOR U.S. CITIES

Rank	City, State	Population	Rank	City, State	Population
1.	New York, N.Y.	7,333,253	51.	Colorado Springs, Colo.	316,480
2.	Los Angeles, Calif.	3,448,613	52.	Mesa, Ariz.	313,649
3.	Chicago, Ill.	2,731,743	53.	Buffalo, N.Y.	312,965
4.	Houston, Tex.	1,702,086	54.	Wichita, Kans.	310,236
5.	Philadelphia, Pa.	1,524,249	55.	Santa Ana, Calif.	290,827
6.	San Diego, Calif.	1,151,977	56.	Arlington, Tex.	286,922
7.	Phoenix, Ariz.	1,048,949	57.	Tampa, Fla.	285,523
8.	Dallas, Tex.	1,022,830	58.	Anaheim, Calif.	282,133
9.	San Antonio, Tex.	998,905	59.	Corpus Christi, Tex.	275,419
10.	Detroit, Mich.	992,038	60.	Louisville, Ky.	270,308
11.	San Jose, Calif.	816,884	61.	Birmingham, Ala.	264,527
12.	Indianapolis, Ind.	752,279	62.	St. Paul, Minn.	262,071
13.	San Francisco, Calif.	734,676	63.	Newark, N.J.	258,751
14.	Baltimore, Md.	702,979	64.	Anchorage, Alaska	253,649
15.	Jacksonville, Fla.	665,070	65.	Aurora, Colo.	250,717
16.	Columbus, Ohio	635,913	66.	Riverside, Calif.	241,644
17.	Milwaukee, Wis.	617,044	67.	Norfolk, Va.	241,426
18.	Memphis, Tenn.	614,289	68.	St. Petersburg, Fla.	238,585
19.	El Paso, Tex.	579,307	69.	Lexington-Fayette, Ky.	237,612
20.	Washington, D.C.	567,094	70.	Raleigh, N.C.	236,707
21.	Boston, Mass.	547,725	71.	Rochester, N.Y.	231,170
22.	Seattle, Wash.	520,947	72.	Baton Rouge, La.	227,482
23.	Austin, Tex.	514,013	73.	Jersey City, N.J.	226,022
24.	Nashville-Davidson, Tenn.	504,505	74.	Stockton, Calif.	222,633
25.	Denver, Colo.	493,559	75.	Akron, Ohio	221,886
26.	Cleveland, Ohio	492,901	76.	Mobile, Ala.	204,490
27.	New Orleans, La.	484,149	77.	Lincoln, Nebr.	203,076
28.	Oklahoma City, Okla.	463,201	78.	Richmond, Va.	201,108
29.	Fort Worth, Tex.	451,814	79.	Shreveport, La.	196,982
30.	Portland, Oreg.	450,777	80.	Greensboro, N.C.	196,167
31.	Kansas City, Mo.	443,878	81.	Montgomery, Ala.	195,471
32.	Charlotte, N.C.	437,797	82.	Madison, Wis.	194,586
33.	Tucson, Ariz.	434,726	83.	Lubbock, Tex.	194,467
34.	Long Beach, Calif.	433,852	84.	Garland, Tex.	194,218
35.	Virginia Beach, Va.	430,295	85.	Hialeah, Fla.	194,120
36.	Albuquerque, N. Mex.	411,994	86.	Des Moines, Iowa	193,965
37.	Atlanta, Ga.	396,052	87.	Jackson, Miss.	193,097
38.	Fresno, Calif.	386,551	88.	Spokane, Wash.	192,781
39.	Honolulu, Hawaii	385,881	89.	Bakersfield, Calif.	191,060
40.	Tulsa, Okla.	374,851	90.	Grand Rapids, Mich.	190,395
41.	Sacramento, Calif.	373,964	91.	Huntington Beach, Calif.	189,220
42.	Miami, Fla.	373,024	92.	Columbus, Ga.	186,470
43.	St. Louis, Mo.	368,215	93.	Fremont, Calif.	183,575
44.	Oakland, Calif.	366,926	94.	Yonkers, N.Y.	183,490
45.	Pittsburgh, Pa.	358,883	95.	Fort Wayne, Ind.	183,359
46.	Cincinnati, Ohio	358,170	96.	Tacoma, Wash.	183,060
47.	Minneapolis, Minn.	354,590	97.	San Bernardino, Calif.	181,718
48.	Omaha, Nebr.	345,033	98.	Chesapeake, Va.	180,577
49.	Las Vegas, Nev.	327,878	99.	Newport News, Va.	179,127
50.	Toledo, Ohio	322,550	100.	Dayton, Ohio	178,540

SERMON ON THE MOUNT
FROM THE BOOK OF MATTHEW

Chapter 5

And seeing the multitudes, he went up into a mountain: and when he was set, his disciples came unto him:

2 And he opened his mouth, and taught them, saying,

3 Blessed are the poor in spirit: for theirs is the kingdom of heaven.

4 Blessed are they that mourn: for they shall be comforted.

5 Blessed are the meek: for they shall inherit the earth.

6 Blessed are they which do hunger and thirst after righteousness: for they shall be filled.

7 Blessed are the merciful: for they shall obtain mercy.

8 Blessed are the pure in heart: for they shall see God.

9 Blessed are the peacemakers: for they shall be called the children of God.

10 Blessed are they which are persecuted for righteousness' sake: for theirs is the kingdom of heaven.

11 Blessed are ye, when men shall revile you, and persecute you, and shall say all manner of evil against you falsely, for my sake.

12 Rejoice, and be exceeding glad: for great is your reward in heaven: for so persecuted they the prophets which were before you.

13 Ye are the salt of the earth: but if the salt have lost his savor, wherewith shall it be salted? it is thenceforth good for nothing, but to be cast out, and to be trodden under foot of men.

14 Ye are the light of the world. A city that is set on a hill cannot be hid.

15 Neither do men light a candle, and put it under a bushel, but on a candlestick; and it giveth light unto all that are in the house.

16 Let your light so shine before men, that they may see your good works, and glorify your Father which is in heaven.

17 Think not that I am come to destroy the law, or the prophets: I am not come to destroy, but to fulfil.

18 For verily I say unto you, Till heaven and earth pass, one jot or one tittle shall in no wise pass from the law, till all be fulfilled.

19 Whosoever therefore shall break one of these least commandments, and shall teach men so, he shall be called the least in the kingdom of heaven: but whosoever shall do and teach them, the same shall be called great in the kingdom of heaven.

20 For I say unto you, That except your righteousness shall exceed the righteousness of the scribes and Pharisees, ye shall in no case enter into the kingdom of heaven.

21 Ye have heard that it was said by them of old time, Thou shalt not kill; and whosoever shall kill shall be in danger of the judgment:

22 But I say unto you, That whosoever is angry with his brother without a cause shall be in danger of the judgment: and whosoever shall say to his brother, Raca, shall be in danger of the council: but whosoever shall say, Thou fool, shall be in danger of hell fire.

23 Therefore if thou bring thy gift to the altar, and there rememberest that thy brother hath aught against thee;

24 Leave there thy gift before the altar, and go thy way; first be reconciled to thy brother, and then come and offer thy gift.

25 Agree with thine adversary quickly, while thou art in the way with him; lest at any time the adversary deliver thee to the judge, and the judge deliver thee to the officer, and thou be cast into prison.

26 Verily I say unto thee, Thou shalt by no means come out thence, till thou hast paid the uttermost farthing.

27 Ye have heard that it was said by them of old time, Thou shalt not commit adultery:

28 But I say unto you, That whosoever looketh on a woman to lust after her hath committed adultery with her already in his heart.

29 And if thy right eye offend thee, pluck it out, and cast it from thee: for it is profitable for thee that one of thy members should perish, and not that thy whole body should be cast into hell.

30 And if thy right hand offend thee, cut it off, and cast it from thee: for it is profitable for thee that one of thy members should perish, and not that thy whole body should be cast into hell.

31 It hath been said, Whosoever shall put away his wife, let him give her a writing of divorcement:

32 But I say unto you, That whosoever shall put away his wife, saving for the cause of fornication, causeth her to commit adultery: and whosoever shall marry her that is divorced committeth adultery.

33 Again, ye have heard that it hath been said by them of old time, Thou shalt not forswear thyself, but shalt perform unto the Lord thine oaths:

34 But I say unto you, Swear not at all; neither by heaven; for it is God's throne:

35 Nor by the earth; for it is his footstool: neither by Jerusalem; for it is the city of the great King.

36 Neither shalt thou swear by thy head, because thou canst not make one hair white or black.

37 But let your communication be, Yea, yea; Nay, nay: for whatsoever is more than these cometh of evil.

38 Ye have heard that it hath been said, An eye for an eye, and a tooth for a tooth:

39 But I say unto you, That ye resist not evil: but whosoever shall smite thee on thy right cheek, turn to him the other also.

40 And if any man will sue thee at the law, and take away thy coat, let him have thy cloak also.

41 And whosoever shall compel thee to go a mile, go with him twain.

42 Give to him that asketh thee, and from him that would borrow of thee turn not thou away.

43 Ye have heard that it hath been said, Thou shalt love thy neighbor, and hate thine enemy.

44 But I say unto you, Love your enemies, bless them that curse you, do good to them that hate you, and pray for them which despitefully use you, and persecute you;

45 That ye may be the children of your Father which is in heaven: for he maketh his sun to rise on the evil and on the good, and sendeth rain on the just and on the unjust.

46 For if ye love them which love you, what reward have ye? do not even the publicans the same?

47 And if ye salute your brethren only, what do ye more than others? do not even the publicans so?

48 Be ye therefore perfect, even as your Father which is in heaven is perfect.

Chapter 6

Take heed that ye do not your alms before men, to be seen of them: otherwise ye have no reward of your Father which is in heaven.

2 Therefore when thou doest thine alms, do not sound a trumpet before thee, as the hypocrites do in the synagogues and in the streets, that they may have glory of men. Verily I say unto you, They have their reward.

3 But when thou doest alms, let not thy left hand know what thy right hand doeth:

4 That thine alms may be in secret: and thy Father which seeth in secret himself shall reward thee openly.

5 And when thou prayest, thou shalt not be as the hypocrites are: for they love to pray standing in the synagogues and in the corners of the streets, that they may be seen of men. Verily I say unto you, They have their reward.

6 But thou, when thou prayest, enter into thy closet, and when thou hast shut thy door, pray to thy Father which is in secret; and thy Father which seeth in secret shall reward thee openly.

7 But when ye pray, use not vain repetitions, as the heathen do: for they think that they shall be heard for their much speaking.

8 Be not ye therefore like unto them: for your Father knoweth what things ye have need of, before ye ask him.

9 After this manner therefore pray ye: Our Father which art in heaven, Hallowed be thy name.

10 Thy kingdom come. Thy will be done in earth, as it is in heaven.

11 Give us this day our daily bread.

12 And forgive us our debts, as we forgive our debtors.

13 And lead us not into temptation, but deliver us from evil: For thine is the kingdom, and the power, and the glory, for ever. Amen.

14 For if ye forgive men their trespasses, your heavenly Father will also forgive you:

15 But if ye forgive not men their trespasses, neither will your Father forgive your trespasses.

16 Moreover when ye fast, be not, as the hypocrites, of a sad countenance: for they disfigure their faces, that they may appear unto men to fast. Verily I say unto you, They have their reward.

17 But thou, when thou fastest, anoint thine head, and wash thy face;

18 That thou appear not unto men to fast, but unto thy Father which is in secret: and thy Father which seeth in secret shall reward thee openly.

19 Lay not up for yourselves treasures upon earth, where moth and rust doth corrupt, and where thieves break through and steal:

20 But lay up for yourselves treasures in heaven, where neither moth nor rust doth corrupt, and where thieves do not break through nor steal:

21 For where your treasure is, there will your heart be also.

22 The light of the body is the eye: if therefore thine eye be single, thy whole body shall be full of light.

23 But if thine eye be evil, thy whole body shall be full of darkness. If therefore the light that is in thee be darkness, how great is that darkness!

24 No man can serve two masters: for either he will hate the one, and love the other; or else he will hold to the one, and despise the other. Ye cannot serve God and mammon.

25 Therefore I say unto you, Take no thought for your life, what ye shall eat, or what ye shall drink; nor yet for your body, what ye shall put on. Is not the life more than meat, and the body than raiment?

26 Behold the fowls of the air: for they sow not, neither do they reap, nor gather into barns; yet your heavenly Father feedeth them. Are ye not much better than they?

27 Which of you by taking thought can add one cubit unto his stature?

28 And why take ye thought for raiment? Consider the lilies of the field, how they grow; they toil not, neither do they spin:

29 And yet I say unto you, That even Solomon in all his glory was not arrayed like one of these.

30 Wherefore, if God so clothe the grass of the field, which to-day is, and to-morrow is cast into the oven, shall he not much more clothe you, O ye of little faith?

31 Therefore take no thought, saying, What shall we eat? or, What shall we drink? or, Wherewithal shall we be clothed?

32 (For after all these things do the Gentiles seek:) for your heavenly Father knoweth that ye have need of all these things.

33 But seek ye first the kingdom of God, and his righteousness; and all these things shall be added unto you.

34 Take therefore no thought for the morrow: for the morrow shall take thought for the things of itself. Sufficient unto the day is the evil thereof.

Chapter 7

Judge not, that ye be not judged.

2 For with what judgment ye judge, ye shall be judged: and with what measure ye mete, it shall be measured to you again.

3 And why beholdest thou the mote that is in thy brother's eye, but considerest not the beam that is in thine own eye?

4 Or how wilt thou say to thy brother, Let me pull out the mote out of thine eye; and, behold, a beam is in thine own eye?

5 Thou hypocrite, first cast out the beam out of thine own eye; and then shalt thou see clearly to cast out the mote out of thy brother's eye.

6 Give not that which is holy unto the dogs, neither cast ye your pearls before swine, lest they trample them under their feet, and turn again and rend you.

7 Ask, and it shall be given you; seek, and ye shall find; knock, and it shall be opened unto you:

8 For every one that asketh receiveth; and he that seeketh findeth; and to him that knocketh it shall be opened.

9 Or what man is there of you, whom if his son ask bread, will he give him a stone?

10 Or if he ask a fish, will he give him a serpent?

11 If ye then, being evil, know how to give good gifts unto your children, how much more shall your Father which is in heaven give good things to them that ask him?

12 Therefore all things whatsoever ye would that men should do to you, do ye even so to them: for this is the law and the prophets.

13 Enter ye in at the strait gate: for wide is the gate, and broad is the way, that leadeth to destruction, and many there be which go in thereat:

14 Because strait is the gate, and narrow is the way, which leadeth unto life, and few there be that find it.

15 Beware of false prophets, which come to you in sheep's clothing, but inwardly they are ravening wolves.

16 Ye shall know them by their fruits. Do men gather grapes of thorns, or figs of thistles?

17 Even so every good tree bringeth forth good fruit; but a corrupt tree bringeth forth evil fruit.

18 A good tree cannot bring forth evil fruit, neither can a corrupt tree bring forth good fruit.

19 Every tree that bringeth not forth good fruit is hewn down, and cast into the fire.

20 Wherefore by their fruits ye shall know them.

21 Not every one that saith unto me, Lord, Lord, shall enter into the kingdom of heaven; but he that doeth the will of my Father which is in heaven.

22 Many will say to me in that day, Lord, Lord, have we not prophesied in thy name? and in thy name have cast out devils? and in thy name done many wonderful works?

23 And then will I profess unto them, I never knew you: depart from me, ye that work iniquity.

24 Therefore whosoever heareth these sayings of mine, and doeth them, I will liken him unto a wise man, which built his house upon a rock:

25 And the rain descended, and the floods came, and the winds blew, and beat upon that house; and it fell not: for it was founded upon a rock.

26 And every one that heareth these sayings of mine, and doeth them not, shall be likened unto a foolish man, which built his house upon the sand:

27 And the rain descended, and the floods came, and the winds blew, and beat upon that house; and it fell: and great was the fall of it.

28 And it came to pass, when Jesus had ended these sayings, the people were astonished at his doctrine:

29 For he taught them as one having authority, and not as the scribes.

DECLARATION OF INDEPENDENCE

"We hold these truths to be self-evident"

America's Revolutionary War was in its second year when the Second Continental Congress decided that the uprising would fail unless independence was identified as its goal: "The colonies are, and of right ought to be, free and independent States." The Declaration of Independence, enumerating grievances against the British Crown, was the U.S. "birth certificate." The taciturn, shy Thomas Jefferson (1743–1826), who had a happy talent for composition and a peculiar felicity of expression, drew up the document between June 11 and June 28, 1776, on a custom-made portable desk on the second floor of his temporary lodgings in Philadelphia. His purpose, he said, was to express the American mind, "not to find new principles, or new arguments, never before thought of, not merely to say things which had never been said before; but to place before mankind the common sense of the subject, in terms so plain and firm as to command their assent, and to justify ourselves in the independent stand we are compelled to take..." (Congress deleted Jefferson's indictment of King George III for trafficking in slaves.) On July 2, twelve of the thirteen colonies voted in favor of independence. (The thirteenth, New York, abstained, awaiting approval from its newly elected convention.) The Declaration of Independence was printed during the night of July 4. The capstone of the ocean-wide, decade-long war of words that the colonists had been waging with Britain, the Declaration has become the great American symbol of independence, revolution and liberty. In 1858, Senatorial candidate Abraham Lincoln (1809–1865) described the Founding Fathers' stirring call to throw off the bonds of tyranny as "the electric cord...that links the hearts of patriotic and liberty-loving men together...."

The Declaration of Independence
1776

When in the course of human events, it becomes necessary for one people to dissolve the political bands which have connected them with another, and to assume among the Powers of the earth, the separate and equal station to which the Laws of Nature and of Nature's God entitle them, a decent respect to the opinions of mankind requires that they should declare the causes which impel them to the separation.

We hold these truths to be self-evident, that all men are created equal, that they are endowed by their Creator with certain unalienable Rights, that among these are Life, Liberty and the pursuit of Happiness. That to secure these rights, Governments are instituted among Men, deriving their just powers from the consent of the governed. That whenever any Form of Government becomes destructive of these ends, it is the Right of the People to alter or to abolish it, and to institute new Government, laying its foundation on such principles and organizing its powers in such form, as to them shall seem most likely to effect their Safety and Happiness. Prudence, indeed, will dictate that Governments long established should not be changed for light and transient causes; and accordingly all experience hath shown, that mankind are more disposed to suffer, while evils are sufferable, than to right themselves by abolishing the forms to which they are accustomed. But when a long train of abuses and usurpations, pursuing invariably the same Object evinces a design to reduce them under absolute Despotism, it is their right, it is their duty, to throw off such

Government, and to provide new Guards for their future security.—Such has been the patient sufferance of these Colonies; and such is now the necessity which constrains them to alter their former Systems of Government. The history of the present King of Great Britain is a history of repeated injuries and usurpations, all having in direct object the establishment of an absolute Tyranny over these States. To prove this, let Facts be submitted to a candid world.

He has refused his Assent to Laws, the most wholesome and necessary for the public good.

He has forbidden his Governors to pass Laws of immediate and pressing importance, unless suspended in their operation till his Assent should be obtained; and when so suspended, he has utterly neglected to attend to them.

He has refused to pass other Laws for the accommodation of large districts of people, unless those people would relinquish the right of Representation in the Legislature, a right inestimable to them and formidable to tyrants only.

He has called together legislative bodies at places unusual, uncomfortable, and distant from the depository of their Public Records, for the sole purpose of fatiguing them into compliance with his measures.

He has dissolved Representative Houses repeatedly, for opposing with manly firmness his invasions on the rights of the people.

He has refused for a long time, after such dissolutions, to cause others to be elected; whereby the Legislative Powers, incapable of Annihilation, have returned to the People at large for their exercise; the State remaining in the meantime exposed to all the dangers of invasion from without, and convulsions within.

He has endeavoured to prevent the population of these States; for that purpose obstructing the Laws of Naturalization of Foreigners; refusing to pass others to encourage their migration hither, and raising the conditions of new Appropriations of Lands.

He has obstructed the Administration of Justice, by refusing his Assent to Laws for establishing Judiciary Powers.

He has made Judges dependent on his Will alone, for the tenure of their offices, and the amount and payment of their salaries.

He has erected a multitude of New Offices, and sent hither swarms of Officers to harass our People, and eat out their substance.

He has kept among us, in times of peace, Standing Armies without the Consent of our legislature.

He has affected to render the Military independent of and superior to the Civil Power.

He has combined with others to subject us to a jurisdiction foreign to our constitution, and unacknowledged by our laws; giving his Assent to their acts of pretended legislation:

For quartering large bodies of armed troops among us:

For protecting them, by a mock Trial, from Punishment for any Murders which they should commit on the Inhabitants of these States:

For cutting off our Trade with all parts of the world:

For imposing taxes on us without our Consent:

For depriving us in many cases, of the benefits of Trial by Jury:

For transporting us beyond Seas to be tried for pretended offences:

For abolishing the free System of English Laws in a neighbouring Province, establishing therein an Arbitrary government, and enlarging its Boundaries so as to render it at once an example and fit instrument for introducing the same absolute rule into these Colonies:

For taking away our Charters, abolishing our most valuable Laws, and altering fundamentally the Forms of our Governments:

For suspending our own Legislature, and declaring themselves invested with Power to legislate for us in all cases whatsoever.

He has abdicated Government here, by declaring us out of his Protection and waging War against us.

He has plundered our seas, ravaged our Coasts, burnt our towns, and destroyed the lives of our people.

He is at this time transporting large armies of foreign mercenaries to complete the works of death, desolation and tyranny, already begun with circumstances of Cruelty & perfidy scarcely paralleled in the most barbarous ages, and totally unworthy the Head of a civilized nation.

He has constrained our fellow Citizens taken Captive on the high Seas to bear Arms against their Country, to become the executioners of their friends and Brethren, or to fall themselves by their Hands.

He has excited domestic insurrections amongst us, and has endeavoured to bring on the inhabitants of our frontiers, the merciless Indian Savages, whose known rule of warfare, is an undistinguished destruction of all ages, sexes and conditions.

In every stage of these Oppressions We have Petitioned for Redress in the most humble terms: Our repeated Petitions have been answered only by repeated injury. A Prince, whose character is thus marked by every act which may define a Tyrant, is unfit to be the ruler of a free People.

Nor have We been wanting in attention to our British brethren. We have warned them from time to time of attempts by their legislature to extend an unwarrantable jurisdiction over us. We have reminded them of the circumstances of our emigration and settlement here. We have appealed to their native justice and magnanimity, and we have conjured them by the ties of our common kindred to disavow these usurpations, which, would inevitably interrupt our connections and correspondence. They too have been deaf to the voice of justice and of consaguinity. We must, therefore, acquiesce in the necessity, which denounces our Separation, and hold them, as we hold the rest of mankind, Enemies in War, in Peace Friends.

We, therefore, the Representatives of the United States of America, in General Congress, Assembled, appealing to the Supreme Judge of the world for the rectitude of our intentions, do, in the Name, and by Authority of the good People of these Colonies, solemnly publish and declare, That these United Colonies are and of right ought to be Free and Independent States; that they are Absolved from all Allegiance to the British Crown, and that all political connection between them and the State of Great Britain, is and ought to be totally dissolved; and that as Free and Independent States, they have full Power to levy War, conclude Peace, contract Alliances, establish Commerce, and to do all other Acts and Things which Independent States may of right do. And for the support of the Declaration, with a firm reliance on the Protection of Divine Providence, we mutually pledge to each other our Lives, our Fortunes and our sacred Honor.

John Hancock

New Hampshire
Josiah Bartlett
Wm. Whipple
Matthew Thornton

Massachusetts-Bay
Saml. Adams
John Adams
Robt. Treat Paine
Elbridge Gerry

Rhode Island
Step. Hopkins
William Ellery

Connecticut
Roger Sherman
Sam'el Huntington
Wm. Williams
Oliver Wolcott

New York
Wm. Floyd
Phil. Livingston
Frans. Lewis
Lewis Morris

Pennsylvania
Rbt. Morris
Benjamin Rush
Benja. Franklin
John Morton
Geo. Clymer
Jas. Smith
Geo. Taylor
James Wilson
Geo. Ross

Delaware
Caesar Rodney
Geo. Read
Tho. M'Kean

North Carolina
Wm. Hooper
Joseph Hewes
John Penn

South Carolina
Edward Rutledge
Thos. Heyward, Junr.
Thomas Lynch, Junr.
Arthur Middleton

New Jersey
Richd. Stockton
Jno. Witherspoon
Fras. Hopkinson
John Hart
Abra. Clark

Georgia
Button Gwinnett
Lyman Hall
Geo. Walton

Maryland
Samuel Chase
Wm. Paca
Thos. Stone
Charles Carroll of
    Carrollton

Virginia
George Wythe
Richard Henry Lee
Th. Jefferson
Benja. Harrison
Ths. Nelson, Jr.
Francis Lightfoot Lee
Carter Braxton

AMENDMENTS TO THE U.S. CONSTITUTION

The Constitution of the United States of America was written over the summer of 1787, and took effect in 1788 upon ratification by nine of the original thirteen states. The Constitution in its original form established the structure of the national government and enumerated the powers of each of its branches, but said little about the rights of the people. When Americans speak of "constitutional rights," therefore, they are almost invariably referring not to the original text of the Constitution, but to one or another of its amendments.

By one estimate, ten thousand proposed amendments have been introduced in Congress in a little over two centuries; just twenty-seven have been adopted, and they are summarized here. The year that each amendment became part of the Constitution is given in parentheses.

The first ten amendments were adopted almost immediately to address the widespread concern about the Constitution's general lack of explicit protections for individual rights; these are known as the Bill of Rights. Although these amendments were originally intended only as limitations on the power of the federal government, and for most of the nation's history provided no protection against state laws that violated individual rights, most of the provisions of the Bill of Rights have now been made applicable to state governments by virtue of the incorporation doctrine.

The Thirteenth, Fourteenth, and Fifteenth Amendments represent the nation's effort to embody in its fundamental law the principles of equality and human dignity that emerged from the Civil War, and are often referred to as the Civil War amendments.

Amendments to the U.S. Constitution

Amendment I (1791)

Congress shall make no law respecting an establishment of religion, or prohibiting the free exercise thereof; or abridging the freedom of speech, or of the press, or the right of the people to peaceably assemble, and to petition the government for a redress of grievances.

Guarantees freedom of religion, freedom of speech, freedom of the press, freedom of assembly, and the right of petition.

Amendment II (1791)

A well regulated Militia, being necessary to the security of a free State, the right of the people to keep and bear Arms, shall not be infringed.

Concerns the right to bear arms as an aspect of the maintenance of a well regulated militia; interpreted by some as guaranteeing an individual's right to bear arms as well.

Amendment III (1791)

No Soldier shall, in time of peace be quartered in any house, without the consent of the Owner, nor in time of war, but in a manner to be prescribed by law.

Prohibits the housing of soldiers in private homes without the consent of the owner, except in time of war.

Amendment IV (1791)

The right of the people to be secure in their persons, houses, papers, and effects, against unreasonable searches and seizures, shall not be violated, and no Warrants shall issue, but upon probable cause, supported by Oath or affirmation, and particularly describing the place to be searched, and the persons or things to be seized.

Prohibits unreasonable search and seizure and requires a showing of probable cause for the issuance of any search warrant or arrest warrant.

Amendment V (1791)

No Person shall be held to answer for a capital, or otherwise infamous crime, unless on a presentment or indictment of a Grand Jury, except in cases arising in the land or naval forces, or in the Militia, when in actual service in time of war or public danger; nor shall any person be subject for the same offense to be twice put in jeopardy of life and limb, nor shall be compelled in any criminal case to be a witness against himself, nor be deprived of life, liberty, or property, without due process of law; nor shall private property be taken for public use without just compensation.

Requires indictment by a grand jury before any person can be put on trial for a serious federal crime; bans double jeopardy and compulsory self-incrimination; prohibits the federal government from depriving any person of life, liberty, or property without due process of law; and prohibits the taking of private property for public use without just compensation.

Amendment VI (1791)

In all criminal prosecutions, the accused shall enjoy the right to a speedy and public trial, by an impartial jury of the State and district wherein the crime shall have been committed; which district shall have been previously ascertained by law, and to be informed of the nature and cause of the accusation; to be confronted with the witnesses against him; to have compulsory process for obtaining witnesses in his favor, and to have the assistance of counsel for his defense.

Guarantees criminal defendants the right to a speedy and public trial by jury; also guarantees them the right to be informed of the charges, the right of confrontation of adverse witnesses, the right to use process to compel the attendance of witnesses for the defense, and the right to counsel.

Amendment VII (1791)

In Suits at common law, where the value in controversy shall exceed twenty dollars, the right of trial by jury shall be preserved, and no fact tried by a jury shall be otherwise reexamined in any Court of the United States, than according to the rules of common law.

Preserves for litigants in civil damage actions in the federal courts the common law right of jury trial.

Amendment VIII (1791)

Excessive bail shall not be required, nor excessive fines imposed, nor cruel and unusual punishments inflicted.

Prohibits criminal courts from requiring excessive bail or imposing cruel and unusual punishment.

Amendment IX (1791)

The enumeration in the Constitution of certain rights shall not be construed to deny or disparage others retained by people.

States that the listing of specific rights in the Constitution is not to be interpreted as suggesting that other rights do not exist or are not equally deserving of protection.

Amendment X (1791)

The powers not delegated to the United States by the Constitution, nor prohibited by it to the States, are reserved to the States respectively, or to the people.

Emphasizes that the federal government has only those powers delegated to it by the Constitution.

Summary of Amendments XI–XXVII to the U.S. Constitution

Amendment XI (1798)

Requires federal courts to respect the sovereign immunity of state governments.

Amendment XII (1804)

Revised the electoral college system to reduce the potential for deadlocks in elections for President and Vice President.

Amendment XIII (1865)

Abolished slavery and involuntary servitude, except for forced labor as punishment for a crime.

Amendment XIV (1868)

Extended American citizenship to people of color by declaring that all persons born or naturalized in the United States and subject to United States jurisdiction are citizens of the United States and of the state where they reside. This amendment also prohibits the states from depriving any person of life, liberty, or property without due process of law, and guarantees all persons equal protection of the laws.

Amendment XV (1870)

Extended the vote to people of color by prohibiting the denial or abridgment of the right of citizens to vote on account of race, color, or previous condition of servitude.

Amendment XVI (1913)

Empowered Congress to institute the federal income tax.

Amendment XVII (1913)

Changed the method of electing United States senators from election by state legislatures to direct election by the people.

Amendment XVIII (1919)

The Prohibition Amendment: prohibited the manufacture, sale, or importation of alcoholic beverages in the United States. Repealed in 1933.

Amendment XIX (1920)

The Woman Suffrage Amendment: extended the vote to women in all states by prohibiting the denial or abridgment of the right to vote on account of sex.

Amendment XX (1933)

Revised the starting dates for terms of office of the President, Vice President, and members of Congress, and made provision for various contingencies in presidential succession such as the death of a President-elect before taking office.

Amendment XXI (1933)

Repealed the Prohibition Amendment and gave the individual states the power to regulate the distribution and use of intoxicating liquors within their borders.

Amendment XXII (1951)

Prohibits any individual from being elected President more than twice, or more than once if the individual has already acted as President for more than two years of a term to which someone else was elected.

Amendment XXIII (1961)

Extended the right to vote in presidential elections to residents of the District of Columbia. The nation's capital still has no voting representation in Congress, even though more Americans live in the District of Columbia than in some states, and even though Congress is the ultimate law-making and budgetary authority for the district. A proposed constitutional amendment to allow citizens in the District of Columbia representation and voting rights on an equal footing with citizens of the 50 states was adopted by Congress in 1978 but failed of ratification.

Amendment XXIV (1964)

Abolished the poll tax as a requirement for voting in primary and general elections for national office.

Amendment XXV (1967)

Provides a mechanism for filling vacancies in the office of Vice President, provides that the Vice President will serve as Acting President during periods of presidential disability, and provides procedures for determining whether such a disability exists.

Amendment XXVI (1971)

Lowered the voting age to eighteen.

Amendment XXVII (1992)

Provides that no change voted by Congress in its own compensation may take effect until after the next biennial congressional election.

THE GETTYSBURG ADDRESS

"That these dead shall not have died in vain"

Only 272 words—but what words! Only 10 sentences—but what sentences! The historian Garry Wills (born 1934) has written about President Abraham Lincoln's brief speech at the formal dedication of the 17-acre National Soldiers' Cemetery, in Gettysburg, Pennsylvania:

"The crowd departed with a new thing in its ideological luggage, that new constitution Lincoln had substituted for the one they brought there with them. They walked off, from those curving graves on the hillside, under a changed sky, into a different America. Lincoln had revolutionized the Revolution, giving people a new past to live with that would change their future indefinitely."

In early July, 1863, General Robert E. Lee's army, driving to split the United States in two, had been turned back by the Union soldiers at Gettysburg. Seven thousand Union and Confederate soldiers gave their "last full measure of devotion" in the decisive three-day battle. The Union had "a new birth of freedom," the Southern cause was broken. The Confederate army, thrown into a defensive war, realized it would never win. The nation, "conceived in liberty and dedicated to the proposition that all men are created equal," had endured. Lincoln (1809–1865) worked on the speech the night before delivery and on the platform while waiting hours to be introduced. He spoke it slowly, clearly, and, with his Kentucky accent, in a high voice. It was over so fast that photographers missed it.

Lincoln's Gettysburg Address
1863

Four score and seven years ago our fathers brought forth on this continent a new nation, conceived in liberty and dedicated to the proposition that all men are created equal.

Now we are engaged in a great civil war, testing whether that nation or any nation so conceived and so dedicated can long endure. We are met on a great battlefield of that war. We have come to dedicate a portion of that field as a final resting place for those who here gave their lives that that nation might live. It is altogether fitting and proper that we should do this.

But, in a larger sense, we cannot dedicate—we cannot consecrate—we cannot hallow—this ground. The brave men, living and dead, who struggled here have consecrated it far above our poor power to add or detract. The world will little note nor long remember what we say here, but it can never forget what they did here. It is for us, the living, rather, to be dedicated here to the unfinished work which they who fought here have thus far so nobly advanced.

It is rather for us to be here dedicated to the great task remaining before us—that from these honored dead we take increased devotion to that cause for which they gave the last full measure of devotion; that we here highly resolve that these dead shall not have died in vain; that this nation, under God, shall have a new birth of freedom; and that government of the people, by the people, for the people shall not perish from the earth.

INDEX TO USEFUL FEATURES

HISTORIC SITES OF THE MIDDLE EAST

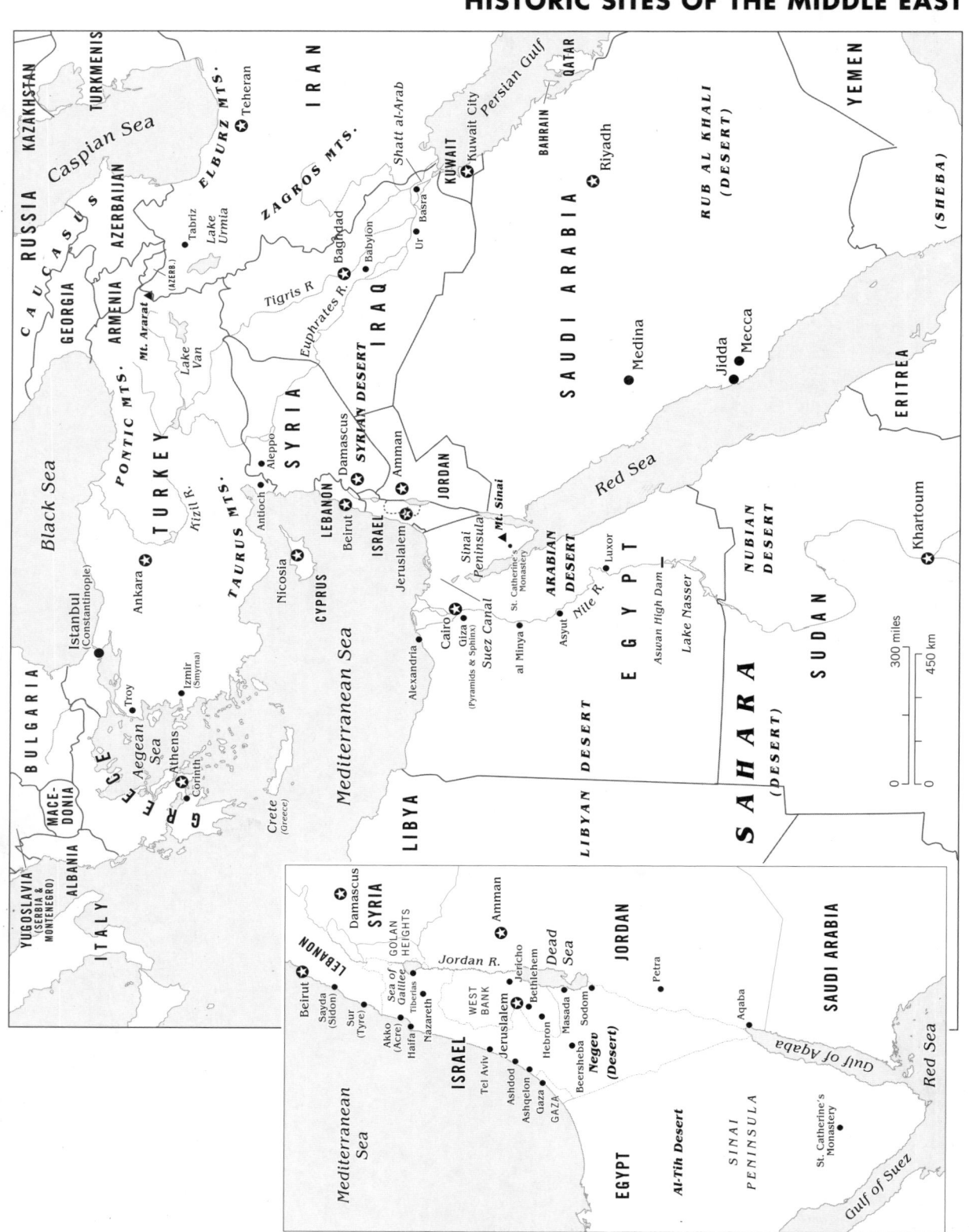